California

PENAL CODE

With Selected Provisions from Other Codes and Rules of Court

Volume 2

Mat# 43075737

ISBN: 978–1–668–71597–0

PREFACE

California Penal Code contains California statutes and rules relating to criminal law and procedure, including the entire text of the Penal Code. Additionally, cross references, Law Revision Commission Comments, references to Witkin's California Criminal Law, Judicial Council Forms, and California Jury Instructions aid the user in construing and applying particular provisions.

WHAT'S NEW

In order to accommodate the growth of this title and to enhance ease of use, it has been divided into two volumes. Includes all laws through c. 997 of the 2022 portion of the 2021–2022 Regular Session, and propositions voted on at the Nov. 8, 2022 election.

The court rules incorporated in this pamphlet reflect all amendments received through October 15, 2022.

ADDITIONAL INFORMATION

All California legislative enactments in 2022 are effective January 1, 2023, unless indicated otherwise. Additions or changes in statutes affected by 2022 legislation are indicated by underlining; deletions are indicated by asterisks. In court rules, additions or changes are indicated by underlining; deletions are indicated by strikethroughs.

Codified legislation which is subject to a governor's veto is followed by an italicized note indicating that fact. For the text of the message, please consult the Historical and Statutory Notes for the provision in *West's Annotated California Codes* or the material pertaining to the legislation affecting the provision in *West's California Legislative Service*.

To facilitate the inclusion of applicable provisions in two portable volumes, repealed statutes and court rules are omitted.

The Uniform Bail and Penalty Schedule referenced in Penal Code § 1269b and Vehicle Code § 40310 is available at http://www.courts.ca.gov/7532.htm.

For official election results, see https://electionresults.sos.ca.gov.

Section captions have been prepared by the publisher, unless specifically indicated otherwise.

CONTACT US

For additional information or research assistance, contact the Reference Attorneys at 1-800-REF-ATTY (1-800-733-2889) or by Live Chat: Access via Westlaw. Contact our U.S. legal editorial department directly with your questions and suggestions by e-mail at editors.us-legal@tr.com.

Thank you for subscribing to this product. Should you have any questions regarding this product, please contact Customer Service at 1-800-328-4880 or by submitting an online request through our Support center on legal.thomsonreuters.com. If you would like to inquire about related publications, or to place an order, please contact us at 1-888-728-7677 or visit us at legal.thomsonreuters.com.

THE PUBLISHER

December 2022

THOMSON REUTERS PROVIEW™

This title is one of many now available on your tablet as an eBook.

Take your research mobile. Powered by the Thomson Reuters ProView™ app, our eBooks deliver the same trusted content as your print resources, but in a compact, on-the-go format.

ProView eBooks are designed for the way you work. You can add your own notes and highlights to the text, and all of your annotations will transfer electronically to every new edition of your eBook.

You can also instantly verify primary authority with built-in links to Westlaw® and KeyCite®, so you can be confident that you're accessing the most current and accurate information.

To find out more about ProView eBooks and available discounts, call 1-800-328-9352.

TABLE OF SECTIONS AFFECTED

This table indicates sections affected by 2022 legislation

Penal Code

Sec.	Effect	Chap.	Sec.
17	Amended	734	2
17.2	Added	775	2
136.2	Amended	87	1
146e	Amended	697	1
			2
186.2	Amended	950	1
186.8	Amended	950	2
186.9	Amended	452	203
192	Amended	626	3
236.1	Amended	87	2
236.14	Amended	776	1
236.15	Amended	776	2
243	Amended	197	12
243.4	Amended	48	70
273.5	Amended	197	13
273.6	Amended	197	14
273.65	Amended	197	15
290.008	Amended	771	13
372.5	Added	487	1
374.3	Amended	784	1
422.92	Amended	48	71
422.94	Added	853	1
457.1	Amended	771	14
487	Amended	22	1
487e	Amended	546	1
487f	Amended	546	2
491	Amended	546	3
538d	Amended	954	1
538e	Amended	954	2
538f	Amended	954	3
538g	Amended	954	4
538h	Amended	954	5
602	Amended	197	16
626	Amended	134	1
626.2	Amended	134	2
626.4	Amended	134	3
626.6	Amended	134	4
629.51	Amended	627	2
629.52	Amended	627	3
631	Amended	27	1
632.7	Amended	27	2
638.50	Amended	627	4

TABLE OF SECTIONS AFFECTED

Sec.	Effect	Chap.	Sec.
638.52	Amended	627	5
647	Amended	882	1
647.3	Amended	86	2
653.20	Repealed	86	3
653.22	Repealed	86	4
653.23	Amended	86	5
653.29	Added	86	6
679.027	Added	771	15
679.06	Added	941	1
679.09	Added	227	1
679.10	Amended	48	72
679.12	Added	994	1
680	Amended	709	1
			1.5
		994	2
			2.5
680.2	Amended	709	2
690.5	Amended	215	5
741	Added	806	2
745	Amended	739	2
786.5	Added	949	1
801.6	Amended	587	1
801.8	Added	587	2
803	Amended	258	115
819	Added	810	9
830.1	Amended	416	1
830.3	Amended	452	204
830.4	Amended	478	63
830.7	Amended	58	4
830.11	Amended	452	205
		474	1
			1.5
832.5	Amended	28	125
832.7	Amended	28	126
		58	5
851.93	Amended	814	3
	Added	814	4
853.6	Amended	856	1
	Added	856	2
977	Amended	57	12
	Added	57	13
977.3	Added	57	14
978.5	Amended	856	3
	Added	856	4
1001.36	Amended	47	38
		735	1
prec. § 1001.81 Pt. 2 Title 6 ch. 2.9D	Added	856	5
1001.81	Added	856	5
1001.82	Added	856	5
1001.95	Amended	58	6
1026	Amended	47	39

TABLE OF SECTIONS AFFECTED

Sec.	Effect	Chap.	Sec.
1026.2	Amended	47	40
1043	Amended	197	17
1043.5	Amended	57	15
	Added	57	16
1127e	Amended	197	18
1170	Amended	744	1
1170.01	Redes. as 1172 and Amended	58	8
1170.02	Amended	744	2
1170.03	Redes. as 1172.1 and Amended	58	9
1170.91	Amended	721	1
1170.95	Redes. as 1172.6 and Amended	58	10
1171	Redes. as 1172.7 and Amended	58	11
1171.1	Redes. as 1172.75 and Amended	58	12
prec. § 1172 Pt. 2 Title 7 ch. 4.5 art. 1.5	Added	58	7
1172	Redes. from 1170.01 and Amended	58	8
1172.1	Redes. from 1170.03 and Amended	58	9
1172.2	Added	744	3
1172.6	Redes. from 1170.95 and Amended	58	10
1172.7	Redes. from 1171 and Amended	58	11
1172.75	Redes. from 1171.1 and Amended	58	12
1192.5	Amended	197	19
1203	Amended	756	1
1203.055	Amended	197	20
1203.097	Amended	197	21
1203.35	Amended	756	2
1203.4	Amended	734	3
1203.4a	Amended	734	4
1203.4b	Amended	197	22
		734	5
		771	16
1203.41	Amended	734	6
		814	5
		842	1
			1.5
1203.42	Amended	734	7
1203.425	Amended	58	13
		814	6
	Added	814	7
	Amended	842	2
			3
1203.426	Added	494	1
1203.427	Added	494	2
1203.45	Amended	734	8
1203.47	Amended	86	7
1203.9	Amended	197	23
1208.2	Amended	57	17
1210.2	Added	856	6
1210.6	Added	734	9
1214.1	Amended	57	18
1233.12	Added	58	14
1269b	Amended	627	6

TABLE OF SECTIONS AFFECTED

Sec.	Effect	Chap.	Sec.
1270.1	Amended	197	24
1299.01	Amended	768	18
	Added	768	19
1299.02	Amended	768	20
	Added	768	21
1299.04	Amended	768	22
	Added	768	23
1326	Amended	810	10
1346.1	Amended	197	25
1369	Amended	47	41
1369.1	Repealed	47	42
1370	Amended	47	43
		197	26
		735	2
		738	11
1370.01	Amended	319	4
			4.5
		735	3
			3.5
1370.6	Amended	47	44
1372	Amended	47	45
1385	Amended	58	15
1387	Amended	197	27
1463	Amended	57	19
1463.001	Amended	57	20
		771	17
1465.9	Amended	57	21
1473	Amended	739	3
			3.5
		982	1
			1.5
1524	Amended	627	7
1524.2	Amended	627	8
1546.5	Added	627	9
1551	Amended	627	10
1602	Amended	47	46
1603	Amended	47	47
1604	Amended	47	48
2067	Amended	58	16
2084.5	Added	827	2
2603	Amended	47	49
2695.5	Amended	379	18
2807	Amended	28	127
3003	Amended	826	1
	Added	826	2
3007.05	Amended	482	4
3408	Amended	628	8
3700	Repealed	795	2
	Redes. from 3700.5 and Amended	795	3
3700.5	Redes. as 3700 and Amended	795	3
3701	Repealed	795	4

TABLE OF SECTIONS AFFECTED

Sec.	Effect	Chap.	Sec.
3701 (Cont'd)	Added	795	5
3702	Repealed	795	6
	Added	795	7
3703	Repealed	795	8
	Added	795	9
3704	Repealed	795	10
3704.5	Repealed	795	11
4013	Amended	255	1
4019	Amended	47	50
		756	3
			4
4024.5	Added	327	1
4852.01	Amended	766	1
4900	Amended	58	17
		771	18
			18.5
	Added	771	19
			19.5
4902	Amended	58	18
4904	Amended	58	19
		771	20
			20.5
	Added	771	21
			21.5
4904.5	Added	58	20
4905	Repealed	58	21
	Added	58	22
5003.7	Repealed	58	23
	Added	58	24
5007.4	Added	58	25
5007.6	Added	837	1
5027	Amended	58	26
5032	Added	58	27
5073	Added	968	2
5076.1	Amended	58	28
6141	Amended	821	1
6401	Added	837	2
6401.5	Added	837	3
6401.8	Added	837	4
10008	Added	802	1
11105	Amended	58	29
	Added	58	30
	Amended	197	28
		814	8
		842	4
			5
11161.2	Amended	557	1
11163.3	Amended	197	29
		986	1
11163.4	Amended	986	2
11163.5	Amended	986	3

TABLE OF SECTIONS AFFECTED

Sec.	Effect	Chap.	Sec.
11163.6	Amended	986	4
11165.2	Amended	770	1
11166	Amended	50	10
		770	2
11167	Amended	770	3
11174.34	Amended	50	11
11177.2	Repealed	734	10
11411	Amended	397	1
13012.4	Added	796	2
13016	Added	899	2
13023	Amended	852	1
13151	Amended	197	30
prec. § 13370 Pt. 4 Title 3 ch. 2 art. 9	Added	787	1
13370	Added	787	1
13511.1	Amended	197	31
13519	Amended	197	32
13660	Added	945	1
prec. § 13680 Pt. 4 Title 4.9	Added	854	1
13680	Added	854	1
13681	Added	854	1
13682	Added	854	1
13683	Added	854	1
13750	Amended	20	1
13777	Amended	58	31
		197	33
13778.2	Added	627	11
13823.16	Amended	197	34
13899	Amended	105	1
14143	Amended	197	35
14306	Amended	58	32
14307	Amended	58	33
14308	Amended	58	34
16515	Added	76	3
16517	Added	76	4
16519	Added	76	5
16520	Amended	76	6
16531	Amended	76	7
16532	Repealed	76	8
17312	Added	76	9
18005	Amended	58	35
18010	Amended	76	10
18122	Repealed	420	29
	Added	420	30
18123	Amended	420	31
18150	Amended	974	1
18170	Amended	974	2
18190	Amended	974	3
18275	Amended	58	36
22295	Amended	287	58
	Added	287	59
23910	Amended	76	11

TABLE OF SECTIONS AFFECTED

Sec.	Effect	Chap.	Sec.
23920	Amended	76	12
23925	Amended	76	13
26715	Amended	995	1
26720	Amended	138	1
26806	Added	995	2
26811	Added	995	3
26835	Amended	76	14
	Added	76	15
26883	Added	141	1
27240	Amended	696	1
27245	Amended	696	2
27305	Amended	696	3
27310	Amended	696	4
27350	Amended	696	5
27510	Amended	76	16
27530	Amended	76	17
27535	Amended	76	18
	Added	76	19
27540	Amended	76	20
	Added	76	21
27573	Added	145	1
27575.1	Added	140	1
29010	Amended	142	1
29180	Amended	76	22
29181	Repealed	76	23
29182	Amended	76	24
29185	Added	76	25
29805	Amended	76	26
		143	1
			1 5
29880	Added	100	1
30372	Added	100	2
30400	Repealed	76	27
	Added	76	28
30401	Added	76	29
30405	Repealed	76	30
30406	Repealed	76	31
30412	Repealed	76	32
30414	Repealed	76	33
30420	Amended	76	34
30442	Repealed	76	35
30445	Repealed	76	35
30447	Repealed	76	35
30448	Repealed	76	35
30450	Repealed	76	35
30452	Repealed	76	35
30454	Repealed	76	35
30456	Repealed	76	35
30470	Repealed	76	36
30472	Added	100	3
30485	Repealed	76	37

TABLE OF SECTIONS AFFECTED

Sec.	Effect	Chap.	Sec.
30490	Repealed	76	37
30495	Repealed	76	37
32000	Amended	452	206
34010	Amended	58	37

TABLE OF CONTENTS

PENAL CODE

Volume 1

TABLE OF CONTENTS

TABLE OF CONTENTS

Volume 2

PENAL PROVISIONS SELECTED FROM CONSTITUTION, OTHER CODES, AND COURT RULES

CONSTITUTION

BUSINESS AND PROFESSIONS CODE

CODE OF CIVIL PROCEDURE

TABLE OF CONTENTS

FAMILY CODE

GOVERNMENT CODE

HEALTH AND SAFETY CODE

TABLE OF CONTENTS

INSURANCE CODE

VEHICLE CODE

WELFARE AND INSTITUTIONS CODE

TABLE OF CONTENTS

CALIFORNIA RULES OF COURT
TITLE 2. TRIAL COURT RULES

TITLE 3. CIVIL RULES

TITLE 4. CRIMINAL RULES

TABLE OF CONTENTS

TABLE OF CONTENTS

INDEX

PENAL CODE

An Act

to

ESTABLISH A PENAL CODE

[Approved February 14, 1872.]

The People of the State of California, represented in Senate and Assembly, do enact as follows:

Part 5

PEACE OFFICERS' MEMORIAL

§ 15001. Construction of memorial to California peace officers; site; funds

(a) The construction of a memorial to California peace officers on the grounds of the State Capitol is hereby authorized. For purposes of this part, the grounds of the State Capitol are that property in the City of Sacramento bounded by Ninth, Fifteenth, "L," and "N" Streets. The actual site for the memorial shall be selected by the commission after consultation with the Department of General Services and the State Office of Historic Preservation.

(b) Funds for the construction of the memorial shall be provided through private contributions for this purpose. *(Added by Stats.1985, c. 1518, § 1.)*

Cross References

Department of General Services, generally, see Government Code § 14600 et seq.

§ 15003. Conduct of peace officer memorial ceremonies

Peace officer memorial ceremonies, including the dedication of the memorial and any subsequent ceremonies, shall be conducted by the California Peace Officers' Memorial Foundation, Inc. *(Added by Stats.1985, c. 1518, § 1. Amended by Stats.1993, c. 29 (S.B.162), § 1; Stats.2016, c. 86 (S.B.1171), § 242, eff. Jan. 1, 2017.)*

Part 6

CONTROL OF DEADLY WEAPONS

Title 1

PRELIMINARY PROVISIONS

Division 1

GENERAL PROVISIONS

§ 16000. Deadly Weapons Recodification Act of 2010; recodification of former Title 2

This act recodifies the provisions of former Title 2 (commencing with Section 12000) of Part 4, which was entitled "Control of Deadly Weapons." The act shall be known and may be cited as the "Deadly Weapons Recodification Act of 2010." *(Added by Stats.2010, c. 711 (S.B.1080), § 6, operative Jan. 1, 2012.)*

Law Revision Commission Comments

Section 16000 provides a convenient means of referring to the recodification of former Sections 12000–12809. For background, see *Nonsubstantive Reorganization of Deadly Weapon Statutes*, 38 Cal. L. Revision Comm'n Reports 217 (2009). [38 Cal.L.Rev.Comm. Reports 217 (2009)].

Research References

2 Witkin, California Criminal Law 4th Crimes Against Public Peace and Welfare § 189 (2021), In General.
2 Witkin, California Criminal Law 4th Crimes Against Public Peace and Welfare § 190 (2021), In General.
2 Witkin, California Criminal Law 4th Crimes Against Public Peace and Welfare § 213 (2021), Concealed Dirk, Dagger, or Explosives.

§ 16005. Nonsubstantive intent of Act

Nothing in the Deadly Weapons Recodification Act of 2010 is intended to substantively change the law relating to deadly weapons. The act is intended to be entirely nonsubstantive in effect. Every provision of this part, of Title 2 (commencing with Section 12001) of Part 4, and every other provision of this act, including, without limitation, every cross-reference in every provision of the act, shall be interpreted consistent with the nonsubstantive intent of the act. *(Added by Stats.2010, c. 711 (S.B.1080), § 6, operative Jan. 1, 2012.)*

Law Revision Commission Comments

Section 16005 makes clear that the Deadly Weapons Recodification Act of 2010 has no substantive impact. The act is intended solely to make the provisions governing control of deadly weapons more user-friendly. For background, see *Nonsubstantive Reorganization of Deadly Weapon Statutes*, 38 Cal.L.Rev.Comm. Reports 217 (2009). [38 Cal.L.Rev.Comm. Reports 217 (2009)].

§ 16010. Provisions as restatement and continuation of former law; references to former provisions and restated and continued provisions

(a) A provision of this part or of Title 2 (commencing with Section 12001) of Part 4, or any other provision of the Deadly Weapons Recodification Act of 2010, insofar as it is substantially the same as a previously existing provision relating to the same subject matter, shall be considered as a restatement and continuation thereof and not as a new enactment.

(b) A reference in a statute to a previously existing provision that is restated and continued in this part or in Title 2 (commencing with Section 12001) of Part 4, or in any other provision of the Deadly Weapons Recodification Act of 2010, shall, unless a contrary intent appears, be deemed a reference to the restatement and continuation.

(c) A reference in a statute to a provision of this part or of Title 2 (commencing with Section 12001) of Part 4, or any other provision of the Deadly Weapons Recodification Act of 2010, which is substantially the same as a previously existing provision, shall, unless a contrary intent appears, be deemed to include a reference to the previously existing provision. *(Added by Stats.2010, c. 711 (S.B. 1080), § 6, operative Jan. 1, 2012.)*

Law Revision Commission Comments

Subdivision (a) of Section 16010 is similar to Section 5, which is a standard provision found in many codes. See, e.g., Bus. & Prof. Code § 2; Corp. Code § 2; Fam. Code § 2; Prob. Code § 2(a); Veh. Code § 2.

Subdivision (b) is drawn from Government Code Section 9604.

Subdivision (c) is drawn from Family Code Section 2. For a specific illustration of the general principle stated in this subdivision, see Section 16015 (determining existence of prior conviction). [38 Cal.L.Rev.Comm. Reports 217 (2009)].

§ 16015. Conviction under previously existing provision as conviction under restatement and continuation of provision

If a previously existing provision is restated and continued in this part, or in Title 2 (commencing with Section 12001) of Part 4, or in any other provision of the Deadly Weapons Recodification Act of 2010, a conviction under that previously existing provision shall, unless a contrary intent appears, be treated as a prior conviction under the restatement and continuation of that provision. *(Added by Stats.2010, c. 711 (S.B.1080), § 6, operative Jan. 1, 2012.)*

Law Revision Commission Comments

Section 16015 makes clear that in determining the existence of a prior conviction that affects the severity of punishment for an offense, a conviction under a former provision that has been restated and continued in the Deadly Weapons Recodification Act of 2010 counts as a prior conviction under the corresponding new provision.

For example, Section 20170 prohibits open display of an imitation firearm in a public place. A first violation of that provision is punishable by a $100 fine, and a second violation is punishable by a $300 fine. See Section 20180. In determining whether to impose a $100 fine or a $300 fine, a violation of the predecessor of Section 20170 (former Section 12256(a)) counts as a prior violation of Section 20170. [38 Cal.L.Rev.Comm. Reports 217 (2009)].

§ 16020. Judicial decision interpreting previously existing provision; relevance

(a) A judicial decision interpreting a previously existing provision is relevant in interpreting any provision of this part, of Title 2 (commencing with Section 12001) of Part 4, or any other provision of the Deadly Weapons Recodification Act of 2010, which restates and continues that previously existing provision.

(b) However, in enacting the Deadly Weapons Recodification Act of 2010, the Legislature has not evaluated the correctness of any judicial decision interpreting a provision affected by the act.

(c) The Deadly Weapons Recodification Act of 2010 is not intended to, and does not, reflect any assessment of any judicial decision interpreting any provision affected by the act. *(Added by Stats.2010, c. 711 (S.B.1080), § 6, operative Jan. 1, 2012.)*

Law Revision Commission Comments

Subdivision (a) of Section 16020 makes clear that case law construing a predecessor provision is relevant in construing its successor in the Deadly Weapons Recodification Act of 2010.

Subdivisions (b) and (c) make clear that in recodifying former Sections 12000–12809, the Legislature has not taken any position on any case interpreting any of those provisions. [38 Cal.L.Rev.Comm. Reports 217 (2009)].

§ 16025. Judicial decision determining constitutionality of previously existing provision; relevance

(a) A judicial decision determining the constitutionality of a previously existing provision is relevant in determining the constitutionality of any provision of this part, of Title 2 (commencing with Section 12001) of Part 4, or any other provision of the Deadly Weapons Recodification Act of 2010, which restates and continues that previously existing provision.

(b) However, in enacting the Deadly Weapons Recodification Act of 2010, the Legislature has not evaluated the constitutionality of any provision affected by the act, or the correctness of any judicial decision determining the constitutionality of any provision affected by the act.

(c) The Deadly Weapons Recodification Act of 2010 is not intended to, and does not, reflect any determination of the constitutionality of any provision affected by the act. *(Added by Stats.2010, c. 711 (S.B.1080), § 6, operative Jan. 1, 2012.)*

Law Revision Commission Comments

Subdivision (a) of Section 16025 makes clear that case law determining the constitutionality of a predecessor provision is relevant in determining the constitutionality of its successor in the Deadly Weapons Recodification Act of 2010.

Subdivisions (b) and (c) make clear that in recodifying former Sections 12000–12809, the Legislature has not taken any position on the constitutionality of any of those provisions. [38 Cal.L.Rev.Comm. Reports 217 (2009)].

Division 2

DEFINITIONS

§ 16100. .50 BMG cartridge defined

Use of the term ".50 BMG cartridge" is governed by Section 30525. *(Added by Stats.2010, c. 711 (S.B.1080), § 6, operative Jan. 1, 2012.)*

Law Revision Commission Comments

Section 16100 is new. It is intended to help persons locate the definition of ".50 BMG cartridge." [38 Cal.L.Rev.Comm. Reports 217 (2009)].

Research References

2 Witkin, California Criminal Law 4th Crimes Against Public Peace and Welfare § 211 (2021), Nature of Crime.

§ 16110. .50 BMG rifle defined

Use of the term ".50 BMG rifle" is governed by Section 30530. *(Added by Stats.2010, c. 711 (S.B.1080), § 6, operative Jan. 1, 2012.)*

Law Revision Commission Comments

Section 16110 is new. It is intended to help persons locate the definition of ".50 BMG rifle." [38 Cal.L.Rev.Comm. Reports 217 (2009)].

§ 16120. Abuse defined

As used in this part, "abuse" means any of the following:

(a) Intentionally or recklessly to cause or attempt to cause bodily injury.

(b) Sexual assault.

(c) To place a person in reasonable apprehension of imminent serious bodily injury to that person or to another.

(d) To molest, attack, strike, stalk, destroy personal property, or violate the terms of a domestic violence protective order issued pursuant to Part 4 (commencing with Section 6300) of Division 10 of the Family Code. *(Added by Stats.2010, c. 711 (S.B.1080), § 6, operative Jan. 1, 2012.)*

Law Revision Commission Comments

Section 16120 continues former Section 12028.5(a)(1) without substantive change. [38 Cal.L.Rev.Comm. Reports 217 (2009)].

§ 16130. Agent defined

As used in Section 26915, "agent" means an employee of the licensee. *(Added by Stats.2010, c. 711 (S.B.1080), § 6, operative Jan. 1, 2012.)*

Law Revision Commission Comments

Section 16130 continues former Section 12071(b)(20)(G)(i) without substantive change. [38 Cal.L.Rev.Comm. Reports 217 (2009)].

§ 16140. Air gauge knife defined

As used in this part, "air gauge knife" means a device that appears to be an air gauge but has concealed within it a pointed, metallic shaft that is designed to be a stabbing instrument which is exposed by mechanical action or gravity which locks into place when extended. *(Added by Stats.2010, c. 711 (S.B.1080), § 6, operative Jan. 1, 2012.)*

Law Revision Commission Comments

Section 16140 continues former Section 12020(c)(18) without substantive change. [38 Cal.L.Rev.Comm. Reports 217 (2009)].

Cross References

Penalty for possession of deadly weapon described in this section within State Capitol, legislative offices, etc., see Penal Code § 171c.
Possession of deadly weapons with intent to assault, see Penal Code § 17500.

§ 16150. Ammunition defined

(a) As used in this part, except in subdivision (a) of Section 30305 and in Section 30306, "ammunition" means one or more loaded cartridges consisting of a primed case, propellant, and with one or more projectiles. "Ammunition" does not include blanks.

(b) As used in subdivision (a) of Section 30305 and in Section 30306, "ammunition" includes, but is not limited to, any bullet, cartridge, magazine, clip, speed loader, autoloader, ammunition feeding device, or projectile capable of being fired from a firearm with a deadly consequence. "Ammunition" does not include blanks.

(c) This section shall become operative on July 1, 2020. *(Added by Stats.2018, c. 780 (S.B.746), § 3, eff. Jan. 1, 2019, operative July 1, 2020.)*

Cross References

Age verification when selling products that are illegal to sell to minor, reasonable steps, products requiring age verification, penalties, see Civil Code § 1798.99.1.
Firearm defined for purposes of this Part, see Penal Code § 16520.
Handgun defined for purposes of this Part, see Penal Code § 16640.
Nuisance caused by illegal conduct involving unlawful weapons or ammunition purpose, unlawful detainer action, see Civil Code § 3485.
Penalty for possession of ammunition as defined in this section within State Capitol, legislative offices, etc., see Penal Code § 171c.

Research References

2 Witkin, California Criminal Law 4th Crimes Against Public Peace and Welfare § 210 (2021), Unlawful Acts Involving Ammunition.
2 Witkin, California Criminal Law 4th Crimes Against Public Peace and Welfare § 256 (2021), Sterile Area of Airport, Passenger Vessel Terminal, or Public Transit Facility.

§ 16151. Ammunition vendor defined

(a) As used in this part, commencing January 1, 2018, "ammunition vendor" means any person, firm, corporation, or other business enterprise that holds a current ammunition vendor license issued pursuant to Section 30385.

(b) Commencing January 1, 2018, a firearms dealer licensed pursuant to Sections 26700 to 26915, inclusive, shall automatically be deemed a licensed ammunition vendor, provided the dealer complies with the requirements of Articles 2 (commencing with Section 30300) and 3 (commencing with Section 30342) of Chapter 1 of Division 10 of Title 4. *(Added by Initiative Measure (Prop. 63, § 8.2, approved Nov. 8, 2016, eff. Nov. 9, 2016).)*

Research References

2 Witkin, California Criminal Law 4th Crimes Against Public Peace and Welfare § 210 (2021), Unlawful Acts Involving Ammunition.
2 Witkin, California Criminal Law 4th Crimes Against Public Peace and Welfare § 228 (2021), Armor Piercing Ammunition.

§ 16160. Antique cannon defined

As used in this part, "antique cannon" means any cannon manufactured before January 1, 1899, which has been rendered incapable of firing or for which ammunition is no longer manufactured in the United States and is not readily available in the ordinary channels of commercial trade. *(Added by Stats.2010, c. 711 (S.B. 1080), § 6, operative Jan. 1, 2012.)*

Law Revision Commission Comments

Section 16160 continues the second sentence of former Section 12301(a)(3) without substantive change. [38 Cal.L.Rev.Comm. Reports 217 (2009)].

§ 16170. Antique firearm defined

(a) As used in Sections 30515 and 30530, "antique firearm" means any firearm manufactured before January 1, 1899.

(b) As used in Section 16520, Section 16650, subdivision (a) of Section 23630, paragraph (1) of subdivision (b) of Section 27505, and subdivision (a) of Section 31615, "antique firearm" has the same meaning as in Section 921(a)(16) of Title 18 of the United States Code.

(c) As used in Sections 16531 and 17700, "antique firearm" means either of the following:

(1) Any firearm not designed or redesigned for using rimfire or conventional center fire ignition with fixed ammunition and manufactured in or before the year 1898. This type of firearm includes any matchlock, flintlock, percussion cap, or similar type of ignition system or replica thereof, whether actually manufactured before or after the year 1898.

(2) Any firearm using fixed ammunition manufactured in or before the year 1898, for which ammunition is no longer manufactured in the United States and is not readily available in the ordinary channels of commercial trade. *(Added by Stats.2010, c. 711 (S.B. 1080), § 6, operative Jan. 1, 2012. Amended by Stats.2019, c. 730 (A.B.879), § 1, eff. Jan. 1, 2020.)*

Law Revision Commission Comments

Subdivision (a) of Section 16170 continues former Section 12276.1(d)(3) and former Section 12278(d) without substantive change.

Subdivision (b) continues without substantive change the definition of "antique firearm" that was used in former Sections 12001(e), 12060(b), 12078(p)(6)(B), 12085(e)(3), 12088.8(a), 12318(b)(2), and 12801(b).

Subdivision (c) continues the second sentence of former Section 12020(b)(5) without substantive change.

See Section 16520 ("firearm"). [38 Cal.L.Rev.Comm. Reports 217 (2009)].

Cross References

Penalty for possession of deadly weapon described in this section within State Capitol, legislative offices, etc., see Penal Code § 171c.
Possession of deadly weapons with intent to assault, see Penal Code § 17500.

Research References

2 Witkin, California Criminal Law 4th Crimes Against Public Peace and Welfare § 262A (2021), (New) Lost or Stolen Firearms.

§ 16180. Antique rifle defined

As used in this part, "antique rifle" means a firearm conforming to the definition of an "antique firearm" in Section 479.11 of Title 27 of the Code of Federal Regulations. *(Added by Stats.2010, c. 711 (S.B.1080), § 6, operative Jan. 1, 2012.)*

Law Revision Commission Comments

Section 16180 continues the third sentence of former Section 12301(a)(3) without substantive change.

See Section 16520 ("firearm"). [38 Cal.L.Rev.Comm. Reports 217 (2009)].

Cross References

Firearm defined for purposes of this Part, see Penal Code § 16520.

§ 16190. Application to purchase defined

As used in this part, "application to purchase" means either of the following:

(a) The initial completion of the register by the purchaser, transferee, or person being loaned a firearm, as required by Section 28210.

(b) The initial completion and transmission to the Department of Justice of the record of electronic or telephonic transfer by the dealer on the purchaser, transferee, or person being loaned a firearm, as required by Section 28215. *(Added by Stats.2010, c. 711 (S.B.1080), § 6, operative Jan. 1, 2012. Amended by Stats.2014, c. 103 (A.B.1798), § 3, eff. Jan. 1, 2015.)*

Law Revision Commission Comments

Section 16190 continues former Section 12001(i) without substantive change.

See Section 16520 ("firearm"). [38 Cal.L.Rev.Comm. Reports 217 (2009)].

Section 16190 is amended to expressly apply the definition of "application to purchase" to the whole of Part 6. This amendment does not effect a substantive change because all of the provisions in Part 6 that use the term "application to purchase" use it with the meaning provided in this section. See, e.g., Sections 26955, 26960, 26965, 27655, 27660, 27665, 28210, 28215, and 28255. [43 Cal.L.Rev.Comm. Reports 63 (2013)].

Cross References

Firearm defined for purposes of this Part, see Penal Code § 16520.

Research References

2 Witkin, California Criminal Law 4th Crimes Against Public Peace and Welfare § 192 (2021), In General.
2 Witkin, California Criminal Law 4th Crimes Against Public Peace and Welfare § 197 (2021), Time and Manner of Delivery by Dealer.

§ 16200. Assault weapon defined

Use of the term "assault weapon" is governed by Sections 30510 and 30515. *(Added by Stats.2010, c. 711 (S.B.1080), § 6, operative Jan. 1, 2012.)*

Law Revision Commission Comments

Section 16200 is new. It is intended to help persons locate the provisions defining "assault weapon." [38 Cal.L.Rev.Comm. Reports 217 (2009)].

§ 16220. Ballistic knife defined

As used in this part, "ballistic knife" means a device that propels a knifelike blade as a projectile by means of a coil spring, elastic material, or compressed gas. Ballistic knife does not include any device that propels an arrow or a bolt by means of any common bow, compound bow, crossbow, or underwater speargun. *(Added by Stats.2010, c. 711 (S.B.1080), § 6, operative Jan. 1, 2012.)*

Law Revision Commission Comments

Section 16220 continues former Section 12020(c)(8) without substantive change. [38 Cal.L.Rev.Comm. Reports 217 (2009)].

Cross References

Penalty for possession of deadly weapon described in this section within State Capitol, legislative offices, etc., see Penal Code § 171c.
Possession of deadly weapons with intent to assault, see Penal Code § 17500.

§ 16230. Ballistics identification system defined

As used in this part, "ballistics identification system" includes, but is not limited to, any automated image analysis system that is capable of storing firearm ballistic markings and tracing those markings to the firearm that produced them. *(Added by Stats.2010, c. 711 (S.B.1080), § 6, operative Jan. 1, 2012.)*

Law Revision Commission Comments

Section 16230 continues former Section 12072.5(a) without substantive change. [38 Cal.L.Rev.Comm. Reports 217 (2009)].

Cross References

Firearm defined for purposes of this Part, see Penal Code § 16520.

§ 16240. Basic firearms safety certificate defined

As used in this part, "basic firearms safety certificate" means a certificate issued before January 1, 2003, by the Department of Justice pursuant to former Article 8 (commencing with Section 12800) of Chapter 6 of Title 2 of Part 4, as that article read at any time from when it became operative on January 1, 1992, to when it was repealed on January 1, 2003. *(Added by Stats.2010, c. 711 (S.B.1080), § 6, operative Jan. 1, 2012.)*

Law Revision Commission Comments

Section 16240 continues former Section 12001(p) without substantive change.

Former Article 8 of Chapter 6 of Title 2 of Part 4, entitled "Basic Firearms Safety Instruction and Certificate," was enacted by 1991 Cal. Stat. ch. 950, § 20, and became operative on January 1, 1992. The article was repealed on January 1, 2003, pursuant to the terms of former Section 12810 (2001 Cal. Stat. ch. 942, § 11).

See Sections 16160 ("antique cannon"), 16180 ("antique rifle"), 16490 ("explosive"). [38 Cal.L.Rev.Comm. Reports 217 (2009)].

Cross References

Firearm defined for purposes of this Part, see Penal Code § 16520.

§ 16250. BB device defined

(a) As used in this part, "BB device" means any instrument that expels a projectile, such as a BB or a pellet, through the force of air pressure, gas pressure, or spring action, or any spot marker gun.

(b) This section shall be operative on January 1, 2016. *(Added by Stats.2014, c. 915 (S.B.199), § 2, eff. Jan. 1, 2015, operative Jan. 1, 2016.)*

Cross References

Manufacture, sale, or possession of imitation firearms, exclusive regulation by Legislature, see Government Code § 53071.5.
Nongame birds, carcass, skin or parts thereof, Native Americans, interruption of salvaging, see Fish and Game Code § 3801.6.
Possession of BB devices in game refuges, notice to department, see Fish and Game Code § 10506.
Prohibited acts in fish or game refuge, firearm, BB device, game refuge, see Fish and Game Code § 10500.
Pupil safety, injurious objects, see Education Code § 49330.
Use of BB devices for hunting while intoxicated, prohibition, see Fish and Game Code § 3001.

Research References

California Jury Instructions - Criminal 16.292, Exhibiting Imitation Firearm.
California Jury Instructions - Criminal 985, Brandishing Imitation Firearm (Pen. Code, §417.4)).
2 Witkin, California Criminal Law 4th Crimes Against Public Peace and Welfare § 196 (2021), Transfers to Specified Persons.

§ 16260. Belt buckle knife defined

As used in this part, "belt buckle knife" is a knife that is made an integral part of a belt buckle and consists of a blade with a length of at least two and one-half inches. *(Added by Stats.2010, c. 711 (S.B.1080), § 6, operative Jan. 1, 2012.)*

Law Revision Commission Comments

Section 16260 continues former Section 12020(c)(13) without substantive change. [38 Cal.L.Rev.Comm. Reports 217 (2009)].

Cross References

Penalty for possession of deadly weapon described in this section within State Capitol, legislative offices, etc., see Penal Code § 171c.
Possession of deadly weapons with intent to assault, see Penal Code § 17500.

§ 16270. Blowgun defined

As used in this part, "blowgun" means a hollow tube designed and intended to be used as a tube through which a dart is propelled by the force of the breath of the user. *(Added by Stats.2010, c. 711 (S.B.1080), § 6, operative Jan. 1, 2012.)*

Law Revision Commission Comments

Section 16270 continues former Section 12580 without substantive change. [38 Cal.L.Rev.Comm. Reports 217 (2009)].

Research References

2 Witkin, California Criminal Law 4th Crimes Against Public Peace and Welfare § 231 (2021), Other Weapons and Devices.

§ 16280. Blowgun ammunition defined

As used in this part, "blowgun ammunition" means a dart designed and intended for use in a blowgun. *(Added by Stats.2010, c. 711 (S.B.1080), § 6, operative Jan. 1, 2012.)*

Law Revision Commission Comments

Section 16280 continues former Section 12581 without substantive change. See Section 16270 ("blowgun"). [38 Cal.L.Rev.Comm. Reports 217 (2009)].

Research References

2 Witkin, California Criminal Law 4th Crimes Against Public Peace and Welfare § 231 (2021), Other Weapons and Devices.

§ 16288. Body armor defined

As used in Section 31360, "body armor" means any bullet-resistant material intended to provide ballistic and trauma protection for the person wearing the body armor. *(Added by Stats.2010, c. 711 (S.B.1080), § 6, operative Jan. 1, 2012.)*

Law Revision Commission Comments

Section 16288 continues former Section 12370(f) without substantive change. [40 Cal.L.Rev.Comm. Reports 107 (2010)].

Research References

2 Witkin, California Criminal Law 4th Crimes Against Public Peace and Welfare § 231 (2021), Other Weapons and Devices.

§ 16290. Body vest defined; body shield defined

As used in this part, "body vest" or "body shield" means any bullet-resistant material intended to provide ballistic and trauma protection for the wearer or holder. *(Added by Stats.2010, c. 711 (S.B.1080), § 6, operative Jan. 1, 2012.)*

Law Revision Commission Comments

Section 16290 continues former Section 12323(c) without substantive change. [38 Cal.L.Rev.Comm. Reports 217 (2009)].

Research References

2 Witkin, California Criminal Law 4th Crimes Against Public Peace and Welfare § 228 (2021), Armor Piercing Ammunition.

§ 16300. Bona fide evidence of identity defined; bona fide evidence of majority and identity defined

As used in this part, "bona fide evidence of identity" or "bona fide evidence of majority and identity" means a document issued by a federal, state, county, or municipal government, or subdivision or agency thereof, including, but not limited to, a motor vehicle operator's license, state identification card, identification card issued to a member of the armed forces, or other form of identification that bears the name, date of birth, description, and picture of the person. *(Added by Stats.2010, c. 711 (S.B.1080), § 6, operative Jan. 1, 2012.)*

Law Revision Commission Comments

Section 16300 continues former Section 12318(b)(1) and the second sentence of former Section 12316(a)(2) without substantive change. [38 Cal.L.Rev. Comm. Reports 217 (2009)].

Research References

2 Witkin, California Criminal Law 4th Crimes Against Public Peace and Welfare § 210 (2021), Unlawful Acts Involving Ammunition.

§ 16310. Boobytrap defined

As used in this part, "boobytrap" means any concealed or camouflaged device designed to cause great bodily injury when triggered by an action of any unsuspecting person coming across the device. Boobytraps may include, but are not limited to, guns, ammunition, or explosive devices attached to trip wires or other triggering mechanisms, sharpened stakes, and lines or wire with hooks attached. *(Added by Stats.2010, c. 711 (S.B.1080), § 6, operative Jan. 1, 2012.)*

Law Revision Commission Comments

Section 16310 continues former Section 12355(c) without substantive change. [38 Cal.L.Rev.Comm. Reports 217 (2009)].

Research References

2 Witkin, California Criminal Law 4th Crimes Against Public Peace and Welfare § 231 (2021), Other Weapons and Devices.

§ 16320. Camouflaging firearm container defined

(a) As used in this part, "camouflaging firearm container" means a container that meets all of the following criteria:

(1) It is designed and intended to enclose a firearm.

(2) It is designed and intended to allow the firing of the enclosed firearm by external controls while the firearm is in the container.

(3) It is not readily recognizable as containing a firearm.

(b) "Camouflaging firearm container" does not include any camouflaging covering used while engaged in lawful hunting or while going to or returning from a lawful hunting expedition. *(Added by Stats.2010, c. 711 (S.B.1080), § 6, operative Jan. 1, 2012.)*

Law Revision Commission Comments

Section 16320 continues former Section 12020(c)(9) without substantive change.

See Section 16520 ("firearm"). [38 Cal.L.Rev.Comm. Reports 217 (2009)].

Cross References

Firearm defined for purposes of this Part, see Penal Code § 16520.

§ 16330. Cane gun defined

As used in this part, "cane gun" means any firearm mounted or enclosed in a stick, staff, rod, crutch, or similar device, designed to be, or capable of being used as, an aid in walking, if the firearm may be fired while mounted or enclosed therein. *(Added by Stats.2010, c. 711 (S.B.1080), § 6, operative Jan. 1, 2012.)*

Law Revision Commission Comments

Section 16330 continues former Section 12020(c)(5) without substantive change.

See Section 16520 ("firearm"). [38 Cal.L.Rev.Comm. Reports 217 (2009)].

Cross References

Firearm defined for purposes of this Part, see Penal Code § 16520.
Penalty for possession of deadly weapon described in this section within State Capitol, legislative offices, etc., see Penal Code § 171c.
Possession of deadly weapons with intent to assault, see Penal Code § 17500.

§ 16340. Cane sword defined

As used in this part, "cane sword" means a cane, swagger stick, stick, staff, rod, pole, umbrella, or similar device, having concealed within it a blade that may be used as a sword or stiletto. *(Added by Stats.2010, c. 711 (S.B.1080), § 6, operative Jan. 1, 2012.)*

Law Revision Commission Comments

Section 16340 continues former Section 12020(c)(15) without substantive change. [38 Cal.L.Rev.Comm. Reports 217 (2009)].

Cross References

Penalty for possession of deadly weapon described in this section within State Capitol, legislative offices, etc., see Penal Code § 171c.
Possession of deadly weapons with intent to assault, see Penal Code § 17500.

§ 16350. Capacity to accept more than 10 rounds defined

As used in Section 30515, "capacity to accept more than 10 rounds" means capable of accommodating more than 10 rounds. The term does not apply to a feeding device that has been permanently altered so that it cannot accommodate more than 10 rounds. *(Added by Stats.2010, c. 711 (S.B.1080), § 6, operative Jan. 1, 2012.)*

Law Revision Commission Comments

Section 16350 continues former Section 12276.1(d)(2) without substantive change. [38 Cal.L.Rev.Comm. Reports 217 (2009)].

§ 16360. CCW defined

As used in this part, "CCW" means "carry concealed weapons." *(Added by Stats.2010, c. 711 (S.B.1080), § 6, operative Jan. 1, 2012.)*

Law Revision Commission Comments

Section 16360 continues former Section 12027(a)(1)(E) without substantive change. [38 Cal.L.Rev.Comm. Reports 217 (2009)].

§ 16370. Certified instructor or DOJ Certified Instructor defined

As used in Sections 31610 to 31700, inclusive, "certified instructor" or "DOJ Certified Instructor" means a person designated as a handgun safety instructor by the Department of Justice pursuant to subdivision (a) of Section 31635. *(Added by Stats.2010, c. 711 (S.B.1080), § 6, operative Jan. 1, 2012.)*

Law Revision Commission Comments

Section 16370 continues former Section 12801(a)(2) without substantive change. [38 Cal.L.Rev.Comm. Reports 217 (2009)].

Cross References

Handgun defined for purposes of this Part, see Penal Code § 16640.

§ 16380. Chamber load indicator defined

As used in this part, "chamber load indicator" means a device that plainly indicates that a cartridge is in the firing chamber. A device satisfies this definition if it is readily visible, has incorporated or adjacent explanatory text or graphics, or both, and is designed and intended to indicate to a reasonably foreseeable adult user of the pistol, without requiring the user to refer to a user's manual or any other resource other than the pistol itself, whether a cartridge is in the firing chamber. *(Added by Stats.2010, c. 711 (S.B.1080), § 6, operative Jan. 1, 2012.)*

Law Revision Commission Comments

Section 16380 continues former Section 12126(c) without substantive change. See also former Section 12130(d)(1)-(2), which used the same definition of "chamber load indicator." [38 Cal.L.Rev.Comm. Reports 217 (2009)].

Cross References

Pistol defined for purposes of this Part, see Penal Code § 16530.

§ 16400. Clear evidence of the person's identity and age defined

As used in this part, "clear evidence of the person's identity and age" means either of the following:

(a) A valid California driver's license.

(b) A valid California identification card issued by the Department of Motor Vehicles. *(Added by Stats.2010, c. 711 (S.B.1080), § 6, operative Jan. 1, 2012.)*

Law Revision Commission Comments

Section 16400 continues former Section 12071(c)(1) without substantive change. [38 Cal.L.Rev.Comm. Reports 217 (2009)].

§ 16405. Composite knuckles defined

As used in this part, "composite knuckles" means any device or instrument made wholly or partially of composite materials, other than a medically prescribed prosthetic, that is not metal knuckles, that is worn for purposes of offense or defense in or on the hand, and that either protects the wearer's hand while striking a blow or increases the force of impact from the blow or injury to the individual receiving the blow. *(Added by Stats.2010, c. 711 (S.B.1080), § 6, operative Jan. 1, 2012.)*

Law Revision Commission Comments

Section 16405 continues the second sentence of former Section 12020.1 without substantive change.

See Sections 16680 ("hard wooden knuckles"), 16920 ("metal knuckles"). [38 Cal.L.Rev.Comm. Reports 217 (2009)].

Cross References

Metal knuckles defined for purposes of this Part, see Penal Code § 16920.

§ 16410. Consultant-evaluator defined

As used in this part, "consultant-evaluator" means a consultant or evaluator who, in the course of that person's profession is loaned firearms from a person licensed pursuant to Chapter 44 (commencing with Section 921) of Title 18 of the United States Code and the regulations issued pursuant thereto, for research or evaluation, and has a current certificate of eligibility issued pursuant to Section 26710. *(Added by Stats.2010, c. 711 (S.B.1080), § 6, operative Jan. 1, 2012.)*

Law Revision Commission Comments

Section 16410 continues former Section 12001(s) without substantive change. [38 Cal.L.Rev.Comm. Reports 217 (2009)].

Cross References

Firearm defined for purposes of this Part, see Penal Code § 16520.

§ 16420. Dagger defined

Use of the term "dagger" is governed by Section 16470. *(Added by Stats.2010, c. 711 (S.B.1080), § 6, operative Jan. 1, 2012.)*

Law Revision Commission Comments

Section 16420 is new. It is intended to help persons locate the definition of "dagger," which is the same as the definition of "dirk." [38 Cal.L.Rev.Comm. Reports 217 (2009)].

§ 16430. Deadly weapon defined

As used in Division 4 (commencing with Section 18250) of Title 2, "deadly weapon" means any weapon, the possession or concealed carrying of which is prohibited by any provision listed in Section 16590. *(Added by Stats.2010, c. 711 (S.B.1080), § 6, operative Jan. 1, 2012.)*

Law Revision Commission Comments

Section 16430 continues former Section 12028.5(a)(3) without substantive change. [38 Cal.L.Rev.Comm. Reports 217 (2009)].

§ 16440. Dealer defined

Use of the term "dealer" is governed by Section 26700. *(Added by Stats.2010, c. 711 (S.B.1080), § 6, operative Jan. 1, 2012.)*

Law Revision Commission Comments

Section 16440 is new. It is intended to help persons locate the definition of "dealer."

See also Section 16790 ("licensed gun dealer"). [38 Cal.L.Rev.Comm. Reports 217 (2009)].

§ 16450. Department defined

As used in Sections 31610 to 31700, inclusive, in Chapter 2 (commencing with Section 29030) of Division 7 of Title 4, and in Article 3 (commencing with Section 30345) of Chapter 1 of Division 10 of Title 4, "department" means the Department of Justice. *(Added by Stats.2010, c. 711 (S.B.1080), § 6, operative Jan. 1, 2012.)*

Law Revision Commission Comments

Section 16450 continues former Sections 12060(a), 12086(a)(2), and 12801(a)(1) without substantive change. [38 Cal.L.Rev.Comm. Reports 217 (2009)].

§ 16460. Destructive device defined

(a) As used in Sections 16510, 16520, and 16780, and in Chapter 1 (commencing with Section 18710) of Division 5 of Title 2, "destructive device" includes any of the following weapons:

(1) Any projectile containing any explosive or incendiary material or any other chemical substance, including, but not limited to, that which is commonly known as tracer or incendiary ammunition, except tracer ammunition manufactured for use in shotguns.

(2) Any bomb, grenade, explosive missile, or similar device or any launching device therefor.

(3) Any weapon of a caliber greater than 0.60 caliber which fires fixed ammunition, or any ammunition therefor, other than a shotgun (smooth or rifled bore) conforming to the definition of a "destructive device" found in subsection (b) of Section 479.11 of Title 27 of the Code of Federal Regulations, shotgun ammunition (single projectile or shot), antique rifle, or an antique cannon.

(4) Any rocket, rocket-propelled projectile, or similar device of a diameter greater than 0.60 inch, or any launching device therefor, and any rocket, rocket-propelled projectile, or similar device containing any explosive or incendiary material or any other chemical substance, other than the propellant for that device, except those

devices as are designed primarily for emergency or distress signaling purposes.

(5) Any breakable container that contains a flammable liquid with a flashpoint of 150 degrees Fahrenheit or less and has a wick or similar device capable of being ignited, other than a device which is commercially manufactured primarily for the purpose of illumination.

(6) Any sealed device containing dry ice (CO_2) or other chemically reactive substances assembled for the purpose of causing an explosion by a chemical reaction.

(b) A bullet containing or carrying an explosive agent is not a destructive device as that term is used in subdivision (a). *(Added by Stats.2010, c. 711 (S.B.1080), § 6, operative Jan. 1, 2012.)*

Law Revision Commission Comments

Subdivision (a) of Section 16460 continues former Section 12301(a)(1)-(2) & (4)-(6) without substantive change. Subdivision (a) also continues the first sentence of former Section 12301(a)(3) without substantive change. See also former Section 12601(b)(6) and the fourth sentence of former Section 12030(d), which used the same definition of "destructive device."

Subdivision (b) continues the second sentence of the second paragraph of former Section 12020(a)(4) without substantive change.

See Sections 16160 ("antique cannon"), 16180 ("antique rifle"), 16490 ("explosive"). [38 Cal.L.Rev.Comm. Reports 217 (2009)].

Cross References

Explosives defined, limits, see Health and Safety Code § 12000.
Firearms, records necessary to identify persons coming within Welfare and Institutions Code §§ 8100 or 8103, availability to Department of Justice, see Welfare and Institutions Code § 8104.
Fireworks and pyrotechnic devices, application of provisions, arms and handguns defined as firearms by the Federal Gun Control Act, see Health and Safety Code § 12540.
Penalty for possession of deadly weapon described in this section within State Capitol, legislative offices, etc., see Penal Code § 171c.
Possession of deadly weapons with intent to assault, see Penal Code § 17500.

Research References

California Jury Instructions - Criminal 12.56, Explosive/Destructive Device—Defined.
2 Witkin, California Criminal Law 4th Crimes Against Public Peace and Welfare § 225 (2021), In General.
1 Witkin California Criminal Law 4th Crimes Against the Person § 147 (2021), Killing by Destructive Device or Explosive.

§ 16470. Dirk defined; dagger defined

As used in this part, "dirk" or "dagger" means a knife or other instrument with or without a handguard that is capable of ready use as a stabbing weapon that may inflict great bodily injury or death. A nonlocking folding knife, a folding knife that is not prohibited by Section 21510, or a pocketknife is capable of ready use as a stabbing weapon that may inflict great bodily injury or death only if the blade of the knife is exposed and locked into position. *(Added by Stats.2010, c. 711 (S.B.1080), § 6, operative Jan. 1, 2012.)*

Law Revision Commission Comments

Section 16470 continues former Section 12020(c)(24) without substantive change. See also former Section 12028(a), which referred to former Section 12020. [38 Cal.L.Rev.Comm. Reports 217 (2009)].

Cross References

Penalty for possession of deadly weapon described in this section within State Capitol, legislative offices, etc., see Penal Code § 171c.
Possession of deadly weapons with intent to assault, see Penal Code § 17500.
Unlawful concealed carrying of dirk or dagger deemed nuisance, see Penal Code § 21390.

Research References

California Jury Instructions - Criminal 12.41, Carrying a Concealed Dagger or Explosive Substance—Weapon Defined.
2 Witkin, California Criminal Law 4th Crimes Against Public Peace and Welfare § 213 (2021), Concealed Dirk, Dagger, or Explosives.
1 Witkin California Criminal Law 4th Introduction to Crimes § 54 (2021), In General.

§ 16480. DOJ Certified Instructor defined

Use of the term "DOJ Certified Instructor" is governed by Section 16370. *(Added by Stats.2010, c. 711 (S.B.1080), § 6, operative Jan. 1, 2012.)*

Law Revision Commission Comments

Section 16480 is new. It is intended to help persons locate the definition of "DOJ Certified Instructor," which is the same as the definition of "certified instructor." [38 Cal.L.Rev.Comm. Reports 217 (2009)].

§ 16490. Domestic violence defined

As used in this part, "domestic violence" means abuse perpetrated against any of the following persons:

(a) A spouse or former spouse.

(b) A cohabitant or former cohabitant, as defined in Section 6209 of the Family Code.

(c) A person with whom the respondent is having or has had a dating or engagement relationship.

(d) A person with whom the respondent has had a child, where the presumption applies that the male parent is the father of the child of the female parent under the Uniform Parentage Act (Part 3 (commencing with Section 7600) of Division 12 of the Family Code).

(e) A child of a party or a child who is the subject of an action under the Uniform Parentage Act, where the presumption applies that the male parent is the father of the child to be protected.

(f) Any other person related by consanguinity or affinity within the second degree. *(Added by Stats.2010, c. 711 (S.B.1080), § 6, operative Jan. 1, 2012.)*

Law Revision Commission Comments

Section 16490 continues former Section 12028.5(a)(2) without substantive change. [38 Cal.L.Rev.Comm. Reports 217 (2009)].

§ 16500. Drop safety requirement for handguns defined

Use of the phrase "drop safety requirement for handguns" is governed by Section 31900. *(Added by Stats.2010, c. 711 (S.B.1080), § 6, operative Jan. 1, 2012.)*

Law Revision Commission Comments

Section 16500 is new. It is intended to help persons locate the definition of "drop safety requirement for handguns." [38 Cal.L.Rev.Comm. Reports 217 (2009)].

Cross References

Handgun defined for purposes of this Part, see Penal Code § 16640.

§ 16505. Encasement defined

For purposes of Chapter 7 (commencing with Section 26400) of Division 5 of Title 4, a firearm is "encased" when that firearm is enclosed in a case that is expressly made for the purpose of containing a firearm and that is completely zipped, snapped, buckled, tied, or otherwise fastened with no part of that firearm exposed. *(Added by Stats.2012, c. 700 (A.B.1527), § 4.)*

§ 16510. Explosive defined

As used in subdivision (a) of Section 16460 and Chapter 1 (commencing with Section 18710) of Division 5 of Title 2, "explosive" means any substance, or combination of substances, the primary or common purpose of which is detonation or rapid combustion, and which is capable of a relatively instantaneous or rapid release of gas and heat, or any substance, the primary purpose of which, when combined with others, is to form a substance capable of a relatively instantaneous or rapid release of gas and heat. "Explosive" includes, but is not limited to, any explosive as defined in Section 841 of Title 18 of the United States Code and published pursuant to Section 555.23 of Title 27 of the Code of Federal Regulations, and any of the following:

(a) Dynamite, nitroglycerine, picric acid, lead azide, fulminate of mercury, black powder, smokeless powder, propellant explosives, detonating primers, blasting caps, or commercial boosters.

(b) Substances determined to be division 1.1, 1.2, 1.3, or 1.6 explosives as classified by the United States Department of Transportation.

(c) Nitro carbo nitrate substances (blasting agent) classified as division 1.5 explosives by the United States Department of Transportation.

(d) Any material designated as an explosive by the State Fire Marshal. The designation shall be made pursuant to the classification standards established by the United States Department of Transportation. The State Fire Marshal shall adopt regulations in accordance with the Government Code to establish procedures for the classification and designation of explosive materials or explosive devices that are not under the jurisdiction of the United States Department of Transportation pursuant to provisions of Section 841 of Title 18 of the United States Code and published pursuant to Section 555.23 of Title 27 of the Code of Federal Regulations that define explosives.

(e) Certain division 1.4 explosives as designated by the United States Department of Transportation when listed in regulations adopted by the State Fire Marshal.

(f) As used in Section 16460 and Chapter 1 (commencing with Section 18710) of Division 5 of Title 2, "explosive" does not include any destructive device, nor does it include ammunition or small arms primers manufactured for use in shotguns, rifles, and pistols. *(Added by Stats.2010, c. 711 (S.B.1080), § 6, operative Jan. 1, 2012.)*

Law Revision Commission Comments

Section 16510 continues former Section 12301(b) without substantive change. To make the provision more easily understandable, the definition of "explosive" in Health and Safety Code Section 12000 is repeated in Section 16510, rather than incorporated by reference as it was in the past. Case law construing the definition in Health and Safety Code Section 12000 is relevant in construing Section 16510.

See Section 16460 ("destructive device"). [38 Cal.L.Rev.Comm. Reports 217 (2009)].

Cross References

Firearms, records necessary to identify persons coming within Welfare and Institutions Code §§ 8100 or 8103, availability to Department of Justice, see Welfare and Institutions Code § 8104.
Fireworks and pyrotechnic devices, application of provisions, see Health and Safety Code § 12540.
Murder, degrees, destructive device, application of definition, see Penal Code § 189.
Pistol defined for purposes of this Part, see Penal Code § 16530.

Research References

California Jury Instructions - Criminal 12.56, Explosive/Destructive Device—Defined.
2 Witkin, California Criminal Law 4th Crimes Against Public Peace and Welfare § 225 (2021), In General.

§ 16515. Federal licensee authorized to serialize firearms defined

"Federal licensee authorized to serialize firearms" means a person, firm, corporation, or other entity that holds any valid federal firearms license that authorizes the person, firm, corporation, or other entity to imprint serial numbers onto firearms pursuant to Chapter 44 (commencing with Section 921) of Title 18 of the United States Code and regulations issued pursuant thereto. *(Added by Stats.2022, c. 76 (A.B.1621), § 3, eff. June 30, 2022.)*

§ 16517. Federally licensed manufacturer or importer defined

"Federally licensed manufacturer or importer" means a person, firm, corporation, or other entity that holds a valid license to manufacture or import firearms issued pursuant to Chapter 44 (commencing with Section 921) of Title 18 of the United States Code and regulations issued pursuant thereto. *(Added by Stats.2022, c. 76 (A.B.1621), § 4, eff. June 30, 2022.)*

§ 16519. Federally regulated firearm precursor part defined

"Federally regulated firearm precursor part" means any firearm precursor part deemed to be a firearm pursuant to Chapter 44 (commencing with Section 921) of Title 18 of the United States Code and regulations issued pursuant thereto, and, if required, has been imprinted with a serial number by a federal licensee authorized to serialize firearms in compliance with all applicable federal laws and regulations. *(Added by Stats.2022, c. 76 (A.B.1621), § 5, eff. June 30, 2022.)*

§ 16520. Firearm defined

(a) As used in this part, "firearm" means a device, designed to be used as a weapon, from which is expelled through a barrel, a projectile by the force of an explosion or other form of combustion.

(b) As used in the following provisions, "firearm" includes the frame or receiver of the weapon, including both a completed frame or receiver, or a firearm precursor part:

(1) Section 136.2.

(2) Section 646.91.

(3) Sections 16515 and 16517.

(4) Section 16550.

(5) Section 16730.

(6) Section 16960.

(7) Section 16990.

(8) Section 17070.

(9) Section 17310.

(10) Sections 18100 to 18500, inclusive.

(11) Section 23690.

(12) Section 23900 to 23925, inclusive.

(13) Sections 26500 to 26590, inclusive.

(14) Sections 26600 to 27140, inclusive.

(15) Sections 27200 to 28490, inclusive.

* * *

(16) Sections 29010 to 29150, inclusive.

(17) Section 29185.

(18) Sections 29610 to 29750, inclusive.

(19) Sections 29800 to 29905, inclusive.

(20) Sections 30150 to 30165, inclusive.

(21) Section 31615.

(22) Sections 31700 to 31830, inclusive.

(23) Sections 34355 to 34370, inclusive.

(24) Sections 527.6 to 527.9, inclusive, of the Code of Civil Procedure.

(25) Sections 8100 * * * to 8108, inclusive, of the Welfare and Institutions Code.

(26) Section 15657.03 of the Welfare and Institutions Code.

(c) As used in the following provisions, "firearm" also includes a rocket, rocket propelled projectile launcher, or similar device containing an explosive or incendiary material, whether or not the device is designed for emergency or distress signaling purposes:

(1) Section 16750.

(2) Subdivision (b) of Section 16840.

(3) Section 25400.

(4) Sections 25850 to 26025, inclusive.

(5) Subdivisions (a), (b), and (c) of Section 26030.

(6) Sections 26035 to 26055, inclusive.

(d) As used in the following provisions, "firearm" does not include an unloaded antique firearm:

(1) Section 16730.

(2) Section 16550.

(3) Section 16960.

(4) Section 17310.

(5) Subdivision (b) of Section 23920.

(6) Section 25135.

(7) Chapter 6 (commencing with Section 26350) of Division 5 of Title 4.

(8) Chapter 7 (commencing with Section 26400) of Division 5 of Title 4.

(9) Sections 26500 to 26588, inclusive.

(10) Sections 26700 to 26915, inclusive.

(11) Section 27510.

(12) Section 27530.

(13) Section 27540.

(14) Section 27545.

(15) Sections 27555 to 27585, inclusive.

(16) Sections 29010 to 29150, inclusive.

* * *

(17) Section 29180.

(e) As used in Sections 34005 and 34010, "firearm" does not include a destructive device.

(f) As used in Sections 17280 and 24680, "firearm" has the same meaning as in Section 922 of Title 18 of the United States Code.

(g) As used in Sections 29180 to 29184, inclusive, "firearm" includes the completed frame or receiver of a weapon * * *.

* * * *(Added by Stats.2021, c. 682 (A.B.1057), § 3, eff. Jan. 1, 2022, operative July 1, 2022. Amended by Stats.2022, c. 76 (A.B.1621), § 6, eff. June 30, 2022.)*

Cross References

Age verification when selling products that are illegal to sell to minor, reasonable steps, products requiring age verification, penalties, see Civil Code § 1798.99.1.

Antique firearm defined, see Penal Code § 16170.

Destructive device defined, see Penal Code § 16460.

Drawing, exhibiting, or using firearm or deadly weapon except in self defense, see Penal Code § 417.

Firearms, records necessary to identify persons coming within Welfare and Institutions Code §§ 8100 or 8103, availability to Department of Justice, see Welfare and Institutions Code § 8104.

Imitation firearms, purchasing, selling, manufacturing, shipping, transporting, distributing, or receiving for commercial purposes prohibited, civil fines, exceptions, see Penal Code § 20165.

Manufacture, sale or possession of imitation firearms, exclusive regulation by Legislature, see Government Code § 53071.5.

Nuisance caused by illegal conduct involving unlawful weapons or ammunition purpose, unlawful detainer action, see Civil Code § 3485.

Penalty for possession of deadly weapon described in this section within State Capitol, legislative offices, etc., see Penal Code § 171c.

Possession of BB devices in game refuges, notice to department, see Fish and Game Code § 10506.

Possession of deadly weapons with intent to assault, see Penal Code § 17500.

Possession of prohibited items in sterile area of public transit facility, firearm defined as specified in this section, see Penal Code § 171.7.

Pupil safety, injurious objects, see Education Code § 49330.

Use of BB devices for hunting while intoxicated, prohibition, see Fish and Game Code § 3001.

Research References

California Jury Instructions - Criminal 12.48, Firearm [Capable of Being Concealed]—Defined.

2 Witkin, California Criminal Law 4th Crimes Against Governmental Authority § 27 (2021), False Reports of Crime.

2 Witkin, California Criminal Law 4th Crimes Against Governmental Authority § 29 (2021), Other False Reports.

2 Witkin, California Criminal Law 4th Crimes Against Public Peace and Welfare § 190 (2021), In General.

2 Witkin, California Criminal Law 4th Crimes Against Public Peace and Welfare § 192 (2021), In General.

2 Witkin, California Criminal Law 4th Crimes Against Public Peace and Welfare § 193 (2021), Sale, Lease, or Transfer by Unlicensed Person.

2 Witkin, California Criminal Law 4th Crimes Against Public Peace and Welfare § 195 (2021), In General.

2 Witkin, California Criminal Law 4th Crimes Against Public Peace and Welfare § 202 (2021), License to Manufacture.

2 Witkin, California Criminal Law 4th Crimes Against Public Peace and Welfare § 205 (2021), Concealment and Possession.

2 Witkin, California Criminal Law 4th Crimes Against Public Peace and Welfare § 232 (2021), Nature and Scope of Statutes.

2 Witkin, California Criminal Law 4th Crimes Against Public Peace and Welfare § 249 (2021), Offenses.

2 Witkin, California Criminal Law 4th Crimes Against Public Peace and Welfare § 253 (2021), Openly Displaying or Carrying Imitation or Unloaded Firearm.

2 Witkin, California Criminal Law 4th Crimes Against Public Peace and Welfare § 253A (2021), (New) Carrying Unloaded Firearm that is Not Handgun in Incorporated Area or Other Public Place.

2 Witkin, California Criminal Law 4th Crimes Against Public Peace and Welfare § 257 (2021), Firearms.

2 Witkin, California Criminal Law 4th Crimes Against Public Peace and Welfare § 262 (2021), Criminal Storage of Firearm.

3 Witkin, California Criminal Law 4th Punishment § 363 (2021), What is Firearm or Weapon.

§ 16530. Firearm capable of being concealed upon the person defined; pistol defined; revolver defined

(a) As used in this part, the terms "firearm capable of being concealed upon the person," "pistol," and "revolver" apply to and include any device designed to be used as a weapon, from which is expelled a projectile by the force of any explosion, or other form of combustion, and that has a barrel less than 16 inches in length. These terms also include any device that has a barrel 16 inches or more in length which is designed to be interchanged with a barrel less than 16 inches in length.

(b) Nothing shall prevent a device defined as a "firearm capable of being concealed upon the person," "pistol," or "revolver" from also being found to be a short-barreled rifle or a short-barreled shotgun. *(Added by Stats.2010, c. 711 (S.B.1080), § 6, operative Jan. 1, 2012.)*

Law Revision Commission Comments

Subdivision (a) of Section 16530 continues former Section 12001(a)(1) without substantive change. See also former Sections 12126(e), 12323(a), and 12601(b)(1), and the introductory clause of former Section 12126, all of which referred to the definition in Section 12001.

With respect to a "firearm capable of being concealed upon the person," "pistol," and "revolver," subdivision (b) continues former Section 12001(f) without substantive change. See also Section 16640(b), which continues former Section 12001(f) with respect to a "handgun."

See Sections 16520 ("firearm"), 17170 ("short-barreled rifle"), 17180 ("short-barreled shotgun"). See also Section 16640 ("handgun" means "any pistol, revolver, or firearm capable of being concealed upon the person"). [38 Cal.L.Rev.Comm. Reports 217 (2009)].

Cross References

Firearm defined for purposes of this Part, see Penal Code § 16520.

Rifle defined, see Penal Code § 17090.
Short-barreled rifle defined, see Penal Code § 17170.
Short-barreled shotgun defined, see Penal Code § 17180.
Shotgun defined, see Penal Code § 17190.
Unlawful carrying and possession of concealed firearm, see Penal Code § 25400.

Research References

California Jury Instructions - Criminal 12.48, Firearm [Capable of Being Concealed]—Defined.
2 Witkin, California Criminal Law 4th Crimes Against Public Peace and Welfare § 190 (2021), In General.
2 Witkin, California Criminal Law 4th Crimes Against Public Peace and Welfare § 205 (2021), Concealment and Possession.
2 Witkin, California Criminal Law 4th Crimes Against Public Peace and Welfare § 211 (2021), Nature of Crime.

§ 16531. Firearm precursor part defined

* * * (a) "Firearm precursor part" means any forging, casting, printing, extrusion, machined body or similar article that has reached a stage in manufacture where it may readily be completed, assembled or converted to be used as the frame or receiver of a functional firearm, or that is marketed or sold to the public to become or be used as the frame or receiver of a functional firearm once completed, assembled or converted.

(b) The Department of Justice, consistent with this section, shall provide written guidance and pictorial diagrams demonstrating * * * examples of firearm precursor * * * parts.

(c) Firearm parts that can only be used on antique firearms, as defined in subdivision (c) of Section 16170, are not firearm precursor parts.

* * * *(Added by Stats.2019, c. 730 (A.B.879), § 2, eff. Jan. 1, 2020. Amended by Stats.2022, c. 76 (A.B.1621), § 7, eff. June 30, 2022.)*

Research References

2 Witkin, California Criminal Law 4th Crimes Against Public Peace and Welfare § 196 (2021), Transfers to Specified Persons.
2 Witkin, California Criminal Law 4th Crimes Against Public Peace and Welfare § 232 (2021), Nature and Scope of Statutes.
2 Witkin, California Criminal Law 4th Crimes Against Public Peace and Welfare § 263 (2021), Nuisances.
3 Witkin, California Criminal Law 4th Punishment § 190 (2021), Noncriminal Actions.

§ 16535. Firearm safety certificate defined

(a) As used in this part, "firearm safety certificate" means a certificate issued by the Department of Justice pursuant to Sections 31610 to 31700, inclusive, or pursuant to former Article 8 (commencing with Section 12800) of Chapter 6 of Title 2 of Part 4, as that article was operative at any time from January 1, 2003, until it was repealed by the Deadly Weapons Recodification Act of 2010.

(b) This section shall become operative on January 1, 2015. *(Added by Stats.2013, c. 761 (S.B.683), § 1, operative Jan. 1, 2015.)*

§ 16540. Firearm safety device defined

As used in this part, "firearm safety device" means a device other than a gun safe that locks and is designed to prevent children and unauthorized users from firing a firearm. The device may be installed on a firearm, be incorporated into the design of the firearm, or prevent access to the firearm. *(Added by Stats.2010, c. 711 (S.B.1080), § 6, operative Jan. 1, 2012. Amended by Stats.2013, c. 737 (A.B.500), § 3; Stats.2014, c. 103 (A.B.1798), § 4, eff. Jan. 1, 2015.)*

Law Revision Commission Comments

Section 16540 continues former Section 12087.6(a) without substantive change.

See Sections 16520 ("firearm"), 16610 ("gun safe"). [38 Cal.L.Rev.Comm. Reports 217 (2009)].

Section 16540 is amended to expressly apply the definition of "firearm safety device" to the whole of Part 6. This amendment does not effect a substantive change because all of the provisions in Part 6 that use the term "firearm safety device" use it with the meaning provided in this section. See, e.g., Sections 26850, 26853, 26856, 26859, and 26915.

Note. The proposed amendment to Section 16540 incorporates a revision made by 2013 Cal. Stat. ch. 737, § 3 (AB 500 (Ammiano)), which will become operative on January 1, 2014. See Cal. Const. art. IV, § 8(c)(1); Gov't Code § 9600(a). [43 Cal.L.Rev.Comm. Reports 63 (2013)].

Cross References

Firearm defined for purposes of this Part, see Penal Code § 16520.
Gun safe defined for purposes of this Part, see Penal Code § 16610.

Research References

2 Witkin, California Criminal Law 4th Crimes Against Public Peace and Welfare § 191 (2021), Safety Devices.
2 Witkin, California Criminal Law 4th Crimes Against Public Peace and Welfare § 262 (2021), Criminal Storage of Firearm.

§ 16550. Firearm transaction record defined

As used in this part, "firearm transaction record" is a record containing the same information referred to in subdivision (a) of Section 478.124, Section 478.124a, and subdivision (e) of Section 478.125 of Title 27 of the Code of Federal Regulations. *(Added by Stats.2010, c. 711 (S.B.1080), § 6, operative Jan. 1, 2012.)*

Law Revision Commission Comments

Section 16550 continues former Section 12071(c)(4)(A) without substantive change. [38 Cal.L.Rev.Comm. Reports 217 (2009)].

Cross References

Firearm defined for purposes of this Part, see Penal Code § 16520.

§ 16560. Firing requirement for handguns defined

Use of the phrase "firing requirement for handguns" is governed by Section 31905. *(Added by Stats.2010, c. 711 (S.B.1080), § 6, operative Jan. 1, 2012.)*

Law Revision Commission Comments

Section 16560 is new. It is intended to help persons locate the definition of "firing requirement for handguns." [38 Cal.L.Rev.Comm. Reports 217 (2009)].

Cross References

Handgun defined for purposes of this Part, see Penal Code § 16640.

§ 16570. Flechette dart defined

As used in this part, "flechette dart" means a dart, capable of being fired from a firearm, that measures approximately one inch in length, with tail fins that take up approximately five-sixteenths of an inch of the body. *(Added by Stats.2010, c. 711 (S.B.1080), § 6, operative Jan. 1, 2012.)*

Law Revision Commission Comments

Section 16570 continues former Section 12020(c)(6) without substantive change.

See Section 16520 ("firearm"). [38 Cal.L.Rev.Comm. Reports 217 (2009)].

Cross References

Firearm defined for purposes of this Part, see Penal Code § 16520.

§ 16575. Continuation of prior law; former Article 4 of Chapter 1 provisions

(a) Except as stated in subdivision (c), the following provisions are continuations of provisions that were included in former Article 4 (commencing with Section 12070) of Chapter 1 of Title 2 of Part 4, entitled "Licenses to Sell Firearms," when that article was repealed by the Deadly Weapons Recodification Act of 2010:

(1) Section 16130.

(2) Subdivision (b) of Section 16170, to the extent that it continues former Sections 12078 and 12085, as those sections read when they were repealed by the Deadly Weapons Recodification Act of 2010.

(3) Section 16230.

(4) Section 16400.

(5) Section 16450, to the extent that it continues subdivision (a) of former Section 12086, as that subdivision read when it was repealed by the Deadly Weapons Recodification Act of 2010.

(6) Subdivisions (b) and (d) of Section 16520, to the extent that they continue subdivision (e) of former Section 12085, as that subdivision read when it was repealed by the Deadly Weapons Recodification Act of 2010.

(7) Subdivision (g) of Section 16520.

(8) Section 16550.

(9) Section 16620.

(10) Section 16720.

(11) Section 16730.

(12) Section 16740, to the extent that it continues subdivision (b) of former Section 12079, as that subdivision read when it was repealed by the Deadly Weapons Recodification Act of 2010.

(13) Section 16800.

(14) Section 16810.

(15) Section 16960.

(16) Section 16990.

(17) Section 17110.

(18) Section 17310.

(19) Sections 26500 to 26588, inclusive.

(20) Sections 26600 to 29150, inclusive.

(21) Chapter 2 (commencing with Section 29500) of Division 8 of Title 4.

(22) Section 30105.

(23) Sections 30150 to 30165, inclusive.

(24) Sections 31705 to 31830, inclusive.

(25) Section 32315.

(26) Section 34205.

(27) Sections 34350 to 34370, inclusive.

(b) Except as stated in subdivision (c), the provisions listed in subdivision (a) may be referred to as "former Article 4 of Chapter 1 provisions."

(c) Subdivision (a) does not include any provision that was first codified in one of the specified numerical ranges after the effective date of the Deadly Weapons Recodification Act of 2010. *(Added by Stats.2010, c. 711 (S.B.1080), § 6, operative Jan. 1, 2012.)*

Law Revision Commission Comments

Section 16575 is new. It provides a convenient means of referring to former Sections 12070–12086.

For a disposition table showing where each provision in former Sections 12070–12086 was recodified, see *Nonsubstantive Reorganization of Deadly Weapon Statutes*, 38 Cal.L.Rev.Comm. Reports 217 (2009). [38 Cal.L.Rev. Comm. Reports 217 (2009)].

§ 16580. Continuation of prior law; former Chapter 1 provisions

(a) Except as stated in subdivision (c), the following provisions are continuations of provisions that were included in former Chapter 1 (commencing with Section 12000) of Title 2 of Part 4, entitled "Firearms," when that chapter was repealed by the Deadly Weapons Recodification Act of 2010:

(1) Sections 12001 to 12022.95, inclusive.

(2) Sections 16120 to 16140, inclusive.

(3) Subdivision (b) of Section 16170, to the extent it continues former Sections 12001, 12060, 12078, 12085, and 12088.8, as those sections read when they were repealed by the Deadly Weapons Recodification Act of 2010.

(4) Subdivision (c) of Section 16170.

(5) Section 16190.

(6) Sections 16220 to 16240, inclusive.

(7) Section 16250, to the extent it continues former Section 12001, as that section read when it was repealed by the Deadly Weapons Recodification Act of 2010.

(8) Section 16260.

(9) Sections 16320 to 16340, inclusive.

(10) Section 16360.

(11) Sections 16400 to 16410, inclusive.

(12) Section 16430.

(13) Section 16450, to the extent it continues former Sections 12060 and 12086, as those sections read when they were repealed by the Deadly Weapons Recodification Act of 2010.

(14) Subdivision (b) of Section 16460.

(15) Section 16470.

(16) Section 16490.

(17) Subdivision (a) of Section 16520, to the extent it continues former Section 12001, as that section read when it was repealed by the Deadly Weapons Recodification Act of 2010.

(18) Subdivisions (b) to (g), inclusive, of Section 16520.

(19) Sections 16530 to 16550, inclusive.

(20) Section 16570.

(21) Sections 16600 to 16640, inclusive.

(22) Section 16650, to the extent it continues former Section 12060, as that section read when it was repealed by the Deadly Weapons Recodification Act of 2010.

(23) Section 16662, to the extent it continues former Section 12060, as that section read when it was repealed by the Deadly Weapons Recodification Act of 2010.

(24) Sections 16670 to 16690, inclusive.

(25) Sections 16720 to 16760, inclusive.

(26) Sections 16800 and 16810.

(27) Sections 16830 to 16870, inclusive.

(28) Sections 16920 to 16960, inclusive.

(29) Sections 16990 and 17000.

(30) Sections 17020 to 17070, inclusive.

(31) Section 17090, to the extent it continues former Section 12020, as that section read when it was repealed by the Deadly Weapons Recodification Act of 2010.

(32) Section 17110.

(33) Section 17125.

(34) Section 17160.

(35) Sections 17170 to 17200, inclusive.

(36) Sections 17270 to 17290, inclusive.

(37) Sections 17310 and 17315.

(38) Sections 17330 to 17505, inclusive.

(39) Sections 17515 to 18500, inclusive.

(40) Sections 19100 to 19290, inclusive.

(41) Sections 20200 to 21390, inclusive.

(42) Sections 21790 to 22490, inclusive.

(43) Sections 23500 to 30290, inclusive.

(44) Sections 30345 to 30365, inclusive.

(45) Sections 31500 to 31590, inclusive.

(46) Sections 31705 to 31830, inclusive.

(47) Sections 32310 to 32450, inclusive.

(48) Sections 32900 to 33320, inclusive.

(49) Sections 33600 to 34370, inclusive.

(b) Except as stated in subdivision (c), the provisions listed in subdivision (a) may be referred to as "former Chapter 1 provisions."

(c) Subdivision (a) does not include any provision that was first codified in one of the specified numerical ranges after the effective date of the Deadly Weapons Recodification Act of 2010. *(Added by Stats.2010, c. 711 (S.B.1080), § 6, operative Jan. 1, 2012.)*

Law Revision Commission Comments

Section 16580 is new. It provides a convenient means of referring to former Sections 12000–12101.

For a disposition table showing where each provision in former Sections 12000–12101 was recodified, see *Nonsubstantive Reorganization of Deadly Weapon Statutes*, 38 Cal.L.Rev.Comm. Reports 217 (2009). [38 Cal.L.Rev. Comm. Reports 217 (2009)].

Research References

2 Witkin, California Criminal Law 4th Crimes Against Public Peace and Welfare § 204 (2021), Punishment.
2 Witkin, California Criminal Law 4th Crimes Against Public Peace and Welfare § 208 (2021), Exempt Activities.
2 Witkin, California Criminal Law 4th Crimes Against Public Peace and Welfare § 250 (2021), Punishment.
2 Witkin, California Criminal Law 4th Crimes Against Public Peace and Welfare § 257 (2021), Firearms.

§ 16585. Continuation of prior law; former Section 12078 provisions

(a) Except as stated in subdivision (d), the following provisions are continuations of provisions that were included in former Section 12078, as that section read when it was repealed by the Deadly Weapons Recodification Act of 2010:

(1) Subdivision (b) of Section 16170, as it pertains to former Section 12078, as that section read when it was repealed by the Deadly Weapons Recodification Act of 2010.

(2) Section 16720.

(3) Subdivision (a) of Section 16730, as it pertains to former Section 12078, as that section read when it was repealed by the Deadly Weapons Recodification Act of 2010.

(4) Subdivision (b) of Section 16730.

(5) Section 16990.

(6) Sections 26600 to 26615, inclusive.

(7) Sections 26950 to 27140, inclusive.

(8) Sections 27400 to 27415, inclusive.

(9) Subdivision (b) of Section 27505, as it pertains to former Section 12078, as that section read when it was repealed by the Deadly Weapons Recodification Act of 2010.

(10) Sections 27600 to 28000, inclusive.

(11) Sections 28400 to 28415, inclusive.

(12) Sections 30150 to 30165, inclusive.

(13) Sections 31705 to 31830, inclusive.

(14) Sections 34355 to 34370, inclusive.

(b) Except as stated in subdivision (d), the provisions listed in subdivision (a) may be referred to as "former Section 12078 provisions."

(c) Except as stated in subdivision (d), the following provisions are continuations of provisions that were included in subdivision (a) of former Section 12078, as that subdivision read when it was repealed by the Deadly Weapons Recodification Act of 2010:

(1) Sections 26600 to 26615, inclusive.

(2) Section 26950.

(3) Sections 27050 to 27065, inclusive.

(4) Sections 27400 to 27415, inclusive.

(5) Sections 27600 to 27615, inclusive.

(6) Section 27650.

(7) Sections 27850 to 27860, inclusive.

(8) Sections 28400 to 28415, inclusive.

(9) Sections 30150 to 30165, inclusive.

(10) Sections 31705 to 31735, inclusive.

(11) Sections 34355 to 34370, inclusive.

(d) Subdivisions (a) and (c) do not include any provision that was first codified in one of the specified numerical ranges after the effective date of the Deadly Weapons Recodification Act of 2010. *(Added by Stats.2010, c. 711 (S.B.1080), § 6, operative Jan. 1, 2012.)*

Law Revision Commission Comments

Section 16585 is new. It provides a convenient means of referring to the provisions that comprised former Section 12078.

For a disposition table showing where each provision in former Section 12078 was recodified, see *Nonsubstantive Recodification of Deadly Weapon Statutes*, 38 Cal.L.Rev.Comm. Reports 217 (2009). [38 Cal.L.Rev.Comm. Reports 217 (2009)].

§ 16590. Generally prohibited weapon defined

As used in this part, "generally prohibited weapon" means any of the following:

(a) An air gauge knife, as prohibited by Section 20310.

(b) Ammunition that contains or consists of a flechette dart, as prohibited by Section 30210.

(c) A ballistic knife, as prohibited by Section 21110.

(d) A belt buckle knife, as prohibited by Section 20410.

(e) A bullet containing or carrying an explosive agent, as prohibited by Section 30210.

(f) A camouflaging firearm container, as prohibited by Section 24310.

(g) A cane gun, as prohibited by Section 24410.

(h) A cane sword, as prohibited by Section 20510.

(i) A concealed dirk or dagger, as prohibited by Section 21310.

(j) A concealed explosive substance, other than fixed ammunition, as prohibited by Section 19100.

(k) A firearm that is not immediately recognizable as a firearm, as prohibited by Section 24510.

(*l*) A large-capacity magazine, as prohibited by Section 32310.

(m) A leaded cane or an instrument or weapon of the kind commonly known as a billy, blackjack, sandbag, sandclub, sap, or slungshot, as prohibited by Section 22210.

(n) A lipstick case knife, as prohibited by Section 20610.

(*o*) Metal knuckles, as prohibited by Section 21810.

(p) A metal military practice handgrenade or a metal replica handgrenade, as prohibited by Section 19200.

(q) A multiburst trigger activator, as prohibited by Section 32900.

(r) A shobi-zue, as prohibited by Section 20710.

(s) A short-barreled rifle or short-barreled shotgun, as prohibited by Section 33215.

(t) A shuriken, as prohibited by Section 22410.

(u) An unconventional pistol, as prohibited by Section 31500.

(v) An undetectable firearm, as prohibited by Section 24610.

(w) A wallet gun, as prohibited by Section 24710.

(x) A writing pen knife, as prohibited by Section 20910.

(y) A zip gun, as prohibited by Section 33600. *(Added by Stats.2010, c. 711 (S.B.1080), § 6, operative Jan. 1, 2012. Amended by Stats.2021, c. 434 (S.B.827), § 22, eff. Jan. 1, 2022.)*

Law Revision Commission Comments

Section 16590 is new. It defines the term "generally prohibited weapon" for drafting convenience. Each of the items listed in this section was formerly listed in subdivision (a) of former Section 12020.

See Sections 16140 ("air gauge knife"), 16220 ("ballistic knife"), 16260 ("belt buckle knife"), 16320 ("camouflaging firearm container"), 16330 ("cane gun"), 16340 ("cane sword"), 16470 ("dirk" or "dagger"), 16510 ("explosive"), 16520 ("firearm"), 16570 ("flechette dart"), 16740 ("large-capacity magazine"), 16760 ("leaded cane"), 16830 ("lipstick case knife"), 16920 ("metal knuckles"), 16930 ("multiburst trigger activator"), 16940 ("nunchaku"), 17160 ("shobi-zue"), 17170 ("short-barreled rifle"), 17180 ("short-barreled shotgun"), 17200 ("shuriken"), 17270 ("unconventional pistol"), 17280 ("undetectable firearm"), 17330 ("wallet gun"), 17350 ("writing pen knife"), 17360 ("zip gun"). [38 Cal.L.Rev.Comm. Reports 217 (2009)].

Cross References

Cane gun defined for purposes of this Part, see Penal Code § 16330.
Confidential information and records, disclosure, consent, comprehensive assessment, see Welfare and Institutions Code § 4514.
Crimes against person by or upon patient, see Welfare and Institutions Code § 5328.4.
Firearm defined for purposes of this Part, see Penal Code § 16520.
Firearms, possession, purchase or receipt by person receiving inpatient treatment for a mental disorder or who has communicated a threat of physical violence to a psychotherapist, violation, see Welfare and Institutions Code § 8100.
Fireworks and pyrotechnic devices, application of provisions, arms and handguns defined as firearms by the Federal Gun Control Act, see Health and Safety Code § 12540.
Fish and Game Commission, publication and distribution of regulations, printing contracts with private entities, see Fish and Game Code § 260.
Health facilities, security and safety assessment, development of security plan, security personnel, assault and battery reports to law enforcement, liability, violation, penalty, see Health and Safety Code § 1257.7.
Large-capacity magazine defined for purposes of this Part, see Penal Code § 16740.
Metal knuckles defined for purposes of this Part, see Penal Code § 16920.
Nunchaku defined for purposes of this Part, see Penal Code § 16940.
Pistol defined for purposes of this Part, see Penal Code § 16530.
Pupil safety, injurious objects, see Education Code § 49330.
Services for the developmentally disabled, confidential information and records, disclosure, see Welfare and Institutions Code § 4514.
Unconventional pistol defined for purposes of this Part, see Penal Code § 17270.
Undetectable firearm defined for purposes of this Part, see Penal Code § 17280.
Wallet gun defined for purposes of this Part, see Penal Code § 17330.
Zip gun defined for purposes of this Part, see Penal Code § 17360.

Research References

2 Witkin, California Criminal Law 4th Crimes Against Public Peace and Welfare § 189 (2021), In General.
2 Witkin, California Criminal Law 4th Crimes Against Public Peace and Welfare § 211 (2021), Nature of Crime.
2 Witkin, California Criminal Law 4th Crimes Against Public Peace and Welfare § 245 (2021), In General.

§ 16600. Great bodily injury defined

As used in Chapter 2 (commencing with Section 25100) of Division 4 of Title 4, "great bodily injury" means a significant or substantial physical injury. *(Added by Stats.2010, c. 711 (S.B.1080), § 6, operative Jan. 1, 2012.)*

Law Revision Commission Comments

Section 16600 continues former Section 12035(a)(4) without substantive change. To make the provision more easily understandable, the definition of "great bodily injury" in Section 12022.7 is repeated in Section 16600, rather than incorporated by reference as it was in the past. Case law construing the definition in Section 12022.7 is relevant in construing Section 16600. [38 Cal.L.Rev.Comm. Reports 217 (2009)].

Research References

2 Witkin, California Criminal Law 4th Crimes Against Public Peace and Welfare § 262 (2021), Criminal Storage of Firearm.

§ 16610. Gun safe defined

As used in this part, "gun safe" means a locking container that fully contains and secures one or more firearms, and that meets the standards for gun safes adopted pursuant to Section 23650. *(Added by Stats.2010, c. 711 (S.B.1080), § 6, operative Jan. 1, 2012.)*

Law Revision Commission Comments

Section 16610 continues former Section 12087.6(b) without substantive change.

See Section 16520 ("firearm"). [38 Cal.L.Rev.Comm. Reports 217 (2009)].

Cross References

Firearm defined for purposes of this Part, see Penal Code § 16520.

§ 16620. Gun Show Trader defined

As used in this part, "Gun Show Trader" means a person described in Section 26525. *(Added by Stats.2010, c. 711 (S.B.1080), § 6, operative Jan. 1, 2012.)*

Law Revision Commission Comments

Section 16620 continues the second paragraph of former Section 12070(b)(5) without substantive change. [38 Cal.L.Rev.Comm. Reports 217 (2009)].

§ 16630. Gunsmith defined

As used in this part, "gunsmith" means any person who is licensed as a dealer pursuant to Chapter 44 (commencing with Section 921) of Title 18 of the United States Code and the regulations issued pursuant thereto, who is engaged primarily in the business of repairing firearms, or making or fitting special barrels, stocks, or trigger mechanisms to firearms, or the agent or employee of that person. *(Added by Stats.2010, c. 711 (S.B.1080), § 6, operative Jan. 1, 2012.)*

Law Revision Commission Comments

Section 16630 continues former Section 12001(r) without substantive change.
See Section 16520 ("firearm"). [38 Cal.L.Rev.Comm. Reports 217 (2009)].

Cross References

Firearm defined for purposes of this Part, see Penal Code § 16520.

§ 16640. Handgun defined

(a) As used in this part, "handgun" means any pistol, revolver, or firearm capable of being concealed upon the person.

(b) Nothing shall prevent a device defined as a "handgun" from also being found to be a short-barreled rifle or a short-barreled shotgun. *(Added by Stats.2010, c. 711 (S.B.1080), § 6, operative Jan. 1, 2012.)*

Law Revision Commission Comments

Subdivision (a) of Section 16640 continues former Section 12001(a)(2) without substantive change. See Sections 16520 ("firearm"), 16530 ("firearm capable of being concealed upon the person," "pistol," and "revolver").

With respect to a "handgun," subdivision (b) continues former Section 12001(f) without substantive change. See also Section 16530(b), which continues former Section 12001(f) with respect to a "firearm capable of being concealed upon the person," "pistol," and "revolver."

See Sections 16520 ("firearm"), 16530 ("firearm capable of being concealed upon the person," "pistol," and "revolver"), 17170 ("short-barreled rifle"), 17180 ("short-barreled shotgun"). [38 Cal.L.Rev.Comm. Reports 217 (2009)].

Cross References

Age verification when selling products that are illegal to sell to minor, reasonable steps, products requiring age verification, penalties, see Civil Code § 1798.99.1.
Firearm capable of being concealed upon the person defined for purposes of this Part, see Penal Code § 16530.
Firearm defined for purposes of this Part, see Penal Code § 16520.
Pistol defined for purposes of this Part, see Penal Code § 16530.
Revolver defined for purposes of this Part, see Penal Code § 16530.
Rifle defined, see Penal Code § 17090.
Short-barreled rifle defined, see Penal Code § 17170.
Short-barreled shotgun defined, see Penal Code § 17180.
Shotgun defined, see Penal Code § 17190.
Unlawful carrying and possession of concealed firearm, see Penal Code § 25400.

Research References

2 Witkin, California Criminal Law 4th Crimes Against Public Peace and Welfare § 190 (2021), In General.
2 Witkin, California Criminal Law 4th Crimes Against Public Peace and Welfare § 197 (2021), Time and Manner of Delivery by Dealer.
2 Witkin, California Criminal Law 4th Crimes Against Public Peace and Welfare § 205 (2021), Concealment and Possession.

§ 16650. Handgun ammunition defined

(a) As used in this part, "handgun ammunition" means ammunition principally for use in pistols, revolvers, and other firearms capable of being concealed upon the person, notwithstanding that the ammunition may also be used in some rifles.

(b) As used in Section 30312 and in Article 3 (commencing with Section 30345) of Chapter 1 of Division 10 of Title 4, "handgun ammunition" does not include either of the following:

(1) Ammunition designed and intended to be used in an antique firearm.

(2) Blanks. *(Added by Stats.2010, c. 711 (S.B.1080), § 6, operative Jan. 1, 2012.)*

Validity

For validity of this section, see Parker v. State (App. 5 Dist. 2013) 164 Cal.Rptr.3d 345, 221 Cal.App.4th 340, review granted and opinion superseded 167 Cal.Rptr.3d 658, 317 P.3d 1184, review dismissed 211 Cal.Rptr.3d 98, 384 P.3d 1242.

Law Revision Commission Comments

Subdivision (a) of Section 16650 continues the first clause of former Section 12060(b), the first clause of former Section 12318(b)(2), and former Section 12323(a) without substantive change.

Subdivision (b) continues the remainder of former Section 12060(b) (except the definition of "antique firearm") and the remainder of former Section 12318(b)(2) (except the definition of "antique firearm") without substantive change.

See Sections 16170 ("antique firearm"), 16520 ("firearm"), 16530 ("firearm capable of being concealed upon the person," "pistol," and "revolver"). [40 Cal. L. Revision Comm'n Reports 107 (2010)].

Cross References

Antique firearm defined, see Penal Code § 16170.
Firearm capable of being concealed upon the person defined for purposes of this Part, see Penal Code § 16530.
Firearm defined for purposes of this Part, see Penal Code § 16520.
Handgun defined for purposes of this Part, see Penal Code § 16640.
Pistol defined for purposes of this Part, see Penal Code § 16530.
Revolver defined for purposes of this Part, see Penal Code § 16530.
Rifle defined, see Penal Code § 17090.

Research References

2 Witkin, California Criminal Law 4th Crimes Against Public Peace and Welfare § 228 (2021), Armor Piercing Ammunition.

§ 16660. Handgun ammunition designed primarily to penetrate metal or armor defined

As used in this part, "handgun ammunition designed primarily to penetrate metal or armor" means any ammunition, except a shotgun shell or ammunition primarily designed for use in a rifle, that is designed primarily to penetrate a body vest or body shield, and has either of the following characteristics:

(a) Has projectile or projectile core constructed entirely, excluding the presence of traces of other substances, from one or a combination of tungsten alloys, steel, iron, brass, beryllium copper, or depleted uranium, or any equivalent material of similar density or hardness.

(b) Is primarily manufactured or designed, by virtue of its shape, cross-sectional density, or any coating applied thereto, including, but not limited to, ammunition commonly known as "KTW ammunition," to breach or penetrate a body vest or body shield when fired from a pistol, revolver, or other firearm capable of being concealed upon the person. *(Added by Stats.2010, c. 711 (S.B.1080), § 6, operative Jan. 1, 2012.)*

Law Revision Commission Comments

Section 16660 continues former Section 12323(b) without substantive change.

See Sections 16290 ("body vest" or "body shield"), 16520 ("firearm"), 16530 ("firearm capable of being concealed upon the person," "pistol," and "revolver"), 16650 ("handgun ammunition"). [38 Cal.L.Rev.Comm. Reports 217 (2009)].

Cross References

Firearm capable of being concealed upon the person defined for purposes of this Part, see Penal Code § 16530.
Firearm defined for purposes of this Part, see Penal Code § 16520.
Handgun ammunition defined, see Penal Code § 16650.
Handgun defined for purposes of this Part, see Penal Code § 16640.
Pistol defined for purposes of this Part, see Penal Code § 16530.
Revolver defined for purposes of this Part, see Penal Code § 16530.
Rifle defined, see Penal Code § 17090.

Research References

2 Witkin, California Criminal Law 4th Crimes Against Public Peace and Welfare § 228 (2021), Armor Piercing Ammunition.

§ 16670. Handgun safety certificate defined

As used in this part, "handgun safety certificate" means a certificate issued by the Department of Justice pursuant to Sections 31610 to 31700, inclusive, or pursuant to former Article 8 (commencing with Section 12800) of Chapter 6 of Title 2 of Part 4, as that article was operative at any time from January 1, 2003, until it was repealed by the Deadly Weapons Recodification Act of 2010. *(Added by Stats.2010, c. 711 (S.B.1080), § 6, operative Jan. 1, 2012.)*

Law Revision Commission Comments

Section 16670 continues former Section 12001(q) without substantive change.

Former Article 8 of Chapter 6 of Title 2 of Part 4, entitled "Handgun Safety Certificate," was enacted by 2001 Cal. Stat. ch. 942, § 10, and became operative on January 1, 2003 (except former Section 12804, which became operative on January 1, 2002). The article was repealed by the Deadly Weapons Recodification Act of 2010, and continued without substantive change in Sections 31610–31700 (except some definitions that are located in "Division 2. Definitions" of Title 1).

See Section 16640 ("handgun"). [38 Cal.L.Rev.Comm. Reports 217 (2009)].

Cross References

Handgun defined for purposes of this Part, see Penal Code § 16640.

§ 16680. Hard wooden knuckles defined

As used in this part, "hard wooden knuckles" means any device or instrument made wholly or partially of wood or paper products that is not metal knuckles, that is worn for purposes of offense or defense in or on the hand, and that either protects the wearer's hand while striking a blow, or increases the force of impact from the blow or injury to the individual receiving the blow. The composite materials, wood, or paper products contained in the device may help support the hand or fist, provide a shield to protect it, or consist of projections or studs that would contact the individual receiving a blow. *(Added by Stats.2010, c. 711 (S.B.1080), § 6, operative Jan. 1, 2012.)*

Law Revision Commission Comments

Section 16680 continues the third and fourth sentences of former Section 12020.1 without substantive change.

See Sections 16405 ("composite knuckles"), 16920 ("metal knuckles"). [38 Cal.L.Rev.Comm. Reports 217 (2009)].

Cross References

Metal knuckles defined for purposes of this Part, see Penal Code § 16920.

§ 16685. Hunting license defined

As used in this part, a valid and unexpired "hunting license" means a hunting license issued by the Department of Fish and Wildlife pursuant to Article 2 (commencing with Section 3031) of Chapter 1 of Part 1 of Division 4 of the Fish and Game Code, for which the time period authorized for the taking of birds or mammals has commenced but not expired. *(Added by Stats.2021, c. 250 (S.B.715), § 5, eff. Jan. 1, 2022.)*

§ 16690. Honorably retired defined

(a) As used in Sections 25650 and 26020, Article 2 (commencing with Section 25450) of Chapter 2 of Division 5 of Title 4, Article 3 (commencing with Section 25900) of Chapter 3 of Division 5 of Title 4, and Section 32406, as added by Chapter 58 of the Statutes of 2016 and as added by Proposition 63, "honorably retired" includes:

(1) A peace officer who has qualified for, and has accepted, a service or disability retirement.

(2) A retired level I reserve officer who meets the requirements specified in paragraph (2) of subdivision (c) of Section 26300.

(b) As used in this section, "honorably retired" does not include an officer who has agreed to a service retirement in lieu of termination. *(Added by Stats.2010, c. 711 (S.B.1080), § 6, operative Jan. 1, 2012. Amended by Stats.2018, c. 63 (A.B.1192), § 1, eff. Jan. 1, 2019.)*

Law Revision Commission Comments

Section 16690 continues the fourth and fifth sentences of former Section 12027(a)(1)(A) without substantive change. [38 Cal.L.Rev.Comm. Reports 217 (2009)].

Research References

2 Witkin, California Criminal Law 4th Crimes Against Public Peace and Welfare § 207 (2021), Exempt Persons.

§ 16700. Imitation firearm defined

(a)(1) As used in this part, "imitation firearm" means any BB device, toy gun, replica of a firearm, or other device that is so substantially similar in coloration and overall appearance to an existing firearm as to lead a reasonable person to perceive that the device is a firearm.

(2) "Imitation firearm" also includes, but is not limited to, a protective case for a cellular telephone that is so substantially similar in coloration and overall appearance to an existing firearm as to lead a reasonable person to perceive that the case is a firearm.

(b) As used in Section 20165, "imitation firearm" does not include any of the following:

(1) A nonfiring collector's replica that is historically significant, and is offered for sale in conjunction with a wall plaque or presentation case.

(2) A spot marker gun which expels a projectile that is greater than 10mm caliber.

(3) A BB device that expels a projectile, such as a BB or pellet, that is other than 6mm or 8mm caliber.

(4) A BB device that is an airsoft gun that expels a projectile, such as a BB or pellet, that is 6mm or 8mm caliber which meets the following:

(A) If the airsoft gun is configured as a handgun, in addition to the blaze orange ring on the barrel required by federal law, the airsoft gun has a trigger guard that has fluorescent coloration over the entire guard, and there is a two centimeter wide adhesive band around the circumference of the protruding pistol grip that has fluorescent coloration.

(B) If the airsoft gun is configured as a rifle or long gun, in addition to the blaze orange ring on the barrel required by federal law, the airsoft gun has a trigger guard that has fluorescent coloration over the entire guard, and there is a two centimeter wide adhesive band with fluorescent coloring around the circumference of any two of the following:

(i) The protruding pistol grip.

(ii) The buttstock.

(iii) A protruding ammunition magazine or clip.

(5) A device where the entire exterior surface of the device is white, bright red, bright orange, bright yellow, bright green, bright blue, bright pink, or bright purple, either singly or as the predominant color in combination with other colors in any pattern, or where the entire device is constructed of transparent or translucent materials which permits unmistakable observation of the device's complete contents.

(c) The adhesive bands described in paragraph (4) of subdivision (b) shall be applied in a manner not intended for removal, and shall be in place on the airsoft gun prior to sale to a customer. *(Added by Stats.2014, c. 915 (S.B.199), § 4, eff. Jan. 1, 2015, operative Jan. 1, 2016. Amended by Stats.2016, c. 198 (A.B.1798), § 1, eff. Jan. 1, 2017.)*

Cross References

Drawing or exhibiting imitation firearms, punishment, exceptions, see Penal Code § 417.4.

Firearm defined for purposes of this Part, see Penal Code § 16520.

Manufacture, sale, or possession of imitation firearms, exclusive regulation by Legislature, see Government Code § 53071.5.

Research References

California Jury Instructions - Criminal 16.292, Exhibiting Imitation Firearm.

2 Witkin, California Criminal Law 4th Crimes Against Public Peace and Welfare § 5 (2021), Unusual Weapons.

2 Witkin, California Criminal Law 4th Crimes Against Public Peace and Welfare § 231 (2021), Other Weapons and Devices.

2 Witkin, California Criminal Law 4th Crimes Against Public Peace and Welfare § 253 (2021), Openly Displaying or Carrying Imitation or Unloaded Firearm.

§ 16720. Immediate family member defined

As used in this part, "immediate family member" means either of the following relationships:

(a) Parent and child.

(b) Grandparent and grandchild. *(Added by Stats.2010, c. 711 (S.B.1080), § 6, operative Jan. 1, 2012.)*

Law Revision Commission Comments

Section 16720 continues former Section 12078(c)(3) without substantive change. [38 Cal.L.Rev.Comm. Reports 217 (2009)].

§ 16730. Infrequent defined; transaction defined

(a) As used in Section 31815 and in Division 6 (commencing with Section 26500) of Title 4, "infrequent" means both of the following are true:

(1) The person conducts less than six transactions per calendar year.

(2) The person sells, leases, or transfers no more than 50 total firearms per calendar year.

(b) As used in this section, "transaction" means a single sale, lease, or transfer of any number of firearms. *(Added by Stats.2010, c. 711 (S.B.1080), § 6, operative Jan. 1, 2012. Amended by Stats.2019, c. 738 (S.B.376), § 5, eff. Jan. 1, 2020.)*

Law Revision Commission Comments

Subdivision (a) of Section 16730 continues the first sentence of former Section 12070(c)(1)(A), former Section 12070(c)(1)(B), and former Section 12078(u)(1) without substantive change.

Subdivision (b) continues the second paragraph of former Section 12078(g)(1) without substantive change.

Subdivision (c) continues the second sentence of former Section 12070(c)(1)(A) without substantive change.

See Sections 16520 ("firearm"), 16640 ("handgun"). [38 Cal.L.Rev.Comm. Reports 217 (2009)].

Cross References

Firearm defined for purposes of this Part, see Penal Code § 16520.
Handgun defined for purposes of this Part, see Penal Code § 16640.

Research References

2 Witkin, California Criminal Law 4th Crimes Against Public Peace and Welfare § 193 (2021), Sale, Lease, or Transfer by Unlicensed Person.

§ 16740. Large-capacity magazine defined

As used in this part, "large-capacity magazine" means any ammunition feeding device with the capacity to accept more than 10 rounds, but shall not be construed to include any of the following:

(a) A feeding device that has been permanently altered so that it cannot accommodate more than 10 rounds.

(b) A .22 caliber tube ammunition feeding device.

(c) A tubular magazine that is contained in a lever-action firearm. *(Added by Stats.2010, c. 711 (S.B.1080), § 6, operative Jan. 1, 2012.)*

Law Revision Commission Comments

Section 16740 continues former Sections 12020(c)(25) and 12079(b) without substantive change. [38 Cal.L.Rev.Comm. Reports 217 (2009)].

Cross References

Firearm defined for purposes of this Part, see Penal Code § 16520.

Research References

California Jury Instructions - Criminal 12.49.7, Possessing or Trafficking in Large Capacity Magazines.

§ 16750. Lawful possession of the firearm defined

(a) As used in Section 25400, "lawful possession of the firearm" means that the person who has possession or custody of the firearm either lawfully owns the firearm or has the permission of the lawful owner or a person who otherwise has apparent authority to possess or have custody of the firearm. A person who takes a firearm without the permission of the lawful owner or without the permission of a person who has lawful custody of the firearm does not have lawful possession of the firearm.

(b) As used in Article 2 (commencing with Section 25850), Article 3 (commencing with Section 25900), and Article 4 (commencing with Section 26000) of Chapter 3 of Division 5 of Title 4, Chapter 6 (commencing with Section 26350) of Division 5 of Title 4, and Chapter 7 (commencing with Section 26400) of Division 5 of Title 4, "lawful possession of the firearm" means that the person who has possession or custody of the firearm either lawfully acquired and lawfully owns the firearm or has the permission of the lawful owner or person who otherwise has apparent authority to possess or have custody of the firearm. A person who takes a firearm without the permission of the lawful owner or without the permission of a person who has lawful custody of the firearm does not have lawful possession of the firearm. *(Added by Stats.2010, c. 711 (S.B.1080), § 6, operative Jan. 1, 2012. Amended by Stats.2011, c. 725 (A.B.144), § 5; Stats.2012, c. 700 (A.B.1527), § 6.)*

Law Revision Commission Comments

Subdivision (a) of Section 16750 continues former Section 12025(g) without substantive change.

Subdivision (b) continues former Section 12031(a)(3) without substantive change.

See Section 16520 ("firearm"). [38 Cal.L.Rev.Comm. Reports 217 (2009)].

Cross References

Firearm defined for purposes of this Part, see Penal Code § 16520.

Research References

2 Witkin, California Criminal Law 4th Crimes Against Public Peace and Welfare § 204 (2021), Punishment.
2 Witkin, California Criminal Law 4th Crimes Against Public Peace and Welfare § 250 (2021), Punishment.

§ 16760. Leaded cane defined

As used in this part, a "leaded cane" means a staff, crutch, stick, rod, pole, or similar device, unnaturally weighted with lead. *(Added by Stats.2010, c. 711 (S.B.1080), § 6, operative Jan. 1, 2012.)*

Law Revision Commission Comments

Section 16760 continues former Section 12020(c)(17) without substantive change. [38 Cal.L.Rev.Comm. Reports 217 (2009)].

Cross References

Penalty for possession of deadly weapon described in this section within State Capitol, legislative offices, etc., see Penal Code § 171c.
Possession of deadly weapons with intent to assault, see Penal Code § 17500.

§ 16770. Less lethal ammunition defined

As used in this part, "less lethal ammunition" means any ammunition that satisfies both of the following requirements:

(a) It is designed to be used in any less lethal weapon or any other kind of weapon (including, but not limited to, any firearm, pistol, revolver, shotgun, rifle, or spring, compressed air, or compressed gas weapon).

(b) When used in a less lethal weapon or other weapon, it is designed to immobilize, incapacitate, or stun a human being through the infliction of any less than lethal impairment of physical condition, function, or senses, including physical pain or discomfort. *(Added by Stats.2010, c. 711 (S.B.1080), § 6, operative Jan. 1, 2012.)*

Law Revision Commission Comments

Section 16770 continues former Section 12601(c) without substantive change.

See Sections 16520 ("firearm"), 16530 ("firearm capable of being concealed upon the person," "pistol," and "revolver"), 16780 ("less lethal weapon"). [38 Cal.L.Rev.Comm. Reports 217 (2009)].

Cross References

Firearm defined for purposes of this Part, see Penal Code § 16520.
Pistol defined for purposes of this Part, see Penal Code § 16530.
Revolver defined for purposes of this Part, see Penal Code § 16530.

Research References

1 Witkin California Criminal Law 4th Crimes Against the Person § 53 (2021), Assault With Stun Gun or Less Lethal Weapon.

§ 16780. Less lethal weapon defined

As used in this part:

(a) "Less lethal weapon" means any device that is designed to or that has been converted to expel or propel less lethal ammunition by any action, mechanism, or process for the purpose of incapacitating, immobilizing, or stunning a human being through the infliction of any less than lethal impairment of physical condition, function, or senses, including physical pain or discomfort. It is not necessary that a weapon leave any lasting or permanent incapacitation, discomfort, pain, or other injury or disability in order to qualify as a less lethal weapon.

(b) Less lethal weapon includes the frame or receiver of any weapon described in subdivision (a), but does not include any of the following unless the part or weapon has been converted as described in subdivision (a):

(1) Pistol, revolver, or firearm.

(2) Machinegun.

(3) Rifle or shotgun using fixed ammunition consisting of standard primer and powder and not capable of being concealed upon the person.

(4) A pistol, rifle, or shotgun that is a firearm having a barrel less than 0.18 inches in diameter and that is designed to expel a projectile by any mechanical means or by compressed air or gas.

(5) When used as designed or intended by the manufacturer, any weapon that is commonly regarded as a toy gun, and that as a toy gun is incapable of inflicting any impairment of physical condition, function, or senses.

(6) A destructive device.

(7) A tear gas weapon.

(8) A bow or crossbow designed to shoot arrows.

(9) A device commonly known as a slingshot.

(10) A device designed for the firing of stud cartridges, explosive rivets, or similar industrial ammunition.

(11) A device designed for signaling, illumination, or safety.

(12) An assault weapon. *(Added by Stats.2010, c. 711 (S.B.1080), § 6, operative Jan. 1, 2012.)*

Law Revision Commission Comments

Section 16780 continues former Section 12601(a)-(b) without substantive change.

See Sections 16460 ("destructive device"), 16520 ("firearm"), 16880 ("machinegun"), 17010 ("pistol"), 17080 ("revolver"), 17250 ("tear gas weapon"), 30510 ("assault weapon"), 30515 (further clarification of "assault weapon"). [38 Cal.L.Rev.Comm. Reports 217 (2009)].

Cross References

Age verification when selling products that are illegal to sell to minor, reasonable steps, products requiring age verification, penalties, see Civil Code § 1798.99.1.
Assault weapon defined for purposes of this Part, see Penal Code §§ 30510, 30515.
Custodial officers, use of less lethal weapons, see Penal Code § 831.
Destructive device defined, see Penal Code § 16460.
Firearm defined for purposes of this Part, see Penal Code § 16520.
Machinegun defined for purposes of this Part, see Penal Code § 16880.
Pistol defined for purposes of this Part, see Penal Code § 16530.
Revolver defined for purposes of this Part, see Penal Code § 16530.
Stun gun or less lethal weapon, assault, punishment, see Penal Code § 244.5.
Tear gas defined for purposes of this Part, see Penal Code § 17240.
Tear gas weapon defined for purposes of this Part, see Penal Code § 17250.

Research References

2 Witkin, California Criminal Law 4th Crimes Against Public Peace and Welfare § 231 (2021), Other Weapons and Devices.
2 Witkin, California Criminal Law 4th Crimes Against Public Peace and Welfare § 258 (2021), Other Weapons.
1 Witkin California Criminal Law 4th Crimes Against the Person § 53 (2021), Assault With Stun Gun or Less Lethal Weapon.

§ 16790. Licensed gun dealer defined

As used in Article 5 (commencing with Section 30900) and Article 7 (commencing with Section 31050) of Chapter 2 of Division 10 of Title 4, "licensed gun dealer" means a person who is licensed pursuant to Sections 26700 to 26915, inclusive, and who has a permit to sell assault weapons or .50 BMG rifles pursuant to Section 31005. *(Added by Stats.2010, c. 711 (S.B.1080), § 6, operative Jan. 1, 2012.)*

Law Revision Commission Comments

Section 16790 continues former Section 12290(c) without substantive change. See also former Section 12285(b)-(c), which used the same definition of "licensed gun dealer."

See Sections 16970 ("person"), 30510 ("assault weapon"), 30515 (further clarification of "assault weapon"), 30530 (".50 BMG rifle").

See also Section 26700 ("dealer," "licensee," or "person licensed pursuant to Sections 26700 to 26915, inclusive"). [38 Cal.L.Rev.Comm. Reports 217 (2009)].

Cross References

.50 BMG rifle defined for purposes of this Part, see Penal Code § 30530.
Person defined, see Penal Code § 16970.

Research References

2 Witkin, California Criminal Law 4th Crimes Against Public Peace and Welfare § 221 (2021), Permits and Conditions for Possession.

§ 16800. Licensed gun show producer defined

As used in this part, "licensed gun show producer" means a person who has been issued a certificate of eligibility by the Department of Justice pursuant to Section 27200. No regulations shall be required to implement this section. *(Added by Stats.2010, c. 711 (S.B.1080), § 6, operative Jan. 1, 2012.)*

Law Revision Commission Comments

Section 16800 continues former Section 12071.1(c) without substantive change. [38 Cal.L.Rev.Comm. Reports 217 (2009)].

§ 16810. Licensed premises defined; licensee's business premises defined; licensee's place of business defined

As used in Article 1 (commencing with Section 26700) and Article 2 (commencing with Section 26800) of Chapter 2 of Division 6 of Title 4, "licensed premises," "licensee's business premises," or "licensee's place of business" means the building designated in the license. *(Added by Stats.2010, c. 711 (S.B.1080), § 6, operative Jan. 1, 2012.)*

Law Revision Commission Comments

Section 16810 continues former Section 12071(c)(3) without substantive change. [38 Cal.L.Rev.Comm. Reports 217 (2009)].

§ 16820. Licensee defined

(a) For purposes of the provisions listed in Section 16580, use of the term "licensee" is governed by Section 26700.

(b) For purposes of Chapter 2 (commencing with Section 29030) of Division 7 of Title 4, use of the term "licensee" is governed by Section 29030. *(Added by Stats.2010, c. 711 (S.B.1080), § 6, operative Jan. 1, 2012.)*

Law Revision Commission Comments

Subdivision (a) of Section 16820 is new. It is intended to help persons locate the definition of "licensee" that relates to firearms dealing and applies for purposes of the specified provisions.

Subdivision (b) is new. It is intended to help persons locate the definition of "licensee" that relates to firearms manufacturing and applies for purposes of key provisions relating to such manufacturing.

See also Section 16790 ("licensed gun dealer"). [38 Cal.L.Rev.Comm. Reports 217 (2009)].

§ 16822. Licensee's business premises defined

Use of the term "licensee's business premises" is governed by Section 16810. *(Added by Stats.2010, c. 711 (S.B.1080), § 6, operative Jan. 1, 2012.)*

Law Revision Commission Comments

Section 16822 is new. It is intended to help persons locate the definition of "licensee's business premises," which is the same as the definition of "licensed premises" in Section 16810. [38 Cal.L.Rev.Comm. Reports 217 (2009)].

§ 16824. Licensee's place of business defined

Use of the term "licensee's place of business" is governed by Section 16810. *(Added by Stats.2010, c. 711 (S.B.1080), § 6, operative Jan. 1, 2012.)*

Law Revision Commission Comments

Section 16824 is new. It is intended to help persons locate the definition of "licensee's place of business," which is the same as the definition of "licensed premises" in Section 16810. [38 Cal.L.Rev.Comm. Reports 217 (2009)].

§ 16830. Lipstick case knife defined

As used in this part, a "lipstick case knife" means a knife enclosed within and made an integral part of a lipstick case. *(Added by Stats.2010, c. 711 (S.B.1080), § 6, operative Jan. 1, 2012.)*

Law Revision Commission Comments

Section 16830 continues former Section 12020(c)(14) without substantive change. [38 Cal.L.Rev.Comm. Reports 217 (2009)].

Cross References

Penalty for possession of deadly weapon described in this section within State Capitol, legislative offices, etc., see Penal Code § 171c.
Possession of deadly weapons with intent to assault, see Penal Code § 17500.

§ 16840. Loaded defined

(a) As used in Section 25800, a firearm shall be deemed to be "loaded" whenever both the firearm and the unexpended ammunition capable of being discharged from the firearm are in the immediate possession of the same person.

(b) As used in Chapter 2 (commencing with Section 25100) of Division 4 of Title 4, in subparagraph (A) of paragraph (6) of subdivision (c) of Section 25400, and in Sections 25850 to 26055, inclusive,

(1) A firearm shall be deemed to be "loaded" when there is an unexpended cartridge or shell, consisting of a case that holds a charge of powder and a bullet or shot, in, or attached in any manner to, the firearm, including, but not limited to, in the firing chamber, magazine, or clip thereof attached to the firearm.

(2) Notwithstanding paragraph (1), a muzzle-loader firearm shall be deemed to be loaded when it is capped or primed and has a powder charge and ball or shot in the barrel or cylinder. *(Added by Stats.2010, c. 711 (S.B.1080), § 6, operative Jan. 1, 2012.)*

Law Revision Commission Comments

Subdivision (a) of Section 16840 continues former Section 12001(j) without substantive change.

Subdivision (b) continues former Sections 12031(g) and 12035(a)(2) without substantive change. See also former Section 12025(b)(6)(A), which used the same definition of "loaded."

See Section 16520 ("firearm").

See also Fish and Game Code § 2006 ("A rifle or shotgun shall be deemed to be loaded for the purposes of this section when there is an unexpended cartridge or shell in the firing chamber but not when the only cartridges or shells are in the magazine."). [38 Cal.L.Rev.Comm. Reports 217 (2009)].

Cross References

Firearm defined for purposes of this Part, see Penal Code § 16520.

Research References

2 Witkin, California Criminal Law 4th Crimes Against Public Peace and Welfare § 100 (2021), Possession in Conjunction With Firearm.
2 Witkin, California Criminal Law 4th Crimes Against Public Peace and Welfare § 249 (2021), Offenses.
2 Witkin, California Criminal Law 4th Crimes Against Public Peace and Welfare § 253 (2021), Openly Displaying or Carrying Imitation or Unloaded Firearm.
2 Witkin, California Criminal Law 4th Crimes Against Public Peace and Welfare § 253A (2021), (New) Carrying Unloaded Firearm that is Not Handgun in Incorporated Area or Other Public Place.
2 Witkin, California Criminal Law 4th Crimes Against Public Peace and Welfare § 261 (2021), Carrying Loaded Firearm With Intent to Commit Felony.
2 Witkin, California Criminal Law 4th Crimes Against Public Peace and Welfare § 262 (2021), Criminal Storage of Firearm.

§ 16850. Locked container defined

As used in this part, "locked container" means a secure container that is fully enclosed and locked by a padlock, keylock, combination lock, or similar locking device. The term "locked container" does not include the utility or glove compartment of a motor vehicle. *(Added by Stats.2010, c. 711 (S.B.1080), § 6, operative Jan. 1, 2012. Amended by Stats.2011, c. 725 (A.B.144), § 6; Stats.2012, c. 700 (A.B.1527), § 7; Stats.2013, c. 737 (A.B.500), § 4; Stats.2014, c. 103 (A.B.1798), § 5, eff. Jan. 1, 2015.)*

Law Revision Commission Comments

Section 16850 continues former Sections 12026.2(d), 12035(a)(5), and 12036(a)(4) without substantive change. See also former Sections 12020(b)(17)(E) and 12094(b)(4)(E), which used the same definition of "locked container." Section 16850 also continues the combined effect of subdivision (c) and the last phrase of paragraph (a)(1) ("other than the utility or glove compartment") of former Section 12026.1 without substantive change.

See Section 16520 ("firearm"). [38 Cal.L.Rev.Comm. Reports 217 (2009)].

Section 16850 is amended to expressly apply the definition of "locked container" to the whole of Part 6. This amendment does not effect a substantive change because all of the provisions in Part 6 that use the term "locked container" use it with the meaning provided in this section. See, e.g., Sections 26815, 27540, and 27560.

Note. The proposed amendment to Section 16850 incorporates a revision made by 2013 Cal. Stat. ch. 737, § 4 (AB 500 (Ammiano)), which will become operative on January 1, 2014. See Cal. Const. art. IV, § 8(c)(1); Gov't Code § 9600(a). [43 Cal.L.Rev.Comm. Reports 63 (2013)].

Cross References

Taking or transferring possession of any assault weapon, .50 BMG rifle, or firearm precursor part, see Business and Professions Code § 22949.63.

Research References

2 Witkin, California Criminal Law 4th Crimes Against Public Peace and Welfare § 207 (2021), Exempt Persons.
2 Witkin, California Criminal Law 4th Crimes Against Public Peace and Welfare § 221 (2021), Permits and Conditions for Possession.
2 Witkin, California Criminal Law 4th Crimes Against Public Peace and Welfare § 257 (2021), Firearms.
2 Witkin, California Criminal Law 4th Crimes Against Public Peace and Welfare § 262 (2021), Criminal Storage of Firearm.

§ 16860. Locking device defined

As used in Sections 16850, 25105, and 25205, "locking device" means a device that is designed to prevent a firearm from functioning and, when applied to the firearm, renders the firearm inoperable. *(Added by Stats.2010, c. 711 (S.B.1080), § 6, operative Jan. 1, 2012.)*

Law Revision Commission Comments

Section 16860 continues former Sections 12035(a)(1) and 12036(a)(1) without substantive change.

See Section 16520 ("firearm"). [38 Cal.L.Rev.Comm. Reports 217 (2009)].

Cross References

Firearm defined for purposes of this Part, see Penal Code § 16520.

Research References

2 Witkin, California Criminal Law 4th Crimes Against Public Peace and Welfare § 262 (2021), Criminal Storage of Firearm.

§ 16865. Long gun defined

As used in Section 26860, "long gun" means any firearm that is not a handgun or a machinegun. *(Added by Stats.2013, c. 761 (S.B.683), § 2.)*

Research References

2 Witkin, California Criminal Law 4th Crimes Against Public Peace and Welfare § 197 (2021), Time and Manner of Delivery by Dealer.

§ 16870. Long-gun safe defined

As used in this part, "long-gun safe" means a locking container designed to fully contain and secure a rifle or shotgun, which has a locking system consisting of either a mechanical combination lock or an electronic combination lock that has at least 1,000 possible unique combinations consisting of a minimum of three numbers, letters, or symbols per combination, and is not listed on the roster maintained pursuant to Section 23655. *(Added by Stats.2010, c. 711 (S.B.1080), § 6, operative Jan. 1, 2012.)*

Law Revision Commission Comments

Section 16870 continues former Section 12087.6(c) without substantive change. See also former Section 12071(b)(20)(G)(ii)(II), which appears to have been subject to the same definition of "long-gun safe" (due to the requirement that the long-gun safe "mee[t] the standards for department-approved gun safes set forth in Section 12088.2").

See Sections 17090 ("rifle"), 17190 ("shotgun"). [38 Cal.L.Rev.Comm. Reports 217 (2009)].

Cross References

Rifle defined, see Penal Code § 17090.
Shotgun defined, see Penal Code § 17190.

§ 16880. Machinegun defined

(a) As used in this part, "machinegun" means any weapon that shoots, is designed to shoot, or can readily be restored to shoot, automatically more than one shot, without manual reloading, by a single function of the trigger.

(b) The term "machinegun" also includes the frame or receiver of any weapon described in subdivision (a), any part designed and intended solely and exclusively, or combination of parts designed and intended, for use in converting a weapon into a machinegun, and any combination of parts from which a machinegun can be assembled if those parts are in the possession or under the control of a person.

(c) The term "machinegun" also includes any weapon deemed by the federal Bureau of Alcohol, Tobacco, Firearms and Explosives as readily convertible to a machinegun under Chapter 53 (commencing with Section 5801) of Title 26 of the United States Code. *(Added by Stats.2010, c. 711 (S.B.1080), § 6, operative Jan. 1, 2012. Amended by Stats.2011, c. 296 (A.B.1023), § 228.)*

Law Revision Commission Comments

Section 16880 continues former Section 12200 without substantive change. See also former Sections 12001(n)(12), 12072(f)(1)(A), 12278(a), and 12601(b)(2), which used the same definition of "machinegun." [38 Cal.L.Rev. Comm. Reports 217 (2009)].

Cross References

Firearm defined for purposes of this Part, see Penal Code § 16520.
Firearms, records necessary to identify persons coming within Welfare and Institutions Code §§ 8100 or 8103, availability to Department of Justice, see Welfare and Institutions Code § 8104.
Pupil safety, injurious objects, see Education Code § 49330.

Research References

2 Witkin, California Criminal Law 4th Crimes Against Public Peace and Welfare § 231 (2021), Other Weapons and Devices.
3 Witkin, California Criminal Law 4th Punishment § 357 (2021), P.C. 12022: Defendant was Armed or Used Dangerous Weapon.
3 Witkin, California Criminal Law 4th Punishment § 358 (2021), P.C. 12022.5: Personal Use of Firearm.

§ 16890. Magazine defined

As used in Section 30515, "magazine" means any ammunition feeding device. *(Added by Stats.2010, c. 711 (S.B.1080), § 6, operative Jan. 1, 2012.)*

Law Revision Commission Comments

Section 16890 continues former Section 12276.1(d)(1) without substantive change. [38 Cal.L.Rev.Comm. Reports 217 (2009)].

§ 16900. Magazine disconnect mechanism defined

As used in this part, "magazine disconnect mechanism" means a mechanism that prevents a semiautomatic pistol that has a detachable magazine from operating to strike the primer of ammunition in the firing chamber when a detachable magazine is not inserted in the semiautomatic pistol. *(Added by Stats.2010, c. 711 (S.B.1080), § 6, operative Jan. 1, 2012.)*

Law Revision Commission Comments

Section 16900 continues former Section 12126(d) without substantive change. See also former Section 12130(d)(1)-(3), which used the same definition of "magazine disconnect mechanism."

See Sections 16530 ("firearm capable of being concealed upon the person," "pistol," and "revolver"), 17140 ("semiautomatic pistol"). [38 Cal.L.Rev. Comm. Reports 217 (2009)].

Cross References

Pistol defined for purposes of this Part, see Penal Code § 16530.

§ 16920. Metal knuckles defined

As used in this part, "metal knuckles" means any device or instrument made wholly or partially of metal that is worn for purposes of offense or defense in or on the hand and that either protects the wearer's hand while striking a blow or increases the force of impact from the blow or injury to the individual receiving the blow. The metal contained in the device may help support the hand or fist, provide a shield to protect it, or consist of projections or studs which would contact the individual receiving a blow. *(Added by Stats.2010, c. 711 (S.B.1080), § 6, operative Jan. 1, 2012.)*

Law Revision Commission Comments

Section 16920 continues former Section 12020(c)(7) without substantive change. See also former Sections 12020.1 and 12029, which referred to former Section 12020. [38 Cal.L.Rev.Comm. Reports 217 (2009)].

Cross References

Penalty for possession of deadly weapon described in this section within State Capitol, legislative offices, etc., see Penal Code § 171c.
Possession of deadly weapons with intent to assault, see Penal Code § 17500.

§ 16930. Multiburst trigger activator defined

(a) As used in this part, a "multiburst trigger activator" means either of the following:

(1) A device designed or redesigned to be attached to, built into, or used in conjunction with, a semiautomatic firearm, which allows

the firearm to discharge two or more shots in a burst by activating the device.

(2) A manual or power-driven trigger activating device constructed and designed so that when attached to, built into, or used in conjunction with, a semiautomatic firearm it increases the rate of fire of that firearm.

(b) "Multiburst trigger activator" includes, but is not limited to, any of the following devices:

(1) A device that uses a spring, piston, or similar mechanism to push back against the recoil of a firearm, thereby moving the firearm in a back-and-forth motion and facilitating the rapid reset and activation of the trigger by a stationary finger. These devices are commonly known as bump stocks, bump fire stocks, or bump fire stock attachments.

(2) A device placed within the trigger guard of a firearm that uses a spring to push back against the recoil of the firearm causing the finger in the trigger guard to move back and forth and rapidly activate the trigger. These devices are commonly known as burst triggers.

(3) A mechanical device that activates the trigger of the firearm in rapid succession by turning a crank. These devices are commonly known as trigger cranks, gat cranks, gat triggers, or trigger actuators.

(4) Any aftermarket trigger or trigger system that, if installed, allows more than one round to be fired with a single depression of the trigger. *(Added by Stats.2010, c. 711 (S.B.1080), § 6, operative Jan. 1, 2012. Amended by Stats.2018, c. 795 (S.B.1346), § 1, eff. Jan. 1, 2019.)*

Law Revision Commission Comments

Section 16930 continues former Section 12020(c)(23) without substantive change.

See Section 16520 ("firearm"). [38 Cal.L.Rev.Comm. Reports 217 (2009)].

Cross References

Firearm defined for purposes of this Part, see Penal Code § 16520.

§ 16940. Nunchaku defined

As used in this part, "nunchaku" means an instrument consisting of two or more sticks, clubs, bars, or rods to be used as handles, connected by a rope, cord, wire, or chain, in the design of a weapon used in connection with the practice of a system of self-defense such as karate. *(Added by Stats.2010, c. 711 (S.B.1080), § 6, operative Jan. 1, 2012.)*

Law Revision Commission Comments

Section 16940 continues former Section 12020(c)(3) without substantive change. See also former Section 12029, which referred to former Section 12020. [38 Cal.L.Rev.Comm. Reports 217 (2009)].

Cross References

Penalty for possession of deadly weapon described in this section within State Capitol, legislative offices, etc., see Penal Code § 171c.
Possession of deadly weapons with intent to assault, see Penal Code § 17500.

§ 16950. Handgun carried openly or exposed

As used in Chapter 6 (commencing with Section 26350) of Division 5 of Title 4, a handgun shall be deemed to be carried openly or exposed if the handgun is not carried concealed within the meaning of Section 25400. *(Added by Stats.2011, c. 725 (A.B.144), § 7.)*

Cross References

Handgun defined for purposes of this Part, see Penal Code § 16640.

Research References

2 Witkin, California Criminal Law 4th Crimes Against Public Peace and Welfare § 253 (2021), Openly Displaying or Carrying Imitation or Unloaded Firearm.

§ 16960. Operation of law defined

As used in Article 1 (commencing with Section 26500) of Chapter 1 of Division 6 of Title 4, "operation of law" includes, but is not limited to, any of the following:

(a) The executor, personal representative, or administrator of an estate, if the estate includes a firearm.

(b) A secured creditor or an agent or employee of a secured creditor when a firearm is possessed as collateral for, or as a result of, a default under a security agreement under the Commercial Code.

(c) A levying officer, as defined in Section 481.140, 511.060, or 680.260 of the Code of Civil Procedure.

(d) A receiver performing the functions of a receiver, if the receivership estate includes a firearm.

(e) A trustee in bankruptcy performing the duties of a trustee, if the bankruptcy estate includes a firearm.

(f) An assignee for the benefit of creditors performing the functions of an assignee, if the assignment includes a firearm.

(g) A transmutation of property between spouses pursuant to Section 850 of the Family Code.

(h) A firearm received by the family of a police officer or deputy sheriff from a local agency pursuant to Section 50081 of the Government Code.

(i) The transfer of a firearm by a law enforcement agency to the person who found the firearm where the delivery is to the person as the finder of the firearm pursuant to Article 1 (commencing with Section 2080) of Chapter 4 of Title 6 of Part 4 of Division 3 of the Civil Code.

(j) The trustee of a trust that includes a firearm and that was part of a will that created the trust.

(k) A person acting pursuant to the person's power of attorney in accordance with Division 4.5 (commencing with Section 4000) of the Probate Code.

(*l*) A limited or general conservator appointed by a court pursuant to the Probate Code or Welfare and Institutions Code.

(m) A guardian ad litem appointed by a court pursuant to Section 372 of the Code of Civil Procedure.

(n) The trustee of a trust that includes a firearm that is under court supervision.

(*o*) A special administrator appointed by a court pursuant to Section 8540 of the Probate Code.

(p) A guardian appointed by a court pursuant to Section 1500 of the Probate Code. *(Added by Stats.2010, c. 711 (S.B.1080), § 6, operative Jan. 1, 2012. Amended by Stats.2019, c. 110 (A.B.1292), § 1, eff. Jan. 1, 2020.)*

Law Revision Commission Comments

Section 16960 continues former Section 12070(c)(2) without substantive change. An incomplete cross-reference to an article in the Civil Code has been corrected. [38 Cal.L.Rev.Comm. Reports 217 (2009)].

Cross References

Firearm defined for purposes of this Part, see Penal Code § 16520.

Research References

2 Witkin, California Criminal Law 4th Crimes Against Public Peace and Welfare § 193 (2021), Sale, Lease, or Transfer by Unlicensed Person.

§ 16965. Passenger's or driver's area defined

As used in this part, "passenger's or driver's area" means that part of a motor vehicle which is designed to carry the driver and passengers, including any interior compartment or space therein. *(Added by Stats.2010, c. 711 (S.B.1080), § 6, operative Jan. 1, 2012.)*

Law Revision Commission Comments

Section 16965 continues the third paragraph of former Section 653k without substantive change. [38 Cal.L.Rev.Comm. Reports 217 (2009)].

§ 16970. Person defined

(a) As used in Sections 16790, 17505, and 30600, "person" means an individual, partnership, corporation, limited liability company, association, or any other group or entity, regardless of how it was created.

(b) As used in Chapter 2 (commencing with Section 30500) of Division 10 of Title 4, except for Section 30600, "person" means an individual. *(Added by Stats.2010, c. 711 (S.B.1080), § 6, operative Jan. 1, 2012. Amended by Stats.2013, c. 729 (A.B.170), § 1; Stats.2014, c. 71 (S.B.1304), § 134, eff. Jan. 1, 2015.)*

Law Revision Commission Comments

Section 16970 continues former Section 12277 without substantive change. See also former Section 12020.5, which used the same definition of "person."

See Section 7 ("the word 'person' includes a corporation as well as a natural person"). [38 Cal.L.Rev.Comm. Reports 217 (2009)].

§ 16980. Person licensed pursuant to Sections 26700 to 26915, inclusive defined

Use of the term "person licensed pursuant to Sections 26700 to 26915, inclusive" is governed by Section 26700. *(Added by Stats. 2010, c. 711 (S.B.1080), § 6, operative Jan. 1, 2012.)*

Law Revision Commission Comments

Section 16980 is new. It is intended to help persons locate the definition of "person licensed pursuant to Sections 26700 to 26915, inclusive."

See also Section 16790 ("licensed gun dealer"). [38 Cal.L.Rev.Comm. Reports 217 (2009)].

§ 16990. A person taking title or possession of a firearm by operation of law defined

As used in any provision listed in subdivision (a) of Section 16585, the phrase "a person taking title or possession of a firearm by operation of law" includes, but is not limited to, any of the following instances in which an individual receives title to, or possession of, a firearm:

(a) The executor, personal representative, or administrator of an estate, if the estate includes a firearm.

(b) A secured creditor or an agent or employee of a secured creditor when the firearm is possessed as collateral for, or as a result of, a default under a security agreement under the Commercial Code.

(c) A levying officer, as defined in Section 481.140, 511.060, or 680.260 of the Code of Civil Procedure.

(d) A receiver performing the functions of a receiver, if the receivership estate includes a firearm.

(e) A trustee in bankruptcy performing the duties of a trustee, if the bankruptcy estate includes a firearm.

(f) An assignee for the benefit of creditors performing the functions of an assignee, if the assignment includes a firearm.

(g) A transmutation of property consisting of a firearm pursuant to Section 850 of the Family Code.

(h) A firearm passing to a surviving spouse pursuant to Chapter 1 (commencing with Section 13500) of Part 2 of Division 8 of the Probate Code.

(i) A firearm received by the family of a police officer or deputy sheriff from a local agency pursuant to Section 50081 of the Government Code.

(j) The transfer of a firearm by a law enforcement agency to the person who found the firearm where the delivery is to the person as the finder of the firearm pursuant to Article 1 (commencing with Section 2080) of Chapter 4 of Title 6 of Part 4 of Division 3 of the Civil Code.

(k) The trustee of a trust that includes a firearm and that was part of a will that created the trust.

(*l*) A firearm passed to a decedent's successor pursuant to Part 1 (commencing with Section 13000) of Division 8 of the Probate Code.

(m) A person acting pursuant to the person's power of attorney in accordance with Division 4.5 (commencing with Section 4000) of the Probate Code.

(n) A limited or general conservator appointed by a court pursuant to the Probate Code or Welfare and Institutions Code.

(*o*) A guardian ad litem appointed by a court pursuant to Section 372 of the Code of Civil Procedure.

(p) The trustee of a trust that includes a firearm that is under court supervision.

(q) The trustee of a trust that is not referenced in subdivisions (k) or (p).

(r) A special administrator appointed by a court pursuant to Section 8540 of the Probate Code.

(s) A guardian appointed by a court pursuant to Section 1500 of the Probate Code. *(Added by Stats.2010, c. 711 (S.B.1080), § 6, operative Jan. 1, 2012. Amended by Stats.2019, c. 110 (A.B.1292), § 2, eff. Jan. 1, 2020.)*

Law Revision Commission Comments

Section 16990 continues former Section 12078(u)(2) without substantive change. [38 Cal.L.Rev.Comm. Reports 217 (2009)].

Cross References

Deliveries or transfers of firearms to dealer by trustee, application of Section 26500, see Penal Code § 26589.
Firearm defined for purposes of this Part, see Penal Code § 16520.

§ 17000. Personal handgun importer and personal firearm importer defined

(a) As used in this part, until January 1, 2014, any reference to the term "personal firearm importer" shall be deemed to mean "personal handgun importer" and, on and after January 1, 2014, any reference to the term "personal handgun importer" shall be deemed to mean "personal firearm importer." A "personal handgun importer," until January 1, 2014, and commencing January 1, 2014, a "personal firearm importer" means an individual who meets all of the following criteria:

(1) The individual is not a person licensed pursuant to Article 1 (commencing with Section 26700) and Article 2 (commencing with Section 26800) of Chapter 2 of Division 6 of Title 4.

(2) The individual is not a licensed manufacturer of firearms pursuant to Chapter 44 (commencing with Section 921) of Title 18 of the United States Code.

(3) The individual is not a licensed importer of firearms pursuant to Chapter 44 (commencing with Section 921) of Title 18 of the United States Code and the regulations issued pursuant thereto.

(4) The individual is the owner of a firearm.

(5) The individual acquired that firearm outside of California.

(6) The individual moved into this state on or after January 1, 1998, in the case of a handgun, or in the case of a firearm that is not a handgun, on or after January 1, 2014, as a resident of this state.

(7) The individual intends to possess that handgun within this state on or after January 1, 1998, or in the case of a firearm that is not a handgun, he or she intends to possess that firearm within this state on or after January 1, 2014.

(8) The firearm was not delivered to the individual by a person licensed pursuant to Article 1 (commencing with Section 26700) and

Article 2 (commencing with Section 26800) of Chapter 2 of Division 6 of Title 4, who delivered that firearm following the procedures set forth in Section 27540 and Article 1 (commencing with Section 26700) and Article 2 (commencing with Section 26800) of Chapter 2 of Division 6 of Title 4.

(9) The individual, while a resident of this state, had not previously reported ownership of that firearm to the Department of Justice in a manner prescribed by the department that included information concerning the individual and a description of the firearm.

(10) The firearm is not a firearm that is prohibited by any provision listed in Section 16590.

(11) The firearm is not an assault weapon.

(12) The firearm is not a machinegun.

(13) The person is 18 years of age or older.

(14) The firearm is not a .50 BMG rifle.

(15) The firearm is not a destructive device.

(b) For purposes of paragraph (6) of subdivision (a):

(1) Except as provided in paragraph (2), residency shall be determined in the same manner as is the case for establishing residency pursuant to Section 12505 of the Vehicle Code.

(2) In the case of a member of the Armed Forces of the United States, residency shall be deemed to be established when the individual was discharged from active service in this state. *(Added by Stats.2010, c. 711 (S.B.1080), § 6, operative Jan. 1, 2012. Amended by Stats.2011, c. 745 (A.B.809), § 3.)*

Law Revision Commission Comments

Subdivision (a) of Section 17000 continues former Section 12001(n) without substantive change. For guidance on what constitutes an assault weapon, see Sections 30510 ("assault weapon") and 30515 (further clarification of "assault weapon"). For guidance on what constitutes a machinegun, see Section 16880 ("machinegun").

Subdivision (b) continues former Section 12001(*o*) without substantive change.

See Sections 16520 ("firearm"), 16640 ("handgun"). [38 Cal.L.Rev.Comm. Reports 217 (2009)].

Cross References

.50 BMG rifle defined for purposes of this Part, see Penal Code § 30530.
Assault weapon defined for purposes of this Part, see Penal Code §§ 30510, 30515.
Firearm defined for purposes of this Part, see Penal Code § 16520.
Handgun defined for purposes of this Part, see Penal Code § 16640.
Machinegun defined for purposes of this Part, see Penal Code § 16880.

Research References

2 Witkin, California Criminal Law 4th Crimes Against Public Peace and Welfare § 199 (2021), Importation Restrictions.

§ 17010. Pistol defined

Use of the term "pistol" is governed by Section 16530. *(Added by Stats.2010, c. 711 (S.B.1080), § 6, operative Jan. 1, 2012.)*

Law Revision Commission Comments

Section 17010 is new. It is intended to help persons locate key rules relating to use of the term "pistol." [38 Cal.L.Rev.Comm. Reports 217 (2009)].

§ 17020. Principal place of employment or business defined

For purposes of this part, a city or county may be considered an applicant's "principal place of employment or business" only if the applicant is physically present in the jurisdiction during a substantial part of the applicant's working hours for purposes of that employment or business. *(Added by Stats.2010, c. 711 (S.B.1080), § 6, operative Jan. 1, 2012.)*

Law Revision Commission Comments

Section 17020 continues former Section 12050(a)(3) without substantive change. [38 Cal.L.Rev.Comm. Reports 217 (2009)].

§ 17030. Prohibited area defined

As used in this part, "prohibited area" means any place where it is unlawful to discharge a weapon. *(Added by Stats.2010, c. 711 (S.B.1080), § 6, operative Jan. 1, 2012.)*

Law Revision Commission Comments

Section 17030 continues former Section 12031(f) without substantive change. [38 Cal.L.Rev.Comm. Reports 217 (2009)].

Research References

2 Witkin, California Criminal Law 4th Crimes Against Public Peace and Welfare § 249 (2021), Offenses.

§ 17040. Public place defined

As used in Chapter 6 (commencing with Section 26350) of Division 5 of Title 4, "public place" has the same meaning as in Section 25850. *(Added by Stats.2011, c. 725 (A.B.144), § 8.)*

Research References

2 Witkin, California Criminal Law 4th Crimes Against Public Peace and Welfare § 253 (2021), Openly Displaying or Carrying Imitation or Unloaded Firearm.

§ 17060. Residence defined

(a) As used in Section 25135, "residence" means any structure intended or used for human habitation, including, but not limited to, houses, condominiums, rooms, motels, hotels, time-shares, and recreational or other vehicles where human habitation occurs.

(b) As used in Sections 27881, 27882, and 27883, "residence" means any structure intended or used for human habitation, including, but not limited to, houses, condominiums, rooms, motels, hotels, and time-shares, but does not include recreational vehicles or other vehicles where human habitation occurs. *(Added by Stats.2013, c. 737 (A.B.500), § 5. Amended by Stats.2019, c. 840 (S.B.172), § 5, eff. Jan. 1, 2020.)*

Research References

2 Witkin, California Criminal Law 4th Crimes Against Public Peace and Welfare § 262 (2021), Criminal Storage of Firearm.

§ 17070. Responsible adult defined

As used in this part, "responsible adult" means a person at least 21 years of age who is not prohibited by state or federal law from possessing, receiving, owning, or purchasing a firearm. *(Added by Stats.2010, c. 711 (S.B.1080), § 6, operative Jan. 1, 2012.)*

Law Revision Commission Comments

Section 17070 continues former Section 12101(e) without substantive change. [38 Cal.L.Rev.Comm. Reports 217 (2009)].

Cross References

Firearm defined for purposes of this Part, see Penal Code § 16520.

Research References

2 Witkin, California Criminal Law 4th Crimes Against Public Peace and Welfare § 243 (2021), Minors.

§ 17080. Revolver defined

Use of the term "revolver" is governed by Section 16530. *(Added by Stats.2010, c. 711 (S.B.1080), § 6, operative Jan. 1, 2012.)*

Law Revision Commission Comments

Section 17080 is new. It is intended to help persons locate key rules relating to use of the term "revolver." [38 Cal.L.Rev.Comm. Reports 217 (2009)].

§ 17090. Rifle defined

As used in Sections 16530, 16640, 16650, 16660, 16870, and 17170, Sections 17720 to 17730, inclusive, Section 17740, subdivision (f) of Section 27555, Article 2 (commencing with Section 30300) of Chapter 1 of Division 10 of Title 4, and Article 1 (commencing with Section 33210) of Chapter 8 of Division 10 of Title 4, "rifle" means a weapon designed or redesigned, made or remade, and intended to be fired from the shoulder and designed or redesigned and made or remade to use the energy of the explosive in a fixed cartridge to fire only a single projectile through a rifled bore for each single pull of the trigger. *(Added by Stats.2010, c. 711 (S.B.1080), § 6, operative Jan. 1, 2012.)*

Law Revision Commission Comments

Section 17090 continues former Sections 12020(c)(20) and 12323(d) without substantive change. See also former Sections 12001(f), 12001.5, 12029, 12072(f)(1)(A), and 12087.6(c), which referred to former Section 12020. [38 Cal.L.Rev.Comm. Reports 217 (2009)].

Cross References

Penalty for possession of deadly weapon described in this section within State Capitol, legislative offices, etc., see Penal Code § 171c.
Possession of deadly weapons with intent to assault, see Penal Code § 17500.

Research References

2 Witkin, California Criminal Law 4th Crimes Against Public Peace and Welfare § 228 (2021), Armor Piercing Ammunition.

§ 17110. Secure facility defined

As used in Section 26890, "secure facility" means a building that meets all of the following specifications:

(a) All perimeter doorways shall meet one of the following:

(1) A windowless steel security door equipped with both a dead bolt and a doorknob lock.

(2) A windowed metal door that is equipped with both a dead bolt and a doorknob lock. If the window has an opening of five inches or more measured in any direction, the window shall be covered with steel bars of at least one-half inch diameter or metal grating of at least nine gauge affixed to the exterior or interior of the door.

(3) A metal grate that is padlocked and affixed to the licensee's premises independent of the door and doorframe.

(b) All windows are covered with steel bars.

(c) Heating, ventilating, air-conditioning, and service openings are secured with steel bars, metal grating, or an alarm system.

(d) Any metal grates have spaces no larger than six inches wide measured in any direction.

(e) Any metal screens have spaces no larger than three inches wide measured in any direction.

(f) All steel bars shall be no further than six inches apart. *(Added by Stats.2010, c. 711 (S.B.1080), § 6, operative Jan. 1, 2012.)*

Law Revision Commission Comments

Section 17110 continues former Section 12071(c)(2) without substantive change.

See also Sections 29141 ("secure facility" for firearm storage by manufacturer), 29142 (special definition of "secure facility" for firearm storage by manufacturer producing fewer than 500 firearms per calendar year). [38 Cal.L.Rev.Comm. Reports 217 (2009)].

§ 17111. Secure facility defined

For purposes of Chapter 2 (commencing with Section 29030) of Division 7 of Title 4, use of the term "secure facility" is governed by Sections 29141 and 29142. *(Added by Stats.2010, c. 711 (S.B.1080), § 6, operative Jan. 1, 2012.)*

Law Revision Commission Comments

Section 17111 is new. It is intended to help persons locate the standard definition of "secure facility" that applies to firearm storage by a manufacturer, and the special definition of "secure facility" that applies to firearm storage by a manufacturer producing fewer than 500 firearms per calendar year. [38 Cal.L.Rev.Comm. Reports 217 (2009)].

§ 17125. Security Exemplar defined

As used in this part, "Security Exemplar" has the same meaning as in Section 922 of Title 18 of the United States Code. *(Added by Stats.2010, c. 711 (S.B.1080), § 6, operative Jan. 1, 2012.)*

Law Revision Commission Comments

With respect to the definition of "Security Exemplar," Section 17125 continues the first paragraph of former Section 12020(c)(22)(C) without substantive change. [38 Cal.L.Rev.Comm. Reports 217 (2009)].

§ 17140. Semiautomatic pistol defined

As used in Sections 16900 and 31910, "semiautomatic pistol" means a pistol with an operating mode that uses the energy of the explosive in a fixed cartridge to extract a fired cartridge and chamber a fresh cartridge with each single pull of the trigger. *(Added by Stats.2010, c. 711 (S.B.1080), § 6, operative Jan. 1, 2012.)*

Law Revision Commission Comments

Section 17140 continues former Section 12126(e) without substantive change.

See Section 16530 ("firearm capable of being concealed upon the person," "pistol," and "revolver"). [38 Cal.L.Rev.Comm. Reports 217 (2009)].

Cross References

Pistol defined for purposes of this Part, see Penal Code § 16530.

§ 17160. Shobi-zue defined

As used in this part, a "shobi-zue" means a staff, crutch, stick, rod, or pole concealing a knife or blade within it, which may be exposed by a flip of the wrist or by a mechanical action. *(Added by Stats.2010, c. 711 (S.B.1080), § 6, operative Jan. 1, 2012.)*

Law Revision Commission Comments

Section 17160 continues former Section 12020(c)(16) without substantive change. [38 Cal.L.Rev.Comm. Reports 217 (2009)].

Cross References

Penalty for possession of deadly weapon described in this section within State Capitol, legislative offices, etc., see Penal Code § 171c.
Possession of deadly weapons with intent to assault, see Penal Code § 17500.

§ 17170. Short-barreled rifle defined

As used in this part, "short-barreled rifle" means any of the following:

(a) A rifle having a barrel or barrels of less than 16 inches in length.

(b) A rifle with an overall length of less than 26 inches.

(c) Any weapon made from a rifle (whether by alteration, modification, or otherwise) if that weapon, as modified, has an overall length of less than 26 inches or a barrel or barrels of less than 16 inches in length.

(d) Any device that may be readily restored to fire a fixed cartridge which, when so restored, is a device defined in subdivisions (a) to (c), inclusive.

(e) Any part, or combination of parts, designed and intended to convert a device into a device defined in subdivisions (a) to (c), inclusive, or any combination of parts from which a device defined in subdivisions (a) to (c), inclusive, may be readily assembled if those parts are in the possession or under the control of the same person. *(Added by Stats.2010, c. 711 (S.B.1080), § 6, operative Jan. 1, 2012. Amended by Stats.2014, c. 103 (A.B.1798), § 6, eff. Jan. 1, 2015.)*

Law Revision Commission Comments

Section 17170 continues former Section 12020(c)(2) without substantive change. See also former Sections 12001(f), 12001.5, 12029, and 12072(f)(1)(A), which used the same definition of "short-barreled rifle."

See Section 17090 ("rifle"). [38 Cal.L.Rev.Comm. Reports 217 (2009)].

Section 17170 is amended to expressly apply the definition of "short-barreled rifle" to the whole of Part 6. This amendment does not effect a substantive change because all of the provisions in Part 6 that use the term "short-barreled rifle" use it with the meaning provided in this section. See, e.g., Sections 16590, 18010, 27140, 27740, 27940, 33300, 33305, 33310, 33315, and 33320. [43 Cal.L.Rev.Comm. Reports 63 (2013)].

Cross References

Manufacture, sale, or possession of short-barreled shotgun or short-barreled rifle, see Penal Code § 33210.
Manufacture, sale or possession of short-barreled shotguns or short-barreled rifles, permits, see Penal Code § 33300.
Penalty for possession of deadly weapon described in this section within State Capitol, legislative offices, etc., see Penal Code § 171c.
Possession of deadly weapons with intent to assault, see Penal Code § 17500.
Rifle defined, see Penal Code § 17090.

Research References

2 Witkin, California Criminal Law 4th Crimes Against Public Peace and Welfare § 212 (2021), Elements of Offense.

§ 17180. Short-barreled shotgun defined

As used in this part, "short-barreled shotgun" means any of the following:

(a) A firearm that is designed or redesigned to fire a fixed shotgun shell and has a barrel or barrels of less than 18 inches in length.

(b) A firearm that has an overall length of less than 26 inches and that is designed or redesigned to fire a fixed shotgun shell.

(c) Any weapon made from a shotgun (whether by alteration, modification, or otherwise) if that weapon, as modified, has an overall length of less than 26 inches or a barrel or barrels of less than 18 inches in length.

(d) Any device that may be readily restored to fire a fixed shotgun shell which, when so restored, is a device defined in subdivisions (a) to (c), inclusive.

(e) Any part, or combination of parts, designed and intended to convert a device into a device defined in subdivisions (a) to (c), inclusive, or any combination of parts from which a device defined in subdivisions (a) to (c), inclusive, can be readily assembled if those parts are in the possession or under the control of the same person. *(Added by Stats.2010, c. 711 (S.B.1080), § 6, operative Jan. 1, 2012. Amended by Stats.2014, c. 103 (A.B.1798), § 7, eff. Jan. 1, 2015.)*

Law Revision Commission Comments

Section 17180 continues former Section 12020(c)(1) without substantive change. See also former Sections 12001(f), 12001.5, 12029, and 12072(f)(1)(A), which used the same definition of "short-barreled shotgun."

See Sections 16520 ("firearm"), 17190 ("shotgun"). [38 Cal.L.Rev.Comm. Reports 217 (2009)].

Section 17180 is amended to expressly apply the definition of "short-barreled shotgun" to the whole of Part 6. This amendment does not effect a substantive change because all of the provisions in Part 6 that use the term "short-barreled shotgun" use it with the meaning provided in this section. See, e.g., Sections 16590, 18010, 27140, 27740, 27940, 33300, 33305, 33310, 33315, and 33320. [43 Cal.L.Rev.Comm. Reports 63 (2013)].

Cross References

Firearm defined for purposes of this Part, see Penal Code § 16520.
Manufacture, sale, or possession of short-barreled shotgun or short-barreled rifle, see Penal Code § 33210.
Manufacture, sale or possession of short-barreled shotguns or short-barreled rifles, permits, see Penal Code § 33300.
Penalty for possession of deadly weapon described in this section within State Capitol, legislative offices, etc., see Penal Code § 171c.
Possession of deadly weapons with intent to assault, see Penal Code § 17500.
Shotgun defined, see Penal Code § 17190.

§ 17190. Shotgun defined

As used in Sections 16530, 16640, 16870, and 17180, Sections 17720 to 17730, inclusive, Section 17740, Section 30215, and Article 1 (commencing with Section 33210) of Chapter 8 of Division 10 of Title 4, "shotgun" means a weapon designed or redesigned, made or remade, and intended to be fired from the shoulder and designed or redesigned and made or remade to use the energy of the explosive in a fixed shotgun shell to fire through a smooth bore either a number of projectiles (ball shot) or a single projectile for each pull of the trigger. *(Added by Stats.2010, c. 711 (S.B.1080), § 6, operative Jan. 1, 2012. Amended by Stats.2014, c. 103 (A.B.1798), § 8, eff. Jan. 1, 2015.)*

Law Revision Commission Comments

Section 17190 continues former Section 12020(c)(21) without substantive change. See also former Sections 12001(f), 12001.5, 12029, 12072(f)(1)(A), and 12087.6(c), which referred to former Section 12020. [38 Cal.L.Rev.Comm. Reports 217 (2009)].

Section 17190 is amended to delete an erroneous cross-reference. [43 Cal.L.Rev.Comm. Reports 63 (2013)].

Cross References

Penalty for possession of deadly weapon described in this section within State Capitol, legislative offices, etc., see Penal Code § 171c.
Possession of deadly weapons with intent to assault, see Penal Code § 17500.

§ 17200. Shuriken defined

As used in this part, a "shuriken" means any instrument, without handles, consisting of a metal plate having three or more radiating points with one or more sharp edges and designed in the shape of a polygon, trefoil, cross, star, diamond, or other geometric shape, for use as a weapon for throwing. *(Added by Stats.2010, c. 711 (S.B.1080), § 6, operative Jan. 1, 2012.)*

Law Revision Commission Comments

Section 17200 continues former Section 12020(c)(11) without substantive change. [38 Cal.L.Rev.Comm. Reports 217 (2009)].

Cross References

Penalty for possession of deadly weapon described in this section within State Capitol, legislative offices, etc., see Penal Code § 171c.
Possession of deadly weapons with intent to assault, see Penal Code § 17500.

§ 17210. Silencer defined

As used in Chapter 9 (commencing with Section 33410) of Division 10 of Title 4, "silencer" means any device or attachment of any kind designed, used, or intended for use in silencing, diminishing, or muffling the report of a firearm. The term "silencer" also includes any combination of parts, designed or redesigned, and intended for use in assembling a silencer or fabricating a silencer and any part intended only for use in assembly or fabrication of a silencer. *(Added by Stats.2010, c. 711 (S.B.1080), § 6, operative Jan. 1, 2012.)*

Law Revision Commission Comments

Section 17210 continues former Section 12500 without substantive change. [38 Cal.L.Rev.Comm. Reports 217 (2009)].

Cross References

Firearm defined for purposes of this Part, see Penal Code § 16520.

Research References

2 Witkin, California Criminal Law 4th Crimes Against Public Peace and Welfare § 231 (2021), Other Weapons and Devices.

§ 17220. SKS rifle defined

Use of the term "SKS rifle" is governed by Section 30710. *(Added by Stats.2010, c. 711 (S.B.1080), § 6, operative Jan. 1, 2012.)*

Law Revision Commission Comments

Section 17220 is new. It is intended to help persons locate the definition of "SKS rifle." [38 Cal.L.Rev.Comm. Reports 217 (2009)].

§ 17230. Stun gun defined

As used in this part, "stun gun" means any item, except a less lethal weapon, used or intended to be used as either an offensive or defensive weapon that is capable of temporarily immobilizing a person by the infliction of an electrical charge. *(Added by Stats.2010, c. 711 (S.B.1080), § 6, operative Jan. 1, 2012.)*

Law Revision Commission Comments

Section 17230 continues former Section 12650 without substantive change. See Section 16780 ("less lethal weapon"). [38 Cal.L.Rev.Comm. Reports 217 (2009)].

Research References

2 Witkin, California Criminal Law 4th Crimes Against Public Peace and Welfare § 231 (2021), Other Weapons and Devices.
2 Witkin, California Criminal Law 4th Crimes Against Public Peace and Welfare § 258 (2021), Other Weapons.

§ 17235. Switchblade knife defined

As used in this part, "switchblade knife" means a knife having the appearance of a pocketknife and includes a spring-blade knife, snap-blade knife, gravity knife, or any other similar type knife, the blade or blades of which are two or more inches in length and which can be released automatically by a flick of a button, pressure on the handle, flip of the wrist or other mechanical device, or is released by the weight of the blade or by any type of mechanism whatsoever. "Switchblade knife" does not include a knife that opens with one hand utilizing thumb pressure applied solely to the blade of the knife or a thumb stud attached to the blade, provided that the knife has a detent or other mechanism that provides resistance that must be overcome in opening the blade, or that biases the blade back toward its closed position. *(Added by Stats.2010, c. 711 (S.B.1080), § 6, operative Jan. 1, 2012.)*

Law Revision Commission Comments

Section 17235 continues the second paragraph of former Section 653k without substantive change. [38 Cal.L.Rev.Comm. Reports 217 (2009)].

Cross References

Pupil safety, injurious objects, see Education Code § 49330.

Research References

2 Witkin, California Criminal Law 4th Crimes Against Public Peace and Welfare § 213 (2021), Concealed Dirk, Dagger, or Explosives.
2 Witkin, California Criminal Law 4th Crimes Against Public Peace and Welfare § 230 (2021), Switchblade Knives.
2 Witkin, California Criminal Law 4th Crimes Against Public Peace and Welfare § 255 (2021), Public Building or Open Meeting.

§ 17240. Tear gas defined

(a) As used in this part, "tear gas" applies to and includes any liquid, gaseous or solid substance intended to produce temporary physical discomfort or permanent injury through being vaporized or otherwise dispersed in the air.

(b) Notwithstanding subdivision (a), "tear gas" does not apply to, and does not include, any substance registered as an economic poison as provided in Chapter 2 (commencing with Section 12751) of Division 7 of the Food and Agricultural Code, provided that the substance is not intended to be used to produce discomfort or injury to human beings. *(Added by Stats.2010, c. 711 (S.B.1080), § 6, operative Jan. 1, 2012.)*

Law Revision Commission Comments

Section 17240 continues former Section 12401 without substantive change. [38 Cal.L.Rev.Comm. Reports 217 (2009)].

Cross References

Advertising, tear gas, see Business and Professions Code § 17533.9.
Penalty for bringing in courtroom, courthouse or court building, see Penal Code § 171b.
Pupil safety, injurious objects, see Education Code § 49330.

Research References

2 Witkin, California Criminal Law 4th Crimes Against Public Peace and Welfare § 229 (2021), Tear Gas.

§ 17250. Tear gas weapon defined

As used in this part, "tear gas weapon" applies to and includes:

(a) Any shell, cartridge, or bomb capable of being discharged or exploded, when the discharge or explosion will cause or permit the release or emission of tear gas.

(b) Any revolver, pistol, fountain pen gun, billy, or other form of device, portable or fixed, intended for the projection or release of tear gas, except those regularly manufactured and sold for use with firearm ammunition. *(Added by Stats.2010, c. 711 (S.B.1080), § 6, operative Jan. 1, 2012.)*

Law Revision Commission Comments

Section 17250 continues former Section 12402 without substantive change. See also former Section 12601(b)(7), which used the same definition of "tear gas weapon." [38 Cal.L.Rev.Comm. Reports 217 (2009)].

Cross References

Advertising, tear gas, see Business and Professions Code § 17533.9.
Firearm defined for purposes of this Part, see Penal Code § 16520.
Nuisance caused by illegal conduct involving unlawful weapons or ammunition purpose, unlawful detainer action, see Civil Code § 3485.
Penalty for bringing in courtroom, courthouse or court building, see Penal Code § 171b.
Pistol defined for purposes of this Part, see Penal Code § 16530.
Pupil safety, injurious objects, see Education Code § 49330.
Revolver defined for purposes of this Part, see Penal Code § 16530.
Tear gas defined for purposes of this Part, see Penal Code § 17240.

Research References

2 Witkin, California Criminal Law 4th Crimes Against Public Peace and Welfare § 229 (2021), Tear Gas.

§ 17270. Unconventional pistol defined

As used in this part, an "unconventional pistol" means a firearm with both of the following characteristics:

(a) It does not have a rifled bore.

(b) It has a barrel or barrels of less than 18 inches in length or has an overall length of less than 26 inches. *(Added by Stats.2010, c. 711 (S.B.1080), § 6, operative Jan. 1, 2012.)*

Law Revision Commission Comments

Section 17270 continues former Section 12020(c)(12) without substantive change.

See Sections 16520 ("firearm"), 16530 ("firearm capable of being concealed upon the person," "pistol," and "revolver"). [38 Cal.L.Rev.Comm. Reports 217 (2009)].

Cross References

Firearm defined for purposes of this Part, see Penal Code § 16520.
Penalty for possession of deadly weapon described in this section within State Capitol, legislative offices, etc., see Penal Code § 171c.
Pistol defined for purposes of this Part, see Penal Code § 16530.
Possession of deadly weapons with intent to assault, see Penal Code § 17500.

§ 17280. Undetectable firearm defined

As used in this part, "undetectable firearm" means any weapon that meets either of the following requirements:

(a) After removal of grips, stocks, and magazines, the weapon is not as detectable as the Security Exemplar, by a walk-through metal detector calibrated and operated to detect the Security Exemplar.

(b) Any major component of the weapon, as defined in Section 922 of Title 18 of the United States Code, when subjected to inspection by the types of X-ray machines commonly used at airports, does not generate an image that accurately depicts the shape of the component. Barium sulfate or other compounds may be used in the fabrication of the component. *(Added by Stats.2010, c. 711 (S.B. 1080), § 6, operative Jan. 1, 2012.)*

Law Revision Commission Comments

Section 17280 continues former Section 12020(c)(22)(A)-(B) without substantive change. With respect to the definition of "major component," Section 17280 also continues former Section 12020(c)(22)(C) without substantive change.

See Sections 16520(a) & (f) ("firearm"), 17125 ("Security Exemplar"). [38 Cal.L.Rev.Comm. Reports 217 (2009)].

Cross References

Firearm defined for purposes of this Part, see Penal Code § 16520.
Penalty for possession of deadly weapon described in this section within State Capitol, legislative offices, etc., see Penal Code § 171c.
Possession of deadly weapons with intent to assault, see Penal Code § 17500.

§ 17290. Undetectable knife defined

As used in this part, "undetectable knife" means any knife or other instrument, with or without a handguard, that satisfies all of the following requirements:

(a) It is capable of ready use as a stabbing weapon that may inflict great bodily injury or death.

(b) It is commercially manufactured to be used as a weapon.

(c) It is not detectable by a metal detector or magnetometer, either handheld or otherwise, which is set at standard calibration. *(Added by Stats.2010, c. 711 (S.B.1080), § 6, operative Jan. 1, 2012.)*

Law Revision Commission Comments

Section 17290 continues the second sentence of former Section 12001.1(a) without substantive change. [38 Cal.L.Rev.Comm. Reports 217 (2009)].

Cross References

Possession of prohibited items in sterile area of public transit facility, undetectable knife as described in this section, see Penal Code § 171.7.

Research References

2 Witkin, California Criminal Law 4th Crimes Against Public Peace and Welfare § 231 (2021), Other Weapons and Devices.

§ 17295. Handgun or other firearm deemed unloaded

(a) For purposes of Chapter 6 (commencing with Section 26350) of Division 5 of Title 4, a handgun shall be deemed "unloaded" if it is not "loaded" within the meaning of subdivision (b) of Section 16840.

(b) For purposes of Chapter 7 (commencing with Section 26400) of Division 5 of Title 4, a firearm that is not a handgun shall be deemed "unloaded" if it is not "loaded" within the meaning of subdivision (b) of Section 16840. *(Added by Stats.2011, c. 725 (A.B.144), § 9. Amended by Stats.2012, c. 700 (A.B.1527), § 8.)*

Cross References

Handgun defined for purposes of this Part, see Penal Code § 16640.

Research References

2 Witkin, California Criminal Law 4th Crimes Against Public Peace and Welfare § 253 (2021), Openly Displaying or Carrying Imitation or Unloaded Firearm.
2 Witkin, California Criminal Law 4th Crimes Against Public Peace and Welfare § 253A (2021), (New) Carrying Unloaded Firearm that is Not Handgun in Incorporated Area or Other Public Place.

§ 17300. Unsafe handgun defined

Use of the phrase "unsafe handgun" is governed by Section 31910. *(Added by Stats.2010, c. 711 (S.B.1080), § 6, operative Jan. 1, 2012.)*

Law Revision Commission Comments

Section 17300 is new. It is intended to help persons locate the definition of "unsafe handgun." [38 Cal.L.Rev.Comm. Reports 217 (2009)].

Cross References

Handgun defined for purposes of this Part, see Penal Code § 16640.

§ 17310. Used firearm defined

As used in this part, "used firearm" means a firearm that has been sold previously at retail and is more than three years old. *(Added by Stats.2010, c. 711 (S.B.1080), § 6, operative Jan. 1, 2012.)*

Law Revision Commission Comments

Section 17310 continues the fourth paragraph of former Section 12070(b)(5) without substantive change.

See Section 16520 ("firearm"). [38 Cal.L.Rev.Comm. Reports 217 (2009)].

Cross References

Firearm defined for purposes of this Part, see Penal Code § 16520.

Research References

2 Witkin, California Criminal Law 4th Crimes Against Public Peace and Welfare § 193 (2021), Sale, Lease, or Transfer by Unlicensed Person.

§ 17312. Valid state or federal serial number or mark of identification defined

"Valid state or federal serial number or mark of identification" means either of the following:

(a) A serial number that has been imprinted by a federal licensee authorized to serialize firearms in accordance with federal law, or that has been assigned to a firearm pursuant to Chapter 53 of Title 26 of the United States Code and the regulations issued pursuant thereto.

(b) A serial number or mark of identification issued by the California Department of Justice pursuant to Section 23910 or 29180. *(Added by Stats.2022, c. 76 (A.B.1621), § 9, eff. June 30, 2022.)*

§ 17315. Vendor defined

As used in Articles 2 through 5 of Chapter 1 of Division 10 of Title 4, "vendor" means an ammunition vendor. *(Added by Stats.2010, c. 711 (S.B.1080), § 6, operative Jan. 1, 2012. Amended by Initiative Measure (Prop. 63, § 8.4, approved Nov. 8, 2016, eff. Nov. 9, 2016).)*

Law Revision Commission Comments

Section 17315 continues the definition of "vendor" in former Section 12060(c) without substantive change.

See Section 16662 ("handgun ammunition vendor"). [38 Cal.L.Rev.Comm. Reports 217 (2009)].

Cross References

Handgun ammunition defined, see Penal Code § 16650.
Handgun defined for purposes of this Part, see Penal Code § 16640.

§ 17320. Violent felony defined

For purposes of Section 31360 only, "violent felony" refers to the specific crimes listed in subdivision (c) of Section 667.5, and to crimes defined under the applicable laws of the United States or any other state, government, or country that are reasonably equivalent to the crimes listed in subdivision (c) of Section 667.5. *(Added by Stats.2010, c. 711 (S.B.1080), § 6, operative Jan. 1, 2012.)*

Law Revision Commission Comments

Section 17320 continues former Section 12370(e) without substantive change. [38 Cal.L.Rev.Comm. Reports 217 (2009)].

Research References

2 Witkin, California Criminal Law 4th Crimes Against Public Peace and Welfare § 231 (2021), Other Weapons and Devices.

§ 17330. Wallet gun defined

As used in this part, "wallet gun" means any firearm mounted or enclosed in a case, resembling a wallet, designed to be or capable of being carried in a pocket or purse, if the firearm may be fired while mounted or enclosed in the case. *(Added by Stats.2010, c. 711 (S.B.1080), § 6, operative Jan. 1, 2012.)*

Law Revision Commission Comments

Section 17330 continues former Section 12020(c)(4) without substantive change.

See Section 16520 ("firearm"). [38 Cal.L.Rev.Comm. Reports 217 (2009)].

Cross References

Firearm defined for purposes of this Part, see Penal Code § 16520.
Penalty for possession of deadly weapon described in this section within State Capitol, legislative offices, etc., see Penal Code § 171c.
Possession of deadly weapons with intent to assault, see Penal Code § 17500.

§ 17340. Wholesaler defined

(a) As used in this part, "wholesaler" means any person who is licensed as a dealer pursuant to Chapter 44 (commencing with Section 921) of Title 18 of the United States Code and the regulations issued pursuant thereto, who sells, transfers, or assigns firearms, or parts of firearms, to persons who are licensed as manufacturers, importers, or gunsmiths pursuant to Chapter 44 (commencing with Section 921) of Title 18 of the United States Code, or persons licensed pursuant to Sections 26700 to 26915, inclusive, and includes persons who receive finished parts of firearms and assemble them into completed or partially completed firearms in furtherance of that purpose.

(b) "Wholesaler" shall not include a manufacturer, importer, or gunsmith who is licensed to engage in those activities pursuant to Chapter 44 (commencing with Section 921) of Title 18 of the United States Code or a person licensed pursuant to Sections 26700 to 26915, inclusive, and the regulations issued pursuant thereto. A wholesaler also does not include a person dealing exclusively in grips, stocks, and other parts of firearms that are not frames or receivers thereof. *(Added by Stats.2010, c. 711 (S.B.1080), § 6, operative Jan. 1, 2012.)*

Law Revision Commission Comments

Section 17340 continues former Section 12001(h) without substantive change.

See Sections 16520 ("firearm"), 16630 ("gunsmith"). [38 Cal.L.Rev.Comm. Reports 217 (2009)].

Cross References

Firearm defined for purposes of this Part, see Penal Code § 16520.
Gunsmith defined for purposes of this Part, see Penal Code § 16630.

Research References

2 Witkin, California Criminal Law 4th Crimes Against Public Peace and Welfare § 193 (2021), Sale, Lease, or Transfer by Unlicensed Person.

§ 17350. Writing pen knife defined

As used in this part, "writing pen knife" means a device that appears to be a writing pen but has concealed within it a pointed, metallic shaft that is designed to be a stabbing instrument which is exposed by mechanical action or gravity which locks into place when extended or the pointed, metallic shaft is exposed by the removal of the cap or cover on the device. *(Added by Stats.2010, c. 711 (S.B.1080), § 6, operative Jan. 1, 2012.)*

Law Revision Commission Comments

Section 17350 continues former Section 12020(c)(19) without substantive change. [38 Cal.L.Rev.Comm. Reports 217 (2009)].

Cross References

Penalty for possession of deadly weapon described in this section within State Capitol, legislative offices, etc., see Penal Code § 171c.
Possession of deadly weapons with intent to assault, see Penal Code § 17500.

§ 17360. Zip gun defined

As used in this part, "zip gun" means any weapon or device that meets all of the following criteria:

(a) It was not imported as a firearm by an importer licensed pursuant to Chapter 44 (commencing with Section 921) of Title 18 of the United States Code and the regulations issued pursuant thereto.

(b) It was not originally designed to be a firearm by a manufacturer licensed pursuant to Chapter 44 (commencing with Section 921) of Title 18 of the United States Code and the regulations issued pursuant thereto.

(c) No tax was paid on the weapon or device nor was an exemption from paying tax on that weapon or device granted under Section 4181 and Subchapters F (commencing with Section 4216) and G (commencing with Section 4221) of Chapter 32 of Title 26 of the United States Code, as amended, and the regulations issued pursuant thereto.

(d) It is made or altered to expel a projectile by the force of an explosion or other form of combustion. *(Added by Stats.2010, c. 711 (S.B.1080), § 6, operative Jan. 1, 2012.)*

Law Revision Commission Comments

Section 17360 continues former Section 12020(c)(10) without substantive change.

See Section 16520 ("firearm"). [38 Cal.L.Rev.Comm. Reports 217 (2009)].

Cross References

Firearm defined for purposes of this Part, see Penal Code § 16520.
Penalty for possession of deadly weapon described in this section within State Capitol, legislative offices, etc., see Penal Code § 171c.
Possession of deadly weapons with intent to assault, see Penal Code § 17500.

Title 2

WEAPONS GENERALLY

Division 1

MISCELLANEOUS RULES RELATING TO WEAPONS GENERALLY

Section

§ 17500. Deadly weapon; possession with intent to assault

Every person having upon the person any deadly weapon, with intent to assault another, is guilty of a misdemeanor. *(Added by Stats.2010, c. 711 (S.B.1080), § 6, operative Jan. 1, 2012.)*

Law Revision Commission Comments

Section 17500 continues former Section 12024 without substantive change. [38 Cal.L.Rev.Comm. Reports 217 (2009)].

Cross References

Assault with deadly weapon, see Penal Code § 245 et seq.
Control of deadly weapons, see Penal Code § 16000 et seq.
Fine where none prescribed, see Penal Code § 672.
Misdemeanor,
Defined, see Penal Code § 17.
Punishment, see Penal Code §§ 19, 19.2.
Threatening crime victim, witness or informant, punishment, see Penal Code § 140.

Research References

California Jury Instructions - Criminal 16.293, Possession of a Deadly Weapon With Intent to Assault.
2 Witkin, California Criminal Law 4th Crimes Against Public Peace and Welfare § 189 (2021), In General.

§ 17505. Advertising of unlawful weapons or devices prohibited

It shall be unlawful for any person, as defined in Section 16970, to advertise the sale of any weapon or device, the possession of which is prohibited by Section 18710, 20110, 30315, 30320, 32625, or 33410, by Article 2 (commencing with Section 30600) of Chapter 2 of Division 10 of Title 4, or by any provision listed in Section 16590, in any newspaper, magazine, circular, form letter, or open publication that is published, distributed, or circulated in this state, or on any billboard, card, label, or other advertising medium, or by means of any other advertising device. *(Added by Stats.2010, c. 711 (S.B.1080), § 6, operative Jan. 1, 2012.)*

Law Revision Commission Comments

Section 17505 continues former Section 12020.5 without substantive change. [38 Cal.L.Rev.Comm. Reports 217 (2009)].

Research References

2 Witkin, California Criminal Law 4th Crimes Against Public Peace and Welfare § 189 (2021), In General.

§ 17510. Carrying firearm or deadly weapon while engaged in labor related picketing prohibited

(a) Any person who does any of the following acts while engaged in picketing, or other informational activities in a public place relating to a concerted refusal to work, is guilty of a misdemeanor:

(1) Carries concealed upon the person, or within any vehicle which is under the person's control or direction, any pistol, revolver, or other firearm capable of being concealed upon the person.

(2) Carries a loaded firearm upon the person or within any vehicle that is under the person's control or direction.

(3) Carries a deadly weapon.

(b) This section shall not be construed to authorize or ratify any picketing or other informational activities not otherwise authorized by law.

(c) The following provisions shall not be construed to authorize any conduct described in paragraph (1) of subdivision (a):

(1) Article 2 (commencing with Section 25450) of Chapter 2 of Division 5 of Title 4.

(2) Sections 25615 to 25655, inclusive.

(d) Sections 25900 to 26020, inclusive, shall not be construed to authorize any conduct described in paragraph (2) of subdivision (a). *(Added by Stats.2010, c. 711 (S.B.1080), § 6, operative Jan. 1, 2012.)*

Law Revision Commission Comments

Subdivision (a) of Section 17510 continues former Section 12590(a)(1)-(3) without substantive change.

With respect to the acts enumerated in subdivision (a), subdivision (b) continues former Section 12590(b) without substantive change. See also Section 830.95(b), which continues former Section 12590(b) with respect to picketing in the uniform of a peace officer.

Subdivisions (c) and (d) continue former Section 12590(c) without substantive change.

See Sections 16520 ("firearm"), 16530 ("firearm capable of being concealed upon the person," "pistol," and "revolver"). [38 Cal.L.Rev.Comm. Reports 217 (2009)].

Cross References

Firearm capable of being concealed upon the person defined for purposes of this Part, see Penal Code § 16530.
Firearm defined for purposes of this Part, see Penal Code § 16520.
Misdemeanors, definition and penalties, see Penal Code §§ 17, 19, 19.2.
Pistol defined for purposes of this Part, see Penal Code § 16530.
Revolver defined for purposes of this Part, see Penal Code § 16530.

Research References

2 Witkin, California Criminal Law 4th Crimes Against Public Peace and Welfare § 64 (2021), Improper Picketing Activity.
2 Witkin, California Criminal Law 4th Crimes Against Public Peace and Welfare § 203 (2021), Nature of Crime.

§ 17512. Permitting person to carry or bring firearm into a motor vehicle

It is a misdemeanor for a driver of any motor vehicle or the owner of any motor vehicle, whether or not the owner of the vehicle is occupying the vehicle, to knowingly permit any other person to carry into or bring into the vehicle a firearm in violation of Section 26350. *(Added by Stats.2011, c. 725 (A.B.144), § 10.)*

Cross References

Firearm defined for purposes of this Part, see Penal Code § 16520.
Misdemeanors, definition and penalties, see Penal Code §§ 17, 19, 19.2.

Research References

2 Witkin, California Criminal Law 4th Crimes Against Public Peace and Welfare § 253 (2021), Openly Displaying or Carrying Imitation or Unloaded Firearm.

§ 17515. Carrying of equipment authorized for the enforcement of law or ordinance

Nothing in any provision listed in Section 16580 prohibits a police officer, special police officer, peace officer, or law enforcement officer from carrying any equipment authorized for the enforcement of law or ordinance in any city or county. *(Added by Stats.2010, c. 711 (S.B.1080), § 6, operative Jan. 1, 2012.)*

Law Revision Commission Comments

With respect to "any equipment authorized for the enforcement of law or ordinance in any city or county," Section 17515 continues former Section 12002(a) without substantive change. The remainder of former Section 12002(a) is continued in Section 22295(a) without substantive change. [38 Cal.L.Rev.Comm. Reports 217 (2009)].

Cross References

Humane officers, authorized to carry firearms, see Corporations Code § 14502.
Machine guns, sale to or possession by police departments, see Penal Code § 32610.
National Guard, commissioned officer to provide himself with prescribed arms, see Military and Veterans Code § 226.
Persons authorized to carry and possess concealed weapons, see Penal Code § 25450 et seq.
Tear gas weapons, exception in favor of peace officers, see Penal Code § 22820.

Division 2

GENERALLY PROHIBITED WEAPONS

CHAPTER 1. EXEMPTIONS

§ 17700. Antique firearm; application of Section 16590

The provisions listed in Section 16590 do not apply to any antique firearm. *(Added by Stats.2010, c. 711 (S.B.1080), § 6, operative Jan. 1, 2012.)*

Law Revision Commission Comments

Section 17700 continues the first sentence of former Section 12020(b)(5) without substantive change.

See Section 16170 ("antique firearm"). [38 Cal.L.Rev.Comm. Reports 217 (2009)].

Cross References

Antique firearm defined, see Penal Code § 16170.
Firearm defined for purposes of this Part, see Penal Code § 16520.

Research References

2 Witkin, California Criminal Law 4th Crimes Against Public Peace and Welfare § 211 (2021), Nature of Crime.
2 Witkin, California Criminal Law 4th Crimes Against Public Peace and Welfare § 263 (2021), Nuisances.

§ 17705. Firearm or ammunition that is curio or relic; prohibited persons obtaining title to firearms or ammunition by bequest or intestate succession; application of Section 16590

(a) The provisions listed in Section 16590 do not apply to any firearm or ammunition that is a curio or relic as defined in Section 478.11 of Title 27 of the Code of Federal Regulations and that is in the possession of a person permitted to possess the items under Chapter 44 (commencing with Section 921) of Title 18 of the United States Code and the regulations issued pursuant thereto.

(b) Any person prohibited by Chapter 1 (commencing with Section 29610), Chapter 2 (commencing with Section 29800), or Chapter 3 (commencing with Section 29900) of Division 9 of Title 4 of this part, or Section 8100 or 8103 of the Welfare and Institutions Code, from possessing firearms or ammunition who obtains title to these items by bequest or intestate succession may retain title for not more than one year, but actual possession of these items at any time is punishable under Chapter 1 (commencing with Section 29610), Chapter 2 (commencing with Section 29800), or Chapter 3 (commencing with Section 29900) of Division 9 of Title 4 of this part, or Section 8100 or 8103 of the Welfare and Institutions Code. Within the year, the person shall transfer title to the firearms or ammunition by sale, gift, or other disposition. Any person who violates this section is in violation of the applicable provision listed in Section 16590. *(Added by Stats.2010, c. 711 (S.B.1080), § 6, operative Jan. 1, 2012.)*

Law Revision Commission Comments

Section 17705 continues former Section 12020(b)(7) without substantive change.

See Section 16520 ("firearm"). [38 Cal.L.Rev.Comm. Reports 217 (2009)].

Cross References

Firearm defined for purposes of this Part, see Penal Code § 16520.
Penalty for possession of deadly weapon described in this section within State Capitol, legislative offices, etc., see Penal Code § 171c.
Possession of deadly weapons with intent to assault, see Penal Code § 17500.

Research References

2 Witkin, California Criminal Law 4th Crimes Against Public Peace and Welfare § 232 (2021), Nature and Scope of Statutes.

§ 17710. Any other weapon in possession of person permitted under federal Gun Control Act of 1968; prohibited persons obtaining title to weapons by bequest or intestate succession; application of Section 16590

(a) The provisions listed in Section 16590 do not apply to "any other weapon" as defined in subsection (e) of Section 5845 of Title 26 of the United States Code, which is in the possession of a person permitted to possess the weapons under the federal Gun Control Act of 1968 (Public Law 90–618),[1] as amended, and the regulations issued pursuant thereto.

(b) Any person prohibited by Chapter 1 (commencing with Section 29610), Chapter 2 (commencing with Section 29800), or Chapter 3 (commencing with Section 29900) of Division 9 of Title 4 of this part, or Section 8100 or 8103 of the Welfare and Institutions Code, from possessing these weapons who obtains title to these weapons by bequest or intestate succession may retain title for not more than one year, but actual possession of these weapons at any time is punishable under Chapter 1 (commencing with Section 29610), Chapter 2 (commencing with Section 29800), or Chapter 3 (commencing with Section 29900) of Division 9 of Title 4 of this part, or Section 8100 or 8103 of the Welfare and Institutions Code. Within the year, the person shall transfer title to the weapons by sale, gift, or other disposition. Any person who violates this section is in violation of the applicable provision listed in Section 16590.

(c) The exemption provided by this section does not apply to a pen gun. *(Added by Stats.2010, c. 711 (S.B.1080), § 6, operative Jan. 1, 2012.)*

1 For public law sections classified to the U.S.C.A., see USCA–Tables.

Law Revision Commission Comments

Section 17710 continues former Section 12020(b)(8) without substantive change. [38 Cal.L.Rev.Comm. Reports 217 (2009)].

Cross References

Penalty for possession of deadly weapon described in this section within State Capitol, legislative offices, etc., see Penal Code § 171c.
Possession of deadly weapons with intent to assault, see Penal Code § 17500.

§ 17715. Instrument or device possessed by historical society, museum, or institutional collection; application of Section 16590

The provisions listed in Section 16590 do not apply to any instrument or device that is possessed by a federal, state, or local historical society, museum, or institutional collection that is open to the public if all of the following conditions are satisfied:

(a) The instrument or device is properly housed.

(b) The instrument or device is secured from unauthorized handling.

(c) If the instrument or device is a firearm, it is unloaded. *(Added by Stats.2010, c. 711 (S.B.1080), § 6, operative Jan. 1, 2012.)*

Law Revision Commission Comments

Section 17715 continues former Section 12020(b)(9) without substantive change.

See Section 16520 ("firearm"). [38 Cal.L.Rev.Comm. Reports 217 (2009)].

Cross References

Firearm defined for purposes of this Part, see Penal Code § 16520.

§ 17720. Instrument or device possessed or used during course of motion picture, television, video production, or entertainment event; application of Section 16590

The provisions listed in Section 16590 do not apply to any instrument or device, other than a short-barreled rifle or a short-barreled shotgun, which is possessed or used during the course of a motion picture, television, or video production or entertainment event by an authorized participant therein in the course of making that production or event or by an authorized employee or agent of the entity producing that production or event. *(Added by Stats.2010, c. 711 (S.B.1080), § 6, operative Jan. 1, 2012.)*

Law Revision Commission Comments

Section 17720 continues former Section 12020(b)(10) without substantive change.

See Sections 17170 ("short-barreled rifle"), 17180 ("short-barreled shotgun"). [38 Cal.L.Rev.Comm. Reports 217 (2009)].

Cross References

Rifle defined, see Penal Code § 17090.
Short-barreled rifle defined, see Penal Code § 17170.
Short-barreled shotgun defined, see Penal Code § 17180.
Shotgun defined, see Penal Code § 17190.

§ 17725. Persons in the business of selling instruments or devices listed in Section 16590 to specified entities; application of Section 16590

The provisions listed in Section 16590 do not apply to any instrument or device, other than a short-barreled rifle or a short-barreled shotgun, which is sold by, manufactured by, exposed or kept for sale by, possessed by, imported by, or lent by a person who is in the business of selling instruments or devices listed in Section 16590 solely to the entities referred to in Sections 17715 and 17720 when engaging in transactions with those entities. *(Added by Stats.2010, c. 711 (S.B.1080), § 6, operative Jan. 1, 2012.)*

Law Revision Commission Comments

Section 17725 continues former Section 12020(b)(11) without substantive change.

See Sections 17170 ("short-barreled rifle"), 17180 ("short-barreled shotgun"). [38 Cal.L.Rev.Comm. Reports 217 (2009)].

Cross References

Rifle defined, see Penal Code § 17090.
Short-barreled rifle defined, see Penal Code § 17170.
Short-barreled shotgun defined, see Penal Code § 17180.
Shotgun defined, see Penal Code § 17190.

§ 17730. Sale to, possession or purchase of weapon, device, or ammunition by law enforcement officer; persons in the business of selling weapons, devices, or ammunition listed in Section 16590 to specified entities; application of Section 16590

The provisions listed in Section 16590 do not apply to any of the following:

(a) The sale to, possession of, or purchase of any weapon, device, or ammunition, other than a short-barreled rifle or a short-barreled shotgun, by any federal, state, county, city and county, or city agency that is charged with the enforcement of any law for use in the discharge of its official duties.

(b) The possession of any weapon, device, or ammunition, other than a short-barreled rifle or short-barreled shotgun, by any peace officer of any federal, state, county, city and county, or city agency that is charged with the enforcement of any law, when the officer is on duty and the use is authorized by the agency and is within the course and scope of the officer's duties.

(c) Any weapon, device, or ammunition, other than a short-barreled rifle or a short-barreled shotgun, that is sold by, manufactured by, exposed or kept for sale by, possessed by, imported by, or lent by, any person who is in the business of selling weapons, devices, and ammunition listed in Section 16590 solely to the entities referred to in subdivision (a) when engaging in transactions with those entities. *(Added by Stats.2010, c. 711 (S.B.1080), § 6, operative Jan. 1, 2012.)*

Law Revision Commission Comments

Subdivisions (a) and (b) of Section 17730 continue former Section 12020(b)(12) without substantive change.

Subdivision (c) continues former Section 12020(b)(13) without substantive change.

See Sections 17170 ("short-barreled rifle"), 17180 ("short-barreled shotgun"). [38 Cal.L.Rev.Comm. Reports 217 (2009)].

Cross References

Rifle defined, see Penal Code § 17090.
Short-barreled rifle defined, see Penal Code § 17170.
Short-barreled shotgun defined, see Penal Code § 17180.
Shotgun defined, see Penal Code § 17190.

§ 17735. Persons meeting specified criteria who possess an instrument, ammunition, weapon, or device that is not a firearm; application of Section 16590

The provisions listed in Section 16590 do not apply to any instrument, ammunition, weapon, or device that is not a firearm and is found and possessed by a person who meets all of the following:

(a) The person is not prohibited from possessing firearms or ammunition under subdivision (a) of Section 30305 or Chapter 2 (commencing with Section 29800) or Chapter 3 (commencing with

Section 29900) of Division 9 of Title 4 of this part, or Section 8100 or 8103 of the Welfare and Institutions Code.

(b) The person possessed the instrument, ammunition, weapon, or device no longer than was necessary to deliver or transport it to a law enforcement agency for that agency's disposition according to law.

(c) If the person is transporting the item, the person is transporting it to a law enforcement agency for disposition according to law. *(Added by Stats.2010, c. 711 (S.B.1080), § 6, operative Jan. 1, 2012.)*

Law Revision Commission Comments

Section 17735 continues former Section 12020(b)(16) without substantive change.

See Section 16520 ("firearm"). [38 Cal.L.Rev.Comm. Reports 217 (2009)].

Cross References

Firearm defined for purposes of this Part, see Penal Code § 16520.

§ 17740. Firearms found and possessed by persons otherwise not prohibited during transport to a law enforcement agency; application of Section 16590

The provisions listed in Section 16590 do not apply to any firearm, other than a short-barreled rifle or short-barreled shotgun, which is found and possessed by a person who meets all of the following:

(a) The person is not prohibited from possessing firearms or ammunition under subdivision (a) of Section 30305 or Chapter 2 (commencing with Section 29800) or Chapter 3 (commencing with Section 29900) of Division 9 of Title 4 of this part, or Section 8100 or 8103 of the Welfare and Institutions Code.

(b) The person possessed the firearm no longer than was necessary to deliver or transport it to a law enforcement agency for that agency's disposition according to law.

(c) If the person is transporting the firearm, the person is transporting it to a law enforcement agency for disposition according to law.

(d) Before transporting the firearm to a law enforcement agency, the person has given prior notice to that law enforcement agency that the person is transporting the firearm to that law enforcement agency for disposition according to law.

(e) The firearm is transported in a locked container as defined in Section 16850. *(Added by Stats.2010, c. 711 (S.B.1080), § 6, operative Jan. 1, 2012.)*

Law Revision Commission Comments

Section 17740 continues former Section 12020(b)(17) without substantive change.

See Sections 16520 ("firearm"), 17170 ("short-barreled rifle"), 17180 ("short-barreled shotgun"). [38 Cal.L.Rev.Comm. Reports 217 (2009)].

Cross References

Firearm defined for purposes of this Part, see Penal Code § 16520.
Rifle defined, see Penal Code § 17090.
Short-barreled rifle defined, see Penal Code § 17170.
Short-barreled shotgun defined, see Penal Code § 17180.
Shotgun defined, see Penal Code § 17190.

§ 17745. Possession of weapon, device, or ammunition by forensic laboratory; application of Section 16590

The provisions listed in Section 16590 do not apply to the possession of any weapon, device, or ammunition by a forensic laboratory or by any authorized agent or employee thereof in the course and scope of the person's authorized activities. *(Added by Stats.2010, c. 711 (S.B.1080), § 6, operative Jan. 1, 2012.)*

Law Revision Commission Comments

Section 17745 continues former Section 12020(b)(18) without substantive change. [38 Cal.L.Rev.Comm. Reports 217 (2009)].

CHAPTER 2. MISCELLANEOUS PROVISIONS

§ 17800. Prohibited weapons; multiple offenses

For purposes of the provisions listed in Section 16590, a violation as to each firearm, weapon, or device enumerated in any of those provisions shall constitute a distinct and separate offense. *(Added by Stats.2010, c. 711 (S.B.1080), § 6, operative Jan. 1, 2012.)*

Law Revision Commission Comments

Section 17800 continues former Section 12001(*l*) without substantive change.

See Section 16520 ("firearm"). [38 Cal.L.Rev.Comm. Reports 217 (2009)].

Cross References

Firearm defined for purposes of this Part, see Penal Code § 16520.

Research References

2 Witkin, California Criminal Law 4th Crimes Against Public Peace and Welfare § 211 (2021), Nature of Crime.
2 Witkin, California Criminal Law 4th Crimes Against Public Peace and Welfare § 213 (2021), Concealed Dirk, Dagger, or Explosives.
2 Witkin, California Criminal Law 4th Crimes Against Public Peace and Welfare § 234 (2021), Effect of Pardon or Dismissal After Fulfillment of Probation Conditions.

Division 3

SURRENDER, DISPOSAL, AND ENJOINING OF WEAPONS CONSTITUTING A NUISANCE

§ 18000. Surrender of weapon to authorities

(a) Any weapon described in Section 19190, 21390, 21590, or 25700, or, upon conviction of the defendant or upon a juvenile court finding that an offense that would be a misdemeanor or felony if committed by an adult was committed or attempted by the juvenile with the use of a firearm, any weapon described in Section 29300, shall be surrendered to one of the following:

(1) The sheriff of a county.

(2) The chief of police or other head of a municipal police department of any city or city and county.

(3) The chief of police of any campus of the University of California or the California State University.

(4) The Commissioner of the California Highway Patrol.

(b) For purposes of this section, the Commissioner of the California Highway Patrol shall receive only weapons that were confiscated by a member of the California Highway Patrol.

(c) A finding that the defendant was guilty of the offense but was insane at the time the offense was committed is a conviction for the purposes of this section. *(Added by Stats.2010, c. 711 (S.B.1080), § 6, operative Jan. 1, 2012.)*

Law Revision Commission Comments

Subdivision (a) of Section 18000 continues the first sentence of former Section 12028(c) without substantive change.

Subdivision (b) continues the second sentence of former Section 12028(c) without substantive change.

In combination with Section 29300(b), subdivision (c) continues the second sentence of former Section 12028(b)(1) without substantive change.

For guidance on disposal of weapons surrendered pursuant to this section, see Section 18005 (disposal of weapons constituting nuisance). For additional guidance on surrender of deadly weapons, see Sections 18010 (treatment of other weapons constituting nuisance), 18250–18500 (seizure of firearm or other deadly weapon at scene of domestic violence), 33800 (receipt for firearm taken into custody by law enforcement officer).

See Section 16520 ("firearm"). [38 Cal.L.Rev.Comm. Reports 217 (2009)].

Cross References

Completion of sale, loan, or transfer of firearm through licensed person, compliance with Section 27545, procedures if dealer cannot legally return firearm to seller, transferor, or person loaning the firearm, see Penal Code § 28050.
Confiscation of firearms or deadly or dangerous weapons owned or possessed by gang members, see Penal Code § 186.22a.
Felonies, definition and penalties, see Penal Code §§ 17, 18.
Firearm defined for purposes of this Part, see Penal Code § 16520.
Misdemeanors, definition and penalties, see Penal Code §§ 17, 19, 19.2.
Sale of firearm precursor parts through licensed firearm precursor part vendor, requirements, exceptions, see Penal Code § 30412.
Transportation of firearm precursor part into the state by a resident, delivery to licensed firearm precursor part vendor, exceptions, see Penal Code § 30414.

Research References

2 Witkin, California Criminal Law 4th Crimes Against Public Peace and Welfare § 10 (2021), Intentional Infliction of Serious Bodily Injury.
2 Witkin, California Criminal Law 4th Crimes Against Public Peace and Welfare § 46 (2021), Place Used by Gang as Nuisance.
2 Witkin, California Criminal Law 4th Crimes Against Public Peace and Welfare § 193 (2021), Sale, Lease, or Transfer by Unlicensed Person.
2 Witkin, California Criminal Law 4th Crimes Against Public Peace and Welfare § 217 (2021), Possession.
2 Witkin, California Criminal Law 4th Crimes Against Public Peace and Welfare § 263 (2021), Nuisances.
3 Witkin, California Criminal Law 4th Punishment § 189 (2021), Criminal Actions.
3 Witkin, California Criminal Law 4th Punishment § 190 (2021), Noncriminal Actions.

§ 18005. Destruction of surrendered weapons; stolen weapons; retention of weapon as evidence

(a) An officer to whom * * * a weapon is surrendered under Section 18000, except upon the certificate of a judge of a court of record, or of the district attorney of the county, that the retention thereof is necessary or proper to the ends of justice, * * * shall destroy that weapon and, if applicable, submit proof of its destruction to the court.

(b) If any weapon has been stolen and is thereafter recovered from the thief or the thief's transferee, or is used in a manner as to constitute a nuisance under Section 19190, 21390, 21590, or 29300, or subdivision (a) of Section 25700 without the prior knowledge of its lawful owner that it would be so used, it shall not be * * * destroyed pursuant to subdivision (a) but shall be restored to the lawful owner, as soon as its use as evidence has been served, upon the lawful owner's identification of the weapon and proof of ownership, and after the law enforcement agency has complied with Chapter 2 (commencing with Section 33850) of Division 11 of Title 4.

* * *

(c) No stolen weapon shall be * * * destroyed pursuant to subdivision (a) * * * unless reasonable notice is given to its lawful owner, if the lawful owner's identity and address can be reasonably ascertained.

(d) If the weapon was evidence in a criminal case, the weapon shall be retained as required by Chapter 13 (commencing with Section 1417) of Title 10 of Part 2. *(Added by Stats.2010, c. 711 (S.B.1080), § 6, operative Jan. 1, 2012. Amended by Stats.2022, c. 58 (A.B.200), § 35, eff. June 30, 2022.)*

Law Revision Commission Comments

Subdivision (a) of Section 18005 continues the third sentence of former Section 12028(c) without substantive change.

Subdivision (b) continues the fourth sentence of former Section 12028(c) without substantive change.

Subdivision (c) continues former Section 12028(d) without substantive change.

Subdivision (d) continues former Section 12028(f) without substantive change.

For additional guidance on disposal of weapons taken into custody by a court or law enforcement agency, see Sections 18010 (treatment of other weapons constituting nuisance), 18250–18500 (seizure of firearm or other deadly weapon at scene of domestic violence), 33800–34010 (firearm in custody of court or law enforcement agency or similar situation). [38 Cal.L.Rev.Comm. Reports 217 (2009)].

Cross References

Completion of sale, loan, or transfer of firearm through licensed person, compliance with Section 27545, procedures if dealer cannot legally return firearm to seller, transferor, or person loaning the firearm, see Penal Code § 28050.
Confiscation of firearms or deadly or dangerous weapons owned or possessed by gang members, see Penal Code § 186.22a.
Possession of assault weapon or .50 BMG rifle, public nuisance, see Penal Code § 30800.
Public nuisances, see Civil Code § 3490 et seq.
Sale of firearm precursor parts through licensed firearm precursor part vendor, requirements, exceptions, see Penal Code § 30412.
Transportation of firearm precursor part into the state by a resident, delivery to licensed firearm precursor part vendor, exceptions, see Penal Code § 30414.

Research References

2 Witkin, California Criminal Law 4th Crimes Against Public Peace and Welfare § 193 (2021), Sale, Lease, or Transfer by Unlicensed Person.
2 Witkin, California Criminal Law 4th Crimes Against Public Peace and Welfare § 223 (2021), Civil Action to Enjoin Possession.
3 Witkin, California Criminal Law 4th Punishment § 190 (2021), Noncriminal Actions.

§ 18010. Weapons constituting nuisance; actions to enjoin; destruction of weapons

(a) The Attorney General, a district attorney, or a city attorney may bring an action to enjoin the manufacture of, importation of, keeping for sale of, offering or exposing for sale, giving, lending, or possession of, any item that constitutes a nuisance under any of the following provisions:

(1) Section 19290, relating to metal handgrenades.

(2) Section 20390, relating to an air gauge knife.

(3) Section 20490, relating to a belt buckle knife.

(4) Section 20590, relating to a cane sword.

(5) Section 20690, relating to a lipstick case knife.

(6) Section 20790, relating to a shobi-zue.

(7) Section 20990, relating to a writing pen knife.

(8) Section 21190, relating to a ballistic knife.

(9) Section 21890, relating to metal knuckles.

(10) Section 22290, relating to a leaded cane or an instrument or weapon of the kind commonly known as a billy, blackjack, sandbag, sandclub, sap, or slungshot.

(11) Section 22490, relating to a shuriken.

(12) Section 24390, relating to a camouflaging firearm container.

(13) Section 24490, relating to a cane gun.

(14) Section 24590, relating to a firearm not immediately recognizable as a firearm.

(15) Section 24690, relating to an undetectable firearm.

(16) Section 24790, relating to a wallet gun.

(17) Section 30290, relating to flechette dart ammunition and to a bullet with an explosive agent.

(18) Section 31590, relating to an unconventional pistol.

(19) Section 32390, relating to a large-capacity magazine.

(20) Section 32990, relating to a multiburst trigger activator.

(21) Section 33290, relating to a short-barreled rifle or a short-barreled shotgun.

(22) Section 33690, relating to a zip gun.

(b) The weapons described in subdivision (a) shall be subject to confiscation and summary destruction whenever found within the state.

(c) The weapons described in subdivision (a) shall be destroyed in the same manner described in Section 18005, except that upon the certification of a judge or of the district attorney that the ends of justice will be served thereby, the weapon shall be preserved until the necessity for its use ceases.

(d)(1) * * * The Attorney General, a district attorney, or a city attorney may bring an action to enjoin the importation into the state or sale or transfer of any firearm precursor part that is unlawfully imported into this state or sold or transferred within this state * * *.

(2) * * * Any firearm precursor parts that are unlawfully imported in this state or unlawfully sold, transferred, or possessed within this state * * * are a nuisance and are subject to confiscation and destruction pursuant to Section 18005. *(Added by Stats.2010, c. 711 (S.B.1080), § 6, operative Jan. 1, 2012. Amended by Stats.2019, c. 730 (A.B.879), § 4, eff. Jan. 1, 2020; Stats.2020, c. 29 (S.B.118), § 22, eff. Aug. 6, 2020; Stats.2021, c. 434 (S.B.827), § 23, eff. Jan. 1, 2022; Stats.2022, c. 76 (A.B.1621), § 10, eff. June 30, 2022.)*

Law Revision Commission Comments

Subdivision (a) of Section 18010 continues the end of the first sentence of former Section 12029 without substantive change.

Subdivision (b) continues the second sentence of former Section 12029 without substantive change.

Subdivision (c) continues the third sentence of former Section 12029 without substantive change.

For additional guidance on surrender and disposal of weapons, see Sections 18000 (surrender of specified weapons constituting nuisance), 18005 (disposal of weapons constituting nuisance), 18250–18500 (seizure of firearm or other deadly weapon at scene of domestic violence), 33800–34010 (firearm in custody of court or law enforcement agency or similar situation). [38 Cal.L.Rev. Comm. Reports 217 (2009)].

Cross References

Attorney General, generally, see Government Code § 12500 et seq.
Cane gun defined for purposes of this Part, see Penal Code § 16330.
Firearm defined for purposes of this Part, see Penal Code § 16520.
Large-capacity magazine defined for purposes of this Part, see Penal Code § 16740.
Metal knuckles defined for purposes of this Part, see Penal Code § 16920.
Nunchaku defined for purposes of this Part, see Penal Code § 16940.
Pistol defined for purposes of this Part, see Penal Code § 16530.
Unconventional pistol defined for purposes of this Part, see Penal Code § 17270.
Undetectable firearm defined for purposes of this Part, see Penal Code § 17280.
Wallet gun defined for purposes of this Part, see Penal Code § 17330.
Zip gun defined for purposes of this Part, see Penal Code § 17360.

Research References

2 Witkin, California Criminal Law 4th Crimes Against Public Peace and Welfare § 263 (2021), Nuisances.
3 Witkin, California Criminal Law 4th Punishment § 190 (2021), Noncriminal Actions.

Division 3.2

GUN VIOLENCE RESTRAINING ORDERS

CHAPTER 1. GENERAL

§ 18100. Gun violence restraining order

(a) A gun violence restraining order is an order, in writing, signed by the court, prohibiting and enjoining a named person from having in his or her custody or control, owning, purchasing, possessing, or receiving any firearms or ammunition. This division establishes a civil restraining order process to accomplish that purpose.

(b) For purposes of this chapter, the term "ammunition" includes a "magazine" as defined in Section 16890. *(Added by Stats.2014, c. 872 (A.B.1014), § 3, eff. Jan. 1, 2015, operative Jan. 1, 2016. Amended by Stats.2018, c. 898 (S.B.1200), § 3, eff. Jan. 1, 2019.)*

Cross References

Issuance of search warrant, grounds, special master, see Penal Code § 1524.

Research References

West's California Judicial Council Forms GV–100, Petition for Gun Violence Restraining Order (Also Available in Chinese, Korean, Spanish, and Vietnamese).
West's California Judicial Council Forms GV–100–INFO, Can a Gun Violence Restraining Order Help Me? (Also Available in Chinese, Korean, Spanish, and Vietnamese).
West's California Judicial Council Forms GV–109, Notice of Court Hearing (Also Available in Chinese, Korean, Spanish, and Vietnamese).

2 Witkin, California Criminal Law 4th Crimes Against Public Peace and Welfare § 242 (2021), Subjects of Protective and Restraining Orders.
4 Witkin, California Criminal Law 4th Illegally Obtained Evidence § 111 (2021), Statutory Grounds.

§ 18105. Petition and order form; promulgation of rules

The Judicial Council shall prescribe the form of the petitions and orders and any other documents, and shall promulgate any rules of court, necessary to implement this division. These forms, orders, and documents shall refer to any order issued pursuant to this chapter as a gun violence restraining order. *(Added by Stats.2014, c. 872 (A.B.1014), § 3, eff. Jan. 1, 2015, operative Jan. 1, 2016. Amended by Stats.2018, c. 898 (S.B.1200), § 4, eff. Jan. 1, 2019.)*

§ 18107. Petition for gun violence restraining order; description of firearms and ammunition

A petition for a gun violence restraining order shall describe the number, types, and locations of any firearms and ammunition presently believed by the petitioner to be possessed or controlled by the subject of the petition. *(Added by Stats.2014, c. 872 (A.B.1014), § 3, eff. Jan. 1, 2015, operative Jan. 1, 2016.)*

§ 18108. Gun violence restraining orders; policies and standards

(a) Each municipal police department and county sheriff's department, the Department of the California Highway Patrol, and the University of California and California State University Police Departments shall, on or before January 1, 2021, develop, adopt, and implement written policies and standards relating to gun violence restraining orders.

(b) The policies and standards shall instruct officers to consider the use of a gun violence restraining order during a domestic disturbance response to any residence which is associated with a firearm registration or record, during a response in which a firearm is present, or during a response in which one of the involved parties owns or possesses a firearm. The policies and standards should encourage the use of gun violence restraining orders in appropriate situations to prevent future violence involving a firearm.

(c) The policies and standards should also instruct officers to consider the use of a gun violence restraining order during a contact with a person exhibiting mental health issues, including suicidal thoughts, statements, or actions, if that person owns or possesses a firearm. The policies and standards shall encourage officers encountering situations in which there is reasonable cause to believe that the person poses an immediate and present danger of causing personal injury to themselves or another person by having custody or control of a firearm to consider obtaining a mental health evaluation of the person by a medically trained professional or to detain the person for mental health evaluation pursuant to agency policy relating to Section 5150 of the Welfare and Institutions Code. The policies and standards should reflect the policy of the agency to prevent access to firearms by persons who, due to mental health issues, pose a danger to themselves or to others by owning or possessing a firearm.

(d) The written policies and standards developed pursuant to this section shall be consistent with any gun violence restraining order training administered by the Commission on Peace Officer Standards and Training, and shall include all of the following:

(1) Standards and procedures for requesting and serving a temporary emergency gun violence restraining order.

(2) Standards and procedures for requesting and serving an ex parte gun violence restraining order.

(3) Standards and procedures for requesting and serving a gun violence restraining order issued after notice and hearing.

(4) Standards and procedures for the seizure of firearms and ammunition at the time of issuance of a temporary emergency gun violence restraining order.

(5) Standards and procedures for verifying the removal of firearms and ammunition from the subject of a gun violence restraining order.

(6) Standards and procedures for obtaining and serving a search warrant for firearms and ammunition.

(7) Responsibility of officers to attend gun violence restraining order hearings.

(8) Standards and procedures for requesting renewals of expiring gun violence restraining orders.

(e) Municipal police departments, county sheriff's departments, the Department of the California Highway Patrol, and the University of California and California State University Police Departments are encouraged, but not required by this section, to train officers on standards and procedures implemented pursuant to this section, and may incorporate these standards and procedures into an academy course, preexisting annual training, or other continuing education program.

(f) In developing these policies and standards, law enforcement agencies are encouraged to consult with gun violence prevention experts and mental health professionals.

(g) Policies developed pursuant to this section shall be made available to the public upon request. *(Added by Stats.2019, c. 727 (A.B.339), § 1, eff. Jan. 1, 2020.)*

§ 18109. Gun violence restraining orders not required in all cases; petition made in the name of law enforcement agency

(a) This division does not require a law enforcement agency or a law enforcement officer to seek a gun violence restraining order in any case, including, but not limited to, in a case in which the agency or officer concludes, after investigation, that the criteria for issuance of a gun violence restraining order are not satisfied.

(b) A petition brought by a law enforcement officer may be made in the name of the law enforcement agency in which the officer is employed.

(c) This section shall become operative on September 1, 2020. *(Added by Stats.2019, c. 724 (A.B.12), § 2, eff. Jan. 1, 2020, operative Sept. 1, 2020.)*

§ 18110. Procedure prior to hearing on issuance, renewal, or termination of order

Prior to a hearing on the issuance, renewal, or termination of an order under Chapter 3 (commencing with Section 18150) or Chapter 4 (commencing with Section 18170), the court shall ensure that a search as described in subdivision (a) of Section 6306 of the Family Code is conducted. After issuing its ruling, the court shall provide the advisement described in subdivision (c) of Section 6306 of the Family Code and shall keep information obtained from a search conducted pursuant to this section confidential in accordance with subdivision (d) of Section 6306 of the Family Code. *(Added by Stats.2014, c. 872 (A.B.1014), § 3, eff. Jan. 1, 2015, operative Jan. 1, 2016.)*

§ 18115. Issuance, dissolution or termination of gun violence restraining order; notification of Department of Justice

(a) The court shall notify the Department of Justice when a gun violence restraining order has been issued or renewed under this division no later than one court day after issuing or renewing the order.

(b) The court shall notify the Department of Justice when a gun violence restraining order has been dissolved or terminated under this division no later than five court days after dissolving or terminating the order. Upon receipt of either a notice of dissolution or a notice of termination of a gun violence restraining order, the Department of Justice shall, within 15 days, document the updated status of any order issued under this division.

(c) The notices required to be submitted to the Department of Justice pursuant to this section shall be submitted in an electronic format, in a manner prescribed by the department.

(d) When notifying the Department of Justice pursuant to subdivision (a) or (b), the court shall indicate in the notice whether the person subject to the gun violence restraining order has filed a relinquishment of firearm rights pursuant to subdivision (d) of Section 18175 or was present in court to be informed of the contents of the order or if the person failed to appear. The person's filing of relinquishment of firearm rights or the person's presence in court constitutes proof of service of notice of the terms of the order.

(e)(1) Within one business day of service, a law enforcement officer who served a gun violence restraining order shall submit the proof of service directly into the California Restraining and Protective Order System, including their name and law enforcement agency, and shall transmit the original proof of service form to the issuing court.

(2) Within one business day of receipt of proof of service by a person other than a law enforcement officer, the clerk of the court shall submit the proof of service of a gun violence restraining order directly into the California Restraining and Protective Order System, including the name of the person who served the order. If the court is unable to provide this notification to the Department of Justice by electronic transmission, the court shall, within one business day of receipt, transmit a copy of the proof of service to a local law enforcement agency. The local law enforcement agency shall submit the proof of service directly into the California Restraining and Protective Order System within one business day of receipt from the court.

(3) Within one business day of issuance of a gun violence restraining order based on a relinquishment of firearm rights pursuant to subdivision (d) of Section 18175, the clerk of the court shall enter the relinquishment of firearm rights form directly into the California Restraining and Protective Order System. If the court is unable to provide this notification to the Department of Justice by electronic transmission, the court shall, within one business day of receipt, transmit a copy of the relinquishment of firearm rights form to a local law enforcement agency. The local law enforcement agency shall submit the relinquishment of firearm rights form directly into the California Restraining and Protective Order System within one business day of receipt from the court. *(Added by Stats.2014, c. 872 (A.B.1014), § 3, eff. Jan. 1, 2015, operative Jan. 1, 2016. Amended by Stats.2015, c. 303 (A.B.731), § 411, eff. Jan. 1, 2016; Stats.2019, c. 733 (A.B.1493), § 1, eff. Jan. 1, 2020.)*

Research References

West's California Judicial Council Forms GV–125, Consent to Gun Violence Restraining Order and Surrender of Firearms.

§ 18120. Persons subject to gun violence restraining order; surrender of firearms and ammunition

(a) A person subject to a gun violence restraining order issued pursuant to this division shall not have in the person's custody or control, own, purchase, possess, or receive any firearms or ammunition while that order is in effect.

(b)(1) Upon issuance of a gun violence restraining order issued pursuant to this division, the court shall order the restrained person to surrender all firearms and ammunition in the restrained person's custody or control, or which the restrained person possesses or owns pursuant to this subdivision.

(2) The surrender ordered pursuant to paragraph (1) shall occur by immediately surrendering all firearms and ammunition in a safe manner, upon request of a law enforcement officer, to the control of the officer, after being served with the restraining order. A law enforcement officer serving a gun violence restraining order that indicates that the restrained person possesses firearms or ammunition shall request that all firearms and ammunition be immediately surrendered.

(3) If the gun violence restraining order is issued as an ex parte order or order after notice and hearing, and is served by a person other than a law enforcement officer, and if no request is made by a law enforcement officer, the surrender shall occur within 24 hours of being served with the order, by surrendering all firearms and ammunition in a safe manner to the control of a local law enforcement agency, selling all firearms and ammunition to a licensed firearms dealer, or transferring all firearms and ammunition to a licensed firearms dealer in accordance with Section 29830.

(4) The law enforcement officer or licensed firearms dealer taking possession of firearms or ammunition pursuant to this subdivision shall issue a receipt to the person surrendering the firearm or firearms or ammunition or both at the time of surrender.

(5) A person ordered to surrender all firearms and ammunition pursuant to this subdivision shall, within 48 hours after being served with the order, do both of the following:

(A) File with the court that issued the gun violence restraining order the original receipt showing all firearms and ammunition have been surrendered to a local law enforcement agency or sold or transferred to a licensed firearms dealer. Failure to timely file a receipt shall constitute a violation of the restraining order.

(B) File a copy of the receipt described in subparagraph (A) with the law enforcement agency, if any, that served the gun violence restraining order. Failure to timely file a copy of the receipt shall constitute a violation of the restraining order.

(c)(1) Except as provided in paragraph (2), firearms or ammunition surrendered to a law enforcement officer or law enforcement agency pursuant to this section shall be retained by the law enforcement agency until the expiration of a gun violence restraining order that has been issued against the restrained person. Upon expiration of an order, the firearms or ammunition shall be returned to the restrained person in accordance with the provisions of Chapter 2 (commencing with Section 33850) of Division 11 of Title 4. Firearms or ammunition that are not claimed are subject to the requirements of Section 34000.

(2) A restrained person who owns firearms or ammunition that are in the custody of a law enforcement agency pursuant to this section is entitled to sell the firearms or ammunition to a licensed firearms dealer or transfer the firearms or ammunition to a licensed firearms dealer in accordance with Section 29830 if the firearm or firearms or ammunition are otherwise legal to own or possess and the restrained person otherwise has right to title of the firearm or firearms or ammunition.

(d) If a person other than the restrained person claims title to firearms or ammunition surrendered pursuant to this section, and the person is determined by the law enforcement agency to be the lawful owner of the firearm or firearms or ammunition, the firearm or firearms or ammunition shall be returned to the person pursuant to Chapter 2 (commencing with Section 33850) of Division 11 of Title 4.

(e) Within one business day of receiving the receipt referred to in paragraph (4) of subdivision (b), the court that issued the order shall transmit a copy of the receipt to the Department of Justice in a manner and pursuant to a process prescribed by the department.

(f) This section shall become operative on September 1, 2020. *(Added by Stats.2019, c. 724 (A.B.12), § 4, eff. Jan. 1, 2020, operative Sept. 1, 2020.)*

Cross References

Retention of records, registry of firearms, dissemination of information in the records by officer, conditions, see Penal Code § 11106.

Research References

West's California Judicial Council Forms GV–800, Proof of Firearms, Ammunition, and Magazines Turned In, Sold, or Stored (Also Available in Chinese, Korean, Spanish, and Vietnamese).

West's California Judicial Council Forms GV–800–INFO, How Do I Turn In, Sell, or Store My Firearms? (Also Available in Chinese, Korean, Spanish, and Vietnamese).

2 Witkin, California Criminal Law 4th Crimes Against Public Peace and Welfare § 242 (2021), Subjects of Protective and Restraining Orders.

§ 18121. Gun violence restraining order; filing fees; fee for subpoena

There is no filing fee for an application, a responsive pleading, or an order to show cause that seeks to obtain, modify, or enforce a gun violence restraining order or other order authorized by this division if the request for the other order is necessary to obtain or give effect to a gun violence restraining order or other order authorized by this division. There is no fee for a subpoena filed in connection with that application, responsive pleading, or order to show cause. There is no fee for any filings related to a petition filed pursuant to this division. *(Added by Stats.2018, c. 898 (S.B.1200), § 6, eff. Jan. 1, 2019. Amended by Stats.2021, c. 686 (S.B.538), § 4, eff. Jan. 1, 2022.)*

Cross References

Acceptance of Judicial Council form, summons, order, or other notices by email, fax, or in-person delivery, fee, court fee waiver or exemption, see Government Code § 26666.5.

§ 18122. Electronic submission of petitions; availability of electronic filing and self-help center information on homepage; adoption of rules and forms for implementation

Section operative July 1, 2023.

(a)(1) A court or court facility that receives petitions for any restraining order under this division or temporary gun violence restraining orders consistent with Chapter 2 (commencing with Section 18125) shall permit those petitions to be submitted electronically. The court or court facility shall, based on the time of receipt, act on these filings consistent with Section 18150.

(2) The request, notice of the court date, copies of the request to serve on the respondent, and the temporary restraining order, if granted, shall be provided to the petitioner electronically, unless the petitioner notes, at the time of electronic filing, that these documents will be picked up from the court or court facility.

(b)(1) Information regarding electronic filing and access to the court's self-help center shall be prominently displayed on each court's homepage.

(2) Each self-help center shall maintain and make available information related to gun violence restraining orders pursuant to this section.

(c) The Judicial Council may adopt or amend rules and forms to implement this section.

(d) This section shall become operative on July 1, 2023. *(Added by Stats.2022, c. 420 (A.B.2960), § 30, eff. Jan. 1, 2023, operative July 1, 2023.)*

§ 18123. Remote appearance of parties and witnesses; development and publication of local rules

* * * A party or witness may appear remotely at the hearing on a petition for a gun violence restraining order. The superior court of each county shall develop local rules and instructions for remote appearances permitted under this section, which shall be posted on its internet website.

* * * *(Added by Stats.2021, c. 686 (S.B.538), § 7, eff. Jan. 1, 2022. Amended by Stats.2022, c. 420 (A.B.2960), § 31, eff. Jan. 1, 2023.)*

CHAPTER 2. TEMPORARY EMERGENCY GUN VIOLENCE RESTRAINING ORDER

Section

§ 18125. Temporary emergency gun violence restraining order; ex parte order; conditions

(a) A temporary emergency gun violence restraining order may be issued on an ex parte basis only if a law enforcement officer asserts, and a judicial officer finds, that there is reasonable cause to believe both of the following:

(1) The subject of the petition poses an immediate and present danger of causing personal injury to himself, herself, or another by having in his or her custody or control, owning, purchasing, possessing, or receiving a firearm or ammunition.

(2) A temporary emergency gun violence restraining order is necessary to prevent personal injury to the subject of the petition or another because less restrictive alternatives either have been tried and found to be ineffective, or have been determined to be inadequate or inappropriate for the circumstances of the subject of the petition.

(b) A temporary emergency gun violence restraining order issued pursuant to this chapter shall prohibit the subject of the petition from having in his or her custody or control, owning, purchasing, possessing, or receiving, or attempting to purchase or receive, a firearm or ammunition, and shall expire 21 days from the date the order is issued. *(Added by Stats.2014, c. 872 (A.B.1014), § 3, eff. Jan. 1, 2015, operative Jan. 1, 2016. Amended by Stats.2018, c. 898 (S.B.1200), § 7, eff. Jan. 1, 2019.)*

Research References

West's California Judicial Council Forms EPO–002, Gun Violence Emergency Protective Order (Also Available in Chinese, Korean, Spanish, and Vietnamese).

West's California Judicial Council Forms GV–020–INFO, How Can I Respond to a Gun Violence Emergency Protective Order (Gun Violence Prevention).

2 Witkin, California Criminal Law 4th Crimes Against Public Peace and Welfare § 242 (2021), Subjects of Protective and Restraining Orders.

§ 18130. Validity of temporary order

A temporary emergency gun violence restraining order is valid only if it is issued by a judicial officer after making the findings required by Section 18125 and pursuant to a specific request by a law enforcement officer. *(Added by Stats.2014, c. 872 (A.B.1014), § 3, eff. Jan. 1, 2015, operative Jan. 1, 2016)*

§ 18135. Contents of temporary order

(a) A temporary emergency gun violence restraining order issued under this chapter shall include all of the following:

(1) A statement of the grounds supporting the issuance of the order.

(2) The date and time the order expires.

(3) The address of the superior court for the county in which the restrained party resides.

(4) The following statement:

"To the restrained person: This order will last until the date and time noted above. You are required to surrender all firearms, ammunition, and magazines that you own or possess in accordance with Section 18120 of the Penal Code and you may not have in your custody or control, own, purchase, possess, or receive, or attempt to purchase or receive any firearm, ammunition, or magazine while this order is in effect. However, a more permanent gun violence restraining order may be obtained from the court. You may seek the advice of an attorney as to any matter connected with the order. The attorney should be consulted promptly so that the attorney may assist you in any matter connected with the order."

(b) When serving a temporary emergency gun violence restraining order, a law enforcement officer shall verbally ask the restrained person if he or she has any firearm, ammunition, or magazine in his or her possession or under his or her custody or control. *(Added by Stats.2014, c. 872 (A.B.1014), § 3, eff. Jan. 1, 2015, operative Jan. 1, 2016. Amended by Stats.2018, c. 898 (S.B.1200), § 8, eff. Jan. 1, 2019.)*

§ 18140. Temporary orders; actions by officer requesting order

A law enforcement officer who requests a temporary emergency gun violence restraining order shall do all of the following:

(a) If the request is made orally, sign a declaration under penalty of perjury reciting the oral statements provided to the judicial officer and memorialize the order of the court on the form approved by the Judicial Council.

(b) Serve the order on the restrained person, if the restrained person can reasonably be located.

(c) File a copy of the order with the court as soon as practicable, but not later than three court days, after issuance.

(d) Have the order entered into the computer database system for protective and restraining orders maintained by the Department of Justice. *(Added by Stats.2014, c. 872 (A.B.1014), § 3, eff. Jan. 1, 2015, operative Jan. 1, 2016. Amended by Stats.2018, c. 873 (A.B. 2526), § 1, eff. Jan. 1, 2019; Stats.2020, c. 286 (A.B.2617), § 1, eff. Jan. 1, 2021.)*

§ 18145. Oral issuance of temporary order; written issuance of temporary order; designation of judge, commissioner, or referee available to issue temporary orders

(a)(1) A judicial officer may issue a temporary emergency gun violence restraining order orally based on the statements of a law enforcement officer made in accordance with subdivision (a) of Section 18140.

(2) If time and circumstances permit, a temporary emergency gun violence restraining order may be obtained in writing and based on a declaration signed under penalty of perjury.

(b) The presiding judge of the superior court of each county shall designate at least one judge, commissioner, or referee who shall be reasonably available to issue temporary emergency gun violence restraining orders when the court is not in session. *(Added by Stats.2014, c. 872 (A.B.1014), § 3, eff. Jan. 1, 2015, operative Jan. 1, 2016. Amended by Stats.2018, c. 873 (A.B.2526), § 2, eff. Jan. 1, 2019.)*

§ 18148. Hearing on issuance of gun violence restraining order

Within 21 days after the date on the order, the court that issued the order or another court in the same jurisdiction, shall hold a hearing pursuant to Section 18175 to determine if a gun violence restraining order should be issued pursuant to Chapter 4 (commencing with Section 18170) after notice and hearing. *(Added by Stats.2018, c. 898 (S.B.1200), § 9, eff. Jan. 1, 2019.)*

Research References

West's California Judicial Council Forms GV–009, Notice of Court Hearing.

CHAPTER 3. EX PARTE GUN VIOLENCE RESTRAINING ORDER

Section

§ 18150. Petition by immediate family member, employer, coworker, teacher, law enforcement officer, roommate, or individual who has dating relationship or child in common

(a)(1) Any of the following individuals may file a petition requesting that the court issue an ex parte gun violence restraining order enjoining the subject of the petition from having in their custody or control, owning, purchasing, possessing, or receiving a firearm or ammunition:

(A) An immediate family member of the subject of the petition.

(B) An employer of the subject of the petition.

(C) A coworker of the subject of the petition, if they have had substantial and regular interactions with the subject for at least one year and have obtained the approval of the employer.

(D) An employee or teacher of a secondary or postsecondary school that the subject has attended in the last six months, if the employee or teacher has obtained the approval of a school administrator or a school administration staff member with a supervisorial role.

(E) A law enforcement officer.

(F) A roommate of the subject of the petition.

(G) An individual who has a dating relationship with the subject of the petition.

(H) An individual who has a child in common with the subject of the petition, if they have had substantial and regular interactions with the subject for at least one year.

(2) For purposes of this subdivision, "dating relationship" has the same meaning as in paragraph (10) of subdivision (f) of Section 243.

(3) For purposes of this subdivision, "immediate family member" * * * means any spouse, whether by marriage or not, domestic partner, parent, child, any person related by consanguinity or affinity within the second degree, or any person related by consanguinity or affinity within the fourth degree who has had substantial and regular interactions with the subject for at least one year.

(4) For purposes of this subdivision, "roommate" means a person who regularly resides in the household, or who, within the prior six months, regularly resided in the household, and who has had substantial and regular interactions with the subject for at least one year.

(5) This chapter does not require a person described in paragraph (1) to seek a gun violence restraining order.

(b) A court may issue an ex parte gun violence restraining order if the petition, supported by an affidavit made in writing and signed by the petitioner under oath, or an oral statement taken pursuant to subdivision (a) of Section 18155, and any additional information provided to the court shows that there is a substantial likelihood that both of the following are true:

(1) The subject of the petition poses a significant danger, in the near future, of causing personal injury to the subject of the petition or another by having in their custody or control, owning, purchasing, possessing, or receiving a firearm as determined by considering the factors listed in Section 18155.

(2) An ex parte gun violence restraining order is necessary to prevent personal injury to the subject of the petition or another because less restrictive alternatives either have been tried and found to be ineffective, or are inadequate or inappropriate for the circumstances of the subject of the petition.

(c) An affidavit supporting a petition for the issuance of an ex parte gun violence restraining order shall set forth the facts tending to establish the grounds of the petition, or the reason for believing that they exist.

(d) An ex parte order under this chapter shall be issued or denied on the same day that the petition is submitted to the court, unless the petition is filed too late in the day to permit effective review, in which case the order shall be issued or denied on the next day of judicial business in sufficient time for the order to be filed that day with the clerk of the court.

(e) This section shall become operative on September 1, 2020. *(Added by Stats.2019, c. 725 (A.B.61), § 2, eff. Jan. 1, 2020, operative Sept. 1, 2020. Amended by Stats.2022, c. 974 (A.B.2870), § 1, eff. Jan. 1, 2023.)*

Cross References

Procedure prior to hearing on issuance, renewal, or termination of order, see Penal Code § 18110.

Research References

West's California Judicial Council Forms GV–110, Temporary Gun Violence Restraining Order (Also Available in Chinese, Korean, Spanish, and Vietnamese).

West's California Judicial Council Forms GV–120–INFO, How Can I Respond to a Petition for Gun Violence Restraining Order? (Also Available in Chinese, Korean, Spanish, and Vietnamese).

2 Witkin, California Criminal Law 4th Crimes Against Governmental Authority § 29 (2021), Other False Reports.

2 Witkin, California Criminal Law 4th Crimes Against Public Peace and Welfare § 242 (2021), Subjects of Protective and Restraining Orders.

§ 18155. Grounds for gun violence restraining order; examination by court

(a)(1) The court, before issuing an ex parte gun violence restraining order, shall examine on oath, the petitioner and any witness the petitioner may produce.

(2) In lieu of examining the petitioner and any witness the petitioner may produce, the court may require the petitioner and any witness to submit a written affidavit signed under oath.

(b)(1) In determining whether grounds for a gun violence restraining order exist, the court shall consider all evidence of the following:

(A) A recent threat of violence or act of violence by the subject of the petition directed toward another.

(B) A recent threat of violence or act of violence by the subject of the petition directed toward himself or herself.

(C) A violation of an emergency protective order issued pursuant to Section 646.91 or Part 3 (commencing with Section 6240) of Division 10 of the Family Code that is in effect at the time the court is considering the petition.

(D) A recent violation of an unexpired protective order issued pursuant to Part 4 (commencing with Section 6300) of Division 10 of the Family Code, Section 136.2, Section 527.6 of the Code of Civil Procedure, or Section 213.5 or 15657.03 of the Welfare and Institutions Code.

(E) A conviction for any offense listed in Section 29805.

(F) A pattern of violent acts or violent threats within the past 12 months, including, but not limited to, threats of violence or acts of violence by the subject of the petition directed toward himself, herself, or another.

(2) In determining whether grounds for a gun violence restraining order exist, the court may consider any other evidence of an increased risk for violence, including, but not limited to, evidence of any of the following:

(A) The unlawful and reckless use, display, or brandishing of a firearm by the subject of the petition.

(B) The history of use, attempted use, or threatened use of physical force by the subject of the petition against another person.

(C) A prior arrest of the subject of the petition for a felony offense.

(D) A history of a violation by the subject of the petition of an emergency protective order issued pursuant to Section 646.91 or Part 3 (commencing with Section 6240) of Division 10 of the Family Code.

(E) A history of a violation by the subject of the petition of a protective order issued pursuant to Part 4 (commencing with Section 6300) of Division 10 of the Family Code, Section 136.2, Section 527.6 of the Code of Civil Procedure, or Section 213.5 or 15657.03 of the Welfare and Institutions Code.

(F) Documentary evidence, including, but not limited to, police reports and records of convictions, of either recent criminal offenses by the subject of the petition that involve controlled substances or alcohol or ongoing abuse of controlled substances or alcohol by the subject of the petition.

(G) Evidence of recent acquisition of firearms, ammunition, or other deadly weapons.

(3) For the purposes of this subdivision, "recent" means within the six months prior to the date the petition was filed.

(c) If the court determines that the grounds to issue an ex parte gun violence restraining order exist, it shall issue an ex parte gun violence restraining order that prohibits the subject of the petition from having in his or her custody or control, owning, purchasing, possessing, or receiving, or attempting to purchase or receive, a firearm or ammunition, and expires no later than 21 days from the date of the order. *(Added by Stats.2014, c. 872 (A.B.1014), § 3, eff. Jan. 1, 2015, operative Jan. 1, 2016. Amended by Stats.2015, c. 303 (A.B.731), § 413, eff. Jan. 1, 2016.)*

§ 18160. Ex parte gun violence restraining order; contents; service

(a) An ex parte gun violence restraining order issued under this chapter shall include all of the following:

(1) A statement of the grounds supporting the issuance of the order.

(2) The date and time the order expires.

(3) The address of the superior court in which a responsive pleading should be filed.

(4) The date and time of the scheduled hearing.

(5) The following statement:

"To the restrained person: This order is valid until the expiration date and time noted above. You are required to surrender all firearms, ammunition, and magazines that you own or possess in accordance with Section 18120 of the Penal Code and you may not have in your custody or control, own, purchase, possess, or receive, or attempt to purchase or receive any firearm, ammunition, or magazine while this order is in effect. A hearing will be held on the date and at the time noted above to determine if a more permanent gun violence restraining order should be issued. Failure to appear at that hearing may result in a court making an order against you that is valid for a period of time between one to five years. You may seek the advice of an attorney as to any matter connected with the order. The attorney should be consulted promptly so that the attorney may assist you in any matter connected with the order."

(b)(1) An ex parte gun violence restraining order shall be personally served on the restrained person by a law enforcement officer, or by a person as provided in Section 414.10 of the Code of Civil Procedure, if the restrained person can reasonably be located.

(2) When serving a gun violence restraining order, a law enforcement officer shall inform the restrained person of the hearing scheduled pursuant to Section 18165.

(3) When serving a gun violence restraining order, a law enforcement officer shall verbally ask the restrained person if the person has a firearm, ammunition, or magazine in the person's possession or under the person's custody or control.

(c) This section shall become operative on September 1, 2020. *(Added by Stats.2019, c. 724 (A.B.12), § 6, eff. Jan. 1, 2020, operative Sept. 1, 2020.)*

Research References

West's California Judicial Council Forms GV–200, Proof of Personal Service (Also Available in Chinese, Korean, Spanish, and Vietnamese).

§ 18165. Hearing to determine issuance of restraining order; timeframe

Within 21 days after the date on the order, before the court that issued the order or another court in the same jurisdiction, the court shall hold a hearing pursuant to Section 18175 to determine if a gun violence restraining order should be issued under Chapter 4 (commencing with Section 18170). *(Added by Stats.2014, c. 872 (A.B. 1014), § 3, eff. Jan. 1, 2015, operative Jan. 1, 2016.)*

CHAPTER 4. GUN VIOLENCE RESTRAINING ORDER ISSUED AFTER NOTICE AND HEARING

Section

§ 18170. Petition to enjoin possession of firearm for one to five years

(a)(1) Any of the following individuals may request that a court, after notice and a hearing, issue a gun violence restraining order enjoining the subject of the petition from having in their custody or control, owning, purchasing, possessing, or receiving a firearm or ammunition for a period of time between one to five years:

(A) An immediate family member of the subject of the petition.

(B) An employer of the subject of the petition.

(C) A coworker of the subject of the petition, if they have had substantial and regular interactions with the subject for at least one year and have obtained the approval of the employer.

(D) An employee or teacher of a secondary or postsecondary school that the subject has attended in the last six months, if the employee or teacher has obtained the approval of a school administrator or a school administration staff member with a supervisorial role.

(E) A law enforcement officer.

(F) A roommate of the subject of the petition.

(G) An individual who has a dating relationship with the subject of the petition.

(H) An individual who has a child in common with the subject of the petition, if they have had substantial and regular interactions with the subject for at least one year.

(2) This chapter does not require a person described in paragraph (1) to seek a gun violence restraining order.

(b) For purposes of this subdivision, "dating relationship" has the same meaning as in paragraph (10) of subdivision (f) of Section 243.

(c) For purposes of this section, "immediate family member" * * * means any spouse, whether by marriage or not, domestic partner, parent, child, any person related by consanguinity or affinity within the second degree, or any person related by consanguinity or affinity within the fourth degree who has had substantial and regular interactions with the subject for at least one year.

(d) For purposes of this subdivision, "roommate" means a person who regularly resides in the household, or who, within the prior six months, regularly resided in the household, and who has had substantial and regular interactions with the subject for at least one year.

(e) This section shall become operative on September 1, 2020. *(Added by Stats.2019, c. 725 (A.B.61), § 4.5, eff. Jan. 1, 2020, operative Sept. 1, 2020. Amended by Stats.2022, c. 974 (A.B.2870), § 2, eff. Jan. 1, 2023.)*

Cross References

Procedure prior to hearing on issuance, renewal, or termination of order, see Penal Code § 18110.

Research References

West's California Judicial Council Forms GV–020, Response to Gun Violence Emergency Protective Order.
West's California Judicial Council Forms GV–025, Proof of Service by Mail.
West's California Judicial Council Forms GV–030, Gun Violence Restraining Order After Hearing on Epo-002 (Clets-HGv).
West's California Judicial Council Forms GV–120, Response to Petition for Gun Violence Restraining Order (Also Available in Chinese, Korean, Spanish, and Vietnamese).
West's California Judicial Council Forms GV–130, Gun Violence Restraining Order After Hearing or Consent to Gun Violence Restraining Order (Clets-Ogv) (Also Available in Chinese, Korean, Spanish, and Vietnamese).
West's California Judicial Council Forms GV–250, Proof of Service by Mail (Also Available in Chinese, Korean, Spanish, and Vietnamese).
2 Witkin, California Criminal Law 4th Crimes Against Governmental Authority § 29 (2021), Other False Reports.
2 Witkin, California Criminal Law 4th Crimes Against Public Peace and Welfare § 242 (2021), Subjects of Protective and Restraining Orders.

§ 18175. Evidence to be considered by court; burden of petitioner; duration of restraining order

(a) In determining whether to issue a gun violence restraining order under this chapter, the court shall consider evidence of the facts identified in paragraph (1) of subdivision (b) of Section 18155 and may consider any other evidence of an increased risk for violence, including, but not limited to, evidence of the facts identified in paragraph (2) of subdivision (b) of Section 18155.

(b) At the hearing, the petitioner has the burden of proving, by clear and convincing evidence, that both of the following are true:

(1) The subject of the petition, or a person subject to a temporary emergency gun violence restraining order or an ex parte gun violence restraining order, as applicable, poses a significant danger of causing personal injury to themselves or another by having in the subject's or

person's custody or control, owning, purchasing, possessing, or receiving a firearm, ammunition, or magazine.

(2) A gun violence restraining order is necessary to prevent personal injury to the subject of the petition, or the person subject to an ex parte gun violence restraining order, as applicable, or another because less restrictive alternatives either have been tried and found to be ineffective, or are inadequate or inappropriate for the circumstances of the subject of the petition, or the person subject to an ex parte gun violence restraining order, as applicable.

(c)(1) If the court finds that there is clear and convincing evidence to issue a gun violence restraining order, the court shall issue a gun violence restraining order that prohibits the subject of the petition from having in the subject's custody or control, owning, purchasing, possessing, or receiving, or attempting to purchase or receive, a firearm, ammunition, or magazine.

(2) If the court finds that there is not clear and convincing evidence to support the issuance of a gun violence restraining order, the court shall dissolve a temporary emergency or ex parte gun violence restraining order then in effect.

(d)(1) The subject of the petition may file a form with the court relinquishing the subject's firearm rights for the duration specified on the petition or, if not stated in the petition, for one year from the date of the proposed hearing, and stating that the subject is not contesting the petition.

(2) If the subject of the petition files a form pursuant to paragraph (1), the court shall issue, without any hearing, the gun violence restraining order at least five court days before the scheduled hearing. If the subject files the form within five court days before the scheduled hearing, the court shall issue, without any hearing, the gun violence restraining order as soon as possible. The court shall provide notice of the order to all parties.

(3) If the subject of the petition files a form pursuant to paragraph (1) and has not already surrendered all firearms, ammunition, and magazines in the subject's custody or control or those that the subject possesses or owns, the subject shall follow the procedures in Section 18120 but shall surrender the firearms, ammunition, and magazines within 48 hours of filing the form relinquishing firearm rights.

(e)(1) The court shall issue a gun violence restraining order under this chapter for a period of time of one to five years, subject to termination by further order of the court at a hearing held pursuant to Section 18185 and renewal by further order of the court pursuant to Section 18190.

(2) In determining the duration of the gun violence restraining order pursuant to paragraph (1), the court shall consider the length of time that the circumstances set forth in subdivision (b) are likely to continue, and shall issue the order based on that determination.

(f) This section shall become operative on September 1, 2020.
(Added by Stats.2019, c. 733 (A.B.1493), § 2.2, eff. Jan. 1, 2020, operative Sept. 1, 2020.)

Cross References

Hearing on issuance of gun violence restraining order, see Penal Code § 18148.
Issuance, dissolution or termination of gun violence restraining order, notification of Department of Justice, see Penal Code § 18115.

Research References

West's California Judicial Council Forms GV–125, Consent to Gun Violence Restraining Order and Surrender of Firearms.

§ 18180. Gun violence restraining order; contents of order

(a) A gun violence restraining order issued pursuant to this chapter shall include all of the following:

(1) A statement of the grounds supporting the issuance of the order.

(2) The date and time the order expires.

(3) The address of the superior court for the county in which the restrained party resides.

(4) The following statement:

"To the restrained person: This order will last until the date and time noted above. If you have not done so already, you must surrender all firearms, ammunition, and magazines that you own or possess in accordance with Section 18120 of the Penal Code. You may not have in your custody or control, own, purchase, possess, or receive, or attempt to purchase or receive a firearm, ammunition, or magazine, while this order is in effect. Pursuant to Section 18185, you have the right to request a hearing on an annual basis to terminate this order during its effective period. You may seek the advice of an attorney as to any matter connected with the order."

(b) If the court issues a gun violence restraining order under this chapter, the court shall inform the restrained person that the person is entitled to a hearing on an annual basis to request a termination of the order, pursuant to Section 18185, and shall provide the restrained person with a form to request a hearing.

(c) This section shall become operative on September 1, 2020.
(Added by Stats.2019, c. 724 (A.B.12), § 12, eff. Jan. 1, 2020, operative Sept. 1, 2020.)

§ 18185. Written request for hearing to terminate order

(a) A person subject to a gun violence restraining order issued under this chapter may submit one written request per year during the effective period of the order for a hearing to terminate the order.

(b) If the court finds after the hearing that there is no longer clear and convincing evidence to believe that paragraphs (1) and (2) of subdivision (b) of Section 18175 are true, the court shall terminate the order.

(c) This section shall become operative on September 1, 2020.
(Added by Stats.2019, c. 724 (A.B.12), § 14, eff. Jan. 1, 2020, operative Sept. 1, 2020.)

Research References

West's California Judicial Council Forms GV–600, Request to Terminate Gun Violence Restraining Order (Also Available in Chinese, Korean, Spanish, and Vietnamese).
West's California Judicial Council Forms GV–610, Notice of Hearing on Request to Terminate Gun Violence Restraining Order (Also Available in Chinese, Korean, Spanish, and Vietnamese).
West's California Judicial Council Forms GV–620, Response to Request to Terminate Gun Violence Restraining Order (Also Available in Chinese, Korean, Spanish, and Vietnamese).
West's California Judicial Council Forms GV–630, Order on Request to Terminate Gun Violence Restraining Order (Also Available in Chinese, Korean, Spanish, and Vietnamese).

§ 18190. Request for renewal of restraining order

(a)(1) Any of the following people may request a renewal of a gun violence restraining order at any time within the three months before the expiration of a gun violence restraining order:

(A) An immediate family member of the subject of the petition.

(B) An employer of the subject of the petition.

(C) A coworker of the subject of the petition, if they have had substantial and regular interactions with the subject for at least one year and have obtained the approval of the employer.

(D) An employee or teacher of a secondary or postsecondary school that the subject has attended in the last six months, if the employee or teacher has obtained the approval of a school administrator or a school administration staff member with a supervisorial role.

(E) A law enforcement officer.

(F) A roommate of the subject of the petition.

(G) An individual who has a dating relationship with the subject of the petition.

(H) An individual who has a child in common with the subject of the petition, if they have had substantial and regular interactions with the subject for at least one year.

(2) For purposes of this subdivision, "dating relationship" has the same meaning as in paragraph (10) of subdivision (f) of Section 243.

(3) For purposes of this subdivision, "immediate family member" * * * means any spouse, whether by marriage or not, domestic partner, parent, child, any person related by consanguinity or affinity within the second degree, or any person related by consanguinity or affinity within the fourth degree who has had substantial and regular interactions with the subject for at least one year.

(4) For purposes of this subdivision, "roommate" means a person who regularly resides in the household, or who, within the prior six months, regularly resided in the household, and who has had substantial and regular interactions with the subject for at least one year.

(5) This chapter does not require a person described in paragraph (1) to seek a gun violence restraining order.

(b) A court may, after notice and a hearing, renew a gun violence restraining order issued under this chapter if the petitioner proves, by clear and convincing evidence, that paragraphs (1) and (2) of subdivision (b) of Section 18175 continue to be true.

(c) In determining whether to renew a gun violence restraining order issued under this chapter, the court shall consider evidence of the facts identified in paragraph (1) of subdivision (b) of Section 18155 and any other evidence of an increased risk for violence, including, but not limited to, evidence of any of the facts identified in paragraph (2) of subdivision (b) of Section 18155.

(d) At the hearing, the petitioner shall have the burden of proving, by clear and convincing evidence, that paragraphs (1) and (2) of subdivision (b) of Section 18175 are true.

(e) If the renewal petition is supported by clear and convincing evidence, the court shall renew the gun violence restraining order issued under this chapter.

(f)(1) The renewal of a gun violence restraining order issued pursuant to this section shall have a duration of between one to five years, subject to termination by further order of the court at a hearing held pursuant to Section 18185 and further renewal by further order of the court pursuant to this section.

(2) In determining the duration of the gun violence restraining order pursuant to paragraph (1), the court shall consider the length of time that the circumstances set forth in subdivision (b) of Section 18175 are likely to continue, and shall issue the order based on that determination.

(g) A gun violence restraining order renewed pursuant to this section shall include the information identified in subdivision (a) of Section 18180.

(h) This section shall become operative on September 1, 2020. *(Added by Stats.2019, c. 725 (A.B.61), § 6.5, eff. Jan. 1, 2020, operative Sept. 1, 2020. Amended by Stats.2022, c. 974 (A.B.2870), § 3, eff. Jan. 1, 2023.)*

Research References

West's California Judicial Council Forms GV–700, Request to Renew Gun Violence Restraining Order (Also Available in Chinese, Korean, Spanish, and Vietnamese).

West's California Judicial Council Forms GV–710, Notice of Hearing on Request to Renew Gun Violence Restraining Order (Also Available in Chinese, Korean, Spanish, and Vietnamese).

West's California Judicial Council Forms GV–720, Response to Request to Renew Gun Violence Restraining Order (Also Available in Chinese, Korean, Spanish, and Vietnamese).

West's California Judicial Council Forms GV–730, Order on Request to Renew Gun Violence Restraining Order (Also Available in Chinese, Korean, Spanish, and Vietnamese).

§ 18195. Continuance of hearing

Any hearing held pursuant to this chapter may be continued upon a showing of good cause. Any existing order issued pursuant to this division shall remain in full force and effect during the period of continuance. *(Added by Stats.2014, c. 872 (A.B.1014), § 3, eff. Jan. 1, 2015, operative Jan. 1, 2016.)*

Research References

West's California Judicial Council Forms GV–115, Request to Continue Court Hearing for Gun Violence Restraining Order (Epo-002 or Temporary Restraining Order) (Also Available in Chinese, Korean, Spanish, and Vietnamese).

West's California Judicial Council Forms GV–116, Order on Request to Continue Hearing (Epo-002 or Temporary Restraining Order) (Clets-EGv or Clets-Tgv) (Also Available in Chinese, Korean, Spanish, and Vietnamese).

§ 18197. Service of restraining order

(a) If a person subject to a gun violence restraining order issued or renewed pursuant to this chapter was not present in court at the time the order was issued or renewed, the gun violence restraining order shall be personally served on the restrained person by a law enforcement officer, or by a person as provided in Section 414.10 of the Code of Civil Procedure, if the restrained person can reasonably be located.

(b) This section shall become operative on September 1, 2020. *(Added by Stats.2019, c. 724 (A.B.12), § 18, eff. Jan. 1, 2020, operative Sept. 1, 2020.)*

CHAPTER 5. OFFENSES

§ 18200. Knowingly filing petitions with false information or with intent to harass; penalty

Every person who files a petition for an ex parte gun violence restraining order pursuant to Chapter 3 (commencing with Section 18150) or a gun violence restraining order issued after notice and a hearing pursuant to Chapter 4 (commencing with Section 18170), knowing the information in the petition to be false or with the intent to harass, is guilty of a misdemeanor. *(Added by Stats.2014, c. 872 (A.B.1014), § 3, eff. Jan. 1, 2015, operative Jan. 1, 2016.)*

Research References

2 Witkin, California Criminal Law 4th Crimes Against Governmental Authority § 29 (2021), Other False Reports.

§ 18205. Possession of firearm or ammunition with knowledge of restraining order; penalty; out-of-state jurisdiction

(a) Every person who owns or possesses a firearm or ammunition with knowledge that they are prohibited from doing so by a temporary emergency gun violence restraining order issued pursuant to Chapter 2 (commencing with Section 18125), an ex parte gun violence restraining order issued pursuant to Chapter 3 (commencing with Section 18150), a gun violence restraining order issued after notice and a hearing issued pursuant to Chapter 4 (commencing with Section 18170), or by a valid order issued by an out-of-state jurisdiction that is similar or equivalent to a gun violence restraining order described in this division, is guilty of a misdemeanor and shall be prohibited from having custody or control of, owning, purchasing, possessing, or receiving, or attempting to purchase or receive, a firearm or ammunition for a five-year period, to commence upon the expiration of the existing gun violence restraining order.

(b) For purposes of this section, a valid order issued by an out-of-state jurisdiction that is similar or equivalent to a gun violence restraining order described in this section must be issued upon a showing by clear and convincing evidence that the person poses a significant danger of causing personal injury to themselves or another because of owning or possessing a firearm or ammunition. *(Added by Stats.2014, c. 872 (A.B.1014), § 3, eff. Jan. 1, 2015, operative Jan. 1, 2016. Amended by Stats.2020, c. 286 (A.B.2617), § 2, eff. Jan. 1, 2021.)*

Research References

2 Witkin, California Criminal Law 4th Crimes Against Public Peace and Welfare § 242 (2021), Subjects of Protective and Restraining Orders.

Division 4

SEIZURE OF FIREARM OR OTHER DEADLY WEAPON AT SCENE OF DOMESTIC VIOLENCE

CHAPTER 1. SEIZURE AND SUBSEQUENT PROCEDURES

§ 18250. Domestic violence incidents, service of specified protective orders, or service of gun violence restraining order; taking of firearms or other deadly weapons into temporary custody

(a) If any of the following persons is at the scene of a domestic violence incident involving a threat to human life or a physical assault, is serving a protective order as defined in Section 6218 of the Family Code, or is serving a gun violence restraining order issued pursuant to Division 3.2 (commencing with Section 18100), that person shall take temporary custody of any firearm or other deadly weapon in plain sight or discovered pursuant to a consensual or other lawful search as necessary for the protection of the peace officer or other persons present:

(1) A sheriff, undersheriff, deputy sheriff, marshal, deputy marshal, or police officer of a city, as defined in subdivision (a) of Section 830.1.

(2) A peace officer of the Department of the California Highway Patrol, as defined in subdivision (a) of Section 830.2.

(3) A member of the University of California Police Department, as defined in subdivision (b) of Section 830.2.

(4) An officer listed in Section 830.6, while acting in the course and scope of the officer's employment as a peace officer.

(5) A member of a California State University Police Department, as defined in subdivision (c) of Section 830.2.

(6) A peace officer of the Department of Parks and Recreation, as defined in subdivision (f) of Section 830.2.

(7) A peace officer, as defined in subdivision (d) of Section 830.31.

(8) A peace officer, as defined in subdivisions (a) and (b) of Section 830.32.

(9) A peace officer, as defined in Section 830.5.

(10) A sworn member of the Department of Justice who is a peace officer, as defined in Section 830.1.

(11) A member of the San Francisco Bay Area Rapid Transit District Police Department, as defined in subdivision (a) of Section 830.33.

(b) This section shall become operative on January 1, 2016. *(Added by Stats.2014, c. 872 (A.B.1014), § 5.5, eff. Jan. 1, 2015, operative Jan. 1, 2016.)*

Cross References

Deadly weapon defined for purposes of this Division, see Penal Code § 16430.
Firearm defined for purposes of this Part, see Penal Code § 16520.
Recordation system for domestic violence calls, confiscation of firearms, see Penal Code § 13730.
Search warrants, grounds for issuance, firearm or deadly weapon at scene of domestic violence incident involving threat to human life or physical assault, see Penal Code § 1524.

Research References

2 Witkin, California Criminal Law 4th Crimes Against Public Peace and Welfare § 193 (2021), Sale, Lease, or Transfer by Unlicensed Person.
4 Witkin, California Criminal Law 4th Illegally Obtained Evidence § 111 (2021), Statutory Grounds.
3 Witkin, California Criminal Law 4th Punishment § 190 (2021), Noncriminal Actions.

§ 18255. Issuance of receipt upon taking firearm or deadly weapon into temporary custody; contents

(a) Upon taking custody of a firearm or other deadly weapon pursuant to this division, the officer shall give the owner or person who possessed the firearm or other deadly weapon a receipt.

(b) The receipt shall describe the firearm or other deadly weapon and list any identification or serial number on the firearm.

(c) The receipt shall indicate where the firearm or other deadly weapon can be recovered, the time limit for recovery as required by this division, and the date after which the owner or possessor can recover the firearm or other deadly weapon.

(d) The receipt shall include the name and residential mailing address of the owner or person who possessed the firearm or other deadly weapon. *(Added by Stats.2010, c. 711 (S.B.1080), § 6, operative Jan. 1, 2012. Amended by Stats.2018, c. 185 (A.B.2176), § 1, eff. Jan. 1, 2019.)*

Law Revision Commission Comments

Subdivision (a) of Section 18255 continues the second sentence of former Section 12028.5(b) without substantive change.

Subdivision (b) continues the third sentence of former Section 12028.5(b) without substantive change.

Subdivision (c) continues the fourth sentence of former Section 12028.5(b) without substantive change.

For what constitutes a deadly weapon, see Section 16430 ("deadly weapon"). See also Section 16520 ("firearm").

See Sections 18250 (seizure of firearm or other deadly weapon at scene of domestic violence), 18260 (delivery of deadly weapon seized by peace officer for community college or school district), 18265 (holding period), 18270 (return of stolen weapon), 18275 (sale or destruction of deadly weapon held longer than one year), 18500 (no liability for act in good faith under this division). For procedures applicable when a law enforcement agency has reasonable cause to believe that return of a weapon would endanger the victim of a domestic violence incident or a person who reported the incident, see Sections 18400–18420.

For additional guidance on surrender and disposal of weapons, see Sections 18000 (surrender of specified weapons constituting nuisance), 18005 (disposal of weapons constituting nuisance), 18010 (treatment of other weapons constituting nuisance), 33800–34010 (firearm in custody of court or law enforcement agency or similar situation). [38 Cal.L.Rev.Comm. Reports 217 (2009)].

Section 18255(a) is amended to add an omitted reference to "other deadly weapon." This is a nonsubstantive change.

Subdivision (d) is new. It provides an opportunity for law enforcement to take the residential mailing address of a person whose weapon is seized. This information is required for the purposes of Section 18405(b). [44 Cal.L.Rev. Comm. Reports 471 (2015)].

Cross References

Deadly weapon defined for purposes of this Division, see Penal Code § 16430.
Firearm defined for purposes of this Part, see Penal Code § 16520.

§ 18260. Delivery of firearm or deadly weapon taken into temporary custody to police department or county sheriff's office

Any peace officer, as defined in subdivisions (a) and (b) of Section 830.32, who takes custody of a firearm or other deadly weapon pursuant to this division, shall deliver the firearm or other deadly weapon within 24 hours to the city police department or county sheriff's office in the jurisdiction where the college or school is located. *(Added by Stats.2010, c. 711 (S.B.1080), § 6, operative Jan. 1, 2012. Amended by Stats.2018, c. 185 (A.B.2176), § 2, eff. Jan. 1, 2019.)*

Law Revision Commission Comments

Section 18260 continues former Section 12028.5(c) without substantive change.

For what constitutes a deadly weapon, see Section 16430 ("deadly weapon"). See also Section 16520 ("firearm").

See Sections 18250 (seizure of firearm or other deadly weapon at scene of domestic violence), 18255 (receipt for weapon), 18265 (holding period), 18270 (return of stolen weapon), 18275 (sale or destruction of deadly weapon held longer than one year), 18500 (no liability for act in good faith under this division). For procedures applicable when a law enforcement agency has reasonable cause to believe that return of a weapon would endanger the victim of a domestic violence incident or a person who reported the incident, see Sections 18400–18420.

For additional guidance on surrender and disposal of weapons, see Sections 18000 (surrender of specified weapons constituting nuisance), 18005 (disposal of weapons constituting nuisance), 18010 (treatment of other weapons constituting nuisance), 33800–34010 (firearm in custody of court or law enforcement agency or similar situation). [38 Cal.L.Rev.Comm. Reports 217 (2009)].

Section 18260 is amended to add a reference to "other deadly weapon." This is a nonsubstantive change. [44 Cal.L.Rev.Comm. Reports 471 (2015)].

Cross References

Deadly weapon defined for purposes of this Division, see Penal Code § 16430.
Firearm defined for purposes of this Part, see Penal Code § 16520.

§ 18265. Time for holding of firearm of deadly weapon taken into temporary custody; civil action for untimely return; awarding of attorney fees to prevailing party

(a) No firearm or other deadly weapon taken into custody pursuant to this division shall be held less than 48 hours.

(b) Except as provided in Section 18400, if a firearm or other deadly weapon is not retained for use as evidence related to criminal charges brought as a result of the domestic violence incident or is not retained because it was illegally possessed, the firearm or other deadly weapon shall be made available to the owner or person who was in lawful possession 48 hours after the seizure, or as soon thereafter as possible, but no later than five business days after the owner or person who was in lawful possession demonstrates compliance with Chapter 2 (commencing with Section 33850) of Division 11 of Title 4.

(c) In any civil action or proceeding for the return of any firearm, ammunition, or other deadly weapon seized by any state or local law enforcement agency and not returned within five business days after the initial seizure, except as provided in Section 18270, the court shall allow reasonable attorney's fees to the prevailing party. *(Added by Stats.2010, c. 711 (S.B.1080), § 6, operative Jan. 1, 2012.)*

Law Revision Commission Comments

Subdivision (a) of Section 18265 continues the fifth sentence of former Section 12028.5(b) without substantive change.

Subdivision (b) continues the sixth sentence of former Section 12028.5(b) without substantive change.

Subdivision (c) continues the seventh sentence of former Section 12028.5(b) without substantive change.

For what constitutes a domestic violence incident, see Sections 16120 ("abuse"), 16490 ("domestic violence"). For what constitutes a deadly weapon, see Section 16430 ("deadly weapon"), see also Section 16520 ("firearm").

See Sections 18250 (seizure of firearm or other deadly weapon at scene of domestic violence), 18255 (receipt for weapon), 18260 (delivery of deadly weapon seized by peace officer for community college or school district), 18270 (return of stolen weapon), 18275 (sale or destruction of deadly weapon held longer than one year), 18500 (no liability for act in good faith under this division). For procedures applicable when a law enforcement agency has reasonable cause to believe that return of a weapon would endanger the victim of a domestic violence incident or a person who reported the incident, see Sections 18400–18420.

For additional guidance on surrender and disposal of weapons, see Sections 18000 (surrender of specified weapons constituting nuisance), 18005 (disposal of weapons constituting nuisance), 18010 (treatment of other weapons constituting nuisance), 33800–34010 (firearm in custody of court or law enforcement agency or similar situation). [38 Cal.L.Rev.Comm. Reports 217 (2009)].

Cross References

Deadly weapon defined for purposes of this Division, see Penal Code § 16430.
Firearm defined for purposes of this Part, see Penal Code § 16520.

§ 18270. Stolen firearm or deadly weapon taken into temporary custody; conditions for return to lawful owner

If a firearm or other deadly weapon has been stolen and has been taken into custody pursuant to this division, it shall be restored to the lawful owner upon satisfaction of all of the following conditions:

(a) Its use for evidence has been served.

(b) The owner identifies the firearm or other deadly weapon and provides proof of ownership.

(c) The law enforcement agency has complied with Chapter 2 (commencing with Section 33850) of Division 11 of Title 4. *(Added by Stats.2010, c. 711 (S.B.1080), § 6, operative Jan. 1, 2012.)*

Law Revision Commission Comments

Section 18270 continues former Section 12028.5(d) without substantive change.

For what constitutes a deadly weapon, see Section 16430 ("deadly weapon"); see also Section 16520 ("firearm").

See Sections 18250 (seizure of firearm or other deadly weapon at scene of domestic violence), 18255 (receipt for weapon), 18260 (delivery of deadly weapon seized by peace officer for community college or school district), 18265 (holding period), 18275 (sale or destruction of deadly weapon held longer than one year), 18500 (no liability for act in good faith under this division). For procedures applicable when a law enforcement agency has reasonable cause to believe that return of a weapon would endanger the victim of a domestic violence incident or a person who reported the incident, see Sections 18400–18420.

For additional guidance on surrender and disposal of weapons, see Sections 18000 (surrender of specified weapons constituting nuisance), 18005 (disposal of weapons constituting nuisance), 18010 (treatment of other weapons constituting nuisance), 33800–34010 (firearm in custody of court or law enforcement agency or similar situation). [38 Cal.L.Rev.Comm. Reports 217 (2009)].

Cross References

Deadly weapon defined for purposes of this Division, see Penal Code § 16430.
Firearm defined for purposes of this Part, see Penal Code § 16520.

§ 18275. Firearm or deadly weapon held for longer than 12 months as nuisance; destruction

(a) Any firearm or other deadly weapon that has been taken into custody and held by any of the following law enforcement authorities for longer than 12 months, and has not been recovered by the owner or person who had lawful possession at the time it was taken into custody, shall be considered a nuisance and * * * destroyed as provided in subdivision (a) * * * of Section 18005:

(1) A police, university police, or sheriff's department.

(2) A marshal's office.

(3) A peace officer of the Department of the California Highway Patrol, as defined in subdivision (a) of Section 830.2.

(4) A peace officer of the Department of Parks and Recreation, as defined in subdivision (f) of Section 830.2.

(5) A peace officer, as defined in subdivision (d) of Section 830.31.

(6) A peace officer, as defined in Section 830.5.

(b) If a firearm or other deadly weapon is not recovered within 12 months due to an extended hearing process as provided in Section 18420, it is not subject to destruction until the court issues a decision, and then only if the court does not order the return of the firearm or other deadly weapon to the owner. *(Added by Stats.2010, c. 711 (S.B.1080), § 6, operative Jan. 1, 2012. Amended by Stats.2022, c. 58 (A.B.200), § 36, eff. June 30, 2022.)*

Law Revision Commission Comments

Section 18275 continues former Section 12028.5(e) without substantive change.

For what constitutes a deadly weapon, see Section 16430 ("deadly weapon"); see also Section 16520 ("firearm").

See Sections 18250 (seizure of firearm or other deadly weapon at scene of domestic violence), 18255 (receipt for weapon), 18260 (delivery of deadly weapon seized by peace officer for community college or school district), 18265 (holding period), 18270 (return of stolen weapon), 18500 (no liability for act in good faith under this division). For procedures applicable when a law enforcement agency has reasonable cause to believe that return of a weapon would endanger the victim of a domestic violence incident or a person who reported the incident, see Sections 18400–18420.

For additional guidance on surrender and disposal of weapons, see Sections 18000 (surrender of specified weapons constituting nuisance), 18005 (disposal of weapons constituting nuisance), 18010 (treatment of other weapons constituting nuisance), 33800–34010 (firearm in custody of court or law enforcement agency or similar situation). [38 Cal.L.Rev.Comm. Reports 217 (2009)].

Cross References

Deadly weapon defined for purposes of this Division, see Penal Code § 16430.
Firearm defined for purposes of this Part, see Penal Code § 16520.

Research References

3 Witkin, California Criminal Law 4th Punishment § 190 (2021), Noncriminal Actions.

CHAPTER 2. PROCEDURE WHERE AGENCY BELIEVES RETURN OF WEAPON WOULD CREATE DANGER

§ 18400. Return of firearm or deadly weapon deemed to endanger victim or person reporting threat; petition to superior court

(a) When a law enforcement agency has reasonable cause to believe that the return of a firearm or other deadly weapon seized under this division would be likely to result in endangering the victim or the person who reported the assault or threat, the agency shall so advise the owner of the firearm or other deadly weapon, and within 60 days of the date of seizure, initiate a petition in superior court to determine if the firearm or other deadly weapon should be returned.

(b) The law enforcement agency may make an ex parte application stating good cause for an order extending the time to file a petition.

(c) Including any extension of time granted in response to an ex parte request, a petition must be filed within 90 days of the date of seizure of the firearm or other deadly weapon. *(Added by Stats.2010, c. 711 (S.B.1080), § 6, operative Jan. 1, 2012.)*

Law Revision Commission Comments

Section 18400 continues former Section 12028.5(f) without substantive change.

For what constitutes a deadly weapon, see Section 16430 ("deadly weapon"); see also Section 16520 ("firearm").

See Sections 18405 (notice of petition), 18410 (hearing on petition), 18415 (order of default), 18420 (petition for second hearing).

See also Sections 18250 (seizure of firearm or other deadly weapon at scene of domestic violence), 18255 (receipt for weapon), 18260 (delivery of deadly weapon seized by peace officer for community college or school district), 18265 (holding period), 18270 (return of stolen weapon), 18275 (sale or destruction of deadly weapon held longer than one year), 18500 (no liability for act in good faith under this division).

For additional guidance on surrender and disposal of weapons, see Sections 18000 (surrender of specified weapons constituting nuisance), 18005 (disposal of weapons constituting nuisance), 18010 (treatment of other weapons constituting nuisance), 33800–34010 (firearm in custody of court or law enforcement agency or similar situation). [38 Cal.L.Rev.Comm. Reports 217 (2009)].

Cross References

Deadly weapon defined for purposes of this Division, see Penal Code § 16430.
Firearm defined for purposes of this Part, see Penal Code § 16520.

§ 18405. Notice of petition regarding return of confiscated firearm or deadly weapon to owner or lawful possessor

(a) If a petition is filed under Section 18400, the law enforcement agency shall inform the owner or person who had lawful possession of the firearm or other deadly weapon, at that person's last known address, by registered mail, return receipt requested, that the person has 30 days from the date of receipt of the notice to respond to the court clerk to confirm the person's desire for a hearing, and that the failure to respond shall result in a default order forfeiting the confiscated firearm or other deadly weapon.

(b) For purposes of this section, the person's last known address shall be presumed to be the address provided to the law enforcement officer by that person at the time of the domestic violence incident.

(c) In the event the person whose firearm or other deadly weapon was seized does not reside at the last address provided to the agency, the agency shall make a diligent, good faith effort to learn the whereabouts of the person and to comply with these notification requirements. *(Added by Stats.2010, c. 711 (S.B.1080), § 6, operative Jan. 1, 2012. Amended by Stats.2018, c. 185 (A.B.2176), § 3, eff. Jan. 1, 2019.)*

Law Revision Commission Comments

Section 18405 continues former Section 12028.5(g) without substantive change.

For what constitutes a deadly weapon, see Section 16430 ("deadly weapon"); see also Section 16520 ("firearm").

See Sections 18400 (petition to determine whether weapon should be returned), 18410 (hearing on petition), 18415 (order of default), 18420 (petition for second hearing).

See also Sections 16120 ("abuse"), 16490 ("domestic violence"), 18250 (seizure of firearm or other deadly weapon at scene of domestic violence), 18255 (receipt for weapon), 18260 (delivery of deadly weapon seized by peace officer for community college or school district), 18265 (holding period), 18270 (return of stolen weapon), 18275 (sale or destruction of deadly weapon held longer than one year), 18500 (no liability for act in good faith under this division).

For additional guidance on surrender and disposal of weapons, see Sections 18000 (surrender of specified weapons constituting nuisance), 18005 (disposal of weapons constituting nuisance), 18010 (treatment of other weapons constituting nuisance), 33800–34010 (firearm in custody of court or law enforcement agency or similar situation). [38 Cal.L.Rev.Comm. Reports 217 (2009)].

Section 18405 is amended to replace an erroneous reference to "family violence" with the defined term "domestic violence." See Section 16490 ("domestic violence" defined). This is a nonsubstantive change. [44 Cal. L.Rev.Comm. Reports 471 (2015)].

Cross References

Deadly weapon defined for purposes of this Division, see Penal Code § 16430.
Firearm defined for purposes of this Part, see Penal Code § 16520.

§ 18410. Request for hearing upon receipt of petition regarding return of confiscated firearm or deadly weapon; burden of proof; attorney fees

(a) If the person who receives a petition under Section 18405 requests a hearing, the court clerk shall set a hearing no later than 30 days from receipt of that request.

(b) The court clerk shall notify the person, the law enforcement agency involved, and the district attorney of the date, time, and place of the hearing.

(c) Unless it is shown by a preponderance of the evidence that the return of the firearm or other deadly weapon would result in endangering the victim or the person reporting the assault or threat, the court shall order the return of the firearm or other deadly weapon and shall award reasonable attorney's fees to the prevailing party. *(Added by Stats.2010, c. 711 (S.B.1080), § 6, operative Jan. 1, 2012.)*

Law Revision Commission Comments

Section 18410 continues former Section 12028.5(h) without substantive change.

For what constitutes a deadly weapon, see Section 16430 ("deadly weapon"); see also Section 16520 ("firearm").

See Sections 18400 (petition to determine whether weapon should be returned), 18405 (notice of petition), 18415 (order of default), 18420 (petition for second hearing).

See also Sections 16120 ("abuse"), 16490 ("domestic violence"), 18250 (seizure of firearm or other deadly weapon at scene of domestic violence), 18255 (receipt for weapon), 18260 (delivery of deadly weapon seized by peace officer for community college or school district), 18265 (holding period), 18270 (return of stolen weapon), 18275 (sale or destruction of deadly weapon held longer than one year), 18500 (no liability for act in good faith under this division).

For additional guidance on surrender and disposal of weapons, see Sections 18000 (surrender of specified weapons constituting nuisance), 18005 (disposal of weapons constituting nuisance), 18010 (treatment of other weapons constituting nuisance), 33800–34010 (firearm in custody of court or law enforcement agency or similar situation). [38 Cal.L.Rev.Comm. Reports 217 (2009)].

Cross References

Deadly weapon defined for purposes of this Division, see Penal Code § 16430.
Firearm defined for purposes of this Part, see Penal Code § 16520.

§ 18415. Petition for order of default; disposal of firearm or deadly weapon

If the person who receives a petition under Section 18405 does not request a hearing or does not otherwise respond within 30 days of the receipt of the notice, the law enforcement agency may file a petition for an order of default and may dispose of the firearm or other deadly weapon as provided in Sections 18000 and 18005. *(Added by Stats.2010, c. 711 (S.B.1080), § 6, operative Jan. 1, 2012.)*

Law Revision Commission Comments

Section 18415 continues former Section 12028.5(i) without substantive change.

For what constitutes a deadly weapon, see Section 16430 ("deadly weapon"); see also Section 16520 ("firearm").

See Sections 18400 (petition to determine whether weapon should be returned), 18405 (notice of petition), 18410 (hearing on petition), 18420 (petition for second hearing).

See also Sections 16120 ("abuse"), 16490 ("domestic violence"), 18250 (seizure of firearm or other deadly weapon at scene of domestic violence), 18255 (receipt for weapon), 18260 (delivery of deadly weapon seized by peace officer for community college or school district), 18265 (holding period), 18270 (return of stolen weapon), 18275 (sale or destruction of deadly weapon held longer than one year), 18500 (no liability for act in good faith under this division).

For additional guidance on surrender and disposal of weapons, see Sections 18000 (surrender of specified weapons constituting nuisance), 18005 (disposal of weapons constituting nuisance), 18010 (treatment of other weapons constituting nuisance), 33800–34010 (firearm in custody of court or law enforcement agency or similar situation). [38 Cal.L.Rev.Comm. Reports 217 (2009)].

Cross References

Deadly weapon defined for purposes of this Division, see Penal Code § 16430.
Firearm defined for purposes of this Part, see Penal Code § 16520.

§ 18420. Petition for second hearing regarding return of confiscated firearm or deadly weapon; time for filing; disposal of confiscated weapon

(a) If, at a hearing under Section 18410, the court does not order the return of the firearm or other deadly weapon to the owner or person who had lawful possession, that person may petition the court for a second hearing within 12 months from the date of the initial hearing.

(b) If there is a petition for a second hearing, unless it is shown by clear and convincing evidence that the return of the firearm or other deadly weapon would result in endangering the victim or the person reporting the assault or threat, the court shall order the return of the firearm or other deadly weapon and shall award reasonable attorney's fees to the prevailing party.

(c) If the owner or person who had lawful possession does not petition the court within this 12–month period for a second hearing or is unsuccessful at the second hearing in gaining return of the firearm or other deadly weapon, the firearm or other deadly weapon may be disposed of as provided in Sections 18000 and 18005. *(Added by Stats.2010, c. 711 (S.B.1080), § 6, operative Jan. 1, 2012.)*

Law Revision Commission Comments

Section 18420 continues former Section 12028.5(j) without substantive change.

For what constitutes a deadly weapon, see Section 16430 ("deadly weapon"); see also Section 16520 ("firearm").

See Sections 18400 (petition to determine whether weapon should be returned), 18405 (notice of petition), 18410 (hearing on petition), 18415 (order of default).

See also Sections 18250 (seizure of firearm or other deadly weapon at scene of domestic violence), 18255 (receipt for weapon), 18260 (delivery of deadly weapon seized by peace officer for community college or school district), 18265 (holding period), 18270 (return of stolen weapon), 18275 (sale or destruction of deadly weapon held longer than one year), 18500 (no liability for act in good faith under this division).

For additional guidance on surrender and disposal of weapons, see Sections 18000 (surrender of specified weapons constituting nuisance), 18005 (disposal of weapons constituting nuisance), 18010 (treatment of other weapons constituting nuisance), 33800–34010 (firearm in custody of court or law enforcement agency or similar situation). [38 Cal.L.Rev.Comm. Reports 217 (2009)].

Cross References

Deadly weapon defined for purposes of this Division, see Penal Code § 16430.
Firearm defined for purposes of this Part, see Penal Code § 16520.

CHAPTER 3. LIABILITY

§ 18500. Liability of law enforcement agency or officer

The law enforcement agency, or the individual law enforcement officer, shall not be liable for any act in the good faith exercise of this division. *(Added by Stats.2010, c. 711 (S.B.1080), § 6, operative Jan. 1, 2012.)*

Law Revision Commission Comments

Section 18500 continues former Section 12028.5(k) without substantive change. [38 Cal.L.Rev.Comm. Reports 217 (2009)].

Division 5

DESTRUCTIVE DEVICES, EXPLOSIVES, AND SIMILAR WEAPONS

CHAPTER 1. DESTRUCTIVE DEVICES AND EXPLOSIVES GENERALLY

ARTICLE 1. PROHIBITED ACTS

§ 18710. Possession of destructive devices prohibited; punishment

(a) Except as provided by this chapter, any person, firm, or corporation who, within this state, possesses any destructive device, other than fixed ammunition of a caliber greater than .60 caliber, is guilty of a public offense.

(b) A person, firm, or corporation who is convicted of an offense under subdivision (a) shall be punished by imprisonment in the county jail for a term not to exceed one year, or in state prison, or by a fine not to exceed ten thousand dollars ($10,000), or by both this fine and imprisonment. *(Added by Stats.2010, c. 711 (S.B.1080), § 6, operative Jan. 1, 2012.)*

Validity

For validity of this section, see People v. Fischer (App. 1 Dist. 2021) 286 Cal.Rptr.3d 613, 71 Cal.App.5th 745.

Law Revision Commission Comments

Section 18710 continues former Section 12303 without substantive change.
See Section 16460 ("destructive device"). [38 Cal.L.Rev.Comm. Reports 217 (2009)].

Cross References

Destructive device defined, see Penal Code § 16460.

Research References

California Jury Instructions - Criminal 12.55, Possession of Destructive Device.
2 Witkin, California Criminal Law 4th Crimes Against Public Peace and Welfare § 189 (2021), In General.
2 Witkin, California Criminal Law 4th Crimes Against Public Peace and Welfare § 225 (2021), In General.
2 Witkin, California Criminal Law 4th Crimes Against Public Peace and Welfare § 226 (2021), Possession or Sale.
3 Witkin, California Criminal Law 4th Punishment § 620 (2021), Other Offenses.

§ 18715. Reckless or malicious possession of destructive device or explosive prohibited; punishment

(a) Every person who recklessly or maliciously has in possession any destructive device or any explosive in any of the following places is guilty of a felony:

(1) On a public street or highway.

(2) In or near any theater, hall, school, college, church, hotel, or other public building.

(3) In or near any private habitation.

(4) In, on, or near any aircraft, railway passenger train, car, cable road, cable car, or vessel engaged in carrying passengers for hire.

(5) In, on, or near any other public place ordinarily passed by human beings.

(b) An offense under subdivision (a) is punishable by imprisonment pursuant to subdivision (h) of Section 1170 for a period of two, four, or six years. *(Added by Stats.2010, c. 711 (S.B.1080), § 6, operative Jan. 1, 2012. Amended by Stats.2011, c. 15 (A.B.109), § 531, eff. April 4, 2011, operative Jan. 1, 2012.)*

Law Revision Commission Comments

Section 18715 continues former Section 12303.2 without substantive change.

See Sections 16460 ("destructive device"), 16510 ("explosive"). [38 Cal. L.Rev.Comm. Reports 217 (2009)].

Cross References

Bringing explosives into area where state prisoners confined, see Penal Code § 4574.
Bringing explosives into Youth Authority institution or camp, or grounds, see Welfare and Institutions Code § 1001.5.
Destructive device defined, see Penal Code § 16460.
Explosive defined, see Penal Code § 16510.
Felonies, definition and penalties, see Penal Code §§ 17, 18.
Firearms, particular persons, weapons restrictions, see Welfare and Institutions Code § 8103.
Maliciously defined for purposes of this Code, see Penal Code § 7.
Order authorizing interception of communications, see Penal Code § 629.52.

Research References

California Jury Instructions - Criminal 12.55.2, Possession of Destructive/Dangerous Device at or Near Certain Places.
2 Witkin, California Criminal Law 4th Crimes Against Public Peace and Welfare § 61 (2021), Terrorism by Weapons of Mass Destruction.
2 Witkin, California Criminal Law 4th Crimes Against Public Peace and Welfare § 226 (2021), Possession or Sale.
1 Witkin California Criminal Law 4th Crimes Against the Person § 195 (2021), Felonies that Are Inherently Dangerous.
1 Witkin California Criminal Law 4th Defenses § 193 (2021), Homicide and Other Crimes.
1 Witkin California Criminal Law 4th Elements § 12 (2021), Recklessness.

§ 18720. Possession without permit of materials to make destructive device or explosive prohibited; punishment

Every person who possesses any substance, material, or any combination of substances or materials, with the intent to make any destructive device or any explosive without first obtaining a valid permit to make that destructive device or explosive, is guilty of a felony, and is punishable by imprisonment pursuant to subdivision (h) of Section 1170 for two, three, or four years. *(Added by Stats.2010, c. 711 (S.B.1080), § 6, operative Jan. 1, 2012. Amended by Stats.2011, c. 15 (A.B.109), § 532, eff. April 4, 2011, operative Jan. 1, 2012.)*

Law Revision Commission Comments

Section 18720 continues former Section 12312 without substantive change.

See Sections 16460 ("destructive device"), 16510 ("explosive"). [38 Cal. L.Rev.Comm. Reports 217 (2009)].

Cross References

Destructive device defined, see Penal Code § 16460.
Explosive defined, see Penal Code § 16510.
Felonies, definition and penalties, see Penal Code §§ 17, 18.
Order authorizing interception of communications, see Penal Code § 629.52.

Research References

California Jury Instructions - Criminal 12.55.8, Possession of Materials With Intent to Make Explosive/Destructive Device.
2 Witkin, California Criminal Law 4th Crimes Against Public Peace and Welfare § 226 (2021), Possession or Sale.

§ 18725. Carrying or placing destructive device or explosive on passenger aircraft, vessel or vehicle prohibited; punishment

Every person who willfully does any of the following is guilty of a felony and is punishable by imprisonment pursuant to subdivision (h) of Section 1170 for two, four, or six years:

(a) Carries any destructive device or any explosive on any vessel, aircraft, car, or other vehicle that transports passengers for hire.

(b) While on board any vessel, aircraft, car, or other vehicle that transports passengers for hire, places or carries any destructive device or any explosive in any hand baggage, roll, or other container.

(c) Places any destructive device or any explosive in any baggage that is later checked with any common carrier. *(Added by Stats.2010, c. 711 (S.B.1080), § 6, operative Jan. 1, 2012. Amended by Stats.2011, c. 15 (A.B.109), § 533, eff. April 4, 2011, operative Jan. 1, 2012.)*

Law Revision Commission Comments

Section 18725 continues former Section 12303.1 without substantive change.

See Sections 16460 ("destructive device"), 16510 ("explosive"). [38 Cal. L.Rev.Comm. Reports 217 (2009)].

Cross References

Common carrier defined, see Public Utilities Code §§ 211, 212.
Destructive device defined, see Penal Code § 16460.
Explosive defined, see Penal Code § 16510.
Felonies, definition and penalties, see Penal Code §§ 17, 18.
Firearms, particular persons, weapons restrictions, see Welfare and Institutions Code § 8103.
Order authorizing interception of communications, see Penal Code § 629.52.
Placing explosives on or near railroad tracks, see Penal Code §§ 214, 218.
Transportation of explosives, see Vehicle Code § 31600.
Willfully defined for purposes of this Code, see Penal Code § 7.

Research References

California Jury Instructions - Criminal 12.55.1, Placing or Carrying Explosive/Destructive Device—Common Carrier.
2 Witkin, California Criminal Law 4th Crimes Against Public Peace and Welfare § 226 (2021), Possession or Sale.

§ 18730. Sale or transportation of destructive devices prohibited; punishment

Except as provided by this chapter, any person, firm, or corporation who, within this state, sells, offers for sale, or knowingly transports any destructive device, other than fixed ammunition of a caliber greater than .60 caliber, is guilty of a felony and is punishable by imprisonment pursuant to subdivision (h) of Section 1170 for two, three, or four years. *(Added by Stats.2010, c. 711 (S.B.1080), § 6, operative Jan. 1, 2012. Amended by Stats.2011, c. 15 (A.B.109), § 534, eff. April 4, 2011, operative Jan. 1, 2012.)*

Law Revision Commission Comments

Section 18730 continues former Section 12303.6 without substantive change.

See Section 16460 ("destructive device"). [38 Cal.L.Rev.Comm. Reports 217 (2009)].

Cross References

Destructive device defined, see Penal Code § 16460.
Felonies, definition and penalties, see Penal Code §§ 17, 18.
Order authorizing interception of communications, see Penal Code § 629.52.

Research References

California Jury Instructions - Criminal 12.55.4, Sale/Transportation of Destructive Device.

2 Witkin, California Criminal Law 4th Crimes Against Public Peace and Welfare § 226 (2021), Possession or Sale.

§ 18735. Sale, possession or transportation of fixed ammunition greater than .60 caliber prohibited; punishment; second and subsequent offenses

(a) Except as provided by this chapter, any person, firm, or corporation who, within this state, sells, offers for sale, possesses or knowingly transports any fixed ammunition of a caliber greater than .60 caliber is guilty of a public offense.

(b) Upon conviction of an offense under subdivision (a), a person, firm, or corporation shall be punished by imprisonment in the county jail for a term not to exceed six months or by a fine not to exceed one thousand dollars ($1,000), or by both this fine and imprisonment.

(c) A second or subsequent conviction shall be punished by imprisonment in the county jail for a term not to exceed one year, or by imprisonment pursuant to subdivision (h) of Section 1170, or by a fine not to exceed three thousand dollars ($3,000), or by both this fine and imprisonment. *(Added by Stats.2010, c. 711 (S.B.1080), § 6, operative Jan. 1, 2012. Amended by Stats.2011, c. 15 (A.B.109), § 535, eff. April 4, 2011, operative Jan. 1, 2012.)*

Law Revision Commission Comments

Section 18735 continues former Section 12304 without substantive change.

A conviction under former Section 12304 counts as a prior conviction in determining the appropriate punishment under this section. See Section 16015 (determining existence of prior conviction). [38 Cal.L.Rev.Comm. Reports 217 (2009)].

Research References

2 Witkin, California Criminal Law 4th Crimes Against Public Peace and Welfare § 226 (2021), Possession or Sale.

§ 18740. Possessing, exploding or igniting destructive device or explosive with intent to injure, intimidate or terrorize prohibited; attempt; punishment

Every person who possesses, explodes, ignites, or attempts to explode or ignite any destructive device or any explosive with intent to injure, intimidate, or terrify any person, or with intent to wrongfully injure or destroy any property, is guilty of a felony, and shall be punished by imprisonment pursuant to subdivision (h) of Section 1170 for a period of three, five, or seven years. *(Added by Stats.2010, c. 711 (S.B.1080), § 6, operative Jan. 1, 2012. Amended by Stats.2011, c. 15 (A.B.109), § 536, eff. April 4, 2011, operative Jan. 1, 2012.)*

Law Revision Commission Comments

Section 18740 continues former Section 12303.3 without substantive change.

See Sections 16460 ("destructive device"), 16510 ("explosive"). [38 Cal. L.Rev.Comm. Reports 217 (2009)].

Cross References

Attempted arson with explosives, see Penal Code § 455.
Burglary with explosives, see Penal Code § 464.
Destructive device defined, see Penal Code § 16460.
Explosive defined, see Penal Code § 16510.
Felonies, definition and penalties, see Penal Code §§ 17, 18.
Firearms, particular persons, weapons restrictions, see Welfare and Institutions Code § 8103.
Fireworks, illegal discharge, see Health and Safety Code § 12680.
Habitual offender, punishment, see Penal Code § 667.7.
Order authorizing interception of communications, see Penal Code § 629.52.

Research References

California Jury Instructions - Criminal 12.55.3, Possession of Destructive Device/Explosive With Intent to Injure.
2 Witkin, California Criminal Law 4th Crimes Against Public Peace and Welfare § 22 (2021), By Arson or Explosives.
2 Witkin, California Criminal Law 4th Crimes Against Public Peace and Welfare § 227 (2021), Injury to Person or Property or Death.
3 Witkin, California Criminal Law 4th Punishment § 479 (2021), Persons Ineligible for Credit.

§ 18745. Igniting or exploding destructive device or explosive with intent to commit murder prohibited; attempt; punishment

Every person who explodes, ignites, or attempts to explode or ignite any destructive device or any explosive with intent to commit murder is guilty of a felony, and shall be punished by imprisonment in the state prison for life with the possibility of parole. *(Added by Stats.2010, c. 711 (S.B.1080), § 6, operative Jan. 1, 2012.)*

Law Revision Commission Comments

Section 18745 continues former Section 12308 without substantive change.

See Sections 16460 ("destructive device"), 16510 ("explosive"). [38 Cal. L.Rev.Comm. Reports 217 (2009)].

Cross References

Destructive device defined, see Penal Code § 16460.
Explosive defined, see Penal Code § 16510.
Felonies, definition and penalties, see Penal Code §§ 17, 18.
Firearms, particular persons, weapons restrictions, see Welfare and Institutions Code § 8103.
Habitual offender, punishment, see Penal Code § 667.7.
Order authorizing interception of communications, see Penal Code § 629.52.
Prison or state prison defined for purposes of this Code, see Penal Code § 6081.

Research References

California Jury Instructions - Criminal 12.55.5, Explosion or Attempt to Explode or Ignite Destructive Device With Intent to Murder.
2 Witkin, California Criminal Law 4th Crimes Against Public Peace and Welfare § 227 (2021), Injury to Person or Property or Death.
3 Witkin, California Criminal Law 4th Punishment § 401 (2021), What Are Violent Felonies.
3 Witkin, California Criminal Law 4th Punishment § 479 (2021), Persons Ineligible for Credit.

§ 18750. Willfully and maliciously exploding or igniting destructive device or explosive and causing bodily injury prohibited; punishment

Every person who willfully and maliciously explodes or ignites any destructive device or any explosive that causes bodily injury to any person is guilty of a felony, and shall be punished by imprisonment in the state prison for a period of five, seven, or nine years. *(Added by Stats.2010, c. 711 (S.B.1080), § 6, operative Jan. 1, 2012.)*

Law Revision Commission Comments

Section 18750 continues former Section 12309 without substantive change.

See Sections 16460 ("destructive device"), 16510 ("explosive"). [38 Cal. L.Rev.Comm. Reports 217 (2009)].

Cross References

Destructive device defined, see Penal Code § 16460.
Explosive defined, see Penal Code § 16510.
Felonies, definition and penalties, see Penal Code §§ 17, 18.
Firearms, particular persons, weapons restrictions, see Welfare and Institutions Code § 8103.
Habitual offender, punishment, see Penal Code § 667.7.
Interceptions relating to crimes not specified in order of authorization, use, crimes involving employment of peace officer, see Penal Code § 629.82.
Order authorizing interception of communications, see Penal Code § 629.52.
Prison or state prison defined for purposes of this Code, see Penal Code § 6081.

Research References

California Jury Instructions - Criminal 12.55.6, Unlawful Explosion/Ignition of Explosive/Destructive Device Causing Bodily Injury.
2 Witkin, California Criminal Law 4th Crimes Against Public Peace and Welfare § 227 (2021), Injury to Person or Property or Death.
4 Witkin, California Criminal Law 4th Illegally Obtained Evidence § 435 (2021), In General.

4 Witkin, California Criminal Law 4th Pretrial Proceedings § 228 (2021), Manner or Means of Committing Offense.
3 Witkin, California Criminal Law 4th Punishment § 479 (2021), Persons Ineligible for Credit.

§ 18755. Willfully or maliciously exploding or igniting destructive device or explosive causing death, mayhem or great bodily injury prohibited; punishment

(a) Every person who willfully and maliciously explodes or ignites any destructive device or any explosive that causes the death of any person is guilty of a felony, and shall be punished by imprisonment in the state prison for life without the possibility of parole.

(b) Every person who willfully and maliciously explodes or ignites any destructive device or any explosive that causes mayhem or great bodily injury to any person is guilty of a felony, and shall be punished by imprisonment in the state prison for life. *(Added by Stats.2010, c. 711 (S.B.1080), § 6, operative Jan. 1, 2012.)*

Law Revision Commission Comments

Section 18755 continues former Section 12310 without substantive change. See Sections 16460 ("destructive device"), 16510 ("explosive"). [38 Cal. L.Rev.Comm. Reports 217 (2009)].

Cross References

Destructive device defined, see Penal Code § 16460.
Explosive defined, see Penal Code § 16510.
Felonies, definition and penalties, see Penal Code §§ 17, 18.
Firearms, particular persons, weapons restrictions, see Welfare and Institutions Code § 8103.
Habitual offender, punishment, see Penal Code § 667.7.
Interceptions relating to crimes not specified in order of authorization, use, crimes involving employment of peace officer, see Penal Code § 629.82.
Order authorizing interception of communications, see Penal Code § 629.52.
Prison or state prison defined for purposes of this Code, see Penal Code § 6081.

Research References

California Jury Instructions - Criminal 12.55.7, Explosion/Ignition of Explosive/Destructive Device Causing Death, Mayhem or Great Bodily Injury.
2 Witkin, California Criminal Law 4th Crimes Against Public Peace and Welfare § 227 (2021), Injury to Person or Property or Death.
4 Witkin, California Criminal Law 4th Illegally Obtained Evidence § 435 (2021), In General.
1 Witkin California Criminal Law 4th Introduction to Crimes § 57 (2021), Meaning Ascertainable from Case Law.
3 Witkin, California Criminal Law 4th Punishment § 524 (2021), Murder by Destructive Device.

§ 18780. Destructive device or explosives violations; ineligibility for probation or suspension of sentence

A person convicted of a violation of this chapter shall not be granted probation, and the execution of the sentence imposed upon that person shall not be suspended by the court. *(Added by Stats.2010, c. 711 (S.B.1080), § 6, operative Jan. 1, 2012.)*

Law Revision Commission Comments

Section 18780 continues former Section 12311 without substantive change. [38 Cal.L.Rev.Comm. Reports 217 (2009)].

Research References

2 Witkin, California Criminal Law 4th Crimes Against Public Peace and Welfare § 225 (2021), In General.
3 Witkin, California Criminal Law 4th Punishment § 620 (2021), Other Offenses.

ARTICLE 2. EXEMPTIONS

Section

§ 18800. Exemptions; peace officers; military forces; firefighters

(a) Nothing in this chapter prohibits the sale to, purchase by, or possession, transportation, storage, or use of, a destructive device or explosive by any of the following:

(1) Any peace officer listed in Section 830.1 or 830.2, or any peace officer in the Department of Justice authorized by the Attorney General, while on duty and acting within the scope and course of employment.

(2) Any member of the Army, Navy, Air Force, or Marine Corps of the United States, or the National Guard, while on duty and acting within the scope and course of employment.

(b) Nothing in this chapter prohibits the sale to, or the purchase, possession, transportation, storage, or use by any person who is a regularly employed and paid officer, employee, or member of a fire department or fire protection or firefighting agency of the federal government, the State of California, a city, county, city and county, district, or other public or municipal corporation or political subdivision of this state, while on duty and acting within the scope and course of employment, of any equipment used by that department or agency in the course of fire suppression. *(Added by Stats.2010, c. 711 (S.B.1080), § 6, operative Jan. 1, 2012.)*

Law Revision Commission Comments

Section 18800 continues former Section 12302 without substantive change. See Sections 16460 ("destructive device"), 16510 ("explosive"). [38 Cal. L.Rev.Comm. Reports 217 (2009)].

Cross References

Attorney General, generally, see Government Code § 12500 et seq.
Destructive device defined, see Penal Code § 16460.
Explosive defined, see Penal Code § 16510.

Research References

2 Witkin, California Criminal Law 4th Crimes Against Public Peace and Welfare § 225 (2021), In General.

ARTICLE 3. PERMIT AND INSPECTION

Section

§ 18900. Permit to conduct business using, or to possess or transport destructive devices; ineligibility; applications

(a) Every dealer, manufacturer, importer, and exporter of any destructive device, or any motion picture or television studio using destructive devices in the conduct of its business, shall obtain a permit for the conduct of that business from the Department of Justice.

(b) Any person, firm, or corporation not mentioned in subdivision (a) shall obtain a permit from the Department of Justice in order to possess or transport any destructive device. No permit shall be issued to any person who meets any of the following criteria:

(1) Has been convicted of any felony.

(2) Is addicted to the use of any narcotic drug.

(3) Is prohibited by state or federal law from possessing, receiving, owning, or purchasing a firearm.

(c) An application for a permit shall comply with all of the following:

(1) It shall be filed in writing.

(2) It shall be signed by the applicant if an individual, or by a member or officer qualified to sign if the applicant is a firm or corporation.

(3) It shall state the name, business in which engaged, business address, and a full description of the use to which the destructive devices are to be put.

(d) Applications and permits shall be uniform throughout the state on forms prescribed by the Department of Justice. *(Added by Stats.2010, c. 711 (S.B.1080), § 6, operative Jan. 1, 2012.)*

Law Revision Commission Comments

Subdivision (a) of Section 18900 continues former Section 12305(a) without substantive change.

Subdivision (b) continues former Section 12305(b) without substantive change.

Subdivision (c) continues former Section 12305(c) without substantive change.

Subdivision (d) continues former Section 12305(d) without substantive change.

See Section 16460 ("destructive device"). [38 Cal.L.Rev.Comm. Reports 217 (2009)].

Cross References

Destructive device defined, see Penal Code § 16460.
Felonies, definition and penalties, see Penal Code §§ 17, 18.
Firearm defined for purposes of this Part, see Penal Code § 16520.
High explosives, permits, see Health and Safety Code § 12101 et seq.

Research References

2 Witkin, California Criminal Law 4th Crimes Against Public Peace and Welfare § 193 (2021), Sale, Lease, or Transfer by Unlicensed Person.
2 Witkin, California Criminal Law 4th Crimes Against Public Peace and Welfare § 225 (2021), In General.
2 Witkin, California Criminal Law 4th Crimes Against Public Peace and Welfare § 228 (2021), Armor Piercing Ammunition.
2 Witkin, California Criminal Law 4th Crimes Against Public Peace and Welfare § 253 (2021), Openly Displaying or Carrying Imitation or Unloaded Firearm.

§ 18905. Permits; fees; renewal

(a) Each applicant for a permit under this article shall pay at the time of filing the application a fee not to exceed the application processing costs of the Department of Justice.

(b) A permit granted under this article may be renewed one year from the date of issuance, and annually thereafter, upon the filing of a renewal application and the payment of a permit renewal fee not to exceed the application processing costs of the Department of Justice.

(c) After the department establishes fees sufficient in amount to cover processing costs, the amount of the fees shall only increase at a rate not to exceed the legislatively approved cost-of-living adjustment for the department. *(Added by Stats.2010, c. 711 (S.B.1080), § 6, operative Jan. 1, 2012.)*

Law Revision Commission Comments

Section 18905 continues former Section 12305(e) without substantive change. [38 Cal.L.Rev.Comm. Reports 217 (2009)].

Cross References

High explosives, permits, see Health and Safety Code § 12101 et seq.

§ 18910. Inspection; security, storage and inventory; frequency

(a) Except as provided in subdivision (b), the Department of Justice shall, for every person, firm, or corporation to whom a permit is issued under this article, annually conduct an inspection for security and safe storage purposes, and to reconcile the inventory of destructive devices.

(b) A person, firm, or corporation with an inventory of fewer than five devices that require any Department of Justice permit shall be subject to an inspection for security and safe storage purposes, and to reconcile inventory, once every five years, or more frequently if determined by the department. *(Added by Stats.2010, c. 711 (S.B.1080), § 6, operative Jan. 1, 2012.)*

Law Revision Commission Comments

Section 18910 continues former Section 12305(f)-(g) without substantive change.

See Section 16460 ("destructive device"). [38 Cal.L.Rev.Comm. Reports 217 (2009)].

Cross References

Destructive device defined, see Penal Code § 16460.
High explosives, permits, see Health and Safety Code § 12101 et seq.

ARTICLE 4. DESTRUCTIVE DEVICE CONSTITUTING NUISANCE

§ 19000. Possession of destructive device; public nuisance; injunction; destruction

(a) Possession of any destructive device in violation of this chapter is a public nuisance.

(b) The Attorney General or district attorney of any city, county, or city and county may bring an action in the superior court to enjoin the possession of any destructive device.

(c) Any destructive device found to be in violation of this chapter shall be surrendered to the Department of Justice, or to the sheriff or chief of police, if the sheriff or chief of police has elected to perform the services required by this section. The department, sheriff, or chief of police shall destroy the destructive device so as to render it unusable and unrepairable as a destructive device, except upon the filing of a certificate with the department by a judge or district attorney stating that the preservation of the destructive device is necessary to serve the ends of justice. *(Added by Stats.2010, c. 711 (S.B.1080), § 6, operative Jan. 1, 2012.)*

Law Revision Commission Comments

Section 19000 continues former Section 12307 without substantive change.

See Section 16460 ("destructive device"). [38 Cal.L.Rev.Comm. Reports 217 (2009)].

Cross References

Attorney General, generally, see Government Code § 12500 et seq.
Destructive device defined, see Penal Code § 16460.

Research References

2 Witkin, California Criminal Law 4th Crimes Against Public Peace and Welfare § 225 (2021), In General.

CHAPTER 2. EXPLOSIVE SUBSTANCE OTHER THAN FIXED AMMUNITION

§ 19100. Carrying of concealed explosive substance; exception; punishment

Except as provided in Chapter 1 (commencing with Section 17700) of Division 2, any person in this state who carries concealed upon the person any explosive substance, other than fixed ammunition, is punishable by imprisonment in a county jail not exceeding one year or imprisonment pursuant to subdivision (h) of Section 1170. *(Added by Stats.2010, c. 711 (S.B.1080), § 6, operative Jan. 1, 2012. Amended by Stats.2012, c. 43 (S.B.1023), § 84, eff. June 27, 2012.)*

Law Revision Commission Comments

Section 19100 continues former Section 12020(a)(3) without substantive change.

For circumstances in which this section is inapplicable, see Sections 16590 ("generally prohibited weapon"), 17700–17745 (exemptions relating to generally prohibited weapons).

See also Sections 17800 (distinct and separate offense), 19190 (concealed explosive substance constituting nuisance). [38 Cal.L.Rev.Comm. Reports 217 (2009)].

Cross References

Penalty for possession of deadly weapon described in this section within State Capitol, legislative offices, etc., see Penal Code § 171c.

Possession of deadly weapons with intent to assault, see Penal Code § 17500.

Research References

California Jury Instructions - Criminal 12.41, Carrying a Concealed Dagger or Explosive Substance—Weapon Defined.

2 Witkin, California Criminal Law 4th Crimes Against Public Peace and Welfare § 213 (2021), Concealed Dirk, Dagger, or Explosives.

2 Witkin, California Criminal Law 4th Crimes Against Public Peace and Welfare § 263 (2021), Nuisances.

§ 19190. Unlawful concealed carrying of explosive substance as nuisance

The unlawful concealed carrying upon the person of any explosive substance other than fixed ammunition, as provided in Section 19100, is a nuisance and is subject to Sections 18000 and 18005. *(Added by Stats.2010, c. 711 (S.B.1080), § 6, operative Jan. 1, 2012.)*

Law Revision Commission Comments

With respect to an explosive substance other than fixed ammunition, Section 19190 continues former Section 12028(a) without substantive change. [38 Cal.L.Rev.Comm. Reports 217 (2009)].

Cross References

Public nuisances, see Civil Code § 3490 et seq.

Research References

2 Witkin, California Criminal Law 4th Crimes Against Public Peace and Welfare § 263 (2021), Nuisances.

CHAPTER 3. HANDGRENADES

§ 19200. Manufacture, import, sale, supply or possession of metal military practice or replica handgrenade; punishment

(a) Except as provided in Section 19205 and Chapter 1 (commencing with Section 17700) of Division 2, any person in this state who manufactures or causes to be manufactured, imports into the state, keeps for sale, or offers or exposes for sale, or who gives, lends, or possesses any metal military practice handgrenade or metal replica handgrenade is punishable by imprisonment in a county jail not exceeding one year or imprisonment pursuant to subdivision (h) of Section 1170.

(b) Notwithstanding subdivision (a), a first offense involving any metal military practice handgrenade or metal replica handgrenade shall be punishable only as an infraction unless the offender is an active participant in a criminal street gang as defined in the Street Terrorism and Enforcement and Prevention Act (Chapter 11 (commencing with Section 186.20) of Title 7 of Part 1). *(Added by Stats.2010, c. 711 (S.B.1080), § 6, operative Jan. 1, 2012. Amended by Stats.2012, c. 43 (S.B.1023), § 85, eff. June 27, 2012.)*

Law Revision Commission Comments

With respect to a metal military practice handgrenade or metal replica handgrenade, subdivision (a) of Section 19200 continues former Section 12020(a)(1) without substantive change.

Subdivision (b) continues the first sentence of the second paragraph of former Section 12020(a)(4) without substantive change.

For circumstances in which this section is inapplicable, see Sections 16590 ("generally prohibited weapon"), 17700–17745 (exemptions relating to generally prohibited weapons), 19205 (toy or permanently inoperative handgrenade).

See also Sections 17800 (distinct and separate offense), 19290 (metal military practice handgrenade or metal replica handgrenade constituting nuisance). [38 Cal.L.Rev.Comm. Reports 217 (2009)].

Research References

2 Witkin, California Criminal Law 4th Crimes Against Public Peace and Welfare § 211 (2021), Nature of Crime.

§ 19205. Plastic toy handgrenade, or inert metal military practice handgrenade or replica; exception to Section 19200

Section 19200 does not apply to any plastic toy handgrenade, or any metal military practice handgrenade or metal replica handgrenade that is a relic, curio, memorabilia, or display item, that is filled with a permanent inert substance, or that is otherwise permanently altered in a manner that prevents ready modification for use as a grenade. *(Added by Stats.2010, c. 711 (S.B.1080), § 6, operative Jan. 1, 2012.)*

Law Revision Commission Comments

Section 19205 continues former Section 12020(b)(15) without substantive change.

For additional circumstances in which Section 19200 is inapplicable, see Sections 16590 ("generally prohibited weapon"), 17700–17745 (exemptions relating to generally prohibited weapons). [38 Cal.L.Rev.Comm. Reports 217 (2009)].

Research References

2 Witkin, California Criminal Law 4th Crimes Against Public Peace and Welfare § 211 (2021), Nature of Crime.

§ 19290. Metal military practice handgrenade or replica as nuisance

Except as provided in Section 19205 and in Chapter 1 (commencing with Section 17700) of Division 2, any metal military practice handgrenade or metal replica handgrenade is a nuisance and is subject to Section 18010. *(Added by Stats.2010, c. 711 (S.B.1080), § 6, operative Jan. 1, 2012.)*

Law Revision Commission Comments

With respect to a metal military practice handgrenade or metal replica handgrenade, Section 19290 continues the first part of the first sentence of former Section 12029 without substantive change. [38 Cal.L.Rev.Comm. Reports 217 (2009)].

Research References

2 Witkin, California Criminal Law 4th Crimes Against Public Peace and Welfare § 263 (2021), Nuisances.

Division 6

LESS LETHAL WEAPONS

§ 19400. Authority to purchase, possess or transport less lethal weapon or ammunition; peace or custodial officers

A person who is a peace officer or a custodial officer, as defined in Chapter 4.5 (commencing with Section 830) of Title 3 of Part 2, may, if authorized by and under the terms and conditions as are specified by the person's employing agency, purchase, possess, or transport any less lethal weapon or ammunition for any less lethal weapon, for official use in the discharge of the person's duties. *(Added by Stats.2010, c. 711 (S.B.1080), § 6, operative Jan. 1, 2012.)*

Law Revision Commission Comments

Section 19400 continues former Section 12600 without substantive change.

See Section 16780 ("less lethal weapon"). [38 Cal.L.Rev.Comm. Reports 217 (2009)].

§ 19405. Sale of less lethal weapon to minor prohibited; punishment

Any person who sells a less lethal weapon to a person under the age of 18 years is guilty of a misdemeanor, punishable by imprisonment in the county jail for up to six months or by a fine of not more than one thousand dollars ($1,000), or by both that imprisonment and fine. *(Added by Stats.2010, c. 711 (S.B.1080), § 6, operative Jan. 1, 2012.)*

Law Revision Commission Comments

Section 19405 continues former Section 12655 without substantive change.

See Section 16780 ("less lethal weapon"). [38 Cal.L.Rev.Comm. Reports 217 (2009)].

Cross References

Age verification when selling products that are illegal to sell to minor, reasonable steps, products requiring age verification, penalties, see Civil Code § 1798.99.1.
Misdemeanors, definition and penalties, see Penal Code §§ 17, 19, 19.2.

Research References

2 Witkin, California Criminal Law 4th Crimes Against Public Peace and Welfare § 231 (2021), Other Weapons and Devices.

Title 3

WEAPONS AND DEVICES OTHER THAN FIREARMS

Division 1

BB DEVICES

§ 19910. Sale of BB device to minor prohibited

Every person who sells any BB device to a minor is guilty of a misdemeanor. *(Added by Stats.2010, c. 711 (S.B.1080), § 6, operative Jan. 1, 2012.)*

Law Revision Commission Comments

Section 19910 continues former Section 12551 without substantive change.

See Section 16250 ("BB device"). [38 Cal.L.Rev.Comm. Reports 217 (2009)].

Cross References

Age verification when selling products that are illegal to sell to minor, reasonable steps, products requiring age verification, penalties, see Civil Code § 1798.99.1.
Misdemeanor,
Defined, see Penal Code § 17.
Punishment, see Penal Code §§ 19, 19.2.

Research References

2 Witkin, California Criminal Law 4th Crimes Against Public Peace and Welfare § 196 (2021), Transfers to Specified Persons.

§ 19915. Furnishing BB device to minor without consent of parent or guardian prohibited; furnishes defined

(a) Every person who furnishes any BB device to any minor, without the express or implied permission of a parent or legal guardian of the minor, is guilty of a misdemeanor.

(b) As used in this section, "furnishes" means either of the following:

(1) A loan.

(2) A transfer that does not involve a sale. *(Added by Stats.2010, c. 711 (S.B.1080), § 6, operative Jan. 1, 2012.)*

Law Revision Commission Comments

Section 19915 continues former Section 12552 without substantive change.

See Section 16250 ("BB device"). [38 Cal.L.Rev.Comm. Reports 217 (2009)].

Cross References

Liability of parent or guardian for injury to person or property caused by discharge of firearm by minor under 18, see Civil Code § 1714.3.
Misdemeanor,
Defined, see Penal Code § 17.
Punishment, see Penal Code §§ 19, 19.2.
Persons who transport or the lending of assault weapon or .50 BMG rifle to a minor, see Penal Code § 30600.
Possession of concealable firearm by minor, see Penal Code § 29610.

Research References

2 Witkin, California Criminal Law 4th Crimes Against Public Peace and Welfare § 196 (2021), Transfers to Specified Persons.

Division 2

BLOWGUNS

§ 20010. Manufacture, sale, possession or use of blowgun or ammunition prohibited

Any person who knowingly manufactures, sells, offers for sale, possesses, or uses a blowgun or blowgun ammunition in this state is guilty of a misdemeanor. *(Added by Stats.2010, c. 711 (S.B.1080), § 6, operative Jan. 1, 2012.)*

Law Revision Commission Comments

Section 20010 continues former Section 12582 without substantive change.

For circumstances in which this section is inapplicable, see Section 20015 (use of blowgun or blowgun ammunition by veterinarian or animal control professional).

See Sections 16270 ("blowgun"), 16280 ("blowgun ammunition"). [38 Cal.L.Rev.Comm. Reports 217 (2009)].

Cross References

Misdemeanors, definition and penalties, see Penal Code §§ 17, 19, 19.2.

Research References

2 Witkin, California Criminal Law 4th Crimes Against Public Peace and Welfare § 231 (2021), Other Weapons and Devices.

§ 20015. Exemptions

Nothing in this division shall prohibit the sale to, purchase by, possession of, or use of any blowgun or blowgun ammunition by zookeepers, animal control officers, Department of Fish and Game personnel, humane officers whose names are maintained in the county record of humane officers pursuant to Section 14502 of the Corporations Code, or veterinarians in the course and scope of their business in order to administer medicine to animals. *(Added by Stats.2010, c. 711 (S.B.1080), § 6, operative Jan. 1, 2012.)*

Law Revision Commission Comments

Section 20015 continues former Section 12583 without substantive change.

See Sections 16270 ("blowgun"), 16280 ("blowgun ammunition"). [38 Cal.L.Rev.Comm. Reports 217 (2009)].

Research References

2 Witkin, California Criminal Law 4th Crimes Against Public Peace and Welfare § 231 (2021), Other Weapons and Devices.

Division 3

BOOBYTRAP

Section

§ 20110. Assembly, placement or possession of boobytrap prohibited; punishment

(a) Except as provided in Chapter 1 (commencing with Section 18710) of Division 5 of Title 2, any person who assembles, maintains, places, or causes to be placed a boobytrap device is guilty of a felony punishable by imprisonment pursuant to subdivision (h) of Section 1170 for two, three, or five years.

(b) Possession of any device with the intent to use the device as a boobytrap is punishable by imprisonment pursuant to subdivision (h) of Section 1170, or in a county jail not exceeding one year, or by a fine not exceeding five thousand dollars ($5,000), or by both that fine and imprisonment. *(Added by Stats.2010, c. 711 (S.B.1080), § 6, operative Jan. 1, 2012. Amended by Stats.2011, c. 15 (A.B.109), § 537, eff. April 4, 2011, operative Jan. 1, 2012; Stats.2012, c. 43 (S.B.1023), § 86, eff. June 27, 2012.)*

Law Revision Commission Comments

Section 20110 continues subdivisions (a) and (b) of former Section 12355 without substantive change.

See Section 16310 ("boobytrap"). [38 Cal.L.Rev.Comm. Reports 217 (2009)].

Cross References

Felonies, definition and penalties, see Penal Code §§ 17, 18.

Research References

2 Witkin, California Criminal Law 4th Crimes Against Public Peace and Welfare § 189 (2021), In General.

2 Witkin, California Criminal Law 4th Crimes Against Public Peace and Welfare § 231 (2021), Other Weapons and Devices.

Division 4

IMITATION FIREARMS

Section

§ 20150. Altering appearance of imitation firearm prohibited; exemptions

(a) Any person who changes, alters, removes, or obliterates any coloration or markings that are required by any applicable state or federal law or regulation, for any imitation firearm, or any device described in subdivision (b) of Section 16700, in a way that makes the imitation firearm or device look more like a firearm, is guilty of a misdemeanor.

(b) This section does not apply to a manufacturer, importer, or distributor of imitation firearms.

(c) This section does not apply to lawful use in theatrical productions, including motion pictures, television, and stage productions. *(Added by Stats.2010, c. 711 (S.B.1080), § 6, operative Jan. 1, 2012.)*

Law Revision Commission Comments

Section 20150 continues former Section 12553(a) without substantive change.

See Sections 16520 ("firearm"), 16700 ("imitation firearm"). [38 Cal.L.Rev. Comm. Reports 217 (2009)].

Cross References

Firearm defined for purposes of this Part, see Penal Code § 16520.
Misdemeanors, definition and penalties, see Penal Code §§ 17, 19, 19.2.

Research References

2 Witkin, California Criminal Law 4th Crimes Against Public Peace and Welfare § 231 (2021), Other Weapons and Devices.

§ 20155. Violation of federal law governing imitation firearms prohibited

Any manufacturer, importer, or distributor of toy, look-alike, or imitation firearms that fails to comply with any applicable federal law or regulation governing the marking of a toy, look-alike, or imitation firearm, is guilty of a misdemeanor. The definition of "imitation firearm" specified in Section 16700 does not apply to this section.

(Added by Stats.2010, c. 711 (S.B.1080), § 6, operative Jan. 1, 2012. Amended by Stats.2018, c. 185 (A.B.2176), § 4, eff. Jan. 1, 2019.)

Law Revision Commission Comments

Section 20155 continues former Section 12553(b) without substantive change.

See Section 16700 ("imitation firearm"). [38 Cal.L.Rev.Comm. Reports 217 (2009)].

Section 20155 is amended to make clear that it is governed by the terminology used in the applicable federal law. See 15 U.S.C. § 5001(c) ("look-alike firearm" defined). This is a nonsubstantive change. [44 Cal. L.Rev.Comm. Reports 471 (2015)].

Cross References

Firearm defined for purposes of this Part, see Penal Code § 16520.
Imitation firearm defined, see Penal Code § 16700.
Misdemeanors, definition and penalties, see Penal Code §§ 17, 19, 19.2.

Research References

2 Witkin, California Criminal Law 4th Crimes Against Public Peace and Welfare § 231 (2021), Other Weapons and Devices.

§ 20160. Written advisory required for sale of imitation firearms; civil fines

(a) Any imitation firearm manufactured after July 1, 2005, shall, at the time of offer for sale in this state, be accompanied by a conspicuous advisory in writing as part of the packaging, but not necessarily affixed to the imitation firearm, to the effect that the product may be mistaken for a firearm by law enforcement officers or others, that altering the coloration or markings required by state or federal law or regulations so as to make the product look more like a firearm is dangerous, and may be a crime, and that brandishing or displaying the product in public may cause confusion and may be a crime.

(b) Any manufacturer, importer, or distributor that fails to comply with this advisory for any imitation firearm manufactured after July 1, 2005, shall be liable for a civil fine for each action brought by a city attorney or district attorney of not more than one thousand dollars ($1,000) for the first action, five thousand dollars ($5,000) for the second action, and ten thousand dollars ($10,000) for the third action and each subsequent action. *(Added by Stats.2010, c. 711 (S.B.1080), § 6, operative Jan. 1, 2012.)*

Law Revision Commission Comments

Section 20160 continues former Section 12554 without substantive change.

In applying subdivision (b), an action under former Section 12554 counts as a prior action under this section. See Section 16010 & Comment (continuation of existing law); see also Section 16015 (determining existence of prior conviction).

See Sections 16520 ("firearm"), 16700 ("imitation firearm"). [38 Cal.L.Rev. Comm. Reports 217 (2009)].

Cross References

Firearm defined for purposes of this Part, see Penal Code § 16520.
Imitation firearm defined, see Penal Code § 16700.

§ 20165. Sale, purchase, manufacture, transportation, receipt or distribution for commercial purposes; fines; exemptions

(a) Any person who, for commercial purposes, purchases, sells, manufactures, ships, transports, distributes, or receives, by mail order or in any other manner, an imitation firearm, except as authorized by this section, is liable for a civil fine in an action brought by the city attorney or the district attorney of not more than ten thousand dollars ($10,000) for each violation.

(b) The manufacture, purchase, sale, shipping, transport, distribution, or receipt, by mail or in any other manner, of an imitation firearm is authorized if the device is manufactured, purchased, sold, shipped, transported, distributed, or received for any of the following purposes:

(1) Solely for export in interstate or foreign commerce.

(2) Solely for lawful use in theatrical productions, including motion picture, television, and stage productions.

(3) For use in a certified or regulated sporting event or competition.

(4) For use in military or civil defense activities, or ceremonial activities.

(5) For public displays authorized by public or private schools. *(Added by Stats.2010, c. 711 (S.B.1080), § 6, operative Jan. 1, 2012.)*

Law Revision Commission Comments

Section 20165 continues former Section 12555(a)-(b) without substantive change.

See Section 16700 ("imitation firearm"), which includes special guidance for interpreting that term in the context of this section. [38 Cal.L.Rev.Comm. Reports 217 (2009)].

Cross References

Firearm defined for purposes of this Part, see Penal Code § 16520.
Imitation firearm defined, see Penal Code § 16700.

Research References

2 Witkin, California Criminal Law 4th Crimes Against Public Peace and Welfare § 231 (2021), Other Weapons and Devices.

§ 20170. Display of imitation firearm in public place prohibited; public place defined

(a) No person may openly display or expose any imitation firearm in a public place.

(b) As used in this section, "public place" means an area open to the public and includes any of the following:

(1) A street.

(2) A sidewalk.

(3) A bridge.

(4) An alley.

(5) A plaza.

(6) A park.

(7) A driveway.

(8) A front yard.

(9) A parking lot.

(10) An automobile, whether moving or not.

(11) A building open to the general public, including one that serves food or drink, or provides entertainment.

(12) A doorway or entrance to a building or dwelling.

(13) A public school.

(14) A public or private college or university. *(Added by Stats. 2010, c. 711 (S.B.1080), § 6, operative Jan. 1, 2012.)*

Law Revision Commission Comments

Subdivision (a) of Section 20170 continues former Section 12556(a) without substantive change.

For circumstances in which this section is inapplicable, see Section 20175 (exemptions). For consequences of violating this section, see Section 20180 (punishment).

Subdivision (b) continues former Section 12556(e) without substantive change.

See Section 16700 ("imitation firearm"). [38 Cal.L.Rev.Comm. Reports 217 (2009)].

Cross References

Firearm defined for purposes of this Part, see Penal Code § 16520.

Imitation firearm defined, see Penal Code § 16700.

Research References

2 Witkin, California Criminal Law 4th Crimes Against Public Peace and Welfare § 253 (2021), Openly Displaying or Carrying Imitation or Unloaded Firearm.

§ 20175. Exemptions to prohibition of public display of imitation firearms

Section 20170 does not apply in any of the following circumstances:

(a) The imitation firearm is packaged or concealed so that it is not subject to public viewing.

(b) The imitation firearm is displayed or exposed in the course of commerce, including a commercial film or video production, or for service, repair, or restoration of the imitation firearm.

(c) The imitation firearm is used in a theatrical production, a motion picture, video, television, or stage production.

(d) The imitation firearm is used in conjunction with a certified or regulated sporting event or competition.

(e) The imitation firearm is used in conjunction with lawful hunting, or a lawful pest control activity.

(f) The imitation firearm is used or possessed at a certified or regulated public or private shooting range.

(g) The imitation firearm is used at a fair, exhibition, exposition, or other similar activity for which a permit has been obtained from a local or state government.

(h) The imitation firearm is used in a military, civil defense, or civic activity, including a flag ceremony, color guard, parade, award presentation, historical reenactment, or memorial.

(i) The imitation firearm is used for a public display authorized by a public or private school or a display that is part of a museum collection.

(j) The imitation firearm is used in a parade, ceremony, or other similar activity for which a permit has been obtained from a local or state government.

(k) The imitation firearm is displayed on a wall plaque or in a presentation case.

(*l*) The imitation firearm is used in an area where the discharge of a firearm is lawful.

(m) The entire exterior surface of the imitation firearm is white, bright red, bright orange, bright yellow, bright green, bright blue, bright pink, or bright purple, either singly or as the predominant color in combination with other colors in any pattern, or the entire device is constructed of transparent or translucent material that permits unmistakable observation of the device's complete contents. Merely having an orange tip as provided in federal law and regulations does not satisfy this requirement. The entire surface must be colored or transparent or translucent. *(Added by Stats.2010, c. 711 (S.B.1080), § 6, operative Jan. 1, 2012.)*

Law Revision Commission Comments

Section 20175 continues former Section 12556(d) without substantive change.

See Section 16700 ("imitation firearm"). [38 Cal.L.Rev.Comm. Reports 217 (2009)].

Cross References

Firearm defined for purposes of this Part, see Penal Code § 16520.
Imitation firearm defined, see Penal Code § 16700.

Research References

2 Witkin, California Criminal Law 4th Crimes Against Public Peace and Welfare § 253 (2021), Openly Displaying or Carrying Imitation or Unloaded Firearm.

§ 20180. Fines; second and subsequent offenses

(a) Except as provided in subdivision (b), violation of Section 20170 is an infraction punishable by a fine of one hundred dollars ($100) for the first offense, and three hundred dollars ($300) for a second offense.

(b) A third or subsequent violation of Section 20170 is punishable as a misdemeanor.

(c) Nothing in Section 20170, 20175, or this section shall be construed to preclude prosecution for a violation of Section 171b, 171.5, or 626.10. *(Added by Stats.2010, c. 711 (S.B.1080), § 6, operative Jan. 1, 2012.)*

Law Revision Commission Comments

Subdivision (a) of Section 20180 continues former Section 12556(b) without substantive change.

Subdivision (b) continues former Section 12556(c) without substantive change.

Subdivision (c) continues former Section 12556 (f) without substantive change.

A violation of the predecessor of Section 20170 (former Section 12556(a)) counts as a prior offense in determining the appropriate punishment under this section. See Section 16015 (determining existence of prior conviction). [38 Cal.L.Rev.Comm. Reports 217 (2009)].

Cross References

Misdemeanors, definition and penalties, see Penal Code §§ 17, 19, 19.2.

Research References

2 Witkin, California Criminal Law 4th Crimes Against Public Peace and Welfare § 253 (2021), Openly Displaying or Carrying Imitation or Unloaded Firearm.

Division 5

KNIVES AND SIMILAR WEAPONS

CHAPTER 1. GENERAL PROVISIONS

§ 20200. Knife carried in sheath worn openly deemed not concealed

A knife carried in a sheath that is worn openly suspended from the waist of the wearer is not concealed within the meaning of Section 16140, 16340, 17350, or 21310. *(Added by Stats.2010, c. 711 (S.B.1080), § 6, operative Jan. 1, 2012.)*

Law Revision Commission Comments

Section 20200 continues former Section 12020(d) without substantive change. [38 Cal.L.Rev.Comm. Reports 217 (2009)].

Cross References

Penalty for possession of deadly weapon described in this section within State Capitol, legislative offices, etc., see Penal Code § 171c.

Possession of deadly weapons with intent to assault, see Penal Code § 17500.

Research References

2 Witkin, California Criminal Law 4th Crimes Against Public Peace and Welfare § 213 (2021), Concealed Dirk, Dagger, or Explosives.

CHAPTER 2. DISGUISED OR MISLEADING APPEARANCE

ARTICLE 1. AIR GAUGE KNIFE

§ 20310. Manufacture, import, sale, supply or possession of air gauge knife; punishment

Except as provided in Chapter 1 (commencing with Section 17700) of Division 2 of Title 2, any person in this state who manufactures or causes to be manufactured, imports into the state, keeps for sale, or offers or exposes for sale, or who gives, lends, or possesses any air gauge knife is punishable by imprisonment in a county jail not exceeding one year or imprisonment pursuant to subdivision (h) of Section 1170. *(Added by Stats.2010, c. 711 (S.B.1080), § 6, operative Jan. 1, 2012. Amended by Stats.2012, c. 43 (S.B.1023), § 87, eff. June 27, 2012.)*

Law Revision Commission Comments

With respect to an air gauge knife, Section 20310 continues former Section 12020(a)(1) without substantive change.

For circumstances in which this section is inapplicable, see Sections 16590 ("generally prohibited weapon"), 17700–17745 (exemptions relating to generally prohibited weapons).

See Section 16140 ("air gauge knife"). See also Sections 17800 (distinct and separate offense), 20390 (air gauge knife constituting nuisance). [38 Cal. L.Rev.Comm. Reports 217 (2009)].

Cross References

Penalty for possession of deadly weapon described in this section within State Capitol, legislative offices, etc., see Penal Code § 171c.

Possession of deadly weapons with intent to assault, see Penal Code § 17500.

Research References

2 Witkin, California Criminal Law 4th Crimes Against Public Peace and Welfare § 211 (2021), Nature of Crime.

§ 20390. Air gauge knife deemed nuisance; exceptions

Except as provided in Chapter 1 (commencing with Section 17700) of Division 2 of Title 2, any air gauge knife is a nuisance and is subject to Section 18010. *(Added by Stats.2010, c. 711 (S.B.1080), § 6, operative Jan. 1, 2012.)*

Law Revision Commission Comments

With respect to an air gauge knife, Section 20390 continues the first part of the first sentence of former Section 12029 without substantive change.

See Section 16140 ("air gauge knife"). [38 Cal.L.Rev.Comm. Reports 217 (2009)].

Research References

2 Witkin, California Criminal Law 4th Crimes Against Public Peace and Welfare § 263 (2021), Nuisances.

ARTICLE 2. BELT BUCKLE KNIFE

§ 20410. Manufacture, import, sale, supply or possession of belt buckle knife; punishment

Except as provided in Chapter 1 (commencing with Section 17700) of Division 2 of Title 2, any person in this state who manufactures or causes to be manufactured, imports into the state, keeps for sale, or offers or exposes for sale, or who gives, lends, or possesses any belt buckle knife is punishable by imprisonment in a county jail not exceeding one year or imprisonment pursuant to subdivision (h) of Section 1170. *(Added by Stats.2010, c. 711 (S.B.1080), § 6, operative Jan. 1, 2012. Amended by Stats.2012, c. 43 (S.B.1023), § 88, eff. June 27, 2012.)*

Law Revision Commission Comments

With respect to a belt buckle knife, Section 20410 continues former Section 12020(a)(1) without substantive change.

For circumstances in which this section is inapplicable, see Sections 16590 ("generally prohibited weapon"), 17700–17745 (exemptions relating to generally prohibited weapons).

See Section 16260 ("belt buckle knife"). See also Sections 17800 (distinct and separate offense), 20490 (belt buckle knife constituting nuisance). [38 Cal.L.Rev.Comm. Reports 217 (2009)].

Cross References

Penalty for possession of deadly weapon described in this section within State Capitol, legislative offices, etc., see Penal Code § 171c.

Possession of deadly weapons with intent to assault, see Penal Code § 17500.

Research References

2 Witkin, California Criminal Law 4th Crimes Against Public Peace and Welfare § 211 (2021), Nature of Crime.

§ 20490. Belt buckle knife deemed nuisance; exceptions

Except as provided in Chapter 1 (commencing with Section 17700) of Division 2 of Title 2, any belt buckle knife is a nuisance and is subject to Section 18010. *(Added by Stats.2010, c. 711 (S.B.1080), § 6, operative Jan. 1, 2012.)*

Law Revision Commission Comments

With respect to a belt buckle knife, Section 20490 continues the first part of the first sentence of former Section 12029 without substantive change.

See Section 16260 ("belt buckle knife"). [38 Cal.L.Rev.Comm. Reports 217 (2009)].

Research References

2 Witkin, California Criminal Law 4th Crimes Against Public Peace and Welfare § 263 (2021), Nuisances.

ARTICLE 3. CANE SWORD

§ 20510. Manufacture, import, sale, supply or possession of cane sword; punishment

Except as provided in Chapter 1 (commencing with Section 17700) of Division 2 of Title 2, any person in this state who manufactures or causes to be manufactured, imports into the state, keeps for sale, or offers or exposes for sale, or who gives, lends, or possesses any cane sword is punishable by imprisonment in a county jail not exceeding one year or imprisonment pursuant to subdivision (h) of Section 1170. *(Added by Stats.2010, c. 711 (S.B.1080), § 6, operative Jan. 1, 2012. Amended by Stats.2012, c. 43 (S.B.1023), § 89, eff. June 27, 2012.)*

Law Revision Commission Comments

With respect to a cane sword, Section 20510 continues former Section 12020(a)(1) without substantive change.

For circumstances in which this section is inapplicable, see Sections 16590 ("generally prohibited weapon"), 17700–17745 (exemptions relating to generally prohibited weapons).

See Section 16340 ("cane sword"). See also Sections 17800 (distinct and separate offense), 20590 (cane sword constituting nuisance). [38 Cal.L.Rev. Comm. Reports 217 (2009)].

Cross References

Penalty for possession of deadly weapon described in this section within State Capitol, legislative offices, etc., see Penal Code § 171c.

Possession of deadly weapons with intent to assault, see Penal Code § 17500.

Research References

2 Witkin, California Criminal Law 4th Crimes Against Public Peace and Welfare § 211 (2021), Nature of Crime.

1 Witkin California Criminal Law 4th Elements § 9 (2021), Facts that Must be Known.

1 Witkin California Criminal Law 4th Elements § 18 (2021), Public Welfare Offenses.

§ 20590. Cane sword deemed nuisance; exceptions

Except as provided in Chapter 1 (commencing with Section 17700) of Division 2 of Title 2, any cane sword is a nuisance and is subject to Section 18010. *(Added by Stats.2010, c. 711 (S.B.1080), § 6, operative Jan. 1, 2012.)*

Law Revision Commission Comments

With respect to a cane sword, Section 20590 continues the first part of the first sentence of former Section 12029 without substantive change.

See Section 16340 ("cane sword"). [38 Cal.L.Rev.Comm. Reports 217 (2009)].

Research References

2 Witkin, California Criminal Law 4th Crimes Against Public Peace and Welfare § 263 (2021), Nuisances.

ARTICLE 4. LIPSTICK CASE KNIFE

§ 20610. Manufacture, import, sale, supply or possession of lipstick case knife; punishment

Except as provided in Chapter 1 (commencing with Section 17700) of Division 2 of Title 2, any person in this state who manufactures or causes to be manufactured, imports into the state, keeps for sale, or offers or exposes for sale, or who gives, lends, or possesses any lipstick case knife is punishable by imprisonment in a county jail not exceeding one year or imprisonment pursuant to subdivision (h) of Section 1170. *(Added by Stats.2010, c. 711 (S.B.1080), § 6, operative Jan. 1, 2012. Amended by Stats.2012, c. 43 (S.B.1023), § 90, eff. June 27, 2012.)*

Law Revision Commission Comments

With respect to a lipstick case knife, Section 20610 continues former Section 12020(a)(1) without substantive change.

For circumstances in which this section is inapplicable, see Sections 16590 ("generally prohibited weapon"), 17700–17745 (exemptions relating to generally prohibited weapons).

See Section 16830 ("lipstick case knife"). See also Sections 17800 (distinct and separate offense), 20690 (lipstick case knife constituting nuisance). [38 Cal.L.Rev.Comm. Reports 217 (2009)].

Cross References

Penalty for possession of deadly weapon described in this section within State Capitol, legislative offices, etc., see Penal Code § 171c.

Possession of deadly weapons with intent to assault, see Penal Code § 17500.

Research References

2 Witkin, California Criminal Law 4th Crimes Against Public Peace and Welfare § 211 (2021), Nature of Crime.

§ 20690. Lipstick case knife deemed nuisance; exceptions

Except as provided in Chapter 1 (commencing with Section 17700) of Division 2 of Title 2, any lipstick case knife is a nuisance and is subject to Section 18010. *(Added by Stats.2010, c. 711 (S.B.1080), § 6, operative Jan. 1, 2012.)*

Law Revision Commission Comments

With respect to a lipstick case knife, Section 20690 continues the first part of the first sentence of former Section 12029 without substantive change.

See Section 16830 ("lipstick case knife"). [38 Cal.L.Rev.Comm. Reports 217 (2009)].

Research References

2 Witkin, California Criminal Law 4th Crimes Against Public Peace and Welfare § 263 (2021), Nuisances.

ARTICLE 5. SHOBI–ZUE

§ 20710. Manufacture, import, sale, supply or possession of shobi-zue; punishment

Except as provided in Chapter 1 (commencing with Section 17700) of Division 2 of Title 2, any person in this state who manufactures or causes to be manufactured, imports into the state, keeps for sale, or offers or exposes for sale, or who gives, lends, or possesses any shobi-zue is punishable by imprisonment in a county jail not exceeding one year or imprisonment pursuant to subdivision (h) of Section 1170. *(Added by Stats.2010, c. 711 (S.B.1080), § 6, operative Jan. 1, 2012. Amended by Stats.2012, c. 43 (S.B.1023), § 91, eff. June 27, 2012.)*

Law Revision Commission Comments

With respect to a shobi-zue, Section 20710 continues former Section 12020(a)(1) without substantive change.

For circumstances in which this section is inapplicable, see Sections 16590 ("generally prohibited weapon"), 17700–17745 (exemptions relating to generally prohibited weapons).

See Section 17160 ("shobi-zue"). See also Sections 17800 (distinct and separate offense), 20790 (shobi-zue constituting nuisance). [38 Cal.L.Rev. Comm. Reports 217 (2009)].

Cross References

Penalty for possession of deadly weapon described in this section within State Capitol, legislative offices, etc., see Penal Code § 171c.

Possession of deadly weapons with intent to assault, see Penal Code § 17500.

Research References

2 Witkin, California Criminal Law 4th Crimes Against Public Peace and Welfare § 211 (2021), Nature of Crime.

§ 20790. Shobi-zue deemed nuisance; exceptions

Except as provided in Chapter 1 (commencing with Section 17700) of Division 2 of Title 2, any shobi-zue is a nuisance and is subject to Section 18010. *(Added by Stats.2010, c. 711 (S.B.1080), § 6, operative Jan. 1, 2012.)*

Law Revision Commission Comments

With respect to a shobi-zue, Section 20790 continues the first part of the first sentence of former Section 12029 without substantive change.

See Section 17160 ("shobi-zue"). [38 Cal.L.Rev.Comm. Reports 217 (2009)].

Research References

2 Witkin, California Criminal Law 4th Crimes Against Public Peace and Welfare § 263 (2021), Nuisances.

ARTICLE 6. UNDETECTABLE KNIFE

§ 20810. Commercial manufacture, import for commercial sale, export or offer for commercial, dealer, wholesaler, or distributor sale of undetectable knives; misdemeanor; manufacture of knives or other instruments to include detectable metal

(a) Any person in this state who commercially manufactures or causes to be commercially manufactured, or who knowingly imports into the state for commercial sale, or who knowingly exports out of this state for commercial, dealer, wholesaler, or distributor sale, or who keeps for commercial sale, or offers or exposes for commercial, dealer, wholesaler, or distributor sale, any undetectable knife is guilty of a misdemeanor.

(b) Notwithstanding any other provision of law, commencing January 1, 2000, all knives or other instrument with or without a handguard that is capable of ready use as a stabbing weapon that may inflict great bodily injury or death that are commercially manufactured in this state that utilize materials that are not detectable by a metal detector or magnetometer, shall be manufactured to include materials that will ensure they are detectable by a metal detector or magnetometer, either handheld or otherwise, that is set at standard calibration. *(Added by Stats.2010, c. 711 (S.B.1080), § 6, operative Jan. 1, 2012.)*

Law Revision Commission Comments

Subdivision (a) of Section 20810 continues the first sentence of former Section 12001.1(a) without change.

Subdivision (b) continues former Section 12001.1(b) without change.

For circumstances in which this section is inapplicable, see Sections 20815 (undetectable knife for law enforcement or military entity), 20820 (undetectable knife for historical society, museum, or institutional collection open to public).

See Section 17290 ("undetectable knife"). [38 Cal.L.Rev.Comm. Reports 217 (2009)].

Cross References

Misdemeanors, definition and penalties, see Penal Code §§ 17, 19, 19.2.
Wholesaler defined for purposes of this Part, see Penal Code § 17340.

Research References

2 Witkin, California Criminal Law 4th Crimes Against Public Peace and Welfare § 231 (2021), Other Weapons and Devices.

§ 20815. Undetectable knives for sale to law enforcement or military entities

Section 20810 does not apply to the manufacture or importation of any undetectable knife for sale to a law enforcement or military entity with a valid agency, department, or unit purchase order, nor does Section 20810 apply to the subsequent sale of any undetectable knife to a law enforcement or military entity. *(Added by Stats.2010, c. 711 (S.B.1080), § 6, operative Jan. 1, 2012.)*

Law Revision Commission Comments

Section 20815 continues former Section 12001.1(c) without substantive change.

See Section 17290 ("undetectable knife"). [38 Cal.L.Rev.Comm. Reports 217 (2009)].

Research References

2 Witkin, California Criminal Law 4th Crimes Against Public Peace and Welfare § 231 (2021), Other Weapons and Devices.

§ 20820. Undetectable knives for sale to historical society, museum, or institutional collection

Section 20810 does not apply to the manufacture or importation of any undetectable knife for sale to a federal, state, or local historical society, museum, or institutional collection that is open to the public, provided that the undetectable knife is properly housed and secured from unauthorized handling, nor does Section 20810 apply to the subsequent sale of the knife to any of these entities. *(Added by Stats.2010, c. 711 (S.B.1080), § 6, operative Jan. 1, 2012.)*

Law Revision Commission Comments

Section 20820 continues former Section 12001.1(d) without substantive change.

See Section 17290 ("undetectable knife"). [38 Cal.L.Rev.Comm. Reports 217 (2009)].

Research References

2 Witkin, California Criminal Law 4th Crimes Against Public Peace and Welfare § 231 (2021), Other Weapons and Devices.

ARTICLE 7. WRITING PEN KNIFE

§ 20910. Manufacture, import, sale, supply or possession of writing pen knife; punishment

Except as provided in Chapter 1 (commencing with Section 17700) of Division 2 of Title 2, any person in this state who manufactures or causes to be manufactured, imports into the state, keeps for sale, or offers or exposes for sale, or who gives, lends, or possesses any writing pen knife is punishable by imprisonment in a county jail not exceeding one year or imprisonment pursuant to subdivision (h) of Section 1170. *(Added by Stats.2010, c. 711 (S.B.1080), § 6, operative Jan. 1, 2012. Amended by Stats.2012, c. 43 (S.B.1023), § 92, eff. June 27, 2012.)*

Law Revision Commission Comments

With respect to a writing pen knife, Section 20910 continues former Section 12020(a)(1) without substantive change.

For circumstances in which this section is inapplicable, see Sections 16590 ("generally prohibited weapon"), 17700–17745 (exemptions relating to generally prohibited weapons).

See Section 17350 ("writing pen knife"). See also Sections 17800 (distinct and separate offense), 20990 (writing pen knife constituting nuisance). [38 Cal.L.Rev.Comm. Reports 217 (2009)].

Cross References

Penalty for possession of deadly weapon described in this section within State Capitol, legislative offices, etc., see Penal Code § 171c.
Possession of deadly weapons with intent to assault, see Penal Code § 17500.

Research References

2 Witkin, California Criminal Law 4th Crimes Against Public Peace and Welfare § 211 (2021), Nature of Crime.

§ 20990. Writing pen knife deemed nuisance; exceptions

Except as provided in Chapter 1 (commencing with Section 17700) of Division 2 of Title 2, any writing pen knife is a nuisance and is subject to Section 18010. *(Added by Stats.2010, c. 711 (S.B.1080), § 6, operative Jan. 1, 2012.)*

Law Revision Commission Comments

With respect to a writing pen knife, Section 20990 continues the first part of the first sentence of former Section 12029 without substantive change.

See Section 17350 ("writing pen knife"). [38 Cal.L.Rev.Comm. Reports 217 (2009)].

Research References

2 Witkin, California Criminal Law 4th Crimes Against Public Peace and Welfare § 263 (2021), Nuisances.

CHAPTER 3. BALLISTIC KNIFE

§ 21110. Manufacture, import, sale, supply or possession of ballistic knife; punishment

Except as provided in Chapter 1 (commencing with Section 17700) of Division 2 of Title 2, any person in this state who manufactures or causes to be manufactured, imports into the state, keeps for sale, or offers or exposes for sale, or who gives, lends, or possesses any ballistic knife is punishable by imprisonment in a county jail not exceeding one year or imprisonment pursuant to subdivision (h) of Section 1170. *(Added by Stats.2010, c. 711 (S.B.1080), § 6, operative Jan. 1, 2012. Amended by Stats.2012, c. 43 (S.B.1023), § 93, eff. June 27, 2012.)*

Law Revision Commission Comments

With respect to a ballistic knife, Section 21110 continues former Section 12020(a)(1) without substantive change.

For circumstances in which this section is inapplicable, see Sections 16590 ("generally prohibited weapon"), 17700–17745 (exemptions relating to generally prohibited weapons).

See Section 16220 ("ballistic knife"). See also Sections 17800 (distinct and separate offense), 21190 (ballistic knife constituting nuisance). [38 Cal.L.Rev. Comm. Reports 217 (2009)].

Cross References

Penalty for possession of deadly weapon described in this section within State Capitol, legislative offices, etc., see Penal Code § 171c.
Possession of deadly weapons with intent to assault, see Penal Code § 17500.

Research References

2 Witkin, California Criminal Law 4th Crimes Against Public Peace and Welfare § 211 (2021), Nature of Crime.

§ 21190. Ballistic knife deemed nuisance; exceptions

Except as provided in Chapter 1 (commencing with Section 17700) of Division 2 of Title 2, any ballistic knife is a nuisance and is subject to Section 18010. *(Added by Stats.2010, c. 711 (S.B.1080), § 6, operative Jan. 1, 2012.)*

Law Revision Commission Comments

With respect to a ballistic knife, Section 21190 continues the first part of the first sentence of former Section 12029 without substantive change.

See Section 16220 ("ballistic knife"). [38 Cal.L.Rev.Comm. Reports 217 (2009)].

Research References

2 Witkin, California Criminal Law 4th Crimes Against Public Peace and Welfare § 263 (2021), Nuisances.

CHAPTER 4. DIRK OR DAGGER

§ 21310. Carrying of concealed dirk or dagger; punishment

Except as provided in Chapter 1 (commencing with Section 17700) of Division 2 of Title 2, any person in this state who carries concealed upon the person any dirk or dagger is punishable by imprisonment in a county jail not exceeding one year or imprisonment pursuant to subdivision (h) of Section 1170. *(Added by Stats.2010, c. 711 (S.B.1080), § 6, operative Jan. 1, 2012. Amended by Stats.2012, c. 43 (S.B.1023), § 94, eff. June 27, 2012.)*

Law Revision Commission Comments

Section 21310 continues the first paragraph of former Section 12020(a)(4) without substantive change.

For circumstances in which this section is inapplicable, see Sections 16590 ("generally prohibited weapon"), 17700–17745 (exemptions relating to generally prohibited weapons), 20200 (circumstances in which knife is not deemed "concealed").

See Section 16470 ("dirk" or "dagger"). See also Sections 17800 (distinct and separate offense), 21390 (concealed dirk or dagger constituting nuisance). [38 Cal.L.Rev.Comm. Reports 217 (2009)].

Cross References

Penalty for possession of deadly weapon described in this section within State Capitol, legislative offices, etc., see Penal Code § 171c.
Possession of deadly weapons with intent to assault, see Penal Code § 17500.
Unlawful concealed carrying of dirk or dagger deemed nuisance, see Penal Code § 21390.

Research References

California Jury Instructions - Criminal 12.41, Carrying a Concealed Dagger or Explosive Substance—Weapon Defined.
2 Witkin, California Criminal Law 4th Crimes Against Public Peace and Welfare § 213 (2021), Concealed Dirk, Dagger, or Explosives.
1 Witkin California Criminal Law 4th Elements § 9 (2021), Facts that Must be Known.
1 Witkin California Criminal Law 4th Introduction to Crimes § 41 (2021), Construction Favoring Validity.
1 Witkin California Criminal Law 4th Introduction to Crimes § 70 (2021), Weapons.

1 Witkin California Criminal Law 4th Introduction to Crimes § 72 (2021), Illustrations: Weapons.

§ 21390. Unlawful concealed carrying of dirk or dagger deemed nuisance

The unlawful concealed carrying upon the person of any dirk or dagger, as provided in Section 21310, is a nuisance and is subject to Sections 18000 and 18005. *(Added by Stats.2010, c. 711 (S.B.1080), § 6, operative Jan. 1, 2012.)*

Law Revision Commission Comments

With respect to a dirk or dagger, Section 21390 continues former Section 12028(a) without substantive change.

See Section 16470 ("dirk" or "dagger"). [38 Cal.L.Rev.Comm. Reports 217 (2009)].

Cross References

Public nuisances, see Civil Code § 3490 et seq.

Research References

2 Witkin, California Criminal Law 4th Crimes Against Public Peace and Welfare § 263 (2021), Nuisances.

CHAPTER 5. SWITCHBLADE KNIFE

§ 21510. Possession, carrying, sale, loan or transfer of switchblade knife prohibited

Every person who does any of the following with a switchblade knife having a blade two or more inches in length is guilty of a misdemeanor:

(a) Possesses the knife in the passenger's or driver's area of any motor vehicle in any public place or place open to the public.

(b) Carries the knife upon the person.

(c) Sells, offers for sale, exposes for sale, loans, transfers, or gives the knife to any other person. *(Added by Stats.2010, c. 711 (S.B.1080), § 6, operative Jan. 1, 2012.)*

Law Revision Commission Comments

Section 21510 continues the first paragraph of former Section 653k without substantive change.

See Sections 16965 ("passenger's or driver's area"), 17235 ("switchblade knife"). [38 Cal.L.Rev.Comm. Reports 217 (2009)].

Cross References

Misdemeanors, definition and penalties, see Penal Code §§ 17, 19, 19.2.

Research References

2 Witkin, California Criminal Law 4th Crimes Against Public Peace and Welfare § 213 (2021), Concealed Dirk, Dagger, or Explosives.
2 Witkin, California Criminal Law 4th Crimes Against Public Peace and Welfare § 230 (2021), Switchblade Knives.
2 Witkin, California Criminal Law 4th Crimes Against Public Peace and Welfare § 263 (2021), Nuisances.
1 Witkin California Criminal Law 4th Introduction to Crimes § 70 (2021), Weapons.
1 Witkin California Criminal Law 4th Introduction to Crimes § 72 (2021), Illustrations: Weapons.

§ 21590. Unlawful possession or carrying of switchblade knife deemed nuisance

The unlawful possession or carrying of any switchblade knife, as provided in Section 21510, is a nuisance and is subject to Sections 18000 and 18005. *(Added by Stats.2010, c. 711 (S.B.1080), § 6, operative Jan. 1, 2012.)*

Law Revision Commission Comments

With respect to a switchblade knife, Section 21590 continues former Section 12028(a) without substantive change.

See Section 17235 ("switchblade knife"). [38 Cal.L.Rev.Comm. Reports 217 (2009)].

Cross References

Public nuisances, see Civil Code § 3490 et seq.
Switch-blade knives having blades two or more inches long, see Penal Code § 653k.

Research References

2 Witkin, California Criminal Law 4th Crimes Against Public Peace and Welfare § 263 (2021), Nuisances.

Division 6

KNUCKLES

CHAPTER 1. COMPOSITE KNUCKLES OR HARD WOODEN KNUCKLES

§ 21710. Manufacture, import, sale, supply or possession of composite or hard wooden knuckles; punishment

Any person in this state who possesses, commercially manufactures or causes to be commercially manufactured, or who knowingly imports into the state for commercial sale, keeps for commercial sale, or offers or exposes for commercial sale, any composite knuckles or hard wooden knuckles is guilty of a misdemeanor. *(Added by Stats.2010, c. 711 (S.B.1080), § 6, operative Jan. 1, 2012.)*

Law Revision Commission Comments

Section 21710 continues the first sentence of former Section 12020.1 without substantive change.

See Sections 16405 ("composite knuckles"), 16680 ("hard wooden knuckles"). [38 Cal.L.Rev.Comm. Reports 217 (2009)].

Cross References

Misdemeanors, see Penal Code §§ 17, 19.

Research References

2 Witkin, California Criminal Law 4th Crimes Against Public Peace and Welfare § 211 (2021), Nature of Crime.

CHAPTER 2. METAL KNUCKLES

§ 21810. Manufacture, import, sale, supply or possession of metal knuckles; punishment

Except as provided in Chapter 1 (commencing with Section 17700) of Division 2 of Title 2, any person in this state who manufactures or causes to be manufactured, imports into the state, keeps for sale, or offers or exposes for sale, or who gives, lends, or possesses any metal knuckles is punishable by imprisonment in a county jail not exceeding one year or imprisonment pursuant to subdivision (h) of Section 1170. *(Added by Stats.2010, c. 711 (S.B.1080), § 6, operative Jan. 1, 2012. Amended by Stats.2012, c. 43 (S.B.1023), § 95, eff. June 27, 2012.)*

Law Revision Commission Comments

With respect to metal knuckles, Section 21810 continues former Section 12020(a)(1) without substantive change.

For circumstances in which this section is inapplicable, see Sections 16590 ("generally prohibited weapon"), 17700–17745 (exemptions relating to generally prohibited weapons).

See Section 16920 ("metal knuckles"). See also Sections 17800 (distinct and separate offense), 21890 (metal knuckles constituting nuisance). [38 Cal. L.Rev.Comm. Reports 217 (2009)].

Cross References

Metal knuckles defined for purposes of this Part, see Penal Code § 16920.
Penalty for possession of deadly weapon described in this section within State Capitol, legislative offices, etc., see Penal Code § 171c.
Possession of deadly weapons with intent to assault, see Penal Code § 17500.

Research References

2 Witkin, California Criminal Law 4th Crimes Against Public Peace and Welfare § 211 (2021), Nature of Crime.
1 Witkin California Criminal Law 4th Elements § 9 (2021), Facts that Must be Known.

§ 21890. Metal knuckles deemed nuisance; exceptions

Except as provided in Chapter 1 (commencing with Section 17700) of Division 2 of Title 2, metal knuckles are a nuisance and are subject to Section 18010. *(Added by Stats.2010, c. 711 (S.B.1080), § 6, operative Jan. 1, 2012.)*

Law Revision Commission Comments

With respect to metal knuckles, Section 21890 continues the first part of the first sentence of former Section 12029 without substantive change.

See Section 16920 ("metal knuckles"). [38 Cal.L.Rev.Comm. Reports 217 (2009)].

Cross References

Metal knuckles defined for purposes of this Part, see Penal Code § 16920.

Research References

2 Witkin, California Criminal Law 4th Crimes Against Public Peace and Welfare § 263 (2021), Nuisances.

Division 7

NUNCHAKU

Division 8

SAPS AND SIMILAR WEAPONS

§ 22210. Manufacture, import, sale, supply or possession of leaded cane, billy, blackjack, sandbag, sandclub, sap, or slungshot; punishment

Except as provided in Section 22215 and Chapter 1 (commencing with Section 17700) of Division 2 of Title 2, any person in this state who manufactures or causes to be manufactured, imports into the state, keeps for sale, or offers or exposes for sale, or who gives, lends, or possesses any leaded cane, or any instrument or weapon of the kind commonly known as a billy, blackjack, sandbag, sandclub, sap, or slungshot, is punishable by imprisonment in a county jail not exceeding one year or imprisonment pursuant to subdivision (h) of Section 1170. *(Added by Stats.2010, c. 711 (S.B.1080), § 6, operative Jan. 1, 2012. Amended by Stats.2012, c. 43 (S.B.1023), § 97, eff. June 27, 2012.)*

Law Revision Commission Comments

With respect to a leaded cane or "any instrument or weapon of the kind commonly known as a blackjack, slungshot, billy, sandclub, sap, or sandbag," Section 22210 continues former Section 12020(a)(1) without substantive change.

For circumstances in which this section is inapplicable, see Sections 16590 ("generally prohibited weapon"), 17700–17745 (exemptions relating to generally prohibited weapons).

See Section 16760 ("leaded cane"). See also Sections 17800 (distinct and separate offense), 22290 (nuisance created by leaded cane or by instrument or weapon of kind commonly known as billy, blackjack, sandbag, sandclub, sap, or slungshot). [38 Cal.L.Rev.Comm. Reports 217 (2009)].

Cross References

Penalty for possession of deadly weapon described in this section within State Capitol, legislative offices, etc., see Penal Code § 171c.
Possession of deadly weapons with intent to assault, see Penal Code § 17500.

Research References

California Jury Instructions - Criminal 12.40, Illegal Possession of Certain Weapons or Explosives.
California Jury Instructions - Criminal 2500, Illegal Possession, etc. of Weapon.
2 Witkin, California Criminal Law 4th Crimes Against Public Peace and Welfare § 211 (2021), Nature of Crime.
2 Witkin, California Criminal Law 4th Crimes Against Public Peace and Welfare § 212 (2021), Elements of Offense.

§ 22215. Wooden clubs or batons for special police officers and uniformed security guards; exception to Section 22210

Section 22210 does not apply to the manufacture for, sale to, exposing or keeping for sale to, importation of, or lending of wooden clubs or batons to special police officers or uniformed security guards authorized to carry any wooden club or baton pursuant to Section 22295 by entities that are in the business of selling wooden clubs or batons to special police officers and uniformed security guards when engaging in transactions with those persons. *(Added by Stats.2010, c. 711 (S.B.1080), § 6, operative Jan. 1, 2012.)*

Law Revision Commission Comments

Section 22215 continues former Section 12020(b)(14) without substantive change.

For additional circumstances in which Section 22210 is inapplicable, see Sections 16590 ("generally prohibited weapon"), 17700–17745 (exemptions relating to generally prohibited weapons). [38 Cal.L.Rev.Comm. Reports 217 (2009)].

Cross References

Carrying and use of wooden club or baton, course of instruction and permit, see Penal Code § 22295.

Research References

2 Witkin, California Criminal Law 4th Crimes Against Public Peace and Welfare § 211 (2021), Nature of Crime.

§ 22290. Leaded cane, billy, blackjack, sandbag, sandclub, sap, or slingshot deemed nuisance; exceptions

Except as provided in Section 22215 and in Chapter 1 (commencing with Section 17700) of Division 2 of Title 2, any leaded cane or any instrument or weapon of the kind commonly known as a billy, blackjack, sandbag, sandclub, sap, or slungshot is a nuisance and is subject to Section 18010. *(Added by Stats.2010, c. 711 (S.B.1080), § 6, operative Jan. 1, 2012.)*

Law Revision Commission Comments

With respect to a leaded cane or "any instrument or weapon of the kind commonly known as a blackjack, slungshot, billy, sandclub, sap, or sandbag," Section 22290 continues the first part of the first sentence of former Section 12029 without substantive change.

See Section 16760 ("leaded cane"). [38 Cal.L.Rev.Comm. Reports 217 (2009)].

Research References

2 Witkin, California Criminal Law 4th Crimes Against Public Peace and Welfare § 263 (2021), Nuisances.

§ 22295. Carrying and use of wooden club or baton; course of instruction and permit

Section operative until Jan. 1, 2024. See, also, § 22295 operative Jan. 1, 2024.

(a) Nothing in any provision listed in Section 16580 prohibits any police officer, special police officer, peace officer, or law enforcement officer from carrying any wooden club or baton.

(b) Nothing in any provision listed in Section 16580 prohibits a uniformed security guard, regularly employed and compensated by a person engaged in any lawful business, while actually employed and engaged in protecting and preserving property or life within the scope of employment, from carrying any wooden club or baton if the uniformed security guard has satisfactorily completed a course of instruction certified by the Department of Consumer Affairs in the carrying and use of the club or baton. The training institution certified by the Department of Consumer Affairs to present this course, whether public or private, is authorized to charge a fee covering the cost of the training.

(c) The Department of Consumer Affairs, in cooperation with the Commission on Peace Officer Standards and Training, shall develop standards for a course in the carrying and use of a club or baton.

(d) Any uniformed security guard who successfully completes a course of instruction under this section is entitled to receive a permit to carry and use a club or baton within the scope of employment, issued by the Department of Consumer Affairs. The department may authorize a certified training institution to issue permits to carry and use a club or baton. A fee in the amount provided by law shall be charged by the Department of Consumer Affairs to offset the costs incurred by the department in course certification, quality control activities associated with the course, and issuance of the permit.

(e) Any person who has received a permit or certificate that indicates satisfactory completion of a club or baton training course approved by the Commission on Peace Officer Standards and Training prior to January 1, 1983, shall not be required to obtain a club or baton permit or complete a course certified by the Department of Consumer Affairs.

(f) Any person employed as a county sheriff's or police security officer, as defined in Section 831.4, shall not be required to obtain a club or baton permit or to complete a course certified by the Department of Consumer Affairs in the carrying and use of a club or baton, provided that the person completes a course approved by the Commission on Peace Officer Standards and Training in the carrying and use of the club or baton, within 90 days of employment.

(g) Nothing in any provision listed in Section 16580 prohibits an animal control officer, as described in Section 830.9, a humane officer, as described in paragraph (5) of subdivision (h) of Section 14502 of the Corporations Code, or an illegal dumping enforcement officer, as described in Section 830.7, from carrying any wooden club or baton if the animal control officer, humane officer, or illegal dumping enforcement officer has satisfactorily completed the course of instruction certified by the Commission on Peace Officer Standards and Training in the carrying and use of the club or baton. The training institution certified by the Commission on Peace Officer Standards and Training to present this course, whether public or private, is authorized to charge a fee covering the cost of the training.

(h) This section shall remain in effect only until January 1, 2024, and as of that date is repealed. *(Added by Stats.2010, c. 711 (S.B.1080), § 6.11, operative Jan. 1, 2012. Amended by Stats.2018, c. 20 (A.B.2349), § 2, eff. Jan. 1, 2019; Stats.2022, c. 287 (A.B.2515), § 58, eff. Jan. 1, 2023.)*

Repeal

For repeal of this section, see its terms.

Law Revision Commission Comments

With respect to a wooden club or baton, subdivision (a) of Section 22295 continues former Section 12002(a) without substantive change. The remainder of former Section 12002(a) is continued in Section 17515 without substantive change.

Subdivisions (b)-(g) continue former Section 12002(b)-(g) without substantive change. [40 Cal.L.Rev.Comm. Reports 107 (2010)].

Cross References

Batons, requirements to carry or use, bureau approval, peace officers, see Business and Professions Code § 7584.1.

Humane officers, authorized to carry firearms, see Corporations Code § 14502.

Machine guns, sale to or possession by police departments, see Penal Code § 32610.

National Guard, commissioned officer to provide himself with prescribed arms, see Military and Veterans Code § 226.

Persons authorized to carry and possess concealed weapons, see Penal Code § 25450 et seq.

Tear gas weapons, exception in favor of peace officers and military and naval forces, see Penal Code § 22820.

§ 22295. Carrying and use of wooden club or baton; course of instruction and permit

Section operative Jan. 1, 2024. See, also, § 22295 operative until Jan. 1, 2024.

(a) Nothing in any provision listed in Section 16580 prohibits any police officer, special police officer, peace officer, or law enforcement officer from carrying any wooden club or baton.

(b) Nothing in any provision listed in Section 16580 prohibits a licensed private patrol operator, a qualified manager of a licensed private patrol operator, or a registered security guard, regularly employed and compensated by a person engaged in any lawful business, while actually employed and engaged in protecting and preserving property or life within the scope of employment, from carrying a baton if they comply with the requirements of Chapter 11.5 (commencing with Section 7580) of Division 3 of the Business and Professions Code relating to the carrying and use of the baton.

(c) Any person who has received a permit or certificate that indicates satisfactory completion of a club or baton training course approved by the Commission on Peace Officer Standards and Training prior to January 1, 1983, shall not be required to obtain a baton permit pursuant to Chapter 11.5 (commencing with Section 7580) of Division 3 of the Business and Professions Code.

(d) Any person employed as a county sheriff's or police security officer, as defined in Section 831.4, shall not be required to obtain a baton permit pursuant to Chapter 11.5 (commencing with Section 7580) of Division 3 of the Business and Professions Code, if the person completes a course approved by the Commission on Peace Officer Standards and Training in the carrying and use of the baton, within 90 days of employment.

(e) Nothing in any provision listed in Section 16580 prohibits an animal control officer, as described in Section 830.9, a humane officer, as described in paragraph (5) of subdivision (h) of Section 14502 of the Corporations Code, or an illegal dumping enforcement officer, as described in Section 830.7, from carrying any wooden club or baton if the animal control officer, humane officer, or illegal dumping enforcement officer has satisfactorily completed the course of instruction certified by the Commission on Peace Officer Standards and Training in the carrying and use of the club or baton. The training institution certified by the Commission on Peace Officer Standards and Training to present this course, whether public or private, is authorized to charge a fee covering the cost of the training.

(f) This section shall become operative on January 1, 2024. *(Added by Stats.2022, c. 287 (A.B.2515), § 59, eff. Jan. 1, 2023, operative Jan. 1, 2024.)*

Cross References

Batons, requirements to carry or use, bureau approval, peace officers, see Business and Professions Code § 7584.1.
Humane officers, authorized to carry firearms, see Corporations Code § 14502.
Machine guns, sale to or possession by police departments, see Penal Code § 32610.
National Guard, commissioned officer to provide himself with prescribed arms, see Military and Veterans Code § 226.
Persons authorized to carry and possess concealed weapons, see Penal Code § 25450 et seq.
Tear gas weapons, exception in favor of peace officers and military and naval forces, see Penal Code § 22820.

§ 22296. Billy, blackjack, or slungshot; nunchaku excluded

As used in this part, a "billy," "blackjack," or "slungshot" does not include a nunchaku. *(Added by Stats.2021, c. 434 (S.B.827), § 27, eff. Jan. 1, 2022.)*

Division 9

SHURIKEN

§ 22410. Manufacture, import, sale, supply or possession of shuriken; punishment

Except as provided in Chapter 1 (commencing with Section 17700) of Division 2 of Title 2, any person in this state who manufactures or causes to be manufactured, imports into the state, keeps for sale, or offers or exposes for sale, or who gives, lends, or possesses any shuriken is punishable by imprisonment in a county jail not exceeding one year or imprisonment pursuant to subdivision (h) of Section 1170. *(Added by Stats.2010, c. 711 (S.B.1080), § 6, operative Jan. 1, 2012. Amended by Stats.2012, c. 43 (S.B.1023), § 98, eff. June 27, 2012.)*

Law Revision Commission Comments

With respect to a shuriken, Section 22410 continues former Section 12020(a)(1) without substantive change.

For circumstances in which this section is inapplicable, see Sections 16590 ("generally prohibited weapon"), 17700–17745 (exemptions relating to generally prohibited weapons).

See Section 17200 ("shuriken"). See also Sections 17800 (distinct and separate offense), 22490 (shuriken constituting nuisance). [38 Cal.L.Rev. Comm. Reports 217 (2009)].

Cross References

Penalty for possession of deadly weapon described in this section within State Capitol, legislative offices, etc., see Penal Code § 171c.
Possession of deadly weapons with intent to assault, see Penal Code § 17500.

Research References

2 Witkin, California Criminal Law 4th Crimes Against Public Peace and Welfare § 211 (2021), Nature of Crime.
2 Witkin, California Criminal Law 4th Crimes Against Public Peace and Welfare § 212 (2021), Elements of Offense.

§ 22490. Shuriken deemed nuisance; exceptions

Except as provided in Chapter 1 (commencing with Section 17700) of Division 2 of Title 2, any shuriken is a nuisance and is subject to Section 18010. *(Added by Stats.2010, c. 711 (S.B.1080), § 6, operative Jan. 1, 2012.)*

Law Revision Commission Comments

With respect to a shuriken, Section 22490 continues the first part of the first sentence of former Section 12029 without substantive change.

See Section 17200 ("shuriken"). [38 Cal.L.Rev.Comm. Reports 217 (2009)].

Research References

2 Witkin, California Criminal Law 4th Crimes Against Public Peace and Welfare § 263 (2021), Nuisances.

Division 10

STUN GUN

§ 22610. Purchase, possession or use of stun gun; exceptions; minors; fines

Notwithstanding any other provision of law, any person may purchase, possess, or use a stun gun, subject to the following requirements:

(a) No person convicted of a felony or any crime involving an assault under the laws of the United States, the State of California, or any other state, government, or country, or convicted of misuse of a stun gun under Section 244.5, shall purchase, possess, or use any stun gun.

(b) No person addicted to any narcotic drug shall purchase, possess, or use a stun gun.

(c)(1) No person shall sell or furnish any stun gun to a minor unless the minor is at least 16 years of age and has the written consent of the minor's parent or legal guardian.

(2) Violation of this subdivision shall be a public offense punishable by a fifty-dollar ($50) fine for the first offense. Any subsequent violation of this subdivision is a misdemeanor.

(d) No minor shall possess any stun gun unless the minor is at least 16 years of age and has the written consent of the minor's parent or legal guardian. *(Added by Stats.2010, c. 711 (S.B.1080), § 6, operative Jan. 1, 2012.)*

Law Revision Commission Comments

Section 22610 continues former Section 12651 without substantive change.

A violation of the predecessor of subdivision (c) (former Section 12651(c)) counts as a prior conviction in determining the appropriate punishment for a violation of that subdivision. See Section 16015 (determining existence of prior conviction).

See Section 17230 ("stun gun"). See also Section 22620 (violation punishable as misdemeanor). [38 Cal.L.Rev.Comm. Reports 217 (2009)].

Cross References

Felonies, definition and penalties, see Penal Code §§ 17, 18.
Misdemeanors, definition and penalties, see Penal Code §§ 17, 19, 19.2.

Research References

2 Witkin, California Criminal Law 4th Crimes Against Public Peace and Welfare § 231 (2021), Other Weapons and Devices.

§ 22615. Manufacturer's name and serial number on stun guns

Each stun gun sold shall contain both of the following:

(a) The name of the manufacturer stamped on the stun gun.

(b) The serial number applied by the manufacturer. *(Added by Stats.2010, c. 711 (S.B.1080), § 6, operative Jan. 1, 2012.)*

Law Revision Commission Comments

Section 22615 continues former Section 12652 without substantive change.

See Section 17230 ("stun gun"). See also Section 22620 (violation punishable as misdemeanor). [38 Cal.L.Rev.Comm. Reports 217 (2009)].

Research References

2 Witkin, California Criminal Law 4th Crimes Against Public Peace and Welfare § 231 (2021), Other Weapons and Devices.

§ 22620. Violation of division; misdemeanor

Unless otherwise specified, any violation of this division is a misdemeanor. *(Added by Stats.2010, c. 711 (S.B.1080), § 6, operative Jan. 1, 2012.)*

Law Revision Commission Comments

Section 22620 continues former Section 12653 without substantive change. [38 Cal.L.Rev.Comm. Reports 217 (2009)].

Cross References

Misdemeanors, definition and penalties, see Penal Code §§ 17, 19, 19.2.

Research References

2 Witkin, California Criminal Law 4th Crimes Against Public Peace and Welfare § 231 (2021), Other Weapons and Devices.

§ 22625. Instruction booklet to accompany sale of stun gun; fines

(a) Each stun gun sold in this state shall be accompanied by an instruction booklet.

(b) Violation of this section shall be a public offense punishable by a fifty-dollar ($50) fine for each weapon sold without the booklet. *(Added by Stats.2010, c. 711 (S.B.1080), § 6, operative Jan. 1, 2012.)*

Law Revision Commission Comments

Section 22625 continues former Section 12654 without substantive change. See Section 17230 ("stun gun"). [38 Cal.L.Rev.Comm. Reports 217 (2009)].

Research References

2 Witkin, California Criminal Law 4th Crimes Against Public Peace and Welfare § 231 (2021), Other Weapons and Devices.

Division 11

TEAR GAS AND TEAR GAS WEAPONS

CHAPTER 1. GENERAL PROVISIONS

§ 22810. Purchase, possession or use of tear gas for self-defense; exceptions; minors; label; instructions; punishment; use against peace officer

Notwithstanding any other provision of law, any person may purchase, possess, or use tear gas or any tear gas weapon for the projection or release of tear gas if the tear gas or tear gas weapon is used solely for self-defense purposes, subject to the following requirements:

(a) No person convicted of a felony or any crime involving an assault under the laws of the United States, the State of California, or any other state, government, or country, or convicted of misuse of tear gas under subdivision (g), shall purchase, possess, or use tear gas or any tear gas weapon.

(b) No person addicted to any narcotic drug shall purchase, possess, or use tear gas or any tear gas weapon.

(c) No person shall sell or furnish any tear gas or tear gas weapon to a minor.

(d) No minor shall purchase, possess, or use tear gas or any tear gas weapon.

(e)(1) No person shall purchase, possess, or use any tear gas weapon that expels a projectile, or that expels the tear gas by any method other than an aerosol spray, or that contains more than 2.5 ounces net weight of aerosol spray.

(2) Every tear gas container and tear gas weapon that may be lawfully purchased, possessed, and used pursuant to this section shall have a label that states: "WARNING: The use of this substance or device for any purpose other than self-defense is a crime under the law. The contents are dangerous—use with care."

(3) After January 1, 1984, every tear gas container and tear gas weapon that may be lawfully purchased, possessed, and used

pursuant to this section shall have a label that discloses the date on which the useful life of the tear gas weapon expires.

(4) Every tear gas container and tear gas weapon that may be lawfully purchased pursuant to this section shall be accompanied at the time of purchase by printed instructions for use.

(f) Effective March 1, 1994, every tear gas container and tear gas weapon that may be lawfully purchased, possessed, and used pursuant to this section shall be accompanied by an insert including directions for use, first aid information, safety and storage information, and explanation of the legal ramifications of improper use of the tear gas container or tear gas product.

(g)(1) Except as provided in paragraph (2), any person who uses tear gas or any tear gas weapon except in self-defense is guilty of a public offense and is punishable by imprisonment pursuant to subdivision (h) of Section 1170 for 16 months, or two or three years or in a county jail not to exceed one year or by a fine not to exceed one thousand dollars ($1,000), or by both the fine and imprisonment.

(2) If the use is against a peace officer, as defined in Chapter 4.5 (commencing with Section 830) of Title 3 of Part 2, engaged in the performance of official duties and the person committing the offense knows or reasonably should know that the victim is a peace officer, the offense is punishable by imprisonment pursuant to subdivision (h) of Section 1170 for 16 months or two or three years or by a fine of one thousand dollars ($1,000), or by both the fine and imprisonment. *(Added by Stats.2010, c. 711 (S.B.1080), § 6, operative Jan. 1, 2012. Amended by Stats.2011, c. 15 (A.B.109), § 538, eff. April 4, 2011, operative Jan. 1, 2012.)*

Law Revision Commission Comments

Section 22810 continues former Section 12403.7 without substantive change.

See Sections 17240 ("tear gas"), 17250 ("tear gas weapon"). [38 Cal.L.Rev. Comm. Reports 217 (2009)].

Cross References

Felonies, definition and penalties, see Penal Code §§ 17, 18.
Illegal sale, possession or transportation of tear gas weapons, see Penal Code § 22900.
Peace officers defined, see Penal Code § 830 et seq.
Tear gas defined for purposes of this Part, see Penal Code § 17240.
Tear gas weapon defined for purposes of this Part, see Penal Code § 17250.
Unauthorized possession of weapon or other instruments in state or local public building, exceptions to prohibition, see Penal Code § 171b.

Research References

2 Witkin, California Criminal Law 4th Crimes Against Public Peace and Welfare § 229 (2021), Tear Gas.
1 Witkin California Criminal Law 4th Introduction to Crimes § 76 (2021), Illustrations: Special Statute is Controlling.

§ 22815. Purchase or possession of tear gas by minor; joint and several liability of parent or guardian for damages resulting from use

(a) Notwithstanding subdivision (d) of Section 22810, a minor who has attained the age of 16 years may purchase and possess tear gas or a tear gas weapon pursuant to this division if the minor is accompanied by a parent or guardian, or has the written consent of a parent or guardian.

(b) Notwithstanding subdivision (c) of Section 22810, a person may sell or furnish tear gas or a tear gas weapon to a minor who has attained the age of 16 years and who is accompanied by a parent or guardian, or who presents a statement of consent signed by the minor's parent or guardian.

(c) Any civil liability of a minor arising out of the minor's use of tear gas or a tear gas weapon other than for self-defense is imposed upon the parent, guardian, or other person who authorized the provision of tear gas to a minor by signing a statement of consent or accompanying the minor, as specified in subdivision (b). That parent, guardian, or other person shall be jointly and severally liable with the minor for any damages proximately resulting from the negligent or wrongful act or omission of the minor in the use of the tear gas or a tear gas weapon. *(Added by Stats.2010, c. 711 (S.B.1080), § 6, operative Jan. 1, 2012. Amended by Stats.2018, c. 185 (A.B.2176), § 5, eff. Jan. 1, 2019.)*

Law Revision Commission Comments

Section 22815 continues former Section 12403.8 without substantive change.

An erroneous cross-reference to former Section 12403.7(a)(4) has been replaced with a cross-reference to Section 22810(d), which continues the substance of former Section 12403.7(d). An erroneous cross-reference to former Section 12403.7(a)(3) has been replaced with a cross-reference to Section 22810(c), which continues the substance of former Section 12403.7(c).

See Sections 17240 ("tear gas"), 17250 ("tear gas weapon"). [38 Cal.L.Rev. Comm. Reports 217 (2009)].

Section 22815 is amended to make clear that civil liability for a minor's use of tear gas or a tear gas weapon may be imposed on any person who authorized the provision of the tear gas or tear gas weapon to the minor. [44 Cal.L.Rev.Comm. Reports 471 (2015)].

Cross References

Tear gas defined for purposes of this Part, see Penal Code § 17240.
Tear gas weapon defined for purposes of this Part, see Penal Code § 17250.

Research References

2 Witkin, California Criminal Law 4th Crimes Against Public Peace and Welfare § 229 (2021), Tear Gas.

§ 22820. Purchase, possession, transportation, or use of tear gas by peace officers; training

Nothing in this division prohibits any person who is a peace officer, as defined in Chapter 4.5 (commencing with Section 830) of Title 3 of Part 2, from purchasing, possessing, transporting, or using any tear gas or tear gas weapon if the person has satisfactorily completed a course of instruction approved by the Commission on Peace Officer Standards and Training in the use of tear gas. *(Added by Stats.2010, c. 711 (S.B.1080), § 6, operative Jan. 1, 2012.)*

Law Revision Commission Comments

Section 22820 continues former Section 12403 without substantive change.

See Sections 17240 ("tear gas"), 17250 ("tear gas weapon"). [38 Cal.L.Rev. Comm. Reports 217 (2009)].

Cross References

Peace officer,
 Defined, see Penal Code § 830 et seq.
 Standards and training commission, see Penal Code § 13500 et seq.
Tear gas defined for purposes of this Part, see Penal Code § 17240.
Tear gas weapon defined for purposes of this Part, see Penal Code § 17250.

Research References

2 Witkin, California Criminal Law 4th Crimes Against Public Peace and Welfare § 229 (2021), Tear Gas.

§ 22825. County custodial officer carrying tear gas weapon

A custodial officer of a county may carry a tear gas weapon pursuant to Section 22820 only while on duty. A custodial officer of a county may carry a tear gas weapon while off duty only in accordance with all other laws. *(Added by Stats.2010, c. 711 (S.B.1080), § 6, operative Jan. 1, 2012.)*

Law Revision Commission Comments

Section 22825 continues former Section 12403.9 without substantive change.

See Sections 17240 ("tear gas"), 17250 ("tear gas weapon"). [38 Cal.L.Rev. Comm. Reports 217 (2009)].

Cross References

Tear gas defined for purposes of this Part, see Penal Code § 17240.

Tear gas weapon defined for purposes of this Part, see Penal Code § 17250.

Research References

2 Witkin, California Criminal Law 4th Crimes Against Public Peace and Welfare § 229 (2021), Tear Gas.

§ 22830. Exemptions for military forces and federal law enforcement officers

Nothing in this division prohibits any member of the military or naval forces of this state or of the United States or any federal law enforcement officer from purchasing, possessing, or transporting any tear gas or tear gas weapon for official use in the discharge of duties. *(Added by Stats.2010, c. 711 (S.B.1080), § 6, operative Jan. 1, 2012.)*

Law Revision Commission Comments

Section 22830 continues former Section 12403.1 without substantive change.

See Sections 17240 ("tear gas"), 17250 ("tear gas weapon"). [38 Cal.L.Rev. Comm. Reports 217 (2009)].

Cross References

Tear gas defined for purposes of this Part, see Penal Code § 17240.
Tear gas weapon defined for purposes of this Part, see Penal Code § 17250.

Research References

2 Witkin, California Criminal Law 4th Crimes Against Public Peace and Welfare § 229 (2021), Tear Gas.

§ 22835. Purchase, possession, or transportation of tear gas for defensive purposes by private investigators or private patrol operators; training

Notwithstanding any other provision of law, a person holding a license as a private investigator pursuant to Chapter 11.3 (commencing with Section 7512) of Division 3 of the Business and Professions Code, or as a private patrol operator pursuant to Chapter 11.5 (commencing with Section 7580) of Division 3 of the Business and Professions Code, or a uniformed patrolperson employee of a private patrol operator, may purchase, possess, or transport any tear gas weapon, if it is used solely for defensive purposes in the course of the activity for which the license was issued and if the person has satisfactorily completed a course of instruction approved by the Department of Consumer Affairs in the use of tear gas. *(Added by Stats.2010, c. 711 (S.B.1080), § 6, operative Jan. 1, 2012.)*

Law Revision Commission Comments

Section 22835 continues former Section 12403.5 without substantive change.

An erroneous cross-reference to "Chapter 11 (commencing with Section 7500), Division 3 of the Business and Professions Code" has been corrected by replacing it with cross-references to "Chapter 11.3 (commencing with Section 7512) of Division 3 of the Business and Professions Code" and "Chapter 11.5 (commencing with Section 7580) of Division 3 of the Business and Professions Code."

See Sections 17240 ("tear gas"), 17250 ("tear gas weapon"). [38 Cal.L.Rev. Comm. Reports 217 (2009)].

Cross References

Alarm companies, firearms permits and permits for other deadly and nonlethal weapons, tear gas or nonlethal chemical agent, course of instruction, see Business and Professions Code § 7596.12.
Private investigators, tear gas or other nonlethal chemical agents, course of instruction, see Business and Professions Code § 7542.1.
Private patrol operators, tear gas or nonlethal chemical agents, training requirements, see Business and Professions Code § 7583.35.
Tear gas defined for purposes of this Part, see Penal Code § 17240.
Tear gas weapon defined for purposes of this Part, see Penal Code § 17250.

Research References

2 Witkin, California Criminal Law 4th Crimes Against Public Peace and Welfare § 229 (2021), Tear Gas.

§ 22840. Unauthorized possession of tear gas in correctional institutions prohibited

Nothing in this division authorizes the possession of tear gas or a tear gas weapon in any institution described in Section 4574, or within the grounds belonging or adjacent to any institution described in Section 4574, except where authorized by the person in charge of the institution. *(Added by Stats.2010, c. 711 (S.B.1080), § 6, operative Jan. 1, 2012.)*

Law Revision Commission Comments

Section 22840 continues former Section 12404 without substantive change.

See Sections 17240 ("tear gas"), 17250 ("tear gas weapon"). [38 Cal.L.Rev. Comm. Reports 217 (2009)].

Cross References

Tear gas defined for purposes of this Part, see Penal Code § 17240.
Tear gas weapon defined for purposes of this Part, see Penal Code § 17250.

CHAPTER 2. UNLAWFUL POSSESSION, SALE, OR TRANSPORTATION

§ 22900. Unlawful sale, possession, or transportation of tear gas; punishment

Any person, firm, or corporation who within this state knowingly sells or offers for sale, possesses, or transports any tear gas or tear gas weapon, except as permitted under the provisions of this division, is guilty of a public offense and upon conviction thereof shall be punishable by imprisonment in the county jail for not exceeding one year or by a fine not to exceed two thousand dollars ($2,000), or by both that fine and imprisonment. *(Added by Stats.2010, c. 711 (S.B.1080), § 6, operative Jan. 1, 2012.)*

Law Revision Commission Comments

Section 22900 continues former Section 12420 without substantive change.

See Sections 17240 ("tear gas"), 17250 ("tear gas weapon"). [38 Cal.L.Rev. Comm. Reports 217 (2009)].

Cross References

Felony defined, see Penal Code § 17.
Public offense defined, see Penal Code § 15.
Tear gas defined for purposes of this Part, see Penal Code § 17240.
Tear gas weapon defined for purposes of this Part, see Penal Code § 17250.

Research References

2 Witkin, California Criminal Law 4th Crimes Against Public Peace and Welfare § 229 (2021), Tear Gas.

§ 22905. Manufacturer's name and serial number required on tear gas weapon

Each tear gas weapon sold, transported, or possessed under the authority of this division shall bear the name of the manufacturer and a serial number applied by the manufacturer. *(Added by Stats.2010, c. 711 (S.B.1080), § 6, operative Jan. 1, 2012.)*

Law Revision Commission Comments

Section 22905 continues former Section 12421 without substantive change.

See Sections 17240 ("tear gas"), 17250 ("tear gas weapon"). [38 Cal.L.Rev. Comm. Reports 217 (2009)].

Cross References

Tear gas defined for purposes of this Part, see Penal Code § 17240.

Tear gas weapon defined for purposes of this Part, see Penal Code § 17250.

Research References

2 Witkin, California Criminal Law 4th Crimes Against Public Peace and Welfare § 229 (2021), Tear Gas.

§ 22910. Removal or alteration of serial number or identification mark on tear gas weapon prohibited; punishment; possessor presumed to have altered weapon

(a) Any person who changes, alters, removes, or obliterates the name of the manufacturer, the serial number, or any other mark of identification on any tear gas weapon is guilty of a public offense and, upon conviction, shall be punished by imprisonment pursuant to subdivision (h) of Section 1170 or by a fine of not more than two thousand dollars ($2,000), or by both that fine and imprisonment.

(b) Possession of any such weapon upon which the same shall have been changed, altered, removed, or obliterated, shall be presumptive evidence that such possessor has changed, altered, removed, or obliterated the same. *(Added by Stats.2010, c. 711 (S.B.1080), § 6, operative Jan. 1, 2012. Amended by Stats.2011, c. 15 (A.B.109), § 539, eff. April 4, 2011, operative Jan. 1, 2012.)*

Law Revision Commission Comments

Subdivision (a) of Section 22910 continues the first paragraph of former Section 12422 without substantive change.

Subdivision (b) continues the second paragraph of former Section 12422 without change. Continuation of this material is not intended to reflect any determination regarding its constitutionality. See Section 16025. For a case discussing the constitutionality of a similar provision, see *In re Christopher K.*, 91 Cal.App.4th 853, 110 Cal.Rptr. 914 (2001).

See Sections 17240 ("tear gas"), 17250 ("tear gas weapon"). [38 Cal.L.Rev. Comm. Reports 217 (2009)].

Cross References

Felony defined, see Penal Code § 17.
Public offense defined, see Penal Code § 15.
Tear gas defined for purposes of this Part, see Penal Code § 17240.
Tear gas weapon defined for purposes of this Part, see Penal Code § 17250.

Research References

2 Witkin, California Criminal Law 4th Crimes Against Public Peace and Welfare § 229 (2021), Tear Gas.

CHAPTER 3. PERMITS

Section

§ 23000. Permits for possession and transportation of tear gas not intended for personal self-defense; protective systems using tear gas

The Department of Justice may issue a permit for the possession and transportation of tear gas or a tear gas weapon that is not intended or certified for personal self-defense purposes, upon proof that good cause exists for issuance of the permit to the applicant. The permit may also allow the applicant to install, maintain, and operate a protective system involving the use of tear gas or a tear gas weapon in any place that is accurately and completely described in the permit application. *(Added by Stats.2010, c. 711 (S.B.1080), § 6, operative Jan. 1, 2012.)*

Law Revision Commission Comments

Section 23000 continues former Section 12423 without substantive change.

See Sections 17240 ("tear gas"), 17250 ("tear gas weapon"). [38 Cal.L.Rev. Comm. Reports 217 (2009)].

Cross References

Authority of Department of Justice and Attorney General in criminal identification and investigation, see Penal Code §§ 11006, 11050, 11051.
Tear gas defined for purposes of this Part, see Penal Code § 17240.
Tear gas weapon defined for purposes of this Part, see Penal Code § 17250.

Research References

2 Witkin, California Criminal Law 4th Crimes Against Public Peace and Welfare § 229 (2021), Tear Gas.

§ 23005. Applications for permits for tear gas not intended for personal self-defense; protective systems

(a) An application for a permit shall satisfy all of the following requirements:

(1) It shall be filed in writing.

(2) It shall be signed by the applicant if an individual, or by a member or officer qualified to sign if the applicant is a firm or corporation.

(3) It shall state the applicant's name, business in which engaged, business address, and a full description of the place or vehicle in which the tear gas or tear gas weapon is to be transported, kept, installed, or maintained.

(b) If the tear gas or tear gas weapon is to be used in connection with, or to constitute, a protective system, the application shall also contain the name of the person who is to install the protective system.

(c) Applications and permits shall be uniform throughout the state upon forms prescribed by the Department of Justice. *(Added by Stats.2010, c. 711 (S.B.1080), § 6, operative Jan. 1, 2012.)*

Law Revision Commission Comments

Section 23005 continues the first three paragraphs of former Section 12424 without substantive change.

See Sections 17240 ("tear gas"), 17250 ("tear gas weapon"). [38 Cal.L.Rev. Comm. Reports 217 (2009)].

Cross References

Tear gas defined for purposes of this Part, see Penal Code § 17240.
Tear gas weapon defined for purposes of this Part, see Penal Code § 17250.

§ 23010. Fees for permits for tear gas not intended for personal self-defense; renewal

(a) Each applicant for a permit shall pay, at the time of filing the application, a fee determined by the Department of Justice, not to exceed the application processing costs of the Department of Justice.

(b) A permit granted pursuant to this chapter may be renewed one year from the date of issuance, and annually thereafter, upon the filing of a renewal application and the payment of a permit renewal fee, not to exceed the application processing costs of the Department of Justice.

(c) After the department establishes fees sufficient to reimburse the department for processing costs, fees charged shall increase at a rate not to exceed the legislatively approved annual cost-of-living adjustments for the department's budget. *(Added by Stats.2010, c. 711 (S.B.1080), § 6, operative Jan. 1, 2012.)*

Law Revision Commission Comments

Section 23010 continues the fourth paragraph of former Section 12424 without substantive change.

See Sections 17240 ("tear gas"), 17250 ("tear gas weapon"). [38 Cal.L.Rev. Comm. Reports 217 (2009)].

§ 23015. Financial institutions with multiple offices or branches; applications and permits for tear gas not intended for personal self-defense

(a) Notwithstanding Section 23000, a bank, a savings and loan association, a credit union, or an industrial loan company that maintains more than one office or branch may make a single annual application for a permit.

(b) In addition to the requirements set forth in this chapter, an application under this section shall separately state the business address and a full description of each office or branch in which the tear gas or tear gas weapon is to be kept, installed, or maintained. Any location addition or deletion as to an office or branch shall be reported to the department within 60 days of the change.

(c) A single permit issued under this section shall allow for the possession, operation, and maintenance of tear gas at each office or branch named in the application, including any location change. *(Added by Stats.2010, c. 711 (S.B.1080), § 6, operative Jan. 1, 2012.)*

Law Revision Commission Comments

Section 23015 continues former Section 12424.5 without substantive change.

See Sections 17240 ("tear gas"), 17250 ("tear gas weapon"). [38 Cal.L.Rev. Comm. Reports 217 (2009)].

Cross References

Tear gas defined for purposes of this Part, see Penal Code § 17240.
Tear gas weapon defined for purposes of this Part, see Penal Code § 17250.

§ 23020. Carrying and keeping of permit for tear gas not intended for personal self-defense; inspection

Every person, firm, or corporation to whom a permit is issued shall either carry the permit upon the person or keep it in the place described in the permit. The permit shall be open to inspection by any peace officer or other person designated by the authority issuing the permit. *(Added by Stats.2010, c. 711 (S.B.1080), § 6, operative Jan. 1, 2012.)*

Law Revision Commission Comments

Section 23020 continues former Section 12425 without substantive change. [38 Cal.L.Rev.Comm. Reports 217 (2009)].

Cross References

Inspection of public records, see Government Code § 6250 et seq.

§ 23025. Revocation or suspension of permit for tear gas not intended for personal self-defense

A permit issued in accordance with this chapter may be revoked or suspended by the issuing authority at any time when it appears that the need for the possession or transportation of the tear gas or tear gas weapon or protective system involving the use thereof, has ceased, or that the holder of the permit has engaged in an unlawful business or occupation or has wrongfully made use of the tear gas or tear gas weapon or the permit issued. *(Added by Stats.2010, c. 711 (S.B.1080), § 6, operative Jan. 1, 2012.)*

Law Revision Commission Comments

Section 23025 continues former Section 12426 without substantive change.

See Sections 17240 ("tear gas"), 17250 ("tear gas weapon"). [38 Cal.L.Rev. Comm. Reports 217 (2009)].

Cross References

Tear gas defined for purposes of this Part, see Penal Code § 17240.
Tear gas weapon defined for purposes of this Part, see Penal Code § 17250.

Title 4

FIREARMS

Division 1

PRELIMINARY PROVISIONS

§ 23500. Short title of Section 16580

The provisions listed in Section 16580 shall be known and may be cited as "The Dangerous Weapons Control Law." *(Added by Stats.2010, c. 711 (S.B.1080), § 6, operative Jan. 1, 2012.)*

Law Revision Commission Comments

Section 23500 continues former Section 12000 without substantive change. [38 Cal.L.Rev.Comm. Reports 217 (2009)].

Cross References

Firearms, records necessary to identify persons coming within Welfare and Institutions Code §§ 8100 or 8103, availability to Department of Justice, see Welfare and Institutions Code § 8104.

§ 23505. Severability of provisions listed in Section 16580

If any section, subdivision, paragraph, subparagraph, sentence, clause, or phrase of any provision listed in Section 16580 is for any reason held unconstitutional, that decision does not affect the validity of any other provision listed in Section 16580. The Legislature hereby declares that it would have passed the provisions listed in Section 16580 and each section, subdivision, paragraph, subparagraph, sentence, clause, and phrase of those provisions, irrespective of the fact that any one or more other sections, subdivisions, paragraphs, subparagraphs, sentences, clauses, or phrases be declared unconstitutional. *(Added by Stats.2010, c. 711 (S.B.1080), § 6, operative Jan. 1, 2012. Amended by Stats.2011, c. 285 (A.B.1402), § 25.)*

Law Revision Commission Comments

Section 23505 continues former Section 12003 without substantive change.

See also Section 12003, to the same effect as this provision. [38 Cal.L.Rev. Comm. Reports 217 (2009)].

Section 23505 is amended to make terminological corrections and a grammatical correction. This is not a substantive change. [41 Cal.L.Rev. Comm. Reports 135 (2011)].

§ 23510. Distinct and separate offenses under sections using term "any firearm"

(a) For purposes of Sections 25400 and 26500, Sections 27500 to 27590, inclusive, Section 28100, Sections 29610 to 29750, inclusive, Sections 29800 to 29905, inclusive, and Section 31615 of this code, and any provision listed in subdivision (a) of Section 16585 of this code, and Sections 8100, 8101, and 8103 of the Welfare and Institutions Code, notwithstanding the fact that the term "any firearm" may be used in those sections, each firearm or the frame or receiver of each firearm constitutes a distinct and separate offense under those sections.

(b) For purposes of Section 25135, notwithstanding the fact that the term "any firearm" may be used in that section, each firearm constitutes a distinct and separate offense under that section. *(Added by Stats.2010, c. 711 (S.B.1080), § 6, operative Jan. 1, 2012. Amended by Stats.2013, c. 737 (A.B.500), § 6.)*

Law Revision Commission Comments

Section 23510 continues former Section 12001(k) without substantive change.

See Section 16520 ("firearm"). [38 Cal.L.Rev.Comm. Reports 217 (2009)].

Cross References

Firearm defined for purposes of this Part, see Penal Code § 16520.

Research References

2 Witkin, California Criminal Law 4th Crimes Against Public Peace and Welfare § 192 (2021), In General.
2 Witkin, California Criminal Law 4th Crimes Against Public Peace and Welfare § 193 (2021), Sale, Lease, or Transfer by Unlicensed Person.
2 Witkin, California Criminal Law 4th Crimes Against Public Peace and Welfare § 195 (2021), In General.
2 Witkin, California Criminal Law 4th Crimes Against Public Peace and Welfare § 203 (2021), Nature of Crime.
2 Witkin, California Criminal Law 4th Crimes Against Public Peace and Welfare § 232 (2021), Nature and Scope of Statutes.
2 Witkin, California Criminal Law 4th Crimes Against Public Peace and Welfare § 234 (2021), Effect of Pardon or Dismissal After Fulfillment of Probation Conditions.
2 Witkin, California Criminal Law 4th Crimes Against Public Peace and Welfare § 262 (2021), Criminal Storage of Firearm.
3 Witkin, California Criminal Law 4th Punishment § 248 (2021), Nature and Purpose of Statute.

§ 23515. Offenses involving violent use of firearm

As used in the provisions listed in Section 16580, an offense that involves the violent use of a firearm includes any of the following:

(a) A violation of paragraph (2) or (3) of subdivision (a) of Section 245 or a violation of subdivision (d) of Section 245.

(b) A violation of Section 246.

(c) A violation of paragraph (2) of subdivision (a) of Section 417.

(d) A violation of subdivision (c) of Section 417. *(Added by Stats.2010, c. 711 (S.B.1080), § 6, operative Jan. 1, 2012.)*

Law Revision Commission Comments

Section 23515 continues former Section 12001.6 without substantive change.
See Section 16520 ("firearm"). [38 Cal.L.Rev.Comm. Reports 217 (2009)].

Cross References

Firearm defined for purposes of this Part, see Penal Code § 16520.

Research References

2 Witkin, California Criminal Law 4th Crimes Against Public Peace and Welfare § 204 (2021), Punishment.
2 Witkin, California Criminal Law 4th Crimes Against Public Peace and Welfare § 233 (2021), Prohibitions.
2 Witkin, California Criminal Law 4th Crimes Against Public Peace and Welfare § 239 (2021), Misdemeanants.
2 Witkin, California Criminal Law 4th Crimes Against Public Peace and Welfare § 250 (2021), Punishment.

§ 23520. Fingerprints required for applications requiring firearm eligibility determination

Each application that requires any firearms eligibility determination involving the issuance of any license, permit, or certificate pursuant to this part shall include two copies of the applicant's fingerprints on forms prescribed by the Department of Justice. One copy of the fingerprints may be submitted to the United States Federal Bureau of Investigation. *(Added by Stats.2010, c. 711 (S.B.1080), § 6, operative Jan. 1, 2012.)*

Law Revision Commission Comments

Section 23520 continues former Section 12001(m) without substantive change.

See Section 16520 ("firearm"). [38 Cal.L.Rev.Comm. Reports 217 (2009)].

Cross References

Firearm defined for purposes of this Part, see Penal Code § 16520.

Division 2

FIREARM SAFETY DEVICES, GUN SAFES, AND RELATED WARNINGS

§ 23620. Short title of division and Sections 16540, 16610 and 16870

This division and Sections 16540, 16610, and 16870 shall be known and may be cited as the "Aroner–Scott–Hayden Firearms Safety Act of 1999." *(Added by Stats.2010, c. 711 (S.B.1080), § 6, operative Jan. 1, 2012.)*

Law Revision Commission Comments

Section 23620 continues former Section 12087 without substantive change. [38 Cal.L.Rev.Comm. Reports 217 (2009)].

Cross References

Firearm defined for purposes of this Part, see Penal Code § 16520.

§ 23625. Legislative findings

The Legislature makes the following findings:

(a) In the years 1987 to 1996, nearly 2,200 children in the United States under the age of 15 years died in unintentional shootings. In 1996 alone, 138 children were shot and killed unintentionally. Thus, more than 11 children every month, or one child every three days, were shot or killed unintentionally in firearms-related incidents.

(b) The United States leads the industrialized world in the rates of children and youth lost to unintentional, firearms-related deaths. A 1997 study from the federal Centers for Disease Control and Prevention reveals that for unintentional firearm-related deaths for children under the age of 15, the rate in the United States was nine times higher than in 25 other industrialized countries combined.

(c) While the number of unintentional deaths from firearms is an unacceptable toll on America's children, nearly eight times that number are treated in U.S. hospital emergency rooms each year for nonfatal unintentional gunshot wounds.

(d) A study of unintentional firearm deaths among children in California found that unintentional gunshot wounds most often involve handguns.

(e) A study in the December 1995 issue of the Archives of Pediatric and Adolescent Medicine found that children as young as three years old are strong enough to fire most commercially available handguns. The study revealed that 25 percent of three to four year olds and 70 percent of five to six year olds had sufficient finger strength to fire 59 (92 percent) of the 64 commonly available handguns referenced in the study.

(f) The Government Accounting Office (GAO), in its March 1991 study, "Accidental Shootings: Many Deaths and Injuries Caused by Firearms Could be Prevented," estimates that 31 percent of accidental deaths caused by firearms might be prevented by the addition of two safety devices: a child-resistant safety device that automatically engages and a device that indicates whether the gun is loaded. According to the study results, of the 107 unintentional firearms-related fatalities the GAO examined for the calendar years 1988 and 1989, 8 percent could have been prevented had the firearm been equipped with a child-resistant safety device. This 8 percent represents instances in which children under the age of six unintentionally shot and killed themselves or other persons.

(g) Currently, firearms are the only products manufactured in the United States that are not subject to minimum safety standards.

(h) A 1997 public opinion poll conducted by the National Opinion Research Center at the University of Chicago in conjunction with the Johns Hopkins Center for Gun Policy and Research found that 74 percent of Americans support safety regulation of the firearms industry.

(i) Some currently available trigger locks and other similar devices are inadequate to prevent the accidental discharge of the firearms to which they are attached, or to prevent children from gaining access to the firearm. *(Added by Stats.2010, c. 711 (S.B.1080), § 6, operative Jan. 1, 2012.)*

Law Revision Commission Comments

Section 23625 continues former Section 12087.5 without substantive change.

See Sections 16520 ("firearm"), 16640 ("handgun"). [38 Cal.L.Rev.Comm. Reports 217 (2009)].

Cross References

Firearm defined for purposes of this Part, see Penal Code § 16520.
Handgun defined for purposes of this Part, see Penal Code § 16640.

§ 23630. Exemptions; antique firearms; peace officers

(a) This division does not apply to the commerce of any antique firearm.

(b)(1) This division does not apply to the commerce of any firearm intended to be used by a salaried, full-time peace officer, as defined in Chapter 4.5 (commencing with Section 830) of Title 3 of Part 2, for purposes of law enforcement.

(2) Nothing in this division precludes a local government, local agency, or state law enforcement agency from requiring its peace officers to store their firearms in gun safes or attach firearm safety devices to those firearms. *(Added by Stats.2010, c. 711 (S.B.1080), § 6, operative Jan. 1, 2012.)*

Law Revision Commission Comments

In combination with Section 16170(b) ("antique firearm"), Section 23630 continues former Section 12088.8 without substantive change.

See Sections 16520 ("firearm"), 16540 ("firearm safety device"), 16610 ("gun safe"). [38 Cal.L.Rev.Comm. Reports 217 (2009)].

Cross References

Antique firearm defined, see Penal Code § 16170.
Firearm defined for purposes of this Part, see Penal Code § 16520.
Firearm safety device defined for purposes of this Division, see Penal Code § 16540.
Gun safe defined for purposes of this Part, see Penal Code § 16610.

§ 23635. Safety device required for firearms sold or transferred by licensed dealers; exemptions; proof of gun safe or safety device ownership; warnings on long-gun safes; warning regarding child safety

(a) Any firearm sold or transferred in this state by a licensed firearms dealer, including a private transfer through a dealer, and any firearm manufactured in this state, shall include or be accompanied by a firearm safety device that is listed on the Department of Justice's roster of approved firearm safety devices and that is identified as appropriate for that firearm by reference to either the manufacturer and model of the firearm, or to the physical characteristics of the firearm that match those listed on the roster for use with the device.

(b) The sale or transfer of a firearm shall be exempt from subdivision (a) if both of the following apply:

(1) The purchaser or transferee owns a gun safe that meets the standards set forth in Section 23650. Gun safes shall not be required to be tested, and therefore may meet the standards without appearing on the Department of Justice roster.

(2) The purchaser or transferee presents an original receipt for purchase of the gun safe, or other proof of purchase or ownership of the gun safe as authorized by the Attorney General, to the firearms dealer. The dealer shall maintain a copy of this receipt or proof of purchase with the dealer's record of sales of firearms.

(c) The sale or transfer of a firearm shall be exempt from subdivision (a) if all of the following apply:

(1) The purchaser or transferee purchases an approved safety device no more than 30 days prior to the day the purchaser or transferee takes possession of the firearm.

(2) The purchaser or transferee presents the approved safety device to the firearms dealer when picking up the firearm.

(3) The purchaser or transferee presents an original receipt to the firearms dealer, which shows the date of purchase, the name, and the model number of the safety device.

(4) The firearms dealer verifies that the requirements in paragraphs (1) to (3), inclusive, have been satisfied.

(5) The firearms dealer maintains a copy of the receipt along with the dealer's record of sales of firearms.

(d)(1) Any long-gun safe commercially sold or transferred in this state, or manufactured in this state for sale in this state, that does not meet the standards for gun safes adopted pursuant to Section 23650 shall be accompanied by the following warning:

"WARNING: This gun safe does not meet the safety standards for gun safes specified in California Penal Code Section 23650. It does not satisfy the requirements of Penal Code Section 23635, which mandates that all firearms sold in California be accompanied by a firearm safety device or proof of ownership, as required by law, of a gun safe that meets the Section 23650 minimum safety standards developed by the California Attorney General."

(2) This warning shall be conspicuously displayed in its entirety on the principal display panel of the gun safe's package, on any descriptive materials that accompany the gun safe, and on a label affixed to the front of the gun safe.

(3) This warning shall be displayed in both English and Spanish, in conspicuous and legible type in contrast by typography, layout, or color with other printed matter on the package or descriptive materials, in a manner consistent with Part 1500.121 of Title 16 of the Code of Federal Regulations, or successor regulations thereto.

(e) Any firearm sold or transferred in this state by a licensed firearms dealer, including a private transfer through a dealer, and any firearm manufactured in this state, shall be accompanied by warning language or a label as described in Section 23640. *(Added by Stats.2010, c. 711 (S.B.1080), § 6, operative Jan. 1, 2012.)*

Law Revision Commission Comments

Subdivision (a) of Section 23635 continues former Section 12088.1(a) without substantive change.

Subdivision (b) continues former Section 12088.1(d) without substantive change.

Subdivision (c) continues former Section 12088.1(e) without substantive change.

Subdivision (d) continues former Section 12088.1(c) without substantive change.

Subdivision (e) continues former Section 12088.1(b) without substantive change.

See Sections 16520 ("firearm"), 16540 ("firearm safety device"), 16610 ("gun safe"), 16870 ("long-gun safe"), 26700 ("dealer," "licensee," or "person licensed pursuant to Sections 26700 to 26915, inclusive"). [38 Cal.L.Rev. Comm. Reports 217 (2009)].

Cross References

Attorney General, generally, see Government Code § 12500 et seq.
Firearm defined for purposes of this Part, see Penal Code § 16520.
Firearm safety device defined for purposes of this Division, see Penal Code § 16540.
Gun safe defined for purposes of this Part, see Penal Code § 16610.

Research References

2 Witkin, California Criminal Law 4th Crimes Against Public Peace and Welfare § 191 (2021), Safety Devices.

§ 23640. Warning label required for firearms regarding child safety

(a)(1) The packaging of any firearm and any descriptive materials that accompany any firearm sold or transferred in this state, or delivered for sale in this state, by any licensed manufacturer or licensed dealer, shall bear a label containing the following warning statement:

WARNING

Firearms must be handled responsibly and securely stored to prevent access by children and other unauthorized users. California has strict laws pertaining to firearms, and you may be fined or imprisoned if you fail to comply with them. Visit the website of the California Attorney General at https://oag.ca.gov/firearms for information on firearm laws applicable to you and how you can comply.

Prevent child access by always keeping guns locked away and unloaded when not in use. If you keep a loaded firearm where a child obtains and improperly uses it, you may be fined or sent to prison.

If you or someone you know is contemplating suicide, please call the national suicide prevention lifeline at 1–800–273–TALK (8255).

(2) A yellow triangle containing an exclamation mark shall appear immediately before the word "Warning" on the label.

(b) If the firearm is sold or transferred without accompanying packaging, the warning label or notice shall be affixed to the firearm itself by a method to be prescribed by regulation of the Attorney General.

(c) The warning statement required under subdivisions (a) and (b) shall satisfy both of the following requirements:

(1) It shall be displayed in its entirety on the principal display panel of the firearm's package, and on any descriptive materials that accompany the firearm.

(2) It shall be displayed in both English and Spanish, in conspicuous and legible type in contrast by typography, layout, or color with other printed matter on that package or descriptive materials, in a manner consistent with Section 1500.121 of Title 16 of the Code of Federal Regulations, or successor regulations thereto.

(3) This section shall become operative on June 1, 2020. *(Added by Stats.2019, c. 729 (A.B.645), § 2, eff. Jan. 1, 2020, operative June 1, 2020.)*

Cross References

Attorney General, generally, see Government Code § 12500 et seq.
Firearm defined for purposes of this Part, see Penal Code § 16520.

§ 23645. Safety device and warning label violations; punishment; second and subsequent violations

(a) Any violation of Section 23635 or Section 23640 is punishable by a fine of one thousand dollars ($1,000).

(b) On a second violation of any of those sections, a licensed firearm manufacturer shall be ineligible to manufacture, or a licensed firearm dealer shall be ineligible to sell, firearms in this state for 30 days, and shall be punished by a fine of one thousand dollars ($1,000).

(c)(1) On a third violation of any of those sections, a firearm manufacturer shall be permanently ineligible to manufacture firearms in this state.

(2) On a third violation of any of those sections, a licensed firearm dealer shall be permanently ineligible to sell firearms in this state. *(Added by Stats.2010, c. 711 (S.B.1080), § 6, operative Jan. 1, 2012.)*

Law Revision Commission Comments

Section 23645 continues former Section 12088.6 without substantive change.

A violation of the predecessor of Section 23635 (former Section 12088.1) or the predecessor of Section 23640 (former Section 12088.3) counts as a prior violation in determining the appropriate punishment under this section. See Section 16015 (determining existence of prior conviction).

See Sections 16520 ("firearm"), 26700 ("dealer," "licensee," or "person licensed pursuant to Sections 26700 to 26915, inclusive"). [38 Cal.L.Rev. Comm. Reports 217 (2009)].

Cross References

Firearm defined for purposes of this Part, see Penal Code § 16520.

Research References

2 Witkin, California Criminal Law 4th Crimes Against Public Peace and Welfare § 191 (2021), Safety Devices.

§ 23650. Standards for firearm safety devices and gun safes to reduce injuries to children; rules and regulations; use of federal test protocols

(a) The Attorney General shall develop regulations to implement a minimum safety standard for firearm safety devices and gun safes to significantly reduce the risk of firearm-related injuries to children 17 years of age and younger. The final standard shall do all of the following:

(1) Address the risk of injury from unintentional gunshot wounds.

(2) Address the risk of injury from self-inflicted gunshot wounds by unauthorized users.

(3) Include provisions to ensure that all firearm safety devices and gun safes are reusable and of adequate quality and construction to prevent children and unauthorized users from firing the firearm and to ensure that these devices cannot be readily removed from the firearm or that the firearm cannot be readily removed from the gun safe except by an authorized user utilizing the key, combination, or other method of access intended by the manufacturer of the device.

(4) Include additional provisions as appropriate.

(b) The Attorney General may consult, for the purposes of guidance in development of the standards, test protocols such as those described in Title 16 (commencing with Part 1700) of the Code of Federal Regulations, relating to poison prevention packaging standards. These protocols may be consulted to provide suggestions for potential methods to utilize in developing standards and shall serve as guidance only. The Attorney General shall also give appropriate consideration to the use of devices that are not detachable, but are permanently installed and incorporated into the design of a firearm.

(c) The Attorney General shall commence development of regulations under this section no later than January 1, 2000. The Attorney General shall adopt and issue regulations implementing a final standard no later than January 1, 2001. The Attorney General shall report to the Legislature on these standards by January 1, 2001. The final standard shall be effective January 1, 2002. *(Added by Stats.2010, c. 711 (S.B.1080), § 6, operative Jan. 1, 2012.)*

Law Revision Commission Comments

Section 23650 continues former Section 12088.2 without substantive change.

See Sections 16520 ("firearm"), 16540 ("firearm safety device"), 16610 ("gun safe"). [38 Cal.L.Rev.Comm. Reports 217 (2009)].

Cross References

Attorney General, generally, see Government Code § 12500 et seq.
Firearm defined for purposes of this Part, see Penal Code § 16520.
Firearm safety device defined for purposes of this Division, see Penal Code § 16540.
Gun safe defined for purposes of this Part, see Penal Code § 16610.
Safety device required for firearms sold or transferred by licensed dealers, exemptions, proof of gun safe or safety device ownership, warnings on long-gun safes, warning regarding child safety, see Penal Code § 23635.

Research References

2 Witkin, California Criminal Law 4th Crimes Against Public Peace and Welfare § 191 (2021), Safety Devices.

§ 23655. Certification of laboratories to test firearm safety devices; certification fees; testing expenses; notice of results; list of tested devices; random retesting

(a) The Department of Justice shall certify laboratories to verify compliance with standards for firearm safety devices set forth in Section 23650.

(b) The Department of Justice may charge any laboratory that is seeking certification to test firearm safety devices a fee not exceeding the costs of certification, including costs associated with the development and approval of regulations and standards pursuant to Section 23650.

(c) The certified laboratory shall, at the manufacturer's or dealer's expense, test a firearm safety device and submit a copy of the final test report directly to the Department of Justice, along with the firearm safety device. The department shall notify the manufacturer or dealer of its receipt of the final test report and the department's determination as to whether the firearm safety device tested may be sold in this state.

(d) Commencing on July 1, 2001, the Department of Justice shall compile, publish, and maintain a roster listing all of the firearm safety devices that have been tested by a certified testing laboratory, have been determined to meet the department's standards for firearm safety devices, and may be sold in this state.

(e) The roster shall list, for each firearm safety device, the manufacturer, model number, and model name.

(f) The department may randomly retest samples obtained from sources other than directly from the manufacturer of the firearm safety device listed on the roster to ensure compliance with the requirements of this division.

(g) Firearm safety devices used for random sample testing and obtained from sources other than the manufacturer shall be in new, unused condition, and still in the manufacturer's original and unopened package. *(Added by Stats.2010, c. 711 (S.B.1080), § 6, operative Jan. 1, 2012.)*

Law Revision Commission Comments

Section 23655 continues former Section 12088 without substantive change.

See Sections 16520 ("firearm"), 16540 ("firearm safety device"), 26700 ("dealer," "licensee," or "person licensed pursuant to Sections 26700 to 26915, inclusive"). [38 Cal.L.Rev.Comm. Reports 217 (2009)].

Cross References

Firearm defined for purposes of this Part, see Penal Code § 16520.
Firearm safety device defined for purposes of this Division, see Penal Code § 16540.

§ 23660. Sale or distribution of firearm safety devices not listed as being tested and verified or not complying with standards prohibited

(a) No person shall keep for commercial sale, offer, or expose for commercial sale, or commercially sell any firearm safety device that is not listed on the roster maintained pursuant to subdivision (d) of Section 23655, or that does not comply with the standards for firearm safety devices adopted pursuant to Section 23650.

(b) No person may distribute as part of an organized firearm safety program, with or without consideration, any firearm safety device that is not listed on the roster maintained pursuant to subdivision (d) of Section 23655, or that does not comply with the standards for firearm safety devices adopted pursuant to Section 23650. *(Added by Stats.2010, c. 711 (S.B.1080), § 6, operative Jan. 1, 2012.)*

Law Revision Commission Comments

Subdivision (a) of Section 23660 continues former Section 12088.15(a) without substantive change.

Subdivision (b) continues former Section 12088.15(b) without substantive change.

See Sections 16520 ("firearm"), 16540 ("firearm safety device"). [38 Cal.L.Rev.Comm. Reports 217 (2009)].

Cross References

Firearm defined for purposes of this Part, see Penal Code § 16520.
Firearm safety device defined for purposes of this Division, see Penal Code § 16540.

Research References

2 Witkin, California Criminal Law 4th Crimes Against Public Peace and Welfare § 191 (2021), Safety Devices.

§ 23665. Long-gun safes to be labeled by manufacturer as meeting standards; sale of long-gun safe that does not meet standards prohibited unless safe is labeled; removal of label prohibited; punishment

(a) No long-gun safe may be manufactured in this state for sale in this state that does not comply with the standards for gun safes adopted pursuant to Section 23650, unless the long-gun safe is labeled by the manufacturer consistent with the requirements of Section 23635.

(b)(1) Any person who keeps for commercial sale, offers, or exposes for commercial sale, or who commercially sells a long-gun safe that does not comply with the standards for gun safes adopted pursuant to Section 23650, and who knows or has reason to know, that the long-gun safe in question does not meet the standards for gun safes adopted pursuant to Section 23650, is in violation of this section, and is punishable as provided in Section 23670, unless the long-gun safe is labeled pursuant to Section 23635.

(2) Any person who keeps for commercial sale, offers, or exposes for commercial sale, or who commercially sells a long-gun safe that does not comply with the standards for gun safes adopted pursuant to Section 23650, and who removes or causes to be removed, from the long-gun safe, the label required pursuant to Section 23635, is in violation of this section, and is punishable as provided in Section 23670. *(Added by Stats.2010, c. 711 (S.B.1080), § 6, operative Jan. 1, 2012.)*

Law Revision Commission Comments

Subdivision (a) of Section 23665 continues former Section 12088.15(c) without substantive change.

Subdivision (b) continues former Section 12088.15(d) without substantive change.

See Sections 16610 ("gun safe"), 16870 ("long-gun safe"). [38 Cal.L.Rev. Comm. Reports 217 (2009)].

Cross References

Gun safe defined for purposes of this Part, see Penal Code § 16610.

§ 23670. Fines for unlawful sale or distribution of firearm safety device or unlawful sale of long-gun safe; second and subsequent offenses

(a)(1) A violation of Section 23660 or 23665 is punishable by a civil fine of up to five hundred dollars ($500).

(2) A second violation of any of those sections, which occurs within five years of the date of a previous offense, is punishable by a civil fine of up to one thousand dollars ($1,000) and, if the violation is committed by a licensed firearms dealer, the dealer shall be ineligible to sell firearms in this state for 30 days.

(3) A third or subsequent violation that occurs within five years of two or more previous offenses is punishable by a civil fine of up to five thousand dollars ($5,000) and, if the violation is committed by a licensed firearms dealer, the firearms dealer shall be permanently ineligible to sell firearms in this state.

(b) The Attorney General, a district attorney, or a city attorney may bring a civil action for a violation of Section 23660 or 23665. *(Added by Stats.2010, c. 711 (S.B.1080), § 6, operative Jan. 1, 2012.)*

Law Revision Commission Comments

Subdivision (a) of Section 23670 continues former Section 12088.15(e) without substantive change.

Subdivision (b) continues former Section 12088.15(f) without substantive change.

A violation of the predecessor of Section 23660 (former Section 12088.15(a)-(b)) or the predecessor of Section 23665 (former Section 12088.15(c)-(d)) counts as a prior violation in determining the appropriate punishment under this section. See Section 16015 (determining existence of prior conviction).

See Sections 16520 ("firearm"), 26700 ("dealer," "licensee," or "person licensed pursuant to Sections 26700 to 26915, inclusive"). [38 Cal.L.Rev. Comm. Reports 217 (2009)].

Cross References

Attorney General, generally, see Government Code § 12500 et seq.
Firearm defined for purposes of this Part, see Penal Code § 16520.

§ 23675. Liability imposed by common law, statutory law, or local ordinance

Compliance with the requirements set forth in this division does not relieve any person from liability to any other person as may be imposed pursuant to common law, statutory law, or local ordinance. *(Added by Stats.2010, c. 711 (S.B.1080), § 6, operative Jan. 1, 2012.)*

Law Revision Commission Comments

Section 23675 continues former Section 12088.7 without substantive change. [38 Cal.L.Rev.Comm. Reports 217 (2009)].

§ 23680. Nonconforming firearm safety devices and gun safes; recall and replacement; order requiring conformity

(a) If at any time the Attorney General determines that a gun safe or firearm safety device subject to the provisions of this division and sold after January 1, 2002, does not conform with the standards required by subdivision (a) of Section 23635 or Section 23650, the Attorney General may order the recall and replacement of the gun safe or firearm safety device, or order that the gun safe or firearm safety device be brought into conformity with those requirements.

(b) If the firearm safety device can be separated and reattached to the firearm without damaging the firearm, the licensed manufacturer or licensed firearms dealer shall immediately provide a conforming replacement as instructed by the Attorney General.

(c) If the firearm safety device cannot be separated from the firearm without damaging the firearm, the Attorney General may order the recall and replacement of the firearm. *(Added by Stats.2010, c. 711 (S.B.1080), § 6, operative Jan. 1, 2012.)*

Law Revision Commission Comments

Section 23680 continues former Section 12088.4 without substantive change.

See Sections 16520 ("firearm"), 16540 ("firearm safety device"), 16610 ("gun safe"), 26700 ("dealer," "licensee," or "person licensed pursuant to Sections 26700 to 26915, inclusive"). [38 Cal.L.Rev.Comm. Reports 217 (2009)].

Cross References

Attorney General, generally, see Government Code § 12500 et seq.
Firearm defined for purposes of this Part, see Penal Code § 16520.
Firearm safety device defined for purposes of this Division, see Penal Code § 16540.

Gun safe defined for purposes of this Part, see Penal Code § 16610.

§ 23685. Report required when minor is wounded by accidental or self-inflicted gunshot

Each lead law enforcement agency investigating an incident shall report to the State Department of Health Services any information obtained that reasonably supports the conclusion that a child 18 years of age or younger suffered an unintentional or self-inflicted gunshot wound inflicted by a firearm that was sold or transferred in this state, or manufactured in this state. The report shall also indicate whether as a result of that incident the child died, suffered serious injury, or was treated for an injury by a medical professional. *(Added by Stats.2010, c. 711 (S.B.1080), § 6, operative Jan. 1, 2012. Amended by Stats.2018, c. 185 (A.B.2176), § 6, eff. Jan. 1, 2019.)*

Law Revision Commission Comments

Section 23685 continues former Section 12088.5 without change.

See Section 16520 ("firearm"). [38 Cal.L.Rev.Comm. Reports 217 (2009)].

Section 23685 is amended for clarity. This is a nonsubstantive change. [44 Cal.L.Rev.Comm. Reports 471 (2015)].

Cross References

Department of Health Care Services, generally, see Health and Safety Code § 100100 et seq.

Firearm defined for purposes of this Part, see Penal Code § 16520.

§ 23690. Dealer fee authorized; Firearm Safety Account created

(a)(1) The Department of Justice may require each dealer to charge each firearm purchaser or transferee a fee not to exceed one dollar ($1) for each firearm transaction, except that the Department of Justice may increase the fee at a rate not to exceed any increase in the California Consumer Price Index, as compiled and reported by the Department of Industrial Relations, and not to exceed the reasonable cost of regulation to the Department of Justice.

(2) The fee shall be for the purpose of supporting department program costs related to this act, including the establishment, maintenance, and upgrading of related database systems and public rosters.

(b)(1) There is hereby created within the General Fund the Firearm Safety Account.

(2) Revenue from the fee imposed by subdivision (a) shall be deposited into the Firearm Safety Account and shall be available for expenditure by the Department of Justice upon appropriation by the Legislature.

(3) Expenditures from the Firearm Safety Account shall be limited to program expenditures as defined by subdivision (a). *(Added by Stats.2010, c. 711 (S.B.1080), § 6, operative Jan. 1, 2012. Amended by Stats.2016, c. 33 (S.B.843), § 37, eff. June 27, 2016.)*

Law Revision Commission Comments

Section 23690 continues former Section 12088.9 without substantive change.

See Sections 16520 ("firearm"), 26700 ("dealer," "licensee," or "person licensed pursuant to Sections 26700 to 26915, inclusive"). [38 Cal.L.Rev. Comm. Reports 217 (2009)].

Cross References

Firearm defined for purposes of this Part, see Penal Code § 16520.

Division 3

DISGUISED OR MISLEADING APPEARANCE

CHAPTER 1. MISCELLANEOUS PROVISIONS

§ 23800. Manufacture, import, sale, supply or possession of firearm with bright orange or bright green coloration; punishment

Any person who, for commercial purposes, purchases, sells, manufactures, ships, transports, distributes, or receives a firearm, where the coloration of the entire exterior surface of the firearm is bright orange or bright green, either singly, in combination, or as the predominant color in combination with other colors in any pattern, is liable for a civil fine in an action brought by the city attorney of the city, or the district attorney for the county, of not more than ten thousand dollars ($10,000). *(Added by Stats.2010, c. 711 (S.B.1080), § 6, operative Jan. 1, 2012.)*

Law Revision Commission Comments

Section 23800 continues former Section 12020.3 without substantive change.

See Section 16520 ("firearm"). [38 Cal.L.Rev.Comm. Reports 217 (2009)].

Cross References

Firearm defined for purposes of this Part, see Penal Code § 16520.

Research References

2 Witkin, California Criminal Law 4th Crimes Against Public Peace and Welfare § 211 (2021), Nature of Crime.

CHAPTER 2. OBLITERATION OF IDENTIFICATION MARKS

§ 23900. Alteration, removal, or obliteration of firearm identification numbers or marks without prior written permission prohibited; punishment

Any person who changes, alters, removes, or obliterates the name of the maker, model, manufacturer's number, or other mark of identification, including any distinguishing number or mark assigned by the Department of Justice, on any pistol, revolver, or any other firearm, without first having secured written permission from the department to make that change, alteration, or removal shall be punished by imprisonment pursuant to subdivision (h) of Section 1170. *(Added by Stats.2010, c. 711 (S.B.1080), § 6, operative Jan. 1,*

2012. Amended by Stats.2011, c. 15 (A.B.109), § 540, eff. April 4, 2011, operative Jan. 1, 2012.)

Law Revision Commission Comments

Section 23900 continues former Section 12090 without substantive change.

See Sections 16520 ("firearm"), 16530 ("firearm capable of being concealed upon the person," "pistol," and "revolver"). [38 Cal.L.Rev.Comm. Reports 217 (2009)].

Cross References

Firearm defined for purposes of this Part, see Penal Code § 16520.
Pistol defined for purposes of this Part, see Penal Code § 16530.
Revolver defined for purposes of this Part, see Penal Code § 16530.

Research References

2 Witkin, California Criminal Law 4th Crimes Against Public Peace and Welfare § 190 (2021), In General.

§ 23910. Assignment of new firearm identification number or mark when original number or mark is missing or obliterated

The Department of Justice, upon request, may assign a distinguishing number or mark of identification to any firearm whenever the firearm lacks a manufacturer's number or other mark of identification. Whenever the manufacturer's number or other mark of identification or a distinguishing number or mark assigned by the department has been destroyed or obliterated, the Department of Justice, upon request, may assign a distinguishing number or mark of identification to any firearm in accordance with Section 29182. *(Added by Stats.2010, c. 711 (S.B.1080), § 6, operative Jan. 1, 2012. Amended by Stats.2016, c. 60 (A.B.857), § 3, eff. Jan. 1, 2017; Stats.2022, c. 76 (A.B.1621), § 11, eff. June 30, 2022.)*

Law Revision Commission Comments

Section 23910 continues former Section 12092 without substantive change.

See Section 16520 ("firearm"). [38 Cal.L.Rev.Comm. Reports 217 (2009)].

Cross References

Firearm defined for purposes of this Part, see Penal Code § 16520.

Research References

2 Witkin, California Criminal Law 4th Crimes Against Public Peace and Welfare § 190 (2021), In General.
2 Witkin, California Criminal Law 4th Crimes Against Public Peace and Welfare § 200 (2021), Reporting and Identification Requirements for Concealable Firearms.
2 Witkin, California Criminal Law 4th Crimes Against Public Peace and Welfare § 202 (2021), License to Manufacture.
2 Witkin, California Criminal Law 4th Crimes Against Public Peace and Welfare § 208 (2021), Exempt Activities.

§ 23915. Stamping additional identification number or mark on firearm; restoration of original mark or number

(a) Any person may place or stamp on any pistol, revolver, or other firearm any number or identifying indicium, provided the number or identifying indicium does not change, alter, remove, or obliterate the manufacturer's name, number, model, or other mark of identification.

(b) This section does not prohibit restoration by the owner of the name of the maker or model, or of the original manufacturer's number or other mark of identification, when that restoration is authorized by the department.

(c) This section does not prevent any manufacturer from placing in the ordinary course of business the name of the maker, model, manufacturer's number, or other mark of identification upon a new firearm. *(Added by Stats.2010, c. 711 (S.B.1080), § 6, operative Jan. 1, 2012.)*

Law Revision Commission Comments

Section 23915 continues former Section 12093 without substantive change.

See Sections 16520 ("firearm"), 16530 (firearm capable of being concealed upon the person, pistol, and revolver). [38 Cal.L.Rev.Comm. Reports 217 (2009)].

Cross References

Firearm defined for purposes of this Part, see Penal Code § 16520.
Pistol defined for purposes of this Part, see Penal Code § 16530.
Revolver defined for purposes of this Part, see Penal Code § 16530.

Research References

2 Witkin, California Criminal Law 4th Crimes Against Public Peace and Welfare § 190 (2021), In General.

§ 23920. Purchase, sale, possession, or transfer of unmarked firearm, or invalid serial number or mark of identification prohibited

(a) Except as provided in Section 23925, any person who, with knowledge of any change, alteration, removal, or obliteration described in this section, buys, receives, disposes of, sells, offers for sale, or has in possession any pistol, revolver, or other firearm that has had the name of the maker or model, or the manufacturer's number or other mark of identification, including any distinguishing number or mark assigned by the Department of Justice, changed, altered, removed, or obliterated, is guilty of a misdemeanor.

(b) Except as provided in Section 23925, any person who, on or after January 1, 2024, knowingly possesses any firearm that does not have a valid state or federal serial number or mark of identification is guilty of a misdemeanor. *(Added by Stats.2010, c. 711 (S.B.1080), § 6, operative Jan. 1, 2012. Amended by Stats.2022, c. 76 (A.B.1621), § 12, eff. June 30, 2022.)*

Law Revision Commission Comments

Section 23920 continues former Section 12094(a) without substantive change.

For circumstances in which this section is inapplicable, see Section 23925 (exemptions).

See Sections 16520 ("firearm"), 16530 (firearm capable of being concealed upon the person, pistol, and revolver). [38 Cal.L.Rev.Comm. Reports 217 (2009)].

Cross References

Firearm defined for purposes of this Part, see Penal Code § 16520.
Misdemeanors, definition and penalties, see Penal Code §§ 17, 19, 19.2.
Pistol defined for purposes of this Part, see Penal Code § 16530.
Revolver defined for purposes of this Part, see Penal Code § 16530.

Research References

2 Witkin, California Criminal Law 4th Crimes Against Public Peace and Welfare § 190 (2021), In General.

§ 23925. Exception to prohibition against purchase, sale, possession, or transfer of unmarked firearms, or invalid serial numbers or marks of identification

(a) Section 23920 does not apply to any of the following:

(1) The acquisition or possession of a firearm described in Section 23920 by any member of the military forces of this state or of the United States, while on duty and acting within the scope and course of employment.

(2) The acquisition or possession of a firearm described in Section 23920 by any peace officer described in Chapter 4.5 (commencing with Section 830) of Title 3 of Part 2, while on duty and acting within the scope and course of employment.

(3) The acquisition or possession of a firearm described in Section 23920 by any employee of a forensic laboratory, while on duty and acting within the scope and course of employment.

(4) The possession and disposition of a firearm described in Section 23920 by a person who meets all of the following:

(A) The person is not prohibited by state or federal law from possessing, receiving, owning, or purchasing a firearm.

(B) The person possessed the firearm no longer than was necessary to deliver it to a law enforcement agency for that agency's disposition according to law.

(C) If the person is transporting the firearm, the person is transporting it to a law enforcement agency in order to deliver it to the agency for the agency's disposition according to law.

(D) If the person is transporting the firearm to a law enforcement agency, the person has given prior notice to the agency that the person is transporting the firearm to that agency for the agency's disposition according to law.

(E) The firearm is transported in a locked container as defined in Section 16850.

(b) Subdivision (b) of Section 23920 does not apply to any of the following:

(1) The possession of a firearm that was made or assembled prior to December 16, 1968, and is not a handgun.

(2) The possession of a firearm that has been entered, before July 1, 2018, into the centralized registry set forth in Section 11106, as being owned by a specific individual or entity, if that firearm has assigned to it a distinguishing number or mark of identification because the department accepted entry of that firearm into the centralized registry.

(3) The possession of a firearm that is a curio or relic, or an antique firearm, as those terms are defined in Section 479.11 of Title 27 of the Code of Federal Regulations.

(4) The possession of a firearm by a federally licensed firearms manufacturer or importer, or any other federal licensee authorized to serialize firearms.

(5) The possession of a firearm by a person who, before January 1, 2024, has applied to the Department of Justice for a unique serial number or mark of identification, pursuant to Section 29180, and fully complies with the provisions of that section, including imprinting the serial number or mark of identification onto the firearm within 10 days after receiving the serial number or mark of identification from the department.

(6)(A) The possession of a firearm by a new resident who, pursuant to Section 29180, applies for a unique serial number or other mark of identification from the Department of Justice within 60 days after arrival in the state, for any firearm the resident wishes to legally possess in the state that does not have a valid state or federal serial number or mark of identification, and who fully complies with the provisions of that section, including imprinting the serial number or mark of identification onto the firearm within 10 days after receiving the serial number or mark of identification from the department.

(B) The good faith effort by a new resident to apply for a unique serial number or other mark of identification after the expiration of the 60-day period specified in this paragraph, or any other person's good faith effort to apply for a unique serial number or mark of identification for a firearm that does not have a valid state or federal serial number or other mark of identification, shall not constitute probable cause for a violation of Section 23920.

(7) The possession of a firearm by a nonresident of this state who is traveling with a firearm in this state in accordance with the provisions of Section 926A of Title 18 of the United States Code, or who possesses or imports a firearm into this state exclusively for use in an organized sport shooting event or competition. *(Added by Stats.2010, c. 711 (S.B.1080), § 6, operative Jan. 1, 2012. Amended by Stats.2022, c. 76 (A.B.1621), § 13, eff. June 30, 2022.)*

Law Revision Commission Comments

Section 23925 continues former Section 12094(b) without substantive change.

See Section 16520 ("firearm"). [38 Cal.L.Rev.Comm. Reports 217 (2009)].

Cross References

Firearm defined for purposes of this Part, see Penal Code § 16520.

CHAPTER 3. CAMOUFLAGING FIREARM CONTAINER

Section

§ 24310. Manufacture, import, sale, supply or possession of camouflaging firearm container; punishment

Except as provided in Chapter 1 (commencing with Section 17700) of Division 2 of Title 2, any person in this state who manufactures or causes to be manufactured, imports into the state, keeps for sale, or offers or exposes for sale, or who gives, lends, or possesses any camouflaging firearm container is punishable by imprisonment in a county jail not exceeding one year or imprisonment pursuant to subdivision (h) of Section 1170. *(Added by Stats.2010, c. 711 (S.B.1080), § 6, operative Jan. 1, 2012. Amended by Stats.2012, c. 43 (S.B.1023), § 99, eff. June 27, 2012.)*

Law Revision Commission Comments

With respect to a camouflaging firearm container, Section 24310 continues former Section 12020(a)(1) without substantive change.

For circumstances in which this section is inapplicable, see Sections 16590 ("generally prohibited weapon"), 17700–17745 (exemptions relating to generally prohibited weapons).

See Section 16320 ("camouflaging firearm container"). See also Sections 17800 (distinct and separate offense), 24390 (camouflaging firearm container constituting nuisance). [38 Cal.L.Rev.Comm. Reports 217 (2009)].

Cross References

Firearm defined for purposes of this Part, see Penal Code § 16520.

Research References

2 Witkin, California Criminal Law 4th Crimes Against Public Peace and Welfare § 211 (2021), Nature of Crime.

§ 24390. Camouflaging firearm container deemed nuisance; exceptions

Except as provided in Chapter 1 (commencing with Section 17700) of Division 2 of Title 2, any camouflaging firearm container is a nuisance and is subject to Section 18010. *(Added by Stats.2010, c. 711 (S.B.1080), § 6, operative Jan. 1, 2012.)*

Law Revision Commission Comments

With respect to a camouflaging firearm container, Section 24390 continues the first part of the first sentence of former Section 12029 without substantive change.

See Section 16320 ("camouflaging firearm container"). [38 Cal.L.Rev. Comm. Reports 217 (2009)].

Cross References

Firearm defined for purposes of this Part, see Penal Code § 16520.

Research References

2 Witkin, California Criminal Law 4th Crimes Against Public Peace and Welfare § 263 (2021), Nuisances.

CHAPTER 4. CANE GUN

Section

§ 24410. Manufacture, import, sale, supply or possession of cane gun; punishment

Except as provided in Chapter 1 (commencing with Section 17700) of Division 2 of Title 2, any person in this state who manufactures or causes to be manufactured, imports into the state, keeps for sale, or offers or exposes for sale, or who gives, lends, or possesses any cane gun is punishable by imprisonment in a county jail not exceeding one year or imprisonment pursuant to subdivision (h) of Section 1170. *(Added by Stats.2010, c. 711 (S.B.1080), § 6, operative Jan. 1, 2012. Amended by Stats.2012, c. 43 (S.B.1023), § 100, eff. June 27, 2012.)*

Law Revision Commission Comments

With respect to a cane gun, Section 24410 continues former Section 12020(a)(1) without substantive change.

For circumstances in which this section is inapplicable, see Sections 16590 ("generally prohibited weapon"), 17700–17745 (exemptions relating to generally prohibited weapons).

See Section 16330 ("cane gun"). See also Sections 17800 (distinct and separate offense), 24490 (cane gun constituting nuisance). [38 Cal.L.Rev.Comm. Reports 217 (2009)].

Cross References

Cane gun defined for purposes of this Part, see Penal Code § 16330.
Penalty for possession of deadly weapon described in this section within State Capitol, legislative offices, etc., see Penal Code § 171c.
Possession of deadly weapons with intent to assault, see Penal Code § 17500.

Research References

2 Witkin, California Criminal Law 4th Crimes Against Public Peace and Welfare § 211 (2021), Nature of Crime.

§ 24490. Cane gun deemed nuisance; exceptions

Except as provided in Chapter 1 (commencing with Section 17700) of Division 2 of Title 2, any cane gun is a nuisance and is subject to Section 18010. *(Added by Stats.2010, c. 711 (S.B.1080), § 6, operative Jan. 1, 2012.)*

Law Revision Commission Comments

With respect to a cane gun, Section 24490 continues the first part of the first sentence of former Section 12029 without substantive change.

See Section 16330 ("cane gun"). [38 Cal.L.Rev.Comm. Reports 217 (2009)].

Cross References

Cane gun defined for purposes of this Part, see Penal Code § 16330.

Research References

2 Witkin, California Criminal Law 4th Crimes Against Public Peace and Welfare § 263 (2021), Nuisances.

CHAPTER 5. FIREARM NOT IMMEDIATELY RECOGNIZABLE AS A FIREARM

§ 24510. Manufacture, import, sale, supply or possession of firearm not immediately recognizable as firearm; punishment

Except as provided in Chapter 1 (commencing with Section 17700) of Division 2 of Title 2, any person in this state who manufactures or causes to be manufactured, imports into the state, keeps for sale, or offers or exposes for sale, or who gives, lends, or possesses any firearm not immediately recognizable as a firearm is punishable by imprisonment in a county jail not exceeding one year or imprisonment pursuant to subdivision (h) of Section 1170. *(Added by Stats.2010, c. 711 (S.B.1080), § 6, operative Jan. 1, 2012. Amended by Stats.2012, c. 43 (S.B.1023), § 101, eff. June 27, 2012.)*

Law Revision Commission Comments

With respect to a firearm that is not immediately recognizable as a firearm, Section 24510 continues former Section 12020(a)(1) without substantive change.

For circumstances in which this section is inapplicable, see Sections 16590 ("generally prohibited weapon"), 17700–17745 (exemptions relating to generally prohibited weapons).

See Section 16520 ("firearm"). See also Sections 17800 (distinct and separate offense), 24590 (firearm not immediately recognizable as such constitutes nuisance). [38 Cal.L.Rev.Comm. Reports 217 (2009)].

Cross References

Firearm defined for purposes of this Part, see Penal Code § 16520.
Penalty for possession of deadly weapon described in this section within State Capitol, legislative offices, etc., see Penal Code § 171c.
Possession of deadly weapons with intent to assault, see Penal Code § 17500.

Research References

2 Witkin, California Criminal Law 4th Crimes Against Public Peace and Welfare § 211 (2021), Nature of Crime.

§ 24590. Firearm not immediately recognizable as firearm deemed nuisance; exceptions

Except as provided in Chapter 1 (commencing with Section 17700) of Division 2 of Title 2, any firearm not immediately recognizable as a firearm is a nuisance and is subject to Section 18010. *(Added by Stats.2010, c. 711 (S.B.1080), § 6, operative Jan. 1, 2012.)*

Law Revision Commission Comments

With respect to a firearm that is not immediately recognizable as a firearm, Section 24590 continues the first part of the first sentence of former Section 12029 without substantive change.

See Section 16520 ("firearm"). [38 Cal.L.Rev.Comm. Reports 217 (2009)].

Cross References

Firearm defined for purposes of this Part, see Penal Code § 16520.

Research References

2 Witkin, California Criminal Law 4th Crimes Against Public Peace and Welfare § 263 (2021), Nuisances.

CHAPTER 6. UNDETECTABLE FIREARM AND FIREARM DETECTION EQUIPMENT

§ 24610. Manufacture, import, sale, supply or possession of undetectable firearm; punishment

Except as provided in Chapter 1 (commencing with Section 17700) of Division 2 of Title 2, any person in this state who manufactures or causes to be manufactured, imports into the state, keeps for sale, or offers or exposes for sale, or who gives, lends, or possesses any undetectable firearm is punishable by imprisonment in a county jail not exceeding one year or imprisonment pursuant to subdivision (h) of Section 1170. *(Added by Stats.2010, c. 711 (S.B.1080), § 6, operative Jan. 1, 2012. Amended by Stats.2012, c. 43 (S.B.1023), § 102, eff. June 27, 2012.)*

Law Revision Commission Comments

With respect to an undetectable firearm, Section 24610 continues former Section 12020(a)(1) without substantive change.

For circumstances in which this section is inapplicable, see Sections 16590 ("generally prohibited weapon"), 17700–17745 (exemptions relating to generally prohibited weapons).

See Section 17280 ("undetectable firearm"). See also Sections 17800 (distinct and separate offense), 24690 (undetectable firearm constituting nuisance). [38 Cal.L.Rev.Comm. Reports 217 (2009)].

Cross References

Firearm defined for purposes of this Part, see Penal Code § 16520.
Penalty for possession of deadly weapon described in this section within State Capitol, legislative offices, etc., see Penal Code § 171c.
Possession of deadly weapons with intent to assault, see Penal Code § 17500.
Undetectable firearm defined for purposes of this Part, see Penal Code § 17280.

Research References

2 Witkin, California Criminal Law 4th Crimes Against Public Peace and Welfare § 211 (2021), Nature of Crime.

§ 24680. Firearm detection equipment newly installed in nonfederal public building; requirements

Any firearm detection equipment newly installed in a nonfederal public building in this state shall be of a type identified by either the United States Attorney General, the Secretary of Transportation, or the Secretary of the Treasury, as appropriate, as available state-of-the-art equipment capable of detecting an undetectable firearm, while distinguishing innocuous metal objects likely to be carried on one's person sufficient for reasonable passage of the public. *(Added by Stats.2010, c. 711 (S.B.1080), § 6, operative Jan. 1, 2012.)*

Law Revision Commission Comments

Section 24680 continues the second paragraph of former Section 12020(c)(22)(C) without substantive change.

See Sections 16520 ("firearm"), 17280 ("undetectable firearm"). [38 Cal.L.Rev.Comm. Reports 217 (2009)].

Cross References

Attorney General, generally, see Government Code § 12500 et seq.
Firearm defined for purposes of this Part, see Penal Code § 16520.
Undetectable firearm defined for purposes of this Part, see Penal Code § 17280.

§ 24690. Undetectable firearm deemed nuisance; exceptions

Except as provided in Chapter 1 (commencing with Section 17700) of Division 2 of Title 2, any undetectable firearm is a nuisance and is subject to Section 18010. *(Added by Stats.2010, c. 711 (S.B.1080), § 6, operative Jan. 1, 2012.)*

Law Revision Commission Comments

With respect to an undetectable firearm, Section 24690 continues the first part of the first sentence of former Section 12029 without substantive change.

See Section 17280 ("undetectable firearm"). [38 Cal.L.Rev.Comm. Reports 217 (2009)].

Cross References

Firearm defined for purposes of this Part, see Penal Code § 16520.
Undetectable firearm defined for purposes of this Part, see Penal Code § 17280.

Research References

2 Witkin, California Criminal Law 4th Crimes Against Public Peace and Welfare § 263 (2021), Nuisances.

CHAPTER 7. WALLET GUN

§ 24710. Manufacture, import, sale, supply or possession of wallet gun; punishment

Except as provided in Chapter 1 (commencing with Section 17700) of Division 2 of Title 2, any person in this state who manufactures or causes to be manufactured, imports into the state, keeps for sale, or offers or exposes for sale, or who gives, lends, or possesses any wallet gun is punishable by imprisonment in a county jail not exceeding one year or imprisonment pursuant to subdivision (h) of Section 1170. *(Added by Stats.2010, c. 711 (S.B.1080), § 6, operative Jan. 1, 2012. Amended by Stats.2012, c. 43 (S.B.1023), § 103, eff. June 27, 2012.)*

Law Revision Commission Comments

With respect to a wallet gun, Section 24710 continues former Section 12020(a)(1) without substantive change.

For circumstances in which this section is inapplicable, see Sections 16590 ("generally prohibited weapon"), 17700–17745 (exemptions relating to generally prohibited weapons).

See Section 17330 ("wallet gun"). See also Sections 17800 (distinct and separate offense), 24790 (wallet gun constituting nuisance). [38 Cal.L.Rev. Comm. Reports 217 (2009)].

Cross References

Penalty for possession of deadly weapon described in this section within State Capitol, legislative offices, etc., see Penal Code § 171c.
Possession of deadly weapons with intent to assault, see Penal Code § 17500.
Wallet gun defined for purposes of this Part, see Penal Code § 17330.

Research References

2 Witkin, California Criminal Law 4th Crimes Against Public Peace and Welfare § 211 (2021), Nature of Crime.

§ 24790. Wallet gun deemed nuisance; exceptions

Except as provided in Chapter 1 (commencing with Section 17700) of Division 2 of Title 2, any wallet gun is a nuisance and is subject to Section 18010. *(Added by Stats.2010, c. 711 (S.B.1080), § 6, operative Jan. 1, 2012.)*

Law Revision Commission Comments

With respect to a wallet gun, Section 24790 continues the first part of the first sentence of former Section 12029 without substantive change.

See Section 17330 ("wallet gun"). [38 Cal.L.Rev.Comm. Reports 217 (2009)].

Cross References

Wallet gun defined for purposes of this Part, see Penal Code § 17330.

Research References

2 Witkin, California Criminal Law 4th Crimes Against Public Peace and Welfare § 263 (2021), Nuisances.

Division 4

STORAGE OF FIREARMS

CHAPTER 1. PRELIMINARY PROVISIONS

§ 25000. Child defined

As used in this division, "child" means a person under 18 years of age. *(Added by Stats.2010, c. 711 (S.B.1080), § 6, operative Jan. 1, 2012.)*

Law Revision Commission Comments

Section 25000 continues former Sections 12035(a)(3) and 12036(a)(2) without substantive change. [38 Cal.L.Rev.Comm. Reports 217 (2009)].

Cross References

Notice to parents and guardians relating to safe storage of firearms, method of notice, development of model language, immunity from civil liability, definitions, construction with other laws, see Education Code § 48986.

Research References

2 Witkin, California Criminal Law 4th Crimes Against Public Peace and Welfare § 262 (2021), Criminal Storage of Firearm.

CHAPTER 2. CRIMINAL STORAGE OF FIREARM

§ 25100. Criminal storage of firearm accessible to child; elements of crime

(a) Except as provided in Section 25105, a person commits the crime of "criminal storage of a firearm in the first degree" if all of the following conditions are satisfied:

(1) The person keeps any firearm within any premises that are under the person's custody or control.

(2) The person knows or reasonably should know that a child is likely to gain access to the firearm without the permission of the child's parent or legal guardian, or that a person prohibited from possessing a firearm or deadly weapon pursuant to state or federal law is likely to gain access to the firearm.

(3) The child obtains access to the firearm and thereby causes death or great bodily injury to the child or any other person, or the person prohibited from possessing a firearm or deadly weapon pursuant to state or federal law obtains access to the firearm and thereby causes death or great bodily injury to themselves or any other person.

(b) Except as provided in Section 25105, a person commits the crime of "criminal storage of a firearm in the second degree" if all of the following conditions are satisfied:

(1) The person keeps any firearm within any premises that are under the person's custody or control.

(2) The person knows or reasonably should know that a child is likely to gain access to the firearm without the permission of the child's parent or legal guardian, or that a person prohibited from possessing a firearm or deadly weapon pursuant to state or federal law is likely to gain access to the firearm.

(3) The child obtains access to the firearm and thereby causes injury, other than great bodily injury, to the child or any other person, or carries the firearm either to a public place or in violation of Section 417, or the person prohibited from possessing a firearm or deadly weapon pursuant to state or federal law obtains access to the firearm and thereby causes injury, other than great bodily injury, to themselves or any other person, or carries the firearm either to a public place or in violation of Section 417.

(c) Except as provided in Section 25105, a person commits the crime of "criminal storage of a firearm in the third degree" if the person keeps any firearm within any premises that are under the person's custody or control and negligently stores or leaves a firearm in a location where the person knows, or reasonably should know, that a child is likely to gain access to the firearm without the permission of the child's parent or legal guardian, unless reasonable action is taken by the person to secure the firearm against access by the child. *(Added by Stats.2010, c. 711 (S.B.1080), § 6, operative Jan. 1, 2012. Amended by Stats.2013, c. 730 (A.B.231), § 1; Stats.2013, c. 758 (S.B.363), § 1.5; Stats.2019, c. 840 (S.B.172), § 6, eff. Jan. 1, 2020.)*

Law Revision Commission Comments

Subdivision (a) of Section 25100 continues former Section 12035(b)(1) without substantive change.

Subdivision (b) continues former Section 12035(b)(2) without substantive change.

For a provision requiring a firearms dealer to post a notice with warnings about firearm storage, see Section 26835.

See Sections 16520 ("firearm"), 16600 ("great bodily injury"), 16840 ("loaded" and "loaded firearm"), 25000 ("child"). [38 Cal.L.Rev.Comm. Reports 217 (2009)].

Cross References

Child defined for purposes of this Division, see Penal Code § 25000.
Firearm defined for purposes of this Part, see Penal Code § 16520.
Loaded defined, see Penal Code § 16840.

Research References

2 Witkin, California Criminal Law 4th Crimes Against Public Peace and Welfare § 239 (2021), Misdemeanants.

2 Witkin, California Criminal Law 4th Crimes Against Public Peace and Welfare § 262 (2021), Criminal Storage of Firearm.

§ 25105. Exceptions to criminal storage of firearm accessible to child

Section 25100 does not apply whenever any of the following occurs:

(a) The child obtains the firearm as a result of an illegal entry to any premises by any person.

(b) The firearm is kept in a locked container or in a location that a reasonable person would believe to be secure.

(c) The firearm is carried on the person or within close enough proximity thereto that the individual can readily retrieve and use the firearm as if carried on the person.

(d) The firearm is locked with a locking device, as defined in Section 16860, which has rendered the firearm inoperable.

(e) The person is a peace officer or a member of the Armed Forces or the National Guard and the child obtains the firearm during, or incidental to, the performance of the person's duties.

(f) The child obtains, or obtains and discharges, the firearm in a lawful act of self-defense or defense of another person.

(g) The person who keeps a firearm on premises that are under the person's custody or control has no reasonable expectation, based on objective facts and circumstances, that a child is likely to be present on the premises. *(Added by Stats.2010, c. 711 (S.B.1080), § 6, operative Jan. 1, 2012. Amended by Stats.2011, c. 296 (A.B.1023), § 229; Stats.2011, c. 285 (A.B.1402), § 26; Stats.2019, c. 840 (S.B.172), § 7, eff. Jan. 1, 2020.)*

Law Revision Commission Comments

Section 25105 continues former Section 12035(c) without substantive change.

See Sections 16520 ("firearm"), 16840 ("loaded" and "loaded firearm"), 16850 ("locked container"), 25000 ("child"). [38 Cal.L.Rev.Comm. Reports 217 (2009)].

Section 25105 is amended to make a grammatical correction. This is not a substantive change. [41 Cal.L.Rev.Comm. Reports 135 (2011)].

Cross References

Child defined for purposes of this Division, see Penal Code § 25000.
Firearm defined for purposes of this Part, see Penal Code § 16520.
Loaded defined, see Penal Code § 16840.

Research References

2 Witkin, California Criminal Law 4th Crimes Against Public Peace and Welfare § 262 (2021), Criminal Storage of Firearm.

§ 25110. Criminal storage of firearm; punishment

(a) Criminal storage of a firearm in the first degree is punishable by imprisonment pursuant to subdivision (h) of Section 1170 for 16 months, or two or three years, by a fine not exceeding ten thousand dollars ($10,000), or by both that imprisonment and fine; or by imprisonment in a county jail not exceeding one year, by a fine not exceeding one thousand dollars ($1,000), or by both that imprisonment and fine.

(b) Criminal storage of a firearm in the second degree is punishable by imprisonment in a county jail not exceeding one year, by a fine not exceeding one thousand dollars ($1,000), or by both that imprisonment and fine.

(c) Criminal storage of a firearm in the third degree is punishable as a misdemeanor. *(Added by Stats.2010, c. 711 (S.B.1080), § 6, operative Jan. 1, 2012. Amended by Stats.2011, c. 15 (A.B.109), § 541, eff. April 4, 2011, operative Jan. 1, 2012; Stats.2013, c. 730 (A.B.231), § 2.)*

Law Revision Commission Comments

Section 25110 continues former Section 12035(d) without substantive change.

See Section 25100 (criminal storage of firearm). [38 Cal.L.Rev.Comm. Reports 217 (2009)].

Cross References

Firearm defined for purposes of this Part, see Penal Code § 16520.

Research References

2 Witkin, California Criminal Law 4th Crimes Against Public Peace and Welfare § 262 (2021), Criminal Storage of Firearm.

§ 25115. Criminal storage of firearm by parent or guardian of child injured or killed as result of accidental shooting; prosecution; legislative intent

If a person who allegedly violated Section 25100 is the parent or guardian of a child who is injured or who dies as the result of an accidental shooting, the district attorney shall consider, among other factors, the impact of the injury or death on the person alleged to have violated Section 25100 when deciding whether to prosecute the alleged violation. It is the Legislature's intent that a parent or guardian of a child who is injured or who dies as the result of an accidental shooting shall be prosecuted only in those instances in which the parent or guardian behaved in a grossly negligent manner or where similarly egregious circumstances exist. This section shall not otherwise restrict, in any manner, the factors that a district attorney may consider when deciding whether to prosecute an alleged violation of Section 25100. *(Added by Stats.2010, c. 711 (S.B.1080), § 6, operative Jan. 1, 2012.)*

Law Revision Commission Comments

Section 25115 continues former Section 12035(e) without substantive change.

See Section 25000 ("child"). [38 Cal.L.Rev.Comm. Reports 217 (2009)].

Cross References

Child defined for purposes of this Division, see Penal Code § 25000.

Research References

2 Witkin, California Criminal Law 4th Crimes Against Public Peace and Welfare § 262 (2021), Criminal Storage of Firearm.

§ 25120. Criminal storage of firearm by parent or guardian of child injured or killed as result of accidental shooting; time for arrest

(a) If a person who allegedly violated Section 25100 is the parent or guardian of a child who was injured or who died as the result of an accidental shooting, no arrest of the person for the alleged violation of Section 25100 shall occur until at least seven days after the date upon which the accidental shooting occurred.

(b) In addition to the limitation stated in subdivision (a), before arresting a person for a violation of Section 25100, a law enforcement officer shall consider the health status of a child who suffered great bodily injury as the result of an accidental shooting, if the person to be arrested is the parent or guardian of the injured child. The intent of this section is to encourage law enforcement officials to delay the arrest of a parent or guardian of a seriously injured child while the child remains on life-support equipment or is in a similarly critical medical condition. *(Added by Stats.2010, c. 711 (S.B.1080), § 6, operative Jan. 1, 2012.)*

Law Revision Commission Comments

Section 25120 continues former Section 12035(f) without substantive change.

See Sections 16600 ("great bodily injury"), 25000 ("child"). [38 Cal.L.Rev. Comm. Reports 217 (2009)].

Cross References

Child defined for purposes of this Division, see Penal Code § 25000.

Research References

2 Witkin, California Criminal Law 4th Crimes Against Public Peace and Welfare § 262 (2021), Criminal Storage of Firearm.

§ 25125. Attendance at firearm safety training course as mitigating factor in deciding whether to prosecute criminal storage of firearm; evidence of attendance admissible at trial

(a) The fact that a person who allegedly violated Section 25100 attended a firearm safety training course prior to the purchase of the firearm that was obtained by a child in violation of Section 25100 shall be considered a mitigating factor by a district attorney when deciding whether to prosecute the alleged violation.

(b) In any action or trial commenced under Section 25100, the fact that the person who allegedly violated Section 25100 attended a firearm safety training course prior to the purchase of the firearm that was obtained by a child in violation of Section 25100 is admissible. *(Added by Stats.2010, c. 711 (S.B.1080), § 6, operative Jan. 1, 2012.)*

Law Revision Commission Comments

Section 25125 continues former Section 12035(g) without substantive change.

See Sections 16520 ("firearm"), 25000 ("child"). [38 Cal.L.Rev.Comm. Reports 217 (2009)].

Cross References

Child defined for purposes of this Division, see Penal Code § 25000.
Firearm defined for purposes of this Part, see Penal Code § 16520.

Research References

2 Witkin, California Criminal Law 4th Crimes Against Public Peace and Welfare § 262 (2021), Criminal Storage of Firearm.

§ 25130. Licensed dealers required to post notice of duties regarding storage of firearms accessible to children

Every person licensed under Sections 26700 to 26915, inclusive, shall post within the licensed premises the notice required by Section 26835, disclosing the duty imposed by this chapter upon any person who keeps a loaded firearm. *(Added by Stats.2010, c. 711 (S.B.1080), § 6, operative Jan. 1, 2012.)*

Law Revision Commission Comments

Section 25130 continues former Section 12035(h) without substantive change.

See Sections 16520 ("firearm"), 16840 ("loaded" and "loaded firearm"). [38 Cal.L.Rev.Comm. Reports 217 (2009)].

Cross References

Firearm defined for purposes of this Part, see Penal Code § 16520.
Loaded defined, see Penal Code § 16840.

Research References

2 Witkin, California Criminal Law 4th Crimes Against Public Peace and Welfare § 262 (2021), Criminal Storage of Firearm.

§ 25135. Persons with firearm in residence where another resident is prohibited from possessing firearms; requirements for retaining firearm; violation

(a) A person who is 18 years of age or older, and who is the owner, lessee, renter, or other legal occupant of a residence, who owns a firearm and who knows or has reason to know that another person also residing therein is prohibited by state or federal law from possessing, receiving, owning, or purchasing a firearm shall not keep in that residence any firearm that he or she owns unless one of the following applies:

(1) The firearm is maintained within a locked container.

(2) The firearm is disabled by a firearm safety device.

(3) The firearm is maintained within a locked gun safe.

(4) The firearm is maintained within a locked trunk.

(5) The firearm is locked with a locking device as described in Section 16860, which has rendered the firearm inoperable.

(6) The firearm is carried on the person or within close enough proximity thereto that the individual can readily retrieve and use the firearm as if carried on the person.

(b) A violation of this section is a misdemeanor.

(c) The provisions of this section are cumulative, and do not restrict the application of any other law. However, an act or omission punishable in different ways by different provisions of law shall not be punished under more than one provision. *(Added by Stats.2013, c. 737 (A.B.500), § 7.)*

Research References

2 Witkin, California Criminal Law 4th Crimes Against Public Peace and Welfare § 239 (2021), Misdemeanants.

2 Witkin, California Criminal Law 4th Crimes Against Public Peace and Welfare § 262 (2021), Criminal Storage of Firearm.

§ 25140. Handgun left in unattended vehicle; requirement to lock handgun in trunk or locked container; peace officers; violation and penalty; exception

(a) Except as otherwise provided in subdivision (b), a person shall, when leaving a handgun in an unattended vehicle, lock the handgun in the vehicle's trunk, lock the handgun in a locked container and place the container out of plain view, lock the handgun in a locked container that is permanently affixed to the vehicle's interior and not in plain view, or lock the handgun in a locked toolbox or utility box.

(b) A peace officer, when leaving a handgun in an unattended vehicle not equipped with a trunk, may, if unable to otherwise comply with subdivision (a), lock the handgun out of plain view within the center utility console of that motor vehicle with a padlock, keylock, combination lock, or other similar locking device.

(c) A violation of subdivision (a) is an infraction punishable by a fine not exceeding one thousand dollars ($1,000).

(d)(1) As used in this section, the following definitions shall apply:

(A) "Locked container" means a secure container that is fully enclosed and locked by a padlock, keylock, combination lock, or similar locking device. The term "locked container" does not include the utility or glove compartment of a motor vehicle.

(B) "Locked toolbox or utility box" means a fully enclosed container that is permanently affixed to the bed of a pickup truck or vehicle that does not contain a trunk, and is locked by a padlock, keylock, combination lock, or other similar locking device.

(C) "Peace officer" means a sworn officer described in Chapter 4.5 (commencing with Section 830) of Title 3 of Part 2, or a sworn federal law enforcement officer, who is authorized to carry a firearm in the course and scope of that officer's duties, while that officer is on duty or off duty.

(D) "Trunk" means the fully enclosed and locked main storage or luggage compartment of a vehicle that is not accessible from the passenger compartment. A trunk does not include the rear of a hatchback, station wagon, or sport utility vehicle, any compartment which has a window, or a toolbox or utility box attached to the bed of a pickup truck.

(E) "Vehicle" has the same meaning as specified in Section 670 of the Vehicle Code.

(2) For purposes of this section, a vehicle is unattended when a person who is lawfully carrying or transporting a handgun in a vehicle is not within close enough proximity to the vehicle to reasonably prevent unauthorized access to the vehicle or its contents.

(3) For purposes of this section, plain view includes any area of the vehicle that is visible by peering through the windows of the vehicle, including windows that are tinted, with or without illumination.

(e) This section does not apply to a peace officer during circumstances requiring immediate aid or action that are within the course of his or her official duties.

(f) This section does not supersede any local ordinance that regulates the storage of handguns in unattended vehicles if the ordinance was in effect before September 26, 2016. *(Added by Stats.2016, c. 651 (S.B.869), § 1, eff. Jan. 1, 2017. Amended by Stats.2017, c. 809 (S.B.497), § 1, eff. Jan. 1, 2018; Stats.2018, c. 94 (S.B.1382), § 1, eff. Jan. 1, 2019.)*

Cross References

Carrying concealed firearms, leaving handgun in unattended vehicle, requirements for securing the handgun, see Penal Code §§ 25452, 25612.

Research References

2 Witkin, California Criminal Law 4th Crimes Against Public Peace and Welfare § 262 (2021), Criminal Storage of Firearm.

CHAPTER 3. STORAGE OF FIREARM WHERE CHILD OBTAINS ACCESS AND CARRIES FIREARM OFF–PREMISES

§ 25200. Storage of firearms accessed by children or prohibited persons and carried off-premises; punishment; firearm deemed as used in the commission of any misdemeanor as provided in this code or any felony; "off-premises" defined

(a) If all of the following conditions are satisfied, a person shall be punished by imprisonment in a county jail not exceeding one year, by a fine not exceeding one thousand dollars ($1,000), or by both that imprisonment and fine:

(1) The person keeps a firearm, loaded or unloaded, within any premises that are under the person's custody or control.

(2) The person knows or reasonably should know that a child is likely to gain access to that firearm without the permission of the child's parent or legal guardian, or that a person prohibited from possessing a firearm or deadly weapon pursuant to state or federal law is likely to gain access to the firearm.

(3) The child or the prohibited person obtains access to that firearm and thereafter carries that firearm off-premises.

(b) If all of the following conditions are satisfied, a person shall be punished by imprisonment in a county jail not exceeding one year, by a fine not exceeding five thousand dollars ($5,000), or by both that imprisonment and fine:

(1) The person keeps any firearm within any premises that are under the person's custody or control.

(2) The person knows or reasonably should know that a child is likely to gain access to the firearm without the permission of the child's parent or legal guardian, or that a person prohibited from possessing a firearm or deadly weapon pursuant to state or federal law is likely to gain access to the firearm.

(3) The child or the prohibited person obtains access to the firearm and thereafter carries that firearm off-premises to any public or private preschool, elementary school, middle school, high school, or to any school-sponsored event, activity, or performance, whether occurring on school grounds or elsewhere.

(c) A firearm that a child or prohibited person gains access to and carries off-premises in violation of this section shall be deemed "used in the commission of any misdemeanor as provided in this code or any felony" for the purpose of Section 29300 regarding the authority to confiscate firearms and other deadly weapons as a nuisance.

(d) As used in this section, "off-premises" means premises other than the premises where the firearm was stored. *(Added by Stats.2010, c. 711 (S.B.1080), § 6, operative Jan. 1, 2012. Amended by Stats.2013, c. 758 (S.B.363), § 2; Stats.2019, c. 840 (S.B.172), § 8, eff. Jan. 1, 2020.)*

Law Revision Commission Comments

Subdivision (a) of Section 25200 continues former Section 12036(b) without substantive change.

Subdivision (b) continues former Section 12036(c) without substantive change.

Subdivision (c) continues former Section 12036(d) without substantive change.

Subdivision (d) continues former Section 12036(a)(3) without substantive change.

For circumstances in which this section does not apply, see Section 25205. For a provision requiring a firearms dealer to post a notice with warnings about firearm storage, see Section 26835.

See Sections 16520 ("firearm"), 16530 ("firearm capable of being concealed upon the person," "pistol," and "revolver"), 25000 ("child"). [38 Cal.L.Rev. Comm. Reports 217 (2009)].

Cross References

Child defined for purposes of this Division, see Penal Code § 25000.
Felonies, definition and penalties, see Penal Code §§ 17, 18.
Firearm capable of being concealed upon the person defined for purposes of this Part, see Penal Code § 16530.
Firearm defined for purposes of this Part, see Penal Code § 16520.
Misdemeanors, definition and penalties, see Penal Code §§ 17, 19, 19.2.
Pistol defined for purposes of this Part, see Penal Code § 16530.
Revolver defined for purposes of this Part, see Penal Code § 16530.

Research References

2 Witkin, California Criminal Law 4th Crimes Against Public Peace and Welfare § 239 (2021), Misdemeanants.
2 Witkin, California Criminal Law 4th Crimes Against Public Peace and Welfare § 262 (2021), Criminal Storage of Firearm.

§ 25205. Exceptions to unlawful storage of firearm accessed by child and carried off-premises

Section 25200 does not apply if any of the following are true:

(a) The child obtains the firearm as a result of an illegal entry into any premises by any person.

(b) The firearm is kept in a locked container or in a location that a reasonable person would believe to be secure.

(c) The firearm is locked with a locking device, as defined in Section 16860, which has rendered the firearm inoperable.

(d) The firearm is carried on the person within close enough range that the individual can readily retrieve and use the firearm as if carried on the person.

(e) The person is a peace officer or a member of the Armed Forces or National Guard and the child obtains the firearm during, or incidental to, the performance of the person's duties.

(f) The child obtains, or obtains and discharges, the firearm in a lawful act of self-defense or defense of another person.

(g) The person who keeps a firearm has no reasonable expectation, based on objective facts and circumstances, that a child is likely to be present on the premises. *(Added by Stats.2010, c. 711 (S.B.1080), § 6, operative Jan. 1, 2012.)*

Law Revision Commission Comments

Section 25205 continues former Section 12036(e) without substantive change.

See Sections 16520 ("firearm"), 16850 ("locked container"), 25000 ("child"). [38 Cal.L.Rev.Comm. Reports 217 (2009)].

Cross References

Child defined for purposes of this Division, see Penal Code § 25000.
Firearm defined for purposes of this Part, see Penal Code § 16520.

§ 25210. Prosecution of parent or guardian of child who is injured or killed as result of accidental shooting; impact of injury or death considered; legislative intent

If a person who allegedly violated Section 25200 is the parent or guardian of a child who is injured or who dies as the result of an accidental shooting, the district attorney shall consider, among other factors, the impact of the injury or death on the person alleged to have violated Section 25200 when deciding whether to prosecute the alleged violation. It is the Legislature's intent that a parent or guardian of a child who is injured or who dies as the result of an accidental shooting shall be prosecuted only in those instances in which the parent or guardian behaved in a grossly negligent manner or where similarly egregious circumstances exist. This section shall not otherwise restrict, in any manner, the factors that a district attorney may consider when deciding whether to prosecute alleged violations of Section 25200. *(Added by Stats.2010, c. 711 (S.B.1080), § 6, operative Jan. 1, 2012.)*

Law Revision Commission Comments

Section 25210 continues former Section 12036(f) without substantive change.

See Section 25000 ("child"). [38 Cal.L.Rev.Comm. Reports 217 (2009)].

Cross References

Child defined for purposes of this Division, see Penal Code § 25000.

§ 25215. Arrest of parent or guardian of child injured or killed as result of accidental shooting; time for arrest

(a) If a person who allegedly violated Section 25200 is the parent or guardian of a child who was injured or who died as the result of an accidental shooting, no arrest of the person for the alleged violation of Section 25200 shall occur until at least seven days after the date upon which the accidental shooting occurred.

(b) In addition to the limitation contained in subdivision (a), before arresting a person for a violation of Section 25200, a law enforcement officer shall consider the health status of a child who suffers great bodily injury as the result of an accidental shooting, if the person to be arrested is the parent or guardian of the injured child. The intent of this section is to encourage law enforcement officials to delay the arrest of a parent or guardian of a seriously injured child while the child remains on life-support equipment or is in a similarly critical medical condition. *(Added by Stats.2010, c. 711 (S.B.1080), § 6, operative Jan. 1, 2012.)*

Law Revision Commission Comments

Section 25215 continues former Section 12036(g) without substantive change.

See Sections 16600 ("great bodily injury"), 25000 ("child"). [38 Cal.L.Rev. Comm. Reports 217 (2009)].

Cross References

Child defined for purposes of this Division, see Penal Code § 25000.

§ 25220. Attendance at firearm safety training course as mitigating factor in deciding whether to prosecute for child accessing firearm and carrying it off-premises; evidence of attendance admissible at trial

(a) The fact that the person who allegedly violated Section 25200 attended a firearm safety training course prior to the purchase of the firearm that is obtained by a child in violation of Section 25200 shall be considered a mitigating factor by a district attorney when deciding whether to prosecute the alleged violation.

(b) In any action or trial commenced under Section 25200, the fact that the person who allegedly violated Section 25200 attended a firearm safety training course prior to the purchase of the firearm that was obtained by a child in violation of Section 25200 is admissible. *(Added by Stats.2010, c. 711 (S.B.1080), § 6, operative Jan. 1, 2012.)*

Law Revision Commission Comments

Section 25220 continues former Section 12036(h) without substantive change.

See Sections 16520 ("firearm"), 25000 ("child"). [38 Cal.L.Rev.Comm. Reports 217 (2009)].

Cross References

Child defined for purposes of this Division, see Penal Code § 25000.
Firearm defined for purposes of this Part, see Penal Code § 16520.

§ 25225. Licensed dealers to post notice regarding children accessing firearms and carrying off-premises

Every person licensed under Sections 26700 to 26915, inclusive, shall post within the licensed premises the notice required by Section 26835, disclosing the duty imposed by this chapter upon any person who keeps any firearm. *(Added by Stats.2010, c. 711 (S.B.1080), § 6, operative Jan. 1, 2012.)*

Law Revision Commission Comments

Section 25225 continues former Section 12036(i) without substantive change.

See Section 16520 ("firearm"). [38 Cal.L.Rev.Comm. Reports 217 (2009)].

Cross References

Firearm defined for purposes of this Part, see Penal Code § 16520.

Research References

2 Witkin, California Criminal Law 4th Crimes Against Public Peace and Welfare § 262 (2021), Criminal Storage of Firearm.

Division 4.5

LOST OR STOLEN FIREARMS

§ 25250. Loss or theft of firearm; report to local law enforcement agency

(a) Commencing July 1, 2017, every person shall report the loss or theft of a firearm he or she owns or possesses to a local law enforcement agency in the jurisdiction in which the theft or loss occurred within five days of the time he or she knew or reasonably should have known that the firearm had been stolen or lost.

(b) Every person who has reported a firearm lost or stolen under subdivision (a) shall notify the local law enforcement agency in the jurisdiction in which the theft or loss occurred within five days if the firearm is subsequently recovered by the person.

(c) Notwithstanding subdivision (a), a person shall not be required to report the loss or theft of a firearm that is an antique firearm within the meaning of subdivision (c) of Section 16170. *(Added by Initiative Measure (Prop. 63, § 4.1, approved Nov. 8, 2016, eff. Nov. 9, 2016).)*

Research References

2 Witkin, California Criminal Law 4th Crimes Against Public Peace and Welfare § 262A (2021), (New) Lost or Stolen Firearms.

§ 25255. Exceptions to reporting requirements

Section 25250 shall not apply to the following:

(a) Any law enforcement agency or peace officer acting within the course and scope of his or her employment or official duties if he or she reports the loss or theft to his or her employing agency.

(b) Any United States marshal or member of the Armed Forces of the United States or the National Guard, while engaged in his or her official duties.

(c) Any person who is licensed, pursuant to Chapter 44 (commencing with Section 921) of Title 18 of the United States Code and the regulations issued pursuant thereto, and who reports the theft or loss in accordance with Section 923(g)(6) of Title 18 of the United States Code, or the successor provision thereto, and applicable regulations issued thereto.

(d) Any person whose firearm was lost or stolen prior to July 1, 2017. *(Added by Initiative Measure (Prop. 63, § 4.1, approved Nov. 8, 2016, eff. Nov. 9, 2016).)*

Research References

2 Witkin, California Criminal Law 4th Crimes Against Public Peace and Welfare § 262A (2021), (New) Lost or Stolen Firearms.

§ 25260. Submission of description of firearms reported lost or stolen

Pursuant to Section 11108.2, every sheriff or police chief shall submit a description of each firearm that has been reported lost or stolen directly into the Department of Justice Automated Firearms System. *(Added by Initiative Measure (Prop. 63, § 4.1, approved Nov. 8, 2016, eff. Nov. 9, 2016). Amended by Stats.2018, c. 864 (A.B.2222), § 6, eff. Jan. 1, 2019.)*

§ 25265. Violations and penalties

(a) Every person who violates Section 25250 is, for a first violation, guilty of an infraction, punishable by a fine not to exceed one hundred dollars ($100).

(b) Every person who violates Section 25250 is, for a second violation, guilty of an infraction, punishable by a fine not to exceed one thousand dollars ($1,000).

(c) Every person who violates Section 25250 is, for a third or subsequent violation, guilty of a misdemeanor, punishable by imprisonment in a county jail not exceeding six months, or by a fine not to exceed one thousand dollars ($1,000), or by both that fine and imprisonment. *(Added by Initiative Measure (Prop. 63, § 4.1, approved Nov. 8, 2016, eff. Nov. 9, 2016).)*

Research References

2 Witkin, California Criminal Law 4th Crimes Against Public Peace and Welfare § 262A (2021), (New) Lost or Stolen Firearms.

§ 25270. Information required when reporting lost or stolen firearm

Every person reporting a lost or stolen firearm pursuant to Section 25250 shall report the make, model, and serial number of the firearm, if known by the person, and any additional relevant information required by the local law enforcement agency taking the report. *(Added by Initiative Measure (Prop. 63, § 4.1, approved Nov. 8, 2016, eff. Nov. 9, 2016).)*

Research References

2 Witkin, California Criminal Law 4th Crimes Against Public Peace and Welfare § 262A (2021), (New) Lost or Stolen Firearms.

§ 25275. False report of lost or stolen firearm; violation and penalty

(a) No person shall report to a local law enforcement agency that a firearm has been lost or stolen, knowing the report to be false. A violation of this section is an infraction, punishable by a fine not exceeding two hundred fifty dollars ($250) for a first offense, and by a fine not exceeding one thousand dollars ($1,000) for a second or subsequent offense.

(b) This section shall not preclude prosecution under any other law. *(Added by Initiative Measure (Prop. 63, § 4.1, approved Nov. 8, 2016, eff. Nov. 9, 2016).)*

Research References

2 Witkin, California Criminal Law 4th Crimes Against Public Peace and Welfare § 262A (2021), (New) Lost or Stolen Firearms.

Division 5

CARRYING FIREARMS

CHAPTER 1. MISCELLANEOUS RULES RELATING TO CARRYING FIREARMS

§ 25300. Carrying firearm in public place or street while masked prohibited; punishment; exceptions

(a) A person commits criminal possession of a firearm when the person carries a firearm in a public place or on any public street while masked so as to hide the person's identity.

(b) Criminal possession of a firearm is punishable by imprisonment pursuant to subdivision (h) of Section 1170 or by imprisonment in a county jail not to exceed one year.

(c) Subdivision (a) does not apply to any of the following:

(1) A peace officer in performance of the officer's duties.

(2) A full-time paid peace officer of another state or the federal government who is carrying out official duties while in this state.

(3) Any person summoned by any of the officers enumerated in paragraph (1) or (2) to assist in making an arrest or preserving the peace while that person is actually engaged in assisting that officer.

(4) The possession of an unloaded firearm or a firearm loaded with blank ammunition by an authorized participant in, or while

rehearsing for, a motion picture, television, video production, entertainment event, entertainment activity, or lawfully organized and conducted activity when the participant lawfully uses the firearm as part of that production, event, or activity.

(5) The possession of a firearm by a licensed hunter while actually engaged in lawful hunting, or while going directly to or returning directly from the hunting expedition. *(Added by Stats.2010, c. 711 (S.B.1080), § 6, operative Jan. 1, 2012. Amended by Stats.2011, c. 15 (A.B.109), § 542, eff. April 4, 2011, operative Jan. 1, 2012.)*

Law Revision Commission Comments

Section 25300 continues former Section 12040 without substantive change. See Section 16520 ("firearm"). [38 Cal.L.Rev.Comm. Reports 217 (2009)].

Cross References

Firearm defined for purposes of this Part, see Penal Code § 16520.

Research References

2 Witkin, California Criminal Law 4th Crimes Against Public Peace and Welfare § 252 (2021), Carrying Firearm While Masked.

CHAPTER 2. CARRYING A CONCEALED FIREARM

ARTICLE 1. CRIME OF CARRYING A CONCEALED FIREARM

§ 25400. Carrying concealed firearm; punishment; minimum sentence

(a) A person is guilty of carrying a concealed firearm when the person does any of the following:

(1) Carries concealed within any vehicle that is under the person's control or direction any pistol, revolver, or other firearm capable of being concealed upon the person.

(2) Carries concealed upon the person any pistol, revolver, or other firearm capable of being concealed upon the person.

(3) Causes to be carried concealed within any vehicle in which the person is an occupant any pistol, revolver, or other firearm capable of being concealed upon the person.

(b) A firearm carried openly in a belt holster is not concealed within the meaning of this section.

(c) Carrying a concealed firearm in violation of this section is punishable as follows:

(1) If the person previously has been convicted of any felony, or of any crime made punishable by a provision listed in Section 16580, as a felony.

(2) If the firearm is stolen and the person knew or had reasonable cause to believe that it was stolen, as a felony.

(3) If the person is an active participant in a criminal street gang, as defined in subdivision (a) of Section 186.22, under the Street Terrorism Enforcement and Prevention Act (Chapter 11 (commencing with Section 186.20) of Title 7 of Part 1), as a felony.

(4) If the person is not in lawful possession of the firearm or the person is within a class of persons prohibited from possessing or acquiring a firearm pursuant to Chapter 2 (commencing with Section 29800) or Chapter 3 (commencing with Section 29900) of Division 9 of this title, or Section 8100 or 8103 of the Welfare and Institutions Code, as a felony.

(5) If the person has been convicted of a crime against a person or property, or of a narcotics or dangerous drug violation, by imprisonment pursuant to subdivision (h) of Section 1170, or by imprisonment in a county jail not to exceed one year, by a fine not to exceed one thousand dollars ($1,000), or by both that imprisonment and fine.

(6) If both of the following conditions are met, by imprisonment pursuant to subdivision (h) of Section 1170, or by imprisonment in a county jail not to exceed one year, by a fine not to exceed one thousand dollars ($1,000), or by both that fine and imprisonment:

(A) The pistol, revolver, or other firearm capable of being concealed upon the person is loaded, or both it and the unexpended ammunition capable of being discharged from it are in the immediate possession of the person or readily accessible to that person.

(B) The person is not listed with the Department of Justice pursuant to paragraph (1) of subdivision (c) of Section 11106 as the registered owner of that pistol, revolver, or other firearm capable of being concealed upon the person.

(7) In all cases other than those specified in paragraphs (1) to (6), inclusive, by imprisonment in a county jail not to exceed one year, by a fine not to exceed one thousand dollars ($1,000), or by both that imprisonment and fine.

(d)(1) Every person convicted under this section who previously has been convicted of a misdemeanor offense enumerated in Section 23515 shall be punished by imprisonment in a county jail for at least three months and not exceeding six months, or, if granted probation, or if the execution or imposition of sentence is suspended, it shall be a condition thereof that the person be imprisoned in a county jail for at least three months.

(2) Every person convicted under this section who has previously been convicted of any felony, or of any crime made punishable by a provision listed in Section 16580, if probation is granted, or if the execution or imposition of sentence is suspended, it shall be a condition thereof that the person be imprisoned in a county jail for not less than three months.

(e) The court shall apply the three-month minimum sentence as specified in subdivision (d), except in unusual cases where the interests of justice would best be served by granting probation or suspending the imposition or execution of sentence without the minimum imprisonment required in subdivision (d) or by granting probation or suspending the imposition or execution of sentence with conditions other than those set forth in subdivision (d), in which case, the court shall specify on the record and shall enter on the minutes the circumstances indicating that the interests of justice would best be served by that disposition.

(f) A peace officer may arrest a person for a violation of paragraph (6) of subdivision (c) if the peace officer has probable cause to believe that the person is not listed with the Department of Justice pursuant to paragraph (1) of subdivision (c) of Section 11106 as the registered owner of the pistol, revolver, or other firearm capable of being concealed upon the person, and one or more of the conditions in subparagraph (A) of paragraph (6) of subdivision (c) is met. *(Added by Stats.2010, c. 711 (S.B.1080), § 6, operative Jan. 1, 2012. Amended by Stats.2011, c. 15 (A.B.109), § 543, eff. April 4, 2011, operative Jan. 1, 2012.)*

Validity

For validity of this section, see Peruta v. County of San Diego, C.A.9 (Cal.)2014, 742 F.3d 1144, on rehearing en banc

824 F.3d 919, certiorari denied 137 S.Ct. 1995, 198 L.Ed.2d 746.

Law Revision Commission Comments

Subdivision (a) of Section 25400 continues former Section 12025(a) without substantive change.

Subdivision (b) continues former Section 12025(f) without substantive change.

Subdivision (c) continues former Section 12025(b) without substantive change. Subdivision (d) continues former Section 12025(d) without substantive change. For guidance in applying paragraphs (c)(1) and (d)(2), see Section 16015 (determining existence of prior conviction).

Subdivision (e) continues former Section 12025(e) without substantive change.

Subdivision (f) continues former Section 12025(c) without substantive change.

Former Section 12025(g) is continued in Section 16750 ("lawful possession of the firearm").

Former Section 12025(h) was repealed by its own terms on January 1, 2005, so it is not continued. See 1999 Cal. Stat. ch. 571, § 2.

See Sections 16520 ("firearm"), 16530 ("firearm capable of being concealed upon the person," "pistol," and "revolver"), 16750 ("lawful possession of the firearm"), 16840 ("loaded" and "loaded firearm"). [38 Cal.L.Rev.Comm. Reports 217 (2009)].

Cross References

Felonies, definition and penalties, see Penal Code §§ 17, 18.
Firearm capable of being concealed upon the person defined for purposes of this Part, see Penal Code § 16530.
Firearm defined for purposes of this Part, see Penal Code § 16520.
Licenses to carry concealed weapons, see Penal Code § 26150 et seq.
Loaded defined, see Penal Code § 16840.
Misdemeanors, definition and penalties, see Penal Code §§ 17, 19, 19.2.
Persons exempt from this section and provisions relating to openly carrying unloaded handgun, see Penal Code § 25605.
Pistol defined for purposes of this Part, see Penal Code § 16530.
Possession of prohibited items in sterile area of public transit facility, see Penal Code § 171.7.
Revolver defined for purposes of this Part, see Penal Code § 16530.
Switch-blade knives having blades two or more inches long, possession in motor vehicle, see Penal Code § 653k.

Research References

California Jury Instructions - Criminal 12.46, Concealable Firearm—Concealed Within Vehicle Controlled by Felon.
California Jury Instructions - Criminal 12.46.1, Concealable Firearm—Concealed Within Vehicle Controlled by Defendant.
California Jury Instructions - Criminal 12.46.2, Concealable Weapons—Defendant Admits Priors, etc.
California Jury Instructions - Criminal 12.47, Concealable Firearm—Possession by Person Convicted of Crime Against Person, Property or Drug Violation.
California Jury Instructions - Criminal 12.47.1, Concealable Firearm—Carried on the Person.
California Jury Instructions - Criminal 12.47.2, Concealed Weapons—Unregistered Loaded Firearm.
California Jury Instructions - Criminal 12.47.5, Concealable Firearm—Concealed Within Vehicle Occupied by Ex-Felon.
California Jury Instructions - Criminal 12.47.6, Concealable Firearm—Concealed Within Vehicle Occupied by Prohibited Person.
California Jury Instructions - Criminal 16.460, Concealed Weapons.
2 Witkin, California Criminal Law 4th Crimes Against Public Peace and Welfare § 64 (2021), Improper Picketing Activity.
2 Witkin, California Criminal Law 4th Crimes Against Public Peace and Welfare § 203 (2021), Nature of Crime.
2 Witkin, California Criminal Law 4th Crimes Against Public Peace and Welfare § 204 (2021), Punishment.
2 Witkin, California Criminal Law 4th Crimes Against Public Peace and Welfare § 205 (2021), Concealment and Possession.
2 Witkin, California Criminal Law 4th Crimes Against Public Peace and Welfare § 206 (2021), Operability of Firearm.
2 Witkin, California Criminal Law 4th Crimes Against Public Peace and Welfare § 207 (2021), Exempt Persons.
2 Witkin, California Criminal Law 4th Crimes Against Public Peace and Welfare § 208 (2021), Exempt Activities.
2 Witkin, California Criminal Law 4th Crimes Against Public Peace and Welfare § 209 (2021), Justifiable Violation of Statute.
2 Witkin, California Criminal Law 4th Crimes Against Public Peace and Welfare § 233 (2021), Prohibitions.
2 Witkin, California Criminal Law 4th Crimes Against Public Peace and Welfare § 243 (2021), Minors.
2 Witkin, California Criminal Law 4th Crimes Against Public Peace and Welfare § 250 (2021), Punishment.
2 Witkin, California Criminal Law 4th Crimes Against Public Peace and Welfare § 253 (2021), Openly Displaying or Carrying Imitation or Unloaded Firearm.
2 Witkin, California Criminal Law 4th Crimes Against Public Peace and Welfare § 257 (2021), Firearms.
2 Witkin, California Criminal Law 4th Crimes Against Public Peace and Welfare § 259 (2021), Playground or Youth Center.
2 Witkin, California Criminal Law 4th Crimes Against Public Peace and Welfare § 263 (2021), Nuisances.
1 Witkin California Criminal Law 4th Introduction to Crimes § 72 (2021), Illustrations: Weapons.
1 Witkin California Criminal Law 4th Introduction to Crimes § 77 (2021), Illustrations: Special Statute is Not Controlling.
4 Witkin, California Criminal Law 4th Pretrial Proceedings § 33 (2021), Other Exceptions.

ARTICLE 2. PEACE OFFICER EXEMPTION

Section

§ 25450. Carrying of concealed firearm by peace officers

As provided in this article, Section 25400 does not apply to, or affect, any of the following:

(a) Any peace officer, listed in Section 830.1 or 830.2, or subdivision (a) of Section 830.33, whether active or honorably retired.

(b) Any other duly appointed peace officer.

(c) Any honorably retired peace officer listed in subdivision (c) of Section 830.5.

(d) Any other honorably retired peace officer who during the course and scope of his or her appointment as a peace officer was authorized to, and did, carry a firearm.

(e) Any full-time paid peace officer of another state or the federal government who is carrying out official duties while in California.

(f) Any person summoned by any of these officers to assist in making arrests or preserving the peace while the person is actually engaged in assisting that officer. *(Added by Stats.2010, c. 711 (S.B.1080), § 6, operative Jan. 1, 2012. Amended by Stats.2013, c. 267 (A.B.703), § 1.)*

Law Revision Commission Comments

Section 25450 continues the first sentence of former Section 12027(a)(1)(A) without substantive change.

For an exemption relating to honorably retired federal officers and agents, see Section 25650.

For guidance on a retired peace officer carrying a loaded firearm, see Sections 25900–25925. For guidance on a retired peace officer carrying a concealed and loaded firearm, see Sections 26300–26325.

See Sections 16520 ("firearm"), 16690 ("honorably retired"). [38 Cal. L.Rev.Comm. Reports 217 (2009)].

Cross References

Carrying of equipment authorized for the enforcement of law or ordinance, see Penal Code § 17515.
Firearm defined for purposes of this Part, see Penal Code § 16520.
Honorably retired defined, see Penal Code § 16690.
Penalty for possession of loaded firearms or enumerated prohibited weapons within State Capitol, legislative offices, etc., exception for retired peace officer with authorization to carry concealed weapons, see Penal Code § 171c.
Proprietary private security officer registration provisions, exemptions to officers carrying unloaded and exposed handguns, see Business and Professions Code § 7574.14.

Research References

2 Witkin, California Criminal Law 4th Crimes Against Public Peace and Welfare § 64 (2021), Improper Picketing Activity.
2 Witkin, California Criminal Law 4th Crimes Against Public Peace and Welfare § 207 (2021), Exempt Persons.
2 Witkin, California Criminal Law 4th Crimes Against Public Peace and Welfare § 210 (2021), Unlawful Acts Involving Ammunition.
2 Witkin, California Criminal Law 4th Crimes Against Public Peace and Welfare § 256 (2021), Sterile Area of Airport, Passenger Vessel Terminal, or Public Transit Facility.

§ 25452. Leaving handgun in unattended vehicle; requirements for securing the handgun

A peace officer and an honorably retired peace officer shall, when leaving a handgun in an unattended vehicle, secure the handgun in the vehicle pursuant to Section 25140. *(Added by Stats.2016, c. 651 (S.B.869), § 2, eff. Jan. 1, 2017.)*

§ 25455. Honorably retired peace officer; issuance of identification certificate; fee; concealed firearm endorsement

(a) Any peace officer described in Section 25450 who has been honorably retired shall be issued an identification certificate by the law enforcement agency from which the officer retired.

(b) The issuing agency may charge a fee necessary to cover any reasonable expenses incurred by the agency in issuing certificates pursuant to this article.

(c) Any officer, except an officer listed in Section 830.1 or 830.2, subdivision (a) of Section 830.33, or subdivision (c) of Section 830.5 who retired prior to January 1, 1981, shall have an endorsement on the identification certificate stating that the issuing agency approves the officer's carrying of a concealed firearm.

(d) An honorably retired peace officer listed in Section 830.1 or 830.2, subdivision (a) of Section 830.33, or subdivision (c) of Section 830.5 who retired prior to January 1, 1981, shall not be required to obtain an endorsement from the issuing agency to carry a concealed firearm. *(Added by Stats.2010, c. 711 (S.B.1080), § 6, operative Jan. 1, 2012.)*

Law Revision Commission Comments

Subdivision (a) of Section 25455 continues the second sentence of former Section 12027(a)(1)(A) without substantive change.

Subdivision (b) continues the third sentence of former Section 12027(a)(1)(A) without substantive change.

Subdivision (c) continues former Section 12027(a)(1)(B) without substantive change.

Subdivision (d) continues the second sentence of former Section 12027(a)(2) without substantive change.

For guidance on a retired peace officer carrying a loaded firearm, see Sections 25900–25925. For guidance on a retired peace officer carrying a concealed and loaded firearm, see Sections 26300–26325.

See Sections 16520 ("firearm"), 16690 ("honorably retired"). [38 Cal. L.Rev.Comm. Reports 217 (2009)].

Cross References

Firearm defined for purposes of this Part, see Penal Code § 16520.
Honorably retired defined, see Penal Code § 16690.
Identification issued to retired peace officers, see Penal Code § 538d.
Penalty for possession of loaded firearms or enumerated prohibited weapons within State Capitol, legislative offices, etc., exception for retired peace officer with authorization to carry concealed weapons, see Penal Code § 171c.

§ 25460. Endorsement or renewal endorsement; format

(a) Except as provided in subdivision (b), no endorsement or renewal endorsement issued pursuant to Section 25465 shall be effective unless it is in the format set forth in subdivision (c).

(b) Any peace officer listed in subdivision (f) of Section 830.2 or in subdivision (c) of Section 830.5, who retired between January 2, 1981, and on or before December 31, 1988, and who is authorized to carry a concealed firearm pursuant to this article, shall not be required to have an endorsement in the format set forth in subdivision (c) until the time of the issuance, on or after January 1, 1989, of a renewal endorsement pursuant to Section 25465.

(c) A certificate issued pursuant to Section 25455 for any person who is not listed in Section 830.1 or 830.2, subdivision (a) of Section 830.33, or subdivision (c) of Section 830.5, or for any person retiring after January 1, 1981, shall be in the following format: it shall be on a 2x3 inch card, bear the photograph of the retiree, include the retiree's name, date of birth, the date that the retiree retired, and the name and address of the agency from which the retiree retired, and have stamped on it the endorsement "CCW Approved" and the date the endorsement is to be renewed. A certificate issued pursuant to Section 25455 shall not be valid as identification for the sale, purchase, or transfer of a firearm. *(Added by Stats.2010, c. 711 (S.B.1080), § 6, operative Jan. 1, 2012.)*

Law Revision Commission Comments

Subdivisions (a) and (b) of Section 25460 continue former Section 12027(a)(1)(C) without substantive change.

Subdivision (c) continues former Section 12027(a)(1)(D) without substantive change.

See Sections 16360 ("CCW"), 16520 ("firearm"). [38 Cal.L.Rev.Comm. Reports 217 (2009)].

Cross References

Firearm defined for purposes of this Part, see Penal Code § 16520.
Identification issued to retired peace officers, see Penal Code § 538d.
Penalty for possession of loaded firearms or enumerated prohibited weapons within State Capitol, legislative offices, etc., exception for retired peace officer with authorization to carry concealed weapons, see Penal Code § 171c.

§ 25465. Retired peace officers; petition to renew privilege to carry concealed firearm

Every five years, a retired peace officer, except an officer listed in Section 830.1 or 830.2, subdivision (a) of Section 830.33, or subdivision (c) of Section 830.5 who retired prior to January 1, 1981, shall petition the issuing agency for renewal of the officer's privilege to carry a concealed firearm. *(Added by Stats.2010, c. 711 (S.B.1080), § 6, operative Jan. 1, 2012.)*

Law Revision Commission Comments

Section 25465 continues the first sentence of former Section 12027(a)(2) without substantive change.

See Section 16520 ("firearm"). [38 Cal.L.Rev.Comm. Reports 217 (2009)].

Cross References

Firearm defined for purposes of this Part, see Penal Code § 16520.

Penalty for possession of loaded firearms or enumerated prohibited weapons within State Capitol, legislative offices, etc., exception for retired peace officer with authorization to carry concealed weapons, see Penal Code § 171c.

§ 25470. Denial or revocation of privilege to carry concealed firearm

(a) The agency from which a peace officer is honorably retired may, upon initial retirement of that peace officer, or at any time subsequent thereto, deny or revoke for good cause the retired officer's privilege to carry a concealed firearm.

(b) A peace officer who is listed in Section 830.1 or 830.2, subdivision (a) of Section 830.33, or subdivision (c) of Section 830.5 who retired prior to January 1, 1981, shall have the privilege to carry a concealed firearm denied or revoked by having the agency from which the officer retired stamp on the officer's identification certificate "No CCW privilege." *(Added by Stats.2010, c. 711 (S.B.1080), § 6, operative Jan. 1, 2012.)*

Law Revision Commission Comments

Subdivision (a) of Section 25470 continues the third sentence of former Section 12027(a)(2) without substantive change.

Subdivision (b) continues the fourth sentence of former Section 12027(a)(2) without substantive change.

See Sections 16360 ("CCW"), 16520 ("firearm"), 16690 ("honorably retired"). [38 Cal.L.Rev.Comm. Reports 217 (2009)].

Cross References

Firearm defined for purposes of this Part, see Penal Code § 16520.
Honorably retired defined, see Penal Code § 16690.
Identification issued to retired peace officers, see Penal Code § 538d.
Penalty for possession of loaded firearms or enumerated prohibited weapons within State Capitol, legislative offices, etc., exception for retired peace officer with authorization to carry concealed weapons, see Penal Code § 171c.

§ 25475. Honorably retired peace officers authorized to carry a concealed firearm; training requirements; annual qualification

(a) An honorably retired peace officer who is listed in subdivision (c) of Section 830.5 and authorized to carry a concealed firearm by this article shall meet the training requirements of Section 832 and shall qualify with the firearm at least annually.

(b) The individual retired peace officer shall be responsible for maintaining eligibility to carry a concealed firearm.

(c) The Department of Justice shall provide subsequent arrest notification pursuant to Section 11105.2 regarding honorably retired peace officers listed in subdivision (c) of Section 830.5 to the agency from which the officer has retired. *(Added by Stats.2010, c. 711 (S.B.1080), § 6, operative Jan. 1, 2012.)*

Law Revision Commission Comments

Section 25475 continues former Section 12027(a)(3) without substantive change.

See Sections 16520 ("firearm"), 16690 ("honorably retired"). [38 Cal. L.Rev.Comm. Reports 217 (2009)].

Cross References

Firearm defined for purposes of this Part, see Penal Code § 16520.
Honorably retired defined, see Penal Code § 16690.
Penalty for possession of loaded firearms or enumerated prohibited weapons within State Capitol, legislative offices, etc., exception for retired peace officer with authorization to carry concealed weapons, see Penal Code § 171c.

ARTICLE 3. CONDITIONAL EXEMPTIONS

§ 25505. Transportation of unloaded firearm in locked container; course of travel

In order for a firearm to be exempted under this article, while being transported to or from a place, the firearm shall be unloaded and kept in a locked container, and the course of travel shall include only those deviations between authorized locations as are reasonably necessary under the circumstances. *(Added by Stats.2010, c. 711 (S.B.1080), § 6, operative Jan. 1, 2012.)*

Law Revision Commission Comments

Section 25505 continues former Section 12026.2(b) without substantive change.

For another provision on transporting a firearm in a locked container, see Section 25610 (carrying firearm in locked container).

See Sections 16520 ("firearm"), 16850 ("locked container"). [38 Cal.L.Rev. Comm. Reports 217 (2009)].

Cross References

Firearm defined for purposes of this Part, see Penal Code § 16520.

Research References

2 Witkin, California Criminal Law 4th Crimes Against Public Peace and Welfare § 208 (2021), Exempt Activities.

§ 25510. Firearms used in motion picture, television, video production, or entertainment event; authorized possession and transportation

Section 25400 does not apply to, or affect, any of the following:

(a) The possession of a firearm by an authorized participant in a motion picture, television, or video production, or an entertainment event, when the participant lawfully uses the firearm as part of that production or event, or while going directly to, or coming directly from, that production or event.

(b) The transportation of a firearm by an authorized employee or agent of a supplier of firearms when going directly to, or coming directly from, a motion picture, television, or video production, or an entertainment event, for the purpose of providing that firearm to an authorized participant to lawfully use as a part of that production or event. *(Added by Stats.2010, c. 711 (S.B.1080), § 6, operative Jan. 1, 2012.)*

Law Revision Commission Comments

Subdivision (a) of Section 25510 continues former Section 12026.2(a)(1) without substantive change.

Subdivision (b) continues former Section 12026.2(a)(8) without substantive change.

For conditions on invoking these exemptions, see Section 25505. For a provision on the effect of this article, see Section 25595.

See Section 16520 ("firearm"). [38 Cal.L.Rev.Comm. Reports 217 (2009)].

Cross References

Firearm defined for purposes of this Part, see Penal Code § 16520.

Research References

2 Witkin, California Criminal Law 4th Crimes Against Public Peace and Welfare § 208 (2021), Exempt Activities.

§ 25515. Possession of firearm in locked container by member of organization or club that lawfully collects and displays firearms

Section 25400 does not apply to, or affect, the possession of a firearm in a locked container by a member of any club or organization, organized for the purpose of lawfully collecting and lawfully displaying pistols, revolvers, or other firearms, while the member is at a meeting of the club or organization or while going directly to, and coming directly from, a meeting of the club or organization. *(Added by Stats.2010, c. 711 (S.B.1080), § 6, operative Jan. 1, 2012.)*

Law Revision Commission Comments

Section 25515 continues former Section 12026.2(a)(2) without substantive change.

For conditions on invoking this exemption, see Section 25505. For an exemption relating to transportation of a curio or relic brought into the state by licensed collector, see Section 25580. For a provision on the effect of this article, see Section 25595.

See Sections 16520 ("firearm"), 16530 ("firearm capable of being concealed upon the person," "pistol," and "revolver"), 16850 ("locked container"). [38 Cal.L.Rev.Comm. Reports 217 (2009)].

Cross References

Firearm defined for purposes of this Part, see Penal Code § 16520.
Pistol defined for purposes of this Part, see Penal Code § 16530.
Revolver defined for purposes of this Part, see Penal Code § 16530.

Research References

2 Witkin, California Criminal Law 4th Crimes Against Public Peace and Welfare § 208 (2021), Exempt Activities.

§ 25520. Transportation of firearm by participant in safety or hunter safety class, or recognized sporting event

Section 25400 does not apply to, or affect, the transportation of a firearm by a participant when going directly to, or coming directly from, a recognized safety or hunter safety class, or a recognized sporting event involving that firearm. *(Added by Stats.2010, c. 711 (S.B.1080), § 6, operative Jan. 1, 2012.)*

Law Revision Commission Comments

Section 25520 continues former Section 12026.2(a)(3) without substantive change.

For conditions on invoking this exemption, see Section 25505. For another exemption relating to hunting, see Section 25640 (licensed hunters or fishermen). For a provision on the effect of this article, see Section 25595.

See Section 16520 ("firearm"). [38 Cal.L.Rev.Comm. Reports 217 (2009)].

Cross References

Firearm defined for purposes of this Part, see Penal Code § 16520.

Research References

2 Witkin, California Criminal Law 4th Crimes Against Public Peace and Welfare § 208 (2021), Exempt Activities.

§ 25525. Place of residence, place of business, and private property; authorized transportation of firearm

(a) Section 25400 does not apply to, or affect, the transportation of a firearm by any citizen of the United States or legal resident over the age of 18 years who resides or is temporarily within this state, and who is not within the excepted classes prescribed by Chapter 2 (commencing with Section 29800) or Chapter 3 (commencing with Section 29900) of Division 9 of this title, or Section 8100 or 8103 of the Welfare and Institutions Code, directly between any of the following places:

(1) The person's place of residence.

(2) The person's place of business.

(3) Private property owned or lawfully possessed by the person.

(b) Section 25400 does not apply to, or affect, the transportation of a firearm by a person listed in subdivision (a) when going directly from the place where that person lawfully received that firearm to that person's place of residence or place of business or to private property owned or lawfully possessed by that person. *(Added by Stats.2010, c. 711 (S.B.1080), § 6, operative Jan. 1, 2012.)*

Law Revision Commission Comments

Subdivision (a) of Section 25525 continues former Section 12026.2(a)(4) without substantive change. Former Section 12026.2(a)(4) referred to "a person listed in Section 12026" and "the places mentioned in Section 12026." To make subdivision (a) of Section 25525 readily understandable, those references have been replaced with the pertinent language from former Section 12026, which is continued in Section 25605.

Subdivision (b) continues former Section 12026.2(a)(6) without substantive change. Former Section 12026.2(a)(6) referred to "a person listed in Section 12026." To make subdivision (b) of Section 25525 readily understandable, that reference has been replaced with a reference to "a person listed in subdivision (a)." This is equivalent to the previous reference, because subdivision (a) includes the pertinent language from former Section 12026.

For conditions on invoking these exemptions, see Section 25505. For an exemption relating to carrying or possession of a firearm at one's place of residence, place of business, or other private property, see Section 25605. For a provision on the effect of this article, see Section 25595.

See Section 16520 ("firearm"). [38 Cal.L.Rev.Comm. Reports 217 (2009)].

Cross References

Firearm defined for purposes of this Part, see Penal Code § 16520.

Research References

2 Witkin, California Criminal Law 4th Crimes Against Public Peace and Welfare § 208 (2021), Exempt Activities.

§ 25530. Transportation related to lawful repair, sale, loan, or transfer of firearm

Section 25400 does not apply to, or affect, the transportation of a firearm by a person when going directly to, or coming directly from, a fixed place of business or private residential property for the purpose of the lawful repair or the lawful sale, loan, or transfer of that firearm. *(Added by Stats.2010, c. 711 (S.B.1080), § 6, operative Jan. 1, 2012.)*

Law Revision Commission Comments

Section 25530 continues former Section 12026.2(a)(5) without substantive change.

For conditions on invoking this exemption, see Section 25505. For a provision on the effect of this article, see Section 25595.

See Section 16520 ("firearm"). [38 Cal.L.Rev.Comm. Reports 217 (2009)].

Cross References

Firearm defined for purposes of this Part, see Penal Code § 16520.

Research References

2 Witkin, California Criminal Law 4th Crimes Against Public Peace and Welfare § 208 (2021), Exempt Activities.

§ 25535. Gun show, swap meet, or similar event; authorized transportation of firearm

Section 25400 does not apply to, or affect, any of the following:

(a) The transportation of a firearm by a person when going directly to, or coming directly from, a gun show, swap meet, or similar event to which the public is invited, for the purpose of displaying that firearm in a lawful manner.

(b) The transportation of a firearm by a person when going directly to, or coming directly from, a gun show or event, as defined in Section 478.100 of Title 27 of the Code of Federal Regulations, for the purpose of lawfully transferring, selling, or loaning that firearm in accordance with Section 27545. *(Added by Stats.2010, c. 711 (S.B.1080), § 6, operative Jan. 1, 2012.)*

Law Revision Commission Comments

Subdivision (a) of Section 25535 continues former Section 12026.2(a)(7) without substantive change.

Subdivision (b) continues former Section 12026.2(a)(14) without substantive change.

For conditions on invoking these exemptions, see Section 25505. For a provision on the effect of this article, see Section 25595.

See Section 16520 ("firearm"). [38 Cal.L.Rev.Comm. Reports 217 (2009)].

Cross References

Firearm defined for purposes of this Part, see Penal Code § 16520.

Research References

2 Witkin, California Criminal Law 4th Crimes Against Public Peace and Welfare § 208 (2021), Exempt Activities.

§ 25540. Transportation to or from target range

Section 25400 does not apply to, or affect, the transportation of a firearm by a person when going directly to, or coming directly from, a target range, which holds a regulatory or business license, for the purposes of practicing shooting at targets with that firearm at that target range. *(Added by Stats.2010, c. 711 (S.B.1080), § 6, operative Jan. 1, 2012.)*

Law Revision Commission Comments

Section 25540 continues former Section 12026.2(a)(9) without substantive change.

For conditions on invoking this exemption, see Section 25505. For another exemption relating to practicing at a target range, see Section 25635 (member of club or organization for purpose of practicing at established target ranges). For a provision on the effect of this article, see Section 25595.

See Section 16520 ("firearm"). [38 Cal.L.Rev.Comm. Reports 217 (2009)].

Cross References

Firearm defined for purposes of this Part, see Penal Code § 16520.

Research References

2 Witkin, California Criminal Law 4th Crimes Against Public Peace and Welfare § 208 (2021), Exempt Activities.

§ 25545. Transportation of firearm to or from licensing agency

Section 25400 does not apply to, or affect, the transportation of a firearm by a person when going directly to, or coming directly from, a place designated by a person authorized to issue licenses pursuant to Section 26150, 26155, 26170, or 26215, when done at the request of the issuing agency so that the issuing agency can determine whether or not a license should be issued to that person to carry that firearm. *(Added by Stats.2010, c. 711 (S.B.1080), § 6, operative Jan. 1, 2012.)*

Law Revision Commission Comments

Section 25545 continues former Section 12026.2(a)(10) without substantive change.

For conditions on invoking this exemption, see Section 25505. For an exemption relating to a person with a license to carry a concealed pistol, revolver, or other firearm capable of being concealed upon the person, see Section 25655. For a provision on the effect of this article, see Section 25595.

See Section 16520 ("firearm"). [38 Cal.L.Rev.Comm. Reports 217 (2009)].

Cross References

Firearm defined for purposes of this Part, see Penal Code § 16520.

Research References

2 Witkin, California Criminal Law 4th Crimes Against Public Peace and Welfare § 208 (2021), Exempt Activities.

§ 25550. Transportation of firearm to or from lawful camping activity; authority of Department of Parks and Recreation

(a) Section 25400 does not apply to, or affect, the transportation of a firearm by a person when going directly to, or coming directly from, a lawful camping activity for the purpose of having that firearm available for lawful personal protection while at the lawful campsite.

(b) This section shall not be construed to override the statutory authority granted to the Department of Parks and Recreation or any other state or local governmental agencies to promulgate rules and regulations governing the administration of parks and campgrounds. *(Added by Stats.2010, c. 711 (S.B.1080), § 6, operative Jan. 1, 2012.)*

Law Revision Commission Comments

Section 25550 continues former Section 12026.2(a)(11) without substantive change.

For conditions on invoking this exemption, see Section 25505. For a provision on the effect of this article, see Section 25595.

See Section 16520 ("firearm"). [38 Cal.L.Rev.Comm. Reports 217 (2009)].

Cross References

Firearm defined for purposes of this Part, see Penal Code § 16520.

Research References

2 Witkin, California Criminal Law 4th Crimes Against Public Peace and Welfare § 208 (2021), Exempt Activities.

§ 25555. Transportation of firearm in order to comply with specified provisions

(a) Section 25400 does not apply to, or affect, the transportation of a firearm by a person in order to comply with Section 26556, 27870, 27875, 27915, 27920, 27925, 29810, or 29830, as it pertains to that firearm.

(b) Section 25400 does not apply to or affect the transportation of a firearm by a person in order to comply with paragraph (2) of subdivision (e) of Section 32000 as it pertains to that firearm.

(c) Section 25400 does not apply to, or affect the transportation of, a firearm by a person in order to comply with Section 6389 of the Family Code. *(Added by Stats.2010, c. 711 (S.B.1080), § 6, operative Jan. 1, 2012. Amended by Stats.2019, c. 738 (S.B.376), § 6, eff. Jan. 1, 2020; Stats.2020, c. 289 (A.B.2699), § 2, eff. Jan. 1, 2021; Stats.2021, c. 685 (S.B.320), § 9, eff. Jan. 1, 2022.)*

Law Revision Commission Comments

Section 25555 continues former Section 12026.2(a)(12) without substantive change.

For conditions on invoking this exemption, see Section 25505. For a provision on the effect of this article, see Section 25595.

See Section 16520 ("firearm"). [38 Cal.L.Rev.Comm. Reports 217 (2009)].

Cross References

Firearm defined for purposes of this Part, see Penal Code § 16520.

Research References

2 Witkin, California Criminal Law 4th Crimes Against Public Peace and Welfare § 208 (2021), Exempt Activities.

§ 25560. Transportation of firearm to utilize Section 28000

Section 25400 does not apply to, or affect, the transportation of a firearm by a person in order to utilize Section 28000 as it pertains to that firearm. *(Added by Stats.2010, c. 711 (S.B.1080), § 6, operative Jan. 1, 2012.)*

Law Revision Commission Comments

Section 25560 continues former Section 12026.2(a)(13) without substantive change.

For conditions on invoking this exemption, see Section 25505. For a provision on the effect of this article, see Section 25595.

See Section 16520 ("firearm"). [38 Cal.L.Rev.Comm. Reports 217 (2009)].

Cross References

Firearm defined for purposes of this Part, see Penal Code § 16520.

Research References

2 Witkin, California Criminal Law 4th Crimes Against Public Peace and Welfare § 208 (2021), Exempt Activities.

§ 25565. Sale, delivery, or transfer of firearm to government representative; authorized transportation

Section 25400 does not apply to, or affect, the transportation of a firearm by a person in order to sell, deliver, or transfer the firearm as specified in Section 27850 or 31725 to an authorized representative of a city, city and county, county, or state or federal government that is acquiring the weapon as part of an authorized, voluntary program in which the entity is buying or receiving weapons from private individuals. *(Added by Stats.2010, c. 711 (S.B.1080), § 6, operative Jan. 1, 2012.)*

Law Revision Commission Comments

Section 25565 continues former Section 12026.2(a)(15) without substantive change. Former Section 12026.2(a)(15) referred to "transportation of a firearm by a person in order to utilize paragraph (6) of subdivision (a) of Section 12078 as it pertains to that firearm." To make Section 25565 readily understandable, that reference has been replaced by pertinent language from former Section 12078(a)(6) and cross-references to Sections 27850 and 31725, which continue former Section 12078(a)(6).

For conditions on invoking this exemption, see Section 25505. For a provision on the effect of this article, see Section 25595.

See Section 16520 ("firearm"). [38 Cal.L.Rev.Comm. Reports 217 (2009)].

Cross References

Firearm defined for purposes of this Part, see Penal Code § 16520.

Research References

2 Witkin, California Criminal Law 4th Crimes Against Public Peace and Welfare § 208 (2021), Exempt Activities.

§ 25570. Transportation of found firearm to law enforcement agency

Section 25400 does not apply to, or affect, any of the following:

(a) The transportation of a firearm by a person who finds the firearm, if the person is transporting the firearm in order to comply with Article 1 (commencing with Section 2080) of Chapter 4 of Division 3 of the Civil Code as it pertains to that firearm, and, if the person is transporting the firearm to a law enforcement agency, the person gives prior notice to the law enforcement agency that the person is transporting the firearm to the law enforcement agency.

(b) The transportation of a firearm by a person who finds the firearm and is transporting it to a law enforcement agency for disposition according to law, if the person gives prior notice to the law enforcement agency that the person is transporting the firearm to the law enforcement agency for disposition according to law.

(c) The transportation of a firearm by a person who took the firearm from a person who was committing a crime against the person who took the firearm, and is transporting it to a law enforcement agency for disposition according to law, if the person gives prior notice to the law enforcement agency that the person is transporting the firearm to the law enforcement agency for disposition according to law. *(Added by Stats.2010, c. 711 (S.B.1080), § 6, operative Jan. 1, 2012. Amended by Stats.2019, c. 110 (A.B.1292), § 3, eff. Jan. 1, 2020.)*

Law Revision Commission Comments

Subdivision (a) of Section 25570 continues former Section 12026.2(a)(16) without substantive change.

Subdivision (b) continues former Section 12026.2(a)(18) without substantive change.

For conditions on invoking these exemptions, see Section 25505. For a provision on the effect of this article, see Section 25595.

See Section 16520 ("firearm"). [38 Cal.L.Rev.Comm. Reports 217 (2009)].

Cross References

Firearm defined for purposes of this Part, see Penal Code § 16520.

Research References

California Jury Instructions - Criminal 12.43.1, Justifiable Violations.

2 Witkin, California Criminal Law 4th Crimes Against Public Peace and Welfare § 208 (2021), Exempt Activities.

2 Witkin, California Criminal Law 4th Crimes Against Public Peace and Welfare § 232 (2021), Nature and Scope of Statutes.

§ 25575. Transportation of firearm in order to comply with Section 27560

Section 25400 does not apply to, or affect, the transportation of a firearm by a person in order to comply with Section 27560 as it pertains to that firearm. *(Added by Stats.2010, c. 711 (S.B.1080), § 6, operative Jan. 1, 2012.)*

Law Revision Commission Comments

Section 25575 continues former Section 12026.2(a)(17) without substantive change.

For conditions on invoking this exemption, see Section 25505. For an exemption relating to transportation of unloaded handguns by a licensed manufacturer, importer, wholesaler, repairer, or dealer, see Section 25615. For a provision on the effect of this article, see Section 25595.

See Section 16520 ("firearm"). [38 Cal.L.Rev.Comm. Reports 217 (2009)].

Cross References

Firearm defined for purposes of this Part, see Penal Code § 16520.

Research References

2 Witkin, California Criminal Law 4th Crimes Against Public Peace and Welfare § 208 (2021), Exempt Activities.

§ 25580. Firearm that is curio or relic; authorized transportation

Section 25400 does not apply to, or affect, the transportation of a firearm that is a curio or relic, as defined in Section 478.11 of Title 27 of the Code of Federal Regulations, by a person in order to comply with Section 27565 as it pertains to that firearm. *(Added by Stats.2010, c. 711 (S.B.1080), § 6, operative Jan. 1, 2012.)*

Law Revision Commission Comments

Section 25580 continues former Section 12026.2(a)(19) without substantive change. Former Section 12026.2(a)(19) referred to "transportation of a firearm by a person in order to comply with paragraph (3) of subdivision (f) of Section 12072." To make Section 25580 readily understandable, that reference has been replaced by key language from former Section 12072(f)(3) and a cross-reference to Sections 27565, which continues former Section 12072(f)(3).

For conditions on invoking this exemption, see Section 25505. For an exemption relating to a club or organization for lawfully collecting and displaying firearms, see Section 25515. For a provision on the effect of this article, see Section 25595.

See Section 16520 ("firearm"). [38 Cal.L.Rev.Comm. Reports 217 (2009)].

Cross References

Firearm defined for purposes of this Part, see Penal Code § 16520.

Research References

2 Witkin, California Criminal Law 4th Crimes Against Public Peace and Welfare § 208 (2021), Exempt Activities.

§ 25585. Transportation of firearm to obtain identification number or mark

Section 25400 does not apply to, or affect, the transportation of a firearm by a person for the purpose of obtaining an identification number or mark assigned to that firearm from the Department of Justice pursuant to Section 23910. *(Added by Stats.2010, c. 711 (S.B.1080), § 6, operative Jan. 1, 2012.)*

Law Revision Commission Comments

Section 25585 continues former Section 12026.2(a)(20) without substantive change.

For conditions on invoking this exemption, see Section 25505. For a provision on the effect of this article, see Section 25595.

See Section 16520 ("firearm"). [38 Cal.L.Rev.Comm. Reports 217 (2009)].

Cross References

Firearm defined for purposes of this Part, see Penal Code § 16520.

Research References

2 Witkin, California Criminal Law 4th Crimes Against Public Peace and Welfare § 208 (2021), Exempt Activities.

§ 25590. Transportation of firearm between places set forth in specified provisions

Section 25400 does not apply to, or affect, the transportation of a firearm by a person if done directly between any of the places set forth below:

(a) A place where the person may carry that firearm pursuant to an exemption from the prohibition set forth in subdivision (a) of Section 25400.

(b) A place where that person may carry that firearm pursuant to an exemption from the prohibition set forth in subdivision (a) of Section 25850, or a place where the prohibition set forth in subdivision (a) of Section 25850 does not apply.

(c) A place where that person may carry a firearm pursuant to an exemption from the prohibition set forth in subdivision (a) of Section 26350, or a place where the prohibition set forth in subdivision (a) of Section 26350 does not apply. *(Added by Stats.2011, c. 725 (A.B. 144), § 11.)*

Cross References

Firearm defined for purposes of this Part, see Penal Code § 16520.

Research References

2 Witkin, California Criminal Law 4th Crimes Against Public Peace and Welfare § 208 (2021), Exempt Activities.

§ 25595. Otherwise lawful carrying or transportation of handgun; application of article

This article does not prohibit or limit the otherwise lawful carrying or transportation of any handgun in accordance with the provisions listed in Section 16580. *(Added by Stats.2010, c. 711 (S.B.1080), § 6, operative Jan. 1, 2012. Amended by Stats.2011, c. 725 (A.B.144), § 12.)*

Law Revision Commission Comments

Section 25595 continues former Section 12026.2(c) without substantive change.

See Section 16530 ("firearm capable of being concealed upon the person," "pistol," and "revolver"). [38 Cal.L.Rev.Comm. Reports 217 (2009)].

Cross References

Handgun defined for purposes of this Part, see Penal Code § 16640.

Research References

2 Witkin, California Criminal Law 4th Crimes Against Public Peace and Welfare § 208 (2021), Exempt Activities.

ARTICLE 4. OTHER EXEMPTIONS

§ 25600. Reasonable belief of grave danger; justifiable violation of Section 25400

(a) A violation of Section 25400 is justifiable when a person who possesses a firearm reasonably believes that person is in grave danger because of circumstances forming the basis of a current restraining order issued by a court against another person who has been found to pose a threat to the life or safety of the person who possesses the firearm. This section may not apply when the circumstances involve a mutual restraining order issued pursuant to Division 10 (commencing with Section 6200) of the Family Code absent a factual finding of a specific threat to the person's life or safety. It is not the intent of the Legislature to limit, restrict, or narrow the application of current statutory or judicial authority to apply this or other justifications to a defendant charged with violating Section 25400 or committing another similar offense.

(b) Upon trial for violating Section 25400, the trier of fact shall determine whether the defendant was acting out of a reasonable belief that the defendant was in grave danger. *(Added by Stats.2010, c. 711 (S.B.1080), § 6, operative Jan. 1, 2012.)*

Law Revision Commission Comments

Section 25600 continues former Section 12025.5 without substantive change. See Section 16520 ("firearm"). [38 Cal.L.Rev.Comm. Reports 217 (2009)].

Cross References

Firearm defined for purposes of this Part, see Penal Code § 16520.

Research References

2 Witkin, California Criminal Law 4th Crimes Against Public Peace and Welfare § 209 (2021), Justifiable Violation of Statute.

§ 25605. Carrying of handgun within place of residence, place of business, or on private property; application of Section 25400 and provisions relating to openly carrying unloaded handgun

(a) Section 25400 and Chapter 6 (commencing with Section 26350) of Division 5 shall not apply to or affect any citizen of the United States or legal resident over the age of 18 years who resides or is temporarily within this state, and who is not within the excepted classes prescribed by Chapter 2 (commencing with Section 29800) or Chapter 3 (commencing with Section 29900) of Division 9 of this title, or Section 8100 or 8103 of the Welfare and Institutions Code, who carries, either openly or concealed, anywhere within the citizen's or legal resident's place of residence, place of business, or on private property owned or lawfully possessed by the citizen or legal resident, any handgun.

(b) No permit or license to purchase, own, possess, keep, or carry, either openly or concealed, shall be required of any citizen of the United States or legal resident over the age of 18 years who resides or is temporarily within this state, and who is not within the excepted classes prescribed by Chapter 2 (commencing with Section 29800) or Chapter 3 (commencing with Section 29900) of Division 9 of this title, or Section 8100 or 8103 of the Welfare and Institutions Code, to purchase, own, possess, keep, or carry, either openly or concealed, a handgun within the citizen's or legal resident's place of residence, place of business, or on private property owned or lawfully possessed by the citizen or legal resident.

(c) Nothing in this section shall be construed as affecting the application of Sections 25850 to 26055, inclusive. *(Added by Stats.2010, c. 711 (S.B.1080), § 6, operative Jan. 1, 2012. Amended by Stats.2011, c. 725 (A.B.144), § 13.)*

Law Revision Commission Comments

Section 25605 continues former Section 12026 without substantive change.

For an exemption relating to transportation of a firearm by the owner or a person in lawful possession of the firearm to that person's place of residence, place of business, or other private property, see Section 25525.

See Section 16530 ("firearm capable of being concealed upon the person," "pistol," and "revolver"). [38 Cal.L.Rev.Comm. Reports 217 (2009)].

Cross References

Handgun defined for purposes of this Part, see Penal Code § 16640.
Licenses to carry concealed weapons, see Penal Code § 26150 et seq.

Research References

2 Witkin, California Criminal Law 4th Crimes Against Public Peace and Welfare § 207 (2021), Exempt Persons.
2 Witkin, California Criminal Law 4th Crimes Against Public Peace and Welfare § 250 (2021), Punishment.
2 Witkin, California Criminal Law 4th Crimes Against Public Peace and Welfare § 257 (2021), Firearms.
1 Witkin California Criminal Law 4th Introduction to Crimes § 65 (2021), Where Direct Conflict Exists.
1 Witkin California Criminal Law 4th Introduction to Crimes § 70 (2021), Weapons.

§ 25610. Authority to transport or carry concealable firearms

(a) Section 25400 shall not be construed to prohibit any citizen of the United States over the age of 18 years who resides or is temporarily within this state, and who is not prohibited by state or federal law from possessing, receiving, owning, or purchasing a firearm, from transporting or carrying any pistol, revolver, or other firearm capable of being concealed upon the person, provided that the following applies to the firearm:

(1) The firearm is within a motor vehicle and it is locked in the vehicle's trunk or in a locked container in the vehicle.

(2) The firearm is carried by the person directly to or from any motor vehicle for any lawful purpose and, while carrying the firearm, the firearm is contained within a locked container.

(b) The provisions of this section do not prohibit or limit the otherwise lawful carrying or transportation of any pistol, revolver, or other firearm capable of being concealed upon the person in accordance with the provisions listed in Section 16580. *(Added by Stats.2010, c. 711 (S.B.1080), § 6, operative Jan. 1, 2012.)*

Law Revision Commission Comments

Subdivision (a) of Section 25610 continues former Section 12026.1(a) without substantive change, except for the last phrase of paragraph (a)(1) (other than the utility or glove compartment). That phrase and former Section 12026.1(c) are continued in Section 16850 ("locked container").

Subdivision (b) continues former Section 12026.1(b) without substantive change.

For another provision on transporting a firearm in a locked container, see Section 25505 (conditions for Article 3 exemptions to apply).

See Sections 16520 ("firearm"), 16530 ("firearm capable of being concealed upon the person," "pistol," and "revolver"), 16850 ("locked container"). [38 Cal.L.Rev.Comm. Reports 217 (2009)].

Cross References

Firearm capable of being concealed upon the person defined for purposes of this Part, see Penal Code § 16530.
Firearm defined for purposes of this Part, see Penal Code § 16520.
Pistol defined for purposes of this Part, see Penal Code § 16530.
Revolver defined for purposes of this Part, see Penal Code § 16530.
Taking or transferring possession of any assault weapon, .50 BMG rifle, or firearm precursor part, see Business and Professions Code § 22949.63.

Research References

2 Witkin, California Criminal Law 4th Crimes Against Public Peace and Welfare § 205 (2021), Concealment and Possession.
2 Witkin, California Criminal Law 4th Crimes Against Public Peace and Welfare § 207 (2021), Exempt Persons.

§ 25612. Leaving handgun in unattended vehicle; requirements for securing the handgun

A person shall, when leaving a handgun in an unattended vehicle, secure the handgun in the vehicle pursuant to Section 25140. *(Added by Stats.2016, c. 651 (S.B.869), § 3, eff. Jan. 1, 2017.)*

§ 25615. Possession or transportation of unloaded firearms in lawful course of business; application of Section 25400

Section 25400 does not apply to, or affect, the possession or transportation of unloaded pistols, revolvers, or other firearms capable of being concealed upon the person as merchandise by a person who is engaged in the business of manufacturing, importing, wholesaling, repairing, or dealing in firearms and who is licensed to engage in that business, or the authorized representative or authorized agent of that person, while engaged in the lawful course of the business. *(Added by Stats.2010, c. 711 (S.B.1080), § 6, operative Jan. 1, 2012.)*

Law Revision Commission Comments

Section 25615 continues former Section 12027(b) without substantive change.

For an exemption relating to compliance with restrictions on importation of handguns by a personal handgun importer, see Section 25575.

See Section 16530 ("firearm capable of being concealed upon the person," "pistol," and "revolver"). [38 Cal.L.Rev.Comm. Reports 217 (2009)].

Cross References

Firearm capable of being concealed upon the person defined for purposes of this Part, see Penal Code § 16530.
Firearm defined for purposes of this Part, see Penal Code § 16520.
Pistol defined for purposes of this Part, see Penal Code § 16530.
Revolver defined for purposes of this Part, see Penal Code § 16530.

Research References

2 Witkin, California Criminal Law 4th Crimes Against Public Peace and Welfare § 64 (2021), Improper Picketing Activity.
2 Witkin, California Criminal Law 4th Crimes Against Public Peace and Welfare § 257 (2021), Firearms.

§ 25620. Members of Army, Navy, Air Force, Coast Guard, Marine Corps, or National Guard; application of Section 25400

Section 25400 does not apply to, or affect, any member of the Army, Navy, Air Force, Coast Guard, or Marine Corps of the United States, or the National Guard, when on duty, or any organization that is by law authorized to purchase or receive those weapons from the United States or this state. *(Added by Stats.2010, c. 711 (S.B.1080), § 6, operative Jan. 1, 2012.)*

Law Revision Commission Comments

Section 25620 continues former Section 12027(c) without substantive change.

For an exemption relating to parading by a duly authorized military or civil organization, or traveling to a meeting of such an organization, see Section 25625. [38 Cal.L.Rev.Comm. Reports 217 (2009)].

Cross References

Machine guns, sale to or possession by police departments, sheriffs, marshals and military and naval forces, see Penal Code § 12201.

Research References

2 Witkin, California Criminal Law 4th Crimes Against Public Peace and Welfare § 207 (2021), Exempt Persons.

§ 25625. Carrying of unloaded firearms by authorized military or civil organization member in relation to parading; application of Section 25400

Section 25400 does not apply to, or affect, the carrying of unloaded pistols, revolvers, or other firearms capable of being concealed upon the person by duly authorized military or civil organizations while parading, or the members thereof when going to and from the places of meeting of their respective organizations. *(Added by Stats.2010, c. 711 (S.B.1080), § 6, operative Jan. 1, 2012.)*

Law Revision Commission Comments

Section 25625 continues former Section 12027(d) without substantive change.

For an exemption relating to a member of the military on duty or an organization authorized by law to purchase or receive weapons, see Section 25620.

See Section 16530 ("firearm capable of being concealed upon the person," "pistol," and "revolver"). [38 Cal.L.Rev.Comm. Reports 217 (2009)].

Cross References

Firearm capable of being concealed upon the person defined for purposes of this Part, see Penal Code § 16530.
Firearm defined for purposes of this Part, see Penal Code § 16520.
Pistol defined for purposes of this Part, see Penal Code § 16530.
Revolver defined for purposes of this Part, see Penal Code § 16530.

§ 25630. Guard or messenger of common carrier, bank, or financial institution while shipping thing of value; application of Section 25400

Section 25400 does not apply to, or affect, any guard or messenger of any common carrier, bank, or other financial institution, while actually employed in and about the shipment, transportation, or delivery of any money, treasure, bullion, bonds, or other thing of value within this state. *(Added by Stats.2010, c. 711 (S.B.1080), § 6, operative Jan. 1, 2012.)*

Law Revision Commission Comments

Section 25630 continues former Section 12027(e) without substantive change.

For another exemption relating to common carriers, see Section 25645 (transportation of unloaded firearms by person operating licensed common carrier). [38 Cal.L.Rev.Comm. Reports 217 (2009)].

Cross References

Private patrol officers, assessment of administrative fines, prohibited acts, concealed weapons, see Business and Professions Code § 7583.37.

Research References

2 Witkin, California Criminal Law 4th Crimes Against Public Peace and Welfare § 207 (2021), Exempt Persons.

§ 25635. Use or transport of firearms for use at target ranges; application of Section 25400

Section 25400 does not apply to, or affect, members of any club or organization organized for the purpose of practicing shooting at targets upon established target ranges, whether public or private, while the members are using pistols, revolvers, or other firearms capable of being concealed upon the person upon the target ranges, or transporting these firearms unloaded when going to and from the ranges. *(Added by Stats.2010, c. 711 (S.B.1080), § 6, operative Jan. 1, 2012.)*

Law Revision Commission Comments

Section 25635 continues former Section 12027(f) without substantive change.

For another exemption relating to practicing at a target range, see Section 25540 (target range).

See Section 16530 ("firearm capable of being concealed upon the person," "pistol," and "revolver"). [38 Cal.L.Rev.Comm. Reports 217 (2009)].

Cross References

Firearm capable of being concealed upon the person defined for purposes of this Part, see Penal Code § 16530.
Firearm defined for purposes of this Part, see Penal Code § 16520.
Pistol defined for purposes of this Part, see Penal Code § 16530.
Revolver defined for purposes of this Part, see Penal Code § 16530.

Research References

2 Witkin, California Criminal Law 4th Crimes Against Public Peace and Welfare § 207 (2021), Exempt Persons.

§ 25640. Licensed hunters or fishermen; application of Section 25400

Section 25400 does not apply to, or affect, licensed hunters or fishermen carrying pistols, revolvers, or other firearms capable of being concealed upon the person while engaged in hunting or fishing, or transporting those firearms unloaded when going to or returning from the hunting or fishing expedition. *(Added by Stats.2010, c. 711 (S.B.1080), § 6, operative Jan. 1, 2012.)*

Law Revision Commission Comments

Section 25640 continues former Section 12027(g) without substantive change.

For another exemption relating to hunting, see Section 25520 (recognized sporting event or safety or hunter safety class).

See Section 16530 ("firearm capable of being concealed upon the person," "pistol," and "revolver"). [38 Cal.L.Rev.Comm. Reports 217 (2009)].

Cross References

Firearm capable of being concealed upon the person defined for purposes of this Part, see Penal Code § 16530.
Firearm defined for purposes of this Part, see Penal Code § 16520.
Pistol defined for purposes of this Part, see Penal Code § 16530.
Revolver defined for purposes of this Part, see Penal Code § 16530.

Research References

2 Witkin, California Criminal Law 4th Crimes Against Public Peace and Welfare § 207 (2021), Exempt Persons.

§ 25645. Transport of firearms by common carrier; application of Sections 25140 and 25400

Sections 25140 and 25400 do not apply to, or affect, the transportation of unloaded firearms by a person operating a licensed common carrier or an authorized agent or employee thereof when the firearms are transported in conformance with applicable federal law. *(Added by Stats.2010, c. 711 (S.B.1080), § 6, operative Jan. 1, 2012. Amended by Stats.2016, c. 651 (S.B.869), § 4, eff. Jan. 1, 2017.)*

Law Revision Commission Comments

Section 25645 continues former Section 12027(h) without substantive change.

For another exemption relating to common carriers, see Section 25630 (guard or messenger of common carrier, bank, or financial institution, when involved in shipping, transporting, or delivering money or other thing of value).

See Section 16520 ("firearm"). [38 Cal.L.Rev.Comm. Reports 217 (2009)].

Cross References

Firearm defined for purposes of this Part, see Penal Code § 16520.

§ 25650. Honorably retired federal officer or agent; application of Section 25400; permit

(a) Upon approval of the sheriff of the county in which the retiree resides, Section 25400 does not apply to, or affect, any honorably retired federal officer or agent of any federal law enforcement agency, including, but not limited to, the Federal Bureau of Investigation, the United States Secret Service, the United States Customs Service, the federal Bureau of Alcohol, Tobacco, Firearms and Explosives, the Federal Bureau of Narcotics, the United States Drug Enforcement Administration, the United States Border Patrol, and any officer or agent of the Internal Revenue Service who was authorized to carry weapons while on duty, who was assigned to duty within the state for a period of not less than one year, or who retired from active service in the state.

(b) A retired federal officer or agent shall provide the sheriff with certification from the agency from which the officer or agent retired certifying that person's service in the state, stating the nature of that person's retirement, and indicating the agency's concurrence that the retired federal officer or agent should be accorded the privilege of carrying a concealed firearm.

(c) Upon that approval, the sheriff shall issue a permit to the retired federal officer or agent indicating that the retiree may carry a concealed firearm in accordance with this section. The permit shall be valid for a period not exceeding five years, shall be carried by the retiree while carrying a concealed firearm, and may be revoked for good cause.

(d) The sheriff of the county in which the retired federal officer or agent resides may require recertification prior to a permit renewal, and may suspend the privilege for cause. The sheriff may charge a fee necessary to cover any reasonable expenses incurred by the county. *(Added by Stats.2010, c. 711 (S.B.1080), § 6, operative Jan. 1, 2012. Amended by Stats.2011, c. 296 (A.B.1023), § 230.)*

Law Revision Commission Comments

Section 25650 continues former Section 12027(i) without substantive change.

For an exemption relating to honorably retired peace officers, see Section 25450 (peace officer exemption).

For an honorably retired federal officer or agent carrying a loaded firearm, see Section 26020.

See Section 16520 ("firearm"). [38 Cal.L.Rev.Comm. Reports 217 (2009)].

Cross References

Firearm defined for purposes of this Part, see Penal Code § 16520.
Honorably retired defined, see Penal Code § 16690.
Identification issued to retired peace officers, see Penal Code § 538d.
Penalty for possession of loaded firearms or enumerated prohibited weapons within State Capitol, legislative offices, etc., exception for retired peace officer with authorization to carry concealed weapons, see Penal Code § 171c.
Private patrol officers, assessment of administrative fines, prohibited acts, concealed weapons, see Business and Professions Code § 7583.37.

§ 25655. Person authorized to carry concealed weapon; application of Section 25400

Section 25400 does not apply to, or affect, the carrying of a pistol, revolver, or other firearm capable of being concealed upon the person by a person who is authorized to carry that weapon in a concealed manner pursuant to Chapter 4 (commencing with Section 26150). *(Added by Stats.2010, c. 711 (S.B.1080), § 6, operative Jan. 1, 2012.)*

Law Revision Commission Comments

Section 25655 continues former Section 12027(j) without substantive change.

For an exemption relating to transportation of a firearm to a place designated by a person who is authorized to issue licenses to carry firearms, see Section 25545.

See Section 16530 ("firearm capable of being concealed upon the person," "pistol," and "revolver"). [38 Cal.L.Rev.Comm. Reports 217 (2009)].

Cross References

Firearm capable of being concealed upon the person defined for purposes of this Part, see Penal Code § 16530.
Firearm defined for purposes of this Part, see Penal Code § 16520.
Pistol defined for purposes of this Part, see Penal Code § 16530.
Revolver defined for purposes of this Part, see Penal Code § 16530.

Research References

2 Witkin, California Criminal Law 4th Crimes Against Public Peace and Welfare § 207 (2021), Exempt Persons.

ARTICLE 5. CONCEALED CARRYING OF FIREARM AS A NUISANCE

§ 25700. Unlawful carrying of handgun as nuisance; application of Section 25400

(a) The unlawful carrying of any handgun in violation of Section 25400 is a nuisance and is subject to Sections 18000 and 18005.

(b) This section does not apply to any of the following:

(1) Any firearm in the possession of the Department of Fish and Game.

(2) Any firearm that was used in the violation of any provision of the Fish and Game Code or any regulation adopted pursuant thereto.

(3) Any firearm that is forfeited pursuant to Section 5008.6 of the Public Resources Code. *(Added by Stats.2010, c. 711 (S.B.1080), § 6, operative Jan. 1, 2012.)*

Law Revision Commission Comments

With respect to unlawful concealed carrying of a handgun, subdivision (a) of Section 25700 continues former Section 12028(a) without substantive change.

With respect to unlawful concealed carrying of a handgun, subdivision (b) continues former Section 12028(e) without substantive change.

See Sections 16520 ("firearm"), 16640 ("handgun"). [38 Cal.L.Rev.Comm. Reports 217 (2009)].

Cross References

Confiscation of firearms or deadly or dangerous weapons owned or possessed by gang members, see Penal Code § 186.22a.
Firearm defined for purposes of this Part, see Penal Code § 16520.
Handgun defined for purposes of this Part, see Penal Code § 16640.
Licenses to carry concealed weapons, see Penal Code § 26150 et seq.
Public nuisances, see Civil Code § 3490 et seq.

Research References

2 Witkin, California Criminal Law 4th Crimes Against Public Peace and Welfare § 263 (2021), Nuisances.

CHAPTER 3. CARRYING A LOADED FIREARM

ARTICLE 1. ARMED CRIMINAL ACTION

§ 25800. Armed criminal action; punishment

(a) Every person who carries a loaded firearm with the intent to commit a felony is guilty of armed criminal action.

(b) Armed criminal action is punishable by imprisonment in a county jail not exceeding one year, or in the state prison. *(Added by Stats.2010, c. 711 (S.B.1080), § 6, operative Jan. 1, 2012.)*

Law Revision Commission Comments

Section 25800 continues former Section 12023 without substantive change.

The definition of "loaded" for armed criminal action differs from the definition of "loaded" for the crime of carrying a loaded firearm in public. See Section 16840 ("loaded" and "loaded firearm"). For yet another definition of "loaded," see Fish and Game Code § 2006 ("A rifle or shotgun shall be deemed to be loaded for the purposes of this section when there is an unexpended cartridge or shell in the firing chamber but not when the only cartridges or shells are in the magazine.").

See also Section 16520 ("firearm"). [38 Cal.L.Rev.Comm. Reports 217 (2009)].

Cross References

Felony defined, see Penal Code § 17.
Firearm defined for purposes of this Part, see Penal Code § 16520.
Licenses to carry concealed weapons, see Penal Code § 26150 et seq.
Loaded defined, see Penal Code § 16840.
Possession of deadly weapon with intent to assault another, see Penal Code § 17500.
Prison or state prison defined for purposes of this Code, see Penal Code § 6081.

Research References

California Jury Instructions - Criminal 12.53, Armed Criminal Action.
2 Witkin, California Criminal Law 4th Crimes Against Public Peace and Welfare § 64 (2021), Improper Picketing Activity.
2 Witkin, California Criminal Law 4th Crimes Against Public Peace and Welfare § 261 (2021), Carrying Loaded Firearm With Intent to Commit Felony.
3 Witkin, California Criminal Law 4th Punishment § 358 (2021), P.C. 12022.5: Personal Use of Firearm.

ARTICLE 2. CRIME OF CARRYING A LOADED FIREARM IN PUBLIC

§ 25850. Carrying a loaded firearm in public; examination of firearm by peace officer; punishment; arrest without warrant

(a) A person is guilty of carrying a loaded firearm when the person carries a loaded firearm on the person or in a vehicle while in any public place or on any public street in an incorporated city or in any public place or on any public street in a prohibited area of unincorporated territory.

(b) In order to determine whether or not a firearm is loaded for the purpose of enforcing this section, peace officers are authorized to examine any firearm carried by anyone on the person or in a vehicle while in any public place or on any public street in an incorporated city or prohibited area of an unincorporated territory. Refusal to allow a peace officer to inspect a firearm pursuant to this section constitutes probable cause for arrest for violation of this section.

(c) Carrying a loaded firearm in violation of this section is punishable, as follows:

(1) Where the person previously has been convicted of any felony, or of any crime made punishable by a provision listed in Section 16580, as a felony.

(2) Where the firearm is stolen and the person knew or had reasonable cause to believe that it was stolen, as a felony.

(3) Where the person is an active participant in a criminal street gang, as defined in subdivision (a) of Section 186.22, under the Street Terrorism Enforcement and Prevention Act (Chapter 11 (commencing with Section 186.20) of Title 7 of Part 1), as a felony.

(4) Where the person is not in lawful possession of the firearm, or is within a class of persons prohibited from possessing or acquiring a firearm pursuant to Chapter 2 (commencing with Section 29800) or Chapter 3 (commencing with Section 29900) of Division 9 of this title, or Section 8100 or 8103 of the Welfare and Institutions Code, as a felony.

(5) Where the person has been convicted of a crime against a person or property, or of a narcotics or dangerous drug violation, by imprisonment pursuant to subdivision (h) of Section 1170, or by imprisonment in a county jail not to exceed one year, by a fine not to exceed one thousand dollars ($1,000), or by both that imprisonment and fine.

(6) Where the person is not listed with the Department of Justice pursuant to Section 11106 as the registered owner of the handgun, by imprisonment pursuant to subdivision (h) of Section 1170, or by imprisonment in a county jail not to exceed one year, or by a fine not to exceed one thousand dollars ($1,000), or both that fine and imprisonment.

(7) In all cases other than those specified in paragraphs (1) to (6), inclusive, as a misdemeanor, punishable by imprisonment in a county jail not to exceed one year, by a fine not to exceed one thousand dollars ($1,000), or by both that imprisonment and fine.

(d)(1) Every person convicted under this section who has previously been convicted of an offense enumerated in Section 23515, or of any crime made punishable under a provision listed in Section 16580, shall serve a term of at least three months in a county jail, or, if granted probation or if the execution or imposition of sentence is suspended, it shall be a condition thereof that the person be imprisoned for a period of at least three months.

(2) The court shall apply the three-month minimum sentence except in unusual cases where the interests of justice would best be served by granting probation or suspending the imposition or execution of sentence without the minimum imprisonment required in this section or by granting probation or suspending the imposition or execution of sentence with conditions other than those set forth in this section, in which case, the court shall specify on the record and shall enter on the minutes the circumstances indicating that the interests of justice would best be served by that disposition.

(e) A violation of this section that is punished by imprisonment in a county jail not exceeding one year shall not constitute a conviction of a crime punishable by imprisonment for a term exceeding one year for the purposes of determining federal firearms eligibility under Section 922(g)(1) of Title 18 of the United States Code.

(f) Nothing in this section, or in Article 3 (commencing with Section 25900) or Article 4 (commencing with Section 26000), shall preclude prosecution under Chapter 2 (commencing with Section 29800) or Chapter 3 (commencing with Section 29900) of Division 9 of this title, Section 8100 or 8103 of the Welfare and Institutions Code, or any other law with a greater penalty than this section.

(g) Notwithstanding paragraphs (2) and (3) of subdivision (a) of Section 836, a peace officer may make an arrest without a warrant:

(1) When the person arrested has violated this section, although not in the officer's presence.

(2) Whenever the officer has reasonable cause to believe that the person to be arrested has violated this section, whether or not this section has, in fact, been violated.

(h) A peace officer may arrest a person for a violation of paragraph (6) of subdivision (c), if the peace officer has probable cause to believe that the person is carrying a handgun in violation of this section and that person is not listed with the Department of Justice pursuant to paragraph (1) of subdivision (c) of Section 11106 as the registered owner of that handgun. *(Added by Stats.2010, c. 711 (S.B.1080), § 6, operative Jan. 1, 2012. Amended by Stats.2011, c. 15 (A.B.109), § 544, eff. April 4, 2011, operative Jan. 1, 2012.)*

Validity

For validity of this section, see Peruta v. County of San Diego, C.A.9 (Cal.)2014, 742 F.3d 1144, on rehearing en banc 824 F.3d 919, certiorari denied 137 S.Ct. 1995, 198 L.Ed.2d 746.

Law Revision Commission Comments

Subdivision (a) of Section 25850 continues former Section 12031(a)(1) without substantive change.

Subdivision (b) continues former Section 12031(e) without substantive change.

Subdivision (c) continues former Section 12031(a)(2) without substantive change. Subdivision (d) continues former Section 12031(a)(6) without substantive change. For guidance in applying paragraphs (c)(1) and (d)(1), see Section 16015 (determining existence of prior conviction).

Subdivision (e) continues former Section 12031(a)(7) without substantive change.

Subdivision (f) continues former Section 12031(a)(4) without substantive change.

Subdivision (g) continues former Section 12031(a)(5)(A) without substantive change.

Subdivision (h) continues former Section 12031(a)(5)(B) without substantive change.

The definition of "loaded" for the crime of carrying a loaded firearm in public differs from the definition of "loaded" for armed criminal action. See Section 16840 ("loaded" and "loaded firearm"). For yet another definition of "loaded," see Fish and Game Code § 2006 ("A rifle or shotgun shall be deemed to be loaded for the purposes of this section when there is an unexpended cartridge or shell in the firing chamber but not when the only cartridges or shells are in the magazine.").

See also Sections 16520 ("firearm"), 16640 ("handgun"), 16750 ("lawful possession of the firearm"), 17030 ("prohibited area"). [38 Cal.L.Rev.Comm. Reports 217 (2009)].

Cross References

Felonies, definition and penalties, see Penal Code §§ 17, 18.
Firearm defined for purposes of this Part, see Penal Code § 16520.
Handgun defined for purposes of this Part, see Penal Code § 16640.
Loaded defined, see Penal Code § 16840.
Misdemeanor, violation of this section while committing act relative to threatening crime victim, witness or informant, punishment, see Penal Code § 140.
Misdemeanors, definition and penalties, see Penal Code §§ 17, 19, 19.2.
Possession of loaded firearms, within state capitol or legislative offices, see Penal Code §§ 171c, 171d.
Prohibition against carrying firearm or deadly weapon while engaged in labor related picketing, see Penal Code § 17510.

Research References

California Jury Instructions - Criminal 12.54, Carrying Loaded Firearm.
California Jury Instructions - Criminal 12.54.1, Carrying Loaded Firearm—Gang Member.
California Jury Instructions - Criminal 16.470, Carrying Loaded Firearm.
2 Witkin, California Criminal Law 4th Crimes Against Public Peace and Welfare § 208 (2021), Exempt Activities.
2 Witkin, California Criminal Law 4th Crimes Against Public Peace and Welfare § 249 (2021), Offenses.
2 Witkin, California Criminal Law 4th Crimes Against Public Peace and Welfare § 250 (2021), Punishment.
2 Witkin, California Criminal Law 4th Crimes Against Public Peace and Welfare § 251 (2021), Exemptions.
2 Witkin, California Criminal Law 4th Crimes Against Public Peace and Welfare § 253 (2021), Openly Displaying or Carrying Imitation or Unloaded Firearm.
2 Witkin, California Criminal Law 4th Crimes Against Public Peace and Welfare § 257 (2021), Firearms.
2 Witkin, California Criminal Law 4th Crimes Against Public Peace and Welfare § 259 (2021), Playground or Youth Center.
2 Witkin, California Criminal Law 4th Crimes Against Public Peace and Welfare § 260 (2021), Motor Vehicle.
4 Witkin, California Criminal Law 4th Illegally Obtained Evidence § 343 (2021), Search for Dangerous Weapon.
4 Witkin, California Criminal Law 4th Pretrial Proceedings § 26 (2021), Determining Probable Cause.
4 Witkin, California Criminal Law 4th Pretrial Proceedings § 33 (2021), Other Exceptions.

ARTICLE 3. PEACE OFFICER EXEMPTION TO THE CRIME OF CARRYING A LOADED FIREARM IN PUBLIC

Section

§ 25900. Peace officers exempt from application of Section 25850

As provided in this article, Section 25850 does not apply to any of the following:

(a) Any peace officer, listed in Section 830.1 or 830.2, or subdivision (a) of Section 830.33, whether active or honorably retired.

(b) Any other duly appointed peace officer.

(c) Any honorably retired peace officer listed in subdivision (c) of Section 830.5.

(d) Any other honorably retired peace officer who during the course and scope of his or her appointment as a peace officer was authorized to, and did, carry a firearm.

(e) Any full-time paid peace officer of another state or the federal government who is carrying out official duties while in California.

(f) Any person summoned by any of these officers to assist in making arrests or preserving the peace while the person is actually engaged in assisting that officer. *(Added by Stats.2010, c. 711 (S.B.1080), § 6, operative Jan. 1, 2012. Amended by Stats.2013, c. 267 (A.B.703), § 2.)*

Law Revision Commission Comments

Section 25900 continues the first sentence of the first paragraph of former Section 12031(b)(1) without substantive change.

For an exemption relating to honorably retired federal officers and agents, see Section 26020.

For guidance on a retired peace officer carrying a concealed firearm, see Sections 25450–25475. For guidance on a retired peace officer carrying a concealed and loaded firearm, see Sections 26300–26325.

See Sections 16520 ("firearm"), 16690 ("honorably retired"). [38 Cal. L.Rev.Comm. Reports 217 (2009)].

Cross References

Firearm defined for purposes of this Part, see Penal Code § 16520.
Honorably retired defined, see Penal Code § 16690.
Proprietary private security officer registration provisions, exemptions to officers carrying unloaded and exposed handguns, see Business and Professions Code § 7574.14.
Retired peace officers, see Business and Professions Code § 7582.2.

Research References

2 Witkin, California Criminal Law 4th Crimes Against Public Peace and Welfare § 64 (2021), Improper Picketing Activity.
2 Witkin, California Criminal Law 4th Crimes Against Public Peace and Welfare § 251 (2021), Exemptions.

§ 25905. Identification certificate for retired peace officer; endorsement for carrying a loaded firearm

(a)(1) Any peace officer described in Section 25900 who has been honorably retired shall be issued an identification certificate by the law enforcement agency from which the officer has retired.

(2) If the agency from which the officer has retired is no longer providing law enforcement services or the relevant governmental body is dissolved, the agency that subsequently provides law enforcement services for that jurisdiction shall issue the identification certificate to that peace officer. This paragraph shall apply only if the following conditions are met:

(A) The successor agency is in possession of the retired officer's complete personnel records or can otherwise verify the retired officer's honorably retired status.

(B) The retired officer is in compliance with all the requirements of the successor agency for the issuance of a retirement identification card and concealed weapon endorsement.

(b) The issuing agency may charge a fee necessary to cover any reasonable expenses incurred by the agency in issuing certificates pursuant to Sections 25900, 25910, 25925, and this section.

(c) Any officer, except an officer listed in Section 830.1 or 830.2, subdivision (a) of Section 830.33, or subdivision (c) of Section 830.5 who retired prior to January 1, 1981, shall have an endorsement on the identification certificate stating that the issuing agency approves the officer's carrying of a loaded firearm.

(d) An honorably retired peace officer listed in Section 830.1 or 830.2, subdivision (a) of Section 830.33, or subdivision (c) of Section 830.5 who retired prior to January 1, 1981, shall not be required to obtain an endorsement from the issuing agency to carry a loaded firearm. *(Added by Stats.2010, c. 711 (S.B.1080), § 6, operative Jan. 1, 2012. Amended by Stats.2013, c. 149 (S.B.303), § 1.)*

Law Revision Commission Comments

Subdivision (a) of Section 25905 continues the second sentence of the first paragraph of former Section 12031(b)(1) without substantive change.

Subdivision (b) continues the third sentence of the first paragraph of former Section 12031(b)(1) without substantive change.

Subdivision (c) continues the second paragraph of former Section 12031(b)(1) without substantive change.

Subdivision (d) continues the second sentence of former Section 12031(b)(2) without substantive change.

For guidance on a retired peace officer carrying a concealed firearm, see Sections 25450–25475. For guidance on a retired peace officer carrying a concealed and loaded firearm, see Sections 26300–26325.

See Sections 16520 ("firearm"), 16690 ("honorably retired"), 16840 ("loaded" and "loaded firearm"). [38 Cal.L.Rev.Comm. Reports 217 (2009)].

Cross References

Firearm defined for purposes of this Part, see Penal Code § 16520.
Honorably retired defined, see Penal Code § 16690.
Loaded defined, see Penal Code § 16840.
Retired peace officers, see Business and Professions Code § 7582.2.

§ 25910. Required endorsement format

(a) Except as provided in subdivision (b), no endorsement or renewal endorsement issued pursuant to Section 25915 shall be effective unless it is in the format set forth in subdivision (c) of Section 25460.

(b) Any peace officer listed in subdivision (f) of Section 830.2 or in subdivision (c) of Section 830.5, who is retired between January 2, 1981, and on or before December 31, 1988, and who is authorized to carry a loaded firearm pursuant to this article, shall not be required to have an endorsement in the format set forth in subdivision (c) of Section 25460 until the time of the issuance, on or after January 1, 1989, of a renewal endorsement pursuant to Section 25915. *(Added by Stats.2010, c. 711 (S.B.1080), § 6, operative Jan. 1, 2012.)*

Law Revision Commission Comments

Section 25910 continues the third paragraph of former Section 12031(b)(1) without substantive change.

See Sections 16520 ("firearm"), 16840 ("loaded" and "loaded firearm"). [38 Cal.L.Rev.Comm. Reports 217 (2009)].

Cross References

Firearm defined for purposes of this Part, see Penal Code § 16520.
Loaded defined, see Penal Code § 16840.
Retired peace officers, see Business and Professions Code § 7582.2.

§ 25915. Renewal of retired peace officer's privilege to carry loaded firearm

Every five years, a retired peace officer, except an officer listed in Section 830.1 or 830.2, subdivision (a) of Section 830.33, or subdivision (c) of Section 830.5 who retired prior to January 1, 1981, shall petition the issuing agency, or a successor agency pursuant to paragraph (2) of subdivision (a) of Section 25905, for renewal of the privilege to carry a loaded firearm. *(Added by Stats.2010, c. 711 (S.B.1080), § 6, operative Jan. 1, 2012. Amended by Stats.2013, c. 149 (S.B.303), § 2.)*

Law Revision Commission Comments

Section 25915 continues the first sentence of former Section 12031(b)(2) without substantive change.

See Sections 16520 ("firearm"), 16840 ("loaded" and "loaded firearm"). [38 Cal.L.Rev.Comm. Reports 217 (2009)].

Cross References

Firearm defined for purposes of this Part, see Penal Code § 16520.
Loaded defined, see Penal Code § 16840.
Retired peace officers, see Business and Professions Code § 7582.2.

§ 25920. Denial or revocation of retired peace officer's privilege to carry loaded firearm

(a) The agency from which a peace officer is honorably retired, or a successor agency pursuant to paragraph (2) of subdivision (a) of Section 25905, may, upon initial retirement of the peace officer, or at any time subsequent thereto, deny or revoke for good cause the retired officer's privilege to carry a loaded firearm.

(b) A peace officer who is listed in Section 830.1 or 830.2, subdivision (a) of Section 830.33, or subdivision (c) of Section 830.5 who is retired prior to January 1, 1981, shall have the privilege to carry a loaded firearm denied or revoked by having the agency from which the officer retired, or a successor agency pursuant to paragraph (2) of subdivision (a) of Section 25905, stamp on the officer's identification certificate "No CCW privilege." *(Added by Stats.2010, c. 711 (S.B.1080), § 6, operative Jan. 1, 2012. Amended by Stats.2013, c. 149 (S.B.303), § 3.)*

Law Revision Commission Comments

Subdivision (a) of Section 25920 continues the third sentence of former Section 12031(b)(2) without substantive change.

Subdivision (b) continues the fourth sentence of former Section 12031(b)(2) without substantive change.

See Sections 16360 ("CCW"), 16520 ("firearm"), 16690 ("honorably retired"), 16840 ("loaded" and "loaded firearm"). [38 Cal.L.Rev.Comm. Reports 217 (2009)].

Cross References

Firearm defined for purposes of this Part, see Penal Code § 16520.
Honorably retired defined, see Penal Code § 16690.
Loaded defined, see Penal Code § 16840.
Retired peace officers, see Business and Professions Code § 7582.2.

§ 25925. Firearm training and qualification requirements for retired peace officers; responsibility to maintain eligibility

(a) An honorably retired peace officer who is listed in subdivision (c) of Section 830.5 and authorized to carry a loaded firearm by this article shall meet the training requirements of Section 832 and shall qualify with the firearm at least annually.

(b) The individual retired peace officer shall be responsible for maintaining eligibility to carry a loaded firearm.

(c) The Department of Justice shall provide subsequent arrest notification pursuant to Section 11105.2 regarding honorably retired peace officers listed in subdivision (c) of Section 830.5 to the agency from which the officer has retired, or a successor agency pursuant to paragraph (2) of subdivision (a) of Section 25905. *(Added by Stats.2010, c. 711 (S.B.1080), § 6, operative Jan. 1, 2012. Amended by Stats.2013, c. 149 (S.B.303), § 4.)*

Law Revision Commission Comments

Section 25925 continues former Section 12031(b)(3) without substantive change.

See Sections 16520 ("firearm"), 16690 ("honorably retired"), 16840 ("loaded" and "loaded firearm"). [38 Cal.L.Rev.Comm. Reports 217 (2009)].

Cross References

Firearm defined for purposes of this Part, see Penal Code § 16520.
Honorably retired defined, see Penal Code § 16690.
Loaded defined, see Penal Code § 16840.
Retired peace officers, see Business and Professions Code § 7582.2.

ARTICLE 4. OTHER EXEMPTIONS TO THE CRIME OF CARRYING A LOADED FIREARM IN PUBLIC

Section

§ 26000. Members of military forces exempt from application of Section 25850

Section 25850 does not apply to members of the military forces of this state or of the United States engaged in the performance of their duties. *(Added by Stats.2010, c. 711 (S.B.1080), § 6, operative Jan. 1, 2012.)*

Law Revision Commission Comments

Section 26000 continues former Section 12031(b)(4) without substantive change. [38 Cal.L.Rev.Comm. Reports 217 (2009)].

Research References

2 Witkin, California Criminal Law 4th Crimes Against Public Peace and Welfare § 251 (2021), Exemptions.
2 Witkin, California Criminal Law 4th Crimes Against Public Peace and Welfare § 257 (2021), Firearms.

§ 26005. Persons using target ranges; members of shooting clubs; exemption from application of Section 25850

Section 25850 does not apply to either of the following:

(a) Persons who are using target ranges for the purpose of practice shooting with a firearm.

(b) Members of shooting clubs while hunting on the premises of those clubs. *(Added by Stats.2010, c. 711 (S.B.1080), § 6, operative Jan. 1, 2012.)*

Law Revision Commission Comments

Section 26005 continues former Section 12031(b)(5) without substantive change.

See Section 16520 ("firearm"). [38 Cal.L.Rev.Comm. Reports 217 (2009)].

Cross References

Firearm defined for purposes of this Part, see Penal Code § 16520.

Research References

2 Witkin, California Criminal Law 4th Crimes Against Public Peace and Welfare § 251 (2021), Exemptions.

§ 26010. Carrying of handgun pursuant to Chapter 4 of Division 5 exempt from application of Section 25850

Section 25850 does not apply to the carrying of any handgun by any person as authorized pursuant to Chapter 4 (commencing with Section 26150) of Division 5. *(Added by Stats.2010, c. 711 (S.B. 1080), § 6, operative Jan. 1, 2012.)*

Law Revision Commission Comments

Section 26010 continues former Section 12031(b)(6) without substantive change.

See Section 16640 ("handgun"). [38 Cal.L.Rev.Comm. Reports 217 (2009)].

Cross References

Handgun defined for purposes of this Part, see Penal Code § 16640.

Research References

2 Witkin, California Criminal Law 4th Crimes Against Public Peace and Welfare § 251 (2021), Exemptions.

§ 26015. Armored vehicle guards exempt from application of Section 25850

Section 25850 does not apply to any armored vehicle guard, as defined in Section 7582.1 of the Business and Professions Code, if either of the following conditions is satisfied:

(a) The guard was hired prior to January 1, 1977, and is acting within the course and scope of employment.

(b) The guard was hired on or after January 1, 1977, has received a firearms qualification card from the Department of Consumer Affairs, and is acting within the course and scope of employment. *(Added by Stats.2010, c. 711 (S.B.1080), § 6, operative Jan. 1, 2012.)*

Law Revision Commission Comments

Section 26015 continues former Section 12031(b)(7) without substantive change. An erroneous cross-reference to Business and Professions Code Section 7521 has been corrected. [38 Cal.L.Rev.Comm. Reports 217 (2009)].

Cross References

Firearm defined for purposes of this Part, see Penal Code § 16520.
Private security services, regulation, licensing, and registration, see Business and Professions Code § 7582 et seq.

Research References

2 Witkin, California Criminal Law 4th Crimes Against Public Peace and Welfare § 251 (2021), Exemptions.

§ 26020. Retired federal officers exempt from application of Section 25850; certification; permit renewal; suspension

(a) Upon approval of the sheriff of the county in which the retiree resides, Section 25850 does not apply to any honorably retired federal officer or agent of any federal law enforcement agency, including, but not limited to, the Federal Bureau of Investigation, the United States Secret Service, the United States Customs Service, the federal Bureau of Alcohol, Tobacco, Firearms and Explosives, the Federal Bureau of Narcotics, the United States Drug Enforcement Administration, the United States Border Patrol, and any officer or agent of the Internal Revenue Service who was authorized to carry weapons while on duty, who was assigned to duty within the state for a period of not less than one year, or who retired from active service in the state.

(b) A retired federal officer or agent shall provide the sheriff with certification from the agency from which the officer or agent retired certifying that person's service in the state, stating the nature of that person's retirement, and indicating the agency's concurrence that the retired federal officer or agent should be accorded the privilege of carrying a loaded firearm.

(c) Upon approval, the sheriff shall issue a permit to the retired federal officer or agent indicating that the retiree may carry a loaded firearm in accordance with this section. The permit shall be valid for a period not exceeding five years, shall be carried by the retiree while carrying a loaded firearm, and may be revoked for good cause.

(d) The sheriff of the county in which the retired federal officer or agent resides may require recertification prior to a permit renewal, and may suspend the privilege for cause. The sheriff may charge a fee necessary to cover any reasonable expenses incurred by the county. *(Added by Stats.2010, c. 711 (S.B.1080), § 6, operative Jan. 1, 2012. Amended by Stats.2011, c. 296 (A.B.1023), § 231.)*

Law Revision Commission Comments

Section 26020 continues former Section 12031(b)(8) without substantive change.

For an exemption relating to honorably retired peace officers, see Section 25900 (peace officer exemption).

For an honorably retired federal officer or agent carrying a concealed firearm, see Section 25650.

See Sections 16520 ("firearm"), 16840 ("loaded" and "loaded firearm"). [38 Cal.L.Rev.Comm. Reports 217 (2009)].

Cross References

Firearm defined for purposes of this Part, see Penal Code § 16520.
Honorably retired defined, see Penal Code § 16690.
Loaded defined, see Penal Code § 16840.
Retired peace officers, see Business and Professions Code § 7582.2.

Research References

2 Witkin, California Criminal Law 4th Crimes Against Public Peace and Welfare § 251 (2021), Exemptions.

§ 26025. Completion of course in firearms training; other exemptions from application of Section 25850

Section 25850 does not apply to any of the following who have completed a regular course in firearms training approved by the Commission on Peace Officer Standards and Training:

(a) Patrol special police officers appointed by the police commission of any city, county, or city and county under the express terms of its charter who also, under the express terms of the charter, satisfy all of the following requirements:

(1) They are subject to suspension or dismissal after a hearing on charges duly filed with the commission after a fair and impartial trial.

(2) They are not less than 18 years of age or more than 40 years of age.

(3) They possess physical qualifications prescribed by the commission.

(4) They are designated by the police commission as the owners of a certain beat or territory as may be fixed from time to time by the police commission.

(b) Animal control officers or zookeepers, regularly compensated in that capacity by a governmental agency, when carrying weapons while acting in the course and scope of their employment and when designated by a local ordinance or, if the governmental agency is not authorized to act by ordinance, by a resolution, either individually or by class, to carry the weapons.

(c) Persons who are authorized to carry the weapons pursuant to Section 14502 of the Corporations Code, while actually engaged in the performance of their duties pursuant to that section.

(d) Harbor police officers designated pursuant to Section 663.5 of the Harbors and Navigation Code. *(Added by Stats.2010, c. 711 (S.B.1080), § 6, operative Jan. 1, 2012.)*

Law Revision Commission Comments

Section 26025 continues former Section 12031(c) without substantive change. [38 Cal.L.Rev.Comm. Reports 217 (2009)].

Cross References

Firearm defined for purposes of this Part, see Penal Code § 16520.

Research References

2 Witkin, California Criminal Law 4th Crimes Against Public Peace and Welfare § 251 (2021), Exemptions.

§ 26030. Completion of courses in carrying and use of firearms and exercise of powers of arrest; exemption from application of Section 25850

(a) Section 25850 does not apply to any of the following who have been issued a certificate pursuant to subdivision (d):

(1) Guards or messengers of common carriers, banks, and other financial institutions, while actually employed in and about the shipment, transportation, or delivery of any money, treasure, bullion, bonds, or other thing of value within this state.

(2) Guards of contract carriers operating armored vehicles pursuant to California Highway Patrol and Public Utilities Commission authority, if they were hired prior to January 1, 1977.

(3) Guards of contract carriers operating armored vehicles pursuant to California Highway Patrol and Public Utilities Commission authority, if they were hired on or after January 1, 1977, and they have completed a course in the carrying and use of firearms that meets the standards prescribed by the Department of Consumer Affairs.

(4) Private investigators licensed pursuant to Chapter 11.3 (commencing with Section 7512) of Division 3 of the Business and Professions Code, while acting within the course and scope of their employment.

(5) Uniformed employees of private investigators licensed pursuant to Chapter 11.3 (commencing with Section 7512) of Division 3 of the Business and Professions Code, while acting within the course and scope of their employment.

(6) Private patrol operators licensed pursuant to Chapter 11.5 (commencing with Section 7580) of Division 3 of the Business and Professions Code, while acting within the course and scope of their employment.

(7) Uniformed employees of private patrol operators licensed pursuant to Chapter 11.5 (commencing with Section 7580) of Division 3 of the Business and Professions Code, while acting within the course and scope of their employment.

(8) Alarm company operators licensed pursuant to Chapter 11.6 (commencing with Section 7590) of Division 3 of the Business and Professions Code, while acting within the course and scope of their employment.

(9) Uniformed security guards or night watch persons employed by any public agency, while acting within the scope and course of their employment.

(10) Uniformed security guards, regularly employed and compensated in that capacity by persons engaged in any lawful business, and uniformed alarm agents employed by an alarm company operator, while actually engaged in protecting and preserving the property of their employers, or on duty or en route to or from their residences or their places of employment, and security guards and alarm agents en route to or from their residences or employer-required range training.

(b) Nothing in paragraph (10) of subdivision (a) shall be construed to prohibit cities and counties from enacting ordinances requiring alarm agents to register their names.

(c) A certificate under this section shall not be required of any person who is a peace officer, who has completed all training required by law for the exercise of the person's power as a peace officer, and who is employed while not on duty as a peace officer.

(d) The Department of Consumer Affairs may issue a certificate to any person referred to in this section, upon notification by the school where the course was completed, that the person has successfully completed a course in the carrying and use of firearms and a course of training in the exercise of the powers of arrest, which meet the standards prescribed by the department pursuant to Section 7583.5 of the Business and Professions Code. *(Added by Stats.2010, c. 711 (S.B.1080), § 6, operative Jan. 1, 2012.)*

Law Revision Commission Comments

The introductory clause of subdivision (a) of Section 26030 continues the first sentence of the introductory paragraph of former Section 12031(d) without substantive change.

Subdivision (a)(1) continues former Section 12031(d)(1) without substantive change.

Subdivision (a)(2)-(3) continues former Section 12031(d)(2) without substantive change.

With respect to licensed private investigators, subdivision (a)(4) continues former Section 12031(d)(3) without substantive change. An erroneous cross-reference to "Chapter 11.5 (commencing with Section 7512) of Division 3 of the Business and Professions Code" has been corrected.

With respect to uniformed employees of licensed private investigators, subdivision (a)(5) continues former Section 12031(d)(6) without substantive change. An erroneous cross-reference to "Chapter 11.5 (commencing with Section 7512) of Division 3 of the Business and Professions Code" has been corrected.

With respect to licensed private patrol operators, subdivision (a)(6) continues former Section 12031(d)(3) without substantive change. An erroneous cross-reference to "Chapter 11.5 (commencing with Section 7512) of Division 3 of the Business and Professions Code" has been corrected.

With respect to uniformed employees of licensed private patrol operators, subdivision (a)(7) continues former Section 12031(d)(6) without substantive change. An erroneous cross-reference to "Chapter 11.5 (commencing with Section 7512) of Division 3 of the Business and Professions Code" has been corrected.

With respect to licensed alarm company operators, subdivision (a)(8) continues former Section 12031(d)(3) without substantive change.

Subdivision (a)(9) continues former Section 12031(d)(4) without substantive change.

Subdivision (a)(10) continues the first sentence of former Section 12031(d)(5) without substantive change.

Subdivision (b) continues the second sentence of former Section 12031(d)(5) without substantive change.

Subdivision (c) continues the second sentence of the introductory paragraph of former Section 12031(d) without substantive change.

Subdivision (d) continues former Section 12033 without substantive change.

See Section 16520 ("firearm"). [38 Cal.L.Rev.Comm. Reports 217 (2009)].

Cross References

Firearm defined for purposes of this Part, see Penal Code § 16520.
Private investigators, possession of firearms, see Business and Professions Code §§ 7542, 7583.29.
Private patrol operators, security guards or patrol persons, see Business and Professions Code § 7581.
Private security services, regulation, licensing, and registration, see Business and Professions Code § 7582 et seq.
Proprietary private security officer registration provisions, exemptions to officers carrying unloaded and exposed handguns, see Business and Professions Code § 7574.14.

Research References

2 Witkin, California Criminal Law 4th Crimes Against Public Peace and Welfare § 251 (2021), Exemptions.

§ 26035. Carrying of loaded firearm at place of business, private property exempt from application of Section 25850

Nothing in Section 25850 shall prevent any person engaged in any lawful business, including a nonprofit organization, or any officer, employee, or agent authorized by that person for lawful purposes connected with that business, from having a loaded firearm within the person's place of business, or any person in lawful possession of private property from having a loaded firearm on that property. *(Added by Stats.2010, c. 711 (S.B.1080), § 6, operative Jan. 1, 2012.)*

Law Revision Commission Comments

Section 26035 continues former Section 12031(h) without substantive change.

See Sections 16520 ("firearm"), 16840 ("loaded" and "loaded firearm"). [38 Cal.L.Rev.Comm. Reports 217 (2009)].

Cross References

Firearm defined for purposes of this Part, see Penal Code § 16520.
Loaded defined, see Penal Code § 16840.

Research References

2 Witkin, California Criminal Law 4th Crimes Against Public Peace and Welfare § 251 (2021), Exemptions.

§ 26040. Lawful hunting exempt from application of Section 25850

Nothing in Section 25850 shall prevent any person from carrying a loaded firearm in an area within an incorporated city while engaged in hunting, provided that the hunting at that place and time is not prohibited by the city council. *(Added by Stats.2010, c. 711 (S.B. 1080), § 6, operative Jan. 1, 2012.)*

Law Revision Commission Comments

Section 26040 continues former Section 12031(i) without substantive change.

See Sections 16520 ("firearm"), 16840 ("loaded" and "loaded firearm"). [38 Cal.L.Rev.Comm. Reports 217 (2009)].

Cross References

Firearm defined for purposes of this Part, see Penal Code § 16520.
Loaded defined, see Penal Code § 16840.

Research References

2 Witkin, California Criminal Law 4th Crimes Against Public Peace and Welfare § 251 (2021), Exemptions.

§ 26045. Carrying of weapon to protect person or property; persons under threat from subject of restraining order; exempt from application of Section 25850

(a) Nothing in Section 25850 is intended to preclude the carrying of any loaded firearm, under circumstances where it would otherwise be lawful, by a person who reasonably believes that any person or the property of any person is in immediate, grave danger and that the carrying of the weapon is necessary for the preservation of that person or property.

(b) A violation of Section 25850 is justifiable when a person who possesses a firearm reasonably believes that person is in grave danger because of circumstances forming the basis of a current restraining order issued by a court against another person who has been found to pose a threat to the life or safety of the person who possesses the firearm. This subdivision may not apply when the circumstances involve a mutual restraining order issued pursuant to Division 10 (commencing with Section 6200) of the Family Code absent a factual finding of a specific threat to the person's life or safety. It is not the intent of the Legislature to limit, restrict, or narrow the application of current statutory or judicial authority to apply this or other justifications to a defendant charged with violating Section 25850 or committing another similar offense. Upon trial for violating Section 25850, the trier of fact shall determine whether the defendant was acting out of a reasonable belief that the defendant was in grave danger.

(c) As used in this section, "immediate" means the brief interval before and after the local law enforcement agency, when reasonably possible, has been notified of the danger and before the arrival of its assistance. *(Added by Stats.2010, c. 711 (S.B.1080), § 6, operative Jan. 1, 2012. Amended by Stats.2018, c. 185 (A.B.2176), § 7, eff. Jan. 1, 2019.)*

Law Revision Commission Comments

Subdivision (a) of Section 26045 continues the first sentence of former Section 12031(j)(1) without substantive change.

Subdivision (b) continues former Section 12031(j)(2) without substantive change.

Subdivision (c) continues the second sentence of former Section 12031(j)(1) without substantive change.

See Sections 16520 ("firearm"), 16840 ("loaded" and "loaded firearm"). [38 Cal.L.Rev.Comm. Reports 217 (2009)].

Section 26045 is amended to correct an erroneous cross-reference. This is a nonsubstantive change. [44 Cal.L.Rev.Comm. Reports 471 (2015)].

Cross References

Firearm defined for purposes of this Part, see Penal Code § 16520.
Loaded defined, see Penal Code § 16840.

Research References

2 Witkin, California Criminal Law 4th Crimes Against Public Peace and Welfare § 251 (2021), Exemptions.

§ 26050. Persons making lawful arrest exempt from application of Section 25850

Nothing in Section 25850 is intended to preclude the carrying of a loaded firearm by any person while engaged in the act of making or attempting to make a lawful arrest. *(Added by Stats.2010, c. 711 (S.B.1080), § 6, operative Jan. 1, 2012.)*

Law Revision Commission Comments

Section 26050 continues former Section 12031(k) without substantive change.

See Sections 16520 ("firearm"), 16840 ("loaded" and "loaded firearm"). [38 Cal.L.Rev.Comm. Reports 217 (2009)].

Cross References

Firearm defined for purposes of this Part, see Penal Code § 16520.
Loaded defined, see Penal Code § 16840.

Research References

2 Witkin, California Criminal Law 4th Crimes Against Public Peace and Welfare § 251 (2021), Exemptions.

§ 26055. Possession of loaded weapon at place of residence exempt from application of Section 25850

Nothing in Section 25850 shall prevent any person from having a loaded weapon, if it is otherwise lawful, at the person's place of residence, including any temporary residence or campsite. *(Added by Stats.2010, c. 711 (S.B.1080), § 6, operative Jan. 1, 2012.)*

Law Revision Commission Comments

Section 26055 continues former Section 12031(*l*) without substantive change.

See Section 16840 ("loaded" and "loaded firearm"). [38 Cal.L.Rev.Comm. Reports 217 (2009)].

Cross References

Loaded defined, see Penal Code § 16840.

Research References

2 Witkin, California Criminal Law 4th Crimes Against Public Peace and Welfare § 251 (2021), Exemptions.

§ 26060. Rocket propelled launcher aboard vessel or aircraft for emergency signaling purposes exempt from application of Section 25850

Nothing in Section 25850 shall prevent any person from storing aboard any vessel or aircraft any loaded or unloaded rocket, rocket propelled projectile launcher, or similar device designed primarily for emergency or distress signaling purposes, or from possessing that type of a device while in a permitted hunting area or traveling to or from a permitted hunting area and carrying a valid California permit or license to hunt. *(Added by Stats.2010, c. 711 (S.B.1080), § 6, operative Jan. 1, 2012.)*

Law Revision Commission Comments

Section 26060 continues former Section 12031.1 without substantive change. [38 Cal.L.Rev.Comm. Reports 217 (2009)].

Research References

2 Witkin, California Criminal Law 4th Crimes Against Public Peace and Welfare § 249 (2021), Offenses.

ARTICLE 5. LOADED FIREARM IN A MOTOR VEHICLE

§ 26100. Permitting loaded firearm in motor vehicle; discharge of firearm from motor vehicle; punishment

(a) It is a misdemeanor for a driver of any motor vehicle or the owner of any motor vehicle, whether or not the owner of the vehicle is occupying the vehicle, knowingly to permit any other person to carry into or bring into the vehicle a firearm in violation of Section 25850 of this code or Section 2006 of the Fish and Game Code.

(b) Any driver or owner of any vehicle, whether or not the owner of the vehicle is occupying the vehicle, who knowingly permits any other person to discharge any firearm from the vehicle is punishable by imprisonment in the county jail for not more than one year or in state prison for 16 months or two or three years.

(c) Any person who willfully and maliciously discharges a firearm from a motor vehicle at another person other than an occupant of a motor vehicle is guilty of a felony punishable by imprisonment in state prison for three, five, or seven years.

(d) Except as provided in Section 3002 of the Fish and Game Code, any person who willfully and maliciously discharges a firearm from a motor vehicle is guilty of a public offense punishable by imprisonment in the county jail for not more than one year or in the state prison. *(Added by Stats.2010, c. 711 (S.B.1080), § 6, operative Jan. 1, 2012.)*

Law Revision Commission Comments

Section 26100 continues former Section 12034 without substantive change. See Section 16520 ("firearm"). [38 Cal.L.Rev.Comm. Reports 217 (2009)].

Cross References

Criminal gang activity, patterns, engaging in acts punishable under this section, see Penal Code § 186.22.
Felonies, definition and penalties, see Penal Code §§ 17, 18.
Firearm defined for purposes of this Part, see Penal Code § 16520.
Juvenile court law, admission of public and persons having interest in case, exceptions, see Welfare and Institutions Code § 676.
Misdemeanors, definition and penalties, see Penal Code §§ 17, 19, 19.2.

Research References

California Jury Instructions - Criminal 9.04, Permitting Shooting from Vehicle.
California Jury Instructions - Criminal 9.05, Shooting from Vehicle at a Person.
California Jury Instructions - Criminal 9.06, Shooting from Vehicle.
California Jury Instructions - Criminal 16.475, Permitting Another to Carry Loaded Firearm Within Motor Vehicle.
2 Witkin, California Criminal Law 4th Crimes Against Public Peace and Welfare § 260 (2021), Motor Vehicle.
2 Witkin, California Criminal Law 4th Crimes Against Public Peace and Welfare § 496 (2021), Dangerous or Injurious Acts.
1 Witkin California Criminal Law 4th Crimes Against the Person § 41 (2021), Nature of Offense.
1 Witkin California Criminal Law 4th Crimes Against the Person § 51 (2021), Discharge of Firearm from Vehicle.
3 Witkin, California Criminal Law 4th Punishment § 359 (2021), P.C. 12022.53: Personal Use of Firearm in Specified Felonies.

CHAPTER 4. LICENSE TO CARRY A PISTOL, REVOLVER, OR OTHER FIREARM CAPABLE OF BEING CONCEALED UPON THE PERSON

§ 26150. Application for license to carry concealed weapon; county sheriff responsibilities; authority to enter into agreement with head of municipal police department

(a) When a person applies for a license to carry a pistol, revolver, or other firearm capable of being concealed upon the person, the sheriff of a county may issue a license to that person upon proof of all of the following:

(1) The applicant is of good moral character.

(2) Good cause exists for issuance of the license.

(3) The applicant is a resident of the county or a city within the county, or the applicant's principal place of employment or business is in the county or a city within the county and the applicant spends a substantial period of time in that place of employment or business.

(4) The applicant has completed a course of training as described in Section 26165.

(b) The sheriff may issue a license under subdivision (a) in either of the following formats:

(1) A license to carry concealed a pistol, revolver, or other firearm capable of being concealed upon the person.

(2) Where the population of the county is less than 200,000 persons according to the most recent federal decennial census, a license to carry loaded and exposed in only that county a pistol, revolver, or other firearm capable of being concealed upon the person.

(c)(1) Nothing in this chapter shall preclude the sheriff of the county from entering into an agreement with the chief or other head of a municipal police department of a city to process all applications for licenses, renewals of licenses, or amendments to licenses pursuant to this chapter, in lieu of the sheriff.

(2) This subdivision shall only apply to applicants who reside within the city in which the chief or other head of the municipal police department has agreed to process applications for licenses, renewals of licenses, and amendments to licenses, pursuant to this chapter. *(Added by Stats.2010, c. 711 (S.B.1080), § 6, operative Jan. 1, 2012. Amended by Stats.2015, c. 785 (A.B.1134), § 2, eff. Jan. 1, 2016.)*

Validity

For validity of this section, see New York State Rifle & Pistol Association, Inc. v. Bruen, 2022, 142 S.Ct. 2111, 213 L.Ed.2d 387.

Law Revision Commission Comments

Section 26150 continues former Section 12050(a)(1)(A) & (D) without substantive change.

See Sections 16520 ("firearm"), 16530 ("firearm capable of being concealed upon the person," "pistol," and "revolver"), 17020 ("principal place of employment or business"). [38 Cal.L.Rev.Comm. Reports 217 (2009)].

Cross References

Alarm companies, carrying concealed weapon without permit, fine, see Business and Professions Code § 7597.6.
Alarm companies, concealed weapons, firearms qualification card, see Business and Professions Code § 7596.6.
Concealed weapons, firearms qualification card, see Business and Professions Code § 7583.31.
Determination of good cause, notification, see Penal Code § 26202.
Exemption of particular records from disclosure, see Government Code § 6254.
Firearm capable of being concealed upon the person defined for purposes of this Part, see Penal Code § 16530.
Firearm defined for purposes of this Part, see Penal Code § 16520.
Pistol defined for purposes of this Part, see Penal Code § 16530.
Private patrol officers, assessment of administrative fines, prohibited acts, concealed weapons, see Business and Professions Code § 7583.37.
Revolver defined for purposes of this Part, see Penal Code § 16530.
Unauthorized possession of weapon or other instruments in state or local public building, exceptions to prohibition, see Penal Code § 171b.

Research References

2 Witkin, California Criminal Law 4th Crimes Against Public Peace and Welfare § 192 (2021), In General.
2 Witkin, California Criminal Law 4th Crimes Against Public Peace and Welfare § 207 (2021), Exempt Persons.
2 Witkin, California Criminal Law 4th Crimes Against Public Peace and Welfare § 208 (2021), Exempt Activities.
2 Witkin, California Criminal Law 4th Crimes Against Public Peace and Welfare § 210 (2021), Unlawful Acts Involving Ammunition.
2 Witkin, California Criminal Law 4th Crimes Against Public Peace and Welfare § 251 (2021), Exemptions.
2 Witkin, California Criminal Law 4th Crimes Against Public Peace and Welfare § 257 (2021), Firearms.
1 Witkin California Criminal Law 4th Introduction to Crimes § 70 (2021), Weapons.
1 Witkin California Criminal Law 4th Introduction to Crimes § 72 (2021), Illustrations: Weapons.

§ 26155. Application for license to carry concealed weapon; responsibility of municipal police department; agreement with county sheriff

(a) When a person applies for a license to carry a pistol, revolver, or other firearm capable of being concealed upon the person, the chief or other head of a municipal police department of any city or city and county may issue a license to that person upon proof of all of the following:

(1) The applicant is of good moral character.

(2) Good cause exists for issuance of the license.

(3) The applicant is a resident of that city.

(4) The applicant has completed a course of training as described in Section 26165.

(b) The chief or other head of a municipal police department may issue a license under subdivision (a) in either of the following formats:

(1) A license to carry concealed a pistol, revolver, or other firearm capable of being concealed upon the person.

(2) Where the population of the county in which the city is located is less than 200,000 persons according to the most recent federal decennial census, a license to carry loaded and exposed in only that county a pistol, revolver, or other firearm capable of being concealed upon the person.

(c) Nothing in this chapter shall preclude the chief or other head of a municipal police department of any city from entering an agreement with the sheriff of the county in which the city is located for the sheriff to process all applications for licenses, renewals of licenses, and amendments to licenses, pursuant to this chapter. *(Added by Stats.2010, c. 711 (S.B.1080), § 6, operative Jan. 1, 2012.)*

Law Revision Commission Comments

Subdivisions (a) and (b) of Section 26155 continue former Section 12050(a)(1)(B) without substantive change.

Subdivision (c) continues former Section 12050(g) without substantive change.

See Sections 16520 ("firearm"), 16530 ("firearm capable of being concealed upon the person," "pistol," and "revolver"). [38 Cal.L.Rev.Comm. Reports 217 (2009)].

Cross References

Alarm companies, carrying concealed weapon without permit, fine, see Business and Professions Code § 7597.6.
Alarm companies, concealed weapons, firearms qualification card, see Business and Professions Code § 7596.6.
Concealed weapons, firearms qualification card, see Business and Professions Code § 7583.31.
Determination of good cause, notification, see Penal Code § 26202.
Exemption of particular records from disclosure, see Government Code § 6254.
Firearm capable of being concealed upon the person defined for purposes of this Part, see Penal Code § 16530.
Firearm defined for purposes of this Part, see Penal Code § 16520.
Pistol defined for purposes of this Part, see Penal Code § 16530.
Private patrol officers, assessment of administrative fines, prohibited acts, concealed weapons, see Business and Professions Code § 7583.37.
Revolver defined for purposes of this Part, see Penal Code § 16530.

§ 26160. Written policy to be made available

Each licensing authority shall publish and make available a written policy summarizing the provisions of Section 26150 and subdivisions (a) and (b) of Section 26155. *(Added by Stats.2010, c. 711 (S.B.1080), § 6, operative Jan. 1, 2012.)*

Law Revision Commission Comments

Section 26160 continues former Section 12050.2 without substantive change. [38 Cal.L.Rev.Comm. Reports 217 (2009)].

Cross References

Determination of good cause, notification, see Penal Code § 26202.

§ 26165. Course of training requirements for new and renewal license applicants

(a) For new license applicants, the course of training for issuance of a license under Section 26150 or 26155 may be any course acceptable to the licensing authority that meets all of the following criteria:

(1) The course shall be no less than eight hours, but shall not be required to exceed 16 hours in length.

(2) The course shall include instruction on firearm safety, firearm handling, shooting technique, and laws regarding the permissible use of a firearm.

(3) The course shall include live-fire shooting exercises on a firing range and shall include a demonstration by the applicant of safe handling of, and shooting proficiency with, each firearm that the applicant is applying to be licensed to carry.

(b) A licensing authority shall establish, and make available to the public, the standards it uses when issuing licenses with regards to the required live-fire shooting exercises, including, but not limited to, a minimum number of rounds to be fired and minimum passing scores from specified firing distances.

(c) Notwithstanding subdivision (a), the licensing authority may require a community college course certified by the Commission on Peace Officer Standards and Training, up to a maximum of 24 hours, but only if required uniformly of all license applicants without exception.

(d) For license renewal applicants, the course of training may be any course acceptable to the licensing authority, shall be no less than four hours, and shall satisfy the requirements of paragraphs (2) and (3) of subdivision (a). No course of training shall be required for any person certified by the licensing authority as a trainer for purposes of this section, in order for that person to renew a license issued pursuant to this article.

(e) The applicant shall not be required to pay for any training courses prior to the determination of good cause being made pursuant to Section 26202. *(Added by Stats.2010, c. 711 (S.B.1080), § 6, operative Jan. 1, 2012. Amended by Stats.2011, c. 741 (S.B.610), § 1; Stats.2018, c. 752 (A.B.2103), § 1, eff. Jan. 1, 2019.)*

Law Revision Commission Comments

Section 26165 continues former Section 12050(a)(1)(E) without substantive change.

See Section 16520 ("firearm"). [38 Cal.L.Rev.Comm. Reports 217 (2009)].

Cross References

Firearm defined for purposes of this Part, see Penal Code § 16520.

§ 26170. Requirements for issuance of license to carry concealed weapon

(a) Upon proof of all of the following, the sheriff of a county, or the chief or other head of a municipal police department of any city or city and county, may issue to an applicant a license to carry concealed a pistol, revolver, or other firearm capable of being concealed upon the person:

(1) The applicant is of good moral character.

(2) Good cause exists for issuance of the license.

(3) The applicant has been deputized or appointed as a peace officer pursuant to subdivision (a) or (b) of Section 830.6 by that sheriff or that chief of police or other head of a municipal police department.

(b) Direct or indirect fees for the issuance of a license pursuant to this section may be waived.

(c) The fact that an applicant for a license to carry a pistol, revolver, or other firearm capable of being concealed upon the person has been deputized or appointed as a peace officer pursuant to subdivision (a) or (b) of Section 830.6 shall be considered only for the purpose of issuing a license pursuant to this section, and shall not be considered for the purpose of issuing a license pursuant to Section 26150 or 26155. *(Added by Stats.2010, c. 711 (S.B.1080), § 6, operative Jan. 1, 2012.)*

Law Revision Commission Comments

Section 26170 continues former Section 12050(a)(1)(C) without substantive change.

See Sections 16520 ("firearm"), 16530 ("firearm capable of being concealed upon the person," "pistol," and "revolver"). [38 Cal.L.Rev.Comm. Reports 217 (2009)].

Cross References

Alarm companies, carrying concealed weapon without permit, fine, see Business and Professions Code § 7597.6.
Alarm companies, concealed weapons, firearms qualification card, see Business and Professions Code § 7596.6.
Concealed weapons, firearms qualification card, see Business and Professions Code § 7583.31.
Exemption of particular records from disclosure, see Government Code § 6254.
Firearm capable of being concealed upon the person defined for purposes of this Part, see Penal Code § 16530.
Firearm defined for purposes of this Part, see Penal Code § 16520.
Pistol defined for purposes of this Part, see Penal Code § 16530.
Private patrol officers, assessment of administrative fines, prohibited acts, concealed weapons, see Business and Professions Code § 7583.37.
Revolver defined for purposes of this Part, see Penal Code § 16530.

§ 26175. Uniformity requirement for license applications; committee to review and revise standard application form; uniform license; requirements

(a)(1) Applications for licenses and applications for amendments to licenses under this article shall be uniform throughout the state, upon forms to be prescribed by the Attorney General.

(2) The Attorney General shall convene a committee composed of one representative of the California State Sheriffs' Association, one representative of the California Police Chiefs Association, and one representative of the Department of Justice to review, and, as deemed appropriate, revise the standard application form for licenses. The committee shall meet for this purpose if two of the committee's members deem that necessary.

(3)(A) The Attorney General shall develop a uniform license that may be used as indicia of proof of licensure throughout the state.

(B) The Attorney General shall approve the use of licenses issued by local agencies that contain all the information required in subdivision (i), including a recent photograph of the applicant, and are deemed to be in substantial compliance with standards developed by the committee described in subparagraph (C), if developed, as they relate to the physical dimensions and general appearance of the licenses. The Attorney General shall retain exemplars of approved licenses and shall maintain a list of agencies issuing local licenses. Approved licenses may be used as indicia of proof of licensure under this chapter in lieu of the uniform license developed by the Attorney General.

(C) A committee composed of two representatives of the California State Sheriffs' Association, two representatives of the California Police Chiefs Association, and one representative of the Department of Justice shall convene to review and revise, as the committee deems appropriate, the design standard for licenses issued by local agencies that may be used as indicia of proof of licensure throughout the state, provided that the design standard meets the requirements of subparagraph (B). The committee shall meet for this purpose if two of the committee's members deem it necessary.

(b) The application shall include a section summarizing the requirements of state law that result in the automatic denial of a license.

(c) The standard application form for licenses described in subdivision (a) shall require information from the applicant, including, but not limited to, the name, occupation, residence, and business address of the applicant, the applicant's age, height, weight, color of eyes and hair, and reason for desiring a license to carry the weapon.

(d) Applications for licenses shall be filed in writing and signed by the applicant.

(e) Applications for amendments to licenses shall be filed in writing and signed by the applicant, and shall state what type of amendment is sought pursuant to Section 26215 and the reason for desiring the amendment.

(f) The forms shall contain a provision whereby the applicant attests to the truth of statements contained in the application.

(g) An applicant shall not be required to complete any additional application or form for a license, or to provide any information other than that necessary to complete the standard application form described in subdivision (a), except to clarify or interpret information provided by the applicant on the standard application form.

(h) The standard application form described in subdivision (a) is deemed to be a local form expressly exempt from the requirements of the Administrative Procedure Act (Chapter 3.5 (commencing with Section 11340) of Part 1 of Division 3 of Title 2 of the Government Code).

(i) Any license issued upon the application shall set forth the licensee's name, occupation, residence and business address, the licensee's age, height, weight, color of eyes and hair, and the reason for desiring a license to carry the weapon, and shall, in addition, contain a description of the weapon or weapons authorized to be carried, giving the name of the manufacturer, the serial number, and the caliber. The license issued to the licensee may be laminated. *(Added by Stats.2010, c. 711 (S.B.1080), § 6, operative Jan. 1, 2012. Amended by Stats.2011, c. 296 (A.B.1023), § 232; Stats.2016, c. 645 (A.B.2510), § 1, eff. Jan. 1, 2017.)*

Law Revision Commission Comments

Subdivision (a) of Section 26175 continues the first, second, and third sentences of former Section 12051(a)(3)(A) without substantive change.

Subdivision (b) continues the fourth sentence of former Section 12051(a)(3)(A) without substantive change.

Subdivision (c) continues the first sentence of former Section 12051(a)(1) without substantive change.

Subdivision (d) continues the second sentence of former Section 12051(a)(1) without substantive change.

Subdivision (e) continues former Section 12051(a)(2) without substantive change.

Subdivision (f) continues former Section 12051(a)(3)(B) without substantive change.

Subdivision (g) continues former Section 12051(a)(3)(C) without substantive change.

Subdivision (h) continues former Section 12051(a)(3)(D) without substantive change.

Subdivision (i) continues the third and fourth sentences of former Section 12051(a)(1) without substantive change. [38 Cal.L.Rev.Comm. Reports 217 (2009)].

Cross References

Attorney General, generally, see Government Code § 12500 et seq.
Licenses to sell firearms, generally, see Penal Code § 26700 et seq.

§ 26180. Filing of false application

(a) Any person who files an application required by Section 26175 knowing that any statement contained therein is false is guilty of a misdemeanor.

(b) Any person who knowingly makes a false statement on the application regarding any of the following is guilty of a felony:

(1) The denial or revocation of a license, or the denial of an amendment to a license, issued pursuant to this article.

(2) A criminal conviction.

(3) A finding of not guilty by reason of insanity.

(4) The use of a controlled substance.

(5) A dishonorable discharge from military service.

(6) A commitment to a mental institution.

(7) A renunciation of United States citizenship. *(Added by Stats.2010, c. 711 (S.B.1080), § 6, operative Jan. 1, 2012.)*

Law Revision Commission Comments

Subdivision (a) of Section 26180 continues former Section 12051(b) without substantive change.

Subdivision (b) continues former Section 12051(c) without substantive change. [38 Cal.L.Rev.Comm. Reports 217 (2009)].

Cross References

Felonies, definition and penalties, see Penal Code §§ 17, 18.
Licenses to sell firearms, generally, see Penal Code § 26700 et seq.
Misdemeanors, definition and penalties, see Penal Code §§ 17, 19, 19.2.

§ 26185. Fingerprint report

(a)(1) The fingerprints of each applicant shall be taken and two copies on forms prescribed by the Department of Justice shall be forwarded to the department.

(2) Upon receipt of the fingerprints and the fee as prescribed in Section 26190, the department shall promptly furnish the forwarding licensing authority a report of all data and information pertaining to any applicant of which there is a record in its office, including information as to whether the person is prohibited by state or federal law from possessing, receiving, owning, or purchasing a firearm.

(3) No license shall be issued by any licensing authority until after receipt of the report from the department.

(b) Notwithstanding subdivision (a), if the license applicant has previously applied to the same licensing authority for a license to carry firearms pursuant to this article and the applicant's fingerprints and fee have been previously forwarded to the Department of Justice, as provided by this section, the licensing authority shall note the previous identification numbers and other data that would provide positive identification in the files of the Department of Justice on the copy of any subsequent license submitted to the department in conformance with Section 26225 and no additional application form or fingerprints shall be required.

(c) If the license applicant has a license issued pursuant to this article and the applicant's fingerprints have been previously forwarded to the Department of Justice, as provided in this section, the licensing authority shall note the previous identification numbers and other data that would provide positive identification in the files of the Department of Justice on the copy of any subsequent license submitted to the department in conformance with Section 26225 and no additional fingerprints shall be required. *(Added by Stats.2010, c. 711 (S.B.1080), § 6, operative Jan. 1, 2012.)*

Law Revision Commission Comments

Section 26185 continues former Section 12052 without substantive change. See Section 16520 ("firearm"). [38 Cal.L.Rev.Comm. Reports 217 (2009)].

Cross References

Firearm defined for purposes of this Part, see Penal Code § 16520.

§ 26190. Application fee; processing fee; cost of psychological testing

(a)(1) An applicant for a new license or for the renewal of a license shall pay at the time of filing the application a fee determined by the Department of Justice. The fee shall not exceed the application processing costs of the Department of Justice for the direct costs of furnishing the report required by Section 26185.

(2) After the department establishes fees sufficient to reimburse the department for processing costs, fees charged shall increase at a rate not to exceed the legislatively approved annual cost-of-living adjustments for the department's budget.

(3) The officer receiving the application and the fee shall transmit the fee, with the fingerprints if required, to the Department of Justice.

(b)(1) The licensing authority of any city, city and county, or county shall charge an additional fee in an amount equal to the reasonable costs for processing the application for a new license, issuing the license, and enforcing the license, including any required notices, excluding fingerprint and training costs, and shall transmit the additional fee, if any, to the city, city and county, or county treasury.

(2) The first 20 percent of this additional local fee may be collected upon filing of the initial application. The balance of the fee shall be collected only upon issuance of the license.

(c) The licensing authority may charge an additional fee, not to exceed twenty-five dollars ($25), for processing the application for a license renewal, and shall transmit an additional fee, if any, to the city, city and county, or county treasury.

(d) These local fees may be increased at a rate not to exceed any increase in the California Consumer Price Index as compiled and reported by the Department of Industrial Relations.

(e)(1) In the case of an amended license pursuant to Section 26215, the licensing authority of any city, city and county, or county may charge a fee, not to exceed ten dollars ($10), for processing the amended license.

(2) This fee may be increased at a rate not to exceed any increase in the California Consumer Price Index as compiled and reported by the Department of Industrial Relations.

(3) The licensing authority shall transmit the fee to the city, city and county, or county treasury.

(f)(1) If psychological testing on the initial application is required by the licensing authority, the license applicant shall be referred to a licensed psychologist used by the licensing authority for the psychological testing of its own employees. The applicant may be charged for the actual cost of the testing in an amount not to exceed one hundred fifty dollars ($150).

(2) Additional psychological testing of an applicant seeking license renewal shall be required only if there is compelling evidence to indicate that a test is necessary. The cost to the applicant for this additional testing shall not exceed one hundred fifty dollars ($150).

(g) Except as authorized pursuant to this section, a requirement, charge, assessment, fee, or condition that requires the payment of any additional funds by the applicant, or requires the applicant to obtain liability insurance, may not be imposed by any licensing authority as a condition of the application for a license. *(Added by Stats.2010, c. 711 (S.B.1080), § 6, operative Jan. 1, 2012. Amended by Stats.2011, c. 741 (S.B.610), § 2; Stats.2019, c. 732 (A.B.1297), § 1, eff. Jan. 1, 2020.)*

Law Revision Commission Comments

Subdivision (a) of Section 26190 continues the first, second, and third sentences of the first paragraph of former Section 12054(a) without substantive change.

Subdivision (b) continues the fourth, fifth, and sixth sentences of the first paragraph of former Section 12054(a) without substantive change.

Subdivision (c) continues the first sentence of the second paragraph of former Section 12054(a) without substantive change.

Subdivision (d) continues the second sentence of the second paragraph of former Section 12054(a) without substantive change.

Subdivision (e) continues former Section 12054(b) without substantive change.

Subdivision (f) continues former Section 12054(c) without substantive change.

Subdivision (g) continues former Section 12054(d) without substantive change. [38 Cal.L.Rev.Comm. Reports 217 (2009)].

Cross References

State summary criminal history information, see Penal Code § 11105.

§ 26195. Refusal to issue license; revocation of license; notification

(a) A license under this article shall not be issued if the Department of Justice determines that the person is prohibited by state or federal law from possessing, receiving, owning, or purchasing a firearm.

(b)(1) A license under this article shall be revoked by the local licensing authority if at any time either the local licensing authority is notified by the Department of Justice that a licensee is prohibited by state or federal law from owning or purchasing firearms, or the local licensing authority determines that the person is prohibited by state or federal law from possessing, receiving, owning, or purchasing a firearm.

(2) If at any time the Department of Justice determines that a licensee is prohibited by state or federal law from possessing, receiving, owning, or purchasing a firearm, the department shall immediately notify the local licensing authority of the determination.

(3) If the local licensing authority revokes the license, the Department of Justice shall be notified of the revocation pursuant to Section 26225. The licensee shall also be immediately notified of the revocation in writing. *(Added by Stats.2010, c. 711 (S.B.1080), § 6, operative Jan. 1, 2012.)*

Law Revision Commission Comments

Subdivision (a) of Section 26195 continues former Section 12050(d) without substantive change.

Subdivision (b) continues former Section 12050(e) without substantive change. [38 Cal.L.Rev.Comm. Reports 217 (2009)].

Cross References

Firearm defined for purposes of this Part, see Penal Code § 16520.

§ 26200. Restrictions on license

(a) A license issued pursuant to this article may include any reasonable restrictions or conditions that the issuing authority deems warranted, including restrictions as to the time, place, manner, and circumstances under which the licensee may carry a pistol, revolver, or other firearm capable of being concealed upon the person.

(b) Any restrictions imposed pursuant to subdivision (a) shall be indicated on any license issued. *(Added by Stats.2010, c. 711 (S.B.1080), § 6, operative Jan. 1, 2012.)*

Law Revision Commission Comments

Subdivision (a) of Section 26200 continues former Section 12050(b) without substantive change.

Subdivision (b) continues former Section 12050(c) without substantive change.

See Section 16530 ("firearm capable of being concealed upon the person," "pistol," and "revolver"). [38 Cal.L.Rev.Comm. Reports 217 (2009)].

Cross References

Firearm capable of being concealed upon the person defined for purposes of this Part, see Penal Code § 16530.
Firearm defined for purposes of this Part, see Penal Code § 16520.
Pistol defined for purposes of this Part, see Penal Code § 16530.
Revolver defined for purposes of this Part, see Penal Code § 16530.

Research References

1 Witkin California Criminal Law 4th Introduction to Crimes § 72 (2021), Illustrations: Weapons.

§ 26202. Determination of good cause; notification

Upon making the determination of good cause pursuant to Section 26150 or 26155, the licensing authority shall give written notice to the applicant of the licensing authority's determination. If the licensing authority determines that good cause exists, the notice shall inform the applicants to proceed with the training requirements specified in Section 26165. If the licensing authority determines that good cause does not exist, the notice shall inform the applicant that the request for a license has been denied and shall state the reason from the department's published policy, described in Section 26160, as to why the determination was made. *(Added by Stats.2011, c. 741 (S.B.610), § 3.)*

Cross References

Payment of training courses prior to determination of good cause, see Penal Code § 26165.

§ 26205. Written notification to applicant

The licensing authority shall give written notice to the applicant indicating if the license under this article is approved or denied. The licensing authority shall give this notice within 90 days of the initial application for a new license or a license renewal, or 30 days after receipt of the applicant's criminal background check from the Department of Justice, whichever is later. If the license is denied, the notice shall state which requirement was not satisfied. *(Added by Stats.2010, c. 711 (S.B.1080), § 6, operative Jan. 1, 2012. Amended by Stats.2011, c. 741 (S.B.610), § 4.)*

Law Revision Commission Comments

Section 26205 continues former Section 12052.5 without substantive change. [38 Cal.L.Rev.Comm. Reports 217 (2009)].

§ 26210. Change of address; notification; issuance of license based on place of residence; effect

(a) When a licensee under this article has a change of address, the license shall be amended to reflect the new address and a new license shall be issued pursuant to subdivision (b) of Section 26215.

(b) The licensee shall notify the licensing authority in writing within 10 days of any change in the licensee's place of residence.

(c) If both of the following conditions are satisfied, a license to carry a concealed handgun may not be revoked solely because the licensee's place of residence has changed to another county:

(1) The licensee has not breached any of the conditions or restrictions set forth in the license.

(2) The licensee has not become prohibited by state or federal law from possessing, receiving, owning, or purchasing a firearm.

(d) Notwithstanding subdivision (c), if a licensee's place of residence was the basis for issuance of a license, any license issued pursuant to Section 26150 or 26155 shall expire 90 days after the licensee moves from the county of issuance.

(e) If the license is one to carry loaded and exposed a pistol, revolver, or other firearm capable of being concealed upon the person, the license shall be revoked immediately upon a change of the licensee's place of residence to another county. *(Added by Stats.2010, c. 711 (S.B.1080), § 6, operative Jan. 1, 2012.)*

Law Revision Commission Comments

Subdivision (a) of Section 26210 continues former Section 12050(f)(2) without substantive change.

Subdivision (b) continues former Section 12050(f)(4)(A) without substantive change.

Subdivisions (c) and (d) continue former Section 12050(f)(4)(B) without substantive change.

Subdivision (e) continues former Section 12050(f)(4)(C) without substantive change.

See Section 16530 ("firearm capable of being concealed upon the person," "pistol," and "revolver"). [38 Cal.L.Rev.Comm. Reports 217 (2009)].

Cross References

Firearm capable of being concealed upon the person defined for purposes of this Part, see Penal Code § 16530.
Firearm defined for purposes of this Part, see Penal Code § 16520.
Handgun defined for purposes of this Part, see Penal Code § 16640.
Pistol defined for purposes of this Part, see Penal Code § 16530.
Revolver defined for purposes of this Part, see Penal Code § 16530.

§ 26215. Application for amendment to license; effect on expiration

(a) A person issued a license pursuant to this article may apply to the licensing authority for an amendment to the license to do one or more of the following:

(1) Add or delete authority to carry a particular pistol, revolver, or other firearm capable of being concealed upon the person.

(2) Authorize the licensee to carry concealed a pistol, revolver, or other firearm capable of being concealed upon the person.

(3) If the population of the county is less than 200,000 persons according to the most recent federal decennial census, authorize the licensee to carry loaded and exposed in only that county a pistol, revolver, or other firearm capable of being concealed upon the person.

(4) Change any restrictions or conditions on the license, including restrictions as to the time, place, manner, and circumstances under which the person may carry a pistol, revolver, or other firearm capable of being concealed upon the person.

(b) If the licensing authority amends the license, a new license shall be issued to the licensee reflecting the amendments.

(c) An amendment to the license does not extend the original expiration date of the license and the license shall be subject to renewal at the same time as if the license had not been amended.

(d) An application to amend a license does not constitute an application for renewal of the license. *(Added by Stats.2010, c. 711 (S.B.1080), § 6, operative Jan. 1, 2012.)*

Law Revision Commission Comments

Subdivision (a) of Section 26215 continues former Section 12050(f)(1) without substantive change.

Subdivision (b) continues former Section 12050(f)(3) without substantive change.

Subdivision (c) continues former Section 12050(f)(5) without substantive change.

Subdivision (d) continues former Section 12050(f)(6) without substantive change.

See Section 16530 ("firearm capable of being concealed upon the person," "pistol," and "revolver"). [38 Cal.L.Rev.Comm. Reports 217 (2009)].

Cross References

Alarm companies, concealed weapons, firearms qualification card, see Business and Professions Code § 7596.6.
Concealed weapons, firearms qualification card, see Business and Professions Code § 7583.31.
Exemption of particular records from disclosure, see Government Code § 6254.
Firearm capable of being concealed upon the person defined for purposes of this Part, see Penal Code § 16530.
Firearm defined for purposes of this Part, see Penal Code § 16520.
Pistol defined for purposes of this Part, see Penal Code § 16530.
Private patrol officers, assessment of administrative fines, prohibited acts, concealed weapons, see Business and Professions Code § 7583.37.
Revolver defined for purposes of this Part, see Penal Code § 16530.

§ 26220. Validity of license; period of time

(a) Except as otherwise provided in this section and in subdivision (c) of Section 26210, a license issued pursuant to Section 26150 or 26155 is valid for any period of time not to exceed two years from the date of the license.

(b) If the licensee's place of employment or business was the basis for issuance of a license pursuant to Section 26150, the license is valid for any period of time not to exceed 90 days from the date of the license. The license shall be valid only in the county in which the license was originally issued. The licensee shall give a copy of this license to the licensing authority of the city, county, or city and county in which the licensee resides. The licensing authority that originally issued the license shall inform the licensee verbally and in writing in at least 16–point type of this obligation to give a copy of the license to the licensing authority of the city, county, or city and county of residence. Any application to renew or extend the validity of, or reissue, the license may be granted only upon the concurrence of the licensing authority that originally issued the license and the licensing authority of the city, county, or city and county in which the licensee resides.

(c) A license issued pursuant to Section 26150 or 26155 is valid for any period of time not to exceed three years from the date of the license if the license is issued to any of the following individuals:

(1) A judge of a California court of record.

(2) A full-time court commissioner of a California court of record.

(3) A judge of a federal court.

(4) A magistrate of a federal court.

(d) A license issued pursuant to Section 26150 or 26155 is valid for any period of time not to exceed four years from the date of the license if the license is issued to a custodial officer who is an employee of the sheriff as provided in Section 831.5, except that the license shall be invalid upon the conclusion of the person's employment pursuant to Section 831.5 if the four-year period has not otherwise expired or any other condition imposed pursuant to this article does not limit the validity of the license to a shorter time period.

(e) A license issued pursuant to Section 26170 to a peace officer appointed pursuant to Section 830.6 is valid for any period of time not to exceed four years from the date of the license, except that the license shall be invalid upon the conclusion of the person's appointment pursuant to Section 830.6 if the four-year period has not otherwise expired or any other condition imposed pursuant to this article does not limit the validity of the license to a shorter time period. *(Added by Stats.2010, c. 711 (S.B.1080), § 6, operative Jan. 1, 2012.)*

Law Revision Commission Comments

Subdivision (a) of Section 26220 continues former Section 12050(a)(2)(A)(i) without substantive change.

Subdivision (b) continues former Section 12050(a)(2)(A)(ii) without substantive change.

Subdivision (c) continues former Section 12050(a)(2)(C) without substantive change.

Subdivision (d) continues former Section 12050(a)(2)(D) without substantive change.

Subdivision (e) continues former Section 12050(a)(2)(B) without substantive change. [38 Cal.L.Rev.Comm. Reports 217 (2009)].

§ 26225. Maintenance of records; report to Attorney General

(a) A record of the following shall be maintained in the office of the licensing authority:

(1) The denial of a license.

(2) The denial of an amendment to a license.

(3) The issuance of a license.

(4) The amendment of a license.

(5) The revocation of a license.

(b) Copies of each of the following shall be filed immediately by the issuing officer or authority with the Department of Justice:

(1) The denial of a license.

(2) The denial of an amendment to a license.

(3) The issuance of a license.

(4) The amendment of a license.

(5) The revocation of a license.

(c)(1) Commencing on or before January 1, 2000, and annually thereafter, each licensing authority shall submit to the Attorney General the total number of licenses issued to peace officers pursuant to Section 26170, and to judges pursuant to Section 26150 or 26155.

(2) The Attorney General shall collect and record the information submitted pursuant to this subdivision by county and licensing authority. *(Added by Stats.2010, c. 711 (S.B.1080), § 6, operative Jan. 1, 2012.)*

Law Revision Commission Comments

Section 26225 continues former Section 12053 without substantive change. [38 Cal.L.Rev.Comm. Reports 217 (2009)].

Cross References

Attorney General,
Generally, see Government Code § 12500 et seq.
Keeping of copies of applications of licenses to carry concealed weapons, see Penal Code § 11106.
Custody of records by county clerk, see Government Code § 26803.
Inspection of public records, see Government Code § 6250 et seq.

CHAPTER 5. RETIRED PEACE OFFICER CARRYING A CONCEALED AND LOADED FIREARM

§ 26300. Retired peace officer authorized to carry concealed and loaded firearm; endorsement on identification certificate; application to retired reserve officer

(a) Any peace officer listed in Section 830.1 or 830.2 or subdivision (c) of Section 830.5 who retired prior to January 1, 1981, is authorized to carry a concealed and loaded firearm if the agency issued the officer an identification certificate and the certificate has not been stamped as specified in Section 25470.

(b) Any peace officer employed by an agency and listed in Section 830.1 or 830.2 or subdivision (c) of Section 830.5 who retired after January 1, 1981, shall have an endorsement on the officer's identification certificate stating that the issuing agency approves the officer's carrying of a concealed and loaded firearm.

(c)(1) Any peace officer not listed in subdivision (a) or (b) who was authorized to, and did, carry a firearm during the course and scope of his or her appointment as a peace officer shall have an endorsement on the officer's identification certificate stating that the issuing agency approves the officer's carrying of a concealed and loaded firearm.

(2) This subdivision applies to a retired reserve officer if the retired reserve officer satisfies the requirements of paragraph (1), was a level I reserve officer as described in paragraph (1) of subdivision (a) of Section 832.6, and he or she served in the aggregate the minimum amount of time as specified by the retiree's agency's policy as a level I reserve officer, provided that the policy shall not set an aggregate term requirement that is less than 10 years or more than

20 years. Service as a reserve officer, other than a level I reserve officer prior to January 1, 1997, shall not count toward the accrual of time required by this section. A law enforcement agency shall have the discretion to revoke or deny an endorsement issued under this subdivision pursuant to Section 26305. *(Added by Stats.2010, c. 711 (S.B.1080), § 6, operative Jan. 1, 2012. Amended by Stats.2013, c. 267 (A.B.703), § 3.)*

Law Revision Commission Comments

Subdivision (a) of Section 26300 continues former Section 12027.1(a)(1)(A)(ii) without substantive change.

Subdivision (b) continues former Section 12027.1(a)(1)(A)(i) without substantive change.

Subdivision (c) continues former Section 12027.1(a)(1)(A)(iii) without substantive change.

Section 26300 and the other provisions in this article provide guidance on a retired peace officer carrying a concealed and loaded firearm. For guidance on a retired peace officer carrying a concealed firearm, see Sections 25450–25475. For guidance on a retired peace officer carrying a loaded firearm, see Sections 25900–25925.

See Section 16520 ("firearm"). [38 Cal.L.Rev.Comm. Reports 217 (2009)].

Cross References

Firearm defined for purposes of this Part, see Penal Code § 16520.

Research References

2 Witkin, California Criminal Law 4th Crimes Against Public Peace and Welfare § 207 (2021), Exempt Persons.

§ 26305. Peace officer retired due to psychological disability; prohibition on issuance of endorsement; revocation or denial of endorsement

(a) No peace officer who is retired after January 1, 1989, because of a psychological disability shall be issued an endorsement to carry a concealed and loaded firearm pursuant to this article.

(b) A retired peace officer may have the privilege to carry a concealed and loaded firearm revoked or denied by violating any departmental rule, or state or federal law that, if violated by an officer on active duty, would result in that officer's arrest, suspension, or removal from the agency.

(c) An identification certificate authorizing the officer to carry a concealed and loaded firearm or an endorsement on the certificate may be immediately and temporarily revoked by the issuing agency when the conduct of a retired peace officer compromises public safety.

(d) An identification certificate authorizing the officer to carry a concealed and loaded firearm or an endorsement may be permanently revoked or denied by the issuing agency only upon a showing of good cause. Good cause shall be determined at a hearing, as specified in Section 26320. *(Added by Stats.2010, c. 711 (S.B.1080), § 6, operative Jan. 1, 2012.)*

Law Revision Commission Comments

Subdivision (a) of Section 26305 continues former Section 12027.1(e) without substantive change.

Subdivision (b) continues former Section 12027.1(a)(2) without substantive change.

Subdivision (c) continues the first sentence of former Section 12027.1(a)(1)(C) without substantive change.

Subdivision (d) continues former Section 12027.1(a)(1)(B) & (b)(1) without substantive change.

See Section 16520 ("firearm"). [38 Cal.L.Rev.Comm. Reports 217 (2009)].

Cross References

Firearm defined for purposes of this Part, see Penal Code § 16520.

§ 26310. Denial of identification certificate or endorsement prior to hearing

(a) Issuance of an identification certificate authorizing the officer to carry a concealed and loaded firearm or an endorsement may be denied prior to a hearing.

(b) If a hearing is not conducted prior to the denial of an endorsement, a retired peace officer, within 15 days of the denial, shall have the right to request a hearing. A retired peace officer who fails to request a hearing pursuant to this section shall forfeit the right to a hearing. *(Added by Stats.2010, c. 711 (S.B.1080), § 6, operative Jan. 1, 2012.)*

Law Revision Commission Comments

Section 26310 continues former Section 12027.1(b)(3) without substantive change.

See Section 16520 ("firearm"). [38 Cal.L.Rev.Comm. Reports 217 (2009)].

Cross References

Firearm defined for purposes of this Part, see Penal Code § 16520.

§ 26312. Notice of temporary revocation of identification certificate or endorsement; hearing

(a) Notice of a temporary revocation shall be effective upon personal service or upon receipt of a notice that was sent by first-class mail, postage prepaid, return receipt requested, to the retiree's last known place of residence.

(b) The retiree shall have 15 days to respond to the notification and request a hearing to determine if the temporary revocation should become permanent.

(c) A retired peace officer who fails to respond to the notice of hearing within the 15–day period shall forfeit the right to a hearing and the authority of the officer to carry a firearm shall be permanently revoked. The retired officer shall immediately return the identification certificate to the issuing agency.

(d) If a hearing is requested, good cause for permanent revocation shall be determined at a hearing, as specified in Section 26320. The hearing shall be held no later than 120 days after the request by the retired officer for a hearing is received.

(e) A retiree may waive the right to a hearing and immediately return the identification certificate to the issuing agency. *(Added by Stats.2010, c. 711 (S.B.1080), § 6, operative Jan. 1, 2012.)*

Law Revision Commission Comments

Section 26312 continues the second through eighth sentences of former Section 12027.1(a)(1)(C) without substantive change.

See Section 16520 ("firearm"). [38 Cal.L.Rev.Comm. Reports 217 (2009)].

Cross References

Firearm defined for purposes of this Part, see Penal Code § 16520.

§ 26315. Permanent revocation of identification certificate or endorsement; hearing

(a) An identification certificate authorizing the officer to carry a concealed and loaded firearm or an endorsement may be permanently revoked only after a hearing, as specified in Section 26320.

(b) Any retired peace officer whose identification certificate authorizing the officer to carry a concealed and loaded firearm or an endorsement is to be revoked shall receive notice of the hearing. Notice of the hearing shall be served either personally on the retiree or sent by first-class mail, postage prepaid, return receipt requested to the retiree's last known place of residence.

(c) From the date the retiree signs for the notice or upon the date the notice is served personally on the retiree, the retiree shall have 15 days to respond to the notification. A retired peace officer who fails to respond to the notice of the hearing shall forfeit the right to a hearing and the authority of the officer to carry a firearm shall be permanently revoked. The retired officer shall immediately return the identification certificate to the issuing agency.

(d) If a hearing is requested, good cause for permanent revocation shall be determined at the hearing, as specified in Section 26320. The hearing shall be held no later than 120 days after the request by the retired officer for a hearing is received.

(e) The retiree may waive the right to a hearing and immediately return the identification certificate to the issuing agency. *(Added by Stats.2010, c. 711 (S.B.1080), § 6, operative Jan. 1, 2012.)*

Law Revision Commission Comments

Section 26315 continues former Section 12027.1(b)(2) without substantive change.

See Section 16520 ("firearm"). [38 Cal.L.Rev.Comm. Reports 217 (2009)].

Cross References

Firearm defined for purposes of this Part, see Penal Code § 16520.

§ 26320. Hearing; three-member board; effect of decision

(a) Any hearing conducted under this article shall be held before a three-member hearing board. One member of the board shall be selected by the agency and one member shall be selected by the retired peace officer or his or her employee organization. The third member shall be selected jointly by the agency and the retired peace officer or his or her employee organization.

(b) Any decision by the board shall be binding on the agency and the retired peace officer. *(Added by Stats.2010, c. 711 (S.B.1080), § 6, operative Jan. 1, 2012.)*

Law Revision Commission Comments

Section 26320 continues former Section 12027.1(d) without substantive change. [38 Cal.L.Rev.Comm. Reports 217 (2009)].

§ 26325. Surrender of identification certificate upon revocation of privilege to carry concealed firearm; issuance of new certificate without endorsement

(a) A retired peace officer, when notified of the revocation of the privilege to carry a concealed and loaded firearm, after the hearing, or upon forfeiting the right to a hearing, shall immediately surrender to the issuing agency the officer's identification certificate.

(b) The issuing agency shall reissue a new identification certificate without an endorsement.

(c) Notwithstanding subdivision (b), if the peace officer retired prior to January 1, 1981, and was at the time of retirement a peace officer listed in Section 830.1 or 830.2 or subdivision (c) of Section 830.5, the issuing agency shall stamp on the identification certificate "No CCW privilege." *(Added by Stats.2010, c. 711 (S.B.1080), § 6, operative Jan. 1, 2012.)*

Law Revision Commission Comments

Section 26325 continues former Section 12027.1(c) without substantive change.

See Sections 16360 ("CCW"), 16520 ("firearm"). [38 Cal.L.Rev.Comm. Reports 217 (2009)].

Cross References

Firearm defined for purposes of this Part, see Penal Code § 16520.

CHAPTER 6. OPENLY CARRYING AN UNLOADED HANDGUN

ARTICLE 1. CRIME OF OPENLY CARRYING AN UNLOADED HANDGUN

§ 26350. Openly carrying an unloaded handgun; penalties; definition

(a)(1) A person is guilty of openly carrying an unloaded handgun when that person carries upon his or her person an exposed and unloaded handgun outside a vehicle while in or on any of the following:

(A) A public place or public street in an incorporated city or city and county.

(B) A public street in a prohibited area of an unincorporated area of a county or city and county.

(C) A public place in a prohibited area of a county or city and county.

(2) A person is guilty of openly carrying an unloaded handgun when that person carries an exposed and unloaded handgun inside or on a vehicle, whether or not on his or her person, while in or on any of the following:

(A) A public place or public street in an incorporated city or city and county.

(B) A public street in a prohibited area of an unincorporated area of a county or city and county.

(C) A public place in a prohibited area of a county or city and county.

(b)(1) Except as specified in paragraph (2), a violation of this section is a misdemeanor.

(2) A violation of subparagraph (A) of paragraph (1) of subdivision (a) is punishable by imprisonment in a county jail not exceeding one year, or by a fine not to exceed one thousand dollars ($1,000), or by both that fine and imprisonment, if both of the following conditions exist:

(A) The handgun and unexpended ammunition capable of being discharged from that handgun are in the immediate possession of that person.

(B) The person is not in lawful possession of that handgun.

(c)(1) Nothing in this section shall preclude prosecution under Chapter 2 (commencing with Section 29800) or Chapter 3 (commencing with Section 29900) of Division 9, Section 8100 or 8103 of the Welfare and Institutions Code, or any other law with a penalty greater than is set forth in this section.

(2) The provisions of this section are cumulative and shall not be construed as restricting the application of any other law. However, an act or omission punishable in different ways by different provisions of law shall not be punished under more than one provision.

(d) Notwithstanding the fact that the term "an unloaded handgun" is used in this section, each handgun shall constitute a distinct and separate offense under this section. *(Added by Stats.2011, c. 725 (A.B.144), § 14.)*

Cross References

Delivery or transportation of firearm to law enforcement agency, application of this section, see Penal Code § 26392.

Handgun defined for purposes of this Part, see Penal Code § 16640.

Misdemeanors, definition and penalties, see Penal Code §§ 17, 19, 19.2.

Research References

2 Witkin, California Criminal Law 4th Crimes Against Public Peace and Welfare § 208 (2021), Exempt Activities.
2 Witkin, California Criminal Law 4th Crimes Against Public Peace and Welfare § 253 (2021), Openly Displaying or Carrying Imitation or Unloaded Firearm.
2 Witkin, California Criminal Law 4th Crimes Against Public Peace and Welfare § 257 (2021), Firearms.

ARTICLE 2. EXEMPTIONS

§ 26361. Exemption for peace officer or any honorably retired peace officer

Section 26350 does not apply to, or affect, the open carrying of an unloaded handgun by any peace officer or any honorably retired peace officer if that officer may carry a concealed firearm pursuant to Article 2 (commencing with Section 25450) of Chapter 2, or a loaded firearm pursuant to Article 3 (commencing with Section 25900) of Chapter 3. *(Added by Stats.2011, c. 725 (A.B.144), § 14.)*

Cross References

Firearm defined for purposes of this Part, see Penal Code § 16520.
Handgun defined for purposes of this Part, see Penal Code § 16640.

Research References

2 Witkin, California Criminal Law 4th Crimes Against Public Peace and Welfare § 253 (2021), Openly Displaying or Carrying Imitation or Unloaded Firearm.
2 Witkin, California Criminal Law 4th Crimes Against Public Peace and Welfare § 257 (2021), Firearms.

§ 26362. Exemption for person who may openly carry a loaded handgun

Section 26350 does not apply to, or affect, the open carrying of an unloaded handgun by any person to the extent that person may openly carry a loaded handgun pursuant to Article 4 (commencing with Section 26000) of Chapter 3. *(Added by Stats.2011, c. 725 (A.B.144), § 14.)*

Cross References

Handgun defined for purposes of this Part, see Penal Code § 16640.

§ 26363. Exemption for person engaged in business of manufacturing, importing, wholesaling, repairing, or dealing in firearms or authorized representative or agent

Section 26350 does not apply to, or affect, the open carrying of an unloaded handgun as merchandise by a person who is engaged in the business of manufacturing, importing, wholesaling, repairing, or dealing in firearms and who is licensed to engage in that business, or the authorized representative or authorized agent of that person, while engaged in the lawful course of the business. *(Added by Stats.2011, c. 725 (A.B.144), § 14.)*

Cross References

Firearm defined for purposes of this Part, see Penal Code § 16520.
Handgun defined for purposes of this Part, see Penal Code § 16640.

§ 26364. Exemption for duly authorized military or civil organization or its members

Section 26350 does not apply to, or affect, the open carrying of an unloaded handgun by a duly authorized military or civil organization, or the members thereof, while parading or while rehearsing or practicing parading, when at the meeting place of the organization. *(Added by Stats.2011, c. 725 (A.B.144), § 14.)*

Cross References

Handgun defined for purposes of this Part, see Penal Code § 16640.

§ 26365. Exemption for member of club or organization for practicing shooting at established target range

Paragraph (1) of subdivision (a) of Section 26350 does not apply to, or affect, the open carrying of an unloaded handgun by a member of any club or organization organized for the purpose of practicing shooting at targets upon established target ranges, whether public or private, while the members are using handguns upon the target ranges or incident to the use of a handgun at that target range. *(Added by Stats.2011, c. 725 (A.B.144), § 14.)*

Cross References

Handgun defined for purposes of this Part, see Penal Code § 16640.

§ 26366. Exemption for licensed hunter engaged in hunting

Section 26350 does not apply to, or affect, the open carrying of an unloaded handgun by a licensed hunter while engaged in hunting or while transporting that handgun when going to or returning from that hunting expedition. *(Added by Stats.2011, c. 725 (A.B.144), § 14.)*

Cross References

Handgun defined for purposes of this Part, see Penal Code § 16640.

§ 26366.5. Exemption for licensed hunter engaged in training a dog

Section 26350 does not apply to, or affect, the open carrying of an unloaded handgun by a licensed hunter while actually engaged in training a dog for the purpose of using the dog in hunting that is not prohibited by law, or while transporting the firearm while going to or returning from that training. *(Added by Stats.2012, c. 700 (A.B.1527), § 9.)*

§ 26367. Exemption for person operating licensed common carrier or authorized agent or employee

Section 26350 does not apply to, or affect, the open carrying of an unloaded handgun incident to transportation of a handgun by a person operating a licensed common carrier, or by an authorized agent or employee thereof, when transported in conformance with applicable federal law. *(Added by Stats.2011, c. 725 (A.B.144), § 14.)*

Cross References

Handgun defined for purposes of this Part, see Penal Code § 16640.

§ 26368. Exemption for member of organization chartered by Congress or nonprofit mutual or public benefit corporation

Section 26350 does not apply to, or affect, the open carrying of an unloaded handgun by a member of an organization chartered by the Congress of the United States or a nonprofit mutual or public benefit corporation organized and recognized as a nonprofit tax-exempt organization by the Internal Revenue Service while on official parade duty or ceremonial occasions of that organization or while rehearsing or practicing for official parade duty or ceremonial occasions. *(Added by Stats.2011, c. 725 (A.B.144), § 14.)*

Cross References

Handgun defined for purposes of this Part, see Penal Code § 16640.

§ 26369. Exemption for person within gun show

Paragraph (1) of subdivision (a) of Section 26350 does not apply to, or affect, the open carrying of an unloaded handgun within a gun show conducted pursuant to Article 1 (commencing with Section 27200) and Article 2 (commencing with Section 27300) of Chapter 3 of Division 6. *(Added by Stats.2011, c. 725 (A.B.144), § 14.)*

Cross References

Handgun defined for purposes of this Part, see Penal Code § 16640.

§ 26370. Exemption for person within school zone

Section 26350 does not apply to, or affect, the open carrying of an unloaded handgun within a school zone, as defined in Section 626.9, if that carrying is not prohibited by Section 626.9. *(Added by Stats.2011, c. 725 (A.B.144), § 14. Amended by Stats.2017, c. 779 (A.B.424), § 2, eff. Jan. 1, 2018.)*

Cross References

Handgun defined for purposes of this Part, see Penal Code § 16640.

§ 26371. Exemption pursuant to Section 171b

Section 26350 does not apply to, or affect, the open carrying of an unloaded handgun when in accordance with the provisions of Section 171b. *(Added by Stats.2011, c. 725 (A.B.144), § 14.)*

Cross References

Handgun defined for purposes of this Part, see Penal Code § 16640.

§ 26372. Exemption for person engaged in act of making or attempting to make lawful arrest

Section 26350 does not apply to, or affect, the open carrying of an unloaded handgun by any person while engaged in the act of making or attempting to make a lawful arrest. *(Added by Stats.2011, c. 725 (A.B.144), § 14.)*

Cross References

Handgun defined for purposes of this Part, see Penal Code § 16640.

§ 26373. Exemption incident to loaning, selling, or transferring handgun

Section 26350 does not apply to, or affect, the open carrying of an unloaded handgun incident to loaning, selling, or transferring that handgun in accordance with Article 1 (commencing with Section 27500) of Chapter 4 of Division 6, or in accordance with any of the exemptions from Section 27545, so long as that handgun is possessed within private property and the possession and carrying is with the permission of the owner or lessee of that private property. *(Added by Stats.2011, c. 725 (A.B.144), § 14.)*

Cross References

Handgun defined for purposes of this Part, see Penal Code § 16640.

§ 26374. Exemption for person engaged in firearms-related activities

Section 26350 does not apply to, or affect, the open carrying of an unloaded handgun by a person engaged in firearms-related activities, while on the premises of a fixed place of business that is licensed to conduct and conducts, as a regular course of its business, activities related to the sale, making, repair, transfer, pawn, or the use of firearms, or related to firearms training. *(Added by Stats.2011, c. 725 (A.B.144), § 14.)*

Cross References

Firearm defined for purposes of this Part, see Penal Code § 16520.
Handgun defined for purposes of this Part, see Penal Code § 16640.

§ 26375. Exemption for authorized participant in or employee or agent of supplier of firearms for entertainment

Section 26350 does not apply to, or affect, the open carrying of an unloaded handgun by an authorized participant in, or an authorized employee or agent of a supplier of firearms for, a motion picture, television or video production, or entertainment event, when the participant lawfully uses the handgun as part of that production or event, as part of rehearsing or practicing for participation in that production or event, or while the participant or authorized employee or agent is at that production or event, or rehearsal or practice for that production or event. *(Added by Stats.2011, c. 725 (A.B.144), § 14.)*

Cross References

Firearm defined for purposes of this Part, see Penal Code § 16520.
Handgun defined for purposes of this Part, see Penal Code § 16640.

§ 26376. Exemption incident to obtaining identification number or mark

Paragraph (1) of subdivision (a) of Section 26350 does not apply to, or affect, the open carrying of an unloaded handgun incident to obtaining an identification number or mark assigned for that handgun from the Department of Justice pursuant to Section 23910. *(Added by Stats.2011, c. 725 (A.B.144), § 14.)*

Cross References

Handgun defined for purposes of this Part, see Penal Code § 16640.

§ 26377. Exemption for person using handgun at established target range

Paragraph (1) of subdivision (a) of Section 26350 does not apply to, or affect, the open carrying of an unloaded handgun at any established target range, whether public or private, while the person is using the handgun upon the target range. *(Added by Stats.2011, c. 725 (A.B.144), § 14.)*

Cross References

Handgun defined for purposes of this Part, see Penal Code § 16640.

§ 26378. Exemption for person summoned by peace officer to assist in making arrests or preserving the peace

Section 26350 does not apply to, or affect, the open carrying of an unloaded handgun by a person when that person is summoned by a peace officer to assist in making arrests or preserving the peace, while the person is actually engaged in assisting that officer. *(Added by Stats.2011, c. 725 (A.B.144), § 14.)*

Cross References

Handgun defined for purposes of this Part, see Penal Code § 16640.

§ 26379. Exemption pursuant to specified sections

Paragraph (1) of subdivision (a) of Section 26350 does not apply to, or affect, the open carrying of an unloaded handgun incident to any of the following:

(a) Complying with Section 27560 or 27565, as it pertains to that handgun.

(b) Section 28000, as it pertains to that handgun.

(c) Section 27850 or 31725, as it pertains to that handgun.

(d) Complying with Section 27870 or 27875, as it pertains to that handgun.

(e) Complying with Section 26556, 27915, 27920, 27925, 29810, or 29830, as it pertains to that handgun.

(f) Complying with paragraph (2) of subdivision (e) of Section 32000, as it pertains to that handgun.

(g) Complying with Section 6389 of the Family Code, as it pertains to that handgun. *(Added by Stats.2011, c. 725 (A.B.144), § 14. Amended by Stats.2019, c. 738 (S.B.376), § 7, eff. Jan. 1, 2020; Stats.2020, c. 289 (A.B.2699), § 3, eff. Jan. 1, 2021; Stats.2021, c. 685 (S.B.320), § 10, eff. Jan. 1, 2022.)*

Cross References

Handgun defined for purposes of this Part, see Penal Code § 16640.

§ 26380. Exemption for individual training to become sworn peace officer

Section 26350 does not apply to, or affect, the open carrying of an unloaded handgun incident to, and in the course and scope of, training of or by an individual to become a sworn peace officer as part of a course of study approved by the Commission on Peace Officer Standards and Training. *(Added by Stats.2011, c. 725 (A.B.144), § 14.)*

Cross References

Handgun defined for purposes of this Part, see Penal Code § 16640.

§ 26381. Exemption for individual training to become licensed pursuant to Chapter 4

Section 26350 does not apply to, or affect, the open carrying of an unloaded handgun incident to, and in the course and scope of, training of or by an individual to become licensed pursuant to Chapter 4 (commencing with Section 26150) as part of a course of study necessary or authorized by the person authorized to issue the license pursuant to that chapter. *(Added by Stats.2011, c. 725 (A.B.144), § 14.)*

Cross References

Handgun defined for purposes of this Part, see Penal Code § 16640.

§ 26382. Exemption incident to and at request of head of municipal police department

Section 26350 does not apply to, or affect, the open carrying of an unloaded handgun incident to and at the request of a sheriff or chief or other head of a municipal police department. *(Added by Stats.2011, c. 725 (A.B.144), § 14.)*

Cross References

Handgun defined for purposes of this Part, see Penal Code § 16640.

§ 26383. Exemption for person within place of business, within place of residence, or on private property

Paragraph (1) of subdivision (a) of Section 26350 does not apply to, or affect, the open carrying of an unloaded handgun by a person when done within a place of business, a place of residence, or on private property, if done with the permission of a person who, by virtue of subdivision (a) of Section 25605, may carry openly an unloaded handgun within that place of business, place of residence, or on that private property owned or lawfully possessed by that person. *(Added by Stats.2011, c. 725 (A.B.144), § 14.)*

Cross References

Handgun defined for purposes of this Part, see Penal Code § 16640.

§ 26384. Exemption for auction, raffle, or similar event of nonprofit public benefit or mutual benefit corporation; delivery by licensed person

Paragraph (1) of subdivision (a) of Section 26350 does not apply to, or affect, the open carrying of an unloaded handgun if all of the following conditions are satisfied:

(a) The open carrying occurs at an auction, raffle, or similar event of a nonprofit public benefit or mutual benefit corporation, at which firearms are auctioned or otherwise sold to fund the activities of that corporation or the local chapters of that corporation.

(b) The unloaded handgun is to be auctioned or otherwise sold for that nonprofit public benefit or mutual benefit corporation.

(c) The unloaded handgun is to be delivered by a person licensed pursuant to, and operating in accordance with, Sections 26700 to 26915, inclusive. *(Added by Stats.2011, c. 725 (A.B.144), § 14.*

Amended by Stats.2013, c. 738 (A.B.538), § 1; Stats.2019, c. 738 (S.B.376), § 8, eff. Jan. 1, 2020.)

Cross References

Firearm defined for purposes of this Part, see Penal Code § 16520.
Handgun defined for purposes of this Part, see Penal Code § 16640.

§ 26385. Exemption pursuant to Section 171c

Section 26350 does not apply to, or affect, the open carrying of an unloaded handgun pursuant to paragraph (3) of subdivision (b) of Section 171c. *(Added by Stats.2011, c. 725 (A.B.144), § 14.)*

Cross References

Handgun defined for purposes of this Part, see Penal Code § 16640.

§ 26386. Exemption pursuant to Section 171d

Section 26350 does not apply to, or affect, the open carrying of an unloaded handgun pursuant to Section 171d. *(Added by Stats.2011, c. 725 (A.B.144), § 14.)*

Cross References

Handgun defined for purposes of this Part, see Penal Code § 16640.

§ 26387. Exemption pursuant to Section 171.7

Section 26350 does not apply to, or affect, the open carrying of an unloaded handgun pursuant to subparagraph (F) of paragraph (1) subdivision (c) of Section 171.7. *(Added by Stats.2011, c. 725 (A.B.144), § 14.)*

Cross References

Handgun defined for purposes of this Part, see Penal Code § 16640.

§ 26388. Exemption for person on publicly owned land

Section 26350 does not apply to, or affect, the open carrying of an unloaded handgun on publicly owned land, if the possession and use of a handgun is specifically permitted by the managing agency of the land and the person carrying that handgun is in lawful possession of that handgun. *(Added by Stats.2011, c. 725 (A.B.144), § 14.)*

Cross References

Handgun defined for purposes of this Part, see Penal Code § 16640.

§ 26389. Exemption for handgun carried in locked trunk of motor vehicle or locked container

Section 26350 does not apply to, or affect, the carrying of an unloaded handgun if the handgun is carried either in the locked trunk of a motor vehicle or in a locked container. *(Added by Stats.2011, c. 725 (A.B.144), § 14.)*

Cross References

Handgun defined for purposes of this Part, see Penal Code § 16640.

§ 26390. Exemption for person holding permit to possess, manufacture, transport, sell, or conduct business using destructive devices, assault weapons, .50 BMG rifles, machineguns, or short-barreled rifles or shotguns

Section 26350 does not apply to, or affect, the open carrying of an unloaded handgun in any of the following circumstances:

(a) The open carrying of an unloaded handgun that is regulated pursuant to Chapter 1 (commencing with Section 18710) of Division 5 of Title 2 by a person who holds a permit issued pursuant to Article 3 (commencing with Section 18900) of that chapter, if the carrying of that handgun is conducted in accordance with the terms and conditions of the permit.

(b) The open carrying of an unloaded handgun that is regulated pursuant to Chapter 2 (commencing with Section 30500) of Division 10 by a person who holds a permit issued pursuant to Section 31005, if the carrying of that handgun is conducted in accordance with the terms and conditions of the permit.

(c) The open carrying of an unloaded handgun that is regulated pursuant to Chapter 6 (commencing with Section 32610) of Division 10 by a person who holds a permit issued pursuant to Section 32650, if the carrying is conducted in accordance with the terms and conditions of the permit.

(d) The open carrying of an unloaded handgun that is regulated pursuant to Article 2 (commencing with Section 33300) of Chapter 8 of Division 10 by a person who holds a permit issued pursuant to Section 33300, if the carrying of that handgun is conducted in accordance with the terms and conditions of the permit. *(Added by Stats.2012, c. 700 (A.B.1527), § 10.)*

Research References

2 Witkin, California Criminal Law 4th Crimes Against Public Peace and Welfare § 253 (2021), Openly Displaying or Carrying Imitation or Unloaded Firearm.

§ 26391. Exemption pursuant to Section 171.5

Section 26350 does not apply to, or affect, the open carrying of an unloaded handgun when done in accordance with the provisions of subdivision (d) of Section 171.5. *(Added by Stats.2012, c. 700 (A.B.1527), § 11.)*

Research References

2 Witkin, California Criminal Law 4th Crimes Against Public Peace and Welfare § 253 (2021), Openly Displaying or Carrying Imitation or Unloaded Firearm.

§ 26392. Delivery or transportation of firearm to law enforcement agency; application of Section 26350

Paragraph (1) of subdivision (a) of Section 26350 does not apply to, or affect, the open carrying of an unloaded handgun in any of the following circumstances:

(a) By a person who finds that handgun, if the person is transporting the handgun in order to comply with Article 1 (commencing with Section 2080) of Chapter 4 of Title 6 of Part 4 of Division 3 of the Civil Code as it pertains to that firearm, and, if the person is transporting the firearm to a law enforcement agency, the person gives prior notice to the law enforcement agency that the person is transporting the handgun to the law enforcement agency.

(b) By a person who finds that handgun and is transporting it to a law enforcement agency for disposition according to law, if the person gives prior notice to the law enforcement agency that the person is transporting the firearm to the law enforcement agency for disposition according to law.

(c) By a person who took the firearm from a person who was committing a crime against the person and is transporting it to a law enforcement agency for disposition according to law, if the person gives prior notice to the law enforcement agency that the person is transporting that handgun to the law enforcement agency for disposition according to law. *(Added by Stats.2019, c. 110 (A.B. 1292), § 4, eff. Jan. 1, 2020.)*

CHAPTER 7. CARRYING AN UNLOADED FIREARM THAT IS NOT A HANDGUN

ARTICLE 1. CRIME OF CARRYING AN UNLOADED FIREARM THAT IS NOT A HANDGUN

§ 26400. Carrying an unloaded firearm that is not a handgun; penalties; definition

(a) A person is guilty of carrying an unloaded firearm that is not a handgun when that person carries upon his or her person an unloaded firearm that is not a handgun outside a vehicle while in any of the following areas:

(1) An incorporated city or city and county.

(2) A public place or a public street in a prohibited area of an unincorporated area of a county.

(b)(1) Except as specified in paragraph (2), a violation of this section is a misdemeanor.

(2) A violation of subdivision (a) is punishable by imprisonment in a county jail not exceeding one year, or by a fine not to exceed one thousand dollars ($1,000), or by both that fine and imprisonment, if the firearm and unexpended ammunition capable of being discharged from that firearm are in the immediate possession of the person and the person is not in lawful possession of that firearm.

(c)(1) Nothing in this section shall preclude prosecution under Chapter 2 (commencing with Section 29800) or Chapter 3 (commencing with Section 29900) of Division 9, Section 8100 or 8103 of the Welfare and Institutions Code, or any other law with a penalty greater than is set forth in this section.

(2) The provisions of this section are cumulative and shall not be construed as restricting the application of any other law. However, an act or omission punishable in different ways by different provisions of law shall not be punished under more than one provision.

(d) Notwithstanding the fact that the term "an unloaded firearm that is not a handgun" is used in this section, each individual firearm shall constitute a distinct and separate offense under this section. *(Added by Stats.2012, c. 700 (A.B.1527), § 12. Amended by Stats. 2017, c. 734 (A.B.7), § 3, eff. Jan. 1, 2018.)*

Cross References

Encased firearm defined for purposes of this Chapter, see Penal Code § 16505.

Research References

2 Witkin, California Criminal Law 4th Crimes Against Public Peace and Welfare § 253A (2021), (New) Carrying Unloaded Firearm that is Not Handgun in Incorporated Area or Other Public Place.

2 Witkin, California Criminal Law 4th Crimes Against Public Peace and Welfare § 257 (2021), Firearms.

ARTICLE 2. EXEMPTIONS

§ 26405. Carrying an unloaded firearm that is not a handgun in an incorporated city or city and county; exemptions

Section 26400 does not apply to, or affect, the carrying of an unloaded firearm that is not a handgun in any of the following circumstances:

(a) By a person when carried within a place of business, a place of residence, or on private real property, if that person, by virtue of subdivision (a) of Section 25605, may carry a firearm within that place of business, place of residence, or on that private real property owned or lawfully occupied by that person.

(b) By a person when carried within a place of business, a place of residence, or on private real property, if done with the permission of a person who, by virtue of subdivision (a) of Section 25605, may carry a firearm within that place of business, place of residence, or on that private real property owned or lawfully occupied by that person.

(c) When the firearm is either in a locked container or encased and it is being transported directly between places where a person is not prohibited from possessing that firearm and the course of travel shall include only those deviations between authorized locations as are reasonably necessary under the circumstances.

(d) If the person possessing the firearm reasonably believes that they are in grave danger because of circumstances forming the basis of a current restraining order issued by a court against another person or persons who has or have been found to pose a threat to the person's life or safety. This subdivision may not apply when the circumstances involve a mutual restraining order issued pursuant to Division 10 (commencing with Section 6200) of the Family Code absent a factual finding of a specific threat to the person's life or safety. Upon a trial for violating Section 26400, the trier of fact shall determine whether the defendant was acting out of a reasonable belief that they were in grave danger.

(e) By a peace officer or an honorably retired peace officer if that officer may carry a concealed firearm pursuant to Article 2 (commencing with Section 25450) of Chapter 2, or a loaded firearm pursuant to Article 3 (commencing with Section 25900) of Chapter 3.

(f) By a person to the extent that person may openly carry a loaded firearm that is not a handgun pursuant to Article 4 (commencing with Section 26000) of Chapter 3.

(g) As merchandise by a person who is engaged in the business of manufacturing, importing, wholesaling, repairing, or dealing in firearms and who is licensed to engage in that business, or the authorized representative or authorized agent of that person, while engaged in the lawful course of the business.

(h) By a duly authorized military or civil organization, or the members thereof, while parading or while rehearsing or practicing parading, when at the meeting place of the organization.

(i) By a member of a club or organization organized for the purpose of practicing shooting at targets upon established target ranges, whether public or private, while the members are using firearms that are not handguns upon the target ranges or incident to the use of a firearm that is not a handgun at that target range.

(j) By a licensed hunter while engaged in hunting or while transporting that firearm when going to or returning from that hunting expedition.

(k) Incident to transportation of a handgun by a person operating a licensed common carrier, or by an authorized agent or employee thereof, when transported in conformance with applicable federal law.

(*l*) By a member of an organization chartered by the Congress of the United States or a nonprofit mutual or public benefit corporation organized and recognized as a nonprofit tax-exempt organization by the Internal Revenue Service while on official parade duty or ceremonial occasions of that organization or while rehearsing or practicing for official parade duty or ceremonial occasions.

(m) Within a gun show conducted pursuant to Article 1 (commencing with Section 27200) and Article 2 (commencing with Section 27300) of Chapter 3 of Division 6.

(n) Within a school zone, as defined in Section 626.9, if that carrying is not prohibited by Section 626.9.

(*o*) When in accordance with the provisions of Section 171b.

(p) By a person while engaged in the act of making or attempting to make a lawful arrest.

(q) By a person engaged in firearms-related activities, while on the premises of a fixed place of business that is licensed to conduct and conducts, as a regular course of its business, activities related to the sale, making, repair, transfer, pawn, or the use of firearms, or related to firearms training.

(r) By an authorized participant in, or an authorized employee or agent of a supplier of firearms for, a motion picture, television, or video production or entertainment event, when the participant lawfully uses that firearm as part of that production or event, as part of rehearsing or practicing for participation in that production or event, or while the participant or authorized employee or agent is at that production or event, or rehearsal or practice for that production or event.

(s) Incident to obtaining an identification number or mark assigned for that firearm from the Department of Justice pursuant to Section 23910.

(t) At an established public target range while the person is using that firearm upon that target range.

(u) By a person when that person is summoned by a peace officer to assist in making arrests or preserving the peace, while the person is actually engaged in assisting that officer.

(v) Incident to any of the following:

(1) Complying with Section 27560 or 27565, as it pertains to that firearm.

(2) Section 28000, as it pertains to that firearm.

(3) Section 27850 or 31725, as it pertains to that firearm.

(4) Complying with Section 27870 or 27875, as it pertains to that firearm.

(5) Complying with Section 26556, 27915, 27920, 27925, 27966, 29810, or 29830, as it pertains to that firearm.

(6) Complying with Section 6389 of the Family Code, as it pertains to that firearm.

(w) Incident to, and in the course and scope of, training of, or by an individual to become a sworn peace officer as part of a course of study approved by the Commission on Peace Officer Standards and Training.

(x) Incident to, and in the course and scope of, training of, or by an individual to become licensed pursuant to Chapter 4 (commencing with Section 26150) as part of a course of study necessary or authorized by the person authorized to issue the license pursuant to that chapter.

(y) Incident to and at the request of a sheriff, chief, or other head of a municipal police department.

(z) If all of the following conditions are satisfied:

(1) The open carrying occurs at an auction, raffle, or similar event of a nonprofit public benefit or mutual benefit corporation at which firearms are auctioned, raffled, or otherwise sold to fund the activities of that corporation or the local chapters of that corporation.

(2) The unloaded firearm that is not a handgun is to be auctioned, raffled, or otherwise sold for that nonprofit public benefit or mutual benefit corporation.

(3) The unloaded firearm that is not a handgun is to be delivered by a person licensed pursuant to, and operating in accordance with, Sections 26700 to 26915, inclusive.

(aa) Pursuant to paragraph (3) of subdivision (b) of Section 171c.

(ab) Pursuant to Section 171d.

(ac) Pursuant to subparagraph (F) of paragraph (1) of subdivision (c) of Section 171.7.

(ad) On publicly owned land, if the possession and use of an unloaded firearm that is not a handgun is specifically permitted by the managing agency of the land and the person carrying that firearm is in lawful possession of that firearm.

(ae) By any of the following:

(1) The carrying of an unloaded firearm that is not a handgun that is regulated pursuant to Chapter 1 (commencing with Section 18710) of Division 5 of Title 2 by a person who holds a permit issued pursuant to Article 3 (commencing with Section 18900) of that chapter, if the carrying of that firearm is conducted in accordance with the terms and conditions of the permit.

(2) The carrying of an unloaded firearm that is not a handgun that is regulated pursuant to Chapter 2 (commencing with Section 30500) of Division 10 by a person who holds a permit issued pursuant to Section 31005, if the carrying of that firearm is conducted in accordance with the terms and conditions of the permit.

(3) The carrying of an unloaded firearm that is not a handgun that is regulated pursuant to Chapter 6 (commencing with Section 32610) of Division 10 by a person who holds a permit issued pursuant to Section 32650, if the carrying of that firearm is conducted in accordance with the terms and conditions of the permit.

(4) The carrying of an unloaded firearm that is not a handgun that is regulated pursuant to Article 2 (commencing with Section 33300) of Chapter 8 of Division 10 by a person who holds a permit issued pursuant to Section 33300, if the carrying of that firearm is conducted in accordance with the terms and conditions of the permit.

(af) By a licensed hunter while actually engaged in training a dog for the purpose of using the dog in hunting that is not prohibited by law, or while transporting the firearm while going to or returning from that training.

(ag) Pursuant to the provisions of subdivision (d) of Section 171.5.

(ah) By a person who is engaged in the business of manufacturing ammunition and who is licensed to engage in that business, or the authorized representative or authorized agent of that person, while the firearm is being used in the lawful course and scope of the licensee's activities as a person licensed pursuant to Chapter 44 (commencing with Section 921) of Title 18 of the United States Code and regulations issued pursuant thereto.

(ai) On the navigable waters of this state that are held in public trust, if the possession and use of an unloaded firearm that is not a handgun is not prohibited by the managing agency thereof and the person carrying the firearm is in lawful possession of the firearm. *(Added by Stats.2012, c. 700 (A.B.1527), § 12. Amended by Stats. 2013, c. 738 (A.B.538), § 2; Stats.2017, c. 779 (A.B.424), § 3, eff. Jan. 1, 2018; Stats.2019, c. 738 (S.B.376), § 9, eff. Jan. 1, 2020; Stats.2021, c. 685 (S.B.320), § 11, eff. Jan. 1, 2022.)*

Cross References

Encased firearm defined for purposes of this Chapter, see Penal Code § 16505.

Research References

2 Witkin, California Criminal Law 4th Crimes Against Public Peace and Welfare § 253A (2021), (New) Carrying Unloaded Firearm that is Not Handgun in Incorporated Area or Other Public Place.

2 Witkin, California Criminal Law 4th Crimes Against Public Peace and Welfare § 257 (2021), Firearms.

§ 26406. Transportation and delivery of firearm to law enforcement agency; application of Section 26400

Section 26400 does not apply to, or affect, the carrying of an unloaded firearm that is not a handgun in any of the following circumstances:

(a) By a person who finds that firearm, if the person is carrying the firearm in order to comply with Article 1 (commencing with Section 2080) of Chapter 4 of Title 6 of Part 4 of Division 3 of the Civil Code as it pertains to that firearm, and, if the person is transporting the firearm to a law enforcement agency, the person gives prior notice to the law enforcement agency that the person is transporting the firearm to the law enforcement agency.

(b) By a person who finds that firearm and is transporting it to a law enforcement agency for disposition according to law, if the person gives prior notice to the law enforcement agency that the person is transporting the firearm to the law enforcement agency for disposition according to law.

(c) By a person who took the firearm from a person who was committing a crime against the person and is transporting it to a law enforcement agency for disposition according to law, if the person gives prior notice to the law enforcement agency that the person is transporting the firearm to the law enforcement agency for disposition according to law. *(Added by Stats.2019, c. 110 (A.B.1292), § 5, eff. Jan. 1, 2020. Amended by Stats.2021, c. 250 (S.B.715), § 6, eff. Jan. 1, 2022.)*

Research References

2 Witkin, California Criminal Law 4th Crimes Against Public Peace and Welfare § 253A (2021), (New) Carrying Unloaded Firearm that is Not Handgun in Incorporated Area or Other Public Place.

Division 6

SALE, LEASE, OR TRANSFER OF FIREARMS

CHAPTER 1. LICENSE REQUIREMENT FOR SALE, LEASE, OR TRANSFER OF FIREARMS

ARTICLE 1. LICENSE REQUIREMENT AND MISCELLANEOUS EXCEPTIONS

§ 26500. License required to sell, lease, or transfer firearms

(a) No person shall sell, lease, or transfer firearms unless the person has been issued a license pursuant to Article 1 (commencing with Section 26700) and Article 2 (commencing with Section 26800) of Chapter 2.

(b) Any person violating this article is guilty of a misdemeanor. *(Added by Stats.2010, c. 711 (S.B.1080), § 6, operative Jan. 1, 2012.)*

Law Revision Commission Comments

Section 26500 continues former Section 12070(a) without substantive change.

See Section 16520 ("firearm"). [38 Cal.L.Rev.Comm. Reports 217 (2009)].

Cross References

Centralized list of exempted federal firearms licensees, see Penal Code § 28450.
Community care facilities, acceptance or storage of client's firearm does not constitute loan, sale, receipt, or transfer, see Health and Safety Code § 1567.94.
Firearm defined for purposes of this Part, see Penal Code § 16520.
Loan of firearm to person enrolled in peace officer training program for purposes of course participation, see Penal Code § 26625.
Machineguns, license to sell, see Penal Code § 32700 et seq.
Misdemeanors, definition and penalties, see Penal Code §§ 17, 19, 19.2.
Residential care facilities for persons with chronic life-threatening illness, acceptance or storage of resident's firearm does not constitute loan, sale, receipt, or transfer, see Health and Safety Code § 1568.099.
Residential care facilities for the elderly, acceptance or storage of resident's firearm does not constitute loan, sale, receipt, or transfer, see Health and Safety Code § 1569.284.
Return or transfer of firearm in custody or control of court or law enforcement agency, authorization of ineligible applicant to sell or transfer firearm to licensed dealer, see Penal Code § 33870.

Research References

2 Witkin, California Criminal Law 4th Crimes Against Public Peace and Welfare § 193 (2021), Sale, Lease, or Transfer by Unlicensed Person.

§ 26505. Exemptions from application of Section 26500

Section 26500 does not apply to the sale, lease, or transfer of any firearm by any of the following:

(a) A person acting pursuant to operation of law.

(b) A person acting pursuant to a court order.

(c) A person acting pursuant to the Enforcement of Judgments Law (Title 9 (commencing with Section 680.010) of Part 2 of the Code of Civil Procedure).

(d) A person who liquidates a personal firearm collection to satisfy a court judgment. *(Added by Stats.2010, c. 711 (S.B.1080), § 6, operative Jan. 1, 2012.)*

Law Revision Commission Comments

Section 26505 continues former Section 12070(b)(1) without substantive change.

See Sections 16520 ("firearm"), 16960 ("operation of law"). [38 Cal.L.Rev. Comm. Reports 217 (2009)].

Cross References

Firearm defined for purposes of this Part, see Penal Code § 16520.

Research References

2 Witkin, California Criminal Law 4th Crimes Against Public Peace and Welfare § 193 (2021), Sale, Lease, or Transfer by Unlicensed Person.

§ 26510. Person acting pursuant to Sections 186.22a, 18000 or 18005; application of Section 26500

Section 26500 does not apply to a person acting pursuant to subdivision (f) of Section 186.22a or Section 18000 or 18005. *(Added by Stats.2010, c. 711 (S.B.1080), § 6, operative Jan. 1, 2012.)*

Law Revision Commission Comments

Section 26510 continues former Section 12070(b)(2) without substantive change. An erroneous cross-reference to Section 186.22a(e) has been corrected by replacing it with a cross-reference to Section 186.22a(f). [38 Cal.L.Rev. Comm. Reports 217 (2009)].

Research References

2 Witkin, California Criminal Law 4th Crimes Against Public Peace and Welfare § 193 (2021), Sale, Lease, or Transfer by Unlicensed Person.

§ 26515. Certain sales, leases, or transfers; application of Section 26500

Section 26500 does not apply to the sale, lease, or transfer of a firearm if both of the following conditions are satisfied:

(a) The sale, lease, or transfer is made by a person who obtains title to the firearm by any of the following means:

(1) Intestate succession or bequest.

(2) As the beneficiary of a trust that includes a firearm.

(3) As a surviving spouse pursuant to Chapter 1 (commencing with Section 13500) of Part 2 of Division 8 of the Probate Code.

(4) As decedent's successor pursuant to Part 1 (commencing with Section 13000) of Division 8 of the Probate Code.

(b) The person disposes of the firearm within 60 days of receipt of the firearm. *(Added by Stats.2010, c. 711 (S.B.1080), § 6, operative Jan. 1, 2012. Amended by Stats.2019, c. 738 (S.B.376), § 10, eff. Jan. 1, 2020.)*

Law Revision Commission Comments

Section 26515 continues former Section 12070(b)(3) without substantive change.

See Section 16520 ("firearm"). [38 Cal.L.Rev.Comm. Reports 217 (2009)].

Cross References

Firearm defined for purposes of this Part, see Penal Code § 16520.

Research References

2 Witkin, California Criminal Law 4th Crimes Against Public Peace and Welfare § 193 (2021), Sale, Lease, or Transfer by Unlicensed Person.

§ 26520. Infrequent sale, lease, or transfer of firearms; application of Section 26500

(a) Section 26500 does not apply to the infrequent sale, lease, or transfer of firearms.

(b) As used in this section, "infrequent" has the meaning provided in Section 16730. *(Added by Stats.2010, c. 711 (S.B.1080), § 6, operative Jan. 1, 2012.)*

Law Revision Commission Comments

Section 26520 continues former Section 12070(b)(4) without substantive change.

See Section 16520 ("firearm"). [38 Cal.L.Rev.Comm. Reports 217 (2009)].

Cross References

Firearm defined for purposes of this Part, see Penal Code § 16520.

Research References

2 Witkin, California Criminal Law 4th Crimes Against Public Peace and Welfare § 193 (2021), Sale, Lease, or Transfer by Unlicensed Person.

§ 26525. Sale, lease, or transfer of used firearms by holder of federal license at gun shows; application of Section 26500; limitations

(a) Section 26500 does not apply to the sale, lease, or transfer of used firearms, other than handguns, at gun shows or events, as specified in Article 1 (commencing with Section 26700) and Article 2 (commencing with Section 26800) of Chapter 2, by a person other than a licensee or dealer, provided the person has a valid federal firearms license and a current certificate of eligibility issued by the Department of Justice, as specified in Section 26710, and provided all the sales, leases, or transfers fully comply with Section 27545. However, the person shall not engage in the sale, lease, or transfer of used firearms other than handguns at more than 12 gun shows or events in any calendar year and shall not sell, lease, or transfer more than 15 used firearms other than handguns at any single gun show or event. In no event shall the person sell more than 75 used firearms other than handguns in any calendar year.

(b) The Department of Justice shall adopt regulations to administer this program and shall recover the full costs of administration from fees assessed applicants. *(Added by Stats.2010, c. 711 (S.B. 1080), § 6, operative Jan. 1, 2012.)*

Law Revision Commission Comments

Subdivision (a) of Section 26525 continues the first paragraph of former Section 12070(b)(5) without substantive change. A person who meets the description in subdivision (a) is known as a Gun Show Trader. See Section 16620 ("Gun Show Trader").

Subdivision (b) continues the third paragraph of former Section 12070(b)(5) without substantive change.

See Sections 16520 ("firearm"), 16640 ("handgun"), 17310 ("used firearm"), 26700 ("dealer," "licensee," or "person licensed pursuant to Sections 26700 to 26915, inclusive"). [38 Cal.L.Rev.Comm. Reports 217 (2009)].

Cross References

Firearm defined for purposes of this Part, see Penal Code § 16520.
Handgun defined for purposes of this Part, see Penal Code § 16640.

Research References

2 Witkin, California Criminal Law 4th Crimes Against Public Peace and Welfare § 193 (2021), Sale, Lease, or Transfer by Unlicensed Person.

§ 26530. Sales, deliveries, or transfers of firearms between licensed importers and manufacturers; application of Section 26500

Section 26500 does not apply to sales, deliveries, or transfers of firearms between or to importers and manufacturers of firearms licensed to engage in that business pursuant to Chapter 44 (commencing with Section 921) of Title 18 of the United States Code and the regulations issued pursuant thereto. *(Added by Stats.2010, c. 711 (S.B.1080), § 6, operative Jan. 1, 2012.)*

Law Revision Commission Comments

Section 26530 continues former Section 12070(b)(6) without substantive change.

See Section 16520 ("firearm"). [38 Cal.L.Rev.Comm. Reports 217 (2009)].

Cross References

Firearm defined for purposes of this Part, see Penal Code § 16520.

Research References

2 Witkin, California Criminal Law 4th Crimes Against Public Peace and Welfare § 193 (2021), Sale, Lease, or Transfer by Unlicensed Person.

§ 26535. Sale, delivery, or transfer of firearms between licensed importer or manufacturer and dealer or wholesaler; application of Section 26500

Section 26500 does not apply to any sale, delivery, or transfer of firearms that satisfies both of the following conditions:

(a) It is made by an importer or manufacturer licensed pursuant to Chapter 44 (commencing with Section 921) of Title 18 of the United States Code and the regulations issued pursuant thereto.

(b) It is made to a dealer or wholesaler. *(Added by Stats.2010, c. 711 (S.B.1080), § 6, operative Jan. 1, 2012.)*

Law Revision Commission Comments

Section 26535 continues former Section 12070(b)(7) without substantive change.

See Sections 16520 ("firearm"), 17340 ("wholesaler"), 26700 ("dealer," "licensee," or "person licensed pursuant to Sections 26700 to 26915, inclusive"). [38 Cal.L.Rev.Comm. Reports 217 (2009)].

Cross References

Dealer defined, see Penal Code § 26700.
Firearm defined for purposes of this Part, see Penal Code § 16520.
Wholesaler defined for purposes of this Part, see Penal Code § 17340.

Research References

2 Witkin, California Criminal Law 4th Crimes Against Public Peace and Welfare § 193 (2021), Sale, Lease, or Transfer by Unlicensed Person.

§ 26537. Sale, delivery, or transfer of firearms between manufacturers of ammunition; application of Section 26500

(a) Section 26500 does not apply to the sale, delivery, or transfer of firearms that satisfies both of the following conditions:

(1) The sale, delivery, or transfer is made by a manufacturer of ammunition licensed pursuant to Chapter 44 (commencing with Section 921) of Title 18 of the United States Code and the regulations issued pursuant thereto.

(2) The sale, delivery, or transfer is made to a dealer or wholesaler.

(b) Section 26500 does not apply to the sale, delivery, or transfer of firearms between or to manufacturers of ammunition licensed to engage in that business pursuant to Chapter 44 (commencing with Section 921) of Title 18 of the United States Code and the regulations issued pursuant thereto, where those firearms are to be used in the course and scope of the licensee's activities as a person licensed pursuant to Chapter 44 (commencing with Section 921) of Title 18 of the United States Code and the regulations issued pursuant thereto. *(Added by Stats.2021, c. 250 (S.B.715), § 7, eff. Jan. 1, 2022.)*

§ 26540. Certain sales, deliveries, transfers, or returns of firearms; application of Section 26500

(a) Section 26500 does not apply to sales, deliveries, transfers, or returns of firearms made pursuant to any of the following:

(1) Sections 18000 and 18005.

(2) Division 4 (commencing with Section 18250) of Title 2.

(3) Section 29810.

(4) Chapter 2 (commencing with Section 33850) of Division 11.

(5) Sections 34005 and 34010.

(b) Section 26500 does not apply to the sale, delivery, or transfer of a firearm to a dealer to comply with Section 6389 of the Family Code. *(Added by Stats.2010, c. 711 (S.B.1080), § 6, operative Jan. 1, 2012. Amended by Stats.2019, c. 738 (S.B.376), § 11, eff. Jan. 1, 2020; Stats.2021, c. 685 (S.B.320), § 12, eff. Jan. 1, 2022.)*

Law Revision Commission Comments

Section 26540 continues former Section 12070(b)(8) without substantive change.

See Section 16520 ("firearm"). [38 Cal.L.Rev.Comm. Reports 217 (2009)].

Cross References

Firearm defined for purposes of this Part, see Penal Code § 16520.

Research References

2 Witkin, California Criminal Law 4th Crimes Against Public Peace and Welfare § 193 (2021), Sale, Lease, or Transfer by Unlicensed Person.

§ 26545. Loan of firearm for shooting targets at a target facility; application of Section 26500

Section 26500 does not apply to the loan of a firearm for the purposes of shooting at targets, if the loan occurs on the premises of a target facility that holds a business or regulatory license or on the premises of any club or organization organized for the purposes of practicing shooting at targets upon established ranges, whether public or private, if the firearm is at all times kept within the premises of the target range or on the premises of the club or organization. *(Added by Stats.2010, c. 711 (S.B.1080), § 6, operative Jan. 1, 2012.)*

Law Revision Commission Comments

Section 26545 continues former Section 12070(b)(9) without substantive change.

See Section 16520 ("firearm"). [38 Cal.L.Rev.Comm. Reports 217 (2009)].

Cross References

Firearm defined for purposes of this Part, see Penal Code § 16520.

Research References

2 Witkin, California Criminal Law 4th Crimes Against Public Peace and Welfare § 193 (2021), Sale, Lease, or Transfer by Unlicensed Person.

§ 26550. Sale, delivery, or transfer by manufacturer, importer, or wholesaler to person outside of state; application of Section 26500

Section 26500 does not apply to any sale, delivery, or transfer of firearms that satisfies all of the following requirements:

(a) It is made by a manufacturer, importer, or wholesaler licensed pursuant to Chapter 44 (commencing with Section 921) of Title 18 of the United States Code and the regulations issued pursuant thereto.

(b) It is made to a person who resides outside this state and is licensed pursuant to Chapter 44 (commencing with Section 921) of Title 18 of the United States Code and the regulations issued pursuant thereto.

(c) It is made in accordance with Chapter 44 (commencing with Section 921) of Title 18 of the United States Code and the regulations issued pursuant thereto. *(Added by Stats.2010, c. 711 (S.B.1080), § 6, operative Jan. 1, 2012.)*

Law Revision Commission Comments

Section 26550 continues former Section 12070(b)(10) without substantive change.

See Sections 16520 ("firearm"), 17340 ("wholesaler"). [38 Cal.L.Rev. Comm. Reports 217 (2009)].

Cross References

Firearm defined for purposes of this Part, see Penal Code § 16520.
Wholesaler defined for purposes of this Part, see Penal Code § 17340.

Research References

2 Witkin, California Criminal Law 4th Crimes Against Public Peace and Welfare § 193 (2021), Sale, Lease, or Transfer by Unlicensed Person.

§ 26555. Sale, delivery, or transfer to manufacturer, importer, or wholesaler by person outside of state; application of Section 26500

Section 26500 does not apply to any sale, delivery, or transfer of firearms that satisfies all of the following requirements:

(a) It is made by a person who resides outside this state and is licensed outside this state pursuant to Chapter 44 (commencing with Section 921) of Title 18 of the United States Code and the regulations issued pursuant thereto.

(b) It is made to a manufacturer, importer, or wholesaler.

(c) It is made in accordance with Chapter 44 (commencing with Section 921) of Title 18 of the United States Code and the regulations issued pursuant thereto. *(Added by Stats.2010, c. 711 (S.B.1080), § 6, operative Jan. 1, 2012.)*

Law Revision Commission Comments

Section 26555 continues former Section 12070(b)(11) without substantive change.

See Sections 16520 ("firearm"), 17340 ("wholesaler"). [38 Cal.L.Rev. Comm. Reports 217 (2009)].

Cross References

Firearm defined for purposes of this Part, see Penal Code § 16520.
Wholesaler defined for purposes of this Part, see Penal Code § 17340.

Research References

2 Witkin, California Criminal Law 4th Crimes Against Public Peace and Welfare § 193 (2021), Sale, Lease, or Transfer by Unlicensed Person.

§ 26556. Sale, delivery, or transfer to manufacturer, importer, or wholesaler by person who has ceased operations as a dealer; application of Section 26500

Section 26500 does not apply to the sale, delivery, or transfer of a firearm that satisfies all of the following requirements:

(a) It is made by a person who has ceased operations as a dealer.

(b) It is made to a dealer, a manufacturer, importer, or wholesaler.

(c) It is made in accordance with Chapter 44 (commencing with Section 921) of Title 18 of the United States Code and the regulations issued pursuant thereto.

(d) The transaction is reported to the Department of Justice in a manner and format prescribed by the department. *(Added by Stats.2019, c. 738 (S.B.376), § 12, eff. Jan. 1, 2020.)*

Research References

2 Witkin, California Criminal Law 4th Crimes Against Public Peace and Welfare § 208 (2021), Exempt Activities.

§ 26560. Sale, delivery, or transfer of firearms by wholesaler to dealer; application of Section 26500

Section 26500 does not apply to any sale, delivery, or transfer of firearms by a wholesaler to a dealer. *(Added by Stats.2010, c. 711 (S.B.1080), § 6, operative Jan. 1, 2012.)*

Law Revision Commission Comments

Section 26560 continues former Section 12070(b)(12) without substantive change.

See Sections 16520 ("firearm"), 17340 ("wholesaler"), 26700 ("dealer," "licensee," or "person licensed pursuant to Sections 26700 to 26915, inclusive"). [38 Cal.L.Rev.Comm. Reports 217 (2009)].

Cross References

Dealer defined, see Penal Code § 26700.
Firearm defined for purposes of this Part, see Penal Code § 16520.
Wholesaler defined for purposes of this Part, see Penal Code § 17340.

Research References

2 Witkin, California Criminal Law 4th Crimes Against Public Peace and Welfare § 193 (2021), Sale, Lease, or Transfer by Unlicensed Person.

§ 26565. Sale, delivery, or transfer of firearms by person outside of state to certain licensed person; application of Section 26500

Section 26500 does not apply to any sale, delivery, or transfer of firearms that satisfies all of the following conditions:

(a) It is made by a person who resides outside this state.

(b) It is made to a person licensed pursuant to Sections 26700 to 26915, inclusive.

(c) It is made in accordance with Chapter 44 (commencing with Section 921) of Title 18 of the United States Code and the regulations issued pursuant thereto. *(Added by Stats.2010, c. 711 (S.B.1080), § 6, operative Jan. 1, 2012.)*

Law Revision Commission Comments

Section 26565 continues former Section 12070(b)(13) without substantive change.

See Sections 16520 ("firearm"), 26700 ("dealer," "licensee," or "person licensed pursuant to Sections 26700 to 26915, inclusive"). [38 Cal.L.Rev. Comm. Reports 217 (2009)].

Cross References

Firearm defined for purposes of this Part, see Penal Code § 16520.

Research References

2 Witkin, California Criminal Law 4th Crimes Against Public Peace and Welfare § 193 (2021), Sale, Lease, or Transfer by Unlicensed Person.

§ 26570. Sale, delivery, or transfer by person outside of state to dealer; application of Section 26500

Section 26500 does not apply to any sale, delivery, or transfer of firearms that satisfies all of the following conditions:

(a) It is made by a person who resides outside this state and is licensed pursuant to Chapter 44 (commencing with Section 921) of Title 18 of the United States Code and the regulations issued pursuant thereto.

(b) It is made to a dealer.

(c) It is made in accordance with Chapter 44 (commencing with Section 921) of Title 18 of the United States Code and the regulations issued pursuant thereto. *(Added by Stats.2010, c. 711 (S.B.1080), § 6, operative Jan. 1, 2012.)*

Law Revision Commission Comments

Section 26570 continues former Section 12070(b)(14) without substantive change.

See Sections 16520 ("firearm"), 26700 ("dealer," "licensee," or "person licensed pursuant to Sections 26700 to 26915, inclusive"). [38 Cal.L.Rev. Comm. Reports 217 (2009)].

Cross References

Dealer defined, see Penal Code § 26700.
Firearm defined for purposes of this Part, see Penal Code § 16520.

Research References

2 Witkin, California Criminal Law 4th Crimes Against Public Peace and Welfare § 193 (2021), Sale, Lease, or Transfer by Unlicensed Person.

§ 26575. Sale, delivery, or transfer of unloaded firearm between wholesalers for use as merchandise; application of Section 26500

Section 26500 does not apply to the sale, delivery, or transfer of an unloaded firearm by one wholesaler to another wholesaler if that firearm is intended as merchandise in the receiving wholesaler's business. *(Added by Stats.2010, c. 711 (S.B.1080), § 6, operative Jan. 1, 2012.)*

Law Revision Commission Comments

Section 26575 continues former Section 12070(b)(15) without substantive change.

See Sections 16520 ("firearm"), 17340 ("wholesaler"). [38 Cal.L.Rev. Comm. Reports 217 (2009)].

Cross References

Firearm defined for purposes of this Part, see Penal Code § 16520.
Wholesaler defined for purposes of this Part, see Penal Code § 17340.

Research References

2 Witkin, California Criminal Law 4th Crimes Against Public Peace and Welfare § 193 (2021), Sale, Lease, or Transfer by Unlicensed Person.

§ 26576. Sale, delivery, or transfer to authorized representative of a city, city and county, county, state government, or federal government as part of buyback program; application of Section 26500

(a) Section 26500 does not apply to a sale, delivery, or transfer of firearms if both of the following requirements are satisfied:

(1) The sale, delivery, or transfer is to an authorized representative of a city, city and county, county, or state government, or of the federal government, and is for the governmental entity.

(2) The entity is acquiring the firearm as part of an authorized, voluntary program in which the entity is buying or receiving firearms from private individuals.

(b) Any weapons acquired pursuant to subdivision (a) of this section shall be disposed of pursuant to the applicable provisions of Section 34000 or Sections 18000 and 18005. *(Added by Stats.2019, c. 738 (S.B.376), § 13, eff. Jan. 1, 2020.)*

Research References

2 Witkin, California Criminal Law 4th Crimes Against Public Peace and Welfare § 193 (2021), Sale, Lease, or Transfer by Unlicensed Person.

§ 26577. Delivery or transfer of firearms to dealer for storage; application of Section 26500

Section 26500 does not apply to a delivery or transfer of firearms made to a dealer pursuant to Section 29830 for storage by that dealer. *(Added by Stats.2019, c. 738 (S.B.376), § 14, eff. Jan. 1, 2020.)*

Research References

2 Witkin, California Criminal Law 4th Crimes Against Public Peace and Welfare § 193 (2021), Sale, Lease, or Transfer by Unlicensed Person.

§ 26580. Loan of unloaded firearm or firearm loaded with blank cartridges for use as prop; application of Section 26500

Section 26500 does not apply to the loan of an unloaded firearm or the loan of a firearm loaded with blank cartridges for use solely as a prop for a motion picture, television, or video production or entertainment or theatrical event. *(Added by Stats.2010, c. 711 (S.B.1080), § 6, operative Jan. 1, 2012.)*

Law Revision Commission Comments

Section 26580 continues former Section 12070(b)(16) without substantive change.

See Section 16520 ("firearm"). [38 Cal.L.Rev.Comm. Reports 217 (2009)].

Cross References

Firearm defined for purposes of this Part, see Penal Code § 16520.

Research References

2 Witkin, California Criminal Law 4th Crimes Against Public Peace and Welfare § 193 (2021), Sale, Lease, or Transfer by Unlicensed Person.

§ 26581. Sale, delivery, or transfer of unloaded firearm to dealer by nonprofit public benefit or mutual benefit corporation as part of auction, raffle, or similar event; application of Section 26500

Section 26500 does not apply to the delivery, sale, or transfer of an unloaded firearm that is not a handgun to a dealer if the delivery, sale, or transfer satisfies both of the following conditions:

(a) The delivery, sale, or transfer is made by a nonprofit public benefit or mutual benefit corporation, including a local chapter of the same nonprofit corporation, organized pursuant to the Corporations Code.

(b) The sale or other transfer of ownership of that firearm is to occur as part of an auction, raffle, or similar event conducted by that nonprofit public benefit or mutual benefit corporation organized pursuant to the Corporations Code. *(Added by Stats.2019, c. 738 (S.B.376), § 15, eff. Jan. 1, 2020.)*

Research References

2 Witkin, California Criminal Law 4th Crimes Against Public Peace and Welfare § 193 (2021), Sale, Lease, or Transfer by Unlicensed Person.

§ 26582. Deliveries or transfers of firearms to law enforcement agency; application of Section 26500

Section 26500 does not apply to delivery or transfer of a firearm to a law enforcement agency made in accordance with Section 27922. *(Added by Stats.2019, c. 110 (A.B.1292), § 6, eff. Jan. 1, 2020.)*

Research References

2 Witkin, California Criminal Law 4th Crimes Against Public Peace and Welfare § 193 (2021), Sale, Lease, or Transfer by Unlicensed Person.

§ 26585. Delivery of unloaded firearm that is curio or relic by collector; application of Section 26500

Section 26500 does not apply to the delivery of an unloaded firearm that is a curio or relic, as defined in Section 478.11 of Title 27 of the Code of Federal Regulations, if the delivery satisfies all of the following conditions:

(a) It is made by a person licensed as a collector pursuant to Chapter 44 (commencing with Section 921) of Title 18 of the United States Code and the regulations issued pursuant thereto.

(b) It is made by a person with a current certificate of eligibility issued pursuant to Section 26710.

(c) It is made to a dealer. *(Added by Stats.2010, c. 711 (S.B.1080), § 6, operative Jan. 1, 2012.)*

Law Revision Commission Comments

Section 26585 continues former Section 12070(b)(17) without substantive change.

See Section 16520 ("firearm"). [38 Cal.L.Rev.Comm. Reports 217 (2009)].

Cross References

Dealer defined, see Penal Code § 26700.
Firearm defined for purposes of this Part, see Penal Code § 16520.

Research References

2 Witkin, California Criminal Law 4th Crimes Against Public Peace and Welfare § 193 (2021), Sale, Lease, or Transfer by Unlicensed Person.

§ 26587. Loan of firearm to gunsmith for repair; application of Section 26500

Section 26500 does not apply to either of the following:

(a) A loan of a firearm to a gunsmith for service or repair.

(b) The return of the firearm by the gunsmith. *(Added by Stats.2010, c. 711 (S.B.1080), § 6, operative Jan. 1, 2012.)*

Law Revision Commission Comments

Section 26587 continues former Section 12070(b)(18) without substantive change.

See Sections 16520 ("firearm"), 16630 ("gunsmith"). [38 Cal.L.Rev.Comm. Reports 217 (2009)].

Cross References

Firearm defined for purposes of this Part, see Penal Code § 16520.
Gunsmith defined for purposes of this Part, see Penal Code § 16630.

Research References

2 Witkin, California Criminal Law 4th Crimes Against Public Peace and Welfare § 193 (2021), Sale, Lease, or Transfer by Unlicensed Person.

§ 26588. Sale, delivery, transfer, or return of firearm regulated under certain laws; application of Section 26500

Section 26500 does not apply to any of the following:

(a) The sale, delivery, transfer, or return of a firearm regulated pursuant to Chapter 1 (commencing with Section 18710) of Division 5 of Title 2 by a person who holds a permit issued pursuant to Article 3 (commencing with Section 18900) of that chapter, if the sale, delivery, transfer, or return is conducted in accordance with the terms and conditions of the permit.

(b) The sale, delivery, transfer, or return of a firearm regulated pursuant to Chapter 2 (commencing with Section 30500) of Division 10 by a person who holds a permit issued pursuant to Section 31005, if the sale, delivery, transfer, or return is conducted in accordance with the terms and conditions of the permit.

(c) The sale, delivery, transfer, or return of a firearm regulated pursuant to Chapter 6 (commencing with Section 32610) of Division 10 by a person who holds a permit issued pursuant to Section 32650, if the sale, delivery, transfer, or return is conducted in accordance with the terms and conditions of the permit.

(d) The sale, delivery, transfer, or return of a firearm regulated pursuant to Article 2 (commencing with Section 33300) of Chapter 8 of Division 10 by a person who holds a permit issued pursuant to Section 33300, if the sale, delivery, transfer, or return is conducted in accordance with the terms and conditions of the permit. *(Added by Stats.2010, c. 711 (S.B.1080), § 6, operative Jan. 1, 2012.)*

Law Revision Commission Comments

Section 26588 continues former Section 12070(b)(19) without substantive change.

See Section 16520 ("firearm"). [38 Cal.L.Rev.Comm. Reports 217 (2009)].

Cross References

Firearm defined for purposes of this Part, see Penal Code § 16520.

Research References

2 Witkin, California Criminal Law 4th Crimes Against Public Peace and Welfare § 193 (2021), Sale, Lease, or Transfer by Unlicensed Person.

§ 26589. Delivery or transfer of firearms to dealer by trustee; application of Section 26500

Section 26500 does not apply to the delivery or transfer of a firearm to a dealer by the trustee of a trust if the delivery or transfer satisfies both of the following conditions:

(a) The trust is not of the type described in either subdivision (k) or (p) of Section 16990.

(b) The trustee is acting within the course and scope of their duties as the trustee of that trust. *(Added by Stats.2019, c. 110 (A.B.1292), § 7, eff. Jan. 1, 2020.)*

Research References

2 Witkin, California Criminal Law 4th Crimes Against Public Peace and Welfare § 193 (2021), Sale, Lease, or Transfer by Unlicensed Person.

§ 26590. Deliveries, transfers, or returns of firearms in custody or control of a court or law enforcement agency; application of Section 26500

Section 26500 does not apply to deliveries, transfers, or returns of firearms made by a court or a law enforcement agency pursuant to Chapter 2 (commencing with Section 33850) of Division 11. *(Added by Stats.2010, c. 711 (S.B.1080), § 6, operative Jan. 1, 2012.)*

Law Revision Commission Comments

Section 26590 continues former Section 12021.3(i)(3) without substantive change.

See Section 16520 ("firearm"). [38 Cal.L.Rev.Comm. Reports 217 (2009)].

Cross References

Firearm defined for purposes of this Part, see Penal Code § 16520.

ARTICLE 2. EXCEPTIONS RELATING TO LAW ENFORCEMENT

§ 26600. Sale, delivery, or transfer of firearms to authorized law enforcement representative for use by governmental agency; application of Section 26500; written authorization; recorded as institutional weapon

(a) Section 26500 does not apply to any sale, delivery, or transfer of firearms made to an authorized law enforcement representative of any city, county, city and county, or state, or of the federal government, for exclusive use by that governmental agency if, prior to the sale, delivery, or transfer of these firearms, written authorization from the head of the agency authorizing the transaction is presented to the person from whom the purchase, delivery, or transfer is being made.

(b) Proper written authorization is defined as verifiable written certification from the head of the agency by which the purchaser or transferee is employed, identifying the employee as an individual authorized to conduct the transaction, and authorizing the transaction for the exclusive use of the agency by which that person is employed.

(c) Within 10 days of the date a handgun, and commencing January 1, 2014, any firearm, is acquired by the agency, a record of the same shall be entered as an institutional weapon into the Automated Firearms System (AFS) via the California Law Enforcement Telecommunications System (CLETS) by the law enforcement or state agency. Any agency without access to AFS shall arrange with the sheriff of the county in which the agency is located to input this information via this system. *(Added by Stats.2010, c. 711 (S.B.1080), § 6, operative Jan. 1, 2012. Amended by Stats.2011, c. 745 (A.B.809), § 4.)*

Law Revision Commission Comments

Section 26600 continues former Section 12078(a)(2) without substantive change, as that provision applied to former Section 12070 (through its reference to "the preceding provisions of this article").

See Sections 16520 ("firearm"), 16640 ("handgun"). [38 Cal.L.Rev.Comm. Reports 217 (2009)].

Cross References

Firearm defined for purposes of this Part, see Penal Code § 16520.
Handgun defined for purposes of this Part, see Penal Code § 16640.

§ 26605. Loan of firearm by law enforcement officer to peace officer; application of Section 26500

Section 26500 does not apply to the loan of a firearm if all of the following conditions are satisfied:

(a) The loan is made by an authorized law enforcement representative of a city, county, or city and county, or of the state or federal government.

(b) The loan is made to a peace officer employed by that agency and authorized to carry a firearm.

(c) The loan is made for the carrying and use of that firearm by that peace officer in the course and scope of the officer's duties. *(Added by Stats.2010, c. 711 (S.B.1080), § 6, operative Jan. 1, 2012.)*

Law Revision Commission Comments

Section 26605 continues former Section 12078(a)(3) without substantive change, as that provision applied to former Section 12070 (through its reference to "the preceding provisions of this article").

See Section 16520 ("firearm"). [38 Cal.L.Rev.Comm. Reports 217 (2009)].

Cross References

Firearm defined for purposes of this Part, see Penal Code § 16520.

§ 26610. Sale, delivery, or transfer of firearm by law enforcement agency to peace officer pursuant to Section 10334 of Public Contract Code; application of Section 26500

(a) Section 26500 does not apply to the sale, delivery, or transfer of a firearm by a law enforcement agency to a peace officer pursuant to Section 10334 of the Public Contract Code.

(b) Within 10 days of the date that a handgun, and commencing January 1, 2014, any firearm, is sold, delivered, or transferred pursuant to Section 10334 of the Public Contract Code to that peace officer, the name of the officer and the make, model, serial number, and other identifying characteristics of the firearm being sold, delivered, or transferred shall be entered into the Automated Firearms System (AFS) via the California Law Enforcement Telecommunications System (CLETS) by the law enforcement or state agency that sold, delivered, or transferred the firearm, provided, however, that if the firearm is not a handgun and does not have a serial number, identification number, or identification mark assigned to it, that fact shall be noted in AFS. Any agency without access to AFS shall arrange with the sheriff of the county in which the agency is located to input this information via this system. *(Added by Stats.2010, c. 711 (S.B.1080), § 6, operative Jan. 1, 2012. Amended by Stats.2011, c. 745 (A.B.809), § 5.)*

Law Revision Commission Comments

Section 26610 continues former Section 12078(a)(4) without substantive change, as that provision applied to former Section 12070 (through its reference to "the preceding provisions of this article").

See Sections 16520 ("firearm"), 16640 ("handgun"). [38 Cal.L.Rev.Comm. Reports 217 (2009)].

Cross References

Firearm defined for purposes of this Part, see Penal Code § 16520.
Handgun defined for purposes of this Part, see Penal Code § 16640.

§ 26613. Delivery of firearm by law enforcement agency pursuant to Section 10334 of Public Contract Code to dealer for spouse or domestic partner of peace officer who died in the line of duty; application of Section 26500

Section 26500 does not apply to the delivery of a firearm by a law enforcement agency to a dealer in order for that dealer to deliver the firearm to the spouse or domestic partner of a peace officer who died in the line of duty if the sale of that firearm to the spouse or domestic partner is made in accordance with subdivision (d) of Section 10334 of the Public Contract Code. *(Added by Stats.2013, c. 16 (A.B.685), § 1.)*

§ 26615. Sale, delivery, or transfer of firearm by law enforcement agency to retiring peace officer; application of Section 26500

(a) Section 26500 does not apply to the sale, delivery, or transfer of a firearm by a law enforcement agency to a retiring peace officer who is authorized to carry a firearm pursuant to Chapter 5 (commencing with Section 26300) of Division 5.

(b) Within 10 days of the date that a handgun, and commencing January 1, 2014, any firearm, is sold, delivered, or transferred to that retiring peace officer, the name of the officer and the make, model, serial number, and other identifying characteristics of the firearm being sold, delivered, or transferred shall be entered into the Automated Firearms System (AFS) via the California Law Enforcement Telecommunications System (CLETS) by the law enforcement or state agency that sold, delivered, or transferred the firearm, provided, however, that if the firearm is not a handgun and does not have a serial number, identification number, or identification mark assigned to it, that fact shall be noted in AFS. Any agency without access to AFS shall arrange with the sheriff of the county in which the agency is located to input this information via this system. *(Added by Stats.2010, c. 711 (S.B.1080), § 6, operative Jan. 1, 2012. Amended by Stats.2011, c. 745 (A.B.809), § 6.)*

Law Revision Commission Comments

Section 26615 continues former Section 12078(a)(5) without substantive change, as that provision applied to former Section 12070 (through its reference to "the preceding provisions of this article").

See Sections 16520 ("firearm"), 16640 ("handgun"). [38 Cal.L.Rev.Comm. Reports 217 (2009)].

Cross References

Firearm defined for purposes of this Part, see Penal Code § 16520.
Handgun defined for purposes of this Part, see Penal Code § 16640.

§ 26620. Sale, delivery, or transfer of firearm by authorized law enforcement representative; application of Section 26500

Section 26500 does not apply to the sale, delivery, or transfer of a firearm when made by an authorized law enforcement representative of a city, county, city and county, or of the state or federal government, if all of the following requirements are met:

(a) The sale, delivery, or transfer is made to one of the following:

(1) A person licensed pursuant to Sections 26700 to 26915, inclusive.

(2) A wholesaler.

(3) A manufacturer or importer of firearms or ammunition licensed to engage in that business pursuant to Chapter 44 (commencing with Section 921) of Title 18 of the United States Code and the regulations issued pursuant thereto.

(b) The sale, delivery, or transfer of the firearm is not subject to the procedures set forth in Section 18000, 18005, 34000, or 34005.

(c) If the authorized law enforcement representative sells, delivers, or transfers a firearm that the governmental agency owns to a person licensed pursuant to Sections 26700 to 26915, inclusive, within 10 days of the date that the firearm is delivered to that licensee pursuant to this section by that agency, the agency has entered a record of the delivery into the Automated Firearms System (AFS) via the California Law Enforcement Telecommunications System (CLETS). Any agency without access to the AFS shall arrange with the sheriff of the county in which the agency is located to input this information via this system. *(Added by Stats.2013, c. 738 (A.B.538), § 3.)*

Cross References

Delivery, sale, or transfer of firearms by authorized law enforcement representative, application of section requiring handgun safety certificate, conditions, see Penal Code § 31835.

§ 26625. Loan of firearm to person enrolled in peace officer training program for purposes of course participation; application of Section 26500

Section 26500 does not apply to the loan of a firearm if the loan of the firearm is to a person enrolled in the course of basic training prescribed by the Commission on Peace Officer Standards and Training, or any other course certified by the commission, for purposes of participation in the course. *(Added by Stats.2017, c. 783 (A.B.693), § 1, eff. Oct. 14, 2017.)*

Research References

2 Witkin, California Criminal Law 4th Crimes Against Public Peace and Welfare § 193 (2021), Sale, Lease, or Transfer by Unlicensed Person.

CHAPTER 2. ISSUANCE, FORFEITURE, AND CONDITIONS OF LICENSE TO SELL, LEASE, OR TRANSFER FIREARMS AT RETAIL

ARTICLE 1. LICENSE TO SELL, LEASE, OR TRANSFER FIREARMS AT RETAIL

§ 26700. Definitions

As used in this division, and in any other provision listed in Section 16580, "dealer," "licensee," or "person licensed pursuant to Sections 26700 to 26915, inclusive" means a person who satisfies all of the following requirements:

(a) Has a valid federal firearms license.

(b) Has any regulatory or business license, or licenses, required by local government.

(c) Has a valid seller's permit issued by the State Board of Equalization.

(d) Has a certificate of eligibility issued by the Department of Justice pursuant to Section 26710.

(e) Has a license issued in the format prescribed by subdivision (c) of Section 26705.

(f) Is among those recorded in the centralized list specified in Section 26715. *(Added by Stats.2010, c. 711 (S.B.1080), § 6, operative Jan. 1, 2012.)*

Law Revision Commission Comments

Section 26700 continues former Section 12071(a)(1) without substantive change.

See also Section 16790 ("licensed gun dealer"). [38 Cal.L.Rev.Comm. Reports 217 (2009)].

Cross References

Firearm defined for purposes of this Part, see Penal Code § 16520.
Protective orders and other domestic violence prevention orders, registration and enforcement of orders, firearm ownership, possession, purchase, or receipt, see Family Code § 6389.

Relinquishment of firearms, persons subject to protective orders, see Code of Civil Procedure § 527.9.

Research References

2 Witkin, California Criminal Law 4th Crimes Against Public Peace and Welfare § 192 (2021), In General.
2 Witkin, California Criminal Law 4th Crimes Against Public Peace and Welfare § 198 (2021), Transfers by Persons Not Licensed in California.
2 Witkin, California Criminal Law 4th Crimes Against Public Peace and Welfare § 199 (2021), Importation Restrictions.
2 Witkin, California Criminal Law 4th Crimes Against Public Peace and Welfare § 221 (2021), Permits and Conditions for Possession.
2 Witkin, California Criminal Law 4th Crimes Against Public Peace and Welfare § 262 (2021), Criminal Storage of Firearm.
1 Witkin California Criminal Law 4th Introduction to Crimes § 72 (2021), Illustrations: Weapons.

§ 26705. Application for license to sell firearms at retail; requirements; form of license; fees

(a) The duly constituted licensing authority of a city, county, or a city and county shall accept applications for, and may grant licenses permitting, licensees to sell firearms at retail within the city, county, or city and county. The duly constituted licensing authority shall inform applicants who are denied licenses of the reasons for the denial in writing.

(b) No license shall be granted to any applicant who fails to provide a copy of the applicant's valid federal firearms license, valid seller's permit issued by the State Board of Equalization, and the certificate of eligibility described in Section 26710.

(c) A license granted by the duly constituted licensing authority of any city, county, or city and county, shall be valid for not more than one year from the date of issuance and shall be in one of the following forms:

(1) In the form prescribed by the Attorney General.

(2) A regulatory or business license that states on its face "Valid for Retail Sales of Firearms" and is endorsed by the signature of the issuing authority.

(3) A letter from the duly constituted licensing authority having primary jurisdiction for the applicant's intended business location stating that the jurisdiction does not require any form of regulatory or business license or does not otherwise restrict or regulate the sale of firearms.

(d) Local licensing authorities may assess fees to recover their full costs of processing applications for licenses. *(Added by Stats.2010, c. 711 (S.B.1080), § 6, operative Jan. 1, 2012.)*

Law Revision Commission Comments

Subdivision (a) of Section 26705 continues former Section 12071(a)(2) without substantive change.

Subdivision (b) continues former Section 12071(a)(3) without substantive change.

Subdivision (c) continues former Section 12071(a)(6) without substantive change.

Subdivision (d) continues former Section 12071(a)(7) without substantive change.

For exceptions to this provision, see Article 5 (commencing with Section 27050) and Article 6 (commencing with Section 27100).

See Section 16520 ("firearm"). [38 Cal.L.Rev.Comm. Reports 217 (2009)].

Cross References

Attorney General, generally, see Government Code § 12500 et seq.
Firearm defined for purposes of this Part, see Penal Code § 16520.
Licensee defined, see Penal Code § 26700.

§ 26710. Certificate of eligibility; determination by Department of Justice; administration; fees

(a) A person may request a certificate of eligibility from the Department of Justice.

(b) The Department of Justice shall examine its records and records available to the department in the National Instant Criminal Background Check System in order to determine if the applicant is prohibited by state or federal law from possessing, receiving, owning, or purchasing a firearm.

(c) The department shall issue a certificate to an applicant if the department's records indicate that the applicant is not a person who is prohibited by state or federal law from possessing firearms.

(d) The department shall adopt regulations to administer the certificate of eligibility program and shall recover the full costs of administering the program by imposing fees assessed to applicants who apply for those certificates. *(Added by Stats.2010, c. 711 (S.B.1080), § 6, operative Jan. 1, 2012.)*

Law Revision Commission Comments

Subdivisions (a)-(c) of Section 26710 continue former Section 12071(a)(4) without substantive change.

Subdivision (d) continues former Section 12071(a)(5) without substantive change.

For exceptions to this provision, see Article 5 (commencing with Section 27050) and Article 6 (commencing with Section 27100).

See Section 16520 ("firearm"). [38 Cal.L.Rev.Comm. Reports 217 (2009)].

Cross References

Centralized list of exempted federal firearms licensees, see Penal Code § 28450.
Certificate of eligibility requirement for agents or employees who handle, sell, or deliver firearm precursor parts, see Penal Code § 30447.
Electronic approval of purchase or transfer of firearm precursor parts by department, determination of eligibility of purchaser or transferee, development of approval procedure for single firearm precursor part transaction or purchase, see Penal Code § 30470.
Firearm defined for purposes of this Part, see Penal Code § 16520.
Flamethrowing devices, permits, issuance or renewal, see Health and Safety Code § 12757.
Flamethrowing devices, regulations, standards for background investigation of applicants, permitholder required to possess valid certificate of eligibility, see Health and Safety Code § 12756.
High explosives, permits, activities covered, applications, conditions of use, duration, limitations on issuing permits if display of placards is required, persons unqualified to apply, see Health and Safety Code § 12101.
Sale, loan or transfer of firearm to licensed collector, application of Section 27545, see Penal Code § 27966.

Research References

2 Witkin, California Criminal Law 4th Crimes Against Public Peace and Welfare § 193 (2021), Sale, Lease, or Transfer by Unlicensed Person.

§ 26715. List of persons licensed to sell firearms at retail; availability; use of information

(a) Except as otherwise provided in paragraphs (1) and (3) of subdivision (b), the Department of Justice shall keep a centralized list of all persons licensed pursuant to subdivisions (a) to (e), inclusive, of Section 26700.

(b)(1) The department may remove from this list any person who knowingly or with gross negligence violates a provision listed in Section 16575.

(2) The department shall remove from the centralized list any person whose federal firearms license has expired or has been revoked.

(3) The department shall remove from the centralized list any person or entity who has failed to provide certification of compliance with Section 26806 pursuant to subdivision (d) of Section 26806.

(4) Upon removal of a dealer from this list, notification shall be provided to local law enforcement and licensing authorities in the jurisdiction where the dealer's business is located.

(c) Information compiled from the list shall be made available, upon request, for the following purposes only:

(1) For law enforcement purposes.

(2) When the information is requested by a person licensed pursuant to Chapter 44 (commencing with Section 921) of Title 18 of the United States Code for determining the validity of the license for firearm shipments.

(3) When information is requested by a person promoting, sponsoring, operating, or otherwise organizing a show or event as defined in Section 478.100 of Title 27 of the Code of Federal Regulations, or its successor, who possesses a valid certificate of eligibility issued pursuant to Article 1 (commencing with Section 27200) of Chapter 3, if that information is requested by the person to determine the eligibility of a prospective participant in a gun show or event to conduct transactions as a firearms dealer pursuant to subdivision (b) of Section 26805.

(d) Information provided pursuant to subdivision (c) shall be limited to information necessary to corroborate an individual's current license status as being one of the following:

(1) A person licensed pursuant to subdivisions (a) to (e), inclusive, of Section 26700.

(2) A person who is licensed pursuant to Chapter 44 (commencing with Section 921) of Title 18 of the United States Code, and who is not subject to the requirement of being licensed pursuant to subdivisions (a) to (e), inclusive, of Section 26700. *(Added by Stats.2010, c. 711 (S.B.1080), § 6, operative Jan. 1, 2012. Amended by Stats.2022, c. 995 (S.B.1384), § 1, eff. Jan. 1, 2023.)*

Law Revision Commission Comments

Subdivision (a) of Section 26715 continues the first sentence of former Section 12071(e)(1) without substantive change.

Subdivision (b)(1) continues the second sentence of former Section 12071(e)(1) without substantive change.

Subdivision (b)(2) continues former Section 12071(e)(2) without substantive change.

Subdivision (b)(3) continues the third sentence of former Section 12071(e)(1) without substantive change.

Subdivision (c) continues former Section 12071(e)(3) without substantive change.

Subdivision (d) continues former Section 12071(e)(4) without substantive change.

For exceptions to this provision, see Article 5 (commencing with Section 27050) and Article 6 (commencing with Section 27100).

See Section 16520 ("firearm"). [38 Cal.L.Rev.Comm. Reports 217 (2009)].

Cross References

Firearm defined for purposes of this Part, see Penal Code § 16520.

§ 26720. Inspection of dealers; fee; exemption

(a) The Department of Justice may * * * conduct inspections of dealers at least every three years to ensure compliance with * * * Section 16575.

(1) Commencing on January 1, 2024, the department shall conduct inspections of all dealers, except a dealer specified in subdivision (c), at least once every three years, to ensure compliance with Section 16575.

(2) Inspections of dealers pursuant to this subdivision shall include an audit of dealer records that includes a sampling of at least 25 percent but no more than 50 percent of each record type.

(b) The department may assess an annual fee, not to exceed one hundred fifteen dollars ($115), to cover the reasonable cost of maintaining the list described in Section 26715, including the cost of inspections.

(c) * * * A dealer whose place of business is located in a jurisdiction that has adopted an inspection program to ensure compliance with firearms law * * * is exempt from that portion of the department's fee that relates to the cost of inspections. The applicant is responsible for providing evidence to the department that the jurisdiction in which the business is located has the inspection program. The department may inspect a dealer who is exempt from mandatory inspections under subdivision (b) to ensure compliance with Section 16575. *(Added by Stats.2010, c. 711 (S.B.1080), § 6, operative Jan. 1, 2012. Amended by Stats.2022, c. 138 (A.B.228), § 1, eff. Jan. 1, 2023.)*

Law Revision Commission Comments

Section 26720 continues former Section 12071(f) without substantive change.

For exceptions to this provision, see Article 5 (commencing with Section 27050) and Article 6 (commencing with Section 27100).

See Sections 16520 ("firearm"), 26700 ("dealer," "licensee," or "person licensed pursuant to Sections 26700 to 26915, inclusive"). [38 Cal.L.Rev. Comm. Reports 217 (2009)].

Cross References

Dealer defined, see Penal Code § 26700.
Firearm defined for purposes of this Part, see Penal Code § 16520.

§ 26725. Availability of inspection information

The Department of Justice shall maintain and make available upon request information concerning all of the following:

(a) The number of inspections conducted and the amount of fees collected pursuant to Section 26720.

(b) A listing of exempted jurisdictions, as defined in Section 26720.

(c) The number of dealers removed from the centralized list defined in Section 26715.

(d) The number of dealers found to have violated a provision listed in Section 16575 with knowledge or gross negligence. *(Added by Stats.2010, c. 711 (S.B.1080), § 6, operative Jan. 1, 2012.)*

Law Revision Commission Comments

Section 26725 continues former Section 12071(g) without substantive change.

For exceptions to this provision, see Article 5 (commencing with Section 27050) and Article 6 (commencing with Section 27100).

See Section 26700 ("dealer," "licensee," or "person licensed pursuant to Sections 26700 to 26915, inclusive"). [38 Cal.L.Rev.Comm. Reports 217 (2009)].

Cross References

Dealer defined, see Penal Code § 26700.

ARTICLE 2. GROUNDS FOR FORFEITURE OF LICENSE

Section

§ 26800. Grounds for forfeiture of license

Section operative until July 1, 2022. See, also, § 26800 operative July 1, 2022.

(a) A license under this chapter is subject to forfeiture for a violation of any of the prohibitions and requirements of this article, except those stated in the following provisions:

(1) Subdivision (c) of Section 26890.

(2) Subdivision (d) of Section 26890.

(3) Subdivision (b) of Section 26900.

(b) This section shall become inoperative on July 1, 2022, and, as of January 1, 2023, is repealed. *(Added by Stats.2010, c. 711 (S.B.1080), § 6, operative Jan. 1, 2012. Amended by Stats.2020, c. 284 (A.B.2362), § 1, eff. Jan. 1, 2021.)*

Inoperative Date and Repeal

For inoperative date and repeal of this section, see its terms.

Law Revision Commission Comments

Section 26800 continues the introductory clause of former Section 12071(b) without substantive change. [38 Cal.L.Rev.Comm. Reports 217 (2009)].

Research References

2 Witkin, California Criminal Law 4th Crimes Against Public Peace and Welfare § 192 (2021), In General.
2 Witkin, California Criminal Law 4th Crimes Against Public Peace and Welfare § 199 (2021), Importation Restrictions.

§ 26800. Grounds for forfeiture of license; civil fines; deposit in Dealers' Record of Sale Special Account

Section operative July 1, 2022. See, also, § 26800 operative until July 1, 2022.

(a) A license under this chapter is subject to forfeiture for a violation of any of the prohibitions and requirements of this article, except those stated in the following provisions:

(1) Subdivision (c) of Section 26890.

(2) Subdivision (d) of Section 26890.

(3) Subdivision (b) of Section 26900.

(b) The department may assess a civil fine against a licensee, in an amount not to exceed one thousand dollars ($1,000), for any breach of a prohibition or requirement of this article that subjects the license to forfeiture under subdivision (a). The department may assess a civil fine, in an amount not to exceed three thousand dollars ($3,000), for a violation of a prohibition or requirement of this article that subjects the license to forfeiture under subdivision (a), for either of the following:

(1) The licensee has received written notification from the department regarding the violation and subsequently failed to take corrective action in a timely manner.

(2) The licensee is otherwise determined by the department to have knowingly or with gross negligence violated the prohibition or requirement.

(c) The department may adopt regulations setting fine amounts and providing a process for a licensee to appeal a fine assessed pursuant to subdivision (b).

(d) Moneys received by the department pursuant to this section shall be deposited into the Dealers' Record of Sale Special Account of the General Fund, to be available, upon appropriation, for expenditure by the department to offset the reasonable costs of firearms-related regulatory and enforcement activities related to the sale, purchase, manufacturing, lawful or unlawful possession, loan, or transfer of firearms pursuant to any provision listed in Section 16580.

(e) This section shall become operative on July 1, 2022. *(Added by Stats.2020, c. 284 (A.B.2362), § 2, eff. Jan. 1, 2021, operative July 1, 2022.)*

Research References

2 Witkin, California Criminal Law 4th Crimes Against Public Peace and Welfare § 192 (2021), In General.
2 Witkin, California Criminal Law 4th Crimes Against Public Peace and Welfare § 199 (2021), Importation Restrictions.

§ 26805. Where licensee may conduct business; types of firearms; acceptance of delivery of firearms

(a) Except as provided in subdivisions (b) and (c), the business of a licensee shall be conducted only in the buildings designated in the license.

(b)(1) A person licensed pursuant to Sections 26700 and 26705 may take possession of firearms and commence preparation of registers for the sale, delivery, or transfer of firearms at any gun show or event, as defined in Section 478.100 of Title 27 of the Code of Federal Regulations, or its successor, if the gun show or event is not conducted from any motorized or towed vehicle. A person conducting business pursuant to this subdivision shall be entitled to conduct business as authorized herein at any gun show or event in the state, without regard to the jurisdiction within this state that issued the license pursuant to Sections 26700 and 26705, provided the person complies with all applicable laws, including, but not limited to, the waiting period specified in subdivision (a) of Section 26815, and all applicable local laws, regulations, and fees, if any.

(2) A person conducting business pursuant to this subdivision shall publicly display the person's license issued pursuant to Sections 26700 and 26705, or a facsimile thereof, at any gun show or event, as specified in this subdivision.

(c)(1) A person licensed pursuant to Sections 26700 and 26705 may engage in the sale and transfer of firearms other than handguns, at events specified in Sections 27900 and 27905, subject to the prohibitions and restrictions contained in those sections.

(2) A person licensed pursuant to Sections 26700 and 26705 may also accept delivery of firearms other than handguns, outside the building designated in the license, provided the firearm is being donated for the purpose of sale or transfer at an auction, raffle, or similar event specified in Section 27900.

(d) The firearm may be delivered to the purchaser, transferee, or person being loaned the firearm at one of the following places:

(1) The building designated in the license.

(2) The places specified in subdivision (b) or (c).

(3) The place of residence of, the fixed place of business of, or on private property owned or lawfully possessed by, the purchaser, transferee, or person being loaned the firearm. *(Added by Stats. 2010, c. 711 (S.B.1080), § 6, operative Jan. 1, 2012. Amended by Stats.2011, c. 745 (A.B.809), § 7; Stats.2019, c. 738 (S.B.376), § 16, eff. Jan. 1, 2020.)*

Law Revision Commission Comments

Section 26805 continues former Section 12071(b)(1) without substantive change.

For exceptions to this provision, see Article 4 (commencing with Section 27000), Article 5 (commencing with Section 27050), and Article 6 (commencing with Section 27100).

For the consequences of violating this section, see Section 26800 (forfeiture of license).

See Sections 16520 ("firearm"), 16530 ("firearm capable of being concealed upon the person," "pistol," and "revolver"), 26700 ("dealer," "licensee," or "person licensed pursuant to Sections 26700 to 26915, inclusive"). [38 Cal.L.Rev.Comm. Reports 217 (2009)].

Cross References

Firearm defined for purposes of this Part, see Penal Code § 16520.
Handgun defined for purposes of this Part, see Penal Code § 16640.
Secondhand dealers, licenses, application, fee, grounds for denial, grant, see Business and Professions Code § 21641.

§ 26806. Digital video surveillance system; requirements; access to recordings; signage

(a) Commencing January 1, 2024, a licensee shall ensure that its business premises are monitored by a digital video surveillance system that meets all of the following requirements:

(1) The system shall clearly record images and, for systems located inside the premises, audio, of the area under surveillance.

(2) Each camera shall be permanently mounted in a fixed location. Cameras shall be placed in locations that allow the camera to clearly record activity occurring in all areas described in paragraph (3) and reasonably produce recordings that allow for the clear identification of any person.

(3) The areas recorded shall include, without limitation, all of the following:

(A) Interior views of all entries or exits to the premises.

(B) All areas where firearms are displayed.

(C) All points of sale, sufficient to identify the parties involved in the transaction.

(4) The system shall continuously record 24 hours per day at a frame rate no less than 15 frames per second.

(5) The media or device on which recordings are stored shall be secured in a manner to protect the recording from tampering, unauthorized access or use, or theft.

(6) Recordings shall be maintained for a minimum of one year.

(7) Recorded images shall clearly and accurately display the date and time.

(8) The system shall be equipped with a failure notification system that provides notification to the licensee of any interruption or failure of the system or storage device.

(b) A licensee shall not use, share, allow access, or otherwise release recordings, to any person except as follows:

(1) A licensee shall allow access to the system to an agent of the department or a licensing authority conducting an inspection of the licensee's premises, for the purpose of inspecting the system for compliance with this section, and only if a warrant or court order would not generally be required for that access.

(2) A licensee shall allow access to the system or release recordings to any person pursuant to search warrant or other court order.

(3) A licensee may allow access to the system or release recordings to any person in response to an insurance claim or as part of the civil discovery process, including, but not limited to, in response to subpoenas, request for production or inspection, or other court order.

(c) The licensee shall post a sign in a conspicuous place at each entrance to the premises that states in block letters not less than one inch in height:

"THESE PREMISES ARE UNDER VIDEO AND AUDIO SURVEILLANCE. YOUR IMAGE AND CONVERSATIONS MAY BE RECORDED."

(d) A licensee shall, on an annual basis, provide certification to the department, in a manner prescribed by the department, that its video surveillance system is in proper working order.

(e) This section does not preclude any local authority or local governing body from adopting or enforcing local laws or policies regarding video surveillance that do not contradict or conflict with the requirements of this section. *(Added by Stats.2022, c. 995 (S.B.1384), § 2, eff. Jan. 1, 2023.)*

Cross References

List of persons licensed to sell firearms at retail, availability, use of information, see Penal Code § 26715.

§ 26810. Display of license

A person's license under this chapter, or a copy thereof certified by the issuing authority, shall be displayed on the premises where it can easily be seen. *(Added by Stats.2010, c. 711 (S.B.1080), § 6, operative Jan. 1, 2012.)*

Law Revision Commission Comments

Section 26810 continues former Section 12071(b)(2) without substantive change.

For exceptions to this provision, see Article 4 (commencing with Section 27000), Article 5 (commencing with Section 27050), and Article 6 (commencing with Section 27100).

For the consequences of violating this section, see Section 26800 (forfeiture of license). [38 Cal.L.Rev.Comm. Reports 217 (2009)].

§ 26811. General liability insurance policy; local requirements

(a) Commencing July 1, 2023, a licensee shall carry a general liability insurance policy providing at least one million dollars ($1,000,000) of coverage per incident.

(b) This section does not preclude any local authority from requiring a more stringent requirement regarding the maintenance of liability insurance. *(Added by Stats.2022, c. 995 (S.B.1384), § 3, eff. Jan. 1, 2023.)*

§ 26815. Delivery of firearms by dealer; requirements

No firearm shall be delivered:

(a) Within 10 days of the application to purchase, or, after notice by the department pursuant to Section 28220, within 10 days of the submission to the department of any correction to the application, or within 10 days of the submission to the department of any fee required pursuant to Section 28225, whichever is later.

(b) Unless unloaded and securely wrapped or unloaded and in a locked container.

(c) Unless the purchaser, transferee, or person being loaned the firearm presents clear evidence of the person's identity and age to the dealer.

(d) Whenever the dealer is notified by the Department of Justice that the person is prohibited by state or federal law from processing, owning, purchasing, or receiving a firearm. The dealer shall make available to the person in the prohibited class a prohibited notice and transfer form, provided by the department, stating that the person is prohibited from owning or possessing a firearm, and that the person may obtain from the department the reason for the prohibition. *(Added by Stats.2010, c. 711 (S.B.1080), § 6, operative Jan. 1, 2012.)*

Law Revision Commission Comments

Section 26815 continues former Section 12071(b)(3) without substantive change.

For exceptions to this provision, see Article 3 (commencing with Section 26950), Article 4 (commencing with Section 27000), Article 5 (commencing with Section 27050), and Article 6 (commencing with Section 27100).

For the consequences of violating this section, see Section 26800 (forfeiture of license).

See Sections 16190 ("application to purchase"), 16400 ("clear evidence of the person's identity and age"), 16520 ("firearm"), 26700 ("dealer," "licensee," or "person licensed pursuant to Sections 26700 to 26915, inclusive"). [38 Cal.L.Rev.Comm. Reports 217 (2009)].

Cross References

Completion of sale, loan, or transfer of firearm through licensed person, compliance with Section 27545, procedures if dealer cannot legally return firearm to seller, transferor, or person loaning the firearm, see Penal Code § 28050.
Dealer defined, see Penal Code § 26700.
Firearm defined for purposes of this Part, see Penal Code § 16520.
Firearm restocking or return-related fees, see Penal Code § 26883.

§ 26820. Display of handgun, imitation handgun, or advertisement where prohibited

No handgun or imitation handgun, or placard advertising the sale or other transfer thereof, shall be displayed in any part of the premises where it can readily be seen from the outside. *(Added by Stats.2010, c. 711 (S.B.1080), § 6, operative Jan. 1, 2012. Amended by Stats.2011, c. 745 (A.B.809), § 8.)*

Validity

For validity of this section, see Tracy Rifle and Pistol LLC v. Harris (E.D.Cal.2018), 339 F.Supp.3d 1007.

Law Revision Commission Comments

Section 26820 continues former Section 12071(b)(4) without substantive change.

For exceptions to this provision, see Article 4 (commencing with Section 27000), Article 5 (commencing with Section 27050), and Article 6 (commencing with Section 27100).

For the consequences of violating this section, see Section 26800 (forfeiture of license).

See Section 16530 ("firearm capable of being concealed upon the person," "pistol," and "revolver"). [38 Cal.L.Rev.Comm. Reports 217 (2009)].

Cross References

Handgun defined for purposes of this Part, see Penal Code § 16640.

§ 26825. Prompt processing of firearms transactions

A licensee shall agree to and shall act properly and promptly in processing firearms transactions pursuant to Chapter 5 (commencing with Section 28050). *(Added by Stats.2010, c. 711 (S.B.1080), § 6, operative Jan. 1, 2012.)*

Law Revision Commission Comments

Section 26825 continues former Section 12071(b)(5) without substantive change.

For exceptions to this provision, see Article 4 (commencing with Section 27000), Article 5 (commencing with Section 27050), and Article 6 (commencing with Section 27100).

For the consequences of violating this section, see Section 26800 (forfeiture of license).

See Sections 16520 ("firearm"), 26700 ("dealer," "licensee," or "person licensed pursuant to Sections 26700 to 26915, inclusive"). [38 Cal.L.Rev. Comm. Reports 217 (2009)].

Cross References

Firearm defined for purposes of this Part, see Penal Code § 16520.
Licensee defined, see Penal Code § 26700.

§ 26830. Compliance with other laws

A licensee shall comply with all of the following:

(a) Sections 27500 to 27535, inclusive.

(b) Section 27555.

(c) Section 28100.

(d) Article 2 (commencing with Section 28150) of Chapter 6.

(e) Article 3 (commencing with Section 28200) of Chapter 6.

(f) Section 30300. *(Added by Stats.2010, c. 711 (S.B.1080), § 6, operative Jan. 1, 2012.)*

Law Revision Commission Comments

Section 26830 continues former Section 12071(b)(6) without substantive change.

For exceptions to this provision, see Article 4 (commencing with Section 27000), Article 5 (commencing with Section 27050), and Article 6 (commencing with Section 27100).

For the consequences of violating this section, see Section 26800 (forfeiture of license).

See Section 26700 ("dealer," "licensee," or "person licensed pursuant to Sections 26700 to 26915, inclusive"). [38 Cal.L.Rev.Comm. Reports 217 (2009)].

Cross References

Licensee defined, see Penal Code § 26700.

§ 26835. Posting of warnings required

Section operative until Jan. 1, 2024. See, also, § 26835 operative Jan. 1, 2024.

(a) A licensee shall conspicuously post within the licensed premises the following warnings in block letters not less than one inch in height:

(1) "FIREARMS MUST BE HANDLED RESPONSIBLY AND SECURELY STORED TO PREVENT ACCESS BY CHILDREN AND OTHER UNAUTHORIZED USERS. CALIFORNIA HAS STRICT LAWS PERTAINING TO FIREARMS, AND YOU MAY BE FINED OR IMPRISONED IF YOU FAIL TO COMPLY WITH THEM. VISIT THE WEBSITE OF THE CALIFORNIA ATTORNEY GENERAL AT HTTPS: //OAG.CA.GOV/FIREARMS FOR INFORMATION ON FIREARM LAWS APPLICABLE TO YOU AND HOW YOU CAN COMPLY."

(2) "IF YOU KEEP A FIREARM WITHIN ANY PREMISES UNDER YOUR CUSTODY OR CONTROL, AND A PERSON UNDER 18 YEARS OF AGE OBTAINS IT AND USES IT, RESULTING IN INJURY OR DEATH, OR CARRIES IT TO A PUBLIC PLACE, YOU MAY BE GUILTY OF A MISDEMEANOR OR A FELONY UNLESS YOU STORED THE FIREARM IN A LOCKED CONTAINER OR LOCKED THE FIREARM WITH

A LOCKING DEVICE TO KEEP IT FROM TEMPORARILY FUNCTIONING."

(3) "CHILDREN MAY BE UNABLE TO DISTINGUISH FIREARMS FROM TOYS AND MAY OPERATE FIREARMS, CAUSING SEVERE INJURIES OR DEATH. IF YOU KEEP A FIREARM WITHIN ANY PREMISES UNDER YOUR CUSTODY OR CONTROL, AND A PERSON UNDER 18 YEARS OF AGE GAINS ACCESS TO THE FIREARM AND CARRIES IT OFF–PREMISES, YOU MAY BE GUILTY OF A MISDEMEANOR, UNLESS YOU STORED THE FIREARM IN A LOCKED CONTAINER, OR LOCKED THE FIREARM WITH A LOCKING DEVICE TO KEEP IT FROM TEMPORARILY FUNCTIONING."

(4) "YOU MAY BE GUILTY OF A MISDEMEANOR, INCLUDING A SIGNIFICANT FINE OR IMPRISONMENT, IF YOU KEEP A FIREARM WHERE A MINOR IS LIKELY TO ACCESS IT OR IF A MINOR OBTAINS AND IMPROPERLY USES IT, OR CARRIES IT OFF OF THE PREMISES TO A SCHOOL OR SCHOOL–SPONSORED EVENT, UNLESS YOU STORED THE FIREARM IN A LOCKED CONTAINER OR LOCKED THE FIREARM WITH A LOCKING DEVICE."

(5) "IF YOU NEGLIGENTLY STORE OR LEAVE A FIREARM WITHIN ANY PREMISES UNDER YOUR CUSTODY OR CONTROL WHERE A PERSON UNDER 18 YEARS OF AGE IS LIKELY TO ACCESS IT, YOU MAY BE GUILTY OF A MISDEMEANOR, INCLUDING A SIGNIFICANT FINE, UNLESS YOU STORED THE FIREARM IN A LOCKED CONTAINER OR LOCKED THE FIREARM WITH A LOCKING DEVICE."

(6) "DISCHARGING FIREARMS IN POORLY VENTILATED AREAS, CLEANING FIREARMS, OR HANDLING AMMUNITION MAY RESULT IN EXPOSURE TO LEAD, A SUBSTANCE KNOWN TO CAUSE BIRTH DEFECTS, REPRODUCTIVE HARM, AND OTHER SERIOUS PHYSICAL INJURY. HAVE ADEQUATE VENTILATION AT ALL TIMES. WASH HANDS THOROUGHLY AFTER EXPOSURE."

(7) "FEDERAL REGULATIONS PROVIDE THAT IF YOU DO NOT TAKE PHYSICAL POSSESSION OF THE FIREARM THAT YOU ARE ACQUIRING OWNERSHIP OF WITHIN 30 DAYS AFTER YOU COMPLETE THE INITIAL BACKGROUND CHECK PAPERWORK, THEN YOU HAVE TO GO THROUGH THE BACKGROUND CHECK PROCESS A SECOND TIME IN ORDER TO TAKE PHYSICAL POSSESSION OF THAT FIREARM."

(8) "NO PERSON SHALL MAKE AN APPLICATION TO PURCHASE MORE THAN ONE HANDGUN OR SEMIAUTOMATIC CENTERFIRE RIFLE WITHIN ANY 30–DAY PERIOD AND NO DELIVERY SHALL BE MADE TO ANY PERSON WHO HAS MADE AN APPLICATION TO PURCHASE MORE THAN ONE HANDGUN OR SEMIAUTOMATIC CENTERFIRE RIFLE WITHIN ANY 30–DAY PERIOD."

(9) "IF A FIREARM YOU OWN OR POSSESS IS LOST OR STOLEN, YOU MUST REPORT THE LOSS OR THEFT TO A LOCAL LAW ENFORCEMENT AGENCY WHERE THE LOSS OR THEFT OCCURRED WITHIN FIVE DAYS OF THE TIME YOU KNEW OR REASONABLY SHOULD HAVE KNOWN THAT THE FIREARM HAD BEEN LOST OR STOLEN."

(b) In addition to the notice required by subdivision (a), a licensee shall post conspicuously within the licensed premises, in block letters not less than one inch in height, an additional notice, including, but not limited to, a notice provided by a suicide prevention program, containing the following statement:

"IF YOU OR SOMEONE YOU KNOW IS CONTEMPLATING SUICIDE, PLEASE CALL THE NATIONAL SUICIDE PREVENTION LIFELINE AT 1–800–273–TALK (8255)."

(c) This section shall * * * remain in effect until January 1, 2024, and as of that date is repealed. *(Added by Stats.2019, c. 840 (S.B.172), § 9.6, eff. Jan. 1, 2020, operative July 1, 2021. Amended by Stats.2022, c. 76 (A.B.1621), § 14, eff. June 30, 2022.)*

Repeal

For repeal of this section, see its terms.

Cross References

Felonies, definition and penalties, see Penal Code §§ 17, 18.
Firearm capable of being concealed upon the person defined for purposes of this Part, see Penal Code § 16530.
Firearm defined for purposes of this Part, see Penal Code § 16520.
Licensee defined, see Penal Code § 26700.
Misdemeanors, definition and penalties, see Penal Code §§ 17, 19, 19.2.
Pistol defined for purposes of this Part, see Penal Code § 16530.
Revolver defined for purposes of this Part, see Penal Code § 16530.

Research References

2 Witkin, California Criminal Law 4th Crimes Against Public Peace and Welfare § 262 (2021), Criminal Storage of Firearm.

§ 26835. Posting of warnings required

Section operative Jan. 1, 2024. See, also, § 26835 operative until Jan. 1, 2024.

(a) A licensee shall conspicuously post within the licensed premises the following warnings in block letters not less than one inch in height:

(1) "FIREARMS MUST BE HANDLED RESPONSIBLY AND SECURELY STORED TO PREVENT ACCESS BY CHILDREN AND OTHER UNAUTHORIZED USERS. CALIFORNIA HAS STRICT LAWS PERTAINING TO FIREARMS, AND YOU MAY BE FINED OR IMPRISONED IF YOU FAIL TO COMPLY WITH THEM. VISIT THE WEBSITE OF THE CALIFORNIA ATTORNEY GENERAL AT HTTPS: //OAG.CA.GOV/FIREARMS FOR INFORMATION ON FIREARM LAWS APPLICABLE TO YOU AND HOW YOU CAN COMPLY."

(2) "IF YOU KEEP A FIREARM WITHIN ANY PREMISES UNDER YOUR CUSTODY OR CONTROL, AND A PERSON UNDER 18 YEARS OF AGE OBTAINS IT AND USES IT, RESULTING IN INJURY OR DEATH, OR CARRIES IT TO A PUBLIC PLACE, YOU MAY BE GUILTY OF A MISDEMEANOR OR A FELONY UNLESS YOU STORED THE FIREARM IN A LOCKED CONTAINER OR LOCKED THE FIREARM WITH A LOCKING DEVICE TO KEEP IT FROM TEMPORARILY FUNCTIONING."

(3) "CHILDREN MAY BE UNABLE TO DISTINGUISH FIREARMS FROM TOYS AND MAY OPERATE FIREARMS, CAUSING SEVERE INJURIES OR DEATH. IF YOU KEEP A FIREARM WITHIN ANY PREMISES UNDER YOUR CUSTODY OR CONTROL, AND A PERSON UNDER 18 YEARS OF AGE GAINS ACCESS TO THE FIREARM AND CARRIES IT OFF–PREMISES, YOU MAY BE GUILTY OF A MISDEMEANOR, UNLESS YOU STORED THE FIREARM IN A LOCKED CONTAINER, OR LOCKED THE FIREARM WITH A LOCKING DEVICE TO KEEP IT FROM TEMPORARILY FUNCTIONING."

(4) "YOU MAY BE GUILTY OF A MISDEMEANOR, INCLUDING A SIGNIFICANT FINE OR IMPRISONMENT, IF YOU KEEP A FIREARM WHERE A MINOR IS LIKELY TO ACCESS IT OR IF A MINOR OBTAINS AND IMPROPERLY USES IT, OR CARRIES IT OFF OF THE PREMISES TO A SCHOOL OR SCHOOL–SPONSORED EVENT, UNLESS YOU STORED THE FIREARM IN A LOCKED CONTAINER OR LOCKED THE FIREARM WITH A LOCKING DEVICE."

(5) "IF YOU NEGLIGENTLY STORE OR LEAVE A FIREARM WITHIN ANY PREMISES UNDER YOUR CUSTODY OR

CONTROL WHERE A PERSON UNDER 18 YEARS OF AGE IS LIKELY TO ACCESS IT, YOU MAY BE GUILTY OF A MISDEMEANOR, INCLUDING A SIGNIFICANT FINE, UNLESS YOU STORED THE FIREARM IN A LOCKED CONTAINER OR LOCKED THE FIREARM WITH A LOCKING DEVICE."

(6) "DISCHARGING FIREARMS IN POORLY VENTILATED AREAS, CLEANING FIREARMS, OR HANDLING AMMUNITION MAY RESULT IN EXPOSURE TO LEAD, A SUBSTANCE KNOWN TO CAUSE BIRTH DEFECTS, REPRODUCTIVE HARM, AND OTHER SERIOUS PHYSICAL INJURY. HAVE ADEQUATE VENTILATION AT ALL TIMES. WASH HANDS THOROUGHLY AFTER EXPOSURE."

(7) "FEDERAL REGULATIONS PROVIDE THAT IF YOU DO NOT TAKE PHYSICAL POSSESSION OF THE FIREARM THAT YOU ARE ACQUIRING OWNERSHIP OF WITHIN 30 DAYS AFTER YOU COMPLETE THE INITIAL BACKGROUND CHECK PAPERWORK, THEN YOU HAVE TO GO THROUGH THE BACKGROUND CHECK PROCESS A SECOND TIME IN ORDER TO TAKE PHYSICAL POSSESSION OF THAT FIREARM."

(8) "NO PERSON SHALL MAKE AN APPLICATION TO PURCHASE MORE THAN ONE FIREARM WITHIN ANY 30–DAY PERIOD AND NO DELIVERY SHALL BE MADE TO ANY PERSON WHO HAS MADE AN APPLICATION TO PURCHASE MORE THAN ONE FIREARM WITHIN ANY 30–DAY PERIOD."

(9) "IF A FIREARM YOU OWN OR POSSESS IS LOST OR STOLEN, YOU MUST REPORT THE LOSS OR THEFT TO A LOCAL LAW ENFORCEMENT AGENCY WHERE THE LOSS OR THEFT OCCURRED WITHIN FIVE DAYS OF THE TIME YOU KNEW OR REASONABLY SHOULD HAVE KNOWN THAT THE FIREARM HAD BEEN LOST OR STOLEN."

(b) In addition to the notice required by subdivision (a), a licensee shall post conspicuously within the licensed premises, in block letters not less than one inch in height, an additional notice, including, but not limited to, a notice provided by a suicide prevention program, containing the following statement:

"IF YOU OR SOMEONE YOU KNOW IS CONTEMPLATING SUICIDE, PLEASE CALL THE NATIONAL SUICIDE PREVENTION LIFELINE AT 1–800–273–TALK (8255)."

(c) This section shall become operative on January 1, 2024. *(Added by Stats.2022, c. 76 (A.B.1621), § 15, eff. June 30, 2022, operative Jan. 1, 2024.)*

Cross References

Felonies, definition and penalties, see Penal Code §§ 17, 18.
Firearm capable of being concealed upon the person defined for purposes of this Part, see Penal Code § 16530.
Firearm defined for purposes of this Part, see Penal Code § 16520.
Licensee defined, see Penal Code § 26700.
Misdemeanors, definition and penalties, see Penal Code §§ 17, 19, 19.2.
Pistol defined for purposes of this Part, see Penal Code § 16530.
Revolver defined for purposes of this Part, see Penal Code § 16530.

§ 26840. Delivery of firearm; valid firearm safety certificate or unexpired handgun safety certificate requirement

(a) A dealer shall not deliver a firearm unless the person receiving the firearm presents to the dealer a valid firearm safety certificate, or, in the case of a handgun, an unexpired handgun safety certificate. The firearms dealer shall retain a photocopy of the firearm safety certificate as proof of compliance with this requirement.

(b) This section shall become operative on January 1, 2015. *(Added by Stats.2013, c. 761 (S.B.683), § 4, operative Jan. 1, 2015.)*

Cross References

Dealer defined, see Penal Code § 26700.
Firearm defined for purposes of this Part, see Penal Code § 16520.
Handgun defined for purposes of this Part, see Penal Code § 16640.
Handgun safety certificate defined for purposes of this Part, see Penal Code § 16670.

§ 26845. Proof of California residence required

(a) No handgun may be delivered unless the purchaser, transferee, or person being loaned the firearm presents documentation indicating that the person is a California resident.

(b) Satisfactory documentation shall include a utility bill from within the last three months, a residential lease, a property deed, or military permanent duty station orders indicating assignment within this state, or other evidence of residency as permitted by the Department of Justice.

(c) The firearms dealer shall retain a photocopy of the documentation as proof of compliance with this requirement. *(Added by Stats.2010, c. 711 (S.B.1080), § 6, operative Jan. 1, 2012. Amended by Stats.2011, c. 745 (A.B.809), § 10.)*

Law Revision Commission Comments

Section 26845 continues former Section 12071(b)(8)(C) without substantive change.

For exceptions to this provision, see Article 4 (commencing with Section 27000), Article 5 (commencing with Section 27050), and Article 6 (commencing with Section 27100).

For the consequences of violating this section, see Section 26800 (forfeiture of license).

See Sections 16520 ("firearm"), 16640 ("handgun"), 26700 ("dealer," "licensee," or "person licensed pursuant to Sections 26700 to 26915, inclusive"). [38 Cal.L.Rev.Comm. Reports 217 (2009)].

Cross References

Dealer defined, see Penal Code § 26700.
Firearm defined for purposes of this Part, see Penal Code § 16520.
Handgun defined for purposes of this Part, see Penal Code § 16640.

§ 26850. Recipient required to perform safe handling demonstration with handgun being delivered; instruction on rendering handgun safe; affidavit of dealer; demonstration for department-certified instructor; exemptions

(a) Except as authorized by the department, no firearms dealer may deliver a handgun unless the recipient performs a safe handling demonstration with that handgun.

(b) The safe handling demonstration shall commence with the handgun unloaded and locked with the firearm safety device with which it is required to be delivered, if applicable. While maintaining muzzle awareness, that is, the firearm is pointed in a safe direction, preferably down at the ground, and trigger discipline, that is, the trigger finger is outside of the trigger guard and along side of the handgun frame, at all times, the handgun recipient shall correctly and safely perform the following:

(1) If the handgun is a semiautomatic pistol, the steps listed in Section 26853.

(2) If the handgun is a double-action revolver, the steps listed in Section 26856.

(3) If the handgun is a single-action revolver, the steps listed in Section 26859.

(c) The recipient shall receive instruction regarding how to render that handgun safe in the event of a jam.

(d) The firearms dealer shall sign and date an affidavit stating that the requirements of subdivisions (a) and (b) have been met. The firearms dealer shall additionally obtain the signature of the handgun purchaser on the same affidavit. The firearms dealer shall retain the original affidavit as proof of compliance with this requirement.

(e) The recipient shall perform the safe handling demonstration for a department-certified instructor.

(f) No demonstration shall be required if the dealer is returning the handgun to the owner of the handgun.

(g) Department-certified instructors who may administer the safe handling demonstration shall meet the requirements set forth in subdivision (b) of Section 31635.

(h) The persons who are exempt from the requirements of subdivision (a) of Section 31615, pursuant to Section 31700, are also exempt from performing the safe handling demonstration. *(Added by Stats.2010, c. 711 (S.B.1080), § 6, operative Jan. 1, 2012. Amended by Stats.2011, c. 745 (A.B.809), § 11.)*

Law Revision Commission Comments

Subdivisions (a) and (b) of Section 26850, in combination with Sections 26853, 26856, and 26859, continue former Section 12071(b)(8)(D) without substantive change.

Subdivision (c) continues former Section 12071(b)(8)(E) without substantive change.

Subdivision (d) continues former Section 12071(b)(8)(F) without substantive change.

Subdivision (e) continues former Section 12071(b)(8)(G) without substantive change.

Subdivision (f) continues former Section 12071(b)(8)(H) without substantive change.

Subdivision (g) continues former Section 12071(b)(8)(I) without substantive change.

Subdivision (h) continues former Section 12071(b)(8)(J) without substantive change.

For exceptions to this provision, see Article 4 (commencing with Section 27000), Article 5 (commencing with Section 27050), and Article 6 (commencing with Section 27100).

For the consequences of violating this section, see Section 26800 (forfeiture of license).

See Sections 16520 ("firearm"), 16530 ("firearm capable of being concealed upon the person," "pistol," and "revolver"), 16640 ("handgun"), 26700 ("dealer," "licensee," or "person licensed pursuant to Sections 26700 to 26915, inclusive"). [38 Cal.L.Rev.Comm. Reports 217 (2009)].

Cross References

Dealer defined, see Penal Code § 26700.
Firearm defined for purposes of this Part, see Penal Code § 16520.
Handgun defined for purposes of this Part, see Penal Code § 16640.
Pistol defined for purposes of this Part, see Penal Code § 16530.
Revolver defined for purposes of this Part, see Penal Code § 16530.

§ 26853. Safe handling demonstration; semiautomatic pistol

To comply with Section 26850, a safe handling demonstration for a semiautomatic pistol shall include all of the following steps:

(a) Remove the magazine.

(b) Lock the slide back. If the model of firearm does not allow the slide to be locked back, pull the slide back, visually and physically check the chamber to ensure that it is clear.

(c) Visually and physically inspect the chamber, to ensure that the handgun is unloaded.

(d) Remove the firearm safety device, if applicable. If the firearm safety device prevents any of the previous steps, remove the firearm safety device during the appropriate step.

(e) Load one bright orange, red, or other readily identifiable dummy round into the magazine. If no readily identifiable dummy round is available, an empty cartridge casing with an empty primer pocket may be used.

(f) Insert the magazine into the magazine well of the firearm.

(g) Manipulate the slide release or pull back and release the slide.

(h) Remove the magazine.

(i) Visually inspect the chamber to reveal that a round can be chambered with the magazine removed.

(j) Lock the slide back to eject the bright orange, red, or other readily identifiable dummy round. If the handgun is of a model that does not allow the slide to be locked back, pull the slide back and physically check the chamber to ensure that the chamber is clear. If no readily identifiable dummy round is available, an empty cartridge casing with an empty primer pocket may be used.

(k) Apply the safety, if applicable.

(*l*) Apply the firearm safety device, if applicable. This requirement shall not apply to an Olympic competition pistol if no firearm safety device, other than a cable lock that the department has determined would damage the barrel of the pistol, has been approved for the pistol, and the pistol is either listed in subdivision (b) of Section 32105 or is subject to subdivision (c) of Section 32105. *(Added by Stats.2010, c. 711 (S.B.1080), § 6, operative Jan. 1, 2012.)*

Law Revision Commission Comments

In combination with Section 26850(a)-(b), Section 26853 continues former Section 12071(b)(8)(D) without substantive change, as it pertained to a semiautomatic pistol.

For exceptions to this provision, see Article 4 (commencing with Section 27000), Article 5 (commencing with Section 27050), and Article 6 (commencing with Section 27100).

For the consequences of violating this section, see Section 26800 (forfeiture of license).

See Sections 16520 ("firearm"), 16530 ("firearm capable of being concealed upon the person," "pistol," and "revolver"), 16640 ("handgun"). [38 Cal. L.Rev.Comm. Reports 217 (2009)].

Cross References

Firearm defined for purposes of this Part, see Penal Code § 16520.
Handgun defined for purposes of this Part, see Penal Code § 16640.
Pistol defined for purposes of this Part, see Penal Code § 16530.

§ 26856. Safe handling demonstration; double-action revolver

To comply with Section 26850, a safe handling demonstration for a double-action revolver shall include all of the following steps:

(a) Open the cylinder.

(b) Visually and physically inspect each chamber, to ensure that the revolver is unloaded.

(c) Remove the firearm safety device. If the firearm safety device prevents any of the previous steps, remove the firearm safety device during the appropriate step.

(d) While maintaining muzzle awareness and trigger discipline, load one bright orange, red, or other readily identifiable dummy round into a chamber of the cylinder and rotate the cylinder so that the round is in the next-to-fire position. If no readily identifiable dummy round is available, an empty cartridge casing with an empty primer pocket may be used.

(e) Close the cylinder.

(f) Open the cylinder and eject the round.

(g) Visually and physically inspect each chamber to ensure that the revolver is unloaded.

(h) Apply the firearm safety device, if applicable. This requirement shall not apply to an Olympic competition pistol if no firearm safety device, other than a cable lock that the department has determined would damage the barrel of the pistol, has been approved for the pistol, and the pistol is either listed in subdivision (b) of Section 32105 or is subject to subdivision (c) of Section 32105. *(Added by Stats.2010, c. 711 (S.B.1080), § 6, operative Jan. 1, 2012.)*

Law Revision Commission Comments

In combination with Section 26850(a)-(b), Section 26856 continues former Section 12071(b)(8)(D) without substantive change, as it pertained to a double-action revolver.

For exceptions to this provision, see Article 4 (commencing with Section 27000), Article 5 (commencing with Section 27050), and Article 6 (commencing with Section 27100).

For the consequences of violating this section, see Section 26800 (forfeiture of license).

See Section 16530 ("firearm capable of being concealed upon the person," "pistol," and "revolver"). [38 Cal.L.Rev.Comm. Reports 217 (2009)].

Cross References

Firearm defined for purposes of this Part, see Penal Code § 16520.
Pistol defined for purposes of this Part, see Penal Code § 16530.
Revolver defined for purposes of this Part, see Penal Code § 16530.

§ 26859. Safe handling demonstration; single-action revolver

To comply with Section 26850, a safe handling demonstration for a single-action revolver shall include all of the following steps:

(a) Open the loading gate.

(b) Visually and physically inspect each chamber, to ensure that the revolver is unloaded.

(c) Remove the firearm safety device required to be sold with the handgun. If the firearm safety device prevents any of the previous steps, remove the firearm safety device during the appropriate step.

(d) Load one bright orange, red, or other readily identifiable dummy round into a chamber of the cylinder, close the loading gate and rotate the cylinder so that the round is in the next-to-fire position. If no readily identifiable dummy round is available, an empty cartridge casing with an empty primer pocket may be used.

(e) Open the loading gate and unload the revolver.

(f) Visually and physically inspect each chamber to ensure that the revolver is unloaded.

(g) Apply the firearm safety device, if applicable. This requirement shall not apply to an Olympic competition pistol if no firearm safety device, other than a cable lock that the department has determined would damage the barrel of the pistol, has been approved for the pistol, and the pistol is either listed in subdivision (b) of Section 32105 or is subject to subdivision (c) of Section 32105. *(Added by Stats.2010, c. 711 (S.B.1080), § 6, operative Jan. 1, 2012.)*

Law Revision Commission Comments

In combination with Section 26850(a)-(b), Section 26859 continues former Section 12071(b)(8)(D) without substantive change, as it pertained to a single-action revolver.

For exceptions to this provision, see Article 4 (commencing with Section 27000), Article 5 (commencing with Section 27050), and Article 6 (commencing with Section 27100).

For the consequences of violating this section, see Section 26800 (forfeiture of license).

See Sections 16530 ("firearm capable of being concealed upon the person," "pistol," and "revolver"), 16640 ("handgun"). [38 Cal.L.Rev.Comm. Reports 217 (2009)].

Cross References

Firearm defined for purposes of this Part, see Penal Code § 16520.
Handgun defined for purposes of this Part, see Penal Code § 16640.
Pistol defined for purposes of this Part, see Penal Code § 16530.
Revolver defined for purposes of this Part, see Penal Code § 16530.

§ 26860. Delivery of long gun; safe handling demonstration requirement

(a) Except as authorized by the department, commencing January 1, 2015, a firearms dealer shall not deliver a long gun unless the recipient performs a safe handling demonstration with that long gun.

(b) The department shall, not later than January 1, 2015, adopt regulations establishing a long gun safe handling demonstration that shall include, at a minimum, loading and unloading the long gun.

(c) The firearms dealer shall sign and date an affidavit stating that the requirements of subdivision (a) and the regulations adopted pursuant to subdivision (b) have been met. The firearms dealer shall additionally obtain the signature of the long gun purchaser on the same affidavit. The firearms dealer shall retain the original affidavit as proof of compliance with this section.

(d) The recipient shall perform the safe handling demonstration for a department-certified instructor.

(e) A demonstration is not required if the dealer is returning the long gun to the owner of the long gun.

(f) Department-certified instructors who may administer the safe handling demonstration shall meet the requirements set forth in subdivision (b) of Section 31635.

(g) An individual who is exempt from the requirements of subdivision (a) of Section 31615, pursuant to Section 31700, is also exempt from performing the safe handling demonstration. *(Added by Stats.2013, c. 761 (S.B.683), § 5.)*

Research References

2 Witkin, California Criminal Law 4th Crimes Against Public Peace and Welfare § 197 (2021), Time and Manner of Delivery by Dealer.

§ 26865. Offer of firearm pamphlet

A licensee shall offer to provide the purchaser or transferee of a firearm, or person being loaned a firearm, with a copy of the pamphlet described in Section 34205, and may add the cost of the pamphlet, if any, to the sales price of the firearm. *(Added by Stats.2010, c. 711 (S.B.1080), § 6, operative Jan. 1, 2012. Amended by Stats.2011, c. 745 (A.B.809), § 12.)*

Law Revision Commission Comments

Section 26865 continues former Section 12071(b)(9) without substantive change.

For exceptions to this provision, see Article 4 (commencing with Section 27000), Article 5 (commencing with Section 27050), and Article 6 (commencing with Section 27100).

For the consequences of violating this section, see Section 26800 (forfeiture of license).

See Sections 16520 ("firearm"), 26700 ("dealer," "licensee," or "person licensed pursuant to Sections 26700 to 26915, inclusive"). [38 Cal.L.Rev. Comm. Reports 217 (2009)].

Cross References

Firearm defined for purposes of this Part, see Penal Code § 16520.
Licensee defined, see Penal Code § 26700.

§ 26870. Collusion by licensee prohibited

A licensee shall not commit an act of collusion as defined in Section 27550. *(Added by Stats.2010, c. 711 (S.B.1080), § 6, operative Jan. 1, 2012.)*

Law Revision Commission Comments

Section 26870 continues former Section 12071(b)(10) without substantive change.

For exceptions to this provision, see Article 4 (commencing with Section 27000), Article 5 (commencing with Section 27050), and Article 6 (commencing with Section 27100).

For the consequences of violating this section, see Section 26800 (forfeiture of license).

See Section 26700 ("dealer," "licensee," or "person licensed pursuant to Sections 26700 to 26915, inclusive"). [38 Cal.L.Rev.Comm. Reports 217 (2009)].

Cross References

Licensee defined, see Penal Code § 26700.

§ 26875. Posting of charges and fees

A licensee shall post conspicuously within the licensed premises a detailed list of each of the following:

(a) All charges required by governmental agencies for processing firearm transfers required by Section 12806, Chapter 5 (commencing with Section 28050), and Article 3 (commencing with Section 28200) of Chapter 6.

(b) All fees that the licensee charges pursuant to Section 12806 and Chapter 5 (commencing with Section 28050). *(Added by Stats.2010, c. 711 (S.B.1080), § 6, operative Jan. 1, 2012.)*

Law Revision Commission Comments

Section 26875 continues former Section 12071(b)(11) without substantive change.

For exceptions to this provision, see Article 4 (commencing with Section 27000), Article 5 (commencing with Section 27050), and Article 6 (commencing with Section 27100).

For the consequences of violating this section, see Section 26800 (forfeiture of license).

See Sections 16520 ("firearm"), 16810 ("licensed premises," "licensee's business premises," and "licensee's place of business"), 26700 ("dealer," "licensee," or "person licensed pursuant to Sections 26700 to 26915, inclusive"). [38 Cal.L.Rev.Comm. Reports 217 (2009)].

Cross References

Firearm defined for purposes of this Part, see Penal Code § 16520.
Licensee defined, see Penal Code § 26700.

§ 26880. Misstatement of government fees prohibited

A licensee shall not misstate the amount of fees charged by a governmental agency pursuant to Section 12806, Chapter 5 (commencing with Section 28050), and Article 3 (commencing with Section 28200) of Chapter 6. *(Added by Stats.2010, c. 711 (S.B.1080), § 6, operative Jan. 1, 2012.)*

Law Revision Commission Comments

Section 26880 continues former Section 12071(b)(12) without substantive change.

For exceptions to this provision, see Article 4 (commencing with Section 27000), Article 5 (commencing with Section 27050), and Article 6 (commencing with Section 27100).

For the consequences of violating this section, see Section 26800 (forfeiture of license).

See Section 26700 ("dealer," "licensee," or "person licensed pursuant to Sections 26700 to 26915, inclusive"). [38 Cal.L.Rev.Comm. Reports 217 (2009)].

Cross References

Licensee defined, see Penal Code § 26700.

§ 26883. Firearm restocking or return-related fees

(a) A licensee shall not charge a restocking or other return-related fee of more than 5 percent of the purchase price of the firearm if the buyer decides to cancel the purchase of the firearm during the 10–day period imposed pursuant to Section 26815.

(b) This section shall not apply to a special order firearm by the buyer.

(c) For purposes of this section, "special order" means a specific request by the buyer for the licensee to order a firearm that is not available to the licensee. *(Added by Stats.2022, c. 141 (A.B.1842), § 1, eff. Jan. 1, 2023.)*

§ 26885. Firearm inventory to be kept at licensed location; report of loss or theft of firearm or ammunition

(a) Except as provided in subdivisions (b) and (c) of Section 26805, all firearms that are in the inventory of a licensee shall be kept within the licensed location.

(b) Within 48 hours of discovery, a licensee shall report the loss or theft of any of the following items to the appropriate law enforcement agency in the city, county, or city and county where the licensee's business premises are located:

(1) Any firearm or ammunition that is merchandise of the licensee.

(2) Any firearm or ammunition that the licensee takes possession of pursuant to Chapter 5 (commencing with Section 28050), or pursuant to Section 30312.

(3) Any firearm or ammunition kept at the licensee's place of business. *(Added by Stats.2010, c. 711 (S.B.1080), § 6, operative Jan. 1, 2012. Amended by Initiative Measure (Prop. 63, § 7.1, approved Nov. 8, 2016, eff. Nov. 9, 2016).)*

Law Revision Commission Comments

Section 26885 continues former Section 12071(b)(13) without substantive change.

For exceptions to this provision, see Article 4 (commencing with Section 27000), Article 5 (commencing with Section 27050), and Article 6 (commencing with Section 27100).

For the consequences of violating this section, see Section 26800 (forfeiture of license).

See Sections 16520 ("firearm"), 16810 ("licensed premises," "licensee's business premises," and "licensee's place of business"), 26700 ("dealer," "licensee," or "person licensed pursuant to Sections 26700 to 26915, inclusive"). [38 Cal.L.Rev.Comm. Reports 217 (2009)].

Cross References

Firearm defined for purposes of this Part, see Penal Code § 16520.
Licensee defined, see Penal Code § 26700.

§ 26890. Storing of firearms inventory when licensee not open for business; methods of securing; imposition of security requirements; exemptions

(a) Except as provided in subdivisions (b) and (c) of Section 26805, any time when the licensee is not open for business, all inventory firearms shall be stored in the licensed location. All firearms shall be secured using one of the following methods as to each particular firearm:

(1) Store the firearm in a secure facility that is a part of, or that constitutes, the licensee's business premises.

(2) Secure the firearm with a hardened steel rod or cable of at least one-eighth inch in diameter through the trigger guard of the firearm. The steel rod or cable shall be secured with a hardened steel lock that has a shackle. The lock and shackle shall be protected or shielded from the use of a boltcutter and the rod or cable shall be anchored in a manner that prevents the removal of the firearm from the premises.

(3) Store the firearm in a locked fireproof safe or vault in the licensee's business premises.

(b) The licensing authority in an unincorporated area of a county or within a city may impose security requirements that are more strict or are at a higher standard than those specified in subdivision (a).

(c) Upon written request from a licensee, the licensing authority may grant an exemption from compliance with the requirements of subdivision (a) if the licensee is unable to comply with those requirements because of local ordinances, covenants, lease conditions, or similar circumstances not under the control of the licensee.

(d) Subdivisions (a) and (b) shall not apply to a licensee organized as a nonprofit public benefit corporation pursuant to Part 2 (commencing with Section 5110) of Division 2 of Title 1 of the Corporations Code, or as a mutual benefit corporation pursuant to Part 3 (commencing with Section 7110) of Division 2 of Title 1 of the Corporations Code, if both of the following conditions are satisfied:

(1) The nonprofit public benefit or mutual benefit corporation obtained the dealer's license solely and exclusively to assist that corporation or local chapters of that corporation in conducting auctions, raffles, or similar events at which firearms are auctioned or raffled off to fund the activities of that corporation or the local chapters of the corporation.

(2) The firearms are not handguns. *(Added by Stats.2010, c. 711 (S.B.1080), § 6, operative Jan. 1, 2012. Amended by Stats.2011, c. 745 (A.B.809), § 13; Stats.2018, c. 185 (A.B.2176), § 8, eff. Jan. 1, 2019; Stats.2019, c. 738 (S.B.376), § 17, eff. Jan. 1, 2020.)*

Law Revision Commission Comments

Subdivision (a) of Section 26890 continues former Section 12071(b)(14) without substantive change.

Subdivision (b) continues former Section 12071(b)(15) without substantive change.

Subdivision (c) continues former Section 12071(d) without substantive change.

Subdivision (d) continues former Section 12071(h) without substantive change.

For exceptions to this provision, see Article 4 (commencing with Section 27000), Article 5 (commencing with Section 27050), and Article 6 (commencing with Section 27100).

For the consequences of violating this section, see Section 26800 (forfeiture of license).

See Sections 16520 ("firearm"), 16530 ("firearm capable of being concealed upon the person," "pistol," and "revolver"), 16810 ("licensed premises," "licensee's business premises," and "licensee's place of business"), 17110 ("secure facility" for firearm storage by dealer), 26700 ("dealer," "licensee," or "person licensed pursuant to Sections 26700 to 26915, inclusive"). [38 Cal.L.Rev.Comm. Reports 217 (2009)].

Section 26890(d) is amended to correct an erroneous use of "or." This is a nonsubstantive change. [44 Cal.L.Rev.Comm. Reports 471 (2015)].

Cross References

Dealer defined, see Penal Code § 26700.
Firearm defined for purposes of this Part, see Penal Code § 16520.
Handgun defined for purposes of this Part, see Penal Code § 16640.
Licensee defined, see Penal Code § 26700.

§ 26895. Copy of license to be submitted to Department of Justice

Commencing January 1, 1994, a licensee shall, upon the issuance or renewal of a license, submit a copy of it to the Department of Justice. *(Added by Stats.2010, c. 711 (S.B.1080), § 6, operative Jan. 1, 2012.)*

Law Revision Commission Comments

Section 26895 continues former Section 12071(b)(16) without substantive change.

For exceptions to this provision, see Article 4 (commencing with Section 27000), Article 5 (commencing with Section 27050), and Article 6 (commencing with Section 27100).

For the consequences of violating this section, see Section 26800 (forfeiture of license).

See Section 26700 ("dealer," "licensee," or "person licensed pursuant to Sections 26700 to 26915, inclusive"). [38 Cal.L.Rev.Comm. Reports 217 (2009)].

Cross References

Licensee defined, see Penal Code § 26700.

§ 26900. Firearm transaction record; availability for inspection

(a) A licensee shall maintain and make available for inspection during business hours to any peace officer, authorized local law enforcement employee, or Department of Justice employee designated by the Attorney General, upon the presentation of proper identification, a firearm transaction record, as defined in Section 16550.

(b) A licensee shall be in compliance with the provisions of subdivision (a) if the licensee maintains and makes available for inspection during business hours to any peace officer, authorized local law enforcement employee, or Department of Justice employee designated by the Attorney General, upon the presentation of proper identification, the bound book containing the same information referred to in Section 478.124a and subdivision (e) of Section 478.125 of Title 27 of the Code of Federal Regulations and the records referred to in subdivision (a) of Section 478.124 of Title 27 of the Code of Federal Regulations. *(Added by Stats.2010, c. 711 (S.B. 1080), § 6, operative Jan. 1, 2012.)*

Law Revision Commission Comments

Subdivision (a) of Section 26900 continues former Section 12071(b)(17) without substantive change.

Subdivision (b) continues former Section 12071(c)(4)(B) without substantive change.

For exceptions to this provision, see Article 4 (commencing with Section 27000), Article 5 (commencing with Section 27050), and Article 6 (commencing with Section 27100).

For the consequences of violating this section, see Section 26800 (forfeiture of license).

See Section 26700 ("dealer," "licensee," or "person licensed pursuant to Sections 26700 to 26915, inclusive"). [38 Cal.L.Rev.Comm. Reports 217 (2009)].

Cross References

Attorney General, generally, see Government Code § 12500 et seq.
Firearm defined for purposes of this Part, see Penal Code § 16520.
Licensee defined, see Penal Code § 26700.

§ 26905. Receipt of handgun or firearm; report to Department of Justice; exemptions

(a) On the date of receipt, a licensee shall report to the Department of Justice, in a format prescribed by the department, the acquisition by the licensee of the ownership of a handgun, and commencing January 1, 2014, of any firearm.

(b) The provisions of this section shall not apply to any of the following transactions:

(1) A transaction subject to the provisions of Sections 26960 and 27660.

(2) The dealer acquired the firearm from a wholesaler.

(3) The dealer acquired the firearm from a person who is licensed as a manufacturer or importer to engage in those activities pursuant to Chapter 44 (commencing with Section 921) of Title 18 of the United States Code and any regulations issued pursuant thereto.

(4) The dealer acquired the firearm from a person who resides outside this state who is licensed pursuant to Chapter 44 (commencing with Section 921) of Title 18 of the United States Code and any regulations issued pursuant thereto.

(5) The dealer is also licensed as a secondhand dealer pursuant to Article 4 (commencing with Section 21625) of Chapter 9 of Division 8 of the Business and Professions Code, acquires a handgun, and, commencing January 1, 2014, any firearm, and reports its acquisition pursuant to Section 21628.2 of the Business and Professions Code. *(Added by Stats.2010, c. 711 (S.B.1080), § 6, operative Jan. 1, 2012. Amended by Stats.2011, c. 745 (A.B.809), § 14.)*

Law Revision Commission Comments

Section 26905 continues former Section 12071(b)(18) without substantive change.

For exceptions to this provision, see Article 4 (commencing with Section 27000), Article 5 (commencing with Section 27050), and Article 6 (commencing with Section 27100).

For the consequences of violating this section, see Section 26800 (forfeiture of license).

See Sections 16520 ("firearm"), 16530 ("firearm capable of being concealed upon the person," "pistol," and "revolver"), 17340 ("wholesaler"), 26700 ("dealer," "licensee," or "person licensed pursuant to Sections 26700 to 26915, inclusive"). [38 Cal.L.Rev.Comm. Reports 217 (2009)].

Cross References

Dealer defined, see Penal Code § 26700.
Firearm defined for purposes of this Part, see Penal Code § 16520.
Handgun defined for purposes of this Part, see Penal Code § 16640.
Licensee defined, see Penal Code § 26700.

Wholesaler defined for purposes of this Part, see Penal Code § 17340.

Research References

2 Witkin, California Criminal Law 4th Crimes Against Public Peace and Welfare § 200 (2021), Reporting and Identification Requirements for Concealable Firearms.

§ 26910. Report to Department of Justice of firearm not delivered within time period required by federal regulations

A licensee shall forward, in a format prescribed by the Department of Justice, information as required by the department on any firearm that is not delivered within the time period set forth in Section 478.102(c) of Title 27 of the Code of Federal Regulations. *(Added by Stats.2010, c. 711 (S.B.1080), § 6, operative Jan. 1, 2012.)*

Law Revision Commission Comments

Section 26910 continues former Section 12071(b)(19) without substantive change.

For exceptions to this provision, see Article 4 (commencing with Section 27000), Article 5 (commencing with Section 27050), and Article 6 (commencing with Section 27100).

For the consequences of violating this section, see Section 26800 (forfeiture of license).

See Sections 16520 ("firearm"), 26700 ("dealer," "licensee," or "person licensed pursuant to Sections 26700 to 26915, inclusive"). [38 Cal.L.Rev. Comm. Reports 217 (2009)].

Cross References

Firearm defined for purposes of this Part, see Penal Code § 16520.
Licensee defined, see Penal Code § 26700.

Research References

2 Witkin, California Criminal Law 4th Crimes Against Public Peace and Welfare § 200 (2021), Reporting and Identification Requirements for Concealable Firearms.
1 Witkin California Criminal Law 4th Introduction to Crimes § 77 (2021), Illustrations: Special Statute is Not Controlling.

§ 26915. Certificate of eligibility requirement for agent or employee of firearms dealer; notification of ineligibility; background check; prohibition from contact with unsecured firearms by ineligible agent; additional conditions imposed by local government ordinance

(a) Commencing January 1, 2018, a firearms dealer shall require any agent or employee who handles, sells, or delivers firearms to obtain and provide to the dealer a certificate of eligibility from the Department of Justice pursuant to Section 26710. On the application for the certificate, the agent or employee shall provide the name and California firearms dealer number of the firearms dealer with whom the person is employed.

(b) The department shall notify the firearms dealer in the event that the agent or employee who has a certificate of eligibility is or becomes prohibited from possessing firearms.

(c) If the local jurisdiction requires a background check of the agents or employees of a firearms dealer, the agent or employee shall obtain a certificate of eligibility pursuant to subdivision (a).

(d)(1) Nothing in this section shall be construed to preclude a local jurisdiction from conducting an additional background check pursuant to Section 11105. The local jurisdiction may not charge a fee for the additional criminal history check.

(2) Nothing in this section shall be construed to preclude a local jurisdiction from prohibiting employment based on criminal history that does not appear as part of obtaining a certificate of eligibility.

(e) The licensee shall prohibit any agent who the licensee knows or reasonably should know is within a class of persons prohibited from possessing firearms pursuant to Chapter 2 (commencing with Section 29800) or Chapter 3 (commencing with Section 29900) of Division 9 of this title, or Section 8100 or 8103 of the Welfare and Institutions Code, from coming into contact with any firearm that is not secured and from accessing any key, combination, code, or other means to open any of the locking devices described in subdivision (g).

(f) Nothing in this section shall be construed as preventing a local government from enacting an ordinance imposing additional conditions on licensees with regard to agents or employees.

(g) For purposes of this article, "secured" means a firearm that is made inoperable in one or more of the following ways:

(1) The firearm is inoperable because it is secured by a firearm safety device listed on the department's roster of approved firearm safety devices pursuant to subdivision (d) of Section 23655.

(2) The firearm is stored in a locked gun safe or long-gun safe that meets the standards for department-approved gun safes set forth in Section 23650.

(3) The firearm is stored in a distinct locked room or area in the building that is used to store firearms, which can only be unlocked by a key, a combination, or similar means.

(4) The firearm is secured with a hardened steel rod or cable that is at least one-eighth of an inch in diameter through the trigger guard of the firearm. The steel rod or cable shall be secured with a hardened steel lock that has a shackle. The lock and shackle shall be protected or shielded from the use of a boltcutter and the rod or cable shall be anchored in a manner that prevents the removal of the firearm from the premises. *(Added by Stats.2010, c. 711 (S.B.1080), § 6, operative Jan. 1, 2012. Amended by Initiative Measure (Prop. 63, § 7.2, approved Nov. 8, 2016, eff. Nov. 9, 2016).)*

Law Revision Commission Comments

Subdivisions (a) through (f) of Section 26915 continue former Section 12071(b)(20)(A)-(F) without substantive change.

Subdivision (g) continues former Section 12071(b)(20)(G)(ii) without substantive change.

For exceptions to this provision, see Article 4 (commencing with Section 27000), Article 5 (commencing with Section 27050), and Article 6 (commencing with Section 27100).

For the consequences of violating this section, see Section 26800 (forfeiture of license).

See Sections 16130 ("agent"), 16520 ("firearm"), 16610 ("gun safe"), 16870 ("long-gun safe"), 26700 ("dealer," "licensee," or "person licensed pursuant to Sections 26700 to 26915, inclusive"). [38 Cal.L.Rev.Comm. Reports 217 (2009)].

Cross References

Dealer defined, see Penal Code § 26700.
Firearm defined for purposes of this Part, see Penal Code § 16520.
Gun safe defined for purposes of this Part, see Penal Code § 16610.
Licensee defined, see Penal Code § 26700.
Vendor to provide information to gun show producer, availability of information, see Penal Code § 27320.

ARTICLE 3. EXCEPTIONS EXTENDING ONLY TO WAITING PERIOD

§ 26950. Peace officer authorized to carry firearms in performance of duties; application of Section 26815

(a) The waiting period described in Section 26815 does not apply to the sale, delivery, or transfer of firearms made to any person who satisfies both of the following requirements:

(1) The person is properly identified as a full-time paid peace officer, as defined in Chapter 4.5 (commencing with Section 830) of Title 3 of Part 2.

(2) The officer's employer has authorized the officer to carry firearms while in the performance of duties.

(b)(1) Proper identification is defined as verifiable written certification from the head of the agency by which the purchaser or transferee is employed, identifying the purchaser or transferee as a peace officer who is authorized to carry firearms while in the performance of duties, and authorizing the purchase or transfer.

(2) The certification shall be delivered to the dealer at the time of purchase or transfer and the purchaser or transferee shall identify himself or herself as the person authorized in the certification.

(3) The dealer shall keep the certification with the record of sale.

(4) On the date that the sale, delivery, or transfer is made, the dealer delivering the firearm shall transmit to the Department of Justice an electronic or telephonic report of the transaction as is indicated in Section 28160 or 28165. *(Added by Stats.2010, c. 711 (S.B.1080), § 6, operative Jan. 1, 2012.)*

Law Revision Commission Comments

Section 26950 continues former Section 12078(a)(1) without substantive change, as that provision applied to the waiting period in former Section 12071.

For other exceptions relating to law enforcement, see Sections 27050–27065.

See Sections 16520 ("firearm"), 26700 ("dealer," "licensee," or "person licensed pursuant to Sections 26700 to 26915, inclusive"). [38 Cal.L.Rev. Comm. Reports 217 (2009)].

Cross References

Dealer defined, see Penal Code § 26700.
Firearm defined for purposes of this Part, see Penal Code § 16520.

§ 26960. Delivery of handgun or firearm by dealer; application of Section 26815

(a) The waiting period described in Section 26815 does not apply to the sale, delivery, or transfer of a handgun, and commencing January 1, 2014, a firearm that is not a handgun, by a dealer in either of the following situations:

(1) The dealer is delivering the firearm to another dealer, the firearm is not intended as merchandise in the receiving dealer's business, and the requirements of subdivisions (b) and (c) are satisfied.

(2) The dealer is delivering the firearm to himself or herself, the firearm is not intended as merchandise in the dealer's business, and the requirements of subdivision (c) are satisfied.

(b) If the dealer is receiving the firearm from another dealer, the dealer receiving the firearm shall present proof to the dealer delivering the firearm that the receiving dealer is licensed pursuant to Article 1 (commencing with Section 26700) and Article 2 (commencing with Section 26800). This shall be done by complying with Section 27555.

(c)(1) Regardless of whether the dealer is selling, delivering, or transferring the firearm to another dealer or to himself or herself, on the date that the application to purchase is completed, the dealer delivering the firearm shall forward by prepaid mail to the Department of Justice a report of the application and the type of information concerning the purchaser or transferee as is indicated in Section 28160.

(2) Where electronic or telephonic transfer of applicant information is used, on the date that the application to purchase is completed, the dealer delivering the firearm shall transmit an electronic or telephonic report of the application and the type of information concerning the purchaser or transferee as is indicated in Section 28160. *(Added by Stats.2010, c. 711 (S.B.1080), § 6, operative Jan. 1, 2012. Amended by Stats.2011, c. 745 (A.B.809), § 16.)*

Law Revision Commission Comments

Section 26960 continues former Section 12078(n) without substantive change, as that provision applied to the waiting period in former Section 12071.

See Sections 16190 ("application to purchase"), 16520 ("firearm"), 16640 ("handgun"), 26700 ("dealer," "licensee," or "person licensed pursuant to Sections 26700 to 26915, inclusive"). [38 Cal.L.Rev.Comm. Reports 217 (2009)].

Cross References

Firearm defined for purposes of this Part, see Penal Code § 16520.
Handgun defined for purposes of this Part, see Penal Code § 16640.

§ 26965. Sale, delivery, or transfer of firearm to holder of special weapons permit; application of Section 26815

(a) The waiting period described in Section 26815 does not apply to the sale, delivery, or transfer of a firearm to the holder of a special weapons permit issued by the Department of Justice pursuant to Section 32650 or 33300, pursuant to Article 3 (commencing with Section 18900) of Chapter 1 of Division 5 of Title 2, or pursuant to Article 4 (commencing with Section 32700) of Chapter 6 of Division 10.

(b) On the date that the application to purchase is completed, the dealer delivering the firearm shall transmit to the Department of Justice an electronic or telephonic report of the application as is indicated in Section 28160 or 28165, as applicable. *(Added by Stats.2010, c. 711 (S.B.1080), § 6, operative Jan. 1, 2012. Amended by Stats.2011, c. 745 (A.B.809), § 17.)*

Law Revision Commission Comments

Section 26965 continues former Section 12078(r) without substantive change, as that provision applied to the waiting period in former Section 12071.

See Sections 16190 ("application to purchase"), 16520 ("firearm"), 26700 ("dealer," "licensee," or "person licensed pursuant to Sections 26700 to 26915, inclusive"). [38 Cal.L.Rev.Comm. Reports 217 (2009)].

Cross References

Dealer defined, see Penal Code § 26700.
Firearm defined for purposes of this Part, see Penal Code § 16520.

§ 26970. Sale, delivery, loan, or transfer of firearm that is curio or relic; application of Section 26815

(a) The waiting period described in Section 26815 does not apply to the sale, delivery, loan, or transfer of a firearm if all of the following conditions are satisfied:

(1) The firearm is a curio or relic, as defined in Section 478.11 of Title 27 of the Code of Federal Regulations, or its successor.

(2) The sale, delivery, loan, or transfer is made by a dealer.

(3) The sale, delivery, loan, or transfer is made to a person who is licensed as a collector pursuant to Chapter 44 (commencing with Section 921) of Title 18 of the United States Code and the regulations issued pursuant thereto.

(4) The licensed collector has a current certificate of eligibility issued by the Department of Justice pursuant to Section 26710.

(b) On the date that the sale, delivery, or transfer is made, the dealer delivering the firearm shall transmit to the Department of Justice an electronic or telephonic report of the transaction as is indicated in Section 28160 or 28165. *(Added by Stats.2010, c. 711 (S.B.1080), § 6, operative Jan. 1, 2012.)*

Law Revision Commission Comments

Section 26970 continues former Section 12078(t)(1) without substantive change, as that provision applied to the waiting period in former Section 12071.

See Sections 16520 ("firearm"), 26700 ("dealer," "licensee," or "person licensed pursuant to Sections 26700 to 26915, inclusive"). [38 Cal.L.Rev. Comm. Reports 217 (2009)].

Cross References

Dealer defined, see Penal Code § 26700.
Firearm defined for purposes of this Part, see Penal Code § 16520.

ARTICLE 4. EXCEPTIONS EXTENDING ONLY TO GROUNDS FOR FORFEITURE OF LICENSE

§ 27000. Loan of firearm for use as prop; application of Article 2

(a) Article 2 (commencing with Section 26800) does not apply to the loan of a firearm if all of the following conditions are satisfied:

(1) The firearm is unloaded.

(2) The loan is made by a dealer.

(3) The loan is made to a person who possesses a valid entertainment firearms permit issued pursuant to Chapter 2 (commencing with Section 29500) of Division 8.

(4) The firearm is loaned solely for use as a prop in a motion picture, television, video, theatrical, or other entertainment production or event.

(b) The dealer shall retain a photocopy of the entertainment firearms permit as proof of compliance with this requirement. *(Added by Stats.2010, c. 711 (S.B.1080), § 6, operative Jan. 1, 2012.)*

Law Revision Commission Comments

Section 27000 continues former Section 12078(s)(3) without substantive change, as that provision applied to former Section 12071(b).

See Sections 16520 ("firearm"), 26700 ("dealer," "licensee," or "person licensed pursuant to Sections 26700 to 26915, inclusive"). [38 Cal.L.Rev. Comm. Reports 217 (2009)].

Cross References

Dealer defined, see Penal Code § 26700.
Firearm defined for purposes of this Part, see Penal Code § 16520.

§ 27005. Loan of unloaded firearm to consultant-evaluator; application of Article 2

(a) Article 2 (commencing with Section 26800) does not apply to the loan of an unloaded firearm to a consultant-evaluator by a person licensed pursuant to Sections 26700 to 26915, inclusive, if the loan does not exceed 45 days from the date of delivery.

(b) At the time of the loan, the consultant-evaluator shall provide the following information, which the dealer shall retain for two years:

(1) A photocopy of a valid, current, government-issued identification to determine the consultant-evaluator's identity, including, but not limited to, a California driver's license, identification card, or passport.

(2) A photocopy of the consultant-evaluator's valid, current certificate of eligibility.

(3) A letter from the person licensed as an importer, manufacturer, or dealer pursuant to Chapter 44 (commencing with Section 921) of Title 18 of the United States Code, with whom the consultant-evaluator has a bona fide business relationship. The letter shall detail the bona fide business purposes for which the firearm is being loaned and confirm that the consultant-evaluator is being loaned the firearm as part of a bona fide business relationship.

(4) The signature of the consultant-evaluator on a form indicating the date the firearm is loaned and the last day the firearm may be returned. *(Added by Stats.2010, c. 711 (S.B.1080), § 6, operative Jan. 1, 2012.)*

Law Revision Commission Comments

Section 27005 continues former Section 12078(s)(4) without substantive change, as that provision applied to former Section 12071(b).

See Sections 16410 ("consultant-evaluator"), 16520 ("firearm"), 26700 ("dealer," "licensee," or "person licensed pursuant to Sections 26700 to 26915, inclusive"). [38 Cal.L.Rev.Comm. Reports 217 (2009)].

Cross References

Consultant-evaluator defined for purposes of this Part, see Penal Code § 16410.
Firearm defined for purposes of this Part, see Penal Code § 16520.

ARTICLE 5. EXCEPTIONS RELATING TO LAW ENFORCEMENT

§ 27050. Sale, delivery, or transfer of firearm to law enforcement representative; application of Articles 1 and 2

(a) Article 1 (commencing with Section 26700) and Article 2 (commencing with Section 26800) do not apply to any sale, delivery, or transfer of firearms made to an authorized law enforcement representative of any city, county, city and county, or state, or of the federal government, for exclusive use by that governmental agency if, prior to the sale, delivery, or transfer of these firearms, written authorization from the head of the agency authorizing the transaction is presented to the person from whom the purchase, delivery, or transfer is being made.

(b) Proper written authorization is defined as verifiable written certification from the head of the agency by which the purchaser or transferee is employed, identifying the employee as an individual authorized to conduct the transaction, and authorizing the transaction for the exclusive use of the agency by which that person is employed.

(c) Within 10 days of the date a handgun, and commencing January 1, 2014, any firearm, is acquired by the agency, a record of the same shall be entered as an institutional weapon into the Automated Firearms System (AFS) via the California Law Enforcement Telecommunications System (CLETS) by the law enforcement or state agency. Any agency without access to AFS shall arrange with the sheriff of the county in which the agency is located to input this information via this system. *(Added by Stats.2010, c. 711 (S.B.1080), § 6, operative Jan. 1, 2012. Amended by Stats.2011, c. 745 (A.B.809), § 18.)*

Law Revision Commission Comments

Section 27050 continues former Section 12078(a)(2) without substantive change, as that provision applied to former Section 12071 (through its reference to "the preceding provisions of this article").

For other exceptions relating to law enforcement, see Sections 26950, 27055–27065.

See Sections 16520 ("firearm"), 16640 ("handgun"). [38 Cal.L.Rev.Comm. Reports 217 (2009)].

Cross References

Firearm defined for purposes of this Part, see Penal Code § 16520.
Handgun defined for purposes of this Part, see Penal Code § 16640.

§ 27055. Loan of firearm by law enforcement representative to peace officer; application of Articles 1 and 2

Article 1 (commencing with Section 26700) and Article 2 (commencing with Section 26800) do not apply to the loan of a firearm if all of the following conditions are satisfied:

(a) The loan is made by an authorized law enforcement representative of a city, county, or city and county, or of the state or federal government.

(b) The loan is made to a peace officer employed by that agency and authorized to carry a firearm.

(c) The loan is made for the carrying and use of that firearm by that peace officer in the course and scope of the officer's duties. *(Added by Stats.2010, c. 711 (S.B.1080), § 6, operative Jan. 1, 2012.)*

Law Revision Commission Comments

Section 27055 continues former Section 12078(a)(3) without substantive change, as that provision applied to former Section 12071 (through its reference to "the preceding provisions of this article").

For other exceptions relating to law enforcement, see Sections 26950, 27050, 27060–27065.

See Section 16520 ("firearm"). [38 Cal.L.Rev.Comm. Reports 217 (2009)].

Cross References

Firearm defined for purposes of this Part, see Penal Code § 16520.

§ 27060. Sale, delivery, or transfer of firearm by law enforcement agency to peace officer pursuant to Section 10334 of Public Contract Code; application of Articles 1 and 2

(a) Article 1 (commencing with Section 26700) and Article 2 (commencing with Section 26800) do not apply to the sale, delivery, or transfer of a firearm by a law enforcement agency to a peace officer pursuant to Section 10334 of the Public Contract Code.

(b) Within 10 days of the date that a handgun, and commencing January 1, 2014, any firearm, is sold, delivered, or transferred pursuant to Section 10334 of the Public Contract Code to that peace officer, the name of the officer and the make, model, serial number, and other identifying characteristics of the firearm being sold, delivered, or transferred shall be entered into the Automated Firearms System (AFS) via the California Law Enforcement Telecommunications System (CLETS) by the law enforcement or state agency that sold, delivered, or transferred the firearm, provided, however, that if the firearm is not a handgun and does not have a serial number, identification number, or identification mark assigned to it, that fact shall be noted in AFS. Any agency without access to AFS shall arrange with the sheriff of the county in which the agency is located to input this information via this system. *(Added by Stats.2010, c. 711 (S.B.1080), § 6, operative Jan. 1, 2012. Amended by Stats.2011, c. 745 (A.B.809), § 19.)*

Law Revision Commission Comments

Section 27060 continues former Section 12078(a)(4) without substantive change, as that provision applied to former Section 12071 (through its reference to "the preceding provisions of this article").

For other exceptions relating to law enforcement, see Sections 26950, 27050–27055, 27065.

See Sections 16520 ("firearm"), 16640 ("handgun"). [38 Cal.L.Rev.Comm. Reports 217 (2009)].

Cross References

Firearm defined for purposes of this Part, see Penal Code § 16520.
Handgun defined for purposes of this Part, see Penal Code § 16640.
Sale, delivery, or transfer of firearm by persons licensed pursuant to Chapter 44, Title 18 of U.S. Code, review of centralized lists of firearms dealers, licensees, and manufacturers, see Penal Code § 27555.

§ 27065. Sale, delivery, or transfer of firearm by law enforcement agency to retiring peace officer; application of Articles 1 and 2

(a) Article 1 (commencing with Section 26700) and Article 2 (commencing with Section 26800) do not apply to the sale, delivery, or transfer of a firearm by a law enforcement agency to a retiring peace officer who is authorized to carry a firearm pursuant to Chapter 5 (commencing with Section 26300) of Division 5.

(b) Within 10 days of the date that a handgun, and commencing January 1, 2014, any firearm, is sold, delivered, or transferred to that retiring peace officer, the name of the officer and the make, model, serial number, and other identifying characteristics of the firearm being sold, delivered, or transferred shall be entered into the Automated Firearms System (AFS) via the California Law Enforcement Telecommunications System (CLETS) by the law enforcement or state agency that sold, delivered, or transferred the firearm, provided, however, that if the firearm is not a handgun and does not have a serial number, identification number, or identification mark assigned to it, that fact shall be noted in AFS. Any agency without access to AFS shall arrange with the sheriff of the county in which the agency is located to input this information via this system. *(Added by Stats.2010, c. 711 (S.B.1080), § 6, operative Jan. 1, 2012. Amended by Stats.2011, c. 745 (A.B.809), § 20.)*

Law Revision Commission Comments

Section 27065 continues former Section 12078(a)(5) without substantive change, as that provision applied to former Section 12071 (through its reference to "the preceding provisions of this article").

For other exceptions relating to law enforcement, see Sections 26950, 27050–27060.

See Sections 16520 ("firearm"), 16640 ("handgun"). [38 Cal.L.Rev.Comm. Reports 217 (2009)].

Cross References

Firearm defined for purposes of this Part, see Penal Code § 16520.
Handgun defined for purposes of this Part, see Penal Code § 16640.

ARTICLE 6. OTHER EXCEPTIONS

§ 27100. Sales, deliveries, or transfers of firearms between or to importers and manufacturers; application of Articles 1 and 2

Article 1 (commencing with Section 26700) and Article 2 (commencing with Section 26800) do not apply to sales, deliveries, or transfers of firearms between or to importers and manufacturers of firearms licensed to engage in that business pursuant to Chapter 44 (commencing with Section 921) of Title 18 of the United States Code and the regulations issued pursuant thereto. *(Added by Stats.2010, c. 711 (S.B.1080), § 6, operative Jan. 1, 2012.)*

Law Revision Commission Comments

Section 27100 continues former Section 12078(b)(1) without substantive change, as that provision applied to former Section 12071.

See Section 16520 ("firearm"). [38 Cal.L.Rev.Comm. Reports 217 (2009)].

Cross References

Firearm defined for purposes of this Part, see Penal Code § 16520.

§ 27105. Delivery of firearm to gunsmith for repair; application of Articles 1 and 2

Article 1 (commencing with Section 26700) and Article 2 (commencing with Section 26800) do not apply to the delivery of a firearm to a gunsmith for service or repair, or to the return of the firearm to its owner by the gunsmith, or to the delivery of a firearm by a gunsmith to a person licensed pursuant to Chapter 44 (commencing with Section 921) of Title 18 of the United States Code for service or repair and the return of the firearm to the gunsmith. *(Added by Stats.2010, c. 711 (S.B.1080), § 6, operative Jan. 1, 2012.)*

Law Revision Commission Comments

Section 27105 continues former Section 12078(e)(1) without substantive change, as that provision applied to former Section 12071.

See Sections 16520 ("firearm"), 16630 ("gunsmith"). [38 Cal.L.Rev.Comm. Reports 217 (2009)].

Cross References

Firearm defined for purposes of this Part, see Penal Code § 16520.
Gunsmith defined for purposes of this Part, see Penal Code § 16630.

§ 27115. Sale, delivery, or transfer of unloaded firearm by dealer to person residing outside of state; application of Articles 1 and 2

Article 1 (commencing with Section 26700) and Article 2 (commencing with Section 26800) do not apply to the sale, delivery, or transfer of unloaded firearms by a dealer to a person who resides outside this state and is licensed pursuant to Chapter 44 (commencing with Section 921) of Title 18 of the United States Code and the regulations issued pursuant thereto. *(Added by Stats.2010, c. 711 (S.B.1080), § 6, operative Jan. 1, 2012.)*

Law Revision Commission Comments

Section 27115 continues former Section 12078(k)(2) without substantive change, as that provision applied to former Section 12071.

See Sections 16520 ("firearm"), 26700 ("dealer," "licensee," or "person licensed pursuant to Sections 26700 to 26915, inclusive"). [38 Cal.L.Rev.Comm. Reports 217 (2009)].

Cross References

Firearm defined for purposes of this Part, see Penal Code § 16520.

§ 27120. Sale, delivery, or transfer of unloaded firearms to wholesaler; application of Articles 1 and 2

Article 1 (commencing with Section 26700) and Article 2 (commencing with Section 26800) do not apply to the sale, delivery, or transfer of unloaded firearms to a wholesaler if the firearms are being returned to the wholesaler and are intended as merchandise in the wholesaler's business. *(Added by Stats.2010, c. 711 (S.B.1080), § 6, operative Jan. 1, 2012.)*

Law Revision Commission Comments

Section 27120 continues former Section 12078(k)(3) without substantive change, as that provision applied to former Section 12071.

See Sections 16520 ("firearm"), 17340 ("wholesaler"), 26700 ("dealer," "licensee," or "person licensed pursuant to Sections 26700 to 26915, inclusive"). [40 Cal. L.Rev.Comm. Reports 107 (2010)].

Cross References

Firearm defined for purposes of this Part, see Penal Code § 16520.
Wholesaler defined for purposes of this Part, see Penal Code § 17340.

§ 27125. Sale, delivery, or transfer of firearms between dealers; application of Articles 1 and 2

Article 1 (commencing with Section 26700) and Article 2 (commencing with Section 26800) do not apply to the sale, delivery, or transfer of firearms if all of the following conditions are satisfied:

(a) The firearms are unloaded.

(b) The sale, delivery, or transfer is made by one dealer to another dealer, upon proof of compliance with the requirements of Section 27555.

(c) The firearms are intended as merchandise in the receiving dealer's business. *(Added by Stats.2010, c. 711 (S.B.1080), § 6, operative Jan. 1, 2012.)*

Law Revision Commission Comments

Section 27125 continues former Section 12078(k)(4) without substantive change, as that provision applied to former Section 12071.

See Sections 16520 ("firearm"), 26700 ("dealer," "licensee," or "person licensed pursuant to Sections 26700 to 26915, inclusive"). [38 Cal.L.Rev. Comm. Reports 217 (2009)].

Cross References

Firearm defined for purposes of this Part, see Penal Code § 16520.

§ 27130. Sale, delivery, or transfer of unloaded firearm by dealer to himself or herself; application of Articles 1 and 2

Until January 1, 2014, Article 1 (commencing with Section 26700) and Article 2 (commencing with Section 26800) do not apply to the sale, delivery, or transfer of an unloaded firearm, other than a handgun, by a dealer to himself or herself. *(Added by Stats.2010, c. 711 (S.B.1080), § 6, operative Jan. 1, 2012. Amended by Stats.2011, c. 745 (A.B.809), § 22.)*

Law Revision Commission Comments

Section 27130 continues former Section 12078(k)(5) without substantive change, as that provision applied to former Section 12071.

See Sections 16520 ("firearm"), 16640 ("handgun"), 26700 ("dealer," "licensee," or "person licensed pursuant to Sections 26700 to 26915, inclusive"). [38 Cal.L.Rev.Comm. Reports 217 (2009)].

Cross References

Firearm defined for purposes of this Part, see Penal Code § 16520.
Handgun defined for purposes of this Part, see Penal Code § 16640.

§ 27135. Loan of unloaded firearm on premises of licensed target facility for target shooting; application of Articles 1 and 2

Article 1 (commencing with Section 26700) and Article 2 (commencing with Section 26800) do not apply to the loan of an unloaded firearm by a dealer who also operates a target facility that holds a business or regulatory license on the premises of the building designated in the license or whose building designated in the license is on the premises of any club or organization organized for the purposes of practicing shooting at targets upon established ranges, whether public or private, to a person at that target facility or that club or organization, if the firearm is at all times kept within the premises of the target range or on the premises of the club or organization. *(Added by Stats.2010, c. 711 (S.B.1080), § 6, operative Jan. 1, 2012.)*

Law Revision Commission Comments

Section 27135 continues former Section 12078(k)(6) without substantive change, as that provision applied to former Section 12071.

See Sections 16520 ("firearm"), 26700 ("dealer," "licensee," or "person licensed pursuant to Sections 26700 to 26915, inclusive"). [38 Cal.L.Rev. Comm. Reports 217 (2009)].

Cross References

Firearm defined for purposes of this Part, see Penal Code § 16520.

§ 27140. Sale, delivery, or transfer of firearm pursuant to particular statutes; application of Articles 1 and 2

Article 1 (commencing with Section 26700) and Article 2 (commencing with Section 26800) do not apply to the sale, delivery, or transfer of a firearm regulated pursuant to any of the following statutes, if the sale, delivery, or transfer of that firearm is conducted in accordance with the applicable provisions of the statute:

(a) Chapter 1 (commencing with Section 18710) of Division 5 of Title 2, relating to destructive devices and explosives.

(b) Section 24410, relating to cane guns, and the exemptions in Chapter 1 (commencing with Section 17700) of Title 2, as they relate to cane guns.

(c) Section 24510, relating to firearms that are not immediately recognizable as firearms, and the exemptions in Chapter 1 (commencing with Section 17700) of Title 2, as they relate to firearms that are not immediately recognizable as firearms.

(d) Sections 24610 and 24680, relating to undetectable firearms, and the exemptions in Chapter 1 (commencing with Section 17700) of Title 2, as they relate to undetectable firearms.

(e) Section 24710, relating to wallet guns, and the exemptions in Chapter 1 (commencing with Section 17700) of Title 2, as they relate to wallet guns.

(f) Chapter 2 (commencing with Section 30500) of Division 10, relating to assault weapons.

(g) Section 31500, relating to unconventional pistols, and the exemptions in Chapter 1 (commencing with Section 17700) of Title 2, as they relate to unconventional pistols.

(h) Sections 33215 to 33225, inclusive, relating to short-barreled rifles and short-barreled shotguns, and the exemptions in Chapter 1 (commencing with Section 17700) of Title 2, as they relate to short-barreled rifles and short-barreled shotguns.

(i) Chapter 6 (commencing with Section 32610) of Division 10, relating to machineguns.

(j) Section 33600, relating to zip guns, and the exemptions in Chapter 1 (commencing with Section 17700) of Title 2, as they relate to zip guns. *(Added by Stats.2010, c. 711 (S.B.1080), § 6, operative Jan. 1, 2012.)*

Law Revision Commission Comments

Section 27140 continues former Section 12078(*o*) without substantive change, as that provision applied to former Section 12071.

See Sections 16330 ("cane gun"), 16460 ("destructive device"), 16510 ("explosive"), 16520 ("firearm"), 16880 ("machinegun"), 17170 ("short-barreled rifle"), 17180 ("short-barreled shotgun"), 17270 ("unconventional pistol"), 17280 ("undetectable firearm"), 17330 ("wallet gun"), 17360 ("zip gun"), 30510 ("assault weapon"), 30515 (further clarification of "assault weapon"). [38 Cal.L.Rev.Comm. Reports 217 (2009)].

Cross References

Cane gun defined for purposes of this Part, see Penal Code § 16330.
Firearm defined for purposes of this Part, see Penal Code § 16520.
Machinegun defined for purposes of this Part, see Penal Code § 16880.
Pistol defined for purposes of this Part, see Penal Code § 16530.
Unconventional pistol defined for purposes of this Part, see Penal Code § 17270.
Undetectable firearm defined for purposes of this Part, see Penal Code § 17280.
Wallet gun defined for purposes of this Part, see Penal Code § 17330.
Zip gun defined for purposes of this Part, see Penal Code § 17360.

CHAPTER 3. GUN SHOW OR EVENT

ARTICLE 1. GUN SHOW OR EVENT

§ 27200. Gun show or event; valid certificate of eligibility required; notification of event; regulations; fees; application of Section 26710

(a) No person shall produce, promote, sponsor, operate, or otherwise organize a gun show or event, as specified in subdivision (b) of Section 26805, unless that person possesses a valid certificate of eligibility from the Department of Justice.

(b) Unless the department's records indicate that the applicant is a person prohibited from possessing firearms, a certificate of eligibility shall be issued by the Department of Justice to an applicant provided the applicant does all of the following:

(1) Certifies that the applicant is familiar with the provisions of this article and Article 2 (commencing with Section 27300).

(2) Ensures that liability insurance is in effect for the duration of an event or show in an amount of not less than one million dollars ($1,000,000).

(3) Provides an annual list of the gun shows or events that the applicant plans to promote, produce, sponsor, operate, or otherwise organize during the year for which the certificate of eligibility is issued, including the date, time, and location of the gun shows or events.

(c) If during that year the information required by paragraph (3) of subdivision (b) changes, or additional gun shows or events will be promoted, produced, sponsored, operated, or otherwise organized by the applicant, the producer shall notify the Department of Justice no later than 30 days prior to the gun show or event.

(d) The Department of Justice shall adopt regulations to administer the certificate of eligibility program under this section.

(e) The Department of Justice shall recover the full costs of administering the certificate of eligibility program by fees assessed applicants who apply for certificates. A licensed gun show producer shall be assessed an annual fee of eighty-five dollars ($85) by the department.

(f) It is the intent of the Legislature that the certificate of eligibility program established pursuant to this section be incorporated into the certificate of eligibility program established pursuant to Section 26710 to the maximum extent practicable. *(Added by Stats.2010, c. 711 (S.B.1080), § 6, operative Jan. 1, 2012.)*

Law Revision Commission Comments

Subdivision (a) of Section 27200 continues the first sentence of former Section 12071.1(a) without substantive change.

Subdivision (b) continues the second sentence of former Section 12071.1(a) without substantive change.

Subdivision (c) continues former Section 12071.1(b) without substantive change.

Subdivisions (d) and (e) continue former Section 12071.1(d) without substantive change.

Subdivision (f) continues former Section 12071.1(q) without substantive change.

For exceptions to provisions in this article and Article 2 (commencing with Section 27300), see Article 3 (commencing with Section 27400).

For the consequences of violating this article, see Section 27245 (punishment).

See Sections 16520 ("firearm"), 16800 ("licensed gun show producer"). [38 Cal.L.Rev.Comm. Reports 217 (2009)].

Cross References

Firearm defined for purposes of this Part, see Penal Code § 16520.

Research References

2 Witkin, California Criminal Law 4th Crimes Against Public Peace and Welfare § 192 (2021), In General.

2 Witkin, California Criminal Law 4th Crimes Against Public Peace and Welfare § 255 (2021), Public Building or Open Meeting.

§ 27205. Provision of list of gun show or event participants to law enforcement agency; other information to be provided

(a) Before commencement of a gun show or event, the producer thereof shall, upon written request from a law enforcement agency with jurisdiction over the facility, make available to that agency, within 48 hours or a later time specified by the agency, a complete and accurate list of all persons, entities, and organizations that have leased or rented, or are known to the producer to intend to lease or rent, any table, display space, or area at the gun show or event for the purpose of selling, leasing, or transferring firearms, or processing the sale or transfer of ammunition.

(b) The producer shall thereafter, upon written request, for every day the gun show or event operates, within 24 hours or a later time specified by the requesting law enforcement agency, make available to that agency an accurate, complete, and current list of the persons, entities, and organizations that have leased or rented, or are known to the producer to intend to lease or rent, any table, display space, or area at the gun show or event for the purpose of selling, leasing, or transferring firearms, or processing the sale or transfer of ammunition.

(c) Subdivisions (a) and (b) apply to any person, entity, or organization, regardless of whether that person, entity, or organization participates in the entire gun show or event, or only a portion thereof.

(d) The information that may be requested by the law enforcement agency with jurisdiction over the facility, and that shall be provided by the producer upon request, includes, but is not limited to, the following information relative to a vendor who offers for sale any firearms manufactured after December 31, 1898, or any ammunition:

(1) The vendor's complete name.

(2) A driver's license or identification card number. *(Added by Stats.2010, c. 711 (S.B.1080), § 6, operative Jan. 1, 2012. Amended by Stats.2019, c. 736 (A.B.1669), § 1, eff. Jan. 1, 2020.)*

Law Revision Commission Comments

Subdivision (a) of Section 27205 continues the first paragraph of former Section 12071.1(f) without substantive change.

Subdivision (b) continues the second paragraph of former Section 12071.1(f) without substantive change.

Subdivision (c) continues the third paragraph of former Section 12071.1(f) without substantive change.

Subdivision (d) continues former Section 12071.1(g) without substantive change.

For exceptions to provisions in this article and Article 2 (commencing with Section 27300), see Article 3 (commencing with Section 27400).

For the consequences of violating this article, see Section 27245 (punishment).

See Section 16520 ("firearm"). [38 Cal.L.Rev.Comm. Reports 217 (2009)].

Cross References

Firearm defined for purposes of this Part, see Penal Code § 16520.

§ 27210. Event and security plan and schedule required; submission to law enforcement agency; approval by facility manager

(a) The producer and facility's manager of a gun show or event shall prepare an annual event and security plan and schedule that shall include, at a minimum, the following information for each show or event:

(1) The type of show or event, including, but not limited to, antique or general firearms and ammunition.

(2) The estimated number of vendors offering firearms or ammunition for sale or display.

(3) The estimated number of attendees.

(4) The number of entrances and exits at the gun show or event site.

(5) The location, dates, and times of the show or event.

(6) The contact person and telephone number for both the producer and the facility.

(7) The number of sworn peace officers employed by the producer or the facility's manager who will be present at the show or event.

(8) The number of nonsworn security personnel employed by the producer or the facility's manager who will be present at the show or event.

(b) The annual event and security plan shall be submitted by either the producer or the facility's manager to the Department of Justice and the law enforcement agency with jurisdiction over the facility.

(c) If significant changes have been made since the annual plan was submitted, the producer shall, not later than 15 days before commencement of the gun show or event, submit to the department, the law enforcement agency with jurisdiction over the facility site, and the facility's manager, a revised event and security plan, including a revised list of vendors that the producer knows, or reasonably should know, will be renting tables, space, or otherwise participating in the gun show or event.

(d) The event and security plan shall be approved by the facility's manager before the event or show, after consultation with the law enforcement agency with jurisdiction over the facility.

(e) A gun show or event shall not commence unless the requirements of subdivisions (b), (c), and (d) are met. *(Added by Stats.2010, c. 711 (S.B.1080), § 6, operative Jan. 1, 2012. Amended by Stats.2014, c. 103 (A.B.1798), § 9, eff. Jan. 1, 2015; Stats.2015, c. 303 (A.B.731), § 415, eff. Jan. 1, 2016; Stats.2019, c. 736 (A.B.1669), § 2, eff. Jan. 1, 2020.)*

Law Revision Commission Comments

Subdivision (a) of Section 27210 continues former Section 12071.1(h) without substantive change.

Subdivision (b) continues the first sentence of former Section 12071.1(i) without substantive change.

Subdivision (c) continues the second sentence of former Section 12071.1(i) without substantive change.

Subdivision (d) continues the third sentence of former Section 12071.1(i) without substantive change.

Subdivision (e) continues the fourth sentence of former Section 12071.1(i) without substantive change.

For exceptions to provisions in this article and Article 2 (commencing with Section 27300), see Article 3 (commencing with Section 27400).

For the consequences of violating this article, see Section 27245 (punishment).

See Section 16520 ("firearm"). [38 Cal.L.Rev.Comm. Reports 217 (2009)].

Section 27210 is amended to standardize the references to the facility's manager for the site of the gun show or event. [43 Cal.L.Rev.Comm. Reports 63 (2013)].

Cross References

Firearm defined for purposes of this Part, see Penal Code § 16520.

§ 27215. Producer of gun show responsible for informing vendors of requirements

The producer of a gun show or event shall be responsible for informing prospective gun show vendors of the requirements of this article and of Article 2 (commencing with Section 27300) that apply to vendors. *(Added by Stats.2010, c. 711 (S.B.1080), § 6, operative Jan. 1, 2012.)*

Law Revision Commission Comments

Section 27215 continues former Section 12071.1(j) without substantive change.

For exceptions to provisions in this article and Article 2 (commencing with Section 27300), see Article 3 (commencing with Section 27400).

For the consequences of violating this article, see Section 27245 (punishment). [38 Cal.L.Rev.Comm. Reports 217 (2009)].

§ 27220. Submission of list of vendors and designated firearms transfer agents to Department of Justice; verification of licenses

(a) Within seven calendar days of the commencement of a gun show or event, but not later than noon on Friday for a show or event held on a weekend, the producer shall submit a list of all prospective vendors and designated firearms transfer agents who are licensed firearms dealers or ammunition vendors to the Department of Justice for the purpose of determining whether these prospective vendors and designated firearms transfer agents possess valid licenses and are thus eligible to participate as licensed dealers or ammunition vendors at the show or event.

(b) The department shall examine its records and if it determines that a dealer's or vendor's license is not valid, it shall notify the show or event producer of that fact before the show or event commences. *(Added by Stats.2010, c. 711 (S.B.1080), § 6, operative Jan. 1, 2012. Amended by Stats.2019, c. 736 (A.B.1669), § 3, eff. Jan. 1, 2020.)*

Law Revision Commission Comments

Subdivision (a) of Section 27220 continues the first sentence of former Section 12071.1(k) without substantive change.

Subdivision (b) continues the second sentence of former Section 12071.1(k) without substantive change.

For exceptions to provisions in this article and Article 2 (commencing with Section 27300), see Article 3 (commencing with Section 27400).

For the consequences of violating this article, see Section 27245 (punishment).

See Sections 16520 ("firearm"), 26700 ("dealer," "licensee," or "person licensed pursuant to Sections 26700 to 26915, inclusive"). [38 Cal.L.Rev. Comm. Reports 217 (2009)].

Cross References

Dealer defined, see Penal Code § 26700.
Firearm defined for purposes of this Part, see Penal Code § 16520.

§ 27225. Failure of firearms dealer or ammunition vendor to cooperate or comply with this Article or Article 2

If a licensed firearms dealer or ammunition vendor fails to cooperate with a producer of a gun show or event, or fails to comply with the applicable requirements of this article or Article 2 (commencing with Section 27300), that person shall not be allowed to participate in that show or event. *(Added by Stats.2010, c. 711 (S.B.1080), § 6, operative Jan. 1, 2012. Amended by Stats.2019, c. 736 (A.B.1669), § 4, eff. Jan. 1, 2020.)*

Law Revision Commission Comments

Section 27225 continues former Section 12071.1(*l*) without substantive change.

For exceptions to provisions in this article and Article 2 (commencing with Section 27300), see Article 3 (commencing with Section 27400).

For the consequences of violating this article, see Section 27245 (punishment).

See Sections 16520 ("firearm"), 26700 ("dealer," "licensee," or "person licensed pursuant to Sections 26700 to 26915, inclusive"). [38 Cal.L.Rev. Comm. Reports 217 (2009)].

Cross References

Dealer defined, see Penal Code § 26700.
Firearm defined for purposes of this Part, see Penal Code § 16520.

§ 27230. Failure of producer to comply with Section 27215 or 27220

If a producer fails to comply with Section 27215 or 27220, the gun show or event shall not commence until those requirements are met. *(Added by Stats.2010, c. 711 (S.B.1080), § 6, operative Jan. 1, 2012.)*

Law Revision Commission Comments

Section 27230 continues former Section 12071.1(m) without substantive change.

For exceptions to provisions in this article and Article 2 (commencing with Section 27300), see Article 3 (commencing with Section 27400).

For the consequences of violating this article, see Section 27245 (punishment). [38 Cal.L.Rev.Comm. Reports 217 (2009)].

§ 27235. Written contracts with firearms or ammunition vendors required

Every producer of a gun show or event shall have a written contract with each gun show vendor selling firearms or ammunition at the show or event. *(Added by Stats.2010, c. 711 (S.B.1080), § 6, operative Jan. 1, 2012. Amended by Stats.2019, c. 736 (A.B.1669), § 5, eff. Jan. 1, 2020.)*

Law Revision Commission Comments

Section 27235 continues former Section 12071.1(n) without substantive change.

For exceptions to provisions in this article and Article 2 (commencing with Section 27300), see Article 3 (commencing with Section 27400).

For the consequences of violating this article, see Section 27245 (punishment).

See Section 16520 ("firearm"). [38 Cal.L.Rev.Comm. Reports 217 (2009)].

Cross References

Firearm defined for purposes of this Part, see Penal Code § 16520.

§ 27240. Signs to be posted at gun show or event

(a) The producer of a gun show or event shall require that signs be posted in a readily visible location at each public entrance to the show containing, but not limited to, the following notice:

"(1) This gun show follows all federal, state, and local firearms, ammunition, and weapons laws, without exception.

(2) Any firearm carried onto the premises by any member of the public will be checked, cleared of any ammunition, and secured in a manner that prevents it from being operated, and an identification tag or sticker will be attached to the firearm before the person is allowed admittance to the show.

(3) No member of the public under the age of 18 years shall be admitted to the show unless accompanied by a parent, grandparent, or legal guardian.

(4) All firearms transfers between private parties at the show shall be conducted through a licensed dealer in accordance with applicable state and federal laws.

(5) Persons possessing firearms of [1] ammunition at this facility shall have in their immediate possession government-issued photo identification, and display it upon request to any security officer or any peace officer, as defined in Section 830.

(6) All ammunition transfers between private parties at the show shall be conducted through a licensed dealer or ammunition vendor in accordance with applicable state and federal laws.

(7) Firearms must be handled responsibly and securely stored to prevent access by children and other unauthorized users. California has strict laws pertaining to firearms, and you may be fined or imprisoned if you fail to comply with them. Visit the internet website of the California Attorney General at https://oag.ca.gov/firearms for information on firearm laws applicable to you and how you can comply.

(8) Children may be unable to distinguish firearms from toys and may operate firearms, causing severe injury or death. If you keep a firearm within any premises under your custody or control, and a person under 18 years of age gains access to the firearm and carries it off-premises, you may be guilty of a misdemeanor, unless you stored the firearm in a locked container, or locked the firearm with a locking device.

(9) You may be guilty of a misdemeanor, including a significant fine or imprisonment, if you keep a firearm where a minor is likely to access it or if a minor obtains and improperly uses it, or carries it off of the premises to a school or school-sponsored event, unless you stored the firearm in a locked container or locked the firearm with a locking device.

(10) If you negligently store or leave a firearm within any premises under your custody or control where a person under 18 years of age is likely to access it, you may be guilty of a misdemeanor, including a significant fine, unless you stored the firearm in a locked container or locked the firearm with a locking device.

(11) Discharging firearms in poorly ventilated areas, cleaning firearms, or handling ammunition may result in exposure to lead, a substance known to cause birth defects, reproductive harm, and other serious physical injury. Have adequate ventilation when discharging or cleaning firearms or handling ammunition. Wash hands thoroughly after exposure.

(12) Federal regulations provide that if you do not take physical possession of the firearm that you are acquiring ownership of within 30 days after you complete the initial background check paperwork, then you must complete the background check process a second time in order to take physical possession of that firearm.

(13) No person shall make an application to purchase more than one handgun or semiautomatic centerfire rifle within any 30–day period and no delivery shall be made to any person who has made an application to purchase more than one handgun or semiautomatic centerfire rifle within any 30–day period.

(14) If a firearm you own or possess is lost or stolen, you must report the loss or theft to a local law enforcement agency where the loss or theft occurred within five days of the time you knew or reasonably should have known that the firearm had been lost or stolen."

(b) The show producer shall post, in a readily visible location at each entrance to the parking lot at the show, signage that states: "The transfer of firearms or ammunition on the parking lot of this facility is a crime." *(Added by Stats.2010, c. 711 (S.B.1080), § 6, operative Jan. 1, 2012. Amended by Stats.2019, c. 736 (A.B.1669), § 6, eff. Jan. 1, 2020; Stats.2022, c. 696 (A.B.2552), § 1, eff. Jan. 1, 2023.)*

[1] So in enrolled bill.

Law Revision Commission Comments

Subdivision (a) of Section 27240 continues former Section 12071.1(*o*) without substantive change.

Subdivision (b) continues former Section 12071.1(p) without substantive change.

For exceptions to provisions in this article and Article 2 (commencing with Section 27300), see Article 3 (commencing with Section 27400).

For the consequences of violating this article, see Section 27245 (punishment).

See Sections 16520 ("firearm"), 26700 ("dealer," "licensee," or "person licensed pursuant to Sections 26700 to 26915, inclusive"). [38 Cal.L.Rev. Comm. Reports 217 (2009)].

Cross References

Dealer defined, see Penal Code § 26700.
Firearm defined for purposes of this Part, see Penal Code § 16520.

§ 27245. Failure of producer to comply with Article; punishment

(a) A willful failure by a gun show producer to comply with any of the requirements of this article, except for the posting of required signs, shall be a misdemeanor punishable by a fine not to exceed four thousand dollars ($4,000) and shall render the producer ineligible for a gun show producer license for * * * two years from the date of the conviction.

(b) A willful failure of a gun show producer to post signs as required by this article shall be a misdemeanor punishable by a fine not to exceed two thousand dollars ($2,000) for the first offense and not to exceed four thousand dollars ($4,000) for the second or subsequent offense, and with respect to the second or subsequent offense, shall render the producer ineligible for a gun show producer license for * * * two years from the date of the conviction.

(c) Multiple violations charged pursuant to subdivision (a) arising from more than one gun show or event shall be grounds for suspension of a producer's certificate of eligibility, issued pursuant to Section 27200, pending adjudication of the violations. *(Added by Stats.2010, c. 711 (S.B.1080), § 6, operative Jan. 1, 2012. Amended by Stats.2022, c. 696 (A.B.2552), § 2, eff. Jan. 1, 2023.)*

Law Revision Commission Comments

Subdivision (a) of Section 27245 continues former Section 12071.1(e)(1) without substantive change.

Subdivision (b) continues former Section 12071.1(e)(2) without substantive change.

Subdivision (c) continues former Section 12071.1(e)(3) without substantive change.

A violation of the predecessor of this article (former Section 12071.1) counts as a prior offense in determining the appropriate punishment under this section. See Section 16015 (determining existence of prior conviction).

For exceptions to provisions in this article and Article 2 (commencing with Section 27300), see Article 3 (commencing with Section 27400). [38 Cal. L.Rev.Comm. Reports 217 (2009)].

Cross References

Misdemeanors, definition and penalties, see Penal Code §§ 17, 19, 19.2.

ARTICLE 2. GUN SHOW ENFORCEMENT AND SECURITY ACT OF 2000

§ 27300. Short title

This article shall be known, and may be cited as, the Gun Show Enforcement and Security Act of 2000. *(Added by Stats.2010, c. 711 (S.B.1080), § 6, operative Jan. 1, 2012.)*

Law Revision Commission Comments

Section 27300 continues former Section 12071.4(a) without substantive change. [38 Cal.L.Rev.Comm. Reports 217 (2009)].

Research References

2 Witkin, California Criminal Law 4th Crimes Against Public Peace and Welfare § 192 (2021), In General.

2 Witkin, California Criminal Law 4th Crimes Against Public Peace and Welfare § 255 (2021), Public Building or Open Meeting.

§ 27305. Vendor certification in writing; contents

All gun show or event vendors shall certify in writing to the producer that they:

(a) Will not display, possess, or offer for sale any firearms, ammunition, knives, or weapons for which possession or sale is prohibited.

(b) Will not display, possess, or offer for sale any unserialized frame or receiver, including an unfinished frame or receiver.

(c) Will not display, possess, or offer for sale any attachment or conversion kit designed to convert a handgun into a short-barreled rifle or into an assault weapon.

(d) Acknowledge that they are responsible for knowing and complying with all applicable federal, state, and local laws dealing with the possession and transfer of firearms or ammunition.

(e) Will not engage in activities that incite or encourage hate crimes.

(f) Will process all transfers of firearms through licensed firearms dealers as required by state law.

(g) Will process all sales or transfers of ammunition through licensed firearms dealers or ammunition vendors as required by state law.

(h) Will verify that all firearms in their possession at the show or event will be unloaded, and that the firearms will be secured in a manner that prevents them from being operated except for brief periods when the mechanical condition of a firearm is being demonstrated to a prospective buyer.

(i) Have complied with the requirements of Section 27320.

(j) Will not display or possess black powder, or offer it for sale. *(Added by Stats.2010, c. 711 (S.B.1080), § 6, operative Jan. 1, 2012. Amended by Stats.2019, c. 736 (A.B.1669), § 7, eff. Jan. 1, 2020; Stats.2022, c. 696 (A.B.2552), § 3, eff. Jan. 1, 2023.)*

Law Revision Commission Comments

Section 27305 continues former Section 12071.4(b) without substantive change.

For exceptions to provisions in this article and Article 1 (commencing with Section 27200), see Article 3 (commencing with Section 27400).

For the consequences of violating this article, see Section 27350 (punishment).

See Sections 16520 ("firearm"), 26700 ("dealer," "licensee," or "person licensed pursuant to Sections 26700 to 26915, inclusive"). [38 Cal.L.Rev. Comm. Reports 217 (2009)].

Cross References

Dealer defined, see Penal Code § 26700.
Firearm defined for purposes of this Part, see Penal Code § 16520.

§ 27310. Firearms and ammunition transfers and sales at gun shows; compliance with state and federal law; inspections; violations posted on website; annual reports

(a) All * * * firearm, ammunition, and firearm precursor part transfers or sales at a gun show or event shall be conducted in accordance with applicable state and federal laws.

(b) * * * The Department of Justice may inspect any firearms dealers, ammunition vendors, firearm precursor part vendors, or manufacturers participating in a gun show or event in order to ensure compliance with subdivision (a). The department may adopt regulations to administer the application and enforcement provisions of this chapter.

(c) Commencing July 1, 2023, the department shall annually conduct enforcement and inspection of a minimum of one-half of all gun shows or events in the state to ensure compliance with this article and with Article 1 (commencing with Section 27200).

(d) The department shall post any violation of subdivision (a) by a firearms dealer, firearm precursor part vendor, or ammunition vendor discovered during an inspection of a gun show or event on its internet website for a period of 90 days after an inspection.

(e)(1) By no later than May 1, 2024, and annually thereafter, the department shall prepare and submit a report to the Legislature summarizing their enforcement efforts pursuant to this section.

(2) The report to be submitted pursuant to this subdivision shall be submitted in compliance with Section 9795 of the Government Code. *(Added by Stats.2010, c. 711 (S.B.1080), § 6, operative Jan. 1, 2012. Amended by Stats.2019, c. 736 (A.B.1669), § 8, eff. Jan. 1, 2020; Stats.2020, c. 273 (A.B.2061), § 1, eff. Jan. 1, 2021; Stats.2022, c. 696 (A.B.2552), § 4, eff. Jan. 1, 2023.)*

Law Revision Commission Comments

Section 27310 continues former Section 12071.4(c) without substantive change.

For exceptions to provisions in this article and Article 1 (commencing with Section 27200), see Article 3 (commencing with Section 27400).

For the consequences of violating this article, see Section 27350 (punishment).

See Section 16520 ("firearm"). [38 Cal.L.Rev.Comm. Reports 217 (2009)].

Cross References

Firearm defined for purposes of this Part, see Penal Code § 16520.

§ 27315. Sales of ammunition at gun show; compliance with Sections 30347, 30348, 30350, 30352, and 30360

Sales of ammunition at a gun show or event shall comply with all applicable laws, including Sections 30347, 30348, 30350, 30352, and 30360. *(Added by Stats.2010, c. 711 (S.B.1080), § 6, operative Jan. 1, 2012. Amended by Stats.2019, c. 736 (A.B.1669), § 9, eff. Jan. 1, 2020.)*

Law Revision Commission Comments

Section 27315 continues former Section 12071.4(d) without substantive change.

For exceptions to provisions in this article and Article 1 (commencing with Section 27200), see Article 3 (commencing with Section 27400).

For the consequences of violating this article, see Section 27350 (punishment). [38 Cal.L.Rev.Comm. Reports 217 (2009)].

§ 27320. Vendor to provide information to gun show producer; availability of information

(a) Before commencement of a gun show or event, each vendor who will offer for sale any firearms manufactured after December 31, 1898, or any ammunition, shall provide to the producer all of the following information relative to the vendor, the vendor's employees, and other persons, compensated or not, who will be working or otherwise providing services to the public at the vendor's display space:

(1) The person's complete name.

(2) The person's driver's license or state-issued identification card number.

(3) The person's date of birth.

(4) The person's certificate of eligibility number pursuant to Section 26915 or 30347 of the Penal Code.

(b) The producer shall keep the information at the onsite headquarters of the show or event for the duration of the show or event, and at the producer's regular place of business for two weeks after the conclusion of the show or event. The producer shall make the information available upon request to any sworn peace officer for purposes of the officer's official law enforcement duties. *(Added by Stats.2010, c. 711 (S.B.1080), § 6, operative Jan. 1, 2012. Amended by Stats.2019, c. 736 (A.B.1669), § 10, eff. Jan. 1, 2020.)*

Law Revision Commission Comments

Section 27320 continues former Section 12071.4(e) without substantive change.

For exceptions to provisions in this article and Article 1 (commencing with Section 27200), see Article 3 (commencing with Section 27400).

For the consequences of violating this article, see Section 27350 (punishment).

See Section 16520 ("firearm"). [38 Cal.L.Rev.Comm. Reports 217 (2009)].

Cross References

Firearm defined for purposes of this Part, see Penal Code § 16520.

§ 27325. Name tags required

At any gun show or event, each vendor and each employee of a vendor shall wear a name tag indicating first and last name. *(Added by Stats.2010, c. 711 (S.B.1080), § 6, operative Jan. 1, 2012.)*

Law Revision Commission Comments

Section 27325 continues former Section 12071.4(f) without substantive change.

For exceptions to provisions in this article and Article 1 (commencing with Section 27200), see Article 3 (commencing with Section 27400).

For the consequences of violating this article, see Section 27350 (punishment). [38 Cal.L.Rev.Comm. Reports 217 (2009)].

§ 27330. Possession of firearm and ammunition at gun show prohibited; exemptions

No person at a gun show or event, other than security personnel or sworn peace officers, shall possess at the same time both a firearm and ammunition that is designed to be fired in the firearm. Vendors having those items at the show for sale or exhibition are exempt from this prohibition. *(Added by Stats.2010, c. 711 (S.B.1080), § 6, operative Jan. 1, 2012.)*

Law Revision Commission Comments

Section 27330 continues former Section 12071.4(g) without substantive change.

For exceptions to provisions in this article and Article 1 (commencing with Section 27200), see Article 3 (commencing with Section 27400).

For the consequences of violating this article, see Section 27350 (punishment).

See Section 16520 ("firearm"). [38 Cal.L.Rev.Comm. Reports 217 (2009)].

Cross References

Firearm defined for purposes of this Part, see Penal Code § 16520.

§ 27335. Attendee of gun show must be 18 years of age or accompanied by parent or legal guardian

No member of the public who is under the age of 18 years shall be admitted to, or be permitted to remain at, a gun show or event unless accompanied by a parent or legal guardian. Any member of the public who is under the age of 18 years shall be accompanied by that person's parent, grandparent, or legal guardian while at the show or event. *(Added by Stats.2010, c. 711 (S.B.1080), § 6, operative Jan. 1, 2012.)*

Law Revision Commission Comments

Section 27335 continues former Section 12071.4(h) without substantive change.

For exceptions to provisions in this article and Article 1 (commencing with Section 27200), see Article 3 (commencing with Section 27400).

For the consequences of violating this article, see Section 27350 (punishment). [38 Cal.L.Rev.Comm. Reports 217 (2009)].

§ 27340. Signing of tags on firearms and ammunition brought into gun show; requirements for carrying firearm and ammunition on premises

(a) Persons other than show or event security personnel, sworn peace officers, or vendors, who bring any firearm or any ammunition that is separate from a firearm onto the gun show or event premises shall sign in ink the tag or sticker that is attached to the firearm prior to being allowed admittance to the show or event, as provided for in subdivision (b) and (c).

(b) All firearms carried onto the premises of a gun show or event by members of the public shall be checked, cleared of any ammunition, secured in a manner that prevents them from being operated, and an identification tag or sticker shall be attached to the firearm, prior to the person being allowed admittance to the show. The identification tag or sticker shall state that all firearms transfers between private parties at the show or event shall be conducted through a licensed dealer in accordance with applicable state and federal laws. The person possessing the firearm shall complete the following information on the tag before it is attached to the firearm:

(1) The gun owner's signature.

(2) The gun owner's printed name.

(3) The identification number from the gun owner's government-issued photo identification.

(c) Any ammunition carried onto the premises of a gun show or event by members of the public shall be checked and secured in a manner that prevents the ammunition from being discharged. An identification tag or sticker shall be attached to the ammunition prior to the person being allowed admittance to the show. The identification tag or sticker shall state that all ammunition transfers between private parties at the show or event shall be conducted through a licensed dealer or ammunition vendor in accordance with applicable state and federal laws. The person possessing the ammunition shall complete the following information on the tag before it is attached to the ammunition:

(1) The ammunition owner's signature.

(2) The ammunition owner's printed name.

(3) The identification number from the ammunition owner's government-issued photo identification. *(Added by Stats.2010, c. 711 (S.B.1080), § 6, operative Jan. 1, 2012. Amended by Stats.2019, c. 736 (A.B.1669), § 11, eff. Jan. 1, 2020.)*

Law Revision Commission Comments

Subdivision (a) of Section 27340 continues former Section 12071.4(i) without substantive change.

Subdivision (b) continues former Section 12071.4(j) without substantive change.

For exceptions to provisions in this article and Article 1 (commencing with Section 27200), see Article 3 (commencing with Section 27400).

For the consequences of violating this article, see Section 27350 (punishment).

See Section 16520 ("firearm"). [38 Cal.L.Rev.Comm. Reports 217 (2009)].

Cross References

Dealer defined, see Penal Code § 26700.
Firearm defined for purposes of this Part, see Penal Code § 16520.

§ 27345. Photo identification required

Any person who possesses a firearm or ammunition at a gun show or event shall have government-issued photo identification in immediate possession, and shall display it upon request to any security officer or peace officer. *(Added by Stats.2010, c. 711 (S.B.1080), § 6, operative Jan. 1, 2012. Amended by Stats.2019, c. 736 (A.B.1669), § 12, eff. Jan. 1, 2020.)*

Law Revision Commission Comments

Section 27345 continues former Section 12071.4(k) without substantive change.

For exceptions to provisions in this article and Article 1 (commencing with Section 27200), see Article 3 (commencing with Section 27400).

For the consequences of violating this article, see Section 27350 (punishment).

See Section 16520 ("firearm"). [38 Cal.L.Rev.Comm. Reports 217 (2009)].

Cross References

Firearm defined for purposes of this Part, see Penal Code § 16520.

§ 27350. Violation of Article; punishment

(a) Unless otherwise specified, a first violation of this article is an infraction.

(b) Any second or subsequent violation of this article is * * * punishable by imprisonment in a county jail not to exceed six months, by a fine of one thousand dollars ($1,000), or by both such fine and imprisonment. Additionally, the department shall prohibit the person from participating as a vendor at any gun show or event for a period of one year.

(c) Any person who commits an act the person knows to be a violation of this article * * * shall, for a first offense, be punished by imprisonment in a county jail not to exceed six months, by a fine of two thousand dollars ($2,000), or by both such fine and imprisonment, and shall be prohibited from participating as a vendor at any gun show or event for a period of one year. *(Added by Stats.2010, c. 711 (S.B.1080), § 6, operative Jan. 1, 2012. Amended by Stats.2022, c. 696 (A.B.2552), § 5, eff. Jan. 1, 2023.)*

Law Revision Commission Comments

Section 27350 continues former Section 12071.4(*l*) without substantive change.

A violation of the predecessor of this article (former Section 12071.4(k)) counts as a prior offense in determining the appropriate punishment under this section. See Section 16015 (determining existence of prior conviction).

For exceptions to provisions in this article and Article 1 (commencing with Section 27200), see Article 3 (commencing with Section 27400). [38 Cal.L.Rev.Comm. Reports 217 (2009)].

Cross References

Misdemeanors, definition and penalties, see Penal Code §§ 17, 19, 19.2.

ARTICLE 3. EXCEPTIONS RELATING TO LAW ENFORCEMENT

Section

§ 27400. Sale, delivery, or transfer of firearms to law enforcement representative for use by government agency; written authorization; recorded as institutional weapon; application of Articles 1 and 2

(a) Article 1 (commencing with Section 27200) and Article 2 (commencing with Section 27300) do not apply to any sale, delivery, or transfer of firearms made to an authorized law enforcement representative of any city, county, city and county, or state, or of the federal government, for exclusive use by that governmental agency if, prior to the sale, delivery, or transfer of these firearms, written authorization from the head of the agency authorizing the transaction is presented to the person from whom the purchase, delivery, or transfer is being made.

(b) Proper written authorization is defined as verifiable written certification from the head of the agency by which the purchaser or transferee is employed, identifying the employee as an individual authorized to conduct the transaction, and authorizing the transaction for the exclusive use of the agency by which that person is employed.

(c) Within 10 days of the date a handgun, and commencing January 1, 2014, any firearm, is acquired by the agency, a record of the same shall be entered as an institutional weapon into the Automated Firearms System (AFS) via the California Law Enforcement Telecommunications System (CLETS) by the law enforcement or state agency. Any agency without access to AFS shall arrange with the sheriff of the county in which the agency is located to input this information via this system. *(Added by Stats.2010, c. 711 (S.B.1080), § 6, operative Jan. 1, 2012. Amended by Stats.2011, c. 745 (A.B.809), § 23.)*

Law Revision Commission Comments

Section 27400 continues former Section 12078(a)(2) without substantive change, as that provision applied to former Sections 12071.1 and 12071.4 (through its reference to the preceding provisions of this article).

See Sections 16520 ("firearm"), 16640 ("handgun"). [38 Cal.L.Rev.Comm. Reports 217 (2009)].

Cross References

Firearm defined for purposes of this Part, see Penal Code § 16520.
Handgun defined for purposes of this Part, see Penal Code § 16640.

§ 27405. Loan of firearm by law enforcement representative; application of Articles 1 and 2

Article 1 (commencing with Section 27200) and Article 2 (commencing with Section 27300) do not apply to the loan of a firearm if all of the following conditions are satisfied:

(a) The loan is made by an authorized law enforcement representative of a city, county, or city and county, or of the state or federal government.

(b) The loan is made to a peace officer employed by that agency and authorized to carry a firearm.

(c) The loan is made for the carrying and use of that firearm by that peace officer in the course and scope of the officer's duties. *(Added by Stats.2010, c. 711 (S.B.1080), § 6, operative Jan. 1, 2012.)*

Law Revision Commission Comments

Section 27405 continues former Section 12078(a)(3) without substantive change, as that provision applied to former Sections 12071.1 and 12071.4 (through its reference to "the preceding provisions of this article").

See Section 16520 ("firearm"). [38 Cal.L.Rev.Comm. Reports 217 (2009)].

Cross References

Firearm defined for purposes of this Part, see Penal Code § 16520.

§ 27410. Sale, delivery, or transfer of firearm by law enforcement agency to peace officer pursuant to Section 10334 of Public Contract Code; entry into Automated Firearms System; application of Articles 1 and 2

(a) Article 1 (commencing with Section 27200) and Article 2 (commencing with Section 27300) do not apply to the sale, delivery, or transfer of a firearm by a law enforcement agency to a peace officer pursuant to Section 10334 of the Public Contract Code.

(b) Within 10 days of the date that a handgun, and commencing January 1, 2014, any firearm, is sold, delivered, or transferred pursuant to Section 10334 of the Public Contract Code to that peace officer, the name of the officer and the make, model, serial number, and other identifying characteristics of the firearm being sold, delivered, or transferred shall be entered into the Automated Firearms System (AFS) via the California Law Enforcement Telecommunications System (CLETS) by the law enforcement or state agency that sold, delivered, or transferred the firearm, provided, however, that if the firearm is not a handgun and does not have a serial number, identification number, or identification mark assigned to it, that fact shall be noted in AFS. Any agency without access to AFS shall arrange with the sheriff of the county in which the agency is located to input this information via this system. *(Added by Stats.2010, c. 711 (S.B.1080), § 6, operative Jan. 1, 2012. Amended by Stats.2011, c. 745 (A.B.809), § 24.)*

Law Revision Commission Comments

Section 27410 continues former Section 12078(a)(4) without substantive change, as that provision applied to former Sections 12071.1 and 12071.4 (through its reference to "the preceding provisions of this article").

See Sections 16520 ("firearm"), 16640 ("handgun"). [38 Cal.L.Rev.Comm. Reports 217 (2009)].

Cross References

Firearm defined for purposes of this Part, see Penal Code § 16520.
Handgun defined for purposes of this Part, see Penal Code § 16640.

§ 27415. Sale, delivery, or transfer of firearm by law enforcement agency to retiring peace officer; entry into Automated Firearms System; application of Articles 1 and 2

(a) Article 1 (commencing with Section 27200) and Article 2 (commencing with Section 27300) do not apply to the sale, delivery, or transfer of a firearm by a law enforcement agency to a retiring peace officer who is authorized to carry a firearm pursuant to Chapter 5 (commencing with Section 26300) of Division 5.

(b) Within 10 days of the date that a handgun, and commencing January 1, 2014, any firearm, is sold, delivered, or transferred to that retiring peace officer, the name of the officer and the make, model, serial number, and other identifying characteristics of the firearm being sold, delivered, or transferred shall be entered into the Automated Firearms System (AFS) via the California Law Enforcement Telecommunications System (CLETS) by the law enforcement or state agency that sold, delivered, or transferred the firearm, provided, however, that if the firearm is not a handgun and does not have a serial number, identification number, or identification mark assigned to it, that fact shall be noted in AFS. Any agency without access to AFS shall arrange with the sheriff of the county in which the agency is located to input this information via this system. *(Added by Stats.2010, c. 711 (S.B.1080), § 6, operative Jan. 1, 2012. Amended by Stats.2011, c. 745 (A.B.809), § 25.)*

Law Revision Commission Comments

Section 27415 continues former Section 12078(a)(5) without substantive change, as that provision applied to former Sections 12071.1 and 12071.4 (through its reference to "the preceding provisions of this article").

See Sections 16520 ("firearm"), 16640 ("handgun"). [38 Cal.L.Rev.Comm. Reports 217 (2009)].

Cross References

Firearm defined for purposes of this Part, see Penal Code § 16520.
Handgun defined for purposes of this Part, see Penal Code § 16640.

CHAPTER 4. CRIMES RELATING TO SALE, LEASE, OR TRANSFER OF FIREARMS

ARTICLE 1. CRIMES RELATING TO SALE, LEASE, OR TRANSFER OF FIREARMS

§ 27500. Sale or delivery of firearms to persons in prohibited classes

(a) No person, corporation, or firm shall knowingly sell, supply, deliver, or give possession or control of a firearm to any person within any of the classes prohibited by Chapter 2 (commencing with Section 29800) or Chapter 3 (commencing with Section 29900) of Division 9.

(b) No person, corporation, or dealer shall sell, supply, deliver, or give possession or control of a firearm to anyone whom the person, corporation, or dealer has cause to believe is within any of the classes prohibited by Chapter 2 (commencing with Section 29800) or Chapter 3 (commencing with Section 29900) of Division 9 of this title, or Section 8100 or 8103 of the Welfare and Institutions Code. *(Added by Stats.2010, c. 711 (S.B.1080), § 6, operative Jan. 1, 2012.)*

Law Revision Commission Comments

Subdivision (a) of Section 27500 continues former Section 12072(a)(1) without substantive change.

Subdivision (b) continues former Section 12072(a)(2) without substantive change.

For exceptions to this provision, see Article 2 (commencing with Section 27600).

For the consequences of violating this section, see Section 27590 (punishment for violation of article).

See Sections 16520 ("firearm"), 26700 ("dealer," "licensee," or "person licensed pursuant to Sections 26700 to 26915, inclusive"). [38 Cal.L.Rev. Comm. Reports 217 (2009)].

Cross References

Centralized list of exempted federal firearms licensees, see Penal Code § 28450.
Dealer defined, see Penal Code § 26700.
Firearm defined for purposes of this Part, see Penal Code § 16520.
Handgun safety certificate, basic familiarity, safe handling and storage of firearms, see Penal Code § 31610.
Protective orders and other domestic violence prevention orders, registration and enforcement of orders, firearm ownership, possession, purchase, or receipt, see Family Code § 6389.
Return or transfer of firearm in custody or control of court or law enforcement agency, sale or transfer of firearm to licensed dealer, see Penal Code § 33850.
Sale of BB device to minors, see Penal Code § 19910.
Special business regulations, secondhand goods, secondhand dealer, see Business and Professions Code § 21626.

Research References

2 Witkin, California Criminal Law 4th Crimes Against Public Peace and Welfare § 195 (2021), In General.
2 Witkin, California Criminal Law 4th Crimes Against Public Peace and Welfare § 196 (2021), Transfers to Specified Persons.
2 Witkin, California Criminal Law 4th Crimes Against Public Peace and Welfare § 198 (2021), Transfers by Persons Not Licensed in California.
2 Witkin, California Criminal Law 4th Crimes Against Public Peace and Welfare § 201 (2021), Punishment.

§ 27505. Sale, loan, or transfer of firearm to individual under 21 years of age prohibited; exceptions

(a) No person, corporation, or firm shall sell, loan, or transfer a firearm to a minor, nor sell a handgun to an individual under 21 years of age.

(b) Subdivision (a) shall not apply to or affect the following circumstances:

(1) The sale of a handgun, if the handgun is an antique firearm and the sale is to a person at least 18 years of age.

(2) The loan of a firearm to a minor by the minor's parent or legal guardian, if both of the following requirements are satisfied:

(A) The minor is being loaned the firearm for the purposes of engaging in a lawful, recreational sport, including, but not limited to, competitive shooting, or agricultural, ranching, or hunting activity or hunting education, or a motion picture, television, or video production, or entertainment or theatrical event, the nature of which involves the use of a firearm.

(B) The duration of the loan does not exceed the amount of time that is reasonably necessary to engage in the lawful, recreational sport, including, but not limited to, competitive shooting, or agricultural, ranching, or hunting activity or hunting education, or a motion picture, television, or video production, or entertainment or theatrical event, the nature of which involves the use of a firearm.

(3) The loan of a semiautomatic centerfire rifle or handgun to a minor by a person who is not the minor's parent or legal guardian, if all of the following requirements are satisfied:

(A) The minor is accompanied by the minor's parent or legal guardian when the loan is made, or the minor has the written consent of the minor's parent or legal guardian, which is presented at the time of the loan, or earlier.

(B) The minor is being loaned the firearm for the purpose of engaging in a lawful, recreational sport, including, but not limited to, competitive shooting, or agricultural, ranching, or hunting activity or hunting education, or a motion picture, television, or video production, or entertainment or theatrical event, the nature of which involves the use of a firearm.

(C) The duration of the loan does not exceed the amount of time that is reasonably necessary to engage in the lawful, recreational sport, including, but not limited to, competitive shooting, or agricultural, ranching, or hunting activity or hunting education, or a motion picture, television, or video production, or entertainment or theatrical event, the nature of which involves the use of a firearm.

(D) The duration of the loan does not, in any event, exceed 10 days.

(4) The loan of a firearm other than a semiautomatic centerfire rifle or a handgun to a minor who is 16 years of age or older, by a person who is not the minor's parent or legal guardian, if all of the following conditions apply:

(A) The loan is with the express permission of the minor's parent or legal guardian.

(B) The minor is being loaned the firearm for the purpose of engaging in a lawful, recreational sport, including, but not limited to, competitive shooting, or agricultural, ranching, or hunting activity or hunting education, the nature of which involves the use of a firearm.

(C) The duration of the loan does not exceed the amount of time that is reasonably necessary to engage in the lawful, recreational sport, including, but not limited to, competitive shooting, or agricultural, ranching, or hunting activity or hunting education, the nature of which involves the use of a firearm.

(D) The duration of the loan does not, in any event, exceed 5 days, unless express permission is provided in the manner described in subparagraph (A) of paragraph (3), in which case the duration of the loan shall not, in any event, exceed 10 days.

(5) The loan of a firearm other than a semiautomatic centerfire rifle or a handgun to a minor under 16 years of age by a person who is not the minor's parent or legal guardian, if all of the following conditions apply:

(A) The loan is with the express permission of the minor's parent or legal guardian.

(B) The minor is being loaned the firearm for the purpose of engaging in a lawful, recreational sport, including, but not limited to, competitive shooting, or agricultural, ranching, or hunting activity or hunting education, the nature of which involves the use of a firearm.

(C) The duration of the loan does not exceed the amount of time that is reasonably necessary to engage in the lawful, recreational sport, including, but not limited to, competitive shooting, or agricultural, ranching, or hunting activity or hunting education, the nature of which involves the use of a firearm.

(D) The minor accompanied at all times by a responsible adult.

(E) The duration of the loan does not, in any event, exceed 5 days, unless express permission is provided in the manner described in subparagraph (A) of paragraph (3), in which case the duration of the loan shall not, in any event, exceed 10 days. *(Added by Stats.2010, c. 711 (S.B.1080), § 6, operative Jan. 1, 2012. Amended by Stats.2021, c. 250 (S.B.715), § 8, eff. Jan. 1, 2022.)*

Law Revision Commission Comments

Subdivision (a) of Section 27505 continues former Section 12072(a)(3)(A) without substantive change.

Subdivision (b) continues without substantive change former Section 12072(a)(3)(B) and former Section 12078(p), as it pertained to former Section 12072(a)(3). See Section 16170 ("antique firearm").

For exceptions to this provision, see Article 2 (commencing with Section 27600).

For the consequences of violating this section, see Section 27590 (punishment for violation of article).

See also Sections 16520 ("firearm"), 16640 ("handgun"). [38 Cal.L.Rev. Comm. Reports 217 (2009)].

Cross References

Age verification when selling products that are illegal to sell to minor, reasonable steps, products requiring age verification, penalties, see Civil Code § 1798.99.1.

Antique firearm defined, see Penal Code § 16170.

Firearm defined for purposes of this Part, see Penal Code § 16520.

Handgun defined for purposes of this Part, see Penal Code § 16640.

Research References

2 Witkin, California Criminal Law 4th Crimes Against Public Peace and Welfare § 196 (2021), Transfers to Specified Persons.

2 Witkin, California Criminal Law 4th Crimes Against Public Peace and Welfare § 201 (2021), Punishment.

§ 27510. Sale, supply, delivery, or giving possession of firearm by licensed person to individual under 21 years of age prohibited; exceptions

(a) A person licensed under Sections 26700 to 26915, inclusive, shall not sell, supply, deliver, or give possession or control of a firearm to any person who is under 21 years of age.

(b)(1) Subdivision (a) does not apply to or affect the sale, supplying, delivery, or giving possession or control of a firearm that is not a handgun * * *, semiautomatic centerfire rifle, completed frame or receiver, or firearm precursor part to a person 18 years of age or older who possesses a valid, unexpired hunting license issued by the Department of Fish and Wildlife.

(2) Subdivision (a) does not apply to or affect the sale, supplying, delivery, or giving possession or control of a firearm that is not a handgun or a semiautomatic centerfire rifle to a person who is 18 years of age or older and provides proper identification of being an honorably discharged member of the United States Armed Forces, the National Guard, the Air National Guard, or the active reserve components of the United States. For purposes of this subparagraph, proper identification includes an Armed Forces Identification Card or other written documentation certifying that the individual is an honorably discharged member [1]

(3) Subdivision (a) does not apply to or affect the sale, supplying, delivery, or giving possession or control of a firearm that is not a handgun to any of the following persons who are 18 years of age or older:

(A) An active peace officer, as described in Chapter 4.5 (commencing with Section 830) of Title 3 of Part 2, who is authorized to carry a firearm in the course and scope of employment.

(B) An active federal officer or law enforcement agent who is authorized to carry a firearm in the course and scope of employment.

(C) A reserve peace officer, as defined in Section 832.6, who is authorized to carry a firearm in the course and scope of employment as a reserve peace officer.

(D) A person who provides proper identification of active membership in the United States Armed Forces, the National Guard, the Air National Guard, or active reserve components of the United States. For purposes of this subparagraph, proper identification includes an Armed Forces Identification Card or other written documentation certifying that the individual is an active member. *(Added by Stats.2010, c. 711 (S.B.1080), § 6, operative Jan. 1, 2012. Amended by Stats.2018, c. 894 (S.B.1100), § 1, eff. Jan. 1, 2019; Stats.2019, c. 737 (S.B.61), § 3, eff. Jan. 1, 2020; Stats.2022, c. 76 (A.B.1621), § 16, eff. June 30, 2022.)*

[1] So in chaptered copy.

Law Revision Commission Comments

Section 27510 continues former Section 12072(b) without substantive change.

For exceptions to this provision, see Article 2 (commencing with Section 27600).

For the consequences of violating this section, see Section 27590 (punishment for violation of article).

See Sections 16520 firearm, 16640 ("handgun"). [38 Cal.L.Rev.Comm. Reports 217 (2009)].

Cross References

Firearm defined for purposes of this Part, see Penal Code § 16520.

Handgun defined for purposes of this Part, see Penal Code § 16640.

Sale, lease, or transfer of firearms, electronic or telephonic transfer of purchaser information, inspection and recording of hunting license, see Penal Code § 28215.
Sale, lease, or transfer of firearms, use of register to record sale, inspection and recording of hunting license, see Penal Code § 28210.

Research References

2 Witkin, California Criminal Law 4th Crimes Against Public Peace and Welfare § 195 (2021), In General.
2 Witkin, California Criminal Law 4th Crimes Against Public Peace and Welfare § 196 (2021), Transfers to Specified Persons.
2 Witkin, California Criminal Law 4th Crimes Against Public Peace and Welfare § 201 (2021), Punishment.

§ 27515. Sale, loan, or transfer of firearm to someone other than actual purchaser or transferee prohibited

No person, corporation, or dealer shall sell, loan, or transfer a firearm to anyone whom the person, corporation, or dealer knows or has cause to believe is not the actual purchaser or transferee of the firearm, or to anyone who is not the one actually being loaned the firearm, if the person, corporation, or dealer has either of the following:

(a) Knowledge that the firearm is to be subsequently sold, loaned, or transferred to avoid the provisions of Section 27540 or 27545.

(b) Knowledge that the firearm is to be subsequently sold, loaned, or transferred to avoid the requirements of any exemption to the provisions of Section 27540 or 27545. *(Added by Stats.2010, c. 711 (S.B.1080), § 6, operative Jan. 1, 2012.)*

Law Revision Commission Comments

Section 27515 continues former Section 12072(a)(4) without substantive change.

For exceptions to this provision, see Article 2 (commencing with Section 27600).

For the consequences of violating this section, see Section 27590 (punishment for violation of article).

See Sections 16520 ("firearm"), 26700 ("dealer," "licensee," or "person licensed pursuant to Sections 26700 to 26915, inclusive"). [38 Cal.L.Rev. Comm. Reports 217 (2009)].

Cross References

Dealer defined, see Penal Code § 26700.
Firearm defined for purposes of this Part, see Penal Code § 16520.

Research References

2 Witkin, California Criminal Law 4th Crimes Against Public Peace and Welfare § 196 (2021), Transfers to Specified Persons.
2 Witkin, California Criminal Law 4th Crimes Against Public Peace and Welfare § 198 (2021), Transfers by Persons Not Licensed in California.
2 Witkin, California Criminal Law 4th Crimes Against Public Peace and Welfare § 201 (2021), Punishment.

§ 27520. Acquisition of firearm for purpose of selling, loaning, or transferring; when prohibited

No person, corporation, or dealer shall acquire a firearm for the purpose of selling, loaning, or transferring the firearm, if the person, corporation, or dealer has either of the following:

(a) In the case of a dealer, intent to violate Section 27510 or 27540.

(b) In any other case, intent to avoid either of the following:

(1) The provisions of Section 27545.

(2) The requirements of any exemption to the provisions of Section 27545. *(Added by Stats.2010, c. 711 (S.B.1080), § 6, operative Jan. 1, 2012.)*

Law Revision Commission Comments

Section 27520 continues former Section 12072(a)(5) without substantive change.

For exceptions to this provision, see Article 2 (commencing with Section 27600).

For the consequences of violating this section, see Section 27590 (punishment for violation of article).

See Sections 16520 ("firearm"), 26700 ("dealer," "licensee," or "person licensed pursuant to Sections 26700 to 26915, inclusive"). [38 Cal.L.Rev. Comm. Reports 217 (2009)].

Cross References

Dealer defined, see Penal Code § 26700.
Firearm defined for purposes of this Part, see Penal Code § 16520.

Research References

2 Witkin, California Criminal Law 4th Crimes Against Public Peace and Welfare § 195 (2021), In General.
2 Witkin, California Criminal Law 4th Crimes Against Public Peace and Welfare § 201 (2021), Punishment.

§ 27525. Dealer compliance with Sections 26905 and 26910

(a) A dealer shall comply with Section 26905.

(b) A dealer shall comply with Section 26910. *(Added by Stats. 2010, c. 711 (S.B.1080), § 6, operative Jan. 1, 2012.)*

Law Revision Commission Comments

Subdivision (a) of Section 27525 continues former Section 12072(a)(6), relating to reporting of handgun acquisitions. without substantive change.

Subdivision (b) continues former Section 12072(a)(7), relating to reporting of information on a firearm that is not timely delivered, without substantive change.

For exceptions to this provision, see Article 2 (commencing with Section 27600).

For the consequences of violating this section, see Section 27590 (punishment for violation of article).

See Sections 16520 ("firearm"), 16640 ("handgun"), 26700 ("dealer," "licensee," or "person licensed pursuant to Sections 26700 to 26915, inclusive"). [38 Cal.L.Rev.Comm. Reports 217 (2009)].

Cross References

Dealer defined, see Penal Code § 26700.

§ 27530. Sale or transfer of firearm; exceptions

(a) No person shall sell or otherwise transfer ownership of a * * * firearm * * * that is not imprinted with a serial number imprinted by a federal licensee authorized to serialize firearms.

* * *

(b) This section does not apply to any of the following:

(1) A firearm made or assembled prior to December 16, 1968, that is not a handgun.

(2) A firearm that is a curio or relic, or an antique firearm, as those terms are defined in Section 479.11 of Title 27 of the Code of Federal Regulations.

(3) A firearm that has been entered, before July 1, 2018, into the centralized registry set forth in Section 11106, as being owned by a specific individual or entity, if that firearm has assigned to it a distinguishing number or mark of identification because the department accepted entry of that firearm into the centralized registry.

(4) The transfer, surrender, or sale of a firearm to a law enforcement agency.

(5) The sale or transfer of ownership of a firearm to a federally licensed firearms manufacturer or importer, or any other federal licensee authorized to serialize firearms. *(Added by Stats.2010, c. 711 (S.B.1080), § 6, operative Jan. 1, 2012. Amended by Stats.2022, c. 76 (A.B.1621), § 17, eff. June 30, 2022.)*

Law Revision Commission Comments

Section 27530 continues former Section 12072(a)(8) without substantive change.

For exceptions to this provision, see Article 2 (commencing with Section 27600).

For the consequences of violating this section, see Section 27590 (punishment for violation of article).

See Sections 16520 ("firearm"), 16640 ("handgun"). [38 Cal.L.Rev.Comm. Reports 217 (2009)].

Cross References

Firearm defined for purposes of this Part, see Penal Code § 16520.
Handgun defined for purposes of this Part, see Penal Code § 16640.

Research References

2 Witkin, California Criminal Law 4th Crimes Against Public Peace and Welfare § 195 (2021), In General.
2 Witkin, California Criminal Law 4th Crimes Against Public Peace and Welfare § 200 (2021), Reporting and Identification Requirements for Concealable Firearms.

§ 27535. Application to purchase more than one handgun or semiautomatic centerfire rifle during 30-day period prohibited; exceptions

Section operative until Jan. 1, 2024. See, also, § 27535 operative Jan. 1, 2024.

(a) A person shall not make an application to purchase more than one handgun or semiautomatic centerfire rifle within any 30–day period. This subdivision does not authorize a person to make an application to purchase both a handgun and semiautomatic centerfire rifle within the same 30–day period.

(b) Subdivision (a) does not apply to any of the following:

(1) Any law enforcement agency.

(2) Any agency duly authorized to perform law enforcement duties.

(3) Any state or local correctional facility.

(4) Any private security company licensed to do business in California.

(5) Any person who is properly identified as a full-time paid peace officer, as defined in Chapter 4.5 (commencing with Section 830) of Title 3 of Part 2, and who is authorized to, and does carry a firearm during the course and scope of employment as a peace officer.

(6) Any motion picture, television, or video production company or entertainment or theatrical company whose production by its nature involves the use of a firearm.

(7) Any person who may, pursuant to Article 2 (commencing with Section 27600), Article 3 (commencing with Section 27650), or Article 4 (commencing with Section 27700), claim an exemption from the waiting period set forth in Section 27540.

(8) Any transaction conducted through a licensed firearms dealer pursuant to Chapter 5 (commencing with Section 28050).

(9) Any person who is licensed as a collector pursuant to Chapter 44 (commencing with Section 921) of Title 18 of the United States Code and the regulations issued pursuant thereto, and has a current certificate of eligibility issued by the Department of Justice pursuant to Article 1 (commencing with Section 26700) of Chapter 2.

(10) The exchange of a handgun or semiautomatic centerfire rifle where the dealer purchased that firearm from the person seeking the exchange within the 30–day period immediately preceding the date of exchange or replacement.

(11) The replacement of a handgun or semiautomatic centerfire rifle when the person's firearm was lost or stolen, and the person reported that firearm lost or stolen pursuant to Section 25250 prior to the completion of the application to purchase the replacement.

(12) The return of any handgun or semiautomatic centerfire rifle to its owner.

(13) A community college that is certified by the Commission on Peace Officer Standards and Training to present the law enforcement academy basic course or other commission-certified law enforcement training.

(c) This section shall * * * remain in effect until January 1, 2024, and as of that date is repealed. *(Added by Stats.2019, c. 737 (S.B.61), § 5, eff. Jan. 1, 2020, operative July 1, 2021. Amended by Stats.2022, c. 76 (A.B.1621), § 18, eff. June 30, 2022.)*

Repeal

For repeal of this section, see its terms.

Cross References

Firearm defined for purposes of this Part, see Penal Code § 16520.
Handgun defined for purposes of this Part, see Penal Code § 16640.

Research References

2 Witkin, California Criminal Law 4th Crimes Against Public Peace and Welfare § 196 (2021), Transfers to Specified Persons.
2 Witkin, California Criminal Law 4th Crimes Against Public Peace and Welfare § 197 (2021), Time and Manner of Delivery by Dealer.
2 Witkin, California Criminal Law 4th Crimes Against Public Peace and Welfare § 201 (2021), Punishment.

§ 27535. Application to purchase more than one handgun or semiautomatic centerfire rifle during 30-day period prohibited; exceptions

Section operative Jan. 1, 2024. See, also, § 27535 operative until Jan. 1, 2024.

(a) A person shall not make an application to purchase more than one firearm within any 30–day period. This subdivision does not authorize a person to make an application to purchase a combination of firearms, completed frames or receivers, or firearm precursor parts within the same 30–day period.

(b) Subdivision (a) does not apply to any of the following:

(1) Any law enforcement agency.

(2) Any agency duly authorized to perform law enforcement duties.

(3) Any state or local correctional facility.

(4) Any private security company licensed to do business in California.

(5) Any person who is properly identified as a full-time paid peace officer, as defined in Chapter 4.5 (commencing with Section 830) of Title 3 of Part 2, and who is authorized to, and does carry a firearm during the course and scope of employment as a peace officer.

(6) Any motion picture, television, or video production company or entertainment or theatrical company whose production by its nature involves the use of a firearm.

(7) Any person who may, pursuant to Article 2 (commencing with Section 27600), Article 3 (commencing with Section 27650), or Article 4 (commencing with Section 27700), claim an exemption from the waiting period set forth in Section 27540.

(8) Any transaction conducted through a licensed firearms dealer pursuant to Chapter 5 (commencing with Section 28050).

(9) Any person who is licensed as a collector pursuant to Chapter 44 (commencing with Section 921) of Title 18 of the United States Code and the regulations issued pursuant thereto, and has a current certificate of eligibility issued by the Department of Justice pursuant to Article 1 (commencing with Section 26700) of Chapter 2.

(10) The exchange of a firearm where the dealer purchased that firearm from the person seeking the exchange within the 30–day period immediately preceding the date of exchange or replacement.

(11) The replacement of a firearm when the person's firearm was lost or stolen, and the person reported that firearm lost or stolen

pursuant to Section 25250 prior to the completion of the application to purchase the replacement.

(12) The return of any firearm to its owner.

(13) A community college that is certified by the Commission on Peace Officer Standards and Training to present the law enforcement academy basic course or other commission-certified law enforcement training.

(c) This section shall become operative on January 1, 2024. *(Added by Stats.2022, c. 76 (A.B.1621), § 19, eff. June 30, 2022, operative Jan. 1, 2024.)*

Cross References

Firearm defined for purposes of this Part, see Penal Code § 16520.
Handgun defined for purposes of this Part, see Penal Code § 16640.

§ 27540. Delivery of firearm by dealer; requirements

Section operative until Jan. 1, 2024. See, also, § 27540 operative Jan. 1, 2024.

A dealer, whether or not acting pursuant to Chapter 5 (commencing with Section 28050), shall not deliver a firearm to a person, as follows:

(a) Within 10 days of the application to purchase, or, after notice by the department pursuant to Section 28220, within 10 days of the submission to the department of any correction to the application, or within 10 days of the submission to the department of any fee required pursuant to Section 28225, whichever is later.

(b) Unless unloaded and securely wrapped or unloaded and in a locked container.

(c) Unless the purchaser, transferee, or person being loaned the firearm presents clear evidence of the person's identity and age to the dealer.

(d) Whenever the dealer is notified by the Department of Justice that the person is prohibited by state or federal law from possessing, receiving, owning, or purchasing a firearm.

(e) A firearm, including a handgun, shall not be delivered unless the purchaser, transferee, or person being loaned the firearm presents a firearm safety certificate to the dealer, except that in the case of a handgun, an unexpired handgun safety certificate may be presented.

(f) Until July 1, 2021, a handgun shall not be delivered whenever the dealer is notified by the Department of Justice that within the preceding 30–day period the purchaser has made another application to purchase a handgun and that the previous application to purchase did not involve any of the entities or circumstances specified in subdivision (b) of Section 27535.

(g) * * * A handgun or semiautomatic centerfire rifle shall not be delivered whenever the dealer is notified by the Department of Justice that within the preceding 30–day period, the purchaser has made another application to purchase either a handgun or semiautomatic centerfire rifle and that the previous application to purchase did not involve any of the entities or circumstances specified in subdivision (b) of Section 27535.

(h) This section shall remain in effect until January 1, 2024, and as of that date is repealed. *(Added by Stats.2010, c. 711 (S.B.1080), § 6, operative Jan. 1, 2012. Amended by Stats.2011, c. 745 (A.B.809), § 26; Stats.2013, c. 761 (S.B.683), § 6; Stats.2019, c. 737 (S.B.61), § 6, eff. Jan. 1, 2020; Stats.2022, c. 76 (A.B.1621), § 20, eff. June 30, 2022.)*

Repeal

For repeal of this section, see its terms.

Law Revision Commission Comments

Section 27540 continues former Section 12072(c) without substantive change.

For exceptions to this provision, see Article 2 (commencing with Section 27600), Article 3 (commencing with Section 27650), and Article 4 (commencing with Section 27700).

For the consequences of violating this section, see Section 27590 (punishment for violation of article).

See Sections 16190 ("application to purchase"), 16240 ("basic firearms safety certificate"), 16400 ("clear evidence of the person's identity and age"), 16520 ("firearm"), 16640 ("handgun"), 16670 ("handgun safety certificate"), 26700 ("dealer," "licensee," or "person licensed pursuant to Sections 26700 to 26915, inclusive"). [38 Cal.L.Rev.Comm. Reports 217 (2009)].

Cross References

Completion of sale, loan, or transfer of firearm through licensed person, compliance with Section 27545, procedures if dealer cannot legally return firearm to seller, transferor, or person loaning the firearm, see Penal Code § 28050.
Dealer defined, see Penal Code § 26700.
Firearm defined for purposes of this Part, see Penal Code § 16520.
Handgun defined for purposes of this Part, see Penal Code § 16640.
Handgun safety certificate defined for purposes of this Part, see Penal Code § 16670.
Persons prohibited from owning or possessing firearm, transfer of firearm to firearms dealer for storage, return of firearm, see Penal Code § 29830.
Sale, lease, or transfer of firearms, electronic or telephonic transfer of purchaser information, copy of record to purchaser requirement, see Penal Code § 28215.
Sale, lease, or transfer of firearms, use of register to record sale, photocopy to purchaser at time of delivery, see Penal Code § 28210.

Research References

2 Witkin, California Criminal Law 4th Crimes Against Public Peace and Welfare § 195 (2021), In General.
2 Witkin, California Criminal Law 4th Crimes Against Public Peace and Welfare § 196 (2021), Transfers to Specified Persons.
2 Witkin, California Criminal Law 4th Crimes Against Public Peace and Welfare § 197 (2021), Time and Manner of Delivery by Dealer.
2 Witkin, California Criminal Law 4th Crimes Against Public Peace and Welfare § 199 (2021), Importation Restrictions.
2 Witkin, California Criminal Law 4th Crimes Against Public Peace and Welfare § 201 (2021), Punishment.

§ 27540. Delivery of firearm by dealer; requirements

Section operative Jan. 1, 2024. See, also, § 27540 operative until Jan. 1, 2024.

A dealer, whether or not acting pursuant to Chapter 5 (commencing with Section 28050), shall not deliver a firearm to a person, as follows:

(a) Within 10 days of the application to purchase, or, after notice by the department pursuant to Section 28220, within 10 days of the submission to the department of any correction to the application, or within 10 days of the submission to the department of any fee required pursuant to Section 28225, whichever is later.

(b) Unless unloaded and securely wrapped or unloaded and in a locked container.

(c) Unless the purchaser, transferee, or person being loaned the firearm presents clear evidence of the person's identity and age to the dealer.

(d) Whenever the dealer is notified by the Department of Justice that the person is prohibited by state or federal law from possessing, receiving, owning, or purchasing a firearm.

(e) A firearm, including a handgun, shall not be delivered unless the purchaser, transferee, or person being loaned the firearm presents a firearm safety certificate to the dealer, except that in the case of a handgun, an unexpired handgun safety certificate may be presented.

(f) A firearm shall not be delivered whenever the dealer is notified by the Department of Justice that within the preceding 30–day period, the purchaser has made another application to purchase a handgun, semiautomatic centerfire rifle, completed frame or receiver, or firearm precursor part, and that the previous application to purchase did not involve any of the entities or circumstances specified in subdivision (b) of Section 27535.

(g) This section shall become operative on January 1, 2024. *(Added by Stats.2022, c. 76 (A.B.1621), § 21, eff. June 30, 2022, operative Jan. 1, 2024.)*

Cross References

Completion of sale, loan, or transfer of firearm through licensed person, compliance with Section 27545, procedures if dealer cannot legally return firearm to seller, transferor, or person loaning the firearm, see Penal Code § 28050.
Dealer defined, see Penal Code § 26700.
Firearm defined for purposes of this Part, see Penal Code § 16520.
Handgun defined for purposes of this Part, see Penal Code § 16640.
Handgun safety certificate defined for purposes of this Part, see Penal Code § 16670.
Persons prohibited from owning or possessing firearm, transfer of firearm to firearms dealer for storage, return of firearm, see Penal Code § 29830.
Sale, lease, or transfer of firearms, electronic or telephonic transfer of purchaser information, copy of record to purchaser requirement, see Penal Code § 28215.
Sale, lease, or transfer of firearms, use of register to record sale, photocopy to purchaser at time of delivery, see Penal Code § 28210.

§ 27545. Sale, loan, or transfer of firearm; completion through licensed dealer

Where neither party to the transaction holds a dealer's license issued pursuant to Sections 26700 to 26915, inclusive, the parties to the transaction shall complete the sale, loan, or transfer of that firearm through a licensed firearms dealer pursuant to Chapter 5 (commencing with Section 28050). *(Added by Stats.2010, c. 711 (S.B.1080), § 6, operative Jan. 1, 2012.)*

Law Revision Commission Comments

Section 27545 continues former Section 12072(d) without substantive change.

For exceptions to this provision, see Article 2 (commencing with Section 27600) and Article 6 (commencing with Section 27850). See also Section 28000 (circumstances that may be reported to Department of Justice in prescribed format).

For the consequences of violating this section, see Section 27590 (punishment for violation of article).

See Sections 16520 ("firearm"), 26700 ("dealer," "licensee," or "person licensed pursuant to Sections 26700 to 26915, inclusive"). [38 Cal.L.Rev. Comm. Reports 217 (2009)].

Cross References

Application to Department of Justice to have firearm returned, contents of application, sale or transfer of firearm, see Penal Code § 33850.
Community care facilities, acceptance or storage of client's firearm does not constitute loan, sale, receipt, or transfer, see Health and Safety Code § 1567.94.
Failure to report sale or transfer of unsafe handgun, penalties, exemptions, see Penal Code § 32000.
Firearm defined for purposes of this Part, see Penal Code § 16520.
Loan of firearm to person enrolled in peace officer training program for purposes of course participation, see Penal Code § 27970.
Residential care facilities for persons with chronic life-threatening illness, acceptance or storage of resident's firearm does not constitute loan, sale, receipt, or transfer, see Health and Safety Code § 1568.099.
Residential care facilities for the elderly, acceptance or storage of resident's firearm does not constitute loan, sale, receipt, or transfer, see Health and Safety Code § 1569.284.
Return of firearm not subject to the requirements of this section, see Family Code § 6389.
Sale, delivery, or transfer of firearms between or to manufacturers of ammunition, application of this section, see Penal Code § 27963.
Secondhand dealer, coin dealer, licensed dealer, gun show trader, see Business and Professions Code § 21626.
State employee, acquisition of goods from state, handgun of peace officer who died in the line of duty, see Public Contract Code § 10334.

Research References

2 Witkin, California Criminal Law 4th Crimes Against Public Peace and Welfare § 195 (2021), In General.
2 Witkin, California Criminal Law 4th Crimes Against Public Peace and Welfare § 196 (2021), Transfers to Specified Persons.
2 Witkin, California Criminal Law 4th Crimes Against Public Peace and Welfare § 198 (2021), Transfers by Persons Not Licensed in California.
2 Witkin, California Criminal Law 4th Crimes Against Public Peace and Welfare § 199 (2021), Importation Restrictions.
2 Witkin, California Criminal Law 4th Crimes Against Public Peace and Welfare § 201 (2021), Punishment.
2 Witkin, California Criminal Law 4th Crimes Against Public Peace and Welfare § 208 (2021), Exempt Activities.

§ 27550. Collusion relating to Sections 31610 to 31700 prohibited; proof of collusion

(a) No person may commit an act of collusion relating to Sections 31610 to 31700, inclusive.

(b) For purposes of this section and Section 26870, collusion may be proven by any one of the following factors:

(1) Answering a test applicant's questions during an objective test relating to firearms safety.

(2) Knowingly grading the examination falsely.

(3) Providing an advance copy of the test to an applicant.

(4) Taking or allowing another person to take the basic firearms safety course for one who is the applicant for a basic firearms safety certificate or a handgun safety certificate.

(5) Allowing another to take the objective test for the applicant, purchaser, or transferee.

(6) Using or allowing another to use one's identification, proof of residency, or thumbprint.

(7) Allowing others to give unauthorized assistance during the examination.

(8) Reference to unauthorized materials during the examination and cheating by the applicant.

(9) Providing originals or photocopies of the objective test, or any version thereof, to any person other than as authorized by the department. *(Added by Stats.2010, c. 711 (S.B.1080), § 6, operative Jan. 1, 2012.)*

Law Revision Commission Comments

Section 27550 continues former Section 12072(e) without substantive change.

For exceptions to this provision, see Article 2 (commencing with Section 27600).

For the consequences of violating this section, see Section 27590 (punishment for violation of article).

See Sections 16240 ("basic firearms safety certificate"), 16520 ("firearm"), 16670 ("handgun safety certificate"). [38 Cal.L.Rev.Comm. Reports 217 (2009)].

Cross References

Firearm defined for purposes of this Part, see Penal Code § 16520.
Handgun defined for purposes of this Part, see Penal Code § 16640.
Handgun safety certificate defined for purposes of this Part, see Penal Code § 16670.

Research References

2 Witkin, California Criminal Law 4th Crimes Against Public Peace and Welfare § 195 (2021), In General.

2 Witkin, California Criminal Law 4th Crimes Against Public Peace and Welfare § 201 (2021), Punishment.

§ 27555. Sale, delivery, or transfer of firearm by persons licensed pursuant to Chapter 44, Title 18 of U.S. Code; verification number required; review of centralized lists of firearms dealers, licensees, and manufacturers

(a)(1) Commencing July 1, 2008, a person who is licensed pursuant to Chapter 44 (commencing with Section 921) of Title 18 of the United States Code may not sell, deliver, or transfer a firearm to a person in California who is licensed pursuant to Chapter 44 (commencing with Section 921) of Title 18 of the United States Code unless, prior to delivery, the person intending to sell, deliver, or transfer the firearm obtains a verification number via the Internet for the intended sale, delivery, or transfer, from the Department of Justice.

(2) If Internet service is unavailable to either the department or the licensee due to a technical or other malfunction, or a federal firearms licensee who is located outside of California does not possess a computer or have Internet access, alternate means of communication, including facsimile or telephone, shall be made available for a licensee to obtain a verification number in order to comply with this section.

(b) For every verification number request received pursuant to this section, the department shall determine whether the intended recipient is on the centralized list of firearms dealers pursuant to Section 26715, or the centralized list of exempted federal firearms licensees pursuant to Section 28450, or the centralized list of firearms manufacturers pursuant to Section 29060.

(c)(1) If the department finds after the reviews specified in subdivision (b) that the intended recipient is authorized to receive the firearm shipment, the department shall issue to the inquiring party, a unique verification number for the intended sale, delivery, or transfer. One verification number shall be issued for each sale, delivery, or transfer, which may involve multiple firearms.

(2) In addition to the unique verification number, the department may provide to the inquiring party information necessary for determining the eligibility of the intended recipient to receive the firearm.

(3) The person intending to sell, deliver, or transfer the firearm shall provide the unique verification number to the recipient along with the firearm upon delivery, in a manner to be determined by the department.

(d) If the department finds after the reviews specified in subdivision (b) that the intended recipient is not authorized to receive the firearm shipment, the department shall notify the inquiring party that the intended recipient is ineligible to receive the shipment.

(e) The department shall prescribe the manner in which the verification numbers may be requested via the Internet, or by alternate means of communication, such as by facsimile or telephone, including all required enrollment information and procedures. *(Added by Stats.2010, c. 711 (S.B.1080), § 6, operative Jan. 1, 2012.)*

Law Revision Commission Comments

Section 27555 continues former Section 12072(f)(1) without substantive change. An erroneous reference to "this section" in former Section 12072(f)(1)(B) has been replaced with a reference to Section 26715, which continues former Section 12071(e).

For exceptions to this provision, see Article 2 (commencing with Section 27600) and Article 5 (commencing with Section 27805).

For the consequences of violating this section, see Section 27590 (punishment for violation of article).

See Sections 16520 ("firearm"), 26700 ("dealer," "licensee," or "person licensed pursuant to Sections 26700 to 26915, inclusive"). [38 Cal.L.Rev. Comm. Reports 217 (2009)].

Cross References

Dealer defined, see Penal Code § 26700.
Firearm defined for purposes of this Part, see Penal Code § 16520.
Licensee defined, see Penal Code § 26700.

Research References

2 Witkin, California Criminal Law 4th Crimes Against Public Peace and Welfare § 195 (2021), In General.
2 Witkin, California Criminal Law 4th Crimes Against Public Peace and Welfare § 198 (2021), Transfers by Persons Not Licensed in California.

§ 27560. Bringing handgun or firearm into state; requirements; effect on other laws; education and notification program; reports; notice; how to transport

(a) Within 60 days of bringing a handgun, and commencing January 1, 2014, any firearm, into this state, a personal firearm importer shall do one of the following:

(1) Forward by prepaid mail or deliver in person to the Department of Justice, a report prescribed by the department including information concerning that individual and a description of the firearm in question.

(2) Sell or transfer the firearm in accordance with the provisions of Section 27545 or in accordance with the provisions of an exemption from Section 27545.

(3) Sell or transfer the firearm to a dealer licensed pursuant to Article 1 (commencing with Section 26700) and Article 2 (commencing with Section 26800) of Chapter 2.

(4) Sell or transfer the firearm to a sheriff or police department.

(b) If all of the following requirements are satisfied, the personal firearm importer shall have complied with the provisions of this section:

(1) The personal firearm importer sells or transfers the firearm pursuant to Section 27545.

(2) The sale or transfer cannot be completed by the dealer to the purchaser or transferee.

(3) The firearm can be returned to the personal firearm importer.

(c)(1) The provisions of this section are cumulative and shall not be construed as restricting the application of any other law.

(2) However, an act or omission punishable in different ways by this article and different provisions of the Penal Code shall not be punished under more than one provision.

(d) The department shall conduct a public education and notification program regarding this section to ensure a high degree of publicity of the provisions of this section.

(e) As part of the public education and notification program described in this section, the department shall do all of the following:

(1) Work in conjunction with the Department of Motor Vehicles to ensure that any person who is subject to this section is advised of the provisions of this section, and provided with blank copies of the report described in paragraph (1) of subdivision (a), at the time when that person applies for a California driver's license or registers a motor vehicle in accordance with the Vehicle Code.

(2) Make the reports referred to in paragraph (1) of subdivision (a) available to dealers licensed pursuant to Article 1 (commencing with Section 26700) and Article 2 (commencing with Section 26800) of Chapter 2.

(3) Make the reports referred to in paragraph (1) of subdivision (a) available to law enforcement agencies.

(4) Make persons subject to the provisions of this section aware of all of the following:

(A) The report referred to in paragraph (1) of subdivision (a) may be completed at either a law enforcement agency or the licensed premises of a dealer licensed pursuant to Article 1 (commencing with

Section 26700) and Article 2 (commencing with Section 26800) of Chapter 2.

(B) It is advisable to do so for the sake of accuracy and completeness of the report.

(C) Before transporting a firearm to a law enforcement agency to comply with subdivision (a), the person should give notice to the law enforcement agency that the person is doing so.

(D) In any event, the handgun should be transported unloaded and in a locked container and a firearm that is not a handgun should be transported unloaded.

(f) Any costs incurred by the department to implement this section shall be absorbed by the department within its existing budget and the fees in the Dealers' Record of Sale Special Account allocated for implementation of subdivisions (d) and (e) of this section pursuant to Section 28235. *(Added by Stats.2010, c. 711 (S.B.1080), § 6, operative Jan. 1, 2012. Amended by Stats.2011, c. 745 (A.B.809), § 27.)*

Law Revision Commission Comments

Section 27560 continues former Section 12072(f)(2) without substantive change.

For guidance in applying this section, see Section 27570 (rules for applying Sections 27560 and 27565).

For exceptions to this provision, see Article 2 (commencing with Section 27600).

For the consequences of violating this section, see Section 27590 (punishment for violation of article).

See Sections 16520 ("firearm"), 16640 ("handgun"), 17000 ("personal handgun importer"), 26700 ("dealer," "licensee," or "person licensed pursuant to Sections 26700 to 26915, inclusive"). [38 Cal.L.Rev.Comm. Reports 217 (2009)].

Cross References

Firearm defined for purposes of this Part, see Penal Code § 16520.
Firearm sale crimes, punishment, prior convictions, see Penal Code § 27590.
Handgun defined for purposes of this Part, see Penal Code § 16640.

Research References

2 Witkin, California Criminal Law 4th Crimes Against Public Peace and Welfare § 199 (2021), Importation Restrictions.
2 Witkin, California Criminal Law 4th Crimes Against Public Peace and Welfare § 208 (2021), Exempt Activities.

§ 27565. Collector bringing curio or relic into state; requirements

(a) This section applies in the following circumstances:

(1) A person is licensed as a collector pursuant to Chapter 44 (commencing with Section 921) of Title 18 of the United States Code and the regulations issued pursuant thereto.

(2) The licensed premises of that person are within this state.

(3) The licensed collector acquires, outside of this state, a handgun, and commencing January 1, 2014, any firearm.

(4) The licensed collector takes actual possession of that firearm outside of this state pursuant to the provisions of subsection (j) of Section 923 of Title 18 of the United States Code, as amended by Public Law 104–208, and transports the firearm into this state.

(5) The firearm is a curio or relic, as defined in Section 478.11 of Title 27 of the Code of Federal Regulations.

(b) Within five days of transporting a firearm into this state under the circumstances described in subdivision (a), the licensed collector shall report the acquisition of that firearm to the department in a format prescribed by the department. *(Added by Stats.2010, c. 711 (S.B.1080), § 6, operative Jan. 1, 2012. Amended by Stats.2011, c. 745 (A.B.809), § 28.)*

Law Revision Commission Comments

Section 27565 continues former Section 12072(f)(3) without substantive change.

For guidance in applying this section, see Section 27570 (rules for applying Sections 27560 and 27565).

For exceptions to this provision, see Article 2 (commencing with Section 27600).

For the consequences of violating this section, see Section 27590 (punishment for violation of article).

See Sections 16520 ("firearm"), 16640 ("handgun"). [38 Cal.L.Rev.Comm. Reports 217 (2009)].

Cross References

Firearm defined for purposes of this Part, see Penal Code § 16520.
Firearm sale crimes, punishment, prior convictions, see Penal Code § 27590.
Handgun defined for purposes of this Part, see Penal Code § 16640.

Research References

2 Witkin, California Criminal Law 4th Crimes Against Public Peace and Welfare § 199 (2021), Importation Restrictions.
2 Witkin, California Criminal Law 4th Crimes Against Public Peace and Welfare § 208 (2021), Exempt Activities.

§ 27570. Violation of Section 27560 or 27565 not continuing offense; statute of limitations; exception

(a) It is the intent of the Legislature that a violation of Section 27560 or 27565 shall not constitute a "continuing offense" and the statute of limitations for commencing a prosecution for a violation of Section 27560 or 27565 commences on the date that the applicable grace period specified in Section 27560 or 27565 expires.

(b) Sections 27560 and 27565 shall not apply to a person who reports ownership of a firearm after the applicable grace period specified in Section 27560 or 27565 expires if evidence of that violation arises only as the result of the person submitting the report described in Section 27560 or 27565. *(Added by Stats.2010, c. 711 (S.B.1080), § 6, operative Jan. 1, 2012. Amended by Stats.2021, c. 250 (S.B.715), § 9, eff. Jan. 1, 2022.)*

Law Revision Commission Comments

Section 27570 continues former Section 12072(f)(4) without substantive change.

See Section 16640 ("handgun"). [38 Cal.L.Rev.Comm. Reports 217 (2009)].

Cross References

Handgun defined for purposes of this Part, see Penal Code § 16640.

Research References

2 Witkin, California Criminal Law 4th Crimes Against Public Peace and Welfare § 199 (2021), Importation Restrictions.

§ 27573. Firearm sales on state property; exceptions

(a) A state officer or employee, or operator, lessee, or licensee of any state property, shall not contract for, authorize, or allow the sale of any firearm, firearm precursor part, or ammunition on state property or in the buildings that sit on state property or property otherwise owned, leased, occupied, or operated by the state.

(b) This section does not apply to any of the following:

(1) A gun buyback event held by a law enforcement agency.

(2) The sale of a firearm by a public administrator, public conservator, or public guardian within the course of their duties.

(3) The sale of a firearm, firearm precursor part, or ammunition on state property that occurs pursuant to a contract that was entered into before January 1, 2023.

(4) The purchase of firearms, firearm precursor parts, or ammunition on state property by a law enforcement agency in the course of its regular duties.

(5) The sale or purchase of a firearm pursuant to subdivision (b) or (c) of Section 10334 of the Public Contract Code. *(Added by Stats.2022, c. 145 (S.B.915), § 1, eff. Jan. 1, 2023.)*

§ 27575. Prohibition to contract for, authorize, or allow the sale of any firearm, firearm precursor part, or ammunition on the property or in the buildings that comprise the OC Fair and Event Center, in the County of Orange, the City of Costa Mesa, or any successor or additional property owned, leased, or otherwise occupied or operated by the district

(a) Notwithstanding any other law, an officer, employee, operator, lessee, or licensee of the 32nd District Agricultural Association, as defined in Section 3884 of the Food and Agricultural Code, shall not contract for, authorize, or allow the sale of any firearm, firearm precursor part, or ammunition on the property or in the buildings that comprise the OC Fair and Event Center, in the County of Orange, the City of Costa Mesa, or any successor or additional property owned, leased, or otherwise occupied or operated by the district.

(b) This section does not apply to any of the following:

(1) A gun buyback event held by a law enforcement agency.

(2) The sale of a firearm by a public administrator, public conservator, or public guardian within the course of their duties.

(3) The sale of a firearm, firearm precursor part, or ammunition on state property that occurs pursuant to a contract that was entered into before January 1, 2022.

(4) The purchase of ammunition on state property by a law enforcement agency in the course of its regular duties. *(Added by Stats.2021, c. 684 (S.B.264), § 2, eff. Jan. 1, 2022.)*

§ 27575.1. Ventura County Fair and Event Center; sale of firearm, firearm precursor part, or ammunition on property prohibited; exceptions

(a) Notwithstanding any other law, an officer, employee, operator, lessee, or licensee of the 31st District Agricultural Association, as defined in Section 3883 of the Food and Agricultural Code, shall not contract for, authorize, or allow the sale of any firearm, firearm precursor part, or ammunition on the property or in the buildings that comprise the Ventura County Fair and Event Center, in the County of Ventura, the City of Ventura, or any successor or additional property owned, leased, or otherwise occupied or operated by the district.

(b) This section does not apply to any of the following:

(1) A gun buyback event held by a law enforcement agency.

(2) The sale of a firearm by a public administrator, public conservator, or public guardian within the course of their duties.

(3) The sale of a firearm, firearm precursor part, or ammunition on state property that occurs pursuant to a contract that was entered into before January 1, 2023.

(4) The purchase of ammunition on state property by a law enforcement agency in the course of its regular duties. *(Added by Stats.2022, c. 140 (A.B.1769), § 1, eff. Jan. 1, 2023.)*

§ 27585. Importation, transportation or bringing of firearms into the state; residents required to take delivery from a state dealer; exceptions

(a) Commencing January 1, 2015, a resident of this state shall not import into this state, bring into this state, or transport into this state, any firearm that the person purchased or otherwise obtained on or after January 1, 2015, from outside of this state unless the person first has that firearm delivered to a dealer in this state for delivery to that resident pursuant to the procedures set forth in Section 27540 and Article 1 (commencing with Section 26700) and Article 2 (commencing with Section 26800) of Chapter 2.

(b) Subdivision (a) does not apply to or affect any of the following:

(1) A licensed collector who is subject to and complies with Section 27565.

(2) A dealer, if the dealer is acting in the course and scope of their activities as a dealer.

(3) A wholesaler, if the wholesaler is acting in the course and scope of their activities as a wholesaler.

(4) A person licensed as an importer of firearms or ammunition or licensed as a manufacturer of firearms or ammunition, pursuant to Section 921 et seq. of Title 18 of the United States Code and the regulations issued pursuant thereto if the importer or manufacturer is acting in the course and scope of their activities as a licensed importer or manufacturer.

(5) A personal firearm importer who is subject to and complies with Section 27560.

(6) A person who complies with subdivision (b) of Section 27875.

(7) A person who complies with subdivision (b), (c), or (d) of Section 27920.

(8) A person who is on the centralized list of exempted federal firearms licensees pursuant to Section 28450 if that person is acting in the course and scope of their activities as a licensee.

(9) A firearm regulated pursuant to Chapter 1 (commencing with Section 18710) of Division 5 of Title 2 acquired by a person who holds a permit issued pursuant to Article 3 (commencing with Section 18900) of Chapter 1 of Division 5 of Title 2, if that person is acting within the course and scope of their activities as a licensee and in accordance with the terms and conditions of the permit.

(10) A firearm regulated pursuant to Chapter 2 (commencing with Section 30500) of Division 10 acquired by a person who holds a permit issued pursuant to Section 31005, if that person is acting within the course and scope of their activities as a licensee and in accordance with the terms and conditions of the permit.

(11) A firearm regulated pursuant to Chapter 6 (commencing with Section 32610) of Division 10 acquired by a person who holds a permit issued pursuant to Section 32650, if that person is acting within the course and scope of their activities as a licensee and in accordance with the terms and conditions of the permit.

(12) A firearm regulated pursuant to Article 2 (commencing with Section 33300) of Chapter 8 of Division 10 acquired by a person who holds a permit issued pursuant to Section 33300, if that person is acting within the course and scope of their activities as a licensee and in accordance with the terms and conditions of the permit.

(13) The importation of a firearm into the state, bringing a firearm into the state, or transportation of a firearm into the state, that is regulated by any of the following statutes, if the acquisition of that firearm occurred outside of California and is conducted in accordance with the applicable provisions of the following statutes:

(A) Chapter 1 (commencing with Section 18710) of Division 5 of Title 2, relating to destructive devices and explosives.

(B) Section 24410, relating to cane guns.

(C) Section 24510, relating to firearms that are not immediately recognizable as firearms.

(D) Sections 24610 and 24680, relating to undetectable firearms.

(E) Section 24710, relating to wallet guns.

(F) Chapter 2 (commencing with Section 30500) of Division 10, relating to assault weapons.

(G) Section 31500, relating to unconventional pistols.

(H) Sections 33215 to 33225, inclusive, relating to short-barreled rifles and short-barreled shotguns.

(I) Chapter 6 (commencing with Section 32610) of Division 10, relating to machineguns.

(J) Section 33600, relating to zip guns, and the exemptions in Chapter 1 (commencing with Section 17700) of Division 2 of Title 2, as they relate to zip guns.

(14) The importation, transportation, or bringing of a firearm into the state by a person who meets any of the following criteria:

(A) The person is listed in the registry set forth in Section 11106 as the owner of the firearm.

(B) The person has been issued documentation by the Department of Justice pursuant to subdivision (b) of Section 11106 that indicates the person is listed in the centralized registry as owning that firearm.

(C) The person has a copy of a Dealer's Record of Sale that shows that the person received that firearm from the dealer listed in that Dealer's Record of Sale and is listed as the owner of the firearm.

(D) If the firearm is a handgun, the person has a license to carry that handgun pursuant to Chapter 4 (commencing with Section 26150) of Division 5 and the person is licensed to carry that handgun.

(15) A licensed common carrier or an authorized agent or employee of a licensed common carrier, when acting in the course and scope of duties incident to the delivery of or receipt of that firearm in accordance with federal law.

(c) The provisions of this section are cumulative and do not restrict the application of any other law. However, an act or omission punishable in different ways by this section and different provisions of this code shall not be punished under more than one provision. *(Added by Stats.2014, c. 878 (A.B.1609), § 4, eff. Jan. 1, 2015. Amended by Stats.2019, c. 730 (A.B.879), § 5, eff. Jan. 1, 2020.)*

Research References

2 Witkin, California Criminal Law 4th Crimes Against Public Peace and Welfare § 199 (2021), Importation Restrictions.
2 Witkin, California Criminal Law 4th Crimes Against Public Peace and Welfare § 201 (2021), Punishment.

§ 27590. Violation of article; punishment; additional punishment

(a) Except as provided in subdivision (b), (c), or (e), a violation of this article is a misdemeanor.

(b) If any of the following circumstances apply, a violation of this article is punishable by imprisonment pursuant to subdivision (h) of Section 1170 for two, three, or four years:

(1) If the violation is of subdivision (a) of Section 27500.

(2) If the defendant has a prior conviction of violating the provisions, other than Section 27535, Section 27560 involving a firearm that is not a handgun, or Section 27565 involving a firearm that is not a handgun, of this article or former Section 12100 of this code, as Section 12100 read at any time from when it was enacted by Section 3 of Chapter 1386 of the Statutes of 1988 to when it was repealed by Section 18 of Chapter 23 of the Statutes of 1994, or Section 8101 of the Welfare and Institutions Code.

(3) If the defendant has a prior conviction of violating any offense specified in Section 29905 or of a violation of Section 32625 or 33410, or of former Section 12560, as that section read at any time from when it was enacted by Section 4 of Chapter 931 of the Statutes of 1965 to when it was repealed by Section 14 of Chapter 9 of the Statutes of 1990, or of any provision listed in Section 16590.

(4) If the defendant is in a prohibited class described in Chapter 2 (commencing with Section 29800) or Chapter 3 (commencing with Section 29900) of Division 9 of this title, or Section 8100 or 8103 of the Welfare and Institutions Code.

(5) A violation of this article by a person who actively participates in a "criminal street gang" as defined in Section 186.22.

(6) A violation of Section 27510 involving the delivery of any firearm to a person who the dealer knows, or should know, is a minor.

(c) If any of the following circumstances apply, a violation of this article shall be punished by imprisonment in a county jail not exceeding one year or pursuant to subdivision (h) of Section 1170, or by a fine not to exceed one thousand dollars ($1,000), or by both that fine and imprisonment:

(1) A violation of Section 27515, 27520, or subdivision (b) of Section 27500.

(2) A violation of Section 27505 involving the sale, loan, or transfer of a handgun to a minor.

(3) A violation of Section 27510 involving the delivery of a handgun.

(4) A violation of subdivision (a), (c), (d), (e), or (f) of Section 27540 involving a handgun.

(5) A violation of Section 27545 involving a handgun.

(6) A violation of Section 27550.

(7) A violation of Section 27585 involving a handgun.

(d) If both of the following circumstances apply, an additional term of imprisonment pursuant to subdivision (h) of Section 1170 for one, two, or three years shall be imposed in addition and consecutive to the sentence prescribed:

(1) A violation of Section 27510 or subdivision (b) of Section 27500.

(2) The firearm transferred in violation of Section 27510 or subdivision (b) of Section 27500 is used in the subsequent commission of a felony for which a conviction is obtained and the prescribed sentence is imposed.

(e)(1) A first violation of Section 27535 is an infraction punishable by a fine of fifty dollars ($50).

(2) A second violation of Section 27535 is an infraction punishable by a fine of one hundred dollars ($100).

(3) A third or subsequent violation of Section 27535 is a misdemeanor.

(4)(A) Until July 1, 2021, for purposes of this subdivision, each application to purchase a handgun in violation of Section 27535 is a separate offense.

(B) Commencing July 1, 2021, for purposes of this subdivision, each application to purchase a handgun or semiautomatic centerfire rifle in violation of Section 27535 is a separate offense. *(Added by Stats.2010, c. 711 (S.B.1080), § 6, operative Jan. 1, 2012. Amended by Stats.2011, c. 15 (A.B.109), § 545, eff. April 4, 2011, operative Jan. 1, 2012; Stats.2011, c. 745 (A.B.809), § 29.5; Stats.2014, c. 878 (A.B. 1609), § 5, eff. Jan. 1, 2015; Stats.2019, c. 737 (S.B.61), § 7, eff. Jan. 1, 2020.)*

Law Revision Commission Comments

Section 27590 continues former Section 12072(g) without substantive change.

For guidance in applying paragraphs (b)(2), (b)(3), (e)(2), and (e)(3), see Section 16015 (determining existence of prior conviction).

See Sections 16520 ("firearm"), 16530 ("firearm capable of being concealed upon the person," "pistol," and "revolver"), 16640 ("handgun"). [38 Cal. L.Rev.Comm. Reports 217 (2009)].

Cross References

Dealer defined, see Penal Code § 26700.
Felonies, definition and penalties, see Penal Code §§ 17, 18.
Firearm defined for purposes of this Part, see Penal Code § 16520.
Handgun defined for purposes of this Part, see Penal Code § 16640.
Misdemeanors, definition and penalties, see Penal Code §§ 17, 19, 19.2.

Research References

2 Witkin, California Criminal Law 4th Crimes Against Public Peace and Welfare § 201 (2021), Punishment.

3 Witkin, California Criminal Law 4th Punishment § 621 (2021), P.C. 1203.

ARTICLE 2. EXCEPTIONS RELATING TO LAW ENFORCEMENT

§ 27600. Sale, delivery, or transfer of firearm by law enforcement representative for use by governmental agency; written authorization; application of Article 1; entry of firearm acquisition or destruction into Automated Firearms System

(a) Article 1 (commencing with Section 27500) does not apply to any sale, delivery, or transfer of firearms made to, or the importation of firearms by, an authorized law enforcement representative of any city, county, city and county, or state, or of the federal government, for exclusive use by that governmental agency if, prior to the sale, delivery, transfer, or importation of these firearms, written authorization from the head of the agency authorizing the transaction is presented to the person from whom the purchase, delivery, or transfer is being made or from whom the firearm is being imported.

(b) Proper written authorization is defined as verifiable written certification from the head of the agency by which the purchaser or transferee is employed, identifying the employee as an individual authorized to conduct the transaction, and authorizing the transaction for the exclusive use of the agency by which that person is employed.

(c) Within 10 days of the date a firearm is acquired by the agency, a record of the same shall be entered as an institutional weapon into the Automated Firearms System (AFS) via the California Law Enforcement Telecommunications System (CLETS) by the law enforcement or state agency. Any agency without access to the AFS shall arrange with the sheriff of the county in which the agency is located to input this information via this system.

(d) Any agency that is the registered owner of an institutional weapon in accordance with subdivision (c) that subsequently destroys that weapon shall enter information that the weapon has been destroyed into the Automated Firearms System (AFS) via the California Law Enforcement Telecommunications System (CLETS) within 10 days of the destruction in accordance with procedures prescribed by the Department of Justice. Any agency without access to the AFS shall arrange with the sheriff of the county in which the agency is located to input this information via this system. *(Added by Stats.2010, c. 711 (S.B.1080), § 6, operative Jan. 1, 2012. Amended by Stats.2011, c. 745 (A.B.809), § 30; Stats.2013, c. 738 (A.B.538), § 4; Stats.2014, c. 878 (A.B.1609), § 6, eff. Jan. 1, 2015.)*

Law Revision Commission Comments

Section 27600 continues former Section 12078(a)(2) without substantive change, as that provision applied to former Section 12072 (through its reference to "the preceding provisions of this article").

See Sections 16520 ("firearm"), 16640 ("handgun"). [38 Cal.L.Rev.Comm. Reports 217 (2009)].

Cross References

Firearm defined for purposes of this Part, see Penal Code § 16520.
Handgun defined for purposes of this Part, see Penal Code § 16640.

§ 27605. Loan of firearm by law enforcement representative to peace officer; application of Article 1

Article 1 (commencing with Section 27500) does not apply to the loan of a firearm if all of the following conditions are satisfied:

(a) The loan is made by an authorized law enforcement representative of a city, county, or city and county, or of the state or federal government.

(b) The loan is made to a peace officer employed by that agency and authorized to carry a firearm.

(c) The loan is made for the carrying and use of that firearm by that peace officer in the course and scope of the officer's duties. *(Added by Stats.2010, c. 711 (S.B.1080), § 6, operative Jan. 1, 2012.)*

Law Revision Commission Comments

Section 27605 continues former Section 12078(a)(3) without substantive change, as that provision applied to former Section 12072 (through its reference to "the preceding provisions of this article").

See Section 16520 ("firearm"). [38 Cal.L.Rev.Comm. Reports 217 (2009)].

Cross References

Firearm defined for purposes of this Part, see Penal Code § 16520.

§ 27610. Sale, delivery, or transfer of firearm by law enforcement agency to peace officer pursuant to Section 10334 of Public Contract Code; application of Article 1

(a) Article 1 (commencing with Section 27500) does not apply to the sale, delivery, or transfer of a firearm by a law enforcement agency to a peace officer pursuant to Section 10334 of the Public Contract Code.

(b) Within 10 days of the date that a handgun, and commencing January 1, 2014, any firearm, is sold, delivered, or transferred pursuant to Section 10334 of the Public Contract Code to that peace officer, the name of the officer and the make, model, serial number, and other identifying characteristics of the firearm being sold, delivered, or transferred shall be entered into the Automated Firearms System (AFS) via the California Law Enforcement Telecommunications System (CLETS) by the law enforcement or state agency that sold, delivered, or transferred the firearm, provided, however, that if the firearm is not a handgun and does not have a serial number, identification number, or identification mark assigned to it, that fact shall be noted in AFS. Any agency without access to AFS shall arrange with the sheriff of the county in which the agency is located to input this information via this system. *(Added by Stats.2010, c. 711 (S.B.1080), § 6, operative Jan. 1, 2012. Amended by Stats.2011, c. 745 (A.B.809), § 31.)*

Law Revision Commission Comments

Section 27610 continues former Section 12078(a)(4) without substantive change, as that provision applied to former Section 12072 (through its reference to "the preceding provisions of this article").

See Sections 16520 ("firearm"), 16640 ("handgun"). [38 Cal.L.Rev.Comm. Reports 217 (2009)].

Cross References

Firearm defined for purposes of this Part, see Penal Code § 16520.

Handgun defined for purposes of this Part, see Penal Code § 16640.

§ 27615. Sale, delivery, or transfer of firearm by law enforcement agency to retiring peace officer; application of Article 1; entry into Automated Firearms System

(a) Article 1 (commencing with Section 27500) does not apply to the sale, delivery, or transfer of a firearm by a law enforcement agency to a retiring peace officer who is authorized to carry a firearm pursuant to Chapter 5 (commencing with Section 26300) of Division 5.

(b) Within 10 days of the date that a handgun, and commencing January 1, 2014, any firearm, is sold, delivered, or transferred to that retiring peace officer, the name of the officer and the make, model, serial number, and other identifying characteristics of the firearm being sold, delivered, or transferred shall be entered into the Automated Firearms System (AFS) via the California Law Enforcement Telecommunications System (CLETS) by the law enforcement or state agency that sold, delivered, or transferred the firearm, provided, however, that if the firearm is not a handgun and does not have a serial number, identification number, or identification mark assigned to it, that fact shall be noted in AFS. Any agency without access to AFS shall arrange with the sheriff of the county in which the agency is located to input this information via this system. *(Added by Stats.2010, c. 711 (S.B.1080), § 6, operative Jan. 1, 2012. Amended by Stats.2011, c. 745 (A.B.809), § 32.)*

Law Revision Commission Comments

Section 27615 continues former Section 12078(a)(5) without substantive change, as that provision applied to former Section 12072 (through its reference to "the preceding provisions of this article").

See Sections 16520 ("firearm"), 16640 ("handgun"). [38 Cal.L.Rev.Comm. Reports 217 (2009)].

Cross References

Firearm defined for purposes of this Part, see Penal Code § 16520.
Handgun defined for purposes of this Part, see Penal Code § 16640.

§ 27620. Sale, delivery, or transfer of firearm by authorized law enforcement representative; application of section requiring completion through licensed firearms dealer; requirements

Section 27545 does not apply to the sale, delivery, or transfer of a firearm when made by an authorized law enforcement representative of a city, county, city and county, or of the state or federal government, if all of the following conditions are met:

(a) The sale, delivery, or transfer is made to one of the following:

(1) A wholesaler.

(2) A manufacturer or importer of firearms or ammunition licensed to engage in that business pursuant to Chapter 44 (commencing with Section 921) of Title 18 of the United States Code and the regulations issued pursuant thereto.

(b) The sale, delivery, or transfer of the firearm is not subject to the procedures set forth in Section 18000, 18005, 34000, or 34005.

(c) Within 10 days of the date that any firearm is delivered pursuant to this section, the governmental agency has entered a record of the delivery into the Automated Firearms System (AFS) via the California Law Enforcement Telecommunications System (CLETS). Any agency without access to the AFS shall arrange with the sheriff of the county in which the agency is located to input this information via this system. *(Added by Stats.2013, c. 738 (A.B.538), § 5.)*

Cross References

Firearm defined for purposes of this Part, see Penal Code § 16520.

ARTICLE 3. EXCEPTIONS EXTENDING ONLY TO WAITING PERIOD

§ 27650. Sale, delivery, or transfer of firearm to peace officer; application of waiting period requirements

(a) The waiting period described in Section 27540 does not apply to the sale, delivery, or transfer of firearms made to any person who satisfies both of the following requirements:

(1) The person is properly identified as a full-time paid peace officer, as defined in Chapter 4.5 (commencing with Section 830) of Title 3 of Part 2.

(2) The officer's employer has authorized the officer to carry firearms while in the performance of duties.

(b)(1) Proper identification is defined as verifiable written certification from the head of the agency by which the purchaser or transferee is employed, identifying the purchaser or transferee as a peace officer who is authorized to carry firearms while in the performance of duties, and authorizing the purchase or transfer.

(2) The certification shall be delivered to the dealer at the time of purchase or transfer and the purchaser or transferee shall identify himself or herself as the person authorized in the certification.

(3) The dealer shall keep the certification with the record of sale.

(4) On the date that the sale, delivery, or transfer is made, the dealer delivering the firearm shall transmit to the Department of Justice an electronic or telephonic report of the transaction as is indicated in Section 28160 or 28165. *(Added by Stats.2010, c. 711 (S.B.1080), § 6, operative Jan. 1, 2012.)*

Law Revision Commission Comments

Section 27650 continues former Section 12078(a)(1) without substantive change, as that provision applied to the waiting period in former Section 12072.

For other exceptions relating to law enforcement, see Sections 27600–27615.

See Sections 16520 ("firearm"), 26700 ("dealer," "licensee," or "person licensed pursuant to Sections 26700 to 26915, inclusive"). [38 Cal.L.Rev. Comm. Reports 217 (2009)].

Cross References

Dealer defined, see Penal Code § 26700.
Firearm defined for purposes of this Part, see Penal Code § 16520.

§ 27660. Sale, delivery, or transfer of handgun or firearm by dealer to another dealer or to himself or herself; application of waiting period requirements

(a) The waiting period described in Section 27540 does not apply to the sale, delivery, or transfer of a handgun, and commencing January 1, 2014, any firearm, by a dealer in either of the following situations:

(1) The dealer is delivering the firearm to another dealer, the firearm is not intended as merchandise in the receiving dealer's business, and the requirements of subdivisions (b) and (c) are satisfied.

(2) The dealer is delivering the firearm to himself or herself, the firearm is not intended as merchandise in the dealer's business, and the requirements of subdivision (c) are satisfied.

(b) If the dealer is receiving the firearm from another dealer, the dealer receiving the firearm shall present proof to the dealer delivering the firearm that the receiving dealer is licensed pursuant to Article 1 (commencing with Section 26700) and Article 2 (commencing with Section 26800). This shall be done by complying with Section 27555.

(c)(1) Regardless of whether the dealer is selling, delivering, or transferring the firearm to another dealer or to himself or herself, on the date that the application to purchase is completed, the dealer delivering the firearm shall forward by prepaid mail to the Department of Justice a report of the application and the type of information concerning the purchaser or transferee as is indicated in Section 28160.

(2) Where electronic or telephonic transfer of applicant information is used, on the date that the application to purchase is completed, the dealer delivering the firearm shall transmit an electronic or telephonic report of the application and the type of information concerning the purchaser or transferee as is indicated in Section 28160. *(Added by Stats.2010, c. 711 (S.B.1080), § 6, operative Jan. 1, 2012. Amended by Stats.2011, c. 745 (A.B.809), § 34.)*

Law Revision Commission Comments

Section 27660 continues former Section 12078(n) without substantive change, as that provision applied to the waiting period in former Section 12072.

See Sections 16190 ("application to purchase"), 16520 ("firearm"), 16640 ("handgun"), 26700 ("dealer," "licensee," or "person licensed pursuant to Sections 26700 to 26915, inclusive"). [38 Cal.L.Rev.Comm. Reports 217 (2009)].

Cross References

Firearm defined for purposes of this Part, see Penal Code § 16520.
Handgun defined for purposes of this Part, see Penal Code § 16640.

§ 27665. Sale, delivery, or transfer of firearm to holder of special weapons permit; application of waiting period requirements; report

(a) The waiting period described in Section 27540 does not apply to the sale, delivery, or transfer of a firearm to the holder of a special weapons permit issued by the Department of Justice pursuant to Section 32650 or 33300, pursuant to Article 3 (commencing with Section 18900) of Chapter 1 of Division 5 of Title 2, or pursuant to Article 4 (commencing with Section 32700) of Chapter 6 of Division 10.

(b) On the date that the application to purchase is completed, the dealer delivering the firearm shall transmit to the Department of Justice an electronic or telephonic report of the application as is indicated in Section 28160 or 28165, as applicable. *(Added by Stats.2010, c. 711 (S.B.1080), § 6, operative Jan. 1, 2012. Amended by Stats.2011, c. 745 (A.B.809), § 35.)*

Law Revision Commission Comments

Section 27665 continues former Section 12078(r) without substantive change, as that provision applied to the waiting period in former Section 12072.

See Sections 16190 ("application to purchase"), 16520 ("firearm"), 26700 ("dealer," "licensee," or "person licensed pursuant to Sections 26700 to 26915, inclusive"). [38 Cal.L.Rev.Comm. Reports 217 (2009)].

Cross References

Dealer defined, see Penal Code § 26700.
Firearm defined for purposes of this Part, see Penal Code § 16520.

§ 27670. Sale, delivery, or transfer of curio or relic firearm; application of waiting period requirements

(a) The waiting period described in Section 27540 does not apply to the sale, delivery, loan, or transfer of a firearm if all of the following conditions are satisfied:

(1) The firearm is a curio or relic, as defined in Section 478.11 of Title 27 of the Code of Federal Regulations, or its successor.

(2) The sale, delivery, loan, or transfer is made by a dealer.

(3) The sale, delivery, loan, or transfer is made to a person who is licensed as a collector pursuant to Chapter 44 (commencing with Section 921) of Title 18 of the United States Code and the regulations issued pursuant thereto.

(4) The licensed collector has a current certificate of eligibility issued by the Department of Justice pursuant to Section 26710.

(b) On the date that the sale, delivery, or transfer is made, the dealer delivering the firearm shall transmit to the Department of Justice an electronic or telephonic report of the transaction as is indicated in Section 28160 or 28165. *(Added by Stats.2010, c. 711 (S.B.1080), § 6, operative Jan. 1, 2012.)*

Law Revision Commission Comments

Section 27670 continues former Section 12078(t)(1) without substantive change, as that provision applied to the waiting period in former Section 12072.

See Sections 16520 ("firearm"), 26700 ("dealer," "licensee," or "person licensed pursuant to Sections 26700 to 26915, inclusive"). [38 Cal.L.Rev. Comm. Reports 217 (2009)].

Cross References

Dealer defined, see Penal Code § 26700.
Firearm defined for purposes of this Part, see Penal Code § 16520.

ARTICLE 4. EXCEPTIONS TO RESTRICTIONS ON DELIVERY OF A FIREARM

Section

§ 27700. Sales, deliveries, or transfers of firearms between or to importers and manufacturers; application of Section 27540

Section 27540 does not apply to sales, deliveries, or transfers of firearms between or to importers and manufacturers of firearms licensed to engage in that business pursuant to Chapter 44 (commencing with Section 921) of Title 18 of the United States Code and the regulations issued pursuant thereto. *(Added by Stats.2010, c. 711 (S.B.1080), § 6, operative Jan. 1, 2012.)*

Law Revision Commission Comments

Section 27700 continues former Section 12078(b)(1) without substantive change, as that provision applied to former Section 12072(c).

See Section 16520 ("firearm"). [38 Cal.L.Rev.Comm. Reports 217 (2009)].

Cross References

Firearm defined for purposes of this Part, see Penal Code § 16520.

Research References

2 Witkin, California Criminal Law 4th Crimes Against Public Peace and Welfare § 197 (2021), Time and Manner of Delivery by Dealer.

§ 27705. Delivery of firearm to gunsmith for repair; application of Section 27540

Section 27540 does not apply to the delivery of a firearm to a gunsmith for service or repair, or to the return of the firearm to its owner by the gunsmith, or to the delivery of a firearm by a gunsmith to a person licensed pursuant to Chapter 44 (commencing with Section 921) of Title 18 of the United States Code for service or repair and the return of the firearm to the gunsmith. *(Added by Stats.2010, c. 711 (S.B.1080), § 6, operative Jan. 1, 2012.)*

Law Revision Commission Comments

Section 27705 continues former Section 12078(e)(1) without substantive change, as that provision applied to former Section 12072(c).

See Sections 16520 ("firearm"), 16630 ("gunsmith"). [38 Cal.L.Rev.Comm. Reports 217 (2009)].

Cross References

Firearm defined for purposes of this Part, see Penal Code § 16520.
Gunsmith defined for purposes of this Part, see Penal Code § 16630.

§ 27715. Sale, delivery, or transfer of firearms by dealer to person outside of state; application of Section 27540

Section 27540 does not apply to the sale, delivery, or transfer of unloaded firearms by a dealer to a person who resides outside this state and is licensed pursuant to Chapter 44 (commencing with Section 921) of Title 18 of the United States Code and the regulations issued pursuant thereto. *(Added by Stats.2010, c. 711 (S.B.1080), § 6, operative Jan. 1, 2012.)*

Law Revision Commission Comments

Section 27715 continues former Section 12078(k)(2) without substantive change, as that provision applied to former Section 12072(c).

See Sections 16520 ("firearm"), 26700 ("dealer," "licensee," or "person licensed pursuant to Sections 26700 to 26915, inclusive"). [38 Cal.L.Rev. Comm. Reports 217 (2009)].

Cross References

Dealer defined, see Penal Code § 26700.
Firearm defined for purposes of this Part, see Penal Code § 16520.

§ 27720. Sale, delivery, or transfer of firearms being returned to wholesaler for use as merchandise; application of Section 27540

Section 27540 does not apply to the sale, delivery, or transfer of unloaded firearms to a wholesaler if the firearms are being returned to the wholesaler and are intended as merchandise in the wholesaler's business. *(Added by Stats.2010, c. 711 (S.B.1080), § 6, operative Jan. 1, 2012.)*

Law Revision Commission Comments

Section 27720 continues former Section 12078(k)(3) without substantive change, as that provision applied to former Section 12072(c).

See Sections 16520 ("firearm"), 17340 ("wholesaler"), 26700 ("dealer," "licensee," or "person licensed pursuant to Sections 26700 to 26915, inclusive"). [38 Cal.L.Rev.Comm. Reports 217 (2009)].

Cross References

Firearm defined for purposes of this Part, see Penal Code § 16520.
Wholesaler defined for purposes of this Part, see Penal Code § 17340.

§ 27725. Sale, delivery, or transfer of firearms between dealers for use as merchandise; application of Section 27540

Section 27540 does not apply to the sale, delivery, or transfer of firearms if all of the following conditions are satisfied:

(a) The firearms are unloaded.

(b) The sale, delivery, or transfer is made by one dealer to another dealer, upon proof of compliance with the requirements of Section 27555.

(c) The firearms are intended as merchandise in the receiving dealer's business. *(Added by Stats.2010, c. 711 (S.B.1080), § 6, operative Jan. 1, 2012.)*

Law Revision Commission Comments

Section 27725 continues former Section 12078(k)(4) without substantive change, as that provision applied to former Section 12072(c).

See Sections 16520 ("firearm"), 26700 ("dealer," "licensee," or "person licensed pursuant to Sections 26700 to 26915, inclusive"). [38 Cal.L.Rev. Comm. Reports 217 (2009)].

Cross References

Dealer defined, see Penal Code § 26700.
Firearm defined for purposes of this Part, see Penal Code § 16520.

§ 27730. Sale, delivery, or transfer of firearm by dealer to himself or herself; application of Section 27540

Until January 1, 2014, Section 27540 does not apply to the sale, delivery, or transfer of an unloaded firearm, other than a handgun, by a dealer to himself or herself. *(Added by Stats.2010, c. 711 (S.B.1080), § 6, operative Jan. 1, 2012. Amended by Stats.2011, c. 745 (A.B.809), § 37.)*

Law Revision Commission Comments

Section 27730 continues former Section 12078(k)(5) without substantive change, as that provision applied to former Section 12072(c).

See Sections 16520 ("firearm"), 16640 ("handgun"), 26700 ("dealer," "licensee," or "person licensed pursuant to Sections 26700 to 26915, inclusive"). [38 Cal.L.Rev.Comm. Reports 217 (2009)].

Cross References

Dealer defined, see Penal Code § 26700.
Firearm defined for purposes of this Part, see Penal Code § 16520.
Handgun defined for purposes of this Part, see Penal Code § 16640.

§ 27735. Loan of firearm by dealer who operates target facility for use in target shooting; application of Section 27540

Section 27540 does not apply to the loan of an unloaded firearm by a dealer who also operates a target facility that holds a business or regulatory license on the premises of the building designated in the license or whose building designated in the license is on the premises of any club or organization organized for the purposes of practicing shooting at targets upon established ranges, whether public or private, to a person at that target facility or that club or organization, if the firearm is at all times kept within the premises of the target range or on the premises of the club or organization. *(Added by Stats.2010, c. 711 (S.B.1080), § 6, operative Jan. 1, 2012.)*

Law Revision Commission Comments

Section 27735 continues former Section 12078(k)(6) without substantive change, as that provision applied to former Section 12072(c).

See Sections 16520 ("firearm"), 26700 ("dealer," "licensee," or "person licensed pursuant to Sections 26700 to 26915, inclusive"). [38 Cal.L.Rev. Comm. Reports 217 (2009)].

Cross References

Dealer defined, see Penal Code § 26700.

Firearm defined for purposes of this Part, see Penal Code § 16520.

§ 27740. Sale, delivery, or transfer of firearm regulated by particular statutes; application of Section 27540

Section 27540 does not apply to the sale, delivery, or transfer of a firearm regulated pursuant to any of the following statutes, if the sale, delivery, or transfer of that firearm is conducted in accordance with the applicable provisions of the statute:

(a) Chapter 1 (commencing with Section 18710) of Division 5 of Title 2, relating to destructive devices and explosives.

(b) Section 24410, relating to cane guns, and the exemptions in Chapter 1 (commencing with Section 17700) of Title 2, as they relate to cane guns.

(c) Section 24510, relating to firearms that are not immediately recognizable as firearms, and the exemptions in Chapter 1 (commencing with Section 17700) of Title 2, as they relate to firearms that are not immediately recognizable as firearms.

(d) Sections 24610 and 24680, relating to undetectable firearms, and the exemptions in Chapter 1 (commencing with Section 17700) of Title 2, as they relate to undetectable firearms.

(e) Section 24710, relating to wallet guns, and the exemptions in Chapter 1 (commencing with Section 17700) of Title 2, as they relate to wallet guns.

(f) Chapter 2 (commencing with Section 30500) of Division 10, relating to assault weapons.

(g) Section 31500, relating to unconventional pistols, and the exemptions in Chapter 1 (commencing with Section 17700) of Title 2, as they relate to unconventional pistols.

(h) Sections 33215 to 33225, inclusive, relating to short-barreled rifles and short-barreled shotguns, and the exemptions in Chapter 1 (commencing with Section 17700) of Title 2, as they relate to short-barreled rifles and short-barreled shotguns.

(i) Chapter 6 (commencing with Section 32610) of Division 10, relating to machineguns.

(j) Section 33600, relating to zip guns, and the exemptions in Chapter 1 (commencing with Section 17700) of Title 2, as they relate to zip guns. *(Added by Stats.2010, c. 711 (S.B.1080), § 6, operative Jan. 1, 2012.)*

Law Revision Commission Comments

Section 27740 continues former Section 12078(*o*) without substantive change, as that provision applied to former Section 12072(c).

See Sections 16330 ("cane gun"), 16460 ("destructive device"), 16510 ("explosive"), 16520 ("firearm"), 16880 ("machinegun"), 17170 ("short-barreled rifle"), 17180 ("short-barreled shotgun"), 17270 ("unconventional pistol"), 17280 ("undetectable firearm"), 17330 ("wallet gun"), 17360 ("zip gun"), 30510 ("assault weapon"), 30515 (further clarification of "assault weapon"). [38 Cal.L.Rev.Comm. Reports 217 (2009)].

Cross References

Cane gun defined for purposes of this Part, see Penal Code § 16330.
Firearm defined for purposes of this Part, see Penal Code § 16520.
Machinegun defined for purposes of this Part, see Penal Code § 16880.
Pistol defined for purposes of this Part, see Penal Code § 16530.
Unconventional pistol defined for purposes of this Part, see Penal Code § 17270.
Undetectable firearm defined for purposes of this Part, see Penal Code § 17280.
Wallet gun defined for purposes of this Part, see Penal Code § 17330.
Zip gun defined for purposes of this Part, see Penal Code § 17360.

§ 27745. Loan of firearm by dealer for use as prop; application of Section 27540

(a) Section 27540 does not apply to the loan of a firearm if all of the following conditions are satisfied:

(1) The firearm is unloaded.

(2) The loan is made by a dealer.

(3) The loan is made to a person who possesses a valid entertainment firearms permit issued pursuant to Chapter 2 (commencing with Section 29500) of Division 8.

(4) The firearm is loaned solely for use as a prop in a motion picture, television, video, theatrical, or other entertainment production or event.

(b) The dealer shall retain a photocopy of the entertainment firearms permit as proof of compliance with this requirement. *(Added by Stats.2010, c. 711 (S.B.1080), § 6, operative Jan. 1, 2012.)*

Law Revision Commission Comments

Section 27745 continues former Section 12078(s)(3) without substantive change, as that provision applied to former Section 12072(c).

See Sections 16520 ("firearm"), 26700 ("dealer," "licensee," or "person licensed pursuant to Sections 26700 to 26915, inclusive"). [38 Cal.L.Rev. Comm. Reports 217 (2009)].

Cross References

Dealer defined, see Penal Code § 26700.
Firearm defined for purposes of this Part, see Penal Code § 16520.

§ 27750. Loan of firearm to consultant-evaluator; application of Section 27540

(a) Section 27540 does not apply to the loan of an unloaded firearm to a consultant-evaluator by a person licensed pursuant to Sections 26700 to 26915, inclusive, if the loan does not exceed 45 days from the date of delivery.

(b) At the time of the loan, the consultant-evaluator shall provide the following information, which the dealer shall retain for two years:

(1) A photocopy of a valid, current, government-issued identification to determine the consultant-evaluator's identity, including, but not limited to, a California driver's license, identification card, or passport.

(2) A photocopy of the consultant-evaluator's valid, current certificate of eligibility.

(3) A letter from the person licensed as an importer, manufacturer, or dealer pursuant to Chapter 44 (commencing with Section 921) of Title 18 of the United States Code, with whom the consultant-evaluator has a bona fide business relationship. The letter shall detail the bona fide business purposes for which the firearm is being loaned and confirm that the consultant-evaluator is being loaned the firearm as part of a bona fide business relationship.

(4) The signature of the consultant-evaluator on a form indicating the date the firearm is loaned and the last day the firearm may be returned. *(Added by Stats.2010, c. 711 (S.B.1080), § 6, operative Jan. 1, 2012.)*

Law Revision Commission Comments

Section 27750 continues former Section 12078(s)(4) without substantive change, as that provision applied to former Section 12072(c).

See Sections 16410 ("consultant-evaluator"), 16520 ("firearm"), 26700 ("dealer," "licensee," or "person licensed pursuant to Sections 26700 to 26915, inclusive"). [38 Cal.L.Rev.Comm. Reports 217 (2009)].

Cross References

Consultant-evaluator defined for purposes of this Part, see Penal Code § 16410.
Firearm defined for purposes of this Part, see Penal Code § 16520.

ARTICLE 5. EXCEPTIONS TO THE REQUIREMENT OF OBTAINING A VERIFICATION NUMBER

Section

§ 27805. Loan of firearm for use as prop; application of Section 27555

(a) Section 27555 does not apply to the loan of a firearm if all of the following conditions are satisfied:

(1) The firearm is unloaded.

(2) The loan is made by a dealer.

(3) The loan is made to a person who possesses a valid entertainment firearms permit issued pursuant to Chapter 2 (commencing with Section 29500) of Division 8.

(4) The firearm is loaned solely for use as a prop in a motion picture, television, video, theatrical, or other entertainment production or event.

(b) The dealer shall retain a photocopy of the entertainment firearms permit as proof of compliance with this requirement. *(Added by Stats.2010, c. 711 (S.B.1080), § 6, operative Jan. 1, 2012.)*

Law Revision Commission Comments

Section 27805 continues former Section 12078(s)(3) without substantive change, as that provision applied to former Section 12072(f)(1).

See Sections 16520 ("firearm"), 26700 ("dealer," "licensee," or "person licensed pursuant to Sections 26700 to 26915, inclusive"). [38 Cal.L.Rev. Comm. Reports 217 (2009)].

Cross References

Dealer defined, see Penal Code § 26700.
Firearm defined for purposes of this Part, see Penal Code § 16520.

§ 27810. Loan of firearm to federal firearms licensee; application of Section 27555

(a) Section 27555 does not apply to the loan of a firearm if all of the following requirements are satisfied:

(1) The firearm is unloaded.

(2) The loan is made by a person who is not a dealer but is a federal firearms licensee pursuant to Chapter 44 of Title 18 (commencing with Section 921) of the United States Code.

(3) The loan is made to a person who possesses a valid entertainment firearms permit issued pursuant to Chapter 2 (commencing with Section 29500) of Division 8.

(4) The firearm is loaned for use solely as a prop in a motion picture, television, video, theatrical, or other entertainment production or event.

(b) The person loaning the firearm pursuant to this section shall retain a photocopy of the entertainment firearms permit as proof of compliance with this requirement. *(Added by Stats.2010, c. 711 (S.B.1080), § 6, operative Jan. 1, 2012.)*

Law Revision Commission Comments

Section 27810 continues former Section 12078(s)(2) without substantive change, as that provision applied to former Section 12072(f)(1).

See Sections 16520 ("firearm"), 26700 ("dealer," "licensee," or "person licensed pursuant to Sections 26700 to 26915, inclusive"). [38 Cal.L.Rev. Comm. Reports 217 (2009)].

Cross References

Dealer defined, see Penal Code § 26700.
Firearm defined for purposes of this Part, see Penal Code § 16520.
Licensee defined, see Penal Code § 26700.

§ 27815. Loan of firearm to consultant-evaluator; application of Section 27555

(a) Section 27555 does not apply to the loan of an unloaded firearm to a consultant-evaluator by a person licensed pursuant to Sections 26700 to 26915, inclusive, if the loan does not exceed 45 days from the date of delivery.

(b) At the time of the loan, the consultant-evaluator shall provide the following information, which the dealer shall retain for two years:

(1) A photocopy of a valid, current, government-issued identification to determine the consultant-evaluator's identity, including, but not limited to, a California driver's license, identification card, or passport.

(2) A photocopy of the consultant-evaluator's valid, current certificate of eligibility.

(3) A letter from the person licensed as an importer, manufacturer, or dealer pursuant to Chapter 44 (commencing with Section 921) of Title 18 of the United States Code, with whom the consultant-evaluator has a bona fide business relationship. The letter shall detail the bona fide business purposes for which the firearm is being loaned and confirm that the consultant-evaluator is being loaned the firearm as part of a bona fide business relationship.

(4) The signature of the consultant-evaluator on a form indicating the date the firearm is loaned and the last day the firearm may be returned. *(Added by Stats.2010, c. 711 (S.B.1080), § 6, operative Jan. 1, 2012.)*

Law Revision Commission Comments

Section 27815 continues former Section 12078(s)(4) without substantive change, as that provision applied to former Section 12072(f)(1).

See Sections 16410 ("consultant-evaluator"), 16520 ("firearm"), 26700 ("dealer," "licensee," or "person licensed pursuant to Sections 26700 to 26915, inclusive"). [38 Cal.L.Rev.Comm. Reports 217 (2009)].

Cross References

Consultant-evaluator defined for purposes of this Part, see Penal Code § 16410.
Firearm defined for purposes of this Part, see Penal Code § 16520.

§ 27820. Sale, loan, or transfer of firearm by or to collector; sale, loan, or transfer of firearm by or to importer or manufacturer; application of Section 27555

(a) Section 27555 does not apply to the sale, loan, or transfer of a firearm by or to a person who is licensed as a collector pursuant to Chapter 44 (commencing with Section 921) of Title 18 of the United States Code and the regulations issued pursuant thereto who is not otherwise licensed as a dealer, manufacturer, or importer of firearms licensed to engage in that business pursuant to Chapter 44 (commencing with Section 921) of Title 18 of the United States Code and the regulations issued pursuant thereto.

(b) Section 27555 does not apply to the sale, loan, or transfer of a firearm if both of the following conditions apply:

(1) The sale, loan, or transfer is by or to a person who is licensed as an importer or manufacturer of ammunition licensed to engage in business pursuant to Chapter 44 (commencing with Section 921) of Title 18 of the United States Code and the regulations issued pursuant thereto.

(2) The person selling, loaning, or transferring the firearm or purchasing that firearm, being transferred that firearm, or being

loaned that firearm is not also licensed as an importer or manufacturer of firearms who is licensed to engage in business pursuant to Chapter 44 (commencing with Section 921) of Title 18 of the United States Code and the regulations issued pursuant thereto. *(Added by Stats.2019, c. 738 (S.B.376), § 21, eff. Jan. 1, 2020.)*

Cross References

Firearm defined for purposes of this Part, see Penal Code § 16520.
Handgun defined for purposes of this Part, see Penal Code § 16640.

§ 27825. Delivery of firearm to gunsmith for repair; application of Section 27555

Section 27555 does not apply to the delivery of a firearm to a gunsmith for service or repair, or to the return of the firearm to its owner by the gunsmith, or to the delivery of a firearm by a gunsmith to a person licensed pursuant to Chapter 44 (commencing with Section 921) of Title 18 of the United States Code for service or repair and the return of the firearm to the gunsmith. *(Added by Stats.2010, c. 711 (S.B.1080), § 6, operative Jan. 1, 2012.)*

Law Revision Commission Comments

Section 27825 continues former Section 12078(e)(1) without substantive change, as that provision applied to former Section 12072(f)(1).

See Sections 16520 ("firearm"), 16630 ("gunsmith"). [38 Cal.L.Rev.Comm. Reports 217 (2009)].

Cross References

Firearm defined for purposes of this Part, see Penal Code § 16520.
Gunsmith defined for purposes of this Part, see Penal Code § 16630.

§ 27830. Transfer of firearm where transferor and transferee are same; application of Section 27555

Section 27555 does not apply where the transferor and the transferee are the same person or corporation. *(Added by Stats.2010, c. 711 (S.B.1080), § 6, operative Jan. 1, 2012.)*

Law Revision Commission Comments

Section 27830 continues former Section 12078(e)(2)(A) without substantive change. [38 Cal.L.Rev.Comm. Reports 217 (2009)].

§ 27835. Transfer of firearm for use as prop; application of Section 27555

Section 27555 does not apply where the transfer is to or from a person who has a valid entertainment firearms permit and the transfer involves the loan or return of a firearm used solely as a prop in a television, film, or theatrical production. *(Added by Stats.2010, c. 711 (S.B.1080), § 6, operative Jan. 1, 2012.)*

Law Revision Commission Comments

Section 27835 continues former Section 12078(e)(2)(B) without substantive change.

For the provisions governing issuance of an entertainment firearms permit, see Sections 29500–29535. [38 Cal.L.Rev.Comm. Reports 217 (2009)].

Cross References

Firearm defined for purposes of this Part, see Penal Code § 16520.

ARTICLE 6. EXCEPTIONS TO THE REQUIREMENT OF USING A DEALER FOR A PRIVATE PARTY FIREARMS TRANSACTION

§ 27850. Sale, delivery, or transfer of firearm to authorized representative of government entity as part of authorized program; application of Section 27545

(a) Section 27545 does not apply to a sale, delivery, or transfer of firearms if both of the following requirements are satisfied:

(1) The sale, delivery, or transfer is to an authorized representative of a city, city and county, county, or state government, or of the federal government, and is for the governmental entity.

(2) The entity is acquiring the weapon as part of an authorized, voluntary program in which the entity is buying or receiving weapons from private individuals.

(b) Any weapons acquired pursuant to this section shall be disposed of pursuant to the applicable provisions of Section 34000 or Sections 18000 and 18005. *(Added by Stats.2010, c. 711 (S.B.1080), § 6, operative Jan. 1, 2012.)*

Law Revision Commission Comments

Section 27850 continues former Section 12078(a)(6) without substantive change, as that provision applied to former Section 12072(d).

See Section 16520 ("firearm"). [38 Cal.L.Rev.Comm. Reports 217 (2009)].

Cross References

Firearm defined for purposes of this Part, see Penal Code § 16520.

Research References

2 Witkin, California Criminal Law 4th Crimes Against Public Peace and Welfare § 198 (2021), Transfers by Persons Not Licensed in California.
2 Witkin, California Criminal Law 4th Crimes Against Public Peace and Welfare § 208 (2021), Exempt Activities.

§ 27855. Sale, delivery, loan, or transfer of firearm by law enforcement representative to certain entities; application of Section 27545

Section 27545 does not apply to the sale, delivery, loan, or transfer of a firearm made by an authorized law enforcement representative of a city, county, city and county, or state, or of the federal government, to any public or private nonprofit historical society, museum, or institutional collection, or the purchase or receipt of that firearm by that public or private nonprofit historical society, museum, or institutional collection, if all of the following conditions are met:

(a) The entity receiving the firearm is open to the public.

(b) The firearm prior to delivery is deactivated or rendered inoperable.

(c) The firearm is not subject to any of the following:

(1) Sections 18000 and 18005.

(2) Division 4 (commencing with Section 18250) of Title 2.

(3) Section 34000.

(4) Sections 34005 and 34010.

(d) The firearm is not prohibited by other provisions of law from being sold, delivered, or transferred to the public at large.

(e) Prior to delivery, the entity receiving the firearm submits a written statement to the law enforcement representative stating that the firearm will not be restored to operating condition, and will either remain with that entity, or if subsequently disposed of, will be transferred in accordance with the applicable provisions listed in Section 16575 and, if applicable, with Section 31615.

(f) Within 10 days of the date that the firearm is sold, loaned, delivered, or transferred to that entity, all of the following information shall be reported to the department in a manner prescribed by the department:

(1) The name of the government entity delivering the firearm.

(2) The make, model, serial number, and other identifying characteristics of the firearm.

(3) The name of the person authorized by the entity to take possession of the firearm.

(g) In the event of a change in the status of the designated representative, the entity shall notify the department of a new representative within 30 days. *(Added by Stats.2010, c. 711 (S.B. 1080), § 6, operative Jan. 1, 2012.)*

Law Revision Commission Comments

Section 27855 continues former Section 12078(a)(7) without substantive change, as that provision applied to former Section 12072(d).

See Section 16520 ("firearm"). [38 Cal.L.Rev.Comm. Reports 217 (2009)].

Cross References

Firearm defined for purposes of this Part, see Penal Code § 16520.

§ 27860. Sale, delivery, loan, or transfer of firearm by person other than law enforcement representative to certain entities; application of Section 27545

Section 27545 does not apply to the sale, delivery, loan, or transfer of a firearm made by any person other than a representative of an authorized law enforcement agency to any public or private nonprofit historical society, museum, or institutional collection, if all of the following conditions are met:

(a) The entity receiving the firearm is open to the public.

(b) The firearm is deactivated or rendered inoperable prior to delivery.

(c) The firearm is not of a type prohibited from being sold, delivered, or transferred to the public.

(d) Prior to delivery, the entity receiving the firearm submits a written statement to the person selling, loaning, or transferring the firearm stating that the firearm will not be restored to operating condition, and will either remain with that entity, or if subsequently disposed of, will be transferred in accordance with the applicable provisions listed in Section 16575 and, if applicable, with Section 31615.

(e) If title to a handgun, and commencing January 1, 2014, any firearm, is being transferred to the public or private nonprofit historical society, museum, or institutional collection, then the designated representative of that entity shall, within 30 days of taking possession of that firearm, forward by prepaid mail or deliver in person to the Department of Justice, a single report signed by both parties to the transaction, which includes all of the following information:

(1) Information identifying the person representing the public or private historical society, museum, or institutional collection.

(2) Information on how title was obtained and from whom.

(3) A description of the firearm in question.

(4) A copy of the written statement referred to in subdivision (d).

(f) The report forms that are to be completed pursuant to this section shall be provided by the Department of Justice.

(g) In the event of a change in the status of the designated representative, the entity shall notify the department of a new representative within 30 days. *(Added by Stats.2010, c. 711 (S.B. 1080), § 6, operative Jan. 1, 2012. Amended by Stats.2011, c. 745 (A.B.809), § 38.)*

Law Revision Commission Comments

Section 27860 continues former Section 12078(a)(8) without substantive change, as that provision applied to former Section 12072(d).

See Sections 16520 ("firearm"), 16640 ("handgun"). [38 Cal.L.Rev.Comm. Reports 217 (2009)].

Cross References

Firearm defined for purposes of this Part, see Penal Code § 16520.

Handgun defined for purposes of this Part, see Penal Code § 16640.

§ 27865. Sale, delivery, or transfer of firearms between or to importers or manufacturers; application of Section 27545

Section 27545 does not apply to sales, deliveries, or transfers of firearms between or to importers and manufacturers of firearms licensed to engage in that business pursuant to Chapter 44 (commencing with Section 921) of Title 18 of the United States Code and the regulations issued pursuant thereto. *(Added by Stats.2010, c. 711 (S.B.1080), § 6, operative Jan. 1, 2012.)*

Law Revision Commission Comments

Section 27865 continues former Section 12078(b)(1) without substantive change, as that provision applied to former Section 12072(d).

See Section 16520 ("firearm"). [38 Cal.L.Rev.Comm. Reports 217 (2009)].

Cross References

Firearm defined for purposes of this Part, see Penal Code § 16520.

§ 27875. Transfer of firearm by gift or bequest; application of Section 27545; importation, bringing or transportation of firearm into the state

(a) Section 27545 does not apply to the transfer of a firearm by gift, bequest, intestate succession, or other means from one individual to another, if all of the following requirements are met:

(1) The transfer is infrequent, as defined in Section 16730.

(2) The transfer is between members of the same immediate family.

(3) Within 30 days of taking possession of the firearm, the person to whom it is transferred shall submit a report to the Department of Justice, in a manner prescribed by the department, that includes information concerning the individual taking possession of the firearm, how title was obtained and from whom, and a description of the firearm in question. The reports that individuals complete pursuant to this subdivision shall be made available to them in a format prescribed by the department.

(4) Until January 1, 2015, the person taking title to the firearm shall first obtain a valid handgun safety certificate if the firearm is a handgun, and commencing January 1, 2015, a valid firearm safety certificate for any firearm, except that in the case of a handgun, a valid unexpired handgun safety certificate may be used.

(5) The person receiving the firearm is 18 years of age or older.

(b) Subdivision (a) of Section 27585 does not apply to a person who imports a firearm into this state, brings a firearm into this state, or transports a firearm into this state if all of the following requirements are met:

(1) The person acquires ownership of the firearm from an immediate family member by bequest or intestate succession.

(2) The person has obtained a valid firearm safety certificate, except that in the case of a handgun, a valid unexpired handgun safety certificate may be used.

(3) The receipt of any firearm by the individual by bequest or intestate succession is infrequent, as defined in Section 16730.

(4) The person acquiring ownership of the firearm by bequest or intestate succession is 18 years of age or older.

(5) Within 30 days of that person taking possession of the firearm and importing, bringing, or transporting it into this state, the person shall submit a report to the Department of Justice, in a manner prescribed by the department, that includes information concerning the individual taking possession of the firearm, how title was obtained and from whom, and a description of the firearm in question. The reports that individuals complete pursuant to this subdivision shall be made available to them in a format prescribed by the department. *(Added by Stats.2010, c. 711 (S.B.1080), § 6, operative Jan. 1, 2012. Amended by Stats.2011, c. 745 (A.B.809), § 40; Stats.2013, c. 761 (S.B.683), § 7; Stats.2014, c. 878 (A.B.1609), § 7, eff. Jan. 1, 2015.)*

Law Revision Commission Comments

Section 27875 continues former Section 12078(c)(2) without substantive change.

See Sections 16520 ("firearm"), 16640 ("handgun"), 16670 ("handgun safety certificate"), 16720 ("immediate family member"). [38 Cal.L.Rev.Comm. Reports 217 (2009)].

Cross References

Firearm defined for purposes of this Part, see Penal Code § 16520.
Handgun defined for purposes of this Part, see Penal Code § 16640.
Handgun safety certificate defined for purposes of this Part, see Penal Code § 16670.

Research References

2 Witkin, California Criminal Law 4th Crimes Against Public Peace and Welfare § 199 (2021), Importation Restrictions.

§ 27880. Loan of firearm between spouses, registered domestic partners, or other specified relations; application of Section 27545

Section 27545 does not apply to the loan of a firearm if all of the following requirements are satisfied:

(a) The loan is to a spouse, registered domestic partner, or any of the following relations, whether by consanguinity, adoption, or steprelation:

(1) Parent.

(2) Child.

(3) Sibling.

(4) Grandparent.

(5) Grandchild.

(b) The loan is infrequent, as defined in Section 16730.

(c) The loan is for any lawful purpose.

(d) The loan does not exceed 30 days in duration.

(e) Until January 1, 2015, if the firearm is a handgun, the individual being loaned the firearm shall have a valid handgun safety certificate. Commencing January 1, 2015, for any firearm, the individual being loaned the firearm shall have a valid firearm safety certificate, except that in the case of a handgun, an unexpired handgun safety certificate may be used.

(f) If the firearm being loaned is a handgun, the handgun is registered to the person making the loan pursuant to Section 11106. *(Added by Stats.2010, c. 711 (S.B.1080), § 6, operative Jan. 1, 2012. Amended by Stats.2011, c. 745 (A.B.809), § 41; Stats.2013, c. 761 (S.B.683), § 8; Stats.2016, c. 41 (A.B.1511), § 1, eff. Jan. 1, 2017.)*

Law Revision Commission Comments

Section 27880 continues former Section 12078(d)(1) without substantive change.

See Sections 16520 ("firearm"), 16640 ("handgun"), 16670 ("handgun safety certificate"). [38 Cal.L.Rev.Comm. Reports 217 (2009)].

Cross References

Firearm defined for purposes of this Part, see Penal Code § 16520.
Handgun defined for purposes of this Part, see Penal Code § 16640.
Handgun safety certificate defined for purposes of this Part, see Penal Code § 16670.

§ 27881. Loan within lender's place of residence or other real property; application of Section 27545

Section 27545 does not apply to the loan of a firearm if all of the following conditions are met:

(a) If the firearm being loaned is a handgun, the handgun is registered to the person making the loan pursuant to Section 11106.

(b) The loan occurs within the lender's place of residence or other real property, except for property that is zoned for commercial, retail, or industrial activity.

(c) The individual receiving the firearm is not prohibited by state or federal law from possessing, receiving, owning, or purchasing a firearm.

(d) The individual receiving the firearm is 18 years of age or older.

(e) The firearm does not leave the real property upon which the loan occurs. *(Added by Stats.2019, c. 840 (S.B.172), § 10, eff. Jan. 1, 2020.)*

§ 27882. Transfer for safekeeping to prevent suicide; application of Section 27545

(a) Section 27545 does not apply to the transfer of a firearm if all of the following conditions are satisfied:

(1) The firearm is voluntarily and temporarily transferred to another person who is 18 years of age or older for safekeeping to prevent it from being accessed or used to attempt suicide by the transferor or another person that may gain access to it in the transferor's household.

(2) The transferee does not use the firearm for any purpose and, except when transporting the firearm to the transferee's residence or when returning it to the transferor, keeps the firearm unloaded and secured in the transferee's residence in one of the following ways:

(A) Secured in a locked container.

(B) Disabled by a firearm safety device.

(C) Secured within a locked gun safe.

(D) Locked with a locking device as described in Section 16860 that has rendered the firearm inoperable.

(3) The duration of the loan is limited to that amount of time reasonably necessary to prevent the harm described in paragraph (1).

(b)(1) If a firearm that has been transferred pursuant to this section cannot be returned to the owner because the owner is prohibited from possessing a firearm, the person in possession of the firearm shall deliver the firearm to a law enforcement agency without delay.

(2) Section 27545 does not apply to the transfer of a firearm to a law enforcement agency pursuant to this subdivision. This section does not authorize the possession of a firearm by any person prohibited from possessing a firearm pursuant to any other law. *(Added by Stats.2019, c. 840 (S.B.172), § 11, eff. Jan. 1, 2020.)*

§ 27883. Loan stored in receiver's place of residence or enclosed structure on receiver's private property; application of Section 27545

Section 27545 does not apply to the loan of a firearm provided all of the following requirements are met:

(a) The firearm being loaned is registered to the person making the loan pursuant to Section 11106.

(b) The firearm being loaned is stored in the receiver's place of residence or in an enclosed structure on the receiver's private property, which is not zoned for commercial, retail, or industrial activity.

(c) The firearm at all times stays within the receiver's place of residence or in an enclosed structure on the receiver's private property, which is not zoned for commercial, retail, or industrial activity.

(d) The individual receiving the firearm is not prohibited by state or federal law from possessing, receiving, owning, or purchasing a firearm.

(e) The individual receiving the firearm is 18 years of age or older.

(f) One of the following applies:

(1) The firearm is maintained within a locked container.

(2) The firearm is disabled by a firearm safety device.

(3) The firearm is maintained within a locked gun safe.

(4) The firearm is locked with a locking device, as defined in Section 16860, which has rendered the firearm inoperable.

(g) The loan does not exceed 120 days in duration.

(h) The loan is made without consideration.

(i) There is a written document in a format prescribed by the Department of Justice that explains the obligations imposed by this section that is signed by both the party loaning the firearm for storage and the person receiving the firearm.

(j) Both parties to the loan have signed copies of the written document required by subdivision (i). *(Added by Stats.2019, c. 840 (S.B.172), § 12, eff. Jan. 1, 2020.)*

§ 27885. Loan of firearm; application of Section 27545

Section 27545 does not apply to the loan of a firearm if all of the following conditions exist:

(a) The person loaning the firearm is at all times within the presence of the person being loaned the firearm.

(b) The loan is for a lawful purpose.

(c) The loan does not exceed three days in duration.

(d) The individual receiving the firearm is not prohibited by state or federal law from possessing, receiving, owning, or purchasing a firearm.

(e) The person loaning the firearm is 18 years of age or older.

(f) The person being loaned the firearm is 18 years of age or older. *(Added by Stats.2010, c. 711 (S.B.1080), § 6, operative Jan. 1, 2012.)*

Law Revision Commission Comments

Section 27885 continues former Section 12078(d)(2) without substantive change, as that provision applied to former Section 12072(d).

See Section 16520 ("firearm"). [38 Cal.L.Rev.Comm. Reports 217 (2009)].

Cross References

Firearm defined for purposes of this Part, see Penal Code § 16520.

§ 27890. Delivery of firearm to gunsmith for repair; application of Section 27545

Section 27545 does not apply to the delivery of a firearm to a gunsmith for service or repair, or to the return of the firearm to its owner by the gunsmith, or to the delivery of a firearm by a gunsmith to a person licensed pursuant to Chapter 44 (commencing with Section 921) of Title 18 of the United States Code for service or repair and the return of the firearm to the gunsmith. *(Added by Stats.2010, c. 711 (S.B.1080), § 6, operative Jan. 1, 2012.)*

Law Revision Commission Comments

Section 27890 continues former Section 12078(e)(1) without substantive change, as that provision applied to former Section 12072(d).

See Sections 16520 ("firearm"), 16630 ("gunsmith"). [38 Cal.L.Rev.Comm. Reports 217 (2009)].

Cross References

Firearm defined for purposes of this Part, see Penal Code § 16520.
Gunsmith defined for purposes of this Part, see Penal Code § 16630.

§ 27895. Sale, delivery, or transfer of firearms by person in state to person outside of state; application of Section 27545

Section 27545 does not apply to the sale, delivery, or transfer of firearms if all of the following requirements are satisfied:

(a) The sale, delivery, or transfer is made by a person who resides in this state.

(b) The sale, delivery, or transfer is made to a person who resides outside this state and is licensed pursuant to Chapter 44 (commencing with Section 921) of Title 18 of the United States Code and the regulations issued pursuant thereto.

(c) The sale, delivery, or transfer is in accordance with Chapter 44 (commencing with Section 921) of Title 18 of the United States Code and the regulations issued pursuant thereto. *(Added by Stats.2010, c. 711 (S.B.1080), § 6, operative Jan. 1, 2012.)*

Law Revision Commission Comments

Section 27895 continues former Section 12078(f) without substantive change, as that provision applied to former Section 12072(d).

See Section 16520 ("firearm"). [38 Cal.L.Rev.Comm. Reports 217 (2009)].

Cross References

Firearm defined for purposes of this Part, see Penal Code § 16520.

§ 27900. Loan of firearm other than handgun at certain auctions, raffles, or similar events; application of Section 27545

Section 27545 does not apply to the loan of a firearm other than a handgun at an auction, raffle, or similar event conducted by a nonprofit public benefit or mutual benefit corporation organized pursuant to the Corporations Code if all of the following apply:

(a) The firearm at all times remains on the premises where the auction, raffle, or similar event occurs.

(b) The firearm is to be auctioned, raffled, or otherwise sold for the benefit of that nonprofit public benefit or mutual benefit corporation.

(c) The firearm, when sold or otherwise transferred, is delivered to a person licensed pursuant to, and operating in accordance with, Sections 26700 to 26915, inclusive, for sale or other transfer to the person who purchased or otherwise acquired ownership of the firearm. *(Added by Stats.2019, c. 738 (S.B.376), § 23, eff. Jan. 1, 2020.)*

Cross References

Firearm defined for purposes of this Part, see Penal Code § 16520.
Handgun defined for purposes of this Part, see Penal Code § 16640.

§ 27905. Transfer of firearm; donation to auction, raffle, or similar event; application of Section 27545

Section 27545 does not apply to the transfer of a firearm if all of the following requirements are satisfied:

(a) The firearm is not a handgun.

(b) The firearm is donated for an auction, raffle, or similar event described in Section 27900.

(c) The firearm is delivered to the nonprofit corporation immediately preceding, or contemporaneous with, the auction, raffle, or similar event. *(Added by Stats.2010, c. 711 (S.B.1080), § 6, operative Jan. 1, 2012. Amended by Stats.2019, c. 738 (S.B.376), § 24, eff. Jan. 1, 2020.)*

Law Revision Commission Comments

Section 27905 continues former Section 12078(g)(2) without substantive change.

See Sections 16520 ("firearm"), 16640 ("handgun"). [38 Cal.L.Rev.Comm. Reports 217 (2009)].

Cross References

Firearm defined for purposes of this Part, see Penal Code § 16520.
Handgun defined for purposes of this Part, see Penal Code § 16640.

§ 27910. Loan of firearm to person 18 years of age or older for target shooting at target facility; application of Section 27545

Section 27545 does not apply to the loan of a firearm to a person 18 years of age or older for the purposes of shooting at targets if the loan occurs on the premises of a target facility that holds a business or regulatory license or on the premises of any club or organization organized for the purposes of practicing shooting at targets upon established ranges, whether public or private, if the firearm is at all times kept within the premises of the target range or on the premises of the club or organization. *(Added by Stats.2010, c. 711 (S.B.1080), § 6, operative Jan. 1, 2012.)*

Law Revision Commission Comments

Section 27910 continues former Section 12078(h) without substantive change, as that provision applied to former Section 12072(d).

See Section 16520 ("firearm"). [38 Cal.L.Rev.Comm. Reports 217 (2009)].

Cross References

Firearm defined for purposes of this Part, see Penal Code § 16520.

§ 27920. Taking title or possession of firearm by operation of law; application of Section 27545; importation, bringing or transportation of firearm into the state

(a) Section 27545 does not apply to a person who takes title or possession of a firearm by operation of law if the person is not prohibited by state or federal law from possessing, receiving, owning, or purchasing a firearm and all of the following conditions are met:

(1) If the person taking title or possession is neither a levying officer as defined in Section 481.140, 511.060, or 680.260 of the Code of Civil Procedure, nor a person who is receiving that firearm pursuant to subdivision (g), (h), (i), (j), (*l*), or (q) of Section 16990, the person shall, within 30 days of taking possession, submit a report to the Department of Justice, in a manner prescribed by the department, that includes information concerning the individual taking possession of the firearm, how title or possession was obtained and from whom, and a description of the firearm in question.

(2) If the person taking title or possession is receiving the firearm pursuant to subdivision (g), (h), (*l*), or (q) of Section 16990, the person shall do both of the following:

(A) Within 30 days of taking possession, submit a report to the Department of Justice, in a manner prescribed by the department, that includes information concerning the individual taking possession of the firearm, how title or possession was obtained and from whom, and a description of the firearm in question.

(B) Prior to taking title or possession of the firearm, the person shall obtain a valid firearm safety certificate, except that in the case of a handgun, a valid unexpired handgun safety certificate may be presented.

(3) Where the person receiving title or possession of the firearm is a person described in subdivision (i) of Section 16990, on the date that the person is delivered the firearm, the name and other information concerning the person taking possession of the firearm, how title or possession of the firearm was obtained and from whom, and a description of the firearm by make, model, serial number, and other identifying characteristics shall be entered into the Automated Firearms System (AFS) via the California Law Enforcement Telecommunications System (CLETS) by the law enforcement or state agency that transferred or delivered the firearm, provided, however, that if the firearm is not a handgun and does not have a serial number, identification number, or identification mark assigned to it, that fact shall be noted in AFS. An agency without access to AFS shall arrange with the sheriff of the county in which the agency is located to input this information via this system.

(4) Where the person receiving title or possession of the firearm is a person described in subdivision (j) of Section 16990, on the date that the person is delivered the firearm, the name and other information concerning the person taking possession of the firearm, how title or possession of the firearm was obtained and from whom, and a description of the firearm by make, model, serial number, and other identifying characteristics shall be entered into the AFS via the CLETS by the law enforcement or state agency that transferred or

delivered the firearm, provided, however, that if the firearm is not a handgun and does not have a serial number, identification number, or identification mark assigned to it, that fact shall be noted in AFS. An agency without access to AFS shall arrange with the sheriff of the county in which the agency is located to input this information via this system. In addition, that law enforcement agency shall not deliver the firearm to the person referred to in this subdivision unless, prior to the delivery of the firearm, the person presents proof to the agency that the person is the holder of a valid firearm safety certificate, except that in the case of a handgun, a valid unexpired handgun safety certificate may be presented.

(b) Subdivision (a) of Section 27585 does not apply to a person who imports a firearm into this state, brings a firearm into this state, or transports a firearm into this state if all of the following requirements are met:

(1) The person acquires ownership of the firearm as an executor, personal representative, or administrator of an estate, or as the trustee of a trust that includes a firearm and that was part of a will that created the trust.

(2) If acquisition of the firearm had occurred within this state, the receipt of the firearm by the executor, personal representative, trustee, or administrator would be exempt from the provisions of Section 27545 pursuant to paragraph (1) of subdivision (a).

(3) Within 30 days of taking possession of the firearm and importing, bringing, or transporting it into this state, the person shall submit a report to the Department of Justice, in a manner prescribed by the department, that includes information concerning the individual taking possession of the firearm, how title was obtained and from whom, and a description of the firearm in question.

(4) If the executor, personal representative, trustee, or administrator subsequently acquires ownership of that firearm in an individual capacity, prior to transferring ownership to themselves, they shall obtain a valid firearm safety certificate, except that in the case of a handgun, a valid unexpired handgun safety certificate may be used.

(5) The executor, personal representative, trustee, or administrator is 18 years of age or older.

(c) Subdivision (a) of Section 27585 does not apply to a person who imports a firearm into this state, brings a firearm into this state, or transports a firearm into this state if all of the following requirements are met:

(1) The person acquires ownership of the firearm by bequest or intestate succession as a surviving spouse or as the surviving registered domestic partner of the decedent who owned that firearm.

(2) If acquisition of the firearm had occurred within this state, the receipt of the firearm by the surviving spouse or registered domestic partner would be exempt from the provisions of Section 27545 pursuant to paragraph (2) of subdivision (a) by virtue of subdivision (h) of Section 16990.

(3) Within 30 days of taking possession of the firearm and importing, bringing, or transporting it into this state, the person shall submit a report to the Department of Justice, in a manner prescribed by the department, that includes information concerning the individual taking possession of the firearm, how title was obtained and from whom, and a description of the firearm in question.

(4) The person has obtained a valid firearm safety certificate, except that in the case of a handgun, a valid unexpired handgun safety certificate may be used.

(d) Subdivision (a) of Section 27585 does not apply to a person who imports a firearm into this state, brings a firearm into this state, or transports a firearm into this state if all of the following requirements are met:

(1) The firearm is imported into this country pursuant to provisions of Section 925(a)(4) of Title 18 of the United States Code.

(2) The person is not subject to the requirements of Section 27560.

(3) The firearm is not a firearm that is prohibited by any provision listed in Section 16590.

(4) The firearm is not an assault weapon.

(5) The firearm is not a machinegun.

(6) The firearm is not a .50 BMG rifle.

(7) The firearm is not a destructive device.

(8) The person is 18 years of age or older.

(9) Within 30 days of that person taking possession of the firearm and importing, bringing, or transporting it into this state, the person shall submit a report to the Department of Justice, in a manner prescribed by the department, that includes information concerning the individual taking possession of the firearm, how title was obtained and from whom, and a description of the firearm in question.

(e) The reports that individuals complete pursuant to this section shall be made available to them in a format prescribed by the Department of Justice. *(Added by Stats.2010, c. 711 (S.B.1080), § 6, operative Jan. 1, 2012. Amended by Stats.2011, c. 745 (A.B.809), § 43; Stats.2013, c. 761 (S.B.683), § 9; Stats.2014, c. 878 (A.B.1609), § 8, eff. Jan. 1, 2015; Stats.2019, c. 110 (A.B.1292), § 8, eff. Jan. 1, 2020.)*

Law Revision Commission Comments

Section 27920 continues former Section 12078(i)(2) without substantive change. An erroneous cross-reference to Code of Civil Procedure Section 680.210 has been corrected by replacing it with a cross-reference to Code of Civil Procedure Section 680.260.

See Sections 16520 ("firearm"), 16640 ("handgun"), 16990 ("person taking title or possession of a firearm by operation of law"). [38 Cal.L.Rev.Comm. Reports 217 (2009)].

Cross References

Firearm defined for purposes of this Part, see Penal Code § 16520.
Handgun defined for purposes of this Part, see Penal Code § 16640.
Handgun safety certificate defined for purposes of this Part, see Penal Code § 16670.

§ 27922. Taking possession of firearm; delivery or return of firearm to law enforcement agency; application of Section 27545

(a) Section 27545 does not apply to a person who takes possession of a firearm and subsequently delivers that firearm to a law enforcement agency if all of the following requirements are met:

(1) The person found the firearm or took the firearm from a person who was committing a crime against the person who took the firearm.

(2) The person taking possession of that firearm subsequently delivers the firearm to a law enforcement agency.

(3) The person gives prior notice to the law enforcement agency that the person is transporting the firearm to the law enforcement agency for disposition according to law.

(b) Except as provided in paragraph (4) of subdivision (a) of Section 27920, any firearms that are delivered to a law enforcement agency pursuant to this section that are not subject to the applicable provisions of Sections 18000, 18005, or 34000, shall, if the person has requested the firearm and is eligible to receive it, be returned to that person in accordance with Chapter 2 (commencing with Section 33850) of Division 11. *(Added by Stats.2019, c. 110 (A.B.1292), § 9, eff. Jan. 1, 2020.)*

Research References

2 Witkin, California Criminal Law 4th Crimes Against Public Peace and Welfare § 193 (2021), Sale, Lease, or Transfer by Unlicensed Person.

§ 27925. Taking possession of firearm by operation of law in representative capacity; transfer to himself or herself in individual capacity; application of Section 27545

(a) Section 27545 does not apply to a person who takes possession of a firearm by operation of law in a representative capacity who subsequently transfers ownership of the firearm to himself or herself in an individual capacity.

(b) Until January 1, 2015, in the case of a handgun, the individual shall obtain a handgun safety certificate prior to transferring ownership to himself or herself, or taking possession of a handgun in an individual capacity. Beginning January 1, 2015, the individual shall obtain a firearm safety certificate prior to transferring ownership to himself or herself, or taking possession of a firearm in an individual capacity, except that in the case of a handgun, an unexpired handgun safety certificate may be used. *(Added by Stats.2010, c. 711 (S.B.1080), § 6, operative Jan. 1, 2012. Amended by Stats.2013, c. 761 (S.B.683), § 10.)*

Law Revision Commission Comments

Section 27925 continues former Section 12078(i)(3) without substantive change.

See Sections 16520 ("firearm"), 16640 ("handgun"), 16670 ("handgun safety certificate"), 16990 ("person taking title or possession of a firearm by operation of law"). [38 Cal.L.Rev.Comm. Reports 217 (2009)].

Cross References

Firearm defined for purposes of this Part, see Penal Code § 16520.
Handgun defined for purposes of this Part, see Penal Code § 16640.
Handgun safety certificate defined for purposes of this Part, see Penal Code § 16670.

§ 27930. Delivery, transfer, or return of firearm under certain statutes; application of Section 27545

Section 27545 does not apply to deliveries, transfers, or returns of firearms made pursuant to any of the following:

(a) Sections 18000 and 18005.

(b) Division 4 (commencing with Section 18250) of Title 2.

(c) Chapter 2 (commencing with Section 33850) of Division 11.

(d) Sections 34005 and 34010.

(e) Section 29810. *(Added by Stats.2010, c. 711 (S.B.1080), § 6, operative Jan. 1, 2012. Amended by Initiative Measure (Prop. 63, § 10.2, approved Nov. 8, 2016, eff. Nov. 9, 2016).)*

Law Revision Commission Comments

Section 27930 continues former Section 12078(j) without substantive change, as that provision applied to former Section 12072(d).

See Section 16520 ("firearm"). [38 Cal.L.Rev.Comm. Reports 217 (2009)].

Cross References

Firearm defined for purposes of this Part, see Penal Code § 16520.

§ 27935. Sale, delivery, or transfer of firearm to wholesaler as merchandise; application of Section 27545

Section 27545 does not apply to the sale, delivery, or transfer of unloaded firearms to a wholesaler as merchandise in the wholesaler's business by a manufacturer or importer licensed to engage in that business pursuant to Chapter 44 (commencing with Section 921) of Title 18 of the United States Code and the regulations issued pursuant thereto, or by another wholesaler, if the sale, delivery, or transfer is made in accordance with Chapter 44 (commencing with Section 921) of Title 18 of the United States Code. *(Added by Stats.2010, c. 711 (S.B.1080), § 6, operative Jan. 1, 2012.)*

Law Revision Commission Comments

Section 27935 continues former Section 12078(m) without substantive change, as that provision applied to former Section 12072(d).

See Sections 16520 ("firearm"), 17340 ("wholesaler"). [38 Cal.L.Rev. Comm. Reports 217 (2009)].

Cross References

Firearm defined for purposes of this Part, see Penal Code § 16520.
Wholesaler defined for purposes of this Part, see Penal Code § 17340.

§ 27937. Sale, delivery, or transfer to manufacturer, importer, or wholesaler by person who has ceased operations as a dealer; application of Section 27545

Section 27545 does not apply to sales, deliveries, or transfers of firearms made pursuant to Section 26556. *(Added by Stats.2019, c. 738 (S.B.376), § 25, eff. Jan. 1, 2020.)*

§ 27940. Sale, delivery, or transfer of firearm regulated pursuant to certain statutes; application of Section 27545

Section 27545 does not apply to the sale, delivery, or transfer of a firearm regulated pursuant to any of the following statutes, if the sale, delivery, or transfer of that firearm is conducted in accordance with the applicable provisions of the statute:

(a) Chapter 1 (commencing with Section 18710) of Division 5 of Title 2, relating to destructive devices and explosives.

(b) Section 24410, relating to cane guns, and the exemptions in Chapter 1 (commencing with Section 17700) of Title 2, as they relate to cane guns.

(c) Section 24510, relating to firearms that are not immediately recognizable as firearms, and the exemptions in Chapter 1 (commencing with Section 17700) of Title 2, as they relate to firearms that are not immediately recognizable as firearms.

(d) Sections 24610 and 24680, relating to undetectable firearms, and the exemptions in Chapter 1 (commencing with Section 17700) of Title 2, as they relate to undetectable firearms.

(e) Section 24710, relating to wallet guns, and the exemptions in Chapter 1 (commencing with Section 17700) of Title 2, as they relate to wallet guns.

(f) Chapter 2 (commencing with Section 30500) of Division 10, relating to assault weapons.

(g) Section 31500, relating to unconventional pistols, and the exemptions in Chapter 1 (commencing with Section 17700) of Title 2, as they relate to unconventional pistols.

(h) Sections 33215 to 33225, inclusive, relating to short-barreled rifles and short-barreled shotguns, and the exemptions in Chapter 1 (commencing with Section 17700) of Title 2, as they relate to short-barreled rifles and short-barreled shotguns.

(i) Chapter 6 (commencing with Section 32610) of Division 10, relating to machineguns.

(j) Section 33600, relating to zip guns, and the exemptions in Chapter 1 (commencing with Section 17700) of Title 2, as they relate to zip guns. *(Added by Stats.2010, c. 711 (S.B.1080), § 6, operative Jan. 1, 2012.)*

Law Revision Commission Comments

Section 27940 continues former Section 12078(*o*) without substantive change, as that provision applied to former Section 12072(d).

See Sections 16330 ("cane gun"), 16460 ("destructive device"), 16510 ("explosive"), 16520 ("firearm"), 16880 ("machinegun"), 17170 ("short-barreled rifle"), 17180 ("short-barreled shotgun"), 17270 ("unconventional pistol"), 17280 ("undetectable firearm"), 17330 ("wallet gun"), 17360 ("zip gun"), 30510 ("assault weapon"), 30515 (further clarification of "assault weapon"). [38 Cal.L.Rev.Comm. Reports 217 (2009)].

Cross References

Cane gun defined for purposes of this Part, see Penal Code § 16330.

Firearm defined for purposes of this Part, see Penal Code § 16520.
Machinegun defined for purposes of this Part, see Penal Code § 16880.
Pistol defined for purposes of this Part, see Penal Code § 16530.
Unconventional pistol defined for purposes of this Part, see Penal Code § 17270.
Undetectable firearm defined for purposes of this Part, see Penal Code § 17280.
Wallet gun defined for purposes of this Part, see Penal Code § 17330.
Zip gun defined for purposes of this Part, see Penal Code § 17360.

Research References

2 Witkin, California Criminal Law 4th Crimes Against Public Peace and Welfare § 201 (2021), Punishment.

§ 27945. Loan of firearm to minor; application of Section 27545

Section 27545 does not apply to the loan of a firearm to a minor in compliance with the applicable exemptions set forth in Section 27505. *(Added by Stats.2021, c. 250 (S.B.715), § 11, eff. Jan. 1, 2022.)*

Cross References

Firearm defined for purposes of this Part, see Penal Code § 16520.
Handgun defined for purposes of this Part, see Penal Code § 16640.

§ 27950. Loan of firearm to licensed hunter during hunting season; application of Section 27545

Section 27545 does not apply to the loan of a firearm, other than a handgun, to a licensed hunter for use by that hunter for a period of time not to exceed the duration of the hunting season for which the firearm is to be used. *(Added by Stats.2010, c. 711 (S.B.1080), § 6, operative Jan. 1, 2012.)*

Law Revision Commission Comments

Section 27950 continues former Section 12078(q) without substantive change.

See Sections 16520 ("firearm"), 16640 ("handgun"). [38 Cal.L.Rev.Comm. Reports 217 (2009)].

Cross References

Firearm defined for purposes of this Part, see Penal Code § 16520.
Handgun defined for purposes of this Part, see Penal Code § 16640.

§ 27955. Loan of firearm for use as prop; application of Section 27545

Section 27545 does not apply to the loan of a firearm if all of the following requirements are satisfied:

(a) The loan is infrequent, as defined in Section 16730.

(b) The firearm is unloaded.

(c) The loan is made by a person who is neither a dealer nor a federal firearms licensee pursuant to Chapter 44 (commencing with Section 921) of Title 18 of the United States Code.

(d) The loan is made to a person 18 years of age or older.

(e) The loan is for use solely as a prop in a motion picture, television, video, theatrical, or other entertainment production or event. *(Added by Stats.2010, c. 711 (S.B.1080), § 6, operative Jan. 1, 2012.)*

Law Revision Commission Comments

Section 27955 continues former Section 12078(s)(1) without substantive change, as that provision applied to former Section 12072(d).

See Sections 16520 ("firearm"), 26700 ("dealer," "licensee," or "person licensed pursuant to Sections 26700 to 26915, inclusive"). [38 Cal.L.Rev. Comm. Reports 217 (2009)].

Cross References

Dealer defined, see Penal Code § 26700.
Firearm defined for purposes of this Part, see Penal Code § 16520.
Licensee defined, see Penal Code § 26700.

§ 27960. Loan of firearm by federal firearms licensee for use as prop; application of Section 27545

(a) Section 27545 does not apply to the loan of a firearm if all of the following requirements are satisfied:

(1) The firearm is unloaded.

(2) The loan is made by a person who is not a dealer but is a federal firearms licensee pursuant to Chapter 44 (commencing with Section 921) of Title 18 of the United States Code.

(3) The loan is made to a person who possesses a valid entertainment firearms permit issued pursuant to Chapter 2 (commencing with Section 29500) of Division 8.

(4) The firearm is loaned for use solely as a prop in a motion picture, television, video, theatrical, or other entertainment production or event.

(b) The person loaning the firearm pursuant to this section shall retain a photocopy of the entertainment firearms permit as proof of compliance with this requirement. *(Added by Stats.2010, c. 711 (S.B.1080), § 6, operative Jan. 1, 2012.)*

Law Revision Commission Comments

Section 27960 continues former Section 12078(s)(2) without substantive change, as that provision applied to former Section 12072(d).

See Sections 16520 ("firearm"), 26700 ("dealer," "licensee," or "person licensed pursuant to Sections 26700 to 26915, inclusive"). [38 Cal.L.Rev. Comm. Reports 217 (2009)].

Cross References

Dealer defined, see Penal Code § 26700.
Firearm defined for purposes of this Part, see Penal Code § 16520.
Licensee defined, see Penal Code § 26700.

§ 27963. Sale, delivery, or transfer of firearms between or to manufacturers of ammunition; application of Section 27545

Section 27545 does not apply to the sale, delivery, or transfer of firearms between or to manufacturers of ammunition licensed to engage in that business pursuant to Chapter 44 (commencing with Section 921) of Title 18 of the United States Code and the regulations issued pursuant thereto where those firearms are to be used in the course and scope of the licensee's activities as a person licensed pursuant to Chapter 44 (commencing with Section 921) of Title 18 of the United States Code and the regulations issued pursuant thereto. *(Added by Stats.2021, c. 250 (S.B.715), § 12, eff. Jan. 1, 2022.)*

§ 27966. Sale, loan, or transfer of firearm to licensed collector; application of Section 27545

If all of the following requirements are satisfied, Section 27545 shall not apply to the sale, loan, or transfer of a firearm:

(a) The firearm is not a handgun.

(b) The firearm is a curio or relic, as defined in Section 478.11 of Title 27 of the Code of Federal Regulations, or its successor.

(c) The person receiving the firearm has a current certificate of eligibility issued pursuant to Section 26710.

(d) The person receiving the firearm is licensed as a collector pursuant to Chapter 44 of Title 18 of the United States Code and the regulations issued thereto.

(e) Within 30 days of taking possession of the firearm, the person to whom it is transferred shall forward by prepaid mail, or deliver in person to the Department of Justice, a report that includes information concerning the individual taking possession of the firearm, how title was obtained and from whom, and a description of the firearm in question. The report forms that individuals complete pursuant to this section shall be provided to them by the department. *(Added by*

Stats.2011, c. 745 (A.B.809), § 45. Amended by Stats.2019, c. 738 (S.B.376), § 26, eff. Jan. 1, 2020.)

Cross References

Firearm defined for purposes of this Part, see Penal Code § 16520.
Handgun defined for purposes of this Part, see Penal Code § 16640.

§ 27970. Loan of firearm to person enrolled in peace officer training program for purposes of course participation; application of Section 27545

Section 27545 does not apply to the loan of a firearm if the loan of the firearm is to a person enrolled in the course of basic training prescribed by the Commission on Peace Officer Standards and Training, or any other course certified by the commission, for purposes of participation in the course. *(Added by Stats.2017, c. 783 (A.B.693), § 2, eff. Oct. 14, 2017.)*

ARTICLE 7. REPORT TO DEPARTMENT OF JUSTICE

§ 28000. Report to Department of Justice by persons otherwise exempt

A person who is exempt from Section 27545 or is otherwise not required by law to report acquisition, ownership, destruction, or disposal of a firearm, or who moves out of this state with the person's firearm, may report that information to the Department of Justice in a format prescribed by the department. *(Added by Stats.2010, c. 711 (S.B.1080), § 6, operative Jan. 1, 2012. Amended by Stats.2011, c. 745 (A.B.809), § 46; Stats.2013, c. 738 (A.B.538), § 6.)*

Law Revision Commission Comments

Section 28000 continues former Section 12078(*l*) without substantive change. See Section 16640 ("handgun"). [38 Cal.L.Rev.Comm. Reports 217 (2009)].

Cross References

Firearm defined for purposes of this Part, see Penal Code § 16520.
Firearm register or record of electronic transfer, required information, see Penal Code § 28160.
Handgun defined for purposes of this Part, see Penal Code § 16640.

Research References

2 Witkin, California Criminal Law 4th Crimes Against Public Peace and Welfare § 208 (2021), Exempt Activities.

CHAPTER 4.1. REGISTRATION AND ASSIGNMENT OF FIREARMS BY PRIVATE PATROL OPERATORS

§ 28010. Ownership and registration of firearms by licensed Private Patrol Operators (PPOs); legislative findings, declarations, and intent; definitions

(a) The Legislature finds and declares that current practices and statutes authorize the purchase, registration, and ownership of firearms by an individual, but not by a business entity.

(b) It is the intent of the Legislature in enacting this chapter to allow business ownership and registration of firearms in the case of licensed Private Patrol Operators (PPOs) who are actively providing armed private contract security services. It is further the intent of the Legislature to establish procedures whereby a PPO may assign firearms it owns to its employees who are licensed to carry firearms and that assignment of a firearm by a PPO to that employee would not constitute a loan, sale, or transfer of a firearm.

(c) It is the intent of the Legislature to require notification of the Bureau of Security and Investigative Services any time a security guard is listed on the Prohibited Armed Persons File so that the bureau may proceed with appropriate action regarding the licensing of the employee.

(d) For purposes of this chapter, the following definitions apply:

(1) "Bureau" means the Bureau of Security and Investigative Services within the Department of Consumer Affairs.

(2) "Department" means the Department of Justice.

(3) "Director" means the Director of the Department of Consumer Affairs.

(4) "Private patrol operator" or "PPO" means a private patrol operator licensed pursuant to Chapter 11.5 (commencing with Section 7580) of Division 3 of the Business and Professions Code whose license is not suspended, revoked, expired, inactive, delinquent, or canceled.

(5) "Security guard" means a security guard registered pursuant to Chapter 11.5 (commencing with Section 7580) of Division 3 of the Business and Professions Code whose registration is not suspended, revoked, expired, inactive, delinquent, or canceled. *(Added by Stats.2014, c. 423 (A.B.2220), § 6, eff. Jan. 1, 2015, operative July 1, 2016.)*

§ 28012. Private Patrol Operator as registered owner of firearm; modification of Dealers' Record of Sale form; firearms custodian; assignment of firearm to security guard; Certificate of Assignment; notification that security guard is prohibited from being armed

(a) A PPO may be the registered owner of a firearm if the PPO is registered with the department pursuant to procedures established by the department.

(b) The department shall modify the department's Dealers' Record of Sale (DROS) form to allow a PPO to be listed as the purchaser and registered owner of a firearm. The form shall also require the PPO to identify its type of business formation and to include any tax identification number or other identifying number of the PPO that may be required by the department.

(c)(1) The department shall modify the department's DROS form to require the PPO to designate a "firearms custodian" for the firearm owned by the PPO that is listed in the DROS. A firearms custodian shall possess a valid firearms qualification permit issued by the bureau. A firearms custodian is responsible for the tracking, safekeeping, and inventory of those firearms of the PPO for which the custodian is designated, and shall serve as a point of contact for the department regarding the firearms for which the custodian is designated.

(2) If a firearms custodian is no longer employed by the PPO in that capacity, or otherwise becomes ineligible to be the firearms

custodian, the PPO shall notify the department of that fact within seven days in a manner prescribed by the department, and the PPO shall notify the department of the designated replacement firearms custodian within 20 days of the original notice.

(d) A security guard shall possess a valid firearm qualification permit issued by the bureau prior to receiving a firearm from a PPO pursuant to a Certificate of Assignment (COA). A firearm shall be assigned by a PPO to a security guard who is employed to work for the PPO only when that employment requires the security guard to be armed.

(e)(1)(A) The department shall prescribe a "Certificate of Assignment" or "COA." The COA may include fields that are in the DROS form, and shall be used to identify the employee of the PPO who has been assigned a PPO-owned firearm by the PPO pursuant to this chapter.

(B) The COA shall also be used to identify an employee of the PPO who will use his or her own firearm in the course of his or her duties as a security guard. The COA shall not require specific information regarding an employee-owned firearm.

(2) A PPO shall register a PPO-owned firearm acquired prior to July 1, 2016, as a PPO-owned firearm in a manner prescribed by the department prior to filing a COA for that firearm.

(3) Upon the PPO assigning a firearm to an employee who is a security guard, the PPO shall complete the COA and file it with the department in a timely manner as prescribed by the department.

(f) The department shall cause the information contained on the COA to be entered into the Automated Firearms System in a timely manner. Upon termination of the employment assignment that requires the security guard to be armed and the transfer of the firearm from the security guard back to the PPO, the PPO shall complete a COA indicating that the firearm is no longer assigned to the employee and that the firearm is in the possession of the PPO and shall file the COA with the department in a timely manner, as prescribed.

(g) If a security guard becomes listed on the Prohibited Armed Persons File, the department shall immediately notify the bureau of the listing by secured electronic delivery. Upon that notification, the bureau shall take appropriate action regarding the security guard. In addition, the department shall notify the PPO, in the manner the department deems appropriate, that the PPO employee is prohibited from being armed. This chapter does not prohibit the department from also notifying the bureau if a security guard has been arrested and charged with an offense that, upon conviction, would constitute a basis for revocation of a firearms qualification permit or security guard registration. *(Added by Stats.2014, c. 423 (A.B.2220), § 6, eff. Jan. 1, 2015, operative July 1, 2016.)*

§ 28014. Fees; deposit into Dealers' Record of Sale Special Account

The department shall charge a fee not to exceed the reasonable costs to the department for filing and processing a COA, and for the costs incurred in the implementation and administration of this chapter, including, but not limited to, entering information obtained pursuant to this chapter into the Automated Firearms System and other databases as deemed necessary by the department. The fee shall be deposited in the Dealers' Record of Sale Special Account. *(Added by Stats.2014, c. 423 (A.B.2220), § 6, eff. Jan. 1, 2015, operative July 1, 2016.)*

§ 28016. Sale or transfer of PPO-owned firearms

(a) If the PPO ceases to do business, ceases to possess a valid PPO license issued by the bureau that is not suspended, revoked, expired, inactive, delinquent, or canceled, ceases as a business entity, or changes its type of business formation, the PPO shall, within 30 days and unless otherwise prohibited by law, lawfully sell or transfer all PPO-owned firearms.

(b) A PPO shall notify the department of the sale or transfer of a PPO-owned firearm within five business days of the transaction in a manner prescribed by the department. This subdivision shall not apply if the sale or transfer was made to or through a licensed firearms dealer pursuant to Chapter 5 (commencing with Section 28050). *(Added by Stats.2014, c. 423 (A.B.2220), § 6, eff. Jan. 1, 2015, operative July 1, 2016.)*

§ 28018. Nature of assignment of firearm

Notwithstanding any other law, an assignment of a firearm pursuant to this chapter shall not constitute a loan, sale, or transfer of a firearm. *(Added by Stats.2014, c. 423 (A.B.2220), § 6, eff. Jan. 1, 2015, operative July 1, 2016.)*

§ 28020. Return of firearm by security guard to PPO; grounds; failure to comply

(a) Within 48 hours of the PPO's request, for any reason, or within 48 hours of separation of employment or revocation of the firearm qualification card, the security guard shall return to the PPO the firearm owned by the PPO and listed on a COA.

(b) The failure of a security guard to comply with subdivision (a) is a misdemeanor.

(c) If a security guard employed by a PPO does not comply with subdivision (a), the PPO shall notify the bureau within seven business days from the date that the security guard was required to return the firearm to the PPO.

(d) This chapter does not limit the right of a security guard to use, possess, or otherwise lawfully carry a firearm owned by that security guard. *(Added by Stats.2014, c. 423 (A.B.2220), § 6, eff. Jan. 1, 2015, operative July 1, 2016.)*

§ 28022. Administrative fine; deposit into Private Security Service Fund; appeal

(a) The director, through his or her designee, may assess an administrative fine of up to one thousand dollars ($1,000) against a PPO or a security guard for each willful violation of this chapter. All fines collected pursuant to this chapter shall be deposited in the Private Security Services Fund.

(b) An assessment imposed pursuant to this section may be appealed pursuant to Section 7581.3 of the Business and Professions Code. *(Added by Stats.2014, c. 423 (A.B.2220), § 6, eff. Jan. 1, 2015, operative July 1, 2016.)*

§ 28024. Operative date of chapter

This chapter shall become operative on July 1, 2016. *(Added by Stats.2014, c. 423 (A.B.2220), § 6, eff. Jan. 1, 2015, operative July 1, 2016.)*

CHAPTER 5. PROCEDURE FOR A PRIVATE PARTY FIREARMS TRANSACTION

Section

§ 28050. Completion of sale, loan, or transfer of firearm through licensed person; compliance with Section 27545; procedures if dealer cannot legally return firearm to seller, transferor, or person loaning the firearm

(a) A person shall complete any sale, loan, or transfer of a firearm through a person licensed pursuant to Sections 26700 to 26915, inclusive, in accordance with this chapter in order to comply with Section 27545.

(b) The seller or transferor or the person loaning the firearm shall deliver the firearm to the dealer who shall retain possession of that firearm.

(c) The dealer shall then deliver the firearm to the purchaser or transferee or the person being loaned the firearm, if it is not prohibited, in accordance with Section 27540.

(d) If the dealer cannot legally deliver the firearm to the purchaser or transferee or the person being loaned the firearm, the dealer shall forthwith, without waiting for the conclusion of the waiting period described in Sections 26815 and 27540, return the firearm to the transferor or seller or the person loaning the firearm. The dealer shall not return the firearm to the seller or transferor or the person loaning the firearm when to do so would constitute a violation of Section 27500, 27505, 27515, 27520, 27525, 27530, or 27535.

(e) Until July 1, 2024, if the dealer cannot legally return the firearm to the transferor or seller or the person loaning the firearm, then the dealer shall forthwith deliver the firearm to the sheriff of the county or the chief of police or other head of a municipal police department of any city or city and county, who shall then dispose of the firearm in the manner provided by Sections 18005 and 34000.

(f) If Commencing July 1, 2024, if the dealer cannot legally return the firearm to the seller, transferor, or person loaning the firearm, then the following procedure shall apply:

(1) The seller, transferor, or person loaning the firearm may request, and the dealer shall grant, that the dealer retain possession of the firearm for a period of up to 45 days so that the transferor or seller or the person loaning the firearm may designate a person to take possession of that firearm in accordance with Section 27540. This 45-day period shall be in addition to the waiting period described in Sections 26815 and 27540, and any time necessary to process a transaction.

(2) If, before the end of the 45-day period, the seller, transferor, or person loaning the firearm designates a person to receive the firearm and that person completes an application to purchase, the dealer shall process the transaction in accordance with the provisions of Section 27540.

(3) If the seller, transferor, or person loaning the firearm, does not request that the firearm be held by the dealer pursuant to this subdivision, or the firearm cannot be delivered to the designated person, the dealer, shall forthwith deliver the firearm to the sheriff of the county or the chief of police or other head of a municipal police department of any city or city and county, where the dealership is located, who shall then dispose of the firearm in the manner provided by Sections 18000, 18005, and 34000.

(g)(1) If a dealer retains possession of a firearm pursuant to subdivision (f), the dealer shall within 72 hours after retaining possession of the firearm, notify the Department of Justice in a manner and format prescribed by the department.

(2) If a dealer delivers possession a firearm to a law enforcement agency pursuant to subdivision (e) or (f), the dealer shall notify the Department of Justice within 72 hours after the delivery of the firearm in a manner and format prescribed by the department. *(Added by Stats.2010, c. 711 (S.B.1080), § 6, operative Jan. 1, 2012. Amended by Stats.2021, c. 250 (S.B.715), § 13, eff. Jan. 1, 2022.)*

Law Revision Commission Comments

Section 28050 continues the first six sentences of former Section 12082(a) without substantive change.

See Sections 16520 ("firearm"), 26700 ("dealer," "licensee," or "person licensed pursuant to Sections 26700 to 26915, inclusive"). [38 Cal.L.Rev. Comm. Reports 217 (2009)].

Cross References

Fees charged by Department of Justice, maximum rate, see Penal Code § 28230.
Firearm defined for purposes of this Part, see Penal Code § 16520.
Firearms reported stolen, lost, found, recovered, held for safekeeping, surrendered, relinquished, or under observation, entry into Department of Justice Automated Firearms System, see Penal Code § 11108.2.
Register or record of transfers, exemption for delivery of unloaded firearm to law enforcement agency pursuant to this section, see Penal Code § 28100.

Research References

2 Witkin, California Criminal Law 4th Crimes Against Public Peace and Welfare § 192 (2021), In General.
2 Witkin, California Criminal Law 4th Crimes Against Public Peace and Welfare § 198 (2021), Transfers by Persons Not Licensed in California.

§ 28055. Sale, loan, or transfer of firearm pursuant to this chapter; fees

(a) For a sale, loan, or transfer conducted pursuant to this chapter, the purchaser or transferee or person being loaned the firearm may be required by the dealer to pay a fee not to exceed ten dollars ($10) per firearm.

(b) For temporary storage of a firearm pursuant to subdivision (f) of Section 28050, the seller, transferor, or person loaning a firearm may be required by the dealer to pay a fee not to exceed ten dollars ($10) per firearm.

(c) No other fee may be charged by the dealer for a sale, loan, or transfer of a firearm conducted pursuant to this chapter, except for the applicable fees that may be charged pursuant to Sections 23690 and 28300 and Article 3 (commencing with Section 28200) of Chapter 6 and forwarded to the Department of Justice, and the fees set forth in Section 31650.

(d) The dealer may not charge any additional fees.

(e) Nothing in these provisions shall prevent a dealer from charging a smaller fee. *(Added by Stats.2010, c. 711 (S.B.1080), § 6, operative Jan. 1, 2012. Amended by Stats.2021, c. 250 (S.B.715), § 14, eff. Jan. 1, 2022.)*

Law Revision Commission Comments

Subdivisions (a) and (b) of Section 28055 continue the seventh sentence of former Section 12082(a) without substantive change.

Subdivision (c) continues the ninth sentence of former Section 12082(a) without substantive change.

Subdivision (d) continues the eighth sentence of former Section 12082(a) without substantive change.

See Sections 16520 ("firearm"), 26700 ("dealer," "licensee," or "person licensed pursuant to Sections 26700 to 26915, inclusive"). [38 Cal.L.Rev. Comm. Reports 217 (2009)].

Cross References

Dealer defined, see Penal Code § 26700.
Firearm defined for purposes of this Part, see Penal Code § 16520.

§ 28060. Attorney General to adopt regulations

The Attorney General shall adopt regulations under this chapter to do all of the following:

(a) Allow the seller or transferor or the person loaning the firearm, and the purchaser or transferee or the person being loaned the firearm, to complete a sale, loan, or transfer through a dealer, and to allow those persons and the dealer to preserve the confidentiality of those records and to comply with the requirements of this chapter and all of the following:

(1) Article 1 (commencing with Section 26700) and Article 2 (commencing with Section 26800) of Chapter 2.

(2) Article 1 (commencing with Section 27500) of Chapter 4.

(3) Article 2 (commencing with Section 28150) of Chapter 6.

(4) Article 3 (commencing with Section 28200) of Chapter 6.

(b) Record sufficient information for purposes of Section 11106 in the instance where a firearm is returned to a personal firearm importer because a sale or transfer of that firearm by the personal firearm importer could not be completed.

(c) Ensure that the register or record of electronic transfer shall state all of the following:

(1) The name and address of the seller or transferor of the firearm or the person loaning the firearm.

(2) Whether or not the person is a personal firearm importer.

(3) Any other information required by Article 2 (commencing with Section 28150) of Chapter 6. *(Added by Stats.2010, c. 711 (S.B.1080), § 6, operative Jan. 1, 2012. Amended by Stats.2011, c. 745 (A.B.809), § 47.)*

Law Revision Commission Comments

Section 28060 continues former Section 12082(b) without substantive change.

See Sections 16520 ("firearm"), 16530 ("firearm capable of being concealed upon the person," "pistol," and "revolver"), 17000 ("personal handgun importer"), 26700 ("dealer," "licensee," or "person licensed pursuant to Sections 26700 to 26915, inclusive"). [38 Cal.L.Rev.Comm. Reports 217 (2009)].

Cross References

Attorney General, generally, see Government Code § 12500 et seq.
Firearm defined for purposes of this Part, see Penal Code § 16520.

§ 28065. Dealer not required to process private party transfers of handguns

Notwithstanding any other provision of law, a dealer who does not sell, transfer, or keep an inventory of handguns is not required to process private party transfers of handguns. *(Added by Stats.2010, c. 711 (S.B.1080), § 6, operative Jan. 1, 2012.)*

Law Revision Commission Comments

Section 28065 continues former Section 12082(c) without substantive change.

See Sections 16640 ("handgun"), 26700 ("dealer," "licensee," or "person licensed pursuant to Sections 26700 to 26915, inclusive"). [38 Cal.L.Rev. Comm. Reports 217 (2009)].

Cross References

Dealer defined, see Penal Code § 26700.
Handgun defined for purposes of this Part, see Penal Code § 16640.

§ 28070. Violation of chapter; punishment

A violation of this chapter by a dealer is a misdemeanor. *(Added by Stats.2010, c. 711 (S.B.1080), § 6, operative Jan. 1, 2012.)*

Law Revision Commission Comments

Section 28070 continues former Section 12082(d) without substantive change.

See Section 26700 ("dealer," "licensee," or "person licensed pursuant to Sections 26700 to 26915, inclusive"). [38 Cal.L.Rev.Comm. Reports 217 (2009)].

Cross References

Dealer defined, see Penal Code § 26700.
Misdemeanors, definition and penalties, see Penal Code §§ 17, 19, 19.2.

CHAPTER 6. RECORDKEEPING, BACKGROUND CHECKS, AND FEES RELATING TO SALE, LEASE, OR TRANSFER OF FIREARMS

ARTICLE 1. GENERAL PROVISIONS RELATING TO THE REGISTER OR THE RECORD OF ELECTRONIC OR TELEPHONIC TRANSFER

§ 28100. Register or record of transfers; application of Article 2; violation; punishment

(a) As required by the Department of Justice, every dealer shall keep a register or record of electronic or telephonic transfer in which shall be entered the information prescribed in Article 2 (commencing with Section 28150).

(b) This section shall not apply to any of the following transactions:

(1) The loan of an unloaded firearm by a dealer to a person who possesses a valid entertainment firearms permit issued pursuant to Chapter 2 (commencing with Section 29500) of Division 8, for use solely as a prop in a motion picture, television, video, theatrical, or other entertainment production or event.

(2) The delivery of an unloaded firearm by a dealer to a gunsmith for service or repair.

(3) Until January 1, 2014, the sale, delivery, or transfer of an unloaded firearm, other than a handgun, by a dealer to another dealer, upon proof of compliance with the requirements of Section 27555.

(4) The sale, delivery, or transfer of an unloaded firearm by a dealer who sells, delivers, or transfers the firearm to a person who resides outside this state and is licensed pursuant to Chapter 44 (commencing with Section 921) of Title 18 of the United States Code and any regulations issued pursuant thereto.

(5) The sale, delivery, or transfer of an unloaded firearm by a dealer to a wholesaler if that firearm is being returned to the wholesaler and is intended as merchandise in the wholesaler's business.

(6) The sale, delivery, or transfer of an unloaded firearm by a dealer to another dealer, upon proof of compliance with the requirements of Section 27555, if the firearm is intended as merchandise in the receiving dealer's business.

(7) Until January 1, 2014, the sale, delivery, or transfer of an unloaded firearm, other than a handgun, by a dealer to themselves.

(8) The loan of an unloaded firearm by a dealer who also operates a target facility which holds a business or regulatory license on the premises of the building designated in the license or whose building designated in the license is on the premises of any club or organization organized for the purpose of practicing shooting at targets upon established ranges, whether public or private, to a person at that target facility or club or organization, if the firearm is kept at all times within the premises of the target range or on the premises of the club or organization.

(9) The loan of an unloaded firearm by a dealer to a consultant-evaluator, if the loan does not exceed 45 days from the date of delivery of the firearm by the dealer to the consultant-evaluator.

(10) The return of an unloaded firearm to the owner of that firearm by a dealer, if the owner initially delivered the firearm to the dealer for service or repair.

(11) The sale, delivery, or transfer of an unloaded firearm by a dealer to a person licensed as an importer or manufacturer pursuant to Chapter 44 (commencing with Section 921) of Title 18 of the United States Code and any regulations issued pursuant thereto.

(12) The delivery of an unloaded firearm to a law enforcement agency pursuant to subdivision (e) or (f) of Section 28050.

(c) A violation of this section is a misdemeanor. *(Added by Stats.2010, c. 711 (S.B.1080), § 6, operative Jan. 1, 2012. Amended by Stats.2011, c. 745 (A.B.809), § 48; Stats.2021, c. 250 (S.B.715), § 15, eff. Jan. 1, 2022.)*

Law Revision Commission Comments

Section 28100 continues former Section 12073 without substantive change.

For exceptions to provisions in this article and in Article 2 (commencing with Section 28150), Article 3 (commencing with Section 28200), and Article 4 (commencing with Section 28300), see Article 5 (commencing with Section 28400).

See Sections 16410 ("consultant-evaluator"), 16520 ("firearm"), 16630 ("gunsmith"), 16640 ("handgun"), 17340 ("wholesaler"), 26700 ("dealer," "licensee," or "person licensed pursuant to Sections 26700 to 26915, inclusive"). [38 Cal.L.Rev.Comm. Reports 217 (2009)].

Cross References

Consultant-evaluator defined for purposes of this Part, see Penal Code § 16410.
Dealer defined, see Penal Code § 26700.
Firearm defined for purposes of this Part, see Penal Code § 16520.
Gunsmith defined for purposes of this Part, see Penal Code § 16630.
Handgun defined for purposes of this Part, see Penal Code § 16640.
Misdemeanors, definition and penalties, see Penal Code §§ 17, 19, 19.2.
Wholesaler defined for purposes of this Part, see Penal Code § 17340.

Research References

2 Witkin, California Criminal Law 4th Crimes Against Public Peace and Welfare § 192 (2021), In General.

§ 28105. Register to be prepared by and obtained from State Printer; costs; standards

(a)(1) The register required by Section 28100 shall be prepared by and obtained from the State Printer.

(2) The State Printer shall furnish the register only to dealers on application, at a cost to be determined by the Department of General Services.

(3) The Department of General Services shall determine the cost for each 100 leaves in quadruplicate, one original and three duplicates for the making of carbon copies.

(4) The original and duplicate copies shall differ in color, and shall be in the form provided by this chapter.

(b) Where the electronic transfer of applicant information is used, the Department of Justice shall develop the standards for all appropriate electronic equipment and telephone numbers to effect the transfer of information to the department. *(Added by Stats.2010, c. 711 (S.B.1080), § 6, operative Jan. 1, 2012.)*

Law Revision Commission Comments

Section 28105 continues former Section 12074 without substantive change.

For exceptions to provisions in this article and in Article 2 (commencing with Section 28150), Article 3 (commencing with Section 28200), and Article 4 (commencing with Section 28300), see Article 5 (commencing with Section 28400).

See Section 26700 ("dealer," "licensee," or "person licensed pursuant to Sections 26700 to 26915, inclusive"). [38 Cal.L.Rev.Comm. Reports 217 (2009)].

Cross References

Dealer defined, see Penal Code § 26700.
Department of General Services, generally, see Government Code § 14600 et seq.

§ 28110. State Printer to forward information to Department of Justice

(a) The State Printer upon issuing a register shall forward to the Department of Justice both of the following:

(1) The name and business address of the dealer.

(2) The series and sheet numbers of the register.

(b) The register shall not be transferable.

(c) If the dealer moves the business to a different location, the dealer shall notify the department of that fact in writing within 48 hours. *(Added by Stats.2010, c. 711 (S.B.1080), § 6, operative Jan. 1, 2012.)*

Law Revision Commission Comments

Section 28110 continues former Section 12075 without substantive change.

For exceptions to provisions in this article and in Article 2 (commencing with Section 28150), Article 3 (commencing with Section 28200), and Article 4 (commencing with Section 28300), see Article 5 (commencing with Section 28400).

See Section 26700 ("dealer," "licensee," or "person licensed pursuant to Sections 26700 to 26915, inclusive"). [38 Cal.L.Rev.Comm. Reports 217 (2009)].

Cross References

Dealer defined, see Penal Code § 26700.

ARTICLE 2. FORM OF THE REGISTER OR THE RECORD OF ELECTRONIC TRANSFER

Section

§ 28150. Definitions

As used in this article, the following words have the following meanings:

(a) "Purchase" means the purchase, loan, or transfer of a firearm.

(b) "Purchaser" means the purchaser or transferee of a firearm or the person being loaned a firearm.

(c) "Sale" means the sale, loan, or transfer of a firearm. *(Added by Stats.2010, c. 711 (S.B.1080), § 6, operative Jan. 1, 2012.)*

Law Revision Commission Comments

Section 28150 continues former Section 12077(g) without substantive change.

See Section 16520 ("firearm"). [38 Cal.L.Rev.Comm. Reports 217 (2009)].

Cross References

Firearm defined for purposes of this Part, see Penal Code § 16520.

§ 28155. Form of register and record of electronic transfer

The Department of Justice shall prescribe the form of the register and the record of electronic transfer pursuant to Section 28105. *(Added by Stats.2010, c. 711 (S.B.1080), § 6, operative Jan. 1, 2012.)*

Law Revision Commission Comments

Section 28155 continues former Section 12077(a) without substantive change. [38 Cal.L.Rev.Comm. Reports 217 (2009)].

§ 28160. Firearm register or record of electronic transfer; required information; thumbprint; delivery date; purchaser signature

(a) For all firearms, the register or record of electronic transfer shall include all of the following information:

(1) The date and time of sale.

(2) The make of firearm.

(3) Peace officer exemption status pursuant to the provisions listed in subdivision (c) of Section 16585, and the agency name.

(4) Any applicable waiting period exemption information.

(5) California Firearms Dealer number issued pursuant to Article 1 (commencing with Section 26700) of Chapter 2.

(6) For transactions occurring on or after January 1, 2003, the purchaser's handgun safety certificate number issued pursuant to Article 2 (commencing with Section 31610) of Chapter 4 of Division 10 of this title, or pursuant to former Article 8 (commencing with Section 12800) of Chapter 6 of Title 2 of Part 4, as that article read at any time from when it became operative on January 1, 2003, to when it was repealed by the Deadly Weapons Recodification Act of 2010.

(7) Manufacturer's name if stamped on the firearm.

(8) Model name or number, if stamped on the firearm.

(9) Serial number, if applicable.

(10) Other number, if more than one serial number is stamped on the firearm.

(11) Any identification number or mark assigned to the firearm pursuant to Section 23910.

(12) If the firearm is not a handgun and does not have a serial number, identification number, or mark assigned to it, a notation as to that fact.

(13) Caliber.

(14) Type of firearm.

(15) If the firearm is new or used.

(16) Barrel length.

(17) Color of the firearm.

(18) Full name of purchaser.

(19) Purchaser's complete date of birth.

(20) Purchaser's local address.

(21) If current address is temporary, complete permanent address of purchaser.

(22) Identification of purchaser.

(23) Purchaser's place of birth (state or country).

(24) Purchaser's complete telephone number.

(25) Purchaser's occupation.

(26) Purchaser's gender.

(27) Purchaser's physical description.

(28) All legal names and aliases ever used by the purchaser.

(29) Yes or no answer to questions that prohibit purchase, including, but not limited to, conviction of a felony as described in Chapter 2 (commencing with Section 29800) or an offense described in Chapter 3 (commencing with Section 29900) of Division 9 of this title, the purchaser's status as a person described in Section 8100 of the Welfare and Institutions Code, whether the purchaser is a person who has been adjudicated by a court to be a danger to others or found not guilty by reason of insanity, and whether the purchaser is a person who has been found incompetent to stand trial or placed under conservatorship by a court pursuant to Section 8103 of the Welfare and Institutions Code.

(30) Signature of purchaser.

(31) Signature of salesperson, as a witness to the purchaser's signature.

(32) Salesperson's certificate of eligibility number, if the salesperson has obtained a certificate of eligibility.

(33) Name and complete address of the dealer or firm selling the firearm as shown on the dealer's license.

(34) The establishment number, if assigned.

(35) The dealer's complete business telephone number.

(36) Any information required by Chapter 5 (commencing with Section 28050).

(37) Any information required to determine whether subdivision (f) of Section 27540 applies.

(38) A statement of the penalties for signing a fictitious name or address, knowingly furnishing any incorrect information, or knowingly omitting any information required to be provided for the register.

(39) A statement informing the purchaser, after his or her ownership of a firearm, of all of the following:

(A) Upon his or her application, the Department of Justice shall furnish him or her any information reported to the department as it relates to his or her ownership of that firearm.

(B) The purchaser is entitled to file a report of his or her acquisition, disposition, or ownership of a firearm with the department pursuant to Section 28000.

(C) Instructions for accessing the department's Internet Web site for more information.

(40) For transactions on and after January 1, 2015, the purchaser's firearm safety certificate number, except that in the case of a handgun, the number from an unexpired handgun safety certificate may be used.

(b) The purchaser shall provide the purchaser's right thumbprint on the register in a manner prescribed by the department. No exception to this requirement shall be permitted except by regulations adopted by the department.

(c) The firearms dealer shall record on the register or record of electronic transfer the date that the firearm is delivered, together with the firearm dealer's signature indicating delivery of the firearm.

(d) The purchaser shall sign the register or the record of electronic transfer on the date that the firearm is delivered to him or her. *(Added by Stats.2010, c. 711 (S.B.1080), § 6, operative Jan. 1, 2012. Amended by Stats.2011, c. 745 (A.B.809), § 49; Stats.2013, c. 738 (A.B.538), § 7; Stats.2013, c. 761 (S.B.683), § 11.5.)*

Law Revision Commission Comments

Section 28160 continues former Section 12077(b) without substantive change.

For exceptions to provisions in this article and in Article 1 (commencing with Section 28100), Article 3 (commencing with Section 28200), and Article 4 (commencing with Section 28300), see Article 5 (commencing with Section 28400).

See Sections 16240 ("basic firearms safety certificate"), 16520 ("firearm"), 16640 ("handgun"), 16670 ("handgun safety certificate"), 26700 ("dealer," "licensee," or "person licensed pursuant to Sections 26700 to 26915, inclusive"), 28150 ("purchase," "purchaser," and "sale"). [38 Cal.L.Rev.Comm. Reports 217 (2009)].

Cross References

Availability of mental health records to Department of Justice, see Welfare and Institutions Code § 8104.
Felonies, definition and penalties, see Penal Code §§ 17, 18.
Firearm defined for purposes of this Part, see Penal Code § 16520.
Handgun defined for purposes of this Part, see Penal Code § 16640.
Handgun safety certificate defined for purposes of this Part, see Penal Code § 16670.
Possession of a firearm by persons adjudicated by a court to be dangerous to others as result of a mental disorder or mental illness, see Welfare and Institutions Code § 8103.
Possession of a firearm by persons receiving inpatient treatment for mental disorders, see Welfare and Institutions Code § 8100.
Submission of information identifying certain persons receiving inpatient treatment for mental disorders, see Welfare and Institutions Code § 8105.

§ 28170. Register of sale; requirements when used

Where the register is used, the following shall apply:

(a) Dealers shall use ink to complete each document.

(b) The dealer or salesperson making a sale shall ensure that all information is provided legibly. The dealer and salespersons shall be informed that incomplete or illegible information will delay sales.

(c) Each dealer shall be provided instructions regarding the procedure for completion of the form and routing of the form. Dealers shall comply with these instructions, which shall include the information set forth in this section.

(d) One firearm transaction shall be reported on each record of sale document. *(Added by Stats.2010, c. 711 (S.B.1080), § 6, operative Jan. 1, 2012. Amended by Stats.2011, c. 745 (A.B.809), § 51.)*

Law Revision Commission Comments

Section 28170 continues former Section 12077(d) without substantive change.

For exceptions to provisions in this article and in Article 1 (commencing with Section 28100), Article 3 (commencing with Section 28200), and Article 4 (commencing with Section 28300), see Article 5 (commencing with Section 28400).

See Sections 16520 ("firearm"), 16640 ("handgun"), 26700 ("dealer," "licensee," or "person licensed pursuant to Sections 26700 to 26915, inclusive"), 28150 ("purchase," "purchaser," and "sale"). [38 Cal.L.Rev.Comm. Reports 217 (2009)].

Cross References

Dealer defined, see Penal Code § 26700.
Firearm defined for purposes of this Part, see Penal Code § 16520.

§ 28175. Dealer or salesperson to ensure that purchaser information is complete

The dealer or salesperson making a sale shall ensure that all required information has been obtained from the purchaser. The dealer and all salespersons shall be informed that incomplete information will delay sales. *(Added by Stats.2010, c. 711 (S.B.1080), § 6, operative Jan. 1, 2012.)*

Law Revision Commission Comments

Section 28175 continues former Section 12077(e) without substantive change.

For exceptions to provisions in this article and in Article 1 (commencing with Section 28100), Article 3 (commencing with Section 28200), and Article 4 (commencing with Section 28300), see Article 5 (commencing with Section 28400).

See Sections 26700 ("dealer," "licensee," or "person licensed pursuant to Sections 26700 to 26915, inclusive"), 28150 ("purchase," "purchaser," and "sale"). [38 Cal.L.Rev.Comm. Reports 217 (2009)].

Cross References

Dealer defined, see Penal Code § 26700.

§ 28180. Name, birth date and identification number of purchaser to be obtained from magnetic strip of driver's license or identification; exceptions

(a) The purchaser's name, date of birth, and driver's license or identification number shall be obtained electronically from the magnetic strip on the purchaser's driver's license or identification and shall not be supplied by any other means, except as authorized by the department.

(b) The requirement of subdivision (a) shall not apply in either of the following cases:

(1) The purchaser's identification consists of a military identification card.

(2) Due to technical limitations, the magnetic strip reader is unable to obtain the required information from the purchaser's identification. In those circumstances, the firearms dealer shall obtain a photocopy of the identification as proof of compliance.

(c) In the event that the dealer has reported to the department that the dealer's equipment has failed, information pursuant to this section shall be obtained by an alternative method to be determined by the department. *(Added by Stats.2010, c. 711 (S.B.1080), § 6, operative Jan. 1, 2012. Amended by Stats.2011, c. 745 (A.B.809), § 52.)*

Law Revision Commission Comments

Section 28180 continues former Section 12077(f) without substantive change.

For exceptions to provisions in this article and in Article 1 (commencing with Section 28100), Article 3 (commencing with Section 28200), and Article 4 (commencing with Section 28300), see Article 5 (commencing with Section 28400).

See Sections 16520 ("firearm"), 26700 ("dealer," "licensee," or "person licensed pursuant to Sections 26700 to 26915, inclusive"), 28150 ("purchase," "purchaser," and "sale"). [38 Cal.L.Rev.Comm. Reports 217 (2009)].

Cross References

Dealer defined, see Penal Code § 26700.
Electronic approval of purchase or transfer of firearm precursor parts by department, determination of eligibility of purchaser or transferee, development of approval procedure for single firearm precursor part transaction or purchase, see Penal Code § 30470.
Firearm defined for purposes of this Part, see Penal Code § 16520.

ARTICLE 3. SUBMISSION OF FEES AND FIREARM PURCHASER INFORMATION TO THE DEPARTMENT OF JUSTICE

Section

§ 28200. Definitions

As used in this article, the following words have the following meanings:

(a) "Purchase" means the purchase, loan, or transfer of a firearm.

(b) "Purchaser" means the purchaser or transferee of a firearm or the person being loaned a firearm.

(c) "Sale" means the sale, loan, or transfer of a firearm.

(d) "Seller" means, if the transaction is being conducted pursuant to Chapter 5 (commencing with Section 28050), the person selling, loaning, or transferring the firearm. *(Added by Stats.2010, c. 711 (S.B.1080), § 6, operative Jan. 1, 2012.)*

Law Revision Commission Comments

Section 28200 continues former Section 12076(*l*) without substantive change. [38 Cal.L.Rev.Comm. Reports 217 (2009)].

Cross References

Firearm defined for purposes of this Part, see Penal Code § 16520.

Research References

2 Witkin, California Criminal Law 4th Crimes Against Public Peace and Welfare § 192 (2021), In General.

2 Witkin, California Criminal Law 4th Crimes Against Public Peace and Welfare § 233 (2021), Prohibitions.

§ 28205. Formats for submitting firearm purchaser information; electronic transfer exclusive means after Jan. 1, 2003

(a) Until January 1, 1998, the Department of Justice shall determine the method by which a dealer shall submit firearm purchaser information to the department. The information shall be in one of the following formats:

(1) Submission of the register described in Article 2 (commencing with Section 28150).

(2) Electronic or telephonic transfer of the information contained in the register described in Article 2 (commencing with Section 28150).

(b) On or after January 1, 1998, electronic or telephonic transfer, including voice or facsimile transmission, shall be the exclusive means by which purchaser information is transmitted to the department.

(c) On or after January 1, 2003, except as permitted by the department, electronic transfer shall be the exclusive means by which information is transmitted to the department. Telephonic transfer shall not be permitted for information regarding sales of any firearms. *(Added by Stats.2010, c. 711 (S.B.1080), § 6, operative Jan. 1, 2012.)*

Law Revision Commission Comments

Section 28205 continues former Section 12076(a) without substantive change.

For exceptions to provisions in this article and in Article 1 (commencing with Section 28100), Article 2 (commencing with Section 28150), and Article 4 (commencing with Section 28300), see Article 5 (commencing with Section 28400).

For the consequences of violating this article, see Section 28250.

See Sections 16520 ("firearm"), 26700 ("dealer," "licensee," or "person licensed pursuant to Sections 26700 to 26915, inclusive"), 28200 ("purchase," "purchaser," "sale," and "seller"). [38 Cal.L.Rev.Comm. Reports 217 (2009)].

Cross References

Dealer defined, see Penal Code § 26700.
Firearm defined for purposes of this Part, see Penal Code § 16520.
Purchaser defined for purposes of this Article, see Penal Code § 28200.
Register of sale or transfer, necessity for, see Penal Code § 28100.
Sale defined for purposes of this Article, see Penal Code § 28200.

§ 28210. Use of register to record sale; requirements and contents; fraud and punishment; retention of original register; copies to be sent to Department of Justice; photocopy to purchaser at time of delivery; private party transfers

(a)(1) Where the register is used, the purchaser of any firearm shall be required to present to the dealer clear evidence of the person's identity and age.

(2) The dealer shall require the purchaser to sign the purchaser's current legal name and affix the purchaser's residence address and date of birth to the register in quadruplicate.

(3) For the sale or transfer of a firearm to a person under 21 years of age pursuant to subdivision (b) of Section 27510, the salesperson shall visually inspect the hunting license to confirm that it is valid and unexpired and shall record the document number, GO ID, and dates valid.

(4) The salesperson shall sign the register in quadruplicate, as a witness to the signature and identification of the purchaser.

(b) Any person furnishing a fictitious name or address, knowingly furnishing any incorrect information, or knowingly omitting any information required to be provided for the register shall be punished as provided in Section 28250.

(c)(1) The original of the register shall be retained by the dealer in consecutive order.

(2) Each book of 50 originals shall become the permanent register of transactions, which shall be retained for not less than three years from the date of the last transaction.

(3) Upon presentation of proper identification, the permanent register of transactions shall be available for inspection by any peace officer, Department of Justice employee designated by the Attorney General, or agent of the federal Bureau of Alcohol, Tobacco, Firearms and Explosives. Until January 1, 2014, no information shall be compiled therefrom regarding the purchasers or other transferees of firearms that are not handguns.

(d) On the date of the application to purchase, two copies of the original sheet of the register shall be placed in the mail, postage prepaid, and properly addressed to the Department of Justice.

(e)(1) A photocopy of the register shall be provided to the purchaser by the dealer at the time of delivery of the firearm and after the dealer notes the date of delivery and the dealer's signature indicating delivery of the firearm, and the purchaser acknowledges the receipt of the firearm.

(2) The requirements of this subdivision apply if a dealer is delivering a firearm pursuant to Section 27540 or Chapter 5 (commencing with Section 28050).

(f) If the transaction is a private party transfer conducted pursuant to Chapter 5 (commencing with Section 28050), a photocopy of the original shall be provided to the seller by the dealer at the time the register is signed by the seller. The dealer shall redact all of the purchaser's personal information, as required pursuant to subdivision (a) of Section 28160 and subdivision (a) of Section 28165, from the seller's copy, and the seller's personal information from the purchaser's copy. *(Added by Stats.2010, c. 711 (S.B.1080), § 6, operative Jan. 1, 2012. Amended by Stats.2011, c. 745 (A.B.809), § 53; Stats.2013, c. 738 (A.B.538), § 8; Stats.2021, c. 250 (S.B.715), § 16, eff. Jan. 1, 2022.)*

Law Revision Commission Comments

Subdivision (a) of Section 28210 continues the first and second sentences of former Section 12076(b)(1) without substantive change.

Subdivision (b) cross-refers to Section 28250, which continues the third sentence of former Section 12076(b)(1) and the third sentence of former Section 12076(c)(1) without substantive change.

Subdivision (c) continues former Section 12076(b)(2) without substantive change.

Subdivision (d) continues former Section 12076(b)(3) without substantive change.

Subdivision (e) continues former Section 12076(b)(4) without change.

Subdivision (f) continues former Section 12076(b)(5) without substantive change.

For exceptions to provisions in this article and in Article 1 (commencing with Section 28100), Article 2 (commencing with Section 28150), and Article 4 (commencing with Section 28300), see Article 5 (commencing with Section 28400).

See Sections 16400 ("clear evidence of the person's identity and age"), 16520 ("firearm"), 26700 ("dealer," "licensee," or "person licensed pursuant to Sections 26700 to 26915, inclusive"), 28200 ("purchase," "purchaser," "sale," and "seller"). [38 Cal.L.Rev.Comm. Reports 217 (2009)].

Cross References

Attorney General, generally, see Government Code § 12500 et seq.
Dealer defined, see Penal Code § 26700.
Firearm defined for purposes of this Part, see Penal Code § 16520.
Handgun defined for purposes of this Part, see Penal Code § 16640.
Purchaser defined for purposes of this Article, see Penal Code § 28200.
Register of sale or transfer, necessity for, see Penal Code § 28100.

Research References

1 Witkin California Criminal Law 4th Introduction to Crimes § 76 (2021), Illustrations: Special Statute is Controlling.

§ 28215. Electronic or telephonic transfer of purchaser information; evidence of identity and age required; signatures; fraud; punishment; original records; inspection of records; applicant information transmission to Department of Justice; copy of record to purchaser requirement; private party transfer; redaction

(a)(1) Where the electronic or telephonic transfer of applicant information is used, the purchaser shall be required to present to the dealer clear evidence of the person's identity and age.

(2) The dealer shall require the purchaser to sign the purchaser's current legal name to the record of electronic or telephonic transfer.

(3) The salesperson shall sign the record of electronic or telephonic transfer, as a witness to the signature and identification of the purchaser.

(4) For the sale or transfer of a firearm to a person under 21 years of age pursuant to subdivision (b) of Section 27510, the salesperson shall visually inspect the hunting license to confirm that it is valid and unexpired and shall record the document number, GO ID, and dates valid.

(5) For the sale or transfer of a firearm to a person under 21 years of age pursuant to subdivision (b) of Section 27510, or to a person without a valid firearm safety certificate pursuant to subdivision (c) of Section 31700, if the dealer or salesperson, upon visual inspection of the hunting license, is unable to confirm that it is valid and unexpired, they shall not deliver the firearm.

(b) Any person furnishing a fictitious name or address, knowingly furnishing any incorrect information, or knowingly omitting any information required to be provided for the electronic or telephonic transfer shall be punished as provided in Section 28250.

(c)(1) The original of each record of electronic or telephonic transfer shall be retained by the dealer in consecutive order.

(2) Each original shall become the permanent record of the transaction, which shall be retained for not less than three years from the date of the last transaction.

(3) Upon presentation of proper identification, the permanent record of the transaction shall be provided for inspection by any peace officer, Department of Justice employee designated by the Attorney General, or agent of the federal Bureau of Alcohol, Tobacco, Firearms and Explosives.

(d) On the date of the application to purchase, the record of applicant information shall be transmitted to the Department of Justice by electronic or telephonic transfer.

(e)(1) A copy of the record of electronic or telephonic transfer shall be provided to the purchaser by the dealer at the time of delivery of the firearm and after the dealer notes the date of delivery and the dealer's signature indicating delivery of the firearm, and the purchaser acknowledges the receipt of the firearm.

(2) The requirements of this subdivision apply if a dealer is delivering a firearm pursuant to Section 27540 or Chapter 5 (commencing with Section 28050).

(f) If the transaction is a private party transfer conducted pursuant to Chapter 5 (commencing with Section 28050), a copy shall be provided to the seller by the dealer at the time the record of electronic or telephonic transfer is signed by the seller. The dealer shall redact all of the purchaser's personal information, as required pursuant to subdivision (a) of Section 28160 and subdivision (a) of Section 28165, from the seller's copy, and the seller's personal information from the purchaser's copy. *(Added by Stats.2010, c. 711 (S.B.1080), § 6, operative Jan. 1, 2012. Amended by Stats.2011, c. 745 (A.B.809), § 54; Stats.2013, c. 738 (A.B.538), § 9; Stats.2021, c. 250 (S.B.715), § 17, eff. Jan. 1, 2022.)*

Law Revision Commission Comments

Subdivision (a) of Section 28215 continues the first and second sentences of former Section 12076(c)(1) without substantive change.

Subdivision (b) cross-refers to Section 28250, which continues the third sentence of former Section 12076(b)(1) and the third sentence of former Section 12076(c)(1) without substantive change.

Subdivision (c) continues former Section 12076(c)(3) without substantive change.

Subdivision (d) continues former Section 12076(c)(2) without substantive change.

Subdivision (e) continues former Section 12076(c)(4) without change.

Subdivision (f) continues former Section 12076(c)(5) without substantive change.

For exceptions to provisions in this article and in Article 1 (commencing with Section 28100), Article 2 (commencing with Section 28150), and Article 4 (commencing with Section 28300), see Article 5 (commencing with Section 28400).

See Sections 16400 ("clear evidence of the person's identity and age"), 16520 ("firearm"), 26700 ("dealer," "licensee," or "person licensed pursuant to Sections 26700 to 26915, inclusive"), 28200 ("purchase," "purchaser," "sale," and "seller"). [38 Cal.L.Rev.Comm. Reports 217 (2009)].

Cross References

Attorney General, generally, see Government Code § 12500 et seq.
Dealer defined, see Penal Code § 26700.
Firearm defined for purposes of this Part, see Penal Code § 16520.
Handgun defined for purposes of this Part, see Penal Code § 16640.
Purchaser defined for purposes of this Article, see Penal Code § 28200.

Research References

2 Witkin, California Criminal Law 4th Crimes Against Public Peace and Welfare § 194 (2021), Furnishing Erroneous Firearm Purchaser Information.

§ 28220. Firearm purchaser information; examination of records; criminal background check; prohibited sales; notice; incomplete, inaccurate or illegible information; failure to submit fee; delay of transfer of firearm to purchaser following receipt of purchaser information; submission of information to the National Instant Criminal Background Check System Index, Denied Persons Files

(a)(1) Upon submission of firearm purchaser information, the Department of Justice shall examine its records, as well as those records that it is authorized to request from the State Department of State Hospitals pursuant to Section 8104 of the Welfare and Institutions Code, in order to determine if the purchaser is a person described in subdivision (a) of Section 27535, or is prohibited by state or federal law from possessing, receiving, owning, or purchasing a firearm.

(2) Commencing July 1, 2025, for the sale or transfer of a firearm to a person under 21 years of age pursuant to subdivision (b) of Section 27510, the Department of Justice shall verify the validity of the purchaser's hunting license with the Department of Fish and Wildlife.

(b) The Department of Justice shall participate in the National Instant Criminal Background Check System (NICS), as described in subsection (t) of Section 922 of Title 18 of the United States Code, and shall notify the dealer and the chief of the police department of the city or city and county in which the sale was made, or if the sale was made in a district in which there is no municipal police department, the sheriff of the county in which the sale was made, that the purchaser is a person prohibited from acquiring a firearm under federal law.

(c) If the department determines that the purchaser is prohibited by state or federal law from possessing, receiving, owning, or purchasing a firearm or is a person described in subdivision (a) of Section 27535, it shall immediately notify the dealer and the chief of the police department of the city or city and county in which the sale was made, or if the sale was made in a district in which there is no municipal police department, the sheriff of the county in which the sale was made, of that fact.

(d) If the department determines that the copies of the register submitted to it pursuant to subdivision (d) of Section 28210 contain any blank spaces or inaccurate, illegible, or incomplete information, preventing identification of the purchaser or the handgun or other firearm to be purchased, or if any fee required pursuant to Section 28225 is not submitted by the dealer in conjunction with submission of copies of the register, the department may notify the dealer of that fact. Upon notification by the department, the dealer shall submit corrected copies of the register to the department, or shall submit any fee required pursuant to Section 28225, or both, as appropriate and, if notification by the department is received by the dealer at any time prior to delivery of the firearm to be purchased, the dealer shall withhold delivery until the conclusion of the waiting period described in Sections 26815 and 27540.

(e) If the department determines that the information transmitted to it pursuant to Section 28215 contains inaccurate or incomplete information preventing identification of the purchaser or the handgun or other firearm to be purchased, or if the fee required pursuant to Section 28225 is not transmitted by the dealer in conjunction with transmission of the electronic or telephonic record, the department may notify the dealer of that fact. Upon notification by the department, the dealer shall transmit corrections to the record of electronic or telephonic transfer to the department, or shall transmit any fee required pursuant to Section 28225, or both, as appropriate, and if notification by the department is received by the dealer at any time prior to delivery of the firearm to be purchased, the dealer shall withhold delivery until the conclusion of the waiting period described in Sections 26815 and 27540.

(f)(1)(A) The department shall immediately notify the dealer to delay the transfer of the firearm to the purchaser if the records of the department, or the records available to the department in the National Instant Criminal Background Check System, indicate one of the following:

(i) The purchaser has been taken into custody and placed in a facility for mental health treatment or evaluation and may be a person described in Section 8100 or 8103 of the Welfare and Institutions Code and the department is unable to ascertain whether the purchaser is a person who is prohibited from possessing, receiving, owning, or purchasing a firearm, pursuant to Section 8100 or 8103 of the Welfare and Institutions Code, prior to the conclusion of the waiting period described in Sections 26815 and 27540.

(ii) The purchaser has been arrested for, or charged with, a crime that would make the purchaser, if convicted, a person who is prohibited by state or federal law from possessing, receiving, owning, or purchasing a firearm, and the department is unable to ascertain whether the purchaser was convicted of that offense prior to the conclusion of the waiting period described in Sections 26815 and 27540.

(iii) The purchaser may be a person described in subdivision (a) of Section 27535, and the department is unable to ascertain whether the purchaser, in fact, is a person described in subdivision (a) of Section 27535, prior to the conclusion of the waiting period described in Sections 26815 and 27540.

(B) The dealer shall provide the purchaser with information about the manner in which the purchaser may contact the department regarding the delay described in subparagraph (A).

(2) The department shall notify the purchaser by mail regarding the delay and explain the process by which the purchaser may obtain a copy of the criminal or mental health record the department has on file for the purchaser. Upon receipt of that criminal or mental health record, the purchaser shall report any inaccuracies or incompleteness to the department on an approved form.

(3) If the department ascertains the final disposition of the arrest or criminal charge, or the outcome of the mental health treatment or evaluation, or the purchaser's eligibility to purchase a firearm, as described in paragraph (1), after the waiting period described in Sections 26815 and 27540, but within 30 days of the dealer's original submission of the purchaser information to the department pursuant to this section, the department shall do the following:

(A) If the purchaser is not a person described in subdivision (a) of Section 27535, and is not prohibited by state or federal law, including, but not limited to, Section 8100 or 8103 of the Welfare and Institutions Code, from possessing, receiving, owning, or purchasing a firearm, the department shall immediately notify the dealer of that fact and the dealer may then immediately transfer the firearm to the purchaser, upon the dealer's recording on the register or record of electronic transfer the date that the firearm is transferred, the dealer signing the register or record of electronic transfer indicating delivery of the firearm to that purchaser, and the purchaser signing the register or record of electronic transfer acknowledging the receipt of the firearm on the date that the firearm is delivered to the purchaser.

(B) If the purchaser is a person described in subdivision (a) of Section 27535, or is prohibited by state or federal law, including, but not limited to, Section 8100 or 8103 of the Welfare and Institutions Code, from possessing, receiving, owning, or purchasing a firearm, the department shall immediately notify the dealer and the chief of the police department in the city or city and county in which the sale was made, or if the sale was made in a district in which there is no municipal police department, the sheriff of the county in which the sale was made, of that fact in compliance with subdivision (c) of Section 28220.

(4) If the department is unable to ascertain the final disposition of the arrest or criminal charge, or the outcome of the mental health treatment or evaluation, or the purchaser's eligibility to purchase a firearm, as described in paragraph (1), within 30 days of the dealer's original submission of purchaser information to the department pursuant to this section, the department shall immediately notify the dealer and the dealer may then immediately transfer the firearm to the purchaser, upon the dealer's recording on the register or record of electronic transfer the date that the firearm is transferred, the dealer signing the register or record of electronic transfer indicating delivery of the firearm to that purchaser, and the purchaser signing the register or record of electronic transfer acknowledging the receipt of the firearm on the date that the firearm is delivered to the purchaser.

(5) Commencing July 1, 2025, if the department is unable to ascertain the validity of a hunting license required pursuant to Section 27510, the department shall immediately notify the dealer to cancel the sale of the firearm. The department shall notify the purchaser by mail that the hunting license was not valid and unexpired or the Department of Fish and Wildlife was unable to verify the license based upon the information provided.

(g)(1) Commencing July 1, 2017, upon receipt of information demonstrating that a person is prohibited from possessing a firearm pursuant to federal or state law, the department shall submit the name, date of birth, and physical description of the person to the National Instant Criminal Background Check System Index, Denied Persons Files. The information provided shall remain privileged and confidential, and shall not be disclosed, except for the purpose of enforcing federal or state firearms laws.

(2) This subdivision does not prohibit the department from sharing information pertaining to a person that is prohibited from possessing a firearm if the department is otherwise expressly authorized or required by state law to share that information with the recipient party. *(Added by Stats.2010, c. 711 (S.B.1080), § 6, operative Jan. 1, 2012. Amended by Stats.2011, c. 745 (A.B.809), § 55; Stats.2012, c. 24 (A.B.1470), § 56, eff. June 27, 2012; Stats.2013, c. 737 (A.B.500), § 8.1; Initiative Measure (Prop. 63, § 5.1, approved Nov. 8, 2016, eff. Nov. 9, 2016); Stats.2021, c. 253 (A.B.173), § 9, eff. Sept. 23, 2021; Stats.2021, c. 250 (S.B.715), § 18, eff. Jan. 1, 2022; Stats.2021, c. 253 (A.B.173), § 9.5, eff. Sept. 23, 2021, operative Jan. 1, 2022.)*

Law Revision Commission Comments

Section 28220 continues former Section 12076(d) without substantive change.

For exceptions to provisions in this article and in Article 1 (commencing with Section 28100), Article 2 (commencing with Section 28150), and Article 4 (commencing with Section 28300), see Article 5 (commencing with Section 28400).

For the consequences of violating this article, see Section 28250.

See Sections 16520 ("firearm"), 16530 ("firearm capable of being concealed upon the person," "pistol," and "revolver"), 26700 ("dealer," "licensee," or "person licensed pursuant to Sections 26700 to 26915, inclusive"), 28200 ("purchase," "purchaser," "sale," and "seller"). [38 Cal.L.Rev.Comm. Reports 217 (2009)].

Cross References

Dealer defined, see Penal Code § 26700.
Firearm defined for purposes of this Part, see Penal Code § 16520.
Firearm precursor part vendors, information to be recorded upon delivery of firearm precursor parts, form, electronic submission to department, persons authorized to purchase firearm precursor parts, see Penal Code § 30452.
Handgun defined for purposes of this Part, see Penal Code § 16640.
Possession of firearms by persons adjudicated by a court to be dangerous to others as result of a mental disorder or mental illness, see Welfare and Institutions Code § 8103.
Possession of firearms by persons receiving inpatient treatment for mental disorder, see Welfare and Institutions Code § 8100.
Purchaser defined for purposes of this Article, see Penal Code § 28200.
Sale defined for purposes of this Article, see Penal Code § 28200.
Submission of information identifying certain persons receiving inpatient treatment for mental disorders, see Welfare and Institutions Code § 8105.

§ 28225. Fee charged to firearm purchaser for processing information; maximum rate

(a) The Department of Justice may require the dealer to charge each firearm purchaser a fee not to exceed one dollar ($1), except that the fee may be increased at a rate not to exceed any increase in the California Consumer Price Index as compiled and reported by the Department of Industrial Relations.

(b) The fee under subdivision (a) shall be no more than is necessary to fund the following:

(1) The department for the cost of furnishing this information.

(2) The department for the cost of meeting its obligations under paragraph (2) of subdivision (b) of Section 8100 of the Welfare and Institutions Code.

(3) Local mental health facilities for state-mandated local costs resulting from the reporting requirements imposed by Section 8103 of the Welfare and Institutions Code.

(4) The State Department of State Hospitals for the costs resulting from the requirements imposed by Section 8104 of the Welfare and Institutions Code.

(5) Local mental hospitals, sanitariums, and institutions for state-mandated local costs resulting from the reporting requirements imposed by Section 8105 of the Welfare and Institutions Code.

(6) Local law enforcement agencies for state-mandated local costs resulting from the notification requirements set forth in subdivision (a) of Section 6385 of the Family Code.

(7) Local law enforcement agencies for state-mandated local costs resulting from the notification requirements set forth in subdivision (c) of Section 8105 of the Welfare and Institutions Code.

(8) For the actual costs associated with the electronic or telephonic transfer of information pursuant to Section 28215.

(9) The Department of Food and Agriculture for the costs resulting from the notification provisions set forth in Section 5343.5 of the Food and Agricultural Code.

(10) The department for the costs associated with subdivisions (d) and (e) of Section 27560.

(c) The fee established pursuant to this section shall not exceed the sum of the actual processing costs of the department, the estimated reasonable costs of the local mental health facilities for complying with the reporting requirements imposed by paragraph (3) of subdivision (b), the costs of the State Department of State Hospitals for complying with the requirements imposed by paragraph (4) of subdivision (b), the estimated reasonable costs of local mental hospitals, sanitariums, and institutions for complying with the reporting requirements imposed by paragraph (5) of subdivision (b), the estimated reasonable costs of local law enforcement agencies for complying with the notification requirements set forth in subdivision (a) of Section 6385 of the Family Code, the estimated reasonable costs of local law enforcement agencies for complying with the notification requirements set forth in subdivision (c) of Section 8105 of the Welfare and Institutions Code imposed by paragraph (7) of subdivision (b), the estimated reasonable costs of the Department of Food and Agriculture for the costs resulting from the notification provisions set forth in Section 5343.5 of the Food and Agricultural Code, and the estimated reasonable costs of the department for the costs associated with subdivisions (d) and (e) of Section 27560 * * *.

(d) Where the electronic or telephonic transfer of applicant information is used, the department shall establish a system to be used for the submission of the fees described in this section to the department. *(Added by Stats.2010, c. 711 (S.B.1080), § 6, operative Jan. 1, 2012. Amended by Stats.2011, c. 743 (S.B.819), § 2; Stats. 2012, c. 24 (A.B.1470), § 57, eff. June 27, 2012; Stats.2019, c. 736 (A.B.1669), § 13, eff. Jan. 1, 2020.)*

Law Revision Commission Comments

Subdivisions (a)-(c) of Section 28225 continue former Section 12076(e) without substantive change.

Subdivision (d) continues former Section 12076(h) without substantive change.

For exceptions to provisions in this article and in Article 1 (commencing with Section 28100), Article 2 (commencing with Section 28150), and Article 4 (commencing with Section 28300), see Article 5 (commencing with Section 28400).

For the consequences of violating this article, see Section 28250.

See Sections 16520 ("firearm"), 26700 ("dealer," "licensee," or "person licensed pursuant to Sections 26700 to 26915, inclusive"), 28200 ("purchase," "purchaser," "sale," and "seller"). [38 Cal.L.Rev.Comm. Reports 217 (2009)].

Cross References

Dealer defined, see Penal Code § 26700.

Electronic approval of purchase or transfer of firearm precursor parts by department, determination of eligibility of purchaser or transferee, development of approval procedure for single firearm precursor part transaction or purchase, see Penal Code § 30470.

Firearm defined for purposes of this Part, see Penal Code § 16520.

Firearms reported stolen, lost, found, recovered, held for safekeeping, or under observation, entry into Department of Justice Automated Firearms System, retention of information, implementation costs, see Penal Code § 11108.2.

Purchaser defined for purposes of this Article, see Penal Code § 28200.

Sale defined for purposes of this Article, see Penal Code § 28200.

§ 28230. Fees charged by Department of Justice; maximum rate

(a) The Department of Justice may charge a fee sufficient to reimburse it for each of the following but not to exceed fourteen dollars ($14), except that the fee may be increased at a rate not to exceed any increase in the California Consumer Price Index as compiled and reported by the Department of Industrial Relations:

(1) For the actual costs associated with the preparation, sale, processing, and filing of forms or reports required or utilized pursuant to any provision listed in subdivision (a) of Section 16585.

(2) For the actual costs associated with the preparation, sale, processing, and filing of reports utilized pursuant to Section 26556, 26905, 27565, 27875, 27966, or 28000, paragraph (1) of subdivision (a) of Section 27560, or paragraphs (1) and (2) of subdivision (a) of, or subdivisions (b), (c), and (d) of, Section 27920, Section 28050, or paragraph (2) of subdivision (e) of Section 32000.

(3) For the actual costs associated with the electronic or telephonic transfer of information pursuant to Section 28215.

(b) Any costs incurred by the Department of Justice to implement this section shall be reimbursed from fees collected and charged pursuant to this section. No fees shall be charged to the dealer pursuant to Section 28225 for implementing this section. *(Added by Stats.2010, c. 711 (S.B.1080), § 6, operative Jan. 1, 2012. Amended by Stats.2011, c. 745 (A.B.809), § 56; Stats.2014, c. 878 (A.B.1609), § 9, eff. Jan. 1, 2015; Stats.2019, c. 738 (S.B.376), § 27, eff. Jan. 1, 2020; Stats.2020, c. 289 (A.B.2699), § 4, eff. Jan. 1, 2021; Stats.2021, c. 250 (S.B.715), § 19, eff. Jan. 1, 2022.)*

Law Revision Commission Comments

Section 28230 continues former Section 12076(f) without substantive change.

For exceptions to provisions in this article and in Article 1 (commencing with Section 28100), Article 2 (commencing with Section 28150), and Article 4 (commencing with Section 28300), see Article 5 (commencing with Section 28400).

See Sections 26700 ("dealer," "licensee," or "person licensed pursuant to Sections 26700 to 26915, inclusive"), 28200 ("purchase," "purchaser," "sale," and "seller"). [38 Cal.L.Rev.Comm. Reports 217 (2009)].

Cross References

Dealer defined, see Penal Code § 26700.

Firearms reported stolen, lost, found, recovered, held for safekeeping, or under observation, entry into Department of Justice Automated Firearms System, retention of information, implementation costs, see Penal Code § 11108.2.

Register of sale or transfer, necessity for, see Penal Code § 28100.

Sale defined for purposes of this Article, see Penal Code § 28200.

§ 28233. Fees charged to firearm purchaser in addition to those in Sections 28225 and 28230; deposit and expenditure of moneys; increase of fees

(a) The Department of Justice may, in addition to the fee described in Sections 28225 and 28230, require a dealer to charge each firearm purchaser a fee in the amount of thirty-one dollars and nineteen cents ($31.19).

(b) Moneys received by the department pursuant to this section shall be deposited in the Dealers' Record of Sale Supplemental Subaccount, within the Dealers' Record of Sale Special Account of the General Fund, which is hereby created, to be available, upon appropriation by the Legislature, for expenditure by the department to offset the reasonable costs of firearms-related regulatory and enforcement activities related to the sale, purchase, manufacturing, lawful or unlawful possession, loan, or transfer of firearms pursuant to any provision listed in Section 16580.

(c) The fee described in subdivision (a) may be increased at a rate no more than any increase in the California Consumer Price Index as compiled and reported by the Department of Industrial Relations, but not to exceed the reasonable cost of regulation to the department. *(Added by Stats.2019, c. 736 (A.B.1669), § 14, eff. Jan. 1, 2020.)*

Cross References

Assault weapon, registration, contents of registration, fee, see Penal Code § 30900.

§ 28235. Fees; disposition

Except as otherwise provided in Section 28233, moneys received by the department pursuant to this article shall be deposited in the Dealers' Record of Sale Special Account of the General Fund, which is hereby created, to be available, upon appropriation by the Legislature, for expenditure by the department to offset the costs incurred pursuant to any of the following:

(a) This article.

(b) Section 18910.

(c) Section 27555.

(d) Subdivisions (d) and (e) of Section 27560.

(e) Chapter 4.1 (commencing with Section 28010).

(f) Article 6 (commencing with Section 28450).

(g) Section 31110.

(h) Section 31115.

(i) Subdivision (a) of Section 32020.

(j) Section 32670.

(k) Section 33320. *(Added by Stats.2010, c. 711 (S.B.1080), § 6, operative Jan. 1, 2012. Amended by Stats.2014, c. 423 (A.B.2220), § 7, eff. Jan. 1, 2015; Stats.2019, c. 736 (A.B.1669), § 15, eff. Jan. 1, 2020.)*

Law Revision Commission Comments

Section 28235 continues former Section 12076(g) without substantive change. [38 Cal.L.Rev.Comm. Reports 217 (2009)].

Cross References

Dealer defined, see Penal Code § 26700.
Register of sale or transfer, necessity for, see Penal Code § 28100.
Sale defined for purposes of this Article, see Penal Code § 28200.

§ 28240. Fees charged one for single firearm transaction

Each fee prescribed in this article shall only be charged once for a single transaction on the same date for taking title or possession of any number of firearms. *(Added by Stats.2010, c. 711 (S.B.1080), § 6, operative Jan. 1, 2012. Amended by Stats.2011, c. 745 (A.B.809), § 57; Stats.2012, c. 691 (A.B.1559), § 1; Stats.2019, c. 736 (A.B. 1669), § 16, eff. Jan. 1, 2020.)*

Law Revision Commission Comments

Subdivisions (a) and (b) of Section 28240 continue former Section 12076(i) without substantive change.

Subdivision (c) continues former Section 12076(j) without substantive change.

For exceptions to provisions in this article and in Article 1 (commencing with Section 28100), Article 2 (commencing with Section 28150), and Article 4 (commencing with Section 28300), see Article 5 (commencing with Section 28400).

For the consequences of violating this article, see Section 28250.

See Sections 16520 ("firearm"), 16530 ("firearm capable of being concealed upon the person," "pistol," and "revolver"), 28200 ("purchase," "purchaser," "sale," and "seller"). [38 Cal.L.Rev.Comm. Reports 217 (2009)].

Cross References

Firearm defined for purposes of this Part, see Penal Code § 16520.
Handgun defined for purposes of this Part, see Penal Code § 16640.
Sale defined for purposes of this Article, see Penal Code § 28200.

§ 28245. Acts relating to firearms other than handguns deemed discretionary under Government Claims Act

Whenever the Department of Justice acts pursuant to this article as it pertains to firearms other than handguns, the department's acts or omissions shall be deemed to be discretionary within the meaning of the Government Claims Act pursuant to Division 3.6 (commencing with Section 810) of Title 1 of the Government Code. *(Added by Stats.2010, c. 711 (S.B.1080), § 6, operative Jan. 1, 2012. Amended by Stats.2011, c. 745 (A.B.809), § 58; Stats.2012, c. 759 (A.B.2690), § 8.)*

Law Revision Commission Comments

Section 28245 continues former Section 12076(k) without substantive change.

See Sections 16520 ("firearm"), 16530 ("firearm capable of being concealed upon the person," "pistol," and "revolver"). [38 Cal.L.Rev.Comm. Reports 217 (2009)].

Section 28245 is amended to more accurately refer to the content of Division 3.6 (commencing with Section 810) of Title 1 of the Government Code. See City of Stockton v. Superior Court, 42 Cal. 4th 730, 734, 741–42, 171 P.3d 20, 68 Cal. Rptr. 3d 295 (2007); see also Gov't Code § 810 (stating that Division 3.6 of Title 1 of the Government Code may be referred to as "Government Claims Act"). [41 Cal.L.Rev.Comm. Reports 285 (2011)].

Cross References

Firearm defined for purposes of this Part, see Penal Code § 16520.
Handgun defined for purposes of this Part, see Penal Code § 16640.

§ 28250. Furnishing false information or omitting information; other violations; punishment

(a) Any person who does any of the following is guilty of a misdemeanor:

(1) Furnishing a fictitious name or address for the register under Section 28210 or the electronic or telephonic transfer under Section 28215.

(2) Knowingly furnishing any incorrect information for the register under Section 28210 or the electronic or telephonic transfer under Section 28215.

(3) Knowingly omitting any information required to be provided for the register under Section 28210 or the electronic or telephonic transfer under Section 28215.

(4) Violating any provision of this article.

(b) Notwithstanding subdivision (a), any person who is prohibited from obtaining a firearm pursuant to Chapter 2 (commencing with Section 29800) or Chapter 3 (commencing with Section 29900) of Division 9 of this title, or Section 8100 or 8103 of the Welfare and Institutions Code, who does any of the following shall be punished by imprisonment in a county jail not exceeding one year or imprisonment pursuant to subdivision (h) of Section 1170 for a term of 8, 12, or 18 months:

(1) Knowingly furnishes a fictitious name or address for the register under Section 28210 or the electronic or telephonic transfer under Section 28215.

(2) Knowingly furnishes any incorrect information for the register under Section 28210 or the electronic or telephonic transfer under Section 28215.

(3) Knowingly omits any information required to be provided for the register under Section 28210 or the electronic or telephonic transfer under Section 28215. *(Added by Stats.2010, c. 711 (S.B. 1080), § 6, operative Jan. 1, 2012. Amended by Stats.2011, c. 15 (A.B.109), § 546, eff. April 4, 2011, operative Jan. 1, 2012.)*

Law Revision Commission Comments

Section 28250 continues the third sentence of former Section 12076(b)(1) and the third sentence of former Section 12076(c)(1) without substantive change. An erroneous reference to "the register" in former Section 12076(c)(1) has been replaced with a reference to "the electronic or telephonic transfer."

For exceptions to provisions in this article and in Article 1 (commencing with Section 28100), Article 2 (commencing with Section 28150), and Article 4 (commencing with Section 28300), see Article 5 (commencing with Section 28400). [38 Cal.L.Rev.Comm. Reports 217 (2009)].

Cross References

Availability of mental health records to Department of Justice, see Welfare and Institutions Code § 8104.
Firearm defined for purposes of this Part, see Penal Code § 16520.
Misdemeanors, definition and penalties, see Penal Code §§ 17, 19, 19.2.
Register of sale or transfer, necessity for, see Penal Code § 28100.
Submission of information identifying certain persons receiving inpatient treatment for mental disorders, see Welfare and Institutions Code § 8105.

Research References

2 Witkin, California Criminal Law 4th Crimes Against Public Peace and Welfare § 194 (2021), Furnishing Erroneous Firearm Purchaser Information.

§ 28255. Notification of firearm possession following conclusion of waiting period

Commencing January 1, 2014, if after the conclusion of the waiting period described in Sections 26815 and 27540, the individual named in the application as the purchaser of the firearm takes possession of the firearm set forth in the application to purchase, the dealer shall notify the Department of Justice of that fact in a manner and within a time period specified by the department, and with sufficient information to identify the purchaser and the firearm that the purchaser took possession of. *(Added by Stats.2013, c. 737 (A.B.500), § 9.)*

Cross References

Criminal identification and statistics, retention of records, firearms, see Penal Code § 11106.

Research References

2 Witkin, California Criminal Law 4th Crimes Against Public Peace and Welfare § 197 (2021), Time and Manner of Delivery by Dealer.

ARTICLE 4. FIREARMS SAFETY AND ENFORCEMENT SPECIAL FUND

§ 28300. Firearms Safety and Enforcement Special Fund established; fee for dealer firearm transactions

(a) The Firearms Safety and Enforcement Special Fund is hereby established in the State Treasury and shall be administered by the Department of Justice.

(b) The Department of Justice may require firearms dealers to charge each person who obtains a firearm a fee not to exceed five dollars ($5) for each transaction, except that the fee may be increased at a rate not to exceed any increase in the California Consumer Price Index as compiled and reported by the Department of Industrial Relations, and not to exceed the reasonable cost of regulation to the department. Revenues from this fee shall be deposited in the Firearms Safety and Enforcement Special Fund.

(c) Revenue deposited into the Firearms Safety and Enforcement Special Fund shall be available for expenditure by the Department of Justice upon appropriation by the Legislature for the purpose of implementing and enforcing the provisions of Article 2 (commencing with Section 31610) of Chapter 4 of Division 10, enforcing Section 830.95, Title 2 (commencing with Section 12001) of Part 4, Sections 16000 to 16960, inclusive, Sections 16970 to 17230, inclusive, Sections 17240 to 21390, inclusive, and Sections 21590 to 34370, inclusive, and for the establishment, maintenance, and upgrading of equipment and services necessary for firearms dealers to comply with Article 2 (commencing with Section 28150). *(Added by Stats.2010, c. 711 (S.B.1080), § 6, operative Jan. 1, 2012. Amended by Stats.2016, c. 33 (S.B.843), § 38, eff. June 27, 2016.)*

Law Revision Commission Comments

Section 28300 continues former Section 12076.5 without substantive change.

For exceptions to provisions in this article and in Article 1 (commencing with Section 28100), Article 2 (commencing with Section 28150), and Article 3 (commencing with Section 28200), see Article 5 (commencing with Section 28400).

See Sections 16520 ("firearm"), 26700 ("dealer," "licensee," or "person licensed pursuant to Sections 26700 to 26915, inclusive"). [38 Cal.L.Rev. Comm. Reports 217 (2009)].

Cross References

Dealer defined, see Penal Code § 26700.
Firearm defined for purposes of this Part, see Penal Code § 16520.

ARTICLE 5. EXCEPTIONS RELATING TO LAW ENFORCEMENT

§ 28400. Sale, delivery or transfer of firearm to authorized law enforcement representative; proper written authorization defined; record required for handgun or firearm transaction

(a) Article 1 (commencing with Section 28100), Article 2 (commencing with Section 28150), Article 3 (commencing with Section 28200), and Article 4 (commencing with Section 28300) do not apply to any sale, delivery, or transfer of firearms made to an authorized law enforcement representative of any city, county, city and county, or state, or of the federal government, for exclusive use by that governmental agency if, prior to the sale, delivery, or transfer of these firearms, written authorization from the head of the agency authorizing the transaction is presented to the person from whom the purchase, delivery, or transfer is being made.

(b) Proper written authorization is defined as verifiable written certification from the head of the agency by which the purchaser or transferee is employed, identifying the employee as an individual authorized to conduct the transaction, and authorizing the transaction for the exclusive use of the agency by which that person is employed.

(c) Within 10 days of the date a handgun, and commencing January 1, 2014, any firearm, is acquired by the agency, a record of the same shall be entered as an institutional weapon into the Automated Firearms System (AFS) via the California Law Enforcement Telecommunications System (CLETS) by the law enforcement or state agency. Any agency without access to AFS shall arrange with the sheriff of the county in which the agency is located to input this information via this system. *(Added by Stats.2010, c. 711 (S.B.1080), § 6, operative Jan. 1, 2012. Amended by Stats.2011, c. 745 (A.B.809), § 59.)*

Law Revision Commission Comments

Section 28400 continues former Section 12078(a)(2) without substantive change, as that provision applied to former Sections 12073, 12074, 12075, 12076, 12076.5, and 12077 (through its reference to "the preceding provisions of this article").

See Sections 16520 ("firearm"), 16640 ("handgun"). [38 Cal.L.Rev.Comm. Reports 217 (2009)].

Cross References

Firearm defined for purposes of this Part, see Penal Code § 16520.
Handgun defined for purposes of this Part, see Penal Code § 16640.

§ 28405. Firearm loaned to authorized law enforcement representative or peace officer

Article 1 (commencing with Section 28100), Article 2 (commencing with Section 28150), Article 3 (commencing with Section 28200), and Article 4 (commencing with Section 28300) do not apply to the loan of a firearm if all of the following conditions are satisfied:

(a) The loan is made by an authorized law enforcement representative of a city, county, or city and county, or of the state or federal government.

(b) The loan is made to a peace officer employed by that agency and authorized to carry a firearm.

(c) The loan is made for the carrying and use of that firearm by that peace officer in the course and scope of the officer's duties. *(Added by Stats.2010, c. 711 (S.B.1080), § 6, operative Jan. 1, 2012.)*

Law Revision Commission Comments

Section 28405 continues former Section 12078(a)(3) without substantive change, as that provision applied to former Sections 12073, 12074, 12075, 12076, 12076.5, and 12077 (through its reference to "the preceding provisions of this article").

See Section 16520 ("firearm"). [38 Cal.L.Rev.Comm. Reports 217 (2009)].

Cross References

Firearm defined for purposes of this Part, see Penal Code § 16520.

§ 28410. Sale, delivery or transfer of firearm by law enforcement agency to peace officer; information required for handgun or firearm transaction

(a) Article 1 (commencing with Section 28100), Article 2 (commencing with Section 28150), Article 3 (commencing with Section 28200), and Article 4 (commencing with Section 28300) do not apply to the sale, delivery, or transfer of a firearm by a law enforcement agency to a peace officer pursuant to Section 10334 of the Public Contract Code.

(b) Within 10 days of the date that a handgun, and commencing January 1, 2014, any firearm, is sold, delivered, or transferred pursuant to Section 10334 of the Public Contract Code to that peace officer, the name of the officer and the make, model, serial number, and other identifying characteristics of the firearm being sold, delivered, or transferred shall be entered into the Automated Firearms System (AFS) via the California Law Enforcement Telecommunications System (CLETS) by the law enforcement or state agency that sold, delivered, or transferred the firearm, provided, however, that if the firearm is not a handgun and does not have a serial number, identification number, or identification mark assigned to it, that fact shall be noted in AFS. Any agency without access to AFS shall arrange with the sheriff of the county in which the agency is located to input this information via this system. *(Added by Stats.2010, c. 711 (S.B.1080), § 6, operative Jan. 1, 2012. Amended by Stats.2011, c. 745 (A.B.809), § 60.)*

Law Revision Commission Comments

Section 28410 continues former Section 12078(a)(4) without substantive change, as that provision applied to former Sections 12073, 12074, 12075, 12076, 12076.5, and 12077 (through its reference to "the preceding provisions of this article").

See Sections 16520 ("firearm"), 16640 ("handgun"). [38 Cal.L.Rev.Comm. Reports 217 (2009)].

Cross References

Firearm defined for purposes of this Part, see Penal Code § 16520.
Handgun defined for purposes of this Part, see Penal Code § 16640.

§ 28415. Sale, delivery or transfer of firearm by law enforcement agency to retiring peace officer; information required for handgun or firearm transaction

(a) Article 1 (commencing with Section 28100), Article 2 (commencing with Section 28150), Article 3 (commencing with Section 28200), and Article 4 (commencing with Section 28300) do not apply to the sale, delivery, or transfer of a firearm by a law enforcement agency to a retiring peace officer who is authorized to carry a firearm pursuant to Chapter 5 (commencing with Section 26300) of Division 5.

(b) Within 10 days of the date that a handgun, and commencing January 1, 2014, any firearm, is sold, delivered, or transferred to that retiring peace officer, the name of the officer and the make, model, serial number, and other identifying characteristics of the firearm being sold, delivered, or transferred shall be entered into the Automated Firearms System (AFS) via the California Law Enforcement Telecommunications System (CLETS) by the law enforcement or state agency that sold, delivered, or transferred the firearm, provided, however, that if the firearm is not a handgun and does not have a serial number, identification number, or identification mark assigned to it, that fact shall be noted in AFS. Any agency without access to AFS shall arrange with the sheriff of the county in which the agency is located to input this information via this system. *(Added by Stats.2010, c. 711 (S.B.1080), § 6, operative Jan. 1, 2012. Amended by Stats.2011, c. 745 (A.B.809), § 61.)*

Law Revision Commission Comments

Section 28415 continues former Section 12078(a)(5) without substantive change, as that provision applied to former Sections 12073, 12074, 12075, 12076, 12076.5, and 12077 (through its reference to "the preceding provisions of this article").

See Sections 16520 ("firearm"), 16640 ("handgun"). [38 Cal.L.Rev.Comm. Reports 217 (2009)].

Cross References

Firearm defined for purposes of this Part, see Penal Code § 16520.
Handgun defined for purposes of this Part, see Penal Code § 16640.

ARTICLE 6. CENTRALIZED LIST OF EXEMPTED FEDERAL FIREARMS LICENSEES

§ 28450. Centralized list of exempted federal firearms licensees; qualifications

(a) Commencing January 1, 2008, the Department of Justice shall keep a centralized list of persons who identify themselves as being licensed pursuant to Chapter 44 (commencing with Section 921) of Title 18 of the United States Code as a dealer, importer, or manufacturer of firearms whose licensed premises are within this state and who declare to the department an exemption from the firearms dealer licensing requirements of Section 26500.

(b) The list shall be known as the centralized list of exempted federal firearms licensees.

(c) To qualify for placement on the centralized list, an applicant shall do all of the following:

(1) Possess a valid federal firearms license pursuant to Chapter 44 (commencing with Section 921) of Title 18 of the United States Code as a dealer, importer, or manufacturer of firearms.

(2) Possess a current, valid certificate of eligibility pursuant to Section 26710.

(3) Maintain with the department a signed declaration enumerating the applicant's statutory exemptions from licensing requirements of Section 26500. *(Added by Stats.2010, c. 711 (S.B.1080), § 6, operative Jan. 1, 2012.)*

Law Revision Commission Comments

Section 28450 continues former Section 12083(a) without substantive change, except the second sentence of paragraph (a)(3), which is continued without substantive change in Section 28455.

See Sections 16520 ("firearm"), 26700 ("dealer," "licensee," or "person licensed pursuant to Sections 26700 to 26915, inclusive"). [38 Cal.L.Rev. Comm. Reports 217 (2009)].

Cross References

Dealer defined, see Penal Code § 26700.
Firearm defined for purposes of this Part, see Penal Code § 16520.
Licensee defined, see Penal Code § 26700.
Sale, delivery, or transfer of firearm by persons licensed pursuant to Chapter 44, Title 18 of U.S. Code, review of centralized list of exempted federal firearms licensees, see Penal Code § 27555.

Research References

2 Witkin, California Criminal Law 4th Crimes Against Public Peace and Welfare § 192 (2021), In General.

§ 28455. Furnishing of fictitious or incorrect information on declaration; misdemeanor

Any person furnishing a fictitious name, knowingly furnishing any incorrect information, or knowingly omitting any information for the declaration under paragraph (3) of subdivision (c) of Section 28450 shall be guilty of a misdemeanor. *(Added by Stats.2010, c. 711 (S.B.1080), § 6, operative Jan. 1, 2012.)*

Law Revision Commission Comments

Section 28455 continues the second sentence of former Section 12083(a)(3) without substantive change. [38 Cal.L.Rev.Comm. Reports 217 (2009)].

Cross References

Misdemeanors, definition and penalties, see Penal Code §§ 17, 19, 19.2.

§ 28460. Annual administrative fee

(a) Commencing January 1, 2008, the department shall assess an annual fee of one hundred fifteen dollars ($115) to cover its costs of maintaining the centralized list of exempted federal firearms licensees prescribed by Section 28450, conducting inspections in accordance with this article, and for the cost of maintaining the firearm shipment verification number system described in Section 27555.

(b) The department may increase the fee at a rate not to exceed the increase in the California Consumer Price Index as compiled and reported by the Department of Industrial Relations.

(c) The fees collected shall be deposited in the Dealers' Record of Sale Special Account.

(d) A person who satisfies all of the following conditions shall not be charged a fee:

(1) The person is not licensed pursuant to Sections 26700 to 26915, inclusive.

(2) The person has been issued a permit pursuant to Section 31005, 32650, or 33300, or pursuant to Article 3 (commencing with Section 18900) of Chapter 1 of Division 5 of Title 2.

(3) The person is placed on the centralized list of exempted federal firearms licensees. *(Added by Stats.2010, c. 711 (S.B.1080), § 6, operative Jan. 1, 2012.)*

Law Revision Commission Comments

Section 28460 continues former Section 12083(b) without substantive change.

For the provision establishing the Dealers' Record of Sale Special Account, see Section 28235.

See Section 16520 ("firearm"). [38 Cal.L.Rev.Comm. Reports 217 (2009)].

Cross References

Firearm defined for purposes of this Part, see Penal Code § 16520.

§ 28465. Importation or receipt of firearms; necessity of inclusion on centralized list; violation

(a) Any person licensed pursuant to Chapter 44 (commencing with Section 921) of Title 18 of the United States Code as a dealer, importer, or manufacturer of firearms whose licensed premises are within this state shall not import or receive firearms from any source unless listed on the centralized list of firearms dealers pursuant to Section 26715, or the centralized list of exempted federal firearms licensees pursuant to Section 28450, or the centralized list of firearms manufacturers pursuant to Section 29060.

(b) A violation of this section is a misdemeanor. *(Added by Stats.2010, c. 711 (S.B.1080), § 6, operative Jan. 1, 2012.)*

Law Revision Commission Comments

Section 28465 continues former Section 12083(c) without substantive change.

See Section 16520 ("firearm"). [38 Cal.L.Rev.Comm. Reports 217 (2009)].

Cross References

Dealer defined, see Penal Code § 26700.
Firearm defined for purposes of this Part, see Penal Code § 16520.
Licensee defined, see Penal Code § 26700.
Misdemeanors, definition and penalties, see Penal Code §§ 17, 19, 19.2.

§ 28470. Persons on centralized list of exempted federal firearms licensees; recordation of verification numbers accompanying firearms received from other licensees; violation

(a) All persons on the centralized list of exempted federal firearms licensees prescribed by Section 28450 shall record and keep on file for three years, the verification number that shall accompany firearms received from other federal firearms licensees pursuant to Section 27555.

(b) A violation of this section is cause for immediate removal from the centralized list. *(Added by Stats.2010, c. 711 (S.B.1080), § 6, operative Jan. 1, 2012.)*

Law Revision Commission Comments

Section 28470 continues former Section 12083(d) without substantive change.

For another provision authorizing removal from the centralized list in specified circumstances, see Section 28485.

See Section 16520 ("firearm"). [38 Cal.L.Rev.Comm. Reports 217 (2009)].

Cross References

Firearm defined for purposes of this Part, see Penal Code § 16520.
Licensee defined, see Penal Code § 26700.

§ 28475. Availability of information from centralized list of exempted federal firearms licensees

Information compiled from the list described in Section 28450 shall be made available for the following purposes:

(a) Requests from local, state, and federal law enforcement agencies and the duly constituted city, county, and city and county licensing authorities.

(b) When the information is requested by a person licensed pursuant to Chapter 44 (commencing with Section 921) of Title 18 of the United States Code for determining the validity of the license for firearm shipments. *(Added by Stats.2010, c. 711 (S.B.1080), § 6, operative Jan. 1, 2012.)*

Law Revision Commission Comments

Section 28475 continues former Section 12083(e) without substantive change.

See Section 16520 ("firearm"). [38 Cal.L.Rev.Comm. Reports 217 (2009)].

Cross References

Firearm defined for purposes of this Part, see Penal Code § 16520.

§ 28480. Onsite inspections; consultation with federal Bureau of Alcohol, Tobacco, Firearms and Explosives; availability of records for inspection

(a) The department may conduct onsite inspections at the business premises of a person on the centralized list described in Section 28450 to determine compliance with firearms laws pursuant to the provisions listed in Section 16575.

(b) The department shall work in consultation with the federal Bureau of Alcohol, Tobacco, Firearms and Explosives to ensure that licensees are not subject to duplicative inspections.

(c) During the inspection the following firearm records shall be made available for review:

(1) Federal records referred to in subdivision (a) of Section 478.125 of Title 27 of the Code of Federal Regulations and the bound book containing the same information referred to in Section 478.124a and subdivision (e) of Section 478.125 of Title 27 of the Code of Federal Regulations.

(2) Verification numbers issued pursuant to Section 27555.

(3) Any other records requested by the department to determine compliance with the provisions listed in Section 16575. *(Added by Stats.2010, c. 711 (S.B.1080), § 6, operative Jan. 1, 2012. Amended by Stats.2014, c. 103 (A.B.1798), § 10, eff. Jan. 1, 2015.)*

Law Revision Commission Comments

Section 28480 continues former Section 12083(f) without substantive change. See Section 16520 ("firearm"). [38 Cal.L.Rev.Comm. Reports 217 (2009)].

Section 28480 is amended to conform to the practice of referring to the Bureau as the "federal Bureau of Alcohol, Tobacco, Firearms and Explosives." [43 Cal.L.Rev.Comm. Reports 63 (2013)].

Cross References

Firearm defined for purposes of this Part, see Penal Code § 16520.
Licensee defined, see Penal Code § 26700.

§ 28485. Removal from centralized list

The department may remove from the centralized list described in Section 28450 any person who violates a provision listed in Section 16575. *(Added by Stats.2010, c. 711 (S.B.1080), § 6, operative Jan. 1, 2012.)*

Law Revision Commission Comments

Section 28485 continues former Section 12083(g) without substantive change.

See also Section 28470, which requires recording and retention of verification numbers and states that violation of that requirement is cause for immediate removal from the centralized list of exempted federal firearms licensees. [38 Cal.L.Rev.Comm. Reports 217 (2009)].

§ 28490. Adoption of regulations; consultation with federal Bureau of Alcohol, Tobacco, Firearms and Explosives

The department may adopt regulations as necessary to carry out the provisions of this article, Article 1 (commencing with Section 26700) and Article 2 (commencing with Section 26800) of Chapter 2, and Sections 27555 to 27570, inclusive. The department shall work in consultation with the federal Bureau of Alcohol, Tobacco, Firearms and Explosives to ensure that state regulations are not duplicative of federal regulations. *(Added by Stats.2010, c. 711 (S.B.1080), § 6, operative Jan. 1, 2012. Amended by Stats.2014, c. 103 (A.B.1798), § 11, eff. Jan. 1, 2015.)*

Law Revision Commission Comments

Section 28490 continues former Section 12083(h) without substantive change. [38 Cal.L.Rev.Comm. Reports 217 (2009)].

Section 28490 is amended to conform to the practice of referring to the Bureau as the "federal Bureau of Alcohol, Tobacco, Firearms and Explosives." [43 Cal.L.Rev.Comm. Reports 63 (2013)].

Cross References

Firearm defined for purposes of this Part, see Penal Code § 16520.

Division 7

MANUFACTURE OF FIREARMS

CHAPTER 1. LICENSE REQUIREMENT FOR MANUFACTURE OF FIREARMS

§ 29010. Manufacture of firearms; necessity of license under Chapter 2; cessation of operations

(a) A person, firm, or corporation * * * shall not manufacture more than three firearms within this state in a calendar year unless that person, firm, or corporation is licensed pursuant to Chapter 2 (commencing with Section 29030).

(b) * * * A person, firm, or corporation shall not use a three-dimensional printer to manufacture * * * any firearm, including a frame or receiver, or any firearm precursor part, unless that person, firm, or corporation is licensed pursuant to Chapter 2 (commencing with Section * * * 29030). As used in this section, "three-dimensional printer" means a computer-aided manufacturing device capable of producing a three-dimensional object from a three-dimensional digital model through an additive manufacturing process that involves the layering of two-dimensional cross sections formed of a resin or similar material that are fused together to form a three-dimensional object.

(c) If a person, firm, or corporation required to be licensed pursuant to Chapter 2 (commencing with Section 29030) ceases operations, then the records required pursuant to Section 29130 and subdivision (b) of Section 29115 shall be forwarded to the federal Bureau of Alcohol, Tobacco, Firearms and Explosives within three days of the closure of business.

(d) A violation of this section is a misdemeanor. *(Added by Stats.2010, c. 711 (S.B.1080), § 6, operative Jan. 1, 2012. Amended by Stats.2011, c. 296 (A.B.1023), § 233; Stats.2019, c. 738 (S.B.376), § 28, eff. Jan. 1, 2020; Stats.2022, c. 142 (A.B.2156), § 1, eff. Jan. 1, 2023.)*

Law Revision Commission Comments

Section 29010 continues subdivisions (a)-(d) of former Section 12085 without substantive change.

See Section 16520 ("firearm"). [38 Cal.L.Rev.Comm. Reports 217 (2009)].

Cross References

Firearm defined for purposes of this Part, see Penal Code § 16520.

Misdemeanors, definition and penalties, see Penal Code §§ 17, 19, 19.2.

Research References

2 Witkin, California Criminal Law 4th Crimes Against Public Peace and Welfare § 202 (2021), License to Manufacture.

CHAPTER 2. ISSUANCE, FORFEITURE, AND CONDITIONS OF LICENSE TO MANUFACTURE FIREARMS

ARTICLE 1. PRELIMINARY PROVISIONS

§ 29030. "Licensee" defined

In this chapter, "licensee" means a person, firm, or corporation that satisfies both of the following:

(a) Has a license issued pursuant to subdivision (b) of Section 29050.

(b) Is among those recorded in the centralized list specified in Section 29060. *(Added by Stats.2010, c. 711 (S.B.1080), § 6, operative Jan. 1, 2012.)*

Law Revision Commission Comments

Section 29030 continues former Section 12086(a)(1) without substantive change. [38 Cal.L.Rev.Comm. Reports 217 (2009)].

Research References

2 Witkin, California Criminal Law 4th Crimes Against Public Peace and Welfare § 202 (2021), License to Manufacture.

ARTICLE 2. LICENSING PROCESS

§ 29050. Manufacture of firearms; acceptance of applications and granting of licenses by Department of Justice; proof required by applicant; time of validity and form of license; notification of denial

(a) The Department of Justice shall accept applications for, and shall grant licenses permitting, the manufacture of firearms within this state.

(b) No license shall be granted by the department unless and until the applicant presents proof that the applicant has all of the following:

(1) A valid license to manufacture firearms issued pursuant to Chapter 44 (commencing with Section 921) of Title 18 of the United States Code.

(2) Any regulatory or business license required by local government.

(3) A valid seller's permit or resale certificate issued by the State Board of Equalization, if applicable.

(4) A certificate of eligibility issued by the Department of Justice pursuant to Section 26710.

(c) A license granted by the department shall be valid for no more than one year from the date of issuance and shall be in the form prescribed by the Attorney General.

(d) The department shall inform applicants who are denied licenses of the reasons for the denial in writing. *(Added by Stats.2010, c. 711 (S.B.1080), § 6, operative Jan. 1, 2012.)*

Law Revision Commission Comments

Subdivision (a) of Section 29050 continues the first sentence of former Section 12086(b)(1) without substantive change.

Subdivision (b) continues former Section 12086(b)(2) without substantive change.

Subdivision (c) continues former Section 12086(b)(4) without substantive change.

Subdivision (d) continues the second sentence of former Section 12086(b)(1) without substantive change.

See Sections 16450 ("department"), 16520 ("firearm"). [38 Cal.L.Rev. Comm. Reports 217 (2009)].

Cross References

Attorney General, generally, see Government Code § 12500 et seq.
Department defined, see Penal Code § 16450.
Firearm defined for purposes of this Part, see Penal Code § 16520.

§ 29055. Administration of this chapter and Chapter 1; adoption of regulations; fees

(a) The department shall adopt regulations to administer this chapter and Chapter 1 (commencing with Section 29010).

(b) The department shall recover the full costs of administering the program by collecting fees from license applicants. Recoverable costs shall include, but not be limited to, the costs of inspections and maintaining a centralized list of licensed firearm manufacturers.

(c) The fee for licensed manufacturers who produce fewer than 500 firearms in a calendar year within this state shall not exceed two hundred fifty dollars ($250) per year or the actual costs of inspections and maintaining a centralized list of firearm manufacturers and any other duties of the department required pursuant to this chapter and Chapter 1 (commencing with Section 29010), whichever is less. *(Added by Stats.2010, c. 711 (S.B.1080), § 6, operative Jan. 1, 2012.)*

Law Revision Commission Comments

Section 29055 continues former Section 12086(b)(3) without substantive change.

See Sections 16450 ("department"), 16520 ("firearm"). [38 Cal.L.Rev. Comm. Reports 217 (2009)].

Cross References

Department defined, see Penal Code § 16450.
Firearm defined for purposes of this Part, see Penal Code § 16520.

§ 29060. Centralized list of licensees; maintenance by Department of Justice; annual provision of list to police departments and county sheriffs

(a) Except as otherwise provided in subdivisions (a) and (b) of Section 20965, the Department of Justice shall maintain a centralized list of all persons licensed pursuant to subdivision (b) of Section 29050.

(b) The centralized list shall be provided annually to each police department and county sheriff within the state. *(Added by Stats. 2010, c. 711 (S.B.1080), § 6, operative Jan. 1, 2012.)*

Law Revision Commission Comments

Section 29060 continues former Section 12086(f)(1) without substantive change. [38 Cal.L.Rev.Comm. Reports 217 (2009)].

Cross References

Department defined, see Penal Code § 16450.

§ 29065. Revocation of license for violation of chapter

(a) Except as provided in subdivision (b), the license of any licensee who violates this chapter may be revoked.

(b) The license of any licensee who knowingly or with gross negligence violates this chapter or violates this chapter three times shall be revoked, and that person, firm, or corporation shall become permanently ineligible to obtain a license pursuant to this chapter.

(c) Upon the revocation of the license, notification shall be provided to local law enforcement authorities in the jurisdiction where the licensee's business is located and to the federal Bureau of Alcohol, Tobacco, Firearms and Explosives. *(Added by Stats.2010, c. 711 (S.B.1080), § 6, operative Jan. 1, 2012. Amended by Stats.2011, c. 296 (A.B.1023), § 234.)*

Law Revision Commission Comments

Subdivision (a) of Section 29065 continues former Section 12086(f)(2) without substantive change.

Subdivision (b) continues former Section 12086(f)(3) without substantive change. For guidance in applying this subdivision, see Section 16010 (continuation of existing law). See also Section 16015 (determining existence of prior conviction).

Subdivision (c) continues former Section 12086(g)(1) without substantive change.

See Section 29030 ("licensee"). [38 Cal.L.Rev.Comm. Reports 217 (2009)].

Cross References

Firearm defined for purposes of this Part, see Penal Code § 16520.
Licensee defined for purposes of this Chapter, see Penal Code § 29030.

§ 29070. Availability of licensee information

(a) The department shall make information concerning the location and name of a licensee available, upon request, for the following purposes only:

(1) Law enforcement.

(2) When the information is requested by a person licensed pursuant to Chapter 44 (commencing with Section 921) of Title 18 of the United States Code for determining the validity of the license for firearm shipments.

(b) Notwithstanding subdivision (a), the department shall make the name and business address of a licensee available to any person upon written request. *(Added by Stats.2010, c. 711 (S.B.1080), § 6, operative Jan. 1, 2012.)*

Law Revision Commission Comments

Subdivision (a) of Section 29070 continues former Section 12086(g)(2) without substantive change.

Subdivision (b) continues former Section 12086(g)(3) without substantive change.

See Sections 16450 ("department"), 16520 ("firearm"), 29030 ("licensee"). [38 Cal.L.Rev.Comm. Reports 217 (2009)].

Cross References

Department defined, see Penal Code § 16450.
Firearm defined for purposes of this Part, see Penal Code § 16520.
Licensee defined for purposes of this Chapter, see Penal Code § 29030.

§ 29075. Duties of Department of Justice regarding availability of information

The Department of Justice shall maintain and make available upon request information concerning all of the following:

(a) The number of inspections conducted and the amount of fees collected pursuant to Section 29055.

(b) The number of licensees removed from the centralized list described in Sections 29060 and 29065.

(c) The number of licensees found to have violated this chapter. *(Added by Stats.2010, c. 711 (S.B.1080), § 6, operative Jan. 1, 2012.)*

Law Revision Commission Comments

Section 29075 continues former Section 12086(h) without substantive change.

See Section 29030 ("licensee"). [38 Cal.L.Rev.Comm. Reports 217 (2009)].

Cross References

Licensee defined for purposes of this Chapter, see Penal Code § 29030.

ARTICLE 3. PROHIBITIONS AND REQUIREMENTS APPLICABLE TO LICENSEE

Section

§ 29100. Mandatory compliance by licensee

A licensee shall comply with the prohibitions and requirements described in this article. *(Added by Stats.2010, c. 711 (S.B.1080), § 6, operative Jan. 1, 2012.)*

Law Revision Commission Comments

Section 29100 continues the introductory clause of former Section 12086(c) without substantive change.

See Section 29030 ("licensee"). [38 Cal.L.Rev.Comm. Reports 217 (2009)].

Cross References

Licensee defined for purposes of this Chapter, see Penal Code § 29030.

§ 29105. Conduct of business in designated buildings

The business of a licensee shall be conducted only in the buildings designated in the license. *(Added by Stats.2010, c. 711 (S.B.1080), § 6, operative Jan. 1, 2012.)*

Law Revision Commission Comments

Section 29105 continues former Section 12086(c)(1) without substantive change.

See Section 29030 ("licensee"). See also Section 29100 (compliance with prohibitions and requirements). [38 Cal.L.Rev.Comm. Reports 217 (2009)].

Cross References

Licensee defined for purposes of this Chapter, see Penal Code § 29030.

§ 29110. Display of license

A licensee shall display the license or a copy thereof, certified by the department, on the premises where it can easily be seen. *(Added by Stats.2010, c. 711 (S.B.1080), § 6, operative Jan. 1, 2012.)*

Law Revision Commission Comments

Section 29110 continues former Section 12086(c)(2) without substantive change.

See Sections 16450 ("department"), 29030 ("licensee"). See also Section 29100 (compliance with prohibitions and requirements). [38 Cal.L.Rev. Comm. Reports 217 (2009)].

Cross References

Department defined, see Penal Code § 16450.
Licensee defined for purposes of this Chapter, see Penal Code § 29030.

§ 29115. Missing or stolen firearms; records and reports

(a) Whenever a licensee discovers that a firearm has been stolen or is missing from the licensee's premises, the licensee shall report the loss or theft within 48 hours of the discovery to all of the following:

(1) The Department of Justice, in a manner prescribed by the department.

(2) The federal Bureau of Alcohol, Tobacco, Firearms and Explosives.

(3) The police department in the city or city and county where the building designated in the license is located.

(4) If there is no police department in the city or city and county where the building designated in the license is located, the sheriff of the county where the building designated in the license is located.

(b) For at least 10 years, the licensee shall maintain records of all firearms that are lost or stolen, as prescribed by the Department of Justice. *(Added by Stats.2010, c. 711 (S.B.1080), § 6, operative Jan. 1, 2012. Amended by Stats.2011, c. 296 (A.B.1023), § 235.)*

Law Revision Commission Comments

Subdivision (a) of Section 29115 continues former Section 12086(c)(3) without substantive change.

Subdivision (b) continues former Section 12086(c)(10) without substantive change.

See Sections 16520 ("firearm"), 29030 ("licensee"). See also Section 29100 (compliance with prohibitions and requirements). [38 Cal.L.Rev.Comm. Reports 217 (2009)].

Cross References

Department defined, see Penal Code § 16450.
Firearm defined for purposes of this Part, see Penal Code § 16520.
Licensee defined for purposes of this Chapter, see Penal Code § 29030.

§ 29120. Employee contact with firearms; certificates of eligibility; prohibited contact

(a) A licensee shall require that each employee obtain a certificate of eligibility pursuant to Section 26710, which shall be renewed annually, before being allowed to come into contact with any firearm.

(b) A licensee shall prohibit any employee who the licensee knows or reasonably should know is prohibited by state or federal law from possessing, receiving, owning, or purchasing a firearm from coming into contact with any firearm. *(Added by Stats.2010, c. 711 (S.B. 1080), § 6, operative Jan. 1, 2012.)*

Law Revision Commission Comments

Section 29120 continues former Section 12086(c)(4) without substantive change.

See Sections 16520 ("firearm"), 29030 ("licensee"). See also Section 29100 (compliance with prohibitions and requirements). [38 Cal.L.Rev.Comm. Reports 217 (2009)].

Cross References

Firearm defined for purposes of this Part, see Penal Code § 16520.
Licensee defined for purposes of this Chapter, see Penal Code § 29030.

§ 29125. Identification of firearm by unique serial number

(a) Each firearm a licensee manufactures in this state shall be identified with a unique serial number stamped onto the firearm utilizing the method of compression stamping.

(b) Licensed manufacturers who produce fewer than 500 firearms in a calendar year within this state may serialize long guns only by utilizing a method of compression stamping or by engraving the serial number onto the firearm.

(c) The licensee shall stamp the serial number onto the firearm within one business day of the time the frame or receiver is manufactured.

(d) The licensee shall not use the same serial number for more than one firearm. *(Added by Stats.2010, c. 711 (S.B.1080), § 6, operative Jan. 1, 2012.)*

Law Revision Commission Comments

Section 29125 continues former Section 12086(c)(5) without substantive change.

See Sections 16520 ("firearm"), 29030 ("licensee"). See also Section 29100 (compliance with prohibitions and requirements). [38 Cal.L.Rev.Comm. Reports 217 (2009)].

Cross References

Firearm defined for purposes of this Part, see Penal Code § 16520.
Licensee defined for purposes of this Chapter, see Penal Code § 29030.

§ 29130. Required maintenance of records

(a) A licensee shall record the type, model, caliber, or gauge, and serial number of each firearm manufactured or acquired, and the date of the manufacture or acquisition, within one business day of the manufacture or acquisition.

(b) The licensee shall maintain permanently within the building designated in the license the records required pursuant to subdivision (a).

(c) Backup copies of the records described in subdivision (a), whether electronic or hard copy, shall be made at least once a month. These backup records shall be maintained in a facility separate from the one in which the primary records are stored. *(Added by Stats.2010, c. 711 (S.B.1080), § 6, operative Jan. 1, 2012.)*

Law Revision Commission Comments

Section 29130 continues former Section 12086(c)(6) without substantive change.

See Sections 16520 ("firearm"), 29030 ("licensee"). See also Section 29100 (compliance with prohibitions and requirements). [38 Cal.L.Rev.Comm. Reports 217 (2009)].

Cross References

Firearm defined for purposes of this Part, see Penal Code § 16520.
Licensee defined for purposes of this Chapter, see Penal Code § 29030.

Research References

2 Witkin, California Criminal Law 4th Crimes Against Public Peace and Welfare § 202 (2021), License to Manufacture.

§ 29135. Compliance inspections of buildings designated in license

(a) A licensee shall allow the department to inspect the building designated in the license to ensure compliance with the requirements of this chapter.

(b) A licensee shall allow any peace officer, authorized law enforcement employee, or Department of Justice employee designated by the Attorney General, upon the presentation of proper identification, to inspect facilities and records during business hours to ensure compliance with the requirements of this chapter. *(Added by Stats.2010, c. 711 (S.B.1080), § 6, operative Jan. 1, 2012.)*

Law Revision Commission Comments

Section 29135 continues former Section 12086(c)(7) without substantive change.

See Section 29030 ("licensee"). See also Section 29100 (compliance with prohibitions and requirements). [38 Cal.L.Rev.Comm. Reports 217 (2009)].

Cross References

Attorney General, generally, see Government Code § 12500 et seq.
Department defined, see Penal Code § 16450.
Licensee defined for purposes of this Chapter, see Penal Code § 29030.

§ 29140. Storage of firearms and firearm barrels in secure facility

A licensee shall store in a secure facility all firearms manufactured and all barrels for firearms manufactured. *(Added by Stats.2010, c. 711 (S.B.1080), § 6, operative Jan. 1, 2012.)*

Law Revision Commission Comments

Section 29140 continues former Section 12086(c)(8) without substantive change.

See Sections 16520 ("firearm"), 29141 ("secure facility" for firearm storage by manufacturer), 29142 (special definition of "secure facility" for firearm storage by manufacturer producing fewer than 500 firearms per calendar year). See also Section 29100 (compliance with prohibitions and requirements). [38 Cal.L.Rev.Comm. Reports 217 (2009)].

Cross References

Firearm defined for purposes of this Part, see Penal Code § 16520.
Licensee defined for purposes of this Chapter, see Penal Code § 29030.

§ 29141. "Secure facility" defined

Except as otherwise provided in Section 29142, as used in this chapter, "secure facility" means that the facility satisfies all of the following:

(a) The facility is equipped with a burglar alarm with central monitoring.

(b) All perimeter entries to areas in which firearms are stored other than doors, including windows and skylights, are secured with steel window guards or an audible, silent, or sonic alarm to detect entry.

(c) All perimeter doorways are designed in one of the following ways:

(1) A windowless steel security door equipped with both a deadbolt and a doorknob lock.

(2) A windowed metal door equipped with both a deadbolt and a doorknob lock. If the window has an opening of five inches or more measured in any direction, the window is covered with steel bars of at least one-half inch diameter or metal grating of at least nine gauge affixed to the exterior or interior of the door.

(3) A metal grate that is padlocked and affixed to the licensee's premises independent of the door and doorframe.

(4) Hinges and hasps attached to doors by welding, riveting, or bolting with nuts on the inside of the door.

(5) Hinges and hasps installed so that they cannot be removed when the doors are closed and locked.

(d) Heating, ventilating, air-conditioning, and service openings are secured with steel bars, metal grating, or an alarm system.

(e) No perimeter metal grates are capable of being entered by any person.

(f) Steel bars used to satisfy the requirements of this section are not capable of being entered by any person.

(g) Perimeter walls of rooms in which firearms are stored are constructed of concrete or at least 10–gauge expanded steel wire mesh utilized along with typical wood frame and drywall construction. If firearms are not stored in a vault, the facility shall use an exterior security-type door along with a high security, single-key deadbolt, or other door that is more secure. All firearms shall be stored in a separate room away from any general living area or work area. Any door to the storage facility shall be locked while unattended.

(h) Perimeter doorways, including the loading dock area, are locked at all times when not attended by paid employees or contracted employees, including security guards.

(i) Except when a firearm is currently being tested, any ammunition on the premises is removed from all manufactured guns and stored in a separate and locked room, cabinet, or box away from the storage area for the firearms. Ammunition may be stored with a weapon only in a locked safe. *(Added by Stats.2010, c. 711 (S.B.1080), § 6, operative Jan. 1, 2012.)*

Law Revision Commission Comments

Section 29141 continues former Section 12086(d) without substantive change.

See Section 16520 ("firearm"). See also Sections 17110 ("secure facility" for firearm storage by dealer), 29142 (special definition of "secure facility" for firearm storage by manufacturer producing fewer than 500 firearms per calendar year). [38 Cal.L.Rev.Comm. Reports 217 (2009)].

Cross References

Firearm defined for purposes of this Part, see Penal Code § 16520.
Licensee defined for purposes of this Chapter, see Penal Code § 29030.

§ 29142. Manufacturers of fewer than 500 firearms annually; security plans

(a) For purposes of this chapter, any licensed manufacturer who produces fewer than 500 firearms in a calendar year within this state may maintain a "secure facility" by complying with all of the requirements described in Section 29141, or may design a security plan that is approved by the Department of Justice or the federal Bureau of Alcohol, Tobacco, Firearms and Explosives.

(b) If a security plan is approved by the federal Bureau of Alcohol, Tobacco, Firearms and Explosives, the approved plan, along with proof of approval, shall be filed with the Department of Justice and the local police department. If there is no police department, the filing shall be with the county sheriff's office.

(c) If a security plan is approved by the Department of Justice, the approved plan, along with proof of approval, shall be filed with the local police department. If there is no police department, the filing shall be with the county sheriff's office. *(Added by Stats.2010, c. 711 (S.B.1080), § 6, operative Jan. 1, 2012. Amended by Stats.2011, c. 296 (A.B.1023), § 236.)*

Law Revision Commission Comments

Section 29142 continues former Section 12086(e) without substantive change.

See Section 16520 ("firearm"). See also Sections 17110 ("secure facility" for firearm storage by dealer), 29141 ("secure facility" for firearm storage by manufacturer). [38 Cal.L.Rev.Comm. Reports 217 (2009)].

Cross References

Department defined, see Penal Code § 16450.
Firearm defined for purposes of this Part, see Penal Code § 16520.

§ 29150. Notice to local law enforcement authorities of location of firearms manufacturing facility

(a) A licensee shall notify the chief of police or other head of the municipal police department in the city or city and county where the building designated in the license is located that the licensee is manufacturing firearms within that city or city and county and the location of the licensed premises.

(b) If there is no police department in the city or city and county where the building designated in the license is located, the licensee shall notify the sheriff of the county where the building designated in the license is located that the licensee is manufacturing firearms within that county and the location of the licensed premises. *(Added by Stats.2010, c. 711 (S.B.1080), § 6, operative Jan. 1, 2012.)*

Law Revision Commission Comments

Section 29150 continues former Section 12086(c)(9) without substantive change.

See Sections 16520 ("firearm"), 29030 ("licensee"). See also Section 29100 (compliance with prohibitions and requirements). [38 Cal.L.Rev.Comm. Reports 217 (2009)].

Cross References

Firearm defined for purposes of this Part, see Penal Code § 16520.
Licensee defined for purposes of this Chapter, see Penal Code § 29030.

CHAPTER 3. ASSEMBLY OF FIREARMS

§ 29180. Manufacture or assembly of firearm; application for unique serial number or mark of identification; affixing number or mark to the firearm; requirements for firearms without a valid serial number; prohibitions and penalties

(a) For purposes of this chapter, "manufacturing" or "assembling" a firearm means to fabricate or construct a firearm, including through additive, subtractive, or other processes, or to fit together the component parts of a firearm to construct a firearm.

(b) * * * Before manufacturing or assembling a firearm, a person manufacturing or assembling the firearm shall, for any firearm that does not have a valid state or federal serial number or mark of identification imprinted on the frame or receiver, do all of the following:

(1)(A) Apply to the Department of Justice for a unique serial number or other mark of identification pursuant to Section 29182.

(B) Each application shall contain a description of the firearm that the applicant intends to assemble, the applicant's full name, address, date of birth, and any other information that the department may deem appropriate.

(2)(A) Within 10 days of manufacturing or assembling a firearm in accordance with paragraph (1), the unique serial number or other mark of identification provided by the department shall be engraved or permanently affixed to the firearm in a manner that meets or exceeds the requirements imposed on licensed importers and licensed manufacturers of firearms pursuant to subsection (i) of Section 923 of Title 18 of the United States Code and regulations issued pursuant thereto.

(B) If the firearm is manufactured or assembled from polymer plastic, 3.7 ounces of material type 17–4 PH stainless steel shall be embedded within the plastic upon fabrication or construction with the unique serial number engraved or otherwise permanently affixed in a manner that meets or exceeds the requirements imposed on licensed importers and licensed manufacturers of firearms pursuant to subsection (i) of Section 923 of Title 18 of the United States Code and regulations issued pursuant thereto.

(3) After the serial number provided by the department is engraved or otherwise permanently affixed to the firearm, the person shall notify the department of that fact in a manner and within a time period specified by the department, and with sufficient information to identify the owner of the firearm, the unique serial number or mark of identification provided by the department, and the firearm in a manner prescribed by the department.

(c) * * * Any person who owns a firearm or firearm precursor part that does not bear a valid state or federal serial number * * * or * * * mark of identification shall be deemed to be in compliance with subdivision (b) of Section 23920 if they comply with all of the following:

(1)* * * (A) By no later than January 1, 2024, or if a new resident of the state, within 60 days after arriving in the state with a firearm that does not have a valid state or federal serial number or mark of identification, apply to the Department of Justice for a unique serial number or other mark of identification pursuant to Section 29182.

(B) An application to the department for a serial number or mark of identification for a firearm precursor part shall include, in a manner prescribed by the department, information identifying the applicant and a description of the firearm that the applicant intends to manufacture or assemble with the firearm precursor part, and any other information that the department may deem appropriate.

(2) Within 10 days of receiving a unique serial number or other mark of identification from the department, * * * engrave or permanently affix that serial number or * * * mark of identification * * * to the firearm in accordance with regulations prescribed by the department pursuant to Section 29182 and in a manner that meets or exceeds the requirements imposed on licensed importers and licensed manufacturers of firearms pursuant to subsection (i) of Section 923 of Title 18 of the United States Code and regulations issued pursuant thereto. If the firearm is manufactured or assembled from polymer plastic, 3.7 ounces of material type 17–4 PH stainless steel shall be embedded within the plastic upon fabrication or construction.

(3) After the serial number provided by the department is engraved or otherwise permanently affixed to the firearm, * * * notify the department of that fact in a manner and within a time period specified by the department and with sufficient information to identify the owner of the firearm, the unique serial number or mark of identification provided by the department, and the firearm in a manner prescribed by the department.

(d)(1) * * * Except by operation of law, a person, corporation, or firm that is not a federally licensed firearms manufacturer shall not sell or transfer * * * ownership of a firearm * * *, as defined in subdivision (g) of Section 16520, if any of the following are true:

(A) That person, corporation, or firm manufactured or assembled the firearm.

(B) That person, corporation, or firm knowingly caused the firearm to be manufactured or assembled by a person, corporation, or firm that is not a federally licensed firearms manufacturer.

(C) That person, corporation, or firm is aware that the firearm was manufactured or assembled by a person, corporation, or firm that is not a federally licensed firearms manufacturer.

(2) Paragraph (1) does not apply to the transfer, surrender, or sale of a firearm to a law enforcement agency.

(3) Any firearms confiscated by law enforcement that do not bear an engraved serial number or other mark of identification pursuant to subdivision (b) or (c), or a firearm surrendered, transferred, or sold to a law enforcement agency pursuant to paragraph (2) shall be destroyed as provided in Section 18005.

(4) Sections 26500 and 27545, and subdivision (a) of Section 31615, do not apply to the transfer, sale, or surrender of firearms to a law enforcement agency pursuant to paragraph (2).

* * *

(e) A person, corporation, or firm shall not knowingly allow, facilitate, aid, or abet the manufacture or assembling of a firearm * * * by a person who is within any of the classes identified by Chapter 2 (commencing with Section 29800) or Chapter 3 (commencing with Section 29900) of Division 9 of this code, or Section 8100 or 8103 of the Welfare and Institutions Code.

(f) A person, corporation, or firm shall not knowingly manufacture or assemble, or knowingly cause, allow, facilitate, aid, or abet the manufacture or assembling of, a firearm that is not imprinted with a valid state or federal serial number or mark of identification.

(g) If the firearm is a handgun, a violation of this section is punishable by imprisonment in a county jail not to exceed one year, or by a fine not to exceed one thousand dollars ($1,000), or by both that fine and imprisonment. For all other firearms, a violation of this section is punishable by imprisonment in a county jail not to exceed six months, or by a fine not to exceed one thousand dollars ($1,000), or by both that fine and imprisonment. Each firearm found to be in violation of this section constitutes a distinct and separate offense. This section does not preclude prosecution under any other law providing for a greater penalty. *(Added by Stats.2016, c. 60 (A.B.857), § 4, eff. Jan. 1, 2017. Amended by Stats.2017, c. 561 (A.B.1516), § 200, eff. Jan. 1, 2018; Stats.2018, c. 780 (S.B.746), § 4, eff. Jan. 1, 2019; Stats.2022, c. 76 (A.B.1621), § 22, eff. June 30, 2022.)*

Cross References

Community care facilities, prohibited acceptance, retention, or storage of firearms, exceptions, see Health and Safety Code § 1567.93.
Residential care facilities for persons with chronic life-threatening illness, prohibited acceptance, retention, or storage of firearms, exceptions, see Health and Safety Code § 1568.098.
Residential care facilities for the elderly, prohibited acceptance, retention, or storage of firearms, exceptions, see Health and Safety Code § 1569.283.
Special firearms rules, firearms eligibility check requirement or request, see Penal Code § 30105.

Research References

2 Witkin, California Criminal Law 4th Crimes Against Public Peace and Welfare § 202 (2021), License to Manufacture.
2 Witkin, California Criminal Law 4th Crimes Against Public Peace and Welfare § 208 (2021), Exempt Activities.

§ 29182. Applications from persons wishing to own a firearm without valid serial number or mark of identification; requirements for granting applications; reasons for denial

(a) * * * The Department of Justice may accept applications from, and may grant applications in the form of serial numbers pursuant to Sections 23910 and 29180 to, persons who wish to * * * own a firearm or firearm precursor part that does not have a valid state or federal serial number or mark of identification.

* * *

(b) An application made pursuant to subdivision (a) shall only be granted by the department if the applicant does all of the following:

(1) For each transaction, completes a firearms eligibility check pursuant to Section 28220 demonstrating that the applicant is not prohibited by state or federal law from possessing, receiving, owning, or purchasing a firearm.

(2) * * * Presents proof of age and identity as specified in Section 16400 * * * demonstrating that person is 21 years of age or older * * *.

* * *

(3) Provides a description of the firearm that * * * the applicant owns or intends to manufacture or assemble, in a manner prescribed by the department.

(4) Has a valid firearm safety * * * certificate.

(c) The department shall inform applicants who are denied an application of the reasons for the denial in writing. The reason for denial may include, without limitation, any of the following:

(1) Based on a firearm eligibility check conducted pursuant to Section 28220, the department has determined that the applicant is prohibited by state or federal law from possessing, receiving, owning, or purchasing a firearm.

(2) Based on a firearm eligibility check conducted pursuant to Section 28220, the department is unable to ascertain the disposition of an arrest or criminal charge, is unable to ascertain the outcome of a mental health evaluation or treatment, or otherwise is unable to conclusively determine that the applicant is not ineligible.

(3) The applicant's description of the firearm that the applicant owns or intends to manufacture or assemble indicates that the firearm would be considered any of the following:

(A) An unsafe handgun.

(B) An assault weapon, as defined in Section 30510 or 30515.

(C) A machinegun.

(D) A .50 BMG rifle.

(E) A destructive device, as defined in Section 16460.

(F) A short-barreled rifle or short-barreled shotgun.

(G) An unconventional pistol.

(H) Any other firearm prohibited by this part.

(d)(1) All applications received on or after January 1, 2024, shall be granted or denied within 90 calendar days after the receipt of the application by the department.

(2) Any application received before January 1, 2024, may be granted or denied within a period of time prescribed by the department.

(e)(1) This chapter does not authorize a person to manufacture, assemble, or possess a weapon prohibited under Section 16590, an assault weapon as defined in Section 30510 or 30515, a machinegun as defined in Section 16880, a .50 BMG rifle as defined in Section 30530, or a destructive device as defined in Section 16460.

(2) This chapter does not authorize a person * * * to manufacture or assemble an unsafe handgun, as defined in Section 31910.

(f) The department shall adopt regulations to administer this chapter. *(Added by Stats.2016, c. 60 (A.B.857), § 4, eff. Jan. 1, 2017. Amended by Stats.2017, c. 561 (A.B.1516), § 202, eff. Jan. 1, 2018; Stats.2018, c. 780 (S.B.746), § 5, eff. Jan. 1, 2019; Stats.2018, c. 894 (S.B.1100), § 2.5, eff. Jan. 1, 2019; Stats.2022, c. 76 (A.B.1621), § 24, eff. June 30, 2022.)*

Cross References

Special firearms rules, firearms eligibility check requirement or request, see Penal Code § 30105.

§ 29183. Fee for issuing distinguishing number or mark

The Department of Justice may charge an applicant a fee for each distinguishing number or mark it issues in an amount sufficient to reimburse it for the actual costs associated with assigning a distinguishing number or mark to a firearm pursuant to Sections 29180 and 29182 and for conducting a firearms eligibility check pursuant to paragraph (1) of subdivision (b) of Section 29182. All money received pursuant to this section shall be deposited in the Dealers' Record of Sale Special Account of the General Fund, to be available upon appropriation by the Legislature. *(Added by Stats.2016, c. 60 (A.B.857), § 4, eff. Jan. 1, 2017. Amended by Stats.2018, c. 780 (S.B.746), § 6, eff. Jan. 1, 2019.)*

§ 29184. Maintenance of information regarding serial numbers and arrests for violations

The Department of Justice shall maintain and make available upon request information concerning both of the following:

(a) The number of serial numbers issued pursuant to Section 29182.

(b) The number of arrests for violations of Section 29180. *(Added by Stats.2016, c. 60 (A.B.857), § 4, eff. Jan. 1, 2017.)*

§ 29185. CNC milling machine; prohibitions; requirements

(a) No person, firm, or corporation, other than a federally licensed firearms manufacturer or importer, shall use a computer numerical control (CNC) milling machine to manufacture a firearm, including a completed frame or receiver or a firearm precursor part.

(b) It is unlawful to sell, offer to sell, or transfer a CNC milling machine that has the sole or primary function of manufacturing firearms to any person in this state, other than a federally licensed firearms manufacturer or importer.

(c) It is unlawful for any person in this state other than a federally licensed firearms manufacturer or importer to possess, purchase, or receive a CNC milling machine that has the sole or primary function of manufacturing firearms.

(d) Subdivisions (b) and (c) do not apply to any of the following:

(1) A person who is engaged in the business of selling manufacturing equipment to a federally licensed firearms manufacturer or importer who possesses a CNC milling machine with the intent to sell or transfer the CNC milling machine to a federally licensed firearms manufacturer or importer.

(2) A common carrier licensed under state law, or a motor carrier, air carrier or carrier affiliated with an air carrier through common controlling interest that is subject to Title 49 of the United States Code, or an authorized agent of any such carrier, when acting in the course and scope of duties incident to the receipt, processing, transportation, or delivery of property.

(3) A person who, before the effective date of the act that added this section, possessed a CNC milling machine that has the sole or primary function of manufacturing firearms and who, within 90 days after that date, does one of the following:

(A) Sells or transfers the machine to a federally licensed firearms manufacturer or importer.

(B) Sells or transfers the machine to a person described in paragraph (1).

(C) Removes the machine from this state.

(D) Relinquished the machine to a law enforcement agency.

(E) Otherwise lawfully terminates possession of the machine.

(e) This section does not apply to any member of the Armed Forces of the United States or the National Guard, while on duty and acting within the scope and course of employment, or any law enforcement agency or forensic laboratory.

(f) A violation of this section is punishable as a misdemeanor. *(Added by Stats.2022, c. 76 (A.B.1621), § 25, eff. June 30, 2022.)*

Division 8

MISCELLANEOUS RULES RELATING TO FIREARMS GENERALLY

CHAPTER 1. MISCELLANEOUS PROVISIONS

Section

§ 29300. Firearms owned or possessed in violation of specified provisions as nuisance

(a) Except as provided in subdivision (c), a firearm of any nature owned or possessed in violation of Chapter 1 (commencing with Section 29610), Chapter 2 (commencing with Section 29800), or Chapter 3 (commencing with Section 29900) of Division 9 of this title, or Chapter 3 (commencing with Section 8100) of Division 5 of the Welfare and Institutions Code, or used in the commission of any misdemeanor as provided in this code, any felony, or an attempt to commit any misdemeanor as provided in this code or any felony, is, upon a conviction of the defendant or upon a juvenile court finding that an offense which would be a misdemeanor or felony if committed by an adult was committed or attempted by the juvenile with the use of a firearm, a nuisance, and is subject to Sections 18000 and 18005.

(b) A finding that the defendant was guilty of the offense but was insane at the time the offense was committed is a conviction for the purposes of this section.

(c) A firearm is not a nuisance pursuant to this section if the firearm owner disposes of the firearm pursuant to Section 29810.

(d) This section does not apply to any of the following:

(1) Any firearm in the possession of the Department of Fish and Game.

(2) Any firearm that was used in the violation of any provision of the Fish and Game Code or any regulation adopted pursuant thereto.

(3) Any firearm that is forfeited pursuant to Section 5008.6 of the Public Resources Code. *(Added by Stats.2010, c. 711 (S.B.1080), § 6, operative Jan. 1, 2012.)*

Law Revision Commission Comments

Subdivision (a) of Section 29300 continues the first sentence of former Section 12028(b)(1) without substantive change.

In combination with Section 18000(c), subdivision (b) continues the second sentence of former Section 12028(b)(1) without substantive change.

Subdivision (c) continues former Section 12028(b)(2) without substantive change.

In combination with Section 25700, subdivision (d) continues former Section 12028(e) without substantive change.

See Section 16520 ("firearm"). [38 Cal.L.Rev.Comm. Reports 217 (2009)].

Cross References

Confiscation of firearms or deadly or dangerous weapons owned or possessed by gang members, see Penal Code § 186.22a.
Felonies, definition and penalties, see Penal Code §§ 17, 18.
Firearm defined for purposes of this Part, see Penal Code § 16520.
Misdemeanors, definition and penalties, see Penal Code §§ 17, 19, 19.2.
Possession of assault weapon or .50 BMG rifle, public nuisance, see Penal Code § 30800.

Public nuisances, see Civil Code § 3490 et seq.

Research References

2 Witkin, California Criminal Law 4th Crimes Against Public Peace and Welfare § 262 (2021), Criminal Storage of Firearm.
2 Witkin, California Criminal Law 4th Crimes Against Public Peace and Welfare § 263 (2021), Nuisances.
3 Witkin, California Criminal Law 4th Punishment § 189 (2021), Criminal Actions.

CHAPTER 2. ENTERTAINMENT FIREARMS PERMIT

§ 29500. Entertainment firearms permits

Any person who is at least 21 years of age may apply for an entertainment firearms permit from the Department of Justice. An entertainment firearms permit authorizes the permitholder to possess firearms loaned to the permitholder for use solely as a prop in a motion picture, television, video, theatrical, or other entertainment production or event. *(Added by Stats.2010, c. 711 (S.B.1080), § 6, operative Jan. 1, 2012.)*

Law Revision Commission Comments

Section 29500 continues the first sentence of former Section 12081(a) without substantive change.

See Section 16520 ("firearm"). [38 Cal.L.Rev.Comm. Reports 217 (2009)].

Cross References

Firearm defined for purposes of this Part, see Penal Code § 16520.

Research References

2 Witkin, California Criminal Law 4th Crimes Against Public Peace and Welfare § 192 (2021), In General.

§ 29505. Entertainment firearms permit requests; contents; fee

(a) Requests for entertainment firearms permits shall be made on application forms prescribed by the Department of Justice that require applicant information, including, but not limited to, the following:

(1) Complete name.

(2) Residential and mailing address.

(3) Telephone number.

(4) Date of birth.

(5) Place of birth.

(6) Country of citizenship and, if other than United States, United States Citizenship and Immigration Services-assigned number.

(7) Valid driver's license number or valid identification card number issued by the California Department of Motor Vehicles.

(8) Social security number.

(9) Signature.

(b) All applications must be submitted with the appropriate fee as specified in Section 29510. *(Added by Stats.2010, c. 711 (S.B.1080), § 6, operative Jan. 1, 2012. Amended by Stats.2021, c. 296 (A.B.1096), § 52, eff. Jan. 1, 2022.)*

Law Revision Commission Comments

Subdivision (a) of Section 29505 continues former Section 12081(b)(1) without substantive change.

Subdivision (b) continues former Section 12081(b)(2) without substantive change. [38 Cal.L.Rev.Comm. Reports 217 (2009)].

Cross References

Firearm defined for purposes of this Part, see Penal Code § 16520.

§ 29510. Entertainment firearms permit program fees; allocation and deposit; review and adjustments

(a) The Department of Justice shall recover the full costs of administering the entertainment firearms permit program by assessing the following application fees:

(1) For the initial application: one hundred four dollars ($104). Of this sum, fifty-six dollars ($56) shall be deposited into the Fingerprint Fee Account, and forty-eight dollars ($48) shall be deposited into the Dealers' Record of Sale Special Account.

(2) For each annual renewal application: twenty-nine dollars ($29), which shall be deposited into the Dealers' Record of Sale Special Account.

(b) The department shall annually review and shall adjust the fees specified in subdivision (a), if necessary, to fully fund, but not to exceed the actual costs of, the permit program provided for by this chapter, including enforcement of the program. *(Added by Stats. 2010, c. 711 (S.B.1080), § 6, operative Jan. 1, 2012. Amended by Stats.2011, c. 296 (A.B.1023), § 237; Stats.2011, c. 285 (A.B.1402), § 27.)*

Law Revision Commission Comments

Subdivision (a) of Section 29510 continues former Section 12081(c) without substantive change.

Subdivision (b) continues former Section 12081(e) without substantive change. [38 Cal.L.Rev.Comm. Reports 217 (2009)].

Section 29510 is amended to replace "Dealer Record of Sale Account" with "Dealers' Record of Sale Special Account." This conforms to the terminology used in other provisions that refer to the same account. See Sections 27560(f), 28235, 28460, 30900, 30905, 31115, 33860. [41 Cal.L.Rev.Comm. Reports 135 (2011)].

Cross References

Firearm defined for purposes of this Part, see Penal Code § 16520.

§ 29515. Entertainment firearms permits; applications and renewals; criminal history and mental health records checks; issuance

(a) Upon receipt of an initial or renewal application submitted as specified in Sections 29505, 29520, and 29525, the department shall examine its records, records the department is authorized to request from the State Department of State Hospitals pursuant to Section 8104 of the Welfare and Institutions Code, and records of the National Instant Criminal Background Check System as described in subsection (t) of Section 922 of Title 18 of the United States Code, in order to determine if the applicant is prohibited from possessing or receiving firearms.

(b) The department shall issue an entertainment firearms permit only if the records indicate that the applicant is not prohibited from possessing or receiving firearms pursuant to any federal, state, or local law. *(Added by Stats.2010, c. 711 (S.B.1080), § 6, operative Jan. 1, 2012. Amended by Stats.2012, c. 24 (A.B.1470), § 58, eff. June 27, 2012.)*

Law Revision Commission Comments

Section 29515 continues the second and third sentences of former Section 12081(a) without substantive change.

See Section 16520 ("firearm"). [38 Cal.L.Rev.Comm. Reports 217 (2009)].

Cross References

Firearm defined for purposes of this Part, see Penal Code § 16520.

§ 29520. Entertainment firearms permits; initial applications; fingerprints; review of criminal offender records

(a) An initial application for an entertainment firearms permit shall require the submission of fingerprint images and related information in a manner prescribed by the department, for the purpose of obtaining information as to the existence and nature of a record of state or federal level convictions and state or federal level arrests for which the department establishes that the individual was released on bail or on the individual's own recognizance pending trial as needed to determine whether the applicant may be issued the permit. Requests for federal level criminal offender record information received by the Department of Justice pursuant to this chapter shall be forwarded by the department to the Federal Bureau of Investigation.

(b) The Department of Justice shall review the criminal offender record information specified in subdivision (*l*) of Section 11105 for entertainment firearms permit applicants.

(c) The Department of Justice shall review subsequent arrests, pursuant to Section 11105.2, to determine the continuing validity of the permit as specified in Section 29530 for all entertainment firearms permitholders. *(Added by Stats.2010, c. 711 (S.B.1080), § 6, operative Jan. 1, 2012.)*

Law Revision Commission Comments

Subdivision (a) of Section 29520 continues former Section 12081(b)(3) without substantive change.

Subdivision (b) continues former Section 12081(b)(4) without substantive change.

Subdivision (c) continues former Section 12081(b)(5) without substantive change. An erroneous cross-reference to former Section 12081(d) has been replaced with a cross-reference to Section 29530, which continues the substance of former Section 12081(f). [38 Cal.L.Rev.Comm. Reports 217 (2009)].

Cross References

Firearm defined for purposes of this Part, see Penal Code § 16520.

§ 29525. Furnishing fictitious name or address; knowingly furnishing incorrect information or omitting required information; penalty

Any person who furnishes a fictitious name or address or knowingly furnishes any incorrect information or knowingly omits any information required to be provided on an application for an entertainment firearms permit is guilty of a misdemeanor. *(Added by Stats.2010, c. 711 (S.B.1080), § 6, operative Jan. 1, 2012.)*

Law Revision Commission Comments

Section 29525 continues former Section 12081(b)(6) without substantive change. [38 Cal.L.Rev.Comm. Reports 217 (2009)].

Cross References

Firearm defined for purposes of this Part, see Penal Code § 16520.
Misdemeanors, definition and penalties, see Penal Code §§ 17, 19, 19.2.

§ 29530. Entertainment firearms permits; expiration

(a) An entertainment firearms permit issued by the Department of Justice shall be valid for one year from the date of issuance.

(b) If at any time during that year the permitholder becomes prohibited from possessing or receiving firearms pursuant to any federal, state, or local law, the entertainment firearms permit shall be no longer valid. *(Added by Stats.2010, c. 711 (S.B.1080), § 6, operative Jan. 1, 2012.)*

Law Revision Commission Comments

Section 29530 continues former Section 12081(f) without substantive change.

See Section 16520 ("firearm"). [38 Cal.L.Rev.Comm. Reports 217 (2009)].

Cross References

Firearm defined for purposes of this Part, see Penal Code § 16520.

§ 29535. Exemption from Administrative Procedure Act

The implementation of Sections 29500, 29505, 29515, 29520, and 29525, and of subdivision (a) of Section 29510, by the department is exempt from the Administrative Procedure Act (Chapter 3.5 (commencing with Section 11340) of Part 1 of Division 3 of Title 2 of the Government Code). *(Added by Stats.2010, c. 711 (S.B.1080), § 6, operative Jan. 1, 2012.)*

Law Revision Commission Comments

Section 29535 continues former Section 12081(d) without substantive change. [38 Cal.L.Rev.Comm. Reports 217 (2009)].

Division 9

SPECIAL FIREARM RULES RELATING TO PARTICULAR PERSONS

CHAPTER 1. JUVENILE

ARTICLE 1. POSSESSION OF FIREARM

§ 29610. Minors; possession of handguns, semiautomatic centerfire rifles, or firearms prohibited

(a) A minor shall not possess a handgun.

(b) A minor shall not possess a semiautomatic centerfire rifle.

(c) Commencing July 1, 2023, a minor shall not possess any firearm.

(d) The provisions of this section are cumulative, and shall not be construed as restricting the application of any other law. However, an act or omission punishable in different ways by different provisions of this code shall not be punished under more than one provision. *(Added by Stats.2010, c. 711 (S.B.1080), § 6, operative Jan. 1, 2012. Amended by Stats.2021, c. 250 (S.B.715), § 21, eff. Jan. 1, 2022.)*

Law Revision Commission Comments

Section 29610 continues former Section 12101(a)(1) without substantive change.

For exceptions to this provision, see Section 29615 (exceptions). For the consequences of violating this provision, see Sections 29700 (punishment for violation of chapter), 29705 (compulsory participation in parenting education).

For further guidance on firearm restrictions relating to minors and persons under age 21, see Sections 27505 (person, corporation, or firm that sells, loans, or transfers firearm to minor or handgun to person under age 21), 27510 (dealer that supplies, delivers, or gives possession or control of firearm to minor or handgun to person under age 21), 27945 (exception for certain situations involving minor), 29650 (prohibition on possession of live ammunition by minor), 29655 (exceptions).

See Section 16530 ("firearm capable of being concealed upon the person," "pistol," and "revolver"). [38 Cal.L.Rev.Comm. Reports 217 (2009)].

Cross References

Firearm capable of being concealed upon the person defined for purposes of this Part, see Penal Code § 16530.
Firearm defined for purposes of this Part, see Penal Code § 16520.
Minor, see Family Code § 6500.
Misdemeanor, committing act relative to threatening crime victim, witness or informant, punishment, see Penal Code § 140.
Pistol defined for purposes of this Part, see Penal Code § 16530.
Revolver defined for purposes of this Part, see Penal Code § 16530.
Sale of BB device to minor without written consent of parent, see Penal Code §§ 19910, 19915.

Research References

2 Witkin, California Criminal Law 4th Crimes Against Public Peace and Welfare § 196 (2021), Transfers to Specified Persons.
2 Witkin, California Criminal Law 4th Crimes Against Public Peace and Welfare § 203 (2021), Nature of Crime.
2 Witkin, California Criminal Law 4th Crimes Against Public Peace and Welfare § 204 (2021), Punishment.
2 Witkin, California Criminal Law 4th Crimes Against Public Peace and Welfare § 210 (2021), Unlawful Acts Involving Ammunition.
2 Witkin, California Criminal Law 4th Crimes Against Public Peace and Welfare § 232 (2021), Nature and Scope of Statutes.
2 Witkin, California Criminal Law 4th Crimes Against Public Peace and Welfare § 243 (2021), Minors.
2 Witkin, California Criminal Law 4th Crimes Against Public Peace and Welfare § 250 (2021), Punishment.
2 Witkin, California Criminal Law 4th Crimes Against Public Peace and Welfare § 263 (2021), Nuisances.
3 Witkin, California Criminal Law 4th Punishment § 666 (2021), Other Express Conditions.

§ 29615. Exemptions to prohibition on possession of handguns, semiautomatic centerfire rifle, or firearms by minors

Section 29610 shall not apply if one of the following circumstances exists:

(a) The minor is accompanied by a parent or legal guardian, and the minor is actively engaged in, or is in direct transit to or from, a lawful, recreational sport, including, but not limited to, competitive shooting, or agricultural, ranching, or hunting activity or hunting education, or a motion picture, television, or video production, or entertainment or theatrical event, the nature of which involves this use of a firearm.

(b) The minor is accompanied by a responsible adult, the minor has the prior written consent of a parent or legal guardian, and the minor is actively engaged in, or is in direct transit to or from, a lawful, recreational sport, including, but not limited to, competitive shooting, or agricultural, ranching, or hunting activity or hunting education, or a motion picture, television, or video production, or entertainment or theatrical event, the nature of which involves the use of a firearm.

(c) The minor is at least 16 years of age, the minor has the prior written consent of a parent or legal guardian, and the minor is actively engaged in, or is in direct transit to or from, a lawful recreational sport, including, but not limited to, competitive shooting, or agricultural, ranching, or hunting activity or hunting education, or a motion picture, television, or video production, or entertainment or theatrical event, the nature of which involves the use of a firearm.

(d) The minor has the prior written consent of a parent or legal guardian, the minor is on lands owned or lawfully possessed by the parent or legal guardian, and the minor is actively engaged in, or is in direct transit to or from, a lawful, recreational sport, including, but not limited to, competitive shooting, or agricultural, ranching, or hunting activity, or a motion picture, television, or video production, or entertainment or theatrical event, the nature of which involves the use of a firearm.

(e) The minor possesses, with the express permission of their parent or legal guardian, a firearm, other than a handgun or semiautomatic centerfire rifle, and both of the following are true:

(1) The minor is actively engaged in, or in direct transit to or from, a lawful, recreational sport, including, but not limited to, competitive shooting, or an agricultural, ranching, or hunting activity or hunting education, the nature of which involves the use of a firearm.

(2) The minor is 16 years of age or older or is accompanied by a responsible adult at all times while the minor is possessing the firearm. *(Added by Stats.2010, c. 711 (S.B.1080), § 6, operative Jan. 1, 2012. Amended by Stats.2011, c. 296 (A.B.1023), § 238; Stats. 2021, c. 250 (S.B.715), § 22, eff. Jan. 1, 2022.)*

Law Revision Commission Comments

Section 29615 continues former Section 12101(a)(2) without substantive change.

See Sections 16520 ("firearm"), 17070 ("responsible adult"). [38 Cal.L.Rev. Comm. Reports 217 (2009)].

Cross References

Firearm defined for purposes of this Part, see Penal Code § 16520.
Minor, see Family Code § 6500.
Misdemeanor, committing act relative to threatening crime victim, witness or informant, punishment, see Penal Code § 140.
Sale of BB device to minor without written consent of parent, see Penal Code §§ 19910, 19915.

Research References

2 Witkin, California Criminal Law 4th Crimes Against Public Peace and Welfare § 243 (2021), Minors.

ARTICLE 2. POSSESSION OF LIVE AMMUNITION

Section

§ 29650. Possession of live ammunition by minor prohibited

A minor shall not possess live ammunition. *(Added by Stats.2010, c. 711 (S.B.1080), § 6, operative Jan. 1, 2012.)*

Law Revision Commission Comments

Section 29650 continues former Section 12101(b)(1) without substantive change.

For exceptions to this provision, see Section 29655 (exceptions). For the consequences of violating this provision, see Sections 29700 (punishment for violation of chapter), 29705 (compulsory participation in parenting education).

For further guidance on firearm restrictions relating to minors and persons under age 21, see Sections 27505 (person, corporation, or firm that sells, loans, or transfers firearm to minor or handgun to person under age 21), 27510 (dealer that supplies, delivers, or gives possession or control of firearm to minor or handgun to person under age 21), 27945 (exception for certain situations involving minor), 29610 (prohibition on possession of handgun by minor), 29615 (exceptions). [38 Cal.L.Rev.Comm. Reports 217 (2009)].

Research References

2 Witkin, California Criminal Law 4th Crimes Against Public Peace and Welfare § 243 (2021), Minors.

1 Witkin California Criminal Law 4th Introduction to Crimes § 38 (2021), Illustrations.

§ 29655. Exceptions to prohibition on possession of live ammunition by a minor

Section 29650 shall not apply if one of the following circumstances exists:

(a) The minor has the written consent of a parent or legal guardian to possess live ammunition.

(b) The minor is accompanied by a parent or legal guardian.

(c) The minor is actively engaged in, or is going to or from, a lawful, recreational sport, including, but not limited to, competitive shooting, or agricultural, ranching, or hunting activity, the nature of which involves the use of a firearm. *(Added by Stats.2010, c. 711 (S.B.1080), § 6, operative Jan. 1, 2012.)*

Law Revision Commission Comments

Section 29655 continues former Section 12101(b)(2) without substantive change.

See Section 16520 ("firearm"). [38 Cal.L.Rev.Comm. Reports 217 (2009)].

Cross References

Firearm defined for purposes of this Part, see Penal Code § 16520.

ARTICLE 3. PUNISHMENT

§ 29700. Penalties for violations of chapter by minors

Every minor who violates this chapter shall be punished as follows:

(a) By imprisonment pursuant to subdivision (h) of Section 1170 or in a county jail if one of the following applies:

(1) The minor has been found guilty previously of violating this chapter.

(2) The minor has been found guilty previously of an offense specified in Section 29905, 32625, or 33410, or an offense specified in any provision listed in Section 16590.

(3) The minor has been found guilty of possessing a handgun in violation of Section 29610.

(b) Violations of this chapter other than those violations specified in subdivision (a) shall be punishable as a misdemeanor. *(Added by Stats.2010, c. 711 (S.B.1080), § 6, operative Jan. 1, 2012. Amended by Stats.2011, c. 15 (A.B.109), § 547, eff. April 4, 2011, operative Jan. 1, 2012; Stats.2021, c. 250 (S.B.715), § 23, eff. Jan. 1, 2022.)*

Law Revision Commission Comments

Section 29700 continues former Section 12101(c) without substantive change. A cross-reference to former Section 12560 has not been continued, because that provision was repealed in 1990. See 1990 Cal. Stat. ch. 9, § 14.

For guidance in applying paragraphs (a)(1) and (a)(2), see Section 16015 (determining existence of prior conviction). For requirements a court may impose on a parent or guardian of a minor who violates this chapter, see Section 29705 (compulsory participation in parenting education). [38 Cal. L.Rev.Comm. Reports 217 (2009)].

Cross References

Misdemeanors, definition and penalties, see Penal Code §§ 17, 19, 19.2.

Research References

2 Witkin, California Criminal Law 4th Crimes Against Public Peace and Welfare § 243 (2021), Minors.

§ 29705. Custodial parent or legal guardian of minor in violation of firearms or ammunition possession restrictions; parenting education classes

In a proceeding to enforce this chapter brought pursuant to Article 14 (commencing with Section 601) of Chapter 2 of Part 1 of Division 2 of the Welfare and Institutions Code, the court may require the custodial parent or legal guardian of a minor who violates this chapter to participate in classes on parenting education that meet the requirements established in Section 16507.7 of the Welfare and Institutions Code. *(Added by Stats.2010, c. 711 (S.B.1080), § 6, operative Jan. 1, 2012.)*

Law Revision Commission Comments

Section 29705 continues former Section 12101(d) without substantive change. An incomplete cross-reference to an article in the Welfare and Institutions Code has been corrected.

For guidance on punishment of a minor who violates this chapter, see Section 29700 (punishment). [38 Cal.L.Rev.Comm. Reports 217 (2009)].

Research References

2 Witkin, California Criminal Law 4th Crimes Against Public Peace and Welfare § 243 (2021), Minors.

ARTICLE 4. LEGISLATIVE INTENT

§ 29750. Legislative intent regarding expanding or narrowing application of statutory or judicial authority in relation to the rights of minors to be loaned or possess live ammunition or firearms for defensive purposes

(a) In enacting the amendments to former Sections 12078 and 12101 by Section 10 of Chapter 33 of the Statutes of 1994, First Extraordinary Session, it was not the intent of the Legislature to expand or narrow the application of the then-existing statutory and judicial authority as to the rights of minors to be loaned or to possess live ammunition or a firearm for the purpose of self-defense or the defense of others.

(b) In enacting the act that adds this subdivision,[1] it is not the intent of the Legislature to expand or narrow the application of existing statutory and judicial authority as to the rights of minors to be loaned or to possess live ammunition or a firearm for the purpose of self-defense or the defense of others. *(Added by Stats.2010, c. 711 (S.B.1080), § 6, operative Jan. 1, 2012. Amended by Stats.2021, c. 250 (S.B.715), § 24, eff. Jan. 1, 2022.)*

[1] Stats.2021, c. 250 (S.B.715).

Law Revision Commission Comments

Section 29750 continues former Section 12101(f) without substantive change. See Section 16520 ("firearm"). [38 Cal.L.Rev.Comm. Reports 217 (2009)].

Cross References

Firearm defined for purposes of this Part, see Penal Code § 16520.

Research References

2 Witkin, California Criminal Law 4th Crimes Against Public Peace and Welfare § 243 (2021), Minors.

CHAPTER 2. PERSON CONVICTED OF SPECIFIED OFFENSE, ADDICTED TO NARCOTIC, OR SUBJECT TO COURT ORDER

ARTICLE 1. PROHIBITIONS ON FIREARM ACCESS

§ 29800. Specified convictions or outstanding warrants; narcotic addiction; restriction on firearm possession; punishment

(a)(1) Any person who has been convicted of a felony under the laws of the United States, the State of California, or any other state, government, or country, or of an offense enumerated in subdivision (a), (b), or (d) of Section 23515, or who is addicted to the use of any narcotic drug, and who owns, purchases, receives, or has in possession or under custody or control any firearm is guilty of a felony.

(2) Any person who has two or more convictions for violating paragraph (2) of subdivision (a) of Section 417 and who owns, purchases, receives, or has in possession or under custody or control any firearm is guilty of a felony.

(3) Any person who has an outstanding warrant for any offense listed in this subdivision and who has knowledge of the outstanding warrant, and who owns, purchases, receives, or has in possession or under custody or control any firearm is guilty of a felony.

(b) Notwithstanding subdivision (a), any person who has been convicted of a felony or of an offense enumerated in Section 23515, when that conviction results from certification by the juvenile court for prosecution as an adult in an adult court under Section 707 of the Welfare and Institutions Code, and who owns or has in possession or under custody or control any firearm is guilty of a felony.

(c) Subdivision (a) shall not apply to a conviction or warrant for a felony under the laws of the United States unless either of the following criteria, as applicable, is satisfied:

(1) Conviction of a like offense under California law can only result in imposition of felony punishment.

(2) The defendant was sentenced to a federal correctional facility for more than 30 days, or received a fine of more than one thousand dollars ($1,000), or received both punishments. *(Added by Stats. 2010, c. 711 (S.B.1080), § 6, operative Jan. 1, 2012. Amended by Stats.2017, c. 17 (A.B.103), § 44, eff. June 27, 2017; Stats.2020, c. 306 (S.B.723), § 1, eff. Jan. 1, 2021.)*

Law Revision Commission Comments

Subdivision (a) of Section 29800 continues former Section 12021(a) without substantive change.

Subdivision (b) continues former Section 12021(b) without substantive change.

For an exemption from the prohibitions in subdivisions (a) and (b), see Section 29850 (justifiable violation of Section 29800, 29805, 29815, or 29820). For a notice requirement relating to those prohibitions, see Section 29810 (notice to person who is subject to Section 29800 or 29805).

Subdivision (c) continues former Section 12021(f) without substantive change.

See Section 16520 ("firearm"). [38 Cal.L.Rev.Comm. Reports 217 (2009)].

Cross References

Felonies, definition and penalties, see Penal Code §§ 17, 18.
Firearm defined for purposes of this Part, see Penal Code § 16520.
Persons prohibited from obtaining firearms, providing fictitious or incorrect information, see Penal Code § 28250.

Research References

California Jury Instructions - Criminal 12.43, Firearm—Possession by Person Convicted of a Felony—No Stipulation of Status.
California Jury Instructions - Criminal 12.44, Firearm—Possession by Person Convicted of a Felony—Status Stipulated.
California Jury Instructions - Criminal 12.45, Firearm—Possession by Narcotic Addict.
2 Witkin, California Criminal Law 4th Crimes Against Public Peace and Welfare § 169 (2021), Drug Treatment Program.
2 Witkin, California Criminal Law 4th Crimes Against Public Peace and Welfare § 194 (2021), Furnishing Erroneous Firearm Purchaser Information.
2 Witkin, California Criminal Law 4th Crimes Against Public Peace and Welfare § 196 (2021), Transfers to Specified Persons.
2 Witkin, California Criminal Law 4th Crimes Against Public Peace and Welfare § 202 (2021), License to Manufacture.
2 Witkin, California Criminal Law 4th Crimes Against Public Peace and Welfare § 204 (2021), Punishment.
2 Witkin, California Criminal Law 4th Crimes Against Public Peace and Welfare § 207 (2021), Exempt Persons.
2 Witkin, California Criminal Law 4th Crimes Against Public Peace and Welfare § 210 (2021), Unlawful Acts Involving Ammunition.
2 Witkin, California Criminal Law 4th Crimes Against Public Peace and Welfare § 232 (2021), Nature and Scope of Statutes.
2 Witkin, California Criminal Law 4th Crimes Against Public Peace and Welfare § 233 (2021), Prohibitions.
2 Witkin, California Criminal Law 4th Crimes Against Public Peace and Welfare § 234 (2021), Effect of Pardon or Dismissal After Fulfillment of Probation Conditions.
2 Witkin, California Criminal Law 4th Crimes Against Public Peace and Welfare § 235 (2021), Felon's Use of Firearm in Self-Defense.
2 Witkin, California Criminal Law 4th Crimes Against Public Peace and Welfare § 236 (2021), Knowledge of Status as Felon.
2 Witkin, California Criminal Law 4th Crimes Against Public Peace and Welfare § 237 (2021), Temporary Possession for Disposal.
2 Witkin, California Criminal Law 4th Crimes Against Public Peace and Welfare § 239 (2021), Misdemeanants.
2 Witkin, California Criminal Law 4th Crimes Against Public Peace and Welfare § 248 (2021), Knowledge and Intent as Elements.
2 Witkin, California Criminal Law 4th Crimes Against Public Peace and Welfare § 250 (2021), Punishment.
2 Witkin, California Criminal Law 4th Crimes Against Public Peace and Welfare § 253A (2021), (New) Carrying Unloaded Firearm that is Not Handgun in Incorporated Area or Other Public Place.
2 Witkin, California Criminal Law 4th Crimes Against Public Peace and Welfare § 257 (2021), Firearms.
2 Witkin, California Criminal Law 4th Crimes Against Public Peace and Welfare § 263 (2021), Nuisances.
1 Witkin California Criminal Law 4th Defenses § 69 (2021), Prisoners and Ex-Felons.
4 Witkin, California Criminal Law 4th Illegally Obtained Evidence § 111 (2021), Statutory Grounds.
4 Witkin, California Criminal Law 4th Pretrial Proceedings § 85E (2021), (New) Limitations on Sealing Order.
4 Witkin, California Criminal Law 4th Pretrial Proceedings § 310 (2021), Where Rule Does Not Apply.

3 Witkin, California Criminal Law 4th Punishment § 100 (2021), Discharge.
3 Witkin, California Criminal Law 4th Punishment § 248 (2021), Nature and Purpose of Statute.
3 Witkin, California Criminal Law 4th Punishment § 252 (2021), In General.
3 Witkin, California Criminal Law 4th Punishment § 308C (2021), (New) Offense is Misdemeanor for All Purposes.
3 Witkin, California Criminal Law 4th Punishment § 446 (2021), Effect of Defendant's Admission.
3 Witkin, California Criminal Law 4th Punishment § 719 (2021), Remaining Effects of Conviction.
3 Witkin, California Criminal Law 4th Punishment § 720B (2021), (New) Automatic Conviction Record Relief.

§ 29805. Specified convictions or outstanding warrants; restriction on firearm possession; punishment

(a)(1) Except as provided in Section 29855, subdivision (a) of Section 29800, or subdivision (b), any person who has been convicted of a misdemeanor violation of Section 71, 76, 136.1, 136.5, or 140, subdivision (d) of Section 148, subdivision (f) of Section 148.5, Section 171b, paragraph (1) of subdivision (a) of Section 171c, Section 171d, 186.28, 240, 241, 242, 243, 243.4, 244.5, 245, 245.5, 246.3, 247, 273.5, 273.6, 417, 417.6, 422, 422.6, 626.9, 646.9, 830.95, 17500, 17510, 25300, 25800, 30315, or 32625, subdivision (b) or (d) of Section 26100, or Section 27510, or Section 8100, 8101, or 8103 of the Welfare and Institutions Code, any firearm-related offense pursuant to Sections 871.5 and 1001.5 of the Welfare and Institutions Code, Section 487 if the property taken was a firearm, or of the conduct punished in subdivision (c) of Section 27590, and who, within 10 years of the conviction, owns, purchases, receives, or has in possession or under custody or control, any firearm is guilty of a public offense, punishable by imprisonment in a county jail not exceeding one year or in the state prison, by a fine not exceeding one thousand dollars ($1,000), or by both that imprisonment and fine.

(2) Any person who has an outstanding warrant for any misdemeanor offense described in this subdivision, and who has knowledge of the outstanding warrant, and who owns, purchases, receives, or has in possession or under custody or control any firearm is guilty of a public offense, punishable by imprisonment in a county jail not exceeding one year or in the state prison, by a fine not exceeding one thousand dollars ($1,000), or by both that imprisonment and fine.

(b) Any person who is convicted, on or after January 1, 2019, of a misdemeanor violation of Section 273.5, and who subsequently owns, purchases, receives, or has in possession or under custody or control, any firearm is guilty of a public offense, punishable by imprisonment in a county jail not exceeding one year or in the state prison, by a fine not exceeding one thousand dollars ($1,000), or by both that imprisonment and fine.

(c) * * * Any person who is convicted on or after January 1, 2020, of a misdemeanor violation of Section 25100, 25135, or 25200, and who, within 10 years of the conviction owns, purchases, receives, or has in possession or under custody or control, any firearm is guilty of a public offense, punishable by imprisonment in a county jail not exceeding one year or in the state prison, by a fine not exceeding one thousand dollars ($1,000), or by both that fine and imprisonment.

(d) Any person who is convicted on or after January 1, 2023, of a misdemeanor violation of Section 273a, subdivision (b), (c), or (f) of Section 368, or subdivision (e) or (f) of Section 29180, and who, within 10 years of the conviction owns, purchases, receives, or has in possession or under custody or control, any firearm is guilty of a public offense, punishable by imprisonment in a county jail not exceeding one year or in the state prison, by a fine not exceeding one thousand dollars ($1,000), or by both that fine and imprisonment.

(e) The court, on forms prescribed by the Department of Justice, shall notify the department of persons subject to this section. However, the prohibition in this section may be reduced, eliminated, or conditioned as provided in Section 29855 or 29860. *(Added by Stats.2010, c. 711 (S.B.1080), § 6.76, operative Jan. 1, 2012. Amended by Initiative Measure (Prop. 63, § 11.2, approved Nov. 8, 2016, eff. Nov. 9, 2016); Stats.2017, c. 17 (A.B.103), § 45, eff. June 27, 2017; Stats.2017, c. 784 (A.B.785), § 1, eff. Jan. 1, 2018; Stats.2018, c. 883 (A.B.3129), § 1, eff. Jan. 1, 2019; Stats.2019, c. 256 (S.B.781), § 13, eff. Jan. 1, 2020; Stats.2019, c. 840 (S.B.172), § 13, eff. Jan. 1, 2020; Stats.2020, c. 306 (S.B.723), § 2, eff. Jan. 1, 2021; Stats.2022, c. 76 (A.B.1621), § 26, eff. June 30, 2022; Stats.2022, c. 143 (A.B.2239), § 1.5, eff. Jan. 1, 2023.)*

Law Revision Commission Comments

Section 29805 continues former Section 12021(c)(1) without substantive change.

For an exemption from this provision, see Section 29850 (justifiable violation of Section 29800, 29805, 29815, or 29820). For guidance on petitioning for relief from this provision, see Sections 29855 (petition by peace officer for relief from prohibition in Section 29805) and 29860 (petition by person who was convicted of offense before that offense was added to Section 29805). For guidance on false arrest arising from enforcement of this provision, see Section 29865 (immunity from liability for false arrest). For a notice requirement relating to this provision, see Section 29810 (notice to person who is subject to Section 29800 or 29805).

See Section 16520 ("firearm"). [40 Cal.L.Rev.Comm. Reports 107 (2010)].

Cross References

Conditions for transfer of student convicted of misdemeanor listed in this section, see Education Code § 48929.
Firearm defined for purposes of this Part, see Penal Code § 16520.
Misdemeanors, definition and penalties, see Penal Code §§ 17, 19, 19.2.
Persons prohibited from obtaining firearms, providing fictitious or incorrect information, see Penal Code § 28250.

Research References

2 Witkin, California Criminal Law 4th Crimes Against Public Peace and Welfare § 232 (2021), Nature and Scope of Statutes.
2 Witkin, California Criminal Law 4th Crimes Against Public Peace and Welfare § 239 (2021), Misdemeanants.
4 Witkin, California Criminal Law 4th Illegally Obtained Evidence § 111 (2021), Statutory Grounds.

§ 29810. Persons subject to firearm possession restrictions upon conviction for specified offenses; relinquishment of firearms; use of Prohibited Persons Relinquishment Form

(a)(1) Upon conviction of any offense that renders a person subject to Section 29800 or Section 29805, the person shall relinquish all firearms he or she owns, possesses, or has under his or her custody or control in the manner provided in this section.

(2) The court shall, upon conviction of a defendant for an offense described in subdivision (a), instruct the defendant that he or she is prohibited from owning, purchasing, receiving, possessing, or having under his or her custody or control, any firearms, ammunition, and ammunition feeding devices, including but not limited to magazines, and shall order the defendant to relinquish all firearms in the manner provided in this section. The court shall also provide the defendant with a Prohibited Persons Relinquishment Form developed by the Department of Justice.

(3) Using the Prohibited Persons Relinquishment Form, the defendant shall name a designee and grant the designee power of attorney for the purpose of transferring or disposing of any firearms. The designee shall be either a local law enforcement agency or a consenting third party who is not prohibited from possessing firearms under state or federal law. The designee shall, within the time periods specified in subdivisions (d) and (e), surrender the firearms to the control of a local law enforcement agency, sell the firearms to a licensed firearms dealer, or transfer the firearms for storage to a firearms dealer pursuant to Section 29830.

(b) The Prohibited Persons Relinquishment Form shall do all of the following:

(1) Inform the defendant that he or she is prohibited from owning, purchasing, receiving, possessing, or having under his or her custody or control, any firearms, ammunition, and ammunition feeding

devices, including but not limited to magazines, and that he or she shall relinquish all firearms through a designee within the time periods set forth in subdivision (d) or (e) by surrendering the firearms to the control of a local law enforcement agency, selling the firearms to a licensed firearms dealer, or transferring the firearms for storage to a firearms dealer pursuant to Section 29830.

(2) Inform the defendant that any cohabitant of the defendant who owns firearms must store those firearms in accordance with Section 25135.

(3) Require the defendant to declare any firearms that he or she owned, possessed, or had under his or her custody or control at the time of his or her conviction, and require the defendant to describe the firearms and provide all reasonably available information about the location of the firearms to enable a designee or law enforcement officials to locate the firearms.

(4) Require the defendant to name a designee, if the defendant declares that he or she owned, possessed, or had under his or her custody or control any firearms at the time of his or her conviction, and grant the designee power of attorney for the purpose of transferring or disposing of all firearms.

(5) Require the designee to indicate his or her consent to the designation and, except a designee that is a law enforcement agency, to declare under penalty of perjury that he or she is not prohibited from possessing any firearms under state or federal law.

(6) Require the designee to state the date each firearm was relinquished and the name of the party to whom it was relinquished, and to attach receipts from the law enforcement officer or licensed firearms dealer who took possession of the relinquished firearms.

(7) Inform the defendant and the designee of the obligation to submit the completed Prohibited Persons Relinquishment Form to the assigned probation officer within the time periods specified in subdivisions (d) and (e).

(c)(1) When a defendant is convicted of an offense described in subdivision (a), the court shall immediately assign the matter to a probation officer to investigate whether the Automated Firearms System or other credible information, such as a police report, reveals that the defendant owns, possesses, or has under his or her custody or control any firearms. The assigned probation officer shall receive the Prohibited Persons Relinquishment Form from the defendant or the defendant's designee, as applicable, and ensure that the Automated Firearms System has been properly updated to indicate that the defendant has relinquished those firearms.

(2) Prior to final disposition or sentencing in the case, the assigned probation officer shall report to the court whether the defendant has properly complied with the requirements of this section by relinquishing all firearms identified by the probation officer's investigation or declared by the defendant on the Prohibited Persons Relinquishment Form, and by timely submitting a completed Prohibited Persons Relinquishment Form. The probation officer shall also report to the Department of Justice on a form to be developed by the department whether the Automated Firearms System has been updated to indicate which firearms have been relinquished by the defendant.

(3) Prior to final disposition or sentencing in the case, the court shall make findings concerning whether the probation officer's report indicates that the defendant has relinquished all firearms as required, and whether the court has received a completed Prohibited Persons Relinquishment Form, along with the receipts described in paragraph (1) of subdivision (d) or paragraph (1) of subdivision (e). The court shall ensure that these findings are included in the abstract of judgment. If necessary to avoid a delay in sentencing, the court may make and enter these findings within 14 days of sentencing.

(4) If the court finds probable cause that the defendant has failed to relinquish any firearms as required, the court shall order the search for and removal of any firearms at any location where the judge has probable cause to believe the defendant's firearms are located. The court shall state with specificity the reasons for and scope of the search and seizure authorized by the order.

(5) Failure by a defendant to timely file the completed Prohibited Persons Relinquishment Form with the assigned probation officer shall constitute an infraction punishable by a fine not exceeding one hundred dollars ($100).

(d) The following procedures shall apply to any defendant who is a prohibited person within the meaning of paragraph (1) of subdivision (a) who does not remain in custody at any time within the five-day period following conviction:

(1) The designee shall dispose of any firearms the defendant owns, possesses, or has under his or her custody or control within five days of the conviction by surrendering the firearms to the control of a local law enforcement agency, selling the firearms to a licensed firearms dealer, or transferring the firearms for storage to a firearms dealer pursuant to Section 29830, in accordance with the wishes of the defendant. Any proceeds from the sale of the firearms shall become the property of the defendant. The law enforcement officer or licensed dealer taking possession of any firearms pursuant to this subdivision shall issue a receipt to the designee describing the firearms and listing any serial number or other identification on the firearms at the time of surrender.

(2) If the defendant owns, possesses, or has under his or her custody or control any firearms to relinquish, the defendant's designee shall submit the completed Prohibited Persons Relinquishment Form to the assigned probation officer within five days following the conviction, along with the receipts described in paragraph (1) of subdivision (d) showing the defendant's firearms were surrendered to a local law enforcement agency or sold or transferred to a licensed firearms dealer.

(3) If the defendant does not own, possess, or have under his or her custody or control any firearms to relinquish, he or she shall, within five days following conviction, submit the completed Prohibited Persons Relinquishment Form to the assigned probation officer, with a statement affirming that he or she has no firearms to be relinquished.

(e) The following procedures shall apply to any defendant who is a prohibited person within the meaning of paragraph (1) of subdivision (a) who is in custody at any point within the five-day period following conviction:

(1) The designee shall dispose of any firearms the defendant owns, possesses, or has under his or her custody or control within 14 days of the conviction by surrendering the firearms to the control of a local law enforcement agency, selling the firearms to a licensed firearms dealer, or transferring the firearms for storage to a firearms dealer pursuant to Section 29830, in accordance with the wishes of the defendant. Any proceeds from the sale of the firearms shall become the property of the defendant. The law enforcement officer or licensed dealer taking possession of any firearms pursuant to this subdivision shall issue a receipt to the designee describing the firearms and listing any serial number or other identification on the firearms at the time of surrender.

(2) If the defendant owns, possesses, or has under his or her custody or control any firearms to relinquish, the defendant's designee shall submit the completed Prohibited Persons Relinquishment Form to the assigned probation officer, within 14 days following conviction, along with the receipts described in paragraph (1) of subdivision (e) showing the defendant's firearms were surrendered to a local law enforcement agency or sold or transferred to a licensed firearms dealer.

(3) If the defendant does not own, possess, or have under his or her custody or control any firearms to relinquish, he or she shall, within 14 days following conviction, submit the completed Prohibited Persons Relinquishment Form to the assigned probation officer, with

a statement affirming that he or she has no firearms to be relinquished.

(4) If the defendant is released from custody during the 14 days following conviction and a designee has not yet taken temporary possession of each firearm to be relinquished as described above, the defendant shall, within five days following his or her release, relinquish each firearm required to be relinquished pursuant to paragraph (1) of subdivision (d).

(f) For good cause, the court may shorten or enlarge the time periods specified in subdivisions (d) and (e), enlarge the time period specified in paragraph (3) of subdivision (c), or allow an alternative method of relinquishment.

(g) The defendant shall not be subject to prosecution for unlawful possession of any firearms declared on the Prohibited Persons Relinquishment Form if the firearms are relinquished as required.

(h) Any firearms that would otherwise be subject to relinquishment by a defendant under this section, but which are lawfully owned by a cohabitant of the defendant, shall be exempt from relinquishment, provided the defendant is notified that the cohabitant must store the firearm in accordance with Section 25135.

(i) A law enforcement agency shall update the Automated Firearms System to reflect any firearms that were relinquished to the agency pursuant to this section. A law enforcement agency shall retain a firearm that was relinquished to the agency pursuant to this section for 30 days after the date the firearm was relinquished. After the 30–day period has expired, the firearm is subject to destruction, retention, sale or other transfer by the agency, except upon the certificate of a judge of a court of record, or of the district attorney of the county, that the retention of the firearm is necessary or proper to the ends of justice, or if the defendant provides written notice of an intent to appeal a conviction for an offense described in subdivision (a), or if the Automated Firearms System indicates that the firearm was reported lost or stolen by the lawful owner. If the firearm was reported lost or stolen, the firearm shall be restored to the lawful owner, as soon as its use as evidence has been served, upon the lawful owner's identification of the weapon and proof of ownership, and after the law enforcement agency has complied with Chapter 2 (commencing with Section 33850) of Division 11 of Title 4. The agency shall notify the Department of Justice of the disposition of relinquished firearms pursuant to Section 34010.

(j) A city, county, or city and county, or a state agency may adopt a regulation, ordinance, or resolution imposing a charge equal to its administrative costs relating to the seizure, impounding, storage, or release of a firearm pursuant to Section 33880.

(k) This section shall become operative on January 1, 2018. *(Added by Initiative Measure (Prop. 63, § 10.4, approved Nov. 8, 2016, eff. Nov. 9, 2016, operative Jan. 1, 2018).)*

Cross References

Firearm defined for purposes of this Part, see Penal Code § 16520.
Taking or transferring possession of any assault weapon, .50 BMG rifle, or firearm precursor part, see Business and Professions Code § 22949.63.

Research References

West's California Judicial Council Forms CR–210, Prohibited Persons Relinquishment Form Findings.
2 Witkin, California Criminal Law 4th Crimes Against Public Peace and Welfare § 193 (2021), Sale, Lease, or Transfer by Unlicensed Person.
2 Witkin, California Criminal Law 4th Crimes Against Public Peace and Welfare § 233 (2021), Prohibitions.
2 Witkin, California Criminal Law 4th Crimes Against Public Peace and Welfare § 239 (2021), Misdemeanants.
2 Witkin, California Criminal Law 4th Crimes Against Public Peace and Welfare § 263 (2021), Nuisances.
4 Witkin, California Criminal Law 4th Illegally Obtained Evidence § 111 (2021), Statutory Grounds.
3 Witkin, California Criminal Law 4th Punishment § 189 (2021), Criminal Actions.

§ 29815. Probation condition restricting possession of firearm; punishment for violation; notice to department of persons subject to this section

(a) Any person who, as an express condition of probation, is prohibited or restricted from owning, possessing, controlling, receiving, or purchasing a firearm and who owns, purchases, receives, or has in possession or under custody or control, any firearm, but who is not subject to Section 29805 or subdivision (a) of Section 29800, is guilty of a public offense, which shall be punishable by imprisonment in a county jail not exceeding one year or in the state prison, by a fine not exceeding one thousand dollars ($1,000), or by both that imprisonment and fine.

(b) The court, on forms provided by the Department of Justice, shall notify the department of persons subject to this section. The notice shall include a copy of the order of probation and a copy of any minute order or abstract reflecting the order and conditions of probation. *(Added by Stats.2010, c. 711 (S.B.1080), § 6, operative Jan. 1, 2012.)*

Law Revision Commission Comments

Subdivision (a) of Section 29815 continues the first sentence of former Section 12021(d)(1) without substantive change. For an exemption from this provision, see Section 29850 (justifiable violation of Section 29800, 29805, 29815, or 29820).

Subdivision (b) continues the second and third sentences of former Section 12021(d)(1) without substantive change.

See Section 16520 ("firearm"). [38 Cal.L.Rev.Comm. Reports 217 (2009)].

Cross References

Firearm defined for purposes of this Part, see Penal Code § 16520.

Research References

2 Witkin, California Criminal Law 4th Crimes Against Public Peace and Welfare § 232 (2021), Nature and Scope of Statutes.
2 Witkin, California Criminal Law 4th Crimes Against Public Peace and Welfare § 240 (2021), Probationers.

§ 29820. Prohibition on possession of a firearm under the age of 30 for those convicted of or alleged to have committed certain offenses; controlled substances violations; punishment for violation

(a) This section applies to a person who satisfies both of the following requirements:

(1) The person meets one of the following:

(A) The person is alleged to have committed an offense listed in subdivision (b) of Section 707 of the Welfare and Institutions Code.

(B) The person was convicted of violating Section 11351 or 11351.5 of the Health and Safety Code by possessing for sale, or Section 11352 of the Health and Safety Code by selling, a substance containing 28.5 grams or more of cocaine as specified in paragraph (6) of subdivision (b) of Section 11055 of, or cocaine base as specified in paragraph (1) of subdivision (f) of Section 11054 of, the Health and Safety Code, or 57 grams or more of a substance containing at least 5 grams of cocaine as specified in paragraph (6) of subdivision (b) of Section 11055 of, or cocaine base as specified in paragraph (1) of subdivision (f) of Section 11054 of, the Health and Safety Code.

(C) The person was convicted of violating Section 11378 of the Health and Safety Code by possessing for sale, or Section 11379 of the Health and Safety Code by selling, a substance containing 28.5 grams or more of methamphetamine or 57 grams or more of a substance containing methamphetamine.

(D) The person was convicted of violating subdivision (a) of Section 11379.6 of the Health and Safety Code, except those who manufacture phencyclidine, or who is convicted of an act that is punishable under subdivision (b) of Section 11379.6 of the Health and Safety Code, except those who offer to perform an act that aids in the manufacture of phencyclidine.

(E) Except as otherwise provided in Section 1203.07, the person was convicted of violating Section 11353 or 11380 of the Health and Safety Code by using, soliciting, inducing, encouraging, or intimidating a minor to manufacture, compound, or sell heroin, cocaine base as specified in paragraph (1) of subdivision (f) of Section 11054 of the Health and Safety Code, cocaine as specified in paragraph (6) of subdivision (b) of Section 11055 of the Health and Safety Code, or methamphetamine.

(F) The person was convicted of violating Section 11379.6, 11382, or 11383 of the Health and Safety Code with respect to methamphetamine, if the person has one or more prior convictions for a violation of Section 11378, 11379, 11379.6, 11380, 11382, or 11383 of the Health and Safety Code with respect to methamphetamine.

(G) The person was alleged to have committed an offense enumerated in Section 29805 or an offense described in Section 25850, subdivision (a) of Section 25400, or subdivision (a) of Section 26100.

(2) The person is subsequently adjudged a ward of the juvenile court within the meaning of Section 602 of the Welfare and Institutions Code because the person committed an offense listed in paragraph (1).

(b) A person described in subdivision (a) shall not own, or have in possession or under custody or control, a firearm until the person is 30 years of age or older.

(c) A violation of this section shall be punishable by imprisonment in a county jail not exceeding one year or in the state prison, by a fine not exceeding one thousand dollars ($1,000), or by both that imprisonment and fine.

(d) The juvenile court, on forms prescribed by the Department of Justice, shall notify the department of persons subject to this section. Notwithstanding any other law, the forms required to be submitted to the department pursuant to this section may be used to determine eligibility to acquire a firearm. *(Added by Stats.2010, c. 711 (S.B.1080), § 6, operative Jan. 1, 2012. Amended by Stats.2021, c. 537 (S.B.73), § 5, eff. Jan. 1, 2022.)*

Law Revision Commission Comments

Subdivisions (a) and (b) of Section 29820 continue the first sentence of former Section 12021(e) without substantive change.

Subdivision (c) continues the second sentence of former Section 12021(e) without substantive change.

Subdivision (d) continues the third and fourth sentences of former Section 12021(e) without substantive change.

For an exemption from this provision, see Section 29850 (justifiable violation of Section 29800, 29805, 29815, or 29820).

See Section 16520 ("firearm"). [38 Cal.L.Rev.Comm. Reports 217 (2009)].

Cross References

Firearm defined for purposes of this Part, see Penal Code § 16520.

Research References

2 Witkin, California Criminal Law 4th Crimes Against Public Peace and Welfare § 232 (2021), Nature and Scope of Statutes.

2 Witkin, California Criminal Law 4th Crimes Against Public Peace and Welfare § 241 (2021), Juvenile Offenders.

§ 29825. Persons restricted from purchasing, receiving, owning, or possessing firearm by temporary restraining order, injunction, or protective order; punishment for violation; probation; notice of restriction on protective order

(a) A person who purchases or receives, or attempts to purchase or receive, a firearm knowing that the person is prohibited from doing so in any jurisdiction by a temporary restraining order or injunction issued pursuant to Section 527.6, 527.8, or 527.85 of the Code of Civil Procedure, a protective order as defined in Section 6218 of the Family Code, a protective order issued pursuant to Section 136.2 or 646.91 of this code, a protective order issued pursuant to Section 15657.03 of the Welfare and Institutions Code, or by a valid order issued by an out-of-state jurisdiction that is similar or equivalent to a temporary restraining order, injunction, or protective order specified in this subdivision, that includes a prohibition from owning or possessing a firearm, is guilty of a public offense, punishable by imprisonment in a county jail not exceeding one year or in the state prison, by a fine not exceeding one thousand dollars ($1,000), or by both that imprisonment and fine.

(b) A person who owns or possesses a firearm knowing that the person is prohibited from doing so in any jurisdiction by a temporary restraining order or injunction issued pursuant to Section 527.6, 527.8, or 527.85 of the Code of Civil Procedure, a protective order as defined in Section 6218 of the Family Code, a protective order issued pursuant to Section 136.2 or 646.91 of this code, a protective order issued pursuant to Section 15657.03 of the Welfare and Institutions Code, or by a valid order issued by an out-of-state jurisdiction that is similar or equivalent to a temporary restraining order, injunction, or protective order specified in this subdivision, that includes a prohibition from owning or possessing a firearm, is guilty of a public offense, punishable by imprisonment in a county jail not exceeding one year, by a fine not exceeding one thousand dollars ($1,000), or by both that imprisonment and fine.

(c) If probation is granted upon conviction of a violation of this section, the court shall impose probation consistent with Section 1203.097.

(d) The Judicial Council shall provide notice on all protective orders issued within the state that the respondent is prohibited from owning, possessing, purchasing, receiving, or attempting to purchase or receive a firearm while the protective order is in effect. The order shall also state that a firearm owned or possessed by the person shall be relinquished to the local law enforcement agency for that jurisdiction, sold to a licensed firearms dealer, or transferred to a licensed firearms dealer pursuant to Section 29830 for the duration of the period that the protective order is in effect, and that proof of surrender or sale shall be filed within a specified time of receipt of the order. The order shall state the penalties for a violation of the prohibition. The order shall also state on its face the expiration date for relinquishment. *(Added by Stats.2010, c. 711 (S.B.1080), § 6.77, operative Jan. 1, 2012. Amended by Stats.2013, c. 739 (A.B.539), § 3; Stats.2019, c. 726 (A.B.164), § 1, eff. Jan. 1, 2020.)*

Law Revision Commission Comments

Subdivision (a) of Section 29825 continues former Section 12021(g)(1) without substantive change.

Subdivision (b) continues former Section 12021(g)(2) without substantive change.

Subdivision (c) continues former Section 12021(g)(4) without substantive change.

Subdivision (d) continues former Section 12021(g)(3) without substantive change.

See Sections 16520 ("firearm"), 26700 ("dealer," "licensee," or "person licensed pursuant to Sections 26700 to 26915, inclusive"). [40 Cal.L.Rev. Comm. Reports 107 (2010)].

Cross References

Contempt of court, conduct constituting, see Penal Code § 166.

Elder Abuse and Dependent Adult Civil Protection Act, protective orders, see Welfare and Institutions Code § 15657.03.

Employees subject to unlawful violence or threat of violence at the workplace, temporary restraining order, injunction, see Code of Civil Procedure § 527.8.

Firearm defined for purposes of this Part, see Penal Code § 16520.

Firearm or ammunition ownership, possession, purchase, or receipt, relinquishment order, see Family Code § 6389.

Harassment, temporary restraining order and injunction, see Code of Civil Procedure § 527.6.

Officers authorized to maintain order on school campus or facility, threat of violence made off school campus, temporary restraining order and injunction, violation of restraining order, see Code of Civil Procedure § 527.85.

Proof of protective orders, purchase or receipt of firearm, see Family Code § 6385.

Research References

West's California Judicial Council Forms JV–250, Notice of Hearing and Temporary Restraining Order—Juvenile (Also Available in Chinese, Korean, Spanish, and Vietnamese).

West's California Judicial Council Forms JV–255, Restraining Order—Juvenile (Clets—Juv) (Also Available in Chinese, Korean, Spanish, and Vietnamese).

2 Witkin, California Criminal Law 4th Crimes Against Governmental Authority § 10 (2021), Orders, Protocol, and Sanctions.

2 Witkin, California Criminal Law 4th Crimes Against Governmental Authority § 31 (2021), Offenses Constituting Contempt.

2 Witkin, California Criminal Law 4th Crimes Against Public Peace and Welfare § 242 (2021), Subjects of Protective and Restraining Orders.

§ 29830. Persons prohibited from owning or possessing firearms, ammunition feeding devices, or ammunition; transfer of firearm, ammunition feeding device, or ammunition to firearms dealer or ammunition vendor for storage; storage fee; notice to Department of Justice; return of firearms or ammunition

(a) A person who is prohibited from owning or possessing a firearm, ammunition feeding device, or ammunition pursuant to any law, may transfer or cause to be transferred, any firearm, ammunition feeding device, or ammunition in his or her possession, or of which he or she is the owner, to a firearms dealer licensed pursuant to Sections 26700 to 26915, inclusive, or may transfer ammunition to an ammunition vendor, licensed pursuant to Sections 30385 to 30395, inclusive, for storage during the duration of the prohibition, if the prohibition on owning or possessing the firearm, ammunition feeding device, or ammunition will expire on a specific ascertainable date, whether or not specified in the court order, or pursuant to Section 29800, 29805, or 29810.

(b) A firearms dealer or ammunition vendor who stores a firearm, ammunition feeding device, or ammunition pursuant to subdivision (a), may charge the owner a reasonable fee for the storage of the firearm, ammunition feeding device, or ammunition.

(c) A firearms dealer or ammunition vendor who stores a firearm, ammunition feeding device, or ammunition pursuant to subdivision (a) shall notify the Department of Justice of the date that the firearms dealer or ammunition vendor has taken possession of the firearm, ammunition feeding device, or ammunition.

(d) Any firearm that is returned by a dealer to the owner of the firearm pursuant to this section shall be returned in accordance with the procedures set forth in Section 27540 and Article 1 (commencing with Section 26700) and Article 2 (commencing with Section 26800) of Chapter 2 of Division 6.

(e) Any ammunition that is returned by a firearms dealer or ammunition vendor to the owner of the ammunition pursuant to this section shall be returned in accordance with the procedures set forth in Article 4 (commencing with Section 30370) of Chapter 1 of Division 10.

(f) This section shall become operative on July 1, 2020. *(Added by Stats.2018, c. 780 (S.B.746), § 8, eff. Jan. 1, 2019, operative July 1, 2020.)*

Cross References

Criminal identification and statistics, retention of records, firearms, see Penal Code § 11106.

Persons subject to gun violence restraining order, surrender of firearms and ammunition, see Penal Code § 18120.

Return of firearm, ineligible applicants, authorization to sell or transfer firearm to licensed dealer for storage, see Penal Code § 33870.

Taking or transferring possession of any assault weapon, .50 BMG rifle, or firearm precursor part, see Business and Professions Code § 22949.63.

Research References

West's California Judicial Council Forms CH–800, Proof of Firearms Turned In, Sold, or Stored.

West's California Judicial Council Forms EA–800, Proof of Firearms Turned In, Sold, or Stored.

West's California Judicial Council Forms SV–800, Proof of Firearms Turned In, Sold, or Stored.

2 Witkin, California Criminal Law 4th Crimes Against Public Peace and Welfare § 193 (2021), Sale, Lease, or Transfer by Unlicensed Person.

2 Witkin, California Criminal Law 4th Crimes Against Public Peace and Welfare § 208 (2021), Exempt Activities.

2 Witkin, California Criminal Law 4th Crimes Against Public Peace and Welfare § 232 (2021), Nature and Scope of Statutes.

2 Witkin, California Criminal Law 4th Crimes Against Public Peace and Welfare § 233 (2021), Prohibitions.

2 Witkin, California Criminal Law 4th Crimes Against Public Peace and Welfare § 239 (2021), Misdemeanants.

ARTICLE 2. EXEMPTION OR PETITION FOR RELIEF

Section

§ 29850. Justifiable violation of provisions restricting firearm possession; consideration of exemption at trial; burden of proof

(a) A violation of Section 29800, 29805, 29815, or 29820 is justifiable where all of the following conditions are met:

(1) The person found the firearm or took the firearm from a person who was committing a crime against the person who found or took the firearm.

(2) The person possessed the firearm no longer than was necessary to deliver or transport the firearm to a law enforcement agency for that agency's disposition according to law or to a licensed firearms dealer for transfer or for storage pursuant to Section 29830.

(3) If the firearm was transported to a law enforcement agency or to a licensed firearms dealer, it was transported in accordance with subdivision (b) of Section 25570.

(4) If the firearm is being transported to a law enforcement agency or to a licensed firearms dealer, the person transporting the firearm has given prior notice to the law enforcement agency or to the licensed firearms dealer that the person is transporting the firearm to the law enforcement agency or the licensed firearms dealer for disposition according to law.

(b) Upon the trial for violating Section 29800, 29805, 29815, or 29820, the trier of fact shall determine whether the defendant was acting within the provisions of the exemption created by this section.

(c) The defendant has the burden of proving by a preponderance of the evidence that the defendant comes within the provisions of the exemption created by this section. *(Added by Stats.2010, c. 711*

(S.B.1080), § 6, operative Jan. 1, 2012. Amended by Stats.2013, c. 739 (A.B.539), § 5.)

Law Revision Commission Comments

Section 29850 continues former Section 12021(h) without substantive change.

See Section 16520 ("firearm"). [38 Cal.L.Rev.Comm. Reports 217 (2009)].

Cross References

Firearm defined for purposes of this Part, see Penal Code § 16520.

Research References

California Jury Instructions - Criminal 12.43.1, Justifiable Violations.
2 Witkin, California Criminal Law 4th Crimes Against Public Peace and Welfare § 232 (2021), Nature and Scope of Statutes.

§ 29855. Peace officers subject to prohibition imposed by Section 29805; petition for relief from prohibition; hearing; required findings and other duties of court with respect to granting of relief

(a) Any person employed as a peace officer described in Section 830.1, 830.2, 830.31, 830.32, 830.33, or 830.5 whose employment or livelihood is dependent on the ability to legally possess a firearm, who is subject to the prohibition imposed by Section 29805 because of a conviction under Section 273.5, 273.6, or 646.9, may petition the court only once for relief from this prohibition.

(b) The petition shall be filed with the court in which the petitioner was sentenced. If possible, the matter shall be heard before the same judge who sentenced the petitioner.

(c) Upon filing the petition, the clerk of the court shall set the hearing date and shall notify the petitioner and the prosecuting attorney of the date of the hearing.

(d) Upon making each of the following findings, the court may reduce or eliminate the prohibition, impose conditions on reduction or elimination of the prohibition, or otherwise grant relief from the prohibition as the court deems appropriate:

(1) Finds by a preponderance of the evidence that the petitioner is likely to use a firearm in a safe and lawful manner.

(2) Finds that the petitioner is not within a prohibited class as specified in Section 29815, 29820, 29825, or 29900, or subdivision (a) or (b) of Section 29800, and the court is not presented with any credible evidence that the petitioner is a person described in Section 8100 or 8103 of the Welfare and Institutions Code.

(3) Finds that the petitioner does not have a previous conviction under Section 29805, no matter when the prior conviction occurred.

(e) In making its decision, the court shall consider the petitioner's continued employment, the interest of justice, any relevant evidence, and the totality of the circumstances. The court shall require, as a condition of granting relief from the prohibition under Section 29805, that the petitioner agree to participate in counseling as deemed appropriate by the court. Relief from the prohibition shall not relieve any other person or entity from any liability that might otherwise be imposed. It is the intent of the Legislature that courts exercise broad discretion in fashioning appropriate relief under this section in cases in which relief is warranted. However, nothing in this section shall be construed to require courts to grant relief to any particular petitioner. It is the intent of the Legislature to permit persons who were convicted of an offense specified in Section 273.5, 273.6, or 646.9 to seek relief from the prohibition imposed by Section 29805. *(Added by Stats.2010, c. 711 (S.B.1080), § 6, operative Jan. 1, 2012. Amended by Stats.2011, c. 296 (A.B.1023), § 239.)*

Law Revision Commission Comments

Section 29855 continues former Section 12021(c)(2) without substantive change.

For guidance on false arrest arising from the enforcement of Section 29805, see Section 29865 (immunity from liability for false arrest).

See Section 16520 ("firearm"). [38 Cal.L.Rev.Comm. Reports 217 (2009)].

Cross References

Firearm defined for purposes of this Part, see Penal Code § 16520.
Specified convictions or outstanding warrants, restriction on firearm possession, punishment, see Penal Code § 29805.

Research References

2 Witkin, California Criminal Law 4th Crimes Against Public Peace and Welfare § 239 (2021), Misdemeanants.

§ 29860. Persons subject to Section 29805 prohibition due to conviction for offense prior to offense being added to Section 29805; petition for relief; hearing; required findings and duties of court with respect to granting of relief

(a) Any person who is subject to the prohibition imposed by Section 29805 because of a conviction of an offense prior to that offense being added to Section 29805 may petition the court only once for relief from this prohibition.

(b) The petition shall be filed with the court in which the petitioner was sentenced. If possible, the matter shall be heard before the same judge that sentenced the petitioner.

(c) Upon filing the petition, the clerk of the court shall set the hearing date and notify the petitioner and the prosecuting attorney of the date of the hearing.

(d) Upon making each of the following findings, the court may reduce or eliminate the prohibition, impose conditions on reduction or elimination of the prohibition, or otherwise grant relief from the prohibition as the court deems appropriate:

(1) Finds by a preponderance of the evidence that the petitioner is likely to use a firearm in a safe and lawful manner.

(2) Finds that the petitioner is not within a prohibited class as specified in Section 29815, 29820, 29825, or 29900, or subdivision (a) or (b) of Section 29800, and the court is not presented with any credible evidence that the petitioner is a person described in Section 8100 or 8103 of the Welfare and Institutions Code.

(3) Finds that the petitioner does not have a previous conviction under Section 29805, no matter when the prior conviction occurred.

(e) In making its decision, the court may consider the interest of justice, any relevant evidence, and the totality of the circumstances. It is the intent of the Legislature that courts exercise broad discretion in fashioning appropriate relief under this section in cases in which relief is warranted. However, nothing in this section shall be construed to require courts to grant relief to any particular petitioner. *(Added by Stats.2010, c. 711 (S.B.1080), § 6, operative Jan. 1, 2012.)*

Law Revision Commission Comments

Section 29860 continues former Section 12021(c)(3) without substantive change.

For guidance on false arrest arising from enforcement of Section 29805, see Section 29865 (immunity from liability for false arrest).

See Section 16520 ("firearm"). [38 Cal.L.Rev.Comm. Reports 217 (2009)].

Cross References

Firearm defined for purposes of this Part, see Penal Code § 16520.

Research References

2 Witkin, California Criminal Law 4th Crimes Against Public Peace and Welfare § 239 (2021), Misdemeanants.

§ 29865. Enforcement of Section 29805 prohibition by law enforcement officer against person to whom relief has been granted; immunity from liability for false arrest

Law enforcement officials who enforce the prohibition specified in Section 29805 against a person who has been granted relief pursuant to Section 29855 or 29860 shall be immune from any liability for false arrest arising from the enforcement of Section 29805 unless the person has in possession a certified copy of the court order that granted the person relief from the prohibition. This immunity from liability shall not relieve any person or entity from any other liability that might otherwise be imposed. *(Added by Stats.2010, c. 711 (S.B.1080), § 6, operative Jan. 1, 2012.)*

Law Revision Commission Comments

Section 29865 continues former Section 12021(c)(4) without substantive change. [38 Cal.L.Rev.Comm. Reports 217 (2009)].

Research References

2 Witkin, California Criminal Law 4th Crimes Against Public Peace and Welfare § 239 (2021), Misdemeanants.

ARTICLE 3. MISCELLANEOUS PROVISIONS

§ 29875. Protocol to facilitate enforcement of firearm ownership restrictions; development by Attorney General

Subject to available funding, the Attorney General, working with the Judicial Council, the California Alliance Against Domestic Violence, prosecutors, and law enforcement, probation, and parole officers, shall develop a protocol for the implementation of the provisions of Section 12021, as it reads in Section 2 of Chapter 830 of the Statutes of 2002, and as later amended at any time before completion of the protocol. The protocol shall be designed to facilitate the enforcement of restrictions on firearm ownership, including provisions for giving notice to defendants who are restricted, provisions for informing those defendants of the procedures by which defendants shall dispose of firearms when required to do so, provisions explaining how defendants shall provide proof of the lawful disposition of firearms, and provisions explaining how defendants may obtain possession of seized firearms when legally permitted to do so pursuant to any provision of law. The protocol shall be completed on or before January 1, 2005. *(Added by Stats.2010, c. 711 (S.B.1080), § 6, operative Jan. 1, 2012.)*

Law Revision Commission Comments

Section 29875 continues former Section 12021(i) without substantive change. See Section 16520 ("firearm"). [38 Cal.L.Rev.Comm. Reports 217 (2009)].

Cross References

Attorney General, generally, see Government Code § 12500 et seq.
Firearm defined for purposes of this Part, see Penal Code § 16520.

§ 29880. Prohibited persons; attempt to acquire or report acquisition or ownership of firearm; notice to local law enforcement agency; notice to county department of mental health

(a) If the Department of Justice determines that a person prohibited from owning, purchasing, receiving, or possessing a firearm by this chapter, Chapter 3 (commencing with Section 29900), or Section 8100 or 8103 of the Welfare and Institutions Code has attempted to acquire a firearm, or has attempted to report their acquisition or ownership of a firearm in order to have it listed in the registry set forth in Section 11106 as owned by that person, whether the report is mandated by this part or made pursuant to Section 28000, the department shall notify the local law enforcement agency with primary jurisdiction over the area in which the person was last known to reside of the attempt in a manner and format prescribed by the Department of Justice.

(b) If a person described in subdivision (a) is prohibited from owning or possessing a firearm pursuant to Section 8100 or 8103 of the Welfare and Institutions Code, the department shall also notify the county department of mental health in the county in which the person was last known to reside. *(Added by Stats.2022, c. 100 (A.B.2551), § 1, eff. Jan. 1, 2023.)*

CHAPTER 3. PERSON CONVICTED OF VIOLENT OFFENSE

§ 29900. Prior conviction of certain violent offenses; prohibited ownership or possession of firearm; punishment; condition of probation; suspension of imposition or execution of sentence

(a)(1) Notwithstanding subdivision (a) of Section 29800, any person who has been previously convicted of any of the offenses listed in Section 29905 and who owns or has in possession or under custody or control any firearm is guilty of a felony.

(2) A dismissal of an accusatory pleading pursuant to Section 1203.4a involving an offense set forth in Section 29905 does not affect the finding of a previous conviction.

(3) If probation is granted, or if the imposition or execution of sentence is suspended, it shall be a condition of the probation or suspension that the defendant serve at least six months in a county jail.

(b)(1) Any person previously convicted of any of the offenses listed in Section 29905 which conviction results from certification by the juvenile court for prosecution as an adult in adult court under the provisions of Section 707 of the Welfare and Institutions Code, who owns or has in possession or under custody or control any firearm, is guilty of a felony.

(2) If probation is granted, or if the imposition or execution of sentence is suspended, it shall be a condition of the probation or suspension that the defendant serve at least six months in a county jail.

(c) The court shall apply the minimum sentence as specified in subdivisions (a) and (b) except in unusual cases where the interests of justice would best be served by granting probation or suspending the imposition or execution of sentence without the imprisonment required by subdivisions (a) and (b), or by granting probation or suspending the imposition or execution of sentence with conditions other than those set forth in subdivisions (a) and (b), in which case the court shall specify on the record and shall enter on the minutes the circumstances indicating that the interests of justice would best be served by the disposition. *(Added by Stats.2010, c. 711 (S.B.1080), § 6, operative Jan. 1, 2012.)*

Law Revision Commission Comments

Subdivision (a) of Section 29900 continues former Section 12021.1(a) without substantive change.

Subdivision (b) continues former Section 12021.1(c) without substantive change.

Subdivision (c) continues former Section 12021.1(d) without substantive change.

See Section 16520 ("firearm"). [38 Cal.L.Rev.Comm. Reports 217 (2009)].

Cross References

Custodial or transportation officers, notification to state or local agency of restrictions on firearm possession, see Penal Code § 832.17.
Denial to issue, refusal to renew, automatic revocation of permits, to alarm companies, see Business and Professions Code §§ 7596.8, 7596.81, 7596.83.
Felonies, definition and penalties, see Penal Code §§ 17, 18.
Firearm defined for purposes of this Part, see Penal Code § 16520.
Misdemeanor violation, threatening crime victim, witness or informant, punishment, see Penal Code § 140.
Notification to agencies employing or taking applications for peace officers authorized to carry firearms, see Penal Code §§ 832.15, 832.16.
Penalty for possession of loaded firearms or enumerated prohibited weapons within State Capitol, legislative offices, etc., prosecution not precluded under this section, see Penal Code § 171c.
Protective orders and other domestic violence prevention orders, registration and enforcement of orders, firearm ownership, possession, purchase, or receipt, see Family Code § 6389.
Public housing authority, access to criminal history for convictions under this section, see Penal Code § 11105.03.
Relinquishment of firearms, persons subject to protective orders, see Code of Civil Procedure § 527.9.

Research References

California Jury Instructions - Criminal 12.43, Firearm—Possession by Person Convicted of a Felony—No Stipulation of Status.
California Jury Instructions - Criminal 12.44, Firearm—Possession by Person Convicted of a Felony—Status Stipulated.
2 Witkin, California Criminal Law 4th Crimes Against Governmental Authority § 8 (2021), Threat of Force by Convicted Felon.
2 Witkin, California Criminal Law 4th Crimes Against Public Peace and Welfare § 194 (2021), Furnishing Erroneous Firearm Purchaser Information.
2 Witkin, California Criminal Law 4th Crimes Against Public Peace and Welfare § 196 (2021), Transfers to Specified Persons.
2 Witkin, California Criminal Law 4th Crimes Against Public Peace and Welfare § 202 (2021), License to Manufacture.
2 Witkin, California Criminal Law 4th Crimes Against Public Peace and Welfare § 204 (2021), Punishment.
2 Witkin, California Criminal Law 4th Crimes Against Public Peace and Welfare § 207 (2021), Exempt Persons.
2 Witkin, California Criminal Law 4th Crimes Against Public Peace and Welfare § 210 (2021), Unlawful Acts Involving Ammunition.
2 Witkin, California Criminal Law 4th Crimes Against Public Peace and Welfare § 232 (2021), Nature and Scope of Statutes.
2 Witkin, California Criminal Law 4th Crimes Against Public Peace and Welfare § 238 (2021), Violent Crimes Offenders.
2 Witkin, California Criminal Law 4th Crimes Against Public Peace and Welfare § 250 (2021), Punishment.
2 Witkin, California Criminal Law 4th Crimes Against Public Peace and Welfare § 253A (2021), (New) Carrying Unloaded Firearm that is Not Handgun in Incorporated Area or Other Public Place.
2 Witkin, California Criminal Law 4th Crimes Against Public Peace and Welfare § 257 (2021), Firearms.
2 Witkin, California Criminal Law 4th Crimes Against Public Peace and Welfare § 263 (2021), Nuisances.
3 Witkin, California Criminal Law 4th Punishment § 100 (2021), Discharge.
3 Witkin, California Criminal Law 4th Punishment § 248 (2021), Nature and Purpose of Statute.
3 Witkin, California Criminal Law 4th Punishment § 252 (2021), In General.

§ 29905. Violent offenses

(a) As used in this chapter, a violent offense includes any of the following:

(1) Murder or voluntary manslaughter.

(2) Mayhem.

(3) Rape.

(4) Sodomy by force, violence, duress, menace, or threat of great bodily harm.

(5) Oral copulation by force, violence, duress, menace, or threat of great bodily harm.

(6) Lewd acts on a child under the age of 14 years.

(7) Any felony punishable by death or imprisonment in the state prison for life.

(8) Any other felony in which the defendant inflicts great bodily injury on any person, other than an accomplice, that has been charged and proven, or any felony in which the defendant uses a firearm which use has been charged and proven.

(9) Attempted murder.

(10) Assault with intent to commit rape or robbery.

(11) Assault with a deadly weapon or instrument on a peace officer.

(12) Assault by a life prisoner on a noninmate.

(13) Assault with a deadly weapon by an inmate.

(14) Arson.

(15) Exploding a destructive device or any explosive with intent to injure.

(16) Exploding a destructive device or any explosive causing great bodily injury.

(17) Exploding a destructive device or any explosive with intent to murder.

(18) Robbery.

(19) Kidnapping.

(20) Taking of a hostage by an inmate of a state prison.

(21) Attempt to commit a felony punishable by death or imprisonment in the state prison for life.

(22) Any felony in which the defendant personally used a dangerous or deadly weapon.

(23) Escape from a state prison by use of force or violence.

(24) Assault with a deadly weapon or force likely to produce great bodily injury.

(25) Any felony violation of Section 186.22.

(26) Any offense enumerated in subdivision (a), (b), or (d) of Section 23515.

(27) Carjacking.

(28) Any offense enumerated in subdivision (c) of Section 23515 if the person has two or more convictions for violating paragraph (2) of subdivision (a) of Section 417.

(b) As used in this chapter, a violent offense also includes any attempt to commit a crime listed in subdivision (a) other than an assault. *(Added by Stats.2010, c. 711 (S.B.1080), § 6, operative Jan. 1, 2012.)*

Law Revision Commission Comments

Section 29905 continues former Section 12021.1(b) without substantive change.

See Section 16520 ("firearm"). [38 Cal.L.Rev.Comm. Reports 217 (2009)].

Cross References

Custodial or transportation officers, notification to state or local agency of restrictions on firearm possession, see Penal Code § 832.17.
Denial to issue, refusal to renew, automatic revocation of permits, to alarm companies, see Business and Professions Code §§ 7596.8, 7596.81, 7596.83.
Felonies, definition and penalties, see Penal Code §§ 17, 18.
Firearm defined for purposes of this Part, see Penal Code § 16520.
Misdemeanor violation, threatening crime victim, witness or informant, punishment, see Penal Code § 140.
Notification to agencies employing or taking applications for peace officers authorized to carry firearms, see Penal Code §§ 832.15, 832.16.
Penalty for possession of loaded firearms or enumerated prohibited weapons within State Capitol, legislative offices, etc., prosecution not precluded under this section, see Penal Code § 171c.

Protective orders and other domestic violence prevention orders, registration and enforcement of orders, firearm ownership, possession, purchase, or receipt, see Family Code § 6389.
Public housing authority, access to criminal history for convictions under this section, see Penal Code § 11105.03.
Relinquishment of firearms, persons subject to protective orders, see Code of Civil Procedure § 527.9.

Research References

2 Witkin, California Criminal Law 4th Crimes Against Public Peace and Welfare § 238 (2021), Violent Crimes Offenders.
2 Witkin, California Criminal Law 4th Crimes Against Public Peace and Welfare § 243 (2021), Minors.
1 Witkin California Criminal Law 4th Introduction to Crimes § 134 (2021), In General.
3 Witkin, California Criminal Law 4th Punishment § 382 (2021), In General.
3 Witkin, California Criminal Law 4th Punishment § 720 (2021), Without Probation.

CHAPTER 4. PROHIBITED ARMED PERSONS FILE

§ 30000. Prohibited Armed Persons File online database; establishment and maintenance; availability of information

(a) The Attorney General shall establish and maintain an online database to be known as the Prohibited Armed Persons File. The purpose of the file is to cross-reference persons who have ownership or possession of a firearm on or after January 1, 1996, as indicated by a record in the Consolidated Firearms Information System, and who, subsequent to the date of that ownership or possession of a firearm, fall within a class of persons who are prohibited from owning or possessing a firearm.

(b) Except as provided in subdivision (c), the information contained in the Prohibited Armed Persons File shall only be available to those entities specified in, and pursuant to, subdivision (b) or (c) of Section 11105, through the California Law Enforcement Telecommunications System, for the purpose of determining if persons are armed and prohibited from possessing firearms.

(c) The information contained in the Prohibited Armed Persons File shall be available to researchers affiliated with the California Firearm Violence Research Center at UC Davis following approval by the institution's governing institutional review board, when required. At the department's discretion, and subject to Section 14240, the data may be provided to any other nonprofit bona fide research institution accredited by the United States Department of Education or the Council for Higher Education Accreditation for the study of the prevention of violence, following approval by the institution's governing institutional review board or human subjects committee, when required, for academic and policy research purposes. Material identifying individuals shall only be provided for research or statistical activities and shall not be transferred, revealed, or used for purposes other than research or statistical activities, and reports or publications derived therefrom shall not identify specific individuals. Reasonable costs to the department associated with the department's processing of that data may be billed to the researcher. If a request for data or letter of support for research using the data is denied, the department shall provide a written statement of the specific reasons for the denial. *(Added by Stats.2010, c. 711 (S.B.1080), § 6, operative Jan. 1, 2012. Amended by Stats.2014, c. 182 (A.B.2300), § 1, eff. Jan. 1, 2015; Stats.2021, c. 253 (A.B.173), § 10, eff. Sept. 23, 2021.)*

Law Revision Commission Comments

Section 30000 continues former Section 12010 without substantive change. See Section 16520 ("firearm"). [38 Cal.L.Rev.Comm. Reports 217 (2009)].

Cross References

Attorney General, generally, see Government Code § 12500 et seq.
Firearm defined for purposes of this Part, see Penal Code § 16520.

§ 30005. Function of Prohibited Armed Persons File database

The Prohibited Armed Persons File database shall function as follows:

(a) Upon entry into the Automated Criminal History System of a disposition for a conviction of any felony, a conviction for any firearms-prohibiting charge specified in Chapter 2 (commencing with Section 29800), a conviction for an offense described in Chapter 3 (commencing with Section 29900), a firearms prohibition pursuant to Section 8100 or 8103 of the Welfare and Institutions Code, or any firearms possession prohibition identified by the federal National Instant Criminal Background Check System, the Department of Justice shall determine if the subject has an entry in the Consolidated Firearms Information System indicating possession or ownership of a firearm on or after January 1, 1996, or an assault weapon registration, or a .50 BMG rifle registration.

(b) Upon an entry into any department automated information system that is used for the identification of persons who are prohibited by state or federal law from acquiring, owning, or possessing firearms, the department shall determine if the subject has an entry in the Consolidated Firearms Information System indicating ownership or possession of a firearm on or after January 1, 1996, or an assault weapon registration, or a .50 BMG rifle registration.

(c) If the department determines that, pursuant to subdivision (a) or (b), the subject has an entry in the Consolidated Firearms Information System indicating possession or ownership of a firearm on or after January 1, 1996, or an assault weapon registration, or a .50 BMG rifle registration, the following information shall be entered into the Prohibited Armed Persons File:

(1) The subject's name.

(2) The subject's date of birth.

(3) The subject's physical description.

(4) Any other identifying information regarding the subject that is deemed necessary by the Attorney General.

(5) The basis of the firearms possession prohibition.

(6) A description of all firearms owned or possessed by the subject, as reflected by the Consolidated Firearms Information System. *(Added by Stats.2010, c. 711 (S.B.1080), § 6, operative Jan. 1, 2012. Amended by Stats.2014, c. 182 (A.B.2300), § 2, eff. Jan. 1, 2015.)*

Law Revision Commission Comments

Section 30005 continues former Section 12011 without substantive change. See Section 16520 ("firearm"). [38 Cal.L.Rev.Comm. Reports 217 (2009)].

Cross References

.50 BMG rifle defined for purposes of this Part, see Penal Code § 30530.
Attorney General, generally, see Government Code § 12500 et seq.
Felonies, definition and penalties, see Penal Code §§ 17, 18.

Firearm defined for purposes of this Part, see Penal Code § 16520.

§ 30010. Attorney General; investigative assistance

The Attorney General shall provide investigative assistance to local law enforcement agencies to better ensure the investigation of individuals who are armed and prohibited from possessing a firearm. *(Added by Stats.2010, c. 711 (S.B.1080), § 6, operative Jan. 1, 2012.)*

Law Revision Commission Comments

Section 30010 continues former Section 12012 without substantive change. See Section 16520 ("firearm"). [38 Cal.L.Rev.Comm. Reports 217 (2009)].

Cross References

Attorney General, generally, see Government Code § 12500 et seq.
Firearm defined for purposes of this Part, see Penal Code § 16520.

§ 30012. Annual report on Armed Prohibited Persons System (APPS); contents

(a) No later than April 1, 2020, and no later than April 1 of each year thereafter, the Department of Justice shall report to the Joint Legislative Budget Committee and the fiscal committees of each house of the Legislature all of the following information for the immediately preceding calendar year:

(1) The total number of individuals in the Armed Prohibited Persons System (APPS) and the number of cases which are active and pending, as follows:

(A)(i) For active cases, the department shall report the status of each case for which the department has initiated an investigation. This information shall include, at a minimum, the number of cases that have not been actively investigated for 12 months or longer, along with a breakdown of the time period that has elapsed since a case was added to the system.

(ii) For purposes of this paragraph, "investigation" means any work conducted by sworn or nonsworn staff to determine whether a prohibited person possesses one or more firearms, whether to remove the person from the database, or whether to shift the person to the pending caseload.

(B) For pending cases, the department shall separately report the number of cases that are unable to be cleared, unable to be located, related to out-of-state individuals, related to only federal firearms prohibitions, and related to incarcerated individuals.

(2) The number of individuals added to the APPS database.

(3) The number of individuals removed from the APPS database, including a breakdown of the basis on which they were removed. At a minimum, this information shall separately report those cases that were removed because the individual is deceased, had prohibitions expire or removed, or had their cases resolved as a result of department firearm seizure activities.

(4) The degree to which the backlog in the APPS has been reduced or eliminated. For purposes of this section, "backlog" means the number of cases for which the department did not initiate an investigation within six months of the case being added to the APPS or has not completed investigatory work within six months of initiating an investigation on the case.

(5) The number of individuals in the APPS before and after the relevant reporting period, including a breakdown of why each individual in the APPS is prohibited from possessing a firearm.

(6) The number of agents and other staff hired for enforcement of the APPS.

(7) The number of firearms recovered due to enforcement of the APPS.

(8) The number of contacts made during the APPS enforcement efforts.

(9) Information regarding task forces or collaboration with local law enforcement on reducing the APPS file or backlog.

(b) For purposes of this section, "Armed Prohibited Persons System" means the "Prohibited Armed Persons File," as described in Section 30000. *(Added by Stats.2019, c. 25 (S.B.94), § 52, eff. June 27, 2019.)*

§ 30015. Armed Prohibited Persons System (APPS); appropriation to address backlog; report to Joint Legislative Budget Committee

(a) The sum of twenty-four million dollars ($24,000,000) is hereby appropriated from the Dealers' Record of Sale Special Account of the General Fund to the Department of Justice to address the backlog in the Armed Prohibited Persons System (APPS) and the illegal possession of firearms by those prohibited persons.

(b) No later than March 1, 2015, and no later than March 1 each year thereafter, the department shall report to the Joint Legislative Budget Committee all of the following for the immediately preceding calendar year:

(1) The degree to which the backlog in the APPS has been reduced or eliminated.

(2) The number of agents hired for enforcement of the APPS.

(3) The number of people cleared from the APPS.

(4) The number of people added to the APPS.

(5) The number of people in the APPS before and after the relevant reporting period, including a breakdown of why each person in the APPS is prohibited from possessing a firearm.

(6) The number of firearms recovered due to enforcement of the APPS.

(7) The number of contacts made during the APPS enforcement efforts.

(8) Information regarding task forces or collaboration with local law enforcement on reducing the APPS backlog.

(c)(1) The requirement for submitting a report imposed under subdivision (b) is inoperative on March 1, 2019, pursuant to Section 10231.5 of the Government Code.

(2) A report to be submitted pursuant to subdivision (b) shall be submitted in compliance with Section 9795 of the Government Code. *(Added by Stats.2013, c. 2 (S.B.140), § 2, eff. May 1, 2013.)*

§ 30020. Initial review of match within daily queue of Armed Prohibited Persons System (APPS); timing

(a) The Department of Justice shall complete an initial review of a match in the daily queue of the Armed Prohibited Persons System within seven days of the match being placed in the queue and shall periodically reassess whether the department can complete those reviews more efficiently.

(b)(1) For the purpose of this section, "Armed Prohibited Persons System" means the "Prohibited Armed Persons File," as described in Section 30000.

(2) For the purpose of this section, "match" means the entry into the Automated Criminal History System or into any department automated information system of the name and other information of an individual who may be prohibited from acquiring, owning, or possessing a firearm, and a corresponding record of ownership or possession of a firearm by that individual, as described in Section 30005. *(Added by Stats.2016, c. 638 (A.B.1999), § 1, eff. Jan. 1, 2017.)*

CHAPTER 5. FIREARMS ELIGIBILITY CHECK

ARTICLE 1. FIREARMS ELIGIBILITY CHECK

§ 30105. Firearms eligibility check

(a) An individual may request that the Department of Justice perform a firearms eligibility check for that individual. The applicant requesting the eligibility check shall provide the personal information required by Section 28160 or 28165, as applicable, but not any information regarding any firearm, to the department, in an application specified by the department.

(b) The department shall charge a fee of twenty dollars ($20) for performing the eligibility check authorized by this section, but not to exceed the actual processing costs of the department. After the department establishes fees sufficient to reimburse the department for processing costs, fees charged may increase at a rate not to exceed the legislatively approved cost-of-living adjustment for the department's budget or as otherwise increased through the Budget Act.

(c) An applicant for the eligibility check pursuant to subdivision (a) shall complete the application, have it notarized by any licensed California Notary Public, and submit it by mail to the department.

(d) Upon receipt of a notarized application and fee, the department shall do all of the following:

(1) Examine its records, and the records it is authorized to request from the State Department of State Hospitals pursuant to Section 8104 of the Welfare and Institutions Code, to determine if the purchaser is prohibited by state or federal law from possessing, receiving, owning, or purchasing a firearm.

(2) Notify the applicant by mail of its determination of whether the applicant is prohibited by state or federal law from possessing, receiving, owning, or purchasing a firearm. The department's notification shall state either "eligible to possess firearms as of the date the check was completed" or "ineligible to possess firearms as of the date the check was completed."

(e) If the department determines that the information submitted to it in the application contains any blank spaces, or inaccurate, illegible, or incomplete information, preventing identification of the applicant, or if the required fee is not submitted, the department shall not be required to perform the firearms eligibility check.

(f) The department shall make applications to conduct a firearms eligibility check as described in this section available to licensed firearms dealers and on the department's Internet Web site.

(g) The department shall be immune from any liability arising out of the performance of the firearms eligibility check, or any reliance upon the firearms eligibility check.

(h) Except as provided in Sections 29180 and 29182, a person or agency shall not require or request an individual to obtain a firearms eligibility check or notification of a firearms eligibility check pursuant to this section. A violation of this subdivision is a misdemeanor.

(i) The department shall include on the application specified in subdivision (a) and the notification of eligibility specified in subdivision (d) the following statements:

"No person or agency may require or request an individual to obtain a firearms eligibility check or notification of firearms eligibility check pursuant to Section 30105 of the Penal Code. A violation of these provisions is a misdemeanor."

"If the applicant for a firearms eligibility check purchases, transfers, or receives a firearm through a licensed dealer as required by law, a waiting period and background check are both required." *(Added by Stats.2010, c. 711 (S.B.1080), § 6, operative Jan. 1, 2012. Amended by Stats.2011, c. 296 (A.B.1023), § 240; Stats.2011, c. 745 (A.B.809), § 62; Stats.2012, c. 24 (A.B.1470), § 59, eff. June 27, 2012; Stats.2016, c. 60 (A.B.857), § 5, eff. Jan. 1, 2017.)*

Law Revision Commission Comments

Section 30105 continues former Section 12077.5 without substantive change.

See Sections 16520 ("firearm"), 26700 ("dealer," "licensee," or "person licensed pursuant to Sections 26700 to 26915, inclusive"). [38 Cal.L.Rev. Comm. Reports 217 (2009)].

Cross References

Firearm defined for purposes of this Part, see Penal Code § 16520.
Misdemeanors, definition and penalties, see Penal Code §§ 17, 19, 19.2.

ARTICLE 2. EXCEPTIONS RELATING TO LAW ENFORCEMENT

§ 30150. Application of firearms eligibility check to sales, deliveries, or transfers of firearms to authorized law enforcement representatives; records of handgun or firearm acquisitions by law enforcement agencies

(a) Section 30105 does not apply to any sale, delivery, or transfer of firearms made to an authorized law enforcement representative of any city, county, city and county, or state, or of the federal government, for exclusive use by that governmental agency if, prior to the sale, delivery, or transfer of these firearms, written authorization from the head of the agency authorizing the transaction is presented to the person from whom the purchase, delivery, or transfer is being made.

(b) Proper written authorization is defined as verifiable written certification from the head of the agency by which the purchaser or transferee is employed, identifying the employee as an individual authorized to conduct the transaction, and authorizing the transaction for the exclusive use of the agency by which that person is employed.

(c) Within 10 days of the date a handgun, and commencing January 1, 2014, any firearm, is acquired by the agency, a record of the same shall be entered as an institutional weapon into the Automated Firearms System (AFS) via the California Law Enforcement Telecommunications System (CLETS) by the law enforcement or state agency. Any agency without access to AFS shall arrange with the sheriff of the county in which the agency is located to input this information via this system. *(Added by Stats.2010, c. 711 (S.B.1080), § 6, operative Jan. 1, 2012. Amended by Stats.2011, c. 745 (A.B.809), § 63.)*

Law Revision Commission Comments

Section 30150 continues former Section 12078(a)(2) without substantive change, as that provision applied to former Section 12077.5 (through its reference to the preceding provisions of this article).

For other exceptions relating to law enforcement, see Sections 30155–30165.

See Sections 16520 ("firearm"), 16640 ("handgun"). [38 Cal.L.Rev.Comm. Reports 217 (2009)].

Cross References

Firearm defined for purposes of this Part, see Penal Code § 16520.
Handgun defined for purposes of this Part, see Penal Code § 16640.

§ 30155. Specified firearms loans; exemption from application of firearms eligibility check

Section 30105 does not apply to the loan of a firearm if all of the following conditions are satisfied:

(a) The loan is made by an authorized law enforcement representative of a city, county, or city and county, or of the state or federal government.

(b) The loan is made to a peace officer employed by that agency and authorized to carry a firearm.

(c) The loan is made for the carrying and use of that firearm by that peace officer in the course and scope of the officer's duties. *(Added by Stats.2010, c. 711 (S.B.1080), § 6, operative Jan. 1, 2012.)*

Law Revision Commission Comments

Section 30155 continues former Section 12078(a)(3) without substantive change, as that provision applied to former Section 12077.5 (through its reference to "the preceding provisions of this article").

For other exceptions relating to law enforcement, see Sections 30150, 30160–30165.

See Section 16520 ("firearm"). [38 Cal.L.Rev.Comm. Reports 217 (2009)].

Cross References

Firearm defined for purposes of this Part, see Penal Code § 16520.

§ 30160. Sale, delivery, or transfer of firearm by law enforcement agency to peace officer; exemption from application of firearms eligibility check; Automated Firearms System (AFS) records

(a) Section 30105 does not apply to the sale, delivery, or transfer of a firearm by a law enforcement agency to a peace officer pursuant to Section 10334 of the Public Contract Code.

(b) Within 10 days of the date that a handgun, and commencing January 1, 2014, any firearm, is sold, delivered, or transferred pursuant to Section 10334 of the Public Contract Code to that peace officer, the name of the officer and the make, model, serial number, and other identifying characteristics of the firearm being sold, delivered, or transferred shall be entered into the Automated Firearms System (AFS) via the California Law Enforcement Telecommunications System (CLETS) by the law enforcement or state agency that sold, delivered, or transferred the firearm, provided, however, that if the firearm is not a handgun and does not have a serial number, identification number, or identification mark assigned to it, that fact shall be noted in AFS. Any agency without access to AFS shall arrange with the sheriff of the county in which the agency is located to input this information via this system. *(Added by Stats.2010, c. 711 (S.B.1080), § 6, operative Jan. 1, 2012. Amended by Stats.2011, c. 745 (A.B.809), § 64.)*

Law Revision Commission Comments

Section 30160 continues former Section 12078(a)(4) without substantive change, as that provision applied to former Section 12077.5 (through its reference to "the preceding provisions of this article").

For other exceptions relating to law enforcement, see Sections 30150–30155, 30165.

See Sections 16520 ("firearm"), 16640 ("handgun"). [38 Cal.L.Rev.Comm. Reports 217 (2009)].

Cross References

Firearm defined for purposes of this Part, see Penal Code § 16520.
Handgun defined for purposes of this Part, see Penal Code § 16640.

§ 30165. Sale, delivery, or transfer of firearm by law enforcement agency to retiring peace officer; exemption from application of firearms eligibility check; Automated Firearms System (AFS) records

(a) Section 30105 does not apply to the sale, delivery, or transfer of a firearm by a law enforcement agency to a retiring peace officer who is authorized to carry a firearm pursuant to Chapter 5 (commencing with Section 26300) of Division 5.

(b) Within 10 days of the date that a handgun, and commencing January 1, 2014, any firearm, is sold, delivered, or transferred to that retiring peace officer, the name of the officer and the make, model, serial number, and other identifying characteristics of the firearm being sold, delivered, or transferred shall be entered into the Automated Firearms System (AFS) via the California Law Enforcement Telecommunications System (CLETS) by the law enforcement or state agency that sold, delivered, or transferred the firearm, provided, however, that if the firearm is not a handgun and does not have a serial number, identification number, or identification mark assigned to it, that fact shall be noted in AFS. Any agency without access to AFS shall arrange with the sheriff of the county in which the agency is located to input this information via this system. *(Added by Stats.2010, c. 711 (S.B.1080), § 6, operative Jan. 1, 2012. Amended by Stats.2011, c. 745 (A.B.809), § 65.)*

Law Revision Commission Comments

Section 30165 continues former Section 12078(a)(5) without substantive change, as that provision applied to former Section 12077.5 (through its reference to "the preceding provisions of this article").

For other exceptions relating to law enforcement, see Sections 30150–30160.

See Sections 16520 ("firearm"), 16640 ("handgun"). [38 Cal.L.Rev.Comm. Reports 217 (2009)].

Cross References

Firearm defined for purposes of this Part, see Penal Code § 16520.
Handgun defined for purposes of this Part, see Penal Code § 16640.

Division 10

SPECIAL RULES RELATING TO PARTICULAR TYPES OF FIREARMS OR FIREARM EQUIPMENT

CHAPTER 1. AMMUNITION

ARTICLE 1. FLECHETTE DART AMMUNITION OR BULLET CONTAINING OR CARRYING AN EXPLOSIVE AGENT

§ 30210. Manufacture, import, sale, supply or possession of ammunition containing any flechette dart or bullets containing an explosive agent; punishment

Except as provided in Section 30215 and Chapter 1 (commencing with Section 17700) of Division 2 of Title 2, any person in this state who manufactures or causes to be manufactured, imports into the state, keeps for sale, or offers or exposes for sale, or who gives, lends, or possesses either of the following is punishable by imprisonment in a county jail not exceeding one year or imprisonment pursuant to subdivision (h) of Section 1170:

(a) Any ammunition that contains or consists of any flechette dart.

(b) Any bullet containing or carrying an explosive agent. *(Added by Stats.2010, c. 711 (S.B.1080), § 6, operative Jan. 1, 2012. Amended by Stats.2012, c. 43 (S.B.1023), § 104, eff. June 27, 2012.)*

Law Revision Commission Comments

With respect to "any ammunition that contains or consists of any flechette dart" and "any bullet containing or carrying an explosive agent," Section 30210 continues former Section 12020(a)(1) without substantive change.

For circumstances in which this section is inapplicable, see Sections 16590 ("generally prohibited weapon"), 17700–17745 (exemptions relating to generally prohibited weapons), 30215 (exemption for tracer ammunition manufactured for use in shotgun).

See Section 16570 ("flechette dart"). See also Sections 16460(b) (bullet with explosive agent is not destructive device), 17800 (distinct and separate offense), 30290 (flechette dart ammunition or bullet with explosive agent constituting nuisance). [38 Cal.L.Rev.Comm. Reports 217 (2009)].

Research References

California Jury Instructions - Criminal 12.49.7, Possessing or Trafficking in Large Capacity Magazines.

2 Witkin, California Criminal Law 4th Crimes Against Public Peace and Welfare § 211 (2021), Nature of Crime.

§ 30215. Tracer ammunition; application of Section 30210

Section 30210 does not apply to tracer ammunition manufactured for use in a shotgun. *(Added by Stats.2010, c. 711 (S.B.1080), § 6, operative Jan. 1, 2012.)*

Law Revision Commission Comments

Section 30215 continues former Section 12020(b)(6) without substantive change.

For additional circumstances in which Section 30210 is inapplicable, see Sections 16590 ("generally prohibited weapon"), 17700–17745 (exemptions relating to generally prohibited weapons).

See Section 17190 ("shotgun"). [38 Cal.L.Rev.Comm. Reports 217 (2009)].

Cross References

Shotgun defined, see Penal Code § 17190.

§ 30290. Nuisances; ammunition containing flechette darts; bullets containing explosive agents

Except as provided in Section 30215 and in Chapter 1 (commencing with Section 17700) of Division 2 of Title 2, any ammunition that contains or consists of any flechette dart, or any bullet containing or carrying an explosive agent, is a nuisance and is subject to Section 18010. *(Added by Stats.2010, c. 711 (S.B.1080), § 6, operative Jan. 1, 2012.)*

Law Revision Commission Comments

With respect to "any ammunition that contains or consists of any flechette dart" and "any bullet containing or carrying an explosive agent," Section 30290 continues the first part of the first sentence of former Section 12029 without substantive change.

See Section 16570 ("flechette dart"). [38 Cal.L.Rev.Comm. Reports 217 (2009)].

Research References

2 Witkin, California Criminal Law 4th Crimes Against Public Peace and Welfare § 263 (2021), Nuisances.

ARTICLE 2. OTHER RESTRICTIONS RELATING TO AMMUNITION

§ 30300. Offenses related to sale or supply of ammunition to underage persons; penalties

(a) Any person, corporation, or dealer who does any of the following shall be punished by imprisonment in a county jail for a term not to exceed six months, or by a fine not to exceed one thousand dollars ($1,000), or by both the imprisonment and fine:

(1) Sells any ammunition or reloaded ammunition to a person under 18 years of age.

(2) Sells any ammunition or reloaded ammunition designed and intended for use in a handgun to a person under 21 years of age. Where ammunition or reloaded ammunition may be used in both a rifle and a handgun, it may be sold to a person who is at least 18 years of age, but less than 21 years of age, if the vendor reasonably believes that the ammunition is being acquired for use in a rifle and not a handgun.

(3) Supplies, delivers, or gives possession of any ammunition to any minor who the person, corporation, or dealer knows, or using reasonable care should know, is prohibited from possessing that ammunition at that time pursuant to Chapter 1 (commencing with Section 29610) of Division 9 of Title 4 of Part 6.

(b) Proof that a person, corporation, or dealer, or his or her agent or employee, demanded, was shown, and acted in reasonable reliance upon, bona fide evidence of majority and identity shall be a defense to any criminal prosecution under this section. *(Added by Stats.2010, c. 711 (S.B.1080), § 6, operative Jan. 1, 2012.)*

Law Revision Commission Comments

Subdivision (a) of Section 30300 continues former Section 12316(a)(1)(A), the first and third sentences of former Section 12316(a)(1)(B), and former Section 12316(a)(1)(C) without substantive change.

Subdivision (b) continues the first sentence of former Section 12316(a)(2) without substantive change.

For limitations on the effect of this article, see Sections 30330 (effect of article on member of military, police agency, forensic laboratory, or holder of permit for destructive device), 30335 (effect of article on permanently deactivated ammunition), 30340 (effect of article on ammunition manufactured under contract approved by government agency).

For further guidance on firearm restrictions relating to minors and persons under age 21, see Sections 27505 (person, corporation, or firm that sells, loans, or transfers firearm to minor or handgun to person under age 21), 27510 (dealer that supplies, delivers, or gives possession or control of firearm to minor or handgun to person under age 21), 27945 (exception for certain situations involving minor), and 29610–29750 (juvenile).

See Sections 16150 ("ammunition"), 16300 ("bona fide evidence of identity" or "bona fide evidence of majority and identity"), 16640 ("handgun"), 16650 ("handgun ammunition"), 17090 ("rifle"). [38 Cal.L.Rev.Comm. Reports 217 (2009)].

Cross References

Age verification when selling products that are illegal to sell to minor, reasonable steps, products requiring age verification, penalties, see Civil Code § 1798.99.1.
Handgun defined for purposes of this Part, see Penal Code § 16640.
Nuisance caused by illegal conduct involving unlawful weapons or ammunition purpose, unlawful detainer action, see Civil Code § 3485.
Rifle defined, see Penal Code § 17090.

Research References

2 Witkin, California Criminal Law 4th Crimes Against Public Peace and Welfare § 210 (2021), Unlawful Acts Involving Ammunition.

§ 30305. Possession of ammunition by persons prohibited from owning or possessing a firearm; penalties; burden of proof in proving exemption

(a)(1) No person prohibited from owning or possessing a firearm under Chapter 2 (commencing with Section 29800) or Chapter 3 (commencing with Section 29900) of Division 9 of this title, or Section 8100 or 8103 of the Welfare and Institutions Code, shall own, possess, or have under custody or control, any ammunition or reloaded ammunition.

(2) A violation of this subdivision is punishable by imprisonment in a county jail not to exceed one year or in the state prison, by a fine not to exceed one thousand dollars ($1,000), or by both the fine and imprisonment.

(b)(1) A person who is not prohibited by subdivision (a) from owning, possessing, or having under the person's custody or control, any ammunition or reloaded ammunition, but who is enjoined from engaging in activity pursuant to an injunction issued pursuant to Section 3479 of the Civil Code against that person as a member of a criminal street gang, as defined in Section 186.22, may not own, possess, or have under the person's custody or control, any ammunition or reloaded ammunition.

(2) A violation of this subdivision is a misdemeanor.

(c) A violation of subdivision (a) or (b) is justifiable where all of the following conditions are met:

(1) The person found the ammunition or reloaded ammunition or took the ammunition or reloaded ammunition from a person who was committing a crime against the person who found or took the ammunition or reloaded ammunition.

(2) The person possessed the ammunition or reloaded ammunition no longer than was necessary to deliver or transport the ammunition or reloaded ammunition to a law enforcement agency for that agency's disposition according to law.

(3) The person is prohibited from possessing any ammunition or reloaded ammunition solely because that person is prohibited from owning or possessing a firearm only by virtue of Chapter 2 (commencing with Section 29800) of Division 9 or ammunition or reloaded ammunition because of subdivision (b).

(d) Upon the trial for violating subdivision (a) or (b), the trier of fact shall determine whether the defendant is subject to the exemption created by subdivision (c). The defendant has the burden of proving by a preponderance of the evidence that the defendant is subject to the exemption provided by subdivision (c). *(Added by Stats.2010, c. 711 (S.B.1080), § 6, operative Jan. 1, 2012.)*

Law Revision Commission Comments

Subdivision (a) of Section 30305 continues former Section 12316(b)(1) & (3) without substantive change.

Subdivision (b) continues former Section 12316(b)(4)-(5) without substantive change.

Subdivision (c) continues former Section 12316(d)(1) without substantive change.

Subdivision (d) continues former Section 12316(d)(2)-(3) without substantive change.

For limitations on the effect of this article, see Sections 30330 (effect of article on member of military, police agency, forensic laboratory, or holder of permit for destructive device), 30335 (effect of article on permanently deactivated ammunition), 30340 (effect of article on ammunition manufactured under contract approved by government agency).

See Sections 16150 ("ammunition"), 16520 ("firearm"). [38 Cal.L.Rev. Comm. Reports 217 (2009)].

Cross References

Attempt to acquire ammunition by prohibited person, notice to local law enforcement agency, investigation, see Penal Code § 30372.
Firearm defined for purposes of this Part, see Penal Code § 16520.
Misdemeanors, definition and penalties, see Penal Code §§ 17, 19, 19.2.
Nuisance caused by illegal conduct involving unlawful weapons or ammunition purpose, unlawful detainer action, see Civil Code § 3485.
Prison or state prison defined for purposes of this Code, see Penal Code § 6081.

Research References

California Jury Instructions - Criminal 12.49, Illegal Possession of Ammunition.
California Jury Instructions - Criminal 12.49.5, Illegal Possession of Ammunition—Defense of Justification.
2 Witkin, California Criminal Law 4th Crimes Against Public Peace and Welfare § 210 (2021), Unlawful Acts Involving Ammunition.

§ 30306. Sale or supply of ammunition to person prohibited from possession, or to person who will make subsequent transfer to person prohibited from possession; penalties

(a) Any person, corporation, firm, or other business enterprise who supplies, delivers, sells, or gives possession or control of, any ammunition to any person who he or she knows or using reasonable care should know is prohibited from owning, possessing, or having under custody or control, any ammunition or reloaded ammunition pursuant to subdivision (a) or (b) of Section 30305, is guilty of a misdemeanor, punishable by imprisonment in a county jail not exceeding one year, or a fine not exceeding one thousand dollars ($1,000), or by both that fine and imprisonment.

(b) Any person, corporation, firm, or other business enterprise who supplies, delivers, sells, or gives possession or control of, any ammunition to any person whom the person, corporation, firm, or other business enterprise knows or has cause to believe is not the actual purchaser or transferee of the ammunition, with knowledge or cause to believe that the ammunition is to be subsequently sold or transferred to a person who is prohibited from owning, possessing, or having under custody or control any ammunition or reloaded ammunition pursuant to subdivision (a) or (b) of Section 30305, is guilty of a misdemeanor, punishable by imprisonment in a county jail not exceeding one year, or a fine not exceeding one thousand dollars ($1,000), or by both that fine and imprisonment.

(c) The provisions of this section are cumulative and shall not be construed as restricting the application of any other law. However, an act or omission punishable in different ways by this section and another provision of law shall not be punished under more than one provision. *(Added by Stats.2010, c. 711 (S.B.1080), § 6, operative Jan. 1, 2012. Amended by Initiative Measure (Prop. 63, § 8.5, approved Nov. 8, 2016, eff. Nov. 9, 2016).)*

Law Revision Commission Comments

Section 30306 continues former Section 12317(a)-(b) without substantive change.

See Section 16150 ("ammunition"). [38 Cal.L.Rev.Comm. Reports 217 (2009)].

Cross References

Misdemeanors, definition and penalties, see Penal Code §§ 17, 19, 19.2.

Research References

2 Witkin, California Criminal Law 4th Crimes Against Public Peace and Welfare § 210 (2021), Unlawful Acts Involving Ammunition.

§ 30310. Ammunition on school grounds prohibited; penalties; exemptions

(a) Unless it is with the written permission of the school district superintendent, the superintendent's designee, or equivalent school authority, no person shall carry ammunition or reloaded ammunition onto school grounds, except sworn law enforcement officers acting within the scope of their duties.

(b) This section shall not apply to any of the following:

(1) A duly appointed peace officer as defined in Chapter 4.5 (commencing with Section 830) of Title 3 of Part 2.

(2) A full-time paid peace officer of another state or the federal government who is carrying out official duties while in California.

(3) Any person summoned by any of these officers to assist in making an arrest or preserving the peace while that person is actually engaged in assisting the officer.

(4) A member of the military forces of this state or of the United States who is engaged in the performance of that person's duties.

(5) An armored vehicle guard, who is engaged in the performance of that person's duties, as defined in subdivision (d) of Section 7582.1 of the Business and Professions Code.

(6) Any peace officer, listed in Section 830.1 or 830.2, or subdivision (a) of Section 830.33, whether active or honorably retired.

(7) Any other duly appointed peace officer.

(8) Any honorably retired peace officer listed in subdivision (c) of Section 830.5.

(9) Any other honorably retired peace officer who during the course and scope of his or her appointment as a peace officer was authorized to, and did, carry a firearm.

(10)(A) A person carrying ammunition or reloaded ammunition onto school grounds that is in a motor vehicle at all times and is within a locked container or within the locked trunk of the vehicle.

(B) For purposes of this paragraph, the term "locked container" has the same meaning as set forth in Section 16850.

(c) A violation of this section is punishable by imprisonment in a county jail for a term not to exceed six months, a fine not to exceed one thousand dollars ($1,000), or both the imprisonment and fine. *(Added by Stats.2010, c. 711 (S.B.1080), § 6, operative Jan. 1, 2012. Amended by Stats.2015, c. 766 (S.B.707), § 2, eff. Jan. 1, 2016.)*

Law Revision Commission Comments

Section 30310 continues former Section 12316(c) without substantive change. An erroneous cross-reference to Business and Professions Code Section 7521(e) has been corrected by replacing it with a cross-reference to Business and Professions Code Section 7582.1(d).

For limitations on the effect of this article, see Sections 30330 (effect of article on member of military, police agency, forensic laboratory, or holder of permit for destructive device), 30335 (effect of article on permanently deactivated ammunition), 30340 (effect of article on ammunition manufactured under contract approved by government agency).

For other provisions relating to weapons on school grounds, see Sections 626.9 (Gun–Free School Zone Act) and 626.10 (miscellaneous weapons on school grounds).

See Section 16520 ("firearm"). [38 Cal.L.Rev.Comm. Reports 217 (2009)].

Cross References

Firearm defined for purposes of this Part, see Penal Code § 16520.
Nuisance caused by illegal conduct involving unlawful weapons or ammunition purpose, unlawful detainer action, see Civil Code § 3485.

Research References

2 Witkin, California Criminal Law 4th Crimes Against Public Peace and Welfare § 210 (2021), Unlawful Acts Involving Ammunition.

§ 30312. Sale of ammunition through licensed ammunition vendor; requirements; exceptions; violation

(a)(1) Commencing January 1, 2018, the sale of ammunition by any party shall be conducted by or processed through a licensed ammunition vendor.

(2) When neither party to an ammunition sale is a licensed ammunition vendor, the seller shall deliver the ammunition to a vendor to process the transaction. The ammunition vendor shall promptly and properly deliver the ammunition to the purchaser, if the sale is not prohibited, as if the ammunition were the vendor's own merchandise. If the ammunition vendor cannot legally deliver the ammunition to the purchaser, the vendor shall forthwith return the ammunition to the seller. The ammunition vendor may charge the purchaser an administrative fee to process the transaction, in an amount to be set by the Department of Justice, in addition to any applicable fees that may be charged pursuant to the provisions of this title.

(b) Commencing January 1, 2018, the sale, delivery, or transfer of ownership of ammunition by any party may only occur in a face-to-face transaction with the seller, deliverer, or transferor, provided, however, that ammunition may be purchased or acquired over the Internet or through other means of remote ordering if a licensed ammunition vendor initially receives the ammunition and processes the transaction in compliance with this section and Article 3 (commencing with Section 30342) of Chapter 1 of Division 10 of Title 4 of this part.

(c) Subdivisions (a) and (b) shall not apply to the sale, delivery, or transfer of ammunition to any of the following:

(1) An authorized law enforcement representative of a city, county, city and county, or state or federal government, if the sale, delivery, or transfer is for exclusive use by that government agency and, prior to the sale, delivery, or transfer of the ammunition, written authorization from the head of the agency employing the purchaser or transferee is obtained, identifying the employee as an individual authorized to conduct the transaction, and authorizing the transaction for the exclusive use of the agency employing the individual.

(2) A sworn peace officer, as defined in Chapter 4.5 (commencing with Section 830) of Title 3 of Part 2, or sworn federal law enforcement officer, who is authorized to carry a firearm in the course and scope of the officer's duties.

(3) An importer or manufacturer of ammunition or firearms who is licensed to engage in business pursuant to Chapter 44 (commencing with Section 921) of Title 18 of the United States Code and the regulations issued pursuant thereto.

(4) A person who is on the centralized list of exempted federal firearms licensees maintained by the Department of Justice pursuant to Article 6 (commencing with Section 28450) of Chapter 6 of Division 6 of this title.

(5) A person whose licensed premises are outside this state and who is licensed as a dealer or collector of firearms pursuant to Chapter 44 (commencing with Section 921) of Title 18 of the United States Code and the regulations issued pursuant thereto.

(6) A person who is licensed as a collector of firearms pursuant to Chapter 44 (commencing with Section 921) of Title 18 of the United States Code and the regulations issued pursuant thereto, whose licensed premises are within this state, and who has a current certificate of eligibility issued by the Department of Justice pursuant to Section 26710.

(7) An ammunition vendor.

(8) A consultant-evaluator.

(9) A person who purchases or receives ammunition at a target facility holding a business or other regulatory license, provided that the ammunition is at all times kept within the facility's premises.

(10) A person who purchases or receives ammunition from a spouse, registered domestic partner, or immediate family member as defined in Section 16720.

(11) A person enrolled in the basic training academy for peace officers or any other course certified by the Commission on Peace Officer Standards and Training, an instructor of the academy or course, or a staff member of the academy or entity providing the course, who is purchasing the ammunition for the purpose of participation or use in the course.

(d) A violation of this section is a misdemeanor. *(Added by Stats.2010, c. 711 (S.B.1080), § 6, operative Jan. 1, 2012. Amended by Initiative Measure (Prop. 63, § 8.6, approved Nov. 8, 2016, eff. Nov. 9, 2016); Stats.2017, c. 783 (A.B.693), § 3, eff. Oct. 14, 2017.)*

Validity

For validity of this section, see Parker v. State (App. 5 Dist. 2013) 164 Cal.Rptr.3d 345, 221 Cal.App.4th 340, review granted and opinion superseded 167 Cal.Rptr.3d 658, 317 P.3d 1184, review dismissed 211 Cal.Rptr.3d 98, 384 P.3d 1242 and Rhode v. Becerra, S.D.Cal.2020, 445 F.Supp.3d 902, order stayed 2020 WL 2049091, opinion issued 2020 WL 9938296.

Law Revision Commission Comments

Subdivision (a) of Section 30312 continues the first sentence of former Section 12318(a) without substantive change.

Subdivision (b) continues former Section 12318(c) without substantive change.

Subdivision (c) continues the second sentence of former Section 12318(a) without substantive change.

See Sections 16300 ("bona fide evidence of identity" or "bona fide evidence of majority and identity"), 16410 ("consultant-evaluator"), 16520 ("firearm"), 16650 ("handgun ammunition"), 16662 ("handgun ammunition vendor"). [38 Cal.L.Rev.Comm. Reports 217 (2009)].

Cross References

Consultant-evaluator defined for purposes of this Part, see Penal Code § 16410.
Firearm defined for purposes of this Part, see Penal Code § 16520.
Handgun ammunition defined, see Penal Code § 16650.
Handgun defined for purposes of this Part, see Penal Code § 16640.
Misdemeanors, definition and penalties, see Penal Code §§ 17, 19, 19.2.

Research References

2 Witkin, California Criminal Law 4th Crimes Against Public Peace and Welfare § 210 (2021), Unlawful Acts Involving Ammunition.

§ 30314. Transportation of ammunition into the state by a resident; delivery to licensed ammunition vendor; exceptions; violation

(a) Commencing January 1, 2018, a resident of this state shall not bring or transport into this state any ammunition that he or she purchased or otherwise obtained from outside of this state unless he or she first has that ammunition delivered to a licensed ammunition vendor for delivery to that resident pursuant to the procedures set forth in Section 30312.

(b) Subdivision (a) does not apply to any of the following:

(1) An ammunition vendor.

(2) A sworn peace officer, as defined in Chapter 4.5 (commencing with Section 830) of Title 3 of Part 2, or sworn federal law enforcement officer, who is authorized to carry a firearm in the course and scope of the officer's duties.

(3) An importer or manufacturer of ammunition or firearms who is licensed to engage in business pursuant to Chapter 44 (commencing with Section 921) of Title 18 of the United States Code and the regulations issued pursuant thereto.

(4) A person who is on the centralized list of exempted federal firearms licensees maintained by the Department of Justice pursuant to Article 6 (commencing with Section 28450) of Chapter 6 of Division 6.

(5) A person who is licensed as a collector of firearms pursuant to Chapter 44 (commencing with Section 921) of Title 18 of the United States Code and the regulations issued pursuant thereto, whose licensed premises are within this state, and who has a current certificate of eligibility issued by the Department of Justice pursuant to Section 26710.

(6) A person who acquired the ammunition from a spouse, registered domestic partner, or immediate family member as defined in Section 16720.

(c) A violation of this section is an infraction for any first time offense, and either an infraction or a misdemeanor for any subsequent offense. *(Added by Initiative Measure (Prop. 63, § 8.7, approved Nov. 8, 2016, eff. Nov. 9, 2016).)*

Validity

For validity of this section, see Rhode v. Becerra, S.D.Cal. 2020, 445 F.Supp.3d 902, order stayed 2020 WL 2049091, opinion issued 2020 WL 9938296.

Research References

2 Witkin, California Criminal Law 4th Crimes Against Public Peace and Welfare § 210 (2021), Unlawful Acts Involving Ammunition.

§ 30315. Possession of metal or armor piercing ammunition; penalties

Any person, firm, or corporation who, within this state knowingly possesses any handgun ammunition designed primarily to penetrate metal or armor is guilty of a public offense and upon conviction thereof shall be punished by imprisonment pursuant to subdivision (h) of Section 1170, or in the county jail for a term not to exceed one year, or by a fine not to exceed five thousand dollars ($5,000), or by both that fine and imprisonment. *(Added by Stats.2010, c. 711 (S.B.1080), § 6, operative Jan. 1, 2012. Amended by Stats.2011, c. 15 (A.B.109), § 548, eff. April 4, 2011, operative Jan. 1, 2012.)*

Law Revision Commission Comments

Section 30315 continues former Section 12320 without substantive change.

For an exception to this provision, see Section 30325 (transporting handgun ammunition designed primarily to penetrate metal or armor to law enforcement agency).

For other limitations on the effect of this article, see Sections 30330 (effect of article on member of military, police agency, forensic laboratory, or holder of permit for destructive device), 30335 (effect of article on permanently deactivated ammunition), 30340 (effect of article on ammunition manufactured under contract approved by government agency).

See Section 16660 ("handgun ammunition designed primarily to penetrate metal or armor"). [38 Cal.L.Rev.Comm. Reports 217 (2009)].

Cross References

Handgun ammunition defined, see Penal Code § 16650.
Handgun defined for purposes of this Part, see Penal Code § 16640.
Murder by use of ammunition designed to penetrate metal or armor, see Penal Code § 189.

Research References

2 Witkin, California Criminal Law 4th Crimes Against Public Peace and Welfare § 189 (2021), In General.
2 Witkin, California Criminal Law 4th Crimes Against Public Peace and Welfare § 228 (2021), Armor Piercing Ammunition.
1 Witkin California Criminal Law 4th Crimes Against the Person § 149 (2021), Killing by Armor-Piercing Ammunition.

§ 30320. Manufacture, import, sale, or transportation of metal or armor piercing ammunition; penalties

Any person, firm, or corporation who, within this state, manufactures, imports, sells, offers to sell, or knowingly transports any handgun ammunition designed primarily to penetrate metal or armor is guilty of a felony and upon conviction thereof shall be punished by imprisonment in state prison, or by a fine not to exceed five thousand dollars ($5,000), or by both that fine and imprisonment. *(Added by Stats.2010, c. 711 (S.B.1080), § 6, operative Jan. 1, 2012.)*

Law Revision Commission Comments

Section 30320 continues former Section 12321 without substantive change.

For an exception to this provision, see Section 30325 (transporting handgun ammunition designed primarily to penetrate metal or armor to law enforcement agency).

For other limitations on the effect of this article, see Sections 30330 (effect of article on member of military, police agency, forensic laboratory, or holder of permit for destructive device), 30335 (effect of article on permanently deactivated ammunition), 30340 (effect of article on ammunition manufactured under contract approved by government agency).

See Section 16660 ("handgun ammunition designed primarily to penetrate metal or armor"). [38 Cal.L.Rev.Comm. Reports 217 (2009)].

Cross References

Felonies, definition and penalties, see Penal Code §§ 17, 18.
Handgun ammunition defined, see Penal Code § 16650.
Handgun defined for purposes of this Part, see Penal Code § 16640.

Research References

2 Witkin, California Criminal Law 4th Crimes Against Public Peace and Welfare § 228 (2021), Armor Piercing Ammunition.

§ 30325. Application to found metal or armor piercing ammunition being transported to law enforcement agency for disposition

Nothing in this article shall apply to or affect the possession of handgun ammunition designed primarily to penetrate metal or armor by a person who found the ammunition, if that person is not prohibited from possessing firearms or ammunition pursuant to subdivision (a) of Section 30305, Chapter 2 (commencing with Section 29800) or Chapter 3 (commencing with Section 29900) of Division 9 of this title, or Section 8100 or 8103 of the Welfare and Institutions Code, and the person is transporting the ammunition to a law enforcement agency for disposition according to law. *(Added by Stats.2010, c. 711 (S.B.1080), § 6, operative Jan. 1, 2012.)*

Law Revision Commission Comments

Section 30325 continues former Section 12322(b) without substantive change.

See Section 16660 ("handgun ammunition designed primarily to penetrate metal or armor"). [38 Cal.L.Rev.Comm. Reports 217 (2009)].

Cross References

Firearm defined for purposes of this Part, see Penal Code § 16520.
Handgun ammunition defined, see Penal Code § 16650.
Handgun defined for purposes of this Part, see Penal Code § 16640.

Research References

2 Witkin, California Criminal Law 4th Crimes Against Public Peace and Welfare § 228 (2021), Armor Piercing Ammunition.

§ 30330. Application of article to sale, purchase, possession, or use of ammunition by military forces, police agencies, forensic laboratories, or permit-holders

Nothing in this article shall apply to or affect the sale to, purchase by, possession of, or use of any ammunition by any member of the Army, Navy, Air Force, or Marine Corps of the United States, or the National Guard, while on duty and acting within the scope and course of employment, or any police agency or forensic laboratory or any person who is the holder of a valid permit issued pursuant to Article 3 (commencing with Section 18900) of Chapter 1 of Division 5 of Title 2. *(Added by Stats.2010, c. 711 (S.B.1080), § 6, operative Jan. 1, 2012.)*

Law Revision Commission Comments

Section 30330 continues former Section 12322(a) without substantive change. [38 Cal.L.Rev.Comm. Reports 217 (2009)].

Research References

2 Witkin, California Criminal Law 4th Crimes Against Public Peace and Welfare § 228 (2021), Armor Piercing Ammunition.

§ 30335. Possession, importation, sale, or transport of deactivated ammunition

Nothing in this article shall prohibit the possession, importation, sale, attempted sale, or transport of ammunition from which the propellant has been removed and the primer has been permanently deactivated. *(Added by Stats.2010, c. 711 (S.B.1080), § 6, operative Jan. 1, 2012.)*

Law Revision Commission Comments

Section 30335 continues former Section 12324 without substantive change. [38 Cal.L.Rev.Comm. Reports 217 (2009)].

Research References

2 Witkin, California Criminal Law 4th Crimes Against Public Peace and Welfare § 228 (2021), Armor Piercing Ammunition.

§ 30340. Manufacture of ammunition under state or federal contracts

Nothing in this article shall prohibit the manufacture of ammunition under contracts approved by agencies of the state or federal government. *(Added by Stats.2010, c. 711 (S.B.1080), § 6, operative Jan. 1, 2012.)*

Law Revision Commission Comments

Section 30340 continues former Section 12325 without substantive change. [38 Cal.L.Rev.Comm. Reports 217 (2009)].

Research References

2 Witkin, California Criminal Law 4th Crimes Against Public Peace and Welfare § 228 (2021), Armor Piercing Ammunition.

ARTICLE 3. AMMUNITION VENDORS

§ 30342. Persons or business enterprises selling more than 500 rounds of ammunition in 30–day period; vendor license requirement; violation

(a) Commencing January 1, 2018, a valid ammunition vendor license shall be required for any person, firm, corporation, or other business enterprise to sell more than 500 rounds of ammunition in any 30–day period.

(b) Subdivision (a) does not apply to, or affect the sale of, ammunition to a person who holds a valid ammunition vendor license by a person in order to comply with Section 6389 of the Family Code.

(c) A violation of this section is a misdemeanor. *(Added by Initiative Measure (Prop. 63, § 8.9, approved Nov. 8, 2016, eff. Nov. 9, 2016). Amended by Stats.2021, c. 685 (S.B.320), § 13, eff. Jan. 1, 2022.)*

Research References

2 Witkin, California Criminal Law 4th Crimes Against Public Peace and Welfare § 210 (2021), Unlawful Acts Involving Ammunition.

§ 30345. Compliance; inspections

(a) A vendor shall comply with all of the conditions, requirements, and prohibitions stated in this article.

(b) Commencing July 1, 2022, the Department of Justice may inspect ammunition vendors to ensure compliance with subdivision (a) and any other applicable state or federal firearms laws. The department may adopt regulations to administer the application and enforcement provisions of this chapter. *(Added by Stats.2010, c. 711 (S.B.1080), § 6, operative Jan. 1, 2012. Amended by Stats.2020, c. 273 (A.B.2061), § 2, eff. Jan. 1, 2021.)*

Validity

For validity of this section, see Parker v. State (App. 5 Dist. 2013) 164 Cal.Rptr.3d 345, 221 Cal.App.4th 340, review granted and opinion superseded 167 Cal.Rptr.3d 658, 317 P.3d 1184, review dismissed 211 Cal.Rptr.3d 98, 384 P.3d 1242.

Law Revision Commission Comments

Section 30345 continues the introductory clause of former Section 12061(a) without substantive change.

See Section 17315 ("vendor"). [38 Cal.L.Rev.Comm. Reports 217 (2009)].

Cross References

Vendor defined for purposes of this Article, see Penal Code § 17315.

§ 30346. Inoperative

Addition of a section of this number by Stats.2016, c. 55 (A.B.1235), § 11, failed to become operative under the provisions of § 19 (a) of that Act.

§ 30347. Certificate of eligibility requirement for agents or employees who handle, sell, or deliver ammunition; notice if agent or employee become prohibited from possessing ammunition; prohibition against specified agents or employees handling ammunition

(a) An ammunition vendor shall require any agent or employee who handles, sells, delivers, or has under his or her custody or control any ammunition, to obtain and provide to the vendor a certificate of eligibility from the Department of Justice issued pursuant to Section 26710. On the application for the certificate, the agent or employee shall provide the name and address of the ammunition vendor with whom the person is employed, or the name and California firearms dealer number of the ammunition vendor if applicable.

(b) The department shall notify the ammunition vendor in the event that the agent or employee who has a certificate of eligibility is or becomes prohibited from possessing ammunition under subdivision (a) of Section 30305 or federal law.

(c) An ammunition vendor shall not permit any agent or employee who the vendor knows or reasonably should know is a person described in Chapter 2 (commencing with Section 29800) or Chapter 3 (commencing with Section 29900) of Division 9 of this title or Section 8100 or 8103 of the Welfare and Institutions Code to handle, sell, deliver, or have under his or her custody or control, any ammunition in the course and scope of employment. *(Added by Stats.2010, c. 711 (S.B.1080), § 6, operative Jan. 1, 2012. Amended by Initiative Measure (Prop. 63, § 8.10, approved Nov. 8, 2016, eff. Nov. 9, 2016).)*

Validity

For validity of a prior version of this section, see Parker v. State (App. 5 Dist. 2013) 164 Cal.Rptr.3d 345, 221 Cal.App.4th 340, review granted and opinion superseded 167 Cal.Rptr.3d 658, 317 P.3d 1184, review dismissed 211 Cal.Rptr.3d 98, 384 P.3d 1242.

Law Revision Commission Comments

Section 30347 continues former Section 12061(a)(1) without substantive change.

See Sections 16650 ("handgun ammunition"), 17315 ("vendor"). [38 Cal.L.Rev.Comm. Reports 217 (2009)].

Cross References

Handgun ammunition defined, see Penal Code § 16650.
Handgun defined for purposes of this Part, see Penal Code § 16640.
Sales of ammunition at gun show, compliance with Sections 30347, 30348, 30350, 30352, and 30360, see Penal Code § 27315.
Vendor defined for purposes of this Article, see Penal Code § 17315.

Vendor to provide information to gun show producer, availability of information, see Penal Code § 27320.

§ 30348. Location for sales of ammunition by a licensed vendor; sales at gun shows or events

(a) Except as provided in subdivision (b), the sale of ammunition by a licensed vendor shall be conducted at the location specified in the license.

(b) A vendor may sell ammunition at a gun show or event if the gun show or event is not conducted from any motorized or towed vehicle.

(c) For purposes of this section, "gun show or event" means a function sponsored by any national, state, or local organization, devoted to the collection, competitive use, or other sporting use of firearms, or an organization or association that sponsors functions devoted to the collection, competitive use, or other sporting use of firearms in the community.

(d) Sales of ammunition at a gun show or event shall comply with all applicable laws including Sections 30347, 30350, 30352, and 30360. *(Added by Initiative Measure (Prop. 63, § 8.11, approved Nov. 8, 2016, eff. Nov. 9, 2016).)*

Cross References

Sales of ammunition at gun show, compliance with Sections 30347, 30348, 30350, 30352, and 30360, see Penal Code § 27315.

§ 30350. Accessibility of ammunition to purchaser or transferee without vendor assistance

An ammunition vendor shall not sell or otherwise transfer ownership of, offer for sale or otherwise offer to transfer ownership of, or display for sale or display for transfer of ownership of any ammunition in a manner that allows that ammunition to be accessible to a purchaser or transferee without the assistance of the vendor or an employee of the vendor. *(Added by Stats.2010, c. 711 (S.B.1080), § 6, operative Jan. 1, 2012. Amended by Initiative Measure (Prop. 63, § 8.12, approved Nov. 8, 2016, eff. Nov. 9, 2016).)*

Validity

For validity of this section, see Parker v. State (App. 5 Dist. 2013) 164 Cal.Rptr.3d 345, 221 Cal.App.4th 340, review granted and opinion superseded 167 Cal.Rptr.3d 658, 317 P.3d 1184, review dismissed 211 Cal.Rptr.3d 98, 384 P.3d 1242.

Law Revision Commission Comments

Section 30350 continues former Section 12061(a)(2) without substantive change.

See Sections 16650 ("handgun ammunition"), 17315 ("vendor"). [38 Cal.L.Rev.Comm. Reports 217 (2009)].

Cross References

Handgun ammunition defined, see Penal Code § 16650.
Handgun defined for purposes of this Part, see Penal Code § 16640.
Sales of ammunition at gun show, compliance with Sections 30347, 30348, 30350, 30352, and 30360, see Penal Code § 27315.
Vendor defined for purposes of this Article, see Penal Code § 17315.

§ 30352. Information to be recorded upon delivery of ammunition; form; electronic submission to department; persons authorized to purchase ammunition

(a) Commencing July 1, 2019, an ammunition vendor shall not sell or otherwise transfer ownership of any ammunition without, at the time of delivery, legibly recording the following information on a form to be prescribed by the Department of Justice:

(1) The date of the sale or other transfer.

(2) The purchaser's or transferee's driver's license or other identification number and the state in which it was issued.

(3) The brand, type, and amount of ammunition sold or otherwise transferred.

(4) The purchaser's or transferee's full name and signature.

(5) The name of the salesperson who processed the sale or other transaction.

(6) The purchaser's or transferee's full residential address and telephone number.

(7) The purchaser's or transferee's date of birth.

(b)(1) Commencing July 1, 2019, an ammunition vendor shall electronically submit to the department the information required by subdivision (a) for all sales and transfers of ownership of ammunition. The department shall retain this information in a database to be known as the Ammunition Purchase Records File. Except as provided in paragraph (2), this information shall remain confidential and may be used by the department and those entities specified in, and pursuant to, subdivision (b) or (c) of Section 11105, through the California Law Enforcement Telecommunications System, only for law enforcement purposes. The ammunition vendor shall not use, sell, disclose, or share the information for any other purpose other than the submission required by this subdivision without the express written consent of the purchaser or transferee.

(2) The information collected by the department as provided in paragraph (1) shall be available to researchers affiliated with the California Firearm Violence Research Center at UC Davis following approval by the institution's governing institutional review board, when required. At the department's discretion, and subject to Section 14240, the data may be provided to any other nonprofit bona fide research institution accredited by the United States Department of Education or the Council for Higher Education Accreditation for the study of the prevention of violence, following approval by the institution's governing institutional review board or human subjects committee, when required, for academic and policy research purposes. Material identifying individuals shall only be provided for research or statistical activities and shall not be transferred, revealed, or used for purposes other than research or statistical activities, and reports or publications derived therefrom shall not identify specific individuals. Reasonable costs to the department associated with the department's processing of that data may be billed to the researcher. If a request for data or letter of support for research using the data is denied, the department shall provide a written statement of the specific reasons for the denial.

(c) Commencing on July 1, 2019, only those persons listed in this subdivision, or those persons or entities listed in subdivision (e), shall be authorized to purchase ammunition. Prior to delivering any ammunition, an ammunition vendor shall require bona fide evidence of identity to verify that the person who is receiving delivery of the ammunition is a person or entity listed in subdivision (e) or one of the following:

(1) A person authorized to purchase ammunition pursuant to Section 30370.

(2) A person who was approved by the department to receive a firearm from the ammunition vendor, pursuant to Section 28220, if that vendor is a licensed firearms dealer, and the ammunition is delivered to the person in the same transaction as the firearm.

(d) Commencing July 1, 2019, the ammunition vendor shall verify with the department, in a manner prescribed by the department, that the person is authorized to purchase ammunition. If the person is not listed as an authorized ammunition purchaser, the vendor shall deny the sale or transfer.

(e) Subdivisions (a) and (d) shall not apply to sales or other transfers of ownership of ammunition by ammunition vendors to any of the following, if properly identified:

(1) An ammunition vendor.

(2) A person who is on the centralized list of exempted federal firearms licensees maintained by the department pursuant to Article 6 (commencing with Section 28450) of Chapter 6 of Division 6 of Title 4 of Part 6.

(3) A person who purchases or receives ammunition at a target facility holding a business or other regulatory license, provided that the ammunition is at all times kept within the facility's premises.

(4) A gunsmith.

(5) A wholesaler.

(6) A manufacturer or importer of firearms or ammunition licensed pursuant to Chapter 44 (commencing with Section 921) of Part I of Title 18 of the United States Code, and the regulations issued pursuant thereto.

(7) An authorized law enforcement representative of a city, county, city and county, or state or federal government, if the sale or other transfer of ownership is for exclusive use by that government agency, and, prior to the sale, delivery, or transfer of the handgun ammunition, written authorization from the head of the agency authorizing the transaction is presented to the person from whom the purchase, delivery, or transfer is being made. Proper written authorization is defined as verifiable written certification from the head of the agency by which the purchaser, transferee, or person otherwise acquiring ownership is employed, identifying the employee as an individual authorized to conduct the transaction, and authorizing the transaction for the exclusive use of the agency by which that individual is employed.

(8)(A) A properly identified sworn peace officer, as defined in Chapter 4.5 (commencing with Section 830) of Title 3 of Part 2, or properly identified sworn federal law enforcement officer, who is authorized to carry a firearm in the course and scope of the officer's duties.

(B)(i) Proper identification is defined as verifiable written certification from the head of the agency by which the purchaser or transferee is employed, identifying the purchaser or transferee as a full-time paid peace officer who is authorized to carry a firearm in the course and scope of the officer's duties.

(ii) The certification shall be delivered to the vendor at the time of purchase or transfer and the purchaser or transferee shall provide bona fide evidence of identity to verify that the purchaser transferee is the person authorized in the certification.

(iii) The vendor shall keep the certification with the record of sale and submit the certification to the department.

(f) The department is authorized to adopt regulations to implement the provisions of this section. *(Added by Stats.2010, c. 711 (S.B.1080), § 6, operative Jan. 1, 2012. Amended by Initiative Measure (Prop. 63, § 8.13, approved Nov. 8, 2016, eff. Nov. 9, 2016); Stats.2016, c. 55 (S.B.1235), § 12, eff. Jan. 1, 2017; Stats.2021, c. 253 (A.B.173), § 11, eff. Sept. 23, 2021.)*

Validity

For validity of this section, see Parker v. State (App. 5 Dist. 2013) 164 Cal.Rptr.3d 345, 221 Cal.App.4th 340, review granted and opinion superseded 167 Cal.Rptr.3d 658, 317 P.3d 1184, review dismissed 211 Cal.Rptr.3d 98, 384 P.3d 1242 and Rhode v. Becerra, S.D.Cal.2020, 445 F.Supp.3d 902, order stayed 2020 WL 2049091, opinion issued 2020 WL 9938296.

Law Revision Commission Comments

Subdivision (a) of Section 30352 continues former Section 12061(a)(3) without substantive change.

Subdivision (b) continues former Section 12061(b) without substantive change.

See Sections 16520 ("firearm"), 16630 ("gunsmith"), 16650 ("handgun ammunition"), 16662 ("handgun ammunition vendor"), 17315 ("vendor"), 17340 ("wholesaler"). [38 Cal.L.Rev.Comm. Reports 217 (2009)].

Cross References

Department defined, see Penal Code § 16450.
Firearm defined for purposes of this Part, see Penal Code § 16520.
Gunsmith defined for purposes of this Part, see Penal Code § 16630.
Handgun ammunition defined, see Penal Code § 16650.
Handgun defined for purposes of this Part, see Penal Code § 16640.
Sales of ammunition at gun show, compliance with Sections 30347, 30348, 30350, 30352, and 30360, see Penal Code § 27315.
Vendor defined for purposes of this Article, see Penal Code § 17315.
Wholesaler defined for purposes of this Part, see Penal Code § 17340.

Research References

2 Witkin, California Criminal Law 4th Crimes Against Public Peace and Welfare § 228 (2021), Armor Piercing Ammunition.

§ 30355. Record maintenance period

Commencing February 1, 2011, the records required by this article shall be maintained on the premises of the vendor for a period of not less than five years from the date of the recorded transfer. *(Added by Stats.2010, c. 711 (S.B.1080), § 6, operative Jan. 1, 2012.)*

Validity

For validity of this section, see Parker v. State (App. 5 Dist. 2013) 164 Cal.Rptr.3d 345, 221 Cal.App.4th 340, review granted and opinion superseded 167 Cal.Rptr.3d 658, 317 P.3d 1184, review dismissed 211 Cal.Rptr.3d 98, 384 P.3d 1242.

Law Revision Commission Comments

Section 30355 continues former Section 12061(a)(4) without substantive change.

See Section 17315 ("vendor"). [38 Cal.L.Rev.Comm. Reports 217 (2009)].

Cross References

Vendor defined for purposes of this Article, see Penal Code § 17315.

Research References

2 Witkin, California Criminal Law 4th Crimes Against Public Peace and Welfare § 228 (2021), Armor Piercing Ammunition.

§ 30356. Inoperative

Addition of a section of this number by § 13 of Stats.2016, c. 55 (S.B.1235), failed to become operative under the provisions of § 19 (a) of that Act.

§ 30357. Inspection of records

(a) Commencing February 1, 2011, the records referred to in Section 30352 shall be subject to inspection at any time during normal business hours by any peace officer employed by a sheriff, city police department, or district attorney as provided in subdivision (a) of Section 830.1, or employed by the department as provided in subdivision (b) of Section 830.1, provided that the officer is conducting an investigation where access to those records is or may be relevant, is seeking information about persons prohibited from owning a firearm or ammunition, or is engaged in ensuring compliance with the Dangerous Weapons Control Law, as defined in Section 23500, or any other laws pertaining to firearms or ammunition.

(b) The records referred to in Section 30352 shall also be subject to inspection at any time during normal business hours by any other employee of the department, provided that the employee is conducting an investigation where access to those records is or may be relevant, is seeking information about persons prohibited from owning a firearm or ammunition, or is engaged in ensuring compliance with the Dangerous Weapons Control Law, as defined in Section 23500, or any other laws pertaining to firearms or ammunition. *(Added by Stats.2010, c. 711 (S.B.1080), § 6, operative Jan. 1, 2012.)*

Validity

For validity of this section, see Parker v. State (App. 5 Dist. 2013) 164 Cal.Rptr.3d 345, 221 Cal.App.4th 340, review granted and opinion superseded 167 Cal.Rptr.3d 658, 317 P.3d 1184, review dismissed 211 Cal.Rptr.3d 98, 384 P.3d 1242.

Law Revision Commission Comments

Section 30357 continues former Section 12061(a)(5) without substantive change.

See Section 16520 ("firearm"). [38 Cal.L.Rev.Comm. Reports 217 (2009)].

Cross References

Department defined, see Penal Code § 16450.
Firearm defined for purposes of this Part, see Penal Code § 16520.

§ 30360. False or missing record entries; fingerprints

Commencing February 1, 2011, a vendor shall not knowingly make a false entry in, fail to make a required entry in, fail to obtain the required thumbprint, or otherwise fail to maintain in the required manner, records prepared in accordance with Section 30352. If the right thumbprint is not available, then the vendor shall have the purchaser or transferee use the left thumb, or any available finger, and shall so indicate on the form. *(Added by Stats.2010, c. 711 (S.B.1080), § 6, operative Jan. 1, 2012.)*

Validity

For validity of this section, see Parker v. State (App. 5 Dist. 2013) 164 Cal.Rptr.3d 345, 221 Cal.App.4th 340, review granted and opinion superseded 167 Cal.Rptr.3d 658, 317 P.3d 1184, review dismissed 211 Cal.Rptr.3d 98, 384 P.3d 1242.

Law Revision Commission Comments

Section 30360 continues former Section 12061(a)(6) without substantive change. An erroneous cross-reference to former Section 12316(a)(2) has been replaced with a reference to Section 30352, which continues former Section 12316(a)(3).

See Section 17315 ("vendor"). [38 Cal.L.Rev.Comm. Reports 217 (2009)].

Cross References

Sales of ammunition at gun show, compliance with Sections 30347, 30348, 30350, 30352, and 30360, see Penal Code § 27315.
Vendor defined for purposes of this Article, see Penal Code § 17315.

§ 30362. Inspections; vendor prohibited from refusing examination or use of records by authorized persons

(a) Commencing February 1, 2011, no vendor shall, during any inspection conducted pursuant to this article, refuse to permit a person authorized under Section 30357 to examine any record prepared in accordance with this article.

(b) Commencing February 1, 2011, no vendor shall refuse to permit the use of any record or information by a person authorized under Section 30357. *(Added by Stats.2010, c. 711 (S.B.1080), § 6, operative Jan. 1, 2012.)*

Validity

For validity of this section, see Parker v. State (App. 5 Dist. 2013) 164 Cal.Rptr.3d 345, 221 Cal.App.4th 340, review granted and opinion superseded 167 Cal.Rptr.3d 658, 317 P.3d 1184, review dismissed 211 Cal.Rptr.3d 98, 384 P.3d 1242.

Law Revision Commission Comments

Section 30362 continues former Section 12061(a)(7) without substantive change.

See Section 17315 ("vendor"). [38 Cal.L.Rev.Comm. Reports 217 (2009)].

Cross References

Vendor defined for purposes of this Article, see Penal Code § 17315.

Research References

2 Witkin, California Criminal Law 4th Crimes Against Public Peace and Welfare § 228 (2021), Armor Piercing Ammunition.

§ 30363. Report of loss or theft of ammunition by vendor

Within 48 hours of discovery, an ammunition vendor shall report the loss or theft of any of the following items to the appropriate law enforcement agency in the city, county, or city and county where the vendor's business premises are located:

(1) Any ammunition that is merchandise of the vendor.

(2) Any ammunition that the vendor takes possession of pursuant to Section 30312.

(3) Any ammunition kept at the vendor's place of business. *(Added by Initiative Measure (Prop. 63, § 8.14, approved Nov. 8, 2016, eff. Nov. 9, 2016).)*

§ 30365. Penalty for record keeping violations; construction of section in relation to other laws

(a) A violation of Section 30352, 30355, 30360, or 30362 is a misdemeanor.

(b) The provisions of this section are cumulative, and shall not be construed as restricting the application of any other law. However, an act or omission punishable in different ways by different provisions of law shall not be punished under more than one provision. *(Added by Stats.2010, c. 711 (S.B.1080), § 6, operative Jan. 1, 2012.)*

Validity

For validity of this section, see Parker v. State (App. 5 Dist. 2013) 164 Cal.Rptr.3d 345, 221 Cal.App.4th 340, review granted and opinion superseded 167 Cal.Rptr.3d 658, 317 P.3d 1184, review dismissed 211 Cal.Rptr.3d 98, 384 P.3d 1242 and Rhode v. Becerra, S.D.Cal.2020, 445 F.Supp.3d 902, order stayed 2020 WL 9938296.

Law Revision Commission Comments

Section 30365 continues former Section 12061(c) without substantive change. [38 Cal.L.Rev.Comm. Reports 217 (2009)].

Cross References

Misdemeanors, definition and penalties, see Penal Code §§ 17, 19, 19.2.

Research References

2 Witkin, California Criminal Law 4th Crimes Against Public Peace and Welfare § 228 (2021), Armor Piercing Ammunition.

§§ 30366 to 30369. Inoperative

Addition of sections 30366, 30367, 30368, and 30369 by § 14 of Stats.2016, c. 55 (S.B.1235), failed to become operative under the provisions of § 19 (a) of that Act.

ARTICLE 4. AMMUNITION PURCHASE AUTHORIZATIONS

Section

§ 30370. Electronic approval of purchase or transfer of ammunition by department; determination of eligibility of purchaser or transferee; development of approval procedure for single ammunition transaction or purchase; provision of ammunition by vendor without approval prohibited; transaction fee; Ammunition Safety and Enforcement Special Fund; regulations

(a) Commencing July 1, 2019, the department shall electronically approve the purchase or transfer of ammunition through a vendor, as defined in Section 16151, except as otherwise specified. This approval shall occur at the time of purchase or transfer, prior to the purchaser or transferee taking possession of the ammunition. Pursuant to the authorization specified in paragraph (1) of subdivision (c) of Section 30352, the following persons are authorized to purchase ammunition:

(1) A purchaser or transferee whose information matches an entry in the Automated Firearms System (AFS) and who is eligible to possess ammunition as specified in subdivision (b).

(2) A purchaser or transferee who has a current certificate of eligibility issued by the department pursuant to Section 26710.

(3) A purchaser or transferee who is not prohibited from purchasing or possessing ammunition in a single ammunition transaction or purchase made pursuant to the procedure developed pursuant to subdivision (c).

(b) To determine if the purchaser or transferee is eligible to purchase or possess ammunition pursuant to paragraph (1) of subdivision (a), the department shall cross-reference the ammunition purchaser's or transferee's name, date of birth, current address, and driver's license or other government identification number, as described in Section 28180, with the information maintained in the AFS. If the purchaser's or transferee's information does not match an AFS entry, the transaction shall be denied. If the purchaser's or transferee's information matches an AFS entry, the department shall determine if the purchaser or transferee falls within a class of persons who are prohibited from owning or possessing ammunition by cross-referencing with the Prohibited Armed Persons File. If the purchaser or transferee is prohibited from owning or possessing a firearm, the transaction shall be denied.

(c) The department shall develop a procedure in which a person who is not prohibited from purchasing or possessing ammunition may be approved for a single ammunition transaction or purchase. The department shall recover the cost of processing and regulatory and enforcement activities related to this section by charging the ammunition transaction or purchase applicant a fee not to exceed the fee charged for the department's Dealers' Record of Sale (DROS) process, as described in Section 28225 and not to exceed the department's reasonable costs.

(d) A vendor is prohibited from providing a purchaser or transferee ammunition without department approval. If a vendor cannot electronically verify a person's eligibility to purchase or possess ammunition via an Internet connection, the department shall provide a telephone line to verify eligibility. This option is available to ammunition vendors who can demonstrate legitimate geographical and telecommunications limitations in submitting the information electronically and who are approved by the department to use the telephone line verification.

(e) The department shall recover the reasonable cost of regulatory and enforcement activities related to this article by charging ammunition purchasers and transferees a per transaction fee not to exceed one dollar ($1), provided, however, that the fee may be increased at a rate not to exceed any increases in the California Consumer Price Index as compiled and reported by the Department of Industrial Relations, not to exceed the reasonable regulatory and enforcement costs.

(f) A fund to be known as the "Ammunition Safety and Enforcement Special Fund" is hereby created within the State Treasury. All fees received pursuant to this section shall be deposited into the Ammunition Safety and Enforcement Special Fund and, notwithstanding Section 13340 of the Government Code, are continuously appropriated for purposes of implementing, operating, and enforcing the ammunition authorization program provided for in this section and Section 30352 and for repaying the start-up loan provided for in Section 30371.

(g) The Department of Justice is authorized to adopt regulations to implement this section. *(Added by Stats.2016, c. 55 (S.B.1235), § 15, eff. Jan. 1, 2017.)*

Validity

For validity of this section, see Rhode v. Becerra, S.D.Cal. 2020, 445 F.Supp.3d 902, order stayed 2020 WL 9938296.

Research References

2 Witkin, California Criminal Law 4th Crimes Against Public Peace and Welfare § 210 (2021), Unlawful Acts Involving Ammunition.

§ 30371. Appropriation for ammunition authorization program costs

(a) There is hereby appropriated twenty-five million dollars ($25,000,000) from the General Fund as a loan for the start-up costs of implementing, operating and enforcing the provisions of the ammunition authorization program provided for in Sections 30352 and 30370.

(b) For purposes of repaying the loan, the Controller shall, after disbursing moneys necessary to implement, operate and enforce the ammunition authorization program provided for in Sections 30352 and 30370, transfer all proceeds from fees received by the Ammunition Safety and Enforcement Special Fund up to the amount of the loan provided by this section, including interest at the pooled money investment account rate, to the General Fund. *(Added by Initiative Measure (Prop. 63, § 8.15, approved Nov. 8, 2016, eff. Nov. 9, 2016).)*

§ 30372. Attempt to acquire ammunition by prohibited person; notice to local law enforcement agency; investigation

(a) If a person attempts to purchase or otherwise acquire ammunition and the sale or other transfer is not approved by the Department of Justice pursuant to Section 30370 because the person is prohibited from possessing ammunition pursuant to Section 30305, the department shall notify the local law enforcement agency with primary jurisdiction in which the person was last known to reside of the attempt.

(b) A local law enforcement agency that receives a notification pursuant to subdivision (a) may investigate whether the person is in unlawful possession of a firearm. However, the law enforcement agency shall not contact the person until it has attempted to confirm both of the following:

(1) That the person is prohibited from possessing ammunition pursuant to Section 30305.

(2) That the person did in fact attempt to make the reported purchase.

(c) Subdivision (a) does not apply if the sale or other transfer is not approved only because the address in the Automated Firearms System does not match the address on the person's identification, if there is a matching file with the same name, date of birth, and identification number.

(d) This section does not authorize a law enforcement agency to conduct a search without a warrant. *(Added by Stats.2022, c. 100 (A.B.2551), § 2, eff. Jan. 1, 2023.)*

ARTICLE 5. AMMUNITION VENDOR LICENSES

§ 30385. Issuance of ammunition vendor licenses by the Department of Justice

(a) The Department of Justice is authorized to issue ammunition vendor licenses pursuant to this article. The department shall, commencing July 1, 2017, commence accepting applications for ammunition vendor licenses. If an application is denied, the department shall inform the applicant of the reason for denial in writing.

(b) The ammunition vendor license shall be issued in a form prescribed by the department and shall be valid for a period of one year. The department may adopt regulations to administer the application and enforcement provisions of this article. The license shall allow the licensee to sell ammunition at the location specified in the license or at a gun show or event as set forth in Section 30348.

(c)(1) In the case of an entity other than a natural person, the department shall issue the license to the entity, but shall require a responsible person to pass the background check pursuant to Section 30395.

(2) For purposes of this article, "responsible person" means a person having the power to direct the management, policies, and practices of the entity as it pertains to ammunition.

(d) Commencing January 1, 2018, a firearms dealer licensed pursuant to Sections 26700 to 26915, inclusive, shall automatically be deemed a licensed ammunition vendor, provided the dealer complies with the requirements of Article 2 (commencing with Section 30300) and Article 3 (commencing with Section 30342). *(Added by Initiative Measure (Prop. 63, § 8.16, approved Nov. 8, 2016, eff. Nov. 9, 2016).)*

§ 30390. License applicant fees

(a) The Department of Justice may charge ammunition vendor license applicants a reasonable fee sufficient to reimburse the department for the reasonable, estimated costs of administering the license program, including the enforcement of this program and maintenance of the registry of ammunition vendors.

(b) The fees received by the department pursuant to this article shall be deposited in the Ammunition Vendors Special Account, which is hereby created. Notwithstanding Section 13340 of the Government Code, the revenue in the fund is continuously appropriated for use by the department for the purpose of implementing, administering and enforcing the provisions of this article, and for collecting and maintaining information submitted pursuant to Section 30352.

(c) The revenue in the Firearms Safety and Enforcement Special Fund shall also be available upon appropriation to the department for the purpose of implementing and enforcing the provisions of this article. *(Added by Initiative Measure (Prop. 63, § 8.16, approved Nov. 8, 2016, eff. Nov. 9, 2016).)*

§ 30395. Issuance of ammunition vendor licenses to qualified applicants; registry of licensed vendors; forfeiture of license

(a) The Department of Justice is authorized to issue ammunition vendor licenses to applicants who the department has determined, either as an individual or a responsible person, are not prohibited from possessing, receiving, owning, or purchasing ammunition under subdivision (a) of Section 30305 or federal law, and who provide a copy of any regulatory or business license required by local government, a valid seller's permit issued by the State Board of Equalization, a federal firearms license if the person is federally licensed, and a certificate of eligibility issued by the department.

(b) The department shall keep a registry of all licensed ammunition vendors. Law enforcement agencies shall be provided access to the registry for law enforcement purposes.

(c) An ammunition vendor license is subject to forfeiture for a breach of any of the prohibitions and requirements of Article 2 (commencing with Section 30300) or Article 3 (commencing with Section 30342). *(Added by Initiative Measure (Prop. 63, § 8.16, approved Nov. 8, 2016, eff. Nov. 9, 2016).)*

CHAPTER 1.5. FIREARM PRECURSOR PARTS

ARTICLE 1. RESTRICTIONS RELATING TO FIREARM PRECURSOR PARTS

§ 30400. Prohibition of selling, offering to sell, or transfer of firearm precursor part not federally regulated; exceptions

(a) Except as provided in subdivision (b) and in Section 30420, or except by operation of law, it shall be unlawful for a person to purchase, sell, offer to sell, or transfer ownership of any firearm precursor part in this state that is not a federally regulated firearm precursor part.

(b) This section does not apply to either of the following:

(1) The purchase of a firearm precursor part that is not a federally regulated firearm precursor part by a federally licensed firearms manufacturer or importer, or by a federal licensee authorized to serialize firearms.

(2) The sale, offer to sell, or transfer of ownership of a firearm precursor part that is not a federally regulated firearm precursor part to a federally licensed firearms manufacturer or importer, or to a federal licensee authorized to serialize firearms. *(Added by Stats. 2022, c. 76 (A.B.1621), § 28, eff. June 30, 2022.)*

§ 30401. Determination of firearm precursor part

(a) The department may, upon receipt of a written request or form prescribed by the department, issue a determination to a person regarding whether an item or kit is a firearm precursor part.

(b) Any request or form submitted pursuant to subdivision (a) shall be executed under the penalty of perjury with a complete and accurate description of the item or kit, the name and address of the manufacturer or importer thereof, and a sample of the item or kit for examination.

(c) The sample of the item or kit shall include all accessories and attachments relevant to the firearm precursor part determination as each determination is limited to the submitted sample. The sample shall include any associated templates, jigs, molds, equipment, or tools that are made available by the seller, distributor, or manufacturer of the item or kit to the purchaser or recipient of the item or kit, and any instructions, guides, or marketing materials if they will be made available by the seller, distributor, or manufacturer with the item or kit.

(d) Upon completion of the examination, the department may return the sample to the person who made the request unless a determination is made that return of the sample would be a, or would place the person in, violation of the law. Unless otherwise stated by the department, a determination made by the department pursuant to this section shall not be deemed by any person to be applicable to, or authoritative with respect to, any other sample, design, model, or configuration. *(Added by Stats.2022, c. 76 (A.B.1621), § 29, eff. June 30, 2022.)*

§ 30420. Application of article; exceptions

This article does not apply to any of the following persons:

* * * (a) A member of the * * * Armed Forces * * * of the United States or the National Guard, while on duty and acting within the scope and course of employment, or any * * * law enforcement agency or forensic laboratory * * *.

(b) A common carrier licensed under state law, or a motor carrier, air carrier or carrier affiliated with an air carrier through common controlling interest that is subject to Title 49 of the United States Code, or an authorized agent of any such carrier, when acting in the course and scope of duties incident to the receipt, processing, transportation, or delivery of property.

(c) An authorized representative of a city, county, city and county, or state or federal government that receives an unserialized firearm precursor part as part of an authorized, voluntary program in which the governmental entity is buying or receiving firearms or firearm precursor parts from private individuals. *(Added by Stats.2019, c. 730 (A.B.879), § 6, eff. Jan. 1, 2020. Amended by Stats.2022, c. 76 (A.B.1621), § 34, eff. June 30, 2022.)*

§ 30425. Manufacture of firearm precursor parts under state or federal contracts

This article does not prohibit the manufacture of firearm precursor parts under contracts approved by agencies of the state or federal government. *(Added by Stats.2019, c. 730 (A.B.879), § 6, eff. Jan. 1, 2020.)*

CHAPTER 2. ASSAULT WEAPONS AND .50 BMG RIFLES

ARTICLE 1. GENERAL PROVISIONS

§ 30500. Short title

This chapter shall be known as the Roberti–Roos Assault Weapons Control Act of 1989 and the .50 Caliber BMG Regulation Act of 2004. *(Added by Stats.2010, c. 711 (S.B.1080), § 6, operative Jan. 1, 2012.)*

Law Revision Commission Comments

Section 30500 continues former Section 12275 without substantive change. [38 Cal.L.Rev.Comm. Reports 217 (2009)].

Cross References

Assault weapon defined for purposes of this Part, see Penal Code §§ 30510, 30515.

Research References

2 Witkin, California Criminal Law 4th Crimes Against Public Peace and Welfare § 214 (2021), Statutory Development.

2 Witkin, California Criminal Law 4th Crimes Against Public Peace and Welfare § 223 (2021), Civil Action to Enjoin Possession.

§ 30505. Legislative findings and declarations

(a) The Legislature hereby finds and declares that the proliferation and use of assault weapons poses a threat to the health, safety, and security of all citizens of this state. The Legislature has restricted the assault weapons specified in Section 30510 based upon finding that each firearm has such a high rate of fire and capacity for firepower that its function as a legitimate sports or recreational firearm is substantially outweighed by the danger that it can be used to kill and injure human beings. It is the intent of the Legislature in enacting this chapter to place restrictions on the use of assault weapons and to establish a registration and permit procedure for their lawful sale and possession. It is not, however, the intent of the Legislature by this chapter to place restrictions on the use of those weapons which are primarily designed and intended for hunting, target practice, or other legitimate sports or recreational activities.

(b) The Legislature hereby finds and declares that the proliferation and use of .50 BMG rifles poses a clear and present terrorist threat to the health, safety, and security of all residents of, and visitors to, this state, based upon findings that those firearms have such a high capacity for long distance and highly destructive firepower that they pose an unacceptable risk to the death and serious injury of human beings, destruction or serious damage of vital public and private buildings, civilian, police and military vehicles, power generation and transmission facilities, petrochemical production and storage facilities, and transportation infrastructure. It is the intent of the Legislature in enacting this chapter to place restrictions on the use of these rifles and to establish a registration and permit procedure for their lawful sale and possession. *(Added by Stats.2010, c. 711 (S.B.1080), § 6, operative Jan. 1, 2012.)*

Law Revision Commission Comments

Section 30505 continues former Section 12275.5 without substantive change.

See Sections 16520 ("firearm"), 30510 ("assault weapon"), 30515 (further clarification of "assault weapon"), 30530 (".50 BMG rifle"). [38 Cal.L.Rev. Comm. Reports 217 (2009)].

Cross References

.50 BMG rifle defined for purposes of this Part, see Penal Code § 30530.

Firearm defined for purposes of this Part, see Penal Code § 16520.

Research References

2 Witkin, California Criminal Law 4th Crimes Against Public Peace and Welfare § 214 (2021), Statutory Development.

§ 30510. "Assault weapon" and "series" defined

As used in this chapter and in Sections 16780, 17000, and 27555, "assault weapon" means the following designated semiautomatic firearms:

(a) All of the following specified rifles:

(1) All AK series including, but not limited to, the models identified as follows:

(A) Made in China AK, AKM, AKS, AK47, AK47S, 56, 56S, 84S, and 86S.

(B) Norinco 56, 56S, 84S, and 86S.

(C) Poly Technologies AKS and AK47.

(D) MAADI AK47 and ARM.

(2) UZI and Galil.

(3) Beretta AR–70.

(4) CETME Sporter.

(5) Colt AR–15 series.

(6) Daewoo K–1, K–2, Max 1, Max 2, AR 100, and AR 110C.

(7) Fabrique Nationale FAL, LAR, FNC, 308 Match, and Sporter.

(8) MAS 223.

(9) HK–91, HK–93, HK–94, and HK–PSG–1.

(10) The following MAC types:

(A) RPB Industries Inc. sM10 and sM11.

(B) SWD Incorporated M11.

(11) SKS with detachable magazine.

(12) SIG AMT, PE–57, SG 550, and SG 551.

(13) Springfield Armory BM59 and SAR–48.

(14) Sterling MK 6.

(15) Steyer AUG.

(16) Valmet M62S, M71S, and M78S.

(17) Armalite AR–180.

(18) Bushmaster Assault Rifle.

(19) Calico M–900.

(20) J&R ENG M–68.

(21) Weaver Arms Nighthawk.

(b) All of the following specified pistols:

(1) UZI.

(2) Encom MP–9 and MP–45.

(3) The following MAC types:

(A) RPB Industries Inc. sM10 and sM11.

(B) SWD Incorporated M–11.

(C) Advance Armament Inc. M–11.

(D) Military Armament Corp. Ingram M–11.

(4) Intratec TEC–9.

(5) Sites Spectre.

(6) Sterling MK–7.

(7) Calico M–950.

(8) Bushmaster Pistol.

(c) All of the following specified shotguns:

(1) Franchi SPAS 12 and LAW 12.

(2) Striker 12.

(3) The Streetsweeper type S/S Inc. SS/12.

(d) Any firearm declared to be an assault weapon by the court pursuant to former Section 12276.5, as it read in Section 3 of Chapter 19 of the Statutes of 1989, Section 1 of Chapter 874 of the Statutes of 1990, or Section 3 of Chapter 954 of the Statutes of 1991, which is specified as an assault weapon in a list promulgated pursuant to former Section 12276.5, as it read in Section 3 of Chapter 954 of the Statutes of 1991.

(e) This section is declaratory of existing law and a clarification of the law and the Legislature's intent which bans the weapons enumerated in this section, the weapons included in the list promulgated by the Attorney General pursuant to former Section 12276.5, as it read in Section 3 of Chapter 954 of the Statutes of 1991, and any other models that are only variations of those weapons with minor differences, regardless of the manufacturer. The Legislature has defined assault weapons as the types, series, and models listed in this section because it was the most effective way to identify and restrict a specific class of semiautomatic weapons.

(f) As used in this section, "series" includes all other models that are only variations, with minor differences, of those models listed in subdivision (a), regardless of the manufacturer. *(Added by Stats. 2010, c. 711 (S.B.1080), § 6, operative Jan. 1, 2012.)*

Law Revision Commission Comments

Subdivisions (a)-(d) and the introductory clause of Section 30510 continue former Section 12276(a)-(d) and its introductory clause without substantive change. See also former Sections 12001(n)(11), 12072(f)(1)(A), 12282, and 12601(b)(12), which cross-referred to the definition in former Section 12276.

Subdivision (e) continues former Section 12276(f) without substantive change.

Subdivisions (d) and (e) refer to former Section 12276.5, which (1) prescribed a procedure by which a court could classify a weapon as an assault weapon, and, as amended in 1991, (2) directed the Attorney General to promulgate a list of the weapons classified as assault weapons by statute or by a court. See 1991 Cal. Stat. ch. 954, § 3; 1990 Cal. Stat. ch. 874, § 1; 1989 Cal. Stat. ch. 19, § 3. Those procedures were discontinued as of January 1, 2007. See 2006 Cal. Stat. ch. 793, § 1. As so amended, former Section 12276.5 is continued in Section 30520 (duties of Attorney General).

Subdivision (f) continues former Section 12276(e) without substantive change.

See Section 30515 (further clarification of "assault weapon"). [38 Cal. L.Rev.Comm. Reports 217 (2009)].

Cross References

Attorney General, generally, see Government Code § 12500 et seq.
Firearm defined for purposes of this Part, see Penal Code § 16520.
Firearms, records necessary to identify persons coming within Welfare and Institutions Code § 8100 or 8103, availability to Department of Justice, see Welfare and Institutions Code § 8104.
Juvenile court law, admission of public and persons having interest in case, exceptions, see Welfare and Institutions Code § 676.
Nuisance caused by illegal conduct involving unlawful weapons or ammunition purpose, unlawful detainer action, see Civil Code § 3485.
Pistol defined for purposes of this Part, see Penal Code § 16530.
Possession of assault weapon or .50 BMG rifle, public nuisance, see Penal Code § 30800.
Registration of assault weapons and .50 BMG rifles and related rules, see Penal Code § 30900 et seq.

Research References

2 Witkin, California Criminal Law 4th Crimes Against Public Peace and Welfare § 215 (2021), What Constitutes Assault Weapon Or.50 Bmg Rifle.
3 Witkin, California Criminal Law 4th Punishment § 357 (2021), P.C. 12022: Defendant was Armed or Used Dangerous Weapon.

3 Witkin, California Criminal Law 4th Punishment § 358 (2021), P.C. 12022.5: Personal Use of Firearm.

§ 30515. "Assault weapon" further defined

(a) Notwithstanding Section 30510, "assault weapon" also means any of the following:

(1) A semiautomatic, centerfire rifle that does not have a fixed magazine but has any one of the following:

(A) A pistol grip that protrudes conspicuously beneath the action of the weapon.

(B) A thumbhole stock.

(C) A folding or telescoping stock.

(D) A grenade launcher or flare launcher.

(E) A flash suppressor.

(F) A forward pistol grip.

(2) A semiautomatic, centerfire rifle that has a fixed magazine with the capacity to accept more than 10 rounds.

(3) A semiautomatic, centerfire rifle that has an overall length of less than 30 inches.

(4) A semiautomatic pistol that does not have a fixed magazine but has any one of the following:

(A) A threaded barrel, capable of accepting a flash suppressor, forward handgrip, or silencer.

(B) A second handgrip.

(C) A shroud that is attached to, or partially or completely encircles, the barrel that allows the bearer to fire the weapon without burning the bearer's hand, except a slide that encloses the barrel.

(D) The capacity to accept a detachable magazine at some location outside of the pistol grip.

(5) A semiautomatic pistol with a fixed magazine that has the capacity to accept more than 10 rounds.

(6) A semiautomatic shotgun that has both of the following:

(A) A folding or telescoping stock.

(B) A pistol grip that protrudes conspicuously beneath the action of the weapon, thumbhole stock, or vertical handgrip.

(7) A semiautomatic shotgun that does not have a fixed magazine.

(8) Any shotgun with a revolving cylinder.

(9) A semiautomatic centerfire firearm that is not a rifle, pistol, or shotgun, that does not have a fixed magazine, but that has any one of the following:

(A) A pistol grip that protrudes conspicuously beneath the action of the weapon.

(B) A thumbhole stock.

(C) A folding or telescoping stock.

(D) A grenade launcher or flare launcher.

(E) A flash suppressor.

(F) A forward pistol grip.

(G) A threaded barrel, capable of accepting a flash suppressor, forward handgrip, or silencer.

(H) A second handgrip.

(I) A shroud that is attached to, or partially or completely encircles, the barrel that allows the bearer to fire the weapon without burning the bearer's hand, except a slide that encloses the barrel.

(J) The capacity to accept a detachable magazine at some location outside of the pistol grip.

(10) A semiautomatic centerfire firearm that is not a rifle, pistol, or shotgun, that has a fixed magazine with the capacity to accept more than 10 rounds.

(11) A semiautomatic centerfire firearm that is not a rifle, pistol, or shotgun, that has an overall length of less than 30 inches.

(b) For purposes of this section, "fixed magazine" means an ammunition feeding device contained in, or permanently attached to, a firearm in such a manner that the device cannot be removed without disassembly of the firearm action.

(c) The Legislature finds a significant public purpose in exempting from the definition of "assault weapon" pistols that are designed expressly for use in Olympic target shooting events. Therefore, those pistols that are sanctioned by the International Olympic Committee and by USA Shooting, the national governing body for international shooting competition in the United States, and that were used for Olympic target shooting purposes as of January 1, 2001, and that would otherwise fall within the definition of "assault weapon" pursuant to this section are exempt, as provided in subdivision (d).

(d) "Assault weapon" does not include either of the following:

(1) Any antique firearm.

(2) Any of the following pistols, because they are consistent with the significant public purpose expressed in subdivision (c):

MANUFACTURER	MODEL	CALIBER
BENELLI	MP90	.22LR
BENELLI	MP90	.32 S&W LONG
BENELLI	MP95	.22LR
BENELLI	MP95	.32 S&W LONG
HAMMERLI	280	.22LR
HAMMERLI	280	.32 S&W LONG
HAMMERLI	SP20	.22LR
HAMMERLI	SP20	.32 S&W LONG
PARDINI	GPO	.22 SHORT
PARDINI	GP–SCHUMANN	.22 SHORT
PARDINI	HP	.32 S&W LONG
PARDINI	MP	.32 S&W LONG
PARDINI	SP	.22LR
PARDINI	SPE	.22LR
WALTHER	GSP	.22LR
WALTHER	GSP	.32 S&W LONG
WALTHER	OSP	.22 SHORT
WALTHER	OSP–2000	.22 SHORT

(3) The Department of Justice shall create a program that is consistent with the purposes stated in subdivision (c) to exempt new models of competitive pistols that would otherwise fall within the definition of "assault weapon" pursuant to this section from being classified as an assault weapon. The exempt competitive pistols may be based on recommendations by USA Shooting consistent with the regulations contained in the USA Shooting Official Rules or may be based on the recommendation or rules of any other organization that the department deems relevant.

(e) The provisions of this section are severable. If any provision of this section or its application is held invalid, that invalidity shall not affect other provisions or applications that can be given effect without the invalid provision or application. *(Added by Stats.2010, c. 711 (S.B.1080), § 6, operative Jan. 1, 2012. Amended by Stats.2016, c. 40 (A.B.1135), § 1, eff. Jan. 1, 2017; Stats.2016, c. 48 (S.B.880), § 1, eff. Jan. 1, 2017; Stats.2020, c. 29 (S.B.118), § 38, eff. Aug. 6, 2020.)*

Validity

For validity of this section, see Miller v. Bonta, S.D.Cal. 2021, 542 F.Supp.3d 1009, vacated and remanded 2022 WL 3095986.

Law Revision Commission Comments

Section 30515 continues former Section 12276.1(a)-(c) without substantive change. See also former Sections 12001(n)(11), 12072(f)(1)(A), 12282, and 12601(b)(12), which cross-referred to the definitional material in former Section 12276.1.

See Sections 16170 ("antique firearm"), 16350 ("capacity to accept more than 10 rounds"), 16890 ("magazine"), 30510 ("assault weapon"). [38 Cal.L.Rev.Comm. Reports 217 (2009)].

Cross References

Antique firearm defined, see Penal Code § 16170.
Applicability of section 30605 to the possession of an assault rifle, conditions, see Penal Code § 30685.
Firearm defined for purposes of this Part, see Penal Code § 16520.
Nuisance caused by illegal conduct involving unlawful weapons or ammunition purpose, unlawful detainer action, see Civil Code § 3485.
Pistol defined for purposes of this Part, see Penal Code § 16530.
Possession of assault weapon or .50 BMG rifle, public nuisance, see Penal Code § 30800.
Registration of assault weapons and .50 BMG rifles and related rules, see Penal Code § 30900 et seq.

Research References

2 Witkin, California Criminal Law 4th Crimes Against Public Peace and Welfare § 215 (2021), What Constitutes Assault Weapon Or.50 Bmg Rifle.

§ 30520. Duties of Attorney General; description and picture of designated assault weapons; promulgation of list of designated assault weapons; adoption of rules and regulations

(a) The Attorney General shall prepare a description for identification purposes, including a picture or diagram, of each assault weapon listed in Section 30510, and any firearm declared to be an assault weapon pursuant to former Section 12276.5, as it read in Section 3 of Chapter 19 of the Statutes of 1989, Section 1 of Chapter 874 of the Statutes of 1990, or Section 3 of Chapter 954 of the Statutes of 1991, and shall distribute the description to all law enforcement agencies responsible for enforcement of this chapter. Those law enforcement agencies shall make the description available to all agency personnel.

(b)(1) Until January 1, 2007, the Attorney General shall promulgate a list that specifies all firearms designated as assault weapons in former Section 12276, as it read in Section 2 of Chapter 954 of the Statutes of 1991, Section 134 of Chapter 427 of the Statutes of 1992, or Section 19 of Chapter 606 of the Statutes of 1993, or declared to be assault weapons pursuant to former Section 12276.5, as it read in Section 3 of Chapter 19 of the Statutes of 1989, Section 1 of Chapter 874 of the Statutes of 1990, or Section 3 of Chapter 954 of the Statutes of 1991. The Attorney General shall file that list with the Secretary of State for publication in the California Code of Regulations. Any declaration that a specified firearm is an assault weapon shall be implemented by the Attorney General who, within 90 days, shall promulgate an amended list which shall include the specified firearm declared to be an assault weapon. The Attorney General shall file the amended list with the Secretary of State for publication in the California Code of Regulations. Any firearm declared to be an assault weapon prior to January 1, 2007, shall remain on the list filed with the Secretary of State.

(2) Chapter 3.5 (commencing with Section 11340) of Part 1 of Division 3 of Title 2 of the Government Code, pertaining to the adoption of rules and regulations, shall not apply to any list of assault weapons promulgated pursuant to this section.

(c) The Attorney General shall adopt those rules and regulations that may be necessary or proper to carry out the purposes and intent of this chapter. *(Added by Stats.2010, c. 711 (S.B.1080), § 6, operative Jan. 1, 2012.)*

Law Revision Commission Comments

Section 30520 continues former Section 12276.5 without substantive change. An incomplete cross-reference to a chapter in the Government Code has been corrected. See also former Sections 12072(f)(1)(A) and 12282, which cross-referred to the definitional material in former Section 12276.5.

As originally enacted, former Section 12276.5 prescribed a procedure by which a court could classify a weapon as an assault weapon. See 1989 Cal. Stat. ch. 19, § 3. The provision was later amended to direct the Attorney General to promulgate a list of the weapons classified as assault weapons by a court or by former Section 12276 (which is continued in Section 30510). See 1991 Cal. Stat. ch. 954, § 3. Still later, the provision was amended to discontinue both of those procedures as of January 1, 2007. See 2006 Cal. Stat. ch. 793, § 1. This section continues former Section 12276.5 as so amended.

See Sections 16520 ("firearm"), 30510 ("assault weapon"), 30515 (further clarification of "assault weapon"). See also Section 16010 (continuation of existing law). [38 Cal.L.Rev.Comm. Reports 217 (2009)].

Cross References

Attorney General, generally, see Government Code § 12500 et seq.
Firearm defined for purposes of this Part, see Penal Code § 16520.
Nuisance caused by illegal conduct involving unlawful weapons or ammunition purpose, unlawful detainer action, see Civil Code § 3485.
Possession of assault weapon or .50 BMG rifle, public nuisance, see Penal Code § 30800.
Registration of assault weapons and .50 BMG rifles and related rules, see Penal Code § 30900 et seq.

Research References

2 Witkin, California Criminal Law 4th Crimes Against Public Peace and Welfare § 214 (2021), Statutory Development.
2 Witkin, California Criminal Law 4th Crimes Against Public Peace and Welfare § 215 (2021), What Constitutes Assault Weapon Or.50 Bmg Rifle.

§ 30525. ".50 BMG cartridge" defined

As used in this part, ".50 BMG cartridge" means a cartridge that is designed and intended to be fired from a center fire rifle and that meets all of the following criteria:

(a) It has an overall length of 5.54 inches from the base to the tip of the bullet.

(b) The bullet diameter for the cartridge is from .510 to, and including, .511 inch.

(c) The case base diameter for the cartridge is from .800 inch to, and including, .804 inch.

(d) The cartridge case length is 3.91 inches. *(Added by Stats.2010, c. 711 (S.B.1080), § 6, operative Jan. 1, 2012.)*

Law Revision Commission Comments

Section 30525 continues former Section 12278(b) without substantive change. [38 Cal.L.Rev.Comm. Reports 217 (2009)].

Cross References

Assault with a deadly weapon or force likely to produce great bodily injury, punishment, see Penal Code § 245.
Nuisance caused by illegal conduct involving unlawful weapons or ammunition purpose, unlawful detainer action, see Civil Code § 3485.
Possession of assault weapon or .50 BMG rifle, public nuisance, see Penal Code § 30800.
Registration of assault weapons and .50 BMG rifles and related rules, see Penal Code § 30900 et seq.
Terms of imprisonment for committing or attempting felony or violation while armed with firearm or using deadly or dangerous weapon, application to principals in commission of offense or attempted offense, see Penal Code § 12022.

§ 30530. ".50 BMG rifle" defined

(a) As used in this part, ".50 BMG rifle" means a center fire rifle that can fire a .50 BMG cartridge and is not already an assault weapon or a machinegun.

(b) A ".50 BMG rifle" does not include any antique firearm, nor any curio or relic as defined in Section 478.11 of Title 27 of the Code of Federal Regulations. *(Added by Stats.2010, c. 711 (S.B.1080), § 6, operative Jan. 1, 2012.)*

Law Revision Commission Comments

Subdivision (a) of Section 30530 continues former Section 12278(a) without substantive change.

Subdivision (b) continues former Section 12278(c) without substantive change. See Section 16170 ("antique firearm"). A cross-reference to nonexistent Section 178.11 of Title 27 of the Code of Federal Regulations has been replaced with a cross-reference to Section 478.11 of the Code of Federal Regulations. See Sections 16880 ("machinegun"), 30510 ("assault weapon"), 30515 (further clarification of "assault weapon"), 30525 (".50 BMG cartridge"). [38 Cal.L.Rev.Comm. Reports 217 (2009)].

Cross References

Antique firearm defined, see Penal Code § 16170.
Assault weapon defined for purposes of this Part, see Penal Code §§ 30510, 30515.
Assault with a deadly weapon or force likely to produce great bodily injury, punishment, see Penal Code § 245.
Firearm defined for purposes of this Part, see Penal Code § 16520.
Machinegun defined for purposes of this Part, see Penal Code § 16880.
Nuisance caused by illegal conduct involving unlawful weapons or ammunition purpose, unlawful detainer action, see Civil Code § 3485.
Possession of assault weapon or .50 BMG rifle, public nuisance, see Penal Code § 30800.
Registration of assault weapons and .50 BMG rifles and related rules, see Penal Code § 30900 et seq.
Terms of imprisonment for committing or attempting felony or violation while armed with firearm or using deadly or dangerous weapon, application to principals in commission of offense or attempted offense, see Penal Code § 12022.

Research References

2 Witkin, California Criminal Law 4th Crimes Against Public Peace and Welfare § 215 (2021), What Constitutes Assault Weapon Or.50 Bmg Rifle.
3 Witkin, California Criminal Law 4th Punishment § 357 (2021), P.C. 12022: Defendant was Armed or Used Dangerous Weapon.

ARTICLE 2. UNLAWFUL ACTS RELATING TO ASSAULT WEAPONS AND .50 BMG RIFLES

§ 30600. Manufacture, distribution, transportation, importation, sale, gift, or loan of assault weapon or .50 BMG rifle; penalties

(a) Any person who, within this state, manufactures or causes to be manufactured, distributes, transports, or imports into the state, keeps for sale, or offers or exposes for sale, or who gives or lends any assault weapon or any .50 BMG rifle, except as provided by this chapter, is guilty of a felony, and upon conviction shall be punished by imprisonment pursuant to subdivision (h) of Section 1170 for four, six, or eight years.

(b) In addition and consecutive to the punishment imposed under subdivision (a), any person who transfers, lends, sells, or gives any assault weapon or any .50 BMG rifle to a minor in violation of subdivision (a) shall receive an enhancement of imprisonment pursuant to subdivision (h) of Section 1170 of one year.

(c) Except in the case of a first violation involving not more than two firearms as provided in Sections 30605 and 30610, for purposes of this article, if more than one assault weapon or .50 BMG rifle is involved in any violation of this article, there shall be a distinct and separate offense for each. *(Added by Stats.2010, c. 711 (S.B.1080), § 6, operative Jan. 1, 2012. Amended by Stats.2011, c. 15 (A.B.109), § 549, eff. April 4, 2011, operative Jan. 1, 2012.)*

Validity

For validity of this section, see Miller v. Bonta, S.D.Cal. 2021, 542 F.Supp.3d 1009, vacated and remanded 2022 WL 3095986.

Law Revision Commission Comments

Section 30600 continues former Section 12280(a) without substantive change.

A conviction under former Chapter 2.3 of Title 2 of Part 4 (former Sections 12275–12290) counts as a prior conviction in determining the appropriate punishment under this section. See Section 16015 (determining existence of prior conviction); see also Section 16010 (continuation of existing law). For further guidance on punishment for a violation of this section, see Section 30615 (sentence enhancement for committing another crime while violating this article).

For exemptions to this provision, see Sections 30625–30675. For guidance in determining when a firearm has become an assault weapon for purposes of this chapter, see Section 30620 (date that firearm becomes assault weapon).

See Sections 16520 ("firearm"), 16970 ("person"), 30510 ("assault weapon"), 30515 (further clarification of "assault weapon"), 30530 (".50 BMG rifle"). [38 Cal.L.Rev.Comm. Reports 217 (2009)].

Cross References

.50 BMG rifle defined for purposes of this Part, see Penal Code § 30530.
Assault weapon defined for purposes of this Part, see Penal Code §§ 30510, 30515.
Control of deadly weapons, person defined, see Penal Code § 16970.
Felonies, definition and penalties, see Penal Code §§ 17, 18.
Firearm defined for purposes of this Part, see Penal Code § 16520.
Juvenile court law, admission of public and persons having interest in case, exceptions, see Welfare and Institutions Code § 676.
Person defined, see Penal Code § 16970.
Printing of fish and game regulations, prohibition of advertising of certain tobacco, alcohol, firearm, and other devices, see Fish and Game Code § 260.

Registration of assault weapons and .50 BMG rifles, forgiveness period, see Penal Code § 30960.

Research References

2 Witkin, California Criminal Law 4th Crimes Against Public Peace and Welfare § 189 (2021), In General.
2 Witkin, California Criminal Law 4th Crimes Against Public Peace and Welfare § 216 (2021), Manufacture, Distribution, Sale, etc.
2 Witkin, California Criminal Law 4th Crimes Against Public Peace and Welfare § 217 (2021), Possession.
2 Witkin, California Criminal Law 4th Crimes Against Public Peace and Welfare § 218 (2021), Commission of Another Crime While Violating Act.
2 Witkin, California Criminal Law 4th Crimes Against Public Peace and Welfare § 219 (2021), Exceptions.
2 Witkin, California Criminal Law 4th Crimes Against Public Peace and Welfare § 220 (2021), Registration Requirements.
2 Witkin, California Criminal Law 4th Crimes Against Public Peace and Welfare § 221 (2021), Permits and Conditions for Possession.

§ 30605. Possession of assault weapon; penalties

(a) Any person who, within this state, possesses any assault weapon, except as provided in this chapter, shall be punished by imprisonment in a county jail for a period not exceeding one year, or by imprisonment pursuant to subdivision (h) of Section 1170.

(b) Notwithstanding subdivision (a), a first violation of these provisions is punishable by a fine not exceeding five hundred dollars ($500) if the person was found in possession of no more than two firearms in compliance with Section 30945 and the person meets all of the following conditions:

(1) The person proves that he or she lawfully possessed the assault weapon prior to the date it was defined as an assault weapon.

(2) The person has not previously been convicted of a violation of this article.

(3) The person was found to be in possession of the assault weapon within one year following the end of the one-year registration period established pursuant to Section 30900.

(4) The person relinquished the firearm pursuant to Section 31100, in which case the assault weapon shall be destroyed pursuant to Sections 18000 and 18005. *(Added by Stats.2010, c. 711 (S.B. 1080), § 6, operative Jan. 1, 2012. Amended by Stats.2011, c. 15 (A.B.109), § 550, eff. April 4, 2011, operative Jan. 1, 2012.)*

Validity

For validity of this section, see Miller v. Bonta, S.D.Cal. 2021, 542 F.Supp.3d 1009, vacated and remanded 2022 WL 3095986.

Law Revision Commission Comments

Section 30605 continues former Section 12280(b) without substantive change.

A conviction under former Chapter 2.3 of Title 2 of Part 4 (former Sections 12275–12290) counts as a prior conviction in determining the appropriate punishment under this section. See Section 16015 (determining existence of prior conviction). For further guidance on punishment for a violation of this section, see Section 30615 (sentence enhancement for committing another crime while violating this article).

For exemptions to this provision, see Sections 30625–30675. For guidance in determining when a firearm has become an assault weapon for purposes of this chapter, see Section 30620 (date that firearm becomes assault weapon).

See Sections 16520 ("firearm"), 16970 ("person"), 30510 ("assault weapon"), 30515 (further clarification of "assault weapon"). See also Section 16010 (continuation of existing law). [38 Cal.L.Rev.Comm. Reports 217 (2009)].

Cross References

Applicability of this section to possession of an assault weapon, conditions, see Penal Code § 30685.
Assault weapon defined for purposes of this Part, see Penal Code §§ 30510, 30515.
Firearm defined for purposes of this Part, see Penal Code § 16520.
Person defined, see Penal Code § 16970.
Registration of assault weapons and .50 BMG rifles, forgiveness period, see Penal Code § 30960.

Research References

2 Witkin, California Criminal Law 4th Crimes Against Public Peace and Welfare § 214 (2021), Statutory Development.
2 Witkin, California Criminal Law 4th Crimes Against Public Peace and Welfare § 216 (2021), Manufacture, Distribution, Sale, etc.
2 Witkin, California Criminal Law 4th Crimes Against Public Peace and Welfare § 217 (2021), Possession.
2 Witkin, California Criminal Law 4th Crimes Against Public Peace and Welfare § 219 (2021), Exceptions.
1 Witkin California Criminal Law 4th Elements § 9 (2021), Facts that Must be Known.
1 Witkin California Criminal Law 4th Introduction to Crimes § 81 (2021), Valid State Statutes.

§ 30610. Possession of .50 BMG rifle; penalties

(a) Any person who, within this state, possesses any .50 BMG rifle, except as provided in this chapter, shall be punished by a fine of one thousand dollars ($1,000), imprisonment in a county jail for a period not to exceed one year, or by both that fine and imprisonment.

(b) Notwithstanding subdivision (a), a first violation of these provisions is punishable by a fine not exceeding five hundred dollars ($500) if the person was found in possession of no more than two firearms in compliance with Section 30905 and the person satisfies all of the following conditions:

(1) The person proves that he or she lawfully possessed the .50 BMG rifle prior to January 1, 2005.

(2) The person has not previously been convicted of a violation of this article.

(3) The person was found to be in possession of the .50 BMG rifle within one year following the end of the .50 BMG rifle registration period established pursuant to Section 30905.

(c) Firearms seized pursuant to this section from persons who meet all of the conditions in paragraphs (1), (2), and (3) of subdivision (b) shall be returned unless the court finds in the interest of public safety, after notice and hearing, that the .50 BMG rifle should be destroyed pursuant to Sections 18000 and 18005. Firearms seized from persons who do not meet the conditions set forth in paragraphs (1), (2), and (3) of subdivision (b) shall be destroyed pursuant to Sections 18000 and 18005. *(Added by Stats.2010, c. 711 (S.B.1080), § 6, operative Jan. 1, 2012.)*

Law Revision Commission Comments

Section 30610 continues former Section 12280(c) without substantive change.

A conviction under former Chapter 2.3 of Title 2 of Part 4 (former Sections 12275–12290) counts as a prior conviction in determining the appropriate punishment under this section. See Section 16015 (determining existence of prior conviction). For further guidance on punishment for a violation of this section, see Section 30615 (sentence enhancement for committing another crime while violating this article).

For exemptions to this provision, see Sections 30625–30675.

See Sections 16520 ("firearm"), 16970 ("person"), 30530 (".50 BMG rifle"). See also Section 16010 (continuation of existing law). [38 Cal.L.Rev.Comm. Reports 217 (2009)].

Cross References

.50 BMG rifle defined for purposes of this Part, see Penal Code § 30530.
Firearm defined for purposes of this Part, see Penal Code § 16520.
Person defined, see Penal Code § 16970.
Registration of assault weapons and .50 BMG rifles, forgiveness period, see Penal Code § 30960.

Research References

2 Witkin, California Criminal Law 4th Crimes Against Public Peace and Welfare § 214 (2021), Statutory Development.

2 Witkin, California Criminal Law 4th Crimes Against Public Peace and Welfare § 217 (2021), Possession.

§ 30615. Commission of another crime; additional, consecutive punishment

Notwithstanding Section 654 or any other provision of law, any person who commits another crime while violating this article may receive an additional, consecutive punishment of one year for violating this article, in addition and consecutive to the punishment, including enhancements, which is prescribed for the other crime. *(Added by Stats.2010, c. 711 (S.B.1080), § 6, operative Jan. 1, 2012.)*

Law Revision Commission Comments

Section 30615 continues former Section 12280(d) without substantive change.

See Section 16970 ("person"). [38 Cal.L.Rev.Comm. Reports 217 (2009)].

Cross References

Person defined, see Penal Code § 16970.

Research References

2 Witkin, California Criminal Law 4th Crimes Against Public Peace and Welfare § 218 (2021), Commission of Another Crime While Violating Act.

§ 30620. Date firearm is assault weapon

As used in this chapter, the date a firearm is an assault weapon is the earliest of the following:

(a) The effective date of an amendment to Section 30510 or to former Section 12276 that adds the designation of the specified firearm.

(b) The effective date of the list promulgated pursuant to former Section 12276.5, as that section read in Section 3 of Chapter 954 of the Statutes of 1991, which adds or changes the designation of the specified firearm.

(c) January 1, 2000, which was the operative date of former Section 12276.1, as enacted by Section 7 of Chapter 129 of the Statutes of 1999. *(Added by Stats.2010, c. 711 (S.B.1080), § 6, operative Jan. 1, 2012.)*

Law Revision Commission Comments

Section 30620 continues former Section 12280(u) without substantive change.

Subdivision (a) refers to former Section 12276. That section is continued in Section 30510 ("assault weapon"), which is also referred to in subdivision (a).

Subdivision (b) refers to the list promulgated pursuant to former Section 12276.5. In the past, that section (1) prescribed a procedure by which a court could classify a weapon as an assault weapon, and, as amended in 1991, (2) directed the Attorney General to promulgate a list of the weapons classified as assault weapons by Section 12276 or by a court. See 1991 Cal. Stat. ch. 954, § 3; 1990 Cal. Stat. ch. 874, § 1; 1989 Cal. Stat. ch. 19, § 3. Those procedures were discontinued as of January 1, 2007. See 2006 Cal. Stat. ch. 793, § 1. As so amended, former Section 12276.5 is continued in Section 30520 (duties of Attorney General).

Subdivision (c) refers to the operative date of former Section 12276.1 (i.e., January 1, 2000). As subsequently amended to exempt certain weapons, that section is continued in Section 30515 (further clarification of "assault weapon").

See Sections 16520 ("firearm"), 30510 ("assault weapon"), 30515 (further clarification of "assault weapon"), 30530 (".50 BMG rifle"). [38 Cal.L.Rev. Comm. Reports 217 (2009)].

Cross References

Firearm defined for purposes of this Part, see Penal Code § 16520.

Research References

2 Witkin, California Criminal Law 4th Crimes Against Public Peace and Welfare § 217 (2021), Possession.

§ 30625. Exemption for Department of Justice, law enforcement agencies, military forces, or other specified entities

Sections 30600, 30605, and 30610 do not apply to the sale of an assault weapon or .50 BMG rifle to, or the purchase, importation, or possession of an assault weapon or a .50 BMG rifle by, the Department of Justice, police departments, sheriffs' offices, marshals' offices, the Department of Corrections and Rehabilitation, the Department of the California Highway Patrol, district attorneys' offices, the Department of Fish and Wildlife, the Department of Parks and Recreation, the Department of Cannabis Control, or the military or naval forces of this state or of the United States, or any federal law enforcement agency for use in the discharge of their official duties. *(Added by Stats.2010, c. 711 (S.B.1080), § 6, operative Jan. 1, 2012. Amended by Stats.2015, c. 303 (A.B.731), § 416, eff. Jan. 1, 2016; Stats.2021, c. 70 (A.B.141), § 108, eff. July 12, 2021.)*

Law Revision Commission Comments

Section 30625 continues former Section 12280(e) without substantive change.

See Sections 30510 ("assault weapon"), 30515 (further clarification of "assault weapon"), 30530 (".50 BMG rifle"). [38 Cal.L.Rev.Comm. Reports 217 (2009)].

Cross References

.50 BMG rifle defined for purposes of this Part, see Penal Code § 30530.
Assault weapon defined for purposes of this Part, see Penal Code §§ 30510, 30515.
Department of Corrections and Rehabilitation, generally, see Penal Code § 5000 et seq.

Research References

2 Witkin, California Criminal Law 4th Crimes Against Public Peace and Welfare § 219 (2021), Exceptions.

§ 30630. Possession by peace officers for law enforcement purposes; sale, delivery, or transfer; authorization and registration; application to federal law enforcement personnel

(a) Sections 30605 and 30610 shall not prohibit the possession or use of assault weapons or a .50 BMG rifle by sworn peace officer members of those agencies specified in Section 30625 for law enforcement purposes, whether on or off duty.

(b)(1) Sections 30600, 30605, and 30610 shall not prohibit the sale, delivery, or transfer of an assault weapon or a .50 BMG rifle to, or the possession of an assault weapon or a .50 BMG rifle by, a sworn peace officer member of an agency specified in Section 30625 if the peace officer is authorized by the officer's employer to possess or receive the assault weapon or the .50 BMG rifle. Required authorization is defined as verifiable written certification from the head of the agency, identifying the recipient or possessor of the assault weapon as a peace officer and authorizing that person to receive or possess the specific assault weapon.

(2) For this exemption to apply, in the case of a peace officer who possesses or receives the assault weapon prior to January 1, 2002, the officer shall register the assault weapon on or before April 1, 2002, pursuant to former Section 12285, as it read at any time from when it was enacted by Section 3 of Chapter 19 of the Statutes of 1989, to and including when it was amended by Section 9 of Chapter 129 of the Statutes of 1999. In the case of a peace officer who possesses or receives the assault weapon on or after January 1, 2002, the officer shall, not later than 90 days after possession or receipt, register the assault weapon pursuant to Article 5 (commencing with Section 30900), or pursuant to former Section 12285, as it read at any time from when it was amended by Section 9 of Chapter 129 of the Statutes of 1999 to when it was repealed by the Deadly Weapons Recodification Act of 2010. In the case of a peace officer who possesses or receives a .50 BMG rifle on or before January 1, 2005, the officer shall register the .50 BMG rifle on or before April 30, 2006. In the case of a peace officer who possesses or receives a .50 BMG rifle after January 1, 2005, the officer shall register the .50 BMG rifle not later than one year after possession or receipt.

(3) With the registration, the peace officer shall include a copy of the authorization required pursuant to this subdivision.

(c) Nothing in this article shall be construed to limit or prohibit the sale, delivery, or transfer of an assault weapon or a .50 BMG rifle to, or the possession of an assault weapon or a .50 BMG rifle by, a member of a federal law enforcement agency provided that person is authorized by the employing agency to possess the assault weapon or .50 BMG rifle. *(Added by Stats.2010, c. 711 (S.B.1080), § 6, operative Jan. 1, 2012.)*

Law Revision Commission Comments

Subdivision (a) of Section 30630 continues former Section 12280(f)(1) without substantive change.

Subdivision (b) continues former Section 12280(f)(2) without substantive change. Subdivision (b) refers to the former Section 12285 that was enacted by 1989 Cal. Stat. ch. 19, § 3, amended several times, and then repealed by the Deadly Weapons Recodification Act. That provision is continued in Article 5 (Sections 30900–30965). Another Section 12285 was added by 1989 Cal. Stat. ch. 18, § 4, and repealed by 1989 Cal. Stat. ch. 19, § 2.5.

Subdivision (c) continues former Section 12280(f)(3) without substantive change.

See Sections 16970 ("person"), 30510 ("assault weapon"), 30515 (further clarification of "assault weapon"), 30530 (".50 BMG rifle"). See also Section 16010 (continuation of existing law). [38 Cal.L.Rev.Comm. Reports 217 (2009)].

Cross References

.50 BMG rifle defined for purposes of this Part, see Penal Code § 30530.
Assault weapon defined for purposes of this Part, see Penal Code §§ 30510, 30515.
Person defined, see Penal Code § 16970.
Prohibition of manufacturing, distributing, transporting, importing into state, to keep for sale, offer or expose for sale, or give or lend of any assault weapon, .50 BMG rifle, or unserialized firearm, exceptions, see Business and Professions Code § 22949.62.

Research References

2 Witkin, California Criminal Law 4th Crimes Against Public Peace and Welfare § 219 (2021), Exceptions.
2 Witkin, California Criminal Law 4th Crimes Against Public Peace and Welfare § 220 (2021), Registration Requirements.

§ 30635. Possession of assault weapon during specified time periods following classification as assault weapon

Section 30605 shall not apply to the possession of an assault weapon during the 90–day period immediately after the date it was specified as an assault weapon pursuant to former Section 12276.5, as that section read in Section 3 of Chapter 19 of the Statutes of 1989, Section 1 of Chapter 874 of the Statutes of 1990, or Section 3 of Chapter 954 of the Statutes of 1991, or during the one-year period after the date it was defined as an assault weapon pursuant to former Section 12276.1, as that section read at any time from when it was enacted by Section 7 of Chapter 129 of the Statutes of 1999 to when it was repealed by the Deadly Weapons Recodification Act of 2010, if all of the following are applicable:

(a) At the time of the possession in question, the person was eligible under the then-applicable version of former Chapter 2.3 (commencing with Section 12275) of Title 2 of Part 4 to register the particular assault weapon.

(b) The person lawfully possessed the particular assault weapon prior to the date it was specified as an assault weapon pursuant to former Section 12276.5, or prior to the date it was defined as an assault weapon pursuant to former Section 12276.1.

(c) At the time of the possession in question, the person was otherwise in compliance with the then-applicable version of former Chapter 2.3 (commencing with Section 12275) of Title 2 of Part 4. *(Added by Stats.2010, c. 711 (S.B.1080), § 6, operative Jan. 1, 2012.)*

Law Revision Commission Comments

Section 30635 continues former Section 12280(g) without substantive change.

The introductory clause and subdivision (b) refer to the date that a weapon "was specified as an assault weapon pursuant to *former Section 12276.5.*" (Emphasis added.) In the past, that section (1) prescribed a procedure by which a court could classify a weapon as an assault weapon, and (2) directed the Attorney General to promulgate a list of the weapons classified as assault weapons by statute or by a court. See 1991 Cal. Stat. ch. 954, § 3; 1990 Cal. Stat. ch. 874, § 1; 1989 Cal. Stat. ch. 19, § 3. Those procedures were discontinued as of January 1, 2007. See 2006 Cal. Stat. ch. 793, § 1. As so amended, former Section 12276.5 is continued in Section 30520 (duties of Attorney General).

The introductory clause and subdivision (b) also refer to the date that a weapon "was defined as an assault weapon pursuant to *former Section 12276.1.*" (Emphasis added.) That section became operative on January 1, 2000. As subsequently amended to exempt certain weapons, it is continued in Section 30515 (further clarification of "assault weapon").

Subdivisions (a) and (c) refer to former Chapter 2.3 of Title 2 of Part 4 (former Sections 12275–12290). That former chapter is continued in this chapter (Sections 30500–31115).

See Sections 16970 ("person"), 30510 ("assault weapon"), 30515 (further clarification of "assault weapon"). See also Section 16010 (continuation of existing law). [38 Cal.L.Rev.Comm. Reports 217 (2009)].

Cross References

Assault weapon defined for purposes of this Part, see Penal Code §§ 30510, 30515.
Person defined, see Penal Code § 16970.

Research References

2 Witkin, California Criminal Law 4th Crimes Against Public Peace and Welfare § 219 (2021), Exceptions.

§ 30640. Exemption to prohibition of .50 BMG rifles for rifles lawfully owned and possessed under former law

Section 30610 shall not apply to the possession of a .50 BMG rifle, which was not defined or specified as an assault weapon pursuant to the then-applicable version of the former Chapter 2.3 (commencing with Section 12275) of Title 2 of Part 4 that was added to this code by Section 3 of Chapter 19 of the Statutes of 1989, by any person prior to May 1, 2006, if all of the following are applicable:

(a) At the time of the possession in question, the person was eligible under the then-applicable version of former Chapter 2.3 (commencing with Section 12275) of Title 2 of Part 4 to register that .50 BMG rifle.

(b) The person lawfully possessed the .50 BMG rifle prior to January 1, 2005.

(c) At the time of the possession in question, the person was otherwise in compliance with the then-applicable version of former Chapter 2.3 (commencing with Section 12275) of Title 2 of Part 4. *(Added by Stats.2010, c. 711 (S.B.1080), § 6, operative Jan. 1, 2012.)*

Law Revision Commission Comments

Section 30640 continues former Section 12280(s) without substantive change.

The introductory clause and subdivisions (a) and (c) refer to the former Chapter 2.3 of Title 2 of Part 4 (former Sections 12275–12290) that was added to this code by 1989 Cal. Stat. ch. 19, § 3. That former chapter is continued in this chapter (Sections 30500–31115). Another Chapter 2.3, also entitled "Roberti–Roos Assault Weapons Control Act of 1989," was added by 1989 Cal. Stat. ch. 18, § 4, and repealed by 1989 Cal. Stat. ch. 19, § 2,5.

See Sections 16970 ("person"), 30510 ("assault weapon"), 30515 (further clarification of "assault weapon"), 30530 (".50 BMG rifle"). See also Section 16010 (continuation of existing law). [38 Cal.L.Rev.Comm. Reports 217 (2009)].

Cross References

.50 BMG rifle defined for purposes of this Part, see Penal Code § 30530.
Assault weapon defined for purposes of this Part, see Penal Code §§ 30510, 30515.

Person defined, see Penal Code § 16970.

Research References

2 Witkin, California Criminal Law 4th Crimes Against Public Peace and Welfare § 217 (2021), Possession.

§ 30645. Exemption to assault weapon and .50 BMG rifle prohibition for manufacturers with permit for sales to specified entities

Sections 30600, 30605, and 30610 shall not apply to the manufacture by any person who is issued a permit pursuant to Section 31005 of assault weapons or .50 BMG rifles for sale to the following:

(a) Exempt entities listed in Section 30625.

(b) Entities and persons who have been issued permits pursuant to Section 31000 or 31005.

(c) Federal military and law enforcement agencies.

(d) Law enforcement and military agencies of other states.

(e) Foreign governments and agencies approved by the United States State Department.

(f) Entities outside the state who have, in effect, a federal firearms dealer's license solely for the purpose of distribution to an entity listed in subdivisions (c) to (e), inclusive. *(Added by Stats.2010, c. 711 (S.B.1080), § 6, operative Jan. 1, 2012.)*

Law Revision Commission Comments

Section 30645 continues former Section 12280(h) without substantive change.

See Sections 16520 ("firearm"), 16970 ("person"), 30510 ("assault weapon"), 30515 (further clarification of "assault weapon"), 30530 (".50 BMG rifle"). [38 Cal.L.Rev.Comm. Reports 217 (2009)].

Cross References

.50 BMG rifle defined for purposes of this Part, see Penal Code § 30530.
Assault weapon defined for purposes of this Part, see Penal Code §§ 30510, 30515.
Firearm defined for purposes of this Part, see Penal Code § 16520.
Person defined, see Penal Code § 16970.

Research References

2 Witkin, California Criminal Law 4th Crimes Against Public Peace and Welfare § 219 (2021), Exceptions.

§ 30650. Exemption from assault weapon or .50 BMG rifle prohibition for sales to specified entities by persons issued permits under applicable law

Sections 30600, 30605, and 30610 shall not apply to the sale of assault weapons or .50 BMG rifles by persons who are issued permits pursuant to Section 31005 to any of the following:

(a) Exempt entities listed in Section 30625.

(b) Entities and persons who have been issued permits pursuant to Section 31000 or 31005.

(c) Federal military and law enforcement agencies.

(d) Law enforcement and military agencies of other states.

(e) Foreign governments and agencies approved by the United States State Department.

(f) Officers described in Section 30630 who are authorized to possess assault weapons or .50 BMG rifles pursuant to Section 30630. *(Added by Stats.2010, c. 711 (S.B.1080), § 6, operative Jan. 1, 2012.)*

Law Revision Commission Comments

Section 30650 continues former Section 12280(t) without substantive change.

See Sections 16970 ("person"), 30510 ("assault weapon"), 30515 (further clarification of "assault weapon"), 30530 (".50 BMG rifle"). [38 Cal.L.Rev. Comm. Reports 217 (2009)].

Cross References

.50 BMG rifle defined for purposes of this Part, see Penal Code § 30530.
Assault weapon defined for purposes of this Part, see Penal Code §§ 30510, 30515.
Person defined, see Penal Code § 16970.

Research References

2 Witkin, California Criminal Law 4th Crimes Against Public Peace and Welfare § 219 (2021), Exceptions.

§ 30655. Application of assault weapon or .50 BMG rifle prohibition to executors or administrators of estates containing restricted weapon

(a) Section 30600 shall not apply to a person who is the executor or administrator of an estate that includes an assault weapon or a .50 BMG rifle registered under Article 5 (commencing with Section 30900) or that was possessed pursuant to subdivision (a) of Section 30630 that is disposed of as authorized by the probate court, if the disposition is otherwise permitted by this chapter.

(b) Sections 30605 and 30610 shall not apply to a person who is the executor or administrator of an estate that includes an assault weapon or a .50 BMG rifle registered under Article 5 (commencing with Section 30900) or that was possessed pursuant to subdivision (a) of Section 30630, if the assault weapon or .50 BMG rifle is possessed at a place set forth in subdivision (a) of Section 30945 or as authorized by the probate court. *(Added by Stats.2010, c. 711 (S.B.1080), § 6, operative Jan. 1, 2012.)*

Law Revision Commission Comments

Subdivision (a) of Section 30655 continues former Section 12280(i) without substantive change.

Subdivision (b) continues former Section 12280(j) without substantive change.

See Sections 16520 ("firearm"), 16970 ("person"), 30510 ("assault weapon"), 30515 (further clarification of "assault weapon"), 30530 (".50 BMG rifle"). See also Section 16010 (continuation of existing law). [38 Cal.L.Rev. Comm. Reports 217 (2009)].

Cross References

.50 BMG rifle defined for purposes of this Part, see Penal Code § 30530.
Assault weapon defined for purposes of this Part, see Penal Code §§ 30510, 30515.
Person defined, see Penal Code § 16970.

Research References

2 Witkin, California Criminal Law 4th Crimes Against Public Peace and Welfare § 219 (2021), Exceptions.

§ 30660. Loan of assault weapon or .50 BMG rifle by lawful possessor to another person; application of law

(a) Section 30600 shall not apply to a person who lawfully possesses and has registered an assault weapon or .50 BMG rifle pursuant to this chapter who lends that assault weapon or .50 BMG rifle to another person, if all the following requirements are satisfied:

(1) The person to whom the assault weapon or .50 BMG rifle is lent is 18 years of age or over and is not prohibited by state or federal law from possessing, receiving, owning, or purchasing a firearm.

(2) The person to whom the assault weapon or .50 BMG rifle is lent remains in the presence of the registered possessor of the assault weapon or .50 BMG rifle.

(3) The assault weapon or .50 BMG rifle is possessed at any of the following locations:

(A) While on a target range that holds a regulatory or business license for the purpose of practicing shooting at that target range.

(B) While on the premises of a target range of a public or private club or organization organized for the purpose of practicing shooting at targets.

(C) While attending any exhibition, display, or educational project that is about firearms and that is sponsored by, conducted under the auspices of, or approved by a law enforcement agency or a nationally or state recognized entity that fosters proficiency in, or promotes education about, firearms.

(b) Section 30600 shall not apply to the return of an assault weapon or .50 BMG rifle to the registered possessor, or the lawful possessor, which is lent by that registered or lawful possessor pursuant to subdivision (a).

(c) Sections 30605 and 30610 shall not apply to the possession of an assault weapon or .50 BMG rifle by a person to whom an assault weapon or .50 BMG rifle is lent pursuant to subdivision (a). *(Added by Stats.2010, c. 711 (S.B.1080), § 6, operative Jan. 1, 2012.)*

Law Revision Commission Comments

Subdivisions (a) and (b) of Section 30660 continue former Section 12280(k) without substantive change.

Subdivision (c) continues former Section 12280(*l*) without substantive change.

See Sections 16520 ("firearm"), 16970 ("person"), 30510 ("assault weapon"), 30515 (further clarification of "assault weapon"), 30530 (".50 BMG rifle"). [38 Cal.L.Rev.Comm. Reports 217 (2009)].

Cross References

.50 BMG rifle defined for purposes of this Part, see Penal Code § 30530.
Assault weapon defined for purposes of this Part, see Penal Code §§ 30510, 30515.
Firearm defined for purposes of this Part, see Penal Code § 16520.
Person defined, see Penal Code § 16970.

Research References

2 Witkin, California Criminal Law 4th Crimes Against Public Peace and Welfare § 219 (2021), Exceptions.

§ 30665. Possession or importation of assault weapon or .50 BMG rifle by nonresident; application of law

Sections 30600, 30605, and 30610 shall not apply to the possession and importation of an assault weapon or a .50 BMG rifle into this state by a nonresident if all of the following conditions are met:

(a) The person is attending or going directly to or coming directly from an organized competitive match or league competition that involves the use of an assault weapon or a .50 BMG rifle.

(b) The competition or match is conducted on the premises of one of the following:

(1) A target range that holds a regulatory or business license for the purpose of practicing shooting at that target range.

(2) A target range of a public or private club or organization that is organized for the purpose of practicing shooting at targets.

(c) The match or competition is sponsored by, conducted under the auspices of, or approved by, a law enforcement agency or a nationally or state recognized entity that fosters proficiency in, or promotes education about, firearms.

(d) The assault weapon or .50 BMG rifle is transported in accordance with Section 25610 or Article 3 (commencing with Section 25505) of Chapter 2 of Division 5.

(e) The person is 18 years of age or over and is not in a class of persons prohibited from possessing firearms by virtue of Chapter 2 (commencing with Section 29800) or Chapter 3 (commencing with Section 29900) of Division 9 of this code or Section 8100 or 8103 of the Welfare and Institutions Code. *(Added by Stats.2010, c. 711 (S.B.1080), § 6, operative Jan. 1, 2012.)*

Law Revision Commission Comments

Section 30665 continues former Section 12280(m) without substantive change.

See Sections 16520 ("firearm"), 16970 ("person"), 30510 ("assault weapon"), 30515 (further clarification of "assault weapon"), 30530 (".50 BMG rifle"). [38 Cal.L.Rev.Comm. Reports 217 (2009)].

Cross References

.50 BMG rifle defined for purposes of this Part, see Penal Code § 30530.
Assault weapon defined for purposes of this Part, see Penal Code §§ 30510, 30515.
Firearm defined for purposes of this Part, see Penal Code § 16520.
Person defined, see Penal Code § 16970.

Research References

2 Witkin, California Criminal Law 4th Crimes Against Public Peace and Welfare § 219 (2021), Exceptions.

§ 30670. Importation of assault weapon or .50 BMG rifle by registered owner; application of law

(a) Section 30600 shall not apply to the importation into this state of an assault weapon or a .50 BMG rifle by the registered owner of that assault weapon or a .50 BMG rifle if it is in accordance with the provisions of Section 30945.

(b) Section 30600 shall not apply during the first 180 days of the 2005 calendar year to the importation into this state of a .50 BMG rifle by a person who lawfully possessed that .50 BMG rifle in this state prior to January 1, 2005. *(Added by Stats.2010, c. 711 (S.B.1080), § 6, operative Jan. 1, 2012.)*

Law Revision Commission Comments

Subdivision (a) of Section 30670 continues former Section 12280(q) without substantive change.

Subdivision (b) continues former Section 12280(r) without substantive change.

See Sections 16970 ("person"), 30510 ("assault weapon"), 30515 (further clarification of "assault weapon"), 30530 (".50 BMG rifle"). See also Section 16010 (continuation of existing law). [38 Cal.L.Rev.Comm. Reports 217 (2009)].

Cross References

.50 BMG rifle defined for purposes of this Part, see Penal Code § 30530.
Assault weapon defined for purposes of this Part, see Penal Code §§ 30510, 30515.
Person defined, see Penal Code § 16970.

Research References

2 Witkin, California Criminal Law 4th Crimes Against Public Peace and Welfare § 219 (2021), Exceptions.

§ 30675. Exemptions from application of specified assault weapon and .50 BMG rifle provisions

(a) Sections 30605 and 30610 shall not apply to any of the following persons:

(1) A person acting in accordance with Section 31000 or 31005.

(2) A person who has a permit to possess an assault weapon or a .50 BMG rifle issued pursuant to Section 31000 or 31005 when that person is acting in accordance with Section 31000 or 31005 or Article 5 (commencing with Section 30900).

(b) Sections 30600, 30605, and 30610 shall not apply to any of the following persons:

(1) A person acting in accordance with Article 5 (commencing with Section 30900).

(2) A person acting in accordance with Section 31000, 31005, 31050, or 31055.

(c) Sections 30605 and 30610 shall not apply to the registered owner of an assault weapon or a .50 BMG rifle possessing that firearm in accordance with Section 30945. *(Added by Stats.2010, c. 711 (S.B.1080), § 6, operative Jan. 1, 2012.)*

Law Revision Commission Comments

Subdivision (a) of Section 30675 continues former Section 12280(n) without substantive change.

Subdivision (b) continues former Section 12280(*o*) without substantive change.

Subdivision (c) continues former Section 12280(p) without substantive change.

See Sections 16520 ("firearm"), 16970 ("person"), 30510 ("assault weapon"), 30515 (further clarification of "assault weapon"), 30530 (".50 BMG rifle"). [38 Cal.L.Rev.Comm. Reports 217 (2009)].

Cross References

.50 BMG rifle defined for purposes of this Part, see Penal Code § 30530.
Assault weapon defined for purposes of this Part, see Penal Code §§ 30510, 30515.
Firearm defined for purposes of this Part, see Penal Code § 16520.
Person defined, see Penal Code § 16970.

Research References

2 Witkin, California Criminal Law 4th Crimes Against Public Peace and Welfare § 219 (2021), Exceptions.

§ 30680. Exception to assault weapon prohibition for possession of assault weapon prior to January 1, 2017

Section added by Stats.2016, c. 40 (A.B.1135), § 2, eff. Jan. 1, 2017. See, also, another section of the same number added by Stats.2016, c. 48 (S.B.880), § 2, eff. Jan. 1, 2017.

Section 30605 does not apply to the possession of an assault weapon by a person who has possessed the assault weapon prior to January 1, 2017, if all of the following are applicable:

(a) Prior to January 1, 2017, the person would have been eligible to register that assault weapon pursuant to subdivision (b) of Section 30900.

(b) The person lawfully possessed that assault weapon prior to January 1, 2017.

(c) The person registers the assault weapon by July 1, 2018, in accordance with subdivision (b) of Section 30900. *(Added by Stats.2016, c. 40 (A.B.1135), § 2, eff. Jan. 1, 2017. Amended by Stats.2017, c. 17 (A.B.103), § 47, eff. June 27, 2017.)*

Research References

2 Witkin, California Criminal Law 4th Crimes Against Public Peace and Welfare § 219 (2021), Exceptions.

§ 30680. Exception to assault weapon prohibition for possession of assault weapon prior to January 1, 2017

Section added by Stats.2016, c. 48 (S.B.880), § 2, eff. Jan. 1, 2017. See, also, another section of the same number added by Stats.2016, c. 40 (A.B.1135), § 2, eff. Jan. 1, 2017.

Section 30605 does not apply to the possession of an assault weapon by a person who has possessed the assault weapon prior to January 1, 2017, if all of the following are applicable:

(a) Prior to January 1, 2017, the person was eligible to register that assault weapon pursuant to subdivision (b) of Section 30900.

(b) The person lawfully possessed that assault weapon prior to January 1, 2017.

(c) The person registers the assault weapon by July 1, 2018, in accordance with subdivision (b) of Section 30900. *(Added by Stats.2016, c. 48 (S.B.880), § 2, eff. Jan. 1, 2017. Amended by Stats.2017, c. 17 (A.B.103), § 48, eff. June 27, 2017.)*

Research References

2 Witkin, California Criminal Law 4th Crimes Against Public Peace and Welfare § 219 (2021), Exceptions.

§ 30685. Applicability of § 30605 to possession of an assault weapon; conditions

Section 30605 does not apply to the possession of an assault weapon as defined by paragraph (9), (10), or (11) of subdivision (a) of Section 30515 by a person who has possessed the assault weapon prior to September 1, 2020, if all of the following are applicable:

(a) Prior to September 1, 2020, the person would have been eligible to register that assault weapon pursuant to subdivision (c) of Section 30900.

(b) The person lawfully possessed that assault weapon prior to September 1, 2020.

(c) The person registers the assault weapon by January 1, 2022, in accordance with subdivision (c) of Section 30900. *(Added by Stats.2020, c. 29 (S.B.118), § 39, eff. Aug. 6, 2020.)*

Research References

2 Witkin, California Criminal Law 4th Crimes Against Public Peace and Welfare § 219 (2021), Exceptions.

ARTICLE 3. SKS RIFLES

§ 30710. "SKS rifle" defined

Notwithstanding paragraph (11) of subdivision (a) of Section 30510, an "SKS rifle" under this article means all SKS rifles commonly referred to as "SKS Sporter" versions, manufactured to accept a detachable AK–47 magazine and imported into this state and sold by a licensed gun dealer, or otherwise lawfully possessed in this state by a resident of this state who is not a licensed gun dealer, between January 1, 1992, and December 19, 1997. *(Added by Stats.2010, c. 711 (S.B.1080), § 6, operative Jan. 1, 2012.)*

Law Revision Commission Comments

Section 30710 continues former Section 12281(i) without substantive change.

See Section 16010 (continuation of existing law). [38 Cal.L.Rev.Comm. Reports 217 (2009)].

§ 30715. Immunity from prosecution for persons, firms, companies, or corporations involved in manufacture, distribution, transportation, possession, sale, transfer, gift, or loan of SKS rifles during specified time frames; retroactive application; SKS rifles not subject to seizure; reopening of convictions and withdrawal of pleas of guilty or nolo contendere under prior law for assertion of immunity

(a)(1) Any person who, or firm, company, or corporation that operated a retail or other commercial firm, company, or corporation, and manufactured, distributed, transported, imported, possessed, possessed for sale, offered for sale, or transferred, for commercial purpose, an SKS rifle in California between January 1, 1992, and December 19, 1997, shall be immune from criminal prosecution under Article 2 (commencing with Section 30600) or former Section 12280.

(2) The immunity provided in this subdivision shall apply retroactively to any person who, or firm, company, or corporation that, is or was charged by complaint or indictment with a violation of former Section 12280 for conduct related to an SKS rifle, whether or not the case of that person, firm, company, or corporation is final.

(b)(1) Any person who possessed, gave, loaned, or transferred an SKS rifle in California between January 1, 1992, and December 19, 1997, shall be immune from criminal prosecution under Article 2 (commencing with Section 30600) or former Section 12280.

(2) The immunity provided in this subdivision shall apply retroactively to any person who was charged by complaint or indictment with a violation of former Section 12280 for conduct related to an SKS rifle, whether or not the case of that person is final.

(c) Any SKS rifle in the possession of any person who, or firm, company, or corporation that, is described in subdivision (a) or (b), shall not be subject to seizure by law enforcement for violation of Article 2 (commencing with Section 30600) or former Section 12280 prior to January 1, 2000.

(d) Any person, firm, company, or corporation, convicted under former Section 12280 for conduct relating to an SKS rifle, shall be permitted to withdraw a plea of guilty or nolo contendere, or to reopen the case and assert the immunities provided in this article, if the court determines that the allowance of the immunity is in the interests of justice. The court shall interpret this article liberally to the benefit of the defendant.

(e) For purposes of this section, "former Section 12280" refers to former Section 12280, as added by Section 3 of Chapter 19 of the Statutes of 1989 or as subsequently amended. *(Added by Stats.2010, c. 711 (S.B.1080), § 6, operative Jan. 1, 2012.)*

Law Revision Commission Comments

Section 30715 continues former Section 12281(a)-(d) without substantive change.

In a number of places, Section 30715 refers to "former Section 12280." Subdivision (e) makes clear that these are references to former Section 12280, as added by 1989 Cal. Stat. ch. 19, § 3, or as subsequently amended. That provision is continued in Article 2 (Sections 30600–30675). Another Section 12280 was added by 1989 Cal. Stat. ch. 18, § 4, and repealed by 1989 Cal. Stat. ch. 19, § 2.5.

See Sections 16970 ("person"), 30710 ("SKS rifle"). See also Section 16010 (continuation of existing law). [38 Cal.L.Rev.Comm. Reports 217 (2009)].

Cross References

Person defined, see Penal Code § 16970.

§ 30720. Relinquishment or disposal of SKS rifles by persons, firms, companies, or corporations in possession

(a) Any person, firm, company, or corporation that is in possession of an SKS rifle shall do one of the following on or before January 1, 2000:

(1) Relinquish the SKS rifle to the Department of Justice pursuant to subdivision (h) of former Section 12281.

(2) Relinquish the SKS rifle to a law enforcement agency pursuant to former Section 12288, as added by Section 3 of Chapter 19 of the Statutes of 1989.

(3) Dispose of the SKS rifle as permitted by former Section 12285, as it read in Section 20 of Chapter 23 of the Statutes of 1994.

(b) Any person who has obtained title to an SKS rifle by bequest or intestate succession shall be required to comply with paragraph (1) or (2) of subdivision (a) unless that person otherwise complies with paragraph (1) of subdivision (b) of former Section 12285, as it read in Section 20 of Chapter 23 of the Statutes of 1994, or as subsequently amended.

(c) Any SKS rifle relinquished to the department pursuant to this section shall be in a manner prescribed by the department. *(Added by Stats.2010, c. 711 (S.B.1080), § 6, operative Jan. 1, 2012.)*

Law Revision Commission Comments

Section 30720 continues former Section 12281(f)(1)-(3) without substantive change.

For the consequences of complying or failing to comply with this provision, see Section 30725.

Subdivision (a)(1) refers to former Section 12281(h), which is continued in Section 30730(a).

Subdivision (a)(2) refers to former Section 12288, as it read from when former Section 12281 became operative (January 1, 1999) until the deadline for relinquishment or disposal of an SKS rifle (January 1, 2000). Former Section 12288, as subsequently amended, is continued in Section 31100 (relinquishment of assault weapon or .50 BMG rifle).

Subdivision (a)(3) refers to former Section 12285, as it read from when former Section 12281 became operative (January 1, 1989) until the deadline for relinquishment or disposal of an SKS rifle (January 1, 2000). Former Section 12285, as subsequently amended, is continued in Article 5 (Sections 30900–30965).

Subdivision (b) refers to former Section 12285(b)(1), as it read when former Section 12281 became operative on January 1, 1989, or thereafter. Former Section 12285(b)(1) is continued in Sections 30910 (restriction on sale or transfer of assault weapon), 30915 (assault weapon obtained by bequest or intestate succession), and 30920 (firearm lawfully possessed before it was classified as "assault weapon").

See Sections 16970 ("person"), 30710 ("SKS rifle"). See also Section 16010 (continuation of existing law). [38 Cal.L.Rev.Comm. Reports 217 (2009)].

Cross References

Person defined, see Penal Code § 16970.

§ 30725. Exemption from prohibitions related to conduct involved in relinquishment of SKS rifles; penalties for failure to relinquish rifles

(a) Any person who complies with Section 30720 shall be exempt from the prohibitions set forth in Section 30600 or 30605 for those acts by that person associated with complying with the requirements of Section 30720.

(b) Failure to comply with Section 30720 is a public offense punishable by imprisonment pursuant to subdivision (h) of Section 1170, or in a county jail, not exceeding one year. *(Added by Stats.2010, c. 711 (S.B.1080), § 6, operative Jan. 1, 2012. Amended by Stats.2011, c. 15 (A.B.109), § 551, eff. April 4, 2011, operative Jan. 1, 2012.)*

Law Revision Commission Comments

Subdivision (a) of Section 30725 continues former Section 12281(g) without substantive change.

Subdivision (b) continues former Section 12281(j) without substantive change.

See Sections 16970 ("person"), 30710 ("SKS rifle"). See also Section 16010 (continuation of existing law). [38 Cal.L.Rev.Comm. Reports 217 (2009)].

Cross References

Person defined, see Penal Code § 16970.

§ 30730. Purchase program; reimbursement of persons relinquishing possession of SKS rifles

(a)(1) The department shall purchase any SKS rifle relinquished pursuant to Section 30720 from funds appropriated for this purpose by the act amending former Section 12281 in the 1997–98 Regular Session of the Legislature or by subsequent budget acts or other legislation.

(2) The department shall adopt regulations for this purchase program that include, but are not limited to, the manner of delivery, the reimbursement to be paid, and the manner in which persons shall be informed of the state purchase program.

(3) Any person who relinquished possession of an SKS rifle to a law enforcement agency pursuant to any version of former Section 12288 prior to the effective date of the purchase program set forth in paragraph (1) shall be eligible to be reimbursed from the purchase program. The procedures for reimbursement pursuant to this paragraph shall be part of the regulations adopted by the department pursuant to paragraph (2).

(b) In addition to the regulations required pursuant to subdivision (a), emergency regulations for the purchase program described in subdivision (a) shall be adopted pursuant to Chapter 3.5 (commencing with Section 11340) of Part 1 of Division 3 of Title 2 of the Government Code. *(Added by Stats.2010, c. 711 (S.B.1080), § 6, operative Jan. 1, 2012.)*

Law Revision Commission Comments

Subdivision (a) of Section 30730 continues former Section 12281(h) without substantive change. Subdivision (a)(3) refers to former Section 12288. That provision is continued in Section 31100 (relinquishment of assault weapon or .50 BMG rifle).

Subdivision (b) continues former Section 12281(k) without substantive change.

See Sections 16970 ("person"), 30710 ("SKS rifle"). See also Section 16010 (continuation of existing law). [38 Cal.L.Rev.Comm. Reports 217 (2009)].

Cross References

Person defined, see Penal Code § 16970.

§ 30735. Notification of district attorneys of provisions relating to immunity for SKS rifle violations, reopening of prosecutions, withdrawal of guilty and nolo contendere pleas, and relinquishment of rifles; notice to defense counsel or defendants; public education and notification program

(a) The Department of Justice shall notify all district attorneys on or before January 31, 1999, of the provisions of former Section 12281.

(b) The department shall identify all criminal prosecutions in the state for conduct related to SKS rifles on or before April 1, 1999. In all cases so identified by the Attorney General, the district attorneys shall inform defense counsel, or the defendant if the defendant is in propria persona, in writing, of the provisions of former Section 12281 on or before May 1, 1999.

(c) Commencing no later than January 1, 1999, the department shall conduct a public education and notification program as described in Section 31115 or in former Section 12289, as added by Section 6 of Chapter 954 of the Statutes of 1991 or as subsequently amended. *(Added by Stats.2010, c. 711 (S.B.1080), § 6, operative Jan. 1, 2012.)*

Law Revision Commission Comments

Subdivisions (a) and (b) of Section 30735 continue former Section 12281(e) without substantive change. Both subdivisions refer to former Section 12281, which is continued in this article (Sections 30710–30735).

Subdivision (c) continues former Section 12281(f)(4) without substantive change. Subdivision (c) refers to former Section 12289, which is continued in Section 31115.

See Section 30710 ("SKS rifle"). See also Section 16010 (continuation of existing law). [38 Cal.L.Rev.Comm. Reports 217 (2009)].

Cross References

Attorney General, generally, see Government Code § 12500 et seq.

ARTICLE 4. ASSAULT WEAPON OR .50 BMG RIFLE CONSTITUTING NUISANCE

§ 30800. Possession as constituting a nuisance; civil action or compromise enjoining possession in lieu of criminal prosecution; civil fine; destruction of firearm deemed nuisance

(a)(1) Except as provided in Article 2 (commencing with Section 30600), possession of any assault weapon or of any .50 BMG rifle in violation of this chapter is a public nuisance, solely for purposes of this section and subdivision (c) of Section 18005.

(2) The Attorney General, any district attorney, or any city attorney, may, in lieu of criminal prosecution, bring a civil action or reach a civil compromise in any superior court to enjoin the manufacture of, importation of, keeping for sale of, offering or exposing for sale, giving, lending, or possession of an assault weapon or .50 BMG rifle that is a public nuisance.

(b)(1) Upon motion of the Attorney General, district attorney, or city attorney, a superior court may impose a civil fine not to exceed five hundred dollars ($500) for the manufacture of, importation of, keeping for sale of, offering or exposing for sale, giving, or lending of an assault weapon or .50 BMG rifle that is a public nuisance pursuant to subdivision (a) and up to two hundred dollars ($200) for each additional assault weapon or .50 BMG that is a public nuisance pursuant to subdivision (a).

(2) Upon motion of the Attorney General, district attorney, or city attorney, a superior court may impose a civil fine not to exceed three hundred dollars ($300) for the possession of an assault weapon or .50 BMG rifle that is a public nuisance pursuant to subdivision (a) and up to one hundred dollars ($100) for each additional assault weapon or .50 BMG rifle possessed, that is a public nuisance pursuant to subdivision (a).

(c) Any assault weapon or .50 BMG rifle deemed a public nuisance under subdivision (a) shall be destroyed in a manner so that it may no longer be used, except upon a finding by a court, or a declaration from the Department of Justice, district attorney, or city attorney stating that the preservation of the assault weapon or .50 BMG rifle is in the interest of justice.

(d) Upon conviction of any misdemeanor or felony involving the illegal possession or use of an assault weapon, the assault weapon shall be deemed a public nuisance and disposed of pursuant to subdivision (c) of Section 18005. *(Added by Stats.2010, c. 711 (S.B.1080), § 6, operative Jan. 1, 2012. Amended by Stats.2019, c. 730 (A.B.879), § 7, eff. Jan. 1, 2020.)*

Validity

For validity of this section, see Miller v. Bonta, S.D.Cal. 2021, 542 F.Supp.3d 1009, vacated and remanded 2022 WL 3095986.

Law Revision Commission Comments

Section 30800 continues former Section 12282 without substantive change.

See Sections 30510 ("assault weapon"), 30515 (further clarification of "assault weapon"), 30530 (".50 BMG rifle"). [38 Cal.L.Rev.Comm. Reports 217 (2009)].

Cross References

.50 BMG rifle defined for purposes of this Part, see Penal Code § 30530.
Assault weapon defined for purposes of this Part, see Penal Code §§ 30510, 30515.
Attorney General, generally, see Government Code § 12500 et seq.
Felonies, definition and penalties, see Penal Code §§ 17, 18.
Misdemeanors, definition and penalties, see Penal Code §§ 17, 19, 19.2.

Research References

2 Witkin, California Criminal Law 4th Crimes Against Public Peace and Welfare § 223 (2021), Civil Action to Enjoin Possession.

ARTICLE 5. REGISTRATION OF ASSAULT WEAPONS AND .50 BMG RIFLES AND RELATED RULES

§ 30900. Registration; contents of registration; fee

(a)(1) Any person who, prior to June 1, 1989, lawfully possessed an assault weapon, as defined in former Section 12276, as added by Section 3 of Chapter 19 of the Statutes of 1989, shall register the firearm by January 1, 1991, and any person who lawfully possessed an assault weapon prior to the date it was specified as an assault weapon pursuant to former Section 12276.5, as added by Section 3 of Chapter 19 of the Statutes of 1989 or as amended by Section 1 of Chapter 874 of the Statutes of 1990 or Section 3 of Chapter 954 of the Statutes of 1991, shall register the firearm within 90 days with the Department of Justice pursuant to those procedures that the department may establish.

(2) Except as provided in Section 30600, any person who lawfully possessed an assault weapon prior to the date it was defined as an assault weapon pursuant to former Section 12276.1, as it read in Section 7 of Chapter 129 of the Statutes of 1999, and which was not specified as an assault weapon under former Section 12276, as added by Section 3 of Chapter 19 of the Statutes of 1989 or as amended at any time before January 1, 2001, or former Section 12276.5, as added by Section 3 of Chapter 19 of the Statutes of 1989 or as amended at any time before January 1, 2001, shall register the firearm by January 1, 2001, with the department pursuant to those procedures that the department may establish.

(3) The registration shall contain a description of the firearm that identifies it uniquely, including all identification marks, the full name, address, date of birth, and thumbprint of the owner, and any other information that the department may deem appropriate.

(4) The department may charge a fee for registration of up to twenty dollars ($20) per person but not to exceed the reasonable processing costs of the department. After the department establishes fees sufficient to reimburse the department for processing costs, fees charged shall increase at a rate not to exceed the legislatively approved annual cost-of-living adjustment for the department's budget or as otherwise increased through the Budget Act but not to exceed the reasonable costs of the department. The fees shall be deposited into the Dealers' Record of Sale Special Account.

(b)(1) Any person who, from January 1, 2001, to December 31, 2016, inclusive, lawfully possessed an assault weapon that does not have a fixed magazine, as defined in Section 30515, including those weapons with an ammunition feeding device that can be readily removed from the firearm with the use of a tool, shall register the firearm before July 1, 2018, but not before the effective date of the regulations adopted pursuant to paragraph (5), with the department pursuant to those procedures that the department may establish by regulation pursuant to paragraph (5).

(2) Registrations shall be submitted electronically via the Internet utilizing a public-facing application made available by the department.

(3) The registration shall contain a description of the firearm that identifies it uniquely, including all identification marks, the date the firearm was acquired, the name and address of the individual from whom, or business from which, the firearm was acquired, as well as the registrant's full name, address, telephone number, date of birth, sex, height, weight, eye color, hair color, and California driver's license number or California identification card number.

(4) The department may charge a fee in an amount of up to fifteen dollars ($15) per person but not to exceed the reasonable processing costs of the department. The fee shall be paid by debit or credit card at the time that the electronic registration is submitted to the department. The fee shall be deposited in the Dealers' Record of Sale Special Account to be used for purposes of this section.

(5) The department shall adopt regulations for the purpose of implementing this subdivision. These regulations are exempt from the Administrative Procedure Act (Chapter 3.5 (commencing with Section 11340) of Part 1 of Division 3 of Title 2 of the Government Code).

(c)(1) Any person who, prior to September 1, 2020, lawfully possessed an assault weapon as defined by paragraph (9), (10), or (11) of subdivision (a) of Section 30515, and is eligible to register an assault weapon as set forth in Section 30950, shall submit an application to register the firearm before January 1, 2022, but not before the effective date of the regulations adopted pursuant to paragraph (5), with the department pursuant to those procedures that the department may establish by regulation pursuant to paragraph (5).

(2) Registration applications shall be submitted in a manner and format to be specified by the department in regulations adopted pursuant to paragraph (5).

(3) The registration application shall contain a description of the firearm that identifies it uniquely, including all identification marks, the date the firearm was acquired, the name and address of the individual from whom, or business from which, the firearm was acquired, as well as the registrant's full name, address, telephone number, date of birth, sex, height, weight, eye color, hair color, and California driver's license number or California identification card number, and any other information that the department may deem appropriate. The registration application shall also contain photographs of the firearm, as specified by the department in regulations adopted pursuant to paragraph (5).

(4) For each registration application, the department may charge a fee that consists of the amount the department is authorized to require a dealer to charge each firearm purchaser under subdivision (a) of Section 28233, not to exceed the reasonable processing costs of the department. For registration applications seeking to register multiple firearms, the fee shall increase by up to five dollars ($5) for each additional firearm after the first, not to exceed the reasonable processing costs of the department. The fee shall be paid in a manner specified by the department in regulations adopted pursuant to paragraph (5) at the time the registration application is submitted to the department. The fee shall be deposited in the Dealers' Record of Sale Special Account to be used for purposes of this section.

(5) The department shall adopt regulations for the purpose of implementing this subdivision and paragraphs (9), (10), and (11) of subdivision (a) of Section 30515. These regulations are exempt from the Administrative Procedure Act (Chapter 3.5 (commencing with

Section 11340) of Part 1 of Division 3 of Title 2 of the Government Code). *(Added by Stats.2010, c. 711 (S.B.1080), § 6, operative Jan. 1, 2012. Amended by Stats.2016, c. 40 (A.B.1135), § 3, eff. Jan. 1, 2017; Stats.2016, c. 48 (S.B.880), § 3, eff. Jan. 1, 2017; Stats.2017, c. 17 (A.B.103), § 49, eff. June 27, 2017; Stats.2020, c. 29 (S.B.118), § 40, eff. Aug. 6, 2020.)*

Law Revision Commission Comments

Section 30900 continues former Section 12285(a)(1) without substantive change.

Under subdivision (a), a person "who, prior to June 1, 1989, lawfully possessed an assault weapon, *as defined in former Section 12276*, ... shall register the firearm by January 1, 1991 ...." (Emphasis added.) For the text of former Section 12276 during this registration period, see 1989 Cal. Stat. ch. 19, § 3. The provision was subsequently amended on several occasions. See 1993 Cal. Stat. ch. 606, § 19; 1992 Cal. Stat. ch. 427, § 134; 1991 Cal. Stat. ch. 954, § 2. As so amended, former Section 12276 is continued in Section 30510 ("assault weapon").

Subdivision (a) also refers to the date that a weapon "was specified as an assault weapon *pursuant to former Section 12276.5*." (Emphasis added.) In the past, that section (1) prescribed a procedure by which a court could classify a weapon as an assault weapon, and (2) directed the Attorney General to promulgate a list of the weapons classified as assault weapons by statute or by a court. See 1991 Cal. Stat. ch. 954, § 3; 1990 Cal. Stat. ch. 874, § 1; 1989 Cal. Stat. ch. 19, § 3. Those procedures were discontinued as of January 1, 2007. See 2006 Cal. Stat. ch. 793, § 1. As so amended, former Section 12276.5 is continued in Section 30520 (duties of Attorney General).

Under subdivision (b), a person "who lawfully possessed an assault weapon prior to the date it was defined as an assault weapon *pursuant to former Section 12276.1*, ... and which was not specified as an assault weapon under former Section 12276, ... or former Section 12276.5, ... shall register the firearm by January 1, 2001 ...." (Emphasis added.) Former Section 12276.1 was enacted as 1999 Cal. Stat. ch. 129, § 7, and became operative on January 1, 2000. That version of the statute remained in effect through the registration deadline of January 1, 2001. As subsequently amended to exempt certain weapons, it is continued in Section 30515 (further clarification of "assault weapon").

See Sections 16520 ("firearm"), 16970 ("person"). See also Section 16010 (continuation of existing law). [38 Cal.L.Rev.Comm. Reports 217 (2009)].

Cross References

Applicability of section 30605 to the possession of an assault weapon, conditions, see Penal Code § 30685.
Assault weapon defined for purposes of this Part, see Penal Code §§ 30510, 30515.
Exception to assault weapon prohibition for possession of assault weapon prior to January 1, 2017, see Penal Code § 30680.
Firearm defined for purposes of this Part, see Penal Code § 16520.
Joint registration, see Penal Code § 30955.
Person defined, see Penal Code § 16970.

Research References

2 Witkin, California Criminal Law 4th Crimes Against Public Peace and Welfare § 217 (2021), Possession.
2 Witkin, California Criminal Law 4th Crimes Against Public Peace and Welfare § 219 (2021), Exceptions.
2 Witkin, California Criminal Law 4th Crimes Against Public Peace and Welfare § 220 (2021), Registration Requirements.
2 Witkin, California Criminal Law 4th Crimes Against Public Peace and Welfare § 221 (2021), Permits and Conditions for Possession.

§ 30905. Lawful possession before specified date of .50 BMG rifle not designated as assault weapon; registration; contents of registration; fee

(a) Except as provided in Section 30600, any person who lawfully possesses any .50 BMG rifle prior to January 1, 2005, that is not specified as an assault weapon under former Section 12276, as it reads in Section 19 of Chapter 606 of the Statutes of 1993, or former Section 12276.5, as it reads in Section 3 of Chapter 954 of the Statutes of 1991, or defined as an assault weapon pursuant to former Section 12276.1, as it reads in Section 3 of Chapter 911 of the Statutes of 2002, shall register the .50 BMG rifle with the department no later than April 30, 2006, pursuant to those procedures that the department may establish.

(b) The registration shall contain a description of the firearm that identifies it uniquely, including all identification marks, the full name, address, date of birth, and thumbprint of the owner, and any other information that the department may deem appropriate.

(c) The department may charge a fee for registration of twenty-five dollars ($25) per person to cover the actual processing and public education campaign costs of the department. The fees shall be deposited into the Dealers' Record of Sale Special Account. Data-processing costs associated with modifying the department's data system to accommodate .50 caliber BMG rifles shall not be paid from the Dealers' Record of Sale Special Account. *(Added by Stats.2010, c. 711 (S.B.1080), § 6, operative Jan. 1, 2012.)*

Law Revision Commission Comments

Section 30905 continues former Section 12285(a)(2) without substantive change.

Under subdivision (a), a person "who lawfully possesses any .50 BMG rifle prior to January 1, 2005, that is not specified as an assault weapon under *former Section 12276, ... or former Section 12276.5*, ... or defined as an assault weapon pursuant to *former Section 12276.1*, shall register the .50 BMG rifle with the department no later than April 30, 2006 ...." (Emphasis added.) For the text of former Section 12276 during this registration period, see 1993 Cal. Stat. ch. 606, § 19, which is continued in Section 30510 ("assault weapon"). For the text of former Section 12276.1 during this registration period, see 2002 Cal. Stat. ch. 911, § 3, which is continued in Section 30515 (further clarification of "assault weapon"). For the text of former Section 12276.5 during this registration period, see 1991 Cal. Stat. ch. 954, § 3. Former Section 12276.5 was subsequently amended. As so amended, it is continued in Section 30520 (duties of Attorney General).

See Sections 16520 ("firearm"), 16970 ("person"), 30530 (".50 BMG rifle"). See also Section 16010 (continuation of existing law). [38 Cal.L.Rev.Comm. Reports 217 (2009)].

Cross References

.50 BMG rifle defined for purposes of this Part, see Penal Code § 30530.
Assault weapon defined for purposes of this Part, see Penal Code §§ 30510, 30515.
Firearm defined for purposes of this Part, see Penal Code § 16520.
Person defined, see Penal Code § 16970.

Research References

2 Witkin, California Criminal Law 4th Crimes Against Public Peace and Welfare § 217 (2021), Possession.
2 Witkin, California Criminal Law 4th Crimes Against Public Peace and Welfare § 220 (2021), Registration Requirements.

§ 30910. Sale of assault weapon

Except as provided in Section 30925, no assault weapon possessed pursuant to this article may be sold or transferred on or after January 1, 1990, to anyone within this state other than to a licensed gun dealer or as provided in Section 31100. *(Added by Stats.2010, c. 711 (S.B.1080), § 6, operative Jan. 1, 2012.)*

Law Revision Commission Comments

Section 30910 continues the first sentence of former Section 12285(b)(1) without substantive change.

See Section 16790 ("licensed gun dealer"), 30510 ("assault weapon"), 30515 (further clarification of "assault weapon"). See also Section 16010 (continuation of existing law). [38 Cal.L.Rev.Comm. Reports 217 (2009)].

Cross References

Assault weapon defined for purposes of this Part, see Penal Code §§ 30510, 30515.

Research References

2 Witkin, California Criminal Law 4th Crimes Against Public Peace and Welfare § 220 (2021), Registration Requirements.

2 Witkin, California Criminal Law 4th Crimes Against Public Peace and Welfare § 221 (2021), Permits and Conditions for Possession.

§ 30915. Assault weapons obtained through bequest or intestate succession; requirements

Any person who obtains title to an assault weapon registered under this article or that was possessed pursuant to subdivision (a) of Section 30630 by bequest or intestate succession shall, within 90 days, do one or more of the following:

(a) Render the weapon permanently inoperable.

(b) Sell the weapon to a licensed gun dealer.

(c) Obtain a permit from the Department of Justice in the same manner as specified in Article 3 (commencing with Section 32650) of Chapter 6.

(d) Remove the weapon from this state. *(Added by Stats.2010, c. 711 (S.B.1080), § 6, operative Jan. 1, 2012.)*

Validity

For validity of this section, see Miller v. Bonta, S.D.Cal. 2021, 542 F.Supp.3d 1009, vacated and remanded 2022 WL 3095986.

Law Revision Commission Comments

In combination with Section 30920(a), Section 30915 continues the second sentence of former Section 12285(b)(1) without substantive change.

See Sections 16520 ("firearm"), 16790 ("licensed gun dealer"), 16970 ("person"), 30510 ("assault weapon"), 30515 (further clarification of "assault weapon"). See also Section 16010 (continuation of existing law). [38 Cal.L.Rev.Comm. Reports 217 (2009)].

Cross References

Assault weapon defined for purposes of this Part, see Penal Code §§ 30510, 30515.
Person defined, see Penal Code § 16970.

Research References

2 Witkin, California Criminal Law 4th Crimes Against Public Peace and Welfare § 220 (2021), Registration Requirements.

§ 30920. Lawfully possessed firearms subsequently declared assault weapons by specified laws; actions required

(a) Any person who lawfully possessed a firearm subsequently declared to be an assault weapon pursuant to former Section 12276.5, as it reads in Section 3 of Chapter 19 of the Statutes of 1989, Section 1 of Chapter 874 of the Statutes of 1990, or Section 3 of Chapter 954 of the Statutes of 1991, or subsequently defined as an assault weapon pursuant to former Section 12276.1, as that section read at any time from when it was enacted by Section 7 of Chapter 129 of the Statutes of 1999 to when it was repealed by the Deadly Weapons Recodification Act of 2010, shall, within 90 days, do one or more of the following:

(1) Render the weapon permanently inoperable.

(2) Sell the weapon to a licensed gun dealer.

(3) Obtain a permit from the Department of Justice in the same manner as specified in Article 3 (commencing with Section 32650) of Chapter 6.

(4) Remove the weapon from this state.

(b) Notwithstanding subdivision (a), a person who lawfully possessed a firearm that was subsequently declared to be an assault weapon pursuant to former Section 12276.5 may alternatively register the firearm within 90 days of the declaration issued pursuant to subdivision (f) of former Section 12276.5, as it reads in Section 3 of Chapter 19 of the Statutes of 1989, Section 1 of Chapter 874 of the Statutes of 1990, or Section 3 of Chapter 954 of the Statutes of 1991. *(Added by Stats.2010, c. 711 (S.B.1080), § 6, operative Jan. 1, 2012.)*

Law Revision Commission Comments

In combination with Section 30915, subdivision (a) of Section 30920 continues the second sentence of former Section 12285(b)(1) without substantive change. Subdivision (b) continues the third sentence of former Section 12285(b)(1) without substantive change.

Subdivision (a) refers to former Section 12276.1. That section was enacted as 1999 Cal. Stat. ch. 129, § 7, and became operative on January 1, 2000. It was later amended to provide for certain exemptions. See 2000 Cal. Stat. ch. 967, § 3; 2002 Cal. Stat. ch. 911, § 3. It is continued in Section 30515 (further clarification of "assault weapon").

Subdivisions (a) and (b) refer to former Section 12276.5, which (1) prescribed a procedure by which a court could classify a weapon as an assault weapon, and (2) directed the Attorney General to promulgate a list of the weapons classified as assault weapons by statute or by a court. See 1991 Cal. Stat. ch. 954, § 3; 1990 Cal. Stat. ch. 874, § 1; 1989 Cal. Stat. ch. 19, § 3. Those procedures were discontinued as of January 1, 2007. See 2006 Cal. Stat. ch. 793, § 1. As so amended, former Section 12276.5 is continued in Section 30520 (duties of Attorney General).

See Sections 16520 ("firearm"), 16790 ("licensed gun dealer"), 16970 ("person"). See also Section 16010 (continuation of existing law). [38 Cal.L.Rev.Comm. Reports 217 (2009)].

Cross References

Assault weapon defined for purposes of this Part, see Penal Code §§ 30510, 30515.
Firearm defined for purposes of this Part, see Penal Code § 16520.
Person defined, see Penal Code § 16970.

Research References

2 Witkin, California Criminal Law 4th Crimes Against Public Peace and Welfare § 220 (2021), Registration Requirements.

§ 30925. Persons moving into the state while in lawful possession of assault weapons; required actions; permits; delivery to licensed gun dealer

A person moving into this state, otherwise in lawful possession of an assault weapon, shall do one of the following:

(a) Prior to bringing the assault weapon into this state, that person shall first obtain a permit from the Department of Justice in the same manner as specified in Article 3 (commencing with Section 32650) of Chapter 6.

(b) The person shall cause the assault weapon to be delivered to a licensed gun dealer in this state in accordance with Chapter 44 (commencing with Section 921) of Title 18 of the United States Code and the regulations issued pursuant thereto. If the person obtains a permit from the Department of Justice in the same manner as specified in Article 3 (commencing with Section 32650) of Chapter 6, the dealer shall redeliver that assault weapon to the person. If the licensed gun dealer is prohibited from delivering the assault weapon to a person pursuant to this section, the dealer shall possess or dispose of the assault weapon as allowed by this chapter. *(Added by Stats.2010, c. 711 (S.B.1080), § 6, operative Jan. 1, 2012.)*

Validity

For validity of this section, see Miller v. Bonta, S.D.Cal. 2021, 542 F.Supp.3d 1009, vacated and remanded 2022 WL 3095986.

Law Revision Commission Comments

Section 30925 continues former Section 12285(b)(2) without substantive change.

See Sections 16790 ("licensed gun dealer"), 16970 ("person"), 30510 ("assault weapon"), 30515 (further clarification of "assault weapon"). [38 Cal.L.Rev.Comm. Reports 217 (2009)].

Cross References

Assault weapon defined for purposes of this Part, see Penal Code §§ 30510, 30515.

Person defined, see Penal Code § 16970.

Research References

2 Witkin, California Criminal Law 4th Crimes Against Public Peace and Welfare § 220 (2021), Registration Requirements.

§ 30930. Sale or transfer of .50 BMG rifle after specified date

Except as provided in Section 30940, no .50 BMG rifle possessed pursuant to this article may be sold or transferred on or after January 1, 2005, to anyone within this state other than to a licensed gun dealer or as provided in Section 31100. *(Added by Stats.2010, c. 711 (S.B.1080), § 6, operative Jan. 1, 2012.)*

Law Revision Commission Comments

Section 30930 continues the first sentence of former Section 12285(b)(3) without substantive change.

See Sections 16790 ("licensed gun dealer"), 30530 (".50 BMG rifle"). [38 Cal.L.Rev.Comm. Reports 217 (2009)].

Cross References

.50 BMG rifle defined for purposes of this Part, see Penal Code § 30530.

Research References

2 Witkin, California Criminal Law 4th Crimes Against Public Peace and Welfare § 220 (2021), Registration Requirements.

§ 30935. Persons obtaining title to .50 BMG rifle through bequest or intestate succession; required actions

Any person who obtains title to a .50 BMG rifle registered under this article or that was possessed pursuant to subdivision (a) of Section 30630 by bequest or intestate succession shall, within 180 days of receipt, do one or more of the following:

(a) Render the weapon permanently inoperable.

(b) Sell the weapon to a licensed gun dealer.

(c) Obtain a permit from the Department of Justice in the same manner as specified in Article 3 (commencing with Section 32650) of Chapter 6.

(d) Remove the weapon from this state. *(Added by Stats.2010, c. 711 (S.B.1080), § 6, operative Jan. 1, 2012.)*

Law Revision Commission Comments

Section 30935 continues the second sentence of former Section 12285(b)(3) without substantive change.

See Sections 16790 ("licensed gun dealer"), 16970 ("person"), 30530 (".50 BMG rifle"). [38 Cal.L.Rev.Comm. Reports 217 (2009)].

Cross References

.50 BMG rifle defined for purposes of this Part, see Penal Code § 30530.
Person defined, see Penal Code § 16970.

Research References

2 Witkin, California Criminal Law 4th Crimes Against Public Peace and Welfare § 220 (2021), Registration Requirements.

§ 30940. Persons moving to the state while in lawful possession of .50 BMG rifles; actions required; permit; transfer to licensed gun dealer

A person moving into this state, otherwise in lawful possession of a .50 BMG rifle, shall do one of the following:

(a) Prior to bringing the .50 BMG rifle into this state, that person shall first obtain a permit from the Department of Justice in the same manner as specified in Article 3 (commencing with Section 32650) of Chapter 6.

(b) The person shall cause the .50 BMG rifle to be delivered to a licensed gun dealer in this state in accordance with Chapter 44 (commencing with Section 921) of Title 18 of the United States Code and the regulations issued pursuant thereto. If the person obtains a permit from the Department of Justice in the same manner as specified in Article 3 (commencing with Section 32650) of Chapter 6, the dealer shall redeliver that .50 BMG rifle to the person. If the licensed gun dealer is prohibited from delivering the .50 caliber BMG rifle to a person pursuant to this section, the dealer shall dispose of the .50 BMG rifle as allowed by this chapter. *(Added by Stats.2010, c. 711 (S.B.1080), § 6, operative Jan. 1, 2012.)*

Law Revision Commission Comments

Section 30940 continues former Section 12285(b)(4) without substantive change.

See Sections 16790 ("licensed gun dealer"), 16970 ("person"), 30530 (".50 BMG rifle"). [38 Cal.L.Rev.Comm. Reports 217 (2009)].

Cross References

.50 BMG rifle defined for purposes of this Part, see Penal Code § 30530.
Person defined, see Penal Code § 16970.

Research References

2 Witkin, California Criminal Law 4th Crimes Against Public Peace and Welfare § 220 (2021), Registration Requirements.

§ 30945. Registered assault weapons or .50 BMG rifles; conditions for possession

Unless a permit allowing additional uses is first obtained under Section 31000, a person who has registered an assault weapon or registered a .50 BMG rifle under this article may possess it only under any of the following conditions:

(a) At that person's residence, place of business, or other property owned by that person, or on property owned by another with the owner's express permission.

(b) While on the premises of a target range of a public or private club or organization organized for the purpose of practicing shooting at targets.

(c) While on a target range that holds a regulatory or business license for the purpose of practicing shooting at that target range.

(d) While on the premises of a shooting club that is licensed pursuant to the Fish and Game Code.

(e) While attending any exhibition, display, or educational project that is about firearms and that is sponsored by, conducted under the auspices of, or approved by a law enforcement agency or a nationally or state recognized entity that fosters proficiency in, or promotes education about, firearms.

(f) While on publicly owned land, if the possession and use of a firearm described in Section 30510, 30515, 30520, or 30530, is specifically permitted by the managing agency of the land.

(g) While transporting the assault weapon or .50 BMG rifle between any of the places mentioned in this section, or to any licensed gun dealer, for servicing or repair pursuant to Section 31050, if the assault weapon is transported as required by Sections 16850 and 25610. *(Added by Stats.2010, c. 711 (S.B.1080), § 6, operative Jan. 1, 2012.)*

Validity

For validity of this section, see Miller v. Bonta, S.D.Cal. 2021, 542 F.Supp.3d 1009, vacated and remanded 2022 WL 3095986.

Law Revision Commission Comments

Section 30945 continues former Section 12285(c) without substantive change.

See Sections 16520 ("firearm"), 16790 ("licensed gun dealer"), 16970 ("person"), 30510 ("assault weapon"), 30515 (further clarification of "assault weapon"), 30530 (".50 BMG rifle"). [38 Cal.L.Rev.Comm. Reports 217 (2009)].

Cross References

Firearm defined for purposes of this Part, see Penal Code § 16520.

Person defined, see Penal Code § 16970.

Research References

2 Witkin, California Criminal Law 4th Crimes Against Public Peace and Welfare § 217 (2021), Possession.

2 Witkin, California Criminal Law 4th Crimes Against Public Peace and Welfare § 219 (2021), Exceptions.

2 Witkin, California Criminal Law 4th Crimes Against Public Peace and Welfare § 221 (2021), Permits and Conditions for Possession.

§ 30950. Persons prohibited from registering or possessing an assault weapon or .50 BMG rifle

No person who is under the age of 18 years, and no person who is prohibited by state or federal law from possessing, receiving, owning, or purchasing a firearm, may register or possess an assault weapon or .50 BMG rifle. *(Added by Stats.2010, c. 711 (S.B.1080), § 6, operative Jan. 1, 2012.)*

Validity

For validity of this section, see Miller v. Bonta, S.D.Cal. 2021, 542 F.Supp.3d 1009, vacated and remanded 2022 WL 3095986.

Law Revision Commission Comments

Section 30950 continues former Section 12285(d) without substantive change.

See Sections 16520 ("firearm"), 16970 ("person"), 30510 ("assault weapon"), 30515 (further clarification of "assault weapon"), 30530 (".50 BMG rifle"). [38 Cal.L.Rev.Comm. Reports 217 (2009)].

Cross References

.50 BMG rifle defined for purposes of this Part, see Penal Code § 30530.

Assault weapon, registration, contents of registration, fee, see Penal Code § 30900.

Assault weapon defined for purposes of this Part, see Penal Code §§ 30510, 30515.

Firearm defined for purposes of this Part, see Penal Code § 16520.

Person defined, see Penal Code § 16970.

Research References

2 Witkin, California Criminal Law 4th Crimes Against Public Peace and Welfare § 220 (2021), Registration Requirements.

§ 30955. Joint registration

(a) The department's registration procedures shall provide the option of joint registration for any assault weapon or .50 BMG rifle owned by family members residing in the same household.

(b) Notwithstanding subdivision (a), for registration of assault weapons in accordance with subdivision (c) of Section 30900, joint registration is not permitted. *(Added by Stats.2010, c. 711 (S.B.1080), § 6, operative Jan. 1, 2012. Amended by Stats.2020, c. 29 (S.B.118), § 41, eff. Aug. 6, 2020.)*

Law Revision Commission Comments

Section 30955 continues former Section 12285(e) without substantive change.

See Sections 30510 ("assault weapon"), 30515 (further clarification of "assault weapon"), 30530 (".50 BMG rifle"). [38 Cal.L.Rev.Comm. Reports 217 (2009)].

Cross References

.50 BMG rifle defined for purposes of this Part, see Penal Code § 30530.

Assault weapon defined for purposes of this Part, see Penal Code §§ 30510, 30515.

Research References

2 Witkin, California Criminal Law 4th Crimes Against Public Peace and Welfare § 220 (2021), Registration Requirements.

§ 30960. Forgiveness period

(a) For 90 days following January 1, 1992, a forgiveness period shall exist to allow any person specified in subdivision (b) of former Section 12280, as it reads in Section 4.5 of Chapter 954 of the Statutes of 1991, to register with the Department of Justice any assault weapon that the person lawfully possessed prior to June 1, 1989.

(b)(1) Any person who registers an assault weapon during the 90-day forgiveness period described in subdivision (a), and any person whose registration form was received by the Department of Justice after January 1, 1991, and who was issued a temporary registration prior to the end of the forgiveness period, shall not be charged with a violation of subdivision (b) of former Section 12280, as added by Section 3 of Chapter 19 of the Statutes of 1989 or as subsequently amended, if law enforcement becomes aware of that violation only as a result of the registration of the assault weapon.

(2) This section shall have no effect upon any person charged prior to January 1, 1992, with a violation of subdivision (b) of former Section 12280 as added by Section 3 of Chapter 19 of the Statutes of 1989 or as subsequently amended, provided that law enforcement was aware of the violation before the weapon was registered. *(Added by Stats.2010, c. 711 (S.B.1080), § 6, operative Jan. 1, 2012.)*

Law Revision Commission Comments

Subdivision (a) of Section 30960 continues former Section 12285(f) without substantive change.

Subdivision (b) continues former Section 12285(h) without substantive change.

Subdivisions (a) and (b) refer to former Section 12280(b). For the text of that provision during the forgiveness period, see 1991 Cal. Stat. ch. 954, § 4.5. As subsequently amended, the provision is continued in Section 30605 (unlawful possession of assault weapons).

See Sections 16970 ("person"), 30510 ("assault weapon"), 30515 (further clarification of "assault weapon"). See also Section 16010 (continuation of existing law). [38 Cal.L.Rev.Comm. Reports 217 (2009)].

Cross References

Assault weapon defined for purposes of this Part, see Penal Code §§ 30510, 30515.

Person defined, see Penal Code § 16970.

§ 30965. Registration under prior law deemed effective under current law

(a) Any person who registered a firearm as an assault weapon pursuant to the provisions of law in effect prior to January 1, 2000, where the assault weapon is thereafter defined as an assault weapon pursuant to Section 30515 or former Section 12276.1, as that section read at any time from when it was enacted by Section 7 of Chapter 129 of the Statutes of 1999 to when it was repealed by the Deadly Weapons Recodification Act of 2010, shall be deemed to have registered the weapon for purposes of this chapter and shall not be required to reregister the weapon pursuant to this article.

(b) Any person who legally registered a firearm as an assault weapon pursuant to the provisions of law in effect prior to January 1, 2005, where the assault weapon is thereafter defined as a .50 caliber BMG rifle pursuant to Section 30530 or former Section 12278, shall be deemed to have registered the weapon for purposes of this chapter and shall not be required to reregister the weapon pursuant to this article. *(Added by Stats.2010, c. 711 (S.B.1080), § 6, operative Jan. 1, 2012.)*

Law Revision Commission Comments

Section 30965 continues former Section 12285(g) without substantive change.

Subdivision (a) refers to former Section 12276.1, which became operative on January 1, 2000. As subsequently amended to exempt certain weapons, it is continued in Section 30515 (further clarification of "assault weapon"), which is also referred to in subdivision (a).

Subdivision (b) refers to a weapon "defined as a .50 BMG caliber rifle pursuant to ... former Section 12278." Former Section 12278 was enacted as 2004 Cal. Stat. ch. 494, § 7, and never amended. The definition of ".50 BMG rifle" in former Section 12278 is continued in Section 30530 (".50 BMG rifle"), which is also referred to in subdivision (b).

See Sections 16520 ("firearm"), 16970 ("person"), 30510 ("assault weapon"), 30515 (further clarification of "assault weapon"), 30530 (".50 BMG rifle"). See also Section 16010 (continuation of existing law). [38 Cal.L.Rev. Comm. Reports 217 (2009)].

Cross References

Assault weapon defined for purposes of this Part, see Penal Code §§ 30510, 30515.
Firearm defined for purposes of this Part, see Penal Code § 16520.
Person defined, see Penal Code § 16970.

Research References

2 Witkin, California Criminal Law 4th Crimes Against Public Peace and Welfare § 220 (2021), Registration Requirements.

ARTICLE 6. PERMITS FOR ASSAULT WEAPONS AND .50 BMG RIFLES

§ 31000. Permit for additional uses; permit for assault weapon lawfully acquired during specified time period; permit for acquisition of assault weapon after specified date; new permits prohibited after January 1, 2014

(a) Any person who lawfully acquired an assault weapon before June 1, 1989, or a .50 BMG rifle before January 1, 2005, and wishes to use it in a manner different than specified in Section 30945 shall first obtain a permit from the Department of Justice in the same manner as specified in Article 3 (commencing with Section 32650) of Chapter 6.

(b) Any person who lawfully acquired an assault weapon between June 1, 1989, and January 1, 1990, and wishes to keep it after January 1, 1990, shall first obtain a permit from the Department of Justice in the same manner as specified in Article 3 (commencing with Section 32650) of Chapter 6.

(c) Any person who wishes to acquire an assault weapon after January 1, 1990, or a .50 BMG rifle after January 1, 2005, shall first obtain a permit from the Department of Justice in the same manner as specified in Article 3 (commencing with Section 32650) of Chapter 6.

(d) On and after January 1, 2014, no partnership, corporation, limited liability company, association, or any other group or entity, regardless of how the entity was created, may be issued a permit to possess an assault weapon or a .50 BMG rifle. *(Added by Stats.2010, c. 711 (S.B.1080), § 6, operative Jan. 1, 2012. Amended by Stats.2013, c. 729 (A.B.170), § 2; Stats.2014, c. 54 (S.B.1461), § 16, eff. Jan. 1, 2015.)*

Law Revision Commission Comments

Section 31000 continues former Section 12286 without substantive change.

See Sections 16970 ("person"), 30510 ("assault weapon"), 30515 (further clarification of "assault weapon"), 30530 (".50 BMG rifle"). [38 Cal.L.Rev. Comm. Reports 217 (2009)].

Cross References

.50 BMG rifle defined for purposes of this Part, see Penal Code § 30530.
Assault weapon defined for purposes of this Part, see Penal Code §§ 30510, 30515.
High explosives, permits, activities covered, applications, conditions of use, duration, limitations on issuing permits if display of placards is required, persons unqualified to apply, see Health and Safety Code § 12101.
Person defined, see Penal Code § 16970.

Research References

2 Witkin, California Criminal Law 4th Crimes Against Public Peace and Welfare § 219 (2021), Exceptions.
2 Witkin, California Criminal Law 4th Crimes Against Public Peace and Welfare § 221 (2021), Permits and Conditions for Possession.

§ 31005. Permit to manufacture or sell assault weapons or .50 BMG rifles to specified entities

(a) The Department of Justice may, upon a finding of good cause, issue permits for the manufacture or sale of assault weapons or .50 BMG rifles for the sale to, purchase by, or possession of assault weapons or .50 BMG rifles by, any of the following:

(1) The agencies listed in Section 30625, and the officers described in Section 30630.

(2) Entities and persons who have been issued permits pursuant to this section or Section 31000.

(3) Federal law enforcement and military agencies.

(4) Law enforcement and military agencies of other states.

(5) Foreign governments and agencies approved by the United States State Department.

(6) Entities outside the state who have, in effect, a federal firearms dealer's license solely for the purpose of distribution to an entity listed in paragraphs (3) to (5), inclusive.

(b) Application for the permits, the keeping and inspection thereof, and the revocation of permits shall be undertaken in the same manner as specified in Article 3 (commencing with Section 32650) of Chapter 6. *(Added by Stats.2010, c. 711 (S.B.1080), § 6, operative Jan. 1, 2012.)*

Law Revision Commission Comments

Section 31005 continues former Section 12287 without substantive change.

See Sections 16970 ("person"), 30510 ("assault weapon"), 30515 (further clarification of "assault weapon"), 30530 (".50 BMG rifle"). [38 Cal.L.Rev. Comm. Reports 217 (2009)].

Cross References

.50 BMG rifle defined for purposes of this Part, see Penal Code § 30530.
Assault weapon defined for purposes of this Part, see Penal Code §§ 30510, 30515.
Firearm defined for purposes of this Part, see Penal Code § 16520.
Person defined, see Penal Code § 16970.

Research References

2 Witkin, California Criminal Law 4th Crimes Against Public Peace and Welfare § 193 (2021), Sale, Lease, or Transfer by Unlicensed Person.
2 Witkin, California Criminal Law 4th Crimes Against Public Peace and Welfare § 219 (2021), Exceptions.
2 Witkin, California Criminal Law 4th Crimes Against Public Peace and Welfare § 221 (2021), Permits and Conditions for Possession.
2 Witkin, California Criminal Law 4th Crimes Against Public Peace and Welfare § 253 (2021), Openly Displaying or Carrying Imitation or Unloaded Firearm.

ARTICLE 7. LICENSED GUN DEALERS

§ 31050. Possession of assault weapon or .50 BMG rifle for service or repair; permissible transfers for gunsmithing purposes; license requirements for gunsmith

(a) Any licensed gun dealer may take possession of any assault weapon or .50 BMG rifle for the purposes of servicing or repair from any person to whom it is legally registered or who has been issued a permit to possess it pursuant to this chapter.

(b) Any licensed gun dealer may transfer possession of any assault weapon or .50 BMG rifle received pursuant to subdivision (a), to a gunsmith for purposes of accomplishing service or repair of that weapon. A transfer is permissible only to the following persons:

(1) A gunsmith who is in the dealer's employ.

(2) A gunsmith with whom the dealer has contracted for gunsmithing services.

(c) In order for paragraph (2) of subdivision (b) to apply, the gunsmith receiving the assault weapon or .50 BMG rifle shall hold all of the following:

(1) A dealer's license issued pursuant to Chapter 44 (commencing with Section 921) of Title 18 of the United States Code and the regulations issued pursuant thereto.

(2) Any business license required by a state or local governmental entity. *(Added by Stats.2010, c. 711 (S.B.1080), § 6, operative Jan. 1, 2012.)*

Law Revision Commission Comments

Section 31050 continues former Section 12290(b) without substantive change.

See Sections 16630 ("gunsmith"), 16790 ("licensed gun dealer"), 16970 ("person"), 30510 ("assault weapon"), 30515 (further clarification of "assault weapon"), 30530 (".50 BMG rifle"). [38 Cal.L.Rev.Comm. Reports 217 (2009)].

Cross References

.50 BMG rifle defined for purposes of this Part, see Penal Code § 30530.
Assault weapon defined for purposes of this Part, see Penal Code §§ 30510, 30515.
Gunsmith defined for purposes of this Part, see Penal Code § 16630.
Person defined, see Penal Code § 16970.

Research References

2 Witkin, California Criminal Law 4th Crimes Against Public Peace and Welfare § 221 (2021), Permits and Conditions for Possession.

§ 31055. Lawful actions involving transportation, display, and sale of assault weapons or .50 BMG rifles

In addition to the uses allowed in Article 5 (commencing with Section 30900), any licensed gun dealer who lawfully possesses an assault weapon or .50 BMG rifle pursuant to Article 5 (commencing with Section 30900) may do any of the following:

(a) Transport the firearm between dealers or out of the state if that person is permitted pursuant to the National Firearms Act. Any transporting allowed by this section or Section 31050 shall be done as required by Sections 16850 and 25610.

(b) Display the firearm at any gun show licensed by a state or local governmental entity.

(c) Sell the firearm to a resident outside the state.

(d) Sell the firearm to a person who has been issued a permit pursuant to Section 31000. *(Added by Stats.2010, c. 711 (S.B.1080), § 6, operative Jan. 1, 2012.)*

Law Revision Commission Comments

Section 31055 continues former Section 12290(a) without substantive change.

See Sections 16790 ("licensed gun dealer"), 16970 ("person"), 30510 ("assault weapon"), 30515 (further clarification of "assault weapon"), 30530 (".50 BMG rifle"). [38 Cal.L.Rev.Comm. Reports 217 (2009)].

Cross References

.50 BMG rifle defined for purposes of this Part, see Penal Code § 30530.
Assault weapon defined for purposes of this Part, see Penal Code §§ 30510, 30515.
Firearm defined for purposes of this Part, see Penal Code § 16520.
Person defined, see Penal Code § 16970.

Research References

2 Witkin, California Criminal Law 4th Crimes Against Public Peace and Welfare § 221 (2021), Permits and Conditions for Possession.

ARTICLE 8. MISCELLANEOUS PROVISIONS

§ 31100. Relinquishment of assault weapon or .50 BMG rifle to police or sheriff's department; transportation

Any individual may arrange in advance to relinquish an assault weapon or a .50 BMG rifle to a police or sheriff's department. The assault weapon or .50 BMG rifle shall be transported in accordance with Sections 16850 and 25610. *(Added by Stats.2010, c. 711 (S.B.1080), § 6, operative Jan. 1, 2012.)*

Law Revision Commission Comments

Section 31100 continues former Section 12288 without substantive change.

See Sections 30510 ("assault weapon"), 30515 (further clarification of "assault weapon"), 30530 (".50 BMG rifle"). [38 Cal.L.Rev.Comm. Reports 217 (2009)].

Cross References

.50 BMG rifle defined for purposes of this Part, see Penal Code § 30530.
Assault weapon defined for purposes of this Part, see Penal Code §§ 30510, 30515.

Research References

2 Witkin, California Criminal Law 4th Crimes Against Public Peace and Welfare § 217 (2021), Possession.
2 Witkin, California Criminal Law 4th Crimes Against Public Peace and Welfare § 220 (2021), Registration Requirements.
2 Witkin, California Criminal Law 4th Crimes Against Public Peace and Welfare § 221 (2021), Permits and Conditions for Possession.

§ 31105. Identification over police radio of individual registering assault weapon or .50 BMG rifle; exceptions

(a) No peace officer or dispatcher shall broadcast over a police radio that an individual has registered, or has obtained a permit to possess, an assault weapon or .50 BMG rifle pursuant to this chapter, unless there exists a reason to believe in good faith that one of the following conditions exist:

(1) The individual has engaged, or may be engaged, in criminal conduct.

(2) The police are responding to a call in which the person allegedly committing a criminal violation may gain access to the assault weapon or .50 BMG rifle.

(3) The victim, witness, or person who reported the alleged criminal violation may be using the assault weapon or .50 BMG rifle to hold the person allegedly committing the criminal violation, or may be using the weapon in defense of self or another person.

(b) This section shall not prohibit a peace officer or dispatcher from broadcasting over a police radio that an individual has not registered, or has not obtained a permit to possess, an assault weapon or .50 BMG rifle pursuant to this chapter.

(c) This section does not limit the transmission of an assault weapon or a .50 BMG rifle ownership status via law enforcement computers or any other medium that is legally accessible only to peace officers or other authorized personnel. *(Added by Stats.2010, c. 711 (S.B.1080), § 6, operative Jan. 1, 2012.)*

Law Revision Commission Comments

Section 31105 continues former Section 12288.5 without substantive change.

See Sections 16970 ("person"), 30510 ("assault weapon"), 30515 (further clarification of "assault weapon"), 30530 (".50 BMG rifle"). [38 Cal.L.Rev. Comm. Reports 217 (2009)].

Cross References

.50 BMG rifle defined for purposes of this Part, see Penal Code § 30530.
Assault weapon defined for purposes of this Part, see Penal Code §§ 30510, 30515.
Person defined, see Penal Code § 16970.

Research References

2 Witkin, California Criminal Law 4th Crimes Against Public Peace and Welfare § 222 (2021), Police Radio Broadcasts.

§ 31110. Inspection of permit holders for security, safe storage, and inventory reconciliation; time frames

(a) Except as provided in subdivision (b), the Department of Justice shall, for every person to whom a permit is issued pursuant to this article, annually conduct an inspection for security and safe storage purposes, and to reconcile the inventory of assault weapons.

(b) A person, firm, or corporation with an inventory of fewer than five devices that require any Department of Justice permit shall be subject to an inspection for security and safe storage purposes, and to reconcile inventory, once every five years, or more frequently if determined by the department. *(Added by Stats.2010, c. 711 (S.B.1080), § 6, operative Jan. 1, 2012. Amended by Stats.2013, c. 729 (A.B.170), § 3.)*

Law Revision Commission Comments

Section 31110 continues former Section 12289.5 without substantive change.

See Sections 16970 ("person"), 30510 ("assault weapon"), 30515 (further clarification of "assault weapon"). [38 Cal.L.Rev.Comm. Reports 217 (2009)].

Cross References

Assault weapon defined for purposes of this Part, see Penal Code §§ 30510, 30515.
Person defined, see Penal Code § 16970.

Research References

2 Witkin, California Criminal Law 4th Crimes Against Public Peace and Welfare § 221 (2021), Permits and Conditions for Possession.

§ 31115. Education and notification program regarding registration of assault weapons and .50 BMG rifles

(a) The Department of Justice shall conduct a public education and notification program regarding the registration of assault weapons and the definition of the weapons set forth in Section 30515 and former Section 12276.1, as it read at any time from when it was added by Section 7 of Chapter 129 of the Statutes of 1999 to when it was repealed by the Deadly Weapons Recodification Act of 2010.

(b) The public education and notification program shall include outreach to local law enforcement agencies and utilization of public service announcements in a variety of media approaches, to ensure maximum publicity of the limited forgiveness period of the registration requirement specified in subdivision (f) of former Section 12285, as that subdivision read in Section 5 of Chapter 954 of the Statutes of 1991, and the consequences of nonregistration. The department shall develop posters describing gunowners' responsibilities under former Chapter 2.3 (commencing with Section 12275) of Title 2 of Part 4, as that chapter read when the forgiveness period commenced on January 1, 1992, which shall be posted in a conspicuous place in every licensed gun store in the state during the forgiveness period.

(c) For .50 BMG rifles, the department's education campaign shall provide materials to dealers of .50 BMG rifles, and to recognized national associations that specialize in .50 BMG rifles.

(d) Any costs incurred by the Department of Justice to implement this section, which cannot be absorbed by the department, shall be funded from the Dealers' Record of Sale Special Account, as set forth in Section 28235, or former Section 12076 as it read at any time from when it was amended by Section 1.7 of Chapter 954 of the Statutes of 1991 to when it was repealed by Section 12 of Chapter 606 of the Statutes of 1993, or former Section 12076 as it read at any time from when it was enacted by Section 13 of Chapter 606 of the Statutes of 1993 to when it was repealed by the Deadly Weapons Recodification Act of 2010, upon appropriation by the Legislature. *(Added by Stats.2010, c. 711 (S.B.1080), § 6, operative Jan. 1, 2012.)*

Law Revision Commission Comments

Section 31115 continues former Section 12289 without substantive change.

Subdivision (a) refers to former Section 12276.1, which became operative on January 1, 2000. As subsequently amended to exempt certain weapons, it is continued in Section 30515 (further clarification of "assault weapon").

Subdivision (b) refers to former Section 12285(f), as it existed when the forgiveness period commenced on January 1, 1992. As subsequently amended, that provision is continued in Section 30960(a).

Subdivision (b) also refers to "former Chapter 2.3 (commencing with Section 12275) of Title 2 of Part 4, as that chapter read when the forgiveness period commenced on January 1, 1992." As subsequently amended, former Chapter 2.3 (former Sections 12275–12290) is continued in this chapter (except some definitions that are located in "Division 2. Definitions" of Title 1).

Subdivision (d) refers to the language in former Section 12076 relating to the Dealers' Record of Sale Special Account. That language was originally located in subdivision (d) of former Section 12076. See 1991 Cal. Stat. ch. 954, § 1.7. It was later relabeled as subdivision (f). See 1992 Cal. Stat. ch. 1326, § 8. Section 12076 was then repealed and replaced by a new Section 12076. Again, the language relating to the Dealers' Record of Sale Special Account was located in subdivision (f). See 1993 Cal. Stat. ch. 606, §§ 12, 13. It was later relabeled as subdivision (g) and remained so labeled until it was repealed by the Deadly Weapons Recodification Act of 2010. See 1997 Cal. Stat. ch. 462, § 6; 2008 Cal. Stat. ch. 698, § 18.

As originally enacted, former Section 12289 referred to "the Dealers' Record of Sale Special Account, as set forth in *subdivision (d)* of Section 12076." See 1991 Cal. Stat. ch. 954, § 6 (emphasis added). The cross-reference to subdivision (d) was correct at that time, but it was never revised to reflect the subsequent relabeling of the language relating to the Dealers' Record of Sale Special Account. See 1999 Cal. Stat. ch. 129, § 11; 2004 Cal. Stat. ch. 494, § 14.

That problem is corrected in this section. Specifically, subdivision (d) does not cross-refer to Section 28220, which continues former Section 12076(d). Instead, subdivision (d) cross-refers to Section 28235, which continues the language from former Section 12076 relating to the Dealers' Record of Sale Special Account.

See Sections 16970 ("person"), 30510 ("assault weapon"), 30515 (further clarification of "assault weapon"), 30530 (".50 BMG rifle"). See also Section 16010 (continuation of existing law). [38 Cal.L.Rev.Comm. Reports 217 (2009)].

Cross References

.50 BMG rifle defined for purposes of this Part, see Penal Code § 30530.
Assault weapon defined for purposes of this Part, see Penal Code §§ 30510, 30515.

CHAPTER 3. BODY ARMOR

Section

§ 31310. Certification requirement

No body armor shall be acquired by the commissioner pursuant to Section 2259.5 of the Vehicle Code unless, pursuant to subdivision (a) of Section 31315, the Department of Justice has certified the body armor. *(Added by Stats.2010, c. 711 (S.B.1080), § 6, operative Jan. 1, 2012.)*

Law Revision Commission Comments

Section 31310 continues former Section 12360 without substantive change. [38 Cal.L.Rev.Comm. Reports 217 (2009)].

§ 31315. Establishment of body armor standards; certification

(a) Before any body armor may be purchased for use by state peace officers, the Department of Justice, after consultation with the Department of the California Highway Patrol, shall establish minimum ballistic performance standards, and shall determine that the armor satisfies those standards.

(b) Only body armor that meets state requirements under subdivision (a) for acquisition or purchase shall be eligible for testing for certification under the ballistic performance standards established by the Department of Justice.

(c) Only body armor that is certified as acceptable by the department shall be purchased for use by state peace officers. *(Added by Stats.2010, c. 711 (S.B.1080), § 6, operative Jan. 1, 2012. Amended by Stats.2011, c. 296 (A.B.1023), § 241.)*

Law Revision Commission Comments

Section 31315 continues former Section 12361 without substantive change. [38 Cal.L.Rev.Comm. Reports 217 (2009)].

§ 31320. Manufacturers and sellers of body armor; application for certification; reimbursement of state for testing and certification expenses

(a) Any person engaged in the manufacture or sale of body armor may apply to the Department of Justice for certification that a particular type of body armor manufactured or sold by that person is acceptable.

(b) The applicant shall reimburse the state for any actual expenses incurred by the state in testing and certifying a particular type of body armor. *(Added by Stats.2010, c. 711 (S.B.1080), § 6, operative Jan. 1, 2012.)*

Law Revision Commission Comments

Section 31320 continues former Section 12362 without substantive change. [38 Cal.L.Rev.Comm. Reports 217 (2009)].

§ 31325. Applications for certification; contents

Any application submitted pursuant to Section 31320 shall contain all of the following:

(a) Full written reports of any investigation conducted for the purpose of determining whether the body armor is acceptable.

(b) A full written statement of the design of the body armor.

(c) A full written statement of the methods used in, and the facilities and controls used for, the manufacture of the body armor.

(d) Any samples of the body armor and its components as the Department of Justice may require.

(e) Specimens of the instructions and advertisements used or proposed to be used for the body armor. *(Added by Stats.2010, c. 711 (S.B.1080), § 6, operative Jan. 1, 2012.)*

Law Revision Commission Comments

Section 31325 continues former Section 12363 without substantive change. [38 Cal.L.Rev.Comm. Reports 217 (2009)].

§ 31330. Ballistic testing schedule for body armor certification

The Department of Justice, in cooperation with the office of procurement of the Department of General Services, shall establish a schedule for ballistic testing for certification pursuant to subdivision (b) of Section 31315. *(Added by Stats.2010, c. 711 (S.B.1080), § 6, operative Jan. 1, 2012.)*

Law Revision Commission Comments

Section 31330 continues former Section 12364 without substantive change. [38 Cal.L.Rev.Comm. Reports 217 (2009)].

Cross References

Department of General Services, generally, see Government Code § 14600 et seq.

§ 31335. Conditions requiring order refusing to certify body armor

The Department of Justice shall issue an order refusing to certify a body armor as acceptable if, after due notice to the applicant, the department finds any of the following:

(a) That the body armor does not satisfy the ballistic performance standards established by the department pursuant to subdivision (b) of Section 31315.

(b) That the application contains any misrepresentation of a material fact.

(c) That the application is materially incomplete.

(d) That the applicant has failed to reimburse the state as required by Section 31320. *(Added by Stats.2010, c. 711 (S.B.1080), § 6, operative Jan. 1, 2012.)*

Law Revision Commission Comments

Section 31335 continues former Section 12365 without substantive change. [38 Cal.L.Rev.Comm. Reports 217 (2009)].

§ 31340. Order of revocation for certification of body armor; conditions justifying

The Department of Justice shall issue an order revoking certification of a body armor if, after due notice to the applicant, the department finds any of the following:

(a) The experience or additional testing show that the body armor does not comply with the department's ballistic performance standards.

(b) The application contains any misrepresentation of a material fact.

(c) The body armor must be retested for certification under new department standards. *(Added by Stats.2010, c. 711 (S.B.1080), § 6, operative Jan. 1, 2012.)*

Law Revision Commission Comments

Section 31340 continues former Section 12366 without substantive change. [38 Cal.L.Rev.Comm. Reports 217 (2009)].

§ 31345. Purchases of certified body armor on behalf of state agencies or departments; availability to peace officers of Department of Justice

(a) All purchases of certified body armor under the provisions of this chapter shall be made by the Department of General Services on behalf of an authorized state agency or department. Purchases of body armor shall be based upon written requests submitted by an authorized state agency or department to the Department of General Services.

(b) The Department of General Services shall make certified body armor available to peace officers of the Department of Justice, as defined by Section 830.3, while engaged in law enforcement activities. *(Added by Stats.2010, c. 711 (S.B.1080), § 6, operative Jan. 1, 2012.)*

Law Revision Commission Comments

Section 31345 continues former Section 12368 without substantive change. [38 Cal.L.Rev.Comm. Reports 217 (2009)].

Cross References

Department of General Services, generally, see Government Code § 14600 et seq.

§ 31350. Definition of enforcement activities; development of standards regarding what constitutes sufficient wear to necessitate replacement of body armor

The Department of General Services shall, pursuant to departmental regulation, after consultation with the Department of the California Highway Patrol, define the term "enforcement activities" for purposes of this chapter, and develop standards regarding what constitutes sufficient wear on body armor to necessitate replacement of the body armor. *(Added by Stats.2010, c. 711 (S.B.1080), § 6, operative Jan. 1, 2012.)*

Law Revision Commission Comments

Section 31350 continues former Section 12369 without substantive change. See also Sections 31330 (schedule for ballistic testing), 31355 (Department of Justice regulations). [38 Cal.L.Rev.Comm. Reports 217 (2009)].

Cross References

Department of General Services, generally, see Government Code § 14600 et seq.

§ 31355. Regulations

The Department of Justice shall adopt and promulgate regulations for the fair and efficient enforcement of this chapter. *(Added by Stats.2010, c. 711 (S.B.1080), § 6, operative Jan. 1, 2012.)*

Law Revision Commission Comments

Section 31355 continues former Section 12367 without substantive change. See also Sections 31330 (schedule for ballistic testing), 31350 (process for defining "enforcement activities" and developing standards for replacement of body armor). [38 Cal.L.Rev.Comm. Reports 217 (2009)].

§ 31360. Purchase, ownership, or possession of body armor by persons convicted of violent felonies; penalties; exemptions

(a) A person who has been convicted of a violent felony under the laws of the United States, the State of California, or any other state, government, or country, who purchases, owns, or possesses body armor, as defined in Section 16288, except as authorized under subdivision (b), is guilty of a felony, punishable by imprisonment in state prison for 16 months, or two or three years.

(b) A person whose employment, livelihood, or safety is dependent on the ability to legally possess and use body armor, who is subject to the prohibition imposed by subdivision (a) due to a prior violent felony conviction, may file a petition for an exception to this prohibition with the chief of police or county sheriff of the jurisdiction in which that person seeks to possess and use the body armor. The chief of police or sheriff may reduce or eliminate the prohibition, impose conditions on reduction or elimination of the prohibition, or otherwise grant relief from the prohibition as the chief of police or sheriff deems appropriate, based on the following:

(1) A finding that the petitioner is likely to use body armor in a safe and lawful manner.

(2) A finding that the petitioner has a reasonable need for this type of protection under the circumstances.

In making its decision, the chief of police or sheriff shall consider the petitioner's continued employment, the interests of justice, any relevant evidence, and the totality of the circumstances. It is the intent of the Legislature that law enforcement officials exercise broad discretion in fashioning appropriate relief under this paragraph in cases in which relief is warranted. However, this paragraph may not be construed to require law enforcement officials to grant relief to any particular petitioner. Relief from this prohibition does not relieve any other person or entity from any liability that might otherwise be imposed.

(c) The chief of police or sheriff shall require, as a condition of granting an exception under subdivision (b), that the petitioner agree to maintain on the petitioner's person a certified copy of the law enforcement official's permission to possess and use body armor, including any conditions or limitations.

(d) Law enforcement officials who enforce the prohibition specified in subdivision (a) against a person who has been granted relief pursuant to subdivision (b), shall be immune from any liability for false arrest arising from the enforcement of this subdivision unless the person has in possession a certified copy of the permission granting the person relief from the prohibition, as required by subdivision (c). This immunity from liability does not relieve any person or entity from any other liability that might otherwise be imposed. *(Added by Stats.2010, c. 711 (S.B.1080), § 6, operative Jan. 1, 2012. Amended by Stats.2011, c. 15 (A.B.109), § 552, eff. April 4, 2011, operative Jan. 1, 2012; Stats.2012, c. 43 (S.B.1023), § 105, eff. June 27, 2012.)*

Law Revision Commission Comments

Section 31360 continues former Section 12370(a)-(d) without substantive change.

See Sections 16288 ("body armor"), 17320 ("violent felony"). [40 Cal. L.Rev.Comm. Reports 107 (2010)].

Cross References

Felonies, definition and penalties, see Penal Code §§ 17, 18.

Research References

California Jury Instructions - Criminal 12.57, Unlawful Possession of Body Armor.

2 Witkin, California Criminal Law 4th Crimes Against Public Peace and Welfare § 231 (2021), Other Weapons and Devices.

CHAPTER 4. HANDGUNS AND FIREARM SAFETY

ARTICLE 1. UNCONVENTIONAL PISTOL

§ 31500. Manufacture, import, sale, supply or possession of unconventional pistol; punishment

Except as provided in Chapter 1 (commencing with Section 17700) of Division 2 of Title 2, any person in this state who manufactures or causes to be manufactured, imports into the state, keeps for sale, or offers or exposes for sale, or who gives, lends, or possesses any unconventional pistol is punishable by imprisonment in a county jail not exceeding one year or imprisonment pursuant to subdivision (h) of Section 1170. *(Added by Stats.2010, c. 711 (S.B.1080), § 6, operative Jan. 1, 2012. Amended by Stats.2012, c. 43 (S.B.1023), § 106, eff. June 27, 2012.)*

Law Revision Commission Comments

With respect to an unconventional pistol, Section 31500 continues former Section 12020(a)(1) without substantive change.

For circumstances in which this section is inapplicable, see Sections 16590 ("generally prohibited weapon"), 17700–17745 (exemptions relating to generally prohibited weapons).

See Section 17270 ("unconventional pistol"). See also Sections 17800 (distinct and separate offense), 31590 (unconventional pistol constituting nuisance).

In addition to the provisions in this chapter, a number of other provisions within this part pertain specifically to handguns. For example, see Sections 25400–25700 (carrying concealed firearm), 26010 (person licensed to carry pistol, revolver, or other firearm capable of being concealed upon the person), 26300–26325 (retired peace officer carrying concealed and loaded firearm), 26820 (display of handgun or imitation or placard advertising handgun), 26840 (presentation of basic firearms safety certificate or handgun safety certificate to dealer), 26845 (no handgun delivery without proof of California residency), 26850–26859 (safe handling demonstration with handgun), 26905 (reporting of handgun acquisitions), 26960 (waiting period exception for sale, delivery, or transfer of handgun, not intended as merchandise, by dealer to self or another dealer), 27505 (transfer of handgun to person under age 21), 27510 (dealer that supplies, delivers, or gives possession or control of handgun to person under age 21), 27530 (transfer of handgun that lacks identifying information), 27560 (restrictions on personal handgun importer), 27565 (handgun that is curio or relic, transported into California by licensed collector), 27660 (waiting period exception for sale, delivery, or transfer of handgun, not intended as merchandise, by dealer to self or another dealer), 27875 (exception for infrequent transfer of handgun between members of same immediate family), 27920 (exception for person who takes title or possession of handgun by operation of law), 28160 (form for handgun), 29610–29615 (possession of handgun by minor). See also Sections 30300 (providing ammunition to minors and other young people), 30312 (delivery or transfer of ownership of handgun ammunition), 30315–30325 (restrictions relating to handgun ammunition designed primarily to penetrate metal or armor), 30345–30365 (handgun ammunition vendors). [38 Cal.L.Rev.Comm. Reports 217 (2009)].

Cross References

Penalty for possession of deadly weapon described in this section within State Capitol, legislative offices, etc., see Penal Code § 171c.
Pistol defined for purposes of this Part, see Penal Code § 16530.
Possession of deadly weapons with intent to assault, see Penal Code § 17500.
Unconventional pistol defined for purposes of this Part, see Penal Code § 17270.

Research References

2 Witkin, California Criminal Law 4th Crimes Against Public Peace and Welfare § 211 (2021), Nature of Crime.

§ 31590. Nuisance

Except as provided in Chapter 1 (commencing with Section 17700) of Division 2 of Title 2, any unconventional pistol is a nuisance and is subject to Section 18010. *(Added by Stats.2010, c. 711 (S.B.1080), § 6, operative Jan. 1, 2012.)*

Law Revision Commission Comments

With respect to an unconventional pistol, Section 31590 continues the first part of the first sentence of former Section 12029 without substantive change.

See Section 17270 ("unconventional pistol"). [38 Cal.L.Rev.Comm. Reports 217 (2009)].

Cross References

Pistol defined for purposes of this Part, see Penal Code § 16530.
Unconventional pistol defined for purposes of this Part, see Penal Code § 17270.

Research References

2 Witkin, California Criminal Law 4th Crimes Against Public Peace and Welfare § 263 (2021), Nuisances.

ARTICLE 2. FIREARM SAFETY CERTIFICATE

§ 31610. Legislative intent

(a) It is the intent of the Legislature in enacting this article to require that persons who obtain firearms have a basic familiarity with those firearms, including, but not limited to, the safe handling and storage of those firearms. It is not the intent of the Legislature to require a firearm safety certificate for the mere possession of a firearm.

(b) This section shall become operative on January 1, 2015. *(Added by Stats.2013, c. 761 (S.B.683), § 15, operative Jan. 1, 2015.)*

Cross References

Firearm defined for purposes of this Part, see Penal Code § 16520.
Handgun defined for purposes of this Part, see Penal Code § 16640.
Handgun safety certificate defined for purposes of this Part, see Penal Code § 16670.

Research References

2 Witkin, California Criminal Law 4th Crimes Against Public Peace and Welfare § 195 (2021), In General.
2 Witkin, California Criminal Law 4th Crimes Against Public Peace and Welfare § 197 (2021), Time and Manner of Delivery by Dealer.

§ 31615. Prohibition on purchase or receipt of, or sale, delivery, loan, or transfer of a firearm to a person lacking a valid safety certificate; penalties

(a) A person shall not do either of the following:

(1) Purchase or receive any firearm, except an antique firearm, without a valid firearm safety certificate, except that in the case of a handgun, an unexpired handgun safety certificate may be used.

(2) Sell, deliver, loan, or transfer any firearm, except an antique firearm, to any person who does not have a valid firearm safety certificate, except that in the case of a handgun, an unexpired handgun safety certificate may be used.

(b) Any person who violates subdivision (a) is guilty of a misdemeanor.

(c) The provisions of this section are cumulative, and shall not be construed as restricting the application of any other law. However, an act or omission punishable in different ways by different provisions of this code shall not be punished under more than one provision.

(d) This section shall become operative on January 1, 2015. *(Added by Stats.2013, c. 761 (S.B.683), § 17, operative Jan. 1, 2015.)*

Cross References

Antique firearm defined, see Penal Code § 16170.
Community care facilities, acceptance or storage of client's firearm does not constitute loan, sale, receipt, or transfer, see Health and Safety Code § 1567.94.
Firearm defined for purposes of this Part, see Penal Code § 16520.
Handgun defined for purposes of this Part, see Penal Code § 16640.
Handgun safety certificate defined for purposes of this Part, see Penal Code § 16670.
Loan of firearm other than handgun or semiautomatic centerfire rifle to minor, application of this section, see Penal Code § 31833.
Misdemeanors, definition and penalties, see Penal Code §§ 17, 19, 19.2.
Residential care facilities for persons with chronic life-threatening illness, acceptance or storage of resident's firearm does not constitute loan, sale, receipt, or transfer, see Health and Safety Code § 1568.099.
Residential care facilities for the elderly, acceptance or storage of resident's firearm does not constitute loan, sale, receipt, or transfer, see Health and Safety Code § 1569.284.
Sales, deliveries, or transfers of firearms between or to importers and manufacturers of ammunition, application of this section, see Penal Code § 31834.

§ 31620. Acts of collusion, alteration, counterfeiting, or falsification relating to firearm or handgun safety certificates or use thereof; penalties

(a) A person shall not commit an act of collusion as specified in Section 27550.

(b) Any person who alters, counterfeits, or falsifies a handgun safety certificate, or who uses or attempts to use any altered, counterfeited, or falsified handgun safety certificate to purchase a handgun, is guilty of a misdemeanor.

(c) Commencing January 1, 2015, any person who alters, counterfeits, or falsifies a firearm safety certificate, or who uses or attempts to use any altered, counterfeited, or falsified firearm safety certificate to purchase a firearm, is guilty of a misdemeanor.

(d) The provisions of this section are cumulative and shall not be construed as restricting the application of any other law. However, an act or omission punishable in different ways by this section and different provisions of this code shall not be punished under more than one provision. *(Added by Stats.2010, c. 711 (S.B.1080), § 6, operative Jan. 1, 2012. Amended by Stats.2013, c. 761 (S.B.683), § 18.)*

Law Revision Commission Comments

Section 31620 continues former Section 12802 without substantive change.

See Sections 16640 ("handgun"), 16670 ("handgun safety certificate"). [38 Cal.L.Rev.Comm. Reports 217 (2009)].

Cross References

Handgun defined for purposes of this Part, see Penal Code § 16640.
Handgun safety certificate defined for purposes of this Part, see Penal Code § 16670.
Misdemeanors, definition and penalties, see Penal Code §§ 17, 19, 19.2.

§ 31625. Issuance of firearm safety certificate; proof of compliance with article; age limitation; violation

(a) A certified instructor shall not issue a firearm safety certificate to any person who has not complied with this article. Proof of compliance shall be forwarded to the department by certified instructors as frequently as the department may determine.

(b) A certified instructor shall not issue a firearm safety certificate to any person who is under 18 years of age.

(c) A violation of this section shall be grounds for the department to revoke the instructor's certification to issue firearm safety certificates.

(d) This section shall become operative on January 1, 2015. *(Added by Stats.2013, c. 761 (S.B.683), § 20, operative Jan. 1, 2015.)*

Cross References

Certified instructor defined, see Penal Code § 16370.
Department defined, see Penal Code § 16450.
Handgun defined for purposes of this Part, see Penal Code § 16640.
Handgun safety certificate defined for purposes of this Part, see Penal Code § 16670.

§ 31630. Firearm safety certificate instructional materials

(a) The department shall develop an instruction manual in English and in Spanish. The department shall make the instruction manual available to firearm dealers licensed pursuant to Sections 26700 to 26915, inclusive, who shall make it available to the general public. Essential portions of the manual may be included in the pamphlet described in Section 34205.

(b) The department shall develop audiovisual materials in English and in Spanish to be issued to instructors certified by the department.

(c) The department shall solicit input from any reputable association or organization, including any law enforcement association that has as one of its objectives the promotion of firearm safety, in the development of the firearm safety certificate instructional materials.

(d) The instruction manual shall prominently include the following firearm safety warning:

Firearms must be handled responsibly and securely stored to prevent access by children and other unauthorized users. California has strict laws pertaining to firearms, and you can be fined or imprisoned if you fail to comply with them. Visit the Web site of the California Attorney General at https://oag.ca.gov/firearms for information on firearm laws applicable to you and how you can comply. *(Added by Stats.2013, c. 761 (S.B.683), § 22, operative Jan. 1, 2015. Amended by Stats.2017, c. 825 (A.B.1525), § 4, eff. Jan. 1, 2018; Stats.2018, c. 92 (S.B.1289), § 170, eff. Jan. 1, 2019.)*

Cross References

Department defined, see Penal Code § 16450.
Firearm defined for purposes of this Part, see Penal Code § 16520.
Handgun defined for purposes of this Part, see Penal Code § 16640.
Handgun safety certificate defined for purposes of this Part, see Penal Code § 16670.

§ 31635. Instructors; minimum skill, knowledge, and competency; entities from whom instructor applicants may receive training certification

(a) The department shall prescribe a minimum level of skill, knowledge, and competency to be required of all firearm safety certificate instructors.

(b) Department Certified Instructor applicants shall have a certification to provide training from one of the following organizations, as specified, or any entity found by the department to give comparable instruction in firearms safety, or the applicant shall have similar or equivalent training to that provided by the following, as determined by the department:

(1) Department of Consumer Affairs, State of California–Firearm Training Instructor.

(2) Director of Civilian Marksmanship, Instructor or Rangemaster.

(3) Federal Government, Certified Rangemaster or Firearm Instructor.

(4) Federal Law Enforcement Training Center, Firearm Instructor Training Program or Rangemaster.

(5) United States Military, Military Occupational Specialty (MOS) as marksmanship or firearms instructor. Assignment as Range Officer or Safety Officer is not sufficient.

(6) National Rifle Association–Certified Instructor, Law Enforcement Instructor, Rangemaster, or Training Counselor.

(7) Commission on Peace Officer Standards and Training (POST), State of California–Firearm Instructor or Rangemaster.

(8) Authorization from a State of California accredited school to teach a firearm training course.

(c) This section shall become operative on January 1, 2015. *(Added by Stats.2013, c. 761 (S.B.683), § 24, operative Jan. 1, 2015.)*

Cross References

Certified instructor defined, see Penal Code § 16370.
Department defined, see Penal Code § 16450.
Firearm defined for purposes of this Part, see Penal Code § 16520.
Handgun defined for purposes of this Part, see Penal Code § 16640.
Handgun safety certificate defined for purposes of this Part, see Penal Code § 16670.

§ 31640. Written test; contents; warning

(a) The department shall develop a written objective test, in English and in Spanish, and prescribe its content, form, and manner, to be administered by an instructor certified by the department.

(b) If the person taking the test is unable to read, the test shall be administered orally. If the person taking the test is unable to read English or Spanish, the test may be administered orally by a translator.

(c) The test shall cover, but not be limited to, all of the following:

(1) The laws applicable to carrying and handling firearms, particularly handguns.

(2) The responsibilities of ownership of firearms, particularly handguns.

(3) Current law as it relates to the private sale and transfer of firearms.

(4) Current law as it relates to the permissible use of lethal force.

(5) What constitutes safe firearm storage.

(6) Issues associated with bringing a firearm into the home, including suicide.

(7) Prevention strategies to address issues associated with bringing firearms into the home.

(d) Commencing January 1, 2019, the test shall require the applicant to be provided with, and acknowledge receipt of, the following warning information:

(1) "Firearms must be handled responsibly and securely stored to prevent access by children and other unauthorized users. California has strict laws pertaining to firearms and you can be fined or imprisoned if you fail to comply with them. Visit the website of the California Attorney General at https://oag.ca.gov/firearms for information on firearm laws applicable to you and how you can comply."

(2) "If you decide to sell or give your firearm to someone, you must generally complete a 'Dealer Record of Sale (DROS)' form and conduct the transfer through a licensed firearms dealer. Remember, it is generally a crime to transfer a firearm without first filling out this form. If the police recover a firearm that was involved in a crime, the firearm's previous owner may be prosecuted if the previous owner did not fill out the DROS form. Please make sure you go to a licensed firearms dealer and fill out that form if you want to sell or give away your firearm."

(3) "If you or someone you know is contemplating suicide, please call the national suicide prevention lifeline at 1–800–273–TALK (8255)."

(e)(1) The department shall update test materials related to this article at least once every five years.

(2) The department shall update the internet website referenced in subdivision (d) regularly to reflect current laws and regulations.

(f) A dealer licensed pursuant to Sections 26700 to 26915, inclusive, or an employee, or a managing officer or partner certified as an instructor pursuant to this article, shall designate a separate room or partitioned area for a person to take the objective test, and maintain adequate supervision to ensure that no acts of collusion occur while the objective test is being administered.

(g) This section shall become operative on June 1, 2020. *(Added by Stats.2019, c. 729 (A.B.645), § 6, eff. Jan. 1, 2020, operative June 1, 2020.)*

Cross References

Department defined, see Penal Code § 16450.
Firearm defined for purposes of this Part, see Penal Code § 16520.
Handgun defined for purposes of this Part, see Penal Code § 16640.

§ 31645. Written test; minimum passing grade; issuance of certificate; retaking test after failure to pass

(a) An applicant for a firearm safety certificate shall successfully pass the objective test referred to in Section 31640, with a passing grade of at least 75 percent. Any person receiving a passing grade on the objective test shall immediately be issued a firearm safety certificate by the instructor, provided that, commencing January 1, 2019, the applicant has acknowledged receipt of the firearm safety warning required by subdivision (d) of Section 31640.

(b) An applicant who fails to pass the objective test upon the first attempt shall be offered additional instructional materials by the instructor, such as a videotape or booklet. The person may not retake the objective test under any circumstances until 24 hours have elapsed after the failure to pass the objective test upon the first attempt. The person failing the test on the first attempt shall take another version of the test upon the second attempt. All tests shall be taken from the same instructor except upon permission by the department, which shall be granted only for good cause shown. The instructor shall make himself or herself available to the applicant during regular business hours in order to retake the test. *(Added by Stats.2013, c. 761 (S.B.683), § 28, operative Jan. 1, 2015. Amended by Stats.2017, c. 825 (A.B.1525), § 6, eff. Jan. 1, 2018.)*

Cross References

Department defined, see Penal Code § 16450.
Handgun defined for purposes of this Part, see Penal Code § 16640.
Handgun safety certificate defined for purposes of this Part, see Penal Code § 16670.

§ 31650. Fees

(a) The certified instructor may charge a fee of twenty-five dollars ($25), fifteen dollars ($15) of which is to be paid to the department pursuant to subdivision (c).

(b) An applicant to renew a firearm safety certificate shall be required to pass the objective test. The certified instructor may charge a fee of twenty-five dollars ($25), fifteen dollars ($15) of which is to be forwarded to the department pursuant to subdivision (c).

(c) The department may charge the certified instructor up to fifteen dollars ($15) for each firearm safety certificate issued by that instructor to cover the department's cost in carrying out and enforcing this article, and enforcing the provisions listed in subdivision (e), as determined annually by the department.

(d) All money received by the department pursuant to this article shall be deposited into the Firearms Safety and Enforcement Special Fund created pursuant to Section 28300.

(e) The department shall conduct enforcement activities, including, but not limited to, law enforcement activities to ensure compliance with the following provisions:

(1) Section 830.95.

(2) Title 2 (commencing with Section 12001) of Part 4.

(3) This part, except Sections 16965, 17235, and 21510.

(f) This section shall become operative on January 1, 2015. *(Added by Stats.2013, c. 761 (S.B.683), § 30, operative Jan. 1, 2015.)*

Cross References

Certified instructor defined, see Penal Code § 16370.
Department defined, see Penal Code § 16450.
Firearm defined for purposes of this Part, see Penal Code § 16520.
Handgun defined for purposes of this Part, see Penal Code § 16640.
Handgun safety certificate defined for purposes of this Part, see Penal Code § 16670.

§ 31655. Certificates; contents; expiration

(a) The department shall develop firearm safety certificates to be issued by instructors certified by the department to those persons who have complied with this article.

(b) A firearm safety certificate shall include, but not be limited to, the following information:

(1) A unique firearm safety certificate identification number.

(2) The holder's full name.

(3) The holder's date of birth.

(4) The holder's driver's license or identification number.

(5) The holder's signature.

(6) The signature of the issuing instructor.

(7) The date of issuance.

(c) The firearm safety certificate shall expire five years after the date that it was issued by the certified instructor.

(d) This section shall become operative on January 1, 2015. *(Added by Stats.2013, c. 761 (S.B.683), § 32, operative Jan. 1, 2015.)*

Cross References

Certified instructor defined, see Penal Code § 16370.
Department defined, see Penal Code § 16450.
Handgun defined for purposes of this Part, see Penal Code § 16640.
Handgun safety certificate defined for purposes of this Part, see Penal Code § 16670.

§ 31660. Duplicate certificates; fees

(a) In the case of loss or destruction of a firearm safety certificate, the issuing instructor shall issue a duplicate certificate upon request and proof of identification to the certificate holder.

(b) In the case of loss or destruction of a handgun safety certificate, the issuing instructor shall issue a duplicate certificate upon request and proof of identification to the certificate holder, which shall be valid only for the balance of the unexpired term of the original certificate.

(c) The department may authorize the issuing instructor to charge a fee, not to exceed fifteen dollars ($15), for a duplicate certificate. Revenues from this fee shall be deposited in the Firearms Safety and Enforcement Special Fund created pursuant to Section 28300.

(d) This section shall become operative on January 1, 2015. *(Added by Stats.2013, c. 761 (S.B.683), § 34, operative Jan. 1, 2015.)*

Cross References

Department defined, see Penal Code § 16450.
Firearm defined for purposes of this Part, see Penal Code § 16520.
Handgun defined for purposes of this Part, see Penal Code § 16640.
Handgun safety certificate defined for purposes of this Part, see Penal Code § 16670.

§ 31665. Immunity from liability

The department shall be immune from any liability arising from implementing Sections 31630, 31635, 31640, and subdivision (a) of Section 31655. *(Added by Stats.2010, c. 711 (S.B.1080), § 6, operative Jan. 1, 2012.)*

Law Revision Commission Comments

Section 31665 continues former Section 12804(h) without substantive change.

See Section 16450 ("department"). [38 Cal.L.Rev.Comm. Reports 217 (2009)].

Cross References

Department defined, see Penal Code § 16450.

§ 31670. Operative date of former Article 8 (commencing with Section 12800)

Except for the provisions of former Section 12804, former Article 8 (commencing with Section 12800) of Chapter 6 of Title 2 of Part 4, as added by Section 10 of Chapter 942 of the Statutes of 2001, became operative on January 1, 2003. *(Added by Stats.2010, c. 711 (S.B. 1080), § 6, operative Jan. 1, 2012.)*

Law Revision Commission Comments

Section 31670 continues former Section 12809 without substantive change.

Former Article 8 of Chapter 6 of Title 2 of Part 4, entitled "Handgun Safety Certificate," consisted of former Sections 12800–12809. One provision in that article, former Section 12804, became operative on January 1, 2002. It is continued in Sections 31630, 31635, 31640, 31655(a), and 31665. The remainder of the article had a delayed operative date of January 1, 2003. Those provisions are continued in Sections 31610–31625, 31645–31650, 31655(b)-(c), 31660, and 31700. [38 Cal.L.Rev.Comm. Reports 217 (2009)].

ARTICLE 3. EXCEPTIONS TO FIREARM SAFETY CERTIFICATE REQUIREMENT

Section

§ 31700. Persons exempt

(a) The following persons, properly identified, are exempted from the firearm safety certificate requirement in subdivision (a) of Section 31615:

(1) Any active or honorably retired peace officer, as defined in Chapter 4.5 (commencing with Section 830) of Title 3 of Part 2.

(2) Any active or honorably retired federal officer or law enforcement agent.

(3) Any reserve peace officer, as defined in Section 832.6.

(4) Any person who has successfully completed the course of training specified in Section 832.

(5) A firearms dealer licensed pursuant to Sections 26700 to 26915, inclusive, who is acting in the course and scope of that person's activities as a person licensed pursuant to Sections 26700 to 26915, inclusive.

(6) A federally licensed collector who is acquiring or being loaned a firearm that is a curio or relic, as defined in Section 478.11 of Title 27 of the Code of Federal Regulations, who has a current certificate of eligibility issued by the department pursuant to Section 26710.

(7) Except as provided in subdivision (d), a person to whom a firearm is being returned, where the person receiving the firearm is the owner of the firearm.

(8) A family member of a peace officer or deputy sheriff from a local agency who receives a firearm pursuant to Section 50081 of the Government Code.

(9) Any individual who has a valid concealed weapons permit issued pursuant to Chapter 4 (commencing with Section 26150) of Division 5.

(10) An active or honorably retired member of the United States Armed Forces, the National Guard, the Air National Guard, or the active reserve components of the United States, where individuals in those organizations are properly identified. For purposes of this section, proper identification includes the Armed Forces Identification Card or other written documentation certifying that the individual is an active or honorably retired member.

(11) Any person who is authorized to carry loaded firearms pursuant to Section 26025 or 26030.

(12) Persons who are the holders of a special weapons permit issued by the department pursuant to Section 32650 or 33300, pursuant to Article 3 (commencing with Section 18900) of Chapter 1 of Division 5 of Title 2, or pursuant to Article 4 (commencing with Section 32700) of Chapter 6 of this division.

(b) The following persons who take title or possession of a firearm by operation of law in a representative capacity, until or unless they transfer title ownership of the firearm to themselves in a personal capacity, are exempted from the firearm safety certificate requirement in subdivision (a) of Section 31615:

(1) The executor, personal representative, or administrator of an estate.

(2) A secured creditor or an agent or employee thereof when the firearms are possessed as collateral for, or as a result of, a default under a security agreement under the Commercial Code.

(3) A levying officer, as defined in Section 481.140, 511.060, or 680.260 of the Code of Civil Procedure.

(4) A receiver performing the functions of a receiver.

(5) A trustee in bankruptcy performing the duties of a trustee.

(6) An assignee for the benefit of creditors performing the functions of an assignee.

(7) The trustee of a trust that includes a firearm and that was part of a will that created the trust.

(8) A person acting pursuant to the person's power of attorney in accordance with Division 4.5 (commencing with Section 4000) of the Probate Code.

(9) A limited or general conservator appointed by a court pursuant to the Probate Code or Welfare and Institutions Code.

(10) A guardian ad litem appointed by a court pursuant to Section 372 of the Code of Civil Procedure.

(11) The trustee of a trust that includes a firearm that is under court supervision.

(12) A special administrator appointed by a court pursuant to Section 8540 of the Probate Code.

(13) A guardian appointed by a court pursuant to Section 1500 of the Probate Code.

(c) A person, 18 years of age or older, validly identified, who has been issued a valid hunting license that is unexpired is exempt from the firearm safety certificate requirement in subdivision (a) of Section 31615, except as to handguns.

(d) A person who takes possession of a firearm and complies with Section 27922 by delivering the firearm to a law enforcement agency is exempted from the firearm safety certificate requirement in subdivision (a) of Section 31615. The exemption set forth in paragraph (7) of subdivision (a) shall not apply to the return of that firearm to that person, if the person has requested the firearm and is eligible to receive it.

(e) The firearm safety certificate requirement in subdivision (a) of Section 31615 shall not apply to a person taking possession of a firearm pursuant to Section 27882 or 27883. *(Added by Stats.2013, c. 761 (S.B.683), § 37, operative Jan. 1, 2015. Amended by Stats.2018, c. 185 (A.B.2176), § 10, eff. Jan. 1, 2019; Stats.2019, c. 110 (A.B.1292), § 10, eff. Jan. 1, 2020; Stats.2019, c. 840 (S.B.172), § 14.5, eff. Jan. 1, 2020; Stats.2021, c. 250 (S.B.715), § 25, eff. Jan. 1, 2022.)*

Law Revision Commission Comments

Section 31700(b)(2) is amended to delete duplicative language. This is a nonsubstantive change.

Subdivision (c) is amended to correct a typographical error. [44 Cal.L.Rev. Comm. Reports 471 (2015)].

Cross References

Department defined, see Penal Code § 16450.
Firearm defined for purposes of this Part, see Penal Code § 16520.
Handgun defined for purposes of this Part, see Penal Code § 16640.
Handgun safety certificate defined for purposes of this Part, see Penal Code § 16670.

§ 31705. Sales, deliveries, or transfers of firearms to authorized law enforcement representatives of state or federal government; proper written authorization defined; entry of record into Automated Firearms System (AFS)

(a) Subdivision (a) of Section 31615 does not apply to any sale, delivery, or transfer of firearms made to an authorized law enforcement representative of any city, county, city and county, or state, or of the federal government, for exclusive use by that governmental agency if, prior to the sale, delivery, or transfer of these firearms, written authorization from the head of the agency authorizing the transaction is presented to the person from whom the purchase, delivery, or transfer is being made.

(b) Proper written authorization is defined as verifiable written certification from the head of the agency by which the purchaser or transferee is employed, identifying the employee as an individual authorized to conduct the transaction, and authorizing the transaction for the exclusive use of the agency by which that person is employed.

(c) Within 10 days of the date a handgun, and commencing January 1, 2014, any firearm, is acquired by the agency, a record of the same shall be entered as an institutional weapon into the Automated Firearms System (AFS) via the California Law Enforcement Telecommunications System (CLETS) by the law enforcement or state agency. Any agency without access to AFS shall arrange with the sheriff of the county in which the agency is located to input this information via this system. *(Added by Stats.2010, c. 711 (S.B.1080), § 6, operative Jan. 1, 2012. Amended by Stats.2011, c. 745 (A.B.809), § 66.)*

Law Revision Commission Comments

Section 31705 continues former Section 12078(a)(2) without substantive change, as that provision applied to former Section 12801(b).

For other exceptions relating to law enforcement, see Sections 31700, 31710–31720, 31730.

See Sections 16520 ("firearm"), 16640 ("handgun"). [38 Cal.L.Rev.Comm. Reports 217 (2009)].

Cross References

Firearm defined for purposes of this Part, see Penal Code § 16520.
Handgun defined for purposes of this Part, see Penal Code § 16640.

§ 31710. Loans of firearms by law enforcement agencies to peace officers for use in course and scope of officer's duties

Subdivision (a) of Section 31615 does not apply to the loan of a firearm if all of the following conditions are satisfied:

(a) The loan is made by an authorized law enforcement representative of a city, county, or city and county, or of the state or federal government.

(b) The loan is made to a peace officer employed by that agency and authorized to carry a firearm.

(c) The loan is made for the carrying and use of that firearm by that peace officer in the course and scope of the officer's duties. *(Added by Stats.2010, c. 711 (S.B.1080), § 6, operative Jan. 1, 2012.)*

Law Revision Commission Comments

Section 31710 continues former Section 12078(a)(3) without substantive change, as that provision applied to former Section 12801(b).

For other exceptions relating to law enforcement, see Sections 31700–31705, 31715–31720, 31730.

See Section 16520 ("firearm"). [38 Cal.L.Rev.Comm. Reports 217 (2009)].

Cross References

Firearm defined for purposes of this Part, see Penal Code § 16520.

§ 31715. Sale, delivery, or transfer of firearm by law enforcement agency to peace officer; entry of record into Automated Firearms System (AFS)

(a) Subdivision (a) of Section 31615 does not apply to the sale, delivery, or transfer of a firearm by a law enforcement agency to a peace officer pursuant to Section 10334 of the Public Contract Code.

(b) Within 10 days of the date that a handgun, and commencing January 1, 2014, any firearm, is sold, delivered, or transferred pursuant to Section 10334 of the Public Contract Code to that peace officer, the name of the officer and the make, model, serial number, and other identifying characteristics of the firearm being sold, delivered, or transferred shall be entered into the Automated Firearms System (AFS) via the California Law Enforcement Telecommunications System (CLETS) by the law enforcement or state agency that sold, delivered, or transferred the firearm, provided, however, that if the firearm is not a handgun and does not have a serial number, identification number, or identification mark assigned to it, that fact shall be noted in AFS. Any agency without access to AFS shall arrange with the sheriff of the county in which the agency is located to input this information via this system. *(Added by Stats.2010, c. 711 (S.B.1080), § 6, operative Jan. 1, 2012. Amended by Stats.2011, c. 745 (A.B.809), § 67.)*

Law Revision Commission Comments

Section 31715 continues former Section 12078(a)(4) without substantive change, as that provision applied to former Section 12801(b).

For other exceptions relating to law enforcement, see Sections 31700–31710, 31720, 31730.

See Sections 16520 ("firearm"), 16640 ("handgun"). [38 Cal.L.Rev.Comm. Reports 217 (2009)].

Cross References

Firearm defined for purposes of this Part, see Penal Code § 16520.
Handgun defined for purposes of this Part, see Penal Code § 16640.

§ 31720. Sales, deliveries, or transfers of firearms to retiring peace officers; entry of record in Automated Firearms System (AFS)

(a) Subdivision (a) of Section 31615 does not apply to the sale, delivery, or transfer of a firearm by a law enforcement agency to a retiring peace officer who is authorized to carry a firearm pursuant to Chapter 5 (commencing with Section 26300) of Division 5.

(b) Within 10 days of the date that a handgun, and commencing January 1, 2014, any firearm, is sold, delivered, or transferred to that retiring peace officer, the name of the officer and the make, model, serial number, and other identifying characteristics of the firearm being sold, delivered, or transferred shall be entered into the Automated Firearms System (AFS) via the California Law Enforcement Telecommunications System (CLETS) by the law enforcement or state agency that sold, delivered, or transferred the firearm, provided, however, that if the firearm is not a handgun and does not have a serial number, identification number, or identification mark assigned to it, that fact shall be noted in AFS. Any agency without access to AFS shall arrange with the sheriff of the county in which the agency is located to input this information via this system. *(Added by Stats.2010, c. 711 (S.B.1080), § 6, operative Jan. 1, 2012. Amended by Stats.2011, c. 745 (A.B.809), § 68.)*

Law Revision Commission Comments

Section 31720 continues former Section 12078(a)(5) without substantive change, as that provision applied to former Section 12801(b).

For other exceptions relating to law enforcement, see Sections 31700–31715, 31730.

See Sections 16520 ("firearm"), 16640 ("handgun"). [38 Cal.L.Rev.Comm. Reports 217 (2009)].

Cross References

Firearm defined for purposes of this Part, see Penal Code § 16520.
Handgun defined for purposes of this Part, see Penal Code § 16640.

§ 31725. Firearms buy-back programs

(a) Subdivision (a) of Section 31615 does not apply to a sale, delivery, or transfer of firearms if both of the following requirements are satisfied:

(1) The sale, delivery, or transfer is to an authorized representative of a city, city and county, county, or state government, or of the federal government, and is for the governmental entity.

(2) The entity is acquiring the weapon as part of an authorized, voluntary program in which the entity is buying or receiving weapons from private individuals.

(b) Any weapons acquired pursuant to this section shall be disposed of pursuant to the applicable provisions of Section 34000 or Sections 18000 and 18005. *(Added by Stats.2010, c. 711 (S.B.1080), § 6, operative Jan. 1, 2012.)*

Law Revision Commission Comments

Section 31725 continues former Section 12078(a)(6) without substantive change, as that provision applied to former Section 12801(b).

See Section 16520 ("firearm"). [38 Cal.L.Rev.Comm. Reports 217 (2009)].

Cross References

Firearm defined for purposes of this Part, see Penal Code § 16520.

§ 31730. Sales, deliveries, loans, or transfers from law enforcement agencies to historical societies, museums, or institutional collections; conditions

Subdivision (a) of Section 31615 does not apply to the sale, delivery, loan, or transfer of a firearm made by an authorized law enforcement representative of a city, county, city and county, or state, or of the federal government, to any public or private nonprofit historical society, museum, or institutional collection, or the purchase or receipt of that firearm by that public or private nonprofit historical society, museum, or institutional collection, if all of the following conditions are met:

(a) The entity receiving the firearm is open to the public.

(b) The firearm prior to delivery is deactivated or rendered inoperable.

(c) The firearm is not subject to any of the following:

(1) Sections 18000 and 18005.

(2) Division 4 (commencing with Section 18250) of Title 2.

(3) Section 34000.

(4) Sections 34005 and 34010.

(d) The firearm is not prohibited by other provisions of law from being sold, delivered, or transferred to the public at large.

(e) Prior to delivery, the entity receiving the firearm submits a written statement to the law enforcement representative stating that the firearm will not be restored to operating condition, and will either remain with that entity, or if subsequently disposed of, will be transferred in accordance with the applicable provisions listed in Section 16575 and, if applicable, Section 31615.

(f) Within 10 days of the date that the firearm is sold, loaned, delivered, or transferred to that entity, all of the following information shall be reported to the department in a manner prescribed by the department:

(1) The name of the government entity delivering the firearm.

(2) The make, model, serial number, and other identifying characteristics of the firearm.

(3) The name of the person authorized by the entity to take possession of the firearm.

(g) In the event of a change in the status of the designated representative, the entity shall notify the department of a new representative within 30 days. *(Added by Stats.2010, c. 711 (S.B. 1080), § 6, operative Jan. 1, 2012.)*

Law Revision Commission Comments

Section 31730 continues former Section 12078(a)(7) without substantive change, as that provision applied to former Section 12801(b).

For other exceptions relating to law enforcement, see Sections 31700–31720. For another exception relating to a nonprofit historical society, museum, or institutional collection, see Section 31735.

See Section 16520 ("firearm"). [38 Cal.L.Rev.Comm. Reports 217 (2009)].

Cross References

Firearm defined for purposes of this Part, see Penal Code § 16520.

§ 31735. Sales, deliveries, loans, or transfers of firearms to historical societies, museums, or institutional collections by personnel other than representatives of law enforcement agencies; conditions

Subdivision (a) of Section 31615 does not apply to the sale, delivery, loan, or transfer of a firearm made by any person other than a representative of an authorized law enforcement agency to any public or private nonprofit historical society, museum, or institutional collection, if all of the following conditions are met:

(a) The entity receiving the firearm is open to the public.

(b) The firearm is deactivated or rendered inoperable prior to delivery.

(c) The firearm is not of a type prohibited from being sold, delivered, or transferred to the public.

(d) Prior to delivery, the entity receiving the firearm submits a written statement to the person selling, loaning, or transferring the firearm stating that the firearm will not be restored to operating condition, and will either remain with that entity, or if subsequently disposed of, will be transferred in accordance with the applicable provisions listed in Section 16575 and, if applicable, with Section 31615.

(e) If title to a handgun, and commencing January 1, 2014, any firearm, is being transferred to the public or private nonprofit historical society, museum, or institutional collection, then the designated representative of that entity shall, within 30 days of taking possession of that firearm, forward by prepaid mail or deliver in person to the Department of Justice, a single report signed by both parties to the transaction, which includes all of the following information:

(1) Information identifying the person representing the public or private historical society, museum, or institutional collection.

(2) Information on how title was obtained and from whom.

(3) A description of the firearm in question.

(4) A copy of the written statement referred to in subdivision (d).

(f) The report forms that are to be completed pursuant to this section shall be provided by the Department of Justice.

(g) In the event of a change in the status of the designated representative, the entity shall notify the department of a new representative within 30 days. *(Added by Stats.2010, c. 711 (S.B. 1080), § 6, operative Jan. 1, 2012. Amended by Stats.2011, c. 745 (A.B.809), § 69.)*

Law Revision Commission Comments

Section 31735 continues former Section 12078(a)(8) without substantive change, as that provision applied to former Section 12801(b).

For another exception relating to a nonprofit historical society, museum, or institutional collection, see Section 31730.

See Sections 16520 ("firearm"), 16640 ("handgun"). [38 Cal.L.Rev.Comm. Reports 217 (2009)].

Cross References

Firearm defined for purposes of this Part, see Penal Code § 16520.
Handgun defined for purposes of this Part, see Penal Code § 16640.

§ 31740. Sales, deliveries, or transfers of firearms between or to licensed importers and manufacturers of firearms

Subdivision (a) of Section 31615 does not apply to sales, deliveries, or transfers of firearms between or to importers and manufacturers of firearms licensed to engage in that business pursuant to Chapter 44 (commencing with Section 921) of Title 18 of the United States Code and the regulations issued pursuant thereto. *(Added by Stats.2010, c. 711 (S.B.1080), § 6, operative Jan. 1, 2012.)*

Law Revision Commission Comments

Section 31740 continues former Section 12078(b)(1) without substantive change, as that provision applied to former Section 12801(b).

See Section 16520 ("firearm"). [38 Cal.L.Rev.Comm. Reports 217 (2009)].

Cross References

Firearm defined for purposes of this Part, see Penal Code § 16520.

§ 31745. Sale, delivery, or transfer of handgun to person licensed under specified provisions

Subdivision (a) of Section 31615 shall not apply to the sale, delivery, or transfer of a handgun to a person licensed pursuant to Sections 26700 to 26915, inclusive, where the licensee is receiving the handgun in the course and scope of the licensee's activities as a person licensed pursuant to Sections 26700 to 26915, inclusive. *(Added by Stats.2010, c. 711 (S.B.1080), § 6, operative Jan. 1, 2012.)*

Law Revision Commission Comments

Section 31745 continues former Section 12078(b)(2) without substantive change.

See Sections 16640 ("handgun"), 26700 ("dealer," "licensee," or "person licensed pursuant to Sections 26700 to 26915, inclusive"). [38 Cal.L.Rev. Comm. Reports 217 (2009)].

Cross References

Handgun defined for purposes of this Part, see Penal Code § 16640.

§ 31750. Loan of firearm; conditions

Subdivision (a) of Section 31615 does not apply to the loan of a firearm if all of the following conditions exist:

(a) The person loaning the firearm is at all times within the presence of the person being loaned the firearm.

(b) The loan is for a lawful purpose.

(c) The loan does not exceed three days in duration.

(d) The individual receiving the firearm is not prohibited by state or federal law from possessing, receiving, owning, or purchasing a firearm.

(e) The person loaning the firearm is 18 years of age or older.

(f) The person being loaned the firearm is 18 years of age or older. *(Added by Stats.2010, c. 711 (S.B.1080), § 6, operative Jan. 1, 2012.)*

Law Revision Commission Comments

Section 31750 continues former Section 12078(d)(2) without substantive change, as that provision applied to former Section 12801(b).

See Section 16520 ("firearm"). [38 Cal.L.Rev.Comm. Reports 217 (2009)].

Cross References

Firearm defined for purposes of this Part, see Penal Code § 16520.

§ 31755. Delivery of firearm to gunsmith; return of firearm by gunsmith

Subdivision (a) of Section 31615 does not apply to the delivery of a firearm to a gunsmith for service or repair, or to the return of the firearm to its owner by the gunsmith, or to the delivery of a firearm by a gunsmith to a person licensed pursuant to Chapter 44 (commencing with Section 921) of Title 18 of the United States Code for service or repair and the return of the firearm to the gunsmith. *(Added by Stats.2010, c. 711 (S.B.1080), § 6, operative Jan. 1, 2012.)*

Law Revision Commission Comments

Section 31755 continues former Section 12078(e)(1) without substantive change, as that provision applied to former Section 12801(b).

See Sections 16520 ("firearm"), 16630 ("gunsmith"). [38 Cal.L.Rev.Comm. Reports 217 (2009)].

Cross References

Firearm defined for purposes of this Part, see Penal Code § 16520.
Gunsmith defined for purposes of this Part, see Penal Code § 16630.

§ 31760. Sale, delivery, or transfer of firearm by resident to licensed nonresident

Subdivision (a) of Section 31615 does not apply to the sale, delivery, or transfer of firearms if all of the following requirements are satisfied:

(a) The sale, delivery, or transfer is made by a person who resides in this state.

(b) The sale, delivery, or transfer is made to a person who resides outside this state and is licensed pursuant to Chapter 44 (commencing with Section 921) of Title 18 of the United States Code and the regulations issued pursuant thereto.

(c) The sale, delivery, or transfer is in accordance with Chapter 44 (commencing with Section 921) of Title 18 of the United States Code and the regulations issued pursuant thereto. *(Added by Stats.2010, c. 711 (S.B.1080), § 6, operative Jan. 1, 2012.)*

Law Revision Commission Comments

Section 31760 continues former Section 12078(f) without substantive change, as that provision applied to former Section 12801(b).

See Section 16520 ("firearm"). [38 Cal.L.Rev.Comm. Reports 217 (2009)].

Cross References

Firearm defined for purposes of this Part, see Penal Code § 16520.

§ 31765. Loans for target shooting purposes; conditions

Subdivision (a) of Section 31615 does not apply to the loan of a firearm to a person 18 years of age or older for the purposes of shooting at targets if the loan occurs on the premises of a target facility that holds a business or regulatory license or on the premises of any club or organization organized for the purposes of practicing shooting at targets upon established ranges, whether public or private, if the firearm is at all times kept within the premises of the target range or on the premises of the club or organization. *(Added by Stats.2010, c. 711 (S.B.1080), § 6, operative Jan. 1, 2012.)*

Law Revision Commission Comments

Section 31765 continues former Section 12078(h) without substantive change, as that provision applied to former Section 12801(b).

For another exception relating to target shooting, see Section 31800.

See Section 16520 ("firearm"). [38 Cal.L.Rev.Comm. Reports 217 (2009)].

Cross References

Firearm defined for purposes of this Part, see Penal Code § 16520.

§ 31770. Deliveries, transfers, or returns made pursuant to specified provisions

Subdivision (a) of Section 31615 does not apply to deliveries, transfers, or returns of firearms made pursuant to any of the following:

(a) Sections 18000 and 18005.

(b) Division 4 (commencing with Section 18250) of Title 2.

(c) Chapter 2 (commencing with Section 33850) of Division 11.

(d) Sections 34005 and 34010. *(Added by Stats.2010, c. 711 (S.B.1080), § 6, operative Jan. 1, 2012.)*

Law Revision Commission Comments

Section 31770 continues former Section 12078(j) without substantive change, as that provision applied to former Section 12801(b).

See Section 16520 ("firearm"). [38 Cal.L.Rev.Comm. Reports 217 (2009)].

Cross References

Firearm defined for purposes of this Part, see Penal Code § 16520.

§ 31780. Sales, deliveries, or transfers by dealers to federally licensed nonresidents

Subdivision (a) of Section 31615 does not apply to the sale, delivery, or transfer of unloaded firearms by a dealer to a person who resides outside this state and is licensed pursuant to Chapter 44 (commencing with Section 921) of Title 18 of the United States Code and the regulations issued pursuant thereto. *(Added by Stats.2010, c. 711 (S.B.1080), § 6, operative Jan. 1, 2012.)*

Law Revision Commission Comments

Section 31780 continues former Section 12078(k)(2) without substantive change, as that provision applied to former Section 12801(b).

See Sections 16520 ("firearm"), 26700 ("dealer," "licensee," or "person licensed pursuant to Sections 26700 to 26915, inclusive"). [38 Cal.L.Rev. Comm. Reports 217 (2009)].

Cross References

Firearm defined for purposes of this Part, see Penal Code § 16520.

§ 31785. Sales, deliveries, or transfers to wholesalers

Subdivision (a) of Section 31615 does not apply to the sale, delivery, or transfer of unloaded firearms to a wholesaler if the firearms are being returned to the wholesaler and are intended as merchandise in the wholesaler's business. *(Added by Stats.2010, c. 711 (S.B.1080), § 6, operative Jan. 1, 2012.)*

Law Revision Commission Comments

Section 31785 continues former Section 12078(k)(3) without substantive change, as that provision applied to former Section 12801(b).

See Sections 16520 ("firearm"), 17340 ("wholesaler"), 26700 ("dealer," "licensee," or "person licensed pursuant to Sections 26700 to 26915, inclusive"). [38 Cal.L.Rev.Comm. Reports 217 (2009)].

Cross References

Firearm defined for purposes of this Part, see Penal Code § 16520.
Wholesaler defined for purposes of this Part, see Penal Code § 17340.

§ 31790. Sale, delivery, or transfer of firearm from dealer to dealer for use as merchandise in receiving dealer's business

Subdivision (a) of Section 31615 does not apply to the sale, delivery, or transfer of firearms if all of the following conditions are satisfied:

(a) The firearms are unloaded.

(b) The sale, delivery, or transfer is made by one dealer to another dealer, upon proof of compliance with the requirements of Section 27555.

(c) The firearms are intended as merchandise in the receiving dealer's business. *(Added by Stats.2010, c. 711 (S.B.1080), § 6, operative Jan. 1, 2012.)*

Law Revision Commission Comments

Section 31790 continues former Section 12078(k)(4) without substantive change, as that provision applied to former Section 12801(b).

See Sections 16520 ("firearm"), 26700 ("dealer," "licensee," or "person licensed pursuant to Sections 26700 to 26915, inclusive"). [38 Cal.L.Rev. Comm. Reports 217 (2009)].

Cross References

Firearm defined for purposes of this Part, see Penal Code § 16520.

§ 31800. Loans by dealers for target shooting on premises

Subdivision (a) of Section 31615 does not apply to the loan of an unloaded firearm by a dealer who also operates a target facility that holds a business or regulatory license on the premises of the building designated in the license or whose building designated in the license is on the premises of any club or organization organized for the purposes of practicing shooting at targets upon established ranges, whether public or private, to a person at that target facility or that club or organization, if the firearm is at all times kept within the premises of the target range or on the premises of the club or organization. *(Added by Stats.2010, c. 711 (S.B.1080), § 6, operative Jan. 1, 2012.)*

Law Revision Commission Comments

Section 31800 continues former Section 12078(k)(6) without substantive change, as that provision applied to former Section 12801(b).

For another exception relating to target shooting, see Section 31765.

See Sections 16520 ("firearm"), 26700 ("dealer," "licensee," or "person licensed pursuant to Sections 26700 to 26915, inclusive"). [38 Cal.L.Rev. Comm. Reports 217 (2009)].

Cross References

Firearm defined for purposes of this Part, see Penal Code § 16520.

§ 31805. Sale, delivery, or transfer of firearm by licensed manufacturer or importer to wholesaler as merchandise

Subdivision (a) of Section 31615 does not apply to the sale, delivery, or transfer of unloaded firearms to a wholesaler as merchandise in the wholesaler's business by a manufacturer or importer licensed to engage in that business pursuant to Chapter 44 (commencing with Section 921) of Title 18 of the United States Code and the regulations issued pursuant thereto, or by another wholesaler, if the sale, delivery, or transfer is made in accordance with Chapter 44 (commencing with Section 921) of Title 18 of the United States Code. *(Added by Stats.2010, c. 711 (S.B.1080), § 6, operative Jan. 1, 2012.)*

Law Revision Commission Comments

Section 31805 continues former Section 12078(m) without substantive change, as that provision applied to former Section 12801(b).

See Sections 16520 ("firearm"), 17340 ("wholesaler"). [38 Cal.L.Rev. Comm. Reports 217 (2009)].

Cross References

Firearm defined for purposes of this Part, see Penal Code § 16520.
Wholesaler defined for purposes of this Part, see Penal Code § 17340.

§ 31810. Loan of handgun or firearm to minor; conditions

Subdivision (a) of Section 31615 does not apply to or affect the following circumstances:

(a) The loan of a handgun, and commencing January 1, 2015, any firearm, to a minor by the minor's parent or legal guardian, if both of the following requirements are satisfied:

(1) The minor is being loaned the firearm for the purposes of engaging in a lawful, recreational sport, including, but not limited to, competitive shooting, or agricultural, ranching, or hunting activity or hunting education, or a motion picture, television, or video production, or entertainment or theatrical event, the nature of which involves the use of a firearm.

(2) The duration of the loan does not exceed the amount of time that is reasonably necessary to engage in the lawful, recreational sport, including, but not limited to, competitive shooting, or agricultural, ranching, or hunting activity or hunting education, or a motion picture, television, or video production, or entertainment or theatrical event, the nature of which involves the use of a firearm.

(b) The loan of a handgun, and commencing January 1, 2015, any firearm, to a minor by a person who is not the minor's parent or legal guardian, if all of the following requirements are satisfied:

(1) The minor is accompanied by the minor's parent or legal guardian when the loan is made, or the minor has the written consent of the minor's parent or legal guardian, which is presented at the time of the loan, or earlier.

(2) The minor is being loaned the firearm for the purpose of engaging in a lawful, recreational sport, including, but not limited to, competitive shooting, or agricultural, ranching, or hunting activity or hunting education, or a motion picture, television, or video production, or entertainment or theatrical event, the nature of which involves the use of a firearm.

(3) The duration of the loan does not exceed the amount of time that is reasonably necessary to engage in the lawful, recreational sport, including, but not limited to, competitive shooting, or agricultural, ranching, or hunting activity or hunting education, or a motion picture, television, or video production, or entertainment or theatrical event, the nature of which involves the use of a firearm.

(4) The duration of the loan does not, in any event, exceed 10 days. *(Added by Stats.2010, c. 711 (S.B.1080), § 6, operative Jan. 1, 2012. Amended by Stats.2013, c. 761 (S.B.683), § 38.)*

Law Revision Commission Comments

Subdivision (a) of Section 31810 continues former Section 12078(p)(3) without substantive change, as that provision applied to former Section 12801(b).

Subdivision (b) continues former Section 12078(p)(2) without substantive change, as that provision applied to former Section 12801(b).

See Sections 16520 ("firearm"), 16640 ("handgun"). [38 Cal.L.Rev.Comm. Reports 217 (2009)].

Cross References

Firearm defined for purposes of this Part, see Penal Code § 16520.
Handgun defined for purposes of this Part, see Penal Code § 16640.

§ 31815. Loan of firearm for use as prop in motion picture, television, video, theatrical, or other entertainment production or event; conditions

Subdivision (a) of Section 31615 does not apply to the loan of a firearm if all of the following requirements are satisfied:

(a) The loan is infrequent, as defined in Section 16730.

(b) The firearm is unloaded.

(c) The loan is made by a person who is neither a dealer nor a federal firearms licensee pursuant to Chapter 44 (commencing with Section 921) of Title 18 of the United States Code.

(d) The loan is made to a person 18 years of age or older.

(e) The loan is for use solely as a prop in a motion picture, television, video, theatrical, or other entertainment production or event. *(Added by Stats.2010, c. 711 (S.B.1080), § 6, operative Jan. 1, 2012.)*

Law Revision Commission Comments

Section 31815 continues former Section 12078(s)(1) without substantive change, as that provision applied to former Section 12801(b).

For other exceptions pertaining to firearms used as props, see Sections 31820–31825.

See Sections 16520 ("firearm"), 26700 ("dealer," "licensee," or "person licensed pursuant to Sections 26700 to 26915, inclusive"). [38 Cal.L.Rev. Comm. Reports 217 (2009)].

Cross References

Firearm defined for purposes of this Part, see Penal Code § 16520.

§ 31820. Loan of firearm by federal firearms licensee to valid entertainment firearms permit holder for use as prop in motion picture, television, video, theatrical, or other entertainment production or event; conditions

(a) Subdivision (a) of Section 31615 does not apply to the loan of a firearm if all of the following requirements are satisfied:

(1) The firearm is unloaded.

(2) The loan is made by a person who is not a dealer but is a federal firearms licensee pursuant to Chapter 44 (commencing with Section 921) of Title 18 of the United States Code.

(3) The loan is made to a person who possesses a valid entertainment firearms permit issued pursuant to Chapter 2 (commencing with Section 29500) of Division 8.

(4) The firearm is loaned for use solely as a prop in a motion picture, television, video, theatrical, or other entertainment production or event.

(b) The person loaning the firearm pursuant to this section shall retain a photocopy of the entertainment firearms permit as proof of compliance with this requirement. *(Added by Stats.2010, c. 711 (S.B.1080), § 6, operative Jan. 1, 2012.)*

Law Revision Commission Comments

Section 31820 continues former Section 12078(s)(2) without substantive change, as that provision applied to former Section 12801(b).

For other exceptions pertaining to firearms used as props, see Sections 31815 and 31825.

See Sections 16520 ("firearm"), 26700 ("dealer," "licensee," or "person licensed pursuant to Sections 26700 to 26915, inclusive"). [38 Cal.L.Rev. Comm. Reports 217 (2009)].

Cross References

Firearm defined for purposes of this Part, see Penal Code § 16520.

§ 31825. Loan of firearm by dealer to valid entertainment firearms permit holder for use as prop in motion picture, television, video, theatrical, or other entertainment production or event; conditions

(a) Subdivision (a) of Section 31615 does not apply to the loan of a firearm if all of the following conditions are satisfied:

(1) The firearm is unloaded.

(2) The loan is made by a dealer.

(3) The loan is made to a person who possesses a valid entertainment firearms permit issued pursuant to Chapter 2 (commencing with Section 29500) of Division 8.

(4) The firearm is loaned solely for use as a prop in a motion picture, television, video, theatrical, or other entertainment production or event.

(b) The dealer shall retain a photocopy of the entertainment firearms permit as proof of compliance with this requirement. *(Added by Stats.2010, c. 711 (S.B.1080), § 6, operative Jan. 1, 2012.)*

Law Revision Commission Comments

Section 31825 continues former Section 12078(s)(3) without substantive change, as that provision applied to former Section 12801(b).

For other exceptions pertaining to firearms used as props, see Sections 31815–31820.

See Sections 16520 ("firearm"), 26700 ("dealer," "licensee," or "person licensed pursuant to Sections 26700 to 26915, inclusive"). [38 Cal.L.Rev. Comm. Reports 217 (2009)].

Cross References

Firearm defined for purposes of this Part, see Penal Code § 16520.

§ 31830. Loan to consultant-evaluator; conditions

(a) Subdivision (a) of Section 31615 does not apply to the loan of an unloaded firearm to a consultant-evaluator by a person licensed pursuant to Sections 26700 to 26915, inclusive, if the loan does not exceed 45 days from the date of delivery.

(b) At the time of the loan, the consultant-evaluator shall provide the following information, which the dealer shall retain for two years:

(1) A photocopy of a valid, current, government-issued identification to determine the consultant-evaluator's identity, including, but not limited to, a California driver's license, identification card, or passport.

(2) A photocopy of the consultant-evaluator's valid, current certificate of eligibility.

(3) A letter from the person licensed as an importer, manufacturer, or dealer pursuant to Chapter 44 (commencing with Section 921) of Title 18 of the United States Code, with whom the consultant-evaluator has a bona fide business relationship. The letter shall detail the bona fide business purposes for which the firearm is being loaned and confirm that the consultant-evaluator is being loaned the firearm as part of a bona fide business relationship.

(4) The signature of the consultant-evaluator on a form indicating the date the firearm is loaned and the last day the firearm may be returned. *(Added by Stats.2010, c. 711 (S.B.1080), § 6, operative Jan. 1, 2012.)*

Law Revision Commission Comments

Section 31830 continues former Section 12078(s)(4) without substantive change, as that provision applied to former Section 12801(b).

See Sections 16410 ("consultant-evaluator"), 16520 ("firearm"), 26700 ("dealer," "licensee," or "person licensed pursuant to Sections 26700 to 26915, inclusive"). [38 Cal.L.Rev.Comm. Reports 217 (2009)].

Cross References

Consultant-evaluator defined for purposes of this Part, see Penal Code § 16410.
Firearm defined for purposes of this Part, see Penal Code § 16520.

§ 31833. Loan of firearm other than handgun or semiautomatic centerfire rifle to minor; conditions

(a) Section 31615 does not apply to the loan of a firearm other than a handgun or semiautomatic centerfire rifle to a minor that complies with all of the conditions set forth in paragraph (4) of subdivision (b) of Section 27505.

(b) Section 31615 does not apply to the loan of a firearm other than a handgun or semiautomatic centerfire rifle to a minor that complies with all of the conditions set forth in paragraph (5) of subdivision (b) of Section 27505. *(Added by Stats.2021, c. 250 (S.B.715), § 26, eff. Jan. 1, 2022.)*

§ 31834. Sales, deliveries, or transfers of firearms between or to importers and manufacturers of ammunition

Section 31615 does not apply to sales, deliveries, or transfers of firearms between or to importers and manufacturers of ammunition licensed to engage in that business pursuant to Chapter 44 (commencing with Section 921) of Title 18 of the United States Code and the regulations issued pursuant thereto, where those firearms are to be used in the course and scope of the licensee's activities as a person licensed pursuant to Chapter 44 (commencing with Section 921) of Title 18 of the United States Code and the regulations issued pursuant thereto. *(Added by Stats.2021, c. 250 (S.B.715), § 27, eff. Jan. 1, 2022.)*

§ 31835. Delivery, sale, or transfer of firearms by authorized law enforcement representative; application of section requiring handgun safety certificate; conditions

Subdivision (a) of Section 31615 does not apply to the delivery, sale, or transfer of firearms when made by authorized law enforcement representatives for cities, counties, cities and counties, or of the state or federal government, if all of the following conditions are met:

(a) The sale, delivery, or transfer is made to one of the persons or entities identified in subdivision (a) of Section 26620.

(b) The sale, delivery, or transfer of the firearm is not subject to the procedures set forth in Section 18000, 18005, 34000, or 34005.

(c) The sale, delivery, or transfer of the firearm follows the procedures set forth in subdivision (c) of Section 26620. *(Added by Stats.2013, c. 738 (A.B.538), § 10.)*

ARTICLE 4. "UNSAFE HANDGUN" AND RELATED DEFINITIONS

Section

§ 31900. "Drop safety requirement for handguns" defined

As used in this part, the "drop safety requirement for handguns" means that at the conclusion of the firing requirements for handguns described in Section 31905, the same certified independent testing laboratory shall subject the same three handguns of the make and model for which certification is sought, to the following test:

(a) A primed case (no powder or projectile) shall be inserted into the chamber. For a pistol, the slide shall be released, allowing it to move forward under the impetus of the recoil spring, and an empty magazine shall be inserted. For both a pistol and a revolver, the weapon shall be placed in a drop fixture capable of dropping the pistol from a drop height of 1m + 1cm (39.4 + 0.4 in.) onto the largest side of a slab of solid concrete having minimum dimensions of 7.5 x 15 x 15 cm (3 x 6 x 6 in.). The drop distance shall be measured from the lowermost portion of the weapon to the top surface of the slab. The weapon shall be dropped from a fixture and not from the hand. The weapon shall be dropped in the condition that it would be in if it were dropped from a hand (cocked with no manual safety applied). If the pistol is designed so that upon leaving the hand a "safety" is automatically applied by the pistol, this feature shall not be defeated. An approved drop fixture is a short piece of string with the weapon attached at one end and the other end held in an air vise until the drop is initiated.

(b) The following six drops shall be performed:

(1) Normal firing position with barrel horizontal.

(2) Upside down with barrel horizontal.

(3) On grip with barrel vertical.

(4) On muzzle with barrel vertical.

(5) On either side with barrel horizontal.

(6) If there is an exposed hammer or striker, on the rearmost point of that device, otherwise on the rearmost point of the weapon.

(c) The primer shall be examined for indentations after each drop. If indentations are present, a fresh primed case shall be used for the next drop.

(d) The handgun shall pass this test if each of the three test guns does not fire the primer. *(Added by Stats.2010, c. 711 (S.B.1080), § 6, operative Jan. 1, 2012.)*

Law Revision Commission Comments

Section 31900 continues former Section 12128 without substantive change.

For the definition of "unsafe handgun," see Section 31910. For rules governing unsafe handguns, see Sections 32000–32030. For exceptions to those rules, see Sections 32100 (exception for single-shot pistol or single-action revolver meeting certain specifications), 32105 (exception for pistols used in Olympic target shooting events), 32110 (other exceptions).

See Sections 16530 ("firearm capable of being concealed upon the person," "pistol," and "revolver"), 16640 ("handgun"). [38 Cal.L.Rev.Comm. Reports 217 (2009)].

Cross References

Exceptions to rules governing unsafe handguns, single-shot pistols meeting certain specifications, see Penal Code § 32100.
Handgun defined for purposes of this Part, see Penal Code § 16640.
Pistol defined for purposes of this Part, see Penal Code § 16530.
Revolver defined for purposes of this Part, see Penal Code § 16530.

§ 31905. "Firing requirement for handguns" defined

(a) As used in this part, "firing requirement for handguns" means a test in which the manufacturer provides three handguns of the make and model for which certification is sought to an independent testing laboratory certified by the Attorney General pursuant to Section 32010. These handguns may not be refined or modified in any way from those that would be made available for retail sale if certification is granted. The magazines of a tested pistol shall be identical to those that would be provided with the pistol to a retail customer.

(b) The test shall be conducted as follows:

(1) The laboratory shall fire 600 rounds from each gun, stopping after each series of 50 rounds has been fired for 5 to 10 minutes to allow the weapon to cool, stopping after each series of 100 rounds has been fired to tighten any loose screws and clean the gun in accordance with the manufacturer's instructions, and stopping as needed to refill the empty magazine or cylinder to capacity before continuing.

(2) The ammunition used shall be of the type recommended by the handgun manufacturer in the user manual, or if none is recommended, any standard ammunition of the correct caliber in new condition that is commercially available.

(c) A handgun shall pass this test if each of the three test guns meets both of the following:

(1) Fires the first 20 rounds without a malfunction that is not due to ammunition that fails to detonate.

(2) Fires the full 600 rounds with no more than six malfunctions that are not due to ammunition that fails to detonate and without any crack or breakage of an operating part of the handgun that increases the risk of injury to the user.

(d) If a pistol or revolver fails the requirements of either paragraph (1) or (2) of subdivision (c) due to ammunition that fails to detonate, the pistol or revolver shall be retested from the beginning of the "firing requirement for handguns" test. A new model of the pistol or revolver that failed due to ammunition that fails to detonate may be submitted for the test to replace the pistol or revolver that failed.

(e) As used in this section, "malfunction" means a failure to properly feed, fire, or eject a round, or failure of a pistol to accept or eject the magazine, or failure of a pistol's slide to remain open after the magazine has been expended. *(Added by Stats.2010, c. 711 (S.B.1080), § 6, operative Jan. 1, 2012.)*

Law Revision Commission Comments

Section 31905 continues former Section 12127 without substantive change.

For the definition of "unsafe handgun," see Section 31910. For rules governing unsafe handguns, see Sections 32000–32030. For exceptions to those rules, see Sections 32100 (exception for single-shot pistol or single-action revolver meeting certain specifications), 32105 (exception for pistols used in Olympic target shooting events), 32110 (other exceptions).

See Sections 16530 ("firearm capable of being concealed upon the person," "pistol," and "revolver"), 16640 ("handgun"). [38 Cal.L.Rev.Comm. Reports 217 (2009)].

Cross References

Attorney General, generally, see Government Code § 12500 et seq.
Handgun defined for purposes of this Part, see Penal Code § 16640.
Pistol defined for purposes of this Part, see Penal Code § 16530.
Revolver defined for purposes of this Part, see Penal Code § 16530.

§ 31910. "Unsafe handgun" defined

As used in this part, "unsafe handgun" means any pistol, revolver, or other firearm capable of being concealed upon the person, for which any of the following is true:

(a) For a revolver:

(1) It does not have a safety device that, either automatically in the case of a double-action firing mechanism, or by manual operation in the case of a single-action firing mechanism, causes the hammer to retract to a point where the firing pin does not rest upon the primer of the cartridge.

(2) It does not meet the firing requirement for handguns.

(3) It does not meet the drop safety requirement for handguns.

(b) For a pistol:

(1) It does not have a positive manually operated safety device, as determined by standards relating to imported guns promulgated by the federal Bureau of Alcohol, Tobacco, Firearms and Explosives.

(2) It does not meet the firing requirement for handguns.

(3) It does not meet the drop safety requirement for handguns.

(4) Commencing July 1, 2022, for all centerfire semiautomatic pistols that are not already listed on the roster pursuant to Section 32015, it does not have a chamber load indicator.

(5) Commencing July 1, 2022, for all centerfire or rimfire semiautomatic pistols that are not already listed on the roster pursuant to Section 32015, it does not have a magazine disconnect mechanism if it has a detachable magazine.

(6)(A) Commencing July 1, 2022, for all semiautomatic pistols that are not already listed on the roster pursuant to Section 32015, it is not designed and equipped with a microscopic array of characters used to identify the make, model, and serial number of the pistol, etched or otherwise imprinted in one or more places on the interior surface or internal working parts of the pistol, and that are transferred by imprinting on each cartridge case when the firearm is fired.

(B) The Attorney General may also approve a method of equal or greater reliability and effectiveness in identifying the specific serial number of a firearm from spent cartridge casings discharged by that firearm than that which is set forth in this paragraph, to be thereafter required as otherwise set forth by this paragraph where the Attorney General certifies that this new method is also unencumbered by any patent restrictions. Approval by the Attorney General shall include notice of that fact via regulations adopted by the Attorney General for purposes of implementing that method for purposes of this paragraph.

(C) The microscopic array of characters required by this section shall not be considered the name of the maker, model, manufacturer's number, or other mark of identification, including any distinguishing number or mark assigned by the Department of Justice, within the meaning of Sections 23900 and 23920.

(7) The Department of Justice shall, for each semiautomatic pistol newly added to the roster pursuant to Section 32015, remove from the roster exactly three semiautomatic pistols lacking one or more of the applicable features described in paragraphs (4), (5), and (6) of subdivision (b) and added to the roster before July 1, 2022. Notwithstanding those paragraphs, each semiautomatic pistol removed from the roster pursuant to this subdivision shall be considered an unsafe handgun. The Attorney General shall remove semiautomatic pistols from the roster pursuant to this subdivision in reverse order of their dates of addition to the roster, beginning with the semiautomatic pistol added to the roster on the earliest date and continuing until each semiautomatic pistol on the roster includes each of the applicable features described in those paragraphs. *(Added by Stats.2010, c. 711 (S.B.1080), § 6, operative Jan. 1, 2012. Amended by Stats.2011, c. 296 (A.B.1023), § 242; Stats.2020, c. 292 (A.B.2847), § 2, eff. Jan. 1, 2021.)*

Law Revision Commission Comments

Section 31910 continues the introductory clause and subdivisions (a) and (b) of former Section 12126 without substantive change.

For rules governing unsafe handguns, see Sections 32000–32030. For exceptions to those rules, see Sections 32100 (exception for single-shot pistol or single-action revolver meeting certain specifications), 32105 (exception for pistols used in Olympic target shooting events), 32110 (other exceptions).

See Sections 16380 ("chamber load indicator"), 16520 ("firearm"), 16530 ("firearm capable of being concealed upon the person," "pistol," and "revolver"), 16640 ("handgun"), 16900 ("magazine disconnect mechanism"), 17140 ("semiautomatic pistol"), 31900 ("drop safety requirement for handguns"), 31905 ("firing requirement for handguns"). [38 Cal.L.Rev.Comm. Reports 217 (2009)].

Cross References

Attorney General, generally, see Government Code § 12500 et seq.
Firearm capable of being concealed upon the person defined for purposes of this Part, see Penal Code § 16530.
Firearm defined for purposes of this Part, see Penal Code § 16520.
Handgun defined for purposes of this Part, see Penal Code § 16640.
Pistol defined for purposes of this Part, see Penal Code § 16530.
Revolver defined for purposes of this Part, see Penal Code § 16530.

Research References

2 Witkin, California Criminal Law 4th Crimes Against Public Peace and Welfare § 224 (2021), Unsafe Handguns.

ARTICLE 5. RULES GOVERNING UNSAFE HANDGUNS

§ 32000. Manufacture, importation, sale, gift, or loan of unsafe handgun; failure to report sale or transfer of unsafe handgun; penalties; exemptions

(a)(1) A person in this state who manufactures or causes to be manufactured, imports into the state for sale, keeps for sale, offers or exposes for sale, gives, or lends an unsafe handgun shall be punished by imprisonment in a county jail not exceeding one year.

(2) The failure to report to the Department of Justice in accordance with the provisions of paragraph (2) of subdivision (e) the sale or transfer of an unsafe handgun obtained pursuant to paragraph (4), (6), or (7) of subdivision (b) may be subject to a civil penalty not to exceed ten thousand dollars ($10,000).

(3) In addition to any criminal penalty provided in paragraph (1), the unlawful sale or transfer of an unsafe handgun obtained pursuant to paragraph (4), (6), or (7) of subdivision (b) may be subject to a civil penalty not to exceed ten thousand dollars ($10,000).

(b) This section shall not apply to any of the following:

(1) The manufacture in this state, or importation into this state, of a prototype handgun when the manufacture or importation is for the sole purpose of allowing an independent laboratory certified by the Department of Justice pursuant to Section 32010 to conduct an independent test to determine whether that handgun is prohibited by Sections 31900 to 32110, inclusive, and, if not, allowing the department to add the firearm to the roster of handguns that may be sold in this state pursuant to Section 32015.

(2) The importation or lending of a handgun by employees or authorized agents of entities determining whether the weapon is prohibited by this section.

(3) Firearms listed as curios or relics, as defined in Section 478.11 of Title 27 of the Code of Federal Regulations.

(4) The sale or purchase of a handgun, if the handgun is sold to, or purchased by, the Department of Justice, a police department, a sheriff's official, a marshal's office, the Department of Corrections and Rehabilitation, the Department of the California Highway Patrol, any district attorney's office, any federal law enforcement agency, or the military or naval forces of this state or of the United States for use in the discharge of their official duties. This section does not prohibit the sale to, or purchase by, sworn members of these agencies of a handgun.

(5) The sale, purchase, or delivery of a handgun, if the sale, purchase, or delivery of the handgun is made pursuant to subdivision (d) of Section 10334 of the Public Contract Code.

(6) Subject to the limitations set forth in subdivision (c), the sale or purchase of a handgun for use as a service weapon, if the handgun is sold to, or purchased by, any of the following entities for use by, or sold to or purchased by, sworn members of these entities who have satisfactorily completed the POST basic course or, before January 1, 2021, have satisfactorily completed the firearms portion of a training course prescribed by the Commission on Peace Officer Standards and Training (POST) pursuant to Section 832, and who, as a condition of carrying that handgun, complete a live-fire qualification prescribed by their employing entity at least once every six months:

(A) The Department of Parks and Recreation.

(B) The Department of Alcoholic Beverage Control.

(C) The Division of Investigation of the Department of Consumer Affairs.

(D) The Department of Motor Vehicles.

(E) The Fraud Division of the Department of Insurance.

(F) The State Department of State Hospitals.

(G) The Department of Fish and Wildlife.

(H) The State Department of Developmental Services.

(I) The Department of Forestry and Fire Protection.

(J) A county probation department.

(K) The Los Angeles World Airports, as defined in Section 830.15.

(L) A K–12 public school district for use by a school police officer, as described in Section 830.32.

(M) A municipal water district for use by a park ranger, as described in Section 830.34.

(N) A county for use by a welfare fraud investigator or inspector, as described in Section 830.35.

(O) A county for use by the coroner or the deputy coroner, as described in Section 830.35.

(P) The Supreme Court and the courts of appeal for use by marshals of the Supreme Court and bailiffs of the courts of appeal, and coordinators of security for the judicial branch, as described in Section 830.36.

(Q) A fire department or fire protection agency of a county, city, city and county, district, or the state for use by either of the following:

(i) A member of an arson-investigating unit, regularly paid and employed in that capacity pursuant to Section 830.37.

(ii) A member other than a member of an arson-investigating unit, regularly paid and employed in that capacity pursuant to Section 830.37.

(R) The University of California Police Department, or the California State University Police Departments, as described in Section 830.2.

(S) A California Community College police department, as described in Section 830.32.

(T) A harbor or port district or other entity employing peace officers described in subdivision (b) of Section 830.33, the San Diego Unified Port District Harbor Police, and the Harbor Department of the City of Los Angeles.

(U) A local agency employing park rangers described in subdivision (b) of Section 830.31.

(V) The Department of Cannabis Control.

(7)(A) Subject to the limitations set forth in subdivision (c), the sale or purchase of a handgun, if the handgun is sold to, or purchased by, any of the following entities for use as a service weapon by the sworn members of these entities who have satisfactorily completed the POST basic course or, before January 1, 2021, have satisfactorily completed the firearms portion of a training course prescribed by the POST pursuant to Section 832, and who, as a condition of carrying that handgun, complete a live-fire qualification prescribed by their employing entity at least once every six months:

(i) The California Horse Racing Board.

(ii) The State Department of Health Care Services.

(iii) The State Department of Public Health.

(iv) The State Department of Social Services.

(v) The Department of Toxic Substances Control.

(vi) The Office of Statewide Health Planning and Development.

(vii) The Public Employees' Retirement System.

(viii) The Department of Housing and Community Development.

(ix) Investigators of the Department of * * * Financial Protection and Innovation.

(x) The Law Enforcement Branch of the Office of Emergency Services.

(xi) The California State Lottery.

(xii) The Franchise Tax Board.

(B) This paragraph does not authorize the sale to, or purchase by, sworn members of the entities specified in subparagraph (A) in a personal capacity.

(c)(1) Notwithstanding Section 26825, a person licensed pursuant to Sections 26700 to 26915, inclusive, shall not process the sale or transfer of an unsafe handgun between a person who has obtained an unsafe handgun pursuant to an exemption specified in paragraph (6) or (7) of subdivision (b) and a person who is not exempt from the requirements of this section.

(2)(A) A person who obtains or has use of an unsafe handgun pursuant to paragraph (6) or (7) of subdivision (b) shall, when leaving the handgun in an unattended vehicle, lock the handgun in the vehicle's trunk, lock the handgun in a locked container and place the container out of plain view, or lock the handgun in a locked container that is permanently affixed to the vehicle's interior and not in plain view.

(B) A violation of subparagraph (A) is an infraction punishable by a fine not exceeding one thousand dollars ($1,000).

(C) For purposes of this paragraph, the following definitions shall apply:

(i) "Vehicle" has the same meaning as defined in Section 670 of the Vehicle Code.

(ii) A vehicle is "unattended" when a person who is lawfully carrying or transporting a handgun in the vehicle is not within close proximity to the vehicle to reasonably prevent unauthorized access to the vehicle or its contents.

(iii) "Locked container" has the same meaning as defined in Section 16850.

(D) Subparagraph (A) does not apply to a peace officer during circumstances requiring immediate aid or action that are within the course of their official duties.

(E) This paragraph does not supersede any local ordinance that regulates the storage of handguns in unattended vehicles if the ordinance was in effect before January 1, 2017.

(d) Violations of subdivision (a) are cumulative with respect to each handgun and shall not be construed as restricting the application of any other law. However, an act or omission punishable in different ways by this section and other provisions of law shall not be punished under more than one provision, but the penalty to be imposed shall be determined as set forth in Section 654.

(e)(1) The Department of Justice shall maintain a database of unsafe handguns obtained pursuant to paragraph (4), (6), or (7) of subdivision (b). This requirement shall apply retroactively to include information in the department's possession. The department may satisfy this requirement by maintaining this information in any existing firearm database that reasonably facilitates compliance with this subdivision.

(2) A person or entity that is in possession of an unsafe handgun obtained pursuant to paragraph (4), (6), or (7) of subdivision (b), shall notify the department of any sale or transfer of that handgun within 72 hours of the sale or transfer in a manner and format prescribed by the department. This requirement shall be deemed satisfied if the sale or transfer is processed through a licensed firearms dealer pursuant to Section 27545. A sale or transfer accomplished through an exception to Section 27545 is not exempt from this reporting requirement.

(3) By no later than March 1, 2021, the department shall provide a notification to persons or entities possessing an unsafe handgun pursuant to paragraph (4), (6), or (7) of subdivision (b) regarding the

prohibitions on the sale or transfer of that handgun contained in this section. Thereafter, the department shall, upon notification of sale or transfer, provide the same notification to the purchaser or transferee of any unsafe handgun sold or transferred pursuant to those provisions. *(Added by Stats.2010, c. 711 (S.B.1080), § 6, operative Jan. 1, 2012. Amended by Stats.2013, c. 758 (S.B.363), § 3; Stats.2015, c. 203 (A.B.892), § 1, eff. Jan. 1, 2016; Stats.2016, c. 640 (A.B.2165), § 1, eff. Jan. 1, 2017; Stats.2018, c. 56 (A.B.1872), § 1, eff. Jan. 1, 2019; Stats.2020, c. 289 (A.B.2699), § 5, eff. Jan. 1, 2021; Stats.2021, c. 70 (A.B.141), § 109, eff. July 12, 2021; Stats.2021, c. 250 (S.B.715), § 28, eff. Jan. 1, 2022; Stats.2022, c. 452 (S.B.1498), § 206, eff. Jan. 1, 2023.)*

Law Revision Commission Comments

Section 32000 continues former Section 12125 without substantive change.

For exceptions to the rules stated in this article, see Sections 32100 (exception for single-shot pistol or single-action revolver meeting certain specifications), 32105 (exception for pistols used in Olympic target shooting events), 32110 (other exceptions).

See Sections 16520 ("firearm"), 16530 ("firearm capable of being concealed upon the person," "pistol," and "revolver"), 16640 ("handgun"), 31910 ("unsafe handgun").

In addition to the provisions in this chapter, a number of other provisions within this part pertain specifically to handguns. For example, see Sections 25400–25700 (carrying concealed firearm), 26010 (person licensed to carry pistol, revolver, or other firearm capable of being concealed upon the person), 26300–26325 (retired peace officer carrying concealed and loaded firearm), 26820 (display of handgun or imitation or placard advertising handgun), 26840 (presentation of basic firearms safety certificate or handgun safety certificate to dealer), 26845 (no handgun delivery without proof of California residency), 26850–26859 (safe handling demonstration with handgun), 26905 (reporting of handgun acquisitions), 26960 (waiting period exception for sale, delivery, or transfer of handgun, not intended as merchandise, by dealer to self or another dealer), 27505 (transfer of handgun to person under age 21), 27510 (dealer that supplies, delivers, or gives possession or control of handgun to person under age 21), 27530 (transfer of handgun that lacks identifying information), 27560 (restrictions on personal handgun importer), 27565 (handgun that is curio or relic, transported into California by licensed collector), 27660 (waiting period exception for sale, delivery, or transfer of handgun, not intended as merchandise, by dealer to self or another dealer), 27875 (exception for infrequent transfer of handgun between members of same immediate family), 27920 (exception for person who takes title or possession of handgun by operation of law), 28160 (form for handgun), 29610–29615 (possession of handgun by minor). See also Sections 30300 (providing ammunition to minors and other young people), 30312 (delivery or transfer of ownership of handgun ammunition), 30315–30325 (restrictions relating to handgun ammunition designed primarily to penetrate metal or armor), 30345–30365 (handgun ammunition vendors). [38 Cal.L.Rev.Comm. Reports 217 (2009)].

Cross References

Criminal identification and statistics, retention of records, firearms, see Penal Code § 11106.
Exceptions to rules governing unsafe handguns, single shot pistols meeting certain specifications, see Penal Code § 32100.
Firearm capable of being concealed upon the person defined for purposes of this Part, see Penal Code § 16530.
Firearm defined for purposes of this Part, see Penal Code § 16520.
Handgun defined for purposes of this Part, see Penal Code § 16640.
Pistol defined for purposes of this Part, see Penal Code § 16530.
Revolver defined for purposes of this Part, see Penal Code § 16530.
Transportation of firearm in order to comply with specified provisions, see Penal Code § 25555.

Research References

2 Witkin, California Criminal Law 4th Crimes Against Public Peace and Welfare § 208 (2021), Exempt Activities.
2 Witkin, California Criminal Law 4th Crimes Against Public Peace and Welfare § 224 (2021), Unsafe Handguns.
1 Witkin California Criminal Law 4th Introduction to Crimes § 70 (2021), Weapons.

§ 32005. Manufacturers and importers; certification that no model of manufactured or imported concealable firearm is unsafe handgun

(a) Every person who is licensed as a manufacturer of firearms pursuant to Chapter 44 (commencing with Section 921) of Title 18 of the United States Code and who manufactures firearms in this state shall certify under penalty of perjury and any other remedy provided by law that every model, kind, class, style, or type of pistol, revolver, or other firearm capable of being concealed upon the person that the person manufactures is not an unsafe handgun as prohibited by Sections 31900 to 32110, inclusive.

(b) Every person who imports into the state for sale, keeps for sale, or offers or exposes for sale any firearm shall certify under penalty of perjury and any other remedy provided by law that every model, kind, class, style, or type of pistol, revolver, or other firearm capable of being concealed upon the person that the person imports, keeps, or exposes for sale is not an unsafe handgun as prohibited by Sections 31900 to 32110, inclusive. *(Added by Stats.2010, c. 711 (S.B.1080), § 6, operative Jan. 1, 2012.)*

Law Revision Commission Comments

Section 32005 continues former Section 12129 without substantive change.

For exceptions to the rules stated in this article, see Sections 32100 (exception for single-shot pistol or single-action revolver meeting certain specifications), 32105 (exception for pistols used in Olympic target shooting events), 32110 (other exceptions).

See Sections 16520 ("firearm"), 16530 ("firearm capable of being concealed upon the person," "pistol," and "revolver"), 31910 ("unsafe handgun"). [38 Cal.L.Rev.Comm. Reports 217 (2009)].

Cross References

Firearm capable of being concealed upon the person defined for purposes of this Part, see Penal Code § 16530.
Firearm defined for purposes of this Part, see Penal Code § 16520.
Handgun defined for purposes of this Part, see Penal Code § 16640.
Pistol defined for purposes of this Part, see Penal Code § 16530.
Revolver defined for purposes of this Part, see Penal Code § 16530.

Research References

2 Witkin, California Criminal Law 4th Crimes Against Public Peace and Welfare § 224 (2021), Unsafe Handguns.

§ 32010. Standards testing of concealable firearms manufactured, imported, or offered for sale in California; certification of testing laboratories; fees; prerequisites for submitting specified handgun types

(a) Any pistol, revolver, or other firearm capable of being concealed upon the person manufactured in this state, imported into the state for sale, kept for sale, or offered or exposed for sale, shall be tested within a reasonable period of time by an independent laboratory certified pursuant to subdivision (b) to determine whether that pistol, revolver, or other firearm capable of being concealed upon the person meets or exceeds the standards defined in Section 31910.

(b) On or before October 1, 2000, the Department of Justice shall certify laboratories to verify compliance with the standards defined in Section 31910. The department may charge a fee to certify a laboratory to test any pistol, revolver, or other firearm capable of being concealed upon the person pursuant to Sections 31900 to 32110, inclusive. The fee shall not exceed the costs of certification.

(c) The certified testing laboratory shall, at the manufacturer's or importer's expense, test the firearm and submit a copy of the final test report directly to the Department of Justice along with a prototype of the weapon to be retained by the department. The department shall notify the manufacturer or importer of its receipt of the final test report and the department's determination as to whether the firearm tested may be sold in this state.

(d)(1) Commencing January 1, 2006, no center-fire semiautomatic pistol may be submitted for testing pursuant to Sections 31900 to 32110, inclusive, if it does not have either a chamber load indicator, or a magazine disconnect mechanism if it has a detachable magazine.

(2) Commencing January 1, 2007, no center-fire semiautomatic pistol may be submitted for testing pursuant to Sections 31900 to 32110, inclusive, if it does not have both a chamber load indicator and a magazine disconnect mechanism.

(3) Commencing January 1, 2006, no rimfire semiautomatic pistol may be submitted for testing pursuant to Sections 31900 to 32110, inclusive, if it has a detachable magazine, and does not have a magazine disconnect mechanism. *(Added by Stats.2010, c. 711 (S.B.1080), § 6, operative Jan. 1, 2012. Amended by Stats.2018, c. 185 (A.B.2176), § 11, eff. Jan. 1, 2019.)*

Law Revision Commission Comments

Section 32010 continues former Section 12130 without substantive change.

For exceptions to the rules stated in this article, see Sections 32100 (exception for single-shot pistol or single-action revolver meeting certain specifications), 32105 (exception for pistols used in Olympic target shooting events), 32110 (other exceptions).

See Sections 16380 ("chamber load indicator"), 16520 ("firearm"), 16530 ("firearm capable of being concealed upon the person," "pistol," and "revolver"), 16900 ("magazine disconnect mechanism"), 17140 ("semiautomatic pistol"). [38 Cal.L.Rev.Comm. Reports 217 (2009)].

Section 32010(b) is amended for clarity. This is a nonsubstantive change. [44 Cal.L.Rev.Comm. Reports 471 (2015)].

Cross References

Firearm capable of being concealed upon the person defined for purposes of this Part, see Penal Code § 16530.
Firearm defined for purposes of this Part, see Penal Code § 16520.
Pistol defined for purposes of this Part, see Penal Code § 16530.
Revolver defined for purposes of this Part, see Penal Code § 16530.

Research References

2 Witkin, California Criminal Law 4th Crimes Against Public Peace and Welfare § 224 (2021), Unsafe Handguns.

§ 32015. Roster of tested handguns determined not to be unsafe; contents

(a) On and after January 1, 2001, the Department of Justice shall compile, publish, and thereafter maintain a roster listing all of the handguns that have been tested by a certified testing laboratory, have been determined not to be unsafe handguns, and may be sold in this state pursuant to this part. The roster shall list, for each firearm, the manufacturer, model number, and model name.

(b)(1) The department may charge every person in this state who is licensed as a manufacturer of firearms pursuant to Chapter 44 (commencing with Section 921) of Title 18 of the United States Code, and any person in this state who manufactures or causes to be manufactured, imports into the state for sale, keeps for sale, or offers or exposes for sale any handgun in this state, an annual fee not exceeding the costs of preparing, publishing, and maintaining the roster pursuant to subdivision (a) and the costs of research and development, report analysis, firearms storage, and other program infrastructure costs necessary to implement Sections 31900 to 32110, inclusive. Commencing January 1, 2015, the annual fee shall be paid on January 1, or the next business day, of every year.

(2) Any handgun that is manufactured by a manufacturer who manufactures or causes to be manufactured, imports into the state for sale, keeps for sale, or offers or exposes for sale any handgun in this state, and who fails to pay any fee required pursuant to paragraph (1), may be excluded from the roster.

(3) If a purchaser has initiated a transfer of a handgun that is listed on the roster as not unsafe, and prior to the completion of the transfer, the handgun is removed from the roster of not unsafe handguns because of failure to pay the fee required to keep that handgun listed on the roster, the handgun shall be deliverable to the purchaser if the purchaser is not otherwise prohibited from purchasing or possessing the handgun. However, if a purchaser has initiated a transfer of a handgun that is listed on the roster as not unsafe, and prior to the completion of the transfer, the handgun is removed from the roster pursuant to subdivision (d) of Section 32020, the handgun shall not be deliverable to the purchaser. *(Added by Stats.2010, c. 711 (S.B.1080), § 6, operative Jan. 1, 2012. Amended by Stats.2013, c. 758 (S.B.363), § 4.)*

Law Revision Commission Comments

Section 32015 continues former Section 12131(a)-(b) without substantive change.

For exceptions to the rules stated in this article, see Sections 32100 (exception for single-shot pistol or single-action revolver meeting certain specifications), 32105 (exception for pistols used in Olympic target shooting events), 32110 (other exceptions).

See Sections 16520 ("firearm"), 16530 ("firearm capable of being concealed upon the person," "pistol," and "revolver"), 16640 ("handgun"), 31910 ("unsafe handgun"). [38 Cal.L.Rev.Comm. Reports 217 (2009)].

Cross References

Firearm capable of being concealed upon the person defined for purposes of this Part, see Penal Code § 16530.
Firearm defined for purposes of this Part, see Penal Code § 16520.
Handgun defined for purposes of this Part, see Penal Code § 16640.
Pistol defined for purposes of this Part, see Penal Code § 16530.
Revolver defined for purposes of this Part, see Penal Code § 16530.

§ 32020. Retesting of handgun models; removal of failed models from roster

(a) The Attorney General may annually retest up to 5 percent of the handgun models that are listed on the roster described in subdivision (a) of Section 32015.

(b) The retesting of a handgun model pursuant to subdivision (a) shall conform to the following:

(1) The Attorney General shall obtain from retail or wholesale sources, or both, three samples of the handgun model to be retested.

(2) The Attorney General shall select the certified laboratory to be used for the retesting.

(3) The ammunition used for the retesting shall be of a type recommended by the manufacturer in the user manual for the handgun. If the user manual for the handgun model makes no ammunition recommendation, the Attorney General shall select the ammunition to be used for the retesting. The ammunition shall be of the proper caliber for the handgun, commercially available, and in new condition.

(c) The retest shall be conducted in the same manner as the testing prescribed in Sections 31900 and 31905.

(d) If the handgun model fails retesting, the Attorney General shall remove the handgun model from the roster maintained pursuant to subdivision (a) of Section 32015. *(Added by Stats.2010, c. 711 (S.B.1080), § 6, operative Jan. 1, 2012.)*

Law Revision Commission Comments

Section 32020 continues former Section 12131(c)-(f) without substantive change.

For exceptions to the rules stated in this article, see Sections 32100 (exception for single-shot pistol or single-action revolver meeting certain specifications), 32105 (exception for pistols used in Olympic target shooting events), 32110 (other exceptions).

See Section 16640 ("handgun"). [38 Cal.L.Rev.Comm. Reports 217 (2009)].

Cross References

Attorney General, generally, see Government Code § 12500 et seq.

Handgun defined for purposes of this Part, see Penal Code § 16640.

§ 32025. Reinstatement of models removed from roster; conditions

A handgun model removed from the roster pursuant to subdivision (d) of Section 32020 may be reinstated on the roster if all of the following are met:

(a) The manufacturer petitions the Attorney General for reinstatement of the handgun model.

(b) The manufacturer pays the Department of Justice for all of the costs related to the reinstatement testing of the handgun model, including the purchase price of the handguns, prior to reinstatement testing.

(c) The reinstatement testing of the handguns shall be in accordance with subdivisions (b) and (c) of Section 32020.

(d) The three handgun samples shall be tested only once for reinstatement. If the sample fails it may not be retested.

(e) If the handgun model successfully passes testing for reinstatement, and if the manufacturer of the handgun is otherwise in compliance with Sections 31900 to 32110, inclusive, the Attorney General shall reinstate the handgun model on the roster maintained pursuant to subdivision (a) of Section 32015.

(f) The manufacturer shall provide the Attorney General with the complete testing history for the handgun model.

(g) Notwithstanding subdivision (a) of Section 32020, the Attorney General may, at any time, further retest any handgun model that has been reinstated to the roster. *(Added by Stats.2010, c. 711 (S.B. 1080), § 6, operative Jan. 1, 2012.)*

Law Revision Commission Comments

Section 32025 continues former Section 12131(g) without substantive change.

For exceptions to the rules stated in this article, see Sections 32100 (exception for single-shot pistol or single-action revolver meeting certain specifications), 32105 (exception for pistols used in Olympic target shooting events), 32110 (other exceptions).

See Section 16640 ("handgun"). [38 Cal.L.Rev.Comm. Reports 217 (2009)].

Cross References

Attorney General, generally, see Government Code § 12500 et seq.
Handgun defined for purposes of this Part, see Penal Code § 16640.

§ 32030. Firearms deemed to satisfy testing requirements due to similarity to tested models

(a) A firearm shall be deemed to satisfy the requirements of subdivision (a) of Section 32015 if another firearm made by the same manufacturer is already listed and the unlisted firearm differs from the listed firearm only in one or more of the following features:

(1) Finish, including, but not limited to, bluing, chrome-plating, oiling, or engraving.

(2) The material from which the grips are made.

(3) The shape or texture of the grips, so long as the difference in grip shape or texture does not in any way alter the dimensions, material, linkage, or functioning of the magazine well, the barrel, the chamber, or any of the components of the firing mechanism of the firearm.

(4) Any other purely cosmetic feature that does not in any way alter the dimensions, material, linkage, or functioning of the magazine well, the barrel, the chamber, or any of the components of the firing mechanism of the firearm.

(b) Any manufacturer seeking to have a firearm listed under this section shall provide to the Department of Justice all of the following:

(1) The model designation of the listed firearm.

(2) The model designation of each firearm that the manufacturer seeks to have listed under this section.

(3) A statement, under oath, that each unlisted firearm for which listing is sought differs from the listed firearm only in one or more of the ways identified in subdivision (a) and is in all other respects identical to the listed firearm.

(c) The department may, in its discretion and at any time, require a manufacturer to provide to the department any model for which listing is sought under this section, to determine whether the model complies with the requirements of this section. *(Added by Stats.2010, c. 711 (S.B.1080), § 6, operative Jan. 1, 2012.)*

Law Revision Commission Comments

Section 32030 continues former Section 12131.5 without substantive change.

For exceptions to the rules stated in this article, see Sections 32100 (exception for single-shot pistol or single-action revolver meeting certain specifications), 32105 (exception for pistols used in Olympic target shooting events), 32110 (other exceptions).

See Section 16520 ("firearm"). [38 Cal.L.Rev.Comm. Reports 217 (2009)].

Cross References

Firearm defined for purposes of this Part, see Penal Code § 16520.

ARTICLE 6. EXCEPTIONS TO RULES GOVERNING UNSAFE HANDGUNS

Section

§ 32100. Single-action revolvers having curio or relic status or meeting certain specifications; single shot pistols meeting certain specifications

(a) Article 4 (commencing with Section 31900) and Article 5 (commencing with Section 32000) shall not apply to a single-action revolver that has at least a five-cartridge capacity with a barrel length of not less than three inches, and meets any of the following specifications:

(1) Was originally manufactured prior to 1900 and is a curio or relic, as defined in Section 478.11 of Title 27 of the Code of Federal Regulations.

(2) Has an overall length measured parallel to the barrel of at least seven and one-half inches when the handle, frame or receiver, and barrel are assembled.

(3) Has an overall length measured parallel to the barrel of at least seven and one-half inches when the handle, frame or receiver, and barrel are assembled and that is currently approved for importation into the United States pursuant to the provisions of paragraph (3) of subsection (d) of Section 925 of Title 18 of the United States Code.

(b) Article 4 (commencing with Section 31900) and Article 5 (commencing with Section 32000) shall not apply to a single-shot pistol with a break top or bolt action and a barrel length of not less than six inches and that has an overall length of at least 10½ inches when the handle, frame or receiver, and barrel are assembled. However, Article 4 (commencing with Section 31900) and Article 5 (commencing with Section 32000) shall apply to a semiautomatic pistol that has been temporarily or permanently altered so that it will not fire in a semiautomatic mode. *(Added by Stats.2010, c. 711 (S.B.1080), § 6, operative Jan. 1, 2012. Amended by Stats.2014, c. 147 (A.B.1964), § 1, eff. Jan. 1, 2015.)*

Law Revision Commission Comments

Section 32100 continues former Section 12133 without substantive change.

See Section 16530 ("firearm capable of being concealed upon the person," "pistol," and "revolver"). [38 Cal.L.Rev.Comm. Reports 217 (2009)].

Cross References

Pistol defined for purposes of this Part, see Penal Code § 16530.
Revolver defined for purposes of this Part, see Penal Code § 16530.

Research References

2 Witkin, California Criminal Law 4th Crimes Against Public Peace and Welfare § 224 (2021), Unsafe Handguns.

§ 32105. Olympic target shooting pistols

(a) The Legislature finds a significant public purpose in exempting pistols that are designed expressly for use in Olympic target shooting events. Therefore, those pistols that are sanctioned by the International Olympic Committee and by USA Shooting, the national governing body for international shooting competition in the United States, and that were used for Olympic target shooting purposes as of January 1, 2001, and that fall within the definition of "unsafe handgun" pursuant to paragraph (3) of subdivision (b) of Section 31910 shall be exempt, as provided in subdivisions (b) and (c).

(b) Article 4 (commencing with Section 31900) and Article 5 (commencing with Section 32000) shall not apply to any of the following pistols, because they are consistent with the significant public purpose expressed in subdivision (a):

MANUFACTURER	MODEL	CALIBER
ANSCHUTZ	FP	.22LR
BENELLI	MP90	.22LR
BENELLI	MP90	.32 S&W LONG
BENELLI	MP95	.22LR
BENELLI	MP95	.32 S&W LONG
DRULOV	FP	.22LR
GREEN	ELECTROARM	.22LR
HAMMERLI	100	.22LR
HAMMERLI	101	.22LR
HAMMERLI	102	.22LR
HAMMERLI	162	.22LR
HAMMERLI	280	.22LR
HAMMERLI	280	.32 S&W LONG
HAMMERLI	FP10	.22LR
HAMMERLI	MP33	.22LR
HAMMERLI	SP20	.22LR
HAMMERLI	SP20	.32 S&W LONG
MORINI	CM102E	.22LR
MORINI	22M	.22LR
MORINI	32M	.32 S&W LONG
MORINI	CM80	.22LR
PARDINI	GP	.22 SHORT
PARDINI	GPO	.22 SHORT
PARDINI	GP–SCHUMANN	.22 SHORT
PARDINI	HP	.32 S&W LONG
PARDINI	K22	.22LR
PARDINI	MP	.32 S&W LONG
PARDINI	PGP75	.22LR
PARDINI	SP	.22LR
PARDINI	SPE	.22LR
SAKO	FINMASTER	.22LR
STEYR	FP	.22LR
VOSTOK	IZH NO. 1	.22LR
VOSTOK	MU55	.22LR
VOSTOK	TOZ35	.22LR
WALTHER	FP	.22LR
WALTHER	GSP	.22LR
WALTHER	GSP	.32 S&W LONG
WALTHER	OSP	.22 SHORT
WALTHER	OSP–2000	.22 SHORT

(c) The department shall create a program that is consistent with the purpose stated in subdivision (a) to exempt new models of competitive firearms from Article 4 (commencing with Section 31900) and Article 5 (commencing with Section 32000). The exempt competitive firearms may be based on recommendations by USA Shooting consistent with the regulations contained in the USA Shooting Official Rules or may be based on the recommendation or rules of any other organization that the department deems relevant. *(Added by Stats.2010, c. 711 (S.B.1080), § 6, operative Jan. 1, 2012. Amended by Stats.2011, c. 296 (A.B.1023), § 243.)*

Law Revision Commission Comments

Section 32105 continues former Section 12132(h) without substantive change.

See Sections 16520 ("firearm"), 16530 ("firearm capable of being concealed upon the person," "pistol," and "revolver"). [38 Cal.L.Rev.Comm. Reports 217 (2009)].

Cross References

Firearm defined for purposes of this Part, see Penal Code § 16520.
Handgun defined for purposes of this Part, see Penal Code § 16640.
Pistol defined for purposes of this Part, see Penal Code § 16530.

§ 32110. Miscellaneous exemptions

Article 4 (commencing with Section 31900) and Article 5 (commencing with Section 32000) shall not apply to any of the following:

(a) The sale, loan, or transfer of any firearm pursuant to Chapter 5 (commencing with Section 28050) of Division 6 in order to comply with Section 27545.

(b) The sale, loan, or transfer of any firearm that is exempt from the provisions of Section 27545 pursuant to any applicable exemption contained in Article 2 (commencing with Section 27600) or Article 6 (commencing with Section 27850) of Chapter 4 of Division 6, if the sale, loan, or transfer complies with the requirements of that applicable exemption to Section 27545.

(c) The sale, loan, or transfer of any firearm as described in paragraph (3) of subdivision (b) of Section 32000.

(d) The delivery of a pistol, revolver, or other firearm capable of being concealed upon the person to a person licensed pursuant to Sections 26700 to 26915, inclusive, for the purposes of the service or repair of that firearm.

(e) The return of a pistol, revolver, or other firearm capable of being concealed upon the person by a person licensed pursuant to Sections 26700 to 26915, inclusive, to its owner where that firearm was initially delivered in the circumstances set forth in subdivision (a), (d), (f), or (i).

(f) The delivery of a pistol, revolver, or other firearm capable of being concealed upon the person to a person licensed pursuant to Sections 26700 to 26915, inclusive, for the purpose of a consignment sale or as collateral for a pawnbroker loan.

(g) The sale, loan, or transfer of any pistol, revolver, or other firearm capable of being concealed upon the person listed as a curio or relic, as defined in Section 478.11 of Title 27 of the Code of Federal Regulations.

(h) The sale, loan, or transfer of any semiautomatic pistol that is to be used solely as a prop during the course of a motion picture, television, or video production by an authorized participant therein in the course of making that production or event or by an authorized employee or agent of the entity producing that production or event.

(i) The delivery of a pistol, revolver, or other firearm capable of being concealed upon the person to a person licensed pursuant to Sections 26700 to 26915, inclusive, where the firearm is being loaned by the licensee to a consultant-evaluator.

(j) The delivery of a pistol, revolver, or other firearm capable of being concealed upon the person by a person licensed pursuant to

Sections 26700 to 26915, inclusive, where the firearm is being loaned by the licensee to a consultant-evaluator.

(k) The return of a pistol, revolver, or other firearm capable of being concealed upon the person to a person licensed pursuant to Sections 26700 to 26915, inclusive, where it was initially delivered pursuant to subdivision (j). *(Added by Stats.2010, c. 711 (S.B.1080), § 6, operative Jan. 1, 2012.)*

Law Revision Commission Comments

Subdivisions (a)-(g) of Section 32110 continue former Section 12132(a)-(g) without substantive change. A cross-reference to nonexistent Section 178.11 of the Code of Federal Regulations has been replaced with a cross-reference to Section 478.11 of Title 27 of the Code of Federal Regulations.

Subdivisions (h)-(k) continue former Section 12132(i)-(*l*) without substantive change.

See Sections 16410 ("consultant-evaluator"), 16520 ("firearm"), 16530 ("firearm capable of being concealed upon the person," "pistol," and "revolver"). [38 Cal.L.Rev.Comm. Reports 217 (2009)].

Cross References

Consultant-evaluator defined for purposes of this Part, see Penal Code § 16410.
Firearm capable of being concealed upon the person defined for purposes of this Part, see Penal Code § 16530.
Firearm defined for purposes of this Part, see Penal Code § 16520.
Pistol defined for purposes of this Part, see Penal Code § 16530.
Revolver defined for purposes of this Part, see Penal Code § 16530.

CHAPTER 5. LARGE–CAPACITY MAGAZINE

ARTICLE 1. RULES GOVERNING LARGE–CAPACITY MAGAZINES

§ 32310. Prohibition on manufacture, import, sale, gift, loan, purchase, receipt, or possession of large-capacity magazines; punishment

(a) Except as provided in Article 2 (commencing with Section 32400) of this chapter and in Chapter 1 (commencing with Section 17700) of Division 2 of Title 2, any person in this state who manufactures or causes to be manufactured, imports into the state, keeps for sale, or offers or exposes for sale, or who gives, lends, buys, or receives any large-capacity magazine is punishable by imprisonment in a county jail not exceeding one year or imprisonment pursuant to subdivision (h) of Section 1170.

(b) For purposes of this section, "manufacturing" includes both fabricating a magazine and assembling a magazine from a combination of parts, including, but not limited to, the body, spring, follower, and floor plate or end plate, to be a fully functioning large-capacity magazine.

(c) Except as provided in Article 2 (commencing with Section 32400) of this chapter and in Chapter 1 (commencing with Section 17700) of Division 2 of Title 2, commencing July 1, 2017, any person in this state who possesses any large-capacity magazine, regardless of the date the magazine was acquired, is guilty of an infraction punishable by a fine not to exceed one hundred dollars ($100) per large-capacity magazine, or is guilty of a misdemeanor punishable by a fine not to exceed one hundred dollars ($100) per large-capacity magazine, by imprisonment in a county jail not to exceed one year, or by both that fine and imprisonment.

(d) Any person who may not lawfully possess a large-capacity magazine commencing July 1, 2017 shall, prior to July 1, 2017:

(1) Remove the large-capacity magazine from the state;

(2) Sell the large-capacity magazine to a licensed firearms dealer; or

(3) Surrender the large-capacity magazine to a law enforcement agency for destruction. *(Added by Stats.2010, c. 711 (S.B.1080), § 6, operative Jan. 1, 2012. Amended by Stats.2012, c. 43 (S.B.1023), § 107, eff. June 27, 2012; Stats.2013, c. 728 (A.B.48), § 1; Stats.2016, c. 58 (S.B.1446), § 1, eff. Jan. 1, 2017; Initiative Measure (Prop. 63, § 6.1, approved Nov. 8, 2016, eff. Nov. 9, 2016).)*

Validity

For validity of this section, see Duncan v. Becerra, S.D.Cal. 2019, 366 F.Supp.3d 1131, affirmed 970 F.3d 1133; Duncan v. Becerra, C.A.9 (Cal.)2020, 970 F.3d 1133, rehearing en banc granted, opinion vacated by Duncan v. Becerra, 9th Cir.(Cal.), February 25, 2021, 988 F.3d 1209.

For an order enjoining implementation and enforcement of subdivisions (c) and (d) of this section, as enacted by Initiative Measure (Prop. 63, approved Nov. 8, 2016, eff. Nov. 9, 2016), see Duncan v. Becerra, S.D.Cal.2017, 265 F.Supp.3d 1106, affirmed 742 Fed.Appx. 218, 2018 WL 3433828.

Law Revision Commission Comments

Section 32310 continues former Section 12020(a)(2) without substantive change.

For circumstances in which this section is inapplicable, see Sections 16590 ("generally prohibited weapon"), 17700–17745 (exemptions relating to generally prohibited weapons), 32400–32450 (exceptions relating specifically to large-capacity magazines).

See Section 16740 ("large-capacity magazine"). See also Sections 17800 (distinct and separate offense), 32315 (permit for possession, transportation, or sale of large-capacity magazines between dealer and out-of-state client), 32390 (large-capacity magazine constituting nuisance). [38 Cal.L.Rev.Comm. Reports 217 (2009)].

Cross References

Large-capacity magazine defined for purposes of this Part, see Penal Code § 16740.
Sale, gift, or loan of large-capacity magazine to person enrolled in peace officer training course, see Penal Code § 32455.

Research References

California Jury Instructions - Criminal 12.49.7, Possessing or Trafficking in Large Capacity Magazines.
2 Witkin, California Criminal Law 4th Crimes Against Public Peace and Welfare § 211 (2021), Nature of Crime.

§ 32311. Large capacity magazine conversion kits; prohibition on manufacture, import, sale, gift, loan, purchase, or receipt; penalties

(a) Except as provided in Article 2 (commencing with Section 32400) of this chapter and in Chapter 1 (commencing with Section 17700) of Division 2 of Title 2, commencing January 1, 2014, any person in this state who knowingly manufactures or causes to be manufactured, imports into the state, keeps for sale, or offers or exposes for sale, or who gives, lends, buys, or receives any large capacity magazine conversion kit is punishable by a fine of not more than one thousand dollars ($1,000) or imprisonment in a county jail not to exceed six months, or by both that fine and imprisonment. This section does not apply to a fully assembled large-capacity magazine, which is governed by Section 32310.

(b) For purposes of this section, a "large capacity magazine conversion kit" is a device or combination of parts of a fully functioning large-capacity magazine, including, but not limited to, the body, spring, follower, and floor plate or end plate, capable of converting an ammunition feeding device into a large-capacity magazine. *(Added by Stats.2013, c. 728 (A.B.48), § 2.)*

Research References

2 Witkin, California Criminal Law 4th Crimes Against Public Peace and Welfare § 211 (2021), Nature of Crime.

§ 32315. Permits for possession, transportation, or sale of large-capacity magazines between licensed individuals and out-of-state clients

Upon a showing that good cause exists, the Department of Justice may issue permits for the possession, transportation, or sale between a person licensed pursuant to Sections 26700 to 26915, inclusive, and an out-of-state client, of large-capacity magazines. *(Added by Stats.2010, c. 711 (S.B.1080), § 6, operative Jan. 1, 2012.)*

Law Revision Commission Comments

Section 32315 continues former Section 12079(a) without substantive change.

See Sections 16740 ("large-capacity magazine"), 26700 ("dealer," "licensee," or "person licensed pursuant to Sections 26700 to 26915, inclusive"). See also Section 32430 (exception for importation or sale of large-capacity magazine by person with permit). [38 Cal.L.Rev.Comm. Reports 217 (2009)].

Cross References

Large-capacity magazine defined for purposes of this Part, see Penal Code § 16740.

Research References

2 Witkin, California Criminal Law 4th Crimes Against Public Peace and Welfare § 192 (2021), In General.

§ 32390. Nuisance status of large-capacity magazines

Except as provided in Article 2 (commencing with Section 32400) of this chapter and in Chapter 1 (commencing with Section 17700) of Division 2 of Title 2, any large-capacity magazine is a nuisance and is subject to Section 18010. *(Added by Stats.2010, c. 711 (S.B.1080), § 6, operative Jan. 1, 2012.)*

Law Revision Commission Comments

With respect to a large-capacity magazine, Section 32390 continues the first part of the first sentence of former Section 12029 without substantive change.

See Section 16740 ("large-capacity magazine"). [38 Cal.L.Rev.Comm. Reports 217 (2009)].

Cross References

Large-capacity magazine defined for purposes of this Part, see Penal Code § 16740.

Research References

2 Witkin, California Criminal Law 4th Crimes Against Public Peace and Welfare § 263 (2021), Nuisances.

ARTICLE 2. EXCEPTIONS RELATING SPECIFICALLY TO LARGE–CAPACITY MAGAZINES

§ 32400. Large-capacity magazines for use by law enforcement agency employees; application of Section 32310

Section 32310 does not apply to the sale of, giving of, lending of, possession of, importation into this state of, or purchase of, any large-capacity magazine to or by any federal, state, county, city and county, or city agency that is charged with the enforcement of any law, for use by agency employees in the discharge of their official duties, whether on or off duty, and where the use is authorized by the agency and is within the course and scope of their duties. *(Added by Stats.2010, c. 711 (S.B.1080), § 6, operative Jan. 1, 2012. Amended by Stats.2016, c. 58 (S.B.1446), § 2, eff. Jan. 1, 2017; Initiative Measure (Prop. 63, § 6.2, approved Nov. 8, 2016, eff. Nov. 9, 2016).)*

Law Revision Commission Comments

Section 32400 continues former Section 12020(b)(19) without substantive change.

See Section 16740 ("large-capacity magazine"). [38 Cal.L.Rev.Comm. Reports 217 (2009)].

Cross References

Large-capacity magazine defined for purposes of this Part, see Penal Code § 16740.

Research References

2 Witkin, California Criminal Law 4th Crimes Against Public Peace and Welfare § 211 (2021), Nature of Crime.

§ 32405. Large-capacity magazines sold to or purchased by sworn peace officer; application of Section 32310

Section 32310 does not apply to the sale to, lending to, transfer to, purchase by, receipt of, possession of, or importation into this state of, a large-capacity magazine by a sworn peace officer, as defined in Chapter 4.5 (commencing with Section 830) of Title 3 of Part 2, or sworn federal law enforcement officer, who is authorized to carry a firearm in the course and scope of that officer's duties. *(Added by Stats.2010, c. 711 (S.B.1080), § 6, operative Jan. 1, 2012. Amended by Stats.2016, c. 58 (S.B.1446), § 3, eff. Jan. 1, 2017; Initiative Measure (Prop. 63, § 6.3, approved Nov. 8, 2016, eff. Nov. 9, 2016).)*

Law Revision Commission Comments

Section 32405 continues former Section 12020(b)(20) without substantive change.

See Sections 16520 ("firearm"), 16740 ("large-capacity magazine"). [38 Cal.L.Rev.Comm. Reports 217 (2009)].

Cross References

Firearm defined for purposes of this Part, see Penal Code § 16520.
Large-capacity magazine defined for purposes of this Part, see Penal Code § 16740.

§ 32406. Infraction relating to possession of large-capacity magazine; exception for honorably retired sworn peace or federal law enforcement officers

Section added by Initiative Measure (Prop. 63, § 6.4, approved Nov. 8, 2016, eff. Nov. 9, 2016). See, also, another section of the same number added by Stats.2016, c. 58 (S.B.1446), § 4, eff. Jan. 1, 2017.

Subdivision (c) of Section 32310 does not apply to an honorably retired sworn peace officer, as defined in Chapter 4.5 (commencing with Section 830) of Title 3 of Part 2, or honorably retired sworn federal law enforcement officer, who was authorized to carry a firearm in the course and scope of that officer's duties. "Honorably retired" shall have the same meaning as provided in Section 16690. *(Added by Initiative Measure (Prop. 63, § 6.4, approved Nov. 8, 2016, eff. Nov. 9, 2016).)*

Cross References

Honorably retired defined, see Penal Code § 16690.

§ 32406. Large-capacity magazines; retired sworn peace officers, historical societies, forensic laboratories, estates, and certain others in possession

Section added by Stats.2016, c. 58 (S.B.1446), § 4, eff. Jan. 1, 2017. See, also, another section of the same number added by Initiative Measure (Prop. 63, § 6.4, approved Nov. 8, 2016, eff. Nov. 9, 2016).

Subdivisions (b) and (c) of Section 32310 do not apply to the following:

(a) An individual who honorably retired from being a sworn peace officer, as defined in Chapter 4.5 (commencing with Section 830) of Title 3 of Part 2, or an individual who honorably retired from being a sworn federal law enforcement officer, who was authorized to carry a firearm in the course and scope of that officer's duties. For purposes of this section, "honorably retired" has the same meaning as provided in Section 16690.

(b) A federal, state, or local historical society, museum or institutional society, or museum or institutional collection, that is open to the public, provided that the large-capacity magazine is unloaded, properly housed within secured premises, and secured from unauthorized handling.

(c) A person who finds a large-capacity magazine, if the person is not prohibited from possessing firearms or ammunition, and possessed it no longer than necessary to deliver or transport it to the nearest law enforcement agency.

(d) A forensic laboratory, or an authorized agent or employee thereof in the course and scope of his or her authorized activities.

(e) The receipt or disposition of a large-capacity magazine by a trustee of a trust, or an executor or administrator of an estate, including an estate that is subject to probate, that includes a large-capacity magazine.

(f) A person lawfully in possession of a firearm that the person obtained prior to January 1, 2000, if no magazine that holds 10 or fewer rounds of ammunition is compatible with that firearm and the person possesses the large-capacity magazine solely for use with that firearm. *(Added by Stats.2016, c. 58 (S.B.1446), § 4, eff. Jan. 1, 2017.)*

Cross References

Honorably retired defined, see Penal Code § 16690.

§ 32410. Large-capacity magazines sold to, purchased by, or possessed by persons licensed pursuant to specified provisions; application of Section 32310

Section 32310 does not apply to the sale, purchase, or possession of any large-capacity magazine to or by a person licensed pursuant to Sections 26700 to 26915, inclusive. *(Added by Stats.2010, c. 711 (S.B.1080), § 6, operative Jan. 1, 2012. Amended by Stats.2016, c. 58 (S.B.1446), § 5, eff. Jan. 1, 2017; Initiative Measure (Prop. 63, § 6.5, approved Nov. 8, 2016, eff. Nov. 9, 2016).)*

Law Revision Commission Comments

Section 32410 continues former Section 12020(b)(21) without substantive change.

See Sections 16740 ("large-capacity magazine"), 26700 ("dealer," "licensee," or "person licensed pursuant to Sections 26700 to 26915, inclusive"). [38 Cal.L.Rev.Comm. Reports 217 (2009)].

Cross References

Large-capacity magazine defined for purposes of this Part, see Penal Code § 16740.

§ 32415. Loan of lawfully possessed large-capacity magazine between two individuals; application of Section 32310

Section 32310 does not apply to the loan of a lawfully possessed large-capacity magazine between two individuals if all of the following conditions are met:

(a) The person being loaned the large-capacity magazine is not prohibited by Chapter 1 (commencing with Section 29610), Chapter 2 (commencing with Section 29800), or Chapter 3 (commencing with Section 29900) of Division 9 of this title or Section 8100 or 8103 of the Welfare and Institutions Code from possessing firearms or ammunition.

(b) The loan of the large-capacity magazine occurs at a place or location where the possession of the large-capacity magazine is not otherwise prohibited, and the person who lends the large-capacity magazine remains in the accessible vicinity of the person to whom the large-capacity magazine is loaned. *(Added by Stats.2010, c. 711 (S.B.1080), § 6, operative Jan. 1, 2012.)*

Law Revision Commission Comments

Section 32415 continues former Section 12020(b)(22) without substantive change.

See Sections 16520 ("firearm"), 16740 ("large-capacity magazine"). [38 Cal.L.Rev.Comm. Reports 217 (2009)].

Cross References

Firearm defined for purposes of this Part, see Penal Code § 16520.

Large-capacity magazine defined for purposes of this Part, see Penal Code § 16740.

§ 32425. Loaning or giving large-capacity magazine to persons licensed pursuant to specified provisions, or to gunsmith, or possession or return of magazine by such persons; application of Section 32310

Section 32310 does not apply to any of the following:

(a) The lending or giving of any large-capacity magazine to a person licensed pursuant to Sections 26700 to 26915, inclusive, or to a gunsmith, for the purposes of maintenance, repair, or modification of that large-capacity magazine.

(b) The possession of any large-capacity magazine by a person specified in subdivision (a) for the purposes specified in subdivision (a).

(c) The return to its owner of any large-capacity magazine by a person specified in subdivision (a). *(Added by Stats.2010, c. 711 (S.B.1080), § 6, operative Jan. 1, 2012. Amended by Stats.2016, c. 58 (S.B.1446), § 7, eff. Jan. 1, 2017; Initiative Measure (Prop. 63, § 6.7, approved Nov. 8, 2016, eff. Nov. 9, 2016).)*

Law Revision Commission Comments

Subdivision (a) of Section 32425 continues former Section 12020(b)(24) without substantive change.

Subdivision (b) continues former Section 12020(b)(25) without substantive change.

See Sections 16630 ("gunsmith"), 16740 ("large-capacity magazine"), 26700 ("dealer," "licensee," or "person licensed pursuant to Sections 26700 to 26915, inclusive"). [38 Cal.L.Rev.Comm. Reports 217 (2009)].

Cross References

Gunsmith defined for purposes of this Part, see Penal Code § 16630.
Large-capacity magazine defined for purposes of this Part, see Penal Code § 16740.

§ 32430. Possession, importation, or sale of large-capacity magazine by person with permit; application of Section 32310

Section 32310 does not apply to the possession of, importation into this state of, or sale of, any large-capacity magazine by a person who has been issued a permit to engage in those activities pursuant to Section 32315, when those activities are in accordance with the terms and conditions of that permit. *(Added by Stats.2010, c. 711 (S.B. 1080), § 6, operative Jan. 1, 2012. Amended by Stats.2016, c. 58 (S.B.1446), § 8, eff. Jan. 1, 2017.)*

Law Revision Commission Comments

Section 32430 continues former Section 12020(b)(26) without substantive change.

See Section 16740 ("large-capacity magazine"). [38 Cal.L.Rev.Comm. Reports 217 (2009)].

Cross References

Large-capacity magazine defined for purposes of this Part, see Penal Code § 16740.

§ 32435. Large-capacity magazines; entity that operates armored vehicle business; application of Section 32310

Section 32310 does not apply to any of the following:

(a) The sale of, giving of, lending of, possession of, importation into this state of, or purchase of, any large-capacity magazine, to or by any entity that operates an armored vehicle business pursuant to the laws of this state.

(b) The lending of large-capacity magazines by an entity specified in subdivision (a) to its authorized employees, while in the course and scope of employment for purposes that pertain to the entity's armored vehicle business.

(c) The possession of any large-capacity magazines by the employees of an entity specified in subdivision (a) for purposes that pertain to the entity's armored vehicle business.

(d) The return of those large-capacity magazines to the entity specified in subdivision (a) by those employees specified in subdivision (b). *(Added by Stats.2010, c. 711 (S.B.1080), § 6, operative Jan. 1, 2012. Amended by Stats.2016, c. 58 (S.B.1446), § 9, eff. Jan. 1, 2017; Initiative Measure (Prop. 63, § 6.8, approved Nov. 8, 2016, eff. Nov. 9, 2016).)*

Law Revision Commission Comments

Subdivision (a) of Section 32435 continues former Section 12020(b)(27) without substantive change.

Subdivision (b) continues former Section 12020(b)(28) without substantive change.

Subdivision (c) continues former Section 12020(b)(29) without substantive change.

See Section 16740 ("large-capacity magazine"). [38 Cal.L.Rev.Comm. Reports 217 (2009)].

Cross References

Large-capacity magazine defined for purposes of this Part, see Penal Code § 16740.

§ 32440. Large-capacity magazines manufactured for law enforcement agency, sworn peace officer, government agency, or military; application of Section 32310

Section 32310 does not apply to any of the following:

(a) The manufacture of a large-capacity magazine for any federal, state, county, city and county, or city agency that is charged with the enforcement of any law, for use by agency employees in the discharge of their official duties, whether on or off duty, and where the use is authorized by the agency and is within the course and scope of their duties.

(b) The manufacture of a large-capacity magazine for use by a sworn peace officer, as defined in Chapter 4.5 (commencing with Section 830) of Title 3 of Part 2, who is authorized to carry a firearm in the course and scope of that officer's duties.

(c) The manufacture of a large-capacity magazine for export or for sale to government agencies or the military pursuant to applicable federal regulations. *(Added by Stats.2010, c. 711 (S.B.1080), § 6, operative Jan. 1, 2012.)*

Law Revision Commission Comments

Section 32440 continues former Section 12020(b)(30) without substantive change.

See Sections 16520 ("firearm"), 16740 ("large-capacity magazine"). [38 Cal.L.Rev.Comm. Reports 217 (2009)].

Cross References

Firearm defined for purposes of this Part, see Penal Code § 16520.
Large-capacity magazine defined for purposes of this Part, see Penal Code § 16740.

§ 32445. Large-capacity magazines loaned for use as motion picture, television, or video production prop; application of Section 32310

Section 32310 does not apply to the loan of a large-capacity magazine for use solely as a prop for a motion picture, television, or video production. *(Added by Stats.2010, c. 711 (S.B.1080), § 6, operative Jan. 1, 2012.)*

Law Revision Commission Comments

Section 32445 continues former Section 12020(b)(31) without substantive change.

See Section 16740 ("large-capacity magazine"). [38 Cal.L.Rev.Comm. Reports 217 (2009)].

Cross References

Large-capacity magazine defined for purposes of this Part, see Penal Code § 16740.

§ 32450. Purchase or possession of large-capacity magazines by special weapons permit holder; application of Section 32310

Section 32310 does not apply to the purchase or possession of a large-capacity magazine by the holder of a special weapons permit issued pursuant to Section 31000, 32650, or 33300, or pursuant to Article 3 (commencing with Section 18900) of Chapter 1 of Division 5 of Title 2, or pursuant to Article 4 (commencing with Section 32700) of Chapter 6 of this division, for any of the following purposes:

(a) For use solely as a prop for a motion picture, television, or video production.

(b) For export pursuant to federal regulations.

(c) For resale to law enforcement agencies, government agencies, or the military, pursuant to applicable federal regulations. *(Added by Stats.2010, c. 711 (S.B.1080), § 6, operative Jan. 1, 2012. Amended by Stats.2016, c. 58 (S.B.1446), § 10, eff. Jan. 1, 2017; Initiative Measure (Prop. 63, § 6.9, approved Nov. 8, 2016, eff. Nov. 9, 2016).)*

Law Revision Commission Comments

Section 32450 continues former Section 12020(b)(32) without substantive change.

See Section 16740 ("large-capacity magazine"). [38 Cal.L.Rev.Comm. Reports 217 (2009)].

Cross References

Large-capacity magazine defined for purposes of this Part, see Penal Code § 16740.

§ 32455. Sale, gift, or loan of large-capacity magazine to person enrolled in peace officer training course; application of Section 32310

Section 32310 does not apply to the sale, gift, or loan of a large-capacity magazine to a person enrolled in the course of basic training prescribed by the Commission on Peace Officer Standards and Training, or any other course certified by the commission, nor to the possession of, or purchase by, the person, for purposes of participation in the course during his or her period of enrollment. Upon completion of the course the large-capacity magazine shall be removed from the state, sold to a licensed firearms dealer, or surrendered to a law enforcement agency, unless another exemption to Section 32310 applies. *(Added by Stats.2017, c. 783 (A.B.693), § 4, eff. Oct. 14, 2017.)*

CHAPTER 6. MACHINEGUNS

ARTICLE 1. GENERAL PROVISIONS

§ 32610. Application of chapter to sale to, or purchase or possession by, law enforcement, military forces, and peace officers acting within scope of duties

Nothing in this chapter shall affect or apply to any of the following:

(a) The sale to, purchase by, or possession of machineguns by a police department, a sheriff's office, a marshal's office, a district attorney's office, the California Highway Patrol, the Department of Justice, the Department of Corrections for use by the department's Special Emergency Response Teams and Law Enforcement Liaison/Investigations Unit, or the military or naval forces of this state or of the United States for use in the discharge of their official duties, provided, however, that any sale to these entities be transacted by a person who is permitted pursuant to Section 32650 and licensed pursuant to Article 4 (commencing with Section 32700).

(b) The possession of machineguns by regular, salaried, full-time peace officer members of a police department, sheriff's office, marshal's office, district attorney's office, the California Highway Patrol, the Department of Justice, or the Department of Corrections for use by the department's Special Emergency Response Teams and Law Enforcement Liaison/Investigations Unit, when on duty and if the use is within the scope of their duties. *(Added by Stats.2010, c. 711 (S.B.1080), § 6, operative Jan. 1, 2012.)*

Law Revision Commission Comments

Section 32610 continues former Section 12201 without substantive change.

See Section 16880 ("machinegun"). [38 Cal.L.Rev.Comm. Reports 217 (2009)].

Cross References

Carrying a concealed firearm, peace officer exemption, see Penal Code § 25450 et seq.

Department of Corrections and Rehabilitation, generally, see Penal Code § 5000 et seq.

Machinegun defined for purposes of this Part, see Penal Code § 16880.

Research References

2 Witkin, California Criminal Law 4th Crimes Against Public Peace and Welfare § 231 (2021), Other Weapons and Devices.

ARTICLE 2. UNLAWFUL ACTS RELATING TO MACHINEGUNS

§ 32625. Unauthorized possession or transportation of machinegun; conversion into or manufacture of machineguns; fines and penalties

(a) Any person, firm, or corporation, who within this state possesses or knowingly transports a machinegun, except as authorized by this chapter, is guilty of a public offense and upon conviction thereof shall be punished by imprisonment pursuant to subdivision (h) of Section 1170, or by a fine not to exceed ten thousand dollars ($10,000), or by both that fine and imprisonment.

(b) Any person, firm, or corporation who within this state intentionally converts a firearm into a machinegun, or who sells, or offers for sale, or knowingly manufactures a machinegun, except as authorized by this chapter, is punishable by imprisonment pursuant to subdivision (h) of Section 1170 for four, six, or eight years. *(Added by Stats.2010, c. 711 (S.B.1080), § 6, operative Jan. 1, 2012. Amended by Stats.2011, c. 15 (A.B.109), § 553, eff. April 4, 2011, operative Jan. 1, 2012.)*

Law Revision Commission Comments

Section 32625 continues former Section 12220 without substantive change.

See Sections 16520 ("firearm"), 16880 ("machinegun"). [38 Cal.L.Rev. Comm. Reports 217 (2009)].

Cross References

Firearm defined for purposes of this Part, see Penal Code § 16520.

Fish and Game Commission, printing, permitted advertisements, private contract exceptions, see Fish and Game Code § 260.
Machinegun defined for purposes of this Part, see Penal Code § 16880.
Order for care, supervision, custody, conduct, maintenance and support of ward of court, extracurricular, enrichment, and social activities placement, counseling, parental participation, see Welfare and Institutions Code § 727.
Public offense defined, see Penal Code § 15.
Pupil safety, injurious objects, see Education Code § 49330.

Research References

2 Witkin, California Criminal Law 4th Crimes Against Public Peace and Welfare § 189 (2021), In General.
2 Witkin, California Criminal Law 4th Crimes Against Public Peace and Welfare § 231 (2021), Other Weapons and Devices.
1 Witkin California Criminal Law 4th Elements § 8 (2021), In General.
1 Witkin California Criminal Law 4th Introduction to Crimes § 81 (2021), Valid State Statutes.
3 Witkin, California Criminal Law 4th Punishment § 621 (2021), P.C. 1203.

ARTICLE 3. PERMITS

Section

§ 32650. Issuance of permit for possession, manufacture, or transportation of machineguns; good cause showing; age restrictions; permits limited to individuals

(a) The Department of Justice may issue permits for the possession, manufacture, and transportation or possession, manufacture, or transportation of machineguns, upon a satisfactory showing that good cause exists for the issuance of the permit to the applicant. No permit shall be issued to a person who is under 18 years of age.

(b) A permit for possession issued pursuant to this section may only be issued to an individual, and may not be issued to a partnership, corporation, limited liability company, association, or any other group or entity, regardless of how that entity was created. *(Added by Stats.2010, c. 711 (S.B.1080), § 6, operative Jan. 1, 2012. Amended by Stats.2013, c. 729 (A.B.170), § 4.)*

Law Revision Commission Comments

Section 32650 continues former Section 12230 without substantive change. See Section 16880 ("machinegun"). [38 Cal.L.Rev.Comm. Reports 217 (2009)].

Cross References

Authority of Department of Justice and Attorney General in criminal identification and investigation, see Penal Code §§ 11050, 11051.
High explosives, permits, activities covered, applications, conditions of use, duration, limitations on issuing permits if display of placards is required, persons unqualified to apply, see Health and Safety Code § 12101.
Machinegun defined for purposes of this Part, see Penal Code § 16880.

Research References

2 Witkin, California Criminal Law 4th Crimes Against Public Peace and Welfare § 193 (2021), Sale, Lease, or Transfer by Unlicensed Person.
2 Witkin, California Criminal Law 4th Crimes Against Public Peace and Welfare § 220 (2021), Registration Requirements.
2 Witkin, California Criminal Law 4th Crimes Against Public Peace and Welfare § 231 (2021), Other Weapons and Devices.
2 Witkin, California Criminal Law 4th Crimes Against Public Peace and Welfare § 253 (2021), Openly Displaying or Carrying Imitation or Unloaded Firearm.

§ 32655. Application for permit; requirements; fees

(a) An application for a permit under this article shall satisfy all of the following conditions:

(1) It shall be filed in writing.

(2) It shall be signed by the applicant if an individual, or by a member or officer qualified to sign if the applicant is a firm or corporation.

(3) It shall state the applicant's name.

(4) It shall state the business in which the applicant is engaged.

(5) It shall state the applicant's business address.

(6) It shall include a full description of the use to which the firearms are to be put.

(b) Applications and permits shall be uniform throughout the state on forms prescribed by the Department of Justice.

(c) Each applicant for a permit shall pay at the time of filing the application a fee determined by the Department of Justice. The fee shall not exceed the application processing costs of the Department of Justice.

(d) A permit granted pursuant to this article may be renewed one year from the date of issuance, and annually thereafter, upon the filing of a renewal application and the payment of a permit renewal fee, which shall not exceed the application processing costs of the Department of Justice.

(e) After the department establishes fees sufficient to reimburse the department for processing costs, fees charged shall increase at a rate not to exceed the legislatively approved annual cost-of-living adjustments for the department's budget. *(Added by Stats.2010, c. 711 (S.B.1080), § 6, operative Jan. 1, 2012.)*

Law Revision Commission Comments

Section 32655 continues former Section 12231 without substantive change. See Section 16520 ("firearm"). [38 Cal.L.Rev.Comm. Reports 217 (2009)].

Cross References

Criminal identification and statistics, custody of applications for licenses to possess dangerous weapons, see Penal Code § 11106.
Firearm defined for purposes of this Part, see Penal Code § 16520.

§ 32660. Location where permit is to be kept; inspections

Every person, firm, or corporation to whom a permit is issued under this article shall keep it on the person or at the place where the firearms are kept. The permit shall be open to inspection by any peace officer or any other person designated by the authority issuing the permit. *(Added by Stats.2010, c. 711 (S.B.1080), § 6, operative Jan. 1, 2012.)*

Law Revision Commission Comments

Section 32660 continues former Section 12232 without substantive change. See Section 16520 ("firearm"). [38 Cal.L.Rev.Comm. Reports 217 (2009)].

Cross References

Firearm defined for purposes of this Part, see Penal Code § 16520.
Inspection of public records, see Government Code § 6250 et seq.

§ 32665. Revocation of permit

A permit issued in accordance with this chapter may be revoked by the issuing authority at any time, when it appears that the need for the firearms has ceased or that the holder of the permit has used the firearms for purposes other than those allowed by the permit or that the holder of the permit has not exercised great care in retaining custody of any weapons possessed under the permit. *(Added by Stats.2010, c. 711 (S.B.1080), § 6, operative Jan. 1, 2012.)*

Law Revision Commission Comments

Section 32665 continues former Section 12233 without substantive change. See Section 16520 ("firearm"). [38 Cal.L.Rev.Comm. Reports 217 (2009)].

Cross References

Firearm defined for purposes of this Part, see Penal Code § 16520.

§ 32670. Inspections for security, safe storage, and inventory reconciliation

(a) Except as provided in subdivision (b), the Department of Justice shall, for every person, firm, or corporation to whom a permit is issued pursuant to this article, annually conduct an inspection for security and safe storage purposes, and to reconcile the inventory of machineguns.

(b) A person, firm, or corporation with an inventory of fewer than five devices that require any Department of Justice permit shall be subject to an inspection for security and safe storage purposes, and to reconcile inventory, once every five years, or more frequently if determined by the department. *(Added by Stats.2010, c. 711 (S.B.1080), § 6, operative Jan. 1, 2012.)*

Law Revision Commission Comments

Section 32670 continues former Section 12234 without substantive change.

See Section 16880 ("machinegun"). [38 Cal.L.Rev.Comm. Reports 217 (2009)].

Cross References

Machinegun defined for purposes of this Part, see Penal Code § 16880.

ARTICLE 4. LICENSES TO SELL MACHINEGUNS

§ 32700. Conditions for issuance of license

The Department of Justice may grant a license to permit the sale of machineguns at the place specified in the license, subject to all of the following conditions:

(a) The business shall be carried on only in the place designated in the license.

(b) The license or a certified copy of the license must be displayed on the premises in a place where it may easily be read.

(c) No machinegun shall be delivered to any person not authorized to receive the machinegun under the provisions of this chapter.

(d) A complete record must be kept of sales made under the authority of the license, showing the name and address of the purchaser, the descriptions and serial numbers of the weapons purchased, the number and date of issue of the purchaser's permit, if any, and the signature of the purchaser or purchasing agent. This record shall be open to the inspection of any peace officer or other person designated by the Attorney General. *(Added by Stats.2010, c. 711 (S.B.1080), § 6, operative Jan. 1, 2012.)*

Law Revision Commission Comments

Section 32700 continues former Section 12250(a)(1)-(4) without substantive change. In combination with Sections 32710 and 32720, Section 32700 also continues the introductory clause of former Section 12250(a) without substantive change.

See Section 16880 ("machinegun"). [38 Cal.L.Rev.Comm. Reports 217 (2009)].

Cross References

Attorney General, generally, see Government Code § 12500 et seq.
Authority of Department of Justice and Attorney General in criminal identification and investigation, see Penal Code §§ 11050, 11051.
Machinegun defined for purposes of this Part, see Penal Code § 16880.

Research References

2 Witkin, California Criminal Law 4th Crimes Against Public Peace and Welfare § 231 (2021), Other Weapons and Devices.

§ 32705. Applications; requirements

An application for a license under this article shall satisfy all of the following conditions:

(a) It shall be filed in writing.

(b) It shall be signed by the applicant if an individual, or by a member or officer qualified to sign if the applicant is a firm or corporation.

(c) It shall state the applicant's name.

(d) It shall state the business in which the applicant is engaged.

(e) It shall state the applicant's business address.

(f) It shall include a full description of the use to which the firearms are to be put. *(Added by Stats.2010, c. 711 (S.B.1080), § 6, operative Jan. 1, 2012.)*

Law Revision Commission Comments

Section 32705 continues the first paragraph of former Section 12250(b) without substantive change.

See Section 16520 ("firearm"). [38 Cal.L.Rev.Comm. Reports 217 (2009)].

Cross References

Firearm defined for purposes of this Part, see Penal Code § 16520.

§ 32710. Uniformity of applications and licenses; forms; effective period of license

(a) Applications and licenses under this article shall be uniform throughout the state, on forms prescribed by the Department of Justice.

(b) A license under this article shall be effective for not more than one year from the date of issuance. *(Added by Stats.2010, c. 711 (S.B.1080), § 6, operative Jan. 1, 2012.)*

Law Revision Commission Comments

Subdivision (a) of Section 32710 continues the second paragraph of former Section 12250(b) without substantive change. Subdivision (a) also continues part of the introductory clause of former Section 12250(a) without substantive change.

Subdivision (b) continues part of the introductory clause of former Section 12250(a) without substantive change. [38 Cal.L.Rev.Comm. Reports 217 (2009)].

§ 32715. Fees; license renewal

(a) Each applicant for a license under this article shall pay at the time of filing the application a fee determined by the Department of Justice. The fee shall not exceed the application processing costs of the Department of Justice.

(b) A license granted pursuant to this article may be renewed one year from the date of issuance, and annually thereafter, upon the filing of a renewal application and the payment of a license renewal fee, which shall not exceed the application processing costs of the Department of Justice.

(c) After the department establishes fees sufficient to reimburse the department for processing costs, fees charged shall increase at a rate not to exceed the legislatively approved annual cost-of-living adjustments for the department's budget. *(Added by Stats.2010, c. 711 (S.B.1080), § 6, operative Jan. 1, 2012.)*

Law Revision Commission Comments

Section 32715 continues the third paragraph of former Section 12250(b) without substantive change. [38 Cal.L.Rev.Comm. Reports 217 (2009)].

§ 32720. Revocation for breach of required conditions

Upon breach of any of the conditions stated in Section 32700, a license under this article shall be revoked. *(Added by Stats.2010, c. 711 (S.B.1080), § 6, operative Jan. 1, 2012.)*

Law Revision Commission Comments

Section 32720 continues part of the introductory clause of former Section 12250(a) without substantive change. [38 Cal.L.Rev.Comm. Reports 217 (2009)].

ARTICLE 5. MACHINEGUN CONSTITUTING NUISANCE

§ 32750. Unlawful possession of machinegun as public nuisance; injunctions; surrender and destruction of machinegun

(a) It shall be a public nuisance to possess any machinegun in violation of this chapter.

(b) The Attorney General, any district attorney, or any city attorney may bring an action before the superior court to enjoin the possession of any machinegun in violation of this chapter.

(c) Any machinegun found to be in violation of this chapter shall be surrendered to the Department of Justice. The department shall destroy the machinegun so as to render it unusable and unrepairable as a machinegun, except upon the filing of a certificate with the department by a judge or district attorney stating that the preservation of the machinegun is necessary to serve the ends of justice. *(Added by Stats.2010, c. 711 (S.B.1080), § 6, operative Jan. 1, 2012.)*

Law Revision Commission Comments

Section 32750 continues former Section 12251 without substantive change.

See Section 16880 ("machinegun"). [38 Cal.L.Rev.Comm. Reports 217 (2009)].

Cross References

Attorney General, generally, see Government Code § 12500 et seq.
Machinegun defined for purposes of this Part, see Penal Code § 16880.

Research References

2 Witkin, California Criminal Law 4th Crimes Against Public Peace and Welfare § 231 (2021), Other Weapons and Devices.

CHAPTER 7. MULTIBURST TRIGGER ACTIVATOR

§ 32900. Manufacture, import, sale, supply or possession of multiburst trigger activator; punishment

Except as provided in Chapter 1 (commencing with Section 17700) of Division 2 of Title 2, any person in this state who manufactures or causes to be manufactured, imports into the state, keeps for sale, or offers or exposes for sale, or who gives, lends, or possesses any multiburst trigger activator is punishable by imprisonment in a county jail not exceeding one year or imprisonment pursuant to subdivision (h) of Section 1170. *(Added by Stats.2010, c. 711 (S.B.1080), § 6, operative Jan. 1, 2012. Amended by Stats.2012, c. 43 (S.B.1023), § 108, eff. June 27, 2012.)*

Law Revision Commission Comments

With respect to a multiburst trigger activator, Section 32900 continues former Section 12020(a)(1) without substantive change.

For circumstances in which this section is inapplicable, see Sections 16590 ("generally prohibited weapon"), 17700–17745 (exemptions relating to generally prohibited weapons).

See Section 16930 ("multiburst trigger activator"). See also Sections 17800 (distinct and separate offense), 32990 (multiburst trigger activator constituting nuisance). [38 Cal.L.Rev.Comm. Reports 217 (2009)].

Research References

2 Witkin, California Criminal Law 4th Crimes Against Public Peace and Welfare § 211 (2021), Nature of Crime.

§ 32990. Nuisance status of multiburst trigger activators

Except as provided in Chapter 1 (commencing with Section 17700) of Division 2 of Title 2, any multiburst trigger activator is a nuisance and is subject to Section 18010. *(Added by Stats.2010, c. 711 (S.B.1080), § 6, operative Jan. 1, 2012.)*

Law Revision Commission Comments

With respect to a multiburst trigger activator, Section 32990 continues the first part of the first sentence of former Section 12029 without substantive change.

See Section 16930 ("multiburst trigger activator"). [38 Cal.L.Rev.Comm. Reports 217 (2009)].

Research References

2 Witkin, California Criminal Law 4th Crimes Against Public Peace and Welfare § 263 (2021), Nuisances.

CHAPTER 8. SHORT–BARRELED RIFLE OR SHORT–BARRELED SHOTGUN

ARTICLE 1. RESTRICTIONS RELATING TO SHORT–BARRELED RIFLE OR SHORT–BARRELED SHOTGUN

§ 33210. Manufacture, sale or possession of short-barreled shotgun or short-barreled rifle

Except as expressly provided in Sections 33215 to 33225, inclusive, and in Chapter 1 (commencing with Section 17700) of Division 2 of Title 2, and solely in accordance with those provisions, no person may manufacture, import into this state, keep for sale, offer for sale, give, lend, or possess any short-barreled rifle or short-barreled shotgun.

Nothing else in any provision listed in Section 16580 shall be construed as authorizing the manufacture, importation into the state, keeping for sale, offering for sale, or giving, lending, or possession of any short-barreled rifle or short-barreled shotgun. *(Added by Stats.2010, c. 711 (S.B.1080), § 6, operative Jan. 1, 2012.)*

Law Revision Commission Comments

Section 33210 continues former Section 12001.5 without substantive change.

See Sections 17170 ("short-barreled rifle"), 17180 ("short-barreled shotgun"). [38 Cal.L.Rev.Comm. Reports 217 (2009)].

Cross References

Rifle defined, see Penal Code § 17090.
Short-barreled rifle defined, see Penal Code § 17170.
Short-barreled shotgun defined, see Penal Code § 17180.
Shotgun defined, see Penal Code § 17190.

Research References

2 Witkin, California Criminal Law 4th Crimes Against Public Peace and Welfare § 211 (2021), Nature of Crime.

§ 33215. Manufacture, import, sale, supply or possession of short-barreled rifle or short-barreled shotgun; punishment

Except as provided in Sections 33220 and 33225 and in Chapter 1 (commencing with Section 17700) of Division 2 of Title 2, any person in this state who manufactures or causes to be manufactured, imports into the state, keeps for sale, or offers or exposes for sale, or who gives, lends, or possesses any short-barreled rifle or short-barreled shotgun is punishable by imprisonment in a county jail not exceeding one year or imprisonment pursuant to subdivision (h) of Section 1170. *(Added by Stats.2010, c. 711 (S.B.1080), § 6, operative Jan. 1, 2012. Amended by Stats.2012, c. 43 (S.B.1023), § 109, eff. June 27, 2012.)*

Law Revision Commission Comments

With respect to short-barreled rifles and short-barreled shotguns, Section 33215 continues former Section 12020(a)(1) without substantive change.

For circumstances in which this section is inapplicable, see Sections 16590 ("generally prohibited weapon"), 17700–17745 (exemptions relating to generally prohibited weapons), 33220 (exceptions relating to law enforcement), 33225 (exception for use authorized by permit).

See Sections 17170 ("short-barreled rifle"), 17180 ("short-barreled shotgun"). See also Sections 17800 (distinct and separate offense), 33290 (short-barreled rifle or short-barreled shotgun constituting nuisance). [38 Cal.L.Rev. Comm. Reports 217 (2009)].

Cross References

Manufacture, sale or possession of short-barreled shotguns or short-barreled rifles, permits, see Penal Code § 33300.
Penalty for possession of deadly weapon described in this section within State Capitol, legislative offices, etc., see Penal Code § 171c.
Possession of deadly weapons with intent to assault, see Penal Code § 17500.
Rifle defined, see Penal Code § 17090.
Short-barreled rifle defined, see Penal Code § 17170.
Short-barreled shotgun defined, see Penal Code § 17180.
Shotgun defined, see Penal Code § 17190.

Research References

2 Witkin, California Criminal Law 4th Crimes Against Public Peace and Welfare § 211 (2021), Nature of Crime.
2 Witkin, California Criminal Law 4th Crimes Against Public Peace and Welfare § 212 (2021), Elements of Offense.
1 Witkin California Criminal Law 4th Elements § 9 (2021), Facts that Must be Known.
3 Witkin, California Criminal Law 4th Punishment § 621 (2021), P.C. 1203.

§ 33220. Short-barreled rifles or short-barreled shotguns; sale to, purchase by, or possession of by enumerated law enforcement, military, or naval officers; application of Section 33215

Section 33215 does not apply to either of the following:

(a) The sale to, purchase by, or possession of short-barreled rifles or short-barreled shotguns by a police department, sheriff's office, marshal's office, the California Highway Patrol, the Department of Justice, the Department of Corrections and Rehabilitation, or the military or naval forces of this state or of the United States, for use in the discharge of their official duties.

(b) The possession of short-barreled rifles and short-barreled shotguns by peace officer members of a police department, sheriff's office, marshal's office, the California Highway Patrol, the Department of Justice, or the Department of Corrections and Rehabilitation, when on duty and the use is authorized by the agency and is within the course and scope of their duties, and the officers have completed a training course in the use of these weapons certified by the Commission on Peace Officer Standards and Training. *(Added by Stats.2010, c. 711 (S.B.1080), § 6, operative Jan. 1, 2012.)*

Law Revision Commission Comments

Section 33220 continues former Section 12020(b)(1) without substantive change.

See Sections 17170 ("short-barreled rifle"), 17180 ("short-barreled shotgun"). [38 Cal.L.Rev.Comm. Reports 217 (2009)].

Cross References

Department of Corrections and Rehabilitation, generally, see Penal Code § 5000 et seq.
Rifle defined, see Penal Code § 17090.
Short-barreled rifle defined, see Penal Code § 17170.
Short-barreled shotgun defined, see Penal Code § 17180.
Shotgun defined, see Penal Code § 17190.

Research References

2 Witkin, California Criminal Law 4th Crimes Against Public Peace and Welfare § 211 (2021), Nature of Crime.

§ 33225. Short-barreled rifles or short-barreled shotguns; manufacture, possession, transportation, or sale authorized by Department of Justice; application of Section 33215

Section 33215 does not apply to the manufacture, possession, transportation, or sale of a short-barreled rifle or short-barreled shotgun, when authorized by the Department of Justice pursuant to Article 2 (commencing with Section 33300) and not in violation of federal law. *(Added by Stats.2010, c. 711 (S.B.1080), § 6, operative Jan. 1, 2012.)*

Law Revision Commission Comments

Section 33225 continues former Section 12020(b)(2) without substantive change.

See Sections 17170 ("short-barreled rifle"), 17180 ("short-barreled shotgun"). [38 Cal.L.Rev.Comm. Reports 217 (2009)].

Cross References

Rifle defined, see Penal Code § 17090.
Short-barreled rifle defined, see Penal Code § 17170.
Short-barreled shotgun defined, see Penal Code § 17180.
Shotgun defined, see Penal Code § 17190.

§ 33290. Nuisance status of short-barreled rifles and short-barreled shotguns

Except as provided in Sections 33220 and 33225 and in Chapter 1 (commencing with Section 17700) of Division 2 of Title 2, any short-barreled rifle or short-barreled shotgun is a nuisance and is subject to Section 18010. *(Added by Stats.2010, c. 711 (S.B.1080), § 6, operative Jan. 1, 2012.)*

Law Revision Commission Comments

With respect to short-barreled rifles and short-barreled shotguns, Section 33290 continues the first part of the first sentence of former Section 12029 without substantive change.

See Sections 17170 ("short-barreled rifle"), 17180 ("short-barreled shotgun"). [38 Cal.L.Rev.Comm. Reports 217 (2009)].

Cross References

Rifle defined, see Penal Code § 17090.
Short-barreled rifle defined, see Penal Code § 17170.
Short-barreled shotgun defined, see Penal Code § 17180.
Shotgun defined, see Penal Code § 17190.

Research References

2 Witkin, California Criminal Law 4th Crimes Against Public Peace and Welfare § 263 (2021), Nuisances.

ARTICLE 2. PERMIT FOR SHORT–BARRELED RIFLE OR SHORT–BARRELED SHOTGUN

§ 33300. Issuance for good cause; period of validity; age restriction

(a) Upon a showing that good cause exists for issuance of a permit to the applicant, and if the Department of Justice finds that issuance of the permit does not endanger the public safety, the department may issue a permit for the manufacture, possession, importation, transportation, or sale of short-barreled rifles or short-barreled shotguns. The permit shall be initially valid for a period of one year, and renewable annually thereafter. No permit shall be issued to a person who is under 18 years of age.

(b) Good cause, for the purposes of this section, shall be limited to only the following:

(1) The permit is sought for the manufacture, possession, importation, or use with blank cartridges, of a short-barreled rifle or short-barreled shotgun, solely as a prop for a motion picture, television, or video production or entertainment event.

(2) The permit is sought for the manufacture of, exposing for sale, keeping for sale, sale of, importation or lending of short-barreled rifles or short-barreled shotguns to the entities listed in Section 33220 by persons who are licensed as dealers or manufacturers under the provisions of Chapter 53 (commencing with Section 5801) of Title 26 of the United States Code, as amended, and the regulations issued pursuant thereto. *(Added by Stats.2010, c. 711 (S.B.1080), § 6, operative Jan. 1, 2012. Amended by Stats.2012, c. 691 (A.B.1559), § 2.)*

Law Revision Commission Comments

Section 33300 continues former Section 12095 without substantive change. See Sections 17170 ("short-barreled rifle"), 17180 ("short-barreled shotgun"). [38 Cal.L.Rev.Comm. Reports 217 (2009)].

Cross References

High explosives, permits, activities covered, applications, conditions of use, duration, limitations on issuing permits if display of placards is required, persons unqualified to apply, see Health and Safety Code § 12101.

Research References

2 Witkin, California Criminal Law 4th Crimes Against Public Peace and Welfare § 192 (2021), In General.
2 Witkin, California Criminal Law 4th Crimes Against Public Peace and Welfare § 193 (2021), Sale, Lease, or Transfer by Unlicensed Person.
2 Witkin, California Criminal Law 4th Crimes Against Public Peace and Welfare § 253 (2021), Openly Displaying or Carrying Imitation or Unloaded Firearm.

§ 33305. Application for permit; requirements

(a) An application for a permit under this article shall satisfy all of the following conditions:

(1) It shall be filed in writing.

(2) It shall be signed by the applicant if an individual, or by a member or officer qualified to sign if the applicant is a firm or corporation.

(3) It shall state the applicant's name.

(4) It shall state the business in which the applicant is engaged.

(5) It shall state the applicant's business address.

(6) It shall include a full description of the use to which the short-barreled rifles or short-barreled shotguns are to be put.

(b) Applications and permits shall be uniform throughout the state on forms prescribed by the Department of Justice.

(c) Each applicant for a permit shall pay at the time of filing the application a fee determined by the Department of Justice. The fee shall not exceed the application processing costs of the Department of Justice.

(d) A permit granted pursuant to this article may be renewed one year from the date of issuance, and annually thereafter, upon the filing of a renewal application and the payment of a permit renewal fee, which shall not exceed the application processing costs of the Department of Justice.

(e) After the department establishes fees sufficient to reimburse the department for processing costs, fees charged shall increase at a rate not to exceed the legislatively approved annual cost-of-living adjustments for the department's budget. *(Added by Stats.2010, c. 711 (S.B.1080), § 6, operative Jan. 1, 2012.)*

Law Revision Commission Comments

Section 33305 continues former Section 12096 without substantive change. See Sections 17170 ("short-barreled rifle"), 17180 ("short-barreled shotgun"). [38 Cal.L.Rev.Comm. Reports 217 (2009)].

§ 33310. Location where permit is to be kept; inspection; unique identifying number for short-barreled rifle or short-barreled shotgun

(a) Every person, firm, or corporation to whom a permit is issued under this article shall keep it on the person or at the place where the short-barreled rifles or short-barreled shotguns are kept. The permit shall be open to inspection by any peace officer or any other person designated by the authority issuing the permit.

(b) Every short-barreled rifle or short-barreled shotgun possessed pursuant to the provisions of this article shall bear a unique identifying number. If a weapon does not bear a unique identifying number, the Department of Justice shall assign a number which shall be placed or stamped on that weapon. *(Added by Stats.2010, c. 711 (S.B.1080), § 6, operative Jan. 1, 2012.)*

Law Revision Commission Comments

Section 33310 continues former Section 12097 without substantive change. See Sections 17170 ("short-barreled rifle"), 17180 ("short-barreled shotgun"). [38 Cal.L.Rev.Comm. Reports 217 (2009)].

Cross References

Rifle defined, see Penal Code § 17090.
Short-barreled rifle defined, see Penal Code § 17170.
Short-barreled shotgun defined, see Penal Code § 17180.
Shotgun defined, see Penal Code § 17190.

§ 33315. Revocation of permit

A permit issued in accordance with this article may be revoked by the issuing authority at any time, when it appears that the need for the short-barreled rifles or short-barreled shotguns has ceased or that the holder of the permit has used the short-barreled rifles or short-barreled shotguns for purposes other than those allowed by the permit or that the holder of the permit has not exercised great care in retaining custody of any weapons possessed under the permit. *(Added by Stats.2010, c. 711 (S.B.1080), § 6, operative Jan. 1, 2012.)*

Law Revision Commission Comments

Section 33315 continues former Section 12098 without substantive change. See Sections 17170 ("short-barreled rifle"), 17180 ("short-barreled shotgun"). [38 Cal.L.Rev.Comm. Reports 217 (2009)].

Cross References

Rifle defined, see Penal Code § 17090.
Short-barreled rifle defined, see Penal Code § 17170.
Short-barreled shotgun defined, see Penal Code § 17180.
Shotgun defined, see Penal Code § 17190.

§ 33320. Inspection for security, safe storage, and inventory reconciliation

(a) Except as provided in subdivision (b), the Department of Justice shall, for every person, firm, or corporation to whom a permit is issued pursuant to this article, annually conduct an inspection for security and safe storage purposes, and to reconcile the inventory of short-barreled rifles and short-barreled shotguns.

(b) A person, firm, or corporation with an inventory of fewer than five devices that require any Department of Justice permit shall be subject to an inspection for security and safe storage purposes, and to reconcile inventory, once every five years, or more frequently if determined by the department. *(Added by Stats.2010, c. 711 (S.B.1080), § 6, operative Jan. 1, 2012.)*

Law Revision Commission Comments

Section 33320 continues former Section 12099 without substantive change. See Sections 17170 ("short-barreled rifle"), 17180 ("short-barreled shotgun"). [38 Cal.L.Rev.Comm. Reports 217 (2009)].

Cross References

Rifle defined, see Penal Code § 17090.
Short-barreled rifle defined, see Penal Code § 17170.
Short-barreled shotgun defined, see Penal Code § 17180.
Shotgun defined, see Penal Code § 17190.

CHAPTER 9. SILENCERS

Section

§ 33410. Possession; fines and penalties

Any person, firm, or corporation who within this state possesses a silencer is guilty of a felony and upon conviction thereof shall be punished by imprisonment pursuant to subdivision (h) of Section 1170 or by a fine not to exceed ten thousand dollars ($10,000), or by both that fine and imprisonment. *(Added by Stats.2010, c. 711 (S.B.1080), § 6, operative Jan. 1, 2012. Amended by Stats.2011, c. 15 (A.B.109), § 554, eff. April 4, 2011, operative Jan. 1, 2012.)*

Law Revision Commission Comments

Section 33410 continues former Section 12520 without substantive change. See Section 17210 ("silencer"). [38 Cal.L.Rev.Comm. Reports 217 (2009)].

Cross References

Felonies, definition and penalties, see Penal Code §§ 17, 18.

Research References

2 Witkin, California Criminal Law 4th Crimes Against Public Peace and Welfare § 189 (2021), In General.
2 Witkin, California Criminal Law 4th Crimes Against Public Peace and Welfare § 231 (2021), Other Weapons and Devices.
1 Witkin California Criminal Law 4th Elements § 9 (2021), Facts that Must be Known.
3 Witkin, California Criminal Law 4th Punishment § 621 (2021), P.C. 1203.

§ 33415. Exempt entities

Section 33410 shall not apply to, or affect, any of the following:

(a) The sale to, purchase by, or possession of silencers by agencies listed in Section 830.1, or the military or naval forces of this state or of the United States, for use in the discharge of their official duties.

(b) The possession of silencers by regular, salaried, full-time peace officers who are employed by an agency listed in Section 830.1, or by the military or naval forces of this state or of the United States, when on duty and when the use of silencers is authorized by the agency and is within the course and scope of their duties.

(c) The manufacture, possession, transportation, or sale or other transfer of silencers to an entity described in subdivision (a) by dealers or manufacturers registered under Chapter 53 (commencing with Section 5801) of Title 26 of the United States Code and the regulations issued pursuant thereto. *(Added by Stats.2010, c. 711 (S.B.1080), § 6, operative Jan. 1, 2012.)*

Law Revision Commission Comments

Section 33415 continues former Section 12501 without substantive change. See Section 17210 ("silencer"). [38 Cal.L.Rev.Comm. Reports 217 (2009)].

Research References

2 Witkin, California Criminal Law 4th Crimes Against Public Peace and Welfare § 231 (2021), Other Weapons and Devices.

CHAPTER 10. ZIP GUNS

Section

§ 33600. Manufacture, import, sale, supply or possession of zip gun; punishment

Except as provided in Chapter 1 (commencing with Section 17700) of Division 2 of Title 2, any person in this state who manufactures or causes to be manufactured, imports into the state, keeps for sale, or offers or exposes for sale, or who gives, lends, or possesses any zip gun is punishable by imprisonment in a county jail not exceeding one year or imprisonment pursuant to subdivision (h) of Section 1170. *(Added by Stats.2010, c. 711 (S.B.1080), § 6, operative Jan. 1, 2012. Amended by Stats.2012, c. 43 (S.B.1023), § 110, eff. June 27, 2012.)*

Law Revision Commission Comments

With respect to a zip gun, Section 33600 continues former Section 12020(a)(1) without substantive change.

For circumstances in which this section is inapplicable, see Sections 16590 ("generally prohibited weapon"), 17700–17745 (exemptions relating to generally prohibited weapons).

See Section 17360 ("zip gun"). See also Sections 17800 (distinct and separate offense), 33690 (zip gun constituting nuisance). [38 Cal.L.Rev.Comm. Reports 217 (2009)].

Cross References

Penalty for possession of deadly weapon described in this section within State Capitol, legislative offices, etc., see Penal Code § 171c.
Possession of deadly weapons with intent to assault, see Penal Code § 17500.

Zip gun defined for purposes of this Part, see Penal Code § 17360.

Research References

2 Witkin, California Criminal Law 4th Crimes Against Public Peace and Welfare § 211 (2021), Nature of Crime.

§ 33690. Nuisance status of zip guns

Except as provided in Chapter 1 (commencing with Section 17700) of Division 2 of Title 2, any zip gun is a nuisance and is subject to Section 18010. *(Added by Stats.2010, c. 711 (S.B.1080), § 6, operative Jan. 1, 2012.)*

Law Revision Commission Comments

With respect to a zip gun, Section 33690 continues the first part of the first sentence of former Section 12029 without substantive change.

See Section 17360 ("zip gun"). [38 Cal.L.Rev.Comm. Reports 217 (2009)].

Cross References

Zip gun defined for purposes of this Part, see Penal Code § 17360.

Research References

2 Witkin, California Criminal Law 4th Crimes Against Public Peace and Welfare § 263 (2021), Nuisances.

Division 11

FIREARM IN CUSTODY OF COURT OR LAW ENFORCEMENT AGENCY OR SIMILAR SITUATION

CHAPTER 1. PROCEDURE FOR TAKING FIREARM INTO CUSTODY

§ 33800. Issuance of receipt upon taking firearm into custody

(a) When a firearm is taken into custody by a law enforcement officer, the officer shall issue the person who possessed the firearm a receipt describing the firearm, and listing any serial number or other identification on the firearm.

(b) The receipt shall indicate where the firearm may be recovered, any applicable time limit for recovery, and the date after which the owner or possessor may recover the firearm pursuant to Chapter 2 (commencing with Section 33850).

(c) Nothing in this section is intended to displace any existing law regarding the seizure or return of firearms. *(Added by Stats.2010, c. 711 (S.B.1080), § 6, operative Jan. 1, 2012.)*

Law Revision Commission Comments

Section 33800 continues former Section 12028.7 without substantive change.

For other provisions specifying procedures for taking a firearm into custody, see Sections 18000 (surrender of specified weapons constituting nuisance), 18010 (treatment of other weapons constituting nuisance), 18250–18500 (seizure of firearm or other deadly weapon at scene of domestic violence), 29300 (firearm of any nature constitutes nuisance under specified circumstances). For rules relating to return or transfer of a firearm that is in the custody or control of a court or law enforcement agency, see Sections 33850–33895. For rules governing disposal of firearms that are unclaimed, abandoned, or subject to destruction, see Sections 34000–34010.

See Section 16520 ("firearm"). [38 Cal.L.Rev.Comm. Reports 217 (2009)].

Cross References

Confiscation and custody of firearms or other deadly weapons, procedure for return of weapon, notice, destruction of weapon, see Welfare and Institutions Code § 8102.

Firearm defined for purposes of this Part, see Penal Code § 16520.

CHAPTER 2. RETURN OR TRANSFER OF FIREARM IN CUSTODY OR CONTROL OF COURT OR LAW ENFORCEMENT AGENCY

§ 33850. Application to Department of Justice to have firearm returned; contents of application; sale or transfer of firearm; sale or transfer of ammunition; furnishing of fictitious or incorrect information

(a) Any person who claims title to any firearm, ammunition feeding device, or ammunition that is in the custody or control of a court or law enforcement agency and who wishes to have the firearm, ammunition feeding device, or ammunition returned shall make application for a determination by the Department of Justice as to whether the applicant is eligible to possess a firearm, ammunition feeding device, or ammunition. The application shall be submitted electronically via the California Firearms Application Reporting System (CFARS) and shall include the following:

(1) The applicant's name, date and place of birth, gender, telephone number, and complete address.

(2) Whether the applicant is a United States citizen. If the applicant is not a United States citizen, the application shall also include the applicant's country of citizenship and the applicant's United States Citizenship and Immigration Services-assigned number or I–94 number.

(3) If the seized property is a firearm, the firearm's make, model, caliber, barrel length, type, country of origin, and serial number, provided, however, that if the firearm is not a handgun and does not have a serial number, identification number, or identification mark assigned to it, there shall be a place on the application to note that fact.

(4) For residents of California, the applicant's valid California driver's license number or valid California identification card number issued by the Department of Motor Vehicles. For nonresidents of California, a copy of the applicant's military identification with orders indicating that the individual is stationed in California, or a copy of the applicant's valid driver's license from the applicant's state of residence, or a copy of the applicant's state identification card from the applicant's state of residence. Copies of the documents provided by non-California residents shall be notarized.

(5) The name of the court or law enforcement agency holding the firearm, ammunition feeding device, or ammunition.

(6) The signature of the applicant and the date of signature.

(7) Any person furnishing a fictitious name or address or knowingly furnishing any incorrect information or knowingly omitting any information required to be provided for the application, including any notarized information pursuant to paragraph (4), shall be guilty of a misdemeanor.

(b) A person who owns a firearm that is in the custody of a court or law enforcement agency and who does not wish to obtain possession of the firearm, and the firearm is an otherwise legal firearm, and the person otherwise has right to title of the firearm, shall be entitled to sell or transfer title of the firearm to a licensed dealer or a third party that is not prohibited from possessing that firearm. Any sale or transfer to a third party pursuant to this subdivision shall be conducted pursuant to Section 27545.

(c) A person who owns an ammunition feeding device or ammunition that is in the custody of a court or a law enforcement agency and who does not wish to obtain possession of the ammunition or ammunition feeding device, and the ammunition feeding device or ammunition is otherwise legal, shall be entitled to sell or otherwise transfer the ammunition feeding device or ammunition to a licensed firearms dealer or ammunition vendor or a third party that is not prohibited from possessing that ammunition feeding device or ammunition. Any sale or other transfer of ammunition to a third party pursuant to subdivision (b) shall be conducted through an ammunition vendor in accordance with the procedures set forth in Article 4 (commencing with Section 30370) of Chapter 1 of Division 10.

(d) Any person furnishing a fictitious name or address, or knowingly furnishing any incorrect information or knowingly omitting any information required to be provided for the application, including any notarized information pursuant to paragraph (4) of subdivision (a), is punishable as a misdemeanor.

(e) This section shall become operative on July 1, 2020. *(Added by Stats.2018, c. 780 (S.B.746), § 10, eff. Jan. 1, 2019, operative July 1, 2020. Amended by Stats.2021, c. 296 (A.B.1096), § 53, eff. Jan. 1, 2022.)*

Cross References

Firearm defined for purposes of this Part, see Penal Code § 16520.
Handgun defined for purposes of this Part, see Penal Code § 16640.
Misdemeanors, definition and penalties, see Penal Code §§ 17, 19, 19.2.

Research References

2 Witkin, California Criminal Law 4th Crimes Against Public Peace and Welfare § 192 (2021), In General.
2 Witkin, California Criminal Law 4th Crimes Against Public Peace and Welfare § 193 (2021), Sale, Lease, or Transfer by Unlicensed Person.

§ 33855. Requirements for return of firearm, ammunition feeding device, or ammunition; fees

A law enforcement agency or court that has taken custody of any firearm, ammunition feeding device, or ammunition shall not return the firearm, ammunition feeding device, or ammunition to any individual unless all of the following requirements are satisfied:

(a) The individual presents to the agency or court notification of a determination by the department pursuant to Section 33865 that the person is eligible to possess a firearm, ammunition feeding device, or ammunition.

(b) If the seized property is a firearm and the agency or court has direct access to the Automated Firearms System, the agency or court has verified that the firearm is not listed as stolen pursuant to Section 11108.2, and that the firearm has been recorded in the Automated Firearms System in the name of the individual who seeks its return.

(c) If the firearm has been reported lost or stolen pursuant to Section 11108.2, a law enforcement agency shall notify the owner or person entitled to possession pursuant to Section 11108.5. However, that person shall provide proof of eligibility to possess a firearm pursuant to Section 33865.

(d) This section does not prevent the local law enforcement agency from charging the rightful owner or person entitled to possession of the firearm the fees described in Section 33880. However, an individual who is applying for a background check to retrieve a firearm that came into the custody or control of a court or law enforcement agency pursuant to Section 33850 shall be exempt from the fees in Section 33860, provided that the court or agency determines the firearm was reported stolen to a law enforcement agency prior to the date the firearm came into custody or control of the court or law enforcement agency, or within five business days of the firearm being stolen from its owner. The court or agency shall notify the Department of Justice of this fee exemption in a manner prescribed by the department.

(e) This section shall become operative on July 1, 2020. *(Added by Stats.2018, c. 864 (A.B.2222), § 7.6, eff. Jan. 1, 2019, operative July 1, 2020.)*

Cross References

Firearm defined for purposes of this Part, see Penal Code § 16520.

§ 33860. Fees for processing requests to return firearms; deposit into Dealers' Record of Sale Special Account; review and adjustment of fees

(a) The Department of Justice shall establish a fee of twenty dollars ($20) per request for return of a firearm, ammunition feeding device, or any quantity of ammunition plus a three-dollar ($3) charge for each additional firearm being processed as part of the request to return a firearm, to cover its reasonable costs for processing applications submitted pursuant to this chapter.

(b) The fees collected pursuant to subdivision (a) shall be deposited into the Dealers' Record of Sale Special Account.

(c) The department shall annually review and shall adjust the fees specified in subdivision (a), if necessary, to fully fund, but not to exceed the reasonable costs of processing applications submitted pursuant to this section.

(d) This section shall become operative on July 1, 2020. *(Added by Stats.2018, c. 780 (S.B.746), § 14, eff. Jan. 1, 2019, operative July 1, 2020.)*

Cross References

Firearm defined for purposes of this Part, see Penal Code § 16520.

§ 33865. Applicant eligibility check; time for completion of background check; written notification of eligibility or denial

(a) When the Department of Justice receives a completed application pursuant to Section 33850 accompanied by the fee required pursuant to Section 33860, it shall conduct an eligibility check of the applicant to determine whether the applicant is eligible to possess a firearm, ammunition feeding device, or ammunition.

(b) The department shall have 30 days from the date of receipt to complete the background check, unless the background check is delayed by circumstances beyond the control of the department. The applicant may contact the department via the California Firearms Application Reporting System (CFARS) to inquire about the reason for a delay.

(c) If the department determines that the applicant is eligible to possess the firearm, ammunition feeding device, or ammunition, the department shall provide the applicant with written notification that includes the following:

(1) The identity of the applicant.

(2) A statement that the applicant is eligible to possess a firearm, ammunition feeding device, or ammunition.

(3) If applicable, a description of the firearm by make, model, and serial number, provided, however, that if the firearm is not a handgun and does not have a serial number, identification number, or identification mark assigned to it, that fact shall be noted.

(d) The department shall enter a record of the firearm into the Automated Firearms System (AFS), provided, however, that if the firearm is not a handgun and does not have a serial number, identification number, or identification mark assigned to it, that fact shall be noted in AFS.

(e) If the department denies the application, and the firearm is an otherwise legal firearm, the department shall notify the applicant of the denial and provide a form for the applicant to use to sell or transfer the firearm to a licensed dealer.

(f) If the department denies the application, the applicant shall receive notification via CFARS from the department explaining the reason for the denial and information regarding the appeal process.

(g) This section shall become operative on July 1, 2020. *(Added by Stats.2018, c. 780 (S.B.746), § 16, eff. Jan. 1, 2019, operative July 1, 2020.)*

Cross References

Firearm defined for purposes of this Part, see Penal Code § 16520.
Handgun defined for purposes of this Part, see Penal Code § 16640.

§ 33870. Ineligible applicants; authorization to sell or transfer firearm, ammunition feeding device, or ammunition to licensed firearms dealer or licensed ammunition vendor; storage of firearm, ammunition feeding device, or ammunition during prohibition period; lost or stolen firearm, ammunition feeding device, or ammunition; fees

(a) If a law enforcement agency determines that the applicant is the legal owner of any firearm, ammunition feeding device, or ammunition deposited with the agency, that the applicant is prohibited from possessing any firearm, ammunition feeding device, or ammunition, and that the firearm, ammunition feeding device, or ammunition is otherwise legal, the applicant shall be entitled to sell or transfer the firearm, ammunition feeding device, or ammunition to a licensed firearms dealer, or licensed ammunition vendor, as applicable. If a law enforcement agency determines that the applicant is prohibited from owning or possessing any firearm, ammunition feeding device, or ammunition and the prohibition will expire on a specific ascertainable date, whether or not that date is specified in a court order, the applicant shall be entitled to have the firearm, ammunition feeding device, or ammunition stored by a licensed firearms dealer or licensed ammunition vendor, as applicable, for the duration of the prohibition period pursuant to Section 29830.

(b) If the firearm, ammunition feeding device, or ammunition has been lost or stolen, it shall be restored to the lawful owner pursuant to Section 11108.5 upon the owner's identification of the property, proof of ownership, and proof of eligibility to possess a firearm, ammunition feeding device, or ammunition pursuant to Section 33865.

(c) This section does not prevent the local law enforcement agency from charging the rightful owner of the property the fees described in Section 33880.

(d) This section shall become operative on July 1, 2020. *(Added by Stats.2018, c. 780 (S.B.746), § 18, eff. Jan. 1, 2019, operative July 1, 2020.)*

Cross References

Confiscation and custody of firearms or other deadly weapons, procedure for return of weapon, notice, destruction of weapon, see Welfare and Institutions Code § 8102.
Firearm defined for purposes of this Part, see Penal Code § 16520.

§ 33875. Time of retention of firearm, ammunition feeding device, or ammunition after notification has been made; disposal of unclaimed firearm, ammunition feeding device, or ammunition

(a) Notwithstanding any other law, no law enforcement agency or court shall be required to retain any firearm, ammunition feeding device, or ammunition for more than 180 days after the owner has been notified by the court or law enforcement agency that the property has been made available for return. An unclaimed firearm, ammunition feeding device, or ammunition may be disposed of after the 180–day period has expired.

(b) This section shall become operative on July 1, 2020. *(Added by Stats.2018, c. 780 (S.B.746), § 20, eff. Jan. 1, 2019, operative July 1, 2020.)*

Cross References

Confiscation and custody of firearms or other deadly weapons, procedure for return of weapon, notice, destruction of weapon, see Welfare and Institutions Code § 8102.
Firearm defined for purposes of this Part, see Penal Code § 16520.

§ 33880. Seizure, impounding, storage, or release of firearm, ammunition feeding device, or ammunition; imposition of charge to recover administrative costs; waiver; poststorage hearing or appeal

(a) A city, county, or city and county, or a state agency may adopt a regulation, ordinance, or resolution imposing a charge equal to its administrative costs relating to the seizure, impounding, storage, or release of any firearm, ammunition feeding device, or ammunition.

(b) The fee under subdivision (a) shall not exceed the actual costs incurred for the expenses directly related to taking possession of any firearm, ammunition feeding device, or ammunition, storing it, and surrendering possession of it to a licensed firearms dealer or to the owner.

(c) The administrative costs described in subdivisions (a) and (b) may be waived by the local or state agency upon verifiable proof that the firearm, ammunition feeding device, or ammunition was reported stolen at the time it came into the custody or control of the law enforcement agency.

(d) The following apply to any charges imposed for administrative costs pursuant to this section:

(1) The charges shall only be imposed on the person claiming title to the firearm, ammunition feeding device, or ammunition.

(2) Any charges shall be collected by the local or state authority only from the person claiming title to the firearm, ammunition feeding device, or ammunition.

(3) The charges shall be in addition to any other charges authorized or imposed pursuant to this code.

(4) A charge shall not be imposed for a hearing or appeal relating to the removal, impound, storage, or release of any firearm, ammunition feeding device, or ammunition, unless that hearing or appeal was requested in writing by the legal owner of the property. In addition, the charge may be imposed only upon the person requesting that hearing or appeal.

(e) Costs for a hearing or appeal related to the release of any firearm, ammunition feeding device, or ammunition shall not be charged to the legal owner who redeems the property, unless the legal owner voluntarily requests the poststorage hearing or appeal. A city, county, city and county, or state agency shall not require a legal owner to request a poststorage hearing as a requirement for release of the firearm, ammunition feeding device, or ammunition to the legal owner.

(f) This section shall become operative on July 1, 2020. *(Added by Stats.2018, c. 780 (S.B.746), § 22, eff. Jan. 1, 2019, operative July 1, 2020.)*

Cross References

Firearm defined for purposes of this Part, see Penal Code § 16520.

§ 33885. Law enforcement agency as defendant or cross-defendant in proceeding for return of firearm, ammunition feeding device, or ammunition; award of reasonable attorney fees to prevailing party

(a) In a proceeding for the return of any firearm, ammunition feeding device, or ammunition seized and not returned pursuant to this chapter, where the defendant or cross-defendant is a law enforcement agency, the court shall award reasonable attorney's fees to the prevailing party.

(b) This section shall become operative on July 1, 2020. *(Added by Stats.2018, c. 780 (S.B.746), § 24, eff. Jan. 1, 2019, operative July 1, 2020.)*

Cross References

Firearm defined for purposes of this Part, see Penal Code § 16520.

§ 33895. Application of Section 27545 to deliveries, transfers, or returns of firearms; application of Sections 30312 and 30342 to deliveries or transfers of returns of ammunition or ammunition feeding devices

(a) Section 27545 does not apply to deliveries, transfers, or returns of firearms made pursuant to this chapter.

(b) Sections 30312 and 30342 do not apply to deliveries or transfers of returns of ammunition or ammunition feeding devices by a court or law enforcement agency made pursuant to this chapter.

(c) This section shall become operative on July 1, 2020. *(Added by Stats.2018, c. 780 (S.B.746), § 26, eff. Jan. 1, 2019, operative July 1, 2020.)*

Cross References

Firearm defined for purposes of this Part, see Penal Code § 16520.

CHAPTER 3. FIREARMS THAT ARE UNCLAIMED, ABANDONED, OR SUBJECT TO DESTRUCTION

Section

§ 34000. Firearms no longer needed as exhibits in criminal actions or proceedings; firearms that are unclaimed or abandoned property; sale or destruction; exemption for firearms in possession of Department of Fish and Game

(a) Notwithstanding any provision of law or of any local ordinance to the contrary, when any firearm is in the possession of any officer of the state, or of a county, city, or city and county, or of any campus of the University of California or the California State University, and the firearm is an exhibit filed in any criminal action or proceeding which is no longer needed or is unclaimed or abandoned property, which has been in the possession of the officer for at least 180 days, the firearm shall be sold, or destroyed, as provided for in Sections 18000 and 18005.

(b) This section does not apply to any firearm in the possession of the Department of Fish and Game, or which was used in the violation of any provision in the Fish and Game Code, or any regulation under that code. *(Added by Stats.2010, c. 711 (S.B.1080), § 6, operative Jan. 1, 2012.)*

Law Revision Commission Comments

Section 34000 continues former Section 12032 without substantive change.

For guidance on whether a firearm can be considered unclaimed, see Section 33875 (unclaimed firearm). For a notification requirement relating to destruction of a firearm pursuant to Sections 18000 and 18005, see Section 34010 (notification of Department of Justice).

See Section 16520 ("firearm"). [38 Cal.L.Rev.Comm. Reports 217 (2009)].

Cross References

Completion of sale, loan, or transfer of firearm through licensed person, compliance with Section 27545, procedures if dealer cannot legally return firearm to seller, transferor, or person loaning the firearm, see Penal Code § 28050.

Firearm defined for purposes of this Part, see Penal Code § 16520.

Sale of firearm precursor parts through licensed firearm precursor part vendor, requirements, exceptions, see Penal Code § 30412.

Transportation of firearm precursor part into the state by a resident, delivery to licensed firearm precursor part vendor, exceptions, see Penal Code § 30414.

Research References

3 Witkin, California Criminal Law 4th Punishment § 190 (2021), Noncriminal Actions.

§ 34005. Alternatives to destruction of firearms and parts

(a)(1) An officer having custody of any firearm that may be useful to the California National Guard, the Coast Guard Auxiliary, or to any military or naval agency of the federal or state government, including, but not limited to, the California State Military Museum and Resource Center, located in Sacramento, and at branch museums located at the California National Guard facilities at Camp Roberts, Camp San Luis Obispo, and Los Alamitos Armed Forces Reserve Center, may, upon the authority of the legislative body of the city, city and county, or county by which the officer is employed and the approval of the Adjutant General, deliver the firearm to the commanding officer of a unit of the California National Guard, the Coast Guard Auxiliary, or any other military agency of the state or federal government, in lieu of destruction as required by any of the provisions listed in Section 16580.

(2) Any state agency, county, municipality, or special purpose district may offer any excess military weapons or equipment, such as historical war equipment like artillery, tanks, or armored vehicles, to

the California State Military Museum and Resource Center or any branch museum described in paragraph (1).

(3) The officer delivering a firearm pursuant to this subdivision shall take a receipt for it, which contains a complete description of the firearm, and shall keep the receipt on file in his or her office as a public record.

(b) Any law enforcement agency that has custody of any firearms, or any parts of any firearms, which are subject to destruction as required by any of the provisions listed in Section 16580, may, in lieu of destroying the weapons, retain and use any of them as may be useful in carrying out the official duties of the agency. Alternatively, upon approval of a court, the agency may do either of the following:

(1) Release the weapons to any other law enforcement agency for use in carrying out the official duties of that agency.

(2) Turn over to the criminalistics laboratory of the Department of Justice or the criminalistics laboratory of a police department, sheriff's office, or district attorney's office, any weapons that may be useful in carrying out the official duties of the respective agencies.

(c)(1) Any firearm, or part of any firearm, which, rather than being destroyed, is used for official purposes pursuant to this section, shall be destroyed by the agency using the weapon when it is no longer needed by the agency for use in carrying out its official duties.

(2) Firearms or weaponry donated to the California State Military Museum and Resource Center may be disposed of pursuant to Section 179 of the Military and Veterans Code.

(d)(1) Any law enforcement agency that has custody of any firearms, or any parts of any firearms, which are subject to destruction as required by any of the provisions listed in Section 16580, may, in lieu of destroying the firearms, obtain an order from the superior court directing the release of the firearms to the sheriff.

(2) The sheriff shall enter those weapons into the Automated Firearms System (AFS), via the California Law Enforcement Telecommunications System, with a complete description of each weapon, including the make, type, category, caliber, and serial number of the firearms, and the name of the academy receiving the weapon entered into the AFS miscellaneous field.

(3) The sheriff shall then release the firearms to the basic training academy certified by the Commission on Peace Officer Standards and Training, so that the firearms may be used for instructional purposes in the certified courses. All firearms released to an academy shall be under the care, custody, and control of the particular academy.

(4) Any firearm, or part of any firearm, which is not destroyed, and is used for the purposes authorized by this section, shall be returned to the law enforcement agency that had original custody of the firearm when it is no longer needed by the basic training academy, or when the basic training academy is no longer certified by the commission.

(5) When those firearms are returned, the law enforcement agency to which the firearms are returned, shall on the date of the return, enter into the Automated Firearms System (AFS), via the California Law Enforcement Telecommunications System, a complete description of each weapon, including the make, type, category, caliber, and serial number of the firearms, and the name of the entity returning the firearm. *(Added by Stats.2010, c. 711 (S.B.1080), § 6, operative Jan. 1, 2012. Amended by Stats.2013, c. 698 (S.B.759), § 1.)*

Law Revision Commission Comments

Subdivision (a) of Section 34005 continues former Section 12030(a) without substantive change.

Subdivision (b) continues former Section 12030(b) without substantive change.

Subdivision (c) continues former Section 12030(c) without substantive change.

Subdivision (d) continues the first, second, third, and fifth sentences of the first paragraph of former Section 12030(d) without substantive change. Subdivision (d) also continues the second paragraph of former Section 12030(d) without substantive change.

For a notice requirement relating to retention of a firearm pursuant to this section, see Section 34010 (notification of Department of Justice).

For rules relating to return or transfer of a firearm that is in the custody or control of a court or law enforcement agency, see Sections 33850–33895. For other provisions on disposal of a firearm in custody, see Sections 18005 (disposal of weapons constituting nuisance), 18010 (treatment of other weapons constituting nuisance), 18250–18500 (seizure of firearm or other deadly weapon at scene of domestic violence), 29300 (firearm of any nature constitutes nuisance under specified circumstances), 34000 (unclaimed firearm or firearm no longer needed as exhibit in criminal case).

See Section 16520 ("firearm"). [38 Cal.L.Rev.Comm. Reports 217 (2009)].

Cross References

California State Military Museum and Resource Center, see Military and Veterans Code § 179.

Confiscation and custody of firearms or other deadly weapons, procedure for return of weapon, notice, destruction of weapon, see Welfare and Institutions Code § 8102.

Disarming prisoner and delivery of weapon to magistrate, see Penal Code § 846.

Firearm defined for purposes of this Part, see Penal Code § 16520.

Machine guns, sale to or possession by police departments, sheriffs, marshals and military and naval forces, see Penal Code § 32610.

Tear gas weapons, official use by peace officers, see Penal Code § 22820.

Research References

2 Witkin, California Criminal Law 4th Crimes Against Public Peace and Welfare § 193 (2021), Sale, Lease, or Transfer by Unlicensed Person.

§ 34010. Notice of retention or destruction; contents

Any law enforcement agency that retains custody of any firearm pursuant to Section 34005, or that destroys a firearm pursuant to Sections 18000 and 18005, shall notify the Department of Justice, and, if applicable, the superior court and any parties to any civil or criminal action related to the firearm, of the retention or destruction. This notification shall consist of a complete description of each firearm, including the name of the manufacturer or brand name, model, caliber, and serial number. *(Added by Stats.2010, c. 711 (S.B.1080), § 6, operative Jan. 1, 2012. Amended by Stats.2022, c. 58 (A.B.200), § 37, eff. June 30, 2022.)*

Law Revision Commission Comments

Section 34010 continues former Section 12030(e) without substantive change.

See Section 16520 ("firearm"). [38 Cal.L.Rev.Comm. Reports 217 (2009)].

Cross References

Firearm defined for purposes of this Part, see Penal Code § 16520.

Research References

2 Witkin, California Criminal Law 4th Crimes Against Public Peace and Welfare § 193 (2021), Sale, Lease, or Transfer by Unlicensed Person.

Division 12

MISCELLANEOUS DUTIES OF THE DEPARTMENT OF JUSTICE

Chapter **Section**

CHAPTER 1. MISCELLANEOUS REPORTS AND PUBLICATIONS

§ 34200. Report on types of firearms used in crimes; contents

The Attorney General shall provide the Legislature on or before April 15 of each year, commencing in 1998, a written report on the specific types of firearms used in the commission of crimes based upon information obtained from state and local crime laboratories. The report shall include all of the following information regarding crimes in which firearms were used:

(a) A description of the relative occurrence of firearms most frequently used in the commission of violent crimes, distinguishing whether the firearms used were handguns, rifles, shotguns, assault weapons, or other related types of weapons.

(b) A description of specific types of firearms that are used in homicides or street gang and drug trafficking crimes.

(c) The frequency with which stolen firearms were used in the commission of the crimes.

(d) The frequency with which fully automatic firearms were used in the commission of the crimes.

(e) Any trends of importance such as those involving specialized ammunition or firearms modifications, such as conversion to a fully automatic weapon, removal of serial number, shortening of barrel, or use of a suppressor. *(Added by Stats.2010, c. 711 (S.B.1080), § 6, operative Jan. 1, 2012.)*

Law Revision Commission Comments

Section 34200 continues former Section 12039 without substantive change.

See Sections 16520 ("firearm"), 16640 ("handgun"), 17090 ("rifle"), 17190 ("shotgun"), 30510 ("assault weapon"), 30515 (further clarification of "assault weapon"). [38 Cal.L.Rev.Comm. Reports 217 (2009)].

Cross References

Attorney General, generally, see Government Code § 12500 et seq.
Firearm defined for purposes of this Part, see Penal Code § 16520.
Handgun defined for purposes of this Part, see Penal Code § 16640.

§ 34205. Pamphlet on California firearms laws; contents

(a) The Department of Justice shall prepare a pamphlet that summarizes California firearms laws as they pertain to persons other than law enforcement officers or members of the armed services.

(b) The pamphlet shall include the following matters:

(1) Lawful possession.

(2) Licensing procedures.

(3) Transportation and use of firearms.

(4) Acquisition of hunting licenses.

(5) The safe handling and use of firearms.

(6) Various methods of safe storage and child proofing of firearms.

(7) The availability of firearms safety programs and devices.

(8) The responsibilities of firearms ownership.

(9) The operation of various types of firearms.

(10) The lawful use of deadly force.

(c) The department shall offer copies of the pamphlet at actual cost to firearms dealers licensed pursuant to Sections 26700 to 26915, inclusive, who shall have copies of the most current version available for sale to retail purchasers or transferees of firearms. The cost of the pamphlet, if any, may be added to the sale price of the firearm. Other interested parties may purchase copies directly from the Department of General Services.

(d) The pamphlet shall declare that it is merely intended to provide a general summary of laws applicable to firearms and is not designed to provide individual guidance for specific areas. Individuals having specific questions shall be directed to contact their local law enforcement agency or private counsel.

(e) The Department of Justice or any other public entity shall be immune from any liability arising from the drafting, publication, or dissemination of the pamphlet or any reliance upon it. All receipts from the sale of these pamphlets shall be deposited as reimbursements to the support appropriation for the Department of Justice. *(Added by Stats.2010, c. 711 (S.B.1080), § 6, operative Jan. 1, 2012.)*

Law Revision Commission Comments

Section 34205 continues former Section 12080 without substantive change.

See Sections 16520 ("firearm"), 26700 ("dealer," "licensee," or "person licensed pursuant to Sections 26700 to 26915, inclusive"). [38 Cal.L.Rev. Comm. Reports 217 (2009)].

Cross References

Department of General Services, generally, see Government Code § 14600 et seq.
Firearm defined for purposes of this Part, see Penal Code § 16520.

CHAPTER 2. BALLISTICS IDENTIFICATION SYSTEM

§ 34350. Study to evaluate ballistics identification systems; report to Legislature

(a) The Attorney General shall conduct a study to evaluate ballistics identification systems to determine the feasibility and potential benefits to law enforcement of utilizing a statewide ballistics identification system capable of maintaining a database of ballistic images and information from test fired and sold firearms. The study shall include an evaluation of ballistics identification systems currently used by state and federal law enforcement agencies and the firearms industry. The Attorney General shall consult with law enforcement agencies, firearms industry representatives, private technology providers, and other appropriate parties in conducting the study.

(b) In evaluating ballistics identification systems to determine the feasibility of utilizing a statewide system as required pursuant to subdivision (a), the Attorney General shall consider, at a minimum, the following:

(1) The development of methods by which firearm manufacturers, importers, and dealers may potentially capture ballistic images from

firearms prior to sale in California and forward that information to the Attorney General.

(2) The development of methods by which the Attorney General will receive, store, and make available to law enforcement ballistic images submitted by firearm manufacturers, importers, and dealers prior to sale in California.

(3) The potential financial costs to the Attorney General of implementing and operating a statewide ballistics identification system, including the process for receipt of information from firearm manufacturers, importers, and dealers.

(4) The capability of a ballistics identification system maintaining a database of ballistic images and information from test fired firearms for all firearms sold in California.

(5) The compatibility of a ballistics identification system with ballistics identification systems that are currently used by law enforcement agencies in California.

(6) A method to ensure that state and local law enforcement agencies can forward ballistic identification information to the Attorney General for inclusion in a statewide ballistics identification system.

(7) The feasibility and potential benefits to law enforcement of requiring firearm manufacturers, importers, and dealers to provide the Attorney General with ballistic images from any, or a selected number of, test fired firearms prior to the sale of those firearms in California.

(c) The Attorney General shall submit a report to the Legislature with the results of the study not later than June 1, 2001. In the event the report includes a determination that a ballistics identification system and database is feasible and would benefit law enforcement, the report shall also recommend a strategy for implementation. *(Added by Stats.2010, c. 711 (S.B.1080), § 6, operative Jan. 1, 2012.)*

Law Revision Commission Comments

Section 34350 continues former Section 12072.5(b)-(d) without substantive change.

For other provisions relating to identification of firearms, see Sections 23900–23925 (obliteration of identification marks), 31910(b)(7) (identification of serial number of pistol or other firearm from spent cartridge casings).

See Sections 16230 ("ballistics identification system"), 16520 ("firearm"), 26700 ("dealer," "licensee," or "person licensed pursuant to Sections 26700 to 26915, inclusive"). [38 Cal.L.Rev.Comm. Reports 217 (2009)].

Cross References

Attorney General, generally, see Government Code § 12500 et seq.
Firearm defined for purposes of this Part, see Penal Code § 16520.

§ 34355. Application of Section 34350 to sales, deliveries, or transfers of firearms to authorized law enforcement representatives of local, state and federal governments; records of handguns and firearms acquired by agencies to be entered into Automated Firearms System (AFS)

(a) Section 34350 does not apply to any sale, delivery, or transfer of firearms made to an authorized law enforcement representative of any city, county, city and county, or state, or of the federal government, for exclusive use by that governmental agency if, prior to the sale, delivery, or transfer of these firearms, written authorization from the head of the agency authorizing the transaction is presented to the person from whom the purchase, delivery, or transfer is being made.

(b) Proper written authorization is defined as verifiable written certification from the head of the agency by which the purchaser or transferee is employed, identifying the employee as an individual authorized to conduct the transaction, and authorizing the transaction for the exclusive use of the agency by which that person is employed.

(c) Within 10 days of the date a handgun, and commencing January 1, 2014, any firearm, is acquired by the agency, a record of the same shall be entered as an institutional weapon into the Automated Firearms System (AFS) via the California Law Enforcement Telecommunications System (CLETS) by the law enforcement or state agency. Any agency without access to AFS shall arrange with the sheriff of the county in which the agency is located to input this information via this system. *(Added by Stats.2010, c. 711 (S.B.1080), § 6, operative Jan. 1, 2012. Amended by Stats.2011, c. 745 (A.B.809), § 76.)*

Law Revision Commission Comments

Section 34355 continues former Section 12078(a)(2) without substantive change, as that provision applied to former Section 12072.5.

For other exceptions relating to law enforcement, see Sections 34360 (exception for loan of firearm to peace officer employee for use in performing official duties), 34365 (exception for sale, delivery, or transfer by law enforcement agency to peace officer pursuant to Public Contract Code), 34370 (exception for sale, delivery, or transfer by law enforcement agency to retiring peace officer authorized to carry concealed and loaded firearm).

See Sections 16520 ("firearm"), 16640 ("handgun"). [38 Cal.L.Rev.Comm. Reports 217 (2009)].

Cross References

Firearm defined for purposes of this Part, see Penal Code § 16520.
Handgun defined for purposes of this Part, see Penal Code § 16640.

§ 34360. Application of Section 34350 to firearms loaned by law enforcement representatives to peace officers for use in course and scope of their duties

Section 34350 does not apply to the loan of a firearm if all of the following conditions are satisfied:

(a) The loan is made by an authorized law enforcement representative of a city, county, or city and county, or of the state or federal government.

(b) The loan is made to a peace officer employed by that agency and authorized to carry a firearm.

(c) The loan is made for the carrying and use of that firearm by that peace officer in the course and scope of the officer's duties. *(Added by Stats.2010, c. 711 (S.B.1080), § 6, operative Jan. 1, 2012.)*

Law Revision Commission Comments

Section 34360 continues former Section 12078(a)(3) without substantive change, as that provision applied to former Section 12072.5.

For other exceptions relating to law enforcement, see Sections 34355 (exception for sale, delivery, or transfer to authorized law enforcement representative of city, county, city and county, or state or federal government), 34365 (exception for sale, delivery, or transfer by law enforcement agency to peace officer pursuant to Public Contract Code), 34370 (exception for sale, delivery, or transfer by law enforcement agency to retiring peace officer authorized to carry concealed and loaded firearm).

See Section 16520 ("firearm"). [38 Cal.L.Rev.Comm. Reports 217 (2009)].

Cross References

Firearm defined for purposes of this Part, see Penal Code § 16520.

§ 34365. Application of Section 34350 to sale, delivery, or transfer of firearm to peace officer by law enforcement agency; records of handguns and firearms to be entered into Automated Firearms System (AFS)

(a) Section 34350 does not apply to the sale, delivery, or transfer of a firearm by a law enforcement agency to a peace officer pursuant to Section 10334 of the Public Contract Code.

(b) Within 10 days of the date that a handgun, and commencing January 1, 2014, any firearm, is sold, delivered, or transferred pursuant to Section 10334 of the Public Contract Code to that peace officer, the name of the officer and the make, model, serial number, and other identifying characteristics of the firearm being sold, delivered, or transferred shall be entered into the Automated

Firearms System (AFS) via the California Law Enforcement Telecommunications System (CLETS) by the law enforcement or state agency that sold, delivered, or transferred the firearm, provided, however, that if the firearm is not a handgun and does not have a serial number, identification number, or identification mark assigned to it, that fact shall be noted in AFS. Any agency without access to AFS shall arrange with the sheriff of the county in which the agency is located to input this information via this system. *(Added by Stats.2010, c. 711 (S.B.1080), § 6, operative Jan. 1, 2012. Amended by Stats.2011, c. 745 (A.B.809), § 77.)*

Law Revision Commission Comments

Section 34365 continues former Section 12078(a)(4) without substantive change, as that provision applied to former Section 12072.5.

For other exceptions relating to law enforcement, see Sections 34355 (exception for sale, delivery, or transfer to authorized law enforcement representative of city, county, city and county, or state or federal government), 34360 (exception for loan of firearm to peace officer employee for use in performing official duties), 34370 (exception for sale, delivery, or transfer by law enforcement agency to retiring peace officer authorized to carry concealed and loaded firearm).

See Sections 16520 ("firearm"), 16640 ("handgun"). [38 Cal.L.Rev.Comm. Reports 217 (2009)].

Cross References

Firearm defined for purposes of this Part, see Penal Code § 16520.
Handgun defined for purposes of this Part, see Penal Code § 16640.

§ 34370. Sale, delivery, or transfer of firearm by law enforcement agency to retiring peace officer; records of handguns and firearms to be entered into Automated Firearms System (AFS)

(a) Section 34350 does not apply to the sale, delivery, or transfer of a firearm by a law enforcement agency to a retiring peace officer who is authorized to carry a firearm pursuant to Chapter 5 (commencing with Section 26300) of Division 5.

(b) Within 10 days of the date that a handgun, and commencing January 1, 2014, any firearm, is sold, delivered, or transferred to that retiring peace officer, the name of the officer and the make, model, serial number, and other identifying characteristics of the firearm being sold, delivered, or transferred shall be entered into the Automated Firearms System (AFS) via the California Law Enforcement Telecommunications System (CLETS) by the law enforcement or state agency that sold, delivered, or transferred the firearm, provided, however, that if the firearm is not a handgun and does not have a serial number, identification number, or identification mark assigned to it, that fact shall be noted in AFS. Any agency without access to AFS shall arrange with the sheriff of the county in which the agency is located to input this information via this system. *(Added by Stats.2010, c. 711 (S.B.1080), § 6, operative Jan. 1, 2012. Amended by Stats.2011, c. 745 (A.B.809), § 78.)*

Law Revision Commission Comments

Section 34370 continues former Section 12078(a)(5) without substantive change, as that provision applied to former Section 12072.5.

For other exceptions relating to law enforcement, see Sections 34355 (exception for sale, delivery, or transfer to authorized law enforcement representative of city, county, city and county, or state or federal government), 34360 (exception for loan of firearm to peace officer employee for use in performing official duties), 34365 (exception for sale, delivery, or transfer by law enforcement agency to peace officer pursuant to Public Contract Code).

See Sections 16520 ("firearm"), 16640 ("handgun"). [38 Cal.L.Rev.Comm. Reports 217 (2009)].

Cross References

Firearm defined for purposes of this Part, see Penal Code § 16520.
Handgun defined for purposes of this Part, see Penal Code § 16640.

CONSTITUTION OF THE STATE OF CALIFORNIA 1879

ARTICLE I. DECLARATION OF RIGHTS

§ 1. Inalienable rights

Section 1. All people are by nature free and independent and have inalienable rights. Among these are enjoying and defending life and liberty, acquiring, possessing, and protecting property, and pursuing and obtaining safety, happiness, and privacy. *(Added Nov. 5, 1974.)*

Cross References

Acquisition of property, see Civil Code § 1000 et seq.
Adoption of unmarried minors, hearings, see Family Code § 8611.
Advertising, unsolicited and unwanted telephone solicitations, legislative findings and declarations, see Business and Professions Code § 17590.
Business records, protection of privacy, dissemination of information, see Civil Code § 1799.
Civil rights, see Civil Code § 51 et seq.
Criminal procedure,
  Arrest, resistance, see Penal Code § 834a.
  Arrest with or without a warrant, see Penal Code § 836.
  Warrant of arrest, complaints, see Penal Code § 813.
Deeds, invalidity of racial restrictions, see Civil Code § 782.
Due process and equal protection, privileges and immunities, requirements, see Cal. Const. Art. 1, § 7.
Force, right to use, see Civil Code § 50.
General personal rights, see Civil Code § 43.
Initiative and referendum, reservation of powers, see Cal. Const. Art. 4, § 1.
Installation or maintenance of two-way mirrors in restrooms, hotels, and toilets, see Penal Code § 653n.
Invasion of privacy, penal provisions, see Penal Code § 630 et seq.
Investigation and control of crimes and criminals, national search of criminal records, disclosure of confidential information, see Penal Code § 11149.4.
Involuntary servitude, see Cal. Const. Art. 1, § 6; Penal Code § 181.
Justifiable homicide, defense of property or person, see Penal Code § 197.
Lawful resistance, see Penal Code §§ 692 et seq.
Obligations arising from particular transactions, Information Practices Act of 1977,
  Invasion of privacy, see Civil Code § 1798.53.
  Legislative findings and declarations, see Civil Code § 1798.1.
  Privacy and constitutional rights, see Civil Code § 1798.73.
Opportunity to seek, obtain and hold employment without discrimination as civil right, see Government Code § 12921.
Ownership, see Civil Code §§ 654, 669 et seq.
Personal data, protection of privacy, dissemination of personal information, see Civil Code § 1798.
Personal relations, see Civil Code § 49.
Protection and advocacy agency, access to information and records, confidentiality, see Welfare and Institutions Code § 4903.
Real estate, law governing, see Civil Code § 755.
Right to instruct representatives, petition, and assembly, and right of access to government information, see Cal. Const. Art. 1, § 3.
Rights retained by the people, see Cal. Const. Art. 1, § 24.
Sex, race, creed, color, national or ethnic origin not a disqualification for any business, profession, vocation, or employment, see Cal. Const. Art. 1, § 8.
Slavery, prohibition, see Const. Art. 1, § 6; Penal Code § 181.
States rights,
  Over individuals, see Government Code § 200 et seq.
  Over property, see Government Code § 180 et seq.
Uniform Single Publication Act, one cause of action, see Civil Code § 3425.3.
Use of rights, see Civil Code §§ 1708, 3514.

Research References

California Jury Instructions-Civil, 8th Edition 7.25.1, Violation of State Constitutional Right of Privacy.
2 Witkin, California Criminal Law 4th Crimes Against Public Peace and Welfare § 508 (2021), In General.
1 Witkin California Criminal Law 4th Crimes Against the Person § 116 (2021), Suicide.
6 Witkin, California Criminal Law 4th Criminal Judgment § 58 (2021), Case Law.
4 Witkin, California Criminal Law 4th Illegally Obtained Evidence § 44 (2021), California Constitution.
4 Witkin, California Criminal Law 4th Illegally Obtained Evidence § 363 (2021), Use of Binoculars.
4 Witkin, California Criminal Law 4th Illegally Obtained Evidence § 401 (2021), Applicants for Government Employment or Promotion.
4 Witkin, California Criminal Law 4th Illegally Obtained Evidence § 404 (2021), College Athletes.
4 Witkin, California Criminal Law 4th Illegally Obtained Evidence § 427 (2021), Interception Permitted Under Former or Other Law.
4 Witkin, California Criminal Law 4th Illegally Obtained Evidence § 429 (2021), Illegal Disclosure After Legal Interception.
4 Witkin, California Criminal Law 4th Pretrial Proceedings § 82 (2021), No Constitutional Right to Destruction of Records.
2 Witkin, California Criminal Law 4th Sex Offenses and Crimes Against Decency § 22 (2021), In General.

§ 1.1. Reproductive freedom

Section operative if Stats.2022, Res. c. 97 (S.C.A.10) (Prop. 1) is approved at the Nov. 8, 2022 election.

SEC. 1.1. The state shall not deny or interfere with an individual's reproductive freedom in their most intimate decisions, which includes their fundamental right to choose to have an abortion and their fundamental right to choose or refuse contraceptives. This section is intended to further the constitutional right to privacy guaranteed by Section 1, and the constitutional right to not be denied equal protection guaranteed by Section 7. Nothing herein narrows or limits the right to privacy or equal protection. *(Added by Stats.2022, Res. c. 97 (S.C.A.10), (Prop. 1, operative if approved at the Nov. 8, 2022 election).)*

§ 2. Liberty of speech or of the press; responsibility for abuse; right to refuse to disclose source of information by member of news media

Sec. 2. (a) Every person may freely speak, write and publish his or her sentiments on all subjects, being responsible for the abuse of this right. A law may not restrain or abridge liberty of speech or press.

(b) A publisher, editor, reporter, or other person connected with or employed upon a newspaper, magazine, or other periodical publication, or by a press association or wire service, or any person who has been so connected or employed, shall not be adjudged in contempt by a judicial, legislative, or administrative body, or any other body having the power to issue subpoenas, for refusing to disclose the source of any information procured while so connected or employed for publication in a newspaper, magazine or other periodical publication, or for refusing to disclose any unpublished information obtained or prepared in gathering, receiving or processing of information for communication to the public.

Nor shall a radio or television news reporter or other person connected with or employed by a radio or television station, or any person who has been so connected or employed, be so adjudged in contempt for refusing to disclose the source of any information procured while so connected or employed for news or news commentary purposes on radio or television, or for refusing to disclose any unpublished information obtained or prepared in gathering, receiving or processing of information for communication to the public.

As used in this subdivision, "unpublished information" includes information not disseminated to the public by the person from whom disclosure is sought, whether or not related information has been disseminated and includes, but is not limited to, all notes, outtakes, photographs, tapes or other data of whatever sort not itself disseminated to the public through a medium of communication, whether or not published information based upon or related to such material has been disseminated. *(Added Nov. 5, 1974. Amended June 3, 1980.)*

Cross References

Consumer Credit Reporting Agencies Act, actions for damages, remedies available, see Civil Code § 1785.31.
Freedom of assembly, see Cal. Const. Art. 1, § 3.
Incitement to riot, see Penal Code § 404.6.
Interruption of communication service, entry of ex parte order, requirements, see Penal Code § 11473.

Legislative findings and declarations regarding California Anti-SLAPP Law, application to certain actions, exception for persons enumerated in this section, see Code of Civil Procedure § 425.17.
Libel and slander, see Civil Code §§ 43, 44 et seq.; Code of Civil Procedure §§ 340, 460 et seq.
Obscene matter, see Penal Code § 311 et seq.
Political reform, lobbyists, exemptions, see Government Code § 86300.
Postsecondary education, liaisons between campus law enforcement agencies and students exercising freedom of speech for purpose of promoting peaceful campus demonstrations, see Education Code § 66303.
Production of evidence, testimony given by journalist under subpoena; immunity rights, see Code of Civil Procedure § 1986.1.
Pupil rights and responsibilities, student exercise of free expression, see Education Code § 48907.
Uniform Single Publication Act, see Civil Code § 3425.1 et seq.
Veterans' institutions, veterans home residents, right to complain and voice grievances, see Military and Veterans Code § 1044.5.
Writ of habeas corpus, persons authorized to prosecute writ, see Penal Code § 1473.

Research References

3 Witkin, California Criminal Law 4th Punishment § 73 (2021), Profits from Crime.

§ 4. Religious liberty

Sec. 4. Free exercise and enjoyment of religion without discrimination or preference are guaranteed. This liberty of conscience does not excuse acts that are licentious or inconsistent with the peace or safety of the State. The Legislature shall make no law respecting an establishment of religion.

A person is not incompetent to be a witness or juror because of his or her opinions on religious beliefs. *(Added Nov. 5, 1974.)*

Cross References

Business establishments, discrimination, see Civil Code § 51 et seq.
Civil service,
Generally, see Government Code § 19700 et seq.
Notations or entries pertaining to religion, see Government Code § 19704.
Religious opinions or affiliations, see Government Code § 19703.
Community college buildings, use by religious groups, see Education Code § 82542.
Community development and housing, residential rehabilitation, equal opportunity in employment and contracts, see Health and Safety Code § 37923.
Credibility of witnesses, see Evidence Code § 780.
Credit card issuance, see Civil Code § 1747.80.
Criminal procedure,
Arrest with or without a warrant, see Penal Code § 836.
Warrant of arrest, complaints, see Penal Code § 813.
Department of youth authority, religious freedom for persons in custody, see Welfare and Institutions Code § 1705.
Disease immunizations, exemptions, see Health and Safety Code § 120365.
Education,
Absence of pupils from school for religious instruction, see Education Code § 46014.
Public money for religious and private schools, teaching religious doctrine, see Cal. Const. Art. 9, § 8.
Sectarian doctrine and publications included in courses of study, see Education Code § 51511.
Environmental health, common drinking cups, see Health and Safety Code § 118375.
Lobbying, see Government Code § 86300.
Malicious mischief, prohibition of bullfights, penalty, see Penal Code § 597m.
Marriage, non-conformity to religious requirements, see Family Code § 420.
Medical practice regulations, interference with religion, see Business and Professions Code § 2063.
Mentally ill persons' rights, see Welfare and Institutions Code § 5325.1.
Nursing in connection with religious practices, persons not licensed as nurses, see Business and Professions Code § 2731.
Opportunity to seek, obtain and hold employment without discrimination as civil right, see Government Code § 12921.
Posting or displaying religious items, landlord not to prohibit, exceptions, location, size, see Civil Code § 1940.45.
Prisoners' rights, see Penal Code §§ 4027, 5009.
Public finance, aid of religious purposes or institutions, see Cal. Const. Art. 16, § 5.
Qualifications,
Jurors, see Code of Civil Procedure § 198 et seq.
Real estate, religious restrictions in transfer or use, see Civil Code § 53.
Religious discrimination in employment on public works, see Labor Code § 1735.
Religious meetings, disturbance, see Penal Code § 302.
School required courses of study, exemptions, see Education Code § 51240 et seq.
State civil service, see Government Code § 19700 et seq.
State government, questions on race, religion, etc. in applications, see Government Code § 8310.
Witnesses, see Evidence Code § 700 et seq.
Writ of habeas corpus, persons authorized to prosecute writ, see Penal Code § 1473.
Zoning and planning, see Government Code § 65008.

§ 6. Slavery; involuntary servitude

Sec. 6. Slavery is prohibited. Involuntary servitude is prohibited except to punish crime. *(Added Nov. 5, 1974.)*

Cross References

Abduction,
Generally, see Penal Code § 265 et seq.
Person under 18, see Penal Code § 267.
Bail, admission to bail generally, see Penal Code § 1268.
Kidnapping,
Jurisdiction, see Penal Code § 784.
Slavery, purpose of, see Penal Code §§ 207, 208.
Sale of persons, prostitution or immoral purposes, see Penal Code § 266d et seq.
Slavery, see Penal Code § 181.

Research References

3 Witkin, California Criminal Law 4th Punishment § 485 (2021), Early Cases.
3 Witkin, California Criminal Law 4th Punishment § 788 (2021), No Right to Bail.

§ 7. Due process and equal protection; pupil school assignment or transportation; privileges and immunities

Sec. 7. (a) A person may not be deprived of life, liberty, or property without due process of law or denied equal protection of the laws; provided, that nothing contained herein or elsewhere in this Constitution imposes upon the State of California or any public entity, board, or official any obligations or responsibilities which exceed those imposed by the Equal Protection Clause of the 14th Amendment to the United States Constitution with respect to the use of pupil school assignment or pupil transportation. In enforcing this subdivision or any other provision of this Constitution, no court of this state may impose upon the State of California or any public entity, board, or official any obligation or responsibility with respect to the use of pupil school assignment or pupil transportation, (1) except to remedy a specific violation by such party that would also constitute a violation of the Equal Protection Clause of the 14th Amendment to the United States Constitution, and (2) unless a federal court would be permitted under federal decisional law to impose that obligation or responsibility upon such party to remedy the specific violation of the Equal Protection Clause of the 14th Amendment of the United States Constitution.

Except as may be precluded by the Constitution of the United States, every existing judgment, decree, writ, or other order of a court of this state, whenever rendered, which includes provisions regarding pupil school assignment or pupil transportation, or which requires a plan including any such provisions shall, upon application to a court having jurisdiction by any interested person, be modified to conform to the provisions of this subdivision as amended, as applied to the facts which exist at the time of such modification.

In all actions or proceedings arising under or seeking application of the amendments to this subdivision proposed by the Legislature at its 1979–80 Regular Session, all courts, wherein such actions or proceedings are or may hereafter be pending, shall give such actions or proceedings first precedence over all other civil actions therein.

Nothing herein shall prohibit the governing board of a school district from voluntarily continuing or commencing a school integration plan after the effective date of this subdivision as amended.

In amending this subdivision, the Legislature and people of the State of California find and declare that this amendment is necessary to serve compelling public interests, including those of making the most effective use of the limited financial resources now and prospectively available to support public education, maximizing the educational opportunities and protecting the health and safety of all public school pupils, enhancing the ability of parents to participate in the educational process, preserving harmony and tranquility in this state and its public schools, preventing the waste of scarce fuel resources, and protecting the environment.

(b) A citizen or class of citizens may not be granted privileges or immunities not granted on the same terms to all citizens. Privileges or immunities granted by the Legislature may be altered or revoked. *(Added Nov. 4, 1974. Amended Nov. 6, 1979.)*

Cross References

Acquisition of property, title by prescription, adverse possession, see Civil Code § 1007.
Aliens, equal property rights, see Cal. Const. Art. 1, § 20.
Birth certificates,
 Adopted children, color or race listing, see Health and Safety Code § 102645.
 Sex change, name change, see Health and Safety Code § 103430.
California department of health services, adjudicative hearings leading to final decisions; procedures, see Health and Safety Code § 100171.
California Voting Rights Act of 2001, see Elections Code § 14025 et seq.
Civil Rights Act, see Civil Code § 51 et seq.
Commencing action for the recovery of real property, adverse possession, occupancy of land, see Code of Civil Procedure § 325.
Community redevelopment projects, prohibited discrimination, see Health and Safety Code §§ 33050, 33435, 33436.
Credit cards, issuance, discrimination, see Civil Code § 1747.80.
Criminal procedure,
 Arrest with or without a warrant, see Penal Code § 836.
 Pleadings and proceedings before trial, issues of fact, see Penal Code § 1042.
 Warrant of arrest, complaints, see Penal Code § 813.
Criminal prosecutions, rights of defendants, see Cal. Const. Art. 1, § 15.
Disqualification from profession or occupation, sex, race, etc., see Cal. Const. Art. 1, § 8.
Educational funds, private organizations, discriminatory membership practices, see Education Code §§ 72014, 89757, 92150.
Fair Employment and Housing Act, see Government Code § 12900 et seq.
Holden Act, housing financial discrimination, see Health and Safety Code § 35800.
Housing and infrastructure finance agency, affirmative action, equal opportunity housing development, see Health and Safety Code § 50955.
Local or special laws where general statute applicable, see Cal. Const. Art. 4, § 16.
Mobilehome park tenancy, discrimination, see Civil Code § 798.20.
Personal rights, in general, see Civil Code § 43 et seq.
Political rights and duties, see Government Code § 270 et seq.
Prisoners, civil rights, see Penal Code §§ 2600, 2601.
Public beach access, see Government Code § 54090 et seq.
Right to instruct representatives, petition, and assembly, and right of access to government information, see Cal. Cal. Const. Art. 1, § 3.
Slavery and involuntary servitude prohibited, see Cal. Const. Art. 1, § 6.
State civil service, prohibited discrimination, see Government Code § 19700 et seq.
State funded activities or programs, denial of benefits, discrimination based on ethnic group, religion, etc., see Government Code § 11135 et seq.
State housing policy, low or moderate income persons, see Health and Safety Code § 50006.
Uniform general laws, see Cal. Const. Art. 4, § 16.
Writ of habeas corpus, persons authorized to prosecute writ, see Penal Code § 1473.

Research References

California Jury Instructions - Criminal 17.50, Concluding Instruction.
California Jury Instructions-Civil, 8th Edition 15.50, Concluding Instruction—General Verdict Without Special Findings.
2 Witkin, California Criminal Law 4th Crimes Against Public Peace and Welfare § 183 (2021), Jury Trial on Issue of Addiction.
2 Witkin, California Criminal Law 4th Crimes Against Public Peace and Welfare § 184 (2021), Revocation of Inpatient Status.
4 Witkin, California Criminal Law 4th Pretrial Proceedings § 198 (2021), No Postindictment Preliminary Hearing.
3 Witkin, California Criminal Law 4th Punishment § 450 (2021), Effect of Reversal for Insufficient Evidence.
3 Witkin, California Criminal Law 4th Punishment § 736 (2021), In General.
3 Witkin, California Criminal Law 4th Punishment § 817 (2021), Placement of Inmates in Program.

§ 7.5. Marriage; validity and recognition

Sec. 7.5. Only marriage between a man and a woman is valid or recognized in California. *(Added by Initiative Measure (Prop. 8, § 2, approved Nov. 4, 2008, eff. Nov. 5, 2008).)*

Validity

For validity of this section, see Perry v. Schwarzenegger, N.D.Cal.2010, 704 F.Supp.2d 921, affirmed by Perry v. Brown, C.A.9 (Cal.)2012, 671 F.3d 1052, vacated and remanded by Hollingsworth v. Perry, 133 S.Ct. 2652, on remand 725 F.3d 1140.

§ 9. Bill of attainder; ex post facto laws; obligation of contracts

Sec. 9. A bill of attainder, ex post facto law, or law impairing the obligation of contracts may not be passed. *(Added Nov. 5, 1974.)*

Validity

This section was held preempted as conflicting with the federal Bankruptcy Code in the decision of In re City of Vallejo, Bkrtcy.E.D.Cal.2009, 403 B.R. 72, affirmed 432 B.R. 262.

Cross References

Bail, admission to bail generally, see Penal Code § 1268.
Certificates of public convenience and necessity, specified utilities, commission authority, see Public Utilities Code § 1007.5.
Community colleges and education facilities, school sites, investigation, see Education Code § 81033.
Contracts, see Civil Code § 1549 et seq.
Criminal procedure,
 Arrest with or without a warrant, see Penal Code § 836.
 Warrant of arrest, complaints, see Penal Code § 813.
Local agencies,
 Obligation of contract, legislative findings and declarations, see Government Code § 53996.
 Payment guarantee, evidences of indebtedness by school districts and education boards, see Government Code § 53830.5.
Nature of a contract, object unlawful or impermissible, see Civil Code § 1598.
Retroactivity in Penal Code provisions, see Penal Code § 3.
State teachers' retirement system, investments, see Education Code § 22362.

Research References

1 Witkin California Criminal Law 4th Introduction to Crimes § 9 (2021), In General.
1 Witkin California Criminal Law 4th Introduction to Crimes § 11 (2021), Nature of Protection.

§ 10. Detention of witnesses; imprisonment for debt, tort, or militia fine

Sec. 10. Witnesses may not be unreasonably detained. A person may not be imprisoned in a civil action for debt or tort, or in peacetime for a militia fine. *(Added Nov. 5, 1974.)*

Cross References

Attachment, words and phrases, see Code of Civil Procedure § 481.010.
Bail, admission to bail generally, see Penal Code § 1268.
Criminal procedure,
 Arrest with or without a warrant, see Penal Code § 836.
 Examination of the case, material witnesses, see Penal Code § 882.
 Warrant of arrest, complaints, see Penal Code § 813.

Dead bodies, detaining for debt, see Health and Safety Code § 7053.
Detention of witnesses, see Penal Code § 881.
Fair debt collection practices, general provisions, see Civil Code § 1788.
Imprisonment for debt or tort, see Code of Civil Procedure § 501.
Militia fines, see Military and Veterans Code § 456 et seq.
Public bonds and obligations, municipal securities, owners' risks and contractual rights, see Government Code § 5854.
Unlawful detention of witness as contempt, see Code of Civil Procedure § 1209.
Writ of habeas corpus, persons authorized to prosecute writ, see Penal Code § 1473.

Research References

2 Witkin, California Criminal Law 4th Crimes Against Governmental Authority § 138 (2021), Failing to Withhold, Collect, or Pay Over.
2 Witkin, California Criminal Law 4th Crimes Against Property § 46 (2021), Nature of Offense.
2 Witkin, California Criminal Law 4th Crimes Against Property § 261 (2021), Rent Skimming.

§ 11. Habeas corpus; suspension

Sec. 11. Habeas corpus may not be suspended unless required by public safety in cases of rebellion or invasion. *(Added Nov. 5, 1974.)*

Cross References

Habeas corpus, see Penal Code § 1473 et seq.
Original jurisdiction in habeas corpus proceedings, see Cal. Const. Art. 6, § 10.
Writ of habeas corpus, persons authorized to prosecute writ, see Penal Code § 1473.

Research References

6 Witkin, California Criminal Law 4th Criminal Writs § 10 (2021), Nature and Purpose.

§ 12. Bail; release; exception for certain crimes; excessive bail; recognizance

Sec. 12. A person shall be released on bail by sufficient sureties, except for:

(a) Capital crimes when the facts are evident or the presumption great;

(b) Felony offenses involving acts of violence on another person, or felony sexual assault offenses on another person, when the facts are evident or the presumption great and the court finds based upon clear and convincing evidence that there is a substantial likelihood the person's release would result in great bodily harm to others; or

(c) Felony offenses when the facts are evident or the presumption great and the court finds based on clear and convincing evidence that the person has threatened another with great bodily harm and that there is a substantial likelihood that the person would carry out the threat if released.

Excessive bail may not be required. In fixing the amount of bail, the court shall take into consideration the seriousness of the offense charged, the previous criminal record of the defendant, and the probability of his or her appearing at the trial or hearing of the case.

A person may be released on his or her own recognizance in the court's discretion. *(Added Nov. 5, 1974. Amended June 8, 1982. Amended by Stats.1994, Res. ch. 95 (A.C.A.37) (Prop. 189, approved Nov. 8, 1994).)*

Cross References

Admission to bail as matter of right, see Penal Code §§ 1271, 1272.
Amount of bail, see Penal Code §§ 815a, 1275.
Bail,
  Generally, see Penal Code § 1268 et seq.
  Acceptance of bail, forfeiture, see Penal Code § 1269b.
  Increase or reduction of bail, determination by magistrate, see Penal Code § 1269c.
Capital offenses, see Penal Code § 1285.
Crimes against nature, sex offenses deemed felony offense involving act of violence and great bodily harm, denial of bail, see Penal Code § 292.
Criminal procedure,
  Arrest with or without a warrant, see Penal Code § 836.
  Inquiry into the competence of the defendant, resolution of question of mental competence, see Penal Code § 1370.
  Warrant of arrest, complaints, see Penal Code § 813.
Inquiry into the competence of the defendant, developmental disability of defendant, procedure, see Penal Code § 1370.1.
Judicial commitments, mentally disordered sex offenders, see Welfare and Institutions Code § 6300.
Non-capital cases, bail, see Penal Code § 1284.
Writ of habeas corpus, persons authorized to prosecute writ, see Penal Code § 1473.

Research References

5 Witkin, California Criminal Law 4th Criminal Trial § 843 (2021), In General.
4 Witkin, California Criminal Law 4th Pretrial Proceedings § 88 (2021), Purpose of Bail.
4 Witkin, California Criminal Law 4th Pretrial Proceedings § 89 (2021), Constitutional and Statutory Framework.
4 Witkin, California Criminal Law 4th Pretrial Proceedings § 90 (2021), Bail as Matter of Right.
4 Witkin, California Criminal Law 4th Pretrial Proceedings § 91 (2021), No Right to Bail.
4 Witkin, California Criminal Law 4th Pretrial Proceedings § 92 (2021), What Constitutes Capital Crime.
4 Witkin, California Criminal Law 4th Pretrial Proceedings § 93 (2021), Public Safety Exception.
4 Witkin, California Criminal Law 4th Pretrial Proceedings § 98 (2021), In General.
4 Witkin, California Criminal Law 4th Pretrial Proceedings § 103 (2021), Excessive Bail and Reduction.
4 Witkin, California Criminal Law 4th Pretrial Proceedings § 135 (2021), In General.
4 Witkin, California Criminal Law 4th Pretrial Proceedings § 136 (2021), Hearing.
3 Witkin, California Criminal Law 4th Punishment § 788 (2021), No Right to Bail.

§ 13. Searches and seizures; warrant

Sec. 13. The right of the people to be secure in their persons, houses, papers, and effects against unreasonable seizures and searches may not be violated; and a warrant may not issue except on probable cause, supported by oath or affirmation, particularly describing the place to be searched and the persons and things to be seized. *(Added Nov. 5, 1974.)*

Cross References

Admitting and excluding evidence,
  Preliminary determinations, procedure, see Evidence Code § 402.
  Relevant evidence, see Evidence Code § 350.
Affidavits, use, see Code of Civil Procedure § 2009.
Alcoholic beverages, seizure and forfeiture of property, restrictions, see Business and Professions Code § 25350.
Arrest,
  Felony, see Penal Code § 821.
  Force, see Penal Code § 843 et seq.
  Fresh pursuit, see Penal Code § 852 et seq.
  Misdemeanor, see Penal Code § 822.
  Procedure, see Penal Code § 833 et seq.
Attachment, see Code of Civil Procedure § 481.010 et seq.; Health and Safety Code § 7053.
Breaking building, doors, windows, etc., to effect,
  Arrest, see Penal Code §§ 844, 845, 855.
  Search, see Penal Code §§ 1531, 1532.
Complaints before magistrates, see Penal Code § 806.
Conspiracy to cause arrest, see Penal Code § 182.
County jails,
  Female deputy sheriffs, female prisoners, see Penal Code § 4020.8.
  Trained female custodial persons, searches of rooms, see Penal Code § 4021.
Crimes against property, theft of retail merchandise or library materials, civil liability and punishment, see Penal Code § 490.5.
Criminal procedure,
  Arrest with or without a warrant, see Penal Code § 836.
  Warrant of arrest, complaints, see Penal Code § 813.

Deceased persons, search of person or property, see Government Code § 27491.3.
Execution, see Code of Civil Procedure § 699.010 et seq.
Forcible entry and detainer, see Code of Civil Procedure § 1159 et seq.
Governmental access to financial records, see Government Code § 7460 et seq.
Government access to financial records, confidentiality, requests for disclosure, see Government Code § 7470.
Informers, disclosure of identity, see Evidence Code §§ 1041, 1042.
Inspection warrants, see Code of Civil Procedure § 1822.50 et seq.
Pleadings and proceedings before trial,
Arraignment, presence of defendant, see Penal Code § 977.
Indictment or information, grounds for setting aside, see Penal Code § 995.
Presumptions and inferences, burden of proof, official duty, see Evidence Code § 664.
Schools, searches, evidence seized by teachers or school officials, see Penal Code § 626.11.
Search warrants, see Penal Code § 1523 et seq.
Security to keep the peace, see Penal Code § 697 et seq.
Seizure of property without lawful authority, misdemeanor, see Penal Code § 146.
Setting aside indictment or information, see Penal Code § 995 et seq.
Special criminal proceedings, search warrants, motion to return property or suppress evidence, see Penal Code § 1538.5.
Time for search, see Penal Code §§ 1533, 1534.
Treatment of prisoners, organic therapy, proceedings on petition, see Penal Code § 2678.
Warrant of arrest,
Generally, see Penal Code § 813 et seq.
Bench warrant, see Penal Code §§ 979 et seq., 986.
Telegraphic, see Penal Code §§ 850, 851.
Writ of habeas corpus, persons authorized to prosecute writ, see Penal Code § 1473.

Research References

California Jury Instructions - Criminal 2.60, Defendant Not Testifying—No Inference of Guilt May be Drawn.
California Jury Instructions - Criminal 2.62, Defendant Testifying—When Adverse Inference May be Drawn.
California Jury Instructions - Criminal 9.24, Lawful Arrest by Peace Officer—Defined.
California Jury Instructions - Criminal 16.104, "Lawful Arrest"—Defined.
5 Witkin, California Criminal Law 4th Criminal Trial § 742 (2021), Scope of Power.
1 Witkin California Criminal Law 4th Defenses § 250 (2021), John Doe DNA Arrest Warrant May Commence Prosecution.
4 Witkin, California Criminal Law 4th Illegally Obtained Evidence § 2 (2021), Types of Excludable Evidence.
4 Witkin, California Criminal Law 4th Illegally Obtained Evidence § 25 (2021), Abolition of Independent Grounds Doctrine.
4 Witkin, California Criminal Law 4th Illegally Obtained Evidence § 44 (2021), California Constitution.
4 Witkin, California Criminal Law 4th Illegally Obtained Evidence § 120 (2021), In General.
4 Witkin, California Criminal Law 4th Illegally Obtained Evidence § 149 (2021), General Requirements.
4 Witkin, California Criminal Law 4th Illegally Obtained Evidence § 151 (2021), In General.
4 Witkin, California Criminal Law 4th Illegally Obtained Evidence § 153 (2021), Particularity Requirement.
4 Witkin, California Criminal Law 4th Illegally Obtained Evidence § 175 (2021), Use of Motorized Battering Ram.
4 Witkin, California Criminal Law 4th Illegally Obtained Evidence § 243 (2021), Telephone and Similar Records.
4 Witkin, California Criminal Law 4th Illegally Obtained Evidence § 244 (2021), Financial and Other Records.
4 Witkin, California Criminal Law 4th Illegally Obtained Evidence § 361 (2021), Flight Over Curtilage.
4 Witkin, California Criminal Law 4th Illegally Obtained Evidence § 407A (2021), (New) DNA Profiling of Suspects and Offenders.
4 Witkin, California Criminal Law 4th Illegally Obtained Evidence § 412 (2021), Exclusionary Rule Under California Constitution.
4 Witkin, California Criminal Law 4th Illegally Obtained Evidence § 413 (2021), Effect of Proposition 8.
4 Witkin, California Criminal Law 4th Pretrial Proceedings § 20 (2021), Failure to Identify Defendant.
4 Witkin, California Criminal Law 4th Pretrial Proceedings § 62 (2021), Booking, Fingerprinting, and Photographing.

§ 14. Felony prosecutions; indictment or information; proceedings before magistrate; right to counsel; interpreter

Sec. 14. Felonies shall be prosecuted as provided by law, either by indictment or, after examination and commitment by a magistrate, by information.

A person charged with a felony by complaint subscribed under penalty of perjury and on file in a court in the county where the felony is triable shall be taken without unnecessary delay before a magistrate of that court. The magistrate shall immediately give the defendant a copy of the complaint, inform the defendant of the defendant's right to counsel, allow the defendant a reasonable time to send for counsel, and on the defendant's request read the complaint to the defendant. On the defendant's request the magistrate shall require a peace officer to transmit within the county where the court is located a message to counsel named by defendant.

A person unable to understand English who is charged with a crime has a right to an interpreter throughout the proceedings. *(Added Nov. 5, 1974.)*

Cross References

Actions against public entities and public employees, actions for taking or damaging private property, work done by department of water resources, see Government Code § 955.8.
Arraignment, see Penal Code § 976 et seq.
Complaint, see Penal Code § 806.
Counsel,
Advisement of right at arraignment, see Penal Code § 987.
Allowance in criminal actions, see Penal Code § 686.
Criminal cases, attendance of witnesses, counsel, see Cal. Const. Art. 1, § 15 Clause 3.
Criminal procedure,
Arrest with or without a warrant, see Penal Code § 836.
Examination of the case, plea procedure in non-capital felony, see Penal Code § 859a.
Pleadings, forms, see Penal Code § 948.
Warrant of arrest, complaints, see Penal Code § 813.
Criminal procedure, pleadings and proceedings before trial,
Arraignment of defendant, see Penal Code § 988.
Indictment or information, see Penal Code § 995.
Grand jury proceedings, investigation into county matters, see Penal Code § 888.
Indictment and information, see Penal Code §§ 737 et seq., 940 et seq.
Informing defendant of charge and right of counsel, see Penal Code §§ 858, 859.
Magistrates, designation, see Penal Code § 808.
Refusal or neglect to allow attorney to visit prisoner, see Penal Code § 825.
Taking of defendant before magistrate without unnecessary delay, see Penal Code § 825.
Writ of habeas corpus, persons authorized to prosecute writ, see Penal Code § 1473.

Research References

5 Witkin, California Criminal Law 4th Criminal Trial § 174 (2021), Protection Under California Law.
5 Witkin, California Criminal Law 4th Criminal Trial § 638 (2021), Defendant or Witness With Communication Problems.
4 Witkin, California Criminal Law 4th Pretrial Proceedings § 68 (2021), Nature and Purpose of Requirement.
4 Witkin, California Criminal Law 4th Pretrial Proceedings § 73 (2021), Complaint in Another County.
4 Witkin, California Criminal Law 4th Pretrial Proceedings § 140 (2021), Nature and Purpose.
4 Witkin, California Criminal Law 4th Pretrial Proceedings § 145 (2021), Opportunity to Obtain Chosen Counsel.
4 Witkin, California Criminal Law 4th Pretrial Proceedings § 166 (2021), In General.

4 Witkin, California Criminal Law 4th Pretrial Proceedings § 199 (2021), Nature and Requisites.

§ 14.1. Felony prosecuted by indictment; postindictment preliminary hearing

Sec. 14.1. If a felony is prosecuted by indictment, there shall be no postindictment preliminary hearing. *(Added by Initiative Measure (Prop. 115), approved June 5, 1990, eff. June 6, 1990.)*

Research References

1 Witkin California Criminal Law 4th Introduction to Crimes § 133 (2021), Application to Pending Cases.
4 Witkin, California Criminal Law 4th Pretrial Proceedings § 198 (2021), No Postindictment Preliminary Hearing.

§ 15. Criminal cases; speedy public trial; compel attendance of witnesses; appearance and defense; counsel; depositions; double jeopardy; self-incrimination; due process

Sec. 15. The defendant in a criminal cause has the right to a speedy public trial, to compel attendance of witnesses in the defendant's behalf, to have the assistance of counsel for the defendant's defense, to be personally present with counsel, and to be confronted with the witnesses against the defendant. The Legislature may provide for the deposition of a witness in the presence of the defendant and the defendant's counsel.

Persons may not twice be put in jeopardy for the same offense, be compelled in a criminal cause to be a witness against themselves, or be deprived of life, liberty, or property without due process of law. *(Added Nov. 5, 1974.)*

Cross References

Cross references may be found under the clauses of Cal. Const. Art. 1, § 15.

Research References

2 Witkin, California Criminal Law 4th Crimes Against Governmental Authority § 30 (2021), In General.
2 Witkin, California Criminal Law 4th Crimes Against Public Peace and Welfare § 184 (2021), Revocation of Inpatient Status.
5 Witkin, California Criminal Law 4th Criminal Trial § 31 (2021), Early Development.
5 Witkin, California Criminal Law 4th Criminal Trial § 35 (2021), Provisions Are Constitutional.
5 Witkin, California Criminal Law 4th Criminal Trial § 174 (2021), Protection Under California Law.
5 Witkin, California Criminal Law 4th Criminal Trial § 232 (2021), In General.
5 Witkin, California Criminal Law 4th Criminal Trial § 235 (2021), Pope Case.
5 Witkin, California Criminal Law 4th Criminal Trial § 236 (2021), Strickland Case.
5 Witkin, California Criminal Law 4th Criminal Trial § 239 (2021), Attorney Who Has Resigned from Bar.
5 Witkin, California Criminal Law 4th Criminal Trial § 317 (2021), Policy and Right.
5 Witkin, California Criminal Law 4th Criminal Trial § 319 (2021), Under California Constitution.
5 Witkin, California Criminal Law 4th Criminal Trial § 326 (2021), Under California Constitution.
5 Witkin, California Criminal Law 4th Criminal Trial § 402 (2021), In General.
5 Witkin, California Criminal Law 4th Criminal Trial § 403 (2021), No Exclusion of Public.
5 Witkin, California Criminal Law 4th Criminal Trial § 491 (2021), Constitutional and Statutory Right.
5 Witkin, California Criminal Law 4th Criminal Trial § 633 (2021), In General.
5 Witkin, California Criminal Law 4th Criminal Trial § 636 (2021), Constitutional and Statutory Provisions.
1 Witkin California Criminal Law 4th Defenses § 115 (2021), Constitutional and Statutory Provisions.
1 Witkin California Criminal Law 4th Defenses § 117 (2021), Federal and State Standards Are Both Applicable.
1 Witkin California Criminal Law 4th Defenses § 143 (2021), Motion Based on Prosecutorial Misconduct.
1 Witkin California Criminal Law 4th Introduction to Crimes § 36 (2021), Rule of Expressio Unius Est Exclusio Alterius.
3 Witkin, California Criminal Law 4th Punishment § 589 (2021), Possibility of Clemency or Change in Law.
3 Witkin, California Criminal Law 4th Punishment § 817 (2021), Placement of Inmates in Program.

§ 16. Jury trial; three-fourths verdict; waiver of jury trial; number of jurors

Sec. 16. Trial by jury is an inviolate right and shall be secured to all, but in a civil cause three-fourths of the jury may render a verdict. A jury may be waived in a criminal cause by the consent of both parties expressed in open court by the defendant and the defendant's counsel. In a civil cause a jury may be waived by the consent of the parties expressed as prescribed by statute.

In civil causes the jury shall consist of 12 persons or a lesser number agreed on by the parties in open court. In civil causes other than causes within the appellate jurisdiction of the court of appeal the Legislature may provide that the jury shall consist of eight persons or a lesser number agreed on by the parties in open court.

In criminal actions in which a felony is charged, the jury shall consist of 12 persons. In criminal actions in which a misdemeanor is charged, the jury shall consist of 12 persons or a lesser number agreed on by the parties in open court. *(Added Nov. 5, 1974. Amended Nov. 4, 1980. Amended by Stats.1996, Res. c. 36 (S.C.A.4), (Prop. 220, approved June 2, 1998, eff. June 3, 1998).)*

Law Revision Commission Comments

For background relating to the amendment to Section 16 of Article I of the California Constitution made by Proposition 220 (approved by the electors June 2, 1998), see *Trial Court Unification: Constitutional Revision (SCA 3)*, 24 Cal. L. Revision Comm'n Reports 1 (1994). [28 Cal.L.Rev.Comm. Reports App. 8 (1998)].

Cross References

Actions triable by jury, issues of fact, see Code of Civil Procedure § 592.
Community mental health services, involuntary treatment, time for hearing, see Welfare and Institutions Code § 5303.
Conduct of jury trial, see Code of Civil Procedure § 607 et seq.
Criminal cases, see Penal Code § 689.
Criminal procedure,
 Arrest with or without a warrant, see Penal Code § 836.
 Pleadings and proceedings before trial, jury formation, see Penal Code § 1046.
 Warrant of arrest, complaints, see Penal Code § 813.
Definitions of jury, see Code of Civil Procedure § 193.
Eminent domain, compensation for private property to be ascertained by jury, see Cal. Const. Art. 1, § 19.
Felonies, definition and penalties, see Penal Code §§ 17, 18.
Forcible entry and unlawful detainer, jury trial, see Code of Civil Procedure § 1171.
Judicial, municipal courts unification with superior courts, see Cal. Const. Art. 6, § 23.
Misdemeanors, definition and penalties, see Penal Code §§ 17, 19 and 19.2.
Narcotic addiction, jury trial, see Welfare and Institutions Code § 3108.
Number of jurors, see Code of Civil Procedure § 194.
Persons with judicial powers, Trial Jury Selection and Management Act, generally, see Code of Civil Procedure § 190.
Persons with judicial powers, Trial Jury Selection and Management Act, challenges, see Code of Civil Procedure § 225.
Persons with judicial powers, Trial Jury Selection and Management Act, number of jurors, see Code of Civil Procedure § 220.
Pleadings and proceedings before trial, arraignment, presence of defendant, see Penal Code § 977.
Purpose of amendments by Stats.1996, Res. c. 36 (S.C.A.4), see Cal. Const. Art. 6, § 23.
School facilities, development fees and charges, levies against manufactured home or mobilehome by school districts, see Education Code § 17625.
Verdict, see Code of Civil Procedure § 624 et seq.; Penal Code § 1147 et seq.
Waiver, see Code of Civil Procedure §§ 631, 1171; Penal Code § 689.
Writ of habeas corpus, persons authorized to prosecute writ, see Penal Code § 1473.

Youth authority, jury trial of whether person detained is physically dangerous to the public, see Welfare and Institutions Code § 1801.5.

Research References

2 Witkin, California Criminal Law 4th Crimes Against Public Peace and Welfare § 183 (2021), Jury Trial on Issue of Addiction.
6 Witkin, California Criminal Law 4th Criminal Judgment § 6 (2021), Change of Foreperson.
5 Witkin, California Criminal Law 4th Criminal Trial § 511 (2021), California Law.
5 Witkin, California Criminal Law 4th Criminal Trial § 514 (2021), Size of Jury.
5 Witkin, California Criminal Law 4th Criminal Trial § 515 (2021), Unanimous Verdict Requirement.
5 Witkin, California Criminal Law 4th Criminal Trial § 535 (2021), In General.
5 Witkin, California Criminal Law 4th Criminal Trial § 544 (2021), Requirement that Jury be Drawn from Vicinage.
5 Witkin, California Criminal Law 4th Criminal Trial § 545 (2021), In General.
5 Witkin, California Criminal Law 4th Criminal Trial § 546 (2021), Necessity of Express Waiver.
5 Witkin, California Criminal Law 4th Criminal Trial § 547 (2021), Consent of Prosecutor and Defense Counsel.
5 Witkin, California Criminal Law 4th Criminal Trial § 589 (2021), Under California Constitution: Wheeler Case.
5 Witkin, California Criminal Law 4th Criminal Trial § 615 (2021), Substitution After Submission.
5 Witkin, California Criminal Law 4th Criminal Trial § 646 (2021), Required Waivers and Advisements.
4 Witkin, California Criminal Law 4th Pretrial Proceedings § 302 (2021), California Rule: Express Advice and Waiver of Rights.

§ 17. Cruel or unusual punishment; excessive fines

Sec. 17. Cruel or unusual punishment may not be inflicted or excessive fines imposed. *(Added Nov. 5, 1974.)*

Cross References

Crimes against the person, homicide,
  Expeditious imposition of sentences, see Penal Code § 190.6.
  Punishment, see Penal Code § 190.
Criminal procedure,
  Arrest with or without a warrant, see Penal Code § 836.
  Warrant of arrest, complaints, see Penal Code § 813.
Cruel and unusual punishments, treatment impairing health, see Penal Code § 673.
Cruel or unusual punishment forbidden, see Penal Code § 2652.
Execution of death penalty, delivery and detention of male person pending execution, see Penal Code § 3600.
Judgment and execution, felony cases, presence or absence of defendant, see Penal Code § 1193.
Judicial commitments, sexually violent predators, see Welfare and Institutions Code § 6600.
Proceedings after commencement of trial and before judgment, initial sentencing, two or more felony convictions, see Penal Code § 1170.1.
Sentencing for driving while under the influence, second or subsequent offense involving alcohol or drugs, minimum confinement, see Vehicle Code § 23580.
Sex offenders, fleeing from state, punishment, see Penal Code § 289.5.

Research References

3 Witkin, California Criminal Law 4th Punishment § 145 (2021), In General.
3 Witkin, California Criminal Law 4th Punishment § 193 (2021), In General.
3 Witkin, California Criminal Law 4th Punishment § 228 (2021), Constitutional and Statutory Provisions.
3 Witkin, California Criminal Law 4th Punishment § 233 (2021), Sentencing of Minors.
3 Witkin, California Criminal Law 4th Punishment § 247 (2021), Punishment for Disease or Status.
3 Witkin, California Criminal Law 4th Punishment § 485 (2021), Early Cases.
3 Witkin, California Criminal Law 4th Punishment § 486 (2021), California Constitution and Statutes.

§ 23. Grand jury

Sec. 23. One or more grand juries shall be drawn and summoned at least once a year in each county. *(Added Nov. 5, 1974.)*

Cross References

Grand jury, see Penal Code § 893 et seq.
Grand jury proceedings,
  Impaneling of grand jury, challenges, see Penal Code § 910.
  Impaneling of grand jury, order directing drawing of grand jury, see Penal Code § 904.
  Investigation into county matters of civil concern, see Penal Code § 888.
  Listing and selection of grand juries, estimate of number of jurors needed, see Penal Code § 895.
  Powers and duties of grand jury, charge by court, see Penal Code § 914.
  Powers and duties of grand jury, private sessions, see Penal Code § 939.
  Powers and duties of grand jury, willful disclosure of making of indictment or information, see Penal Code § 924.
Persons with judicial powers, Trial Jury Selection and Management Act, kinds of juries, see Code of Civil Procedure § 193.

Research References

4 Witkin, California Criminal Law 4th Introduction to Criminal Procedure § 33 (2021), Nature.
4 Witkin, California Criminal Law 4th Introduction to Criminal Procedure § 39 (2021), Impaneling.

§ 24. Rights not dependent on federal constitution; criminal cases; construction of laws consistent with federal constitution; rights reserved to the people

Sec. 24. Rights guaranteed by this Constitution are not dependent on those guaranteed by the United States Constitution.

In criminal cases the rights of a defendant to equal protection of the laws, to due process of law, to the assistance of counsel, to be personally present with counsel, to a speedy and public trial, to compel the attendance of witnesses, to confront the witnesses against him or her, to be free from unreasonable searches and seizures, to privacy, to not be compelled to be a witness against himself or herself, to not be placed twice in jeopardy for the same offense, and to not suffer the imposition of cruel or unusual punishment, shall be construed by the courts of this State in a manner consistent with the Constitution of the United States. This Constitution shall not be construed by the courts to afford greater rights to criminal defendants than those afforded by the Constitution of the United States, nor shall it be construed to afford greater rights to minors in juvenile proceedings on criminal causes than those afforded by the Constitution of the United States.

This declaration of rights may not be construed to impair or deny others retained by the people. *(Added Nov. 5, 1974. Amended by Initiative Measure (Prop. 115, approved June 5, 1990, eff. June 6, 1990).)*

Validity

Amendment of this section by Prop. 115, which inserted the second paragraph relating to the rights of a defendant in criminal cases, was held unconstitutional in the case of Raven v. Deukmejian (1990) 276 Cal.Rptr. 326, 801 P.2d 1077, 52 Cal.3d 336, rehearing denied.

Cross References

Initiative and referendum, see Cal. Const. Art. 2, § 8 et seq.

Research References

5 Witkin, California Criminal Law 4th Criminal Trial § 323 (2021), Relationship Between State and Federal Guarantees.
4 Witkin, California Criminal Law 4th Illegally Obtained Evidence § 25 (2021), Abolition of Independent Grounds Doctrine.
1 Witkin California Criminal Law 4th Introduction to Crimes § 131 (2021), Construction of Rights Under United States Constitution.
1 Witkin California Criminal Law 4th Introduction to Crimes § 132 (2021), Constitutional Challenges.

§ 26. Mandatory and prohibitory provisions

Sec. 26. The provisions of this Constitution are mandatory and prohibitory, unless by express words they are declared to be otherwise. *(Formerly Art. 1, § 28, added Nov. 7, 1972. Renumbered Art. 1, § 26, June 8, 1976.)*

§ 27. Death penalty

Sec. 27. All statutes of this State in effect on February 17, 1972, requiring, authorizing, imposing, or relating to the death penalty are in full force and effect, subject to legislative amendment or repeal by statute, initiative, or referendum.

The death penalty provided for under those statutes shall not be deemed to be, or to constitute, the infliction of cruel or unusual punishments within the meaning of Article 1, Section 6 nor shall such punishment for such offenses be deemed to contravene any other provision of this constitution. *(Added Nov. 7, 1972.)*

Cross References

Assault with deadly weapon by life prisoner, death penalty, see Penal Code § 4500.
Attempts to kill, train derailing or wrecking, punishment, see Penal Code § 219.
Crimes against the person, homicide,
Death penalty or life imprisonment without parole, see Penal Code § 190.2.
Punishment, execution of death penalty, see Penal Code § 190.
Cruel or unusual punishment, excessive fines, see Cal. Const. Art. 1, § 17.
Execution, judgment of death, see Penal Code § 1217 et seq.
Execution of death penalty,
Delivery and detention of male person pending execution, see Penal Code § 3600.
Suspension of execution, persons authorized to suspend execution, see Penal Code § 3700.
Homicide, death penalty or life imprisonment, aggravating and mitigating circumstances, see Penal Code § 190.3.
Murder, death penalty, see Penal Code §§ 190, 190.1.
Perjury, procuring death of innocent person, see Penal Code § 128.
Treason, death penalty, see Penal Code § 37.
Writ of habeas corpus, persons authorized to prosecute writ, see Penal Code § 1473.

Research References

3 Witkin, California Criminal Law 4th Punishment § 486 (2021), California Constitution and Statutes.
3 Witkin, California Criminal Law 4th Punishment § 509 (2021), Former Law.

§ 28. Findings and declarations; rights of victims; enforcement

Sec. 28. (a) The People of the State of California find and declare all of the following:

(1) Criminal activity has a serious impact on the citizens of California. The rights of victims of crime and their families in criminal prosecutions are a subject of grave statewide concern.

(2) Victims of crime are entitled to have the criminal justice system view criminal acts as serious threats to the safety and welfare of the people of California. The enactment of comprehensive provisions and laws ensuring a bill of rights for victims of crime, including safeguards in the criminal justice system fully protecting those rights and ensuring that crime victims are treated with respect and dignity, is a matter of high public importance. California's victims of crime are largely dependent upon the proper functioning of government, upon the criminal justice system and upon the expeditious enforcement of the rights of victims of crime described herein, in order to protect the public safety and to secure justice when the public safety has been compromised by criminal activity.

(3) The rights of victims pervade the criminal justice system. These rights include personally held and enforceable rights described in paragraphs (1) through (17) of subdivision (b).

(4) The rights of victims also include broader shared collective rights that are held in common with all of the People of the State of California and that are enforceable through the enactment of laws and through good-faith efforts and actions of California's elected, appointed, and publicly employed officials. These rights encompass the expectation shared with all of the people of California that persons who commit felonious acts causing injury to innocent victims will be appropriately and thoroughly investigated, appropriately detained in custody, brought before the courts of California even if arrested outside the State, tried by the courts in a timely manner, sentenced, and sufficiently punished so that the public safety is protected and encouraged as a goal of highest importance.

(5) Victims of crime have a collectively shared right to expect that persons convicted of committing criminal acts are sufficiently punished in both the manner and the length of the sentences imposed by the courts of the State of California. This right includes the right to expect that the punitive and deterrent effect of custodial sentences imposed by the courts will not be undercut or diminished by the granting of rights and privileges to prisoners that are not required by any provision of the United States Constitution or by the laws of this State to be granted to any person incarcerated in a penal or other custodial facility in this State as a punishment or correction for the commission of a crime.

(6) Victims of crime are entitled to finality in their criminal cases. Lengthy appeals and other post-judgment proceedings that challenge criminal convictions, frequent and difficult parole hearings that threaten to release criminal offenders, and the ongoing threat that the sentences of criminal wrongdoers will be reduced, prolong the suffering of crime victims for many years after the crimes themselves have been perpetrated. This prolonged suffering of crime victims and their families must come to an end.

(7) Finally, the People find and declare that the right to public safety extends to public and private primary, elementary, junior high, and senior high school, and community college, California State University, University of California, and private college and university campuses, where students and staff have the right to be safe and secure in their persons.

(8) To accomplish the goals it is necessary that the laws of California relating to the criminal justice process be amended in order to protect the legitimate rights of victims of crime.

(b) In order to preserve and protect a victim's rights to justice and due process, a victim shall be entitled to the following rights:

(1) To be treated with fairness and respect for his or her privacy and dignity, and to be free from intimidation, harassment, and abuse, throughout the criminal or juvenile justice process.

(2) To be reasonably protected from the defendant and persons acting on behalf of the defendant.

(3) To have the safety of the victim and the victim's family considered in fixing the amount of bail and release conditions for the defendant.

(4) To prevent the disclosure of confidential information or records to the defendant, the defendant's attorney, or any other person acting on behalf of the defendant, which could be used to locate or harass the victim or the victim's family or which disclose confidential communications made in the course of medical or counseling treatment, or which are otherwise privileged or confidential by law.

(5) To refuse an interview, deposition, or discovery request by the defendant, the defendant's attorney, or any other person acting on behalf of the defendant, and to set reasonable conditions on the conduct of any such interview to which the victim consents.

(6) To reasonable notice of and to reasonably confer with the prosecuting agency, upon request, regarding, the arrest of the defendant if known by the prosecutor, the charges filed, the determination whether to extradite the defendant, and, upon request, to be notified of and informed before any pretrial disposition of the case.

(7) To reasonable notice of all public proceedings, including delinquency proceedings, upon request, at which the defendant and the prosecutor are entitled to be present and of all parole or other

post-conviction release proceedings, and to be present at all such proceedings.

(8) To be heard, upon request, at any proceeding, including any delinquency proceeding, involving a post-arrest release decision, plea, sentencing, post-conviction release decision, or any proceeding in which a right of the victim is at issue.

(9) To a speedy trial and a prompt and final conclusion of the case and any related post-judgment proceedings.

(10) To provide information to a probation department official conducting a pre-sentence investigation concerning the impact of the offense on the victim and the victim's family and any sentencing recommendations before the sentencing of the defendant.

(11) To receive, upon request, the pre-sentence report when available to the defendant, except for those portions made confidential by law.

(12) To be informed, upon request, of the conviction, sentence, place and time of incarceration, or other disposition of the defendant, the scheduled release date of the defendant, and the release of or the escape by the defendant from custody.

(13) To restitution.

(A) It is the unequivocal intention of the People of the State of California that all persons who suffer losses as a result of criminal activity shall have the right to seek and secure restitution from the persons convicted of the crimes causing the losses they suffer.

(B) Restitution shall be ordered from the convicted wrongdoer in every case, regardless of the sentence or disposition imposed, in which a crime victim suffers a loss.

(C) All monetary payments, monies, and property collected from any person who has been ordered to make restitution shall be first applied to pay the amounts ordered as restitution to the victim.

(14) To the prompt return of property when no longer needed as evidence.

(15) To be informed of all parole procedures, to participate in the parole process, to provide information to the parole authority to be considered before the parole of the offender, and to be notified, upon request, of the parole or other release of the offender.

(16) To have the safety of the victim, the victim's family, and the general public considered before any parole or other post-judgment release decision is made.

(17) To be informed of the rights enumerated in paragraphs (1) through (16).

(c)(1) A victim, the retained attorney of a victim, a lawful representative of the victim, or the prosecuting attorney upon request of the victim, may enforce the rights enumerated in subdivision (b) in any trial or appellate court with jurisdiction over the case as a matter of right. The court shall act promptly on such a request.

(2) This section does not create any cause of action for compensation or damages against the State, any political subdivision of the State, any officer, employee, or agent of the State or of any of its political subdivisions, or any officer or employee of the court.

(d) The granting of these rights to victims shall not be construed to deny or disparage other rights possessed by victims. The court in its discretion may extend the right to be heard at sentencing to any person harmed by the defendant. The parole authority shall extend the right to be heard at a parole hearing to any person harmed by the offender.

(e) As used in this section, a "victim" is a person who suffers direct or threatened physical, psychological, or financial harm as a result of the commission or attempted commission of a crime or delinquent act. The term "victim" also includes the person's spouse, parents, children, siblings, or guardian, and includes a lawful representative of a crime victim who is deceased, a minor, or physically or psychologically incapacitated. The term "victim" does not include a person in custody for an offense, the accused, or a person whom the court finds would not act in the best interests of a minor victim.

(f) In addition to the enumerated rights provided in subdivision (b) that are personally enforceable by victims as provided in subdivision (c), victims of crime have additional rights that are shared with all of the People of the State of California. These collectively held rights include, but are not limited to, the following:

(1) Right to Safe Schools. All students and staff of public primary, elementary, junior high, and senior high schools, and community colleges, colleges, and universities have the inalienable right to attend campuses which are safe, secure and peaceful.

(2) Right to Truth-in-Evidence. Except as provided by statute hereafter enacted by a two-thirds vote of the membership in each house of the Legislature, relevant evidence shall not be excluded in any criminal proceeding, including pretrial and post conviction motions and hearings, or in any trial or hearing of a juvenile for a criminal offense, whether heard in juvenile or adult court. Nothing in this section shall affect any existing statutory rule of evidence relating to privilege or hearsay, or Evidence Code Sections 352, 782 or 1103. Nothing in this section shall affect any existing statutory or constitutional right of the press.

(3) Public Safety Bail. A person may be released on bail by sufficient sureties, except for capital crimes when the facts are evident or the presumption great. Excessive bail may not be required. In setting, reducing or denying bail, the judge or magistrate shall take into consideration the protection of the public, the safety of the victim, the seriousness of the offense charged, the previous criminal record of the defendant, and the probability of his or her appearing at the trial or hearing of the case. Public safety and the safety of the victim shall be the primary considerations.

A person may be released on his or her own recognizance in the court's discretion, subject to the same factors considered in setting bail.

Before any person arrested for a serious felony may be released on bail, a hearing may be held before the magistrate or judge, and the prosecuting attorney and the victim shall be given notice and reasonable opportunity to be heard on the matter.

When a judge or magistrate grants or denies bail or release on a person's own recognizance, the reasons for that decision shall be stated in the record and included in the court's minutes.

(4) Use of Prior Convictions. Any prior felony conviction of any person in any criminal proceeding, whether adult or juvenile, shall subsequently be used without limitation for purposes of impeachment or enhancement of sentence in any criminal proceeding. When a prior felony conviction is an element of any felony offense, it shall be proven to the trier of fact in open court.

(5) Truth in Sentencing. Sentences that are individually imposed upon convicted criminal wrongdoers based upon the facts and circumstances surrounding their cases shall be carried out in compliance with the courts' sentencing orders, and shall not be substantially diminished by early release policies intended to alleviate overcrowding in custodial facilities. The legislative branch shall ensure sufficient funding to adequately house inmates for the full terms of their sentences, except for statutorily authorized credits which reduce those sentences.

(6) Reform of the parole process. The current process for parole hearings is excessive, especially in cases in which the defendant has been convicted of murder. The parole hearing process must be reformed for the benefit of crime victims.

(g) As used in this article, the term "serious felony" is any crime defined in subdivision (c) of Section 1192.7 of the Penal Code, or any successor statute. *(Added by Initiative Measure, approved by the people, June 8, 1982. Amended by Initiative Measure (Prop. 9, § 4.1, approved Nov. 4, 2008, eff. Nov. 5, 2008).)*

CA Const.

Cross References

Bail, see Cal. Const. Art. 1, § 12.
Crimes against public justice, witnesses, see Penal Code § 132.5.
Criminal Justice Planning Committee for State Judicial System, local assistance centers, Victim–Witness Assistance Fund, see Penal Code § 13835.7.
Criminal procedure,
Arrest with or without a warrant, see Penal Code § 836.
Judgment and execution, notice to victim, see Penal Code § 1191.2.
Warrant of arrest, complaints, see Penal Code § 813.
Felonies, definition and penalties, see Penal Code §§ 17, 18.
Hearsay evidence, see Evidence Code § 1200 et seq.
Illegal evidence, effect of constitutional right to truth-in-evidence provision, see Vehicle Code § 40808.
Judgment and execution, probation, suspension of sentence, see Penal Code § 1203.1.
Juvenile court law, wards and hearings, victims' rights to presence at proceedings, see Welfare and Institutions Code § 676.5.
Medical parole, conditions, effect on other types of parole, see Penal Code § 3550.
Members of the military, mitigation of certain criminal sentences where mental health problems stem from service, recall of sentence, see Penal Code § 1170.91.
Proceedings after the commencement of the trial and before judgment, sexual assault prosecution; prohibition against psychiatric or psychological examination to test witness credibility, see Penal Code § 1112.
Reversal for error resulting in miscarriage of justice, see Cal. Const. Art. 6, § 13.
Rights of victims and witnesses of crimes,
Legislative intent, see Penal Code § 679.
Statutory rights, see Penal Code § 679.02.
State Board of Control, indemnification of private citizens, declaration of public interest, see Government Code § 13959.
Victims of crime, indemnification of victims of crime, public purpose, see Government Code § 29631.
Victim's Rights Cards, see Penal Code § 679.08.
Writ of habeas corpus, persons authorized to prosecute writ, see Penal Code § 1473.

Research References

California Jury Instructions - Criminal 2.23, Believability of Witness—Conviction of a Felony.
California Jury Instructions - Criminal 2.24, Believability of Witness—Evidence of Character for Honesty or Truthfulness.
California Jury Instructions - Criminal 12.44, Firearm—Possession by Person Convicted of a Felony—Status Stipulated.
2 Witkin, California Criminal Law 4th Crimes Against Governmental Authority § 13 (2021), Disclosure of Information by Prospective Witness for Consideration.
2 Witkin, California Criminal Law 4th Crimes Against Public Peace and Welfare § 233 (2021), Prohibitions.
2 Witkin, California Criminal Law 4th Crimes Against Public Peace and Welfare § 279 (2021), In General.
5 Witkin, California Criminal Law 4th Criminal Trial § 109 (2021), Proposition 8: Abrogation of State Constitutional Basis for Rule.
5 Witkin, California Criminal Law 4th Criminal Trial § 155 (2021), California Decisions.
5 Witkin, California Criminal Law 4th Criminal Trial § 174 (2021), Protection Under California Law.
5 Witkin, California Criminal Law 4th Criminal Trial § 326 (2021), Under California Constitution.
5 Witkin, California Criminal Law 4th Criminal Trial § 429 (2021), In General.
5 Witkin, California Criminal Law 4th Criminal Trial § 430 (2021), Nature of Trial or Hearing.
5 Witkin, California Criminal Law 4th Criminal Trial § 431 (2021), Where Codefendant Testifies.
5 Witkin, California Criminal Law 4th Criminal Trial § 442 (2021), Test for Harmless or Reversible Error.
5 Witkin, California Criminal Law 4th Criminal Trial § 443 (2021), Reversible Error.
5 Witkin, California Criminal Law 4th Criminal Trial § 475 (2021), In General.
5 Witkin, California Criminal Law 4th Criminal Trial § 618 (2021), Bifurcation to Determine Validity of Prior Convictions.
1 Witkin California Criminal Law 4th Elements § 47 (2021), What Constitutes Corpus Delicti.
1 Witkin California Criminal Law 4th Elements § 48 (2021), No Proof by Extrajudicial Admission or Confession Alone.
1 Witkin California Criminal Law 4th Elements § 49 (2021), Rule is Not Abrogated by Truth in Evidence Provision of Proposition 8.
1 Witkin California Criminal Law 4th Elements § 53 (2021), Prima Facie Showing.
4 Witkin, California Criminal Law 4th Illegally Obtained Evidence § 25 (2021), Abolition of Independent Grounds Doctrine.
4 Witkin, California Criminal Law 4th Illegally Obtained Evidence § 144 (2021), In General.
4 Witkin, California Criminal Law 4th Illegally Obtained Evidence § 168 (2021), Presentation of Warrant.
4 Witkin, California Criminal Law 4th Illegally Obtained Evidence § 324 (2021), Detention of Student on School Grounds.
4 Witkin, California Criminal Law 4th Illegally Obtained Evidence § 392 (2021), Search Under Established School Policy.
4 Witkin, California Criminal Law 4th Illegally Obtained Evidence § 420 (2021), Application in State Cases.
1 Witkin California Criminal Law 4th Introduction to Crimes § 75 (2021), General Principles.
1 Witkin California Criminal Law 4th Introduction to Crimes § 124 (2021), Constitutional Provisions and Statutes.
1 Witkin California Criminal Law 4th Introduction to Crimes § 125 (2021), Declaration of Intent.
1 Witkin California Criminal Law 4th Introduction to Crimes § 126 (2021), Enumerated Rights.
1 Witkin California Criminal Law 4th Introduction to Crimes § 134 (2021), In General.
4 Witkin, California Criminal Law 4th Introduction to Criminal Procedure § 21 (2021), Citizen May Not Compel or Intervene in Prosecution.
4 Witkin, California Criminal Law 4th Pretrial Proceedings § 31 (2021), Intoxication and Motor Vehicles.
4 Witkin, California Criminal Law 4th Pretrial Proceedings § 88 (2021), Purpose of Bail.
4 Witkin, California Criminal Law 4th Pretrial Proceedings § 89 (2021), Constitutional and Statutory Framework.
4 Witkin, California Criminal Law 4th Pretrial Proceedings § 93 (2021), Public Safety Exception.
4 Witkin, California Criminal Law 4th Pretrial Proceedings § 98 (2021), In General.
4 Witkin, California Criminal Law 4th Pretrial Proceedings § 103 (2021), Excessive Bail and Reduction.
4 Witkin, California Criminal Law 4th Pretrial Proceedings § 135 (2021), In General.
4 Witkin, California Criminal Law 4th Pretrial Proceedings § 136 (2021), Hearing.
3 Witkin, California Criminal Law 4th Punishment § 2 (2021), Current Emphasis.
3 Witkin, California Criminal Law 4th Punishment § 18 (2021), Nature of Confinement.
3 Witkin, California Criminal Law 4th Punishment § 36 (2021), Deductions from Sentence.
3 Witkin, California Criminal Law 4th Punishment § 40 (2021), In General.
3 Witkin, California Criminal Law 4th Punishment § 116 (2021), Constitutional Right.
3 Witkin, California Criminal Law 4th Punishment § 118 (2021), Definition of Victim.
3 Witkin, California Criminal Law 4th Punishment § 119 (2021), Rights of Third Parties.
3 Witkin, California Criminal Law 4th Punishment § 120 (2021), Damages Recoverable.
3 Witkin, California Criminal Law 4th Punishment § 308B (2021), (New) in General.
3 Witkin, California Criminal Law 4th Punishment § 309 (2021), State Prison Term.
3 Witkin, California Criminal Law 4th Punishment § 398 (2021), What Constitutes Prior Conviction.
3 Witkin, California Criminal Law 4th Punishment § 405 (2021), Nature of Enhancement.
3 Witkin, California Criminal Law 4th Punishment § 413 (2021), Dual Use of Prior Conviction.
3 Witkin, California Criminal Law 4th Punishment § 421B (2021), (New) in General.
3 Witkin, California Criminal Law 4th Punishment § 446 (2021), Effect of Defendant's Admission.

3 Witkin, California Criminal Law 4th Punishment § 830 (2021), In General.

§ 29. Due process; speedy and public trial; criminal cases

Sec. 29. In a criminal case, the people of the State of California have the right to due process of law and to a speedy and public trial. *(Added by Initiative Measure (Prop. 115, approved June 5, 1990, eff. June 6, 1990).)*

Cross References

Criminal cases, speedy and public trial, see Cal. Const. Art. 1, § 15, cl. 1.
Due process and equal protection, privileges and immunities, see Cal. Const. Art. 1, § 7.
Writ of habeas corpus, persons authorized to prosecute writ, see Penal Code § 1473.

Research References

5 Witkin, California Criminal Law 4th Criminal Trial § 317 (2021), Policy and Right.
5 Witkin, California Criminal Law 4th Criminal Trial § 319 (2021), Under California Constitution.
5 Witkin, California Criminal Law 4th Criminal Trial § 402 (2021), In General.
5 Witkin, California Criminal Law 4th Criminal Trial § 408 (2021), Right of Press and Public.
5 Witkin, California Criminal Law 4th Criminal Trial § 633 (2021), In General.
1 Witkin California Criminal Law 4th Introduction to Crimes § 129 (2021), Constitutional Provisions and Statutes.
1 Witkin California Criminal Law 4th Introduction to Crimes § 133 (2021), Application to Pending Cases.

§ 30. Joining of criminal cases; protection of victims and witnesses; hearsay evidence; admissibility; discovery

Sec. 30. (a) This Constitution shall not be construed by the courts to prohibit the joining of criminal cases as prescribed by the Legislature or by the people through the initiative process.

(b) In order to protect victims and witnesses in criminal cases, hearsay evidence shall be admissible at preliminary hearings, as prescribed by the Legislature or by the people through the initiative process.

(c) In order to provide for fair and speedy trials, discovery in criminal cases shall be reciprocal in nature, as prescribed by the Legislature or by the people through the initiative process. *(Added by Initiative Measure (Prop. 115, approved June 5, 1990, eff. June 6, 1990).)*

Cross References

Hearsay evidence, hearsay rule, see Evidence Code § 1200.
Pleadings and proceedings before trial, discovery, purpose, see Penal Code § 1054.

Research References

5 Witkin, California Criminal Law 4th Criminal Trial § 32 (2021), Enactment.
5 Witkin, California Criminal Law 4th Criminal Trial § 35 (2021), Provisions Are Constitutional.
5 Witkin, California Criminal Law 4th Criminal Trial § 85 (2021), In General.
5 Witkin, California Criminal Law 4th Criminal Trial § 421 (2021), Normal Requirement of Joint Trial.
5 Witkin, California Criminal Law 4th Criminal Trial § 451 (2021), Pertinent Factors.
5 Witkin, California Criminal Law 4th Criminal Trial § 658 (2021), Scope of Rule.
1 Witkin California Criminal Law 4th Introduction to Crimes § 133 (2021), Application to Pending Cases.
4 Witkin, California Criminal Law 4th Pretrial Proceedings § 155 (2021), Continuance as to Fewer Than All Defendants.
4 Witkin, California Criminal Law 4th Pretrial Proceedings § 167 (2021), When Permitted.
4 Witkin, California Criminal Law 4th Pretrial Proceedings § 168 (2021), Double Hearsay is Prohibited.

§ 31. Discrimination based on race, sex, color, ethnicity, or national origin; gender-based qualifications in public employment, education, or contracting

Sec. 31. (a) The State shall not discriminate against, or grant preferential treatment to, any individual or group on the basis of race, sex, color, ethnicity, or national origin in the operation of public employment, public education, or public contracting.

(b) This section shall apply only to action taken after the section's effective date.

(c) Nothing in this section shall be interpreted as prohibiting bona fide qualifications based on sex which are reasonably necessary to the normal operation of public employment, public education, or public contracting.

(d) Nothing in this section shall be interpreted as invalidating any court order or consent decree which is in force as of the effective date of this section.

(e) Nothing in this section shall be interpreted as prohibiting action which must be taken to establish or maintain eligibility for any federal program, where ineligibility would result in a loss of federal funds to the State.

(f) For the purposes of this section, "State" shall include, but not necessarily be limited to, the State itself, any city, county, city and county, public university system, including the University of California, community college district, school district, special district, or any other political subdivision or governmental instrumentality of or within the State.

(g) The remedies available for violations of this section shall be the same, regardless of the injured party's race, sex, color, ethnicity, or national origin, as are otherwise available for violations of then-existing California antidiscrimination law.

(h) This section shall be self-executing. If any part or parts of this section are found to be in conflict with federal law or the United States Constitution, the section shall be implemented to the maximum extent that federal law and the United States Constitution permit. Any provision held invalid shall be severable from the remaining portions of this section. *(Added by Initiative Measure (Prop. 209, approved Nov. 5, 1996, eff. Nov. 6, 1996).)*

Cross References

Effective date, conflicting measures, and amendment or repeal of initiative statutes, see Cal. Const. Art. 2, § 10.
International Convention on the Elimination of All Forms of Racial Discrimination, private causes of action and requiring government to prove racial discrimination pursuant to this section, see Government Code § 8315.
Public sector outreach and recruitment programs directed to minority groups and women by state and local government agencies, permitted activities, see Government Code § 11139.6.

§ 32. Public Safety and Rehabilitation Act of 2016

SEC. 32. (a) The following provisions are hereby enacted to enhance public safety, improve rehabilitation, and avoid the release of prisoners by federal court order, notwithstanding anything in this article or any other provision of law:

(1) Parole Consideration: Any person convicted of a nonviolent felony offense and sentenced to state prison shall be eligible for parole consideration after completing the full term for his or her primary offense.

(A) For purposes of this section only, the full term for the primary offense means the longest term of imprisonment imposed by the court for any offense, excluding the imposition of an enhancement, consecutive sentence, or alternative sentence.

(2) Credit Earning: The Department of Corrections and Rehabilitation shall have authority to award credits earned for good behavior and approved rehabilitative or educational achievements.

(b) The Department of Corrections and Rehabilitation shall adopt regulations in furtherance of these provisions, and the Secretary of the Department of Corrections and Rehabilitation shall certify that these regulations protect and enhance public safety. *(Added by Initiative Measure (Prop. 57, § 3, approved Nov. 8, 2016, eff. Nov. 9, 2016).)*

Research References

6 Witkin, California Criminal Law 4th Criminal Appeal § 72 (2021), Orders After Judgment.
3 Witkin, California Criminal Law 4th Punishment § 476 (2021), Eligibility for Credit.
3 Witkin, California Criminal Law 4th Punishment § 726 (2021), In General.

ARTICLE IV. LEGISLATIVE

Section

§ 15. Dishonest influence of legislator; offense

Sec. 15. A person who seeks to influence the vote or action of a member of the Legislature in the member's legislative capacity by bribery, promise of reward, intimidation, or other dishonest means, or a member of the Legislature so influenced, is guilty of a felony. *(Added Nov. 8, 1966. Amended Nov. 5, 1974.)*

Cross References

Asking or receiving bribe, see Penal Code § 86.
Bribe to procure election, see Cal. Const. Art. 7, § 8.
Bribery or corrupt influencing of legislator, see Penal Code § 85.
Crimes against public justice, bribery, council members, see Penal Code § 165.
Crimes by and against the executive power of the state, bribes, punishment, see Penal Code § 67.
Felonies, definition and penalties, see Penal Code §§ 17, 18.
Forfeiture and disqualification from holding office, see Cal. Const. Art. 7, § 8; Government Code § 9055; Penal Code §§ 86, 88.
Lobbying, see Government Code § 86100 et seq.
Obtaining thing of value on claim of ability to improperly influence legislator, see Government Code § 9054.
Soliciting or accepting pay for opposing measure after having secured its introduction, see Government Code § 9056.

Research References

2 Witkin, California Criminal Law 4th Crimes Against Governmental Authority § 37 (2021), Legislative Officers.
2 Witkin, California Criminal Law 4th Crimes Against Governmental Authority § 132 (2021), Illegal Lobbying and Related Offenses.

ARTICLE V. EXECUTIVE

Section

§ 8. Governor; reprieves, pardons, and commutations; review of parole decisions; report to Legislature

Sec. 8. (a) Subject to application procedures provided by statute, the Governor, on conditions the Governor deems proper, may grant a reprieve, pardon, and commutation, after sentence, except in case of impeachment. The Governor shall report to the Legislature each reprieve, pardon, and commutation granted, stating the pertinent facts and the reasons for granting it. The Governor may not grant a pardon or commutation to a person twice convicted of a felony except on recommendation of the Supreme Court, 4 judges concurring.

(b) No decision of the parole authority of this state with respect to the granting, denial, revocation, or suspension of parole of a person sentenced to an indeterminate term upon conviction of murder shall become effective for a period of 30 days, during which the Governor may review the decision subject to procedures provided by statute. The Governor may only affirm, modify, or reverse the decision of the parole authority on the basis of the same factors which the parole authority is required to consider. The Governor shall report to the Legislature each parole decision affirmed, modified, or reversed, stating the pertinent facts and reasons for the action. *(Adopted Nov. 8, 1966. Amended Nov. 7, 1972; Nov. 5, 1974; Nov. 8, 1988.)*

Cross References

Death penalty, Governor's power to suspend, see Penal Code § 3700 et seq.
Executive power, see Cal. Const. Art. 5, § 1.
Legislative power, see Cal. Const. Art. 4, § 1.
Register of application for pardon or commutation of sentence, see Government Code § 12030.
Statutory provisions, see Penal Code § 4800 et seq.
Supreme Court, jurisdiction, see Cal. Const. Art. 6, §§ 10, 11.

Research References

1 Witkin California Criminal Law 4th Introduction to Crimes § 18 (2021), Changes Involving Parole and Probation.
1 Witkin California Criminal Law 4th Introduction to Crimes § 126 (2021), Enumerated Rights.
3 Witkin, California Criminal Law 4th Punishment § 589 (2021), Possibility of Clemency or Change in Law.
3 Witkin, California Criminal Law 4th Punishment § 747 (2021), In General.
3 Witkin, California Criminal Law 4th Punishment § 748 (2021), Scope of Review Power.
3 Witkin, California Criminal Law 4th Punishment § 778 (2021), In General.
3 Witkin, California Criminal Law 4th Punishment § 808 (2021), In General.
3 Witkin, California Criminal Law 4th Punishment § 810 (2021), Development of Standard.
3 Witkin, California Criminal Law 4th Punishment § 824 (2021), Nature of Powers.
3 Witkin, California Criminal Law 4th Punishment § 829 (2021), Decision and Report by Governor.

ARTICLE VI. JUDICIAL

Section

§ 10. Jurisdiction; habeas corpus and proceedings for extraordinary relief; original jurisdiction of superior courts; comments on evidence and credibility of witnesses

Sec. 10. The Supreme Court, courts of appeal, superior courts, and their judges have original jurisdiction in habeas corpus proceedings. Those courts also have original jurisdiction in proceedings for extraordinary relief in the nature of mandamus, certiorari, and prohibition. The appellate division of the superior court has original jurisdiction in proceedings for extraordinary relief in the nature of mandamus, certiorari, and prohibition directed to the superior court in causes subject to its appellate jurisdiction.

Superior courts have original jurisdiction in all other causes.

The court may make any comment on the evidence and the testimony and credibility of any witness as in its opinion is necessary for the proper determination of the cause. *(Added Nov. 8, 1966. Amended by Stats.1996, Res. c. 36 (S.C.A.4), (Prop. 220, approved June 2, 1998, eff. June 3, 1998); Stats.2002, Res. c. 88 (A.C.A.15), § 5 (Prop. 48, approved Nov. 5, 2002, eff. Nov. 6, 2002).)*

Law Revision Commission Comments

For background relating to the amendment to Section 10 of Article VI of the California Constitution made by Proposition 220 (approved by the electors June 2, 1998), see *Trial Court Unification: Constitutional Revision (SCA 3)*, 24 Cal. L. Revision Comm'n Reports 1 (1994). [28 Cal.L.Rev.Comm. Reports App. 8 (1998)].

Section 10 is amended to reflect unification of the municipal and superior courts pursuant to former Section 5(e). This amendment does not affect the power of the Legislature to establish divisions within the superior court, such as the small claims court or the juvenile court, or to create administrative tribunals that make adjudicative decisions, subject to judicial review. [32 Cal.L.Rev.Comm. Reports 50 (2002)].

Cross References

Acknowledgment or proof of instrument, correction of, see Civil Code §§ 1202, 1203.
Appellate division of superior court, composition, jurisdiction and powers, procedure, see Code of Civil Procedure § 77.
Ballots, correction of errors, see Elections Code § 13314.
Bridge, road, ferry, wharf, etc., franchise or license for, hearing on, see Government Code § 26003.
Bridge and highway district formation protest, hearing on, see Streets and Highways Code § 27104 et seq.
Certiorari, writ of, see Code of Civil Procedure § 1067.
Civil cases,
  Appealable judgments and orders in limited civil cases, see Code of Civil Procedure § 904.2.
  Limitations of actions, see Code of Civil Procedure § 312 et seq.
  Place of trial, see Code of Civil Procedure § 392 et seq.
Comment and charge as to law, power of judge, see Penal Code § 1093.
Comments by court,
  Jury instructions for civil trials, see Code of Civil Procedure § 607a.
  Jury instructions for criminal trials, see Penal Code § 1127.
Contempt, power to punish,
  Generally, see Code of Civil Procedure § 178.
  Legislature, of witness subpoenaed by, see Government Code § 9408.
  State Bar of California, by witnesses called by, see Business and Professions Code § 6051.
  Workers' Compensation Appeals Board, by witness subpoenaed by, see Labor Code § 132.
Corporations, winding up and involuntary dissolution, see Corporations Code § 1806.
Counties, one court for each, see Cal. Const. Art. 6, § 4.
Courts of Appeal, appellate jurisdiction, see Cal. Const. Art. 6, § 11.
Credibility of witnesses, see Evidence Code § 785.
Criminal cases,
  Appeals from inferior courts, see Penal Code § 1466 et seq.
  Determination of law and fact questions, see Penal Code § 1126.
  Instructions, comments by court and credibility, see Penal Code § 1127.
  Limitations of actions, see Penal Code § 799 et seq.
Death, establishment of fact of, see Probate Code § 200 et seq.
Declaratory relief, see Code of Civil Procedure § 1060 et seq.
Default judgment, see Code of Civil Procedure § 585.
Director of corporation,
  Provisional, when appointed, see Corporations Code § 308.
  Removal for fraud, etc., see Corporations Code § 304.
  Validity of election, action by shareholder, see Corporations Code §§ 601 et seq., 701 et seq., 1508.
Dissenting shareholders, suit by, see Corporations Code § 1304 et seq.
Easements, application for arbitrator to apportion cost of maintaining, see Civil Code § 845.
Eminent domain, generally, see Cal. Const. Art. 1, § 19; Code of Civil Procedure § 1240.010 et seq.
Estates of decedents, administration, see Probate Code §§ 7000, 7001.
Evidence, jury as judges of effect, see Evidence Code § 312.
Further instructions after retirement of jury for deliberation, see Code of Civil Procedure § 614.
Habeas corpus,
  Petition for, see Penal Code §§ 1474, 1475.
  Suspension of writ, see Cal. Const. Art. 1, § 11.
Holidays, open for what purposes, see Code of Civil Procedure §§ 134, 135.
Homestead, sale, insufficient bids, see Code of Civil Procedure § 704.800.
Impeachment, see Cal. Const. Art. 4, § 18; Government Code § 3020 et seq.
Improvement Act of 1911,
  Lien for unpaid claim, enforcement of, see Public Contract Code § 20460.
  Validity of proceedings and contracts, determination of, see Public Contract Code § 20434.
Incompetent spouse, proceedings relating to community realty, see Probate Code § 3100 et seq.
Indictment or information required for offenses triable in, exceptions, see Penal Code §§ 682, 737, 859a.
Injunction, see Code of Civil Procedure § 525 et seq.
Inspection of corporate records, suit by stockholders for, see Corporations Code § 1603.
Instructions for jury,
  Civil trials, see Code of Civil Procedure § 607a et seq.
  Criminal trials, see Penal Code § 1127.
Insurance,
  Commissioner's application for order, method of service, see Insurance Code § 1039.
  Insolvency proceedings, powers relating to, see Insurance Code § 1058.
  Law or order, enjoining violation, see Insurance Code § 12928.6.
Irrigation district,
  Bond issue or assessment, validation of, see Water Code § 22670.
  Formation election, contest of, see Water Code § 20933.
Judicial Council,
  Adoption of rules, see Cal. Const. Art. 6, § 6; Government Code § 68072.
  Court's own rules to conform to rules of, see Government Code § 68070.
Judicial holidays, see Code of Civil Procedure § 135.
Judicial power, see Cal. Const. Art. 6, § 1; Code of Civil Procedure § 128.
Jurisdiction,
  Abatement of placer mining contrary to law, see Public Resources Code § 3967.
  Administration of estates, see Probate Code § 7050 et seq.
  Care of old cemeteries, see Health and Safety Code § 8702.
  Cemetery, removal of dedication, see Health and Safety Code § 8580.
  Cemetery, transfer of funds on vacation of, see Health and Safety Code § 7932.
  Change of names, applications for, see Code of Civil Procedure §§ 1275, 1276.
  Criminally insane, proceedings for release of, see Penal Code § 1026 et seq.
  Dentistry practice, injunctive proceedings against unlicensed, see Business and Professions Code § 1705.
  Disbarment proceedings, see Business and Professions Code § 6100.
  Disinterment of human remains, see Health and Safety Code § 7526.
  Division of Labor Standards Enforcement, review of rulings, see Labor Code § 1296.
  Elevator, enjoining operation of, see Labor Code § 7303.
  Employee housing, abatement proceedings, see Health and Safety Code § 17060.
  False containers, condemnation of, see Business and Professions Code § 12606.
  Family conciliation court, see Family Code § 1830.
  Food condemnation proceedings, see Health and Safety Code § 111895.
  Foreclosure of bond lien under Improvement Act of 1911, see Streets and Highways Code § 6612.
  Gambling machines, etc., seizure and summary destruction of, see Penal Code § 335a.
  Guardianship proceedings, see Probate Code § 2200.
  Improvement Bond Act of 1915, foreclosure of liens, see Streets and Highways Code § 8830.
  Medical school or applicant for licensure, disapproval or rejection by Division of Licensing, review, see Business and Professions Code § 2087.
  Mentally abnormal sex offender, commitment of, see Welfare and Institutions Code § 4135.
  Mentally ill persons, order for examination or detention of, see Welfare and Institutions Code §§ 5002, 6250.
  Minor's claim for money, compromise of, see Probate Code § 3500.
  Municipal and inferior courts, see Cal. Const. Art. 6, §§ 10, 11; Code of Civil Procedure § 86.
  Newspaper of general circulation, determining fact of, see Government Code § 6020.
  Oath of county board of public welfare member, administration of, see Welfare and Institutions Code § 18103.
  Oil and gas conservation orders and rulings, review of, see Public Resources Code § 3354.
  Public officer, proceedings for removal, see Government Code § 3060 et seq.
  Real property ownership for taxation purposes, determination of, see Revenue and Taxation Code §§ 457, 458.
  Rights of way for utilities, actions between municipal corporations, see Public Utilities Code §§ 10104, 10107.

Salvage dispute, see Harbors and Navigation Code § 532.
Separation of grade district proceedings, determination of legality, see Streets and Highways Code § 8265.
Transfer of actions within jurisdiction of lower court, see Code of Civil Procedure § 396.
Waste of gas, enjoining, see Public Resources Code §§ 3310, 3312.
Workers' compensation, abate business conducted without security for, see Labor Code § 3712.
Jury instructions,
Conduct of civil trials, see Code of Civil Procedure § 607a et seq.
Conduct of criminal trials, see Penal Code § 1127.
Juvenile hall, sessions in township where located, see Code of Civil Procedure § 73e.
Limited civil cases, jurisdiction, see Code of Civil Procedure § 86.
Local laws relating to practice of courts prohibited, see Cal. Const. Art. 4, § 16.
Mandate, writ of, see Code of Civil Procedure § 1084 et seq.
Marriage,
Validity of, see Family Code § 300 et seq.
Void, petition to declare, see Family Code § 2250.
Mentally disordered persons, release from state hospital before recovery, see Welfare and Institutions Code § 7361.
Mentally disordered sex offenders, proceedings relating to, see Welfare and Institutions Code § 6300 et seq.
Minors, orders relating to custody, see Family Code § 3022.
Missing persons, administration of estates,
Persons missing over 5 years, see Probate Code § 12401 et seq.
Trustees of estates of persons missing over 90 days, see Probate Code § 1845 et seq.
Naturalization records of clerk, see Government Code § 69847.
Pay for transacting judicial business, exceptions, see Code of Civil Procedure § 133 et seq.
Pilots, suspension, etc., review, see Harbors and Navigation Code § 1183.
Postponement of trial, see Code of Civil Procedure § 594a et seq.
Powers in conducting proceedings, see Code of Civil Procedure §§ 128, 177.
Private trials and hearings,
Generally, see Family Code § 214.
Adoption proceedings, see Family Code § 8611.
Prohibition, writ of, see Code of Civil Procedure § 1102 et seq.
Property taxes, assessed by two or more counties, proceedings on, see Revenue and Taxation Code § 4988.
Proposed jury instructions, see Code of Civil Procedure § 607a.
Public lands,
Contests relating to, see Public Resources Code § 7921 et seq.
Held in violation of statute, forfeiture of, see Public Resources Code § 6802.
Swamp, overflowed or tide lands, determine right to apply for, see Public Resources Code § 7526 et seq.
Pupils, twenty-four-hour elementary school, commitment to, see Education Code § 48600 et seq.
Purpose of amendments by Stats.1996, Res. c. 36 (S.C.A.4), see Government Code §§ 70200-70219.
Question of fact, determination by jury, see Evidence Code § 312.
Question of law, determination by court, see Evidence Code §§ 310, 400 et seq., 457; Penal Code § 1124.
Quo warranto, writ of, see Code of Civil Procedure § 803.
Receiver, power to appoint, see Code of Civil Procedure § 564.
Record, court of, see Cal. Const. Art. 6, § 1.
Review, writ of, see Code of Civil Procedure § 1067 et seq.
Rules,
Filing, public inspection, see Government Code § 68071.
Power to make, limitations on, see Government Code § 68070.
School employee's dismissal, proceedings for, see Education Code § 44932 et seq.
Share certificate lost, stolen or destroyed, action relating to, see Corporations Code § 419.
Special administrators, see Probate Code § 8540 et seq.
Special instructions, see Code of Civil Procedure § 609.
Style of process, see Government Code § 100.
Summary judgment, see Code of Civil Procedure § 437c.
Trial, how issue brought to, see Code of Civil Procedure § 594.
Trusts, administration of, see Probate Code § 16000 et seq.
Unclaimed property,
Escheat proceedings on, see Code of Civil Procedure § 1410.
Jurisdiction to determine title, see Code of Civil Procedure § 1353.
Vacancy,
Judgeship, no effect on pending proceedings, see Code of Civil Procedure § 184.
Trusteeship, filling of, see Probate Code §§ 370, 15660.
Waters,
Permit, review of revocation, see Water Code § 1410.
Settlement of stream system users' rights, review of board order, see Water Code § 2750.
Wrecked property,
Sale, orders relating to salvage and expense of, see Harbors and Navigation Code § 518.
Salvage and expenses for delivery of, see Harbors and Navigation Code § 514.
Written statements of points of law, furnished to either party upon request, see Code of Civil Procedure § 608.

Research References

California Jury Instructions - Criminal 17.30, Jury Not to Take Cue from the Judge.
California Jury Instructions - Criminal 17.32, Judge's Comment on Evidence.
California Jury Instructions-Civil, 8th Edition 15.20, Jury Not to Take Cue from Judge.
California Jury Instructions-Civil, 8th Edition 15.21, Judge's Comment on Evidence.
5 Witkin, California Criminal Law 4th Criminal Trial § 741 (2021), Nature of Power.
5 Witkin, California Criminal Law 4th Criminal Trial § 744 (2021), Impartiality is Required.
5 Witkin, California Criminal Law 4th Criminal Trial § 745 (2021), Comment to Deadlocked Jury.
5 Witkin, California Criminal Law 4th Criminal Trial § 746 (2021), Comment on Guilt of Defendant.
6 Witkin, California Criminal Law 4th Criminal Writs § 11 (2021), Courts With Original Jurisdiction.
6 Witkin, California Criminal Law 4th Criminal Writs § 13 (2021), Territorial Jurisdiction is Unlimited.
6 Witkin, California Criminal Law 4th Criminal Writs § 24 (2021), Failure to Seek Relief in Lower Court.
6 Witkin, California Criminal Law 4th Criminal Writs § 67B (2021), (New) Constitutionality.
4 Witkin, California Criminal Law 4th Jurisdiction and Venue § 14 (2021), Original Jurisdiction in All Causes.
3 Witkin, California Criminal Law 4th Punishment § 552 (2021), Comment by Judge.

§ 11. Appellate jurisdiction

Sec. 11. (a) The Supreme Court has appellate jurisdiction when judgment of death has been pronounced. With that exception courts of appeal have appellate jurisdiction when superior courts have original jurisdiction in causes of a type within the appellate jurisdiction of the courts of appeal on June 30, 1995, and in other causes prescribed by statute. When appellate jurisdiction in civil causes is determined by the amount in controversy, the Legislature may change the appellate jurisdiction of the courts of appeal by changing the jurisdictional amount in controversy.

(b) Except as provided in subdivision (a), the appellate division of the superior court has appellate jurisdiction in causes prescribed by statute.

(c) The Legislature may permit courts exercising appellate jurisdiction to take evidence and make findings of fact when jury trial is waived or not a matter of right. *(Added Nov. 8, 1966. Amended by Stats.1994, Res. c. 113 (S.C.A.7) (Prop. 191, approved Nov. 8, 1994, operative Jan. 1, 1995); Stats.1996, Res. c. 36 (S.C.A.4), (Prop. 220, approved June 2, 1998, eff. June 3, 1998).)*

Law Revision Commission Comments

For background relating to the amendment to Section 11 of Article VI of the California Constitution made by Proposition 220 (approved by the electors June 2, 1998), see *Trial Court Unification: Constitutional Revision (SCA 3)*, 24 Cal. L. Revision Comm'n Reports 1 (1994). [28 Cal.L.Rev.Comm. Reports App. 8 (1998)].

Cross References

Appeals,
Death penalty, automatic, see Penal Code § 1239.
Habeas corpus where judgment of death rendered, see Penal Code § 1506.

Municipal court, from, additional findings of fact, evidence, see Code of Civil Procedure § 909.
Superior courts, from, generally, see Code of Civil Procedure § 904.1; Penal Code § 1235 et seq.
Appellate departments,
Establishment, designation of judges, see Code of Civil Procedure § 77.
Jurisdiction, rules of practice, see Code of Civil Procedure § 77.
Arbitration, powers and duties of neutral arbitrator, see Code of Civil Procedure § 1282.
Certiorari or writ of review, see Code of Civil Procedure § 1067 et seq.
Chambers, powers of justices at, see Code of Civil Procedure § 165.
Courts of record, see Cal. Const. Art. 6, § 1.
Decisions in writing, see Cal. Const. Art. 6, § 14.
Disbarment proceedings, review of, see Business and Professions Code § 6082.
Election contest, preference to, see Code of Civil Procedure § 44.
Eminent domain, see Cal. Const. Art. 1, § 19; Code of Civil Procedure § 1230.010 et seq.
Evidence, taking of, see Cal. Const. Art. 6, § 11; Code of Civil Procedure § 909.
Habeas corpus, see Cal. Const. Art. 1, § 5; Penal Code § 1473 et seq.
Incidental powers and duties of judicial officers, see Code of Civil Procedure § 177 et seq.
Interchange of appeals with Supreme Court, see Cal. Const. Art. 6, § 12.
Judgment, remitted in appeal case, see Code of Civil Procedure § 43.
Mandamus, see Code of Civil Procedure § 1084 et seq.
New trials, see Code of Civil Procedure § 656 et seq.
Open for business, when, see Code of Civil Procedure § 134.
Powers,
Appealed cases, see Code of Civil Procedure §§ 43, 906 et seq.
Conducting proceedings, see Code of Civil Procedure §§ 128, 177.
Preference to certain appeals, see Code of Civil Procedure § 44.
Prohibition, writ of, see Code of Civil Procedure § 1102 et seq.
Public, sittings shall be, see Code of Civil Procedure § 124.
Publication of opinions, see Cal. Const. Art. 6, § 14.
Purpose of amendments by Stats.1996, Res. c. 36 (S.C.A.4), see Government Code §§ 70200-70219.
Remedial powers, see Code of Civil Procedure §§ 43, 906 et seq.
Reprieves, pardons and commutations, functions relating to, see Penal Code § 4850 et seq.
Rules of practice and procedure, see Government Code §§ 68070, 68072; Penal Code § 1247k.
Safety in employment, orders, etc., see Labor Code § 6600 et seq.
School employee's dismissal, appeal from judgment, see Education Code § 44945.
Small claims court, appeals from, see Code of Civil Procedure § 116.110 et seq.
Transfers to Supreme Court, see Cal. Const. Art. 6, § 12.
Workers' compensation proceedings, review of, see Labor Code § 5955.

Research References

6 Witkin, California Criminal Law 4th Criminal Appeal § 1 (2021), Appellate Jurisdiction.
6 Witkin, California Criminal Law 4th Criminal Appeal § 56 (2021), In General.
6 Witkin, California Criminal Law 4th Criminal Appeal § 149 (2021), Procedure.
6 Witkin, California Criminal Law 4th Criminal Writs § 67B (2021), (New) Constitutionality.
3 Witkin, California Criminal Law 4th Punishment § 598 (2021), In General.

§ 12. Supreme Court; transfer of causes; review of court of appeals decisions

Sec. 12. (a) The Supreme Court may, before decision, transfer to itself a cause in a court of appeal. It may, before decision, transfer a cause from itself to a court of appeal or from one court of appeal or division to another. The court to which a cause is transferred has jurisdiction.

(b) The Supreme Court may review the decision of a court of appeal in any cause.

(c) The Judicial Council shall provide, by rules of court, for the time and procedure for transfer and for review, including, among other things, provisions for the time and procedure for transfer with instructions, for review of all or part of a decision, and for remand as improvidently granted.

(d) This section shall not apply to an appeal involving a judgment of death. *(Added Nov. 8, 1966. Amended Nov. 6, 1984, eff. May 6, 1985.)*

Research References

6 Witkin, California Criminal Law 4th Criminal Appeal § 1 (2021), Appellate Jurisdiction.

§ 13. Reversal for error resulting in miscarriage of justice

Sec. 13. No judgment shall be set aside, or new trial granted, in any cause, on the ground of misdirection of the jury, or of the improper admission or rejection of evidence, or for any error as to any matter of pleading, or for any error as to any matter of procedure, unless, after an examination of the entire cause, including the evidence, the court shall be of the opinion that the error complained of has resulted in a miscarriage of justice. *(Added Nov. 8, 1966.)*

Cross References

Errors not affecting substantial rights disregarded, reversal only for prejudicial error, presumptions, see Code of Civil Procedure § 475.
Technical errors not affecting substantial rights to be disregarded, see Penal Code § 1258.

Research References

California Jury Instructions - Criminal 17.10, Conviction of Lesser Included or Lesser Related Offense—Implied Acquittal—First.
California Jury Instructions - Criminal App C.
6 Witkin, California Criminal Law 4th Criminal Judgment § 44 (2021), Allen Instruction Disapproved.
5 Witkin, California Criminal Law 4th Criminal Trial § 566 (2021), In General.
5 Witkin, California Criminal Law 4th Criminal Trial § 680 (2021), In General.
4 Witkin, California Criminal Law 4th Pretrial Proceedings § 219 (2021), Doctrine of Nonprejudicial Error.
4 Witkin, California Criminal Law 4th Pretrial Proceedings § 319 (2021), Remedy for Failure to Advise.
6 Witkin, California Criminal Law 4th Reversible Error § 1 (2021), Theory and Scope of Doctrine.
6 Witkin, California Criminal Law 4th Reversible Error § 17 (2021), Error Harmless Beyond Reasonable Doubt.
6 Witkin, California Criminal Law 4th Reversible Error § 23 (2021), Development of Concept.
6 Witkin, California Criminal Law 4th Reversible Error § 24 (2021), Limitation of Concept.
6 Witkin, California Criminal Law 4th Reversible Error § 31 (2021), In General.
6 Witkin, California Criminal Law 4th Reversible Error § 34 (2021), Defendant Not Charged With Death of Victim.
6 Witkin, California Criminal Law 4th Reversible Error § 59 (2021), Bad Faith as Factor.
6 Witkin, California Criminal Law 4th Reversible Error § 60 (2021), Bad Faith Alone Insufficient.

BUSINESS AND PROFESSIONS CODE

GENERAL PROVISIONS

§ 7. Convictions

Any conviction for a crime under any act repealed by this code, which crime is continued as a public offense by this code, constitutes a conviction under this code for any purpose for which it constituted a conviction under the act repealed. *(Stats.1937, c. 399, p. 1230, § 7.)*

Cross References

Effect of Penal Code upon acts or omissions commenced before or after effective date, see Penal Code § 6.
Termination or suspension of law creating offense, see Government Code § 9608.

§ 7.5. "Conviction" defined; authority

(a) A conviction within the meaning of this code means a judgment following a plea or verdict of guilty or a plea of nolo contendere or finding of guilt. Any action which a board is permitted to take following the establishment of a conviction may be taken when the time for appeal has elapsed, or the judgment of conviction has been affirmed on appeal or when an order granting probation is made suspending the imposition of sentence. However, a board may not deny a license to an applicant who is otherwise qualified pursuant to subdivision (b) or (c) of Section 480.

(b)(1) Nothing in this section shall apply to the licensure of persons pursuant to Chapter 4 (commencing with Section 6000) of Division 3.

(2) This section does not in any way modify or otherwise affect the existing authority of the following entities in regard to licensure:

(A) The State Athletic Commission.

(B) The Bureau for Private Postsecondary Education.

(C) The California Horse Racing Board.

(c) Except as provided in subdivision (b), this section controls over and supersedes the definition of conviction contained within individual practice acts under this code.

(d) This section shall become operative on July 1, 2020. *(Added by Stats.2018, c. 995 (A.B.2138), § 2, eff. Jan. 1, 2019, operative July 1, 2020.)*

Cross References

Accountants, disciplinary proceedings, conviction defined, see Business and Professions Code § 5106.
Acupuncture, enforcement, conviction of crime, see Business and Professions Code § 4956.
Alarm companies, denial of license, certificate, or registration, conviction of crime, see Business and Professions Code § 7591.10.
Architecture, disciplinary proceedings, conviction of certain crimes, see Business and Professions Code § 5577.
Attorneys, disciplinary authority of the courts, immediate suspension and subsequent disbarment upon conviction of crime, see Business and Professions Code § 6102.
Automotive repair,
  Denial, suspension and revocation, conviction defined, see Business and Professions Code § 9889.4.
  Denial of license, grounds, see Business and Professions Code § 9889.2.
Barbering and cosmetology, disciplinary proceedings, convictions, see Business and Professions Code § 7405.
Board defined for purposes of this Code, see Business and Professions Code § 22.
Cemeteries, disciplinary proceedings, conviction defined, see Business and Professions Code § 9727.2.
Clinical laboratory technology, denial, revocation and suspension of licenses, conviction defined, see Business and Professions Code § 1321.
Contractors, disciplinary proceedings, conviction defined, see Business and Professions Code § 7124.
Denial of licenses, acts disqualifying applicant, see Business and Professions Code § 480.
Dentistry, suspension and revocation of licenses, conviction of crime as ground for discipline, see Business and Professions Code § 1670.1.
Dentists, unprofessional conduct, see Business and Professions Code § 1681.
Disciplinary authority of the courts, immediate suspension and subsequent disbarment upon conviction of crime, see Business and Professions Code § 6102.
Electronic and appliance repair dealers, offenses against the chapter, conviction, see Business and Professions Code § 9853.
Funeral directors and embalmers, disciplinary proceedings, conviction defined, see Business and Professions Code § 7709.
Geologists and geophysicists, disciplinary proceedings, suspension or revocation, see Business and Professions Code § 7863.
Guide dogs for the blind, disciplinary action, conviction defined, see Business and Professions Code § 7211.2.
Land surveyors, disciplinary proceedings, conviction defined, see Business and Professions Code § 8783.
Landscape architecture, discipline, conviction defined, see Business and Professions Code § 5676.
Locksmiths, disciplinary proceedings and administrative citations, see Business and Professions Code § 6980.71.
Marriage, family and child counselors, denial, suspension and revocation, unprofessional conduct, see Business and Professions Code § 4982.
Medicine,
  Conviction of violation of federal or state laws or regulations regulating dangerous drugs or controlled substances, see Business and Professions Code § 2237.
  Incarceration following conviction of a felony, automatic suspension of certificate, penalty hearing, see Business and Professions Code § 2236.1.
  Misuse of controlled substances, dangerous drugs or alcohol, unprofessional conduct, see Business and Professions Code § 2239.
Nursing, disciplinary proceedings, conviction defined, see Business and Professions Code § 2765.
Optometry, conviction defined, authority to suspend, revoke, or refuse license, see Business and Professions Code § 3107.
Pharmacy, disciplinary proceedings,
  Felony convictions, see Business and Professions Code § 4311.
  Unprofessional conduct, see Business and Professions Code § 4301.
Physical therapy, suspension, revocation and reinstatement of license, conviction defined, see Business and Professions Code § 2661.
Physician assistants, conviction, defined, grounds for denial, suspension or revocation, see Business and Professions Code § 3531.
Private investigators, disciplinary proceedings, guilty pleas or convictions, see Business and Professions Code § 7562.
Private security services, disciplinary proceedings, guilty pleas or convictions, see Business and Professions Code § 7587.5
Professional engineers, disciplinary proceedings, conviction defined, see Business and Professions Code § 6779.
Psychiatric technicians, disciplinary proceedings, conviction defined, see Business and Professions Code § 4523.
Psychologists,
  Denial, suspension and revocation, felony conviction, see Business and Professions Code § 2966.
  Suspension, revocation or refusal to issue license, see Business and Professions Code § 2963.
Real estate regulations, disciplinary action, grounds, see Business and Professions Code § 10177.
Registered dispensing opticians, suspension or revocation of certificate, conviction of specified crime, see Business and Professions Code § 2555.1.
Repossessors,
  Denial of license, criteria, see Business and Professions Code § 7501.8.
  Disciplinary proceedings, record of conviction, see Business and Professions Code § 7510.4

Respiratory therapy, suspension, revocation, and reinstatement of certificates, conviction of offense related to duties, see Business and Professions Code § 3752.
Shorthand reporters, disciplinary proceedings, conviction defined, see Business and Professions Code § 8026.
Social workers, unprofessional conduct, effect on licensee or registrant, see Business and Professions Code § 4992.3.
Speech–language pathologists and audiologists, conviction, discipline or denial of license, see Business and Professions Code § 2533.1.
Structural pest control operators, disciplinary proceedings, conviction defined, see Business and Professions Code § 8655.
Suspension and revocation of licenses, conviction of crime, relationship of crime to licensed activity, see Business and Professions Code § 490.
Veterinary medicine, revocation and suspension,
Conviction defined, see Business and Professions Code § 4885.
Grounds, see Business and Professions Code § 4883.
Vocational nursing, disciplinary proceedings, conviction defined, see Business and Professions Code § 2878.6.

Division 9

ALCOHOLIC BEVERAGES

CHAPTER 16. REGULATORY PROVISIONS

ARTICLE 1. IN GENERAL

§ 25600. Premiums, gifts, or free goods; refunds or exchanges to customers; donations to nonprofit charitable organizations; advertising specialties; free or discounted transportation

(a)(1) No licensee shall, directly or indirectly, give any premium, gift, or free goods in connection with the sale or distribution of any alcoholic beverage, except as provided by rules that shall be adopted by the department to implement this section or as authorized by this division.

(2)(A) Notwithstanding paragraph (1), for purposes of this section, a refund to, or exchange of products for, a dissatisfied consumer by a licensee authorized to sell to consumers shall not be deemed a premium, gift, or free goods given in connection with the sale or distribution of an alcoholic beverage.

(B) A winegrower may advertise or otherwise offer consumers a guarantee of product satisfaction only in newsletters or other publications of the winegrower or at the winegrower's premises. A winegrower may refund to a dissatisfied consumer the entire purchase price of wine produced by that winegrower and sold to that consumer, regardless of where the wine was purchased.

(3)(A) Notwithstanding paragraph (1), a winegrower, a beer manufacturer, a distilled spirits manufacturer, a craft distiller, a brandy manufacturer, a rectifier, or a wine rectifier may donate a portion of the purchase price of an alcoholic beverage to a nonprofit charitable organization in connection with the sale or distribution of an alcohol beverage, subject to all of the following limitations:

(i) The donation is only in connection with the sale or distribution of alcoholic beverages in manufacturer-sealed containers.

(ii) Promotion or advertisement of the donation shall not directly encourage or reference the consumption of alcoholic beverages.

(iii) A donation shall not benefit a retail licensee, or benefit a nonprofit charitable organization established for the specific purpose of benefiting the employees of retail licensees and the advertisement or promotion of a donation, shall not, directly or indirectly, advertise, promote, or reference any retail licensee. This is not intended to preclude the identification of licensed retailers as permitted by Section 25500.1.

(B) This paragraph shall be inoperative on January 1, 2025.

(b)(1) Except as provided in paragraph (2), no rule of the department may permit a licensee to give any premium, gift, or free goods of greater than inconsequential value in connection with the sale or distribution of beer. With respect to beer, premiums, gifts, or free goods, including advertising specialties that have no significant utilitarian value other than advertising, shall be deemed to have greater than inconsequential value if they cost more than twenty-five cents ($0.25) per unit, or cost more than fifteen dollars ($15) in the aggregate for all those items given by a single supplier to a single retail premises per calendar year.

(2)(A) No rule of the department may impose a dollar limit for consumer advertising specialties furnished by a beer manufacturer to the general public other than three dollars ($3) per unit original cost to the beer manufacturer who purchased it.

(B) With respect to beer, a beer manufacturer may give consumer advertising specialties to the general public that do not exceed three dollars ($3) per unit original cost to the beer manufacturer who purchased it. For purposes of this paragraph, "beer manufacturer" includes a holder of a beer manufacturer's license, a holder of an out-of-state beer manufacturer's certificate, an out-of-state vendor that holds a certificate of compliance, or a holder of a beer and wine importer's general license. A licensee authorized to give consumer advertising specialties pursuant to this paragraph shall not be precluded from doing so on the basis of holding any other type of alcoholic beverage license.

(C) A beer manufacturer, as defined in subparagraph (B) of paragraph (2) shall not require a beer wholesaler to fund the purchase of consumer advertising specialties that beer manufacturers are permitted to give under paragraph (2).

(D) Consumer advertising specialties furnished by a beer manufacturer are intended only for adults of legal drinking age. Coin banks, toys, balloons, magic tricks, miniature bottles or cans, confections, dolls, or other items that appeal to minors or underage drinkers may not be used in connection with the merchandising of beer.

(c) With respect to distilled spirits and wines, a licensee may furnish, give, rent, loan, or sell advertising specialties to a retailer, provided those items bear conspicuous advertising required of a sign and the total value of all retailer advertising specialties furnished by a supplier, directly or indirectly, to a retailer do not exceed fifty dollars ($50) per brand in any one calendar year per retail premises. The value of a retailer advertising specialty is the actual cost of that item to the supplier who initially purchased it, excluding transportation and installation costs. The furnishing or giving of any retailer advertising specialty shall not be conditioned upon the purchase of the supplier's product. Retail advertising specialties given or furnished free of charge may not be sold by the retail licensee. No rule of the department may impose a dollar limit for consumer advertising specialties furnished by a distilled spirits supplier to a retailer or to the general public of less than five dollars ($5) per unit original cost to the supplier who purchased it. A rule or decision of the department may not approve glassware as an authorized retailer advertising specialty for distilled spirits or wine under this section.

(d)(1) Notwithstanding any other provision of this division, a beer manufacturer or distilled spirits manufacturer may provide directly to consumers free or discounted rides through taxicabs, transportation network companies, or any other ride service for the purpose of furthering public safety. The free or discounted rides may be provided by vouchers, codes, or any other method to deliver the free or discounted ride. A free or discounted ride, or the provision of a voucher, code, or other method of delivery, shall not be conditioned upon the purchase of an alcoholic beverage. A beer and wine wholesaler or distilled spirits importer general that holds a wholesaler's or retailer's license only as an additional license shall not directly or indirectly underwrite, share in, or contribute to, the costs of free or discounted rides or serve as an agent of a beer manufacturer or distilled spirits manufacturer to provide free or discounted rides to consumers. Nothing in this provision authorizes a beer manufacturer or distilled spirits manufacturer to provide a gift or anything of value directly or indirectly to a retail licensee.

(2) For purposes of this section:

(A) "Beer manufacturer" has the same meaning as defined in subparagraph (B) of paragraph (2) of subdivision (b).

(B) "Distilled spirits manufacturer" means a distilled spirits manufacturer, holder of a distilled spirits rectifier's general license, distilled spirits manufacturer's agent, brandy manufacturer, holder of an out-of-state distilled spirits shipper's certificate, holder of a distilled spirits importer general's license, or craft distiller.

(C) "Glassware" means a single-service glass container or nonglass container capable of holding no more than 23 ounces of liquid volume or a decanter, chalice, infusion jar, or similar container of any size and made of any material. *(Added by Stats.1953, c. 152, p. 1020, § 1. Amended by Stats.1983, c. 215, § 2, eff. July 13, 1983; Stats.1985, c. 803, § 1; Stats.1988, c. 1080, § 1; Stats.1994, c. 392 (A.B.3329), § 1; Stats.1995, c. 91 (S.B.975), § 15; Stats.1997, c. 544 (S.B.993), § 3; Stats.2008, c. 629 (A.B.1245), § 1; Stats.2009, c. 521 (A.B.1282), § 1, eff. Oct. 11, 2009; Stats.2017, c. 226 (A.B.711), § 1, eff. Jan. 1, 2018; Stats.2018, c. 689 (S.B.973), § 2, eff. Jan. 1, 2019; Stats.2018, c. 727 (A.B.3264), § 3.5, eff. Jan. 1, 2019; Stats.2021, c. 207 (A.B.1267), § 1, eff. Jan. 1, 2022.)*

Cross References

Brandy manufacturer's license, authority to conduct tastings, conditions, liability, see Business and Professions Code § 23363.3.

Distilled spirits manufacturer's license, authority to conduct tastings, conditions, liability, see Business and Professions Code § 23363.1.

Limitation as to time of filing accusations, see Business and Professions Code §§ 24206, 24208.

Purchase of advertising space, conditions, penalties, see Business and Professions Code § 25503.6.

Raffle prizes, special temporary on-sale or off-sale beer or wine licenses, issuance to nonprofit corporations, see Business and Professions Code § 24045.6.

Samples permitted in some instances, see Business and Professions Code § 23386.

Special on-sale general license to facility partially located in County of Placer and County of Washoe, facility requirements, special provisions, see Business and Professions Code § 23399.52.

Research References

2 Witkin, California Criminal Law 4th Crimes Against Public Peace and Welfare § 363 (2021), Time, Place, and Manner of Sale.

§ 25600.05. Beer manufacturers; retail advertising glassware restrictions

(a) For purposes of this section:

(1) "Beer manufacturer" has the same meaning as that term is defined in subparagraph (B) of paragraph (2) of subdivision (b) of Section 25600.

(2) "Case" means a box containing up to 24 pieces of glassware.

(3) "Glassware" means a single-service glass container or nonglass container capable of holding no more than 23 ounces of liquid volume and which is intended for the service of beer.

(4) "Retail advertising glassware" means glassware that bears conspicuous advertising of beer required of a sign.

(b) Notwithstanding Section 25500, Section 25600, or any other law to the contrary:

(1) A beer manufacturer, without direct or indirect charge, may give up to five cases of retail advertising glassware to an on-sale retail licensee, per licensed location, each calendar year for use at the licensed location. The giving of retail advertising glassware shall not be conditioned, directly or indirectly, upon the purchase or sale of any product, including, without limitation, any beer manufactured, produced, imported, sold, marketed, or in any other way promoted or represented by the beer manufacturer giving the retail advertising glassware. Retail advertising glassware provided pursuant to this section shall only be delivered by the beer manufacturer providing it to the licensed premises of the retailer receiving the retail advertising glassware. No more than five cases of retail advertising glassware shall be delivered by the beer manufacturer to any single on-sale retail licensed premises.

(2) An on-sale retail licensee may accept, without direct or indirect charge, up to 10 cases of retail advertising glassware, per licensed location, from licensed beer manufacturers each calendar year for use at the licensed location. The on-sale retail licensee shall not sell the retail advertising glassware, give it away, or return it to a manufacturer for cash, credit, or replacement. The on-sale retail licensee shall not condition the purchase of a beer manufacturer's product or products on the giving of retail advertising glassware by that beer manufacturer.

(c) A beer wholesaler shall not directly or indirectly underwrite, share in, or contribute to the costs of glassware or any costs of transportation or shipping or serve as the agent of the beer manufacturer to deliver, stock, or store glassware for an on-sale retailer.

(d) A licensee authorized to give retail advertising glassware pursuant to this section shall not be precluded from doing so on the basis of having an interest in any other type of alcoholic beverage license within or outside of the state.

(e) A beer manufacturer shall file with the department, in a manner prescribed by the department, records related to glassware provided to an on-sale retail licensee pursuant to this section within 30 days of the delivery of the glassware. In addition, a beer manufacturer shall keep and maintain records for a three-year period of all glassware given pursuant to this section.

(f) An on-sale retail licensee shall keep and maintain records for a three-year period of all glassware received pursuant to this section and of all other retail advertising glassware purchased or otherwise received. Such records shall be maintained by the on-sale retail licensee at the licensed premises to which the beer manufacturer delivers the glassware authorized by this section. The on-sale retail licensee shall produce records to the department promptly upon request.

(g) This section shall remain in effect only until January 1, 2026, and as of that date is repealed. *(Added by Stats.2019, c. 623 (A.B.1133), § 1, eff. Jan. 1, 2020. Amended by Stats.2022, c. 296 (A.B.2971), § 6, eff. Jan. 1, 2023.)*

Repeal

For repeal of this section, see its terms.

§ 25600.1. Consumer contests; conditions; prohibited contests; monetary limitations; penalties

(a) An authorized licensee may conduct consumer contests, subject to the following conditions:

(1)(A) Entry or extra chances in a contest shall not be made available via the purchase of an alcoholic beverage.

(B) Entry into or participation in a contest shall be limited to persons 21 years of age or older.

(C) No contest shall involve consumption of alcoholic beverages by a participant.

(D) A contest may not be conducted for the benefit of any permanent retail licensee.

(2)(A) Closures, caps, cap liners, corks, labels, cartons, cases, packaging, or other similar material shall not be used as an entry to a contest or as a means of determining the amount or size of the prize or the winner in a contest, except as provided in subparagraphs (D) and (F).

(B) The authorized licensee shall provide an alternative means of entry that does not require a visit to a licensed premises.

(C) Except as provided in subparagraph (D), removable entry forms shall not be used on alcoholic beverage labels, containers, packaging, cases, or cartons.

(D) Removable entry forms that are neck hangers shall be used only on bottles of wine or distilled spirits, and shall not require purchase of the product. Removable neck hangers shall be used only if other entry forms are available at the point of sale or if an alternative means of entry is also available.

(E) Entry forms may be provided through electronic or other media, including point of sale.

(F) Codes that may be scanned or electronically entered by a consumer where the authorized licensee has permanently affixed the codes as part of the original alcoholic beverage label, container, packaging, case, or carton, and where the codes are not removable and not required to be removed are permitted as a form of entry.

(G) All permitted means of entry, including the use of electronic or scanner codes, shall clearly indicate that no purchase is required to enter.

(3) A contest shall not provide for the instant or immediate awarding of a prize or prizes. Instant or immediate notification to the consumer that he or she is a winner is permissible.

(4) Except for providing a means of entry, a contest authorized by this section shall not be conducted at the premises of a retail licensee or the premises of a winegrower or beer manufacturer operating under a duplicate license for a branch office.

(5) Alcoholic beverages or anything redeemable for alcoholic beverages shall not be awarded as a contest prize. This paragraph shall not prohibit a contest in which the prize is cash or cash equivalent, the awarding of cash or cash equivalent, or the inclusion of alcoholic beverages as an incidental part of a prize package.

(6) A retail licensee shall not serve as the agent of an authorized licensee by collecting or forwarding entries or awarding prizes to, or redeeming prizes for, a contest winner.

(7) A licensee that is not an authorized licensee shall not directly or indirectly underwrite, share in, or contribute to, the costs of a contest authorized by this section or serve as the agent of an

authorized licensee to collect or forward entries or to furnish any prize to a contest winner.

(8)(A) Advertising of a contest shall comply with the signage and advertising restrictions contained in this chapter, Chapter 15 (commencing with Section 25500), and any regulations issued by the department.

(B) Advertising or promotion of a contest shall not identify or refer to any retail licensee.

(C) A retail licensee shall only advertise or promote a contest authorized by this section in the manner specified in subparagraph (A).

(D) Advertising or promotion of a contest shall only be conducted on the premises of a retail licensee when such advertisement or promotion involves a minimum of three unaffiliated retail licensees. For purposes of this subparagraph, "unaffiliated retail licensees" shall not include any retail licensee owned or controlled in whole or in part by an authorized licensee or any officer, director, or agent of that licensee.

(E) Placement of signs or other advertising of a contest in a licensed retail premises shall not be conditioned upon the following:

(i) The placement of any product within the licensed premises or the restriction, in any way, of the purchase of a product by a licensee, the removal of a product from the sales area of a licensed premises, or the resetting or repositioning of a product within the licensed premises.

(ii) The purchase or sale of any product produced, imported, distributed, represented, or promoted by an authorized licensee or its agent.

(F) An agreement, whether written or oral, entered into, by, and between a retail licensee and an authorized licensee or its agent that precludes the advertisement or promotion of a contest on the premises of the retail licensee by another authorized licensee is prohibited.

(9) Contest prizes shall not be awarded to an authorized licensee, retail licensee, or wholesale licensee or agent, officer, employee, or family member of an authorized licensee, retail licensee, or wholesale licensee. For the purposes of this paragraph, "family member" means a spouse, parent, sibling, child, son-in-law, daughter-in-law, and lineal descendants, including those by adoption. An authorized licensee shall maintain all records pertaining to a contest for three years following the completion of a contest. This section shall not apply to contests conducted by an authorized licensee as part of a sales incentive program for wholesale licensees or their employees or an authorized licensee's employees.

(b) Nothing in this section shall preclude licensees from sponsoring contests as permitted by regulations of the department.

(c) For purposes of this section:

(1)(A) "Authorized licensee" means a winegrower, beer and wine importer general, beer manufacturer, out-of-state beer manufacturer certificate holder, distilled spirits manufacturer, distilled spirits manufacturer's agent, distilled spirits importer general, distilled spirits general rectifier, rectifier, out-of-state distilled spirits shipper's certificate holder, brandy manufacturer, and brandy importer. An authorized licensee may conduct a consumer contest pursuant to this section regardless of whether the licensee holds any additional license not included in this paragraph.

(B) An "authorized licensee" shall not include a beer and wine wholesaler, a beer and wine importer general, or distilled spirits importer general that only holds a wholesaler's or retailer's license as an additional license.

(2) "Contest" means a game, contest, puzzle, or similar activity that holds out or offers to participants the opportunity to receive or compete for gifts, prizes, gratuities, or other things of value as determined by skill, knowledge, or ability rather than upon random selection. Skill, knowledge, or ability does not include the consumption or use of alcoholic beverages.

(d) Nothing in this section authorizes conducting any contest where consumers are entitled to an allotment or accumulation of points based on purchases made over a period of time that can be redeemed for prizes, things of value, or additional contest entries.

(e) A prize awarded for a contest conducted pursuant to this section shall not be subject to the monetary limitation imposed by Section 25600 or a regulation of the department.

(f) An authorized licensee that violates this section, in addition to any other penalty imposed by this division, may be prohibited by the department from offering a contest to California residents for a period of 12 months. *(Added by Stats.2012, c. 489 (S.B.778), § 1. Amended by Stats.2015, c. 311 (S.B.796), § 4, eff. Jan. 1, 2016.)*

Cross References

Special on-sale general license to facility partially located in County of Placer and County of Washoe, facility requirements, special provisions, see Business and Professions Code § 23399.52.

Research References

2 Witkin, California Criminal Law 4th Crimes Against Public Peace and Welfare § 363 (2021), Time, Place, and Manner of Sale.

§ 25600.2. Consumer sweepstakes; conditions; prohibited sweepstakes; monetary limitations; penalties

(a) An authorized licensee may conduct or sponsor consumer sweepstakes, subject to the following conditions:

(1)(A) No entry fee may be charged to participate in a sweepstakes authorized by this subdivision. Entry or extra chances in a sweepstakes shall not be made available via the purchase of an alcoholic beverage.

(B) Entry into or participation in a sweepstakes shall be limited to persons 21 years of age or older.

(C) No sweepstakes shall involve consumption of alcoholic beverages by a participant.

(D) Subject to subparagraph (B), any sweepstakes offered in California shall be open to all residents of California.

(E) A sweepstakes may not be conducted for the benefit of any permanent retail license.

(2)(A) Closures, caps, cap liners, corks, labels, cartons, cases, packaging, or other similar material shall not be used as an entry to a sweepstakes or as a means of determining the amount or size of the prize or the winner in a sweepstakes, except as provided in subparagraphs (D) and (F).

(B) The authorized licensee shall provide an alternative means of entry that does not require a visit to a licensed premises.

(C) Except as provided in subparagraph (D), removable entry forms shall not be used on alcoholic beverage labels, containers, packaging, cases, or cartons.

(D) Removable entry forms that are neck hangers shall be used only on bottles of wine or distilled spirits, and shall not require purchase of the product. Removable neck hangers shall be used only if other entry forms are available at the point of sale or if an alternative means of entry is also available.

(E) Entry forms may be provided through electronic or other media, including point of sale.

(F) Codes that may be scanned or electronically entered by a consumer where the authorized licensee has permanently affixed the codes as part of the original alcoholic beverage label, container, packaging, case, or carton and where the codes are not removable and not required to be removed are permitted as a form of entry.

Bus. & Prof.

(G) All permitted means of entry, including the use of electronic or scanner codes, shall clearly indicate that no purchase is required to enter.

(H) All sweepstakes entries shall provide the entrant with an equal odds of winning.

(3) A sweepstakes shall not provide for the instant or immediate awarding of a prize or prizes. Instant or immediate notification to the consumer that he or she is a winner is permissible.

(4) Except for providing a means of entry, a sweepstakes authorized by this section shall not be conducted at the premises of a retail licensee or the premises of a winegrower or beer manufacturer operating under a duplicate license for a branch office.

(5) Alcoholic beverages or anything redeemable for alcoholic beverages shall not be awarded as a sweepstakes prize. This paragraph shall not prohibit a sweepstakes in which the prize is cash or cash equivalent, the awarding of cash or cash equivalent, or the inclusion of alcoholic beverages as an incidental part of a prize package.

(6) A retail licensee shall not serve as the agent of an authorized licensee by collecting or forwarding entries or awarding prizes to, or redeeming prizes for, a sweepstakes winner. The matching of entries with numbers or pictures on the point-of-sale materials at retail licensed premises is permitted only if entrants are also offered the opportunity to use an alternative means to determine prize-winning status. An authorized licensee may furnish and maintain a deposit box on a retail licensed premises for the collection and forwarding of sweepstakes entry forms.

(7) A licensee that is not an authorized licensee shall not directly or indirectly underwrite, share in, or contribute to, the costs of a sweepstakes authorized by this section or serve as the agent of an authorized licensee to collect or forward entries or to furnish any prize to a sweepstakes winner.

(8)(A) Advertising of a sweepstakes shall comply with the signage and advertising restrictions contained in this chapter, Chapter 15 (commencing with Section 25500), and any regulations issued by the department.

(B) Advertising or promotion of a sweepstakes shall not identify or refer to a retail licensee.

(C) A retail licensee shall only advertise or promote a sweepstakes authorized by this section in the manner specified in subparagraph (A).

(D) Advertising or promotion of a sweepstakes shall only be conducted on the premises of a retail licensee when such advertisement or promotion involves a minimum of three unaffiliated retail licensees. For purposes of this subparagraph, "unaffiliated retail licensees" shall not include a retail licensee owned or controlled in whole or in part by an authorized licensee or any officer, director, or agent of that licensee.

(E) Placement of signs or other advertising of a sweepstakes in a licensed retail premises shall not be conditioned upon the following:

(i) The placement of a product within the licensed premises or the restriction, in any way, of the purchase of a product by a licensee, the removal of a product from the sales area of a licensed premises, or the resetting or repositioning of a product within the licensed premises.

(ii) The purchase or sale of a product produced, imported, distributed, represented, or promoted by an authorized licensee or its agent.

(F) An agreement, whether written or oral, entered into, by, and between a retail licensee and an authorized licensee that precludes the advertisement or promotion of a sweepstakes on the premises of the retail licensee by another authorized licensee or its agent is prohibited.

(9) Sweepstakes prizes shall not be awarded to an authorized licensee, retail licensee, or wholesale licensee or agent, officer, employee, or family member of an authorized licensee, retail licensee, or wholesale licensee. For the purposes of this paragraph, "family member" means a spouse, parent, sibling, child, son-in-law, daughter-in-law, and lineal descendants, including those by adoption. An authorized licensee shall maintain all records pertaining to a sweepstakes for three years following the completion of a sweepstakes.

(b) For purposes of this section:

(1)(A) "Authorized licensee" means a winegrower, beer and wine importer general, beer manufacturer, out-of-state beer manufacturer certificate holder, distilled spirits manufacturer, distilled spirits manufacturer's agent, distilled spirits importer general, distilled spirits general rectifier, rectifier, out-of-state distilled spirits shipper's certificate holder, brandy manufacturer, and brandy importer. An authorized licensee may conduct, sponsor, or participate in a sweepstakes pursuant to this section regardless of whether the licensee holds an additional license not included in this paragraph.

(B) An "authorized licensee" shall not include a beer and wine wholesaler, a beer and wine importer general, or distilled spirits importer general that only holds a wholesaler's or retailer's license as an additional license.

(2) "Sweepstakes" means a procedure, activity, or event for the distribution of anything of value by lot, chance, or random selection where the odds for winning a prize are equal for each entry.

(c) Nothing in this section authorizes conducting sweepstakes where consumers are entitled to an allotment or accumulation of points based on purchases made over a period of time that can be redeemed for prizes, things of value, or additional sweepstakes entries.

(d) A prize awarded for a sweepstakes conducted pursuant to this section shall not be subject to the monetary limitation imposed by Section 25600 or a regulation of the department.

(e) An authorized licensee that violates this section, in addition to any other penalty imposed by this division, may be prohibited by the department from offering a sweepstakes to California residents for a period of 12 months. *(Added by Stats.2012, c. 489 (S.B.778), § 2. Amended by Stats.2013, c. 76 (A.B.383), § 8; Stats.2015, c. 311 (S.B.796), § 5, eff. Jan. 1, 2016.)*

Cross References

Special on-sale general license to facility partially located in County of Placer and County of Washoe, facility requirements, special provisions, see Business and Professions Code § 23399.52.

Research References

2 Witkin, California Criminal Law 4th Crimes Against Public Peace and Welfare § 363 (2021), Time, Place, and Manner of Sale.

§ 25600.3. Nonretail licensees; use of coupons prohibited; definitions

(a) A nonretail licensee shall not offer, fund, produce, sponsor, promote, furnish, or redeem any type of coupon.

(b) A licensee authorized to sell alcoholic beverages at retail shall not accept, redeem, possess, or utilize any type of coupon that is funded, produced, sponsored, promoted, or furnished by a nonretail licensee.

(c) For purposes of this section:

(1) "Nonretail licensee" means any person who own or holds any interest, directly or indirectly, in any license, authorization, or permit issued pursuant to this division that authorizes the manufacture, production, rectification, importation, or wholesaling of alcoholic beverages, except for a brewpub restaurant license issued pursuant to Section 23396.3.

(2) "Cider" has the same meaning set forth in Section 4.21(e)(5) of the Code of Federal Regulations.

(3) "Perry" has the same meaning set forth in Section 4.21(e)(5) of the Code of Federal Regulations.

(4) "Coupon" means any method by which a consumer receives a discount on the purchase of any item that is funded, produced, sponsored, promoted, or furnished, either directly or indirectly, by a nonretail licensee, including, but not limited to, a paper coupon, a digital coupon, an instant redeemable coupon (IRC), or a mail-in rebate or mail-in discount, except as otherwise provided, or an electronic coupon commonly referred to as a scan or scanback. "Coupon" does not include:

(A)(i) A mail-in rebate or electronic or digital rebate where all of the following apply:

(I) The consumer must submit a request for the rebate to the nonretail licensee or its vendor after the purchase of a qualifying product.

(II) The rebate is paid to the consumer after the purchase of the qualifying product and receipt of the consumer's request with any required information.

(III) The rebate is paid and funded by the nonretail licensee.

(ii) A retail licensee shall not act as the vendor or intermediary for the nonretail licensee or the consumer.

(iii) For purposes of this subparagraph, "nonretail license" and "vendor" shall not include an importer or wholesaler that holds only wholesaler or importer licenses, or both, that primarily sells beer, nonalcoholic beer, malt beverages, cider, or perry to retail licensees.

(B) A discount or rebate that is offered, funded, produced, sponsored, promoted, or furnished by a distilled spirits manufacturer, distilled manufacturer's agent, brandy manufacturer, brandy importer, distilled spirits rectifier general, holder of an out-of-state distilled spirits shipper certificate, distilled spirits importer general, distilled spirits importer, rectifier, brandy wholesaler, distilled spirits wholesaler, or a holder of a craft distiller's license, regardless of other licenses held, that offers a discount or rebate on the purchase of any item so long as no nonalcoholic beer, beer, malt beverages, or wine products are advertised or promoted by these licensees in connection with the discount or rebate.

(C) A discount that is offered and funded by a beer manufacturer on the purchase of beer, malt beverages, cider, or perry at the licensed premises of production or other licensed premises owned or leased and operated by the beer manufacturer.

(D) A discount that is offered and funded by a winegrower on the purchase of wine sold directly by the winegrower to a consumer at or from the licensed premises of production or other licensed premises owned or leased and operated by the winegrower or through the Internet where a consumer buys directly from a winegrower.

(d) Nothing in this section is intended to preclude or prevent or otherwise restrict an on-sale or off-sale retail licensee that is not also a nonretail licensee from offering, funding, producing, sponsoring, promoting, furnishing, or redeeming a discount to consumers on the purchase of alcoholic beverages that is not otherwise prohibited by this section or any other provision of law. *(Added by Stats.2014, c. 145 (A.B.1928), § 1, eff. Jan. 1, 2015. Amended by Stats.2016, c. 194 (S.B.1032), § 1, eff. Jan. 1, 2017; Stats.2017, c. 561 (A.B.1516), § 14, eff. Jan. 1, 2018; Stats.2017, c. 419 (A.B.1722), § 2, eff. Jan. 1, 2018.)*

Cross References

Special on-sale general license to facility partially located in County of Placer and County of Washoe, facility requirements, special provisions, see Business and Professions Code § 23399.52.

§ 25600.5. Invitation-only events in connection with sale of wine or spirits; conditions and limitations; legislative findings

Notwithstanding any other provision of this division, a manufacturer of distilled spirits, distilled spirits manufacturer's agent, out-of-state distilled spirits shipper's certificate holder, winegrower, rectifier, or distiller, or its authorized unlicensed agent, may provide, free of charge, entertainment, food, and distilled spirits, wine, or nonalcoholic beverages to consumers at an invitation-only event in connection with the sale or distribution of wine or distilled spirits, subject to the following conditions:

(a) No licensee, other than those specified in this section, may conduct or participate in any portion of an event authorized by this section. A licensee authorized to conduct an event pursuant to this section shall not be precluded from doing so on the basis of holding any other type of alcoholic beverage license.

(b) An event authorized by this section shall be conducted on either the:

(1) Premises for which a caterer's authorization has been issued, except that any event held on the premises of a licensed winegrower shall not be authorized to provide any distilled spirits other than brandy.

(2) Premises of a hotel holding an on-sale beer and wine or on-sale general license, except an event shall not be conducted in the lobby area of a hotel or in any portion of a hotel that is identified, promoted, or otherwise designated by the hotel as a club, nightclub, or other similar entertainment venue. For purposes of this paragraph, "hotel" means any hotel, motel, resort, bed and breakfast inn, or other similar transient lodging establishment, but it does not include any residential hotel as defined in Section 50519 of the Health and Safety Code.

(c) A hotel where the event authorized by this section is being conducted shall maintain, during all times while exercising its license privileges, other areas within the licensed premises that shall be made readily available to the public not attending the authorized event.

(d) Except as provided in paragraph (2) of subdivision (b), an event authorized by this section shall not be conducted on premises for which a permanent retail license has been issued.

(e) Except for fair market value payments authorized pursuant to this section, a retail licensee, including the licensed caterer or the licensed hotel, shall not receive, nor shall the licensee conducting the event give, any other item of value or benefit in connection with events authorized by this section.

(f) The person authorized by this section to provide, free of charge, entertainment, food, and beverages shall be present during the event.

(g) The person authorized by this section to provide, free of charge, entertainment, food, and beverages shall have sole responsibility for providing payment for the entertainment, food, beverages, and rental fees at the event. Payments for entertainment, food, beverages, and rental fees shall not exceed fair market value. No other licensed person shall be authorized, under this section, to provide any portion of these payments.

(h) Requests for attendance at the event shall be by invitation sent to consumers over 21 years of age at a specific address via mail or email, by telephone, or presented in person. Invitations or other advertisements of the event shall not be disseminated by any other means. Invitations shall not be sent by the authorized person or their authorized unlicensed agent inviting all of the employees of a retail licensee or a chain of retail licensees under common ownership to an authorized event.

(i) Attendance at the event shall be limited to consumers who receive and accept an invitation to the event. Invited consumers may each invite one guest. All attendees shall be over 21 years of age. The total number of consumers and their guests allowed at any event authorized by this section shall not exceed 600 people. Admittance to the event shall be controlled by a list containing the names of consumers who accepted the invitation and their guests. The persons identified in this section shall be responsible for compliance.

(j) No premium, gift, free goods, or other thing of value may be given away in connection with the event, except as authorized by this division.

(k) The duration of any event authorized by this section shall not exceed four hours.

(*l*)(1) Subject to paragraph (3), a person authorized to conduct events pursuant to this section shall not conduct more than 12 events in a calendar year where the consumers and guests in attendance exceed 100 people, and not more than 24 events in a calendar year where the consumers and guests in attendance is 100 people or fewer.

(2) The limitation on events authorized by this section shall be by person, whether that person holds a single license or multiple licenses. If a person holds multiple licenses, the limitation shall be applied to the person holding the license, not by type of license.

(3) A licensee authorized to conduct events pursuant to this section shall not conduct more than two events in a calendar year on the premises of any single licensed hotel or other licensed hotel under the same or common ownership.

(4) The licensee conducting the event shall not advertise any retail licensee. If the event is held on the premises of a retail licensee as permitted by this section, the licensee conducting the event may list the retailer's name and address in the invitation and any related advertising for the sole purpose of identifying the location of the event. The listing of the retailer's name and address shall be the only reference to the retail licensee and shall be relatively inconspicuous in relation to the invitation or advertisement as a whole. Pictures or illustrations of the retailer's premises, or laudatory references to the retailer, shall not be permitted.

(5)(A) Other than as specifically authorized by this section, alcoholic beverage promotions of any sort shall not be conducted by any licensee in conjunction with an event held on the premises of a retail licensee pursuant to this section. This restriction includes any discounted drink specials offered by the retail licensee to consumers.

(B) For purposes of this paragraph, "in conjunction with" means during an event and any period within 24 hours before and 24 hours following an event.

(6) A retail licensee shall conspicuously offer for sale alcoholic beverages other than the products produced, distributed, bottled, or otherwise offered for sale by the licensee conducting the event.

(m) At least 30 days prior to an event, the licensee, or its authorized unlicensed agent, authorized to conduct the event shall apply to the department for a permit authorizing the event. In addition to any other information required by the department, the licensee shall provide the department all of the following information:

(1) The name of the company authorized to conduct the event.

(2) The number of people planned to be in attendance.

(3) The start and end times for the event.

(4) The location of the event.

(5) The name of the caterer, if required, obtaining the caterer's authorization for the event.

(n) All alcoholic beverages provided pursuant to this section shall be purchased from the holder of the caterer's permit or the licensed hotel, as applicable.

(*o*) All alcoholic beverages served at an event authorized by this section shall be served in accordance with Sections 25631 and 25632.

(p) No person authorized to conduct an event pursuant to this section shall hold such an event at the same location more than eight times in a calendar year.

(q) The person authorized to conduct an event under this section may provide attendees at the event with a free ride home. The free rides shall only constitute free ground transportation to attendees' homes or to hotels or motels where attendees are staying.

(r) In addition to the prescribed fee imposed upon a licensed caterer to conduct an event authorized by this section, a fee of two hundred dollars ($200) shall be collected by the department from the licensee, or its authorized unlicensed agent, authorized by this section to provide, free of charge, entertainment, and beverages at an authorized event. This fee may be adjusted by the department pursuant to subdivisions (d) and (e) of Section 23320.

(s) All licensees involved in events held pursuant to this section shall be responsible for compliance with this section, and with all other provisions of this division in connection with these events, and each may be subject to discipline for violation of this division.

(t) The Legislature finds and declares both of the following:

(1) That it is necessary and proper to require a separation between manufacturing interests, wholesale interests, and retail interests in the production and distribution of alcoholic beverages in order to prevent suppliers from dominating local markets through vertical integration and to prevent excessive sales of alcoholic beverages produced by overly aggressive marketing techniques.

(2) Any exception established by the Legislature to the general prohibition against tied interests must be limited to the express terms of the exception so as to not undermine the general prohibitions.

(u) This section shall remain in effect only until January 1, 2028, and as of that date is repealed. *(Added by Stats.2008, c. 638 (A.B.2293), § 1. Amended by Stats.2012, c. 153 (A.B.252), § 1; Stats.2013, c. 461 (A.B.1116), § 1; Stats.2017, c. 295 (A.B.609), § 1, eff. Jan. 1, 2018; Stats.2019, c. 29 (S.B.82), § 70, eff. June 27, 2019; Stats.2022, c. 296 (A.B.2971), § 7, eff. Jan. 1, 2023.)*

Repeal

For repeal of this section, see its terms.

Cross References

Special on-sale general license to facility partially located in County of Placer and County of Washoe, facility requirements, special provisions, see Business and Professions Code § 23399.52.

§ 25601. Disorderly houses; places of disturbance, etc.

Every licensee, or agent or employee of a licensee, who keeps, permits to be used, or suffers to be used, in conjunction with a licensed premises, any disorderly house or place in which people abide or to which people resort, to the disturbance of the neighborhood, or in which people abide or to which people resort for purposes which are injurious to the public morals, health, convenience, or safety, is guilty of a misdemeanor. *(Added by Stats.1953, c. 152, p. 1020, § 1.)*

Cross References

Keeping of a disorderly house, see Penal Code § 316.
Limitations as to time of filing accusations, see Business and Professions Code §§ 24207, 24208.
Suspension or revocation of license, grounds, see Business and Professions Code § 24200.

Research References

2 Witkin, California Criminal Law 4th Crimes Against Public Peace and Welfare § 363 (2021), Time, Place, and Manner of Sale.
1 Witkin California Criminal Law 4th Introduction to Crimes § 60 (2021), Meaning Defined by Court.

2 Witkin, California Criminal Law 4th Sex Offenses and Crimes Against Decency § 79 (2021), Keeping House and Related Offenses.

§ 25602. Sales to drunkard or intoxicated person; offense; civil liability

(a) Every person who sells, furnishes, gives, or causes to be sold, furnished, or given away, any alcoholic beverage to any habitual or common drunkard or to any obviously intoxicated person is guilty of a misdemeanor.

(b) No person who sells, furnishes, gives, or causes to be sold, furnished, or given away, any alcoholic beverage pursuant to subdivision (a) of this section shall be civilly liable to any injured person or the estate of such person for injuries inflicted on that person as a result of intoxication by the consumer of such alcoholic beverage.

(c) The Legislature hereby declares that this section shall be interpreted so that the holdings in cases such as Vesely v. Sager (5 Cal.3d 153), Bernhard v. Harrah's Club (16 Cal.3d 313) and Coulter v. Superior Court (_____ Cal.3d _____)[1] be abrogated in favor of prior judicial interpretation finding the consumption of alcoholic beverages rather than the serving of alcoholic beverages as the proximate cause of injuries inflicted upon another by an intoxicated person. *(Added by Stats.1953, c. 152, p. 1020, § 1. Amended by Stats.1978, c. 929, p. 2903, § 1.)*

[1] See 21 Cal.3rd 144, 577 P.2d 669, 145 Cal.Rptr. 534.

Cross References

Brandy manufacturer's license, authority to conduct tastings, conditions, liability, see Business and Professions Code § 23363.3.
Civil liability, see Civil Code § 1714.
Distilled spirits manufacturer's license, authority to conduct tastings, conditions, liability, see Business and Professions Code § 23363.1.
Limitation as to time of filing accusations, see Business and Professions Code §§ 24206, 24208.
Principals in crime of drunkard defined as persons causing drunkenness, see Penal Code § 31.
Responsible beverage service training program, sale and service of alcoholic beverages, duties of a licensee, see Business and Professions Code § 25686.
Suspension or revocation of license, grounds, see Business and Professions Code § 24200.

Research References

California Jury Instructions-Civil, 8th Edition 4.50, Selling Liquor to an Obviously Intoxicated Minor—Essential Elements.
2 Witkin, California Criminal Law 4th Crimes Against Public Peace and Welfare § 362 (2021), Furnishing Liquor to Specified Persons.

§ 25602.1. Sales to intoxicated minors; cause of action for injury or death

Notwithstanding subdivision (b) of Section 25602, a cause of action may be brought by or on behalf of any person who has suffered injury or death against any person licensed, or required to be licensed, pursuant to Section 23300, or any person authorized by the federal government to sell alcoholic beverages on a military base or other federal enclave, who sells, furnishes, gives or causes to be sold, furnished or given away any alcoholic beverage, and any other person who sells, or causes to be sold, any alcoholic beverage, to any obviously intoxicated minor where the furnishing, sale or giving of that beverage to the minor is the proximate cause of the personal injury or death sustained by that person. *(Added by Stats.1978, c. 930, p. 2905, § 1. Amended by Stats.1986, c. 289, § 1.)*

Research References

California Jury Instructions - Criminal 1.25, "Minor"—Defined.
California Jury Instructions-Civil, 8th Edition 4.50, Selling Liquor to an Obviously Intoxicated Minor—Essential Elements.

§ 25602.2. Injunctive relief; procedure; presumptions

The director may bring an action to enjoin a violation or the threatened violation of subdivision (a) of Section 25602. Such action may be brought in the county in which the violation occurred or is threatened to occur. Any proceeding brought hereunder shall conform to the requirements of Chapter 3 (commencing with Section 525) of Title 7 of Part 2 of the Code of Civil Procedure, except that it shall be presumed that there is no adequate remedy at law, and that irreparable damage will occur if the continued or threatened violation is not restrained or enjoined. *(Added by Stats.1978, c. 930, p. 2905, § 2.)*

§ 25602.3. Second and subsequent offenses; offer in compromise; prohibition

Notwithstanding any other provision of this division, no licensee may petition the department for an offer in compromise pursuant to Section 23095 for a second or any subsequent violation of subdivision (a) of Section 25602 which occurs within 36 months of the initial violation. *(Added by Stats.1978, c. 930, p. 2905, § 3.)*

§ 25603. Bringing alcoholic beverage into prison, jail, or reformatory

Every person, not authorized by law, who brings into any state prison, city or county jail, city and county jail, or reformatory in this State, or within the grounds belonging to any such institution, any alcoholic beverage is guilty of a felony. *(Added by Stats.1953, c. 152, p. 1020, § 1.)*

Cross References

Controlled substances, similar provision, see Penal Code § 4573.
Suspension or revocation of license, grounds, see Business and Professions Code § 24200.

Research References

2 Witkin, California Criminal Law 4th Crimes Against Public Peace and Welfare § 362 (2021), Furnishing Liquor to Specified Persons.

§ 25604. Unlicensed premises; nuisance; "consideration" defined; abatement action

It is a public nuisance for any person to maintain any club room in which any alcoholic beverage is received or kept, or to which any alcoholic beverage is brought, for consumption on the premises by members of the public or of any club, corporation, or association, unless the person and premises are licensed under this division. It is a public nuisance for any person to keep, maintain, operate or lease any premises for the purpose of providing therein for a consideration a place for the drinking of alcoholic beverages by members of the public or other persons, unless the person and premises are licensed under this division. As used herein "consideration" includes cover charge, the sale of food, ice, mixers or other liquids used with alcoholic beverage drinks, or the furnishing of glassware or other containers for use in the consumption of alcoholic beverage drinks.

The Attorney General or any district attorney may bring an action in the name of the people to abate the nuisance, and the Attorney General shall, upon request of the department, bring the action. *(Added by Stats.1953, c. 152, p. 1020, § 1. Amended by Stats.1953, c. 1331, p. 2893, § 17; Stats.1955, c. 447, p. 925, § 130.)*

Cross References

Club licenses, see Business and Professions Code § 23425 et seq.
Public nuisance defined, see Civil Code § 3480; Penal Code § 370.
Remedies and abatement, see Civil Code § 3491 et seq.

Research References

2 Witkin, California Criminal Law 4th Crimes Against Public Peace and Welfare § 361 (2021), In General.

§ 25605. Delivery of alcoholic beverages pursuant to telephone orders or other electronic means; proof of age and identity

No off-sale licensee shall deliver any alcoholic beverages pursuant to orders received for alcoholic beverages by telephone or other electronic means unless upon delivery the recipient shall be able to furnish proof of age and identity to indicate that he or she is 21 years of age or over. *(Added by Stats.1963, c. 1410, p. 2947, § 1. Amended by Stats.2013, c. 337 (S.B.818), § 5.)*

Research References

2 Witkin, California Criminal Law 4th Crimes Against Public Peace and Welfare § 364 (2021), Furnishing Liquor to Minors.

§ 25606. Vehicles transporting beverages or property subject to seizure; punishment; seizure

It is unlawful for any person to use any automobile or other vehicle to conceal, convey, carry, or transport any alcoholic beverages which are subject to seizure under this division, or any stills or parts thereof subject to seizure under this division, or any materials or supplies capable of and intended for use in the manufacture or production of alcoholic beverages with the design to evade the excise taxes or license fees imposed by this division. This section does not apply to any person who uses an automobile or other vehicle to transport distilled spirits for lawful use in the trades, professions, or industries. Any person violating the provisions of this section is guilty of a misdemeanor and shall be punished by a fine of not more than one thousand dollars ($1,000) or by imprisonment in the county jail for not more than one year, or by both such fine and imprisonment.

The department may seize any automobile or other vehicle used contrary to the provisions of this section. *(Added by Stats.1953, c. 152, p. 1021, § 1. Amended by Stats.1955, c. 447, p. 925, § 131; Stats.1983, c. 1092, § 59, eff. Sept. 27, 1983, operative Jan. 1, 1984.)*

Cross References

Common carriers exempt, see Business and Professions Code § 25374.
Excise taxes, see Revenue and Taxation Code § 32001 et seq.
Seizure and forfeiture of property, see Business and Professions Code § 25350 et seq.
Still defined, see Business and Professions Code § 23034.

Research References

2 Witkin, California Criminal Law 4th Crimes Against Public Peace and Welfare § 361 (2021), In General.
3 Witkin, California Criminal Law 4th Punishment § 190 (2021), Noncriminal Actions.

§ 25607. Possession of beverages unauthorized for sale; presumption; seizure; exception; shared common licensed areas; multiple licenses; shared common licensed area between manufacturer and multiple retailers

(a) Except as provided in subdivisions (b), (c), (d), * * * (e), and (f), it is unlawful for any person or licensee to have upon any premises for which a license has been issued any alcoholic beverages other than the alcoholic beverage that the licensee is authorized to sell at the premises under their license. It shall be presumed that all alcoholic beverages found or located upon premises for which licenses have been issued belong to the person or persons to whom the licenses were issued. Any person * * * who violates the provisions of this section is guilty of a misdemeanor. The department may seize any alcoholic beverages found in violation of this section.

(b) Except as provided in subdivision (c), a bona fide public eating place for which an on-sale beer and wine license has been issued may have upon the premises brandy, rum, or liqueurs for use solely for cooking purposes.

(c)(1) A licensed winegrower, licensed beer manufacturer that holds a small beer manufacturer's license, and a licensed craft distiller, in any combination, whose licensed premises of production are immediately adjacent to each other and that are not branch offices, may, with the approval of the department and under such conditions as the department may require, share a common licensed area in which the consumption of alcoholic beverages is permitted, only under all of the following circumstances:

(A) The shared common licensed area is adjacent and contiguous to the licensed premises of the licensees.

(B) The licensed premises of the licensees are not branch offices.

(C) The shared common licensed area shall be readily accessible from the premises of the licensees without the necessity of using a public street, alley, or sidewalk.

(D) Except as otherwise authorized by this division, the alcoholic beverages that may be consumed in the shared common licensed area shall be purchased by the consumer only from the licensed winegrower, the licensed beer manufacturer, or the licensed craft distiller.

(E) The licensed winegrower, the licensed beer manufacturer, and the licensed craft distiller shall be jointly responsible for compliance with the provisions of this division and for any violations that may occur within the shared common licensed area.

(2) Nothing in this subdivision is intended to authorize the licensed winegrower, the licensed beer manufacturer, or the licensed craft distiller to sell, furnish, give, or have upon their respective licensed premises any alcoholic beverages, or to engage in any other activity, not otherwise authorized by this division, including, without limitation, the consumption on the premises of any distilled spirits purchased by consumers for consumption off the premises pursuant to Section 23504 or the consumption of distilled spirits other than as permitted by Section 23363.1.

(d) The holder of a beer manufacturer's license, winegrower's license, brandy manufacturer's license, distilled spirits manufacturer's license, craft distiller's license, any rectifier's license, any importer's license, or any wholesaler's license, that holds more than one of those licenses for a single premises, may have alcoholic beverages that are authorized under those licenses at the same time anywhere within the premises for purposes of production and storage, if the holder of the licenses maintains records of production and storage that identify the specific location of each alcoholic beverage product within the premises. Nothing in this subdivision is intended to allow a licensee to hold licenses, alone or in combination, or to exercise any license privileges, not otherwise provided for or authorized by this division.

(e) Notwithstanding any provision to the contrary, a licensed manufacturer may share a common licensed area with multiple licensed retailers, subject to the provisions of this subdivision.

(1) No retail licensee sharing the common licensed area with a licensed manufacturer shall sell or serve any alcoholic beverages that are manufactured, produced, bottled, processed, imported, rectified, distributed, represented, or sold by the manufacturer, directly or indirectly. This prohibition shall apply to all licensed premises owned or operated, in whole or in part, by the retail licensee anywhere in the state. No wholesaler shall be responsible for compliance with this paragraph.

(2) The licensed manufacturer may, in connection with the operation of the shared common area only, advertise or promote the common licensed area, including, but not limited to, any advertising or promotion related to the licensed retailers sharing the common licensed area, provided that each retailer pays its pro rata share of the costs of that advertising or promotion. The cost attributed to each retailer's pro rata share shall not be less than the current market price for that advertising or promotion.

(3) The licensed manufacturer may, in connection with the operation of the shared common area only, pay its pro rata share of the cost of the operation of the shared common area, including, but not limited to, the cost of renting, utilities, or any other operating costs for the area.

(4) Except as provided in paragraphs (2) and (3), no other thing of value may be given or furnished by the manufacturer to the retailers.

(5) The manufacturer may have on the area of its licensed premises that encompass the shared common licensed area alcoholic beverages that would not otherwise be permitted on the manufacturer's licensed premises. This provision does not authorize the possession of alcoholic beverages not otherwise permitted on the manufacturer's licensed premises that is not part of the shared common licensed area.

(6) All retailers sharing the common licensed area shall hold the same license type. Nothing in this subdivision shall authorize any of the retailers to exercise license privileges that are not authorized by their license.

(7) All licensees holding licenses within the shared common licensed area shall be jointly responsible for compliance with all laws that may subject their license to discipline.

(8) A wholesaler does not directly or indirectly underwrite, share in, or contribute to any costs related to the common licensed area.

(9) The manufacturer maintains records necessary to establish its compliance with this section.

(10)(A) This subdivision does not authorize a licensed manufacturer to share a common licensed area with a single retailer or with multiple retailers under common ownership, in whole or in part.

(B) This subdivision is intended to be a narrow exception to the separation of manufacturers and retailers. This subdivision shall be narrowly construed.

(11) The Legislature finds and declares both of the following:

(A) It is necessary and proper to require a separation between manufacturing interests, wholesale interests, and retail interests in the production and distribution of alcoholic beverages in order to prevent suppliers from dominating local markets through vertical integration and to prevent excessive sales of alcoholic beverages produced by overly aggressive marketing techniques.

(B) Any exception established by the Legislature to the general prohibition against tied interests must be limited to the express terms of the exception so as to not undermine the general prohibitions.

(f)(1) Notwithstanding any provision to the contrary, the holder of a beer manufacturer's license and a winegrower's license that holds both of those licenses for a single premises may have alcoholic beverages that are authorized under those licenses at the same time anywhere within the premises and may maintain a designated area upon that premises where retail sales and consumption authorized under those licenses may occur.

(2) The privileges described in paragraph (1) may be exercised by the licensee only if all of the following apply:

(A) The licenses are held under identical ownership.

(B) The manufacturer's licenses for the single premises are either both master licenses or both branch offices, and not a combination of a master license and a branch office.

(C) For overlapping branch offices, only alcoholic beverages produced by the licensee are sold.

(3) Nothing in this subdivision is intended to allow a licensee to hold licenses, alone or in combination, or to exercise any license privileges, not otherwise provided for or authorized by this division. *(Added by Stats.1953, c. 152, p. 1021, § 1. Amended by Stats.1955, c. 447, p. 926, § 132; Stats.1984, c. 382, § 1; Stats.2017, c. 788 (A.B.997), § 1, eff. Jan. 1, 2018; Stats.2018, c. 293 (A.B.1890), § 1, eff. Jan. 1, 2019; Stats.2019, c. 696 (A.B.1825), § 2, eff. Jan. 1, 2020; Stats.2021, c. 656 (S.B.314), § 3, eff. Oct. 8, 2021; Stats.2022, c. 175 (A.B.1734), § 1, eff. Jan. 1, 2023.)*

Cross References

Limitation as to time of filing accusations, see Business and Professions Code §§ 24206, 24208.
Misdemeanor, generally, see Penal Code §§ 17, 19.
Revocation or suspension of licenses, see Business and Professions Code § 24200.
Rights and obligation of licensees, see Business and Professions Code § 23355 et seq.
Seizure or forfeiture of property, see Business and Professions Code § 25350 et seq.
Types of licenses, see Business and Professions Code § 23320.

Research References

2 Witkin, California Criminal Law 4th Crimes Against Public Peace and Welfare § 361 (2021), In General.

§ 25607.5. Nonprofit corporation; authorized receipt and possession of donated beer or wine

A nonprofit corporation that is required to obtain a license to sell beer or wine under Section 23300 may receive and possess beer or wine donated to it if, at the time of receipt of the beer or wine, the nonprofit corporation has submitted an application with the department for a license to sell the donated beer or wine. Nothing in this section is intended to affect or otherwise limit the application of Section 25503.9. *(Added by Stats.2008, c. 71 (A.B.1964), § 3. Amended by Stats.2015, c. 107 (A.B.774), § 3, eff. Jan. 1, 2016.)*

§ 25608. Public schoolhouses or grounds; penalties; exceptions; bar from privilege of using public school property

(a) Every person who possesses, consumes, sells, gives, or delivers to another person an alcoholic beverage in or on a public schoolhouse or the grounds of the schoolhouse, is guilty of a misdemeanor. This section does not, however, make it unlawful for a person to acquire, possess, or use an alcoholic beverage in or on a public schoolhouse, or on the grounds of the schoolhouse, if any of the following applies:

(1) The alcoholic beverage possessed, consumed, or sold, pursuant to a license obtained under this division, is wine or beer that is produced by a bonded winery or brewery owned or operated as part of an instructional program in viticulture and enology or brewing.

(2) The alcoholic beverage is acquired, possessed, or used in connection with a course of instruction given at the school and the person has been authorized to acquire, possess, or use it by the governing body or other administrative head of the school.

(3) The public schoolhouse is surplus school property and the grounds of the schoolhouse are leased to a lessee that is a general law city with a population of less than 50,000, or the public schoolhouse is surplus school property and the grounds of the schoolhouse are located in an unincorporated area and are leased to a lessee that is a civic organization, and the property is to be used for community center purposes and no public school education is to be conducted on the property by either the lessor or the lessee and the property is not being used by persons under the age of 21 years for recreational purposes at any time during which alcoholic beverages are being sold or consumed on the premises.

(4) The alcoholic beverages are acquired, possessed, or used during events at a college-owned or college-operated veterans stadium with a capacity of over 12,000 people, located in a county with a population of over 6,000,000 people. As used in this paragraph, "events" mean football games sponsored by a college, other than a public community college, or other events sponsored by noncollege groups.

(5) The alcoholic beverages are acquired, possessed, or used during an event not sponsored by any college at a performing arts facility built on property owned by a community college district and leased to a nonprofit organization that is a public benefit corporation formed under Part 2 (commencing with Section 5110) of Division 2 of Title 1 of the Corporations Code. As used in this paragraph, "performing arts facility" means an auditorium with more than 300 permanent seats.

(6) The alcoholic beverage is wine for sacramental or other religious purposes and is used only during authorized religious services held on or before January 1, 1995.

(7) The alcoholic beverages are acquired, possessed, or used during an event at a community center owned by a community services district or a city and the event is not held at a time when students are attending a public school-sponsored activity at the center.

(8) The alcoholic beverage is wine that is acquired, possessed, or used during an event sponsored by a community college district or an organization operated for the benefit of the community college district where the college district maintains both an instructional program in viticulture on no less than five acres of land owned by the district and an instructional program in enology, which includes sales and marketing.

(9) The alcoholic beverage is acquired, possessed, or used at a professional minor league baseball game conducted at the stadium of a community college located in a county with a population of less than 250,000 inhabitants, and the baseball game is conducted pursuant to a contract between the community college district and a professional sports organization.

(10) The alcoholic beverages are acquired, possessed, or used during events at a college-owned or college-operated stadium or other facility. As used in this paragraph, "events" means fundraisers held to benefit a nonprofit corporation that has obtained a license pursuant to this division for the event. "Events" does not include football games or other athletic contests sponsored by any college or public community college. This paragraph does not apply to any public education facility in which any grade from kindergarten to grade 12, inclusive, is schooled.

(11) The alcoholic beverages are possessed, consumed, or sold, pursuant to a license, permit, or authorization obtained under this division, for an event held at an overnight retreat facility owned and operated by a county office of education or a school district at times when pupils are not on the grounds.

(12) The grounds of the public schoolhouse on which the alcoholic beverage is acquired, possessed, used, or consumed is property that has been developed and is used for residential facilities or housing that is offered for rent, lease, or sale exclusively to faculty or staff of a public school or community college.

(13) The grounds of a public schoolhouse on which the alcoholic beverage is acquired, possessed, used, or consumed is property of a community college that is leased, licensed, or otherwise provided for use as a water conservation demonstration garden and community passive recreation resource by a joint powers agency comprised of public agencies, including the community college, and the event at which the alcoholic beverage is acquired, possessed, used, or consumed is conducted pursuant to a written policy adopted by the governing body of the joint powers agency and no public funds are used for the purchase or provision of the alcoholic beverage.

(14) The alcoholic beverage is beer or wine acquired, possessed, used, sold, or consumed only in connection with a course of instruction, sponsored dinner, or meal demonstration given as part of a culinary arts program at a campus of a California community college and the person has been authorized to acquire, possess, use, sell, or consume the beer or wine by the governing body or other administrative head of the school.

(15) The alcoholic beverages are possessed, consumed, or sold, pursuant to a license or permit obtained under this division for special events held at the facilities of a public community college during the special event. As used in this paragraph, "special event" means events that are held with the permission of the governing board of the community college district that are festivals, shows, private parties, concerts, theatrical productions, and other events held on the premises of the public community college and for which the principal attendees are members of the general public or invited guests and not students of the public community college.

(16) The alcoholic beverages are acquired, possessed, or used during an event at a community college-owned facility in which any grade from kindergarten to grade 12, inclusive, is schooled, if the event is held at a time when students in any grades from kindergarten to grade 12, inclusive, are not present at the facility. As used in this paragraph, "events" include fundraisers held to benefit a nonprofit corporation that has obtained a license pursuant to this division for the event.

(17) The alcoholic beverages are acquired, possessed, used, or consumed pursuant to a license or permit obtained under this division for special events held at facilities owned and operated by an educational agency, a county office of education, superintendent of schools, school district, or community college district at a time when pupils are not on the grounds. As used in this paragraph, "facilities" include, but are not limited to, office complexes, conference centers, or retreat facilities.

(b) Any person convicted of a violation of this section shall, in addition to the penalty imposed for the misdemeanor, be barred from having or receiving any privilege of the use of public school property that is accorded by Article 2 (commencing with Section 82537) of Chapter 8 of Part 49 of Division 7 of Title 3 the Education Code.

(Added by Stats.1953, c. 152, p. 1021, § 1. Amended by Stats.1963, c. 1040, p. 2334, § 17; Stats.1963, c. 1557, p. 3141, § 1; Stats.1981, c. 605, p. 2326, § 1; Stats.1983, c. 216, § 1; Stats.1985, c. 188, § 1; Stats.1986, c. 248, § 14; Stats.1986, c. 1123, § 1; Stats.1987, c. 685, § 1; Stats.1989, c. 112, § 1; Stats.1989, c. 543, § 1; Stats.1993, c. 238 (S.B.113), § 2; Stats.1997, c. 90 (S.B.572), § 1, eff. July 21, 1997; Stats.1998, c. 639 (A.B.2416), § 14; Stats.2005, c. 203 (S.B.220), § 1, eff. Sept. 6, 2005; Stats.2005, c. 204 (A.B.767), § 2; Stats.2006, c. 72 (S.B.1486), § 2; Stats.2007, c. 149 (A.B.1598), § 1; Stats.2008, c. 508 (A.B.3071), § 3; Stats.2009, c. 398 (A.B.172), § 1; Stats.2009, c. 399 (A.B.1448), § 1; Stats.2010, c. 79 (A.B.1643), § 1, eff. July 15, 2010; Stats.2010, c. 84 (A.B.1748), § 1; Stats.2010, c. 239 (A.B.1860), § 1.7, eff. Sept. 24, 2010; Stats.2011, c. 296 (A.B.1023), § 30; Stats.2011, c. 672 (A.B.319), § 1; Stats.2011, c. 702 (S.B.339), § 3.5; Stats.2014, c. 235 (A.B.2073), § 1, eff. Jan. 1, 2015; Stats.2015, c. 303 (A.B.731), § 24, eff. Jan. 1, 2016; Stats.2017, c. 119 (S.B.228), § 1, eff. Jan. 1, 2018.)

Cross References

Suspension or revocation of license, grounds, see Business and Professions Code § 24200.

Research References

2 Witkin, California Criminal Law 4th Crimes Against Public Peace and Welfare § 363 (2021), Time, Place, and Manner of Sale.

§ 25608.5. Possession of alcoholic beverages on Lower American River; "container" defined; punishment; notice

(a) On the portion of the Lower American River, as defined in Section 5841 of the Public Resources Code, from the Hazel Avenue Bridge to the Watt Avenue Bridge, a person in a nonmotorized vessel shall not possess a container with an alcoholic beverage, whether opened or closed, during the summer holiday periods that the Sacramento County Board of Supervisors prohibits the consumption or possession of an open alcoholic beverage container on the land portions along the river.

(b) For purposes of this section, "container" means bottle, can, or other receptacle.

(c) A violation of this section is punishable as an infraction pursuant to subdivision (b) of Section 25132 of the Government Code.

(d) Sacramento County shall provide notice on the land portions along the river described in subdivision (a) that a violation of this section is punishable as an infraction. *(Added by Stats.2007, c. 19 (A.B.951), § 1, eff. June 28, 2007.)*

§ 25608.10. Possession of alcoholic beverages on Truckee River; "container" defined; punishment; notice

(a) On the portion of the Truckee River, from the outfall of Lake Tahoe upstream of the Highway 89 Bridge in Tahoe City to the Alpine Meadows Bridge, a person in a vessel, as defined by Section 651 of the Harbors and Navigation Code, or a bather, as defined by Section 651.1 of the Harbors and Navigation Code, shall not possess a container with an alcoholic beverage, whether opened or closed, during the summer holiday periods that the Placer County Board of Supervisors prohibits the consumption of an alcoholic beverage or possession of an open alcoholic beverage container on the land portions along this portion of the river.

(b) For purposes of this section, "container" means a bottle, can, or other receptacle.

(c) A violation of this section is punishable as an infraction pursuant to subdivision (b) of Section 25132 of the Government Code.

(d) Placer County shall provide notice on the land portions along the Truckee River described in subdivision (a) that a violation of this section is punishable as an infraction. *(Added by Stats.2008, c. 44 (S.B.1159), § 1, eff. June 30, 2008.)*

§ 25608.12. Possession of alcoholic beverages on Sacramento River; "container" defined; punishment; notice

(a) On the portion of the Sacramento River, from the Highway 32 Bridge to the mouth of Big Chico Creek, a person in a vessel, as defined by Section 651 of the Harbors and Navigation Code, or a bather, as defined by Section 651.1 of the Harbors and Navigation Code, shall not possess a container with an alcoholic beverage, whether opened or closed, during the summer holiday periods that the Glenn County Board of Supervisors and the Butte County Board of Supervisors prohibit the consumption of an alcoholic beverage or possession of an open alcoholic beverage container on the land portions along this portion of the Sacramento River.

(b) For purposes of this section, "container" means a bottle, can, or other receptacle.

(c) A violation of this section is punishable as an infraction pursuant to subdivision (b) of Section 25132 of the Government Code.

(d) Glenn County and Butte County shall provide notice on the land portions along the Sacramento River described in subdivision (a) that a violation of this section is punishable as an infraction. *(Added by Stats.2011, c. 158 (A.B.494), § 1, eff. Aug. 1, 2011.)*

§ 25609. Offer of substitute brand

Every person who, in response to an inquiry or request for any brand, type, or character of alcoholic beverages, sells or offers for sale under an on-sale license a different brand, type, or character without first informing the purchaser of the difference is guilty of a misdemeanor. *(Added by Stats.1953, c. 152, p. 1021, § 1.)*

Cross References

Labels and containers in general, see Business and Professions Code § 25170 et seq.
Limitation as to time of filing accusations, see Business and Professions Code §§ 24206, 24208.

Research References

2 Witkin, California Criminal Law 4th Crimes Against Public Peace and Welfare § 363 (2021), Time, Place, and Manner of Sale.

§ 25610. Obliteration, etc., of marks on package

(a) Any person who erases, removes, obliterates, destroys, or renders illegible in any manner any serial numbers, stamps, marks, brands, legends, or other information required by federal or state law to be attached or placed upon any packages or original cases containing alcoholic beverages, before the contents of such packages or cases have been entirely removed, is guilty of a misdemeanor.

(b) Any licensee who possesses any original unopened package or case containing alcoholic beverages on which or from which any serial number required by federal or state law to be attached or placed has been erased, removed, obliterated, destroyed, or rendered illegible in any manner, is guilty of a misdemeanor. *(Added by Stats.1953, c. 152, p. 1022, § 1. Amended by Stats.1963, c. 775, p. 1805, § 1.)*

Cross References

Limitation as to time of filing accusations, see Business and Professions Code §§ 24206, 24208.

Research References

2 Witkin, California Criminal Law 4th Crimes Against Public Peace and Welfare § 363 (2021), Time, Place, and Manner of Sale.

§ 25611.1. Signs; manufacturers, winegrowers, agents, and other associates; authority to furnish

Any manufacturer, winegrower, manufacturer's agent, rectifier, distiller, bottler, importer, or wholesaler, or any officer, director, or agent of any of these persons may furnish, give, lend, sell, or rent:

(a) Interior signs, advertising either wine or distilled spirits, for use in on-sale retail premises, each of which shall not exceed 630 square inches in size. This limitation on the size of interior signs, advertising either wine or distilled spirits, shall not be applicable to off-sale retail premises.

(b) Interior signs advertising beer in on-sale or off-sale retail premises which shall bear conspicuous notice of the beer manufacturer's name, brand name, trade name, slogans, markings, trademarks, or other symbols commonly associated with and generally used by the beer manufacturer in identifying the beer manufacturer's name or product, and which may bear graphic or pictorial advertising representations. These signs shall include, but are not limited to, posters, placards, stickers, decals, shelf strips, wall panels, plaques, shadow boxes, mobiles, dummy bottles, bottle toppers, case wrappers, brand-identifying statuettes, tap markers, and table tents. These interior signs advertising beer shall not be deemed of intrinsic or utilitarian value and shall remain the property of the beer wholesaler who authorized and furnished them, unless given or sold to the retail licensee.

(c) Interior signs advertising beer for use in on-sale or off-sale retail premises, which are illuminated or mechanized, and which shall principally bear a conspicuous notice of the beer manufacturer's name, brand name, trade name, slogans, markings, trademarks, or other symbols commonly associated with and generally used by the beer manufacturer in identifying the beer manufacturer's name or product, and which may bear graphic or pictorial advertising representations. These illuminated or mechanized interior signs advertising beer shall not be deemed of intrinsic or utilitarian value and shall remain the property of the beer wholesaler who authorized and furnished them, unless given or sold to the retail licensee.

(d) Signs or other advertising matter for exterior use at any on-sale or off-sale retail premises as may be permitted by this division and rules of the department adopted pursuant thereto. *(Added by Stats.1957, c. 1987, p. 3533, § 2. Amended by Stats.1965, c. 721, p. 2123, § 2; Stats.1968, c. 653, p. 1336, § 1; Stats.1996, c. 99 (A.B.3144), § 1; Stats.1997, c. 26 (A.B.973), § 1; Stats.2001, c. 207 (A.B.395), § 1.)*

Cross References

Special on-sale general license to facility partially located in County of Placer and County of Washoe, facility requirements, special provisions, see Business and Professions Code § 23399.52.

Bus. & Prof.

Research References

2 Witkin, California Criminal Law 4th Crimes Against Public Peace and Welfare § 363 (2021), Time, Place, and Manner of Sale.

§ 25611.2. Electronic data services; manufacturers and winegrowers; authority to furnish

Nothing in this chapter shall prohibit any alcoholic beverage manufacturer, manufacturer's agent, winegrower, or wholesaler from furnishing or giving electronic data services to a licensed retail premises. For purposes of this section, "electronic data services" are limited to the transmission by telephone line, microwave, or other electronic means of data relating to retailer inventory of the manufacturer's, winegrower's, or wholesaler's brands, monitoring of brand sales performance, electronic invoice transmissions, and electronic funds transfer. *(Added by Stats.1994, c. 171 (S.B.1618), § 1. Amended by Stats.1996, c. 99 (A.B.3144), § 2.)*

Cross References

Special on-sale general license to facility partially located in County of Placer and County of Washoe, facility requirements, special provisions, see Business and Professions Code § 23399.52.

§ 25611.3. Beer wholesalers; exterior advertisement signs

A beer wholesaler may sell or rent exterior signs advertising beer for use at any on-sale or off-sale retail premises. Exterior signs include, but are not limited to, signs, inflatables, and banners used to advertise a beer manufacturer's product. Exterior signs must be sold or rented at not less than cost, as defined in Section 17026. An exterior sign that is customized for a retailer must be sold, and may not be rented. *(Added by Stats.2008, c. 395 (S.B.1246), § 1.)*

Cross References

Special on-sale general license to facility partially located in County of Placer and County of Washoe, facility requirements, special provisions, see Business and Professions Code § 23399.52.

§ 25612. Signs; retail premises

Signs or other advertising matter used in connection with the licensed premises of any retailer of alcoholic beverages shall not be of any obnoxious, gaudy, blatant, or offensive nature and shall in no manner contrary to the rules of the department obstruct the view of the interior of the premises from the street. *(Added by Stats.1953, c. 152, p. 1022, § 1. Amended by Stats.1955, c. 447, p. 926, § 133.)*

Cross References

Limitation as to time of filing accusations, see Business and Professions Code §§ 24206, 24208.

Rules and regulations, see Business and Professions Code § 25750.

Special on-sale general license to facility partially located in County of Placer and County of Washoe, facility requirements, special provisions, see Business and Professions Code § 23399.52.

Research References

2 Witkin, California Criminal Law 4th Crimes Against Public Peace and Welfare § 363 (2021), Time, Place, and Manner of Sale.

§ 25612.5. Retail licensee; operating standards; local regulations

(a) This section shall apply to licensees other than a retail on-sale licensee or on-sale beer and wine licensee who is licensed and operates as a bona fide public eating place, as defined in Section 23038, 23038.1, or 23038.2, or as a hotel, motel, or similar lodging establishment, as defined in subdivision (b) of Section 25503.16; a winegrowers license; a licensed beer manufacturer, as defined in Section 23357; a retail licensee who concurrently holds an off-sale retail beer and wine license and a beer manufacturer's license for those same or contiguous premises; and a retail on-sale licensee or on-sale beer and wine licensee who is licensed and operates as a bona fide public eating place, as defined in Section 23038, 23038.1, or 23038.2, or as a hotel, motel, or similar lodging establishment, as defined in subdivision (b) of Section 25503.16, a licensed beer manufacturer, as defined in Section 23357, or a winegrowers license, who sells off-sale beer and wine under the on-sale license on those same or contiguous premises.

(b) The Legislature finds and declares that it is in the interest of the public health, safety, and welfare to adopt operating standards as set forth in this section for specified retail premises licensed by the department. The standards set forth in this section are state standards that do not preclude the adoption and implementation of more stringent local regulations that are otherwise authorized by law.

(c) Other than as provided in subdivision (a), each retail licensee shall comply with all of the following:

(1) A prominent, permanent sign or signs stating "NO LOITERING IS ALLOWED ON OR IN FRONT OF THESE PREMISES" shall be posted in a place that is clearly visible to patrons of the licensee. The size, format, form, placement, and languages of the sign or signs shall be determined by the department. This paragraph shall apply to a licensee only upon written notice to the licensee from the department. The department shall issue this written notice only upon a request, from the local law enforcement agency in whose jurisdiction the premises are located, that is supported by substantial evidence that there is loitering adjacent to the premises.

(2) A prominent, permanent sign or signs stating "NO OPEN ALCOHOLIC BEVERAGE CONTAINERS ARE ALLOWED ON THESE PREMISES" shall be posted in a place that is clearly visible to patrons of the licensee. The size, format, form, placement, and languages of the sign or signs shall be determined by the department. This paragraph shall apply to a licensee only upon written notice to the licensee from the department. The department shall issue this written notice only upon a request, from the local law enforcement agency in whose jurisdiction the premises are located, that is supported by substantial evidence that there is drinking in public adjacent to the premises.

(3) No alcoholic beverages shall be consumed on the premises of an off-sale retail establishment, and no alcoholic beverages shall be consumed outside the edifice of an on-sale retail establishment.

(4) The exterior of the premises, including adjacent public sidewalks and all parking lots under the control of the licensee, shall be illuminated during all hours of darkness during which the premises are open for business in a manner so that persons standing in those areas at night are identifiable by law enforcement personnel. However, the required illumination shall be placed so as to minimize interference with the quiet enjoyment of nearby residents of their property.

(5) Litter shall be removed daily from the premises, including adjacent public sidewalks and all parking lots under the control of the licensee. These areas shall be swept or cleaned, either mechanically or manually, on a weekly basis to control debris.

(6) Graffiti shall be removed from the premises and all parking lots under the control of the licensee within 72 hours of application. If the graffiti occurs on a Friday or weekend day, or on a holiday, the licensee shall remove the graffiti 72 hours following the beginning of the next weekday.

(7) No more than 33 percent of the square footage of the windows and clear doors of an off-sale premises shall bear advertising or signs of any sort, and all advertising and signage shall be placed and maintained in a manner that ensures that law enforcement personnel have a clear and unobstructed view of the interior of the premises, including the area in which the cash registers are maintained, from the exterior public sidewalk or entrance to the premises. However, this latter requirement shall not apply to premises where there are no windows, or where existing windows are located at a height that precludes a view of the interior of the premises to a person standing outside the premises.

(8) Upon request of the local law enforcement agency in whose jurisdiction the licensed premises are located or at the discretion of the department, each public telephone located on off-sale premises (or located in an adjacent area under the control of the off-sale licensee) shall be equipped with devices or mechanisms that prevent persons from calling into that public telephone.

(9) Every licensed retailer who sells or rents video recordings of harmful matter, as defined by Section 313 of the Penal Code, shall create an area within his or her business establishment for the placement of video recordings of harmful matter and for any material that advertises the sale or rental of these video recordings. This area shall be labeled "adults only." The licensed retailer shall make reasonable efforts to arrange the video recordings in this area in such a way that minors may not readily access the video recordings or view the video box covers. The failure to create and label the "adults only" area is an infraction punishable by a fine of not more than one hundred dollars ($100). The failure to place a video recording or advertisement, regardless of its content, in this area shall not constitute an infraction.

(10) A copy of the applicable operating standards shall be available during normal business hours for viewing by the general public. *(Added by Stats.1994, c. 629 (A.B.2742), § 4. Amended by Stats.1995, c. 743 (A.B.683), § 5, eff. Oct. 10, 1995; Stats.1999, c. 787 (A.B.749), § 2.)*

Cross References

Instructional tasting license at premises of off-sale retail license, limitations on issuance and use, application and fee, see Business and Professions Code § 23396.6.

Special on-sale general license to facility partially located in County of Placer and County of Washoe, facility requirements, special provisions, see Business and Professions Code § 23399.52.

Suspension and revocation of alcoholic beverages licenses, additional grounds, see Business and Professions Code § 24200.1.

Research References

2 Witkin, California Criminal Law 4th Crimes Against Public Peace and Welfare § 363 (2021), Time, Place, and Manner of Sale.

§ 25613. Draught beer; tap signs; placards or markers

Every holder of an on-sale retail license who gives, sells, or otherwise dispenses any draught beer shall, upon the faucet, spigot, or outlet from which the beer is drawn, attach and keep posted a clear and legible notice, placard, or marker which shall in the English language indicate and declare the name or brand adopted by the manufacturer of the draught beer so given, sold, or dispensed by the licensee. If the faucet, spigot, or other drawing device is in a location not within the room of the place of service and consumption of the beer, there shall also be kept posted a similar notice, placard, or marker in the place of service and consumption of the beer which shall truthfully state and indicate only the kinds and brands of draught beer actually on sale in the premises of the on-sale licensee. *(Added by Stats.1953, c. 152, p. 1022, § 1. Amended by Stats.1965, c. 78, p. 1019, § 3.)*

Cross References

Illegal dispensing or display, draught beer, see Business and Professions Code § 25206.

Special on-sale general license to facility partially located in County of Placer and County of Washoe, facility requirements, special provisions, see Business and Professions Code § 23399.52.

§ 25614. Beer violations

Any person who violates any of the provisions of Sections 25611 to 25613, inclusive, or substitutes another or different brand of draught beer from that indicated by any of the required notices, placards, or markers, or substitutes one brand of beer for another, or misrepresents the brand or kind of beer served to a consumer is guilty of a misdemeanor. *(Added by Stats.1953, c. 152, p. 1022, § 1.)*

Cross References

Suspension or revocation of license, grounds, see Business and Professions Code § 24200.

§ 25616. False reports; refusal to permit inspection; falsification of records, etc.; punishment

Any person who knowingly or willfully files a false license fee report with the department, and any person who refuses to permit the department or any of its representatives to make any inspection or examination for which provision is made in this division, or who fails to keep books of account as prescribed by the department, or who fails to preserve such books for the inspection of the department for such time as the department deems necessary, or who alters, cancels, or obliterates entries in such books of account for the purpose of falsifying the records of sales of alcoholic beverages made under this division is guilty of a misdemeanor and shall be punished by a fine of not less than two hundred dollars ($200) nor more than one thousand dollars ($1,000), or by imprisonment in the county jail for not less than one month nor more than six months, or by both such fine and imprisonment. *(Added by Stats.1953, c. 152, p. 1023, § 1. Amended by Stats.1955, c. 447, p. 926, § 134; Stats.1955, c. 1842, p. 3412, § 17; Stats.1983, c. 1092, § 60, eff. Sept. 27, 1983, operative Jan. 1, 1984.)*

Cross References

Alcoholic Beverage Tax Law, in general, see Revenue and Taxation Code § 32001 et seq.

Failure to make reports concerning license fees, see Business and Professions Code § 23328.

Fees for licensees, see Business and Professions Code § 23320.

Inspection of premises and examination of books, see Business and Professions Code § 25753.

Limitations as to time of filing accusations, see Business and Professions Code §§ 24207, 24208.

Suspension or revocation of licenses, grounds, see Business and Professions Code § 24200.

§ 25617. Offense and punishment not otherwise specified

Every person convicted for a violation of any of the provisions of this division for which another penalty or punishment is not specifically provided for in this division is guilty of a misdemeanor and shall be punished by a fine of not more than one thousand dollars ($1,000) or by imprisonment in the county jail for not more than six months, or by both such fine and imprisonment. *(Added by Stats.1953, c. 152, p. 1023, § 1. Amended by Stats.1983, c. 1092, § 61, eff. Sept. 27, 1983, operative Jan. 1, 1984.)*

Cross References

Wine direct shipper permits, enforcement, see Business and Professions Code § 23661.3.

Research References

2 Witkin, California Criminal Law 4th Crimes Against Public Peace and Welfare § 361 (2021), In General.

1 Witkin California Criminal Law 4th Introduction to Crimes § 5 (2021), Necessity of Punishment.

3 Witkin, California Criminal Law 4th Punishment § 306 (2021), Where Punishment is Not Specified.

§ 25618. Punishment for felony not otherwise specified

Every person convicted of a felony for a violation of any of the provisions of this division for which another punishment is not specifically provided for in this division shall be punished by a fine of not more than ten thousand dollars ($10,000), imprisonment in a county jail for not more than one year, imprisonment pursuant to subdivision (h) of Section 1170 of the Penal Code, or by both that fine and imprisonment. *(Added by Stats.1953, c. 152, p. 1023, § 1. Amended by Stats.1983, c. 1092, § 62, eff. Sept. 27, 1983, operative Jan. 1, 1984; Stats.2006, c. 347 (A.B.2367), § 1; Stats.2011, c. 15 (A.B.109), § 30, eff. April 4, 2011, operative Oct. 1, 2011.)*

Research References

2 Witkin, California Criminal Law 4th Crimes Against Public Peace and Welfare § 361 (2021), In General.

§ 25619. Enforcement duties; nonenforcement as offense

Every peace officer and every district attorney in this State shall enforce the provisions of this division and shall inform against and diligently prosecute persons whom they have reasonable cause to believe offenders against the provisions of this division. Every such officer refusing or neglecting to do so is guilty of a misdemeanor. *(Added by Stats.1953, c. 152, p. 1023, § 1.)*

Cross References

Peace officers specified, see Penal Code § 830 et seq.
Seizure of property as evidence, see Business and Professions Code § 25373.

§ 25620. Possession of open containers; local ordinances; exceptions

(a) Any person possessing any can, bottle, or other receptacle containing any alcoholic beverage that has been opened, or a seal broken, or the contents of which have been partially removed, in any city, county, or city and county owned park or other city, county, or city and county owned public place, or any recreation and park district, or any regional park or open-space district shall be guilty of an infraction if the city, county, or city and county has enacted an ordinance that prohibits the possession of those containers in those areas or the consumption of alcoholic beverages in those areas.

(b) This section does not apply where the possession is within premises located in a park or other public place for which a license has been issued pursuant to this division.

(c) This section does not apply when an individual is in possession of an alcoholic beverage container for the purpose of recycling or other related activity. *(Added by Stats.1980, c. 255, p. 529, § 1, eff. June 28, 1980. Amended by Stats.2000, c. 381 (A.B.2187), § 1.)*

§ 25621. Punishment for purchase, sale, or possession of vaporized alcohol or alcohol vaporizing device

(a) No person shall purchase, offer for sale, or use any vaporized form of alcohol produced by an alcohol vaporizing device.

(b) For purposes of this section, "alcohol vaporizing device" means any device, machine, or process that mixes spirits, liquor, or other alcohol product with pure oxygen or other gas to produce a vaporized product for the purpose of consumption by inhalation.

(c)(1) Any person who sells or offers for sale any vaporized form of alcohol produced by an alcohol vaporizing device is guilty of a misdemeanor that shall be punishable by a fine of not more than one thousand dollars ($1,000) or by imprisonment in the county jail for not more than six months, or by both.

(2) Any person who purchases or uses any vaporized form of alcohol produced by an alcohol vaporizing device is subject to a fine of two hundred fifty dollars ($250).

(d) Any person who possesses, sells, or offers for sale any alcohol vaporizing device shall be guilty of a misdemeanor. *(Added by Stats.2006, c. 29 (A.B.273), § 1.)*

Research References

2 Witkin, California Criminal Law 4th Crimes Against Public Peace and Welfare § 363 (2021), Time, Place, and Manner of Sale.

§ 25621.5. Prohibition against sale of cannabis, cannabis product, or alcoholic beverage containing cannabis by alcoholic beverage licensee; disciplinary action

(a) A licensee shall not, at its licensed premises, sell, offer, or provide cannabis or cannabis products, as defined in Section 26001, including an alcoholic beverage that contains cannabis or a cannabis product, and no alcoholic beverage shall be manufactured, sold, or offered for sale if it contains tetrahydrocannabinol or cannabinoids, regardless of source.

(b) The department shall take disciplinary action against a licensee that violates this section, including, but not limited to, suspension or revocation of the license. *(Added by Stats.2018, c. 827 (A.B.2914), § 1, eff. Jan. 1, 2019.)*

Research References

2 Witkin, California Criminal Law 4th Crimes Against Public Peace and Welfare § 363 (2021), Time, Place, and Manner of Sale.

§ 25622. Beer in which caffeine has been directly added; prohibitions; enforcement authority; confidential and proprietary information

(a) Beer to which caffeine has been directly added as a separate ingredient shall not be imported into this state, produced, manufactured, or distributed within this state, or sold by a licensed retailer within this state.

(b) The department may require licensees to submit product formulas as it determines to be necessary to implement and enforce this section. Any information required to be provided by any licensee to the department pursuant to this section shall be considered confidential and corporate proprietary information. This information shall not be subject to disclosure under the California Public Records Act (Division 10 (commencing with Section 7920.000) of Title 1 of the Government Code). *(Added by Stats.2011, c. 140 (S.B.39), § 1. Amended by Stats.2020, c. 370 (S.B.1371), § 19, eff. Jan. 1, 2021; Stats.2021, c. 615 (A.B.474), § 39, eff. Jan. 1, 2022, operative Jan. 1, 2023.)*

Law Revision Commission Comments

Section 25622 is amended to reflect nonsubstantive recodification of the California Public Records Act. See California Public Records Act Clean-Up, 46 Cal. L. Revision Comm'n Reports 207 (2019). [48 Cal.L.Rev.Comm. Reports __ (2021) [2021-22 AR Appx. 6]].

Research References

2 Witkin, California Criminal Law 4th Crimes Against Public Peace and Welfare § 363 (2021), Time, Place, and Manner of Sale.

§ 25623. Prohibition against possession, purchase, sale, offer for sale, manufacture, distribution, or use of powdered alcohol; violation and penalty

(a) A person shall not possess, purchase, sell, offer for sale, manufacture, distribute, or use powdered alcohol.

(b) Any person who sells, offers for sale, manufactures, or distributes powdered alcohol is guilty of an infraction that shall be punishable by a fine of not more than five hundred dollars ($500). *(Added by Stats.2016, c. 778 (S.B.819), § 5, eff. Jan. 1, 2017.)*

Research References

2 Witkin, California Criminal Law 4th Crimes Against Public Peace and Welfare § 363 (2021), Time, Place, and Manner of Sale.

§ 25623.5. Possession, purchase, sale, manufacture, distribution, or use of powdered alcohol; penalty

(a) A person shall not possess, purchase, sell, offer for sale, manufacture, distribute, or use powdered alcohol.

(b) Any person who purchases, possesses, or uses powdered alcohol is guilty of an infraction and subject to a fine of one hundred twenty-five dollars ($125). *(Added by Stats.2016, c. 742 (A.B.1554), § 5, eff. Jan. 1, 2017.)*

Research References

2 Witkin, California Criminal Law 4th Crimes Against Public Peace and Welfare § 363 (2021), Time, Place, and Manner of Sale.

ARTICLE 3. WOMEN AND MINORS

§ 25657. Employment of persons to procure or encourage purchase or sale of drinks; persons begging or soliciting drinks

It is unlawful:

(a) For any person to employ, upon any licensed on-sale premises, any person for the purpose of procuring or encouraging the purchase or sale of alcoholic beverages, or to pay any such person a percentage or commission on the sale of alcoholic beverages for procuring or encouraging the purchase or sale of alcoholic beverages on such premises.

(b) In any place of business where alcoholic beverages are sold to be consumed upon the premises, to employ or knowingly permit anyone to loiter in or about said premises for the purpose of begging or soliciting any patron or customer of, or visitor in, such premises to purchase any alcoholic beverages for the one begging or soliciting.

Every person who violates the provisions of this section is guilty of a misdemeanor. *(Added by Stats.1953, c. 152, p. 1024, § 1. Amended by Stats.1953, c. 1591, p. 3272, § 3; Stats.1971, c. 151, p. 203, § 1.)*

Cross References

Grounds for revocation or suspension of license, see Business and Professions Code § 24200.

Limitations as to time of filing accusations, see Business and Professions Code §§ 24207, 24208.

Punishment for misdemeanor, see Business and Professions Code § 25617.

Research References

2 Witkin, California Criminal Law 4th Crimes Against Public Peace and Welfare § 363 (2021), Time, Place, and Manner of Sale.

§ 25658. Providing alcoholic beverages to persons under 21 years of age; prohibition; criminal punishment; law enforcement decoys; additional punishment

(a) Except as otherwise provided in subdivision (c), every person who sells, furnishes, gives, or causes to be sold, furnished, or given away any alcoholic beverage to any person under 21 years of age is guilty of a misdemeanor.

(b) Except as provided in Section 25667 or 25668, any person under 21 years of age who purchases any alcoholic beverage, or any person under 21 years of age who consumes any alcoholic beverage in any on-sale premises, is guilty of a misdemeanor.

(c) Any person who violates subdivision (a) by purchasing any alcoholic beverage for, or furnishing, giving, or giving away any alcoholic beverage to, a person under 21 years of age, and the person under 21 years of age thereafter consumes the alcohol and thereby proximately causes great bodily injury or death to themselves or any other person, is guilty of a misdemeanor.

(d) Any on-sale licensee who knowingly permits a person under 21 years of age to consume any alcoholic beverage in the on-sale premises, whether or not the licensee has knowledge that the person is under 21 years of age, is guilty of a misdemeanor.

(e)(1) Except as otherwise provided in paragraph (2) or (3), or Section 25667 or 25668, any person who violates this section shall be punished by a fine of two hundred fifty dollars ($250), no part of which shall be suspended, or the person shall be required to perform not less than 24 hours or more than 32 hours of community service during hours when the person is not employed and is not attending school, or a combination of a fine and community service as determined by the court. A second or subsequent violation of subdivision (b), where prosecution of the previous violation was not barred pursuant to Section 25667 or 25668, shall be punished by a fine of not more than five hundred dollars ($500), or the person shall be required to perform not less than 36 hours or more than 48 hours of community service during hours when the person is not employed and is not attending school, or a combination of a fine and community service as determined by the court. It is the intent of the Legislature that the community service requirements prescribed in this section require service at an alcohol or drug treatment program or facility or at a county coroner's office, if available, in the area where the violation occurred or where the person resides.

(2) Except as provided in paragraph (3), any person who violates subdivision (a) by furnishing an alcoholic beverage, or causing an alcoholic beverage to be furnished, to a minor shall be punished by a fine of one thousand dollars ($1,000), no part of which shall be suspended, and the person shall be required to perform not less than 24 hours of community service during hours when the person is not employed and is not attending school.

(3) Any person who violates subdivision (c) shall be punished by imprisonment in a county jail for a minimum term of six months not to exceed one year, by a fine of one thousand dollars ($1,000), or by both imprisonment and fine.

(f) Persons under 21 years of age may be used by peace officers in the enforcement of this section to apprehend licensees, or employees or agents of licensees, or other persons who sell or furnish alcoholic beverages to minors. Notwithstanding subdivision (b), any person under 21 years of age who purchases or attempts to purchase any alcoholic beverage while under the direction of a peace officer is immune from prosecution for that purchase or attempt to purchase an alcoholic beverage. Guidelines with respect to the use of persons under 21 years of age as decoys shall be adopted and published by the department in accordance with the rulemaking portion of the Administrative Procedure Act (Chapter 3.5 (commencing with Section 11340) of Part 1 of Division 3 of Title 2 of the Government Code). Law enforcement-initiated minor decoy programs in operation prior to the effective date of regulatory guidelines adopted by the department shall be authorized as long as the minor decoy displays to the seller of alcoholic beverages the appearance of a person under 21 years of age. This subdivision shall not be construed to prevent the department from taking disciplinary action against a licensee who sells alcoholic beverages to a minor decoy prior to the department's final adoption of regulatory guidelines. After the completion of every minor decoy program performed under this subdivision, the law enforcement agency using the decoy shall notify licensees within 72 hours of the results of the program. When the use of a minor decoy results in the issuance of a citation, the notification required shall be given to licensees and the department within 72 hours of the issuance of the citation. A law enforcement agency may comply with this requirement by leaving a written notice at the licensed premises addressed to the licensee, or by mailing a notice addressed to the licensee.

(g) The penalties imposed by this section do not preclude prosecution or the imposition of penalties under any other provision of law, including, but not limited to, Section 272 of the Penal Code.
(Added by Stats.1953, c. 152, p. 1025, § 1. Amended by Stats.1957, c. 2152, p. 3810, § 1; Stats.1959, c. 866, p. 2901, § 1; Stats.1983, c. 1092, § 63, eff. Sept. 27, 1983, operative Jan. 1, 1984; Stats.1984, c. 403, § 1; Stats.1990, c. 695 (A.B.3448), § 2; Stats.1994, c. 1205 (A.B.3805), § 1, eff. Sept. 30, 1994; Stats.1997, c. 357 (S.B.805), § 1; Stats.1998, c. 441 (A.B.1204), § 1; Stats.1998, c. 565 (S.B.1696), § 1.5; Stats.1999, c. 786 (S.B.340), § 1; Stats.1999, c. 787 (A.B.749), § 3; Stats.2004, c. 291 (A.B.2037), § 1; Stats.2005, c. 22 (S.B.1108), § 10; Stats.2007, c. 743 (A.B.1658), § 1; Stats.2007, c. 744 (A.B. 1739), § 4.5; Stats.2010, c. 245 (A.B.1999), § 1; Stats.2011, c. 296 (A.B.1023), § 31; Stats.2014, c. 162 (A.B.1989), § 1, eff. Jan. 1, 2015; Stats.2019, c. 505 (S.B.485), § 1, eff. Jan. 1, 2020.)

Cross References

Alcohol sold or furnished to intoxicated person, violations, punishment, see Business and Professions Code § 25602.
Criminal offenses,
  Allowing minor under eighteen to gamble in drinking place, see Penal Code § 336.
  Sending minor under eighteen years of age into saloon, see Penal Code § 273f.
Grounds for suspension or revocation, see Business and Professions Code § 24200.
Limitation as to time of filing accusations, see Business and Professions Code §§ 24206, 24208.
Majority and identity, evidence, see Business and Professions Code § 25660.
Punishment for misdemeanor, see Business and Professions Code § 25617.
Special on-sale general license to facility partially located in County of Placer and County of Washoe, facility requirements, special provisions, see Business and Professions Code § 23399.52.
Stay of suspension, petition to make offer of compromise for retail and nonretail licensees, grounds for stay, see Business and Professions Code § 23095.

Research References

California Jury Instructions - Criminal 16.010, Selling Liquor to Person Under 21.
California Jury Instructions - Criminal 16.011, Purchase or Consumption of Liquor by Minor.
California Jury Instructions - Criminal 16.012, Reliance on Proof of Majority.
California Jury Instructions - Criminal 16.013, Purchase of Liquor for Minor, Resulting in Great Bodily Injury.
California Jury Instructions - Criminal 16.013.1, Mistake of Fact as to Age.
California Jury Instructions-Civil, 8th Edition 4.50, Selling Liquor to an Obviously Intoxicated Minor—Essential Elements.
2 Witkin, California Criminal Law 4th Crimes Against Public Peace and Welfare § 362 (2021), Furnishing Liquor to Specified Persons.
2 Witkin, California Criminal Law 4th Crimes Against Public Peace and Welfare § 364 (2021), Furnishing Liquor to Minors.
2 Witkin, California Criminal Law 4th Crimes Against Public Peace and Welfare § 365 (2021), Purchase of Liquor by Minors.
2 Witkin, California Criminal Law 4th Crimes Against Public Peace and Welfare § 366 (2021), Evidence of Age.
2 Witkin, California Criminal Law 4th Crimes Against Public Peace and Welfare § 367 (2021), Employing Minors in Liquor Business.
2 Witkin, California Criminal Law 4th Crimes Against Public Peace and Welfare § 368 (2021), Use of Minors in Enforcement of Liquor Laws.
1 Witkin California Criminal Law 4th Defenses § 47 (2021), Mistake Negating Criminal Intent or Knowledge.
1 Witkin California Criminal Law 4th Defenses § 111 (2021), Illustrations of Defense Rejected.
1 Witkin California Criminal Law 4th Elements § 18 (2021), Public Welfare Offenses.
1 Witkin California Criminal Law 4th Introduction to Crimes § 90 (2021), Misdemeanor-Infraction.

§ 25658.1. Petition for offer in compromise for third or subsequent violation; revocation of license for third violation; determination of penalty

(a) Notwithstanding any other provision of this division, no licensee may petition the department for an offer in compromise pursuant to Section 23095 for a third or any subsequent violation of Section 25658 that occurs within 36 months of the initial violation.

(b) Notwithstanding Section 24200, the department may revoke a license for a third violation of Section 25658 that occurs within any 36–month period. This provision shall not be construed to limit the department's authority and discretion to revoke a license prior to a third violation when the circumstances warrant that penalty.

(c) For purposes of this section, no violation may be considered for purposes of determination of the penalty until it has become final.
(Added by Stats.1994, c. 627 (A.B.463), § 7. Amended by Stats.1999, c. 786 (S.B.340), § 2; Stats.2004, c. 227 (S.B.1102), § 8, eff. Aug. 16, 2004.)

§ 25658.2. Parent or legal guardian who knowingly permits his or her child or person in company of child to consume alcoholic beverage or use controlled substance at his or her home

(a) A parent or legal guardian who knowingly permits his or her child, or a person in the company of the child, or both, who are under the age of 18 years, to consume an alcoholic beverage or use a controlled substance at the home of the parent or legal guardian is guilty of misdemeanor if all of the following occur:

(1) As the result of the consumption of an alcoholic beverage or use of a controlled substance at the home of the parent or legal guardian, the child or other underage person has a blood-alcohol concentration of 0.05 percent or greater, as measured by a chemical test, or is under the influence of a controlled substance.

(2) The parent knowingly permits that child or other underage person, after leaving the parent's or legal guardian's home, to drive a vehicle.

(3) That child or underage person is found to have caused a traffic collision while driving the vehicle.

(b) A person who violates subdivision (a) shall be punished by imprisonment in a county jail for a term not to exceed one year, by a fine not exceeding one thousand dollars ($1,000), or by both imprisonment and fine. *(Added by Stats.2003, c. 625 (A.B.1301), § 1.)*

Cross References

Misdemeanor, definition, penalties, see Penal Code §§ 17, 19 and 19.2.

Research References

California Jury Instructions - Criminal 16.016, Parent/Guardian Knowingly Permitting Minor's Use or Consumption of Alcohol or Controlled Substance in the Home.

2 Witkin, California Criminal Law 4th Crimes Against Public Peace and Welfare § 369 (2021), Consumption of Alcohol or Drugs by Minor Who Later Causes Traffic Collision.

§ 25658.4. Off sale of alcoholic beverages requiring executed sworn application and acknowledgment; form and contents; notice; adoption of rules and fees

(a) No clerk shall make an off sale of alcoholic beverages unless the clerk executes under penalty of perjury on the first day of that sale an application and acknowledgment. The application and acknowledgment shall be in a form understandable to the clerk.

(1) The department shall specify the form of the application and acknowledgment, which shall include at a minimum a summary of this division pertaining to the following:

(A) The prohibitions contained in Sections 25658 and 25658.5 pertaining to the sale to, and purchase of, alcoholic beverages by persons under 21 years of age.

(B) Bona fide evidence of majority as provided in Section 25660.

(C) Hours of operation as provided in Article 2 (commencing with Section 25631).

(D) The prohibitions contained in subdivision (a) of Section 25602 and Section 25602.1 pertaining to sales to an intoxicated person.

(E) Sections 23393 and 23394 as they pertain to on-premises consumption of alcoholic beverages in an off-sale premises.

(F) The requirements and prohibitions contained in Section 25659.5 pertaining to sales of keg beer for consumption off licensed premises.

(2) The application and acknowledgment shall also include a statement that the clerk has read and understands the summary, a statement that the clerk has never been convicted of violating this division or, if convicted, an explanation of the circumstances of each conviction, and a statement that the application and acknowledgment is executed under penalty of perjury.

(3) The licensee shall keep the executed application and acknowledgment on the premises at all times and available for inspection by the department. A licensee with more than one licensed off-sale premises in the state may comply with this subdivision by maintaining an executed application and acknowledgment at a designated licensed premises, regional office, or headquarters office in the state. An executed application and acknowledgment maintained at the designated locations shall be valid for all licensed off-sale premises owned by the licensee. Any licensee maintaining an application and acknowledgment at a designated site other than the individual licensed off-sale premises shall notify the department in advance and in writing of the site where the application and acknowledgment shall be maintained and available for inspection. A licensee electing to maintain an application and acknowledgments at a designated site other than the licensed premises shall maintain at each licensed premises a notice of where the executed application and acknowledgments are located. Any licensee with more than one licensed off-sale premises who elects to maintain the application and acknowledgments at a designated site other than each licensed premises shall provide the department, upon written demand, a copy of any employee's executed application and acknowledgment within 10 business days. A violation of this subdivision by a licensee constitutes grounds for discipline by the department.

(b) The licensee shall post a notice that contains and describes, in concise terms, prohibited sales of alcoholic beverages, a statement that the off-sale seller will refuse to make a sale if the seller reasonably suspects that the Alcoholic Beverage Control Act may be violated. The notice shall be posted at an entrance or at a point of sale in the licensed premises or in any other location that is visible to purchasers of alcoholic beverages and to the off-sale seller.

(c) A retail licensee shall post a notice that contains and describes, in concise terms, the fines and penalties for any violation of Section 25658, relating to the sale of alcoholic beverages to, or the purchase of alcoholic beverages by, any person under 21 years of age.

(d) Nonprofit organizations or licensees may obtain video recordings and other training materials from the department on the Licensee Education on Alcohol and Drugs (LEAD) program. The video recordings and training materials may be updated periodically and may be provided in English and other languages, and when made available by the department, shall be provided at cost.

(e) As used in this section:

(1) "Off–sale seller" means any person holding a retail off-sale license issued by the department and any person employed by that licensee who in the course of that employment sells alcoholic beverages.

(2) "Clerk" means an off-sale seller who is not a licensee.

(f) The department may adopt rules and appropriate fees for licensees that it determines necessary for the administration of this section. *(Added by Stats.1991, c. 726 (A.B.1784), § 4. Amended by Stats.1997, c. 357 (S.B.805), § 2; Stats.1997, c. 774 (A.B.1082), § 3.5; Stats.1999, c. 786 (S.B.340), § 3; Stats.2009, c. 88 (A.B.176), § 11; Stats.2010, c. 328 (S.B.1330), § 27; Stats.2019, c. 505 (S.B.485), § 2, eff. Jan. 1, 2020.)*

Law Revision Commission Comments

Subdivision (a)(1)(C) of Section 25658.4 is amended to correct a cross-reference. Former Section 25630, the first section of Article 2 of Chapter 16, was repealed by 1969 Cal. Stat. ch. 614, § 1.

Subdivision (d) is amended to reflect advances in recording technology and for consistency of terminology. For a similar reform, see 2002 Cal. Stat. ch. 1068 (replacing numerous references to "audiotape" in Civil Discovery Act with either "audio technology," "audio recording," or "audio record," as context required). [37 Cal. L. Revision Comm'n Reports 211 (2007)].

§ 25658.5. Minors; attempts to purchase; punishment

(a) Any person under 21 years of age who attempts to purchase any alcoholic beverage from a licensee, or the licensee's agent or employee, is guilty of an infraction and shall be punished by a fine of not more than two hundred fifty dollars ($250), or the person shall be required to perform not less than 24 hours or more than 32 hours of community service during hours when the person is not employed or is not attending school, or a combination of fine and community service as determined by the court. A second or subsequent violation of this section shall be punished by a fine of not more than five hundred dollars ($500), or the person shall be required to perform not less than 36 hours or more than 48 hours of community service during hours when the person is not employed or is not attending school, or a combination of fine and community service, as the court deems just. It is the intent of the Legislature that the community service requirements prescribed in this section require service at an alcohol or drug treatment program or facility or at a county coroner's office, if available, in the area where the violation occurred or where the person resides.

(b) The penalties imposed by this section do not preclude prosecution or the imposition of penalties under any other provision of law. *(Added by Stats.1987, c. 583, § 1. Amended by Stats.1999, c. 787 (A.B.749), § 4; Stats.2007, c. 743 (A.B.1658), § 2; Stats.2019, c. 505 (S.B.485), § 3, eff. Jan. 1, 2020.)*

Research References

2 Witkin, California Criminal Law 4th Crimes Against Public Peace and Welfare § 365 (2021), Purchase of Liquor by Minors.
1 Witkin California Criminal Law 4th Introduction to Crimes § 90 (2021), Misdemeanor-Infraction.

§ 25659. Proof of age; authority to require

For the purpose of preventing the violation of Section 25658, any licensee, or his or her agent or employee, may refuse to sell or serve alcoholic beverages to any person who is unable to produce adequate written evidence that he or she is over the age of 21 years. A licensee, or his or her agent or employee, may seize any identification presented by a person that shows the person to be under the age of 21 years or that is false, so long as a receipt is given to the person from whom the identification is seized and the seized identification is given within 24 hours of seizure to the local law enforcement agency that has jurisdiction over the licensed premises. A licensee, his or her agent or employees decision to not seize a license shall not create any civil or criminal liability. *(Added by Stats.1953, c. 152, p. 1025, § 1. Amended by Stats.1998, c. 565 (S.B.1696), § 2.)*

Cross References

Controlled access alcoholic beverage cabinet in hotel or motel, use, see Business and Professions Code § 23355.2.

Research References

2 Witkin, California Criminal Law 4th Crimes Against Public Peace and Welfare § 366 (2021), Evidence of Age.

§ 25659.5. Keg beer identification tag; placement on sale; signature on receipt; violations; misdemeanor; fees to state; disposition

(a) Retail licensees selling keg beer for consumption off licensed premises shall place an identification tag on all kegs of beer at the time of sale and shall require the signing of a receipt for the keg of beer by the purchaser in order to allow kegs to be traced if the contents are used in violation of this article. The keg identification shall be in the form of a numbered label prescribed and supplied by the department that identifies the seller. The receipt shall be on a form prescribed and supplied by the department and shall include the name and address of the purchaser and the purchaser's driver's license number or equivalent form of identification number. A retailer shall not return any deposit upon the return of any keg that does not have the identification label required pursuant to subdivision (a).

(b) Any licensee selling keg beer for off premise consumption who fails to require the signing of a receipt at the time of sale and fails to place a numbered identification label on the keg shall be subject to disciplinary action pursuant to this division. The licensee shall retain a copy of the receipt, which shall be retained on the licensed premise for a period of six months. The receipt records shall be available for inspection and copying by the department or other authorized law enforcement agency.

(c) Possession of a keg containing beer with knowledge that the keg is not identified as required by subdivision (a) is a misdemeanor.

(d) Any purchaser of keg beer who knowingly provides false information as required by subdivision (a) is guilty of a misdemeanor.

(e) The identification label required pursuant to subdivision (a) shall be constructed of material and made attachable in such a manner as to make the label easily removable for the purpose of cleaning and reusing the keg by a beer manufacturer.

(f) The department is authorized to charge fees for supplying receipt forms and identification labels pursuant to subdivision (a). The fees for receipt forms and identification labels shall be ten dollars ($10) and twenty-five dollars ($25), respectively, and may be adjusted by the department pursuant to subdivisions (d) and (e) of Section 23320. Fees collected pursuant to this subdivision shall be deposited in the Alcohol Beverage Control Fund.

(g) As used in this section, "keg" means any brewery-sealed, individual container of beer having a liquid capacity of six gallons or more. *(Added by Stats.1993, c. 270 (A.B.8), § 1. Amended by Stats.2019, c. 29 (S.B.82), § 71, eff. June 27, 2019.)*

Research References

2 Witkin, California Criminal Law 4th Crimes Against Public Peace and Welfare § 363 (2021), Time, Place, and Manner of Sale.

§ 25660. Bona fide evidence of majority and identity; defense to criminal prosecutions

(a) Bona fide evidence of majority and identity of the person is any of the following:

(1) A document issued by a federal, state, county, or municipal government, or subdivision or agency thereof, including, but not limited to, a valid motor vehicle operator's license, that contains the name, date of birth, description, and picture of the person.

(2) A valid passport issued by the United States or by a foreign government.

(3) A valid identification card issued to a member of the Armed Forces that includes a date of birth and a picture of the person.

(b) Proof that the defendant-licensee, or his or her employee or agent, demanded, was shown, and acted in reliance upon bona fide evidence in any transaction, employment, use, or permission forbidden by Section 25658, 25663, or 25665 shall be a defense to any criminal prosecution therefor or to any proceedings for the suspension or revocation of any license based thereon. *(Added by Stats.1953, c. 152, p. 1025, § 1. Amended by Stats.1955, c. 627, p. 1127, § 1; Stats.1959, c. 550, p. 2512, § 1; Stats.1987, c. 67, § 1; Stats.2005, c. 68 (A.B.764), § 1; Stats.2006, c. 538 (S.B.1852), § 35; Stats.2009, c. 142 (A.B.1191), § 2; Stats.2009, c. 405 (A.B.59), § 1.5; Stats.2010, c. 165 (A.B.1896), § 1.)*

Research References

California Jury Instructions - Criminal 16.012, Reliance on Proof of Majority.
2 Witkin, California Criminal Law 4th Crimes Against Public Peace and Welfare § 364 (2021), Furnishing Liquor to Minors.
2 Witkin, California Criminal Law 4th Crimes Against Public Peace and Welfare § 366 (2021), Evidence of Age.

§ 25660.5. Minors; selling or furnishing false evidence of majority and identity to

Any person who sells, gives, or furnishes to any person under the age of 21 years any false or fraudulent written, printed, or photostatic evidence of the majority and identity of such person or who sells, gives or furnishes to any person under the age of 21 years evidence of majority and identification of any other person is guilty of a misdemeanor. *(Added by Stats.1957, c. 1274, p. 2575, § 1. Amended by Stats.1965, c. 1216, p. 3035, § 1.)*

Cross References

Punishment for misdemeanor, see Business and Professions Code § 25617.

Research References

2 Witkin, California Criminal Law 4th Crimes Against Public Peace and Welfare § 366 (2021), Evidence of Age.

§ 25661. False evidence of age and identity; use; possession

(a) Any person under 21 years of age who presents or offers to any licensee, or agent or employee of a licensee, any written, printed, or photostatic evidence of age and identity which is false, fraudulent or not actually their own for the purpose of ordering, purchasing, attempting to purchase or otherwise procuring or attempting to procure, the serving of any alcoholic beverage, or who possesses any false or fraudulent written, printed, or photostatic evidence of age and identity, is guilty of a misdemeanor and shall be punished by a fine of at least two hundred fifty dollars ($250), no part of which shall be suspended; or the person shall be required to perform not less than 24 hours nor more than 32 hours of community service during hours when the person is not employed and is not attending school, or a combination of fine and community service as determined by the court. A second or subsequent violation of this section shall be punished by a fine of not more than five hundred dollars ($500), or the person shall be required to perform not less than 36 hours or more than 48 hours of community service during hours when the person is not employed or is not attending school, or a combination of fine and community service, as the court deems just. It is the intent of the Legislature that the community service requirements prescribed in this section require service at an alcohol or drug treatment program or facility or at a county coroner's office, if available, in the area where the violation occurred or where the person resides.

(b) The penalties imposed by this section do not preclude prosecution or the imposition of penalties under any other provision of law. *(Added by Stats.1953, c. 152, p. 1025, § 1. Amended by Stats.1957, c. 1274, p. 2576, § 2; Stats.1959, c. 868, p. 2902, § 1; Stats.1983, c. 1092, § 64, eff. Sept. 27, 1983, operative Jan. 1, 1984; Stats.1989, c. 110, § 1; Stats.1999, c. 787 (A.B.749), § 5; Stats.2007, c. 743 (A.B.1658), § 3; Stats.2019, c. 505 (S.B.485), § 4, eff. Jan. 1, 2020.)*

Cross References

Punishment for misdemeanor, see Business and Professions Code § 25617.

Research References

2 Witkin, California Criminal Law 4th Crimes Against Public Peace and Welfare § 365 (2021), Purchase of Liquor by Minors.
1 Witkin California Criminal Law 4th Introduction to Crimes § 90 (2021), Misdemeanor-Infraction.

§ 25662. Possession of beverage by minor; authorization of peace officers to seize beverages; disposition of seized beverages

(a) Except as provided in Section 25667 or 25668, any person under 21 years of age who possesses any alcoholic beverage on any street or highway or in any public place or in any place open to the public is guilty of a misdemeanor and shall be punished by a fine of two hundred fifty dollars ($250) or the person shall be required to perform not less than 24 hours or more than 32 hours of community service during hours when the person is not employed or is not attending school. A second or subsequent violation shall be punishable as a misdemeanor and the person shall be fined not more than five hundred dollars ($500), or required to perform not less than 36 hours or more than 48 hours of community service during hours when the person is not employed or is not attending school, or a combination of fine and community service as the court deems just. It is the intent of the Legislature that the community service requirements prescribed in this section require service at an alcohol or drug treatment program or facility or at a county coroner's office, if available, in the area where the violation occurred or where the person resides. This section does not apply to possession by a person under 21 years of age making a delivery of an alcoholic beverage in pursuance of the order of a parent, responsible adult relative, or any other adult designated by the parent or legal guardian, or in pursuance of employment. That person shall have a complete defense if they were following, in a timely manner, the reasonable instructions of a parent, legal guardian, responsible adult relative, or adult designee relating to disposition of the alcoholic beverage.

(b) Unless otherwise provided by law, where a peace officer has lawfully entered the premises, the peace officer may seize any alcoholic beverage in plain view that is in the possession of, or provided to, a person under 21 years of age at social gatherings, when those gatherings are open to the public, 10 or more persons under 21 years of age are participating, persons under 21 years of age are consuming alcoholic beverages, and there is no supervision of the social gathering by a parent or guardian of one or more of the participants.

Where a peace officer has seized alcoholic beverages pursuant to this subdivision, the officer may destroy any alcoholic beverage contained in an opened container and in the possession of, or provided to, a person under 21 years of age, and, with respect to alcoholic beverages in unopened containers, the officer shall impound those beverages for a period not to exceed seven working days pending a request for the release of those beverages by a person 21 years of age or older who is the lawful owner or resident of the property upon which the alcoholic beverages were seized. If no one requests release of the seized alcoholic beverages within that period, those beverages may be destroyed.

(c) The penalties imposed by this section do not preclude prosecution or the imposition of penalties under any other provision of law. *(Added by Stats.1953, c. 152, p. 1025, § 1. Amended by Stats.1963, c. 396, p. 1203, § 1; Stats.1988, c. 680, § 1; Stats.1990, c. 1697 (S.B.2635), § 1; Stats.1996, c. 124 (A.B.3470), § 6; Stats.1997, c. 17 (S.B.947), § 13; Stats.1999, c. 787 (A.B.749), § 6; Stats.2007, c. 743 (A.B.1658), § 4; Stats.2010, c. 245 (A.B.1999), § 2; Stats.2014, c. 162 (A.B.1989), § 2, eff. Jan. 1, 2015; Stats.2019, c. 505 (S.B.485), § 5, eff. Jan. 1, 2020.)*

Cross References

Possession of alcoholic beverage in vehicle, persons under twenty-one, see Vehicle Code § 23224.
Punishment for misdemeanor, see Business and Professions Code § 25617.

Research References

California Jury Instructions - Criminal 16.020, Possession of Liquor by Minor.
2 Witkin, California Criminal Law 4th Crimes Against Public Peace and Welfare § 365 (2021), Purchase of Liquor by Minors.
1 Witkin California Criminal Law 4th Introduction to Crimes § 90 (2021), Misdemeanor-Infraction.

§ 25663. Employment of minor; on-sale and off-sale premises; sanctions

(a) Except as provided in subdivision (c), no licensee that sells or serves alcoholic beverages for consumption on the premises shall employ any person under 21 years of age for the purpose of preparing or serving alcoholic beverages. Every person who employs or uses the services of any person under the age of 21 years in or on that portion of any premises, during business hours, which are primarily designed and used for the sale and service of alcoholic beverages for consumption on the premises is guilty of a misdemeanor.

(b) Any off-sale licensee who employs or uses the services of any person under the age of 18 years for the sale of alcoholic beverages shall be subject to suspension or revocation of his or her license, except that a person under the age of 18 years may be employed or used for those purposes if that person is under the continuous supervision of a person 21 years of age or older.

(c) Any person between 18 and 21 years of age employed in any bona fide public eating place, as defined in Sections 23038 and 23038.1, which is licensed for the on-sale of alcoholic beverages, may serve alcoholic beverages to consumers only under the following circumstances: such service occurs in an area primarily designed and used for the sale and service of food for consumption on the premises; and the primary duties of the employee shall be the service of meals to guests, with the service of alcoholic beverages being incidental to such duties. For purposes of this subdivision, "serve" or "service" includes the delivery, presentation, opening, or pouring of an alcoholic beverage. *(Added by Stats.1953, c. 152, p. 1025, § 1. Amended by Stats.1955, c. 1258, p. 2291, § 1; Stats.1959, c. 543, p. 2509, § 1; Stats.1984, c. 770, § 1; Stats.2008, c. 508 (A.B.3071), § 4.)*

Cross References

Limitation as to time of filing accusations, see Business and Professions Code §§ 24206, 24208.
Punishment for misdemeanor, see Business and Professions Code § 25617.

Research References

2 Witkin, California Criminal Law 4th Crimes Against Public Peace and Welfare § 367 (2021), Employing Minors in Liquor Business.

§ 25663.5. Employment of minor in on-sale premises; musicians

Notwithstanding Section 25663 or any other provision of law, persons 18 to 21 years of age may be employed as musicians, for entertainment purposes only, during business hours on premises which are primarily designed and used for the sale and service of alcoholic beverages for consumption on the premises, if live acts, demonstrations, or exhibitions which involve the exposure of the private parts or buttocks of any participant or the breasts of any female participant are not allowed on such premises. However, the area of such employment shall be limited to a portion of the premises that is restricted to the use exclusively of musicians or entertainers in the performance of their functions, and no alcoholic beverages shall be sold, served, consumed, or taken into that area. *(Added by Stats.1971, c. 1761, p. 3810, § 1.)*

Research References

2 Witkin, California Criminal Law 4th Crimes Against Public Peace and Welfare § 367 (2021), Employing Minors in Liquor Business.

§ 25664. Advertisements encouraging minors to drink

(a)(1) The use, in any advertisement of alcoholic beverages, of any subject matter, language, or slogan addressed to and intended to encourage minors to drink the alcoholic beverages, is prohibited.

(2) Signage or flyers advertising an establishment that serves alcoholic beverages to individuals under the age of 21 years are prohibited under paragraph (1) if one of the establishment's principal business activities is the selling of alcoholic beverages, and the advertisement expressly states that the jurisdiction in which the establishment is located has a legal drinking age of under 21 years or that individuals under the age of 21 years may patronize the establishment.

(3) Nothing in this section shall be deemed to restrict or prohibit any advertisement of alcoholic beverages to those persons of legal drinking age.

(b) The department may adopt rules as it determines to be necessary for the administration of this section. *(Added by Stats. 1953, c. 152, p. 1025, § 1. Amended by Stats.1985, c. 803, § 2, operative July 1, 1986; Stats.2003, c. 771 (A.B.1398), § 3.)*

Cross References

False advertising, see Business and Professions Code § 17500 et seq.
Limitation as to time of filing accusations, see Business and Professions Code §§ 24206, 24208.

Research References

2 Witkin, California Criminal Law 4th Crimes Against Public Peace and Welfare § 367 (2021), Employing Minors in Liquor Business.

§ 25665. Minors entering and remaining on premises

Any licensee under an on-sale license issued for public premises, as defined in Section 23039, who permits a person under the age of 21 years to enter and remain in the licensed premises without lawful business therein is guilty of a misdemeanor. Any person under the age of 21 years who enters and remains in the licensed public premises without lawful business therein is guilty of a misdemeanor and shall be punished by a fine of not less than two hundred dollars ($200), no part of which shall be suspended. *(Added by Stats.1955, c. 1779, p. 3287, § 11, operative Jan. 1, 1957. Amended by Stats.1957, c. 2152, p. 3810, § 2; Stats.1959, c. 867, p. 2901, § 1; Stats.1983, c. 1092, § 65, eff. Sept. 27, 1983, operative Jan. 1, 1984.)*

Cross References

Limitation as to time of filing accusations, see Business and Professions Code §§ 24206, 24208.
Punishment for misdemeanor, see Business and Professions Code § 25617.

Research References

2 Witkin, California Criminal Law 4th Crimes Against Public Peace and Welfare § 365 (2021), Purchase of Liquor by Minors.
2 Witkin, California Criminal Law 4th Crimes Against Public Peace and Welfare § 367 (2021), Employing Minors in Liquor Business.

§ 25666. Examination of minor decoy; depositions

(a) In a hearing on an accusation charging a licensee with a violation of Section 25658, the department shall produce the minor decoy alleged in the accusation for examination at the hearing unless the minor decoy is unavailable as a witness because they are dead or unable to attend the hearing because of a then-existing physical or mental illness or infirmity, or unless the licensee has waived, in writing, the appearance of the minor decoy. When a minor decoy is absent because of a then-existing physical or mental illness or infirmity, a reasonable continuance shall be granted to allow for the appearance of the minor decoy if the administrative law judge finds that it is reasonably likely that the minor decoy can be produced within a reasonable amount of time.

(b)(1) Nothing in this section shall prevent the department from taking testimony of the minor decoy as provided in Section 11511 of the Government Code.

(2) This section is not intended to preclude the continuance of a hearing because of the unavailability of a minor decoy for any other reason pursuant to Section 11524 of the Government Code.

(c) For purposes of this section, "minor decoy" means a person under 21 years of age used by peace officers in the enforcement of Section 25658 to apprehend licensees, or employees or agents of licensees, or other persons who sell or furnish alcoholic beverages to minors. *(Added by Stats.1963, c. 1562, p. 3144, § 1. Amended by Stats.1987, c. 81, § 1; Stats.2015, c. 519 (A.B.776), § 5, eff. Jan. 1, 2016; Stats.2021, c. 208 (A.B.1275), § 1, eff. Jan. 1, 2022.)*

§ 25666.5. Violations by minors; participation in youthful drunk driver visitation program as term and condition of probation

If a person is convicted of a violation of subdivision (b) of Section 25658, or Section 25658.5, 25661, or 25662 and is granted probation, the court may order, with the consent of the defendant, as a term and condition of probation, in addition to any other term and condition required or authorized by law, that the defendant participate in the program prescribed in Article 3 (commencing with Section 23509) of Chapter 12 of Division 11.5 of the Vehicle Code. *(Added by Stats.1992, c. 432 (A.B.2361), § 1. Amended by Stats.1998, c. 118 (S.B.1186), § 1, operative July 1, 1999.)*

Research References

2 Witkin, California Criminal Law 4th Crimes Against Public Peace and Welfare § 365 (2021), Purchase of Liquor by Minors.

§ 25667. Immunity from criminal prosecution under specified minor consumption provisions

(a) Any person under the age of 21 years shall be immune from criminal prosecution under subdivision (a) of Section 25662 and subdivision (b) of Section 25658, where the person establishes all of the following:

(1) The underage person called 911 and reported that either himself or herself or another person was in need of medical assistance due to alcohol consumption.

(2) The underage person was the first person to make the 911 report.

(3) The underage person, who reported that another person was in need of medical assistance, remained on the scene with the other person until that medical assistance arrived and cooperated with medical assistance and law enforcement personnel on the scene.

(b) This section shall not provide immunity from criminal prosecution for any offense that involves activities made dangerous by the consumption of alcoholic beverages, including, but not limited to, a violation of Section 23103 of the Vehicle Code, as specified by Section 23103.5 of the Vehicle Code, or a violation of Sections 23152 and 23153 of the Vehicle Code. *(Added by Stats.2010, c. 245 (A.B.1999), § 3.)*

Research References

2 Witkin, California Criminal Law 4th Crimes Against Public Peace and Welfare § 365 (2021), Purchase of Liquor by Minors.

§ 25668. Students enrolled in an established Associate's degree or Bachelor's degree program in hotel management, culinary arts, enology, or brewing; authority to "taste" an alcoholic beverage

(a) A qualified student may taste an alcoholic beverage, and both the student and the qualified academic institution in which the student is enrolled shall not be subject to criminal prosecution under subdivision (a) of Section 25658 and subdivision (a) of Section 25662, if all of the following criteria are met:

(1) The qualified student tastes the alcoholic beverage while enrolled in a qualified academic institution.

(2) The qualified academic institution has established an associate's degree or bachelor's degree program in any of the following:

(A) Hotel management.

(B) Culinary arts.

(C) Enology or brewing that is designed to train industry professionals in the production of wine or beer.

(3) The qualified student tastes the alcoholic beverage for educational purposes as part of the instruction in a course required for an associate's degree or bachelor's degree.

(4) The alcoholic beverage remains in the control of an authorized instructor of the qualified academic institution who is at least 21 years of age.

(b) This section shall not be construed to allow a student under 21 years of age to receive an alcoholic beverage unless it is delivered as part of the student's curriculum requirements.

(c) A license or permit is not required to be held by a qualified academic institution engaging in the activities authorized by this section, provided an extra fee or charge is not imposed for the alcoholic beverages tasted.

(d) For the purposes of this section, the following terms have the following meanings:

(1) "Qualified academic institution" means a public college or university accredited by a commission recognized by the United States Department of Education.

(2) "Qualified student" means a student enrolled in a qualified academic institution who is at least 18 years of age.

(3) "Taste" means to draw an alcoholic beverage into the mouth, but does not include swallowing or otherwise consuming the alcoholic beverage. *(Added by Stats.2014, c. 162 (A.B.1989), § 3, eff. Jan. 1, 2015. Amended by Stats.2019, c. 457 (A.B.1308), § 1, eff. Jan. 1, 2020; Stats.2020, c. 370 (S.B.1371), § 20, eff. Jan. 1, 2021.)*

Research References

2 Witkin, California Criminal Law 4th Crimes Against Public Peace and Welfare § 364 (2021), Furnishing Liquor to Minors.

2 Witkin, California Criminal Law 4th Crimes Against Public Peace and Welfare § 365 (2021), Purchase of Liquor by Minors.

CODE OF CIVIL PROCEDURE

Part 1

OF COURTS OF JUSTICE

Title 2

JUDICIAL OFFICERS

CHAPTER 3. DISQUALIFICATIONS OF JUDGES

§ 170. Duty to decide

A judge has a duty to decide any proceeding in which he or she is not disqualified. *(Added by Stats.1984, c. 1555, § 2.)*

Cross References

Action for refund of taxes by public agency, disqualification of judges, see Revenue and Taxation Code § 5161.
Affinity defined, see Code of Civil Procedure § 17.
Change of place of trial, see Code of Civil Procedure §§ 397, 398.
Definitions applicable to this section, see Code of Civil Procedure § 170.5.
Degree of consanguineous relationship, see Probate Code § 6402 et seq.
Disqualification of arbitrator, application of this section, see Code of Civil Procedure § 1141.18.
Disqualification of judge in probate proceedings, see Probate Code § 7060.
Eminent domain, see Code of Civil Procedure § 1230.010 et seq.; Cal. Const. Art. 1, § 19.
Judge as relative or partner of appraiser of estate, see Probate Code § 8923.
Juvenile court, disqualification of referee, reassignment of matter, see Welfare and Institutions Code § 247.5.
Juvenile court rules related to this section, see California Rules of Court, Rule 5.536.
Practice of law by judges, see Government Code § 68082.
Prejudice against party, attorney or interest thereof, cumulative remedy, see Code of Civil Procedure § 170.6.
Relationship between judge and receiver, see Code of Civil Procedure § 566.

Research References

5 Witkin, California Criminal Law 4th Criminal Trial § 2 (2021), In General.

§ 170.1. Grounds for disqualification

(a) A judge shall be disqualified if any one or more of the following are true:

(1)(A) The judge has personal knowledge of disputed evidentiary facts concerning the proceeding.

(B) A judge shall be deemed to have personal knowledge within the meaning of this paragraph if the judge, or the spouse of the judge, or a person within the third degree of relationship to either of them, or the spouse of such a person is to the judge's knowledge likely to be a material witness in the proceeding.

(2)(A) The judge served as a lawyer in the proceeding, or in any other proceeding involving the same issues he or she served as a lawyer for a party in the present proceeding or gave advice to a party in the present proceeding upon a matter involved in the action or proceeding.

(B) A judge shall be deemed to have served as a lawyer in the proceeding if within the past two years:

(i) A party to the proceeding, or an officer, director, or trustee of a party, was a client of the judge when the judge was in the private practice of law or a client of a lawyer with whom the judge was associated in the private practice of law.

(ii) A lawyer in the proceeding was associated in the private practice of law with the judge.

(C) A judge who served as a lawyer for, or officer of, a public agency that is a party to the proceeding shall be deemed to have served as a lawyer in the proceeding if he or she personally advised or in any way represented the public agency concerning the factual or legal issues in the proceeding.

(3)(A) The judge has a financial interest in the subject matter in a proceeding or in a party to the proceeding.

(B) A judge shall be deemed to have a financial interest within the meaning of this paragraph if:

(i) A spouse or minor child living in the household has a financial interest.

(ii) The judge or the spouse of the judge is a fiduciary who has a financial interest.

(C) A judge has a duty to make reasonable efforts to inform himself or herself about his or her personal and fiduciary interests and those of his or her spouse and the personal financial interests of children living in the household.

(4) The judge, or the spouse of the judge, or a person within the third degree of relationship to either of them, or the spouse of such a person is a party to the proceeding or an officer, director, or trustee of a party.

(5) A lawyer or a spouse of a lawyer in the proceeding is the spouse, former spouse, child, sibling, or parent of the judge or the judge's spouse or if such a person is associated in the private practice of law with a lawyer in the proceeding.

(6)(A) For any reason:

(i) The judge believes his or her recusal would further the interests of justice.

(ii) The judge believes there is a substantial doubt as to his or her capacity to be impartial.

(iii) A person aware of the facts might reasonably entertain a doubt that the judge would be able to be impartial.

(B) Bias or prejudice toward a lawyer in the proceeding may be grounds for disqualification.

(7) By reason of permanent or temporary physical impairment, the judge is unable to properly perceive the evidence or is unable to properly conduct the proceeding.

(8)(A) The judge has a current arrangement concerning prospective employment or other compensated service as a dispute resolution neutral or is participating in, or, within the last two years has participated in, discussions regarding prospective employment or service as a dispute resolution neutral, or has been engaged in that employment or service, and any of the following applies:

(i) The arrangement is, or the prior employment or discussion was, with a party to the proceeding.

(ii) The matter before the judge includes issues relating to the enforcement of either an agreement to submit a dispute to an alternative dispute resolution process or an award or other final decision by a dispute resolution neutral.

(iii) The judge directs the parties to participate in an alternative dispute resolution process in which the dispute resolution neutral will be an individual or entity with whom the judge has the arrangement, has previously been employed or served, or is discussing or has discussed the employment or service.

(iv) The judge will select a dispute resolution neutral or entity to conduct an alternative dispute resolution process in the matter before the judge, and among those available for selection is an individual or entity with whom the judge has the arrangement, with whom the judge has previously been employed or served, or with whom the judge is discussing or has discussed the employment or service.

(B) For the purposes of this paragraph, all of the following apply:

(i) "Participating in discussions" or "has participated in discussion" means that the judge solicited or otherwise indicated an interest in accepting or negotiating possible employment or service as an alternative dispute resolution neutral, or responded to an unsolicited statement regarding, or an offer of, that employment or service by expressing an interest in that employment or service, making an inquiry regarding the employment or service, or encouraging the person making the statement or offer to provide additional information about that possible employment or service. If a judge's response to an unsolicited statement regarding, a question about, or offer of, prospective employment or other compensated service as a dispute resolution neutral is limited to responding negatively, declining the offer, or declining to discuss that employment or service, that response does not constitute participating in discussions.

(ii) "Party" includes the parent, subsidiary, or other legal affiliate of any entity that is a party and is involved in the transaction, contract, or facts that gave rise to the issues subject to the proceeding.

(iii) "Dispute resolution neutral" means an arbitrator, mediator, temporary judge appointed under Section 21 of Article VI of the California Constitution, referee appointed under Section 638 or 639, special master, neutral evaluator, settlement officer, or settlement facilitator.

(9)(A) The judge has received a contribution in excess of one thousand five hundred dollars ($1500) from a party or lawyer in the proceeding, and either of the following applies:

(i) The contribution was received in support of the judge's last election, if the last election was within the last six years.

(ii) The contribution was received in anticipation of an upcoming election.

(B) Notwithstanding subparagraph (A), the judge shall be disqualified based on a contribution of a lesser amount if subparagraph (A) of paragraph (6) applies.

(C) The judge shall disclose any contribution from a party or lawyer in a matter that is before the court that is required to be reported under subdivision (f) of Section 84211 of the Government Code, even if the amount would not require disqualification under this paragraph. The manner of disclosure shall be the same as that provided in Canon 3E of the Code of Judicial Ethics.

(D) Notwithstanding paragraph (1) of subdivision (b) of Section 170.3, the disqualification required under this paragraph may be waived by the party that did not make the contribution unless there are other circumstances that would prohibit a waiver pursuant to paragraph (2) of subdivision (b) of Section 170.3.

(b) A judge before whom a proceeding was tried or heard shall be disqualified from participating in any appellate review of that proceeding.

(c) At the request of a party or on its own motion an appellate court shall consider whether in the interests of justice it should direct that further proceedings be heard before a trial judge other than the judge whose judgment or order was reviewed by the appellate court. *(Added by Stats.1984, c. 1555, § 5. Amended by Stats.2002, c. 1094 (A.B.2504), § 1; Stats.2005, c. 332 (A.B.1322), § 1, eff. Sept. 22, 2005; Stats.2010, c. 686 (A.B.2487), § 1.)*

Cross References

Action defined, see Code of Civil Procedure § 22.
Affinity defined, see Code of Civil Procedure § 17.
Arbitration, generally, see Code of Civil Procedure § 1281 et seq.
Arbitration, neutral arbitrators, disclosure of information and disqualification, see Code of Civil Procedure § 1281.9.
Definitions applicable to this section, see Code of Civil Procedure § 170.5.
Disqualification of neutral arbitrator, see Code of Civil Procedure § 1281.91.
Each generation a degree, see Probate Code § 6402.
Judicial disqualification on relationship grounds, see Code of Civil Procedure § 170 et seq.
Witnesses, competency, judges, arbitrators or mediators as witnesses, see Evidence Code § 703.5.
Workers' compensation and insurance, selection of arbitrator, see Labor Code § 5271.

Research References

6 Witkin, California Criminal Law 4th Criminal Appeal § 54 (2021), In General.
5 Witkin, California Criminal Law 4th Criminal Trial § 3 (2021), In General.
5 Witkin, California Criminal Law 4th Criminal Trial § 4 (2021), Procedure.

§ 170.2. Circumstances not constituting grounds for disqualification

It shall not be grounds for disqualification that the judge:

(a) Is or is not a member of a racial, ethnic, religious, sexual or similar group and the proceeding involves the rights of such a group.

(b) Has in any capacity expressed a view on a legal or factual issue presented in the proceeding, except as provided in paragraph (2) of subdivision (a) of, or subdivision (b) or (c) of, Section 170.1.

(c) Has as a lawyer or public official participated in the drafting of laws or in the effort to pass or defeat laws, the meaning, effect or application of which is in issue in the proceeding unless the judge believes that his or her prior involvement was so well known as to raise a reasonable doubt in the public mind as to his or her capacity to be impartial. *(Added by Stats.1984, c. 1555, § 6.)*

Cross References

Definitions applicable to this section, see Code of Civil Procedure § 170.5.

§ 170.3. Proceedings; waiver; failure or refusal to withdraw

(a)(1) If a judge determines himself or herself to be disqualified, the judge shall notify the presiding judge of the court of his or her recusal and shall not further participate in the proceeding, except as provided in Section 170.4, unless his or her disqualification is waived by the parties as provided in subdivision (b).

(2) If the judge disqualifying himself or herself is the only judge or the presiding judge of the court, the notification shall be sent to the person having authority to assign another judge to replace the disqualified judge.

(b)(1) A judge who determines himself or herself to be disqualified after disclosing the basis for his or her disqualification on the record may ask the parties and their attorneys whether they wish to waive the disqualification, except where the basis for disqualification is as provided in paragraph (2). A waiver of disqualification shall recite the basis for the disqualification, and is effective only when signed by all parties and their attorneys and filed in the record.

(2) There shall be no waiver of disqualification if the basis therefor is either of the following:

(A) The judge has a personal bias or prejudice concerning a party.

(B) The judge served as an attorney in the matter in controversy, or the judge has been a material witness concerning that matter.

(3) The judge shall not seek to induce a waiver and shall avoid any effort to discover which lawyers or parties favored or opposed a waiver of disqualification.

(4) If grounds for disqualification are first learned of or arise after the judge has made one or more rulings in a proceeding, but before the judge has completed judicial action in a proceeding, the judge shall, unless the disqualification be waived, disqualify himself or herself, but in the absence of good cause the rulings he or she has made up to that time shall not be set aside by the judge who replaces the disqualified judge.

(c)(1) If a judge who should disqualify himself or herself refuses or fails to do so, any party may file with the clerk a written verified statement objecting to the hearing or trial before the judge and setting forth the facts constituting the grounds for disqualification of the judge. The statement shall be presented at the earliest practicable opportunity after discovery of the facts constituting the ground for disqualification. Copies of the statement shall be served on each party or his or her attorney who has appeared and shall be personally served on the judge alleged to be disqualified, or on his or her clerk, provided that the judge is present in the courthouse or in chambers.

(2) Without conceding his or her disqualification, a judge whose impartiality has been challenged by the filing of a written statement may request any other judge agreed upon by the parties to sit and act in his or her place.

(3) Within 10 days after the filing or service, whichever is later, the judge may file a consent to disqualification in which case the judge shall notify the presiding judge or the person authorized to appoint a replacement of his or her recusal as provided in subdivision (a), or the judge may file a written verified answer admitting or denying any or all of the allegations contained in the party's statement and setting forth any additional facts material or relevant to the question of disqualification. The clerk shall forthwith transmit a copy of the judge's answer to each party or his or her attorney who has appeared in the action.

(4) A judge who fails to file a consent or answer within the time allowed shall be deemed to have consented to his or her disqualification and the clerk shall notify the presiding judge or person authorized to appoint a replacement of the recusal as provided in subdivision (a).

(5) A judge who refuses to recuse himself or herself shall not pass upon his or her own disqualification or upon the sufficiency in law, fact, or otherwise, of the statement of disqualification filed by a party. In that case, the question of disqualification shall be heard and determined by another judge agreed upon by all the parties who have appeared or, in the event they are unable to agree within five days of notification of the judge's answer, by a judge selected by the chairperson of the Judicial Council, or if the chairperson is unable to act, the vice chairperson. The clerk shall notify the executive officer of the Judicial Council of the need for a selection. The selection shall be made as expeditiously as possible. No challenge pursuant to this subdivision or Section 170.6 may be made against the judge selected to decide the question of disqualification.

(6) The judge deciding the question of disqualification may decide the question on the basis of the statement of disqualification and answer and any written arguments as the judge requests, or the judge may set the matter for hearing as promptly as practicable. If a hearing is ordered, the judge shall permit the parties and the judge alleged to be disqualified to argue the question of disqualification and shall for good cause shown hear evidence on any disputed issue of fact. If the judge deciding the question of disqualification determines that the judge is disqualified, the judge hearing the question shall notify the presiding judge or the person having authority to appoint a replacement of the disqualified judge as provided in subdivision (a).

(d) The determination of the question of the disqualification of a judge is not an appealable order and may be reviewed only by a writ of mandate from the appropriate court of appeal sought only by the parties to the proceeding. The petition for the writ shall be filed and served within 10 days after service of written notice of entry of the court's order determining the question of disqualification. If the notice of entry is served by mail, that time shall be extended as provided in subdivision (a) of Section 1013. *(Added by Stats.1984, c. 1555, § 7. Amended by Stats.1990, c. 910 (S.B.2316), § 1; Stats.2006, c. 567 (A.B.2303), § 4.)*

Cross References

Action defined, see Code of Civil Procedure § 22.
Attorneys, State Bar Act, see Business and Professions Code § 6000.
Computation of time, see Code of Civil Procedure §§ 12, 12a, 12b; Government Code § 6800 et seq.
Definitions applicable to this section, see Code of Civil Procedure § 170.5.
Discovery, generally, see Code of Civil Procedure § 2016 et seq.
Judicial Council, see Government Code § 68500 et seq.
Mandamus, purpose of writ of mandate, courts which may issue writ and parties to whom issued, see Code of Civil Procedure § 1085.
Notice, actual and constructive, defined, see Civil Code § 18.
Writ and process defined, see Code of Civil Procedure § 17.

Research References

6 Witkin, California Criminal Law 4th Criminal Appeal § 54 (2021), In General.
6 Witkin, California Criminal Law 4th Criminal Appeal § 71 (2021), Orders Before Judgment.
5 Witkin, California Criminal Law 4th Criminal Trial § 2 (2021), In General.
5 Witkin, California Criminal Law 4th Criminal Trial § 4 (2021), Procedure.

§ 170.4. Powers of disqualified judges

(a) A disqualified judge, notwithstanding his or her disqualification may do any of the following:

(1) Take any action or issue any order necessary to maintain the jurisdiction of the court pending the assignment of a judge not disqualified.

(2) Request any other judge agreed upon by the parties to sit and act in his or her place.

(3) Hear and determine purely default matters.

(4) Issue an order for possession prior to judgment in eminent domain proceedings.

(5) Set proceedings for trial or hearing.

(6) Conduct settlement conferences.

(b) Notwithstanding paragraph (5) of subdivision (c) of Section 170.3, if a statement of disqualification is untimely filed or if on its face it discloses no legal grounds for disqualification, the trial judge against whom it was filed may order it stricken.

(c)(1) If a statement of disqualification is filed after a trial or hearing has commenced by the start of voir dire, by the swearing of the first witness or by the submission of a motion for decision, the judge whose impartiality has been questioned may order the trial or hearing to continue, notwithstanding the filing of the statement of disqualification. The issue of disqualification shall be referred to another judge for decision as provided in subdivision (a) of Section 170.3, and if it is determined that the judge is disqualified, all orders and rulings of the judge found to be disqualified made after the filing of the statement shall be vacated.

(2) For the purposes of this subdivision, if (A) a proceeding is filed in a single judge court or has been assigned to a single judge for comprehensive disposition, and (B) the proceeding has been set for trial or hearing 30 or more days in advance before a judge whose name was known at the time, the trial or hearing shall be deemed to have commenced 10 days prior to the date scheduled for trial or hearing as to any grounds for disqualification known before that time.

(3) A party may file no more than one statement of disqualification against a judge unless facts suggesting new grounds for disqualification are first learned of or arise after the first statement of disqualification was filed. Repetitive statements of disqualification not alleging facts suggesting new grounds for disqualification shall be stricken by the judge against whom they are filed.

(d) Except as provided in this section, a disqualified judge shall have no power to act in any proceeding after his or her disqualification or after the filing of a statement of disqualification until the question of his or her disqualification has been determined. *(Added by Stats.1984, c. 1555, § 8.)*

Cross References

Action, defined, see Code of Civil Procedure § 22.
Computation of time, see Code of Civil Procedure §§ 12, 12a, 12b; Government Code § 6800 et seq.
Definitions applicable to this section, see Code of Civil Procedure § 170.5.
Eminent domain, generally, see Cal. Const. Art. 1, § 19; Code of Civil Procedure § 1240.010 et seq.; Government Code §§ 15850 et seq., 40404; Public Utilities Code § 619.

§ 170.5. Definitions

For the purposes of Sections 170 to 170.5, inclusive, the following definitions apply:

(a) "Judge" means judges of the superior courts, and court commissioners and referees.

(b) "Financial interest" means ownership of more than a 1 percent legal or equitable interest in a party, or a legal or equitable interest in a party of a fair market value in excess of one thousand five hundred dollars ($1,500), or a relationship as director, advisor or other active participant in the affairs of a party, except as follows:

(1) Ownership in a mutual or common investment fund that holds securities is not a "financial interest" in those securities unless the judge participates in the management of the fund.

(2) An office in an educational, religious, charitable, fraternal, or civic organization is not a "financial interest" in securities held by the organization.

(3) The proprietary interest of a policyholder in a mutual insurance company, or a depositor in a mutual savings association, or a similar proprietary interest, is a "financial interest" in the organization only if the outcome of the proceeding could substantially affect the value of the interest.

(c) "Officer of a public agency" does not include a Member of the Legislature or a state or local agency official acting in a legislative capacity.

(d) The third degree of relationship shall be calculated according to the civil law system.

(e) "Private practice of law" includes a fee for service, retainer, or salaried representation of private clients or public agencies, but excludes lawyers as full-time employees of public agencies or lawyers working exclusively for legal aid offices, public defender offices, or similar nonprofit entities whose clientele is by law restricted to the indigent.

(f) "Proceeding" means the action, case, cause, motion, or special proceeding to be tried or heard by the judge.

(g) "Fiduciary" includes any executor, trustee, guardian, or administrator. *(Added by Stats.1984, c. 1555, § 9. Amended by Stats.1998, c. 931 (S.B.2139), § 47, eff. Sept. 28, 1998; Stats.2002, c. 784 (S.B.1316), § 35.)*

Law Revision Commission Comments

Section 170.5 is amended to reflect the elimination of the justice court. Cal. Const. art. VI, §§ 1, 5(b). [28 Cal.L.Rev.Comm. Reports 51 (1998)].

Subdivision (a) of Section 170.5 is amended to reflect unification of the municipal and superior courts pursuant to Article VI, Section 5(e), of the California Constitution. [32 Cal.L.Rev.Comm. Reports 99 (2002)].

Cross References

Action defined, see Code of Civil Procedure § 22.
Restrictions against private arbitration company from administering consumer arbitration or related services, presence of financial interest, see Code of Civil Procedure § 1281.92.
Special proceeding defined, see Code of Civil Procedure § 23.
State and United States as including District of Columbia and territories, see Code of Civil Procedure § 17.

Research References

5 Witkin, California Criminal Law 4th Criminal Trial § 3 (2021), In General.

§ 170.6. Prejudice against party, attorney or interest thereof; motion and affidavit; assignment of another judge, court commissioner or referee; number of motions; continuance; cumulative remedy; severability

(a)(1) A judge, court commissioner, or referee of a superior court of the State of California shall not try a civil or criminal action or special proceeding of any kind or character nor hear any matter therein that involves a contested issue of law or fact when it is established as provided in this section that the judge or court commissioner is prejudiced against a party or attorney or the interest of a party or attorney appearing in the action or proceeding.

(2) A party to, or an attorney appearing in, an action or proceeding may establish this prejudice by an oral or written motion without prior notice supported by affidavit or declaration under penalty of perjury, or an oral statement under oath, that the judge, court commissioner, or referee before whom the action or proceeding is pending, or to whom it is assigned, is prejudiced against a party or attorney, or the interest of the party or attorney, so that the party or attorney cannot, or believes that he or she cannot, have a fair and impartial trial or hearing before the judge, court commissioner, or referee. If the judge, other than a judge assigned to the case for all purposes, court commissioner, or referee assigned to, or who is scheduled to try, the cause or hear the matter is known at least 10 days before the date set for trial or hearing, the motion shall be made at least 5 days before that date. If directed to the trial of a cause with a master calendar, the motion shall be made to the judge supervising the master calendar not later than the time the cause is assigned for trial. If directed to the trial of a criminal cause that has been assigned to a judge for all purposes, the motion shall be made to the assigned judge or to the presiding judge by a party within 10 days after notice of the all purpose assignment, or if the party has not yet appeared in the action, then within 10 days after the appearance. If directed to the trial of a civil cause that has been assigned to a judge for all purposes, the motion shall be made to the assigned judge or to the presiding judge by a party within 15 days after notice of the all purpose assignment, or if the party has not yet appeared in the action, then within 15 days after the appearance. If the court in which the action is pending is authorized to have no more than one judge, and the motion claims that the duly elected or appointed judge of that court is prejudiced, the motion shall be made before the expiration of 30 days from the date of the first appearance in the action of the party who is making the motion or whose attorney is making the motion. In no event shall a judge, court commissioner, or referee entertain the motion if it is made after the drawing of the name of the first juror, or if there is no jury, after the making of an

opening statement by counsel for plaintiff, or if there is no opening statement by counsel for plaintiff, then after swearing in the first witness or the giving of any evidence or after trial of the cause has otherwise commenced. If the motion is directed to a hearing, other than the trial of a cause, the motion shall be made not later than the commencement of the hearing. In the case of trials or hearings not specifically provided for in this paragraph, the procedure specified herein shall be followed as nearly as possible. The fact that a judge, court commissioner, or referee has presided at, or acted in connection with, a pretrial conference or other hearing, proceeding, or motion prior to trial, and not involving a determination of contested fact issues relating to the merits, shall not preclude the later making of the motion provided for in this paragraph at the time and in the manner herein provided.

A motion under this paragraph may be made following reversal on appeal of a trial court's decision, or following reversal on appeal of a trial court's final judgment, if the trial judge in the prior proceeding is assigned to conduct a new trial on the matter. Notwithstanding paragraph (4), the party who filed the appeal that resulted in the reversal of a final judgment of a trial court may make a motion under this section regardless of whether that party or side has previously done so. The motion shall be made within 60 days after the party or the party's attorney has been notified of the assignment.

(3) A party to a civil action making that motion under this section shall serve notice on all parties no later than five days after making the motion.

(4) If the motion is duly presented, and the affidavit or declaration under penalty of perjury is duly filed or an oral statement under oath is duly made, thereupon and without any further act or proof, the judge supervising the master calendar, if any, shall assign some other judge, court commissioner, or referee to try the cause or hear the matter. In other cases, the trial of the cause or the hearing of the matter shall be assigned or transferred to another judge, court commissioner, or referee of the court in which the trial or matter is pending or, if there is no other judge, court commissioner, or referee of the court in which the trial or matter is pending, the Chair of the Judicial Council shall assign some other judge, court commissioner, or referee to try the cause or hear the matter as promptly as possible. Except as provided in this section, no party or attorney shall be permitted to make more than one such motion in any one action or special proceeding pursuant to this section. In actions or special proceedings where there may be more than one plaintiff or similar party or more than one defendant or similar party appearing in the action or special proceeding, only one motion for each side may be made in any one action or special proceeding.

(5) Unless required for the convenience of the court or unless good cause is shown, a continuance of the trial or hearing shall not be granted by reason of the making of a motion under this section. If a continuance is granted, the cause or matter shall be continued from day to day or for other limited periods upon the trial or other calendar and shall be reassigned or transferred for trial or hearing as promptly as possible.

(6) Any affidavit filed pursuant to this section shall be in substantially the following form:

(Here set forth court and cause)
State of California, ss. PEREMPTORY CHALLENGE
County of ______

______, being duly sworn, deposes and says: That he or she is a party (or attorney for a party) to the within action (or special proceeding). That ____ the judge, court commissioner, or referee before whom the trial of the (or a hearing in the) action (or special proceeding) is pending (or to whom it is assigned) is prejudiced against the party (or his or her attorney) or the interest of the party (or his or her attorney) so that affiant cannot or believes that he or she cannot have a fair and impartial trial or hearing before the judge, court commissioner, or referee.

Subscribed and sworn to before me this
______ day of ______, 20____.
(Clerk or notary public or other
officer administering oath)

(7) Any oral statement under oath or declaration under penalty of perjury made pursuant to this section shall include substantially the same contents as the affidavit above.

(b) Nothing in this section shall affect or limit Section 170 or Title 4 (commencing with Section 392) of Part 2, and this section shall be construed as cumulative thereto.

(c) If any provision of this section or the application to any person or circumstance is held invalid, that invalidity shall not affect other provisions or applications of the section that can be given effect without the invalid provision or application and, to this end, the provisions of this section are declared to be severable. *(Added by Stats.1957, c. 1055, p. 2288, § 1. Amended by Stats.1959, c. 640, p. 2620, § 1; Stats.1961, c. 526, p. 1628, § 1; Stats.1965, c. 1442, p. 3375, § 1; Stats.1967, c. 1602, p. 3832, § 2; Stats.1976, c. 1071, p. 4815, § 1; Stats.1981, c. 192, § 1; Stats.1982, c. 1644, p. 6682, § 2; Stats.1985, c. 715, § 1; Stats.1989, c. 537, § 1; Stats.1998, c. 167 (A.B.1199), § 1; Stats.2002, c. 784 (S.B.1316), § 36; Stats.2003, c. 62 (S.B.600), § 22; Stats.2010, c. 131 (A.B.1894), § 1.)*

Law Revision Commission Comments

Subdivision (1) of Section 170.6 is amended to reflect the elimination of the justice court. Cal. Const. art. VI, §§ 1, 5(b). [28 Cal.L.Rev.Comm. Reports 51 (1998)].

Subdivision (1) of Section 170.6 is amended to reflect unification of the municipal and superior courts pursuant to Article VI, Section 5(e), of the California Constitution. [32 Cal.L.Rev.Comm. Reports 100 (2002)].

Cross References

Action defined, see Code of Civil Procedure § 22.
Attorneys, State Bar Act, see Business and Professions Code § 6000.
Challenge, removal of action or proceeding from delay reduction program, see Government Code § 68607.5.
Classes of judicial remedies, see Code of Civil Procedure § 21.
Computation of time, see Code of Civil Procedure §§ 12, 12a, 12b; Government Code § 6800 et seq.
Disqualification of arbitrator, application of this section, see Code of Civil Procedure § 1141.18.
Disqualification of judges, see Code of Civil Procedure § 170.
Judicial Council, see Government Code § 68500 et seq.; Cal. Const. Art. 6, § 6.
Juvenile court, disqualification of referee, reassignment of matter, see Welfare and Institutions Code § 247.5.
Juvenile court law, parent or guardian, notice to appear, see Welfare and Institutions Code § 792.
Kinds of actions, see Code of Civil Procedure § 24.
Minimum time periods for certain actions, see Government Code § 68616.
Notice, actual and constructive, defined, see Civil Code § 18.
Oath defined, see Penal Code § 119.
Petition for coordination of cases, right to file peremptory challenge under this section limited upon grant of petition, see California Rules of Court, Rule 3.532.
Special proceeding, defined, see Code of Civil Procedure § 23.
"State" and "United States" as including District of Columbia and territories, see Code of Civil Procedure § 17.
Statement under oath, perjury, see Penal Code § 118 et seq.
Wards,
  Commencement of proceedings, notice, see Welfare and Institutions Code § 661.
  Commencement of proceedings, petition, see Welfare and Institutions Code § 656.
  Hearings, compulsory education violations, see Welfare and Institutions Code § 700.2.

Research References

West's California Judicial Council Forms JV–611, Child Habitually Truant §601(B) (Also Available in Spanish).
5 Witkin, California Criminal Law 4th Criminal Trial § 5 (2021), In General.
5 Witkin, California Criminal Law 4th Criminal Trial § 6 (2021), Form and Time of Motion.
5 Witkin, California Criminal Law 4th Criminal Trial § 7 (2021), Number of Challenges.
5 Witkin, California Criminal Law 4th Criminal Trial § 194 (2021), Appointment in Lieu of Alternative Counsel.
5 Witkin, California Criminal Law 4th Criminal Trial § 484 (2021), Consent.
5 Witkin, California Criminal Law 4th Criminal Trial § 486 (2021), Refiled Case is Not Continuation of Dismissed Case.
6 Witkin, California Criminal Law 4th Criminal Writs § 68 (2021), In General.
6 Witkin, California Criminal Law 4th Criminal Writs § 94 (2021), Reference.
4 Witkin, California Criminal Law 4th Illegally Obtained Evidence § 459 (2021), Felony Prosecution: Limitations on Subsequent Proceedings.

§ 170.7. Judge serving on appellate division; application of § 170.6

Section 170.6 does not apply to a judge designated or assigned to serve on the appellate division of a superior court in the judge's capacity as a judge of that division. *(Added by Stats.1963, c. 872, p. 2120, § 1. Amended by Stats.1998, c. 931 (S.B.2139), § 48, eff. Sept. 28, 1998.)*

Law Revision Commission Comments

Section 170.7 is amended to refer more precisely to the appellate division. See Cal. Const. art. VI, § 4. [28 Cal.L.Rev.Comm. Reports 51 (1998)].

§ 170.8. No qualified judge; assignment of judge

When there is no judge of a court qualified to hear an action or proceeding, the clerk shall forthwith notify the Chairman of the Judicial Council of that fact. The judge assigned by the Chairman of the Judicial Council shall hear the action or proceeding at the time fixed therefor or, if no time has been fixed or good cause appears for changing the time theretofore fixed, the judge shall fix a time for hearing in accordance with law and rules and hear the action or proceeding at the time so fixed. *(Added by Stats.1963, c. 872, p. 2120, § 2. Amended by Stats.1989, c. 1417, § 2.)*

Cross References

Action defined, see Code of Civil Procedure § 22.
Judicial Council, see Government Code § 68500 et seq.

§ 170.9. Acceptance of gifts; value limit; exceptions; adjustments; travel expenses

(a) A judge shall not accept gifts from a single source in a calendar year with a total value of more than two hundred fifty dollars ($250). This section shall not be construed to authorize the receipt of gifts that would otherwise be prohibited by the Code of Judicial Ethics adopted by the California Supreme Court or any other law.

(b) This section shall not prohibit or limit the following:

(1) Payments, advances, or reimbursements for travel and related lodging and subsistence permitted by subdivision (e).

(2) Wedding gifts and gifts exchanged between individuals on birthdays, holidays, and other similar occasions, if the gifts exchanged are not substantially disproportionate in value.

(3) A gift, bequest, favor, or loan from a person whose preexisting relationship with a judge would prevent the judge from hearing a case involving that person, under the Code of Judicial Ethics adopted by the California Supreme Court.

(c) For purposes of this section, "judge" includes all of the following:

(1) Judges of the superior courts.

(2) Justices of the courts of appeal and the Supreme Court.

(3) Subordinate judicial officers, as defined in Section 71601 of the Government Code.

(d) The gift limitation amounts in this section shall be adjusted biennially by the Commission on Judicial Performance to reflect changes in the Consumer Price Index, rounded to the nearest ten dollars ($10).

(e) Payments, advances, or reimbursements for travel, including actual transportation and related lodging and subsistence that is reasonably related to a judicial or governmental purpose, or to an issue of state, national, or international public policy, are not prohibited or limited by this section if any of the following apply:

(1) The travel is in connection with a speech, practice demonstration, or group or panel discussion given or participated in by the judge, the lodging and subsistence expenses are limited to the day immediately preceding, the day of, and the day immediately following the speech, demonstration, or discussion, and the travel is within the United States.

(2) The travel is provided by a government, a governmental agency or authority, a foreign government, a foreign bar association, an international service organization, a bona fide public or private educational institution, as defined in Section 203 of the Revenue and Taxation Code, or a nonprofit charitable or religious organization that is exempt from taxation under Section 501(c)(3) of the Internal Revenue Code,[1] or by a person domiciled outside the United States who substantially satisfies the requirements for tax-exempt status under Section 501(c)(3) of the Internal Revenue Code.

For purposes of this section, "foreign bar association" means an association of attorneys located outside the United States (A) that performs functions substantially equivalent to those performed by state or local bar associations in this state and (B) that permits membership by attorneys in that country representing various legal specialties and does not limit membership to attorneys generally representing one side or another in litigation. "International service organization" means a bona fide international service organization of which the judge is a member. A judge who accepts travel payments from an international service organization pursuant to this subdivision shall not preside over or participate in decisions affecting that organization, its state or local chapters, or its local members.

(3) The travel is provided by a state or local bar association or judges professional association in connection with testimony before a governmental body or attendance at any professional function hosted by the bar association or judges professional association, the lodging and subsistence expenses are limited to the day immediately preceding, the day of, and the day immediately following the professional function.

(f) Payments, advances, and reimbursements for travel not described in subdivision (e) are subject to the limit in subdivision (a).

(g) No judge shall accept any honorarium.

(h) "Honorarium" means a payment made in consideration for any speech given, article published, or attendance at a public or private conference, convention, meeting, social event, meal, or like gathering.

(i) "Honorarium" does not include earned income for personal services that are customarily provided in connection with the practice of a bona fide business, trade, or profession, such as teaching or writing for a publisher, and does not include fees or other things of value received pursuant to Section 94.5 of the Penal Code for performance of a marriage.

For purposes of this section, "teaching" shall include presentations to impart educational information to lawyers in events qualifying for credit under mandatory continuing legal education, to students in bona fide educational institutions, and to associations or groups of judges.

(j) Subdivisions (a) and (e) shall apply to all payments, advances, and reimbursements for travel and related lodging and subsistence.

(k) This section does not apply to any honorarium that is not used and, within 30 days after receipt, is either returned to the donor or delivered to the Controller for deposit in the General Fund without being claimed as a deduction from income for tax purposes.

(*l*) "Gift" means a payment to the extent that consideration of equal or greater value is not received and includes a rebate or discount in the price of anything of value unless the rebate or discount is made in the regular course of business to members of the public without regard to official status. A person, other than a defendant in a criminal action, who claims that a payment is not a gift by reason of receipt of consideration has the burden of proving that the consideration received is of equal or greater value. However, the term "gift" does not include any of the following:

(1) Informational material such as books, reports, pamphlets, calendars, periodicals, cassettes and discs, or free or reduced-price admission, tuition, or registration, for informational conferences or seminars. No payment for travel or reimbursement for any expenses shall be deemed "informational material."

(2) Gifts that are not used and, within 30 days after receipt, are returned to the donor or delivered to a charitable organization without being claimed as a charitable contribution for tax purposes.

(3) Gifts from a judge's spouse, child, parent, grandparent, grandchild, brother, sister, parent-in-law, brother-in-law, sister-in-law, nephew, niece, aunt, uncle, or first cousin or the spouse of any such person. However, a gift from any of those persons shall be considered a gift if the donor is acting as an agent or intermediary for a person not covered by this paragraph.

(4) Campaign contributions required to be reported under Chapter 4 (commencing with Section 84100) of Title 9 of the Government Code.

(5) Any devise or inheritance.

(6) Personalized plaques and trophies with an individual value of less than two hundred fifty dollars ($250).

(7) Admission to events hosted by state or local bar associations or judges professional associations, and provision of related food and beverages at those events, when attendance does not require "travel," as described in paragraph (3) of subdivision (e).

(m) The Commission on Judicial Performance shall enforce the prohibitions of this section with regard to judges of the superior courts and justices of the courts of appeal and the Supreme Court. With regard to subordinate judicial officers, consistent with Section 18.1 of Article VI of the California Constitution, the court employing the subordinate judicial officer shall exercise initial jurisdiction to enforce the prohibitions of this section, and the Commission on Judicial Performance shall exercise discretionary jurisdiction with respect to the enforcement of the prohibitions of this section. *(Added by Stats.1994, c. 1238 (A.B.3638), § 1. Amended by Stats. 1995, c. 378 (S.B.353), § 1; Stats.1996, c. 557 (S.B.1589), § 1; Stats.2002, c. 784 (S.B.1316), § 37; Stats.2010, c. 206 (A.B.2116), § 1; Stats.2011, c. 296 (A.B.1023), § 36.)*

1 Internal Revenue Code sections are in Title 26 of the U.S.C.A.

Law Revision Commission Comments

Subdivision (c) of Section 170.9 is amended to reflect unification of the municipal and superior courts pursuant to Article VI, Section 5(e), of the California Constitution. [32 Cal.L.Rev.Comm. Reports 103 (2002)].

Cross References

Action defined, see Code of Civil Procedure § 22.
Attorneys, State Bar Act, see Business and Professions Code § 6000.
Computation of time, see Code of Civil Procedure §§ 12, 12a, 12b; Government Code § 6800 et seq.
Holidays defined for purposes of this Code, see Code of Civil Procedure § 10.
Kinds of actions, see Code of Civil Procedure § 24.
"State" and "United States" as including District of Columbia and territories, see Code of Civil Procedure § 17.
State Controller, generally, see Government Code § 12402 et seq.
Travel payments, advances and reimbursements, see Government Code § 89506.

Title 3

PERSONS SPECIALLY INVESTED WITH POWERS OF A JUDICIAL NATURE

CHAPTER 1. TRIAL JURY SELECTION AND MANAGEMENT ACT

Section

§ 190. Citation

This chapter shall be known and may be cited as the Trial Jury Selection and Management Act. *(Added by Stats.1988, c. 1245, § 2.)*

Cross References

Grand jury, see Penal Code § 888 et seq.
Trial by jury, see Cal. Const. Art. 1, § 16.
Uniform Controlled Substances Act, seizure and disposition, claim of interest procedure, see Health and Safety Code § 11488.5.

Research References

5 Witkin, California Criminal Law 4th Criminal Trial § 553 (2021), In General.

§ 191. State policy; random selection; opportunity and obligation to serve

The Legislature recognizes that trial by jury is a cherished constitutional right, and that jury service is an obligation of citizenship.

It is the policy of the State of California that all persons selected for jury service shall be selected at random from the population of the area served by the court; that all qualified persons have an equal opportunity, in accordance with this chapter, to be considered for jury service in the state and an obligation to serve as jurors when summoned for that purpose; and that it is the responsibility of jury commissioners to manage all jury systems in an efficient, equitable, and cost-effective manner, in accordance with this chapter. *(Added by Stats.1988, c. 1245, § 2.)*

Cross References

"Court" defined for purposes of this Chapter, see Code of Civil Procedure § 194.
"Random" defined for purposes of this Chapter, see Code of Civil Procedure § 194.
"State" and "United States" as including District of Columbia and territories, see Code of Civil Procedure § 17.
Uniform Controlled Substances Act, seizure and disposition, claim of interest procedure, see Health and Safety Code § 11488.5.

Research References

5 Witkin, California Criminal Law 4th Criminal Trial § 535 (2021), In General.

§ 192. Application of chapter

This chapter applies to the selection of jurors, and the formation of trial juries, for both civil and criminal cases, in all trial courts of the state. *(Added by Stats.1988, c. 1245, § 2.)*

Cross References

"Court" defined for purposes of this Chapter, see Code of Civil Procedure § 194.
Formation of grand jury, see Penal Code § 893 et seq.
Grand jury must be drawn at least once a year in each county, see Cal. Const. Art. 1, § 23.
Impaneling grand jurors, see Penal Code § 904 et seq.
Powers and duties of grand jury, see Penal Code § 914 et seq.
"State" and "United States" as including District of Columbia and territories, see Code of Civil Procedure § 17.
"Trial jury" defined for purposes of this Chapter, see Code of Civil Procedure § 194.
Uniform Controlled Substances Act, seizure and disposition, claim of interest procedure, see Health and Safety Code § 11488.5.

§ 193. Kinds of juries

Juries are of three kinds:

(a) Grand juries established pursuant to Title 4 (commencing with Section 888) of Part 2 of the Penal Code.

(b) Trial juries.

(c) Juries of inquest. *(Added by Stats.1988, c. 1245, § 2.)*

Cross References

Criminal procedure, formation of trial jury, see Penal Code § 1046.
Grand juries,
  Formation, see Penal Code § 893 et seq.
  "Grand jury" defined, see Penal Code § 888.
  Grand jury must be drawn at least once a year in each county, see Cal. Const. Art. 1, § 23.
  Impaneling grand jurors, see Penal Code § 904 et seq.
  Powers and duties, see Penal Code § 914 et seq.
  Proceedings, generally, see Penal Code § 888 et seq.
Juries of inquest,
  Duties, see Code of Civil Procedure § 236.
  Selection of jurors, see Code of Civil Procedure § 235.
"Jury of inquest" defined for purposes of this Chapter, see Code of Civil Procedure § 194.
Trial by jury, see Cal. Const. Art. 1, § 16.
"Trial jury" defined for purposes of this Chapter, see Code of Civil Procedure § 194.
Uniform Controlled Substances Act, seizure and disposition, claim of interest procedure, see Health and Safety Code § 11488.5.

§ 194. Definitions

The following definitions govern the construction of this chapter:

(a) "County" means any county or any coterminous city and county.

(b) "Court" means a superior court of this state, and includes, when the context requires, any judge of the court.

(c) "Deferred jurors" are those prospective jurors whose request to reschedule their service to a more convenient time is granted by the jury commissioner.

(d) "Excused jurors" are those prospective jurors who are excused from service by the jury commissioner for valid reasons based on statute, state or local court rules, and policies.

(e) "Juror pool" means the group of prospective qualified jurors appearing for assignment to trial jury panels.

(f) "Jury of inquest" is a body of persons summoned from the citizens before the sheriff, coroner, or other ministerial officers, to inquire of particular facts.

(g) "Master list" means a list of names randomly selected from the source lists.

(h) "Potential juror" means any person whose name appears on a source list.

(i) "Prospective juror" means a juror whose name appears on the master list.

(j) "Qualified juror" means a person who meets the statutory qualifications for jury service.

(k) "Qualified juror list" means a list of qualified jurors.

(*l*) "Random" means that which occurs by mere chance indicating an unplanned sequence of selection where each juror's name has substantially equal probability of being selected.

(m) "Source list" means a list used as a source of potential jurors.

(n) "Summons list" means a list of prospective or qualified jurors who are summoned to appear or to be available for jury service.

(*o*) "Trial jurors" are those jurors sworn to try and determine by verdict a question of fact.

(p) "Trial jury" means a body of persons selected from the citizens of the area served by the court and sworn to try and determine by verdict a question of fact.

(q) "Trial jury panel" means a group of prospective jurors assigned to a courtroom for the purpose of voir dire. *(Added by Stats.1988, c. 1245, § 2. Amended by Stats.1998, c. 931 (S.B.2139), § 50, eff. Sept. 28, 1998; Stats.2002, c. 784 (S.B.1316), § 39.)*

Law Revision Commission Comments

Subdivision (b) of Section 194 is amended to reflect the elimination of the justice court. Cal. Const. art. VI, §§ 1, 5(b). [28 Cal.L.Rev.Comm. Reports 51 (1998)].

Subdivision (b) of Section 194 is amended to reflect unification of the municipal and superior courts pursuant to Article VI, Section 5(e), of the California Constitution. [32 Cal.L.Rev.Comm. Reports 107 (2002)].

Cross References

"Sheriff" as including "marshal", see Code of Civil Procedure § 17.
"State" and "United States" as including District of Columbia and territories, see Code of Civil Procedure § 17.
Uniform Controlled Substances Act, seizure and disposition, claim of interest procedure, see Health and Safety Code § 11488.5.

§ 195. Jury commissioners; appointment; term; ex officio commissioners; clerk/administrators; salaries; duties

(a) In each county, there shall be one jury commissioner who shall be appointed by, and serve at the pleasure of, a majority of the judges of the superior court. In any county where there is a superior court administrator or executive officer, that person shall serve as ex officio jury commissioner. In any court jurisdiction where any person other than a court administrator or clerk/administrator is serving as jury commissioner on the effective date of this section, that person shall continue to so serve at the pleasure of a majority of the judges of the appointing court.

(b) Any jury commissioner may, whenever the business of court requires, appoint deputy jury commissioners. Salaries and benefits of those deputies shall be fixed in the same manner as salaries and benefits of other court employees.

(c) The jury commissioner shall be primarily responsible for managing the jury system under the general supervision of the court in conformance with the purpose and scope of this act. He or she shall have authority to establish policies and procedures necessary to fulfill this responsibility. *(Added by Stats.1988, c. 1245, § 2. Amended by Stats.1998, c. 931 (S.B.2139), § 51, eff. Sept. 28, 1998; Stats.2002, c. 784 (S.B.1316), § 40.)*

Law Revision Commission Comments

Section 195 is amended to reflect the elimination of the justice court. Cal. Const. art. VI, §§ 1, 5(b). [28 Cal.L.Rev.Comm. Reports 51 (1998)].

Subdivision (a) of Section 195 is amended to reflect unification of the municipal and superior courts pursuant to Article VI, Section 5(e), of the California Constitution.

Subdivision (b) is amended to reflect enactment of the Trial Court Employment Protection and Governance Act. See Gov't Code §§ 71620 (trial court personnel), 71623 (salaries). [32 Cal.L.Rev.Comm. Reports 108 (2002)].

Cross References

County defined for purposes of this Chapter, see Code of Civil Procedure § 194.
"Court" defined for purposes of this Chapter, see Code of Civil Procedure § 194.
Criminal procedure, grand jury formation, powers and duties of jury commissioner, see Penal Code § 903.1 et seq.
Orientation for new jurors, see Code of Civil Procedure § 214.
Records maintained by jury commissioner, see Code of Civil Procedure § 207.
Uniform Controlled Substances Act, seizure and disposition, claim of interest procedure, see Health and Safety Code § 11488.5.

§ 196. Jury commissioners; inquiry into qualifications; oaths; travel expenses; failure of prospective to respond; summons

(a) The jury commissioner or the court shall inquire as to the qualifications of persons on the master list or source list who are or may be summoned for jury service. The commissioner or the court may require any person to answer, under oath, orally or in written form, all questions as may be addressed to that person, regarding the person's qualifications and ability to serve as a prospective trial juror. The commissioner and his or her assistants shall have power to administer oaths and shall be allowed actual traveling expenses incurred in the performance of their duties.

(b) Response to the jury commissioner or the court concerning an inquiry or summons may be made by any person having knowledge that the prospective juror is unable to respond to such inquiry or summons.

(c) Any person who fails to respond to jury commissioner or court inquiry as instructed, may be summoned to appear before the jury commissioner or the court to answer the inquiry, or may be deemed to be qualified for jury service in the absence of a response to the inquiry. Any information thus acquired by the court or jury commissioner shall be noted in jury commissioner or court records. *(Added by Stats.1988, c. 1245, § 2. Amended by Stats.2003, c. 149 (S.B.79), § 6.)*

Law Revision Commission Comments

Subdivision (a) of Section 196 is amended to reflect enactment of the Trial Court Funding Act. See Gov't Code §§ 77003 ("court operations" defined), 77200 (state funding of trial court operations). *Cf.* Cal. R. Ct. 810(d), Function 2 (jury services). Subdivision (a) is also amended to reflect enactment of Government Code Section 69505 (business-related travel expenses of trial court judges and employees). [33 Cal.L.Rev.Comm. Reports 189 (2003)].

Cross References

"Court" defined for purposes of this Chapter, see Code of Civil Procedure § 194.
Criminal procedure, grand juries, inquiry into qualifications by jury commissioners, see Penal Code § 903.2.
"Master list" defined for purposes of this Chapter, see Code of Civil Procedure § 194.
"Prospective juror" defined for purposes of this Chapter, see Code of Civil Procedure § 194.

"Source list" defined for purposes of this Chapter, see Code of Civil Procedure § 194.
Uniform Controlled Substances Act, seizure and disposition, claim of interest procedure, see Health and Safety Code § 11488.5.

§ 197. Source lists of jurors; contents; data from department of motor vehicles; confidentiality

(a) All persons selected for jury service shall be selected at random, from a source or sources inclusive of a representative cross section of the population of the area served by the court. Sources may include, in addition to other lists, customer mailing lists, telephone directories, or utility company lists.

(b)(1) The list of registered voters and the Department of Motor Vehicles' list of licensed drivers and identification cardholders resident within the area served by the court, are appropriate source lists for selection of jurors. Until January 1, 2022, only these two source lists, when substantially purged of duplicate names, shall be considered inclusive of a representative cross section of the population, within the meaning of subdivision (a).

(2) The list of resident state tax filers is an appropriate source list for selection of jurors. Beginning on January 1, 2022, the list of resident state tax filers, the list of registered voters, and the Department of Motor Vehicles' list of licensed drivers and identification cardholders resident within the area served by the court, when substantially purged of duplicate names, shall be considered inclusive of a representative cross section of the population, within the meaning of subdivision (a).

(c) The Department of Motor Vehicles shall furnish the jury commissioner of each county with the current list of the names, addresses, and other identifying information of persons residing in the county who are age 18 years or older and who are holders of a current driver's license or identification card issued pursuant to Article 3 (commencing with Section 12800) of, or Article 5 (commencing with Section 13000) of, Chapter 1 of Division 6 of the Vehicle Code. The conditions under which these lists shall be compiled semiannually shall be determined by the director, consistent with any rules which may be adopted by the Judicial Council. This service shall be provided by the Department of Motor Vehicles pursuant to Section 1812 of the Vehicle Code. The jury commissioner shall not disclose the information furnished by the Department of Motor Vehicles pursuant to this section to any person, organization, or agency.

(d)(1) The Franchise Tax Board shall annually furnish the jury commissioner of each county with a list of resident state tax filers for their county in consultation with the Judicial Council.

(2) The list of resident state tax filers shall be submitted to the jury commissioner of each county by November 1, 2021, and each November 1 thereafter.

(3)(A) For purposes of this section, "list of resident state tax filers" means a list that includes the name, date of birth, principal residence address, and county of principal residence, of persons who are 18 years of age or older and have filed a California resident income tax return for the preceding taxable year.

(B) For purposes of this paragraph, "county of principal residence" means the county in which the taxpayer has their principal residence on the date that the taxpayer filed their California resident income tax return.

(C) For the purposes of this paragraph, "principal residence" is used in the same manner it is used in Section 121 of the Internal Revenue Code.[1] *(Added by Stats.1988, c. 1245, § 2. Amended by Stats.2020, c. 230 (S.B.592), § 1, eff. Jan. 1, 2021.)*

[1] Internal Revenue Code sections are in Title 26 of the U.S.C.A.

Cross References

County defined for purposes of this Chapter, see Code of Civil Procedure § 194.
"Court" defined for purposes of this Chapter, see Code of Civil Procedure § 194.
Grand jury proceedings,
  Furnishing jury lists, see Penal Code § 903.1.
  Inquiry into qualifications, see Penal Code § 903.2.
  Listing and selection of jurors, see Penal Code § 895 et seq.
Inspection of public records, exemptions from disclosure, see Government Code § 6276.28.
Judicial Council, see Government Code § 68500 et seq.
"Random" defined for purposes of this Chapter, see Code of Civil Procedure § 194.
"Source list" defined for purposes of this Chapter, see Code of Civil Procedure § 194.
Uniform Controlled Substances Act, seizure and disposition, claim of interest procedure, see Health and Safety Code § 11488.5.

Research References

5 Witkin, California Criminal Law 4th Criminal Trial § 535 (2021), In General.

§ 198. Master and qualified juror lists; random selection; use of lists

(a) Random selection shall be utilized in creating master and qualified juror lists, commencing with selection from source lists, and continuing through selection of prospective jurors for voir dire.

(b) The jury commissioner shall, at least once in each 12–month period, randomly select names of prospective trial jurors from the source list or lists, to create a master list.

(c) The master jury list shall be used by the jury commissioner, as provided by statute and state and local court rules, for the purpose of (1) mailing juror questionnaires and subsequent creation of a qualified juror list, and (2) summoning prospective jurors to respond or appear for qualification and service. *(Added by Stats.1988, c. 1245, § 2.)*

Civ. Pro.

Cross References

Grand jury proceedings,
  Furnishing jury lists, see Penal Code § 903.1.
  Listing and selection of grand jurors, see Penal Code § 895 et seq.
"Master list" defined for purposes of this Chapter, see Code of Civil Procedure § 194.
Month defined, see Code of Civil Procedure § 17.
Persons qualified to be prospective jurors, see Code of Civil Procedure § 203.
"Prospective juror" defined for purposes of this Chapter, see Code of Civil Procedure § 194.
"Qualified juror" defined for purposes of this Chapter, see Code of Civil Procedure § 194.
"Qualified juror list" defined for purposes of this Chapter, see Code of Civil Procedure § 194.
"Random" defined for purposes of this Chapter, see Code of Civil Procedure § 194.
Religious qualifications for jurors, see Cal. Const. Art. 1, § 4.
"Source list" defined for purposes of this Chapter, see Code of Civil Procedure § 194.
"State" and "United States" as including District of Columbia and territories, see Code of Civil Procedure § 17.
Summoning qualified citizens to complete panel when no available prospective jurors remain, see Code of Civil Procedure § 211.
"Trial jurors" defined for purposes of this Chapter, see Code of Civil Procedure § 194.
Uniform Controlled Substances Act, seizure and disposition, claim of interest procedure, see Health and Safety Code § 11488.5.

§ 198.5. Selection of master jury lists and qualified jury lists to serve in session of superior court from area where session is held pursuant to local superior court rule

If sessions of the superior court are held in a location other than the county seat, the names for master jury lists and qualified jury lists to serve in a session may be selected from the area in which the session is held, pursuant to a local superior court rule that divides the county in a manner that provides all qualified persons in the county an equal opportunity to be considered for jury service. Nothing in this section precludes the court, in its discretion, from ordering a countywide venire in the interest of justice. *(Added by Stats.1988, c. 1245, § 2. Amended by Stats.1998, c. 931 (S.B.2139), § 52, eff. Sept. 28, 1998; Stats.2002, c. 784 (S.B.1316), § 41, operative Jan. 1, 2004; Stats.2003, c. 449 (A.B.1712), § 6.)*

Law Revision Commission Comments

Section 198.5 is amended to accommodate unification of the municipal and superior courts in a county. Cal. Const. art. VI, § 5(e). Subdivision (b) is drawn from Section 191 (policy of state to select jury from population of area served by court; all qualified persons to have an equal opportunity to be considered for jury service). A local rule promulgated pursuant to subdivision (b) may differentiate between misdemeanors and limited civil cases, on the one hand, and felonies and civil cases other than limited civil cases, on the other. See Code Civ. Proc. § 85 (limited civil cases) & Comment; Penal Code § 691 (definitions) & Comment. [28 Cal.L.Rev.Comm. Reports 51 (1998)].

Section 198.5 is amended, effective January 1, 2004, to reflect unification of the municipal and superior courts pursuant to Article VI, Section 5(e), of the California Constitution. It incorporates provisions drawn from Sections 199 (El Dorado County venires), 199.2 (Placer County venires), 199.3 (Nevada County venires), and 199.5 (Santa Barbara County venires). [32 Cal.L.Rev.Comm. Reports 109 (2002)].

Cross References

County defined for purposes of this Chapter, see Code of Civil Procedure § 194.
"Court" defined for purposes of this Chapter, see Code of Civil Procedure § 194.
Uniform Controlled Substances Act, seizure and disposition, claim of interest procedure, see Health and Safety Code § 11488.5.

§ 201. Superior courts; separate trial jury panels; use of jurors from one panel on another

In any superior court, a separate trial jury panel may be drawn, summoned, and impaneled for each judge, or any one panel may be drawn, summoned, and impaneled by any one of the judges, for use in the trial of cases before any of the judges, as occasion may require. In those courts, when a panel of jurors is in attendance for service before one or more of the judges, whether impaneled for common use or not, the whole or any number of the jurors from such panel may be required to attend and serve in the trial of cases, or to complete a panel, or jury, before any other of the judges. *(Added by Stats.1988, c. 1245, § 2. Amended by Stats.2002, c. 784 (S.B.1316), § 47.)*

Law Revision Commission Comments

Section 201 is amended to reflect unification of the municipal and superior courts pursuant to Article VI, Section 5(e), of the California Constitution.

The section is also amended to reflect the fact that every superior court has at least two judgeships as a result of trial court unification. See Gov't Code § 69580 *et seq.* (number of judges). [32 Cal.L.Rev.Comm. Reports 112 (2002)].

Cross References

Challenges to the jury or jurors, see Code of Civil Procedure § 225 et seq.
"Court" defined for purposes of this Chapter, see Code of Civil Procedure § 194.
Summoning jurors, see Code of Civil Procedure § 208 et seq.
"Trial jury panel" defined for purposes of this Chapter, see Code of Civil Procedure § 194.
Uniform Controlled Substances Act, seizure and disposition, claim of interest procedure, see Health and Safety Code § 11488.5.

§ 202. Mechanical, electric, or electronic equipment

Mechanical, electric, or electronic equipment, which in the opinion of the jury commissioner is satisfactory therefor, may be used in the performance of any function specified by this chapter for the selection and drawing of jurors. *(Added by Stats.1988, c. 1245, § 2.)*

Cross References

Judicial Council, provisions relating to,
Electronic collection of court data, see Government Code § 68500.1.
Mechanical or electronic entry, storage, and retrieval of court records, see Government Code § 68511.2.
Uniform entry, storage, and retrieval of court data, see Government Code § 68513.
Uniform Controlled Substances Act, seizure and disposition, claim of interest procedure, see Health and Safety Code § 11488.5.

§ 203. Persons qualified to be trial jurors; exceptions; severability

(a) All persons are eligible and qualified to be prospective trial jurors, except the following:

(1) Persons who are not citizens of the United States.

(2) Persons who are less than 18 years of age.

(3) Persons who are not domiciliaries of the State of California, as determined pursuant to Article 2 (commencing with Section 2020) of Chapter 1 of Division 2 of the Elections Code.

(4) Persons who are not residents of the jurisdiction wherein they are summoned to serve.

(5) Persons who have been convicted of malfeasance in office and whose civil rights have not been restored.

(6) Persons who are not possessed of sufficient knowledge of the English language, provided that no person shall be deemed incompetent solely because of the loss of sight or hearing in any degree or other disability which impedes the person's ability to communicate or which impairs or interferes with the person's mobility.

(7) Persons who are serving as grand or trial jurors in any court of this state.

(8) Persons who are the subject of conservatorship.

(9) Persons while they are incarcerated in any prison or jail.

(10) Persons who have been convicted of a felony and are currently on parole, postrelease community supervision, felony probation, or mandated supervision for the conviction of a felony.

(11) Persons who are currently required to register as a sex offender pursuant to Section 290 of the Penal Code based on a felony conviction.

(b) No person shall be excluded from eligibility for jury service in the State of California, for any reason other than those reasons provided by this section.

(c) The provisions of this section are severable. If any provision of this section or its application is held invalid, that invalidity shall not affect other provisions or applications that can be given effect without the invalid provision or application. *(Added by Stats.1988, c. 1245, § 2. Amended by Stats.1994, c. 923 (S.B.1546), § 1; Stats.2019, c. 591 (S.B.310), § 1, eff. Jan. 1, 2020.)*

Cross References

Convicted felons, exclusion from jury service, see Cal. Const. Art. 7, § 3.
"Court" defined for purposes of this Chapter, see Code of Civil Procedure § 194.
Disabled jurors, appointment of service providers to facilitate communication or participation, see Code of Civil Procedure § 224.
English language requirement, proceedings in courts of justice, see Code of Civil Procedure § 185.
Felonies, definition and penalties, see Penal Code §§ 17, 18.
Grand jurors, competency, see Penal Code § 893.
Hearing impaired persons, assistive listening systems in civil or criminal proceedings, see Civil Code § 54.8.
No religious qualifications for juror, see Cal. Const. Art. 1, § 4.
Residence, see Government Code § 243 et seq.
Selection of jurors for voir dire, exemption of peace officers, see Code of Civil Procedure § 219.
"State" and "United States" as including District of Columbia and territories, see Code of Civil Procedure § 17.
State militia, active members, exemption from jury duty, see Military and Veterans Code § 391.
"Trial jurors" defined for purposes of this Chapter, see Code of Civil Procedure § 194.

Uniform Controlled Substances Act, seizure and disposition, claim of interest procedure, see Health and Safety Code § 11488.5.

Research References

5 Witkin, California Criminal Law 4th Criminal Trial § 535 (2021), In General.
3 Witkin, California Criminal Law 4th Punishment § 182 (2021), Loss of Civil Rights.

§ 204. Exemptions and excuses from jury service

(a) No eligible person shall be exempt from service as a trial juror by reason of occupation, economic status, or any characteristic listed or defined in Section 11135 of the Government Code, or for any other reason. No person shall be excused from service as a trial juror except as specified in subdivision (b).

(b) An eligible person may be excused from jury service only for undue hardship, upon themselves or upon the public, as defined by the Judicial Council. *(Added by Stats.1988, c. 1245, § 2. Amended by Stats.2000, c. 43 (A.B.2418), § 2; Stats.2007, c. 568 (A.B.14), § 15.)*

Cross References

Grand jurors, exemptions, see Penal Code § 894.
Grand jury, qualifications, exemptions and excuses, see Penal Code § 894.
Judicial Council, see Government Code § 68500 et seq.
No religious qualifications for juror, see Cal. Const. Art. 1, § 4.
Selection of jurors for voir dire, exemption of peace officers, see Code of Civil Procedure § 219.
State militia, active members, exemption from jury duty, see Military and Veterans Code § 391.
Uniform Controlled Substances Act, seizure and disposition, claim of interest procedure, see Health and Safety Code § 11488.5.
Written excuses of jurors, see Code of Civil Procedure § 218.

Research References

5 Witkin, California Criminal Law 4th Criminal Trial § 535 (2021), In General.
5 Witkin, California Criminal Law 4th Criminal Trial § 538 (2021), Social or Economic Discrimination.
4 Witkin, California Criminal Law 4th Introduction to Criminal Procedure § 38 (2021), Formation.

§ 205. Juror questionnaires; contents; use; additional questionnaires

(a) If a jury commissioner requires a person to complete a questionnaire, the questionnaire shall ask only questions related to juror identification, qualification, and ability to serve as a prospective juror.

(b) Except as ordered by the court, the questionnaire referred to in subdivision (a) shall be used solely for qualifying prospective jurors, and for management of the jury system, and not for assisting in the courtroom voir dire process of selecting trial jurors for specific cases.

(c) The court may require a prospective juror to complete such additional questionnaires as may be deemed relevant and necessary for assisting in the voir dire process or to ascertain whether a fair cross section of the population is represented as required by law, if such procedures are established by local court rule.

(d) The trial judge may direct a prospective juror to complete additional questionnaires as proposed by counsel in a particular case to assist the voir dire process. *(Added by Stats.1988, c. 1245, § 2.)*

Cross References

"Court" defined for purposes of this Chapter, see Code of Civil Procedure § 194.
Criminal cases, voir dire, see Code of Civil Procedure § 223.
Grand jurors,
  Inquiry into qualifications, see Penal Code § 903.2.
  Selection and listing by court, see Penal Code § 896.
Inquiry in qualifications of prospective jurors, see Code of Civil Procedure § 196.
"Prospective juror" defined for purposes of this Chapter, see Code of Civil Procedure § 194.
"Trial jurors" defined for purposes of this Chapter, see Code of Civil Procedure § 194.
Uniform Controlled Substances Act, seizure and disposition, claim of interest procedure, see Health and Safety Code § 11488.5.

Research References

West's California Judicial Council Forms JURY–001, Juror Questionnaire for Civil Cases.
West's California Judicial Council Forms JURY–002, Juror Questionnaire for Criminal Cases/Capital Case Supplement.
5 Witkin, California Criminal Law 4th Criminal Trial § 569 (2021), Pre-Voir Dire Conference.

§ 206. Criminal actions; discussion of deliberation or verdict after discharge of jury; informing jury; violations

(a) Prior to discharging the jury from the case, the judge in a criminal action shall inform the jurors that they have an absolute right to discuss or not to discuss the deliberation or verdict with anyone. The judge shall also inform the jurors of the provisions set forth in subdivisions (b), (d), and (e).

(b) Following the discharge of the jury in a criminal case, the defendant, or his or her attorney or representative, or the prosecutor, or his or her representative, may discuss the jury deliberation or verdict with a member of the jury, provided that the juror consents to the discussion and that the discussion takes place at a reasonable time and place.

(c) If a discussion of the jury deliberation or verdict with a member of the jury pursuant to subdivision (b) occurs at any time more than 24 hours after the verdict, prior to discussing the jury deliberation or verdict with a member of a jury pursuant to subdivision (b), the defendant or his or her attorney or representative, or the prosecutor or his or her representative, shall inform the juror of the identity of the case, the party in that case which the person represents, the subject of the interview,[1] the absolute right of the juror to discuss or not discuss the deliberations or verdict in the case with the person, and the juror's right to review and have a copy of any declaration filed with the court.

(d) Any unreasonable contact with a juror by the defendant, or his or her attorney or representative, or by the prosecutor, or his or her representative, without the juror's consent shall be immediately reported to the trial judge.

(e) Any violation of this section shall be considered a violation of a lawful court order and shall be subject to reasonable monetary sanctions in accordance with Section 177.5 of the Code of Civil Procedure.

(f) Nothing in the section shall prohibit a peace officer from investigating an allegation of criminal conduct.

(g) Pursuant to Section 237, a defendant or defendant's counsel may, following the recording of a jury's verdict in a criminal proceeding, petition the court for access to personal juror identifying information within the court's records necessary for the defendant to communicate with jurors for the purpose of developing a motion for new trial or any other lawful purpose. This information consists of jurors' names, addresses, and telephone numbers. The court shall consider all requests for personal juror identifying information pursuant to Section 237. *(Added by Stats.1988, c. 1245, § 2. Amended by Stats.1992, c. 971 (S.B.1299), § 2; Stats.1993, c. 632 (A.B.1915), § 1; Stats.1995, c. 964 (S.B.508), § 2; Stats.1996, c. 636 (S.B.2123), § 1, eff. Sept. 19, 1996; Stats.2000, c. 242 (A.B.2567), § 1.)*

[1] So in chaptered copy.

Cross References

Action defined, see Code of Civil Procedure § 22.
Attorneys, State Bar Act, see Business and Professions Code § 6000.
Classes of judicial remedies, see Code of Civil Procedure § 21.

Civ. Pro.

"Court" defined for purposes of this Chapter, see Code of Civil Procedure § 194.
Criminal actions, Penal Code as defining and providing for prosecution of, see Code of Civil Procedure § 31.
Kinds of actions, see Code of Civil Procedure § 24.
Peace officers, generally, Penal Code § 830 et seq.
Threatening juror after verdict has been rendered in a criminal proceeding, see Penal Code § 95.1.
Time for discharge of jury in criminal case, see Penal Code § 1140.
Uniform Controlled Substances Act, seizure and disposition, claim of interest procedure, see Health and Safety Code § 11488.5.

Research References

California Jury Instructions - Criminal 17.60, Post Verdict Juror Admonition/Order.
2 Witkin, California Criminal Law 4th Crimes Against Governmental Authority § 15 (2021), Disclosure or Solicitation of Juror Information.
6 Witkin, California Criminal Law 4th Criminal Judgment § 56 (2021), Information Conveyed to Jurors.
6 Witkin, California Criminal Law 4th Criminal Judgment § 57 (2021), Statutory Procedure.
6 Witkin, California Criminal Law 4th Criminal Judgment § 58 (2021), Case Law.
6 Witkin, California Criminal Law 4th Criminal Judgment § 133 (2021), Juror Testimony.

§ 207. Records; maintenance; preservation

(a) The jury commissioner shall maintain records regarding selection, qualification, and assignment of prospective jurors.

(b) The jury commissioner shall maintain records providing a clear audit trail regarding a juror's attendance, jury fees, and mileage.

(c) All records and papers maintained or compiled by the jury commissioner in connection with the selection or service of a juror may be kept on an electronic or microfilm medium and such records shall be preserved for at least three years after the list used in their selection is prepared, or for any longer period ordered by the court or the jury commissioner. *(Added by Stats.1988, c. 1245, § 2.)*

Cross References

"Court" defined for purposes of this Chapter, see Code of Civil Procedure § 194.
"Prospective juror" defined for purposes of this Chapter, see Code of Civil Procedure § 194.
Uniform Controlled Substances Act, seizure and disposition, claim of interest procedure, see Health and Safety Code § 11488.5.

§ 208. Summoning jurors; methods of serving summons

The jury commissioner shall estimate the number of prospective jurors that may be required to serve the needs of the court, and shall summon prospective jurors for service. Prospective jurors shall be summoned by mailing a summons by first-class mail or by personal service or, in urgency situations, as elsewhere provided by law. The summons, when served by mail, shall be mailed at least 10 days prior to the date of required appearance. Once a prospective juror has been summoned, the date, time, or place of appearance may be modified or further specified by the jury commissioner, by means of written, telegraphic, telephonic, or direct oral communication with the prospective juror. *(Added by Stats.1988, c. 1245, § 2. Amended by Stats.2003, c. 149 (S.B.79), § 7.)*

Law Revision Commission Comments

Section 208 is amended to reflect unification of the municipal and superior courts pursuant to former Section 5(e) of Article VI of the California Constitution. [33 Cal.L.Rev.Comm. Reports 189 (2003)].

Cross References

Computation of time, see Code of Civil Procedure §§ 12, 12a, 12b; Government Code § 6800 et seq.
"Court" defined for purposes of this Chapter, see Code of Civil Procedure § 194.
Grand jury proceedings, estimate of number of jurors needed, see Penal Code § 895.
"Prospective juror" defined for purposes of this Chapter, see Code of Civil Procedure § 194.
Service of summons, see Code of Civil Procedure § 415.10 et seq.
Uniform Controlled Substances Act, seizure and disposition, claim of interest procedure, see Health and Safety Code § 11488.5.
Use of master and qualified juror lists, see Code of Civil Procedure § 198.

§ 209. Failure to respond to summons; attachment; compelling attendance; contempt

(a) Any prospective trial juror who has been summoned for service, and who fails to attend as directed or to respond to the court or jury commissioner and to be excused from attendance, may be attached and compelled to attend. Following an order to show cause hearing, the court may find the prospective juror in contempt of court, punishable by fine, incarceration, or both, as otherwise provided by law.

(b) In lieu of imposing sanctions for contempt as set forth in subdivision (a), the court may impose reasonable monetary sanctions, as provided in this subdivision, on a prospective juror who has not been excused pursuant to Section 204 after first providing the prospective juror with notice and an opportunity to be heard. If a juror fails to respond to the initial summons the court may issue a second summons indicating that the person failed to appear in response to a previous summons and ordering the person to appear for jury duty. The second summons may be issued no earlier than 90 days after the initial failure to appear. Upon the failure of the juror to appear in response to the second summons, the court may issue a failure to appear notice informing the person that failure to respond may result in the imposition of money sanctions. If the prospective juror does not attend the court within the time period as directed by the failure to appear notice, the court shall issue an order to show cause. Payment of monetary sanctions imposed pursuant to this subdivision does not relieve the person of his or her obligation to perform jury duty.

(c)(1) The court may give notice of its intent to impose sanctions by either of the following means:

(A) Verbally to a prospective juror appearing in person in open court.

(B) The issuance on its own motion of an order to show cause requiring the prospective juror to demonstrate reasons for not imposing sanctions. The court may serve the order to show cause by certified or first-class mail.

(2) The monetary sanctions imposed pursuant to subdivision (b) may not exceed two hundred fifty dollars ($250) for the first violation, seven hundred fifty dollars ($750) for the second violation, and one thousand five hundred dollars ($1,500) for the third and any subsequent violation. Monetary sanctions may not be imposed on a prospective juror more than once during a single juror pool cycle. The prospective juror may be excused from paying sanctions pursuant to subdivision (b) of Section 204 or in the interests of justice. The full amount of any sanction paid shall be deposited in a bank account established for this purpose by the Administrative Office of the Courts and transmitted from that account monthly to the Controller for deposit in the Trial Court Trust Fund, as provided in Section 68085.1 of the Government Code. It is the intent of the Legislature that the funds derived from the monetary sanctions authorized in this section be allocated, to the extent feasible, to the family courts and the civil courts. The Judicial Council shall, by rule, provide for a procedure by which a prospective juror against whom a sanction has been imposed by default may move to set aside the default. *(Added by Stats.1988, c. 1245, § 2. Amended by Stats.2003, c. 359 (A.B.1180), § 1; Stats.2005, c. 75 (A.B.145), § 28, eff. July 19, 2005, operative Jan. 1, 2006; Stats.2006, c. 567 (A.B.2303), § 5; Stats.2009, c. 44 (S.B.319), § 1.)*

Cross References

"Court" defined for purposes of this Chapter, see Code of Civil Procedure § 194.
Judicial Council, see Government Code § 68500 et seq.
"Juror pool" defined for purposes of this Chapter, see Code of Civil Procedure § 194.
Legislative intent, construction of statutes, see Code of Civil Procedure § 1859.
Month defined, see Code of Civil Procedure § 17.
Notice, actual and constructive, defined, see Civil Code § 18.
Organization and government of courts, collection of fees and fines pursuant to this section, deposits, see Government Code § 68085.1.
"Prospective juror" defined for purposes of this Chapter, see Code of Civil Procedure § 194.
State Controller, generally, see Government Code § 12402 et seq.
Uniform Controlled Substances Act, seizure and disposition, claim of interest procedure, see Health and Safety Code § 11488.5.

Research References

West's California Judicial Council Forms JURY–010, Juror's Motion to Set Aside Sanctions and Order.

§ 210. Summons; contents

The summons shall contain the date, time, and place of appearance required of the prospective juror or, alternatively, instructions as to the procedure for calling the jury commissioner for telephonic instructions for appearance as well as such additional juror information as deemed appropriate by the jury commissioner. *(Added by Stats.1988, c. 1245, § 2.)*

Cross References

"Prospective juror" defined for purposes of this Chapter, see Code of Civil Procedure § 194.
Uniform Controlled Substances Act, seizure and disposition, claim of interest procedure, see Health and Safety Code § 11488.5.

§ 210.5. Standardized jury summons

The Judicial Council shall adopt a standardized jury summons for use, with appropriate modifications, around the state, that is understandable and has consumer appeal. The standardized jury summons shall include a specific reference to the rules for breast-feeding mothers. The use of the standardized jury summons shall be voluntary, unless otherwise prescribed by the rules of court. *(Added by Stats.2000, c. 266 (A.B.1814), § 2.)*

Cross References

Judicial Council, see Government Code § 68500 et seq.
"State" and "United States" as including District of Columbia and territories, see Code of Civil Procedure § 17.
Uniform Controlled Substances Act, seizure and disposition, claim of interest procedure, see Health and Safety Code § 11488.5.

§ 211. Additional jurors; summoning qualified citizens to complete panel

When a court has no prospective jurors remaining available for voir dire from panels furnished by, or available from, the jury commissioner, and finds that not proceeding with voir dire will place a party's right to a trial by jury in jeopardy, the court may direct the sheriff or marshal to summon, serve, and immediately attach the person of a sufficient number of citizens having the qualifications of jurors, to complete the panel. *(Added by Stats.1988, c. 1245, § 2. Amended by Stats.1996, c. 872 (A.B.3472), § 7.)*

Cross References

Additional grand jurors, applicability of this section, see Penal Code § 908.
"Court" defined for purposes of this Chapter, see Code of Civil Procedure § 194.
Elisor, power and duties, see Code of Civil Procedure § 262.8 et seq.
Grand jury proceedings, impaneling of grand jury,
Filling of vacancies, see Penal Code § 908.1.
Number of persons constituting jury, see Penal Code § 908.
"Prospective juror" defined for purposes of this Chapter, see Code of Civil Procedure § 194.
"Sheriff" as including "marshal", see Code of Civil Procedure § 17.
Uniform Controlled Substances Act, seizure and disposition, claim of interest procedure, see Health and Safety Code § 11488.5.

§ 213. Availability of jurors on telephone notice

Unless excused by reason of undue hardship, all or any portion of the summoned prospective jurors shall be available on one-hour notice by telephone to appear for service, when the jury commissioner determines that it will efficiently serve the operational requirements of the court.

Jurors available on one-hour telephone notice shall receive credit for each day of such availability towards their jury service obligation, but they shall not be paid unless they are actually required to make an appearance. *(Added by Stats.1988, c. 1245, § 2.)*

Cross References

"Court" defined for purposes of this Chapter, see Code of Civil Procedure § 194.
Notice, actual and constructive, defined, see Civil Code § 18.
"Prospective juror" defined for purposes of this Chapter, see Code of Civil Procedure § 194.
Undue hardship, excuse from jury service, see Code of Civil Procedure § 204.
Uniform Controlled Substances Act, seizure and disposition, claim of interest procedure, see Health and Safety Code § 11488.5.

§ 214. Orientation for new jurors; notice of rights under Labor Code

The jury commissioner shall provide orientation for new jurors, which shall include necessary basic information concerning jury service. The jury commissioner shall notify each juror of the provisions of Section 230 of the Labor Code. *(Added by Stats.1988, c. 1245, § 2. Amended by Stats.1989, c. 1416, § 8.)*

Cross References

Jury commissioners, powers and duties, see Code of Civil Procedure § 195.
Notice, actual and constructive, defined, see Civil Code § 18.
Uniform Controlled Substances Act, seizure and disposition, claim of interest procedure, see Health and Safety Code § 11488.5.

§ 215. Fees for jurors; mileage; public transit services

(a) Except as provided in subdivision (b), on and after July 1, 2000, the fee for jurors in the superior court, in civil and criminal cases, is fifteen dollars ($15) a day for each day's attendance as a juror after the first day.

(b) A juror who is employed by a federal, state, or local government entity, or by any other public entity as defined in Section 481.200, and who receives regular compensation and benefits while performing jury service, shall not be paid the fee described in subdivision (a).

(c) All jurors in the superior court, in civil and criminal cases, shall be reimbursed for mileage at the rate of thirty-four cents ($0.34) per mile for each mile actually traveled in attending and returning from court as a juror after the first day * * *.

(d) All jurors and prospective jurors who have been summoned shall be provided with access to existing public transit services at no cost utilizing one of the following options:

(1) Courts may partner with public transit operators in their county to create new programs or continue existing public transit programs that provide no-cost service for jurors and prospective jurors who have been summoned.

(2) A method of reimbursement determined by the court up to a daily maximum of twelve dollars ($12).

(e) Subdivision (d) does not apply to a court in an area where a public transit operator does not provide existing service that is reasonably available to the court facility.

(f) In determining whether transit service is reasonably available to the court facility, the court shall consider factors that include, but are not limited to, all of the following:

(1) Proximity of transit service to the court location.

(2) Hours of operation of transit service in the vicinity of the court location.

(3) Frequency of operation of transit service in the vicinity of the court location.

(4) Availability of transit access to all areas of the court's jurisdiction from which a potential juror may reside.

(g) Prior to determining that transit service is not reasonably available to the court facility, the court shall contact the public transit operator to inquire whether new transit options may be implemented near the court. *(Added by Stats.1988, c. 1245, § 2. Amended by Stats.1998, c. 931 (S.B.2139), § 54, eff. Sept. 28, 1998; Stats.2000, c. 127 (A.B.2866), § 1, eff. July 10, 2000; Stats.2002, c. 784 (S.B.1316), § 48; Stats.2002, c. 144 (A.B.2925), § 1; Stats.2004, c. 227 (S.B. 1102), § 9, eff. Aug. 16, 2004; Stats.2022, c. 326 (A.B.1981), § 2, eff. Jan. 1, 2023.)*

Law Revision Commission Comments

Subdivision (a) of Section 215 is amended to reflect the elimination of the justice court. Cal. Const. art. VI, §§ 1, 5(b). [28 Cal.L.Rev.Comm. Reports 51 (1998)].

References to the municipal courts are deleted from subdivisions (a) and (b) of Section 215 to reflect unification of the municipal and superior courts pursuant to Article VI, Section 5(e), of the California Constitution.

Cross References

Alternate jurors, fees and expenses, see Code of Civil Procedure § 234.
Civil actions, allowable costs, jury food and lodging, see Code of Civil Procedure § 1033.5
"Court" defined for purposes of this Chapter, see Code of Civil Procedure § 194.
Grand jurors, fees, see Penal Code § 890.
Juries of inquest, compensation, see Code of Civil Procedure § 235.
"State" and "United States" as including District of Columbia and territories, see Code of Civil Procedure § 17.
Uniform Controlled Substances Act, seizure and disposition, claim of interest procedure, see Health and Safety Code § 11488.5.

§ 216. Deliberation rooms; restriction of jury assembly facilities

(a) At each court facility where jury cases are heard, the court shall provide a deliberation room or rooms for use of jurors when they have retired for deliberation. The deliberation rooms shall be designed to minimize unwarranted intrusions by other persons in the court facility, shall have suitable furnishings, equipment, and supplies, and shall also have restroom accommodations for male and female jurors.

(b) Unless authorized by the jury commissioner, jury assembly facilities shall be restricted to use by jurors and jury commissioner staff. *(Added by Stats.1988, c. 1245, § 2. Amended by Stats.1996, c. 872 (A.B.3472), § 8; Stats.2020, c. 210 (A.B.1984), § 1, eff. Jan. 1, 2021.)*

Law Revision Commission Comments

Section 216 is amended to reflect enactment of the Trial Court Funding Act of 1997 and the related Trial Court Facilities Act of 2002. See Sections 77003 ("court operations" defined), 77200 (state funding of trial court operations). See also Sections 70311-70312 (responsibility for court operations & facilities), 70391 (Judicial Council responsibility & authority for court facilities). [46 Cal.L.Rev.Comm. Reports 25 (2019)].

Cross References

County defined for purposes of this Chapter, see Code of Civil Procedure § 194.
"Court" defined for purposes of this Chapter, see Code of Civil Procedure § 194.
Criminal proceedings,
Decision in court or deliberation by jury, see Penal Code § 1128.
Information for jury after retirement, see Penal Code § 1138.
Papers and evidence which jury may take with them upon retiring for deliberation, see Penal Code § 1137.
"Sheriff" as including "marshal", see Code of Civil Procedure § 17.
Submission of case to jury, decision in court or deliberation, see Code of Civil Procedure § 613.
Uniform Controlled Substances Act, seizure and disposition, claim of interest procedure, see Health and Safety Code § 11488.5.

§ 217. Criminal cases; food, lodging, and necessities for jurors; expenses

In criminal cases only, while the jury is kept together, either during the progress of the trial or after their retirement for deliberation, the court may direct the sheriff or marshal to provide the jury with suitable and sufficient food and lodging, or other reasonable necessities. The expenses incurred under this section shall be charged against the Trial Court Operations Fund of the county in which the court is held. All those expenses shall be paid on the order of the court. *(Added by Stats.1988, c. 1245, § 2. Amended by Stats.1996, c. 872 (A.B.3472), § 9; Stats.1998, c. 931 (S.B.2139), § 55, eff. Sept. 28, 1998; Stats.2002, c. 784 (S.B.1316), § 49.)*

Law Revision Commission Comments

Section 217 is amended to reflect the elimination of the justice court. Cal. Const. art. VI, §§ 1, 5(b). [28 Cal.L.Rev.Comm. Reports 51 (1998)].

Section 217 is amended to reflect unification of the municipal and superior courts pursuant to Article VI, Section 5(e), of the California Constitution.

The section is also amended to reflect enactment of the Trial Court Funding Act. See Gov't Code §§ 77003 ("court operations" defined), 77009 (Trial Court Operations Fund), 77200 (state funding of trial court operations). [32 Cal.L.Rev.Comm. Reports 113 (2002)].

Cross References

Alternate jurors, fees and expenses, see Code of Civil Procedure § 234.
Civil actions, allowable costs, jury food and lodging, see Code of Civil Procedure § 1033.5
County defined for purposes of this Chapter, see Code of Civil Procedure § 194.
"Court" defined for purposes of this Chapter, see Code of Civil Procedure § 194.
Grand jurors, fees, see Penal Code § 890.
Juries of inquest, compensation, see Code of Civil Procedure § 235.
"Sheriff" as including "marshal", see Code of Civil Procedure § 17.
Uniform Controlled Substances Act, seizure and disposition, claim of interest procedure, see Health and Safety Code § 11488.5.

§ 218. Written excuses of jurors; acceptance by commissioner

The jury commissioner shall hear the excuses of jurors summoned, in accordance with the standards prescribed by the Judicial Council. It shall be left to the discretion of the jury commissioner to accept an excuse under subdivision (b) of Section 204 without a personal appearance. All excuses shall be in writing setting forth the basis of the request and shall be signed by the juror. *(Added by Stats.1988, c. 1245, § 2.)*

Cross References

Grand jury, qualifications, exemptions and excuses, see Penal Code § 894.
Judicial Council, see Government Code § 68500 et seq.
Persons qualified to be trial jurors, see Code of Civil Procedure § 203.
Uniform Controlled Substances Act, seizure and disposition, claim of interest procedure, see Health and Safety Code § 11488.5.

Research References

5 Witkin, California Criminal Law 4th Criminal Trial § 538 (2021), Social or Economic Discrimination.

§ 219. Selection of jurors for voir dire; exemption of peace officers

(a) Except as provided in subdivision (b), the jury commissioner shall randomly select jurors for jury panels to be sent to courtrooms for voir dire.

(b)(1) Notwithstanding subdivision (a), no peace officer, as defined in Section 830.1, subdivision (a) of Section 830.2, and subdivision (a) of Section 830.33, of the Penal Code, shall be selected for voir dire in civil or criminal matters.

(2) Notwithstanding subdivision (a), no peace officer, as defined in subdivisions (b) and (c) of Section 830.2 of the Penal Code, shall be selected for voir dire in criminal matters. *(Added by Stats.1988, c. 1245, § 2. Amended by Stats.1992, c. 324 (A.B.2577), § 1; Stats. 1994, c. 742 (S.B.2066), § 2; Stats.1998, c. 606 (S.B.1880), § 1; Stats.2001, c. 55 (S.B.303), § 1.)*

Cross References

Grand jury, qualifications, exemptions and excuses, see Penal Code § 894.
Peace officers, generally, Penal Code § 830 et seq.
Uniform Controlled Substances Act, seizure and disposition, claim of interest procedure, see Health and Safety Code § 11488.5.

§ 219.5. Adoption by Judicial Council of rule of court requiring trial courts to establish procedures for jury service giving peace officers scheduling accommodations when necessary

The Judicial Council shall adopt a rule of court, on or before January 1, 2005, requiring the trial courts to establish procedures for jury service that gives peace officers, as defined by Section 830.5 of the Penal Code, scheduling accommodations when necessary. *(Added by Stats.2003, c. 353 (A.B.513), § 1.)*

Cross References

"Court" defined for purposes of this Chapter, see Code of Civil Procedure § 194.
Formation of trial jury and calendar of issues for trial, see Penal Code § 1046.
Judicial Council, see Government Code § 68500 et seq.
Peace officers, generally, Penal Code § 830 et seq.
Trial by jury, conduct of trial, see Code of Civil Procedure § 607 et seq.
Trial jury selection and management, see Code of Civil Procedure § 190 et seq.
Uniform Controlled Substances Act, seizure and disposition, claim of interest procedure, see Health and Safety Code § 11488.5.

§ 220. Number of jurors

A trial jury shall consist of 12 persons, except that in civil actions and cases of misdemeanor, it may consist of 12 or any number less than 12, upon which the parties may agree. *(Added by Stats.1988, c. 1245, § 2.)*

Cross References

Action defined, see Code of Civil Procedure § 22.
Civil action defined, see Code of Civil Procedure § 30.
Civil action, origin, see Code of Civil Procedure § 25.
Classes of judicial remedies, see Code of Civil Procedure § 21.
Discharge of juror unable to perform duties, prior to verdict, see Code of Civil Procedure § 233.
Kinds of actions, see Code of Civil Procedure § 24.
Misdemeanors, definition and penalties, see Penal Code §§ 17, 19, and 19.2.
Trial jury defined for purposes of this Chapter, see Code of Civil Procedure § 194.
Uniform Controlled Substances Act, seizure and disposition, claim of interest procedure, see Health and Safety Code § 11488.5.

§ 222. Selection for voir dire; panel list; seating

(a) Except as provided in subdivision (b), when an action is called for trial by jury, the clerk shall randomly select the names of the jurors for voir dire, until the jury is selected or the panel is exhausted.

(b) When the jury commissioner has provided the court with a listing of the trial jury panel in random order, the court shall seat prospective jurors for voir dire in the order provided by the panel list. *(Added by Stats.1988, c. 1245, § 2. Amended by Stats.2007, c. 263 (A.B.310), § 4.)*

Law Revision Commission Comments

Section 222 is amended to delete unnecessary language authorizing the judge to substitute for the clerk if there is no clerk. See Code Civ. Proc. § 167 (judge may perform any act court clerk may perform); Government Code §§ 69840–69848 (duties of clerk of superior court), 71620(b) (executive or administrative officer has authority of clerk of court). [35 Cal.L.Rev.Comm. Reports 219 (2006)].

Cross References

Action defined, see Code of Civil Procedure § 22.
"Court" defined for purposes of this Chapter, see Code of Civil Procedure § 194.
"Prospective juror" defined for purposes of this Chapter, see Code of Civil Procedure § 194.
"Random" defined for purposes of this Chapter, see Code of Civil Procedure § 194.
"Trial jury panel" defined for purposes of this Chapter, see Code of Civil Procedure § 194.
Uniform Controlled Substances Act, seizure and disposition, claim of interest procedure, see Health and Safety Code § 11488.5.

Research References

5 Witkin, California Criminal Law 4th Criminal Trial § 553 (2021), In General.

§ 222.5. Prospective jurors; examination; opening statements; questionnaires

(a) To select a fair and impartial jury in a civil jury trial, the trial judge shall conduct an initial examination of prospective jurors. At the final status conference or at the first practical opportunity prior to voir dire, whichever comes first, the trial judge shall consider and discuss with counsel the form and subject matter of voir dire questions. Before voir dire by the trial judge, the parties may submit questions to the trial judge. The trial judge may include additional questions requested by the parties as the trial judge deems proper.

(b)(1) Upon completion of the trial judge's initial examination, counsel for each party shall have the right to examine, by oral and direct questioning, any of the prospective jurors in order to enable counsel to intelligently exercise both peremptory challenges and challenges for cause. The scope of the examination conducted by counsel shall be within reasonable limits prescribed by the trial judge in the judge's sound discretion subject to the provisions of this chapter. During any examination conducted by counsel for the parties, the trial judge shall permit liberal and probing examination calculated to discover bias or prejudice with regard to the circumstances of the particular case before the court. The fact that a topic has been included in the trial judge's examination shall not preclude appropriate followup questioning in the same area by counsel. The trial judge shall permit counsel to conduct voir dire examination without requiring prior submission of the questions unless a particular counsel engages in improper questioning.

(2) The trial judge shall not impose specific unreasonable or arbitrary time limits or establish an inflexible time limit policy for voir dire.

(3) For purposes of this section, an "improper question" is any question that, as its dominant purpose, attempts to precondition the prospective jurors to a particular result, indoctrinate the jury, or question the prospective jurors concerning the pleadings or the applicable law.

(c)(1) In exercising the judge's sound discretion, the trial judge shall give due consideration to all of the following:

(A) The amount of time requested by trial counsel.

(B) Any unique or complex elements, legal or factual, in the case.

(C) Length of the trial.

(D) Number of parties.

(E) Number of witnesses.

(F) Whether the case is designated as a complex or long cause.

(2) As voir dire proceeds, the judge shall permit supplemental time for questioning based on any of the following:

(A) Individual responses or conduct of jurors that may evince attitudes inconsistent with suitability to serve as a fair and impartial juror in the particular case.

(B) Composition of the jury panel.

(C) An unusual number of for cause challenges.

(d) Upon the request of a party, the trial judge shall allow a brief opening statement by counsel for each party prior to the commencement of the oral questioning phase of the voir dire process.

(e) In civil cases, the trial judge may, upon stipulation by counsel for all the parties appearing in the action, permit counsel to examine the prospective jurors outside a judge's presence.

(f) A trial judge shall not arbitrarily or unreasonably refuse to submit reasonable written questionnaires, the contents of which are determined by the court in its sound discretion, when requested by counsel. If a questionnaire is utilized, the parties shall be given reasonable time to evaluate the responses to the questionnaires before oral questioning commences.

(g) To help facilitate the jury selection process, at the earliest practical time, the judge in a civil trial shall provide the parties with both the alphabetical list and the list of prospective jurors in the order in which they will be called. *(Added by Stats.1990, c. 1232 (A.B.3820), § 1.5. Amended by Stats.2011, c. 409 (A.B.1403), § 1; Stats.2017, c. 337 (S.B.658), § 1, eff. Jan. 1, 2018.)*

Cross References

Action defined, see Code of Civil Procedure § 22.
"Court" defined for purposes of this Chapter, see Code of Civil Procedure § 194.
"Prospective juror" defined for purposes of this Chapter, see Code of Civil Procedure § 194.
Uniform Controlled Substances Act, seizure and disposition, claim of interest procedure, see Health and Safety Code § 11488.5.

§ 223. Criminal cases; voir dire examination by court and counsel

(a) To select a fair and impartial jury in a criminal jury trial, the trial judge shall conduct an initial examination of prospective jurors. At the first practical opportunity prior to voir dire, the trial judge shall consider the form and subject matter of voir dire questions. Before voir dire by the trial judge, the parties may submit questions to the trial judge. The trial judge may include additional questions requested by the parties as the trial judge deems proper.

(b)(1) Upon completion of the trial judge's initial examination, counsel for each party shall have the right to examine, by oral and direct questioning, any of the prospective jurors. The scope of the examination conducted by counsel shall be within reasonable limits prescribed by the trial judge in the judge's sound discretion subject to the provisions of this chapter. During any examination conducted by counsel for the parties, the trial judge shall permit liberal and probing examination calculated to discover bias or prejudice with regard to the circumstances of the particular case or the parties before the court. The fact that a topic has been included in the trial judge's examination shall not preclude appropriate followup questioning in the same area by counsel. The trial judge should permit counsel to conduct voir dire examination without requiring prior submission of the questions unless a particular counsel engages in improper questioning.

(2) The trial judge shall not impose specific unreasonable or arbitrary time limits or establish an inflexible time limit policy for voir dire. As voir dire proceeds, the trial judge shall permit supplemental time for questioning based on individual responses or conduct of jurors that may evince attitudes inconsistent with suitability to serve as a fair and impartial juror in the particular case.

(3) For purposes of this section, an "improper question" is any question that, as its dominant purpose, attempts to precondition the prospective jurors to a particular result or indoctrinate the jury.

(c) In exercising the judge's sound discretion, the trial judge shall consider all of the following:

(1) The amount of time requested by trial counsel.

(2) Any unique or complex legal or factual elements in the case.

(3) The length of the trial.

(4) The number of parties.

(5) The number of witnesses.

(d) Voir dire of any prospective jurors shall, where practicable, take place in the presence of the other jurors in all criminal cases, including death penalty cases. Examination of prospective jurors shall be conducted only in aid of the exercise of challenges for cause.

(e) The trial judge shall, in his or her sound discretion, consider reasonable written questionnaires when requested by counsel. If a questionnaire is utilized, the parties shall be given reasonable time to evaluate the responses to the questionnaires before oral questioning commences.

(f) To help facilitate the jury selection process, at the earliest practical time, the trial judge in a criminal trial shall provide the parties with the list of prospective jurors in the order in which they will be called.

(g) The trial judge's exercise of discretion in the manner in which voir dire is conducted, including any limitation on the time that will be allowed for direct questioning of prospective jurors by counsel and any determination that a question is not in aid of the exercise of challenges for cause, is not cause for a conviction to be reversed, unless the exercise of that discretion results in a miscarriage of justice, as specified in Section 13 of Article VI of the California Constitution. *(Added by Stats.2017, c. 302 (A.B.1541), § 2, eff. Jan. 1, 2018.)*

Cross References

"Court" defined for purposes of this Chapter, see Code of Civil Procedure § 194.
"Prospective juror" defined for purposes of this Chapter, see Code of Civil Procedure § 194.

Research References

5 Witkin, California Criminal Law 4th Criminal Trial § 566 (2021), In General.
5 Witkin, California Criminal Law 4th Criminal Trial § 567 (2021), Examination by Judge.
5 Witkin, California Criminal Law 4th Criminal Trial § 568 (2021), Examination by Counsel.
5 Witkin, California Criminal Law 4th Criminal Trial § 570 (2021), In Camera and Sequestered Voir Dire.
5 Witkin, California Criminal Law 4th Criminal Trial § 574 (2021), Questions Must Relate to Challenge for Cause.
1 Witkin California Criminal Law 4th Introduction to Crimes § 133 (2021), Application to Pending Cases.

§ 224. Disabled jurors; presence of service providers; instructions; appointment

(a) If a party does not cause the removal by challenge of an individual juror who is deaf, hard of hearing, blind, visually impaired, or speech impaired and who requires auxiliary services to facilitate communication, the party shall stipulate to the presence of a service provider in the jury room during jury deliberations, and prepare and deliver to the court proposed jury instructions to the service provider.

(b) As used in this section, "service provider" includes, but is not limited to, a person who is a sign language interpreter, oral interpreter, deaf-blind interpreter, reader, or speech interpreter. If auxiliary services are required during the course of jury deliberations, the court shall instruct the jury and the service provider that the service provider for the juror with a disability is not to participate in the jury's deliberations in any manner except to facilitate communication between the juror with a disability and other jurors.

(c) The court shall appoint a service provider whose services are needed by a juror with a disability to facilitate communication or participation. A sign language interpreter, oral interpreter, or deaf-blind interpreter appointed pursuant to this section shall be a qualified interpreter, as defined in subdivision (f) of Section 754 of the Evidence Code. Service providers appointed by the court under this subdivision shall be compensated in the same manner as provided in subdivision (i) of Section 754 of the Evidence Code. *(Added by Stats.1988, c. 1245, § 2. Amended by Stats.1992, c. 913 (A.B.1077), § 9; Stats.1993, c. 1214 (A.B.551), § 3; Stats.2016, c. 94 (A.B.1709), § 3, eff. Jan. 1, 2017.)*

Cross References

"Court" defined for purposes of this Chapter, see Code of Civil Procedure § 194.
Court interpreter services, see Government Code § 68560 et seq.
Hearing impaired persons, use of assistive listening systems in civil or criminal proceedings, see Civil Code § 54.8.
Persons qualified to be trial jurors, see Code of Civil Procedure § 203.
Uniform Controlled Substances Act, seizure and disposition, claim of interest procedure, see Health and Safety Code § 11488.5.

Research References

California Jury Instructions - Criminal 1.08, Sign Language or Cart Interpreter in Jury Room.

§ 225. Challenges; definition; classes and types

A challenge is an objection made to the trial jurors that may be taken by any party to the action, and is of the following classes and types:

(a) A challenge to the trial jury panel for cause.

(1) A challenge to the panel may only be taken before a trial jury is sworn. The challenge shall be reduced to writing, and shall plainly and distinctly state the facts constituting the ground of challenge.

(2) Reasonable notice of the challenge to the jury panel shall be given to all parties and to the jury commissioner, by service of a copy thereof.

(3) The jury commissioner shall be permitted the services of legal counsel in connection with challenges to the jury panel.

(b) A challenge to a prospective juror by either:

(1) A challenge for cause, for one of the following reasons:

(A) General disqualification—that the juror is disqualified from serving in the action on trial.

(B) Implied bias—as, when the existence of the facts as ascertained, in judgment of law disqualifies the juror.

(C) Actual bias—the existence of a state of mind on the part of the juror in reference to the case, or to any of the parties, which will prevent the juror from acting with entire impartiality, and without prejudice to the substantial rights of any party.

(2) A peremptory challenge to a prospective juror. *(Added by Stats.1988, c. 1245, § 2.)*

Cross References

Action defined, see Code of Civil Procedure § 22.
Notice, actual and constructive, defined, see Civil Code § 18.
"Prospective juror" defined for purposes of this Chapter, see Code of Civil Procedure § 194.
"Trial jurors" defined for purposes of this Chapter, see Code of Civil Procedure § 194.
"Trial jury" defined for purposes of this Chapter, see Code of Civil Procedure § 194.
"Trial jury panel" defined for purposes of this Chapter, see Code of Civil Procedure § 194.
Uniform Controlled Substances Act, seizure and disposition, claim of interest procedure, see Health and Safety Code § 11488.5.

Research References

5 Witkin, California Criminal Law 4th Criminal Trial § 554 (2021), Nature and Grounds.
5 Witkin, California Criminal Law 4th Criminal Trial § 555 (2021), Procedure.
5 Witkin, California Criminal Law 4th Criminal Trial § 556 (2021), Nature and Grounds.
5 Witkin, California Criminal Law 4th Criminal Trial § 557 (2021), In General.
5 Witkin, California Criminal Law 4th Criminal Trial § 564 (2021), Sufficient Showing.
5 Witkin, California Criminal Law 4th Criminal Trial § 573 (2021), In General.
5 Witkin, California Criminal Law 4th Criminal Trial § 580 (2021), In General.
5 Witkin, California Criminal Law 4th Criminal Trial § 582 (2021), Statement, Notice, and Trial of Challenge.
5 Witkin, California Criminal Law 4th Criminal Trial § 605 (2021), Excusing Juror on Judge's Own Motion.

§ 226. Challenges to individual jurors; time; form; exclusion on peremptory challenge

(a) A challenge to an individual juror may only be made before the jury is sworn.

(b) A challenge to an individual juror may be taken orally or may be made in writing, but no reason need be given for a peremptory challenge, and the court shall exclude any juror challenged peremptorily.

(c) All challenges for cause shall be exercised before any peremptory challenges may be exercised.

(d) All challenges to an individual juror, except a peremptory challenge, shall be taken, first by the defendants, and then by the people or plaintiffs. *(Added by Stats.1988, c. 1245, § 2.)*

Cross References

"Court" defined for purposes of this Chapter, see Code of Civil Procedure § 194.
Criminal procedure, challenging the jury, see Penal Code § 1065 et seq.
Uniform Controlled Substances Act, seizure and disposition, claim of interest procedure, see Health and Safety Code § 11488.5.

Research References

5 Witkin, California Criminal Law 4th Criminal Trial § 580 (2021), In General.
5 Witkin, California Criminal Law 4th Criminal Trial § 581 (2021), Order of Challenges.
5 Witkin, California Criminal Law 4th Criminal Trial § 589 (2021), Under California Constitution: Wheeler Case.
5 Witkin, California Criminal Law 4th Criminal Trial § 592 (2021), Statutory Prohibition.

§ 227. Challenges for cause; time; order

The challenges of either party for cause need not all be taken at once, but they may be taken separately, in the following order, including in each challenge all the causes of challenge belonging to the same class and type:

(a) To the panel.

(b) To an individual juror, for a general disqualification.

(c) To an individual juror, for an implied bias.

(d) To an individual juror, for an actual bias. *(Added by Stats.1988, c. 1245, § 2.)*

Cross References

Criminal procedure, challenging the jury, see Penal Code § 1065 et seq.

Uniform Controlled Substances Act, seizure and disposition, claim of interest procedure, see Health and Safety Code § 11488.5.

Research References

5 Witkin, California Criminal Law 4th Criminal Trial § 581 (2021), Order of Challenges.

§ 228. Challenges for general disqualification; grounds

Challenges for general disqualification may be taken on one or both of the following grounds, and for no other:

(a) A want of any of the qualifications prescribed by this code to render a person competent as a juror.

(b) The existence of any incapacity which satisfies the court that the challenged person is incapable of performing the duties of a juror in the particular action without prejudice to the substantial rights of the challenging party. *(Added by Stats.1988, c. 1245, § 2. Amended by Stats.2002, c. 1008 (A.B.3028), § 1.)*

Cross References

Action defined, see Code of Civil Procedure § 22.
"Court" defined for purposes of this Chapter, see Code of Civil Procedure § 194.
Court interpreter services, see Government Code § 68560 et seq.
Criminal procedure, challenging the jury, see Penal Code § 1065 et seq.
Hearing impaired persons, use of assistive listening systems in civil or criminal proceedings, see Civil Code § 54.8.
Persons qualified to be trial jurors, see Code of Civil Procedure § 203.
Uniform Controlled Substances Act, seizure and disposition, claim of interest procedure, see Health and Safety Code § 11488.5.

Research References

5 Witkin, California Criminal Law 4th Criminal Trial § 556 (2021), Nature and Grounds.

§ 229. Challenges for implied bias; causes

A challenge for implied bias may be taken for one or more of the following causes, and for no other:

(a) Consanguinity or affinity within the fourth degree to any party, to an officer of a corporation which is a party, or to any alleged witness or victim in the case at bar.

(b) Standing in the relation of, or being the parent, spouse, or child of one who stands in the relation of, guardian and ward, conservator and conservatee, master and servant, employer and clerk, landlord and tenant, principal and agent, or debtor and creditor, to either party or to an officer of a corporation which is a party, or being a member of the family of either party; or a partner in business with either party; or surety on any bond or obligation for either party, or being the holder of bonds or shares of capital stock of a corporation which is a party; or having stood within one year previous to the filing of the complaint in the action in the relation of attorney and client with either party or with the attorney for either party. A depositor of a bank or a holder of a savings account in a savings and loan association shall not be deemed a creditor of that bank or savings and loan association for the purpose of this paragraph solely by reason of his or her being a depositor or account holder.

(c) Having served as a trial or grand juror or on a jury of inquest in a civil or criminal action or been a witness on a previous or pending trial between the same parties, or involving the same specific offense or cause of action; or having served as a trial or grand juror or on a jury within one year previously in any criminal or civil action or proceeding in which either party was the plaintiff or defendant or in a criminal action where either party was the defendant.

(d) Interest on the part of the juror in the event of the action, or in the main question involved in the action, except his or her interest as a member or citizen or taxpayer of a county, city and county, incorporated city or town, or other political subdivision of a county, or municipal water district.

(e) Having an unqualified opinion or belief as to the merits of the action founded upon knowledge of its material facts or of some of them.

(f) The existence of a state of mind in the juror evincing enmity against, or bias towards, either party.

(g) That the juror is party to an action pending in the court for which he or she is drawn and which action is set for trial before the panel of which the juror is a member.

(h) If the offense charged is punishable with death, the entertaining of such conscientious opinions as would preclude the juror finding the defendant guilty; in which case the juror may neither be permitted nor compelled to serve. *(Added by Stats.1988, c. 1245, § 2.)*

Cross References

Action defined, see Code of Civil Procedure § 22.
Affinity defined, see Code of Civil Procedure § 17.
Attorneys, State Bar Act, see Business and Professions Code § 6000.
Bond and Undertaking Law, bonds or undertakings given as security, see Code of Civil Procedure § 995.010 et seq.
Civil action defined, see Code of Civil Procedure § 30.
Civil action, origin, see Code of Civil Procedure § 25.
County defined for purposes of this Chapter, see Code of Civil Procedure § 194.
"Court" defined for purposes of this Chapter, see Code of Civil Procedure § 194.
Criminal procedure, challenging the jury, see Penal Code § 1065 et seq.
Criminal proceedings, juror's personal knowledge of fact in controversy, see Penal Code § 1120.
"Jury of inquest" defined for purposes of this Chapter, see Code of Civil Procedure § 194.
Kinds of actions, see Code of Civil Procedure § 24.
Obligation defined, see Code of Civil Procedure § 26.
"State" and "United States" as including District of Columbia and territories, see Code of Civil Procedure § 17.
Uniform Controlled Substances Act, seizure and disposition, claim of interest procedure, see Health and Safety Code § 11488.5.

Research References

5 Witkin, California Criminal Law 4th Criminal Trial § 557 (2021), In General.
5 Witkin, California Criminal Law 4th Criminal Trial § 558 (2021), In General.

§ 230. Challenges for cause; trial; witnesses

Challenges for cause shall be tried by the court. The juror challenged and any other person may be examined as a witness in the trial of the challenge, and shall truthfully answer all questions propounded to them. *(Added by Stats.1988, c. 1245, § 2.)*

Cross References

"Court" defined for purposes of this Chapter, see Code of Civil Procedure § 194.
Criminal procedure, challenging the jury, see Penal Code § 1065 et seq.
Uniform Controlled Substances Act, seizure and disposition, claim of interest procedure, see Health and Safety Code § 11488.5.

Research References

5 Witkin, California Criminal Law 4th Criminal Trial § 582 (2021), Statement, Notice, and Trial of Challenge.
5 Witkin, California Criminal Law 4th Criminal Trial § 583 (2021), Discretion of Trial Judge.

§ 231. Peremptory challenges; joint defendants; passing peremptory challenges

(a) In criminal cases, if the offense charged is punishable with death, or with imprisonment in the state prison for life, the defendant is entitled to 20 and the people to 20 peremptory challenges. Except as provided in subdivision (b), in a trial for any other offense, the defendant is entitled to 10 and the state to 10 peremptory challenges. When two or more defendants are jointly tried, their challenges shall be exercised jointly, but each defendant shall also be entitled to five additional challenges which may be exercised separately, and the people shall also be entitled to additional challenges equal to the number of all the additional separate challenges allowed the defendants.

(b) If the offense charged is punishable with a maximum term of imprisonment of 90 days or less, the defendant is entitled to six and the state to six peremptory challenges. When two or more defendants are jointly tried, their challenges shall be exercised jointly, but each defendant shall also be entitled to four additional challenges which may be exercised separately, and the state shall also be entitled to additional challenges equal to the number of all the additional separate challenges allowed the defendants.

(c) In civil cases, each party shall be entitled to six peremptory challenges. If there are more than two parties, the court shall, for the purpose of allotting peremptory challenges, divide the parties into two or more sides according to their respective interests in the issues. Each side shall be entitled to eight peremptory challenges. If there are several parties on a side, the court shall divide the challenges among them as nearly equally as possible. If there are more than two sides, the court shall grant such additional peremptory challenges to a side as the interests of justice may require, provided that the peremptory challenges of one side shall not exceed the aggregate number of peremptory challenges of all other sides. If any party on a side does not use his or her full share of peremptory challenges, the unused challenges may be used by the other party or parties on the same side.

(d) Peremptory challenges shall be taken or passed by the sides alternately, commencing with the plaintiff or people, and each party shall be entitled to have the panel full before exercising any peremptory challenge. When each side passes consecutively, the jury shall then be sworn, unless the court, for good cause, shall otherwise order. The number of peremptory challenges remaining with a side shall not be diminished by any passing of a peremptory challenge.

(e) If all the parties on both sides pass consecutively, the jury shall then be sworn, unless the court, for good cause, shall otherwise order. The number of peremptory challenges remaining with a side shall not be diminished by any passing of a peremptory challenge.

(f) This section shall become operative on January 1, 2021. *(Added by Stats.2016, c. 33 (S.B.843), § 3, eff. June 27, 2016, operative Jan. 1, 2021.)*

Cross References

Computation of time, see Code of Civil Procedure §§ 12, 12a, 12b; Government Code § 6800 et seq.

"Court" defined for purposes of this Chapter, see Code of Civil Procedure § 194.

Criminal procedure, challenging the jury, see Penal Code § 1065 et seq.

Expedited jury trial cases, number of jurors, peremptory challenges, see Code of Civil Procedure § 630.04.

"State" and "United States" as including District of Columbia and territories, see Code of Civil Procedure § 17.

Uniform Controlled Substances Act, seizure and disposition, claim of interest procedure, see Health and Safety Code § 11488.5.

Research References

5 Witkin, California Criminal Law 4th Criminal Trial § 580 (2021), In General.

5 Witkin, California Criminal Law 4th Criminal Trial § 586 (2021), Time and Method.

5 Witkin, California Criminal Law 4th Criminal Trial § 587 (2021), Number.

3 Witkin, California Criminal Law 4th Punishment § 161 (2021), In General.

§ 231.5. Peremptory challenges to remove prospective jurors; bias

A party shall not use a peremptory challenge to remove a prospective juror on the basis of an assumption that the prospective juror is biased merely because of a characteristic listed or defined in Section 11135 of the Government Code, or similar grounds. *(Added by Stats.2000, c. 43 (A.B.2418), § 3. Amended by Stats.2015, c. 115 (A.B.87), § 1, eff. Jan. 1, 2016.)*

Cross References

"Prospective juror" defined for purposes of this Chapter, see Code of Civil Procedure § 194.

Uniform Controlled Substances Act, seizure and disposition, claim of interest procedure, see Health and Safety Code § 11488.5.

Research References

5 Witkin, California Criminal Law 4th Criminal Trial § 592 (2021), Statutory Prohibition.

5 Witkin, California Criminal Law 4th Criminal Trial § 595 (2021), What Constitutes Cognizable Group.

§ 231.7. Prohibition of peremptory challenge on the basis of race, ethnicity, gender, gender identity, sexual orientation, national origin, or religious affiliation; actual or perceived membership in any group; motion

Section operative until Jan. 1, 2026. See, also, § 231.7 operative Jan. 1, 2026.

(a) A party shall not use a peremptory challenge to remove a prospective juror on the basis of the prospective juror's race, ethnicity, gender, gender identity, sexual orientation, national origin, or religious affiliation, or the perceived membership of the prospective juror in any of those groups.

(b) A party, or the trial court on its own motion, may object to the improper use of a peremptory challenge under subdivision (a). After the objection is made, any further discussion shall be conducted outside the presence of the panel. The objection shall be made before the jury is impaneled, unless information becomes known that could not have reasonably been known before the jury was impaneled.

(c) Notwithstanding Section 226, upon objection to the exercise of a peremptory challenge pursuant to this section, the party exercising the peremptory challenge shall state the reasons the peremptory challenge has been exercised.

(d)(1) The court shall evaluate the reasons given to justify the peremptory challenge in light of the totality of the circumstances. The court shall consider only the reasons actually given and shall not speculate on, or assume the existence of, other possible justifications for the use of the peremptory challenge. If the court determines there is a substantial likelihood that an objectively reasonable person would view race, ethnicity, gender, gender identity, sexual orientation, national origin, or religious affiliation, or perceived membership in any of those groups, as a factor in the use of the peremptory challenge, then the objection shall be sustained. The court need not find purposeful discrimination to sustain the objection. The court shall explain the reasons for its ruling on the record. A motion brought under this section shall also be deemed a sufficient presentation of claims asserting the discriminatory exclusion of jurors in violation of the United States and California Constitutions.

(2)(A) For purposes of this section, an objectively reasonable person is aware that unconscious bias, in addition to purposeful discrimination, have resulted in the unfair exclusion of potential jurors in the State of California.

(B) For purposes of this section, a "substantial likelihood" means more than a mere possibility but less than a standard of more likely than not.

(C) For purposes of this section, "unconscious bias" includes implicit and institutional biases.

(3) In making its determination, the circumstances the court may consider include, but are not limited to, any of the following:

(A) Whether any of the following circumstances exist:

(i) The objecting party is a member of the same perceived cognizable group as the challenged juror.

(ii) The alleged victim is not a member of that perceived cognizable group.

Civ. Pro.

(iii) Witnesses or the parties are not members of that perceived cognizable group.

(B) Whether race, ethnicity, gender, gender identity, sexual orientation, national origin, or religious affiliation, or perceived membership in any of those groups, bear on the facts of the case to be tried.

(C) The number and types of questions posed to the prospective juror, including, but not limited to, any the following:

(i) Consideration of whether the party exercising the peremptory challenge failed to question the prospective juror about the concerns later stated by the party as the reason for the peremptory challenge pursuant to subdivision (c).

(ii) Whether the party exercising the peremptory challenge engaged in cursory questioning of the challenged potential juror.

(iii) Whether the party exercising the peremptory challenge asked different questions of the potential juror against whom the peremptory challenge was used in contrast to questions asked of other jurors from different perceived cognizable groups about the same topic or whether the party phrased those questions differently.

(D) Whether other prospective jurors, who are not members of the same cognizable group as the challenged prospective juror, provided similar, but not necessarily identical, answers but were not the subject of a peremptory challenge by that party.

(E) Whether a reason might be disproportionately associated with a race, ethnicity, gender, gender identity, sexual orientation, national origin, or religious affiliation, or perceived membership in any of those groups.

(F) Whether the reason given by the party exercising the peremptory challenge was contrary to or unsupported by the record.

(G) Whether the counsel or counsel's office exercising the challenge has used peremptory challenges disproportionately against a given race, ethnicity, gender, gender identity, sexual orientation, national origin, or religious affiliation, or perceived membership in any of those groups, in the present case or in past cases, including whether the counsel or counsel's office who made the challenge has a history of prior violations under Batson v. Kentucky (1986) 476 U.S. 79, People v. Wheeler (1978) 22 Cal.3d 258, Section 231.5, or this section.

(e) A peremptory challenge for any of the following reasons is presumed to be invalid unless the party exercising the peremptory challenge can show by clear and convincing evidence that an objectively reasonable person would view the rationale as unrelated to a prospective juror's race, ethnicity, gender, gender identity, sexual orientation, national origin, or religious affiliation, or perceived membership in any of those groups, and that the reasons articulated bear on the prospective juror's ability to be fair and impartial in the case:

(1) Expressing a distrust of or having a negative experience with law enforcement or the criminal legal system.

(2) Expressing a belief that law enforcement officers engage in racial profiling or that criminal laws have been enforced in a discriminatory manner.

(3) Having a close relationship with people who have been stopped, arrested, or convicted of a crime.

(4) A prospective juror's neighborhood.

(5) Having a child outside of marriage.

(6) Receiving state benefits.

(7) Not being a native English speaker.

(8) The ability to speak another language.

(9) Dress, attire, or personal appearance.

(10) Employment in a field that is disproportionately occupied by members listed in subdivision (a) or that serves a population disproportionately comprised of members of a group or groups listed in subdivision (a).

(11) Lack of employment or underemployment of the prospective juror or prospective juror's family member.

(12) A prospective juror's apparent friendliness with another prospective juror of the same group as listed in subdivision (a).

(13) Any justification that is similarly applicable to a questioned prospective juror or jurors, who are not members of the same cognizable group as the challenged prospective juror, but were not the subject of a peremptory challenge by that party. The unchallenged prospective juror or jurors need not share any other characteristics with the challenged prospective juror for peremptory challenge relying on this justification to be considered presumptively invalid.

(f) For purposes of subdivision (e), the term "clear and convincing" refers to the degree of certainty the factfinder must have in determining whether the reasons given for the exercise of a peremptory challenge are unrelated to the prospective juror's cognizable group membership, bearing in mind conscious and unconscious bias. To determine that a presumption of invalidity has been overcome, the factfinder shall determine that it is highly probable that the reasons given for the exercise of a peremptory challenge are unrelated to conscious or unconscious bias and are instead specific to the juror and bear on that juror's ability to be fair and impartial in the case.

(g)(1) The following reasons for peremptory challenges have historically been associated with improper discrimination in jury selection:

(A) The prospective juror was inattentive, or staring or failing to make eye contact.

(B) The prospective juror exhibited either a lack of rapport or problematic attitude, body language, or demeanor.

(C) The prospective juror provided unintelligent or confused answers.

(2) The reasons set forth in paragraph (1) are presumptively invalid unless the trial court is able to confirm that the asserted behavior occurred, based on the court's own observations or the observations of counsel for the objecting party. Even with that confirmation, the counsel offering the reason shall explain why the asserted demeanor, behavior, or manner in which the prospective juror answered questions matters to the case to be tried.

(h) Upon a court granting an objection to the improper exercise of a peremptory challenge, the court shall do one or more of the following:

(1) Quash the jury venire and start jury selection anew. This remedy shall be provided if requested by the objecting party.

(2) If the motion is granted after the jury has been impaneled, declare a mistrial and select a new jury if requested by the defendant.

(3) Seat the challenged juror.

(4) Provide the objecting party additional challenges.

(5) Provide another remedy as the court deems appropriate.

(i) This section applies in all jury trials in which jury selection begins on or after January 1, 2022.

(j) The denial of an objection made under this section shall be reviewed by the appellate court de novo, with the trial court's express factual findings reviewed for substantial evidence. The appellate court shall not impute to the trial court any findings, including findings of a prospective juror's demeanor, that the trial court did not expressly state on the record. The reviewing court shall consider only reasons actually given under subdivision (c) and shall not speculate as to or consider reasons that were not given to explain either the party's use of the peremptory challenge or the party's failure to challenge similarly situated jurors who are not members of the same cognizable group as the challenged juror, regardless of whether the moving party made a comparative analysis argument in the trial court. Should the appellate court determine that the objection was erroneously denied, that error shall be deemed prejudicial, the judgment shall be reversed, and the case remanded for a new trial.

(k) This section shall not apply to civil cases.

(*l*) It is the intent of the Legislature that enactment of this section shall not, in purpose or effect, lower the standard for judging challenges for cause or expand use of challenges for cause.

(m) The provisions of this section are severable. If any provision of this section or its application is held invalid, that invalidity shall not affect other provisions or applications that can be given effect without the invalid provision or application.

(n) This section shall remain in effect only until January 1, 2026, and as of that date is repealed. *(Added by Stats.2020, c. 318 (A.B.3070), § 2, eff. Jan. 1, 2021.)*

Repeal

For repeal of this section, see its terms.

Research References

5 Witkin, California Criminal Law 4th Criminal Trial § 592 (2021), Statutory Prohibition.

5 Witkin, California Criminal Law 4th Criminal Trial § 595 (2021), What Constitutes Cognizable Group.

§ 231.7. Prohibition of peremptory challenge on the basis of race, ethnicity, gender, gender identity, sexual orientation, national origin, or religious affiliation; actual or perceived membership in any group; motion

Section operative Jan. 1, 2026. See, also, § 231.7 operative until Jan. 1, 2026.

(a) A party shall not use a peremptory challenge to remove a prospective juror on the basis of the prospective juror's race, ethnicity, gender, gender identity, sexual orientation, national origin, or religious affiliation, or the perceived membership of the prospective juror in any of those groups.

(b) A party, or the trial court on its own motion, may object to the improper use of a peremptory challenge under subdivision (a). After the objection is made, any further discussion shall be conducted outside the presence of the panel. The objection shall be made before the jury is impaneled, unless information becomes known that could not have reasonably been known before the jury was impaneled.

(c) Notwithstanding Section 226, upon objection to the exercise of a peremptory challenge pursuant to this section, the party exercising the peremptory challenge shall state the reasons the peremptory challenge has been exercised.

(d)(1) The court shall evaluate the reasons given to justify the peremptory challenge in light of the totality of the circumstances. The court shall consider only the reasons actually given and shall not speculate on, or assume the existence of, other possible justifications for the use of the peremptory challenge. If the court determines there is a substantial likelihood that an objectively reasonable person would view race, ethnicity, gender, gender identity, sexual orientation, national origin, or religious affiliation, or perceived membership in any of those groups, as a factor in the use of the peremptory challenge, then the objection shall be sustained. The court need not find purposeful discrimination to sustain the objection. The court shall explain the reasons for its ruling on the record. A motion brought under this section shall also be deemed a sufficient presentation of claims asserting the discriminatory exclusion of jurors in violation of the United States and California Constitutions.

(2)(A) For purposes of this section, an objectively reasonable person is aware that unconscious bias, in addition to purposeful discrimination, have resulted in the unfair exclusion of potential jurors in the State of California.

(B) For purposes of this section, a "substantial likelihood" means more than a mere possibility but less than a standard of more likely than not.

(C) For purposes of this section, "unconscious bias" includes implicit and institutional biases.

(3) In making its determination, the circumstances the court may consider include, but are not limited to, any of the following:

(A) Whether any of the following circumstances exist:

(i) The objecting party is a member of the same perceived cognizable group as the challenged juror.

(ii) The alleged victim is not a member of that perceived cognizable group.

(iii) Witnesses or the parties are not members of that perceived cognizable group.

(B) Whether race, ethnicity, gender, gender identity, sexual orientation, national origin, or religious affiliation, or perceived membership in any of those groups, bear on the facts of the case to be tried.

(C) The number and types of questions posed to the prospective juror, including, but not limited to, any the following:

(i) Consideration of whether the party exercising the peremptory challenge failed to question the prospective juror about the concerns later stated by the party as the reason for the peremptory challenge pursuant to subdivision (c).

(ii) Whether the party exercising the peremptory challenge engaged in cursory questioning of the challenged potential juror.

(iii) Whether the party exercising the peremptory challenge asked different questions of the potential juror against whom the peremptory challenge was used in contrast to questions asked of other jurors from different perceived cognizable groups about the same topic or whether the party phrased those questions differently.

(D) Whether other prospective jurors, who are not members of the same cognizable group as the challenged prospective juror, provided similar, but not necessarily identical, answers but were not the subject of a peremptory challenge by that party.

(E) Whether a reason might be disproportionately associated with a race, ethnicity, gender, gender identity, sexual orientation, national origin, or religious affiliation, or perceived membership in any of those groups.

(F) Whether the reason given by the party exercising the peremptory challenge was contrary to or unsupported by the record.

(G) Whether the counsel or counsel's office exercising the challenge has used peremptory challenges disproportionately against a given race, ethnicity, gender, gender identity, sexual orientation, national origin, or religious affiliation, or perceived membership in any of those groups, in the present case or in past cases, including whether the counsel or counsel's office who made the challenge has a history of prior violations under Batson v. Kentucky (1986) 476 U.S. 79, People v. Wheeler (1978) 22 Cal.3d 258, Section 231.5, or this section.

(e) A peremptory challenge for any of the following reasons is presumed to be invalid unless the party exercising the peremptory challenge can show by clear and convincing evidence that an objectively reasonable person would view the rationale as unrelated to a prospective juror's race, ethnicity, gender, gender identity, sexual orientation, national origin, or religious affiliation, or perceived membership in any of those groups, and that the reasons articulated bear on the prospective juror's ability to be fair and impartial in the case:

(1) Expressing a distrust of or having a negative experience with law enforcement or the criminal legal system.

(2) Expressing a belief that law enforcement officers engage in racial profiling or that criminal laws have been enforced in a discriminatory manner.

(3) Having a close relationship with people who have been stopped, arrested, or convicted of a crime.

(4) A prospective juror's neighborhood.

(5) Having a child outside of marriage.

(6) Receiving state benefits.

(7) Not being a native English speaker.

(8) The ability to speak another language.

(9) Dress, attire, or personal appearance.

(10) Employment in a field that is disproportionately occupied by members listed in subdivision (a) or that serves a population disproportionately comprised of members of a group or groups listed in subdivision (a).

(11) Lack of employment or underemployment of the prospective juror or prospective juror's family member.

(12) A prospective juror's apparent friendliness with another prospective juror of the same group as listed in subdivision (a).

(13) Any justification that is similarly applicable to a questioned prospective juror or jurors, who are not members of the same cognizable group as the challenged prospective juror, but were not the subject of a peremptory challenge by that party. The unchallenged prospective juror or jurors need not share any other characteristics with the challenged prospective juror for peremptory challenge relying on this justification to be considered presumptively invalid.

(f) For purposes of subdivision (e), the term "clear and convincing" refers to the degree of certainty the factfinder must have in determining whether the reasons given for the exercise of a peremptory challenge are unrelated to the prospective juror's cognizable group membership, bearing in mind conscious and unconscious bias. To determine that a presumption of invalidity has been overcome, the factfinder shall determine that it is highly probable that the reasons given for the exercise of a peremptory challenge are unrelated to conscious or unconscious bias and are instead specific to the juror and bear on that juror's ability to be fair and impartial in the case.

(g)(1) The following reasons for peremptory challenges have historically been associated with improper discrimination in jury selection:

(A) The prospective juror was inattentive, or staring or failing to make eye contact.

(B) The prospective juror exhibited either a lack of rapport or problematic attitude, body language, or demeanor.

(C) The prospective juror provided unintelligent or confused answers.

(2) The reasons set forth in paragraph (1) are presumptively invalid unless the trial court is able to confirm that the asserted behavior occurred, based on the court's own observations or the observations of counsel for the objecting party. Even with that confirmation, the counsel offering the reason shall explain why the asserted demeanor, behavior, or manner in which the prospective juror answered questions matters to the case to be tried.

(h) Upon a court granting an objection to the improper exercise of a peremptory challenge, the court shall do one or more of the following:

(1) Quash the jury venire and start jury selection anew. This remedy shall be provided if requested by the objecting party.

(2) If the motion is granted after the jury has been impaneled, declare a mistrial and select a new jury if requested by the defendant.

(3) Seat the challenged juror.

(4) Provide the objecting party additional challenges.

(5) Provide another remedy as the court deems appropriate.

(i) This section applies in all jury trials in which jury selection begins on or after January 1, 2022.

(j) The denial of an objection made under this section shall be reviewed by the appellate court de novo, with the trial court's express factual findings reviewed for substantial evidence. The appellate court shall not impute to the trial court any findings, including findings of a prospective juror's demeanor, that the trial court did not expressly state on the record. The reviewing court shall consider only reasons actually given under subdivision (c) and shall not speculate as to or consider reasons that were not given to explain either the party's use of the peremptory challenge or the party's failure to challenge similarly situated jurors who are not members of the same cognizable group as the challenged juror, regardless of whether the moving party made a comparative analysis argument in the trial court. Should the appellate court determine that the objection was erroneously denied, that error shall be deemed prejudicial, the judgment shall be reversed, and the case remanded for a new trial.

(k) It is the intent of the Legislature that enactment of this section shall not, in purpose or effect, lower the standard for judging challenges for cause or expand use of challenges for cause.

(*l*) The provisions of this section are severable. If any provision of this section or its application is held invalid, that invalidity shall not affect other provisions or applications that can be given effect without the invalid provision or application.

(m) This section shall become operative January 1, 2026. *(Added by Stats.2020, c. 318 (A.B.3070), § 3, eff. Jan. 1, 2021, operative Jan. 1, 2026.)*

Research References

5 Witkin, California Criminal Law 4th Criminal Trial § 592 (2021), Statutory Prohibition.

5 Witkin, California Criminal Law 4th Criminal Trial § 595 (2021), What Constitutes Cognizable Group.

§ 232. Perjury acknowledgement and agreement

(a) Prior to the examination of prospective trial jurors in the panel assigned for voir dire, the following perjury acknowledgement and agreement shall be obtained from the panel, which shall be acknowledged by the prospective jurors with the statement "I do":

"Do you, and each of you, understand and agree that you will accurately and truthfully answer, under penalty of perjury, all questions propounded to you concerning your qualifications and competency to serve as a trial juror in the matter pending before this court; and that failure to do so may subject you to criminal prosecution."

(b) As soon as the selection of the trial jury is completed, the following acknowledgment and agreement shall be obtained from the trial jurors, which shall be acknowledged by the statement "I do":

"Do you and each of you understand and agree that you will well and truly try the cause now pending before this court, and a true verdict render according only to the evidence presented to you and to the instructions of the court." *(Added by Stats.1988, c. 1245, § 2. Amended by Stats.1989, c. 1416, § 10.)*

Cross References

"Court" defined for purposes of this Chapter, see Code of Civil Procedure § 194.

Grand jury proceedings, oath taken by grand jury members, see Penal Code § 911.

"Prospective juror" defined for purposes of this Chapter, see Code of Civil Procedure § 194.
"Trial jurors" defined for purposes of this Chapter, see Code of Civil Procedure § 194.
"Trial jury" defined for purposes of this Chapter, see Code of Civil Procedure § 194.
Uniform Controlled Substances Act, seizure and disposition, claim of interest procedure, see Health and Safety Code § 11488.5.

Research References

5 Witkin, California Criminal Law 4th Criminal Trial § 553 (2021), In General.

§ 233. Discharge of juror unable to perform duties; alternate jurors; discharge of jury

If, before the jury has returned its verdict to the court, a juror becomes sick or, upon other good cause shown to the court, is found to be unable to perform his or her duty, the court may order the juror to be discharged. If any alternate jurors have been selected as provided by law, one of them shall then be designated by the court to take the place of the juror so discharged. If after all alternate jurors have been made regular jurors or if there is no alternate juror, a juror becomes sick or otherwise unable to perform the juror's duty and has been discharged by the court as provided in this section, the jury shall be discharged and a new jury then or afterwards impaneled, and the cause may again be tried. Alternatively, with the consent of all parties, the trial may proceed with only the remaining jurors, or another juror may be sworn and the trial begin anew. *(Added by Stats.1988, c. 1245, § 2.)*

Cross References

"Court" defined for purposes of this Chapter, see Code of Civil Procedure § 194.
Discharge of jury without verdict or prevention from giving verdict, retrial, see Code of Civil Procedure § 616.
Number of jurors on trial jury, see Code of Civil Procedure § 220.
Uniform Controlled Substances Act, seizure and disposition, claim of interest procedure, see Health and Safety Code § 11488.5.

Research References

5 Witkin, California Criminal Law 4th Criminal Trial § 607 (2021), In General.
5 Witkin, California Criminal Law 4th Criminal Trial § 608 (2021), In General.
5 Witkin, California Criminal Law 4th Criminal Trial § 609 (2021), Delayed Discovery of Ground of Disqualification.
5 Witkin, California Criminal Law 4th Criminal Trial § 610 (2021), Juror's Misconduct.
5 Witkin, California Criminal Law 4th Criminal Trial § 616 (2021), Exhaustion of Alternates.
1 Witkin California Criminal Law 4th Defenses § 149 (2021), Illness, Incapacity, or Absence of Juror.

§ 234. Alternate jurors; drawing and examining; qualifications; attendance; confinement; replacing original juror; fees and expenses

Whenever, in the opinion of a judge of a superior court about to try a civil or criminal action or proceeding, the trial is likely to be a protracted one, or upon stipulation of the parties, the court may cause an entry to that effect to be made in the minutes of the court and thereupon, immediately after the jury is impaneled and sworn, the court may direct the calling of one or more additional jurors, in its discretion, to be known as "alternate jurors."

These alternate jurors shall be drawn from the same source, and in the same manner, and have the same qualifications, as the jurors already sworn, and shall be subject to the same examination and challenges. However, each side, or each defendant, as provided in Section 231, shall be entitled to as many peremptory challenges to the alternate jurors as there are alternate jurors called.

The alternate jurors shall be seated so as to have equal power and facilities for seeing and hearing the proceedings in the case, and shall take the same oath as the jurors already selected, and shall, unless excused by the court, attend at all times upon the trial of the cause in company with the other jurors, but shall not participate in deliberation unless ordered by the court, and for a failure to do so are liable to be punished for contempt.

They shall obey the orders of and be bound by the admonition of the court, upon each adjournment of the court; but if the regular jurors are ordered to be kept in the custody of the sheriff or marshal during the trial of the cause, the alternate jurors shall also be kept in confinement with the other jurors; and upon final submission of the case to the jury, the alternate jurors shall be kept in the custody of the sheriff or marshal who shall not suffer any communication to be made to them except by order of the court, and shall not be discharged until the original jurors are discharged, except as provided in this section.

If at any time, whether before or after the final submission of the case to the jury, a juror dies or becomes ill, or upon other good cause shown to the court is found to be unable to perform his or her duty, or if a juror requests a discharge and good cause appears therefor, the court may order the juror to be discharged and draw the name of an alternate, who shall then take his or her place in the jury box, and be subject to the same rules and regulations as though he or she had been selected as one of the original jurors.

All laws relative to fees, expenses, and mileage or transportation of jurors shall be applicable to alternate jurors, except that in civil cases the sums for fees and mileage or transportation need not be deposited until the judge directs alternate jurors to be impaneled. *(Added by Stats.1988, c. 1245, § 2. Amended by Stats.1996, c. 872 (A.B.3472), § 10; Stats.1998, c. 931 (S.B.2139), § 56, eff. Sept. 28, 1998; Stats.2002, c. 784 (S.B.1316), § 50; Stats.2010, c. 328 (S.B. 1330), § 33.)*

Civ. Pro.

Law Revision Commission Comments

Section 234 is amended to reflect the elimination of the justice court. Cal. Const. art. VI, §§ 1, 5(b). [28 Cal.L.Rev.Comm. Reports 51 (1998)].

Section 234 is amended to reflect unification of the municipal and superior courts pursuant to Article VI, Section 5(e), of the California Constitution. [32 Cal.L.Rev.Comm. Reports 114 (2002)].

Cross References

Action defined, see Code of Civil Procedure § 22.
"Court" defined for purposes of this Chapter, see Code of Civil Procedure § 194.
Criminal procedure, alternate jurors, see Penal Code § 1089.
Discharge of jury without verdict or prevention from giving verdict, retrial, see Code of Civil Procedure § 616.
Kinds of actions, see Code of Civil Procedure § 24.
Number of jurors on trial jury, see Code of Civil Procedure § 220.
"Sheriff" as including "marshal", see Code of Civil Procedure § 17.
Uniform Controlled Substances Act, seizure and disposition, claim of interest procedure, see Health and Safety Code § 11488.5.

Research References

5 Witkin, California Criminal Law 4th Criminal Trial § 587 (2021), Number.
5 Witkin, California Criminal Law 4th Criminal Trial § 606 (2021), In General.
5 Witkin, California Criminal Law 4th Criminal Trial § 607 (2021), In General.
5 Witkin, California Criminal Law 4th Criminal Trial § 612 (2021), Request of Juror on Good Cause.
5 Witkin, California Criminal Law 4th Criminal Trial § 615 (2021), Substitution After Submission.

§ 235. Juries of inquest; selection; compensation

At the request of the sheriff, coroner, or other ministerial officer, the jury commissioner shall provide such prospective jurors as may be required to form a jury of inquest. Prospective jurors so provided shall be selected, obligated, and compensated in the same manner as other jurors selected under the provisions of this chapter. *(Added by Stats.1988, c. 1245, § 2.)*

Cross References

Coroner, inquests, see Government Code § 27490 et seq.

"Jury of inquest" defined for purposes of this Chapter, see Code of Civil Procedure § 194.
Kinds of juries, see Code of Civil Procedure § 193.
"Prospective juror" defined for purposes of this Chapter, see Code of Civil Procedure § 194.
"Sheriff" as including "marshal", see Code of Civil Procedure § 17.

§ 236. Juries of inquest; oath; duties

When six or more prospective jurors of inquest attend, they shall be sworn by the coroner to inquire who the person was, and when, where, and by what means the person came to his or her death, to inquire into the circumstances attending the death, and to render a true verdict thereon, according to the evidence offered them or arising from the inspection of the body. *(Added by Stats.1988, c. 1245, § 2.)*

Cross References

Coroner, inquests, see Government Code § 27490 et seq.
"Jury of inquest" defined for purposes of this Chapter, see Code of Civil Procedure § 194.
Kinds of juries, see Code of Civil Procedure § 193.
"Prospective juror" defined for purposes of this Chapter, see Code of Civil Procedure § 194.

§ 237. Access to juror information; sealed records; violations

(a)(1) The names of qualified jurors drawn from the qualified juror list for the superior court shall be made available to the public upon request unless the court determines that a compelling interest, as defined in subdivision (b), requires that this information should be kept confidential or its use limited in whole or in part.

(2) Upon the recording of a jury's verdict in a criminal jury proceeding, the court's record of personal juror identifying information of trial jurors, as defined in Section 194, consisting of names, addresses, and telephone numbers, shall be sealed until further order of the court as provided by this section.

(3) For purposes of this section, "sealed" or "sealing" means extracting or otherwise removing the personal juror identifying information from the court record.

(4) This subdivision applies only to cases in which a jury verdict was returned on or after January 1, 1996.

(b) Any person may petition the court for access to these records. The petition shall be supported by a declaration that includes facts sufficient to establish good cause for the release of the juror's personal identifying information. The court shall set the matter for hearing if the petition and supporting declaration establish a prima facie showing of good cause for the release of the personal juror identifying information, but shall not set the matter for hearing if there is a showing on the record of facts that establish a compelling interest against disclosure. A compelling interest includes, but is not limited to, protecting jurors from threats or danger of physical harm. If the court does not set the matter for hearing, the court shall by minute order set forth the reasons and make express findings either of a lack of a prima facie showing of good cause or the presence of a compelling interest against disclosure.

(c) If a hearing is set pursuant to subdivision (b), the petitioner shall provide notice of the petition and the time and place of the hearing at least 20 days prior to the date of the hearing to the parties in the criminal action. The court shall provide notice to each affected former juror by personal service or by first-class mail, addressed to the last known address of the former juror as shown in the records of the court. In a capital case, the petitioner shall also serve notice on the Attorney General. Any affected former juror may appear in person, in writing, by telephone, or by counsel to protest the granting of the petition. A former juror who wishes to appear at the hearing to oppose the unsealing of the personal juror identifying information may request the court to close the hearing in order to protect the former juror's anonymity.

(d) After the hearing, the records shall be made available as requested in the petition, unless a former juror's protest to the granting of the petition is sustained. The court shall sustain the protest of the former juror if, in the discretion of the court, the petitioner fails to show good cause, the record establishes the presence of a compelling interest against disclosure as defined in subdivision (b), or the juror is unwilling to be contacted by the petitioner. The court shall set forth reasons and make express findings to support the granting or denying of the petition to disclose. The court may require the person to whom disclosure is made, or his or her agent or employee, to agree not to divulge jurors' identities or identifying information to others; the court may otherwise limit disclosure in any manner it deems appropriate.

(e) Any court employee who has legal access to personal juror identifying information sealed under subdivision (a), who discloses the information, knowing it to be a violation of this section or a court order issued under this section, is guilty of a misdemeanor.

(f) Any person who intentionally solicits another to unlawfully access or disclose personal juror identifying information contained in records sealed under subdivision (a), knowing that the records have been sealed, or who, knowing that the information was unlawfully secured, intentionally discloses it to another person is guilty of a misdemeanor. *(Added by Stats.1992, c. 971 (S.B.1299), § 3. Amended by Stats.1993, c. 632 (A.B.1915), § 2; Stats.1995, c. 964 (S.B.508), § 3; Stats.1996, c. 636 (S.B.2123), § 2, eff. Sept. 19, 1996.)*

Cross References

Action defined, see Code of Civil Procedure § 22.
Attorney General, generally, see Government Code § 12500 et seq.
Attorneys, State Bar Act, see Business and Professions Code § 6000.
Computation of time, see Code of Civil Procedure §§ 12, 12a, 12b; Government Code § 6800 et seq.
"Court" defined for purposes of this Chapter, see Code of Civil Procedure § 194.
Kinds of actions, see Code of Civil Procedure § 24.
Misdemeanors, definition and penalties, see Penal Code §§ 17, 19, and 19.2.
Notice, actual and constructive, defined, see Civil Code § 18.
Private investigators providing juror information to defendant without authorization, violation, see Penal Code § 95.3.
"Qualified juror" defined for purposes of this Chapter, see Code of Civil Procedure § 194.
"Qualified juror list" defined for purposes of this Chapter, see Code of Civil Procedure § 194.
Sealed records, violation for juror information provided to defendant without authorization, see Penal Code § 95.2.
Threatening jurors, punishment, see Penal Code § 95.1.
"Trial jurors" defined for purposes of this Chapter, see Code of Civil Procedure § 194.
Uniform Controlled Substances Act, seizure and disposition, claim of interest procedure, see Health and Safety Code § 11488.5.

Research References

California Jury Instructions - Criminal 17.60, Post Verdict Juror Admonition/Order.
2 Witkin, California Criminal Law 4th Crimes Against Governmental Authority § 15 (2021), Disclosure or Solicitation of Juror Information.
6 Witkin, California Criminal Law 4th Criminal Appeal § 137 (2021), Juror Identifying Information.
6 Witkin, California Criminal Law 4th Criminal Judgment § 57 (2021), Statutory Procedure.
6 Witkin, California Criminal Law 4th Criminal Judgment § 58 (2021), Case Law.

Part 4

MISCELLANEOUS PROVISIONS

Title 4

CIVIL DISCOVERY ACT

CHAPTER 4. ATTORNEY WORK PRODUCT

§ 2018.010. "Client" defined

For purposes of this chapter, "client" means a "client" as defined in Section 951 of the Evidence Code. *(Added by Stats.2004, c. 182 (A.B.3081), § 23, operative July 1, 2005.)*

Law Revision Commission Comments

Section 2018.010 continues the second paragraph of former Section 2018(f) without substantive change. [33 Cal.L.Rev.Comm. Reports 820 (2004)].

Cross References

Administrative adjudication, see Government Code § 11511.
Arbitration proceedings, see Code of Civil Procedure § 1283 et seq.
Attorneys, depositions in disciplinary proceedings, see Business and Professions Code § 6115.
Executive department, employment of outside counsel and consent from Attorney General, written notification, see Government Code § 11045.
Privileged communications, see Evidence Code § 911 et seq.
Refusal to obey subpoena as contempt, see Code of Civil Procedure § 2031.
Untimely response to a demand for inspection, objection on the basis of attorney work product, relief from waiver of objection under certain conditions, see Code of Civil Procedure § 2031.300.

Research References

4 Witkin, California Criminal Law 4th Illegally Obtained Evidence § 118 (2021), Where Attorney is Suspected of Crime.

§ 2018.020. Policy of the state

It is the policy of the state to do both of the following:

(a) Preserve the rights of attorneys to prepare cases for trial with that degree of privacy necessary to encourage them to prepare their cases thoroughly and to investigate not only the favorable but the unfavorable aspects of those cases.

(b) Prevent attorneys from taking undue advantage of their adversary's industry and efforts. *(Added by Stats.2004, c. 182 (A.B.3081), § 23, operative July 1, 2005.)*

Law Revision Commission Comments

Section 2018.020 continues former Section 2018(a) without substantive change. [33 Cal.L.Rev.Comm. Reports 820 (2004)].

§ 2018.030. Writings and written documentation

(a) A writing that reflects an attorney's impressions, conclusions, opinions, or legal research or theories is not discoverable under any circumstances.

(b) The work product of an attorney, other than a writing described in subdivision (a), is not discoverable unless the court determines that denial of discovery will unfairly prejudice the party seeking discovery in preparing that party's claim or defense or will result in an injustice. *(Added by Stats.2004, c. 182 (A.B.3081), § 23, operative July 1, 2005.)*

Law Revision Commission Comments

Subdivision (a) of Section 2018.030 continues former Section 2018(c) without substantive change.

Subdivision (b) continues former Section 2018(b) without substantive change. [33 Cal.L.Rev.Comm. Reports 821 (2004)].

Cross References

Court defined for purposes of this Title, see Code of Civil Procedure § 2016.020.
Criminal procedure, search warrants, see Penal Code § 1054.6.
Discovery, generally, see Code of Civil Procedure § 2016.010 et seq.
Writing defined for purposes of this Title, see Code of Civil Procedure § 2016.020.

Research References

5 Witkin, California Criminal Law 4th Criminal Trial § 39 (2021), Matters Outside Scope of Discovery Statutes.
5 Witkin, California Criminal Law 4th Criminal Trial § 44A (2021), (New) Discovery from Codefendants.

§ 2018.040. Restatement of existing law

This chapter is intended to be a restatement of existing law relating to protection of work product. It is not intended to expand or reduce the extent to which work product is discoverable under existing law in any action. *(Added by Stats.2004, c. 182 (A.B.3081), § 23, operative July 1, 2005.)*

Law Revision Commission Comments

Section 2018.040 continues the first and second sentences of former Section 2018(d) without change, except to replace section with chapter. [33 Cal.L.Rev. Comm. Reports 821 (2004)].

Cross References

Action defined for purposes of this Title, see Code of Civil Procedure § 2016.020.

§ 2018.050. Participation in crime or fraud

Notwithstanding Section 2018.040, when a lawyer is suspected of knowingly participating in a crime or fraud, there is no protection of work product under this chapter in any official investigation by a law enforcement agency or proceeding or action brought by a public prosecutor in the name of the people of the State of California if the services of the lawyer were sought or obtained to enable or aid anyone to commit or plan to commit a crime or fraud. *(Added by Stats.2004, c. 182 (A.B.3081), § 23, operative July 1, 2005.)*

Law Revision Commission Comments

Section 2018.050 continues the third sentence of former Section 2018(d) without substantive change. [33 Cal.L.Rev.Comm. Reports 821 (2004)].

Cross References

Action defined for purposes of this Title, see Code of Civil Procedure § 2016.020.

Fraud, actual or constructive, see Civil Code §§ 1572 to 1574.

Research References

5 Witkin, California Criminal Law 4th Criminal Trial § 39 (2021), Matters Outside Scope of Discovery Statutes.

§ 2018.060. In camera hearings

Nothing in this chapter is intended to limit an attorney's ability to request an in camera hearing as provided for in People v. Superior Court (Laff) (2001) 25 Cal.4th 703.[1] *(Added by Stats.2004, c. 182 (A.B.3081), § 23, operative July 1, 2005.)*

1 107 Cal.Rptr.2d 328.

Law Revision Commission Comments

Section 2018.060 continues the fourth sentence of former Section 2018(d) without change, except to replace section with chapter. [33 Cal.L.Rev.Comm. Reports 822 (2004)].

Cross References

Court defined for purposes of this Title, see Code of Civil Procedure § 2016.020.

§ 2018.070. Disciplinary proceedings

(a) The State Bar may discover the work product of an attorney against whom disciplinary charges are pending when it is relevant to issues of breach of duty by the lawyer and requisite client approval has been granted.

(b) Where requested and for good cause, discovery under this section shall be subject to a protective order to ensure the confidentiality of the work product except for its use by the State Bar in disciplinary investigations and its consideration under seal in State Bar Court proceedings.

(c) For purposes of this chapter, whenever a client has initiated a complaint against an attorney, the requisite client approval shall be deemed to have been granted. *(Added by Stats.2004, c. 182 (A.B.3081), § 23, operative July 1, 2005.)*

Law Revision Commission Comments

Subdivisions (a) and (b) of Section 2018.070 continue the first sentence of former Section 2018(e) without substantive change.

Subdivision (c) continues the second sentence of former Section 2018(e) without change, except to replace section with chapter. [33 Cal.L.Rev.Comm. Reports 822 (2004)].

Cross References

Client defined for purposes of this Chapter, see Code of Civil Procedure § 2018.010.

Court defined for purposes of this Title, see Code of Civil Procedure § 2016.020.

Discovery, generally, see Code of Civil Procedure § 2016.010 et seq.

§ 2018.080. Breach of duty; actions against attorney by client or former client

In an action between an attorney and a client or a former client of the attorney, no work product privilege under this chapter exists if the work product is relevant to an issue of breach by the attorney of a duty to the client arising out of the attorney-client relationship. *(Added by Stats.2004, c. 182 (A.B.3081), § 23, operative July 1, 2005.)*

Law Revision Commission Comments

Section 2018.080 continues the first paragraph of former Section 2018(f) without substantive change. [33 Cal.L.Rev.Comm. Reports 822 (2004)].

Cross References

Action defined for purposes of this Title, see Code of Civil Procedure § 2016.020.

Client defined for purposes of this Chapter, see Code of Civil Procedure § 2018.010.

FAMILY CODE

Division 10

PREVENTION OF DOMESTIC VIOLENCE

Part 1

SHORT TITLE AND DEFINITIONS

§ 6200. Short title

This division may be cited as the Domestic Violence Prevention Act. *(Added by Stats.1993, c. 219 (A.B.1500), § 154.)*

Law Revision Commission Comments

Section 6200 continues former Code of Civil Procedure Section 541 without substantive change.

This division collects the substantive provisions for issuance of restraining orders intended to prevent domestic violence. Formerly these substantive provisions were duplicated in substantial part in the former Family Law Act, the Domestic Violence Prevention Act, and the Uniform Parentage Act. Now that these bodies of law have been consolidated in the Family Code, these duplicative provisions have been consolidated and continued in this division.

The orders that may be issued under this division may be issued in a proceeding brought pursuant to this division. These orders may also be issued in a proceeding for dissolution, nullity, or legal separation, and in an action brought pursuant to the Uniform Parentage Act. See Section 6221 (application of this division). See also Sections 2045, 2047, 2049 (restraining orders in dissolution, nullity, or legal separation proceeding), 7710, 7720, 7730 (restraining orders in Uniform Parentage Act proceeding).

See also Welf. & Inst. Code § 213.5 (protective orders during pendency of proceeding to declare minor dependent). [23 Cal.L.Rev.Comm. Reports 1 (1993)].

Cross References

Unemployment compensation benefits, eligibility, leaving work for good cause due to domestic violence, see Unemployment Insurance Code § 1256.

Research References

West's California Judicial Council Forms DV–100, Request for Domestic Violence Restraining Order (Also Available in Chinese, Korean, Spanish, and Vietnamese).

West's California Judicial Council Forms DV–101, Description of Abuse (Also Available in Chinese, Korean, Spanish, and Vietnamese).

West's California Judicial Council Forms DV–110, Temporary Restraining Order (Clets—Tro) (Also Available in Chinese, Korean, Spanish, and Vietnamese).

West's California Judicial Council Forms DV–120, Response to Request for Domestic Violence Restraining Order (Also Available in Korean, Spanish, and Vietnamese).

West's California Judicial Council Forms DV–130, Restraining Order After Hearing (Clets—Oah) (Order of Protection) (Also Available in Korean, Spanish, and Vietnamese).

West's California Judicial Council Forms FL–311, Child Custody and Visitation (Parenting Time) Application Attachment (Also Available in Spanish).

2 Witkin, California Criminal Law 4th Crimes Against Public Peace and Welfare § 209 (2021), Justifiable Violation of Statute.

2 Witkin, California Criminal Law 4th Crimes Against Public Peace and Welfare § 251 (2021), Exemptions.

2 Witkin, California Criminal Law 4th Crimes Against Public Peace and Welfare § 257 (2021), Firearms.

4 Witkin, California Criminal Law 4th Pretrial Proceedings § 32 (2021), Domestic Violence.

§ 6201. Construction of code; application of definitions

Unless the provision or context otherwise requires, the definitions in this part govern the construction of this code. *(Added by Stats.1993, c. 219 (A.B.1500), § 154.)*

Law Revision Commission Comments

Section 6201 continues without substantive change and generalizes the introductory clause of former Code of Civil Procedure Section 542. The introductory clause of this section has been added for conformity with other sections in this code. See Section 50 & Comment.

For provisions outside this division that use the definitions in this division, see Sections 213 (responding party's request for affirmative relief alternative to moving party's requested relief), 3064 (limitation on ex parte order granting or modifying custody order), 3100 (visitation rights of a parent), 3101 (visitation rights of stepparent), 3103 (visitation rights of grandparent), 3113 (separate meetings with court appointed investigator), 3181 (separate meetings with mediator), 3192 (separate meetings with counselor appointed in custody proceeding). [23 Cal.L.Rev.Comm. Reports 1 (1993)].

§ 6203. "Abuse" defined

(a) For purposes of this act, "abuse" means any of the following:

(1) To intentionally or recklessly cause or attempt to cause bodily injury.

(2) Sexual assault.

(3) To place a person in reasonable apprehension of imminent serious bodily injury to that person or to another.

(4) To engage in any behavior that has been or could be enjoined pursuant to Section 6320.

(b) Abuse is not limited to the actual infliction of physical injury or assault. *(Added by Stats.1993, c. 219 (A.B.1500), § 154. Amended by Stats.1998, c. 581 (A.B.2801), § 16; Stats.2014, c. 635 (A.B.2089), § 2, eff. Jan. 1, 2015; Stats.2015, c. 303 (A.B.731), § 149, eff. Jan. 1, 2016.)*

Law Revision Commission Comments

Section 6203 continues former Code of Civil Procedure Section 542(a) without substantive change. For provisions adopting this definition by reference, see Section 3011 (determining best interest of child in custody proceeding); Evid. Code § 1107 (admissibility of expert witness testimony regarding battered women's syndrome). [23 Cal.L.Rev.Comm. Reports 1 (1993)].

Cross References

Abandonment and neglect of children, criminal history search, prior restraining orders, see Penal Code § 273.75.

Child abuse and neglect reporting, child abuse or neglect defined, see Penal Code § 11165.6.

Criminal history, use when setting bond or considering plea agreement, see Penal Code § 273.75.
Domestic violence, interagency death review teams, reporting procedures, see Penal Code § 11163.3.
Emergency protective orders, grounds for issuance, persons in danger of domestic violence or abuse, see Family Code § 6250.
Evidence of character, habit, or custom, battered women's syndrome, abuse and domestic violence, see Evidence Code § 1107.
Person defined for purposes of this Code, see Family Code § 105.
Presumption against persons perpetrating domestic violence, custody of children, see Family Code § 3044.
Protective orders to prevent domestic violence, issuance of order upon affidavit, see Family Code § 6300.
Protective orders to prevent domestic violence, persons who may be granted order, see Family Code § 6301.
Rights of victims and witnesses, domestic violence or abuse counselors, presence at law enforcement interviews, see Penal Code § 679.05.

§ 6205. "Affinity" defined

"Affinity," when applied to the marriage relation, signifies the connection existing in consequence of marriage between each of the married persons and the blood relatives of the other. *(Added by Stats.1993, c. 219 (A.B.1500), § 154.)*

Law Revision Commission Comments

Section 6205 is a new provision drawn from Code of Civil Procedure Section 17(9). [23 Cal.L.Rev.Comm. Reports 1 (1993)].

Cross References

Person defined for purposes of this Code, see Family Code § 105.
References to husband, wife, spouses and married persons, persons included for purposes of this Code, see Family Code § 11.

§ 6209. "Cohabitant" defined

"Cohabitant" means a person who regularly resides in the household. "Former cohabitant" means a person who formerly regularly resided in the household. *(Added by Stats.1993, c. 219 (A.B.1500), § 154.)*

Law Revision Commission Comments

Section 6209 continues former Code of Civil Procedure Section 542(c) without change. [23 Cal.L.Rev.Comm. Reports 1 (1993)].

Cross References

Arrest with and without warrant, citizen's arrest by domestic victim, protective or restraining order, see Penal Code § 836.
Domestic violence incidents, temporary custody of firearms by officers, subsequent procedures, see Penal Code § 18250.
Person defined for purposes of this Code, see Family Code § 105.

§ 6210. "Dating relationship" defined

"Dating relationship" means frequent, intimate associations primarily characterized by the expectation of affection or sexual involvement independent of financial considerations. *(Added by Stats.2001, c. 110 (A.B.362), § 1.)*

Cross References

Battery committed against former spouse, fiancee, or victim who has or had dating relationship with defendant, see Penal Code § 243.

§ 6211. "Domestic violence" defined

"Domestic violence" is abuse perpetrated against any of the following persons:

(a) A spouse or former spouse.

(b) A cohabitant or former cohabitant, as defined in Section 6209.

(c) A person with whom the respondent is having or has had a dating or engagement relationship.

(d) A person with whom the respondent has had a child, where the presumption applies that the male parent is the father of the child of the female parent under the Uniform Parentage Act (Part 3 (commencing with Section 7600) of Division 12).

(e) A child of a party or a child who is the subject of an action under the Uniform Parentage Act, where the presumption applies that the male parent is the father of the child to be protected.

(f) Any other person related by consanguinity or affinity within the second degree. *(Added by Stats.1993, c. 219 (A.B.1500), § 154.)*

Law Revision Commission Comments

Subdivisions (a)-(d) and (f) of Section 6211 continue without substantive change and broaden former Code of Civil Procedure Section 542(b). In subdivision (c), the reference to an ongoing dating or engagement relationship has been added. This is drawn from the definition of domestic violence in Penal Code Section 13700. In subdivision (f), the reference to any "adult" person related by consanguinity or affinity has been omitted. This is consistent with the addition of children in subdivision (e).

Subdivision (e) is drawn from former Civil Code Section 7020 and eliminates any implication that children are not covered by this statute. Former Civil Code Section 7020 authorized restraining orders to protect children who are the subject of a proceeding pursuant to the Uniform Parentage Act. The former Domestic Violence Protection Act protected "cohabitants" but did not specifically mention children. See former Code Civ. Proc. § 542(b)-(c). Subdivision (e) continues the protection explicit in the former Uniform Parentage Act and extends it explicitly to include a child of a party to the proceeding in which the orders are sought. See Section 6221 (application of division).

Where a child has been declared a dependent of the juvenile court, that court may issue orders to protect the child from violence pursuant to the Welfare and Institutions Code. See, e.g., Welf. & Inst. Code §§ 213.5 (ex parte orders during pendency of proceeding to declare child a dependent), 304 (juvenile court authority to issue protective orders sua sponte). See also Section 6221(b) (nothing in this division affects the jurisdiction of the juvenile court).

See Sections 6320 (ex parte order enjoining harassment, threats, and violence), 6321 (ex parte order excluding party from dwelling), 6340 (orders that may be issued after notice and hearing); see also Sections 6203 ("abuse" defined), 6205 ("affinity" defined), 6209 ("cohabitant" and "former cohabitant" defined); Welf. & Inst. Code § 213.5 (issuance of restraining order during pendency of proceeding to determine minor dependent).

For provisions adopting this definition by reference, see Sections 3064 (limitation on ex parte order granting or modifying custody order), 3113 (separate meetings with court appointed investigator), 3181 (separate meetings with mediator), 3192 (separate meetings with counselor appointed in custody proceeding); Code Civ. Proc. §§ 128 (contempt powers of court), 1219 (punishment for contempt); Evid. Code §§ 1037.7 (victim-counselor privilege), 1107 (admissibility of expert witness testimony regarding battered women's syndrome); Penal Code §§ 273.6 (penalty for violation of protective order), 977 (appearance in misdemeanors), 1377 (compromise of misdemeanors).

For other domestic violence provisions, see, e.g., Penal Code §§ 136.2 (penalty for intimidation of witness), 273.83 (individuals subject to prosecution by district attorney's "spousal abuser" unit), 277 (penalty for child abduction), 653m (penalty for annoying telephone calls), 853.6 (citation and release not automatically available for misdemeanor violation of order to prevent domestic violence), 1000.6 (diversion of misdemeanant to counseling), 12028.5 (confiscating weapons at scene of domestic violence), 13700 (law enforcement response to domestic violence); Welf. & Inst. Code § 18291 ("domestic violence" defined for purposes of the Domestic Violence Centers Act). [23 Cal.L.Rev.Comm. Reports 1 (1993)].

Cross References

Action for damages suffered as result of domestic violence, see Code of Civil Procedure § 340.15.
Address confidentiality for victims of domestic violence and stalking, definitions, see Government Code § 6205.5.
Arraignment of the defendant, presence of defendant, domestic violence, see Penal Code § 977.
Authority to compromise misdemeanors for which victim has civil action, see Penal Code § 1377.
Cancellation and failure to renew certain property insurance, victims of domestic violence, see Insurance Code § 676.9.
Change of names, orders to show cause, publication or posting, see Code of Civil Procedure § 1277.

Child abuse and neglect reporting, child abuse or neglect defined, see Penal Code § 11165.6.
Community conflict resolution programs, referral of cases by district attorney, considerations, see Penal Code § 14152.
Conditions preventing deferral of sentencing from being offered, see Penal Code § 1001.98.
Criminal history, use when setting bond or considering plea agreement, see Penal Code § 273.75.
Domestic violence, admissibility of other acts evidence, see Evidence Code § 1109.
Domestic violence, interagency death review teams, reporting procedures, see Penal Code § 11163.3.
Domestic violence incidents, temporary custody of firearms, domestic violence defined, see Penal Code §§ 16490, 18250.
Domestic violence offenses, community conflict resolution program referrals prohibited, see Penal Code § 14152.
Domestic violence offenses, compromise prohibited, see Penal Code § 1377.
Domestic violence victim–Counselor privilege, see Evidence Code § 1037.7.
Emergency protective orders, grounds for issuance, persons in danger of domestic violence or abuse, see Family Code § 6250.
Evidence of character, habit, or custom, battered women's syndrome, abuse and domestic violence, see Evidence Code § 1107.
Imprisonment to compel performance of acts, exemption of sexual assault and domestic violence victims who refuse to testify, see Code of Civil Procedure § 1219.
Lease not to be terminated based on domestic or sexual assault against tenant, landlord's liability for compliance, form for affirmative defense to unlawful detainer action, see Code of Civil Procedure § 1161.3.
Legal actions by domestic violence and sexual assault victims, see Labor Code § 230.
Life and disability insurance,
Discriminatory practices, victims of domestic violence, see Insurance Code § 10144.3.
Victims of domestic violence, health care service plans, see Insurance Code § 10144.2.
Notification to victim or witness of release of person convicted of stalking or domestic violence, see Penal Code § 646.92.
Offer of diversion to misdemeanor defendant, charged offenses not eligible for diversion, see Penal Code § 1001.95.
Payment of wages, employers with twenty-five or more employees, domestic violence and sexual assault victims, see Labor Code § 230.1.
Person defined for purposes of this Code, see Family Code § 105.
Point–of–service health care service plan contracts, victims of domestic violence, see Health and Safety Code § 1374.75.
Powers and duties of housing authorities, annual report of activities to department, see Health and Safety Code § 34328.1.
Powers of courts, contempt orders, execution of sentence and stay pending appeal, see Code of Civil Procedure § 128.
Presumption against persons perpetrating domestic violence, custody of children, see Family Code § 3044.
Probation revocation or modification, discharge, conditions, see Penal Code § 1203.3.
Protective orders to prevent domestic violence, issuance of order upon affidavit, see Family Code § 6300.
Protective orders to prevent domestic violence, persons who may be granted order, see Family Code § 6301.
References to husband, wife, spouses and married persons, persons included for purposes of this Code, see Family Code § 11.
Respondent defined for purposes of this Code, see Family Code § 127.
Rights of victims and witnesses, domestic violence or abuse counselors, presence at law enforcement interviews, see Penal Code § 679.05.
Summoning law enforcement assistance or emergency assistance by victim of abuse, victim of crime, or individual in emergency, local agency ordinance, etc. limiting right prohibited, see Government Code § 53165.
Summoning law enforcement assistance or emergency assistance, lease or rental agreement provisions prohibiting or limiting right void, see Civil Code § 1946.8.
Suspension of money judgment or order for support of a child, exceptions, resumption of obligation, administrative adjustment, evaluation, see Family Code § 4007.5.
Temporary or permanent support, spouse convicted of domestic violence, presumption disfavoring award, see Family Code § 4325.
Terms of probation for crime of domestic violence, see Penal Code § 1203.097.
Unlawful detainer, commission of nuisance upon premises, see Code of Civil Procedure § 1161.
Victims of domestic violence, notice and conditions of perpetrator's parole, see Penal Code § 3053.2.
Victims of domestic violence, sexual assault, or stalking, written notice to terminate tenancy, requirements, see Civil Code § 1946.7.
Violent sexual felony, domestic violence felony, prohibited awards, see Family Code § 4324.5.

Research References

California Jury Instructions - Criminal 2.50.02, Evidence of Other Domestic Violence.
2 Witkin, California Criminal Law 4th Crimes Against Governmental Authority § 10 (2021), Orders, Protocol, and Sanctions.
2 Witkin, California Criminal Law 4th Crimes Against Governmental Authority § 25 (2021), Prohibited Compromises.
1 Witkin California Criminal Law 4th Crimes Against the Person § 330 (2021), Exception: Belief that Child Will Suffer Injury or Harm.
1 Witkin California Criminal Law 4th Crimes Against the Person § 337 (2021), Notice of Release or Escape.
6 Witkin, California Criminal Law 4th Criminal Judgment § 147 (2021), No Requirement in Misdemeanor Case.
5 Witkin, California Criminal Law 4th Criminal Trial § 508 (2021), Misdemeanor Cases.
4 Witkin, California Criminal Law 4th Pretrial Proceedings § 254 (2021), Presence of Defendant.
3 Witkin, California Criminal Law 4th Punishment § 664 (2021), Counseling, Treatment, and Education.
3 Witkin, California Criminal Law 4th Punishment § 683 (2021), Procedure.
3 Witkin, California Criminal Law 4th Punishment § 752 (2021), Discretionary Conditions.
3 Witkin, California Criminal Law 4th Punishment § 753 (2021), Mandatory Conditions.

§ 6215. "Emergency protective order" defined

"Emergency protective order" means an order issued under Part 3 (commencing with Section 6240). *(Added by Stats.1993, c. 219 (A.B.1500), § 154.)*

Law Revision Commission Comments

Section 6215 is a new provision included for drafting convenience. [23 Cal.L.Rev.Comm. Reports 1 (1993)].

Cross References

Judgment and order defined for purposes of this Code, see Family Code § 100.

§ 6216. "Firearm" and "firearm precursor part" defined

* * * For the purposes of this division, "firearm" includes the frame or receiver of the weapon * * *, including a completed frame or receiver or a firearm precursor part. "Firearm precursor part" has the same meaning as in subdivision (a) of Section 16531 of the Penal Code.

* * * *(Added by Stats.2021, c. 682 (A.B.1057), § 1, eff. Jan. 1, 2022, operative July 1, 2022. Amended by Stats.2022, c. 76 (A.B.1621), § 2, eff. June 30, 2022.)*

§ 6218. "Protective order" defined

"Protective order" means an order that includes any of the following restraining orders, whether issued ex parte, after notice and hearing, or in a judgment:

(a) An order described in Section 6320 enjoining specific acts of abuse.

(b) An order described in Section 6321 excluding a person from a dwelling.

(c) An order described in Section 6322 enjoining other specified behavior. *(Added by Stats.1993, c. 219 (A.B.1500), § 154.)*

Law Revision Commission Comments

Section 6218 restates former Code of Civil Procedure Section 542(d) and expands the definition to include orders described in Sections 6321 and 6322. As revised, this term describes the three orders that most directly protect a victim of domestic violence from abuse. These are the orders to prevent specific acts of abuse, such as contacting, molesting, and striking, to exclude a party from a dwelling, and to enjoin other specified behaviors necessary to

Family

effectuate the first two orders. See Sections 6320 (enjoining harassment, threats, and violence), 6321 (exclusion from dwelling), 6322 (enjoining additional specified behaviors).

In this division, the term "protective order" is used in Sections 6252 (orders included in emergency protective order), 6303 (support person for victim of domestic violence), 6304 (court to provide information to parties concerning terms and effect of order), 6343 (participation in counseling), 6360 (orders included in judgment), 6385 (notice to Department of Justice), 6386 (appointment of counsel and payment if fees and costs to enforce order), 6388 (criminal penalty for violation of order).

For provisions adopting this definition by reference, see Sections 213 (responding party's request for affirmative relief alternative to moving party's requested relief), 2045, 2047, 2049 (restraining orders in proceeding for dissolution, nullity, and legal separation), 3100 (visitation rights of a parent), 3101 (visitation rights of stepparent), 3113 (separate meetings with court appointed investigator), 3103 (visitation rights of grandparent), 3181 (separate meetings with mediator), 3192 (separate meetings with counselor appointed in custody proceeding), 7710, 7720, 7730 (restraining orders in action pursuant to the Uniform Parentage Act); Gov't Code § 26841 (fees for protective order); Penal Code §§ 273.6 (willful violation of court order), 12021 (firearms), 14152 (referrals by district attorney to community conflict resolution program); Welf. & Inst. Code §§ 304 (custody of dependent children of the court), 362.4 (juvenile court order concerning custody or visitation). [23 Cal.L.Rev.Comm. Reports 1 (1993)].

Cross References

Abandonment and neglect of children, intentional and knowing violation of court order to prevent harassment, disturbing the peace, or threats or acts of violence, see Penal Code § 273.6.
Community conflict resolution programs, referral of cases by district attorney, considerations, see Penal Code § 14152.
Contempt of court, conduct constituting, see Penal Code § 166.
Criminal identification and statistics, public housing authorities, access to information, see Penal Code § 11105.03.
Dependent children, jurisdiction, custody of child, restraining order, see Welfare and Institutions Code § 304.
Judgment and order defined for purposes of this Code, see Family Code § 100.
Juvenile court law, protective order, parentage, custody, or visitation order, see Welfare and Institutions Code § 726.5.
License plates, application for new and different plates by domestic violence victims, conditions for issuance, see Vehicle Code § 4467.
Person defined for purposes of this Code, see Family Code § 105.
Relinquishment of firearms, persons subject to restraining orders, see Code of Civil Procedure § 527.9.
Search warrants, grounds for issuance, firearm owned by, in possession of, or in custody and control of person against whom protective order has been issued under this section, see Penal Code § 1524.
Termination of juvenile court jurisdiction, pending proceedings relating to parental marriage or custody order, see Welfare and Institutions Code § 362.4.
Unlawful carrying and possession of firearms, specified convictions, see Penal Code §§ 29800 to 29875.

Research References

West's California Judicial Council Forms JV–245, Request for Restraining Order—Juvenile (Also Available in Chinese, Korean, Spanish, and Vietnamese).
West's California Judicial Council Forms JV–250, Notice of Hearing and Temporary Restraining Order—Juvenile (Also Available in Chinese, Korean, Spanish, and Vietnamese).
West's California Judicial Council Forms JV–255, Restraining Order—Juvenile (Clets—Juv) (Also Available in Chinese, Korean, Spanish, and Vietnamese).
2 Witkin, California Criminal Law 4th Crimes Against Governmental Authority § 31 (2021), Offenses Constituting Contempt.
2 Witkin, California Criminal Law 4th Crimes Against Public Peace and Welfare § 242 (2021), Subjects of Protective and Restraining Orders.
4 Witkin, California Criminal Law 4th Illegally Obtained Evidence § 111 (2021), Statutory Grounds.

§ 6219. Demonstration project to identify best practices in domestic violence court cases; participation in project; findings and recommendations

Subject to adequate, discretionary funding from a city or a county, the superior courts in San Diego County and in Santa Clara County may develop a demonstration project to identify the best practices in civil, juvenile, and criminal court cases involving domestic violence. The superior courts in any other county that is able and willing may also participate in the demonstration project. The superior courts participating in this demonstration project shall report their findings and recommendations to the Judicial Council and the Legislature on or before May 1, 2004. The Judicial Council may make those recommendations available to any court or county. *(Added by Stats.2002, c. 192 (A.B.1909), § 1.)*

Cross References

County defined for purposes of this Code, see Family Code § 67.

Part 2

GENERAL PROVISIONS

§ 6220. Purpose

The purpose of this division is to prevent acts of domestic violence, abuse, and sexual abuse and to provide for a separation of the persons involved in the domestic violence for a period sufficient to enable these persons to seek a resolution of the causes of the violence. *(Added by Stats.1993, c. 219 (A.B.1500), § 154. Amended by Stats.2014, c. 635 (A.B.2089), § 3, eff. Jan. 1, 2015.)*

Law Revision Commission Comments

Section 6220 continues former Code of Civil Procedure Section 540 without substantive change. The list of persons in the former section has been omitted. This is not a substantive change, since the list is duplicated in the definition of domestic violence that applies to this section. See Section 6211 ("domestic violence" defined). [23 Cal.L.Rev.Comm. Reports 1 (1993)].

Cross References

Domestic violence defined for purposes of this Code, see Family Code § 6211.
Person defined for purposes of this Code, see Family Code § 105.
Prevention of domestic violence, issuance of order upon affidavit or testimony, see Family Code § 6300.
Protective orders and other domestic violence protection orders, confidentiality of information relating to minors, see Family Code § 6301.5.

§ 6221. Application of division; forms for issuance of orders

(a) Unless the provision or context otherwise requires, this division applies to any order described in this division, whether the order is issued in a proceeding brought pursuant to this division, in an action brought pursuant to the Uniform Parentage Act (Part 3 (commencing with Section 7600) of Division 12), or in a proceeding for dissolution of marriage, for nullity of marriage, or for legal separation of the parties.

(b) Nothing in this division affects the jurisdiction of the juvenile court.

(c) Any order issued by a court to which this division applies shall be issued on forms adopted by the Judicial Council of California and that have been approved by the Department of Justice pursuant to subdivision (i) of Section 6380. However, the fact that an order issued by a court pursuant to this section was not issued on forms adopted by the Judicial Council and approved by the Department of Justice shall not, in and of itself, make the order unenforceable. *(Added by Stats.1993, c. 219 (A.B.1500), § 154. Amended by Stats.1999, c. 661 (A.B.825), § 4.)*

Law Revision Commission Comments

Subdivision (a) of Section 6221 is new and is added to make clear that the provisions of this division are applicable not only to proceedings brought pursuant to this division, but also in proceedings for dissolution, nullity, and legal separation and in actions brought pursuant to the Uniform Parentage Act.

Subdivision (b) is new [and] is added to help to ensure that conflicts of jurisdiction between the family court and the juvenile court do not arise. [23 Cal.L.Rev.Comm. Reports 1 (1993)].

Cross References

Court interpreter services provided in civil actions, reimbursement by Judicial Council, prioritization where funding is insufficient, see Evidence Code § 756.
Electronic transmission of data filed with the court with respect to protective orders, see Family Code § 6380.
Judgment and order defined for purposes of this Code, see Family Code § 100.
Proceeding defined for purposes of this Code, see Family Code § 110.
Witnesses, interpreters and translators, hearings or proceedings related to domestic violence, see Evidence Code § 756.

§ 6222. Application, responsive pleading, or show cause order seeking to acquire, modify, or enforce a protective order; subpoena filed in connection; fees

There is no filing fee for an application, a responsive pleading, or an order to show cause that seeks to obtain, modify, or enforce a protective order or other order authorized by this division when the request for the other order is necessary to obtain or give effect to a protective order. There is no fee for a subpoena filed in connection with that application, responsive pleading, or order to show cause. There is no fee for any filings related to a petition filed pursuant to Part 4 (commencing with 6300) of this division. *(Added by Stats. 2002, c. 1009 (A.B.2030), § 4, operative Jan. 1, 2007. Amended by Stats.2006, c. 476 (A.B.2695), § 3; Stats.2021, c. 686 (S.B.538), § 1, eff. Jan. 1, 2022.)*

Cross References

Harassment, temporary restraining order or injunction, fee waiver, see Code of Civil Procedure § 527.6.
Judgment and order defined for purposes of this Code, see Family Code § 100.
Petitioner defined for purposes of this Code, see Family Code § 126.
Proceeding defined for purposes of this Code, see Family Code § 110.
Protective order defined for purposes of this Code, see Family Code § 6218.

§ 6223. Custody or visitation order; application of Part 2 of Division 8

A custody or visitation order issued in a proceeding brought pursuant to this division is subject to Part 2 (commencing with Section 3020) of Division 8 (custody of children). *(Added by Stats.1993, c. 219 (A.B.1500), § 154.)*

Law Revision Commission Comments

Section 6223 is a new provision that provides a cross-reference to the main custody statute in Division 8. This section makes clear that, where a custody or visitation order is issued in a proceeding brought pursuant to the Domestic Violence Prevention Act, the court is to apply the same substantive and procedural rules as would be applied in any other proceeding in which these issues may be determined.

For sections of particular importance in situations involving domestic violence, see Sections 3030 (custody and unsupervised visitation prohibited where parent convicted under certain Penal Code provisions), 3031 (custody or visitation should not be inconsistent with restraining orders), 3100(b) (limiting visitation to situation where third party present), 3131 (action by district attorney where child taken or detained in violation of visitation order). [23 Cal.L.Rev.Comm. Reports 1 (1993)].

Cross References

Judgment and order defined for purposes of this Code, see Family Code § 100.
Proceeding defined for purposes of this Code, see Family Code § 110.

§ 6224. Statement on face of order; expiration date and notice

An order described in this division shall state on its face the date of expiration of the order and the following statements in substantially the following form:

"This order is effective when made. The law enforcement agency shall enforce it immediately on receipt. It is enforceable anywhere in California by any law enforcement agency that has received the order or is shown a copy of the order. If proof of service on the restrained person has not been received, the law enforcement agency shall advise the restrained person of the terms of the order and then shall enforce it." *(Added by Stats.1993, c. 219 (A.B.1500), § 154.)*

Law Revision Commission Comments

Section 6224 continues without substantive change former Code of Civil Procedure Section 552, the third paragraph of former Civil Code Section 4359(a), the first sentence of former Civil Code Section 4359(c), and former Civil Code Section 7020(c). This section generalizes the requirements of the former sections to apply to all orders issued pursuant to this division. This is not a substantive change. See Cal. R. Ct. 1285.05 (rev. July 1, 1987) (temporary restraining order in dissolution, nullity, or legal separation proceeding), 1296.10 (rev. Jan. 1, 1991) (order to show cause and temporary restraining order in proceeding pursuant to Domestic Violence Prevention Act or Uniform Parentage Act), 1296.29 (new July 1, 1991) (restraining order after hearing in dissolution, nullity, or legal separation or in proceedings under Domestic Violence Prevention Act or Uniform Parentage Act). [23 Cal.L.Rev.Comm. Reports 1 (1993)].

Cross References

Intentional and knowing violations of court orders to prevent harassment or domestic violence, see Penal Code § 273.6.
Judgment and order defined for purposes of this Code, see Family Code § 100.
Person defined for purposes of this Code, see Family Code § 105.
State defined for purposes of this Code, see Family Code § 145.
Temporary restraining orders or injunctions, victims of domestic violence, see Code of Civil Procedure § 527.6.

Research References

West's California Judicial Council Forms FL–300, Request for Order (Also Available in Spanish).

§ 6225. Explicit statement of address not required

A petition for an order described in this division is valid and the order is enforceable without explicitly stating the address of the petitioner or the petitioner's place of residence, school, employment, the place where the petitioner's child is provided child care services, or the child's school. *(Added by Stats.1993, c. 219 (A.B.1500), § 154.)*

Law Revision Commission Comments

Section 6225 generalizes and continues the last sentence of former Code of Civil Procedure Section 545 without substantive change. This section has been expanded to apply to orders contained in a judgment. The references to "petitioner" have been substituted for the former references to "applicant." These are not substantive changes. [23 Cal.L.Rev.Comm. Reports 1 (1993)].

Cross References

Judgment and order defined for purposes of this Code, see Family Code § 100.

Petitioner defined for purposes of this Code, see Family Code § 126.

§ 6226. Forms and instructions; promulgation by Judicial Council

The Judicial Council shall prescribe the form of the orders and any other documents required by this division and shall promulgate forms and instructions for applying for orders described in this division. *(Added by Stats.1993, c. 219 (A.B.1500), § 154.)*

Law Revision Commission Comments

Section 6226 continues without substantive change former Code of Civil Procedure Section 543, the first sentence of the third paragraph of subdivision (b) and the first sentence of the fourth paragraph of subdivision (c) of former Code of Civil Procedure Section 546, and the last paragraph of former Civil Code Section 4359(a). [23 Cal.L.Rev.Comm. Reports 1 (1993)].

Cross References

Judgment and order defined for purposes of this Code, see Family Code § 100.

Research References

West's California Judicial Council Forms FL–300, Request for Order (Also Available in Spanish).

§ 6226.5. Confidentiality program provision in "Can a Domestic Violence Restraining Order Help Me?" form

(a) On or before January 1, 2023, the Judicial Council shall amend the Judicial Council form entitled "Can a Domestic Violence Restraining Order Help Me?" to include a brief description of the address confidentiality program established under Chapter 3.1 (commencing with Section 6205) of Division 7 of Title 1 of the Government Code, the benefits of enrollment in the program for victims of domestic violence, and the internet address for the Secretary of State's internet web page that contains more detailed information about the program.

(b) On or before January 1, 2023, the Judicial Council shall make the Judicial Council form available in English and in at least the other languages described in Section 1632 of the Civil Code. The Judicial Council may make the form available in additional languages. *(Added by Stats.2021, c. 457 (A.B.277), § 1, eff. Jan. 1, 2022.)*

§ 6227. Remedies in this chapter additional to other remedies

The remedies provided in this division are in addition to any other civil or criminal remedies that may be available to the petitioner. *(Added by Stats.1993, c. 219 (A.B.1500), § 154.)*

Law Revision Commission Comments

Section 6227 continues former Code of Civil Procedure Section 549 without substantive change. The word "petitioner" has been substituted for "plaintiff" to conform to revisions made in former law. See 1990 Cal. Stat. ch. 752. [23 Cal.L.Rev.Comm. Reports 1 (1993)].

Cross References

Petitioner defined for purposes of this Code, see Family Code § 126.

§ 6228. Access to Domestic Violence Reports Act of 1999

(a) State and local law enforcement agencies shall provide, upon request and without charging a fee, one copy of all incident report face sheets, one copy of all incident reports, or both, to a victim, or the victim's representative as defined in subdivision (g), of a crime that constitutes an act of any of the following:

(1) Domestic violence, as defined in Section 6211.

(2) Sexual assault, as defined in Sections 261, 261.5, 262, 265, 266, 266a, 266b, 266c, 266g, 266j, 267, 269, 273.4, 285, 286, 287, 288, 288.5, 289, or 311.4 of, or former Section 288a of, the Penal Code.

(3) Stalking, as defined in Section 1708.7 of the Civil Code or Section 646.9 of the Penal Code.

(4) Human trafficking, as defined in Section 236.1 of the Penal Code.

(5) Abuse of an elder or a dependent adult, as defined in Section 15610.07 of the Welfare and Institutions Code.

(b)(1) A copy of an incident report face sheet shall be made available during regular business hours to a victim or the victim's representative no later than 48 hours after being requested, unless the state or local law enforcement agency informs the victim or the victim's representative of the reasons why, for good cause, the incident report face sheet is not available, in which case the incident report face sheet shall be made available no later than five working days after the request is made.

(2) A copy of the incident report shall be made available during regular business hours to a victim or the victim's representative no later than five working days after being requested, unless the state or local law enforcement agency informs the victim or the victim's representative of the reasons why, for good cause, the incident report is not available, in which case the incident report shall be made available no later than 10 working days after the request is made.

(c) A person requesting copies under this section shall present state or local law enforcement with the person's identification, including a current, valid driver's license, a state-issued identification card, or a passport. If the person is a representative of the victim and the victim is deceased, the representative shall also present a certified copy of the death certificate or other satisfactory evidence of the death of the victim at the time a request is made. If the person is a representative of the victim and the victim is alive and not the subject of a conservatorship, the representative shall also present a written authorization, signed by the victim, making the person the victim's personal representative.

(d)(1) This section shall apply to requests for domestic violence face sheets or incident reports made within five years from the date of completion of the incident report.

(2) This section shall apply to requests for sexual assault, stalking, human trafficking, or abuse of an elder or a dependent adult face sheets or incident reports made within two years from the date of completion of the incident report.

(e) This section shall be known and may be cited as the Access to Domestic Violence Reports Act of 1999.

(f) For purposes of this section, "victim" includes a minor who is 12 years of age or older.

(g)(1) For purposes of this section, if the victim is deceased, a "representative of the victim" means any of the following:

(A) The surviving spouse.

(B) A surviving child of the decedent who has attained 18 years of age.

(C) A domestic partner, as defined in subdivision (a) of Section 297.

(D) A surviving parent of the decedent.

(E) A surviving adult relative.

(F) The personal representative of the victim, as defined in Section 58 of the Probate Code, if one is appointed.

(G) The public administrator if one has been appointed.

(2) For purposes of this section, if the victim is not deceased, a "representative of the victim" means any of the following:

(A) A parent, guardian, or adult child of the victim, or an adult sibling of a victim 12 years of age or older, who shall present to law enforcement identification pursuant to subdivision (c). A guardian shall also present to law enforcement a copy of the letters of guardianship demonstrating that the person is the appointed guardian of the victim.

(B) An attorney for the victim, who shall present to law enforcement identification pursuant to subdivision (c) and written proof that the person is the attorney for the victim.

(C) A conservator of the victim who shall present to law enforcement identification pursuant to subdivision (c) and a copy of the letters of conservatorship demonstrating that the person is the appointed conservator of the victim.

(3) A representative of the victim does not include any person who has been convicted of murder in the first degree, as defined in Section 189 of the Penal Code, of the victim, or any person identified in the incident report face sheet as a suspect. *(Added by Stats.1999, c. 1022 (A.B.403), § 1. Amended by Stats.2002, c. 377 (S.B.1265), § 1; Stats.2010, c. 363 (A.B.1738), § 1; Stats.2011, c. 296 (A.B.1023), § 93; Stats.2016, c. 875 (A.B.1678), § 1, eff. Jan. 1, 2017; Stats.2018, c. 423 (S.B.1494), § 24, eff. Jan. 1, 2019; Stats.2019, c. 115 (A.B. 1817), § 59, eff. Jan. 1, 2020.)*

Cross References

Adult defined for purposes of this Code, see Family Code § 6501.
Person defined for purposes of this Code, see Family Code § 105.
References to husband, wife, spouses and married persons, persons included for purposes of this Code, see Family Code § 11.
State defined for purposes of this Code, see Family Code § 145.

§ 6229. Minor under 12 years of age appearing without counsel

A minor, under 12 years of age, accompanied by a duly appointed and acting guardian ad litem, shall be permitted to appear in court without counsel for the limited purpose of requesting or opposing a request for a temporary restraining order or injunction, or both, under this division as provided in Section 374 of the Code of Civil Procedure. *(Added by Stats.2010, c. 572 (A.B.1596), § 12, operative Jan. 1, 2012.)*

Part 3

EMERGENCY PROTECTIVE ORDERS

CHAPTER 1. GENERAL PROVISIONS

§ 6240. Definitions

As used in this part:

(a) "Judicial officer" means a judge, commissioner, or referee designated under Section 6241.

(b) "Law enforcement officer" means one of the following officers who requests or enforces an emergency protective order under this part:

(1) A police officer.

(2) A sheriff's officer.

(3) A peace officer of the Department of the California Highway Patrol.

(4) A peace officer of the University of California Police Department.

(5) A peace officer of the California State University and College Police Departments.

(6) A peace officer of the Department of Parks and Recreation, as defined in subdivision (f) of Section 830.2 of the Penal Code.

(7) A peace officer of the Department of General Services of the City of Los Angeles, as defined in subdivision (c) of Section 830.31 of the Penal Code.

(8) A housing authority patrol officer, as defined in subdivision (d) of Section 830.31 of the Penal Code.

(9) A peace officer for a district attorney, as defined in Section 830.1 or 830.35 of the Penal Code.

(10) A parole officer, probation officer, or deputy probation officer, as defined in Section 830.5 of the Penal Code.

(11) A peace officer of a California Community College police department, as defined in subdivision (a) of Section 830.32.

(12) A peace officer employed by a police department of a school district, as defined in subdivision (b) of Section 830.32.

(c) "Abduct" means take, entice away, keep, withhold, or conceal. *(Added by Stats.1993, c. 219 (A.B.1500), § 154. Amended by Stats.1993, c. 1229 (A.B.224), § 1; Gov.Reorg.Plan No. 1 of 1995, § 4, eff. July 12, 1995; Stats.1996, c. 305 (A.B.3103), § 5; Stats.1996, c. 988 (A.B.2936), § 3; Stats.1999, c. 659 (S.B.355), § 1; Stats.2004, c. 250 (S.B.1391), § 1.)*

Law Revision Commission Comments

Section 6240 is a new section that defines terms for the purposes of this part relating exclusively to emergency protective orders. The terms "judicial officer" and "law enforcement officer" are consistent with the Judicial Council form for the emergency protective order. See Cal. R. Ct. 1295.90 (rev. Jan. 1, 1992). See also Section 6215 ("emergency protective order" defined).

In this part, provisions concerning emergency protective orders relating to domestic violence from former Code of Civil Procedure Section 546(b) and provisions concerning emergency protective orders relating to child abuse from former Code of Civil Procedure Section 546(c) have been unified to the extent practicable. This approach is consistent with the unified Judicial Council form for the emergency protective order. [23 Cal.L.Rev.Comm. Reports 1 (1993)].

Cross References

Emergency protective order defined for purposes of this Code, see Family Code § 6215.
Freedom from parental custody and control, stay of proceedings and effect upon jurisdiction under these provisions, see Family Code § 7807.
Judgment and order defined for purposes of this Code, see Family Code § 100.
State defined for purposes of this Code, see Family Code § 145.

Research References

West's California Judicial Council Forms EPO–001, Emergency Protective Order (CLETS-EPO) (Also Available in Chinese, Korean, Spanish, and Vietnamese).

§ 6241. Designation of judge, commissioner, or referee to orally issue emergency protective orders

The presiding judge of the superior court in each county shall designate at least one judge, commissioner, or referee to be reasonably available to issue orally, by telephone or otherwise, emergency protective orders at all times whether or not the court is in session. *(Added by Stats.1993, c. 219 (A.B.1500), § 154.)*

Law Revision Commission Comments

Section 6241 continues without substantive change the first sentence of the first paragraph of former Code of Civil Procedure Section 546(b). See Section 6240(a) ("judicial officer" defined by reference to this section). See also Section 6215 ("emergency protective order" defined). [23 Cal.L.Rev.Comm. Reports 1 (1993)].

Cross References

County defined for purposes of this Code, see Family Code § 67.
Emergency protective order defined for purposes of this Code, see Family Code § 6215.
Judgment and order defined for purposes of this Code, see Family Code § 100.

CHAPTER 2. ISSUANCE AND EFFECT OF EMERGENCY PROTECTIVE ORDER

§ 6250. Grounds for issuance

A judicial officer may issue an ex parte emergency protective order where a law enforcement officer asserts reasonable grounds to believe any of the following:

(a) That a person is in immediate and present danger of domestic violence, based on the person's allegation of a recent incident of abuse or threat of abuse by the person against whom the order is sought.

(b) That a child is in immediate and present danger of abuse by a family or household member, based on an allegation of a recent incident of abuse or threat of abuse by the family or household member.

(c) That a child is in immediate and present danger of being abducted by a parent or relative, based on a reasonable belief that a person has an intent to abduct the child or flee with the child from the jurisdiction or based on an allegation of a recent threat to abduct the child or flee with the child from the jurisdiction.

(d) That an elder or dependent adult is in immediate and present danger of abuse as defined in Section 15610.07 of the Welfare and Institutions Code, based on an allegation of a recent incident of abuse or threat of abuse by the person against whom the order is sought, except that no emergency protective order shall be issued based solely on an allegation of financial abuse. *(Added by Stats.1993, c. 219 (A.B.1500), § 154. Amended by Stats.1996, c. 988 (A.B.2936), § 4; Stats.1999, c. 561 (A.B.59), § 1; Stats.2003, c. 468 (S.B.851), § 3.)*

Law Revision Commission Comments

Section 6250 continues without substantive change the second sentence of the first paragraph of subdivision (b) and the first sentence of the first paragraph of subdivision (c) of former Code of Civil Procedure Section 546. In subdivision (a), the phrase "by the person against whom the order is sought" has been added. This is not a substantive change. See Sections 6203 ("abuse" defined), 6211 ("domestic violence" defined).

See also Sections 6215 ("emergency protective order" defined), 6240(a) ("judicial officer" defined). [23 Cal.L.Rev.Comm. Reports 1 (1993)].

Cross References

Adult defined for purposes of this Code, see Family Code § 6501.
Domestic violence defined for purposes of this Code, see Family Code § 6211.
Emergency protective order defined for purposes of this Code, see Family Code § 6215.
Judgment and order defined for purposes of this Code, see Family Code § 100.
Officer to inform that order may be sought, request for person in immediate and present danger, see Family Code § 6275.
Person defined for purposes of this Code, see Family Code § 105.

Research References

2 Witkin, California Criminal Law 4th Crimes Against Governmental Authority § 10 (2021), Orders, Protocol, and Sanctions.

§ 6250.3. Valid orders

An emergency protective order is valid only if it is issued by a judicial officer after making the findings required by Section 6251 and pursuant to a specific request by a law enforcement officer. *(Added by Stats.2006, c. 82 (A.B.1787), § 1.)*

§ 6250.5. Issuance of ex parte emergency protective orders to peace officers

A judicial officer may issue an ex parte emergency protective order to a peace officer defined in subdivisions (a) and (b) of Section 830.32 if the issuance of that order is consistent with an existing memorandum of understanding between the college or school police department where the peace officer is employed and the sheriff or police chief of the city in whose jurisdiction the peace officer's college or school is located and the peace officer asserts reasonable grounds to believe that there is a demonstrated threat to campus safety. *(Added by Stats.1999, c. 659 (S.B.355), § 1.5.)*

Cross References

Emergency protective order defined for purposes of this Code, see Family Code § 6215.
Judgment and order defined for purposes of this Code, see Family Code § 100.

§ 6251. Findings of court

An emergency protective order may be issued only if the judicial officer finds both of the following:

(a) That reasonable grounds have been asserted to believe that an immediate and present danger of domestic violence exists, that a child is in immediate and present danger of abuse or abduction, or that an elder or dependent adult is in immediate and present danger of abuse as defined in Section 15610.07 of the Welfare and Institutions Code.

(b) That an emergency protective order is necessary to prevent the occurrence or recurrence of domestic violence, child abuse, child abduction, or abuse of an elder or dependent adult. *(Added by Stats.1993, c. 219 (A.B.1500), § 154. Amended by Stats.1996, c. 988 (A.B.2936), § 5; Stats.1999, c. 561 (A.B.59), § 2.)*

Law Revision Commission Comments

Section 6251 continues without substantive change the first sentence of the second paragraph of subdivision (b) and the first sentence of the second paragraph of subdivision (c) of former Code of Civil Procedure Section 546. See also Sections 6203 ("abuse" defined), 6211 ("domestic violence" defined), 6215 ("emergency protective order" defined), 6240(a) ("judicial officer" defined). [23 Cal.L.Rev.Comm. Reports 1 (1993)].

Cross References

Abuse defined for purposes of the Domestic Violence Protection Act, see Family Code § 6203.
Adult defined for purposes of this Code, see Family Code § 6501.
Domestic violence defined for purposes of this Code, see Family Code § 6211.
Emergency protective order defined for purposes of this Code, see Family Code § 6215.
Judgment and order defined for purposes of this Code, see Family Code § 100.

§ 6252. Inclusion of other orders

An emergency protective order may include any of the following specific orders, as appropriate:

(a) A protective order, as defined in Section 6218.

(b) An order determining the temporary care and control of any minor child of the endangered person and the person against whom the order is sought.

(c) An order authorized in Section 213.5 of the Welfare and Institutions Code, including provisions placing the temporary care and control of the endangered child and any other minor children in the family or household with the parent or guardian of the endangered child who is not a restrained party.

(d) An order determining the temporary care and control of any minor child who is in danger of being abducted.

(e) An order authorized by Section 15657.03 of the Welfare and Institutions Code. *(Added by Stats.1993, c. 219 (A.B.1500), § 154. Amended by Stats.1996, c. 988 (A.B.2936), § 6; Stats.1999, c. 561 (A.B.59), § 3.)*

Law Revision Commission Comments

The introductory clause and subdivisions (a) and (b) of Section 6252 continue without substantive change the third sentence of the first paragraph of former Code of Civil Procedure Section 546(b). A reference to "child" has been substituted for "children." This is not a substantive change. See Section 10 (singular includes plural).

The introductory clause and subdivision (c) continue without substantive change the second sentence of the first paragraph of former Code of Civil Procedure Section 546(c). The reference to the "legal" guardian has been omitted as surplus. This conforms with terminology in the Probate Code. See Prob. Code §§ 2350(b), 2400(b) ("guardian" defined).

See also Sections 6203 ("abuse" defined), 6211 ("domestic violence" defined), 6215 ("emergency protective order" defined). [23 Cal.L.Rev.Comm. Reports 1 (1993)].

Cross References

Emergency protective order defined for purposes of this Code, see Family Code § 6215.
Guardian, defined, see Probate Code §§ 2350, 2400.
Judgment and order defined for purposes of this Code, see Family Code § 100.
Minor defined for purposes of this Code, see Family Code § 6500.
Parent or guardian, defined, see Family Code § 6903.
Person defined for purposes of this Code, see Family Code § 105.

§ 6252.5. Addresses or locations of persons protected under court order; prohibition upon certain enjoined parties from acting to obtain such information

(a) The court shall order that any party enjoined pursuant to an order issued under this part be prohibited from taking any action to obtain the address or location of a protected party or a protected party's family members, caretakers, or guardian, unless there is good cause not to make that order.

(b) The Judicial Council shall promulgate forms necessary to effectuate this section. *(Added by Stats.2005, c. 472 (A.B.978), § 2.)*

§ 6253. Contents of orders

An emergency protective order shall include all of the following:

(a) A statement of the grounds asserted for the order.

(b) The date and time the order expires.

(c) The address of the superior court for the district or county in which the endangered person or child in danger of being abducted resides.

(d) The following statements, which shall be printed in English and Spanish:

(1) "To the Protected Person: This order will last only until the date and time noted above. If you wish to seek continuing protection, you will have to apply for an order from the court, at the address noted above. You may seek the advice of an attorney as to any matter connected with your application for any future court orders. The attorney should be consulted promptly so that the attorney may assist you in making your application."

(2) "To the Restrained Person: This order will last until the date and time noted above. The protected party may, however, obtain a more permanent restraining order from the court. You may seek the advice of an attorney as to any matter connected with the application. The attorney should be consulted promptly so that the attorney may assist you in responding to the application."

(e) In the case of an endangered child, the following statement, which shall be printed in English and Spanish: "This order will last only until the date and time noted above. You may apply for a more permanent restraining order under Section 213.5 of the Welfare and Institutions Code from the court at the address noted above. You may seek the advice of an attorney in connection with the application for a more permanent restraining order."

(f) In the case of a child in danger of being abducted, the following statement, which shall be printed in English and Spanish: "This order will last only until the date and time noted above. You may apply for a child custody order from the court, at the address noted above. You may seek the advice of an attorney as to any matter connected with the application. The attorney should be consulted promptly so that the attorney may assist you in responding to the application." *(Added by Stats.1993, c. 219 (A.B.1500), § 154. Amended by Stats.1996, c. 988 (A.B.2936), § 7.)*

Law Revision Commission Comments

Section 6253 continues without substantive change the parts of the second paragraphs of subdivisions (b) and (c) of former Code of Civil Procedure Section 546 that enumerated the contents of an emergency protective order, and the last sentence of the third paragraph of subdivision (b) and the last sentence of the fourth paragraph of subdivision (c) of former Code of Civil Procedure Section 546. The language concerning attorney advice in subdivision (e) has been conformed to the language of subdivision (d)(1). See also Section 6215 ("emergency protective order" defined). [23 Cal.L.Rev.Comm. Reports 1 (1993)].

Cross References

County defined for purposes of this Code, see Family Code § 67.
Emergency protective order defined for purposes of this Code, see Family Code § 6215.
Judgment and order defined for purposes of this Code, see Family Code § 100.
Person defined for purposes of this Code, see Family Code § 105.

§ 6254. Availability of orders; effect of vacation of household

The fact that the endangered person has left the household to avoid abuse does not affect the availability of an emergency protective order. *(Added by Stats.1993, c. 219 (A.B.1500), § 154.)*

Law Revision Commission Comments

Section 6254 continues without substantive change the seventh paragraph of subdivision (b) and the seventh paragraph of subdivision (c) of former Code of Civil Procedure Section 546. The endangered person may be an adult or a child. See also Section 6203 ("abuse" defined), 6215 ("emergency protective order" defined). [23 Cal.L.Rev.Comm. Reports 1 (1993)].

Cross References

Abuse defined for purposes of the Domestic Violence Protection Act, see Family Code § 6203.
Emergency protective order defined for purposes of this Code, see Family Code § 6215.
Judgment and order defined for purposes of this Code, see Family Code § 100.
Person defined for purposes of this Code, see Family Code § 105.

§ 6255. Issuance of orders without prejudice

An emergency protective order shall be issued without prejudice to any person. *(Added by Stats.1993, c. 219 (A.B.1500), § 154.)*

Law Revision Commission Comments

Section 6255 continues without substantive change the last sentence of the first paragraph of subdivision (b) and the last sentence of the first paragraph of subdivision (c) of former Code of Civil Procedure Section 546. See also Section 6215 ("emergency protective order" defined). [23 Cal.L.Rev.Comm. Reports 1 (1993)].

Cross References

Emergency protective order defined for purposes of this Code, see Family Code § 6215.
Judgment and order defined for purposes of this Code, see Family Code § 100.
Person defined for purposes of this Code, see Family Code § 105.

§ 6256. Expiration of orders

An emergency protective order expires at the earlier of the following times:

(a) The close of judicial business on the fifth court day following the day of its issuance.

(b) The seventh calendar day following the day of its issuance. *(Added by Stats.1993, c. 219 (A.B.1500), § 154. Amended by Stats.1993, c. 1229 (A.B.224), § 2.)*

Law Revision Commission Comments

Section 6256 supersedes the sixth paragraph of subdivision (b) and the third sentence of the first paragraph of subdivision (c) of former Code of Civil Procedure Section 546. See also Section 6215 ("emergency protective order" defined). [23 Cal.L.Rev.Comm. Reports 1 (1993)].

Cross References

Emergency protective order defined for purposes of this Code, see Family Code § 6215.
Judgment and order defined for purposes of this Code, see Family Code § 100.

§ 6257. Application for restraining orders under Welfare and Institutions Code § 213.5

If an emergency protective order concerns an endangered child, the child's parent or guardian who is not a restrained person, or a person having temporary custody of the endangered child, may apply to the court for a restraining order under Section 213.5 of the Welfare and Institutions Code. *(Added by Stats.1993, c. 219 (A.B. 1500), § 154.)*

Law Revision Commission Comments

Section 6257 continues the third paragraph of former Code of Civil Procedure Section 546(c) without substantive change. For provisions relating to orders concerning endangered children, see Section 6250(b), 6251(a), 6252(b)-(c). See also Section 6215 ("emergency protective order" defined). The reference to the "legal" guardian has been omitted as surplus. This conforms with terminology in the Probate Code. See Prob. Code §§ 2350(b), 2400(b) ("guardian" defined). [23 Cal.L.Rev.Comm. Reports 1 (1993)].

Cross References

Emergency protective order defined for purposes of this Code, see Family Code § 6215.
Guardian, defined, see Probate Code §§ 2350, 2400.
Judgment and order defined for purposes of this Code, see Family Code § 100.
Parent or guardian, defined, see Family Code § 6903.
Person defined for purposes of this Code, see Family Code § 105.

CHAPTER 3. DUTIES OF LAW ENFORCEMENT OFFICER

§ 6270. Reduction of orders to writing

A law enforcement officer who requests an emergency protective order shall reduce the order to writing and sign it. *(Added by Stats.1993, c. 219 (A.B.1500), § 154.)*

Law Revision Commission Comments

Section 6270 continues without substantive change the second sentence of the second paragraph of subdivision (b) and the second sentence of the second paragraph of subdivision (c) of former Code of Civil Procedure Section 546. The requirement of this section is satisfied by use of the Judicial Council form. See Cal. R. Ct. 1295.90 (rev. Jan. 1, 1992). See also Sections 6215 ("emergency protective order" defined), 6240(b) ("law enforcement officer" defined). [23 Cal.L.Rev.Comm. Reports 1 (1993)].

Cross References

Emergency protective order defined for purposes of this Code, see Family Code § 6215.
Judgment and order defined for purposes of this Code, see Family Code § 100.

§ 6271. Duties of officer who requested order

A law enforcement officer who requests an emergency protective order shall do all of the following:

(a) Serve the order on the restrained person, if the restrained person can reasonably be located.

(b) Give a copy of the order to the protected person or, if the protected person is a minor child, to a parent or guardian of the endangered child who is not a restrained person, if the parent or guardian can reasonably be located, or to a person having temporary custody of the endangered child.

(c) File a copy of the order with the court as soon as practicable after issuance.

(d) Have the order entered into the computer database system for protective and restraining orders maintained by the Department of Justice. *(Added by Stats.1993, c. 219 (A.B.1500), § 154. Amended by Stats.2013, c. 145 (A.B.238), § 1.)*

Law Revision Commission Comments

Section 6271 continues without substantive change the fifth paragraph of subdivision (b) and the sixth paragraph of subdivision (c) of former Code of Civil Procedure Section 546. References to the "legal" guardian have been omitted as surplus. This conforms with terminology in the Probate Code. See Prob. Code §§ 2350(b), 2400(b) ("guardian" defined).

See Section 6252 (b)–(c) (orders concerning endangered child); see also Sections 6215 ("emergency protective order" defined), 6240(b) ("law enforcement officer" defined). [23 Cal.L.Rev.Comm. Reports 1 (1993)].

Cross References

Emergency protective order defined for purposes of this Code, see Family Code § 6215.
Guardian, defined, see Probate Code §§ 2350, 2400.
Judgment and order defined for purposes of this Code, see Family Code § 100.
Minor defined for purposes of this Code, see Family Code § 6500.
Parent or guardian, defined, see Family Code § 6903.
Person defined for purposes of this Code, see Family Code § 105.

§ 6272. Enforcement of orders; liability of officers enforcing orders

(a) A law enforcement officer shall use every reasonable means to enforce an emergency protective order.

(b) A law enforcement officer who acts in good faith to enforce an emergency protective order is not civilly or criminally liable. *(Added by Stats.1993, c. 219 (A.B.1500), § 154.)*

Law Revision Commission Comments

Section 6272 restates without substantive change the last paragraph of subdivision (b) and the last paragraph of subdivision (c) of former Code of Civil Procedure Section 546. See also Sections 6215 ("emergency protective order" defined), 6240(b) ("law enforcement officer" defined). [23 Cal.L.Rev. Comm. Reports 1 (1993)].

Cross References

Emergency protective order defined for purposes of this Code, see Family Code § 6215.
Judgment and order defined for purposes of this Code, see Family Code § 100.

§ 6274. Stalking; emergency protective order

A peace officer, as defined in Section 830.1 or 830.2 of the Penal Code, may seek an emergency protective order relating to stalking under Section 646.91 of the Penal Code if the requirements of that section are complied with. *(Added by Stats.1997, c. 169 (A.B.350), § 1.)*

Cross References

Emergency protective order defined for purposes of this Code, see Family Code § 6215.
Judgment and order defined for purposes of this Code, see Family Code § 100.

§ 6275. Conditions under which an officer is to inform a person for whom emergency protective order may be sought

(a) A law enforcement officer who responds to a situation in which the officer believes that there may be grounds for the issuance of an emergency protective order pursuant to Section 6250 of this code or Section 646.91 of the Penal Code, shall inform the person for whom an emergency protective order may be sought, or, if that person is a minor, the minor's parent or guardian, provided that the parent or guardian is not the person against whom the emergency protective order may be obtained, that the person may request the officer to request an emergency protective order pursuant to this part.

(b) Notwithstanding Section 6250, and pursuant to this part, an officer shall request an emergency protective order if the officer believes that the person requesting an emergency protective order is in immediate and present danger. *(Added by Stats.2006, c. 479 (A.B.2139), § 1. Amended by Stats.2019, c. 115 (A.B.1817), § 60, eff. Jan. 1, 2020.)*

Research References

West's California Judicial Council Forms EPO–001, Emergency Protective Order (CLETS-EPO) (Also Available in Chinese, Korean, Spanish, and Vietnamese).

Part 4

PROTECTIVE ORDERS AND OTHER DOMESTIC VIOLENCE PREVENTION ORDERS

CHAPTER 1. GENERAL PROVISIONS

§ 6300. Issuance of order upon affidavit or testimony

(a) An order may be issued under this part to restrain any person for the purpose specified in Section 6220, if an affidavit or testimony and any additional information provided to the court pursuant to Section 6306, shows, to the satisfaction of the court, reasonable proof of a past act or acts of abuse. The court may issue an order under this part based solely on the affidavit or testimony of the person requesting the restraining order.

(b) An ex parte restraining order issued pursuant to Article 1 (commencing with Section 6320) shall not be denied solely because the other party was not provided with notice. *(Added by Stats.1993, c. 219 (A.B.1500), § 154. Amended by Stats.2001, c. 572 (S.B.66), § 2; Stats.2014, c. 635 (A.B.2089), § 4, eff. Jan. 1, 2015; Stats.2018, c. 219 (A.B.2694), § 1, eff. Jan. 1, 2019.)*

Law Revision Commission Comments

Section 6300 continues without substantive change and generalizes the first sentence of former Code of Civil Procedure Section 545 and supersedes the fourth sentence of Section 545. A reference to an order issued under "this part" has been substituted for the former reference to a "temporary" restraining order. This is not a substantive change. See also Sections 6203 ("abuse" defined), 6211 ("domestic violence" defined).

For general provisions relating to ex parte restraining orders, see Part 4 (commencing with Section 240) of Division 2. [23 Cal.L.Rev.Comm. Reports 1 (1993)].

Cross References

Abuse defined for purposes of the Domestic Violence Protection Act, see Family Code § 6203.
Domestic violence defined for purposes of this Code, see Family Code § 6211.
Judgment and order defined for purposes of this Code, see Family Code § 100.
Person defined for purposes of this Code, see Family Code § 105.

§ 6301. Persons who may be granted order

(a) An order under this part may be granted to any person described in Section 6211, including a minor pursuant to subdivision (b) of Section 372 of the Code of Civil Procedure.

(b) The right to petition for relief shall not be denied because the petitioner has vacated the household to avoid abuse, and in the case of a marital relationship, notwithstanding that a petition for dissolution of marriage, for nullity of marriage, or for legal separation of the parties has not been filed.

(c) The length of time since the most recent act of abuse is not, by itself, determinative. The court shall consider the totality of the circumstances in determining whether to grant or deny a petition for relief. *(Added by Stats.1993, c. 219 (A.B.1500), § 154. Amended by Stats.1996, c. 727 (A.B.2155), § 3; Stats.2014, c. 635 (A.B.2089), § 5, eff. Jan. 1, 2015; Stats.2015, c. 303 (A.B.731), § 150, eff. Jan. 1, 2016.)*

Law Revision Commission Comments

Section 6301 continues the second and third sentences of former Code of Civil Procedure Section 545 without substantive change. A reference to Section 6211 has been substituted for the reference to former Code of Civil Procedure Section 542. This is not a substantive change, since the relevant part of the former section is continued in Section 6211. The former reference to a "temporary" restraining order has been omitted, for consistency with other sections in this part. This is not a substantive change. See also Section 6203 ("abuse" defined). [23 Cal.L.Rev.Comm. Reports 1 (1993)].

Cross References

Abuse defined for purposes of the Domestic Violence Protection Act, see Family Code § 6203.
Judgment and order defined for purposes of this Code, see Family Code § 100.
Minor defined for purposes of this Code, see Family Code § 6500.
Person defined for purposes of this Code, see Family Code § 105.
Petitioner defined for purposes of this Code, see Family Code § 126.

§ 6301.5. Confidentiality of information relating to minors

(a) A minor or the minor's legal guardian may petition the court to have information regarding a minor that was obtained in connection with a request for a protective order pursuant to this division, including, but not limited to, the minor's name, address, and the circumstances surrounding the request for a protective order with respect to that minor, be kept confidential, except as provided in subdivision (d).

(b) The court may order the information specified in subdivision (a) be kept confidential if the court expressly finds all of the following:

Family

(1) The minor's right to privacy overcomes the right of public access to the information.

(2) There is a substantial probability that the minor's interest will be prejudiced if the information is not kept confidential.

(3) The order to keep the information confidential is narrowly tailored.

(4) No less restrictive means exist to protect the minor's privacy.

(c)(1) If the request is granted, except as provided in subdivision (d), information regarding the minor shall be maintained in a confidential case file and shall not become part of the public file in the proceeding, any other proceeding initiated under the Family Code, or any other civil proceeding between the parties. Except as provided in paragraph (2), if the court determines that disclosure of confidential information has been made without a court order, the court may impose a sanction of up to one thousand dollars ($1,000). The minor who has alleged abuse as defined under this division shall not be sanctioned for disclosure of the confidential information. If the court imposes a sanction, the court shall first determine whether the person has, or is reasonably likely to have, the ability to pay.

(2) Confidential information may be disclosed without a court order pursuant to subdivision (d) only in the following circumstances:

(A) By the minor's legal guardian who petitioned to keep the information confidential pursuant to this section or the protected party in an order pursuant to this division, provided that the disclosure effectuates the purpose of this division specified in Section 6220 or is in the minor's best interest. A legal guardian or a protected party who makes a disclosure under this subparagraph is subject to the sanction in paragraph (1) only if the disclosure was malicious.

(B) By a person to whom confidential information is disclosed, provided that the disclosure effectuates the purpose of this division specified in Section 6220 or is in the best interest of the minor, no more information than necessary is disclosed, and a delay would be caused by first obtaining a court order to authorize the disclosure of the information. A person who makes a disclosure pursuant to this subparagraph is subject to the sanction in paragraph (1) if the person discloses the information in a manner that recklessly or maliciously disregards these requirements.

(d)(1) Confidential information shall be made available to both of the following:

(A) Law enforcement pursuant to Section 6380, to the extent necessary and only for the purpose of enforcing the protective order.

(B) The respondent to allow the respondent to comply with the order for confidentiality and to allow the respondent to comply with and respond to the protective order. A notice shall be provided to the respondent that identifies the specific information that has been made confidential and shall include a statement that disclosure is punishable by a monetary fine.

(2) At any time, the court on its own may authorize a disclosure of any portion of the confidential information to certain individuals or entities as necessary to effectuate the purpose of this division specified in Section 6220, including implementation of the protective order, or if it is in the best interest of the minor, including, but not limited to, disclosure to educational institutions, childcare providers, medical or mental health providers, professional or nonprofessional supervisors for visitation, the Department of Child Support Services, attorneys for the parties or the minor, judicial officers, court employees, child custody evaluators, family court mediators, and court reporters.

(3) The court may authorize a disclosure of any portion of the confidential information to any person that files a petition if the court determines disclosure would effectuate the purpose of this division specified in Section 6220 or if the court determines that disclosure is in the best interest of the minor. The party who petitioned the court to keep the information confidential pursuant to this section shall be served personally or by first-class mail with a copy of the petition and afforded an opportunity to object to the disclosure. *(Added by Stats.2017, c. 384 (A.B.953), § 2, eff. Jan. 1, 2018. Amended by Stats.2019, c. 294 (A.B.925), § 2, eff. Jan. 1, 2020.)*

Research References

West's California Judicial Council Forms DV–160, Request to Keep Minor's Information Confidential (Domestic Violence Prevention) (Also Available in Chinese, Korean, Spanish, and Vietnamese).

West's California Judicial Council Forms DV–160–INFO, Privacy Protection for a Minor (Person Under 18 Years Old) (Domestic Violence Prevention).

West's California Judicial Council Forms DV–165, Order on Request to Keep Minor's Information Confidential (Also Available in Chinese, Korean, Spanish, and Vietnamese).

West's California Judicial Council Forms DV–170, Notice of Order Protecting Information of Minor (Domestic Violence Prevention) (Also Available in Chinese, Korean, Spanish, and Vietnamese).

West's California Judicial Council Forms DV–175, Cover Sheet for Confidential Information (Domestic Violence Prevention) (Also Available in Chinese, Korean, Spanish, and Vietnamese).

West's California Judicial Council Forms DV–176, Request for Release of Minor's Confidential Information.

West's California Judicial Council Forms DV–177, Notice of Request for Release of Minor's Confidential Information.

West's California Judicial Council Forms DV–178, Response to Request for Release of Minor's Confidential Information.

West's California Judicial Council Forms DV–179, Order on Request for Release of Minor's Confidential Information.

§ 6302. Notice of hearing

A notice of hearing under this part shall notify the respondent that, if the respondent does not attend the hearing, the court may make orders against the respondent that could last up to five years. *(Added by Stats.2010, c. 572 (A.B.1596), § 14, operative Jan. 1, 2012. Amended by Stats.2019, c. 115 (A.B.1817), § 61, eff. Jan. 1, 2020.)*

§ 6303. Support persons for victims of domestic violence; powers and duties; discretion of court

(a) It is the function of a support person to provide moral and emotional support for a person who alleges to be a victim of domestic violence. The person who alleges to be a victim of domestic violence may select any individual to act as a support person. No certification, training, or other special qualification is required for an individual to act as a support person. The support person shall assist the person in feeling more confident that the person will not be injured or threatened by the other party during the proceedings where the person and the other party must be present in close proximity. The support person is not present as a legal adviser and shall not give legal advice.

(b) A support person shall be permitted to accompany either party to any proceeding to obtain a protective order, as defined in Section 6218. Where the party is not represented by an attorney, the support person may sit with the party at the table that is generally reserved for the party and the party's attorney.

(c) Notwithstanding any other law to the contrary, if a court has issued a protective order, a support person shall be permitted to accompany a party protected by the order during any mediation orientation or mediation session, including separate mediation sessions, held pursuant to a proceeding described in Section 3021. Family Court Services, and any agency charged with providing family court services, shall advise the party protected by the order of the right to have a support person during mediation. A mediator may exclude a support person from a mediation session if the support person participates in the mediation session, or acts as an advocate, or the presence of a particular support person is disruptive or disrupts the process of mediation. The presence of the support person does not waive the confidentiality of the mediation, and the support person is bound by the confidentiality of the mediation.

(d) In a proceeding subject to this section, a support person shall be permitted to accompany a party in court where there are allegations or threats of domestic violence and, where the party is not represented by an attorney, may sit with the party at the table that is generally reserved for the party and the party's attorney.

(e) This section does not preclude a court from exercising its discretion to remove a person from the courtroom when it would be in the interest of justice to do so, or when the court believes the person is prompting, swaying, or influencing the party protected by the order. *(Added by Stats.1993, c. 219 (A.B.1500), § 154. Amended by Stats.1996, c. 761 (S.B.1995), § 7; Stats.2012, c. 470 (A.B.1529), § 21; Stats.2019, c. 115 (A.B.1817), § 62, eff. Jan. 1, 2020.)*

Law Revision Commission Comments

Section 6303 continues without substantive change and generalizes former Civil Code Section 4351.6. Subdivision (a) has been revised to refer to the function of a support person, rather than the legislative intent regarding that function. This is not a substantive change. Duplicative references to "the person who alleges he or she is a victim of domestic violence" have been omitted and references to "the person" substituted. In subdivisions (b) and (c), the term "protective order" has been substituted for the references to orders under specific sections formerly in the Civil Code and the Code of Civil Procedure. Section 6218 defines "protective order" to include the orders formerly listed, except as to orders under Code of Civil Procedure 527.6, which provides for similar orders in situations not covered by this division. This is not a substantive change, since, insofar as former Civil Code Section 4351.6 applied to Code of Civil Procedure Section 527.6, the former section is continued in new subdivision (f) of Code of Civil Procedure Section 527.6. See Code Civ. Proc. § 527.6 (civil harassment orders) & Comment. See also Section 6211 ("domestic violence" defined).

In subdivision (c), a reference to a "proceeding described in Section 3021" has been substituted for the narrower reference to an "action or proceeding under this part," meaning the former Family Law Act (former Part 5 (commencing with former Section 4000) of Division 4 of the Civil Code). See Section 3021 Comment.

Former Civil Code Section 4351.6(e) has been omitted. This is not a substantive change, since the former subdivision duplicated a provision that is continued in Section 6303(a). [23 Cal.L.Rev.Comm. Reports 1 (1993)].

Subdivision (c) of Section 6303 is amended to reflect enactment of the Lockyer–Isenberg Trial Court Funding Act, 1997 Cal. Stat. ch. 850 (see generally Gov't Code §§ 77000–77655). See, e.g., Gov't Code §§ 77001 (local trial court management), 77003 ("court operations" defined), 77200 (state funding of "court operations"); see also Fam. Code § 3170(b) (requiring domestic violence cases to be handled by Family Court Services according to approved protocol by Judicial Council); Cal. R. Ct. 5.215(b) ("This rule sets forth protocol for Family Court Services' handling of domestic violence cases consistent with requirement of Family Code section 3170(b)."), Cal. R. Ct. 5.215(h)(1) ("Family Court Services staff must advise the party protected by a protective order of the right to have a support person attend any mediation orientation or mediation sessions, including separate mediation sessions, under Family Code section 6303."). [39 Cal.L.Rev.Comm. Reports 157 (2009)].

Cross References

Domestic violence defined for purposes of this Code, see Family Code § 6211.
Judgment and order defined for purposes of this Code, see Family Code § 100.
Person defined for purposes of this Code, see Family Code § 105.
Proceeding defined for purposes of this Code, see Family Code § 110.
Support defined for purposes of this Code, see Family Code § 150.

§ 6304. Protective orders; court to inform parties of terms of orders

When making a protective order, as defined in Section 6218, where both parties are present in court, the court shall inform both the petitioner and the respondent of the terms of the order, including notice that the respondent is prohibited from owning, possessing, purchasing, or receiving or attempting to own, possess, purchase, or receive a firearm or ammunition, and including notice of the penalty for violation. Information provided shall include how any firearms or ammunition still in the restrained party's possession are to be relinquished, according to local procedures, and the process for submitting a receipt to the court showing proof of relinquishment. *(Added by Stats.1993, c. 219 (A.B.1500), § 154. Amended by Stats.1999, c. 662 (S.B.218), § 2; Stats.2010, c. 572 (A.B.1596), § 15, operative Jan. 1, 2012; Stats.2021, c. 685 (S.B.320), § 3, eff. Jan. 1, 2022.)*

Law Revision Commission Comments

Section 6304 continues former Code of Civil Procedure Section 550(f) without substantive change. The reference to "protective order" has been substituted for the reference to an order "predicated on" what are now Sections 6320–6322. This is not a substantive change, since "protective order" has been defined to include the same orders. See Section 6218 ("protective order" defined). See also Penal Code § 12021 (penalty for violation of firearm prohibition in restraining order). [23 Cal.L.Rev.Comm. Reports 1 (1993)].

Cross References

Intentional and knowing violation of court order to prevent harassment or domestic violence, penalties, see Penal Code § 273.6.
Judgment and order defined for purposes of this Code, see Family Code § 100.
Petitioner defined for purposes of this Code, see Family Code § 126.
Respondent defined for purposes of this Code, see Family Code § 127.
Unlawful ownership or possession of firearms in violation of protective order, penalties, see Penal Code §§ 29800 to 29875.

§ 6305. Mutual orders; personal appearance of parties; application for relief

(a) The court shall not issue a mutual order enjoining the parties from specific acts of abuse described in Section 6320 unless both of the following apply:

(1) Both parties personally appear and each party presents written evidence of abuse or domestic violence in an application for relief using a mandatory Judicial Council restraining order application form. For purposes of this paragraph, written evidence of abuse or domestic violence in a responsive pleading does not satisfy the party's obligation to present written evidence of abuse or domestic violence. By July 1, 2016, the Judicial Council shall modify forms as necessary to provide notice of this information.

(2) The court makes detailed findings of fact indicating that both parties acted as a primary aggressor and that neither party acted primarily in self-defense.

(b) For purposes of subdivision (a), in determining if both parties acted primarily as aggressors, the court shall consider the provisions concerning dominant aggressors set forth in paragraph (3) of subdivision (c) of Section 836 of the Penal Code. *(Added by Stats.1993, c. 219 (A.B.1500), § 154. Amended by Stats.1995, c. 246 (S.B.591), § 2; Stats.2014, c. 635 (A.B.2089), § 6, eff. Jan. 1, 2015; Stats.2015, c. 73 (A.B.536), § 1, eff. Jan. 1, 2016.)*

Law Revision Commission Comments

Section 6305 continues without substantive change former Code of Civil Procedure Section 545.5, the second paragraph of former Civil Code Section 4359(a), and former Civil Code Section 7020(f). The references in the former sections to the definition of domestic violence have been omitted. These are not substantive changes, since the definition applicable to this section is the same. See Section 6211 ("domestic violence" defined); see also Section 6302 ("abuse" defined). A reference to Section 6320 has been substituted for a specific list of acts. This is not a substantive change, since Section 6320 duplicates the omitted list. [23 Cal.L.Rev.Comm. Reports 1 (1993)].

Cross References

Abuse defined for purposes of the Domestic Violence Protection Act, see Family Code § 6203.
Domestic violence defined for purposes of this Code, see Family Code § 6211.
Intentional and knowing violation of court order to prevent harassment or domestic violence, penalties, see Penal Code § 273.6.
Judgment and order defined for purposes of this Code, see Family Code § 100.

§ 6306. Criminal history search; prior restraining orders

(a) Prior to a hearing on the issuance or denial of an order under this part, the court shall ensure that a search is or has been conducted to determine if the subject of the proposed order has a prior criminal conviction for a violent felony specified in Section 667.5 of the Penal Code or a serious felony specified in Section 1192.7 of the Penal Code; has a misdemeanor conviction involving domestic violence, weapons, or other violence; has an outstanding warrant; is currently on parole or probation; has a registered firearm; or has a prior restraining order or a violation of a prior restraining order. The search shall be conducted of all records and databases readily available and reasonably accessible to the court, including, but not limited to, the following:

(1) The California Sex and Arson Registry (CSAR).

(2) The Supervised Release File.

(3) State summary criminal history information maintained by the Department of Justice pursuant to Section 11105 of the Penal Code.

(4) The Federal Bureau of Investigation's nationwide database.

(5) Locally maintained criminal history records or databases.

However, a record or database need not be searched if the information available in that record or database can be obtained as a result of a search conducted in another record or database.

(b)(1) Prior to deciding whether to issue an order under this part or when determining appropriate temporary custody and visitation orders, the court shall consider the following information obtained pursuant to a search conducted under subdivision (a): a conviction for a violent felony specified in Section 667.5 of the Penal Code or a serious felony specified in Section 1192.7 of the Penal Code; a misdemeanor conviction involving domestic violence, weapons, or other violence; an outstanding warrant; parole or probation status; a prior restraining order; and a violation of a prior restraining order.

(2) Information obtained as a result of the search that does not involve a conviction described in this subdivision shall not be considered by the court in making a determination regarding the issuance of an order pursuant to this part. That information shall be destroyed and shall not become part of the public file in this or any other civil proceeding.

(c)(1) After issuing its ruling, the court shall advise the parties that they may request the information described in subdivision (b) upon which the court relied. The court shall admonish the party seeking the proposed order that it is unlawful, pursuant to Sections 11142 and 13303 of the Penal Code, to willfully release the information, except as authorized by law.

(2) Upon the request of either party to obtain the information described in subdivision (b) upon which the court relied, the court shall release the information to the parties or, upon either party's request, to the party's attorney in that proceeding.

(3) The party seeking the proposed order may release the information to the party's counsel, court personnel, and court-appointed mediators for the purpose of seeking judicial review of the court's order or for purposes of court proceedings under Section 213.5 of the Welfare and Institutions Code.

(d) Information obtained as a result of the search conducted pursuant to subdivision (a) and relied upon by the court shall be maintained in a confidential case file and shall not become part of the public file in the proceeding or any other civil proceeding. However, the contents of the confidential case file shall be disclosed to the court-appointed mediator assigned to the case or to a child custody evaluator appointed by the court pursuant to Section 3111 of this code or Section 730 of the Evidence Code. All court-appointed mediators and child custody evaluators appointed or contracted by the court pursuant to Section 3111 of this code or Section 730 of the Evidence Code who receive information from the search conducted pursuant to subdivision (a) shall be subject to, and shall comply with, the California Law Enforcement Telecommunications System policies, practices, and procedures adopted pursuant to Section 15160 of the Government Code.

(e) If the results of the search conducted pursuant to subdivision (a) indicate that an outstanding warrant exists against the subject of the order, the court shall order the clerk of the court to immediately notify, by the most effective means available, appropriate law enforcement officials of the issuance and contents of a protective order and of any other information obtained through the search that the court determines is appropriate. The law enforcement officials so notified shall take all actions necessary to execute any outstanding warrants or any other actions, with respect to the restrained person, as appropriate and as soon as practicable.

(f) If the results of the search conducted pursuant to subdivision (a) indicate that the subject of the order owns a registered firearm or if the court receives evidence of the subject's possession of a firearm or ammunition, the court shall make a written record as to whether the subject has relinquished the firearm or ammunition and provided proof of the required storage, sale, or relinquishment of the firearm or ammunition. If evidence of compliance with firearms prohibitions is not provided pursuant to subdivision (c) of Section 6389, the court shall order the clerk of the court to immediately notify, by the most effective means available, appropriate law enforcement officials of the issuance and contents of a protective order, information about the firearm or ammunition, and of any other information obtained through the search that the court determines is appropriate. The law enforcement officials so notified shall take all actions necessary to obtain those and any other firearms or ammunition owned, possessed, or controlled by the restrained person and to address any violation of the order with respect to firearms or ammunition as appropriate and as soon as practicable.

(g) If the results of the search conducted pursuant to subdivision (a) indicate that the subject of the order is currently on parole or probation, the court shall order the clerk of the court to immediately notify, by the most effective means available, the appropriate parole or probation officer of the issuance and contents of a protective order issued by the court and of any other information obtained through the search that the court determines is appropriate. That officer shall take all actions necessary to revoke parole or probation, or any other actions, with respect to the restrained person, as appropriate and as soon as practicable.

(h) This section shall not delay the granting of an application for an order that may otherwise be granted without the information resulting from the database search. If the court finds that a protective order under this part should be granted on the basis of the affidavit presented with the petition, the court shall issue the protective order and shall then ensure that a search is conducted pursuant to subdivision (a) prior to the hearing. *(Added by Stats.2001, c. 572 (S.B.66), § 3. Amended by Stats.2012, c. 765 (S.B.1433), § 1; Stats.2014, c. 54 (S.B.1461), § 2, eff. Jan. 1, 2015; Stats.2019, c. 115 (A.B.1817), § 63, eff. Jan. 1, 2020; Stats.2021, c. 685 (S.B.320), § 4, eff. Jan. 1, 2022.)*

Cross References

Domestic violence defined for purposes of this Code, see Family Code § 6211.
Felonies, definition and penalties, see Penal Code §§ 17, 18.
Judgment and order defined for purposes of this Code, see Family Code § 100.
Juvenile court law, proceedings to declare a minor child a dependent child, see Welfare and Institutions Code § 213.5.
Misdemeanors, definition and penalties, see Penal Code §§ 17, 19, 19.2.
Person defined for purposes of this Code, see Family Code § 105.
Procedure prior to hearing on issuance, renewal, or termination of order, see Penal Code § 18110.
Proceeding defined for purposes of this Code, see Family Code § 110.
Protective order defined for purposes of this Code, see Family Code § 6218.
State defined for purposes of this Code, see Family Code § 145.

§ 6306.5. Electronically submitted petitions seeking domestic violence restraining orders

(a)(1) Petitions seeking domestic violence restraining orders under Chapter 2 (commencing with Section 6320) and domestic violence temporary restraining orders under Part 4 (commencing with Section 240) of Division 2 may be submitted electronically in every trial court. Courts shall accept these filings consistent with the timeframe in Section 246.

(2) The notice of court date, copies of the request to mail on respondent, and the temporary restraining order, if granted, shall be remitted to the petitioner electronically.

(3) Notwithstanding paragraph (2), the petitioner may elect to receive documents by regular mail or to retrieve documents from the court.

(b) The Judicial Council shall develop or amend rules and forms as necessary to implement this section.

(c) There shall be no fee for any filings related to a petition submitted electronically in accordance with this section.

(d) This section shall become operative only upon an appropriation of funds for this purpose in the annual Budget Act or other statute. *(Added by Stats.2021, c. 681 (A.B.887), § 1, eff. Jan. 1, 2022.)*

Contingent Operation

Operation of this section is contingent upon availability of funding in the annual Budget Act, by its own terms.

§ 6306.6. Domestic violence restraining orders visible on superior court's internet website

(a) Information about access to self-help services regarding domestic violence restraining orders shall be prominently visible on the superior court's internet website.

(b) The Judicial Council shall develop or amend rules as necessary to implement this section. *(Added by Stats.2021, c. 681 (A.B.887), § 2, eff. Jan. 1, 2022.)*

§ 6307. Electronic submission of petitions and filings; availability of electronic filing and self-help center information on homepage; adoption of rules and forms for implementation

Section operative July 1, 2023.

(a)(1) A court or court facility that receives petitions for domestic violence restraining orders under this part or domestic violence temporary restraining orders under Part 4 (commencing with Section 240) of Division 2 shall permit those petitions and any filings related to those petitions to be submitted electronically. The court or court facility shall, based on the time of receipt, act on these filings consistent with Section 246.

(2) The request, notice of the court date, copies of the request to serve on the respondent, and the temporary restraining order, if granted, shall be provided to the petitioner electronically, unless the petitioner notes, at the time of electronic filing, that these documents will be picked up from the court or court facility.

(b)(1) Information regarding electronic filing and access to the court's self-help center shall be prominently displayed on each court's homepage.

(2) Each self-help center shall maintain and make available information related to domestic violence restraining orders pursuant to this section.

(c) The Judicial Council may adopt or amend rules and forms to implement this section.

(d) This section shall become operative on July 1, 2023. *(Added by Stats.2022, c. 420 (A.B.2960), § 17, eff. Jan. 1, 2023, operative July 1, 2023.)*

§ 6308. Remote appearance of party, support person, and witness; development and publication of local rules

* * * A party, support person as defined in Section 6303, or witness may appear remotely at the hearing on a petition for a domestic violence restraining order. The superior court of each county shall develop local rules and instructions for remote appearances permitted under this section, which shall be posted on its internet website.

* * * *(Added by Stats.2021, c. 686 (S.B.538), § 3, eff. Jan. 1, 2022. Amended by Stats.2022, c. 420 (A.B.2960), § 18, eff. Jan. 1, 2023.)*

CHAPTER 2. ISSUANCE OF ORDERS

ARTICLE 1. EX PARTE ORDERS

§ 6320. Ex parte order enjoining contact, credibly or falsely impersonating, or destroying personal property; protection for companion animals

(a) The court may issue an ex parte order enjoining a party from molesting, attacking, striking, stalking, threatening, sexually assaulting, battering, credibly impersonating as described in Section 528.5 of the Penal Code, falsely personating as described in Section 529 of the Penal Code, harassing, telephoning, including, but not limited to, making annoying telephone calls as described in Section 653m of the Penal Code, destroying personal property, contacting, either directly or indirectly, by mail or otherwise, coming within a specified distance of, or disturbing the peace of the other party, and, in the discretion of the court, on a showing of good cause, of other named family or household members.

(b) On a showing of good cause, the court may include in a protective order a grant to the petitioner of the exclusive care, possession, or control of any animal owned, possessed, leased, kept, or held by either the petitioner or the respondent or a minor child residing in the residence or household of either the petitioner or the respondent. The court may order the respondent to stay away from the animal and forbid the respondent from taking, transferring, encumbering, concealing, molesting, attacking, striking, threatening, harming, or otherwise disposing of the animal.

(c) As used in this subdivision (a), "disturbing the peace of the other party" refers to conduct that, based on the totality of the circumstances, destroys the mental or emotional calm of the other party. This conduct may be committed directly or indirectly, including through the use of a third party, and by any method or through any means including, but not limited to, telephone, online

Family

accounts, text messages, internet-connected devices, or other electronic technologies. This conduct includes, but is not limited to, coercive control, which is a pattern of behavior that in purpose or effect unreasonably interferes with a person's free will and personal liberty. Examples of coercive control include, but are not limited to, unreasonably engaging in any of the following:

(1) Isolating the other party from friends, relatives, or other sources of support.

(2) Depriving the other party of basic necessities.

(3) Controlling, regulating, or monitoring the other party's movements, communications, daily behavior, finances, economic resources, or access to services.

(4) Compelling the other party by force, threat of force, or intimidation, including threats based on actual or suspected immigration status, to engage in conduct from which the other party has a right to abstain or to abstain from conduct in which the other party has a right to engage.

(5) Engaging in reproductive coercion, which consists of control over the reproductive autonomy of another through force, threat of force, or intimidation, and may include, but is not limited to, unreasonably pressuring the other party to become pregnant, deliberately interfering with contraception use or access to reproductive health information, or using coercive tactics to control, or attempt to control, pregnancy outcomes.

(d) This section does not limit any remedies available under this act or any other provision of law. *(Added by Stats.2013, c. 260 (A.B.157), § 2, operative July 1, 2014. Amended by Stats.2020, c. 248 (S.B.1141), § 2, eff. Jan. 1, 2021; Stats.2021, c. 135 (S.B.374), § 1, eff. Jan. 1, 2022.)*

Cross References

Abandonment and neglect of children, intentional and knowing violation of court order to prevent harassment, disturbing the peace, or threats or acts of violence, see Penal Code § 273.6.
Contempt of court, conduct constituting, see Penal Code § 166.
Court orders available in response to good cause belief of harm to, intimidation of, or dissuasion of victim or witness, see Penal Code § 136.2.
Interstate enforcement of domestic violence protection orders, more than one order issued, enforcement of no-contact order, see Family Code § 6405.
Judgment and order defined for purposes of this Code, see Family Code § 100.
More than one order issued, enforcement of no-contact order, see Family Code § 6383.
Property defined for purposes of this Code, see Family Code § 113.
Suspension of money judgment or order for support of a child, exceptions, resumption of obligation, administrative adjustment, evaluation, see Family Code § 4007.5.
Uniform Recognition and Enforcement of Canadian Domestic Violence Protection Orders Act, multiple protective orders, priority of enforcement, see Family Code § 6457.

Research References

West's California Judicial Council Forms FL–300, Request for Order (Also Available in Spanish).
West's California Judicial Council Forms JV–245, Request for Restraining Order—Juvenile (Also Available in Chinese, Korean, Spanish, and Vietnamese).
2 Witkin, California Criminal Law 4th Crimes Against Governmental Authority § 10 (2021), Orders, Protocol, and Sanctions.

§ 6320.5. Order denying petition for ex parte order; reasons; right to noticed hearing; right to waive hearing

(a) An order denying a petition for an ex parte order pursuant to Section 6320 shall include the reasons for denying the petition.

(b) An order denying a jurisdictionally adequate petition for an ex parte order, pursuant to Section 6320, shall provide the petitioner the right to a noticed hearing on the earliest date that the business of the court will permit, but not later than 21 days or, if good cause appears to the court, 25 days from the date of the order. The petitioner shall serve on the respondent, at least five days before the hearing, copies of all supporting papers filed with the court, including the application and affidavits.

(c) Notwithstanding subdivision (b), upon the denial of the ex parte order pursuant to Section 6320, the petitioner shall have the option of waiving the right to a noticed hearing. However, this section does not preclude a petitioner who waives the right to a noticed hearing from refiling a new petition, without prejudice, at a later time. *(Added by Stats.2008, c. 263 (A.B.2553), § 1. Amended by Stats.2010, c. 572 (A.B.1596), § 17, operative Jan. 1, 2012; Stats.2019, c. 115 (A.B.1817), § 64, eff. Jan. 1, 2020.)*

Research References

West's California Judicial Council Forms DV–112, Waiver of Hearing on Denied Request for Temporary Restraining Order (Also Available in Chinese, Korean, Spanish, and Vietnamese).

§ 6321. Ex parte order excluding party from dwelling

(a) The court may issue an ex parte order excluding a party from the family dwelling, the dwelling of the other party, the common dwelling of both parties, or the dwelling of the person who has care, custody, and control of a child to be protected from domestic violence for the period of time and on the conditions the court determines, regardless of which party holds legal or equitable title or is the lessee of the dwelling.

(b) The court may issue an order under subdivision (a) only on a showing of all of the following:

(1) Facts sufficient for the court to ascertain that the party who will stay in the dwelling has a right under color of law to possession of the premises.

(2) That the party to be excluded has assaulted or threatens to assault the other party or any other person under the care, custody, and control of the other party, or any minor child of the parties or of the other party.

(3) That physical or emotional harm would otherwise result to the other party, to any person under the care, custody, and control of the other party, or to any minor child of the parties or of the other party. *(Added by Stats.1993, c. 219 (A.B.1500), § 154.)*

Law Revision Commission Comments

Section 6321 restates without substantive change part of the first sentence of Code of Civil Procedure Section 546(a), and continues without substantive change the last paragraph of former Code of Civil Procedure Section 546(a) and former Civil Code Sections 4359(a)(3) and 7020(a)(2). This section supersedes the third part of former Civil Code Section 5102(a). The reference to "the common dwelling of both parties" is drawn from former Civil Code Section 7020(b). This is not a substantive change, but rather is added to clarify application of the section to unmarried persons. A reference to the "superior" court has been omitted as surplus. See Section 200 (jurisdiction in superior court). The former reference to Code of Civil Procedure Section 527 has been omitted. This is not a substantive change. See Section 240 & Comment.

For general provisions relating to ex parte restraining orders, see Part 4 (commencing with Section 240) of Division 2. [23 Cal.L.Rev.Comm. Reports 1 (1993)].

Cross References

Domestic violence defined for purposes of this Code, see Family Code § 6211.
Ex parte temporary restraining orders, generally, see Family Code § 240 et seq.
Exclusion of spouse from other's dwelling, see Family Code § 753.
Judgment and order defined for purposes of this Code, see Family Code § 100.
Minor defined for purposes of this Code, see Family Code § 6500.
Nullity, dissolution, and legal separation, ex parte protective orders, generally, see Family Code § 2045.
Person defined for purposes of this Code, see Family Code § 105.
Uniform Parentage Act, issuance of ex parte orders, see Family Code § 7710.

Research References

West's California Judicial Council Forms JV–245, Request for Restraining Order—Juvenile (Also Available in Chinese, Korean, Spanish, and Vietnamese).

§ 6322. Ex parte order enjoining specified behavior

The court may issue an ex parte order enjoining a party from specified behavior that the court determines is necessary to effectuate orders under Section 6320 or 6321. *(Added by Stats.1993, c. 219 (A.B.1500), § 154.)*

Law Revision Commission Comments

Section 6322 restates without substantive change part of the first sentence of former Code of Civil Procedure Section 546(a), and continues without substantive change former Civil Code Sections 4359(a)(6) and 7020(a)(3). A reference to the "superior" court has been omitted as surplus. See Section 200 (jurisdiction in superior court). The former reference to Code of Civil Procedure Section 527 has been omitted. This is not a substantive change. See Section 240 & Comment.

For general provisions relating to ex parte restraining orders, see Part 4 (commencing with Section 240) of Division 2. [23 Cal.L.Rev.Comm. Reports 1 (1993)].

Cross References

Ex parte temporary restraining orders, generally, see Family Code § 240 et seq.
Judgment and order defined for purposes of this Code, see Family Code § 100.
Nullity, dissolution, and legal separation, ex parte protective orders, generally, see Family Code § 2045.
Uniform Parentage Act, issuance of ex parte orders, see Family Code § 7710.

Research References

West's California Judicial Council Forms JV–245, Request for Restraining Order—Juvenile (Also Available in Chinese, Korean, Spanish, and Vietnamese).

§ 6322.5. Restrained person having firearm or ammunition; determination of violation of Section 6389

(a) When relevant information is presented to the court at a noticed hearing that a restrained person has a firearm or ammunition, the court shall consider that information and determine, by a preponderance of the evidence, whether the person subject to a protective order has a firearm or ammunition in, or subject to, their immediate possession or control in violation of Section 6389.

(b)(1) In making the determination required pursuant to subdivision (a), the court may consider whether the restrained person filed a firearm relinquishment, storage, or sales receipt or if an exemption from the firearm prohibition was granted pursuant to subdivision (h) of Section 6389.

(2) The court may make the determination at a noticed hearing when a domestic violence protective order is issued, at a subsequent review hearing, or at any subsequent family or juvenile law hearing while the order remains in effect.

(3) If the court makes a determination that the restrained person has a firearm or ammunition in violation of Section 6389, the court shall make a written record of the determination and provide a copy to any party who is present at the hearing and, upon request, to any party not present at the hearing.

(c)(1) When presented with information pursuant to subdivision (a), the court may set a review hearing to determine whether there has been a violation of Section 6389.

(2) The review hearing shall be held within 10 court days after the noticed hearing at which the information was presented. If the restrained person is not present when the court sets the review hearing, the protected person shall provide notice of the review hearing to the restrained person at least two court days before the review hearing, in accordance with Section 414.10 of the Code of Civil Procedure, by personal service or by mail to the restrained person's last known address.

(3) The court may, for good cause, extend the date of the review hearing for a reasonable period or remove it from the calendar.

(4) The court shall order the restrained person to appear at the hearing.

(5) The court may conduct the review hearing in the absence of the protected person.

(6) This section does not prohibit the court from permitting a party or witness to appear through technology that enables remote appearances, as determined by the court.

(d) The determination made pursuant to this section may be considered by the court in issuing an order to show cause for contempt pursuant to paragraph (5) of subdivision (a) of Section 1209 of the Code of Civil Procedure or an order for monetary sanctions pursuant to Section 177.5 of the Code of Civil Procedure. *(Added by Stats.2021, c. 685 (S.B.320), § 5, eff. Jan. 1, 2022.)*

Cross References

Custody of children, presumption against person perpetrating domestic violence, see Family Code § 3044.
Proceedings to declare a minor child a dependent child, ex parte orders, see Welfare and Institutions Code § 213.5.

§ 6322.7. Addresses or locations of persons protected under court order; prohibition upon certain enjoined parties from acting to obtain such information

(a) The court shall order that any party enjoined pursuant to an order issued under this part be prohibited from taking any action to obtain the address or location of any protected person, unless there is good cause not to make that order.

(b) The Judicial Council shall develop forms necessary to effectuate this section. *(Added by Stats.2005, c. 472 (A.B.978), § 3. Amended by Stats.2010, c. 572 (A.B.1596), § 18, operative Jan. 1, 2012.)*

§ 6323. Ex parte orders regarding temporary custody and visitation of minor children; stipulation of parentage; considerations

(a) Subject to Section 3064:

(1) The court may issue an ex parte order determining the temporary custody and visitation of a minor child, on the conditions the court determines, to a party who has established a parent and child relationship pursuant to paragraph (2). The parties shall inform the court if a custody or visitation order has already been issued in any other proceeding.

(2)(A) In making a determination of the best interest of the child, in order to limit the child's exposure to potential domestic violence, and to ensure the safety of all family members, if the party who has obtained the restraining order has established a parent and child relationship and the other party has not established that relationship, the court may award temporary sole legal and physical custody to the party to whom the restraining order was issued and may make an order of no visitation to the other party pending the establishment of a parent and child relationship between the child and the other party.

(B) A party may establish a parent and child relationship for purposes of subparagraph (A) only by offering proof of any of the following:

(i) The party gave birth to the child.

(ii) The child is conclusively presumed to be a child of the marriage between the parties, pursuant to Section 7540, or the party has been determined by a court to be a parent of the child, pursuant to Section 7541.

(iii) Legal adoption or pending legal adoption of the child by the party.

(iv) The party has signed a valid voluntary declaration of paternity, which has been in effect more than 60 days prior to the issuance of the restraining order, and that declaration has not been rescinded or set aside.

(v) A determination made by the juvenile court that there is a parent and child relationship between the party offering the proof and the child.

Family

(vi) A determination of parentage made in a proceeding to determine custody or visitation in a case brought by the local child support agency pursuant to Chapter 2 (commencing with Section 17400) of Division 17.

(vii) The party has been determined to be the parent of the child through a proceeding under the Uniform Parentage Act (Part 3 (commencing with Section 7600) of Division 12).

(viii) Both parties stipulate, in writing or on the record, for purposes of this proceeding, that they are the parents of the child.

(b)(1) Except as provided in paragraph (2), the court shall not make a finding of paternity in this proceeding, and an order issued pursuant to this section shall be without prejudice in any other action brought to establish a parent and child relationship.

(2) The court may accept a stipulation of paternity by the parties and, if paternity is uncontested, enter a judgment establishing paternity, subject to the set-aside provisions in Section 7646.

(c) When making an order for custody or visitation pursuant to this section, the court's order shall specify the time, day, place, and manner of transfer of the child for custody or visitation to limit the child's exposure to potential domestic conflict or violence and to ensure the safety of all family members. If the court finds a party is staying in a place designated as a shelter for victims of domestic violence or other confidential location, the court's order for time, day, place, and manner of transfer of the child for custody or visitation shall be designed to prevent disclosure of the location of the shelter or other confidential location.

(d) When making an order for custody or visitation pursuant to this section, the court shall consider whether the best interest of the child, based upon the circumstances of the case, requires that a visitation or custody arrangement shall be limited to situations in which a third person, specified by the court, is present, or whether visitation or custody shall be suspended or denied.

(e) When determining whether visitation should be suspended, denied, or limited to situations in which a third person is present pursuant to subdivision (d), the court shall consider a determination made pursuant to Section 6322.5 that the party is a restrained person in possession or control of a firearm or ammunition in violation of Section 6389. *(Added by Stats.1993, c. 219 (A.B.1500), § 154. Amended by Stats.1994, c. 320 (A.B.356), § 3; Stats.1997, c. 396 (S.B.564), § 2; Stats.2010, c. 352 (A.B.939), § 18; Stats.2019, c. 497 (A.B.991), § 111, eff. Jan. 1, 2020; Stats.2019, c. 115 (A.B.1817), § 65, eff. Jan. 1, 2020; Stats.2021, c. 685 (S.B.320), § 6, eff. Jan. 1, 2022.)*

Law Revision Commission Comments

Section 6323 restates without substantive change part of the first sentence of Code of Civil Procedure Section 546(a), and continues without substantive change former Civil Code Sections 4359(a)(4) and 7020(a)(4). The intention of this section is to continue the prior law and practice. The reference to Section 3064 has been added. To the extent that the court's authority to issue custody orders ex parte is limited by Section 3064, this limitation also applies to visitation. A reference to the "superior" court has been omitted as surplus. See Section 200 (jurisdiction in superior court). The former reference to Code of Civil Procedure Section 527 has been omitted. This is not a substantive change. See Section 240 & Comment.

Section 6223 requires that procedural and substantive rules contained in Part 2 (commencing with Section 3020) of Division 8 of this code be applied where a court determines custody or visitation in a proceeding brought pursuant to the Domestic Violence Prevention Act. For sections of particular importance in situations involving domestic violence, see Sections 3030 (custody and unsupervised visitation prohibited where parent convicted under certain Penal Code provisions), 3031 (custody or visitation should not be inconsistent with restraining orders), 3100(b) (limiting visitation to situation where third party present), 3131 (action by district attorney where child taken or detained in violation of visitation order). See also Cal. R. Ct. 1285.05 (rev. July 1, 1991) (temporary restraining order), 1296.10 (rev. Jan. 1, 1991) (order to show cause and temporary restraining order).

For general provisions relating to ex parte restraining orders, see Part 4 (commencing with Section 240) of Division 2. See also Section 3021 (Part 2 of Division 8 applicable to proceeding for dissolution, nullity, and legal separation and to action pursuant to the Uniform Parentage Act). [23 Cal.L.Rev.Comm. Reports 1 (1993)].

Cross References

Custody or visitation orders, proceedings to declare a minor child a dependent child of the court, required procedures, see Welfare and Institutions Code § 213.5.
Destruction of court records, notice, retention periods, see Government Code § 68152.
Domestic violence defined for purposes of this Code, see Family Code § 6211.
Ex parte temporary restraining orders, generally, see Family Code § 240 et seq.
Judgment and order defined for purposes of this Code, see Family Code § 100.
Minor defined for purposes of this Code, see Family Code § 6500.
Nullity, dissolution, and legal separation, ex parte protective orders, generally, see Family Code § 2045.
Person defined for purposes of this Code, see Family Code § 105.
Proceeding defined for purposes of this Code, see Family Code § 110.
Uniform Parentage Act, issuance of ex parte orders, see Family Code § 7710.

Research References

West's California Judicial Council Forms DV–180, Agreement and Judgment of Parentage (Also Available in Chinese, Korean, Spanish, and Vietnamese).

§ 6323.5. Ex parte provision restraining a party from accessing records and information pertaining to the health care, education, daycare, recreational activities, or employment of a minor child of the parties; protocols relating to the provider's compliance; release of information or records

(a) For purposes of this section, the following definitions apply:

(1) "Discretionary services organization" includes any organization that provides nonessential services to children, such as recreational activities, entertainment, and summer camps. "Discretionary services organization" also includes a place of employment of a minor described in subdivision (b).

(2) "Essential care provider" includes a public or private school, health care facility, daycare facility, dental facility, or other similar organization that frequently provides essential social, health, or care services to children.

(b)(1) Notwithstanding Section 3025, and in accordance with Section 6322, a court may include in an ex parte order a provision restraining a party from accessing records and information pertaining to the health care, education, daycare, recreational activities, or employment of a minor child of the parties.

(2) A parent or guardian may provide a copy of an order with a provision specified in paragraph (1) to an essential care provider or a discretionary services organization, or both.

(c)(1)(A) An essential care provider shall, on or before February 1, 2023, develop protocols relating to the provider's compliance with the order described in subdivision (b), including, at a minimum, designating the appropriate personnel responsible for receiving the protective order, establishing a means of ensuring that the restrained party is not able to access the records or information, and implementing a procedure for submission of a copy of an order and for providing the party that submits the copy of the order with documentation indicating when, and to whom, the copy of the order was submitted.

(B) A discretionary services organization that is provided an order described in subdivision (b), shall develop the protocols specified in paragraph (1) within 30 days of receipt of the first order.

(2) If an essential care provider or discretionary services organization is provided with a copy of an order described in subdivision (b), the essential care provider or discretionary services organization shall not release information or records pertaining to the child to the restrained party. This requirement applies regardless of whether the

essential care provider or discretionary services organization has finalized the protocols described in paragraph (1).

(d) The Judicial Council shall develop or update any forms or rules of court that are necessary to implement this section.

(e) This section shall become operative on January 1, 2023. *(Added by Stats.2021, c. 129 (S.B.24), § 2, eff. Jan. 1, 2022, operative Jan. 1, 2023.)*

§ 6324. Ex parte order regarding real or personal property

The court may issue an ex parte order determining the temporary use, possession, and control of real or personal property of the parties and the payment of any liens or encumbrances coming due during the period the order is in effect. *(Added by Stats.1993, c. 219 (A.B.1500), § 154.)*

Law Revision Commission Comments

Section 6324 restates part of the first sentence of Code of Civil Procedure Section 546(a) without substantive change, and continues part of former Civil Code Section 4359(a)(5) without substantive change. Former Code of Civil Procedure Section 546(a) did not provide for issuance of an ex parte order determining temporary the use of property and the payment of debts for unmarried parties. This section has been generalized to allow issuance of the order in cases where the parties are not married, both in a proceeding brought pursuant to the Domestic Violence Prevention Act and in an action brought pursuant to the Uniform Parentage Act. Authorizing the court to issue an order determining the use of the property of unmarried parties is not a substantive change, since the Judicial Council form allows this order. See Cal. R. Ct. 1296.10 (rev. Jan. 1, 1991) (order to show cause and temporary restraining order). A reference to the "superior" court has been omitted as surplus. See Section 200 (jurisdiction in superior court). The former reference to Code of Civil Procedure Section 527 has been omitted. This is not a substantive change. See Section 240 & Comment.

For general provisions relating to ex parte restraining orders, see Part 4 (commencing with Section 240) of Division 2. [23 Cal.L.Rev.Comm. Reports 1 (1993)].

Cross References

Ex parte temporary restraining orders, generally, see Family Code § 240 et seq.
Judgment and order defined for purposes of this Code, see Family Code § 100.
Nullity, dissolution, and legal separation, ex parte protective orders, generally, see Family Code § 2045.
Property defined for purposes of this Code, see Family Code § 113.
Uniform Parentage Act, issuance of ex parte orders, see Family Code § 7710.

Research References

West's California Judicial Council Forms DV–250, Proof of Service by Mail (CLETS) (Domestic Violence Prevention) (Also Available in Chinese, Korean, Spanish, and Vietnamese).
West's California Judicial Council Forms FL–344, Property Order Attachment to Findings and Order After Hearing (Also Available in Spanish).

§ 6325. Ex parte order regarding community, quasi-community and separate property

The court may issue an ex parte order restraining a married person from specified acts in relation to community, quasi-community, and separate property as provided in Section 2045. *(Added by Stats.1993, c. 219 (A.B.1500), § 154.)*

Law Revision Commission Comments

Section 6325 restates part of the first sentence of Code of Civil Procedure Section 546(a) without substantive change.

For general provisions relating to ex parte restraining orders, see Part 4 (commencing with Section 240) of Division 2. See also Section 11 (reference to married person includes formerly married person). [23 Cal.L.Rev.Comm. Reports 1 (1993)].

Cross References

Ex parte temporary restraining orders, generally, see Family Code § 240 et seq.
Judgment and order defined for purposes of this Code, see Family Code § 100.
Nullity, dissolution, and legal separation, ex parte protective orders, generally, see Family Code § 2045.
Person defined for purposes of this Code, see Family Code § 105.
Property defined for purposes of this Code, see Family Code § 113.
References to husband, wife, spouses and married persons, persons included for purposes of this Code, see Family Code § 11.
Separate property defined for purposes of this Code, see Family Code § 130.
Uniform Parentage Act, issuance of ex parte orders, see Family Code § 7710.

§ 6325.5. Ex parte order regarding insurance coverage

(a) The court may issue an ex parte order restraining any party from cashing, borrowing against, canceling, transferring, disposing of, or changing the beneficiaries of any insurance or other coverage held for the benefit of the parties, or their child or children, if any, for whom support may be ordered, or both.

(b) This section shall become operative on July 1, 2014. *(Added by Stats.2013, c. 261 (A.B.161), § 1, operative July 1, 2014.)*

§ 6326. Issuance or denial on date application submitted

An ex parte order under this article shall be issued or denied on the same day that the application is submitted to the court, unless the application is filed too late in the day to permit effective review, in which case the order shall be issued or denied on the next day of judicial business in sufficient time for the order to be filed that day with the clerk of the court. A petition for an ex parte order pursuant to this article shall not be denied solely because the other party was not provided with notice. *(Added by Stats.1993, c. 148 (A.B.1331), § 2. Amended by Stats.2018, c. 219 (A.B.2694), § 2, eff. Jan. 1, 2019.)*

Cross References

Ex parte temporary restraining orders, generally, see Family Code § 240 et seq.
Judgment and order defined for purposes of this Code, see Family Code § 100.
Nullity, dissolution, and legal separation, ex parte protective orders, generally, see Family Code § 2045.
Uniform Parentage Act, issuance of ex parte orders, see Family Code § 7710.

Research References

West's California Judicial Council Forms FL–300, Request for Order (Also Available in Spanish).

§ 6327. Ex parte orders; application of Part 4 of Division 2

Part 4 (commencing with Section 240) of Division 2 applies to the issuance of any ex parte order under this article, other than an order under Section 6322.5. *(Formerly § 6326, added by Stats.1993, c. 219 (A.B.1500), § 154. Renumbered § 6327 and amended by Stats.1993, c. 876 (S.B.1068), § 27.2, eff. Oct. 6, 1993, operative Jan. 1, 1994. Amended by Stats.1998, c. 511 (A.B.1900), § 6.)*

Law Revision Commission Comments

Section 6327 makes clear that the general rules concerning issuance of temporary restraining orders apply to this article. [23 Cal.L.Rev.Comm. Reports 1 (1993)].

Cross References

Judgment and order defined for purposes of this Code, see Family Code § 100.

ARTICLE 2. ORDERS ISSUABLE AFTER NOTICE AND HEARING

§ 6340. Ex parte orders; survival of custody, visitation, or support order following expiration of protective order; alternative methods of service; court statement upon denial

(a)(1) The court may issue any of the orders described in Article 1 (commencing with Section 6320) after notice and a hearing. When determining whether to make any orders under this subdivision, the court shall consider whether failure to make any of these orders may jeopardize the safety of the petitioner and the children for whom the custody or visitation orders are sought. If the court makes any order for custody, visitation, or support, that order shall survive the termination of any protective order. The Judicial Council shall provide notice of this provision on any Judicial Council forms related to this subdivision.

(2)(A) If at the time of a hearing with respect to an order issued pursuant to this part based on an ex parte temporary restraining order, the court determines that, after diligent effort, the petitioner has been unable to accomplish personal service, and that there is reason to believe that the restrained party is evading service, the court may permit an alternative method of service designed to give reasonable notice of the action to the respondent. Alternative methods of service include, but are not limited to, the following:

(i) Service by publication pursuant to the standards set forth in Section 415.50 of the Code of Civil Procedure.

(ii) Service by first-class mail sent to the respondent at the most current address for the respondent that is available to the court or delivering a copy of the pleadings and orders at the respondent's home or place of employment, pursuant to the standards set forth in Sections 415.20 to 415.40, inclusive, of the Code of Civil Procedure.

(B) If the court permits an alternative method of service under this paragraph, the court shall grant a continuance to allow for the alternative service pursuant to Section 245.

(b) The court shall, upon denying a petition under this part, provide a brief statement of the reasons for the decision in writing or on the record. A decision stating "denied" is insufficient.

(c) The court may issue an order described in Section 6321 excluding a person from a dwelling if the court finds that physical or emotional harm would otherwise result to the other party, to a person under the care, custody, and control of the other party, or to a minor child of the parties or of the other party. *(Added by Stats.1993, c. 219 (A.B.1500), § 154. Amended by Stats.2004, c. 472 (A.B.2148), § 4; Stats.2010, c. 352 (A.B.939), § 19; Stats.2014, c. 635 (A.B.2089), § 7, eff. Jan. 1, 2015; Stats.2018, c. 219 (A.B.2694), § 3, eff. Jan. 1, 2019.)*

Law Revision Commission Comments

Section 6340 generalizes and continues without substantive change former Code of Civil Procedure Section 547(a), the last part of former Civil Code Section 5102(a), and the first two sentences of former Civil Code Section 7020(b). In subdivision (b), the phrase "if the court finds" has been substituted for inconsistent references in the former sections to a "showing" by the petitioner and a "finding" by the court.

This section generalizes the former sections as follows:

(1) The former Family Law Act, applicable to proceedings for dissolution, nullity, and legal separation, did not contain a provision for orders after hearing, except in the case of former Civil Code Section 5102 which provided for orders excluding a party from a dwelling. This section makes clear that any of the orders described in Section 6320 may be issued after notice and hearing in a proceeding for dissolution, nullity, or legal separation. This is not a substantive change. See Cal. R. Ct. 1296.29 (July 1, 1991) (restraining order after hearing).

(2) Former Civil Code Section 7020(b) did not provide for orders determining the temporary use of property or payment of debts in a proceeding under the Uniform Parentage Act. This section generalizes former Code of Civil Procedure Section 547(a) which provided for these orders as between unmarried parties in a proceeding under the Domestic Violence Prevention Act. This is not a substantive change. See Cal. R. Ct. 1296.31E (Jan. 1, 1992) (domestic violence miscellaneous orders attachment). [23 Cal.L.Rev.Comm. Reports 1 (1993)].

Cross References

Determination of amount due for spousal support, considerations, see Family Code § 4320.
Ex parte temporary restraining orders, generally, see Family Code § 240 et seq.
Intentional and knowing violations of court orders to prevent harassment or domestic violence, penalties, see Penal Code § 273.6.
Judgment and order defined for purposes of this Code, see Family Code § 100.
Minor defined for purposes of this Code, see Family Code § 6500.
Nullity, dissolution, and legal separation, ex parte protective orders, generally, see Family Code § 2045.
Person defined for purposes of this Code, see Family Code § 105.
Uniform Parentage Act, issuance of ex parte orders, see Family Code § 7710.

Research References

West's California Judicial Council Forms DV–117, Order Granting Alternative Service.
West's California Judicial Council Forms DV–140, Child Custody and Visitation Order (Also Available in Chinese, Korean, Spanish, and Vietnamese).
West's California Judicial Council Forms DV–205–INFO, What If the Person I Want Protection from is Avoiding (Evading) Service?
West's California Judicial Council Forms DV–210, Summons (Domestic Violence Prevention).
West's California Judicial Council Forms DV–250, Proof of Service by Mail (CLETS) (Domestic Violence Prevention) (Also Available in Chinese, Korean, Spanish, and Vietnamese).
West's California Judicial Council Forms FL–341, Child Custody and Visitation (Parenting Time) Order Attachment (Also Available in Spanish).

§ 6341. Married parties with no other child support order; presumptive father; considerations; order to pay child support; order to pay spousal support; considerations; effect of order in proceedings for dissolution, nullity of marriage or legal separation

(a) If the parties are married to each other and no other child support order exists or if there is a presumption under Section 7611 that the respondent is the natural father of a minor child and the child is in the custody of the petitioner, after notice and a hearing, the court may, if requested by the petitioner, order a party to pay an amount necessary for the support and maintenance of the child if the order would otherwise be authorized in an action brought pursuant to Division 9 (commencing with Section 3500) or the Uniform Parentage Act (Part 3 (commencing with Section 7600) of Division 12). When determining whether to make any orders under this subdivision, the court shall consider whether failure to make any of these orders may jeopardize the safety of the petitioner and the children for whom child support is requested, including safety concerns related to the financial needs of the petitioner and the children. The Judicial Council shall provide notice of this provision on any Judicial Council forms related to this subdivision.

(b) An order issued pursuant to subdivision (a) of this section shall be without prejudice in an action brought pursuant to the Uniform Parentage Act (Part 3 (commencing with Section 7600) of Division 12).

(c) If the parties are married to each other and no spousal support order exists, after notice and a hearing, the court may order the respondent to pay spousal support in an amount, if any, that would otherwise be authorized in an action pursuant to Part 1 (commencing with Section 3500) or Part 3 (commencing with Section 4300) of Division 9. When determining whether to make any orders under this subdivision, the court shall consider whether failure to make any of these orders may jeopardize the safety of the petitioner, including safety concerns related to the financial needs of the petitioner. The Judicial Council shall provide notice of this provision on any Judicial Council forms related to this subdivision.

(d) An order issued pursuant to subdivision (c) shall be without prejudice in a proceeding for dissolution of marriage, nullity of marriage, or legal separation of the parties. *(Added by Stats.1993, c. 219 (A.B.1500), § 154. Amended by Stats.1999, c. 980 (A.B.1671), § 13; Stats.2004, c. 472 (A.B.2148), § 5; Stats.2005, c. 22 (S.B.1108), § 63.)*

Law Revision Commission Comments

Section 6341 continues former Code of Civil Procedure Section 547(b) without substantive change. [23 Cal.L.Rev.Comm. Reports 1 (1993)].

Cross References

Judgment and order defined for purposes of this Code, see Family Code § 100.
Minor defined for purposes of this Code, see Family Code § 6500.
Petitioner defined for purposes of this Code, see Family Code § 126.
Respondent defined for purposes of this Code, see Family Code § 127.
Support defined for purposes of this Code, see Family Code § 150.
Support order defined for purposes of this Code, see Family Code § 155.

§ 6342. Orders for restitution

(a) After notice and a hearing, the court may issue any of the following orders:

(1) An order that restitution be paid to the petitioner for loss of earnings and out-of-pocket expenses, including, but not limited to, expenses for medical care and temporary housing, incurred as a direct result of the abuse inflicted by the respondent or any actual physical injuries sustained from the abuse.

(2) An order that restitution be paid by the petitioner for out-of-pocket expenses incurred by a party as a result of an ex parte order that is found by the court to have been issued on facts shown at a noticed hearing to be insufficient to support the order.

(3) An order that restitution be paid by the respondent to any public or private agency for the reasonable cost of providing services to the petitioner required as a direct result of the abuse inflicted by the respondent or any actual injuries sustained therefrom.

(b) An order for restitution under this section shall not include damages for pain and suffering. *(Added by Stats.1993, c. 219 (A.B.1500), § 154.)*

Law Revision Commission Comments

Section 6342 continues former Code of Civil Procedure Section 547(c) and the last two sentences of former Civil Code Section 7020(b) without substantive change. References to "petitioner" have been substituted for the former references to "family or household member" in the former Code of Civil Procedure section. References to "petitioner" have been substituted for references to "plaintiff" in the former Civil Code section. These are not substantive changes. See also Section 6203 ("abuse" defined). [23 Cal.L.Rev. Comm. Reports 1 (1993)].

Cross References

Abuse defined for purposes of the Domestic Violence Protection Act, see Family Code § 6203.
Judgment and order defined for purposes of this Code, see Family Code § 100.
Petitioner defined for purposes of this Code, see Family Code § 126.
Respondent defined for purposes of this Code, see Family Code § 127.
Support defined for purposes of this Code, see Family Code § 150.

§ 6342.5. Order determining use, possession, and control of real or personal property; debts incurred as result of domestic violence

(a) After notice and a hearing, the court may issue an order determining the use, possession, and control of real or personal property of the parties during the period the order is in effect and the payment of any liens or encumbrances coming due during that period.

(b) The order described in subdivision (a) may include a finding that specific debts were incurred as the result of domestic violence and without the consent of a party. For purposes of this subdivision, the acts that may support this finding include, but are not limited to, the crimes proscribed by Section 530.5 of the Penal Code. This finding does not affect the priority of any lien or other security interest.

(c) The Judicial Council shall adopt appropriate forms and modify existing forms, as necessary, to effectuate this section.

(d) This section shall be operative on January 1, 2022. *(Added by Stats.2020, c. 245 (A.B.2517), § 1, eff. Jan. 1, 2021, operative Jan. 1, 2022.)*

§ 6343. Batterer's program; order to participate; enrollment; resource list

(a) After notice and a hearing, the court may issue an order requiring the restrained party to participate in a batterer's program approved by the probation department as provided in Section 1203.097 of the Penal Code.

(b)(1) Commencing July 1, 2016, if the court orders a restrained party to participate in a batterer's program pursuant to subdivision (a), the restrained party shall do all of the following:

(A) Register for the program by the deadline ordered by the court. If no deadline is ordered by the court, the restrained party shall register no later than 30 days from the date the order was issued.

(B) At the time of enrollment, sign all necessary program consent forms for the program to release proof of enrollment, attendance records, and completion or termination reports to the court and the protected party, or the protected party's attorney. The court and the protected party may provide to the program a fax number or mailing address for purposes of receiving proof of enrollment, attendance records, and completion or termination reports.

(C) Provide the court and the protected party with the name, address, and telephone number of the program.

(2) By July 1, 2016, the Judicial Council shall revise or promulgate forms as necessary to effectuate this subdivision.

(c) The courts shall, in consultation with local domestic violence shelters and programs, develop a resource list of referrals to appropriate community domestic violence programs and services to be provided to each applicant for an order under this section. *(Added by Stats.1993, c. 219 (A.B.1500), § 154. Amended by Stats.1993, c. 876 (S.B.1068), § 27.3, eff. Oct. 6, 1993, operative Jan. 1, 1994; Stats.1999, c. 662 (S.B.218), § 3; Stats.2015, c. 72 (A.B.439), § 1, eff. Jan. 1, 2016; Stats.2019, c. 115 (A.B.1817), § 66, eff. Jan. 1, 2020.)*

Law Revision Commission Comments

Section 6343 continues former Code of Civil Procedure Section 547(d) without substantive change and includes 1993 amendments. See 1993 Cal. Stat. ch. 197, § 2 (amending repealed Fam. Code § 5754). The requirements for meeting separately with the counselor have been revised to provide that either a history of violence or the existence of a protective order is sufficient. This is consistent with other sections in the code. See Sections 3113 (separate meetings with court appointed investigator), 3181 (separate meetings with mediator), 3192 (separate meetings with counselor appointed in custody

Family

proceeding). See also Sections 6211 ("domestic violence" defined), 6218 ("protective order" defined). [23 Cal.L.Rev.Comm. Reports 1 (1993)].

Cross References

Domestic violence defined for purposes of this Code, see Family Code § 6211.
Judgment and order defined for purposes of this Code, see Family Code § 100.

Research References

West's California Judicial Council Forms DV–805, Proof of Enrollment for Batterer Intervention Program (Also Available in Chinese, Korean, Spanish, and Vietnamese).
West's California Judicial Council Forms DV–815, Batterer Intervention Program Progress Report (Also Available in Chinese, Korean, Spanish, and Vietnamese).

§ 6344. Order for payment of attorney's fees and costs; grounds for determination

(a) After notice and a hearing, a court, upon request, shall issue an order for the payment of attorney's fees and costs for a prevailing petitioner.

(b) After notice and a hearing, the court, upon request, may issue an order for the payment of attorney's fees and costs for a prevailing respondent only if the respondent establishes by a preponderance of the evidence that the petition or request is frivolous or solely intended to abuse, intimidate, or cause unnecessary delay.

(c) Before a court awards attorney's fees and costs pursuant to this section, the court shall first determine pursuant to Section 270 that the party ordered to pay has, or is reasonably likely to have, the ability to pay. *(Added by Stats.2022, c. 591 (A.B.2369), § 2, eff. Jan. 1, 2023.)*

Cross References

Custody of children, award of attorney's fees and costs, see Family Code § 3121.
Dissolution and separation, award of attorney's fees and costs, see Family Code §§ 2030, 2031.
Judgment and order defined for purposes of this Code, see Family Code § 100.
Payment of appointed counsel's fees and costs, enforcement of protective order, see Family Code § 6386.
Uniform Parentage Act, child custody and visitation proceedings, award of attorney's fees and costs, see Family Code § 7605.

§ 6345. Duration of orders

(a) In the discretion of the court, the personal conduct, stay-away, and residence exclusion orders contained in a court order issued after notice and a hearing under this article may have a duration of not more than five years, subject to termination or modification by further order of the court either on written stipulation filed with the court or on the motion of a party. These orders may be renewed, upon the request of a party, either for five or more years, or permanently, at the discretion of the court, without a showing of further abuse since the issuance of the original order * * *. Renewals and subsequent renewals shall be subject to termination * * *, modification, or subsequent renewal by further order of the court either on written stipulation filed with the court or on the motion of a party. The request for renewal may be brought at any time within the three months before the expiration of the orders.

(b) Notwithstanding subdivision (a), the duration of any orders, other than the protective orders described in subdivision (a), that are also contained in a court order issued after notice and a hearing under this article, including, but not limited to, orders for custody, visitation, support, and disposition of property, shall be governed by the law relating to those specific subjects.

(c) The failure to state the expiration date on the face of the form creates an order with a duration of three years from the date of issuance.

(d) If an action is filed for the purpose of terminating or modifying a protective order prior to the expiration date specified in the order by a party other than the protected party, the party who is protected by the order shall be given notice, pursuant to subdivision (b) of Section 1005 of the Code of Civil Procedure, of the proceeding by personal service or, if the protected party has satisfied the requirements of Chapter 3.1 (commencing with Section 6205) of Division 7 of Title 1 of the Government Code, by service on the Secretary of State. If the party who is protected by the order cannot be notified prior to the hearing for modification or termination of the protective order, the court shall deny the motion to modify or terminate the order without prejudice or continue the hearing until the party who is protected can be properly noticed and may, upon a showing of good cause, specify another method for service of process that is reasonably designed to afford actual notice to the protected party. The protected party may waive the right to notice if the protected party is physically present in court and does not challenge the sufficiency of the notice. *(Added by Stats.1993, c. 219 (A.B.1500), § 154. Amended by Stats.1995, c. 907 (A.B.935), § 2; Stats.2005, c. 125 (A.B.99), § 1; Stats.2010, c. 572 (A.B.1596), § 19, operative Jan. 1, 2012; Stats.2011, c. 101 (A.B.454), § 4; Stats.2019, c. 115 (A.B.1817), § 67, eff. Jan. 1, 2020; Stats.2022, c. 88 (S.B.935), § 1, eff. Jan. 1, 2023.)*

Law Revision Commission Comments

Section 6345 continues without substantive change and generalizes former Code of Civil Procedure Section 548 and the third sentence of former Civil Code Section 7020(b). In subdivision (a), the requirement that the stipulation be written has been generalized. Former Civil Code Section 7020(b) did not contain a writing requirement, but rather allowed stipulation by "mutual consent." In subdivision (c), the reference to the former Family Law Act (former Part 5 (commencing with former Section 4000) of Division 4 of the Civil Code) has been omitted. This expands application of this subdivision to all orders that may be issued after notice and a hearing under this article, whether issued in a proceeding for dissolution, nullity, or legal separation, in an action brought pursuant to the Uniform Parentage Act, or in a proceeding brought pursuant to the Domestic Violence Prevention Act. [23 Cal.L.Rev. Comm. Reports 1 (1993)].

Cross References

Abuse defined for purposes of the Domestic Violence Protection Act, see Family Code § 6203.
Judgment and order defined for purposes of this Code, see Family Code § 100.
Property defined for purposes of this Code, see Family Code § 113.
Protective order defined for purposes of this Code, see Family Code § 6218.
State defined for purposes of this Code, see Family Code § 145.
Support defined for purposes of this Code, see Family Code § 150.

Research References

West's California Judicial Council Forms DV–200, Proof of Personal Service (CLETS) (Also Available in Korean, Spanish, and Vietnamese).
West's California Judicial Council Forms DV–400, Findings and Order to Terminate Restraining Order After Hearing (Clets—Cancel) (Also Available in Spanish).
West's California Judicial Council Forms DV–700, Request to Renew Restraining Order (Also Available in Chinese, Korean, Spanish, and Vietnamese).
West's California Judicial Council Forms DV–710, Notice of Hearing to Renew Restraining Order (Also Available in Chinese, Korean, Spanish, and Vietnamese).
West's California Judicial Council Forms DV–720, Response to Request to Renew Restraining Order (Also Available in Chinese, Korean, Spanish, and Vietnamese).
West's California Judicial Council Forms DV–730, Order to Renew Domestic Violence Restraining Order (Also Available in Chinese, Korean, Spanish, and Vietnamese).

§ 6346. Custody and visitation orders; notice and hearing

The court may make appropriate custody and visitation orders pursuant to the Uniform Parentage Act (Part 3 (commencing with Section 7600) of Division 12) after notice and a hearing under this section when the party who has requested custody or visitation has not established a parent and child relationship under subparagraph (B) of paragraph (2) of subdivision (a) of Section 6323, but has taken steps to establish that relationship by filing an action under the Uniform Parentage Act. *(Added by Stats.1997, c. 396 (S.B.564), § 3.)*

Cross References

Judgment and order defined for purposes of this Code, see Family Code § 100.

§ 6347. Order directing wireless telephone service provider to transfer billing responsibility and rights to requesting party

(a) Commencing July 1, 2016, in order to ensure that the requesting party can maintain an existing wireless telephone number, and the wireless numbers of any minor children in the care of the requesting party, the court may issue an order, after notice and a hearing, directing a wireless telephone service provider to transfer the billing responsibility for and rights to the wireless telephone number or numbers to the requesting party, if the requesting party is not the accountholder.

(b)(1) The order transferring billing responsibility for and rights to the wireless telephone number or numbers to a requesting party shall be a separate order that is directed to the wireless telephone service provider. The order shall list the name and billing telephone number of the accountholder, the name and contact information of the person to whom the telephone number or numbers will be transferred, and each telephone number to be transferred to that person. The court shall ensure that the contact information of the requesting party is not provided to the accountholder in proceedings held pursuant to Division 10 (commencing with Section 6200).

(2) The order shall be served on the wireless service provider's agent for service of process listed with the Secretary of State.

(3) Where the wireless service provider cannot operationally or technically effectuate the order due to certain circumstances, including, but not limited to, any of the following, the wireless service provider shall notify the requesting party within 72 hours of receipt of the order:

(A) When the accountholder has already terminated the account.

(B) When differences in network technology prevent the functionality of a device on the network.

(C) When there are geographic or other limitations on network or service availability.

(c)(1) Upon transfer of billing responsibility for and rights to a wireless telephone number or numbers to a requesting party pursuant to subdivision (b) by a wireless telephone service provider, the requesting party shall assume all financial responsibility for the transferred wireless telephone number or numbers, monthly service costs, and costs for any mobile device associated with the wireless telephone number or numbers.

(2) This section shall not preclude a wireless service provider from applying any routine and customary requirements for account establishment to the requesting party as part of this transfer of billing responsibility for a wireless telephone number or numbers and any devices attached to that number or numbers, including, but not limited to, identification, financial information, and customer preferences.

(d) This section shall not affect the ability of the court to apportion the assets and debts of the parties as provided for in law, or the ability to determine the temporary use, possession, and control of personal property pursuant to Sections 6324 and 6340.

(e) No cause of action shall lie against any wireless telephone service provider, its officers, employees, or agents, for actions taken in accordance with the terms of a court order issued pursuant to this section.

(f) The Judicial Council shall, on or before July 1, 2016, develop any forms or rules necessary to effectuate this section. *(Added by Stats.2015, c. 415 (A.B.1407), § 2, eff. Jan. 1, 2016.)*

Research References

West's California Judicial Council Forms DV–900, Order Transferring Wireless Phone Account (Also Available in Chinese, Korean, Spanish, and Vietnamese).

West's California Judicial Council Forms DV–901, Attachment to Order Transferring Wireless Phone Account (Also Available in Chinese, Korean, Spanish, and Vietnamese).

ARTICLE 3. ORDERS INCLUDED IN JUDGMENT

§ 6360. Judgments which may include protective orders

A judgment entered in a proceeding for dissolution of marriage, for nullity of marriage, for legal separation of the parties, in a proceeding brought pursuant to this division, or in an action brought pursuant to the Uniform Parentage Act (Part 3 (commencing with Section 7600) of Division 12) may include a protective order as defined in Section 6218. *(Added by Stats.1993, c. 219 (A.B.1500), § 154.)*

Law Revision Commission Comments

Section 6360 continues without substantive change and generalizes the first sentences of former Civil Code Sections 4458, 4516, and 7021. The former sections applied only to judgments pursuant to the former Family Law Act and the Uniform Parentage Act, whereas this section allows the inclusion of these orders in a judgment in a proceeding brought pursuant to the Domestic Violence Prevention Act. The reference to a "protective order" has been substituted for the former reference to orders that may be issued pursuant to what are now Sections 6320–6322. This is not a substantive change, since "protective order" has been defined to include the same orders. See Section 6218 ("protective order" defined). See also Sections 6380 (transmittal to local law enforcement agency), 6388 (criminal penalty for violation of order). [23 Cal.L.Rev.Comm. Reports 1 (1993)].

Cross References

Judgment and order defined for purposes of this Code, see Family Code § 100.
Proceeding defined for purposes of this Code, see Family Code § 110.

§ 6361. Statements on face of order included in judgment

If an order is included in a judgment pursuant to this article, the judgment shall state on its face both of the following:

(a) Which provisions of the judgment are the orders.

(b) The date of expiration of the orders, which shall be not more than five years from the date the judgment is issued, unless extended by the court after notice and a hearing. *(Added by Stats.1993, c. 219 (A.B.1500), § 154. Amended by Stats.2005, c. 125 (A.B.99), § 2.)*

Law Revision Commission Comments

Section 6361 continues without substantive change and generalizes the second sentences of former Civil Code Sections 4458, 4516, and 7021. The former sections applied only to judgments pursuant to the former Family Law Act and the Uniform Parentage Act, whereas this section allows the inclusion of these orders in any judgment under this code. See also Sections 6380 (transmittal to local law enforcement agency), 6388 (criminal penalty for violation of order). [23 Cal.L.Rev.Comm. Reports 1 (1993)].

Cross References

Judgment and order defined for purposes of this Code, see Family Code § 100.
State defined for purposes of this Code, see Family Code § 145.

CHAPTER 3. REGISTRATION AND ENFORCEMENT OF ORDERS

§ 6380. California Law Enforcement Telecommunications System; information transmitted to Department of Justice; California Restraining and Protective Order System

(a) Each county, with the approval of the Department of Justice, shall, by July 1, 1996, develop a procedure, using existing systems, for the electronic transmission of data, as described in subdivision (b), to the Department of Justice. The data shall be electronically transmitted through the California Law Enforcement Telecommunications System (CLETS) of the Department of Justice by law enforcement personnel, or with the approval of the Department of Justice, court personnel, or another appropriate agency capable of maintaining and preserving the integrity of both the CLETS and the California Restraining and Protective Order System, as described in subdivision (e). Data entry is required to be entered only once under the requirements of this section, unless the order is served at a later time. A portion of all fees payable to the Department of Justice under subdivision (a) of Section 1203.097 of the Penal Code for the entry of the information required under this section, based upon the proportion of the costs incurred by the local agency and those incurred by the Department of Justice, shall be transferred to the local agency actually providing the data. All data with respect to criminal court protective orders issued, modified, extended, or terminated under Section 136.2 of the Penal Code, and all data filed with the court on the required Judicial Council forms with respect to protective orders, including their issuance, modification, extension, or termination, to which this division applies pursuant to Section 6221, shall be transmitted by the court or its designee within one business day to law enforcement personnel by either one of the following methods:

(1) Transmitting a physical copy of the order to a local law enforcement agency authorized by the Department of Justice to enter orders into CLETS.

(2) With the approval of the Department of Justice, entering the order into CLETS directly.

(b) Upon the issuance of a protective order to which this division applies pursuant to Section 6221, or the issuance of a temporary restraining order or injunction relating to harassment, unlawful violence, or the threat of violence pursuant to Section 527.6, 527.8, or 527.85 of the Code of Civil Procedure, or the issuance of a criminal court protective order under Section 136.2 of the Penal Code, or the issuance of a juvenile court restraining order related to domestic violence pursuant to Section 213.5, 304, or 362.4 of the Welfare and Institutions Code, or the issuance of a protective order pursuant to Section 15657.03 of the Welfare and Institutions Code, or upon registration with the court clerk of a domestic violence protective or restraining order issued by the tribunal of another state, as defined in Section 6401, and including any of the foregoing orders issued in connection with an order for modification of a custody or visitation order issued pursuant to a dissolution, legal separation, nullity, or paternity proceeding the Department of Justice shall be immediately notified of the contents of the order and the following information:

(1) The name, race, date of birth, and other personal descriptive information of the respondent as required by a form prescribed by the Department of Justice.

(2) The names of the protected persons.

(3) The date of issuance of the order.

(4) The duration or expiration date of the order.

(5) The terms and conditions of the protective order, including stay-away, no-contact, residency exclusion, custody, and visitation provisions of the order.

(6) The department or division number and the address of the court.

(7) Whether or not the order was served upon the respondent.

(8) The terms and conditions of any restrictions on the ownership or possession of firearms.

All available information shall be included; however, the inability to provide all categories of information shall not delay the entry of the information available.

(c) The information conveyed to the Department of Justice shall also indicate whether the respondent was present in court to be informed of the contents of the court order. The respondent's presence in court shall provide proof of service of notice of the terms of the protective order. The respondent's failure to appear shall also be included in the information provided to the Department of Justice.

(d)(1) Within one business day of service, a law enforcement officer who served a protective order shall submit the proof of service directly into the Department of Justice California Restraining and Protective Order System, including the officer's name and law enforcement agency, and shall transmit the original proof of service form to the issuing court.

(2) Within one business day of receipt of proof of service by a person other than a law enforcement officer, the clerk of the court shall submit the proof of service of a protective order directly into the Department of Justice California Restraining and Protective Order System, including the name of the person who served the order. If the court is unable to provide this notification to the Department of Justice by electronic transmission, the court shall, within one business day of receipt, transmit a copy of the proof of service to a local law enforcement agency. The local law enforcement agency shall submit the proof of service directly into the Department of Justice California Restraining and Protective Order System within one business day of receipt from the court.

(e) The Department of Justice shall maintain a California Restraining and Protective Order System and shall make available to court clerks and law enforcement personnel, through computer access, all information regarding the protective and restraining orders and injunctions described in subdivision (b), whether or not served upon the respondent.

(f) If a court issues a modification, extension, or termination of a protective order, it shall be on forms adopted by the Judicial Council of California and that have been approved by the Department of Justice, and the transmitting agency for the county shall immediately notify the Department of Justice, by electronic transmission, of the terms of the modification, extension, or termination.

(g) The Judicial Council shall assist local courts charged with the responsibility for issuing protective orders by developing informational packets describing the general procedures for obtaining a domestic violence restraining order and indicating the appropriate Judicial

Council forms. The informational packets shall include a design, that local courts shall complete, that describes local court procedures and maps to enable applicants to locate filing windows and appropriate courts, and shall also include information on how to return proofs of service, including mailing addresses and fax numbers. The court clerk shall provide a fee waiver form to all applicants for domestic violence protective orders. The court clerk shall provide all Judicial Council forms required by this chapter to applicants free of charge. The informational packet shall also contain a statement that the protective order is enforceable in any state, as defined in Section 6401, and general information about agencies in other jurisdictions that may be contacted regarding enforcement of an order issued by a court of this state.

(h) For the purposes of this part, "electronic transmission" shall include computer access through the California Law Enforcement Telecommunications System (CLETS).

(i) Only protective and restraining orders issued on forms adopted by the Judicial Council of California and that have been approved by the Department of Justice shall be transmitted to the Department of Justice. However, this provision does not apply to a valid protective or restraining order related to domestic or family violence issued by a tribunal of another state, as defined in Section 6401. Those orders shall, upon request, be registered pursuant to Section 6404.

(j)(1) All protective orders subject to transmittal to CLETS pursuant to this section are required to be so transmitted.

(2) This subdivision does not constitute a change in, but is declaratory of, existing law. *(Added by Stats.1994, c. 872 (A.B.3034), § 2. Amended by Stats.1995, c. 731 (A.B.233), § 1; Stats.1996, c. 1139 (A.B.2647), § 1; Stats.1996, c. 1140 (A.B.2231), § 1.5; Stats. 1998, c. 187 (A.B.1531), § 1; Stats.1998, c. 581 (A.B.2801), § 17; Stats.1998, c. 702 (A.B.2177), § 1; Stats.1998, c. 707 (S.B.1682), § 2.7; Stats.1999, c. 83 (S.B.966), § 52; Stats.1999, c. 561 (A.B.59), § 4; Stats.1999, c. 661 (A.B.825), § 5.5; Stats.2001, c. 698 (A.B.160), § 2; Stats.2001, c. 816 (A.B.731), § 1.5; Stats.2002, c. 265 (S.B.1627), § 1; Stats.2005, c. 631 (S.B.720), § 2; Stats.2010, c. 572 (A.B.1596), § 20, operative Jan. 1, 2012; Stats.2018, c. 89 (S.B.1089), § 2, eff. Jan. 1, 2019; Stats.2019, c. 497 (A.B.991), § 112, eff. Jan. 1, 2020; Stats.2019, c. 115 (A.B.1817), § 68, eff. Jan. 1, 2020.)*

Cross References

Arrest with and without warrant, citizen's arrest by domestic victim, protective or restraining order, see Penal Code § 836.
County defined for purposes of this Code, see Family Code § 67.
Court orders available in response to good cause belief of harm to, intimidation of, or dissuasion of victim or witness, see Penal Code § 136.2.
Criminal procedure, judgment and execution, domestic violence victims, see Penal Code § 1203.097.
Domestic violence defined for purposes of this Code, see Family Code § 6211.
Domestic violence prevention order, contempt for failure to comply, see Code of Civil Procedure § 1218.
Employees subject to unlawful violence or threat of violence at the workplace, temporary restraining order, injunction, see Code of Civil Procedure § 527.8.
Judgment and order defined for purposes of this Code, see Family Code § 100.
Juvenile court law, proceedings to declare a minor child a dependent child, see Welfare and Institutions Code § 213.5.
Officers authorized to maintain order on school campus or facility, threat of violence made off school campus, temporary restraining order and injunction, violation of restraining order, see Code of Civil Procedure § 527.85.
Person defined for purposes of this Code, see Family Code § 105.
Proceeding defined for purposes of this Code, see Family Code § 110.
Protective order defined for purposes of this Code, see Family Code § 6218.
Registration of Canadian domestic violence protection order, see Family Code § 6454.
Respondent defined for purposes of this Code, see Family Code § 127.
State defined for purposes of this Code, see Family Code § 145.
Temporary restraining order and injunction, domestic violence, see Code of Civil Procedure § 527.6.

Research References

West's California Judicial Council Forms JV–250, Notice of Hearing and Temporary Restraining Order—Juvenile (Also Available in Chinese, Korean, Spanish, and Vietnamese).
West's California Judicial Council Forms JV–255, Restraining Order—Juvenile (Clets—Juv) (Also Available in Chinese, Korean, Spanish, and Vietnamese).
4 Witkin, California Criminal Law 4th Introduction to Criminal Procedure § 13 (2021), Department of Justice.

§ 6381. Enforceability of orders; receipt of copy by law enforcement agency; California Restraining and Protective Order System

(a) Notwithstanding Section 6380 and subject to subdivision (b), an order issued under this part is enforceable in any place in this state.

(b) An order issued under this part is not enforceable by a law enforcement agency of a political subdivision unless that law enforcement agency has received a copy of the order, or the officer enforcing the order has been shown a copy of the order or has obtained information, through the California Restraining and Protective Order System maintained by the Department of Justice, of the contents of the order, as described in subdivision (b).

(c) The data contained in the California Restraining and Protective Order System shall be deemed to be original, self-authenticating, documentary evidence of the court orders. Oral notification of the terms of the orders shall be sufficient notice for enforcement under subdivision (g) of Section 136.2 and Section 273.6 of the Penal Code. *(Added by Stats.1993, c. 219 (A.B.1500), § 154. Amended by Stats.1994, c. 872 (A.B.3034), § 3; Stats.1999, c. 661 (A.B.825), § 7; Stats.2019, c. 115 (A.B.1817), § 69, eff. Jan. 1, 2020.)*

Law Revision Commission Comments

Section 6381 continues without substantive change and generalizes the last paragraph of former Civil Code Section 4359(b). The former section applied only to the former Family Law Act. [23 Cal.L.Rev.Comm. Reports 1 (1993)].

Cross References

Domestic violence defined for purposes of this Code, see Family Code § 6211.
Judgment and order defined for purposes of this Code, see Family Code § 100.
State defined for purposes of this Code, see Family Code § 145.

§ 6382. Availability of information concerning orders; law enforcement officers

Each appropriate law enforcement agency shall make available to any law enforcement officer responding to the scene of reported domestic violence, through an existing system for verification, information as to the existence, terms, and current status of an order issued under this part. *(Added by Stats.1993, c. 219 (A.B.1500), § 154.)*

Law Revision Commission Comments

Section 6382 continues without substantive change the first sentence of the second paragraph of former Code of Civil Procedure Section 550(a), the last sentence of the first paragraph of former Civil Code Section 4359(b), and the last sentence of former Civil Code Section 7020(e). See also Section 6211 ("domestic violence" defined). [23 Cal.L.Rev.Comm. Reports 1 (1993)].

Cross References

Domestic violence defined for purposes of this Code, see Family Code § 6211.
Judgment and order defined for purposes of this Code, see Family Code § 100.

§ 6383. Service of order; verification; verbal notice; report; civil liability

(a) A temporary restraining order or emergency protective order issued under this part shall, on request of the petitioner, be served on the respondent, whether or not the respondent has been taken into

Family

custody, by a law enforcement officer who is present at the scene of reported domestic violence involving the parties to the proceeding.

(b) The petitioner shall provide the officer with an endorsed copy of the order and a proof of service that the officer shall complete and transmit to the issuing court.

(c) It is a rebuttable presumption that the proof of service was signed on the date of service.

(d) Upon receiving information at the scene of a domestic violence incident that a protective order has been issued under this part, or that a person who has been taken into custody is the respondent to that order, if the protected person cannot produce an endorsed copy of the order, a law enforcement officer shall immediately inquire of the California Restraining and Protective Order System to verify the existence of the order.

(e) If the law enforcement officer determines that a protective order has been issued, but not served, the officer shall immediately notify the respondent of the terms of the order and where a written copy of the order can be obtained, and the officer shall, at that time, also enforce the order. The law enforcement officer's verbal notice of the terms of the order shall constitute service of the order and is sufficient notice for the purposes of this section and for the purposes of Sections 273.6 and 29825 of the Penal Code.

(f) If a report is required under Section 13730 of the Penal Code, or if no report is required, then in the daily incident log, the officer shall provide the name and assignment of the officer notifying the respondent pursuant to subdivision (e) and the case number of the order.

(g) Upon service of the order outside of the court, a law enforcement officer shall advise the respondent to go to the local court to obtain a copy of the order containing the full terms and conditions of the order.

(h)(1) There shall be no civil liability on the part of, and no cause of action for false arrest or false imprisonment against, a peace officer who makes an arrest pursuant to a protective or restraining order that is regular upon its face, if the peace officer, in making the arrest, acts in good faith and has reasonable cause to believe that the person against whom the order is issued has notice of the order and has committed an act in violation of the order.

(2) If there is more than one order issued and one of the orders is an emergency protective order that has precedence in enforcement pursuant to paragraph (1) of subdivision (c) of Section 136.2 of the Penal Code, the peace officer shall enforce the emergency protective order. If there is more than one order issued, none of the orders issued is an emergency protective order that has precedence in enforcement, and one of the orders issued is a no-contact order, as described in Section 6320, the peace officer shall enforce the no-contact order. If there is more than one civil order regarding the same parties and neither an emergency protective order that has precedence in enforcement nor a no-contact order has been issued, the peace officer shall enforce the order that was issued last. If there are both civil and criminal orders regarding the same parties and neither an emergency protective order that has precedence in enforcement nor a no-contact order has been issued, the peace officer shall enforce the criminal order issued last, subject to the provisions of subdivisions (h) and (i) of Section 136.2 of the Penal Code. This section does not exonerate a peace officer from liability for the unreasonable use of force in the enforcement of the order. The immunities afforded by this section shall not affect the availability of any other immunity that may apply, including, but not limited to, Sections 820.2 and 820.4 of the Government Code. *(Added by Stats.1993, c. 219 (A.B.1500), § 154. Amended by Stats.1994, c. 872 (A.B.3034), § 4; Stats.1997, c. 347 (A.B.356), § 1; Stats.1999, c. 661 (A.B.825), § 8; Stats.2001, c. 698 (A.B.160), § 3; Stats.2005, c. 467 (A.B.429), § 2; Stats.2010, c. 178 (S.B.1115), § 24, operative Jan. 1, 2012; Stats.2013, c. 263 (A.B.176), § 2, operative July 1, 2014; Stats.2014, c. 71 (S.B.1304), § 54, eff. Jan. 1, 2015; Stats.2019, c. 115 (A.B.1817), § 70, eff. Jan. 1, 2020.)*

Law Revision Commission Comments

Section 6383 continues without substantive change and generalizes the last two sentences of the second paragraph of former Code of Civil Procedure Section 550(a), former Code of Civil Procedure Section 550(h), former Civil Code Section 4359(e), and former Civil Code Section 7020(g). See also Section 6211 ("domestic violence" defined). [23 Cal.L.Rev.Comm. Reports 1 (1993)].

Subdivision (e) of Section 6383 is amended to reflect nonsubstantive reorganization of the statutes governing control of deadly weapons. [38 Cal.L.Rev.Comm. Reports 217 (2009)].

Cross References

Domestic violence defined for purposes of this Code, see Family Code § 6211.
Emergency protective order defined for purposes of this Code, see Family Code § 6215.
Judgment and order defined for purposes of this Code, see Family Code § 100.
Person defined for purposes of this Code, see Family Code § 105.
Petitioner defined for purposes of this Code, see Family Code § 126.
Proceeding defined for purposes of this Code, see Family Code § 110.
Respondent defined for purposes of this Code, see Family Code § 127.

§ 6384. Personal service of order not required; forms for orders

(a) If a respondent named in an order issued under this part after a hearing has not been served personally with the order but has received actual notice of the existence and substance of the order through personal appearance in court to hear the terms of the order from the court, no additional proof of service is required for enforcement of the order.

If a respondent named in a temporary restraining order or emergency protective order is personally served with the order and notice of hearing with respect to a restraining order or protective order based on the temporary restraining order or emergency protective order, but the respondent does not appear at the hearing either in person or by counsel, and the terms and conditions of the restraining order or protective order issued at the hearing are identical to the temporary restraining or emergency protective order, except for the duration of the order, the restraining order or protective order issued at the hearing may be served on the respondent by first-class mail sent to the respondent at the most current address for the respondent that is available to the court.

(b) The Judicial Council forms for orders issued under this part shall contain a statement in substantially the following form:

"If you have been personally served with a temporary restraining order and notice of hearing, but you do not appear at the hearing either in person or by a lawyer, and a restraining order that is the same as this temporary restraining order except for the expiration date is issued at the hearing, a copy of the order will be served on you by mail at the following address: ____.

If that address is not correct or you wish to verify that the temporary restraining order was converted to a restraining order at the hearing without substantive change and to find out the duration of that order, contact the clerk of the court." *(Added by Stats.1993, c. 219 (A.B.1500), § 154. Amended by Stats.1997, c. 347 (A.B.356), § 2; Stats.2010, c. 572 (A.B.1596), § 21, operative Jan. 1, 2012.)*

Law Revision Commission Comments

Subdivision (a) of Section 6384 continues former Code of Civil Procedure Section 550(e) without substantive change. In subdivision (a), a reference to an order issued under "this part" has been substituted for the former reference to "this section." The former reference was unclear, since former Code of Civil Procedure Section 550 did not provide for the issuance of orders. The reference has been corrected to include any of the orders issued under Part 4 of this division.

Subdivision (b) of Section 6384 continues former Code of Civil Procedure Section 550(g) without substantive change. The former reference to "temporary restraining orders or restraining orders issued after a hearing" has been replaced by a reference to orders issued under "this part." This is not a substantive change. [23 Cal.L.Rev.Comm. Reports 1 (1993)].

Cross References

Emergency protective order defined for purposes of this Code, see Family Code § 6215.
Judgment and order defined for purposes of this Code, see Family Code § 100.
Person defined for purposes of this Code, see Family Code § 105.

§ 6385. Proof of service of protective orders; personal descriptive information; purchase or receipt of firearm

(a) Proof of service of the protective order is not required for the purposes of Section 6380 if the order indicates on its face that both parties were personally present at the hearing at which the order was issued and that, for the purpose of Section 6384, no proof of service is required, or if the order was served by a law enforcement officer pursuant to Section 6383.

(b) The failure of the petitioner to provide the Department of Justice with the personal descriptive information regarding the person restrained does not invalidate the protective order.

(c) There is no civil liability on the part of, and no cause of action arises against, an employee of a local law enforcement agency, a court, or the Department of Justice, acting within the scope of employment, if a person described in Section 29825 of the Penal Code unlawfully purchases or receives or attempts to purchase or receive a firearm and a person is injured by that firearm or a person who is otherwise entitled to receive a firearm is denied a firearm and either wrongful action is due to a failure of a court to provide the notification provided for in this chapter. *(Added by Stats.1993, c. 219 (A.B.1500), § 154. Amended by Stats.1994, c. 872 (A.B.3034), § 5; Stats.1995, c. 731 (A.B.233), § 2; Stats.2002, c. 265 (S.B.1627), § 2; Stats.2010, c. 178 (S.B.1115), § 25, operative Jan. 1, 2012.)*

Law Revision Commission Comments

Section 6385 continues former Code of Civil Procedure Section 550(b)–(d) without substantive change. The word "petitioner" has been substituted for "plaintiff" to conform to revisions made to former law. See 1990 Cal. Stat. ch. 752. The reference to "protective order" has been substituted for the reference to an order based on what are now Sections 6320–6322. This is not a substantive change, since "protective order" has been defined to include the same orders. See Section 6218 ("protective order" defined). In subdivision (c), a reference to providing information to the "Department of Justice" has been substituted for the reference to "local law enforcement," since the purpose of this section is the provision of information to the Department of Justice. This is not a substantive change.

See also Section 6304 (court to provide information to parties concerning terms and effect of order); Penal Code § 12021 (criminal penalty for acquiring firearm while subject to restraining order against domestic violence). [23 Cal.L.Rev.Comm. Reports 1 (1993)].

Subdivision (c) of Section 6385 is amended to reflect nonsubstantive reorganization of the statutes governing control of deadly weapons. [38 Cal.L.Rev.Comm. Reports 217 (2009)].

Cross References

Judgment and order defined for purposes of this Code, see Family Code § 100.
Person defined for purposes of this Code, see Family Code § 105.
Petitioner defined for purposes of this Code, see Family Code § 126.
Protective order defined for purposes of this Code, see Family Code § 6218.
Transmission of firearm purchaser information, procedures, see Penal Code §§ 28200 to 28250.

§ 6386. Appointment of counsel; payment of attorney fees and costs

(a) The court may, in its discretion, appoint counsel to represent the petitioner in a proceeding to enforce the terms of a protective order, as defined in Section 6218.

(b) In a proceeding in which private counsel was appointed by the court pursuant to subdivision (a), the court may order the respondent to pay reasonable attorney's fees and costs incurred by the petitioner. *(Added by Stats.1993, c. 219 (A.B.1500), § 154.)*

Law Revision Commission Comments

Section 6386 restates former Code of Civil Procedure Section 553 without substantive change. The words "petitioner" and "respondent" have been substituted for "plaintiff" and "defendant" to conform to revisions made to former law. See 1990 Cal. Stat. ch. 752. The reference to "protective order" has been substituted for the reference to an order based on what are now Sections 6320–6322. This is not a substantive change, since "protective order" has been defined to include the same orders. See Section 6218 ("protective order" defined). See also Sections 270–272 (general provisions for attorney's fees and costs). [23 Cal.L.Rev.Comm. Reports 1 (1993)].

Cross References

Judgment and order defined for purposes of this Code, see Family Code § 100.
Petitioner defined for purposes of this Code, see Family Code § 126.
Proceeding defined for purposes of this Code, see Family Code § 110.
Respondent defined for purposes of this Code, see Family Code § 127.

§ 6387. Copies of order to be provided to petitioner

The court shall order the clerk of the court to provide to a petitioner, without cost, up to three certified, stamped, and endorsed copies of any order issued under this part, and of an extension, modification, or termination of the order. *(Added by Stats.1993, c. 219 (A.B.1500), § 154. Amended by Stats.2001, c. 176 (S.B.210), § 5; Stats.2010, c. 572 (A.B.1596), § 22, operative Jan. 1, 2012.)*

Law Revision Commission Comments

Section 6387 continues without substantive change the last sentence of the first paragraph of former Code of Civil Procedure Section 550(a). [23 Cal.L.Rev.Comm. Reports 1 (1993)].

Cross References

Judgment and order defined for purposes of this Code, see Family Code § 100.
Petitioner defined for purposes of this Code, see Family Code § 126.

§ 6388. Willful and knowing violation of order; penalty

A willful and knowing violation of a protective order, as defined in Section 6218, is a crime punishable as provided by Section 273.6 of the Penal Code. *(Added by Stats.1993, c. 219 (A.B.1500), § 154.)*

Law Revision Commission Comments

Section 6388 continues without substantive change former Code of Civil Procedure Section 551, the last sentence of former Civil Code Section 4359(c), former Civil Code Section 7020(h), and the last sentences of former Civil Code Section 4458, 4516, and 7021. The reference to "protective order" has been substituted for the reference to an order based on what are now Sections 6320–6322. This is not a substantive change, since "protective order" has been defined to include the same orders. See Section 6218 ("protective order" defined). [23 Cal.L.Rev.Comm. Reports 1 (1993)].

Cross References

Judgment and order defined for purposes of this Code, see Family Code § 100.

§ 6389. Firearm or ammunition ownership, possession, purchase, or receipt; relinquishment order; use immunity; storage fee; order content; exemption; sale; penalty

(a) A person subject to a protective order, as defined in Section 6218, shall not own, possess, purchase, or receive a firearm or ammunition while that protective order is in effect. A person who owns, possesses, purchases, or receives, or attempts to purchase or receive a firearm or ammunition while the protective order is in effect is punishable pursuant to Section 29825 of the Penal Code.

(b) On all forms providing notice that a protective order has been requested or granted, the Judicial Council shall include a notice that, upon service of the order, the respondent shall be ordered to relinquish possession or control of any firearms or ammunition and not to purchase or receive or attempt to purchase or receive any firearms or ammunition for a period not to exceed the duration of the restraining order.

(c)(1) Upon issuance of a protective order, as defined in Section 6218, the court shall order the respondent to relinquish any firearm or ammunition in the respondent's immediate possession or control or subject to the respondent's immediate possession or control.

(2) The relinquishment ordered pursuant to paragraph (1) shall occur by immediately surrendering the firearm or ammunition in a safe manner, upon request of a law enforcement officer, to the control of the officer, after being served with the protective order. A law enforcement officer serving a protective order that indicates that the respondent possesses weapons or ammunition shall request that the firearm or ammunition be immediately surrendered. Alternatively, if a request is not made by a law enforcement officer, the relinquishment shall occur within 24 hours of being served with the order, by either surrendering the firearm or ammunition in a safe manner to the control of local law enforcement officials, or by selling, transferring, or relinquishing for storage pursuant to Section 29830 of the Penal Code, the firearm or ammunition to a licensed gun dealer, as specified in Article 1 (commencing with Section 26700) and Article 2 (commencing with Section 26800) of Chapter 2 of Division 6 of Title 4 of Part 6 of the Penal Code. The law enforcement officer or licensed gun dealer taking possession of the firearm or ammunition pursuant to this subdivision shall issue a receipt to the person relinquishing the firearm or ammunition at the time of relinquishment. A person ordered to relinquish a firearm or ammunition pursuant to this subdivision shall, within 48 hours after being served with the order, do both of the following:

(A) File, with the court that issued the protective order, the receipt showing the firearm or ammunition was surrendered to a local law enforcement agency or sold to a licensed gun dealer. Failure to timely file a receipt shall constitute a violation of the protective order.

(B) File a copy of the receipt described in subparagraph (A) with the law enforcement agency that served the protective order. Failure to timely file a copy of the receipt shall constitute a violation of the protective order.

(3) The forms for protective orders adopted by the Judicial Council and approved by the Department of Justice shall require the petitioner to describe the number, types, and locations of any firearms or ammunition presently known by the petitioner to be possessed or controlled by the respondent.

(4) A court holding a hearing on this matter shall review the file to determine whether the receipt has been filed and inquire of the respondent whether they have complied with the requirement. Violations of the firearms prohibition of any restraining order under this section shall be reported to the prosecuting attorney in the jurisdiction where the order has been issued within two business days of the court hearing unless the restrained party provides a receipt showing compliance at a subsequent hearing or by direct filing with the clerk of the court.

(5) Every law enforcement agency in the state shall develop, adopt, and implement written policies and standards for law enforcement officers who request immediate relinquishment of firearms or ammunition.

(d) If the respondent declines to relinquish possession of a firearm or ammunition based on the assertion of the right against self-incrimination, as provided by the Fifth Amendment to the United States Constitution and Section 15 of Article I of the California Constitution, the court may grant use immunity for the act of relinquishing the firearm or ammunition required under this section.

(e) A local law enforcement agency may charge the respondent a fee for the storage of a firearm or ammunition pursuant to this section. This fee shall not exceed the actual cost incurred by the local law enforcement agency for the storage of the firearm or ammunition. For purposes of this subdivision, "actual cost" means expenses directly related to taking possession of a firearm or ammunition, storing the firearm or ammunition, and surrendering possession of the firearm or ammunition to a licensed dealer as defined in Section 26700 of the Penal Code or to the respondent.

(f) The restraining order requiring a person to relinquish a firearm or ammunition pursuant to subdivision (c) shall state on its face that the respondent is prohibited from owning, possessing, purchasing, or receiving a firearm or ammunition while the protective order is in effect and that the firearm or ammunition shall be relinquished to the local law enforcement agency for that jurisdiction or sold to a licensed gun dealer, and that proof of surrender or sale shall be filed with the court within a specified period of receipt of the order. The order shall also state on its face the expiration date for relinquishment. This section does not limit a respondent's right under existing law to petition the court at a later date for modification of the order.

(g) The restraining order requiring a person to relinquish a firearm or ammunition pursuant to subdivision (c) shall prohibit the person from possessing or controlling a firearm or ammunition for the duration of the order. At the expiration of the order, the local law enforcement agency shall return possession of the surrendered firearm or ammunition to the respondent, within five days after the expiration of the relinquishment order, unless the local law enforcement agency determines that (1) the firearm or ammunition has been stolen, (2) the respondent is prohibited from possessing a firearm or ammunition because the respondent is in a prohibited class for the possession of firearms or ammunition, as defined in Chapter 2 (commencing with Section 29800) and Chapter 3 (commencing with Section 29900) of Division 9 of Title 4 of Part 6 of the Penal Code, Section 30305 of the Penal Code, and Sections 8100 and 8103 of the Welfare and Institutions Code, or (3) another successive restraining order is issued against the respondent under this section. If the local law enforcement agency determines that the respondent is the legal owner of a firearm or ammunition deposited with the local law enforcement agency and is prohibited from possessing a firearm or ammunition, the respondent shall be entitled to sell or transfer the firearm or ammunition to a licensed dealer as defined in Section 26700 of the Penal Code. If the firearm or ammunition has been stolen, the firearm or ammunition shall be restored to the lawful owner upon the owner identifying the firearm and ammunition and providing proof of ownership.

(h) The court may, as part of the relinquishment order, grant an exemption from the relinquishment requirements of this section for a particular firearm or ammunition if the respondent can show that a particular firearm or ammunition is necessary as a condition of continued employment and that the current employer is unable to reassign the respondent to another position where a firearm or ammunition is unnecessary. If an exemption is granted pursuant to this subdivision, the order shall provide that the firearm or ammunition shall be in the physical possession of the respondent only during scheduled work hours and during travel to and from the place of employment. When a peace officer is required, as a condition of employment, to carry a firearm or ammunition and whose personal safety depends on the ability to carry a firearm or ammunition a court may allow the peace officer to continue to carry a firearm or ammunition, either on duty or off duty, if the court finds by a preponderance of the evidence that the officer does not pose a threat of harm. Prior to making this finding, the court shall require a mandatory psychological evaluation of the peace officer and may require the peace officer to enter into counseling or other remedial treatment program to deal with any propensity for domestic violence.

(i) During the period of the relinquishment order, a respondent is entitled to make one sale of all firearms or ammunition that are in the possession of a local law enforcement agency pursuant to this section. A licensed gun dealer, who presents a local law enforcement agency with a bill of sale indicating that all firearms or ammunition owned by the respondent that are in the possession of the local law enforcement agency have been sold by the respondent to the licensed gun dealer, shall be given possession of those firearms or ammunition, at the location where a respondent's firearms or ammunition are stored, within five days of presenting the local law enforcement agency with a bill of sale.

(j) The disposition of any unclaimed property under this section shall be made pursuant to Section 1413 of the Penal Code.

(k) The relinquishment of a firearm to a law enforcement agency pursuant to subdivision (g) or the return of a firearm to a person pursuant to subdivision (g) shall not be subject to the requirements of Section 27545 of the Penal Code.

(*l*) If the respondent notifies the court that the respondent owns a firearm or ammunition that is not in their immediate possession, the court may limit the order to exclude that firearm or ammunition if the judge is satisfied the respondent is unable to gain access to that firearm or ammunition while the protective order is in effect.

(m) A respondent to a protective order who violates an order issued pursuant to this section shall be punished under the provisions of Section 29825 of the Penal Code. *(Added by Stats.1994, c. 871 (S.B.1278), § 2. Amended by Stats.1999, c. 662 (S.B.218), § 5; Stats.2003, c. 498 (S.B.226), § 5; Stats.2004, c. 250 (S.B.1391), § 2; Stats.2006, c. 467 (S.B.585), § 1; Stats.2010, c. 178 (S.B.1115), § 26, operative Jan. 1, 2012; Stats.2010, c. 572 (A.B.1596), § 23, operative Jan. 1, 2012; Stats.2011, c. 285 (A.B.1402), § 6; Stats.2012, c. 765 (S.B.1433), § 2; Stats.2019, c. 115 (A.B.1817), § 71, eff. Jan. 1, 2020; Stats.2021, c. 685 (S.B.320), § 7, eff. Jan. 1, 2022.)*

Law Revision Commission Comments

Subdivisions (a), (c), (g), (k), and (m) of Section 6389 (as it reads in 2010 Cal. Stat. ch. 572, § 23) are amended to reflect nonsubstantive reorganization of the statutes governing control of deadly weapons. [41 Cal.L.Rev.Comm. Reports 135 (2011)].

Cross References

Abandonment and neglect of children, intentional and knowing violation of court order to prevent harassment, disturbing the peace, or threats or acts of violence, see Penal Code § 273.6.
Carrying an unloaded firearm that is not a handgun in an incorporated city or city and county, exemption for complying with this section, see Penal Code § 26405.
Certain sales, deliveries, transfers, or returns of firearms, application of Penal Code § 26500, see Penal Code § 26540.
Contempt of court, conduct constituting, see Penal Code § 166.
Criminal history search, prior restraining orders, see Family Code § 6306.
Custody of children, presumption against person perpetrating domestic violence, see Family Code § 3044.
Domestic violence defined for purposes of this Code, see Family Code § 6211.
Ex parte orders, restrained person having firearm or ammunition, determination of violation of this section, see Family Code § 6322.5.
Ex parte orders regarding temporary custody and visitation of minor children, stipulation of parentage, considerations, see Family Code § 6323.
Firearms reported stolen, lost, found, recovered, held for safekeeping, surrendered, relinquished, or under observation, entry into Department of Justice Automated Firearms System, see Penal Code § 11108.2.
Judgment and order defined for purposes of this Code, see Family Code § 100.
Open carrying of unloaded handgun, exemption pursuant to this section, see Penal Code § 26379.
Person defined for purposes of this Code, see Family Code § 105.
Persons or business enterprises selling more than 500 rounds of ammunition in 30-day period, vendor license requirement, exemption for compliance with this section, see Penal Code § 30342.
Proceedings to declare a minor child a dependent child, ex parte orders, see Welfare and Institutions Code § 213.5.
Property defined for purposes of this Code, see Family Code § 113.
Respondent defined for purposes of this Code, see Family Code § 127.
Search warrants, grounds for issuance, firearm owned by, in possession of, or in custody and control of person subject to firearms prohibition under this section, see Penal Code § 1524.
State defined for purposes of this Code, see Family Code § 145.
Transportation of firearm in order to comply with specified provisions, see Penal Code § 25555.

Research References

West's California Judicial Council Forms DV–800, Proof of Firearms Turned In, Sold, or Stored.
West's California Judicial Council Forms JV–250, Notice of Hearing and Temporary Restraining Order—Juvenile (Also Available in Chinese, Korean, Spanish, and Vietnamese).
West's California Judicial Council Forms JV–255, Restraining Order—Juvenile (Clets—Juv) (Also Available in Chinese, Korean, Spanish, and Vietnamese).
2 Witkin, California Criminal Law 4th Crimes Against Governmental Authority § 31 (2021), Offenses Constituting Contempt.
2 Witkin, California Criminal Law 4th Crimes Against Public Peace and Welfare § 242 (2021), Subjects of Protective and Restraining Orders.
4 Witkin, California Criminal Law 4th Illegally Obtained Evidence § 40 (2021), In General.
4 Witkin, California Criminal Law 4th Illegally Obtained Evidence § 111 (2021), Statutory Grounds.

Part 5

UNIFORM INTERSTATE ENFORCEMENT OF DOMESTIC VIOLENCE PROTECTION ORDERS ACT

Section

§ 6400. Short title

This part may be cited as the Uniform Interstate Enforcement of Domestic Violence Protection Orders Act. *(Added by Stats.2001, c. 816 (A.B.731), § 3.)*

Cross References

Freedom from parental custody and control, stay of proceedings and effect upon jurisdiction under these provisions, see Family Code § 7807.
Judgment and order defined for purposes of this Code, see Family Code § 100.
Uniform act, construction of provisions, see Family Code § 3.

§ 6401. Definitions

In this part:

(1) "Foreign protection order" means a protection order issued by a tribunal of another state.

(2) "Issuing state" means the state whose tribunal issues a protection order.

(3) "Mutual foreign protection order" means a foreign protection order that includes provisions in favor of both the protected individual seeking enforcement of the order and the respondent.

(4) "Protected individual" means an individual protected by a protection order.

(5) "Protection order" means an injunction or other order, issued by a tribunal under the domestic violence, family violence, or antistalking laws of the issuing state, to prevent an individual from engaging in violent or threatening acts against, harassment of, contact or communication with, or physical proximity to, another individual.

(6) "Respondent" means the individual against whom enforcement of a protection order is sought.

(7) "State" means a state of the United States, the District of Columbia, Puerto Rico, the United States Virgin Islands, or any

Family

territory or insular possession subject to the jurisdiction of the United States. The term includes an Indian tribe or band, or any branch of the United States military, that has jurisdiction to issue protection orders.

(8) "Tribunal" means a court, agency, or other entity authorized by law to issue or modify a protection order. *(Added by Stats.2001, c. 816 (A.B.731), § 3. Amended by Stats.2003, c. 134 (S.B.399), § 1.)*

Cross References

Domestic violence defined for purposes of this Code, see Family Code § 6211.
Judgment and order defined for purposes of this Code, see Family Code § 100.
Respondent defined for purposes of this Code, see Family Code § 127.
State defined for purposes of this Code, see Family Code § 145.
Uniform act, construction of provisions, see Family Code § 3.

§ 6402. Judicial enforcement of order

(a) A person authorized by the law of this state to seek enforcement of a protection order may seek enforcement of a valid foreign protection order in a tribunal of this state. The tribunal shall enforce the terms of the order, including terms that provide relief that a tribunal of this state would lack power to provide but for this section. The tribunal shall enforce the order, whether the order was obtained by independent action or in another proceeding, if it is an order issued in response to a complaint, petition, or motion filed by or on behalf of an individual seeking protection. In a proceeding to enforce a foreign protection order, the tribunal shall follow the procedures of this state for the enforcement of protection orders.

(b) A tribunal of this state may not enforce a foreign protection order issued by a tribunal of a state that does not recognize the standing of a protected individual to seek enforcement of the order.

(c) A tribunal of this state shall enforce the provisions of a valid foreign protection order which govern custody and visitation, if the order was issued in accordance with the jurisdictional requirements governing the issuance of custody and visitation orders in the issuing state.

(d) A foreign protection order is valid if it meets all of the following criteria:

(1) Identifies the protected individual and the respondent.

(2) Is currently in effect.

(3) Was issued by a tribunal that had jurisdiction over the parties and subject matter under the law of the issuing state.

(4) Was issued after the respondent was given reasonable notice and had an opportunity to be heard before the tribunal issued the order or, in the case of an order ex parte, the respondent was given notice and has had or will have an opportunity to be heard within a reasonable time after the order was issued, in a manner consistent with the rights of the respondent to due process.

(e) A foreign protection order valid on its face is prima facie evidence of its validity.

(f) Absence of any of the criteria for validity of a foreign protection order is an affirmative defense in an action seeking enforcement of the order.

(g) A tribunal of this state may enforce provisions of a mutual foreign protection order which favor a respondent only if both of the following are true:

(1) The respondent filed a written pleading seeking a protection order from the tribunal of the issuing state.

(2) The tribunal of the issuing state made specific findings in favor of the respondent. *(Added by Stats.2001, c. 816 (A.B.731), § 3. Amended by Stats.2003, c. 134 (S.B.399), § 2.)*

Cross References

Judgment and order defined for purposes of this Code, see Family Code § 100.
Person defined for purposes of this Code, see Family Code § 105.
Prima facie evidence, see Evidence Code § 602.
Proceeding defined for purposes of this Code, see Family Code § 110.
Respondent defined for purposes of this Code, see Family Code § 127.
State defined for purposes of this Code, see Family Code § 145.
Uniform act, construction of provisions, see Family Code § 3.

§ 6403. Nonjudicial enforcement of order

(a) A law enforcement officer of this state, upon determining that there is probable cause to believe that a valid foreign protection order exists and that the order has been violated, shall enforce the order as if it were the order of a tribunal of this state. Presentation of a protection order that identifies both the protected individual and the respondent and, on its face, is currently in effect constitutes, in and of itself, probable cause to believe that a valid foreign protection order exists. For the purposes of this section, the protection order may be inscribed on a tangible medium or may have been stored in an electronic or other medium if it is retrievable in perceivable form. Presentation of a certified copy of a protection order is not required for enforcement.

(b) If a foreign protection order is not presented, a law enforcement officer of this state may consider other information in determining whether there is probable cause to believe that a valid foreign protection order exists.

(c) If a law enforcement officer of this state determines that an otherwise valid foreign protection order cannot be enforced because the respondent has not been notified or served with the order, the officer shall inform the respondent of the order, make a reasonable effort to serve the order upon the respondent, and allow the respondent a reasonable opportunity to comply with the order before enforcing the order. Verbal notice of the terms of the order is sufficient notice for the purposes of this section.

(d) Registration or filing of an order in this state is not required for the enforcement of a valid foreign protection order pursuant to this part. *(Added by Stats.2001, c. 816 (A.B.731), § 3.)*

Cross References

Judgment and order defined for purposes of this Code, see Family Code § 100.
Respondent defined for purposes of this Code, see Family Code § 127.
State defined for purposes of this Code, see Family Code § 145.
Uniform act, construction of provisions, see Family Code § 3.

§ 6404. Registration of order

(a) A foreign protection order shall, upon request of the person in possession of the order, be registered with a court of this state in order to be entered in the California Restraining and Protective Order System established under Section 6380. The Judicial Council shall adopt rules of court to do the following:

(1) Set forth the process whereby a person in possession of a foreign protection order may voluntarily register the order with a court of this state for entry into the California Restraining and Protective Order System.

(2) Require the sealing of foreign protection orders and provide access only to law enforcement, the person who registered the order upon written request with proof of identification, the defense after arraignment on criminal charges involving an alleged violation of the order, or upon further order of the court.

(b) A fee shall not be charged for the registration of a foreign protection order. The court clerk shall provide all Judicial Council forms required by this part to a person in possession of a foreign protection order free of charge. *(Added by Stats.2001, c. 816 (A.B.731), § 3. Amended by Stats.2019, c. 115 (A.B.1817), § 72, eff. Jan. 1, 2020.)*

Cross References

Domestic violence defined for purposes of this Code, see Family Code § 6211.
Judgment and order defined for purposes of this Code, see Family Code § 100.
Person defined for purposes of this Code, see Family Code § 105.

Registration of Canadian domestic violence protection order, see Family Code § 6454.
State defined for purposes of this Code, see Family Code § 145.
Uniform act, construction of provisions, see Family Code § 3.

Research References

West's California Judicial Council Forms DV–600, Order to Register Out-Of-State or Tribal Court Protective/Restraining Order (Also Available in Chinese, Korean, Spanish, and Vietnamese).

§ 6405. Immunity from civil liability; multiple orders; precedence in enforcement; unreasonable use of force

(a) There shall be no civil liability on the part of, and no cause of action for false arrest or false imprisonment against, a peace officer who makes an arrest pursuant to a foreign protection order that is regular upon its face, if the peace officer, in making the arrest, acts in good faith and has reasonable cause to believe that the person against whom the order is issued has notice of the order and has committed an act in violation of the order.

(b) If there is more than one order issued and one of the orders is an emergency protective order that has precedence in enforcement pursuant to paragraph (1) of subdivision (c) of Section 136.2 of the Penal Code, the peace officer shall enforce the emergency protective order. If there is more than one order issued, none of the orders issued is an emergency protective order that has precedence in enforcement, and one of the orders issued is a no-contact order, as described in Section 6320, the peace officer shall enforce the no-contact order. If there is more than one civil order regarding the same parties and neither an emergency protective order that has precedence in enforcement nor a no-contact order has been issued, the peace officer shall enforce the order that was issued last. If there are both civil and criminal orders regarding the same parties and neither an emergency protective order that has precedence in enforcement nor a no-contact order has been issued, the peace officer shall enforce the criminal order issued last.

(c) Nothing in this section shall be deemed to exonerate a peace officer from liability for the unreasonable use of force in the enforcement of the order. The immunities afforded by this section shall not affect the availability of any other immunity that may apply, including, but not limited to, Sections 820.2 and 820.4 of the Government Code. *(Added by Stats.2001, c. 816 (A.B.731), § 3. Amended by Stats.2013, c. 263 (A.B.176), § 3, operative July 1, 2014.)*

Cross References

Judgment and order defined for purposes of this Code, see Family Code § 100.
Person defined for purposes of this Code, see Family Code § 105.
Uniform act, construction of provisions, see Family Code § 3.

§ 6406. Other remedies

A protected individual who pursues remedies under this part is not precluded from pursuing other legal or equitable remedies against the respondent. *(Added by Stats.2001, c. 816 (A.B.731), § 3.)*

Cross References

Respondent defined for purposes of this Code, see Family Code § 127.
Uniform act, construction of provisions, see Family Code § 3.

§ 6407. Uniformity of application and construction

In applying and construing this part, consideration shall be given to the need to promote uniformity of the law with respect to its subject matter among states that also have adopted the act cited in Section 6400. *(Added by Stats.2001, c. 816 (A.B.731), § 3.)*

Cross References

State defined for purposes of this Code, see Family Code § 145.
Uniform act, construction of provisions, see Family Code § 3.

§ 6408. Severability clause

If any provision of this part or its application to any person or circumstance is held invalid, the invalidity does not affect other provisions or applications of this part which can be given effect without the invalid provision or application, and to this end the provisions of this part are severable. *(Added by Stats.2001, c. 816 (A.B.731), § 3.)*

Cross References

Person defined for purposes of this Code, see Family Code § 105.
Uniform act, construction of provisions, see Family Code § 3.

§ 6409. Application of Part

This part applies to protection orders issued before January 1, 2002, and to continuing actions for enforcement of foreign protection orders commenced before January 1, 2002. A request for enforcement of a foreign protection order made on or after January 1, 2002, for violations of a foreign protection order occurring before January 1, 2002, is governed by this part. *(Added by Stats.2001, c. 816 (A.B.731), § 3.)*

Cross References

Judgment and order defined for purposes of this Code, see Family Code § 100.
Uniform act, construction of provisions, see Family Code § 3.

Part 6

UNIFORM RECOGNITION AND ENFORCEMENT OF CANADIAN DOMESTIC VIOLENCE PROTECTION ORDERS ACT

Section

§ 6450. Short title

This part may be cited as the Uniform Recognition and Enforcement of Canadian Domestic Violence Protection Orders Act. *(Added by Stats.2017, c. 98 (S.B.204), § 1, eff. Jan. 1, 2018.)*

§ 6451. Definitions

In this part:

(a) "Canadian domestic violence protection order" means a judgment or part of a judgment or order issued in English in a civil proceeding by a court of Canada under law of the issuing jurisdiction that relates to domestic violence and prohibits a respondent from doing any of the following:

(1) Being in physical proximity to a protected individual or following a protected individual.

(2) Directly or indirectly contacting or communicating with a protected individual or other individual described in the order.

Family

(3) Being within a certain distance of a specified place or location associated with a protected individual.

(4) Molesting, annoying, harassing, or engaging in threatening conduct directed at a protected individual.

(b) "Domestic protection order" means an injunction or other order issued by a tribunal that relates to domestic or family violence laws to prevent an individual from engaging in violent or threatening acts against, harassment of, direct or indirect contact or communication with, or being in physical proximity to, another individual.

(c) "Issuing court" means the court that issues a Canadian domestic violence protection order.

(d) "Law enforcement officer" means an individual authorized by law of this state to enforce a domestic protection order.

(e) "Person" means an individual, estate, business or nonprofit entity, public corporation, government or governmental subdivision, agency, or instrumentality, or other legal entity.

(f) "Protected individual" means an individual protected by a Canadian domestic violence protection order.

(g) "Record" means information that is inscribed on a tangible medium or that is stored in an electronic or other medium and is retrievable in perceivable form.

(h) "Respondent" means an individual against whom a Canadian domestic violence protection order is issued.

(i) "State" means a state of the United States, the District of Columbia, Puerto Rico, the United States Virgin Islands, or any territory or insular possession subject to the jurisdiction of the United States. The term includes a federally recognized Indian tribe.

(j) "Tribunal" means a court, agency, or other entity authorized by law to establish, enforce, or modify a domestic protection order. *(Added by Stats.2017, c. 98 (S.B.204), § 1, eff. Jan. 1, 2018.)*

§ 6452. Enforcement of Canadian domestic violence protection order by law enforcement officer

(a) If a law enforcement officer determines under subdivision (b) or (c) that there is probable cause to believe a valid Canadian domestic violence protection order exists and the order has been violated, the officer shall enforce the terms of the Canadian domestic violence protection order as if the terms were in an order of a tribunal of this state. Presentation to a law enforcement officer of a certified copy of a Canadian domestic violence protection order is not required for enforcement.

(b) Presentation to a law enforcement officer of a record of a Canadian domestic violence protection order that identifies both a protected individual and a respondent and on its face is in effect constitutes probable cause to believe that a valid order exists.

(c) If a record of a Canadian domestic violence protection order is not presented as provided in subdivision (b), a law enforcement officer may consider other information in determining whether there is probable cause to believe that a valid Canadian domestic violence protection order exists.

(d) If a law enforcement officer determines that an otherwise valid Canadian domestic violence protection order cannot be enforced because the respondent has not been notified of or served with the order, the officer shall notify the protected individual that the officer will make reasonable efforts to contact the respondent, consistent with the safety of the protected individual. After notice to the protected individual and consistent with the safety of the individual, the officer shall make a reasonable effort to inform the respondent of the order, notify the respondent of the terms of the order, provide a record of the order, if available, to the respondent, and allow the respondent a reasonable opportunity to comply with the order before the officer enforces the order. Verbal notice of the terms of the order is sufficient for purposes of this subdivision.

(e) If a law enforcement officer determines that an individual is a protected individual, the officer shall inform the individual of available local victim services. *(Added by Stats.2017, c. 98 (S.B.204), § 1, eff. Jan. 1, 2018.)*

§ 6453. Enforcement of Canadian domestic violence protection order by tribunal

(a) A tribunal of this state may issue an order enforcing or refusing to enforce a Canadian domestic violence protection order on application of any of the following:

(1) A protected party or other person authorized by law of this state other than this part to seek enforcement of a domestic protection order.

(2) A respondent.

(b) In a proceeding under subdivision (a), the tribunal of this state shall follow the procedures of this state for enforcement of a domestic protection order. An order entered under this section is limited to the enforcement of the terms of the Canadian domestic violence protection order as described in subdivision (a) of Section 6451.

(c) A Canadian domestic violence protection order is enforceable under this section if all of the following apply:

(1) The order identifies a protected individual and a respondent.

(2) The order is valid and in effect.

(3) The issuing court had jurisdiction over the parties and the subject matter under law applicable in the issuing court.

(4) The order was issued after either of the following:

(A) The respondent was given reasonable notice and had an opportunity to be heard before the court issued the order.

(B) In the case of an ex parte order, the respondent was given reasonable notice and had or will have an opportunity to be heard within a reasonable time after the order was issued, in a manner consistent with the right of the respondent to due process.

(d) A Canadian domestic violence protection order valid on its face is prima facie evidence of its enforceability under this section.

(e) A claim that a Canadian domestic violence protection order does not comply with subdivision (c) is an affirmative defense in a proceeding seeking enforcement of the order. If the tribunal of this state determines that the order is not enforceable, the tribunal of this state shall issue an order that the Canadian domestic violence protection order is not enforceable under this section and Section 6452 and may not be registered under Section 6454.

(f) This section applies to enforcement of a provision of a Canadian domestic violence protection order against a party to the order in which each party is a protected individual and respondent only if both of the following apply:

(1) The party seeking enforcement of the order filed a pleading requesting the order from the issuing court.

(2) The court made detailed findings of fact indicating that both parties acted as a primary aggressor and that neither party acted primarily in self-defense. *(Added by Stats.2017, c. 98 (S.B.204), § 1, eff. Jan. 1, 2018.)*

§ 6454. Registration of Canadian domestic violence protection order

(a) An individual may register a Canadian domestic violence protection order in this state. To register the order, the individual must present a certified copy of the order to a court of this state to be entered into the California Restraining and Protective Order System established under Section 6380, pursuant to procedures set forth in Section 6404.

(b) A fee shall not be charged for the registration of a Canadian domestic violence protection order under this section.

(c) Registration in this state or filing under law of this state other than this part of a Canadian domestic violence protection order is not required for its enforcement under this part. *(Added by Stats.2017, c. 98 (S.B.204), § 1, eff. Jan. 1, 2018. Amended by Stats.2019, c. 115 (A.B.1817), § 73, eff. Jan. 1, 2020.)*

Research References

West's California Judicial Council Forms DV–630, Order to Register Canadian Domestic Violence Protective/Restraining Order (Also Available in Chinese, Korean, Spanish, and Vietnamese).

§ 6455. Immunity

(a) There shall be no civil liability on the part of, and no cause of action for false arrest or false imprisonment against, a law enforcement officer who makes an arrest pursuant to a Canadian domestic violence protection order that is regular upon its face, if the law enforcement officer, in making the arrest, acts in good faith and has reasonable cause to believe that the person against whom the order is issued has notice of the order and has committed an act in violation of the order.

(b) Nothing in this section shall be deemed to exonerate a law enforcement officer from liability for the unreasonable use of force in the enforcement of the order. The immunities afforded by this section shall not affect the availability of any other immunity that may apply, including, but not limited to, Sections 820.2 and 820.4 of the Government Code. *(Added by Stats.2017, c. 98 (S.B.204), § 1, eff. Jan. 1, 2018.)*

§ 6456. Other remedies

An individual who seeks a remedy under this part may seek other legal or equitable remedies. *(Added by Stats.2017, c. 98 (S.B.204), § 1, eff. Jan. 1, 2018.)*

§ 6457. Multiple protective orders; priority of enforcement

If there is more than one order issued and one of the orders is an emergency protective order that has precedence in enforcement pursuant to paragraph (1) of subdivision (c) of Section 136.2 of the Penal Code, the law enforcement officer shall enforce the emergency protective order. If there is more than one order issued, none of the orders issued is an emergency protective order that has precedence in enforcement, and one of the orders issued is a no-contact order, as described in Section 6320, the law enforcement officer shall enforce the no-contact order. If there is more than one civil order regarding the same parties and neither an emergency protective order that has precedence in enforcement nor a no-contact order has been issued, the law enforcement officer shall enforce the order that was issued last. If there are both civil and criminal orders regarding the same parties and neither an emergency protective order that has precedence in enforcement nor a no-contact order has been issued, the law enforcement officer shall enforce the criminal order issued last. *(Added by Stats.2017, c. 98 (S.B.204), § 1, eff. Jan. 1, 2018.)*

§ 6458. Relation to Electronic Signatures in Global and National Commerce Act

This part modifies, limits, or supersedes the federal Electronic Signatures in Global and National Commerce Act (15 U.S.C. Sec. 7001 et seq.), but does not modify, limit, or supersede Section 101(c) of that act (15 U.S.C. Sec. 7001(c)), or authorize electronic delivery of any of the notices described in Section 103(b) of that act (15 U.S.C. Sec. 7003(b)). *(Added by Stats.2017, c. 98 (S.B.204), § 1, eff. Jan. 1, 2018.)*

§ 6459. Transition

This part applies to a Canadian domestic violence protection order issued before, on, or after January 1, 2018, and to a continuing action for enforcement of a Canadian domestic violence protection order commenced before, on, or after January 1, 2018. A request for enforcement of a Canadian domestic violence protection order made on or after January 1, 2018, for a violation of the order occurring before, on, or after January 1, 2018, is governed by this part. *(Added by Stats.2017, c. 98 (S.B.204), § 1, eff. Jan. 1, 2018.)*

§ 6460. Severability

If any provision of this part or its application to any person or circumstance is held invalid, the invalidity does not affect other provisions or applications of this part that can be given effect without the invalid provision or application, and to this end the provisions of this part are severable. *(Added by Stats.2017, c. 98 (S.B.204), § 1, eff. Jan. 1, 2018.)*

GOVERNMENT CODE

Title 2

GOVERNMENT OF THE STATE OF CALIFORNIA

Division 3

EXECUTIVE DEPARTMENT

Part 4

CALIFORNIA VICTIM COMPENSATION BOARD

CHAPTER 5. INDEMNIFICATION OF VICTIMS OF CRIME

ARTICLE 1. GENERAL PROVISIONS

§ 13950. Declaration of public interest; application of chapter

(a) The Legislature finds and declares that it is in the public interest to assist residents of the State of California in obtaining compensation for the pecuniary losses they suffer as a direct result of criminal acts.

(b) This chapter shall govern the procedure by which crime victims may obtain compensation from the Restitution Fund.

(c) Any reference in statute or regulations to Article 1 (commencing with Section 13959) of Chapter 5, as it read on December 31, 2002, shall be construed to refer to this chapter. *(Added by Stats.2002, c. 1141 (S.B.1423), § 2.)*

Cross References

Counties or cities, indemnification of victims of crime, see Government Code § 29631 et seq.
Crime, defined for purposes of this Chapter, see Government Code § 13951.
Restitution fines, victim defined, persons included in definition, see Penal Code § 1202.4.
Victim, defined for purposes of this Chapter, see Government Code § 13951.

Research References

1 Witkin California Criminal Law 4th Introduction to Crimes § 121 (2021), Victims of Crime.
3 Witkin, California Criminal Law 4th Punishment § 110 (2021), In General.
3 Witkin, California Criminal Law 4th Punishment § 117 (2021), Statutory Requirement.
3 Witkin, California Criminal Law 4th Punishment § 118 (2021), Definition of Victim.
3 Witkin, California Criminal Law 4th Punishment § 657 (2021), Definitions.

§ 13951. Definitions

As used in this chapter, the following definitions shall apply:

(a) "Board" means the California Victim Compensation Board.

(b)(1) "Crime" means a crime or public offense, wherever it may take place, that would constitute a misdemeanor or a felony if the crime had been committed in California by a competent adult.

(2) "Crime" includes an act of terrorism, as defined in Section 2331 of Title 18 of the United States Code, committed against a resident of the state, whether or not the act occurs within the state.

(c) "Derivative victim" means an individual who sustains pecuniary loss as a result of injury or death to a victim.

(d) "Law enforcement" means every district attorney, municipal police department, sheriff's department, district attorney's office, county probation department, and social services agency, the Department of Justice, the Department of Corrections, the Department of the Youth Authority, the Department of the California Highway Patrol, the police department of any campus of the University of California, California State University, or community college, and every agency of the State of California expressly authorized by statute to investigate or prosecute law violators.

(e) "Pecuniary loss" means an economic loss or expense resulting from an injury or death to a victim of crime that has not been and will not be reimbursed from any other source.

(f) "Peer counseling" means counseling offered by a provider of mental health counseling services who has completed a specialized course in rape crisis counseling skills development, participates in continuing education in rape crisis counseling skills development, and provides rape crisis counseling within the State of California.

(g) "Victim" means an individual who sustains injury or death as a direct result of a crime as specified in subdivision (e) of Section 13955.

(h) "Victim center" means a victim and witness assistance center that receives funds pursuant to Section 13835.2 of the Penal Code. *(Added by Stats.2002, c. 1141 (S.B.1423), § 2. Amended by Stats. 2016, c. 31 (S.B.836), § 118, eff. June 27, 2016.)*

Cross References

Department of Corrections, generally, see Penal Code § 5000 et seq.
Employers with 25 or more employees, victims of crime or abuse, employer prohibited from discharging or discriminating against employee for taking time off for specific purposes, advance notice, confidentiality, reinstatement and reimbursement, right to file complaint with Division of Labor Standards Enforcement, compensatory time off or unpaid leave, see Labor Code § 230.1.
Felonies, definition and penalties, see Penal Code §§ 17, 18.
Jury duty, legal actions by victims of crime or abuse, employer prohibited from discharging or discriminating against employee for taking time off for court appearance or due to employee's status as a victim, advance notice for time off, reasonable accommodation, reinstatement and reimbursement, right to file complaint with Division of Labor Standards Enforcement, compensatory time off, see Labor Code § 230.
Misdemeanors, definition and penalties, see Penal Code §§ 17, 19, 19.2.
Restitution fines, victim defined, persons included in definition, see Penal Code § 1202.4.

Research References

1 Witkin California Criminal Law 4th Introduction to Crimes § 121 (2021), Victims of Crime.
3 Witkin, California Criminal Law 4th Punishment § 118 (2021), Definition of Victim.
3 Witkin, California Criminal Law 4th Punishment § 657 (2021), Definitions.

ARTICLE 2. APPLICATIONS FOR COMPENSATION

§ 13952. Filing; verified application; additional information; authorized representatives

(a) An application for compensation shall be filed with the board in the manner determined by the board.

(b)(1) The application for compensation shall be verified under penalty of perjury by the individual who is seeking compensation, who may be the victim or derivative victim, or an individual seeking reimbursement for burial, funeral, or crime scene cleanup expenses pursuant to subdivision (a) of Section 13957. If the individual seeking compensation is a minor or is incompetent, the application shall be verified under penalty of perjury or on information and belief by the parent with legal custody, guardian, conservator, or relative caregiver of the victim or derivative victim for whom the application is made. However, if a minor seeks compensation only for expenses for medical, medical-related, psychiatric, psychological, or other mental health counseling-related services and the minor is authorized by statute to consent to those services, the minor may verify the application for compensation under penalty of perjury.

(2) For purposes of this subdivision, "relative caregiver" means a relative as defined in paragraph (2) of subdivision (h) of Section 6550 of the Family Code, who assumed primary responsibility for the child while the child was in the relative's care and control, and who is not a biological or adoptive parent.

(c)(1) The board may require submission of additional information supporting the application that is reasonably necessary to verify the application and determine eligibility for compensation.

(2) The staff of the board shall determine whether an application for compensation contains all of the information required by the board. If the staff determines that an application does not contain all of the required information, the staff shall communicate that determination to the applicant with a brief statement of the additional information required. The applicant, within 30 calendar days of being notified that the application is incomplete, may either supply the additional information or appeal the staff's determination to the board, which shall review the application to determine whether it is complete.

(3) The board shall not require an applicant to submit documentation from the Internal Revenue Service, the Franchise Tax Board, the State Board of Equalization, the Social Security Administration, or the Employment Development Department to determine eligibility for compensation. The board may require and use documentation from these entities to verify the amount of compensation for income or support loss.

(d)(1) The board may recognize an authorized representative of the victim or derivative victim, who shall represent the victim or derivative victim pursuant to rules adopted by the board.

(2) For purposes of this subdivision, "authorized representative" means any of the following:

(A) Any person who has written authorization by the victim or derivative victim. However, a medical or mental health provider, or agent of the medical or mental health provider, who has provided services to the victim or derivative victim shall not be allowed to be an authorized representative.

(B) Any person designated by law including, but not limited to, a legal guardian, conservator, or social worker.

(3) Except for attorney's fees awarded under this chapter, no authorized representative described in paragraph (2) shall charge, demand, receive, or collect any amount for services rendered under this subdivision.

(4) The initial application materials sent by the board to an applicant shall be written in English, Spanish, Chinese, Vietnamese, Korean, East Armenian, Tagalog, Russian, Arabic, Farsi, Hmong, Khmer, Punjabi, and Lao. If the applicant selects one of the languages listed in this subdivision, the board shall send all subsequent communications in that language. *(Added by Stats.2002, c. 1141 (S.B.1423), § 2. Amended by Stats.2003, c. 281 (A.B.976), § 1; Stats.2006, c. 582 (A.B.2869), § 1; Stats.2007, c. 130 (A.B.299), § 116; Stats.2012, c. 870 (S.B.1299), § 1; Stats.2015, c. 569 (A.B. 1140), § 1, eff. Jan. 1, 2016.)*

Cross References

Board defined for purposes of this Chapter, see Government Code § 13951.
Crime, defined for purposes of this Chapter, see Government Code § 13951.
Derivative victim, defined for purposes of this Chapter, see Government Code § 13951.
Victim, defined for purposes of this Chapter, see Government Code § 13951.

Research References

1 Witkin California Criminal Law 4th Introduction to Crimes § 121 (2021), Victims of Crime.

§ 13952.5. Emergency awards

(a) An emergency award shall be available to a person eligible for compensation pursuant to this chapter if the board determines that such an award is necessary to avoid or mitigate substantial hardship that may result from delaying compensation until complete and final consideration of an application.

(b) The board shall establish the method for requesting an emergency award, which may include, but need not be limited to, requiring submission of the regular application as provided for in Section 13952.

(c)(1) The board may grant an emergency award based solely on the application of the victim or derivative victim. The board may refuse to grant an emergency award where it has reason to believe that the applicant will not be eligible for compensation under this chapter.

(2) By mutual agreement between the staff of the board and the applicant or the applicant's representative, the staff of the board may take additional 10–day periods to verify the emergency award claim and make payment.

(3) The board may delegate authority to designated staff persons and designated agencies, including, but not limited to, district attorneys, probation departments, victim centers, and other victim service providers approved by the board and under contract with the board, who shall use guidelines established by the board, to grant and disburse emergency awards.

(d) Disbursements of funds for emergency awards shall be made within 30 calendar days of application.

(e)(1) If an application for an emergency award is denied, the board shall notify the applicant in writing of the reasons for the denial.

(2) An applicant for an emergency award shall not be entitled to a hearing before the board to contest a denial of an emergency award. However, denial of an emergency award shall not prevent further consideration of the application for a regular award and shall not affect the applicant's right to a hearing pursuant to Section 13959 if staff recommends denial of a regular award.

(f)(1) If upon final disposition of the regular application, it is found that the applicant is not eligible for compensation from the board, the applicant shall reimburse the board for the emergency award pursuant to an agreed-upon repayment schedule.

(2) If upon a final disposition of the application, the board grants compensation to the applicant, the amount of the emergency award shall be deducted from the final award of compensation. If the amount of the compensation is less than the amount of the

emergency award, the excess amount shall be treated as an overpayment pursuant to Section 13965.

(3) "Final disposition," for the purposes of this section, shall mean the final decision of the board with respect to the victim's or derivative victim's application, before any action for judicial review is instituted.

(g) The amount of an emergency award shall be dependent upon the immediate needs of the victim or derivative victim subject to rates and limitations established by the board. *(Added by Stats.2002, c. 1141 (S.B.1423), § 2.)*

Cross References

Board defined for purposes of this Chapter, see Government Code § 13951.
Derivative victim, defined for purposes of this Chapter, see Government Code § 13951.
Victim, defined for purposes of this Chapter, see Government Code § 13951.
Victim center, defined for purposes of this Chapter, see Government Code § 13951.

Research References

1 Witkin California Criminal Law 4th Introduction to Crimes § 121 (2021), Victims of Crime.

§ 13953. Time to file; extension of time; tolling

(a) An application for compensation shall be filed within seven years of the date of the crime, seven years after the victim attains 21 years of age, or seven years of the time the victim or derivative victim knew or in the exercise of ordinary diligence could have discovered that an injury or death had been sustained as a direct result of crime, whichever is later.

(b) The board may for good cause grant an extension of the time period in subdivision (a). In making this determination, the board shall consider both of the following:

(1) Whether the victim or derivative victim incurs emotional harm or a pecuniary loss while testifying during the prosecution or in the punishment of the person accused or convicted of the crime.

(2) Whether the victim or derivative victim incurs emotional harm or a pecuniary loss when the person convicted of the crime is scheduled for a parole hearing or released from incarceration.

(c) The period prescribed in this section for filing an application by or on behalf of a derivative victim shall be tolled when the board accepts the application filed by a victim of the same qualifying crime. *(Added by Stats.2002, c. 1141 (S.B.1423), § 2. Amended by Stats. 2008, c. 582 (A.B.717), § 1; Stats.2012, c. 870 (S.B.1299), § 2; Stats.2018, c. 38 (A.B.1824), § 2, eff. June 27, 2018; Stats.2018, c. 983 (S.B.1232), § 1, eff. Jan. 1, 2019; Stats.2019, c. 592 (S.B.375), § 1, eff. Jan. 1, 2020.)*

Cross References

Board defined for purposes of this Chapter, see Government Code § 13951.
Crime, defined for purposes of this Chapter, see Government Code § 13951.
Derivative victim, defined for purposes of this Chapter, see Government Code § 13951.
Law enforcement, defined for purposes of this Chapter, see Government Code § 13951.
Pecuniary loss, defined for purposes of this Chapter, see Government Code § 13951.
Victim, defined for purposes of this Chapter, see Government Code § 13951.

Research References

1 Witkin California Criminal Law 4th Introduction to Crimes § 121 (2021), Victims of Crime.

§ 13954. Verification of claims; training sessions for center personnel; obligation to provide information; confidentiality

(a) The board shall verify with hospitals, physicians, law enforcement officials, or other interested parties involved, the treatment of the victim or derivative victim, circumstances of the crime, amounts paid or received by or for the victim or derivative victim, and any other pertinent information deemed necessary by the board. Verification information shall be returned to the board within 10 business days after a request for verification has been made by the board. Verification information shall be provided at no cost to the applicant, the board, or victim centers. When requesting verification information, the board shall certify that a signed authorization by the applicant is retained in the applicant's file and that this certification constitutes actual authorization for the release of information, notwithstanding any other provision of law. If requested by a physician or mental health provider, the board shall provide a copy of the signed authorization for the release of information.

(b)(1) The applicant shall cooperate with the staff of the board or the victim center in the verification of the information contained in the application. Failure to cooperate shall be reported to the board, which, in its discretion, may reject the application solely on this ground.

(2) An applicant may be found to have failed to cooperate with the board if any of the following occur:

(A) The applicant has information, or there is information that he or she may reasonably obtain, that is needed to process the application or supplemental claim, and the applicant failed to provide the information after being requested to do so by the board. The board shall take the applicant's economic, psychosocial, and postcrime traumatic circumstances into consideration, and shall not unreasonably reject an application solely for failure to provide information.

(B) The applicant provided, or caused another to provide, false information regarding the application or supplemental claim.

(C) The applicant refused to apply for other benefits potentially available to him or her from other sources besides the board including, but not limited to, worker's compensation, state disability insurance, social security benefits, and unemployment insurance.

(D) The applicant threatened violence or bodily harm to a member of the board or staff.

(c) The board may contract with victim centers to provide verification of applications processed by the centers pursuant to conditions stated in subdivision (a). The board and its staff shall cooperate with the Office of Criminal Justice Planning and victim centers in conducting training sessions for center personnel and shall cooperate in the development of standardized verification procedures to be used by the victim centers in the state. The board and its staff shall cooperate with victim centers in disseminating standardized board policies and findings as they relate to the centers.

(d)(1) Notwithstanding Section 827 of the Welfare and Institutions Code or any other provision of law, every law enforcement and social service agency in the state shall provide to the board or to victim centers that have contracts with the board pursuant to subdivision (c), upon request, a complete copy of the law enforcement report and any supplemental reports involving the crime or incident giving rise to a claim, a copy of a petition filed in a juvenile court proceeding, reports of the probation officer, and any other document made available to the probation officer or to the judge, referee, or other hearing officer, for the specific purpose of determining the eligibility of a claim filed pursuant to this chapter.

(2) The board and victim centers receiving records pursuant to this subdivision may not disclose a document that personally identifies a minor to anyone other than the minor who is so identified, his or her custodial parent or guardian, the attorneys for those parties, and any other persons that may be designated by court order. Any information received pursuant to this section shall be received in confidence for the limited purpose for which it was provided and may not be further disseminated. A violation of this subdivision is a misdemeanor punishable by a fine not to exceed five hundred dollars ($500).

(3) The law enforcement agency supplying information pursuant to this section may withhold the names of witnesses or informants from the board, if the release of those names would be detrimental to the parties or to an investigation in progress.

(e) Notwithstanding any other provision of law, every state agency, upon receipt of a copy of a release signed in accordance with the Information Practices Act of 1977 (Chapter 1 (commencing with Section 1798) of Title 1.8 of Part 4 of Division 3 of the Civil Code) by the applicant or other authorized representative, shall provide to the board or victim center the information necessary to complete the verification of an application filed pursuant to this chapter.

(f) The Department of Justice shall furnish, upon application of the board, all information necessary to verify the eligibility of any applicant for benefits pursuant to subdivision (c) of Section 13956, to recover any restitution fine or order obligations that are owed to the Restitution Fund or to any victim of crime, or to evaluate the status of any criminal disposition.

(g) A privilege is not waived under Section 912 of the Evidence Code by an applicant consenting to disclosure of an otherwise privileged communication if that disclosure is deemed necessary by the board for verification of the application.

(h) Any verification conducted pursuant to this section shall be subject to the time limits specified in Section 13958.

(i) Any county social worker acting as the applicant for a child victim or elder abuse victim shall not be required to provide personal identification, including, but not limited to, the applicant's date of birth or social security number. County social workers acting in this capacity shall not be required to sign a promise of repayment to the board. *(Added by Stats.2002, c. 1141 (S.B.1423), § 2. Amended by Stats.2012, c. 870 (S.B.1299), § 3; Stats.2015, c. 569 (A.B.1140), § 2, eff. Jan. 1, 2016.)*

Cross References

Board defined for purposes of this Chapter, see Government Code § 13951.
Crime, defined for purposes of this Chapter, see Government Code § 13951.
Derivative victim, defined for purposes of this Chapter, see Government Code § 13951.
Law enforcement, defined for purposes of this Chapter, see Government Code § 13951.
Misdemeanors, definition and penalties, see Penal Code §§ 17, 19, 19.2.
State agency defined for purposes of this Division, see Government Code § 11000.
Victim, defined for purposes of this Chapter, see Government Code § 13951.
Victim center, defined for purposes of this Chapter, see Government Code § 13951

ARTICLE 3. ELIGIBILITY FOR COMPENSATION

§ 13955. Requirements; persons and derivative victims

Except as provided in Section 13956, a person shall be eligible for compensation when all of the following requirements are met:

(a) The person for whom compensation is being sought is any of the following:

(1) A victim.

(2) A derivative victim.

(3)(A) A person who is entitled to reimbursement for funeral, burial, or crime scene cleanup expenses pursuant to paragraph (9) or (10) of subdivision (a) of Section 13957.

(B) This paragraph applies without respect to any felon status of the victim.

(b) Either of the following conditions is met:

(1) The crime occurred in California. This paragraph shall apply only during those time periods during which the board determines that federal funds are available to the state for the compensation of victims of crime.

(2) Whether or not the crime occurred in California, the victim was any of the following:

(A) A resident of California.

(B) A member of the military stationed in California.

(C) A family member living with a member of the military stationed in California.

(c) If compensation is being sought for a derivative victim, the derivative victim is a resident of California, or any other state, who is any of the following:

(1) At the time of the crime was the parent, grandparent, sibling, spouse, child, or grandchild of the victim.

(2) At the time of the crime was living in the household of the victim.

(3) At the time of the crime was a person who had previously lived in the household of the victim for a period of not less than two years in a relationship substantially similar to a relationship listed in paragraph (1).

(4) Is another family member of the victim, including, but not limited to, the victim's fiancé or fiancée, and who witnessed the crime.

(5) Is the primary caretaker of a minor victim, but was not the primary caretaker at the time of the crime.

(d) The application is timely pursuant to Section 13953.

(e)(1) Except as provided in paragraph (2), the injury or death was a direct result of a crime.

(2) Notwithstanding paragraph (1), no act involving the operation of a motor vehicle, aircraft, or water vehicle that results in injury or death constitutes a crime for the purposes of this chapter, except when the injury or death from such an act was any of the following:

(A) Intentionally inflicted through the use of a motor vehicle, aircraft, or water vehicle.

(B) Caused by a driver who fails to stop at the scene of an accident in violation of Section 20001 of the Vehicle Code.

(C) Caused by a person who is under the influence of any alcoholic beverage or drug.

(D) Caused by a driver of a motor vehicle in the immediate act of fleeing the scene of a crime in which he or she knowingly and willingly participated.

(E) Caused by a person who commits vehicular manslaughter in violation of subdivision (b) of Section 191.5, subdivision (c) of Section 192, or Section 192.5 of the Penal Code.

(F) Caused by any party where a peace officer is operating a motor vehicle in an effort to apprehend a suspect, and the suspect is evading, fleeing, or otherwise attempting to elude the peace officer.

(f) As a direct result of the crime, the victim or derivative victim sustained one or more of the following:

(1) Physical injury. The board may presume a child who has been the witness of a crime of domestic violence has sustained physical injury. A child who resides in a home where a crime or crimes of domestic violence have occurred may be presumed by the board to have sustained physical injury, regardless of whether the child has witnessed the crime.

(2) Emotional injury and a threat of physical injury.

(3) Emotional injury, where the crime was a violation of any of the following provisions:

Government

(A) Section 236.1, 261, 262, 271, 273a, 273d, 285, 286, 287, or 288 of, former Section 288a of, Section 288.5, 289, or 653.2 of, or subdivision (b) or (c) of Section 311.4 of, the Penal Code.

(B) Section 270 of the Penal Code, where the emotional injury was a result of conduct other than a failure to pay child support, and criminal charges were filed.

(C) Section 261.5 of the Penal Code, and criminal charges were filed.

(D) Section 278 or 278.5 of the Penal Code, and criminal charges were filed. For purposes of this paragraph, the child, and not the nonoffending parent or other caretaker, shall be deemed the victim.

(4) Injury to, or the death of, a guide, signal, or service dog, as defined in Section 54.1 of the Civil Code, as a result of a violation of Section 600.2 or 600.5 of the Penal Code.

(5) Emotional injury to a victim who is a minor incurred as a direct result of the nonconsensual distribution of pictures or video of sexual conduct in which the minor appears.

(g) The injury or death has resulted or may result in pecuniary loss within the scope of compensation pursuant to Sections 13957 to 13957.7, inclusive. *(Added by Stats.2002, c. 1141 (S.B.1423), § 4. Amended by Stats.2005, c. 485 (S.B.719), § 2; Stats.2006, c. 582 (A.B.2869), § 2; Stats.2007, c. 130 (A.B.299), § 117; Stats.2007, c. 747 (A.B.678), § 1; Stats.2012, c. 870 (S.B.1299), § 4; Stats.2013, c. 147 (S.B.60), § 1; Stats.2014, c. 502 (A.B.2264), § 1, eff. Jan. 1, 2015; Stats.2015, c. 569 (A.B.1140), § 3, eff. Jan. 1, 2016; Stats.2018, c. 423 (S.B.1494), § 29, eff. Jan. 1, 2019.)*

Cross References

Board defined for purposes of this Chapter, see Government Code § 13951.
Crime, defined for purposes of this Chapter, see Government Code § 13951.
Derivative victim, defined for purposes of this Chapter, see Government Code § 13951.
Fleeing a police officer while operating a motor vehicle, penalty, see Vehicle Code § 2800.1.
Pecuniary loss, defined for purposes of this Chapter, see Government Code § 13951.
Vehicle pursuit reports filed by law enforcement agency, contents, see Vehicle Code § 14602.1.
Victim, defined for purposes of this Chapter, see Government Code § 13951.

Research References

1 Witkin California Criminal Law 4th Introduction to Crimes § 121 (2021), Victims of Crime.

§ 13956. Disqualification from eligibility

Section operative until July 1, 2024. See, also, § 13956 operative July 1, 2024, subject to appropriation.

Notwithstanding Section 13955, a person shall not be eligible for compensation under the following conditions:

(a) An application may be denied, in whole or in part, if the board finds that denial is appropriate because of the nature of the victim's or other applicant's involvement in the events leading to the crime, or the involvement of the person whose injury or death gives rise to the application.

(1) Factors that may be considered in determining whether the victim or derivative victim was involved in the events leading to the qualifying crime include, but are not limited to:

(A) The victim or derivative victim initiated the qualifying crime, or provoked or aggravated the suspect into initiating the qualifying crime.

(B) The qualifying crime was a reasonably foreseeable consequence of the conduct of the victim or derivative victim.

(C) The victim or derivative victim was committing a crime that could be charged as a felony and reasonably lead to the victim being victimized. However, committing a crime shall not be considered involvement if the victim's injury or death occurred as a direct result of a crime committed in violation of Section 261, 273.5, or former Section 262 of, or for a crime of unlawful sexual intercourse with a minor in violation of subdivision (d) of Section 261.5 of, the Penal Code.

(2) If the victim is determined to have been involved in the events leading to the qualifying crime, factors that may be considered to mitigate or overcome involvement include, but are not limited to:

(A) The victim's injuries were significantly more serious than reasonably could have been expected based on the victim's level of involvement.

(B) A third party interfered in a manner not reasonably foreseeable by the victim or derivative victim.

(C) The board shall consider the victim's age, physical condition, and psychological state, as well as any compelling health and safety concerns, in determining whether the application should be denied pursuant to this section. The application of a derivative victim of domestic violence under 18 years of age or derivative victim of trafficking under 18 years of age shall not be denied on the basis of the denial of the victim's application under this subdivision.

(b)(1) An application shall be denied if the board finds that the victim or, if compensation is sought by, or on behalf of, a derivative victim, either the victim or derivative victim failed to cooperate reasonably with a law enforcement agency in the apprehension and conviction of a criminal committing the crime. In determining whether cooperation has been reasonable, the board shall consider the victim's or derivative victim's age, physical condition, and psychological state, cultural or linguistic barriers, any compelling health and safety concerns, including, but not limited to, a reasonable fear of retaliation or harm that would jeopardize the well-being of the victim or the victim's family or the derivative victim or the derivative victim's family, and giving due consideration to the degree of cooperation of which the victim or derivative victim is capable in light of the presence of any of these factors. A victim of domestic violence shall not be determined to have failed to cooperate based on the victim's conduct with law enforcement at the scene of the crime. Lack of cooperation shall also not be found solely because a victim of sexual assault, domestic violence, or human trafficking delayed reporting the qualifying crime.

(2) An application for a claim based on domestic violence shall not be denied solely because a police report was not made by the victim. The board shall adopt guidelines that allow the board to consider and approve applications for assistance based on domestic violence relying upon evidence other than a police report to establish that a domestic violence crime has occurred. Factors evidencing that a domestic violence crime has occurred may include, but are not limited to, medical records documenting injuries consistent with allegations of domestic violence, mental health records, or that the victim has obtained a permanent restraining order.

(3) An application for a claim based on a sexual assault shall not be denied solely because a police report was not made by the victim. The board shall adopt guidelines that allow it to consider and approve applications for assistance based on a sexual assault relying upon evidence other than a police report to establish that a sexual assault crime has occurred. Factors evidencing that a sexual assault crime has occurred may include, but are not limited to, medical records documenting injuries consistent with allegations of sexual assault, mental health records, or that the victim received a sexual assault examination.

(4) An application for a claim based on human trafficking as defined in Section 236.1 of the Penal Code shall not be denied solely because a police report was not made by the victim. The board shall adopt guidelines that allow the board to consider and approve applications for assistance based on human trafficking relying upon evidence other than a police report to establish that a human trafficking crime has occurred. That evidence may include any

reliable corroborating information approved by the board, including, but not limited to, the following:

(A) A Law Enforcement Agency Endorsement issued pursuant to Section 236.5 of the Penal Code.

(B) A human trafficking caseworker, as identified in Section 1038.2 of the Evidence Code, has attested by affidavit that the individual was a victim of human trafficking.

(5)(A) An application for a claim by a military personnel victim based on a sexual assault by another military personnel shall not be denied solely because it was not reported to a superior officer or law enforcement at the time of the crime.

(B) Factors that the board shall consider for purposes of determining if a claim qualifies for compensation include, but are not limited to, the evidence of the following:

(i) Restricted or unrestricted reports to a military victim advocate, sexual assault response coordinator, chaplain, attorney, or other military personnel.

(ii) Medical or physical evidence consistent with sexual assault.

(iii) A written or oral report from military law enforcement or a civilian law enforcement agency concluding that a sexual assault crime was committed against the victim.

(iv) A letter or other written statement from a sexual assault counselor, as defined in Section 1035.2 of the Evidence Code, licensed therapist, or mental health counselor, stating that the victim is seeking services related to the allegation of sexual assault.

(v) A credible witness to whom the victim disclosed the details that a sexual assault crime occurred.

(vi) A restraining order from a military or civilian court against the perpetrator of the sexual assault.

(vii) Other behavior by the victim consistent with sexual assault.

(C) For purposes of this subdivision, the sexual assault at issue shall have occurred during military service, including deployment.

(D) For purposes of this subdivision, the sexual assault may have been committed off base.

(E) For purposes of this subdivision, a "perpetrator" means an individual who is any of the following at the time of the sexual assault:

(i) An active duty military personnel from the United States Army, Navy, Marine Corps, Air Force, or Coast Guard.

(ii) A civilian employee of any military branch specified in clause (i), military base, or military deployment.

(iii) A contractor or agent of a private military or private security company.

(iv) A member of the California National Guard.

(F) For purposes of this subdivision, "sexual assault" means an offense included in Section 261, 264.1, 286, 287, formerly 288a, or Section 289 of the Penal Code, as of January 1, 2015.

(c)(1) Notwithstanding Section 13955, a person who is convicted of a violent felony listed in subdivision (c) of Section 667.5 of the Penal Code shall not be granted compensation until that person has been discharged from probation or has been released from a correctional institution and has been discharged from parole, or has been discharged from postrelease community supervision or mandatory supervision, if any, for that violent crime. Compensation shall not be granted to an applicant pursuant to this chapter during any period of time the applicant is held in a correctional institution or while an applicant is required to register as a sex offender pursuant to Section 290 of the Penal Code.

(2) A person who has been convicted of a violent felony listed in subdivision (c) of Section 667.5 of the Penal Code may apply for compensation pursuant to this chapter at any time, but the award of that compensation may not be considered until the applicant meets the requirements for compensation set forth in paragraph (1).

(d)(1) This section shall become inoperative on July 1, 2024, only if General Fund moneys over the multiyear forecasts beginning in the 2024–25 fiscal year are available to support ongoing augmentations and actions, and if an appropriation is made to backfill the Restitution Fund to support the actions in this section. If those conditions are met, this section is repealed January 1, 2025.

(2) The amendments made by the act adding this subdivision [1] shall become operative on January 1, 2023. *(Added by Stats.2002, c. 1141 (S.B.1423), § 2. Amended by Stats.2005, c. 240 (A.B.22), § 5; Stats.2014, c. 506 (A.B.2545), § 1, eff. Jan. 1, 2015; Stats.2015, c. 303 (A.B.731), § 194, eff. Jan. 1, 2016; Stats.2015, c. 569 (A.B.1140), § 4, eff. Jan. 1, 2016; Stats.2018, c. 423 (S.B.1494), § 30, eff. Jan. 1, 2019; Stats.2021, c. 626 (A.B.1171), § 12, eff. Jan. 1, 2022; Stats.2022, c. 771 (A.B.160), § 2, eff. Sept. 29, 2022, operative Jan. 1, 2023.)*

1 Stats.2022, c. 771 (A.B.160).

Inoperative Date and Repeal

For inoperative date and repeal of this section, see its terms.

Cross References

Board defined for purposes of this Chapter, see Government Code § 13951.
Crime, defined for purposes of this Chapter, see Government Code § 13951.
Derivative victim, defined for purposes of this Chapter, see Government Code § 13951.
Disclosure of applicant's identity, closed hearings conducted pursuant to this section, see Government Code § 11125.8.
Felonies, definition and penalties, see Penal Code §§ 17, 18.
Law enforcement, defined for purposes of this Chapter, see Government Code § 13951.
Pecuniary loss, defined for purposes of this Chapter, see Government Code § 13951.
Victim, defined for purposes of this Chapter, see Government Code § 13951.

Research References

1 Witkin California Criminal Law 4th Introduction to Crimes § 121 (2021), Victims of Crime.

§ 13956. Disqualification from eligibility

Section operative July 1, 2024, subject to appropriation. See, also, § 13956 operative until July 1, 2024.

Notwithstanding Section 13955, a person shall not be eligible for compensation under the following conditions:

(a) An application may be denied, in whole or in part, if the board finds that denial is appropriate because of the nature of the victim's or other applicant's involvement in the events leading to the crime, or the involvement of the person whose injury or death gives rise to the application.

(1) Factors that may be considered in determining whether the victim or derivative victim was involved in the events leading to the qualifying crime include, but are not limited to:

(A) The victim or derivative victim initiated the qualifying crime, or provoked or aggravated the suspect into initiating the qualifying crime.

(B) The qualifying crime was a reasonably foreseeable consequence of the conduct of the victim or derivative victim.

(C) The victim or derivative victim was committing a crime that could be charged as a felony and reasonably lead to the victim being victimized. However, committing a crime shall not be considered involvement if the victim's injury or death occurred as a direct result of a crime committed in violation of Section 261, 273.5, or former Section 262 of, or for a crime of unlawful sexual intercourse with a minor in violation of subdivision (d) of Section 261.5 of, the Penal Code.

(2) If the victim is determined to have been involved in the events leading to the qualifying crime, factors that may be considered to mitigate or overcome involvement include, but are not limited to:

(A) The victim's injuries were significantly more serious than reasonably could have been expected based on the victim's level of involvement.

(B) A third party interfered in a manner not reasonably foreseeable by the victim or derivative victim.

(C) The board shall consider the victim's age, physical condition, and psychological state, as well as any compelling health and safety concerns, in determining whether the application should be denied pursuant to this section. The application of a derivative victim of domestic violence under 18 years of age or derivative victim of trafficking under 18 years of age shall not be denied on the basis of the denial of the victim's application under this subdivision.

(b)(1) An application shall be denied if the board finds that the victim or, if compensation is sought by, or on behalf of, a derivative victim, either the victim or derivative victim failed to cooperate reasonably with a law enforcement agency in the apprehension and conviction of a criminal committing the crime. In determining whether cooperation has been reasonable, the board shall consider the victim's or derivative victim's age, physical condition, and psychological state, cultural or linguistic barriers, any compelling health and safety concerns, including, but not limited to, a reasonable fear of retaliation or harm that would jeopardize the well-being of the victim or the victim's family or the derivative victim or the derivative victim's family, and giving due consideration to the degree of cooperation of which the victim or derivative victim is capable in light of the presence of any of these factors. A victim shall not be determined to have failed to cooperate based on the victim's conduct with law enforcement at the scene of the crime. Lack of cooperation shall also not be found solely because a victim delayed reporting the qualifying crime.

(2) An application for a claim based on domestic violence shall not be denied solely because a police report was not made by the victim. The board shall adopt guidelines that allow the board to consider and approve applications for assistance based on domestic violence relying upon evidence other than a police report to establish that a domestic violence crime has occurred. Factors evidencing that a domestic violence crime has occurred may include, but are not limited to, medical records documenting injuries consistent with allegations of domestic violence, mental health records, or that the victim has obtained a permanent restraining order.

(3) An application for a claim based on a sexual assault shall not be denied solely because a police report was not made by the victim. The board shall adopt guidelines that allow it to consider and approve applications for assistance based on a sexual assault relying upon evidence other than a police report to establish that a sexual assault crime has occurred. Factors evidencing that a sexual assault crime has occurred may include, but are not limited to, medical records documenting injuries consistent with allegations of sexual assault, mental health records, or that the victim received a sexual assault examination.

(4) An application for a claim based on human trafficking as defined in Section 236.1 of the Penal Code shall not be denied solely because a police report was not made by the victim. The board shall adopt guidelines that allow the board to consider and approve applications for assistance based on human trafficking relying upon evidence other than a police report to establish that a human trafficking crime has occurred. That evidence may include any reliable corroborating information approved by the board, including, but not limited to, the following:

(A) A Law Enforcement Agency Endorsement issued pursuant to Section 236.5 of the Penal Code.

(B) A human trafficking caseworker, as identified in Section 1038.2 of the Evidence Code, has attested by affidavit that the individual was a victim of human trafficking.

(5)(A) An application for a claim by a military personnel victim based on a sexual assault by another military personnel shall not be denied solely because it was not reported to a superior officer or law enforcement at the time of the crime.

(B) Factors that the board shall consider for purposes of determining if a claim qualifies for compensation include, but are not limited to, the evidence of the following:

(i) Restricted or unrestricted reports to a military victim advocate, sexual assault response coordinator, chaplain, attorney, or other military personnel.

(ii) Medical or physical evidence consistent with sexual assault.

(iii) A written or oral report from military law enforcement or a civilian law enforcement agency concluding that a sexual assault crime was committed against the victim.

(iv) A letter or other written statement from a sexual assault counselor, as defined in Section 1035.2 of the Evidence Code, licensed therapist, or mental health counselor, stating that the victim is seeking services related to the allegation of sexual assault.

(v) A credible witness to whom the victim disclosed the details that a sexual assault crime occurred.

(vi) A restraining order from a military or civilian court against the perpetrator of the sexual assault.

(vii) Other behavior by the victim consistent with sexual assault.

(C) For purposes of this subdivision, the sexual assault at issue shall have occurred during military service, including deployment.

(D) For purposes of this subdivision, the sexual assault may have been committed off base.

(E) For purposes of this subdivision, a "perpetrator" means an individual who is any of the following at the time of the sexual assault:

(i) An active duty military personnel from the United States Army, Navy, Marine Corps, Air Force, or Coast Guard.

(ii) A civilian employee of any military branch specified in clause (i), military base, or military deployment.

(iii) A contractor or agent of a private military or private security company.

(iv) A member of the California National Guard.

(F) For purposes of this subdivision, "sexual assault" means an offense included in Section 261, 264.1, 286, 287, formerly 288a, or Section 289 of the Penal Code, as of January 1, 2015.

(c)(1) Notwithstanding Section 13955, a person who is convicted of a violent felony listed in subdivision (c) of Section 667.5 of the Penal Code shall not be granted compensation until that person has been released from a correctional institution. Compensation shall not be granted to an applicant pursuant to this chapter during any period of time the applicant is held in a correctional institution or while an applicant is required to register as a sex offender pursuant to Section 290 of the Penal Code.

(2) A person who has been convicted of a violent felony listed in subdivision (c) of Section 667.5 of the Penal Code may apply for compensation pursuant to this chapter at any time, but the award of that compensation may not be considered until the applicant meets the requirements for compensation set forth in paragraph (1).

(d) This section shall become operative on July 1, 2024, only if General Fund moneys over the multiyear forecasts beginning in the 2024–25 fiscal year are available to support ongoing augmentations and actions, and if an appropriation is made to backfill the Restitution Fund to support the actions in this section. *(Added by*

Stats.2022, c. 771 (A.B.160), § 3, eff. Sept. 29, 2022, operative July 1, 2024.)

Contingent Operation

Operation of this section is contingent upon availability of funding, by its own terms.

Cross References

Board defined for purposes of this Chapter, see Government Code § 13951.
Crime, defined for purposes of this Chapter, see Government Code § 13951.
Derivative victim, defined for purposes of this Chapter, see Government Code § 13951.
Disclosure of applicant's identity, closed hearings conducted pursuant to this section, see Government Code § 11125.8.
Felonies, definition and penalties, see Penal Code §§ 17, 18.
Law enforcement, defined for purposes of this Chapter, see Government Code § 13951.
Pecuniary loss, defined for purposes of this Chapter, see Government Code § 13951.
Victim, defined for purposes of this Chapter, see Government Code § 13951.

ARTICLE 4. SCOPE OF COMPENSATION

§ 13957. Reimbursement for pecuniary loss; discretion of board; specific losses; limitation upon amount disbursed

Section operative until July 1, 2024. See, also, § 13957 operative July 1, 2024, subject to appropriation.

(a) The board may grant for pecuniary loss, when the board determines it will best aid the person seeking compensation, as follows:

(1) Subject to the limitations set forth in Section 13957.2, reimburse the amount of medical or medical-related expenses incurred by the victim for services that were provided by a licensed medical provider, including, but not limited to, eyeglasses, hearing aids, dentures, or any prosthetic device taken, lost, or destroyed during the commission of the crime, or the use of which became necessary as a direct result of the crime.

(2) Subject to the limitations set forth in Section 13957.2, reimburse the amount of outpatient psychiatric, psychological, or other mental health counseling-related expenses incurred by the victim or derivative victim, including peer counseling services provided by a rape crisis center as defined by Section 13837 of the Penal Code, and including family psychiatric, psychological, or mental health counseling for the successful treatment of the victim provided to family members of the victim in the presence of the victim, whether or not the family member relationship existed at the time of the crime, that became necessary as a direct result of the crime, subject to the following conditions:

(A) The following persons may be reimbursed for the expense of their outpatient mental health counseling in an amount not to exceed ten thousand dollars ($10,000):

(i) A victim.

(ii) A derivative victim who is the surviving parent, grandparent, sibling, child, grandchild, spouse, or fiance of a victim of a crime that directly resulted in the death of the victim.

(iii) A derivative victim, as described in paragraphs (1) to (4), inclusive, of subdivision (c) of Section 13955, who is the primary caretaker of a minor victim whose claim is not denied or reduced pursuant to Section 13956 in a total amount not to exceed ten thousand dollars ($10,000) for not more than two derivative victims.

(B) The following persons may be reimbursed for the expense of their outpatient mental health counseling in an amount not to exceed five thousand dollars ($5,000):

(i) A derivative victim not eligible for reimbursement pursuant to subparagraph (A), provided that mental health counseling of a derivative victim described in paragraph (5) of subdivision (c) of Section 13955, shall be reimbursed only if that counseling is necessary for the treatment of the victim.

(ii) A minor who suffers emotional injury as a direct result of witnessing a violent crime and who is not eligible for reimbursement of the costs of outpatient mental health counseling under any other provision of this chapter. To be eligible for reimbursement under this clause, the minor must have been in close proximity to the victim when the minor witnessed the crime.

(C) The board may reimburse a victim or derivative victim for outpatient mental health counseling in excess of that authorized by subparagraph (A) or (B) or for inpatient psychiatric, psychological, or other mental health counseling if the claim is based on dire or exceptional circumstances that require more extensive treatment, as approved by the board.

(D) Expenses for psychiatric, psychological, or other mental health counseling-related services may be reimbursed only if the services were provided by either of the following individuals:

(i) A person who would have been authorized to provide those services pursuant to former Article 1 (commencing with Section 13959) as it read on January 1, 2002.

(ii) A person who is licensed in * * * the state in which the victim lives to provide those services, or who is properly supervised by a person who is licensed in * * * the state in which the victim lives to provide those services, subject to the board's approval and subject to the limitations and restrictions the board may impose.

(3) Subject to the limitations set forth in Section 13957.5, authorize compensation equal to the loss of income or loss of support, or both, that a victim or derivative victim incurs as a direct result of the victim's or derivative victim's injury or the victim's death. If the qualifying crime is a violation of Section 236.1 of the Penal Code, the board may authorize compensation equal to loss of income or support that a victim incurs as a direct result of the victim's deprivation of liberty during the crime, not to exceed the amount set forth in Section 13957.5. If the victim or derivative victim requests that the board give priority to reimbursement of loss of income or support, the board may not pay medical expenses, or mental health counseling expenses, except upon the request of the victim or derivative victim or after determining that payment of these expenses will not decrease the funds available for payment of loss of income or support.

(4) Authorize a cash payment to or on behalf of the victim for job retraining or similar employment-oriented services.

(5) Reimburse the expense of installing or increasing residential security, not to exceed one thousand dollars ($1,000). Installing or

increasing residential security may include, but need not be limited to, both of the following:

(A) Home security device or system.

(B) Replacing or increasing the number of locks.

(6) Reimburse the expense of renovating or retrofitting a victim's residence, or the expense of modifying or purchasing a vehicle, to make the residence or the vehicle accessible or operational by a victim upon verification that the expense is medically necessary for a victim who is permanently disabled as a direct result of the crime, whether the disability is partial or total.

(7)(A) Authorize a cash payment or reimbursement not to exceed three thousand four hundred and eighteen dollars ($3,418) to a victim for expenses incurred in relocating, if the expenses are determined by law enforcement to be necessary for the personal safety of the victim or by a mental health treatment provider to be necessary for the emotional well-being of the victim. For purposes of this paragraph, "expenses incurred in relocating" may include the costs of temporary housing for any pets belonging to the victim upon immediate relocation.

(B) The cash payment or reimbursement made under this paragraph shall only be awarded to one claimant per crime giving rise to the relocation. The board may authorize more than one relocation per crime if necessary for the personal safety or emotional well-being of the claimant. However, the total cash payment or reimbursement for all relocations due to the same crime shall not exceed three thousand four hundred and eighteen dollars ($3,418). For purposes of this paragraph, a claimant is the crime victim, or, if the victim is deceased, a person who resided with the deceased at the time of the crime.

(C) The board may, under compelling circumstances, award a second cash payment or reimbursement to a victim for another crime if both of the following conditions are met:

(i) The crime occurs more than three years from the date of the crime giving rise to the initial relocation cash payment or reimbursement.

(ii) The crime does not involve the same offender.

(D) When a relocation payment or reimbursement is provided to a victim of sexual assault or domestic violence and the identity of the offender is known to the victim, the victim shall agree not to inform the offender of the location of the victim's new residence and not to allow the offender on the premises at any time, or shall agree to seek a restraining order against the offender. A victim may be required to repay the relocation payment or reimbursement to the board if the victim violates the terms set forth in this paragraph.

(E) Notwithstanding subparagraphs (A) and (B), the board may increase the cash payment or reimbursement for expenses incurred in relocating to an amount greater than three thousand four hundred and eighteen dollars ($3,418) if the board finds this amount is appropriate due to the unusual, dire, or exceptional circumstances of a particular claim.

(F) If a security deposit, pet deposit, or both is required for relocation, the board shall be named as the recipient and receive the funds upon expiration of the victim's rental agreement.

(8) When a victim dies as a result of a crime, the board may reimburse any individual who voluntarily, and without anticipation of personal gain, pays or assumes the obligation to pay any of the following expenses:

(A) The medical expenses incurred as a direct result of the crime in an amount not to exceed the rates or limitations established by the board.

(B) The funeral and burial expenses incurred as a direct result of the crime, not to exceed twelve thousand eight hundred and eighteen dollars ($12,818). The board shall not create or comply with a regulation or policy that mandates a lower maximum potential amount of an award pursuant to this subparagraph for less than twelve thousand eight hundred and eighteen dollars ($12,818).

(9) When the crime occurs in a residence or inside a vehicle, the board may reimburse any individual who voluntarily, and without anticipation of personal gain, pays or assumes the obligation to pay the reasonable costs to clean the scene of the crime in an amount not to exceed one thousand seven hundred and nine dollars ($1,709). Services reimbursed pursuant to this subdivision shall be performed by persons registered with the State Department of Public Health as trauma scene waste practitioners in accordance with Chapter 9.5 (commencing with Section 118321) of Part 14 of Division 104 of the Health and Safety Code.

(10) When the crime is a violation of Section 600.2 or 600.5 of the Penal Code, the board may reimburse the expense of veterinary services, replacement costs, or other reasonable expenses, as ordered by the court pursuant to Section 600.2 or 600.5 of the Penal Code, in an amount not to exceed ten thousand dollars ($10,000).

(11) An award of compensation pursuant to paragraph (5) of subdivision (f) of Section 13955 shall be limited to compensation to provide mental health counseling and shall not limit the eligibility of a victim for an award that the victim may be otherwise entitled to receive under this part. A derivative victim shall not be eligible for compensation under this provision.

(b) The total award to or on behalf of each victim or derivative victim may not exceed thirty-five thousand dollars ($35,000), except that this award may be increased to an amount not exceeding seventy thousand dollars ($70,000) if federal funds for that increase are available.

(c)(1) This section shall become inoperative on July 1, 2024, only if General Fund moneys over the multiyear forecasts beginning in the 2024–25 fiscal year are available to support ongoing augmentations and actions, and if an appropriation is made to backfill the Restitution Fund to support the actions in this section. If those conditions are met, this section is repealed January 1, 2025.

(2) The amendments made by the act adding this subdivision [1] shall become operative on January 1, 2023. *(Added by Stats.2002, c. 1141 (S.B.1423), § 2. Amended by Stats.2006, c. 539 (A.B.105), § 1; Stats.2006, c. 571 (A.B.2413), § 2; Stats.2007, c. 564 (S.B.883), § 1; Stats.2008, c. 582 (A.B.717), § 2; Stats.2008, c. 587 (A.B.2809), § 2; Stats.2009, c. 578 (S.B.314), § 2; Stats.2013, c. 147 (S.B.60), § 2; Stats.2014, c. 502 (A.B.2264), § 2, eff. Jan. 1, 2015; Stats.2015, c. 569 (A.B.1140), § 5, eff. Jan. 1, 2016; Stats.2019, c. 572 (A.B.415), § 1, eff. Jan. 1, 2020; Stats.2019, c. 575 (A.B.629), § 1.5, eff. Jan. 1, 2020; Stats.2020, c. 370 (S.B.1371), § 143, eff. Jan. 1, 2021; Stats.2022, c. 48 (S.B.189), § 41, eff. June 30, 2022; Stats.2022, c. 707 (S.B.877), § 1, eff. Jan. 1, 2023; Stats.2022, c. 771 (A.B.160), § 4, eff. Sept. 29, 2022, operative Jan. 1, 2023; Stats.2022, c. 771 (A.B.160), § 4.5, eff. Sept. 29, 2022, operative Jan. 1, 2023.)*

[1] Stats.2022, c. 771 (A.B.160).

Inoperative Date and Repeal

For inoperative date and repeal of this section, see its terms.

Cross References

Board defined for purposes of this Chapter, see Government Code § 13951.
Crime, defined for purposes of this Chapter, see Government Code § 13951.
Department of Health Care Services, generally, see Health and Safety Code § 100100 et seq.
Derivative victim, defined for purposes of this Chapter, see Government Code § 13951.
Law enforcement, defined for purposes of this Chapter, see Government Code § 13951.
Pecuniary loss, defined for purposes of this Chapter, see Government Code § 13951.
Peer counseling, defined for purposes of this Chapter, see Government Code § 13951.

Victim, defined for purposes of this Chapter, see Government Code § 13951.

Research References

1 Witkin California Criminal Law 4th Introduction to Crimes § 121 (2021), Victims of Crime.

§ 13957. Reimbursement for pecuniary loss; discretion of board; specific losses; limitation upon amount disbursed

Section operative July 1, 2024, subject to appropriation. See, also, § 13957 operative until July 1, 2024.

(a) The board may grant for pecuniary loss, when the board determines it will best aid the person seeking compensation, as follows:

(1) Subject to the limitations set forth in Section 13957.2, reimburse the amount of medical or medical-related expenses incurred by the victim for services that were provided by a licensed medical provider, including, but not limited to, eyeglasses, hearing aids, dentures, or any prosthetic device taken, lost, or destroyed during the commission of the crime, or the use of which became necessary as a direct result of the crime.

(2) Subject to the limitations set forth in Section 13957.2, reimburse the amount of psychiatric, psychological, or other mental health counseling-related expenses incurred by the victim or derivative victim, including peer counseling services provided by a rape crisis center as defined by Section 13837 of the Penal Code, and including family psychiatric, psychological, or mental health counseling for the successful treatment of the victim provided to family members of the victim in the presence of the victim, whether or not the family member relationship existed at the time of the crime, that became necessary as a direct result of the crime, subject to the following conditions:

(A) The following persons may be reimbursed for the expense of their outpatient mental health counseling:

(i) A victim.

(ii) A derivative victim who is the surviving parent, grandparent, sibling, child, grandchild, spouse, or fiance of a victim of a crime that directly resulted in the death of the victim.

(iii) A derivative victim, as described in paragraphs (1) to (4), inclusive, of subdivision (c) of Section 13955, who is the primary caretaker of a minor victim whose claim is not denied or reduced pursuant to Section 13956 for not more than two derivative victims.

(iv) A derivative victim not eligible for reimbursement pursuant to clause (iii), provided that mental health counseling of a derivative victim described in paragraph (5) of subdivision (c) of Section 13955, shall be reimbursed only if that counseling is necessary for the treatment of the victim.

(v) A minor who suffers emotional injury as a direct result of witnessing a violent crime and who is not eligible for reimbursement of the costs of outpatient mental health counseling under any other provision of this chapter. To be eligible for reimbursement under this clause, the minor must have been in close proximity to the victim when the minor witnessed the crime.

(B) The board may reimburse a victim or derivative victim for inpatient psychiatric, psychological, or other mental health counseling if the claim is based on dire or exceptional circumstances that require more extensive treatment, as approved by the board.

(C) Expenses for psychiatric, psychological, or other mental health counseling-related services may be reimbursed only if the services were provided by either of the following individuals:

(i) A person who would have been authorized to provide those services pursuant to former Article 1 (commencing with Section 13959) as it read on January 1, 2002.

(ii) A person who is licensed in the state in which the victim lives to provide those services, or who is properly supervised by a person who is licensed in the state in which the victim lives to provide those services, subject to the board's approval and subject to the limitations and restrictions the board may impose.

(3) Subject to the limitations set forth in Section 13957.5, authorize compensation equal to the loss of income or loss of support, or both, that a victim or derivative victim incurs as a direct result of the victim's or derivative victim's injury or the victim's death. If the qualifying crime is a violation of Section 236.1 of the Penal Code, the board may authorize compensation equal to loss of income or support that a victim incurs as a direct result of the victim's deprivation of liberty during the crime, not to exceed the amount set forth in Section 13957.5. If the victim or derivative victim requests that the board give priority to reimbursement of loss of income or support, the board may not pay medical expenses, or mental health counseling expenses, except upon the request of the victim or derivative victim or after determining that payment of these expenses will not decrease the funds available for payment of loss of income or support.

(4) Authorize a cash payment to or on behalf of the victim for job retraining or similar employment-oriented services.

(5) Reimburse the expense of installing or increasing residential security, not to exceed one thousand dollars ($1,000). Installing or increasing residential security may include, but need not be limited to, both of the following:

(A) Home security device or system.

(B) Replacing or increasing the number of locks.

(6) Reimburse the expense of renovating or retrofitting a victim's residence, or the expense of modifying or purchasing a vehicle, to make the residence or the vehicle accessible or operational by a victim upon verification that the expense is medically necessary for a victim who is permanently disabled as a direct result of the crime, whether the disability is partial or total.

(7)(A) Authorize a cash payment or reimbursement not to exceed seven thousand five hundred dollars ($7,500) to a victim for expenses incurred in relocating, if the expenses are determined by law enforcement to be necessary for the personal safety of the victim or by a mental health treatment provider to be necessary for the emotional well-being of the victim. For purposes of this paragraph, "expenses incurred in relocating" may include the costs of temporary housing for any pets belonging to the victim upon immediate relocation.

(B) The cash payment or reimbursement made under this paragraph shall only be awarded to one claimant per crime giving rise to the relocation. The board may authorize more than one relocation per crime if necessary for the personal safety or emotional well-being of the claimant. However, the total cash payment or reimbursement for all relocations due to the same crime shall not exceed seven thousand five hundred dollars ($7,500). For purposes of this paragraph, a claimant is the crime victim, or, if the victim is deceased, a person who resided with the deceased at the time of the crime.

(C) The board may, under compelling circumstances, award a second cash payment or reimbursement to a victim for another crime if both of the following conditions are met:

(i) The crime occurs more than three years from the date of the crime giving rise to the initial relocation cash payment or reimbursement.

(ii) The crime does not involve the same offender.

(D) When a relocation payment or reimbursement is provided to a victim of sexual assault or domestic violence and the identity of the offender is known to the victim, the victim shall agree not to inform the offender of the location of the victim's new residence and not to allow the offender on the premises at any time, or shall agree to seek a restraining order against the offender. A victim may be required to repay the relocation payment or reimbursement to the board if the victim violates the terms set forth in this paragraph.

(E) Notwithstanding subparagraphs (A) and (B), the board may increase the cash payment or reimbursement for expenses incurred in relocating to an amount greater than seven thousand five hundred dollars ($7,500) if the board finds this amount is appropriate due to the unusual, dire, or exceptional circumstances of a particular claim.

(F) If a security deposit, pet deposit, or both is required for relocation, the board shall be named as the recipient and receive the funds upon expiration of the victim's rental agreement.

(8) When a victim dies as a result of a crime, the board may reimburse any individual who voluntarily, and without anticipation of personal gain, pays or assumes the obligation to pay any of the following expenses:

(A) The medical expenses incurred as a direct result of the crime in an amount not to exceed the rates or limitations established by the board.

(B) The funeral and burial expenses incurred as a direct result of the crime, not to exceed twenty thousand dollars ($20,000). The board shall not create or comply with a regulation or policy that mandates a lower maximum potential amount of an award pursuant to this subparagraph for less than twenty thousand dollars ($20,000).

(9) When the crime occurs in a residence or inside a vehicle, the board may reimburse any individual who voluntarily, and without anticipation of personal gain, pays or assumes the obligation to pay the reasonable costs to clean the scene of the crime in an amount not to exceed one thousand seven hundred and nine dollars ($1,709). Services reimbursed pursuant to this subdivision shall be performed by persons registered with the State Department of Public Health as trauma scene waste practitioners in accordance with Chapter 9.5 (commencing with Section 118321) of Part 14 of Division 104 of the Health and Safety Code.

(10) When the crime is a violation of Section 600.2 or 600.5 of the Penal Code, the board may reimburse the expense of veterinary services, replacement costs, or other reasonable expenses, as ordered by the court pursuant to Section 600.2 or 600.5 of the Penal Code, in an amount not to exceed ten thousand dollars ($10,000).

(11) An award of compensation pursuant to paragraph (5) of subdivision (f) of Section 13955 shall be limited to compensation to provide mental health counseling and shall not limit the eligibility of a victim for an award that the victim may be otherwise entitled to receive under this part. A derivative victim shall not be eligible for compensation under this provision.

(b) The total award to or on behalf of each victim or derivative victim shall not exceed one hundred thousand dollars ($100,000).

(c) This section shall become operative on July 1, 2024, only if General Fund moneys over the multiyear forecasts beginning in the 2024–25 fiscal year are available to support ongoing augmentations and actions, and if an appropriation is made to backfill the Restitution Fund to support the actions in this section. *(Added by Stats.2022, c. 771 (A.B.160), § 5.5, eff. Sept. 29, 2022, operative July 1, 2024.)*

Contingent Operation

Operation of this section is contingent upon availability of funding, by its own terms.

Cross References

Board defined for purposes of this Chapter, see Government Code § 13951.
Crime, defined for purposes of this Chapter, see Government Code § 13951.
Department of Health Care Services, generally, see Health and Safety Code § 100100 et seq.
Derivative victim, defined for purposes of this Chapter, see Government Code § 13951.
Law enforcement, defined for purposes of this Chapter, see Government Code § 13951.
Pecuniary loss, defined for purposes of this Chapter, see Government Code § 13951.
Peer counseling, defined for purposes of this Chapter, see Government Code § 13951.
Victim, defined for purposes of this Chapter, see Government Code § 13951.

§ 13957.2. Medical and medical-related services and mental health and counseling services; maximum rates and service limitations for reimbursement

(a) The board may establish maximum rates and service limitations for reimbursement of medical and medical-related services and for mental health and counseling services. The adoption, amendment, and repeal of these service limitations and maximum rates shall not be subject to the rulemaking provision of the Administrative Procedure Act (Chapter 3.5 (commencing with Section 11340) of Part 1). An informational copy of the service limitations and maximum rates shall be filed with the Secretary of State upon adoption by the board. Any reduction in the maximum rates or service limitations shall not affect payment or reimbursement of losses incurred prior to three months after the adoption of the reduction. A provider who accepts payment from the program for a service shall accept the program's rates as payment in full and shall not accept any payment on account of the service from any other source if the total of payments accepted would exceed the maximum rate set by the board for that service. A provider shall not charge a victim or derivative victim for any difference between the cost of a service provided to a victim or derivative victim and the program's payment for that service. To ensure service limitations that are uniform and appropriate to the levels of treatment required by the victim or derivative victim, the board may review all claims for these services as necessary to ensure their medical necessity.

(b) The board may request an independent examination and report from any provider of medical or medical-related services or psychological or psychiatric treatment or mental health counseling services, if it believes there is a reasonable basis for requesting an additional evaluation. The victim or derivative victim shall be notified of the name of the provider who is to perform the evaluation within 30 calendar days of that determination. In cases where the crime involves sexual assault, the provider shall have expertise in the needs of sexual assault victims. In cases where the crime involves child abuse or molestation, the provider shall have expertise in the needs of victims of child abuse or molestation, as appropriate. When a reevaluation is requested, payments shall not be discontinued prior to completion of the reevaluation.

(c) Reimbursement for any medical, medical-related, or mental health services shall, if the application has been approved, be paid by the board within an average of 90 days from receipt of the claim for payment. Payments to a medical or mental health provider may not be discontinued prior to completion of any reevaluation. Whether or not a reevaluation is obtained, if the board determines that payments to a provider will be discontinued, the board shall notify the provider of their discontinuance within 30 calendar days of its determination. *(Added by Stats.2002, c. 1141 (S.B.1423), § 2. Amended by Stats.2007, c. 564 (S.B.883), § 2; Stats.2012, c. 870 (S.B.1299), § 5.)*

Cross References

Board defined for purposes of this Chapter, see Government Code § 13951.
Crime, defined for purposes of this Chapter, see Government Code § 13951.
Derivative victim, defined for purposes of this Chapter, see Government Code § 13951.
Victim, defined for purposes of this Chapter, see Government Code § 13951.

Research References

1 Witkin California Criminal Law 4th Introduction to Crimes § 121 (2021), Victims of Crime.

§ 13957.5. Loss of income or support; permissible board action; limitation upon amount

Section operative until July 1, 2024. See, also, § 13957.5 operative July 1, 2024, subject to appropriation.

(a) In authorizing compensation for loss of income and support pursuant to paragraph (3) of subdivision (a) of Section 13957, the board may take any of the following actions:

(1) Compensate the victim for loss of income directly resulting from the injury, except that loss of income may not be paid by the board for more than five years following the crime, unless the victim is disabled as defined in Section 416(i) of Title 42 of the United States Code, as a direct result of the injury.

(2) Compensate an adult derivative victim for loss of income, subject to all of the following:

(A) The derivative victim is the parent or legal guardian of a victim, who at the time of the crime was under 18 years of age and is hospitalized as a direct result of the crime.

(B) The minor victim's treating physician certifies in writing that the presence of the victim's parent or legal guardian at the hospital is necessary for the treatment of the victim.

(C) Reimbursement for loss of income under this paragraph may not exceed the total value of the income that would have been earned by the adult derivative victim during a 30–day period.

(3) Compensate an adult derivative victim for loss of income, subject to all of the following:

(A) The derivative victim is the parent or legal guardian of a victim who at the time of the crime was under 18 years of age.

(B) The victim died as a direct result of the crime.

(C) The board shall pay for loss of income under this paragraph for not more than 30 calendar days from the date of the victim's death.

(4) Compensate a derivative victim who was legally dependent on the victim at the time of the crime for the loss of support incurred by that person as a direct result of the crime, subject to both of the following:

(A) Loss of support shall be paid by the board for income lost by an adult for a period up to, but not more than, five years following the date of the crime.

(B) Loss of support shall not be paid by the board on behalf of a minor for a period beyond the child's attaining 18 years of age.

(5)(A) If the qualifying crime is a violation of Section 236.1 of the Penal Code, and the victim has not been and will not be compensated from any other source, compensate the victim for loss of income or support directly resulting from the deprivation of liberty during the crime based upon the value of the victim's labor as guaranteed under California law at the time that the services were performed for the number of hours that the services were performed, for up to 40 hours per week.

(B) On or before July 1, 2020, the board shall adopt guidelines that allow it to rely on evidence other than official employment documentation in considering and approving an application for that compensation. The evidence may include any reliable corroborating information approved by the board, including, but not limited to, a statement under penalty of perjury from the applicant, a human trafficking caseworker as defined in Section 1038.2 of the Evidence Code, a licensed attorney, or a witness to the circumstances of the crime.

(C) Compensation for loss of income paid by the board pursuant to this paragraph shall not exceed ten thousand dollars ($10,000) per year that the services were performed, for a maximum of two years.

(D) If the victim is a minor at the time of application, the board shall distribute payment under this paragraph when the minor reaches 18 years of age.

(b) The total amount payable to all derivative victims pursuant to this section as the result of one crime shall not exceed seventy thousand dollars ($70,000).

(c)(1) This section shall become inoperative on July 1, 2024, only if General Fund moneys over the multiyear forecasts beginning in the 2024–25 fiscal year are available to support ongoing augmentations and actions, and if an appropriation is made to backfill the Restitution Fund to support the actions in this section. If those conditions are met, this section is repealed January 1, 2025.

(2) The amendments made by the act adding this subdivision [1] shall become operative on January 1, 2023. *(Added by Stats.2002, c. 1141 (S.B.1423), § 2. Amended by Stats.2015, c. 569 (A.B.1140), § 6, eff. Jan. 1, 2016; Stats.2019, c. 575 (A.B.629), § 2, eff. Jan. 1, 2020; Stats.2022, c. 771 (A.B.160), § 6, eff. Sept. 29, 2022, operative Jan. 1, 2023.)*

[1] Stats.2022, c. 771 (A.B.160).

Inoperative Date and Repeal

For inoperative date and repeal of this section, see its terms.

Cross References

Board defined for purposes of this Chapter, see Government Code § 13951.
Crime, defined for purposes of this Chapter, see Government Code § 13951.
Derivative victim, defined for purposes of this Chapter, see Government Code § 13951.
Victim, defined for purposes of this Chapter, see Government Code § 13951.

§ 13957.5. Loss of income or support; permissible board action; guidelines for accepting evidence; limitation upon amount

Section operative July 1, 2024, subject to appropriation.
See, also, § 13957.5 operative until July 1, 2024.

(a) In authorizing compensation for loss of income and support pursuant to paragraph (3) of subdivision (a) of Section 13957, the board may take any of the following actions:

(1) Subject to paragraph (7), and calculated as provided in paragraph (8), compensate the victim for loss of income directly resulting from the injury, except that loss of income shall not be paid by the board for more than five years following the crime, unless the victim is disabled as defined in Section 416(i) of Title 42 of the United States Code, as a direct result of the injury.

(2) Compensate an adult derivative victim for loss of income, subject to all of the following:

(A) The derivative victim is the parent, legal guardian, or spouse of the victim, or if no parent, legal guardian, or spouse of the victim is present at the hospital, is another derivative victim, who is present at the hospital during the period the victim is hospitalized as a direct result of the crime.

(B) The victim's treating physician certifies in writing that the presence of the derivative victim at the hospital is reasonably necessary for the treatment of the victim, or is reasonably necessary for the victim's psychological well-being.

(C) Reimbursement for loss of income under this paragraph shall not exceed the total value of the income that would have been earned, calculated as described in paragraph (8), by the adult derivative victim during a 30–day period.

(3) Compensate an adult derivative victim for loss of income, subject to all of the following:

(A) The victim died as a direct result of the crime.

(B)(i) If the derivative victim is the spouse of the victim, is the parent of the victim, was living in the household of the victim at the time of the crime, was the legal guardian of the victim at the time of the crime, or was the legal guardian of the victim when the victim was under 18 years of age, the board shall pay for loss of income under this paragraph, calculated as provided by paragraph (8), for not more than 30 calendar days occurring within 90 calendar days of the victim's death.

(ii) For a derivative victim not included in clause (i), the board shall pay for loss of income under this paragraph, calculated as

Government

provided by paragraph (8), for not more than seven calendar days occurring within 90 calendar days of the victim's death.

(4) Compensate a derivative victim who was legally dependent on the victim at the time of the crime for the loss of support incurred by that person as a direct result of the crime, calculated as provided in paragraph (8), subject to both of the following:

(A) Loss of support shall be paid by the board for income lost by an adult for a period up to, but not more than, five years following the date of the crime.

(B) Loss of support shall not be paid by the board on behalf of a minor for a period beyond the child's attaining 18 years of age.

(5)(A) If the qualifying crime is a violation of Section 236.1 of the Penal Code, and the victim has not been and will not be compensated from any other source, compensate the victim for loss of income or support directly resulting from the deprivation of liberty during the crime based upon the value of the victim's labor as guaranteed under California law at the time that the services were performed for the number of hours that the services were performed, for up to 40 hours per week.

(B) On or before July 1, 2020, the board shall adopt guidelines that allow it to rely on evidence other than official employment documentation in considering and approving an application for that compensation. The evidence may include any reliable corroborating information approved by the board, including, but not limited to, a statement under penalty of perjury from the applicant, a human trafficking caseworker as defined in Section 1038.2 of the Evidence Code, a licensed attorney, or a witness to the circumstances of the crime.

(C) Compensation for loss of income paid by the board pursuant to this paragraph shall not exceed ten thousand dollars ($10,000) per year that the services were performed, for a maximum of two years.

(D) If the victim is a minor at the time of application, the board shall distribute payment under this paragraph when the minor reaches 18 years of age.

(6) If the victim is a minor at the time of the crime, the victim shall be eligible for future loss of income due to disability from future employment directly resulting from the injury at a rate an employee would earn if employed for 35 hours per week at the minimum wage required at the time of the crime by Section 1182.12 of the Labor Code for a maximum of one year.

(7)(A) A victim or derivative victim who is otherwise eligible for loss of income under paragraph (1), (2), or (3) shall be eligible for loss of income if they were employed or receiving earned income benefits at the time of the crime. If an otherwise eligible adult victim or derivative victim was not employed or receiving earned income benefits at the time of the crime, they shall be eligible for loss of income under paragraph (1), (2), or (3) if the victim or derivative victim was fully or partially employed or receiving income benefits for a total of at least two weeks in the 12 months preceding the qualifying crime, or had an offer of employment at the time of the crime and was unable to begin employment as a result of the crime.

(B) A derivative victim who is otherwise eligible for loss of support under paragraph (4) shall be eligible for loss of support if the victim was employed or receiving earned income benefits at the time of the crime. If the victim was not employed or receiving earned income benefits at the time of the crime, the derivative victim shall be eligible if the victim was fully or partially employed or receiving earned income benefits for a total of at least two weeks in the 12 months preceding the qualifying crime, or if the victim had an offer of employment at the time of the crime and was unable to begin employment as a result of the crime.

(8)(A) Except as provided by subparagraph (B), loss of income or support under paragraph (1), (2), (3), or (4) shall be based on the actual loss the victim or derivative victim, as applicable, sustains or the wages the victim or derivative victim, as applicable, would have earned if employed for 35 hours per week at the minimum wage required by Section 1182.12 of the Labor Code during the applicable period, whichever is greater.

(B) For victims who are under 18 years of age at the time of the crime, loss of income under paragraph (1) shall be based upon the actual loss the victim sustains.

(b) By July 1, 2025, the board shall adopt new guidelines for accepting evidence that may be available to the victim or derivative victim in considering and approving a claim for loss of income or support under this section, which shall require the board to accept any form of reliable corroborating information approved by the board regarding the victim or derivative victim's income, including, but not limited to, all of the following:

(1) A statement from the employer.

(2) A pattern of deposits into a bank or credit union account of the victim or derivative victim.

(3) Pay stubs or copies of checks received as payment.

(4) A copy of a job offer letter from an employer.

(5) Income tax records.

(6) Verification through a vendor, if the employer contracts with a vendor for employment verification.

(7) Information related to eligibility or enrollment from any of the following:

(A) The CalFresh program pursuant to Chapter 10 (commencing with Section 18900) of Part 6 of Division 9 of the Welfare and Institution Code.

(B) The CalWORKs program.

(C) The state's children's health insurance program under Title XXI of the federal Social Security Act (42 U.S.C. Sec. 1397aa et seq.).

(D) The California Health Benefit Exchange established pursuant to Title 22 (commencing with Section 100500) of the Government Code.

(E) The electronic service established in accordance with Section 435.949 of Title 42 of the Code of Federal Regulations.

(F) Records from the Employment Development Department.

(c) The total amount payable to all derivative victims pursuant to this section as the result of one crime shall not exceed one hundred thousand dollars ($100,000).

(d) This section shall become operative on July 1, 2024, only if General Fund moneys over the multiyear forecasts beginning in the 2024–25 fiscal year are available to support ongoing augmentations and actions, and if an appropriation is made to backfill the Restitution Fund to support the actions in this section. *(Added by Stats.2022, c. 771 (A.B.160), § 7, eff. Sept. 29, 2022, operative July 1, 2024.)*

Contingent Operation

Operation of this section is contingent upon availability of funding, by its own terms.

Cross References

Board defined for purposes of this Chapter, see Government Code § 13951.
Crime, defined for purposes of this Chapter, see Government Code § 13951.
Derivative victim, defined for purposes of this Chapter, see Government Code § 13951.
Victim, defined for purposes of this Chapter, see Government Code § 13951.

§ 13957.7. Limitation upon time for reimbursement; exception; payments; construction with other public assistance funding; attorney's fees

(a) No reimbursement may be made for any expense that is submitted more than three years after it is incurred by the victim or derivative victim. However, reimbursement may be made for an expense submitted more than three years after the date it is incurred if the victim or derivative victim has affirmed the debt and is liable for the debt at the time the expense is submitted for reimbursement, or has paid the expense as a direct result of a crime for which a timely application has been filed or has paid the expense as a direct result of a crime for which an application has been filed and approved.

(b) Compensation made pursuant to this chapter may be on a one-time or periodic basis. If periodic, the board may increase, reduce, or terminate the amount of compensation according to the applicant's need, subject to the maximum limits provided in this chapter.

(c)(1) The board may authorize direct payment to a provider of services that are reimbursable pursuant to this chapter and may make those payments prior to verification. However, the board may not, without good cause, authorize a direct payment to a provider over the objection of the victim or derivative victim.

(2) Reimbursement on the initial claim for any psychological, psychiatric, or mental health counseling services shall, if the application has been approved, be paid by the board within 90 days of the date of receipt of the claim for payment, with subsequent payments to be made to the provider within one month of the receipt of a claim for payment.

(d) Payments for peer counseling services provided by a rape crisis center may not exceed fifteen dollars ($15) for each hour of services provided. Those services shall be limited to in-person counseling for a period not to exceed 10 weeks plus one series of facilitated support group counseling sessions.

(e) The board shall develop procedures to ensure that a victim is using compensation for job retraining or relocation only for its intended purposes. The procedures may include, but need not be limited to, requiring copies of receipts, agreements, or other documents as requested, or developing a method for direct payment.

(f) Compensation granted pursuant to this chapter shall not disqualify an otherwise eligible applicant from participation in any other public assistance program.

(g) The board shall pay attorney's fees representing the reasonable value of legal services rendered to the applicant, in an amount equal to 10 percent of the amount of the award, or five hundred dollars ($500), whichever is less, for each victim and each derivative victim. The board may request that an attorney provide verification of legal services provided to an applicant and the board may contact an applicant to verify that legal services were provided. An attorney receiving fees from another source may waive the right to receive fees under this subdivision. Payments under this subdivision shall be in addition to any amount authorized or ordered under subdivision (b) of Section 13960. An attorney may not charge, demand, receive, or collect any amount for services rendered in connection with any proceedings under this chapter except as awarded under this chapter.

(h) A private nonprofit agency shall be reimbursed for its services at the level of the normal and customary fee charged by the private nonprofit agency to clients with adequate means of payment for its services, except that this reimbursement may not exceed the maximum reimbursement rates set by the board and may be made only to the extent that the victim otherwise qualifies for compensation under this chapter and that other reimbursement or direct subsidies are not available to serve the victim. *(Added by Stats.2002, c. 1141 (S.B. 1423), § 2. Amended by Stats.2012, c. 870 (S.B.1299), § 6; Stats. 2015, c. 569 (A.B.1140), § 7, eff. Jan. 1, 2016.)*

Cross References

Board defined for purposes of this Chapter, see Government Code § 13951.
Crime, defined for purposes of this Chapter, see Government Code § 13951.
Derivative victim, defined for purposes of this Chapter, see Government Code § 13951.
Peer counseling, defined for purposes of this Chapter, see Government Code § 13951.
Victim, defined for purposes of this Chapter, see Government Code § 13951.

Research References

1 Witkin California Criminal Law 4th Introduction to Crimes § 121 (2021), Victims of Crime.

§ 13958. Approval or denial of application; time requirements

The board shall approve or deny applications, based on recommendations of the board staff, within an average of 90 calendar days and no later than 180 calendar days of acceptance by the board or victim center.

(a) If the board does not meet the 90–day average standard prescribed in this subdivision, the board shall, thereafter, report to the Legislature, on a quarterly basis, its progress and its current average time of processing applications. These quarterly reports shall continue until the board meets the 90–day average standard for two consecutive quarters.

(b) If the board fails to approve or deny an individual application within 180 days of the date it is accepted, pursuant to this subdivision, the board shall advise the applicant and his or her representative, in writing, of the reason for the failure to approve or deny the application. *(Added by Stats.2002, c. 1141 (S.B.1423), § 2.)*

Cross References

Board defined for purposes of this Chapter, see Government Code § 13951.
Victim, defined for purposes of this Chapter, see Government Code § 13951.
Victim center, defined for purposes of this Chapter, see Government Code § 13951.

Research References

1 Witkin California Criminal Law 4th Introduction to Crimes § 121 (2021), Victims of Crime.

ARTICLE 5. HEARINGS AND JUDICIAL REVIEW

§ 13959. Hearing on denial of compensation; date; process; decision; reconsideration

Section operative until July 1, 2024. See, also, § 13959 operative July 1, 2024, subject to appropriation.

(a) The board shall grant a hearing to an applicant who contests a staff recommendation to deny compensation in whole or in part.

(b) The board shall notify the applicant not less than 10 days prior to the date of the hearing. Notwithstanding Section 11123, if the appeal that the board is considering involves either a crime against a minor, a crime of sexual assault, or a crime of domestic violence, the board may exclude from the hearing all persons other than board members and members of its staff, the applicant for benefits, a minor applicant's parents or guardians, the applicant's representative, witnesses, and other persons of the applicant's choice to provide assistance to the applicant during the hearing. However, the board shall not exclude persons from the hearing if the applicant or applicant's representative requests that the hearing be open to the public.

(c) At the hearing, the person seeking compensation shall have the burden of establishing, by a preponderance of the evidence, the elements for eligibility under Section 13955.

(d) Except as otherwise provided by law, in making determinations of eligibility for compensation and in deciding upon the amount of

Government

compensation, the board shall apply the law in effect as of the date an application was submitted.

(e)(1) The hearing shall be informal and need not be conducted according to the technical rules relating to evidence and witnesses. The board may rely on any relevant evidence if it is the sort of evidence on which responsible persons are accustomed to rely in the conduct of serious affairs, regardless of the existence of a common law or statutory rule that might make improper the admission of the evidence over objection in a civil action. The board may rely on written reports prepared for the board, or other information received, from public agencies responsible for investigating the crime. If the applicant or the applicant's representative chooses not to appear at the hearing, the board may act solely upon the application for compensation, the staff's report, and other evidence that appears in the record.

(2) The board shall allow a service animal to accompany and support a witness while testifying at a hearing.

(f) Hearings shall be held in various locations with the frequency necessary to provide for the speedy adjudication of the appeals. If the applicant's presence is required at the hearing, the board shall schedule the applicant's hearing in as convenient a location as possible or conduct the hearing by telephone.

(g) The board may delegate the hearing of appeals to hearing officers.

(h) The decisions of the board shall be in writing within six months of the date the board received the appeal unless the board determines that there was insufficient information to make a decision. If the board determines that there was insufficient information to make a decision, the board shall notify the applicant in writing within six months of the date the board received the appeal. Copies of the decisions shall be delivered to the applicant or to * * * the applicant's representative personally or sent to * * * them by mail.

(i) The board may order a reconsideration of all or part of a decision on written request of the applicant. The board shall not grant more than one request for reconsideration with respect to any one decision on an appeal for compensation. The board shall not consider any request for reconsideration filed with the board more than 30 calendar days after the personal delivery or 60 calendar days after the mailing of the original decision.

(j) The board may order a reconsideration of all or part of a decision on its own motion, at its discretion, at any time.

(k) Evidence submitted after the board has denied a request for reconsideration shall not be considered unless the board chooses to reconsider its decision on its own motion.

(*l*)(1) This section shall become inoperative on July 1, 2024, only if General Fund moneys over the multiyear forecasts beginning in the 2024–25 fiscal year are available to support ongoing augmentations and actions, and if an appropriation is made to backfill the Restitution Fund to support the actions in this section. If those conditions are met, this section is repealed January 1, 2025.

(2) The amendments made by the act adding this subdivision [1] shall become operative on January 1, 2023. *(Added by Stats.2002, c. 1141 (S.B.1423), § 2. Amended by Stats.2007, c. 564 (S.B.883), § 3; Stats.2008, c. 179 (S.B.1498), § 96; Stats.2015, c. 569 (A.B.1140), § 9, eff. Jan. 1, 2016; Stats.2016, c. 121 (A.B.1563), § 1, eff. Jan. 1, 2017; Stats.2022, c. 771 (A.B.160), § 8, eff. Sept. 29, 2022, operative Jan. 1, 2023.)*

[1] Stats.2022, c. 771 (A.B.160).

Inoperative Date and Repeal

For inoperative date and repeal of this section, see its terms.

Cross References

Board defined for purposes of this Chapter, see Government Code § 13951.

Crime, defined for purposes of this Chapter, see Government Code § 13951.

Research References

1 Witkin California Criminal Law 4th Introduction to Crimes § 121 (2021), Victims of Crime.

3 Witkin, California Criminal Law 4th Punishment § 657 (2021), Definitions.

§ 13959. Hearing on denial of compensation; date; process; decision; reconsideration

Section operative July 1, 2024, subject to appropriation. See, also, § 13959 operative until July 1, 2024.

(a) The board shall grant a hearing to an applicant who contests a staff recommendation to deny compensation in whole or in part.

(b) The board shall notify the applicant not less than 10 days prior to the date of the hearing. Notwithstanding Section 11123, if the appeal that the board is considering involves either a crime against a minor, a crime of sexual assault, or a crime of domestic violence, the board may exclude from the hearing all persons other than board members and members of its staff, the applicant for benefits, a minor applicant's parents or guardians, the applicant's representative, witnesses, and other persons of the applicant's choice to provide assistance to the applicant during the hearing. However, the board shall not exclude persons from the hearing if the applicant or applicant's representative requests that the hearing be open to the public.

(c) At the hearing, the person seeking compensation shall have the burden of establishing, by a preponderance of the evidence, the elements for eligibility under Section 13955.

(d) Except as otherwise provided by law, in making determinations of eligibility for compensation and in deciding upon the amount of compensation, the board shall apply the law in effect as of the date an application was submitted.

(e)(1) The hearing shall be informal and need not be conducted according to the technical rules relating to evidence and witnesses. The board may rely on any relevant evidence if it is the sort of evidence on which responsible persons are accustomed to rely on the conduct of serious affairs, regardless of the existence of a common law or statutory rule that might make improper the admission of the evidence over objection in a civil action. The board may rely on written reports prepared for the board, or other information received, from public agencies responsible for investigating the crime. If the applicant or the applicant's representative chooses not to appear at the hearing, the board may act solely upon the application for compensation, the staff's report, and other evidence that appears in the record.

(2) The board shall allow a service animal to accompany and support a witness while testifying at a hearing.

(f) Hearings shall be held in various locations with the frequency necessary to provide for the speedy adjudication of the appeals. If the applicant's presence is required at the hearing, the board shall schedule the applicant's hearing in as convenient a location as possible or conduct the hearing by telephone.

(g) The board may delegate the hearing of appeals to hearing officers.

(h) The decisions of the board shall be in writing within four months of the date the board received the appeal unless the board determines that there was insufficient information to make a decision. If the board determines that there was insufficient information to make a decision, the board shall notify the applicant in writing within four months of the date the board received the appeal. Copies of the decisions shall be delivered to the applicant or to the applicant's representative personally or sent to them by mail.

(i) The board may order a reconsideration of all or part of a decision on written request of the applicant. The board shall not grant more than one request for reconsideration with respect to any one decision on an appeal for compensation. The board shall not consider any request for reconsideration filed with the board more than 365 calendar days after the personal delivery or the mailing of the original decision.

(j) The board may order a reconsideration of all or part of a decision on its own motion, at its discretion, at any time.

(k) Evidence submitted after the board has denied a request for reconsideration shall not be considered unless the board chooses to reconsider its decision on its own motion.

(*l*) This section shall become operative on July 1, 2024, only if General Fund moneys over the multiyear forecasts beginning in the 2024–25 fiscal year are available to support ongoing augmentations and actions, and if an appropriation is made to backfill the Restitution Fund to support the actions in this section. *(Added by Stats.2022, c. 771 (A.B.160), § 9, eff. Sept. 29, 2022, operative July 1, 2024.)*

Contingent Operation

Operation of this section is contingent upon availability of funding, by its own terms.

Cross References

Board defined for purposes of this Chapter, see Government Code § 13951.
Crime, defined for purposes of this Chapter, see Government Code § 13951.

§ 13960. Writ of mandate

(a) Judicial review of a final decision made pursuant to this chapter may be had by filing a petition for a writ of mandate in accordance with Section 1094.5 of the Code of Civil Procedure. The right to petition shall not be affected by the failure to seek reconsideration before the board. The petition shall be filed as follows:

(1) Where no request for reconsideration is made, within 30 calendar days of personal delivery or within 60 calendar days of the mailing of the board's decision on the application for compensation.

(2) Where a timely request for reconsideration is filed and rejected by the board, within 30 calendar days of personal delivery or within 60 calendar days of the mailing of the notice of rejection.

(3) Where a timely request for reconsideration is filed and granted by the board, or reconsideration is ordered by the board, within 30 calendar days of personal delivery or within 60 calendar days of the mailing of the final decision on the reconsidered application.

(b)(1) In an action resulting in the issuance of a writ of mandate pursuant to this section the court may order the board to pay to the applicant's attorney reasonable attorney's fees or one thousand dollars ($1,000), whichever is less. If action is taken by the board in favor of the applicant in response to the filing of the petition, but prior to a judicial determination, the board shall pay the applicant's costs of filing the petition.

(2) In case of appeal by the board of a decision on the petition for writ of mandate that results in a decision in favor of the applicant, the court may order the board to pay to the applicant's attorney reasonable attorney fees.

(3) Nothing in this section shall be construed to prohibit or limit an award of attorney's fees pursuant to Section 1021.5 of the Code of Civil Procedure. *(Added by Stats.2002, c. 1141 (S.B.1423), § 2.)*

Cross References

Board defined for purposes of this Chapter, see Government Code § 13951.
Mandamus, purpose of writ of mandate, courts which may issue writ and parties to whom issued, see Code of Civil Procedure § 1085.
Writ of mandate, see Code of Civil Procedure § 1085 et seq.

Research References

1 Witkin California Criminal Law 4th Introduction to Crimes § 121 (2021), Victims of Crime.

ARTICLE 6. ADMINISTRATION

§ 13962. Board publication of program availability; duties of local law enforcement agencies; training and outreach duties of board; required affirmations regarding program availability for gang members and suspected gang members; required affirmations regarding program availability regardless of documentation or immigration status

Section operative until July 1, 2024. See, also, § 13962 operative July 1, 2024, subject to appropriation.

(a) The board shall publicize through the board, law enforcement agencies, victim centers, hospitals, medical, mental health or other counseling service providers, and other public or private agencies, the existence of the program established pursuant to this chapter, including the procedures for obtaining compensation under the program.

(b) It shall be the duty of every local law enforcement agency to inform crime victims of the provisions of this chapter, of the existence of victim centers, and in counties where no victim center exists, to provide application forms to victims who desire to seek compensation pursuant to this chapter. The board shall provide application forms and all other documents that local law enforcement agencies and victim centers may require to comply with this section. The board, in cooperation with victim centers, shall set standards to be followed by local law enforcement agencies for this purpose and may require them to file with the board a description of the procedures adopted by each agency to comply with the standards. The board shall conduct outreach to local law enforcement agencies about their duties under this section.

(c) Every local law enforcement agency shall annually provide to the board contact information for the Victims of Crime Liaison Officer designated pursuant to Section 649.36 of Title 2 of the California Code of Regulations.

(d) The board shall annually make available to the Victims of Crime Liaison Officer at every local law enforcement agency one hour of training on victim compensation in California and materials to educate the officers and staff in their law enforcement agencies and publicize the program within their jurisdictions.

(e) The board's outreach pursuant to subdivision (a) and training pursuant to subdivision (d) shall affirm that neither access to information about victim compensation, nor an application for compensation, shall be denied on the basis of the victim's or derivative victim's membership in, association with, or affiliation with, a gang, or on the basis of the victim's or derivative victim's designation as a suspected gang member, associate, or affiliate in a shared gang database, as defined in Section 186.34 of the Penal Code.

(f) The board's outreach pursuant to subdivision (a) and training pursuant to subdivision (d) shall affirm that neither access to information about victim compensation, nor an application for compensation, shall be denied on the basis of the victim's or derivative victim's documentation or immigration status.

(g)(1) This section shall become inoperative on July 1, 2024, only if General Fund moneys over the multiyear forecasts beginning in the 2024–25 fiscal year are available to support ongoing augmentations and actions, and if an appropriation is made to backfill the Restitution Fund to support the actions in this section. If those conditions are met, this section is repealed January 1, 2025.

(2) The amendments made by the act adding this subdivision [1] shall become operative on January 1, 2023. *(Added by Stats.2002, c. 1141 (S.B.1423), § 2. Amended by Stats.2018, c. 161 (A.B.1639), § 3, eff. Jan. 1, 2019; Stats.2022, c. 771 (A.B.160), § 10, eff. Sept. 29, 2022, operative Jan. 1, 2023.)*

[1] Stats.2022, c. 771 (A.B.160).

Inoperative Date and Repeal

For inoperative date and repeal of this section, see its terms.

Cross References

Board defined for purposes of this Chapter, see Government Code § 13951.
Crime, defined for purposes of this Chapter, see Government Code § 13951.
Law enforcement, defined for purposes of this Chapter, see Government Code § 13951.
Rules and regulations of state agencies, see Government Code § 11342.1 et seq.
Victim, defined for purposes of this Chapter, see Government Code § 13951.
Victim center, defined for purposes of this Chapter, see Government Code § 13951.

Research References

1 Witkin California Criminal Law 4th Introduction to Crimes § 121 (2021), Victims of Crime.

§ 13962. Board publication of program availability; duties of local law enforcement agencies; training and outreach duties of board; required affirmations regarding program availability for gang members and suspected gang members; required affirmations regarding program availability regardless of documentation or immigration status; documents to be provided to general acute care hospitals

Section operative July 1, 2024, subject to appropriation.
See, also, § 13962 operative until July 1, 2024.

(a) The board shall publicize through the board, law enforcement agencies, victim centers, hospitals, medical, mental health or other counseling service providers, and other public or private agencies, the existence of the program established pursuant to this chapter, including the procedures for obtaining compensation under the program.

(b) It shall be the duty of every local law enforcement agency to inform crime victims of the provisions of this chapter, of the existence of victim centers, and of the existence of trauma recovery centers as described under Section 13963.1, and to provide application forms to victims who desire to seek compensation pursuant to this chapter. The board shall provide application forms and all other documents that local law enforcement agencies and victim centers may require to comply with this section. The board, in cooperation with victim centers, shall set standards to be followed by local law enforcement agencies for this purpose and may require them to file with the board a description of the procedures adopted by each agency to comply with the standards. The board shall conduct outreach to local law enforcement agencies about their duties under this section.

(c) Every local law enforcement agency shall annually provide to the board contact information for the Victims of Crime Liaison Officer designated pursuant to Section 649.36 of Title 2 of the California Code of Regulations.

(d) The board shall annually make available to the Victims of Crime Liaison Officer at every local law enforcement agency one hour of training on victim compensation in California and materials to educate the officers and staff in their law enforcement agencies and publicize the program within their jurisdictions.

(e) The board's outreach pursuant to subdivision (a) and training pursuant to subdivision (d) shall affirm that neither access to information about victim compensation, nor an application for compensation, shall be denied on the basis of the victim's or derivative victim's membership in, association with, or affiliation with, a gang, or on the basis of the victim's or derivative victim's designation as a suspected gang member, associate, or affiliate in a shared gang database, as defined in Section 186.34 of the Penal Code.

(f) The board's outreach pursuant to subdivision (a) and training pursuant to subdivision (d) shall affirm that neither access to information about victim compensation, nor an application for compensation, shall be denied on the basis of the victim's or derivative victim's documentation or immigration status.

(g)(1) The board shall provide every general acute care hospital in the state that operates an emergency department with both of the following:

(A) A poster developed by the board describing the existence of the program established pursuant to this chapter, including the procedures for obtaining compensation under the program.

(B) Application forms to distribute to victims, derivative victims, and their family members who desire to seek compensation pursuant to this chapter.

(2) It shall be the duty of every general acute care hospital to display a poster provided to the hospital pursuant to subparagraph (A) of paragraph (1) prominently in the lobby or waiting area of its emergency department.

(3) At the request of the hospital, the board shall provide the documents described in paragraph (1) in any of the languages listed in paragraph (4) of subdivision (d) of Section 13952.

(h) This section shall become operative on July 1, 2024, only if General Fund moneys over the multiyear forecasts beginning in the 2024–25 fiscal year are available to support ongoing augmentations and actions, and if an appropriation is made to backfill the Restitution Fund to support the actions in this section. *(Added by Stats.2022, c. 771 (A.B.160), § 11, eff. Sept. 29, 2022, operative July 1, 2024.)*

Contingent Operation

Operation of this section is contingent upon availability of funding, by its own terms.

Cross References

Board defined for purposes of this Chapter, see Government Code § 13951.
Crime, defined for purposes of this Chapter, see Government Code § 13951.
Law enforcement, defined for purposes of this Chapter, see Government Code § 13951.
Rules and regulations of state agencies, see Government Code § 11342.1 et seq.
Victim, defined for purposes of this Chapter, see Government Code § 13951.
Victim center, defined for purposes of this Chapter, see Government Code § 13951.

§ 13963. Subrogation; lien; action or claim by recipient; disposition of proceeds; action prosecuted by recipient alone; payment of costs and attorney's fees

(a) The board shall be subrogated to the rights of the recipient to the extent of any compensation granted by the board. The subrogation rights shall be against the perpetrator of the crime or any person liable for the losses suffered as a direct result of the crime which was the basis for receipt of compensation, including an insurer held liable in accordance with the provision of a policy of insurance issued pursuant to Section 11580.2 of the Insurance Code.

(b) The board shall also be entitled to a lien on any judgment, award, or settlement in favor of or on behalf of the recipient for losses suffered as a direct result of the crime that was the basis for receipt of compensation in the amount of the compensation granted by the board. The board may recover this amount in a separate action, or may intervene in an action brought by or on behalf of the recipient. If a claim is filed within one year of the date of recovery, the board shall pay 25 percent of the amount of the recovery that is subject to a lien on the judgment, award, or settlement, to the recipient responsible for recovery if the recipient notified the board of the action prior to receiving any recovery. The remaining amount, and any amount not claimed within one year pursuant to this section, shall be deposited in the Restitution Fund.

(c) The board may compromise or settle and release any lien pursuant to this chapter if it is found that the action is in the best interest of the state or the collection would cause undue hardship upon the recipient. Repayment obligations to the Restitution Fund shall be enforceable as a summary judgment.

(d) No judgment, award, or settlement in any action or claim by a recipient, where the board has an interest, shall be satisfied without first giving the board notice and a reasonable opportunity to perfect and satisfy the lien. The notice shall be given to the board in Sacramento except in cases where the board specifies that the notice shall be given otherwise. The notice shall include the complete terms of the award, settlement, or judgment, and the name and address of any insurer directly or indirectly providing for the satisfaction.

(e)(1) If the recipient brings an action or asserts a claim for damages against the person or persons liable for the injury or death giving rise to an award by the board under this chapter, notice of the institution of legal proceedings, notice of all hearings, conferences, and proceedings, and notice of settlement shall be given to the board in Sacramento except in cases where the board specifies that notice shall be given to the Attorney General. Notice of the institution of legal proceedings shall be given to the board within 30 days of filing the action. All notices shall be given by the attorney employed to bring the action for damages or by the recipient if no attorney is employed.

(2) Notice shall include all of the following:

(A) Names of all parties to the claim or action.

(B) The address of all parties to the claim or action except for those persons represented by attorneys and in that case the name of the party and the name and address of the attorney.

(C) The nature of the claim asserted or action brought.

(D) In the case of actions before courts or administrative agencies, the full title of the case including the identity of the court or agency, the names of the parties, and the case or docket number.

(3) When the recipient or his or her attorney has reason to believe that a person from whom damages are sought is receiving a defense provided in whole or in part by an insurer, or is insured for the injury caused to the recipient, notice shall include a statement of that fact and the name and address of the insurer. Upon request of the board, a person obligated to provide notice shall provide the board with a copy of the current written claim or complaint.

(f) The board shall pay the county probation department or other county agency responsible for collection of funds owed to the Restitution Fund under Section 13967, as operative on or before September 28, 1994, Section 1202.4 of the Penal Code, Section 1203.04 of the Penal Code, as operative on or before August 2, 1995, or Section 730.6 of the Welfare and Institutions Code, 10 percent of the funds so owed and collected by the county agency and deposited in the Restitution Fund. This payment shall be made only when the funds are deposited in the Restitution Fund within 45 days of the end of the month in which the funds are collected. Receiving 10 percent of the moneys collected as being owed to the Restitution Fund shall be considered an incentive for collection efforts and shall be used for furthering these collection efforts. The 10–percent rebates shall be used to augment the budgets for the county agencies responsible for collection of funds owed to the Restitution Fund, as provided in Section 13967, as operative on or before September 28, 1994, Section 1202.4 of the Penal Code, Section 1203.04 of the Penal Code, operative on or before August 2, 1995, or Section 730.6 of the Welfare and Institutions Code. The 10–percent rebates shall not be used to supplant county funding.

(g) In the event of judgment or award in a suit or claim against a third party or insurer, if the action or claim is prosecuted by the recipient alone, the court or agency shall first order paid from any judgment or award the reasonable litigation expenses incurred in preparation and prosecution of the action or claim, together with reasonable attorney's fees when an attorney has been retained. After payment of the expenses and attorney's fees, the court or agency shall, on the application of the board, allow as a lien against the amount of the judgment or award, the amount of the compensation granted by the board to the recipient for losses sustained as a result of the same incident upon which the settlement, award, or judgment is based.

(h) For purposes of this section, "recipient" means any person who has received compensation or will be provided compensation pursuant to this chapter, including the victim's guardian, conservator or other personal representative, estate, and survivors.

(i) In accordance with subparagraph (B) of paragraph (4) of subdivision (f) of Section 1202.4 of the Penal Code, a representative of the board may provide the probation department, district attorney, and court with information relevant to the board's losses prior to the imposition of a sentence. *(Added by Stats.2002, c. 1141 (S.B.1423), § 2. Amended by Stats.2014, c. 508 (A.B.2685), § 1, eff. Jan. 1, 2015; Stats.2015, c. 569 (A.B.1140), § 10, eff. Jan. 1, 2016.)*

Cross References

Actions for damages against defendant arising from felony offense, limitation of actions, stay of judgment, restitution, see Code of Civil Procedure § 340.3.
Actions for damages to victims of human trafficking, see Civil Code § 52.5.
Attorney General, generally, see Government Code § 12500 et seq.
Board defined for purposes of this Chapter, see Government Code § 13951.
Carry over of unexpended funds by trial courts, funds excluded from calculation of amount authorized to be carried over commencing June 30, 2014, see Government Code § 77203.
Crime, defined for purposes of this Chapter, see Government Code § 13951.
Restitution fines, applicability to provisions in this section, see Penal Code § 1202.4.

Subcutaneous implanting of identification device, judgment, award or settlement obtained subject to provisions of this section, see Civil Code § 52.7.
Victim, defined for purposes of this Chapter, see Government Code § 13951.

§ 13963.1. Grants to trauma recovery centers; legislative findings and declarations; criteria; requirements

(a) The Legislature finds and declares all of the following:

(1) Without treatment, approximately 50 percent of people who survive a traumatic, violent injury experience lasting or extended psychological or social difficulties. Untreated psychological trauma often has severe economic consequences, including overuse of costly medical services, loss of income, failure to return to gainful employment, loss of medical insurance, and loss of stable housing.

(2) Victims of crime should receive timely and effective mental health treatment.

(3) The board shall administer a program to evaluate applications and award grants to trauma recovery centers.

(b) The board shall award a grant only to a trauma recovery center that meets all of the following criteria:

(1) The trauma recovery center demonstrates that it serves as a community resource by providing services, including, but not limited to, making presentations and providing training to law enforcement, community-based agencies, and other health care providers on the identification and effects of violent crime.

(2) Any other related criteria required by the board.

(3) The trauma recovery center uses the core elements established in Section 13963.2.

(c) It is the intent of the Legislature to provide an annual appropriation of two million dollars ($2,000,000) per year from the Restitution Fund.

(d) The board may award a grant providing funding for up to a maximum period of three years. Any portion of a grant that a trauma recovery center does not use within the specified grant period shall revert to the Restitution Fund. The board may award consecutive grants to a trauma recovery center to prevent a lapse in funding.

(e) The board, when considering grant applications, shall give preference to a trauma recovery center that conducts outreach to, and serves, both of the following:

(1) Crime victims who typically are unable to access traditional services, including, but not limited to, victims who are homeless, chronically mentally ill, of diverse ethnicity, members of immigrant and refugee groups, disabled, who have severe trauma-related symptoms or complex psychological issues, or juvenile victims, including minors who have had contact with the juvenile dependency or justice system.

(2) Victims of a wide range of crimes, including, but not limited to, victims of sexual assault, domestic violence, physical assault, shooting, stabbing, human trafficking, and vehicular assault, and family members of homicide victims.

(f) The trauma recovery center sites shall be selected by the board through a well-defined selection process that takes into account the rate of crime and geographic distribution to serve the greatest number of victims.

(g) A trauma recovery center that is awarded a grant shall do both of the following:

(1) Report to the board annually on how grant funds were spent, how many clients were served (counting an individual client who receives multiple services only once), units of service, staff productivity, treatment outcomes, and patient flow throughout both the clinical and evaluation components of service.

(2) In compliance with federal statutes and rules governing federal matching funds for victims' services, each center shall submit any forms and data requested by the board to allow the board to receive the 60 percent federal matching funds for eligible victim services and allowable expenses.

(h) For purposes of this section, a trauma recovery center provides, including, but not limited to, all of the following resources, treatments, and recovery services to crime victims:

(1) Mental health services.

(2) Assertive community-based outreach and clinical case management.

(3) Coordination of care among medical and mental health care providers, law enforcement agencies, and other social services.

(4) Services to family members and loved ones of homicide victims.

(5) A multidisciplinary staff of clinicians that includes psychiatrists, psychologists, and social workers, and may include case managers and peer counselors. *(Added by Stats.2013, c. 28 (S.B.71), § 13, eff. June 27, 2013. Amended by Stats.2014, c. 28 (S.B.854), § 30, eff. June 20, 2014; Stats.2017, c. 587 (A.B.1384), § 2, eff. Jan. 1, 2018.)*

Cross References

Informing crime victims of their rights, Victim Protections and Resources card, see Penal Code § 679.027.

§ 13963.2. Selection, establishment, and implementation of Trauma Recovery Centers (TRCs); use of Integrated Trauma Recovery Services (ITRS) model developed by State Pilot Trauma Recovery Center (State Pilot TRC); requirements of TRCs

The Trauma Recovery Center at the San Francisco General Hospital, University of California, San Francisco, is recognized as the State Pilot Trauma Recovery Center (State Pilot TRC). The California Victim Compensation Board shall use the evidence-informed Integrated Trauma Recovery Services (ITRS) model developed by the State Pilot TRC when it selects, establishes, and implements Trauma Recovery Centers (TRCs) pursuant to Section 13963.1. All TRCs funded through the Restitution Fund or Safe Neighborhoods and Schools Fund shall do all of the following:

(a) Provide outreach and services to crime victims who typically are unable to access traditional services, including, but not limited to, victims who are homeless, chronically mentally ill, members of immigrant and refugee groups, disabled, who have severe trauma-related symptoms or complex psychological issues, are of diverse ethnicity or origin, or are juvenile victims, including minors who have had contact with the juvenile dependency or justice system.

(b) Serve victims of a wide range of crimes, including, but not limited to, victims of sexual assault, domestic violence, battery, crimes of violence, vehicular assault, and human trafficking, as well as family members of homicide victims.

(c) Offer evidence-based and evidence-informed mental health services and support services that include individual and group treatment, medication management, substance abuse treatment, case management, and assertive outreach. This care shall be provided in a manner that increases access to services and removes barriers to care for victims of violent crime, and may include providing services to a victim in his or her home, in the community, or at other locations conducive to maintaining quality treatment and confidentiality.

(d) Be comprised of a staff that includes a multidisciplinary team of clinicians made up of at least one psychologist, one social worker, and additional staff. Clinicians are not required to work full-time as a member of the multidisciplinary team. At least one psychiatrist shall be available to the team to assist with medication management, provide consultation, and assist with treatment to meet the clinical needs of the victim. The psychiatrist may be on staff or on contract. A clinician shall be either a licensed clinician or a supervised clinician engaged in completion of the applicable licensure process. Clinical supervision and other supports shall be provided to staff regularly to ensure the highest quality of care and to help staff constructively manage vicarious trauma they experience as service providers to victims of violent crime. Clinicians shall meet the training or certification requirements for the evidence-based practices they use.

(e) Offer mental health services and case management that are coordinated through a single point of contact for the victim, with support from an integrated multidisciplinary treatment team. Each client receiving mental health services shall have a treatment plan in place, which is periodically reviewed by the multidisciplinary team. Examples of primary treatment goals include, but are not limited to, a decrease in psychosocial distress, minimizing long-term disability, improving overall quality of life, reducing the risk of future victimization, and promoting post-traumatic growth.

(f) Deliver services that include assertive outreach and case management including, but not limited to, accompanying a client to court proceedings, medical appointments, or other appointments as needed, assistance with filing an application for assistance to the California Victim Compensation Board, filing police reports or filing restraining orders, assistance with obtaining safe housing and financial benefits, helping a client obtain medical care, providing assistance securing employment, and working as a liaison to other community agencies, law enforcement, or other supportive service providers as needed. TRCs shall offer outreach and case management services to clients without regard to whether clients choose to access mental health services.

(g) Ensure that no person is excluded from services solely on the basis of emotional or behavioral issues resulting from trauma, including, but not limited to, substance abuse problems, low initial motivation, or high levels of anxiety.

(h) Utilize established, evidence-based and evidence-informed practices in treatment. These practices may include, but are not limited to, motivational interviewing, harm reduction, seeking safety, cognitive behavioral therapy, and trauma-focused cognitive processing therapy.

(i) Ensure that no person is excluded from services based on immigration status. *(Added by Stats.2017, c. 587 (A.B.1384), § 3, eff. Jan. 1, 2018.)*

§ 13964. Restitution Fund; continuous appropriation; annual review; emergency awards

(a) Claims under this chapter shall be paid from the Restitution Fund.

(b) Notwithstanding Section 13340, except for funds to support trauma recovery center grants pursuant to Section 13963.1, the proceeds in the Restitution Fund are hereby continuously appropriated to the board, without regard to fiscal years, for the purposes of this chapter. However, the funds appropriated pursuant to this section for administrative costs of the board shall be subject to annual review through the State Budget process.

(c) A sum not to exceed 15 percent of the amount appropriated annually to pay claims pursuant to this chapter may be withdrawn from the Restitution Fund, to be used as a revolving fund by the board for the payment of emergency awards pursuant to Section 13961. *(Added by Stats.2002, c. 1141 (S.B.1423), § 2. Amended by Stats.2013, c. 28 (S.B.71), § 14, eff. June 27, 2013.)*

Cross References

Board defined for purposes of this Chapter, see Government Code § 13951.
Conservation work of persons committed to youth authority, see Welfare and Institutions Code § 1760.5.
Deductions from wages of persons committed to youth authority, see Welfare and Institutions Code § 1752.83.
False information to pawnbrokers, restitution, see Penal Code § 484.1.
Payment of restitution fine as condition of liberty from Youth Authority, see Welfare and Institutions Code § 1766.1.
Persons providing information leading to location of missing children, awards from Restitution Fund, see Government Code § 13974.1.
Probation, see Penal Code § 1203.

Research References

1 Witkin California Criminal Law 4th Introduction to Crimes § 121 (2021), Victims of Crime.
3 Witkin, California Criminal Law 4th Punishment § 73 (2021), Profits from Crime.

§ 13965. Liability for overpayments; exception

(a) Any recipient of an overpayment pursuant to this chapter is liable to repay the board that amount unless both of the following facts exist:

(1) The overpayment was not due to fraud, misrepresentation, or willful nondisclosure on the part of the recipient.

(2) The overpayment was received without fault on the part of the recipient, and its recovery would be against equity and good conscience.

(b) All actions to collect overpayments shall commence within seven years from the date of the overpayment. However, an action to collect an overpayment due to fraud, misrepresentation, or willful nondisclosure by the recipient may be commenced at any time.

(c) Any recipient of an overpayment is authorized to contest the staff recommendation of an overpayment pursuant to the hearing procedures in Section 13959. If a final determination is made by the board that an overpayment exists, the board may collect the overpayment in any manner prescribed by law.

(d) All overpayments exceeding two thousand dollars ($2,000) shall be reported to the Legislature pursuant to Section 13928 and the relief from liability described in subdivision (a) shall be subject to legislative approval. *(Added by Stats.2002, c. 1141 (S.B.1423), § 2. Amended by Stats.2015, c. 569 (A.B.1140), § 11, eff. Jan. 1, 2016.)*

Research References

1 Witkin California Criminal Law 4th Introduction to Crimes § 121 (2021), Victims of Crime.

§ 13966. Restitution Fund; recovery of monies owed to fund

The board may do all of the following to recover moneys owed to the Restitution Fund:

(a) File a civil action against the liable person for the recovery of the amount of moneys owed. This action shall be filed within one year of either of the following events, or within three years of either of the following events if the liable person was overpaid benefits due to fraud, misrepresentation, or nondisclosure as described in paragraph (1) of subdivision (a) of Section 13965:

(1) The mailing or personal service of the notice of the moneys owed if the person affected does not file an appeal with the board or person designated by the board.

(2) The mailing of the decision of the board if the person affected does not initiate a further appeal.

(b)(1) Initiate proceedings for a summary judgment against the liable person. However, this subdivision shall apply only where the board has found, pursuant to Section 13965, that the overpayment may not be waived. The board may, not later than three years after the overpayment became final, file with the clerk of the proper court in the county from which the overpayment of benefits was paid or in the county in which the claimant resides, a certificate containing all of the following:

(A) The amount due, plus interest from the date that the initial determination of the moneys owed was made.

(B) A statement that the board has complied with all the provisions of this chapter prior to the filing of the certificate.

Government

(C) A request that the judgment be entered against the liable person in the amount set forth in the certificate.

(2) The clerk, immediately upon the filing of the certificate, shall enter a judgment for the state against the liable person in the amount set forth in the certificate. *(Added by Stats.2002, c. 1141 (S.B.1423), § 2.)*

Cross References

Board defined for purposes of this Chapter, see Government Code § 13951.

HEALTH AND SAFETY CODE

Division 10

UNIFORM CONTROLLED SUBSTANCES ACT

CHAPTER 1. GENERAL PROVISIONS AND DEFINITIONS

§ 11000. Short title

This division shall be known as the "California Uniform Controlled Substances Act." *(Added by Stats.1972, c. 1407, p. 2987, § 3.)*

Cross References

Healing arts, optometry, admission to practice, practice of optometry, permitted activities, see Business and Professions Code § 3041.

Research References

2 Witkin, California Criminal Law 4th Crimes Against Public Peace and Welfare § 84 (2021), California Statutes and General Law.
2 Witkin, California Criminal Law 4th Crimes Against Public Peace and Welfare § 155 (2021), Drug Paraphernalia.
2 Witkin, California Criminal Law 4th Crimes Against Public Peace and Welfare § 159 (2021), Money Associated With Unlawful Transactions.
2 Witkin, California Criminal Law 4th Crimes Against Public Peace and Welfare § 176 (2021), In General.
1 Witkin California Criminal Law 4th Defenses § 120 (2021), Civil Forfeiture.
1 Witkin California Criminal Law 4th Defenses § 277 (2021), Narcotics Offenses.
1 Witkin California Criminal Law 4th Introduction to Crimes § 10 (2021), Penal Code and Uniform Laws.
1 Witkin California Criminal Law 4th Introduction to Crimes § 46 (2021), Other Rules.
3 Witkin, California Criminal Law 4th Punishment § 196 (2021), In General.
3 Witkin, California Criminal Law 4th Punishment § 211 (2021), Discretionary Suspension.
3 Witkin, California Criminal Law 4th Punishment § 721 (2021), In General.
3 Witkin, California Criminal Law 4th Punishment § 725 (2021), Where Minor was Not Convicted.

§ 11001. Application of definitions

Unless the context otherwise requires, the definitions in this chapter govern the construction of this division. *(Added by Stats. 1972, c. 1407, p. 2987, § 3.)*

Cross References

Minors using narcotics or restricted dangerous drugs, see Welfare and Institutions Code § 359.

§ 11002. Administer

"Administer" means the direct application of a controlled substance, whether by injection, inhalation, ingestion, or any other means, to the body of a patient for his immediate needs or to the body of a research subject by any of the following:

(a) A practitioner or, in his presence, by his authorized agent.

(b) The patient or research subject at the direction and in the presence of the practitioner. *(Added by Stats.1972, c. 1407, p. 2987, § 3.)*

Cross References

Agent defined for purposes of this Division, see Health and Safety Code § 11003.
Children who are exposed to alcohol or drugs or who are HIV positive, placement, see Welfare and Institutions Code § 16525.30.
Controlled substance defined for purposes of this Division, see Health and Safety Code § 11007.
Practitioner defined for purposes of this Division, see Health and Safety Code § 11026.

Research References

California Jury Instructions - Criminal 12.07, Administer—Defined.
California Jury Instructions - Criminal 17.26.13, Administering of Controlled Substance to Victim.

§ 11003. Agent

"Agent" means an authorized person who acts on behalf of or at the direction of a manufacturer, distributor, or dispenser. It does not include a common or contract carrier, public warehouseman, or employee of the carrier or warehouseman. *(Added by Stats.1972, c. 1407, p. 2988, § 3.)*

Cross References

Dispenser defined for purposes of this Division, see Health and Safety Code § 11011.
Distributor defined for purposes of this Division, see Health and Safety Code § 11013.
Manufacturer defined for purposes of this Division, see Health and Safety Code § 11017.
Person defined for purposes of this Division, see Health and Safety Code § 11022.

§ 11004. Attorney general

"Attorney General" means the Attorney General of the State of California. *(Added by Stats.1972, c. 1407, p. 2988, § 3.)*

Cross References

Attorney General, generally, see Government Code § 12500 et seq.

§ 11005. Board of pharmacy

"Board of Pharmacy" means the California State Board of Pharmacy. *(Added by Stats.1972, c. 1407, p. 2988, § 3.)*

Cross References

State board of pharmacy, see Business and Professions Code § 4001 et seq.

§ 11006.5. Concentrated cannabis

"Concentrated cannabis" means the separated resin, whether crude or purified, obtained from cannabis. *(Added by Stats.1975, c. 248, p. 641, § 1. Amended by Stats.2017, c. 27 (S.B.94), § 113, eff. June 27, 2017.)*

Cross References

Marijuana defined for purposes of this Division, see Health and Safety Code § 11018.
Rules of the road, public offenses, offenses involving alcohol and drugs, possession of open container containing alcoholic beverage or marijuana while driving a motor vehicle, see Vehicle Code § 23222.

Research References

California Jury Instructions - Criminal 12.20, Marijuana—Concentrated Cannabis—Unlawful Possession as Felony/Misdemeanor.
2 Witkin, California Criminal Law 4th Crimes Against Public Peace and Welfare § 91 (2021), Definition.

§ 11007. Controlled substance

"Controlled substance," unless otherwise specified, means a drug, substance, or immediate precursor which is listed in any schedule in Section 11054, 11055, 11056, 11057, or 11058. *(Added by Stats.1987, c. 1174, § 1, eff. Sept. 26, 1987.)*

Cross References

Children, delinquents and wards of the juvenile court, juvenile court law, wards and dependent children—records, school district police or security department, disclosure of juvenile criminal records, protection of vulnerable school staff and other students, see Welfare and Institutions Code § 828.1.
Drug defined for purposes of this Division, see Health and Safety Code § 11014.
Liability for compensation, conditions of compensation, credits against judgment or settlement, see Labor Code § 3600.
Of crimes and punishments, miscellaneous crimes, schools, drug offenders, presence on school grounds, see Penal Code § 626.85.

Research References

2 Witkin, California Criminal Law 4th Crimes Against Public Peace and Welfare § 58 (2021), Drug Offenders.
2 Witkin, California Criminal Law 4th Crimes Against Public Peace and Welfare § 86 (2021), In General.

§ 11008. Customs broker

"Customs broker" means a person in this state who is authorized to act as a broker for any of the following:

(a) A person in this state who is licensed to sell, distribute, or otherwise possess any controlled substance.

(b) A person in any other state who ships any controlled substance into this state.

(c) A person in this state or any other state who ships or transfers any controlled substance through this state. *(Added by Stats.1972, c. 1407, p. 2988, § 3.)*

Cross References

Controlled substance defined for purposes of this Division, see Health and Safety Code § 11007.
Distribute defined for purposes of this Division, see Health and Safety Code § 11012.
Person defined for purposes of this Division, see Health and Safety Code § 11022.

§ 11009. Deliver or delivery

"Deliver" or "delivery" means the actual, constructive, or attempted transfer from one person to another of a controlled substance, whether or not there is an agency relationship. *(Added by Stats.1972, c. 1407, p. 2988, § 3.)*

Cross References

Controlled substance defined for purposes of this Division, see Health and Safety Code § 11007.
Person defined for purposes of this Division, see Health and Safety Code § 11022.

§ 11010. Dispense

"Dispense" means to deliver a controlled substance to an ultimate user or research subject by or pursuant to the lawful order of a practitioner, including the prescribing, furnishing, packaging, labeling, or compounding necessary to prepare the substance for that delivery. *(Added by Stats.1972, c. 1407, p. 2987, § 3.)*

Cross References

Controlled substance defined for purposes of this Division, see Health and Safety Code § 11007.
Deliver or delivery defined for purposes of this Division, see Health and Safety Code § 11009.
Practitioner defined for purposes of this Division, see Health and Safety Code § 11026.
Ultimate user defined for purposes of this Division, see Health and Safety Code § 11030.

§ 11011. Dispenser

"Dispenser" means a practitioner who dispenses. *(Added by Stats.1972, c. 1407, p. 2988, § 3.)*

Cross References

Dispense defined for purposes of this Division, see Health and Safety Code § 11010.
Practitioner defined for purposes of this Division, see Health and Safety Code § 11026.

§ 11012. Distribute

"Distribute" means to deliver other than by administering or dispensing a controlled substance. *(Added by Stats.1972, c. 1407, p. 2988, § 3.)*

Cross References

Controlled substance defined for purposes of this Division, see Health and Safety Code § 11007.
Deliver or delivery defined for purposes of this Division, see Health and Safety Code § 11009.

§ 11013. Distributor

"Distributor" means a person who distributes. The term distributor also includes warehousemen handling or storing controlled substances and customs brokers. *(Added by Stats.1972, c. 1407, p. 2988, § 3.)*

Cross References

Controlled substance defined for purposes of this Division, see Health and Safety Code § 11007.
Customs broker defined for purposes of this Division, see Health and Safety Code § 11008.
Distribute defined for purposes of this Division, see Health and Safety Code § 11012.
Person defined for purposes of this Division, see Health and Safety Code § 11022.

§ 11014. Drug

"Drug" means (a) substances recognized as drugs in the official United States Pharmacopoeia, official Homeopathic Pharmacopoeia of the United States, or official National Formulary, or any supplement to any of them; (b) substances intended for use in the diagnosis, cure, mitigation, treatment, or prevention of disease in man or animals; (c) substances (other than food) intended to affect the structure or any function of the body of man or animals; and (d) substances intended for use as a component of any article specified in subdivision (a), (b), or (c) of this section. It does not include devices or their components, parts, or accessories. *(Added by Stats.1972, c. 1407, p. 2988, § 3.)*

Research References

2 Witkin, California Criminal Law 4th Crimes Against Public Peace and Welfare § 86 (2021), In General.

§ 11014.5. Drug paraphernalia

(a) "Drug paraphernalia" means all equipment, products and materials of any kind which are designed for use or marketed for use, in planting, propagating, cultivating, growing, harvesting, manufacturing, compounding, converting, producing, processing, preparing, testing, analyzing, packaging, repackaging, storing, containing, concealing, injecting, ingesting, inhaling, or otherwise introducing into the human body a controlled substance in violation of this division. It includes, but is not limited to:

(1) Kits designed for use or marketed for use in planting, propagating, cultivating, growing, or harvesting of any species of plant which is a controlled substance or from which a controlled substance can be derived.

(2) Kits designed for use or marketed for use in manufacturing, compounding, converting, producing, processing, or preparing controlled substances.

(3) Isomerization devices designed for use or marketed for use in increasing the potency of any species of plant which is a controlled substance.

(4) Testing equipment designed for use or marketed for use in identifying, or in analyzing the strength, effectiveness, or purity of controlled substances, except as otherwise provided in subdivision (d).

(5) Scales and balances designed for use or marketed for use in weighing or measuring controlled substances.

(6) Containers and other objects designed for use or marketed for use in storing or concealing controlled substances.

(7) Hypodermic syringes, needles, and other objects designed for use or marketed for use in parenterally injecting controlled substances into the human body.

(8) Objects designed for use or marketed for use in ingesting, inhaling, or otherwise introducing cannabis, cocaine, hashish, or hashish oil into the human body, such as:

(A) Carburetion tubes and devices.

(B) Smoking and carburetion masks.

(C) Roach clips, meaning objects used to hold burning material, such as a cannabis cigarette, that has become too small or too short to be held in the hand.

(D) Miniature cocaine spoons, and cocaine vials.

(E) Chamber pipes.

(F) Carburetor pipes.

(G) Electric pipes.

(H) Air-driven pipes.

(I) Chillums.

(J) Bongs.

(K) Ice pipes or chillers.

(b) For the purposes of this section, the phrase "marketed for use" means advertising, distributing, offering for sale, displaying for sale, or selling in a manner which promotes the use of equipment, products, or materials with controlled substances.

(c) In determining whether an object is drug paraphernalia, a court or other authority may consider, in addition to all other logically relevant factors, the following:

(1) Statements by an owner or by anyone in control of the object concerning its use.

(2) Instructions, oral or written, provided with the object concerning its use for ingesting, inhaling, or otherwise introducing a controlled substance into the human body.

(3) Descriptive materials accompanying the object which explain or depict its use.

(4) National and local advertising concerning its use.

(5) The manner in which the object is displayed for sale.

(6) Whether the owner, or anyone in control of the object, is a legitimate supplier of like or related items to the community, such as a licensed distributor or dealer of tobacco products.

(7) Expert testimony concerning its use.

(d) Notwithstanding paragraph (4) of subdivision (a), "drug paraphernalia" does not include any testing equipment designed, marketed, intended to be used, or used, to test a substance for the presence of fentanyl, ketamine, gamma hydroxybutyric acid, or any analog of fentanyl.

(e) If any provision of this section or the application thereof to any person or circumstance is held invalid, it is the intent of the Legislature that the invalidity shall not affect other provisions or applications of the section which can be given effect without the invalid provision or application and to this end the provisions of this section are severable. *(Added by Stats.1982, c. 1278, p. 4725, § 1. Amended by Stats.2017, c. 27 (S.B.94), § 114, eff. June 27, 2017; Stats.2022, c. 201 (A.B.1598), § 1, eff. Jan. 1, 2023.)*

Cross References

Controlled substance defined for purposes of this Division, see Health and Safety Code § 11007.
Distributor defined for purposes of this Division, see Health and Safety Code § 11013.
Elementary and secondary education, instruction and services, pupils, pupil rights and responsibilities, suspension or expulsion, grounds for suspension or expulsion, legislative intent, see Education Code § 48900.
Marijuana defined for purposes of this Division, see Health and Safety Code § 11018.
Person defined for purposes of this Division, see Health and Safety Code § 11022.

Research References

2 Witkin, California Criminal Law 4th Crimes Against Public Peace and Welfare § 155 (2021), Drug Paraphernalia.

§ 11015. Federal bureau

"Federal bureau" means the Drug Enforcement Administration of the United States Department of Justice, or its successor agency.

(Added by Stats.1972, c. 1407, p. 2988, § 3. Amended by Stats.1992, c. 978 (S.B.1822), § 2.)

§ 11016. Furnish

"Furnish" has the same meaning as provided in Section 4048.5 of the Business and Professions Code. *(Added by Stats.1972, c. 1407, p. 2989, § 3.)*

§ 11017. Manufacturer

"Manufacturer" has the same meaning as provided in Section 4034 of the Business and Professions Code. *(Added by Stats.1972, c. 1407, p. 2987, § 3.)*

§ 11018. Cannabis

"Cannabis" means all parts of the plant Cannabis sativa L., whether growing or not; the seeds thereof; the resin extracted from any part of the plant; and every compound, manufacture, salt, derivative, mixture, or preparation of the plant, its seeds or resin. It does not include either of the following:

(a) Industrial hemp, as defined in Section 11018.5.

(b) The weight of any other ingredient combined with cannabis to prepare topical or oral administrations, food, drink, or other product. *(Added by Stats.1972, c. 1407, p. 2989, § 3. Amended by Initiative Measure (Prop. 64, § 4.1, approved Nov. 8, 2016, eff. Nov. 9, 2016); Stats.2017, c. 27 (S.B.94), § 115, eff. June 27, 2017.)*

Research References

California Jury Instructions - Criminal 12.24.4, Lawful Uses—Definitions.
California Jury Instructions - Criminal 12.31, "Marijuana"—Defined.
California Jury Instructions - Criminal 16.030, Concentrated Cannabis or Marijuana—Illegal Possession.
2 Witkin, California Criminal Law 4th Crimes Against Public Peace and Welfare § 91 (2021), Definition.

§ 11018.1. Cannabis products

"Cannabis products" means cannabis that has undergone a process whereby the plant material has been transformed into a concentrate, including, but not limited to, concentrated cannabis, or an edible or topical product containing cannabis or concentrated cannabis and other ingredients. *(Added by Initiative Measure (Prop. 64, § 4.2, approved Nov. 8, 2016, eff. Nov. 9, 2016). Amended by Stats.2017, c. 27 (S.B.94), § 116, eff. June 27, 2017.)*

Research References

California Jury Instructions - Criminal 12.24.4, Lawful Uses—Definitions.
2 Witkin, California Criminal Law 4th Crimes Against Public Peace and Welfare § 91 (2021), Definition.
2 Witkin, California Criminal Law 4th Crimes Against Public Peace and Welfare § 303 (2021), Drinking or Possessing Alcohol or Marijuana.

§ 11018.2. Cannabis accessories

"Cannabis accessories" means any equipment, products or materials of any kind which are used, intended for use, or designed for use in planting, propagating, cultivating, growing, harvesting, manufacturing, compounding, converting, producing, processing, preparing, testing, analyzing, packaging, repackaging, storing, smoking, vaporizing, or containing cannabis, or for ingesting, inhaling, or otherwise introducing cannabis or cannabis products into the human body. *(Added by Initiative Measure (Prop. 64, § 4.3, approved Nov. 8, 2016, eff. Nov. 9, 2016). Amended by Stats.2017, c. 27 (S.B.94), § 117, eff. June 27, 2017.)*

Research References

California Jury Instructions - Criminal 12.24.4, Lawful Uses—Definitions.
2 Witkin, California Criminal Law 4th Crimes Against Public Peace and Welfare § 91 (2021), Definition.

§ 11018.5. Industrial hemp; hemp

(a) "Industrial hemp" or "hemp" means an agricultural product, whether growing or not, that is limited to types of the plant Cannabis sativa L. and any part of that plant, including the seeds of the plant and all derivatives, extracts, the resin extracted from any part of the plant, cannabinoids, isomers, acids, salts, and salts of isomers, with a delta–9 tetrahydrocannabinol concentration of no more than 0.3 percent on a dry weight basis.

(b) Industrial hemp shall not be subject to the provisions of this division or of Division 10 (commencing with Section 26000) of the Business and Professions Code, but instead shall be regulated by the Department of Food and Agriculture in accordance with the provisions of Division 24 (commencing with Section 81000) of the Food and Agricultural Code, inclusive. *(Added by Stats.2013, c. 398 (S.B.566), § 6, operative Jan. 1, 2017. Amended by Initiative Measure (Prop. 64, § 9.1, approved Nov. 8, 2016, eff. Nov. 9, 2016); Stats.2017, c. 27 (S.B.94), § 118, eff. June 27, 2017; Stats.2018, c. 986 (S.B.1409), § 8, eff. Jan. 1, 2019; Stats.2021, c. 576 (A.B.45), § 2, eff. Oct. 6, 2021.)*

Cross References

Cannabidiol products, compliance with federal law deemed to be compliance with state law, exception for products regulated pursuant to this section, see Health and Safety Code § 11150.2.

Research References

California Jury Instructions - Criminal 12.24.4, Lawful Uses—Definitions.

§ 11019. Narcotic drug

"Narcotic drug" means any of the following, whether produced directly or indirectly by extraction from substances of vegetable origin, or independently by means of chemical synthesis, or by a combination of extraction and chemical synthesis:

(a) Opium and opiate, and any salt, compound, derivative, or preparation of opium or opiate.

(b) Any salt, compound, isomer, or derivative, whether natural or synthetic, of the substances referred to in subdivision (a), but not including the isoquinoline alkaloids of opium.

(c) Opium poppy and poppy straw.

(d) Coca leaves and any salt, compound, derivative, or preparation of coca leaves, but not including decocainized coca leaves or extractions of coca leaves which do not contain cocaine or ecgonine.

(e) Cocaine, whether natural or synthetic, or any salt, isomer, derivative, or preparation thereof.

(f) Ecgonine, whether natural or synthetic, or any salt, isomer, derivative, or preparation thereof.

(g) Acetylfentanyl, the thiophene analog thereof, derivatives of either, and any salt, compound, isomer, or preparation of acetylfentanyl or the thiophene analog thereof. *(Added by Stats.1972, c. 1407, p. 2989, § 3. Amended by Stats.1985, c. 21, § 1, eff. April 2, 1985; Stats.1985, c. 1098, § 1, eff. Sept. 27, 1985.)*

Cross References

Isomer defined for purposes of this Division, see Health and Safety Code § 11033.
Opiate defined for purposes of this Division, see Health and Safety Code § 11020.
Opium poppy defined for purposes of this Division, see Health and Safety Code § 11021.

Poppy straw defined for purposes of this Division, see Health and Safety Code § 11025.

Research References

California Jury Instructions - Criminal 12.05, Narcotics—Forgery of Prescription.
California Jury Instructions - Criminal 12.20, Marijuana—Concentrated Cannabis—Unlawful Possession as Felony/Misdemeanor.
2 Witkin, California Criminal Law 4th Crimes Against Public Peace and Welfare § 87 (2021), Substances Formerly Classified as Narcotics.
2 Witkin, California Criminal Law 4th Crimes Against Public Peace and Welfare § 176 (2021), In General.

§ 11020. Opiate

"Opiate" means any substance having an addiction-forming or addiction-sustaining liability similar to morphine or being capable of conversion into a drug having addiction-forming or addiction-sustaining liability. It does not include, unless specifically designated as controlled under Chapter 2 (commencing with Section 11053) of this division, the dextrorotatory isomer of 3-methoxy-n-methylmorphinan and its salts (dextromethorphan). It does include its racemic and levorotatory forms. *(Added by Stats.1972, c. 1407, p. 2989, § 3.)*

Cross References

Drug defined for purposes of this Division, see Health and Safety Code § 11014.
Isomer defined for purposes of this Division, see Health and Safety Code § 11033.

§ 11021. Opium poppy

"Opium poppy" means the plant of the species Papaver somniferum L., except its seeds. *(Added by Stats.1972, c. 1407, p. 2989, § 3.)*

§ 11022. Person

"Person" means individual, corporation, government or governmental subdivision or agency, business trust, estate, trust, partnership, limited liability company, or association, or any other legal entity. *(Added by Stats.1972, c. 1407, p. 2989, § 3. Amended by Stats.1994, c. 1010 (S.B.2053), § 159.)*

§ 11023. Pharmacy

"Pharmacy" has the same meaning as provided in Section 4035 of the Business and Professions Code. *(Added by Stats.1972, c. 1407, p. 2989, § 3.)*

§ 11024. Physician, dentist, podiatrist, pharmacist, veterinarian, optometrist

"Physician," "dentist," "podiatrist," "pharmacist," "veterinarian," and "optometrist" means persons who are licensed to practice their respective professions in this state. *(Added by Stats.1972, c. 1407, p. 2989, § 3. Amended by Stats.2000, c. 676 (S.B.929), § 6.)*

Cross References

Person defined for purposes of this Division, see Health and Safety Code § 11022.

§ 11025. Poppy straw

"Poppy straw" means all parts, except the seeds, of the opium poppy, after mowing. *(Added by Stats.1972, c. 1407, p. 2990, § 3.)*

Cross References

Opium poppy defined for purposes of this Division, see Health and Safety Code § 11021.

§ 11026. Practitioner

"Practitioner" means any of the following:

(a) A physician, dentist, veterinarian, podiatrist, or pharmacist acting within the scope of a project authorized under Article 1 (commencing with Section 128125) of Chapter 3 of Part 3 of Division 107, a registered nurse acting within the scope of a project authorized under Article 1 (commencing with Section 128125) of Chapter 3 of Part 3 of Division 107, a certified nurse-midwife acting within the scope of Section 2746.51 of the Business and Professions Code, a nurse practitioner acting within the scope of Section 2836.1 of the Business and Professions Code, or a physician assistant acting within the scope of a project authorized under Article 1 (commencing with Section 128125) of Chapter 3 of Part 3 of Division 107 or Section 3502.1 of the Business and Professions Code, or an optometrist acting within the scope of Section 3041 of the Business and Professions Code.

(b) A pharmacy, hospital, or other institution licensed, registered, or otherwise permitted to distribute, dispense, conduct research with respect to, or to administer, a controlled substance in the course of professional practice or research in this state.

(c) A scientific investigator, or other person licensed, registered, or otherwise permitted, to distribute, dispense, conduct research with respect to, or administer, a controlled substance in the course of professional practice or research in this state. *(Added by Stats.1972, c. 1407, p. 2990, § 3. Amended by Stats.1976, c. 896, p. 2056, § 1; Stats.1977, c. 843, p. 2532, § 16; Stats.1986, c. 1042, § 1, eff. Sept. 23, 1986; Stats.1996, c. 1023 (S.B.1497), § 196, eff. Sept. 29, 1996; Stats.1999, c. 749 (S.B.816), § 7; Stats.2000, c. 676 (S.B.929), § 7; Stats.2001, c. 289 (S.B.298), § 10.)*

Cross References

Administer defined for purposes of this Division, see Health and Safety Code § 11002.
Controlled substance defined for purposes of this Division, see Health and Safety Code § 11007.
Dispense defined for purposes of this Division, see Health and Safety Code § 11010.
Distribute defined for purposes of this Division, see Health and Safety Code § 11012.
Imitation controlled substances, lawful manufacture, distribution, or possession, see Health and Safety Code § 109585.
Person defined for purposes of this Division, see Health and Safety Code § 11022.
Pharmacy defined for purposes of this Division, see Health and Safety Code § 11023.
Physician, dentist, podiatrist, pharmacist, veterinarian, and optometrist defined for purposes of this Division, see Health and Safety Code § 11024.
Prevention of crimes and apprehension of criminals, investigation and control of crimes and criminals, prevention and abatement of unlawful activities, the Hertzberg–Alarcon California Prevention of Terrorism Act, possession of restricted biological agents, penalties, exemptions, see Penal Code § 11419.

Research References

2 Witkin, California Criminal Law 4th Crimes Against Public Peace and Welfare § 61 (2021), Terrorism by Weapons of Mass Destruction.

§ 11027. Prescription; electronic transmission prescription

(a) "Prescription" means an oral order or electronic transmission prescription for a controlled substance given individually for the person(s) for whom prescribed, directly from the prescriber to the furnisher or indirectly by means of a written order of the prescriber.

(b) "Electronic transmission prescription" includes both image and data prescriptions. "Electronic image transmission prescription" is any prescription order for which a facsimile of the order is received by a pharmacy from a licensed prescriber. "Electronic data transmission prescription" is any prescription order, other than an electronic image transmission prescription, which is electronically transmitted from a licensed prescriber to a pharmacy. *(Added by Stats.1972, c. 1407, p. 2990, § 3. Amended by Stats.1976, c. 896, p. 2056, § 2; Stats.1979, c. 634, p. 1960, § 3; Stats.1994, c. 26 (A.B.1807), § 241, eff. March 30, 1994.)*

Cross References

Controlled substance defined for purposes of this Division, see Health and Safety Code § 11007.
Person defined for purposes of this Division, see Health and Safety Code § 11022.
Pharmacy defined for purposes of this Division, see Health and Safety Code § 11023.

Research References

California Jury Instructions - Criminal 12.30.2, Controlled Substance (Sched. I–V)—Burden of Proof as to Prescription.
2 Witkin, California Criminal Law 4th Crimes Against Public Peace and Welfare § 152 (2021), In General.

§ 11029. Production

"Production" includes the manufacture, planting, cultivation, growing, or harvesting of a controlled substance. *(Added by Stats. 1972, c. 1407, p. 2990, § 3.)*

Cross References

Controlled substance defined for purposes of this Division, see Health and Safety Code § 11007.

§ 11029.5. "Security printer" defined

"Security printer" means a person approved to produce controlled substance prescription forms pursuant to Section 11161.5. *(Added by Stats.2003, c. 406 (S.B.151), § 2.)*

Cross References

Controlled substance defined for purposes of this Division, see Health and Safety Code § 11007.
Person defined for purposes of this Division, see Health and Safety Code § 11022.
Prescription or electronic transmission prescription defined for purposes of this Division, see Health and Safety Code § 11027.

§ 11030. Ultimate user

"Ultimate user" means a person who lawfully possesses a controlled substance for his own use or for the use of a member of his household or for administering to an animal owned by him or by a member of his household. *(Added by Stats.1972, c. 1407, p. 2990, § 3.)*

Cross References

Controlled substance defined for purposes of this Division, see Health and Safety Code § 11007.
Person defined for purposes of this Division, see Health and Safety Code § 11022.

§ 11031. Wholesaler

"Wholesaler" has the same meaning as provided in Section 4038 of the Business and Professions Code. *(Added by Stats.1972, c. 1407, p. 2990, § 3.)*

§ 11032. Narcotics, restricted dangerous drugs and marijuana; construction of terms used outside division

If reference is made to the term "narcotics" in any law not in this division, unless otherwise expressly provided, it means those controlled substances classified in Schedules I and II, as defined in this division. If reference is made to "restricted dangerous drugs" not in this division, unless otherwise expressly provided, it means those controlled substances classified in Schedules III and IV. If reference is made to the term "marijuana" in any law not in this division, unless otherwise expressly provided, it means cannabis as defined in this division. *(Added by Stats.1972, c. 1407, p. 2990, § 3. Amended by Stats.2017, c. 27 (S.B.94), § 119, eff. June 27, 2017.)*

Cross References

Controlled substance defined for purposes of this Division, see Health and Safety Code § 11007.
Courses on drug education required for accreditation of teacher education institution, see Education Code § 51261.
Elementary and secondary education, instruction and services,
General instructional programs, required courses of study, general provisions, instruction on alcohol, narcotics and restricted dangerous drugs, see Education Code § 51203.
Instructional materials and testing, instructional materials, requirements, materials, ecological systems and their protection, use of tobacco, alcohol, drugs, and other dangerous substances, see Education Code § 60041.
Marijuana defined for purposes of this Division, see Health and Safety Code § 11018.
Minors using narcotics or restricted dangerous drugs, see Welfare and Institutions Code § 359.

§ 11033. Isomer

As used in this division, except as otherwise defined, the term "isomer" includes optical and geometrical (diastereomeric) isomers. *(Added by Stats.1985, c. 21, § 2, eff. April 2, 1985.)*

CHAPTER 2. STANDARDS AND SCHEDULES

Section

§ 11053. Alternative names

The controlled substances listed or to be listed in the schedules in this chapter are included by whatever official, common, usual, chemical, or trade name designated. *(Added by Stats.1972, c. 1407, p. 2990, § 3.)*

Cross References

Children, delinquents and wards of the juvenile court, juvenile court law, wards—judgments and orders, juvenile court law,
Judgment, see Welfare and Institutions Code § 725.
Order for care, supervision, custody, maintenance and support of ward of court, see Welfare and Institutions Code § 727.
Controlled substance defined for purposes of this Division, see Health and Safety Code § 11007.
Imitation Controlled Substances Act, see Health and Safety Code § 109525 et seq.
Of criminal procedure, of judgment and execution, the judgment, see Penal Code § 1203.1ab.

Research References

2 Witkin, California Criminal Law 4th Crimes Against Public Peace and Welfare § 84 (2021), California Statutes and General Law.

§ 11054. Schedule I; substances included

(a) The controlled substances listed in this section are included in Schedule I.

(b) Opiates. Unless specifically excepted or unless listed in another schedule, any of the following opiates, including their isomers, esters, ethers, salts, and salts of isomers, esters, and ethers whenever the existence of those isomers, esters, ethers, and salts is possible within the specific chemical designation:

(1) Acetylmethadol.

(2) Allylprodine.

(3) Alphacetylmethadol (except levoalphacetylmethadol, also known as levo-alpha- acetylmethadol, levomethadyl acetate, or LAAM).

(4) Alphameprodine.
(5) Alphamethadol.
(6) Benzethidine.
(7) Betacetylmethadol.
(8) Betameprodine.
(9) Betamethadol.
(10) Betaprodine.
(11) Clonitazene.
(12) Dextromoramide.
(13) Diampromide.
(14) Diethylthiambutene.
(15) Difenoxin.
(16) Dimenoxadol.
(17) Dimepheptanol.
(18) Dimethylthiambutene.
(19) Dioxaphetyl butyrate.
(20) Dipipanone.
(21) Ethylmethylthiambutene.
(22) Etonitazene.
(23) Etoxeridine.
(24) Furethidine.
(25) Hydroxypethidine.
(26) Ketobemidone.
(27) Levomoramide.
(28) Levophenacylmorphan.
(29) Morpheridine.
(30) Noracymethadol.
(31) Norlevorphanol.
(32) Normethadone.
(33) Norpipanone.
(34) Phenadoxone.
(35) Phenampromide.
(36) Phenomorphan.
(37) Phenoperidine.
(38) Piritramide.
(39) Proheptazine.
(40) Properidine.
(41) Propiram.
(42) Racemoramide.
(43) Tilidine.
(44) Trimeperidine.

(45) Any substance which contains any quantity of acetylfentanyl (N–[1–phenethyl–4–piperidinyl] acetanilide) or a derivative thereof.

(46) Any substance which contains any quantity of the thiophene analog of acetylfentanyl (N–[1–[2–(2–thienyl)ethyl]–4–piperidinyl] acetanilide) or a derivative thereof.

(47) 1–Methyl–4–Phenyl–4–Propionoxypiperidine (MPPP).

(48) 1–(2–Phenethyl)–4–Phenyl–4–Acetyloxypiperidine (PEPAP).

(c) Opium derivatives. Unless specifically excepted or unless listed in another schedule, any of the following opium derivatives, its salts, isomers, and salts of isomers whenever the existence of those salts, isomers, and salts of isomers is possible within the specific chemical designation:

(1) Acetorphine.
(2) Acetyldihydrocodeine.
(3) Benzylmorphine.
(4) Codeine methylbromide.
(5) Codeine–N–Oxide.
(6) Cyprenorphine.
(7) Desomorphine.
(8) Dihydromorphine.
(9) Drotebanol.
(10) Etorphine (except hydrochloride salt).
(11) Heroin.
(12) Hydromorphinol.
(13) Methyldesorphine.
(14) Methyldihydromorphine.
(15) Morphine methylbromide.
(16) Morphine methylsulfonate.
(17) Morphine–N–Oxide.
(18) Myrophine.
(19) Nicocodeine.
(20) Nicomorphine.
(21) Normorphine.
(22) Pholcodine.
(23) Thebacon.

(d) Hallucinogenic substances. Unless specifically excepted or unless listed in another schedule, any material, compound, mixture, or preparation, which contains any quantity of the following hallucinogenic substances, or which contains any of its salts, isomers, and salts of isomers whenever the existence of those salts, isomers, and salts of isomers is possible within the specific chemical designation (for purposes of this subdivision only, the term "isomer" includes the optical, position, and geometric isomers):

(1) 4–bromo–2,5–dimethoxy–amphetamine—Some trade or other names: 4–bromo–2,5–dimethoxy–alpha–methylphenethylamine; 4–bromo–2,5–DMA.

(2) 2,5–dimethoxyamphetamine—Some trade or other names: 2,5–dimethoxy–alpha–methylphenethylamine; 2,5–DMA.

(3) 4–methoxyamphetamine—Some trade or other names: 4–methoxy–alpha–methylphenethylamine, paramethoxyamphetamine, PMA.

(4) 5–methoxy–3,4–methylenedioxy–amphetamine.

(5) 4–methyl–2,5–dimethoxy–amphetamine—Some trade or other names: 4–methyl–2,5–dimethoxy–alpha–methylphenethylamine; "DOM"; and "STP."

(6) 3,4–methylenedioxy amphetamine.

(7) 3,4,5–trimethoxy amphetamine.

(8) Bufotenine—Some trade or other names: 3–(beta–dimethylaminoethyl)–5–hydroxyindole; 3–(2–dimethylaminoethyl)–5 indolol; N,N–dimethylserolonin, 5–hydroxy–N,N–dimethyltryptamine; mappine.

(9) Diethyltryptamine—Some trade or other names: N,N–Diethyltryptamine; DET.

(10) Dimethyltryptamine—Some trade or other names: DMT.

(11) Ibogaine—Some trade or other names: 7–Ethyl–6,6beta, 7,8,9,10,12,13–octahydro–2–methoxy–6,9–methano–5H–pyrido [1',2':1,2] azepino [5,4–b] indole; Tabernantheiboga.

(12) Lysergic acid diethylamide.

(13) Cannabis.

(14) Mescaline.

(15) Peyote—Meaning all parts of the plant presently classified botanically as Lophophora williamsii Lemaire, whether growing or not, the seeds thereof, any extract from any part of the plant, and every compound, manufacture, salts, derivative, mixture, or preparation of the plant, its seeds or extracts (interprets 21 U.S.C. Sec. 812(c), Schedule 1(c)(12)).

(16) N–ethyl–3–piperidyl benzilate.

(17) N–methyl–3–piperidyl benzilate.

(18) Psilocybin.

(19) Psilocyn.

(20) Tetrahydrocannabinols. Synthetic equivalents of the substances contained in the plant, or in the resinous extractives of Cannabis, sp. and/or synthetic substances, derivatives, and their isomers with similar chemical structure and pharmacological activity such as the following: delta 1 cis or trans tetrahydrocannabinol, and their optical isomers; delta 6 cis or trans tetrahydrocannabinol, and their optical isomers; delta 3,4 cis or trans tetrahydrocannabinol, and its optical isomers.

Because nomenclature of these substances is not internationally standardized, compounds of these structures, regardless of numerical designation of atomic positions covered.

(21) Ethylamine analog of phencyclidine—Some trade or other names: N–ethyl–1–phenylcyclohexylamine, (1–phenylcyclohexyl) ethylamine, N–(1–phenylcyclohexyl) ethylamine, cyclohexamine, PCE.

(22) Pyrrolidine analog of phencyclidine—Some trade or other names: 1–(1–phenylcyclohexyl)–pyrrolidine, PCP, PHP.

(23) Thiophene analog of phencyclidine—Some trade or other names: 1–[1–(2 thienyl)–cyclohexyl]–piperidine, 2–thienyl analog of phencyclidine, TPCP, TCP.

(e) Depressants. Unless specifically excepted or unless listed in another schedule, any material, compound, mixture, or preparation which contains any quantity of the following substances having a depressant effect on the central nervous system, including its salts, isomers, and salts of isomers whenever the existence of those salts, isomers, and salts of isomers is possible within the specific chemical designation:

(1) Mecloqualone.

(2) Methaqualone.

(3) Gamma hydroxybutyric acid (also known by other names such as GHB; gamma hydroxy butyrate; 4–hydroxybutyrate; 4–hydroxybutanoic acid; sodium oxybate; sodium oxybutyrate), including its immediate precursors, isomers, esters, ethers, salts, and salts of isomers, esters, and ethers, including, but not limited to, gammabutyrolactone, for which an application has not been approved under Section 505 of the Federal Food, Drug, and Cosmetic Act (21 U.S.C. Sec. 355).

(f) Unless specifically excepted or unless listed in another schedule, any material, compound, mixture, or preparation which contains any quantity of the following substances having a stimulant effect on the central nervous system, including its isomers:

(1) Cocaine base.

(2) Fenethylline, including its salts.

(3) N–Ethylamphetamine, including its salts. *(Added by Stats. 1984, c. 1635, § 44.5. Amended by Stats.1985, c. 290, § 1; Stats.1985, c. 1098, § 1.2, eff. Sept. 27, 1985; Stats.1986, c. 1044, § 1; Stats.1987, c. 1174, § 1.5, eff. Sept. 26, 1987; Stats.1995, c. 455 (A.B.1113), § 3, eff. Sept. 5, 1995; Stats.2001, c. 841 (A.B.258), § 1; Stats.2002, c. 664 (A.B.3034), § 130; Stats.2017, c. 27 (S.B.94), § 120, eff. June 27, 2017.)*

Cross References

Administering controlled substance against victim's will, additional punishment, see Penal Code § 12022.75.

Analogs considered identical with controlled substance for punishment purposes, see Health and Safety Code §§ 11400, 11401.

Cocaine base, possession or purchase for sale, punishment, see Health and Safety Code § 11351.5.

Controlled substance defined for purposes of this Division, see Health and Safety Code § 11007.

Convicted persons, prohibition of probation or suspension of sentence for specified controlled substance violations, see Penal Code § 1203.07.

Criminal gang activity, sale or manufacture of controlled substances defined by this section, see Penal Code § 186.22.

Drug endangered children, law enforcement and social services agencies' response, development of policies and standards for narcotic crime scenes, see Penal Code § 13879.80 et seq.

Elementary and secondary education, instruction and services, pupils, pupil rights and responsibilities, suspension or expulsion, expulsion relating to controlled substances or alcohol, enrollment in drug rehabilitation program, see Education Code § 48916.5.

Illegal dumping of waste matter, impoundment, see Vehicle Code § 23112.7.

Isomer defined for purposes of this Division, see Health and Safety Code § 11033.

Local agencies, cities and counties, powers and duties common to cities and counties, massage, massage, grounds for denial of license, see Government Code § 51032.

Manufacturing, compounding, converting, producing, etc., terms of imprisonment, see Health and Safety Code § 11379.6.

Marijuana defined for purposes of this Division, see Health and Safety Code § 11018.

Of criminal procedure, of judgment and execution, the judgment, felony convictions for controlled substances violations involving cocaine, cocaine base, methamphetamine, phencyclidine or heroin, probation and sentencing, see Penal Code § 1203.073.

Opiate defined for purposes of this Division, see Health and Safety Code § 11020.

Persons illegally obtaining substances listed in this section, mandatory jail term, see Health and Safety Code § 11550.

Possession of moneys or negotiable instruments in excess of $100,000 involved in unlawful sale or purchase of a controlled substance listed in this section, punishment, see Health and Safety Code § 11370.6.

Probation requirements for nonviolent drug offenders, exception for possession of controlled substances while armed with a deadly weapon, see Penal Code § 1210.1.

Prohibition on possession of a firearm under the age of 30 for those convicted of or alleged to have committed certain offenses, controlled substances violations, punishment for violation, see Penal Code § 29820.

School district certificated employees, leave of absence when charged with offense under this section, see Education Code § 44940.

Spores or mycelium capable of producing mushrooms or other material containing controlled substances, cultivation for production prohibited, see Health and Safety Code § 11390.

Research References

California Jury Instructions - Criminal 12.00, Controlled Substance (Sched. I–V)—Unlawful Possession as Felony/Misdemeanor.

California Jury Instructions - Criminal 16.062, Misdemeanor Unlawful Possession of Controlled Substance.

2 Witkin, California Criminal Law 4th Crimes Against Public Peace and Welfare § 85 (2021), Uniform Controlled Substances Act.

2 Witkin, California Criminal Law 4th Crimes Against Public Peace and Welfare § 86 (2021), In General.

2 Witkin, California Criminal Law 4th Crimes Against Public Peace and Welfare § 87 (2021), Substances Formerly Classified as Narcotics.

2 Witkin, California Criminal Law 4th Crimes Against Public Peace and Welfare § 88 (2021), Substances Formerly Classified as Restricted Dangerous Drugs.

2 Witkin, California Criminal Law 4th Crimes Against Public Peace and Welfare § 89 (2021), Analogs of Controlled Substances.

2 Witkin, California Criminal Law 4th Crimes Against Public Peace and Welfare § 93 (2021), Specified Narcotics and Restricted Dangerous Drugs.

2 Witkin, California Criminal Law 4th Crimes Against Public Peace and Welfare § 97 (2021), In General.

2 Witkin, California Criminal Law 4th Crimes Against Public Peace and Welfare § 101 (2021), Possession for Sale.

2 Witkin, California Criminal Law 4th Crimes Against Public Peace and Welfare § 115 (2021), Statutory Prohibitions.
2 Witkin, California Criminal Law 4th Crimes Against Public Peace and Welfare § 124 (2021), Substances Formerly Classified as Narcotics.
2 Witkin, California Criminal Law 4th Crimes Against Public Peace and Welfare § 131 (2021), Cultivating, Harvesting, or Processing.
2 Witkin, California Criminal Law 4th Crimes Against Public Peace and Welfare § 164 (2021), In General.
3 Witkin, California Criminal Law 4th Punishment § 374 (2021), In General.
3 Witkin, California Criminal Law 4th Punishment § 375 (2021), Value or Amount.

§ 11055. Schedule II; substances included

(a) The controlled substances listed in this section are included in Schedule II.

(b) Any of the following substances, except those narcotic drugs listed in other schedules, whether produced directly or indirectly by extraction from substances of vegetable origin, or independently by means of chemical synthesis, or by combination of extraction and chemical synthesis:

(1) Opium, opiate, and any salt, compound, derivative, or preparation of opium or opiate, with the exception of naloxone hydrochloride (N–allyl–14–hydroxy–nordihydromorphinone hydrochloride), but including the following:

(A) Raw opium.

(B) Opium extracts.

(C) Opium fluid extracts.

(D) Powdered opium.

(E) Granulated opium.

(F) Tincture of opium.

(G) Codeine.

(H) Ethylmorphine.

(I)(i) Hydrocodone.

(ii) Hydrocodone combination products with not more than 300 milligrams of dihydrocodeinone per 100 milliliters or not more than 15 milligrams per dosage unit, with one or more active nonnarcotic ingredients in recognized therapeutic amounts.

(iii) Oral liquid preparations of dihydrocodeinone containing the above specified amounts that contain, as its nonnarcotic ingredients, two or more antihistamines in combination with each other.

(iv) Hydrocodone combination products with not more than 300 milligrams of dihydrocodeinone per 100 milliliters or not more than 15 milligrams per dosage unit, with a fourfold or greater quantity of an isoquinoline alkaloid of opium.

(J) Hydromorphone.

(K) Metopon.

(L) Morphine.

(M) Oxycodone.

(N) Oxymorphone.

(O) Thebaine.

(2) Any salt, compound, isomer, or derivative, whether natural or synthetic, of the substances referred to in paragraph (1), but not including the isoquinoline alkaloids of opium.

(3) Opium poppy and poppy straw.

(4) Coca leaves and any salt, compound, derivative, or preparation of coca leaves, but not including decocainized coca leaves or extractions which do not contain cocaine or ecgonine.

(5) Concentrate of poppy straw (the crude extract of poppy straw in either liquid, solid, or powder form which contains the phenanthrene alkaloids of the opium poppy).

(6) Cocaine, except as specified in Section 11054.

(7) Ecgonine, whether natural or synthetic, or any salt, isomer, derivative, or preparation thereof.

(c) Opiates. Unless specifically excepted or unless in another schedule, any of the following opiates, including its isomers, esters, ethers, salts, and salts of isomers, esters, and ethers whenever the existence of those isomers, esters, ethers, and salts is possible within the specific chemical designation, dextrorphan and levopropoxyphene excepted:

(1) Alfentanyl.

(2) Alphaprodine.

(3) Anileridine.

(4) Bezitramide.

(5) Bulk dextropropoxyphene (nondosage forms).

(6) Dihydrocodeine.

(7) Diphenoxylate.

(8) Fentanyl.

(9) Isomethadone.

(10) Levoalphacetylmethadol, also known as levo-alpha-acetylmethadol, levomethadyl acetate, or LAAM. This substance is authorized for the treatment of narcotic addicts under federal law (see Part 291 (commencing with Section 291.501) and Part 1308 (commencing with Section 1308.01) of Title 21 of the Code of Federal Regulations).

(11) Levomethorphan.

(12) Levorphanol.

(13) Metazocine.

(14) Methadone.

(15) Methadone–Intermediate, 4–cyano–2–dimethylamino–4, 4–diphenyl butane.

(16) Moramide–Intermediate, 2–methyl–3–morpholino–1, 1–diphenylpropane–carboxylic acid.

(17) Pethidine (meperidine).

(18) Pethidine–Intermediate–A, 4–cyano–1–methyl–4–phenylpiperidine.

(19) Pethidine–Intermediate–B, ethyl–4–phenylpiperidine–4–carboxylate.

(20) Pethidine–Intermediate–C, 1–methyl–4–phenylpiperidine–4–carboxylic acid.

(21) Phenazocine.

(22) Piminodine.

(23) Racemethorphan.

(24) Racemorphan.

(25) Sufentanyl.

(d) Stimulants. Unless specifically excepted or unless listed in another schedule, any material, compound, mixture, or preparation which contains any quantity of the following substances having a stimulant effect on the central nervous system:

(1) Amphetamine, its salts, optical isomers, and salts of its optical isomers.

(2) Methamphetamine, its salts, isomers, and salts of its isomers.

(3) Dimethylamphetamine (N,N–dimethylamphetamine), its salts, isomers, and salts of its isomers.

(4) N–Ethylmethamphetamine (N–ethyl, N–methylamphetamine), its salts, isomers, and salts of its isomers.

(5) Phenmetrazine and its salts.

(6) Methylphenidate.

(7) Khat, which includes all parts of the plant classified botanically as Catha Edulis, whether growing or not, the seeds thereof, any extract from any part of the plant, and every compound, manufacture, salt, derivative, mixture, or preparation of the plant, its seeds, or extracts.

(8) Cathinone (also known as alpha-aminopropiophenone, 2–aminopropiophenone, and norephedrone).

(e) Depressants. Unless specifically excepted or unless listed in another schedule, any material, compound, mixture, or preparation which contains any quantity of the following substances having a depressant effect on the central nervous system, including its salts, isomers, and salts of isomers whenever the existence of those salts, isomers, and salts of isomers is possible within the specific chemical designation:

(1) Amobarbital.

(2) Pentobarbital.

(3) Phencyclidines, including the following:

(A) 1–(1–phenylcyclohexyl) piperidine (PCP).

(B) 1–(1–phenylcyclohexyl) morpholine (PCM).

(C) Any analog of phencyclidine which is added by the Attorney General by regulation pursuant to this paragraph.

The Attorney General, or his or her designee, may, by rule or regulation, add additional analogs of phencyclidine to those enumerated in this paragraph after notice, posting, and hearing pursuant to Chapter 3.5 (commencing with Section 11340) of Part 1 of Division 3 of Title 2 of the Government Code. The Attorney General shall, in the calendar year of the regular session of the Legislature in which the rule or regulation is adopted, submit a draft of a proposed bill to each house of the Legislature which would incorporate the analogs into this code. No rule or regulation shall remain in effect beyond January 1 after the calendar year of the regular session in which the draft of the proposed bill is submitted to each house. However, if the draft of the proposed bill is submitted during a recess of the Legislature exceeding 45 calendar days, the rule or regulation shall be effective until January 1 after the next calendar year.

(4) Secobarbital.

(5) Glutethimide.

(f) Immediate precursors. Unless specifically excepted or unless listed in another schedule, any material, compound, mixture, or preparation which contains any quantity of the following substances:

(1) Immediate precursor to amphetamine and methamphetamine:

(A)[1] Phenylacetone. Some trade or other names: phenyl–2 propanone; P2P; benzyl methyl ketone; methyl benzyl ketone.

(2) Immediate precursors to phencyclidine (PCP):

(A) 1–phenylcyclohexylamine.

(B) 1–piperidinocyclohexane carbonitrile (PCC). *(Added by Stats. 1984, c. 1635, § 45.5. Amended by Stats.1985, c. 3, § 1, eff. Jan. 29, 1985; Stats.1985, c. 21, § 3, eff. April 2, 1985; Stats.1985, c. 1098, § 1.4, eff. Sept. 27, 1985; Stats.1986, c. 384, § 2, eff. July 17, 1986; Stats.1986, c. 1042, § 3, eff. Sept. 23, 1986; Stats.1986, c. 1044, § 2.5; Stats.1987, c. 1174, § 2, eff. Sept. 26, 1987; Stats.1988, c. 712, § 1, eff. Aug. 29, 1988; Stats.1995, c. 455 (A.B.1113), § 4, eff. Sept. 5, 1995; Stats.1997, c. 560 (A.B.6), § 1, eff. Sept. 29, 1997; Stats.1997, c. 714 (S.B.3), § 1, eff. Oct. 6, 1997; Stats.1999, c. 975 (A.B.924), § 1; Stats.2000, c. 8 (S.B.550), § 1, eff. March 29, 2000; Stats.2001, c. 841 (A.B.258), § 2; Stats.2008, c. 292 (A.B.1141), § 1; Stats.2010, c. 76 (A.B.1414), § 1; Stats.2018, c. 589 (A.B.2783), § 1, eff. Jan. 1, 2019.)*

[1] No subd. (f)(1)(B) in enrolled bill.

Cross References

Administering controlled substance against victim's will, additional punishment, see Penal Code § 12022.75.

Analogs considered identical with controlled substance for punishment purposes, see Health and Safety Code §§ 11400, 11401.

Attorney General, generally, see Government Code § 12500 et seq.

Attorney General defined for purposes of this Division, see Health and Safety Code § 11004.

Controlled substance defined for purposes of this Division, see Health and Safety Code § 11007.

Criminal gang activity, sale or manufacture of controlled substances defined by this section, see Penal Code § 186.22.

Drug endangered children, law enforcement and social services agencies' response, development of policies and standards for narcotic crime scenes, see Penal Code § 13879.80 et seq.

Elementary and secondary education, instruction and services, pupils, pupil rights and responsibilities, suspension or expulsion, expulsion relating to controlled substances or alcohol, enrollment in drug rehabilitation program, see Education Code § 48916.5.

Healing arts, nursing, nurse–midwives, nurse-midwives, furnishing or ordering drugs or devices, see Business and Professions Code § 2746.51.

Illegal dumping of waste matter, impoundment, see Vehicle Code § 23112.7.

Isomer defined for purposes of this Division, see Health and Safety Code § 11033.

Local agencies, cities and counties, powers and duties common to cities and counties, massage, massage, grounds for denial of license, see Government Code § 51032.

Manufacturing, compounding, converting, producing, etc., terms of imprisonment, see Health and Safety Code § 11379.6.

Minors, medical treatment, consent by minor, diagnosis or treatment of drug and alcohol abuse, liability for cost of services, disclosure of medical information, see Family Code § 6929.

Narcotic drug defined for purposes of this Division, see Health and Safety Code § 11019.

Nurse-midwives, furnishing or ordering drugs or devices, see Business and Professions Code § 2746.51.

Of criminal procedure, of judgment and execution, the judgment,

Controlled substances violations, use of minors as agents, see Penal Code § 1203.07.

Felony convictions for controlled substances violations involving cocaine, cocaine base, methamphetamine, phencyclidine or heroin, probation and sentencing, see Penal Code § 1203.073.

Legislative intent regarding prosecution of violent sex crimes, see Penal Code § 1192.7.

Opiate defined for purposes of this Division, see Health and Safety Code § 11020.

Opium poppy defined for purposes of this Division, see Health and Safety Code § 11021.

Persons illegally obtaining substances listed in this section, mandatory jail term, see Health and Safety Code § 11550.

Poppy straw defined for purposes of this Division, see Health and Safety Code § 11025.

Possession of moneys or negotiable instruments in excess of $100,000 involved in unlawful sale or purchase of a controlled substance listed in this section, punishment, see Health and Safety Code § 11370.6.

Probation requirements for nonviolent drug offenders, exception for possession of controlled substances while armed with a deadly weapon, see Penal Code § 1210.1.

Prohibition on possession of a firearm under the age of 30 for those convicted of or alleged to have committed certain offenses, controlled substances violations, punishment for violation, see Penal Code § 29820.

School district certificated employees, leave of absence when charged with offense under this section, see Education Code § 44940.

Research References

California Jury Instructions - Criminal 12.09.5, Possession With Intent to Manufacture Methamphetamine.

California Jury Instructions - Criminal 12.09.7, Possession of Ephedrine, etc., With Intent to Sell for Purpose of Manufacture of Methamphetamine.

2 Witkin, California Criminal Law 4th Crimes Against Public Peace and Welfare § 85 (2021), Uniform Controlled Substances Act.

2 Witkin, California Criminal Law 4th Crimes Against Public Peace and Welfare § 87 (2021), Substances Formerly Classified as Narcotics.

2 Witkin, California Criminal Law 4th Crimes Against Public Peace and Welfare § 88 (2021), Substances Formerly Classified as Restricted Dangerous Drugs.

2 Witkin, California Criminal Law 4th Crimes Against Public Peace and Welfare § 93 (2021), Specified Narcotics and Restricted Dangerous Drugs.

2 Witkin, California Criminal Law 4th Crimes Against Public Peace and Welfare § 118 (2021), Sufficient Quantity.

3 Witkin, California Criminal Law 4th Punishment § 375 (2021), Value or Amount.

§ 11056. Schedule III; substances included

(a) The controlled substances listed in this section are included in Schedule III.

(b) Stimulants. Unless specifically excepted or unless listed in another schedule, any material, compound, mixture, or preparation that contains any quantity of the following substances having a stimulant effect on the central nervous system, including its salts, isomers (whether optical, position, or geometric), and salts of those isomers whenever the existence of those salts, isomers, and salts of isomers is possible within the specific chemical designation:

(1) Those compounds, mixtures, or preparations in dosage unit form containing any stimulant substances listed in Schedule II which compounds, mixtures, or preparations were listed on August 25, 1971, as excepted compounds under Section 1308.32 of Title 21 of the Code of Federal Regulations, and any other drug of the quantitative composition shown in that list for those drugs or that is the same except that it contains a lesser quantity of controlled substances.

(2) Benzphetamine.

(3) Chlorphentermine.

(4) Clortermine.

(5) Mazindol.

(6) Phendimetrazine.

(c) Depressants. Unless specifically excepted in Section 11059 or elsewhere, or unless listed in another schedule, any material, compound, mixture, or preparation that contains any quantity of the following substances having a depressant effect on the central nervous system:

(1) Any compound, mixture, or preparation containing any of the following:

(A) Amobarbital.

(B) Secobarbital.

(C) Pentobarbital

or any salt thereof and one or more other active medicinal ingredients that are not listed in any schedule.

(2) Any suppository dosage form containing any of the following:

(A) Amobarbital.

(B) Secobarbital.

(C) Pentobarbital

or any salt of any of these drugs and approved by the federal Food and Drug Administration for marketing only as a suppository.

(3) Any substance that contains any quantity of a derivative of barbituric acid or any salt thereof.

(4) Chlorhexadol.

(5) Lysergic acid.

(6) Lysergic acid amide.

(7) Methyprylon.

(8) Sulfondiethylmethane.

(9) Sulfonethylmethane.

(10) Sulfonmethane.

(11) Gamma hydroxybutyric acid, and its salts, isomers, and salts of isomers, contained in a drug product for which an application has been approved under Section 505 of the Federal Food, Drug, and Cosmetic Act (21 U.S.C. Sec. 355).

(d) Nalorphine.

(e) Narcotic drugs. Unless specifically excepted or unless listed in another schedule, any material, compound, mixture, or preparation containing any of the following narcotic drugs, or their salts calculated as the free anhydrous base or alkaloid, in limited quantities as set forth below:

(1) Not more than 1.8 grams of codeine per 100 milliliters or not more than 90 milligrams per dosage unit, with an equal or greater quantity of an isoquinoline alkaloid of opium.

(2) Not more than 1.8 grams of codeine per 100 milliliters or not more than 90 milligrams per dosage unit, with one or more active, nonnarcotic ingredients in recognized therapeutic amounts.

(3) Not more than 1.8 grams of dihydrocodeine per 100 milliliters or not more than 90 milligrams per dosage unit, with one or more active nonnarcotic ingredients in recognized therapeutic amounts.

(4) Not more than 300 milligrams of ethylmorphine per 100 milliliters or not more than 15 milligrams per dosage unit, with one or more active, nonnarcotic ingredients in recognized therapeutic amounts.

(5) Not more than 500 milligrams of opium per 100 milliliters or per 100 grams or not more than 25 milligrams per dosage unit, with one or more active, nonnarcotic ingredients in recognized therapeutic amounts.

(6) Not more than 50 milligrams of morphine per 100 milliliters or per 100 grams, with one or more active, nonnarcotic ingredients in recognized therapeutic amounts.

(f) Anabolic steroids and chorionic gonadotropin. Any material, compound, mixture, or preparation containing chorionic gonadotropin or an anabolic steroid (excluding anabolic steroid products listed in the "Table of Exempt Anabolic Steroid Products" (Section 1308.34 of Title 21 of the Code of Federal Regulations), as exempt from the federal Controlled Substances Act (Section 801 and following of Title 21 of the United States Code)), including, but not limited to, the following:

(1) Androisoxazole.

(2) Androstenediol.

(3) Bolandiol.

(4) Bolasterone.

(5) Boldenone.

(6) Chloromethandienone.

(7) Clostebol.

(8) Dihydromesterone.

(9) Ethylestrenol.

(10) Fluoxymesterone.

(11) Formyldienolone.

(12) 4–Hydroxy–19–nortestosterone.

(13) Mesterolone.

(14) Methandriol.

(15) Methandrostenolone.

(16) Methenolone.

(17) 17–Methyltestosterone.

(18) Methyltrienolone.

(19) Nandrolone.

(20) Norbolethone.

(21) Norethandrolone.

(22) Normethandrolone.

(23) Oxandrolone.

(24) Oxymesterone.

(25) Oxymetholone.

(26) Quinbolone.

(27) Stanolone.

(28) Stanozolol.

(29) Stenbolone.

(30) Testosterone.

(31) Trenbolone.

(32) Human chorionic gonadotropin (hCG), except when possessed by, sold to, purchased by, transferred to, or administered by a licensed veterinarian, or a licensed veterinarian's designated agent, exclusively for veterinary use.

(g) Ketamine. Any material, compound, mixture, or preparation containing ketamine.

(h) Hallucinogenic substances. Any of the following hallucinogenic substances: dronabinol (synthetic) in sesame oil and encapsulated in a soft gelatin capsule in a drug product approved by the federal Food and Drug Administration. *(Added by Stats.1984, c. 1635, § 46.5. Amended by Stats.1986, c. 384, § 3, eff. July 17, 1986; Stats.1986, c. 534, § 1, eff. Aug. 20, 1986; Stats.1986, c. 1033, § 1; Stats.1989, c. 567, § 1; Stats.1991, c. 294 (A.B.444), § 1; Stats.1995, c. 59 (S.B.491), § 1; Stats.2000, c. 8 (S.B.550), § 2, eff. March 29, 2000; Stats.2001, c. 841 (A.B.258), § 3; Stats.2018, c. 81 (A.B.2589), § 1, eff. Jan. 1, 2019; Stats.2018, c. 589 (A.B.2783), § 2.5, eff. Jan. 1, 2019; Stats.2019, c. 497 (A.B.991), § 157, eff. Jan. 1, 2020; Stats.2021, c. 618 (A.B.527), § 1, eff. Jan. 1, 2022.)*

Cross References

Administering controlled substance against victim's will, additional punishment, see Penal Code § 12022.75.

Anabolic steroids, unlawful possession, misdemeanor for persons without previous convictions, see Health and Safety Code § 11377.

Controlled substance defined for purposes of this Division, see Health and Safety Code § 11007.

Criminal gang activity, sale or manufacture of controlled substances defined by this section, see Penal Code § 186.22.

Elementary and secondary education, instruction and services, pupils, pupil rights and responsibilities, suspension or expulsion, expulsion relating to controlled substances or alcohol, enrollment in drug rehabilitation program, see Education Code § 48916.5.

General business regulations, representations to the public, advertising, particular offenses, advertising sale of anabolic steroids, penalty, see Business and Professions Code § 17533.10.

Healing arts, naturopathic doctors act, application of Chapter, furnishing or ordering drugs, conditions, see Business and Professions Code § 3640.5.

Illegal dumping of waste matter, impoundment, see Vehicle Code § 23112.7.

Isomer defined for purposes of this Division, see Health and Safety Code § 11033.

Local agencies, cities and counties, powers and duties common to cities and counties, massage, massage, grounds for denial of license, see Government Code § 51032.

Manufacturing, compounding, converting, producing, etc., terms of imprisonment, see Health and Safety Code § 11379.6.

Narcotic drug defined for purposes of this Division, see Health and Safety Code § 11019.

Naturopathic doctors, furnishing or ordering of Schedule III controlled substances as defined by this section, requirements, see Business and Professions Code § 3640.5.

Nurse-midwives, furnishing or ordering drugs or devices, see Business and Professions Code § 2746.51.

Possession of moneys or negotiable instruments in excess of $100,000 involved in unlawful sale or purchase of a controlled substance listed in this section, punishment, see Health and Safety Code § 11370.6.

Probation requirements for nonviolent drug offenders, exception for possession of controlled substances while armed with a deadly weapon, see Penal Code § 1210.1.

School district certificated employees, leave of absence when charged with offense under this section, see Education Code § 44940.

Research References

2 Witkin, California Criminal Law 4th Crimes Against Public Peace and Welfare § 85 (2021), Uniform Controlled Substances Act.

2 Witkin, California Criminal Law 4th Crimes Against Public Peace and Welfare § 87 (2021), Substances Formerly Classified as Narcotics.

2 Witkin, California Criminal Law 4th Crimes Against Public Peace and Welfare § 88 (2021), Substances Formerly Classified as Restricted Dangerous Drugs.

2 Witkin, California Criminal Law 4th Crimes Against Public Peace and Welfare § 93 (2021), Specified Narcotics and Restricted Dangerous Drugs.

2 Witkin, California Criminal Law 4th Crimes Against Public Peace and Welfare § 97 (2021), In General.

2 Witkin, California Criminal Law 4th Crimes Against Public Peace and Welfare § 101 (2021), Possession for Sale.

2 Witkin, California Criminal Law 4th Crimes Against Public Peace and Welfare § 115 (2021), Statutory Prohibitions.

2 Witkin, California Criminal Law 4th Crimes Against Public Peace and Welfare § 157 (2021), Visiting or Using Place for Unlawful Activity.

2 Witkin, California Criminal Law 4th Crimes Against Public Peace and Welfare § 162 (2021), Advertising Anabolic Steroids.

§ 11057. Schedule IV; substances included

(a) The controlled substances listed in this section are included in Schedule IV.

(b) Schedule IV shall consist of the drugs and other substances, by whatever official name, common or usual name, chemical name, or brand name designated, listed in this section.

(c) Narcotic drugs. Unless specifically excepted or unless listed in another schedule, any material, compound, mixture, or preparation containing any of the following narcotic drugs, or their salts calculated as the free anhydrous base or alkaloid, in limited quantities as set forth below:

(1) Not more than 1 milligram of difenoxin and not less than 25 micrograms of atropine sulfate per dosage unit.

(2) Dextropropoxyphene (alpha-(+)-4-dimethylamino-1, 2-diphenyl-3-methyl-2-propionoxybutane).

(3) Butorphanol.

(d) Depressants. Unless specifically excepted in Section 11059 or elsewhere, or unless listed in another schedule, any material, compound, mixture, or preparation which contains any quantity of the following substances, including its salts, isomers, and salts of isomers whenever the existence of those salts, isomers, and salts of isomers is possible within the specific chemical designation:

(1) Alprazolam.

(2) Barbital.

(3) Chloral betaine.

(4) Chloral hydrate.

(5) Chlordiazepoxide.

(6) Clobazam.

(7) Clonazepam.

(8) Clorazepate.

(9) Diazepam.

(10) Estazolam.

(11) Ethchlorvynol.

(12) Ethinamate.

(13) Flunitrazepam.

(14) Flurazepam.

(15) Halazepam.

(16) Lorazepam.

(17) Mebutamate.

(18) Meprobamate.

(19) Methohexital.

(20) Methylphenobarbital (Mephobarbital).

(21) Midazolam.

(22) Nitrazepam.

(23) Oxazepam.

(24) Paraldehyde.

(25) Petrichoral.

(26) Phenobarbital.

(27) Prazepam.

(28) Quazepam.

(29) Temazepam.

(30) Triazolam.

(31) Zaleplon.

(32) Zolpidem.

(e) Fenfluramine. Any material, compound, mixture, or preparation which contains any quantity of the following substances, including its salts, isomers (whether optical, position, or geometric), and salts of those isomers, whenever the existence of those salts, isomers, and salts of isomers is possible:

(1)[1] Fenfluramine.

(f) Stimulants. Unless specifically excepted or unless listed in another schedule, any material, compound, mixture, or preparation which contains any quantity of the following substances having a stimulant effect on the central nervous system, including its salts, isomers (whether optical, position, or geometric), and salts of those isomers is possible within the specific chemical designation:

(1) Diethylpropion.

(2) Mazindol.

(3) Modafinil.

(4) Phentermine.

(5) Pemoline (including organometallic complexes and chelates thereof).

(6) Pipradrol.

(7) SPA ((-)–1–dimethylamino–1,2–diphenylethane).

(8) Cathine ((+)-norpseudoephedrine).

(g) Other substances. Unless specifically excepted or unless listed in another schedule, any material, compound, mixture, or preparation which contains any quantity of pentazocine, including its salts. *(Added by Stats.1984, c. 1635, § 47.5. Amended by Stats.1985, c. 290, § 2; Stats.1992, c. 616 (S.B.2013), § 1; Stats.1996, c. 109 (S.B.1426), § 1, eff. July 1, 1996; Stats.1996, c. 846 (S.B.2164), § 2; Stats.2002, c. 1013 (S.B.2026), § 86; Stats.2008, c. 292 (A.B.1141), § 2; Stats.2021, c. 618 (A.B.527), § 2, eff. Jan. 1, 2022.)*

[1] No subd. (e)(2) in enrolled bill.

Cross References

Administering controlled substance against victim's will, additional punishment, see Penal Code § 12022.75.
Controlled substance defined for purposes of this Division, see Health and Safety Code § 11007.
Criminal gang activity, sale or manufacture of controlled substances defined by this section, see Penal Code § 186.22.
Drug endangered children, law enforcement and social services agencies' response, development of policies and standards for narcotic crime scenes, see Penal Code § 13879.80 et seq.
Elementary and secondary education, instruction and services, pupils, pupil rights and responsibilities, suspension or expulsion, expulsion relating to controlled substances or alcohol, enrollment in drug rehabilitation program, see Education Code § 48916.5.
Illegal dumping of waste matter, impoundment, see Vehicle Code § 23112.7.
Isomer defined for purposes of this Division, see Health and Safety Code § 11033.
Local agencies, cities and counties, powers and duties common to cities and counties, massage, massage, grounds for denial of license, see Government Code § 51032.
Manufacturing, compounding, converting, producing, etc., terms of imprisonment, see Health and Safety Code § 11379.6.
Narcotic drug defined for purposes of this Division, see Health and Safety Code § 11019.
Possession of moneys or negotiable instruments in excess of $100,000 involved in unlawful sale or purchase of a controlled substance listed in this section, punishment, see Health and Safety Code § 11370.6.
Probation requirements for nonviolent drug offenders, exception for possession of controlled substances while armed with a deadly weapon, see Penal Code § 1210.1.

Research References

2 Witkin, California Criminal Law 4th Crimes Against Public Peace and Welfare § 85 (2021), Uniform Controlled Substances Act.

§ 11058. Schedule V; substances included

(a) The controlled substances listed in this section are included in Schedule V.

(b) Schedule V shall consist of the drugs and other substances, by whatever official name, common or usual name, chemical name, or brand name designated, listed in this section.

(c) Narcotic drugs containing nonnarcotic active medicinal ingredients. Any compound, mixture, or preparation containing any of the following narcotic drugs, or their salts calculated as the free anhydrous base or alkaloid, in limited quantities as set forth below, which shall include one or more nonnarcotic active medicinal ingredients in sufficient proportion to confer upon the compound, mixture, or preparation valuable medicinal qualities other than those possessed by narcotic drugs alone:

(1) Not more than 200 milligrams of codeine per 100 milliliters or per 100 grams.

(2) Not more than 100 milligrams of dihydrocodeine per 100 milliliters or per 100 grams.

(3) Not more than 100 milligrams of ethylmorphine per 100 milliliters or per 100 grams.

(4) Not more than 2.5 milligrams of diphenoxylate and not less than 25 micrograms of atropine sulfate per dosage unit.

(5) Not more than 100 milligrams of opium per 100 milliliters or per 100 grams.

(6) Not more than 0.5 milligram of difenoxin and not less than 25 micrograms of atropine sulfate per dosage unit.

(d) Buprenorphine. *(Added by Stats.1984, c. 1635, § 48.5. Amended by Stats.1985, c. 1098, § 1.2, eff. Sept. 27, 1985; Stats.1986, c. 63, § 1, eff. April 23, 1986.)*

Cross References

Administering controlled substance against victim's will, additional punishment, see Penal Code § 12022.75.
Controlled substance defined for purposes of this Division, see Health and Safety Code § 11007.
Criminal gang activity, sale or manufacture of controlled substances defined by this section, see Penal Code § 186.22.
Drug endangered children, law enforcement and social services agencies' response, development of policies and standards for narcotic crime scenes, see Penal Code § 13879.80 et seq.
Elementary and secondary education, instruction and services, pupils, pupil rights and responsibilities, suspension or expulsion, expulsion relating to controlled substances or alcohol, enrollment in drug rehabilitation program, see Education Code § 48916.5.
Illegal dumping of waste matter, impoundment, see Vehicle Code § 23112.7.
Local agencies, cities and counties, powers and duties common to cities and counties, massage, massage, grounds for denial of license, see Government Code § 51032.
Manufacturing, compounding, converting, producing, etc., terms of imprisonment, see Health and Safety Code § 11379.6.
Narcotic drug defined for purposes of this Division, see Health and Safety Code § 11019.

Possession of moneys or negotiable instruments in excess of $100,000 involved in unlawful sale or purchase of a controlled substance listed in this section, punishment, see Health and Safety Code § 11370.6.

Probation requirements for nonviolent drug offenders, exception for possession of controlled substances while armed with a deadly weapon, see Penal Code § 1210.1.

Research References

California Jury Instructions - Criminal 12.00, Controlled Substance (Sched. I–V)—Unlawful Possession as Felony/Misdemeanor.

California Jury Instructions - Criminal 16.062, Misdemeanor Unlawful Possession of Controlled Substance.

2 Witkin, California Criminal Law 4th Crimes Against Public Peace and Welfare § 85 (2021), Uniform Controlled Substances Act.

§ 11059. Specific compounds, mixtures, or preparations that contain a nonnarcotic controlled substance; exemptions from scheduling

(a) Specific compounds, mixtures, or preparations that contain a nonnarcotic controlled substance in combination with a derivative of barbituric acid or any salt thereof that are listed in the federal Table of Exempted Prescription Products and have been exempted pursuant to federal law or regulation (Section 1308.32 of Title 21 of the Code of Federal Regulations or its successors), are excepted from scheduling under subdivision (c) of Section 11056.

(b) Specific compounds, mixtures, or preparations that contain a nonnarcotic controlled substance in combination with a chlordiazepoxide or phenobarbital that are listed in the federal Table of Exempted Prescription Products and have been exempted from scheduling under federal law or regulation (Section 1308.32 of Title 21 of the Code of Federal Regulations or its successors) are excepted from scheduling under subdivision (d) of Section 11057. *(Added by Stats.2021, c. 618 (A.B.527), § 3, eff. Jan. 1, 2022.)*

CHAPTER 3. REGULATION AND CONTROL

ARTICLE 1. REPORTING

§ 11100. Transactions reported; exemptions; punishment; offenses involving minors

(a) Any manufacturer, wholesaler, retailer, or other person or entity in this state that sells, transfers, or otherwise furnishes any of the following substances to any person or entity in this state or any other state shall submit a report to the Department of Justice of all of those transactions:

(1) Phenyl–2–propanone.

(2) Methylamine.

(3) Ethylamine.

(4) D–lysergic acid.

(5) Ergotamine tartrate.

(6) Diethyl malonate.

(7) Malonic acid.

(8) Ethyl malonate.

(9) Barbituric acid.

(10) Piperidine.

(11) N–acetylanthranilic acid.

(12) Pyrrolidine.

(13) Phenylacetic acid.

(14) Anthranilic acid.

(15) Morpholine.

(16) Ephedrine.

(17) Pseudoephedrine.

(18) Norpseudoephedrine.

(19) Phenylpropanolamine.

(20) Propionic anhydride.

(21) Isosafrole.

(22) Safrole.

(23) Piperonal.

(24) Thionyl chloride.

(25) Benzyl cyanide.

(26) Ergonovine maleate.

(27) N–methylephedrine.

(28) N–ethylephedrine.

(29) N–methylpseudoephedrine.

(30) N–ethylpseudoephedrine.

(31) Chloroephedrine.

(32) Chloropseudoephedrine.

(33) Hydriodic acid.

(34) Gamma–butyrolactone, including butyrolactone; butyrolactone gamma; 4–butyrolactone; 2(3H)–furanone dihydro; dihydro–2(3H)–furanone; tetrahydro–2–furanone; 1,2–butanolide; 1,4–butanolide; 4–butanolide; gamma-hydroxybutyric acid lactone; 3–hy-

droxybutyric acid lactone and 4–hydroxybutanoic acid lactone with Chemical Abstract Service number (96–48–0).

(35) 1,4–butanediol, including butanediol; butane–1,4–diol; 1,4–butylene glycol; butylene glycol; 1,4–dihydroxybutane; 1,4–tetramethylene glycol; tetramethylene glycol; tetramethylene 1,4–diol with Chemical Abstract Service number (110–63–4).

(36) Red phosphorus, including white phosphorus, hypophosphorous acid and its salts, ammonium hypophosphite, calcium hypophosphite, iron hypophosphite, potassium hypophosphite, manganese hypophosphite, magnesium hypophosphite, sodium hypophosphite, and phosphorous acid and its salts.

(37) Iodine or tincture of iodine.

(38) Any of the substances listed by the Department of Justice in regulations promulgated pursuant to subdivision (b).

(b) The Department of Justice may adopt rules and regulations in accordance with Chapter 3.5 (commencing with Section 11340) of Part 1 of Division 3 of Title 2 of the Government Code that add substances to subdivision (a) if the substance is a precursor to a controlled substance and delete substances from subdivision (a). However, no regulation adding or deleting a substance shall have any effect beyond March 1 of the year following the calendar year during which the regulation was adopted.

(c)(1)(A) Any manufacturer, wholesaler, retailer, or other person or entity in this state, prior to selling, transferring, or otherwise furnishing any substance specified in subdivision (a) to any person or business entity in this state or any other state, shall require (i) a letter of authorization from that person or business entity that includes the currently valid business license number or federal Drug Enforcement Administration (DEA) registration number, the address of the business, and a full description of how the substance is to be used, and (ii) proper identification from the purchaser. The manufacturer, wholesaler, retailer, or other person or entity in this state shall retain this information in a readily available manner for three years. The requirement for a full description of how the substance is to be used does not require the person or business entity to reveal their chemical processes that are typically considered trade secrets and proprietary information.

(B) For the purposes of this paragraph, "proper identification" for in-state or out-of-state purchasers includes two or more of the following: federal tax identification number; seller's permit identification number; city or county business license number; license issued by the State Department of Public Health; registration number issued by the federal Drug Enforcement Administration; precursor business permit number issued by the Department of Justice; driver's license; or other identification issued by a state.

(2)(A) Any manufacturer, wholesaler, retailer, or other person or entity in this state that exports a substance specified in subdivision (a) to any person or business entity located in a foreign country shall, on or before the date of exportation, submit to the Department of Justice a notification of that transaction, which notification shall include the name and quantity of the substance to be exported and the name, address, and, if assigned by the foreign country or subdivision thereof, business identification number of the person or business entity located in a foreign country importing the substance.

(B) The department may authorize the submission of the notification on a monthly basis with respect to repeated, regular transactions between an exporter and an importer involving a substance specified in subdivision (a), if the department determines that a pattern of regular supply of the substance exists between the exporter and importer and that the importer has established a record of utilization of the substance for lawful purposes.

(d)(1) Any manufacturer, wholesaler, retailer, or other person or entity in this state that sells, transfers, or otherwise furnishes a substance specified in subdivision (a) to a person or business entity in this state or any other state shall, not less than 21 days prior to delivery of the substance, submit a report of the transaction, which includes the identification information specified in subdivision (c), to the Department of Justice. The Department of Justice may authorize the submission of the reports on a monthly basis with respect to repeated, regular transactions between the furnisher and the recipient involving the substance or substances if the Department of Justice determines that a pattern of regular supply of the substance or substances exists between the manufacturer, wholesaler, retailer, or other person or entity that sells, transfers, or otherwise furnishes the substance or substances and the recipient of the substance or substances, and the recipient has established a record of utilization of the substance or substances for lawful purposes.

(2) The person selling, transferring, or otherwise furnishing any substance specified in subdivision (a) shall affix his or her signature or otherwise identify himself or herself as a witness to the identification of the purchaser or purchasing individual, and shall, if a common carrier is used, maintain a manifest of the delivery to the purchaser for three years.

(e) This section shall not apply to any of the following:

(1) Any pharmacist or other authorized person who sells or furnishes a substance upon the prescription of a physician, dentist, podiatrist, or veterinarian.

(2) Any physician, dentist, podiatrist, or veterinarian who administers or furnishes a substance to his or her patients.

(3) Any manufacturer or wholesaler licensed by the California State Board of Pharmacy that sells, transfers, or otherwise furnishes a substance to a licensed pharmacy, physician, dentist, podiatrist, or veterinarian, or a retail distributor as defined in subdivision (h), provided that the manufacturer or wholesaler submits records of any suspicious sales or transfers as determined by the Department of Justice.

(4) Any analytical research facility that is registered with the federal Drug Enforcement Administration of the United States Department of Justice.

(5) A state-licensed health care facility that administers or furnishes a substance to its patients.

(6)(A) Any sale, transfer, furnishing, or receipt of any product that contains ephedrine, pseudoephedrine, norpseudoephedrine, or phenylpropanolamine and which is lawfully sold, transferred, or furnished over the counter without a prescription pursuant to the federal Food, Drug, and Cosmetic Act (21 U.S.C. Sec. 301 et seq.) or regulations adopted thereunder. However, this section shall apply to preparations in solid or liquid dosage form, except pediatric liquid forms, as defined, containing ephedrine, pseudoephedrine, norpseudoephedrine, or phenylpropanolamine where the individual transaction involves more than three packages or nine grams of ephedrine, pseudoephedrine, norpseudoephedrine, or phenylpropanolamine.

(B) Any ephedrine, pseudoephedrine, norpseudoephedrine, or phenylpropanolamine product subsequently removed from exemption pursuant to Section 814 of Title 21 of the United States Code shall similarly no longer be exempt from any state reporting or permitting requirement, unless otherwise reinstated pursuant to subdivision (d) or (e) of Section 814 of Title 21 of the United States Code as an exempt product.

(7) The sale, transfer, furnishing, or receipt of any betadine or povidone solution with an iodine content not exceeding 1 percent in containers of eight ounces or less, or any tincture of iodine not exceeding 2 percent in containers of one ounce or less, that is sold over the counter.

(8) Any transfer of a substance specified in subdivision (a) for purposes of lawful disposal as waste.

(f)(1) Any person specified in subdivision (a) or (d) who does not submit a report as required by that subdivision or who knowingly submits a report with false or fictitious information shall be punished by imprisonment in a county jail not exceeding six months, by a fine not exceeding five thousand dollars ($5,000), or by both the fine and imprisonment.

(2) Any person specified in subdivision (a) or (d) who has previously been convicted of a violation of paragraph (1) shall, upon a subsequent conviction thereof, be punished by imprisonment pursuant to subdivision (h) of Section 1170 of the Penal Code, or by imprisonment in a county jail not exceeding one year, by a fine not exceeding one hundred thousand dollars ($100,000), or by both the fine and imprisonment.

(g)(1) Except as otherwise provided in subparagraph (A) of paragraph (6) of subdivision (e), it is unlawful for any manufacturer, wholesaler, retailer, or other person to sell, transfer, or otherwise furnish a substance specified in subdivision (a) to a person under 18 years of age.

(2) Except as otherwise provided in subparagraph (A) of paragraph (6) of subdivision (e), it is unlawful for any person under 18 years of age to possess a substance specified in subdivision (a).

(3) Notwithstanding any other law, it is unlawful for any retail distributor to (i) sell in a single transaction more than three packages of a product that he or she knows to contain ephedrine, pseudoephedrine, norpseudoephedrine, or phenylpropanolamine, or (ii) knowingly sell more than nine grams of ephedrine, pseudoephedrine, norpseudoephedrine, or phenylpropanolamine, other than pediatric liquids as defined. Except as otherwise provided in this section, the three package per transaction limitation or nine gram per transaction limitation imposed by this paragraph shall apply to any product that is lawfully sold, transferred, or furnished over the counter without a prescription pursuant to the federal Food, Drug, and Cosmetic Act (21 U.S.C. Sec. 301 et seq.), or regulations adopted thereunder, unless exempted from the requirements of the federal Controlled Substances Act by the federal Drug Enforcement Administration pursuant to Section 814 of Title 21 of the United States Code.

(4)(A) A first violation of this subdivision is a misdemeanor.

(B) Any person who has previously been convicted of a violation of this subdivision shall, upon a subsequent conviction thereof, be punished by imprisonment in a county jail not exceeding one year, by a fine not exceeding ten thousand dollars ($10,000), or by both the fine and imprisonment.

(h) For the purposes of this article, the following terms have the following meanings:

(1) "Drug store" is any entity described in Code 5912 of the Standard Industrial Classification (SIC) Manual published by the United States Office of Management and Budget, 1987 edition.

(2) "General merchandise store" is any entity described in Codes 5311 to 5399, inclusive, and Code 5499 of the Standard Industrial Classification (SIC) Manual published by the United States Office of Management and Budget, 1987 edition.

(3) "Grocery store" is any entity described in Code 5411 of the Standard Industrial Classification (SIC) Manual published by the United States Office of Management and Budget, 1987 edition.

(4) "Pediatric liquid" means a nonencapsulated liquid whose unit measure according to product labeling is stated in milligrams, ounces, or other similar measure. In no instance shall the dosage units exceed 15 milligrams of phenylpropanolamine or pseudoephedrine per five milliliters of liquid product, except for liquid products primarily intended for administration to children under two years of age for which the recommended dosage unit does not exceed two milliliters and the total package content does not exceed one fluid ounce.

(5) "Retail distributor" means a grocery store, general merchandise store, drugstore, or other related entity, the activities of which, as a distributor of ephedrine, pseudoephedrine, norpseudoephedrine, or phenylpropanolamine products, are limited exclusively to the sale of ephedrine, pseudoephedrine, norpseudoephedrine, or phenylpropanolamine products for personal use both in number of sales and volume of sales, either directly to walk-in customers or in face-to-face transactions by direct sales. "Retail distributor" includes an entity that makes a direct sale, but does not include the parent company of that entity if the company is not involved in direct sales regulated by this article.

(6) "Sale for personal use" means the sale in a single transaction to an individual customer for a legitimate medical use of a product containing ephedrine, pseudoephedrine, norpseudoephedrine, or phenylpropanolamine in dosages at or below that specified in paragraph (3) of subdivision (g). "Sale for personal use" also includes the sale of those products to employers to be dispensed to employees from first-aid kits or medicine chests.

(i) It is the intent of the Legislature that this section shall preempt all local ordinances or regulations governing the sale by a retail distributor of over-the-counter products containing ephedrine, pseudoephedrine, norpseudoephedrine, or phenylpropanolamine. *(Added by Stats.1986, c. 1028, § 3, operative Oct. 1, 1987. Amended by Stats.1987, c. 5, § 2, eff. March 17, 1987, operative April 1, 1987; Stats.1988, c. 73, § 1; Stats.1988, c. 712, § 2, eff. Aug. 29, 1988; Stats.1989, c. 1133, § 1; Stats.1992, c. 978 (S.B.1822), § 3; Stats.1993, c. 589 (A.B.2211), § 88; Stats.1997, c. 397 (A.B.1173), § 1; Stats. 1999, c. 975 (A.B.924), § 2; Stats.1999, c. 978 (A.B.162), § 1.5; Stats.2001, c. 841 (A.B.258), § 4; Stats.2003, c. 369 (S.B.276), § 1, eff. Sept. 12, 2003; Stats.2004, c. 405 (S.B.1796), § 4; Stats.2005, c. 468 (A.B.465), § 1; Stats.2011, c. 15 (A.B.109), § 145, eff. April 4, 2011, operative Oct. 1, 2011; Stats.2012, c. 867 (S.B.1144), § 3.)*

Cross References

Administer defined for purposes of this Division, see Health and Safety Code § 11002.
Controlled substance defined for purposes of this Division, see Health and Safety Code § 11007.
Deliver or delivery defined for purposes of this Division, see Health and Safety Code § 11009.
Department of Health Care Services, generally, see Health and Safety Code § 100100 et seq.
Distributor defined for purposes of this Division, see Health and Safety Code § 11013.
Furnish defined for purposes of this Division, see Health and Safety Code § 11016.
Manufacturer defined for purposes of this Division, see Health and Safety Code § 11017.
Misdemeanors, definition and penalties, see Penal Code §§ 17, 19 and 19.2.
Of criminal procedure, of judgment and execution, the judgment, legislative intent regarding prosecution of violent sex crimes, see Penal Code § 1192.7.
Person defined for purposes of this Division, see Health and Safety Code § 11022.
Physician, dentist, podiatrist, pharmacist, veterinarian, and optometrist defined for purposes of this Division, see Health and Safety Code § 11024.
Prescription or electronic transmission prescription defined for purposes of this Division, see Health and Safety Code § 11027.
Uniform controlled substances act, regulation and control, reporting, drug cleanup fines, transfer of funds, see Health and Safety Code § 11100.05.
Wholesaler defined for purposes of this Division, see Health and Safety Code § 11031.

Research References

2 Witkin, California Criminal Law 4th Crimes Against Public Peace and Welfare § 133 (2021), In General.
2 Witkin, California Criminal Law 4th Crimes Against Public Peace and Welfare § 152 (2021), In General.

§ 11100.05. Drug cleanup fines; transfer of funds

(a) In addition to any fine or imprisonment imposed under subdivision (f) of Section 11100 or subdivision (j) of Section 11106 of the Health and Safety Code, the following drug cleanup fine shall be imposed:

(1) Ten thousand dollars ($10,000) for violations described in paragraph (1) of subdivision (f) of Section 11100.

(2) One hundred thousand dollars ($100,000) for violations described in paragraph (2) of subdivision (f) of Section 11100.

(3) Ten thousand dollars ($10,000) for violations described in subdivision (j) of Section 11106.

(b) At least once a month, all fines collected under this section shall be transferred to the State Treasury for deposit in the Clandestine Drug Lab Clean-up Account. The transmission to the State Treasury shall be carried out in the same manner as fines collected for the state by a county. *(Added by Stats.1987, c. 1295, § 1, eff. Sept. 28, 1987. Amended by Stats.2005, c. 468 (A.B.465), § 2.)*

§ 11100.1. Obtaining substances from sources outside state; violation; punishment

(a) Any manufacturer, wholesaler, retailer, or other person or entity in this state that obtains from a source outside of this state any substance specified in subdivision (a) of Section 11100 shall submit a report of that transaction to the Department of Justice 21 days in advance of obtaining the substance. However, the Department of Justice may authorize the submission of reports within 72 hours, or within a timeframe and in a manner acceptable to the Department of Justice, after the actual physical obtaining of a specified substance with respect to repeated transactions between a furnisher and an obtainer involving the substances, if the Department of Justice determines that the obtainer has established a record of utilization of the substances for lawful purposes. This section does not apply to any person whose prescribing or dispensing activities are subject to the reporting requirements set forth in Section 11164; any manufacturer or wholesaler who is licensed by the California State Board of Pharmacy and also registered with the federal Drug Enforcement Administration of the United States Department of Justice; any analytical research facility that is registered with the federal Drug Enforcement Administration of the United States Department of Justice; or any state-licensed health care facility.

(b)(1) Any person specified in subdivision (a) who does not submit a report as required by that subdivision shall be punished by imprisonment in a county jail not exceeding six months, by a fine not exceeding five thousand dollars ($5,000), or by both that fine and imprisonment.

(2) Any person specified in subdivision (a) who has been previously convicted of a violation of subdivision (a) who subsequently does not submit a report as required by subdivision (a) shall be punished by imprisonment pursuant to subdivision (h) of Section 1170 of the Penal Code, or by imprisonment in a county jail not exceeding one year, by a fine not exceeding one hundred thousand dollars ($100,-000), or by both that fine and imprisonment. *(Added by Stats.1980, c. 950, p. 2996, § 1. Amended by Stats.1982, c. 1279, p. 4729, § 2; Stats.1989, c. 1133, § 2; Stats.1992, c. 978 (S.B.1822), § 4; Stats.1997, c. 397 (A.B.1173), § 2; Stats.2003, c. 369 (S.B.276), § 2, eff. Sept. 12, 2003; Stats.2005, c. 468 (A.B.465), § 3; Stats.2011, c. 15 (A.B.109), § 146, eff. April 4, 2011, operative Oct. 1, 2011.)*

Cross References

Manufacturer defined for purposes of this Division, see Health and Safety Code § 11017.
Person defined for purposes of this Division, see Health and Safety Code § 11022.
Wholesaler defined for purposes of this Division, see Health and Safety Code § 11031.

§ 11101. Transferor's reporting form

The State Department of Justice shall provide a common reporting form for the substances in Section 11100 which contains at least the following information:

(a) Name of the substance.

(b) Quantity of the substance sold, transferred, or furnished.

(c) The date the substance was sold, transferred, or furnished.

(d) The name and address of the person buying or receiving such substance.

(e) The name and address of the manufacturer, wholesaler, retailer, or other person selling, transferring, or furnishing such substance. *(Added by Stats.1972, c. 1407, p. 2996, § 3. Amended by Stats.1974, c. 1072, § 2.)*

Cross References

Manufacturer defined for purposes of this Division, see Health and Safety Code § 11017.
Person defined for purposes of this Division, see Health and Safety Code § 11022.
Wholesaler defined for purposes of this Division, see Health and Safety Code § 11031.

§ 11102. Regulations

The Department of Justice may adopt all regulations necessary to carry out the provisions of this part. *(Added by Stats.1974, c. 1072, § 3.)*

§ 11103. Theft, loss and discrepancy reports

The theft or loss of any substance regulated pursuant to Section 11100 discovered by any permittee or any person regulated by the provisions of this chapter shall be reported in writing to the Department of Justice within three days after the discovery.

Any difference between the quantity of any substance regulated pursuant to Section 11100 received and the quantity shipped shall be reported in writing to the Department of Justice within three days of the receipt of actual knowledge of the discrepancy.

Any report made pursuant to this section shall also include the name of the common carrier or person who transports the substance and date of shipment of the substance. *(Formerly § 11105, added by Stats.1972, c. 1407, p. 2987, § 3. Renumbered § 11103 and amended by Stats.1974, c. 1072, § 6. Amended by Stats.1997, c. 397 (A.B.1173), § 3.)*

Cross References

Person defined for purposes of this Division, see Health and Safety Code § 11022.

§ 11104. Furnishing § 11100(a) substances, laboratory glassware or apparatus, or chemical reagent or solvent for manufacturing purposes; violations

(a) Any manufacturer, wholesaler, retailer, or other person or entity that sells, transfers, or otherwise furnishes any of the substances listed in subdivision (a) of Section 11100 with knowledge or the intent that the recipient will use the substance to unlawfully manufacture a controlled substance is guilty of a felony.

(b) Any manufacturer, wholesaler, retailer, or other person or entity that sells, transfers, or otherwise furnishes any laboratory glassware or apparatus, any chemical reagent or solvent, or any combination thereof, or any chemical substance specified in Section 11107.1, with knowledge that the recipient will use the goods or chemical substance to unlawfully manufacture a controlled substance, is guilty of a misdemeanor.

(c) Any person who receives or distributes any substance listed in subdivision (a) of Section 11100, or any laboratory glassware or apparatus, any chemical reagent or solvent, or any combination thereof, or any chemical substance specified in Section 11107.1, with the intent of causing the evasion of the recordkeeping or reporting requirements of this article, is guilty of a misdemeanor. *(Added by Stats.1978, c. 699, p. 2211, § 2.3. Amended by Stats.1984, c. 1547, § 1; Stats.1992, c. 580 (S.B.1820), § 1, eff. Aug. 31, 1992; Stats.2003, c. 369 (S.B.276), § 3, eff. Sept. 12, 2003; Stats.2005, c. 468 (A.B.465), § 4.)*

Cross References

Controlled substance defined for purposes of this Division, see Health and Safety Code § 11007.
"Distribute" defined for purposes of this Division, see Health and Safety Code § 11012.
Felonies, definition and penalties, see Penal Code §§ 17, 18.
"Furnish" defined for purposes of this Division, see Health and Safety Code § 11016.
"Manufacturer" defined for purposes of this Division, see Health and Safety Code § 11017.
Misdemeanor, definition, penalties, see Penal Code §§ 17, 19, 19.2.
Person defined for purposes of this Division, see Health and Safety Code § 11022.
"Wholesaler" defined for purposes of this Division, see Health and Safety Code § 11031.

Research References

2 Witkin, California Criminal Law 4th Crimes Against Public Peace and Welfare § 133 (2021), In General.
1 Witkin California Criminal Law 4th Elements § 65 (2021), General Principles.

§ 11104.5. Possession of § 11107.1 substances, laboratory glassware or apparatus, or chemical reagent or solvent for manufacturing purposes; misdemeanor

Any person who knowingly or intentionally possesses any laboratory glassware or apparatus, any chemical reagent or solvent, or any combination thereof, or any chemical substance specified in paragraph (36) or (37) of subdivision (a) of Section 11100, Section 11107, or Section 11107.1, with the intent to manufacture a controlled substance, is guilty of a misdemeanor. *(Added by Stats.1992, c. 580 (S.B.1820), § 2, eff. Aug. 31, 1992. Amended by Stats.2005, c. 468 (A.B.465), § 5.)*

Cross References

Controlled substance defined for purposes of this Division, see Health and Safety Code § 11007.
Misdemeanors, definition and penalties, see Penal Code §§ 17, 19 and 19.2.
Person defined for purposes of this Division, see Health and Safety Code § 11022.

Research References

2 Witkin, California Criminal Law 4th Crimes Against Public Peace and Welfare § 133 (2021), In General.

§ 11105. False statement in connection with report or record; penalty

(a) It is unlawful for any person to knowingly make a false statement in connection with any report or record required under this article.

(b)(1) Any person who violates this section shall be punished by imprisonment pursuant to subdivision (h) of Section 1170 of the Penal Code, or by imprisonment in a county jail not exceeding one year, or by a fine not exceeding five thousand dollars ($5,000), or by both that fine and imprisonment.

(2) Any person who has been previously convicted of violating this section and who subsequently violates this section shall be punished by imprisonment pursuant to subdivision (h) of Section 1170 of the Penal Code for two, three, or four years, or by a fine not exceeding one hundred thousand dollars ($100,000), or by both that fine and imprisonment. *(Added by Stats.1978, c. 699, p. 2211, § 2.5. Amended by Stats.1979, c. 784, p. 2674, § 2; Stats.1982, c. 1279, § 3; Stats.2011, c. 15 (A.B.109), § 147, eff. April 4, 2011, operative Oct. 1, 2011.)*

Cross References

Person defined for purposes of this Division, see Health and Safety Code § 11022.

§ 11106. Permit for conduct of business; exemptions; applications; site inspection and audit; denial of application or suspension of permit; forms; fees; renewal; violations

(a)(1)(A) Any manufacturer, wholesaler, retailer, or any other person or entity in this state that sells, transfers, or otherwise furnishes any substance specified in subdivision (a) of Section 11100 to a person or business entity in this state or any other state or who obtains from a source outside of the state any substance specified in subdivision (a) of Section 11100 shall submit an application to, and obtain a permit for the conduct of that business from, the Department of Justice. For any substance added to the list set forth in subdivision (a) of Section 11100 on or after January 1, 2002, the Department of Justice may postpone the effective date of the requirement for a permit for a period not to exceed six months from the listing date of the substance.

(B) An intracompany transfer does not require a permit if the transferor is a permittee. Transfers between company partners or between a company and an analytical laboratory do not require a permit if the transferor is a permittee and a report as to the nature and extent of the transfer is made to the Department of Justice pursuant to Section 11100 or 11100.1.

(C) This paragraph shall not apply to any manufacturer, wholesaler, or wholesale distributor who is licensed by the California State Board of Pharmacy and also registered with the federal Drug Enforcement Administration of the United States Department of Justice; any pharmacist or other authorized person who sells or furnishes a substance upon the prescription of a physician, dentist, podiatrist, or veterinarian; any state-licensed health care facility, physician, dentist, podiatrist, veterinarian, or veterinary food-animal drug retailer licensed by the California State Board of Pharmacy that administers or furnishes a substance to a patient; or any analytical research facility that is registered with the federal Drug Enforcement Administration of the United States Department of Justice.

(D) This paragraph shall not apply to the sale, transfer, furnishing, or receipt of any betadine or povidone solution with an iodine content not exceeding 1 percent in containers of eight ounces or less, or any tincture of iodine not exceeding 2 percent in containers of one ounce or less, that is sold over the counter.

(2) Except as provided in paragraph (3), no permit shall be required of any manufacturer, wholesaler, retailer, or other person or entity for the sale, transfer, furnishing, or obtaining of any product which contains ephedrine, pseudoephedrine, norpseudoephedrine, or phenylpropanolamine and which is lawfully sold, transferred, or furnished over the counter without a prescription or by a prescription pursuant to the federal Food, Drug, and Cosmetic Act (21 U.S.C. Sec. 301 et seq.) or regulations adopted thereunder.

(3) A permit shall be required for the sale, transfer, furnishing, or obtaining of preparations in solid or liquid dosage form containing ephedrine, pseudoephedrine, norpseudoephedrine, or phenylpropanolamine, unless (A) the transaction involves the sale of ephedrine, pseudoephedrine, norpseudoephedrine, or phenylpropanolamine products by retail distributors as defined by this article over the counter and without a prescription, or (B) the transaction is made by a person or business entity exempted from the permitting requirements of this subdivision under paragraph (1).

(b)(1) The department shall provide application forms, which are to be completed under penalty of perjury, in order to obtain information relating to the identity of any applicant applying for a permit, including, but not limited to, the business name of the applicant or the individual name, and if a corporate entity, the names of its board of directors, the business in which the applicant is engaged, the business address of the applicant, a full description of any substance to be sold, transferred, or otherwise furnished or to be obtained, the specific purpose for the use, sale, or transfer of those substances specified in subdivision (a) of Section 11100, the training, experience, or education relating to this use, and any additional information requested by the department relating to possible grounds for denial as set forth in this section, or by applicable regulations adopted by the department.

(2) The requirement for the specific purpose for the use, sale, or transfer of those substances specified in subdivision (a) of Section 11100 does not require applicants or permittees to reveal their chemical processes that are typically considered trade secrets and proprietary business information.

(c) Applicants and permittees shall authorize the department, or any of its duly authorized representatives, as a condition of being permitted, to make any examination of the books and records of any applicant, permittee, or other person, or visit and inspect the business premises of any applicant or permittee during normal business hours, as deemed necessary to enforce this chapter.

(d) An application may be denied, or a permit may be revoked or suspended, for reasons which include, but are not limited to, the following:

(1) Materially falsifying an application for a permit or an application for the renewal of a permit.

(2) If any individual owner, manager, agent, representative, or employee for the applicant who has direct access, management, or control for any substance listed under subdivision (a) of Section 11100, is or has been convicted of a misdemeanor or felony relating to any of the substances listed under subdivision (a) of Section 11100, any misdemeanor drug-related offense, or any felony under the laws of this state or the United States.

(3) Failure to maintain effective controls against the diversion of precursors to unauthorized persons or entities.

(4) Failure to comply with this article or any regulations of the department adopted thereunder.

(5) Failure to provide the department, or any duly authorized federal or state official, with access to any place for which a permit has been issued, or for which an application for a permit has been submitted, in the course of conducting a site investigation, inspection, or audit; or failure to promptly produce for the official conducting the site investigation, inspection, or audit any book, record, or document requested by the official.

(6) Failure to provide adequate documentation of a legitimate business purpose involving the applicant's or permittee's use of any substance listed in subdivision (a) of Section 11100.

(7) Commission of any act which would demonstrate actual or potential unfitness to hold a permit in light of the public safety and welfare, which act is substantially related to the qualifications, functions, or duties of a permitholder.

(8) If any individual owner, manager, agent, representative, or employee for the applicant who has direct access, management, or control for any substance listed under subdivision (a) of Section 11100, willfully violates or has been convicted of violating, any federal, state, or local criminal statute, rule, or ordinance regulating the manufacture, maintenance, disposal, sale, transfer, or furnishing of any of those substances.

(e) Notwithstanding any other provision of law, an investigation of an individual applicant's qualifications, or the qualifications of an applicant's owner, manager, agent, representative, or employee who has direct access, management, or control of any substance listed under subdivision (a) of Section 11100, for a permit may include review of his or her summary criminal history information pursuant to Sections 11105 and 13300 of the Penal Code, including, but not limited to, records of convictions, regardless of whether those convictions have been expunged pursuant to Section 1203.4 of the Penal Code, and any arrests pending adjudication.

(f) The department may retain jurisdiction of a canceled or expired permit in order to proceed with any investigation or disciplinary action relating to a permittee.

(g) The department may grant permits on forms prescribed by it, which shall be effective for not more than one year from the date of issuance and which shall not be transferable. Applications and permits shall be uniform throughout the state, on forms prescribed by the department.

(h) Each applicant shall pay at the time of filing an application for a permit a fee determined by the department which shall not exceed the application processing costs of the department.

(i) A permit granted pursuant to this article may be renewed one year from the date of issuance, and annually thereafter, following the timely filing of a complete renewal application with all supporting documents, the payment of a permit renewal fee not to exceed the application processing costs of the department, and a review of the application by the department.

(j) Selling, transferring, or otherwise furnishing or obtaining any substance specified in subdivision (a) of Section 11100 without a permit is a misdemeanor or a felony.

(k)(1) No person under 18 years of age shall be eligible for a permit under this section.

(2) No business for which a permit has been issued shall employ a person under 18 years of age in the capacity of a manager, agent, or representative.

(*l*)(1) An applicant, or an applicant's employees who have direct access, management, or control of any substance listed under subdivision (a) of Section 11100, for an initial permit shall submit with the application one set of 10–print fingerprints for each individual acting in the capacity of an owner, manager, agent, or representative for the applicant, unless the applicant's employees are exempted from this requirement by the Department of Justice. These exemptions may only be obtained upon the written request of the applicant.

(2) In the event of subsequent changes in ownership, management, or employment, the permittee shall notify the department in writing within 15 calendar days of the changes, and shall submit one set of 10–print fingerprints for each individual not previously fingerprinted under this section. *(Added by Stats.1986, c. 1028, § 2, operative April 1, 1987. Amended by Stats.1987, c. 5, § 3, eff. March 17, 1987, operative April 1, 1987; Stats.1988, c. 73, § 2; Stats.1989, c. 1133, § 3; Stats.1992, c. 579 (S.B.1821), § 1, eff. Aug. 31, 1992; Stats.1997, c. 397 (A.B.1173), § 4; Stats.1999, c. 978 (A.B.162), § 2; Stats.2002, c. 13 (A.B.154), § 1, eff. March 21, 2002; Stats.2003, c. 369 (S.B.276), § 4, eff. Sept. 12, 2003; Stats.2005, c. 468 (A.B.465), § 6.)*

Cross References

Administer defined for purposes of this Division, see Health and Safety Code § 11002.
Agent defined for purposes of this Division, see Health and Safety Code § 11003.
Distributor defined for purposes of this Division, see Health and Safety Code § 11013.
Felonies, definition and penalties, see Penal Code §§ 17, 18.
Furnish defined for purposes of this Division, see Health and Safety Code § 11016.
Manufacturer defined for purposes of this Division, see Health and Safety Code § 11017.
Misdemeanors, definition and penalties, see Penal Code §§ 17, 19 and 19.2.
Person defined for purposes of this Division, see Health and Safety Code § 11022.
Physician, dentist, podiatrist, pharmacist, veterinarian, and optometrist defined for purposes of this Division, see Health and Safety Code § 11024.
Prescription or electronic transmission prescription defined for purposes of this Division, see Health and Safety Code § 11027.
Uniform controlled substances act, regulation and control, reporting, drug cleanup fines, transfer of funds, see Health and Safety Code § 11100.05.

Wholesaler defined for purposes of this Division, see Health and Safety Code § 11031.

§ 11106.5. Interim orders suspending permittee or imposing permit restrictions

(a) The Department of Justice, or an administrative law judge sitting alone as provided in subdivision (h), may upon petition issue an interim order suspending any permittee or imposing permit restrictions. The petition shall include affidavits that demonstrate, to the satisfaction of the department, both of the following:

(1) The permittee has engaged in acts or omissions constituting a violation of this code or has been convicted of a crime substantially related to the permitted activity.

(2) Permitting the permittee to operate, or to continue to operate without restrictions, would endanger the public health, safety, or welfare.

(b) No interim order provided for in this section shall be issued without notice to the permittee, unless it appears from the petition and supporting documents that serious injury would result to the public before the matter could be heard on notice.

(c) Except as provided in subdivision (b), the permittee shall be given at least 15 days' notice of the hearing on the petition for an interim order. The notice shall include documents submitted to the department in support of the petition. If the order was initially issued without notice as provided in subdivision (b), the permittee shall be entitled to a hearing on the petition within 20 days of the issuance of the interim order without notice. The permittee shall be given notice of the hearing within two days after issuance of the initial interim order, and shall receive all documents in support of the petition. The failure of the department to provide a hearing within 20 days following issuance of the interim order without notice, unless the permittee waives his or her right to the hearing, shall result in the dissolution of the interim order by operation of law.

(d) At the hearing on the petition for an interim order, the permittee may do the following:

(1) Be represented by counsel.

(2) Have a record made of the proceedings, copies of which shall be available to the permittee upon payment of costs computed in accordance with the provisions for transcript costs for judicial review contained in Section 11523 of the Government Code.

(3) Present affidavits and other documentary evidence.

(4) Present oral argument.

(e) The department, or an administrative law judge sitting alone as provided in subdivision (h), shall issue a decision on the petition for interim order within five business days following submission of the matter. The standard of proof required to obtain an interim order pursuant to this section shall be a preponderance of the evidence standard. If the interim order was previously issued without notice, the department shall determine whether the order shall remain in effect, be dissolved, or be modified.

(f) The department shall file an accusation within 15 days of the issuance of an interim order. In the case of an interim order issued without notice, the time shall run from the date of the order issued after the noticed hearing. If the permittee files a notice of defense, the hearing shall be held within 30 days of the agency's receipt of the notice of defense. A decision shall be rendered on the accusation no later than 30 days after submission of the matter. Failure to comply with any of the requirements in this subdivision shall dissolve the interim order by operation of law.

(g) Interim orders shall be subject to judicial review pursuant to Section 1094.5 of the Code of Civil Procedure and shall be heard only in the superior court in and for the County of Sacramento, San Francisco, Los Angeles, or San Diego. The review of an interim order shall be limited to a determination of whether the department abused its discretion in the issuance of the interim order. Abuse of discretion is established if the respondent department has not proceeded in the manner required by law, or if the court determines that the interim order is not supported by substantial evidence in light of the whole record.

(h) The department may, in its sole discretion, delegate the hearing on any petition for an interim order to an administrative law judge in the Office of Administrative Hearings. If the department hears the noticed petition itself, an administrative law judge shall preside at the hearing, rule on the admission and exclusion of evidence, and advise the department on matters of law. The department shall exercise all other powers relating to the conduct of the hearing, but may delegate any or all of them to the administrative law judge. When the petition has been delegated to an administrative law judge, he or she shall sit alone and exercise all of the powers of the department relating to the conduct of the hearing. A decision issued by an administrative law judge sitting alone shall be final when it is filed with the department. If the administrative law judge issues an interim order without notice, he or she shall preside at the noticed hearing, unless unavailable, in which case another administrative law judge may hear the matter. The decision of the administrative law judge sitting alone on the petition for an interim order is final, subject only to judicial review in accordance with subdivision (g).

(i)(1) Failure to comply with an interim order issued pursuant to subdivision (a) or (b) shall constitute a separate cause for disciplinary action against any permittee, and may be heard at, and as a part of, the noticed hearing provided for in subdivision (f). Allegations of noncompliance with the interim order may be filed at any time prior to the rendering of a decision on the accusation. Violation of the interim order is established upon proof that the permittee was on notice of the interim order and its terms, and that the order was in effect at the time of the violation. The finding of a violation of an interim order made at the hearing on the accusation shall be reviewed as a part of any review of a final decision of the department.

(2) If the interim order issued by the department provides for anything less than a complete suspension of the permittee and the permittee violates the interim order prior to the hearing on the accusation provided for in subdivision (f), the department may, upon notice to the permittee and proof of violation, modify or expand the interim order.

(j) A plea or verdict of guilty or a conviction after a plea of nolo contendere is deemed to be a conviction within the meaning of this section. A certified record of the conviction shall be conclusive evidence of the fact that the conviction occurred. The department may take action under this section notwithstanding the fact that an appeal of the conviction may be taken.

(k) The interim orders provided for by this section shall be in addition to, and not a limitation on, the authority to seek injunctive relief provided in any other provision of law. *(Added by Stats.1997, c. 397 (A.B.1173), § 5. Amended by Stats.2012, c. 867 (S.B.1144), § 4.)*

§ 11106.7. Violations of chapter provisions or regulations by permittees; system for issuance of citations; order of abatement or order for payment of assessment of administrative fine

(a) The Department of Justice may establish, by regulation, a system for the issuance to a permittee of a citation which may contain an order of abatement or an order to pay an administrative fine assessed by the Department of Justice, if the permittee is in violation of any provision of this chapter or any regulation adopted by the Department of Justice pursuant to this chapter.

(b) The system shall contain the following provisions:

(1) Citations shall be in writing and shall describe with particularity the nature of the violation, including specific reference to the provision of law or regulation of the department determined to have been violated.

(2) Whenever appropriate, the citation shall contain an order of abatement fixing a reasonable time for abatement of the violation.

(3) In no event shall the administrative fine assessed by the department exceed two thousand five hundred dollars ($2,500) for each violation. In assessing a fine, due consideration shall be given to the appropriateness of the amount of the fine with respect to such factors as the gravity of the violation, the good faith of the permittee, and the history of previous violations.

(4) An order of abatement or a fine assessment issued pursuant to a citation shall inform the permittee that if the permittee desires a hearing to contest the finding of a violation, that hearing shall be requested by written notice to the department within 30 days of the date of issuance of the citation or assessment. Hearings shall be held pursuant to Chapter 5 (commencing with Section 11500) of Part 1 of Division 3 of Title 2 of the Government Code.

(5) In addition to requesting a hearing, the permittee may, within 10 days after service of the citation, request in writing an opportunity for an informal conference with the department regarding the citation. At the conclusion of the informal conference, the department may affirm, modify, or dismiss the citation, including any fine levied or order of abatement issued. The decision shall be deemed to be a final order with regard to the citation issued, including the fine levied and the order of abatement. However, the permittee does not waive its right to request a hearing to contest a citation by requesting an informal conference. If the citation is dismissed after the informal conference, the request for a hearing on the matter of the citation shall be deemed to be withdrawn. If the citation, including any fine levied or order of abatement, is modified, the citation originally issued shall be considered withdrawn and a new citation issued. If a hearing is requested for a subsequent citation, it shall be requested within 30 days of service of that subsequent citation.

(6) Failure of a permittee to pay a fine within 30 days of the date of assessment or comply with an order of abatement within the fixed time, unless the citation is being appealed, may result in disciplinary action being taken by the department. If a citation is not contested and a fine is not paid, the full amount of the assessed fine shall be added to the renewal of the permit. A permit shall not be renewed without payment of the renewal fee and fine.

(c) The system may contain the following provisions:

(1) A citation may be issued without the assessment of an administrative fine.

(2) Assessment of administrative fines may be limited to only particular violations of the law or department regulations.

(d) Notwithstanding any other provision of law, if a fine is paid to satisfy an assessment based on the finding of a violation, payment of the fine shall be represented as satisfactory resolution of the matter for purposes of public disclosure.

(e) Administrative fines collected pursuant to this section shall be deposited in the General Fund.

(f) The sanctions authorized under this section shall be separate from, and in addition to, any other administrative, civil, or criminal remedies; however, a criminal action may not be initiated for a specific offense if a citation has been issued pursuant to this section for that offense, and a citation may not be issued pursuant to this section for a specific offense if a criminal action for that offense has been filed.

(g) Nothing in this section shall be deemed to prevent the department from serving and prosecuting an accusation to suspend or revoke a permit if grounds for that suspension or revocation exist. *(Added by Stats.2003, c. 142 (A.B.709), § 1.)*

§ 11107. Laboratory glassware or apparatus, chemical reagents or solvents; duties of sellers; violations

(a) Any manufacturer, wholesaler, retailer, or other person or entity in this state that sells to any person or entity in this state or any other state, any laboratory glassware or apparatus, any chemical reagent or solvent, or any combination thereof, where the value of the goods sold in the transaction exceeds one hundred dollars ($100) shall do the following:

(1) Notwithstanding any other law, in any face-to-face or will-call sale, the seller shall prepare a bill of sale which identifies the date of sale, cost of product, method of payment, specific items and quantities purchased, and the proper purchaser identification information, all of which shall be entered onto the bill of sale or a legible copy of the bill of sale, and shall also affix on the bill of sale his or her signature as witness to the purchase and identification of the purchaser.

(A) For the purposes of this section, "proper purchaser identification" includes a valid motor vehicle operator's license or other official and valid state-issued identification of the purchaser that contains a photograph of the purchaser, and includes the residential or mailing address of the purchaser, other than a post office box number, the motor vehicle license number of the motor vehicle used by the purchaser at the time of purchase, a description of how the substance is to be used, and the signature of the purchaser.

(B) The seller shall retain the original bill of sale containing the purchaser identification information for five years in a readily presentable manner, and present the bill of sale containing the purchaser identification information upon demand by any law enforcement officer or authorized representative of the Attorney General. Copies of these bills of sale obtained by representatives of the Attorney General shall be maintained by the Department of Justice for a period of not less than five years.

(2)(A) Notwithstanding any other law, in all sales other than face-to- face or will-call sales the seller shall maintain for a period of five years the following sales information: the name and address of the purchaser, date of sale, product description, cost of product, method of payment, method of delivery, delivery address, and valid identifying information.

(B) For the purposes of this paragraph, "valid identifying information" includes two or more of the following: federal tax identification number; resale tax identification number; city or county business license number; license issued by the State Department of Public Health; registration number issued by the federal Drug Enforcement Administration; precursor business permit number issued by the Department of Justice; motor vehicle operator's license; or other identification issued by a state.

(C) The seller shall, upon the request of any law enforcement officer or any authorized representative of the Attorney General, produce a report or record of sale containing the information in a readily presentable manner.

(D) If a common carrier is used, the seller shall maintain a manifest regarding the delivery in a readily presentable manner and for a period of five years.

(b) This section shall not apply to any wholesaler who is licensed by the California State Board of Pharmacy and registered with the federal Drug Enforcement Administration of the United States Department of Justice and who sells laboratory glassware or apparatus, any chemical reagent or solvent, or any combination thereof, to a licensed pharmacy, physician, dentist, podiatrist, or veterinarian.

(c) A violation of this section is a misdemeanor.

(d) For the purposes of this section, the following terms have the following meanings:

(1) "Laboratory glassware" includes, but is not limited to, condensers, flasks, separatory funnels, and beakers.

(2) "Apparatus" includes, but is not limited to, heating mantles, ring stands, and rheostats.

(3) "Chemical reagent" means a chemical that reacts chemically with one or more precursors, but does not become part of the finished product.

(4) "Chemical solvent" means a chemical that does not react chemically with a precursor or reagent and does not become part of the finished product. A "chemical solvent" helps other chemicals mix, cools chemical reactions, and cleans the finished product. *(Added by Stats.1989, c. 1133, § 4. Amended by Stats.1992, c. 578 (S.B.1057), § 1; Stats.1992, c. 580 (S.B.1820), § 3, eff. Aug. 31, 1992; Stats.1997, c. 397 (A.B.1173), § 6; Stats.2003, c. 369 (S.B.276), § 5, eff. Sept. 12, 2003; Stats.2012, c. 867 (S.B.1144), § 5.)*

Cross References

Attorney General, generally, see Government Code § 12500 et seq.
Attorney General defined for purposes of this Division, see Health and Safety Code § 11004.
Deliver or delivery defined for purposes of this Division, see Health and Safety Code § 11009.
Department of Health Care Services, generally, see Health and Safety Code § 100100 et seq.
Manufacturer defined for purposes of this Division, see Health and Safety Code § 11017.
Misdemeanors, definition and penalties, see Penal Code §§ 17, 19 and 19.2.
Person defined for purposes of this Division, see Health and Safety Code § 11022.
Physician, dentist, podiatrist, pharmacist, veterinarian, and optometrist defined for purposes of this Division, see Health and Safety Code § 11024.
Wholesaler defined for purposes of this Division, see Health and Safety Code § 11031.

Research References

2 Witkin, California Criminal Law 4th Crimes Against Public Peace and Welfare § 135 (2021), Duties of Lawful Seller.

§ 11107.1. Sales of specified chemicals; duties of seller; violations

(a) Any manufacturer, wholesaler, retailer, or other person or entity in this state that sells to any person or entity in this state or any other state any quantity of sodium cyanide, potassium cyanide, cyclohexanone, bromobenzene, magnesium turnings, mercuric chloride, sodium metal, lead acetate, palladium black, hydrogen chloride gas, trichlorofluoromethane (fluorotrichloromethane), dichlorodifluoromethane, 1,1,2–trichloro–1,2,2–trifluoroethane (trichlorotrifluoroethane), sodium acetate, or acetic anhydride shall do the following:

(1)(A) Notwithstanding any other provision of law, in any face-to-face or will-call sale, the seller shall prepare a bill of sale which identifies the date of sale, cost of sale, method of payment, the specific items and quantities purchased and the proper purchaser identification information, all of which shall be entered onto the bill of sale or a legible copy of the bill of sale, and shall also affix on the bill of sale his or her signature as witness to the purchase and identification of the purchaser.

(B) For the purposes of this paragraph, "proper purchaser identification" includes a valid driver's license or other official and valid state-issued identification of the purchaser that contains a photograph of the purchaser, and includes the residential or mailing address of the purchaser, other than a post office box number, the motor vehicle license number of the motor vehicle used by the purchaser at the time of purchase, a description of how the substance is to be used, the Environmental Protection Agency certification number or resale tax identification number assigned to the individual or business entity for which the individual is purchasing any chlorofluorocarbon product, and the signature of the purchaser.

(C) The seller shall retain the original bill of sale containing the purchaser identification information for five years in a readily presentable manner, and present the bill of sale containing the purchaser identification information upon demand by any law enforcement officer or authorized representative of the Attorney General. Copies of these bills of sale obtained by representatives of the Attorney General shall be maintained by the Department of Justice for a period of not less than five years.

(2)(A) Notwithstanding any other law, in all sales other than face-to- face or will-call sales the seller shall maintain for a period of five years the following sales information: the name and address of the purchaser, date of sale, product description, cost of product, method of payment, method of delivery, delivery address, and valid identifying information.

(B) For the purposes of this paragraph, "valid identifying information" includes two or more of the following: federal tax identification number; resale tax identification number; city or county business license number; license issued by the State Department of Public Health; registration number issued by the federal Drug Enforcement Administration; precursor business permit number issued by the Department of Justice; driver's license; or other identification issued by a state.

(C) The seller shall, upon the request of any law enforcement officer or any authorized representative of the Attorney General, produce a report or record of sale containing the information in a readily presentable manner.

(D) If a common carrier is used, the seller shall maintain a manifest regarding the delivery in a readily presentable manner for a period of five years.

(b) Any manufacturer, wholesaler, retailer, or other person or entity in this state that purchases any item listed in subdivision (a) of Section 11107.1 shall do the following:

(1) Provide on the record of purchase information on the source of the items purchased, the date of purchase, a description of the specific items, the quantities of each item purchased, and the cost of the items purchased.

(2) Retain the record of purchase for three years in a readily presentable manner and present the record of purchase upon demand to any law enforcement officer or authorized representative of the Attorney General.

(c)(1) A first violation of this section is a misdemeanor.

(2) Any person who has previously been convicted of a violation of this section shall, upon a subsequent conviction thereof, be punished by imprisonment in a county jail not exceeding one year, by a fine not exceeding one hundred thousand dollars ($100,000), or both the fine and imprisonment. *(Added by Stats.1989, c. 1133, § 5. Amended by Stats.1990, c. 352 (S.B.2329), § 1; Stats.1992, c. 580 (S.B.1820), § 4, eff. Aug. 31, 1992; Stats.1997, c. 397 (A.B.1173), § 7; Stats.1998, c. 305 (S.B.1539), § 1; Stats.2003, c. 369 (S.B.276), § 6, eff. Sept. 12, 2003; Stats.2005, c. 468 (A.B.465), § 7; Stats.2012, c. 867 (S.B.1144), § 6.)*

Cross References

Attorney General, generally, see Government Code § 12500 et seq.
Attorney General defined for purposes of this Division, see Health and Safety Code § 11004.
Deliver or delivery defined for purposes of this Division, see Health and Safety Code § 11009.
Department of Health Care Services, generally, see Health and Safety Code § 100100 et seq.
Manufacturer defined for purposes of this Division, see Health and Safety Code § 11017.
Misdemeanors, definition and penalties, see Penal Code §§ 17, 19 and 19.2.
Person defined for purposes of this Division, see Health and Safety Code § 11022.
Wholesaler defined for purposes of this Division, see Health and Safety Code § 11031.

Research References

2 Witkin, California Criminal Law 4th Crimes Against Public Peace and Welfare § 133 (2021), In General.

2 Witkin, California Criminal Law 4th Crimes Against Public Peace and Welfare § 135 (2021), Duties of Lawful Seller.

§ 11107.2. Sale of nonodorized butane prohibited; exemptions; penalties

(a) Except as otherwise provided in subdivision (b), it is unlawful for a manufacturer, wholesaler, reseller, retailer, or other person or entity to sell to any customer any quantity of nonodorized butane.

(b) The limitations in subdivisions (a) shall not apply to any of the following transactions:

(1) Butane sold to manufacturers, wholesalers, resellers, or retailers solely for the purpose of resale.

(2) Butane sold to a person for use in a lawful commercial enterprise, including, but not limited to, a volatile solvent extraction activity licensed under Division 10 (commencing with Section 26000) of the Business and Professions Code or a medical cannabis collective or cooperative described in subdivision (b) of Section 11362.775 of this code, operating in compliance with all applicable state licensing requirements and local regulations governing that type of business.

(3) The sale of pocket lighters, utility lighters, grill lighters, torch lighters, butane gas appliances, refill canisters, gas cartridges, or other products that contain or use nonodorized butane and contain less than 150 milliliters of butane.

(4) The sale of any product in which butane is used as an aerosol propellant.

(c)(1) Any person or business that violates subdivision (a) is subject to a civil penalty of two thousand five hundred dollars ($2,500).

(2) The Attorney General, a city attorney, a county counsel, or a district attorney may bring a civil action to enforce this section.

(3) The civil penalty shall be deposited into the General Fund if the action is brought by the Attorney General. If the action is brought by a city attorney, the civil penalty shall be paid to the treasurer of the city in which the judgment is entered. If the action is brought by a county counsel or district attorney, the civil penalty shall be paid to the treasurer of the county in which the judgment is entered.

(d) As used in this section, the following definitions shall apply:

(1) "Customer" means any person or entity other than those described in paragraphs (1) and (2) of subdivision (b) that purchases or acquires nonodorized butane from a seller during a transaction.

(2) "Nonodorized butane" means iso-butane, n-butane, butane, or a mixture of butane and propane of any power that may also use the words "refined," "pure," "purified," "premium," or "filtered," to describe the butane or butane mixture, which does not contain ethyl mercaptan or a similar odorant.

(3) "Sell" or "sale" means to furnish, give away, exchange, transfer, deliver, surrender, distribute, or supply, in exchange for money or any other consideration.

(4) "Seller" means any person, business entity, or employee thereof that sells nonodorized butane to any customer within this state.

(e) This section shall become operative on July 1, 2019. *(Added by Stats.2018, c. 595 (A.B.3112), § 1, eff. Jan. 1, 2019, operative July 1, 2019.)*

Research References

2 Witkin, California Criminal Law 4th Crimes Against Public Peace and Welfare § 133 (2021), In General.

§ 11110. Supplying drugs containing dextromethorphan to minors; fines; prima facie evidence of violation; proof

(a) It shall be an infraction, punishable by a fine not exceeding two hundred fifty dollars ($250), for any person, corporation, or retail distributor to willfully and knowingly supply, deliver, or give possession of a drug, material, compound, mixture, preparation, or substance containing any quantity of dextromethorphan (the dextrorotatory isomer of 3–methoxy–N–methylmorphinan, including its salts, but not including its racemic or levorotatory forms) to a person under 18 years of age in an over-the-counter sale without a prescription.

(b) It shall be prima facie evidence of a violation of this section if the person, corporation, or retail distributor making the sale does not require and obtain bona fide evidence of majority and identity from the purchaser, unless from the purchaser's outward appearance the person making the sale would reasonably presume the purchaser to be 25 years of age or older.

(c) Proof that a person, corporation, or retail distributor, or his or her agent or employee, demanded, was shown, and acted in reasonable reliance upon, bona fide evidence of majority and identity shall be a defense to any criminal prosecution under this section. As used in this section, "bona fide evidence of majority and identity" means a document issued by a federal, state, county, or municipal government, or subdivision or agency thereof, including, but not limited to, a motor vehicle operator's license, California state identification card, identification card issued to a member of the Armed Forces, or other form of identification that bears the name, date of birth, description, and picture of the person.

(d)(1) Notwithstanding any other provision of this section, a retail clerk who fails to require and obtain proof of age from the purchaser shall not be guilty of an infraction pursuant to subdivision (a) or subject to any civil penalties.

(2) This subdivision shall not apply to a retail clerk who is a willful participant in an ongoing criminal conspiracy to violate this section. *(Added by Stats.2011, c. 199 (S.B.514), § 1.)*

Research References

2 Witkin, California Criminal Law 4th Crimes Against Public Peace and Welfare § 127 (2021), Other Drugs.

§ 11111. Sale of products containing dextromethorphan without prescription; use of cash register equipped with age-verification feature to monitor age-restricted items

A person, corporation, or retail distributor that sells or makes available products containing dextromethorphan, as defined in subdivision (a) of Section 11110, in an over-the-counter sale without a prescription shall, if feasible, use a cash register that is equipped with an age-verification feature to monitor age-restricted items. The cash register shall be programmed to direct the retail clerk making the sale to request bona fide evidence of majority and identity, as described in subdivision (c) of Section 11110, before a product containing dextromethorphan may be purchased. *(Added by Stats. 2011, c. 199 (S.B.514), § 2.)*

Research References

2 Witkin, California Criminal Law 4th Crimes Against Public Peace and Welfare § 127 (2021), Other Drugs.

CHAPTER 4. PRESCRIPTIONS

ARTICLE 1. REQUIREMENTS OF PRESCRIPTIONS

§ 11150. Persons authorized to write or issue prescriptions

No person other than a physician, dentist, podiatrist, or veterinarian, or naturopathic doctor acting pursuant to Section 3640.7 of the Business and Professions Code, or pharmacist acting within the scope of a project authorized under Article 1 (commencing with Section 128125) of Chapter 3 of Part 3 of Division 107 or within the scope of Section 4052.1, 4052.2, or 4052.6 of the Business and Professions Code, a registered nurse acting within the scope of a project authorized under Article 1 (commencing with Section 128125) of Chapter 3 of Part 3 of Division 107, a certified nurse-midwife acting within the scope of Section 2746.51 of the Business and Professions Code, a nurse practitioner acting within the scope of Section 2836.1 of the Business and Professions Code, a physician assistant acting within the scope of a project authorized under Article 1 (commencing with Section 128125) of Chapter 3 of Part 3 of Division 107 or Section 3502.1 of the Business and Professions Code, a naturopathic doctor acting within the scope of Section 3640.5 of the Business and Professions Code, or an optometrist acting within the scope of Section 3041 of the Business and Professions Code, or an out-of-state prescriber acting pursuant to Section 4005 of the Business and Professions Code shall write or issue a prescription. *(Added by Stats.1972, c. 1407, p. 3001, § 3. Amended by Stats.1977, c. 843, p. 2533, § 18; Stats.1981, c. 113, p. 847, § 9; Stats.1996, c. 1023 (S.B.1497), § 198, eff. Sept. 29, 1996; Stats.1997, c. 549 (S.B.1349), § 142; Stats.1999, c. 749 (S.B.816), § 8; Stats.2000, c. 676 (S.B.929), § 8; Stats.2001, c. 289 (S.B.298), § 11; Stats.2004, c. 191 (A.B.2660), § 6; Stats.2005, c. 506 (A.B.302), § 26, eff. Oct. 4, 2005; Stats.2009, c. 308 (S.B.819), § 93; Stats.2014, c. 319 (S.B.1039), § 5, eff. Jan. 1, 2015.)*

Cross References

Conditions authorizing prescription, see Health and Safety Code § 11210.

Controlled Substance Utilization Review and Evaluation System (CURES) fee, creation of CURES Fund, CURES operation and maintenance, see Business and Professions Code § 208.
Controlled substances for self use, see Health and Safety Code § 11170.
Disclosure of Controlled Substance Utilization Review and Evaluation System (CURES) data, see Health and Safety Code § 11165.1.
False representation as physician to obtain prescription drugs, see Business and Professions Code § 4323.
Operation of pharmacy by unauthorized person, see Business and Professions Code § 4328.
Person defined for purposes of this Division, see Health and Safety Code § 11022.
Persons who may write prescriptions, see Business and Professions Code § 4040.
Pharmacy, power to perform procedures and functions, see Business and Professions Code § 4052.
Physician, dentist, podiatrist, pharmacist, veterinarian, and optometrist defined for purposes of this Division, see Health and Safety Code § 11024.
Practitioner defined for purposes of this Division, see Health and Safety Code § 11026.
Prescription or electronic transmission prescription defined for purposes of this Division, see Health and Safety Code § 11027.
Prescriptions by veterinarians, see Health and Safety Code §§ 11240, 11241.

Research References

2 Witkin, California Criminal Law 4th Crimes Against Public Peace and Welfare § 152 (2021), In General.

§ 11150.2. Cannabinoid products; compliance with federal law deemed to be compliance with state law; exception

(a) Notwithstanding any other law, if cannabinoids are excluded from Schedule I of the federal Controlled Substances Act and placed on a schedule of the act other than Schedule I, or if a product composed of cannabinoids is approved by the federal Food and Drug Administration and either placed on a schedule of the act other than Schedule I, or exempted from one or more provisions of the act, so as to permit a physician, pharmacist, or other authorized healing arts licensee acting within their scope of practice, to prescribe, furnish, or dispense that product, the physician, pharmacist, or other authorized healing arts licensee who prescribes, furnishes, or dispenses that product in accordance with federal law shall be deemed to be in compliance with state law governing those acts.

(b) For purposes of this chapter, upon the effective date of one of the changes in federal law described in subdivision (a), notwithstanding any other state law, a product composed of cannabinoids may be prescribed, furnished, dispensed, transferred, transported, possessed, or used in accordance with federal law and is authorized pursuant to state law.

(c) This section does not apply to any product containing cannabinoids that is made or derived from industrial hemp, as defined in Section 11018.5 and regulated pursuant to that section. *(Added by Stats.2018, c. 62 (A.B.710), § 3, eff. July 9, 2018. Amended by Stats.2021, c. 618 (A.B.527), § 4, eff. Jan. 1, 2022.)*

Research References

2 Witkin, California Criminal Law 4th Crimes Against Public Peace and Welfare § 152 (2021), In General.

§ 11150.6. Methaqualone; schedule I substance

Notwithstanding Section 11150.5 or subdivision (a) of Section 11054, methaqualone, its salts, isomers, and salts of its isomers shall be deemed to be classified in Schedule I for the purposes of this chapter. *(Added by Stats.1984, c. 22, § 1, eff. March 1, 1984.)*

Cross References

Isomer defined for purposes of this Division, see Health and Safety Code § 11033.

§ 11151. Prescriptions by unlicensed person authorized to practice

A prescription written by an unlicensed person lawfully practicing medicine pursuant to Section 2065 of the Business and Professions Code, shall be filled only at a pharmacy maintained in the hospital which employs such unlicensed person. *(Added by Stats.1972, c. 1407, p. 3001, § 3. Amended by Stats.1986, c. 248, § 144.)*

Cross References

Person defined for purposes of this Division, see Health and Safety Code § 11022.
Pharmacy defined for purposes of this Division, see Health and Safety Code § 11023.
Prescription or electronic transmission prescription defined for purposes of this Division, see Health and Safety Code § 11027.

§ 11152. Nonconforming prescriptions

No person shall write, issue, fill, compound, or dispense a prescription that does not conform to this division. *(Added by Stats.1972, c. 1407, p. 3001, § 3.)*

Cross References

Dispense defined for purposes of this Division, see Health and Safety Code § 11010.
Forgery of prescription, see Business and Professions Code § 4324.
Person defined for purposes of this Division, see Health and Safety Code § 11022.
Prescriptions defined, see Health and Safety Code § 11027.
Requisites of prescriptions, see Health and Safety Code § 11158.

Research References

2 Witkin, California Criminal Law 4th Crimes Against Public Peace and Welfare § 152 (2021), In General.

§ 11153. Controlled substance prescriptions; issuance; filling; legality; offense; penalties

(a) A prescription for a controlled substance shall only be issued for a legitimate medical purpose by an individual practitioner acting in the usual course of his or her professional practice. The responsibility for the proper prescribing and dispensing of controlled substances is upon the prescribing practitioner, but a corresponding responsibility rests with the pharmacist who fills the prescription. Except as authorized by this division, the following are not legal prescriptions: (1) an order purporting to be a prescription which is issued not in the usual course of professional treatment or in legitimate and authorized research; or (2) an order for an addict or habitual user of controlled substances, which is issued not in the course of professional treatment or as part of an authorized narcotic treatment program, for the purpose of providing the user with controlled substances, sufficient to keep him or her comfortable by maintaining customary use.

(b) Any person who knowingly violates this section shall be punished by imprisonment pursuant to subdivision (h) of Section 1170 of the Penal Code, or in a county jail not exceeding one year, or by a fine not exceeding twenty thousand dollars ($20,000), or by both that fine and imprisonment.

(c) No provision of the amendments to this section enacted during the second year of the 1981–82 Regular Session shall be construed as expanding the scope of practice of a pharmacist. *(Added by Stats.1982, c. 1284, p. 4753, § 3, eff. Sept. 22, 1982. Amended by Stats.1995, c. 455 (A.B.1113), § 5, eff. Sept. 5, 1995; Stats.2011, c. 15 (A.B.109), § 148, eff. April 4, 2011, operative Oct. 1, 2011.)*

Cross References

Conditions authorizing prescription of controlled substance, see Health and Safety Code § 11210.
Controlled substance defined for purposes of this Division, see Health and Safety Code § 11007.
Penalty for violation of provisions of this section, see Health and Safety Code § 11371.
Person defined for purposes of this Division, see Health and Safety Code § 11022.
Pharmacies, unprofessional conduct, licenses procured through misrepresentation, see Business and Professions Code § 4301.

Physician, dentist, podiatrist, pharmacist, veterinarian, and optometrist defined for purposes of this Division, see Health and Safety Code § 11024.
Practitioner defined for purposes of this Division, see Health and Safety Code § 11026.
Prescription or electronic transmission prescription defined for purposes of this Division, see Health and Safety Code § 11027.

Research References

2 Witkin, California Criminal Law 4th Crimes Against Public Peace and Welfare § 152 (2021), In General.
2 Witkin, California Criminal Law 4th Crimes Against Public Peace and Welfare § 153 (2021), Inducing Minor to Commit Prescription Offenses.

§ 11153.5. Furnishing controlled substances for other than legitimate medical purposes; punishment for violations

(a) No wholesaler or manufacturer, or agent or employee of a wholesaler or manufacturer, shall furnish controlled substances for other than legitimate medical purposes.

(b) Anyone who violates this section knowing, or having a conscious disregard for the fact, that the controlled substances are for other than a legitimate medical purpose shall be punishable by imprisonment pursuant to subdivision (h) of Section 1170 of the Penal Code, or in a county jail not exceeding one year, or by a fine not exceeding twenty thousand dollars ($20,000), or by both that fine and imprisonment.

(c) Factors to be considered in determining whether a wholesaler or manufacturer, or agent or employee of a wholesaler or manufacturer, furnished controlled substances knowing or having a conscious disregard for the fact that the controlled substances are for other than legitimate medical purposes shall include, but not be limited to, whether the use of controlled substances was for purposes of increasing athletic ability or performance, the amount of controlled substances furnished, the previous ordering pattern of the customer (including size and frequency of orders), the type and size of the customer, and where and to whom the customer distributes the product. *(Added by Stats.1986, c. 384, § 4, eff. July 17, 1986. Amended by Stats.1987, c. 181, § 1; Stats.1988, c. 918, § 5; Stats. 2011, c. 15 (A.B.109), § 149, eff. April 4, 2011, operative Oct. 1, 2011.)*

Cross References

Agent defined for purposes of this Division, see Health and Safety Code § 11003.
Controlled substance defined for purposes of this Division, see Health and Safety Code § 11007.
Distribute defined for purposes of this Division, see Health and Safety Code § 11012.
Furnish defined for purposes of this Division, see Health and Safety Code § 11016.
Manufacturer defined for purposes of this Division, see Health and Safety Code § 11017.
Pharmacies, unprofessional conduct, licenses procured through misrepresentation, see Business and Professions Code § 4301.
Wholesaler defined for purposes of this Division, see Health and Safety Code § 11031.

Research References

2 Witkin, California Criminal Law 4th Crimes Against Public Peace and Welfare § 152 (2021), In General.

§ 11154. Prescription, administration or furnishing controlled substances, restrictions

(a) Except in the regular practice of his or her profession, no person shall knowingly prescribe, administer, dispense, or furnish a controlled substance to or for any person or animal which is not under his or her treatment for a pathology or condition other than addiction to a controlled substance, except as provided in this division.

(b) No person shall knowingly solicit, direct, induce, aid, or encourage a practitioner authorized to write a prescription to unlawfully prescribe, administer, dispense, or furnish a controlled substance. *(Added by Stats.1972, c. 1407, p. 3002, § 3. Amended by Stats.1982, c. 1403, p. 5356, § 1.)*

Cross References

Administer defined for purposes of this Division, see Health and Safety Code § 11002.
Children who are exposed to alcohol or drugs or who are HIV positive, placement, see Welfare and Institutions Code § 16525.30.
Controlled substance defined for purposes of this Division, see Health and Safety Code § 11007.
Controlled substances for self use, see Health and Safety Code § 11170.
Dispense defined for purposes of this Division, see Health and Safety Code § 11010.
Furnish defined for purposes of this Division, see Health and Safety Code § 11016.
Lawful medical use, see Health and Safety Code § 11210 et seq.
Penalty for violation of provisions of this section, see Health and Safety Code § 11371.
Person defined for purposes of this Division, see Health and Safety Code § 11022.
Practitioner defined for purposes of this Division, see Health and Safety Code § 11026.
Prescription or electronic transmission prescription defined for purposes of this Division, see Health and Safety Code § 11027.
Veterinarians, prohibition against prescribing controlled substances for human beings, see Health and Safety Code § 11240.

Research References

2 Witkin, California Criminal Law 4th Crimes Against Public Peace and Welfare § 152 (2021), In General.
1 Witkin California Criminal Law 4th Defenses § 220 (2021), Prior Administrative Proceeding.

§ 11155. Physician surrendering controlled substance privileges; prohibited acts

Any physician, who by court order or order of any state or governmental agency, or who voluntarily surrenders his controlled substance privileges, shall not possess, administer, dispense, or prescribe a controlled substance unless and until such privileges have been restored, and he has obtained current registration from the appropriate federal agency as provided by law. *(Added by Stats.1972, c. 1407, p. 3002, § 3.)*

Cross References

Administer defined for purposes of this Division, see Health and Safety Code § 11002.
Controlled substance defined for purposes of this Division, see Health and Safety Code § 11007.
Dispense defined for purposes of this Division, see Health and Safety Code § 11010.
Offense, punishment, see Health and Safety Code § 11371.
Physician, dentist, podiatrist, pharmacist, veterinarian, and optometrist defined for purposes of this Division, see Health and Safety Code § 11024.

Research References

2 Witkin, California Criminal Law 4th Crimes Against Public Peace and Welfare § 152 (2021), In General.

§ 11156. Prescribing, administering or dispensing controlled substances to addict prohibited; exceptions; "addict" defined

(a) Except as provided in Section 2241 of the Business and Professions Code, no person shall prescribe for, or administer, or dispense a controlled substance to, an addict, or to any person representing himself or herself as such, except as permitted by this division.

(b)(1) For purposes of this section, "addict" means a person whose actions are characterized by craving in combination with one or more of the following:

(A) Impaired control over drug use.

(B) Compulsive use.

(C) Continued use despite harm.

(2) Notwithstanding paragraph (1), a person whose drug-seeking behavior is primarily due to the inadequate control of pain is not an addict within the meaning of this section. *(Added by Stats.1972, c. 1407, p. 3002, § 3. Amended by Stats.2006, c. 350 (A.B.2198), § 8.)*

Cross References

Administer defined for purposes of this Division, see Health and Safety Code § 11002.
Controlled substance defined for purposes of this Division, see Health and Safety Code § 11007.
Dispense defined for purposes of this Division, see Health and Safety Code § 11010.
Drug defined for purposes of this Division, see Health and Safety Code § 11014.
Narcotic addict defined, see Welfare and Institutions Code § 3009.
Penalty for violations of provisions of this section, see Health and Safety Code § 11371.
Person defined for purposes of this Division, see Health and Safety Code § 11022.
Treatment of addicts, see Health and Safety Code § 11215 et seq.

Research References

2 Witkin, California Criminal Law 4th Crimes Against Public Peace and Welfare § 152 (2021), In General.

§ 11157. False or fictitious prescription

No person shall issue a prescription that is false or fictitious in any respect. *(Added by Stats.1972, c. 1407, p. 3002, § 3.)*

Cross References

False representation as physician to obtain prescription drugs, see Business and Professions Code § 4323.
Forged or altered prescriptions, punishment, see Health and Safety Code § 11368.
Forgery of prescription, see Business and Professions Code § 4324.
Person defined for purposes of this Division, see Health and Safety Code § 11022.
Prescription defined, see Health and Safety Code § 11027.

Research References

2 Witkin, California Criminal Law 4th Crimes Against Public Peace and Welfare § 152 (2021), In General.

§ 11158. Prescriptions for schedule II, III, IV and V substances; practitioners authorized to administer controlled substances

(a) Except as provided in Section 11159 or in subdivision (b) of this section, no controlled substance classified in Schedule II shall be dispensed without a prescription meeting the requirements of this chapter. Except as provided in Section 11159 or when dispensed directly to an ultimate user by a practitioner, other than a pharmacist or pharmacy, no controlled substance classified in Schedule III, IV, or V may be dispensed without a prescription meeting the requirements of this chapter.

(b) A practitioner specified in Section 11150 may dispense directly to an ultimate user a controlled substance classified in Schedule II in an amount not to exceed a 72-hour supply for the patient in accordance with directions for use given by the dispensing practitioner only where the patient is not expected to require any additional amount of the controlled substance beyond the 72 hours. Practitioners dispensing drugs pursuant to this subdivision shall meet the requirements of subdivision (f) of Section 11164.

(c) Except as otherwise prohibited or limited by law, a practitioner specified in Section 11150, may administer controlled substances in the regular practice of his or her profession. *(Added by Stats.1976, c. 896, p. 2057, § 6. Amended by Stats.1980, c. 1223, p. 4143, § 2.)*

Cross References

Administer defined for purposes of this Division, see Health and Safety Code § 11002.
Controlled substance defined for purposes of this Division, see Health and Safety Code § 11007.
Dispense defined for purposes of this Division, see Health and Safety Code § 11010.
Drug defined for purposes of this Division, see Health and Safety Code § 11014.
Healing arts, pharmacy, surgical clinics, surgical clinics, schedule II controlled substances, see Business and Professions Code § 4194.
Pharmacy defined for purposes of this Division, see Health and Safety Code § 11023.
Physician, dentist, podiatrist, pharmacist, veterinarian, and optometrist defined for purposes of this Division, see Health and Safety Code § 11024.
Practitioner defined for purposes of this Division, see Health and Safety Code § 11026.
Prescription or electronic transmission prescription defined for purposes of this Division, see Health and Safety Code § 11027.
Ultimate user defined for purposes of this Division, see Health and Safety Code § 11030.

Research References

2 Witkin, California Criminal Law 4th Crimes Against Public Peace and Welfare § 152 (2021), In General.

§ 11158.1. Prescription for controlled substance containing opioids; dispensing or issuing to minors; required discussions; exemptions

(a) Except when a patient is being treated as set forth in Sections 11159, 11159.2, and 11167.5, and Article 2 (commencing with Section 11215) of Chapter 5, pertaining to the treatment of addicts, or for a diagnosis of chronic intractable pain as used in Section 124960 of this code and Section 2241.5 of the Business and Professions Code, a prescriber shall discuss all of the following with the minor, the minor's parent or guardian, or another adult authorized to consent to the minor's medical treatment before directly dispensing or issuing for a minor the first prescription in a single course of treatment for a controlled substance containing an opioid:

(1) The risks of addiction and overdose associated with the use of opioids.

(2) The increased risk of addiction to an opioid to an individual who is suffering from both mental and substance abuse disorders.

(3) The danger of taking an opioid with a benzodiazepine, alcohol, or another central nervous system depressant.

(4) Any other information required by law.

(b) This section does not apply in any of the following circumstances:

(1) If the minor's treatment includes emergency services and care as defined in Section 1317.1.

(2) If the minor's treatment is associated with or incident to an emergency surgery, regardless of whether the surgery is performed on an inpatient or outpatient basis.

(3) If, in the prescriber's professional judgment, fulfilling the requirements of subdivision (a) would be detrimental to the minor's health or safety, or in violation of the minor's legal rights regarding confidentiality.

(c) Notwithstanding any other law, including Section 11374, failure to comply with this section shall not constitute a criminal offense. *(Added by Stats.2018, c. 693 (S.B.1109), § 13, eff. Jan. 1, 2019.)*

§ 11159. Order for use by hospital patient; form and contents; record

An order for controlled substances for use by a patient in a county or licensed hospital shall be exempt from all requirements of this article, but shall be in writing on the patient's record, signed by the prescriber, dated, and shall state the name and quantity of the controlled substance ordered and the quantity actually administered. The record of such orders shall be maintained as a hospital record for a minimum of seven years. *(Added by Stats.1972, c. 1407, p. 3002, § 3.)*

Cross References

Controlled substance defined for purposes of this Division, see Health and Safety Code § 11007.
Order for hospital patient as prescription, see Business and Professions Code § 4019.

Research References

2 Witkin, California Criminal Law 4th Crimes Against Public Peace and Welfare § 152 (2021), In General.

§ 11159.1. Order furnished to patients in certain clinics; requirements; record

An order for controlled substances furnished to a patient in a clinic which has a permit issued pursuant to Article 13 (commencing with Section 4180) of Chapter 9 of Division 2 of the Business and Professions Code, except an order for a Schedule II controlled substance, shall be exempt from the prescription requirements of this article and shall be in writing on the patient's record, signed by the prescriber, dated, and shall state the name and quantity of the controlled substance ordered and the quantity actually furnished. The record of the order shall be maintained as a clinic record for a minimum of seven years. This section shall apply only to a clinic that has obtained a permit under the provisions of Article 13 (commencing with Section 4180) of Chapter 9 of Division 2 of the Business and Professions Code.

Clinics that furnish controlled substances shall be required to keep a separate record of the furnishing of those drugs which shall be available for review and inspection by all properly authorized personnel. *(Added by Stats.1984, c. 757, § 3. Amended by Stats. 2004, c. 695 (S.B.1913), § 52.)*

Cross References

Controlled substance defined for purposes of this Division, see Health and Safety Code § 11007.
Drug defined for purposes of this Division, see Health and Safety Code § 11014.
Furnish defined for purposes of this Division, see Health and Safety Code § 11016.
Prescription or electronic transmission prescription defined for purposes of this Division, see Health and Safety Code § 11027.

Research References

2 Witkin, California Criminal Law 4th Crimes Against Public Peace and Welfare § 152 (2021), In General.

§ 11159.2. Treatment of terminally ill patient with controlled substances for pain relief; prescription requirements; technical errors in certification

(a) Notwithstanding any other provision of law, a prescription for a controlled substance for use by a patient who has a terminal illness may be written on a prescription form that does not meet the requirements of Section 11162.1 if the prescription meets the following requirements:

(1) Contain the information specified in subdivision (a) of Section 11164.

(2) Indicate that the prescriber has certified that the patient is terminally ill by the words "11159.2 exemption."

(b) A pharmacist may fill a prescription pursuant to this section when there is a technical error in the certification required by paragraph (2) of subdivision (a), provided that he or she has personal knowledge of the patient's terminal illness, and subsequently returns the prescription to the prescriber for correction within 72 hours.

(c) For purposes of this section, "terminally ill" means a patient who meets all of the following conditions:

(1) In the reasonable medical judgment of the prescribing physician, the patient has been determined to be suffering from an illness that is incurable and irreversible.

(2) In the reasonable medical judgment of the prescribing physician, the patient's illness will, if the illness takes its normal course, bring about the death of the patient within a period of one year.

(3) The patient's treatment by the physician prescribing a controlled substance pursuant to this section primarily is for the control of pain, symptom management, or both, rather than for cure of the illness.

(d) This section shall become operative on July 1, 2004. *(Added by Stats.2003, c. 406 (S.B.151), § 3.5, operative July 1, 2004. Amended by Stats.2005, c. 487 (S.B.734), § 1.)*

Cross References

Controlled substance defined for purposes of this Division, see Health and Safety Code § 11007.
Electronic data transmission prescriptions, see Business and Professions Code § 688.
Healing arts, medicine, enforcement, medicine, prioritization of investigative and prosecutorial resources, annual report requirements, see Business and Professions Code § 2220.05.
Physician, dentist, podiatrist, pharmacist, veterinarian, and optometrist defined for purposes of this Division, see Health and Safety Code § 11024.
Prescriber duties when prescribing an opioid or benzodiazepine medication to a patient, exceptions, see Business and Professions Code § 741.
Prescription or electronic transmission prescription defined for purposes of this Division, see Health and Safety Code § 11027.

§ 11159.3. Controlled substance prescriptions for patients who cannot access medications due to emergency; requirements

(a) Notwithstanding any other law, during a declared local, state, or federal emergency, if the California State Board of Pharmacy issues a notice that the board is waiving the application of the provisions of, or regulations adopted pursuant to, the Pharmacy Law, as specified in subdivision (b) of Section 4062 of the Business and Professions Code, a pharmacist may fill a prescription for a controlled substance for use by a patient who cannot access medications as a result of the declared local, state, or federal emergency, regardless of whether the prescription form meets the requirements of Section 11162.1, if the prescription meets the following requirements:

(1) Contains the information specified in subdivision (a) of Section 11164.

(2) Indicates that the patient is affected by a declared emergency with the words "11159.3 exemption" or a similar statement.

(3) Is written and dispensed within the first two weeks of the notice issued by the board.

(b) A pharmacist filling a prescription pursuant to this section shall do all of the following:

(1) Exercise appropriate professional judgment, including reviewing the patient's activity report from the CURES Prescription Drug Monitoring Program before dispensing the medication.

(2) If the prescription is for a Schedule II controlled substance, dispense no greater than the amount needed for a seven-day supply.

(3) Require the patient to first demonstrate, to the satisfaction of the pharmacist, their inability to access medications. This demonstration may include, but is not limited to, verification of residency within an evacuation area.

(c) A pharmacist shall not refill a prescription that has been dispensed pursuant to this section. *(Added by Stats.2019, c. 705 (S.B.569), § 1, eff. Jan. 1, 2020.)*

Research References

2 Witkin, California Criminal Law 4th Crimes Against Public Peace and Welfare § 152 (2021), In General.

§ 11161. Practitioner named in a warrant or accusatory pleading for certain enumerated felonies; order to surrender prescription forms and prohibit access to additional forms; hearings; motions to vacate

(a) When a practitioner is named in a warrant of arrest or is charged in an accusatory pleading with a felony violation of Section 11153, 11154, 11156, 11157, 11170, 11173, 11350, 11351, 11352, 11353, 11353.5, 11377, 11378, 11378.5, 11379, 11379.5, or 11379.6, the court in which the accusatory pleading is filed or the magistrate who issued the warrant of arrest shall, upon the motion of a law enforcement agency which is supported by reasonable cause, issue an order which requires the practitioner to surrender to the clerk of the court all controlled substance prescription forms in the practitioner's possession at a time set in the order and which prohibits the practitioner from obtaining, ordering, or using any additional prescription forms. The law enforcement agency obtaining the order shall notify the Department of Justice of this order. Except as provided in subdivisions (b) and (e) of this section, the order shall remain in effect until further order of the court. Any practitioner possessing prescription forms in violation of the order is guilty of a misdemeanor.

(b) The order provided by subdivision (a) shall be vacated if the court or magistrate finds that the underlying violation or violations are not supported by reasonable cause at a hearing held within two court days after the practitioner files and personally serves upon the prosecuting attorney and the law enforcement agency that obtained the order, a notice of motion to vacate the order with any affidavits on which the practitioner relies. At the hearing, the burden of proof, by a preponderance of the evidence, is on the prosecution. Evidence presented at the hearing shall be limited to the warrant of arrest with supporting affidavits, the motion to require the defendant to surrender controlled substance prescription forms and to prohibit the defendant from obtaining, ordering, or using controlled substance prescription forms, with supporting affidavits, the sworn complaint together with any documents or reports incorporated by reference thereto which, if based on information and belief, state the basis for the information, or any other documents of similar reliability as well as affidavits and counter affidavits submitted by the prosecution and defense. Granting of the motion to vacate the order is no bar to prosecution of the alleged violation or violations.

(c) The defendant may elect to challenge the order issued under subdivision (a) at the preliminary examination. At that hearing, the evidence shall be limited to that set forth in subdivision (b) and any other evidence otherwise admissible at the preliminary examination.

(d) If the practitioner has not moved to vacate the order issued under subdivision (a) by the time of the preliminary examination and he or she is held to answer on the underlying violation or violations, the practitioner shall be precluded from afterwards moving to vacate the order. If the defendant is not held to answer on the underlying charge or charges at the conclusion of the preliminary examination, the order issued under subdivision (a) shall be vacated.

(e) Notwithstanding subdivision (d), any practitioner who is diverted pursuant to Chapter 2.5 (commencing with Section 1000) of Title 7 of Part 2 of the Penal Code may file a motion to vacate the order issued under subdivision (a).

(f) This section shall become operative on November 1, 2004. *(Added by Stats.2003, c. 406 (S.B.151), § 5, operative July 1, 2004. Amended by Stats.2004, c. 573 (A.B.30), § 2, eff. Sept. 18, 2004, operative Nov. 1, 2004; Stats.2005, c. 487 (S.B.734), § 2.)*

Cross References

Burden of proof, generally, see Evidence Code § 500 et seq.
Controlled substance defined for purposes of this Division, see Health and Safety Code § 11007.
Felonies, definition and penalties, see Penal Code §§ 17, 18.
Misdemeanor, definition, penalties, see Penal Code §§ 17, 19, 19.2.
Practitioner defined for purposes of this Division, see Health and Safety Code § 11026.
Prescription or electronic transmission prescription defined for purposes of this Division, see Health and Safety Code § 11027.

§ 11161.5. Official prescription forms; approval of security printers; submission of exemplar; verification of prescriber license; ordering and delivery records; theft or loss; violations; penalties

(a) Prescription forms for controlled substance prescriptions shall be obtained from security printers approved by the Department of Justice.

(b) The department may approve security printer applications after the applicant has provided the following information:

(1) Name, address, and telephone number of the applicant.

(2) Policies and procedures of the applicant for verifying the identity of the prescriber ordering controlled substance prescription forms.

(3) Policies and procedures of the applicant for verifying delivery of controlled substance prescription forms to prescribers.

(4)(A) The location, names, and titles of the applicant's agent for service of process in this state; all principal corporate officers, if any; all managing general partners, if any; and any individual owner, partner, corporate officer, manager, agent, representative, employee, or subcontractor of the applicant who has direct access to, or management or control of, controlled substance prescription forms.

(B) A report containing this information shall be made on an annual basis and within 30 days after any change of office, principal corporate officers, managing general partner, or of any person described in subparagraph (A).

(5)(A) A signed statement indicating whether the applicant, any principal corporate officer, any managing general partner, or any individual owner, partner, corporate officer, manager, agent, representative, employee, or subcontractor of the applicant who has direct access to, or management or control of, controlled substance prescription forms, has ever been convicted of, or pled no contest to, a violation of any law of a foreign country, the United States, or any state, or of any local ordinance.

(B) The department shall provide the applicant and any individual owner, partner, corporate officer, manager, agent, representative, employee, or subcontractor of the applicant who has direct access to, or management or control of, controlled substance prescription forms, with the means and direction to provide fingerprints and related information, in a manner specified by the department, for the purpose of completing state, federal, or foreign criminal background checks.

(C) Any applicant described in subdivision (b) shall submit his or her fingerprint images and related information to the department, for the purpose of the department obtaining information as to the existence and nature of a record of state, federal, or foreign level convictions and state, federal, or foreign level arrests for which the department establishes that the applicant was released on bail or on his or her own recognizance pending trial, as described in subdivision (*l*) of Section 11105 of the Penal Code. Requests for federal level criminal offender record information received by the department pursuant to this section shall be forwarded to the Federal Bureau of Investigation by the department.

(D) The department shall assess against each security printer applicant a fee determined by the department to be sufficient to cover all processing, maintenance, and investigative costs generated from or associated with completing state, federal, or foreign background checks and inspections of security printers pursuant to this section with respect to that applicant; the fee shall be paid by the applicant at the time he or she submits the security printer application, fingerprints, and related information to the department.

(E) The department shall retain fingerprint impressions and related information for subsequent arrest notification pursuant to Section 11105.2 of the Penal Code for all applicants.

(c) The department may, within 60 calendar days of receipt of the application from the applicant, deny the security printer application.

(d) The department may deny a security printer application on any of the following grounds:

(1) The applicant, any individual owner, partner, corporate officer, manager, agent, representative, employee, or subcontractor for the applicant, who has direct access, management, or control of controlled substance prescription forms, has been convicted of a crime. A conviction within the meaning of this paragraph means a plea or verdict of guilty or a conviction following a plea of nolo contendere. Any action which a board is permitted to take following the establishment of a conviction may be taken when the time for appeal has elapsed, the judgment of conviction has been affirmed on appeal, or when an order granting probation is made suspending the imposition of sentence, irrespective of a subsequent order under the provisions of Section 1203.4 of the Penal Code.

(2) The applicant committed any act involving dishonesty, fraud, or deceit with the intent to substantially benefit himself, herself, or another, or substantially injure another.

(3) The applicant committed any act that would constitute a violation of this division.

(4) The applicant knowingly made a false statement of fact required to be revealed in the application to produce controlled substance prescription forms.

(5) The department determines that the applicant failed to demonstrate adequate security procedures relating to the production and distribution of controlled substance prescription forms.

(6) The department determines that the applicant has submitted an incomplete application.

(7) As a condition for its approval as a security printer, an applicant shall authorize the Department of Justice to make any examination of the books and records of the applicant, or to visit and inspect the applicant during business hours, to the extent deemed necessary by the board or department to properly enforce this section.

(e) An approved applicant shall submit an exemplar of a controlled substance prescription form, with all security features, to the Department of Justice within 30 days of initial production.

(f) The department shall maintain a list of approved security printers and the department shall make this information available to prescribers and other appropriate government agencies, including the Board of Pharmacy.

(g) Before printing any controlled substance prescription forms, a security printer shall verify with the appropriate licensing board that the prescriber possesses a license and current prescribing privileges which permits the prescribing of controlled substances with the federal Drug Enforcement Administration (DEA).

(h) Controlled substance prescription forms shall be provided directly to the prescriber either in person, by certified mail, or by a means that requires a signature signifying receipt of the package and provision of that signature to the security printer. Controlled substance prescription forms provided in person shall be restricted to established customers. Security printers shall obtain a photo identification from the customer and maintain a log of this information. Controlled substance prescription forms shall be shipped only to the prescriber's address on file and verified with the federal Drug Enforcement Administration or the Medical Board of California.

(i) Security printers shall retain ordering and delivery records in a readily retrievable manner for individual prescribers for three years.

(j) Security printers shall produce ordering and delivery records upon request by an authorized officer of the law as defined in Section 4017 of the Business and Professions Code.

(k) Security printers shall report any theft or loss of controlled substance prescription forms to the Department of Justice via fax or email within 24 hours of the theft or loss.

(*l*)(1) The department shall impose restrictions, sanctions, or penalties, subject to subdivisions (m) and (n), against security printers who are not in compliance with this division pursuant to regulations implemented pursuant to this division and shall revoke its approval of a security printer for a violation of this division or action that would permit a denial pursuant to subdivision (d) of this section.

(2) When the department revokes its approval, it shall notify the appropriate licensing boards and remove the security printer from the list of approved security printers.

(m) The following violations by security printers shall be punishable pursuant to subdivision (n):

(1) Failure to comply with the Security Printer Guidelines established by the Security Printer Program as a condition of approval.

(2) Failure to take reasonable precautions to prevent any dishonest act or illegal activity related to the access and control of security prescription forms.

(3) Theft or fraudulent use of a prescriber's identity in order to obtain security prescription forms.

(n) A security printer approved pursuant to subdivision (b) shall be subject to the following penalties for actions leading to the denial of a security printer application specified in subdivision (d) or for a violation specified in subdivision (m):

(1) For a first violation, a fine not to exceed one thousand dollars ($1,000).

(2) For a second or subsequent violation, a fine not to exceed two thousand five hundred dollars ($2,500) for each violation.

(3) For a third or subsequent violation, a filing of an administrative disciplinary action seeking to suspend or revoke security printer approval.

(*o*) In order to facilitate the standardization of all prescription forms and the serialization of prescription forms with unique identifiers, the Department of Justice may cease issuing new approvals of security printers to the extent necessary to achieve these purposes. The department may, pursuant to regulation, reduce the number of currently approved security printers to no fewer than three vendors. The department shall ensure that any reduction or limitation of approved security printers does not impact the ability of vendors to meet demand for prescription forms. *(Added by Stats. 2003, c. 406 (S.B.151), § 6. Amended by Stats.2005, c. 487 (S.B.734), § 3; Stats.2011, c. 418 (S.B.360), § 1; Stats.2018, c. 479 (A.B.1753), § 2, eff. Jan. 1, 2019.)*

Cross References

Agent defined for purposes of this Division, see Health and Safety Code § 11003.

Controlled substance defined for purposes of this Division, see Health and Safety Code § 11007.

Deliver or delivery defined for purposes of this Division, see Health and Safety Code § 11009.

Person defined for purposes of this Division, see Health and Safety Code § 11022.

Prescription or electronic transmission prescription defined for purposes of this Division, see Health and Safety Code § 11027.

Production defined for purposes of this Division, see Health and Safety Code § 11029.

Security printer defined for purposes of this Division, see Health and Safety Code § 11029.5.

§ 11161.7. Prescribers with certain restrictions upon authority to prescribe; availability of restriction information from Board of Pharmacy

(a) When a prescriber's authority to prescribe controlled substances is restricted by civil, criminal, or administrative action, or by an order of the court issued pursuant to Section 11161, the law enforcement agency or licensing board that sought the restrictions shall provide the name, category of licensure, license number, and the nature of the restrictions imposed on the prescriber to security printers, the Department of Justice, and the Board of Pharmacy.

(b) The Board of Pharmacy shall make available the information required by subdivision (a) to pharmacies and security printers to prevent the dispensing of controlled substance prescriptions issued by the prescriber and the ordering of additional controlled substance prescription forms by the restricted prescriber. *(Added by Stats.2003, c. 406 (S.B.151), § 7.)*

Cross References

Controlled substance defined for purposes of this Division, see Health and Safety Code § 11007.
Prescription or electronic transmission prescription defined for purposes of this Division, see Health and Safety Code § 11027.
Security printer defined for purposes of this Division, see Health and Safety Code § 11029.5.

§ 11162.1. Official forms; required features; batch control numbers; form contents; orders by designated prescribers for facility use; submission of information regarding prescription forms delivered

(a) The prescription forms for controlled substances shall be printed with the following features:

(1) A latent, repetitive "void" pattern shall be printed across the entire front of the prescription blank; if a prescription is scanned or photocopied, the word "void" shall appear in a pattern across the entire front of the prescription.

(2) A watermark shall be printed on the backside of the prescription blank; the watermark shall consist of the words "California Security Prescription."

(3) A chemical void protection that prevents alteration by chemical washing.

(4) A feature printed in thermochromic ink.

(5) An area of opaque writing so that the writing disappears if the prescription is lightened.

(6) A description of the security features included on each prescription form.

(7)(A) Six quantity check off boxes shall be printed on the form so that the prescriber may indicate the quantity by checking the applicable box where the following quantities shall appear:

1–24

25–49

50–74

75–100

101–150

151 and over.

(B) In conjunction with the quantity boxes, a space shall be provided to designate the units referenced in the quantity boxes when the drug is not in tablet or capsule form.

(8) Prescription blanks shall contain a statement printed on the bottom of the prescription blank that the "Prescription is void if the number of drugs prescribed is not noted."

(9) The preprinted name, category of licensure, license number, federal controlled substance registration number, and address of the prescribing practitioner.

(10) Check boxes shall be printed on the form so that the prescriber may indicate the number of refills ordered.

(11) The date of origin of the prescription.

(12) A check box indicating the prescriber's order not to substitute.

(13) An identifying number assigned to the approved security printer by the Department of Justice.

(14)(A) A check box by the name of each prescriber when a prescription form lists multiple prescribers.

(B) Each prescriber who signs the prescription form shall identify themselves as the prescriber by checking the box by the prescriber's name.

(15) A uniquely serialized number, in a manner prescribed by the Department of Justice in accordance with Section 11162.2.

(b) Each batch of controlled substance prescription forms shall have the lot number printed on the form and each form within that batch shall be numbered sequentially beginning with the numeral one.

(c)(1) A prescriber designated by a licensed health care facility, a clinic specified in Section 1200, or a clinic specified in subdivision (a) of Section 1206 that has 25 or more physicians or surgeons may order controlled substance prescription forms for use by prescribers when treating patients in that facility without the information required in paragraph (9) of subdivision (a) or paragraph (3).

(2) Forms ordered pursuant to this subdivision shall have the name, category of licensure, license number, and federal controlled substance registration number of the designated prescriber and the name, address, category of licensure, and license number of the licensed health care facility the clinic specified in Section 1200, or the clinic specified in Section 1206 that has 25 or more physicians or surgeons preprinted on the form. Licensed health care facilities or clinics exempt under Section 1206 are not required to preprint the category of licensure and license number of their facility or clinic.

(3) Forms ordered pursuant to this section shall not be valid prescriptions without the name, category of licensure, license number, and federal controlled substance registration number of the prescriber on the form.

(4)(A) Except as provided in subparagraph (B), the designated prescriber shall maintain a record of the prescribers to whom the controlled substance prescription forms are issued, that shall include the name, category of licensure, license number, federal controlled substance registration number, and quantity of controlled substance prescription forms issued to each prescriber. The record shall be maintained in the health facility for three years.

(B) Forms ordered pursuant to this subdivision that are printed by a computerized prescription generation system shall not be subject to subparagraph (A) or paragraph (7) of subdivision (a). Forms printed pursuant to this subdivision that are printed by a computerized prescription generation system may contain the prescriber's name, category of professional licensure, license number, federal controlled substance registration number, and the date of the prescription.

(d) Within the next working day following delivery, a security printer shall submit via web-based application, as specified by the Department of Justice, all of the following information for all prescription forms delivered:

(1) Serial numbers of all prescription forms delivered.

(2) All prescriber names and Drug Enforcement Administration Controlled Substance Registration Certificate numbers displayed on the prescription forms.

Health & Safety

(3) The delivery shipment recipient names.

(4) The date of delivery. *(Added by Stats.2003, c. 406 (S.B.151), § 9, operative July 1, 2004. Amended by Stats.2004, c. 573 (A.B.30), § 3, eff. Sept. 18, 2004; Stats.2005, c. 487 (S.B.734), § 4; Stats.2006, c. 538 (S.B.1852), § 368; Stats.2006, c. 286 (A.B.2986), § 1; Stats. 2007, c. 130 (A.B.299), § 161; Stats.2011, c. 418 (S.B.360), § 2; Stats.2018, c. 479 (A.B.1753), § 3, eff. Jan. 1, 2019; Stats.2019, c. 4 (A.B.149), § 1, eff. March 11, 2019.)*

Cross References

Controlled substance defined for purposes of this Division, see Health and Safety Code § 11007.
Drug defined for purposes of this Division, see Health and Safety Code § 11014.
Medi–Cal Benefits Program, schedule of benefits, tamper resistant prescription form requirement for outpatient prescribed drugs, see Welfare and Institutions Code § 14132.
Physician, dentist, podiatrist, pharmacist, veterinarian, and optometrist defined for purposes of this Division, see Health and Safety Code § 11024.
Practitioner defined for purposes of this Division, see Health and Safety Code § 11026.
Prescription or electronic transmission prescription defined for purposes of this Division, see Health and Safety Code § 11027.
Security printer defined for purposes of this Division, see Health and Safety Code § 11029.5.

§ 11162.2. Uniquely serialized numbers; date when required feature; minimum requirements

(a) Notwithstanding any other law, the uniquely serialized number described in paragraph (15) of subdivision (a) of Section 11162.1 shall not be a required feature in the printing of new prescription forms produced by approved security printers until a date determined by the Department of Justice, which shall be no later than January 1, 2020.

(b) Specifications for the serialized number shall be prescribed by the Department of Justice and shall meet the following minimum requirements:

(1) The serialized number shall be compliant with all state and federal requirements.

(2) The serialized number shall be utilizable as a barcode that may be scanned by dispensers.

(3) The serialized number shall be compliant with current National Council for Prescription Drug Program Standards. *(Added by Stats.2019, c. 4 (A.B.149), § 2, eff. March 11, 2019.)*

§ 11162.5. Official blanks; counterfeit; punishment

(a) Every person who counterfeits a prescription blank purporting to be an official prescription blank prepared and issued pursuant to Section 11161.5, or knowingly possesses more than three counterfeited prescription blanks, shall be punished by imprisonment pursuant to subdivision (h) of Section 1170 of the Penal Code or by imprisonment in a county jail for not more than one year.

(b) Every person who knowingly possesses three or fewer counterfeited prescription blanks purporting to be official prescription blanks prepared and issued pursuant to Section 11161.5, shall be guilty of a misdemeanor punishable by imprisonment in a county jail not exceeding six months, or by a fine not exceeding one thousand dollars ($1,000), or by both that fine and imprisonment. *(Added by Stats.1984, c. 1434, § 1, eff. Sept. 26, 1984. Amended by Stats.2006, c. 901 (S.B.1422), § 1.6; Stats.2011, c. 15 (A.B.109), § 150, eff. April 4, 2011, operative Oct. 1, 2011.)*

Cross References

Misdemeanors, definition and penalties, see Penal Code §§ 17, 19 and 19.2.
Person defined for purposes of this Division, see Health and Safety Code § 11022.
Prescription or electronic transmission prescription defined for purposes of this Division, see Health and Safety Code § 11027.

Research References

2 Witkin, California Criminal Law 4th Crimes Against Public Peace and Welfare § 152 (2021), In General.

§ 11162.6. Counterfeit prescription forms; punishment for creation, possession or use; criminal penalties

(a) Every person who counterfeits a controlled substance prescription form shall be guilty of a misdemeanor punishable by imprisonment in a county jail for not more than one year, by a fine not exceeding one thousand dollars ($1,000), or by both that imprisonment and fine.

(b) Every person who knowingly possesses a counterfeited controlled substance prescription form shall be guilty of a misdemeanor punishable by imprisonment in a county jail not exceeding six months, by a fine not exceeding one thousand dollars ($1,000), or by both that imprisonment and fine.

(c) Every person who attempts to obtain or obtains a controlled substance prescription form under false pretenses shall be guilty of a misdemeanor punishable by imprisonment in a county jail not exceeding six months, by a fine not exceeding one thousand dollars ($1,000), or by both that imprisonment and fine.

(d) Every person who fraudulently produces controlled substance prescription forms shall be guilty of a misdemeanor punishable by imprisonment in a county jail not exceeding six months, by a fine not exceeding one thousand dollars ($1,000), or by both that imprisonment and fine.

(e) This section shall become operative on July 1, 2004. *(Added by Stats.2003, c. 406 (S.B.151), § 10, operative July 1, 2004.)*

Cross References

Controlled substance defined for purposes of this Division, see Health and Safety Code § 11007.
Failure to keep prescription file, penalty, see Business and Professions Code § 4333.
Misdemeanors, definition and penalties, see Penal Code §§ 17, 19 and 19.2.
Person defined for purposes of this Division, see Health and Safety Code § 11022.
Prescription or electronic transmission prescription defined for purposes of this Division, see Health and Safety Code § 11027.

Research References

2 Witkin, California Criminal Law 4th Crimes Against Public Peace and Welfare § 152 (2021), In General.

§ 11164. Execution and contents of prescriptions for schedule II, III, IV and V controlled substances; oral or electronically transmitted prescriptions; record

Except as provided in Section 11167, no person shall prescribe a controlled substance, nor shall any person fill, compound, or dispense a prescription for a controlled substance, unless it complies with the requirements of this section.

(a) Each prescription for a controlled substance classified in Schedule II, III, IV, or V, except as authorized by subdivision (b), shall be made on a controlled substance prescription form as specified in Section 11162.1 and shall meet the following requirements:

(1) The prescription shall be signed and dated by the prescriber in ink and shall contain the prescriber's address and telephone number; the name of the ultimate user or research subject, or contact information as determined by the Secretary of the United States Department of Health and Human Services; refill information, such as the number of refills ordered and whether the prescription is a first-time request or a refill; and the name, quantity, strength, and directions for use of the controlled substance prescribed.

(2) The prescription shall also contain the address of the person for whom the controlled substance is prescribed. If the prescriber does not specify this address on the prescription, the pharmacist filling the prescription or an employee acting under the direction of the pharmacist shall write or type the address on the prescription or maintain this information in a readily retrievable form in the pharmacy.

(b)(1) Notwithstanding paragraph (1) of subdivision (a) of Section 11162.1, any controlled substance classified in Schedule III, IV, or V may be dispensed upon an oral or electronically transmitted prescription, which shall be produced in hard copy form and signed and dated by the pharmacist filling the prescription or by any other person expressly authorized by provisions of the Business and Professions Code. Any person who transmits, maintains, or receives any electronically transmitted prescription shall ensure the security, integrity, authority, and confidentiality of the prescription.

(2) The date of issue of the prescription and all the information required for a written prescription by subdivision (a) shall be included in the written record of the prescription; the pharmacist need not include the address, telephone number, license classification, or federal registry number of the prescriber or the address of the patient on the hard copy, if that information is readily retrievable in the pharmacy.

(3) Pursuant to an authorization of the prescriber, any agent of the prescriber on behalf of the prescriber may orally or electronically transmit a prescription for a controlled substance classified in Schedule III, IV, or V, if in these cases the written record of the prescription required by this subdivision specifies the name of the agent of the prescriber transmitting the prescription.

(c) The use of commonly used abbreviations shall not invalidate an otherwise valid prescription.

(d) Notwithstanding subdivisions (a) and (b), prescriptions for a controlled substance classified in Schedule V may be for more than one person in the same family with the same medical need.

(e)(1) Notwithstanding any other law, a prescription written on a prescription form that was otherwise valid prior to January 1, 2019, but that does not comply with paragraph (15) of subdivision (a) of Section 11162.1, or a valid controlled substance prescription form approved by the Department of Justice as of January 1, 2019, is a valid prescription that may be filled, compounded, or dispensed until January 1, 2021.

(2) If the Department of Justice determines that there is an inadequate availability of compliant prescription forms to meet demand on or before the date described in paragraph (1), the department may extend the period during which prescriptions written on noncompliant prescription forms remain valid for a period no longer than an additional six months. *(Added by Stats.2003, c. 406 (S.B.151), § 13, operative Jan. 1, 2005. Amended by Stats.2005, c. 487 (S.B.734), § 5; Stats.2006, c. 286 (A.B.2986), § 2; Stats.2019, c. 4 (A.B.149), § 3, eff. March 11, 2019.)*

Cross References

Agent defined for purposes of this Division, see Health and Safety Code § 11003.
Clinic permits, dispensing drugs, see Business and Professions Code § 4193.
Conflicts between this section and Business and Professions Code § 4036, this section to prevail, see Business and Professions Code § 4040.
Controlled substance defined for purposes of this Division, see Health and Safety Code § 11007.
Department of Health Care Services, generally, see Health and Safety Code § 100100 et seq.
Dispense defined for purposes of this Division, see Health and Safety Code § 11010.
Furnishing controlled substances by oral or electronically transmitted order to unknown persons, see Business and Professions Code § 4059.
Furnishing or dispensing dangerous drug or device without prescription, see Business and Professions Code § 4059.
Healing arts, pharmacy, scope of practice and exemptions, hospitals with 100 or fewer beds, wholesale purchase of drugs, see Business and Professions Code § 4056.
Nonresident pharmacy registration, denial, revocation, or suspension, see Business and Professions Code § 4303.
Oral prescriptions, see Health and Safety Code § 11167.
Person defined for purposes of this Division, see Health and Safety Code § 11022.
Pharmacy defined for purposes of this Division, see Health and Safety Code § 11023.
Physician, dentist, podiatrist, pharmacist, veterinarian, and optometrist defined for purposes of this Division, see Health and Safety Code § 11024.
Prescription or electronic transmission prescription defined for purposes of this Division, see Health and Safety Code § 11027.
Refilling prescriptions, see Health and Safety Code § 11200.
Sale without prescription, see Health and Safety Code § 11250 et seq.
Ultimate user defined for purposes of this Division, see Health and Safety Code § 11030.
Veterinarian, prescription, contents, see Health and Safety Code § 11241.

Research References

California Jury Instructions - Criminal 12.30.1, Controlled Substance (Sched. I–V)—Burden of Proof as to Prescription.
2 Witkin, California Criminal Law 4th Crimes Against Public Peace and Welfare § 152 (2021), In General.

§ 11164.1. Prescribers in another state for delivery in another state; prescription requirements

(a)(1) Notwithstanding any other law, a prescription for a controlled substance issued by a prescriber in another state for delivery to a patient in another state may be dispensed by a California pharmacy, if the prescription conforms with the requirements for controlled substance prescriptions in the state in which the controlled substance was prescribed.

(2) A prescription for a Schedule II, Schedule III, Schedule IV, or Schedule V controlled substance dispensed pursuant to this subdivision shall be reported by the dispensing pharmacy to the Department of Justice in the manner prescribed by subdivision (d) of Section 11165.

(b) A pharmacy may dispense a prescription for a Schedule III, Schedule IV, or Schedule V controlled substance from an out-of-state prescriber pursuant to Section 4005 of the Business and Professions Code and Section 1717 of Title 16 of the California Code of Regulations.

(c) This section shall become operative on January 1, 2021. *(Added by Stats.2019, c. 677 (A.B.528), § 4, eff. Jan. 1, 2020, operative Jan. 1, 2021.)*

Cross References

Controlled substance defined for purposes of this Division, see Health and Safety Code § 11007.
Deliver or delivery defined for purposes of this Division, see Health and Safety Code § 11009.
Dispense defined for purposes of this Division, see Health and Safety Code § 11010.
Pharmacy defined for purposes of this Division, see Health and Safety Code § 11023.
Prescription or electronic transmission prescription defined for purposes of this Division, see Health and Safety Code § 11027.

§ 11164.5. Maintenance of received or controlled substance dispensing information by pharmacy's or hospital's computer system for the period required by law

(a) Notwithstanding Section 11164, if only recorded and stored electronically, on magnetic media, or in any other computerized form, the pharmacy's or hospital's computer system shall not permit the received information or the controlled substance dispensing information required by this section to be changed, obliterated, destroyed, or disposed of, for the record maintenance period required by law, once the information has been received by the pharmacy or the hospital and once the controlled substance has been dispensed, respectively. Once the controlled substance has been dispensed, if the previously created record is determined to be incorrect, a correcting addition may be made only by or with the approval of a pharmacist. After a pharmacist enters the change or enters his or her approval of the change into the computer, the resulting record shall include the correcting addition and the date it was made to the record, the identity of the person or pharmacist making the correction, and the identity of the pharmacist approving the correction.

(b) Nothing in this section shall be construed to exempt any pharmacy or hospital dispensing Schedule II controlled substances pursuant to electronic transmission prescriptions from existing reporting requirements. *(Added by Stats.2000, c. 293 (A.B.2240), § 4. Amended by Stats.2016, c. 484 (S.B.1193), § 55, eff. Jan. 1, 2017.)*

Cross References

Controlled substance defined for purposes of this Division, see Health and Safety Code § 11007.
Healing arts, pharmacy, requirements for prescriptions,
Electronic prescriptions or orders entered by a prescriber or pharmacist, see Business and Professions Code § 4071.1.
Oral or electronic data transmission prescription, reduction to writing, exception, see Business and Professions Code § 4070.
Person defined for purposes of this Division, see Health and Safety Code § 11022.
Physician, dentist, podiatrist, pharmacist, veterinarian, and optometrist defined for purposes of this Division, see Health and Safety Code § 11024.
Prescription or electronic transmission prescription defined for purposes of this Division, see Health and Safety Code § 11027.

§ 11165. Controlled Substance Utilization Review and Evaluation System (CURES); electronic monitoring of Schedule II, Schedule III, Schedule IV, and Schedule V controlled substances; funding; confidentiality; reporting requirements for dispensers; stakeholder assistance in establishing rules and regulations and identifying CURES upgrades; education on access and use of CURES PDMP; agreements for purposes of interstate data sharing of prescription drug monitoring program information; reporting requirements for veterinarians

(a) To assist health care practitioners in their efforts to ensure appropriate prescribing, ordering, administering, furnishing, and dispensing of controlled substances, law enforcement and regulatory agencies in their efforts to control the diversion and resultant abuse of Schedule II, Schedule III, Schedule IV, and Schedule V controlled substances, and for statistical analysis, education, and research, the Department of Justice shall, contingent upon the availability of adequate funds in the CURES Fund, maintain the Controlled Substance Utilization Review and Evaluation System (CURES) for the electronic monitoring of, and internet access to information regarding, the prescribing and dispensing of Schedule II, Schedule III, Schedule IV, and Schedule V controlled substances by all practitioners authorized to prescribe, order, administer, furnish, or dispense these controlled substances.

(b) The department may seek and use grant funds to pay the costs incurred by the operation and maintenance of CURES. The department shall annually report to the Legislature and make available to the public the amount and source of funds it receives for support of CURES.

(c)(1) The operation of CURES shall comply with all applicable federal and state privacy and security laws and regulations.

(2)(A) CURES shall operate under existing provisions of law to safeguard the privacy and confidentiality of patients. Data obtained from CURES shall only be provided to appropriate state, local, and federal public agencies for disciplinary, civil, or criminal purposes and to other agencies or entities, as determined by the department, for the purpose of educating practitioners and others in lieu of disciplinary, civil, or criminal actions. Data may be provided to public or private entities, as approved by the department, for educational, peer review, statistical, or research purposes, if patient information, including information that may identify the patient, is not compromised. The University of California shall be provided access to identifiable data for research purposes if the requirements of subdivision (t) of Section 1798.24 of the Civil Code are satisfied. Further, data disclosed to an individual or agency as described in this subdivision shall not be disclosed, sold, or transferred to a third party, unless authorized by, or pursuant to, state and federal privacy and security laws and regulations. The department shall establish policies, procedures, and regulations regarding the use, access, evaluation, management, implementation, operation, storage, disclosure, and security of the information within CURES, consistent with this subdivision.

(B) Notwithstanding subparagraph (A), a regulatory board whose licensees do not prescribe, order, administer, furnish, or dispense controlled substances shall not be provided data obtained from CURES.

(3) The department shall, no later than January 1, 2021, adopt regulations regarding the access and use of the information within CURES. The department shall consult with all stakeholders identified by the department during the rulemaking process. The regulations shall, at a minimum, address all of the following in a manner consistent with this chapter:

(A) The process for approving, denying, and disapproving individuals or entities seeking access to information in CURES.

(B) The purposes for which a health care practitioner may access information in CURES.

(C) The conditions under which a warrant, subpoena, or court order is required for a law enforcement agency to obtain information from CURES as part of a criminal investigation.

(D) The process by which information in CURES may be provided for educational, peer review, statistical, or research purposes.

(4) In accordance with federal and state privacy laws and regulations, a health care practitioner may provide a patient with a copy of the patient's CURES patient activity report as long as no additional CURES data are provided and the health care practitioner keeps a copy of the report in the patient's medical record in compliance with subdivision (d) of Section 11165.1.

(d) For each prescription for a Schedule II, Schedule III, Schedule IV, or Schedule V controlled substance, as defined in the controlled substances schedules in federal law and regulations, specifically Sections 1308.12, 1308.13, 1308.14, and 1308.15, respectively, of Title 21 of the Code of Federal Regulations, the dispensing pharmacy, clinic, or other dispenser shall report the following information to the department or contracted prescription data processing vendor as soon as reasonably possible, but not more than one working day after the date a controlled substance is released to the patient or patient's representative, in a format specified by the department:

(1) Full name, address, and, if available, telephone number of the ultimate user or research subject, or contact information as determined by the Secretary of the United States Department of Health and Human Services, and the gender and date of birth of the ultimate user.

(2) The prescriber's category of licensure, license number, national provider identifier (NPI) number, if applicable, the federal controlled substance registration number, and the state medical license number of a prescriber using the federal controlled substance registration number of a government-exempt facility.

(3) Pharmacy prescription number, license number, NPI number, and federal controlled substance registration number.

(4) National Drug Code (NDC) number of the controlled substance dispensed.

(5) Quantity of the controlled substance dispensed.

(6) The International Statistical Classification of Diseases (ICD) Code contained in the most current ICD revision, or any revision deemed sufficient by the State Board of Pharmacy, if available.

(7) Number of refills ordered.

(8) Whether the drug was dispensed as a refill of a prescription or as a first-time request.

(9) Prescribing date of the prescription.

(10) Date of dispensing of the prescription.

(11) The serial number for the corresponding prescription form, if applicable.

(e) The department may invite stakeholders to assist, advise, and make recommendations on the establishment of rules and regulations necessary to ensure the proper administration and enforcement of the CURES database. A prescriber or dispenser invitee shall be licensed by one of the boards or committees identified in subdivision (d) of Section 208 of the Business and Professions Code, in active practice in California, and a regular user of CURES.

(f) The department shall, prior to upgrading CURES, consult with prescribers licensed by one of the boards or committees identified in subdivision (d) of Section 208 of the Business and Professions Code, one or more of the boards or committees identified in subdivision (d) of Section 208 of the Business and Professions Code, and any other stakeholder identified by the department, for the purpose of identifying desirable capabilities and upgrades to the CURES Prescription Drug Monitoring Program (PDMP).

(g) The department may establish a process to educate authorized subscribers of the CURES PDMP on how to access and use the CURES PDMP.

(h)(1) The department may enter into an agreement with an entity operating an interstate data sharing hub, or an agency operating a prescription drug monitoring program in another state, for purposes of interstate data sharing of prescription drug monitoring program information.

(2) Data obtained from CURES may be provided to authorized users of another state's prescription drug monitoring program, as determined by the department pursuant to subdivision (c), if the entity operating the interstate data sharing hub, and the prescription drug monitoring program of that state, as applicable, have entered into an agreement with the department for interstate data sharing of prescription drug monitoring program information.

(3) An agreement entered into by the department for purposes of interstate data sharing of prescription drug monitoring program information shall ensure that all access to data obtained from CURES and the handling of data contained within CURES comply with California law, including regulations, and meet the same patient privacy, audit, and data security standards employed and required for direct access to CURES.

(4) For purposes of interstate data sharing of CURES information pursuant to this subdivision, an authorized user of another state's prescription drug monitoring program shall not be required to register with CURES, if the authorized user is registered and in good standing with that state's prescription drug monitoring program.

(5) The department shall not enter into an agreement pursuant to this subdivision until the department has issued final regulations regarding the access and use of the information within CURES as required by paragraph (3) of subdivision (c).

(i) Notwithstanding subdivision (d), a veterinarian shall report the information required by that subdivision to the department as soon as reasonably possible, but not more than seven days after the date a controlled substance is dispensed.

(j) If the dispensing pharmacy, clinic, or other dispenser experiences a temporary technological or electrical failure, it shall, without undue delay, seek to correct any cause of the temporary technological or electrical failure that is reasonably within its control. The deadline for transmitting prescription information to the department or contracted prescription data processing vendor pursuant to subdivision (d) shall be extended until the failure is corrected. If the dispensing pharmacy, clinic, or other dispenser experiences technological limitations that are not reasonably within its control, or is impacted by a natural or manmade disaster, the deadline for transmitting prescription information to the department or contracted prescription data processing vendor shall be extended until normal operations have resumed. *(Added by Stats.2019, c. 677 (A.B.528), § 6, eff. Jan. 1, 2020, operative Jan. 1, 2021. Amended by Stats.2021, c. 618 (A.B.527), § 5, eff. Jan. 1, 2022.)*

Cross References

Controlled substance defined for purposes of this Division, see Health and Safety Code § 11007.

Department of Health Care Services, generally, see Health and Safety Code § 100100 et seq.

Development and dissemination of information and educational material regarding assessing a patient's risk of abusing or diverting controlled substances and information relating to the Controlled Substance Utilization Review and Evaluation System (CURES), see Business and Professions Code § 2196.8.

Dispense defined for purposes of this Division, see Health and Safety Code § 11010.

Drug defined for purposes of this Division, see Health and Safety Code § 11014.

Healing arts, pharmacy, scope of practice and exemptions, dispensing dangerous drugs to emergency room patients, conditions, responsibility for error, see Business and Professions Code § 4068.

Person defined for purposes of this Division, see Health and Safety Code § 11022.

Pharmacy, dispensing dangerous drugs to emergency room patients, see Business and Professions Code § 4068.

Pharmacy defined for purposes of this Division, see Health and Safety Code § 11023.

Practitioner defined for purposes of this Division, see Health and Safety Code § 11026.

Prescription or electronic transmission prescription defined for purposes of this Division, see Health and Safety Code § 11027.

Ultimate user defined for purposes of this Division, see Health and Safety Code § 11030.

§ 11165.1. Disclosure of Controlled Substance Utilization Review and Evaluation System data; civil or administrative liability

(a)(1)(A)(i) A health care practitioner authorized to prescribe, order, administer, furnish, or dispense Schedule II, Schedule III, Schedule IV, or Schedule V controlled substances pursuant to Section 11150 shall, upon receipt of a federal Drug Enforcement Administration (DEA) registration, submit an application developed by the department to obtain approval to electronically access information regarding the controlled substance history of a patient that is maintained by the department. Upon approval, the department shall release to the practitioner or their delegate the electronic history of controlled substances dispensed to an individual under the practitioner's care based on data contained in the CURES Prescription Drug Monitoring Program (PDMP).

(ii) A pharmacist shall, upon licensure, submit an application developed by the department to obtain approval to electronically access information regarding the controlled substance history of a patient that is maintained by the department. Upon approval, the department shall release to the pharmacist or their delegate the electronic history of controlled substances dispensed to an individual under the pharmacist's care based on data contained in the CURES PDMP.

(iii) A licensed physician and surgeon who does not hold a DEA registration may submit an application developed by the department to obtain approval to electronically access information regarding the controlled substance history of the patient that is maintained by the department. Upon approval, the department shall release to the physician and surgeon or their delegate the electronic history of

Health & Safety

controlled substances dispensed to a patient under their care based on data contained in the CURES PDMP.

(iv) The department shall implement its duties described in clauses (i), (ii), and (iii) upon completion of any technological changes to the CURES database necessary to support clauses (i), (ii), and (iii), or by October 1, 2022, whichever is sooner.

(B) The department may deny an application or suspend a subscriber, for reasons that include, but are not limited to, the following:

(i) Materially falsifying an application to access information contained in the CURES database.

(ii) Failing to maintain effective controls for access to the patient activity report.

(iii) Having their federal DEA registration suspended or revoked.

(iv) Violating a law governing controlled substances or another law for which the possession or use of a controlled substance is an element of the crime.

(v) Accessing information for a reason other than to diagnose or treat a patient, or to document compliance with the law.

(C) An authorized subscriber shall notify the department within 30 days of a change to the subscriber account.

(D) An approved health care practitioner, pharmacist, or a person acting on behalf of a health care practitioner or pharmacist pursuant to subdivision (b) of Section 209 of the Business and Professions Code may use the department's online portal or a health information technology system that meets the criteria required in subparagraph (E) to access information in the CURES database pursuant to this section. A subscriber who uses a health information technology system that meets the criteria required in subparagraph (E) to access the CURES database may submit automated queries to the CURES database that are triggered by predetermined criteria.

(E) An approved health care practitioner or pharmacist may submit queries to the CURES database through a health information technology system if the entity that operates the health information technology system certifies all of the following:

(i) The entity will not use or disclose data received from the CURES database for a purpose other than delivering the data to an approved health care practitioner or pharmacist or performing data processing activities that may be necessary to enable the delivery unless authorized by, and pursuant to, state and federal privacy and security laws and regulations.

(ii) The health information technology system will authenticate the identity of an authorized health care practitioner or pharmacist initiating queries to the CURES database and, at the time of the query to the CURES database, the health information technology system submits the following data regarding the query to CURES:

(I) The date of the query.

(II) The time of the query.

(III) The first and last name of the patient queried.

(IV) The date of birth of the patient queried.

(V) The identification of the CURES user for whom the system is making the query.

(iii) The health information technology system meets applicable patient privacy and information security requirements of state and federal law.

(iv) The entity has entered into a memorandum of understanding with the department that solely addresses the technical specifications of the health information technology system to ensure the security of the data in the CURES database and the secure transfer of data from the CURES database. The technical specifications shall be universal for all health information technology systems that establish a method of system integration to retrieve information from the CURES database. The memorandum of understanding shall not govern, or in any way impact or restrict, the use of data received from the CURES database or impose any additional burdens on covered entities in compliance with the regulations promulgated pursuant to the federal Health Insurance Portability and Accountability Act of 1996 found in Parts 160 and 164 of Title 45 of the Code of Federal Regulations.

(F) No later than October 1, 2018, the department shall develop a programming interface or other method of system integration to allow health information technology systems that meet the requirements in subparagraph (E) to retrieve information in the CURES database on behalf of an authorized health care practitioner or pharmacist.

(G) The department shall not access patient-identifiable information in an entity's health information technology system.

(H) An entity that operates a health information technology system that is requesting to establish an integration with the CURES database shall pay a reasonable fee to cover the cost of establishing and maintaining integration with the CURES database.

(I) The department may prohibit integration or terminate a health information technology system's ability to retrieve information in the CURES database if the health information technology system fails to meet the requirements of subparagraph (E), or the entity operating the health information technology system does not fulfill its obligation under subparagraph (H).

(2) A health care practitioner authorized to prescribe, order, administer, furnish, or dispense Schedule II, Schedule III, Schedule IV, or Schedule V controlled substances pursuant to Section 11150 or a pharmacist shall be deemed to have complied with paragraph (1) if the licensed health care practitioner or pharmacist has been approved to access the CURES database through the process developed pursuant to subdivision (a) of Section 209 of the Business and Professions Code.

(b) A request for, or release of, a controlled substance history pursuant to this section shall be made in accordance with guidelines developed by the department.

(c) In order to prevent the inappropriate, improper, or illegal use of Schedule II, Schedule III, Schedule IV, or Schedule V controlled substances, the department may initiate the referral of the history of controlled substances dispensed to an individual based on data contained in CURES to licensed health care practitioners, pharmacists, or both, providing care or services to the individual.

(d) The history of controlled substances dispensed to an individual based on data contained in CURES that is received by a practitioner or pharmacist from the department pursuant to this section is medical information subject to the provisions of the Confidentiality of Medical Information Act contained in Part 2.6 (commencing with Section 56) of Division 1 of the Civil Code.

(e) Information concerning a patient's controlled substance history provided to a practitioner or pharmacist pursuant to this section shall include prescriptions for controlled substances listed in Sections 1308.12, 1308.13, 1308.14, and 1308.15 of Title 21 of the Code of Federal Regulations.

(f) A health care practitioner, pharmacist, or a person acting on behalf of a health care practitioner or pharmacist, when acting with reasonable care and in good faith, is not subject to civil or administrative liability arising from false, incomplete, inaccurate, or misattributed information submitted to, reported by, or relied upon in the CURES database or for a resulting failure of the CURES database to accurately or timely report that information.

(g) For purposes of this section, the following terms have the following meanings:

(1) "Automated basis" means using predefined criteria to trigger an automated query to the CURES database, which can be attributed to a specific health care practitioner or pharmacist.

(2) "Department" means the Department of Justice.

(3) "Entity" means an organization that operates, or provides or makes available, a health information technology system to a health care practitioner or pharmacist.

(4) "Health information technology system" means an information processing application using hardware and software for the storage, retrieval, sharing of or use of patient data for communication, decisionmaking, coordination of care, or the quality, safety, or efficiency of the practice of medicine or delivery of health care services, including, but not limited to, electronic medical record applications, health information exchange systems, or other interoperable clinical or health care information system.

(h) This section shall become operative on July 1, 2021, or upon the date the department promulgates regulations to implement this section and posts those regulations on its internet website, whichever date is earlier. *(Added by Stats.2019, c. 677 (A.B.528), § 8, eff. Jan. 1, 2020, operative July 1, 2021. Amended by Stats.2021, c. 77 (A.B.137), § 20, eff. July 16, 2021.)*

Cross References

Controlled substance defined for purposes of this Division, see Health and Safety Code § 11007.
Nurse midwives, furnishing or ordering of drugs, see Business and Professions Code § 2746.51.
Physician, dentist, podiatrist, pharmacist, veterinarian, and optometrist defined for purposes of this Division, see Health and Safety Code § 11024.
Practitioner defined for purposes of this Division, see Health and Safety Code § 11026.

§ 11165.2. Audits of the CURES system and its users; citations; fines; abatement

(a) The Department of Justice may conduct audits of the CURES Prescription Drug Monitoring Program system and its users.

(b) The Department of Justice may establish, by regulation, a system for the issuance to a CURES Prescription Drug Monitoring Program subscriber of a citation which may contain an order of abatement, or an order to pay an administrative fine assessed by the Department of Justice if the subscriber is in violation of any provision of this chapter or any regulation adopted by the Department of Justice pursuant to this chapter.

(c) The system shall contain the following provisions:

(1) Citations shall be in writing and shall describe with particularity the nature of the violation, including specific reference to the provision of law or regulation of the department determined to have been violated.

(2) Whenever appropriate, the citation shall contain an order of abatement establishing a reasonable time for abatement of the violation.

(3) In no event shall the administrative fine assessed by the department exceed two thousand five hundred dollars ($2,500) for each violation. In assessing a fine, due consideration shall be given to the appropriateness of the amount of the fine with respect to such factors as the gravity of the violation, the good faith of the subscribers, and the history of previous violations.

(4) An order of abatement or a fine assessment issued pursuant to a citation shall inform the subscriber that if the subscriber desires a hearing to contest the finding of a violation, a hearing shall be requested by written notice to the CURES Prescription Drug Monitoring Program within 30 days of the date of issuance of the citation or assessment. Hearings shall be held pursuant to Chapter 5 (commencing with Section 11500) of Part 1 of Division 3 of Title 2 of the Government Code.

(5) In addition to requesting a hearing, the subscriber may, within 10 days after service of the citation, request in writing an opportunity for an informal conference with the department regarding the citation. At the conclusion of the informal conference, the department may affirm, modify, or dismiss the citation, including any fine levied or order of abatement issued. The decision shall be deemed to be a final order with regard to the citation issued, including the fine levied or the order of abatement which could include permanent suspension to the system, a monetary fine, or both, depending on the gravity of the violation. However, the subscriber does not waive its right to request a hearing to contest a citation by requesting an informal conference. If the citation is affirmed, a formal hearing may be requested within 30 days of the date the citation was affirmed. If the citation is dismissed after the informal conference, the request for a hearing on the matter of the citation shall be deemed to be withdrawn. If the citation, including any fine levied or order of abatement, is modified, the citation originally issued shall be considered withdrawn and a new citation issued. If a hearing is requested for a subsequent citation, it shall be requested within 30 days of service of that subsequent citation.

(6) Failure of a subscriber to pay a fine within 30 days of the date of assessment or comply with an order of abatement within the fixed time, unless the citation is being appealed, may result in disciplinary action taken by the department. If a citation is not contested and a fine is not paid, the subscriber account will be terminated:

(A) A citation may be issued without the assessment of an administrative fine.

(B) Assessment of administrative fines may be limited to only particular violations of law or department regulations.

(d) Notwithstanding any other provision of law, if a fine is paid to satisfy an assessment based on the finding of a violation, payment of the fine shall be represented as a satisfactory resolution of the matter for purposes of public disclosure.

(e) Administrative fines collected pursuant to this section shall be deposited in the CURES Program Special Fund, available upon appropriation by the Legislature. These special funds shall provide support for costs associated with informal and formal hearings, maintenance, and updates to the CURES Prescription Drug Monitoring Program.

(f) The sanctions authorized under this section shall be separate from, and in addition to, any other administrative, civil, or criminal remedies; however, a criminal action may not be initiated for a specific offense if a citation has been issued pursuant to this section for that offense, and a citation may not be issued pursuant to this section for a specific offense if a criminal action for that offense has been filed.

(g) Nothing in this section shall be deemed to prevent the department from serving and prosecuting an accusation to suspend or revoke a subscriber if grounds for that suspension or revocation exist. *(Added by Stats.2011, c. 418 (S.B.360), § 5.)*

§ 11165.3. Reporting of theft or loss of prescription forms

The theft or loss of prescription forms shall be reported immediately by the security printer or affected prescriber to the CURES Prescription Drug Monitoring Program, but no later than three days after the discovery of the theft or loss. This notification may be done in writing utilizing the approved Department of Justice form or may be reported by the authorized subscriber through the CURES Prescription Drug Monitoring Program. *(Added by Stats.2011, c. 418 (S.B.360), § 6. Amended by Stats.2012, c. 867 (S.B.1144), § 7.)*

§ 11165.4. Consultation of CURES database before prescribing Schedule II, Schedule III, or Schedule IV controlled substance; exemptions; failure to comply with provisions

(a)(1)(A)(i) A health care practitioner authorized to prescribe, order, administer, or furnish a controlled substance shall consult the patient activity report or information from the patient activity report obtained from the CURES database to review a patient's controlled substance history for the past 12 months before prescribing a Schedule II, Schedule III, or Schedule IV controlled substance to the patient for the first time and at least once every six months thereafter if the prescriber renews the prescription and the substance remains part of the treatment of the patient.

(ii) If a health care practitioner authorized to prescribe, order, administer, or furnish a controlled substance is not required, pursuant to an exemption described in subdivision (c), to consult the patient activity report from the CURES database the first time the health care practitioner prescribes, orders, administers, or furnishes a controlled substance to a patient, the health care practitioner shall consult the patient activity report from the CURES database to review the patient's controlled substance history before subsequently prescribing a Schedule II, Schedule III, or Schedule IV controlled substance to the patient and at least once every six months thereafter if the prescriber renews the prescription and the substance remains part of the treatment of the patient.

(iii) A health care practitioner who did not directly access the CURES database to perform the required review of the controlled substance use report shall document in the patient's medical record that they reviewed the CURES database generated report within 24 hours of the controlled substance prescription that was provided to them by another authorized user of the CURES database.

(B) For purposes of this paragraph, "first time" means the initial occurrence in which a health care practitioner, in their role as a health care practitioner, intends to prescribe, order, administer, or furnish a Schedule II, Schedule III, or Schedule IV controlled substance to a patient and has not previously prescribed a controlled substance to the patient.

(2) A health care practitioner shall review a patient's controlled substance history that has been obtained from the CURES database no earlier than 24 hours, or the previous business day, before the health care practitioner prescribes, orders, administers, or furnishes a Schedule II, Schedule III, or Schedule IV controlled substance to the patient.

(b) The duty to consult the CURES database, as described in subdivision (a), does not apply to veterinarians or pharmacists.

(c) The duty to consult the CURES database, as described in subdivision (a), does not apply to a health care practitioner in any of the following circumstances:

(1) If a health care practitioner prescribes, orders, or furnishes a controlled substance to be administered to a patient in any of the following facilities or during a transfer between any of the following facilities, or for use while on facility premises:

(A) A licensed clinic, as described in Chapter 1 (commencing with Section 1200) of Division 2.

(B) An outpatient setting, as described in Chapter 1.3 (commencing with Section 1248) of Division 2.

(C) A health facility, as described in Chapter 2 (commencing with Section 1250) of Division 2.

(D) A county medical facility, as described in Chapter 2.5 (commencing with Section 1440) of Division 2.

(E) Another medical facility, including, but not limited to, an office of a health care practitioner and an imaging center.

(F) A correctional clinic, as described in Section 4187 of the Business and Professions Code, or a correctional pharmacy, as described in Section 4021.5 of the Business and Professions Code.

(2) If a health care practitioner prescribes, orders, administers, or furnishes a controlled substance in the emergency department of a general acute care hospital and the quantity of the controlled substance does not exceed a nonrefillable seven-day supply of the controlled substance to be used in accordance with the directions for use.

(3) If a health care practitioner prescribes, orders, administers, or furnishes a controlled substance to a patient as part of the patient's treatment for a surgical, radiotherapeutic, therapeutic, or diagnostic procedure and the quantity of the controlled substance does not exceed a nonrefillable seven-day supply of the controlled substance to be used in accordance with the directions for use, in any of the following facilities:

(A) A licensed clinic, as described in Chapter 1 (commencing with Section 1200) of Division 2.

(B) An outpatient setting, as described in Chapter 1.3 (commencing with Section 1248) of Division 2.

(C) A health facility, as described in Chapter 2 (commencing with Section 1250) of Division 2.

(D) A county medical facility, as described in Chapter 2.5 (commencing with Section 1440) of Division 2.

(E) A place of practice, as defined in Section 1658 of the Business and Professions Code.

(F) Another medical facility where surgical procedures are permitted to take place, including, but not limited to, the office of a health care practitioner.

(4) If a health care practitioner prescribes, orders, administers, or furnishes a controlled substance to a patient who is terminally ill, as defined in subdivision (c) of Section 11159.2.

(5)(A) If all of the following circumstances are satisfied:

(i) It is not reasonably possible for a health care practitioner to access the information in the CURES database in a timely manner.

(ii) Another health care practitioner or designee authorized to access the CURES database is not reasonably available.

(iii) The quantity of controlled substance prescribed, ordered, administered, or furnished does not exceed a nonrefillable seven-day supply of the controlled substance to be used in accordance with the directions for use and no refill of the controlled substance is allowed.

(B) A health care practitioner who does not consult the CURES database under subparagraph (A) shall document the reason they did not consult the database in the patient's medical record.

(6) If the CURES database is not operational, as determined by the department, or cannot be accessed by a health care practitioner because of a temporary technological or electrical failure. A health care practitioner shall, without undue delay, seek to correct the cause of the temporary technological or electrical failure that is reasonably within the health care practitioner's control.

(7) If the CURES database cannot be accessed because of technological limitations that are not reasonably within the control of a health care practitioner.

(8) If consultation of the CURES database would, as determined by the health care practitioner, result in a patient's inability to obtain a prescription in a timely manner and thereby adversely impact the patient's medical condition, provided that the quantity of the controlled substance does not exceed a nonrefillable seven-day supply if the controlled substance were used in accordance with the directions for use.

(d)(1) A health care practitioner who fails to consult the CURES database, as described in subdivision (a), shall be referred to the appropriate state professional licensing board solely for administrative sanctions, as deemed appropriate by that board.

(2) This section does not create a private cause of action against a health care practitioner. This section does not limit a health care practitioner's liability for the negligent failure to diagnose or treat a patient.

(e) All applicable state and federal privacy laws govern the duties required by this section.

(f) The provisions of this section are severable. If any provision of this section or its application is held invalid, that invalidity shall not affect other provisions or applications that can be given effect without the invalid provision or application.

(g) This section shall become operative on July 1, 2021, or upon the date the department promulgates regulations to implement this section and posts those regulations on its internet website, whichever date is earlier. *(Added by Stats.2019, c. 677 (A.B.528), § 10, eff. Jan. 1, 2020, operative July 1, 2021.)*

§ 11165.5. Donations to support Controlled Substance Utilization Review and Evaluation System (CURES)

(a) The Department of Justice may seek voluntarily contributed private funds from insurers, health care service plans, qualified manufacturers, and other donors for the purpose of supporting CURES. Insurers, health care service plans, qualified manufacturers, and other donors may contribute by submitting their payment to the Controller for deposit into the CURES Fund established pursuant to subdivision (c) of Section 208 of the Business and Professions Code. The department shall make information about the amount and the source of all private funds it receives for support of CURES available to the public. Contributions to the CURES Fund pursuant to this subdivision shall be nondeductible for state tax purposes.

(b) For purposes of this section, the following definitions apply:

(1) "Controlled substance" means a drug, substance, or immediate precursor listed in any schedule in Section 11055, 11056, or 11057 of the Health and Safety Code.

(2) "Health care service plan" means an entity licensed pursuant to the Knox–Keene Health Care Service Plan Act of 1975 (Chapter 2.2 (commencing with Section 1340) of Division 2 of the Health and Safety Code).

(3) "Insurer" means an admitted insurer writing health insurance, as defined in Section 106 of the Insurance Code, and an admitted insurer writing workers' compensation insurance, as defined in Section 109 of the Insurance Code.

(4) "Qualified manufacturer" means a manufacturer of a controlled substance, but does not mean a wholesaler or nonresident wholesaler of dangerous drugs, regulated pursuant to Article 11 (commencing with Section 4160) of Chapter 9 of Division 2 of the Business and Professions Code, a veterinary food-animal drug retailer, regulated pursuant to Article 15 (commencing with Section 4196) of Chapter 9 of Division 2 of the Business and Professions Code, or an individual regulated by the Medical Board of California, the Dental Board of California, the California State Board of Pharmacy, the Veterinary Medical Board, the Board of Registered Nursing, the Physician Assistant Committee of the Medical Board of California, the Osteopathic Medical Board of California, the State Board of Optometry, or the California Board of Podiatric Medicine. *(Added by Stats.2013, c. 400 (S.B.809), § 8.)*

§ 11165.6. Prescriber access to CURES database

A prescriber shall be allowed to access the CURES database for a list of patients for whom that prescriber is listed as a prescriber in the CURES database. *(Added by Stats.2018, c. 274 (A.B.2086), § 1, eff. Jan. 1, 2019.)*

§ 11166. Time limit on filling prescription; mutilated, forged, or altered prescription

No person shall fill a prescription for a controlled substance after six months has elapsed from the date written on the prescription by the prescriber. No person shall knowingly fill a mutilated or forged or altered prescription for a controlled substance except for the addition of the address of the person for whom the controlled substance is prescribed as provided by paragraph (3) of subdivision (b) of Section 11164. *(Added by Stats.1976, c. 896, p. 2058, § 13. Amended by Stats.1985, c. 630, § 1; Stats.1998, c. 878 (S.B.2239), § 58; Stats.2003, c. 406 (S.B.151), § 19.)*

Cross References

Controlled substance defined for purposes of this Division, see Health and Safety Code § 11007.
Dating of prescriptions, see Health and Safety Code § 11172.
False or fictitious prescription, see Health and Safety Code § 11157.
Forged or altered prescriptions, punishment, see Health and Safety Code § 11368.
Person defined for purposes of this Division, see Health and Safety Code § 11022.
Prescription or electronic transmission prescription defined for purposes of this Division, see Health and Safety Code § 11027.

Research References

2 Witkin, California Criminal Law 4th Crimes Against Public Peace and Welfare § 152 (2021), In General.

§ 11167. Emergency that may result in death or intense suffering; oral, written, or electronic data transmission order; requirements

Notwithstanding subdivision (a) of Section 11164, in an emergency where failure to issue a prescription may result in loss of life or intense suffering, an order for a controlled substance may be dispensed on an oral order, an electronic data transmission order, or a written order not made on a controlled substance form as specified in Section 11162.1, subject to all of the following requirements:

(a) The order contains all information required by subdivision (a) of Section 11164.

(b) Any written order is signed and dated by the prescriber in ink, and the pharmacy reduces any oral or electronic data transmission order to hard copy form prior to dispensing the controlled substance.

(c) The prescriber provides a written prescription on a controlled substance prescription form that meets the requirements of Section 11162.1, by the seventh day following the transmission of the initial order; a postmark by the seventh day following transmission of the initial order shall constitute compliance.

(d) If the prescriber fails to comply with subdivision (c), the pharmacy shall so notify the Department of Justice in writing within 144 hours of the prescriber's failure to do so and shall make and retain a hard copy, readily retrievable record of the prescription, including the date and method of notification of the Department of Justice.

(e) This section shall become operative on January 1, 2005. *(Added by Stats.2003, c. 406 (S.B.151), § 22, operative Jan. 1, 2005. Amended by Stats.2012, c. 867 (S.B.1144), § 8.)*

Cross References

Controlled substance defined for purposes of this Division, see Health and Safety Code § 11007.
Healing arts, pharmacy, scope of practice and exemptions, hospitals with 100 or fewer beds, wholesale purchase of drugs, see Business and Professions Code § 4056.
Pharmacy defined for purposes of this Division, see Health and Safety Code § 11023.
Prescription or electronic transmission prescription defined for purposes of this Division, see Health and Safety Code § 11027.

§ 11167.5. Hospice care provided by licensed facilities or home health agencies; oral or electronically transmitted prescriptions for Schedule II controlled substances; transaction documentation

(a) An order for a controlled substance classified in Schedule II for a patient of a licensed skilled nursing facility, a licensed intermediate care facility, a licensed home health agency, or a licensed hospice may be dispensed upon an oral or electronically transmitted prescription. If the prescription is transmitted orally, the pharmacist shall, prior to filling the prescription, reduce the prescription to writing in ink in the handwriting of the pharmacist on a form developed by the pharmacy for this purpose. If the prescription is transmitted electronically, the pharmacist shall, prior to filling the prescription, produce, sign, and date a hard copy prescription. The prescriptions shall contain the date the prescription was orally or electronically transmitted by the prescriber, the name of the person for whom the prescription was authorized, the name and address of the licensed skilled nursing facility, licensed intermediate care facility, licensed home health agency, or licensed hospice in which that person is a patient, the name and quantity of the controlled substance prescribed, the directions for use, and the name, address, category of professional licensure, license number, and federal controlled substance registration number of the prescriber. The original shall be properly endorsed by the pharmacist with the pharmacy's state license number, the name and address of the pharmacy, and the signature of the person who received the controlled substances for the licensed skilled nursing facility, licensed intermediate care facility, licensed home health agency, or licensed hospice. A licensed skilled nursing facility, a licensed intermediate care facility, a licensed home health agency, or a licensed hospice shall forward to the dispensing pharmacist a copy of any signed telephone orders, chart orders, or related documentation substantiating each oral or electronically transmitted prescription transaction under this section.

(b) This section shall become operative on July 1, 2004. *(Added by Stats.2003, c. 406 (S.B.151), § 24, operative July 1, 2004.)*

Cross References

Controlled substance defined for purposes of this Division, see Health and Safety Code § 11007.
Person defined for purposes of this Division, see Health and Safety Code § 11022.
Pharmacy defined for purposes of this Division, see Health and Safety Code § 11023.
Physician, dentist, podiatrist, pharmacist, veterinarian, and optometrist defined for purposes of this Division, see Health and Safety Code § 11024.
Prescription or electronic transmission prescription defined for purposes of this Division, see Health and Safety Code § 11027.

§ 11170. Controlled substances for self use

No person shall prescribe, administer, or furnish a controlled substance for himself. *(Added by Stats.1972, c. 1407, p. 3003, § 3.)*

Cross References

Administer defined for purposes of this Division, see Health and Safety Code § 11002.
Controlled substance defined for purposes of this Division, see Health and Safety Code § 11007.
Furnish defined for purposes of this Division, see Health and Safety Code § 11016.
Person defined for purposes of this Division, see Health and Safety Code § 11022.

Research References

2 Witkin, California Criminal Law 4th Crimes Against Public Peace and Welfare § 152 (2021), In General.

§ 11171. Prescription, administration or furnishing controlled substance

No person shall prescribe, administer, or furnish a controlled substance except under the conditions and in the manner provided by this division. *(Added by Stats.1972, c. 1407, p. 3003, § 3.)*

Cross References

Administer defined for purposes of this Division, see Health and Safety Code § 11002.
Controlled substance defined for purposes of this Division, see Health and Safety Code § 11007.
Furnish defined for purposes of this Division, see Health and Safety Code § 11016.
Furnishing controlled substances by oral or electronically transmitted to unknown persons, see Business and Professions Code § 4075.
Person defined for purposes of this Division, see Health and Safety Code § 11022.
Selling, dispensing or compounding drug under influence of dangerous drug, penalty, see Business and Professions Code § 4327.

Research References

2 Witkin, California Criminal Law 4th Crimes Against Public Peace and Welfare § 152 (2021), In General.

§ 11172. Antedating or postdating prescription

No person shall antedate or postdate a prescription. *(Added by Stats.1972, c. 1407, p. 3003, § 3.)*

Cross References

Person defined for purposes of this Division, see Health and Safety Code § 11022.
Prescription or electronic transmission prescription defined for purposes of this Division, see Health and Safety Code § 11027.

Research References

2 Witkin, California Criminal Law 4th Crimes Against Public Peace and Welfare § 152 (2021), In General.

§ 11173. Fraud, deceit, misrepresentations

(a) No person shall obtain or attempt to obtain controlled substances, or procure or attempt to procure the administration of or prescription for controlled substances, (1) by fraud, deceit, misrepresentation, or subterfuge; or (2) by the concealment of a material fact.

(b) No person shall make a false statement in any prescription, order, report, or record, required by this division.

(c) No person shall, for the purpose of obtaining controlled substances, falsely assume the title of, or represent himself to be, a manufacturer, wholesaler, pharmacist, physician, dentist, veterinarian, registered nurse, physician's assistant, or other authorized person.

(d) No person shall affix any false or forged label to a package or receptacle containing controlled substances. *(Added by Stats.1972, c. 1407, p. 3003, § 3. Amended by Stats.1977, c. 843, p. 2533, § 19.)*

Cross References

Controlled substance defined for purposes of this Division, see Health and Safety Code § 11007.
Controlled substance obtained by nonconforming prescription, see Health and Safety Code § 11180.
False or fictitious prescription, see Health and Safety Code § 11157.
False representation as physician to obtain prescription drugs, see Business and Professions Code § 4323; Penal Code § 377.
Forged or altered prescriptions, punishment, see Health and Safety Code § 11368.
Forgery of prescription, see Business and Professions Code § 4324.
Manufacturer defined for purposes of this Division, see Health and Safety Code § 11017.
Person defined for purposes of this Division, see Health and Safety Code § 11022.
Physician, dentist, podiatrist, pharmacist, veterinarian, and optometrist defined for purposes of this Division, see Health and Safety Code § 11024.
Prescription or electronic transmission prescription defined for purposes of this Division, see Health and Safety Code § 11027.
Wholesaler defined for purposes of this Division, see Health and Safety Code § 11031.

Research References

2 Witkin, California Criminal Law 4th Crimes Against Public Peace and Welfare § 152 (2021), In General.
2 Witkin, California Criminal Law 4th Crimes Against Public Peace and Welfare § 153 (2021), Inducing Minor to Commit Prescription Offenses.

§ 11174. False name or address

No person shall, in connection with the prescribing, furnishing, administering, or dispensing of a controlled substance, give a false name or false address. *(Added by Stats.1972, c. 1407, p. 3004, § 3.)*

Cross References

Controlled substance defined for purposes of this Division, see Health and Safety Code § 11007.
Person defined for purposes of this Division, see Health and Safety Code § 11022.

Research References

2 Witkin, California Criminal Law 4th Crimes Against Public Peace and Welfare § 152 (2021), In General.

§ 11175. Possession of noncomplying prescriptions; unlawfully obtained controlled substances

No person shall obtain or possess a prescription that does not comply with this division, nor shall any person obtain a controlled substance by means of a prescription which does not comply with this division or possess a controlled substance obtained by such a prescription. *(Added by Stats.1972, c. 1407, p. 3004, § 3. Amended by Stats.1976, c. 896, p. 2059, § 17.)*

Cross References

Controlled substance defined for purposes of this Division, see Health and Safety Code § 11007.
Person defined for purposes of this Division, see Health and Safety Code § 11022.
Prescription or electronic transmission prescription defined for purposes of this Division, see Health and Safety Code § 11027.

Research References

2 Witkin, California Criminal Law 4th Crimes Against Public Peace and Welfare § 152 (2021), In General.

§ 11179. Filing and retention of prescriptions

A person who fills a prescription shall keep it on file for at least three years from the date of filling it. *(Added by Stats.1972, c. 1407, p. 3004, § 3. Amended by Stats.1976, c. 896, p. 2059, § 21.)*

Cross References

Person defined for purposes of this Division, see Health and Safety Code § 11022.
Pharmacists' records, see Health and Safety Code § 11205 et seq.
Prescription or electronic transmission prescription defined for purposes of this Division, see Health and Safety Code § 11027.
Receipt for pharmacist's copy of prescription removed by officer, see Health and Safety Code § 11195.

§ 11180. Possession of controlled substance obtained by nonconforming prescription

No person shall obtain or possess a controlled substance obtained by a prescription that does not comply with this division. *(Added by Stats.1972, c. 1407, p. 3004, § 3.)*

Cross References

Controlled substance defined for purposes of this Division, see Health and Safety Code § 11007.
Person defined for purposes of this Division, see Health and Safety Code § 11022.
Possession of noncomplying prescription, see Health and Safety Code § 11175.
Prescription or electronic transmission prescription defined for purposes of this Division, see Health and Safety Code § 11027.

ARTICLE 2. PRESCRIBER'S RECORD

Section

§ 11190. Duty to keep record of Schedule II controlled substances; transaction documentation; records of prescriptions for Schedule II, Schedule III, and Schedule IV controlled substances

(a) Every practitioner, other than a pharmacist, who prescribes or administers a controlled substance classified in Schedule II shall make a record that, as to the transaction, shows all of the following:

(1) The name and address of the patient.

(2) The date.

(3) The character, including the name and strength, and quantity of controlled substances involved.

(b) The prescriber's record shall show the pathology and purpose for which the controlled substance was administered or prescribed.

(c)(1) For each prescription for a Schedule II, Schedule III, or Schedule IV controlled substance that is dispensed by a prescriber pursuant to Section 4170 of the Business and Professions Code, the prescriber shall record and maintain the following information:

(A) Full name, address, and the telephone number of the ultimate user or research subject, or contact information as determined by the Secretary of the United States Department of Health and Human Services, and the gender, and date of birth of the patient.

(B) The prescriber's category of licensure and license number; federal controlled substance registration number; and the state medical license number of any prescriber using the federal controlled substance registration number of a government-exempt facility.

(C) NDC (National Drug Code) number of the controlled substance dispensed.

(D) Quantity of the controlled substance dispensed.

(E) ICD–9 (diagnosis code), if available.

(F) Number of refills ordered.

(G) Whether the drug was dispensed as a refill of a prescription or as a first-time request.

(H) Date of origin of the prescription.

(2)(A) Each prescriber that dispenses controlled substances shall provide the Department of Justice the information required by this subdivision on a weekly basis in a format set by the Department of Justice pursuant to regulation.

(B) The reporting requirement in this section shall not apply to the direct administration of a controlled substance to the body of an ultimate user.

(d) This section shall become operative on January 1, 2005.

(e) The reporting requirement in this section for Schedule IV controlled substances shall not apply to any of the following:

(1) The dispensing of a controlled substance in a quantity limited to an amount adequate to treat the ultimate user involved for 48 hours or less.

(2) The administration or dispensing of a controlled substance in accordance with any other exclusion identified by the United States Health and Human Service Secretary for the National All Schedules Prescription Electronic Reporting Act of 2005.

(f) Notwithstanding paragraph (2) of subdivision (c), the reporting requirement of the information required by this section for a Schedule II or Schedule III controlled substance, in a format set by the Department of Justice pursuant to regulation, shall be on a monthly basis for all of the following:

(1) The dispensing of a controlled substance in a quantity limited to an amount adequate to treat the ultimate user involved for 48 hours or less.

(2) The administration or dispensing of a controlled substance in accordance with any other exclusion identified by the United States Health and Human Service Secretary for the National All Schedules Prescription Electronic Reporting Act of 2005. *(Added by Stats.2003,*

Health & Safety

c. 406 (S.B.151), § 29, operative Jan. 1, 2005. Amended by Stats.2004, c. 573 (A.B.30), § 5, eff. Sept. 18, 2004, operative Jan. 1, 2005; Stats.2005, c. 487 (S.B.734), § 7; Stats.2006, c. 286 (A.B.2986), § 5.)

Cross References

Administer defined for purposes of this Division, see Health and Safety Code § 11002.
Controlled substance defined for purposes of this Division, see Health and Safety Code § 11007.
Department of Health Care Services, generally, see Health and Safety Code § 100100 et seq.
Dispense defined for purposes of this Division, see Health and Safety Code § 11010.
Drug defined for purposes of this Division, see Health and Safety Code § 11014.
Pharmacists' records, see Health and Safety Code § 11205 et seq.
Physician, dentist, podiatrist, pharmacist, veterinarian, and optometrist defined for purposes of this Division, see Health and Safety Code § 11024.
Practitioner defined for purposes of this Division, see Health and Safety Code § 11026.
Prescription or electronic transmission prescription defined for purposes of this Division, see Health and Safety Code § 11027.
Prescriptions, generally, see Health and Safety Code § 11150 et seq.
Ultimate user defined for purposes of this Division, see Health and Safety Code § 11030.

§ 11191. Preservation of record; violations

The record shall be preserved for three years.

Every person who violates any provision of this section is guilty of a misdemeanor. *(Added by Stats.1972, c. 1407, p. 3005, § 3. Amended by Stats.1976, c. 896, p. 2059, § 23.)*

Cross References

Misdemeanor,
  Defined, see Penal Code § 17.
  Punishment, see Penal Code §§ 19, 19.2.
Person defined for purposes of this Division, see Health and Safety Code § 11022.

§ 11192. Prima facie evidence of violation

In a prosecution for a violation of Section 11190, proof that a defendant received or has had in his possession at any time a greater amount of controlled substances than is accounted for by any record required by law or that the amount of controlled substances possessed by a defendant is a lesser amount than is accounted for by any record required by law is prima facie evidence of a violation of the section. *(Added by Stats.1972, c. 1407, p. 3005, § 3. Amended by Stats.1976, c. 637, p. 1504, § 1.)*

Cross References

Controlled substance defined for purposes of this Division, see Health and Safety Code § 11007.
Establishment of rebuttable presumption, one fact prima facie evidence of another fact, see Evidence Code § 602.

ARTICLE 3. COPIES OF PRESCRIPTIONS

Section

§ 11195. Receipt for pharmacist's copy of prescription removed by officer

Whenever the pharmacist's copy of a controlled substance prescription is removed by a peace officer, agent of the Attorney General, or inspector of the Board of Pharmacy, or investigator of the Division of Investigation of the Department of Consumer Affairs for the purpose of investigation or as evidence, the officer or inspector or investigator shall give to the pharmacist a receipt in lieu thereof. *(Added by Stats.1972, c. 1407, p. 3005, § 3.)*

Cross References

Agent defined for purposes of this Division, see Health and Safety Code § 11003.
Attorney General, generally, see Government Code § 12500 et seq.
Attorney General defined for purposes of this Division, see Health and Safety Code § 11004.
Controlled substance defined for purposes of this Division, see Health and Safety Code § 11007.
Inspection of records of manufacturer and disposition of dangerous drugs or devices, see Business and Professions Code § 4081.
Physician, dentist, podiatrist, pharmacist, veterinarian, and optometrist defined for purposes of this Division, see Health and Safety Code § 11024.
Prescription or electronic transmission prescription defined for purposes of this Division, see Health and Safety Code § 11027.

ARTICLE 4. REFILLING PRESCRIPTIONS

Section

§ 11200. Restrictions and prohibitions

(a) No person shall dispense or refill a controlled substance prescription more than six months after the date thereof.

(b) No prescription for a Schedule III or IV substance may be refilled more than five times and in an amount, for all refills of that prescription taken together, exceeding a 120-day supply.

(c) No prescription for a Schedule II substance may be refilled. *(Added by Stats.1972, c. 1407, p. 3005, § 3. Amended by Stats.1979, c. 634, p. 1962, § 6; Stats.1991, c. 592 (A.B.1188), § 2; Stats.1992, c. 616 (S.B.2013), § 2.)*

Cross References

Controlled substance defined for purposes of this Division, see Health and Safety Code § 11007.
Dispense defined for purposes of this Division, see Health and Safety Code § 11010.
Person defined for purposes of this Division, see Health and Safety Code § 11022.
Prescription or electronic transmission prescription defined for purposes of this Division, see Health and Safety Code § 11027.

§ 11201. Refilling prescription when prescriber unavailable

A prescription for a controlled substance, except those appearing in Schedule II, may be refilled without the prescriber's authorization if the prescriber is unavailable to authorize the refill and if, in the pharmacist's professional judgment, failure to refill the prescription might present an immediate hazard to the patient's health and welfare or might result in intense suffering. The pharmacist shall refill only a reasonable amount sufficient to maintain the patient until the prescriber can be contacted. The pharmacist shall note on the reverse side of the prescription the date and quantity of the refill and that the prescriber was not available and the basis for his judgment to refill the prescription without the prescriber's authorization. The pharmacist shall inform the patient that the prescription was refilled without the prescriber's authorization, indicating that the prescriber was not available and that, in the pharmacist's professional judgment, failure to provide the drug might result in an immediate hazard to the patient's health and welfare or might result in intense suffering. The pharmacist shall inform the prescriber within a reasonable period of time. Prior to refilling a prescription pursuant to this section, the pharmacist shall make every reasonable effort to contact the prescriber.

The prescriber shall not incur any liability as the result of a refilling of a prescription pursuant to this section. *(Added by Stats.1977, c. 1211, p. 4087, § 2.)*

Cross References

Controlled substance defined for purposes of this Division, see Health and Safety Code § 11007.
Drug defined for purposes of this Division, see Health and Safety Code § 11014.
Physician, dentist, podiatrist, pharmacist, veterinarian, and optometrist defined for purposes of this Division, see Health and Safety Code § 11024.
Prescription or electronic transmission prescription defined for purposes of this Division, see Health and Safety Code § 11027.
Public social services, aid and medical assistance, basic health care, administration, update of allowable drug product prices, notice of reimbursement limitation, see Welfare and Institutions Code § 14105.7.

ARTICLE 5. PHARMACISTS' RECORDS

Section

§ 11205. Controlled substance prescription file

The owner of a pharmacy or any person who purchases a controlled substance upon federal order forms as required pursuant to the provisions of the Federal "Comprehensive Drug Abuse Prevention and Control Act of 1970," (P.L. 91–513, 84 Stat. 1236),[1] relating to the importation, exportation, manufacture, production, compounding, distribution, dispensing, and control of controlled substances, and who sells controlled substances obtained upon such federal order forms in response to prescriptions shall maintain and file such prescriptions in a separate file apart from noncontrolled substances prescriptions. Such files shall be preserved for a period of three years. *(Added by Stats.1972, c. 1407, p. 3006, § 3. Amended by Stats.1976, c. 896, p. 2060, § 24.)*

[1] 21 U.S.C.A. § 801 et seq.

Cross References

Controlled substance defined for purposes of this Division, see Health and Safety Code § 11007.
Person defined for purposes of this Division, see Health and Safety Code § 11022.
Pharmacy defined for purposes of this Division, see Health and Safety Code § 11023.
Prescriber's record, see Health and Safety Code § 11190 et seq.
Prescription, see Health and Safety Code §§ 11027, 11150 et seq.
Production defined for purposes of this Division, see Health and Safety Code § 11029.
Requirements of prescriptions, see Health and Safety Code § 11150 et seq.

§ 11206. Transaction record

Filed prescriptions shall constitute a transaction record that, together with information that is readily retrievable in the pharmacy pursuant to Section 11164 shall show or include the following:

(a) The name(s) and address of the patient(s).

(b) The date.

(c) The character, including the name and strength, quantity, and directions for use of the controlled substance involved.

(d) The name, address, telephone number, category of professional licensure, and the federal controlled substance registration number of the prescriber. *(Added by Stats.1972, c. 1407, p. 3006, § 3. Amended by Stats.1976, c. 896, p. 2060, § 25; Stats.1979, c. 634, p. 1962, § 7; Stats.1988, c. 398, § 5.)*

Cross References

Controlled substance defined for purposes of this Division, see Health and Safety Code § 11007.
Pharmacy defined for purposes of this Division, see Health and Safety Code § 11023.
Prescriptions, see Health and Safety Code §§ 11027, 11150 et seq.
Requirements of prescriptions, see Health and Safety Code § 11150 et seq.

§ 11207. Compounding, preparation, filling or dispensing of controlled substance prescriptions; pharmacists and intern pharmacists

(a) No person other than a pharmacist as defined in Section 4036 of the Business and Professions Code or an intern pharmacist, as defined in Section 4030 of the Business and Professions Code, who is under the personal supervision of a pharmacist, shall compound, prepare, fill or dispense a prescription for a controlled substance.

(b) Notwithstanding subdivision (a), a pharmacy technician may perform those tasks permitted by Section 4115 of the Business and Professions Code when assisting a pharmacist dispensing a prescription for a controlled substance. *(Added by Stats.1972, c. 1407, p. 3006, § 3. Amended by Stats.1976, c. 896, p. 2060, § 26; Stats.2004, c. 695 (S.B.1913), § 53.)*

Cross References

Applications, see Business and Professions Code § 4200 et seq.
Controlled substance defined for purposes of this Division, see Health and Safety Code § 11007.
Dispense defined for purposes of this Division, see Health and Safety Code § 11010.
Person defined for purposes of this Division, see Health and Safety Code § 11022.
Pharmacist defined, see Business and Professions Code § 4040.
Pharmacy defined for purposes of this Division, see Health and Safety Code § 11023.
Physician, dentist, podiatrist, pharmacist, veterinarian, and optometrist defined for purposes of this Division, see Health and Safety Code § 11024.
Prescription, see Health and Safety Code §§ 11027, 11150 et seq.
Records of pharmacists, see Business and Professions Code § 4003.
Statute providing that fact is prima facie evidence of another fact establishes rebuttable presumption, see Evidence Code § 602.

§ 11208. Evidence

In a prosecution under this division, proof that a defendant received or has had in his possession at any time a greater amount of controlled substances than is accounted for by any record required by law or that the amount of controlled substances possessed by the defendant is a lesser amount than is accounted for by any record required by law is prima facie evidence of guilt. *(Added by Stats.1972, c. 1407, p. 3006, § 3.)*

Cross References

Controlled substance defined for purposes of this Division, see Health and Safety Code § 11007.
Prima facie evidence, see Evidence Code § 602.

§ 11209. Delivery of Schedule II, III, or IV controlled substances; signing and retaining receipts; reports of discrepancies

(a) No person shall deliver Schedule II, III, or IV controlled substances to a pharmacy or pharmacy receiving area, nor shall any person receive controlled substances on behalf of a pharmacy unless, at the time of delivery, a pharmacist or authorized receiving personnel signs a receipt showing the type and quantity of the controlled substances received. Any discrepancy between the receipt and the type or quantity of controlled substances actually received shall be reported to the delivering wholesaler or manufacturer by the next business day after delivery to the pharmacy.

(b) The delivery receipt and any record of discrepancy shall be maintained by the wholesaler or manufacturer for a period of three years.

(c) A violation of this section is a misdemeanor.

(d) Nothing in this section shall require a common carrier to label a package containing controlled substances in a manner contrary to federal law or regulation. *(Added by Stats.1986, c. 384, § 5, eff. July 17, 1986. Amended by Stats.1988, c. 918, § 6.)*

Cross References

Controlled substance defined for purposes of this Division, see Health and Safety Code § 11007.
Deliver or delivery defined for purposes of this Division, see Health and Safety Code § 11009.
Manufacturer defined for purposes of this Division, see Health and Safety Code § 11017.
Misdemeanors, definition and penalties, see Penal Code §§ 17, 19 and 19.2.
Person defined for purposes of this Division, see Health and Safety Code § 11022.
Pharmacy defined for purposes of this Division, see Health and Safety Code § 11023.
Physician, dentist, podiatrist, pharmacist, veterinarian, and optometrist defined for purposes of this Division, see Health and Safety Code § 11024.
Wholesaler defined for purposes of this Division, see Health and Safety Code § 11031.

CHAPTER 5. USE OF CONTROLLED SUBSTANCES

ARTICLE 1. LAWFUL MEDICAL USE OTHER THAN TREATMENT OF ADDICTS

§ 11210. Conditions authorizing prescription; quantity; duration

A physician, surgeon, dentist, veterinarian, naturopathic doctor acting pursuant to Section 3640.7 of the Business and Professions Code, or podiatrist, or pharmacist acting within the scope of a project authorized under Article 1 (commencing with Section 128125) of Chapter 3 of Part 3 of Division 107 or within the scope of Section 4052.1, 4052.2, or 4052.6 of the Business and Professions Code, or registered nurse acting within the scope of a project authorized under Article 1 (commencing with Section 128125) of Chapter 3 of Part 3 of Division 107, or physician assistant acting within the scope of a project authorized under Article 1 (commencing with Section 128125) of Chapter 3 of Part 3 of Division 107, or naturopathic doctor acting within the scope of Section 3640.5 of the Business and Professions Code, or an optometrist acting within the scope of Section 3041 of the Business and Professions Code may prescribe for, furnish to, or administer controlled substances to his or her patient when the patient is suffering from a disease, ailment, injury, or infirmities attendant upon old age, other than addiction to a controlled substance.

The physician, surgeon, dentist, veterinarian, naturopathic doctor acting pursuant to Section 3640.7 of the Business and Professions Code, or podiatrist, or pharmacist acting within the scope of a project authorized under Article 1 (commencing with Section 128125) of Chapter 3 of Part 3 of Division 107 or within the scope of Section 4052.1, 4052.2, or 4052.6 of the Business and Professions Code, or registered nurse acting within the scope of a project authorized under Article 1 (commencing with Section 128125) of Chapter 3 of Part 3 of Division 107, or physician assistant acting within the scope of a project authorized under Article 1 (commencing with Section 128125) of Chapter 3 of Part 3 of Division 107, or naturopathic doctor acting within the scope of Section 3640.5 of the Business and Professions Code, or an optometrist acting within the scope of Section 3041 of the Business and Professions Code shall prescribe, furnish, or administer controlled substances only when in good faith he or she believes the disease, ailment, injury, or infirmity requires the treatment.

The physician, surgeon, dentist, veterinarian, or naturopathic doctor acting pursuant to Section 3640.7 of the Business and Professions Code, or podiatrist, or pharmacist acting within the scope of a project authorized under Article 1 (commencing with Section 128125) of Chapter 3 of Part 3 of Division 107 or within the scope of Section 4052.1, 4052.2, or 4052.6 of the Business and Professions Code, or registered nurse acting within the scope of a project authorized under Article 1 (commencing with Section 128125) of Chapter 3 of Part 3 of Division 107, or physician assistant acting within the scope of a project authorized under Article 1 (commencing with Section 128125) of Chapter 3 of Part 3 of Division 107, or a naturopathic doctor acting within the scope of Section 3640.5 of the Business and Professions Code, or an optometrist acting within the scope of Section 3041 of the Business and Professions Code shall prescribe, furnish, or administer controlled substances only in the quantity and for the length of time as are reasonably necessary. *(Added by Stats.1972, c. 1407, p. 3006, § 3. Amended by Stats.1977, c. 843, p. 2534, § 20; Stats.1996, c. 1023 (S.B.1497), § 199, eff. Sept. 29, 1996; Stats.2000, c. 676 (S.B.929), § 9; Stats.2005, c. 506 (A.B.302), § 28, eff. Oct. 4, 2005; Stats.2014, c. 319 (S.B.1039), § 6, eff. Jan. 1, 2015.)*

Cross References

Administer defined for purposes of this Division, see Health and Safety Code § 11002.
Controlled substance defined for purposes of this Division, see Health and Safety Code § 11007.
Conviction for violation of regulations of dangerous drugs or controlled substances as unprofessional conduct, see Business and Professions Code § 2237.
Furnish defined for purposes of this Division, see Health and Safety Code § 11016.
Offense, punishment, see Health and Safety Code § 11371.
Persons authorized to write prescriptions, see Business and Professions Code § 4040; Health and Safety Code § 11150.
Physician, dentist, podiatrist, pharmacist, veterinarian, and optometrist defined for purposes of this Division, see Health and Safety Code § 11024.
Prescription defined for purposes of this Division, see Health and Safety Code § 11027.
Prescription to addicts forbidden, see Health and Safety Code § 11156.
Prescriptions, generally, see Health and Safety Code § 11150 et seq.
Requisites of prescription, see Health and Safety Code § 11158.
Responsibility of practitioner for proper prescription and dispensation of controlled substances, see Health and Safety Code § 11153.
Restrictions on prescription, administration or furnishing controlled substances, see Health and Safety Code § 11154.
Self-prescription, prohibition, see Health and Safety Code § 11170.
Treatment of addicts, see Health and Safety Code § 11215 et seq.

Research References

2 Witkin, California Criminal Law 4th Crimes Against Public Peace and Welfare § 152 (2021), In General.

§ 11211. Purchases by hospitals for emergency cases

In order to provide a supply of controlled substances as may be necessary to handle emergency cases, any hospital which does not employ a resident pharmacist and which is under the supervision of a licensed physician, may purchase controlled substances on federal order forms for such institution, under the name of such hospital, such supply to be made available to a registered nurse for administration to patients in emergency cases, upon direction of a licensed physician. *(Added by Stats.1972, c. 1407, p. 3006, § 3.)*

Cross References

Controlled substance defined for purposes of this Division, see Health and Safety Code § 11007.

Physician, dentist, podiatrist, pharmacist, veterinarian, and optometrist defined for purposes of this Division, see Health and Safety Code § 11024.

§ 11212. Entitlement under federal law to use enumerated controlled substances for research, instruction or analysis

Persons who, under applicable federal laws or regulations, are lawfully entitled to use controlled substances for the purpose of research, instruction, or analysis, may lawfully obtain and use for such purposes those substances classified in paragraphs (45) and (46) of subdivision (b) of Section 11054 of the Health and Safety Code, upon registration with and approval by the California Department of Justice for use of those substances in bona fide research, instruction, or analysis.

That research, instruction, or analysis shall be carried on only under the auspices of the individual identified by the registrant as responsible for the research. Complete records of receipts, stocks at hand, and use of these controlled substances shall be kept.

The Department of Justice may withdraw approval of the use of such substances at any time. The department may obtain and inspect at any time the records required to be maintained by this section. *(Added by Stats.1985, c. 1098, § 1.5, eff. Sept. 27, 1985.)*

Cross References

Controlled substance defined for purposes of this Division, see Health and Safety Code § 11007.
Person defined for purposes of this Division, see Health and Safety Code § 11022.

§ 11213. Use for research, instruction or analysis; approval; records

Persons who, under applicable federal laws or regulations, are lawfully entitled to use controlled substances for the purpose of research, instruction, or analysis, may lawfully obtain and use for such purposes such substances as are defined as controlled substances in this division, upon approval for use of such controlled substances in bona fide research, instruction, or analysis by the Research Advisory Panel established pursuant to Section 11480 and 11481.

Such research, instruction, or analysis shall be carried on only under the auspices of the head of a research project which has been approved by the Research Advisory Panel pursuant to Section 11480 or Section 11481. Complete records of receipts, stocks at hand, and use of these controlled substances shall be kept. *(Added by Stats.1972, c. 1407, p. 3007, § 3.)*

Cross References

Authorization of possession and distribution of controlled substances for research, see Health and Safety Code § 11604.
Controlled substance defined for purposes of this Division, see Health and Safety Code § 11007.
Person defined for purposes of this Division, see Health and Safety Code § 11022.

ARTICLE 2. TREATMENT OF ADDICTS FOR ADDICTION

§ 11215. Administration of narcotics; persons authorized

(a) Except as provided in subdivision (b), any narcotic controlled substance employed in treating an addict for addiction shall be administered by:

(1) A physician and surgeon.

(2) A registered nurse acting under the instruction of a physician and surgeon.

(3) A physician assistant licensed pursuant to Chapter 7.7 (commencing with Section 3500) of Division 2 of the Business and Professions Code acting under the patient-specific authority of his or her physician and surgeon supervisor approved pursuant to Section 3515 of the Business and Professions Code.

(b) When acting under the direction of a physician and surgeon, the following persons may administer a narcotic controlled substance orally in the treatment of an addict for addiction to a controlled substance:

(1) A psychiatric technician licensed pursuant to Chapter 10 (commencing with Section 4500) of Division 2 of the Business and Professions Code.

(2) A vocational nurse licensed pursuant to Chapter 6.5 (commencing with Section 2840) of Division 2 of the Business and Professions Code.

(3) A pharmacist licensed pursuant to Chapter 9 (commencing with Section 4000) of Division 2 of the Business and Professions Code.

(c) Except as permitted in this section, no person shall order, permit, or direct any other person to administer a narcotic controlled substance to a person being treated for addiction to a controlled substance. *(Added by Stats.1972, c. 1407, p. 3007, § 3. Amended by Stats.1973, c. 516, p. 991, § 1; Stats.1976, c. 896, p. 2061, § 27; Stats.1991, c. 176 (A.B.535), § 1; Stats.1994, c. 26 (A.B.1807), § 245, eff. March 30, 1994; Stats.1995, c. 455 (A.B.1113), § 6, eff. Sept. 5, 1995.)*

Cross References

Administer defined for purposes of this Division, see Health and Safety Code § 11002.
Administration or prescription of narcotic to addict forbidden, exceptions, see Health and Safety Code §§ 11153, 11156.
Amount of controlled substance to be used or prescribed in treatment, see Health and Safety Code §§ 11218, 11219.
Controlled substance defined for purposes of this Division, see Health and Safety Code § 11007.
Discontinuance of narcotics, see Health and Safety Code § 11220.
Healing arts, medicine, enforcement, provision of prescription drugs and controlled substances to addicts, conditions, see Business and Professions Code § 2241.
Hypodermic needles and syringes, see Business and Professions Code § 4141 et seq.
Narcotic treatment programs, see Health and Safety Code § 11876.
Person defined for purposes of this Division, see Health and Safety Code § 11022.
Physician, dentist, podiatrist, pharmacist, veterinarian, and optometrist defined for purposes of this Division, see Health and Safety Code § 11024.
Restrictions on prescription, administration or furnishing controlled substances, see Health and Safety Code § 11154.

Research References

2 Witkin, California Criminal Law 4th Crimes Against Public Peace and Welfare § 188 (2021), Treatment of Addicts With Narcotics.

§ 11217. Place of treatment

Except as provided in Section 11223, no person shall treat an addict for addiction to a narcotic drug except in one of the following:

(a) An institution approved by the State Department of Health Care Services, and where the patient is at all times kept under restraint and control.

(b) A city or county jail.

(c) A state prison.

(d) A facility designated by a county and approved by the State Department of Health Care Services pursuant to Division 5 (commencing with Section 5000) of the Welfare and Institutions Code.

(e) A state hospital.

(f) A county hospital.

(g) A facility licensed by the State Department of Health Care Services pursuant to Division 10.5 (commencing with Section 11750).

(h) A facility as defined in subdivision (a) or (b) of Section 1250 and Section 1250.3.

A narcotic controlled substance in the continuing treatment of addiction to a controlled substance shall be used only in those programs licensed by the State Department of Health Care Services pursuant to Article 1 (commencing with Section 11839) of Chapter 10 of Part 2 of Division 10.5 on either an inpatient or outpatient basis, or both.

This section does not apply during emergency treatment, or where the patient's addiction is complicated by the presence of incurable disease, serious accident, or injury, or the infirmities of old age.

Neither this section nor any other provision of this division shall be construed to prohibit the maintenance of a place in which persons seeking to recover from addiction to a controlled substance reside and endeavor to aid one another and receive aid from others in recovering from that addiction, nor does this section or this division prohibit that aid, provided that no person is treated for addiction in a place by means of administering, furnishing, or prescribing of controlled substances. The preceding sentence is declaratory of preexisting law.

Neither this section or any other provision of this division shall be construed to prohibit short-term narcotic detoxification treatment in a controlled setting approved by the director and pursuant to rules and regulations of the director. Facilities and treatment approved by the director under this paragraph shall not be subject to approval or inspection by the Medical Board of California, nor shall persons in those facilities be required to register with, or report the termination of residence with, the police department or sheriff's office. *(Added by Stats.1972, c. 1407, p. 3008, § 3. Amended by Stats.1973, c. 142, p. 398, § 39.4, eff. June 30, 1973, operative July 1, 1973; Stats.1974, c. 1044, § 32.8, eff. Sept. 23, 1974; Stats.1982, c. 932, p. 3388, § 1; Stats.1987, c. 287, § 1; Stats.1987, c. 880, § 2; Stats.1989, c. 886, § 98; Stats.1995, c. 455 (A.B.1113), § 7, eff. Sept. 5, 1995; Stats.2012, c. 34 (S.B.1009), § 25, eff. June 27, 2012; Stats.2013, c. 22 (A.B.75), § 17, eff. June 27, 2013, operative July 1, 2013.)*

Cross References

Controlled substance defined for purposes of this Division, see Health and Safety Code § 11007.

Healing arts, medicine, enforcement, provision of prescription drugs and controlled substances to addicts, conditions, see Business and Professions Code § 2241.

Narcotic drug defined for purposes of this Division, see Health and Safety Code § 11019.

Person defined for purposes of this Division, see Health and Safety Code § 11022.

Research References

2 Witkin, California Criminal Law 4th Crimes Against Public Peace and Welfare § 152 (2021), In General.

2 Witkin, California Criminal Law 4th Crimes Against Public Peace and Welfare § 188 (2021), Treatment of Addicts With Narcotics.

§ 11217.5. Place of treatment by physician; authorized medications

Notwithstanding the provisions of Section 11217, a licensed physician and surgeon may treat an addict for addiction in any office or medical facility which, in the professional judgment of such physician and surgeon, is medically proper for the rehabilitation and treatment of such addict. Such licensed physician and surgeon may administer to an addict, under his direct care, those medications and therapeutic agents which, in the judgment of such physician and surgeon, are medically necessary, provided that nothing in this section shall authorize the administration of any narcotic drug. *(Added by Stats.1972, c. 1407, p. 3009, § 3.)*

Cross References

Administer defined for purposes of this Division, see Health and Safety Code § 11002.

Healing arts, medicine, enforcement, provision of prescription drugs and controlled substances to addicts, conditions, see Business and Professions Code § 2241.

Narcotic drug defined for purposes of this Division, see Health and Safety Code § 11019.

Physician, dentist, podiatrist, pharmacist, veterinarian, and optometrist defined for purposes of this Division, see Health and Safety Code § 11024.

Research References

2 Witkin, California Criminal Law 4th Crimes Against Public Peace and Welfare § 188 (2021), Treatment of Addicts With Narcotics.

§ 11218. Maximum daily amounts for first 15 days of treatment

A physician treating an addict for addiction may not prescribe for or furnish to the addict more than any one of the following amounts of controlled substances during each of the first 15 days of that treatment:

(a) Eight grains of opium.

(b) Four grains of morphine.

(c) Six grains of Pantopon.

(d) One grain of Dilaudid.

(e) Four hundred milligrams of isonipecaine (Demerol). *(Added by Stats.1972, c. 1407, p. 3009, § 3. Amended by Stats.1995, c. 455 (A.B.1113), § 8, eff. Sept. 5, 1995; Stats.2002, c. 543 (S.B.1447), § 1.)*

Cross References

Controlled substance defined for purposes of this Division, see Health and Safety Code § 11007.

Furnish defined for purposes of this Division, see Health and Safety Code § 11016.

Healing arts, medicine, enforcement, provision of prescription drugs and controlled substances to addicts, conditions, see Business and Professions Code § 2241.

Physician, dentist, podiatrist, pharmacist, veterinarian, and optometrist defined for purposes of this Division, see Health and Safety Code § 11024.

Research References

2 Witkin, California Criminal Law 4th Crimes Against Public Peace and Welfare § 188 (2021), Treatment of Addicts With Narcotics.

§ 11219. Maximum daily amounts after 15 days of treatment

After 15 days of treatment, the physician may not prescribe for or furnish to the addict more than any one of the following amounts of controlled substances during each day of the treatment:

(a) Four grains of opium.

(b) Two grains of morphine.

(c) Three grains of Pantopon.

(d) One-half grain of Dilaudid.

(e) Two hundred milligrams of isonipecaine (Demerol). *(Added by Stats.1972, c. 1407, p. 3009, § 3. Amended by Stats.1995, c. 455 (A.B.1113), § 9, eff. Sept. 5, 1995; Stats.2002, c. 543 (S.B.1447), § 2.)*

Cross References

Controlled substance defined for purposes of this Division, see Health and Safety Code § 11007.

Furnish defined for purposes of this Division, see Health and Safety Code § 11016.
Healing arts, medicine, enforcement, provision of prescription drugs and controlled substances to addicts, conditions, see Business and Professions Code § 2241.
Physician, dentist, podiatrist, pharmacist, veterinarian, and optometrist defined for purposes of this Division, see Health and Safety Code § 11024.

§ 11220. Discontinuance of narcotics

At the end of 30 days from the first treatment, the prescribing or furnishing of controlled substances, except medications approved by the federal Food and Drug Administration for the purpose of narcotic replacement treatment or medication-assisted treatment of substance use disorders, shall be discontinued. *(Added by Stats.1972, c. 1407, p. 3009, § 3. Amended by Stats.1995, c. 455 (A.B.1113), § 10, eff. Sept. 5, 1995; Stats.2017, c. 223 (A.B.395), § 1, eff. Jan. 1, 2018.)*

Cross References

Controlled substance defined for purposes of this Division, see Health and Safety Code § 11007.
Healing arts, medicine, enforcement, provision of prescription drugs and controlled substances to addicts, conditions, see Business and Professions Code § 2241.

Research References

2 Witkin, California Criminal Law 4th Crimes Against Public Peace and Welfare § 188 (2021), Treatment of Addicts With Narcotics.

§ 11222. Persons in custody; medical aid; continuation in narcotic treatment program

In any case in which a person is taken into custody by arrest or other process of law and is lodged in a jail or other place of confinement, and there is reasonable cause to believe that the person is addicted to a controlled substance, it is the duty of the person in charge of the place of confinement to provide the person so confined with medical aid as necessary to ease any symptoms of withdrawal from the use of controlled substances.

In any case in which a person, who is participating in a narcotic treatment program, is incarcerated in a jail or other place of confinement, he or she shall, in the discretion of the director of the program, be entitled to continue in the program until conviction. *(Added by Stats.1972, c. 1407, p. 3010, § 3. Amended by Stats.1995, c. 455 (A.B.1113), § 11, eff. Sept. 5, 1995.)*

Cross References

Controlled substance defined for purposes of this Division, see Health and Safety Code § 11007.
Person defined for purposes of this Division, see Health and Safety Code § 11022.
Rights of incarcerated pregnant person, treatment, see Penal Code § 4023.8.

Research References

2 Witkin, California Criminal Law 4th Crimes Against Public Peace and Welfare § 188 (2021), Treatment of Addicts With Narcotics.

§ 11223. Treatment for addiction by federally registered physician and surgeon

Notwithstanding any other provision of law, a physician and surgeon who is registered with the federal Attorney General pursuant to Section 823(g) of Title 21 of the United States Code may provide treatment for addiction pursuant to this federal law. *(Added by Stats.2010, c. 93 (A.B.2268), § 1.)*

ARTICLE 3. VETERINARIANS

Section

§ 11240. Human beings

No veterinarian shall prescribe, administer, or furnish a controlled substance for himself or any other human being. *(Added by Stats.1972, c. 1407, p. 3010, § 3.)*

Cross References

Administer defined for purposes of this Division, see Health and Safety Code § 11002.
Controlled substance defined for purposes of this Division, see Health and Safety Code § 11007.
Furnish defined for purposes of this Division, see Health and Safety Code § 11016.
Persons authorized to write prescriptions, see Health and Safety Code § 11150.

§ 11241. Contents of prescription

A prescription written by a veterinarian shall state the kind of animal for which ordered and the name and address of the owner or person having custody of the animal. *(Added by Stats.1972, c. 1407, p. 2987, § 3.)*

Cross References

Authorization to write prescriptions, see Health and Safety Code § 11150.
Person defined for purposes of this Division, see Health and Safety Code § 11022.
Prescription or electronic transmission prescription defined for purposes of this Division, see Health and Safety Code § 11027.

ARTICLE 4. SALE WITHOUT PRESCRIPTION

Section

§ 11250. Authorized retail sales by pharmacists; execution of orders required by federal law

(a) No prescription is required in case of the sale of controlled substances at retail in pharmacies by pharmacists to any of the following:

(1) Physicians.

(2) Dentists.

(3) Podiatrists.

(4) Veterinarians.

(5) Pharmacists acting within the scope of a project authorized under Article 1 (commencing with Section 128125) of Chapter 3 of Part 3 of Division 107, or registered nurses acting within the scope of a project authorized under Article 1 (commencing with Section 128125) of Chapter 3 of Part 3 of Division 107, or physician assistants acting within the scope of a project authorized under Article 1 (commencing with Section 128125) of Chapter 3 of Part 3 of Division 107.

(6) Optometrist.

(b) In any sale mentioned in this article, there shall be executed any written order that may otherwise be required by federal law relating to the production, importation, exportation, manufacture, compounding, distributing, dispensing, or control of controlled substances. *(Added by Stats.1972, c. 1407, p. 3010, § 3. Amended by Stats.1977, c. 843, p. 2534, § 21; Stats.1996, c. 1023 (S.B.1497), § 200, eff. Sept. 29, 1996; Stats.2003, c. 426 (A.B.186), § 4.)*

Cross References

Controlled substance defined for purposes of this Division, see Health and Safety Code § 11007.
Pharmacy defined for purposes of this Division, see Health and Safety Code § 11023.
Physician, dentist, podiatrist, pharmacist, veterinarian, and optometrist defined for purposes of this Division, see Health and Safety Code § 11024.
Prescription or electronic transmission prescription defined for purposes of this Division, see Health and Safety Code § 11027.
Prescriptions, see Health and Safety Code § 11150 et seq.
Production defined for purposes of this Division, see Health and Safety Code § 11029.

§ 11251. Authorized sales at wholesale

No prescription is required in case of sales at wholesale by pharmacies, jobbers, wholesalers, and manufacturers to any of the following:

(a) Pharmacies as defined in the Business and Professions Code.

(b) Physicians.

(c) Dentists.

(d) Podiatrists.

(e) Veterinarians.

(f) Other jobbers, wholesalers or manufacturers.

(g) Pharmacists acting within the scope of a project authorized under Article 1 (commencing with Section 128125) of Chapter 3 of Part 3 of Division 107, or registered nurses acting within the scope of a project authorized under Article 1 (commencing with Section 128125) of Chapter 3 of Part 3 of Division 107, or physician assistants acting within the scope of a project authorized under Article 1 (commencing with Section 128125) of Chapter 3 of Part 3 of Division 107.

(h) Optometrists. *(Added by Stats.1972, c. 1407, p. 3011, § 3. Amended by Stats.1976, c. 896, p. 2061, § 28; Stats.1977, c. 843, p. 2535, § 22; Stats.1996, c. 1023 (S.B.1497), § 201, eff. Sept. 29, 1996; Stats.2003, c. 426 (A.B.186), § 5.)*

Cross References

Manufacturer defined for purposes of this Division, see Health and Safety Code § 11017.
Pharmacies defined, see Business and Professions Code § 4037.
Pharmacy defined for purposes of this Division, see Health and Safety Code § 11023.
Physician, dentist, podiatrist, pharmacist, veterinarian, and optometrist defined for purposes of this Division, see Health and Safety Code § 11024.
Prescription or electronic transmission prescription defined for purposes of this Division, see Health and Safety Code § 11027.
Wholesaler defined for purposes of this Division, see Health and Safety Code § 11031.

§ 11252. Orders and forms required by federal law

All wholesale jobbers, wholesalers, and manufacturers, mentioned in this division shall keep, in a manner readily accessible, the written orders or blank forms required to be preserved pursuant to federal law relating to the production, importation, exportation, manufacture, compounding, distributing, dispensing, or control of controlled substances. *(Added by Stats.1972, c. 1407, p. 3011, § 3.)*

Cross References

Controlled substance defined for purposes of this Division, see Health and Safety Code § 11007.
Manufacturer defined for purposes of this Division, see Health and Safety Code § 11017.
Production defined for purposes of this Division, see Health and Safety Code § 11029.
Wholesaler defined for purposes of this Division, see Health and Safety Code § 11031.

§ 11253. Preservation of orders and forms

The written orders or blank forms shall be preserved for at least three years after the date of the last entry made. *(Added by Stats.1972, c. 1407, p. 3011, § 3. Amended by Stats.1976, c. 896, p. 2061, § 29.)*

§ 11255. Order, contract or agreement for future delivery as sale

The taking of any order, or making of any contract or agreement, by any traveling representative or employee of any person for future delivery in this state, of any controlled substance constitutes a sale within the meaning of this division. *(Added by Stats.1972, c. 1407, p. 3011, § 3.)*

Cross References

Controlled substance defined for purposes of this Division, see Health and Safety Code § 11007.
Deliver or delivery defined for purposes of this Division, see Health and Safety Code § 11009.
Person defined for purposes of this Division, see Health and Safety Code § 11022.

§ 11256. Transmittal of copy of order, contract or agreement to purchase from foreign wholesaler, etc.

Within 24 hours after any purchaser in this state gives any order for a controlled substance classified in Schedule II to, or makes any contract or agreement for purchases from or sales by, an out-of-state wholesaler or manufacturer of any controlled substances for delivery in this state, the purchaser shall forward to the Attorney General by registered mail a true and correct copy of the order, contract, or agreement. *(Added by Stats.1972, c. 1407, p. 2987, § 3.)*

Cross References

Attorney General, generally, see Government Code § 12500 et seq.
Attorney General defined for purposes of this Division, see Health and Safety Code § 11004.
Controlled substance defined for purposes of this Division, see Health and Safety Code § 11007.
Deliver or delivery defined for purposes of this Division, see Health and Safety Code § 11009.
Manufacturer defined for purposes of this Division, see Health and Safety Code § 11017.
Wholesaler defined for purposes of this Division, see Health and Safety Code § 11031.

CHAPTER 6. OFFENSES AND PENALTIES

ARTICLE 1. OFFENSES INVOLVING CONTROLLED SUBSTANCES FORMERLY CLASSIFIED AS NARCOTICS

Section

§ 11350. Possession of designated controlled substances; punishment and fine; possession by person other than the prescription holder

(a) Except as otherwise provided in this division, every person who possesses (1) any controlled substance specified in subdivision (b), (c), (e), or paragraph (1) of subdivision (f) of Section 11054, specified in paragraph (14), (15), or (20) of subdivision (d) of Section 11054, or specified in subdivision (b) or (c) of Section 11055, or specified in subdivision (h) of Section 11056, or (2) any controlled substance classified in Schedule III, IV, or V which is a narcotic drug, unless upon the written prescription of a physician, dentist, podiatrist, or veterinarian licensed to practice in this state, shall be punished by imprisonment in a county jail for not more than one year, except that such person shall instead be punished pursuant to subdivision (h) of Section 1170 of the Penal Code if that person has one or more prior convictions for an offense specified in clause (iv) of subparagraph (C) of paragraph (2) of subdivision (e) of Section 667 of the Penal Code or for an offense requiring registration pursuant to subdivision (c) of Section 290 of the Penal Code.

(b) Except as otherwise provided in this division, whenever a person who possesses any of the controlled substances specified in subdivision (a), the judge may, in addition to any punishment provided for pursuant to subdivision (a), assess against that person a fine not to exceed seventy dollars ($70) with proceeds of this fine to be used in accordance with Section 1463.23 of the Penal Code. The court shall, however, take into consideration the defendant's ability to pay, and no defendant shall be denied probation because of his or her inability to pay the fine permitted under this subdivision.

(c) Except in unusual cases in which it would not serve the interest of justice to do so, whenever a court grants probation pursuant to a felony conviction under this section, in addition to any other conditions of probation which may be imposed, the following conditions of probation shall be ordered:

(1) For a first offense under this section, a fine of at least one thousand dollars ($1,000) or community service.

(2) For a second or subsequent offense under this section, a fine of at least two thousand dollars ($2,000) or community service.

(3) If a defendant does not have the ability to pay the minimum fines specified in paragraphs (1) and (2), community service shall be ordered in lieu of the fine.

(d) It is not unlawful for a person other than the prescription holder to possess a controlled substance described in subdivision (a) if both of the following apply:

(1) The possession of the controlled substance is at the direction or with the express authorization of the prescription holder.

(2) The sole intent of the possessor is to deliver the prescription to the prescription holder for its prescribed use or to discard the substance in a lawful manner.

(e) This section does not permit the use of a controlled substance by a person other than the prescription holder or permit the distribution or sale of a controlled substance that is otherwise inconsistent with the prescription. *(Added by Stats.1972, c. 1407, p. 2987, § 3. Amended by Stats.1973, c. 1078, p. 2171, § 2, eff. Oct. 1, 1973; Stats.1975, c. 1087, p. 2647, § 1; Stats.1976, c. 1139, p. 5079, § 65, operative July 1, 1977; Stats.1983, c. 790, § 3; Stats.1984, c. 1635, § 50; Stats.1986, c. 1044, § 3; Stats.1987, c. 970, § 1; Stats.1989, c. 534, § 1; Stats.1991, c. 257 (A.B.1706), § 1; Stats.2000, c. 8 (S.B.550), § 3, eff. March 29, 2000; Stats.2011, c. 15 (A.B.109), § 151, eff. April 4, 2011, operative Oct. 1, 2011; Initiative Measure (Prop. 47, § 11, approved Nov. 4, 2014, eff. Nov. 5, 2014); Stats.2017, c. 269 (S.B.811), § 4, eff. Jan. 1, 2018.)*

Cross References

Arrest of teacher or instructor employed in community college district, notices, see Health and Safety Code § 11591.5.
Arrest without warrant of person in traffic accident under combined influence of intoxicating liquor and any drug, see Vehicle Code § 40300.5; Welfare and Institutions Code § 625.
Cannabis, unauthorized possession, see Health and Safety Code § 11357.
Children, delinquents and wards of the juvenile court, juvenile court law, wards, commencement of proceedings,
Eligibility for program of supervision, see Welfare and Institutions Code § 654.3.
Eligibility for program of supervision, application to commence proceedings, see Welfare and Institutions Code § 653.5.
Children, delinquents and wards of the juvenile court, juvenile court law, wards, judgments and orders, order for care, supervision, custody, maintenance and support of ward of court, see Welfare and Institutions Code § 727.
Controlled substance defined for purposes of this Division, see Health and Safety Code § 11007.
Controlled substance offense defined as violation of this section for purposes of Education Code, see Education Code §§ 44011, 87011.
Felonies, definition and penalties, see Penal Code §§ 17, 18.
Felony offense defined for purposes of this Article, see Health and Safety Code § 11356.
Fine in addition to imprisonment for conviction of violation of this section, see Health and Safety Code § 11372.
Fines, increment for each separate offense, see Health and Safety Code § 11372.5.
Further grounds for denial, classes of applicants, and rehabilitation, see Education Code § 44346.
Juvenile court law,
Application to commence proceedings, affidavits, see Welfare and Institutions Code § 653.5.
Eligibility for program of supervision, see Welfare and Institutions Code § 654.3.
Medical assistance exception to controlled substance possession and related offenses, persons experiencing drug-related overdose, no exception to laws prohibiting actions made dangerous by controlled substance use, see Health and Safety Code § 11376.5.
Narcotic drug defined for purposes of this Division, see Health and Safety Code § 11019.
New trial, application prior to commitment of defendant for narcotics addiction, see Penal Code § 1182.
Of criminal procedure, pleadings and proceedings before trial, special proceedings in narcotics and drug abuse cases, application to certain violations, see Penal Code § 1000.
Other taxes, corporation tax law, net income, items not deductible, illegal activities, determination by court on legality of activities, taxable years, see Revenue and Taxation Code § 24436.1.
Person defined for purposes of this Division, see Health and Safety Code § 11022.

Physician, dentist, podiatrist, pharmacist, veterinarian, and optometrist defined for purposes of this Division, see Health and Safety Code § 11024.
Possession of certain drugs without prescription, prohibition, see Business and Professions Code § 4060.
Prescription or electronic transmission prescription defined for purposes of this Division, see Health and Safety Code § 11027.
Prescriptions, requirements, see Health and Safety Code § 11150 et seq.
Presentation of allegations of act or omission by applicant or holder of a credential, circumstances under which committee has jurisdiction to commence initial review, formal review and investigation, report of actions and recommendations, including findings as to probable cause and appropriate adverse action, limitation on inquiries and request for production of information and records, and limitation on presentation of certain convictions, see Education Code § 44242.5.
Prior convictions, answer to charge in accusatory pleading, see Penal Code § 1025.
Recovery of funds expended in investigation, see Health and Safety Code § 11501.
Registration of controlled substance offenders, conviction of offense defined in this section, see Health and Safety Code § 11591 et seq.
Sales without prescriptions, see Health and Safety Code § 11250 et seq.
School employee, arrest for controlled substance offense as described in this section, notice to school authorities, see Health and Safety Code § 11591.
Special proceedings in narcotics and drug abuse cases, see Penal Code § 1000 et seq.
Unauthorized possession of narcotics in prison, camp, or jail, see Penal Code § 4573.6.
Unlawful detainer actions to abate nuisance caused by illegal conduct involving controlled substance purpose, including violations of these provisions, see Civil Code § 3486.

Research References

California Jury Instructions - Criminal 12.00, Controlled Substance (Sched. I–V)—Unlawful Possession as Felony/Misdemeanor.
California Jury Instructions - Criminal 12.30.1, Controlled Substance (Sched. I–V)—Burden of Proof as to Prescription.
California Jury Instructions - Criminal 16.062, Misdemeanor Unlawful Possession of Controlled Substance.
2 Witkin, California Criminal Law 4th Crimes Against Public Peace and Welfare § 73 (2021), For Drug Activities.
2 Witkin, California Criminal Law 4th Crimes Against Public Peace and Welfare § 84 (2021), California Statutes and General Law.
2 Witkin, California Criminal Law 4th Crimes Against Public Peace and Welfare § 86 (2021), In General.
2 Witkin, California Criminal Law 4th Crimes Against Public Peace and Welfare § 87 (2021), Substances Formerly Classified as Narcotics.
2 Witkin, California Criminal Law 4th Crimes Against Public Peace and Welfare § 89 (2021), Analogs of Controlled Substances.
2 Witkin, California Criminal Law 4th Crimes Against Public Peace and Welfare § 91 (2021), Definition.
2 Witkin, California Criminal Law 4th Crimes Against Public Peace and Welfare § 97 (2021), In General.
2 Witkin, California Criminal Law 4th Crimes Against Public Peace and Welfare § 114 (2021), Defenses.
2 Witkin, California Criminal Law 4th Crimes Against Public Peace and Welfare § 115 (2021), Statutory Prohibitions.
2 Witkin, California Criminal Law 4th Crimes Against Public Peace and Welfare § 124 (2021), Substances Formerly Classified as Narcotics.
2 Witkin, California Criminal Law 4th Crimes Against Public Peace and Welfare § 125 (2021), Substances Formerly Classified as Restricted Dangerous Drugs.
2 Witkin, California Criminal Law 4th Crimes Against Public Peace and Welfare § 169 (2021), Drug Treatment Program.
1 Witkin California Criminal Law 4th Introduction to Crimes § 75 (2021), General Principles.
4 Witkin, California Criminal Law 4th Pretrial Proceedings § 98 (2021), In General.
4 Witkin, California Criminal Law 4th Pretrial Proceedings § 374A (2021), (New) Offense Mistakenly Charged and Pleaded as Felony.
4 Witkin, California Criminal Law 4th Pretrial Proceedings § 386 (2021), Offenses and Conditions.
3 Witkin, California Criminal Law 4th Punishment § 212 (2021), Mandatory Suspension.
3 Witkin, California Criminal Law 4th Punishment § 254 (2021), Illustrations.
3 Witkin, California Criminal Law 4th Punishment § 296 (2021), Possession and Other Crimes.
3 Witkin, California Criminal Law 4th Punishment § 308A (2021), (New) in General.
3 Witkin, California Criminal Law 4th Punishment § 616 (2021), Health and Safety Code Provisions.

§ 11350.5. Possession of gamma hydroxybutyric acid (GHB) with intent to commit sexual assault; punishment

(a) Except as otherwise provided in this division, every person who possesses a controlled substance specified in paragraph (3) of subdivision (e) of Section 11054 of this code with the intent to commit sexual assault shall be punished by imprisonment pursuant to subdivision (h) of Section 1170 of the Penal Code.

(b) For purposes of this section, "sexual assault" means conduct in violation of Section 243.4, 261, 262, 286, 287, or 289 of, or former Section 288a of, the Penal Code. *(Added by Stats.2016, c. 893 (S.B.1182), § 2, eff. Jan. 1, 2017. Amended by Stats.2018, c. 423 (S.B.1494), § 35, eff. Jan. 1, 2019.)*

Research References

2 Witkin, California Criminal Law 4th Crimes Against Public Peace and Welfare § 101A (2021), (New) Possession of "Date Rape" Drugs With Intent to Commit Sexual Assault.

§ 11351. Possession or purchase for sale of designated controlled substances; punishment

Except as otherwise provided in this division, every person who possesses for sale or purchases for purposes of sale (1) any controlled substance specified in subdivision (b), (c), or (e) of Section 11054, specified in paragraph (14), (15), or (20) of subdivision (d) of Section 11054, or specified in subdivision (b) or (c) of Section 11055, or specified in subdivision (h) of Section 11056, or (2) any controlled substance classified in Schedule III, IV, or V which is a narcotic drug, shall be punished by imprisonment pursuant to subdivision (h) of Section 1170 of the Penal Code for two, three, or four years. *(Added by Stats.1972, c. 1407, p. 3012, § 3. Amended by Stats.1973, c. 1078, p. 2172, § 3, eff. Oct. 1, 1973; Stats.1975, c. 1087, p. 2648, § 2; Stats.1976, c. 1139, p. 5079, § 66, operative July 1, 1977; Stats.1983, c. 790, § 4; Stats.1984, c. 1635, § 51; Stats.1985, c. 1398, § 1.5; Stats.1987, c. 970, § 2; Stats.2000, c. 8 (S.B.550), § 4, eff. March 29, 2000; Stats.2011, c. 15 (A.B.109), § 152, eff. April 4, 2011, operative Oct. 1, 2011.)*

Cross References

Additional penalty for trafficking violation on grounds of or near drug treatment center, detoxification facility, or homeless shelter, see Health and Safety Code § 11380.7.
Additional term, conviction of this section with respect to substance containing heroin or cocaine, see Health and Safety Code § 11370.4.
Arrest of teacher or instructor employed in community college district, notices, see Health and Safety Code § 11591.5.
Cannabis,
Planting, harvesting, or processing, see Health and Safety Code § 11358.
Possession for sale, see Health and Safety Code § 11359.
Controlled substance defined for purposes of this Division, see Health and Safety Code § 11007.
Controlled substance offense defined as violation of this section for purposes of Education Code, see Education Code §§ 44011, 87011.
Dangerous drug violations, punishment, see Health and Safety Code § 11377 et seq.
Electronic communications interception, authorization order for investigation of violations of this section, see Penal Code § 629.52.
Examination of witnesses conditionally, cases in which authorized, see Penal Code § 1335.
Felony offense defined, see Health and Safety Code § 11356.
Fine in addition to imprisonment for conviction of violation of this section, see Health and Safety Code § 11372.
Fines, increment for each separate offense, see Health and Safety Code § 11372.5.
Hearsay evidence, exceptions to the hearsay rule, declarant unavailable as witness, unavailable declarant, hearsay rule, see Evidence Code § 1350.
Narcotic drug defined for purposes of this Division, see Health and Safety Code § 11019.

Person defined for purposes of this Division, see Health and Safety Code § 11022.
Of criminal procedure,
Miscellaneous proceedings, examination of witnesses conditionally, cases in which authorized, see Penal Code § 1335.
Of judgment and execution, the judgment, felony convictions for controlled substances violations involving cocaine, cocaine base, methamphetamine, phencyclidine or heroin, probation and sentencing, see Penal Code § 1203.073.
Pleadings and proceedings before trial, career criminals, see Penal Code § 999e.
Persons convicted of this section, section 11351.5, or 11352, sentence enhancements for prior conviction of this section, see Health and Safety Code § 11370.2.
Prevention of crimes and apprehension of criminals, California Council on Criminal Justice, California Career Criminal Apprehension Program, individuals subject to apprehension efforts, see Penal Code § 13853.
Probation or suspension of sentence, previous convictions, see Health and Safety Code § 11370.
Probation or suspension of sentence prohibited for persons convicted of violating this section, see Penal Code § 1203.07.
Prohibition on possession of a firearm under the age of 30 for those convicted of or alleged to have committed certain offenses, controlled substances violations, punishment for violation, see Penal Code § 29820.
Registration of controlled substance offenders, conviction of offense defined in this section, see Health and Safety Code § 11591 et seq.
School employee, arrest for controlled substance offense as described in this section, notice to school authorities, see Health and Safety Code § 11591.
Seizure of things of value and believed to be forfeitable, see Health and Safety Code § 11488.
Sentence enhancements for persons with certain prior convictions, see Health and Safety Code § 11370.2.
Unavailable declarant, hearsay rule, see Evidence Code § 1350.
Uniform controlled substances act, offenses and penalties, offenses involving controlled substances formerly classified as narcotics, sale of heroin, fine in addition to imprisonment, see Health and Safety Code § 11352.5.
Unlawful detainer actions to abate nuisance caused by illegal conduct involving controlled substance purpose, including violations of these provisions, see Civil Code § 3486.
Unlawful transportation, importation, sale, or gift of cannabis, see Health and Safety Code § 11360.
Vehicle inspection, see Vehicle Code § 2804 et seq.

Research References

California Jury Instructions - Criminal 12.01, Controlled Substance (Sched. I–V)—Illegal Possession or Purchase for Sale.
2 Witkin, California Criminal Law 4th Crimes Against Public Peace and Welfare § 87 (2021), Substances Formerly Classified as Narcotics.
2 Witkin, California Criminal Law 4th Crimes Against Public Peace and Welfare § 101 (2021), Possession for Sale.
2 Witkin, California Criminal Law 4th Crimes Against Public Peace and Welfare § 115 (2021), Statutory Prohibitions.
3 Witkin, California Criminal Law 4th Punishment § 375 (2021), Value or Amount.
3 Witkin, California Criminal Law 4th Punishment § 615 (2021), Penal Code Provisions.

§ 11351.5. Possession of cocaine base for sale; punishment

Except as otherwise provided in this division, every person who possesses for sale or purchases for purposes of sale cocaine base, which is specified in paragraph (1) of subdivision (f) of Section 11054, shall be punished by imprisonment pursuant to subdivision (h) of Section 1170 of the Penal Code for a period of two, three, or four years. *(Added by Stats.1986, c. 1044, § 4. Amended by Stats.1987, c. 1174, § 3, eff. Sept. 26, 1987; Stats.2011, c. 15 (A.B.109), § 153, eff. April 4, 2011, operative Oct. 1, 2011; Stats.2014, c. 749 (S.B.1010), § 3, eff. Jan. 1, 2015.)*

Cross References

Additional penalty for trafficking violation on grounds of or near drug treatment center, detoxification facility, or homeless shelter, see Health and Safety Code § 11380.7.
Arrest of teacher or instructor employed in community college district, notices, see Health and Safety Code § 11591.5.
Convictions under this section, prohibition on probation or suspension of sentence, see Penal Code § 1203.073.
Electronic communications interception, authorization order for investigation of violations of this section, see Penal Code § 629.52.
Of criminal procedure, pleadings and proceedings before trial, career criminals, see Penal Code § 999e.
Person defined for purposes of this Division, see Health and Safety Code § 11022.
Probation or suspension of sentence prohibited for persons convicted of violating this section, see Penal Code § 1203.07.
Prohibition on possession of a firearm under the age of 30 for those convicted of or alleged to have committed certain offenses, controlled substances violations, punishment for violation, see Penal Code § 29820.
School employee, arrest for controlled substance offense as described in this section, notice to school authorities, see Health and Safety Code § 11591.
Unlawful detainer actions to abate nuisance caused by illegal conduct involving controlled substance purpose, including violations of these provisions, see Civil Code § 3486.

Research References

California Jury Instructions - Criminal 12.01, Controlled Substance (Sched. I–V)—Illegal Possession or Purchase for Sale.
2 Witkin, California Criminal Law 4th Crimes Against Public Peace and Welfare § 87 (2021), Substances Formerly Classified as Narcotics.
2 Witkin, California Criminal Law 4th Crimes Against Public Peace and Welfare § 101 (2021), Possession for Sale.
2 Witkin, California Criminal Law 4th Crimes Against Public Peace and Welfare § 115 (2021), Statutory Prohibitions.
2 Witkin, California Criminal Law 4th Crimes Against Public Peace and Welfare § 129 (2021), Schools.

§ 11352. Transportation, sale, giving away, etc., of designated controlled substances; punishment; definition; prosecution for aiding and abetting

(a) Except as otherwise provided in this division, every person who transports, imports into this state, sells, furnishes, administers, or gives away, or offers to transport, import into this state, sell, furnish, administer, or give away, or attempts to import into this state or transport (1) any controlled substance specified in subdivision (b), (c), or (e), or paragraph (1) of subdivision (f) of Section 11054, specified in paragraph (14), (15), or (20) of subdivision (d) of Section 11054, or specified in subdivision (b) or (c) of Section 11055, or specified in subdivision (h) of Section 11056, or (2) any controlled substance classified in Schedule III, IV, or V which is a narcotic drug, unless upon the written prescription of a physician, dentist, podiatrist, or veterinarian licensed to practice in this state, shall be punished by imprisonment pursuant to subdivision (h) of Section 1170 of the Penal Code for three, four, or five years.

(b) Notwithstanding the penalty provisions of subdivision (a), any person who transports any controlled substances specified in subdivision (a) within this state from one county to another noncontiguous county shall be punished by imprisonment pursuant to subdivision (h) of Section 1170 of the Penal Code for three, six, or nine years.

(c) For purposes of this section, "transports" means to transport for sale.

(d) This section does not preclude or limit the prosecution of an individual for aiding and abetting the commission of, or conspiring to commit, or acting as an accessory to, any act prohibited by this section. *(Added by Stats.1972, c. 1407, p. 3013, § 3. Amended by Stats.1973, c. 1078, p. 2173, § 4, eff. Oct. 1, 1973; Stats.1975, c. 1087, p. 2649, § 3; Stats.1976, c. 1139, p. 5079, § 67, operative July 1, 1977; Stats.1983, c. 790, § 5; Stats.1984, c. 1635, § 52; Stats.1986, c. 1044, § 5; Stats.1987, c. 970, § 3; Stats.1989, c. 1102, § 1; Stats.2000, c. 8 (S.B.550), § 5, eff. March 29, 2000; Stats.2011, c. 15 (A.B.109), § 154, eff. April 4, 2011, operative Oct. 1, 2011; Stats.2013, c. 504 (A.B.721), § 1; Stats.2014, c. 54 (S.B.1461), § 7, eff. Jan. 1, 2015.)*

Cross References

Additional penalty for trafficking violation on grounds of or near drug treatment center, detoxification facility, or homeless shelter, see Health and Safety Code § 11380.7.

Additional term, conviction of this section with respect to substance containing heroin or cocaine, see Health and Safety Code § 11370.4.
Administer defined for purposes of this Division, see Health and Safety Code § 11002.
Arrest of teacher or instructor employed in community college district, notices, see Health and Safety Code § 11591.5.
Controlled substance defined for purposes of this Division, see Health and Safety Code § 11007.
Controlled substances, sale or transfer, aggravation of crime, see Penal Code § 1170.82.
Electronic communications interception, authorization order for investigation of violations of this section, see Penal Code § 629.52.
Employment or use of minors in sale or transportation of narcotics, penalty for, see Health and Safety Code §§ 11353, 11354.
Examination of witnesses conditionally, cases in which authorized, see Penal Code § 1335.
Fine in addition to imprisonment, see Health and Safety Code § 11372.
Fines, increment for each separate offense, see Health and Safety Code § 11372.5.
Furnish defined for purposes of this Division, see Health and Safety Code § 11016.
Hearsay evidence, exceptions to the hearsay rule, declarant unavailable as witness, unavailable declarant, hearsay rule, see Evidence Code § 1350.
Inspection of vehicles, see Vehicle Code §§ 2804 et seq., 2810, 2813.
Narcotic drug defined for purposes of this Division, see Health and Safety Code § 11019.
Of crimes and punishments, miscellaneous crimes, of other and miscellaneous offenses, see Penal Code § 653f.
Of criminal procedure,
  Miscellaneous proceedings, examination of witnesses conditionally, cases in which authorized, see Penal Code § 1335.
  Of proceedings after the commencement of the trial and before judgment, trial court sentencing, initial sentencing, controlled substances, sale or transfer, aggravation of crime, see Penal Code § 1170.82.
  Pleadings and proceedings before trial, career criminals, see Penal Code § 999e.
Of criminal procedure, of judgment and execution, the judgment,
  Felony convictions for controlled substances violations, probation on condition of minimum sentence to county jail, see Penal Code § 1203.076.
  Felony convictions for controlled substances violations involving cocaine, cocaine base, methamphetamine, phencyclidine or heroin, probation and sentencing, see Penal Code § 1203.073.
Person defined for purposes of this Division, see Health and Safety Code § 11022.
Persons convicted of this section, section 11351, or 11351.5, sentence enhancements for prior conviction of this section, see Health and Safety Code § 11370.2.
Physician, dentist, podiatrist, pharmacist, veterinarian, and optometrist defined for purposes of this Division, see Health and Safety Code § 11024.
Prescription or electronic transmission prescription defined for purposes of this Division, see Health and Safety Code § 11027.
Prevention of crimes and apprehension of criminals, California Council on Criminal Justice, California Career Criminal Apprehension Program, individuals subject to apprehension efforts, see Penal Code § 13853.
Probation or suspension of sentence, previous convictions, see Health and Safety Code § 11370.
Probation or suspension of sentence prohibited for persons convicted of violating this section, see Penal Code § 1203.07.
Proceedings in misdemeanor and infraction cases and appeals from such cases, sales of chemicals, drugs, laboratory apparatus or devices to process controlled substances, allocation of fines and forfeitures, see Penal Code § 1463.10.
Prohibition on possession of a firearm under the age of 30 for those convicted of or alleged to have committed certain offenses, controlled substances violations, punishment for violation, see Penal Code § 29820.
School employee, arrest for controlled substance offense as described in this section, notice to school authorities, see Health and Safety Code § 11591.
Seizure of things of value and believed to be forfeitable, see Health and Safety Code § 11488.
Sentence enhancements for persons with certain prior convictions, see Health and Safety Code § 11370.2.
Soliciting commission of certain offenses, punishment, degree of proof, see Penal Code § 653f.
Unavailable declarant, hearsay rule, see Evidence Code § 1350.
Uniform controlled substances act, offenses and penalties, offenses involving controlled substances formerly classified as narcotics, sale of heroin, fine in addition to imprisonment, see Health and Safety Code § 11352.5.
Unlawful detainer actions to abate nuisance caused by illegal conduct involving controlled substance purpose, including violations of these provisions, see Civil Code § 3486.
Unlawful transportation, importation, sale, or gift of cannabis, see Health and Safety Code § 11360.

Research References

California Jury Instructions - Criminal 12.02, Controlled Substance (Sched. I–V)—Illegal Sale, etc.
California Jury Instructions - Criminal 12.03, Controlled Substance (Sched. I–V)—Illegal Offer to Sell, etc.
2 Witkin, California Criminal Law 4th Crimes Against Public Peace and Welfare § 101 (2021), Possession for Sale.
2 Witkin, California Criminal Law 4th Crimes Against Public Peace and Welfare § 115 (2021), Statutory Prohibitions.
2 Witkin, California Criminal Law 4th Crimes Against Public Peace and Welfare § 119 (2021), Illegal Sale Following Lawful Possession.
2 Witkin, California Criminal Law 4th Crimes Against Public Peace and Welfare § 129 (2021), Schools.
1 Witkin California Criminal Law 4th Crimes Against the Person § 192 (2021), Nature of Requirement.
1 Witkin California Criminal Law 4th Crimes Against the Person § 194 (2021), Statute Including Multiple Offenses.
6 Witkin, California Criminal Law 4th Criminal Appeal § 170 (2021), Multiple Theories.
1 Witkin California Criminal Law 4th Defenses § 277 (2021), Narcotics Offenses.
1 Witkin California Criminal Law 4th Elements § 33 (2021), General Solicitation Statute.
3 Witkin, California Criminal Law 4th Punishment § 615 (2021), Penal Code Provisions.
3 Witkin, California Criminal Law 4th Punishment § 654 (2021), Mandatory.

§ 11352.1. Dispensing or furnishing drugs without a license; additional punishment

(a) The Legislature hereby declares that the dispensing and furnishing of prescription drugs, controlled substances, and dangerous drugs or dangerous devices without a license poses a significant threat to the health, safety, and welfare of all persons residing in the state. It is the intent of the Legislature in enacting this provision to enhance the penalties attached to this illicit and dangerous conduct.

(b) Notwithstanding Section 4321 of the Business and Professions Code, and in addition to any other penalties provided by law, any person who knowingly and unlawfully dispenses or furnishes a dangerous drug or dangerous device, or any material represented as, or presented in lieu of, any dangerous drug or dangerous device, as defined in Section 4022 of the Business and Professions Code, or who knowingly owns, manages, or operates a business that dispenses or furnishes a dangerous drug or dangerous device or any material represented as, or presented in lieu of, any dangerous drug or dangerous device, as defined in Section 4022 of the Business and Professions Code without a license to dispense or furnish these products, shall be guilty of a misdemeanor. Upon the first conviction, each violation shall be punishable by imprisonment in a county jail not to exceed one year, or by a fine not to exceed five thousand dollars ($5,000), or by both that fine and imprisonment. Upon a second or subsequent conviction, each violation shall be punishable by imprisonment in a county jail not to exceed one year, or by a fine not to exceed ten thousand dollars ($10,000), or by both that fine and imprisonment. *(Added by Stats.1998, c. 750 (A.B.2687), § 1, eff. Sept. 23, 1998. Amended by Stats.2000, c. 350 (A.B.751), § 1, eff. Sept. 8, 2000.)*

Cross References

Controlled substance defined for purposes of this Division, see Health and Safety Code § 11007.
Dispense defined for purposes of this Division, see Health and Safety Code § 11010.
Drug defined for purposes of this Division, see Health and Safety Code § 11014.
Furnish defined for purposes of this Division, see Health and Safety Code § 11016.

Misdemeanors, definition and penalties, see Penal Code §§ 17, 19, 19.2.
Person defined for purposes of this Division, see Health and Safety Code § 11022.
Prescription or electronic transmission prescription defined for purposes of this Division, see Health and Safety Code § 11027.

Research References

2 Witkin, California Criminal Law 4th Crimes Against Public Peace and Welfare § 371 (2021), Poisons, New or Dangerous Drugs and Devices, and Biologics.

§ 11352.5. Sale of heroin; fine in addition to imprisonment

The court shall impose a fine not exceeding fifty thousand dollars ($50,000), in the absence of a finding that the defendant would be incapable of paying such a fine, in addition to any term of imprisonment provided by law for any of the following persons:

(1) Any person who is convicted of violating Section 11351 of the Health and Safety Code by possessing for sale 14.25 grams or more of a substance containing heroin.

(2) Any person who is convicted of violating Section 11352 of the Health and Safety Code by selling or offering to sell 14.25 grams or more of a substance containing heroin.

(3) Any person convicted of violating Section 11351 of the Health and Safety Code by possessing heroin for sale or convicted of violating Section 11352 of the Health and Safety Code by selling or offering to sell heroin, and who has one or more prior convictions for violating Section 11351 or Section 11352 of the Health and Safety Code. *(Added by Stats.1976, c. 1132, p. 5049, § 1. Amended by Stats.1983, c. 223, § 1.)*

Cross References

Person defined for purposes of this Division, see Health and Safety Code § 11022.

Research References

California Jury Instructions - Criminal 17.22, Possession for Sale/Offering to Sell/Sale of 14.25 Grams or More.
2 Witkin, California Criminal Law 4th Crimes Against Public Peace and Welfare § 101 (2021), Possession for Sale.
2 Witkin, California Criminal Law 4th Crimes Against Public Peace and Welfare § 115 (2021), Statutory Prohibitions.

§ 11353. Adult inducing minor to violate provisions; use or employment of minors; punishment

Every person 18 years of age or over, (a) who in any voluntary manner solicits, induces, encourages, or intimidates any minor with the intent that the minor shall violate any provision of this chapter or Section 11550 with respect to either (1) a controlled substance which is specified in subdivision (b), (c), or (e), or paragraph (1) of subdivision (f) of Section 11054, specified in paragraph (14), (15), or (20) of subdivision (d) of Section 11054, or specified in subdivision (b) or (c) of Section 11055, or specified in subdivision (h) of Section 11056, or (2) any controlled substance classified in Schedule III, IV, or V which is a narcotic drug, (b) who hires, employs, or uses a minor to unlawfully transport, carry, sell, give away, prepare for sale, or peddle any such controlled substance, or (c) who unlawfully sells, furnishes, administers, gives, or offers to sell, furnish, administer, or give, any such controlled substance to a minor, shall be punished by imprisonment in the state prison for a period of three, six, or nine years. *(Added by Stats.1972, c. 1407, p. 3013, § 3. Amended by Stats.1973, c. 1078, p. 2174, § 5, eff. Oct. 1, 1973; Stats.1976, c. 1139, p. 5080, § 68, operative July 1, 1977; Stats.1983, c. 790, § 6; Stats.1984, c. 1635, § 53; Stats.1985, c. 1377, § 1; Stats.1986, c. 1035, § 1; Stats.1986, c. 1044, § 6; Stats.1987, c. 970, § 4; Stats.1990, c. 1664 (A.B.2645), § 1.5; Stats.2000, c. 8 (S.B.550), § 6, eff. March 29, 2000.)*

Cross References

Additional penalty for trafficking violation on grounds of or near drug treatment center, detoxification facility, or homeless shelter, see Health and Safety Code § 11380.7.
Administer defined for purposes of this Division, see Health and Safety Code § 11002.
Adults employing or selling cannabis to minors, see Health and Safety Code § 11361.
Arrest of teacher or instructor employed in community college district, notices, see Health and Safety Code § 11591.5.
Cannabis, sales to minors, etc., see Health and Safety Code § 11361.
Contributing to the delinquency of a minor, see Penal Code § 272.
Controlled substance defined for purposes of this Division, see Health and Safety Code § 11007.
Controlled substance offense defined as violation of this section for purposes of Education Code, see Education Code §§ 44011, 87011.
Denial of probation or suspension of sentence after conviction of violation of this section, prior conviction of certain offenses, see Health and Safety Code § 11370.
Education or treatment programs, condition to probation, see Health and Safety Code § 11373.
Expenditures to obtain evidence, see Health and Safety Code § 11454.
Fine in addition to imprisonment for conviction of violation of this section, see Health and Safety Code § 11372.
Furnish defined for purposes of this Division, see Health and Safety Code § 11016.
Life sentence for person who has served two or more prior terms for certain drug offenses involving minors, see Penal Code § 667.75.
Narcotic drug defined for purposes of this Division, see Health and Safety Code § 11019.
Of criminal procedure, of proceedings after the commencement of the trial and before judgment, trial court sentencing, initial sentencing, crimes involving minors under 11 years of age, circumstance in aggravation, see Penal Code § 1170.72.
Person defined for purposes of this Division, see Health and Safety Code § 11022.
Probation or suspension of sentence, previous convictions, see Health and Safety Code § 11370.
Prohibition on possession of a firearm under the age of 30 for those convicted of or alleged to have committed certain offenses, controlled substances violations, punishment for violation, see Penal Code § 29820.
Recovery of funds expended in investigations, see Health and Safety Code § 11501.
Registration of controlled substance offenders, conviction of offense defined in this section, see Health and Safety Code § 11591 et seq.
School employee, arrest for controlled substance offense as described in this section, notice to school authorities, see Health and Safety Code § 11591.
Seizure of boats, airplanes or vehicles, see Health and Safety Code §§ 11470, 11488.

Research References

California Jury Instructions - Criminal 12.10, Controlled Substance (Sched. I and II)—Illegal Sale, etc., to Minor.
California Jury Instructions - Criminal 12.11, Controlled Substance (Sched. I and II)—Illegal Offer to Sell, etc., to Minor.
California Jury Instructions - Criminal 12.12, Controlled Substance (Sched. I and II)—Employment of Minor to Peddle.
California Jury Instructions - Criminal 12.13, Controlled Substance (Sched. I and II)—Inducing Minor to Violate Controlled Substances Law.
2 Witkin, California Criminal Law 4th Crimes Against Public Peace and Welfare § 124 (2021), Substances Formerly Classified as Narcotics.
2 Witkin, California Criminal Law 4th Crimes Against Public Peace and Welfare § 128 (2021), Parks, Playgrounds, Child Care Facilities, and Religious Facilities.
2 Witkin, California Criminal Law 4th Crimes Against Public Peace and Welfare § 129 (2021), Schools.
1 Witkin California Criminal Law 4th Elements § 5 (2021), In General.
1 Witkin California Criminal Law 4th Elements § 36 (2021), Miscellaneous Solicitation Statutes.
4 Witkin, California Criminal Law 4th Pretrial Proceedings § 212 (2021), Designation of Statute by Number.
3 Witkin, California Criminal Law 4th Punishment § 374 (2021), In General.

§ 11353.1. Enhancement of sentence imposed under § 11353

(a) Notwithstanding any other provision of law, any person 18 years of age or over who is convicted of a violation of Section 11353, in addition to the punishment imposed for that conviction, shall receive an additional punishment as follows:

(1) If the offense involved heroin, cocaine, cocaine base, or any analog of these substances and occurred upon the grounds of, or within, a church or synagogue, a playground, a public or private youth center, a child day care facility, or a public swimming pool, during hours in which the facility is open for business, classes, or school-related programs, or at any time when minors are using the facility, the defendant shall, as a full and separately served enhancement to any other enhancement provided in paragraph (3), be punished by imprisonment in the state prison for one year.

(2) If the offense involved heroin, cocaine, cocaine base, or any analog of these substances and occurred upon, or within 1,000 feet of, the grounds of any public or private elementary, vocational, junior high, or high school, during hours that the school is open for classes or school-related programs, or at any time when minors are using the facility where the offense occurs, the defendant shall, as a full and separately served enhancement to any other enhancement provided in paragraph (3), be punished by imprisonment in the state prison for two years.

(3) If the offense involved a minor who is at least four years younger than the defendant, the defendant shall, as a full and separately served enhancement to any other enhancement provided in this subdivision, be punished by imprisonment in the state prison for one, two, or three years, at the discretion of the court.

(b) The additional punishment provided in this section shall not be imposed unless the allegation is charged in the accusatory pleading and admitted by the defendant or found to be true by the trier of fact.

(c) The additional punishment provided in this section shall be in addition to any other punishment provided by law and shall not be limited by any other provision of law.

(d) Notwithstanding any other provision of law, the court may strike the additional punishment provided for in this section if it determines that there are circumstances in mitigation of the additional punishment and states on the record its reasons for striking the additional punishment.

(e) As used in this section the following definitions shall apply:

(1) "Playground" means any park or recreational area specifically designed to be used by children which has play equipment installed, including public grounds designed for athletic activities such as baseball, football, soccer, or basketball, or any similar facility located on public or private school grounds, or on city, county, or state parks.

(2) "Youth center" means any public or private facility that is primarily used to host recreational or social activities for minors, including, but not limited to, private youth membership organizations or clubs, social service teenage club facilities, video arcades, or similar amusement park facilities.

(3) "Video arcade" means any premises where 10 or more video game machines or devices are operated, and where minors are legally permitted to conduct business.

(4) "Video game machine" means any mechanical amusement device, which is characterized by the use of a cathode ray tube display and which, upon the insertion of a coin, slug, or token in any slot or receptacle attached to, or connected to, the machine, may be operated for use as a game, contest, or amusement.

(5) "Within 1,000 feet of the grounds of any public or private elementary, vocational, junior high, or high school" means any public area or business establishment where minors are legally permitted to conduct business which is located within 1,000 feet of any public or private elementary, vocational, junior high, or high school.

(6) "Child day care facility" has the meaning specified in Section 1596.750.

(f) This section does not require either that notice be posted regarding the proscribed conduct or that the applicable 1,000-foot boundary limit be marked. *(Added by Stats.1989, c. 1178, § 1. Amended by Stats.1990, c. 1663 (A.B.3744), § 1; Stats.1990, c. 1664 (A.B.2645), § 2; Stats.1990, c. 1665 (S.B.2112), § 1; Stats.1993, c. 556 (A.B.312), § 1.)*

Cross References

Additional penalty for trafficking violation on grounds of or near drug treatment center, detoxification facility, or homeless shelter, see Health and Safety Code § 11380.7.

Person defined for purposes of this Division, see Health and Safety Code § 11022.

Research References

2 Witkin, California Criminal Law 4th Crimes Against Public Peace and Welfare § 124 (2021), Substances Formerly Classified as Narcotics.

2 Witkin, California Criminal Law 4th Crimes Against Public Peace and Welfare § 128 (2021), Parks, Playgrounds, Child Care Facilities, and Religious Facilities.

2 Witkin, California Criminal Law 4th Crimes Against Public Peace and Welfare § 130 (2021), Drug Treatment Centers, Detoxification Facilities, and Homeless Shelters.

1 Witkin California Criminal Law 4th Introduction to Crimes § 76 (2021), Illustrations: Special Statute is Controlling.

3 Witkin, California Criminal Law 4th Punishment § 374 (2021), In General.

§ 11353.4. Second or subsequent violations of § 11353 as applied to certain Schedule I substances; additional punishment; violations involving minors age 14 or younger

(a) Any person 18 years of age or older who is convicted for a second or subsequent time of violating Section 11353, as that section applies to paragraph (1) of subdivision (f) of Section 11054, where the previous conviction resulted in a prison sentence, shall, as a full and separately served enhancement to the punishment imposed for that second or subsequent conviction of Section 11353, be punished by imprisonment in the state prison for one, two, or three years.

(b) If the second or subsequent violation of Section 11353, as described in subdivision (a), involved a minor who is 14 years of age or younger, the defendant shall, as a full and separately served enhancement to any other enhancement provided in this section, be punished by imprisonment in the state prison for one, two, or three years, at the discretion of the court.

(c) The additional punishment provided in this section shall not be imposed unless the allegation is charged in the accusatory pleading and admitted by the defendant or found to be true by the trier of fact.

(d) The additional punishment provided in this section shall be in addition to any other punishment provided by law and shall not be limited by any other provision of law.

(e) Notwithstanding any other provision of law, the court may strike the additional punishment provided for in this section if it determines that there are circumstances in mitigation of the additional punishment and states on the record its reasons for striking the additional punishment. *(Added by Stats.1993, c. 586 (A.B.313), § 1.)*

Cross References

Person defined for purposes of this Division, see Health and Safety Code § 11022.

Research References

2 Witkin, California Criminal Law 4th Crimes Against Public Peace and Welfare § 124 (2021), Substances Formerly Classified as Narcotics.

§ 11353.5. Controlled substances given away or sold to minors; locations where children are present; comparative ages of defendant and minor

Except as authorized by law, any person 18 years of age or older who unlawfully prepares for sale upon school grounds or a public playground, a child day care facility, a church, or a synagogue, or sells or gives away a controlled substance, other than a controlled substance described in Section 11353 or 11380, to a minor upon the grounds of, or within, any school, child day care facility, public playground, church, or synagogue providing instruction in preschool, kindergarten, or any of grades 1 to 12, inclusive, or providing child care services, during hours in which those facilities are open for classes, school-related programs, or child care, or at any time when minors are using the facility where the offense occurs, or upon the grounds of a public playground during the hours in which school-related programs for minors are being conducted, or at any time when minors are using the facility where the offense occurs, shall be punished by imprisonment pursuant to subdivision (h) of Section 1170 of the Penal Code for five, seven, or nine years. Application of this section shall be limited to persons at least five years older than the minor to whom he or she prepares for sale, sells, or gives away a controlled substance. *(Added by Stats.1983, c. 951, § 1. Amended by Stats.1986, c. 1038, § 1; Stats.1988, c. 1266, § 1; Stats.1990, c. 1663 (A.B.3744), § 2; Stats.1990, c. 1664 (A.B.2645), § 3; Stats.1990, c. 1665 (S.B.2112), § 2; Stats.1993, c. 556 (A.B.312), § 2; Stats.2011, c. 15 (A.B.109), § 155, eff. April 4, 2011, operative Oct. 1, 2011.)*

Cross References

Additional penalty for trafficking violation on grounds of or near drug treatment center, detoxification facility, or homeless shelter, see Health and Safety Code § 11380.7.

Arrest of teacher or instructor employed in community college district, notices, see Health and Safety Code § 11591.5.

Controlled substance defined for purposes of this Division, see Health and Safety Code § 11007.

Life sentence for person who has served two or more prior terms for certain drug offenses involving minors, see Penal Code § 667.75.

Of criminal procedure, of proceedings after the commencement of the trial and before judgment, trial court sentencing, initial sentencing, crimes involving minors under 11 years of age, circumstance in aggravation, see Penal Code § 1170.72.

Person defined for purposes of this Division, see Health and Safety Code § 11022.

School employee, arrest for controlled substance offense as described in this section, notice to school authorities, see Health and Safety Code § 11591.

Research References

2 Witkin, California Criminal Law 4th Crimes Against Public Peace and Welfare § 128 (2021), Parks, Playgrounds, Child Care Facilities, and Religious Facilities.

2 Witkin, California Criminal Law 4th Crimes Against Public Peace and Welfare § 129 (2021), Schools.

2 Witkin, California Criminal Law 4th Crimes Against Public Peace and Welfare § 130 (2021), Drug Treatment Centers, Detoxification Facilities, and Homeless Shelters.

§ 11353.6. Juvenile Drug Trafficking and Schoolyard Act of 1988; additional punishment

(a) This section shall be known, and may be cited, as the Juvenile Drug Trafficking and Schoolyard Act of 1988.

(b) Any person 18 years of age or over who is convicted of a violation of Section 11351.5, 11352, or 11379.6, as those sections apply to paragraph (1) of subdivision (f) of Section 11054, or of Section 11351, 11352, or 11379.6, as those sections apply to paragraph (11) of subdivision (c) of Section 11054, or of Section 11378, 11379, or 11379.6, as those sections apply to paragraph (2) of subdivision (d) of Section 11055, or of a conspiracy to commit one of those offenses, where the violation takes place upon the grounds of, or within 1,000 feet of, a public or private elementary, vocational, junior high, or high school during hours that the school is open for classes or school-related programs, or at any time when minors are using the facility where the offense occurs, shall receive an additional punishment of three, four, or five years at the court's discretion.

(c) Any person 18 years of age or older who is convicted of a violation pursuant to subdivision (b) which involves a minor who is at least four years younger than that person, as a full and separately served enhancement to that provided in subdivision (b), shall be punished by imprisonment pursuant to subdivision (h) of Section 1170 of the Penal Code for three, four, or five years at the court's discretion.

(d) The additional terms provided in this section shall not be imposed unless the allegation is charged in the accusatory pleading and admitted or found to be true by the trier of fact.

(e) The additional terms provided in this section shall be in addition to any other punishment provided by law and shall not be limited by any other provision of law.

(f) Notwithstanding any other provision of law, the court may strike the additional punishment for the enhancements provided in this section if it determines that there are circumstances in mitigation of the additional punishment and states on the record its reasons for striking the additional punishment.

(g) "Within 1,000 feet of a public or private elementary, vocational, junior high, or high school" means any public area or business establishment where minors are legally permitted to conduct business which is located within 1,000 feet of any public or private elementary, vocational, junior high, or high school. *(Added by Stats.1988, c. 1248, § 1. Amended by Stats.1992, c. 989 (A.B.2124), § 1; Stats.1993, c. 551 (A.B.104), § 1; Stats.2011, c. 15 (A.B.109), § 156, eff. April 4, 2011, operative Oct. 1, 2011.)*

Cross References

Additional penalty for trafficking violation on grounds of or near drug treatment center, detoxification facility, or homeless shelter, see Health and Safety Code § 11380.7.

Person defined for purposes of this Division, see Health and Safety Code § 11022.

Research References

2 Witkin, California Criminal Law 4th Crimes Against Public Peace and Welfare § 128 (2021), Parks, Playgrounds, Child Care Facilities, and Religious Facilities.

2 Witkin, California Criminal Law 4th Crimes Against Public Peace and Welfare § 129 (2021), Schools.

2 Witkin, California Criminal Law 4th Crimes Against Public Peace and Welfare § 130 (2021), Drug Treatment Centers, Detoxification Facilities, and Homeless Shelters.

1 Witkin California Criminal Law 4th Introduction to Crimes § 50 (2021), Enhanced Penalty.

§ 11353.7. Adult preparing for sale, sale or gift of controlled substance to minor in public parks

Except as authorized by law, and except as provided otherwise in Sections 11353.1, 11353.6, and 11380.1 with respect to playgrounds situated in a public park, any person 18 years of age or older who unlawfully prepares for sale in a public park, including units of the state park system and state vehicular recreation areas, or sells or gives away a controlled substance to a minor under the age of 14 years in a public park, including units of the state park system and state vehicular recreation areas, during hours in which the public park, including units of the state park system and state vehicular recreation areas, is open for use, with knowledge that the person is a minor under the age of 14 years, shall be punished by imprisonment in state prison for three, six, or nine years. *(Added by Stats.1988, c. 1177, § 1. Amended by Stats.1990, c. 1665 (S.B.2112), § 3; Stats. 2011, c. 15 (A.B.109), § 157, eff. April 4, 2011, operative Oct. 1, 2011; Stats.2012, c. 43 (S.B.1023), § 13, eff. June 27, 2012.)*

Cross References

Additional penalty for trafficking violation on grounds of or near drug treatment center, detoxification facility, or homeless shelter, see Health and Safety Code § 11380.7.

Arrest of teacher or instructor employed in community college district, notices, see Health and Safety Code § 11591.5.

Controlled substance defined for purposes of this Division, see Health and Safety Code § 11007.

Of criminal procedure, of proceedings after the commencement of the trial and before judgment, trial court sentencing, initial sentencing, crimes involving minors under 11 years of age, circumstance in aggravation, see Penal Code § 1170.72.
Person defined for purposes of this Division, see Health and Safety Code § 11022.
School employee, arrest for controlled substance offense as described in this section, notice to school authorities, see Health and Safety Code § 11591.

Research References

2 Witkin, California Criminal Law 4th Crimes Against Public Peace and Welfare § 128 (2021), Parks, Playgrounds, Child Care Facilities, and Religious Facilities.
2 Witkin, California Criminal Law 4th Crimes Against Public Peace and Welfare § 130 (2021), Drug Treatment Centers, Detoxification Facilities, and Homeless Shelters.

§ 11354. Minor inducing another minor to violate provisions; use or employment of minors; punishment; juvenile court

(a) Every person under the age of 18 years who in any voluntary manner solicits, induces, encourages, or intimidates any minor with the intent that the minor shall violate any provision of this chapter or Section 11550, who hires, employs, or uses a minor to unlawfully transport, carry, sell, give away, prepare for sale, or peddle (1) any controlled substance specified in subdivision (b), (c), or (e), or paragraph (1) of subdivision (f) of Section 11054, specified in paragraph (14), (15), or (20) of subdivision (d) of Section 11054, or specified in subdivision (b) or (c) of Section 11055, or specified in subdivision (h) of Section 11056, or (2) any controlled substance classified in Schedule III, IV, or V which is a narcotic drug, or who unlawfully sells, furnishes, administers, gives, or offers to sell, furnish, administer, or give, any such controlled substance to a minor shall be punished by imprisonment in the state prison.

(b) This section is not intended to affect the jurisdiction of the juvenile court. *(Added by Stats.1972, c. 1407, p. 3014, § 3. Amended by Stats.1973, c. 1078, p. 2175, § 6, eff. Oct. 1, 1973; Stats.1976, c. 1139, p. 5080, § 69, operative July 1, 1977; Stats.1983, c. 790, § 7; Stats.1984, c. 1635, § 54; Stats.1985, c. 1377, § 2; Stats.1986, c. 1044, § 7; Stats.1987, c. 970, § 5; Stats.2000, c. 8 (S.B.550), § 7, eff. March 29, 2000.)*

Cross References

Additional penalty for trafficking violation on grounds of or near drug treatment center, detoxification facility, or homeless shelter, see Health and Safety Code § 11380.7.
Administer defined for purposes of this Division, see Health and Safety Code § 11002.
Arrest of teacher or instructor employed in community college district, notices, see Health and Safety Code § 11591.5.
Controlled substance defined for purposes of this Division, see Health and Safety Code § 11007.
Controlled substance offense defined as violation of this section for purposes of Education Code, see Education Code §§ 44011, 87011.
Education or treatment programs, condition to probation, see Health and Safety Code § 11373.
Expenditures to obtain evidence, see Health and Safety Code § 11454.
Felony offense defined for purposes of this Article, see Health and Safety Code § 11356.
Furnish defined for purposes of this Division, see Health and Safety Code § 11016.
Narcotic drug defined for purposes of this Division, see Health and Safety Code § 11019.
Of criminal procedure, of proceedings after the commencement of the trial and before judgment, trial court sentencing, initial sentencing, crimes involving minors under 11 years of age, circumstance in aggravation, see Penal Code § 1170.72.
Person defined for purposes of this Division, see Health and Safety Code § 11022.
Recovery of funds expended in investigations, see Health and Safety Code § 11501.
Registration of controlled substance offender, conviction of offense defined in this section, see Health and Safety Code § 11591 et seq.
School employee, arrest for controlled substance offense as described in this section, notice to school authorities, see Health and Safety Code § 11591.

Research References

California Jury Instructions - Criminal 12.10, Controlled Substance (Sched. I and II)—Illegal Sale, etc., to Minor.
California Jury Instructions - Criminal 12.11, Controlled Substance (Sched. I and II)—Illegal Offer to Sell, etc., to Minor.
California Jury Instructions - Criminal 12.12, Controlled Substance (Sched. I and II)—Employment of Minor to Peddle.
California Jury Instructions - Criminal 12.13, Controlled Substance (Sched. I and II)—Inducing Minor to Violate Controlled Substances Law.
2 Witkin, California Criminal Law 4th Crimes Against Public Peace and Welfare § 124 (2021), Substances Formerly Classified as Narcotics.

§ 11355. Sale or furnishing substance falsely represented to be a controlled substance; punishment

Every person who agrees, consents, or in any manner offers to unlawfully sell, furnish, transport, administer, or give (1) any controlled substance specified in subdivision (b), (c), or (e), or paragraph (1) of subdivision (f) of Section 11054, specified in paragraph (13), (14), (15), or (20) of subdivision (d) of Section 11054, or specified in subdivision (b) or (c) of Section 11055, or specified in subdivision (h) of Section 11056, or (2) any controlled substance classified in Schedule III, IV, or V which is a narcotic drug to any person, or who offers, arranges, or negotiates to have any such controlled substance unlawfully sold, delivered, transported, furnished, administered, or given to any person and who then sells, delivers, furnishes, transports, administers, or gives, or offers, arranges, or negotiates to have sold, delivered, transported, furnished, administered, or given to any person any other liquid, substance, or material in lieu of any such controlled substance shall be punished by imprisonment in the county jail for not more than one year, or pursuant to subdivision (h) of Section 1170 of the Penal Code. *(Added by Stats.1972, c. 1407, p. 3014, § 3. Amended by Stats.1973, c. 1078, p. 2176, § 7, eff. Oct. 1, 1973; Stats.1976, c. 1139, p. 5080, § 70, operative July 1, 1977; Stats.1983, c. 790, § 8; Stats.1984, c. 1635, § 55; Stats.1986, c. 1044, § 8; Stats.1987, c. 970, § 6; Stats.2000, c. 8 (S.B.550), § 8, eff. March 29, 2000; Stats.2011–2012, 1st Ex.Sess., c. 12 (A.B.17), § 4, eff. Sept. 21, 2011, operative Oct. 1, 2011.)*

Cross References

Administer defined for purposes of this Division, see Health and Safety Code § 11002.
Arrest of teacher or instructor employed in community college district, notices, see Health and Safety Code § 11591.5.
Controlled substance defined for purposes of this Division, see Health and Safety Code § 11007.
Controlled substance offense defined as violation of this section for purposes of Education Code, see Education Code §§ 44011, 87011.
Deliver or delivery defined for purposes of this Division, see Health and Safety Code § 11009.
Expenditures to obtain evidence, see Health and Safety Code § 11454.
Fine in addition to imprisonment for conviction of violation of this section, see Health and Safety Code § 11372.
Fines, increment for each separate offense, see Health and Safety Code § 11372.5.
Furnish defined for purposes of this Division, see Health and Safety Code § 11016.
Narcotic drug defined for purposes of this Division, see Health and Safety Code § 11019.
Person defined for purposes of this Division, see Health and Safety Code § 11022.
Probation or suspension of sentence, previous convictions, see Health and Safety Code § 11370.
Recovery of funds expended in investigations, see Health and Safety Code § 11501.
Registration of controlled substance offender, conviction of offense defined in this section, see Health and Safety Code § 11591 et seq.
School employee, arrest for controlled substance offense as described in this section, notice to school authorities, see Health and Safety Code § 11591.

Seizure of things of value and believed to be forfeitable, see Health and Safety Code § 11488.

Research References

California Jury Instructions - Criminal 12.04, Controlled Substance (Sched. I–V)—Illegal Sale, etc. of Substance in Lieu Thereof.
2 Witkin, California Criminal Law 4th Crimes Against Public Peace and Welfare § 123 (2021), Fraudulent Agreement.

§ 11356. "Felony offense" and "offense punishable as a felony" defined

As used in this article "felony offense," and "offense punishable as a felony" refer to an offense prior to October 1, 2011, for which the law prescribes imprisonment in the state prison, or for an offense on or after October 1, 2011, imprisonment in either the state prison or pursuant to subdivision (h) of Section 1170 of the Penal Code, as either an alternative or the sole penalty, regardless of the sentence the particular defendant received. *(Added by Stats.1972, c. 1407, p. 3015, § 3. Amended by Stats.1974, c. 545, § 59; Stats.2011, c. 15 (A.B.109), § 158, eff. April 4, 2011, operative Oct. 1, 2011; Stats.2011, c. 39 (A.B.117), § 2, eff. June 30, 2011, operative Oct. 1, 2011.)*

Cross References

Felony defined, see Penal Code § 17.
Fish and game generally, importation, transportation, and sheltering of restricted live wild animals, regulation and enforcement, regulations relating to caging standards deemed not building standards, see Fish and Game Code § 2192.
Similar section, cannabis violations, see Health and Safety Code § 11362.

Research References

2 Witkin, California Criminal Law 4th Crimes Against Public Peace and Welfare § 163 (2021), Punishment.

§ 11356.5. Valuation of controlled substances; conviction of or inducing another to violate provisions; additional punishment based on value

(a) Any person convicted of a violation of Section 11351, 11352, 11379.5, or 11379.6 insofar as the latter section relates to phencyclidine or any of its analogs which is specified in paragraph (21), (22), or (23) of subdivision (d) of Section 11054 or in paragraph (3) of subdivision (e) of Section 11055, who, as part of the transaction for which he or she was convicted, has induced another to violate Section 11351, 11352, 11379.5, or 11379.6 insofar as the latter section relates to phencyclidine or its analogs, shall be punished as follows:

(1) By an additional one year in prison if the value of the controlled substance involved in the transaction for which the person was convicted exceeds five hundred thousand dollars ($500,000).

(2) By an additional two years in prison if the value of the controlled substance involved in the transaction for which the person was convicted exceeds two million dollars ($2,000,000).

(3) By an additional three years in prison if the value of the controlled substance involved in the transaction for which the person was convicted exceeds five million dollars ($5,000,000).

(b) For purposes of this section, "value of the controlled substance" means the retail price to the user. *(Added by Stats.1983, c. 716, § 1. Amended by Stats.1985, c. 3, § 2, eff. Jan. 29, 1985; Stats.1995, c. 377 (S.B.1095), § 1.)*

Cross References

Bail schedule, considerations in adopting uniform countywide schedule, see Penal Code § 1269b.
Controlled substance defined for purposes of this Division, see Health and Safety Code § 11007.
Person defined for purposes of this Division, see Health and Safety Code § 11022.

Research References

2 Witkin, California Criminal Law 4th Crimes Against Public Peace and Welfare § 101 (2021), Possession for Sale.
2 Witkin, California Criminal Law 4th Crimes Against Public Peace and Welfare § 115 (2021), Statutory Prohibitions.
2 Witkin, California Criminal Law 4th Crimes Against Public Peace and Welfare § 132 (2021), Manufacture.
3 Witkin, California Criminal Law 4th Punishment § 375 (2021), Value or Amount.

ARTICLE 2. CANNABIS

§ 11357. Possession [1]

(a) Except as authorized by law, possession of not more than 28.5 grams of cannabis, or not more than eight grams of concentrated cannabis, or both, shall be punished or adjudicated as follows:

(1) Persons under 18 years of age are guilty of an infraction and shall be required to:

(A) Upon a finding that a first offense has been committed, complete four hours of drug education or counseling and up to 10 hours of community service over a period not to exceed 60 days.

(B) Upon a finding that a second offense or subsequent offense has been committed, complete six hours of drug education or counseling and up to 20 hours of community service over a period not to exceed 90 days.

(2) Persons at least 18 years of age but less than 21 years of age are guilty of an infraction and punishable by a fine of not more than one hundred dollars ($100).

(b) Except as authorized by law, possession of more than 28.5 grams of cannabis, or more than eight grams of concentrated cannabis, shall be punished as follows:

(1) Persons under 18 years of age who possess more than 28.5 grams of cannabis or more than eight grams of concentrated cannabis, or both, are guilty of an infraction and shall be required to:

(A) Upon a finding that a first offense has been committed, complete eight hours of drug education or counseling and up to 40 hours of community service over a period not to exceed 90 days.

(B) Upon a finding that a second or subsequent offense has been committed, complete 10 hours of drug education or counseling and up to 60 hours of community service over a period not to exceed 120 days.

(2) Persons 18 years of age or older who possess more than 28.5 grams of cannabis, or more than eight grams of concentrated cannabis, or both, shall be punished by imprisonment in a county jail for a period of not more than six months or by a fine of not more than five hundred dollars ($500), or by both that fine and imprisonment.

(c) Except as authorized by law, a person 18 years of age or older who possesses not more than 28.5 grams of cannabis, or not more than eight grams of concentrated cannabis, upon the grounds of, or within, any school providing instruction in kindergarten or any of grades 1 to 12, inclusive, during hours the school is open for classes or school-related programs is guilty of a misdemeanor and shall be punished as follows:

(1) A fine of not more than two hundred fifty dollars ($250), upon a finding that a first offense has been committed.

(2) A fine of not more than five hundred dollars ($500), or by imprisonment in a county jail for a period of not more than 10 days, or both, upon a finding that a second or subsequent offense has been committed.

(d) Except as authorized by law, a person under 18 years of age who possesses not more than 28.5 grams of cannabis, or not more than eight grams of concentrated cannabis, upon the grounds of, or within, any school providing instruction in kindergarten or any of grades 1 to 12, inclusive, during hours the school is open for classes or school-related programs is guilty of an infraction and shall be punished in the same manner provided in paragraph (1) of subdivision (b). *(Added by Stats.1972, c. 1407, p. 3015, § 3. Amended by Stats.1973, c. 1078, p. 2176, § 8, eff. Oct. 1, 1973; Stats.1975, c. 248, p. 641, § 2; Stats.1976, c. 1139, p. 5081, § 71, operative July 1, 1977; Stats.1982, c. 1287, p. 4759, § 1, operative Sept. 1, 1983; Stats.1983, c. 223, § 2; Stats.1983, c. 434, § 1, eff. July 28, 1983; Stats.1983, c. 434, § 1.5, eff. July 28, 1983, operative Jan. 1, 1984; Stats.2010, c. 708 (S.B.1449), § 1; Stats.2011, c. 15 (A.B.109), § 159, eff. April 4, 2011, operative Oct. 1, 2011; Initiative Measure (Prop. 47, § 12, approved Nov. 4, 2014, eff. Nov. 5, 2014); Initiative Measure (Prop. 64, § 8.1, approved Nov. 8, 2016, eff. Nov. 9, 2016); Stats.2017, c. 27 (S.B.94), § 122, eff. June 27, 2017; Stats.2017, c. 253 (A.B.133), § 15, eff. Sept. 16, 2017.)*

1 Section caption supplied by Prop. 64.

Cross References

Arrest, notice to appear and bail, see Penal Code § 853.6.
Cannabis defined for purposes of this Division, see Health and Safety Code § 11018.
Children, delinquents and wards of the juvenile court, juvenile court law, the juvenile court, powers of juvenile hearing officers, see Welfare and Institutions Code § 256.
Concentrated cannabis defined for purposes of this Division, see Health and Safety Code § 11006.5.
Convictions, limitations on employers and penalties, see Labor Code § 432.8.
Designated controlled substances, unauthorized possession, see Health and Safety Code § 11350.
Expenditures to obtain evidence, see Health and Safety Code § 11454.
Fine in addition to imprisonment, see Health and Safety Code § 11372.
Fines, increment for each separate offense, see Health and Safety Code § 11372.5.
Medical assistance exception to controlled substance possession and related offenses, persons experiencing drug-related overdose, no exception to laws prohibiting actions made dangerous by controlled substance use, see Health and Safety Code § 11376.5.
Medical marijuana program, generally, see Health and Safety Code § 11362.7 et seq.
Misdemeanors, definition and penalties, see Penal Code §§ 17, 19, 19.2.
Of criminal procedure, pleadings and proceedings before trial, special proceedings in narcotics and drug abuse cases, application to certain violations, see Penal Code § 1000.
Organization and government of courts, management of trial court records, destruction of records, retention periods, see Government Code § 68152.
Person defined for purposes of this Division, see Health and Safety Code § 11022.
Probation or suspension of sentence, previous convictions, see Health and Safety Code § 11370.
Recovery of funds expended in investigations, see Health and Safety Code § 11501.
Registration of controlled substance offender, conviction of offense defined in this section, see Health and Safety Code § 11591 et seq.
School district certificated employees, leave of absence when charged with offense under this section, see Education Code § 44940.
Special proceedings in prosecutions under this section, see Penal Code § 1000 et seq.
Trade samples, see Business and Professions Code § 26153.1.

Research References

California Jury Instructions - Criminal 12.20, Marijuana—Concentrated Cannabis—Unlawful Possession as Felony/Misdemeanor.
California Jury Instructions - Criminal 16.030, Concentrated Cannabis or Marijuana—Illegal Possession.
2 Witkin, California Criminal Law 4th Crimes Against Public Peace and Welfare § 86 (2021), In General.
2 Witkin, California Criminal Law 4th Crimes Against Public Peace and Welfare § 90 (2021), In General.
2 Witkin, California Criminal Law 4th Crimes Against Public Peace and Welfare § 91B (2021), (New) Restricted and Prohibited Activities.
2 Witkin, California Criminal Law 4th Crimes Against Public Peace and Welfare § 98 (2021), Marijuana.
2 Witkin, California Criminal Law 4th Crimes Against Public Peace and Welfare § 101 (2021), Possession for Sale.
2 Witkin, California Criminal Law 4th Crimes Against Public Peace and Welfare § 111 (2021), Dual Requirement.
2 Witkin, California Criminal Law 4th Crimes Against Public Peace and Welfare § 115 (2021), Statutory Prohibitions.
2 Witkin, California Criminal Law 4th Crimes Against Public Peace and Welfare § 131 (2021), Cultivating, Harvesting, or Processing.
2 Witkin, California Criminal Law 4th Crimes Against Public Peace and Welfare § 138 (2021), Statutory Authorization.
2 Witkin, California Criminal Law 4th Crimes Against Public Peace and Welfare § 149 (2021), Protection from Criminal Liability.
2 Witkin, California Criminal Law 4th Crimes Against Public Peace and Welfare § 163A (2021), (New) Resentencing or Dismissal of Marijuana Conviction.
2 Witkin, California Criminal Law 4th Crimes Against Public Peace and Welfare § 430 (2021), Employment Relationship.
1 Witkin California Criminal Law 4th Introduction to Crimes § 49 (2021), Less Severe Penalty.
1 Witkin California Criminal Law 4th Introduction to Crimes § 86 (2021), In General.
4 Witkin, California Criminal Law 4th Pretrial Proceedings § 386 (2021), Offenses and Conditions.
3 Witkin, California Criminal Law 4th Punishment § 308A (2021), (New) in General.

3 Witkin, California Criminal Law 4th Punishment § 722 (2021), Constitutionality.

§ 11357.5. Synthetic cannabinoid compound or derivative; prohibited sale, dispensing, distribution, etc., or possession for sale; first, second, third or subsequent offense; punishment; exception

(a) Every person who sells, dispenses, distributes, furnishes, administers, or gives, or offers to sell, dispense, distribute, furnish, administer, or give, or possesses for sale any synthetic cannabinoid compound, or any synthetic cannabinoid derivative, to any person, is guilty of a misdemeanor, punishable by imprisonment in a county jail not to exceed six months, or by a fine not to exceed one thousand dollars ($1,000), or by both that fine and imprisonment.

(b) Every person who uses or possesses any synthetic cannabinoid compound, or any synthetic cannabinoid derivative, is guilty of a public offense, punishable as follows:

(1) A first offense is an infraction punishable by a fine not exceeding two hundred fifty dollars ($250).

(2) A second offense is an infraction punishable by a fine not exceeding two hundred fifty dollars ($250) or a misdemeanor punishable by imprisonment in a county jail not exceeding six months, a fine not exceeding five hundred dollars ($500), or by both that fine and imprisonment.

(3) A third or subsequent offense is a misdemeanor punishable by imprisonment in a county jail not exceeding six months, or by a fine not exceeding one thousand dollars ($1,000), or by both that fine and imprisonment.

(c) As used in this section, the term "synthetic cannabinoid compound" refers to any of the following substances or an analog of any of the following substances:

(1) Adamantoylindoles or adamantoylindazoles, which includes adamantyl carboxamide indoles and adamantyl carboxamide indazoles, or any compound structurally derived from 3–(1–adamantoyl)indole, 3–(1–adamantoyl)indazole, 3–(2–adamantoyl)indole, N–(1–adamantyl)–1H–indole–3–carboxamide, or N–(1–adamantyl)–1H–indazole–3–carboxamide by substitution at the nitrogen atom of the indole or indazole ring with alkyl, haloalkyl, alkenyl, cyanoalkyl, hydroxyalkyl, cycloalkylmethyl, cycloalkylethyl, 1–(N–methyl–2–piperidinyl)methyl, 2–(4–morpholinyl)ethyl, or 1–(N–methyl–2–pyrrolidinyl)methyl, 1–(N–methyl–3–morpholinyl)methyl, or (tetrahydropyran–4–yl)methyl group, whether or not further substituted in the indole or indazole ring to any extent and whether or not substituted in the adamantyl ring to any extent, including, but not limited to, 2NE1, 5F–AKB–48, AB–001, AKB–48, AM–1248, JWH–018 adamantyl carboxamide, STS–135.

(2) Benzoylindoles, which includes any compound structurally derived from a 3–(benzoyl)indole structure with substitution at the nitrogen atom of the indole ring with alkyl, haloalkyl, cyanoalkyl, hydroxyalkyl, alkenyl, cycloalkylmethyl, cycloalkylethyl, 1–(N–methyl–2–piperidinyl)methyl, 2–(4–morpholinyl)ethyl, or 1–(N–methyl–2–pyrrolidinyl)methyl, 1–(N–methyl–3–morpholinyl)methyl, or (tetrahydropyran–4–yl)methyl group, whether or not further substituted in the indole ring to any extent and whether or not substituted in the phenyl ring to any extent, including, but not limited to, AM–630, AM–661, AM–679, AM–694, AM–1241, AM–2233, RCS–4, WIN 48,098 (Pravadoline).

(3) Cyclohexylphenols, which includes any compound structurally derived from 2–(3–hydroxycyclohexyl)phenol by substitution at the 5–position of the phenolic ring by alkyl, haloalkyl, cyanoalkyl, hydroxyalkyl, alkenyl, cycloalkylmethyl, cycloalkylethyl, 1–(N–methyl–2–piperidinyl)methyl, 2–(4–morpholinyl)ethyl, or 1–(N–methyl–2–pyrrolidinyl)methyl, 1–(N–methyl–3–morpholinyl)methyl, or (tetrahydropyran–4–yl)methyl group, whether or not further substituted in the cyclohexyl ring to any extent, including, but not limited to, CP 47,497, CP 55,490, CP 55,940, CP 56,667, cannabicyclohexanol.

(4) Cyclopropanoylindoles, which includes any compound structurally derived from 3–(cyclopropylmethanoyl)indole, 3–(cyclopropylmethanone)indole, 3–(cyclobutylmethanone)indole or 3–(cyclopentylmethanone)indole by substitution at the nitrogen atom of the indole ring, whether or not further substituted in the indole ring to any extent, whether or not substituted on the cyclopropyl, cyclobutyl, or cyclopentyl rings to any extent.

(5) Naphthoylindoles, which includes any compound structurally derived from 3–(1–naphthoyl)indole or 1H–indol–3–yl–(1–naphthyl)methane by substitution at the nitrogen atom of the indole ring by alkyl, haloalkyl, cyanoalkyl, hydroxyalkyl, alkenyl, cycloalkylmethyl, cycloalkylethyl, 1–(N–methyl–2–piperidinyl)methyl, 2–(4–morpholinyl)ethyl group, 1–(N–methyl–2–pyrrolidinyl)methyl, 1–(N–methyl–3–morpholinyl)methyl, or (tetrahydropyran–4–yl)methyl group, whether or not further substituted in the naphthyl ring to any extent, including, but not limited to, AM–678, AM–1220, AM–1221, AM–1235, AM–2201, AM–2232, EAM–2201, JWH–004, JWH–007, JWH–009, JWH–011, JWH–015, JWH–016, JWH–018, JWH–019, JWH–020, JWH–022, JWH–046, JWH–047, JWH–048, JWH–049, JWH–050, JWH–070, JWH–071, JWH–072, JWH–073, JWH–076, JWH–079, JWH–080, JWH–081, JWH–082, JWH–094, JWH–096, JWH–098, JWH–116, JWH–120, JWH–122, JWH–148, JWH–149, JWH–164, JWH–166, JWH–180, JWH–181, JWH–182, JWH–189, JWH–193, JWH–198, JWH–200, JWH–210, JWH–211, JWH–212, JWH–213, JWH–234, JWH–235, JWH–236, JWH–239, JWH–240, JWH–241, JWH–242, JWH–258, JWH–262, JWH–386, JWH–387, JWH–394, JWH–395, JWH–397, JWH–398, JWH–399, JWH–400, JWH–412, JWH–413, JWH–414, JWH–415, JWH–424, MAM–2201, WIN 55,212.

(6) Naphthoylnaphthalenes, which includes any compound structurally derived from naphthalene–1–yl–(naphthalene–1–yl) methanone with substitutions on either of the naphthalene rings to any extent, including, but not limited to, CB–13.

(7) Naphthoylpyrroles, which includes any compound structurally derived from 3–(1–naphthoyl)pyrrole by substitution at the nitrogen atom of the pyrrole ring by alkyl, haloalkyl, cyanoalkyl, hydroxyalkyl, alkenyl, cycloalkylmethyl, cycloalkylethyl, 1–(N–methyl–2–piperidinyl)methyl, 2–(4–morpholinyl)ethyl, or 1–(N–methyl–2–pyrrolidinyl)methyl, 1–(N–methyl–3–morpholinyl)methyl, or (tetrahydropyran–4–yl)methyl group, whether or not further substituted in the pyrrole ring to any extent and whether or not substituted in the naphthyl ring to any extent, including, but not limited to, JWH–030, JWH–031, JWH–145, JWH–146, JWH–147, JWH–150, JWH–156, JWH–243, JWH–244, JWH–245, JWH–246, JWH–292, JWH–293, JWH–307, JWH–308, JWH–309, JWH–346, JWH–348, JWH–363, JWH–364, JWH–365, JWH–367, JWH–368, JWH–369, JWH–370, JWH–371, JWH–373, JWH–392.

(8) Naphthylmethylindenes, which includes any compound containing a naphthylideneindene structure or which is structurally derived from 1–(1–naphthylmethyl)indene with substitution at the 3–position of the indene ring by alkyl, haloalkyl, cyanoalkyl, hydroxyalkyl, alkenyl, cycloalkylmethyl, cycloalkylethyl, 1–(N–methyl–2–piperidinyl)methyl, 2–(4–morpholinyl)ethyl, or 1–(N–methyl–2–pyrrolidinyl)methyl, 1–(N–methyl–3–morpholinyl)methyl, or (tetrahydropyran–4–yl)methyl group, whether or not further substituted in the indene ring to any extent and whether or not substituted in the naphthyl ring to any extent, including, but not limited to, JWH–171, JWH–176, JWH–220.

(9) Naphthylmethylindoles, which includes any compound structurally derived from an H–indol–3–yl–(1–naphthyl) methane by substitution at the nitrogen atom of the indole ring by alkyl, haloalkyl, cyanoalkyl, hydroxyalkyl, alkenyl, cycloalkylmethyl, cycloalkylethyl, 1–(N–methyl–2–piperidinyl)methyl, 2–(4–morpholinyl)ethyl, or 1–(N–methyl–2–pyrrolidinyl)methyl, 1–(N–methyl–3–morpholinyl)methyl, or (tetrahydropyran–4–yl)methyl group, whether or not further substituted in the indole ring to any extent and whether or not substituted in the naphthyl ring to any extent, including, but not

limited to, JWH–175, JWH–184, JWH–185, JWH–192, JWH–194, JWH–195, JWH–196, JWH–197, JWH–199.

(10) Phenylacetylindoles, which includes any compound structurally derived from 3–phenylacetylindole by substitution at the nitrogen atom of the indole ring with alkyl, haloalkyl, cyanoalkyl, hydroxyalkyl, alkenyl, cycloalkylmethyl, cycloalkylethyl, 1–(N–methyl–2–piperidinyl)methyl, 2–(4–morpholinyl)ethyl, or 1–(N–methyl–2–pyrrolidinyl)methyl, 1–(N–methyl–3–morpholinyl)methyl, or (tetrahydropyran–4–yl)methyl group, whether or not further substituted in the indole ring to any extent and whether or not substituted in the phenyl ring to any extent, including, but not limited to, cannabipiperidiethanone, JWH–167, JWH–201, JWH–202, JWH–203, JWH–204, JWH–205, JWH–206, JWH–207, JWH–208, JWH–209, JWH–237, JWH–248, JWH–249, JWH–250, JWH–251, JWH–253, JWH–302, JWH–303, JWH–304, JWH–305, JWH–306, JWH–311, JWH–312, JWH–313, JWH–314, JWH–315, JWH–316, RCS–8.

(11) Quinolinylindolecarboxylates, which includes any compound structurally derived from quinolin–8–yl–1H–indole–3–carboxylate by substitution at the nitrogen atom of the indole ring with alkyl, haloalkyl, benzyl, halobenzyl, alkenyl, haloalkenyl, alkoxy, cyanoalkyl, hydroxyalkyl, cycloalkylmethyl, cycloalkylethyl, (N–methylpiperidin–2–yl)alkyl, (4–tetrahydropyran)alkyl, or 2–(4–morpholinyl)alkyl, whether or not further substituted in the indole ring to any extent, whether or not substituted in the quinoline ring to any extent, including, but not limited to, BB–22, 5–Fluoro–PB–22, PB–22.

(12) Tetramethylcyclopropanoylindoles, which includes any compound structurally derived from 3–tetramethylcyclopropanoylindole, 3–(1–tetramethylcyclopropyl)indole, 3–(2,2,3,3–tetramethylcyclopropyl)indole or 3–(2,2,3,3–tetramethylcyclopropylcarbonyl)indole with substitution at the nitrogen atom of the indole ring by an alkyl, haloalkyl, cyanoalkyl, hydroxyalkyl, alkenyl, cycloalkylmethyl, cycloalkylethyl, 1–(N–methyl–2–piperidinyl)methyl, 2–(4–morpholinyl)ethyl, 1–(N–methyl–2–pyrrolidinyl)methyl, 1–(N–methyl–3–morpholinyl)methyl, or (tetrahydropyran–4–yl)methyl group whether or not further substituted in the indole ring to any extent and whether or not substituted in the tetramethylcyclopropanoyl ring to any extent, including, but not limited to, 5–bromo–UR–144, 5–chloro–UR–144, 5–fluoro–UR–144, A–796,260, A–834,735, AB–034, UR–144, XLR11.

(13) Tetramethylcyclopropane-thiazole carboxamides, which includes any compound structurally derived from 2,2,3,3–tetramethyl–N–(thiazol–2–ylidene)cyclopropanecarboxamide by substitution at the nitrogen atom of the thiazole ring by alkyl, haloalkyl, benzyl, halobenzyl, alkenyl, haloalkenyl, alkoxy, cyanoalkyl, hydroxyalkyl, cycloalkylmethyl, cycloalkylethyl, (N–methylpiperidin–2–yl)alkyl, (4–tetrahydropyran)alkyl, or 2–(4–morpholinyl)alkyl, whether or not further substituted in the thiazole ring to any extent, whether or not substituted in the tetramethylcyclopropyl ring to any extent, including, but not limited to, A–836,339.

(14) Unclassified synthetic cannabinoids, which includes all of the following:

(A) AM–087, (6aR,10aR)–3–(2–methyl–6–bromohex–2–yl)–6,6,9–t rimethyl–6a,7,10,10a–tetrahydrobenzo[c]chromen–1–ol.

(B) AM–356, methanandamide, including (5Z,8Z,11Z,14Z)—[(1R)–2–hydroxy–1–methylethyl]icosa–5,8,11,14–tetraenamide and arachidonyl–1'–hydroxy–2'–propylamide.

(C) AM–411, (6aR,10aR)–3–(1–adamantyl)–6,6,9–trimethyl–6 a,7,10,10a–tetrahydrobenzo[c]chromen–1–ol.

(D) AM–855, (4aR,12bR)–8–hexyl 2,5,5–trimethyl–1 ,4,4a,8,9,10,-11,12b–octahydronaphtho[3,2–c]isochromen–12–ol.

(E) AM–905, (6aR,9R,10aR)–3–[(E)–hept–1–enyl]–9–(hydroxymethyl)–6,6–dimethyl–6a,7,8,9,10,10a–hexahydrobenzo[c]chromen-1-ol.

(F) AM–906, (6aR,9R,10aR)–3–[(Z)–hept–1–enyl]–9–(hydroxymethyl)–6,6–dimethyl–6a,7,8,9,10,10a–hexahydrobenzo[c]chromen-1-ol.

(G) AM–2389, (6aR,9R,10aR)–3–(1–hexyl–cyclobut–1–yl)–6 a,7,8,9,10,10a–hexahydro–6,6–dimethyl–6H–dibenzo[b,d]pyran–1,9 diol.

(H) BAY 38–7271, (–)–(R)–3–(2–Hydroxymethylindanyl–4–o xy)phenyl–4,4,4–trifluorobutyl–1–sulfonate.

(I) CP 50,556–1, Levonantradol, including 9–hydroxy–6–methyl–3 –[5–phenylpentan–2–yl]oxy–5,6,6a,7,8,9,10,10a–octahydrophenant hridin–1–yl]acetate; [(6S,6aR,9R, 10aR)–9–hydroxy–6–methyl–3–[(2R)–5–phenylpentan–2–yl]oxy–5,6,6a,7,8,9,10,10a–octahydrophenanthridin–1–yl]acetate; and [9–hydroxy–6–methyl–3–[5–phenylpentan–2–yl]oxy–5,6,6a,7,8,9,10,10a–octahydrophenanthridin–1–yl]acetate.

(J) HU–210, including (6aR,10aR)–9–(hydroxymethyl)–6,6–d imethyl–3–(2–methyloctan–2–yl)–6a,7,10,10a–tetrahydrobenzo[c] chromen–1–ol; [(6aR,10aR)–9–(hydroxymethyl)–6,6–dimethyl–3–(2–methyl octan–2–yl)–6a,7,10,10a–tetrahydrobenzo[c]chromen–1–o l and 1,1–Dimethylheptyl–11–hydroxytetrahydrocannabinol.

(K) HU–211, Dexanabinol, including (6aS, 10aS)–9–(hydroxy methyl)–6,6–dimethyl–3–(2–methyloctan–2–yl)–6a,7,10,10a–t etrahydrobenzo[c]chromen–1–ol and (6aS, 10aS)–9–(hydroxy methyl)–6,6–dimethyl- 3–(2–methyloctan–2–yl)–6a,7,10,10a–t etrahydrobenzo[c]chromen–1–ol.

(L) HU–243, 3–dimethylheptyl–11–hydroxyhexahydrocannabinol.

(M) HU–308, [(91R,2R,5R)–2–[2,6–dimethoxy–4–(2–methyloctan–2 -yl)phenyl]–7,7–dimethyl–4–bicyclo[3.1.1]hept–3–enyl]methanol.

(N) HU–331, 3–hydroxy–2–[(1R,6R)–3–methyl–6–(1–m ethylethenyl)–2–cyclohexen–1–yl]–5–pentyl–2,5–cyclohexadiene–1,4–dione.

(O) HU–336, (6aR,10aR)–6,6,9–trimethyl–3–pentyl–6a,7,10,10a–t etrahydro–1H–benzo[c]chromene–1,4(6H)–dione.

(P) JTE–907, N–(benzol[1,3]dioxol–5–ylmethyl)–7–methoxy–2–o xo–8–pentyloxy–1,2–dihydroquinoline–3–carboxamide.

(Q) JWH–051, ((6aR,10aR)–6,6–dimethyl–3–(2–methyloctan–2–y l)–6a,7,10,10a–tetrahydrobenzo[c]chromen–9–yl)methanol.

(R) JWH–057 (6aR,10aR)–3–(1,1–dimethylheptyl)–6a,7,10,10a–t etrahydro–6,6,9–trimethyl–6H–Dibenzo[b,d]pyran.

(S) JWH–133 (6aR,10aR)–3–(1,1–Dimethylbutyl)–6a,7,10,10a–t etrahydro –6,6,9–trimethyl–6H–dibenzo[b,d]pyran.

(T) JWH–359, (6aR,10aR)- 1–methoxy- 6,6,9–trimethyl- 3–[(2R)–1 ,1,2–trimethylbutyl]- 6a,7,10,10a–tetrahydrobenzo[c]chromene.

(U) URB–597 [3–(3–carbamoylphenyl)phenyl]–N–cyclohexylcarb amate.

(V) URB–602 [1,1'–Biphenyl]–3–yl–carbamic acid, cyclohexyl ester; OR cyclohexyl [1,1'–biphenyl]–3–ylcarbamate.

(W) URB–754 6–methyl–2–[(4–methylphenyl)amino]–4H–3,1–b enzoxazin–4–one.

(X) URB–937 3'–carbamoyl–6–hydroxy–[1,1'–biphenyl]–3–yl cyc lohexylcarbamate.

(Y) WIN 55,212–2, including (R)–(+)–[2,3–dihydro–5–methyl–3 –(4–morpholinylmethyl)pyrrolo[1,2,3–de]–1,4–benzoxazin–6–yl]–1 -napthalenylmethanone and [2,3–Dihydro–5–methyl–3–(4–morp holinylmethyl)pyrrolo[(1,2,3–de)–1,4–benzoxazin–6–yl]–1–n apthalenylmethanone.

(d) The substances or analogs of substances identified in subdivision (c) may be lawfully obtained and used for bona fide research, instruction, or analysis if that possession and use does not violate federal law.

(e) As used in this section, "synthetic cannabinoid compound" does not include either of the following:

(1) Any substance for which there is an approved new drug application, as defined in Section 505 of the federal Food, Drug, and Cosmetic Act (21 U.S.C. Sec. 355) or which is generally recognized as safe and effective for use pursuant to Section 501, 502, and 503 of the federal Food, Drug, and Cosmetic Act and Title 21 of the Code of Federal Regulations.

(2) With respect to a particular person, any substance for which an exemption is in effect for investigational use for that person pursuant to Section 505 of the federal Food, Drug, and Cosmetic Act (21 U.S.C. Sec. 355), to the extent that the conduct with respect to that substance is pursuant to the exemption. *(Added by Stats.2014, c. 372 (S.B.1283), § 2, eff. Jan. 1, 2015, operative Jan. 1, 2016. Amended by Stats.2016, c. 624 (S.B.139), § 2, eff. Sept. 25, 2016.)*

Research References

2 Witkin, California Criminal Law 4th Crimes Against Public Peace and Welfare § 89 (2021), Analogs of Controlled Substances.
2 Witkin, California Criminal Law 4th Crimes Against Public Peace and Welfare § 97 (2021), In General.
2 Witkin, California Criminal Law 4th Crimes Against Public Peace and Welfare § 115 (2021), Statutory Prohibitions.

§ 11358. Planting, Harvesting, or Processing [1]

Each person who plants, cultivates, harvests, dries, or processes cannabis plants, or any part thereof, except as otherwise provided by law, shall be punished as follows:

(a) Each person under the age of 18 who plants, cultivates, harvests, dries, or processes any cannabis plants shall be punished in the same manner provided in paragraph (1) of subdivision (b) of Section 11357.

(b) Each person at least 18 years of age but less than 21 years of age who plants, cultivates, harvests, dries, or processes not more than six living cannabis plants shall be guilty of an infraction and a fine of not more than one hundred dollars ($100).

(c) Each person 18 years of age or over who plants, cultivates, harvests, dries, or processes more than six living cannabis plants shall be punished by imprisonment in a county jail for a period of not more than six months or by a fine of not more than five hundred dollars ($500), or by both that fine and imprisonment.

(d) Notwithstanding subdivision (c), a person 18 years of age or over who plants, cultivates, harvests, dries, or processes more than six living cannabis plants, or any part thereof, except as otherwise provided by law, may be punished by imprisonment pursuant to subdivision (h) of Section 1170 of the Penal Code if any of the following conditions exist:

(1) The person has one or more prior convictions for an offense specified in clause (iv) of subparagraph (C) of paragraph (2) of subdivision (e) of Section 667 of the Penal Code or for an offense requiring registration pursuant to subdivision (c) of Section 290 of the Penal Code.

(2) The person has two or more prior convictions under subdivision (c).

(3) The offense resulted in any of the following:

(A) Violation of Section 1052 of the Water Code relating to illegal diversion of water.

(B) Violation of Section 13260, 13264, 13272, or 13387 of the Water Code relating to discharge of water.

(C) Violation of Section 5650 or 5652 of the Fish and Game Code relating to waters of the state.

(D) Violation of Section 1602 of the Fish and Game Code relating to rivers, streams, and lakes.

(E) Violation of Section 374.8 of the Penal Code relating to hazardous substances or Section 25189.5, 25189.6, or 25189.7 of the Health and Safety Code relating to hazardous waste.

(F) Violation of Section 2080 of the Fish and Game Code relating to endangered and threatened species or Section 3513 of the Fish and Game Code relating to the Migratory Bird Treaty Act, or Section 2000 of the Fish and Game Code relating to the unlawful taking of fish and wildlife.

(G) Intentionally or with gross negligence causing substantial environmental harm to public lands or other public resources. *(Added by Stats.1972, c. 1407, p. 3016, § 3. Amended by Stats.1973, c. 1078, p. 2177, § 9, eff. Oct. 1, 1973; Stats.1976, c. 1139, p. 5082, § 72, operative July 1, 1977; Stats.2011, c. 15 (A.B.109), § 160, eff. April 4, 2011, operative Oct. 1, 2011; Initiative Measure (Prop. 64, § 8.2, approved Nov. 8, 2016, eff. Nov. 9, 2016); Stats.2017, c. 27 (S.B.94), § 123, eff. June 27, 2017.)*

[1] Section caption supplied by Prop. 64.

Cross References

Arrest of teacher or instructor employed in community college district, notices, see Health and Safety Code § 11591.5.
Cannabis defined for purposes of this Division, see Health and Safety Code § 11018.
Fines, increment for each separate offense, see Health and Safety Code § 11372.5.
Medical marijuana program, criminal liability for use of marijuana, application of section, see Health and Safety Code § 11362.765.
Of criminal procedure, pleadings and proceedings before trial, special proceedings in narcotics and drug abuse cases, see Penal Code § 1000.
Person defined for purposes of this Division, see Health and Safety Code § 11022.
Peyote, unauthorized planting, cultivating and harvesting, see Health and Safety Code § 11363.
Public social services, miscellaneous provisions, food stamps, eligibility for convicted drug felons to receive food stamps, see Welfare and Institutions Code § 18901.3.
Registration of controlled substance offender, conviction of offense defined in this section, see Health and Safety Code § 11591 et seq.
School district certificated employees, leave of absence when charged with offense under this section, see Education Code § 44940.
School employee, arrest for controlled substance offense as described in this section, notice to school authorities, see Health and Safety Code § 11591.

Research References

California Jury Instructions - Criminal 12.24, Marijuana—Unlawful Planting, etc.
2 Witkin, California Criminal Law 4th Crimes Against Public Peace and Welfare § 131 (2021), Cultivating, Harvesting, or Processing.
2 Witkin, California Criminal Law 4th Crimes Against Public Peace and Welfare § 132 (2021), Manufacture.
2 Witkin, California Criminal Law 4th Crimes Against Public Peace and Welfare § 138 (2021), Statutory Authorization.
2 Witkin, California Criminal Law 4th Crimes Against Public Peace and Welfare § 149 (2021), Protection from Criminal Liability.
2 Witkin, California Criminal Law 4th Crimes Against Public Peace and Welfare § 163A (2021), (New) Resentencing or Dismissal of Marijuana Conviction.
4 Witkin, California Criminal Law 4th Pretrial Proceedings § 246 (2021), Improper Amendments.
4 Witkin, California Criminal Law 4th Pretrial Proceedings § 374D (2021), (New) Recalled Sentence.
4 Witkin, California Criminal Law 4th Pretrial Proceedings § 386 (2021), Offenses and Conditions.
3 Witkin, California Criminal Law 4th Punishment § 308A (2021), (New) in General.
3 Witkin, California Criminal Law 4th Punishment § 665 (2021), Abstinence from Alcohol or Drugs.

§ 11359. Possession for Sale [1]

Every person who possesses for sale any cannabis, except as otherwise provided by law, shall be punished as follows:

(a) Every person under the age of 18 who possesses cannabis for sale shall be punished in the same manner provided in paragraph (1) of subdivision (b) of Section 11357.

(b) Every person 18 years of age or over who possesses cannabis for sale shall be punished by imprisonment in a county jail for a period of not more than six months or by a fine of not more than five hundred dollars ($500), or by both such fine and imprisonment.

(c) Notwithstanding subdivision (b), a person 18 years of age or over who possesses cannabis for sale may be punished by imprisonment pursuant to subdivision (h) of Section 1170 of the Penal Code if:

(1) The person has one or more prior convictions for an offense specified in clause (iv) of subparagraph (C) of paragraph (2) of subdivision (e) of Section 667 of the Penal Code or for an offense requiring registration pursuant to subdivision (c) of Section 290 of the Penal Code;

(2) The person has two or more prior convictions under subdivision (b); or

(3) The offense occurred in connection with the knowing sale or attempted sale of cannabis to a person under the age of 18 years.

(d) Notwithstanding subdivision (b), a person 21 years of age or over who possesses cannabis for sale may be punished by imprisonment pursuant to subdivision (h) of Section 1170 of the Penal Code if the offense involves knowingly hiring, employing, or using a person 20 years of age or younger in unlawfully cultivating, transporting, carrying, selling, offering to sell, giving away, preparing for sale, or peddling any cannabis. *(Added by Stats.1972, c. 1407, p. 3016, § 3. Amended by Stats.1973, c. 1078, p. 2178, § 10, eff. Oct. 1, 1973; Stats.1976, c. 1139, p. 5082, § 73, operative July 1, 1977; Stats.2011, c. 15 (A.B.109), § 161, eff. April 4, 2011, operative Oct. 1, 2011; Initiative Measure (Prop. 64, § 8.3, approved Nov. 8, 2016, eff. Nov. 9, 2016); Stats.2017, c. 27 (S.B.94), § 124, eff. June 27, 2017.)*

1 Section caption supplied by Prop. 64.

Cross References

Arrest of teacher or instructor employed in community college district, notices, see Health and Safety Code § 11591.5.
Cannabis defined for purposes of this Division, see Health and Safety Code § 11018.
Dangerous drug violations, effect of prior conviction under this section, see Health and Safety Code § 11377 et seq.
Designated controlled substances, possession for sale, see Health and Safety Code § 11351.
Fine in addition to imprisonment for conviction of violation of this section, see Health and Safety Code § 11372.
Fines, increment for each separate offense, see Health and Safety Code § 11372.5.
Medical marijuana program, generally, see Health and Safety Code § 11362.7 et seq.
Person defined for purposes of this Division, see Health and Safety Code § 11022.
Registration of controlled substance offender, conviction of offense defined in this section, see Health and Safety Code § 11591 et seq.
School district certificated employees, leave of absence when charged with offense under this section, see Education Code § 44940.
School employee, arrest for controlled substance offense as described in this section, notice to school authorities, see Health and Safety Code § 11591.
Seizure of things of value and believed to be forfeitable, see Health and Safety Code § 11488.
Unlawful detainer actions to abate nuisance caused by illegal conduct involving controlled substance purpose, including violations of these provisions, see Civil Code § 3486.

Research References

California Jury Instructions - Criminal 12.21, Marijuana—Unlawful Possession for Sale.
2 Witkin, California Criminal Law 4th Crimes Against Public Peace and Welfare § 101 (2021), Possession for Sale.
2 Witkin, California Criminal Law 4th Crimes Against Public Peace and Welfare § 149 (2021), Protection from Criminal Liability.
2 Witkin, California Criminal Law 4th Crimes Against Public Peace and Welfare § 163A (2021), (New) Resentencing or Dismissal of Marijuana Conviction.

§ 11360. Unlawful Transportation, Importation, Sale, or Gift [1]

(a) Except as otherwise provided by this section or as authorized by law, every person who transports, imports into this state, sells, furnishes, administers, or gives away, or offers to transport, import into this state, sell, furnish, administer, or give away, or attempts to import into this state or transport any cannabis shall be punished as follows:

(1) Persons under the age of 18 years shall be punished in the same manner as provided in paragraph (1) of subdivision (b) of Section 11357.

(2) Persons 18 years of age or over shall be punished by imprisonment in a county jail for a period of not more than six months or by a fine of not more than five hundred dollars ($500), or by both such fine and imprisonment.

(3) Notwithstanding paragraph (2), a person 18 years of age or over may be punished by imprisonment pursuant to subdivision (h) of Section 1170 of the Penal Code for a period of two, three, or four years if:

(A) The person has one or more prior convictions for an offense specified in clause (iv) of subparagraph (C) of paragraph (2) of subdivision (e) of Section 667 of the Penal Code or for an offense requiring registration pursuant to subdivision (c) of Section 290 of the Penal Code;

(B) The person has two or more prior convictions under paragraph (2);

(C) The offense involved the knowing sale, attempted sale, or the knowing offer to sell, furnish, administer, or give away cannabis to a person under the age of 18 years; or

(D) The offense involved the import, offer to import, or attempted import into this state, or the transport for sale, offer to transport for sale, or attempted transport for sale out of this state, of more than 28.5 grams of cannabis or more than four grams of concentrated cannabis.

(b) Except as authorized by law, every person who gives away, offers to give away, transports, offers to transport, or attempts to transport not more than 28.5 grams of cannabis, other than concentrated cannabis, is guilty of an infraction and shall be punished by a fine of not more than one hundred dollars ($100). In any case in which a person is arrested for a violation of this subdivision and does not demand to be taken before a magistrate, that person shall be released by the arresting officer upon presentation of satisfactory evidence of identity and giving his or her written promise to appear in court, as provided in Section 853.6 of the Penal Code, and shall not be subjected to booking.

(c) For purposes of this section, "transport" means to transport for sale.

(d) This section does not preclude or limit prosecution for any aiding and abetting or conspiracy offenses. *(Added by Stats.1972, c. 1407, p. 3017, § 3. Amended by Stats.1973, c. 1078, p. 2178, § 11, eff. Oct. 1, 1973; Stats.1975, c. 248, p. 642, § 3; Stats.1976, c. 1139, p. 5082, § 74, operative July 1, 1977; Stats.1983, c. 223, § 3; Stats.2011, c. 15 (A.B.109), § 162, eff. April 4, 2011, operative Oct. 1, 2011; Stats.2015, c. 77 (A.B.730), § 1, eff. Jan. 1, 2016; Initiative Measure (Prop. 64, § 8.4, approved Nov. 8, 2016, eff. Nov. 9, 2016); Stats.2017, c. 27 (S.B.94), § 125, eff. June 27, 2017.)*

1 Section caption supplied by Prop. 64.

Cross References

Administer defined for purposes of this Division, see Health and Safety Code § 11002.
Arrest, notice to appear and bail, see Penal Code § 853.6.
Arrest of teacher or instructor employed in community college district, notices, see Health and Safety Code § 11591.5.
Cannabis defined for purposes of this Division, see Health and Safety Code § 11018.

Concentrated cannabis defined for purposes of this Division, see Health and Safety Code § 11006.5.
Controlled substances, sale or transfer, aggravation of crime, see Penal Code § 1170.82.
Convictions, limitations on employers and penalties, see Labor Code § 432.8.
Fine in addition to imprisonment for conviction of violation of this section, see Health and Safety Code § 11372.
Fines, increment for each separate offense, see Health and Safety Code § 11372.5.
Furnish defined for purposes of this Division, see Health and Safety Code § 11016.
Medical marijuana program, generally, see Health and Safety Code § 11362.7 et seq.
Misdemeanors, definition and penalties, see Penal Code §§ 17, 19, 19.2.
Of criminal procedure,
Of proceedings after the commencement of the trial and before judgment, trial court sentencing, initial sentencing, controlled substances, sale or transfer, aggravation of crime, see Penal Code § 1170.82.
Proceedings in misdemeanor and infraction cases and appeals from such cases, sales of chemicals, drugs, laboratory apparatus or devices to process controlled substances, allocation of fines and forfeitures, see Penal Code § 1463.10.
Organization and government of courts, management of trial court records, destruction of records, retention periods, see Government Code § 68152.
Person defined for purposes of this Division, see Health and Safety Code § 11022.
Registration of controlled substance offender, conviction of offense defined in this section, see Health and Safety Code § 11591 et seq.
School district certificated employees, leave of absence when charged with offense under this section, see Education Code § 44940.
School employee, arrest for controlled substance offense as described in this section, notice to school authorities, see Health and Safety Code § 11591.
Seizure of things of value and believed to be forfeitable, see Health and Safety Code § 11488.
Transportation, sale, giving away, etc. of designated controlled substances, see Health and Safety Code § 11352.
Unlawful detainer actions to abate nuisance caused by illegal conduct involving controlled substance purpose, including violations of these provisions, see Civil Code § 3486.

Research References

California Jury Instructions - Criminal 12.22, Marijuana—Unlawful Sale, etc.
California Jury Instructions - Criminal 12.22.5, Marijuana—Unlawfully Gives Away or Transports More Than 28.5 Grams.
California Jury Instructions - Criminal 12.23, Marijuana—Unlawful Offer to Sell, etc.
California Jury Instructions - Criminal 16.035, Marijuana—Gives Away or Transports Not More Than 28.5 Grams.
2 Witkin, California Criminal Law 4th Crimes Against Public Peace and Welfare § 115 (2021), Statutory Prohibitions.
2 Witkin, California Criminal Law 4th Crimes Against Public Peace and Welfare § 116 (2021), Transportation.
2 Witkin, California Criminal Law 4th Crimes Against Public Peace and Welfare § 141 (2021), Transportation Distinguished.
2 Witkin, California Criminal Law 4th Crimes Against Public Peace and Welfare § 149 (2021), Protection from Criminal Liability.
2 Witkin, California Criminal Law 4th Crimes Against Public Peace and Welfare § 163A (2021), (New) Resentencing or Dismissal of Marijuana Conviction.
4 Witkin, California Criminal Law 4th Pretrial Proceedings § 262 (2021), Illustrations.
4 Witkin, California Criminal Law 4th Pretrial Proceedings § 264 (2021), No Reasonable Cause.

§ 11361. Adults employing or selling to minors; minors under or over 14 years of age; punishments

(a) A person 18 years of age or over who hires, employs, or uses a minor in unlawfully transporting, carrying, selling, giving away, preparing for sale, or peddling any cannabis, who unlawfully sells, or offers to sell, any cannabis to a minor, or who furnishes, administers, or gives, or offers to furnish, administer, or give any cannabis to a minor under 14 years of age, or who induces a minor to use cannabis in violation of law shall be punished by imprisonment in the state prison for a period of three, five, or seven years.

(b) A person 18 years of age or over who furnishes, administers, or gives, or offers to furnish, administer, or give, any cannabis to a minor 14 years of age or older in violation of law shall be punished by imprisonment in the state prison for a period of three, four, or five years. *(Added by Stats.1972, c. 1407, p. 3018, § 3. Amended by Stats.1973, c. 1078, p. 2179, § 12, eff. Oct. 1, 1973; Stats.1976, c. 1139, p. 5082, § 75, operative July 1, 1977; Stats.1986, c. 1035, § 2; Stats.2017, c. 27 (S.B.94), § 126, eff. June 27, 2017.)*

Cross References

Administer defined for purposes of this Division, see Health and Safety Code § 11002.
Adult inducing minor to violate provisions on controlled dangerous substances, see Health and Safety Code § 11353.
Arrest of teacher or instructor employed in community college district, notices, see Health and Safety Code § 11591.5.
Cannabis defined for purposes of this Division, see Health and Safety Code § 11018.
Denial of probation or suspension of sentence after conviction of violation of this section, prior conviction of certain offenses, see Health and Safety Code § 11370.
Fine in addition to imprisonment for conviction of violation of this section, see Health and Safety Code § 11372.
Fines, increment for each separate offense, see Health and Safety Code § 11372.5.
Forfeiture of boats, airplanes or vehicles, see Health and Safety Code § 11470.
Furnish defined for purposes of this Division, see Health and Safety Code § 11016.
Life sentence for person who has served two or more prior terms for certain drug offenses involving minors, see Penal Code § 667.75.
Of criminal procedure, of proceedings after the commencement of the trial and before judgment, trial court sentencing, initial sentencing, crimes involving minors under 11 years of age, circumstance in aggravation, see Penal Code § 1170.72.
Person defined for purposes of this Division, see Health and Safety Code § 11022.
Registration of controlled substance offender, conviction of offense defined in this section, see Health and Safety Code § 11591 et seq.
School district certificated employees, leave of absence when charged with offense under this section, see Education Code § 44940.
School employee, arrest for controlled substance offense as described in this section, notice to school authorities, see Health and Safety Code § 11591.

Research References

California Jury Instructions - Criminal 12.25, Marijuana—Illegal Sale, etc., to Minor.
California Jury Instructions - Criminal 12.26, Marijuana—Illegal Offer to Sell, etc., to Minor.
California Jury Instructions - Criminal 12.27, Marijuana—Employment of Minor to Peddle.
California Jury Instructions - Criminal 12.28, Marijuana—Inducing Minor to Use.
California Jury Instructions - Criminal 12.29, Marijuana—Illegal Furnishing to Minor Fourteen Years or Older.
2 Witkin, California Criminal Law 4th Crimes Against Public Peace and Welfare § 126 (2021), Marijuana.
4 Witkin, California Criminal Law 4th Pretrial Proceedings § 264 (2021), No Reasonable Cause.
4 Witkin, California Criminal Law 4th Pretrial Proceedings § 374D (2021), (New) Recalled Sentence.

§ 11361.1. Drug education and counseling requirements under Sections 11357, 11358, 11359, and 11360

(a) The drug education and counseling requirements under Sections 11357, 11358, 11359, and 11360 shall be:

(1) Mandatory, unless the court finds that such drug education or counseling is unnecessary for the person, or that a drug education or counseling program is unavailable;

(2) Free to participants, and shall consist of at least four hours of group discussion or instruction based on science and evidence-based principles and practices specific to the use and abuse of cannabis and other controlled substances.

(b) For good cause, the court may grant an extension of time not to exceed 30 days for a person to complete the drug education and counseling required under Sections 11357, 11358, 11359, and 11360. *(Added by Initiative Measure (Prop. 64, § 8.5, approved Nov. 8, 2016, eff. Nov. 9, 2016). Amended by Stats.2017, c. 27 (S.B.94), § 127, eff. June 27, 2017.)*

Research References

2 Witkin, California Criminal Law 4th Crimes Against Public Peace and Welfare § 98 (2021), Marijuana.

§ 11361.5. Destruction of Arrest and Conviction Records; Procedure; Exceptions [1]

(a) Records of any court of this state, any public or private agency that provides services upon referral under Section 1000.2 of the Penal Code, or of any state agency pertaining to the arrest or conviction of any person for a violation of Section 11357 or subdivision (b) of Section 11360, or pertaining to the arrest or conviction of any person under the age of 18 for a violation of any provision of this article except Section 11357.5, shall not be kept beyond two years from the date of the conviction, or from the date of the arrest if there was no conviction, except with respect to a violation of subdivision (d) of Section 11357, or any other violation by a person under the age of 18 occurring upon the grounds of, or within, any school providing instruction in kindergarten or any of grades 1 to 12, inclusive, during hours the school is open for classes or school-related programs, the records shall be retained until the offender attains the age of 18 years at which time the records shall be destroyed as provided in this section. A court or agency having custody of the records, including the statewide criminal databases, shall provide for the timely destruction of the records in accordance with subdivision (c), and those records shall also be purged from the statewide criminal databases. As used in this subdivision, "records pertaining to the arrest or conviction" shall include records of arrests resulting in the criminal proceeding and records relating to other offenses charged in the accusatory pleading, whether the defendant was acquitted or charges were dismissed. The two-year period beyond which records shall not be kept pursuant to this subdivision does not apply to any person who is, at the time at which this subdivision would otherwise require record destruction, incarcerated for an offense subject to this subdivision. For such persons, the two-year period shall commence from the date the person is released from custody. The requirements of this subdivision do not apply to records of any conviction occurring before January 1, 1976, or records of any arrest not followed by a conviction occurring before that date, or records of any arrest for an offense specified in subdivision (c) of Section 1192.7, or subdivision (c) of Section 667.5, of the Penal Code.

(b) This subdivision applies only to records of convictions and arrests not followed by conviction occurring before January 1, 1976, for any of the following offenses:

(1) A violation of Section 11357 or a statutory predecessor thereof.

(2) Unlawful possession of a device, contrivance, instrument, or paraphernalia used for unlawfully smoking cannabis, in violation of Section 11364, as it existed before January 1, 1976, or a statutory predecessor thereof.

(3) Unlawful visitation or presence in a room or place in which cannabis is being unlawfully smoked or used, in violation of Section 11365, as it existed before January 1, 1976, or a statutory predecessor thereof.

(4) Unlawfully using or being under the influence of cannabis, in violation of Section 11550, as it existed before January 1, 1976, or a statutory predecessor thereof.

(A) A person subject to an arrest or conviction for those offenses may apply to the Department of Justice for destruction of records pertaining to the arrest or conviction if two or more years have elapsed since the date of the conviction, or since the date of the arrest if not followed by a conviction. The application shall be submitted upon a form supplied by the Department of Justice and shall be accompanied by a fee, which shall be established by the department in an amount which will defray the cost of administering this subdivision and costs incurred by the state under subdivision (c), but which shall not exceed thirty-seven dollars and fifty cents ($37.50). The application form may be made available at every local police or sheriff's department and from the Department of Justice and may require that information which the department determines is necessary for purposes of identification.

(B) The department may request, but not require, the applicant to include a self-administered fingerprint upon the application. If the department is unable to sufficiently identify the applicant for purposes of this subdivision without the fingerprint or without additional fingerprints, it shall so notify the applicant and shall request the applicant to submit any fingerprints which may be required to effect identification, including a complete set if necessary, or, alternatively, to abandon the application and request a refund of all or a portion of the fee submitted with the application, as provided in this section. If the applicant fails or refuses to submit fingerprints in accordance with the department's request within a reasonable time which shall be established by the department, or if the applicant requests a refund of the fee, the department shall promptly mail a refund to the applicant at the address specified in the application or at any other address which may be specified by the applicant. However, if the department has notified the applicant that election to abandon the application will result in forfeiture of a specified amount which is a portion of the fee, the department may retain a portion of the fee which the department determines will defray the actual costs of processing the application, provided the amount of the portion retained shall not exceed ten dollars ($10).

(C) Upon receipt of a sufficient application, the Department of Justice shall destroy records of the department, if any, pertaining to the arrest or conviction in the manner prescribed by subdivision (c) and shall notify the Federal Bureau of Investigation, the law enforcement agency which arrested the applicant, and, if the applicant was convicted, the probation department which investigated the applicant and the Department of Motor Vehicles, of the application.

(c) Destruction of records of arrest or conviction pursuant to subdivision (a) or (b) shall be accomplished by permanent obliteration of all entries or notations upon the records pertaining to the arrest or conviction, and the record shall be prepared again so that it appears that the arrest or conviction never occurred. However, where (1) the only entries upon the record pertain to the arrest or conviction and (2) the record can be destroyed without necessarily effecting the destruction of other records, then the document constituting the record shall be physically destroyed.

(d) Notwithstanding subdivision (a) or (b), written transcriptions of oral testimony in court proceedings and published judicial appellate reports are not subject to this section. Additionally, no records shall be destroyed pursuant to subdivision (a) if the defendant or a codefendant has filed a civil action against the peace officers or law enforcement jurisdiction which made the arrest or instituted the prosecution and if the agency which is the custodian of those records has received a certified copy of the complaint in the civil action, until the civil action has finally been resolved. Immediately following the final resolution of the civil action, records subject to subdivision (a) shall be destroyed pursuant to subdivision (c) if more than two years have elapsed from the date of the conviction or arrest without conviction. *(Added by Stats.1975, c. 248, p. 643, § 4. Amended by Stats.1976, c. 952, p. 2177, § 1; Stats.1980, c. 676, p. 1947, § 163.5; Stats.1981, c. 714, p. 2679, § 222; Stats.1982, c. 1287, p. 4761, § 2; Stats.1983, c. 434, § 2, eff. July 28, 1983; Stats.1984, c. 1635, § 55.5; Stats.1993, c. 59 (S.B.443), § 12, eff. June 30, 1993; Initiative Measure (Prop. 64, § 8.6, approved Nov. 8, 2016, eff. Nov. 9,*

2016); Stats.2017, c. 27 (S.B.94), § 128, eff. June 27, 2017; Stats.2018, c. 92 (S.B.1289), § 140, eff. Jan. 1, 2019.)

Cross References

Cannabis defined for purposes of this Division, see Health and Safety Code § 11018.
Convictions, limitations on employers and penalties, see Labor Code § 432.8.
Organization and government of courts, management of trial court records, destruction of records, retention periods, see Government Code § 68152.
Person defined for purposes of this Division, see Health and Safety Code § 11022.
Schoolbus, school pupil activity bus, general public paratransit vehicle, youth bus, or vehicle for transportation of developmentally disabled persons, grounds to refuse or revoke driver certificate, see Vehicle Code § 13370.

Research References

2 Witkin, California Criminal Law 4th Crimes Against Public Peace and Welfare § 90 (2021), In General.

§ 11361.7. Accuracy, relevancy, timeliness and completeness of record subject to destruction; alteration of records; questions on prior criminal record; application of section

(a) Any record subject to destruction or permanent obliteration pursuant to Section 11361.5, or more than two years of age, or a record of a conviction for an offense specified in subdivision (a) or (b) of Section 11361.5 which became final more than two years previously, shall not be considered to be accurate, relevant, timely, or complete for any purposes by any agency or person. The provisions of this subdivision shall be applicable for purposes of the Privacy Act of 1974 (5 U.S.C. Section 552a) to the fullest extent permissible by law, whenever any information or record subject to destruction or permanent obliteration under Section 11361.5 was obtained by any state agency, local public agency, or any public or private agency that provides services upon referral under Section 1000.2 of the Penal Code, and is thereafter shared with or disseminated to any agency of the federal government.

(b) No public agency shall alter, amend, assess, condition, deny, limit, postpone, qualify, revoke, surcharge, or suspend any certificate, franchise, incident, interest, license, opportunity, permit, privilege, right, or title of any person because of an arrest or conviction for an offense specified in subdivision (a) or (b) of Section 11361.5, or because of the facts or events leading to such an arrest or conviction, on or after the date the records of such arrest or conviction are required to be destroyed by subdivision (a) of Section 11361.5, or two years from the date of such conviction or arrest without conviction with respect to arrests and convictions occurring prior to January 1, 1976. As used in this subdivision, "public agency" includes, but is not limited to, any state, county, city and county, city, public or constitutional corporation or entity, district, local or regional political subdivision, or any department, division, bureau, office, board, commission or other agency thereof.

(c) Any person arrested or convicted for an offense specified in subdivision (a) or (b) of Section 11361.5 may, two years from the date of such a conviction, or from the date of the arrest if there was no conviction, indicate in response to any question concerning his prior criminal record that he was not arrested or convicted for such offense.

(d) The provisions of this section shall be applicable without regard to whether destruction or obliteration of records has actually been implemented pursuant to Section 11361.5. *(Added by Stats. 1976, c. 952, p. 2179, § 2.)*

Cross References

Person defined for purposes of this Division, see Health and Safety Code § 11022.

§ 11361.8. Recall or dismissal of sentence

(a) A person currently serving a sentence for a conviction, whether by trial or by open or negotiated plea, who would not have been guilty of an offense, or who would have been guilty of a lesser offense under the Control, Regulate and Tax Adult Use of Marijuana Act had that act been in effect at the time of the offense may petition for a recall or dismissal of sentence before the trial court that entered the judgment of conviction in their case to request resentencing or dismissal in accordance with Sections 11357, 11358, 11359, 11360, 11362.1, 11362.2, 11362.3, and 11362.4 as those sections have been amended or added by that act.

(b) Upon receiving a petition under subdivision (a), the court shall presume the petitioner satisfies the criteria in subdivision (a) unless the party opposing the petition proves by clear and convincing evidence that the petitioner does not satisfy the criteria. If the petitioner satisfies the criteria in subdivision (a), the court shall grant the petition to recall the sentence or dismiss the sentence because it is legally invalid unless the court determines that granting the petition would pose an unreasonable risk of danger to public safety.

(1) In exercising its discretion, the court may consider, but shall not be limited to evidence provided for in subdivision (b) of Section 1170.18 of the Penal Code.

(2) As used in this section, "unreasonable risk of danger to public safety" has the same meaning as provided in subdivision (c) of Section 1170.18 of the Penal Code.

(c) A person who is serving a sentence and is resentenced pursuant to subdivision (b) shall be given credit for any time already served and shall be subject to supervision for one year following completion of their time in custody or shall be subject to whatever supervision time they would have otherwise been subject to after release, whichever is shorter, unless the court, in its discretion, as part of its resentencing order, releases the person from supervision. Such person is subject to parole supervision under Section 3000.08 of the Penal Code or postrelease community supervision under subdivision (a) of Section 3451 of the Penal Code by the designated agency and the jurisdiction of the court in the county in which the offender is released or resides, or in which an alleged violation of supervision has occurred, for the purpose of hearing petitions to revoke supervision and impose a term of custody.

(d) Under no circumstances may resentencing under this section result in the imposition of a term longer than the original sentence, or the reinstatement of charges dismissed pursuant to a negotiated plea agreement.

(e) A person who has completed their sentence whether by trial or open or negotiated plea, who would not have been guilty of the conviction offense under the Control, Regulate and Tax Adult Use of Marijuana Act had that act been in effect at the time of the offense, may file an application before the trial court that entered the judgment of conviction in their case to have the conviction dismissed and sealed because the prior conviction is now legally invalid or redesignated as a misdemeanor or infraction in accordance with Sections 11357, 11358, 11359, 11360, 11362.1, 11362.2, 11362.3, and 11362.4 as those sections have been amended or added by that act.

(f) The court shall presume the petitioner satisfies the criteria in subdivision (e) unless the party opposing the application proves by clear and convincing evidence that the petitioner does not satisfy the criteria in subdivision (e). Once the applicant satisfies the criteria in subdivision (e), the court shall redesignate the conviction as a misdemeanor or infraction or dismiss and seal the conviction as legally invalid as now established under the Control, Regulate and Tax Adult Use of Marijuana Act.

(g) Unless requested by the applicant, no hearing is necessary to grant or deny an application filed under subdivision (e).

(h) Any felony conviction that is recalled and resentenced under subdivision (b) or designated as a misdemeanor or infraction under subdivision (f) shall be considered a misdemeanor or infraction for all purposes. Any misdemeanor conviction that is recalled and resentenced under subdivision (b) or designated as an infraction under subdivision (f) shall be considered an infraction for all purposes.

(i) If the court that originally sentenced the petitioner is not available, the presiding judge shall designate another judge to rule on the petition or application.

(j) Nothing in this section is intended to diminish or abrogate any rights or remedies otherwise available to the petitioner or applicant.

(k) Nothing in this and related sections is intended to diminish or abrogate the finality of judgments in any case not falling within the purview of the Control, Regulate and Tax Adult Use of Marijuana Act.

(*l*) A resentencing hearing ordered under the Control, Regulate and Tax Adult Use of Marijuana Act shall constitute a "post-conviction release proceeding" under paragraph (7) of subdivision (b) of Section 28 of Article I of the California Constitution (Marsy's Law).

(m) The provisions of this section shall apply equally to juvenile delinquency adjudications and dispositions under Section 602 of the Welfare and Institutions Code if the juvenile would not have been guilty of an offense or would have been guilty of a lesser offense under the Control, Regulate and Tax Adult Use of Marijuana Act.

(n) The Judicial Council shall promulgate and make available all necessary forms to enable the filing of the petitions and applications provided in this section. *(Added by Initiative Measure (Prop. 64, § 8.7, approved Nov. 8, 2016, eff. Nov. 9, 2016). Amended by Stats.2021, c. 434 (S.B.827), § 2, eff. Jan. 1, 2022.)*

Research References

West's California Judicial Council Forms CR–400, Petition/Application (Health and Safety Code, §11361.8) Adult Crime(S).
West's California Judicial Council Forms CR–401, Proof of Service for Petition/Application (Health and Safety Code, §11361.8) Adult Crime(S).
West's California Judicial Council Forms CR–402, Prosecuting Agency Response to Petition/Application (Health and Safety Code, §11361.8) Adult Crime(S).
West's California Judicial Council Forms CR–403, Order After Petition/Application (Health and Safety Code, §11363.8) Adult Crime(S).
West's California Judicial Council Forms JV–744, Request to Reduce Juvenile Marijuana Offense.
West's California Judicial Council Forms JV–744A, Attachment to Request to Reduce Juvenile Marijuana Offense (Health and Safety Code, §11361.8(M)).
West's California Judicial Council Forms JV–745, Prosecuting Agency Response to Request to Reduce Juvenile Marijuana Offense (Health and Safety Code, §11361.8(M)).
West's California Judicial Council Forms JV–746, Order After Request to Reduce Juvenile Marijuana Offense (Health and Safety Code, §11361.8(M)).
2 Witkin, California Criminal Law 4th Crimes Against Public Peace and Welfare § 101 (2021), Possession for Sale.
2 Witkin, California Criminal Law 4th Crimes Against Public Peace and Welfare § 163A (2021), (New) Resentencing or Dismissal of Marijuana Conviction.

§ 11361.9. Criminal history information review by department; recall or dismissal of sentence; sealing or redesignation; notice; challenge by prosecutor; update to state summary criminal history information records; legislative intent

(a) On or before July 1, 2019, the Department of Justice shall review the records in the state summary criminal history information database and shall identify past convictions that are potentially eligible for recall or dismissal of sentence, dismissal and sealing, or redesignation pursuant to Section 11361.8. The department shall notify the prosecution of all cases in their jurisdiction that are eligible for recall or dismissal of sentence, dismissal and sealing, or redesignation.

(b) The prosecution shall have until July 1, 2020, to review all cases and determine whether to challenge the recall or dismissal of sentence, dismissal and sealing, or redesignation.

(c)(1) The prosecution may challenge the resentencing of a person who is still serving a sentence pursuant to this section when the person does not meet the criteria established in Section 11361.8 * * *.

(2) The prosecution may challenge the dismissal and sealing or redesignation of a person pursuant to this section who has completed * * * their sentence for a conviction when the person does not meet the criteria established in Section 11361.8.

(3) On or before July 1, 2020, the prosecution shall inform the court and the public defender's office in their county when they are challenging a particular recall or dismissal of sentence, dismissal and sealing, or redesignation. The prosecution shall inform the court when they are not challenging a particular recall or dismissal of sentence, dismissal and sealing, or redesignation.

(4) The public defender's office, upon receiving notice from the prosecution pursuant to paragraph (3), shall make a reasonable effort to notify the person whose resentencing or dismissal is being challenged.

(d)(1) If the prosecution did not challenge the recall or dismissal of sentence, dismissal and sealing, or redesignation * * * of a conviction on or before July 1, 2020, the conviction shall be deemed unchallenged, recalled, dismissed, and redesignated, as applicable, and the court shall * * * issue an order, recalling or dismissing the sentence, dismissing and sealing, or redesignating the conviction in each case pursuant to Section 11361.8 no later than March 1, 2023. * * *

(2) On or before March 1, 2023, the court shall update its records in accordance with this section, and shall report all convictions that have been recalled, dismissed, redesignated, or sealed to the Department of Justice for adjustment of the state summary criminal history information database.

(3) On or before July 1, 2023, the Department of Justice shall ensure that all of the records in the state summary criminal history information database that have been recalled, dismissed, sealed, or redesignated pursuant to this section have been updated, and shall ensure that inaccurate state summary criminal history is not disseminated. For those individuals whose state summary criminal history information was disseminated pursuant to Section 11105 of the Penal Code in the 30 days prior to an update based on this section, and the requesting entity is still entitled to receive the state summary criminal history information, the Department of Justice shall provide a subsequent notice to the entity.

(e) The * * * Department of Justice shall post general information on its * * * internet website about the recall or dismissal of sentences, dismissal and sealing, or redesignation authorized in this section. The department shall conduct an awareness campaign about the recall or dismissal of sentences, dismissal and sealing, or redesignation authorized in this section, so that individuals that may be impacted by this process are informed of the process pursuant to Article 5 (commencing with Section 11120) of Chapter 1 of Title 1 of Part 4 of the Penal Code, to request their criminal history information to verify the updates or how to contact the courts, prosecution, or public defenders' offices to assist in verifying the updates. If an individual requests their criminal history information to verify updates to their criminal history made pursuant to this section, the department may provide a one-time fee waiver of its fees under Section 11123 of the Penal Code for processing and responding to the request.

(f) A conviction, arrest, or other proceeding that has been ordered sealed pursuant to Section 11361.8, is deemed never to have occurred, and the person may reply accordingly to any inquiry about the events.

(g) Courts that have previously eliminated court records covered by this article pursuant to Sections 68152 and 68153 of the Government Code are compliant with the provisions of subdivision

(c) of Section 11361.5. Courts that have previously eliminated court records covered by this article pursuant to Sections 68152 and 68153 of the Government Code shall report to the Department of Justice, in a manner prescribed by the Department of Justice, that the relevant records have been destroyed and that the record are otherwise reduced, dismissed, or sealed in accordance with this section.

(h) Beginning March 1, 2023, and until June 1, 2024, the Department of Justice, in consultation with the Judicial Council, shall submit quarterly joint progress reports to the Legislature that include, but are not limited to, all of following information:

(1) Total number of cases recalled, dismissed, resentenced, sealed, and redesignated in each county, and the status of the department's update to the state summary criminal history database.

(2) Status of cases challenged by the prosecution, and all relevant statistical information regarding the disposition of the challenged cases in each county.

(3) The number of past convictions in the state summary criminal history database that are potentially eligible for recall or dismissal of sentence, dismissal and sealing, or redesignation pursuant to Section 11361.8.

(4) The status of the department's public awareness campaign to provide notification to impacted individuals.

(i) It is the intent of the Legislature that persons who are currently serving a sentence or who proactively petition for a recall or dismissal of sentence, dismissal and sealing, or redesignation pursuant to Section 11361.8 be prioritized for review. *(Added by Stats.2018, c. 993 (A.B.1793), § 1, eff. Jan. 1, 2019. Amended by Stats.2022, c. 387 (A.B.1706), § 1, eff. Jan. 1, 2023.)*

Research References

2 Witkin, California Criminal Law 4th Crimes Against Public Peace and Welfare § 163A (2021), (New) Resentencing or Dismissal of Marijuana Conviction.

§ 11362. "Felony offense" and offense "punishable as a felony" defined

As used in this article "felony offense," and offense "punishable as a felony" refer to an offense prior to July 1, 2011, for which the law prescribes imprisonment in the state prison, or for an offense on or after July 1, 2011, imprisonment in either the state prison or pursuant to subdivision (h) of Section 1170 of the Penal Code, as either an alternative or the sole penalty, regardless of the sentence the particular defendant received. *(Added by Stats.1972, c. 1407, p. 3018, § 3. Amended by Stats.2011, c. 15 (A.B.109), § 163, eff. April 4, 2011, operative Oct. 1, 2011.)*

Cross References

Felony defined, see Penal Code § 17.

§ 11362.1. Possession of cannabis by persons 21 years of age or older

(a) Subject to Sections 11362.2, 11362.3, 11362.4, and 11362.45, but notwithstanding any other provision of law, it shall be lawful under state and local law, and shall not be a violation of state or local law, for persons 21 years of age or older to:

(1) Possess, process, transport, purchase, obtain, or give away to persons 21 years of age or older without any compensation whatsoever, not more than 28.5 grams of cannabis not in the form of concentrated cannabis;

(2) Possess, process, transport, purchase, obtain, or give away to persons 21 years of age or older without any compensation whatsoever, not more than eight grams of cannabis in the form of concentrated cannabis, including as contained in cannabis products;

(3) Possess, plant, cultivate, harvest, dry, or process not more than six living cannabis plants and possess the cannabis produced by the plants;

(4) Smoke or ingest cannabis or cannabis products; and

(5) Possess, transport, purchase, obtain, use, manufacture, or give away cannabis accessories to persons 21 years of age or older without any compensation whatsoever.

(b) Paragraph (5) of subdivision (a) is intended to meet the requirements of subsection (f) of Section 863 of Title 21 of the United States Code (21 U.S.C. Sec. 863(f)) by authorizing, under state law, any person in compliance with this section to manufacture, possess, or distribute cannabis accessories.

(c) Cannabis and cannabis products involved in any way with conduct deemed lawful by this section are not contraband nor subject to seizure, and no conduct deemed lawful by this section shall constitute the basis for detention, search, or arrest. *(Added by Initiative Measure (Prop. 64, § 4.4, approved Nov. 8, 2016, eff. Nov. 9, 2016). Amended by Stats.2017, c. 27 (S.B.94), § 129, eff. June 27, 2017.)*

Cross References

Commercial cannabis activity, license required, exemption for cultivation in accordance with this section, see Business and Professions Code § 26037.5.

Enactment of administrative fines and penalties, maximum amounts, illegal cannabis cultivation, procedure, review and appeal, see Government Code § 53069.4.

Engaging in commercial cannabis activity without a license, aiding and abetting unlicensed commercial cannabis activity, civil penalties, see Business and Professions Code § 26038.

Research References

California Jury Instructions - Criminal 12.20, Marijuana—Concentrated Cannabis—Unlawful Possession as Felony/Misdemeanor.

California Jury Instructions - Criminal 12.21, Marijuana—Unlawful Possession for Sale.

California Jury Instructions - Criminal 12.22, Marijuana—Unlawful Sale, etc.

California Jury Instructions - Criminal 12.22.5, Marijuana—Unlawfully Gives Away or Transports More Than 28.5 Grams.

California Jury Instructions - Criminal 12.23, Marijuana—Unlawful Offer to Sell, etc.

California Jury Instructions - Criminal 12.24, Marijuana—Unlawful Planting, etc.

California Jury Instructions - Criminal 12.24.3, Lawful Uses.

2 Witkin, California Criminal Law 4th Crimes Against Public Peace and Welfare § 91A (2021), (New) Permitted Activities.

2 Witkin, California Criminal Law 4th Crimes Against Public Peace and Welfare § 91B (2021), (New) Restricted and Prohibited Activities.

2 Witkin, California Criminal Law 4th Crimes Against Public Peace and Welfare § 91C (2021), (New) Effect on Other Laws.

4 Witkin, California Criminal Law 4th Illegally Obtained Evidence § 266 (2021), In General.

§ 11362.2. Personal cultivation of cannabis

(a) Personal cultivation of cannabis under paragraph (3) of subdivision (a) of Section 11362.1 is subject to the following restrictions:

(1) A person shall plant, cultivate, harvest, dry, or process plants in accordance with local ordinances, if any, adopted in accordance with subdivision (b).

(2) The living plants and any cannabis produced by the plants in excess of 28.5 grams are kept within the person's private residence, or upon the grounds of that private residence (e.g., in an outdoor garden area), are in a locked space, and are not visible by normal unaided vision from a public place.

(3) Not more than six living plants may be planted, cultivated, harvested, dried, or processed within a single private residence, or upon the grounds of that private residence, at one time.

(b)(1) A city, county, or city and county may enact and enforce reasonable regulations to regulate the actions and conduct in paragraph (3) of subdivision (a) of Section 11362.1.

(2) Notwithstanding paragraph (1), a city, county, or city and county shall not completely prohibit persons engaging in the actions and conduct under paragraph (3) of subdivision (a) of Section 11362.1 inside a private residence, or inside an accessory structure to a private residence located upon the grounds of a private residence that is fully enclosed and secure.

(3) Notwithstanding paragraph (3) of subdivision (a) of Section 11362.1, a city, county, or city and county may completely prohibit persons from engaging in actions and conduct under paragraph (3) of subdivision (a) of Section 11362.1 outdoors upon the grounds of a private residence.

(4) Paragraph (3) shall become inoperative upon a determination by the California Attorney General that adult use of cannabis is lawful in the State of California under federal law, and an act taken by a city, county, or city and county under paragraph (3) is unenforceable upon the date of that determination by the Attorney General.

(5) For purposes of this section, "private residence" means a house, an apartment unit, a mobile home, or other similar dwelling. *(Added by Initiative Measure (Prop. 64, § 4.5, approved Nov. 8, 2016, eff. Nov. 9, 2016). Amended by Stats.2017, c. 27 (S.B.94), § 130, eff. June 27, 2017.)*

Research References

2 Witkin, California Criminal Law 4th Crimes Against Public Peace and Welfare § 91B (2021), (New) Restricted and Prohibited Activities.

§ 11362.3. Prohibited smoking, ingesting, possession or manufacture of cannabis

(a) Section 11362.1 does not permit any person to:

(1) Smoke or ingest cannabis or cannabis products in a public place, except in accordance with Section 26200 of the Business and Professions Code.

(2) Smoke cannabis or cannabis products in a location where smoking tobacco is prohibited.

(3) Smoke cannabis or cannabis products within 1,000 feet of a school, day care center, or youth center while children are present at the school, day care center, or youth center, except in or upon the grounds of a private residence or in accordance with Section 26200 of the Business and Professions Code and only if such smoking is not detectable by others on the grounds of the school, day care center, or youth center while children are present.

(4) Possess an open container or open package of cannabis or cannabis products while driving, operating, or riding in the passenger seat or compartment of a motor vehicle, boat, vessel, aircraft, or other vehicle used for transportation.

(5) Possess, smoke, or ingest cannabis or cannabis products in or upon the grounds of a school, day care center, or youth center while children are present.

(6) Manufacture concentrated cannabis using a volatile solvent, unless done in accordance with a license under Division 10 (commencing with Section 26000) of the Business and Professions Code.

(7) Smoke or ingest cannabis or cannabis products while driving, operating a motor vehicle, boat, vessel, aircraft, or other vehicle used for transportation.

(8) Smoke or ingest cannabis or cannabis products while riding in the passenger seat or compartment of a motor vehicle, boat, vessel, aircraft, or other vehicle used for transportation except as permitted on a motor vehicle, boat, vessel, aircraft, or other vehicle used for transportation that is operated in accordance with Section 26200 of the Business and Professions Code and while no persons under 21 years of age are present.

(b) For purposes of this section, the following definitions apply:

(1) "Day care center" has the same meaning as in Section 1596.76.

(2) "Smoke" means to inhale, exhale, burn, or carry any lighted or heated device or pipe, or any other lighted or heated cannabis or cannabis product intended for inhalation, whether natural or synthetic, in any manner or in any form. "Smoke" includes the use of an electronic smoking device that creates an aerosol or vapor, in any manner or in any form, or the use of any oral smoking device for the purpose of circumventing the prohibition of smoking in a place.

(3) "Volatile solvent" means a solvent that is or produces a flammable gas or vapor that, when present in the air in sufficient quantities, will create explosive or ignitable mixtures.

(4) "Youth center" has the same meaning as in Section 11353.1.

(c) Nothing in this section shall be construed or interpreted to amend, repeal, affect, restrict, or preempt laws pertaining to the Compassionate Use Act of 1996. *(Added by Initiative Measure (Prop. 64, § 4.6, approved Nov. 8, 2016, eff. Nov. 9, 2016). Amended by Stats.2017, c. 27 (S.B.94), § 131, eff. June 27, 2017.)*

Research References

2 Witkin, California Criminal Law 4th Crimes Against Public Peace and Welfare § 91B (2021), (New) Restricted and Prohibited Activities.

2 Witkin, California Criminal Law 4th Crimes Against Public Peace and Welfare § 91C (2021), (New) Effect on Other Laws.

2 Witkin, California Criminal Law 4th Crimes Against Public Peace and Welfare § 369D (2021), (New) Local Regulation Permitted.

§ 11362.4. Penalties for violations; drug education program

(a) A person who engages in the conduct described in paragraph (1) of subdivision (a) of Section 11362.3 is guilty of an infraction punishable by no more than a one-hundred-dollar ($100) fine; provided, however, that persons under 18 years of age shall instead be required to complete four hours of a drug education program or counseling, and up to 10 hours of community service, over a period not to exceed 60 days once the drug education program or counseling and community service opportunity are made available to the person.

(b) A person who engages in the conduct described in paragraph (2), (3), or (4) of subdivision (a) of Section 11362.3 is guilty of an infraction punishable by no more than a two-hundred-fifty-dollar ($250) fine, unless that activity is otherwise permitted by state and local law; provided, however, that a person under 18 years of age shall instead be required to complete four hours of drug education or counseling, and up to 20 hours of community service, over a period not to exceed 90 days once the drug education program or counseling and community service opportunity are made available to the person.

(c) A person who engages in the conduct described in paragraph (5) of subdivision (a) of Section 11362.3 is subject to the same punishment as provided under subdivision (c) or (d) of Section 11357.

(d) A person who engages in the conduct described in paragraph (6) of subdivision (a) of Section 11362.3 is subject to punishment under Section 11379.6.

(e) A person who violates the restrictions in subdivision (a) of Section 11362.2 is guilty of an infraction punishable by no more than a two-hundred-fifty-dollar ($250) fine.

(f) Notwithstanding subdivision (e), a person under 18 years of age who violates the restrictions in subdivision (a) of Section 11362.2 shall be punished under paragraph (1) of subdivision (b) of Section 11357.

(g)(1) The drug education program or counseling hours required by this section shall be mandatory unless the court makes a finding that the program or counseling is unnecessary for the person or that a drug education program or counseling is unavailable.

(2) The drug education program required by this section for persons under 18 years of age shall be free to participants and

provide at least four hours of group discussion or instruction based on science and evidence-based principles and practices specific to the use and abuse of cannabis and other controlled substances.

(h) Upon a finding of good cause, the court may extend the time for a person to complete the drug education or counseling, and community service required under this section. *(Added by Initiative Measure (Prop. 64, § 4.7, approved Nov. 8, 2016, eff. Nov. 9, 2016). Amended by Stats.2017, c. 27 (S.B.94), § 132, eff. June 27, 2017; Stats.2018, c. 92 (S.B.1289), § 141, eff. Jan. 1, 2019.)*

Research References

2 Witkin, California Criminal Law 4th Crimes Against Public Peace and Welfare § 91B (2021), (New) Restricted and Prohibited Activities.

§ 11362.45. Effect of Section 11362.1 on other laws

Section 11362.1 does not amend, repeal, affect, restrict, or preempt:

(a) Laws making it unlawful to drive or operate a vehicle, boat, vessel, or aircraft, while smoking, ingesting, or impaired by, cannabis or cannabis products, including, but not limited to, subdivision (e) of Section 23152 of the Vehicle Code, or the penalties prescribed for violating those laws.

(b) Laws prohibiting the sale, administering, furnishing, or giving away of cannabis, cannabis products, or cannabis accessories, or the offering to sell, administer, furnish, or give away cannabis, cannabis products, or cannabis accessories to a person younger than 21 years of age.

(c) Laws prohibiting a person younger than 21 years of age from engaging in any of the actions or conduct otherwise permitted under Section 11362.1.

(d) Laws pertaining to smoking or ingesting cannabis or cannabis products on the grounds of, or within, any facility or institution under the jurisdiction of the Department of Corrections and Rehabilitation or the Division of Juvenile Justice, or on the grounds of, or within, any other facility or institution referenced in Section 4573 of the Penal Code.

(e) Laws providing that it would constitute negligence or professional malpractice to undertake any task while impaired from smoking or ingesting cannabis or cannabis products.

(f) The rights and obligations of public and private employers to maintain a drug and alcohol free workplace or require an employer to permit or accommodate the use, consumption, possession, transfer, display, transportation, sale, or growth of cannabis in the workplace, or affect the ability of employers to have policies prohibiting the use of cannabis by employees and prospective employees, or prevent employers from complying with state or federal law.

(g) The ability of a state or local government agency to prohibit or restrict any of the actions or conduct otherwise permitted under Section 11362.1 within a building owned, leased, or occupied by the state or local government agency.

(h) The ability of an individual or private entity to prohibit or restrict any of the actions or conduct otherwise permitted under Section 11362.1 on the individual's or entity's privately owned property.

(i) Laws pertaining to the Compassionate Use Act of 1996. *(Added by Initiative Measure (Prop. 64, § 4.8, approved Nov. 8, 2016, eff. Nov. 9, 2016). Amended by Stats.2017, c. 27 (S.B.94), § 133, eff. June 27, 2017.)*

Cross References

Engaging in commercial cannabis activity without a license, aiding and abetting unlicensed commercial cannabis activity, civil penalties, see Business and Professions Code § 26038.

Research References

2 Witkin, California Criminal Law 4th Crimes Against Public Peace and Welfare § 91C (2021), (New) Effect on Other Laws.

§ 11362.5. Medical use

(a) This section shall be known and may be cited as the Compassionate Use Act of 1996.

(b)(1) The people of the State of California hereby find and declare that the purposes of the Compassionate Use Act of 1996 are as follows:

(A) To ensure that seriously ill Californians have the right to obtain and use marijuana for medical purposes where that medical use is deemed appropriate and has been recommended by a physician who has determined that the person's health would benefit from the use of marijuana in the treatment of cancer, anorexia, AIDS, chronic pain, spasticity, glaucoma, arthritis, migraine, or any other illness for which marijuana provides relief.

(B) To ensure that patients and their primary caregivers who obtain and use marijuana for medical purposes upon the recommendation of a physician are not subject to criminal prosecution or sanction.

(C) To encourage the federal and state governments to implement a plan to provide for the safe and affordable distribution of marijuana to all patients in medical need of marijuana.

(2) Nothing in this section shall be construed to supersede legislation prohibiting persons from engaging in conduct that endangers others, nor to condone the diversion of marijuana for nonmedical purposes.

(c) Notwithstanding any other provision of law, no physician in this state shall be punished, or denied any right or privilege, for having recommended marijuana to a patient for medical purposes.

(d) Section 11357, relating to the possession of marijuana, and Section 11358, relating to the cultivation of marijuana, shall not apply to a patient, or to a patient's primary caregiver, who possesses or cultivates marijuana for the personal medical purposes of the patient upon the written or oral recommendation or approval of a physician.

(e) For the purposes of this section, "primary caregiver" means the individual designated by the person exempted under this section who has consistently assumed responsibility for the housing, health, or safety of that person. *(Added by Initiative Measure (Prop. 215, § 1, approved Nov. 5, 1996).)*

Cross References

Cannabis defined for purposes of this Division, see Health and Safety Code § 11018.
Commercial cannabis activity, license required, exemption for cultivation in accordance with this section, see Business and Professions Code § 26037.5.
Compassionate Access to Medical Cannabis Act or Ryan's Law, legislative intent, see Health and Safety Code § 1649.
Compassionate Access to Medical Cannabis Act or Ryan's Law, medical cannabis recommendation not required, see Health and Safety Code § 1649.4.
Person defined for purposes of this Division, see Health and Safety Code § 11022.
Physician, dentist, podiatrist, pharmacist, veterinarian, and optometrist defined for purposes of this Division, see Health and Safety Code § 11024.

Research References

California Jury Instructions - Criminal 3412, Compassionate Use.
2 Witkin, California Criminal Law 4th Crimes Against Public Peace and Welfare § 98 (2021), Marijuana.
2 Witkin, California Criminal Law 4th Crimes Against Public Peace and Welfare § 114 (2021), Defenses.
2 Witkin, California Criminal Law 4th Crimes Against Public Peace and Welfare § 131 (2021), Cultivating, Harvesting, or Processing.
2 Witkin, California Criminal Law 4th Crimes Against Public Peace and Welfare § 136 (2021), Adoption of Compassionate Use Act.

2 Witkin, California Criminal Law 4th Crimes Against Public Peace and Welfare § 137 (2021), Right of Physician to Recommend Marijuana.
2 Witkin, California Criminal Law 4th Crimes Against Public Peace and Welfare § 138 (2021), Statutory Authorization.
2 Witkin, California Criminal Law 4th Crimes Against Public Peace and Welfare § 139 (2021), Recommendation or Approval.
2 Witkin, California Criminal Law 4th Crimes Against Public Peace and Welfare § 140 (2021), Quantity Allowed.
2 Witkin, California Criminal Law 4th Crimes Against Public Peace and Welfare § 142 (2021), Primary Caregiver.
2 Witkin, California Criminal Law 4th Crimes Against Public Peace and Welfare § 143 (2021), No Right to Grow Marijuana for Cooperative.
2 Witkin, California Criminal Law 4th Crimes Against Public Peace and Welfare § 144 (2021), Return of Confiscated Marijuana.
2 Witkin, California Criminal Law 4th Crimes Against Public Peace and Welfare § 145 (2021), Other Laws Not Affected.
2 Witkin, California Criminal Law 4th Crimes Against Public Peace and Welfare § 147 (2021), Purpose and Validity of Program.
1 Witkin California Criminal Law 4th Elements § 81 (2021), In General.
4 Witkin, California Criminal Law 4th Illegally Obtained Evidence § 266 (2021), In General.
1 Witkin California Criminal Law 4th Introduction to Crimes § 45 (2021), Particular Terms.
1 Witkin California Criminal Law 4th Introduction to Crimes § 51 (2021), Elimination of Criminal Sanctions.

§ 11362.9. California Cannabis Research Program; legislative intent; creation; research proposals; establishment; powers and duties; Scientific Advisory Council

(a)(1) It is the intent of the Legislature that the state commission objective scientific research by the premier research institute of the world, the University of California, regarding the efficacy and safety of administering cannabis, its naturally occurring constituents, and synthetic compounds, as part of medical treatment. If the Regents of the University of California, by appropriate resolution, accept this responsibility, the University of California shall create a program, to be known as the California Cannabis Research Program, hosted by the Center for Medicinal Cannabis Research. Whenever "California Marijuana Research Program" appears in any statute, regulation, or contract, or in any other code, it shall be construed to refer to the California Cannabis Research Program.

(2) The program shall develop and conduct studies intended to ascertain the general medical safety and efficacy of cannabis and, if found valuable, shall develop medical guidelines for the appropriate administration and use of cannabis. The studies may examine the effect of cannabis on motor skills, the health and safety effects of cannabis, cannabinoids, and other related constituents, and other behavioral and health outcomes.

(b) The program may immediately solicit proposals for research projects to be included in the cannabis studies. Program requirements to be used when evaluating responses to its solicitation for proposals shall include, but not be limited to, all of the following:

(1) Proposals shall demonstrate the use of key personnel, including clinicians or scientists and support personnel, who are prepared to develop a program of research regarding the general medical efficacy and safety of cannabis.

(2) Proposals shall contain procedures for outreach to patients with various medical conditions who may be suitable participants in research on cannabis.

(3) Proposals shall contain provisions for a patient registry.

(4) Proposals shall contain provisions for an information system that is designed to record information about possible study participants, investigators, and clinicians, and deposit and analyze data that accrues as part of clinical trials.

(5) Proposals shall contain protocols suitable for research on cannabis, addressing patients diagnosed with acquired immunodeficiency syndrome (AIDS) or human immunodeficiency virus (HIV), cancer, glaucoma, or seizures or muscle spasms associated with a chronic, debilitating condition. The proposal may also include research on other serious illnesses, provided that resources are available and medical information justifies the research.

(6) Proposals shall demonstrate the use of a specimen laboratory capable of housing plasma, urine, and other specimens necessary to study the concentration of cannabinoids in various tissues, as well as housing specimens for studies of toxic effects of cannabis.

(7) Proposals shall demonstrate the use of a laboratory capable of analyzing cannabis, provided to the program under this section, for purity and cannabinoid content and the capacity to detect contaminants.

(c) In order to ensure objectivity in evaluating proposals, the program shall use a peer review process that is modeled on the process used by the National Institutes of Health, and that guards against funding research that is biased in favor of or against particular outcomes. Peer reviewers shall be selected for their expertise in the scientific substance and methods of the proposed research, and their lack of bias or conflict of interest regarding the applicants or the topic of an approach taken in the proposed research. Peer reviewers shall judge research proposals on several criteria, foremost among which shall be both of the following:

(1) The scientific merit of the research plan, including whether the research design and experimental procedures are potentially biased for or against a particular outcome.

(2) Researchers' expertise in the scientific substance and methods of the proposed research, and their lack of bias or conflict of interest regarding the topic of, and the approach taken in, the proposed research.

(d) If the program is administered by the Regents of the University of California, any grant research proposals approved by the program shall also require review and approval by the research advisory panel.

(e) It is the intent of the Legislature that the program be established as follows:

(1) The program shall be located at one or more University of California campuses that have a core of faculty experienced in organizing multidisciplinary scientific endeavors and, in particular, strong experience in clinical trials involving psychopharmacologic agents. The campuses at which research under the auspices of the program is to take place shall accommodate the administrative offices, including the director of the program, as well as a data management unit, and facilities for detection and analysis of various naturally occurring and synthetic cannabinoids, as well as storage of specimens.

(2) When awarding grants under this section, the program shall utilize principles and parameters of the other well-tested statewide research programs administered by the University of California, modeled after programs administered by the National Institutes of Health, including peer review evaluation of the scientific merit of applications.

(3) The scientific and clinical operations of the program shall occur partly at University of California campuses and partly at other postsecondary institutions that have clinicians or scientists with expertise to conduct the required studies. Criteria for selection of research locations shall include the elements listed in subdivision (b) and, additionally, shall give particular weight to the organizational plan, leadership qualities of the program director, and plans to involve investigators and patient populations from multiple sites.

(4) The funds received by the program shall be allocated to various research studies in accordance with a scientific plan developed by the Scientific Advisory Council. As the first wave of studies is completed, it is anticipated that the program will receive requests for funding of additional studies. These requests shall be reviewed by the Scientific Advisory Council.

(5) The size, scope, and number of studies funded shall be commensurate with the amount of appropriated and available program funding.

(f) All personnel involved in implementing approved proposals shall be authorized as required by Section 11604.

(g) Studies conducted pursuant to this section shall include the greatest amount of new scientific research possible on the medical uses of, and medical hazards associated with, cannabis. The program shall consult with the Research Advisory Panel analogous agencies in other states, and appropriate federal agencies in an attempt to avoid duplicative research and the wasting of research dollars.

(h) The program shall make every effort to recruit qualified patients and qualified physicians from throughout the state.

(i) The cannabis studies shall employ state-of-the-art research methodologies.

(j) The program shall ensure that all cannabis used in the studies is of the appropriate medicinal quality. Cannabis used by the program may be obtained from the National Institute on Drug Abuse or any other entity authorized by the appropriate federal agencies, the Attorney General pursuant to Section 11478, or may be cultivated by the program pursuant to applicable federal and state laws and regulations.

(k) The program may review, approve, or incorporate studies and research by independent groups presenting scientifically valid protocols for medical research, regardless of whether the areas of study are being researched by the committee.

(*l*)(1) To enhance understanding of the efficacy and adverse effects of cannabis as a pharmacological agent, the program shall conduct focused controlled clinical trials on the usefulness of cannabis in patients diagnosed with AIDS or HIV, cancer, glaucoma, or seizures or muscle spasms associated with a chronic, debilitating condition. The program may add research on other serious illnesses, provided that resources are available and medical information justifies the research. The studies shall focus on comparisons of both the efficacy and safety of methods of administering the drug to patients, including inhalational, tinctural, and oral, evaluate possible uses of cannabis as a primary or adjunctive treatment, and develop further information on optimal dosage, timing, mode of administration, and variations in the effects of different cannabinoids and varieties of cannabis or synthetic compounds that simulate the effects of naturally occurring cannabinoids. The studies may also focus on examining testing methods for detecting harmful contaminants in cannabis, including, but not limited to, mold, bacteria, and mycotoxins that could cause harm to patients.

(2) The program shall examine the safety of cannabis in patients with various medical disorders, including the interaction of cannabis with other drugs, relative safety of inhalation versus oral forms, and the effects on mental function in medically ill persons.

(3) The program shall be limited to providing for objective scientific research to ascertain the efficacy and safety of cannabis as part of medical treatment, and should not be construed as encouraging or sanctioning the social or recreational use of cannabis.

(m)(1) Subject to paragraph (2), the program shall, prior to approving proposals, seek to obtain research protocol guidelines from the National Institutes of Health and shall, if the National Institutes of Health issues research protocol guidelines, comply with those guidelines.

(2) If, after a reasonable period of time of not less than six months and not more than a year has elapsed from the date the program seeks to obtain guidelines pursuant to paragraph (1), no guidelines have been approved, the program may proceed using the research protocol guidelines it develops.

(n) In order to maximize the scope and size of the cannabis studies, the program may do any of the following:

(1) Solicit, apply for, and accept funds from foundations, private individuals, and all other funding sources that can be used to expand the scope or timeframe of the cannabis studies that are authorized under this section. The program shall not expend more than 5 percent of its General Fund allocation in efforts to obtain money from outside sources.

(2) Include within the scope of the cannabis studies other cannabis research projects that are independently funded and that meet the requirements set forth in subdivisions (a) to (c), inclusive. In no case shall the program accept funds that are offered with any conditions other than that the funds be used to study the efficacy and safety of cannabis as part of medical treatment.

(*o*)(1) Within six months of the effective date of this section, the program shall report to the Legislature, the Governor, and the Attorney General on the progress of the cannabis studies.

(2) Thereafter, the program shall issue a report to the Legislature every 24 months detailing the progress of the studies. The interim reports required under this paragraph shall include, but not be limited to, data on all of the following:

(A) The names and number of diseases or conditions under study.

(B) The number of patients enrolled in each study, by disease.

(C) Any scientifically valid preliminary findings.

(p) If the Regents of the University of California implement this section, the President of the University of California, or the president's designee, shall appoint a multidisciplinary Scientific Advisory Council, not to exceed 15 members, to provide policy guidance in the creation and implementation of the program. Members shall be chosen on the basis of scientific expertise. Members of the council shall serve on a voluntary basis, with reimbursement for expenses incurred in the course of their participation. The members shall be reimbursed for travel and other necessary expenses incurred in their performance of the duties of the council.

(q) No more than 10 percent of the total funds appropriated may be used for all aspects of the administration of this section.

(r) This section shall be implemented only to the extent that funding for its purposes is appropriated by the Legislature.

(s) Money appropriated to the program pursuant to subdivision (e) of Section 34019 of the Revenue and Taxation Code shall only be used as authorized by the Control, Regulate and Tax Adult Use of Marijuana Act (AUMA).

(t) This section does not limit or preclude cannabis-related research activities at any campus of the University of California. *(Added by Stats.1999, c. 750 (S.B.847), § 3. Amended by Stats.2001, c. 854 (S.B.205), § 7; Stats.2003, c. 704 (S.B.295), § 1; Stats.2016, c. 828 (A.B.2679), § 3, eff. Jan. 1, 2017; Stats.2017, c. 27 (S.B.94), § 150, eff. June 27, 2017; Stats.2019, c. 802 (A.B.420), § 1, eff. Oct. 12, 2019.)*

Cross References

Agent defined for purposes of this Division, see Health and Safety Code § 11003.

Attorney General, generally, see Government Code § 12500 et seq.

Attorney General defined for purposes of this Division, see Health and Safety Code § 11004.

Cannabis, required study of impact of cannabis on motor skills, see Business and Professions Code § 26190.5.

Cannabis defined for purposes of this Division, see Health and Safety Code § 11018.

Drug defined for purposes of this Division, see Health and Safety Code § 11014.

Person defined for purposes of this Division, see Health and Safety Code § 11022.

Physician, dentist, podiatrist, pharmacist, veterinarian, and optometrist defined for purposes of this Division, see Health and Safety Code § 11024.

Qualified patient defined for purposes of this Article, see Health and Safety Code § 11362.7.

ARTICLE 2.5. MEDICAL MARIJUANA PROGRAM

§ 11362.7. Definitions

For purposes of this article, the following definitions shall apply:

(a) "Attending physician" means an individual who possesses a license in good standing to practice medicine, podiatry, or osteopathy issued by the Medical Board of California, the California Board of Podiatric Medicine, or the Osteopathic Medical Board of California and who has taken responsibility for an aspect of the medical care, treatment, diagnosis, counseling, or referral of a patient and who has conducted a medical examination of that patient before recording in the patient's medical record the physician's assessment of whether the patient has a serious medical condition and whether the medical use of cannabis is appropriate.

(b) "Department" means the State Department of Public Health.

(c) "Person with an identification card" means an individual who is a qualified patient who has applied for and received a valid identification card pursuant to this article.

(d) "Primary caregiver" means the individual, designated by a qualified patient, who has consistently assumed responsibility for the housing, health, or safety of that patient, and may include any of the following:

(1) In a case in which a qualified patient or person with an identification card receives medical care or supportive services, or both, from a clinic licensed pursuant to Chapter 1 (commencing with Section 1200) of Division 2, a health care facility licensed pursuant to Chapter 2 (commencing with Section 1250) of Division 2, a residential care facility for persons with chronic life-threatening illness licensed pursuant to Chapter 3.01 (commencing with Section 1568.01) of Division 2, a residential care facility for the elderly licensed pursuant to Chapter 3.2 (commencing with Section 1569) of Division 2, a hospice, or a home health agency licensed pursuant to Chapter 8 (commencing with Section 1725) of Division 2, the owner or operator, or no more than three employees who are designated by the owner or operator, of the clinic, facility, hospice, or home health agency, if designated as a primary caregiver by that qualified patient or person with an identification card.

(2) An individual who has been designated as a primary caregiver by more than one qualified patient or person with an identification card, if every qualified patient or person with an identification card who has designated that individual as a primary caregiver resides in the same city or county as the primary caregiver.

(3) An individual who has been designated as a primary caregiver by a qualified patient or person with an identification card who resides in a city or county other than that of the primary caregiver, if the individual has not been designated as a primary caregiver by any other qualified patient or person with an identification card.

(e) A primary caregiver shall be at least 18 years of age, unless the primary caregiver is the parent of a minor child who is a qualified patient or a person with an identification card or the primary caregiver is a person otherwise entitled to make medical decisions under state law pursuant to Section 6922, 7002, 7050, or 7120 of the Family Code.

(f) "Qualified patient" means a person who is entitled to the protections of Section 11362.5, but who does not have an identification card issued pursuant to this article.

(g) "Identification card" means a document issued by the department that identifies a person authorized to engage in the medical use of cannabis and the person's designated primary caregiver, if any.

(h) "Serious medical condition" means all of the following medical conditions:

(1) Acquired immune deficiency syndrome (AIDS).

(2) Anorexia.

(3) Arthritis.

(4) Cachexia.

(5) Cancer.

(6) Chronic pain.

(7) Glaucoma.

(8) Migraine.

(9) Persistent muscle spasms, including, but not limited to, spasms associated with multiple sclerosis.

(10) Seizures, including, but not limited to, seizures associated with epilepsy.

(11) Severe nausea.

(12) Any other chronic or persistent medical symptom that either:

(A) Substantially limits the ability of the person to conduct one or more major life activities as defined in the federal Americans with Disabilities Act of 1990 (Public Law 101–336).[1]

(B) If not alleviated, may cause serious harm to the patient's safety or physical or mental health.

(i) "Written documentation" means accurate reproductions of those portions of a patient's medical records that have been created by the attending physician, that contain the information required by paragraph (2) of subdivision (a) of Section 11362.715, and that the patient may submit as part of an application for an identification card. *(Added by Stats.2003, c. 875 (S.B.420), § 2. Amended by Stats.2017, c. 27 (S.B.94), § 134, eff. June 27, 2017; Stats.2017, c. 775 (S.B.798), § 112, eff. Jan. 1, 2018.)*

1 For public law sections classified to the U.S.C.A., see USCA–Tables.

Cross References

Cannabis defined for purposes of this Division, see Health and Safety Code § 11018.
Department of Health Care Services, generally, see Health and Safety Code § 100100 et seq.
Determination of medically significant cannabis use, see Business and Professions Code § 2228.5.
Health care facilities, duties regarding permitted use of medical cannabis, see Health and Safety Code § 1649.2.
Medical marijuana use by recipient of anatomical gift, discrimination prohibited, see Health and Safety Code § 7151.36.
Person defined for purposes of this Division, see Health and Safety Code § 11022.
Physician, dentist, podiatrist, pharmacist, veterinarian, and optometrist defined for purposes of this Division, see Health and Safety Code § 11024.

Research References

2 Witkin, California Criminal Law 4th Crimes Against Public Peace and Welfare § 126 (2021), Marijuana.
2 Witkin, California Criminal Law 4th Crimes Against Public Peace and Welfare § 137 (2021), Right of Physician to Recommend Marijuana.
2 Witkin, California Criminal Law 4th Crimes Against Public Peace and Welfare § 147 (2021), Purpose and Validity of Program.
2 Witkin, California Criminal Law 4th Crimes Against Public Peace and Welfare § 148 (2021), Identification Cards.
2 Witkin, California Criminal Law 4th Crimes Against Public Peace and Welfare § 149 (2021), Protection from Criminal Liability.
2 Witkin, California Criminal Law 4th Crimes Against Public Peace and Welfare § 150 (2021), Limits on Protection from Criminal Liability.
2 Witkin, California Criminal Law 4th Crimes Against Public Peace and Welfare § 151 (2021), Fraudulent Use of Card.
2 Witkin, California Criminal Law 4th Crimes Against Public Peace and Welfare § 303 (2021), Drinking or Possessing Alcohol or Marijuana.
2 Witkin, California Criminal Law 4th Crimes Against Public Peace and Welfare § 369B (2021), (New) Licensing.
4 Witkin, California Criminal Law 4th Illegally Obtained Evidence § 266 (2021), In General.
1 Witkin California Criminal Law 4th Introduction to Crimes § 81 (2021), Valid State Statutes.

§ 11362.71. Establishment and maintenance of voluntary program for issuance of identification cards to qualified patients; access to necessary information; duties of county health departments; arrests for possession, transportation, delivery or cultivation

For Executive Order N–80–20 (2019 CA EO 80-20), which authorizes local governments to further halt commercial renter evictions, among other COVID-19-related provisions, see Historical and Statutory Notes under Corporations Code § 20.

For Executive Order N–01–21 (2021 CA EO 1-21), which withdraws and supersedes certain portions of Executive Order N–80–20, relating to identification cards for the medical use of cannabis, due to the COVID-19 pandemic, see Historical and Statutory Notes under Health and Safety Code § 11362.745.

(a)(1) The department shall establish and maintain a voluntary program for the issuance of identification cards to qualified patients who satisfy the requirements of this article and voluntarily apply to the identification card program.

(2) The department shall establish and maintain a 24–hour, toll-free telephone number that will enable state and local law enforcement officers to have immediate access to information necessary to verify the validity of an identification card issued by the department, until a cost-effective Internet Web-based system can be developed for this purpose.

(b) Every county health department, or the county's designee, shall do all of the following:

(1) Provide applications upon request to individuals seeking to join the identification card program.

(2) Receive and process completed applications in accordance with Section 11362.72.

(3) Maintain records of identification card programs.

(4) Utilize protocols developed by the department pursuant to paragraph (1) of subdivision (d).

(5) Issue identification cards developed by the department to approved applicants and designated primary caregivers.

(c) The county board of supervisors may designate another health-related governmental or nongovernmental entity or organization to perform the functions described in subdivision (b), except for an entity or organization that cultivates or distributes cannabis.

(d) The department shall develop all of the following:

(1) Protocols that shall be used by a county health department or the county's designee to implement the responsibilities described in subdivision (b), including, but not limited to, protocols to confirm the accuracy of information contained in an application and to protect the confidentiality of program records.

(2) Application forms that shall be issued to requesting applicants.

(3) An identification card that identifies a person authorized to engage in the medical use of cannabis and an identification card that identifies the person's designated primary caregiver, if any. The two identification cards developed pursuant to this paragraph shall be easily distinguishable from each other.

(e) No person or designated primary caregiver in possession of a valid identification card shall be subject to arrest for possession, transportation, delivery, or cultivation of medicinal cannabis in an amount established pursuant to this article, unless there is probable cause to believe that the information contained in the card is false or falsified, the card has been obtained by means of fraud, or the person is otherwise in violation of the provisions of this article.

(f) It shall not be necessary for a person to obtain an identification card in order to claim the protections of Section 11362.5. *(Added by Stats.2003, c. 875 (S.B.420), § 2. Amended by Stats.2017, c. 27 (S.B.94), § 135, eff. June 27, 2017.)*

Cross References

Cannabis defined for purposes of this Division, see Health and Safety Code § 11018.
Deliver or delivery defined for purposes of this Division, see Health and Safety Code § 11009.
Department defined for purposes of this Article, see Health and Safety Code § 11362.7.
Department of Health Care Services, generally, see Health and Safety Code § 100100 et seq.
Distribute defined for purposes of this Division, see Health and Safety Code § 11012.
Exemption from sales and use taxes, medicinal cannabis or medicinal cannabis products, see Revenue and Taxation Code § 6369.6.
Identification card defined for purposes of this Article, see Health and Safety Code § 11362.7.
Person defined for purposes of this Division, see Health and Safety Code § 11022.
Primary caregiver defined for purposes of this Article, see Health and Safety Code § 11362.7.
Qualified patient defined for purposes of this Article, see Health and Safety Code § 11362.7.

Research References

2 Witkin, California Criminal Law 4th Crimes Against Public Peace and Welfare § 147 (2021), Purpose and Validity of Program.
2 Witkin, California Criminal Law 4th Crimes Against Public Peace and Welfare § 149 (2021), Protection from Criminal Liability.

§ 11362.712. Possession of physician's recommendation required

(a) Commencing on January 1, 2018, a qualified patient must possess a physician's recommendation that complies with Article 25 (commencing with Section 2525) of Chapter 5 of Division 2 of the Business and Professions Code. Failure to comply with this requirement shall not, however, affect any of the protections provided to patients or their primary caregivers by Section 11362.5.

(b) A county health department or the county's designee shall develop protocols to ensure that, commencing upon January 1, 2018, all identification cards issued pursuant to Section 11362.71 are supported by a physician's recommendation that complies with Article 25 (commencing with Section 2525) of Chapter 5 of Division 2 of the Business and Professions Code. *(Added by Initiative Measure (Prop. 64, § 5.1, approved Nov. 8, 2016, eff. Nov. 9, 2016).)*

Research References

2 Witkin, California Criminal Law 4th Crimes Against Public Peace and Welfare § 139 (2021), Recommendation or Approval.
2 Witkin, California Criminal Law 4th Crimes Against Public Peace and Welfare § 147 (2021), Purpose and Validity of Program.
2 Witkin, California Criminal Law 4th Crimes Against Public Peace and Welfare § 369C (2021), (New) Consumer Protection and Protection of Minors.

§ 11362.713. Confidential medical information; disclosure

(a) Information identifying the names, addresses, or social security numbers of patients, their medical conditions, or the names of their primary caregivers, received and contained in the records of the State Department of Public Health and by any county public health department are hereby deemed "medical information" within the meaning of the Confidentiality of Medical Information Act (Part 2.6 (commencing with Section 56) of Division 1 of the Civil Code) and shall not be disclosed by the department or by any county public health department except in accordance with the restrictions on disclosure of individually identifiable information under the Confidentiality of Medical Information Act.

(b) Within 24 hours of receiving any request to disclose the name, address, or social security number of a patient, their medical condition, or the name of their primary caregiver, the State Department of Public Health or any county public health agency shall contact the patient and inform the patient of the request and if the request was made in writing, a copy of the request.

(c) Notwithstanding Section 56.10 of the Civil Code, neither the State Department of Public Health, nor any county public health agency, shall disclose, nor shall they be ordered by agency or court to disclose, the names, addresses, or social security numbers of patients, their medical conditions, or the names of their primary caregivers, sooner than the 10th day after which the patient whose records are sought to be disclosed has been contacted.

(d) No identification card application system or database used or maintained by the State Department of Public Health or by any county department of public health or the county's designee as provided in Section 11362.71 shall contain any personal information of any qualified patient, including, but not limited to, the patient's name, address, social security number, medical conditions, or the names of their primary caregivers. Such an application system or database may only contain a unique user identification number, and when that number is entered, the only information that may be provided is whether the card is valid or invalid. *(Added by Initiative Measure (Prop. 64, § 5.2, approved Nov. 8, 2016, eff. Nov. 9, 2016).)*

§ 11362.715. Requirements for issuance of identification cards; legal representatives

(a) A person who seeks an identification card shall pay the fee, as provided in Section 11362.755, and provide all of the following to the county health department or the county's designee on a form developed and provided by the department:

(1) The name of the person and proof of his or her residency within the county.

(2) Written documentation by the attending physician in the person's medical records stating that the person has been diagnosed with a serious medical condition and that the medicinal use of cannabis is appropriate.

(3) The name, office address, office telephone number, and California medical license number of the person's attending physician.

(4) The name and the duties of the primary caregiver.

(5) A government-issued photo identification card of the person and of the designated primary caregiver, if any. If the applicant is a person under 18 years of age, a certified copy of a birth certificate shall be deemed sufficient proof of identity.

(b) If the person applying for an identification card lacks the capacity to make medical decisions, the application may be made by the person's legal representative, including, but not limited to, any of the following:

(1) A conservator with authority to make medical decisions.

(2) An attorney-in-fact under a durable power of attorney for health care or surrogate decisionmaker authorized under another advanced health care directive.

(3) Any other individual authorized by statutory or decisional law to make medical decisions for the person.

(c) The legal representative described in subdivision (b) may also designate in the application an individual, including himself or herself, to serve as a primary caregiver for the person, provided that the individual meets the definition of a primary caregiver.

(d) The person or legal representative submitting the written information and documentation described in subdivision (a) shall retain a copy thereof. *(Added by Stats.2003, c. 875 (S.B.420), § 2. Amended by Stats.2017, c. 27 (S.B.94), § 136, eff. June 27, 2017.)*

Cross References

Attending physician defined for purposes of this Article, see Health and Safety Code § 11362.7.
Cannabis defined for purposes of this Division, see Health and Safety Code § 11018.
Department defined for purposes of this Article, see Health and Safety Code § 11362.7.
Department of Health Care Services, generally, see Health and Safety Code § 100100 et seq.
Health care facilities, duties regarding permitted use of medical cannabis, see Health and Safety Code § 1649.2.
Identification card defined for purposes of this Article, see Health and Safety Code § 11362.7.
Person defined for purposes of this Division, see Health and Safety Code § 11022.
Physician, dentist, podiatrist, pharmacist, veterinarian, and optometrist defined for purposes of this Division, see Health and Safety Code § 11024.
Primary caregiver defined for purposes of this Article, see Health and Safety Code § 11362.7.
Serious medical condition defined for purposes of this Article, see Health and Safety Code § 11362.7.
Written documentation defined for purposes of this Article, see Health and Safety Code § 11362.7.

Research References

2 Witkin, California Criminal Law 4th Crimes Against Public Peace and Welfare § 148 (2021), Identification Cards.

§ 11362.72. Duties of county health department or county's designee after receipt of application for identification card; approval of application; issuance of card

(a) Within 30 days of receipt of an application for an identification card, a county health department or the county's designee shall do all of the following:

(1) For purposes of processing the application, verify that the information contained in the application is accurate. If the person is less than 18 years of age, the county health department or its designee shall also contact the parent with legal authority to make medical decisions, legal guardian, or other person or entity with legal authority to make medical decisions, to verify the information.

(2) Verify with the Medical Board of California or the Osteopathic Medical Board of California that the attending physician has a license in good standing to practice medicine or osteopathy in the state.

(3) Contact the attending physician by facsimile, telephone, or mail to confirm that the medical records submitted by the patient are a true and correct copy of those contained in the physician's office records. When contacted by a county health department or the county's designee, the attending physician shall confirm or deny that the contents of the medical records are accurate.

(4) Take a photograph or otherwise obtain an electronically transmissible image of the applicant and of the designated primary caregiver, if any.

(5) Approve or deny the application. If an applicant who meets the requirements of Section 11362.715 can establish that an identification card is needed on an emergency basis, the county or its designee shall issue a temporary identification card that shall be valid for 30 days from the date of issuance. The county, or its designee, may extend the temporary identification card for no more than 30 days at a time, so long as the applicant continues to meet the requirements of this paragraph.

(b) If the county health department or the county's designee approves the application, it shall, within 24 hours, or by the end of the next working day of approving the application, electronically transmit the following information to the department:

(1) A unique user identification number of the applicant.

(2) The date of expiration of the identification card.

(3) The name and telephone number of the county health department or the county's designee that has approved the application.

(c) The county health department or the county's designee shall issue an identification card to the applicant and to his or her designated primary caregiver, if any, within five working days of approving the application.

(d) In any case involving an incomplete application, the applicant shall assume responsibility for rectifying the deficiency. The county shall have 14 days from the receipt of information from the applicant pursuant to this subdivision to approve or deny the application. *(Added by Stats.2003, c. 875 (S.B.420), § 2.)*

Cross References

Attending physician defined for purposes of this Article, see Health and Safety Code § 11362.7.
Department defined for purposes of this Article, see Health and Safety Code § 11362.7.
Department of Health Care Services, generally, see Health and Safety Code § 100100 et seq.
Identification card defined for purposes of this Article, see Health and Safety Code § 11362.7.
Person defined for purposes of this Division, see Health and Safety Code § 11022.
Physician, dentist, podiatrist, pharmacist, veterinarian, and optometrist defined for purposes of this Division, see Health and Safety Code § 11024.
Primary caregiver defined for purposes of this Article, see Health and Safety Code § 11362.7.

Research References

2 Witkin, California Criminal Law 4th Crimes Against Public Peace and Welfare § 148 (2021), Identification Cards.

§ 11362.735. Serially numbered identification cards; contents; copy given to primary caregiver

(a) An identification card issued by the county health department shall be serially numbered and shall contain all of the following:

(1) A unique user identification number of the cardholder.

(2) The date of expiration of the identification card.

(3) The name and telephone number of the county health department or the county's designee that has approved the application.

(4) A 24–hour, toll-free telephone number, to be maintained by the department, that will enable state and local law enforcement officers to have immediate access to information necessary to verify the validity of the card.

(5) Photo identification of the cardholder.

(b) A separate identification card shall be issued to the person's designated primary caregiver, if any, and shall include a photo identification of the caregiver. *(Added by Stats.2003, c. 875 (S.B. 420), § 2.)*

Cross References

Department defined for purposes of this Article, see Health and Safety Code § 11362.7.
Department of Health Care Services, generally, see Health and Safety Code § 100100 et seq.
Identification card defined for purposes of this Article, see Health and Safety Code § 11362.7.
Person defined for purposes of this Division, see Health and Safety Code § 11022.
Primary caregiver defined for purposes of this Article, see Health and Safety Code § 11362.7.

Research References

2 Witkin, California Criminal Law 4th Crimes Against Public Peace and Welfare § 148 (2021), Identification Cards.

§ 11362.74. Denial of applications; reasons; reapplication after denial; appeals

(a) The county health department or the county's designee may deny an application only for any of the following reasons:

(1) The applicant did not provide the information required by Section 11362.715, and upon notice of the deficiency pursuant to subdivision (d) of Section 11362.72, did not provide the information within 30 days.

(2) The county health department or the county's designee determines that the information provided was false.

(3) The applicant does not meet the criteria set forth in this article.

(b) Any person whose application has been denied pursuant to subdivision (a) may not reapply for six months from the date of denial unless otherwise authorized by the county health department or the county's designee or by a court of competent jurisdiction.

(c) Any person whose application has been denied pursuant to subdivision (a) may appeal that decision to the department. The county health department or the county's designee shall make available a telephone number or address to which the denied applicant can direct an appeal. *(Added by Stats.2003, c. 875 (S.B.420), § 2.)*

Cross References

Department defined for purposes of this Article, see Health and Safety Code § 11362.7.
Department of Health Care Services, generally, see Health and Safety Code § 100100 et seq.
Person defined for purposes of this Division, see Health and Safety Code § 11022.

Research References

2 Witkin, California Criminal Law 4th Crimes Against Public Peace and Welfare § 148 (2021), Identification Cards.

§ 11362.745. Annual renewal of identification cards

For Executive Order N–80–20 (2019 CA EO 80-20), which authorizes local governments to further halt commercial renter evictions, among other COVID-19-related provisions, see Historical and Statutory Notes under Corporations Code § 20.

For Executive Order N–01–21 (2021 CA EO 1-21), which withdraws and supersedes certain portions of Executive Order N–80–20, relating to identification cards for the medical use of cannabis, due to the COVID-19 pandemic, see Historical and Statutory Notes under this section.

(a) An identification card shall be valid for a period of one year.

(b) Upon annual renewal of an identification card, the county health department or its designee shall verify all new information and may verify any other information that has not changed.

(c) The county health department or the county's designee shall transmit its determination of approval or denial of a renewal to the department. *(Added by Stats.2003, c. 875 (S.B.420), § 2.)*

Cross References

Department defined for purposes of this Article, see Health and Safety Code § 11362.7.
Department of Health Care Services, generally, see Health and Safety Code § 100100 et seq.
Identification card defined for purposes of this Article, see Health and Safety Code § 11362.7.

§ 11362.755. Fees; reduced fees for Medi–Cal beneficiaries; waiver; reimbursement for excess administrative costs

(a) Each county health department or the county's designee may charge a fee for all costs incurred by the county or the county's designee for administering the program pursuant to this article.

(b) In no event shall the amount of the fee charged by a county health department exceed one hundred dollars ($100) per application or renewal.

(c) Upon satisfactory proof of participation and eligibility in the Medi–Cal program, a Medi–Cal beneficiary shall receive a 50 percent reduction in the fees established pursuant to this section.

(d) Upon satisfactory proof that a qualified patient, or the legal guardian of a qualified patient under the age of 18, is a medically indigent adult who is eligible for and participates in the County Medical Services Program, the fee established pursuant to this section shall be waived.

(e) In the event the fees charged and collected by a county health department are not sufficient to pay for the administrative costs incurred in discharging the county health department's duties with respect to the mandatory identification card system, the Legislature, upon request by the county health department, shall reimburse the county health department for those reasonable administrative costs in excess of the fees charged and collected by the county health department. *(Added by Stats.2003, c. 875 (S.B.420), § 2. Amended by Initiative Measure (Prop. 64, § 5.3, approved Nov. 8, 2016, eff. Nov. 9, 2016).)*

Cross References

Department defined for purposes of this Article, see Health and Safety Code § 11362.7.
Department of Health Care Services, generally, see Health and Safety Code § 100100 et seq.
Identification card defined for purposes of this Article, see Health and Safety Code § 11362.7.
Medical marijuana program, applications and fees for identification cards, see Health and Safety Code § 11362.715.
Person defined for purposes of this Division, see Health and Safety Code § 11022.

§ 11362.76. Duties and responsibilities of persons to possess identification cards; expiration of card for failure to comply

(a) A person who possesses an identification card shall:

(1) Within seven days, notify the county health department or the county's designee of any change in the person's attending physician or designated primary caregiver, if any.

(2) Annually submit to the county health department or the county's designee the following:

(A) Updated written documentation of the person's serious medical condition.

(B) The name and duties of the person's designated primary caregiver, if any, for the forthcoming year.

(b) If a person who possesses an identification card fails to comply with this section, the card shall be deemed expired. If an identification card expires, the identification card of any designated primary caregiver of the person shall also expire.

(c) If the designated primary caregiver has been changed, the previous primary caregiver shall return his or her identification card to the department or to the county health department or the county's designee.

(d) If the owner or operator or an employee of the owner or operator of a provider has been designated as a primary caregiver pursuant to paragraph (1) of subdivision (d) of Section 11362.7, of the qualified patient or person with an identification card, the owner or operator shall notify the county health department or the county's designee, pursuant to Section 11362.715, if a change in the designated primary caregiver has occurred. *(Added by Stats.2003, c. 875 (S.B.420), § 2.)*

Cross References

Department of Health Care Services, generally, see Health and Safety Code § 100100 et seq.
Person defined for purposes of this Division, see Health and Safety Code § 11022.

Physician, dentist, podiatrist, pharmacist, veterinarian, and optometrist defined for purposes of this Division, see Health and Safety Code § 11024.

§ 11362.765. Criminal liability; application of section; assistance and compensation

(a) Subject to the requirements of this article, the individuals specified in subdivision (b) shall not be subject, on that sole basis, to criminal liability under Section 11357, 11358, 11359, 11360, 11366, 11366.5, or 11570. This section does not authorize the individual to smoke or otherwise consume cannabis unless otherwise authorized by this article, nor shall anything in this section authorize any individual or group to cultivate or distribute cannabis for profit.

(b) Subdivision (a) shall apply to all of the following:

(1) A qualified patient or a person with an identification card who transports or processes cannabis for his or her own personal medical use.

(2) A designated primary caregiver who transports, processes, administers, delivers, or gives away cannabis for medical purposes, in amounts not exceeding those established in subdivision (a) of Section 11362.77, only to the qualified patient of the primary caregiver, or to the person with an identification card who has designated the individual as a primary caregiver.

(3) An individual who provides assistance to a qualified patient or a person with an identification card, or his or her designated primary caregiver, in administering medicinal cannabis to the qualified patient or person or acquiring the skills necessary to cultivate or administer cannabis for medical purposes to the qualified patient or person.

(c) A primary caregiver who receives compensation for actual expenses, including reasonable compensation incurred for services provided to an eligible qualified patient or person with an identification card to enable that person to use cannabis under this article, or for payment for out-of-pocket expenses incurred in providing those services, or both, shall not, on the sole basis of that fact, be subject to prosecution or punishment under Section 11359 or 11360. *(Added by Stats.2003, c. 875 (S.B.420), § 2. Amended by Stats.2017, c. 27 (S.B.94), § 137, eff. June 27, 2017.)*

Cross References

Administer defined for purposes of this Division, see Health and Safety Code § 11002.
Cannabis defined for purposes of this Division, see Health and Safety Code § 11018.
Deliver or delivery defined for purposes of this Division, see Health and Safety Code § 11009.
Distribute defined for purposes of this Division, see Health and Safety Code § 11012.
Identification card defined for purposes of this Article, see Health and Safety Code § 11362.7.
Person defined for purposes of this Division, see Health and Safety Code § 11022.
Person with an identification card defined for purposes of this Article, see Health and Safety Code § 11362.7.
Primary caregiver defined for purposes of this Article, see Health and Safety Code § 11362.7.
Qualified patient defined for purposes of this Article, see Health and Safety Code § 11362.7.

Research References

2 Witkin, California Criminal Law 4th Crimes Against Public Peace and Welfare § 141 (2021), Transportation Distinguished.
2 Witkin, California Criminal Law 4th Crimes Against Public Peace and Welfare § 142 (2021), Primary Caregiver.
2 Witkin, California Criminal Law 4th Crimes Against Public Peace and Welfare § 149 (2021), Protection from Criminal Liability.
2 Witkin, California Criminal Law 4th Crimes Against Public Peace and Welfare § 369B (2021), (New) Licensing.

§ 11362.768. Medicinal cannabis cooperative, collective, dispensary, etc.; proximity to schools restricted; application to specified individuals; exception; storefront or mobile retail outlet requirement; more restrictive local ordinances or policies; preemption

(a) This section shall apply to individuals specified in subdivision (b) of Section 11362.765.

(b) No medicinal cannabis cooperative, collective, dispensary, operator, establishment, or provider who possesses, cultivates, or distributes medicinal cannabis pursuant to this article shall be located within a 600–foot radius of a school.

(c) The distance specified in this section shall be the horizontal distance measured in a straight line from the property line of the school to the closest property line of the lot on which the medicinal cannabis cooperative, collective, dispensary, operator, establishment, or provider is to be located without regard to intervening structures.

(d) This section shall not apply to a medicinal cannabis cooperative, collective, dispensary, operator, establishment, or provider that is also a licensed residential medical or elder care facility.

(e) This section shall apply only to a medicinal cannabis cooperative, collective, dispensary, operator, establishment, or provider that is authorized by law to possess, cultivate, or distribute medicinal cannabis and that has a storefront or mobile retail outlet which ordinarily requires a local business license.

(f) Nothing in this section shall prohibit a city, county, or city and county from adopting ordinances or policies that further restrict the location or establishment of a medicinal cannabis cooperative, collective, dispensary, operator, establishment, or provider.

(g) This section does not preempt local ordinances, adopted prior to January 1, 2011, that regulate the location or establishment of a medicinal cannabis cooperative, collective, dispensary, operator, establishment, or provider.

(h) For the purposes of this section, "school" means any public or private school providing instruction in kindergarten or any of grades 1 to 12, inclusive, but does not include any private school in which education is primarily conducted in private homes. *(Added by Stats.2010, c. 603 (A.B.2650), § 1. Amended by Stats.2017, c. 27 (S.B.94), § 138, eff. June 27, 2017.)*

Research References

2 Witkin, California Criminal Law 4th Crimes Against Public Peace and Welfare § 149 (2021), Protection from Criminal Liability.

§ 11362.769. Cannabis cultivation; environmental impacts; state agency enforcement

Indoor and outdoor medical cannabis cultivation shall be conducted in accordance with state and local laws. State agencies, including, but not limited to, the Department of Food and Agriculture, the State Board of Forestry and Fire Protection, the Department of Fish and Wildlife, the State Water Resources Control Board, the California regional water quality control boards, and traditional state law enforcement agencies shall address environmental impacts of medical cannabis cultivation and shall coordinate, when appropriate, with cities and counties and their law enforcement agencies in enforcement efforts. *(Added by Stats.2015, c. 688 (A.B.243), § 5, eff. Jan. 1, 2016. Amended by Stats.2016, c. 32 (S.B.837), § 66, eff. June 27, 2016.)*

§ 11362.77. Amount qualified patients or caregivers may possess; guidelines

(a) A qualified patient or primary caregiver may possess no more than eight ounces of dried cannabis per qualified patient. In addition, a qualified patient or primary caregiver may also maintain no more than six mature or 12 immature cannabis plants per qualified patient.

(b) If a qualified patient or primary caregiver has a physician's recommendation that this quantity does not meet the qualified patient's medical needs, the qualified patient or primary caregiver may possess an amount of cannabis consistent with the patient's needs.

(c) Counties and cities may retain or enact medicinal cannabis guidelines allowing qualified patients or primary caregivers to exceed the state limits set forth in subdivision (a).

(d) Only the dried mature processed flowers of female cannabis plant or the plant conversion shall be considered when determining allowable quantities of cannabis under this section.

(e) A qualified patient or a person holding a valid identification card, or the designated primary caregiver of that qualified patient or person, may possess amounts of cannabis consistent with this article. *(Added by Stats.2003, c. 875 (S.B.420), § 2. Amended by Stats.2017, c. 27 (S.B.94), § 139, eff. June 27, 2017.)*

Cross References

Attorney General, generally, see Government Code § 12500 et seq.
Attorney General defined for purposes of this Division, see Health and Safety Code § 11004.
Cannabis defined for purposes of this Division, see Health and Safety Code § 11018.
Identification card defined for purposes of this Article, see Health and Safety Code § 11362.7.
Person defined for purposes of this Division, see Health and Safety Code § 11022.
Primary caregiver defined for purposes of this Article, see Health and Safety Code § 11362.7.
Qualified patient defined for purposes of this Article, see Health and Safety Code § 11362.7.

Research References

California Jury Instructions - Criminal 12.24.1, Defense of Compassionate Use.
2 Witkin, California Criminal Law 4th Crimes Against Public Peace and Welfare § 91 (2021), Definition.
2 Witkin, California Criminal Law 4th Crimes Against Public Peace and Welfare § 140 (2021), Quantity Allowed.
2 Witkin, California Criminal Law 4th Crimes Against Public Peace and Welfare § 147 (2021), Purpose and Validity of Program.
2 Witkin, California Criminal Law 4th Crimes Against Public Peace and Welfare § 149 (2021), Protection from Criminal Liability.
2 Witkin, California Criminal Law 4th Crimes Against Public Peace and Welfare § 150 (2021), Limits on Protection from Criminal Liability.

§ 11362.78. Refusal to accept identification card; fraud

A state or local law enforcement agency or officer shall not refuse to accept an identification card issued pursuant to this article unless the state or local law enforcement agency or officer has probable cause to believe that the information contained in the card is false or fraudulent, or the card is being used fraudulently. *(Added by Stats.2003, c. 875 (S.B.420), § 2. Amended by Stats.2017, c. 27 (S.B.94), § 142, eff. June 27, 2017.)*

Cross References

Department defined for purposes of this Article, see Health and Safety Code § 11362.7.
Identification card defined for purposes of this Article, see Health and Safety Code § 11362.7.

§ 11362.785. Accommodation of medicinal use of cannabis at places of employment or penal institutions; permission for prisoners or persons under arrest to apply for identification card; reimbursement for medicinal use of cannabis

(a) Nothing in this article shall require any accommodation of medicinal use of cannabis on the property or premises of a place of employment or during the hours of employment or on the property or premises of a jail, correctional facility, or other type of penal institution in which prisoners reside or persons under arrest are detained.

(b) Notwithstanding subdivision (a), a person shall not be prohibited or prevented from obtaining and submitting the written information and documentation necessary to apply for an identification card on the basis that the person is incarcerated in a jail, correctional facility, or other penal institution in which prisoners reside or persons under arrest are detained.

(c) This article does not prohibit a jail, correctional facility, or other penal institution in which prisoners reside or persons under arrest are detained, from permitting a prisoner or a person under arrest who has an identification card, to use cannabis for medicinal purposes under circumstances that will not endanger the health or safety of other prisoners or the security of the facility.

(d) This article does not require a governmental, private, or any other health insurance provider or health care service plan to be liable for a claim for reimbursement for the medicinal use of cannabis. *(Added by Stats.2003, c. 875 (S.B.420), § 2. Amended by Stats.2017, c. 27 (S.B.94), § 143, eff. June 27, 2017.)*

Cross References

Cannabis defined for purposes of this Division, see Health and Safety Code § 11018.
Identification card defined for purposes of this Article, see Health and Safety Code § 11362.7.
Person defined for purposes of this Division, see Health and Safety Code § 11022.

§ 11362.79. Places where medicinal use of cannabis prohibited

This article does not authorize a qualified patient or person with an identification card to engage in the smoking of medicinal cannabis under any of the following circumstances:

(a) In a place where smoking is prohibited by law.

(b) In or within 1,000 feet of the grounds of a school, recreation center, or youth center, unless the medicinal use occurs within a residence.

(c) On a schoolbus.

(d) While in a motor vehicle that is being operated.

(e) While operating a boat. *(Added by Stats.2003, c. 875 (S.B. 420), § 2. Amended by Stats.2017, c. 27 (S.B.94), § 144, eff. June 27, 2017.)*

Cross References

Cannabis defined for purposes of this Division, see Health and Safety Code § 11018.
Identification card defined for purposes of this Article, see Health and Safety Code § 11362.7.
Person defined for purposes of this Division, see Health and Safety Code § 11022.
Person with an identification card defined for purposes of this Article, see Health and Safety Code § 11362.7.
Qualified patient defined for purposes of this Article, see Health and Safety Code § 11362.7.

Research References

2 Witkin, California Criminal Law 4th Crimes Against Public Peace and Welfare § 150 (2021), Limits on Protection from Criminal Liability.

§ 11362.795. Confirmation by court that criminal defendant is allowed to use medicinal cannabis while on probation, released on bail, or on parole; statement of court's decision and reasons; administrative appeal of decision

(a)(1) Any criminal defendant who is eligible to use cannabis pursuant to Section 11362.5 may request that the court confirm that he or she is allowed to use medicinal cannabis while he or she is on probation or released on bail.

(2) The court's decision and the reasons for the decision shall be stated on the record and an entry stating those reasons shall be made in the minutes of the court.

(3) During the period of probation or release on bail, if a physician recommends that the probationer or defendant use medicinal cannabis, the probationer or defendant may request a modification of the conditions of probation or bail to authorize the use of medicinal cannabis.

(4) The court's consideration of the modification request authorized by this subdivision shall comply with the requirements of this section.

(b)(1) Any person who is to be released on parole from a jail, state prison, school, road camp, or other state or local institution of confinement and who is eligible to use medicinal cannabis pursuant to Section 11362.5 may request that he or she be allowed to use medicinal cannabis during the period he or she is released on parole. A parolee's written conditions of parole shall reflect whether or not a request for a modification of the conditions of his or her parole to use medicinal cannabis was made, and whether the request was granted or denied.

(2) During the period of the parole, where a physician recommends that the parolee use medicinal cannabis, the parolee may request a modification of the conditions of the parole to authorize the use of medicinal cannabis.

(3) Any parolee whose request to use medicinal cannabis while on parole was denied may pursue an administrative appeal of the decision. Any decision on the appeal shall be in writing and shall reflect the reasons for the decision.

(4) The administrative consideration of the modification request authorized by this subdivision shall comply with the requirements of this section. *(Added by Stats.2003, c. 875 (S.B.420), § 2. Amended by Stats.2017, c. 27 (S.B.94), § 145, eff. June 27, 2017.)*

Cross References

Cannabis defined for purposes of this Division, see Health and Safety Code § 11018.
Person defined for purposes of this Division, see Health and Safety Code § 11022.
Physician, dentist, podiatrist, pharmacist, veterinarian, and optometrist defined for purposes of this Division, see Health and Safety Code § 11024.

§ 11362.8. Civil penalty or other disciplinary action against licensee based on role as designated primary caregiver; application of section

A professional licensing board shall not impose a civil penalty or take other disciplinary action against a licensee based solely on the fact that the licensee has performed acts that are necessary or appropriate to carry out the licensee's role as a designated primary caregiver to a person who is a qualified patient or who possesses a lawful identification card issued pursuant to Section 11362.72. However, this section shall not apply to acts performed by a physician relating to the discussion or recommendation of the medical use of cannabis to a patient. These discussions or recommendations, or both, shall be governed by Section 11362.5. *(Added by Stats.2003, c. 875 (S.B.420), § 2. Amended by Stats.2017, c. 27 (S.B.94), § 146, eff. June 27, 2017.)*

Cross References

Cannabis defined for purposes of this Division, see Health and Safety Code § 11018.
Identification card defined for purposes of this Article, see Health and Safety Code § 11362.7.
Person defined for purposes of this Division, see Health and Safety Code § 11022.
Physician, dentist, podiatrist, pharmacist, veterinarian, and optometrist defined for purposes of this Division, see Health and Safety Code § 11024.
Primary caregiver defined for purposes of this Article, see Health and Safety Code § 11362.7.
Qualified patient defined for purposes of this Article, see Health and Safety Code § 11362.7.

§ 11362.81. Penalties; application of section; development and adoption of guidelines to ensure security and nondiversion of cannabis grown for medicinal use

(a) A person specified in subdivision (b) shall be subject to the following penalties:

(1) For the first offense, imprisonment in the county jail for no more than six months or a fine not to exceed one thousand dollars ($1,000), or both.

(2) For a second or subsequent offense, imprisonment in the county jail for no more than one year, or a fine not to exceed one thousand dollars ($1,000), or both.

(b) Subdivision (a) applies to any of the following:

(1) A person who fraudulently represents a medical condition or fraudulently provides any material misinformation to a physician, county health department or the county's designee, or state or local law enforcement agency or officer, for the purpose of falsely obtaining an identification card.

(2) A person who steals or fraudulently uses any person's identification card in order to acquire, possess, cultivate, transport, use, produce, or distribute cannabis.

(3) A person who counterfeits, tampers with, or fraudulently produces an identification card.

(4) A person who breaches the confidentiality requirements of this article to information provided to, or contained in the records of, the department or of a county health department or the county's designee pertaining to an identification card program.

(c) In addition to the penalties prescribed in subdivision (a), a person described in subdivision (b) may be precluded from attempting to obtain, or obtaining or using, an identification card for a period of up to six months at the discretion of the court.

(d) In addition to the requirements of this article, the Attorney General shall develop and adopt appropriate guidelines to ensure the security and nondiversion of cannabis grown for medicinal use by patients qualified under the Compassionate Use Act of 1996. *(Added by Stats.2003, c. 875 (S.B.420), § 2. Amended by Stats.2017, c. 27 (S.B.94), § 147, eff. June 27, 2017.)*

Cross References

Attorney General, generally, see Government Code § 12500 et seq.
Attorney General defined for purposes of this Division, see Health and Safety Code § 11004.
Cannabis defined for purposes of this Division, see Health and Safety Code § 11018.
Department defined for purposes of this Article, see Health and Safety Code § 11362.7.
Department of Health Care Services, generally, see Health and Safety Code § 100100 et seq.
Distribute defined for purposes of this Division, see Health and Safety Code § 11012.
Identification card defined for purposes of this Article, see Health and Safety Code § 11362.7.
Person defined for purposes of this Division, see Health and Safety Code § 11022.
Physician, dentist, podiatrist, pharmacist, veterinarian, and optometrist defined for purposes of this Division, see Health and Safety Code § 11024.

Research References

California Jury Instructions - Criminal 2370, Planting, etc., Marijuana.
2 Witkin, California Criminal Law 4th Crimes Against Public Peace and Welfare § 151 (2021), Fraudulent Use of Card.

§ 11362.82. Separate and distinct provisions

If any section, subdivision, sentence, clause, phrase, or portion of this article is for any reason held invalid or unconstitutional by any court of competent jurisdiction, that portion shall be deemed a separate, distinct, and independent provision, and that holding shall not affect the validity of the remaining portion thereof. *(Added by Stats.2003, c. 875 (S.B.420), § 2.)*

§ 11362.83. Adoption of local ordinances and enforcement of laws consistent with article

Nothing in this article shall prevent a city or other local governing body from adopting and enforcing any of the following:

(a) Adopting local ordinances that regulate the location, operation, or establishment of a medicinal cannabis cooperative or collective.

(b) The civil and criminal enforcement of local ordinances described in subdivision (a).

(c) Enacting other laws consistent with this article. *(Added by Stats.2003, c. 875 (S.B.420), § 2. Amended by Stats.2011, c. 196 (A.B.1300), § 1; Stats.2017, c. 27 (S.B.94), § 148, eff. June 27, 2017.)*

Research References

2 Witkin, California Criminal Law 4th Crimes Against Public Peace and Welfare § 147 (2021), Purpose and Validity of Program.

§ 11362.84. Status and conduct of a qualified patient shall not by itself be used to restrict or abridge custodial or parental rights

The status and conduct of a qualified patient who acts in accordance with the Compassionate Use Act shall not, by itself, be used to restrict or abridge custodial or parental rights to minor children in any action or proceeding under the jurisdiction of family or juvenile court. *(Added by Initiative Measure (Prop. 64, § 5.4, approved Nov. 8, 2016, eff. Nov. 9, 2016).)*

§ 11362.85. Conforming state law to changes in federal law upon determination that federal schedule of controlled substances has reclassified or declassified cannabis

Upon a determination by the California Attorney General that the federal schedule of controlled substances has been amended to reclassify or declassify cannabis, the Legislature may amend or repeal the provisions of this code, as necessary, to conform state law to such changes in federal law. *(Added by Initiative Measure (Prop. 64, § 5.5, approved Nov. 8, 2016, eff. Nov. 9, 2016). Amended by Stats.2017, c. 27 (S.B.94), § 149, eff. June 27, 2017.)*

§ 11362.9. Editorial Note

For a section of this number as added by Stats.1999, c. 750 (S.B.847), § 3, see Health and Safety Code § 11362.9 in Article 2, "Cannabis".

ARTICLE 3. PEYOTE

§ 11363. Planting, cultivating and harvesting; punishment

Every person who plants, cultivates, harvests, dries, or processes any plant of the genus Lophophora, also known as peyote, or any part thereof shall be punished by imprisonment in the county jail for a period of not more than one year or the state prison. *(Added by Stats.1972, c. 1407, p. 3018, § 3. Amended by Stats.1973, c. 1078, p. 2180, § 13, eff. Oct. 1, 1973; Stats.1975, c. 248, p. 644, § 5; Stats.1976, c. 1139, p. 5082, § 76, operative July 1, 1977.)*

Cross References

Arrest of teacher or instructor employed in community college district, notices, see Health and Safety Code § 11591.5.
Expenditures to obtain evidence, see Health and Safety Code § 11454.
Fines, increment for each separate offense, see Health and Safety Code § 11372.5.
Person defined for purposes of this Division, see Health and Safety Code § 11022.
Previous conviction, plea, see Penal Code § 1025.
Recovery of funds expended in investigations, see Health and Safety Code § 11501.
School district certificated employees, leave of absence when charged with offense under this section, see Education Code § 44940.
School employee, arrest for controlled substance offense as described in this section, notice to school authorities, see Health and Safety Code § 11591.
Verdict or finding upon charge of previous conviction, see Penal Code § 1158.

Research References

2 Witkin, California Criminal Law 4th Crimes Against Public Peace and Welfare § 87 (2021), Substances Formerly Classified as Narcotics.
2 Witkin, California Criminal Law 4th Crimes Against Public Peace and Welfare § 131 (2021), Cultivating, Harvesting, or Processing.

ARTICLE 4. MISCELLANEOUS OFFENSES AND PROVISIONS

§ 11364. Opium pipes; instruments for injecting or smoking controlled substances; exceptions for safe disposal and personal use

(a) It is unlawful to possess an opium pipe or any device, contrivance, instrument, or paraphernalia used for unlawfully injecting or smoking (1) a controlled substance specified in subdivision (b), (c), or (e) or paragraph (1) of subdivision (f) of Section 11054, specified in paragraph (14), (15), or (20) of subdivision (d) of Section 11054, specified in subdivision (b) or (c) of Section 11055, or specified in paragraph (2) of subdivision (d) of Section 11055, or (2) a controlled substance that is a narcotic drug classified in Schedule III, IV, or V.

(b) This section shall not apply to hypodermic needles or syringes that have been containerized for safe disposal in a container that meets state and federal standards for disposal of sharps waste.

(c) Until January 1, 2026, as a public health measure intended to prevent the transmission of HIV, viral hepatitis, and other bloodborne diseases among persons who use syringes and hypodermic needles, and to prevent subsequent infection of sexual partners, newborn children, or other persons, this section shall not apply to the possession solely for personal use of hypodermic needles or syringes.

(Added by Stats.1972, c. 1407, p. 3019, § 3. Amended by Stats.1973, c. 1078, p. 2181, § 14, eff. Oct. 1, 1973; Stats.1975, c. 248, p. 645, § 6; Stats.1983, c. 790, § 9; Stats.1984, c. 1635, § 56; Stats.1986, c. 1044, § 9; Stats.1990, c. 544 (S.B.2028), § 1; Stats.1990, c. 1664 (A.B. 2645), § 4; Stats.2004, c. 608 (S.B.1159), § 4; Stats.2010, c. 667 (A.B.1701), § 2; Stats.2011, c. 296 (A.B.1023), § 152; Stats.2011, c. 738 (S.B.41), § 10; Stats.2012, c. 162 (S.B.1171), § 86; Stats.2014, c. 331 (A.B.1743), § 8, eff. Jan. 1, 2015; Stats.2020, c. 274 (A.B.2077), § 4, eff. Jan. 1, 2021.)

Cross References

Controlled substance defined for purposes of this Division, see Health and Safety Code § 11007.
Convictions, limitations on employers and penalties, see Labor Code § 432.8.
Diversion from trial for education, treatment or rehabilitation, see Penal Code § 1000 et seq.
Expenditures to obtain evidence, see Health and Safety Code § 11454.
Fines, increment for each separate offense, see Health and Safety Code § 11372.5.
Hypodermic needles and syringes, see Business and Professions Code § 4141 et seq.
Hypodermic needles or syringes, confiscation of stocks outside of licensed premises and not in possession or control of persons entitled to exemption under this section, see Business and Professions Code § 4148.5.
Opiate defined for purposes of this Division, see Health and Safety Code § 11020.
Opium poppy defined for purposes of this Division, see Health and Safety Code § 11021.
Recovery of funds expended in investigations, see Health and Safety Code § 11501.
School district certificated employees, leave of absence when charged with offense under this section, see Education Code § 44940.
Seizure of equipment or products used for unlawfully using or administering controlled substance, see Health and Safety Code § 11472.

Research References

California Jury Instructions - Criminal 16.040, Possession of Controlled Substance Device.
2 Witkin, California Criminal Law 4th Crimes Against Public Peace and Welfare § 155 (2021), Drug Paraphernalia.
4 Witkin, California Criminal Law 4th Pretrial Proceedings § 386 (2021), Offenses and Conditions.

§ 11364.5. Drug paraphernalia; maintenance or operation of a place of business; exclusion of minors; revocation or denial of license

(a) Except as authorized by law, no person shall maintain or operate any place of business in which drug paraphernalia is kept, displayed or offered in any manner, sold, furnished, transferred or given away unless such drug paraphernalia is completely and wholly kept, displayed or offered within a separate room or enclosure to which persons under the age of 18 years not accompanied by a parent or legal guardian are excluded. Each entrance to such a room or enclosure shall be signposted in reasonably visible and legible words to the effect that drug paraphernalia is kept, displayed or offered in such room or enclosure and that minors, unless accompanied by a parent or legal guardian, are excluded.

(b) Except as authorized by law, no owner, manager, proprietor or other person in charge of any room or enclosure, within any place of business, in which drug paraphernalia is kept, displayed or offered in any manner, sold, furnished, transferred or given away shall permit or allow any person under the age of 18 years to enter, be in, remain in or visit such room or enclosure unless that minor person is accompanied by * * * their parent or legal guardian.

(c) Unless authorized by law, no person under the age of 18 years shall enter, be in, remain in, or visit any room or enclosure in any place of business in which drug paraphernalia is kept, displayed or offered in any manner, sold, furnished, transferred, or given away unless accompanied by * * * their parent or legal guardian.

(d) As used in this section, "drug paraphernalia" means all equipment, products, and materials of any kind which are intended for use or designed for use, in planting, propagating, cultivating, growing, harvesting, manufacturing, compounding, converting, producing, processing, preparing, testing, analyzing, packaging, repackaging, storing, containing, concealing, injecting, ingesting, inhaling, or otherwise introducing into the human body a controlled substance. "Drug paraphernalia" includes, but is not limited to, all of the following:

(1) Kits intended for use or designed for use in planting, propagating, cultivating, growing, or harvesting of any species of plant which is a controlled substance or from which a controlled substance can be derived.

(2) Kits intended for use or designed for use in manufacturing, compounding, converting, producing, processing, or preparing controlled substances.

(3) Isomerization devices intended for use or designed for use in increasing the potency of any species of plant which is a controlled substance.

(4) Testing equipment intended for use or designed for use in identifying, or in analyzing the strength, effectiveness, or purity of controlled substances, except as otherwise provided in subdivision (g).

(5) Scales and balances intended for use or designed for use in weighing or measuring controlled substances.

(6) Diluents and adulterants, such as quinine hydrochloride, mannitol, mannite, dextrose, and lactose, intended for use or designed for use in cutting controlled substances.

(7) Separation gins and sifters intended for use or designed for use in removing twigs and seeds from, or in otherwise cleaning or refining, cannabis.

(8) Blenders, bowls, containers, spoons, and mixing devices intended for use or designed for use in compounding controlled substances.

(9) Capsules, balloons, envelopes, and other containers intended for use or designed for use in packaging small quantities of controlled substances.

(10) Containers and other objects intended for use or designed for use in storing or concealing controlled substances.

(11) Hypodermic syringes, needles, and other objects intended for use or designed for use in parenterally injecting controlled substances into the human body.

(12) Objects intended for use or designed for use in ingesting, inhaling, or otherwise introducing cannabis, cocaine, hashish, or hashish oil into the human body, such as the following:

(A) Metal, wooden, acrylic, glass, stone, plastic, or ceramic pipes with or without screens, permanent screens, hashish heads, or punctured metal bowls.

(B) Water pipes.

(C) Carburetion tubes and devices.

(D) Smoking and carburetion masks.

(E) Roach clips, meaning objects used to hold burning material, such as a cannabis cigarette that has become too small or too short to be held in the hand.

(F) Miniature cocaine spoons, and cocaine vials.

(G) Chamber pipes.

(H) Carburetor pipes.

(I) Electric pipes.

(J) Air-driven pipes.

(K) Chillums.

(L) Bongs.

(M) Ice pipes or chillers.

(e) In determining whether an object is drug paraphernalia, a court or other authority may consider, in addition to all other logically relevant factors, the following:

(1) Statements by an owner or by anyone in control of the object concerning its use.

(2) Prior convictions, if any, of an owner, or of anyone in control of the object, under any state or federal law relating to any controlled substance.

(3) Direct or circumstantial evidence of the intent of an owner, or of anyone in control of the object, to deliver it to persons whom * * * they know, or should reasonably know, intend to use the object to facilitate a violation of this section. The innocence of an owner, or of anyone in control of the object, as to a direct violation of this section shall not prevent a finding that the object is intended for use, or designed for use, as drug paraphernalia.

(4) Instructions, oral or written, provided with the object concerning its use.

(5) Descriptive materials, accompanying the object which explain or depict its use.

(6) National and local advertising concerning its use.

(7) The manner in which the object is displayed for sale.

(8) Whether the owner, or anyone in control of the object, is a legitimate supplier of like or related items to the community, such as a licensed distributor or dealer of tobacco products.

(9) The existence and scope of legitimate uses for the object in the community.

(10) Expert testimony concerning its use.

(f) This section shall not apply to any of the following:

(1) Any pharmacist or other authorized person who sells or furnishes drug paraphernalia described in paragraph (11) of subdivision (d) upon the prescription of a physician, dentist, podiatrist, or veterinarian.

(2) Any physician, dentist, podiatrist, or veterinarian who furnishes or prescribes drug paraphernalia described in paragraph (11) of subdivision (d) to * * * a patient.

(3) Any manufacturer, wholesaler, or retailer licensed by the California State Board of Pharmacy to sell or transfer drug paraphernalia described in paragraph (11) of subdivision (d).

(g) Notwithstanding paragraph (4) of subdivision (d), "drug paraphernalia" does not include any testing equipment designed, marketed, intended to be used, or used, to test a substance for the presence of fentanyl, ketamine, gamma hydroxybutyric acid, or any analog of fentanyl.

(h) Notwithstanding any other provision of law, including Section 11374, violation of this section shall not constitute a criminal offense, but operation of a business in violation of the provisions of this section shall be grounds for revocation or nonrenewal of any license, permit, or other entitlement previously issued by a city, county, or city and county for the privilege of engaging in such business and shall be grounds for denial of any future license, permit, or other entitlement authorizing the conduct of such business or any other business, if the business includes the sale of drug paraphernalia. *(Added by Stats.1980, c. 505, p. 1060, § 1. Amended by Stats.1984, c. 1635, § 57; Stats.2017, c. 27 (S.B.94), § 151, eff. June 27, 2017; Stats.2022, c. 201 (A.B.1598), § 2, eff. Jan. 1, 2023.)*

Cross References

Cannabis defined for purposes of this Division, see Health and Safety Code § 11018.

Controlled substance defined for purposes of this Division, see Health and Safety Code § 11007.
Deliver or delivery defined for purposes of this Division, see Health and Safety Code § 11009.
Distributor defined for purposes of this Division, see Health and Safety Code § 11013.
Drug defined for purposes of this Division, see Health and Safety Code § 11014.
Drug paraphernalia defined for purposes of this Division, see Health and Safety Code § 11014.5.
Furnish defined for purposes of this Division, see Health and Safety Code § 11016.
Manufacturer defined for purposes of this Division, see Health and Safety Code § 11017.
Person defined for purposes of this Division, see Health and Safety Code § 11022.
Pharmacy, confiscation of hypodermic needles and syringes, stocks outside of licensed premises and not in possession or control of authorized persons, see Business and Professions Code § 4148.5.
Physician, dentist, podiatrist, pharmacist, veterinarian, and optometrist defined for purposes of this Division, see Health and Safety Code § 11024.
Prescription or electronic transmission prescription defined for purposes of this Division, see Health and Safety Code § 11027.
Wholesaler defined for purposes of this Division, see Health and Safety Code § 11031.

§ 11364.7. Delivering, furnishing, transferring, possessing or manufacture with intent to deliver, furnish, transfer or manufacture drug paraphernalia; penalties and punishment

(a)(1) Except as authorized by law, any person who delivers, furnishes, or transfers, possesses with intent to deliver, furnish, or transfer, or manufactures with the intent to deliver, furnish, or transfer, drug paraphernalia, knowing, or under circumstances where one reasonably should know, that it will be used to plant, propagate, cultivate, grow, harvest, compound, convert, produce, process, prepare, test, analyze, pack, repack, store, contain, conceal, inject, ingest, inhale, or otherwise introduce into the human body a controlled substance, except as provided in subdivision (b), in violation of this division, is guilty of a misdemeanor.

(2) A public entity, its agents, or employees shall not be subject to criminal prosecution for distribution of hypodermic needles or syringes or any materials deemed by a local or state health department to be necessary to prevent the spread of communicable diseases, or to prevent drug overdose, injury, or disability to participants in clean needle and syringe exchange projects authorized by the public entity pursuant to Chapter 18 (commencing with Section 121349) of Part 4 of Division 105.

(b) Except as authorized by law, any person who manufactures with intent to deliver, furnish, or transfer drug paraphernalia knowing, or under circumstances where one reasonably should know, that it will be used to plant, propagate, cultivate, grow, harvest, manufacture, compound, convert, produce, process, prepare, test, analyze, pack, repack, store, contain, conceal, inject, ingest, inhale, or otherwise introduce into the human body cocaine, cocaine base, heroin, phencyclidine, or methamphetamine in violation of this division shall be punished by imprisonment in a county jail for not more than one year, or in the state prison.

(c) Except as authorized by law, any person, 18 years of age or over, who violates subdivision (a) by delivering, furnishing, or transferring drug paraphernalia to a person under 18 years of age who is at least three years his or her junior, or who, upon the grounds of a public or private elementary, vocational, junior high, or high school, possesses a hypodermic needle, as defined in paragraph (7) of subdivision (a) of Section 11014.5, with the intent to deliver, furnish, or transfer the hypodermic needle, knowing, or under circumstances where one reasonably should know, that it will be used by a person under 18 years of age to inject into the human body a controlled substance, is guilty of a misdemeanor and shall be punished by imprisonment in a county jail for not more than one year, by a fine of not more than one thousand dollars ($1,000), or by both that imprisonment and fine.

(d) The violation, or the causing or the permitting of a violation, of subdivision (a), (b), or (c) by a holder of a business or liquor license issued by a city, county, or city and county, or by the State of California, and in the course of the licensee's business shall be grounds for the revocation of that license.

(e) All drug paraphernalia defined in Section 11014.5 is subject to forfeiture and may be seized by any peace officer pursuant to Section 11471 unless its distribution has been authorized pursuant to subdivision (a).

(f) If any provision of this section or the application thereof to any person or circumstance is held invalid, it is the intent of the Legislature that the invalidity shall not affect other provisions or applications of this section which can be given effect without the invalid provision or application and to this end the provisions of this section are severable. *(Added by Stats.1982, c. 1278, p. 4727, § 2. Amended by Stats.1991, c. 573 (A.B.898), § 1; Stats.1992, c. 983 (A.B.565), § 1; Stats.1999, c. 762 (A.B.136), § 1; Stats.2005, c. 692 (A.B.547), § 2; Stats.2018, c. 34 (A.B.1810), § 7, eff. June 27, 2018.)*

Cross References

Agent defined for purposes of this Division, see Health and Safety Code § 11003.
Alcoholic beverage license, suspension or revocation for furnishing drug paraphernalia, see Business and Professions Code § 24200.6.
Controlled substance defined for purposes of this Division, see Health and Safety Code § 11007.
Deliver or delivery defined for purposes of this Division, see Health and Safety Code § 11009.
Furnish defined for purposes of this Division, see Health and Safety Code § 11016.
Misdemeanors, definition and penalties, see Penal Code §§ 17, 19, 19.2.
Person defined for purposes of this Division, see Health and Safety Code § 11022.

Research References

2 Witkin, California Criminal Law 4th Crimes Against Public Peace and Welfare § 155 (2021), Drug Paraphernalia.

§ 11365. Presence in room or place where designated controlled substances smoked or used; aiding or abetting

(a) It is unlawful to visit or to be in any room or place where any controlled substances which are specified in subdivision (b), (c), or (e), or paragraph (1) of subdivision (f) of Section 11054, specified in paragraph (14), (15), or (20) of subdivision (d) of Section 11054, or specified in subdivision (b) or (c) or paragraph (2) of subdivision (d) of Section 11055, or which are narcotic drugs classified in Schedule III, IV, or V, are being unlawfully smoked or used with knowledge that such activity is occurring.

(b) This section shall apply only where the defendant aids, assists, or abets the perpetration of the unlawful smoking or use of a controlled substance specified in subdivision (a). This subdivision is declaratory of existing law as expressed in People v. Cressey (1970) 2 Cal. 3d 836. *(Added by Stats.1972, c. 1407, p. 3019, § 3. Amended by Stats.1973, c. 1078, p. 2181, § 15, eff. Oct. 1, 1973; Stats.1975, c. 248, p. 645, § 7; Stats.1983, c. 790, § 10; Stats.1984, c. 1635, § 58; Stats.1986, c. 1044, § 10; Stats.1991, c. 551 (A.B.55), § 1.)*

Cross References

Controlled substance defined for purposes of this Division, see Health and Safety Code § 11007.
Convictions, limitations on employers and penalties, see Labor Code § 432.8.
Diversion from trial for education, treatment or rehabilitation, see Penal Code § 1000 et seq.

Narcotic drug defined for purposes of this Division, see Health and Safety Code § 11019.

Research References

California Jury Instructions - Criminal 16.050, Presence Where Controlled Substances Used.

2 Witkin, California Criminal Law 4th Crimes Against Public Peace and Welfare § 157 (2021), Visiting or Using Place for Unlawful Activity.

4 Witkin, California Criminal Law 4th Pretrial Proceedings § 386 (2021), Offenses and Conditions.

§ 11366. Opening or maintenance of unlawful places; punishment

Every person who opens or maintains any place for the purpose of unlawfully selling, giving away, or using any controlled substance which is (1) specified in subdivision (b), (c), or (e), or paragraph (1) of subdivision (f) of Section 11054, specified in paragraph (13), (14), (15), or (20) of subdivision (d) of Section 11054, or specified in subdivision (b), (c), paragraph (1) or (2) of subdivision (d), or paragraph (3) of subdivision (e) of Section 11055, or (2) which is a narcotic drug classified in Schedule III, IV, or V, shall be punished by imprisonment in the county jail for a period of not more than one year or the state prison. *(Added by Stats.1972, c. 1407, p. 3019, § 3. Amended by Stats.1973, c. 1078, p. 2181, § 16, eff. Oct. 1, 1973; Stats.1976, c. 1139, p. 5083, § 77, operative July 1, 1977; Stats.1983, c. 790, § 11; Stats.1984, c. 1635, § 59; Stats.1986, c. 1044, § 11; Stats.1991, c. 492 (S.B.32), § 1.)*

Cross References

Arrest of teacher or instructor employed in community college district, notices, see Health and Safety Code § 11591.5.

Controlled substance defined for purposes of this Division, see Health and Safety Code § 11007.

Controlled substance offense defined as violation of this section for purposes of Education Code, see Education Code §§ 44011, 87011.

Expenditures to obtain evidence, see Health and Safety Code § 11454.

Forfeiture of real property for violating this section, see Health and Safety Code § 11470.

Medical marijuana program, generally, see Health and Safety Code § 11362.7 et seq.

Medical marijuana program, criminal liability for use of marijuana, application of section, see Health and Safety Code § 11362.765.

Narcotic drug defined for purposes of this Division, see Health and Safety Code § 11019.

Person defined for purposes of this Division, see Health and Safety Code § 11022.

Recovery of funds expended in investigations, see Health and Safety Code § 11501.

Registration of controlled substance offender, conviction of offense defined in this section, see Health and Safety Code § 11591 et seq.

School employee, arrest for controlled substance offense as described in this section, notice to school authorities, see Health and Safety Code § 11591.

Unlawful detainer actions to abate nuisance caused by illegal conduct involving controlled substance purpose, including violations of these provisions, see Civil Code § 3486.

Research References

California Jury Instructions - Criminal 12.08, Opening or Maintaining Place for Controlled Substance Sale or Use.

2 Witkin, California Criminal Law 4th Crimes Against Public Peace and Welfare § 149 (2021), Protection from Criminal Liability.

2 Witkin, California Criminal Law 4th Crimes Against Public Peace and Welfare § 157 (2021), Visiting or Using Place for Unlawful Activity.

5 Witkin, California Criminal Law 4th Criminal Trial § 707 (2021), Technical or Specialized Terms.

1 Witkin California Criminal Law 4th Elements § 47 (2021), What Constitutes Corpus Delicti.

4 Witkin, California Criminal Law 4th Illegally Obtained Evidence § 175 (2021), Use of Motorized Battering Ram.

1 Witkin California Criminal Law 4th Introduction to Crimes § 38 (2021), Illustrations.

3 Witkin, California Criminal Law 4th Punishment § 197 (2021), Property Subject to Forfeiture.

3 Witkin, California Criminal Law 4th Punishment § 296 (2021), Possession and Other Crimes.

§ 11366.5. Renting, leasing, or making available for use a building, room, space, or enclosure for unlawful manufacture, storage, or distribution of controlled substance; allowing building, room, space, or enclosure to be fortified to suppress law enforcement entry to further sale of specified controlled substances; punishment

(a) Any person who has under his or her management or control any building, room, space, or enclosure, either as an owner, lessee, agent, employee, or mortgagee, who knowingly rents, leases, or makes available for use, with or without compensation, the building, room, space, or enclosure for the purpose of unlawfully manufacturing, storing, or distributing any controlled substance for sale or distribution shall be punished by imprisonment in the county jail for not more than one year, or pursuant to subdivision (h) of Section 1170 of the Penal Code.

(b) Any person who has under his or her management or control any building, room, space, or enclosure, either as an owner, lessee, agent, employee, or mortgagee, who knowingly allows the building, room, space, or enclosure to be fortified to suppress law enforcement entry in order to further the sale of any amount of cocaine base as specified in paragraph (1) of subdivision (f) of Section 11054, cocaine as specified in paragraph (6) of subdivision (b) of Section 11055, heroin, phencyclidine, amphetamine, methamphetamine, or lysergic acid diethylamide and who obtains excessive profits from the use of the building, room, space, or enclosure shall be punished by imprisonment pursuant to subdivision (h) of Section 1170 of the Penal Code for two, three, or four years.

(c) Any person who violates subdivision (a) after previously being convicted of a violation of subdivision (a) shall be punished by imprisonment pursuant to subdivision (h) of Section 1170 of the Penal Code for two, three, or four years.

(d) For the purposes of this section, "excessive profits" means the receipt of consideration of a value substantially higher than fair market value. *(Added by Stats.1982, c. 1279, p. 4730, § 4. Amended by Stats.1985, c. 1533, § 1; Stats.1986, c. 1026, § 1; Stats.1987, c. 1174, § 4, eff. Sept. 26, 1987; Stats.2011, c. 15 (A.B.109), § 164, eff. April 4, 2011, operative Oct. 1, 2011.)*

Cross References

Agent defined for purposes of this Division, see Health and Safety Code § 11003.

Arrest of teacher or instructor employed in community college district, notices, see Health and Safety Code § 11591.5.

Controlled substance defined for purposes of this Division, see Health and Safety Code § 11007.

Forfeiture of real property for violating this section, see Health and Safety Code § 11470.

Medical marijuana program, generally, see Health and Safety Code § 11362.7 et seq.

Medical marijuana program, criminal liability for use of marijuana, application of section, see Health and Safety Code § 11362.765.

Person defined for purposes of this Division, see Health and Safety Code § 11022.

School employee, arrest for controlled substance offense as described in this section, notice to school authorities, see Health and Safety Code § 11591.

Research References

California Jury Instructions - Criminal 12.09.1, Manufacturing or Offering to Manufacture a Controlled Substance.

2 Witkin, California Criminal Law 4th Crimes Against Public Peace and Welfare § 132 (2021), Manufacture.

2 Witkin, California Criminal Law 4th Crimes Against Public Peace and Welfare § 149 (2021), Protection from Criminal Liability.

2 Witkin, California Criminal Law 4th Crimes Against Public Peace and Welfare § 157 (2021), Visiting or Using Place for Unlawful Activity.

4 Witkin, California Criminal Law 4th Illegally Obtained Evidence § 175 (2021), Use of Motorized Battering Ram.

1 Witkin California Criminal Law 4th Introduction to Crimes § 77 (2021), Illustrations: Special Statute is Not Controlling.

§ 11366.6. Utilizing building, room, space, or enclosure designed to suppress law enforcement entry in order to sell, manufacture, or possess for sale specified controlled substances; punishment

Any person who utilizes a building, room, space, or enclosure specifically designed to suppress law enforcement entry in order to sell, manufacture, or possess for sale any amount of cocaine base as specified in paragraph (1) of subdivision (f) of Section 11054, cocaine as specified in paragraph (6) of subdivision (b) of Section 11055, heroin, phencyclidine, amphetamine, methamphetamine, or lysergic acid diethylamide shall be punished by imprisonment pursuant to subdivision (h) of Section 1170 of the Penal Code for three, four, or five years. *(Added by Stats.1985, c. 1533, § 2. Amended by Stats.1986, c. 1026, § 2; Stats.1986, c. 1044, § 12.5; Stats.1987, c. 1174, § 5, eff. Sept. 26, 1987; Stats.2011, c. 15 (A.B.109), § 165, eff. April 4, 2011, operative Oct. 1, 2011.)*

Cross References

Arrest of teacher or instructor employed in community college district, notices, see Health and Safety Code § 11591.5.
Forfeiture of real property for violating this section, see Health and Safety Code § 11470.
Person defined for purposes of this Division, see Health and Safety Code § 11022.
School employee, arrest for controlled substance offense as described in this section, notice to school authorities, see Health and Safety Code § 11591.
Suspension of sentence and probation for persons convicted of violating this section, see Penal Code § 1203.074.
Unlawful detainer actions to abate nuisance caused by illegal conduct involving controlled substance purpose, including violations of these provisions, see Civil Code § 3486.

Research References

2 Witkin, California Criminal Law 4th Crimes Against Public Peace and Welfare § 157 (2021), Visiting or Using Place for Unlawful Activity.
3 Witkin, California Criminal Law 4th Punishment § 296 (2021), Possession and Other Crimes.

§ 11366.7. Sale of chemical, drug, laboratory apparatus or device with knowledge or intent of use for unlawful manufacture, processing, or preparation of controlled substance

(a) This section shall apply to the following:

(1) Any chemical or drug.

(2) Any laboratory apparatus or device.

(b) Any retailer or wholesaler who sells any item in paragraph (1) or (2) of subdivision (a) with knowledge or the intent that it will be used to unlawfully manufacture, compound, convert, process, or prepare a controlled substance for unlawful sale or distribution, shall be punished by imprisonment in a county jail for not more than one year, or in the state prison, or by a fine not exceeding twenty-five thousand dollars ($25,000), or by both that imprisonment and fine. Any fine collected pursuant to this section shall be distributed as specified in Section 1463.10 of the Penal Code. *(Added by Stats. 1982, c. 1279, p. 4730, § 5. Amended by Stats.1984, c. 1547, § 2; Stats.1990, c. 350 (S.B.2084), § 6; Stats.1994, c. 979 (S.B.937), § 1.)*

Cross References

Controlled substance defined for purposes of this Division, see Health and Safety Code § 11007.
Drug defined for purposes of this Division, see Health and Safety Code § 11014.
Wholesaler defined for purposes of this Division, see Health and Safety Code § 11031.

Research References

2 Witkin, California Criminal Law 4th Crimes Against Public Peace and Welfare § 133 (2021), In General.

§ 11366.8. Construction, possession or use of false compartment with intent to conceal controlled substance; punishment

(a) Every person who possesses, uses, or controls a false compartment with the intent to store, conceal, smuggle, or transport a controlled substance within the false compartment shall be punished by imprisonment in a county jail for a term of imprisonment not to exceed one year or pursuant to subdivision (h) of Section 1170 of the Penal Code.

(b) Every person who designs, constructs, builds, alters, or fabricates a false compartment for, or installs or attaches a false compartment to, a vehicle with the intent to store, conceal, smuggle, or transport a controlled substance shall be punished by imprisonment pursuant to subdivision (h) of Section 1170 of the Penal Code for 16 months or two or three years.

(c) The term "vehicle" means any of the following vehicles without regard to whether the vehicles are private or commercial, including, but not limited to, cars, trucks, buses, aircraft, boats, ships, yachts, and vessels.

(d) The term "false compartment" means any box, container, space, or enclosure that is intended for use or designed for use to conceal, hide, or otherwise prevent discovery of any controlled substance within or attached to a vehicle, including, but not limited to, any of the following:

(1) False, altered, or modified fuel tanks.

(2) Original factory equipment of a vehicle that is modified, altered, or changed.

(3) Compartment, space, or box that is added to, or fabricated, made, or created from, existing compartments, spaces, or boxes within a vehicle. *(Added by Stats.1993, c. 562 (A.B.1760), § 1. Amended by Stats.1994, c. 146 (A.B.3601), § 106; Stats.2011, c. 15 (A.B.109), § 166, eff. April 4, 2011, operative Oct. 1, 2011.)*

Cross References

Controlled substance defined for purposes of this Division, see Health and Safety Code § 11007.
Person defined for purposes of this Division, see Health and Safety Code § 11022.

Research References

California Jury Instructions - Criminal 12.38, False Compartments.
California Jury Instructions - Criminal 12.39, Forfeiture of Cash or Equivalents Under $25,000.00.
2 Witkin, California Criminal Law 4th Crimes Against Public Peace and Welfare § 156 (2021), Concealment in False Compartment.

§ 11367. Immunity from prosecution

All duly authorized peace officers, while investigating violations of this division in performance of their official duties, and any person working under their immediate direction, supervision or instruction, are immune from prosecution under this division. *(Added by Stats.1972, c. 1407, p. 3019, § 3.)*

Cross References

Alcoholic beverage laws, powers of peace officers to enforce, see Business and Professions Code § 25755.
Authorized officers of the law, see Business and Professions Code § 4017.
Department of Justice, see Penal Code § 11052.
Fish and game officers, see Fish and Game Code §§ 851, 878.
Highway patrol members, see Vehicle Code § 2409.
Minimum standards, see Government Code § 1031.
Motor vehicle department officers, see Vehicle Code § 1655.
Peace officers defined, see Government Code § 50920; Penal Code §§ 7, 243, 245, 830 et seq.
Person defined for purposes of this Division, see Health and Safety Code § 11022.
Probation officers, see Penal Code § 1203.71; Welfare and Institutions Code § 283.
Public utilities commission assistants, see Public Utilities Code § 308.
School security patrol, designation as peace officers, see Education Code § 38001.
Sealers, see Business and Professions Code § 12013.
Special agents and investigators, see Government Code § 12571.
State university police, see Education Code § 89560.

Treasurer's guards and messengers, see Government Code § 12304.
University police, see Education Code § 92600.

Research References

1 Witkin California Criminal Law 4th Defenses § 49 (2021), Mistake of Fact Distinguished from Mistake of Law.
1 Witkin California Criminal Law 4th Defenses § 277 (2021), Narcotics Offenses.

§ 11367.5. Immunity from prosecution; peace officers; substance abuse or canine training

(a) Any sheriff, chief of police, the Chief of the Division of Law Enforcement, or the Commissioner of the California Highway Patrol, or a designee thereof, may, in his or her discretion, provide controlled substances in his or her possession and control to any duly authorized peace officer or civilian drug detection canine trainer working under the direction of a law enforcement agency, provided the controlled substances are no longer needed as criminal evidence and provided the person receiving the controlled substances, if required by the federal Drug Enforcement Administration, possesses a current and valid federal Drug Enforcement Administration registration which specifically authorizes the recipient to possess controlled substances while providing substance abuse training to law enforcement or the community or while providing canine drug detection training.

(b) All duly authorized peace officers, while providing substance abuse training to law enforcement or the community or while providing canine drug detection training, in performance of their official duties, and any person working under their immediate direction, supervision, or instruction, are immune from prosecution under this division.

(c)(1) Any person receiving controlled substances pursuant to subdivision (a) shall maintain custody and control of the controlled substances and shall keep records regarding any loss of, or damage to, those controlled substances.

(2) All controlled substances shall be maintained in a secure location approved by the dispensing agency.

(3) Any loss shall be reported immediately to the dispensing agency.

(4) All controlled substances shall be returned to the dispensing agency upon the conclusion of the training or upon demand by the dispensing agency. *(Added by Stats.1992, c. 137 (A.B.2308), § 1. Amended by Stats.2012, c. 867 (S.B.1144), § 9.)*

Cross References

Controlled substance defined for purposes of this Division, see Health and Safety Code § 11007.
Person defined for purposes of this Division, see Health and Safety Code § 11022.

Research References

1 Witkin California Criminal Law 4th Defenses § 277 (2021), Narcotics Offenses.

§ 11368. Forged or altered prescriptions; punishment

Every person who forges or alters a prescription or who issues or utters an altered prescription, or who issues or utters a prescription bearing a forged or fictitious signature for any narcotic drug, or who obtains any narcotic drug by any forged, fictitious, or altered prescription, or who has in possession any narcotic drug secured by a forged, fictitious, or altered prescription, shall be punished by imprisonment in the county jail for not less than six months nor more than one year, or in the state prison. *(Added by Stats.1972, c. 1407, p. 3019, § 3. Amended by Stats.1973, c. 1078, p. 2182, § 17, eff. Oct. 1, 1973; Stats.1976, c. 1139, p. 5083, § 78, operative July 1, 1977; Stats.1990, c. 43 (A.B.1577), § 1.)*

Cross References

Arrest of teacher or instructor employed in community college district, notices, see Health and Safety Code § 11591.5.
Controlled substance offense as including violation of this section, see Education Code §§ 44011, 87011.
Fines, increment for each separate offense, see Health and Safety Code § 11372.5.
Forgery, generally, see Penal Code § 470 et seq.
Forgery of prescription, see Business and Professions Code § 4324.
Narcotic drug defined for purposes of this Division, see Health and Safety Code § 11019.
Of criminal procedure, pleadings and proceedings before trial, special proceedings in narcotics and drug abuse cases, application to certain violations, see Penal Code § 1000.
Person defined for purposes of this Division, see Health and Safety Code § 11022.
Prescription or electronic transmission prescription defined for purposes of this Division, see Health and Safety Code § 11027.
School employee, arrest for controlled substance offense as described in this section, notice to school authorities, see Health and Safety Code § 11591.

Research References

California Jury Instructions - Criminal 12.05, Narcotics—Forgery of Prescription.
California Jury Instructions - Criminal 14.50.1, Shoplifting as Felony/Misdemeanor.
2 Witkin, California Criminal Law 4th Crimes Against Property § 9 (2021), Petty Theft.
2 Witkin, California Criminal Law 4th Crimes Against Property § 15A (2021), (New) Shoplifting.
2 Witkin, California Criminal Law 4th Crimes Against Property § 200 (2021), Miscellaneous Offenses.
2 Witkin, California Criminal Law 4th Crimes Against Public Peace and Welfare § 154 (2021), Forgery or Alteration.
2 Witkin, California Criminal Law 4th Crimes Against Public Peace and Welfare § 164 (2021), In General.
2 Witkin, California Criminal Law 4th Crimes Against Public Peace and Welfare § 408 (2021), Forged Prescriptions and False Representations.
4 Witkin, California Criminal Law 4th Pretrial Proceedings § 386 (2021), Offenses and Conditions.
4 Witkin, California Criminal Law 4th Pretrial Proceedings § 387 (2021), Construction of Statute.
4 Witkin, California Criminal Law 4th Pretrial Proceedings § 398 (2021), Defendant's Satisfactory Performance.
3 Witkin, California Criminal Law 4th Punishment § 308A (2021), (New) in General.
3 Witkin, California Criminal Law 4th Punishment § 437 (2021), Felony-Misdemeanors ("Wobblers").

§ 11370. Probation or suspension of sentence; prior convictions; allegations in information or indictment

(a) A person convicted of violating Section 11353 or 11361, or of committing an offense referred to in those sections, shall not, except as provided in subdivision (e), be granted probation by the trial court or have the execution of the sentence suspended by the court, if the person has been previously convicted of an offense described in subdivision (c).

(b) A person who was 18 years of age or older at the time of the commission of the offense and is convicted for the first time of selling, furnishing, administering, or giving a controlled substance that is (1) specified in subdivision (b), (c), (e), or paragraph (1) of subdivision (f) of Section 11054, specified in paragraph (14), (15), or (20) of subdivision (d) of Section 11054, or specified in subdivision (b) or (c) of Section 11055, or (2) that is a narcotic drug classified in Schedule III, IV, or V, to a minor or inducing a minor to use the controlled substance in violation of law shall not, except as provided in subdivision (e), be granted probation by the trial court or have the execution of the sentence suspended by the court.

(c) A previous conviction of any of the following offenses, or of an offense under the laws of another state or of the United States that, if committed in this state, would have been punishable as that offense, shall render a person ineligible for probation or suspension of sentence pursuant to subdivision (a):

(1) A felony offense described in this division involving a controlled substance specified in subdivision (b), (c), (e), or paragraph (1) of subdivision (f) of Section 11054, specified in paragraph (13), (14), (15), or (20) of subdivision (d) of Section 11054, or specified in subdivision (b) or (c) of Section 11055.

(2) A felony offense described in this division involving a narcotic drug classified in Schedule III, IV, or V.

(d) The existence of a previous conviction or fact that would make a person ineligible for suspension of sentence or probation under this section shall be alleged in the information or indictment, and either admitted by the defendant in open court, or found to be true by the jury trying the issue of guilt or by the court where guilt is established by a plea of guilty or nolo contendere or by trial by the court sitting without a jury.

(e) A person who is made ineligible for probation pursuant to this section may be granted probation only in an unusual case where the interests of justice would best be served. When probation is granted pursuant to this subdivision, the court shall specify on the record the circumstances supporting the finding. *(Added by Stats.1972, c. 1407, p. 3020, § 3. Amended by Stats.1973, c. 1078, p. 2182, § 18, eff. Oct. 1, 1973; Stats.1975, c. 1087, p. 2650, § 4; Stats.1983, c. 790, § 12; Stats.1984, c. 1635, § 60; Stats.1986, c. 1030, § 1; Stats.1986, c. 1044, § 13.5; Stats.2021, c. 537 (S.B.73), § 1, eff. Jan. 1, 2022.)*

Cross References

Controlled substance defined for purposes of this Division, see Health and Safety Code § 11007.
Denial of probation, generally, see Penal Code § 1203.
Felonies, definition and penalties, see Penal Code §§ 17, 18.
Narcotic drug defined for purposes of this Division, see Health and Safety Code § 11019.
Person defined for purposes of this Division, see Health and Safety Code § 11022.

Research References

2 Witkin, California Criminal Law 4th Crimes Against Public Peace and Welfare § 163 (2021), Punishment.
5 Witkin, California Criminal Law 4th Criminal Trial § 475 (2021), In General.
3 Witkin, California Criminal Law 4th Punishment § 616 (2021), Health and Safety Code Provisions.

§ 11370.1. Possession of certain controlled substances while armed with a firearm; punishment; eligibility for diversion or deferred entry of judgment

(a) Notwithstanding Section 11350 or 11377 or any other provision of law, every person who unlawfully possesses any amount of a substance containing cocaine base, a substance containing cocaine, a substance containing heroin, a substance containing methamphetamine, a crystalline substance containing phencyclidine, a liquid substance containing phencyclidine, plant material containing phencyclidine, or a hand-rolled cigarette treated with phencyclidine while armed with a loaded, operable firearm is guilty of a felony punishable by imprisonment in the state prison for two, three, or four years.

As used in this subdivision, "armed with" means having available for immediate offensive or defensive use.

(b) Any person who is convicted under this section shall be ineligible for diversion or deferred entry of judgment under Chapter 2.5 (commencing with Section 1000) of Title 6 of Part 2 of the Penal Code. *(Added by Stats.1989, c. 1041, § 1. Amended by Stats.1990, c. 41 (A.B.664), § 1; Stats.1991, c. 469 (A.B.154), § 1; Stats.1996, c. 1132 (S.B.1369), § 1.)*

Cross References

Arrest of teacher or instructor employed in community college district, notices, see Health and Safety Code § 11591.5.
Felonies, definition and penalties, see Penal Code §§ 17, 18.
Person defined for purposes of this Division, see Health and Safety Code § 11022.
School employee, arrest for controlled substance offense as described in this section, notice to school authorities, see Health and Safety Code § 11591.

Research References

California Jury Instructions - Criminal 12.52, Unlawful Possession of Controlled Substance While Armed With a Firearm.
2 Witkin, California Criminal Law 4th Crimes Against Public Peace and Welfare § 100 (2021), Possession in Conjunction With Firearm.
2 Witkin, California Criminal Law 4th Crimes Against Public Peace and Welfare § 164 (2021), In General.
1 Witkin California Criminal Law 4th Introduction to Crimes § 38 (2021), Illustrations.
3 Witkin, California Criminal Law 4th Punishment § 254 (2021), Illustrations.

§ 11370.2. Sentence enhancements for persons with certain prior convictions

(a) Any person convicted of a violation of, or of a conspiracy to violate, Section 11351, 11351.5, or 11352 shall receive, in addition to any other punishment authorized by law, including Section 667.5 of the Penal Code, a full, separate, and consecutive three-year term for each prior felony conviction of, or for each prior felony conviction of conspiracy to violate, Section 11380, whether or not the prior conviction resulted in a term of imprisonment.

(b) Any person convicted of a violation of, or of a conspiracy to violate, Section 11378.5, 11379.5, 11379.6, or 11383 shall receive, in addition to any other punishment authorized by law, including Section 667.5 of the Penal Code, a full, separate, and consecutive three-year term for each prior felony conviction of, or for each prior felony conviction of conspiracy to violate, Section 11380, whether or not the prior conviction resulted in a term of imprisonment.

(c) Any person convicted of a violation of, or of a conspiracy to violate, Section 11378 or 11379 with respect to any substance containing a controlled substance specified in paragraph (1) or (2) of subdivision (d) of Section 11055 shall receive, in addition to any other punishment authorized by law, including Section 667.5 of the Penal Code, a full, separate, and consecutive three-year term for each prior felony conviction of, or for each prior felony conviction of conspiracy to violate, Section 11380, whether or not the prior conviction resulted in a term of imprisonment.

(d) The enhancements provided for in this section shall be pleaded and proven as provided by law.

(e) The conspiracy enhancements provided for in this section shall not be imposed unless the trier of fact finds that the defendant conspirator was substantially involved in the planning, direction, execution, or financing of the underlying offense.

(f) Prior convictions from another jurisdiction qualify for use under this section pursuant to Section 668. *(Added by Stats.1985, c. 1398, § 2. Amended by Stats.1986, c. 80, § 1; Stats.1986, c. 1044, § 15; Stats.1989, c. 1245, § 1; Stats.1989, c. 1326, § 1.5; Stats.1998, c. 936 (A.B.105), § 1, eff. Sept. 28, 1998; Stats.2017, c. 677 (S.B.180), § 1, eff. Jan. 1, 2018.)*

Cross References

Aggregate term, mitigating circumstances, see Penal Code § 1170.1.
Bail schedule, considerations in adopting uniform countywide schedule, see Penal Code § 1269b.
Commitment of ward who is 14 years of age or older to secure youth treatment facility, maximum term of confinement, see Welfare and Institutions Code § 875.
Controlled substance defined for purposes of this Division, see Health and Safety Code § 11007.
Felonies, definition and penalties, see Penal Code §§ 17, 18.
Invalidity of sentence enhancements imposed pursuant to this section, identification of persons serving enhanced sentences, review and resentencing, waiver of resentencing hearing, see Penal Code § 1171.
Juvenile court law, limitations on parental or guardian control, see Welfare and Institutions Code § 726.

Person defined for purposes of this Division, see Health and Safety Code § 11022.

Research References

2 Witkin, California Criminal Law 4th Crimes Against Public Peace and Welfare § 163 (2021), Punishment.
4 Witkin, California Criminal Law 4th Pretrial Proceedings § 339 (2021), Nature of Plea Bargaining.
4 Witkin, California Criminal Law 4th Pretrial Proceedings § 374E (2021), (New) Change in Law Regarding Sentence Enhancement.
3 Witkin, California Criminal Law 4th Punishment § 255 (2021), In General.
3 Witkin, California Criminal Law 4th Punishment § 404 (2021), Dual Use of Prior Conviction.
3 Witkin, California Criminal Law 4th Punishment § 419 (2021), Controlled Substance Offenses.

§ 11370.4. Convictions under specified sections with respect to substances containing heroin, cocaine base, cocaine, methamphetamine, amphetamine or phencyclidine; additional terms

(a) Any person convicted of a violation of, or of a conspiracy to violate, Section 11351, 11351.5, or 11352 with respect to a substance containing heroin, cocaine base as specified in paragraph (1) of subdivision (f) of Section 11054, or cocaine as specified in paragraph (6) of subdivision (b) of Section 11055 shall receive an additional term as follows:

(1) Where the substance exceeds one kilogram by weight, the person shall receive an additional term of three years.

(2) Where the substance exceeds four kilograms by weight, the person shall receive an additional term of five years.

(3) Where the substance exceeds 10 kilograms by weight, the person shall receive an additional term of 10 years.

(4) Where the substance exceeds 20 kilograms by weight, the person shall receive an additional term of 15 years.

(5) Where the substance exceeds 40 kilograms by weight, the person shall receive an additional term of 20 years.

(6) Where the substance exceeds 80 kilograms by weight, the person shall receive an additional term of 25 years.

The conspiracy enhancements provided for in this subdivision shall not be imposed unless the trier of fact finds that the defendant conspirator was substantially involved in the planning, direction, execution, or financing of the underlying offense.

(b) Any person convicted of a violation of, or of conspiracy to violate, Section 11378, 11378.5, 11379, or 11379.5 with respect to a substance containing methamphetamine, amphetamine, phencyclidine (PCP) and its analogs shall receive an additional term as follows:

(1) Where the substance exceeds one kilogram by weight, or 30 liters by liquid volume, the person shall receive an additional term of three years.

(2) Where the substance exceeds four kilograms by weight, or 100 liters by liquid volume, the person shall receive an additional term of five years.

(3) Where the substance exceeds 10 kilograms by weight, or 200 liters by liquid volume, the person shall receive an additional term of 10 years.

(4) Where the substance exceeds 20 kilograms by weight, or 400 liters by liquid volume, the person shall receive an additional term of 15 years.

In computing the quantities involved in this subdivision, plant or vegetable material seized shall not be included.

The conspiracy enhancements provided for in this subdivision shall not be imposed unless the trier of fact finds that the defendant conspirator was substantially involved in the planning, direction, execution, or financing of the underlying offense.

(c) The additional terms provided in this section shall not be imposed unless the allegation that the weight of the substance containing heroin, cocaine base as specified in paragraph (1) of subdivision (f) of Section 11054, cocaine as specified in paragraph (6) of subdivision (b) of Section 11055, methamphetamine, amphetamine, or phencyclidine (PCP) and its analogs exceeds the amounts provided in this section is charged in the accusatory pleading and admitted or found to be true by the trier of fact.

(d) The additional terms provided in this section shall be in addition to any other punishment provided by law.

(e) Notwithstanding any other provision of law, the court may strike the additional punishment for the enhancements provided in this section if it determines that there are circumstances in mitigation of the additional punishment and states on the record its reasons for striking the additional punishment. *(Added by Stats.1985, c. 1398, § 3. Amended by Stats.1986, c. 80, § 2; Stats.1986, c. 1044, § 17; Stats.1987, c. 991, § 1; Stats.1987, c. 1174, § 6, eff. Sept. 26, 1987; Stats.1987, c. 1174, § 6.5, eff. Sept. 26, 1987, operative Jan. 1, 1988; Stats.1989, c. 1245, § 2; Stats.1989, c. 1326, § 2.5; Stats.1992, c. 680 (S.B.1363), § 1; Stats.1997, c. 505 (A.B.513), § 1; Stats.1998, c. 425 (A.B.2369), § 1.)*

Cross References

Aggregate term, mitigating circumstances, see Penal Code § 1170.1.
Bail schedule, considerations in adopting uniform countywide schedule, see Penal Code § 1269b.
Fine upon person receiving additional term pursuant to this section, see Health and Safety Code § 11372.
Person defined for purposes of this Division, see Health and Safety Code § 11022.

Research References

California Jury Instructions - Criminal 17.21, Finding for Health and Safety Code §11370.4/11379.8 Sentence Enhancements.
2 Witkin, California Criminal Law 4th Crimes Against Public Peace and Welfare § 163 (2021), Punishment.
5 Witkin, California Criminal Law 4th Criminal Trial § 531 (2021), Other Applications.
5 Witkin, California Criminal Law 4th Criminal Trial § 727 (2021), Findings Permitted or Required.
3 Witkin, California Criminal Law 4th Punishment § 347 (2021), Power to Strike Enhancements.
3 Witkin, California Criminal Law 4th Punishment § 375 (2021), Value or Amount.
3 Witkin, California Criminal Law 4th Punishment § 429A (2021), (New) Where Third Strike is Not Serious or Violent Felony.

§ 11370.6. Possession of moneys or negotiable instruments in excess of $100,000 involved in unlawful sale or purchase of any controlled substance; punishment; acceptance of such funds by defense attorneys in payment of legal fees with criminal intent; proof

(a) Every person who possesses any moneys or negotiable instruments in excess of one hundred thousand dollars ($100,000) which have been obtained as the result of the unlawful sale, possession for sale, transportation, manufacture, offer for sale, or offer to manufacture any controlled substance listed in Section 11054, 11055, 11056, 11057, or 11058, with knowledge that the moneys or negotiable instruments have been so obtained, and any person who possesses any moneys or negotiable instruments in excess of one hundred thousand dollars ($100,000) which are intended by that person for the unlawful purchase of any controlled substance listed in Section 11054, 11055, 11056, 11057, or 11058 and who commits an act in substantial furtherance of the unlawful purchase, shall be punished by imprisonment in a county jail for a term not to exceed one year, or by imprisonment pursuant to subdivision (h) of Section 1170 of the Penal Code for two, three, or four years.

(b) In consideration of the constitutional right to counsel afforded by the Sixth Amendment to the United States Constitution and Section 15 of Article 1 of the California Constitution, when a case charged under subdivision (a) involves an attorney who accepts a fee for representing a client in a criminal investigation or proceeding, the prosecution shall additionally be required to prove that the moneys or negotiable instruments were accepted by the attorney with the intent to participate in the unlawful conduct described in subdivision (a) or to disguise or aid in disguising the source of the funds or the nature of the criminal activity.

(c) In determining the guilt or innocence of a person charged under subdivision (a), the trier of fact may consider the following in addition to any other relevant evidence:

(1) The lack of gainful employment by the person charged.

(2) The expert opinion of a qualified controlled substances expert as to the source of the assets.

(3) The existence of documents or ledgers that indicate sales of controlled substances. *(Added by Stats.1988, c. 267, § 1. Amended by Stats.2011, c. 15 (A.B.109), § 167, eff. April 4, 2011, operative Oct. 1, 2011.)*

Cross References

Controlled substance defined for purposes of this Division, see Health and Safety Code § 11007.
Person defined for purposes of this Division, see Health and Safety Code § 11022.

Research References

California Jury Instructions - Criminal 12.35, Unlawful Possession of Moneys/Negotiable Instruments in Excess of $100,000.
California Jury Instructions - Criminal 12.36, Attorney—Unlawful Possession of Money/Negotiable Instruments in Excess of $100,000.
California Jury Instructions - Criminal 12.37, Unlawful Possession of Money/Negotiable Instruments—Factors to Consider.
2 Witkin, California Criminal Law 4th Crimes Against Public Peace and Welfare § 159 (2021), Money Associated With Unlawful Transactions.

§ 11370.9. Proceeds over $25,000 derived from controlled substance offenses; penalties

(a) It is unlawful for any person knowingly to receive or acquire proceeds, or engage in a transaction involving proceeds, known to be derived from any violation of this division or Division 10.1 with the intent to conceal or disguise or aid in concealing or disguising the nature, location, ownership, control, or source of the proceeds or to avoid a transaction reporting requirement under state or federal law.

(b) It is unlawful for any person knowingly to give, sell, transfer, trade, invest, conceal, transport, or maintain an interest in, or otherwise make available, anything of value which that person knows is intended to be used for the purpose of committing, or furthering the commission of, any violation of this division or Division 10.1 with the intent to conceal or disguise or aid in concealing or disguising the nature, location, ownership, control, or source of the proceeds or to avoid a transaction reporting requirement under state or federal law.

(c) It is unlawful for any person knowingly to direct, plan, organize, initiate, finance, manage, supervise, or facilitate the transportation or transfer of proceeds known to be derived from any violation of this division or Division 10.1 with the intent to conceal or disguise or aid in concealing or disguising the nature, location, ownership, control, or source of the proceeds or to avoid a transaction reporting requirement under state or federal law.

(d) It is unlawful for any person knowingly to conduct a transaction involving proceeds derived from a violation of this division or Division 10.1 when the transaction is designed in whole or in part to conceal or disguise the nature, location, source, ownership, or control of the proceeds known to be derived from a violation of this division or Division 10.1 with the intent to conceal or disguise or aid in concealing or disguising the nature, location, ownership, control, or source of the proceeds or to avoid a transaction reporting requirement under state or federal law.

(e) A violation of this section shall be punished by imprisonment in a county jail for not more than one year or in the state prison for a period of two, three, or four years, by a fine of not more than two hundred fifty thousand dollars ($250,000) or twice the value of the proceeds or property involved in the violation, whichever is greater, or by both that imprisonment and fine. Notwithstanding any other provision of law, each violation of this section shall constitute a separate, punishable offense without limitation.

(f) This section shall apply only to a transaction, or series of related transactions within a 30-day period, involving over twenty-five thousand dollars ($25,000) or to proceeds of a value exceeding twenty-five thousand dollars ($25,000).

(g) In consideration of the constitutional right to counsel afforded by the Sixth Amendment to the United States Constitution and Section 15 of Article 1 of the California Constitution, this section is not intended to apply to the receipt of, or a related transaction involving, a fee by an attorney for the purpose of providing advice or representing a person in a criminal investigation or prosecution.

(h) For the purposes of this section, the following terms have the following meanings:

(1) "Proceeds" means property acquired or derived directly or indirectly from, produced through, or realized through any violation of this division or Division 10.1.

(2) "Transaction" includes a purchase, sale, trade, loan, pledge, investment, gift, transfer, transmission, delivery, deposit, withdrawal, payment, electronic, magnetic, or manual transfer between accounts, exchange of currency, extension of credit, purchase or sale of any monetary instrument, or any other acquisition or disposition of property by whatever means effected.

(3) "Represented by a law enforcement officer" means any representation of fact made by a peace officer as defined in Section 7 of the Penal Code, or a federal officer described in subsection (e) of Sections 1956 and 1957 of Title 18 of the United States Code, or by another person at the direction of, or with the approval of, that peace officer or federal officer. *(Added by Stats.1992, c. 503 (S.B.386), § 1. Amended by Stats.1993, c. 589 (A.B.2211), § 89.)*

Cross References

Deliver or delivery defined for purposes of this Division, see Health and Safety Code § 11009.
Person defined for purposes of this Division, see Health and Safety Code § 11022.

Research References

California Jury Instructions - Criminal 12.37.1, Proceeds Over $25,000 Derived from Controlled Substance Crimes (No. 1).
California Jury Instructions - Criminal 12.37.2, Proceeds Over $25,000 Derived from Controlled Substance Crimes (No. 2).
California Jury Instructions - Criminal 12.37.3, Proceeds Over $25,000 Derived from Controlled Substance Crimes (No. 3).
California Jury Instructions - Criminal 12.37.4, Proceeds Over $25,000 Derived from Controlled Substance Crimes (No. 4).
2 Witkin, California Criminal Law 4th Crimes Against Public Peace and Welfare § 159 (2021), Money Associated With Unlawful Transactions.

§ 11371. Prescription violations; inducing minor to violate provisions; punishment

Any person who shall knowingly violate any of the provisions of Section 11153, 11154, 11155, or 11156 with respect to (1) a controlled substance specified in subdivision (b), (c), or (d) of Section 11055, or (2) a controlled substance specified in paragraph (1) of subdivision (b) of Section 11056, or (3) a controlled substance which is a narcotic drug classified in Schedule III, IV, or V, or who in any voluntary manner solicits, induces, encourages or intimidates any minor with the intent that such minor shall commit any such offense, shall be punished by imprisonment pursuant to subdivision (h) of Section 1170 of the Penal Code, or in a county jail not exceeding one year, or by a fine not exceeding twenty thousand dollars ($20,000), or by both such fine and imprisonment. *(Added by Stats.1972, c. 1407, p. 3020, § 3. Amended by Stats.1973, c. 1078, p. 2183, § 19, eff. Oct. 1, 1973; Stats.1976, c. 1136, § 1; Stats.1976, c. 1139, p. 5083, § 80.5, operative*

July 1, 1977; Stats.1979, c. 879, p. 3064, § 2; Stats.1983, c. 790, § 13; Stats.2011, c. 15 (A.B.109), § 168, eff. April 4, 2011, operative Oct. 1, 2011.)

Cross References

Controlled substance defined for purposes of this Division, see Health and Safety Code § 11007.
Narcotic drug defined for purposes of this Division, see Health and Safety Code § 11019.
Person defined for purposes of this Division, see Health and Safety Code § 11022.

Research References

2 Witkin, California Criminal Law 4th Crimes Against Public Peace and Welfare § 152 (2021), In General.
2 Witkin, California Criminal Law 4th Crimes Against Public Peace and Welfare § 153 (2021), Inducing Minor to Commit Prescription Offenses.
2 Witkin, California Criminal Law 4th Crimes Against Public Peace and Welfare § 163 (2021), Punishment.

§ 11371.1. Fraud and false representation; inducing minor to violate provisions; punishment

Any person who shall knowingly violate any of the provisions of Section 11173 or 11174 with respect to (1) a controlled substance specified in subdivision (b), (c), or (d) of Section 11055, or (2) a controlled substance specified in paragraph (1) of subdivision (b) of Section 11056, or (3) a controlled substance which is a narcotic drug classified in Schedule III, IV, or V, or who in any voluntary manner solicits, induces, encourages or intimidates any minor with the intent that such minor shall commit any such offense, shall be punished by imprisonment pursuant to subdivision (h) of Section 1170 of the Penal Code, or in a county jail not exceeding one year. *(Added by Stats.1976, c. 1136, p. 5054, § 4, operative July 1, 1977. Amended by Stats.1979, c. 879, p. 3064, § 3; Stats.1983, c. 790, § 14; Stats.2011, c. 15 (A.B.109), § 169, eff. April 4, 2011, operative Oct. 1, 2011.)*

Cross References

Controlled substance defined for purposes of this Division, see Health and Safety Code § 11007.
Narcotic drug defined for purposes of this Division, see Health and Safety Code § 11019.
Person defined for purposes of this Division, see Health and Safety Code § 11022.

Research References

2 Witkin, California Criminal Law 4th Crimes Against Public Peace and Welfare § 152 (2021), In General.
2 Witkin, California Criminal Law 4th Crimes Against Public Peace and Welfare § 153 (2021), Inducing Minor to Commit Prescription Offenses.

§ 11372. Fines

(a) In addition to the term of imprisonment provided by law for persons convicted of violating Section 11350, 11351, 11351.5, 11352, 11353, 11355, 11359, 11360, or 11361, the trial court may impose a fine not exceeding twenty thousand dollars ($20,000) for each offense. In no event shall a fine be levied in lieu of or in substitution for the term of imprisonment provided by law for any of these offenses.

(b) Any person receiving an additional term pursuant to paragraph (1) of subdivision (a) of Section 11370.4, may, in addition, be fined by an amount not exceeding one million dollars ($1,000,000) for each offense.

(c) Any person receiving an additional term pursuant to paragraph (2) of subdivision (a) of Section 11370.4, may, in addition, be fined by an amount not to exceed four million dollars ($4,000,000) for each offense.

(d) Any person receiving an additional term pursuant to paragraph (3) of subdivision (a) of Section 11370.4, may, in addition, be fined by an amount not to exceed eight million dollars ($8,000,000) for each offense.

(e) The court shall make a finding, prior to the imposition of the fines authorized by subdivisions (b) to (e), inclusive, that there is a reasonable expectation that the fine, or a substantial portion thereof, could be collected within a reasonable period of time, taking into consideration the defendant's income, earning capacity, and financial resources. *(Added by Stats.1972, c. 1407, p. 3020, § 3. Amended by Stats.1986, c. 1044, § 18; Stats.1987, c. 656, § 1; Stats.2002, c. 787 (S.B.1798), § 2.)*

Cross References

Person defined for purposes of this Division, see Health and Safety Code § 11022.

Research References

2 Witkin, California Criminal Law 4th Crimes Against Public Peace and Welfare § 163 (2021), Punishment.

§ 11372.5. Criminal laboratory analysis fee; increase in total fine to include increment; criminalistics laboratories fund; surplus funds

(a) Every person who is convicted of a violation of Section 11350, 11351, 11351.5, 11352, 11355, 11358, 11359, 11361, 11363, 11364, 11368, 11375, 11377, 11378, 11378.5, 11379, 11379.5, 11379.6, 11380, 11380.5, 11382, 11383, 11390, 11391, or 11550 or subdivision (a) or (c) of Section 11357, or subdivision (a) of Section 11360 of this code, or Section 4230 of the Business and Professions Code shall pay a criminal laboratory analysis fee in the amount of fifty dollars ($50) for each separate offense. The court shall increase the total fine necessary to include this increment.

With respect to those offenses specified in this subdivision for which a fine is not authorized by other provisions of law, the court shall, upon conviction, impose a fine in an amount not to exceed fifty dollars ($50), which shall constitute the increment prescribed by this section and which shall be in addition to any other penalty prescribed by law.

(b) The county treasurer shall maintain a criminalistics laboratories fund. The sum of fifty dollars ($50) shall be deposited into the fund for every conviction under Section 11350, 11351, 11351.5, 11352, 11355, 11358, 11359, 11361, 11363, 11364, 11368, 11375, 11377, 11378, 11378.5, 11379, 11379.5, 11379.6, 11380, 11380.5, 11382, 11383, 11390, 11391, or 11550, subdivision (a) or (c) of Section 11357, or subdivision (a) of Section 11360 of this code, or Section 4230 of the Business and Professions Code, in addition to fines, forfeitures, and other moneys which are transmitted by the courts to the county treasurer pursuant to Section 11502. The deposits shall be made prior to any transfer pursuant to Section 11502. The county may retain an amount of this money equal to its administrative cost incurred pursuant to this section. Moneys in the criminalistics laboratories fund shall, except as otherwise provided in this section, be used exclusively to fund (1) costs incurred by criminalistics laboratories providing microscopic and chemical analyses for controlled substances, in connection with criminal investigations conducted within both the incorporated or unincorporated portions of the county, (2) the purchase and maintenance of equipment for use by these laboratories in performing the analyses, and (3) for continuing education, training, and scientific development of forensic scientists regularly employed by these laboratories. Moneys in the criminalistics laboratory fund shall be in addition to any allocations pursuant to existing law. As used in this section, "criminalistics laboratory" means a laboratory operated by, or under contract with, a city, county, or other public agency, including a criminalistics laboratory of the Department of Justice, (1) which has not less than one regularly employed forensic scientist engaged in the analysis of solid-dose controlled substances, and (2) which is registered as an analytical laboratory with the Drug Enforcement Administration of the United States Department of Justice for the possession of all scheduled controlled substances. In counties served by criminalistics laboratories of the Department of Justice, amounts deposited in the criminalistics laboratories fund, after deduction of appropriate and reasonable county overhead charges not to exceed 5 percent attributable to the collection thereof, shall be paid by the county treasurer once a month to the Controller for deposit into the state General Fund, and shall be excepted from the expenditure requirements otherwise prescribed by this subdivision.

(c) The county treasurer shall, at the conclusion of each fiscal year, determine the amount of any funds remaining in the special fund established pursuant to this section after expenditures for that fiscal year have been made for the purposes herein specified. The board of supervisors may, by resolution, assign the treasurer's duty to determine the amount of remaining funds to the auditor or another county officer. The county treasurer shall annually distribute those surplus funds in accordance with the allocation scheme for distribution of fines and forfeitures set forth in Section 11502. *(Added by Stats.1980, c. 1222, p. 4140, § 1. Amended by Stats.1983, c. 101, § 110; Stats.1983, c. 626, § 1; Stats.1985, c. 1098, § 5, eff. Sept. 27, 1985; Stats.1985, c. 1264, § 1; Stats.1986, c. 587, § 1; Stats.1986, c. 1044, § 19.5; Stats.1992, c. 1159 (S.B.1729), § 1; Stats.2005, c. 158 (S.B.966), § 23.)*

Cross References

Allocation and distribution of fines, forfeitures, penalties, fees or assessments collected in any criminal case, see Penal Code § 1464.8.

Controlled substance defined for purposes of this Division, see Health and Safety Code § 11007.

Distribute defined for purposes of this Division, see Health and Safety Code § 11012.

Person defined for purposes of this Division, see Health and Safety Code § 11022.

State Controller, generally, see Government Code § 12402 et seq.

Research References

2 Witkin, California Criminal Law 4th Crimes Against Public Peace and Welfare § 163 (2021), Punishment.

3 Witkin, California Criminal Law 4th Punishment § 103 (2021), State and County Assessments and Surcharges.

3 Witkin, California Criminal Law 4th Punishment § 104 (2021), Additional Assessments, Penalties, and Fees.

§ 11372.7. Persons convicted of violation of this chapter; payment of drug program fee; fee amount; ability to pay; drug program fund

(a) Except as otherwise provided in subdivision (b) or (e), each person who is convicted of a violation of this chapter shall pay a drug program fee in an amount not to exceed one hundred fifty dollars ($150) for each separate offense. The court shall increase the total fine, if necessary, to include this increment, which shall be in addition to any other penalty prescribed by law.

(b) The court shall determine whether or not the person who is convicted of a violation of this chapter has the ability to pay a drug program fee. If the court determines that the person has the ability to pay, the court may set the amount to be paid and order the person to pay that sum to the county in a manner that the court believes is reasonable and compatible with the person's financial ability. In its determination of whether a person has the ability to pay, the court shall take into account the amount of any fine imposed upon that person and any amount that person has been ordered to pay in restitution. If the court determines that the person does not have the ability to pay a drug program fee, the person shall not be required to pay a drug program fee.

(c) The county treasurer shall maintain a drug program fund. For every drug program fee assessed and collected pursuant to subdivisions (a) and (b), an amount equal to this assessment shall be deposited into the fund for every conviction pursuant to this chapter, in addition to fines, forfeitures, and other moneys which are transmitted by the courts to the county treasurer pursuant to Sections 11372.5 and 11502. These deposits shall be made prior to any transfer pursuant to Section 11502. Amounts deposited in the drug program fund shall be allocated by the administrator of the county's drug program to drug abuse programs in the schools and the community, subject to the approval of the board of supervisors, as follows:

(1) The moneys in the fund shall be allocated through the planning process established pursuant to Sections 11983, 11983.1, 11983.2, and 11983.3.

(2) A minimum of 33 percent of the fund shall be allocated to primary prevention programs in the schools and the community. Primary prevention programs developed and implemented under this article shall emphasize cooperation in planning and program implementation among schools and community drug abuse agencies, and shall demonstrate coordination through an interagency agreement among county offices of education, school districts, and the county drug program administrator. These primary prevention programs may include:

(A) School- and classroom-oriented programs, including, but not limited to, programs designed to encourage sound decisionmaking, an awareness of values, an awareness of drugs and their effects, enhanced self-esteem, social and practical skills that will assist students toward maturity, enhanced or improved school climate and relationships among all school personnel and students, and furtherance of cooperative efforts of school- and community-based personnel.

(B) School- or community-based nonclassroom alternative programs, or both, including, but not limited to, positive peer group programs, programs involving youth and adults in constructive activities designed as alternatives to drug use, and programs for special target groups, such as women, ethnic minorities, and other high-risk, high-need populations.

(C) Family-oriented programs, including, but not limited to, programs aimed at improving family relationships and involving parents constructively in the education and nurturing of their children, as well as in specific activities aimed at preventing drug abuse.

(d) Moneys deposited into a county drug program fund pursuant to this section shall supplement, and shall not supplant, any local funds made available to support the county's drug abuse prevention and treatment efforts.

(e) This section shall not apply to any person convicted of a violation of subdivision (b) of Section 11357 of the Health and Safety Code. *(Added by Stats.1986, c. 1027, § 3. Amended by Stats.1987, c. 247, § 1, eff. July 27, 1987; Stats.1987, c. 621, § 4.5; Stats.1993, c. 474 (A.B.855), § 1; Stats.2001, c. 750 (A.B.1107), § 19; Stats.2001, c. 854 (S.B.205), § 8; Stats.2002, c. 545 (S.B.1852), § 1.5.)*

Cross References

Drug defined for purposes of this Division, see Health and Safety Code § 11014.

Person defined for purposes of this Division, see Health and Safety Code § 11022.

Research References

2 Witkin, California Criminal Law 4th Crimes Against Public Peace and Welfare § 163 (2021), Punishment.

3 Witkin, California Criminal Law 4th Punishment § 103 (2021), State and County Assessments and Surcharges.

3 Witkin, California Criminal Law 4th Punishment § 104 (2021), Additional Assessments, Penalties, and Fees.

§ 11373. Education or treatment as a condition of probation

(a) Whenever any person who is otherwise eligible for probation is granted probation by the trial court after conviction for a violation of any controlled substance offense under this division, the trial court shall, as a condition of probation, order that person to secure education or treatment from a local community agency designated by the court, if the service is available and the person is likely to benefit from the service.

If the defendant is a minor, the trial court shall also order his or her parents or guardian to participate in the education or treatment to the extent the court determines that participation will aid the education or treatment of the minor.

If a minor is found by a juvenile court to have been in possession of any controlled substance, in addition to any other order it may make, the juvenile court shall order the minor to receive education or treatment from a local community agency designated by the court, if the service is available and the person is likely to benefit from the service, and it shall also order his or her parents or guardian to participate in the education or treatment to the extent the court determines that participation will aid the education or treatment of the minor.

(b) The willful failure to complete a court ordered education or treatment program shall be a circumstance in aggravation for purposes of sentencing for any subsequent prosecution for a violation of Section 11353, 11354, or 11380. The failure to complete an education or treatment program because of the person's inability to pay the costs of the program or because of the unavailability to the defendant of appropriate programs is not a willful failure to complete the program. *(Added by Stats.1972, c. 1407, p. 3020, § 3. Amended by Stats.1984, c. 1635, § 61; Stats.1992, c. 185 (A.B.1847), § 1.)*

Cross References

Controlled substance defined for purposes of this Division, see Health and Safety Code § 11007.
Person defined for purposes of this Division, see Health and Safety Code § 11022.

Research References

3 Witkin, California Criminal Law 4th Punishment § 664 (2021), Counseling, Treatment, and Education.

§ 11374. Violation of or failure to comply with provisions; misdemeanor

Every person who violates or fails to comply with any provision of this division, except one for which a penalty is otherwise in this division specifically provided, is guilty of a misdemeanor punishable by a fine in a sum not less than thirty dollars ($30) nor more than five hundred dollars ($500), or by imprisonment for not less than 15 nor more than 180 days, or by both. *(Added by Stats.1972, c. 1407, p. 3021, § 3.)*

Cross References

Misdemeanor, definition and penalties, see Penal Code §§ 17, 19, 19.2.
Person defined for purposes of this Division, see Health and Safety Code § 11022.
Prescription for controlled substance containing opioids, dispensing or issuing to minors, required discussions, exemptions, see Health and Safety Code § 11158.1.

Research References

2 Witkin, California Criminal Law 4th Crimes Against Public Peace and Welfare § 155 (2021), Drug Paraphernalia.
2 Witkin, California Criminal Law 4th Crimes Against Public Peace and Welfare § 163 (2021), Punishment.
3 Witkin, California Criminal Law 4th Punishment § 306 (2021), Where Punishment is Not Specified.

§ 11374.5. Manufacturer violating hazardous substance disposal law by disposal of controlled substance or its precursor; punishment; definitions

Section operative until Jan. 1, 2024. See, also, § 11374.5 operative Jan. 1, 2024.

(a) Any manufacturer of a controlled substance who disposes of any hazardous substance that is a controlled substance or a chemical used in, or is a byproduct of, the manufacture of a controlled substance in violation of any law regulating the disposal of hazardous substances or hazardous waste is guilty of a public offense punishable by imprisonment pursuant to subdivision (h) of Section 1170 of the Penal Code for two, three, or four years or in the county jail not exceeding one year.

(b)(1) In addition to any other penalty or liability imposed by law, a person who is convicted of violating subdivision (a), or any person who is convicted of the manufacture, sale, possession for sale, possession, transportation, or disposal of any hazardous substance that is a controlled substance or a chemical used in, or is a byproduct of, the manufacture of a controlled substance in violation of any law, shall pay a penalty equal to the amount of the actual cost incurred by the state or local agency to remove and dispose of the hazardous substance that is a controlled substance or a chemical used in, or is a byproduct of, the manufacture of a controlled substance and to take removal action with respect to any release of the hazardous substance or any items or materials contaminated by that release, if the state or local agency requests the prosecuting authority to seek recovery of that cost. The court shall transmit all penalties collected pursuant to this subdivision to the county treasurer of the county in which the court is located for deposit in a special account in the county treasury. The county treasurer shall pay that money at least once a month to the agency that requested recovery of the cost for the removal action. The county may retain up to 5 percent of any assessed penalty for appropriate and reasonable administrative costs attributable to the collection and disbursement of the penalty.

(2) If the Department of Toxic Substances Control has requested recovery of the cost of removing the hazardous substance that is a controlled substance or a chemical used in, or is a byproduct of, the manufacture of a controlled substance or taking removal action with respect to any release of the hazardous substance, the county treasurer shall transfer funds in the amount of the penalty collected to the Treasurer, who shall deposit the money in the Illegal Drug Lab Cleanup Account, which is hereby created in the General Fund in the State Treasury. The Department of Toxic Substances Control may expend the money in the Illegal Drug Lab Cleanup Account, upon appropriation by the Legislature, to cover the cost of taking removal actions pursuant to Section 25354.5.

(3) If a local agency and the Department of Toxic Substances Control have both requested recovery of removal costs with respect to a hazardous substance that is a controlled substance or a chemical used in, or is a byproduct of, the manufacture of a controlled substance, the county treasurer shall apportion any penalty collected among the agencies involved in proportion to the costs incurred.

(c) As used in this section the following terms have the following meaning:

(1) "Dispose" means to abandon, deposit, intern, or otherwise discard as a final action after use has been achieved or a use is no longer intended.

(2) "Hazardous substance" has the same meaning as defined in Section 25316.

(3) "Hazardous waste" has the same meaning as defined in Section 25117.

(4) For purposes of this section, "remove" or "removal" has the same meaning as set forth in Section 25323. *(Added by Stats.1986, c. 1031, § 1. Amended by Stats.1993, c. 549 (S.B.1175), § 1; Stats.1998, c. 425 (A.B.2369), § 2; Stats.2011, c. 15 (A.B.109), § 170, eff. April 4, 2011, operative Oct. 1, 2011.)*

§ 11374.5. Manufacturer violating hazardous substance disposal law by disposal of controlled substance or its precursor; punishment; definitions

Section operative Jan. 1, 2024. See, also, § 11374.5 operative until Jan. 1, 2024.

(a) Any manufacturer of a controlled substance who disposes of any hazardous substance that is a controlled substance or a chemical used in, or is a byproduct of, the manufacture of a controlled substance in violation of any law regulating the disposal of hazardous substances or hazardous waste is guilty of a public offense punishable by imprisonment pursuant to subdivision (h) of Section 1170 of the Penal Code for two, three, or four years or in the county jail not exceeding one year.

(b)(1) In addition to any other penalty or liability imposed by law, a person who is convicted of violating subdivision (a), or any person who is convicted of the manufacture, sale, possession for sale, possession, transportation, or disposal of any hazardous substance that is a controlled substance or a chemical used in, or is a byproduct of, the manufacture of a controlled substance in violation of any law, shall pay a penalty equal to the amount of the actual cost incurred by the state or local agency to remove and dispose of the hazardous substance that is a controlled substance or a chemical used in, or is a byproduct of, the manufacture of a controlled substance and to take removal action with respect to any release of the hazardous substance or any items or materials contaminated by that release, if the state or local agency requests the prosecuting authority to seek recovery of that cost. The court shall transmit all penalties collected pursuant to this subdivision to the county treasurer of the county in which the court is located for deposit in a special account in the county treasury. The county treasurer shall pay that money at least once a month to the agency that requested recovery of the cost for the removal action. The county may retain up to 5 percent of any assessed penalty for appropriate and reasonable administrative costs attributable to the collection and disbursement of the penalty.

(2) If the Department of Toxic Substances Control has requested recovery of the cost of removing the hazardous substance that is a controlled substance or a chemical used in, or is a byproduct of, the manufacture of a controlled substance or taking removal action with respect to any release of the hazardous substance, the county treasurer shall transfer funds in the amount of the penalty collected to the Treasurer, who shall deposit the money in the Illegal Drug Lab Cleanup Account, which is hereby created in the General Fund in the State Treasury. The Department of Toxic Substances Control may expend the money in the Illegal Drug Lab Cleanup Account, upon appropriation by the Legislature, to cover the cost of taking removal actions pursuant to Article 16 (commencing with Section * * * 79350) of Chapter 5 of Part 2 of Division 45.

(3) If a local agency and the Department of Toxic Substances Control have both requested recovery of removal costs with respect to a hazardous substance that is a controlled substance or a chemical used in, or is a byproduct of, the manufacture of a controlled substance, the county treasurer shall apportion any penalty collected among the agencies involved in proportion to the costs incurred.

(c) As used in this section the following terms have the following meaning:

(1) "Dispose" means to abandon, deposit, intern, or otherwise discard as a final action after use has been achieved or a use is no longer intended.

(2) "Hazardous substance" has the same meaning as defined in subdivision (a) of Section 78075.

(3) "Hazardous waste" has the same meaning as defined in Section 25117.

(4) For purposes of this section, "remove" or "removal" has the same meaning as set forth in Section 78135. *(Added by Stats.1986, c. 1031, § 1. Amended by Stats.1993, c. 549 (S.B.1175), § 1; Stats.1998, c. 425 (A.B.2369), § 2; Stats.2011, c. 15 (A.B.109), § 170, eff. April 4, 2011, operative Oct. 1, 2011; Stats.2022, c. 258 (A.B.2327), § 29, eff. Jan. 1, 2023, operative Jan. 1, 2024.)*

Law Revision Commission Comments

Section 11374.5(b)(2), (c)(2), and (c)(4) are amended to update cross-references in accordance with the nonsubstantive recodification of Chapter 6.8 (commencing with Section 25300) of Division 20 of the Health and Safety Code. [48 Cal.L.Rev.Comm. Reports ＿ (2021)].

Cross References

Controlled substance defined for purposes of this Division, see Health and Safety Code § 11007.
Manufacturer defined for purposes of this Division, see Health and Safety Code § 11017.
Person defined for purposes of this Division, see Health and Safety Code § 11022.

Research References

2 Witkin, California Criminal Law 4th Crimes Against Public Peace and Welfare § 160 (2021), Improper Disposal.

§ 11375. Possession, possession for sale, or sale of designated controlled substances; application of section; punishment

Section operative until the terms of Section 3 of Stats.1996, c. 109 (S.B.1426) are met. See, also, section operative when the terms of Section 3 of Stats.1996, c. 109 (S.B.1426) are met.

(a) As to the substances specified in subdivision (c), this section, and not Sections 11377, 11378, 11379, and 11380, shall apply.

(b)(1) Every person who possesses for sale, or who sells, any substance specified in subdivision (c) shall be punished by imprisonment in the county jail for a period of not more than one year or state prison.

(2) Every person who possesses any controlled substance specified in subdivision (c), unless upon the prescription of a physician, dentist, podiatrist, or veterinarian, licensed to practice in this state, shall be guilty of an infraction or a misdemeanor.

(c) This section shall apply to any material, compound, mixture, or preparation containing any of the following substances:

(1) Chlordiazepoxide.

(2) Clonazepam.

(3) Clorazepate.

(4) Diazepam.

(5) Flurazepam.

(6) Lorazepam.

(7) Mebutamate.

(8) Oxazepam.

(9) Prazepam.

(10) Temazepam.

(11) Halazepam.

(12) Alprazolam.

(13) Propoxyphene.

(14) Diethylpropion.

(15) Phentermine.

(16) Pemoline.

(17) Fenfluramine.

(18) Triazolam. *(Added by Stats.1984, c. 1635, § 63. Amended by Stats.1992, c. 616 (S.B.2013), § 3; Stats.2001, c. 838 (A.B.98), § 2.)*

Cross References

Certified farmers' markets, requirements, see Health and Safety Code § 114371.

Health & Safety

Controlled substance defined for purposes of this Division, see Health and Safety Code § 11007.
Isomer defined for purposes of this Division, see Health and Safety Code § 11033.
Misdemeanors, definition and penalties, see Penal Code §§ 17, 19, 19.2.
Person defined for purposes of this Division, see Health and Safety Code § 11022.
Physician, dentist, podiatrist, pharmacist, veterinarian, and optometrist defined for purposes of this Division, see Health and Safety Code § 11024.
Prescription or electronic transmission prescription defined for purposes of this Division, see Health and Safety Code § 11027.
Special proceedings in narcotics and drug abuse cases, application of Chapter to certain violations, including specified provisions of this section, see Penal Code § 1000.

Research References

2 Witkin, California Criminal Law 4th Crimes Against Public Peace and Welfare § 88 (2021), Substances Formerly Classified as Restricted Dangerous Drugs.
2 Witkin, California Criminal Law 4th Crimes Against Public Peace and Welfare § 97 (2021), In General.
2 Witkin, California Criminal Law 4th Crimes Against Public Peace and Welfare § 101 (2021), Possession for Sale.
2 Witkin, California Criminal Law 4th Crimes Against Public Peace and Welfare § 108 (2021), Possession Inconsistent With Legal Possession.
2 Witkin, California Criminal Law 4th Crimes Against Public Peace and Welfare § 115 (2021), Statutory Prohibitions.
2 Witkin, California Criminal Law 4th Crimes Against Public Peace and Welfare § 125 (2021), Substances Formerly Classified as Restricted Dangerous Drugs.
4 Witkin, California Criminal Law 4th Pretrial Proceedings § 386 (2021), Offenses and Conditions.

§ 11375. Possession, possession for sale, or sale of designated controlled substances; application of section; punishment

Section operative when the terms of Section 3 of Stats.1996, c. 109 (S.B.1426) are met. See, also, section operative until the terms of Section 3 of Stats.1996, c. 109 (S.B.1426) are met.

(a) As to the substances specified in subdivision (c), this section, and not Sections 11377, 11378, 11379, and 11380, shall apply.

(b)(1) Every person who possesses for sale, or who sells, any substance specified in subdivision (c) shall be punished by imprisonment in the county jail for a period of not more than one year or state prison.

(2) Every person who possesses any controlled substance specified in subdivision (c), unless upon the prescription of a physician, dentist, podiatrist, or veterinarian, licensed to practice in this state, shall be guilty of an infraction or a misdemeanor.

(c) This section shall apply to any material, compound, mixture, or preparation containing any of the following substances:

(1) Chlordiazepoxide.

(2) Clonazepam.

(3) Clorazepate.

(4) Diazepam.

(5) Flurazepam.

(6) Lorazepam.

(7) Mebutamate.

(8) Oxazepam.

(9) Prazepam.

(10) Temazepam.

(11) Halazepam.

(12) Alprazolam.

(13) Propoxyphene.

(14) Diethylpropion.

(15) Phentermine.

(16) Pemoline.

(17) Triazolam. *(Added by Stats.1984, c. 1635, § 63. Amended by Stats.1992, c. 616 (S.B.2013), § 3; Stats.1996, c. 109 (S.B.1426), § 2, eff. July 1, 1996; Stats.2001, c. 838 (A.B.98), § 1, operative contingent.)*

Operative Effect

Section 3 of Stats.1996, c. 109 (S.B.1426) provides that "[t]his bill shall not become operative unless fenfluramine and its salts and isomers are removed from Schedule IV of the federal Controlled Substances Act (21 U.S.C.A. Sec. 812; 21 C.F.R. 1308.14)."

Cross References

Certified farmers' markets, requirements, see Health and Safety Code § 114371.
Fines, increment for each separate offense, see Health and Safety Code § 11372.5.
Special proceedings in narcotics and drug abuse cases, application of Chapter to certain violations, including specified provisions of this section, see Penal Code § 1000.

Research References

2 Witkin, California Criminal Law 4th Crimes Against Public Peace and Welfare § 88 (2021), Substances Formerly Classified as Restricted Dangerous Drugs.
2 Witkin, California Criminal Law 4th Crimes Against Public Peace and Welfare § 97 (2021), In General.
2 Witkin, California Criminal Law 4th Crimes Against Public Peace and Welfare § 101 (2021), Possession for Sale.
2 Witkin, California Criminal Law 4th Crimes Against Public Peace and Welfare § 108 (2021), Possession Inconsistent With Legal Possession.
2 Witkin, California Criminal Law 4th Crimes Against Public Peace and Welfare § 115 (2021), Statutory Prohibitions.
2 Witkin, California Criminal Law 4th Crimes Against Public Peace and Welfare § 125 (2021), Substances Formerly Classified as Restricted Dangerous Drugs.
4 Witkin, California Criminal Law 4th Pretrial Proceedings § 386 (2021), Offenses and Conditions.

§ 11375.5. Synthetic stimulant compound or derivative; prohibited sale, dispensing, distribution, etc., or possession for sale; first, second, third or subsequent offense; punishment

(a) Every person who sells, dispenses, distributes, furnishes, administers, or gives, or offers to sell, dispense, distribute, furnish, administer, or give, any synthetic stimulant compound specified in subdivision (c), or any synthetic stimulant derivative, to any person, or who possesses that compound or derivative for sale, is guilty of a misdemeanor, punishable by imprisonment in a county jail not to exceed six months, or by a fine not to exceed one thousand dollars ($1,000), or by both that fine and imprisonment.

(b) Every person who uses or possesses any synthetic stimulant compound specified in subdivision (c), or any synthetic stimulant derivative, is guilty of a public offense, punishable as follows:

(1) A first offense is an infraction punishable by a fine not exceeding two hundred fifty dollars ($250).

(2) A second offense is an infraction punishable by a fine not exceeding two hundred fifty dollars ($250) or a misdemeanor punishable by imprisonment in a county jail not exceeding six months, a fine not exceeding five hundred dollars ($500), or by both that fine and imprisonment.

(3) A third or subsequent offense is a misdemeanor punishable by imprisonment in a county jail not exceeding six months, or by a fine not exceeding one thousand dollars ($1,000), or by both that fine and imprisonment.

(c) Unless specifically excepted, or contained within a pharmaceutical product approved by the United States Food and Drug Administration, or unless listed in another schedule, subdivisions (a) and (b) apply to any material, compound, mixture, or preparation which contains any quantity of a substance or analog of a substance, including its salts, isomers, esters, or ethers, and salts of isomers, esters, or ethers whenever the existence of such salts, isomers, esters, or ethers, and salts of isomers, esters, or ethers is possible, that is structurally derived from 2–amino–1–phenyl–1–propanone by modification in one of the following ways:

(1) By substitution in the phenyl ring to any extent with alkyl, alkoxy, alkylenedioxy, haloalkyl, or halide substituents, whether or not further substituted in the phenyl ring by one or more other univalent substituents.

(2) By substitution at the 3–position with an alkyl substituent.

(3) By substitution at the nitrogen atom with alkyl or dialkyl groups, or by inclusion of the nitrogen atom in a cyclic structure.

(d) This section shall not prohibit prosecution under any other provision of law. *(Added by Stats.2014, c. 372 (S.B.1283), § 4, eff. Jan. 1, 2015, operative Jan. 1, 2016. Amended by Stats.2016, c. 624 (S.B.139), § 3, eff. Sept. 25, 2016.)*

Research References

2 Witkin, California Criminal Law 4th Crimes Against Public Peace and Welfare § 97 (2021), In General.
2 Witkin, California Criminal Law 4th Crimes Against Public Peace and Welfare § 115 (2021), Statutory Prohibitions.

§ 11375.7. Preguilty plea drug court program; eligibility to participate; grounds for exclusion or dismissal from program

(a) Unless otherwise excluded pursuant to this section, a person charged with a misdemeanor pursuant to paragraph (3) of subdivision (b) of Section 11357.5 or paragraph (3) of subdivision (b) of Section 11375.5 shall be eligible to participate in a preguilty plea drug court program, as described in Section 1000.5 of the Penal Code.

(b) Notwithstanding any other law, a positive test for use of a controlled substance, any other drug that may not be possessed without a prescription, or alcohol shall not be grounds for dismissal from the program, unless the person is not making progress in the program. The court shall consider a report or recommendation of the treatment provider in making this determination. It shall be presumed that a person engaged in a program is making progress, unless that presumption is defeated by clear and convincing evidence. The person may offer evidence or an argument that he or she would benefit from and make progress in a different program or mode. If the court so finds, it may place the person in a different treatment program.

(c) Notwithstanding any other law, the following persons are excluded from participation in the program under this section:

(1) A person with a history of violence that indicates that he or she presents a current risk of violent behavior currently or during the treatment program. This ground for exclusion shall be established by clear and convincing evidence.

(2) A person required to register as a sex offender pursuant to Section 290, unless the court finds by clear and convincing evidence that the person does not present a substantial risk of committing sexual offenses currently or through the course of the program and the person would benefit from the program, including that treatment would reduce the risk that the person would sexually reoffend.

(3) A person who the treatment provider concludes is unamenable to any and all forms of drug treatment. The defendant may present evidence that he or she is amenable to treatment and the court may retain the person in the program if the court finds that the person is amenable to treatment through a different provider or a different mode of treatment.

(d) Notwithstanding any other law, a prior conviction for an offense involving a controlled substance or drug that may not be possessed without a prescription, including a substance listed in Section 11357.5 or 11375.5, is not grounds for exclusion from the program, unless the court finds by clear and convincing evidence that the person is likely to engage in drug commerce for financial gain, rather than for purposes of obtaining a drug or drugs for personal use. *(Added by Stats.2016, c. 624 (S.B.139), § 4, eff. Sept. 25, 2016. Amended by Stats.2017, c. 561 (A.B.1516), § 112, eff. Jan. 1, 2018.)*

§ 11376. Counseling or education programs; conditions of sentencing or probation

Upon the diversion or conviction of a person for any offense involving substance abuse, the court may require, in addition to any or all other terms of diversion or imprisonment, fine, or other reasonable conditions of sentencing or probation imposed by the court, that the defendant participate in and complete counseling or education programs, or both, including, but not limited to, parent education or parenting programs operated by community colleges, school districts, other public agencies, or private agencies. *(Added by Stats.1996, c. 210 (S.B.1443), § 1.)*

Cross References

Person defined for purposes of this Division, see Health and Safety Code § 11022.

Research References

2 Witkin, California Criminal Law 4th Crimes Against Public Peace and Welfare § 88 (2021), Substances Formerly Classified as Restricted Dangerous Drugs.
3 Witkin, California Criminal Law 4th Punishment § 664 (2021), Counseling, Treatment, and Education.

§ 11376.5. Medical assistance exception to controlled substance or paraphernalia possession and related offenses; persons experiencing drug-related overdose; no exception to laws prohibiting sales, forcible administration, or liability for actions made dangerous by controlled substance use

(a) Notwithstanding any other law, it shall not be a crime for a person to be under the influence of, or to possess for personal use, a controlled substance, controlled substance analog, or drug paraphernalia, if that person, in good faith, seeks medical assistance for another person experiencing a drug-related overdose that is related to the possession of a controlled substance, controlled substance analog, or drug paraphernalia of the person seeking medical assistance, and that person does not obstruct medical or law enforcement personnel. No other immunities or protections from arrest or prosecution for violations of the law are intended or may be inferred.

(b) Notwithstanding any other law, it shall not be a crime for a person who experiences a drug-related overdose and who is in need of medical assistance to be under the influence of, or to possess for personal use, a controlled substance, controlled substance analog, or drug paraphernalia, if the person or one or more other persons at the scene of the overdose, in good faith, seek medical assistance for the person experiencing the overdose. No other immunities or protections from arrest or prosecution for violations of the law are intended or may be inferred.

(c) This section shall not affect laws prohibiting the selling, providing, giving, or exchanging of drugs, or laws prohibiting the forcible administration of drugs against a person's will.

(d) Nothing in this section shall affect liability for any offense that involves activities made dangerous by the consumption of a controlled substance or controlled substance analog, including, but not limited to, violations of Section 23103 of the Vehicle Code as specified in Section 23103.5 of the Vehicle Code, or violations of Section 23152 or 23153 of the Vehicle Code.

(e) For the purposes of this section, "drug-related overdose" means an acute medical condition that is the result of the ingestion or use by an individual of one or more controlled substances or one or more controlled substances in combination with alcohol, in quantities that are excessive for that individual that may result in death, disability, or serious injury. An individual's condition shall be deemed to be a "drug-related overdose" if a reasonable person of ordinary knowledge would believe the condition to be a drug-related overdose that may result in death, disability, or serious injury. *(Added by Stats.2012, c. 338 (A.B.472), § 2.)*

Research References

2 Witkin, California Criminal Law 4th Crimes Against Public Peace and Welfare § 93 (2021), Specified Narcotics and Restricted Dangerous Drugs.

2 Witkin, California Criminal Law 4th Crimes Against Public Peace and Welfare § 97 (2021), In General.

ARTICLE 5. OFFENSES INVOLVING CONTROLLED SUBSTANCES FORMERLY CLASSIFIED AS RESTRICTED DANGEROUS DRUGS

§ 11377. Unauthorized possession; punishment; possession by person other than the prescription holder

(a) Except as authorized by law and as otherwise provided in subdivision (b) or Section 11375, or in Article 7 (commencing with Section 4211) of Chapter 9 of Division 2 of the Business and Professions Code, every person who possesses any controlled substance which is (1) classified in Schedule III, IV, or V, and which is not a narcotic drug, (2) specified in subdivision (d) of Section 11054, except paragraphs (13), (14), (15), and (20) of subdivision (d), (3) specified in paragraph (11) of subdivision (c) of Section 11056, (4) specified in paragraph (2) or (3) of subdivision (f) of Section 11054, or (5) specified in subdivision (d), (e), or (f) of Section 11055, unless upon the prescription of a physician, dentist, podiatrist, or veterinarian, licensed to practice in this state, shall be punished by imprisonment in a county jail for a period of not more than one year, except that such person may instead be punished pursuant to subdivision (h) of Section 1170 of the Penal Code if that person has one or more prior convictions for an offense specified in clause (iv) of subparagraph (C) of paragraph (2) of subdivision (e) of Section 667 of the Penal Code or for an offense requiring registration pursuant to subdivision (c) of Section 290 of the Penal Code.

(b) The judge may assess a fine not to exceed seventy dollars ($70) against any person who violates subdivision (a), with the proceeds of this fine to be used in accordance with Section 1463.23 of the Penal Code. The court shall, however, take into consideration the defendant's ability to pay, and no defendant shall be denied probation because of his or her inability to pay the fine permitted under this subdivision.

(c) It is not unlawful for a person other than the prescription holder to possess a controlled substance described in subdivision (a) if both of the following apply:

(1) The possession of the controlled substance is at the direction or with the express authorization of the prescription holder.

(2) The sole intent of the possessor is to deliver the prescription to the prescription holder for its prescribed use or to discard the substance in a lawful manner.

(d) This section does not permit the use of a controlled substance by a person other than the prescription holder or permit the distribution or sale of a controlled substance that is otherwise inconsistent with the prescription. *(Added by Stats.1972, c. 1407, p. 3021, § 3. Amended by Stats.1973, c. 1078, p. 2183, § 22, eff. Oct. 1, 1973; Stats.1973, c. 1088, p. 2206, § 3, eff. Oct. 1, 1973; Stats.1976, c. 1139, p. 5084, § 81, operative July 1, 1977; Stats.1977, c. 843, p. 2535, § 23; Stats.1978, c. 699, p. 2212, § 3; Stats.1981, c. 742, p. 2907, § 1; Stats.1984, c. 1635, § 65; Stats.1985, c. 3, § 3, eff. Jan. 29, 1985; Stats.1986, c. 1033, § 2; Stats.1986, c. 1044, § 20.5; Stats.1988, c. 1243, § 3; Stats.1991, c. 294 (A.B.444), § 2; Stats.1998, c. 358 (A.B.1731), § 1; Stats.1999, c. 975 (A.B.924), § 3; Stats.2001, c. 838 (A.B.98), § 3; Stats.2001, c. 841 (A.B.258), § 5.5; Stats.2002, c. 664 (A.B.3034), § 131; Stats.2008, c. 292 (A.B.1141), § 3; Stats.2011, c. 15 (A.B.109), § 171, eff. April 4, 2011, operative Oct. 1, 2011; Initiative Measure (Prop. 47, § 13, approved Nov. 4, 2014, eff. Nov. 5, 2014); Stats.2017, c. 269 (S.B.811), § 6, eff. Jan. 1, 2018.)*

Cross References

Anabolic steroids, advertising sale, penalty, see Business and Professions Code § 17533.10.

Arrest of teacher or instructor employed in community college district, notices, see Health and Safety Code § 11591.5.

Controlled substance defined for purposes of this Division, see Health and Safety Code § 11007.

Controlled substances, quantity, aggravated term, see Penal Code § 1170.73.

Diversion from trial for education, treatment or rehabilitation, see Penal Code § 1000 et seq.

Felony offenses involving crystalline form of methamphetamine, aggravation of crime, see Penal Code § 1170.74.

Fines, increment for each separate offense, see Health and Safety Code § 11372.5.

Further grounds for denial, classes of applicants, and rehabilitation, see Education Code § 44346.

Juvenile court law,

Application to commence proceedings, affidavits, see Welfare and Institutions Code § 653.5.

Eligibility for program of supervision, see Welfare and Institutions Code § 653.5.

Misdemeanors, definition and penalties, see Penal Code §§ 17, 19, 19.2.

Narcotic drug defined for purposes of this Division, see Health and Safety Code § 11019.
Of criminal procedure, pleadings and proceedings before trial, special proceedings in narcotics and drug abuse cases, application to certain violations, see Penal Code § 1000.
Person defined for purposes of this Division, see Health and Safety Code § 11022.
Pharmacy, prescriber dispensing, exemptions, see Business and Professions Code § 4171.
Physician, dentist, podiatrist, pharmacist, veterinarian, and optometrist defined for purposes of this Division, see Health and Safety Code § 11024.
Prescription or electronic transmission prescription defined for purposes of this Division, see Health and Safety Code § 11027.
Presentation of allegations of act or omission by applicant or holder of a credential, circumstances under which committee has jurisdiction to commence initial review, formal review and investigation, report of actions and recommendations, including findings as to probable cause and appropriate adverse action, limitation on inquiries and request for production of information and records, and limitation on presentation of certain convictions, see Education Code § 44242.5.
School employee, arrest for controlled substance offense as described in this section, notice to school authorities, see Health and Safety Code § 11591.
Unlawful detainer actions to abate nuisance caused by illegal conduct involving controlled substance purpose, including violations of these provisions, see Civil Code § 3486.

Research References

California Jury Instructions - Criminal 12.00, Controlled Substance (Sched. I–V)—Unlawful Possession as Felony/Misdemeanor.
California Jury Instructions - Criminal 12.16, Controlled Substance (Sched. III, IV and V)—Inducing Minor to Violate Controlled Substances Law.
California Jury Instructions - Criminal 12.17, Controlled Substance (Sched. III, IV and V)—Using Minor as Agent to Violate Controlled Substances Law.
California Jury Instructions - Criminal 12.30.2, Controlled Substance (Sched. I–V)—Burden of Proof as to Prescription.
California Jury Instructions - Criminal 16.062, Misdemeanor Unlawful Possession of Controlled Substance.
2 Witkin, California Criminal Law 4th Crimes Against Public Peace and Welfare § 86 (2021), In General.
2 Witkin, California Criminal Law 4th Crimes Against Public Peace and Welfare § 97 (2021), In General.
2 Witkin, California Criminal Law 4th Crimes Against Public Peace and Welfare § 108 (2021), Possession Inconsistent With Legal Possession.
2 Witkin, California Criminal Law 4th Crimes Against Public Peace and Welfare § 125 (2021), Substances Formerly Classified as Restricted Dangerous Drugs.
2 Witkin, California Criminal Law 4th Crimes Against Public Peace and Welfare § 162 (2021), Advertising Anabolic Steroids.
4 Witkin, California Criminal Law 4th Pretrial Proceedings § 386 (2021), Offenses and Conditions.
3 Witkin, California Criminal Law 4th Punishment § 104 (2021), Additional Assessments, Penalties, and Fees.
3 Witkin, California Criminal Law 4th Punishment § 308A (2021), (New) in General.
3 Witkin, California Criminal Law 4th Punishment § 308–I (2021), (New) Application to Juveniles.
3 Witkin, California Criminal Law 4th Punishment § 330 (2021), Value or Quantity.
3 Witkin, California Criminal Law 4th Punishment § 437 (2021), Felony-Misdemeanors ("Wobblers").

§ 11377.5. Possession of gamma hydroxybutyric acid (GHB), ketamine, or flunitrazepam (Rohypnol) with intent to commit sexual assault; punishment

(a) Except as otherwise provided in this division, every person who possesses any controlled substance specified in paragraph (11) of subdivision (c) of, or subdivision (g) of, Section 11056 of this code, or paragraph (13) of subdivision (d) of Section 11057 of this code, with the intent to commit sexual assault, shall be punished by imprisonment pursuant to subdivision (h) of Section 1170 of the Penal Code.

(b) For purposes of this section, "sexual assault" means conduct in violation of Section 243.4, 261, 262, 286, 287, or 289 of, or former Section 288a of, the Penal Code. *(Added by Stats.2016, c. 893 (S.B.1182), § 3, eff. Jan. 1, 2017. Amended by Stats.2018, c. 423 (S.B.1494), § 36, eff. Jan. 1, 2019.)*

Research References

2 Witkin, California Criminal Law 4th Crimes Against Public Peace and Welfare § 101A (2021), (New) Possession of "Date Rape" Drugs With Intent to Commit Sexual Assault.

§ 11378. Possession for sale; punishment

Except as otherwise provided in Article 7 (commencing with Section 4110) of Chapter 9 of Division 2 of the Business and Professions Code, a person who possesses for sale a controlled substance that meets any of the following criteria shall be punished by imprisonment pursuant to subdivision (h) of Section 1170 of the Penal Code:

(1) The substance is classified in Schedule III, IV, or V and is not a narcotic drug, except the substance specified in subdivision (g) of Section 11056.

(2) The substance is specified in subdivision (d) of Section 11054, except paragraphs (13), (14), (15), (20), (21), (22), and (23) of subdivision (d).

(3) The substance is specified in paragraph (11) of subdivision (c) of Section 11056.

(4) The substance is specified in paragraph (2) or (3) of subdivision (f) of Section 11054.

(5) The substance is specified in subdivision (d), (e), or (f), except paragraph (3) of subdivision (e) and subparagraphs (A) and (B) of paragraph (2) of subdivision (f), of Section 11055. *(Added by Stats.1972, c. 1407, p. 3028, § 3. Amended by Stats.1973, c. 1078, p. 2184, § 23, eff. Oct. 1, 1973; Stats.1976, c. 1139, p. 5084, § 82, operative July 1, 1977; Stats.1984, c. 1635, § 66; Stats.1985, c. 3, § 4, eff. Jan. 29, 1985; Stats.1986, c. 1044, § 21; Stats.1991, c. 294 (A.B.444), § 3; Stats.2001, c. 841 (A.B.258), § 6; Stats.2011, c. 15 (A.B.109), § 172, eff. April 4, 2011, operative Oct. 1, 2011; Stats.2013, c. 76 (A.B.383), § 110.)*

Cross References

Additional penalty for trafficking violation on grounds of or near drug treatment center, detoxification facility, or homeless shelter, see Health and Safety Code § 11380.7
Additional term for conviction of violating this section with respect to certain substances, see Health and Safety Code § 11370.4.
Anabolic steroids, advertising sale, penalty, see Business and Professions Code § 17533.10.
Arrest of teacher or instructor employed in community college district, notices, see Health and Safety Code § 11591.5.
Cannabis offenses, effect of prior conviction under this section, see Health and Safety Code § 11357 et seq.
Controlled substance defined for purposes of this Division, see Health and Safety Code § 11007.
Controlled substances, quantity, aggravated term, see Penal Code § 1170.73.
Electronic communications interception, authorization order for investigation of violations of this section, see Penal Code § 629.52.
Examination of witnesses conditionally, cases in which authorized, see Penal Code § 1335.
Felony convictions for controlled substances violations involving cocaine, cocaine base, methamphetamine, phencyclidine or heroin, probation and sentencing, see Penal Code § 1203.073.
Felony offenses involving crystalline form of methamphetamine, aggravation of crime, see Penal Code § 1170.74.
Fines, increment for each separate offense, see Health and Safety Code § 11372.5.
Interception of wire communications, authorization order for investigation of violations of this section, see Penal Code § 629.50 et seq.
Narcotic drug defined for purposes of this Division, see Health and Safety Code § 11019.
Of criminal procedure,
Miscellaneous proceedings, examination of witnesses conditionally, cases in which authorized, see Penal Code § 1335.
Pleadings and proceedings before trial, career criminals, see Penal Code § 999e.

Health & Safety

Person defined for purposes of this Division, see Health and Safety Code § 11022.
Persons convicted of this section or section 11379, sentence enhancements for prior conviction of this section, see Health and Safety Code § 11370.2.
Probation or suspension of sentence prohibited for persons convicted of violating this section, see Penal Code § 1203.07.
Prohibition on possession of a firearm under the age of 30 for those convicted of or alleged to have committed certain offenses, controlled substances violations, punishment for violation, see Penal Code § 29820.
School employee, arrest for controlled substance offense as described in this section, notice to school authorities, see Health and Safety Code § 11591.
Seizure of things of value and believed to be forfeitable, see Health and Safety Code § 11488.
Unavailable declarant, hearsay rule, see Evidence Code § 1350.
Unlawful detainer actions to abate nuisance caused by illegal conduct involving controlled substance purpose, including violations of these provisions, see Civil Code § 3486.

Research References

California Jury Instructions - Criminal 12.01, Controlled Substance (Sched. I–V)—Illegal Possession or Purchase for Sale.
California Jury Instructions - Criminal 12.16, Controlled Substance (Sched. III, IV and V)—Inducing Minor to Violate Controlled Substances Law.
California Jury Instructions - Criminal 12.17, Controlled Substance (Sched. III, IV and V)—Using Minor as Agent to Violate Controlled Substances Law.
2 Witkin, California Criminal Law 4th Crimes Against Public Peace and Welfare § 101 (2021), Possession for Sale.
3 Witkin, California Criminal Law 4th Punishment § 375 (2021), Value or Amount.
3 Witkin, California Criminal Law 4th Punishment § 419 (2021), Controlled Substance Offenses.

§ 11378.5. Possession for sale of designated substances including phencyclidine; punishment

Except as otherwise provided in Article 7 (commencing with Section 4211) of Chapter 9 of Division 2 of the Business and Professions Code, every person who possesses for sale phencyclidine or any analog or any precursor of phencyclidine which is specified in paragraph (21), (22), or (23) of subdivision (d) of Section 11054 or in paragraph (3) of subdivision (e) or in subdivision (f), except subparagraph (A) of paragraph (1) of subdivision (f), of Section 11055, shall be punished by imprisonment pursuant to subdivision (h) of Section 1170 of the Penal Code for a period of three, four, or five years. *(Added by Stats.1978, c. 699, p. 2212, § 4. Amended by Stats.1984, c. 1635, § 67; Stats.1985, c. 3, § 5, eff. Jan. 29, 1985; Stats.2011, c. 15 (A.B.109), § 173, eff. April 4, 2011, operative Oct. 1, 2011.)*

Cross References

Additional term for conviction of violating this section with respect to certain substances, see Health and Safety Code § 11370.4.
Arrest of teacher or instructor employed in community college district, notices, see Health and Safety Code § 11591.5.
Controlled substances, quantity, aggravated term, see Penal Code § 1170.73.
Electronic communications interception, authorization order for investigation of violations of this section, see Penal Code § 629.52.
Fines, increment for each separate offense, see Health and Safety Code § 11372.5.
Forfeiture of boats, airplanes or vehicles, see Health and Safety Code § 11470.
Interception of wire communications, authorization order for investigation of violations of this section, see Penal Code § 629.50 et seq.
Person defined for purposes of this Division, see Health and Safety Code § 11022.
Persons convicted of this section, section 11379.5, 11379.6, or 11383, sentence enhancements for prior conviction of this section, see Health and Safety Code § 11370.2.
Probation or suspension of sentence prohibited for persons convicted of violating this section, see Penal Code § 1203.07.
School employee, arrest for controlled substance offense as described in this section, notice to school authorities, see Health and Safety Code § 11591.
Seizure of things of value and believed to be forfeitable, see Health and Safety Code § 11488.
Unlawful detainer actions to abate nuisance caused by illegal conduct involving controlled substance purpose, including violations of these provisions, see Civil Code § 3486.

Research References

California Jury Instructions - Criminal 12.01, Controlled Substance (Sched. I–V)—Illegal Possession or Purchase for Sale.
2 Witkin, California Criminal Law 4th Crimes Against Public Peace and Welfare § 101 (2021), Possession for Sale.
2 Witkin, California Criminal Law 4th Crimes Against Public Peace and Welfare § 102 (2021), In General.
3 Witkin, California Criminal Law 4th Punishment § 615 (2021), Penal Code Provisions.

§ 11379. Transportation, sale, furnishing, etc.; punishment; definition; prosecution under aiding and abetting, accessory, or conspiracy theory

(a) Except as otherwise provided in subdivision (b) and in Article 7 (commencing with Section 4211) of Chapter 9 of Division 2 of the Business and Professions Code, every person who transports, imports into this state, sells, furnishes, administers, or gives away, or offers to transport, import into this state, sell, furnish, administer, or give away, or attempts to import into this state or transport any controlled substance which is (1) classified in Schedule III, IV, or V and which is not a narcotic drug, except subdivision (g) of Section 11056, (2) specified in subdivision (d) of Section 11054, except paragraphs (13), (14), (15), (20), (21), (22), and (23) of subdivision (d), (3) specified in paragraph (11) of subdivision (c) of Section 11056, (4) specified in paragraph (2) or (3) of subdivision (f) of Section 11054, or (5) specified in subdivision (d) or (e), except paragraph (3) of subdivision (e), or specified in subparagraph (A) of paragraph (1) of subdivision (f), of Section 11055, unless upon the prescription of a physician, dentist, podiatrist, or veterinarian, licensed to practice in this state, shall be punished by imprisonment pursuant to subdivision (h) of Section 1170 of the Penal Code for a period of two, three, or four years.

(b) Notwithstanding the penalty provisions of subdivision (a), any person who transports any controlled substances specified in subdivision (a) within this state from one county to another noncontiguous county shall be punished by imprisonment pursuant to subdivision (h) of Section 1170 of the Penal Code for three, six, or nine years.

(c) For purposes of this section, "transports" means to transport for sale.

(d) Nothing in this section is intended to preclude or limit prosecution under an aiding and abetting theory, accessory theory, or a conspiracy theory. *(Added by Stats.1972, c. 1407, p. 3022, § 3. Amended by Stats.1973, c. 1078, p. 2185, § 24, eff. Oct. 1, 1973; Stats.1976, c. 1139, p. 5084, § 83, operative July 1, 1977; Stats.1977, c. 843, p. 2536, § 24; Stats.1984, c. 1635, § 68; Stats.1985, c. 3, § 6, eff. Jan. 29, 1985; Stats.1986, c. 1044, § 22; Stats.1989, c. 1102, § 2; Stats.1991, c. 294 (A.B.444), § 4; Stats.2001, c. 841 (A.B.258), § 7; Stats.2011, c. 15 (A.B.109), § 174, eff. April 4, 2011, operative Oct. 1, 2011; Stats.2013, c. 504 (A.B.721), § 2; Stats.2014, c. 71 (S.B.1304), § 88, eff. Jan. 1, 2015; Stats.2014, c. 54 (S.B.1461), § 8, eff. Jan. 1, 2015.)*

Cross References

Additional penalty for trafficking violation on grounds of or near drug treatment center, detoxification facility, or homeless shelter, see Health and Safety Code § 11380.7
Additional term for conviction of violating this section with respect to certain substances, see Health and Safety Code § 11370.4.
Administer defined for purposes of this Division, see Health and Safety Code § 11002.
Anabolic steroids, advertising sale, penalty, see Business and Professions Code § 17533.10.
Arrest of teacher or instructor employed in community college district, notices, see Health and Safety Code § 11591.5.
Cannabis offenses, effect of prior conviction under this section, see Health and Safety Code § 11357 et seq.

Controlled substance defined for purposes of this Division, see Health and Safety Code § 11007.
Controlled substances, sale or transfer, aggravation of crime, see Penal Code § 1170.82.
Electronic communications interception, authorization order for investigation of violations of this section, see Penal Code § 629.52.
Examination of witnesses conditionally, cases in which authorized, see Penal Code § 1335.
Felony convictions for controlled substances violations involving cocaine, cocaine base, methamphetamine, phencyclidine or heroin, probation and sentencing, see Penal Code § 1203.073.
Felony offenses involving crystalline form of methamphetamine, aggravation of crime, see Penal Code § 1170.74.
Fines, increment for each separate offense, see Health and Safety Code § 11372.5.
Furnish defined for purposes of this Division, see Health and Safety Code § 11016.
Interception of wire communications, authorization order for investigation of violations of this section, see Penal Code § 629.50 et seq.
Narcotic drug defined for purposes of this Division, see Health and Safety Code § 11019.
Of criminal procedure,
Miscellaneous proceedings, examination of witnesses conditionally, cases in which authorized, see Penal Code § 1335.
Of proceedings after the commencement of the trial and before judgment, trial court sentencing, initial sentencing, controlled substances, sale or transfer, aggravation of crime, see Penal Code § 1170.82.
Proceedings in misdemeanor and infraction cases and appeals from such cases, sales of chemicals, drugs, laboratory apparatus or devices to process controlled substances, allocation of fines and forfeitures, see Penal Code § 1463.10.
Person defined for purposes of this Division, see Health and Safety Code § 11022.
Persons convicted of this section or section 11378, sentence enhancements for prior conviction of this section, see Health and Safety Code § 11370.2.
Physician, dentist, podiatrist, pharmacist, veterinarian, and optometrist defined for purposes of this Division, see Health and Safety Code § 11024.
Prescription or electronic transmission prescription defined for purposes of this Division, see Health and Safety Code § 11027.
Probation or suspension of sentence prohibited for persons convicted of violating this section, see Penal Code § 1203.07.
Prohibition on possession of a firearm under the age of 30 for those convicted of or alleged to have committed certain offenses, controlled substances violations, punishment for violation, see Penal Code § 29820.
School employee, arrest for controlled substance offense as described in this section, notice to school authorities, see Health and Safety Code § 11591.
Seizure of things of value and believed to be forfeitable, see Health and Safety Code § 11488.
Soliciting commission of certain offenses, punishment, degree of proof, see Penal Code § 653f.
Unavailable declarant, hearsay rule, see Evidence Code § 1350.
Unlawful detainer actions to abate nuisance caused by illegal conduct involving controlled substance purpose, including violations of these provisions, see Civil Code § 3486.

Research References

California Jury Instructions - Criminal 12.02, Controlled Substance (Sched. I–V)—Illegal Sale, etc.
California Jury Instructions - Criminal 12.03, Controlled Substance (Sched. I–V)—Illegal Offer to Sell, etc.
California Jury Instructions - Criminal 12.16, Controlled Substance (Sched. III, IV and V)—Inducing Minor to Violate Controlled Substances Law.
California Jury Instructions - Criminal 12.17, Controlled Substance (Sched. III, IV and V)—Using Minor as Agent to Violate Controlled Substances Law.
2 Witkin, California Criminal Law 4th Crimes Against Public Peace and Welfare § 115 (2021), Statutory Prohibitions.
2 Witkin, California Criminal Law 4th Crimes Against Public Peace and Welfare § 116 (2021), Transportation.
2 Witkin, California Criminal Law 4th Crimes Against Public Peace and Welfare § 117 (2021), In General.
2 Witkin, California Criminal Law 4th Crimes Against Public Peace and Welfare § 119 (2021), Illegal Sale Following Lawful Possession.
1 Witkin California Criminal Law 4th Elements § 52 (2021), When Rule is Not Applicable.
3 Witkin, California Criminal Law 4th Punishment § 103 (2021), State and County Assessments and Surcharges.
3 Witkin, California Criminal Law 4th Punishment § 419 (2021), Controlled Substance Offenses.

§ 11379.2. Possession for sale or sale of ketamine; punishment

Except as otherwise provided in Article 7 (commencing with Section 4211) of Chapter 9 of Division 2 of the Business and Professions Code, every person who possesses for sale or sells any controlled substance specified in subdivision (g) of Section 11056 shall be punished by imprisonment in the county jail for a period of not more than one year or in the state prison. *(Added by Stats.1991, c. 294 (A.B.444), § 5.)*

Cross References

Controlled substance defined for purposes of this Division, see Health and Safety Code § 11007.
Person defined for purposes of this Division, see Health and Safety Code § 11022.

Research References

2 Witkin, California Criminal Law 4th Crimes Against Public Peace and Welfare § 101 (2021), Possession for Sale.
2 Witkin, California Criminal Law 4th Crimes Against Public Peace and Welfare § 115 (2021), Statutory Prohibitions.

§ 11379.5. Transportation, sale, furnishing, etc. of designated substances including phencyclidine; punishment

(a) Except as otherwise provided in subdivision (b) and in Article 7 (commencing with Section 4211) of Chapter 9 of Division 2 of the Business and Professions Code, every person who transports, imports into this state, sells, furnishes, administers, or gives away, or offers to transport, import into this state, sell, furnish, administer, or give away, or attempts to import into this state or transport phencyclidine or any of its analogs which is specified in paragraph (21), (22), or (23) of subdivision (d) of Section 11054 or in paragraph (3) of subdivision (e) of Section 11055, or its precursors as specified in subparagraph (A) or (B) of paragraph (2) of subdivision (f) of Section 11055, unless upon the prescription of a physician, dentist, podiatrist, or veterinarian licensed to practice in this state, shall be punished by imprisonment pursuant to subdivision (h) of Section 1170 of the Penal Code for a period of three, four, or five years.

(b) Notwithstanding the penalty provisions of subdivision (a), any person who transports for sale any controlled substances specified in subdivision (a) within this state from one county to another noncontiguous county shall be punished by imprisonment pursuant to subdivision (h) of Section 1170 of the Penal Code for three, six, or nine years.

(c) For purposes of this section, "transport" means to transport for sale.

(d) This section does not preclude or limit prosecution for any aiding and abetting or conspiracy offenses. *(Added by Stats.1978, c. 699, p. 2212, § 5. Amended by Stats.1984, c. 1635, § 69; Stats.1985, c. 3, § 7, eff. Jan. 29, 1985; Stats.1989, c. 1102, § 3; Stats.2011, c. 15 (A.B.109), § 175, eff. April 4, 2011, operative Oct. 1, 2011; Stats.2015, c. 77 (A.B.730), § 2, eff. Jan. 1, 2016.)*

Cross References

Additional term for conviction of violating this section with respect to certain substances, see Health and Safety Code § 11370.4.
Administer defined for purposes of this Division, see Health and Safety Code § 11002.
Arrest of teacher or instructor employed in community college district, notices, see Health and Safety Code § 11591.5.
Controlled substance defined for purposes of this Division, see Health and Safety Code § 11007.
Controlled substances, sale or transfer, aggravation of crime, see Penal Code § 1170.82.
Electronic communications interception, authorization order for investigation of violations of this section, see Penal Code § 629.52.
Felony convictions for controlled substances violations, probation on condition of minimum sentence to county jail, see Penal Code § 1203.076.

Fines, increment for each separate offense, see Health and Safety Code § 11372.5.
Forfeiture of boats, airplanes or vehicles, see Health and Safety Code § 11470.
Furnish defined for purposes of this Division, see Health and Safety Code § 11016.
Interception of wire communications, authorization order for investigation of violations of this section, see Penal Code § 629.50 et seq.
Of criminal procedure,
Of proceedings after the commencement of the trial and before judgment, trial court sentencing, initial sentencing, controlled substances, sale or transfer, aggravation of crime, see Penal Code § 1170.82.
Proceedings in misdemeanor and infraction cases and appeals from such cases, sales of chemicals, drugs, laboratory apparatus or devices to process controlled substances, allocation of fines and forfeitures, see Penal Code § 1463.10.
Person defined for purposes of this Division, see Health and Safety Code § 11022.
Persons convicted of this section, section 11378.5, 11379.6, or 11383, sentence enhancements for prior conviction of this section, see Health and Safety Code § 11370.2.
Physician, dentist, podiatrist, pharmacist, veterinarian, and optometrist defined for purposes of this Division, see Health and Safety Code § 11024.
Prescription or electronic transmission prescription defined for purposes of this Division, see Health and Safety Code § 11027.
Probation or suspension of sentence prohibited for persons convicted of violating this section, see Penal Code § 1203.07.
School employee, arrest for controlled substance offense as described in this section, notice to school authorities, see Health and Safety Code § 11591.
Seizure of things of value and believed to be forfeitable, see Health and Safety Code § 11488.
Soliciting commission of certain offenses, punishment, degree of proof, see Penal Code § 653f.
Unlawful detainer actions to abate nuisance caused by illegal conduct involving controlled substance purpose, including violations of these provisions, see Civil Code § 3486.

Research References

2 Witkin, California Criminal Law 4th Crimes Against Public Peace and Welfare § 115 (2021), Statutory Prohibitions.
3 Witkin, California Criminal Law 4th Punishment § 615 (2021), Penal Code Provisions.
3 Witkin, California Criminal Law 4th Punishment § 654 (2021), Mandatory.

§ 11379.6. Manufacturing, compounding, converting, producing, deriving, processing or preparing by chemical extraction or independently by means of chemical synthesis enumerated controlled substances; factor in aggravation; terms of imprisonment; fines

(a) Except as otherwise provided by law, every person who manufactures, compounds, converts, produces, derives, processes, or prepares, either directly or indirectly by chemical extraction or independently by means of chemical synthesis, any controlled substance specified in Section 11054, 11055, 11056, 11057, or 11058 shall be punished by imprisonment pursuant to subdivision (h) of Section 1170 of the Penal Code for three, five, or seven years and by a fine not exceeding fifty thousand dollars ($50,000).

(b) Except when an enhancement pursuant to Section 11379.7 is pled and proved, the fact that a person under 16 years of age resided in a structure in which a violation of this section involving methamphetamine occurred shall be considered a factor in aggravation by the sentencing court.

(c) Except when an enhancement pursuant to Section 11379.7 is pled and proved, the fact that a violation of this section involving methamphetamine occurred within 200 feet of an occupied residence or any structure where another person was present at the time the offense was committed may be considered a factor in aggravation by the sentencing court.

(d) The fact that a violation of this section involving the use of a volatile solvent to chemically extract concentrated cannabis occurred within 300 feet of an occupied residence or any structure where another person was present at the time the offense was committed may be considered a factor in aggravation by the sentencing court.

(e) Except as otherwise provided by law, every person who offers to perform an act which is punishable under subdivision (a) shall be punished by imprisonment pursuant to subdivision (h) of Section 1170 of the Penal Code for three, four, or five years.

(f) All fines collected pursuant to subdivision (a) shall be transferred to the State Treasury for deposit in the Clandestine Drug Lab Clean-up Account, as established by Section 5 of Chapter 1295 of the Statutes of 1987. The transmission to the State Treasury shall be carried out in the same manner as fines collected for the state by the county. *(Added by Stats.1985, c. 3, § 8, eff. Jan. 29, 1985. Amended by Stats.1985, c. 323, § 1, eff. July 29, 1985; Stats.1989, c. 1024, § 1; Stats.2003, c. 620 (A.B.233), § 1; Stats.2011, c. 15 (A.B.109), § 176, eff. April 4, 2011, operative Oct. 1, 2011; Stats.2015, c. 141 (S.B.212), § 1, eff. Jan. 1, 2016.)*

Cross References

Additional penalty for trafficking violation on grounds of or near drug treatment center, detoxification facility, or homeless shelter, see Health and Safety Code § 11380.7
Arrest of teacher or instructor employed in community college district, notices, see Health and Safety Code § 11591.5.
Controlled substance defined for purposes of this Division, see Health and Safety Code § 11007.
Controlled substances violations, use of minors as agents, prohibition of probation or suspension of sentence, see Penal Code § 1203.07.
Electronic communications interception, authorization order for investigation of violations of this section, see Penal Code § 629.52.
Felony offenses involving crystalline form of methamphetamine, aggravation of crime, see Penal Code § 1170.74.
Fines, increment for each separate offense, see Health and Safety Code § 11372.5.
Interception of wire communications, authorization order for investigation of violations of this section, see Penal Code § 629.50 et seq.
Limitation on grant of probation, see Penal Code § 1203.073.
Person defined for purposes of this Division, see Health and Safety Code § 11022.
Persons convicted for violations of this section involving methamphetamine or phencyclidine, additional punishment for crimes involving structures where underage child present, or where great bodily injury is suffered by underage child, see Health and Safety Code § 11379.7.
Persons convicted of this section, section 11378.5, 11379.5, or 11383, sentence enhancements for prior conviction of this section, see Health and Safety Code § 11370.2.
Prohibition on possession of a firearm under the age of 30 for those convicted of or alleged to have committed certain offenses, controlled substances violations, punishment for violation, see Penal Code § 29820.
School employee, arrest for controlled substance offense as described in this section, notice to school authorities, see Health and Safety Code § 11591.
Seizure of boats, airplanes, or vehicles, see Health and Safety Code § 11470.
Soliciting commission of certain offenses, punishment, degree of proof, see Penal Code § 653f.
Unlawful detainer actions to abate nuisance caused by illegal conduct involving controlled substance purpose, including violations of these provisions, see Civil Code § 3486.

Research References

California Jury Instructions - Criminal 12.09.1, Manufacturing or Offering to Manufacture a Controlled Substance.
2 Witkin, California Criminal Law 4th Crimes Against Public Peace and Welfare § 91B (2021), (New) Restricted and Prohibited Activities.
2 Witkin, California Criminal Law 4th Crimes Against Public Peace and Welfare § 129 (2021), Schools.
2 Witkin, California Criminal Law 4th Crimes Against Public Peace and Welfare § 132 (2021), Manufacture.
2 Witkin, California Criminal Law 4th Crimes Against Public Peace and Welfare § 149 (2021), Protection from Criminal Liability.
2 Witkin, California Criminal Law 4th Crimes Against Public Peace and Welfare § 157 (2021), Visiting or Using Place for Unlawful Activity.
1 Witkin California Criminal Law 4th Elements § 58 (2021), Mere Preparation is Insufficient.
1 Witkin California Criminal Law 4th Introduction to Crimes § 77 (2021), Illustrations: Special Statute is Not Controlling.
3 Witkin, California Criminal Law 4th Punishment § 310 (2021), County Jail Sentence and Realignment Legislation.

3 Witkin, California Criminal Law 4th Punishment § 375 (2021), Value or Amount.
3 Witkin, California Criminal Law 4th Punishment § 615 (2021), Penal Code Provisions.

§ 11379.7. Convictions for specified violations involving methamphetamine or phencyclidine; structures where underage child present; great bodily injury suffered by underage child; additional punishment

(a) Except as provided in subdivision (b), any person convicted of a violation of subdivision (a) of Section 11379.6 or Section 11383, or of an attempt to violate subdivision (a) of Section 11379.6 or Section 11383, as those sections relate to methamphetamine or phencyclidine, when the commission or attempted commission of the crime occurs in a structure where any child under 16 years of age is present, shall, in addition and consecutive to the punishment prescribed for the felony of which he or she has been convicted, be punished by an additional term of two years in the state prison.

(b) Any person convicted of a violation of subdivision (a) of Section 11379.6 or Section 11383, or of an attempt to violate subdivision (a) of Section 11379.6 or Section 11383, as those sections relate to methamphetamine or phencyclidine, where the commission of the crime causes any child under 16 years of age to suffer great bodily injury, shall, in addition and consecutive to the punishment prescribed for the felony of which he or she has been convicted, be punished by an additional term of five years in the state prison.

(c) As used in this section, "structure" means any house, apartment building, shop, warehouse, barn, building, vessel, railroad car, cargo container, motor vehicle, housecar, trailer, trailer coach, camper, mine, floating home, or other enclosed structure capable of holding a child and manufacturing equipment.

(d) As used in this section, "great bodily injury" has the same meaning as defined in Section 12022.7 of the Penal Code. *(Added by Stats.1996, c. 871 (A.B.3392), § 1.)*

Cross References

Felonies, definition and penalties, see Penal Code §§ 17, 18.
Person defined for purposes of this Division, see Health and Safety Code § 11022.

Research References

2 Witkin, California Criminal Law 4th Crimes Against Public Peace and Welfare § 132 (2021), Manufacture.
2 Witkin, California Criminal Law 4th Crimes Against Public Peace and Welfare § 134 (2021), Precursors of Methamphetamine and Phencyclidine.
3 Witkin, California Criminal Law 4th Punishment § 310 (2021), County Jail Sentence and Realignment Legislation.

§ 11379.8. Conviction for violation of § 11379.6(a) with respect to any substance containing specified controlled substances; additional term

(a) Any person convicted of a violation of subdivision (a) of Section 11379.6, or of a conspiracy to violate subdivision (a) of Section 11379.6, with respect to any substance containing a controlled substance which is specified in paragraph (21), (22), or (23) of subdivision (d) of Section 11054, or in paragraph (1) or (2) of subdivision (d) or in paragraph (3) of subdivision (e) or in paragraph (2) of subdivision (f) of Section 11055 shall receive an additional term as follows:

(1) Where the substance exceeds three gallons of liquid by volume or one pound of solid substances by weight, the person shall receive an additional term of three years.

(2) Where the substance exceeds 10 gallons of liquid by volume or three pounds of solid substance by weight, the person shall receive an additional term of five years.

(3) Where the substance exceeds 25 gallons of liquid by volume or 10 pounds of solid substance by weight, the person shall receive an additional term of 10 years.

(4) Where the substance exceeds 105 gallons of liquid by volume or 44 pounds of solid substance by weight, the person shall receive an additional term of 15 years.

In computing the quantities involved in this subdivision, plant or vegetable material seized shall not be included.

(b) The additional terms provided in this section shall not be imposed unless the allegation that the controlled substance exceeds the amounts provided in this section is charged in the accusatory pleading and admitted or found to be true by the trier of fact.

(c) The additional terms provided in this section shall be in addition to any other punishment provided by law.

(d) Notwithstanding any other provision of law, the court may strike the additional punishment for the enhancements provided in this section if it determines that there are circumstances in mitigation of the additional punishment and states on the record its reasons for striking the additional punishment.

(e) The conspiracy enhancements provided for in this section shall not be imposed unless the trier of fact finds that the defendant conspirator was substantially involved in the direction or supervision of, or in a significant portion of the financing of, the underlying offense. *(Added by Stats.1985, c. 1398, § 4. Amended by Stats.1986, c. 80, § 3; Stats.1992, c. 578 (S.B.1057), § 2; Stats.1998, c. 425 (A.B.2369), § 3.)*

Cross References

Aggregate term, mitigating circumstances, see Penal Code § 1170.1.
Controlled substance defined for purposes of this Division, see Health and Safety Code § 11007.
Person defined for purposes of this Division, see Health and Safety Code § 11022.

Research References

California Jury Instructions - Criminal 17.21, Finding for Health and Safety Code §11370.4/11379.8 Sentence Enhancements.
2 Witkin, California Criminal Law 4th Crimes Against Public Peace and Welfare § 132 (2021), Manufacture.
3 Witkin, California Criminal Law 4th Punishment § 375 (2021), Value or Amount.

§ 11379.9. Death or great bodily injury of another person; use of methamphetamine or phencyclidine; punishment

(a) Except as provided by Section 11379.7, any person convicted of a violation of, or of an attempt to violate, subdivision (a) of Section 11379.6 or Section 11383, as those sections relate to methamphetamine or phencyclidine, when the commission or attempted commission of the offense causes the death or great bodily injury of another person other than an accomplice, shall, in addition and consecutive to any other punishment authorized by law, be punished by an additional term of one year in the state prison for each death or injury.

(b) Nothing in this section shall preclude prosecution under both this section and Section 187, 192, or 12022.7, or any other provision of law. However, a person who is punished under another provision of law for causing death or great bodily injury as described in subdivision (a) shall not receive an additional term of imprisonment under this section. *(Added by Stats.1997, c. 553 (A.B.904), § 1. Amended by Stats.1998, c. 936 (A.B.105), § 2, eff. Sept. 28, 1998.)*

Cross References

Person defined for purposes of this Division, see Health and Safety Code § 11022.

Research References

2 Witkin, California Criminal Law 4th Crimes Against Public Peace and Welfare § 132 (2021), Manufacture.

2 Witkin, California Criminal Law 4th Crimes Against Public Peace and Welfare § 134 (2021), Precursors of Methamphetamine and Phencyclidine.

§ 11380. Adult using minor as agent; inducing minor to violate provisions; furnishing to minor; punishment

(a) Every person 18 years of age or over who violates any provision of this chapter involving controlled substances which are (1) classified in Schedule III, IV, or V and which are not narcotic drugs or (2) specified in subdivision (d) of Section 11054, except paragraphs (13), (14), (15), and (20) of subdivision (d), specified in paragraph (11) of subdivision (c) of Section 11056, specified in paragraph (2) or (3) or subdivision (f) of Section 11054, or specified in subdivision (d), (e), or (f) of Section 11055, by the use of a minor as agent, who solicits, induces, encourages, or intimidates any minor with the intent that the minor shall violate any provision of this article involving those controlled substances or who unlawfully furnishes, offers to furnish, or attempts to furnish those controlled substances to a minor shall be punished by imprisonment in the state prison for a period of three, six, or nine years.

(b) Nothing in this section applies to a registered pharmacist furnishing controlled substances pursuant to a prescription. *(Added by Stats.1972, c. 1407, p. 3023, § 3. Amended by Stats.1973, c. 1078, p. 2186, § 25, eff. Oct. 1, 1973; Stats.1976, c. 1139, p. 5085, § 84, operative July 1, 1977; Stats.1984, c. 1635, § 70; Stats.1985, c. 3, § 9, eff. Jan. 29, 1985; Stats.1986, c. 248, § 145; Stats.1986, c. 1035, § 3; Stats.1986, c. 1044, § 23; Stats.1990, c. 1664 (A.B.2645), § 5; Stats.1990, c. 1665 (S.B.2112), § 5; Stats.2001, c. 841 (A.B.258), § 8.)*

Cross References

Additional penalty for trafficking violation on grounds of or near drug treatment center, detoxification facility, or homeless shelter, see Health and Safety Code § 11380.7.

Agent defined for purposes of this Division, see Health and Safety Code § 11003.

Arrest of teacher or instructor employed in community college district, notices, see Health and Safety Code § 11591.5.

Cannabis offenses, effect of prior conviction under this section, see Health and Safety Code § 11357 et seq.

Controlled substance defined for purposes of this Division, see Health and Safety Code § 11007.

Controlled substances violations, use of minors as agents, prohibition of probation or suspension of sentence, see Penal Code § 1203.07.

Convictions under this section, prohibition of probation or suspension of sentence, see Penal Code § 1203.07.

Education or treatment programs, condition to probation, see Health and Safety Code § 11373.

Felony convictions for controlled substances violations involving cocaine, cocaine base, methamphetamine, phencyclidine or heroin, probation and sentencing, see Penal Code § 1203.073.

Fines, increment for each separate offense, see Health and Safety Code § 11372.5.

Furnish defined for purposes of this Division, see Health and Safety Code § 11016.

Invalidity of sentence enhancements imposed pursuant to Health and Safety Code § 11370.2, identification of persons serving enhanced sentences, review and resentencing, waiver of resentencing hearing, see Penal Code § 1171.

Life sentence for person who has served two or more prior terms for certain drug offenses involving minors, see Penal Code § 667.75.

Narcotic drug defined for purposes of this Division, see Health and Safety Code § 11019.

Of criminal procedure, of proceedings after the commencement of the trial and before judgment, trial court sentencing, initial sentencing, crimes involving minors under 11 years of age, circumstance in aggravation, see Penal Code § 1170.72.

Person defined for purposes of this Division, see Health and Safety Code § 11022.

Persons convicted of this section, sentence enhancements for prior conviction of this section, see Health and Safety Code § 11370.2.

Peyote offenses, see Health and Safety Code § 11363.

Physician, dentist, podiatrist, pharmacist, veterinarian, and optometrist defined for purposes of this Division, see Health and Safety Code § 11024.

Prescription or electronic transmission prescription defined for purposes of this Division, see Health and Safety Code § 11027.

Prohibition on possession of a firearm under the age of 30 for those convicted of or alleged to have committed certain offenses, controlled substances violations, punishment for violation, see Penal Code § 29820.

School employee, arrest for controlled substance offense as described in this section, notice to school authorities, see Health and Safety Code § 11591.

Research References

California Jury Instructions - Criminal 12.15, Controlled Substance (Sched. III, IV and V)—Illegal Furnishing or Offering to Furnish to Minor.

California Jury Instructions - Criminal 12.16, Controlled Substance (Sched. III, IV and V)—Inducing Minor to Violate Controlled Substances Law.

California Jury Instructions - Criminal 12.17, Controlled Substance (Sched. III, IV and V)—Using Minor as Agent to Violate Controlled Substances Law.

2 Witkin, California Criminal Law 4th Crimes Against Public Peace and Welfare § 124 (2021), Substances Formerly Classified as Narcotics.

2 Witkin, California Criminal Law 4th Crimes Against Public Peace and Welfare § 125 (2021), Substances Formerly Classified as Restricted Dangerous Drugs.

2 Witkin, California Criminal Law 4th Crimes Against Public Peace and Welfare § 128 (2021), Parks, Playgrounds, Child Care Facilities, and Religious Facilities.

2 Witkin, California Criminal Law 4th Crimes Against Public Peace and Welfare § 129 (2021), Schools.

4 Witkin, California Criminal Law 4th Pretrial Proceedings § 212 (2021), Designation of Statute by Number.

3 Witkin, California Criminal Law 4th Punishment § 374 (2021), In General.

3 Witkin, California Criminal Law 4th Punishment § 419 (2021), Controlled Substance Offenses.

3 Witkin, California Criminal Law 4th Punishment § 615 (2021), Penal Code Provisions.

§ 11380.1. Enhancement of sentence imposed under § 11380

(a) Notwithstanding any other provision of law, any person 18 years of age or over who is convicted of a violation of Section 11380, in addition to the punishment imposed for that conviction, shall receive an additional punishment as follows:

(1) If the offense involved phencyclidine (PCP), methamphetamine, lysergic acid diethylamide (LSD), or any analog of these substances and occurred upon the grounds of, or within, a church or synagogue, a playground, a public or private youth center, a child day care facility, or a public swimming pool, during hours in which the facility is open for business, classes, or school-related programs, or at any time when minors are using the facility, the defendant shall, as a full and separately served enhancement to any other enhancement provided in paragraph (3), be punished by imprisonment in the state prison for one year.

(2) If the offense involved phencyclidine (PCP), methamphetamine, lysergic acid diethylamide (LSD), or any analog of these substances and occurred upon, or within 1,000 feet of, the grounds of any public or private elementary, vocational, junior high school, or high school, during hours that the school is open for classes or school-related programs, or at any time when minors are using the facility where the offense occurs, the defendant shall, as a full and separately served enhancement to any other enhancement provided in paragraph (3), be punished by imprisonment in the state prison for two years.

(3) If the offense involved a minor who is at least four years younger than the defendant, the defendant shall, as a full and separately served enhancement to any other enhancement provided in this subdivision, be punished by imprisonment in the state prison for one, two, or three years, at the discretion of the court.

(b) The additional punishment provided in this section shall not be imposed unless the allegation is charged in the accusatory pleading and admitted by the defendant or found to be true by the trier of fact.

(c) The additional punishment provided in this section shall be in addition to any other punishment provided by law and shall not be limited by any other provision of law.

(d) Notwithstanding any other provision of law, the court may strike the additional punishment provided for in this section if it determines that there are circumstances in mitigation of the additional punishment and states on the record its reasons for striking the additional punishment.

(e) The definitions contained in subdivision (e) of Section 11353.1 shall apply to this section.

(f) This section does not require either that notice be posted regarding the proscribed conduct or that the applicable 1,000-foot boundary limit be marked. *(Added by Stats.1990, c. 1665 (S.B.2112), § 6. Amended by Stats.1993, c. 305 (A.B.246), § 1; Stats.1993, c. 556 (A.B.312), § 3.5.)*

Cross References

Additional penalty for trafficking violation on grounds of or near drug treatment center, detoxification facility, or homeless shelter, see Health and Safety Code § 11380.7.

Person defined for purposes of this Division, see Health and Safety Code § 11022.

Research References

2 Witkin, California Criminal Law 4th Crimes Against Public Peace and Welfare § 125 (2021), Substances Formerly Classified as Restricted Dangerous Drugs.

2 Witkin, California Criminal Law 4th Crimes Against Public Peace and Welfare § 128 (2021), Parks, Playgrounds, Child Care Facilities, and Religious Facilities.

2 Witkin, California Criminal Law 4th Crimes Against Public Peace and Welfare § 130 (2021), Drug Treatment Centers, Detoxification Facilities, and Homeless Shelters.

3 Witkin, California Criminal Law 4th Punishment § 374 (2021), In General.

§ 11380.7. Additional penalty for trafficking violation on the grounds of, or within 1,000 feet of, drug treatment center, detoxification facility, or homeless shelter; mitigating factors; definitions

(a) Notwithstanding any other provision of law, any person who is convicted of trafficking in heroin, cocaine, cocaine base, methamphetamine, or phencyclidine (PCP), or of a conspiracy to commit trafficking in heroin, cocaine, cocaine base, methamphetamine, or phencyclidine (PCP), in addition to the punishment imposed for the conviction, shall be imprisoned pursuant to subdivision (h) of Section 1170 of the Penal Code for an additional one year if the violation occurred upon the grounds of, or within 1,000 feet of, a drug treatment center, detoxification facility, or homeless shelter.

(b)(1) The additional punishment provided in this section shall not be imposed unless the allegation is charged in the accusatory pleading and admitted by the defendant or found to be true by the trier of fact.

(2) The additional punishment provided in this section shall not be imposed if any other additional punishment is imposed pursuant to Section 11353.1, 11353.5, 11353.6, 11353.7, or 11380.1.

(c) Notwithstanding any other provision of law, the court may strike the additional punishment provided for in this section if it determines that there are circumstances in mitigation of the additional punishment and states on the record its reasons for striking the additional punishment. In determining whether or not to strike the additional punishment, the court shall consider the following factors and any relevant factors in aggravation or mitigation in Rules 4.421 and 4.423 of the California Rules of Court.

(1) The following factors indicate that the court should exercise its discretion to strike the additional punishment unless these factors are outweighed by factors in aggravation:

(A) The defendant is homeless, or is in a homeless shelter or transitional housing.

(B) The defendant lacks resources for the necessities of life.

(C) The defendant is addicted to or dependent on controlled substances.

(D) The defendant's motive was merely to maintain a steady supply of drugs for personal use.

(E) The defendant was recruited or exploited by a more culpable person to commit the crime.

(2) The following factors indicate that the court should not exercise discretion to strike the additional punishment unless these factors are outweighed by factors in mitigation:

(A) The defendant, in committing the crime, preyed on homeless persons, drug addicts or substance abusers who were seeking treatment, shelter or transitional services.

(B) The defendant's primary motive was monetary compensation.

(C) The defendant induced others, particularly homeless persons, drug addicts and substance abusers, to become involved in trafficking.

(d) For the purposes of this section, the following terms have the following meanings:

(1) "Detoxification facility" means any premises, place, or building in which 24–hour residential nonmedical services are provided to adults who are recovering from problems related to alcohol, drug, or alcohol and drug misuse or abuse, and who need alcohol, drug, or alcohol and drug recovery treatment or detoxification services.

(2) "Drug treatment program" or "drug treatment" has the same meaning set forth in subdivision (b) of Section 1210 of the Penal Code.

(3) "Homeless shelter" includes, but is not limited to, emergency shelter housing, as well as transitional housing, but does not include domestic violence shelters. "Emergency shelter housing" is housing with minimal support services for homeless persons in which residency is limited to six months or less and is not related to the person's ability to pay. "Transitional housing" means housing with supportive services, including self-sufficiency development services, which is exclusively designed and targeted to help recently homeless persons find permanent housing as soon as reasonably possible, limits residency to 24 months, and in which rent and service fees are based on ability to pay.

(4) "Trafficking" means any of the unlawful activities specified in Sections 11351, 11351.5, 11352, 11353, 11354, 11378, 11379, 11379.6, and 11380. It does not include simple possession or drug use. *(Added by Stats.2006, c. 650 (S.B.1318), § 2. Amended by Stats.2011, c. 15 (A.B.109), § 177, eff. April 4, 2011, operative Oct. 1, 2011.)*

Cross References

Controlled substance defined for purposes of this Division, see Health and Safety Code § 11007.

Drug defined for purposes of this Division, see Health and Safety Code § 11014.

Person defined for purposes of this Division, see Health and Safety Code § 11022.

Research References

2 Witkin, California Criminal Law 4th Crimes Against Public Peace and Welfare § 130 (2021), Drug Treatment Centers, Detoxification Facilities, and Homeless Shelters.

3 Witkin, California Criminal Law 4th Punishment § 374 (2021), In General.

§ 11381. "Felony offense" and offense "punishable as a felony" defined

As used in this article "felony offense" and offense "punishable as a felony" refer to an offense prior to October 1, 2011, for which the law prescribes imprisonment in the state prison, or for an offense on or after October 1, 2011, imprisonment in either the state prison or pursuant to subdivision (h) of Section 1170 of the Penal Code, as either an alternative or the sole penalty, regardless of the sentence the particular defendant received. *(Added by Stats.1972, c. 1407, p.*

3024, § 3. Amended by Stats.2011, c. 15 (A.B.109), § 178, eff. April 4, 2011, operative Oct. 1, 2011; Stats.2011, c. 39 (A.B.117), § 3, eff. June 30, 2011, operative Oct. 1, 2011.)

Cross References

Felonies, definition and penalties, see Penal Code §§ 17, 18.

§ 11382. Sale or furnishing substances falsely represented to be a controlled substance; punishment

Every person who agrees, consents, or in any manner offers to unlawfully sell, furnish, transport, administer, or give any controlled substance which is (a) classified in Schedule III, IV, or V and which is not a narcotic drug, or (b) specified in subdivision (d) of Section 11054, except paragraphs (13), (14), (15), and (20) of subdivision (d), specified in paragraph (11) of subdivision (c) of Section 11056, or specified in subdivision (d), (e), or (f) of Section 11055, to any person, or offers, arranges, or negotiates to have that controlled substance unlawfully sold, delivered, transported, furnished, administered, or given to any person and then sells, delivers, furnishes, transports, administers, or gives, or offers, or arranges, or negotiates to have sold, delivered, transported, furnished, administered, or given to any person any other liquid, substance, or material in lieu of that controlled substance shall be punished by imprisonment in the county jail for not more than one year, or pursuant to subdivision (h) of Section 1170 of the Penal Code. *(Added by Stats.1972, c. 1407, p. 3024, § 3. Amended by Stats.1973, c. 1078, p. 2187, § 26, eff. Oct. 1, 1973; Stats.1976, c. 1139, p. 5085, § 85, operative July 1, 1977; Stats.1978, c. 699, p. 2213, § 7; Stats.1984, c. 1635, § 72; Stats.1985, c. 3, § 11, eff. Jan. 29, 1985; Stats.2001, c. 841 (A.B.258), § 9; Stats.2002, c. 664 (A.B.3034), § 132; Stats.2011–2012, 1st Ex.Sess., c. 12 (A.B.17), § 5, eff. Sept. 21, 2011, operative Oct. 1, 2011.)*

Cross References

Administer defined for purposes of this Division, see Health and Safety Code § 11002.
Controlled substance defined for purposes of this Division, see Health and Safety Code § 11007.
Deliver or delivery defined for purposes of this Division, see Health and Safety Code § 11009.
Felony convictions for controlled substances violations involving cocaine, cocaine base, methamphetamine, phencyclidine or heroin, probation and sentencing, see Penal Code § 1203.073.
Fines, increment for each separate offense, see Health and Safety Code § 11372.5.
Furnish defined for purposes of this Division, see Health and Safety Code § 11016.
Narcotic drug defined for purposes of this Division, see Health and Safety Code § 11019.
Person defined for purposes of this Division, see Health and Safety Code § 11022.
Prohibition on possession of a firearm under the age of 30 for those convicted of or alleged to have committed certain offenses, controlled substances violations, punishment for violation, see Penal Code § 29820.
Seizure of things of value and believed to be forfeitable, see Health and Safety Code § 11488.

Research References

California Jury Instructions - Criminal 12.04, Controlled Substance (Sched. I–V)—Illegal Sale, etc. of Substance in Lieu Thereof.
2 Witkin, California Criminal Law 4th Crimes Against Public Peace and Welfare § 123 (2021), Fraudulent Agreement.

§ 11382.5. Identification of manufacturer of controlled substances; exception; application to pharmacists

All controlled substances in Schedules I, II, III, IV, and V, in solid or capsule form, except for such controlled substances in the possession or inventory of a wholesaler, retailer, or pharmacist on January 1, 1975, shall not be sold, furnished, or distributed in this state unless they have on the controlled substance if in solid form, or on the capsule if in capsule form, an identifying device, insignia, or mark of the manufacturer of such controlled substance. However, the exception for such controlled substances in the possession or inventory of a wholesaler, retailer, or pharmacist shall not be available to any wholesaler, retailer, or pharmacist under the control or jurisdiction of a manufacturer of controlled substances.

This section shall not apply to a pharmacist who, in accordance with applicable state law, compounds such controlled substance in the course of his practice as a pharmacist for direct dispensing by him upon a prescription of any person licensed to prescribe such controlled substances. *(Added by Stats.1974, c. 926, § 1.)*

Cross References

Controlled substance defined for purposes of this Division, see Health and Safety Code § 11007.
Manufacturer defined for purposes of this Division, see Health and Safety Code § 11017.
Person defined for purposes of this Division, see Health and Safety Code § 11022.
Physician, dentist, podiatrist, pharmacist, veterinarian, and optometrist defined for purposes of this Division, see Health and Safety Code § 11024.
Prescription or electronic transmission prescription defined for purposes of this Division, see Health and Safety Code § 11027.
Wholesaler defined for purposes of this Division, see Health and Safety Code § 11031.

ARTICLE 6. PRECURSORS OF PHENCYCLIDINE (PCP) AND METHAMPHETAMINE

§ 11383. Possession with intent to manufacture phencyclidine (PCP) or any of its analogs; punishment

(a) Any person who possesses at the same time any of the following combinations, a combination product thereof, or possesses any compound or mixture containing the chemicals listed in the following combinations, with the intent to manufacture phencyclidine (PCP) or any of its analogs specified in subdivision (d) of Section 11054 or subdivision (e) of Section 11055, is guilty of a felony and shall be punished by imprisonment pursuant to subdivision (h) of Section 1170 of the Penal Code for two, four, or six years:

(1) Piperidine and cyclohexanone.

(2) Pyrrolidine and cyclohexanone.

(3) Morpholine and cyclohexanone.

(b) Any person who possesses the optical, positional, or geometric isomer of any of the compounds listed in this section, with the intent to manufacture these controlled substances is guilty of a felony and shall be punished by imprisonment pursuant to subdivision (h) of Section 1170 of the Penal Code for two, four, or six years:

(1) Phencyclidine (PCP).

(2) Any analog of PCP specified in subdivision (d) of Section 11054, or in subdivision (e) of Section 11055.

(c) Any person who possesses any compound or mixture containing piperidine, cyclohexanone, pyrrolidine, morpholine, 1–phenylcyclohexylamine (PCA), 1–piperidinocyclohexanecarbonitrile (PCC), or phenylmagnesium bromide (PMB) with the intent to manufacture phencyclidine, is guilty of a felony and shall be punished by imprisonment pursuant to subdivision (h) of Section 1170 of the Penal Code for two, four, or six years.

(d) Any person who possesses immediate precursors sufficient for the manufacture of piperidine, cyclohexanone, pyrrolidine, morpholine, or phenylmagnesium bromide (PMB) with the intent to manufacture phencyclidine, is guilty of a felony and shall be punished by imprisonment pursuant to subdivision (h) of Section 1170 of the Penal Code for two, four, or six years.

(e) This section does not apply to drug manufacturers licensed by this state or persons authorized by regulation of the Board of Pharmacy to possess those substances or combinations of substances. *(Added by Stats.1972, c. 1407, p. 3024, § 3. Amended by Stats.1976, c. 1116, p. 5015, § 2; Stats.1976, c. 1139, p. 5085, § 86, operative July 1, 1977; Stats.1977, c. 165, p. 640, § 3.6, eff. June 29, 1977, operative July 1, 1977; Stats.1978, c. 699, p. 2213, § 8; Stats.1980, c. 749, p. 2247, § 3, eff. July 28, 1980; Stats.1982, c. 1279, p. 4730, § 6; Stats.1984, c. 1635, § 73; Stats.1985, c. 3, § 12, eff. Jan. 29, 1985; Stats.1987, c. 424, § 1; Stats.1988, c. 712, § 3, eff. Aug. 29, 1988; Stats.1990, c. 1591 (S.B.1894), § 1; Stats.1992, c. 49 (A.B.823), § 1; Stats.1992, c. 578 (S.B.1057), § 3; Stats.1993, c. 1 (S.B.92), § 1, eff. Feb. 8, 1993; Stats.1995, c. 571 (S.B.419), § 1; Stats.2003, c. 619 (A.B.158), § 1; Stats.2006, c. 646 (S.B.1299), § 2; Stats.2011, c. 15 (A.B.109), § 179, eff. April 4, 2011, operative Oct. 1, 2011.)*

Cross References

Arrest of teacher or instructor employed in community college district, notices, see Health and Safety Code § 11591.5.
Controlled substance defined for purposes of this Division, see Health and Safety Code § 11007.
Diversion from trial for education, treatment or rehabilitation, see Penal Code § 1000 et seq.
Drug defined for purposes of this Division, see Health and Safety Code § 11014.
Felonies, definition and penalties, see Penal Code §§ 17, 18.
Felony convictions for controlled substances violations involving cocaine, cocaine base, methamphetamine, phencyclidine or heroin, probation and sentencing, see Penal Code § 1203.073.
Fines, increment for each separate offense, see Health and Safety Code § 11372.5.
Isomer defined for purposes of this Division, see Health and Safety Code § 11033.
Manufacturer defined for purposes of this Division, see Health and Safety Code § 11017.
Methamphetamine or Fentanyl Contaminated Property Cleanup Act, see Health and Safety Code § 25400.10 et seq.
Person defined for purposes of this Division, see Health and Safety Code § 11022.
Persons convicted for violations of this section involving methamphetamine or phencyclidine, additional punishment for crimes involving structures where underage child present, or where great bodily injury is suffered by underage child, see Health and Safety Code § 11379.7.
Persons convicted of this section, section 11378.5, 11379.5, or 11379.6, sentence enhancements for prior conviction of this section, see Health and Safety Code § 11370.2.
Prohibition on possession of a firearm under the age of 30 for those convicted of or alleged to have committed certain offenses, controlled substances violations, punishment for violation, see Penal Code § 29820.
School employee, arrest for controlled substance offense as described in this section, notice to school authorities, see Health and Safety Code § 11591.
Unlawful detainer actions to abate nuisance caused by illegal conduct involving controlled substance purpose, including violations of these provisions, see Civil Code § 3486.

Research References

California Jury Instructions - Criminal 12.09.3, Possession With Intent to Manufacture Pcp.
California Jury Instructions - Criminal 12.09.6, Possession of Methylamine etc. With Intent to Sell for Purpose of Manufacturing Methamphetamine.
2 Witkin, California Criminal Law 4th Crimes Against Public Peace and Welfare § 134 (2021), Precursors of Methamphetamine and Phencyclidine.
3 Witkin, California Criminal Law 4th Punishment § 615 (2021), Penal Code Provisions.

§ 11383.5. Possession with intent to manufacture methamphetamine or N–ethylamphetamine; punishment

(a) Any person who possesses both methylamine and phenyl–2–propanone (phenylacetone) at the same time with the intent to manufacture methamphetamine, or who possesses both ethylamine and phenyl–2–propanone (phenylacetone) at the same time with the intent to manufacture N–ethylamphetamine, is guilty of a felony and shall be punished by imprisonment pursuant to subdivision (h) of Section 1170 of the Penal Code for two, four, or six years.

(b)(1) Any person who, with the intent to manufacture methamphetamine or any of its analogs specified in subdivision (d) of Section 11055, possesses ephedrine or pseudoephedrine, or any salts, isomers, or salts of isomers of ephedrine or pseudoephedrine, or who possesses a substance containing ephedrine or pseudoephedrine, or any salts, isomers, or salts of isomers of ephedrine or pseudoephedrine, or who possesses at the same time any of the following, or a combination product thereof, is guilty of a felony and shall be punished by imprisonment pursuant to subdivision (h) of Section 1170 of the Penal Code for two, four, or six years:

(A) Ephedrine, pseudoephedrine, norpseudoephedrine, N–methylephedrine, N–ethylephedrine, N–methylpseudoephedrine, N–ethylpseudoephedrine, or phenylpropanolamine, plus hydriodic acid.

(B) Ephedrine, pseudoephedrine, norpseudoephedrine, N–methylephedrine, N–ethylephedrine, N–methylpseudoephedrine, N–ethylpseudoephedrine, or phenylpropanolamine, thionyl chloride and hydrogen gas.

(C) Ephedrine, pseudoephedrine, norpseudoephedrine, N–methylephedrine, N–ethylephedrine, N–methylpseudoephedrine, N–ethylpseudoephedrine, or phenylpropanolamine, plus phosphorus pentachloride and hydrogen gas.

(D) Ephedrine, pseudoephedrine, norpseudoephedrine, N–methylephedrine, N–ethylephedrine, N–methylpseudoephedrine, N–ethylpseudoephedrine, chloroephedrine and chloropseudoephedrine, or phenylpropanolamine, plus any reducing agent.

(2) Any person who, with the intent to manufacture methamphetamine or any of its analogs specified in subdivision (d) of Section 11055, possesses hydriodic acid or a reducing agent or any product containing hydriodic acid or a reducing agent is guilty of a felony and shall be punished by imprisonment pursuant to subdivision (h) of Section 1170 of the Penal Code for two, four, or six years.

(c) Any person who possesses the optical, positional, or geometric isomer of any of the compounds listed in this section, with the intent to manufacture any of the following controlled substances, is guilty of a felony and shall be punished by imprisonment pursuant to subdivision (h) of Section 1170 of the Penal Code for two, four, or six years:

(1) Methamphetamine.

(2) Any analog of methamphetamine specified in subdivision (d) of Section 11055.

(3) N–ethylamphetamine.

(d) Any person who possesses immediate precursors sufficient for the manufacture of methylamine, ethylamine, phenyl–2–propanone, ephedrine, pseudoephedrine, norpseudoephedrine, N–methylephedrine, N–ethylephedrine, phenylpropanolamine, hydriodic acid or a reducing agent, thionyl chloride, or phosphorus pentachloride, with the intent to manufacture methamphetamine, is guilty of a felony and shall be punished by imprisonment pursuant to subdivision (h) of Section 1170 of the Penal Code for two, four, or six years.

(e) Any person who possesses essential chemicals sufficient to manufacture hydriodic acid or a reducing agent, with the intent to manufacture methamphetamine, is guilty of a felony and shall be punished by imprisonment pursuant to subdivision (h) of Section 1170 of the Penal Code for two, four, or six years.

(f) Any person who possesses any compound or mixture containing ephedrine, pseudoephedrine, norpseudoephedrine, N–methylephedrine, N– ethylephedrine, phenylpropanolamine, hydriodic acid or a reducing agent, thionyl chloride, or phosphorus pentachloride, with the intent to manufacture methamphetamine, is guilty of a felony and shall be punished by imprisonment pursuant to subdivision (h) of Section 1170 of the Penal Code for two, four, or six years.

(g) For purposes of this section, a "reducing agent" for the purposes of manufacturing methamphetamine means an agent that causes reduction to occur by either donating a hydrogen atom to an organic compound or by removing an oxygen atom from an organic compound.

(h) This section does not apply to drug manufacturers licensed by this state or persons authorized by regulation of the Board of Pharmacy to possess those substances or combinations of substances. *(Added by Stats.2006, c. 646 (S.B.1299), § 3. Amended by Stats.2011, c. 15 (A.B.109), § 180, eff. April 4, 2011, operative Oct. 1, 2011.)*

Cross References

Agent defined for purposes of this Division, see Health and Safety Code § 11003.
Controlled substance defined for purposes of this Division, see Health and Safety Code § 11007.
Drug defined for purposes of this Division, see Health and Safety Code § 11014.
Felonies, definition and penalties, see Penal Code §§ 17, 18.
Isomer defined for purposes of this Division, see Health and Safety Code § 11033.
Manufacturer defined for purposes of this Division, see Health and Safety Code § 11017.
Person defined for purposes of this Division, see Health and Safety Code § 11022.
Persons convicted for violations involving methamphetamine or phencyclidine, additional punishment for crimes involving structures where underage child present, or where great bodily injury is suffered by underage child, see Health and Safety Code § 11379.7.

Research References

California Jury Instructions - Criminal 12.09.2, Possession With Intent to Manufacture.
California Jury Instructions - Criminal 12.09.3, Possession With Intent to Manufacture Pcp.
California Jury Instructions - Criminal 12.09.4, Possession With Intent to Manufacture Methamphetamine.
California Jury Instructions - Criminal 12.09.5, Possession With Intent to Manufacture Methamphetamine.
California Jury Instructions - Criminal 12.09.9, Possession of Isomer With Intent to Manufacture Methamphetamine.
California Jury Instructions - Criminal 12.09.10, Possession of Precursor With Intent to Manufacture Methamphetamine.
California Jury Instructions - Criminal 12.09.11, Possession of Essential Chemicals With Intent to Manufacture Methamphetamine.
California Jury Instructions - Criminal 12.09.12, Possession of Compound or Mixture With Intent to Manufacture Methamphetamine.
2 Witkin, California Criminal Law 4th Crimes Against Public Peace and Welfare § 134 (2021), Precursors of Methamphetamine and Phencyclidine.

§ 11383.6. Possession with intent to sell, transfer or furnish chemicals to persons having intent to manufacture phencyclidine (PCP); punishment

(a) Any person who possesses at the same time any of the following combinations, a combination product thereof, or possesses any compound or mixture containing the chemicals listed in the following combinations, with the intent to sell, transfer, or otherwise furnish those chemicals, combinations, or mixtures to another person with the knowledge that they will be used to manufacture phencyclidine (PCP) or any of its analogs specified in subdivision (d) of Section 11054 or subdivision (e) of Section 11055 is guilty of a felony and shall be punished by imprisonment pursuant to subdivision (h) of Section 1170 of the Penal Code for 16 months, two, or three years:

(1) Piperidine and cyclohexanone.

(2) Pyrrolidine and cyclohexanone.

(3) Morpholine and cyclohexanone.

(b) Any person who possesses the optical, positional, or geometric isomer of any of the compounds listed in this section with the intent to sell, transfer, or otherwise furnish the isomer to another person with the knowledge that they will be used to manufacture these controlled substances is guilty of a felony and shall be punished by imprisonment pursuant to subdivision (h) of Section 1170 of the Penal Code for 16 months, two, or three years:

(1) Phencyclidine (PCP).

(2) Any analog of PCP specified in subdivision (d) of Section 11054, or in subdivision (e) of Section 11055.

(c) Any person who possesses any compound or mixture containing piperidine, cyclohexanone, pyrrolidine, morpholine, 1–phenylcyclohexylamine (PCA), 1–piperidinocyclohexanecarbonitrile (PCC), or phenylmagnesium bromide (PMB) with the intent to sell, transfer, or otherwise furnish the compound or mixture to another person with the knowledge that it will be used to manufacture phencyclidine is guilty of a felony and shall be punished by imprisonment pursuant to subdivision (h) of Section 1170 of the Penal Code for 16 months, two, or three years.

(d) Any person who possesses immediate precursors sufficient for the manufacture of piperidine, cyclohexanone, pyrrolidine, morpholine, or phenylmagnesium bromide (PMB) with the intent to sell, transfer or otherwise furnish the immediate precursors to another person with the knowledge that they will be used to manufacture phencyclidine is guilty of a felony and shall be punished by imprisonment pursuant to subdivision (h) of Section 1170 of the Penal Code for 16 months, two, or three years.

(e) This section does not apply to drug manufacturers licensed by this state or persons authorized by regulation of the Board of Pharmacy to possess those substances or combinations of substances. *(Added by Stats.2006, c. 646 (S.B.1299), § 4. Amended by Stats.2011, c. 15 (A.B.109), § 181, eff. April 4, 2011, operative Oct. 1, 2011.)*

Cross References

Controlled substance defined for purposes of this Division, see Health and Safety Code § 11007.
Drug defined for purposes of this Division, see Health and Safety Code § 11014.
Felonies, definition and penalties, see Penal Code §§ 17, 18.
Furnish defined for purposes of this Division, see Health and Safety Code § 11016.
Isomer defined for purposes of this Division, see Health and Safety Code § 11033.
Manufacturer defined for purposes of this Division, see Health and Safety Code § 11017.
Person defined for purposes of this Division, see Health and Safety Code § 11022.
Persons convicted for violations involving methamphetamine or phencyclidine, additional punishment for crimes involving structures where underage child present, or where great bodily injury is suffered by underage child, see Health and Safety Code § 11379.7.

Research References

California Jury Instructions - Criminal 12.09.13, Possession of Combination Product With Intent to Sell for Manufacturing Pcp.
California Jury Instructions - Criminal 12.09.14, Possession of Compound Isomer With Intent to Sell for Manufacturing Pcp.
California Jury Instructions - Criminal 12.09.15, Possession of Compound/Mixture With Intent to Sell for Manufacturing Pcp.
California Jury Instructions - Criminal 12.09.16, Possession of Precursor With Intent to Sell for Manufacturing Pcp.

2 Witkin, California Criminal Law 4th Crimes Against Public Peace and Welfare § 134 (2021), Precursors of Methamphetamine and Phencyclidine.

§ 11383.7. Possession with intent to sell, transfer or furnish chemicals to persons having intent to manufacture methamphetamine or N–ethylamphetamine; punishment

(a) Any person who possesses both methylamine and phenyl–2–propanone (phenylacetone) at the same time with the intent to sell, transfer, or otherwise furnish those chemicals to another person with the knowledge that they will be used to manufacture methamphetamine, or who possesses both ethylamine and phenyl–2–propanone (phenylacetone) at the same time with the intent to sell, transfer, or otherwise furnish those chemicals to another person with the knowledge that they will be used to manufacture methamphetamine is guilty of a felony and shall be punished by imprisonment pursuant to subdivision (h) of Section 1170 of the Penal Code for 16 months, two, or three years.

(b)(1) Any person who possesses ephedrine or pseudoephedrine, or any salts, isomers, or salts of isomers of ephedrine or pseudoephedrine, or who possesses a substance containing ephedrine or pseudoephedrine, or any salts, isomers, or salts of isomers of ephedrine or pseudoephedrine, or who possesses at the same time any of the following, or a combination product thereof, with the intent to sell, transfer, or otherwise furnish those chemicals, substances, or products to another person with the knowledge that they will be used to manufacture methamphetamine or any of its analogs specified in subdivision (d) of Section 11055 is guilty of a felony and shall be punished by imprisonment pursuant to subdivision (h) of Section 1170 of the Penal Code for 16 months, two, or three years:

(A) Ephedrine, pseudoephedrine, norpseudoephedrine, N–methylephedrine, N–ethylephedrine, N–methylpseudoephedrine, N–ethylpseudoephedrine, or phenylpropanolamine, plus hydriodic acid.

(B) Ephedrine, pseudoephedrine, norpseudoephedrine, N–methylephedrine, N–ethylephedrine, N–methylpseudoephedrine, N–ethylpseudoephedrine, or phenylpropanolamine, thionyl chloride and hydrogen gas.

(C) Ephedrine, pseudoephedrine, norpseudoephedrine, N–methylephedrine, N–ethylephedrine, N–methylpseudoephedrine, N–ethylpseudoephedrine, or phenylpropanolamine, plus phosphorus pentachloride and hydrogen gas.

(D) Ephedrine, pseudoephedrine, norpseudoephedrine, N–methylephedrine, N–ethylephedrine, N–methylpseudoephedrine, N–ethylpseudoephedrine, chloroephedrine and chloropseudoephedrine, or phenylpropanolamine, plus any reducing agent.

(2) Any person who possesses hydriodic acid or a reducing agent or any product containing hydriodic acid or a reducing agent with the intent to sell, transfer, or otherwise furnish that chemical, product, or substance to another person with the knowledge that they will be used to manufacture methamphetamine or any of its analogs specified in subdivision (d) of Section 11055 is guilty of a felony and shall be punished by imprisonment pursuant to subdivision (h) of Section 1170 of the Penal Code for 16 months, two, or three years.

(c) Any person who possesses the optical, positional, or geometric isomer of any of the compounds listed in this section with the intent to sell, transfer, or otherwise furnish any of the compounds to another person with the knowledge that they will be used to manufacture these controlled substances is guilty of a felony and shall be punished by imprisonment pursuant to subdivision (h) of Section 1170 of the Penal Code for 16 months, two, or three years:

(1) Methamphetamine.

(2) Any analog of methamphetamine specified in subdivision (d) of Section 11055.

(3) N–ethylamphetamine.

(d) Any person who possesses immediate precursors sufficient for the manufacture of methylamine, ethylamine, phenyl–2–propanone, ephedrine, pseudoephedrine, norpseudoephedrine, N–methylephedrine, N–ethylephedrine, phenylpropanolamine, hydriodic acid or a reducing agent, thionyl chloride, or phosphorus pentachloride, with the intent to sell, transfer, or otherwise furnish these substances to another person with the knowledge that they will be used to manufacture methamphetamine is guilty of a felony and shall be punished by imprisonment pursuant to subdivision (h) of Section 1170 of the Penal Code for 16 months, two, or three years.

(e) Any person who possesses essential chemicals sufficient to manufacture hydriodic acid or a reducing agent with the intent to sell, transfer, or otherwise furnish those chemicals to another person with the knowledge that they will be used to manufacture methamphetamine is guilty of a felony and shall be punished by imprisonment pursuant to subdivision (h) of Section 1170 of the Penal Code for 16 months, two, or three years.

(f) Any person who possesses any compound or mixture containing ephedrine, pseudoephedrine, norpseudoephedrine, N–methylephedrine, N– ethylephedrine, phenylpropanolamine, hydriodic acid or a reducing agent, thionyl chloride, or phosphorus pentachloride, with the intent to sell, transfer, or otherwise furnish that compound or mixture to another person with the knowledge that they will be used to manufacture methamphetamine is guilty of a felony and shall be punished by imprisonment pursuant to subdivision (h) of Section 1170 of the Penal Code for 16 months, two, or three years.

(g) For purposes of this section, a "reducing agent" for the purposes of manufacturing methamphetamine means an agent that causes reduction to occur by either donating a hydrogen atom to an organic compound or by removing an oxygen atom from an organic compound.

(h) This section does not apply to drug manufacturers licensed by this state or persons authorized by regulation of the Board of Pharmacy to possess those substances or combinations of substances. *(Added by Stats.2006, c. 646 (S.B.1299), § 5. Amended by Stats.2011, c. 15 (A.B.109), § 182, eff. April 4, 2011, operative Oct. 1, 2011.)*

Cross References

Agent defined for purposes of this Division, see Health and Safety Code § 11003.
Controlled substance defined for purposes of this Division, see Health and Safety Code § 11007.
Drug defined for purposes of this Division, see Health and Safety Code § 11014.
Felonies, definition and penalties, see Penal Code §§ 17, 18.
Furnish defined for purposes of this Division, see Health and Safety Code § 11016.
Isomer defined for purposes of this Division, see Health and Safety Code § 11033.
Manufacturer defined for purposes of this Division, see Health and Safety Code § 11017.
Person defined for purposes of this Division, see Health and Safety Code § 11022.
Persons convicted for violations involving methamphetamine or phencyclidine, additional punishment for crimes involving structures where underage child present, or where great bodily injury is suffered by underage child, see Health and Safety Code § 11379.7.

Research References

California Jury Instructions - Criminal 12.09.6, Possession of Methylamine etc. With Intent to Sell for Purpose of Manufacturing Methamphetamine.
California Jury Instructions - Criminal 12.09.7, Possession of Ephedrine, etc., With Intent to Sell for Purpose of Manufacture of Methamphetamine.
California Jury Instructions - Criminal 12.09.8, Possession of Hydriotic Acid, etc., With Intent to Sell for Purpose of Manufacturing Methamphetamine.
2 Witkin, California Criminal Law 4th Crimes Against Public Peace and Welfare § 134 (2021), Precursors of Methamphetamine and Phencyclidine.

§ 11384. Regulations by Board of Pharmacy

The Board of Pharmacy shall, by regulation, authorize such persons to possess any combinations of substance specified in subdivision (a) or (b) of Section 11383 as it determines need and will use such substance for a lawful purpose. *(Added by Stats.1972, c. 1407, p. 3024, § 3. Amended by Stats.1976, c. 1116, p. 5016, § 3.)*

Cross References

Person defined for purposes of this Division, see Health and Safety Code § 11022.

ARTICLE 7. MUSHROOMS

§ 11390. Cultivation of spores or mycelium capable of producing mushrooms or other material containing controlled substance; punishment

Except as otherwise authorized by law, every person who, with intent to produce a controlled substance specified in paragraph (18) or (19) of subdivision (d) of Section 11054, cultivates any spores or mycelium capable of producing mushrooms or other material which contains such a controlled substance shall be punished by imprisonment in the county jail for a period of not more than one year or in the state prison. *(Added by Stats.1985, c. 1264, § 2.)*

Cross References

Controlled substance defined for purposes of this Division, see Health and Safety Code § 11007.
Fines, increment for each separate offense, see Health and Safety Code § 11372.5.
Person defined for purposes of this Division, see Health and Safety Code § 11022.

Research References

2 Witkin, California Criminal Law 4th Crimes Against Public Peace and Welfare § 115 (2021), Statutory Prohibitions.
2 Witkin, California Criminal Law 4th Crimes Against Public Peace and Welfare § 131 (2021), Cultivating, Harvesting, or Processing.

§ 11391. Transporting, importing, selling, furnishing, giving away, etc., spores or mycelium capable of producing mushrooms containing controlled substance to violate § 11390; punishment

(a) Except as otherwise authorized by law, every person who transports, imports into this state, sells, furnishes, gives away, or offers to transport, import into this state, sell, furnish, or give away any spores or mycelium capable of producing mushrooms or other material which contain a controlled substance specified in paragraph (18) or (19) of subdivision (d) of Section 11054 for the purpose of facilitating a violation of Section 11390 shall be punished by imprisonment in the county jail for a period of not more than one year or in the state prison.

(b) For purposes of this section, "transport" means to transport for sale.

(c) This section does not preclude or limit prosecution for any aiding and abetting or conspiracy offenses. *(Added by Stats.1985, c. 1264, § 2. Amended by Stats.2015, c. 77 (A.B.730), § 3, eff. Jan. 1, 2016.)*

Cross References

Controlled substance defined for purposes of this Division, see Health and Safety Code § 11007.
Fines, increment for each separate offense, see Health and Safety Code § 11372.5.
Furnish defined for purposes of this Division, see Health and Safety Code § 11016.
Person defined for purposes of this Division, see Health and Safety Code § 11022.
Soliciting commission of certain offenses, punishment, degree of proof, see Penal Code § 653f.

Research References

2 Witkin, California Criminal Law 4th Crimes Against Public Peace and Welfare § 115 (2021), Statutory Prohibitions.

§ 11392. Spores or mycelium capable of producing mushrooms or other material containing psilocyn or psyocylin; use in research, instruction, or analysis

Spores or mycelium capable of producing mushrooms or other material which contains psilocyn or psyoclyin may be lawfuly[1] obtained and used for bona fide research, instruction, or analysis, if not in violation of federal law, and if the research, instruction, or analysis is approved by the Research Advisory Panel established pursuant to Sections 11480 and 11481. *(Added by Stats.1985, c. 1264, § 2.)*

[1] So in chaptered copy.

CHAPTER 6.5. ANALOGS

§ 11400. Legislative findings and declarations; analogs of controlled substances; punishment

The Legislature finds and declares that the laws of this state which prohibit the possession, possession for sale, offer for sale, sale, manufacturing, and transportation of controlled substances are being circumvented by the commission of those acts with respect to analogs of specified controlled substances which have, are represented to have, or are intended to have effects on the central nervous system which are substantially similar to, or greater than, the controlled substances classified in Sections 11054 and 11055 and the synthetic cannabinoid compounds defined in Section 11357.5, of which they are analogs. These analogs have been synthesized by so-called "street chemists" and imported into this state from other jurisdictions as precursors to, or substitutes for, controlled substances and synthetic cannabinoid compounds, due to the nonexistence of applicable criminal penalties. These analogs present grave dangers to the health and safety of the people of this state. Therefore, it is the intent of the Legislature that a controlled substance or controlled substance analog, as defined in Section 11401, be considered identical, for purposes of the penalties and punishment specified in Chapter 6 (commencing with Section 11350), to the controlled substance in Section 11054 or 11055 or the synthetic cannabinoid compound defined in Section 11357.5 of which it is an analog. *(Added by Stats.1988, c. 712, § 4, eff. Aug. 29, 1988. Amended by Stats.2016, c. 627 (S.B.1036), § 1, eff. Jan. 1, 2017; Stats.2017, c. 561 (A.B.1516), § 113, eff. Jan. 1, 2018.)*

Cross References

Controlled substance defined for purposes of this Division, see Health and Safety Code § 11007.

Research References

2 Witkin, California Criminal Law 4th Crimes Against Public Peace and Welfare § 73 (2021), For Drug Activities.

2 Witkin, California Criminal Law 4th Crimes Against Public Peace and Welfare § 89 (2021), Analogs of Controlled Substances.

§ 11401. "Controlled substance analog" defined; treatment for offenses and penalties

(a) A controlled substance analog shall, for the purposes of Chapter 6 (commencing with Section 11350), be treated the same as the controlled substance classified in Section 11054 or 11055 or the synthetic cannabinoid compound defined in Section 11357.5 of which it is an analog.

(b) Except as provided in subdivision (c), the term "controlled substance analog" means either of the following:

(1) A substance the chemical structure of which is substantially similar to the chemical structure of a controlled substance classified in Section 11054 or 11055 or a synthetic cannabinoid compound defined in Section 11357.5.

(2) A substance that has, is represented as having, or is intended to have a stimulant, depressant, or hallucinogenic effect on the central nervous system that is substantially similar to, or greater than, the stimulant, depressant, or hallucinogenic effect on the central nervous system of a controlled substance classified in Section 11054 or 11055 or a synthetic cannabinoid compound defined in Section 11357.5.

(c) The term "controlled substance analog" does not mean any of the following:

(1) A substance for which there is an approved new drug application as defined under Section 505 of the federal Food, Drug, and Cosmetic Act (21 U.S.C. Sec. 355) or that is generally recognized as safe and effective for use pursuant to Sections 501, 502, and 503 of the federal Food, Drug, and Cosmetic Act (21 U.S.C. Secs. 351, 352, and 353) and Section 330 and following of Title 21 of the Code of Federal Regulations.

(2) With respect to a particular person, a substance for which an exemption is in effect for investigational use for that person under Section 505 of the federal Food, Drug, and Cosmetic Act (21 U.S.C. Sec. 355), to the extent that the conduct with respect to that substance is pursuant to the exemption.

(3) A substance, before an exemption as specified in paragraph (2) takes effect with respect to the substance, to the extent the substance is not intended for human consumption. *(Added by Stats.1988, c. 712, § 4, eff. Aug. 29, 1988. Amended by Stats.2016, c. 627 (S.B.1036), § 2, eff. Jan. 1, 2017; Stats.2017, c. 561 (A.B.1516), § 114, eff. Jan. 1, 2018.)*

Cross References

Controlled substance defined for purposes of this Division, see Health and Safety Code § 11007.
Person defined for purposes of this Division, see Health and Safety Code § 11022.

Research References

2 Witkin, California Criminal Law 4th Crimes Against Public Peace and Welfare § 89 (2021), Analogs of Controlled Substances.

CHAPTER 7. DEPARTMENT OF JUSTICE

§ 11450. Agents and employees of Attorney General

The Attorney General may, in conformity with the State Civil Service Act, Part 2 (commencing with Section 18500), Division 5, Title 2 of the Government Code, employ such agents, chemists, clerical, and other employees as are necessary for the conduct of the affairs of the Department of Justice in carrying out its responsibilities specified in this division. *(Formerly § 11452, added by Stats.1972, c. 1407, p. 3025, § 3. Renumbered § 11450 and amended by Stats.1974, c. 1403, § 5.)*

Cross References

Age limit for narcotic or special agent, see Government Code § 15005.
Agent defined for purposes of this Division, see Health and Safety Code § 11003.
Attorney General, generally, see Government Code § 12500 et seq.
Attorney General defined for purposes of this Division, see Health and Safety Code § 11004.
Officers of Department of Justice, authority of peace officers, see Penal Code § 830.3.
Possession of tear gas weapons, see Penal Code § 22820.
Right to carry concealed or loaded firearms, see Penal Code §§ 25450, 25900 et seq.

Research References

4 Witkin, California Criminal Law 4th Introduction to Criminal Procedure § 14 (2021), Principal Powers and Duties.

§ 11454. Expenditures to obtain evidence

The Attorney General and the agents appointed by him, when authorized so to do by the Attorney General, may expend such sums as the Attorney General deems necessary in the purchase of controlled substances for evidence and in the employment of operators to obtain evidence.

The sums so expended shall be repaid to the officer making the expenditures upon claims approved by the Attorney General and subject to postaudit by the Department of Finance. The claims when approved shall be paid out of the funds appropriated or made available by law for the support or use of the Department of Justice. *(Added by Stats.1972, c. 1407, p. 3025, § 3. Amended by Stats.1974, c. 1403, § 7.)*

Cross References

Agent defined for purposes of this Division, see Health and Safety Code § 11003.
Attorney General, generally, see Government Code § 12500 et seq.
Attorney General defined for purposes of this Division, see Health and Safety Code § 11004.
Controlled substance defined for purposes of this Division, see Health and Safety Code § 11007.
Department of Finance, generally, see Government Code § 13000 et seq.
Recovery of funds expended in investigations, see Health and Safety Code § 11501.

CHAPTER 8. SEIZURE AND DISPOSITION

§ 11469. Guidelines for utilization of seizure and forfeiture laws

In order to ensure the proper utilization of the laws permitting the seizure and forfeiture of property under this chapter, the Legislature hereby establishes the following guidelines:

(a) Law enforcement is the principal objective of forfeiture. Potential revenue must not be allowed to jeopardize the effective investigation and prosecution of criminal offenses, officer safety, the integrity of ongoing investigations, or the due process rights of citizens.

(b) No prosecutor's or sworn law enforcement officer's employment or salary shall be made to depend upon the level of seizures or forfeitures he or she achieves.

(c) Whenever appropriate, prosecutors should seek criminal sanctions as to the underlying criminal acts which give rise to the forfeiture action.

(d) Seizing agencies shall have a manual detailing the statutory grounds for forfeiture and all applicable policies and procedures. The manual shall include procedures for prompt notice to interestholders, the expeditious release of seized property, where appropriate, and the prompt resolution of claims of innocent ownership.

(e) Seizing agencies shall implement training for officers assigned to forfeiture programs, which training should be ongoing.

(f) Seizing agencies shall avoid any appearance of impropriety in the sale or acquisition of forfeited property.

(g) Seizing agencies shall not put any seized or forfeited property into service.

(h) Unless otherwise provided by law, forfeiture proceeds shall be maintained in a separate fund or account subject to appropriate accounting controls and annual financial audits of all deposits and expenditures.

(i) Seizing agencies shall ensure that seized property is protected and its value preserved.

(j) Although civil forfeiture is intended to be remedial by removing the tools and profits from those engaged in the illicit drug trade, it can have harsh effects on property owners in some circumstances. Therefore, law enforcement shall seek to protect the interests of innocent property owners, guarantee adequate notice and due process to property owners, and ensure that forfeiture serves the remedial purpose of the law. *(Added by Stats.1994, c. 314 (A.B.114), § 1, eff. Aug. 19, 1994.)*

Cross References

Drug defined for purposes of this Division, see Health and Safety Code § 11014.
Restitution fines, exception, amounts, see Penal Code § 1202.4.

Research References

3 Witkin, California Criminal Law 4th Punishment § 110 (2021), In General.
3 Witkin, California Criminal Law 4th Punishment § 117 (2021), Statutory Requirement.
3 Witkin, California Criminal Law 4th Punishment § 196 (2021), In General.

§ 11470. Property subject to forfeiture; vesting of personal property with state

The following are subject to forfeiture:

(a) All controlled substances which have been manufactured, distributed, dispensed, or acquired in violation of this division.

(b) All raw materials, products, and equipment of any kind which are used, or intended for use, in manufacturing, compounding, processing, delivering, importing, or exporting any controlled substance in violation of this division.

(c) All property except real property or a boat, airplane, or any vehicle which is used, or intended for use, as a container for property described in subdivision (a) or (b).

(d) All books, records, and research products and materials, including formulas, microfilm, tapes, and data which are used, or intended for use, in violation of this division.

(e) The interest of any registered owner of a boat, airplane, or any vehicle other than an implement of husbandry, as defined in Section 36000 of the Vehicle Code, which has been used as an instrument to facilitate the manufacture of, or possession for sale or sale of 14.25 grams or more of heroin, or a substance containing 14.25 grams or more of heroin, or 14.25 grams or more of a substance containing heroin, or 28.5 grams or more of Schedule I controlled substances except cannabis, peyote, or psilocybin; 10 pounds dry weight or more of cannabis, peyote, or psilocybin; or 28.5 grams or more of cocaine, as specified in paragraph (6) of subdivision (b) of Section 11055, cocaine base as specified in paragraph (1) of subdivision (f) of Section 11054, or methamphetamine; or a substance containing 28.5 grams or more of cocaine, as specified in paragraph (6) of subdivision (b) of Section 11055, cocaine base as specified in paragraph (1) of subdivision (f) of Section 11054, or methamphetamine; or 57 grams or more of a substance containing cocaine, as specified in paragraph (6) of subdivision (b) of Section 11055, cocaine base as specified in paragraph (1) of subdivision (f) of Section 11054, or methamphetamine; or 28.5 grams or more of Schedule II controlled substances. An interest in a vehicle which may be lawfully driven on the highway with a class C, class M1, or class M2 license, as prescribed in Section 12804.9 of the Vehicle Code, shall not be forfeited under this subdivision if there is a community property interest in the vehicle by a person other than the defendant and the vehicle is the sole class C, class M1, or class M2 vehicle available to the defendant's immediate family.

(f) All moneys, negotiable instruments, securities, or other things of value furnished or intended to be furnished by any person in exchange for a controlled substance, all proceeds traceable to such an exchange, and all moneys, negotiable instruments, or securities used or intended to be used to facilitate any violation of Section 11351, 11351.5, 11352, 11355, 11359, 11360, 11378, 11378.5, 11379, 11379.5, 11379.6, 11380, 11382, or 11383 of this code, or Section 182 of the Penal Code, or a felony violation of Section 11366.8 of this code, insofar as the offense involves manufacture, sale, possession for sale, offer for sale, or offer to manufacture, or conspiracy to commit at least one of those offenses, if the exchange, violation, or other conduct which is the basis for the forfeiture occurred within five years of the seizure of the property, or the filing of a petition under this chapter, or the issuance of an order of forfeiture of the property, whichever comes first.

(g) The real property of any property owner who is convicted of violating Section 11366, 11366.5, or 11366.6 with respect to that property. However, property which is used as a family residence or for other lawful purposes, or which is owned by two or more persons, one of whom had no knowledge of its unlawful use, shall not be subject to forfeiture.

(h)(1) Subject to the requirements of Section 11488.5 and except as further limited by this subdivision to protect innocent parties who claim a property interest acquired from a defendant, all right, title, and interest in any personal property described in this section shall vest in the state upon commission of the act giving rise to forfeiture under this chapter, if the state or local governmental entity proves a violation of Section 11351, 11351.5, 11352, 11355, 11359, 11360, 11378, 11378.5, 11379, 11379.5, 11379.6, 11380, 11382, or 11383 of this code, or Section 182 of the Penal Code, or a felony violation of Section 11366.8 of this code, insofar as the offense involves the manufacture, sale, possession for sale, offer for sale, offer to manufacture, or conspiracy to commit at least one of those offenses, in accordance with the burden of proof set forth in paragraph (1) of subdivision (i) of Section 11488.4 or, in the case of cash or negotiable instruments in excess of twenty-five thousand dollars ($25,000), paragraph (4) of subdivision (i) of Section 11488.4.

(2) The operation of the special vesting rule established by this subdivision shall be limited to circumstances where its application will not defeat the claim of any person, including a bona fide purchaser or encumbrancer who, pursuant to Section 11488.5, 11488.6, or 11489, claims an interest in the property seized, notwithstanding that the interest in the property being claimed was acquired from a defendant whose property interest would otherwise have been subject to divestment pursuant to this subdivision. *(Added by Stats.1994, c. 314 (A.B.114), § 3, eff. Aug. 19, 1994. Amended by Stats.1997, c. 241 (S.B.457), § 1; Stats.2012, c. 867 (S.B.1144), § 10.5; Stats.2014, c. 749 (S.B.1010), § 4, eff. Jan. 1, 2015; Stats.2017, c. 27 (S.B.94), § 152, eff. June 27, 2017.)*

Cross References

Burden of proof, generally, see Evidence Code § 500 et seq.
Cannabis defined for purposes of this Division, see Health and Safety Code § 11018.
Controlled substance defined for purposes of this Division, see Health and Safety Code § 11007.
Delivery of controlled substances to designated agency, see Health and Safety Code § 11474.
Felonies, definition and penalties, see Penal Code §§ 17, 18.
Issuance of warrant on probable cause, see Cal. Const. Art. 1, § 13; Penal Code § 1525.
Person defined for purposes of this Division, see Health and Safety Code § 11022.
Search warrants, generally, see Penal Code § 1523 et seq.
Seizure and forfeiture proceeding, see Business and Professions Code § 25375.
Seizure of things of value and believed to be forfeitable, see Health and Safety Code § 11488.
Trial on issue of forfeiture, see Health and Safety Code § 11488.4.

Research References

California Jury Instructions - Criminal 12.39, Forfeiture of Cash or Equivalents Under $25,000.00.
2 Witkin, California Criminal Law 4th Crimes Against Public Peace and Welfare § 158 (2021), Imitation Controlled Substances.
2 Witkin, California Criminal Law 4th Crimes Against Public Peace and Welfare § 163 (2021), Punishment.
5 Witkin, California Criminal Law 4th Criminal Trial § 179 (2021), When Counsel is Not Required.
1 Witkin California Criminal Law 4th Defenses § 120 (2021), Civil Forfeiture.
3 Witkin, California Criminal Law 4th Punishment § 188 (2021), In General.
3 Witkin, California Criminal Law 4th Punishment § 189 (2021), Criminal Actions.
3 Witkin, California Criminal Law 4th Punishment § 197 (2021), Property Subject to Forfeiture.
3 Witkin, California Criminal Law 4th Punishment § 198 (2021), Required Nexus Between Money and Crime.
3 Witkin, California Criminal Law 4th Punishment § 200 (2021), Necessity for Conviction.
3 Witkin, California Criminal Law 4th Punishment § 201 (2021), Commencement of Proceeding.
3 Witkin, California Criminal Law 4th Punishment § 203 (2021), Motion for Return.
3 Witkin, California Criminal Law 4th Punishment § 205 (2021), Hearing and Determination.

§ 11470.1. Civil action for recovery of expenses of seizing, eradicating, destroying or taking remedial action with respect to controlled substance or its precursors; burden of proof; presumption; discharge in bankruptcy; temporary restraining order or preliminary injunction; admissibility of evidence

Section operative until Jan. 1, 2024. See, also, § 11470.1 operative Jan. 1, 2024.

(a) The expenses of seizing, eradicating, destroying, or taking remedial action with respect to, any controlled substance or its precursors shall be recoverable from:

(1) Any person who manufactures or cultivates a controlled substance or its precursors in violation of this division.

(2) Any person who aids and abets or who knowingly profits in any manner from the manufacture or cultivation of a controlled substance or its precursors on property owned, leased, or possessed by the defendant, in violation of this division.

(b) The expenses of taking remedial action with respect to any controlled substance or its precursors shall also be recoverable from any person liable for the costs of that remedial action under Chapter 6.8 (commencing with Section 25300) of Division 20 of the Health and Safety Code.

(c) It shall be necessary to seek or obtain a criminal conviction for the unlawful manufacture or cultivation of any controlled substance or its precursors prior to the entry of judgment for the recovery of expenses. If criminal charges are pending against the defendant for the unlawful manufacture or cultivation of any controlled substance or its precursors, an action brought pursuant to this section shall, upon a defendant's request, be continued while the criminal charges are pending.

(d) The action may be brought by the district attorney, county counsel, city attorney, the State Department of Health Care Services, or Attorney General. All expenses recovered pursuant to this section shall be remitted to the law enforcement agency which incurred them.

(e)(1) The burden of proof as to liability shall be on the plaintiff and shall be by a preponderance of the evidence in an action alleging that the defendant is liable for expenses pursuant to paragraph (1) of subdivision (a). The burden of proof as to liability shall be on the plaintiff and shall be by clear and convincing evidence in an action alleging that the defendant is liable for expenses pursuant to paragraph (2) of subdivision (a). The burden of proof as to the amount of expenses recoverable shall be on the plaintiff and shall be by a preponderance of the evidence in any action brought pursuant to subdivision (a).

(2) Notwithstanding paragraph (1), for any person convicted of a criminal charge of the manufacture or cultivation of a controlled substance or its precursors there shall be a presumption affecting the burden of proof that the person is liable.

(f) Only expenses which meet the following requirements shall be recoverable under this section:

(1) The expenses were incurred in seizing, eradicating, or destroying the controlled substance or its precursors or in taking remedial action with respect to a hazardous substance. These expenses may not include any costs incurred in use of the herbicide paraquat.

(2) The expenses were incurred as a proximate result of the defendant's manufacture or cultivation of a controlled substance in violation of this division.

(3) The expenses were reasonably incurred.

(g) For purposes of this section, "remedial action" shall have the meaning set forth in Section 25322.

(h) For the purpose of discharge in bankruptcy, a judgment for recovery of expenses under this section shall be deemed to be a debt for willful and malicious injury by the defendant to another entity or to the property of another entity.

(i) Notwithstanding Section 526 of the Code of Civil Procedure, the plaintiff may be granted a temporary restraining order or a preliminary injunction, pending or during trial, to restrain the defendant from transferring, encumbering, hypothecating, or otherwise disposing of any assets specified by the court, if it appears by the complaint that the plaintiff is entitled to the relief demanded and it appears that the defendant may dispose of those assets to thwart enforcement of the judgment.

(j) The Legislature finds and declares that civil penalties for the recovery of expenses incurred in enforcing the provisions of this division shall not supplant criminal prosecution for violation of those provisions, but shall be a supplemental remedy to criminal enforcement.

(k) Any testimony, admission, or any other statement made by the defendant in any proceeding brought pursuant to this section, or any evidence derived from the testimony, admission, or other statement, shall not be admitted or otherwise used in any criminal proceeding arising out of the same conduct.

(*l*) No action shall be brought or maintained pursuant to this section against a person who has been acquitted of criminal charges for conduct that is the basis for an action under this section. *(Added by Stats.1983, c. 931, § 1. Amended by Stats.1986, c. 1031, § 1.5; Stats.2016, c. 831 (S.B.443), § 1, eff. Jan. 1, 2017.)*

§ 11470.1. Civil action for recovery of expenses of seizing, eradicating, destroying or taking remedial action with respect to controlled substance or its precursors; burden of proof; presumption; discharge in bankruptcy; temporary restraining order or preliminary injunction; admissibility of evidence

Section operative Jan. 1, 2024. See, also, § 11470.1 operative until Jan. 1, 2024.

(a) The expenses of seizing, eradicating, destroying, or taking remedial action with respect to, any controlled substance or its precursors shall be recoverable from:

(1) Any person who manufactures or cultivates a controlled substance or its precursors in violation of this division.

(2) Any person who aids and abets or who knowingly profits in any manner from the manufacture or cultivation of a controlled substance or its precursors on property owned, leased, or possessed by the defendant, in violation of this division.

(b) The expenses of taking remedial action with respect to any controlled substance or its precursors shall also be recoverable from any person liable for the costs of that remedial action under * * * Part 2 (commencing with Section 78000) of Division * * * 45.

(c) It shall be necessary to seek or obtain a criminal conviction for the unlawful manufacture or cultivation of any controlled substance or its precursors prior to the entry of judgment for the recovery of expenses. If criminal charges are pending against the defendant for the unlawful manufacture or cultivation of any controlled substance or its precursors, an action brought pursuant to this section shall, upon a defendant's request, be continued while the criminal charges are pending.

(d) The action may be brought by the district attorney, county counsel, city attorney, the State Department of Health Care Services, or Attorney General. All expenses recovered pursuant to this section shall be remitted to the law enforcement agency which incurred them.

(e)(1) The burden of proof as to liability shall be on the plaintiff and shall be by a preponderance of the evidence in an action alleging that the defendant is liable for expenses pursuant to paragraph (1) of subdivision (a). The burden of proof as to liability shall be on the plaintiff and shall be by clear and convincing evidence in an action alleging that the defendant is liable for expenses pursuant to paragraph (2) of subdivision (a). The burden of proof as to the amount of expenses recoverable shall be on the plaintiff and shall be by a preponderance of the evidence in any action brought pursuant to subdivision (a).

(2) Notwithstanding paragraph (1), for any person convicted of a criminal charge of the manufacture or cultivation of a controlled substance or its precursors there shall be a presumption affecting the burden of proof that the person is liable.

(f) Only expenses which meet the following requirements shall be recoverable under this section:

(1) The expenses were incurred in seizing, eradicating, or destroying the controlled substance or its precursors or in taking remedial action with respect to a hazardous substance. These expenses may not include any costs incurred in use of the herbicide paraquat.

(2) The expenses were incurred as a proximate result of the defendant's manufacture or cultivation of a controlled substance in violation of this division.

(3) The expenses were reasonably incurred.

(g) For purposes of this section, "remedial action" shall have the meaning set forth in Section 78125.

(h) For the purpose of discharge in bankruptcy, a judgment for recovery of expenses under this section shall be deemed to be a debt for willful and malicious injury by the defendant to another entity or to the property of another entity.

(i) Notwithstanding Section 526 of the Code of Civil Procedure, the plaintiff may be granted a temporary restraining order or a preliminary injunction, pending or during trial, to restrain the defendant from transferring, encumbering, hypothecating, or otherwise disposing of any assets specified by the court, if it appears by the complaint that the plaintiff is entitled to the relief demanded and it appears that the defendant may dispose of those assets to thwart enforcement of the judgment.

(j) The Legislature finds and declares that civil penalties for the recovery of expenses incurred in enforcing the provisions of this division shall not supplant criminal prosecution for violation of those provisions, but shall be a supplemental remedy to criminal enforcement.

(k) Any testimony, admission, or any other statement made by the defendant in any proceeding brought pursuant to this section, or any evidence derived from the testimony, admission, or other statement, shall not be admitted or otherwise used in any criminal proceeding arising out of the same conduct.

(*l*) No action shall be brought or maintained pursuant to this section against a person who has been acquitted of criminal charges for conduct that is the basis for an action under this section. *(Added by Stats.1983, c. 931, § 1. Amended by Stats.1986, c. 1031, § 1.5; Stats.2016, c. 831 (S.B.443), § 1, eff. Jan. 1, 2017; Stats.2022, c. 258 (A.B.2327), § 30, eff. Jan. 1, 2023, operative Jan. 1, 2024.)*

Law Revision Commission Comments

Section 11470.1(b) and (g) are amended to update cross-references in accordance with the nonsubstantive recodification of Chapter 6.8 (commencing with Section 25300) of Division 20 of the Health and Safety Code. [48 Cal.L.Rev.Comm. Reports __ (2021)].

Cross References

Attorney General, generally, see Government Code § 12500 et seq.
Attorney General defined for purposes of this Division, see Health and Safety Code § 11004.
Burden of proof, generally, see Evidence Code § 500 et seq.
Controlled substance defined for purposes of this Division, see Health and Safety Code § 11007.
Department of Health Care Services, generally, see Health and Safety Code § 100100 et seq.
Person defined for purposes of this Division, see Health and Safety Code § 11022.
Seizure and forfeiture proceeding, see Business and Professions Code § 25375.

Research References

3 Witkin, California Criminal Law 4th Punishment § 119 (2021), Rights of Third Parties.
3 Witkin, California Criminal Law 4th Punishment § 196 (2021), In General.

§ 11470.2. Criminal proceeding for recovery of expenses recoverable under § 11470.1; petition in conjunction with criminal proceeding; hearing; burden of proof; discharge in bankruptcy

(a) In lieu of a civil action for the recovery of expenses as provided in Section 11470.1, the prosecuting attorney in a criminal proceeding may, upon conviction of the underlying offense, seek the recovery of all expenses recoverable under Section 11470.1 from:

(1) Any person who manufacturers or cultivates a controlled substance or its precursors in violation of this division.

(2) Any person who aids and abets or who knowingly profits in any manner from the manufacture or cultivation of a controlled substance or its precursors on property owned, leased, or possessed by the defendant, in violation of this division. The trier of fact shall make an award of expenses, if proven, which shall be enforceable as any civil judgment. If probation is granted, the court may order payment of the expenses as a condition of probation. All expenses recovered pursuant to this section shall be remitted to the law enforcement agency which incurred them.

(b) The prosecuting attorney may, in conjunction with the criminal proceeding, file a petition for recovery of expenses with the superior court of the county in which the defendant has been charged with the underlying offense. The petition shall allege that the defendant had manufactured or cultivated a controlled substance in violation of Division 10 (commencing with Section 11000) of the Health and Safety Code and that expenses were incurred in seizing, eradicating, or destroying the controlled substance or its precursors. The petition shall also state the amount to be assessed. The prosecuting attorney shall make service of process of a notice of that petition to the defendant.

(c) The defendant may admit to or deny the petition for recovery of expenses. If the defendant admits the allegations of the petition, the court shall rule for the prosecuting attorney and enter a judgment for recovery of the expenses incurred.

(d) If the defendant denies the petition or declines to admit to it, the petition shall be heard in the superior court in which the underlying criminal offense will be tried and shall be promptly heard following the defendant's conviction on the underlying offense. The hearing shall be held either before the same jury or before a new jury in the discretion of the court, unless waived by the consent of all parties.

(e) At the hearing, the burden of proof as to the amount of expenses recoverable shall be on the prosecuting attorney and shall be by a preponderance of the evidence.

(f) For the purpose of discharge in bankruptcy, a judgment for recovery of expenses under this section shall be deemed to be a debt for willful and malicious injury by the defendant to another entity or to the property of another entity. *(Added by Stats.1983, c. 931, § 2.)*

Cross References

Burden of proof, generally, see Evidence Code § 500 et seq.
Controlled substance defined for purposes of this Division, see Health and Safety Code § 11007.
Manufacturer defined for purposes of this Division, see Health and Safety Code § 11017.
Person defined for purposes of this Division, see Health and Safety Code § 11022.
Seizure and forfeiture proceeding, see Business and Professions Code § 25375.

Research References

5 Witkin, California Criminal Law 4th Criminal Trial § 491 (2021), Constitutional and Statutory Right.
3 Witkin, California Criminal Law 4th Punishment § 119 (2021), Rights of Third Parties.
3 Witkin, California Criminal Law 4th Punishment § 196 (2021), In General.

§ 11470.3. Property of minors; forfeiture procedures applicable; continuance of forfeiture hearing

(a) Section 11470 shall be applicable to property owned by, or in the possession of, minors.

(b) The procedures for the forfeiture of property that comes within Section 11470 shall be applicable to minors.

(c) Notwithstanding the provisions of this chapter, if a petition has been filed alleging that the minor is a person described in Section 602 of the Welfare and Institutions Code because of a violation which is the basis for the seizure and forfeiture of property under this chapter, any related forfeiture hearing shall be continued until the adjudication of the petition. The forfeiture hearing shall not be conducted in juvenile court. *(Added by Stats.1988, c. 1358, § 2.)*

Cross References

Person defined for purposes of this Division, see Health and Safety Code § 11022.
Seizure and forfeiture proceeding, see Business and Professions Code § 25375.

§ 11470.4. Application of chapter to minors found to be persons described in § 602 of Welfare and Institutions Code

The provisions of this chapter apply to any minor who has been found to be a person described in Section 602 of the Welfare and Institutions Code because of a violation of Section 11351, 11351.5, 11352, 11355, 11366, 11366.5, 11366.6, 11378.5, 11379, 11379.5, 11379.6, or 11382. *(Added by Stats.1988, c. 1249, § 1.)*

Cross References

Person defined for purposes of this Division, see Health and Safety Code § 11022.
Seizure and forfeiture proceeding, see Business and Professions Code § 25375.

§ 11471. Seizure of property subject to forfeiture

Property subject to forfeiture under this division may be seized by any peace officer upon process issued by any court having jurisdiction over the property. Seizure without process may be made if any of the following situations exist:

(a) The seizure is incident to an arrest or a search under a search warrant.

(b) The property subject to seizure has been the subject of a prior judgment in favor of the state in a criminal injunction or forfeiture proceeding based upon this division.

(c) There is probable cause to believe that the property is directly or indirectly dangerous to health or safety.

(d) There is probable cause to believe that the property was used or is intended to be used in violation of this division.

(e) Real property subject to forfeiture may not be seized, absent exigent circumstances, without notice to the interested parties and a hearing to determine that seizure is necessary to preserve the property pending the outcome of the proceedings. At the hearing, the prosecution shall bear the burden of establishing that probable cause exists for the forfeiture of the property and that seizure is necessary to preserve the property pending the outcome of the forfeiture proceedings. The court may issue seizure orders pursuant to this section if it finds that seizure is warranted or pendente lite orders pursuant to Section 11492 if it finds that the status quo or value of the property can be preserved without seizure.

(f) Where business records are seized in conjunction with the seizure of property subject to forfeiture, the seizing agency shall, upon request, provide copies of the records to the person, persons, or business entity from whom such records were seized. *(Added by Stats.1972, c. 1407, p. 3026, § 3. Amended by Stats.1980, c. 1019, p. 3269, § 1; Stats.1994, c. 314 (A.B.114), § 4, eff. Aug. 19, 1994.)*

Cross References

Person defined for purposes of this Division, see Health and Safety Code § 11022.
Search warrants, see Penal Code § 1523 et seq.
Searches and seizures, see Cal. Const. Art. 1, § 13.
Seizure and forfeiture proceeding, see Business and Professions Code § 25375.

Research References

2 Witkin, California Criminal Law 4th Crimes Against Public Peace and Welfare § 155 (2021), Drug Paraphernalia.
3 Witkin, California Criminal Law 4th Punishment § 199 (2021), Seizure of Property.

§ 11471.2. Property seized or forfeited under Controlled Substances Act; referral or transfer of property to federal agency, or receipt of equitable share of property prohibited

(a) State or local law enforcement authorities shall not refer or otherwise transfer property seized under state law authorizing the seizure of property to a federal agency seeking the adoption of the seized property by the federal agency for proceeding with federal forfeiture under the federal Controlled Substances Act. Nothing in this section shall be construed to prohibit the federal government, or any of its agencies, from seizing property, seeking forfeiture under federal law, or sharing federally forfeited property with state or local law enforcement agencies when those state or local agencies work with federal agencies in joint investigations arising out of federal law or federal joint task forces comprised of federal and state or local agencies. Nothing in this section shall be construed to prohibit state or local law enforcement agencies from participating in a joint law enforcement operation with federal agencies.

(b) Except as provided in this subdivision and in subdivision (c), a state or local law enforcement agency participating in a joint investigation with a federal agency shall not receive an equitable share from the federal agency of all or a portion of the forfeited property or proceeds from the sale of property forfeited pursuant to the federal Controlled Substances Act unless a defendant is convicted in an underlying or related criminal action of an offense for which property is subject to forfeiture as specified in Section 11470 or Section 11488, or an offense under the federal Controlled Substances Act that includes all of the elements of an offense for which property is subject to forfeiture as specified in Sections 11470 and 11488. In any case in which the forfeited property is cash or negotiable instruments of a value of not less than forty thousand dollars ($40,000) there shall be no requirement of a criminal conviction as a prerequisite to receipt by state or local law enforcement agencies of an equitable share from federal authorities.

(c) If the defendant has been arrested and charged in an underlying or related criminal action or proceeding for an offense described in subdivision (b) and willfully fails to appear as required, intentionally flees to evade prosecution, or is deceased, there shall be no requirement of a criminal conviction as a prerequisite to receipt by state or local law enforcement agencies of an equitable share from federal authorities. *(Added by Stats.2016, c. 831 (S.B.443), § 2, eff. Jan. 1, 2017.)*

Research References

3 Witkin, California Criminal Law 4th Punishment § 196 (2021), In General.

§ 11471.5. Seizure by peace officer; notice to Franchise Tax Board; value of property exceeding $5,000

A peace officer making a seizure pursuant to Section 11471 shall notify the Franchise Tax Board where there is reasonable cause to believe that the value of the seized property exceeds five thousand dollars ($5,000). *(Added by Stats.1987, c. 924, § 1.5, eff. Sept. 22, 1987.)*

Cross References

Seizure and forfeiture proceeding, see Business and Professions Code § 25375.

§ 11472. Seizure by peace officer; search warrant

Controlled substances and any device, contrivance, instrument, or paraphernalia used for unlawfully using or administering a controlled substance, which are possessed in violation of this division, may be seized by any peace officer and in the aid of such seizure a search warrant may be issued as prescribed by law. *(Formerly § 11473, added by Stats.1972, c. 1407, p. 3026, § 3. Renumbered § 11472 and amended by Stats.1980, c. 1019, p. 3269, § 3.)*

Cross References

Controlled substance defined for purposes of this Division, see Health and Safety Code § 11007.
Search warrants, see Penal Code § 1523 et seq.
Seizure and forfeiture proceeding, see Business and Professions Code § 25375.

Research References

4 Witkin, California Criminal Law 4th Illegally Obtained Evidence § 111 (2021), Statutory Grounds.

§ 11473. Order for destruction upon conviction; exceptions

(a) All seizures under provisions of this chapter, except seizures of vehicles, boats, or airplanes, as specified in subdivision (e) of Section 11470, or seizures of moneys, negotiable instruments, securities, or other things of value as specified in subdivision (f) of Section 11470, shall, upon conviction of the owner or defendant, be ordered destroyed by the court in which conviction was had.

(b) Law enforcement may request of the court that certain uncontaminated science equipment be relinquished to a school or school district for science classroom education in lieu of destruction. *(Formerly § 11474, added by Stats.1972, c. 1407, p. 3026, § 3. Amended by Stats.1976, c. 1407, p. 6332, § 2. Renumbered § 11473 and amended by Stats.1980, c. 1019, p. 3269, § 4. Amended by Stats.1982, c. 1289, p. 4768, § 2; Stats.1983, c. 948, § 2; Stats.1988, c. 1492, § 3; Stats.1989, c. 1195, § 1.5; Stats.1983, c. 948, § 2, operative Jan. 1, 1994; Stats.1994, c. 979 (S.B.937), § 2.)*

Cross References

Seizure and forfeiture proceeding, see Business and Professions Code § 25375.
Uniform controlled substances, seizure and disposition, hazardous chemicals and containers, see Health and Safety Code § 11479.5.

Research References

3 Witkin, California Criminal Law 4th Punishment § 196 (2021), In General.

§ 11473.5. Order for destruction; seized property in possession of government official; cases without trials or convictions; exceptions

(a) All seizures of controlled substances, instruments, or paraphernalia used for unlawfully using or administering a controlled substance which are in possession of any city, county, or state official as found property, or as the result of a case in which no trial was had or which has been disposed of by way of dismissal or otherwise than by way of conviction, shall be destroyed by order of the court, unless the court finds that the controlled substances, instruments, or paraphernalia were lawfully possessed by the defendant.

(b) If the court finds that the property was not lawfully possessed by the defendant, law enforcement may request of the court that certain uncontaminated instruments or paraphernalia be relinquished to a school or school district for science classroom education in lieu of destruction. *(Formerly § 11474.5, added by Stats.1972, c. 1407, p. 3026, § 3. Renumbered § 11473.5 and amended by Stats. 1980, c. 1019, p. 3269, § 5. Amended by Stats.1994, c. 979 (S.B.937), § 3.)*

Cross References

Controlled substance defined for purposes of this Division, see Health and Safety Code § 11007.
Seizure and forfeiture proceeding, see Business and Professions Code § 25375.
Uniform controlled substances, seizure and disposition, hazardous chemicals and containers, see Health and Safety Code § 11479.5.

Research References

2 Witkin, California Criminal Law 4th Crimes Against Public Peace and Welfare § 144 (2021), Return of Confiscated Marijuana.
3 Witkin, California Criminal Law 4th Punishment § 196 (2021), In General.

§ 11474. Order for destruction; execution; contents; delivery of controlled substances

A court order for the destruction of controlled substances, instruments, or paraphernalia pursuant to the provisions of Section 11473 or 11473.5 may be carried out by a police or sheriff's department, the Department of Justice, the Department of the California Highway Patrol, the Department of Cannabis Control, or the Department of Alcoholic Beverage Control. The court order shall specify the agency responsible for the destruction. Controlled substances, instruments, or paraphernalia not in the possession of the designated agency at the time the order of the court is issued shall be delivered to the designated agency for destruction in compliance with the order. *(Added by Stats.1980, c. 1019, p. 3270, § 6. Amended by Stats.1996, c. 1154 (A.B.3020), § 5, eff. Sept. 30, 1996; Stats.1999, c. 787 (A.B.749), § 7; Stats.2021, c. 70 (A.B.141), § 105, eff. July 12, 2021.)*

Cross References

Controlled substance defined for purposes of this Division, see Health and Safety Code § 11007.
Seizure and forfeiture proceeding, see Business and Professions Code § 25375.

§ 11475. Schedule I substances as contraband; forfeiture

Controlled substances listed in Schedule I that are possessed, transferred, sold, or offered for sale in violation of this division are contraband and shall be seized and summarily forfeited to the state. Controlled substances listed in Schedule I, which are seized or come into the possession of the state, the owners of which are unknown, are contraband and shall be summarily forfeited to the state. *(Added by Stats.1972, c. 1407, p. 3026, § 3.)*

Cross References

Controlled substance defined for purposes of this Division, see Health and Safety Code § 11007.
Seizure and forfeiture proceeding, see Business and Professions Code § 25375.

§ 11476. Plants from which Schedules I and II substances derived; seizure and forfeiture

Species of plants from which controlled substances in Schedules I and II may be derived which have been planted or cultivated in violation of this division, or of which the owners or cultivators are unknown, or which are wild growths, may be seized and summarily forfeited to the state. *(Added by Stats.1972, c. 1407, p. 3027, § 3.)*

Cross References

Controlled substance defined for purposes of this Division, see Health and Safety Code § 11007.
Seizure and forfeiture proceeding, see Business and Professions Code § 25375.

§ 11477. Plants; authority for seizure and forfeiture

The failure, upon demand by a peace officer of the person in occupancy or in control of land or premises upon which the species of plants are growing or being stored, to produce an appropriate registration, or proof that he is the holder thereof, constitutes authority for the seizure and forfeiture of the plants. *(Added by Stats.1972, c. 1407, p. 3027, § 3. Amended by Stats.1980, c. 1019, p. 3270, § 7.)*

Cross References

Person defined for purposes of this Division, see Health and Safety Code § 11022.

Seizure and forfeiture proceeding, see Business and Professions Code § 25375.

§ 11478. Cannabis; use in research projects; receipts and records; report

Cannabis may be provided by the Attorney General to the heads of research projects which have been registered by the Attorney General, and which have been approved by the research advisory panel pursuant to Section 11480.

The head of the approved research project shall personally receipt for such quantities of cannabis and shall make a record of their disposition. The receipt and record shall be retained by the Attorney General. The head of the approved research project shall also, at intervals and in the manner required by the research advisory panel, report the progress or conclusions of the research project. *(Added by Stats.1972, c. 1407, p. 3027, § 3. Amended by Stats.1974, c. 545, § 60; Stats.1980, c. 1019, p. 3270, § 8; Stats.2017, c. 27 (S.B.94), § 153, eff. June 27, 2017.)*

Cross References

Attorney General, generally, see Government Code § 12500 et seq.
Attorney General defined for purposes of this Division, see Health and Safety Code § 11004.
Cannabis defined for purposes of this Division, see Health and Safety Code § 11018.
Expenditures to obtain evidence, see Health and Safety Code § 11454.
Recovery of funds expended in investigation, see Health and Safety Code § 11501.
Seizure and forfeiture proceeding, see Business and Professions Code § 25375.

§ 11479. Destruction of controlled substances without court order; requirements; special requirements for growing or harvested cannabis

Notwithstanding Sections 11473 and 11473.5, at any time after seizure by a law enforcement agency of a suspected controlled substance, except in the case of growing or harvested cannabis, that amount in excess of 10 pounds in gross weight may be destroyed without a court order by the chief of the law enforcement agency or a designated subordinate. In the case of growing or harvested cannabis, that amount in excess of two pounds, or the amount of cannabis a medicinal cannabis patient or designated caregiver is authorized to possess by ordinance in the city or county where the cannabis was seized, whichever is greater, may be destroyed without a court order by the chief of the law enforcement agency or a designated subordinate. Destruction shall not take place pursuant to this section until all of the following requirements are satisfied:

(a) At least five random and representative samples have been taken, for evidentiary purposes, from the total amount of suspected controlled substances to be destroyed. These samples shall be in addition to the 10 pounds required above. When the suspected controlled substance consists of growing or harvested cannabis plants, at least one 2–pound sample or a sample in the amount of medicinal cannabis a medicinal cannabis patient or designated caregiver is authorized to possess by ordinance in the city or county where the cannabis was seized, whichever is greater, shall be retained. This sample may include stalks, branches, or leaves. In addition, five representative samples of leaves or buds shall be retained for evidentiary purposes from the total amount of suspected controlled substances to be destroyed.

(b) Photographs and videos have been taken that reasonably and accurately demonstrate the total amount of the suspected controlled substance to be destroyed.

(c) The gross weight of the suspected controlled substance has been determined, either by actually weighing the suspected controlled substance or by estimating that weight after dimensional measurement of the total suspected controlled substance.

(d) The chief of the law enforcement agency has determined that it is not reasonably possible to preserve the suspected controlled substance in place, or to remove the suspected controlled substance to another location. In making this determination, the difficulty of transporting and storing the suspected controlled substance to another site and the storage facilities may be taken into consideration.

Subsequent to any destruction of a suspected controlled substance pursuant to this section, an affidavit shall be filed within 30 days in the court that has jurisdiction over any pending criminal proceedings pertaining to that suspected controlled substance, reciting the applicable information required by subdivisions (a), (b), (c), and (d) together with information establishing the location of the suspected controlled substance, and specifying the date and time of the destruction. In the event that there are no criminal proceedings pending that pertain to that suspected controlled substance, the affidavit may be filed in any court within the county that would have jurisdiction over a person against whom those criminal charges might be filed. *(Added by Stats.1979, c. 865, p. 3014, § 2, eff. Sept. 22, 1979. Amended by Stats.1983, c. 946, § 1; Stats.1984, c. 1209, § 1; Stats.1986, c. 1031, § 2; Stats.1989, c. 1072, § 1, eff. Sept. 30, 1989; Stats.2002, c. 787 (S.B.1798), § 3; Stats.2015, c. 713 (S.B.303), § 1, eff. Jan. 1, 2016; Stats.2017, c. 27 (S.B.94), § 154, eff. June 27, 2017.)*

Cross References

Cannabis defined for purposes of this Division, see Health and Safety Code § 11018.
Controlled substance defined for purposes of this Division, see Health and Safety Code § 11007.
Engaging in commercial cannabis activity without a license, aiding and abetting unlicensed commercial cannabis activity, civil penalties, destruction of cannabis in accordance with this section, see Business and Professions Code § 26038.
Person defined for purposes of this Division, see Health and Safety Code § 11022.
Seizure and forfeiture proceeding, see Business and Professions Code § 25375.

Research References

2 Witkin, California Criminal Law 4th Crimes Against Public Peace and Welfare § 369B (2021), (New) Licensing.
3 Witkin, California Criminal Law 4th Punishment § 196 (2021), In General.

§ 11479.1. Phencyclidine or analog thereof; destruction without court order; affidavit

(a) Notwithstanding the provisions of Sections 11473, 11473.5, and 11479, at any time after seizure by a law enforcement agency and identification by a forensic chemist or criminalist of phencyclidine, or an analog thereof, that amount in excess of one gram of a crystalline substance containing phencyclidine or its analog, 10 milliliters of a liquid substance containing phencyclidine or its analog, two grams of plant material containing phencyclidine or its analog, or five hand-rolled cigarettes treated with phencyclidine or its analog, may be destroyed without a court order by the chief of the law enforcement agency or a designated subordinate. Destruction shall not take place pursuant to this section until all of the following requirements are satisfied:

(1) At least one gram of a crystalline substance containing phencyclidine or its analog, 10 milliliters of a liquid substance containing phencyclidine or its analog, two grams of plant material containing phencyclidine or its analog, or five hand-rolled cigarettes treated with phencyclidine or its analog have been taken as samples from the phencyclidine or analog to be destroyed.

(2) Photographs have been taken which reasonably demonstrate the total amount of phencyclidine or its analog to be destroyed.

(3) The gross weight of the phencyclidine or its analog has been determined by actually weighing the phencyclidine or analog.

(b) Subsequent to any destruction of phencyclidine or its analog, an affidavit shall be filed within 30 days in the court which has jurisdiction over any pending criminal proceedings pertaining to that phencyclidine or its analog, reciting the applicable information required by paragraphs (1), (2), and (3) of subdivision (a), together with information establishing the location of the phencyclidine or analog and specifying the date and time of the destruction. In the event that there are no criminal proceedings pending which pertain to that phencyclidine or analog, the affidavit may be filed in any court within the county which would have jurisdiction over a person against whom these criminal charges might be filed. *(Added by Stats.1983, c. 946, § 2. Amended by Stats.2002, c. 787 (S.B.1798), § 4.)*

Cross References

Person defined for purposes of this Division, see Health and Safety Code § 11022.
Seizure and forfeiture proceeding, see Business and Professions Code § 25375.

§ 11479.2. Destruction of controlled substance, except cannabis, with court order; requirements

Notwithstanding the provisions of Sections 11473, 11473.5, 11474, 11479, and 11479.1, at any time after seizure by a law enforcement agency of a suspected controlled substance, except cannabis, any amount, as determined by the court, in excess of 57 grams may, by court order, be destroyed by the chief of a law enforcement agency or a designated subordinate. Destruction shall not take place pursuant to this section until all of the following requirements are satisfied:

(a) At least five random and representative samples have been taken, for evidentiary purposes, from the total amount of suspected controlled substances to be destroyed. Those samples shall be in addition to the 57 grams required above and each sample shall weigh not less than one gram at the time the sample is collected.

(b) Photographs have been taken which reasonably demonstrate the total amount of the suspected controlled substance to be destroyed.

(c) The gross weight of the suspected controlled substance has been determined, either by actually weighing the suspected controlled substance or by estimating such weight after dimensional measurement of the total suspected controlled substance.

(d) In cases involving controlled substances suspected of containing cocaine or methamphetamine, an analysis has determined the qualitative and quantitative nature of the suspected controlled substance.

(e) The law enforcement agency with custody of the controlled substance sought to be destroyed has filed a written motion for the order of destruction in the court which has jurisdiction over any pending criminal proceeding in which a defendant is charged by accusatory pleading with a crime specifically involving the suspected controlled substance sought to be destroyed. The motion shall, by affidavit of the chief of the law enforcement agency or designated subordinate, recite the applicable information required by subdivisions (a), (b), (c), and (d), together with information establishing the location of the suspected controlled substance and the title of any pending criminal proceeding as defined in this subdivision. The motion shall bear proof of service upon all parties to any pending criminal proceeding. No motion shall be made when a defendant is without counsel until the defendant has entered his or her plea to the charges.

(f) The order for destruction shall issue pursuant to this section upon the motion and affidavit in support of the order, unless within 20 days after application for the order, a defendant has requested, in writing, a hearing on the motion. Within 10 days after the filing of that request, or a longer period of time upon good cause shown by either party, the court shall conduct a hearing on the motion in which each party to the motion for destruction shall be permitted to call and examine witnesses. The hearing shall be recorded. Upon conclusion of the hearing, if the court finds that the defendant would not be prejudiced by the destruction, it shall grant the motion and make an order for destruction. In making the order, the court shall ensure that the representative samples to be retained are of sufficient quantities to allow for qualitative analyses by both the prosecution and the defense. Any order for destruction pursuant to this section shall include the applicable information required by subdivisions (a), (b), (c), (d), and (e) and the name of the agency responsible for the destruction. Unless waived, the order shall provide for a 10–day delay prior to destruction in order to allow expert analysis of the controlled substance by the defense.

Subsequent to any destruction of a suspected controlled substance pursuant to this section, an affidavit shall be filed within 30 days in the court which ordered destruction stating the location of the retained, suspected controlled substance and specifying the date and time of destruction.

This section does not apply to seizures involving hazardous chemicals or controlled substances in mixture or combination with hazardous chemicals. *(Added by Stats.1984, c. 1209, § 2. Amended by Stats.1986, c. 1031, § 3; Stats.2017, c. 27 (S.B.94), § 155, eff. June 27, 2017.)*

Cross References

Cannabis defined for purposes of this Division, see Health and Safety Code § 11018.
Controlled substance defined for purposes of this Division, see Health and Safety Code § 11007.
Seizure and forfeiture proceeding, see Business and Professions Code § 25375.

§ 11479.5. Hazardous chemicals, chemical containers, or items contaminated with hazardous substance used in unlawful manufacture of controlled substances; disposal without court order; seizure without a warrant; requirements

(a) Notwithstanding Sections 11473 and 11473.5, at any time after seizure by a law enforcement agency of a suspected hazardous chemical, the chemical's container, or any item contaminated with a hazardous substance believed to have been used or intended to have been used in the unlawful manufacture of controlled substances, that amount in excess of one fluid ounce if liquid, or one avoirdupois ounce if solid, of each different type of suspected hazardous chemical, its container, and any item contaminated with a hazardous substance may be disposed of without a court order by the seizing agency. For the purposes of this section, "hazardous chemical" means any material that is believed by the chief of the law enforcement agency, or his or her designee, to be toxic, carcinogenic, explosive, corrosive, or flammable, and that is believed by the chief of the law enforcement agency, or his or her designee, to have been used or intended to have been used in the unlawful manufacture of controlled substances.

(b) Destruction pursuant to this section of suspected hazardous chemicals or suspected hazardous chemicals and controlled substances in combination, or the chemical containers and items contaminated with a hazardous substance, shall not take place until all of the following requirements are met:

(1) At least a one ounce sample is taken from each different type of suspected hazardous chemical to be destroyed.

(2) At least a one ounce sample has been taken from each container of a mixture of a suspected hazardous chemical with a suspected controlled substance.

(3) Photographs have been taken which reasonably demonstrate the total amount of suspected controlled substances and suspected hazardous chemicals to be destroyed.

(4) The gross weight or volume of the suspected hazardous chemical seized has been determined.

(5) Photographs have been taken of the chemical containers and items contaminated with a hazardous substance that reasonably demonstrate their size.

(c) Subsequent to any disposal of a suspected hazardous chemical, its container, or any item contaminated with a hazardous substance pursuant to this section, the law enforcement agency involved shall maintain records concerning the details of its compliance with, and reciting the applicable information required by paragraphs (1), (2),

(3), (4), and (5) of subdivision (b), together with the information establishing the location of the suspected hazardous chemical, its container, and any item contaminated with a hazardous substance, and specifying the date and time of the disposal.

(d)(1) Subsequent to any destruction of a suspected controlled substance in combination with a hazardous chemical or any item contaminated with a hazardous substance pursuant to this section, an affidavit containing applicable information required by paragraphs (1), (2), (3), (4), and (5) of subdivision (b) shall be filed within 30 days in the court that issued the search warrant.

(2) If the disposed materials were seized without a warrant, an affidavit containing applicable information required by paragraphs (1), (2), (3), (4), and (5) of subdivision (b) shall be filed in the court that has jurisdiction over any criminal proceedings pertaining to the suspected controlled substance after the criminal proceedings are initiated.

(e) A law enforcement agency responsible for the disposal of any hazardous chemical shall comply with the provisions of Chapter 6.5 (commencing with Section 25100) of Division 20 of the Health and Safety Code, as well as all applicable state and federal statutes and regulations. *(Added by Stats.1989, c. 1072, § 2, eff. Sept. 30, 1989. Amended by Stats.2002, c. 787 (S.B.1798), § 5; Stats.2002, c. 443 (A.B.2589), § 1.)*

Cross References

Controlled substance defined for purposes of this Division, see Health and Safety Code § 11007.
Hazardous substance account, illegal controlled substance manufacturing operations, see Health and Safety Code § 25354.5.
Search warrants, see Penal Code § 1523 et seq.
Seizure and forfeiture proceeding, see Business and Professions Code § 25375.

§ 11480. Cannabis and hallucinogenic drug research; Research Advisory Panel; hearings; projects

(a) The Legislature finds that there is a need to encourage further research into the nature and effects of cannabis and hallucinogenic drugs and to coordinate research efforts on such subjects.

(b) There is a Research Advisory Panel that consists of a representative of the State Department of Health Services, a representative of the California State Board of Pharmacy, the State Public Health Officer, a representative of the Attorney General, a representative of the University of California who shall be a pharmacologist, a physician, or a person holding a doctorate degree in the health sciences, a representative of a private university in this state who shall be a pharmacologist, a physician, or a person holding a doctorate degree in the health sciences, a representative of a statewide professional medical society in this state who shall be engaged in the private practice of medicine and shall be experienced in treating controlled substance dependency, a representative appointed by and serving at the pleasure of the Governor who shall have experience in drug abuse, cancer, or controlled substance research and who is either a registered nurse, licensed pursuant to Chapter 6 (commencing with Section 2700) of Division 2 of the Business and Professions Code, or other health professional. The Governor shall annually designate the private university and the professional medical society represented on the panel. Members of the panel shall be appointed by the heads of the entities to be represented, and they shall serve at the pleasure of the appointing power.

(c) The Research Advisory Panel shall appoint two special members to the Research Advisory Panel, who shall serve at the pleasure of the Research Advisory Panel only during the period Article 6 (commencing with Section 11260) of Chapter 5 remains effective.[1] The additional members shall be physicians and surgeons, and who are board certified in oncology, ophthalmology, or psychiatry.

(d) The panel shall annually select a chairperson from among its members.

(e) The panel may hold hearings on, and in other ways study, research projects concerning cannabis or hallucinogenic drugs in this state. Members of the panel shall serve without compensation, but shall be reimbursed for any actual and necessary expenses incurred in connection with the performance of their duties.

(f) The panel may approve research projects, which have been registered by the Attorney General, into the nature and effects of cannabis or hallucinogenic drugs, and shall inform the Attorney General of the head of the approved research projects that are entitled to receive quantities of cannabis pursuant to Section 11478.

(g) The panel may withdraw approval of a research project at any time, and when approval is withdrawn shall notify the head of the research project to return any quantities of cannabis to the Attorney General.

(h) The panel shall report annually to the Legislature and the Governor those research projects approved by the panel, the nature of each research project, and, where available, the conclusions of the research project. *(Added by Stats.1972, c. 1407, p. 3027, § 3. Amended by Stats.1973, c. 142, p. 399, § 39.5, eff. June 30, 1973, operative July 1, 1973; Stats.1974, c. 545, § 61; Stats.1974, c. 1403, § 8; Stats.1979, c. 300, p. 1114, § 2; Stats.1980, c. 374, p. 747, § 1, eff. July 10, 1980; Stats.1983, c. 101, § 111; Stats.2017, c. 27 (S.B.94), § 156, eff. June 27, 2017.)*

[1] Article 6 was repealed on June 30, 1989.

Cross References

Attorney General, generally, see Government Code § 12500 et seq.
Attorney General defined for purposes of this Division, see Health and Safety Code § 11004.
Cannabis defined for purposes of this Division, see Health and Safety Code § 11018.
Controlled substance defined for purposes of this Division, see Health and Safety Code § 11007.
Department of Health Care Services, generally, see Health and Safety Code § 100100 et seq.
Drug defined for purposes of this Division, see Health and Safety Code § 11014.
Educational programs on controlled substances, encouragement of research, see Health and Safety Code § 11601 et seq.
Person defined for purposes of this Division, see Health and Safety Code § 11022.
Physician, dentist, podiatrist, pharmacist, veterinarian, and optometrist defined for purposes of this Division, see Health and Safety Code § 11024.
Seizure and forfeiture proceeding, see Business and Professions Code § 25375.
Spores or mycelium capable of producing mushrooms or other material containing psilocyn or psyocylin, use in research, instruction, or analysis, see Health and Safety Code § 11392.
Use of controlled substances for research, instruction or analysis, see Health and Safety Code § 11213.

§ 11481. Research Advisory Panel; hearings and studies; project approval; reports

The Research Advisory Panel may hold hearings on, and in other ways study, research projects concerning the treatment of abuse of controlled substances.

The panel may approve research projects, which have been registered by the Attorney General, concerning the treatment of abuse of controlled substances and shall inform the chief of such approval. The panel may withdraw approval of a research project at any time and when approval is withdrawn shall so notify the chief.

The panel shall, annually and in the manner determined by the panel, report to the Legislature and the Governor those research projects approved by the panel, the nature of each research project, and where available, the conclusions of the research project. *(Added by Stats.1972, c. 1407, p. 3028, § 3.)*

Cross References

Attorney General, generally, see Government Code § 12500 et seq.

Attorney General defined for purposes of this Division, see Health and Safety Code § 11004.
Controlled substance defined for purposes of this Division, see Health and Safety Code § 11007.
Seizure and forfeiture proceeding, see Business and Professions Code § 25375.
Spores or mycelium capable of producing mushrooms or other material containing psilocyn or psyocylin, use in research, instruction, or analysis, see Health and Safety Code § 11392.

§ 11483. Narcotic treatment programs not prohibited

No provision of this division shall be construed to prohibit the establishment and effective operation of a narcotic treatment program licensed pursuant to Article 4 (commencing with Section 11885) of Chapter 1 of Part 3 of Division 10.5. *(Added by Stats.1972, c. 1407, p. 3028, § 3. Amended by Stats.1974, c. 545, § 63; Stats.1982, c. 932, p. 3389, § 2; Stats.1995, c. 455 (A.B.1113), § 12, eff. Sept. 5, 1995.)*

Cross References

Seizure and forfeiture proceeding, see Business and Professions Code § 25375.

§ 11485. Disposal of seized personal property in the event no defendant is prosecuted

Any peace officer of this state who, incident to a search under a search warrant issued for a violation of Section 11358 with respect to which no prosecution of a defendant results, seizes personal property suspected of being used in the planting, cultivation, harvesting, drying, processing, or transporting of cannabis, shall, if the seized personal property is not being held for evidence or destroyed as contraband, and if the owner of the property is unknown or has not claimed the property, provide notice regarding the seizure and manner of reclamation of the property to any owner or tenant of real property on which the property was seized. In addition, this notice shall be posted at the location of seizure and shall be published at least once in a newspaper of general circulation in the county in which the property was seized. If, after 90 days following the first publication of the notice, no owner appears and proves his or her ownership, the seized personal property shall be deemed to be abandoned and may be disposed of by sale to the public at public auction as set forth in Article 1 (commencing with Section 2080) of Chapter 4 of Title 6 of Part 4 of Division 3 of the Civil Code, or may be disposed of by transfer to a government agency or community service organization. Any profit from the sale or transfer of the property shall be expended for investigative services with respect to crimes involving cannabis. *(Added by Stats.1985, c. 1563, § 2, eff. Oct. 2, 1985. Amended by Stats.2017, c. 27 (S.B.94), § 157, eff. June 27, 2017.)*

Cross References

Cannabis defined for purposes of this Division, see Health and Safety Code § 11018.
Search warrants, see Penal Code § 1523 et seq.
Seizure and forfeiture proceeding, see Business and Professions Code § 25375.

§ 11488. Seizure of items subject to forfeiture; notice to Franchise Tax Board; receipts; presumptions

(a) Any peace officer of this state, subsequent to making or attempting to make an arrest for a violation of Section 11351, 11351.5, 11352, 11355, 11359, 11360, 11378, 11378.5, 11379, 11379.5, 11379.6, or 11382 of this code, or Section 182 of the Penal Code insofar as the offense involves manufacture, sale, purchase for the purpose of sale, possession for sale or offer to manufacture or sell, or conspiracy to commit one of those offenses, may seize any item subject to forfeiture under subdivisions (a) to (f), inclusive, of Section 11470. The peace officer shall also notify the Franchise Tax Board of a seizure where there is reasonable cause to believe that the value of the seized property exceeds five thousand dollars ($5,000).

(b) Receipts for property seized pursuant to this section shall be delivered to any person out of whose possession such property was seized, in accordance with Section 1412 of the Penal Code. In the event property seized was not seized out of anyone's possession, receipt for the property shall be delivered to the individual in possession of the premises at which the property was seized.

(c) There shall be a presumption affecting the burden of proof that the person to whom a receipt for property was issued is the owner thereof. This presumption may, however, be rebutted at the forfeiture hearing specified in Section 11488.5. *(Added by Stats.1994, c. 314 (A.B.114), § 9, eff. Aug. 19, 1994.)*

Cross References

Burden of proof, generally, see Evidence Code § 500 et seq.
Person defined for purposes of this Division, see Health and Safety Code § 11022.
Seizure and forfeiture proceeding, see Business and Professions Code § 25375.
Vesting of personal property with state following violations of controlled substances provisions, see Health and Safety Code § 11470.

Research References

5 Witkin, California Criminal Law 4th Criminal Trial § 512 (2021), In General.
3 Witkin, California Criminal Law 4th Punishment § 199 (2021), Seizure of Property.

§ 11488.1. Seized property; use as evidence; institution of forfeiture proceeding

Property seized pursuant to Section 11488 may, where appropriate, be held for evidence. The Attorney General or the district attorney for the jurisdiction involved shall institute and maintain the proceedings. *(Added by Stats.1982, c. 1289, p. 4769, § 4. Amended by Stats.1988, c. 892, § 1; Stats.1990, c. 1200 (A.B.4251), § 2; Stats. 1994, c. 314 (A.B.114), § 10, eff. Aug. 19, 1994.)*

Cross References

Attorney General, generally, see Government Code § 12500 et seq.
Attorney General defined for purposes of this Division, see Health and Safety Code § 11004.
Seizure and forfeiture proceeding, see Business and Professions Code § 25375.

Research References

3 Witkin, California Criminal Law 4th Punishment § 199 (2021), Seizure of Property.

§ 11488.2. Return of seized property if no authorization to hold

Within 15 days after the seizure, if the peace officer does not hold the property seized pursuant to Section 11488 for evidence or if the law enforcement agency for which the peace officer is employed does not refer the matter in writing for the institution of forfeiture proceedings by the Attorney General or the district attorney pursuant to Section 11488.1, the officer shall comply with any notice to withhold issued with respect to the property by the Franchise Tax Board. If no notice to withhold has been issued with respect to the property by the Franchise Tax Board, the officer shall return the property to the individual designated in the receipt therefor or if the property is a vehicle, boat, or airplane, it shall be returned to the registered owner. *(Added by Stats.1982, c. 1289, p. 4769, § 5. Amended by Stats.1983, c. 948, § 6; Stats.1990, c. 1200 (A.B.4251), § 3.)*

Cross References

Attorney General, generally, see Government Code § 12500 et seq.
Attorney General defined for purposes of this Division, see Health and Safety Code § 11004.
Seizure and forfeiture proceeding, see Business and Professions Code § 25375.

Research References

3 Witkin, California Criminal Law 4th Punishment § 199 (2021), Seizure of Property.

§ 11488.4. Petition of forfeiture; physical seizure of assets; notice of seizure; investigation; publication; motion for return of property; burden of proof

(a)(1) Except as provided in subdivision (j), if the Department of Justice or the local governmental entity determines that the factual circumstances do warrant that the moneys, negotiable instruments, securities, or other things of value seized or subject to forfeiture come within the provisions of subdivisions (a) to (g), inclusive, of Section 11470, and are not automatically made forfeitable or subject to court order of forfeiture or destruction by another provision of this chapter, the Attorney General or district attorney shall file a petition of forfeiture with the superior court of the county in which the defendant has been charged with the underlying criminal offense or in which the property subject to forfeiture has been seized or, if no seizure has occurred, in the county in which the property subject to forfeiture is located. If the petition alleges that real property is forfeitable, the prosecuting attorney shall cause a lis pendens to be recorded in the office of the county recorder of each county in which the real property is located.

(2) A petition of forfeiture under this subdivision shall be filed as soon as practicable, but in any case within one year of the seizure of the property which is subject to forfeiture, or as soon as practicable, but in any case within one year of the filing by the Attorney General or district attorney of a lis pendens or other process against the property, whichever is earlier.

(b) Physical seizure of assets shall not be necessary in order to have that particular asset alleged to be forfeitable in a petition under this section. The prosecuting attorney may seek protective orders for any asset pursuant to Section 11492.

(c) The Attorney General or district attorney shall make service of process regarding this petition upon every individual designated in a receipt issued for the property seized. In addition, the Attorney General or district attorney shall cause a notice of the seizure, if any, and of the intended forfeiture proceeding, as well as a notice stating that any interested party may file a verified claim with the superior court of the county in which the property was seized or if the property was not seized, a notice of the initiation of forfeiture proceedings with respect to any interest in the property seized or subject to forfeiture, to be served by personal delivery or by registered mail upon any person who has an interest in the seized property or property subject to forfeiture other than persons designated in a receipt issued for the property seized. Whenever a notice is delivered pursuant to this section, it shall be accompanied by a claim form as described in Section 11488.5 and directions for the filing and service of a claim.

(d) An investigation shall be made by the law enforcement agency as to any claimant to a vehicle, boat, or airplane whose right, title, interest, or lien is of record in the Department of Motor Vehicles or appropriate federal agency. If the law enforcement agency finds that any person, other than the registered owner, is the legal owner thereof, and that ownership did not arise subsequent to the date and time of arrest or notification of the forfeiture proceedings or seizure of the vehicle, boat, or airplane, it shall forthwith send a notice to the legal owner at his or her address appearing on the records of the Department of Motor Vehicles or appropriate federal agency.

(e) When a forfeiture action is filed, the notices shall be published once a week for three successive weeks in a newspaper of general circulation in the county where the seizure was made or where the property subject to forfeiture is located.

(f) All notices shall set forth the time within which a claim of interest in the property seized or subject to forfeiture is required to be filed pursuant to Section 11488.5. The notices shall explain, in plain language, what an interested party must do and the time in which the person must act to contest the forfeiture in a hearing. The notices shall state what rights the interested party has at a hearing. The notices shall also state the legal consequences for failing to respond to the forfeiture notice.

(g) Nothing contained in this chapter shall preclude a person, other than a defendant, claiming an interest in property actually seized from moving for a return of property if that person can show standing by proving an interest in the property not assigned subsequent to the seizure or filing of the forfeiture petition.

(h)(1) If there is an underlying or related criminal action, a defendant may move for the return of the property on the grounds that there is not probable cause to believe that the property is forfeitable pursuant to subdivisions (a) to (g), inclusive, of Section 11470 and is not automatically made forfeitable or subject to court order of forfeiture or destruction by another provision of this chapter. The motion may be made prior to, during, or subsequent to the preliminary examination. If made subsequent to the preliminary examination, the Attorney General or district attorney may submit the record of the preliminary hearing as evidence that probable cause exists to believe that the underlying or related criminal violations have occurred.

(2) Within 15 days after a defendant's motion is granted, the people may file a petition for a writ of mandate or prohibition seeking appellate review of the ruling.

(i)(1) With respect to property described in subdivisions (e) and (g) of Section 11470 for which forfeiture is sought and as to which forfeiture is contested, the state or local governmental entity shall have the burden of proving beyond a reasonable doubt that the property for which forfeiture is sought was used, or intended to be used, to facilitate a violation of one of the offenses enumerated in subdivision (f) or (g) of Section 11470.

(2) In the case of property described in subdivision (f) of Section 11470, except cash, negotiable instruments, or other cash equivalents of a value of not less than forty thousand dollars ($40,000), for which forfeiture is sought and as to which forfeiture is contested, the state or local governmental entity shall have the burden of proving beyond a reasonable doubt that the property for which forfeiture is sought meets the criteria for forfeiture described in subdivision (f) of Section 11470.

(3) In the case of property described in paragraphs (1) and (2), where forfeiture is contested, a judgment of forfeiture requires as a condition precedent thereto, that a defendant be convicted in an underlying or related criminal action of an offense specified in subdivision (f) or (g) of Section 11470 which offense occurred within five years of the seizure of the property subject to forfeiture or within five years of the notification of intention to seek forfeiture. If the defendant is found guilty of the underlying or related criminal offense, the issue of forfeiture shall be tried before the same jury, if the trial was by jury, or tried before the same court, if trial was by court, unless waived by all parties. The issue of forfeiture shall be bifurcated from the criminal trial and tried after conviction unless waived by all the parties.

(4) In the case of property described in subdivision (f) of Section 11470 that is cash or negotiable instruments of a value of not less than forty thousand dollars ($40,000), the state or local governmental entity shall have the burden of proving by clear and convincing evidence that the property for which forfeiture is sought is such as is described in subdivision (f) of Section 11470. There is no requirement for forfeiture thereof that a criminal conviction be obtained in an underlying or related criminal offense.

(5) If there is an underlying or related criminal action, and a criminal conviction is required before a judgment of forfeiture may be entered, the issue of forfeiture shall be tried in conjunction therewith. In such a case, the issue of forfeiture shall be bifurcated from the criminal trial and tried after conviction unless waived by the parties. Trial shall be by jury unless waived by all parties. If there is no underlying or related criminal action, the presiding judge of the superior court shall assign the action brought pursuant to this chapter for trial.

(j) The Attorney General or the district attorney of the county in which property is subject to forfeiture under Section 11470 may, pursuant to this subdivision, order forfeiture of personal property not exceeding twenty-five thousand dollars ($25,000) in value. The

Attorney General or district attorney shall provide notice of proceedings under this subdivision pursuant to subdivisions (c), (d), (e), and (f), including:

(1) A description of the property.

(2) The appraised value of the property.

(3) The date and place of seizure or location of any property not seized but subject to forfeiture.

(4) The violation of law alleged with respect to forfeiture of the property.

(5)(A) The instructions for filing and serving a claim with the Attorney General or the district attorney pursuant to Section 11488.5 and time limits for filing a claim and claim form.

(B) If no claims are timely filed, the Attorney General or the district attorney shall prepare a written declaration of forfeiture of the subject property to the state and dispose of the property in accordance with Section 11489. A written declaration of forfeiture signed by the Attorney General or district attorney under this subdivision shall be deemed to provide good and sufficient title to the forfeited property. The prosecuting agency ordering forfeiture pursuant to this subdivision shall provide a copy of the declaration of forfeiture to any person listed in the receipt given at the time of seizure and to any person personally served notice of the forfeiture proceedings.

(C) If a claim is timely filed, then the Attorney General or district attorney shall file a petition of forfeiture pursuant to this section within 30 days of the receipt of the claim. The petition of forfeiture shall then proceed pursuant to other provisions of this chapter, except that no additional notice need be given and no additional claim need be filed.

(k) If in any underlying or related criminal action or proceeding, in which a petition for forfeiture has been filed pursuant to this section, and a criminal conviction is required before a judgment of forfeiture may be entered, the defendant willfully fails to appear as required, there shall be no requirement of a criminal conviction as a prerequisite to the forfeiture. In these cases, forfeiture shall be ordered as against the defendant and judgment entered upon default, upon application of the state or local governmental entity. In its application for default, the state or local governmental entity shall be required to give notice to the defendant's attorney of record, if any, in the underlying or related criminal action, and to make a showing of due diligence to locate the defendant. In moving for a default judgment pursuant to this subdivision, the state or local governmental entity shall be required to establish a prima facie case in support of its petition for forfeiture. *(Added by Stats.1994, c. 314 (A.B.114), § 13, eff. Aug. 19, 1994. Amended by Stats.2016, c. 831 (S.B.443), § 3, eff. Jan. 1, 2017.)*

Cross References

Attorney General, generally, see Government Code § 12500 et seq.
Attorney General defined for purposes of this Division, see Health and Safety Code § 11004.
Deliver or delivery defined for purposes of this Division, see Health and Safety Code § 11009.
Mandamus, purpose of writ of mandate, courts which may issue writ and parties to whom issued, see Code of Civil Procedure § 1085.
Person defined for purposes of this Division, see Health and Safety Code § 11022.
Seizure and forfeiture proceeding, see Business and Professions Code § 25375.

Research References

California Jury Instructions - Criminal 12.39, Forfeiture of Cash or Equivalents Under $25,000.00.
4 Witkin, California Criminal Law 4th Illegally Obtained Evidence § 187 (2021), Rights of Third-Party Claimant.
3 Witkin, California Criminal Law 4th Punishment § 197 (2021), Property Subject to Forfeiture.
3 Witkin, California Criminal Law 4th Punishment § 200 (2021), Necessity for Conviction.
3 Witkin, California Criminal Law 4th Punishment § 201 (2021), Commencement of Proceeding.
3 Witkin, California Criminal Law 4th Punishment § 202 (2021), Alternative Procedure for Personal Property.
3 Witkin, California Criminal Law 4th Punishment § 203 (2021), Motion for Return.
3 Witkin, California Criminal Law 4th Punishment § 204 (2021), Third-Party Claim.
3 Witkin, California Criminal Law 4th Punishment § 205 (2021), Hearing and Determination.

§ 11488.5. Claim of interest procedure; default judgment; forfeiture hearing; burden of proof; continuance; order of release

(a)(1) Any person claiming an interest in the property seized pursuant to Section 11488 may, unless for good cause shown the court extends the time for filing, at any time within 30 days from the date of the last publication of the notice of seizure, if that person was not personally served or served by mail, or within 30 days after receipt of actual notice, file with the superior court of the county in which the defendant has been charged with the underlying or related criminal offense or in which the property was seized or, if there was no seizure, in which the property is located, a claim, verified in accordance with Section 446 of the Code of Civil Procedure, stating his or her interest in the property. An endorsed copy of the claim shall be served by the claimant on the Attorney General or district attorney, as appropriate, within 30 days of the filing of the claim. The Judicial Council shall develop and approve official forms for the verified claim that is to be filed pursuant to this section. The official forms shall be drafted in nontechnical language, in English and in Spanish, and shall be made available through the office of the clerk of the appropriate court.

(2) Any person who claims that the property was assigned to him or to her prior to the seizure or notification of pending forfeiture of the property under this chapter, whichever occurs last, shall file a claim with the court and prosecuting agency pursuant to Section 11488.5 declaring an interest in that property and that interest shall be adjudicated at the forfeiture hearing. The property shall remain under control of the law enforcement or prosecutorial agency until the adjudication of the forfeiture hearing. Seized property shall be protected and its value shall be preserved pending the outcome of the forfeiture proceedings.

(3) The clerk of the court shall not charge or collect a fee for the filing of a claim in any case in which the value of the respondent property as specified in the notice is five thousand dollars ($5,000) or less. If the value of the property, as specified in the notice, is more than five thousand dollars ($5,000), the clerk of the court shall charge the filing fee specified in Section 70611 of the Government Code.

(4) The claim of a law enforcement agency to property seized pursuant to Section 11488 or subject to forfeiture shall have priority over a claim to the seized or forfeitable property made by the Franchise Tax Board in a notice to withhold issued pursuant to Section 18817 or 26132 of the Revenue and Taxation Code.

(b)(1) If at the end of the time set forth in subdivision (a) there is no claim on file, the court, upon motion, shall declare the property seized or subject to forfeiture pursuant to subdivisions (a) to (g), inclusive, of Section 11470 forfeited to the state. In moving for a default judgment pursuant to this subdivision, the state or local governmental entity shall be required to establish a prima facie case in support of its petition for forfeiture. There is no requirement for forfeiture thereof that a criminal conviction be obtained in an underlying or related criminal offense.

(2) The court shall order the money forfeited or the proceeds of the sale of property to be distributed as set forth in Section 11489.

(c)(1) If a verified claim is filed, the forfeiture proceeding shall be set for hearing on a day not less than 30 days therefrom, and the proceeding shall have priority over other civil cases. Notice of the hearing shall be given in the same manner as provided in Section 11488.4. Such a verified claim or a claim filed pursuant to

Health & Safety

subdivision (j) of Section 11488.4 shall not be admissible in the proceedings regarding the underlying or related criminal offense set forth in subdivision (a) of Section 11488.

(2) The hearing shall be by jury, unless waived by consent of all parties.

(3) The provisions of the Code of Civil Procedure shall apply to proceedings under this chapter unless otherwise inconsistent with the provisions or procedures set forth in this chapter. However, in proceedings under this chapter, there shall be no joinder of actions, coordination of actions, except for forfeiture proceedings, or cross-complaints, and the issues shall be limited strictly to the questions related to this chapter.

(d)(1) At the hearing, the state or local governmental entity shall have the burden of establishing, pursuant to subdivision (i) of Section 11488.4, that the owner of any interest in the seized property consented to the use of the property with knowledge that it would be or was used for a purpose for which forfeiture is permitted, in accordance with the burden of proof set forth in subdivision (i) of Section 11488.4.

(2) No interest in the seized property shall be affected by a forfeiture decree under this section unless the state or local governmental entity has proven that the owner of that interest consented to the use of the property with knowledge that it would be or was used for the purpose charged. Forfeiture shall be ordered when, at the hearing, the state or local governmental entity has shown that the assets in question are subject to forfeiture pursuant to Section 11470, in accordance with the burden of proof set forth in subdivision (i) of Section 11488.4.

(e) The forfeiture hearing shall be continued upon motion of the prosecution or the defendant until after a verdict of guilty on any criminal charges specified in this chapter and pending against the defendant have been decided. The forfeiture hearing shall be conducted in accordance with Sections 190 to 222.5, inclusive, Sections 224 to 234, inclusive, Section 237, and Sections 607 to 630, inclusive, of the Code of Civil Procedure if a trial by jury, and by Sections 631 to 636, inclusive, of the Code of Civil Procedure if by the court. Unless the court or jury finds that the seized property was used for a purpose for which forfeiture is permitted, the court shall order the seized property released to the person it determines is entitled thereto.

If the court or jury finds that the seized property was used for a purpose for which forfeiture is permitted, but does not find that a person claiming an interest therein, to which the court has determined he or she is entitled, had actual knowledge that the seized property would be or was used for a purpose for which forfeiture is permitted and consented to that use, the court shall order the seized property released to the claimant.

(f) All seized property which was the subject of a contested forfeiture hearing and which was not released by the court to a claimant shall be declared by the court to be forfeited to the state, provided the burden of proof required pursuant to subdivision (i) of Section 11488.4 has been met. The court shall order the forfeited property to be distributed as set forth in Section 11489.

(g) All seized property which was the subject of the forfeiture hearing and which was not forfeited shall remain subject to any order to withhold issued with respect to the property by the Franchise Tax Board. *(Added by Stats.1994, c. 314 (A.B.114), § 15, eff. Aug. 19, 1994. Amended by Stats.1997, c. 241 (S.B.457), § 2; Stats.2008, c. 214 (A.B.1826), § 1; Stats.2016, c. 831 (S.B.443), § 4, eff. Jan. 1, 2017.)*

Cross References

Attorney General, generally, see Government Code § 12500 et seq.
Attorney General defined for purposes of this Division, see Health and Safety Code § 11004.
Burden of proof, generally, see Evidence Code § 500 et seq.
Person defined for purposes of this Division, see Health and Safety Code § 11022.
Presumption that person issued receipt for things of value seized as forfeitable was owner, see Health and Safety Code § 11488.
Seizure and forfeiture proceeding, see Business and Professions Code § 25375.

Research References

West's California Judicial Council Forms MC–200, Claim Opposing Forfeiture.
5 Witkin, California Criminal Law 4th Criminal Trial § 512 (2021), In General.
3 Witkin, California Criminal Law 4th Punishment § 197 (2021), Property Subject to Forfeiture.
3 Witkin, California Criminal Law 4th Punishment § 201 (2021), Commencement of Proceeding.
3 Witkin, California Criminal Law 4th Punishment § 204 (2021), Third-Party Claim.
3 Witkin, California Criminal Law 4th Punishment § 205 (2021), Hearing and Determination.

§ 11488.6. Lien or security interest claims; disposition

(a) If the court or jury at the forfeiture hearing finds that the property is forfeitable pursuant to Section 11470, but does not find that a person having a valid ownership interest, which includes, but is not limited to, a valid lien, mortgage, security interest, or interest under a conditional sales contract acquired such interest with actual knowledge that the property was to be used for a purpose for which forfeiture is permitted, and the amount due such person is less than the appraised value of the property, such person may pay to the state or the local governmental entity which initiated the forfeiture proceeding the amount of the equity, which shall be deemed to be the difference between the appraised value and the amount of the lien, mortgage, security interest, or interest under a conditional sales contract. Upon such payment, the state or local governmental entity shall relinquish all claims to the property. If the holder of the interest elects not to make such payment to the state or local governmental entity, the property shall be deemed forfeited to the state or local governmental entity and the ownership certificate shall be forwarded. The appraised value shall be determined as of the date judgment is entered on a wholesale basis either by agreement between the legal owner and the governmental entity involved, or if they cannot agree, then by the inheritance tax appraiser for the county in which the action is brought. A person having a valid ownership interest, which includes, but is not limited to, a valid lien, mortgage, security interest, or interest under a conditional sales contract shall be paid the appraised value of his or her interest in accordance with the provisions of Section 11489.

(b) If the amount due to a person having a valid ownership interest, which includes, but is not limited to, a valid lien, mortgage, security interest, or interest under a conditional sales contract is less than the value of the property and the person elects not to make payment to the governmental entity, the property shall be sold at public auction by the Department of General Services or by the local governmental entity which shall provide notice of such sale by one publication in a newspaper published and circulated in the city, community, or locality where the sale is to take place.

(c) The proceeds of sale pursuant to subdivision (b) shall be first distributed in accordance with the provisions of Section 11489. *(Added by Stats.1982, c. 1289, p. 4772, § 9. Amended by Stats.1983, c. 948, § 10; Stats.1986, c. 534, § 5, eff. Aug. 20, 1986; Stats.1988, c. 1492, § 13; Stats.1990, c. 1200 (A.B.4251), § 6; Stats.1986, c. 534, § 5, eff. Aug. 20, 1986, operative Jan. 1, 1994; Stats.1994, c. 314 (A.B.114), § 16, eff. Aug. 19, 1994.)*

Cross References

Department of General Services, generally, see Government Code § 14600 et seq.
Person defined for purposes of this Division, see Health and Safety Code § 11022.

Seizure and forfeiture proceeding, see Business and Professions Code § 25375.

Research References

3 Witkin, California Criminal Law 4th Punishment § 205 (2021), Hearing and Determination.

§ 11489. Distribution of funds from forfeitures and seizures

Notwithstanding Section 11502 and except as otherwise provided in Section 11473, in all cases where the property is seized pursuant to this chapter and forfeited to the state or local governmental entity and, where necessary, sold by the Department of General Services or local governmental entity, the money forfeited or the proceeds of sale shall be distributed by the state or local governmental entity as follows:

(a) To the bona fide or innocent purchaser, conditional sales vendor, or mortgagee of the property, if any, up to the amount of their interest in the property, when the court declaring the forfeiture orders a distribution to that person.

(b) The balance, if any, to accumulate, and to be distributed and transferred quarterly in the following manner:

(1) To the state agency or local governmental entity for all expenditures made or incurred by it in connection with the sale of the property, including expenditures for any necessary costs of notice required by Section 11488.4, and for any necessary repairs, storage, or transportation of any property seized under this chapter.

(2) The remaining funds shall be distributed as follows:

(A) Sixty–five percent to the state, local, or state and local law enforcement entities that participated in the seizure distributed so as to reflect the proportionate contribution of each agency.

(i) Fifteen percent of the funds distributed pursuant to this subparagraph shall be deposited in a special fund maintained by the county, city, or city and county of any agency making the seizure or seeking an order for forfeiture. This fund shall be used for the sole purpose of funding programs designed to combat drug abuse and divert gang activity, and shall wherever possible involve educators, parents, community-based organizations and local businesses, and uniformed law enforcement officers. Those programs that have been evaluated as successful shall be given priority. These funds shall not be used to supplant any state or local funds that would, in the absence of this clause, otherwise be made available to the programs.

It is the intent of the Legislature to cause the development and continuation of positive intervention programs for high-risk elementary and secondary schoolage students. Local law enforcement should work in partnership with state and local agencies and the private sector in administering these programs.

(ii) The actual distribution of funds set aside pursuant to clause (i) is to be determined by a panel consisting of the sheriff of the county, a police chief selected by the other chiefs in the county, and the district attorney and the chief probation officer of the county.

(B) Ten percent to the prosecutorial agency that processes the forfeiture action.

(C) Twenty–four percent to the General Fund. Notwithstanding Section 13340 of the Government Code, the moneys are hereby continuously appropriated to the General Fund. Commencing January 1, 1995, all moneys deposited in the General Fund pursuant to this subparagraph, in an amount not to exceed ten million dollars ($10,000,000), shall be made available for school safety and security, upon appropriation by the Legislature, and shall be disbursed pursuant to Senate Bill 1255 of the 1993–94 Regular Session, as enacted.

(D) One percent to the Environmental Enforcement and Training Account, established in Section 14303 of the Penal Code.

(c) Notwithstanding Item 0820–101–469 of the Budget Act of 1985 (Chapter 111 of the Statutes of 1985), all funds allocated to the Department of Justice pursuant to subparagraph (A) of paragraph (2) of subdivision (b) shall be deposited into the Department of Justice Special Deposit Fund–State Asset Forfeiture Account and used for the law enforcement efforts of the state or for state or local law enforcement efforts pursuant to Section 11493.

All funds allocated to the Department of Justice by the federal government under its Federal Asset Forfeiture program authorized by the Comprehensive Crime Control Act of 1984 may be deposited directly into the Narcotics Assistance and Relinquishment by Criminal Offender Fund and used for state and local law enforcement efforts pursuant to Section 11493.

Funds that are not deposited pursuant to the above paragraph shall be deposited into the Department of Justice Special Deposit Fund–Federal Asset Forfeiture Account.

(d) All the funds distributed to the state or local governmental entity pursuant to subparagraphs (A) and (B) of paragraph (2) of subdivision (b) shall not supplant any state or local funds that would, in the absence of this subdivision, be made available to support the law enforcement and prosecutorial efforts of these agencies.

The court shall order the forfeiture proceeds distributed to the state, local, or state and local governmental entities as provided in this section.

For the purposes of this section, "local governmental entity" means any city, county, or city and county in this state.

(e) This section shall become operative on January 1, 1994. *(Added by Stats.1991, c. 641 (A.B.192), § 4, operative Jan. 1, 1994. Amended by Stats.1992, c. 722 (S.B.485), § 7, eff. Sept. 15, 1992, operative Jan. 1, 1994; Stats.1994, c. 314 (A.B.114), § 19, eff. Aug. 19, 1994; Stats.1995, c. 100 (S.B.233), § 1, eff. July 18, 1995; Stats.1997, c. 241 (S.B.457), § 3; Stats.2021, c. 83 (S.B.157), § 2, eff. July 16, 2021.)*

Cross References

Department of General Services, generally, see Government Code § 14600 et seq.

Drug defined for purposes of this Division, see Health and Safety Code § 11014.

Mental health, primary intervention program,

Review of programs, see Welfare and Institutions Code § 4352.

Training of personnel, see Welfare and Institutions Code § 4351.

Person defined for purposes of this Division, see Health and Safety Code § 11022.

Seizure and forfeiture proceeding, notice, probable cause hearing, see Business and Professions Code § 25375.

Vesting of personal property with state following violations of controlled substances provisions, see Health and Safety Code § 11470.

Research References

3 Witkin, California Criminal Law 4th Punishment § 196 (2021), In General.

§ 11490. Inapplicability of provisions on forfeiture to common carrier or employee acting to enforce division

The provisions of this division relative to forfeiture of vehicles, boats, or airplanes shall not apply to a common carrier, or to an employee acting within the scope of his employment in the enforcement of this division. *(Formerly § 11498, added by Stats.1976, c. 1407, p. 6336, § 17. Renumbered § 11490 and amended by Stats. 1983, c. 948, § 29.)*

Cross References

Seizure and forfeiture proceeding, see Business and Professions Code § 25375.

Research References

3 Witkin, California Criminal Law 4th Punishment § 197 (2021), Property Subject to Forfeiture.

§ 11491. Decisional law relating to search and seizure; chapter not construed to extend or change

Nothing in this chapter shall be construed to extend or change decisional law as it relates to the topic of search and seizure.

Health & Safety

(Formerly § 11499, added by Stats.1977, c. 771, p. 2401, § 5. Renumbered § 11491 and amended by Stats.1983, c. 948, § 30.)

Cross References

Seizure and forfeiture proceeding, see Business and Professions Code § 25375.

§ 11492. Pendente lite orders to preserve status quo; preliminary injunctions; surety bonds or undertakings

(a) Concurrent with, or subsequent to, the filing of the petition, the prosecuting agency may move the superior court for the following pendente lite orders to preserve the status quo or value of the property alleged in the petition for forfeiture.

(1) An injunction to restrain all interested parties and enjoin them from transferring, encumbering, hypothecating, or otherwise disposing of that property.

(2) Appointment of a receiver to take possession of, care for, manage, and operate the assets and properties so that the property may be maintained and preserved.

(3) Order an interlocutory sale of the property named in the petition when the property is liable to perish, to waste, or to be significantly reduced in value, or when the expenses of maintaining the property are disproportionate to the value thereof, and the proceeds thereof shall be deposited with the court or as directed by the court pending determination of the forfeiture proceeding.

(b) No preliminary injunction may be granted, receiver appointed, or interlocutory sale ordered without notice to the interested parties and a hearing to determine that the order is necessary to preserve the property named in the petition, pending the outcome of the proceedings, and that there is probable cause to believe that the property is subject to forfeiture under Section 11470. However, a temporary restraining order may issue pending that hearing pursuant to the provisions of Section 527 of the Code of Civil Procedure.

(c) Notwithstanding any other provision of law, the court in granting these motions may order a surety bond or undertaking to preserve the property interests of the interested parties. *(Added by Stats.1983, c. 948, § 22. Amended by Stats.1990, c. 1200 (A.B.4251), § 8; Stats.1994, c. 314 (A.B.114), § 20, eff. Aug. 19, 1994; Stats.1997, c. 241 (S.B.457), § 4.)*

Cross References

Protective orders for property seized for forfeiture, see Health and Safety Code § 11488.4.
Seizure and forfeiture proceeding, notice, probable cause hearing, see Business and Professions Code § 25375.

Research References

3 Witkin, California Criminal Law 4th Punishment § 199 (2021), Seizure of Property.
3 Witkin, California Criminal Law 4th Punishment § 201 (2021), Commencement of Proceeding.

§ 11493. Narcotics Assistance and Relinquishment by Criminal Offender Fund

There is hereby created in the General Fund the Narcotics Assistance and Relinquishment by Criminal Offender Fund. The fund shall be administered by an advisory committee which shall be appointed by the Attorney General and which shall be comprised of three police chiefs, three sheriffs, two district attorneys, one private citizen, and an official of the Department of Justice who shall serve as the executive officer.

The money in the fund shall be available, upon appropriation by the Legislature, for distribution by the advisory committee to local and state law enforcement agencies in support of general narcotic law enforcement efforts. *(Added by Stats.1983, c. 948, § 23.5. Amended by Stats.2007, c. 176 (S.B.82), § 61, eff. Aug. 24, 2007.)*

Cross References

Attorney General, generally, see Government Code § 12500 et seq.
Attorney General defined for purposes of this Division, see Health and Safety Code § 11004.

§ 11494. Property seized or forfeiture proceeding initiated prior to January 1, 1994; applicable law

In the case of any property seized or forfeiture proceeding initiated before January 1, 1994, the proceeding to forfeit the property and the distribution of any forfeited property shall be subject to the provisions of this chapter in effect on December 31, 1993, as if those sections had not been repealed, replaced, or amended. *(Added by Stats.1994, c. 314 (A.B.114), § 22, eff. Aug. 19, 1994.)*

§ 11495. Funds received by law enforcement agencies; deposit; distribution; audits; periodic report

(a) The funds received by the law enforcement agencies under Section 11489 shall be deposited into an account maintained by the Controller, county auditor, or city treasurer. These funds shall be distributed to the law enforcement agencies at their request. The Controller, auditor, or treasurer shall maintain a record of these disbursements which records shall be open to public inspection, subject to the privileges contained in Sections 1040, 1041, and 1042 of the Evidence Code.

(b) Upon request of the governing body of the jurisdiction in which the distributions are made, the Controller, auditor, or treasurer shall conduct an audit of these funds and their use. In the case of the state, the governing body shall be the Legislature.

(c) Each year, the Attorney General shall publish a report that sets forth the following information for the state, each county, each city, and each city and county:

(1) The number of forfeiture actions initiated and administered by state or local agencies under California law, the number of cases adopted by the federal government, and the number of cases initiated by a joint federal-state action that were prosecuted under federal law.

(2) The number of cases and the administrative number or court docket number of each case for which forfeiture was ordered or declared.

(3) The number of suspects charged with a controlled substance violation.

(4) The number of alleged criminal offenses that were under federal or state law.

(5) The disposition of cases, including no charge, dropped charges, acquittal, plea agreement, jury conviction, or other.

(6) The value of the assets forfeited.

(7) The recipients of the forfeited assets, the amounts received, and the date of the disbursement.

(d) The Attorney General shall develop administrative guidelines for the collection and publication of the information required in subdivision (c).

(e) The Attorney General's report shall cover the calendar year and shall be made no later than July 1 of each year. *(Added by Stats.1994, c. 314 (A.B.114), § 23, eff. Aug. 19, 1994. Amended by Stats.2016, c. 831 (S.B.443), § 5, eff. Jan. 1, 2017; Stats.2019, c. 364 (S.B.112), § 9, eff. Sept. 27, 2019.)*

Cross References

Attorney General, generally, see Government Code § 12500 et seq.
Attorney General defined for purposes of this Division, see Health and Safety Code § 11004.

State Controller, generally, see Government Code § 12402 et seq.

CHAPTER 9. COLLECTION AND DISPOSITION OF FINES

§ 11500. Prosecution by district attorney, Attorney General, or special counsel; compensation

The district attorney, or any person designated by him, of the county in which any violation of this division is committed shall conduct all actions and prosecutions for the violation.

However, the Attorney General, or special counsel employed by the Attorney General for that purpose, may take complete charge of the conduct of such actions or prosecutions. The Attorney General may fix the compensation to be paid for the service and may incur such other expense in connection with the conduct of the actions or prosecutions as he may deem necessary. No attorney employed as special counsel shall receive as compensation more than three thousand five hundred dollars ($3,500) in any one year. *(Added by Stats.1972, c. 1407, p. 3029, § 3.)*

Cross References

Attorney General, generally, see Government Code § 12500 et seq.
Attorney General defined for purposes of this Division, see Health and Safety Code § 11004.
Disqualification of district attorney, employment of special counsel, see Government Code § 12553.
District attorney, duties as public prosecutor, see Government Code § 26500 et seq.
Person defined for purposes of this Division, see Health and Safety Code § 11022.
Special proceedings in prosecutions under this section, see Penal Code § 1000 et seq.

Research References

4 Witkin, California Criminal Law 4th Pretrial Proceedings § 211 (2021), Any Words Giving Notice.
4 Witkin, California Criminal Law 4th Pretrial Proceedings § 217 (2021), Conspiracy.

§ 11501. Action to recover funds expended in investigation of violations of controlled substances regulations

The State of California, or any political subdivision thereof, may maintain an action against any person or persons engaged in the unlawful sale of controlled substances for the recovery of any public funds paid over to such person or persons in the course of any investigation of violations of this division. All proceedings under this section shall be instituted in the superior court of the county where the funds were paid over, where the sale was made, or where the defendant resides. Notwithstanding Section 483.010 of the Code of Civil Procedure, in any action under this section, a writ of attachment may be issued, without the showing required by Section 485.010 of the Code of Civil Procedure, in the manner provided by Chapter 5 (commencing with Section 485.010) of Title 6.5 of Part 2 of the Code of Civil Procedure to attach any funds paid over or any other funds on the defendant's person at the time of his arrest. *(Added by Stats.1972, c. 1407, p. 3029, § 3. Amended by Stats.1974, c. 1516, § 30, operative Jan. 1, 1977.)*

Law Revision Commission Comments

Section 11501 is amended to restore the ability of the state to attach any public funds paid over in the course of a narcotics investigation (and other funds on the defendant's person at the time of his arrest). See former Civ.Proc. § 537(6), Cal.Stats.1961, Ch. 1164, § 2. The amendment also makes clear that the attachment may be issued ex parte pursuant to Code of Civil Procedure Sections 485.210–485.540.

Cross References

Controlled substance defined for purposes of this Division, see Health and Safety Code § 11007.
Expenditures to obtain evidence, see Health and Safety Code § 11454.
Person defined for purposes of this Division, see Health and Safety Code § 11022.

§ 11502. Disposition of fines and forfeitures; refunds

(a) All moneys, forfeited bail, or fines received by any court under this division shall as soon as practicable after the receipt thereof be deposited with the county treasurer of the county in which the court is situated. Amounts so deposited shall be paid at least once a month as follows: 75 percent to the State Treasurer by warrant of the county auditor drawn upon the requisition of the clerk or judge of the court to be deposited in the State Treasury on order of the Controller; and 25 percent to the city treasurer of the city, if the offense occurred in a city, otherwise to the treasurer of the county in which the prosecution is conducted.

(b) Any money deposited in the State Treasury under this section that is determined by the Controller to have been erroneously deposited therein shall be refunded by him or her out of any moneys in the State Treasury that are available by law for that purpose. *(Added by Stats.1972, c. 1407, p. 3029, § 3. Amended by Stats.2006, c. 538 (S.B.1852), § 369; Stats.2016, c. 31 (S.B.836), § 161, eff. June 27, 2016.)*

Cross References

Allocation and distribution of fines, forfeitures, penalties, fees or assessments collected in any criminal case, see Penal Code § 1464.8.
Automated administrative systems for management of civil and criminal cases, use of fees for fund, transmittal of fees, see Government Code § 68090.8.
California Victim Compensation and Government Claims Board, see Government Code § 13900 et seq.
Distribution of fines and forfeitures imposed and collected for crimes, see Penal Code § 1463.
Drug program fund, deposits equal to drug program fees, see Health and Safety Code § 11372.7.
Enforcement of collection and transmittal, see Government Code § 68103.
Payment to state, see Government Code § 68101.
State Controller, generally, see Government Code § 12402 et seq.
State Treasurer, generally, see Government Code § 12302 et seq.
Warrants, generally, see Government Code § 29800 et seq.

Research References

2 Witkin, California Criminal Law 4th Crimes Against Public Peace and Welfare § 123 (2021), Fraudulent Agreement.
2 Witkin, California Criminal Law 4th Crimes Against Public Peace and Welfare § 124 (2021), Substances Formerly Classified as Narcotics.

§ 11503. Record of fines and forfeitures

Judges and magistrates who collect fines or forfeitures under this division shall keep a record thereof, and, upon the imposition of any such fine or forfeiture, shall at least monthly transmit a record of it to the county auditor. The county auditor shall transmit a record of the imposition, collection and payment of such fines or forfeitures to the State Controller at the time of transmittal of each warrant to the State Treasurer pursuant to this article. *(Added by Stats.1972, c. 1407, p. 3030, § 3.)*

Cross References

Funds received by judges, deposit, record, see Government Code § 68101.
State Controller, generally, see Government Code § 12402 et seq.
State Treasurer, generally, see Government Code § 12302 et seq.

Research References

2 Witkin, California Criminal Law 4th Crimes Against Public Peace and Welfare § 123 (2021), Fraudulent Agreement.

§ 11504. Fine or forfeiture imposed upon vacation of sentence; accounting

When an imprisonment has been imposed for a violation of this division, and before the termination of the sentence, the defendant is released by the vacation of the sentence of imprisonment and the imposition of a fine or forfeiture instead, the fine or forfeiture shall be recorded and accounted for in the same manner as though it had been imposed in the first instance. *(Added by Stats.1972, c. 1407, p. 3030, § 3.)*

Cross References

Fine authorized in addition to imprisonment, see Penal Code § 672.

§ 11505. Sentence imposed in lieu of fine

Whenever a fine has been imposed for violation of this division, and before the full payment of the fine a sentence of imprisonment is imposed instead, the imprisonment shall be recorded and accounted for to the county auditor. *(Added by Stats.1972, c. 1407, p. 3030, § 3.)*

§ 11506. Examination of reports and records; suit to enforce collection and transmittal of fines and forfeitures

The State Controller shall check the reports and records received by him with the transmittals of fines and forfeitures and whenever it appears that fines or forfeitures have not been transmitted the county auditor shall and the State Controller may bring suit to enforce their collection or transmittal, or both. *(Added by Stats.1972, c. 1407, p. 3030, § 3.)*

Cross References

Disposition of fines and forfeitures, see Health and Safety Code § 11502.
Enforcement of collection and transmittal, see Government Code § 68103.
Payment to state, see Government Code § 68101.
State Controller, generally, see Government Code § 12402 et seq.

§ 11507. Liability on bond of judge or magistrate

The official bond of any judge or magistrate is liable for his failure to transmit the fines or forfeitures imposed by him under this division. *(Added by Stats.1972, c. 1407, p. 3030, § 3.)*

Cross References

County and judicial district officers, liability on bond for nonperformance or malperformance of duties, see Government Code § 1505.
Official bonds, generally, see Government Code § 1450 et seq.

§ 11508. Inspection of records of judges and magistrates

The records kept by a judge or magistrate under this division are open to public inspection, and may be checked by the State Controller, the Attorney General, the district attorney of the particular county, or the state bureau. *(Added by Stats.1972, c. 1407, p. 3030, § 3.)*

Cross References

Attorney General, generally, see Government Code § 12500 et seq.
Attorney General defined for purposes of this Division, see Health and Safety Code § 11004.
Inspection of public records, see Government Code § 6250 et seq.
State Controller, generally, see Government Code § 12402 et seq.

CHAPTER 9.5. LOITERING FOR DRUG ACTIVITIES

§ 11530. Definitions

As used in this subdivision, the following terms have the following meanings:

(a) "Loiter" means to delay or linger without a lawful purpose for being on the property and for the purpose of committing a crime as opportunity may be discovered.

(b) "Public place" means an area open to the public or exposed to public view and includes streets, sidewalks, bridges, alleys, plazas, parks, driveways, parking lots, automobiles, whether moving or not, and buildings open to the general public, including those which serve food or drink, or provide entertainment, and the doorways and entrances to buildings or dwellings and the grounds enclosing them. *(Added by Stats.1995, c. 981 (A.B.1035), § 2.)*

Research References

2 Witkin, California Criminal Law 4th Crimes Against Public Peace and Welfare § 73 (2021), For Drug Activities.
6 Witkin, California Criminal Law 4th Criminal Judgment § 92 (2021), Procedure.

§ 11532. Offense; intent; relevant circumstances

(a) It is unlawful for any person to loiter in any public place in a manner and under circumstances manifesting the purpose and with the intent to commit an offense specified in Chapter 6 (commencing with Section 11350) and Chapter 6.5 (commencing with Section 11400).

(b) Among circumstances that may be considered in determining whether a person has the requisite intent to engage in drug-related activity are that the person:

(1) Acts as a "look-out."

(2) Transfers small objects or packages for currency in a furtive fashion.

(3) Tries to conceal himself or herself or any object that reasonably could be involved in an unlawful drug-related activity.

(4) Uses signals or language indicative of summoning purchasers of illegal drugs.

(5) Repeatedly beckons to, stops, attempts to stop, or engages in conversations with passersby, whether on foot or in a motor vehicle, indicative of summoning purchasers of illegal drugs.

(6) Repeatedly passes to or receives from passersby, whether on foot or in a motor vehicle, money or small objects.

(7) Is under the influence of a controlled substance or possesses narcotic or drug paraphernalia. For the purposes of this paragraph, "narcotic or drug paraphernalia" means any device, contrivance, instrument, or apparatus designed or marketed for the use of smoking, injecting, ingesting, or consuming cannabis, hashish, PCP, or any controlled substance, including, but not limited to, roach clips, cigarette papers, and rollers designed or marketed for use in smoking a controlled substance.

(8) Has been convicted in any court within this state, within five years prior to the arrest under this chapter, of any violation involving the use, possession, or sale of any of the substances referred to in Chapter 6 (commencing with Section 11350) or Chapter 6.5 (commencing with Section 11400), or has been convicted of any violation

of those provisions or substantially similar laws of any political subdivision of this state or of any other state.

(9) Is currently subject to any order prohibiting his or her presence in any high drug activity geographic area.

(10) Has engaged, within six months prior to the date of arrest under this section, in any behavior described in this subdivision, with the exception of paragraph (8), or in any other behavior indicative of illegal drug-related activity.

(c) The list of circumstances set forth in subdivision (b) is not exclusive. The circumstances set forth in subdivision (b) should be considered particularly salient if they occur in an area that is known for unlawful drug use and trafficking, or if they occur on or in premises that have been reported to law enforcement as a place suspected of unlawful drug activity. Any other relevant circumstances may be considered in determining whether a person has the requisite intent. Moreover, no one circumstance or combination of circumstances is in itself determinative of intent. Intent must be determined based on an evaluation of the particular circumstances of each case. *(Added by Stats.1995, c. 981 (A.B.1035), § 2. Amended by Stats.2017, c. 27 (S.B.94), § 158, eff. June 27, 2017.)*

Cross References

Cannabis defined for purposes of this Division, see Health and Safety Code § 11018.
Controlled substance defined for purposes of this Division, see Health and Safety Code § 11007.
Drug defined for purposes of this Division, see Health and Safety Code § 11014.
Drug paraphernalia defined for purposes of this Division, see Health and Safety Code § 11014.5.
Person defined for purposes of this Division, see Health and Safety Code § 11022.
Transit districts, prohibition orders, violations of this section, see Public Utilities Code § 99171.

Research References

2 Witkin, California Criminal Law 4th Crimes Against Public Peace and Welfare § 73 (2021), For Drug Activities.
2 Witkin, California Criminal Law 4th Crimes Against Public Peace and Welfare § 126 (2021), Marijuana.

§ 11534. Severability

If any section, subdivision, sentence, clause, phrase, or portion of this chapter is for any reason held invalid or unconstitutional by any court of competent jurisdiction, that portion shall be deemed a separate, distinct, and independent provision, and that holding shall not affect the validity of the remaining portion thereof. *(Added by Stats.1995, c. 981 (A.B.1035), § 2.)*

§ 11536. Violation; offense

A violation of any provision of this chapter is a misdemeanor. *(Added by Stats.1995, c. 981 (A.B.1035), § 2.)*

Cross References

Misdemeanors, definition and penalties, see Penal Code §§ 17, 19, 19.2.

§ 11538. Local laws; preemption

Nothing in this chapter shall prevent a local governing body from adopting and enforcing laws consistent with this chapter. Where local laws duplicate or supplement this chapter, this chapter shall be construed as providing alternative remedies and not to preempt the field. *(Added by Stats.1995, c. 981 (A.B.1035), § 2.)*

Research References

2 Witkin, California Criminal Law 4th Crimes Against Public Peace and Welfare § 73 (2021), For Drug Activities.

CHAPTER 9.8. TREATMENT

Section

§ 11545. Legislative findings and declarations

The Legislature hereby finds and declares that licensed physicians, experienced in the treatment of addiction, should be allowed and encouraged to treat addiction by all appropriate means. *(Added by Stats.2000, c. 815 (S.B.1807), § 1.)*

Cross References

Physician, dentist, podiatrist, pharmacist, veterinarian, and optometrist defined for purposes of this Division, see Health and Safety Code § 11024.

CHAPTER 10. CONTROL OF USERS OF CONTROLLED SUBSTANCES

ARTICLE 1. ADDICTS

Section

§ 11550. Unlawful acts; penalties; rehabilitation programs; possession of firearms; diversion

(a) A person shall not use, or be under the influence of any controlled substance that is (1) specified in subdivision (b), (c), or (e), or paragraph (1) of subdivision (f) of Section 11054, specified in paragraph (14), (15), (21), (22), or (23) of subdivision (d) of Section 11054, specified in subdivision (b) or (c) of Section 11055, or specified in paragraph (1) or (2) of subdivision (d) or in paragraph (3) of subdivision (e) of Section 11055, or (2) a narcotic drug classified in Schedule III, IV, or V, except when administered by or under the direction of a person licensed by the state to dispense, prescribe, or administer controlled substances. It shall be the burden of the defense to show that it comes within the exception. A person convicted of violating this subdivision is guilty of a misdemeanor and shall be sentenced to serve a term of not more than one year in a county jail. The court may also place a person convicted under this subdivision on probation for a period not to exceed five years.

(b)(1) A person who is convicted of violating subdivision (a) when the offense occurred within seven years of that person being convicted of two or more separate violations of that subdivision, and refuses to complete a licensed drug rehabilitation program offered by the court pursuant to subdivision (c), shall be punished by imprisonment in a county jail for not less than 180 days nor more than one year. In no event does the court have the power to absolve a person convicted of a violation of subdivision (a) who is punishable under this subdivision from the obligation of spending at least 180 days in confinement in a county jail unless there are no licensed drug rehabilitation programs reasonably available.

(2) For the purpose of this section, a drug rehabilitation program is not reasonably available unless the person is not required to pay more than the court determines that he or she is reasonably able to pay in order to participate in the program.

(c)(1) The court may, when it would be in the interest of justice, permit a person convicted of a violation of subdivision (a) punishable under subdivision (a) or (b) to complete a licensed drug rehabilitation program in lieu of part or all of the imprisonment in a county jail. As a condition of sentencing, the court may require the offender to pay all or a portion of the drug rehabilitation program.

(2) In order to alleviate jail overcrowding and to provide recidivist offenders with a reasonable opportunity to seek rehabilitation pursuant to this subdivision, counties are encouraged to include provisions to augment licensed drug rehabilitation programs in their substance abuse proposals and applications submitted to the state for federal and state drug abuse funds.

(d) In addition to any fine assessed under this section, the judge may assess a fine not to exceed seventy dollars ($70) against a person who violates this section, with the proceeds of this fine to be used in accordance with Section 1463.23 of the Penal Code. The court shall, however, take into consideration the defendant's ability to pay, and a defendant shall not be denied probation because of his or her inability to pay the fine permitted under this subdivision.

(e)(1) Notwithstanding subdivisions (a) and (b) or any other law, a person who is unlawfully under the influence of cocaine, cocaine base, heroin, methamphetamine, or phencyclidine while in the immediate personal possession of a loaded, operable firearm is guilty of a public offense punishable by imprisonment in a county jail for not exceeding one year or in state prison.

(2) As used in this subdivision "immediate personal possession" includes, but is not limited to, the interior passenger compartment of a motor vehicle.

(f) Every person who violates subdivision (e) is punishable upon the second and each subsequent conviction by imprisonment in the state prison for two, three, or four years.

(g) This section does not prevent deferred entry of judgment or a defendant's participation in a preguilty plea drug court program under Chapter 2.5 (commencing with Section 1000) of Title 6 of Part 2 of the Penal Code unless the person is charged with violating subdivision (b) or (c) of Section 243 of the Penal Code. A person charged with violating this section by being under the influence of any controlled substance which is specified in paragraph (21), (22), or (23) of subdivision (d) of Section 11054 or in paragraph (3) of subdivision (e) of Section 11055 and with violating either subdivision (b) or (c) of Section 243 of the Penal Code or with a violation of subdivision (e) shall be ineligible for deferred entry of judgment or a preguilty plea drug court program. *(Added by Stats.1972, c. 1407, p. 3031, § 3. Amended by Stats.1973, c. 1078, p. 2187, § 27, eff. Oct. 1, 1973; Stats.1975, c. 248, p. 645, § 8; Stats.1981, c. 948, p. 3620, § 2; Stats.1983, c. 790, § 15; Stats.1984, c. 1635, § 74; Stats.1985, c. 3, § 14, eff. Jan. 29, 1985; Stats.1985, c. 1377, § 3; Stats.1986, c. 1026, § 3; Stats.1986, c. 1036, § 1; Stats.1986, c. 1037, § 1; Stats.1986, c. 1044, § 27.7; Stats.1988, c. 1243, § 4; Stats.1989, c. 1041, § 2; Stats.1990, c. 1096 (A.B.3407), § 1, operative July 1, 1991; Stats.2001, c. 854 (S.B.205), § 9; Stats.2014, c. 819 (A.B.2492), § 1, eff. Jan. 1, 2015.)*

Cross References

Administer defined for purposes of this Division, see Health and Safety Code § 11002.
Arrest of teacher or instructor employed in community college district, notices, see Health and Safety Code § 11591.5.
Burden of producing evidence, see Evidence Code §§ 110, 550.
Controlled substance defined for purposes of this Division, see Health and Safety Code § 11007.
Controlled substance offense as including violation of this section, see Education Code §§ 44011, 87011.
Convictions, limitations on employers and penalties, see Labor Code § 432.8.
Dispense defined for purposes of this Division, see Health and Safety Code § 11010.
Drug endangered children, law enforcement and social services agencies' response, development of policies and standards for narcotic crime scenes, see Penal Code § 13879.80 et seq.
Fines, increment for each separate offense, see Health and Safety Code § 11372.5.
Minor inducing another minor to violate this section, see Health and Safety Code § 11354.
Minor using controlled substances, procedure for disposition by juvenile court judge, see Welfare and Institutions Code § 708.
Misdemeanor defined, see Penal Code § 17.
Narcotic drug defined for purposes of this Division, see Health and Safety Code § 11019.
New trial, application prior to commitment of defendant for narcotics addiction, see Penal Code § 1182.
Of criminal procedure, pleadings and proceedings before trial, special proceedings in narcotics and drug abuse cases, application to certain violations, see Penal Code § 1000.
Ownership or possession of concealable firearm by addict, see Penal Code § 29800.
Person defined for purposes of this Division, see Health and Safety Code § 11022.
Persons authorized to write prescriptions, see Health and Safety Code § 11150.
Registration of controlled substance offenders, see Health and Safety Code § 11591 et seq.
School employee, arrest for controlled substance offense as described in this section, notice to school authorities, see Health and Safety Code § 11591.
Treatment of addicts, see Health and Safety Code § 11215 et seq.

Research References

California Jury Instructions - Criminal 12.13, Controlled Substance (Sched. I and II)—Inducing Minor to Violate Controlled Substances Law.
California Jury Instructions - Criminal 16.060, Use or Under Influence of Controlled Substances—"Under the Influence of Controlled Substance"—Defined.
California Jury Instructions - Criminal 16.061, Use or Under Influence of Controlled Substances—Burden of Proof of Authorized Administration.
2 Witkin, California Criminal Law 4th Crimes Against Public Peace and Welfare § 93 (2021), Specified Narcotics and Restricted Dangerous Drugs.
2 Witkin, California Criminal Law 4th Crimes Against Public Peace and Welfare § 94 (2021), Possession of Firearm While Under the Influence.
2 Witkin, California Criminal Law 4th Crimes Against Public Peace and Welfare § 124 (2021), Substances Formerly Classified as Narcotics.
2 Witkin, California Criminal Law 4th Crimes Against Public Peace and Welfare § 164 (2021), In General.
6 Witkin, California Criminal Law 4th Criminal Appeal § 88 (2021), Miscellaneous Orders.
1 Witkin California Criminal Law 4th Introduction to Crimes § 84 (2021), Distinction: Reenactment.
4 Witkin, California Criminal Law 4th Pretrial Proceedings § 209 (2021), Statutory Language Sufficient.
4 Witkin, California Criminal Law 4th Pretrial Proceedings § 210 (2021), Statutory Language Not Sufficient.
4 Witkin, California Criminal Law 4th Pretrial Proceedings § 303 (2021), Nature and Scope of Requirements.
4 Witkin, California Criminal Law 4th Pretrial Proceedings § 386 (2021), Offenses and Conditions.
3 Witkin, California Criminal Law 4th Punishment § 295 (2021), In General.
3 Witkin, California Criminal Law 4th Punishment § 649 (2021), Misdemeanor Cases.
3 Witkin, California Criminal Law 4th Punishment § 654 (2021), Mandatory.

§ 11551. Tests to determine use of controlled substances as condition of probation or parole; cost of administration; regulations

(a) Whenever any court in this state grants probation to a person who the court has reason to believe is or has been a user of controlled substances, the court may require as a condition to probation that the probationer submit to periodic tests by a city or county health officer, or by a physician and surgeon appointed by the city or county health officer with the approval of the Attorney General, to determine, by whatever means is available, whether the probationer is addicted to a controlled substance.

In any case provided for in this subdivision, the city or county health officer, or the physician and surgeon appointed by the city or county health officer with the approval of the Attorney General shall report the results of the tests to the probation officer.

(b) In any case in which a person is granted parole by a county parole board and the person is or has been a user of controlled substances, a condition of the parole may be that the parolee undergo periodic tests as provided in subdivision (a) and that the county or city health officer, or the physician and surgeon appointed by the city or county health officer with the approval of the Attorney General, shall report the results to the board.

(c) In any case in which any state agency grants a parole to a person who is or has been a user of controlled substances, it may be a condition of the parole that the parolee undergo periodic tests as provided in subdivision (a) and that the county or city health officer, or the physician and surgeon appointed by the city or county health officer with the approval of the Attorney General, shall report the results of the tests to such state agency.

(d) The cost of administering tests pursuant to subdivisions (a) and (b) shall be a charge against the county. The cost of administering tests pursuant to subdivision (c) shall be paid by the state.

(e) The state department, in conjunction with the Attorney General, shall issue regulations governing the administering of the tests provided for in this section and providing the form of the report required by this section. *(Added by Stats.1972, c. 1407, p. 3031, § 3.)*

Cross References

Attorney General, generally, see Government Code § 12500 et seq.
Attorney General defined for purposes of this Division, see Health and Safety Code § 11004.
City health officers, see Health and Safety Code § 101460 et seq.
Controlled substance defined for purposes of this Division, see Health and Safety Code § 11007.
County health officer, see Health and Safety Code § 101000 et seq.
County jail prisoners, work furlough program for drug addicts, see Penal Code § 1208.
Minors, care and treatment for misuse of drugs in program of supervision by probation officer, see Welfare and Institutions Code § 654.
Order placing defendant in diagnostic facility, see Penal Code § 1203.03.
Person defined for purposes of this Division, see Health and Safety Code § 11022.
Physician, dentist, podiatrist, pharmacist, veterinarian, and optometrist defined for purposes of this Division, see Health and Safety Code § 11024.

Research References

2 Witkin, California Criminal Law 4th Crimes Against Public Peace and Welfare § 96 (2021), Testing for Addiction.
3 Witkin, California Criminal Law 4th Punishment § 666 (2021), Other Express Conditions.
3 Witkin, California Criminal Law 4th Punishment § 752 (2021), Discretionary Conditions.

§ 11552. Arrested persons; tests to determine use of controlled substances

In any case in which a person has been arrested for a criminal offense and is suspected of being addicted to a controlled substance, a law enforcement officer having custody of such person may, with the written consent of such person, request the city or county health officer, or physician appointed by such health officer pursuant to Section 11551, to administer to the arrested person a test to determine, by whatever means is available whether the arrested person is addicted to a controlled substance, and such health officer or physician may administer such test to such arrested person. *(Added by Stats.1972, c. 1407, p. 3032, § 3.)*

Cross References

Administer defined for purposes of this Division, see Health and Safety Code § 11002.
Arrest for being under influence of controlled substance or drug, release from custody, see Penal Code §§ 849, 851.6.
Controlled substance defined for purposes of this Division, see Health and Safety Code § 11007.
Court-ordered evaluation for persons impaired by drug abuse, see Welfare and Institutions Code § 5225 et seq.
Person defined for purposes of this Division, see Health and Safety Code § 11022.
Physician, dentist, podiatrist, pharmacist, veterinarian, and optometrist defined for purposes of this Division, see Health and Safety Code § 11024.
State civil service, leave of absence pending investigation of accusations of drug addiction, see Government Code § 19574.5.

Research References

2 Witkin, California Criminal Law 4th Crimes Against Public Peace and Welfare § 96 (2021), Testing for Addiction.
4 Witkin, California Criminal Law 4th Pretrial Proceedings § 63 (2021), Tests for Intoxication or Addiction.

§ 11553. Cannabis use; exemption from §§ 11551, 11552

The fact that a person is or has been, or is suspected of being, a user of cannabis is not alone sufficient grounds upon which to invoke Section 11551 or 11552.

This section shall not be construed to limit the discretion of a judge to invoke Section 11551 or 11552 if the court has reason to believe a person is or has been a user of narcotics or drugs other than cannabis. *(Added by Stats.1972, c. 1407, p. 3032, § 3. Amended by Stats.2017, c. 27 (S.B.94), § 159, eff. June 27, 2017.)*

Cross References

Cannabis defined for purposes of this Division, see Health and Safety Code § 11018.
Drug defined for purposes of this Division, see Health and Safety Code § 11014.
Person defined for purposes of this Division, see Health and Safety Code § 11022.

Research References

2 Witkin, California Criminal Law 4th Crimes Against Public Peace and Welfare § 96 (2021), Testing for Addiction.

§ 11554. Rehabilitation; public policy

The rehabilitation of persons addicted to controlled substances and the prevention of continued addiction to controlled substances is a matter of statewide concern. It is the policy of the state to encourage each county and city and county to make use, whenever applicable, of testing procedures to determine addiction to controlled substances or the absence thereof, and to foster research in means of detecting the existence of addiction to controlled substances and in medical methods and procedures for that purpose. *(Added by Stats.1972, c. 1407, p. 3032, § 3.)*

Cross References

Admission to state hospital for treatment of controlled substances, referral, see Welfare and Institutions Code § 5344.
Controlled substance defined for purposes of this Division, see Health and Safety Code § 11007.
Person defined for purposes of this Division, see Health and Safety Code § 11022.

§ 11555. Promotion of use of article provisions; assistance to local agencies; medical supplies and services

The Attorney General is directed to promote and sponsor the use by agencies of local government of the provisions of this article. The Attorney General may assist such agencies to establish facilities for, and to train personnel to conduct testing procedures pursuant to Section 11551, and may conduct demonstrations thereof for limited periods. For these purposes the Attorney General may procure such medical supplies, equipment, and temporary services of physicians and qualified consultants as may reasonably be necessary. Subject to the availability of funds appropriated for the purpose, the Attorney General may contract with any county or city and county which undertakes to establish facilities and a testing program pursuant to Section 11551, and such contract may provide for payment by the state of such costs of initially establishing and demonstrating such program as the Attorney General may approve. *(Added by Stats. 1972, c. 1407, p. 3032, § 3.)*

Cross References

Attorney General, generally, see Government Code § 12500 et seq.
Attorney General defined for purposes of this Division, see Health and Safety Code § 11004.
Physician, dentist, podiatrist, pharmacist, veterinarian, and optometrist defined for purposes of this Division, see Health and Safety Code § 11024.
Special proceedings in narcotics cases, see Penal Code § 1000 et seq.

ARTICLE 2. SUBSTANCE ABUSE TREATMENT CONTROL UNITS

§ 11560. Authority of departments to establish

The Department of Corrections and the Department of the Youth Authority are authorized to establish substance abuse treatment control units in state correctional facilities or training schools or as separate establishments for any study, research, and treatment that may be necessary for the control of the addiction or habituation, or imminent addiction or habituation, to controlled substances or alcohol of persons committed to the custody of the Director of Corrections or the Director of the Youth Authority. *(Added by Stats.1972, c. 1407, p. 3033, § 3. Amended by Stats.1992, c. 465 (A.B.1874), § 2.)*

Cross References

Controlled substance defined for purposes of this Division, see Health and Safety Code § 11007.
Department of Corrections and Rehabilitation, generally, see Penal Code § 5000 et seq.
Medical facility for confinement, care and treatment of males under custody of department of corrections, see Penal Code § 6102.
Person defined for purposes of this Division, see Health and Safety Code § 11022.

§ 11561. Parole authority; order for detention of male parolee

When the parole authority concludes that there are reasonable grounds for believing that a person on parole is addicted or habituated to, or is in imminent danger of addiction or habituation to, controlled substances or alcohol, it may, in accordance with procedures used to revoke parole, issue an order to detain or place the person in a substance abuse treatment control unit for a period not to exceed 90 days. The order shall be a sufficient warrant for any peace officer or employee of the Department of Corrections to return the person to physical custody. Detention pursuant to the order shall not be deemed a suspension, cancellation, or revocation of parole until the parole authority so orders pursuant to Section 3060 of the Penal Code. A parolee taken into physical custody pursuant to Section 3060 of the Penal Code may be detained in a substance abuse treatment control unit established pursuant to this article.

No person on parole shall be placed in a substance abuse treatment control unit against his or her will. *(Added by Stats.1972, c. 1407, p. 3033, § 3. Amended by Stats.1979, c. 255, p. 548, § 5; Stats.1992, c. 465 (A.B.1874), § 3; Stats.1992, c. 695 (S.B.97), § 5, eff. Sept. 15, 1992; Stats.2003, c. 468 (S.B.851), § 5.)*

Cross References

Controlled substance defined for purposes of this Division, see Health and Safety Code § 11007.
Department of Corrections and Rehabilitation, generally, see Penal Code § 5000 et seq.
Person defined for purposes of this Division, see Health and Safety Code § 11022.

Research References

3 Witkin, California Criminal Law 4th Punishment § 754 (2021), Constructive Custody of Parolee.

§ 11562. Youth Authority; order for detention of parolee

When the Youth Authority concludes that there are reasonable grounds for believing that a person committed to its custody, and on parole, is addicted or habituated to, or is in imminent danger of addiction or habituation to, controlled substances or alcohol, it may, in accordance with procedures used to revoke parole, issue an order to detain or place that person in a substance abuse treatment control unit for not to exceed 90 days. The order shall be a sufficient warrant for any peace officer or employee of the Department of the Youth Authority to return to physical custody that person. Detention pursuant to the order shall not be deemed a suspension, cancellation, or revocation of parole unless the Youth Authority so orders pursuant to Section 1767.3 of the Welfare and Institutions Code.

With the consent of the Director of Corrections, the Director of the Youth Authority may, pursuant to this section, confine the addicted or habituated or potentially addicted or habituated person, over 18 years of age, in a substance abuse treatment control unit established by the Department of Corrections.

No person committed to the custody of the Youth Authority and on parole shall be placed in a substance abuse treatment control unit against his or her will. *(Added by Stats.1972, c. 1407, p. 3033, § 3. Amended by Stats.1992, c. 465 (A.B.1874), § 4.)*

Cross References

Controlled substance defined for purposes of this Division, see Health and Safety Code § 11007.
Department of Corrections and Rehabilitation, generally, see Penal Code § 5000 et seq.
Person defined for purposes of this Division, see Health and Safety Code § 11022.

§ 11563. Parole authority; order for detention of female parolee

When the parole authority concludes that there are reasonable grounds for believing that a woman on parole is addicted or habituated to, or is in imminent danger of addiction or habituation to, controlled substances or alcohol, it may, in accordance with procedures used to revoke parole, issue an order to detain or place the person in a substance abuse treatment control unit for a period not to exceed 90 days. The order shall be a sufficient warrant for any peace officer or employee of the Department of Corrections to return the person to physical custody. Detention pursuant to the order shall not be deemed a suspension, cancellation, or revocation of parole until such time as the parole authority so orders pursuant to Section 3060 of the Penal Code. A parolee taken into physical custody pursuant to Section 3060, 6043, or 6044 of the Penal Code may be detained in a substance abuse treatment control unit established pursuant to this article.

No woman on parole shall be placed in a substance abuse treatment control unit against her will. *(Added by Stats.1972, c. 1407, p. 3033, § 3. Amended by Stats.1979, c. 255, p. 548, § 6; Stats.1992, c. 465 (A.B.1874), § 5; Stats.1992, c. 695 (S.B.97), § 6, eff. Sept. 15, 1992.)*

Cross References

Controlled substance defined for purposes of this Division, see Health and Safety Code § 11007.
Department of Corrections and Rehabilitation, generally, see Penal Code § 5000 et seq.

Person defined for purposes of this Division, see Health and Safety Code § 11022.

§ 11564. Effect of power to detain upon power to revoke parole

The authority granted to the parole authority and to the Department of the Youth Authority in no way limits Sections 3060 and 3325 of the Penal Code. *(Added by Stats.1972, c. 1407, p. 3034, § 3. Amended by Stats.1979, c. 255, p. 549, § 7; Stats.1992, c. 695 (S.B.97), § 7, eff. Sept. 15, 1992.)*

§ 11565. "Parole authority" defined

For purposes of this article, "parole authority" has the same meaning as described in Section 3000 of the Penal Code. *(Added by Stats.1992, c. 695 (S.B.97), § 8, eff. Sept. 15, 1992.)*

ARTICLE 3. ABATEMENT

§ 11570. Nuisance

Every building or place used for the purpose of unlawfully selling, serving, storing, keeping, manufacturing, or giving away any controlled substance, precursor, or analog specified in this division, and every building or place wherein or upon which those acts take place, is a nuisance which shall be enjoined, abated, and prevented, and for which damages may be recovered, whether it is a public or private nuisance. *(Added by Stats.1972, c. 1407, p. 3034, § 3. Amended by Stats.1986, c. 590, § 1; Stats.1986, c. 1043, § 1.5.)*

Cross References

Abatement of nuisance by public body, authority for, see Civil Code § 3494.
Actions for nuisance on real property, see Code of Civil Procedure § 731 et seq.
Controlled substance defined for purposes of this Division, see Health and Safety Code § 11007.
Injunction, generally, see Code of Civil Procedure § 525 et seq.
Medical marijuana program, generally, see Health and Safety Code § 11362.7 et seq.
Medical marijuana program, criminal liability for use of cannabis, application of section, see Health and Safety Code § 11362.765.
Nuisance defined, see Civil Code § 3479 et seq.
Public nuisance defined, see Penal Code § 370.
State Department of Health Care Services, abatement of nuisance, see Health and Safety Code §§ 100170, 100175.

Research References

2 Witkin, California Criminal Law 4th Crimes Against Public Peace and Welfare § 142 (2021), Primary Caregiver.
2 Witkin, California Criminal Law 4th Crimes Against Public Peace and Welfare § 149 (2021), Protection from Criminal Liability.

§ 11571. Nuisance; action to abate; injunction

If there is reason to believe that a nuisance, as described in Section 11570, is kept, maintained, or exists in any county, the district attorney or county counsel of the county, or the city attorney of any incorporated city or of any city and county, in the name of the people, may, or any citizen of the state resident in the county, in his or her own name, may, maintain an action to abate and prevent the nuisance and to perpetually enjoin the person conducting or maintaining it, and the owner, lessee, or agent of the building or place in or upon which the nuisance exists from directly or indirectly maintaining or permitting the nuisance. *(Added by Stats.1992, c. 198 (A.B.2906), § 2, eff. July 14, 1992, operative Jan. 1, 1996. Amended by Stats.1998, c. 613 (A.B.1384), § 1; Stats.2002, c. 1057 (A.B.1868), § 1; Stats.2003, c. 62 (S.B.600), § 182; Stats.2010, c. 570 (A.B.1502), § 3.)*

Cross References

Agent defined for purposes of this Division, see Health and Safety Code § 11003.
City attorneys pursuing drug abatement actions, see Penal Code §§ 11105, 13300.
District attorney to prosecute actions, see Code of Civil Procedure § 731.
Person defined for purposes of this Division, see Health and Safety Code § 11022.
State Department of Health Care Services, actions to enjoin and abate nuisances dangerous to health, see Health and Safety Code § 100170.

§ 11571.1. Local drug abatement laws; adoption and enforcement; construction of article; relief against forfeiture of lease

(a) Nothing in this article shall prevent a local governing body from adopting and enforcing laws, consistent with this article, relating to drug abatement. Where local laws duplicate or supplement this article, this article shall be construed as providing alternative remedies and not preempting the field.

(b) Nothing in this article shall prevent a tenant from receiving relief against a forfeiture of a lease pursuant to Section 1179 of the Code of Civil Procedure. *(Added by Stats.2009, c. 244 (A.B.530), § 7.)*

§ 11571.5. City attorneys or city prosecutors; actions to abate nuisances

For purposes of this article, an action to abate a nuisance may be taken by the city attorney or city prosecutor of the city within which the nuisance exists, is kept, or is maintained. An action by a city attorney or city prosecutor shall be accorded the same precedence as an action maintained by the district attorney of the county. *(Added by Stats.1986, c. 182, § 1.)*

§ 11572. Verification of complaint

Unless filed by the district attorney, or the city attorney of an incorporated city, the complaint in the action shall be verified. *(Added by Stats.1972, c. 1407, p. 3034, § 3. Amended by Stats.1987, c. 1076, § 3.)*

Cross References

Verification of complaint, see Code of Civil Procedure § 431.30.

§ 11573. Temporary restraining order or injunction

(a) If the existence of the nuisance is shown in the action to the satisfaction of the court or judge, either by verified complaint or affidavit, the court or judge shall allow a temporary restraining order or injunction to abate and prevent the continuance or recurrence of the nuisance.

(b) A temporary restraining order or injunction may enjoin subsequent owners, commercial lessees, or agents who acquire the building or place where the nuisance exists with notice of the temporary restraining order or injunction, specifying that the owner of the property subject to the temporary restraining order or injunction shall notify any prospective purchaser, commercial lessee, or other successor in interest of the existence of the order or injunction, and of its application to successors in interest, prior to entering into any agreement to sell or lease the property. The temporary restraining order or injunction shall not constitute a title defect, lien, or encumbrance on the real property. *(Added by Stats.1972, c. 1407, p. 3034, § 3. Amended by Stats.2002, c. 1057 (A.B.1868), § 2.)*

Cross References

Agent defined for purposes of this Division, see Health and Safety Code § 11003.

Preliminary, temporary restraining order injunction, see Code of Civil Procedure § 527.

§ 11573.5. Prior acts or threats of violence; protection of witnesses; closure of premises; tenant assistance

(a) At the time of application for issuance of a temporary restraining order or injunction pursuant to Section 11573, if proof of the existence of the nuisance depends, in whole or part, upon the affidavits of witnesses who are not peace officers, upon a showing of prior threats of violence or acts of violence by any defendant or other person, the court may issue orders to protect those witnesses, including, but not limited to, nondisclosure of the name, address, or any other information which may identify those witnesses.

(b) A temporary restraining order or injunction issued pursuant to Section 11573 may include closure of the premises pending trial when a prior order or injunction does not result in the abatement of the nuisance. The duration of the order or injunction shall be within the court's discretion. In no event shall the total period of closure pending trial exceed one year. Prior to ruling on a request for closure the court may order that some or all of the rent payments owing to the defendant be placed in an escrow account for a period of up to 90 days or until the nuisance is abated. If the court subsequently orders a closure of the premises, the money in the escrow account shall be used to pay for relocation assistance pursuant to subdivision (d). In ruling upon a request for closure, whether for a defined or undefined duration, the court shall consider all of the following factors:

(1) The extent and duration of the nuisance at the time of the request.

(2) Prior efforts by the defendant to comply with previous court orders to abate the nuisance.

(3) The nature and extent of any effect which the nuisance has upon other persons, such as residents or businesses.

(4) Any effect of prior orders placing displaced residents' or occupants' rent payments into an escrow account upon the defendant's efforts to abate the nuisance.

(5) The effect of granting the request upon any resident or occupant of the premises who is not named in the action, including the availability of alternative housing or relocation assistance, the pendency of any action to evict a resident or occupant, and any evidence of participation by a resident or occupant in the nuisance activity.

(c) In making an order of closure pursuant to this section, the court may order the premises vacated and may issue any other orders necessary to effectuate the closure. However, all tenants who may be affected by the order shall be provided reasonable notice and an opportunity to be heard at all hearings regarding the closure request prior to the issuance of any order.

(d) In making an order of closure pursuant to this section, the court shall order the defendant to provide relocation assistance to any tenant ordered to vacate the premises, provided the court determines that the tenant was not actively involved in the nuisance activity. The relocation assistance ordered to be paid by the defendant shall be in the amount necessary to cover moving costs, security deposits for utilities and comparable housing, adjustment in any lost rent, and any other reasonable expenses the court may deem fair and reasonable as a result of the court's order.

(e) At the hearing to order closure pursuant to this section, the court may make the following orders with respect to any displaced tenant not actively involved in the nuisance:

(1) Priority for senior citizens, physically handicapped persons, or persons otherwise suffering from a permanent or temporary disability for claims against money for relocation assistance.

(2) Order the local agency seeking closure pursuant to this section to make reasonable attempts to seek additional sources of funds for relocation assistance to displaced tenants, if deemed necessary.

(3) Appoint a receiver to oversee the disbursement of relocation assistance funds, whose services shall be paid from the escrow fund.

(4) Where a defendant has paid relocation assistance pursuant to subdivision (d), the escrow account under subdivision (b) may be released to the defendant and no appointment under paragraph (3) shall be made.

(f)(1) The remedies set forth pursuant to this section shall be in addition to any other existing remedies for nuisance abatement actions, including, but not limited to, the following:

(A) Capital improvements to the property, such as security gates.

(B) Improved interior or exterior lighting.

(C) Security guards.

(D) Posting of signs.

(E) Owner membership in neighborhood or local merchants' associations.

(F) Attending property management training programs.

(G) Making cosmetic improvements to the property.

(H) Requiring the owner or person in control of the property to reside in the property until the nuisance is abated. The order shall specify the number of hours per day or per week the owner or person in control of the property must be physically present in the property. In determining this amount, the court shall consider the nature and severity of the nuisance.

(2) At all stages of an action brought pursuant to this article, the court has equitable powers to order steps necessary to remedy the problem and enhance the abatement process. *(Added by Stats.1988, c. 1525, § 1. Amended by Stats.1989, c. 1360, § 90; Stats.1991, c. 247 (A.B.666), § 1; Stats.2001, c. 854 (S.B.205), § 10; Stats.2002, c. 1057 (A.B.1868), § 3.)*

Cross References

Person defined for purposes of this Division, see Health and Safety Code § 11022.

§ 11574. Bond

On granting the temporary writ the court or judge shall require an undertaking on the part of the applicant to the effect that the applicant will pay to the defendant enjoined such damages, not exceeding an amount to be specified, as the defendant sustains by reason of the injunction if the court finally decides that the applicant was not entitled to the injunction. *(Added by Stats.1972, c. 1407, p. 3034, § 3. Amended by Stats.1982, c. 517, p. 2397, § 275.)*

Law Revision Commission Comments

Section 11574 is amended to delete provisions duplicated in the Bond and Undertaking Law. See Code Civ. Proc. §§ 995.220 (undertaking not required of public entity), 995.310 (sureties on undertaking), 995.320 (contents of undertaking) (16 Cal.L.Rev. Comm. Reports 501).

Cross References

Bond and Undertaking Law, see Code of Civil Procedure § 995.010 et seq.
Suretyship, see Civil Code § 2787 et seq.
Undertaking on injunction, see Code of Civil Procedure § 529.

§ 11575. Precedence of action

The action shall have precedence over all other actions, except criminal proceedings, election contests, hearings on injunctions, and actions to forfeit vehicles under this division. *(Added by Stats.1972, c. 1407, p. 3034, § 3.)*

§ 11575.5. Evidence of nuisance

In any action for abatement instituted pursuant to this article, all evidence otherwise authorized by law, including evidence of reputation in a community, as provided in the Evidence Code, shall be admissible to prove the existence of a nuisance. *(Added by Stats. 1988, c. 1525, § 2.)*

Cross References

Character and reputation, evidence affected or excluded by extrinsic policies, see Evidence Code § 1100 et seq.

§ 11576. Dismissal for want of prosecution

If the complaint is filed by a citizen it shall not be dismissed by him or for want of prosecution except upon a sworn statement made by him and his attorney, setting forth the reasons why the action should be dismissed, and by dismissal ordered by the court. *(Added by Stats.1972, c. 1407, p. 3034, § 3.)*

§ 11577. Substitution of plaintiff

In case of failure to prosecute the action with reasonable diligence, or at the request of the plaintiff, the court, in its discretion, may substitute any other citizen consenting thereto for the plaintiff. *(Added by Stats.1972, c. 1407, p. 3034, § 3.)*

§ 11578. Costs

If the action is brought by a citizen and the court finds there was no reasonable ground or cause for the action, the costs shall be taxed against him. *(Added by Stats.1972, c. 1407, p. 3035, § 3.)*

Cross References

Costs, see Code of Civil Procedure § 1021 et seq.

§ 11579. Order of abatement; lien for costs

If the existence of the nuisance is established in the action, an order of abatement shall be entered as part of the judgment in the case, and plaintiff's costs in the action are a lien upon the building or place. The lien is enforceable and collectible by execution issued by order of the court. *(Added by Stats.1972, c. 1407, p. 3035, § 3.)*

Cross References

Judgment lien, see Code of Civil Procedure § 697.010 et seq.
Liens, generally, see Civil Code § 2872 et seq.

§ 11580. Violation of injunction or abatement order; penalty

A violation or disobedience of the injunction or order for abatement is punishable as a contempt of court by a fine of not less than five hundred dollars ($500) nor more than ten thousand dollars ($10,000), or by imprisonment in the county jail for not less than one nor more than six months, or by both.

A contempt may be based on a violation of any court order including failure to pay relocation assistance. Notwithstanding any other provision of law, any fines assessed for contempt shall first be held by the court and applied to satisfaction of the court's order for relocation assistance pursuant to subdivision (d) of Section 11573.5.

Evidence concerning the duration and repetitive nature of the violations shall be considered by the court in determining the contempt penalties. *(Added by Stats.1972, c. 1407, p. 3035, § 3. Amended by Stats.1988, c. 1525, § 3.)*

Cross References

Contempts, see Code of Civil Procedure § 1209 et seq.
Lien of fine for contempt, see Health and Safety Code § 11587.

§ 11581. Removal and sale of property; closing of building or place; civil penalty; in lieu damages; fair market rental value

(a) If the existence of the nuisance is established in the action, an order of abatement shall be entered as a part of the judgment, which order shall direct the removal from the building or place of all fixtures, musical instruments, and other movable property used in conducting, maintaining, aiding, or abetting the nuisance and shall direct their sale in the manner provided for the sale of chattels under execution.

(b)(1) The order shall provide for the effectual closing of the building or place against its use for any purpose, and for keeping it closed for a period of one year. This subdivision is intended to give priority to closure. Any alternative to closure may be considered only as provided in this section.

(2) In addition, the court may assess a civil penalty not to exceed twenty-five thousand dollars ($25,000) against any or all of the defendants, based upon the severity of the nuisance and its duration.

(3) One-half of the civil penalties collected pursuant to this section shall be deposited in the Restitution Fund in the State Treasury, the proceeds of which shall be available only upon appropriation by the Legislature to indemnify persons filing claims pursuant to Article 1 (commencing with Section 13959) of Chapter 5 of Part 4 of Division 3 of Title 2 of the Government Code, and one-half of the civil penalties collected shall be paid to the city in which the judgment was entered, if the action was brought by the city attorney or city prosecutor. If the action was brought by a district attorney, one-half of the civil penalties collected shall be paid to the treasurer of the county in which the judgment was entered.

(c)(1) If the court finds that any vacancy resulting from closure of the building or place may create a nuisance or that closure is otherwise harmful to the community, in lieu of ordering the building or place closed, the court may order the person who is responsible for the existence of the nuisance, or the person who knowingly permits controlled substances to be unlawfully sold, served, stored, kept, or given away in or from a building or place he or she owns, to pay damages in an amount equal to the fair market rental value of the building or place for one year to the city or county in whose jurisdiction the nuisance is located for the purpose of carrying out drug abuse treatment, prevention, and education programs. If awarded to a city, eligible programs may include those developed as a result of cooperative programs among schools, community agencies, and the local law enforcement agency. These funds shall not be used to supplant existing city, county, state, or federal resources used for drug prevention and education programs.

(2) For purposes of this subdivision, the actual amount of rent being received for the rental of the building or place, or the existence of any vacancy therein, may be considered, but shall not be the sole

Health & Safety

determinant of the fair market rental value. Expert testimony may be used to determine the fair market rental value.

(d) This section shall become operative on January 1, 1996. *(Added by Stats.1991, c. 572 (A.B.894), § 4, operative Jan. 1, 1996. Amended by Stats.2002, c. 1057 (A.B.1868), § 4; Stats.2003, c. 62 (S.B.600), § 183.)*

Cross References

Controlled substance defined for purposes of this Division, see Health and Safety Code § 11007.
Drug defined for purposes of this Division, see Health and Safety Code § 11014.
Person defined for purposes of this Division, see Health and Safety Code § 11022.

§ 11582. Court custody of building or place

While the order of abatement remains in effect, the building or place is in the custody of the court. *(Added by Stats.1972, c. 1407, p. 3035, § 3.)*

§ 11583. Fees; removal and sale of property; closing of building or place

For removing and selling the movable property, the officer is entitled to charge and receive the same fees as he would for levying upon and selling like property on execution; and for closing the premises and keeping them closed, a reasonable sum shall be allowed by the court. *(Added by Stats.1972, c. 1407, p. 3035, § 3.)*

§ 11584. Disposition of proceeds of sale

The proceeds of the sale of the movable property shall be applied as follows:

First—To the fees and costs of the removal and sale.

Second—To the allowances and costs of closing and keeping closed the building or place.

Third—To the payment of the plaintiff's costs in the action.

Fourth—The balance, if any, to the owner of the property. *(Added by Stats.1972, c. 1407, p. 3035, § 3.)*

§ 11585. Sale of building

If the proceeds of the sale of the movable property do not fully discharge all of the costs, fees, and allowances, the building and place shall then also be sold under execution issued upon the order of the court or judge and the proceeds of the sale shall be applied in like manner. *(Added by Stats.1972, c. 1407, p. 3035, § 3.)*

§ 11586. Release of building to owner

(a) If the owner of the building or place has not been guilty of any contempt of court in the proceedings, and appears and pays all costs, fees, and allowances that are a lien on the building or place and files a bond in the full value of the property conditioned that the owner will immediately abate any nuisance that may exist at the building or place and prevent it from being established or kept thereat within a period of one year thereafter, the court, or judge may, if satisfied of the owner's good faith, order the building or place to be delivered to the owner, and the order of abatement canceled so far as it may relate to the property.

(b) The release of property under the provisions of this division does not release it from any judgment, lien, penalty, or liability to which it may be subject. *(Added by Stats.1972, c. 1407, p. 3035, § 3. Amended by Stats.1982, c. 517, p. 2397, § 276.)*

Law Revision Commission Comments

Section 11586 is amended for consistency with the Bond and Undertaking Law. See Code Civ. Proc. § 995.910 (objections to bonds). The other changes in Section 11586 are technical. (16 Cal.L.Rev. Comm. Reports 501).

Cross References

Bond and Undertaking Law, see Code of Civil Procedure § 995.010 et seq.
Suretyship, see Civil Code § 2787 et seq.

§ 11587. Lien of fine

Whenever the owner of a building or place upon which the act or acts constituting the contempt have been committed, or the owner of any interest therein, has been guilty of a contempt of court, and fined in any proceedings under this division, the fine is a lien upon the building or place to the extent of his interest in it.

The lien is enforceable and collectible by execution issued by order of the court. *(Added by Stats.1972, c. 1407, p. 3036, § 3.)*

Cross References

Liens, see Civil Code § 2872 et seq.

ARTICLE 4. REGISTRATION OF CONTROLLED SUBSTANCE OFFENDERS

Section

§ 11591. School employee; arrest for controlled substance offense; notice to school authorities

Every sheriff, chief of police, or the Commissioner of the California Highway Patrol, upon the arrest for any of the controlled substance offenses described in Section 11350, 11351, 11351.5, 11352, 11353, 11353.5, 11353.7, 11354, 11355, 11358, 11359, 11360, 11361, 11363, 11366, 11366.5, 11366.6, 11368, 11370.1, 11378, 11378.5, 11379, 11379.5, 11379.6, 11380, 11383, or 11550, or subdivision (a) of Section 11377, or Section 11364, insofar as that section relates to paragraph (12) of subdivision (d) of Section 11054, of any school employee, shall, provided that the sheriff, chief of police, or Commissioner of the California Highway Patrol knows that the arrestee is a school employee, do one of the following:

(a) If the school employee is a teacher in any of the public schools of this state, the sheriff, chief of police, or Commissioner of the California Highway Patrol shall immediately notify by telephone the superintendent of schools of the school district employing the teacher and shall immediately give written notice of the arrest to the Commission on Teacher Credentialing and to the superintendent of schools in the county where the person is employed. Upon receipt of the notice, the county superintendent of schools and the Commission on Teacher Credentialing shall immediately notify the governing board of the school district employing the person.

(b) If the school employee is a nonteacher in any of the public schools of this state, the sheriff, chief of police, or Commissioner of the California Highway Patrol shall immediately notify by telephone the superintendent of schools of the school district employing the nonteacher and shall immediately give written notice of the arrest to the governing board of the school district employing the person.

(c) If the school employee is a teacher in any private school of this state, the sheriff, chief of police, or Commissioner of the California Highway Patrol shall immediately notify by telephone the private school authority employing the teacher and shall immediately give written notice of the arrest to the private school authority employing the teacher.

(d) If a person described in subdivision (a) was arrested for an offense defined in Section 11378, 11379, or 11380, this section shall only apply to offenses involving controlled substances specified in paragraph (12) of subdivision (d) of Section 11054 and paragraph (2) of subdivision (d) of Section 11055, and to analogs of these substances, as defined in Section 11401. If a person described in subdivision (a) was arrested for an offense defined in Section 11379 or 11379.5, this section does not apply if the arrest was for transporting, offering to transport, or attempting to transport a controlled substance. This section does not apply to a person who was arrested for a misdemeanor under Section 11360. *(Added by Stats.1972, c. 1407, p. 3036, § 3. Amended by Stats.1973, c. 198, p. 515, § 16; Stats.1973, c. 489, p. 962, § 6, eff. Sept. 17, 1973; Stats.1984, c. 1635, § 75; Stats.2003, c. 536 (A.B.608), § 1; Stats. 2019, c. 580 (A.B.1261), § 3, eff. Jan. 1, 2020.)*

Cross References

Controlled substance defined for purposes of this Division, see Health and Safety Code § 11007.
Person defined for purposes of this Division, see Health and Safety Code § 11022.

Research References

3 Witkin, California Criminal Law 4th Punishment § 225 (2021), Particular Professions.

§ 11591.5. Arrest of teacher or instructor employed in community college district; notices

(a) Every sheriff or chief of police, upon the arrest for any of the controlled substance offenses described in Section 11350, 11351, 11351.5, 11352, 11353, 11353.5, 11353.7, 11354, 11355, 11358, 11359, 11360, 11361, 11363, 11366, 11366.5, 11366.6, 11368, 11370.1, 11378, 11378.5, 11379, 11379.5, 11379.6, 11380, 11383, or 11550, or subdivision (a) of Section 11377, or Section 11364, insofar as that section relates to paragraph (9) of subdivision (d) of Section 11054, of any teacher or instructor employed in any community college district shall immediately notify by telephone the superintendent of the community college district employing the teacher or instructor and shall immediately give written notice of the arrest to the Office of the Chancellor of the California Community Colleges. Upon receipt of that notice, the district superintendent shall immediately notify the governing board of the community college district employing the person.

(b) If a person described in subdivision (a) was arrested for an offense defined in Section 11378, 11379, or 11380, this section shall only apply to offenses involving controlled substances specified in paragraph (12) of subdivision (d) of Section 11054 and paragraph (2) of subdivision (d) of Section 11055, and to analogs of these substances, as defined in Section 11401. If a person described in subdivision (a) was arrested for an offense defined in Section 11379 or 11379.5, this section does not apply if the arrest was for transporting, offering to transport, or attempting to transport a controlled substance. This section does not apply to a person who was arrested for a misdemeanor under Section 11360. *(Added by Stats.1983, c. 1032, § 3. Amended by Stats.2019, c. 580 (A.B.1261), § 4, eff. Jan. 1, 2020.)*

Cross References

Controlled substance defined for purposes of this Division, see Health and Safety Code § 11007.
Person defined for purposes of this Division, see Health and Safety Code § 11022.

§ 11594. Registration requirements; termination; access to information

All registration requirements set forth in this article, as it read on January 1, 2019, are terminated. The statements, photographs, and fingerprints obtained pursuant to this section, as it read on January 1, 2019, are not open to inspection by the public or by any person other than a regularly employed peace or other law enforcement officer. *(Added by Stats.2019, c. 580 (A.B.1261), § 8, eff. Jan. 1, 2020.)*

Research References

2 Witkin, California Criminal Law 4th Crimes Against Public Peace and Welfare § 177 (2021), In General.
2 Witkin, California Criminal Law 4th Crimes Against Public Peace and Welfare § 182 (2021), Commitment of Persons Not Convicted of Crimes.
3 Witkin, California Criminal Law 4th Punishment § 185 (2021), Controlled Substance Offenders.

CHAPTER 13. MISCELLANEOUS

§ 11650. Prosecution for violations of prior law; pending proceedings; application of division

(a) Prosecution for any violation of law occurring prior to the effective date of this division is not affected or abated by this division. If the offense being prosecuted is similar to one set out in Chapter 6 (commencing with Section 11350) of this division, then the penalties under Chapter 6 (commencing with Section 11350) apply if they are less than those under prior law.

(b) Civil seizures or forfeitures and injunctive proceedings commenced prior to effective date of this division are not affected by this division.

(c) All administrative proceedings pending under prior laws which are superseded by this division shall be continued and brought to a final determination in accord with the laws and rules in effect prior to the effective date of this division. Any substance controlled under prior law which is not listed within Schedules I through V, is automatically controlled without further proceedings and shall be listed in the appropriate schedule.

(d) This division applies to violations of law, seizures and forfeiture, injunctive proceedings, administrative proceedings and investigations which occur on or after the effective date of this division. *(Added by Stats.1972, c. 1407, p. 3042, § 3. Amended by Stats.1992, c. 978 (S.B.1822), § 7; Stats.1993, c. 589 (A.B.2211), § 90.)*

§ 11651. Continuation of orders and regulations

Any orders and regulations promulgated pursuant to any law affected by this division and in effect on the effective date of this division, not in conflict with it continue in effect until modified, superseded, or repealed. *(Added by Stats.1972, c. 1407, p. 3042, § 3.)*

Division 10.5

ALCOHOL AND DRUG PROGRAMS

Part 3

STATE GOVERNMENT'S ROLE TO ALLEVIATE PROBLEMS RELATED TO THE USE AND ABUSE OF ALCOHOL AND OTHER DRUGS

CHAPTER 2. COMMUNITY ALCOHOL AND OTHER DRUG ABUSE CONTROL

ARTICLE 1. COMPREHENSIVE DRUG COURT IMPLEMENTATION ACT OF 1999

§ 11970. Short title; oversight; design and implementation

(a) This article shall be known and may be cited as the Comprehensive Drug Court Implementation Act of 1999.

(b) The State Department of Alcohol and Drug Programs shall provide oversight of this article.

(c) The department and the Judicial Council shall design and implement this article through the Drug Court Partnership Executive Steering Committee established under the former Drug Court Partnership Act of 1998 pursuant to former Section 11970, for the purpose of funding cost-effective local drug court systems for adults, juveniles, and parents of children who are detained by, or are dependents of, the juvenile court.

(d) This section shall become inoperative on July 1, 2013. *(Added by Stats.2012, c. 36 (S.B.1014), § 67, eff. June 27, 2012, operative July 1, 2012. Amended by Stats.2013, c. 22 (A.B.75), § 60, eff. June 27, 2013, operative July 1, 2013.)*

Inoperative Date

For inoperative date of this section, see its terms.

§ 11970.5. Short title

(a) This article shall be known and may be cited as the Drug Court Programs Act.

(b) This section shall become operative on July 1, 2013. *(Added by Stats.2013, c. 22 (A.B.75), § 61, eff. June 27, 2013, operative July 1, 2013.)*

§ 11971. Drug court program; use of funds; plan for operation of program

(a)(1) At its option, a county may provide a program authorized by this article. A county that chooses to provide a program shall ensure that any funds used for the program are used in compliance with the requirements for receipt of federal block grant funds for prevention and treatment of substance abuse described in Subchapter XVII of Chapter 6A of Title 42 of the United States Code and other federal provisions governing the receipt of federal funds.

(2) The funds contained in each county's Behavioral Health Subaccount of the Support Services Account of the Local Revenue Fund 2011 may be used to fund the cost of drug court treatment programs for the purpose of applying for federal grant funds from the federal Substance Abuse and Mental Health Services Administration as described in Section 11775.

(b) If a county chooses to provide a drug court program, a county alcohol and drug program administrator and the presiding judge in the county shall develop, as part of the contract for alcohol and other drug abuse services, a plan for the operation of drug court program that shall include the information necessary for the state to ensure a county's compliance with the provisions for receipt of the federal block grant funds for prevention and treatment of substance abuse found at Subchapter XVII of Chapter 6A of Title 42 of the United States Code and other applicable federal provisions for funds.

(c) The plan shall do all of the following:

(1) Describe existing programs that serve substance abusing adults, juveniles, and parents of children who are detained by, or are dependents of, the juvenile court.

(2) Provide a local action plan for implementing cost-effective drug court systems, including any or all of the following drug court systems:

(A) Drug courts operating pursuant to Sections 1000 to 1000.5, inclusive, of the Penal Code.

(B) Drug courts for juvenile offenders.

(C) Drug courts for parents of children who are detained by, or are dependents of, the juvenile court.

(D) Drug courts for parents of children in family law cases involving custody and visitation issues.

(E) Other drug court systems that are approved by the Drug Court Partnership Executive Steering Committee.

(3) Develop information-sharing systems to ensure that county actions are fully coordinated, and to provide data for measuring the success of the local action plan in achieving its goals.

(4) Identify outcome measures that will determine the cost effectiveness of the local action plan. *(Added by Stats.2012, c. 36 (S.B.1014), § 67, eff. June 27, 2012, operative July 1, 2012.)*

§ 11972. Legislative intent regarding design and operation of drug court programs

It is the intent of the Legislature that drug court programs be designed and operated in accordance with the document entitled "Defining Drug Courts: The Key Components," developed by the National Association of Drug Court Professionals and Drug Court Standards Committee (reprinted 2004). It is the intent of the Legislature that the key components of the programs include:

(a) Integration by drug courts of alcohol and other drug treatment services with justice system case processing.

(b) Promotion of public safety, while protecting participants' due process rights, by prosecution and defense counsel using a nonadversarial approach.

(c) Early identification of eligible participants and prompt placement in the drug court program.

(d) Access provided by drug courts to a continuum of alcohol, drug, and other related treatment and rehabilitation services.

(e) Frequent alcohol and other drug testing to monitor abstinence.

(f) A coordinated strategy to govern drug court responses to participants' compliance.

(g) Ongoing judicial interaction with each drug court participant is essential.

(h) Monitoring and evaluation to measure the achievement of program goals and gauge effectiveness.

(i) Continuing interdisciplinary education to promote effective drug court planning, implementation, and operations.

(j) Forging partnerships among drug courts, public agencies, and community-based organizations to generate local support and enhance drug court program effectiveness. *(Added by Stats.2012, c. 36 (S.B.1014), § 67, eff. June 27, 2012, operative July 1, 2012.)*

§ 11973. Legislative intent regarding funding of dependency drug courts; evaluation of cost avoidance

(a) It is the intent of the Legislature that dependency drug courts be funded unless an evaluation of cost avoidance as provided in this section with respect to child welfare services and foster care demonstrates that the program is not cost effective.

(b) The State Department of Social Services, in collaboration with the State Department of Alcohol and Drug Programs and the Judicial Council, shall conduct an evaluation of cost avoidance with respect to child welfare services and foster care pursuant to this section. These parties shall do all of the following:

(1) Consult with legislative staff and at least one representative of an existing dependency drug court program who has experience conducting an evaluation of cost avoidance, to clarify the elements to be reviewed.

(2) Identify requirements, such as specific measures of cost savings and data to be evaluated, and methodology for use of control cases for comparison data.

(3) Whenever possible, use existing evaluation case samples to gather the necessary additional data.

(c) This section shall become inoperative on July 1, 2013. *(Added by Stats.2012, c. 36 (S.B.1014), § 67, eff. June 27, 2012, operative July 1, 2012. Amended by Stats.2013, c. 22 (A.B.75), § 62, eff. June 27, 2013, operative July 1, 2013.)*

Inoperative Date

For inoperative date of this section, see its terms.

§ 11974. Implementation; adoption of emergency regulations

(a) Notwithstanding the rulemaking provisions of Chapter 3.5 (commencing with Section 11340) of Part 1 of Division 3 of Title 2 of the Government Code, the department may implement, interpret, or make specific the amendments to this article made by the act that added this section by means of all-county letters, plan letters, plan or provider bulletins, or similar instructions from the department until regulations are adopted pursuant to that chapter of the Government Code.

(b) The department shall adopt emergency regulations no later than July 1, 2014. The department may subsequently readopt any emergency regulation authorized by this section that is the same as or is substantially equivalent to an emergency regulation previously adopted pursuant to this section.

(c) The initial adoption of emergency regulations implementing this article and the one readoption of emergency regulations authorized by this section shall be deemed an emergency and necessary for the immediate preservation of the public peace, health, safety, or general welfare. Initial emergency regulations and the one readoption of emergency regulations authorized by this section shall be exempt from review by the Office of Administrative Law. The initial emergency regulations and the one readoption of emergency regulations authorized by this section shall be submitted to the Office of Administrative Law for filing with the Secretary of State and each shall remain in effect for no more than 180 days, by which time final regulations may be adopted. *(Added by Stats.2012, c. 36 (S.B.1014), § 67, eff. June 27, 2012, operative July 1, 2012.)*

ARTICLE 2. DRUG COURT PARTNERSHIP ACT OF 2002

Section

§ 11975. Short title; Drug Court Partnership Program; administration; revised multi-agency plans; use of funds; data collection instrument

(a) This article shall be known and may be cited as the Drug Court Partnership Act of 2002.

(b) The Drug Court Partnership Program, as provided for in this article, shall be administered by the State Department of Alcohol and Drug Programs for the purpose of providing assistance to drug courts that accept only defendants who have been convicted of felonies. The department and the Judicial Council shall design and implement this program through the Drug Court Systems Steering Committee as originally established by the department and the Judicial Council to implement the former Drug Court Partnership Act of 1998 (Article 3 (commencing with Section 11970)).

(c)(1) The department shall require counties that participate in the Drug Court Partnership Program to submit a revised multiagency plan that is in conformance with the Drug Court Systems Steering Committee's recommended guidelines. Revised multiagency plans that are reviewed and approved by the department and recommended by the Drug Court Systems Steering Committee shall be funded for the 2002–03 fiscal year under this article. The department, without a renewal of the Drug Court Systems Steering Committee's original recommendation, may disburse future year appropriations to the grantees.

(2) The multiagency plan shall identify the resources and strategies for providing an effective drug court program exclusively for convicted felons who meet the requirements of this article and the guidelines adopted thereunder, and shall set forth the basis for determining eligibility for participation that will maximize savings to the state in avoided prison costs.

(3) The multiagency plan shall include, but not be limited to, all of the following components:

(A) The method by which the drug court will ensure that the target population of felons will be identified and referred to the drug court.

(B) The elements of the treatment and supervision programs.

(C) The method by which the grantee will provide the specific outcomes and data required by the department to determine state prison savings or cost avoidance.

(D) Assurance that funding received pursuant to this article will be used to supplement, rather than supplant, existing programs.

(d) Funds shall be used only for programs that are identified in the approved multiagency plan. Acceptable uses may include, but shall not be limited to, any of the following:

(1) Drug court coordinators.

(2) Training.

(3) Drug testing.

(4) Treatment.

(5) Transportation.

(6) Other costs related to substance abuse treatment.

(e) The department shall identify and design a data collection instrument to determine state prison cost savings and avoidance from this program.

(f) This section shall become inoperative on July 1, 2013. *(Added by Stats.2012, c. 36 (S.B.1014), § 69, eff. June 27, 2012, operative July 1, 2012. Amended by Stats.2013, c. 22 (A.B.75), § 63, eff. June 27, 2013, operative July 1, 2013.)*

Inoperative Date

For inoperative date of this section, see its terms.

Division 104

ENVIRONMENTAL HEALTH

Part 4

DRUGS, DEVICES, AND COSMETICS

CHAPTER 5. IMITATION CONTROLLED SUBSTANCES

ARTICLE 1. PROVISIONS AND DEFINITIONS

§ 109525. Short title

This chapter shall be known as the "California Imitation Controlled Substances Act." *(Added by Stats.1995, c. 415 (S.B.1360), § 6.)*

Research References

2 Witkin, California Criminal Law 4th Crimes Against Public Peace and Welfare § 158 (2021), Imitation Controlled Substances.
2 Witkin, California Criminal Law 4th Crimes Against Public Peace and Welfare § 159 (2021), Money Associated With Unlawful Transactions.

§ 109530. Construction of chapter

Unless the context otherwise requires, the definitions in this article govern the construction of this chapter. *(Added by Stats.1995, c. 415 (S.B.1360), § 6.)*

§ 109535. "Controlled substance" defined

"Controlled substance" means a substance as defined in Section 11007. *(Added by Stats.1995, c. 415 (S.B.1360), § 6.)*

Research References

2 Witkin, California Criminal Law 4th Crimes Against Public Peace and Welfare § 158 (2021), Imitation Controlled Substances.

§ 109540. "Distribute" defined

"Distribute" means the actual, constructive, or attempted transfer, delivery, or dispensing to another of an imitation controlled substance. *(Added by Stats.1995, c. 415 (S.B.1360), § 6.)*

Research References

2 Witkin, California Criminal Law 4th Crimes Against Public Peace and Welfare § 158 (2021), Imitation Controlled Substances.

§ 109545. "Manufacture" defined

"Manufacture" means the production, preparation, compounding, processing, encapsulating, packaging or repackaging, labeling or relabeling, of an imitation controlled substance. *(Added by Stats. 1995, c. 415 (S.B.1360), § 6.)*

Research References

2 Witkin, California Criminal Law 4th Crimes Against Public Peace and Welfare § 158 (2021), Imitation Controlled Substances.

§ 109550. "Imitation controlled substance" defined

"Imitation controlled substance" means (a) a product specifically designed or manufactured to resemble the physical appearance of a controlled substance, that a reasonable person of ordinary knowledge would not be able to distinguish the imitation from the controlled substance by outward appearances, or (b) a product, not a controlled substance, that, by representations made and by dosage unit appearance, including color, shape, size, or markings, would lead a reasonable person to believe that, if ingested, the product would have a stimulant or depressant effect similar to or the same as that of one or more of the controlled substances included in Schedules I through V, inclusive, of the Uniform Controlled Substances Act, pursuant to Chapter 2 (commencing with Section 11053) of Division 10. *(Added by Stats.1995, c. 415 (S.B.1360), § 6.)*

Research References

2 Witkin, California Criminal Law 4th Crimes Against Public Peace and Welfare § 158 (2021), Imitation Controlled Substances.

§ 109555. Cumulative effect; other remedies

The provisions of this chapter are cumulative, and shall not be construed as restricting any remedy, provisional or otherwise, provided by law for the benefit of any party. *(Added by Stats.1995, c. 415 (S.B.1360), § 6.)*

ARTICLE 2. OFFENSES AND PENALTIES

§ 109575. Manufacture, distribution, or possession with intent to distribute imitation controlled substance

Any person who knowingly manufactures, distributes, or possesses with intent to distribute, an imitation controlled substance is guilty of a misdemeanor and shall, if convicted, be subject to imprisonment for not more than six months in the county jail or a fine of not more than one thousand dollars ($1,000), or both the imprisonment and fine. *(Added by Stats.1995, c. 415 (S.B.1360), § 6.)*

Cross References

Misdemeanors, definition and penalties, see Penal Code §§ 17, 19 and 19.2.

Research References

2 Witkin, California Criminal Law 4th Crimes Against Public Peace and Welfare § 158 (2021), Imitation Controlled Substances.

§ 109580. Distribution of imitation controlled substance to person under 18

Any person 18 years of age or over who violates Section 109575 by knowingly distributing an imitation controlled substance to a person under 18 years of age is guilty of a misdemeanor and shall, if convicted, be punished by imprisonment for not more than one year in a county jail or a fine of not more than two thousand dollars ($2,000), or by both that imprisonment and fine. Upon a second or subsequent conviction of this offense, the person shall be subject to imprisonment for not more than one year in a county jail and a fine of not less than six thousand dollars ($6,000). *(Added by Stats.1995, c. 415 (S.B.1360), § 6. Amended by Stats.2001, c. 854 (S.B.205), § 17.)*

Cross References

Misdemeanors, definition and penalties, see Penal Code §§ 17, 19 and 19.2.

Research References

2 Witkin, California Criminal Law 4th Crimes Against Public Peace and Welfare § 158 (2021), Imitation Controlled Substances.

§ 109585. Lawful manufacture, distribution, or possession of imitation controlled substance

No civil or criminal liability shall be imposed by virtue of this chapter on any person registered under the California Uniform Controlled Substances Act who manufactures, distributes, or possesses an imitation controlled substance for use by a practitioner, as defined in Section 11026, in the course of lawful professional practice or research. *(Added by Stats.1995, c. 415 (S.B.1360), § 6.)*

§ 109590. Forfeitures of imitation controlled substances

All imitation controlled substances shall be subject to forfeiture in accordance with the procedures set forth in Chapter 8 (commencing with Section 11470) of Division 10. *(Added by Stats.1995, c. 415 (S.B.1360), § 6.)*

Research References

2 Witkin, California Criminal Law 4th Crimes Against Public Peace and Welfare § 158 (2021), Imitation Controlled Substances.

Division 105

COMMUNICABLE DISEASE PREVENTION AND CONTROL

Part 1

ADMINISTRATION OF COMMUNICABLE DISEASE PREVENTION AND CONTROL

CHAPTER 4. VIOLATIONS

§ 120275. Violation of rule, order, or regulation of state department; offense

Any person who, after notice, violates, or who, upon the demand of any health officer, refuses or neglects to conform to, any rule, order, or regulation prescribed by the department respecting a quarantine or disinfection of persons, animals, things, or places, is guilty of a misdemeanor. *(Added by Stats.1995, c. 415 (S.B.1360), § 7.)*

Cross References

Duty of district attorney to prosecute violations, see Health and Safety Code § 120590.
Health officer defined for purposes of this Division, see Health and Safety Code § 120100.
Misdemeanor,
  Defined, see Penal Code § 17.
  Punishment, see Penal Code §§ 19, 19.2.
Notice, actual and constructive, defined, see Civil Code § 18.

Research References

2 Witkin, California Criminal Law 4th Crimes Against Public Peace and Welfare § 457 (2021), Communicable Diseases.

§ 120280. Refusal to comply with isolation order; offense; confinement by court order; probation

Inasmuch as the orders provided for by Section 121365 are for the protection of the public health, any person who, after service upon him or her of an order of a local health officer as provided in Section 121365 violates or fails to comply with the order, is guilty of a misdemeanor. Upon conviction thereof, in addition to any and all other penalties that may be imposed by law upon the conviction, the person may be ordered by the court confined until the order of the local health officer shall have been fully complied with or terminated by the local health officer, but not exceeding one year from the date of passing judgment upon the conviction, further, the court, upon suitable assurances that the order of the local health officer will be complied with, may place any person convicted of a violation of the order of the local health officer upon probation for a period not to exceed two years, upon condition that the order of the local health officer be fully complied with, further, upon any subsequent violation of the order of the local health officer, the probation shall be terminated and confinement as provided for in this section shall be ordered by the court. Confinement may be accomplished by placement in any appropriate facility, penal institution, or dwelling approved for the specific case by the local health officer. *(Added by Stats.1995, c. 415 (S.B.1360), § 7.)*

Cross References

Burial expenses of persons dying while confined, see Health and Safety Code § 121395.
Health officer defined for purposes of this Division, see Health and Safety Code § 120100.
Misdemeanor,
  Defined, see Penal Code § 17.
  Punishment, see Penal Code §§ 19, 19.2.
Penal institution defined for purposes of this Division, see Health and Safety Code § 120115.

Health & Safety

Release in county other than county of confinement, see Health and Safety Code § 121400.

Research References

2 Witkin, California Criminal Law 4th Crimes Against Public Peace and Welfare § 457 (2021), Communicable Diseases.

§ 120285. Subsequent convictions; punishment

Upon any subsequent conviction under the provisions of Section 120280, the court may order the person confined for a period not exceeding one year for the subsequent conviction, or other penalty as provided by that section. *(Added by Stats.1995, c. 415 (S.B.1360), § 7.)*

Cross References

Prior convictions, form of allegations, see Penal Code § 969.

§ 120290. Intentional transmission of an infectious or communicable disease; elements; exception for pregnancy; misdemeanor offense; anonymity; medical records

(a)(1) A defendant is guilty of intentional transmission of an infectious or communicable disease if all of the following apply:

(A) The defendant knows that he or she or a third party is afflicted with an infectious or communicable disease.

(B) The defendant acts with the specific intent to transmit or cause an afflicted third party to transmit that disease to another person.

(C) The defendant or the afflicted third party engages in conduct that poses a substantial risk of transmission to that person.

(D) The defendant or the third party transmits the infectious or communicable disease to the other person.

(E) If exposure occurs through interaction with the defendant and not a third party, the person exposed to the disease during voluntary interaction with the defendant did not know that the defendant was afflicted with the disease. A person's interaction with the defendant is not involuntary solely on the basis of his or her lack of knowledge that the defendant was afflicted with the disease.

(2) A defendant is guilty of willful exposure to an infectious or communicable disease if a health officer, or the health officer's designee, acting under circumstances that make securing a quarantine or health officer order infeasible, has instructed the defendant not to engage in particularized conduct that poses a substantial risk of transmission of an infectious or communicable disease, and the defendant engages in that conduct within 96 hours of the instruction. A health officer, or the health officer's designee, may issue a maximum of two instructions to a defendant that may result in a violation of this paragraph.

(b) The defendant does not act with the intent required pursuant to subparagraph (B) of paragraph (1) of subdivision (a) if the defendant takes, or attempts to take, practical means to prevent transmission.

(c) Failure to take practical means to prevent transmission alone is insufficient to prove the intent required pursuant to subparagraph (B) of paragraph (1) of subdivision (a).

(d) Becoming pregnant while infected with an infectious or communicable disease, continuing a pregnancy while infected with an infectious or communicable disease, or declining treatment for an infectious or communicable disease during pregnancy does not constitute a crime for purposes of this section.

(e) For purposes of this section, the following definitions shall apply:

(1) "Conduct that poses a substantial risk of transmission" means an activity that has a reasonable probability of disease transmission as proven by competent medical or epidemiological evidence. Conduct posing a low or negligible risk of transmission as proven by competent medical or epidemiological evidence does not meet the definition of conduct posing a substantial risk of transmission.

(2) "Infectious or communicable disease" means a disease that spreads from person to person, directly or indirectly, that has significant public health implications.

(3) "Practical means to prevent transmission" means a method, device, behavior, or activity demonstrated scientifically to measurably limit or reduce the risk of transmission of an infectious or communicable disease, including, but not limited to, the use of a condom, barrier protection or prophylactic device, or good faith compliance with a medical treatment regimen for the infectious or communicable disease prescribed by a health officer or physician.

(f) This section does not preclude a defendant from asserting any common law defense.

(g)(1) A violation of paragraph (1) of subdivision (a) or paragraph (2) of subdivision (a) is a misdemeanor, punishable by imprisonment in a county jail for not more than six months.

(2) A person who attempts to intentionally transmit an infectious or communicable disease by engaging in the conduct described in subparagraphs (A), (B), (C), and (E) of paragraph (1) of subdivision (a) is guilty of a misdemeanor punishable by imprisonment in a county jail for not more than 90 days.

(h)(1) When alleging a violation of subdivision (a), the prosecuting attorney or the grand jury shall substitute a pseudonym for the true name of a complaining witness. The actual name and other identifying characteristics of a complaining witness shall be revealed to the court only in camera, unless the complaining witness requests otherwise, and the court shall seal the information from further disclosure, except by counsel as part of discovery.

(2) Unless the complaining witness requests otherwise, all court decisions, orders, petitions, and other documents, including motions and papers filed by the parties, shall be worded so as to protect the name or other identifying characteristics of the complaining witness from public disclosure.

(3) Unless the complaining witness requests otherwise, a court in which a violation of this section is filed shall, at the first opportunity, issue an order that prohibits counsel, their agents, law enforcement personnel, and court staff from making a public disclosure of the name or any other identifying characteristic of the complaining witness.

(4) Unless the defendant requests otherwise, a court in which a violation of this section is filed, at the earliest opportunity, shall issue an order that counsel and their agents, law enforcement personnel, and court staff, before a finding of guilt, not publicly disclose the name or other identifying characteristics of the defendant, except by counsel as part of discovery or to a limited number of relevant individuals in its investigation of the specific charges under this section. In any public disclosure, a pseudonym shall be substituted for the true name of the defendant.

(5) For purposes of this subdivision, "identifying characteristics" includes, but is not limited to, the name or any part of the name, address or any part of the address, city or unincorporated area of residence, age, marital status, relationship of the defendant and complaining witness, place of employment, or race or ethnic background.

(i)(1) A court, upon a finding of probable cause that an individual has violated this section, shall order the production of the individual's medical records or the attendance of a person with relevant knowledge thereof, so long as the return of the medical records or attendance of the person pursuant to the subpoena is submitted initially to the court for an in-camera inspection. Only upon a finding by the court that the medical records or proffered testimony are relevant to the pleading offense, the information produced pursuant to the court's order shall be disclosed to the prosecuting entity and admissible if otherwise permitted by law.

(2) A defendant's medical records, medications, prescriptions, or medical devices shall not be used as the sole basis of establishing the specific intent required pursuant to subparagraph (B) of paragraph (1) of subdivision (a).

(3) Surveillance reports and records maintained by state and local health officials shall not be subpoenaed or released for the purpose of establishing the specific intent required pursuant to subparagraph (B) of paragraph (1) of subdivision (a).

(4) A court shall take judicial notice of any fact establishing an element of the offense upon the defendant's motion or stipulation.

(5) A defendant is not prohibited from submitting medical evidence to show the absence of the stated intent required pursuant to subparagraph (B) of paragraph (1) of subdivision (a).

(j) Before sentencing, a defendant shall be assessed for placement in one or more community-based programs that provide counseling, supervision, education, and reasonable redress to the victim or victims.

(k)(1) This section does not apply to a person who donates an organ or tissue for transplantation or research purposes.

(2) This section does not apply to a person, whether a paid or volunteer donor, who donates breast milk to a medical center or breast milk bank that receives breast milk for purposes of distribution. *(Added by Stats.2017, c. 537 (S.B.239), § 5, eff. Jan. 1, 2018.)*

Cross References

Misdemeanor,
  Defined, see Penal Code § 17.
  Punishment, see Penal Code §§ 19, 19.2.
Transplantation of tissues, screening tests for infectious diseases of donors, penalties, see Health and Safety Code § 1644.5.

Research References

2 Witkin, California Criminal Law 4th Crimes Against Public Peace and Welfare § 457 (2021), Communicable Diseases.

§ 120295. Violations of duties by local health officers; offense; penalty

Any person who violates Section 120130 or any section in Chapter 3 (commencing with Section 120175, but excluding Section 120195), is guilty of a misdemeanor, punishable by a fine of not less than fifty dollars ($50) nor more than one thousand dollars ($1,000), or by imprisonment for a term of not more than 90 days, or by both. He or she is guilty of a separate offense for each day that the violation continued. *(Added by Stats.1995, c. 415 (S.B.1360), § 7. Amended by Stats.1996, c. 1023 (S.B.1497), § 350.6, eff. Sept. 29, 1997.)*

Cross References

Computation of time, see Code of Civil Procedure §§ 12 and 12a; Government Code § 6800 et seq.
Misdemeanors, definition and penalties, see Penal Code §§ 17, 19 and 19.2.
Property taxation, delinquency penalty, costs or charges, cancellation, findings, documented hardship arising from shelter-in-place order, see Revenue and Taxation Code § 4985.2.

Research References

2 Witkin, California Criminal Law 4th Crimes Against Public Peace and Welfare § 457 (2021), Communicable Diseases.

§ 120300. Prosecution of violations; duty of district attorney

The district attorney of the county where a violation of Sections 121365 and 120280 may be committed, shall prosecute all those violations and, upon the request of a health officer, shall prosecute, as provided in Section 120280, violations of any order of a health officer made and served as provided in Section 121365 or Section 120105. *(Added by Stats.1995, c. 415 (S.B.1360), § 7.)*

Cross References

Attorney General as legal adviser in prosecution, see Government Code § 11157.
District attorney, powers and duties, see Government Code § 26500 et seq.
Health officer defined for purposes of this Division, see Health and Safety Code § 120100.

§ 120305. Illegal possession of intoxicating liquor at treatment facility; offense; exceptions

Every person who possesses any intoxicating liquor in or on any public hospital or sanatorium providing for the treatment of tuberculosis or within the boundaries of the grounds belonging thereto is guilty of a misdemeanor. This section shall not prohibit (a) the possession of any intoxicating liquor used for medicinal purposes when issued pursuant to a written order of a physician licensed to practice medicine under the laws of the State of California, (b) the possession of any intoxicating liquor by personnel for his or her own use who resides at the hospital or sanatorium or on the grounds thereof, (c) the possession of any intoxicating liquor used by a minister of the gospel or priest or rabbi in a religious sacrament or ceremony or (d) the service of wine to a patient as part of the hospital's regular menu or bill of fare if the patient is located in a portion of the premises wholly separate and isolated from patients receiving treatment for tuberculosis. *(Added by Stats.1995, c. 415 (S.B.1360), § 7.)*

Cross References

Misdemeanors, definition and penalties, see Penal Code §§ 17, 19 and 19.2.

Division 112

PUBLIC HEALTH

Part 1

GENERAL PROVISIONS

CHAPTER 2. GENERAL POWERS OF THE DEPARTMENT

ARTICLE 3. ELECTRONIC VIOLENT DEATH REPORTING SYSTEM

§ 131230. California Electronic Violent Death Reporting System

(a) To the extent that funding is appropriated by the Legislature or available through private funds in each fiscal year, the department shall establish and maintain the California Electronic Violent Death Reporting System.

(b) The department shall collect data on violent deaths as reported from data sources, including, but not limited to, death certificates, law enforcement reports, and coroner or medical examiner reports. The department shall post on its Internet Web site a summary and analysis of the collected data.

(c)(1) The department may enter into a contract, grant, or other agreement with a local agency to collect the data specified in subdivision (b) within the agency's jurisdiction.

(2)(A) The department may enter into a contract, grant, or other agreement with a local agency to collect the data specified in subdivision (b) from other local agencies if the following conditions are met:

(i) The local agency entering into the agreement agrees to collect the data from the other local agencies.

(ii) The local agency entering into the agreement is not responsible for reporting to the department data that have not been made available by the other local agencies.

(B) The other local agencies described in subparagraph (A) may also enter into their own agreements with the department pursuant to paragraph (1).

(3) The data collected pursuant to paragraph (1) or (2) shall be limited to data that the local agency entering into the agreement or the other local agencies are authorized to collect within their respective jurisdictions.

(4) A local agency entering into an agreement pursuant to paragraph (1) or (2) shall collect data based on existing or new data elements required by the California Electronic Violent Death Reporting System only to the extent that resources are made available.

(d) To the extent that funding is available for this purpose, a law enforcement agency may report to the department data on the circumstances surrounding all violent deaths from investigative reports and, if available, laboratory toxicology reports to be used by the department for the limited purpose of conducting public health surveillance and epidemiology. Aggregate data shall be public, but individual identifying information shall remain confidential. The collected data shall be based on the data elements of the federal Centers for Disease Control and Prevention's National Violent Death Reporting System.

(e) The department may apply for grants provided under the National Violent Death Reporting System for purposes of implementing this section.

(f) The department may accept private or foundation moneys to implement this section.

(g) This section does not limit data sources that the department may collect, which may include any public agency document that may contain data on violent deaths. *(Added by Stats.2016, c. 712 (S.B.877), § 2, eff. Jan. 1, 2017.)*

Cross References

Sexual orientation and gender identity, collection of data upon completion of training, aggregation, deidentification, and reporting of data, see Health and Safety Code § 102937.

Research References

1 Witkin California Criminal Law 4th Crimes Against the Person § 96 (2021), Crimes Included.

§ 131231. "Violent death" defined

For purposes of this article, "violent death" means a death resulting from the use of physical force or power against oneself, another person, or a group or community, and includes, but is not limited to, homicide, suicide, legal intervention deaths, unintentional firearm deaths, and undetermined intent deaths. *(Added by Stats. 2016, c. 712 (S.B.877), § 2, eff. Jan. 1, 2017.)*

Research References

1 Witkin California Criminal Law 4th Crimes Against the Person § 96 (2021), Crimes Included.

INSURANCE CODE

Division 1

GENERAL RULES GOVERNING INSURANCE

Part 2

THE BUSINESS OF INSURANCE

CHAPTER 5. PRODUCTION AGENCIES

ARTICLE 12. CONDUCT OF LICENSEE

Section

§ 1733. Fiduciaries; theft of funds

All funds received by any person acting as a licensee under this chapter, Chapter 5A (commencing with Section 1759), Chapter 6 (commencing with Section 1760), or Chapter 7 (commencing with Section 1800), as premium or return premium on or under any policy of insurance or undertaking of bail, are received and held by that person in that person's fiduciary capacity. A person who diverts or appropriates those fiduciary funds to that person's own use is guilty of theft and punishable for theft as provided by law. Any premium that a premium financer agrees to advance pursuant to the terms of a premium finance agreement shall constitute fiduciary funds as defined in this section only if actually received by a person licensed in one or more of the capacities herein specified. *(Added by Stats.1959, c. 4, p. 1817, § 2, eff. Feb. 27, 1959. Amended by Stats.1983, c. 356, § 6; Stats.1990, c. 1420 (S.B.2642), § 58, operative Jan. 1, 1992; Stats.2006, c. 740 (A.B.2125), § 8; Stats.2008, c. 300 (A.B.2044), § 6; Stats.2021, c. 133 (S.B.272), § 21, eff. July 23, 2021.)*

Cross References

Bail licenses, application of this section, see Insurance Code § 1821.
Broker defined, see Insurance Code § 33.
Insurance agent defined, see Insurance Code §§ 31, 1621.
Insurance solicitor defined, see Insurance Code §§ 34, 1624.
Life agent defined, see Insurance Code §§ 32, 1622.
Life and disability insurance analyst defined for purposes of this Code, see Insurance Code § 32.5.
Motor club agent defined, see Insurance Code § 12143.
Punishment for theft, see Penal Code §§ 489, 490.
Special lines surplus line broker, see Insurance Code § 1760.5.
Surplus line broker defined for purposes of this Code, see Insurance Code § 47.
Theft, generally, see Penal Code § 484 et seq.

Research References

2 Witkin, California Criminal Law 4th Crimes Against Property § 33 (2021), Other Persons.
2 Witkin, California Criminal Law 4th Crimes Against Public Peace and Welfare § 447 (2021), Other Brokers and Agents.

CHAPTER 12. THE INSURANCE FRAUDS PREVENTION ACT

ARTICLE 1. FALSE AND FRAUDULENT CLAIMS

Section

§ 1871.4. Unlawful conduct; penalties

(a) It is unlawful to do any of the following:

(1) Make or cause to be made a knowingly false or fraudulent material statement or material representation for the purpose of obtaining or denying any compensation, as defined in Section 3207 of the Labor Code.

(2) Present or cause to be presented a knowingly false or fraudulent written or oral material statement in support of, or in opposition to, a claim for compensation for the purpose of obtaining or denying any compensation, as defined in Section 3207 of the Labor Code.

(3) Knowingly assist, abet, conspire with, or solicit a person in an unlawful act under this section.

(4) Make or cause to be made a knowingly false or fraudulent statement with regard to entitlement to benefits with the intent to discourage an injured worker from claiming benefits or pursuing a claim.

For the purposes of this subdivision, "statement" includes, but is not limited to, a notice, proof of injury, bill for services, payment for services, hospital or doctor records, X–ray, test results, medical-legal expense as defined in Section 4620 of the Labor Code, other evidence of loss, injury, or expense, or payment.

(5) Make or cause to be made a knowingly false or fraudulent material statement or material representation for the purpose of obtaining or denying any of the benefits or reimbursement provided in the Return–to–Work Program established under Section 139.48 of the Labor Code.

(6) Make or cause to be made a knowingly false or fraudulent material statement or material representation for the purpose of discouraging an employer from claiming any of the benefits or reimbursement provided in the Return–to–Work Program established under Section 139.48 of the Labor Code.

(b) Every person who violates subdivision (a) shall be punished by imprisonment in a county jail for one year, or pursuant to subdivision (h) of Section 1170 of the Penal Code, for two, three, or five years, or by a fine not exceeding one hundred fifty thousand dollars ($150, 000) or double the value of the fraud, whichever is greater, or by both that imprisonment and fine. Restitution shall be ordered, including restitution for any medical evaluation or treatment services obtained or provided. The court shall determine the amount of restitution and the person or persons to whom the restitution shall be paid. A person convicted under this section may be charged the costs of investigation at the discretion of the court.

(c) A person who violates subdivision (a) and who has a prior felony conviction of that subdivision, of former Section 556, of former Section 1871.1, or of Section 548 or 550 of the Penal Code, shall receive a two-year enhancement for each prior conviction in addition to the sentence provided in subdivision (b).

The existence of any fact that would subject a person to a penalty enhancement shall be alleged in the information or indictment and either admitted by the defendant in open court, or found to be true by the jury trying the issue of guilt or by the court where guilt is established by plea of guilty or nolo contendere or by trial by the court sitting without a jury.

(d) This section may not be construed to preclude the applicability of any other provision of criminal law that applies or may apply to a transaction. *(Added by Stats.1991, c. 116 (S.B.1218), § 13. Amended by Stats.1991, c. 934 (A.B.1673), § 4; Stats.1992, c. 675 (A.B.3067), § 5; Stats.1992, c. 1352 (A.B.3660), § 2, eff. Sept. 30, 1992; Stats. 1992, c. 1352 (A.B.3660), § 2.5, eff. Sept. 30, 1992, operative Jan. 1, 1993; Stats.1993, c. 120 (A.B.1300), § 3, eff. July 16, 1993; Stats.1995, c. 574 (S.B.465), § 1; Stats.2002, c. 6 (A.B.749), § 2.7; Stats.2003, c. 635 (A.B.227), § 8; Stats.2003–2004, 4th Ex.Sess., c. 2 (S.B.2), § 1, eff. March 6, 2005; Stats.2011, c. 15 (A.B.109), § 212, eff. April 4, 2011, operative Oct. 1, 2011.)*

Cross References

Attorneys, disciplinary authority of the courts, insurance claims, fraud, see Business and Professions Code § 6106.5.
Attorneys, disciplinary authority of the courts, investigation, insurance fraud, see Business and Professions Code § 6106.6.
Charging defendant costs of investigation, prosecution, or appeal prohibited, exceptions, see Penal Code § 688.5.
Chiropractors, employment of runners, cappers, steerers to procure patients, see Business and Professions Code § 1003.
Chiropractors, investigation, persons against whom an information or indictment has been filed, see Business and Professions Code § 1004.
Commencing criminal actions, tolling or extension of time periods, see Penal Code § 803.
Criminal procedure, victim, defined, see Penal Code § 1191.10.
Department of Insurance, reported violation of state law concerning illegally provided medical services, license revocation of physician or surgeon, see Business and Professions Code § 2417.
Disclosure or reception of information, immunity from civil liability, see Insurance Code § 1877.5.
Enforcement provisions, see Insurance Code § 1872 et seq.
False or fraudulent claims, disciplinary action, see Business and Professions Code § 810.
False or fraudulent claims against insurers, solicitation, acceptance or referral of business, penalties and restitution, see Penal Code § 549.
False or fraudulent claims or statements, prohibited acts, see Penal Code § 550.
Felonies, definition and penalties, see Penal Code §§ 17, 18.
Medicine, employment of persons to procure patients, see Business and Professions Code § 2273.
Medicine, investigation, persons against whom an information or indictment has been filed, see Business and Professions Code § 2220.6.
Victim restitution, multiple felonies involving fraud or embezzlement, see Penal Code § 186.11.
Violation of this section,
 Commencement of action, see Penal Code § 801.5.
 Investigations, see Insurance Code §§ 1872.3, 1872.83.
Workers' compensation and insurance, compensation, inducements or rewards given to adjuster of claims for the referral or settlement of a claim, see Labor Code § 3219.
Workers' compensation and insurance, conviction of making false or fraudulent statements to obtain or deny workers' compensation, see Labor Code § 5803.5.
Workers' compensation misrepresentations, legislative declarations, prohibited acts, penalties, see Labor Code § 3820.

Research References

2 Witkin, California Criminal Law 4th Crimes Against Property § 225 (2021), Workers' Compensation Claims.
2 Witkin, California Criminal Law 4th Crimes Against Property § 227 (2021), Procuring, Accepting, or Referring Business.
5 Witkin, California Criminal Law 4th Criminal Trial § 729 (2021), Exception: Continuous Course of Conduct.
1 Witkin California Criminal Law 4th Defenses § 252 (2021), Discovery of Crime: Statutory Provisions.
1 Witkin California Criminal Law 4th Introduction to Crimes § 149 (2021), Fraud and Related Offenses.
3 Witkin, California Criminal Law 4th Punishment § 119 (2021), Rights of Third Parties.

ARTICLE 2. BUREAU OF FRAUDULENT CLAIMS

Section

1872.3. Investigation of violations; publication of information; public inspection; cooperation with law enforcement agencies.
1872.4. Insurer's belief of fraudulent claim; reports; failure to prosecute; cooperation of law enforcement agencies.
1872.41. Fraudulent applications; duties of agent or broker.
1872.5. Insurer's tort liability.
1872.51. Written or oral information; liability protection.
1872.6. Investigations by other agencies.

§ 1872.3. Investigation of violations; publication of information; public inspection; cooperation with law enforcement agencies

(a) If, by its own inquiries or as a result of complaints, the Fraud Division has reason to believe that a person has engaged in, or is engaging in, an act or practice that violates Section 1871.4 of this code, or Section 549 or 550 of the Penal Code, the commissioner in his or her discretion may do either or both of the following:

(1) Make those public or private investigations within or outside of this state that he or she deems necessary to determine whether any person has violated or is about to violate any provision of Section 1871.4 of this code, or Section 549 or 550 of the Penal Code, or to aid in the enforcement of this chapter.

(2) Publish information concerning any violation of this chapter or Section 550 of the Penal Code.

(b) For purposes of any investigation under this section, the commissioner or any officer designated by the commissioner may administer oaths and affirmations, subpoena witnesses, compel their attendance, take evidence, and require the production of any books, papers, correspondence, memoranda, agreements, or other documents or records that the commissioner deems relevant or material to the inquiry, as provided by Section 12924.

(c) If any matter that the commissioner seeks to obtain by request is located outside the state, the person so requested may make it available to the commissioner or his or her representative to be examined at the place where it is located. The commissioner may designate representatives, including officials of the state in which the matter is located, to inspect the matter on his or her behalf, and he or she may respond to similar requests from officials of other states.

(d) Except as provided in subdivision (e), the department's papers, documents, reports, or evidence relative to the subject of an investigation under this section shall not be subject to public inspection for so long a period as the commissioner deems reasonably necessary to complete the investigation, to protect the person investigated from unwarranted injury, or to serve the public interest. Furthermore, those papers, documents, reports, or evidence shall not be subject to subpoena or subpoena duces tecum until opened for public inspection by the commissioner, unless the commissioner otherwise consents or, after notice to the commissioner and a hearing, the superior court determines that the public interest and any ongoing investigation by the commissioner would not be unnecessarily jeopardized by compliance with the subpoena duces tecum.

(e) The Fraud Division shall furnish all papers, documents, reports, complaints, or other facts or evidence to any police, sheriff, or other law enforcement agency, when so requested, and shall assist and cooperate with those law enforcement agencies. *(Added by Stats.1989, c. 1119, § 3. Amended by Stats.1991, c. 116 (S.B.1218), § 15; Stats.1991, c. 934 (A.B.1673), § 6; Stats.1992, c. 675 (A.B. 3067), § 7; Stats.2005, c. 717 (A.B.1183), § 3.)*

Cross References

Oath defined for purposes of this Code, see Insurance Code § 17.

§ 1872.4. Insurer's belief of fraudulent claim; reports; failure to prosecute; cooperation of law enforcement agencies

(a) Any company licensed to write insurance in this state that has determined, after the completion of the insurer's special investigative unit investigation, that it reasonably suspects or knows * * * an act of insurance fraud may have occurred or might be occurring shall, within 60 days after that determination by the insurer * * *, send to the Fraud Division, on a form prescribed by the department, the information requested by the form and any additional information relative to the factual circumstances * * * regarding the alleged insurance fraud and person or entity that may have committed or is committing insurance fraud, as specified in Section 2698.38 of Title 10 of the California Code of Regulations. The Fraud Division shall review each report and undertake further investigation it deems necessary and proper to determine the validity of the allegations. Whenever the commissioner is satisfied that fraud, deceit, or intentional misrepresentation of any kind has been committed in the submission of the claim, * * * claims, application, or other insurance transaction, the commissioner shall report the violations of law to the insurer, to the appropriate licensing agency, and to the district attorney of the county in which the offenses were committed, as provided by Sections 12928 and 12930. If the commissioner is satisfied that fraud, deceit, or intentional misrepresentation has not been committed, * * * the commissioner shall report that determination to the insurer. If prosecution by the district attorney concerned is not begun within 60 days of the receipt of the commissioner's report, the district attorney shall inform the commissioner and the insurer as to the reasons for the lack of prosecution regarding the reported violations.

(b) This section shall not require an insurer to submit to the Fraud Division the information specified in subdivision (a) in either of the following instances:

(1) The insurer's initial investigation indicated a potentially fraudulent claim but further investigation revealed that it was not fraudulent.

(2) The insurer and the claimant have reached agreement as to the amount of the claim and the insurer does not have reasonable grounds to believe that claim to be fraudulent.

(c) Nothing contained in this article shall relieve an insurer of its existing obligations to also report suspected violations of law to appropriate local law enforcement agencies.

(d) Any police, sheriff, disciplinary body governed by the provisions of the Business and Professions Code, or other law enforcement agency shall furnish all papers, documents, reports, complaints, or other facts or evidence to the Fraud Division, when so requested, and shall otherwise assist and cooperate with the division.

(e) If an insurer, at the time the insurer, pursuant to subdivision (a) forwards to the Fraud Division information on a claim that appears to be fraudulent, has no evidence to believe the insured on that claim is involved with the fraud or the fraudulent collision, the insurer shall take all necessary steps to assure that no surcharge is added to the insured's premium because of the claim. *(Added by Stats.1989, c. 1119, § 3. Amended by Stats.1999, c. 885 (A.B.1050), § 3; Stats.2005, c. 717 (A.B.1183), § 4; Stats.2022, c. 424 (S.B.1242), § 21, eff. Jan. 1, 2023.)*

Cross References

Insurer defined for purposes of this Article, see Insurance Code § 1872.2.
Insurer defined for purposes of this Chapter, see Insurance Code § 1875.

§ 1872.41. Fraudulent applications; duties of agent or broker

(a) An agent or broker who, before placing an insurance application with an insurer, reasonably suspects or knows that a fraudulent application is being made shall, within 60 days after the determination by the agent or broker that the application appears to be fraudulent, submit to the Fraud Division, using the electronic form within Fraud Division's Consumer Fraud Reporting Portal, the information requested by the form and any additional information relative to the factual circumstances of the application and the alleged material misrepresentations contained in the application. All data fields within the Fraud Division's Consumer Fraud Reporting Portal electronic form shall be completed accurately, to the best of the agent or broker's ability. An agent or broker shall not submit a fraud referral anonymously. The Fraud Division shall review each report and undertake further investigation it deems necessary and proper to determine the validity of the allegations.

(b) An agent or broker who, after an insurance application has been placed with an insurer, reasonably suspects or knows that fraud has been perpetrated shall report that information directly to the insurer's special investigative unit. An agent or broker shall furnish all papers, documents, reports, or other facts or evidence to the insurer's special investigative unit upon request, and shall otherwise assist and cooperate with the insurer's special investigative unit.

(c) An agent or broker shall furnish all papers, documents, reports, or other facts or evidence to the department upon request, and shall otherwise assist and cooperate with the department.

(d)(1) For purposes of this section, an "agent or broker" is a natural person licensed to transact insurance in a capacity described in Section 1625, 1625.5, 1625.55, 1626, or 1758.1 and is not the employee of an insurer.

(2) An agent or broker is not considered a "contracted entity" or "integral antifraud personnel" pursuant to Section 2689.30 of Title 10 of the California Code of Regulations. *(Added by Stats.2022, c. 424 (S.B.1242), § 22, eff. Jan. 1, 2023.)*

§ 1872.5. Insurer's tort liability

No insurer, or the employees or agents of any insurer, shall be subject to civil liability for libel, slander, or any other relevant tort cause of action by virtue of providing any of the following without malice:

(a) Any information or reports relating to suspected fraudulent insurance transaction furnished to law enforcement officials, or licensing officials governed by the Business and Professions Code.

(b) Any reports or information relating to suspected fraudulent insurance transaction furnished to other persons subject to this chapter.

(c) Any information or reports required by this article or required by the commissioner under the authority granted in this chapter. *(Added by Stats.1989, c. 1119, § 3.)*

Cross References

Insurer defined for purposes of this Article, see Insurance Code § 1872.2.
Insurer defined for purposes of this Chapter, see Insurance Code § 1875.

§ 1872.51. Written or oral information; liability protection

(a) An agent or broker who furnishes written or oral information pursuant to Section 1872.41, or an authorized governmental agency, or its employees, that furnishes or receives written or oral information pursuant to Section 1872.41 or assists in an investigation of a suspected insurance fraud violation conducted by an authorized governmental agency, shall not be subject to any civil liability in a cause or action if the insurer, authorized agent, agent or broker, or authorized governmental agency acted in good faith, without malice, and reasonably believes that the action taken was warranted by the then-known facts, obtained by reasonable efforts.

(b) This chapter does not abrogate or lessen the existing common law or statutory privileges and immunities of an insurer, agent authorized by that insurer to act on its behalf, agent or broker, licensed rating organization, or any authorized governmental agency or its employees. *(Added by Stats.2022, c. 424 (S.B.1242), § 23, eff. Jan. 1, 2023.)*

§ 1872.6. Investigations by other agencies

Nothing contained in this article shall:

(a) Preempt the authority of other law enforcement or licensing agencies to investigate and prosecute suspected violations of law.

(b) Prevent or prohibit a person from voluntarily disclosing any information concerning violations of this chapter to any law enforcement or licensing agency governed by the Business and Professions Code.

(c) Limit any of the powers granted to the department or the commissioner to investigate possible violations of the chapter and take appropriate action against wrongdoers. *(Added by Stats.1989, c. 1119, § 3.)*

ARTICLE 5. ARSON INVESTIGATIONS

§ 1875. Definitions

As used in this chapter:

(a) "Authorized agency" means any of the following officers or agencies, or their duly authorized representatives, when investigating or prosecuting arson in connection with a specific fire: the State Fire Marshal, the Director of the Department of Forestry and Fire Protection, the chief of any city or county fire department, the chief of any fire protection district, the Attorney General, any district attorney, or any peace officer, the Department of Insurance, and any federal agency.

(b) "Insurer" means any insurer admitted to write, or otherwise issuing, fire insurance covering property in this state and includes its agents, servants, investigators, and adjusters. "Insurer" includes the California FAIR Plan. *(Added by Stats.1989, c. 1119, § 3. Amended by Stats.1991, c. 602 (A.B.1725), § 2.)*

Cross References

Attorney General, generally, see Government Code § 12500 et seq.
Fire insurance defined, generally, see Insurance Code § 102.

§ 1875.1. Release of information to authorized agency

An authorized agency may, when there is evidence or suspicion that the crime of arson has been committed, request any insurer to release all information in its possession that the authorized agency determines to be relevant to the crime. The insurer shall release the following:

(a) Any insurance policy or any application for such a policy.

(b) Policy premium payment records.

(c) History of previous claims made by the insured for fire loss.

(d) Material relating to the investigation of the loss, including the statement of any person, proof of loss, and any other relevant evidence. *(Added by Stats.1989, c. 1119, § 3.)*

Cross References

Authorized agency defined for purposes of this Chapter, see Insurance Code § 1875.
Insurer defined for purposes of this Chapter, see Insurance Code § 1875.

§ 1875.2. Suspicion of cause of fire by incendiary means; furnishing information to and cooperation with authorized agency by insurer

If any insurer has reason to suspect that a fire loss was caused by incendiary means, the insurer shall furnish an authorized agency with all relevant information acquired during its investigation of the fire loss and cooperate in an investigation by an authorized agency.

The authorized agency provided with the information pursuant to this article may release that information to any of the other authorized agencies. *(Added by Stats.1989, c. 1119, § 3.)*

Cross References

Authorized agency defined for purposes of this Chapter, see Insurance Code § 1875.
Insurer defined for purposes of this Chapter, see Insurance Code § 1875.

§ 1875.3. Notice to insurer; release of information

An authorized agency shall notify the insurer, if known, and at the expense of the insurer, whenever it has reason to believe that a fire loss was not accidentally caused. The agency shall also release to the claimant's insurer specific information regarding the fire loss at the earliest time possible unless it determines that an ongoing investigation would be jeopardized. *(Added by Stats.1989, c. 1119, § 3. Amended by Stats.1991, c. 602 (A.B.1725), § 3.)*

Cross References

Authorized agency defined for purposes of this Chapter, see Insurance Code § 1875.
Insurer defined for purposes of this Chapter, see Insurance Code § 1875.

§ 1875.4. Civil liability

In the absence of fraud or malice, no insurer or person acting in its behalf who (a) furnishes information whether oral or written, pursuant to this article, or (b) assists in any investigation conducted by an authorized agency, shall be liable for damages in a civil action, nor shall any authorized agency which releases information pursuant to this chapter be liable for damages in a civil action.

The act of furnishing information required pursuant to this article shall not constitute an act of fraud or malice. *(Added by Stats.1989, c. 1119, § 3.)*

Cross References

Authorized agency defined for purposes of this Chapter, see Insurance Code § 1875.
Insurer defined for purposes of this Chapter, see Insurance Code § 1875.

§ 1875.5. Insurer's failure to comply

In any case in which an insurer willfully fails to comply with this article, the authorized agency may petition the superior court in an appropriate county for an order requiring compliance. *(Added by Stats.1989, c. 1119, § 3.)*

Cross References

Authorized agency defined for purposes of this Chapter, see Insurance Code § 1875.
Insurer defined for purposes of this Chapter, see Insurance Code § 1875.

§ 1875.6. Agency release of information in connection with criminal or civil proceeding

Any authorized agency that receives any information furnished as required by this article shall not make the information public until the time that its release is required in connection with a criminal or civil proceeding. *(Added by Stats.1989, c. 1119, § 3. Amended by Stats.1991, c. 602 (A.B.1725), § 4.)*

Cross References

Authorized agency defined for purposes of this Chapter, see Insurance Code § 1875.

§ 1875.8. Arson Information Reporting System

(a) There is hereby created the Arson Information Reporting System to permit insurers, law enforcement agencies, fire investigative agencies, and district attorneys to deposit arson case information in a common data base within the Department of Justice. The State Fire Marshal shall oversee the establishment, operation, and maintenance of the Arson Information Reporting System. The Department of Justice shall implement the Arson Information Reporting System in consultation with the State Fire Marshal.

(b) The purpose of the data base is to identify utilization patterns by individual claimants and the methods of operation of individuals, groups, or businesses engaged in the commission of arson, and to prevent the commission of insurance fraud by arson.

(c) The use of the information deposited pursuant to this article shall be made available to law enforcement agencies, fire investigative agencies, district attorneys, and insurers, via modem, for the purpose of investigating and prosecuting arson and arson-related insurance fraud, or evaluating the validity and payment of fire-related insurance claims. The State Fire Marshal shall establish rules governing the access to, and use of, information and the circumstances under which information may be accessed and corrected.

(d) Any information acquired pursuant to this section shall not be a part of any public record. Except as otherwise provided by law, any authorized governmental agency, an insurer, or an agent authorized by an insurer to act on its behalf, which receives any information furnished pursuant to this section, shall not release that information to public inspection until the time that its release is required in connection with a criminal or civil proceeding.

(e) Information submitted to the State Fire Marshal pursuant to this section concerning active cases shall be confidential.

(f) Nothing in this section shall prohibit the accumulation and public distribution by the bureau of statistical data if that data does not reveal the identity of specific claimants, injured parties, attorneys, physicians, or other service providers. *(Added by Stats.1994, c. 420 (A.B.2336), § 1.)*

Cross References

Insurer defined for purposes of this Chapter, see Insurance Code § 1875.

VEHICLE CODE

Division 2

ADMINISTRATION

CHAPTER 4. ADMINISTRATION AND ENFORCEMENT

ARTICLE 1. LAWFUL ORDERS AND INSPECTIONS

§ 2800. Peace officers, Department of California Highway Patrol or authorized enforcement officers; compliance with lawful orders and lawful out-of-service orders; vehicle inspections

(a) It is unlawful to willfully fail or refuse to comply with a lawful order, signal, or direction of a peace officer, as defined in Chapter 4.5 (commencing with Section 830) of Title 3 of Part 2 of the Penal Code, when that peace officer is in uniform and is performing duties pursuant to any of the provisions of this code, or to refuse to submit to a lawful inspection pursuant to this code.

(b)(1) Except as authorized pursuant to Section 24004, it is unlawful to fail or refuse to comply with a lawful out-of-service order issued by an authorized employee of the Department of the California Highway Patrol or by an authorized enforcement officer as described in subdivision (d).

(2) It is unlawful for a driver transporting hazardous materials in a commercial motor vehicle that is required to display a placard pursuant to Section 27903 to violate paragraph (1).

(3) It is unlawful for a driver of a vehicle designed to transport 16 or more passengers, including the driver, to violate paragraph (1).

(c) It is unlawful to fail or refuse to comply with a lawful out-of-service order issued by the United States Secretary of the Department of Transportation.

(d) "Out-of-Service order" means a declaration by an authorized enforcement officer of a federal, state, Canadian, Mexican, or local jurisdiction that a driver, a commercial motor vehicle, or a motor carrier operation is out-of-service pursuant to Section 386.72, 392.5, 392.9a, 395.13, or 396.9 of Title 49 of the Code of Federal Regulations, state law, or the North American Standard Out-of-Service Criteria.

(e) It is unlawful for a driver of a commercial vehicle subject to inspection under this code to fail to comply with any vehicle inspection testing and associated procedures as required by an authorized member of the California Highway Patrol. *(Stats.1959, c. 3, p. 1552, § 2800. Amended by Stats.1981, c. 644, p. 2414, § 1; Stats.1999, c. 724 (A.B.1650), § 29.5; Stats.2004, c. 952 (A.B.3049), § 2, operative Sept. 20, 2005; Stats.2006, c. 288 (A.B.3011), § 1; Stats.2010, c. 491 (S.B.1318), § 36; Stats.2012, c. 670 (A.B.2188), § 1; Stats.2022, c. 295 (A.B.2956), § 3, eff. Jan. 1, 2023.)*

Cross References

Applicability of this section to trolley coaches, see Vehicle Code § 21051.
Authority of highway patrol, see Vehicle Code § 2409.
Commercial motor vehicles, suspension of driving privileges for violations of this section, see Vehicle Code § 15311.
Conditions under which employer prohibited from allowing driver to drive, see Vehicle Code § 15240.
Direction of traffic by members of highway patrol, see Vehicle Code § 2410.
Duration of prohibition against operation of commercial motor vehicle, see Vehicle Code § 15312.
Failure to stop and submit to inspection of equipment or unsafe condition endangering a person, punishment for misdemeanor conviction, see Vehicle Code § 42002.1.
Farm labor vehicles subject to forfeiture as nuisance, and impounding, see Vehicle Code § 34506.5.
Inspections by patrol members, see Vehicle Code § 2804 et seq.
Obedience to traffic control devices and signals, see Vehicle Code §§ 21461, 21462.
Operation of vehicle with unlawful equipment or in unsafe condition, see Vehicle Code § 24002 et seq.
Optional appearance before magistrate, see Vehicle Code § 40303.
Penalty for violations affecting failure to stop and submit to inspection of equipment or for an unsafe condition, see Vehicle Code § 42001.
Possession and display of driver's license, see Vehicle Code § 12951.
Punishment for misdemeanors under this section, see Vehicle Code § 42001 et seq.
Rules of the road, bicycles or animals, see Vehicle Code §§ 21050, 21200.
School safety patrol traffic signals, disregarding, see Education Code § 49307.
Vehicles incidentally operated over highway, applicability of this section, see Vehicle Code § 25802.
Violation a misdemeanor, see Vehicle Code § 40000.7.

Research References

2 Witkin, California Criminal Law 4th Crimes Against Public Peace and Welfare § 267 (2021), Misdemeanors.
2 Witkin, California Criminal Law 4th Crimes Against Public Peace and Welfare § 328 (2021), Failure to Comply With Instructions.

§ 2800.1. Flight from pursuing peace officer

(a) Any person who, while operating a motor vehicle and with the intent to evade, willfully flees or otherwise attempts to elude a pursuing peace officer's motor vehicle, is guilty of a misdemeanor punishable by imprisonment in a county jail for not more than one year if all of the following conditions exist:

(1) The peace officer's motor vehicle is exhibiting at least one lighted red lamp visible from the front and the person either sees or reasonably should have seen the lamp.

(2) The peace officer's motor vehicle is sounding a siren as may be reasonably necessary.

(3) The peace officer's motor vehicle is distinctively marked.

(4) The peace officer's motor vehicle is operated by a peace officer, as defined in Chapter 4.5 (commencing with Section 830) of Title 3 of Part 2 of the Penal Code, and that peace officer is wearing a distinctive uniform.

(b) Any person who, while operating a motor vehicle and with the intent to evade, willfully flees or otherwise attempts to elude a pursuing peace officer's bicycle, is guilty of a misdemeanor punishable by imprisonment in a county jail for not more than one year if the following conditions exist:

(1) The peace officer's bicycle is distinctively marked.

(2) The peace officer's bicycle is operated by a peace officer, as defined in paragraph (4) of subdivision (a), and that peace officer is wearing a distinctive uniform.

(3) The peace officer gives a verbal command to stop.

(4) The peace officer sounds a horn that produces a sound of at least 115 decibels.

(5) The peace officer gives a hand signal commanding the person to stop.

(6) The person is aware or reasonably should have been aware of the verbal command, horn, and hand signal, but refuses to comply with the command to stop. *(Added by Stats.1982, c. 947, p. 3433, § 2. Amended by Stats.1988, c. 504, § 1, eff. Aug. 22, 1988; Stats.1995, c. 68 (S.B.170), § 1; Stats.2005, c. 485 (S.B.719), § 6.)*

Cross References

Commercial motor vehicles, suspension of driving privileges for violations of this section, see Vehicle Code §§ 15300, 15302.
Driver's license examinations, knowledge of risks and punishment associated with fleeing a police officer while operating a motor vehicle, see Vehicle Code § 1666.1.
Indemnification of victims of crime, persons injured where police officer is operating a motor vehicle attempting to apprehend a suspect, see Government Code § 13955.
Vehicle pursuit reports filed by law enforcement agency, contents, see Vehicle Code § 14602.1.
Violation as misdemeanor, see Vehicle Code § 40000.7.

Research References

California Jury Instructions - Criminal 12.85, Flight from Pursuing Peace Officer—Reckless Driving.
California Jury Instructions - Criminal 12.86, Flight from Pursuing Peace Officer Causing Death/Serious Bodily Injury.
California Jury Instructions - Criminal 16.890, Flight from Pursuing Peace Officer.
2 Witkin, California Criminal Law 4th Crimes Against Public Peace and Welfare § 329 (2021), Flight from Pursuing Peace Officer.
1 Witkin California Criminal Law 4th Crimes Against the Person § 191 (2021), Restrictions on Scope of Doctrine.
1 Witkin California Criminal Law 4th Crimes Against the Person § 200 (2021), Fleeing Police Officer.
3 Witkin, California Criminal Law 4th Punishment § 211 (2021), Discretionary Suspension.

§ 2800.2. Driving in willful or wanton disregard for safety of persons or property while fleeing from pursuing police officer; penalties

(a) If a person flees or attempts to elude a pursuing peace officer in violation of Section 2800.1 and the pursued vehicle is driven in a willful or wanton disregard for the safety of persons or property, the person driving the vehicle, upon conviction, shall be punished by imprisonment in the state prison, or by confinement in the county jail for not less than six months nor more than one year. The court may also impose a fine of not less than one thousand dollars ($1,000) nor more than ten thousand dollars ($10,000), or may impose both that imprisonment or confinement and fine.

(b) For purposes of this section, a willful or wanton disregard for the safety of persons or property includes, but is not limited to, driving while fleeing or attempting to elude a pursuing peace officer during which time either three or more violations that are assigned a traffic violation point count under Section 12810 occur, or damage to property occurs. *(Added by Stats.1988, c. 504, § 3, eff. Aug. 22, 1988. Amended by Stats.1996, c. 420 (A.B.1999), § 1; Stats.1998, c. 472 (A.B.2066), § 1.)*

Cross References

Commercial motor vehicles, suspension of driving privileges for violations of this section, see Vehicle Code §§ 15300, 15302.
Traffic violation point count, violation of this section, see Vehicle Code § 12810.

Research References

California Jury Instructions - Criminal 12.85, Flight from Pursuing Peace Officer—Reckless Driving.
California Jury Instructions - Criminal 16.890, Flight from Pursuing Peace Officer.
2 Witkin, California Criminal Law 4th Crimes Against Public Peace and Welfare § 329 (2021), Flight from Pursuing Peace Officer.
1 Witkin California Criminal Law 4th Crimes Against the Person § 200 (2021), Fleeing Police Officer.
1 Witkin California Criminal Law 4th Crimes Against the Person § 214 (2021), Disregard for Human Safety Compared.
5 Witkin, California Criminal Law 4th Criminal Trial § 630 (2021), Prohibition Against Conclusively Presuming Element of Crime.
5 Witkin, California Criminal Law 4th Criminal Trial § 689 (2021), Instructions on Definitions of Statutory Terms.
3 Witkin, California Criminal Law 4th Punishment § 195 (2021), Impounding of Motor Vehicles.

§ 2800.3. Death or serious bodily injury proximately caused by flight from pursuing peace officer; punishment; "serious bodily injury" defined

(a) Whenever willful flight or attempt to elude a pursuing peace officer in violation of Section 2800.1 proximately causes serious bodily injury to any person, the person driving the pursued vehicle, upon conviction, shall be punished by imprisonment in the state prison for three, five, or seven years, by imprisonment in a county jail for not more than one year, or by a fine of not less than two thousand dollars ($2,000) nor more than ten thousand dollars ($10,000), or by both that fine and imprisonment.

(b) Whenever willful flight or attempt to elude a pursuing peace officer in violation of Section 2800.1 proximately causes death to a person, the person driving the pursued vehicle, upon conviction, shall be punished by imprisonment in the state prison for a term of 4, 6, or 10 years.

(c) Nothing in this section shall preclude the imposition of a greater sentence pursuant to Section 190 of the Penal Code or any other provisions of law applicable to punishment for an unlawful death.

(d) For the purposes of this section, "serious bodily injury" has the same meaning as defined in paragraph (4) of subdivision (f) of Section 243 of the Penal Code. *(Formerly § 2800.2, added by Stats.1982, c. 947, p. 3433, § 3. Renumbered § 2800.3, and amended by Stats.1988, c. 504, § 2, eff. Aug. 22, 1988. Amended by Stats.1991, c. 656 (S.B.666), § 1; Stats.1996, c. 420 (A.B.1999), § 2; Stats.1998, c. 256 (A.B.1382), § 1; Stats.2005, c. 485 (S.B.719), § 7.)*

Cross References

Commercial motor vehicles, suspension of driving privileges for violations of this section, see Vehicle Code §§ 15300, 15302.
Driver's license examinations, knowledge of risks and punishment associated with fleeing a police officer while operating a motor vehicle, see Vehicle Code § 1666.1.
Indemnification of victims of crime, persons injured where police officer is operating a motor vehicle attempting to apprehend a suspect, see Government Code § 13955.

Research References

California Jury Instructions - Criminal 12.86, Flight from Pursuing Peace Officer Causing Death/Serious Bodily Injury.
California Jury Instructions - Criminal 16.890, Flight from Pursuing Peace Officer.
2 Witkin, California Criminal Law 4th Crimes Against Public Peace and Welfare § 329 (2021), Flight from Pursuing Peace Officer.
1 Witkin California Criminal Law 4th Crimes Against the Person § 191 (2021), Restrictions on Scope of Doctrine.
1 Witkin California Criminal Law 4th Crimes Against the Person § 200 (2021), Fleeing Police Officer.

3 Witkin, California Criminal Law 4th Punishment § 195 (2021), Impounding of Motor Vehicles.
3 Witkin, California Criminal Law 4th Punishment § 216 (2021), Offenses Involving Injury.
3 Witkin, California Criminal Law 4th Punishment § 350 (2021), General Provision.
3 Witkin, California Criminal Law 4th Punishment § 353 (2021), In Commission of Felony.

§ 2800.4. Willful driving of vehicle on highway in direction opposite lawful traffic during flight from pursuing peace officer; punishment

Whenever a person willfully flees or attempts to elude a pursuing peace officer in violation of Section 2800.1, and the person operating the pursued vehicle willfully drives that vehicle on a highway in a direction opposite to that in which the traffic lawfully moves upon that highway, the person upon conviction is punishable by imprisonment for not less than six months nor more than one year in a county jail or by imprisonment in the state prison, or by a fine of not less than one thousand dollars ($1,000) nor more than ten thousand dollars ($10,000), or by both that fine and imprisonment. *(Added by Stats.2006, c. 688 (S.B.1735), § 1. Amended by Stats.2011, c. 15 (A.B.109), § 599, eff. April 4, 2011, operative Oct. 1, 2011; Stats.2012, c. 43 (S.B.1023), § 111, eff. June 27, 2012.)*

Research References

2 Witkin, California Criminal Law 4th Crimes Against Public Peace and Welfare § 329 (2021), Flight from Pursuing Peace Officer.

§ 2801. Obedience to firemen

It is unlawful to wilfully fail or refuse to comply with any lawful order, signal, or direction of any member of any fire department, paid, volunteer, or company operated, when wearing the badge or insignia of a fireman and when in the course of his duties he is protecting the personnel and fire department equipment. *(Stats. 1959, c. 3, p. 1552, § 2801.)*

Cross References

Failure to stop and submit to inspection of equipment or unsafe condition endangering a person, punishment for misdemeanor conviction, see Vehicle Code § 42002.1.
Penalty for violations affecting failure to stop and submit to inspection of equipment or for an unsafe condition, see Vehicle Code § 42001.
Punishment for misdemeanors under this section, see Vehicle Code § 42001.
Rules of the road, bicycles or animals, see Vehicle Code §§ 21050, 21200.
Violation a misdemeanor, see Vehicle Code § 40000.7.

Research References

2 Witkin, California Criminal Law 4th Crimes Against Public Peace and Welfare § 267 (2021), Misdemeanors.

Division 3

REGISTRATION OF VEHICLES AND CERTIFICATES OF TITLE

CHAPTER 1. ORIGINAL AND RENEWAL OF REGISTRATION; ISSUANCE OF CERTIFICATES OF TITLE

ARTICLE 4. EVIDENCES OF REGISTRATION

§ 4463. Forgery, alteration, counterfeit or falsification of registration, license plate, certificate, license, etc., or disabled person placard; penalties

(a) A person who, with intent to prejudice, damage, or defraud, commits any of the following acts is guilty of a felony and upon conviction thereof shall be punished by imprisonment pursuant to subdivision (h) of Section 1170 of the Penal Code for 16 months, or two or three years, or by imprisonment in a county jail for not more than one year:

(1) Alters, forges, counterfeits, or falsifies a certificate of ownership, registration card, certificate, license, license plate, temporary license plate, device issued pursuant to Sections 4853 and 4854, special plate, or permit provided for by this code or a comparable certificate of ownership, registration card, certificate, license, license plate, temporary license plate, device comparable to that issued pursuant to Sections 4853 and 4854, special plate, or permit provided for by a foreign jurisdiction, or alters, forges, counterfeits, or falsifies the document, device, or plate with intent to represent it as issued by the department, or alters, forges, counterfeits, or falsifies with fraudulent intent an endorsement of transfer on a certificate of ownership or other document evidencing ownership, or with fraudulent intent displays or causes or permits to be displayed or have in * * * their possession a blank, incomplete, canceled, suspended, revoked, altered, forged, counterfeit, or false certificate of ownership, registration card, certificate, license, license plate, temporary license plate, device issued pursuant to Sections 4853 and 4854, special plate, or permit.

(2) Utters, publishes, passes, or attempts to pass, as true and genuine, a false, altered, forged, or counterfeited matter listed in paragraph (1) knowing it to be false, altered, forged, or counterfeited.

(b) A person who, with intent to prejudice, damage, or defraud, commits any of the following acts is guilty of a misdemeanor, and upon conviction thereof shall be punished by imprisonment in a county jail for six months, a fine of not less than five hundred dollars ($500) and not more than one thousand dollars ($1,000), or both that fine and imprisonment, which penalty shall not be suspended:

(1) Forges, counterfeits, or falsifies a disabled person placard or a comparable placard relating to parking privileges for disabled persons provided for by a foreign jurisdiction, or forges, counterfeits, or falsifies a disabled person placard with intent to represent it as issued by the department.

(2) Passes, or attempts to pass, as true and genuine, a false, forged, or counterfeit disabled person placard knowing it to be false, forged, or counterfeited.

(3) Acquires, possesses, sells, or offers for sale a genuine or counterfeit disabled person placard.

(c) A person who, with fraudulent intent, displays or causes or permits to be displayed a forged, counterfeit, or false disabled person placard, is subject to the issuance of a notice of parking violation imposing a civil penalty of not less than two hundred fifty dollars ($250) and not more than one thousand dollars ($1,000), for which enforcement shall be governed by the procedures set forth in Article 3 (commencing with Section 40200) of Chapter 1 of Division 17, or is guilty of a misdemeanor punishable by imprisonment in a county jail for six months, a fine of not less than two hundred fifty dollars ($250) and not more than one thousand dollars ($1,000), or both that fine and imprisonment, which penalty shall not be suspended.

(d) For purposes of subdivision (b) or (c), "disabled person placard" means a placard issued pursuant to Section 22511.55 or 22511.59.

(e) A person who, with intent to prejudice, damage, or defraud, commits any of the following acts is guilty of an infraction, and upon conviction thereof shall be punished by a fine of not less than one hundred dollars ($100) and not more than two hundred fifty dollars ($250) for a first offense, not less than two hundred fifty dollars ($250) and not more than five hundred dollars ($500) for a second offense, and not less than five hundred dollars ($500) and not more than one thousand dollars ($1,000) for a third or subsequent offense, which penalty shall not be suspended:

(1) Forges, counterfeits, or falsifies a Clean Air Sticker or a comparable clean air sticker relating to high-occupancy vehicle lane privileges provided for by a foreign jurisdiction, or forges, counterfeits, or falsifies a Clean Air Sticker with intent to represent it as issued by the department.

(2) Passes, or attempts to pass, as true and genuine, a false, forged, or counterfeit Clean Air Sticker knowing it to be false, forged, or counterfeited.

(3) Acquires, possesses, sells, or offers for sale a counterfeit Clean Air Sticker.

(4) Acquires, possesses, sells, or offers for sale a genuine Clean Air Sticker separate from the vehicle for which the department issued that sticker.

(f) As used in this section, "Clean Air Sticker" means a label or decal issued pursuant to Sections 5205.5 and 21655.9.

* * * *(Added by Stats.2016, c. 90 (A.B.516), § 10, eff. Jan. 1, 2017, operative Jan. 1, 2019. Amended by Stats.2022, c. 746 (A.B.984), § 1, eff. Jan. 1, 2023.)*

Cross References

Certificate of ownership and registration card, see Vehicle Code § 4450.
Cigarette tax stamps or meter impressions, counterfeiting, see Revenue and Taxation Code § 30473.
Counterfeiting, see Penal Code § 470 et seq.
Endorsement of certificate of ownership upon transfer, see Vehicle Code § 5750 et seq.
Fines, disabled parking restrictions, see Penal Code § 1465.6.
Off-highway vehicles, applicability of registration provisions, see Vehicle Code § 38100.
Parking penalties, additional assessments, see Vehicle Code § 40203.6.
Procedure upon registration, see Vehicle Code § 4150 et seq.
Surrender of evidences of registration, see Vehicle Code § 8802.
Suspension, revocation or cancellation of registration, see Vehicle Code § 8800 et seq.
Violation as misdemeanor, see Vehicle Code § 40000.7.

Research References

2 Witkin, California Criminal Law 4th Crimes Against Property § 178 (2021), In General.
2 Witkin, California Criminal Law 4th Crimes Against Property § 192 (2021), Possession of Forged Writing.
2 Witkin, California Criminal Law 4th Crimes Against Property § 199 (2021), Motor Vehicle Items.
1 Witkin California Criminal Law 4th Introduction to Crimes § 149 (2021), Fraud and Related Offenses.

§ 4463.5. Decorative or facsimile license plates; authorization; punishment for violation

(a) No person shall manufacture or sell a decorative or facsimile license plate of a size substantially similar to the license plate issued by the department.

(b) Notwithstanding subdivision (a), the director may authorize the manufacture and sale of decorative or facsimile license plates for special events or media productions.

(c) A violation of this section is a misdemeanor punishable by a fine of not less than five hundred dollars ($500). *(Added by Stats.1986, c. 859, § 1.)*

Cross References

Violation as misdemeanor, see Vehicle Code § 40000.7.

Research References

2 Witkin, California Criminal Law 4th Crimes Against Property § 199 (2021), Motor Vehicle Items.

Division 4

SPECIAL ANTITHEFT LAWS

CHAPTER 1. REPORTS OF STOLEN VEHICLES

Section

§ 10500. Stolen, or unlawfully driven or taken vehicles; leased or rented vehicles; lost or stolen license plates; notification to reporting party

Section operative until Jan. 1, 2024. See, also, § 10500 operative Jan. 1, 2024.

(a) A peace officer, upon receiving a report based on reliable information that a vehicle registered under this code has been stolen, taken, or driven in violation of Section 10851, or that a leased or rented vehicle has not been returned within 72 hours following the expiration of the lease or rental agreement and after the owner attempted to notify the customer pursuant to subdivision (b) of Section 10855, or that license plates for a vehicle have been lost or stolen, shall, immediately after receiving that information, report the information to the Department of Justice Stolen Vehicle System. An officer, upon receiving information of the recovery of a vehicle described in this subdivision, or of the recovery of plates which have been previously reported as lost or stolen, shall immediately report the fact of the recovery to the Department of Justice Stolen Vehicle System. At the same time, the recovering officer shall advise the Department of Justice Stolen Vehicle System and the original reporting law enforcement agency of the location and condition of the vehicle or license plates recovered. The original reporting law enforcement agency, upon receipt of the information from the recovering officer, shall immediately attempt to notify the reporting party by telephone, if the telephone number of the reporting party is available or readily accessible, of the location and condition of the recovered vehicle. If the reporting party's telephone number is unknown, or notification attempts were unsuccessful, the original reporting law enforcement agency shall notify the reporting party by placing, in the mail, a notice providing the location and condition of the recovered vehicle. This written notice shall be mailed within 24 hours of the original reporting law enforcement agency's receipt of the information of the recovery of the vehicle, excluding holidays and weekends.

(b) If the recovered vehicle is subject to parking or storage charges, Section 10652.5 applies.

(c) This section shall remain in effect until January 1, 2024, and as of that date, is repealed. *(Added by Stats.1982, c. 581, p. 2541, § 2, operative Jan. 1, 1989. Amended by Stats.1990, c. 337 (A.B.2717), § 1; Stats.1992, c. 290 (A.B.1583), § 1; Stats.1994, c. 675 (S.B.1741), § 3; Stats.2019, c. 609 (A.B.391), § 1, eff. Jan. 1, 2020.)*

Inoperative Date and Repeal

For inoperative date and repeal of this section, see its terms.

Cross References

Departmental action on report of stolen, taken or driven vehicle, see Vehicle Code § 10504.
Owners' reports of stolen and recovered vehicles, see Vehicle Code § 10502.

Research References

4 Witkin, California Criminal Law 4th Introduction to Criminal Procedure § 51 (2021), In General.

§ 10500. Stolen, or unlawfully driven or taken vehicles; leased or rented vehicles; lost or stolen license plates; notification to reporting party

Section operative Jan. 1, 2024. See, also, § 10500 operative until Jan. 1, 2024.

(a) A peace officer, upon receiving a report based on reliable information that a vehicle registered under this code has been stolen, taken, or driven in violation of Section 10851, or that a leased or rented vehicle has not been returned within five days after its owner has made written demand for its return, by certified or registered mail, following the expiration of the lease or rental agreement, or that license plates for a vehicle have been lost or stolen, shall, immediately after receiving that information, report the information to the Department of Justice Stolen Vehicle System. An officer, upon receiving information of the recovery of a vehicle described in this subdivision, or of the recovery of plates which have been previously reported as lost or stolen, shall immediately report the fact of the recovery to the Department of Justice Stolen Vehicle System. At the same time, the recovering officer shall advise the Department of Justice Stolen Vehicle System and the original reporting law enforcement agency of the location and condition of the vehicle or license plates recovered. The original reporting law enforcement agency, upon receipt of the information from the recovering officer, shall immediately attempt to notify the reporting party by telephone, if the telephone number of the reporting party is available or readily accessible, of the location and condition of the recovered vehicle. If the reporting party's telephone number is unknown, or notification attempts were unsuccessful, the original reporting law enforcement agency shall notify the reporting party by placing, in the mail, a notice providing the location and condition of the recovered vehicle. This written notice shall be mailed within 24 hours of the original reporting law enforcement agency's receipt of the information of the recovery of the vehicle, excluding holidays and weekends.

(b) If the recovered vehicle is subject to parking or storage charges, Section 10652.5 applies.

(c) This section shall become operative on January 1, 2024. *(Added by Stats.2019, c. 609 (A.B.391), § 2, eff. Jan. 1, 2020, operative Jan. 1, 2024.)*

Cross References

Departmental action on report of stolen, taken or driven vehicle, see Vehicle Code § 10504.
Owners' reports of stolen and recovered vehicles, see Vehicle Code § 10502.

Research References

4 Witkin, California Criminal Law 4th Introduction to Criminal Procedure § 51 (2021), In General.

§ 10501. False report of theft; prior conviction; penalty

(a) It is unlawful for any person to make or file a false or fraudulent report of theft of a vehicle required to be registered under this code with any law enforcement agency with intent to deceive.

(b) If a person has been previously convicted of a violation of subdivision (a), he or she is punishable by imprisonment pursuant to subdivision (h) of Section 1170 of the Penal Code for 16 months, or two or three years, or in a county jail for not to exceed one year. *(Stats.1959, c. 3, p. 1594, § 10501. Amended by Stats.1982, c. 958, p. 3458, § 1; Stats.2011, c. 15 (A.B.109), § 601, eff. April 4, 2011, operative Oct. 1, 2011.)*

Cross References

Registration, see Vehicle Code § 4000 et seq.
Violations, see Vehicle Code §§ 40000.9, 42002.

Research References

2 Witkin, California Criminal Law 4th Crimes Against Governmental Authority § 27 (2021), False Reports of Crime.
2 Witkin, California Criminal Law 4th Crimes Against Governmental Authority § 61 (2021), Effect of Special Statute.
2 Witkin, California Criminal Law 4th Crimes Against Property § 265 (2021), Miscellaneous Frauds.
1 Witkin California Criminal Law 4th Introduction to Crimes § 76 (2021), Illustrations: Special Statute is Controlling.

§ 10502. Reports by owners

(a) The owner or legal owner of a vehicle registered under this code which has been stolen or embezzled may notify the Department of the California Highway Patrol of the theft or embezzlement, but in the event of an embezzlement other than an embezzlement as specified in Section 10855, may make the report only after having procured the issuance of a warrant for the arrest of the person charged with the embezzlement.

(b) Every owner or legal owner who has given any notice under subdivision (a) shall notify the Department of the California Highway Patrol of a recovery of the vehicle. *(Stats.1959, c. 3, p. 1595, § 10502. Amended by Stats.1992, c. 290 (A.B.1583), § 2.)*

Cross References

Definitions,
  Legal owner, see Vehicle Code § 370.
  Owner, see Vehicle Code § 460.
  Vehicle, see Vehicle Code § 670.
Effective period of report, see Vehicle Code § 10504.
Embezzlement, see Penal Code § 503 et seq.
Registration, see Vehicle Code § 4000 et seq.

§ 10503. Notice to Department of Motor Vehicles

The Department of Justice upon receiving notice under this chapter that a vehicle has been stolen, or taken or driven in violation of Section 10851, or that a vehicle reported stolen, or taken or driven in violation of Section 10851 has been recovered, shall notify the Department of Motor Vehicles of the reported theft, taking or driving, or recovery. *(Stats.1959, c. 3, p. 1595, § 10503. Amended by Stats.1972, c. 98, p. 133, § 2, eff. May 30, 1972, operative Oct. 1, 1972.)*

§ 10504. Action by department

The department upon receiving a report of a stolen vehicle, or of a vehicle taken or driven in violation of Section 10851, shall place an appropriate notice in the electronic file system which will identify such vehicles during the processing of new certificates of registration, ownership, or registration and ownership. When such vehicles are thus identified, processing shall be discontinued and the Department of Justice shall be notified. New certificates shall not be issued until cleared by the Department of Justice. Notices shall remain in the Department of Motor Vehicles system until a Department of Justice deletion is received.

A report of a stolen vehicle, or of a vehicle taken or driven in violation of Section 10851, is effective for a period of not less than one year from the date first reported or longer as the department may determine. *(Stats.1959, c. 3, p. 1595, § 10504. Amended by Stats.1970, c. 1439, p. 2794, § 11; Stats.1972, c. 98, p. 133, § 3, eff. May 30, 1972, operative Oct. 1, 1972.)*

Cross References

Definitions,
 Department, see Vehicle Code § 290.
 Vehicle, see Vehicle Code § 670.
Registration indices and records, see Vehicle Code § 1800 et seq.

§ 10505. Notification of transfer

Upon the transfer of registration of a vehicle reported as stolen or embezzled, the department shall immediately notify the reporting agency of such fact. *(Stats.1959, c. 3, p. 1595, § 10505.)*

CHAPTER 1.5. REPORTS OF STOLEN VESSELS

§ 10550. Definitions

In this chapter, unless the context clearly requires a different meaning, the terms and definitions set forth in Section 9840 shall apply. *(Added by Stats.1970, c. 1428, p. 2769, § 62. Amended by Stats.1973, c. 759, p. 1371, § 14.)*

§ 10551. Peace officers duty to report to department

Every peace officer upon receiving a report based on reliable information that any undocumented vessel numbered under this code has been stolen shall immediately after receiving such information report the theft to the Department of Justice, Automated Boat System, and such peace officer upon receiving information of the recovery of any such vessel which he has previously reported as stolen, shall immediately report the fact of the recovery to the Department of Justice, Automated Boat System. *(Added by Stats. 1970, c. 1428, p. 2769, § 62. Amended by Stats.1980, c. 617, p. 1700, § 5.)*

Cross References

Peace officers, see Penal Code § 830 et seq.

§ 10551.5. Notice of reported theft or recovery by department of justice

The Department of Justice upon receiving notice under this chapter that a vessel has been stolen or that a vessel reported stolen has been recovered shall notify the Department of Motor Vehicles of the reported theft or recovery. *(Added by Stats.1980, c. 617, p. 1700, § 6.)*

§ 10552. False or fraudulent reports

It is unlawful for any person to make or file a false or fraudulent report of the theft of an undocumented vessel required to be numbered under this code with any law enforcement agents with intent to deceive. *(Added by Stats.1970, c. 1428, p. 2769, § 62.)*

Cross References

False reporting of criminal offense, misdemeanor, see Penal Code § 148.5.

Research References

2 Witkin, California Criminal Law 4th Crimes Against Governmental Authority § 27 (2021), False Reports of Crime.

§ 10553. Report by owner or legal owner

The owner or legal owner of a vessel numbered under this code which has been stolen or embezzled may notify a law enforcement agency of the theft or embezzlement, but in the event of an embezzlement may make the report only after having procured the issuance of a warrant for the arrest of the person charged with such embezzlement. Every owner or legal owner who has given any such notice shall notify the law enforcement agency of a recovery of the vessel. *(Added by Stats.1970, c. 1428, p. 2770, § 62. Amended by Stats.1980, c. 617, p. 1700, § 7.)*

Cross References

Embezzlement, see Penal Code § 503 et seq.
Theft or larceny, see Penal Code § 484 et seq.

§ 10554. Notice in electronic file system; processing of new certificates; duration of effectiveness of reports

The department upon receiving a report of a stolen or embezzled vessel shall place an appropriate notice in the electronic file system which will identify such vessel during the processing of new certificates of number, ownership, or number and ownership. When such vessels are thus identified, processing shall be discontinued and the agency holding the theft report and the Department of Justice shall be notified. New certificates shall not be issued until cleared by the Department of Justice. Notices shall remain in the Department of Motor Vehicles system until a Department of Justice deletion is received.

A report of a stolen or embezzled vessel is effective for a period of not less than one year from the date first reported, or for such longer period as the department may determine. *(Added by Stats.1970, c. 1428, p. 2770, § 62. Amended by Stats.1980, c. 617, p. 1700, § 8.)*

CHAPTER 3. ALTERATION OR REMOVAL OF NUMBERS

§ 10750. Altering or changing vehicle numbers

(a) No person shall intentionally deface, destroy, or alter the motor number, other distinguishing number, or identification mark of a vehicle required or employed for registration purposes without written authorization from the department, nor shall any person place or stamp any serial, motor, or other number or mark upon a vehicle, except one assigned thereto by the department.

(b) This section does not prohibit the restoration by an owner of the original vehicle identification number when the restoration is authorized by the department, nor prevent any manufacturer from placing in the ordinary course of business numbers or marks upon new motor vehicles or new parts thereof. *(Stats.1959, c. 3, p. 1596, § 10750. Amended by Stats.1970, c. 824, p. 1559, § 6.)*

Cross References

Definitions,
  Department, see Vehicle Code § 290.
  Owner, see Vehicle Code § 460.
  Person, see Vehicle Code § 470.
  Vehicle, see Vehicle Code § 670.
Registration indices and records, see Vehicle Code § 1800.
Suspension, cancellation or revocation of registration, see Vehicle Code § 8800.
Violation a misdemeanor, see Vehicle Code § 40000.9.

Research References

2 Witkin, California Criminal Law 4th Crimes Against Property § 308 (2021), Tampering or Injuring.

§ 10751. Manufacturer's serial or identification numbers; disposition; hearing; notice; application of section

(a) No person shall knowingly buy, sell, offer for sale, receive, or have in his or her possession, any vehicle, or component part thereof, from which any serial or identification number, including, but not limited to, any number used for registration purposes, that is affixed by the manufacturer to the vehicle or component part, in whatever manner deemed proper by the manufacturer, has been removed, defaced, altered, or destroyed, unless the vehicle or component part has attached thereto an identification number assigned or approved by the department in lieu of the manufacturer's number.

(b) Whenever a vehicle described in subdivision (a), including a vehicle assembled with any component part which is in violation of subdivision (a), comes into the custody of a peace officer, it shall be destroyed, sold, or otherwise disposed of under the conditions as provided in an order by the court having jurisdiction. No court order providing for disposition shall be issued unless the person from whom the property was seized, and all claimants to the property whose interest or title is on registration records in the Department of Motor Vehicles, are provided a postseizure hearing by the court having jurisdiction within 90 days after the seizure. This subdivision shall not apply with respect to a seized vehicle or component part used as evidence in any criminal action or proceeding. Nothing in this section shall, however, preclude the return of a seized vehicle or a component part to the owner by the seizing agency following presentation of satisfactory evidence of ownership and, if determined necessary, upon the assignment of an identification number to the vehicle or component part by the department.

(c) Whenever a vehicle described in subdivision (a) comes into the custody of a peace officer, the person from whom the property was seized, and all claimants to the property whose interest or title is on registration records in the Department of Motor Vehicles, shall be notified within five days, excluding Saturdays, Sundays, and holidays, after the seizure, of the date, time, and place of the hearing required in subdivision (b). The notice shall contain the information specified in subdivision (d).

(d) Whenever a peace officer seizes a vehicle described in subdivision (a), the person from whom the property was seized shall be provided a notice of impoundment of the vehicle which shall serve as a receipt and contain the following information:

(1) Name and address of person from whom the property was seized.

(2) A statement that the vehicle seized has been impounded for investigation of a violation of Section 10751 of the California Vehicle Code and that the property will be released upon a determination that the serial or identification number has not been removed, defaced, altered, or destroyed, or upon the presentation of satisfactory evidence of ownership of the vehicle or a component part, if no other person claims an interest in the property; otherwise, a hearing regarding the disposition of the vehicle shall take place in the proper court.

(3) A statement that the person from whom the property was seized, and all claimants to the property whose interest or title is on registration records in the Department of Motor Vehicles, will receive written notification of the date, time, and place of the hearing within five days, excluding Saturdays, Sundays, and holidays, after the seizure.

(4) Name and address of the law enforcement agency where evidence of ownership of the vehicle or component part may be presented.

(5) A statement of the contents of Section 10751 of the Vehicle Code.

(e) A hearing on the disposition of the property shall be held by the superior court within 90 days after the seizure. The hearing shall be before the court without a jury. A proceeding under this section is a limited civil case.

(1) If the evidence reveals either that the serial or identification number has not been removed, defaced, altered, or destroyed or that the number has been removed, defaced, altered, or destroyed but satisfactory evidence of ownership has been presented to the seizing agency or court, the property shall be released to the person entitled thereto. Nothing in this section precludes the return of the vehicle or a component part to a good faith purchaser following presentation of satisfactory evidence of ownership thereof upon the assignment of an identification number to the vehicle or component part by the department.

(2) If the evidence reveals that the identification number has been removed, defaced, altered, or destroyed, and satisfactory evidence of ownership has not been presented, the vehicle shall be destroyed, sold, or otherwise disposed of as provided by court order.

(3) At the hearing, the seizing agency has the burden of establishing that the serial or identification number has been removed, defaced, altered, or destroyed and that no satisfactory evidence of ownership has been presented.

(f) This section does not apply to a scrap metal processor engaged primarily in the acquisition, processing, and shipment of ferrous and nonferrous scrap, and who receives dismantled vehicles from licensed dismantlers, licensed junk collectors, or licensed junk dealers as scrap metal for the purpose of recycling the dismantled vehicles for their metallic content, the end product of which is the production of material for recycling and remelting purposes for steel mills, foundries, smelters, and refiners. *(Added by Stats.1981, c. 599, p. 2314, § 2, operative Jan. 1, 1988. Amended by Stats.1990, c. 481 (S.B.2809), § 1; Stats.1991, c. 13 (A.B.37), § 25, eff. Feb. 13, 1991; Stats.1998, c. 931 (S.B.2139), § 455, eff. Sept. 28, 1998; Stats.2002, c. 784 (S.B. 1316), § 596.)*

Law Revision Commission Comments

Section 10751 is amended to accommodate unification of the municipal and superior courts in a county. Cal. Const. art. VI, § 5(e). The section is also amended to reflect elimination of the justice court. Cal. Const. art. VI, §§ 1, 5(b).

A limited civil case is within the original jurisdiction of the municipal court or of the superior court in a county in which there is no municipal court. Cal. Const. art. VI, 10 (superior court jurisdiction); Code Civ. Proc. §§ 85, 85.1 (limited civil cases). See also Code Civ. Proc. §§ 91, 904.2, 1085 (trial procedures and writ and appellate jurisdiction for limited civil cases). [28 Cal.L.Rev.Comm. Reports 51 (1998)].

Subdivision (e) of Section 10751 is amended to reflect unification of the municipal and superior courts pursuant to Article VI, Section 5(e), of the California Constitution. [32 Cal.L.Rev.Comm. Reports 537 (2002)].

Cross References

Alteration or change of vehicle numbers, see Vehicle Code § 10750.
Definitions,
  Department, see Vehicle Code § 290.
  Manufacturer's gross vehicle weight rating, see Vehicle Code § 350.
  Motor vehicle, see Vehicle Code § 415.

Person, see Vehicle Code § 470.
Vehicle, see Vehicle Code § 670.
Punishment for violation of section, see Vehicle Code § 42002.4.
Registration indices and records, see Vehicle Code § 1800.
Suspension, revocation or cancellation of registration, see Vehicle Code § 8800 et seq.
Violation as misdemeanor, see Vehicle Code § 40000.9.

Research References

2 Witkin, California Criminal Law 4th Crimes Against Property § 308 (2021), Tampering or Injuring.
2 Witkin, California Criminal Law 4th Crimes Against Public Peace and Welfare § 267 (2021), Misdemeanors.

§ 10752. Manufacturer's or governmental serial or identification numbers; possession or sale; penalties

(a) No person shall, with intent to prejudice, damage, injure, or defraud, acquire, possess, sell, or offer for sale any genuine or counterfeit manufacturer's serial or identification number from or for, or purporting to be from or for, a vehicle or component part thereof.

(b) No person shall, with intent to prejudice, damage, injure, or defraud, acquire, possess, sell, or offer for sale any genuine or counterfeit serial or identification number issued by the department, the Department of the California Highway Patrol, or the vehicle registration and titling agency of any foreign jurisdiction which is from or for, or purports to be from or for, a vehicle or component part thereof.

(c) Every person convicted of a violation of subdivision (a) or (b) shall be punished by imprisonment pursuant to subdivision (h) of Section 1170 of the Penal Code, or in the county jail for not less than 90 days nor more than one year, and by a fine of not less than two hundred fifty dollars ($250) nor more than five thousand dollars ($5,000). *(Added by Stats.1980, c. 608, p. 1677, § 4. Amended by Stats.1985, c. 623, § 2; Stats.2011, c. 15 (A.B.109), § 602, eff. April 4, 2011, operative Oct. 1, 2011.)*

Research References

2 Witkin, California Criminal Law 4th Crimes Against Property § 265 (2021), Miscellaneous Frauds.
1 Witkin California Criminal Law 4th Introduction to Crimes § 62 (2021), Illustrations.

CHAPTER 3.5. MOTOR VEHICLE CHOP SHOPS

§ 10801. Ownership or operation; punishment

Any person who knowingly and intentionally owns or operates a chop shop is guilty of a public offense and, upon conviction, shall be punished by imprisonment pursuant to subdivision (h) of Section 1170 of the Penal Code for two, three, or four years, or by a fine of not more than fifty thousand dollars ($50,000), or by both the fine and imprisonment, or by up to one year in the county jail, or by a fine of not more than one thousand dollars ($1,000), or by both the fine and imprisonment. *(Added by Stats.1993, c. 386 (S.B.73), § 3, eff. Sept. 8, 1993. Amended by Stats.2011, c. 15 (A.B.109), § 603, eff. April 4, 2011, operative Oct. 1, 2011.)*

Research References

California Jury Instructions - Criminal 14.68, Chop Shop—Ownership/Operation.
2 Witkin, California Criminal Law 4th Crimes Against Property § 309 (2021), Motor Vehicle Chop Shops.
1 Witkin California Criminal Law 4th Introduction to Crimes § 149 (2021), Fraud and Related Offenses.

§ 10802. Vehicle identification numbers; alteration, destruction, forgery or removal; punishment

Any person who knowingly alters, counterfeits, defaces, destroys, disguises, falsifies, forges, obliterates, or removes vehicle identification numbers, with the intent to misrepresent the identity or prevent the identification of motor vehicles or motor vehicle parts, for the purpose of sale, transfer, import, or export, is guilty of a public offense and, upon conviction, shall be punished by imprisonment pursuant to subdivision (h) of Section 1170 of the Penal Code for 16 months, or two or three years, or by a fine of not more than twenty-five thousand dollars ($25, 000), or by both the fine and imprisonment, or by up to one year in the county jail, or by a fine of not more than one thousand dollars ($1,000), or by both the fine and imprisonment. *(Added by Stats.1993, c. 386 (S.B.73), § 3, eff. Sept. 8, 1993. Amended by Stats.2011, c. 15 (A.B.109), § 604, eff. April 4, 2011, operative Oct. 1, 2011.)*

Research References

2 Witkin, California Criminal Law 4th Crimes Against Property § 309 (2021), Motor Vehicle Chop Shops.

§ 10803. Possession, purchase, sale or transfer of more than one motor vehicle or parts; knowledge of altered, destroyed, forged or removed vehicle identification numbers; punishment

(a) Any person who buys with the intent to resell, disposes of, sells, or transfers, more than one motor vehicle or parts from more than one motor vehicle, with the knowledge that the vehicle identification numbers of the motor vehicles or motor vehicle parts have been altered, counterfeited, defaced, destroyed, disguised, falsified, forged, obliterated, or removed for the purpose of misrepresenting the identity or preventing the identification of the motor vehicles or motor vehicle parts, is guilty of a public offense and, upon conviction, shall be punished by imprisonment pursuant to subdivision (h) of Section 1170 of the Penal Code for two, four, or six years, or by a fine of not more than sixty thousand dollars ($60,000), or by both the fine and imprisonment, or by up to one year in the county jail, or by a fine of not more than one thousand dollars ($1,000), or by both the fine and imprisonment.

(b) Any person who possesses, for the purpose of sale, transfer, import, or export, more than one motor vehicle or parts from more than one motor vehicle, with the knowledge that the vehicle identification numbers of the motor vehicles or motor vehicle parts have been altered, counterfeited, defaced, destroyed, disguised, falsified, forged, obliterated, or removed for the purpose of misrepresenting the identity or preventing the identification of the motor vehicles or motor vehicle parts, is guilty of a public offense and, upon conviction, shall be punished by imprisonment pursuant to subdivision (h) of Section 1170 of the Penal Code for 16 months, or two or three years, or by a fine of not more than thirty thousand dollars ($30,000), or by both the fine and imprisonment, or by imprisonment in the county jail not exceeding one year or by a fine of not more than one thousand dollars ($1,000) or by both the fine and imprisonment. *(Added by Stats.1993, c. 386 (S.B.73), § 3, eff. Sept. 8, 1993. Amended by Stats.2011, c. 15 (A.B.109), § 605, eff. April 4, 2011, operative Oct. 1, 2011.)*

Research References

2 Witkin, California Criminal Law 4th Crimes Against Property § 309 (2021), Motor Vehicle Chop Shops.

§ 10804. Exemption; motor vehicle scrap processor; owner or authorized possessor of recovered stolen vehicle

(a) Section 10803 does not apply to a motor vehicle scrap processor who, in the normal legal course of business and in good faith, processes a motor vehicle or motor vehicle part by crushing, compacting, or other similar methods, if any vehicle identification number is not removed from the motor vehicle or motor vehicle part prior to or during the processing.

(b) Section 10803 does not apply to any owner or authorized possessor of a motor vehicle or motor vehicle part which has been recovered by law enforcement authorities after having been stolen or if the condition of the vehicle identification number of the motor vehicle or motor vehicle part is known to, or has been reported to, law enforcement authorities. Law enforcement authorities are presumed to have knowledge of all vehicle identification numbers on a motor vehicle or motor vehicle part which are altered, counterfeited, defaced, disguised, falsified, forged, obliterated, or removed, when law enforcement authorities deliver or return the motor vehicle or motor vehicle part to its owner or an authorized possessor after it has been recovered by law enforcement authorities after having been reported stolen. *(Added by Stats.1993, c. 386 (S.B.73), § 3, eff. Sept. 8, 1993.)*

Research References

2 Witkin, California Criminal Law 4th Crimes Against Property § 309 (2021), Motor Vehicle Chop Shops.

CHAPTER 4. THEFT AND INJURY OF VEHICLES

§ 10850. Application of chapter

The provisions of this chapter apply to vehicles upon the highways and elsewhere throughout the State. *(Stats.1959, c. 3, p. 1597, § 10850.)*

Cross References

Highway defined, see Vehicle Code §§ 360, 590.
Law enforcement, California Highway Patrol, see Vehicle Code § 2400.
Vehicle defined, see Vehicle Code § 670.

Research References

2 Witkin, California Criminal Law 4th Crimes Against Property § 5 (2021), Specified Kinds of Property.

§ 10851. Theft and unlawful driving or taking of a vehicle

(a) Any person who drives or takes a vehicle not his or her own, without the consent of the owner thereof, and with intent either to permanently or temporarily deprive the owner thereof of his or her title to or possession of the vehicle, whether with or without intent to steal the vehicle, or any person who is a party or an accessory to or an accomplice in the driving or unauthorized taking or stealing, is guilty of a public offense and, upon conviction thereof, shall be punished by imprisonment in a county jail for not more than one year or pursuant to subdivision (h) of Section 1170 of the Penal Code or by a fine of not more than five thousand dollars ($5,000), or by both the fine and imprisonment.

(b) If the vehicle is (1) an ambulance, as defined in subdivision (a) of Section 165, (2) a distinctively marked vehicle of a law enforcement agency or fire department, taken while the ambulance or vehicle is on an emergency call and this fact is known to the person driving or taking, or any person who is party or an accessory to or an accomplice in the driving or unauthorized taking or stealing, or (3) a vehicle which has been modified for the use of a disabled veteran or any other disabled person and which displays a distinguishing license plate or placard issued pursuant to Section 22511.5 or 22511.9 and this fact is known or should reasonably have been known to the person driving or taking, or any person who is party or an accessory in the driving or unauthorized taking or stealing, the offense is a felony punishable by imprisonment pursuant to subdivision (h) of Section 1170 of the Penal Code for two, three, or four years or by a fine of not more than ten thousand dollars ($10,000), or by both the fine and imprisonment.

(c) In any prosecution for a violation of subdivision (a) or (b), the consent of the owner of a vehicle to its taking or driving shall not in any case be presumed or implied because of the owner's consent on a previous occasion to the taking or driving of the vehicle by the same or a different person.

(d) The existence of any fact which makes subdivision (b) applicable shall be alleged in the accusatory pleading, and either admitted by the defendant in open court, or found to be true by the jury trying the issue of guilt or by the court where guilt is established by plea of guilty or nolo contendere or by trial by the court sitting without a jury.

(e) Any person who has been convicted of one or more previous felony violations of this section, or felony grand theft of a vehicle in violation of subdivision (d) of Section 487 of the Penal Code, former subdivision (3) of Section 487 of the Penal Code, as that section read prior to being amended by Section 4 of Chapter 1125 of the Statutes of 1993, or Section 487h of the Penal Code, is punishable as set forth in Section 666.5 of the Penal Code. The existence of any fact that would bring a person under Section 666.5 of the Penal Code shall be alleged in the information or indictment and either admitted by the defendant in open court, or found to be true by the jury trying the issue of guilt or by the court where guilt is established by plea of guilty or nolo contendere, or by trial by the court sitting without a jury.

(f) This section shall become operative on January 1, 1997. *(Added by Stats.1993, c. 1125 (A.B.1630), § 14, eff. Oct. 11, 1993, operative Jan. 1, 1997. Amended by Stats.1995, c. 101 (S.B.317), § 4, operative Jan. 1, 1997; Stats.2011, c. 15 (A.B.109), § 606, eff. April 4, 2011, operative Oct. 1, 2011.)*

Cross References

Applicability of this section to trolley coaches, see Vehicle Code § 21051.
Department of Justice reports of theft, taking, driving or recovery, see Vehicle Code § 10503.
Electronic file record of stolen vehicles, withholding registration, see Vehicle Code § 10504.
Grand theft as including taking of automobile, see Penal Code § 487.
Owner defined, see Vehicle Code § 460.
Police reports, see Vehicle Code § 10500.
Revocation of driver's license by department, see Vehicle Code § 13350.
Subsequent conviction of petty theft following conviction of auto theft under this section, punishment, see Penal Code § 666.
Suspension or revocation of driver's license, recommendation of court, see Vehicle Code § 13357.
Taking vehicle for temporary use, see Penal Code § 499b.

Research References

California Jury Instructions - Criminal 1.23, "Consent"—Defined.
California Jury Instructions - Criminal 14.36, Unlawful Vehicle Taking.
California Jury Instructions - Criminal 14.37, Auto Taking—When Acts May Constitute Either or Both Crimes.
California Jury Instructions - Criminal 14.65, Receiving Stolen Property—Defined.
California Jury Instructions - Criminal 17.04, Receiving Stolen Property and Vehicle Code Section 10851—One or Two Crimes Committed.
2 Witkin, California Criminal Law 4th Crimes Against Property § 5 (2021), Specified Kinds of Property.

2 Witkin, California Criminal Law 4th Crimes Against Property § 9 (2021), Petty Theft.
2 Witkin, California Criminal Law 4th Crimes Against Property § 37 (2021), Partners or Spouses.
2 Witkin, California Criminal Law 4th Crimes Against Property § 78 (2021), Dual Conviction.
2 Witkin, California Criminal Law 4th Crimes Against Property § 107 (2021), Nature of Crime.
2 Witkin, California Criminal Law 4th Crimes Against Property § 108 (2021), Distinctions.
2 Witkin, California Criminal Law 4th Crimes Against Property § 109 (2021), What Constitutes Driving or Taking Vehicle.
2 Witkin, California Criminal Law 4th Crimes Against Property § 110 (2021), Lack of Consent by Owner.
2 Witkin, California Criminal Law 4th Crimes Against Property § 111 (2021), Specific Intent.
2 Witkin, California Criminal Law 4th Crimes Against Property § 112 (2021), Relationship to Receiving Stolen Property.
2 Witkin, California Criminal Law 4th Crimes Against Property § 113 (2021), Related Offenses.
2 Witkin, California Criminal Law 4th Crimes Against Property § 114 (2021), In General.
2 Witkin, California Criminal Law 4th Crimes Against Property § 118 (2021), Robbery Distinguished.
2 Witkin, California Criminal Law 4th Crimes Against Public Peace and Welfare § 274 (2021), Felonies.
1 Witkin California Criminal Law 4th Crimes Against the Person § 191 (2021), Restrictions on Scope of Doctrine.
6 Witkin, California Criminal Law 4th Criminal Judgment § 75 (2021), In General.
6 Witkin, California Criminal Law 4th Criminal Judgment § 89 (2021), Appeal by Defendant More Severely Treated.
1 Witkin California Criminal Law 4th Defenses § 47 (2021), Mistake Negating Criminal Intent or Knowledge.
1 Witkin California Criminal Law 4th Elements § 36 (2021), Miscellaneous Solicitation Statutes.
1 Witkin California Criminal Law 4th Introduction to Crimes § 48 (2021), In General.
1 Witkin California Criminal Law 4th Introduction to Crimes § 89 (2021), Where Court Fails to Enter Judgment.
1 Witkin California Criminal Law 4th Introduction to Crimes § 94 (2021), In General.
3 Witkin, California Criminal Law 4th Punishment § 217 (2021), Other Serious Offenses.
3 Witkin, California Criminal Law 4th Punishment § 254 (2021), Illustrations.
3 Witkin, California Criminal Law 4th Punishment § 289 (2021), Theft and Other Crimes.
3 Witkin, California Criminal Law 4th Punishment § 308A (2021), (New) in General.
3 Witkin, California Criminal Law 4th Punishment § 378 (2021), In General.
3 Witkin, California Criminal Law 4th Punishment § 417 (2021), Theft.

§ 10851.5. Theft of binder chains

Any person who takes binder chains, required under regulations adopted pursuant to Section 31510, having a value of nine hundred fifty dollars ($950) or less which chains are not his own, without the consent of the owner thereof, and with intent either permanently or temporarily to deprive the owner thereof of his title to or possession of the binder chains whether with or without intent to steal the same, or any person who is a party or accessory to or an accomplice in the unauthorized taking or stealing is guilty of a misdemeanor, and upon conviction thereof shall be punished by imprisonment in the county jail for not less than six months or by a fine of not less than one thousand dollars ($1,000) or by both such fine and imprisonment. The consent of the owner of the binder chain to its taking shall not in any case be presumed or implied because of such owner's consent on a previous occasion to the taking of the binder chain by the same or a different person. *(Added by Stats.1963, c. 1780, p. 3560, § 1. Amended by Stats.1983, c. 1092, § 380, eff. Sept. 27, 1983, operative Jan. 1, 1984; Stats.2009–2010, 3rd Ex.Sess., c. 28 (S.B.18), § 54, eff. Jan. 25, 2010.)*

Cross References

Misdemeanor, see Penal Code §§ 17, 19, 19.2.
Violation a misdemeanor, see Vehicle Code § 40000.9.

§ 10852. Breaking or removing vehicle parts

No person shall either individually or in association with one or more other persons, wilfully injure or tamper with any vehicle or the contents thereof or break or remove any part of a vehicle without the consent of the owner. *(Stats.1959, c. 3, p. 1597, § 10852.)*

Cross References

Applicability of this section to trolley coaches, see Vehicle Code § 21051.
Procedure on arrest for violation of this section, see Vehicle Code § 40303.
Violation a misdemeanor, see Vehicle Code § 40000.9.
Violation of this section involving vehicle modified for use of disabled person, penalty, see Vehicle Code § 42002.5.

Research References

California Jury Instructions - Criminal 16.620, Tampering With Vehicle.
2 Witkin, California Criminal Law 4th Crimes Against Property § 308 (2021), Tampering or Injuring.
2 Witkin, California Criminal Law 4th Crimes Against Public Peace and Welfare § 267 (2021), Misdemeanors.
1 Witkin California Criminal Law 4th Elements § 94 (2021), Conspiracy to Commit Any Crime.

§ 10852.5. Unlawful purchase of used catalytic converter; lawful sellers

(a) No person shall purchase a used catalytic converter, including for the purpose of dismantling, recycling, or smelting, except from any of the following:

(1) An automobile dismantler licensed pursuant to Chapter 3 (commencing with Section 11500) of Division 5.

(2) A core recycler, as defined in Section 21610 of the Business and Professions Code, that maintains a fixed place of business and has obtained the catalytic converter pursuant to that section.

(3) A motor vehicle manufacturer, dealer, or lessor-retailer licensed pursuant to Division 5 (commencing with Section 11100).

(4) An automotive repair dealer licensed pursuant to Chapter 20.3 (commencing with Section 9880) of Division 3 of the Business and Professions Code.

(5) Any other licensed business that may reasonably generate, possess, or sell used catalytic converters.

(6) An individual possessing documentation that they are the lawful owner of the used catalytic converter, including, but not limited to, a certificate of title or registration that identifies the individual as the legal or registered owner of the vehicle from which the catalytic converter was detached, and that includes a vehicle identification number that matches the vehicle identification number permanently marked on the catalytic converter.

(b) As used in this section, the following terms have the following meanings:

(1) "Permanently marked" means prominently engraved, etched, welded, metal stamped, acid marked, or otherwise permanently displayed using a similarly reliable method of imparting a lasting mark on the exterior case of the catalytic converter.

(2) "Used catalytic converter" means a catalytic converter that has been previously installed on a vehicle and has been detached. It does not include a reconditioned or refurbished catalytic converter being sold at retail.

(c) A violation of this section is punishable as an infraction by a fine, as follows:

(1) For a first offense, by a fine of one thousand dollars ($1,000).

(2) For a second offense, by a fine of two thousand dollars ($2,000).

(3) For a third or subsequent offense, by a fine of four thousand dollars ($4,000). *(Added by Stats.2022, c. 514 (S.B.1087), § 2, eff. Jan. 1, 2023.)*

§ 10853. Malicious mischief to vehicle

No person shall with intent to commit any malicious mischief, injury, or other crime, climb into or upon a vehicle whether it is in motion or at rest, nor shall any person attempt to manipulate any of the levers, starting mechanism, brakes, or other mechanism or device of a vehicle while the same is at rest and unattended, nor shall any person set in motion any vehicle while the same is at rest and unattended. *(Stats.1959, c. 3, p. 1597, § 10853.)*

Cross References

Applicability of this section to trolley coaches, see Vehicle Code § 21051.
Procedure on arrest for violation of this section, see Vehicle Code § 40303.
Violation a misdemeanor, see Vehicle Code § 40000.9.
Violation of this section involving vehicle modified for use of disabled person, penalty, see Vehicle Code § 42002.5.

Research References

2 Witkin, California Criminal Law 4th Crimes Against Property § 308 (2021), Tampering or Injuring.
2 Witkin, California Criminal Law 4th Crimes Against Public Peace and Welfare § 267 (2021), Misdemeanors.

§ 10854. Unlawful use or tampering by bailee

Every person having the storage, care, safe-keeping, custody, or possession of any vehicle of a type subject to registration under this code who, without the consent of the owner, takes, hires, runs, drives, or uses the vehicle or who takes or removes any part thereof is guilty of a misdemeanor and upon conviction shall be punished by a fine of not exceeding one thousand dollars ($1,000) or by imprisonment in the county jail for not exceeding one year or by both. *(Stats.1959, c. 3, p. 1598, § 10854.)*

Cross References

Misdemeanor, see Penal Code §§ 17, 19, 19.2.
Owner defined, see Vehicle Code § 460.
Vehicles subject to registration, see Vehicle Code § 4000 et seq.
Violation a misdemeanor, see Vehicle Code § 40000.9.

Research References

2 Witkin, California Criminal Law 4th Crimes Against Property § 113 (2021), Related Offenses.
2 Witkin, California Criminal Law 4th Crimes Against Property § 308 (2021), Tampering or Injuring.

§ 10855. Leased and rented vehicles; contacting other party

Section operative until Jan. 1, 2024. See, also, § 10855 operative Jan. 1, 2024.

(a)(1) If a person who has leased or rented a vehicle willfully and intentionally fails to return the vehicle to its owner within 72 hours after the lease or rental agreement has expired, the person shall be presumed to have embezzled the vehicle.

(2) If the owner of a vehicle that has been leased or rented discovers that it was procured by fraud, the owner is not required to wait until the expiration of the lease or rental agreement to inform law enforcement pursuant to subdivision (c).

(b) The owner of an embezzled vehicle as described in paragraph (1) of subdivision (a) shall attempt to contact the other party to the lease or rental agreement who has failed to return the vehicle using the contact method designated in the rental agreement for this purpose. If the owner is able to contact the party, the owner shall inform the party that if arrangements for the return of the vehicle that are satisfactory for the owner are not made, the owner may report the vehicle stolen to law enforcement. If the owner is not able to contact the other party after a reasonable number of attempts, or, if upon contacting the other party, the owner is not able to arrange for the satisfactory return of the vehicle, the owner may report the vehicle stolen pursuant to subdivision (c).

(c) The owner of a vehicle that has been embezzled as described in paragraph (1) of subdivision (a), after satisfaction of the requirements of subdivision (b), or of a vehicle that was stolen as described in paragraph (2) of subdivision (a), may report this occurrence to a peace officer.

(d) The lease or rental agreement shall disclose that failure to return the vehicle within 72 hours of the expiration of the lease or rental agreement may result in the owner reporting the vehicle as stolen and shall require the lessee to provide a method to contact the lessee if the vehicle is not returned.

(e) Section 40000.1 does not apply to an owner who fails to comply with this section.

(f) This section shall remain in effect until January 1, 2024, and as of that date, is repealed. *(Stats.1959, c. 3, p. 1598, § 10855. Amended by Stats.2019, c. 609 (A.B.391), § 3, eff. Jan. 1, 2020.)*

Inoperative Date and Repeal

For inoperative date and repeal of this section, see its terms.

Cross References

Embezzlement, see Penal Code §§ 487, 490a, 503 et seq.
Reports of stolen vehicles, leased or rented vehicles, see Vehicle Code § 10500.

Research References

5 Witkin, California Criminal Law 4th Criminal Trial § 631 (2021), Presumptions of Knowledge or Intent.
1 Witkin California Criminal Law 4th Elements § 6 (2021), Evidence and Instructions.

§ 10855. Leased and rented vehicles

Section operative Jan. 1, 2024. See, also, § 10855 operative until Jan. 1, 2024.

(a) If a person who has leased or rented a vehicle willfully and intentionally fails to return the vehicle to its owner within five days after the lease or rental agreement has expired, the person shall be presumed to have embezzled the vehicle.

(b) This section shall become operative on January 1, 2024. *(Added by Stats.2019, c. 609 (A.B.391), § 4, eff. Jan. 1, 2020, operative Jan. 1, 2024.)*

Cross References

Embezzlement, see Penal Code §§ 487, 490a, 503 et seq.
Reports of stolen vehicles, leased or rented vehicles, see Vehicle Code § 10500.

Research References

5 Witkin, California Criminal Law 4th Criminal Trial § 631 (2021), Presumptions of Knowledge or Intent.
1 Witkin California Criminal Law 4th Elements § 6 (2021), Evidence and Instructions.

§ 10856. Interference with transport of vehicle; release of vehicle or collateral to person legally entitled

(a) A person shall not interfere with the transport of a vehicle to a storage facility, auction, or dealer by an individual who is employed by a repossession agency or who is licensed pursuant to Chapter 11 (commencing with Section 7500) of Division 3 of the Business and Professions Code once repossession is complete as provided in Section 7507.12 of the Business and Professions Code. This subdivision shall not apply to a peace officer while acting in an official capacity.

(b) Any tow yard, impounding agency, or governmental agency, or any person acting on behalf of those entities, shall not refuse to release a vehicle or other collateral to anyone that is legally entitled to that vehicle or other collateral. This subdivision shall not apply to a vehicle being held for evidence by law enforcement or a prosecuting attorney. *(Added by Stats.2014, c. 390 (A.B.2503), § 11, eff. Sept. 17, 2014.)*

Division 6

DRIVERS' LICENSES

CHAPTER 1. ISSUANCE OF LICENSES, EXPIRATION, AND RENEWAL

ARTICLE 1. PERSONS REQUIRED TO BE LICENSED, EXEMPTIONS, AND AGE LIMITS

§ 12500. License requirements; motorized scooter engine requirements

(a) A person may not drive a motor vehicle upon a highway, unless the person then holds a valid driver's license issued under this code, except those persons who are expressly exempted under this code.

(b) A person may not drive a motorcycle, motor-driven cycle, or motorized bicycle upon a highway, unless the person then holds a valid driver's license or endorsement issued under this code for that class, except those persons who are expressly exempted under this code, or those persons specifically authorized to operate motorized bicycles or motorized scooters with a valid driver's license of any class, as specified in subdivision (h) of Section 12804.9.

(c) A person may not drive a motor vehicle in or upon any offstreet parking facility, unless the person then holds a valid driver's license of the appropriate class or certification to operate the vehicle. As used in this subdivision, "offstreet parking facility" means any offstreet facility held open for use by the public for parking vehicles and includes any publicly owned facilities for offstreet parking, and privately owned facilities for offstreet parking where no fee is charged for the privilege to park and which are held open for the common public use of retail customers.

(d) A person may not drive a motor vehicle or combination of vehicles that is not of a type for which the person is licensed.

(e) A motorized scooter operated on public streets shall at all times be equipped with an engine that complies with the applicable State Air Resources Board emission requirements. *(Stats.1959, c. 3, p. 1613, § 12500. Amended by Stats.1961, c. 1615, p. 3453, § 5; Stats.1963, c. 74, p. 700, § 2; Stats.1984, c. 621, § 2; Stats.1990, c. 1359 (A.B.55), § 3; Stats.1993, c. 272 (A.B.301), § 17, eff. Aug. 2, 1993; Stats.1993, c. 1292 (S.B.274), § 7; Stats.1996, c. 10 (A.B.1869), § 12, eff. Feb. 9, 1996; Stats.2004, c. 755 (A.B.1878), § 3; Stats.2007, c. 630 (A.B.1728), § 3.)*

Cross References

Certain violations constituting misdemeanors, see Vehicle Code § 40000.11.
Conduct of sobriety checkpoint inspection, vehicle impoundment and release, see Vehicle Code § 2814.2.
Driver license compact, see Vehicle Code § 15000 et seq.
Driver's license defined, see Vehicle Code § 310.
Driving when privileges suspended or revoked, see Vehicle Code § 14601.
Employment of unlicensed motor vehicle attendant, see Vehicle Code § 14605.
Highway defined, see Vehicle Code § 360.
Offense under this section as infraction, see Penal Code § 19.8.
Permitting unlicensed person to drive as offense, see Vehicle Code § 14606.
Removal of vehicle, circumstances permitting, see Vehicle Code § 22651.
Renting vehicle to unlicensed person, see Vehicle Code § 14608.
Transportation of agricultural irrigation supplies, inspection of bills of lading, shipping, or delivery papers, care of apprehended supplies, see Vehicle Code § 2810.2.

Research References

California Jury Instructions - Criminal 16.630, Driving Without Being Licensed.
California Jury Instructions - Criminal 16.840, Reckless Driving.
2 Witkin, California Criminal Law 4th Crimes Against Public Peace and Welfare § 305 (2021), Driving Without Valid License.
2 Witkin, California Criminal Law 4th Crimes Against Public Peace and Welfare § 310 (2021), Unlawful Use of License.
1 Witkin California Criminal Law 4th Elements § 18 (2021), Public Welfare Offenses.
1 Witkin California Criminal Law 4th Introduction to Crimes § 90 (2021), Misdemeanor-Infraction.
4 Witkin, California Criminal Law 4th Pretrial Proceedings § 60 (2021), Juvenile Offenses.
3 Witkin, California Criminal Law 4th Punishment § 289 (2021), Theft and Other Crimes.

§ 12501. Persons exempt

The following persons are not required to obtain a driver's license:

(a) An officer or employee of the United States, while operating a motor vehicle owned or controlled by the United States on the business of the United States, except when the motor vehicle being operated is a commercial motor vehicle, as defined in Section 15210.

(b) Any person while driving or operating implements of husbandry incidentally operated or moved over a highway, except as provided in Section 36300 or 36305.

(c) Any person driving or operating an off-highway motor vehicle subject to identification, as defined in Section 38012, while driving or operating such motor vehicle as provided in Section 38025. Nothing in this subdivision authorizes operation of a motor vehicle by a person without a valid driver's license upon any offstreet parking facility, as defined in subdivision (c) of Section 12500. *(Stats.1959, c. 3, p. 1614, § 12501. Amended by Stats.1959, c. 1685, p. 4084, § 1; Stats.1963, c. 268, p. 1025, § 2; Stats.1963, c. 2149, p. 4487, § 13; Stats.1969, c. 1075, p. 2064, § 8; Stats.1972, c. 973, p. 1758, § 16, eff. Aug. 16, 1972; Stats.1984, c. 621, § 3; Stats.1986, c. 973, § 2; Stats.1990, c. 1360 (S.B.1510), § 10.)*

Cross References

Definitions,
Implement of husbandry, see Vehicle Code § 36000.
Motor vehicle, see Vehicle Code § 415.
Nonresidents exempt, see Vehicle Code § 12502 et seq.
Vehicles exempt from registration, see Vehicle Code §§ 4002, 4006 et seq., 6700 et seq.

Research References

California Jury Instructions - Criminal 16.630, Driving Without Being Licensed.
2 Witkin, California Criminal Law 4th Crimes Against Public Peace and Welfare § 305 (2021), Driving Without Valid License.

§ 12502. Persons who may operate a motor vehicle without obtaining a driver's license; exemption requiring a medical certificate; compliance with medical certificate restrictions

(a) The following persons may operate a motor vehicle in this state without obtaining a driver's license under this code:

(1) A nonresident over the age of 18 years having in his or her immediate possession a valid driver's license issued by a foreign jurisdiction of which he or she is a resident, except as provided in Section 12505.

(2) A nonresident, 21 years of age or older, if transporting hazardous material, as defined in Section 353, in a commercial vehicle, having in his or her immediate possession, a valid license with the appropriate endorsement issued by another state or other jurisdiction that is recognized by the department, or a Canadian driver's license and a copy of his or her current training certificate to transport hazardous material that complies with all federal laws and regulations with respect to hazardous materials, both of which shall be in his or her immediate possession.

(3) A nonresident having in his or her immediate possession a valid driver's license, issued by the Diplomatic Motor Vehicle Office of the Office of Foreign Missions of the United States Department of State, for the type of motor vehicle or combination of vehicles that the person is operating.

(b)(1) A driver required to have a commercial driver's license under Part 383 of Title 49 of the Code of Federal Regulations who submits a current medical examiner's certificate to the licensing state in accordance with Section 383.71(h) of Subpart E of Part 383 of Title 49 of the Code of Federal Regulations, documenting that he or she meets the physical qualification requirements of Section 391.41 of Subpart E of Part 391 of Title 49 of the Code of Federal Regulations, is not required to carry on his or her person the medical examiner's certificate or a copy of that certificate.

(2) A driver may use the date-stamped receipt, given to the driver by the licensing state agency, for up to 15 days after the date stamped on the receipt, as proof of medical certification.

(c) A nonresident possessing a medical certificate in accordance with subdivision (b) shall comply with any restriction of the medical certificate issued to that nonresident.

(d) This section shall become operative on January 31, 2014. *(Added by Stats.2012, c. 670 (A.B.2188), § 2.5, operative Jan. 31, 2014.)*

Cross References

Nonresident defined, see Vehicle Code § 435.
Renting vehicle to nonresident licensed in his own state, see Vehicle Code § 14608.

Research References

California Jury Instructions - Criminal 16.630, Driving Without Being Licensed.

§ 12503. Unlicensed nonresident

A nonresident over the age of 18 years whose home state or country does not require the licensing of drivers may operate a foreign vehicle owned by him for not to exceed 30 days without obtaining a license under this code. *(Stats.1959, c. 3, p. 1614, § 12503. Amended by Stats.1961, c. 1615, p. 3453, § 7; Stats.1971, c. 1748, p. 3763, § 55, operative March 4, 1972.)*

Research References

California Jury Instructions - Criminal 16.630, Driving Without Being Licensed.

§ 12504. Nonresident minors

(a) Sections 12502 and 12503 apply to any nonresident over the age of 16 years but under the age of 18 years. The maximum period during which that nonresident may operate a motor vehicle in this state without obtaining a driver's license is limited to a period of 10 days immediately following the entry of the nonresident into this state except as provided in subdivision (b) of this section.

(b) Any nonresident over the age of 16 years but under the age of 18 years who is a resident of a foreign jurisdiction which requires the licensing of drivers may continue to operate a motor vehicle in this state after 10 days from his or her date of entry into this state if he or she meets both the following:

(1) He or she has a valid driver's license, issued by the foreign jurisdiction, in his or her immediate possession.

(2) He or she has been issued and has in his or her immediate possession a nonresident minor's certificate, which the department issues to a nonresident minor who holds a valid driver's license issued to him or her by his or her home state or country, and who files proof of financial responsibility.

(c) Whenever any of the conditions for the issuance of a nonresident minor's certificate cease to exist, the department shall cancel the certificate and require the minor to surrender it to the department. *(Stats.1959, c. 3, p. 1614, § 12504. Amended by Stats.1963, c. 237, p. 978, § 3; Stats.1963, c. 666, p. 1654, § 3; Stats.1967, c. 478, p. 1683, § 2; Stats.1971, c. 1748, p. 3763, § 56, operative March 4, 1972; Stats.1992, c. 974 (S.B.1600), § 4, eff. Sept. 28, 1992.)*

Cross References

Application of this section to nonresident members of the armed forces under the age of 18, see Vehicle Code § 12518.
Failure to surrender nonresident minor's certificate as ground for refusal to issue or renew a driver's license, see Vehicle Code § 12809.
Permitting unlicensed minor to drive, see Vehicle Code § 14607.
Student licenses if parent or guardian is nonresident, see Vehicle Code § 12650.

§ 12505. Residency

(a)(1) For purposes of this division only and notwithstanding Section 516, residency shall be determined as a person's state of domicile. "State of domicile" means the state where a person has * * * their true, fixed, and permanent home and principal residence and to which * * * the person has manifested the intention of returning whenever * * * they are absent.

Prima facie evidence of residency for driver's licensing purposes includes, but is not limited to, the following:

(A) Address where registered to vote.

(B) Payment of resident tuition at a public institution of higher education.

(C) Filing a homeowner's property tax exemption.

(D) Other acts, occurrences, or events that indicate presence in the state is more than temporary or transient.

(2) California residency is required of a person in order to be issued a commercial driver's license under this code.

(b) The presumption of residency in this state may be rebutted by satisfactory evidence that the licensee's primary residence is in another state.

(c) A person entitled to an exemption under Section 12502, 12503, or 12504 may operate a motor vehicle in this state for not to exceed 10 days from the date * * * the person establishes residence in this state, except that a person shall not operate a motor vehicle for employment in this state after establishing residency without first obtaining a license from the department.

(d) If the State of California is decertified by the federal government and prohibited from issuing an initial, renewal, or upgraded commercial driver's license pursuant to Section 384.405 of Title 49 of the Code of Federal Regulations, the following applies:

(1) An existing commercial driver's license issued pursuant to this code prior to the date that the state is notified of its decertification shall remain valid until its expiration date.

(2) A person who is a resident of this state may obtain a nondomiciled commercial learner's permit or commercial driver's license from any state that elects to issue a nondomiciled commercial learner's permit or commercial driver's license and that complies with the testing and licensing standards contained in subparts F, G, and H of Part 383 of Title 49 of the Code of Federal Regulations.

(3) For the purposes of this subdivision, a nondomiciled commercial learner's permit or commercial driver's license is a commercial learner's permit or commercial driver's license issued by a state to an individual domiciled in a foreign country or in another state.

(e) The department may issue a nondomiciled commercial learner's permit or nondomiciled commercial driver's license to a person who is domiciled in a state or jurisdiction that has been decertified by the federal government or not determined to be in compliance with the testing and licensing standards contained in subparts F, G, and H of Part 383 of Title 49 of the Code of Federal Regulations.

(f) Subject to Section 12504, a person over the age of 16 years who is a resident of a foreign jurisdiction other than a state, territory, or possession of the United States, the District of Columbia, the Commonwealth of Puerto Rico, or Canada, having a valid driver's license issued to * * * the person by any other foreign jurisdiction may operate a motor vehicle in this state without obtaining a license from the department, unless the department determines that the foreign jurisdiction does not meet the licensing standards imposed by this code.

(g) A person who is 18 years of age or older and in possession of a valid commercial learner's permit or commercial driver's license issued by * * * a foreign jurisdiction that meets the licensing standards contained in subparts F, G, and H of Part 383 of Title 49 of the Code of Federal Regulations shall be granted reciprocity to operate vehicles of the appropriate class on the highways of this state.

(h) A person from a foreign jurisdiction that does not meet the licensing standards contained in subparts F, G, and H of Part 383 of Title 49 of the Code of Federal Regulations shall obtain a commercial learner's permit or commercial driver's license from the department before operating on the highways a motor vehicle for which a commercial driver's license is required, as described in Section 12804.9. The medical examination form required for issuance of a commercial driver's license shall be completed by a health care professional, as defined in paragraph (2) of subdivision (a) of Section 12804.9, who is licensed, certified, or registered to perform physical examinations in the United States of America. This subdivision does not apply to (1) drivers of schoolbuses operated in California on a trip for educational purposes or (2) drivers of vehicles used to provide the services of a local public agency.

(i) This section does not authorize the employment of a person in violation of Section 12515. *(Stats.1959, c. 3, p. 1614, § 12505. Amended by Stats.1961, c. 1614, p. 3451, § 1; Stats.1963, c. 209, p. 949, § 5, eff. April 29, 1963; Stats.1963, c. 237, p. 978, § 4; Stats.1963, c. 666, p. 1655, § 4; Stats.1970, c. 166, p. 408, § 1; Stats.1983, c. 1000, § 8; Stats.1991, c. 13 (A.B.37), § 27, eff. Feb. 13, 1991; Stats.1993, c. 272 (A.B.301), § 19, eff. Aug. 2, 1993; Stats.1995, c. 766 (S.B.726), § 10; Stats.2004, c. 952 (A.B.3049), § 3, operative Sept. 20, 2005; Stats.2013, c. 649 (A.B.1047), § 1; Stats.2022, c. 295 (A.B.2956), § 11, eff. Jan. 1, 2023.)*

§ 12506. Temporary licenses

The department may issue a temporary driver's license to any person applying for a driver's license, to any person applying for renewal of a driver's license, or to any licensee whose license is required to be changed, added to, or modified. Notwithstanding paragraph (3) of subdivision (a) of Section 12805, the department may issue a temporary driver's license to an applicant who has previously been licensed in this state or in any other state, territory, or possession of the United States, the District of Columbia, the Commonwealth of Puerto Rico, or the Dominion of Canada, notwithstanding that the applicant has failed the written examination on the person's first attempt.

A temporary license permits the operation of a motor vehicle upon the highways for a period of 60 days, if the licensee has the temporary license in his or her immediate possession, and while the department is completing its investigation and determination of all facts relative to the applicant's right to receive a license. The temporary license is invalid when the applicant's license has been issued or refused. *(Stats.1959, c. 3, p. 1614, § 12506. Amended by Stats.1961, c. 1615, p. 3453, § 9; Stats.1971, c. 1214, p. 2343, § 11, operative May 3, 1972; Stats.1973, c. 891, p. 1661, § 1, eff. Sept. 28, 1973, operative Oct. 1, 1973; Stats.1985, c. 743, § 1; Stats.1987, c. 321, § 2; Stats.2016, c. 339 (S.B.838), § 7, eff. Sept. 13, 2016.)*

Cross References

Application for license, contents, see Vehicle Code § 12800.

§ 12508. Limited term license

When in the opinion of the department it would be in the interest of safety, the department may issue, in individual cases, to any applicant for a driver's license, a license limited in duration to less than the regular term. Upon the expiration of a limited term license the department may extend its duration for an additional period without fee but the duration of the license and extensions shall not exceed the term of a regular license. *(Stats.1959, c. 3, p. 1615, § 12508.)*

Cross References

Expiration of driver's license, see Vehicle Code § 12816.

§ 12509. Instruction permits for certain motor vehicles; duration of permit

(a) Except as otherwise provided in subdivision (f) of Section 12514, the department, for good cause, may issue an instruction permit to a physically and mentally qualified person who meets one of the following requirements and who applies to the department for an instruction permit:

(1) Is 15 years and 6 months of age or older, and has successfully completed approved courses in automobile driver education and driver training as provided in paragraph (3) of subdivision (a) of Section 12814.6.

(2) Is 15 years and 6 months of age or older, and has successfully completed an approved course in automobile driver education and is taking driver training as provided in paragraph (3) of subdivision (a) of Section 12814.6.

(3) Is 15 years and 6 months of age and enrolled and participating in an integrated automobile driver education and training program as provided in subparagraph (B) of paragraph (3) of subdivision (a) of Section 12814.6.

(4) Is over 16 years of age and is applying for a restricted driver's license pursuant to Section 12814.7.

(5) Is over 17 years and 6 months of age.

(b) The applicant shall qualify for, and be issued, an instruction permit within 12 months from the date of the application.

(c) An instruction permit issued pursuant to subdivision (a) shall entitle the applicant to operate a vehicle, subject to the limitations imposed by this section and any other provisions of law, upon the highways for a period not exceeding 24 months from the date of the application.

(d) Except as provided in Section 12814.6, a person, while having in * * * their immediate possession a valid permit issued pursuant to paragraphs (1) to (3), inclusive, of, and paragraph (5) of, subdivision (a), may operate a motor vehicle, other than a motorcycle, motorized scooter, or a motorized bicycle, when accompanied by, and under the immediate supervision of, a California-licensed driver with a valid license of the appropriate class who is 18 years of age or over and whose driving privilege is not subject to probation. An accompanying licensed driver at all times shall occupy a position within the driver's compartment that would enable the accompanying licensed driver to assist the person in controlling the vehicle as may be necessary to avoid a collision and to provide immediate guidance in the safe operation of the vehicle.

(e) A person, while having in * * * their immediate possession a valid permit issued pursuant to paragraph (4) of subdivision (a), may only operate a government-owned motor vehicle, other than a motorcycle, motorized scooter, or a motorized bicycle, when taking driver training instruction administered by the California National Guard.

(f) The department may also issue an instruction permit to a person who has been issued a valid driver's license to authorize the person to obtain driver training instruction and to practice that instruction in order to obtain another class of driver's license or an endorsement.

(g) The department may further restrict permits issued under subdivision (a) as it may determine to be appropriate to ensure the safe operation of a motor vehicle by the permittee. *(Added by Stats.1974, c. 644, p. 1507, § 2. Amended by Stats.1976, c. 645, p. 1594, § 1; Stats.1977, c. 579, p. 1914, § 183; Stats.1995, c. 766 (S.B.726), § 11; Stats.1997, c. 760 (S.B.1329), § 4; Stats.2000, c. 1035 (S.B.1403), § 14; Stats.2001, c. 825 (S.B.290), § 13; Stats.2002, c. 418 (A.B.2273), § 2; Stats.2002, c. 758 (A.B.3024), § 11.5; Stats.2003, c. 62 (S.B.600), § 305; Stats.2003, c. 768 (A.B.1343), § 2; Stats.2004, c. 183 (A.B.3082), § 352; Stats.2004, c. 755 (A.B.1878), § 4; Stats.2005, c. 22 (S.B.1108), § 198; Stats.2006, c. 538 (S.B.1852), § 656; Stats.2010, c. 586 (A.B.1952), § 2; Stats.2011, c. 296 (A.B.1023), § 303; Stats.2022, c. 295 (A.B.2956), § 12, eff. Jan. 1, 2023.)*

Cross References

Provisional driver's licenses, demonstration program, see Vehicle Code § 12814.6.
Provisional restricted class C license for operation of army and national guard vehicles, conditions, see Vehicle Code § 12814.7.
Student licenses, see Vehicle Code § 12650 et seq.

§ 12509.5. Instruction permits; motorcycles, motorized bicycles, moped, etc.

(a) A person shall obtain an instruction permit issued pursuant to this section before operating, or being issued a class M1 or M2 driver's license to operate, a two-wheel motorcycle, motor-driven cycle, motorized bicycle, moped, or bicycle with an attached motor. The person shall meet the following requirements to obtain an instruction permit for purposes of this section:

(1) If age 15 years and 6 months or older, but under the age of 18 years, the applicant shall meet all of the following requirements:

(A) Have a valid class C license or complete driver education and training pursuant to paragraph (3) of subdivision (a) of Section 12814.6.

(B) Successfully complete a motorcyclist safety program that is operated pursuant to Article 2 (commencing with Section 2930) of Chapter 5 of Division 2.

(C) Pass the motorcycle driver's written exam.

(2) If 18 years of age or older, but under 21 years of age, the applicant shall meet both of the following requirements:

(A) Successfully complete a motorcyclist safety program that is operated pursuant to Article 2 (commencing with Section 2930) of Chapter 5 of Division 2.

(B) Pass the motorcycle driver's written exam.

(3) If 21 years of age or older, pass the motorcycle driver's written exam.

(b) A person described in paragraph (1) or (2) of subdivision (a) shall hold an instruction permit issued pursuant to this section for a minimum of six months before being issued a class M1 or M2 license.

(c) A person issued an instruction permit pursuant to this section shall not operate a two-wheel motorcycle, motor-driven cycle, motorized bicycle, moped, or bicycle with an attached motor during the hours of darkness, shall stay off any freeways that have full control of access and have no crossings at grade, and shall not carry any passenger except an instructor licensed under Chapter 1 (commencing with Section 11100) of Division 5 or a qualified instructor as defined in Section 41907 of the Education Code.

(d) An instruction permit issued pursuant to this section shall be valid for a period not exceeding 24 months from the date of application.

(e) The department may perform, during regularly scheduled computer system maintenance and upgrades, any necessary software updates related to the changes made by the addition, during the 2009–10 Regular Session, of this section. *(Added by Stats.2010, c. 586 (A.B.1952), § 3. Amended by Stats.2019, c. 636 (A.B.1810), § 6, eff. Jan. 1, 2020.)*

§ 12511. Licensee entitled to one license

No person shall have in his or her possession or otherwise under his or her control more than one driver's license. *(Added by Stats.1959, c. 298, p. 2207, § 2. Amended by Stats.1961, c. 1615, p. 3453, § 11; Stats.1988, c. 1509, § 4.)*

§ 12512. Issuance of licenses to persons under the age of 18 years

Except as provided in Sections 12513, 12514, and 12814.6, no license to drive shall be issued to a person under the age of 18 years. *(Added by Stats.2000, c. 596 (A.B.2909), § 6.)*

Cross References

Prospective employers of drivers of vehicles requiring certain licenses or certificates, class C license issued pursuant to this section, see Vehicle Code § 1808.1.

§ 12513. Junior permits; issuance

(a) Upon application, successful completion of tests and compliance with Sections 17700 to 17705, inclusive, the department may issue a junior permit to any person 14 years of age, but less than 18, who establishes eligibility as required by this section. A person is eligible when, in the opinion of the department, any one or more of the following circumstances exist:

School or other transportation facilities are inadequate for regular attendance at school and at activities authorized by the school. The application for a junior permit shall be accompanied by a signed statement from the school principal verifying such facts. A junior permit issued under this subsection shall be restricted to operating a vehicle from residence to the school and return.

Reasonable transportation facilities are inadequate and operation of a vehicle by a minor is necessary due to illness of a family member. The application shall be accompanied by a signed statement from a physician familiar with the condition, containing a diagnosis and probable date when sufficient recovery will have been made to terminate the emergency.

Transportation facilities are inadequate, and use of a motor vehicle is necessary in the transportation to and from the employment of the applicant and the applicant's income from such employment is essential in the support of the family, or where the applicant's operation of a motor vehicle is essential to an enterprise from which an appreciable portion of the income of the family will be derived. The application shall be accompanied by a signed statement from the parents or the guardian, setting forth the reasons a permit is necessary under this subsection.

(b) The existence of public transportation at reasonable intervals within one mile of the residence of the applicant may be considered adequate grounds for refusal of a junior permit.

(c) The department shall impose restrictions upon junior permits appropriate to the conditions and area under which they are intended to be used. *(Stats.1959, c. 3, p. 1615, § 12513. Amended by Stats.1959, c. 1996, p. 4624, § 16.5; Stats.1969, c. 947, p. 1891, § 1.)*

§ 12514. Junior permits; duration; revocation

(a) Junior permits issued pursuant to Section 12513 shall not be valid for a period exceeding that established on the original request as the approximate date the minor's operation of a vehicle will no longer be necessary. In any event, no permit shall be valid on or after the 18th birthday of the applicant.

(b) The department may revoke any permit when to do so is necessary for the welfare of the minor or in the interests of safety.

(c) If conditions or location of residence, which required the minor's operation of a vehicle, change prior to expiration of the permit, the department may cancel the permit.

(d) Upon a determination that the permittee has operated a vehicle in violation of restrictions, the department shall revoke the permit.

(e) A junior permit is a form of driver's license that shall include all information required by subdivision (a) of Section 12811 except for an engraved picture or photograph of the permittee, and is subject to all provisions of this code applying to driver's licenses, except as otherwise provided in this section and Section 12513.

(f) An instruction permit valid for a period of not more than six months may be issued after eligibility has been established under Section 12513.

(g) The department shall cancel any permit six months from the date of issuance unless the permittee has complied with one of the conditions prescribed by paragraph (3) of subdivision (a) of Section 12814.6. *(Stats.1959, c. 3, p. 1616, § 12514. Amended by Stats.1959, c. 1996, p. 4624, § 17; Stats.1961, c. 1615, p. 3454, § 13; Stats.1969, c. 947, p. 1893, § 2; Stats.1992, c. 1243 (A.B.3090), § 80, eff. Sept. 30, 1992; Stats.1997, c. 760 (S.B.1329), § 6; Stats.1998, c. 485 (A.B. 2803), § 158; Stats.2000, c. 1035 (S.B.1403), § 15.)*

Cross References

Instruction permits, see Vehicle Code § 12509.

§ 12515. Driving for hire; age limit

(a) No person under the age of 18 years shall be employed for compensation by another for the purpose of driving a motor vehicle on the highways.

(b) No person under the age of 21 years shall be employed for compensation by another to drive, and no person under the age of 21 years may drive a motor vehicle, as defined in Section 34500 or subdivision (b) of Section 15210, that is engaged in interstate commerce, or any motor vehicle that is engaged in the interstate or intrastate transportation of hazardous material, as defined in Section 353. *(Stats.1959, c. 3, p. 1617, § 12515. Amended by Stats.1961, c. 1615, p. 3454, § 14; Stats.1984, c. 779, § 3; Stats.1986, c. 434, § 2; Stats.1988, c. 1509, § 5.)*

Cross References

Parents' or guardian's signature to minor's application for license, see Vehicle Code § 17701.
Permitting unlicensed minor to drive as offense, see Vehicle Code § 14607.
Persons not of legal age, denial of license, see Vehicle Code § 12805.
Prima facie evidence, see Evidence Code § 602.
Violation as misdemeanor, see Vehicle Code § 40000.11.

§ 12516. Age for driving school bus

It is unlawful for any person under the age of 18 years to drive a school bus transporting pupils to or from school. *(Stats.1959, c. 3, p. 1617, § 12516.)*

Cross References

Minimum age, driving for hire license, see Vehicle Code § 12515.
Schoolbus defined, see Vehicle Code § 545.

§ 12517. Schoolbus and pupil activity bus drivers; qualifications; certificates; fees

(a)(1) A person may not operate a schoolbus while transporting pupils unless that person has in his or her immediate possession a valid driver's license for the appropriate class of vehicle to be driven endorsed for schoolbus and passenger transportation.

(2) When transporting one or more pupils at or below the 12th–grade level to or from a public or private school or to or from public

or private school activities, the person described in paragraph (1) shall have in his or her immediate possession a certificate issued by the department to permit the operation of a schoolbus.

(b) A person may not operate a school pupil activity bus unless that person has in his or her immediate possession a valid driver's license for the appropriate class of vehicle to be driven endorsed for passenger transportation. When transporting one or more pupils at or below the 12th–grade level to or from public or private school activities, the person shall also have in his or her immediate possession a certificate issued by the department to permit the operation of school pupil activity buses.

(c) The applicant for a certificate to operate a schoolbus or school pupil activity bus shall meet the eligibility and training requirements specified for schoolbus and school pupil activity busdrivers in this code, the Education Code, and regulations adopted by the Department of the California Highway Patrol, and, in addition to the fee authorized in Section 2427, shall pay a fee of twenty-five dollars ($25) with the application for issuance of an original certificate, and a fee of twelve dollars ($12) for the renewal of that certificate. *(Stats. 1959, c. 3, p. 1617, § 12517. Amended by Stats.1961, c. 1615, p. 3454, § 15; Stats.1982, c. 1233, p. 4544, § 1; Stats.1982, c. 1273, p. 4703, § 16; Stats.1990, c. 104 (S.B.798), § 3, eff. May 23, 1990; Stats.1990, c. 1360 (S.B.1510), § 11; Stats.1996, c. 440 (S.B.1588), § 8; Stats. 2004, c. 952 (A.B.3049), § 4, operative Sept. 20, 2005; Stats.2005, c. 199 (A.B.1748), § 2; Stats.2006, c. 574 (A.B.2520), § 7.)*

Cross References

School pupil activity bus, definition and driver regulations, see Vehicle Code § 546.
Schoolbus and school pupil activity bus driver training course, see Education Code § 40070.
Schoolbus defined, see Vehicle Code § 545.
Traffic violation point count, number giving rise to presumptions of negligence by certificate or license holder, see Vehicle Code § 12810.5.
Training courses for certification under this section, see Education Code § 40080 et seq.
Violation as misdemeanor, see Vehicle Code § 40000.11.

Research References

2 Witkin, California Criminal Law 4th Crimes Against Public Peace and Welfare § 305 (2021), Driving Without Valid License.

§ 12517.1. "Schoolbus accident" defined; investigation

(a) A "schoolbus accident" means any of the following:

(1) A motor vehicle accident resulting in property damage in excess of one thousand dollars ($1,000), or personal injury, on public or private property, and involving a schoolbus, youth bus, school pupil activity bus, or general public paratransit vehicle transporting a pupil.

(2) A collision between a vehicle and a pupil or a schoolbus driver while the pupil or driver is crossing the highway when the schoolbus flashing red signal lamps are required to be operated pursuant to Section 22112 or when the schoolbus is stopped for the purpose of loading or unloading pupils.

(3) Injury of a pupil inside a vehicle described in paragraph (1) as a result of acceleration, deceleration, or other movement of the vehicle.

(b) The Department of the California Highway Patrol shall investigate all schoolbus accidents, except that accidents involving only property damage and occurring entirely on private property shall be investigated only if they involve a violation of this code.

(c) This section shall become operative on January 1, 2017. *(Added by Stats.2015, c. 451 (S.B.491), § 24, eff. Jan. 1, 2016, operative Jan. 1, 2017.)*

§ 12517.2. Bus drivers and farm labor vehicle operators; applications for certificates; medical examination

(a) Applicants for an original or renewal certificate to drive a schoolbus, school pupil activity bus, youth bus, general public paratransit vehicle, or farm labor vehicle shall submit a report of a medical examination of the applicant given not more than two years prior to the date of the application by a physician licensed to practice medicine, a licensed advanced practice registered nurse qualified to perform a medical examination, a licensed physician assistant, or a licensed doctor of chiropractic listed on the most current National Registry of Certified Medical Examiners, as adopted by the United States Department of Transportation, as published by the notice in the Federal Register, Volume 77, Number 77, Friday, April 20, 2012, on pages 24104 to 24135, inclusive, and pursuant to Section 391.42 of Title 49 of the Code of Federal Regulations. The report shall be on a form approved by the department.

(b) Schoolbus drivers, within the same month of reaching 65 years of age and each 12th month thereafter, shall undergo a medical examination, pursuant to Section 12804.9, and shall submit a report of that medical examination on a form as specified in subdivision (a). *(Added by Stats.1990, c. 1360 (S.B.1510), § 13. Amended by Stats. 1993, c. 272 (A.B.301), § 20, eff. Aug. 2, 1993; Stats.2007, c. 158 (A.B.139), § 1; Stats.2012, c. 670 (A.B.2188), § 3; Stats.2013, c. 160 (A.B.722), § 1.)*

§ 12517.3. Fingerprints; bus and ambulance drivers

(a)(1) An applicant for an original certificate to drive a schoolbus, school pupil activity bus, youth bus, or general public paratransit vehicle shall be fingerprinted by the Department of the California Highway Patrol, on a form provided or approved by the Department of the California Highway Patrol for submission to the Department of Justice, utilizing the Applicant Expedite Service or an electronic fingerprinting system.

(2) An applicant fingerprint form shall be processed and returned to the office of the Department of the California Highway Patrol from which it originated not later than 15 working days from the date on which the fingerprint form was received by the Department of Justice, unless circumstances, other than the administrative duties of the Department of Justice, warrant further investigation.

(3) Applicant fingerprints that are submitted by utilizing an electronic fingerprinting system shall be processed and returned to the appropriate office of the Department of the California Highway Patrol within three working days.

(4) The commissioner may utilize the California Law Enforcement Telecommunications System to conduct a preliminary criminal and driver history check to determine an applicant's eligibility to hold an original or renewal certificate to drive a schoolbus, school pupil activity bus, youth bus, or general public paratransit vehicle.

(b)(1) Notwithstanding subdivision (a), an applicant for an original certificate to drive a schoolbus, school pupil activity bus, youth bus, or general public paratransit vehicle may be fingerprinted by a public law enforcement agency, a school district, or a county office of education utilizing an electronic fingerprinting system with terminals managed by the Department of Justice.

(2) The Department of Justice shall provide the fingerprint information processed pursuant to this subdivision to the appropriate office of the Department of the California Highway Patrol within three working days of receipt of the information.

(3) An applicant for an original certificate to drive an ambulance shall submit a completed fingerprint card to the department. *(Added by Stats.1990, c. 1360 (S.B.1510), § 14. Amended by Stats.1997, c. 738 (A.B.1238), § 1; Stats.1999, c. 229 (A.B.128), § 1, eff. Aug. 25, 1999; Stats.2006, c. 311 (S.B.1586), § 7.)*

Cross References

Fingerprint rollers, qualification and certification of persons, necessity of certificate, see Penal Code § 11102.1.

§ 12517.4. Regulations for issuance of certificate to drive a schoolbus, school pupil activity bus, youth bus, paratransit vehicle, or farm labor vehicle

This section governs the issuance of a certificate to drive a schoolbus, school pupil activity bus, youth bus, general public paratransit vehicle, or farm labor vehicle.

(a) The driver certificate shall be issued only to applicants meeting all applicable provisions of this code and passing the examinations prescribed by the department and the Department of the California Highway Patrol. The examinations shall be conducted by the Department of the California Highway Patrol, pursuant to Sections 12517, 12519, 12522, 12523, and 12523.5.

(b) A temporary driver certificate shall be issued by the Department of the California Highway Patrol after an applicant has cleared a criminal history background check by the Department of Justice and, if applicable, the Federal Bureau of Investigation, and has passed the examinations and meets all other applicable provisions of this code.

(c) A permanent driver's certificate shall be issued by the department after an applicant has passed all tests and met all applicable provisions of this code. Certificates are valid for a maximum of five years and shall expire on the fifth birthday following the issuance of an original certificate or the expiration of the certificate renewed.

(d) A holder of a certificate may not violate any restriction placed on the certificate. Depending upon the type of vehicle used in the driving test and the abilities and physical condition of the applicant, the Department of the California Highway Patrol and the department may place restrictions on a certificate to assure the safe operation of a motor vehicle and safe transportation of passengers. These restrictions may include, but are not limited to, all of the following:

(1) Automatic transmission only.

(2) Hydraulic brakes only.

(3) Type 2 bus only.

(4) Conventional or type 2 bus only.

(5) Two-axle motor truck or passenger vehicle only.

(e) A holder of a certificate may not drive a motor vehicle equipped with a two-speed rear axle unless the certificate is endorsed: "May drive vehicle with two-speed rear axle."

(f) This section shall become operative on September 20, 2005. *(Added by Stats.1990, c. 1360 (S.B.1510), § 15. Amended by Stats. 1996, c. 1043 (A.B.2352), § 1; Stats.2004, c. 952 (A.B.3049), § 5, operative Sept. 20, 2005.)*

§ 12517.45. Transporting school pupils; requirements

(a) A person shall not operate a motor vehicle described in subdivision (k) of Section 545 while transporting school pupils at or below the 12th–grade level to or from a public or private school or to or from public or private school activities, unless all of the following requirements are met:

(1) The person has in his or her immediate possession all of the following:

(A) A valid driver's license of a class appropriate to the vehicle driven and that is endorsed for passenger transportation.

(B) Either a certificate to drive a schoolbus as described in Section 40082 of the Education Code, or a certificate to drive a school pupil activity bus as described in Section 40083 of the Education Code, issued by the department in accordance with eligibility and training requirements specified by the department, the State Department of Education, and the Department of the California Highway Patrol.

(C) A parental authorization form for each pupil signed by a parent or a legal guardian of the pupil that gives permission for that pupil to be transported to or from the school or school-related activity.

(2)(A) The motor vehicle has passed an annual inspection conducted by the Department of the California Highway Patrol and is in compliance with the charter-party carrier's responsibilities under Section 5374 of the Public Utilities Code.

(B) The Department of the California Highway Patrol may charge a charter-party carrier a reasonable fee sufficient to cover the costs incurred by the Department of the California Highway Patrol in conducting the annual inspection of a motor vehicle.

(b) A driver of a motor vehicle described in subdivision (k) of Section 545 shall comply with the duties specified in subdivision (a) of Section 5384.1 of the Public Utilities Code. *(Added by Stats.2008, c. 649 (A.B.830), § 4.)*

Cross References

Violation as misdemeanor, see Vehicle Code § 40000.11.

§ 12517.5. Driver of paratransit vehicles; qualifications

A person who is employed as a driver of a paratransit vehicle shall not operate that vehicle unless the person meets both of the following requirements:

(a) Has in his or her immediate possession a valid driver's license of a class appropriate to the vehicle driven.

(b) Successfully completes, during each calendar year, four hours of training administered by, or at the direction of, his or her employer or the employer's agent on the safe operation of paratransit vehicles and four hours of training on the special transportation needs of the persons he or she is employed to transport.

This subdivision may be satisfied if the driver receives transportation training or a certificate, or both, pursuant to Section 40082, 40083, 40085, 40085.5, or 40088 of the Education Code.

The employer shall maintain a record of the current training received by each driver in his or her employ and shall present that record on demand to any authorized representative of the Department of the California Highway Patrol. *(Added by Stats.1998, c. 241 (A.B.1634), § 2. Amended by Stats.1999, c. 1007 (S.B.532), § 18; Stats.2002, c. 664 (A.B.3034), § 217.)*

§ 12518. Nonresident minor member of armed forces

The provisions of Section 12504 shall apply to any nonresident who is under the age of 18 years and who is a member of the armed forces of the United States on active duty within this state, except that the maximum period during which such nonresident may operate a motor vehicle in this state without obtaining a driver's license or a nonresident minor's certificate shall be limited to a period of 60 days immediately following the entry of such nonresident into this state. *(Added by Stats.1959, c. 17, p. 1865, § 2. Amended by Stats.1961, c. 1615, p. 3454, § 16; Stats.1963, c. 237, p. 979, § 5; Stats.1963, c. 666, p. 1655, § 5; Stats.1967, c. 478, p. 1684, § 3; Stats.1971, c. 1748, p. 3764, § 57, operative March 4, 1972.)*

§ 12519. Farm labor vehicle license

(a) No person shall operate a farm labor vehicle unless the person has in his or her possession a driver's license for the appropriate class of vehicle to be driven, endorsed for passenger transportation, and, when transporting one or more farmworker passengers, a certificate issued by the department to permit the operation of farm labor vehicles.

(b) The applicants shall present evidence that they have successfully completed the driver training course developed by the Department of Education pursuant to Section 40081 of the Education Code, and approved by the Department of Motor Vehicles and the

Department of the California Highway Patrol before a permanent certificate will be issued.

(c) The certificate shall be issued only to applicants qualified by examinations prescribed by the Department of Motor Vehicles and the Department of the California Highway Patrol and upon payment of a fee of twelve dollars ($12) to the Department of the California Highway Patrol. The examinations shall be conducted by the Department of the California Highway Patrol.

(d) A person holding a valid certificate to permit the operation of a farm labor vehicle, issued prior to January 1, 1991, shall not be required to reapply for a certificate to satisfy any additional requirements imposed by the act adding this subdivision until the certificate he or she holds expires or is canceled or revoked. *(Added by Stats.1959, c. 679, p. 2650, § 3. Amended by Stats.1961, c. 1615, p. 3454, § 17; Stats.1965, c. 1555, p. 3647, § 1; Stats.1974, c. 1447, p. 3160, § 3, eff. Sept. 26, 1974; Stats.1975, c. 791, p. 1815, § 2, eff. Sept. 16, 1975; Stats.1978, c. 488, p. 1616, § 3; Stats.1981, c. 813, p. 3154, § 9; Stats.1982, c. 1273, p. 4703, § 17; Stats.1990, c. 1360 (S.B.1510), § 17.)*

Cross References

Farm labor contractor or employee operating bus or truck transporting individuals, licenses, see Labor Code § 1696.3.
Farm labor vehicle defined, see Vehicle Code § 322.
Persons driving or operating implements of husbandry, exemption, see Vehicle Code § 36300.
Traffic violation point count, number giving rise to presumptions of negligence by certificate or license holder, see Vehicle Code § 12810.5.
Training courses for certification under this section, see Education Code § 40080 et seq.
Violation as misdemeanor, see Vehicle Code § 40000.11.

§ 12520. Tow truck drivers; necessity of valid driver's license; permanent tow truck driver certificate

(a) No person employed as a tow truck driver, as defined in Section 2430.1, shall operate a tow truck unless that person has, in his or her immediate possession, a valid California driver's license of an appropriate class for the vehicle to be driven, and a tow truck driver certificate issued by the department or a temporary tow truck driver certificate issued by the Department of the California Highway Patrol, to permit the operation of the tow truck.

(b) When notified that the applicant has been cleared through the Department of Justice or the Federal Bureau of Investigation, or both, and if the applicant meets all other applicable provisions of this code, the department shall issue a permanent tow truck driver certificate. The permanent tow truck driver certificate shall be valid for a maximum of five years and shall expire on the same date as that of the applicant's driver's license. *(Added by Stats.1991, c. 488 (A.B.123), § 5. Amended by Stats.1996, c. 1043 (A.B.2352), § 2.)*

Cross References

Liens on vehicles or vessels, enforcement, disposition of proceeds, see Business and Professions Code § 21702.5.

§ 12521. Tour bus operators; use of safety belts; report of accidents

An operator of a tour bus shall, at all times when operating the tour bus, do all the following:

(a) Use a safety belt.

(b) Report any accidents involving the tour bus to the Department of the California Highway Patrol. *(Added by Stats.1990, c. 1360 (S.B.1510), § 22.5.)*

§ 12522. First aid examination for schoolbus or youth bus operator

(a) Every person who operates a schoolbus or youth bus in the transportation of school pupils shall, in addition to any other requirement for a schoolbus or youth bus driver's certificate, qualify by an examination on first aid practices deemed necessary for schoolbus operators or youth bus operators. Standards for examination shall be determined by the Emergency Medical Services Authority after consultation with the State Department of Education, the Department of Motor Vehicles, and the Department of the California Highway Patrol. The local school authority employing the applicant shall provide a course of instruction concerning necessary first aid practices.

(b) The Department of the California Highway Patrol shall conduct the first aid examination as part of the examination of applicants for a schoolbus or youth bus driver's certificate and shall certify to the Department of Motor Vehicles that the applicant has satisfactorily demonstrated his or her qualifications in first aid practices, knowledge of schoolbus or youth bus laws and regulations, and ability to operate a schoolbus or youth bus. The first aid certifications shall be valid for the term of the schoolbus or youth bus driver's certificate.

(c) The first aid examination may be waived if the applicant possesses either of the following minimum qualifications:

(1) A current first aid certificate issued by the American Red Cross or by an organization whose first aid training program is at least equivalent to the American Red Cross first aid training program, as determined by the Emergency Medical Services Authority. The Emergency Medical Services Authority may charge a fee, sufficient to cover its administrative costs of approval, to an organization that applies to have its first aid training program approved for purposes of this paragraph.

(2) A current license as a physician and surgeon, osteopathic physician and surgeon, or registered nurse, or a current certificate as a physician's assistant or emergency medical technician. The first aid certificate or license shall be maintained throughout the term of the schoolbus or youth bus driver's certificate and shall be presented upon demand of any traffic officer. The schoolbus or youth bus driver's certificate shall not be valid during any time that the driver fails to maintain and possess that license or certificate after the first aid examination has been waived. *(Added by Stats.1965, c. 1315, p. 3204, § 1. Amended by Stats.1967, c. 565, p. 1912, § 1; Stats.1969, c. 26, p. 127, § 6; Stats.1974, c. 545, p. 1311, § 162; Stats.1978, c. 429, p. 1436, § 174, eff. July 17, 1978, operative July 1, 1978; Stats.1983, c. 1246, § 45, operative July 1, 1984; Stats.1987, c. 723, § 3, eff. Sept. 18, 1987; Stats.1992, c. 624 (A.B.3144), § 3, eff. Sept. 14, 1992; Stats. 1993, c. 226 (A.B.1987), § 15.)*

Cross References

Youth bus defined, see Vehicle Code § 680.

§ 12523. Youth bus operators; licensing requirements; renewals; applicability of regulations for schoolbus drivers; operating rules

(a) No person shall operate a youth bus without having in possession a valid driver's license of the appropriate class, endorsed for passenger transportation and a certificate issued by the department to permit the operation of a youth bus.

(b) Applicants for a certificate to drive a youth bus shall present evidence that they have successfully completed a driver training course administered by or at the direction of their employer consisting of a minimum of 10 hours of classroom instruction covering applicable laws and regulations and defensive driving practices and a minimum of 10 hours of behind-the-wheel training in a vehicle to be used as a youth bus. Applicants seeking to renew a certificate to drive a youth bus shall present evidence that they have received two hours of refresher training during each 12 months of driver certificate validity.

(c) The driver certificate shall be issued only to applicants qualified by examinations prescribed by the Department of Motor Vehicles and the Department of the California Highway Patrol, and upon payment of a fee of twenty-five dollars ($25) for an original certificate and twelve dollars ($12) for the renewal of that certificate to the Department of the California Highway Patrol. The examinations shall be conducted by the Department of the California Highway Patrol. The Department of Motor Vehicles may deny, suspend, or revoke a certificate valid for driving a youth bus for the causes specified in this code or in regulations adopted pursuant to this code.

(d) An operator of a youth bus shall, at all times when operating a youth bus, do all of the following:

(1) Use seat belts.

(2) Refrain from smoking tobacco products.

(3) Report any accidents reportable under Section 16000 to the Department of the California Highway Patrol.

(e) A person holding a valid certificate to permit the operation of a youth bus, issued prior to January 1, 1991, shall not be required to reapply for a certificate to satisfy any additional requirements imposed by the act adding this subdivision until the certificate he or she holds expires or is canceled or revoked.

(f) For purposes of this section, "smoking" has the same meaning as in subdivision (c) of Section 22950.5 of the Business and Professions Code.

(g) For purposes of this section, "tobacco product" means a product or device as defined in subdivision (d) of Section 22950.5 of the Business and Professions Code. *(Added by Stats.1982, c. 383, p. 1712, § 5, eff. July 4, 1982. Amended by Stats.1990, c. 104 (S.B.798), § 4, eff. May 23, 1990; Stats.1990, c. 1360 (S.B.1510), § 23; Stats. 2015–2016, 2nd Ex.Sess., c. 7 (S.B.5), § 27, eff. June 9, 2016.)*

Cross References

Traffic violation point count, number giving rise to presumptions of negligence by certificate or license holder, see Vehicle Code § 12810.5.
Youth bus defined, see Vehicle Code § 680.

§ 12523.5. Paratransit vehicle operator; driver's license and certificate; fee; qualifications; renewals; operating rules

(a) No person shall operate a general public paratransit vehicle unless he or she has in his or her possession a valid driver's license of the appropriate class endorsed for passenger transportation when operating a vehicle designed, used, or maintained for carrying more than 10 persons including the driver and either (1) a certificate issued by the department to permit the operation of a general public paratransit vehicle, or (2) a certificate issued by the department to drive a schoolbus or school pupil activity bus pursuant to Section 12517.

(b) Applicants for a certificate to drive a general public paratransit vehicle shall pay a fee to the Department of the California Highway Patrol of twenty-five dollars ($25) for an original certificate and twelve dollars ($12) for a renewal certificate. Applicants for an original certificate shall present evidence that they have successfully completed a driver training course consisting of a minimum of 40 hours of instruction within the previous two years. The instruction shall have covered applicable laws and regulations and defensive driving practices, a minimum of eight hours of certified defensive driving, and a minimum of 20 hours of behind-the-wheel training in a vehicle to be used as a general public paratransit vehicle. Applicants seeking to renew a certificate valid for driving a general public paratransit vehicle shall present evidence that they have received two hours of refresher training during each 12 months of driver certificate validity.

(c) The driver certificate shall be issued only to applicants qualified by examinations prescribed by the Department of Motor Vehicles and the Department of the California Highway Patrol. The examinations shall be conducted by the Department of the California Highway Patrol. The Department of Motor Vehicles may deny, suspend, or revoke a certificate valid for driving a general public paratransit vehicle for the causes specified in this code or the Education Code or in regulations adopted pursuant to this code or the Education Code.

(d) An operator of a general public paratransit vehicle shall do all of the following:

(1) Use seatbelts.

(2) Refrain from smoking.

(3) Report any accident reportable under Section 16000 to the Department of the California Highway Patrol.

(e) A person holding a valid certificate to permit the operation of a general public paratransit vehicle, issued prior to January 1, 1991, shall not be required to reapply for a certificate to satisfy any additional requirements imposed by the act adding this subdivision until the certificate he or she holds expires or is canceled or revoked. *(Added by Stats.1987, c. 986, § 4, operative July 1, 1988. Amended by Stats.1988, c. 683, § 4, eff. Aug. 27, 1988, operative Jan. 1, 1989; Stats.1989, c. 1136, § 5, operative July 1, 1990; Stats.1990, c. 104 (S.B.798), § 5, eff. May 23, 1990; Stats.1990, c. 1360 (S.B.1510), § 24.)*

§ 12523.6. Driver of persons with developmental disabilities; special driver certificate

(a)(1) On and after March 1, 1998, no person who is employed primarily as a driver of a motor vehicle that is used for the transportation of persons with developmental disabilities, as defined in subdivision (a) of Section 4512 of the Welfare and Institutions Code, shall operate that motor vehicle unless that person has in his or her possession a valid driver's license of the appropriate class and a valid special driver certificate issued by the department.

(2) This subdivision only applies to a person who is employed by a business, a nonprofit organization, or a state or local public agency.

(b) The special driver certificate shall be issued only to an applicant who has cleared a criminal history background check by the Department of Justice and, if applicable, by the Federal Bureau of Investigation.

(1) In order to determine the applicant's suitability as the driver of a vehicle used for the transportation of persons with developmental disabilities, the Department of the California Highway Patrol shall require the applicant to furnish to that department, on a form provided or approved by that department for submission to the Department of Justice, a full set of fingerprints sufficient to enable a criminal background investigation.

(2) Except as provided in paragraph (3), an applicant shall furnish to the Department of the California Highway Patrol evidence of having resided in this state for seven consecutive years immediately prior to the date of application for the certificate.

(3) If an applicant is unable to furnish the evidence required under paragraph (2), the Department of the California Highway Patrol shall require the applicant to furnish an additional full set of fingerprints. That department shall submit those fingerprint cards to the Department of Justice. The Department of Justice shall, in turn, submit the additional full set of fingerprints required under this paragraph to the Federal Bureau of Investigation for a national criminal history record check.

(4) Applicant fingerprint forms shall be processed and returned to the area office of the Department of the California Highway Patrol from which they originated not later than 15 working days from the date on which the fingerprint forms were received by the Department of Justice, unless circumstances, other than the administrative duties of the Department of Justice, warrant further investigation. Upon implementation of an electronic fingerprinting system with terminals located statewide and managed by the Department of Justice, the Department of Justice shall ascertain the information required pursuant to this subdivision within three working days.

(5) The applicant shall pay, in addition to the fees authorized in Section 2427, a fee of twenty-five dollars ($25) for an original certificate and twelve dollars ($12) for the renewal of that certificate to the Department of the California Highway Patrol.

(c) A certificate issued under this section shall not be deemed a certification to operate a particular vehicle that otherwise requires a driver's license or endorsement for a particular class under this code.

(d) On or after March 1, 1998, no person who operates a business or a nonprofit organization or agency shall employ a person who is employed primarily as a driver of a motor vehicle for hire that is used for the transportation of persons with developmental disabilities unless the employed person operates the motor vehicle in compliance with subdivision (a).

(e) Nothing in this section precludes an employer of persons who are occasionally used as drivers of motor vehicles for the transportation of persons with developmental disabilities from requiring those persons, as a condition of employment, to obtain a special driver certificate pursuant to this section or precludes any volunteer driver from applying for a special driver certificate.

(f) As used in this section, a person is employed primarily as driver if that person performs at least 50 percent of his or her time worked including, but not limited to, time spent assisting persons onto and out of the vehicle, or at least 20 hours a week, whichever is less, as a compensated driver of a motor vehicle for hire for the transportation of persons with developmental disabilities.

(g) This section does not apply to any person who has successfully completed a background investigation prescribed by law, including, but not limited to, health care transport vehicle operators, or to the operator of a taxicab regulated pursuant to Section 21100. This section does not apply to a person who holds a valid certificate, other than a farm labor vehicle driver certificate, issued under Section 12517.4 or 12527. This section does not apply to a driver who provides transportation on a noncommercial basis to persons with developmental disabilities. *(Added by Stats.1997, c. 595 (A.B.1611), § 1, eff. Sept. 30, 1997. Amended by Stats.1998, c. 485 (A.B.2803), § 159; Stats.1998, c. 877 (A.B.2132), § 53.)*

§ 12524. Vehicles hauling highway route controlled quantities of radioactive materials; driver's license and certificate

A class A, class B, or class C driver's licenseholder shall not operate a vehicle hauling highway route controlled quantities of radioactive materials, as defined in Section 173.403 of Title 49 of the Code of Federal Regulations, unless the driver possesses a valid license of the appropriate class and a certificate of training as required in Section 397.101(e) of Title 49 of the Code of Federal Regulations. *(Added by Stats.1990, c. 1360 (S.B.1510), § 25.1. Amended by Stats.1992, c. 1241 (S.B.1615), § 19; Stats.1993, c. 272 (A.B.301), § 21, eff. Aug. 2, 1993; Stats.2017, c. 397 (S.B.810), § 2, eff. Jan. 1, 2018.)*

Cross References

Directing operation of vehicle transporting fissile class III shipments or large quantity radioactive materials by unauthorized driver, see Vehicle Code § 14611.

Medical certificate of person employed to drive class 1 or class 2 vehicle, employer responsibilities, see Vehicle Code § 14606.

§ 12525. Mechanics or other maintenance personnel; operation of certain vehicles requiring endorsement or certificates; exemption

Mechanics or other maintenance personnel may operate vehicles requiring a schoolbus endorsement or certificates issued pursuant to Section 2512, 12517, 12519, 12523, or 12523.5 without obtaining a schoolbus endorsement or those certificates if that operation is within the course of their employment and they do not transport pupils or members of the public. *(Added by Stats.1990, c. 1360 (S.B.1510), § 27. Amended by Stats.2006, c. 574 (A.B.2520), § 8.)*

§ 12527. Ambulance drivers; application for certificate; requirements

In addition to satisfying all requirements specified in this code and in regulations adopted pursuant to this code, an applicant for an ambulance driver certificate shall satisfy all of the following requirements:

(a) Except as otherwise provided, every ambulance driver responding to an emergency call or transporting patients shall be at least 18 years of age, hold a driver's license valid in California, possess a valid ambulance driver certificate, and be trained and competent in ambulance operation and the use of safety and emergency care equipment required by the California Code of Regulations governing ambulances.

(b) Except as provided in subdivision (e), a person shall not operate an ambulance unless the person has in their immediate possession a driver's license for the appropriate class of vehicle to be driven and a certificate issued by the department to permit the operation of an ambulance.

(c) An ambulance driver certificate shall only be issued by the department upon the successful completion of an examination conducted by the department and subject to all of the following conditions:

(1) An applicant for an original or renewal driver certificate shall submit a report of medical examination on a form approved by the department, the Federal Motor Carrier Safety Administration, or the Federal Aviation Administration. The report shall be dated within the two years preceding the application date.

(2) An applicant for an original driver certificate shall submit an acceptable fingerprint card.

(3) The certificate to drive an ambulance shall be valid for a period not exceeding five years and six months and shall expire on the same date as the driver's license. The ambulance driver certificate shall only be valid when both of the following conditions exist:

(A) The certificate is accompanied by a medical examination certificate that was issued within the preceding two years and approved by the department, the Federal Motor Carrier Safety Administration, or the Federal Aviation Administration.

(B) A copy of the medical examination report based upon which the certificate was issued is on file with the department.

(4) The ambulance driver certificate is renewable under conditions prescribed by the department. Except as provided in paragraphs (2) and (3) of subdivision (d), an applicant renewing an ambulance driver certificate shall possess certificates or licenses evidencing compliance with the emergency medical training and educational standards for ambulance attendants established by the Emergency Medical Services Authority.

(d)(1) Every ambulance driver shall have been trained to assist the ambulance attendant in the care and handling of the ill and injured.

Except as provided in paragraph (2), the driver of a California-based ambulance shall, within one year of initial issuance of the driver's ambulance driver certificate, possess a certificate or license evidencing compliance with the emergency medical training and educational standards established for ambulance attendants by the Emergency Medical Services Authority. In those emergencies requiring both the regularly assigned driver and attendant to be utilized in providing patient care, the specialized emergency medical training requirement shall not apply to persons temporarily detailed to drive the ambulance.

(2) Paragraph (1) does not apply to an ambulance driver who is a volunteer driver for a volunteer ambulance service if the service is provided in the unincorporated areas of a county with a population of less than 125,000 persons, as determined by the most recent federal decennial census. The operation of an ambulance subject to this

paragraph shall only apply if the name of the driver and the volunteer ambulance service and facts substantiating the public health necessity for an exemption are submitted to the department by the county board of supervisors and at least one of the following entities in the county where the driver operates the ambulance:

(A) The county health officer.

(B) The county medical care committee.

(C) The local emergency medical services agency coordinator.

(3) The information required by paragraph (2) shall be submitted to the department at the time of application for an ambulance driver certificate. Upon receipt of that information, the department shall restrict the certificate holder to driving an ambulance for the volunteer ambulance service.

(4) The director may terminate any certificate issued pursuant to paragraph (2) at any time the department determines that the qualifying conditions specified no longer exist.

(5) The exemption granted pursuant to paragraph (2) shall expire on the expiration date of the ambulance driver certificate.

(e) An ambulance certificate is not required for persons operating ambulances in the line of duty as salaried, regular, full-time police officers, deputy sheriffs, members of a fire department of a public agency, or members of a fire department of a federally recognized tribe. This exemption excludes volunteers and part-time employees or members of a department whose duties are primarily clerical or administrative. *(Added by Stats.1990, c. 1360 (S.B.1510), § 28. Amended by Stats.1994, c. 954 (A.B.2635), § 1; Stats.1995, c. 766 (S.B.726), § 12; Stats.1996, c. 1043 (A.B.2352), § 3; Stats.2016, c. 208 (A.B.2906), § 11, eff. Jan. 1, 2017; Stats.2018, c. 198 (A.B.3246), § 21, eff. Jan. 1, 2019; Stats.2021, c. 282 (A.B.798), § 4, eff. Jan. 1, 2022.)*

Cross References

Drivers' licenses, issuance and expiration, traffic violation point count, see Vehicle Code § 12810.5.

Prospective employers of drivers of vehicles requiring certain licenses or certificates, pull-notice system and periodic reports, application to vehicles for which certificate under this section is required, see Vehicle Code § 1808.1.

ARTICLE 4. SIGNATURE AND DISPLAY OF LICENSES

§ 12950. Signature of licensee

(a) Every person licensed under this code shall write his or her usual signature with pen and ink in the space provided for that purpose on the license issued to him or her, immediately on receipt thereof, and the license is not valid until so signed, except that if the department issues a form of license which bears the facsimile signature of the applicant as shown upon the application, the license is valid even though not so signed.

(b) For purposes of subdivision (a), signature includes a digitized signature. *(Stats.1959, c. 3, p. 1623, § 12950. Amended by Stats. 2003, c. 819 (A.B.593), § 3.)*

Cross References

Space for signature of licensee, see Vehicle Code § 12811.

Unlawful use of license, see Vehicle Code § 14610.

§ 12950.5. Digitized signatures on driver's license; digitized signatures of persons who register to vote on voter registration cards and change of address information to be provided to Secretary of State

(a) The department shall require digitized signatures on each driver's license. A digitized signature is an electronic representation of a handwritten signature.

(b) The department shall provide to the Secretary of State the digitized signature of every person who registers to vote on the voter registration card provided by the department.

(c) The department shall provide the Secretary of State with change-of-address information for every voter who indicates that he or she desires to have his or her address changed for voter registration purposes. *(Added by Stats.2003, c. 819 (A.B.593), § 4.)*

§ 12951. Possession of valid driver's license

(a) The licensee shall have the valid driver's license issued to him or her in his or her immediate possession at all times when driving a motor vehicle upon a highway.

Any charge under this subdivision shall be dismissed when the person charged produces in court a driver's license duly issued to that person and valid at the time of his or her arrest, except that upon a third or subsequent charge the court in its discretion may dismiss the charge. When a temporary, interim, or duplicate driver's license is produced in court, the charge shall not be dismissed unless the court has been furnished proof by the Department of Motor Vehicles that the temporary, interim, or duplicate license was issued prior to the arrest, that the driving privilege and license had not been suspended or revoked, and that the person was eligible for the temporary, interim, or duplicate license.

(b) The driver of a motor vehicle shall present his or her license for examination upon demand of a peace officer enforcing the provisions of this code. *(Stats.1959, c. 3, p. 1623, § 12951. Amended by Stats.1965, c. 175, p. 1141, § 1; Stats.1965, c. 495, p. 1804, § 1; Stats.1965, c. 1177, p. 2977, § 1; Stats.1968, c. 1192, p. 2257, § 6, operative Jan. 1, 1969; Stats.1993, c. 1292 (S.B.274), § 8.)*

Cross References

Certain violations constituting misdemeanors, see Vehicle Code § 40000.11.

Notice to correct driver's license infraction, see Vehicle Code § 40303.5.

Unlawful use of license, see Vehicle Code § 14610.

Research References

California Jury Instructions - Criminal 16.632, Failure to Present License Upon Demand.

2 Witkin, California Criminal Law 4th Crimes Against Public Peace and Welfare § 305 (2021), Driving Without Valid License.

1 Witkin California Criminal Law 4th Defenses § 203 (2021), Attempting to Create Violation of Prohibition Against Multiple Prosecution.

§ 12952. Display of license to court

A licensee shall display his driver's license upon request of a magistrate or judge before whom he may be brought for violation of any traffic law. *(Stats.1959, c. 3, p. 1623, § 12952.)*

§ 12953. Accidents or violations causing detention of crewmember of train by police; furnishing of license; issuance of citation

In any circumstances involving accidents or violations in which the engineer or any other crewmember of any train is detained by state or local police, the engineer or any other crew member shall not be required to furnish a motor vehicle operator's license, nor shall any citation involving the operation of a train be issued against the motor vehicle operator's license of the engineer or any other crew member of the train. *(Added by Stats.1980, c. 1134, p. 3660, § 11.)*

CHAPTER 2. SUSPENSION OR REVOCATION OF LICENSES

ARTICLE 1. GENERAL PROVISIONS

§ 13100. Cancellation

When used in reference to a driver's license, "cancellation" means that a driver's license certificate is terminated without prejudice and must be surrendered. Any person whose license has been canceled may immediately apply for a license. Cancellation of license may be made only when specifically authorized in this code, when application is made for a license to operate vehicles of a higher class, or when a license has been issued through error or voluntarily surrendered to the department. *(Stats.1959, c. 3, p. 1623, § 13100. Amended by Stats.1961, c. 1615, p. 3457, § 25; Stats.1974, c. 428, p. 1040, § 3.)*

Cross References

Application for license, see Vehicle Code § 12800.
Cancellation of minor's license, see Vehicle Code §§ 17711, 17712.
Records of licenses suspended, revoked and cancelled, see Vehicle Code §§ 1801, 1807.
Renewal of license, see Vehicle Code §§ 12808, 12814.
Seizure of documents and plates, see Vehicle Code § 4460.

§ 13101. Revocation

When used in reference to a driver's license, "revocation" means that the person's privilege to drive a motor vehicle is terminated and a new driver's license may be obtained after the period of revocation. *(Stats.1959, c. 3, p. 1623, § 13101.)*

Cross References

Suspension or revocation of,
Emergency vehicle permit, grounds, see Vehicle Code § 2417.
License by court, see Vehicle Code § 13200 et seq.

Research References

2 Witkin, California Criminal Law 4th Crimes Against Public Peace and Welfare § 265 (2021), In General.
3 Witkin, California Criminal Law 4th Punishment § 210 (2021), In General.

§ 13102. Suspension; examination

When used in reference to a driver's license, "suspension" means that the person's privilege to drive a motor vehicle is temporarily withdrawn. The department may, before terminating any suspension based upon a physical or mental condition of the licensee, require such examination of the licensee as deemed appropriate in relation to evidence of any condition which may affect the ability of the licensee to safely operate a motor vehicle. *(Stats.1959, c. 3, p. 1623, § 13102. Amended by Stats.1976, c. 498, p. 1238, § 1; Stats.1999, c. 724 (A.B.1650), § 31.)*

Cross References

Definitions,
Highway, see Vehicle Code §§ 360, 590.
Motor vehicle, see Vehicle Code § 415.

Research References

3 Witkin, California Criminal Law 4th Punishment § 210 (2021), In General.

§ 13103. Equivalents of conviction

For purposes of this division, a plea of nolo contendere or a plea of guilty or judgment of guilty, whether probation is granted or not, a forfeiture of bail, or a finding reported under Section 1816, constitutes a conviction of any offense prescribed by this code, other than offenses relating to the unlawful parking of vehicles. *(Added by Stats.1959, c. 1622, p. 3991, § 3. Amended by Stats.1972, c. 1207, p. 2333, § 3.)*

Cross References

Forfeiture of bail, see Penal Code § 1305 et seq.
Judgments in criminal cases, see Penal Code § 1191 et seq.
Plea of guilty, see Penal Code § 1016 et seq.

Research References

3 Witkin, California Criminal Law 4th Punishment § 210 (2021), In General.

§ 13105. Conviction of a juvenile

For the purposes of this chapter, "convicted" or "conviction" includes a finding by a judge of a juvenile court, a juvenile hearing officer, or referee of a juvenile court that a person has committed an offense, and "court" includes a juvenile court except as otherwise specifically provided. *(Added by Stats.1972, c. 755, p. 1349, § 2. Amended by Stats.2003, c. 149 (S.B.79), § 81.)*

Law Revision Commission Comments

Section 13105 is amended to reflect the redesignation of traffic hearing officers as juvenile hearing officers. See 1997 Cal. Stat. ch. 679. [33 Cal.L.Rev. Comm. Reports 246 (2003)].

Research References

3 Witkin, California Criminal Law 4th Punishment § 210 (2021), In General.

§ 13106. Notice of suspension or revocation of driving privilege; presumptions; alternative methods for determining whereabouts of drivers

(a) When the privilege of a person to operate a motor vehicle is suspended or revoked, the department shall notify the person by first-class mail * * * of the action taken and of the effective date * * * of that suspension or revocation, except for those persons personally given notice by the department * * *, a court, * * * a peace officer pursuant to Section 13388 or 13382, or otherwise pursuant to this code. It shall be a rebuttable presumption, affecting the burden of proof, that a person has knowledge of the suspension or revocation if notice has been sent by first-class mail by the department pursuant to this section to the most recent address reported to the department pursuant to Section 12800 or 14600, or any more recent address on file if reported by the person, a court, or a law enforcement agency, or to the most recent electronic delivery address provided in accordance with Section 1801.2, and the notice has not been returned to the department as undeliverable or unclaimed. It is the responsibility of a holder of a driver's license to report changes of address to the department pursuant to Section 14600.

(b) The department may utilize alternative methods for determining the whereabouts of a driver * * * whose driving privilege has been suspended or revoked * * * pursuant to this code * * * for the purpose of providing the driver with notice of suspension or revocation. Alternative methods may include, but are not limited to, cooperating with other state agencies that maintain more current address information than the department's driver's license files. *(Added by Stats.1994, c. 1133 (A.B.3148), § 5, operative June 30, 1995. Amended by Stats.1998, c. 683 (A.B.2347), § 2; Stats.1999, c. 22 (S.B.24), § 8, eff. May 26, 1999, operative July 1, 1999; Stats.2002, c. 805 (A.B.2996), § 17, eff. Sept. 23, 2002; Stats.2022, c. 838 (S.B.1193), § 8, eff. Jan. 1, 2023.)*

Cross References

Burden of proof, generally, see Evidence Code § 500 et seq.
Driving after revocation or suspension of driving privilege, mailed notice as presumption affecting burden of proof, see Vehicle Code § 14601 et seq.

Research References

2 Witkin, California Criminal Law 4th Crimes Against Public Peace and Welfare § 308 (2021), Knowledge of Suspension, Revocation, or Restriction.
3 Witkin, California Criminal Law 4th Punishment § 210 (2021), In General.

ARTICLE 2. SUSPENSION OR REVOCATION BY COURT

§ 13200. Speeding or reckless driving

Whenever any person licensed under this code is convicted of a violation of any provision of this code relating to the speed of vehicles or a violation of Section 23103 the court may, unless this code makes mandatory a revocation by the department, suspend the privilege of the person to operate a motor vehicle for a period of not to exceed 30 days upon a first conviction, for a period of not to exceed 60 days upon a second conviction, and for a period of not to exceed six months upon a third or any subsequent conviction. *(Stats.1959, c. 3, p. 1623, § 13200.)*

Cross References

Conviction, equivalents, see Vehicle Code § 13103.
Maximum period of suspension, see Vehicle Code § 13203.
Offenses,
  Driving while intoxicated, see Vehicle Code §§ 23152, 23153.
  Failure to stop after accident, see Vehicle Code § 20001 et seq.
  Reckless driving, see Vehicle Code §§ 23103, 23104.
Seizure of documents and plates, see Vehicle Code § 4460.
Speed laws, see Vehicle Code § 22348 et seq.
Surrender of suspended or revoked licenses, see Vehicle Code § 13550.
Suspension or revocation,
  Emergency vehicle permit, see Vehicle Code § 2417.
  Failure to satisfy judgment, see Vehicle Code § 16370 et seq.
  Failure to stop after accident, see Vehicle Code § 13201.
  Registration of vehicles, see Vehicle Code § 8800 et seq.
  Violating provisions of restricted license, see Vehicle Code §§ 13360, 14603.

Research References

3 Witkin, California Criminal Law 4th Punishment § 211 (2021), Discretionary Suspension.

§ 13200.5. Driving at speeds over 100 m.p.h.; suspension of privilege to operate a motor vehicle

Whenever any person licensed under this code is convicted of a violation of subdivision (b) of Section 22348, the court may, unless this code makes mandatory a revocation by the department, suspend the privilege of the person to operate a motor vehicle for a period of not to exceed 30 days. *(Added by Stats.1983, c. 980, § 1. Amended by Stats.1984, c. 276, § 2.)*

Cross References

Driving at speed greater than 100 miles per hour, see Vehicle Code § 22348.

Research References

2 Witkin, California Criminal Law 4th Crimes Against Public Peace and Welfare § 320 (2021), In General.
3 Witkin, California Criminal Law 4th Punishment § 211 (2021), Discretionary Suspension.

§ 13201. Certain misdemeanors

A court may suspend, for not more than six months, the privilege of a person to operate a motor vehicle upon conviction of any of the following offenses:

(a) Failure of the driver of a vehicle involved in an accident to stop or otherwise comply with Section 20002.

(b) Reckless driving proximately causing bodily injury to a person under Section 23104 or 23105.

(c) Failure of the driver of a vehicle to stop at a railway grade crossing as required by Section 22452.

(d) Evading a peace officer in violation of Section 2800.1 or 2800.2, or in violation of Section 2800.3 if the person's license is not revoked for that violation pursuant to paragraph (3) of subdivision (a) of Section 13351.

(e)(1) Knowingly causing or participating in a vehicular collision, or any other vehicular accident, for the purpose of presenting or causing to be presented any false or fraudulent insurance claim.

(2) In lieu of suspending a person's driving privilege pursuant to paragraph (1), the court may order the privilege to operate a motor vehicle restricted to necessary travel to and from that person's place of employment for not more than six months. If driving a motor vehicle is necessary to perform the duties of the person's employment, the court may restrict the driving privilege to allow driving in that person's scope of employment. Whenever a person's driving privilege is restricted pursuant to this paragraph, the person shall be required to maintain proof of financial responsibility. *(Stats.1959, c. 3, p. 1624, § 13201. Amended by Stats.1971, c. 1530, p. 3024, § 5, operative May 3, 1972; Stats.1972, c. 92, p. 118, § 3; Stats.1975, c. 1133, p. 2804, § 1; Stats.1981, c. 939, p. 3548, § 3; Stats.1981, c. 940, p. 3563, § 2; Stats.1988, c. 504, § 4, eff. Aug. 22, 1988; Stats.1991, c. 656 (S.B.666), § 2; Stats.1992, c. 490 (A.B.2699), § 1; Stats.2007, c. 682 (A.B.430), § 11.)*

Cross References

Grounds for suspension, see Vehicle Code § 13361.

Research References

1 Witkin California Criminal Law 4th Introduction to Crimes § 144 (2021), Enhancement and Punishment Issues.
3 Witkin, California Criminal Law 4th Punishment § 211 (2021), Discretionary Suspension.

§ 13202.5. Drug and alcohol related offenses by person under age of 21, but aged 13 or over; suspension, delay, or restriction of driving privileges

(a)(1) For each conviction of a person for an offense specified in subdivision (d), committed while the person was under 21 years of age, but 13 years of age or older, the court shall suspend the person's driving privilege for one year. If the person convicted does not yet have the privilege to drive, the court shall order the department to delay issuing the privilege to drive for one year subsequent to the time the person becomes legally eligible to drive. However, if there is no further conviction for an offense specified in subdivision (d) in a 12–month period after the conviction, the court, upon petition of the person affected, may modify the order imposing the delay of the privilege. For each successive offense, the court shall suspend the person's driving privilege for those possessing a license or delay the eligibility for those not in possession of a license at the time of their conviction for one additional year.

(2) As used in this section, the term "conviction" includes the findings in juvenile proceedings specified in Section 13105.

(b) Whenever the court suspends driving privileges pursuant to subdivision (a), the court in which the conviction is had shall require all driver's licenses held by the person to be surrendered to the court. The court shall within 10 days following the conviction transmit a certified abstract of the conviction, together with any driver's licenses surrendered, to the department.

(c)(1) After a court has issued an order suspending or delaying driving privileges pursuant to subdivision (a), the court, upon petition of the person affected, may review the order and may impose restrictions on the person's privilege to drive based upon a showing of a critical need to drive.

(2) As used in this section, "critical need to drive" means the circumstances that are required to be shown for the issuance of a junior permit pursuant to Section 12513.

(3) The restriction shall remain in effect for the balance of the period of suspension or restriction in this section. The court shall notify the department of any modification within 10 days of the order of modification.

(d) This section applies to violations involving controlled substances or alcohol contained in the following provisions:

(1) Section 191.5 of, and subdivision (a) or (b) of Section 192.5 of, the Penal Code.

(2) Section 23103 when subject to Section 23103.5, Section 23140, and Article 2 (commencing with Section 23152) of Chapter 12 of Division 11 of this code.

(e) Suspension, restriction, or delay of driving privileges pursuant to this section shall be in addition to any penalty imposed upon conviction of a violation specified in subdivision (d). *(Added by Stats.1984, c. 658, § 1. Amended by Stats.1988, c. 1254, § 3; Stats.1990, c. 1696 (S.B.1756), § 3; Stats.1990, c. 1697 (S.B.2635), § 4; Stats.2007, c. 747 (A.B.678), § 17; Stats.2019, c. 505 (S.B.485), § 12, eff. Jan. 1, 2020.)*

Research References

2 Witkin, California Criminal Law 4th Crimes Against Property § 259 (2021), Offenses Involving Identification Documents.
2 Witkin, California Criminal Law 4th Crimes Against Public Peace and Welfare § 303 (2021), Drinking or Possessing Alcohol or Marijuana.
3 Witkin, California Criminal Law 4th Punishment § 212 (2021), Mandatory Suspension.

§ 13202.8. Ignition interlock device; installation and maintenance; restrictions under § 13202.5

The restrictions specified in Section 13202.5 for the violations specified in that section may include, but are not limited to, the installation and maintenance of a certified ignition interlock device pursuant to Section 13386. Any restriction is subject to the provisions of Section 13202.5 relating to restrictions. *(Formerly § 13202.7, added by Stats.1990, c. 1403 (A.B.2040), § 5, eff. Sept. 28, 1990. Renumbered § 13202.8 and amended by Stats.1991, c. 425 (S.B.558), § 1. Amended by Stats.1998, c. 118 (S.B.1186), § 1.33, operative July 1, 1999.)*

Research References

3 Witkin, California Criminal Law 4th Punishment § 212 (2021), Mandatory Suspension.

§ 13203. Limitation on suspension

In no event shall a court suspend the privilege of any person to operate a motor vehicle or as a condition of probation prohibit the operation of a motor vehicle for a period of time longer than that specified in this code. Any such prohibited order of a court, whether imposed as a condition of probation or otherwise, shall be null and void, and the department shall restore or reissue a license to any person entitled thereto irrespective of any such invalid order of a court. *(Stats.1959, c. 3, p. 1624, § 13203. Amended by Stats.1963, c. 917, p. 2169, § 13; Stats.1967, c. 549, p. 1897, § 2; Stats.1972, c. 755, p. 1349, § 2.5; Stats.1973, c. 903, p. 1683, § 1; Stats.1974, c. 1283, p. 2776, § 1, eff. Sept. 23, 1974.)*

Cross References

Misdemeanors, see Vehicle Code § 13201.

Research References

3 Witkin, California Criminal Law 4th Punishment § 210 (2021), In General.
3 Witkin, California Criminal Law 4th Punishment § 679 (2021), Other Invalid Conditions.

§ 13205. Nonresidents

The privileges of a nonresident to operate vehicles in this State may be suspended or revoked under the provisions of this chapter in the same manner and to the same extent as the privileges of a resident driver. *(Stats.1959, c. 3, p. 1624, § 13205.)*

Cross References

Exemption of nonresidents from license requirements, see Vehicle Code § 12502 et seq.
Nonresident defined, see Vehicle Code § 435.
Registration permits to nonresident owners, see Vehicle Code § 6700 et seq.

Research References

3 Witkin, California Criminal Law 4th Punishment § 210 (2021), In General.

§ 13206. Surrender of license

Whenever a court suspends the privilege of a person to operate a motor vehicle, the court shall require the person's license to be surrendered to it. Unless required by the provisions of Section 13550 to send the license to the department, the court shall retain the license during the period of suspension and return it to the licensee at the end of the period after indorsing thereon a record of the suspension. *(Stats.1959, c. 3, p. 1624, § 13206.)*

Cross References

Surrender of revoked or suspended license by department, see Vehicle Code § 13550.
Suspension and surrender of all licenses, see Vehicle Code § 13207.

Research References

3 Witkin, California Criminal Law 4th Punishment § 210 (2021), In General.

§ 13207. Licenses affected by suspension

Whenever a court suspends the privilege of any person to operate a motor vehicle, the suspension shall apply to all driver's licenses held by him, and all licenses shall be surrendered to the court. *(Stats. 1959, c. 3, p. 1625, § 13207.)*

Cross References

Cancellation, revocation and suspension of license, defined, see Vehicle Code § 13100 et seq.
Surrender of license to court, see Vehicle Code § 13550.

§ 13208. Recommendation of court to department

In any criminal proceeding, without regard to its disposition, wherein the defendant is charged with a violation of Division 11 (commencing with Section 21000), the court may, if it has reason to believe that any of the conditions specified in Section 12805 or 12806 exist, recommend to the department that an investigation be conducted to determine whether the driving privilege of that person should be suspended or revoked. In making the recommendation, the court shall state the basis for the belief that the condition exists and whether the defendant relied upon the condition as a part of his or her defense. The department may provide a form for the court's convenience. *(Added by Stats.1959, c. 1477, p. 3772, § 1. Amended by Stats.1987, c. 321, § 7.)*

Research References

3 Witkin, California Criminal Law 4th Punishment § 220 (2021), Distinction: Investigation and Hearing.

§ 13209. Record of prior conviction

Before sentencing a person upon a conviction of a violation of Section 23152 or 23153, the court shall obtain from the department a record of any prior convictions of that person for traffic violations. The department shall furnish that record upon the written request of the court.

Notwithstanding the provisions of Section 1449 of the Penal Code, in any such criminal action the time for pronouncement of judgment shall not commence to run until the time that the court receives the record of prior convictions from the department. *(Added by Stats.1961, c. 1936, p. 4087, § 1. Amended by Stats.1971, c. 1530, p. 3025, § 6, operative May 3, 1972; Stats.1981, c. 939, p. 3548, § 4.5.)*

Research References

6 Witkin, California Criminal Law 4th Criminal Judgment § 149 (2021), Scope of Right.

§ 13210. Suspensions of driving privileges; commission of assault; road rage

In addition to the penalties set forth in subdivision (a) of Section 245 of the Penal Code, the court may order the suspension of the driving privilege of any operator of a motor vehicle who commits an assault as described in subdivision (a) of Section 245 of the Penal Code on an operator or passenger of another motor vehicle, an operator of a bicycle, or a pedestrian and the offense occurs on a highway. The suspension period authorized under this section for an assault commonly known as "road rage," shall be six months for a first offense and one year for a second or subsequent offense to commence, at the discretion of the court, either on the date of the person's conviction, or upon the person's release from confinement or imprisonment. The court may, in lieu of or in addition to the suspension of the driving privilege, order a person convicted under this section to complete a court-approved anger management or "road rage" course, subsequent to the date of the current violation. *(Added by Stats.2000, c. 642 (A.B.2733), § 4.)*

ARTICLE 3. SUSPENSION AND REVOCATION BY DEPARTMENT

§ 13350. Required revocation; affidavit of understanding; reinstatement

(a) The department immediately shall revoke the privilege of a person to drive a motor vehicle upon receipt of a duly certified abstract of the record of a court showing that the person has been convicted of any of the following crimes or offenses:

(1) Failure of the driver of a vehicle involved in an accident resulting in injury or death to a person to stop or otherwise comply with Section 20001.

(2) A felony in the commission of which a motor vehicle is used, except as provided in Section 13351, 13352, or 13357.

(3) Reckless driving causing bodily injury.

(b) If a person is convicted of a violation of Section 23152 punishable under Section 23546, 23550, or 23550.5, or a violation of Section 23153 punishable under Section 23550.5 or 23566, including a violation of subdivision (b) of Section 191.5 of the Penal Code as provided in Section 193.7 of that code, the court shall, at the time of surrender of the driver's license or temporary permit, require the defendant to sign an affidavit in a form provided by the department acknowledging his or her understanding of the revocation required by paragraph (5), (6), or (7) of subdivision (a) of Section 13352, and an acknowledgment of his or her designation as a habitual traffic offender. A copy of this affidavit shall be transmitted, with the license or temporary permit, to the department within the prescribed 10 days.

(c) The department shall not reinstate the privilege revoked under subdivision (a) until the expiration of one year after the date of revocation and until the person whose privilege was revoked gives proof of financial responsibility as defined in Section 16430. *(Stats. 1959, c. 3, p. 1625, § 13350. Amended by Stats.1959, c. 1048, p. 3089, § 1; Stats.1961, c. 58, p. 1009, § 33; Stats.1965, c. 1060, p. 2706, § 1; Stats.1967, c. 1110, p. 2756, § 7; Stats.1971, c. 1530, p. 3025, § 8, operative May 3, 1972; Stats.1982, c. 655, p. 2671, § 1; Stats.1988, c. 1415, § 1; Stats.1990, c. 44 (A.B.1648), § 2; Stats.1991, c. 656 (S.B.666), § 3; Stats.1992, c. 974 (S.B.1600), § 5, eff. Sept. 28, 1992; Stats.1997, c. 901 (A.B.130), § 1; Stats.1998, c. 118 (S.B.1186), § 1.35, operative July 1, 1999; Stats.1999, c. 22 (S.B.24), § 9, eff. May 26, 1999, operative July 1, 1999; Stats.2002, c. 545 (S.B.1852), § 7; Stats.2007, c. 747 (A.B.678), § 18.)*

Cross References

Commercial motor vehicles, multiple violations, see Vehicle Code § 15302.
Definitions,
Felony, see Penal Code § 17.
Manslaughter in driving of vehicle, see Penal Code § 192.
Driver license compact party states, reported conduct as ground for suspension or revocation, see Vehicle Code § 15023.
Grand theft of motor vehicle, see Penal Code § 487.
Proof of financial responsibility, see Vehicle Code § 16430.
Theft and unlawful driving or taking of a vehicle, see Vehicle Code § 10851.

Research References

2 Witkin, California Criminal Law 4th Crimes Against Public Peace and Welfare § 279 (2021), In General.
2 Witkin, California Criminal Law 4th Crimes Against Public Peace and Welfare § 281 (2021), One Separate Conviction of Related Offense.
2 Witkin, California Criminal Law 4th Crimes Against Public Peace and Welfare § 282 (2021), Two Separate Convictions of Related Offenses.
2 Witkin, California Criminal Law 4th Crimes Against Public Peace and Welfare § 283 (2021), Three or More Separate Convictions of Related Offenses.
2 Witkin, California Criminal Law 4th Crimes Against Public Peace and Welfare § 287 (2021), Two or More Separate Convictions of Related Offenses.
2 Witkin, California Criminal Law 4th Crimes Against Public Peace and Welfare § 289 (2021), Prior Violation Punished as Felony.

1 Witkin California Criminal Law 4th Crimes Against the Person § 267 (2021), Vehicular Manslaughter While Intoxicated.
3 Witkin, California Criminal Law 4th Punishment § 211 (2021), Discretionary Suspension.
3 Witkin, California Criminal Law 4th Punishment § 216 (2021), Offenses Involving Injury.
3 Witkin, California Criminal Law 4th Punishment § 217 (2021), Other Serious Offenses.

§ 13350.5. Conviction of vehicular manslaughter for driving under influence or influence of alcohol and drugs causing bodily injury as conviction of § 23153

Notwithstanding Section 13350, for the purposes of this article, conviction of a violation of subdivision (b) of Section 191.5 of the Penal Code is a conviction of a violation of Section 23153. *(Added by Stats.1983, c. 937, § 3. Amended by Stats.1987, c. 309, § 1; Stats. 1991, c. 656 (S.B.666), § 4; Stats.1998, c. 118 (S.B.1186), § 1.37, operative July 1, 1999; Stats.1999, c. 22 (S.B.24), § 10, eff. May 26, 1999, operative July 1, 1999; Stats.2007, c. 747 (A.B.678), § 19.)*

Research References

3 Witkin, California Criminal Law 4th Punishment § 216 (2021), Offenses Involving Injury.

§ 13351. Required revocation; conviction of manslaughter, three or more violations of §§ 20001, 20002, 23103, 23104 or 23105, or Penal Code §§ 191.5, 192.5, or 2800.3; reinstatement

(a) The department immediately shall revoke the privilege of a person to drive a motor vehicle upon receipt of a duly certified abstract of the record of a court showing that the person has been convicted of any of the following crimes or offenses:

(1) Manslaughter resulting from the operation of a motor vehicle, except when convicted under paragraph (2) of subdivision (c) of Section 192 of the Penal Code.

(2) Conviction of three or more violations of Section 20001, 20002, 23103, 23104, or 23105 within a period of 12 months from the time of the first offense to the third or subsequent offense, or a combination of three or more convictions of violations within the same period.

(3) Violation of subdivision (a) of Section 191.5 or subdivision (a) of Section 192.5 of the Penal Code or of Section 2800.3 causing serious bodily injury resulting in a serious impairment of physical condition, including, but not limited to, loss of consciousness, concussion, serious bone fracture, protracted loss or impairment of function of any bodily member or organ, and serious disfigurement.

(b) The department shall not reinstate the privilege revoked under subdivision (a) until the expiration of three years after the date of revocation and until the person whose privilege was revoked gives proof of financial responsibility, as defined in Section 16430. *(Added by Stats.1982, c. 655, p. 2671, § 3. Amended by Stats.1985, c. 6, § 2, eff. Feb. 21, 1985; Stats.1991, c. 656 (S.B.666), § 5; Stats.1992, c. 974 (S.B.1600), § 6, eff. Sept. 28, 1992; Stats.2007, c. 682 (A.B.430), § 12; Stats.2007, c. 747 (A.B.678), § 20.5.)*

Cross References

Renewal of licenses, see Vehicle Code §§ 12808, 12814.

Research References

3 Witkin, California Criminal Law 4th Punishment § 216 (2021), Offenses Involving Injury.
3 Witkin, California Criminal Law 4th Punishment § 217 (2021), Other Serious Offenses.

§ 13351.5. Vehicle used to commit assault with a deadly weapon or force likely to produce great bodily injury; revocation of driving privilege

(a) Upon receipt of a duly certified abstract of the record of any court showing that a person has been convicted of a felony for a violation of Section 245 of the Penal Code and that a vehicle was found by the court to constitute the deadly weapon or instrument used to commit that offense, the department immediately shall revoke the privilege of that person to drive a motor vehicle.

(b) The department shall not reinstate a privilege revoked under subdivision (a) under any circumstances.

(c) Notwithstanding subdivision (b), the department shall terminate any revocation order issued under this section on or after January 1, 1995, for a misdemeanor conviction of violating Section 245 of the Penal Code. *(Added by Stats.1994, c. 1221 (S.B.1758), § 9. Amended by Stats.1998, c. 606 (S.B.1880), § 15.)*

Cross References

Felonies, definition and penalties, see Penal Code §§ 17, 18.
Misdemeanors, definition and penalties, see Penal Code §§ 17, 19 and 19.2.

Research References

3 Witkin, California Criminal Law 4th Punishment § 217 (2021), Other Serious Offenses.

§ 13351.8. Suspension of driving privilege; receipt of certified abstract of record

Upon receipt of a duly certified abstract of the record of any court showing that the court has ordered the suspension of a driver's license pursuant to Section 13210, on or after January 1, 2001, the department shall suspend the person's driving privilege in accordance with that suspension order commencing either on the date of the person's conviction or upon the person's release from confinement or imprisonment. *(Added by Stats.2000, c. 642 (A.B.2733), § 5.)*

§ 13351.85. Conviction under § 12110; suspension of driving privileges

Upon receipt of a duly certified abstract of any court showing that a person has been convicted of a violation of Section 12110, the department shall suspend that person's driving privilege for four months if the conviction was a first conviction, and for one year, if the conviction was a second or subsequent conviction of a violation of that section that occurred within seven years of the current conviction. *(Added by Stats.2000, c. 641 (A.B.2729), § 2.)*

Research References

2 Witkin, California Criminal Law 4th Crimes Against Public Peace and Welfare § 422 (2021), In General.

§ 13352. Conviction for driving under the influence or engaging in speed contests or exhibitions of speed; terms of suspension or revocation of license; eligibility for restricted license; reinstatement conditions

Section operative until Jan. 1, 2026. See, also, § 13352 operative Jan. 1, 2026.

(a) The department shall immediately suspend or revoke the privilege of a person to operate a motor vehicle upon the receipt of an abstract of the record of a court showing that the person has been convicted of a violation of Section 23152 or 23153, subdivision (a) of Section 23109, or Section 23109.1, or upon the receipt of a report of a judge of the juvenile court, a juvenile traffic hearing officer, or a referee of a juvenile court showing that the person has been found to have committed a violation of Section 23152 or 23153, subdivision (a) of Section 23109, or Section 23109.1. If an offense specified in this section occurs in a vehicle defined in Section 15210, the suspension or revocation specified in this subdivision applies also to the noncommercial driving privilege. The commercial driving privilege shall be disqualified as specified in Sections 15300 to 15302, inclusive. For the purposes of this section, suspension or revocation shall be as follows:

(1)(A) Except as provided in this subparagraph, or as required under Section 13352.1 or 13352.4, upon a conviction or finding of a violation of Section 23152 punishable under Section 23536, the

Vehicle

privilege shall be suspended for a period of six months. The privilege shall not be reinstated until the person gives proof of financial responsibility and gives proof satisfactory to the department of successful completion of a driving-under-the-influence program licensed pursuant to Section 11836 of the Health and Safety Code described in subdivision (b) of Section 23538 of this code. If the court, as authorized under paragraph (3) of subdivision (b) of Section 23646, elects to order a person to enroll in, participate in, and complete either program described in subdivision (b) of Section 23542, the department shall require that program in lieu of the program described in subdivision (b) of Section 23538. For the purposes of this paragraph, enrollment in, participation in, and completion of an approved program shall occur subsequent to the date of the current violation. Credit shall not be given to any program activities completed prior to the date of the current violation. Except when the court has ordered installation of a functioning, certified ignition interlock device pursuant to Section 23575.3, the department shall advise the person that * * * they may apply to the department for a restricted driver's license if the person meets all of the following requirements:

(i) The underlying conviction was not only for the use of drugs, as defined in Section 312, at the time of the violation.

(ii) The person satisfactorily provides to the department, subsequent to the violation date of the current underlying conviction, enrollment in, or completion of, a driving-under-the-influence program licensed pursuant to Section 11836 of the Health and Safety Code, as described in subdivision (b) of Section 23538 of this code.

(iii) The person agrees, as a condition of the restriction, to continue satisfactory participation in the program described in clause (ii).

(iv) The person does both of the following:

(I) Submits the "Verification of Installation" form described in paragraph (2) of subdivision (g) of Section 13386.

(II) Agrees to maintain the functioning, certified ignition interlock device as required under subdivision (i).

(v) The person provides proof of financial responsibility, as defined in Section 16430.

(vi) The person pays all reissue fees and any restriction fee required by the department.

(vii) The person pays to the department a fee sufficient to cover the reasonable costs of administering the requirements of this paragraph, as determined by the department.

(B) The restrictions described in this paragraph shall remain in effect for the period required in subdivision (e).

(2)(A) Except as provided in this paragraph, upon a conviction or finding of a violation of Section 23153 punishable under Section 23554, the privilege shall be suspended for a period of one year. The privilege shall not be reinstated until the person gives proof of financial responsibility and gives proof satisfactory to the department of successful completion of a driving-under-the-influence program licensed pursuant to Section 11836 of the Health and Safety Code as described in subdivision (b) of Section 23556 of this code. If the court, as authorized under paragraph (3) of subdivision (b) of Section 23646, elects to order a person to enroll in, participate in, and complete either program described in subdivision (b) of Section 23542, the department shall require that program in lieu of the program described in Section 23556. For the purposes of this paragraph, enrollment in, participation in, and completion of an approved program shall occur subsequent to the date of the current violation. Credit shall not be given to any program activities completed prior to the date of the current violation. The department shall advise the person that they may apply to the department for a restricted driver's license if the person meets all of the following requirements:

(i) The underlying conviction was not only for the use of drugs, as defined in Section 312, at the time of the violation.

(ii) The person satisfactorily provides, subsequent to the violation date of the current underlying conviction, either of the following:

(I) Proof of enrollment in a driving-under-the-influence program licensed pursuant to Section 11836 of the Health and Safety Code, as described in subdivision (b) of Section 23556 of this code.

(II) Proof of enrollment in a program described in subdivision (b) of Section 23542, if the court has ordered the person to enroll in, participate in, and complete either program described in that section, in which case the person shall not be required to provide the proof described in subclause (I).

(iii) The person agrees, as a condition of the restriction, to continue satisfactory participation in the program described in clause (ii).

(iv) The person complies with Section 23575.3.

(v) The person does both of the following:

(I) Submits the "Verification of Installation" form described in paragraph (2) of subdivision (g) of Section 13386.

(II) Agrees to maintain the functioning, certified ignition interlock device as required under subdivision (i).

(vi) The person provides proof of financial responsibility, as defined in Section 16430.

(vii) The person pays all reissue fees and any restriction fee required by the department.

(viii) The person pays to the department a fee sufficient to cover the reasonable costs of administering the requirements of this paragraph, as determined by the department.

(B) The restriction shall remain in effect for the period required in subdivision (e).

(3)(A) Except as provided in this paragraph or in Section 13352.5, upon a conviction or finding of a violation of Section 23152 punishable under Section 23540, the privilege shall be suspended for two years. The privilege shall not be reinstated until the person gives proof of financial responsibility and gives proof satisfactory to the department of successful completion of a driving-under-the-influence program licensed pursuant to Section 11836 of the Health and Safety Code as described in subdivision (b) of Section 23542 of this code. For the purposes of this paragraph, enrollment in, participation in, and completion of an approved program shall occur subsequent to the date of the current violation. Credit shall not be given to any program activities completed prior to the date of the current violation. The department shall advise the person that they may apply to the department for a restricted driver's license if the person meets all of the following requirements:

(i) Completion of 12 months of the suspension period if the underlying conviction was only for the use of drugs, as defined in Section 312, at the time of the violation.

(ii) The person satisfactorily provides, subsequent to the violation date of the current underlying conviction, either of the following:

(I) Proof of enrollment in an 18–month driving-under-the-influence program licensed pursuant to Section 11836 of the Health and Safety Code if a 30–month program is unavailable in the person's county of residence or employment.

(II) Proof of enrollment in a 30–month driving-under-the-influence program licensed pursuant to Section 11836 of the Health and Safety Code, if available in the county of the person's residence or employment.

(iii) The person agrees, as a condition of the restriction, to continue satisfactory participation in the program described in clause (ii).

(iv) The person complies with Section 23575.3, if the underlying conviction involved the use of alcohol.

(v) The person does both of the following:

(I) Submits the "Verification of Installation" form described in paragraph (2) of subdivision (g) of Section 13386.

(II) Agrees to maintain the functioning, certified ignition interlock device as required under subdivision (i).

(vi) The person provides proof of financial responsibility, as defined in Section 16430.

(vii) The person pays all reissue fees and any restriction fee required by the department.

(viii) The person pays to the department a fee sufficient to cover the reasonable costs of administering the requirements of this paragraph, as determined by the department.

(B) The restriction shall remain in effect for the period required in subdivision (e).

(4)(A) Except as provided in this paragraph, upon a conviction or finding of a violation of Section 23153 punishable under Section 23560, the privilege shall be revoked for a period of three years. The privilege may not be reinstated until the person gives proof of financial responsibility, and the person gives proof satisfactory to the department of successful completion of a driving-under-the-influence program licensed pursuant to Section 11836 of the Health and Safety Code, as described in paragraph (4) of subdivision (b) of Section 23562 of this code. For the purposes of this paragraph, enrollment in, participation in, and completion of an approved program shall occur subsequent to the date of the current violation. Credit shall not be given to any program activities completed prior to the date of the current violation. The department shall advise the person that they may apply to the department for a restricted driver's license if the person meets all of the following requirements:

(i) Completion of 12 months of the suspension period if the underlying conviction was only for the use of drugs, as defined in Section 312, at the time of the violation.

(ii) The person satisfactorily provides, subsequent to the violation date of the current underlying conviction, either of the following:

(I) Proof of enrollment in an 18–month driving-under-the-influence program licensed pursuant to Section 11836 of the Health and Safety Code if a 30–month program is unavailable in the person's county of residence or employment.

(II) Proof of enrollment in a 30–month driving-under-the-influence program licensed pursuant to Section 11836 of the Health and Safety Code, if available in the county of the person's residence or employment.

(iii) The person agrees, as a condition of the restriction, to continue satisfactory participation in the program described in clause (ii).

(iv) The person complies with Section 23575.3, if the underlying conviction involved the use of alcohol.

(v) The person does both of the following:

(I) Submits the "Verification of Installation" form described in paragraph (2) of subdivision (g) of Section 13386.

(II) Agrees to maintain the functioning, certified ignition interlock device as required under subdivision (i).

(vi) The person provides proof of financial responsibility, as defined in Section 16430.

(vii) The person pays all applicable reinstatement or reissue fees and any restriction fee required by the department.

(viii) The person pays to the department a fee sufficient to cover the reasonable costs of administering the requirements of this paragraph, as determined by the department.

(B) The restriction shall remain in effect for the period required in subdivision (e).

(5)(A) Except as provided in this paragraph, upon a conviction or finding of a violation of Section 23152 punishable under Section 23546, the privilege shall be revoked for a period of three years. The privilege shall not be reinstated until the person files proof of financial responsibility and gives proof satisfactory to the department of successful completion of an 18–month driving-under-the-influence program licensed pursuant to Section 11836 of the Health and Safety Code, as described in subdivision (b) or (c) of Section 23548 of this code, if a 30–month program is unavailable in the person's county of residence or employment, or, if available in the county of the person's residence or employment, a 30–month driving-under-the-influence program licensed pursuant to Section 11836 of the Health and Safety Code, or a program specified in Section 8001 of the Penal Code. For the purposes of this paragraph, enrollment in, participation in, and completion of an approved program shall occur subsequent to the date of the current violation. Credit shall not be given to any program activities completed prior to the date of the current violation. The department shall advise the person that they may apply to the department for a restricted driver's license if the person meets all of the following requirements:

(i) Completion of 12 months of the suspension period if the underlying conviction was only for the use of drugs, as defined in Section 312, at the time of the violation.

(ii) The person satisfactorily provides, subsequent to the violation date of the current underlying conviction, either of the following:

(I) Proof of enrollment in an 18–month driving-under-the-influence program licensed pursuant to Section 11836 of the Health and Safety Code if a 30–month program is unavailable in the person's county of residence or employment.

(II) Proof of enrollment in a 30–month driving-under-the-influence program licensed pursuant to Section 11836 of the Health and Safety Code, if available in the county of the person's residence or employment.

(iii) The person agrees, as a condition of the restriction, to continue satisfactory participation in the program described in clause (ii).

(iv) The person complies with Section 23575.3, if the underlying conviction involved the use of alcohol.

(v) The person does both of the following:

(I) Submits the "Verification of Installation" form described in paragraph (2) of subdivision (g) of Section 13386.

(II) Agrees to maintain the functioning, certified ignition interlock device as required under Section 23575.3, if applicable.

(vi) The person provides proof of financial responsibility, as defined in Section 16430.

(vii) An individual convicted of a violation of Section 23152 punishable under Section 23546 may also, at any time after sentencing, petition the court for referral to an 18–month driving-under-the-influence program licensed pursuant to Section 11836 of the Health and Safety Code, or, if available in the county of the person's residence or employment, a 30–month driving-under-the-influence program licensed pursuant to Section 11836 of the Health and Safety Code. Unless good cause is shown, the court shall order the referral.

(viii) The person pays all applicable reinstatement or reissue fees and any restriction fee required by the department.

(ix) The person pays to the department a fee sufficient to cover the reasonable costs of administering the requirements of this paragraph, as determined by the department.

(B) The restriction shall remain in effect for the period required in subdivision (e).

(6)(A) Except as provided in this paragraph, upon a conviction or finding of a violation of Section 23153 punishable under Section 23550.5 or 23566, the privilege shall be revoked for a period of five years. The privilege may not be reinstated until the person gives proof of financial responsibility and gives proof satisfactory to the department of successful completion of a driving-under-the-influence program licensed pursuant to Section 11836 of the Health and Safety Code as described in subdivision (b) of Section 23568 of this code, or if available in the county of the person's residence or employment, a 30–month driving-under-the-influence program licensed pursuant to Section 11836 of the Health and Safety Code, or a program specified in Section 8001 of the Penal Code. For the purposes of this paragraph, enrollment in, participation in, and completion of an approved program shall be subsequent to the date of the current violation. Credit shall not be given to any program activities completed prior to the date of the current violation. The department shall advise the person that they may apply to the department for a restricted driver's license if the person meets all of the following requirements:

(i) Completion of 12 months of the suspension period if the underlying conviction was only for the use of drugs, as defined in Section 312, at the time of the violation.

(ii) The person satisfactorily provides, subsequent to the violation date of the current underlying conviction, either of the following:

(I) Proof of enrollment in a 30–month driving-under-the-influence program licensed pursuant to Section 11836 of the Health and Safety Code, if available in the county of the person's residence or employment.

(II) Proof of enrollment in an 18–month driving-under-the-influence program licensed pursuant to Section 11836 of the Health and Safety Code, if a 30–month program is unavailable in the person's county of residence or employment.

(iii) The person agrees, as a condition of the restriction, to continue satisfactory participation in the program described in clause (ii).

(iv) The person complies with Section 23575.3, if the underlying conviction involved alcohol.

(v) The person does both of the following:

(I) Submits the "Verification of Installation" form described in paragraph (2) of subdivision (g) of Section 13386.

(II) Agrees to maintain the functioning, certified ignition interlock device as required under subdivision (i).

(vi) The person provides proof of financial responsibility, as defined in Section 16430.

(vii) An individual convicted of a violation of Section 23153 punishable under Section 23566 may also, at any time after sentencing, petition the court for referral to an 18–month driving-under-the-influence program licensed pursuant to Section 11836 of the Health and Safety Code, or, if available in the county of the person's residence or employment, a 30–month driving-under-the-influence program licensed pursuant to Section 11836 of the Health and Safety Code. Unless good cause is shown, the court shall order the referral.

(viii) The person pays all applicable reinstatement or reissue fees and any restriction fee required by the department.

(ix) The person pays to the department a fee sufficient to cover the reasonable costs of administering the requirements of this paragraph, as determined by the department.

(B) The restriction shall remain in effect for the period required in subdivision (e).

(7)(A) Except as provided in this paragraph, upon a conviction or finding of a violation of Section 23152 punishable under Section 23550 or 23550.5, or of a violation of Section 23153 punishable under Section 23550.5, the privilege shall be revoked for a period of four years. The privilege shall not be reinstated until the person files proof of financial responsibility and gives proof satisfactory to the department of successful completion of an 18–month driving-under-the-influence program licensed pursuant to Section 11836 of the Health and Safety Code, if a 30–month program is unavailable in the person's county of residence or employment, or, if available in the county of the person's residence or employment, a 30–month driving-under-the-influence program licensed pursuant to Section 11836 of the Health and Safety Code, or a program specified in Section 8001 of the Penal Code. For the purposes of this paragraph, enrollment in, participation in, and completion of an approved program shall occur subsequent to the date of the current violation. Credit shall not be given to any program activities completed prior to the date of the current violation. The department shall advise the person that they may apply to the department for a restricted driver's license if the person meets all of the following requirements:

(i) Completion of 12 months of the suspension period if the underlying conviction was only for the use of drugs, as defined in Section 312, at the time of the violation.

(ii) The person satisfactorily provides, subsequent to the violation date of the current underlying conviction, either of the following:

(I) Proof of enrollment in an 18–month driving-under-the-influence program licensed pursuant to Section 11836 of the Health and Safety Code, if a 30–month program is unavailable in the person's county of residence or employment.

(II) Proof of enrollment in a 30–month driving-under-the-influence program licensed pursuant to Section 11836 of the Health and Safety Code, if available in the county of the person's residence or employment.

(iii) The person agrees, as a condition of the restriction, to continue satisfactory participation in the program described in clause (ii).

(iv) The person complies with Section 23575.3, if the underlying conviction involved alcohol.

(v) The person does both of the following:

(I) Submits the "Verification of Installation" form described in paragraph (2) of subdivision (g) of Section 13386.

(II) Agrees to maintain the functioning, certified ignition interlock device as required under subdivision (i).

(vi) The person provides proof of financial responsibility, as defined in Section 16430.

(vii) An individual convicted of a violation of Section 23152 punishable under Section 23550 may also, at any time after sentencing, petition the court for referral to an 18–month driving-under-the-influence program licensed pursuant to Section 11836 of the Health and Safety Code, or, if available in the county of the person's residence or employment, a 30–month driving-under-the-influence program licensed pursuant to Section 11836 of the Health and Safety Code. Unless good cause is shown, the court shall order the referral.

(viii) The person pays all applicable reinstatement or reissue fees and any restriction fee required by the department.

(ix) The person pays to the department a fee sufficient to cover the reasonable costs of administering the requirements of this paragraph, as determined by the department.

(B) The restriction shall remain in effect for the period required in subdivision (e).

(8)(A) Upon a conviction or finding of a violation of subdivision (a) of Section 23109 that is punishable under subdivision (e) of that section or Section 23109.1, the privilege shall be suspended for a period of 90 days to six months, if ordered by the court. The privilege shall not be reinstated until the person gives proof of financial responsibility, as defined in Section 16430.

(B) Commencing July 1, 2025, upon a finding of a violation of subdivision (c) of Section 23109 for engaging in a motor vehicle exhibition of speed, as described in paragraph (2) of subdivision (i) of Section 23109, the privilege shall be suspended for a period of 90 days to six months, if ordered by the court. The privilege shall not be reinstated until the person gives proof of financial responsibility, as defined in Section 16430.

(9) Upon a conviction or finding of a violation of subdivision (a) of Section 23109 that is punishable under subdivision (f) of that section, the privilege shall be suspended for a period of six months, if ordered by the court. The privilege shall not be reinstated until the person gives proof of financial responsibility, as defined in Section 16430.

(b) For the purposes of paragraphs (2) to (9), inclusive, of subdivision (a), the finding of the juvenile court judge, the juvenile hearing officer, or the referee of a juvenile court of a commission of a violation of Section 23152 or 23153, subdivision (a) of Section 23109, or Section 23109.1, as specified in subdivision (a) of this section, is a conviction.

(c) A judge of a juvenile court, juvenile hearing officer, or referee of a juvenile court shall immediately report the findings specified in subdivision (a) to the department.

(d) A conviction of an offense in a state, territory, or possession of the United States, the District of Columbia, the Commonwealth of Puerto Rico, or Canada that, if committed in this state, would be a violation of Section 23152, is a conviction of Section 23152 for the purposes of this section, and a conviction of an offense that, if committed in this state, would be a violation of Section 23153, is a conviction of Section 23153 for the purposes of this section. The department shall suspend or revoke the privilege to operate a motor vehicle pursuant to this section upon receiving notice of that conviction.

(e)(1) The restricted driving privilege shall become effective when the department receives all of the documents and fees required under paragraphs (1) to (7), inclusive, of subdivision (a) and, except as specified in paragraph (2) or (3), shall remain in effect until all reinstatement requirements are satisfied.

(2) For the purposes of the restriction conditions specified in paragraphs (1) to (7), inclusive, of subdivision (a), the department shall terminate the restriction imposed pursuant to this section and shall suspend or revoke the person's driving privilege upon receipt of notification from the driving-under-the-influence program that the person has failed to comply with the program requirements. The person's driving privilege shall remain suspended or revoked for the remaining period of the original suspension or revocation imposed under this section and until all reinstatement requirements described in this section are met.

(3) The department shall immediately suspend or revoke the privilege to operate a motor vehicle of a person who, with respect to an ignition interlock device installed pursuant to this section attempts to remove, bypass, or tamper with the device, has the device removed prior to the termination date of the restriction, or fails three or more times to comply with any requirement for the maintenance or calibration of the device. The privilege shall remain suspended or revoked for the remaining period of the originating suspension or revocation and until all reinstatement requirements in this section are satisfied, provided, however, that if the person provides proof to the satisfaction of the department that the person is in compliance with the restriction issued pursuant to this section, the department may, in its discretion, restore the privilege to operate a motor vehicle and reimpose the remaining term of the restriction.

(f) Notwithstanding the suspension periods specified in paragraphs (1) to (7), inclusive, of subdivision (a) or Section 13352.1, if the person maintains a functioning, certified ignition interlock device for the mandatory term required under Section 23575.3, inclusive of any term credit earned under Section 13353.6 or 13353.75, the department shall reinstate the person's privilege to operate a motor vehicle at the time the other reinstatement requirements are satisfied.

(g) For the purposes of this section, completion of a program is the following:

(1) Satisfactory completion of all program requirements approved pursuant to program licensure, as evidenced by a certificate of completion issued, under penalty of perjury, by the licensed program.

(2) Certification, under penalty of perjury, by the director of a program specified in Section 8001 of the Penal Code, that the person has completed a program specified in Section 8001 of the Penal Code.

(h)(1) The holder of a commercial driver's license who was operating a motor vehicle other than a commercial vehicle, or a driver who was operating a commercial vehicle, as defined in Section 15210, at the time of the violation that resulted in the suspension of that person's driving privilege pursuant to this section is not eligible for the restricted driver's license authorized under paragraphs (1) to (7), inclusive, of subdivision (a).

(2) Notwithstanding paragraph (1), as authorized under this section, the department shall issue the person a noncommercial driver's license restricted in the same manner and subject to the same conditions and requirements as specified in paragraphs (1) to (7), inclusive, of subdivision (a).

(i) A person whose driving privilege is restricted by the Department of Motor Vehicles pursuant to this section shall arrange for each vehicle with a functioning, certified ignition interlock device to be serviced by the installer at least once every 60 days in order for the installer to recalibrate the device and monitor the operation of the device. The installer shall notify the department if the device is removed or indicates that the person has attempted to remove, bypass, or tamper with the device, or if the person fails three or more times to comply with any requirement for the maintenance or calibration of the ignition interlock device.

(j) The reinstatement of the driving privilege pursuant to this section does not abrogate a person's continuing duty to comply with any restriction imposed pursuant to Section 23575.3.

(k) For purposes of this section, "bypass" means either of the following:

(1) Failure to take any random retest.

(2) Failure to pass a random retest with a breath alcohol concentration not exceeding 0.03 percent, by weight of alcohol, in the person's blood.

(*l*) For purposes of this section, "random retest" means a breath test performed by the driver upon a certified ignition interlock device at random intervals after the initial engine startup breath test and while the vehicle's motor is running.

(m) The restriction conditions specified in paragraphs (1) to (7), inclusive, of subdivision (a) shall apply only to a person who is convicted for a violation of Section 23152 or 23153 that occurred on or after January 1, 2019.

(n) This section shall become operative on January 1, 2019.

(*o*) This section shall remain in effect only until January 1, 2026, and as of that date is repealed, unless a later enacted statute that is enacted before January 1, 2026, deletes or extends that date. *(Added by Stats.2016, c. 783 (S.B.1046), § 5, eff. Jan. 1, 2017, operative Jan. 1, 2019. Amended by Stats.2017, c. 485 (S.B.611), § 3, eff. Jan. 1, 2018, operative Jan. 1, 2019; Stats.2021, c. 611 (A.B.3), § 1, eff. Jan. 1, 2022.)*

Repeal

For repeal of this section, see its terms.

Cross References

Commercial motor vehicles, multiple violations, see Vehicle Code § 15302.
Consecutive imposition of restriction, suspension, or revocation imposed under this section and suspension or revocation for refusing chemical testing, see Vehicle Code § 13353.1.
Conviction and punishment for violation of driving while under the influence of an alcoholic beverage, see Vehicle Code §§ 23612, 23620.
Driving under influence of alcohol or drugs, juvenile court finding in another jurisdiction deemed conviction for purpose of this section, see Vehicle Code § 23521.
Maximum period of suspension in certain cases, see Vehicle Code § 13556.
Participation of convicted person in alcohol services program, see Health and Safety Code § 11837.
Proof of financial responsibility, see Vehicle Code § 16430.
Separate offense involving alcohol or drugs and operation of vessel, etc., as separate offense under this section, see Vehicle Code § 23620.
Surrender of revoked licenses, see Vehicle Code §§ 13207, 13550.

Research References

2 Witkin, California Criminal Law 4th Crimes Against Public Peace and Welfare § 279 (2021), In General.
2 Witkin, California Criminal Law 4th Crimes Against Public Peace and Welfare § 280 (2021), First Violation.
2 Witkin, California Criminal Law 4th Crimes Against Public Peace and Welfare § 281 (2021), One Separate Conviction of Related Offense.
2 Witkin, California Criminal Law 4th Crimes Against Public Peace and Welfare § 282 (2021), Two Separate Convictions of Related Offenses.
2 Witkin, California Criminal Law 4th Crimes Against Public Peace and Welfare § 283 (2021), Three or More Separate Convictions of Related Offenses.
2 Witkin, California Criminal Law 4th Crimes Against Public Peace and Welfare § 285 (2021), First Violation.
2 Witkin, California Criminal Law 4th Crimes Against Public Peace and Welfare § 286 (2021), One Separate Conviction of Related Offense.
2 Witkin, California Criminal Law 4th Crimes Against Public Peace and Welfare § 287 (2021), Two or More Separate Convictions of Related Offenses.
2 Witkin, California Criminal Law 4th Crimes Against Public Peace and Welfare § 290 (2021), Ignition Interlock Device.
2 Witkin, California Criminal Law 4th Crimes Against Public Peace and Welfare § 321 (2021), Speed Contests and Exhibitions.
3 Witkin, California Criminal Law 4th Punishment § 214 (2021), Drunk Driving.
3 Witkin, California Criminal Law 4th Punishment § 215 (2021), Excessive Speed.
3 Witkin, California Criminal Law 4th Punishment § 218 (2021), Effect of Criminal Proceedings.
3 Witkin, California Criminal Law 4th Punishment § 219 (2021), Grounds.
3 Witkin, California Criminal Law 4th Punishment § 221 (2021), In General.

§ 13352. Conviction for driving under the influence or engaging in speed contests or exhibitions of speed; terms of suspension or revocation of license; eligibility for restricted license; reinstatement conditions

Section operative Jan. 1, 2026. See, also, § 13352 operative until Jan. 1, 2026.

(a) The department shall immediately suspend or revoke the privilege of a person to operate a motor vehicle upon the receipt of an abstract of the record of a court showing that the person has been convicted of a violation of Section 23152 or 23153, subdivision (a) of Section 23109, or Section 23109.1, or upon the receipt of a report of a judge of the juvenile court, a juvenile traffic hearing officer, or a referee of a juvenile court showing that the person has been found to have committed a violation of Section 23152 or 23153, subdivision (a) of Section 23109, or Section 23109.1. If an offense specified in this section occurs in a vehicle defined in Section 15210, the suspension or revocation specified in this subdivision also applies to the noncommercial driving privilege. The commercial driving privilege shall be disqualified as specified in Sections 15300 to 15302, inclusive. For the purposes of this section, suspension or revocation shall be as follows:

(1) Except as required under Section 13352.1 or 13352.4, upon a conviction or finding of a violation of Section 23152 punishable under Section 23536, the privilege shall be suspended for a period of six months. The privilege shall not be reinstated until the person gives proof of financial responsibility and gives proof satisfactory to the department of successful completion of a driving-under-the-influence program licensed pursuant to Section 11836 of the Health and Safety Code described in subdivision (b) of Section 23538 of this code. If the court, as authorized under paragraph (3) of subdivision (b) of Section 23646, elects to order a person to enroll in, participate in, and complete either program described in subdivision (b) of Section 23542, the department shall require that program in lieu of the program described in subdivision (b) of Section 23538. For the purposes of this paragraph, enrollment in, participation in, and completion of an approved program shall occur subsequent to the date of the current violation. Credit shall not be given to any program activities completed prior to the date of the current violation.

(2) Upon a conviction or finding of a violation of Section 23153 punishable under Section 23554, the privilege shall be suspended for a period of one year. The privilege shall not be reinstated until the person gives proof of financial responsibility and gives proof satisfactory to the department of successful completion of a driving-under-the-influence program licensed pursuant to Section 11836 of the Health and Safety Code as described in subdivision (b) of Section 23556 of this code. If the court, as authorized under paragraph (3) of subdivision (b) of Section 23646, elects to order a person to enroll in, participate in, and complete either program described in subdivision (b) of Section 23542, the department shall require that program in lieu of the program described in Section 23556. For the purposes of this paragraph, enrollment, participation, and completion of an approved program shall occur subsequent to the date of the current violation. Credit shall not be given to any program activities completed prior to the date of the current violation.

(3) Except as provided in Section 13352.5, upon a conviction or finding of a violation of Section 23152 punishable under Section 23540, the privilege shall be suspended for two years. The privilege shall not be reinstated until the person gives proof of financial responsibility and gives proof satisfactory to the department of successful completion of a driving-under-the-influence program licensed pursuant to Section 11836 of the Health and Safety Code as described in subdivision (b) of Section 23542 of this code. For the purposes of this paragraph, enrollment in, participation in, and completion of an approved program shall be subsequent to the date of the current violation. Credit shall not be given to any program activities completed prior to the date of the current violation. The department shall advise the person that they may apply to the department for a restriction of the driving privilege if the person meets all of the following requirements:

(A) Completion of 12 months of the suspension period, or completion of 90 days of the suspension period if the underlying conviction did not include the use of drugs as defined in Section 312 and the person was found to be only under the influence of an alcoholic beverage at the time of the violation.

(B) The person satisfactorily provides, subsequent to the violation date of the current underlying conviction, either of the following:

(i) Proof of enrollment in an 18–month driving-under-the-influence program licensed pursuant to Section 11836 of the Health and Safety Code if a 30–month program is unavailable in the person's county of residence or employment.

(ii) Proof of enrollment in a 30–month driving-under-the-influence program licensed pursuant to Section 11836 of the Health and Safety Code, if available in the county of the person's residence or employment.

(C) The person agrees, as a condition of the restriction, to continue satisfactory participation in the program described in subparagraph (B).

(D) The person submits the "Verification of Installation" form described in paragraph (2) of subdivision (g) of Section 13386.

(E) The person agrees to maintain the ignition interlock device as required under subdivision (g) of Section 23575.

(F) The person provides proof of financial responsibility, as defined in Section 16430.

(G) The person pays all reissue fees and any restriction fee required by the department.

(H) The person pays to the department a fee sufficient to cover the costs of administration of this paragraph, as determined by the department.

(I) The restriction shall remain in effect for the period required in subdivision (f) of Section 23575.

(4) Except as provided in this paragraph, upon a conviction or finding of a violation of Section 23153 punishable under Section 23560, the privilege shall be revoked for a period of three years. The privilege may not be reinstated until the person gives proof of financial responsibility, and the person gives proof satisfactory to the department of successful completion of a driving-under-the-influence program licensed pursuant to Section 11836 of the Health and Safety Code, as described in paragraph (4) of subdivision (b) of Section 23562 of this code. For the purposes of this paragraph, enrollment in, participation in, and completion of an approved program shall occur subsequent to the date of the current violation. Credit shall not be given to any program activities completed prior to the date of the current violation. The department shall advise the person that after the completion of 12 months of the revocation period, which may include credit for a suspension period served under subdivision (c) of Section 13353.3, they may apply to the department for a restricted driver's license if the person meets all of the following requirements:

(A) The person satisfactorily provides, subsequent to the violation date of the current underlying conviction, either of the following:

(i) The initial 12 months of an 18–month driving-under-the-influence program licensed pursuant to Section 11836 of the Health and Safety Code if a 30–month program is unavailable in the person's county of residence or employment.

(ii) The initial 12 months of a 30–month driving-under-the-influence program licensed pursuant to Section 11836 of the Health and Safety Code, if available in the county of the person's residence or employment.

(B) The person agrees, as a condition of the restriction, to continue satisfactory participation in the program described in subparagraph (A).

(C) The person submits the "Verification of Installation" form described in paragraph (2) of subdivision (g) of Section 13386.

(D) The person agrees to maintain the ignition interlock device as required under subdivision (g) of Section 23575.

(E) The person provides proof of financial responsibility, as defined in Section 16430.

(F) The person pays all applicable reinstatement or reissue fees and any restriction fee required by the department.

(G) The restriction shall remain in effect for the period required in subdivision (f) of Section 23575.

(5) Except as provided in this paragraph, upon a conviction or finding of a violation of Section 23152 punishable under Section 23546, the privilege shall be revoked for a period of three years. The privilege shall not be reinstated until the person files proof of financial responsibility and gives proof satisfactory to the department of successful completion of an 18–month driving-under-the-influence program licensed pursuant to Section 11836 of the Health and Safety Code, as described in subdivision (b) or (c) of Section 23548 of this code, if a 30–month program is unavailable in the person's county of residence or employment, or, if available in the county of the person's residence or employment, a 30–month driving-under-the-influence program licensed pursuant to Section 11836 of the Health and Safety Code, or a program specified in Section 8001 of the Penal Code. For the purposes of this paragraph, enrollment in, participation in, and completion of an approved program shall occur subsequent to the date of the current violation. Credit shall not be given to any program activities completed prior to the date of the current violation. The department shall advise the person that they may apply to the department for a restricted driver's license, which may include credit for a suspension period served under subdivision (c) of Section 13353.3, if the person meets all of the following requirements:

(A) Completion of 12 months of the suspension period, or completion of six months of the suspension period if the underlying conviction did not include the use of drugs as defined in Section 312 and the person was found to be only under the influence of an alcoholic beverage at the time of the violation.

(B) The person satisfactorily provides, subsequent to the violation date of the current underlying conviction, either of the following:

(i) Proof of enrollment in an 18–month driving-under-the-influence program licensed pursuant to Section 11836 of the Health and Safety Code if a 30–month program is unavailable in the person's county of residence or employment.

(ii) Proof of enrollment in a 30–month driving-under-the-influence program licensed pursuant to Section 11836 of the Health and Safety Code, if available in the county of the person's residence or employment.

(C) The person agrees, as a condition of the restriction, to continue satisfactory participation in the program described in subparagraph (B).

(D) The person submits the "Verification of Installation" form described in paragraph (2) of subdivision (g) of Section 13386.

(E) The person agrees to maintain the ignition interlock device as required under subdivision (g) of Section 23575.

(F) The person provides proof of financial responsibility, as defined in Section 16430.

(G) An individual convicted of a violation of Section 23152 punishable under Section 23546 may also, at any time after sentencing, petition the court for referral to an 18–month driving-under-the-influence program licensed pursuant to Section 11836 of the Health and Safety Code, or, if available in the county of the person's residence or employment, a 30–month driving-under-the-influence program licensed pursuant to Section 11836 of the Health and Safety Code. Unless good cause is shown, the court shall order the referral.

(H) The person pays all applicable reinstatement or reissue fees and any restriction fee required by the department.

(I) The person pays to the department a fee sufficient to cover the costs of administration of this paragraph, as determined by the department.

(J) The restriction shall remain in effect for the period required in subdivision (f) of Section 23575.

(6) Except as provided in this paragraph, upon a conviction or finding of a violation of Section 23153 punishable under Section 23550.5 or 23566, the privilege shall be revoked for a period of five years. The privilege may not be reinstated until the person gives proof of financial responsibility and gives proof satisfactory to the department of successful completion of a driving-under-the-influence program licensed pursuant to Section 11836 of the Health and Safety Code as described in subdivision (b) of Section 23568 of this code, or if available in the county of the person's residence or employment, a

30–month driving-under-the-influence program licensed pursuant to Section 11836 of the Health and Safety Code, or a program specified in Section 8001 of the Penal Code. For the purposes of this paragraph, enrollment in, participation in, and completion of an approved program shall be subsequent to the date of the current violation. Credit shall not be given to any program activities completed prior to the date of the current violation. The department shall advise the person that after completion of 12 months of the revocation period, which may include credit for a suspension period served under subdivision (c) of Section 13353.3, they may apply to the department for a restricted driver's license if the person meets all of the following requirements:

(A) The person satisfactorily provides, subsequent to the violation date of the current underlying conviction, either of the following:

(i) Completion of the initial 12 months of a 30–month driving-under-the-influence program licensed pursuant to Section 11836 of the Health and Safety Code, if available in the county of the person's residence or employment.

(ii) Completion of the initial 12 months of an 18–month driving-under-the-influence program licensed pursuant to Section 11836 of the Health and Safety Code, if a 30–month program is unavailable in the person's county of residence or employment.

(B) The person agrees, as a condition of the restriction, to continue satisfactory participation in the program described in subparagraph (A).

(C) The person submits the "Verification of Installation" form described in paragraph (2) of subdivision (g) of Section 13386.

(D) The person agrees to maintain the ignition interlock device as required under subdivision (g) of Section 23575.

(E) The person provides proof of financial responsibility, as defined in Section 16430.

(F) An individual convicted of a violation of Section 23153 punishable under Section 23566 may also, at any time after sentencing, petition the court for referral to an 18–month driving-under-the-influence program licensed pursuant to Section 11836 of the Health and Safety Code, or, if available in the county of the person's residence or employment, a 30–month driving-under-the-influence program licensed pursuant to Section 11836 of the Health and Safety Code. Unless good cause is shown, the court shall order the referral.

(G) The person pays all applicable reinstatement or reissue fees and any restriction fee required by the department.

(H) The restriction shall remain in effect for the period required in subdivision (f) of Section 23575.

(7) Except as provided in this paragraph, upon a conviction or finding of a violation of Section 23152 punishable under Section 23550 or 23550.5, or of a violation of Section 23153 punishable under Section 23550.5, the privilege shall be revoked for a period of four years. The privilege shall not be reinstated until the person files proof of financial responsibility and gives proof satisfactory to the department of successful completion of an 18–month driving-under-the-influence program licensed pursuant to Section 11836 of the Health and Safety Code, if a 30–month program is unavailable in the person's county of residence or employment, or, if available in the county of the person's residence or employment, a 30–month driving-under-the-influence program licensed pursuant to Section 11836 of the Health and Safety Code, or a program specified in Section 8001 of the Penal Code. For the purposes of this paragraph, enrollment in, participation in, and completion of an approved program shall occur subsequent to the date of the current violation. Credit shall not be given to any program activities completed prior to the date of the current violation. The department shall advise the person that after completion of 12 months of the revocation period, which may include credit for a suspension period served under subdivision (c) of Section 13353.3, * * * they may apply to the department for a restricted driver's license if the person meets all of the following requirements:

(A) The person satisfactorily provides, subsequent to the violation date of the current underlying conviction, either of the following:

(i) The initial 12 months of an 18–month driving-under-the-influence program licensed pursuant to Section 11836 of the Health and Safety Code, if a 30–month program is unavailable in the person's county of residence or employment.

(ii) The initial 12 months of a 30–month driving-under-the-influence program licensed pursuant to Section 11836 of the Health and Safety Code, if available in the county of the person's residence or employment.

(B) The person agrees, as a condition of the restriction, to continue satisfactory participation in the program described in subparagraph (A).

(C) The person submits the "Verification of Installation" form described in paragraph (2) of subdivision (g) of Section 13386.

(D) The person agrees to maintain the ignition interlock device as required under subdivision (g) of Section 23575.

(E) The person provides proof of financial responsibility, as defined in Section 16430.

(F) An individual convicted of a violation of Section 23152 punishable under Section 23550 may also, at any time after sentencing, petition the court for referral to an 18–month driving-under-the-influence program licensed pursuant to Section 11836 of the Health and Safety Code, or, if available in the county of the person's residence or employment, a 30–month driving-under-the-influence program licensed pursuant to Section 11836 of the Health and Safety Code. Unless good cause is shown, the court shall order the referral.

(G) The person pays all applicable reinstatement or reissue fees and any restriction fee required by the department.

(H) The restriction shall remain in effect for the period required in subdivision (f) of Section 23575.

(8)(A) Upon a conviction or finding of a violation of subdivision (a) of Section 23109 that is punishable under subdivision (e) of that section or Section 23109.1, the privilege shall be suspended for a period of 90 days to six months, if ordered by the court. The privilege shall not be reinstated until the person gives proof of financial responsibility, as defined in Section 16430.

(B) Upon a finding of a violation of subdivision (c) of Section 23109 for engaging in a motor vehicle exhibition of speed, as described in paragraph (2) of subdivision (i) of Section 23109, the privilege shall be suspended for a period of 90 days to six months, if ordered by the court. The privilege shall not be reinstated until the person gives proof of financial responsibility, as defined in Section 16430.

(9) Upon a conviction or finding of a violation of subdivision (a) of Section 23109 that is punishable under subdivision (f) of that section, the privilege shall be suspended for a period of six months, if ordered by the court. The privilege shall not be reinstated until the person gives proof of financial responsibility, as defined in Section 16430.

(b) For the purpose of paragraphs (2) to (9), inclusive, of subdivision (a), the finding of the juvenile court judge, the juvenile hearing officer, or the referee of a juvenile court of a commission of a violation of Section 23152 or 23153, subdivision (a) of Section 23109, or Section 23109.1, as specified in subdivision (a) of this section, is a conviction.

(c) A judge of a juvenile court, juvenile hearing officer, or referee of a juvenile court shall immediately report the findings specified in subdivision (a) to the department.

(d) A conviction of an offense in a state, territory, or possession of the United States, the District of Columbia, the Commonwealth of

Puerto Rico, or Canada that, if committed in this state, would be a violation of Section 23152, is a conviction of Section 23152 for the purposes of this section, and a conviction of an offense that, if committed in this state, would be a violation of Section 23153, is a conviction of Section 23153 for the purposes of this section. The department shall suspend or revoke the privilege to operate a motor vehicle pursuant to this section upon receiving notice of that conviction.

(e) For the purposes of the restriction conditions specified in paragraphs (3) to (7), inclusive, of subdivision (a), the department shall terminate the restriction imposed pursuant to this section and shall suspend or revoke the person's driving privilege upon receipt of notification from the driving-under-the-influence program that the person has failed to comply with the program requirements. The person's driving privilege shall remain suspended or revoked for the remaining period of the original suspension or revocation imposed under this section and until all reinstatement requirements described in this section are met.

(f) For the purposes of this section, completion of a program is the following:

(1) Satisfactory completion of all program requirements approved pursuant to program licensure, as evidenced by a certificate of completion issued, under penalty of perjury, by the licensed program.

(2) Certification, under penalty of perjury, by the director of a program specified in Section 8001 of the Penal Code, that the person has completed a program specified in Section 8001 of the Penal Code.

(g) The holder of a commercial driver's license who was operating a commercial motor vehicle, as defined in Section 15210, at the time of a violation that resulted in a suspension or revocation of the person's noncommercial driving privilege under this section is not eligible for the restricted driver's license authorized under paragraphs (3) to (7), inclusive, of subdivision (a).

(h) This section shall become operative January 1, 2026. *(Added by Stats.2016, c. 783 (S.B.1046), § 6, eff. Jan. 1, 2017, operative Jan. 1, 2026. Amended by Stats.2021, c. 611 (A.B.3), § 2, eff. Jan. 1, 2022, operative Jan. 1, 2026.)*

Cross References

Commercial motor vehicles, multiple violations, see Vehicle Code § 15302.
Consecutive imposition of restriction, suspension, or revocation imposed under this section and suspension or revocation for refusing chemical testing, see Vehicle Code § 13353.1.
Conviction and punishment for violation of driving while under the influence of an alcoholic beverage, see Vehicle Code §§ 23612, 23620.
Driving under influence of alcohol or drugs, juvenile court finding in another jurisdiction deemed conviction for purpose of this section, see Vehicle Code § 23521.
Maximum period of suspension in certain cases, see Vehicle Code § 13556.
Participation of convicted person in alcohol services program, see Health and Safety Code § 11837.
Proof of financial responsibility, see Vehicle Code § 16430.
Separate offense involving alcohol or drugs and operation of vessel, etc., as separate offense under this section, see Vehicle Code § 23620.
Surrender of revoked licenses, see Vehicle Code §§ 13207, 13550.

Research References

2 Witkin, California Criminal Law 4th Crimes Against Public Peace and Welfare § 279 (2021), In General.
2 Witkin, California Criminal Law 4th Crimes Against Public Peace and Welfare § 280 (2021), First Violation.
2 Witkin, California Criminal Law 4th Crimes Against Public Peace and Welfare § 281 (2021), One Separate Conviction of Related Offense.
2 Witkin, California Criminal Law 4th Crimes Against Public Peace and Welfare § 282 (2021), Two Separate Convictions of Related Offenses.
2 Witkin, California Criminal Law 4th Crimes Against Public Peace and Welfare § 283 (2021), Three or More Separate Convictions of Related Offenses.
2 Witkin, California Criminal Law 4th Crimes Against Public Peace and Welfare § 285 (2021), First Violation.
2 Witkin, California Criminal Law 4th Crimes Against Public Peace and Welfare § 286 (2021), One Separate Conviction of Related Offense.
2 Witkin, California Criminal Law 4th Crimes Against Public Peace and Welfare § 287 (2021), Two or More Separate Convictions of Related Offenses.
2 Witkin, California Criminal Law 4th Crimes Against Public Peace and Welfare § 290 (2021), Ignition Interlock Device.
2 Witkin, California Criminal Law 4th Crimes Against Public Peace and Welfare § 321 (2021), Speed Contests and Exhibitions.
3 Witkin, California Criminal Law 4th Punishment § 214 (2021), Drunk Driving.
3 Witkin, California Criminal Law 4th Punishment § 215 (2021), Excessive Speed.
3 Witkin, California Criminal Law 4th Punishment § 218 (2021), Effect of Criminal Proceedings.
3 Witkin, California Criminal Law 4th Punishment § 219 (2021), Grounds.
3 Witkin, California Criminal Law 4th Punishment § 221 (2021), In General.

§ 13352.1. Conviction or finding of violation of § 23152; ten month suspension of privilege for certain offenders; conditions for reinstatement; eligibility for restricted license

Section operative until Jan. 1, 2026. See, also, § 13352.1 operative Jan. 1, 2026.

(a) Pursuant to subdivision (a) of Section 13352 and except as required under subdivision (c) of this section or Section 13352.4, upon a conviction or finding of a violation of Section 23152 punishable under Section 23536, if the court refers the person to a program pursuant to paragraph (2) of subdivision (b) of Section 23538, the privilege shall be suspended for 10 months.

(b) The privilege may not be reinstated until the person gives proof of financial responsibility and gives proof satisfactory to the department of successful completion of a driving-under-the-influence program licensed pursuant to Section 11836 of the Health and Safety Code described in subdivision (b) of Section 23538 of this code. For the purposes of this subdivision, enrollment, participation, and completion of an approved program shall be subsequent to the date of the current violation. Credit may not be given to any program activities completed prior to the date of the current violation.

(c)(1) Except when the court has ordered installation of a functioning, certified ignition interlock device pursuant to Section 23575.3, the department shall advise the person that he or she may apply to the department for a restricted driver's license if the person meets all of the following requirements:

(A) The underlying conviction was not only for the use of drugs, as defined in Section 312, at the time of the violation.

(B) The person satisfactorily provides to the department, subsequent to the violation date of the current underlying conviction, enrollment in, or completion of, a driving-under-the-influence program licensed pursuant to Section 11836 of the Health and Safety Code, as described in paragraph (2) of subdivision (b) of Section 23538 of this code.

(C) The person agrees, as a condition of the restriction, to continue satisfactory participation in the program described in subparagraph (B).

(D) The person does both of the following:

(i) Submits the "Verification of Installation" form described in paragraph (2) of subdivision (g) of Section 13386.

(ii) Agrees to maintain the functioning, certified ignition interlock device as required under subdivision (e).

(E) The person provides proof of financial responsibility, as defined in Section 16430.

(F) The person pays all reissue fees and any restriction fee required by the department.

(G) The person pays to the department a fee sufficient to cover the reasonable costs of administering the requirements of this paragraph, as determined by the department.

(2) The restriction shall remain in effect for the period required in subdivision (d).

(d)(1) The restricted driving privilege shall become effective when the department receives all of the documents and fees required under subdivision (c) and, except as specified in paragraph (2) or (3), shall remain in effect until all reinstatement requirements are satisfied.

(2) For the purposes of the restriction conditions specified in subdivision (c), the department shall terminate the restriction imposed pursuant to this section and shall suspend or revoke the person's driving privilege upon receipt of notification from the driving-under-the-influence program that the person has failed to comply with the program requirements. The person's driving privilege shall remain suspended or revoked for the remaining period of the original suspension or revocation imposed under this section and until all reinstatement requirements described in this section are met.

(3) The department shall immediately suspend or revoke the privilege to operate a motor vehicle of a person who, with respect to an ignition interlock device installed pursuant to Section 23575.3, attempts to remove, bypass, or tamper with the device, has the device removed prior to the termination date of the restriction, or fails three or more times to comply with any requirement for the maintenance or calibration of the device. The privilege shall remain suspended or revoked for the remaining period of the originating suspension or revocation and until all reinstatement requirements in this section are satisfied, provided, however, that if the person provides proof to the satisfaction of the department that the person is in compliance with the restriction issued pursuant to this section, the department may, in its discretion, restore the privilege to operate a motor vehicle and reimpose the remaining term of the restriction.

(e) A person whose driving privilege is restricted by the department pursuant to this section shall arrange for each vehicle with a functioning, certified ignition interlock device to be serviced by the installer at least once every 60 days in order for the installer to recalibrate the device and monitor the operation of the device. The installer shall notify the Department of Motor Vehicles if the device is removed or indicates that the person has attempted to remove, bypass, or tamper with the device, or if the person fails three or more times to comply with any requirement for the maintenance or calibration of the ignition interlock device.

(f)(1) The holder of a commercial driver's license who was operating a motor vehicle other than a commercial vehicle, or a driver who was operating a commercial vehicle, as defined in Section 15210, at the time of the violation that resulted in the suspension of that person's driving privilege under paragraph (1) of subdivision (a) of Section 13352 or this section is not eligible for the restricted driver's license authorized under this section.

(2) Notwithstanding paragraph (1), as authorized under this section, the department shall issue the person a noncommercial driver's license restricted in the same manner and subject to the same conditions and requirements as specified in subdivision (c).

(g) For the purposes of this section, "bypass" means either of the following:

(1) Failure to take any random retest.

(2) Failure to pass a random retest with a breath alcohol concentration not exceeding 0.03 percent, by weight of alcohol, in the person's blood.

(h) For purposes of this section, "random retest" means a breath test performed by the driver upon a certified ignition interlock device at random intervals after the initial engine startup breath test and while the vehicle's motor is running.

(i) The restriction conditions specified in this section shall apply only to a person who is convicted for a violation of Section 23152, as specified in subdivision (a), that occurred on or after January 1, 2019.

(j) This section shall become operative on January 1, 2019.

(k) This section shall remain in effect only until January 1, 2026, and as of that date is repealed. *(Added by Stats.2017, c. 485 (S.B.611), § 5, eff. Jan. 1, 2018, operative Jan. 1, 2019.)*

Repeal

For repeal of this section, see its terms.

Research References

2 Witkin, California Criminal Law 4th Crimes Against Public Peace and Welfare § 280 (2021), First Violation.
2 Witkin, California Criminal Law 4th Crimes Against Public Peace and Welfare § 290 (2021), Ignition Interlock Device.
3 Witkin, California Criminal Law 4th Punishment § 214 (2021), Drunk Driving.

§ 13352.1. Conviction or finding of violation of § 23152; ten month suspension of privilege for certain offenders; conditions for reinstatement

Section operative Jan. 1, 2026. See, also, § 13352.1 operative until Jan. 1, 2026.

(a) Pursuant to subdivision (a) of Section 13352 and except as required under Section 13352.4, upon a conviction or finding of a violation of Section 23152 punishable under Section 23536, if the court refers the person to a program pursuant to paragraph (2) of subdivision (b) of Section 23538, the privilege shall be suspended for 10 months.

(b) The privilege may not be reinstated until the person gives proof of financial responsibility and gives proof satisfactory to the department of successful completion of a driving-under-the-influence program licensed pursuant to Section 11836 of the Health and Safety Code described in subdivision (b) of Section 23538 of this code. For the purposes of this subdivision, enrollment, participation, and completion of an approved program shall be subsequent to the date of the current violation. Credit may not be given to any program activities completed prior to the date of the current violation.

(c) This section shall become operative on January 1, 2026. *(Added by Stats.2017, c. 485 (S.B.611), § 6, eff. Jan. 1, 2018, operative Jan. 1, 2026.)*

Research References

2 Witkin, California Criminal Law 4th Crimes Against Public Peace and Welfare § 280 (2021), First Violation.
2 Witkin, California Criminal Law 4th Crimes Against Public Peace and Welfare § 290 (2021), Ignition Interlock Device.
3 Witkin, California Criminal Law 4th Punishment § 214 (2021), Drunk Driving.

§ 13352.2. Driving-under-the-influence programs; filing of proof of enrollment and proof of completion by program provider

(a) If a person is required under Section 13352 to provide the department with proof of enrollment in a driving-under-the-influence program licensed pursuant to Section 11836 of the Health and Safety Code, or a program specified in Section 8001 of the Penal Code, the department shall deem that requirement satisfied upon receiving at its headquarters proof of enrollment that is satisfactory to the department and has been forwarded to the department by the program provider.

(b) If a person is required under Section 13352 to provide the department with proof of completion of a driving-under-the-influence program licensed pursuant to Section 11836 of the Health and Safety Code, or a program specified in Section 8001 of the Penal Code, the department shall deem that requirement satisfied upon receiving at its headquarters proof of completion that is satisfactory to the department and has been forwarded to the department by the program provider. *(Added by Stats.2004, c. 403 (S.B.1696), § 1.)*

§ 13352.3. Persons under eighteen years of age convicted of violations of §§ 23152 or 23153; term of revocation; reinstatement of privilege

(a) Notwithstanding any other provision of law, except subdivisions (b), (c), and (d) of Section 13352 and Sections 13367 and 23521, the department immediately shall revoke the privilege of any person to operate a motor vehicle upon receipt of a duly certified abstract of the record of any court showing that the person was convicted of a violation of Section 23152 or 23153 while under 18 years of age, or upon receipt of a report of a judge of the juvenile court, a juvenile hearing officer, or a referee of a juvenile court showing that the person has been found to have committed a violation of Section 23152 or 23153.

(b) The term of the revocation shall be until the person reaches 18 years of age, for one year, or for the period prescribed for restriction, suspension, or revocation specified in subdivision (a) of Section 13352, whichever is longer. The privilege may not be reinstated until the person gives proof of financial responsibility as defined in Section 16430. *(Added by Stats.1983, c. 934, § 2. Amended by Stats.1992, c. 974 (S.B.1600), § 7, eff. Sept. 28, 1992; Stats.1998, c. 118 (S.B.1186), § 3.2, operative July 1, 1999; Stats.2003, c. 149 (S.B.79), § 83.)*

Law Revision Commission Comments

Subdivision (a) of Section 13352.3 is amended to reflect the redesignation of traffic hearing officers as juvenile hearing officers. See 1997 Cal. Stat. ch. 679. [33 Cal.L.Rev.Comm. Reports 257 (2003)].

Cross References

Driving under influence of alcohol or drugs, juvenile court finding in another jurisdiction deemed conviction for purpose of this section, see Vehicle Code § 23521.

Research References

3 Witkin, California Criminal Law 4th Punishment § 214 (2021), Drunk Driving.

§ 13352.4. Restricted driver's licenses

Section operative until Jan. 1, 2026. See, also, § 13352.4 operative Jan. 1, 2026.

(a) Except as provided in subdivision (h), or when the court has ordered installation of a functioning, certified ignition interlock device pursuant to Section 23575.3, the department shall issue a restricted driver's license to a person whose driver's license was suspended under paragraph (1) of subdivision (a) of Section 13352 or Section 13352.1, if the person meets all of the following requirements:

(1) Submits proof satisfactory to the department of either of the following:

(A) Enrollment in a driving-under-the-influence program licensed pursuant to Section 11836 of the Health and Safety Code, as described in subdivision (b) of Section 23538 of this code.

(B) Enrollment in a program described in subdivision (b) of Section 23542, if the court has ordered the person to enroll in, participate in, and complete either program described in that section, in which case the person shall not be required to provide proof of the enrollment described in subparagraph (A).

(2) Submits proof of financial responsibility, as defined in Section 16430.

(3) Pays all applicable reinstatement or reissue fees and any restriction fee required by the department.

(b) The restriction of the driving privilege shall become effective when the department receives all of the documents and fees required under subdivision (a) and shall remain in effect for a period of 12 months and until the date all reinstatement requirements described in Section 13352 or 13352.1 have been met.

(c) The restriction of the driving privilege shall be limited to the hours necessary for driving to and from the person's place of employment, driving during the course of employment, and driving to and from activities required in the driving-under-the-influence program.

(d) Whenever the driving privilege is restricted under this section, proof of financial responsibility, as defined in Section 16430, shall be maintained for three years. If the person does not maintain that proof of financial responsibility at any time during the restriction, the driving privilege shall be suspended until the proof required under Section 16484 is received by the department.

(e) For the purposes of this section, enrollment, participation, and completion of an approved program shall be subsequent to the date of the current violation. Credit may not be given to a program activity completed prior to the date of the current violation.

(f) The department shall terminate the restriction issued under this section and shall suspend the privilege to operate a motor vehicle pursuant to paragraph (1) of subdivision (a) of Section 13352 or Section 13352.1 immediately upon receipt of notification from the driving-under-the-influence program that the person has failed to comply with the program requirements. The privilege shall remain suspended until the final day of the original suspension imposed under paragraph (1) of subdivision (a) of Section 13352 or Section 13352.1, or until the date all reinstatement requirements described in Section 13352 or 13352.1 have been met, whichever date is later.

(g)(1) The holder of a commercial driver's license who was operating a motor vehicle other than a commercial vehicle, or a driver who was operating a commercial vehicle, as defined in Section 15210, at the time of the violation that resulted in the suspension of that person's driving privilege under paragraph (1) of subdivision (a) of Section 13352 or Section 13352.1 is not eligible for the restricted driver's license authorized under this section.

(2) Notwithstanding paragraph (1), as authorized under this section, the department shall issue the person a noncommercial driver's license restricted in the same manner and subject to the same conditions and requirements as specified in subdivision (a).

(h) If, upon conviction, the court has made the determination, as authorized under Section 23536 or paragraph (3) of subdivision (a) of Section 23538, to disallow the issuance of a restricted driver's license, the department may not issue a restricted driver's license under this section.

(i) This section shall become operative on January 1, 2019.

(j) This section shall remain in effect only until January 1, 2026, and as of that date is repealed, unless a later enacted statute, that is enacted before January 1, 2026, deletes or extends that date. *(Added by Stats.2016, c. 783 (S.B.1046), § 8, eff. Jan. 1, 2017, operative Jan. 1, 2019. Amended by Stats.2017, c. 485 (S.B.611), § 7, eff. Jan. 1, 2018, operative Jan. 1, 2019.)*

Repeal

For repeal of this section, see its terms.

Research References

2 Witkin, California Criminal Law 4th Crimes Against Public Peace and Welfare § 280 (2021), First Violation.

3 Witkin, California Criminal Law 4th Punishment § 214 (2021), Drunk Driving.

§ 13352.4. Restricted driver's licenses

Section operative Jan. 1, 2026. See, also, § 13352.4 operative until Jan. 1, 2026.

(a) Except as provided in subdivision (h), the department shall issue a restricted driver's license to a person whose driver's license was suspended under paragraph (1) of subdivision (a) of Section 13352 or Section 13352.1, if the person meets all of the following requirements:

(1) Submits proof satisfactory to the department of either of the following, as applicable:

(A) Enrollment in a driving-under-the-influence program licensed pursuant to Section 11836 of the Health and Safety Code, as described in subdivision (b) of Section 23538 of this code.

(B) Enrollment in a program described in subdivision (b) of Section 23542, if the court has ordered the person to enroll in, participate in, and complete either program described in that section, in which case the person shall not be required to provide proof of the enrollment described in subparagraph (A).

(2) Submits proof of financial responsibility, as defined in Section 16430.

(3) Pays all applicable reinstatement or reissue fees and any restriction fee required by the department.

(b) The restriction of the driving privilege shall become effective when the department receives all of the documents and fees required under subdivision (a) and shall remain in effect until the final day of the original suspension imposed under paragraph (1) of subdivision (a) of Section 13352 or Section 13352.1, or until the date all reinstatement requirements described in Section 13352 or 13352.1 have been met, whichever date is later, and may include credit for any suspension period served under subdivision (c) of Section 13353.3.

(c) The restriction of the driving privilege shall be limited to the hours necessary for driving to and from the person's place of employment, driving during the course of employment, and driving to and from activities required in the driving-under-the-influence program.

(d) Whenever the driving privilege is restricted under this section, proof of financial responsibility, as defined in Section 16430, shall be maintained for three years. If the person does not maintain that proof of financial responsibility at any time during the restriction, the driving privilege shall be suspended until the proof required under Section 16484 is received by the department.

(e) For the purposes of this section, enrollment, participation, and completion of an approved program shall be subsequent to the date of the current violation. Credit may not be given to a program activity completed prior to the date of the current violation.

(f) The department shall terminate the restriction issued under this section and shall suspend the privilege to operate a motor vehicle pursuant to paragraph (1) of subdivision (a) of Section 13352 or Section 13352.1 immediately upon receipt of notification from the driving-under-the-influence program that the person has failed to comply with the program requirements. The privilege shall remain suspended until the final day of the original suspension imposed under paragraph (1) of subdivision (a) of Section 13352 or 13352.1, or until the date all reinstatement requirements described in Section 13352 or Section 13352.1 have been met, whichever date is later.

(g) The holder of a commercial driver's license who was operating a commercial motor vehicle, as defined in Section 15210, at the time of a violation that resulted in a suspension or revocation of the person's noncommercial driving privilege under paragraph (1) of subdivision (a) of Section 13352 or Section 13352.1 is not eligible for the restricted driver's license authorized under this section.

(h) If, upon conviction, the court has made the determination, as authorized under subdivision (d) of Section 23536 or paragraph (3) of subdivision (a) of Section 23538, to disallow the issuance of a restricted driver's license, the department may not issue a restricted driver's license under this section.

(i) This section shall become operative January 1, 2026. *(Added by Stats.2016, c. 783 (S.B.1046), § 9, eff. Jan. 1, 2017, operative Jan. 1, 2026.)*

Research References

2 Witkin, California Criminal Law 4th Crimes Against Public Peace and Welfare § 280 (2021), First Violation.

3 Witkin, California Criminal Law 4th Punishment § 214 (2021), Drunk Driving.

§ 13352.5. Restricted driver's licenses

(a) The department shall issue a restricted driver's license to a person whose driver's license was suspended under paragraph (3) of subdivision (a) of Section 13352, if all of the following requirements have been met:

(1) Proof satisfactory to the department of enrollment in, or completion of, a driving-under-the-influence program licensed pursuant to Section 11836 of the Health and Safety Code, as described in subdivision (b) of Section 23542 has been received in the department's headquarters.

(2) The person submits proof of financial responsibility, as described in Section 16430.

(3) The person completes not less than 12 months of the suspension period imposed under paragraph (3) of subdivision (a) of Section 13352. The 12 months may include credit for any suspension period served under subdivision (c) of Section 13353.3.

(4) The person pays all applicable reinstatement or reissue fees and any restriction fee required by the department.

(b) The restriction of the driving privilege shall become effective when the department receives all of the documents and fees required under subdivision (a) and shall remain in effect until the final day of the original suspension imposed under paragraph (3) of subdivision (a) of Section 13352, or until the date all reinstatement requirements described in Section 13352 have been met, whichever date is later.

(c) The restriction of the driving privilege shall be limited to the hours necessary for driving to and from the person's place of employment, driving during the course of employment, and driving to and from activities required in the driving-under-the-influence program.

(d) Whenever the driving privilege is restricted under this section, proof of financial responsibility, as defined in Section 16430, shall be maintained for three years. If the person does not maintain that proof of financial responsibility at any time during the restriction, the driving privilege shall be suspended until the proof required under Section 16484 is received by the department.

(e) For the purposes of this section, enrollment in, participation in, and completion of an approved program shall be subsequent to the date of the current violation. Credit shall not be given to any program activities completed prior to the date of the current violation.

(f) The department shall terminate the restriction imposed pursuant to this section and shall suspend the privilege to drive under paragraph (3) of subdivision (a) of Section 13352 upon receipt of notification from the driving-under-the-influence program that the person has failed to comply with the program requirements.

(g) If, upon conviction, the court has made the determination, as authorized under subdivision (b) of Section 23540 or subdivision (d) of Section 23542, to disallow the issuance of a restricted driver's license, the department shall not issue a restricted driver's license under this section.

(h) A person restricted pursuant to this section may apply to the department for a restricted driver's license, subject to the conditions specified in paragraph (3) of subdivision (a) of Section 13352. Whenever proof of financial responsibility has already been provided and a restriction fee has been paid in compliance with restrictions described in this section, and the offender subsequently receives an ignition interlock device restriction described in paragraph (3) of subdivision (a) of Section 13352, the proof of financial responsibility period shall not be extended beyond the previously established term and no additional restriction fee shall be required.

(i) This section applies to a person who meets all of the following conditions:

(1) Has been convicted of a violation of Section 23152 that occurred on or before July 1, 1999, and is punishable under Section 23540, or former Section 23165.

(2) Was granted probation for the conviction subject to conditions imposed under subdivision (b) of Section 23542, or under subdivision (b) of former Section 23166.

(3) Is no longer subject to the probation described in paragraph (2).

(4) Has not completed the licensed driving-under-the-influence program under paragraph (3) of subdivision (a) of Section 13352 for reinstatement of the driving privilege.

(5) Has no violations in his or her driving record that would preclude issuance of a restricted driver's license. *(Added by Stats. 2004, c. 551 (S.B.1697), § 6.5, operative Sept. 20, 2005. Amended by Stats.2009, c. 193 (S.B.598), § 2, operative July 1, 2010; Stats.2010, c. 30 (S.B.895), § 1, eff. June 22, 2010, operative July 1, 2010.)*

Cross References

Consecutive imposition of restriction, suspension, or revocation under this section and suspension or revocation for refusing chemical testing, see Vehicle Code § 13353.1.

Driving under influence of alcohol or drugs, juvenile court finding in another jurisdiction deemed conviction for purpose of this section, see Vehicle Code § 23521.

Probation conditions, see Vehicle Code §§ 23542, 23562.

Research References

2 Witkin, California Criminal Law 4th Crimes Against Public Peace and Welfare § 281 (2021), One Separate Conviction of Related Offense.

4 Witkin, California Criminal Law 4th Pretrial Proceedings § 401 (2021), Other Programs.

3 Witkin, California Criminal Law 4th Punishment § 214 (2021), Drunk Driving.

3 Witkin, California Criminal Law 4th Punishment § 218 (2021), Effect of Criminal Proceedings.

§ 13352.6. Conviction of person under 21 drinking and driving; reinstatement; driving-under-the-influence program

(a) The department shall immediately suspend the driving privilege of a person who is 18 years of age or older and is convicted of a violation of Section 23140, upon the receipt of a duly certified abstract of the record of a court showing that conviction. The privilege may not be reinstated until the person provides the department with proof of financial responsibility and until proof satisfactory to the department, of successful completion of a driving-under-the-influence program licensed under Section 11836 of the Health and Safety Code has been received in the department's headquarters. That attendance shall be as follows:

(1) If, within 10 years of the current violation of Section 23140, the person has not been convicted of a separate violation of Section 23140, 23152, or 23153, or of Section 23103, with a plea of guilty under Section 23103.5, or of Section 655 of the Harbors and Navigation Code, or of Section 191.5 of, or subdivision (a) of Section 192.5 of, the Penal Code, the person shall complete, at a minimum, the education component of that licensed driving-under-the-influence program.

(2) If the person does not meet the requirements of paragraph (1), the person shall complete, at a minimum, the program described in paragraph (1) of subdivision (c) of Section 11837 of the Health and Safety Code.

(b) For the purposes of this section, enrollment, participation, and completion of the program shall be subsequent to the date of the current violation. Credit for enrollment, participation, or completion may not be given for any program activities completed prior to the date of the current violation. *(Added by Stats.2000, c. 1063 (A.B.803), § 2. Amended by Stats.2004, c. 403 (S.B.1696), § 3; Stats.2004, c. 550 (S.B.1694), § 5.5; Stats.2007, c. 747 (A.B.678), § 21.)*

Research References

2 Witkin, California Criminal Law 4th Crimes Against Public Peace and Welfare § 279 (2021), In General.

3 Witkin, California Criminal Law 4th Punishment § 214 (2021), Drunk Driving.

§ 13353. Chemical blood, breath, or urine tests

(a) If a person refuses the officer's request to submit to, or fails to complete, a chemical test or tests pursuant to Section 23612, upon receipt of the officer's sworn statement that the officer had reasonable cause to believe the person had been driving a motor vehicle in violation of Section 23140, 23152, or 23153, and that the person had refused to submit to, or did not complete, the test or tests after being requested by the officer, the department shall do one of the following:

(1) Suspend the person's privilege to operate a motor vehicle for a period of one year.

(2) Revoke the person's privilege to operate a motor vehicle for a period of two years if the refusal occurred within 10 years of either (A) a separate violation of Section 23103 as specified in Section 23103.5, or of Section 23140, 23152, or 23153, or of Section 191.5 or subdivision (a) of Section 192.5 of the Penal Code, that resulted in a conviction, or (B) a suspension or revocation of the person's privilege to operate a motor vehicle pursuant to this section or Section 13353.2 for an offense that occurred on a separate occasion.

(3) Revoke the person's privilege to operate a motor vehicle for a period of three years if the refusal occurred within 10 years of any of the following:

(A) Two or more separate violations of Section 23103 as specified in Section 23103.5, or of Section 23140, 23152, or 23153, or of Section 191.5 or subdivision (a) of Section 192.5 of the Penal Code, or any combination thereof, that resulted in convictions.

(B) Two or more suspensions or revocations of the person's privilege to operate a motor vehicle pursuant to this section or Section 13353.2 for offenses that occurred on separate occasions.

(C) Any combination of two or more of those convictions or administrative suspensions or revocations.

The officer's sworn statement shall be submitted pursuant to Section 13380 on a form furnished or approved by the department. The suspension or revocation shall not become effective until 30 days after the giving of written notice thereof, or until the end of a stay of the suspension or revocation, as provided for in Section 13558.

(D) For the purposes of this section, a conviction of an offense in any state, territory, or possession of the United States, the District of Columbia, the Commonwealth of Puerto Rico, or the Dominion of Canada that, if committed in this state, would be a violation of Section 23103, as specified in Section 23103.5, or Section 23140, 23152, or 23153, or Section 191.5 or subdivision (a) of Section 192.5 of the Penal Code, is a conviction of that particular section of the Vehicle Code or Penal Code.

(b) If a person on more than one occasion in separate incidents refuses the officer's request to submit to, or fails to complete, a chemical test or tests pursuant to Section 23612 while driving a motor vehicle, upon the receipt of the officer's sworn statement that the officer had reasonable cause to believe the person had been driving a motor vehicle in violation of Section 23140, 23152, or 23153, the department shall disqualify the person from operating a commercial motor vehicle for the rest of his or her lifetime.

(c) The notice of the order of suspension or revocation under this section shall be served on the person by a peace officer pursuant to Section 23612. The notice of the order of suspension or revocation shall be on a form provided by the department. If the notice of the order of suspension or revocation has not been served by the peace officer pursuant to Section 23612, the department immediately shall notify the person in writing of the action taken. The peace officer who serves the notice, or the department, if applicable, also shall provide, if the officer or department, as the case may be, determines that it is necessary to do so, the person with the appropriate non-English notice developed pursuant to subdivision (d) of Section 14100.

(d) Upon the receipt of the officer's sworn statement, the department shall review the record. For purposes of this section, the scope of the administrative review shall cover all of the following issues:

(1) Whether the peace officer had reasonable cause to believe the person had been driving a motor vehicle in violation of Section 23140, 23152, or 23153.

(2) Whether the person was placed under arrest.

(3) Whether the person refused to submit to, or did not complete, the test or tests after being requested by a peace officer.

(4) Whether, except for a person described in subdivision (a) of Section 23612 who is incapable of refusing, the person had been told that his or her driving privilege would be suspended or revoked if he or she refused to submit to, or did not complete, the test or tests.

(e) The person may request an administrative hearing pursuant to Section 13558. Except as provided in subdivision (e) of Section 13558, the request for an administrative hearing does not stay the order of suspension or revocation.

(f) The suspension or revocation imposed under this section shall run concurrently with any restriction, suspension, or revocation imposed under Section 13352, 13352.4, or 13352.5 that resulted from the same arrest. *(Added by Stats.2004, c. 952 (A.B.3049), § 7.5, operative Sept. 20, 2005. Amended by Stats.2005, c. 279 (S.B.1107), § 21; Stats.2007, c. 747 (A.B.678), § 22.)*

Research References

California Jury Instructions - Criminal 16.835, Liquor Influenced Driving—Refusal to Take Sobriety Test—Consciousness of Guilt.
California Jury Instructions - Criminal 17.29, Willful Refusal to Take or Complete Tests Regarding Driving Under the Influence.
2 Witkin, California Criminal Law 4th Crimes Against Public Peace and Welfare § 295 (2021), Test as Incidental to Lawful Arrest or Detention.
2 Witkin, California Criminal Law 4th Crimes Against Public Peace and Welfare § 297 (2021), Notice of Consequences of Refusal to Submit to Test.
2 Witkin, California Criminal Law 4th Crimes Against Public Peace and Welfare § 301 (2021), Notice of Suspension or Revocation of License.
2 Witkin, California Criminal Law 4th Crimes Against Public Peace and Welfare § 302 (2021), Administrative Sanctions.
2 Witkin, California Criminal Law 4th Crimes Against Public Peace and Welfare § 306 (2021), Reason for Suspension, Revocation, or Restriction.
4 Witkin, California Criminal Law 4th Illegally Obtained Evidence § 193A (2021), (New) Body Search for Blood Alcohol Level.
4 Witkin, California Criminal Law 4th Pretrial Proceedings § 41 (2021), Summoning Assistance.
3 Witkin, California Criminal Law 4th Punishment § 220 (2021), Distinction: Investigation and Hearing.
3 Witkin, California Criminal Law 4th Punishment § 221 (2021), In General.
3 Witkin, California Criminal Law 4th Punishment § 222 (2021), Administrative and Judicial Review.
3 Witkin, California Criminal Law 4th Punishment § 223 (2021), Effect of Criminal Case.

§ 13353.1. Preliminary alcohol screening test; refusal or failure to complete; notice; review

(a) If a person refuses an officer's request to submit to, or fails to complete, a preliminary alcohol screening test pursuant to Section 13388 or 13389, upon the receipt of the officer's sworn statement, submitted pursuant to Section 13380, that the officer had reasonable cause to believe the person had been driving a motor vehicle in violation of Section 23136 or 23154, and that the person had refused to submit to, or did not complete, the test after being requested by the officer, the department shall do one of the following:

(1) Suspend the person's privilege to operate a motor vehicle for a period of one year.

(2) Revoke the person's privilege to operate a motor vehicle for a period of two years if the refusal occurred within 10 years of either of the following:

(A) A separate violation of subdivision (a) of Section 23136, that resulted in a finding of a violation, or a separate violation, that resulted in a conviction, of Section 23103, as specified in Section 23103.5, of Section 23140, 23152, or 23153, or of Section 191.5 or subdivision (a) of Section 192.5 of the Penal Code.

(B) A suspension or revocation of the person's privilege to operate a motor vehicle if that action was taken pursuant to this section or Section 13353 or 13353.2 for an offense that occurred on a separate occasion.

(3) Revoke the person's privilege to operate a motor vehicle for a period of three years if the refusal occurred within 10 years of any of the following:

(A) Two or more separate violations of subdivision (a) of Section 23136, that resulted in findings of violations, or two or more separate violations, that resulted in convictions, of Section 23103, as specified in Section 23103.5, of Section 23140, 23152, or 23153, or of Section 191.5 or subdivision (a) of Section 192.5 of the Penal Code, or any combination thereof.

(B) Two or more suspensions or revocations of the person's privilege to operate a motor vehicle if those actions were taken pursuant to this section, or Section 13353 or 13353.2, for offenses that occurred on separate occasions.

(C) Any combination of two or more of the convictions or administrative suspensions or revocations described in subparagraph (A) or (B).

(b) For the purposes of this section, a conviction of an offense in any state, territory, or possession of the United States, the District of Columbia, the Commonwealth of Puerto Rico, or Canada that, if committed in this state, would be a violation of Section 23103, as specified in Section 23103.5, or Section 23140, 23152, or 23153, or Section 191.5 or subdivision (a) of Section 192.5 of the Penal Code, is a conviction of that particular section of the Vehicle or Penal Code.

(c) The notice of the order of suspension or revocation under this section shall be served on the person by the peace officer pursuant to Section 13388 and shall not become effective until 30 days after the person is served with that notice. The notice of the order of suspension or revocation shall be on a form provided by the department. If the notice of the order of suspension or revocation has not been served by the peace officer pursuant to Section 13388, the department immediately shall notify the person in writing of the action taken. The peace officer who serves the notice, or the department, if applicable, also shall provide, if the officer or department, as the case may be, determines that it is necessary to do so, the person with the appropriate non-English notice developed pursuant to subdivision (d) of Section 14100.

(d) Upon the receipt of the officer's sworn statement, the department shall review the record. For the purposes of this section, the scope of the administrative review shall cover all of the following issues:

(1) Whether the peace officer had reasonable cause to believe the person had been driving a motor vehicle in violation of Section 23136.

(2) Whether the person was lawfully detained.

(3) Whether the person refused to submit to, or did not complete, the test after being requested to do so by a peace officer.

(e) The person may request an administrative hearing pursuant to Section 13558. Except as provided in subdivision (e) of Section 13558, the request for an administrative hearing does not stay the order of suspension or revocation. *(Added by Stats.1993, c. 899 (S.B.689), § 4. Amended by Stats.1994, c. 938 (S.B.1295), § 2, eff. Sept. 28, 1994; Stats.1998, c. 118 (S.B.1186), § 3.10, operative July 1, 1999; Stats.2001, c. 473 (S.B.485), § 19; Stats.2004, c. 550 (S.B.1694), § 7; Stats.2007, c. 747 (A.B.678), § 23; Stats.2007, c. 749 (A.B.1165), § 1.5, operative Jan. 1, 2009.)*

Cross References

Driving motor vehicle following suspension or revocation of license pursuant to this section, punishment, see Vehicle Code § 14601.5.

Research References

California Jury Instructions - Criminal 17.29, Willful Refusal to Take or Complete Tests Regarding Driving Under the Influence.
2 Witkin, California Criminal Law 4th Crimes Against Public Peace and Welfare § 302 (2021), Administrative Sanctions.
4 Witkin, California Criminal Law 4th Illegally Obtained Evidence § 193A (2021), (New) Body Search for Blood Alcohol Level.
3 Witkin, California Criminal Law 4th Punishment § 221 (2021), In General.

§ 13353.2. Immediate suspension; grounds; notice of order of suspension; determination of facts

(a) The department shall immediately suspend the privilege of a person to operate a motor vehicle for any one of the following reasons:

(1) The person was driving a motor vehicle when the person had 0.08 percent or more, by weight, of alcohol in his or her blood.

(2) The person was under 21 years of age and had a blood-alcohol concentration of 0.01 percent or greater, as measured by a preliminary alcohol screening test, or other chemical test.

(3) The person was driving a vehicle that requires a commercial driver's license when the person had 0.04 percent or more, by weight, of alcohol in his or her blood.

(4) The person was driving a motor vehicle when both of the following applied:

(A) The person was on probation for a violation of Section 23152 or 23153.

(B) The person had 0.01 percent or more, by weight, of alcohol in his or her blood, as measured by a preliminary alcohol screening test or other chemical test.

(b) The notice of the order of suspension under this section shall be served on the person by a peace officer pursuant to Section 13382 or 13388. The notice of the order of suspension shall be on a form provided by the department. If the notice of the order of suspension has not been served upon the person by the peace officer pursuant to Section 13382 or 13388, upon the receipt of the report of a peace officer submitted pursuant to Section 13380, the department shall mail written notice of the order of the suspension to the person at the last known address shown on the department's records and, if the address of the person provided by the peace officer's report differs from the address of record, to that address.

(c) The notice of the order of suspension shall specify clearly the reason and statutory grounds for the suspension, the effective date of the suspension, the right of the person to request an administrative hearing, the procedure for requesting an administrative hearing, and the date by which a request for an administrative hearing shall be made in order to receive a determination prior to the effective date of the suspension.

(d) The department shall make a determination of the facts in subdivision (a) on the basis of the report of a peace officer submitted pursuant to Section 13380. The determination of the facts, after administrative review pursuant to Section 13557, by the department is final, unless an administrative hearing is held pursuant to Section 13558 and any judicial review of the administrative determination after the hearing pursuant to Section 13559 is final.

(e) The determination of the facts in subdivision (a) is a civil matter that is independent of the determination of the person's guilt or innocence, shall have no collateral estoppel effect on a subsequent criminal prosecution, and shall not preclude the litigation of the same or similar facts in the criminal proceeding. If a person is acquitted of criminal charges relating to a determination of facts under subdivision (a), or if the person's driver's license was suspended pursuant to Section 13388 and the department finds no basis for a suspension pursuant to that section, the department shall immediately reinstate the person's privilege to operate a motor vehicle if the department has suspended it administratively pursuant to subdivision (a), and the department shall return or reissue for the remaining term any driver's license that has been taken from the person pursuant to Section 13382 or otherwise. Notwithstanding subdivision (b) of Section 13558, if criminal charges under Section 23140, 23152, or 23153 are not filed by the district attorney because of a lack of evidence, or if those charges are filed but are subsequently dismissed by the court because of an insufficiency of evidence, the person has a renewed right to request an administrative hearing before the department. The request for a hearing shall be made within one year from the date of arrest.

(f) The department shall furnish a form that requires a detailed explanation specifying which evidence was defective or lacking and detailing why that evidence was defective or lacking. The form shall be made available to the person to provide to the district attorney. The department shall hold an administrative hearing, and the hearing officer shall consider the reasons for the failure to prosecute given by the district attorney on the form provided by the department. If applicable, the hearing officer shall consider the reasons stated on the record by a judge who dismisses the charges. A fee shall not be imposed pursuant to Section 14905 for the return or reissuing of a driver's license pursuant to this subdivision. The disposition of a suspension action under this section does not affect an action to suspend or revoke the person's privilege to operate a motor vehicle under another provision of this code, including, but not limited to, Section 13352 or 13353, or Chapter 3 (commencing with Section 13800). *(Added by Stats.1989, c. 1460, § 7, operative July 1, 1990. Amended by Stats.1990, c. 431 (S.B.1150), § 4, eff. July 26, 1990; Stats.1992, c. 1281 (A.B.3580), § 4; Stats.1993, c. 899 (S.B.689), § 5; Stats.1993, c. 1244 (S.B.126), § 12.1; Stats.1994, c. 938 (S.B.1295), § 3, eff. Sept. 28, 1994; Stats.1998, c. 118 (S.B.1186), § 3.12, operative July 1, 1999; Stats.1999, c. 22 (S.B.24), § 14, eff. May 26, 1999, operative July 1, 1999; Stats.2006, c. 574 (A.B.2520), § 11; Stats.2007, c. 130 (A.B.299), § 238; Stats.2007, c. 749 (A.B.1165), § 2, operative Jan. 1, 2009; Stats.2008, c. 179 (S.B.1498), § 219.)*

Cross References

Driving with knowledge of suspension, revocation, or restriction of driving privilege, punishment, see Vehicle Code § 14601.5.
Fee for license issued following suspension under this section, see Vehicle Code § 14905.

Research References

California Jury Instructions - Criminal 17.29, Willful Refusal to Take or Complete Tests Regarding Driving Under the Influence.
2 Witkin, California Criminal Law 4th Crimes Against Public Peace and Welfare § 277 (2021), Driving With Unlawful Blood-Alcohol Level.

2 Witkin, California Criminal Law 4th Crimes Against Public Peace and Welfare § 279 (2021), In General.
2 Witkin, California Criminal Law 4th Crimes Against Public Peace and Welfare § 306 (2021), Reason for Suspension, Revocation, or Restriction.
4 Witkin, California Criminal Law 4th Illegally Obtained Evidence § 384 (2021), In General.
4 Witkin, California Criminal Law 4th Illegally Obtained Evidence § 461 (2021), Evidence is Inadmissible.
3 Witkin, California Criminal Law 4th Punishment § 213 (2021), In General.
3 Witkin, California Criminal Law 4th Punishment § 221 (2021), In General.
3 Witkin, California Criminal Law 4th Punishment § 223 (2021), Effect of Criminal Case.

§ 13353.3. Order of suspension under Vehicle Code § 13353.2; effective date, period, and termination of suspension

Section operative until Jan. 1, 2026. See, also, § 13353.3 operative Jan. 1, 2026.

(a) An order of suspension of a person's privilege to operate a motor vehicle pursuant to Section 13353.2 shall become effective 30 days after the person is served with the notice pursuant to Section 13382 or 13388, or subdivision (b) of Section 13353.2.

(b) The period of suspension of a person's privilege to operate a motor vehicle under Section 13353.2 is as follows:

(1)(A) If the person has not been convicted of a separate violation of Section 23103, as specified in Section 23103.5, or Section 23140, 23152, or 23153, or Section 191.5 or subdivision (a) of Section 192.5 of the Penal Code, the person has not been administratively determined to have refused chemical testing pursuant to Section 13353 or 13353.1 of this code, or the person has not been administratively determined to have been driving with an excessive concentration of alcohol pursuant to Section 13353.2 on a separate occasion, which offense or occurrence occurred within 10 years of the occasion in question, the person's privilege to operate a motor vehicle shall be suspended for four months, except as provided in subparagraph (B).

(B) The four-month suspension pursuant to subparagraph (A) shall terminate if the person has been convicted of a violation arising out of the same occurrence and all of the following conditions are met:

(i) The person is eligible for a restricted driver's license pursuant to Section 13352 or 13352.1.

(ii) The person installs a functioning, certified ignition interlock device as required in Section 13352 or 13352.1 for that restricted driver's license.

(iii) The person complies with all other applicable conditions of Section 13352 or 13352.1 for a restricted driver's license.

(2)(A) If the person has been convicted of one or more separate violations of Section 23103, as specified in Section 23103.5, or Section 23140, 23152, or 23153, or Section 191.5 or subdivision (a) of Section 192.5 of the Penal Code, the person has been administratively determined to have refused chemical testing pursuant to Section 13353 or 13353.1 of this code, or the person has been administratively determined to have been driving with an excessive concentration of alcohol pursuant to Section 13353.2 on a separate occasion, which offense or occasion occurred within 10 years of the occasion in question, the person's privilege to operate a motor vehicle shall be suspended for one year, except as provided in subparagraph (B).

(B) The one-year suspension pursuant to subparagraph (A) shall terminate if the person has been convicted of a violation arising out of the same occurrence and all of the following conditions are met:

(i) The person is eligible for a restricted driver's license pursuant to Section 13352 or 13352.1.

(ii) The person installs a functioning, certified ignition interlock device as required in Section 13352 or 13352.1 for that restricted driver's license.

(iii) The person complies with all other applicable conditions of Section 13352 or 13352.1 for a restricted driver's license.

(3) Notwithstanding any other law, if a person has been administratively determined to have been driving in violation of Section 23136 or to have refused chemical testing pursuant to Section 13353.1, the period of suspension shall not be for less than one year.

(c) If a person's privilege to operate a motor vehicle is suspended pursuant to Section 13353.2 and the person is convicted of a violation of Section 23152 or 23153, including, but not limited to, a violation described in Section 23620, arising out of the same occurrence, both the suspension under Section 13353.2 and the suspension or revocation under Section 13352 shall be imposed, except that the periods of suspension or revocation shall run concurrently, and the total period of suspension or revocation shall not exceed the longer of the two suspension or revocation periods.

(d) For the purposes of this section, a conviction of an offense in any state, territory, or possession of the United States, the District of Columbia, the Commonwealth of Puerto Rico, or Canada that, if committed in this state, would be a violation of Section 23103, as specified in Section 23103.5, or Section 23140, 23152, or 23153, or Section 191.5 or subdivision (a) of Section 192.5 of the Penal Code, is a conviction of that particular section of the Vehicle Code or Penal Code.

(e) This section shall become operative on January 1, 2019.

(f) This section shall remain in effect only until January 1, 2026, and as of that date is repealed, unless a later enacted statute, that is enacted before January 1, 2026, deletes or extends that date. *(Added by Stats.2016, c. 783 (S.B.1046), § 11, eff. Jan. 1, 2017, operative Jan. 1, 2019. Amended by Stats.2017, c. 485 (S.B.611), § 9, eff. Jan. 1, 2018, operative Jan. 1, 2019.)*

Repeal

For repeal of this section, see its terms.

Research References

2 Witkin, California Criminal Law 4th Crimes Against Public Peace and Welfare § 279 (2021), In General.
2 Witkin, California Criminal Law 4th Crimes Against Public Peace and Welfare § 290 (2021), Ignition Interlock Device.

§ 13353.3. Order of suspension under Vehicle Code § 13353.2; effective date, period, and termination of suspension

Section operative Jan. 1, 2026. See, also, § 13353.3 operative until Jan. 1, 2026.

(a) An order of suspension of a person's privilege to operate a motor vehicle pursuant to Section 13353.2 shall become effective 30 days after the person is served with the notice pursuant to Section 13382 or 13388, or subdivision (b) of Section 13353.2.

(b) The period of suspension of a person's privilege to operate a motor vehicle under Section 13353.2 is as follows:

(1) If the person has not been convicted of a separate violation of Section 23103, as specified in Section 23103.5, or Section 23140, 23152, or 23153, or Section 191.5 or subdivision (a) of Section 192.5 of the Penal Code, the person has not been administratively determined to have refused chemical testing pursuant to Section 13353 or 13353.1 of this code, or the person has not been administratively determined to have been driving with an excessive concentration of alcohol pursuant to Section 13353.2 on a separate occasion, which offense or occurrence occurred within 10 years of the occasion in question, the person's privilege to operate a motor vehicle shall be suspended for four months.

(2)(A) If the person has been convicted of one or more separate violations of Section 23103, as specified in Section 23103.5, or Section 23140, 23152, or 23153, or Section 191.5 or subdivision (a) of Section 192.5 of the Penal Code, the person has been administratively determined to have refused chemical testing pursuant to Section 13353 or 13353.1 of this code, or the person has been administratively determined to have been driving with an excessive concentration of alcohol pursuant to Section 13353.2 on a separate occasion, which offense or occasion occurred within 10 years of the occasion in question, the person's privilege to operate a motor vehicle shall be suspended for one year, except as provided in subparagraphs (B) and (C).

(B) The one-year suspension pursuant to subparagraph (A) shall terminate if the person has been convicted of a violation arising out of the same occurrence and all of the following conditions are met:

(i) The person is eligible for a restricted driver's license pursuant to Section 13352.

(ii) The person installs a functioning, certified ignition interlock device as required in Section 13352 for that restricted driver's license.

(iii) The person complies with all other applicable conditions of Section 13352 for a restricted driver's license.

(C) The one-year suspension pursuant to subparagraph (A) shall terminate after completion of a 90–day suspension period, and the person shall be eligible for a restricted license if the person has been convicted of a violation of Section 23103, as specified in Section 23103.5, arising out of the same occurrence, has no more than two prior alcohol-related convictions within 10 years, as specified pursuant to subparagraph (A), and all of the following conditions are met:

(i) The person satisfactorily provides, subsequent to the underlying violation date, proof satisfactory to the department of enrollment in a nine-month driving-under-the-influence program licensed pursuant to Chapter 9 (commencing with Section 11836) of Part 2 of Division 10.5 of the Health and Safety Code that consists of at least 60 hours of program activities, including education, group counseling, and individual interview sessions.

(ii) The person agrees, as a condition of the restriction, to continue satisfactory participation in the program described in clause (i).

(iii) The person installs a functioning, certified ignition interlock device and submits the "Verification of Installation" form described in paragraph (2) of subdivision (g) of Section 13386.

(iv) The person agrees to maintain the ignition interlock device as required pursuant to subdivision (g) of Section 23575.

(v) The person provides proof of financial responsibility, as defined in Section 16430.

(vi) The person pays all license fees and any restriction fee required by the department.

(vii) The person pays to the department a fee sufficient to cover the costs of administration of this paragraph, as determined by the department.

(D) The department shall advise those persons that are eligible under subparagraph (C) that after completion of 90 days of the suspension period, the person may apply to the department for a restricted driver's license, subject to the conditions set forth in subparagraph (C).

(E) The restricted driving privilege shall become effective when the department receives all of the documents and fees required under subparagraph (C) and remain in effect for at least the remaining period of the original suspension and until the person provides satisfactory proof to the department of successful completion of a driving-under-the-influence program licensed pursuant to Section 11836 of the Health and Safety Code. The restricted driving privilege shall be subject to the following conditions:

(i) If the driving privilege is restricted under this section, proof of financial responsibility, as described in Section 16430, shall be maintained for three years. If the person does not maintain that proof of financial responsibility at any time during the restriction, the driving privilege shall be suspended until the proof required pursuant to Section 16484 is received by the department.

(ii) For the purposes of this section, enrollment, participation, and completion of an approved program shall occur subsequent to the date of the current violation. Credit may not be given to a program activity completed prior to the date of the current violation.

(iii) The department shall terminate the restriction issued pursuant to this section and shall suspend the privilege to operate a motor vehicle pursuant to subparagraph (A) immediately upon receipt of notification from the driving-under-the-influence program that the person has failed to comply with the program requirements. The privilege shall remain suspended until the final day of the original suspension imposed pursuant to subparagraph (A).

(iv) The department shall suspend the privilege to operate a motor vehicle pursuant to subparagraph (A) immediately upon receipt of notification from the installer that a person has attempted to remove, bypass, or tamper with the ignition interlock device, has removed the device prior to the termination date of the restriction, or fails three or more times to comply with any requirement for the maintenance or calibration of the ignition interlock device ordered pursuant to this section. The privilege shall remain suspended for the remaining period of the original suspension imposed pursuant to subparagraph (A), except that if the person provides proof to the satisfaction of the department that he or she is in compliance with the restriction issued pursuant to this section, the department may, in its discretion, restore the privilege to operate a motor vehicle and reimpose the remaining term of the restriction.

(3) Notwithstanding any other law, if a person has been administratively determined to have been driving in violation of Section 23136 or to have refused chemical testing pursuant to Section 13353.1, the period of suspension shall not be for less than one year.

(c) If a person's privilege to operate a motor vehicle is suspended pursuant to Section 13353.2 and the person is convicted of a violation of Section 23152 or 23153, including, but not limited to, a violation described in Section 23620, arising out of the same occurrence, both the suspension under Section 13353.2 and the suspension or revocation under Section 13352 shall be imposed, except that the periods of suspension or revocation shall run concurrently, and the total period of suspension or revocation shall not exceed the longer of the two suspension or revocation periods.

(d) For the purposes of this section, a conviction of an offense in any state, territory, or possession of the United States, the District of Columbia, the Commonwealth of Puerto Rico, or Canada that, if committed in this state, would be a violation of Section 23103, as specified in Section 23103.5, or Section 23140, 23152, or 23153, or Section 191.5 or subdivision (a) of Section 192.5 of the Penal Code, is a conviction of that particular section of the Vehicle Code or Penal Code.

(e) The holder of a commercial driver's license who was operating a commercial motor vehicle, as defined in Section 15210, at the time of a violation that resulted in a suspension or revocation of the person's noncommercial driving privilege is not eligible for the restricted driver's license authorized pursuant to this section.

(f) This section shall become operative January 1, 2026. *(Added by Stats.2016, c. 783 (S.B.1046), § 12, eff. Jan. 1, 2017, operative Jan. 1, 2026.)*

Research References

2 Witkin, California Criminal Law 4th Crimes Against Public Peace and Welfare § 279 (2021), In General.

2 Witkin, California Criminal Law 4th Crimes Against Public Peace and Welfare § 290 (2021), Ignition Interlock Device.

§ 13353.4. Restoration of driving privilege and issuance of restricted or hardship permit to operate motor vehicle during suspension or revocation period

Section operative until Jan. 1, 2026. See, also, § 13353.4 operative Jan. 1, 2026.

(a) Except as provided in Section 13353.3, 13353.6, 13353.7, or 13353.8, the driving privilege shall not be restored, and a restricted or hardship permit to operate a motor vehicle shall not be issued, to a person during the suspension or revocation period specified in Section 13353, 13353.1, or 13353.3.

(b) The privilege to operate a motor vehicle shall not be restored after a suspension or revocation pursuant to Section 13352, 13353, 13353.1, or 13353.2 until all applicable fees, including the fees prescribed in Section 14905, have been paid and the person gives proof of financial responsibility, as defined in Section 16430, to the department.

(c) This section shall become operative on January 1, 2019.

(d) This section shall remain in effect only until January 1, 2026, and as of that date is repealed, unless a later enacted statute, that is enacted before January 1, 2026, deletes or extends that date. *(Added by Stats.2016, c. 783 (S.B.1046), § 14, eff. Jan. 1, 2017, operative Jan. 1, 2019.)*

Repeal

For repeal of this section, see its terms.

Research References

2 Witkin, California Criminal Law 4th Crimes Against Public Peace and Welfare § 279 (2021), In General.
2 Witkin, California Criminal Law 4th Crimes Against Public Peace and Welfare § 290 (2021), Ignition Interlock Device.
2 Witkin, California Criminal Law 4th Crimes Against Public Peace and Welfare § 302 (2021), Administrative Sanctions.
2 Witkin, California Criminal Law 4th Crimes Against Public Peace and Welfare § 306 (2021), Reason for Suspension, Revocation, or Restriction.
3 Witkin, California Criminal Law 4th Punishment § 214 (2021), Drunk Driving.

§ 13353.4. Restoration of driving privilege and issuance of restricted or hardship permit to operate motor vehicle during suspension or revocation period

Section operative Jan. 1, 2026. See, also, § 13353.4 operative until Jan. 1, 2026.

(a) Except as provided in Section 13353.3, 13353.7, or 13353.8, the driving privilege shall not be restored, and a restricted or hardship permit to operate a motor vehicle shall not be issued, to a person during the suspension or revocation period specified in Section 13353, 13353.1, or 13353.3.

(b) The privilege to operate a motor vehicle shall not be restored after a suspension or revocation pursuant to Section 13352, 13353, 13353.1, or 13353.2 until all applicable fees, including the fees prescribed in Section 14905, have been paid and the person gives proof of financial responsibility, as defined in Section 16430, to the department.

(c) This section shall become operative January 1, 2026. *(Added by Stats.2016, c. 783 (S.B.1046), § 15, eff. Jan. 1, 2017, operative Jan. 1, 2026.)*

Research References

2 Witkin, California Criminal Law 4th Crimes Against Public Peace and Welfare § 279 (2021), In General.
2 Witkin, California Criminal Law 4th Crimes Against Public Peace and Welfare § 290 (2021), Ignition Interlock Device.
2 Witkin, California Criminal Law 4th Crimes Against Public Peace and Welfare § 302 (2021), Administrative Sanctions.
2 Witkin, California Criminal Law 4th Crimes Against Public Peace and Welfare § 306 (2021), Reason for Suspension, Revocation, or Restriction.
3 Witkin, California Criminal Law 4th Punishment § 214 (2021), Drunk Driving.

§ 13353.45. Certificate of completion; fees

The department shall, in consultation with the State Department of Health Care Services, with representatives of the county alcohol program administrators, and with representatives of licensed drinking driver program providers, develop a certificate of completion for the purposes of Sections 13352, 13352.4, and 13352.5 and shall develop, implement, and maintain a system for safeguarding the certificates against misuse. The department may charge a reasonable fee for each blank completion certificate distributed to a drinking driver program. The fee shall be sufficient to cover, but shall not exceed, the costs incurred in administering this section, Sections 13352, 13352.4, and 13352.5 or twelve dollars ($12) per person, whichever is less. *(Added by Stats.1992, c. 1181 (S.B.1650), § 5, eff. Sept. 30, 1992, operative July 1, 1993. Amended by Stats.1994, c. 938 (S.B.1295), § 6, eff. Sept. 28, 1994; Stats.2002, c. 545 (S.B.1852), § 13; Stats.2013, c. 22 (A.B.75), § 86, eff. June 27, 2013, operative July 1, 2013.)*

§ 13353.5. Expiration of suspension or revocation period; out of state residence; reinstatement; conditions

Section operative until Jan. 1, 2026. See, also, § 13353.5 operative Jan. 1, 2026.

(a) If a person whose driving privilege is suspended or revoked under Section 13352, Section 13352.1, former Section 13352.4, Section 13352.4, Section 13352.6, paragraph (1) of subdivision (g) of Section 23247, or paragraph (3) of subdivision (e) of Section 13352 is a resident of another state at the time the mandatory period of suspension or revocation expires, the department may terminate the suspension or revocation, upon written application of the person, for the purpose of allowing the person to apply for a license in his or her state of residence. The application shall include, but need not be limited to, evidence satisfactory to the department that the applicant now resides in another state.

(b) If the person submits an application for a California driver's license within three years after the date of the action to terminate suspension or revocation pursuant to subdivision (a), a license shall not be issued until evidence satisfactory to the department establishes that the person is qualified for reinstatement and no grounds exist including, but not limited to, one or more subsequent convictions for driving under the influence of alcohol or other drugs that would support a refusal to issue a license. The department may waive the three-year requirement if the person provides the department with proof of financial responsibility, as defined in Section 16430, and proof satisfactory to the department of successful completion of a driving-under-the-influence program described in Section 13352, and the driving-under-the-influence program is of the length required under paragraphs (1) to (7), inclusive, of subdivision (a) of Section 13352.

(c) For the purposes of this section, "state" includes a foreign province or country.

(d) This section shall become operative on January 1, 2019.

(e) This section shall remain in effect only until January 1, 2026, and as of that date is repealed, unless a later enacted statute, that is enacted before January 1, 2026, deletes or extends that date. *(Added by Stats.2016, c. 783 (S.B.1046), § 17, eff. Jan. 1, 2017, operative Jan. 1, 2019. Amended by Stats.2017, c. 485 (S.B.611), § 11, eff. Jan. 1, 2018, operative Jan. 1, 2019.)*

Repeal

For repeal of this section, see its terms.

§ 13353.5. Expiration of suspension or revocation period; out of state residence; reinstatement; conditions

Section operative Jan. 1, 2026. See, also, § 13353.5 operative until Jan. 1, 2026.

(a) If a person whose driving privilege is suspended or revoked under Section 13352, Section 13352.1, former Section 13352.4, Section 13352.4, Section 13352.6, paragraph (1) of subdivision (g) of Section 23247, or paragraph (2) of subdivision (f) of Section 23575 is a resident of another state at the time the mandatory period of suspension or revocation expires, the department may terminate the suspension or revocation, upon written application of the person, for the purpose of allowing the person to apply for a license in his or her state of residence. The application shall include, but need not be limited to, evidence satisfactory to the department that the applicant now resides in another state.

(b) If the person submits an application for a California driver's license within three years after the date of the action to terminate suspension or revocation pursuant to subdivision (a), a license shall not be issued until evidence satisfactory to the department establishes that the person is qualified for reinstatement and no grounds exist including, but not limited to, one or more subsequent convictions for driving under the influence of alcohol or other drugs that would support a refusal to issue a license. The department may waive the three-year requirement if the person provides the department with proof of financial responsibility, as defined in Section 16430, and proof satisfactory to the department of successful completion of a driving-under-the-influence program described in Section 13352, and the driving-under-the-influence program is of the length required under paragraphs (1) to (7), inclusive, of subdivision (a) of Section 13352.

(c) For the purposes of this section, "state" includes a foreign province or country.

(d) This section shall become operative January 1, 2026. *(Added by Stats.2016, c. 783 (S.B.1046), § 18, eff. Jan. 1, 2017, operative Jan. 1, 2026. Amended by Stats.2017, c. 485 (S.B.611), § 12, eff. Jan. 1, 2018, operative Jan. 1, 2026.)*

§ 13353.6. Eligibility for restricted driver's license on or after effective date specified in § 13353.3; reinstatement of suspension; credit toward mandatory term required to install functioning, certified ignition interlock device

(a) Notwithstanding any other law, a person whose driving privilege has been suspended under Section 13353.2 and who has not been convicted of, or found to have committed, a separate violation of Section 23103, as specified in Section 23103.5, or Section 23140, 23152, or 23153, or Section 191.5 or subdivision (a) of Section 192.5 of the Penal Code, and if the person's privilege to operate a motor vehicle has not been suspended or revoked pursuant to Section 13353 or 13353.2 for an offense that occurred on a separate occasion within 10 years of the occasion in question, may apply to the department for a restricted driver's license on or after the effective date specified in Section 13353.3, if the person meets all of the following requirements:

(1)(A) The person satisfactorily provides proof of enrollment in a driving-under-the-influence program licensed under Section 11836 of the Health and Safety Code, as described in subdivision (b) of Section 23538.

(B) The program shall report any failure to participate in the program to the department and shall certify successful completion of the program to the department.

(C) If a person who has been issued a restricted license under this section fails at any time to participate in the program, the department shall immediately terminate the restriction and reinstate the suspension of the privilege to operate a motor vehicle. The department shall give notice of the suspension under this paragraph in the same manner as prescribed in subdivision (b) of Section 13353.2 for the period specified in Section 13353.3, that is effective upon receipt by the person.

(D) For the purposes of this section, enrollment, participation, and completion of an approved program shall occur subsequent to the date of the current violation. Credit may not be given to a program activity completed prior to the date of the current violation.

(2) The person installs a functioning, certified ignition interlock device on any vehicle that he or she operates and submits the "Verification of Installation" form described in paragraph (2) of subdivision (g) of Section 13386.

(3) The person agrees to maintain the functioning, certified ignition interlock device as required under subdivision (f).

(4)(A) The person was 21 years of age or older at the time the offense occurred and gives proof of financial responsibility, as defined in Section 16430.

(B) If the driving privilege is restricted under this section, proof of financial responsibility, as described in Section 16430, shall be maintained for three years. If the person does not maintain that proof of financial responsibility at any time during the restriction, the driving privilege shall be suspended until the proof required pursuant to Section 16484 is received by the department.

(5) The person pays all applicable reinstatement or reissue fees.

(b) The restriction under this section shall remain in effect for the remaining period of the original suspension period under Section 13353.3.

(c) The department shall terminate the restriction issued pursuant to this section and shall immediately reinstate the suspension of the privilege to operate a motor vehicle upon receipt of notification from the ignition interlock device installer that a person has attempted to remove, bypass, or tamper with the ignition interlock device, has removed the device prior to the termination date of the restriction, or fails three or more times to comply with any requirement for the maintenance or calibration of the ignition interlock device. The privilege shall remain suspended for the remaining mandatory suspension period imposed pursuant to Section 13353.3, provided, however, that if the person provides proof to the satisfaction of the department that the person is in compliance with the restriction issued pursuant to this section, the department may, in its discretion, restore the privilege to operate a motor vehicle and reimpose the remaining term of the restriction.

(d) Notwithstanding any other law, a person whose driving privilege has been suspended under Section 13353.2, who is eligible for a restricted driver's license as provided for in this section, and who installs a functioning, certified ignition interlock device pursuant to this section, shall receive credit towards the mandatory term the person is required to install a functioning, certified ignition interlock device pursuant to Section 23575.3 for a conviction of a violation arising out of the same occurrence that led to the person's driving privilege being suspended pursuant to Section 13352 equal to the period of time the person installs a functioning, certified ignition interlock device pursuant to this section or Section 13353.75.

(e)(1) The holder of a commercial driver's license who was operating a motor vehicle other than a commercial vehicle, or a driver who was operating a commercial vehicle, as defined in Section 15210, at the time of the violation that resulted in the suspension of that person's driving privilege pursuant to Section 13353.2 is not eligible for the restricted driver's license authorized under this section.

(2) Notwithstanding paragraph (1), as authorized under this section, the department shall issue the person a noncommercial driver's license restricted in the same manner and subject to the same conditions and requirements as specified in subdivision (a).

(f) A person whose driving privilege is restricted by the department pursuant to this section shall arrange for each vehicle with a functioning, certified ignition interlock device to be serviced by the installer at least once every 60 days in order for the installer to recalibrate the device and monitor the operation of the device. The installer shall notify the department if the device is removed or indicates that the person has attempted to remove, bypass, or tamper with the device, or if the person fails three or more times to comply with any requirement for the maintenance or calibration of the ignition interlock device.

(g) For the purposes of this section, the following definitions apply:

(1) "Bypass" means either of the following:

(A) Failure to take any random retest.

(B) Failure to pass a random retest with a breath alcohol concentration not exceeding 0.03 percent, by weight of alcohol, in the person's blood.

(2) "Operates" includes operating a vehicle that is not owned by the person subject to this section.

(3) "Owned" means solely owned or owned in conjunction with another person or legal entity.

(4) "Random retest" means a breath test performed by the driver upon a certified ignition interlock device at random intervals after the initial engine startup breath test and while the vehicle's motor is running.

(5) "Vehicle" does not include a motorcycle until the state certifies an ignition interlock device that can be installed on a motorcycle. A person subject to an ignition interlock device restriction shall not operate a motorcycle for the duration of the ignition interlock device restriction period.

(h) Notwithstanding subdivisions (a) and (b), and upon a conviction under Section 23152 or 23153 for the current offense, the department shall suspend or revoke the person's privilege to operate a motor vehicle under Section 13352 or 13352.1.

(i) The restriction conditions specified in this section shall apply only to a person who is suspended under Section 13353.2 for a violation that occurred on or after January 1, 2019.

(j) This section shall become operative on January 1, 2019.

(k) This section shall remain in effect only until January 1, 2026, and as of that date is repealed, unless a later enacted statute, that is enacted before January 1, 2026, deletes or extends that date. *(Added by Stats.2016, c. 783 (S.B.1046), § 19, eff. Jan. 1, 2017, operative Jan. 1, 2019. Amended by Stats.2017, c. 561 (A.B.1516), § 253, eff. Jan. 1, 2018, operative Jan. 1, 2019; Stats.2017, c. 485 (S.B.611), § 13, eff. Jan. 1, 2018, operative Jan. 1, 2019.)*

Repeal

For repeal of this section, see its terms.

Research References

2 Witkin, California Criminal Law 4th Crimes Against Public Peace and Welfare § 279 (2021), In General.

2 Witkin, California Criminal Law 4th Crimes Against Public Peace and Welfare § 290 (2021), Ignition Interlock Device.

2 Witkin, California Criminal Law 4th Crimes Against Public Peace and Welfare § 302 (2021), Administrative Sanctions.

§ 13353.7. Restricted driver's licenses

(a) Subject to subdivision (c), if the person whose driving privilege has been suspended under Section 13353.2 has not been convicted of, or found to have committed, a separate violation of Section 23103, as specified in Section 23103.5, or Section 23140, 23152, or 23153 of this code, or Section 191.5 or subdivision (a) of Section 192.5 of the Penal Code, and if the person's privilege to operate a motor vehicle has not been suspended or revoked pursuant to Section 13353 or 13353.2 for an offense that occurred on a separate occasion within 10 years of the occasion in question and, if the person subsequently enrolls in a driving-under-the-influence program licensed under Section 11836 of the Health and Safety Code, as described in subdivision (b) of Section 23538, that person, if 21 years of age or older at the time the offense occurred, may apply to the department for a restricted driver's license limited to travel to and from the activities required by the program and to and from and in the course of the person's employment. After receiving proof of enrollment in the program, and if the person has not been arrested subsequent to the offense for which the person's driving privilege has been suspended under Section 13353.2 for a violation of Section 23103, as specified in Section 23103.5, or Section 23140, 23152, or 23153 of this code, or Section 191.5 or subdivision (a) of Section 192.5 of the Penal Code, and if the person's privilege to operate a motor vehicle has not been suspended or revoked pursuant to Section 13353 or 13353.2 for an offense that occurred on a separate occasion, notwithstanding Section 13551, the department shall, after review pursuant to Section 13557, suspend the person's privilege to operate a motor vehicle for 30 days and then issue the person a restricted driver's license under the following conditions:

(1) The program shall report any failure to participate in the program to the department and shall certify successful completion of the program to the department.

(2) The person was 21 years of age or older at the time the offense occurred and gives proof of financial responsibility as defined in Section 16430.

(3) The restriction shall be imposed for a period of five months.

(4) If a person who has been issued a restricted license under this section fails at any time to participate in the program, the department shall suspend the restricted license immediately. The department shall give notice of the suspension under this paragraph in the same manner as prescribed in subdivision (b) of Section 13353.2 for the period specified in Section 13353.3, that is effective upon receipt by the person.

(b) Notwithstanding subdivision (a), and upon a conviction of Section 23152 or 23153, the department shall suspend or revoke the person's privilege to operate a motor vehicle under Section 13352.

(c) If the driver was operating a commercial vehicle, as defined in Section 15210, at the time of the violation that resulted in the suspension of that person's driving privilege under Section 13353.2, the department shall, pursuant to this section, if the person is otherwise eligible, issue the person a class C or class M driver's license restricted in the same manner and subject to the same conditions as specified in subdivision (a), except that the license may not allow travel to and from or in the course of the person's employment.

(d) If the holder of a commercial driver's license was operating a motor vehicle, other than a commercial vehicle as defined in Section 15210, at the time of the violation that resulted in the suspension of that person's driving privilege pursuant to Section 13353.2, the department shall, pursuant to this section, if the person is otherwise eligible, issue the person a class C or class M driver's license restricted in the same manner and subject to the same conditions as specified in subdivision (a).

(e) This section does not apply to a person whose driving privilege has been suspended or revoked pursuant to Section 13353 or 13353.2 for an offense that occurred on a separate occasion, or as a result of a conviction of a separate violation of Section 23103, as specified in Section 23103.5, or Section 23140, 23152, or 23153, when that violation occurred within 10 years of the offense in question. This subdivision shall be operative only so long as a one-year suspension of the driving privilege for a second or subsequent occurrence or offense, with no restricted or hardship licenses permitted, is required by Section 408 or 410 of Title 23 of the United States Code. *(Added by Stats.2004, c. 952 (A.B.3049), § 10.5, operative Sept. 20, 2005. Amended by Stats.2007, c. 747 (A.B.678), § 25; Stats.2012, c. 670 (A.B.2188), § 5.)*

Research References

2 Witkin, California Criminal Law 4th Crimes Against Public Peace and Welfare § 306 (2021), Reason for Suspension, Revocation, or Restriction.

§ 13353.75. Restricted driver's licenses; specified violations; requirements

(a) Subject to subdivision (d), a person whose driving privilege has been suspended under Section 13353.2, and who has been previously convicted of, or found to have committed, a separate violation of Section 23103, as specified in Section 23103.5, or Section 23140, 23152, or 23153, or Section 191.5 or subdivision (a) of Section 192.5 of the Penal Code, or whose privilege to operate a motor vehicle has been suspended or revoked pursuant to Section 13353 or 13353.2 for an offense that occurred on a separate occasion within 10 years of the occasion in question may apply to the department for a restricted driver's license on or after the effective date specified in Section 13353.3, if the person meets all of the following requirements:

(1)(A) The person satisfactorily provides proof of enrollment in a driving-under-the-influence program licensed under Section 11836 of the Health and Safety Code, as described in subdivision (b) of Section 23538 of this code.

(B) The program shall report any failure to participate in the program to the department and shall certify successful completion of the program to the department.

(C) If a person who has been issued a restricted license under this section fails at any time to participate in the program, the department shall immediately terminate the restriction and reinstate the suspension of the privilege to operate a motor vehicle. The department shall give notice of the suspension under this paragraph in the same manner as prescribed in subdivision (b) of Section 13353.2 for the period specified in Section 13353.3, that is effective upon receipt by the person.

(D) For the purposes of this section, enrollment, participation, and completion of an approved program shall occur subsequent to the date of the current violation. Credit may not be given to a program activity completed prior to the date of the current violation.

(2)(A) The person was 21 years of age or older at the time the offense occurred and gives proof of financial responsibility, as defined in Section 16430.

(B) If the driving privilege is restricted under this section, proof of financial responsibility, as described in Section 16430, shall be maintained for three years. If the person does not maintain that proof of financial responsibility at any time during the restriction, the driving privilege shall be suspended until the proof required pursuant to Section 16484 is received by the department.

(3) The person installs a functioning, certified ignition interlock device on any vehicle that he or she operates and submits the "Verification of Installation" form described in paragraph (2) of subdivision (g) of Section 13386.

(4) The person agrees to maintain the functioning, certified ignition interlock device as required under subdivision (g).

(5) The person pays all applicable reinstatement or reissue fees.

(b) The restriction shall remain in effect for the remaining period of the original suspension period under Section 13353.3.

(c) Notwithstanding subdivisions (a) and (b), and upon a conviction under Section 23152 or 23153 for the current offense, the department shall suspend or revoke the person's privilege to operate a motor vehicle under Section 13352 or 13352.1.

(d) (1) The holder of a commercial driver's license who was operating a motor vehicle other than a commercial vehicle, or a driver who was operating a commercial vehicle, as defined in Section 15210, at the time of the violation that resulted in the suspension of that person's driving privilege pursuant to Section 13353.2 is not eligible for the restricted driver's license authorized under this section.

(2) Notwithstanding paragraph (1), as authorized under this section, the department shall issue the person a noncommercial driver's license restricted in the same manner and subject to the same conditions and requirements as specified in subdivision (a).

(e) The department shall terminate the restriction issued pursuant to this section and shall immediately reinstate the suspension of the privilege to operate a motor vehicle upon receipt of notification from the ignition interlock device installer that a person has attempted to remove, bypass, or tamper with the ignition interlock device, has removed the device prior to the termination date of the restriction, or fails three or more times to comply with any requirement for the maintenance or calibration of the ignition interlock device. The privilege shall remain suspended for the remaining mandatory suspension period imposed pursuant to Section 13353.3. However, if the person provides proof to the satisfaction of the department that the person is in compliance with the restriction issued pursuant to this section, the department may, in its discretion, restore the privilege to operate a motor vehicle and reimpose the remaining term of the restriction.

(f) Notwithstanding any other law, a person whose driving privilege has been suspended under Section 13353.2, who is eligible for a restricted driver's license as provided for in this section, and who installs a functioning, certified ignition interlock device pursuant to this section, shall receive credit toward the mandatory term the person is required to install a functioning, certified ignition interlock device pursuant to Section 23575.3 for a conviction of a violation arising out of the same occurrence that led to the person's driving privilege being suspended pursuant to Section 13352 or 13352.1 equal to the period of time the person installs a functioning, certified ignition interlock device pursuant to this section or Section 13353.75.

(g) A person whose driving privilege is restricted by the department pursuant to this section shall arrange for each vehicle with a functioning, certified ignition interlock device to be serviced by the installer at least once every 60 days in order for the installer to recalibrate the device and monitor the operation of the device. The installer shall notify the department if the device is removed or indicates that the person has attempted to remove, bypass, or tamper with the device, or if the person fails three or more times to comply with any requirement for the maintenance or calibration of the ignition interlock device.

(h) For the purposes of this section, the following definitions apply:

(1) "Bypass" means either of the following:

(A) Failure to take any random retest.

(B) Failure to pass a random retest with a breath alcohol concentration not exceeding 0.03 percent, by weight of alcohol, in the person's blood.

(2) "Operates" includes operating a vehicle that is not owned by the person subject to this section.

(3) "Owned" means solely owned or owned in conjunction with another person or legal entity.

(4) "Random retest" means a breath test performed by the driver upon a certified ignition interlock device at random intervals after the initial engine startup breath test and while the vehicle's motor is running.

(5) "Vehicle" does not include a motorcycle until the state certifies an ignition interlock device that can be installed on a motorcycle. A person subject to an ignition interlock device restriction shall not operate a motorcycle for the duration of the ignition interlock device restriction period.

(i) The restriction conditions specified in this section shall apply only to a person who is suspended under Section 13353.2 for a violation that occurred on or after January 1, 2019.

(j) This section shall become operative January 1, 2019.

(k) This section shall remain in effect only until January 1, 2026, and as of that date is repealed, unless a later enacted statute, that is enacted before January 1, 2026, deletes or extends that date. *(Added by Stats.2016, c. 783 (S.B.1046), § 20, eff. Jan. 1, 2017. Amended by Stats.2017, c. 485 (S.B.611), § 14, eff. Jan. 1, 2018, operative Jan. 1, 2019.)*

Repeal

For repeal of this section, see its terms.

Research References

2 Witkin, California Criminal Law 4th Crimes Against Public Peace and Welfare § 290 (2021), Ignition Interlock Device.

§ 13353.8. Order suspending or delaying driving privileges; showing of critical need to drive; review of order; imposition of restrictions on driving privilege

(a) After the department has issued an order suspending or delaying driving privileges as a result of a violation of subdivision (a) of Section 23136, the department, upon the petition of the person affected, may review the order and may impose restrictions on the person's privilege to drive based upon a showing of a critical need to drive, if the department determines that, within 10 years of the current violation of Section 23136, the person has not violated Section 23136 or been convicted of a separate violation of Section 23140, 23152, or 23153, or of Section 23103, with a plea of guilty under Section 23103.5, or of Section 191.5 or subdivision (a) of Section 192.5 of, the Penal Code, and that the person's driving privilege has not been suspended or revoked under Section 13353, 13353.1, or 13353.2 within that 10–year period.

(b) For purposes of this section, a conviction of an offense in a state, territory, or possession of the United States, the District of Columbia, the Commonwealth of Puerto Rico, or the Dominion of Canada that, if committed in this state, would be a violation of Section 23103, as specified in Section 23103.5, or Section 23140, 23152, 23153, or Section 191.5 or subdivision (a) of Section 192.5 of the Penal Code, is a conviction of that particular section of the Vehicle Code or Penal Code.

(c) As used in this section, "critical need to drive" means the circumstances that are required to be shown for the issuance of a junior permit pursuant to Section 12513.

(d) The restriction shall be imposed not earlier than the 31st day after the date the order of suspension became effective and shall remain in effect for the balance of the period of suspension or restriction in this section. *(Added by Stats.1993, c. 899 (S.B.689), § 7. Amended by Stats.1994, c. 938 (S.B.1295), § 8, eff. Sept. 28, 1994; Stats.1995, c. 766 (S.B.726), § 17; Stats.2003, c. 254 (S.B.408), § 1; Stats.2004, c. 550 (S.B.1694), § 10; Stats.2007, c. 747 (A.B.678), § 26.)*

Cross References

Driving motor vehicle following restriction of driving privilege pursuant to this section, punishment, see Vehicle Code § 14601.5.

§ 13355. Driving upon a highway at a speed greater than one hundred miles per hour; suspension of privilege to operate motor vehicle

The department shall immediately suspend the privilege of any person to operate a motor vehicle upon receipt of a duly certified abstract of the record of any court showing that the person has been convicted of a violation of subdivision (b) of Section 22348, or upon a receipt of a report of a judge of a juvenile court, a juvenile hearing officer, or a referee of a juvenile court showing that the person has been found to have committed a violation of subdivision (b) of Section 22348 under the following conditions and for the periods, as follows:

(a) Upon a conviction or finding of an offense under subdivision (b) of Section 22348 that occurred within three years of a prior offense resulting in a conviction of an offense under subdivision (b) of Section 22348, the privilege shall be suspended for a period of six months, or the privilege shall be restricted for six months to necessary travel to and from the person's place of employment and, if driving a motor vehicle is necessary to perform the duties of the person's employment, restricted to driving within the person's scope of employment.

(b) Upon a conviction or finding of an offense under subdivision (b) of Section 22348 that occurred within five years of two or more prior offenses resulting in convictions of offenses under subdivision (b) of Section 22348, the privilege shall be suspended for a period of one year, or the privilege shall be restricted for one year to necessary travel to and from the person's place of employment and, if driving a motor vehicle is necessary to perform the duties of the person's employment, restricted to driving within the person's scope of employment. *(Added by Stats.1983, c. 980, § 2. Amended by Stats.2003, c. 149 (S.B.79), § 84.)*

Law Revision Commission Comments

Section 13355 is amended to reflect the redesignation of traffic hearing officers as juvenile hearing officers. See 1997 Cal. Stat. ch. 679. [33 Cal.L.Rev. Comm. Reports 258 (2003)].

Cross References

Driving at speed greater than 100 miles per hour, see Vehicle Code § 22348.

Research References

2 Witkin, California Criminal Law 4th Crimes Against Public Peace and Welfare § 320 (2021), In General.

3 Witkin, California Criminal Law 4th Punishment § 215 (2021), Excessive Speed.

§ 13357. Revocation or suspension for theft or unlawful taking of a vehicle

Upon the recommendation of the court the department shall suspend or revoke the privilege to operate a motor vehicle of any person who has been found guilty of a violation of Section 10851. *(Added by Stats.1967, c. 1110, p. 2757, § 9.)*

Cross References

Commercial motor vehicles, multiple violations, see Vehicle Code § 15302.

Research References

4 Witkin, California Criminal Law 4th Illegally Obtained Evidence § 384 (2021), In General.

3 Witkin, California Criminal Law 4th Punishment § 217 (2021), Other Serious Offenses.

§ 13359. Grounds for suspension or revocation

The department may suspend or revoke the privilege of any person to operate a motor vehicle upon any of the grounds which authorize the refusal to issue a license. *(Stats.1959, c. 3, p. 1627, § 13359. Amended by Stats.1976, c. 498, p. 1238, § 2.)*

Cross References

Grounds authorizing refusal to issue a license, see Vehicle Code § 12805 et seq.

Research References

3 Witkin, California Criminal Law 4th Punishment § 213 (2021), In General.

§ 13360. Violation of license restrictions

Upon receiving satisfactory evidence of any violation of the restrictions of a driver's license, the department may suspend or revoke the same. *(Stats.1959, c. 3, p. 1627, § 13360.)*

Cross References

Restricted licenses, issuance, see Vehicle Code § 12813.

Research References

3 Witkin, California Criminal Law 4th Punishment § 213 (2021), In General.

§ 13361. Grounds for suspension

The department may suspend the privilege of any person to operate a motor vehicle upon receipt of a duly certified abstract of the record of any court showing that the person has been convicted of any of the following crimes or offenses:

(a) Failure to stop in the event of an accident resulting in damage to property only, or otherwise failing to comply with the requirements of Section 20002.

(b) A second or subsequent conviction of reckless driving.

(c) Manslaughter resulting from the operation of a motor vehicle as provided in paragraph (2) of subdivision (c) of Section 192 of the Penal Code.

In any case under this section the department is authorized to require proof of ability to respond in damages as defined in Section 16430. *(Stats.1959, c. 3, p. 1627, § 13361. Amended by Stats.1959, c. 1048, p. 3089, § 2; Stats.1963, c. 87, p. 715, § 1; Stats.1965, c. 1060, p. 2706, § 2; Stats.1967, c. 236, p. 1371, § 5; Stats.1967, c. 253, p. 1401, § 3; Stats.1982, c. 655, p. 2672, § 4; Stats.1982, c. 1339, p. 4983, § 10, eff. Sept. 24, 1982; Stats.1985, c. 6, § 3, eff. Feb. 21, 1985.)*

Cross References

Proof of financial responsibility, see Vehicle Code § 16430.
Reckless driving, see Vehicle Code §§ 23103, 23104.
Stopping at scene of accident, see Vehicle Code § 20000 et seq.

Research References

3 Witkin, California Criminal Law 4th Punishment § 219 (2021), Grounds.

§ 13362. Surrender of license erroneously issued

The department may require the surrender to it of any driver's license which has been issued erroneously or which contains any erroneous or false statement, or which does not contain any notation required by law or by the department. In the event a licensee does not surrender the license upon proper demand, the department may suspend the licensee's privilege to operate a motor vehicle. The suspension shall continue until the correction of the license by the department or until issuance of another license or temporary license in lieu thereof. *(Stats.1959, c. 3, p. 1627, § 13362.)*

Cross References

Surrender of license during suspension, see Vehicle Code § 13206.

§ 13363. Conviction in another state

(a) The department may, in its discretion, except as provided in Chapter 6 (commencing with Section 15000) of Division 6, of this code, suspend or revoke the privilege of any resident or nonresident to drive a motor vehicle in this State upon receiving notice of the conviction of the person in a state, territory, or possession of the United States, the District of Columbia, the Commonwealth of Puerto Rico, or the Dominion of Canada of an offense therein which, if committed in this State, would be grounds for the suspension or revocation of the privilege to operate a motor vehicle.

(b) Whenever any state, territory, or possession of the United States, the District of Columbia, the Commonwealth of Puerto Rico, or the Dominion of Canada reports the conviction of a violation in such place by a person licensed in this State, the department shall not give effect to such report pursuant to subdivision (a) of this section or Section 15023 unless the department is satisfied that the law of such other place pertaining to the conviction is substantially the same as the law of this State pertaining to such conviction and that the description of the violation from which the conviction arose, is sufficient and that the interpretation and enforcement of such law are substantially the same in such other place as they are in this State. *(Stats.1959, c. 3, p. 1627, § 13363. Amended by Stats.1963, c. 237, p. 980, § 9.)*

Cross References

Definitions,
Conviction, see Vehicle Code § 13103.
Nonresident, see Vehicle Code § 435.

Research References

3 Witkin, California Criminal Law 4th Punishment § 214 (2021), Drunk Driving.
3 Witkin, California Criminal Law 4th Punishment § 219 (2021), Grounds.

§ 13364. Driver's license; suspension; dishonored check; notice; reinstatement

Section operative until Jan. 1, 2027. See, also, § 13364 operative Jan. 1, 2027.

(a) Notwithstanding any other provision of this code, a person's privilege to operate a motor vehicle shall be suspended upon notification by a bank or financial institution that a check has been dishonored when that check was presented to the department for either of the following reasons:

(1) In payment of a fine that resulted from an outstanding violation pursuant to Section 40508 or a suspension pursuant to Section 13365.

(2) In payment of a fee or penalty owed by the person, if the fee or penalty is required by this code for the issuance, reissuance, or return of the person's driver's license after suspension, revocation, or restriction of the driving privilege.

(b) The suspension shall remain in effect until payment of all fines, fees, and penalties is made to the department or to the court, as appropriate, and the person's driving record does not contain any notification of a court order issued pursuant to subdivision (a) of Section 42003 or of a violation of subdivision (a) or (b) of Section 40508.

(c) No suspension imposed pursuant to this section shall become effective until 30 days after the mailing of a written notice of the intent to suspend.

(d) The written notice of a suspension imposed pursuant to this section shall be delivered by certified mail.

(e) If any personal check is offered in payment of fines described in paragraph (1) of subdivision (a) and is returned for any reason, the related notice issued pursuant to former Section 40509 or former Section 40509.5 shall be restored to the person's record.

(f) Notwithstanding any other provision of law, any license that has been suspended pursuant to this section shall immediately be reinstated, and the fees and penalties waived, upon the submission of proof acceptable to the department that the check has been erroneously dishonored by the bank or financial institution.

(g) This section shall remain in effect only until January 1, 2027, and as of that date is repealed. *(Added by Stats.1993, c. 845 (A.B.484), § 1. Amended by Stats.1998, c. 877 (A.B.2132), § 56; Stats.2022, c. 800 (A.B.2746), § 14, eff. Jan. 1, 2023.)*

Repeal

For repeal of this section, see its terms.

Research References

3 Witkin, California Criminal Law 4th Punishment § 213 (2021), In General.

§ 13364. Driver's license; suspension; dishonored check; notice; reinstatement

Section operative Jan. 1, 2027. See, also, § 13364 operative until Jan. 1, 2027.

(a) Notwithstanding any other provision of this code, a person's privilege to operate a motor vehicle shall be suspended upon notification by a bank or financial institution that a check has been dishonored when that check was presented to the department for either of the following reasons:

(1) In payment of a fine that resulted from an outstanding violation pursuant to Section 40508 or a suspension pursuant to former Section 13365.

(2) In payment of a fee or penalty owed by the person, if the fee or penalty is required by this code for the issuance, reissuance, or return of the person's driver's license after suspension, revocation, or restriction of the driving privilege.

(b) The suspension shall remain in effect until payment of all fines, fees, and penalties is made to the department or to the court, as appropriate, and the person's driving record does not contain any notification of a court order issued pursuant to subdivision (a) of Section 42003 or of a violation of subdivision (a) or (b) of Section 40508.

(c) No suspension imposed pursuant to this section shall become effective until 30 days after the mailing of a written notice of the intent to suspend.

(d) The written notice of a suspension imposed pursuant to this section shall be delivered by certified mail.

(e) If any personal check is offered in payment of fines described in paragraph (1) of subdivision (a) and is returned for any reason, the related notice issued pursuant to former Section 40509 or former Section 40509.5 shall be restored to the person's record.

(f) Notwithstanding any other provision of law, any license that has been suspended pursuant to this section shall immediately be reinstated, and the fees and penalties waived, upon the submission of proof acceptable to the department that the check has been erroneously dishonored by the bank or financial institution.

(g) This section shall become operative on January 1, 2027. *(Added by Stats.2022, c. 800 (A.B.2746), § 15, eff. Jan. 1, 2023, operative Jan. 1, 2027.)*

§ 13365. Violation of written promise to appear or lawfully granted continuance of promise to appear

(a) Upon receipt of notification of a violation of subdivision (a) of Section 40508, the department shall take the following action:

(1) If the notice is given pursuant to subdivision (a) of former Section 40509, if the driving record of the person who is the subject of the notice contains one or more prior notifications of a violation issued pursuant to former Section 40509 or former Section 40509.5, and if the person's driving privilege is not currently suspended under this section, the department shall suspend the driving privilege of the person.

(2) If the notice is given pursuant to subdivision (a) of Section 40509.5, and if the driving privilege of the person who is the subject of the notice is not currently suspended under this section, the department shall suspend the driving privilege of the person.

(b)(1) A suspension under this section shall not be effective before a date 60 days after the date of receipt, by the department, of the notice given specified in subdivision (a), and the notice of suspension shall not be mailed by the department before a date 30 days after receipt of the notice given specified in subdivision (a).

(2) The suspension shall continue until the suspended person's driving record does not contain any notification of a violation of subdivision (a) of Section 40508.

(c) This section shall remain in effect only until January 1, 2027, and as of that date is repealed. *(Added by Stats.1963, c. 354, p. 1145, § 1. Amended by Stats.1971, c. 1532, p. 3037, § 2, operative May 3, 1972; Stats.1981, c. 584, p. 2250, § 1, operative July 1, 1982; Stats.1983, c. 983, § 5, eff. Sept. 21, 1983; Stats.1984, c. 858, § 1, operative July 1, 1985; Stats.1990, c. 472 (S.B.1826), § 1; Stats.1998, c. 877 (A.B.2132), § 57; Stats.2017, c. 17 (A.B.103), § 51, eff. June 27, 2017; Stats.2022, c. 800 (A.B.2746), § 16, eff. Jan. 1, 2023.)*

Repeal

For repeal of this section, see its terms.

Cross References

One-time infraction amnesty program, eligibility, see Vehicle Code § 42008.8.

Research References

3 Witkin, California Criminal Law 4th Punishment § 213 (2021), In General.
3 Witkin, California Criminal Law 4th Punishment § 217 (2021), Other Serious Offenses.

§ 13365.2. Persons charged with driving under the influence of drugs or alcohol; failure to make appearance; effective date of suspension

(a) Upon receipt of the notice required under subdivision (b) of former Section 40509.5, the department shall suspend the driving privilege of the person upon whom notice was received and shall continue that suspension until receipt of the certificate required under that subdivision.

(b) The suspension required under subdivision (a) shall become effective on the 45th day after the mailing of written notice by the department.

(c) This section shall remain in effect only until January 1, 2027, and as of that date is repealed. *(Added by Stats.1996, c. 224 (S.B.1579), § 4. Amended by Stats.2017, c. 17 (A.B.103), § 52, eff. June 27, 2017; Stats.2022, c. 800 (A.B.2746), § 17, eff. Jan. 1, 2023.)*

Repeal

For repeal of this section, see its terms.

Research References

4 Witkin, California Criminal Law 4th Pretrial Proceedings § 53 (2021), Failure to Appear.
3 Witkin, California Criminal Law 4th Punishment § 217 (2021), Other Serious Offenses.

§ 13365.5. Notification of willful failure to comply with court order; suspension; effective date of suspension

(a) Upon receipt of a notification issued pursuant to Section 40509.1, the department shall suspend the person's privilege to operate a motor vehicle until compliance with the court order is shown or as prescribed in subdivision (c) of Section 12808. The suspension under this section shall not be effective until 45 days after the giving of written notice by the department.

(b) This section does not apply to a notification of failure to comply with a court order issued for a violation enumerated in paragraph (1), (2), (3), (6), or (7) of subdivision (b) of Section 1803. *(Added by Stats.1993, c. 158 (A.B.392), § 21.7, eff. July 21, 1993.)*

§ 13366. Effective date of suspension or revocation

Whenever in this code the department is required to suspend or revoke the privilege of a person to operate a motor vehicle upon the conviction of such person of violating this code, such suspension or revocation shall begin upon a plea, finding or verdict of guilty. *(Stats.1959, c. 3, p. 1628, § 13366.)*

Cross References

Consecutive imposition of restriction, suspension or revocation for driving under influence or refusing chemical testing, see Vehicle Code § 13353.1.

Research References

3 Witkin, California Criminal Law 4th Punishment § 213 (2021), In General.

§ 13366.5. Commencement of suspension or revocation

(a) Notwithstanding Section 13366, whenever in this code the department is required to disqualify the commercial driving privilege of a person to operate a commercial motor vehicle upon the conviction of that person of a violation of this code, the suspension or revocation shall begin upon receipt by the department of a duly certified abstract of any court record showing that the person has been so convicted.

(b) This section shall become operative on September 20, 2005. *(Added by Stats.2004, c. 952 (A.B.3049), § 11, operative Sept. 20, 2005.)*

Cross References

Commercial vehicles, sanctions, serious traffic violations occurring within three years of two or more separate offenses, see Vehicle Code § 15308.

Research References

3 Witkin, California Criminal Law 4th Punishment § 213 (2021), In General.

§ 13367. Determining minor's suspension

For purposes of the suspension or revocation of any driver's license issued to a minor, the department shall not provide any lighter penalty than would be given to an adult under similar circumstances. *(Added by Stats.1959, c. 562, p. 2524, § 4.)*

§ 13368. Driver training requirement

The department, as a condition to the reinstatement of a suspended license or the issuance of a new license to an individual whose prior license has been revoked, may require the individual to attend the program authorized by the provisions of Section 1659. *(Added by Stats.1965, c. 447, p. 1758, § 2.)*

§ 13369. Certificate or endorsement for specified vehicles

(a) This section applies to the following endorsements and certificates:

(1) Passenger transportation vehicle.

(2) Hazardous materials.

(3) Schoolbus.

(4) School pupil activity bus.

(5) Youth bus.

(6) General public paratransit vehicle.

(7) Farm labor vehicle.

(8) Vehicle used for the transportation of developmentally disabled persons.

(b) The department shall refuse to issue or renew, or shall revoke, the certificate or endorsement of a person who meets the following conditions:

(1) Within three years, has committed any violation that results in a conviction assigned a violation point count of two or more, as defined in Sections 12810 and 12810.5. The department shall not refuse to issue or renew, nor may it revoke, a person's hazardous materials or passenger transportation vehicle endorsement if the violation leading to the conviction occurred in the person's private vehicle and not in a commercial motor vehicle, as defined in Section 15210.

(2) Within three years, has had his or her driving privilege suspended, revoked, or on probation for any reason involving unsafe operation of a motor vehicle. The department shall not refuse to issue or renew, nor may it revoke, a person's passenger transportation vehicle endorsement if the person's driving privilege has, within three years, been placed on probation only for a reason involving unsafe operation of a motor vehicle.

(3) Notwithstanding paragraphs (1) and (2), does not meet the qualifications for issuance of a hazardous materials endorsement set forth in Parts 383, 384, and 1572 of Title 49 of the Code of Federal Regulations.

(c) The department may refuse to issue or renew, or may suspend or revoke, the certificate or endorsement of a person who meets any of the following conditions:

(1) Within 12 months, has been involved as a driver in three accidents in which the driver caused or contributed to the causes of the accidents.

(2) Within 24 months, as a driver, caused or contributed to the cause of an accident resulting in a fatality or serious injury or serious property damage in excess of one thousand dollars ($1,000).

(3) Has violated any provision of this code, or any rule or regulation pertaining to the safe operation of a vehicle for which the certificate or endorsement was issued.

(4) Has violated any restriction of the certificate, endorsement, or commercial driver's license.

(5) Has knowingly made a false statement or failed to disclose a material fact on an application for a certificate or endorsement.

(6) Has been determined by the department to be a negligent or incompetent operator.

(7) Has demonstrated irrational behavior to the extent that a reasonable and prudent person would have reasonable cause to believe that the applicant's ability to perform the duties of a driver may be impaired.

(8) Excessively or habitually uses, or is addicted to, alcoholic beverages, narcotics, or dangerous drugs.

(9) Does not meet the minimum medical standards established or approved by the department.

(d) The department may cancel the certificate or endorsement of any driver who meets any of the following conditions:

(1) Does not have a valid driver's license of the appropriate class.

(2) Has requested cancellation of the certificate or endorsement.

(3) Has failed to meet any of the requirements for issuance or retention of the certificate or endorsement, including, but not limited to, payment of the proper fee, submission of an acceptable medical report and fingerprint cards, and compliance with prescribed training requirements.

(4) Has had his or her driving privilege suspended or revoked for a cause involving other than the safe operation of a motor vehicle.

(e)(1) The department shall refuse to issue or renew, or shall suspend or revoke, the passenger vehicle endorsement of a person who violates subdivision (b) of Section 5387 of the Public Utilities Code.

(2) A person found to be in violation of subdivision (b) of Section 5387 of the Public Utilities Code shall be ineligible for a passenger vehicle endorsement that would permit him or her to drive a bus of any kind, including, but not limited to, a bus, schoolbus, youth bus, school pupil activity bus, trailer bus, or a transit bus, with passengers, for a period of five years.

(f)(1) Reapplication following refusal or revocation under subdivision (b) or (c) may be made after a period of not less than one year from the effective date of denial or revocation, except in cases where a longer period of suspension or revocation is required by law.

(2) Reapplication following cancellation under subdivision (d) may be made at any time without prejudice.

(g) This section shall become operative on January 1, 2017. *(Added by Stats.2015, c. 451 (S.B.491), § 26, eff. Jan. 1, 2016, operative Jan. 1, 2017.)*

§ 13370. Schoolbus, school pupil activity bus, general public paratransit vehicle, youth bus, or vehicle for transportation of developmentally disabled persons; grounds to refuse or revoke driver certificate

(a) The department shall refuse to issue or shall revoke a schoolbus, school pupil activity bus, general public paratransit vehicle, or youth bus driver certificate, or a certificate for a vehicle used for the transportation of developmentally disabled persons, if any of the following causes apply to the applicant or certificate holder:

(1) Has been convicted of a sex offense as defined in Section 44010 of the Education Code.

(2) Has been convicted, within two years, of an offense specified in Section 11361.5 of the Health and Safety Code.

(3) Has failed to meet prescribed training requirements for certificate issuance.

(4) Has failed to meet prescribed testing requirements for certificate issuance.

(5) Has been convicted of a violent felony listed in subdivision (c) of Section 667.5 of the Penal Code, or a serious felony listed in subdivision (c) of Section 1192.7 of the Penal Code. This paragraph shall not be applied to revoke a license that was valid on January 1, 2005, unless the certificate holder is convicted for an offense that is committed on or after that date.

(b) The department may refuse to issue or renew, or may suspend or revoke a schoolbus, school pupil activity bus, general public paratransit vehicle, or youth bus driver certificate, or a certificate for a vehicle used for the transportation of developmentally disabled persons, if any of the following causes apply to the applicant or certificate holder:

(1) Has been convicted of a crime specified in Section 44424 of the Education Code within seven years. This paragraph does not apply if denial is mandatory.

(2) Has committed an act involving moral turpitude.

(3) Has been convicted of an offense, not specified in this section and other than a sex offense, that is punishable as a felony, within seven years.

(4) Has been dismissed as a driver for a cause relating to pupil transportation safety.

(5) Has been convicted, within seven years, of an offense relating to the use, sale, possession, or transportation of narcotics, habit-forming drugs, or dangerous drugs, except as provided in paragraph (3) of subdivision (a).

(6) Has been reported to the Department of Motor Vehicles, pursuant to Section 39843 of the Education Code, for leaving a pupil unattended on a schoolbus, school pupil activity bus, or youth bus.

(c)(1) Reapplication following refusal or revocation under paragraph (1), (2), or (3) of subdivision (a) or any paragraph of subdivision (b) may be made after a period of not less than one year after the effective date of refusal or revocation.

(2) Reapplication following refusal or revocation under paragraph (4) of subdivision (a) may be made after a period of not less than 45 days after the date of the applicant's third testing failure.

(3) An applicant or holder of a certificate may reapply for a certificate whenever a felony or misdemeanor conviction is reversed or dismissed. A termination of probation and dismissal of charges pursuant to Section 1203.4 of the Penal Code or a dismissal of charges pursuant to Section 1203.4a of the Penal Code is not a dismissal for purposes of this section.

(4) A former applicant or holder of a certificate whose certificate was revoked pursuant to paragraph (6) of subdivision (b) may reapply for a certificate if the certificate revocation is reversed or dismissed by the department. *(Added by Stats.1990, c. 1360 (S.B.1510), § 36. Amended by Stats.1998, c. 877 (A.B.2132), § 59; Stats.2003, c. 594 (S.B.315), § 37; Stats.2004, c. 615 (S.B.1233), § 27; Stats.2005, c. 66 (A.B.637), § 2; Stats.2016, c. 721 (S.B.1072), § 6, eff. Jan. 1, 2017.)*

Cross References

Felonies, definition and penalties, see Penal Code §§ 17, 18.

Misdemeanors, definition and penalties, see Penal Code §§ 17, 19 and 19.2.

§ 13371. Schoolbus, activity bus, youth bus, paratransit vehicle, and developmentally disabled person vehicle certificate; hearing

This section applies to schoolbus, school pupil activity bus, youth bus, general public paratransit vehicle certificates, and a certificate for a vehicle used for the transportation of developmentally disabled persons.

(a) Any driver or applicant who has received a notice of refusal, suspension, or revocation, may, within 15 days after the mailing date, submit to the department a written request for a hearing. Failure to demand a hearing within 15 days is a waiver of the right to a hearing.

(1) Upon receipt by the department of the hearing request, the department may stay the action until a hearing is conducted and the final decision has been rendered by the Certificate Action Review Board pursuant to paragraph (2) of subdivision (d). The department shall not stay an action when there is reasonable cause to believe the stay would pose a significant risk to the safety of pupils being transported in a schoolbus, school pupil activity bus, youth bus, or persons being transported in a general public paratransit vehicle.

(2) An applicant or driver is not entitled to a hearing whenever the action by the department is made mandatory by this article or any other applicable law or regulation except where the cause for refusal is based on failure to meet medical standards or excessive and habitual use of or addiction to alcoholic beverages, narcotics, or dangerous drugs.

(b) The department shall appoint a hearing officer to conduct the hearing in accordance with Section 14112. After the hearing, the hearing officer shall prepare and submit findings and recommendations to the department.

(c) The department shall mail, as specified in Section 22, a copy of the hearing officer's findings and recommendations to the driver or applicant and to the driver or applicant's hearing representative, either of whom may file a statement of exception to the findings and recommendations within 24 days after the mailing date.

(d)(1) The Certificate Action Review Board consists of the following three members: a chairperson appointed by the director of the department, a member appointed by the Commissioner of the California Highway Patrol, and a member appointed by the Superintendent of Public Instruction.

(2) After a hearing, the board shall review the findings and recommendations of the hearing officer, and any statement of exception, and make a decision concerning disposition of the action taken by the department, which decision shall be final. At this stage, no evidence shall be heard that was not presented at the hearing, unless the person wishing to present the new evidence establishes, to the satisfaction of the board, that it could not have been obtained with due diligence prior to the hearing. *(Added by Stats.1990, c. 1360 (S.B.1510), § 37. Amended by Stats.1992, c. 731 (S.B.1606), § 1; Stats.1998, c. 877 (A.B.2132), § 60; Stats.2005, c. 66 (A.B.637), § 3.)*

§ 13372. Ambulance driver certificate; refusal to issue or renew; suspension or revocation; grounds; conditions for reapplication

(a) The department shall refuse to issue or renew, or shall suspend or revoke an ambulance driver certificate if any of the following apply to the applicant or certificate holder:

(1) Is required to register as a sex offender under Section 290 of the Penal Code for any offense involving force, violence, threat, or intimidation.

(2) Habitually or excessively uses or is addicted to narcotics or dangerous drugs.

(3) Is on parole or probation for any felony, theft, or any crime involving force, violence, threat, or intimidation.

(b) The department may refuse to issue or renew, or may suspend or revoke an ambulance driver certificate if any of the following apply to the applicant or certificate holder:

(1) Has been convicted within seven years of any offense punishable as a felony or has been convicted during that period of any theft.

(2) Has committed any act involving moral turpitude, including fraud or intentional dishonesty for personal gain, within seven years.

(3) Habitually and excessively uses intoxicating beverages.

(4) Has been convicted within seven years of any offense relating to the use, sale, possession, or transportation of narcotics or addictive or dangerous drugs, or of any misdemeanor involving force, violence, threat, or intimidation.

(5) Is on probation to the department for a cause involving the unsafe operation of a motor vehicle.

(6) Within three years has had his or her driver's license suspended or revoked by the department for a cause involving the unsafe operation of a motor vehicle, or, within the same period, has been convicted of any of the following:

(A) Failing to stop and render aid in an accident involving injury or death.

(B) Driving-under-the-influence of intoxicating liquor, any drug, or under the combined influence of intoxicating liquor and any drug.

(C) Reckless driving, or reckless driving involving bodily injury.

(7) Has knowingly made a false statement or failed to disclose a material fact in his or her application.

(8) Has been involved as a driver in any motor vehicle accident causing death or bodily injury or in three or more motor vehicle accidents within one year.

(9) Does not meet minimum medical standards specified in this code or in regulations adopted pursuant to this code.

(10) Has demonstrated irrational behavior or incurred a physical disability to the extent that a reasonable and prudent person would have reasonable cause to believe that the ability to perform the duties normally expected of an ambulance driver may be impaired.

(11) Has violated any provision of this code or any rule or regulation adopted by the Commissioner of the California Highway Patrol relating to the operation of emergency ambulances within one year.

(12) Has committed any act that warrants dismissal, as provided in Section 13373.

(c)(1) Reapplication following refusal or revocation under subdivision (a) or (b) may be made after a period of not less than one year after the effective date of the refusal or revocation, except in cases where a longer period of refusal, suspension, or revocation is required by law.

(2) Reapplication following refusal or revocation under subdivision (a) or (b) may be made if a felony or misdemeanor conviction supporting the refusal or revocation is reversed or dismissed. A termination of probation and dismissal of charges under Section 1203.4 of the Penal Code or a dismissal of charges under Section 1203.4a of the Penal Code is not a dismissal for purposes of this section. *(Added by Stats.1990, c. 1360 (S.B.1510), § 38. Amended by Stats.2005, c. 66 (A.B.637), § 4.)*

Cross References

Felonies, definition and penalties, see Penal Code §§ 17, 18.
Misdemeanors, definition and penalties, see Penal Code §§ 17, 19 and 19.2.

§ 13373. Dismissal of ambulance drivers or attendants; causes

The receipt of satisfactory evidence of any violation of Article 1 (commencing with Section 1100) of Subchapter 5 of Chapter 2 of Title 13 of the California Code of Regulations, the Vehicle Code, or any other applicable law that would provide grounds for refusal, suspension, or revocation of an ambulance driver's certificate or evidence of an act committed involving intentional dishonesty for personal gain or conduct contrary to justice, honesty, modesty, or good morals, may be sufficient cause for the dismissal of any ambulance driver or attendant. Dismissal of a driver or attendant under this section shall be reported by the employer to the Department of Motor Vehicles at Sacramento within 10 days. *(Added by Stats.1990, c. 1360 (S.B.1510), § 39. Amended by Stats. 2005, c. 66 (A.B.637), § 5.)*

§ 13374. Denial, suspension, or revocation of ambulance drivers license; hearing; request; waiver; findings and recommendations; review committee; final decision

(a) An applicant for, or the holder of, an ambulance driver certificate who has received a notice of refusal, suspension, or revocation may submit, within 15 days after the notice has been mailed by the department, a written request for a hearing. Upon receipt of the request, the department shall appoint a referee who shall conduct an informal hearing in accordance with Section 14104. Failure to request a hearing within 15 days after the notice has been mailed by the department is a waiver of the right to a hearing. A request for a hearing shall not operate to stay the action for which notice is given.

(b) Upon conclusion of an informal hearing, the referee shall prepare and submit findings and recommendations through the department to a committee of three members one each appointed by the Director of the Emergency Medical Service Authority, the director, and the Commissioner of the California Highway Patrol with the appointee of the Commissioner of the California Highway Patrol serving as chairperson. After a review of the findings and recommendations, the committee shall render a final decision on the action taken, and the department shall notify the person involved of the decision. *(Added by Stats.1990, c. 1360 (S.B.1510), § 40. Amended by Stats.2005, c. 66 (A.B.637), § 6.)*

§ 13375. Plea or verdict of guilty or plea of nolo contendere; conviction

For the purposes of this article, any plea or verdict of guilty, plea of nolo contendere, or court finding of guilt in a trial without a jury, or forfeiture of bail, is deemed a conviction, notwithstanding subsequent action under Section 1203.4 or 1203.4a of the Penal Code allowing withdrawal of the plea of guilty and entering a plea of not guilty, setting aside the verdict of guilty, or dismissing the accusation or information. *(Added by Stats.1990, c. 1360 (S.B.1510), § 41.)*

§ 13376. Bus or public paratransit driver certificates; revocation or suspension; positive test result or refusal to submit to test for a controlled substance; sex offense prosecution

(a) This section applies to the following certificates:

(1) Schoolbus.

(2) School pupil activity bus.

(3) Youth bus.

(4) General public paratransit vehicle.

(5) Vehicle used for the transportation of developmentally disabled persons.

(b)(1) The department shall revoke a certificate listed in subdivision (a) for three years if the certificate holder refuses to submit to a test for, fails to comply with the testing requirements for, or receives a positive test for a controlled substance, as specified in Part 382 (commencing with Section 382.101) of Title 49 of the Code of Federal Regulations and Section 34520. However, the department shall not revoke a certificate under this paragraph if the certificate holder is in compliance with any rehabilitation or return to duty program that is imposed by the employer that meets the controlled substances and alcohol use and testing requirements set forth in Part 382 (commencing with Section 382.101) of Title 49 of the Code of

Federal Regulations. The driver shall be allowed to participate in a rehabilitation or return to duty program only once within a three-year period. The employer or program shall report any subsequent positive test result or drop from the program to the department on a form approved by the department.

(2) If an applicant refuses to submit to a test for, fails to comply with the testing requirements for, or receives a positive test for a controlled substance, the department shall refuse the application for a certificate listed in subdivision (a) for three years from the date of the confirmed positive test result.

(3) The carrier that requested the test shall report the refusal, failure to comply, or positive test result to the department not later than five days after receiving notification of the test result on a form approved by the department.

(4) The department shall maintain a record of any action taken for a refusal, failure to comply, or positive test result in the driving record of the applicant or certificate holder for three years from the date of the refusal, failure to comply, or positive test result.

(c)(1) The department may temporarily suspend a schoolbus, school pupil activity bus, youth bus, or general public paratransit driver certificate, or temporarily withhold issuance of a certificate to an applicant, if the holder or applicant is arrested for or charged with any sex offense, as defined in Section 44010 of the Education Code.

(2) Upon receipt of a notice of temporary suspension, or of the department's intent to withhold issuance, of a certificate, the certificate holder or applicant may request a hearing within 10 days of the effective date of the department's action.

(3) The department shall, upon request of the holder of, or applicant for, a certificate, within 10 working days of the receipt of the request, conduct a hearing on whether the public interest requires suspension or withholding of the certificate pursuant to paragraph (1).

(4) If the charge is dismissed or results in a finding of not guilty, the department shall immediately terminate the suspension or resume the application process, and shall expunge the suspension action taken pursuant to this subdivision from the record of the applicant or certificate holder.

(d) An applicant or holder of a certificate may reapply for a certificate whenever a felony or misdemeanor conviction is reversed or dismissed. A termination of probation and dismissal of charges pursuant to Section 1203.4 of the Penal Code or a dismissal of charges pursuant to Section 1203.4a of the Penal Code is not a dismissal for purposes of this section.

(e) The determination of the facts pursuant to this section is a civil matter which is independent of the determination of the person's guilt or innocence, has no collateral estoppel effect on a subsequent criminal prosecution, and does not preclude the litigation of the same or similar facts in a criminal proceeding. *(Added by Stats.1990, c. 741 (A.B.3636), § 1. Amended by Stats.1997, c. 738 (A.B.1238), § 2; Stats.2005, c. 66 (A.B.637), § 7.)*

Cross References

Felonies, definition and penalties, see Penal Code §§ 17, 18.
Misdemeanors, definition and penalties, see Penal Code §§ 17, 19 and 19.2.

§ 13377. Tow truck driver certificates; grounds for revocation or refusal to issue or renew; reapplication for certificate

(a) The department shall not issue or renew, or shall revoke, the tow truck driver certificate of an applicant or holder for any of the following causes:

(1) The tow truck driver certificate applicant or holder has been convicted of a violation of Section 220 of the Penal Code.

(2) The tow truck driver certificate applicant or holder has been convicted of a violation of paragraph (1), (2), (3), or (4) of subdivision (a) of Section 261 of the Penal Code.

(3) The tow truck driver certificate applicant or holder has been convicted of a violation of Section 264.1, 267, 288, or 289 of the Penal Code.

(4) The tow truck driver certificate applicant or holder has been convicted of any felony or three misdemeanors as set forth in subparagraph (B) of paragraph (2) of subdivision (a) of Section 5164 of the Public Resources Code.

(5) The tow truck driver certificate applicant's or holder's driving privilege has been suspended or revoked in accordance with any provisions of this code.

(b) For purposes of this section, a conviction means a plea or verdict of guilty or a conviction following a plea of nolo contendere. For purposes of this section, the record of a conviction, or a copy thereof certified by the clerk of the court or by a judge of the court in which the conviction occurred, is conclusive evidence of the conviction.

(c) Whenever the department receives information from the Department of Justice, or the Federal Bureau of Investigation, that a tow truck driver has been convicted of an offense specified in paragraph (1), (2), (3), or (4) of subdivision (a), the department shall immediately notify the employer and the Department of the California Highway Patrol.

(d) An applicant or holder of a tow truck driver certificate, whose certificate was denied or revoked, may reapply for a certificate whenever the applicable felony or misdemeanor conviction is reversed or dismissed. If the cause for the denial or revocation was based on the suspension or revocation of the applicant's or holder's driving privilege, he or she may reapply for a certificate upon restoration of his or her driving privilege. A termination of probation and dismissal of charges pursuant to Section 1203.4 of the Penal Code or a dismissal of charges pursuant to Section 1203.4a of the Penal Code is not a dismissal for purposes of this section. *(Added by Stats.1991, c. 488 (A.B.123), § 6. Amended by Stats.1992, c. 1243 (A.B.3090), § 86.2, eff. Sept. 30, 1992; Stats.2000, c. 135 (A.B.2539), § 159; Stats.2002, c. 787 (S.B.1798), § 34; Stats.2004, c. 184 (S.B.1314), § 6, eff. July 23, 2004.)*

Cross References

Counties and cities, persons convicted of Penal Code offenses, supervisory or disciplinary authority over minors, see Public Resources Code § 5164.
Felonies, definition and penalties, see Penal Code §§ 17, 18.
Misdemeanors, definition and penalties, see Penal Code §§ 17, 19 and 19.2.

§ 13378. Request for hearing; stay; appointment of hearing officer

(a) Any applicant for, or holder of, a tow truck driver certificate who has received a notice of refusal or revocation, may submit to the department, within 15 days after the mailing of the notice, a written request for a hearing. Failure to request a hearing, in writing, within 15 days is a waiver of the right to a hearing.

(b) Upon receipt by the department of the hearing request, the department may stay the action until a hearing is conducted and the final decision is made by the hearing officer. The department shall not stay the action when there is reasonable cause to believe that the stay would pose a threat to a member of the motoring public who may require the services of the tow truck driver in question.

(c) An applicant for, or a holder of, a tow truck driver certificate, whose certificate has been refused or revoked, is not entitled to a hearing whenever the action by the department is made mandatory by this article or any other applicable law or regulation.

(d) Upon receipt of a request for a hearing, and when the requesting party is entitled to a hearing under this article, the department shall appoint a hearing officer to conduct a hearing in accordance with Section 14112. *(Added by Stats.1991, c. 488 (A.B.123), § 7. Amended by Stats.1996, c. 124 (A.B.3470), § 123; Stats.2005, c. 66 (A.B.637), § 8.)*

§ 13380. Peace officer's report; service of notice of suspension; arrest

(a) If a peace officer serves a notice of an order of suspension pursuant to Section 13388, or arrests any person for a violation of Section 23140, 23152, or 23153, the peace officer shall immediately forward to the department a sworn report of all information relevant to the enforcement action, including information that adequately identifies the person, a statement of the officer's grounds for belief that the person violated Section 23136, 23140, 23152, or 23153, a report of the results of any chemical tests that were conducted on the person or the circumstances constituting a refusal to submit to or complete the chemical testing pursuant to Section 13388 or 23612, a copy of any notice to appear under which the person was released from custody, and, if immediately available, a copy of the complaint filed with the court. For the purposes of this section and subdivision (g) of Section 23612, "immediately" means on or before the end of the fifth ordinary business day following the arrest, except that with respect to Section 13388 only, "immediately" has the same meaning as that term is defined in paragraph (3) of subdivision (b) of Section 13388.

(b) The peace officer's sworn report shall be made on forms furnished or approved by the department.

(c) For the purposes of this section, a report prepared pursuant to subdivision (a) and received pursuant to subdivision (a) of Section 1801, is a sworn report when it bears an entry identifying the maker of the document or a signature that has been affixed by means of an electronic device approved by the department. *(Added by Stats.1998, c. 118 (S.B.1186), § 3.24, operative July 1, 1999.)*

Research References

2 Witkin, California Criminal Law 4th Crimes Against Public Peace and Welfare § 298 (2021), Administration of Test.
2 Witkin, California Criminal Law 4th Crimes Against Public Peace and Welfare § 301 (2021), Notice of Suspension or Revocation of License.

§ 13382. Blood alcohol of specified level; suspension or revocation of driving privilege; notice; confiscation of license; temporary license

(a) If the chemical test results for a person who has been arrested for a violation of Section 23152 or 23153 show that the person has 0.08 percent or more, by weight, of alcohol in the person's blood, or if the chemical test results for a person who has been arrested for a violation of Section 23140 show that the person has 0.05 percent or more, by weight, of alcohol in the person's blood, the peace officer, acting on behalf of the department, shall serve a notice of order of suspension or revocation of the person's privilege to operate a motor vehicle personally on the arrested person.

(b) If the peace officer serves the notice of order of suspension or revocation, the peace officer shall take possession of any driver's license issued by this state which is held by the person. When the officer takes possession of a valid driver's license, the officer shall issue, on behalf of the department, a temporary driver's license. The temporary driver's license shall be an endorsement on the notice of the order of suspension or revocation and shall be valid for 30 days from the date of arrest.

(c) The peace officer shall immediately forward a copy of the completed notice of order of suspension form, and any driver's license taken into possession under subdivision (b), with the report required by Section 13380, to the department. For the purposes of this section, "immediately" means on or before the end of the fifth ordinary business day following the arrest. *(Added by Stats.1998, c. 118 (S.B.1186), § 4, operative July 1, 1999.)*

Research References

2 Witkin, California Criminal Law 4th Crimes Against Public Peace and Welfare § 301 (2021), Notice of Suspension or Revocation of License.

§ 13384. Consent to chemical test of blood, breath or urine

(a) The department shall not issue or renew a driver's license to any person unless the person consents in writing to submit to a chemical test or tests of that person's blood, breath, or urine pursuant to Section 23612, or a preliminary alcohol screening test pursuant to Section 23136, when requested to do so by a peace officer.

(b) All application forms for driver's licenses or driver's license renewal notices shall include a requirement that the applicant sign the following declaration as a condition of licensure:

"I agree to submit to a chemical test of my blood, breath, or urine for the purpose of determining the alcohol or drug content of my blood when testing is requested by a peace officer acting in accordance with Section 13388 or 23612 of the Vehicle Code."

(c) The department is not, incident to this section, required to maintain, copy, or store any information other than that to be incorporated into the standard application form. *(Added by Stats. 1998, c. 118 (S.B.1186), § 5, operative July 1, 1999.)*

Research References

2 Witkin, California Criminal Law 4th Crimes Against Public Peace and Welfare § 302 (2021), Administrative Sanctions.

§ 13385. Driving under the influence; declaration required in application forms or renewal notices as condition of licensure

(a) On or after July 1, 2008, all application forms for driver's licenses or driver's license renewal notices shall include a requirement that the applicant sign the following declaration as a condition of licensure:

"I am hereby advised that being under the influence of alcohol or drugs, or both, impairs the ability to safely operate a motor vehicle. Therefore, it is extremely dangerous to human life to drive while under the influence of alcohol or drugs, or both. If I drive while under the influence of alcohol or drugs, or both, and as a result, a person is killed, I can be charged with murder."

(b) On all application forms for driver's licenses or driver's license renewal notices printed by the department, in English or a language other than English, the department shall include the declaration in the same language as the application or renewal notice.

(c) The department is not, incident to this section, required to maintain, copy, or store any information other than that to be incorporated into the standard application form. *(Added by Stats. 2007, c. 748 (A.B.808), § 2.)*

§ 13386. Certification and list of ignition interlock devices; prohibitions

Section operative until Jan. 1, 2026. See, also, § 13386 operative Jan. 1, 2026.

(a)(1) The department shall certify or cause to be certified ignition interlock devices required by Article 5 (commencing with Section 23575) of Chapter 2 of Division 11.5 and publish a list of approved devices.

(2)(A) The department shall ensure that ignition interlock devices that have been certified according to the requirements of this section continue to meet certification requirements. The department may periodically require manufacturers to indicate in writing whether the devices continue to meet certification requirements.

(B) The department may use denial of certification, suspension or revocation of certification, or decertification of an ignition interlock device in another state as an indication that the certification requirements are not met, if either of the following apply:

(i) The denial of certification, suspension or revocation of certification, or decertification in another state constitutes a violation by the manufacturer of Article 2.55 (commencing with Section 125.00) of Chapter 1 of Division 1 of Title 13 of the California Code of Regulations.

(ii) The denial of certification for an ignition interlock device in another state was due to a failure of an ignition interlock device to meet the standards adopted by the regulation set forth in clause (i), specifically Sections 1 and 2 of the model specification for breath alcohol ignition interlock devices, as published by notice in the Federal Register, Vol. 57, No. 67, Tuesday, April 7, 1992, on pages 11774 to 11787, inclusive, or the model specifications for breath alcohol ignition interlock devices, as published by notice in the Federal Register, Vol. 78, No. 89, Wednesday, May 8, 2013, on pages 25489 to 26867, inclusive.

(C) Failure to continue to meet certification requirements shall result in suspension or revocation of certification of ignition interlock devices.

(b)(1) A manufacturer shall not furnish an installer, service center, technician, or consumer with technology or information that allows a device to be used in a manner that is contrary to the purpose for which it is certified.

(2) Upon a violation of paragraph (1), the department shall suspend or revoke the certification of the ignition interlock device that is the subject of that violation.

(c) An installer, service center, or technician shall not tamper with, change, or alter the functionality of the device from its certified criteria.

(d) The department shall utilize information from an independent, accredited (ISO/IEC 17025) laboratory to certify ignition interlock devices of the manufacturer or manufacturer's agent, in accordance with the guidelines. The cost of certification shall be borne by the manufacturers of ignition interlock devices. If the certification of a device is suspended or revoked, the manufacturer of the device shall be responsible for, and shall bear the cost of, the removal of the device and the replacement of a certified device of the manufacturer or another manufacturer.

(e) A model of ignition interlock device shall not be certified unless it meets the accuracy requirements and specifications provided in the guidelines adopted by the National Highway Traffic Safety Administration.

(f) All manufacturers of ignition interlock devices that meet the requirements of subdivision (e) and are certified in a manner approved by the department, who intend to market the devices in this state, first shall apply to the department on forms provided by that department. The application shall be accompanied by a fee in an amount not to exceed the amount necessary to cover the reasonable costs incurred by the department in carrying out this section.

(g) The department shall ensure that standard forms and procedures are developed for documenting decisions and compliance and communicating results to relevant agencies. These forms shall include all of the following:

(1) An "Option to Install," to be sent by the department to all offenders along with the mandatory order of suspension or revocation. This shall include the alternatives available for early license reinstatement with the installation of a functioning, certified ignition interlock device and shall be accompanied by a toll-free telephone number for each manufacturer of a certified ignition interlock device. Information regarding approved installation locations shall be provided to drivers by manufacturers with ignition interlock devices that have been certified in accordance with this section.

(2) A "Verification of Installation" to be returned to the department by the offender upon application for reinstatement. Copies shall be provided for the manufacturer or the manufacturer's agent.

(3) A "Notice of Noncompliance" and procedures to ensure continued use of the ignition interlock device during the restriction period and to ensure compliance with maintenance requirements. The maintenance period shall be standardized at 60 days to maximize monitoring checks for equipment tampering.

(h) The department shall develop rules under which every manufacturer and manufacturer's agent certified by the department to provide ignition interlock devices shall provide a fee schedule to the department of the manufacturer's standard ignition interlock device program costs, stating the standard charges for installation, service and maintenance, and removal of the manufacturer's device, and shall develop a form to be signed by an authorized representative of the manufacturer pursuant to which the manufacturer agrees to provide functioning, certified ignition interlock devices to applicants at the costs described in subdivision (k) of Section 23575.3. The form shall contain an acknowledgment that the failure of the manufacturer, its agents, or authorized installers to comply with subdivision (k) of Section 23575.3 shall result in suspension or revocation of the department's approval for the manufacturer to market ignition interlock devices in this state.

(i) A person who manufactures, installs, services, or repairs, or otherwise deals in ignition interlock devices shall not disclose, sell, or transfer to a third party any individually identifiable information pertaining to individuals who are required by law to install a functioning, certified ignition interlock device on a vehicle that he or she operates, except to the extent necessary to confirm or deny that an individual has complied with ignition interlock device installation and maintenance requirements.

(j) This section shall become operative on January 1, 2019.

(k) This section shall remain in effect only until January 1, 2026, and as of that date is repealed. *(Added by Stats.2017, c. 485 (S.B.611), § 16, eff. Jan. 1, 2018, operative Jan. 1, 2019.)*

Repeal

For repeal of this section, see its terms.

Cross References

Causing bodily injury to another while driving with license suspended or revoked, reinstatement of driving privileges, application of this section, see Vehicle Code § 14601.4.

Driving with knowledge of suspension, revocation, or restriction of driving privilege, punishment, reinstatement of driving privileges, see Vehicle Code § 14601.5.

Pilot program to reduce driving under the influence offenses, establishment in Alameda, Los Angeles, Sacramento, and Tulare Counties, see Vehicle Code § 23700.

Suspension or revocation of driving privilege for driving under the influence of alcoholic beverages or drugs, compliance with this section, see Vehicle Code § 14601.2.

§ 13386. Certification and list of ignition interlock devices; prohibitions

Section operative Jan. 1, 2026. See, also, § 13386 operative until Jan. 1, 2026.

(a)(1) The department shall certify or cause to be certified ignition interlock devices required by Article 5 (commencing with Section 23575) of Chapter 2 of Division 11.5 and publish a list of approved devices.

(2)(A) The department shall ensure that ignition interlock devices that have been certified according to the requirements of this section continue to meet certification requirements. The department may periodically require manufacturers to indicate in writing whether the devices continue to meet certification requirements.

(B) The department may use denial of certification, suspension or revocation of certification, or decertification of an ignition interlock device in another state as an indication that the certification requirements are not met, if either of the following apply:

(i) The denial of certification, suspension or revocation of certification, or decertification in another state constitutes a violation by the manufacturer of Article 2.55 (commencing with Section 125.00) of Chapter 1 of Division 1 of Title 13 of the California Code of Regulations.

(ii) The denial of certification for an ignition interlock device in another state was due to a failure of an ignition interlock device to meet the standards adopted by the regulation set forth in clause (i), specifically Sections 1 and 2 of the model specification for breath alcohol ignition interlock devices, as published by notice in the Federal Register, Vol. 57, No. 67, Tuesday, April 7, 1992, on pages 11774 to 11787, inclusive, or the Model Specifications for Breath Alcohol Ignition Interlock Devices, as published by notice in the Federal Register, Vol. 78, No. 89, Wednesday, May 8, 2013, on pages 25489 to 26867, inclusive.

(C) Failure to continue to meet certification requirements shall result in suspension or revocation of certification of ignition interlock devices.

(b)(1) A manufacturer shall not furnish an installer, service center, technician, or consumer with technology or information that allows a device to be used in a manner that is contrary to the purpose for which it is certified.

(2) Upon a violation of paragraph (1), the department shall suspend or revoke the certification of the ignition interlock device that is the subject of that violation.

(c) An installer, service center, or technician shall not tamper with, change, or alter the functionality of the device from its certified criteria.

(d) The department shall utilize information from an independent, accredited (ISO/IEC 17025) laboratory to certify ignition interlock devices of the manufacturer or manufacturer's agent, in accordance with the guidelines. The cost of certification shall be borne by the manufacturers of ignition interlock devices. If the certification of a device is suspended or revoked, the manufacturer of the device shall be responsible for, and shall bear the cost of, the removal of the device and the replacement of a certified device of the manufacturer or another manufacturer.

(e) A model of ignition interlock device shall not be certified unless it meets the accuracy requirements and specifications provided in the guidelines adopted by the National Highway Traffic Safety Administration.

(f) All manufacturers of ignition interlock devices that meet the requirements of subdivision (e) and are certified in a manner approved by the department, who intend to sell the devices in this state, first shall apply to the department on forms provided by that department. The application shall be accompanied by a fee in an amount not to exceed the amount necessary to cover the costs incurred by the department in carrying out this section.

(g) The department shall ensure that standard forms and procedures are developed for documenting decisions and compliance and communicating results to relevant agencies. These forms shall include all of the following:

(1) An "Option to Install," to be sent by the department to repeat offenders along with the mandatory order of suspension or revocation. This shall include the alternatives available for early license reinstatement with the installation of an ignition interlock device and shall be accompanied by a toll-free telephone number for each manufacturer of a certified ignition interlock device. Information regarding approved installation locations shall be provided to drivers by manufacturers with ignition interlock devices that have been certified in accordance with this section.

(2) A "Verification of Installation" to be returned to the department by the reinstating offender upon application for reinstatement. Copies shall be provided for the manufacturer or the manufacturer's agent.

(3) A "Notice of Noncompliance" and procedures to ensure continued use of the ignition interlock device during the restriction period and to ensure compliance with maintenance requirements. The maintenance period shall be standardized at 60 days to maximize monitoring checks for equipment tampering.

(h) Every manufacturer and manufacturer's agent certified by the department to provide ignition interlock devices shall adopt fee schedules that provide for the payment of the costs of the device by applicants in amounts commensurate with the applicant's ability to pay.

(i) A person who manufactures, installs, services, or repairs, or otherwise deals in ignition interlock devices shall not disclose, sell, or transfer to a third party any individually identifiable information pertaining to individuals who are required by law to install an ignition interlock device on a vehicle that he or she owns or operates, except to the extent necessary to confirm or deny that an individual has complied with ignition interlock device installation and maintenance requirements.

(j) This section shall become operative January 1, 2026. *(Added by Stats.2016, c. 783 (S.B.1046), § 22, eff. Jan. 1, 2017, operative Jan. 1, 2026.)*

Cross References

Causing bodily injury to another while driving with license suspended or revoked, reinstatement of driving privileges, application of this section, see Vehicle Code § 14601.4.

Driving with knowledge of suspension, revocation, or restriction of driving privilege, punishment, reinstatement of driving privileges, see Vehicle Code § 14601.5.

Pilot program to reduce driving under the influence offenses, establishment in Alameda, Los Angeles, Sacramento, and Tulare Counties, see Vehicle Code § 23700.

Suspension or revocation of driving privilege for driving under the influence of alcoholic beverages or drugs, compliance with this section, see Vehicle Code § 14601.2.

§ 13388. Preliminary alcohol screening test or other chemical testing; procedure upon failure to take or complete test

(a) If a peace officer lawfully detains a person under 21 years of age who is driving a motor vehicle, and the officer has reasonable cause to believe that the person is in violation of Section 23136, the officer shall request that the person take a preliminary alcohol screening test to determine the presence of alcohol in the person, if a preliminary alcohol screening test device is immediately available. If a preliminary alcohol screening test device is not immediately available, the officer may request the person to submit to chemical testing of his or her blood, breath, or urine, conducted pursuant to Section 23612.

(b) If the person refuses to take, or fails to complete, the preliminary alcohol screening test or refuses to take or fails to complete a chemical test if a preliminary alcohol device is not immediately available, or if the person takes the preliminary alcohol screening test and that test reveals a blood-alcohol concentration of 0.01 percent or greater, or if the results of a chemical test reveal a blood-alcohol concentration of 0.01 percent or greater, the officer shall proceed as follows:

(1) The officer, acting on behalf of the department, shall serve the person with a notice of an order of suspension of the person's driving privilege.

(2) The officer shall take possession of any driver's license issued by this state which is held by the person. When the officer takes possession of a valid driver's license, the officer shall issue, on behalf of the department, a temporary driver's license. The temporary driver's license shall be an endorsement on the notice of the order of suspension and shall be valid for 30 days from the date of issuance, or until receipt of the order of suspension from the department, whichever occurs first.

(3) The officer immediately shall forward a copy of the completed notice of order of suspension form, and any driver's license taken into possession under paragraph (2), with the report required by Section 13380, to the department. For the purposes of this paragraph, "immediately" means on or before the end of the fifth ordinary business day after the notice of order of suspension was served.

(c) For the purposes of this section, a preliminary alcohol screening test device is an instrument designed and used to measure the presence of alcohol in a person based on a breath sample. *(Added by Stats.1998, c. 118 (S.B.1186), § 7, operative July 1, 1999.)*

Research References

2 Witkin, California Criminal Law 4th Crimes Against Public Peace and Welfare § 293 (2021), Nature and Scope of Law.
2 Witkin, California Criminal Law 4th Crimes Against Public Peace and Welfare § 301 (2021), Notice of Suspension or Revocation of License.
2 Witkin, California Criminal Law 4th Crimes Against Public Peace and Welfare § 302 (2021), Administrative Sanctions.

§ 13389. Persons previously convicted of driving under the influence; lawful detention during probation; preliminary alcohol screening test; suspension of driving privileges

(a) If a peace officer lawfully detains a person previously convicted of Section 23152 or 23153 who is driving a motor vehicle, while the person is on probation for a violation of Section 23152 or 23153, and the officer has reasonable cause to believe that the person is in violation of Section 23154, the officer shall request that the person take a preliminary alcohol screening test to determine the presence of alcohol in the person, if a preliminary alcohol screening test device is immediately available. If a preliminary alcohol screening test device is not immediately available, the officer may request the person to submit to chemical testing of his or her blood, breath, or urine, conducted pursuant to Section 23612.

(b) If the person refuses to take, or fails to complete, the preliminary alcohol screening test or refuses to take or fails to complete a chemical test if a preliminary alcohol device is not immediately available, or if the person takes the preliminary alcohol screening test and that test reveals a blood-alcohol concentration of 0.01 percent or greater, the officer shall proceed as follows:

(1) The officer, acting on behalf of the department, shall serve the person with a notice of an order of suspension of the person's driving privilege.

(2)(A) The officer shall take possession of any driver's license issued by this state that is held by the person. When the officer takes possession of a valid driver's license, the officer shall issue, on behalf of the department, a temporary driver's license.

(B) The temporary driver's license shall be an endorsement on the notice of the order of suspension and shall be valid for 30 days from the date of issuance, or until receipt of the order of suspension from the department, whichever occurs first.

(3)(A) The officer shall immediately forward a copy of the completed notice of order of suspension form, and any driver's license taken into possession under paragraph (2), with the report required by Section 13380, to the department.

(B) For the purposes of subparagraph (A), "immediately" means on or before the end of the fifth ordinary business day after the notice of order of suspension was served.

(c) For the purposes of this section, a preliminary alcohol screening test device is an instrument designed and used to measure the presence of alcohol in a person based on a breath sample. *(Added by Stats.2007, c. 749 (A.B.1165), § 3, operative Jan. 1, 2009.)*

Cross References

Drivers' licenses, review of suspension or revocation order, see Vehicle Code § 13557.

Research References

2 Witkin, California Criminal Law 4th Crimes Against Public Peace and Welfare § 293 (2021), Nature and Scope of Law.
2 Witkin, California Criminal Law 4th Crimes Against Public Peace and Welfare § 301 (2021), Notice of Suspension or Revocation of License.

§ 13390. Temporary license; information regarding installation of ignition interlock device

(a) A temporary license issued pursuant to Section 13382 or 13389 shall contain a notice that the person may be able to regain driving privileges with the installation of an ignition interlock device, that financial assistance may be available for that purpose, and a contact for obtaining more information regarding the ignition interlock program.

(b) This section shall become operative on January 1, 2019.

(c) This section shall remain in effect only until January 1, 2026, and as of that date is repealed. *(Added by Stats.2017, c. 485 (S.B.611), § 18, eff. Jan. 1, 2018, operative Jan. 1, 2019.)*

Repeal

For repeal of this section, see its terms.

Research References

2 Witkin, California Criminal Law 4th Crimes Against Public Peace and Welfare § 301 (2021), Notice of Suspension or Revocation of License.

§ 13392. Fee for reissuance, return or issuance of license

Any person whose license is suspended or delayed issuance pursuant to Section 13388 shall pay to the department, in addition to any other fees required for the reissuance, return, or issuance of a driver's license, one hundred dollars ($100) for the reissuance, return, or issuance of his or her driver's license. *(Added by Stats.1998, c. 118 (S.B.1186), § 9, operative July 1, 1999.)*

ARTICLE 4. PROCEDURE

Section

§ 13550. Surrender of license or temporary permit to court

Whenever any person is convicted of any offense for which this code makes mandatory the revocation or suspension by the department of the privilege of the person to operate a motor vehicle, the privilege of the person to operate a motor vehicle is suspended or revoked until the department takes the action required by this code, and the court in which the conviction is had shall require the surrender to it of the driver's license or temporary permit issued to the person convicted and the court shall within 10 days after the conviction forward the same with the required report of the conviction to the department. *(Stats.1959, c. 3, p. 1628, § 13550. Amended by Stats.1961, c. 1615, p. 3457, § 26; Stats.1971, c. 1530, p. 3027, § 11, operative May 3, 1972; Stats.1972, c. 1129, p. 2170, § 3; Stats.1990, c. 44 (A.B.1648), § 3.)*

Cross References

Conviction of driving under the influence, first time offense, surrender of license, see Vehicle Code § 23536.
Driving under the influence and causing bodily injury to another, punishment and conditions of probation, surrender of license, see Vehicle Code §§ 23554 to 23568.
Driving while under the influence of alcoholic beverages or drugs, surrender of license for conviction, see Vehicle Code § 23660.
Licenses affected by suspension or revocation, see Vehicle Code § 13207.
Multiple offenses with respect to driving under the influence, punishment and conditions of probation, surrender of license, see Vehicle Code §§ 23550 and 23552.
Retention of license by court during suspension, see Vehicle Code § 13206.
Second offense with respect to driving under the influence, punishment and conditions of probation, surrender of license, see Vehicle Code §§ 23540 and 23542.

Research References

2 Witkin, California Criminal Law 4th Crimes Against Public Peace and Welfare § 280 (2021), First Violation.
2 Witkin, California Criminal Law 4th Crimes Against Public Peace and Welfare § 281 (2021), One Separate Conviction of Related Offense.
2 Witkin, California Criminal Law 4th Crimes Against Public Peace and Welfare § 282 (2021), Two Separate Convictions of Related Offenses.
2 Witkin, California Criminal Law 4th Crimes Against Public Peace and Welfare § 283 (2021), Three or More Separate Convictions of Related Offenses.
2 Witkin, California Criminal Law 4th Crimes Against Public Peace and Welfare § 285 (2021), First Violation.
2 Witkin, California Criminal Law 4th Crimes Against Public Peace and Welfare § 286 (2021), One Separate Conviction of Related Offense.
2 Witkin, California Criminal Law 4th Crimes Against Public Peace and Welfare § 287 (2021), Two or More Separate Convictions of Related Offenses.
2 Witkin, California Criminal Law 4th Crimes Against Public Peace and Welfare § 289 (2021), Prior Violation Punished as Felony.

§ 13551. Surrender of licenses to department

(a) Whenever the department revokes or suspends the privilege of any person to operate a motor vehicle, the revocation or suspension shall apply to all driver's licenses held by that person, and, unless previously surrendered to the court, all of those licenses shall be surrendered to the department, or, pursuant to Section 13388, 23612, or 13382, to a peace officer on behalf of the department. Whenever the department cancels a driver's license, the license shall be surrendered to the department. All suspended licenses shall be retained by the department. The department shall return the license to the licensee, or may issue the person a new license upon the expiration of the period of suspension or revocation, if the person is otherwise eligible for a driver's license.

(b) The department shall return the license to the licensee, or may issue the person a new license, whenever the department determines that the grounds for suspension, revocation, or cancellation did not exist at the time the action was taken, if the person is otherwise eligible for a driver's license. *(Stats.1959, c. 3, p. 1628, § 13551. Amended by Stats.1961, c. 1615, p. 3457, § 27; Stats.1963, c. 154, p. 822, § 1; Stats.1967, c. 769, p. 2157, § 1; Stats.1989, c. 1460, § 12, operative July 1, 1990; Stats.1990, c. 431 (S.B.1150), § 9, eff. July 26, 1990; Stats.1993, c. 899 (S.B.689), § 8; Stats.1998, c. 118 (S.B.1186), § 3.18, operative July 1, 1999.)*

Cross References

Cancellation, revocation and suspension of license, defined, see Vehicle Code § 13100 et seq.
Driver's license,
  Surrender on suspension by court, see Vehicle Code § 13206.
  Suspension for failure to report accident, see Vehicle Code § 16004.
Motor vehicle defined, see Vehicle Code § 415.
Seizure of documents and plates upon expiration, revocation, cancellation or suspension, see Vehicle Code § 4460.
Suspension or revocation of driver's license by,
  Court, see Vehicle Code § 13200 et seq.
  Department, see Vehicle Code § 13350 et seq.

§ 13552. Nonresidents

(a) The privileges of a nonresident to operate vehicles in this state may be suspended or revoked under the provisions of this chapter in the same manner and to the same extent as the privileges of a resident driver.

(b) Any nonresident, whether or not licensed to drive in a foreign jurisdiction, who operates a motor vehicle upon a highway after his privilege of operating a motor vehicle in this state has been suspended or revoked is in violation of Section 14601 or 14601.1.

(c) Whenever the department revokes or suspends the privileges of a nonresident to operate vehicles in this state, it shall send a certified copy of the order to the proper authorities in the state wherein the person is a resident. *(Stats.1959, c. 3, p. 1628, § 13552. Amended by Stats.1971, c. 438, p. 908, § 189, operative May 3, 1972.)*

Cross References

Nonresident defined, see Vehicle Code § 435.
Suspension or revocation,
  Of license by court, provisions applicable to nonresidents, see Vehicle Code § 13205.
  Of privilege of nonresident to drive in this state, see Vehicle Code § 13363.

Research References

3 Witkin, California Criminal Law 4th Punishment § 210 (2021), In General.

§ 13553. Unlicensed persons

Whenever a court or the department suspends or revokes the privilege of any person to operate a motor vehicle and the person does not hold a valid driver's license, or has never applied for or received a driver's license in this State, the person shall be subject to any and all penalties and disabilities provided in this code for a violation of the terms and conditions of a suspension or revocation of the privilege to operate a motor vehicle. *(Stats.1959, c. 3, p. 1629, § 13553.)*

Cross References

Driving when license, suspended or revoked, see Vehicle Code § 14601.
Penalties, generally, see Vehicle Code § 42000 et seq.
Suspension or revocation of license by,
  Court, see Vehicle Code § 13200 et seq.
  Department, see Vehicle Code § 13350.
Violation of code as misdemeanor, see Vehicle Code § 40000.5 et seq.

§ 13555. Termination of probation and dismissal of charges

A termination of probation and dismissal of charges pursuant to Section 1203.4 of, or a dismissal of charges pursuant to Section 1203.4a of, or relief granted pursuant to Section 1203.425 of, the Penal Code does not affect any revocation or suspension of the privilege of the person convicted to drive a motor vehicle under this chapter. Such person's prior conviction shall be considered a conviction for the purpose of revoking or suspending or otherwise limiting such privilege on the ground of two or more convictions. *(Stats.1959, c. 3, p. 1629, § 13555. Amended by Stats.1959, c. 1996, p. 4626, § 18.6; Stats.1963, c. 1994, p. 4075, § 1; Stats.1019, c. 578 (A.B.1076), § 10, eff. Jan. 1, 2020.)*

Research References

3 Witkin, California Criminal Law 4th Punishment § 210 (2021), In General.
3 Witkin, California Criminal Law 4th Punishment § 719 (2021), Remaining Effects of Conviction.

3 Witkin, California Criminal Law 4th Punishment § 720B (2021), (New) Automatic Conviction Record Relief.

§ 13556. Duration of suspension

(a) Unless otherwise specifically provided in this chapter, no suspension of a license by the department shall be for a longer period than six months, except that the department may suspend a license for a maximum period of 12 months in those cases when a discretionary revocation would otherwise be authorized pursuant to this chapter.

(b) Any discretionary suspension, the ending of which is dependent upon an action by the person suspended and which has been in effect for eight years, may be ended at the election of the department.

(c) Notwithstanding any other provisions of this code, a suspension based upon a physical or mental condition shall continue until evidence satisfactory to the department establishes that the cause for which the action was taken has been removed or no longer renders the person incapable of operating a motor vehicle safely. *(Stats. 1959, c. 3, p. 1629, § 13556. Amended by Stats.1976, c. 498, p. 1298, § 3; Stats.1982, c. 612, p. 2596, § 1.)*

Cross References

Grounds for suspension, see Vehicle Code § 13361.

Research References

3 Witkin, California Criminal Law 4th Punishment § 210 (2021), In General.

§ 13557. Review of suspension or revocation order

(a) The department shall review the determination made pursuant to Section 13353, 13353.1, or 13353.2 relating to a person who has received a notice of an order of suspension or revocation of the person's privilege to operate a motor vehicle pursuant to Section 13353, 13353.1, 13353.2, 13382, or 23612, [1]. The department shall consider the sworn report submitted by the peace officer pursuant to Section 23612 or 13380 and any other evidence accompanying the report.

(b)(1) If the department determines in the review of a determination made under Section 13353 or 13353.1, by a preponderance of the evidence, all of the following facts, the department shall sustain the order of suspension or revocation:

(A) The peace officer had reasonable cause to believe that the person had been driving a motor vehicle in violation of Section 23136, 23140, 23152, 23153, or 23154.

(B) The person was placed under arrest or, if the alleged violation was of Section 23136, that the person was lawfully detained.

(C) The person refused or failed to complete the chemical test or tests after being requested by a peace officer.

(D) Except for the persons described in Section 23612 who are incapable of refusing, the person had been told that his or her privilege to operate a motor vehicle would be suspended or revoked if he or she refused to submit to, and complete, the required testing.

(2) If the department determines, by a preponderance of the evidence, that any of the facts required under paragraph (1) were not proven, the department shall rescind the order of suspension or revocation and, if the person is otherwise eligible, return or reissue the person's driver's license pursuant to Section 13551. The determination of the department upon administrative review is final unless a hearing is requested pursuant to Section 13558.

(3) If the department determines in the review of a determination made under Section 13353.2, by the preponderance of the evidence, all of the following facts, the department shall sustain the order of suspension or revocation, or if the person is under 21 years of age and does not yet have a driver's license, the department shall delay issuance of that license for one year:

(A) The peace officer had reasonable cause to believe that the person had been driving a motor vehicle in violation of Section 23136, 23140, 23152, 23153, or 23154.

(B) The person was placed under arrest or, if the alleged violation was of Section 23136, the person was lawfully detained.

(C) The person was driving a motor vehicle under any of the following circumstances:

(i) When the person had 0.08 percent or more, by weight, of alcohol in his or her blood.

(ii) When the person was under 21 years of age and had 0.05 percent or more, by weight, of alcohol in his or her blood.

(iii) When the person was under 21 years of age and had a blood-alcohol concentration of 0.01 percent or greater, as measured by a preliminary alcohol screening test, or other chemical test.

(iv) When the person was driving a vehicle that requires a commercial driver's license and the person had 0.04 percent or more, by weight, of alcohol in his or her blood.

(v) When the person was on probation for a violation of Section 23152 or 23153 and had a blood-alcohol concentration of 0.01 percent or greater, as measured by a preliminary alcohol screening test or other chemical test.

(4) If the department determines that any of those facts required under paragraph (3) were not proven by the preponderance of the evidence, the department shall rescind the order of suspension or revocation and, if the person is otherwise eligible, return or reissue the person's driver's license pursuant to Section 13551. For persons under 21 years of age, the determination of the department pursuant to paragraph (3) is final unless a hearing is requested within 10 days of the determination, which hearing shall be conducted according to Section 13558. For persons over 21 years of age, the determination of the department upon administrative review is final unless a hearing is requested pursuant to Section 13558.

(c) The department shall make the determination upon administrative review before the effective date of the order of suspension or revocation.

(d) The administrative review does not stay the suspension or revocation of a person's privilege to operate a motor vehicle. If the department is unable to make a determination on administrative review within the time limit in subdivision (c), the department shall stay the effective date of the order of suspension or revocation pending the determination and, if the person's driver's license has been taken by the peace officer pursuant to Section 13382, 13388, 13389, or 23612, the department shall notify the person before the expiration date of the temporary permit issued pursuant to Section 13382, 13388, 13389, or 23612, or the expiration date of any previous extension issued pursuant to this subdivision, in a form that permits the person to establish to any peace officer that his or her privilege to operate a motor vehicle is not suspended or revoked.

(e) A person may request and be granted a hearing pursuant to Section 13558 without first receiving the results of an administrative review pursuant to this section. After receiving a request for a hearing, the department is not required to conduct an administrative review of the same matter pursuant to this section.

(f) A determination of facts by the department under this section has no collateral estoppel effect on a subsequent criminal prosecution and does not preclude litigation of those same facts in the criminal proceeding. *(Added by Stats.1989, c. 1460, § 13, operative July 1, 1990. Amended by Stats.1990, c. 431 (S.B.1150), § 10, eff. July 26, 1990; Stats.1992, c. 974 (S.B.1600), § 9, eff. Sept. 28, 1992; Stats.1993, c. 899 (S.B.689), § 9; Stats.1993, c. 1244 (S.B.126), § 15.5; Stats.1994, c. 938 (S.B.1295), § 9, eff. Sept. 28, 1994; Stats.1998, c. 118 (S.B.1186), § 3.20, operative July 1, 1999; Stats.2010, c. 244 (A.B.1928), § 1; Stats.2011, c. 296 (A.B.1023), § 307.)*

[1] So in enrolled bill.

Research References

3 Witkin, California Criminal Law 4th Punishment § 221 (2021), In General.
3 Witkin, California Criminal Law 4th Punishment § 222 (2021), Administrative and Judicial Review.

§ 13558. Hearing on suspension or revocation

(a) Any person, who has received a notice of an order of suspension or revocation of the person's privilege to operate a motor vehicle pursuant to Section 13353, 13353.1, 13353.2, 13388, 23612, or 13382 or a notice pursuant to Section 13557, may request a hearing on the matter pursuant to Article 3 (commencing with Section 14100) of Chapter 3, except as otherwise provided in this section.

(b) If the person wishes to have a hearing before the effective date of the order of suspension or revocation, the request for a hearing shall be made within 10 days of the receipt of the notice of the order of suspension or revocation. The hearing shall be held at a place designated by the department as close as practicable to the place where the arrest occurred, unless the parties agree to a different location. Any evidence at the hearing shall not be limited to the evidence presented at an administrative review pursuant to Section 13557.

(c)(1) The only issues at the hearing on an order of suspension or revocation pursuant to Section 13353 or 13353.1 shall be those facts listed in paragraph (1) of subdivision (b) of Section 13557. Notwithstanding Section 14106, the period of suspension or revocation specified in Section 13353 or 13353.1 shall not be reduced and, notwithstanding Section 14105.5, the effective date of the order of suspension or revocation shall not be stayed pending review at a hearing pursuant to this section.

(2) The only issues at the hearing on an order of suspension pursuant to Section 13353.2 shall be those facts listed in paragraph (3) of subdivision (b) of Section 13557. Notwithstanding Section 14106, the period of suspension specified in Section 13353.3 shall not be reduced.

(d) The department shall hold the administrative hearing before the effective date of the order of suspension or revocation if the request for the hearing is postmarked or received by the department on or before 10 days after the person's receipt of the service of the notice of the order of suspension or revocation pursuant to Section 13353.2, 13388, 23612, or 13382.

(e) A request for an administrative hearing does not stay the suspension or revocation of a person's privilege to operate a motor vehicle. If the department does not conduct an administrative hearing and make a determination after an administrative hearing within the time limit in subdivision (d), the department shall stay the effective date of the order of suspension or revocation pending the determination and, if the person's driver's license has been taken by the peace officer pursuant to Section 13388, 23612, or 13382, the department shall notify the person before the expiration date of the temporary permit issued pursuant to Section 13388, 23612, or 13382, or the expiration date of any previous extension issued pursuant to this subdivision, provided the person is otherwise eligible, in a form that permits the person to establish to any peace officer that his or her privilege to operate a motor vehicle is not suspended or revoked.

(f) The department shall give written notice of its determination pursuant to Section 14105. If the department determines, upon a hearing of the matter, to suspend or revoke the person's privilege to operate a motor vehicle, notwithstanding the term of any temporary permit issued pursuant to Section 13388, 23612, or 13382, the temporary permit shall be revoked and the suspension or revocation of the person's privilege to operate a motor vehicle shall become effective five days after notice is given. If the department sustains the order of suspension or revocation, the department shall include notice that the person has a right to review by the court pursuant to Section 13559.

(g) A determination of facts by the department upon a hearing pursuant to this section has no collateral estoppel effect on a subsequent criminal prosecution and does not preclude litigation of those same facts in the criminal proceeding. *(Added by Stats.1989, c. 1460, § 14, operative July 1, 1990. Amended by Stats.1990, c. 216 (S.B.2510), § 117; Stats.1990, c. 431 (S.B.1150), § 11, eff. July 26, 1990; Stats.1992, c. 974 (S.B.1600), § 10, eff. Sept. 28, 1992; Stats.1993, c. 899 (S.B.689), § 10; Stats.1994, c. 938 (S.B.1295), § 10, eff. Sept. 28, 1994; Stats.1998, c. 118 (S.B.1186), § 3.22, operative July 1, 1999; Stats.2015, c. 451 (S.B.491), § 27, eff. Jan. 1, 2016.)*

Research References

2 Witkin, California Criminal Law 4th Crimes Against Public Peace and Welfare § 302 (2021), Administrative Sanctions.
3 Witkin, California Criminal Law 4th Punishment § 222 (2021), Administrative and Judicial Review.

§ 13559. Blood alcohol content of .08 percent or more, or refusal of chemical test; judicial review of suspension; stay; effect on criminal prosecution

(a) Notwithstanding Section 14400 or 14401, within 30 days of the issuance of the notice of determination of the department sustaining an order of suspension or revocation of the person's privilege to operate a motor vehicle after the hearing pursuant to Section 13558, the person may file a petition for review of the order in the court of competent jurisdiction in the person's county of residence. The filing of a petition for judicial review shall not stay the order of suspension or revocation. The review shall be on the record of the hearing and the court shall not consider other evidence. If the court finds that the department exceeded its constitutional or statutory authority, made an erroneous interpretation of the law, acted in an arbitrary and capricious manner, or made a determination which is not supported by the evidence in the record, the court may order the department to rescind the order of suspension or revocation and return, or reissue a new license to, the person.

(b) A finding by the court after a review pursuant to this section shall have no collateral estoppel effect on a subsequent criminal prosecution and does not preclude litigation of those same facts in the criminal proceeding. *(Added by Stats.1989, c. 1460, § 15, operative July 1, 1990. Amended by Stats.1990, c. 431 (S.B.1150), § 12, eff. July 26, 1990.)*

Research References

3 Witkin, California Criminal Law 4th Punishment § 222 (2021), Administrative and Judicial Review.

CHAPTER 3. INVESTIGATION AND HEARING

ARTICLE 1. INVESTIGATION AND RE–EXAMINATION

§ 13800. Investigations by the department

The department may conduct an investigation to determine whether the privilege of any person to operate a motor vehicle should be suspended or revoked or whether terms or conditions of probation should be imposed upon receiving information or upon a showing by its records:

(a) That the licensee has been involved as a driver in an accident causing death or personal injury or serious damage to property.

(b) That the licensee has been involved in three or more accidents within a period of 12 consecutive months.

(c) That the person in three consecutive years has committed three or more offenses that have resulted in convictions involving the consumption of an alcoholic beverage or drug, or both, while operating a motor vehicle, including, but not limited to, offenses under Section 23103.5, 23152, 23153, 23222, or 23224; has been involved in three or more crashes in which the crash reports show that the person was driving and had consumed alcoholic beverages or drugs, or both; or had any combination of three or more of those offenses and crashes.

(d) That the licensee is a reckless, negligent, or incompetent driver of a motor vehicle.

(e) That the licensee has permitted an unlawful or fraudulent use of their driver's license.

(f) That any ground exists for which a license might be refused. The receipt by the department of an abstract of the record of conviction of any offense involving the use or possession of narcotic controlled substances under Division 10 (commencing with Section 11000) of the Health and Safety Code shall be a sufficient basis for an investigation by the department to determine whether grounds exist for which a license might be refused. *(Stats.1959, c. 3, p. 1629, § 13800. Amended by Stats.1961, c. 1845, p. 3928, § 2; Stats.1972, c. 1407, p. 3045, § 13; Stats.1982, c. 1339, p. 4984, § 11, eff. Sept. 24, 1982; Stats.2022, c. 81 (A.B.2198), § 3, eff. Jan. 1, 2023.)*

Cross References

Grounds permitting refusal of license, see Vehicle Code § 12809.

Research References

3 Witkin, California Criminal Law 4th Punishment § 220 (2021), Distinction: Investigation and Hearing.

§ 13801. Re-examination by department

In addition to the investigation, the department may require the re-examination of the licensee, and shall give 10 days' written notice of the time and place thereof. If the licensee refuses or fails to submit to the re-examination, the department may peremptorily suspend the driving privilege of the person until such time as the licensee shall have submitted to re-examination. The suspension shall be effective upon notice. *(Stats.1959, c. 3, p. 1629, § 13801.)*

Cross References

License examination and driving test, see Vehicle Code § 12804.9.
Method of giving notice, see Vehicle Code § 22 et seq.

§ 13802. Special consideration for amount of use

In applying the provisions of Section 13800 the department shall give due consideration to the amount of use or mileage traveled in the operation of a motor vehicle. *(Stats.1959, c. 3, p. 1630, § 13802. Amended by Stats.1961, c. 1615, p. 3457, § 28.)*

Research References

3 Witkin, California Criminal Law 4th Punishment § 220 (2021), Distinction: Investigation and Hearing.

ARTICLE 2. NOTICE

Section

§ 13950. Notice required

Whenever the department determines upon investigation or re-examination that any of the grounds for re-examination are true, or that the safety of the person investigated or re-examined or other persons upon the highways requires such action, and it proposes to revoke or suspend the driving privilege of the person or proposes to impose terms of probation on his driving privilege, notice and an opportunity to be heard shall be given before taking the action. *(Stats.1959, c. 3, p. 1630, § 13950.)*

Cross References

Hearings by department, see Vehicle Code § 14100 et seq.
Issuance of license, see Vehicle Code § 12800 et seq.
Method of giving notice, see Vehicle Code § 22 et seq.
Renewal of licenses, see Vehicle Code §§ 12808, 12814.

Research References

3 Witkin, California Criminal Law 4th Punishment § 220 (2021), Distinction: Investigation and Hearing.

§ 13951. Notice upon refusal of license

Whenever the department proposes to refuse to issue or renew a driver's license, it shall notify the applicant of such fact and give him an opportunity to be heard. *(Stats.1959, c. 3, p. 1630, § 13951.)*

Cross References

Hearings, see Vehicle Code § 14100 et seq.

§ 13952. Contents of notice

The notice shall contain a statement setting forth the proposed action and the grounds therefor, and notify the person of his right to a hearing as provided in this chapter, or the department, at the time it gives notice of its intention to act may set the date of hearing, giving 10 days' notice thereof. *(Stats.1959, c. 3, p. 1630, § 13952. Amended by Stats.1961, c. 58, p. 1009, § 34, eff. March 31, 1961.)*

Cross References

Hearings, see Vehicle Code § 14100 et seq.

§ 13953. Alternative action

In the alternative to the procedure under Sections 13950, 13951, and 13952 and in the event the department determines upon investigation or reexamination that the safety of the person subject to investigation or reexamination or other persons upon the highways require such action, the department shall forthwith and without hearing suspend or revoke the privilege of the person to operate a motor vehicle or impose reasonable terms and conditions of probation which shall be relative to the safe operation of a motor vehicle. No order of suspension or revocation or the imposition of terms or conditions of probation shall become effective until 30 days after the giving of written notice thereof to the person affected, except that the department shall have authority to make any such order effective immediately upon the giving of notice when in its opinion because of the mental or physical condition of the person such immediate action is required for the safety of the driver or other persons upon the highways. *(Stats.1959, c. 3, p. 1630, § 13953. Amended by Stats. 1959, c. 1996, p. 4626, § 19; Stats.1969, c. 1045, p. 2029, § 1.)*

Research References

3 Witkin, California Criminal Law 4th Punishment § 220 (2021), Distinction: Investigation and Hearing.

§ 13954. Suspension or revocation of license upon crash occurring under specified circumstances; application of section

(a) Notwithstanding any other provision of this code, the department immediately shall suspend or revoke the driving privilege of a person who the department has reasonable cause to believe was in some manner involved in * * * a crash while operating a motor vehicle under the following circumstances at the time of the crash:

(1) The person had 0.08 percent or more, by weight, of alcohol in * * * their blood.

(2) * * * They proximately caused the crash as a result of an act prohibited, or the neglect of any duty imposed, by law.

(3) The crash occurred within five years of the date of a violation of subdivision (b) of Section 191.5 of the Penal Code that resulted in a conviction.

(b) If * * * a crash described in subdivision (a) does not result in a conviction or finding of a violation of Section 23152 or 23153, the department shall suspend the driving privilege under this section for one year from the date of commencement of the original suspension. After the one-year suspension period, the driving privilege may be reinstated if evidence establishes to the satisfaction of the department that no grounds exist that would authorize the refusal to issue a license and that reinstatement of the driving privilege would not jeopardize the safety of the person or other persons upon the highways, and if the person gives proof of financial responsibility, as defined in Section 16430.

(c) If * * * a crash described in subdivision (a) does result in a conviction or finding of a violation of Section 23152 or 23153, the department shall revoke the driving privilege under this section for three years from the date of commencement of the original revocation. After the three-year revocation period, the driving privilege may be reinstated if evidence establishes to the satisfaction of the department that no grounds exist that would authorize the refusal to issue a license and that reinstatement of the driving privilege would not jeopardize the safety of the person or other persons upon the highways, and if the person gives proof of financial responsibility.

(d) Any revocation action under subdivision (c) shall be imposed as follows:

(1) If the crash results in a first conviction of a violation of Section 23152 or 23153, or if the person was convicted of a separate violation of Section 23152 or 23153 that occurred within five years of the crash, the period of revocation under subdivision (c) shall be concurrent with any period of restriction, suspension, or revocation imposed under Section 13352, 13352.4, or 13352.5.

(2) If the person was convicted of two or more separate violations of Section 23152 or 23153, or both, that occurred within five years of the crash, the period of revocation under subdivision (c) shall be cumulative and shall be imposed consecutively with any period of restriction, suspension, or revocation imposed under Section 13352 or 13352.5.

(e) The department immediately shall notify the person in writing of the action taken and, upon the person's request in writing and within 15 days from the date of receipt of that request, shall grant the person an opportunity for a hearing in the same manner and under the same conditions as provided in Article 3 (commencing with Section 14100) of Chapter 3, except as otherwise provided in this section. For purposes of this section, the scope of the hearing shall cover the following issues:

(1) Whether the peace officer had reasonable cause to believe the person had been driving a motor vehicle in violation of Section 23152 or 23153.

(2) Whether the person had been placed under lawful arrest.

(3) Whether a chemical test of the person's blood, breath, or urine indicated that the blood-alcohol level was 0.08 percent or more, by weight, at the time of testing.

If the department determines, upon a hearing of the matter, that the person had not been placed under lawful arrest, or that a chemical test of the person's blood, breath, or urine did not indicate a blood-alcohol level of 0.08 percent or more, by weight, at the time of testing, the suspension or revocation shall be terminated immediately.

(f) This section applies if the crash occurred on or after January 1, 1990, without regard for the dates of the violations referred to in subdivisions (a) and (d).

(g) Notwithstanding subdivision (f), if a person's privilege to operate a motor vehicle is required to be suspended or revoked pursuant to this section as it read before January 1, 1990, as a result of * * * a crash that occurred before January 1, 1990, the privilege shall be suspended or revoked pursuant to this section as it read before January 1, 1990. *(Added by Stats.1985, c. 1071, § 1. Amended by Stats.1989, c. 479, § 2; Stats.1992, c. 974 (S.B.1600), § 11, eff. Sept. 28, 1992; Stats.2004, c. 551 (S.B.1697), § 12, operative Sept. 20, 2005; Stats.2007, c. 747 (A.B.678), § 27; Stats.2022, c. 81 (A.B.2198), § 4, eff. Jan. 1, 2023.)*

Cross References

Chemical testing for blood-alcohol level, see Vehicle Code § 23612.
Grounds permitting refusal to issue license, see Vehicle Code § 12809.

Research References

3 Witkin, California Criminal Law 4th Punishment § 213 (2021), In General.
3 Witkin, California Criminal Law 4th Punishment § 220 (2021), Distinction: Investigation and Hearing.

ARTICLE 3. HEARING

Section

§ 14100. Demand for hearing; application; notice; contents

(a) Whenever the department has given notice, or has taken or proposes to take action under Section 12804.15, 13353, 13353.2, 13950, 13951, 13952, or 13953, the person receiving the notice or subject to the action may, within 10 days, demand a hearing which shall be granted, except as provided in Section 14101.

(b) An application for a hearing does not stay the action by the department for which the notice is given.

(c) The fact that a person has the right to request an administrative hearing within 10 days after receipt of the notice of the order of suspension under this section and Section 16070, and that the request is required to be made within 10 days in order to receive a determination prior to the effective date of the suspension shall be made prominent on the notice.

(d) The department shall make available notices, to accompany the notice provided pursuant to this section, that provide the information required pursuant to subdivision (c) in all non-English languages spoken by a substantial number of the public served by the department, and shall distribute the notices as it determines is appropriate.

(e) The department shall implement the provisions of subdivisions (c) and (d) as soon as practicable, but not later than January 1, 1994. *(Stats.1959, c. 3, p. 1630, § 14100. Amended by Stats.1959, c. 1996, p. 4626, § 20; Stats.1989, c. 1460, § 16, operative July 1, 1990; Stats. 1990, c. 431 (S.B.1150), § 13, eff. July 26, 1990; Stats.1991, c. 13*

(A.B.37), § 31, eff. Feb. 13, 1991; Stats.1992, c. 1281 (A.B.3580), § 7; Stats.2001, c. 658 (A.B.67), § 5, eff. Oct. 10, 2001.)

Research References

3 Witkin, California Criminal Law 4th Punishment § 220 (2021), Distinction: Investigation and Hearing.

§ 14100.1. Denial, suspension, or revocation of passenger transportation vehicle, hazardous materials endorsement, or farm labor vehicle certificate; conduct of hearings

Hearings granted on refusal, suspension, or revocation of a passenger transportation vehicle or hazardous materials endorsement, or farm labor vehicle certificate shall be conducted according to Chapter 3 (commencing with Section 13800) of Division 6. *(Added by Stats.1990, c. 1360 (S.B.1510), § 42.)*

§ 14101. Entitlement to hearing

A person is not entitled to a hearing in either of the following cases:

(a) If the action by the department is made mandatory by this code.

(b) If the person has previously been given an opportunity with appropriate notice for a hearing and failed to request a hearing within the time specified by law. *(Stats.1959, c. 3, p. 1631, § 14101. Amended by Stats.1991, c. 13 (A.B.37), § 32, eff. Feb. 13, 1991.)*

§ 14103. Waiver of hearing

Failure to respond to a notice given under this chapter within 10 days is a waiver of the right to a hearing, and the department may take action without a hearing or may, upon request of the person whose privilege of driving is in question, or at its own option, reopen the question, take evidence, change, or set aside any order previously made, or grant a hearing. *(Stats.1959, c. 3, p. 1631, § 14103. Amended by Stats.1991, c. 13 (A.B.37), § 34, eff. Feb. 13, 1991.)*

§ 14104. Time and place; notice

If the department grants a hearing as provided in this chapter, it shall fix a time and place for the hearing and shall give 10 days' notice of the hearing to the applicant or licensee. The notice of hearing shall also include a statement of the discovery rights of the applicant or licensee to review the department's records prior to the hearing. *(Stats.1959, c. 3, p. 1631, § 14104. Amended by Stats.1961, c. 58, p. 1009, § 35, eff. March 31, 1961; Stats.1991, c. 13 (A.B.37), § 35, eff. Feb. 13, 1991.)*

§ 14104.2. Conduct of hearing; recordings

(a) Any hearing shall be conducted by the director or by a hearing officer or hearing board appointed by him or her from officers or employees of the department.

(b) The entire proceedings at any hearing may be recorded by a phonographic recorder or by mechanical, electronic, or other means capable of reproduction or transcription. *(Added by Stats.1991, c. 13 (A.B.37), § 36, eff. Feb. 13, 1991.)*

§ 14104.5. Subpoenas; issuance

(a) Before a hearing has commenced, the department, or the hearing officer or hearing board, shall issue subpoenas or subpoenas duces tecum, or both, at the request of any party, for attendance or production of documents at the hearing. After the hearing has commenced, the department, if it is hearing the case, or the hearing officer sitting alone, or the hearing board, may issue subpoenas or subpoenas duces tecum, or both.

(b) Notwithstanding Section 11450.20 of the Government Code, subpoenas and subpoenas duces tecum issued in conjunction with the hearings may be served by first-class mail. *(Added by Stats.1976, c. 891, p. 2048, § 1. Amended by Stats.1991, c. 13 (A.B.37), § 37, eff. Feb. 13, 1991; Stats.1999, c. 724 (A.B.1650), § 32.)*

§ 14104.7. Evidence

At any hearing, the department shall consider its official records and may receive sworn testimony. At the hearing, or subsequent to the hearing with the consent of the applicant or licensee, any or all of the following may be submitted as evidence concerning any fact relating to the ability of the applicant or licensee to safely operate a motor vehicle:

(a) Reports of attending or examining physicians and surgeons.

(b) Reports of special investigators appointed by the department to investigate and report upon any facts relating to the ability of the person to operate a vehicle safely.

(c) Properly authenticated reports of hospital records, excerpts from expert testimony received by the department or a hearing board upon similar issues of scientific fact in other cases, and the prior decision of the director upon those issues. *(Added by Stats.1991, c. 13 (A.B.37), § 38, eff. Feb. 13, 1991.)*

§ 14105. Finding and decision; notice; review; correction of errors

(a) Upon the conclusion of a hearing, the hearing officer or hearing board shall make findings and render a decision on behalf of the department and shall notify the person involved. Notice of the decision shall include a statement of the person's right to a review. The decision shall take effect as stated in the notice, but not less than four nor more than 15 days after the notice is mailed.

(b) The decision may be modified at any time after issuance to correct mistakes or clerical errors. *(Stats.1959, c. 3, p. 1631, § 14105. Amended by Stats.1976, c. 891, p. 2048, § 2; Stats.1980, c. 92, p. 230, § 1; Stats.1991, c. 13 (A.B.37), § 39, eff. Feb. 13, 1991; Stats.1999, c. 724 (A.B.1650), § 33.)*

Research References

3 Witkin, California Criminal Law 4th Punishment § 220 (2021), Distinction: Investigation and Hearing.

§ 14105.5. Review of decision; stay; scope; notice; correction of errors

(a) The person subject to a hearing may request a review of the decision taken under Section 14105 within 15 days of the effective date of the decision.

(b) On receipt of a request for review, the department shall stay the action pending a decision on review, unless the hearing followed an action pursuant to Section 13353, 13353.2, or 13953. The review shall include an examination of the hearing report, documentary evidence, and findings. The hearing officer or hearing board conducting the original hearing may not participate in the review process.

(c) Following the review, a written notice of the department's decision shall be mailed to the person involved. If the action has been stayed pending review, the department's decision shall take effect as stated in the notice, but not less than four nor more than 15 days after the notice is mailed.

(d) The decision may be modified at any time after issuance to correct mistakes or clerical errors. *(Added by Stats.1980, c. 92, p. 231, § 2. Amended by Stats.1991, c. 13 (A.B.37), § 40, eff. Feb. 13, 1991; Stats.1999, c. 724 (A.B.1650), § 34.)*

Research References

3 Witkin, California Criminal Law 4th Punishment § 220 (2021), Distinction: Investigation and Hearing.

§ 14106. Reopening case

Following the mailing of the notice of the department's decision pursuant to Section 14105.5, the department, at its own option or upon the request of the person whose privilege of driving is in question, may reopen the question, take further evidence, or change or set aside any order previously made. *(Stats.1959, c. 3, p. 1631, § 14106. Amended by Stats.1991, c. 13 (A.B.37), § 41, eff. Feb. 13, 1991.)*

§ 14112. Procedures; law governing

(a) All matters in a hearing not covered by this chapter shall be governed, as far as applicable, by Chapter 5 (commencing with Section 11500) of Part 1 of Division 3 of Title 2 of the Government Code.

(b) Subdivision (a) of Section 11425.30 of the Government Code does not apply to a proceeding for issuance, denial, revocation, or suspension of a driver's license pursuant to this division. *(Stats.1959, c. 3, p. 1632, § 14112. Amended by Stats.1961, c. 58, p. 1010, § 37, eff. March 31, 1961; Stats.1991, c. 13 (A.B.37), § 47, eff. Feb. 13, 1991; Stats.1995, c. 938 (S.B.523), § 91, operative July 1, 1997; Stats.2004, c. 193 (S.B.111), § 196.)*

Validity

For validity of this section, see California DUI Lawyers Association v. California Department of Motor Vehicles (App. 2 Dist. 2022) 292 Cal.Rptr.3d 608.

Law Revision Commission Comments

Subdivision (b) is added to Section 14112 in recognition of the personnel problem faced by the Department of Motor Vehicles due to the large volume of drivers' licensing cases. Subdivision (b) makes separation of functions requirements inapplicable in drivers' licensing cases, including license classifications and endorsements. However, the separation of functions requirements remain applicable in other Department of Motor Vehicle hearings, including schoolbus and ambulance operation certificate hearings, on which the department is required to report. [25 Cal.L.Rev.Comm. Reports 55 (1995)].

Section 14112 is amended to delete reference to an obsolete reporting requirement. The required report was to be completed by December 31, 1999. [33 Cal.L.Rev.Comm. Reports 495 (2003)].

Research References

3 Witkin, California Criminal Law 4th Punishment § 220 (2021), Distinction: Investigation and Hearing.

ARTICLE 4. PROBATION

Section

§ 14250. Probation

Whenever by any provision of this code the department has discretionary authority to suspend or revoke the privilege of a person to operate a motor vehicle, the department may in lieu of suspension or revocation place the person on probation, the terms of which may include a suspension as a condition of probation, issuing a probationary license with such reasonable terms and conditions as shall be deemed by the department to be appropriate. *(Stats.1959, c. 3, p. 1632, § 14250. Amended by Stats.1963, c. 154, p. 822, § 2.)*

Cross References

Traffic violator schools, instructors' licenses, qualifying requirements, see Vehicle Code § 11206.

Research References

3 Witkin, California Criminal Law 4th Punishment § 219 (2021), Grounds.

§ 14250.5. Driver training requirement

The department, as a condition of probation, may require a person whose privilege to operate a motor vehicle is subject to suspension or revocation to attend, for not to exceed 24 hours, the program authorized by the provisions of Section 1659. *(Added by Stats.1965, c. 447, p. 1758, § 3.)*

§ 14251. Termination or modification of probation

The department shall have authority to terminate or to modify the terms or conditions of any order of probation whenever good cause appears therefor. *(Stats.1959, c. 3, p. 1633, § 14251.)*

§ 14252. Withdrawal of probationary license

The department upon receiving satisfactory evidence of a violation of any of the terms or conditions of probation imposed under this code, may withdraw the probationary license and order the suspension or revocation of the privilege to operate a motor vehicle. *(Stats.1959, c. 3, p. 1633, § 14252.)*

§ 14253. Termination of probation

Unless probation was imposed for a cause which is continuing, the probationer, after not less than one year, may request in writing the termination of the probation and the return of his regular license. Upon a showing that there has been no violation of the terms or conditions of the probation for a period of one year immediately preceding the request, the department shall terminate the probation and either restore to the person his driver's license or require an application for a new license. *(Stats.1959, c. 3, p. 1633, § 14253.)*

Research References

3 Witkin, California Criminal Law 4th Punishment § 219 (2021), Grounds.

ARTICLE 5. REVIEW OF ORDERS

Section

§ 14400. Court review

Nothing in this code shall be deemed to prevent a review or other action as may be permitted by the Constitution and laws of this State by a court of competent jurisdiction of any order of the department refusing, canceling, suspending, or revoking the privilege of a person to operate a motor vehicle. *(Stats.1959, c. 3, p. 1633, § 14400.)*

Cross References

Blood alcohol content of .08 percent or more, or refusal of chemical test, judicial review of suspension, see Vehicle Code § 13559.

Research References

3 Witkin, California Criminal Law 4th Punishment § 213 (2021), In General.

§ 14401. Requirements regarding court review

(a) Any action brought in a court of competent jurisdiction to review any order of the department refusing, canceling, placing on probation, suspending, or revoking the privilege of a person to operate a motor vehicle shall be commenced within 90 days from the date the order is noticed.

(b) Upon final completion of all administrative appeals, the person whose driving privilege was refused, canceled, placed on probation, suspended, or revoked shall be given written notice by the department of his or her right to a review by a court pursuant to subdivision (a). *(Added by Stats.1973, c. 628, p. 1156, § 1. Amended by Stats.1985, c. 1008, § 3.)*

Cross References

Blood alcohol content of .08 percent or more, or refusal of chemical test, judicial review of suspension, see Vehicle Code § 13559.

Research References

3 Witkin, California Criminal Law 4th Punishment § 213 (2021), In General.

CHAPTER 4. VIOLATION OF LICENSE PROVISIONS

Section

§ 14600. Change of address

(a) Whenever any person after applying for or receiving a driver's license moves to a new residence, or acquires a new mailing address different from the address shown in the application or in the license as issued, he or she shall within 10 days thereafter notify the department of both the old and new address. The department may issue a document to accompany the driver's license reflecting the new address of the holder of the license.

(b) When, pursuant to subdivision (b) of Section 12951, a driver presents his or her driver's license to a peace officer, he or she shall, if applicable, also present the document issued pursuant to subdivision (a) if the driver's license does not reflect the driver's current residence or mailing address. *(Stats.1959, c. 3, p. 1633, § 14600. Amended by Stats.1959, c. 964, p. 2995, § 3; Stats.1976, c. 552, p. 1392, § 4; Stats.1992, c. 1243 (A.B.3090), § 86.4, eff. Sept. 30, 1992.)*

Cross References

California New Motor Voter Program, provision of records to Secretary of State, information to be provided, see Elections Code § 2263.
Contents of license, see Vehicle Code §§ 12811, 12813.
Notice of change of address by registered owner, see Vehicle Code § 4159.

§ 14601. Driving when privileges suspended or revoked for certain offenses; knowledge; punishment; driving on private property; requiring installation of ignition interlock device

(a) No person shall drive a motor vehicle at any time when that person's driving privilege is suspended or revoked for reckless driving in violation of Section 23103, 23104, or 23105, any reason listed in subdivision (a) or (c) of Section 12806 authorizing the department to refuse to issue a license, negligent or incompetent operation of a motor vehicle as prescribed in subdivision (e) of Section 12809, or negligent operation as prescribed in Section 12810.5, if the person so driving has knowledge of the suspension or revocation. Knowledge shall be conclusively presumed if mailed notice has been given by the department to the person pursuant to Section 13106. The presumption established by this subdivision is a presumption affecting the burden of proof.

(b) A person convicted under this section shall be punished as follows:

(1) Upon a first conviction, by imprisonment in a county jail for not less than five days or more than six months and by a fine of not less than three hundred dollars ($300) or more than one thousand dollars ($1,000).

(2) If the offense occurred within five years of a prior offense that resulted in a conviction of a violation of this section or Section 14601.1, 14601.2, or 14601.5, by imprisonment in a county jail for not less than 10 days or more than one year and by a fine of not less than five hundred dollars ($500) or more than two thousand dollars ($2,000).

(c) If the offense occurred within five years of a prior offense that resulted in a conviction of a violation of this section or Section 14601.1, 14601.2, or 14601.5, and is granted probation, the court shall impose as a condition of probation that the person be confined in a county jail for at least 10 days.

(d) Nothing in this section prohibits a person from driving a motor vehicle, that is owned or utilized by the person's employer, during the course of employment on private property that is owned or utilized by the employer, except an offstreet parking facility as defined in subdivision (c) of Section 12500.

(e) When the prosecution agrees to a plea of guilty or nolo contendere to a charge of a violation of this section in satisfaction of, or as a substitute for, an original charge of a violation of Section 14601.2, and the court accepts that plea, except, in the interest of justice, when the court finds it would be inappropriate, the court shall, pursuant to Section 23575, require the person convicted, in addition to any other requirements, to install a certified ignition interlock device on any vehicle that the person owns or operates for a period not to exceed three years.

(f) This section also applies to the operation of an off-highway motor vehicle on those lands to which the Chappie-Z'berg Off-Highway Motor Vehicle Law of 1971 (Division 16.5 (commencing with Section 38000)) applies as to off-highway motor vehicles, as described in Section 38001. *(Added by Stats.1968, c. 963, p. 1849, § 3; Stats.1968, c. 1195, p. 2270, § 7. Amended by Stats.1971, c. 1530, p. 3027, § 12, operative May 3, 1972; Stats.1972, c. 618, p. 1148, § 140; Stats.1981, c. 939, p. 3559, § 9; Stats.1981, c. 940, p. 3565, § 7; Stats.1982, c. 53, p. 169, § 19, eff. Feb. 18, 1982; Stats.1982, c. 1339, p. 4984, § 12, eff. Sept. 24, 1982; Stats.1983, c. 1092, § 385, eff. Sept. 27, 1983, operative Jan. 1, 1984; Stats.1985, c. 1522, § 1; Stats.1986, c. 1306, § 9; Stats.1987, c. 321, § 8; Stats.1994, c. 253 (A.B.2416), § 1; Stats.1994, c. 1133 (A.B.3148), § 7, operative June 30, 1995; Stats.1995, c. 91 (S.B.975), § 176; Stats.1995, c. 766 (S.B.726), § 18; Stats.2000, c. 1064 (A.B.2227), § 7, eff. Sept. 30, 2000; Stats.2003, c. 468 (S.B.851), § 26; Stats.2004, c. 908 (A.B. 2666), § 14; Stats.2007, c. 682 (A.B.430), § 14.)*

Cross References

Burden of proof, generally, see Evidence Code § 500 et seq.
Cancellation, suspension and revocation of license by department, see Vehicle Code § 13350 et seq.
Challenging constitutional validity of separate conviction, see Vehicle Code § 41403.
Constitutional challenge to validity of conviction, see Vehicle Code § 23624.
Grounds requiring refusal of license, see Vehicle Code § 12805 et seq.
Guilty plea, see Vehicle Code § 41610.
Nonresidents, effect of operation while driver's license is suspended or revoked, see Vehicle Code § 13552.
Optional appearance before magistrate, see Vehicle Code § 40303.
Presumption affecting burden of proof, see Evidence Code §§ 605, 606.
Removal of vehicle, circumstances permitting, see Vehicle Code § 22651.
Suspension or revocation of license by court, see Vehicle Code § 13200 et seq.
Traffic violation point counts, allocation of points, see Vehicle Code § 12810.
Unlicensed persons, penalties, see Vehicle Code § 13553.
Violation a misdemeanor, see Vehicle Code § 40000.11.

Research References

California Jury Instructions - Criminal 16.640, Driving When License Suspended or Revoked.
California Jury Instructions - Criminal 16.641, Inference of Knowledge of Suspension or Revocation of Driver's License.
2 Witkin, California Criminal Law 4th Crimes Against Public Peace and Welfare § 306 (2021), Reason for Suspension, Revocation, or Restriction.
2 Witkin, California Criminal Law 4th Crimes Against Public Peace and Welfare § 308 (2021), Knowledge of Suspension, Revocation, or Restriction.
5 Witkin, California Criminal Law 4th Criminal Trial § 480 (2021), Vehicle Code Convictions.
1 Witkin California Criminal Law 4th Defenses § 203 (2021), Attempting to Create Violation of Prohibition Against Multiple Prosecution.
3 Witkin, California Criminal Law 4th Punishment § 654 (2021), Mandatory.

§ 14601.1. Driving when privilege revoked or suspended for other reasons

(a) No person shall drive a motor vehicle when his or her driving privilege is suspended or revoked for any reason other than those listed in Section 14601, 14601.2, or 14601.5, if the person so driving has knowledge of the suspension or revocation. Knowledge shall be conclusively presumed if mailed notice has been given by the department to the person pursuant to Section 13106. The presumption established by this subdivision is a presumption affecting the burden of proof.

(b) Any person convicted under this section shall be punished as follows:

(1) Upon a first conviction, by imprisonment in the county jail for not more than six months or by a fine of not less than three hundred dollars ($300) or more than one thousand dollars ($1,000), or by both that fine and imprisonment.

(2) If the offense occurred within five years of a prior offense which resulted in a conviction of a violation of this section or Section 14601, 14601.2, or 14601.5, by imprisonment in the county jail for not less than five days or more than one year and by a fine of not less than five hundred dollars ($500) or more than two thousand dollars ($2,000).

(c) Nothing in this section prohibits a person from driving a motor vehicle, which is owned or utilized by the person's employer, during the course of employment on private property which is owned or utilized by the employer, except an offstreet parking facility as defined in subdivision (d) of Section 12500.

(d) When the prosecution agrees to a plea of guilty or nolo contendere to a charge of a violation of this section in satisfaction of, or as a substitute for, an original charge of a violation of Section 14601.2, and the court accepts that plea, except, in the interest of justice, when the court finds it would be inappropriate, the court shall, pursuant to Section 23575, require the person convicted, in addition to any other requirements, to install a certified ignition interlock device on any vehicle that the person owns or operates for a period not to exceed three years.

(e) This section also applies to the operation of an off-highway motor vehicle on those lands to which the Chappie–Z'berg Off–Highway Motor Vehicle Law of 1971 (Division 16.5 (commencing with Section 38000)) applies as to off-highway motor vehicles, as described in Section 38001. *(Added by Stats.1968, c. 1195, p. 2271, § 8. Amended by Stats.1972, c. 618, p. 1149, § 142; Stats.1981, c. 940, p. 3565, § 8; Stats.1982, c. 53, p. 170, § 20, eff. Feb. 18, 1982; Stats.1982, c. 1339, p. 4985, § 13, eff. Sept. 24, 1982; Stats.1983, c. 1092, § 386, eff. Sept. 27, 1983, operative Jan. 1, 1984; Stats.1984, c. 216, § 9; Stats.1985, c. 1522, § 2; Stats.1986, c. 1306, § 10; Stats.1994, c. 253 (A.B.2416), § 2; Stats.1994, c. 1133 (A.B.3148), § 8, operative June 30, 1995; Stats.1995, c. 91 (S.B.975), § 178; Stats.1995, c. 766 (S.B.726), § 19; Stats.2000, c. 1064 (A.B.2227), § 8, eff. Sept. 30, 2000; Stats.2004, c. 908 (A.B.2666), § 15.)*

Cross References

Burden of proof, generally, see Evidence Code § 500 et seq.
Cancellation, suspension and revocation of license by department, see Vehicle Code § 13350 et seq.
Challenging constitutional validity of separate conviction, see Vehicle Code § 41403.
Guilty plea, see Vehicle Code § 41610.
Nonresident operating vehicle after license suspension or revocation, see Vehicle Code § 13552.
Offense under this section as infraction, see Penal Code § 19.8.
Optional appearance before magistrate, see Vehicle Code § 40303.
Presumption affecting burden of proof, see Evidence Code §§ 605, 606.
Removal of vehicle, circumstances permitting, see Vehicle Code § 22651.
Suspension or revocation of license by court, see Vehicle Code § 13200 et seq.
Traffic violation point counts, allocation of points, see Vehicle Code § 12810.
Violation a misdemeanor, see Vehicle Code § 40000.11.

Research References

California Jury Instructions - Criminal 16.640, Driving When License Suspended or Revoked.
California Jury Instructions - Criminal 16.641, Inference of Knowledge of Suspension or Revocation of Driver's License.
2 Witkin, California Criminal Law 4th Crimes Against Public Peace and Welfare § 306 (2021), Reason for Suspension, Revocation, or Restriction.

1 Witkin California Criminal Law 4th Introduction to Crimes § 90 (2021), Misdemeanor-Infraction.

§ 14601.2. Driving when privilege suspended or revoked for driving under the influence of alcoholic beverage or drug; compliance with restriction; punishment

(a) A person shall not drive a motor vehicle at any time when that person's driving privilege is suspended or revoked for a conviction of a violation of Section 23152 or 23153 if the person so driving has knowledge of the suspension or revocation.

(b) Except in full compliance with the restriction, a person shall not drive a motor vehicle at any time when that person's driving privilege is restricted if the person so driving has knowledge of the restriction.

(c) Knowledge of the suspension or revocation of the driving privilege shall be conclusively presumed if mailed notice has been given by the department to the person pursuant to Section 13106. Knowledge of the restriction of the driving privilege shall be presumed if notice has been given by the court to the person. The presumption established by this subdivision is a presumption affecting the burden of proof.

(d) A person convicted of a violation of this section shall be punished as follows:

(1) Upon a first conviction, by imprisonment in the county jail for not less than 10 days or more than six months and by a fine of not less than three hundred dollars ($300) or more than one thousand dollars ($1,000), unless the person has been designated a habitual traffic offender under subdivision (b) of Section 23546, subdivision (b) of Section 23550, or subdivision (d) of Section 23550.5, in which case the person, in addition, shall be sentenced as provided in paragraph (3) of subdivision (e) of Section 14601.3.

(2) If the offense occurred within five years of a prior offense that resulted in a conviction of a violation of this section or Section 14601, 14601.1, or 14601.5, by imprisonment in the county jail for not less than 30 days or more than one year and by a fine of not less than five hundred dollars ($500) or more than two thousand dollars ($2,000), unless the person has been designated a habitual traffic offender under subdivision (b) of Section 23546, subdivision (b) of Section 23550, or subdivision (d) of Section 23550.5, in which case the person, in addition, shall be sentenced as provided in paragraph (3) of subdivision (e) of Section 14601.3.

(e) If a person is convicted of a first offense under this section and is granted probation, the court shall impose as a condition of probation that the person be confined in the county jail for at least 10 days.

(f) If the offense occurred within five years of a prior offense that resulted in a conviction of a violation of this section or Section 14601, 14601.1, or 14601.5 and is granted probation, the court shall impose as a condition of probation that the person be confined in the county jail for at least 30 days.

(g) If a person is convicted of a second or subsequent offense that results in a conviction of this section within seven years, but over five years, of a prior offense that resulted in a conviction of a violation of this section or Section 14601, 14601.1, or 14601.5 and is granted probation, the court shall impose as a condition of probation that the person be confined in the county jail for at least 10 days.

(h) Pursuant to Section 23575, the court shall require a person convicted of a violation of this section to install a certified ignition interlock device on a vehicle the person owns or operates. Upon receipt of the abstract of a conviction under this section, the department shall not reinstate the privilege to operate a motor vehicle until the department receives proof of either the "Verification of Installation" form as described in paragraph (2) of subdivision (h) of Section 13386 or the Judicial Council Form I.D. 100.

(i) This section does not prohibit a person who is participating in, or has completed, an alcohol or drug rehabilitation program from driving a motor vehicle that is owned or utilized by the person's employer, during the course of employment on private property that is owned or utilized by the employer, except an offstreet parking facility, as defined in subdivision (c) of Section 12500.

(j) This section also applies to the operation of an off-highway motor vehicle on those lands that the Chappie–Z'berg Off–Highway Motor Vehicle Law of 1971 (Division 16.5 (commencing with Section 38000)) applies as to off-highway motor vehicles, as described in Section 38001.

(k) If Section 23573 is applicable, then subdivision (h) is not applicable. *(Added by Stats.2004, c. 908 (A.B.2666), § 16.5, operative Sept. 20, 2005. Amended by Stats.2005, c. 279 (S.B.1107), § 22; Stats.2006, c. 835 (A.B.3045), § 3; Stats.2008, c. 404 (S.B.1388), § 1; Stats.2014, c. 71 (S.B.1304), § 173, eff. Jan. 1, 2015.)*

Cross References

Burden of proof, generally, see Evidence Code § 500 et seq.
Challenging constitutional validity of separate conviction, see Vehicle Code § 41403.
Constitutional challenge to validity of conviction, see Vehicle Code § 23624.
Guilty plea, see Vehicle Code § 41610.
Presumption affecting burden of proof, see Evidence Code §§ 605, 606.
Removal of vehicle, circumstances permitting, see Vehicle Code § 22651.
Traffic violation point counts, allocation of points, see Vehicle Code § 12810.
Violation as misdemeanor, see Vehicle Code § 40000.11.

Research References

California Jury Instructions - Criminal 16.640, Driving When License Suspended or Revoked.
California Jury Instructions - Criminal 16.641, Inference of Knowledge of Suspension or Revocation of Driver's License.
2 Witkin, California Criminal Law 4th Crimes Against Public Peace and Welfare § 290 (2021), Ignition Interlock Device.
2 Witkin, California Criminal Law 4th Crimes Against Public Peace and Welfare § 306 (2021), Reason for Suspension, Revocation, or Restriction.
2 Witkin, California Criminal Law 4th Crimes Against Public Peace and Welfare § 307 (2021), Habitual Traffic Offender.

§ 14601.3. Habitual traffic offender; accumulation of driving record history while driving privilege suspended or revoked; penalty

(a) It is unlawful for a person whose driving privilege has been suspended or revoked to accumulate a driving record history which results from driving during the period of suspension or revocation. A person who violates this subdivision is designated an habitual traffic offender.

For purposes of this section, a driving record history means any of the following, if the driving occurred during any period of suspension or revocation:

(1) Two or more convictions within a 12–month period of an offense given a violation point count of two pursuant to Section 12810.

(2) Three or more convictions within a 12–month period of an offense given a violation point count of one pursuant to Section 12810.

(3) Three or more accidents within a 12–month period that are subject to the reporting requirements of Section 16000.

(4) Any combination of convictions or accidents, as specified in paragraphs (1) to (3), inclusive, which results during any 12–month period in a violation point count of three or more pursuant to Section 12810.

(b) Knowledge of suspension or revocation of the driving privilege shall be conclusively presumed if mailed notice has been given by the department to the person pursuant to Section 13106. The presumption established by this subdivision is a presumption affecting the burden of proof.

(c) The department, within 30 days of receipt of a duly certified abstract of the record of any court or accident report which results in a person being designated an habitual traffic offender, may execute and transmit by mail a notice of that designation to the office of the district attorney having jurisdiction over the location of the person's last known address as contained in the department's records.

(d)(1) The district attorney, within 30 days of receiving the notice required in subdivision (c), shall inform the department of whether or not the person will be prosecuted for being an habitual traffic offender.

(2) Notwithstanding any other provision of this section, any habitual traffic offender designated under subdivision (b) of Section 23546, subdivision (b) of Section 23550, or subdivision (b) of Section 23550.5, who is convicted of violating Section 14601.2 shall be sentenced as provided in paragraph (3) of subdivision (e).

(e) Any person convicted under this section of being an habitual traffic offender shall be punished as follows:

(1) Upon a first conviction, by imprisonment in the county jail for 30 days and by a fine of one thousand dollars ($1,000).

(2) Upon a second or any subsequent offense within seven years of a prior conviction under this section, by imprisonment in the county jail for 180 days and by a fine of two thousand dollars ($2,000).

(3) Any habitual traffic offender designated under Section 193.7 of the Penal Code or under subdivision (b) of Section 23546, subdivision (b) of Section 23550, subdivision (b) of Section 23550.5, or subdivision (d) of Section 23566 who is convicted of a violation of Section 14601.2 shall be punished by imprisonment in the county jail for 180 days and by a fine of two thousand dollars ($2,000). The penalty in this paragraph shall be consecutive to that imposed for the violation of any other law.

(f) This section also applies to the operation of an off-highway motor vehicle on those lands to which the Chappie–Z'berg Off–Highway Motor Vehicle Law of 1971 (Division 16.5 (commencing with Section 38000)) applies as to off-highway motor vehicles, as described in Section 38001. *(Added by Stats.1982, c. 655, p. 2672, § 5. Amended by Stats.1984, c. 239, § 1; Stats.1986, c. 1306, § 12; Stats.1988, c. 1415, § 7; Stats.1990, c. 44 (A.B.1648), § 4; Stats.1994, c. 1133 (A.B.3148), § 10, operative June 30, 1995; Stats.1995, c. 91 (S.B.975), § 179; Stats.1997, c. 901 (A.B.130), § 4; Stats.1998, c. 118 (S.B.1186), § 10.2, operative July 1, 1999; Stats.1999, c. 22 (S.B.24), § 16, eff. May 26, 1999, operative July 1, 1999; Stats.2004, c. 908 (A.B.2666), § 17.)*

Cross References

Burden of proof, generally, see Evidence Code § 500 et seq.
Guilty plea, see Vehicle Code § 41610.
Presumption affecting burden of proof, see Evidence Code §§ 605, 606.
Removal of vehicle, circumstances permitting, see Vehicle Code § 22651.
Traffic violation point counts, allocation of points, see Vehicle Code § 12810.

Research References

2 Witkin, California Criminal Law 4th Crimes Against Public Peace and Welfare § 306 (2021), Reason for Suspension, Revocation, or Restriction.
2 Witkin, California Criminal Law 4th Crimes Against Public Peace and Welfare § 307 (2021), Habitual Traffic Offender.
1 Witkin California Criminal Law 4th Crimes Against the Person § 267 (2021), Vehicular Manslaughter While Intoxicated.

§ 14601.4. Causing bodily injury to another while driving with license suspended or revoked; penalty; reinstatement of driving privileges

(a) It is unlawful for a person, while driving a vehicle with a license suspended or revoked pursuant to Section 14601.2 to do an act forbidden by law or neglect a duty imposed by law in the driving of the vehicle, which act or neglect proximately causes bodily injury to a person other than the driver. In proving the person neglected a duty imposed by law in the driving of the vehicle, it is not necessary to prove that a specific section of this code was violated.

(b) A person convicted under this section shall be imprisoned in the county jail and shall not be released upon work release, community service, or other release program before the minimum period of imprisonment, prescribed in Section 14601.2, is served. If a person is convicted of that offense and is granted probation, the court shall require that the person convicted serve at least the minimum time of imprisonment, as specified in those sections, as a term or condition of probation.

(c) When the prosecution agrees to a plea of guilty or nolo contendere to a charge of a violation of this section in satisfaction of, or as a substitute for, an original charge of a violation of Section 14601.2, and the court accepts that plea, except, in the interest of justice, when the court finds it should be inappropriate, the court shall, pursuant to Section 23575, require the person convicted, in addition to other requirements, to install a certified ignition interlock device on a vehicle that the person owns or operates for a period not to exceed three years.

(d) This section also applies to the operation of an off-highway motor vehicle on those lands that the Chappie–Z'berg Off–Highway Motor Vehicle Law of 1971 (Division 16.5 (commencing with Section 38000)) applies as to off-highway motor vehicles, as described in Section 38001.

(e) Upon receipt of the abstract of a conviction under this section, the department shall not reinstate the privilege to operate a motor vehicle until the department receives proof of either the "Verification of Installation" form as described in paragraph (2) of subdivision (g) of Section 13386 or the Judicial Council Form I.D. 100.

(f) If Section 23573 is applicable, then subdivisions (c) and (e) are not applicable. *(Added by Stats.1988, c. 1254, § 4. Amended by Stats.2000, c. 1064 (A.B.2227), § 9, eff. Sept. 30, 2000; Stats.2004, c. 908 (A.B.2666), § 18; Stats.2006, c. 835 (A.B.3045), § 4; Stats.2008, c. 404 (S.B.1388), § 2.)*

Cross References

Removal of vehicle, circumstances permitting, see Vehicle Code § 22651.

Research References

2 Witkin, California Criminal Law 4th Crimes Against Public Peace and Welfare § 306 (2021), Reason for Suspension, Revocation, or Restriction.

§ 14601.5. Driving with knowledge of suspension, revocation, or restriction of driving privilege; punishment; reinstatement of driving privileges

(a) A person shall not drive a motor vehicle at any time when that person's driving privilege is suspended or revoked pursuant to Section 13353, 13353.1, or 13353.2 and that person has knowledge of the suspension or revocation.

(b) Except in full compliance with the restriction, a person shall not drive a motor vehicle at any time when that person's driving privilege is restricted pursuant to Section 13353.7 or 13353.8 and that person has knowledge of the restriction.

(c) Knowledge of suspension, revocation, or restriction of the driving privilege shall be conclusively presumed if notice has been given by the department to the person pursuant to Section 13106. The presumption established by this subdivision is a presumption affecting the burden of proof.

(d) A person convicted of a violation of this section is punishable, as follows:

(1) Upon a first conviction, by imprisonment in the county jail for not more than six months or by a fine of not less than three hundred dollars ($300) or more than one thousand dollars ($1,000), or by both that fine and imprisonment.

(2) If the offense occurred within five years of a prior offense that resulted in a conviction for a violation of this section or Section 14601, 14601.1, 14601.2, or 14601.3, by imprisonment in the county jail for not less than 10 days or more than one year, and by a fine of not less than five hundred dollars ($500) or more than two thousand dollars ($2,000).

(e) In imposing the minimum fine required by subdivision (d), the court shall take into consideration the defendant's ability to pay the fine and may, in the interest of justice, and for reasons stated in the record, reduce the amount of that minimum fine to less than the amount otherwise imposed.

(f) This section does not prohibit a person who is participating in, or has completed, an alcohol or drug rehabilitation program from driving a motor vehicle, that is owned or utilized by the person's employer, during the course of employment on private property that is owned or utilized by the employer, except an offstreet parking facility as defined in subdivision (c) of Section 12500.

(g) When the prosecution agrees to a plea of guilty or nolo contendere to a charge of a violation of this section in satisfaction of, or as a substitute for, an original charge of a violation of Section 14601.2, and the court accepts that plea, except, in the interest of justice, when the court finds it would be inappropriate, the court shall, pursuant to Section 23575, require the person convicted, in addition to other requirements, to install a certified ignition interlock device on a vehicle that the person owns or operates for a period not to exceed three years.

(h) This section also applies to the operation of an off-highway motor vehicle on those lands that the Chappie–Z'berg Off–Highway Motor Vehicle Law of 1971 (Division 16.5 (commencing with Section 38000)) applies as to off-highway motor vehicles, as described in Section 38001.

(i) Upon receipt of the abstract of a conviction under this section, the department shall not reinstate the privilege to operate a motor vehicle until the department receives proof of either the "Verification of Installation" form as described in paragraph (2) of subdivision (g) of Section 13386 or the Judicial Council Form I.D. 100.

(j) If Section 23573 [1] is applicable, then subdivisions (g) and (i) are not applicable. *(Added by Stats.2004, c. 952 (A.B.3049), § 13.5, operative Sept. 20, 2005. Amended by Stats.2006, c. 835 (A.B.3045), § 5; Stats.2008, c. 404 (S.B.1388), § 3.)*

1 Added by Stats.2008, c. 404 (S.B.1388), § 4, operative July 1, 2009.

Cross References

Burden of proof, generally, see Evidence Code § 500 et seq.

Research References

2 Witkin, California Criminal Law 4th Crimes Against Public Peace and Welfare § 306 (2021), Reason for Suspension, Revocation, or Restriction.

§ 14601.8. Service of sentence

The judge may, in his or her discretion, allow any person convicted of a violation of Section 14601 or 14601.1 to serve his or her sentence on a sufficient number of consecutive weekend days to complete the sentence. *(Formerly § 14601.5, added by Stats.1961, c. 278, § 2. Amended by Stats.1968, c. 1195, § 5. Renumbered § 14601.8 and amended by Stats.1992, c. 982 (S.B.2022), § 1.)*

§ 14602. Release of vehicle to registered owner or agent

In accordance with subdivision (p) of Section 22651, a vehicle removed pursuant to subdivision (c) of Section 2814.2 shall be released to the registered owner or his or her agent at any time the facility to which the vehicle has been removed is open upon presentation of the registered owner's or his or her agent's currently valid driver's license to operate the vehicle and proof of current vehicle registration. *(Added by Stats.2011, c. 653 (A.B.353), § 3.)*

§ 14602.1. Vehicle pursuit reports

(a) Every state and local law enforcement agency, including, but not limited to, city police departments and county sheriffs' offices, shall report to the Department of the California Highway Patrol, on a paper or electronic form developed and approved by the Department of the California Highway Patrol, all motor vehicle pursuit data.

(b) Effective January 1, 2006, the form shall require the reporting of all motor vehicle pursuit data, which shall include, but not be limited to, all of the following:

(1) Whether any person involved in a pursuit or a subsequent arrest was injured, specifying the nature of that injury. For all purposes of this section, the form shall differentiate between the suspect driver, a suspect passenger, and the peace officers involved.

(2) The violations that caused the pursuit to be initiated.

(3) The identity of the peace officers involved in the pursuit.

(4) The means or methods used to stop the suspect being pursued.

(5) All charges filed with the court by the district attorney.

(6) The conditions of the pursuit, including, but not limited to, all of the following:

(A) Duration.

(B) Mileage.

(C) Number of peace officers involved.

(D) Maximum number of law enforcement vehicles involved.

(E) Time of day.

(F) Weather conditions.

(G) Maximum speeds.

(7) Whether a pursuit resulted in a collision, and a resulting injury or fatality to an uninvolved third party, and the corresponding number of persons involved.

(8) Whether the pursuit involved multiple law enforcement agencies.

(9) How the pursuit was terminated.

(c) In order to minimize costs, the department, upon updating the form, shall update the corresponding database to include all of the reporting requirements specified in subdivision (b).

(d) All motor vehicle pursuit data obtained pursuant to subdivision (b) shall be submitted to the Department of the California Highway Patrol no later than 30 days following a motor vehicle pursuit.

(e) The Department of the California Highway Patrol shall submit annually to the Legislature a report that includes, but is not limited to, the following information:

(1) The number of motor vehicle pursuits reported to the Department of the California Highway Patrol during that year.

(2) The number of those motor vehicle pursuits that reportedly resulted in a collision in which an injury or fatality to an uninvolved third party occurred.

(3) The total number of uninvolved third parties who were injured or killed as a result of those collisions during that year. *(Added by Stats.1991, c. 1048 (S.B.185), § 2. Amended by Stats.2001, c. 745 (S.B.1191), § 228, eff. Oct. 12, 2001; Stats.2005, c. 485 (S.B.719), § 9.)*

§ 14602.5. Driving class M1 or M2 motor vehicle while driving privilege suspended or revoked; impounding vehicle

(a) Whenever a person is convicted for driving any class M1 or M2 motor vehicle, while his or her driving privilege has been suspended or revoked, of which vehicle he or she is the owner, or of which the owner permitted the operation, knowing the person's driving privilege was suspended or revoked, the court may, at the time sentence is imposed on the person, order the motor vehicle impounded in any manner as the court may determine, for a period not to exceed six months for a first conviction, and not to exceed 12 months for a second or subsequent conviction. For the purposes of this section, a "second or subsequent conviction" includes a conviction for any offense described in this section. The cost of keeping the vehicle shall be a lien on the vehicle, pursuant to Chapter 6.5 (commencing with Section 3067) of Title 14 of Part 4 of Division 3 of the Civil Code.

(b) Notwithstanding subdivision (a), any motor vehicle impounded pursuant to this section which is subject to a chattel mortgage, conditional sale contract, or lease contract shall, upon the filing of an affidavit by the legal owner that the chattel mortgage, conditional sale contract, or lease contract is in default, be released by the court to the legal owner, and shall be delivered to him or her upon payment of the accrued cost of keeping the motor vehicle. *(Added by Stats.1990, c. 1359 (A.B.55), § 5.)*

Research References

3 Witkin, California Criminal Law 4th Punishment § 195 (2021), Impounding of Motor Vehicles.

§ 14602.6. Driving without a license, while privilege suspended or revoked, or while privilege is restricted and vehicle is not equipped with interlock device; arrest; seizure and impoundment of vehicle; notice to owner; storage hearing; release of vehicle; liability of law enforcement agency and impounding agency

(a)(1) Whenever a peace officer determines that a person was driving a vehicle while his or her driving privilege was suspended or revoked, driving a vehicle while his or her driving privilege is restricted pursuant to Section 13352 or 23575 and the vehicle is not equipped with a functioning, certified interlock device, or driving a vehicle without ever having been issued a driver's license, the peace officer may either immediately arrest that person and cause the removal and seizure of that vehicle or, if the vehicle is involved in a traffic collision, cause the removal and seizure of the vehicle without the necessity of arresting the person in accordance with Chapter 10 (commencing with Section 22650) of Division 11. A vehicle so impounded shall be impounded for 30 days.

(2) The impounding agency, within two working days of impoundment, shall send a notice by certified mail, return receipt requested, to the legal owner of the vehicle, at the address obtained from the department, informing the owner that the vehicle has been impounded. Failure to notify the legal owner within two working days shall prohibit the impounding agency from charging for more than 15 days' impoundment when the legal owner redeems the impounded vehicle. The impounding agency shall maintain a published telephone number that provides information 24 hours a day regarding the impoundment of vehicles and the rights of a registered owner to request a hearing. The law enforcement agency shall be open to issue a release to the registered owner or legal owner, or the agent of either, whenever the agency is open to serve the public for nonemergency business.

(b) The registered and legal owner of a vehicle that is removed and seized under subdivision (a) or their agents shall be provided the opportunity for a storage hearing to determine the validity of, or consider any mitigating circumstances attendant to, the storage, in accordance with Section 22852.

(c) Any period in which a vehicle is subjected to storage under this section shall be included as part of the period of impoundment ordered by the court under subdivision (a) of Section 14602.5.

(d)(1) An impounding agency shall release a vehicle to the registered owner or his or her agent prior to the end of 30 days' impoundment under any of the following circumstances:

(A) When the vehicle is a stolen vehicle.

(B) When the vehicle is subject to bailment and is driven by an unlicensed employee of a business establishment, including a parking service or repair garage.

(C) When the license of the driver was suspended or revoked for an offense other than those included in Article 2 (commencing with Section 13200) of Chapter 2 of Division 6 or Article 3 (commencing with Section 13350) of Chapter 2 of Division 6.

(D) When the vehicle was seized under this section for an offense that does not authorize the seizure of the vehicle.

(E) When the driver reinstates his or her driver's license or acquires a driver's license and proper insurance.

(2) No vehicle shall be released pursuant to this subdivision without presentation of the registered owner's or agent's currently valid driver's license to operate the vehicle and proof of current vehicle registration, or upon order of a court.

(e) The registered owner or his or her agent is responsible for all towing and storage charges related to the impoundment, and any administrative charges authorized under Section 22850.5.

(f) A vehicle removed and seized under subdivision (a) shall be released to the legal owner of the vehicle or the legal owner's agent prior to the end of 30 days' impoundment if all of the following conditions are met:

(1) The legal owner is a motor vehicle dealer, bank, credit union, acceptance corporation, or other licensed financial institution legally operating in this state or is another person, not the registered owner, holding a security interest in the vehicle.

(2)(A) The legal owner or the legal owner's agent pays all towing and storage fees related to the seizure of the vehicle. No lien sale processing fees shall be charged to the legal owner who redeems the vehicle prior to the 15th day of impoundment. Neither the impounding authority nor any person having possession of the vehicle shall collect from the legal owner of the type specified in paragraph (1), or the legal owner's agent any administrative charges imposed pursuant to Section 22850.5 unless the legal owner voluntarily requested a poststorage hearing.

(B) A person operating or in charge of a storage facility where vehicles are stored pursuant to this section shall accept a valid bank credit card or cash for payment of towing, storage, and related fees by a legal or registered owner or the owner's agent claiming the vehicle. A credit card shall be in the name of the person presenting the card. "Credit card" means "credit card" as defined in subdivision (a) of Section 1747.02 of the Civil Code, except, for the purposes of this section, credit card does not include a credit card issued by a retail seller.

(C) A person operating or in charge of a storage facility described in subparagraph (B) who violates subparagraph (B) shall be civilly liable to the owner of the vehicle or to the person who tendered the fees for four times the amount of the towing, storage, and related fees, but not to exceed five hundred dollars ($500).

(D) A person operating or in charge of a storage facility described in subparagraph (B) shall have sufficient funds on the premises of the primary storage facility during normal business hours to accommodate, and make change in, a reasonable monetary transaction.

(E) Credit charges for towing and storage services shall comply with Section 1748.1 of the Civil Code. Law enforcement agencies may include the costs of providing for payment by credit when making agreements with towing companies on rates.

(3) The legal owner or the legal owner's agent presents a copy of the assignment, as defined in subdivision (b) of Section 7500.1 of the Business and Professions Code; a release from the one responsible governmental agency, only if required by the agency; a government-issued photographic identification card; and any one of the following, as determined by the legal owner or the legal owner's agent: a certificate of repossession for the vehicle, a security agreement for

the vehicle, or title, whether paper or electronic, showing proof of legal ownership for the vehicle. Any documents presented may be originals, photocopies, or facsimile copies, or may be transmitted electronically. The law enforcement agency, impounding agency, or any other governmental agency, or any person acting on behalf of those agencies, shall not require any documents to be notarized. The law enforcement agency, impounding agency, or any person acting on behalf of those agencies may require the agent of the legal owner to produce a photocopy or facsimile copy of its repossession agency license or registration issued pursuant to Chapter 11 (commencing with Section 7500) of Division 3 of the Business and Professions Code, or to demonstrate, to the satisfaction of the law enforcement agency, impounding agency, or any person acting on behalf of those agencies, that the agent is exempt from licensure pursuant to Section 7500.2 or 7500.3 of the Business and Professions Code.

No administrative costs authorized under subdivision (a) of Section 22850.5 shall be charged to the legal owner of the type specified in paragraph (1), who redeems the vehicle unless the legal owner voluntarily requests a poststorage hearing. No city, county, city and county, or state agency shall require a legal owner or a legal owner's agent to request a poststorage hearing as a requirement for release of the vehicle to the legal owner or the legal owner's agent. The law enforcement agency, impounding agency, or other governmental agency, or any person acting on behalf of those agencies, shall not require any documents other than those specified in this paragraph. The law enforcement agency, impounding agency, or other governmental agency, or any person acting on behalf of those agencies, shall not require any documents to be notarized. The legal owner or the legal owner's agent shall be given a copy of any documents he or she is required to sign, except for a vehicle evidentiary hold logbook. The law enforcement agency, impounding agency, or any person acting on behalf of those agencies, or any person in possession of the vehicle, may photocopy and retain the copies of any documents presented by the legal owner or legal owner's agent.

(4) A failure by a storage facility to comply with any applicable conditions set forth in this subdivision shall not affect the right of the legal owner or the legal owner's agent to retrieve the vehicle, provided all conditions required of the legal owner or legal owner's agent under this subdivision are satisfied.

(g)(1) A legal owner or the legal owner's agent that obtains release of the vehicle pursuant to subdivision (f) shall not release the vehicle to the registered owner of the vehicle, or the person who was listed as the registered owner when the vehicle was impounded, or any agents of the registered owner, unless the registered owner is a rental car agency, until after the termination of the 30–day impoundment period.

(2) The legal owner or the legal owner's agent shall not relinquish the vehicle to the registered owner or the person who was listed as the registered owner when the vehicle was impounded until the registered owner or that owner's agent presents his or her valid driver's license or valid temporary driver's license to the legal owner or the legal owner's agent. The legal owner or the legal owner's agent or the person in possession of the vehicle shall make every reasonable effort to ensure that the license presented is valid and possession of the vehicle will not be given to the driver who was involved in the original impoundment proceeding until the expiration of the impoundment period.

(3) Prior to relinquishing the vehicle, the legal owner may require the registered owner to pay all towing and storage charges related to the impoundment and any administrative charges authorized under Section 22850.5 that were incurred by the legal owner in connection with obtaining custody of the vehicle.

(4) Any legal owner who knowingly releases or causes the release of a vehicle to a registered owner or the person in possession of the vehicle at the time of the impoundment or any agent of the registered owner in violation of this subdivision shall be guilty of a misdemeanor and subject to a fine in the amount of two thousand dollars ($2,000) in addition to any other penalties established by law.

(5) The legal owner, registered owner, or person in possession of the vehicle shall not change or attempt to change the name of the legal owner or the registered owner on the records of the department until the vehicle is released from the impoundment.

(h)(1) A vehicle removed and seized under subdivision (a) shall be released to a rental car agency prior to the end of 30 days' impoundment if the agency is either the legal owner or registered owner of the vehicle and the agency pays all towing and storage fees related to the seizure of the vehicle.

(2) The owner of a rental vehicle that was seized under this section may continue to rent the vehicle upon recovery of the vehicle. However, the rental car agency may not rent another vehicle to the driver of the vehicle that was seized until 30 days after the date that the vehicle was seized.

(3) The rental car agency may require the person to whom the vehicle was rented to pay all towing and storage charges related to the impoundment and any administrative charges authorized under Section 22850.5 that were incurred by the rental car agency in connection with obtaining custody of the vehicle.

(i) Notwithstanding any other provision of this section, the registered owner and not the legal owner shall remain responsible for any towing and storage charges related to the impoundment, any administrative charges authorized under Section 22850.5, and any parking fines, penalties, and administrative fees incurred by the registered owner.

(j)(1) The law enforcement agency and the impounding agency, including any storage facility acting on behalf of the law enforcement agency or impounding agency, shall comply with this section and shall not be liable to the registered owner for the improper release of the vehicle to the legal owner or the legal owner's agent provided the release complies with the provisions of this section. A law enforcement agency shall not refuse to issue a release to a legal owner or the agent of a legal owner on the grounds that it previously issued a release.

(2)(A) The legal owner of collateral shall, by operation of law and without requiring further action, indemnify and hold harmless a law enforcement agency, city, county, city and county, the state, a tow yard, storage facility, or an impounding yard from a claim arising out of the release of the collateral to a licensed repossessor or licensed repossession agency, and from any damage to the collateral after its release, including reasonable attorney's fees and costs associated with defending a claim, if the collateral was released in compliance with this section.

(B) This subdivision shall apply only when collateral is released to a licensed repossessor, licensed repossession agency, or its officers or employees pursuant to Chapter 11 (commencing with Section 7500) of Division 3 of the Business and Professions Code. *(Added by Stats.1994, c. 1221 (S.B.1758), § 13. Amended by Stats.1995, c. 922 (S.B.833), § 3; Stats.1998, c. 582 (S.B.117), § 5; Stats.2001, c. 480 (A.B.360), § 1; Stats.2001, c. 554 (A.B.783), § 2.5; Stats.2002, c. 664 (A.B.3034), § 219; Stats.2002, c; 402 (A.B.1883), § 7; Stats.2005, c. 646 (A.B.979), § 2; Stats.2006, c. 538 (S.B.1852), § 658; Stats.2006, c. 418 (A.B.2318), § 7; Stats.2007, c. 192 (S.B.659), § 10, eff. Sept. 7, 2007; Stats.2009, c. 322 (A.B.515), § 5; Stats.2015, c. 740 (A.B.281), § 14, eff. Jan. 1, 2016.)*

Cross References

Misdemeanors, definition and penalties, see Penal Code §§ 17, 19 and 19.2.

Research References

4 Witkin, California Criminal Law 4th Illegally Obtained Evidence § 204 (2021), Inventory Search Under Standard Police Procedures.

3 Witkin, California Criminal Law 4th Punishment § 195 (2021), Impounding of Motor Vehicles.

§ 14602.7. Fleeing or evading a peace officer; reckless driving; removal and impoundment

(a) A magistrate presented with the affidavit of a peace officer establishing reasonable cause to believe that a vehicle, described by vehicle type and license number, was an instrumentality used in the peace officer's presence in violation of Section 2800.1, 2800.2, 2800.3, or 23103, shall issue a warrant or order authorizing any peace officer to immediately seize and cause the removal of the vehicle. The warrant or court order may be entered into a computerized database. A vehicle so impounded may be impounded for a period not to exceed 30 days.

The impounding agency, within two working days of impoundment, shall send a notice by certified mail, return receipt requested, to the legal owner of the vehicle, at the address obtained from the department, informing the owner that the vehicle has been impounded and providing the owner with a copy of the warrant or court order. Failure to notify the legal owner within two working days shall prohibit the impounding agency from charging for more than 15 days impoundment when a legal owner redeems the impounded vehicle. The law enforcement agency shall be open to issue a release to the registered owner or legal owner, or the agent of either, whenever the agency is open to serve the public for regular, nonemergency business.

(b)(1) An impounding agency shall release a vehicle to the registered owner or his or her agent prior to the end of the impoundment period and without the permission of the magistrate authorizing the vehicle's seizure under any of the following circumstances:

(A) When the vehicle is a stolen vehicle.

(B) When the vehicle is subject to bailment and is driven by an unlicensed employee of the business establishment, including a parking service or repair garage.

(C) When the registered owner of the vehicle causes a peace officer to reasonably believe, based on the totality of the circumstances, that the registered owner was not the driver who violated Section 2800.1, 2800.2, or 2800.3, the agency shall immediately release the vehicle to the registered owner or his or her agent.

(2) No vehicle shall be released pursuant to this subdivision, except upon presentation of the registered owner's or agent's currently valid driver's license to operate the vehicle and proof of current vehicle registration, or upon order of the court.

(c)(1) Whenever a vehicle is impounded under this section, the magistrate ordering the storage shall provide the vehicle's registered and legal owners of record, or their agents, with the opportunity for a poststorage hearing to determine the validity of the storage.

(2) A notice of the storage shall be mailed or personally delivered to the registered and legal owners within 48 hours after issuance of the warrant or court order, excluding weekends and holidays, by the person or agency executing the warrant or court order, and shall include all of the following information:

(A) The name, address, and telephone number of the agency providing the notice.

(B) The location of the place of storage and a description of the vehicle, which shall include, if available, the name or make, the manufacturer, the license plate number, and the mileage of the vehicle.

(C) A copy of the warrant or court order and the peace officer's affidavit, as described in subdivision (a).

(D) A statement that, in order to receive their poststorage hearing, the owners, or their agents, are required to request the hearing from the magistrate issuing the warrant or court order in person, in writing, or by telephone, within 10 days of the date of the notice.

(3) The poststorage hearing shall be conducted within two court days after receipt of the request for the hearing.

(4) At the hearing, the magistrate may order the vehicle released if he or she finds any of the circumstances described in subdivision (b) or (e) that allow release of a vehicle by the impounding agency. The magistrate may also consider releasing the vehicle when the continued impoundment will cause undue hardship to persons dependent upon the vehicle for employment or to a person with a community property interest in the vehicle.

(5) Failure of either the registered or legal owner, or his or her agent, to request, or to attend, a scheduled hearing satisfies the poststorage hearing requirement.

(6) The agency employing the peace officer who caused the magistrate to issue the warrant or court order shall be responsible for the costs incurred for towing and storage if it is determined in the poststorage hearing that reasonable grounds for the storage are not established.

(d) The registered owner or his or her agent is responsible for all towing and storage charges related to the impoundment, and any administrative charges authorized under Section 22850.5.

(e) A vehicle removed and seized under subdivision (a) shall be released to the legal owner of the vehicle or the legal owner's agent prior to the end of the impoundment period and without the permission of the magistrate authorizing the seizure of the vehicle if all of the following conditions are met:

(1) The legal owner is a motor vehicle dealer, bank, credit union, acceptance corporation, or other licensed financial institution legally operating in this state or is another person, not the registered owner, holding a financial interest in the vehicle.

(2)(A) The legal owner or the legal owner's agent pays all towing and storage fees related to the seizure of the vehicle. No lien sale processing fees shall be charged to the legal owner who redeems the vehicle prior to the 15th day of impoundment. Neither the impounding authority nor any person having possession of the vehicle shall collect from the legal owner of the type specified in paragraph (1), or the legal owner's agent any administrative charges imposed pursuant to Section 22850.5 unless the legal owner voluntarily requested a poststorage hearing.

(B) A person operating or in charge of a storage facility where vehicles are stored pursuant to this section shall accept a valid bank credit card or cash for payment of towing, storage, and related fees by a legal or registered owner or the owner's agent claiming the vehicle. A credit card shall be in the name of the person presenting the card. "Credit card" means "credit card" as defined in subdivision (a) of Section 1747.02 of the Civil Code, except, for the purposes of this section, credit card does not include a credit card issued by a retail seller.

(C) A person operating or in charge of a storage facility described in subparagraph (B) who violates subparagraph (B) shall be civilly liable to the owner of the vehicle or to the person who tendered the fees for four times the amount of the towing, storage and related fees, but not to exceed five hundred dollars ($500).

(D) A person operating or in charge of a storage facility described in subparagraph (B) shall have sufficient funds on the premises of the primary storage facility during normal business hours to accommodate, and make change in, a reasonable monetary transaction.

(E) Credit charges for towing and storage services shall comply with Section 1748.1 of the Civil Code. Law enforcement agencies may include the costs of providing for payment by credit when making agreements with towing companies on rates.

(3) The legal owner or the legal owner's agent presents, to the law enforcement agency, impounding agency, person in possession of the

vehicle, or any person acting on behalf of those agencies, a copy of the assignment, as defined in subdivision (b) of Section 7500.1 of the Business and Professions Code; a release from the one responsible governmental agency, only if required by the agency; a government-issued photographic identification card; and any one of the following, as determined by the legal owner or the legal owner's agent: a certificate of repossession for the vehicle, a security agreement for the vehicle, or title, whether paper or electronic, showing proof of legal ownership for the vehicle. Any documents presented may be originals, photocopies, or facsimile copies, or may be transmitted electronically. The law enforcement agency, impounding agency, or any other governmental agency, or any person acting on behalf of those agencies, shall not require any documents to be notarized. The law enforcement agency, impounding agency, or any person acting on behalf of those agencies, may require the agent of the legal owner to produce a photocopy or facsimile copy of its repossession agency license or registration issued pursuant to Chapter 11 (commencing with Section 7500) of Division 3 of the Business and Professions Code, or to demonstrate, to the satisfaction of the law enforcement agency, impounding agency, or any person acting on behalf of those agencies that the agent is exempt from licensure pursuant to Section 7500.2 or 7500.3 of the Business and Professions Code.

No administrative costs authorized under subdivision (a) of Section 22850.5 shall be charged to the legal owner of the type specified in paragraph (1), who redeems the vehicle unless the legal owner voluntarily requests a poststorage hearing. No city, county, city and county, or state agency shall require a legal owner or a legal owner's agent to request a poststorage hearing as a requirement for release of the vehicle to the legal owner or the legal owner's agent. The law enforcement agency, impounding agency, or other governmental agency, or any person acting on behalf of those agencies, shall not require any documents other than those specified in this paragraph. The law enforcement agency, impounding agency, or other governmental agency, or any person acting on behalf of those agencies, shall not require any documents to be notarized. The legal owner or the legal owner's agent shall be given a copy of any documents he or she is required to sign, except for a vehicle evidentiary hold logbook. The law enforcement agency, impounding agency, or any person acting on behalf of those agencies, or any person in possession of the vehicle, may photocopy and retain the copies of any documents presented by the legal owner or legal owner's agent.

(4) A failure by a storage facility to comply with any applicable conditions set forth in this subdivision shall not affect the right of the legal owner or the legal owner's agent to retrieve the vehicle, provided all conditions required of the legal owner or legal owner's agent under this subdivision are satisfied.

(f)(1) A legal owner or the legal owner's agent that obtains release of the vehicle pursuant to subdivision (e) shall not release the vehicle to the registered owner or the person who was listed as the registered owner when the vehicle was impounded of the vehicle or any agents of the registered owner, unless a registered owner is a rental car agency, until the termination of the impoundment period.

(2) The legal owner or the legal owner's agent shall not relinquish the vehicle to the registered owner or the person who was listed as the registered owner when the vehicle was impounded until the registered owner or that owner's agent presents his or her valid driver's license or valid temporary driver's license to the legal owner or the legal owner's agent. The legal owner or the legal owner's agent shall make every reasonable effort to ensure that the license presented is valid and possession of the vehicle will not be given to the driver who was involved in the original impoundment proceeding until the expiration of the impoundment period.

(3) Prior to relinquishing the vehicle, the legal owner may require the registered owner to pay all towing and storage charges related to the impoundment and the administrative charges authorized under Section 22850.5 that were incurred by the legal owner in connection with obtaining the custody of the vehicle.

(4) Any legal owner who knowingly releases or causes the release of a vehicle to a registered owner or the person in possession of the vehicle at the time of the impoundment or any agent of the registered owner in violation of this subdivision shall be guilty of a misdemeanor and subject to a fine in the amount of two thousand dollars ($2,000) in addition to any other penalties established by law.

(5) The legal owner, registered owner, or person in possession of the vehicle shall not change or attempt to change the name of the legal owner or the registered owner on the records of the department until the vehicle is released from the impoundment.

(g)(1) A vehicle impounded and seized under subdivision (a) shall be released to a rental car agency prior to the end of the impoundment period if the agency is either the legal owner or registered owner of the vehicle and the agency pays all towing and storage fees related to the seizure of the vehicle.

(2) The owner of a rental vehicle that was seized under this section may continue to rent the vehicle upon recovery of the vehicle. However, the rental car agency shall not rent another vehicle to the driver who used the vehicle that was seized to evade a police officer until 30 days after the date that the vehicle was seized.

(3) The rental car agency may require the person to whom the vehicle was rented and who evaded the peace officer to pay all towing and storage charges related to the impoundment and any administrative charges authorized under Section 22850.5 that were incurred by the rental car agency in connection with obtaining custody of the vehicle.

(h) Notwithstanding any other provision of this section, the registered owner and not the legal owner shall remain responsible for any towing and storage charges related to the impoundment and the administrative charges authorized under Section 22850.5 and any parking fines, penalties, and administrative fees incurred by the registered owner.

(i)(1) This section does not apply to vehicles abated under the Abandoned Vehicle Abatement Program pursuant to Sections 22660 to 22668, inclusive, and Section 22710, or to vehicles impounded for investigation pursuant to Section 22655, or to vehicles removed from private property pursuant to Section 22658.

(2) This section does not apply to abandoned vehicles removed pursuant to Section 22669 that are determined by the public agency to have an estimated value of three hundred dollars ($300) or less.

(j) The law enforcement agency and the impounding agency, including any storage facility acting on behalf of the law enforcement agency or impounding agency, shall comply with this section and shall not be liable to the registered owner for the improper release of the vehicle to the legal owner or the legal owner's agent provided the release complies with the provisions of this section. The legal owner shall indemnify and hold harmless a storage facility from any claims arising out of the release of the vehicle to the legal owner or the legal owner's agent and from any damage to the vehicle after its release, including the reasonable costs associated with defending any such claims. A law enforcement agency shall not refuse to issue a release to a legal owner or the agent of a legal owner on the grounds that it previously issued a release. *(Added by Stats.1997, c. 743 (A.B.662), § 1. Amended by Stats.1998, c. 485 (A.B.2803), § 160; Stats.2001, c. 554 (A.B.783), § 3; Stats.2002, c. 664 (A.B.3034), § 220; Stats.2002, c. 402 (A.B.1883), § 8; Stats.2006, c. 418 (A.B.2318), § 8; Stats.2007, c. 192 (S.B.659), § 11, eff. Sept. 7, 2007; Stats.2009, c. 322 (A.B.515), § 6.)*

Cross References

Misdemeanors, definition and penalties, see Penal Code §§ 17, 19 and 19.2.

Research References

2 Witkin, California Criminal Law 4th Crimes Against Public Peace and Welfare § 271 (2021), Reckless Driving.
2 Witkin, California Criminal Law 4th Crimes Against Public Peace and Welfare § 329 (2021), Flight from Pursuing Peace Officer.
3 Witkin, California Criminal Law 4th Punishment § 195 (2021), Impounding of Motor Vehicles.

§ 14602.8. Immediate removal and seizure of vehicle driven by repeat offender; storage and impoundment; vehicle owner's rights and responsibilities

(a)(1) If a peace officer determines that a person has been convicted of a violation of Section 23140, 23152, or 23153, that the violation occurred within the preceding 10 years, and that one or more of the following circumstances applies to that person, the officer may immediately cause the removal and seizure of the vehicle that the person was driving, under either of the following circumstances:

(A) The person was driving a vehicle when the person had 0.10 percent or more, by weight, of alcohol in his or her blood.

(B) The person driving the vehicle refused to submit to or complete a chemical test requested by the peace officer.

(2) A vehicle impounded pursuant to paragraph (1) shall be impounded for the following period of time:

(A) Five days, if the person has been convicted once of violating Section 23140, 23152, or 23153, and the violation occurred within the preceding 10 years.

(B) Fifteen days, if the person has been convicted two or more times of violating Section 23140, 23152, or 23153, or any combination thereof, and the violations occurred within the preceding 10 years.

(3) Within two working days after impoundment, the impounding agency shall send a notice by certified mail, return receipt requested, to the legal owner of the vehicle, at the address obtained from the department, informing the owner that the vehicle has been impounded. Failure to notify the legal owner within two working days shall prohibit the impounding agency from charging for more than five days' impoundment when the legal owner redeems the impounded vehicle. The impounding agency shall maintain a published telephone number that provides information 24 hours a day regarding the impoundment of vehicles and the rights of a registered owner to request a hearing. The law enforcement agency shall be open to issue a release to the registered owner or legal owner, or the agent of either, whenever the agency is open to serve the public for regular, nonemergency business.

(b) The registered and legal owner of a vehicle that is removed and seized under subdivision (a) or his or her agent shall be provided the opportunity for a storage hearing to determine the validity of, or consider any mitigating circumstances attendant to, the storage, in accordance with Section 22852.

(c) Any period during which a vehicle is subjected to storage under this section shall be included as part of the period of impoundment ordered by the court under Section 23594.

(d)(1) The impounding agency shall release the vehicle to the registered owner or his or her agent prior to the end of the impoundment period under any of the following circumstances:

(A) When the vehicle is a stolen vehicle.

(B) When the vehicle is subject to bailment and is driven by an unlicensed employee of a business establishment, including a parking service or repair garage.

(C) When the driver of the vehicle is not the sole registered owner of the vehicle and the vehicle is being released to another registered owner of the vehicle who agrees not to allow the driver to use the vehicle until after the end of the impoundment period.

(2) A vehicle shall not be released pursuant to this subdivision without presentation of the registered owner's or agent's currently valid driver's license to operate the vehicle and proof of current vehicle registration, or upon order of a court.

(e) The registered owner or his or her agent is responsible for all towing and storage charges related to the impoundment, and any administrative charges authorized under Section 22850.5.

(f) A vehicle removed and seized under subdivision (a) shall be released to the legal owner of the vehicle or the legal owner's agent prior to the end of the impoundment period if all of the following conditions are met:

(1) The legal owner is a motor vehicle dealer, bank, credit union, acceptance corporation, or other licensed financial institution legally operating in this state, or is another person who is not the registered owner and holds a security interest in the vehicle.

(2)(A) The legal owner or the legal owner's agent pays all towing and storage fees related to the seizure of the vehicle. A lien sale processing fee shall not be charged to the legal owner who redeems the vehicle prior to the 10th day of impoundment. The impounding authority or any person having possession of the vehicle shall not collect from the legal owner of the type specified in paragraph (1) or the legal owner's agent any administrative charges imposed pursuant to Section 22850.5 unless the legal owner voluntarily requested a poststorage hearing.

(B) A person operating or in charge of a storage facility where vehicles are stored pursuant to this section shall accept a valid bank credit card or cash for payment of towing, storage, and related fees by a legal or registered owner or the owner's agent claiming the vehicle. A credit card shall be in the name of the person presenting the card. "Credit card" means "credit card" as defined in subdivision (a) of Section 1747.02 of the Civil Code, except, for the purposes of this section, credit card does not include a credit card issued by a retail seller.

(C) A person operating or in charge of a storage facility described in subparagraph (B) who violates subparagraph (B) shall be civilly liable to the owner of the vehicle or to the person who tendered the fees for four times the amount of the towing, storage, and other related fees, but not to exceed five hundred dollars ($500).

(D) A person operating or in charge of a storage facility described in subparagraph (B) shall have sufficient funds on the premises of the primary storage facility during normal business hours to accommodate, and make change in, a reasonable monetary transaction.

(E) Credit charges for towing and storage services shall comply with Section 1748.1 of the Civil Code. Law enforcement agencies may include the costs of providing for payment by credit when making agreements with towing companies on rates.

(3)(A) The legal owner or the legal owner's agent presents to the law enforcement agency or impounding agency, or any person acting on behalf of those agencies, a copy of the assignment, as defined in subdivision (b) of Section 7500.1 of the Business and Professions Code; a release from the one responsible governmental agency, only if required by the agency; a government-issued photographic identification card; and any one of the following as determined by the legal owner or the legal owner's agent: a certificate of repossession for the vehicle, a security agreement for the vehicle, or title, whether paper or electronic, showing proof of legal ownership for the vehicle. The law enforcement agency, impounding agency, or any other governmental agency, or any person acting on behalf of those agencies, shall not require the presentation of any other documents.

(B) The legal owner or the legal owner's agent presents to the person in possession of the vehicle, or any person acting on behalf of the person in possession, a copy of the assignment, as defined in subdivision (b) of Section 7500.1 of the Business and Professions

Code; a release from the one responsible governmental agency, only if required by the agency; a government-issued photographic identification card; and any one of the following as determined by the legal owner or the legal owner's agent: a certificate of repossession for the vehicle, a security agreement for the vehicle, or title, whether paper or electronic, showing proof of legal ownership for the vehicle. The person in possession of the vehicle, or any person acting on behalf of the person in possession, shall not require the presentation of any other documents.

(C) All presented documents may be originals, photocopies, or facsimile copies, or may be transmitted electronically. The law enforcement agency, impounding agency, or any person acting on behalf of them, shall not require a document to be notarized. The law enforcement agency, impounding agency, or any person in possession of the vehicle, or anyone acting on behalf of those agencies may require the agent of the legal owner to produce a photocopy or facsimile copy of its repossession agency license or registration issued pursuant to Chapter 11 (commencing with Section 7500) of Division 3 of the Business and Professions Code, or to demonstrate, to the satisfaction of the law enforcement agency, the impounding agency, any other governmental agency, or any person in possession of the vehicle, or anyone acting on behalf of them, that the agent is exempt from licensure pursuant to Section 7500.2 or 7500.3 of the Business and Professions Code.

(D) Administrative costs authorized under subdivision (a) of Section 22850.5 shall not be charged to the legal owner of the type specified in paragraph (1) who redeems the vehicle unless the legal owner voluntarily requests a poststorage hearing. A city, county, city and county, or state agency shall not require a legal owner or a legal owner's agent to request a poststorage hearing as a requirement for release of the vehicle to the legal owner or the legal owner's agent. The law enforcement agency, the impounding agency, any governmental agency, or any person acting on behalf of those agencies shall not require any documents other than those specified in this paragraph. The law enforcement agency, impounding agency, or other governmental agency, or any person acting on behalf of those agencies, shall not require any documents to be notarized. The legal owner or the legal owner's agent shall be given a copy of any documents he or she is required to sign, except for a vehicle evidentiary hold logbook. The law enforcement agency, impounding agency, or any person acting on behalf of those agencies, or any person in possession of the vehicle, may photocopy and retain the copies of any documents presented by the legal owner or legal owner's agent.

(4) A failure by a storage facility to comply with any applicable conditions set forth in this subdivision shall not affect the right of the legal owner or the legal owner's agent to retrieve the vehicle, provided all conditions required of the legal owner or legal owner's agent under this subdivision are satisfied.

(g)(1) A legal owner or the legal owner's agent who obtains release of the vehicle pursuant to subdivision (f) shall not release the vehicle to the registered owner of the vehicle or the person who was listed as the registered owner when the vehicle was impounded or any agents of the registered owner unless the registered owner is a rental car agency, until after the termination of the impoundment period.

(2) The legal owner or the legal owner's agent shall not relinquish the vehicle to the registered owner or the person who was listed as the registered owner when the vehicle was impounded until the registered owner or that owner's agent presents his or her valid driver's license or valid temporary driver's license to the legal owner or the legal owner's agent. The legal owner or the legal owner's agent or the person in possession of the vehicle shall make every reasonable effort to ensure that the license presented is valid and possession of the vehicle will not be given to the driver who was involved in the original impoundment proceeding until the expiration of the impoundment period.

(3) Prior to relinquishing the vehicle, the legal owner may require the registered owner to pay all towing and storage charges related to the impoundment and any administrative charges authorized under Section 22850.5 that were incurred by the legal owner in connection with obtaining custody of the vehicle.

(4) A legal owner who knowingly releases or causes the release of a vehicle to a registered owner or the person in possession of the vehicle at the time of the impoundment or an agent of the registered owner in violation of this subdivision is guilty of a misdemeanor and subject to a fine in the amount of two thousand dollars ($2,000) in addition to any other penalties established by law.

(5) The legal owner, registered owner, or person in possession of the vehicle shall not change or attempt to change the name of the legal owner or the registered owner on the records of the department until the vehicle is released from the impoundment.

(h)(1) A vehicle removed and seized under subdivision (a) shall be released to a rental car agency prior to the end of the impoundment period if the agency is either the legal owner or registered owner of the vehicle and the agency pays all towing and storage fees related to the seizure of the vehicle.

(2) The owner of a rental vehicle that was seized under this section may continue to rent the vehicle upon recovery of the vehicle. However, the rental car agency shall not rent another vehicle to the driver of the vehicle that was seized until the impoundment period has expired.

(3) The rental car agency may require the person to whom the vehicle was rented to pay all towing and storage charges related to the impoundment and any administrative charges authorized under Section 22850.5 that were incurred by the rental car agency in connection with obtaining custody of the vehicle.

(i) Notwithstanding any other provision of this section, the registered owner, and not the legal owner, shall remain responsible for any towing and storage charges related to the impoundment, any administrative charges authorized under Section 22850.5, and any parking fines, penalties, and administrative fees incurred by the registered owner.

(j) The law enforcement agency and the impounding agency, including any storage facility acting on behalf of the law enforcement agency or impounding agency, shall comply with this section and shall not be liable to the registered owner for the improper release of the vehicle to the legal owner or the legal owner's agent provided the release complies with the provisions of this section. The legal owner shall indemnify and hold harmless a storage facility from any claims arising out of the release of the vehicle to the legal owner or the legal owner's agent and from any damage to the vehicle after its release, including the reasonable costs associated with defending any such claims. A law enforcement agency shall not refuse to issue a release to a legal owner or the agent of a legal owner on the grounds that it previously issued a release. *(Added by Stats.2005, c. 656 (S.B.207), § 1. Amended by Stats.2009, c. 322 (A.B.515), § 7; Stats.2011, c. 341 (S.B.565), § 2.)*

Cross References

Misdemeanors, definition and penalties, see Penal Code §§ 17, 19 and 19.2.

Research References

2 Witkin, California Criminal Law 4th Crimes Against Public Peace and Welfare § 279 (2021), In General.
3 Witkin, California Criminal Law 4th Punishment § 195 (2021), Impounding of Motor Vehicles.

§ 14602.9. Charter-party carrier buses; impoundment; notice; storage hearing; release of vehicle; towing and storage charges

(a) For purposes of this section, "peace officer" means a person designated as a peace officer pursuant to Chapter 4.5 (commencing with Section 830) of Title 3 of Part 2 of the Penal Code.

(b) A peace officer may impound a bus or limousine of a charter-party carrier for 30 days if the officer determines that any of the following violations occurred while the driver was operating the bus or limousine of the charter-party carrier:

(1) The driver was operating the bus or limousine of a charter-party carrier when the charter-party carrier did not have a permit or certificate issued by the Public Utilities Commission, pursuant to Section 5375 of the Public Utilities Code.

(2) The driver was operating the bus or limousine of a charter-party carrier when the charter-party carrier was operating with a suspended permit or certificate from the Public Utilities Commission.

(3) The driver was operating the bus or limousine of a charter-party carrier without having a current and valid driver's license of the proper class, a passenger vehicle endorsement, or the required certificate.

(c) A peace officer may impound a bus or limousine belonging to a passenger stage corporation for 30 days if the officer determines any of the following violations occurred while the driver was operating the bus or limousine:

(1) The driver was operating the bus or limousine when the passenger stage corporation did not have a certificate of public convenience and necessity issued by the Public Utilities Commission as required pursuant to Article 2 (commencing with Section 1031) of Chapter 5 of Part 1 of Division 1 of the Public Utilities Code.

(2) The driver was operating the bus or limousine when the operating rights or certificate of public convenience and necessity of a passenger stage corporation was suspended, canceled, or revoked pursuant to Section 1033.5, 1033.7, or 1045 of the Public Utilities Code.

(3) The driver was operating the bus or limousine without having a current and valid driver's license of the proper class.

(d) Within two working days after impoundment, the impounding agency shall send a notice by certified mail, return receipt requested, to the legal owner of the vehicle, at the address obtained from the department, informing the owner that the vehicle has been impounded. Failure to notify the legal owner within two working days shall prohibit the impounding agency from charging for more than 15 day's impoundment when the legal owner redeems the impounded vehicle. The impounding agency shall maintain a published telephone number that provides information 24 hours a day regarding the impoundment of vehicles and the rights of a registered owner to request a hearing.

(e) The registered and legal owner of a vehicle that is removed and seized under subdivision (b) or (c) or his or her agent shall be provided the opportunity for a storage hearing to determine the validity of, or consider any mitigating circumstances attendant to, the storage, in accordance with Section 22852.

(f)(1) The impounding agency shall release the vehicle to the registered owner or his or her agent prior to the end of the impoundment period under any of the following circumstances:

(A) When the vehicle is a stolen vehicle.

(B) When the vehicle is subject to bailment and is driven by an unlicensed employee of a business establishment, including a parking service or repair garage.

(C) When, for a charter-party carrier of passengers, the driver of the vehicle is not the sole registered owner of the vehicle and the vehicle is being released to another registered owner of the vehicle who agrees not to allow the driver to use the vehicle until after the end of the impoundment period and the charter-party carrier has been issued a valid permit from the Public Utilities Commission, pursuant to Section 5375 of the Public Utilities Code.

(D) When, for a passenger stage corporation, the driver of the vehicle is not the sole registered owner of the vehicle and the vehicle is being released to another registered owner of the vehicle who agrees not to allow the driver to use the vehicle until after the end of the impoundment period and the passenger stage corporation has been issued a valid certificate of public convenience and necessity by the Public Utilities Commission, pursuant to Article 2 (commencing with Section 1031) of Chapter 5 of Part 1 of Division 1 of the Public Utilities Code.

(2) A vehicle shall not be released pursuant to this subdivision without presentation of the registered owner's or agent's currently valid driver's license to operate the vehicle and proof of current vehicle registration, or upon order of a court.

(g) The registered owner or his or her agent is responsible for all towing and storage charges related to the impoundment, and any administrative charges authorized under Section 22850.5.

(h) A vehicle removed and seized under subdivision (b) or (c) shall be released to the legal owner of the vehicle or the legal owner's agent prior to the end of the impoundment period if all of the following conditions are met:

(1) The legal owner is a motor vehicle dealer, bank, credit union, acceptance corporation, or other licensed financial institution legally operating in this state, or is another person who is not the registered owner and holds a security interest in the vehicle.

(2) The legal owner or the legal owner's agent pays all towing and storage fees related to the seizure of the vehicle. A lien sale processing fee shall not be charged to the legal owner who redeems the vehicle prior to the 10th day of impoundment. The impounding authority or any person having possession of the vehicle shall not collect from the legal owner of the type specified in paragraph (1), or the legal owner's agent, any administrative charges imposed pursuant to Section 22850.5 unless the legal owner voluntarily requested a poststorage hearing.

(3)(A) The legal owner or the legal owner's agent presents either lawful foreclosure documents or an affidavit of repossession for the vehicle, and a security agreement or title showing proof of legal ownership for the vehicle. All presented documents may be originals, photocopies, or facsimile copies, or may be transmitted electronically. The impounding agency shall not require a document to be notarized. The impounding agency may require the agent of the legal owner to produce a photocopy or facsimile copy of its repossession agency license or registration issued pursuant to Chapter 11 (commencing with Section 7500) of Division 3 of the Business and Professions Code, or to demonstrate, to the satisfaction of the impounding agency, that the agent is exempt from licensure pursuant to Section 7500.2 or 7500.3 of the Business and Professions Code.

(B) Administrative costs authorized under subdivision (a) of Section 22850.5 shall not be charged to the legal owner of the type specified in paragraph (1), who redeems the vehicle unless the legal owner voluntarily requests a poststorage hearing. A city, county, or state agency shall not require a legal owner or a legal owner's agent to request a poststorage hearing as a requirement for release of the vehicle to the legal owner or the legal owner's agent. The impounding agency shall not require any documents other than those specified in this paragraph. The impounding agency shall not require any documents to be notarized.

(C) As used in this paragraph, "foreclosure documents" means an "assignment" as that term is defined in subdivision (b) of Section 7500.1 of the Business and Professions Code.

(i)(1) A legal owner or the legal owner's agent who obtains release of the vehicle pursuant to subdivision (h) may not release the vehicle to the registered owner of the vehicle or any agents of the registered owner, unless the registered owner is a rental car agency, until after the termination of the impoundment period.

(2) The legal owner or the legal owner's agent shall not relinquish the vehicle to the registered owner until the registered owner or that owner's agent presents his or her valid driver's license or valid temporary driver's license to the legal owner or the legal owner's

agent. The legal owner or the legal owner's agent shall make every reasonable effort to ensure that the license presented is valid.

(3) Prior to relinquishing the vehicle, the legal owner may require the registered owner to pay all towing and storage charges related to the impoundment and any administrative charges authorized under Section 22850.5 that were incurred by the legal owner in connection with obtaining custody of the vehicle.

(j)(1) A vehicle removed and seized under subdivision (b) or (c) shall be released to a rental agency prior to the end of the impoundment period if the agency is either the legal owner or registered owner of the vehicle and the agency pays all towing and storage fees related to the seizure of the vehicle.

(2) The owner of a rental vehicle that was seized under this section may continue to rent the vehicle upon recovery of the vehicle. However, the rental agency shall not rent another vehicle to the driver of the vehicle that was seized until the impoundment period has expired.

(3) The rental agency may require the person to whom the vehicle was rented to pay all towing and storage charges related to the impoundment and any administrative charges authorized under Section 22850.5 that were incurred by the rental agency in connection with obtaining custody of the vehicle.

(k) Notwithstanding any other provision of this section, the registered owner, and not the legal owner, shall remain responsible for any towing and storage charges related to the impoundment, any administrative charges authorized under Section 22850.5, and any parking fines, penalties, and administrative fees incurred by the registered owner.

(*l*) The impounding agency is not liable to the registered owner for the improper release of the vehicle to the legal owner or the legal owner's agent provided the release complies with this section.

(m) This section does not authorize the impoundment of privately owned personal vehicles that are not common carriers nor the impoundment of vehicles used in transportation for compensation by charter-party carriers that are not required to carry individual permits.

(n) For the purposes of this section, a "charter-party carrier" means a charter-party carrier of passengers as defined by Section 5360 of the Public Utilities Code.

(*o*) For purposes of this section, a "passenger stage corporation" means a passenger stage corporation as defined by Section 226 of the Public Utilities Code. *(Added by Stats.2009, c. 248 (A.B.636), § 5. Amended by Stats.2015, c. 718 (S.B.541), § 11, eff. Jan. 1, 2016; Stats.2015, c. 740 (A.B.281), § 15.5, eff. Jan. 1, 2016.)*

Cross References

Charter-party carriers, grounds for impounding of bus, see Public Utilities Code § 5387.

§ 14603. Violation of license restrictions

No person shall operate a vehicle in violation of the provisions of a restricted license issued to him. *(Stats.1959, c. 3, p. 1634, § 14603.)*

Cross References

Restricted license, issuance, see Vehicle Code § 12813.

§ 14604. Non-owner driver of vehicle; owner to determine that driver has valid license; standard of inquiry; rental companies

(a) No owner of a motor vehicle may knowingly allow another person to drive the vehicle upon a highway unless the owner determines that the person possesses a valid driver's license that authorizes the person to operate the vehicle. For the purposes of this section, an owner is required only to make a reasonable effort or inquiry to determine whether the prospective driver possesses a valid driver's license before allowing him or her to operate the owner's vehicle. An owner is not required to inquire of the department whether the prospective driver possesses a valid driver's license.

(b) A rental company is deemed to be in compliance with subdivision (a) if the company rents the vehicle in accordance with Sections 14608 and 14609. *(Added by Stats.1994, c. 1221 (S.B.1758), § 14. Amended by Stats.1995, c. 922 (S.B.833), § 3.5.)*

Research References

2 Witkin, California Criminal Law 4th Crimes Against Public Peace and Welfare § 309 (2021), Permitting Unlicensed Person to Drive.

§ 14605. Operation of motor vehicles in offstreet parking facilities

(a) No person who owns or is in control of a motor vehicle shall cause or permit another person to operate the vehicle within or upon an offstreet parking facility if the person has knowledge that the driver does not have a driver's license of the appropriate class or certification to operate the vehicle.

(b) No operator of an offstreet parking facility shall hire or retain in his employment an attendant whose duties involve the operating of motor vehicles unless such attendant, at all times during such employment, is licensed as a driver under the provisions of this code.

(c) As used in this section, "offstreet parking facility" means any offstreet facility held open for use by the public for parking vehicles and includes all publicly owned facilities for offstreet parking, and privately owned facilities for offstreet parking where no fee is charged for the privilege to park and which are held open for the common public use of retail customers. *(Stats.1959, c. 3, p. 1634, § 14605. Amended by Stats.1961, c. 1615, p. 3457, § 30; Stats.1984, c. 621, § 4.)*

Cross References

Regulation in cities over 2,000,000 population, see Vehicle Code § 22950.
Use of street or alley by parking facility operator prohibited, see Vehicle Code § 22951.

Research References

2 Witkin, California Criminal Law 4th Crimes Against Public Peace and Welfare § 309 (2021), Permitting Unlicensed Person to Drive.

§ 14606. Employment of person to drive motor vehicle; license and medical certificate; operation of commercial motor vehicles

(a) A person shall not employ, hire, knowingly permit, or authorize any person to drive a motor vehicle owned by him or her or under his or her control upon the highways unless that person is licensed for the appropriate class of vehicle to be driven.

(b) Whenever a person fails to qualify, on reexamination, to operate a commercial motor vehicle, an employer shall report that failure to the department within 10 days.

(c) An employer shall obtain from a driver required to have a commercial driver's license or commercial endorsement a copy of the driver's medical certification before allowing the driver to operate a commercial motor vehicle. The employer shall retain the certification as part of a driver qualification file.

(d) This section shall become operative on January 30, 2014. *(Added by Stats.2012, c. 670 (A.B.2188), § 7, operative Jan. 1, 2014. Amended by Stats.2013, c. 523 (S.B.788), § 30, operative Jan. 30, 2014.)*

Cross References

Civil liability of owners and operators, see Vehicle Code § 17000 et seq.
Driving school or driving instructor, cancellation revocation or suspension of license for violation of this section, see Vehicle Code § 11110.
Driving without a license, see Vehicle Code § 12500.
Owner, definitions of, see Vehicle Code §§ 370, 460, 505.

Person defined, see Vehicle Code § 470.

Research References

2 Witkin, California Criminal Law 4th Crimes Against Public Peace and Welfare § 309 (2021), Permitting Unlicensed Person to Drive.

§ 14607. Permitting unlicensed minor to drive

No person shall cause or knowingly permit his child, ward, or employee under the age of 18 years to drive a motor vehicle upon the highways unless such child, ward, or employee is then licensed under this code. *(Stats.1959, c. 3, p. 1634, § 14607. Amended by Stats. 1961, c. 1615, p. 3458, § 32; Stats.1971, c. 1748, p. 3764, § 59, operative March 4, 1972.)*

Cross References

Age limit for issuance of license,
 Junior permits, see Vehicle Code §§ 12513, 12514.
Civil liability of persons signing license applications of minors, see Vehicle Code § 17700 et seq.
Definitions,
 Highway, see Vehicle Code §§ 360, 590.
 Motor vehicle, see Vehicle Code § 415.
Licensing of nonresident minors, see Vehicle Code § 12504.

Research References

2 Witkin, California Criminal Law 4th Crimes Against Public Peace and Welfare § 309 (2021), Permitting Unlicensed Person to Drive.

§ 14607.4. Legislative findings and declarations

The Legislature finds and declares all of the following:

(a) Driving a motor vehicle on the public streets and highways is a privilege, not a right.

(b) Of all drivers involved in fatal accidents, more than 20 percent are not licensed to drive. A driver with a suspended license is four times as likely to be involved in a fatal accident as a properly licensed driver.

(c) At any given time, it is estimated by the Department of Motor Vehicles that of some 20 million driver's licenses issued to Californians, 720,000 are suspended or revoked. Furthermore, 1,000,000 persons are estimated to be driving without ever having been licensed at all.

(d) Over 4,000 persons are killed in traffic accidents in California annually, and another 330,000 persons suffer injuries.

(e) Californians who comply with the law are frequently victims of traffic accidents caused by unlicensed drivers. These innocent victims suffer considerable pain and property loss at the hands of people who flaunt the law. The Department of Motor Vehicles estimates that 75 percent of all drivers whose driving privilege has been withdrawn continue to drive regardless of the law.

(f) It is necessary and appropriate to take additional steps to prevent unlicensed drivers from driving, including the civil forfeiture of vehicles used by unlicensed drivers. The state has a critical interest in enforcing its traffic laws and in keeping unlicensed drivers from illegally driving. Seizing the vehicles used by unlicensed drivers serves a significant governmental and public interest, namely the protection of the health, safety, and welfare of Californians from the harm of unlicensed drivers, who are involved in a disproportionate number of traffic incidents, and the avoidance of the associated destruction and damage to lives and property.

(g) The Safe Streets Act of 1994 is consistent with the due process requirements of the United States Constitution and the holding of the Supreme Court of the United States in Calero-Toledo v. Pearson Yacht Leasing Co., 40 L.Ed.2d 452. *(Added by Stats.1994, c. 1133 (A.B.3148), § 11.)*

§ 14607.6. Motor vehicles subject to forfeiture; driving without a license; impoundment; officer's discretion; hearings; release of vehicle; community property interests; surrender; redemption and sale; stolen vehicles; distribution of filing fee

(a) Notwithstanding any other provision of law, and except as provided in this section, a motor vehicle is subject to forfeiture as a nuisance if it is driven on a highway in this state by a driver with a suspended or revoked license, or by an unlicensed driver, who is a registered owner of the vehicle at the time of impoundment and has a previous misdemeanor conviction for a violation of subdivision (a) of Section 12500 or Section 14601, 14601.1, 14601.2, 14601.3, 14601.4, or 14601.5.

(b) A peace officer shall not stop a vehicle for the sole reason of determining whether the driver is properly licensed.

(c)(1) If a driver is unable to produce a valid driver's license on the demand of a peace officer enforcing the provisions of this code, as required by subdivision (b) of Section 12951, the vehicle shall be impounded regardless of ownership, unless the peace officer is reasonably able, by other means, to verify that the driver is properly licensed. Prior to impounding a vehicle, a peace officer shall attempt to verify the license status of a driver who claims to be properly licensed but is unable to produce the license on demand of the peace officer.

(2) A peace officer shall not impound a vehicle pursuant to this subdivision if the license of the driver expired within the preceding 30 days and the driver would otherwise have been properly licensed.

(3) A peace officer may exercise discretion in a situation where the driver without a valid license is an employee driving a vehicle registered to the employer in the course of employment. A peace officer may also exercise discretion in a situation where the driver without a valid license is the employee of a bona fide business establishment or is a person otherwise controlled by such an establishment and it reasonably appears that an owner of the vehicle, or an agent of the owner, relinquished possession of the vehicle to the business establishment solely for servicing or parking of the vehicle or other reasonably similar situations, and where the vehicle was not to be driven except as directly necessary to accomplish that business purpose. In this event, if the vehicle can be returned to or be retrieved by the business establishment or registered owner, the peace officer may release and not impound the vehicle.

(4) A registered or legal owner of record at the time of impoundment may request a hearing to determine the validity of the impoundment pursuant to subdivision (n).

(5) If the driver of a vehicle impounded pursuant to this subdivision was not a registered owner of the vehicle at the time of impoundment, or if the driver of the vehicle was a registered owner of the vehicle at the time of impoundment but the driver does not have a previous conviction for a violation of subdivision (a) of Section 12500 or Section 14601, 14601.1, 14601.2, 14601.3, 14601.4, or 14601.5, the vehicle shall be released pursuant to this code and is not subject to forfeiture.

(d)(1) This subdivision applies only if the driver of the vehicle is a registered owner of the vehicle at the time of impoundment. Except as provided in paragraph (5) of subdivision (c), if the driver of a vehicle impounded pursuant to subdivision (c) was a registered owner of the vehicle at the time of impoundment, the impounding agency shall authorize release of the vehicle if, within three days of impoundment, the driver of the vehicle at the time of impoundment presents his or her valid driver's license, including a valid temporary California driver's license or permit, to the impounding agency. The vehicle shall then be released to a registered owner of record at the time of impoundment, or an agent of that owner authorized in writing, upon payment of towing and storage charges related to the impoundment, and any administrative charges authorized by Section 22850.5, providing that the person claiming the vehicle is properly licensed and the vehicle is properly registered. A vehicle impounded pursuant to the circumstances described in paragraph (3) of subdivision (c) shall be released to a registered owner whether or not the driver of the vehicle at the time of impoundment presents a valid driver's license.

(2) If there is a community property interest in the vehicle impounded pursuant to subdivision (c), owned at the time of impoundment by a person other than the driver, and the vehicle is the only vehicle available to the driver's immediate family that may be operated with a class C driver's license, the vehicle shall be released to a registered owner or to the community property interest owner upon compliance with all of the following requirements:

(A) The registered owner or the community property interest owner requests release of the vehicle and the owner of the community property interest submits proof of that interest.

(B) The registered owner or the community property interest owner submits proof that he or she, or an authorized driver, is properly licensed and that the impounded vehicle is properly registered pursuant to this code.

(C) All towing and storage charges related to the impoundment and any administrative charges authorized pursuant to Section 22850.5 are paid.

(D) The registered owner or the community property interest owner signs a stipulated vehicle release agreement, as described in paragraph (3), in consideration for the nonforfeiture of the vehicle. This requirement applies only if the driver requests release of the vehicle.

(3) A stipulated vehicle release agreement shall provide for the consent of the signator to the automatic future forfeiture and transfer of title to the state of any vehicle registered to that person, if the vehicle is driven by a driver with a suspended or revoked license, or by an unlicensed driver. The agreement shall be in effect for only as long as it is noted on a driving record maintained by the department pursuant to Section 1806.1.

(4) The stipulated vehicle release agreement described in paragraph (3) shall be reported by the impounding agency to the department not later than 10 days after the day the agreement is signed.

(5) No vehicle shall be released pursuant to paragraph (2) if the driving record of a registered owner indicates that a prior stipulated vehicle release agreement was signed by that person.

(e)(1) The impounding agency, in the case of a vehicle that has not been redeemed pursuant to subdivision (d), or that has not been otherwise released, shall promptly ascertain from the department the names and addresses of all legal and registered owners of the vehicle.

(2) The impounding agency, within two days of impoundment, shall send a notice by certified mail, return receipt requested, to all legal and registered owners of the vehicle, at the addresses obtained from the department, informing them that the vehicle is subject to forfeiture and will be sold or otherwise disposed of pursuant to this section. The notice shall also include instructions for filing a claim with the district attorney, and the time limits for filing a claim. The notice shall also inform any legal owner of its right to conduct the sale pursuant to subdivision (g). If a registered owner was personally served at the time of impoundment with a notice containing all the information required to be provided by this paragraph, no further notice is required to be sent to a registered owner. However, a notice shall still be sent to the legal owners of the vehicle, if any. If notice was not sent to the legal owner within two working days, the impounding agency shall not charge the legal owner for more than 15-days' impoundment when the legal owner redeems the impounded vehicle.

(3) No processing charges shall be imposed on a legal owner who redeems an impounded vehicle within 15 days of the impoundment of that vehicle. If no claims are filed and served within 15 days after the mailing of the notice in paragraph (2), or if no claims are filed and served within five days of personal service of the notice specified in paragraph (2), when no other mailed notice is required pursuant to paragraph (2), the district attorney shall prepare a written declaration of forfeiture of the vehicle to the state. A written declaration of forfeiture signed by the district attorney under this subdivision shall be deemed to provide good and sufficient title to the forfeited vehicle. A copy of the declaration shall be provided on request to any person informed of the pending forfeiture pursuant to paragraph (2). A claim that is filed and is later withdrawn by the claimant shall be deemed not to have been filed.

(4) If a claim is timely filed and served, then the district attorney shall file a petition of forfeiture with the appropriate juvenile or superior court within 10 days of the receipt of the claim. The district attorney shall establish an expedited hearing date in accordance with instructions from the court, and the court shall hear the matter without delay. The court filing fee of one hundred dollars ($100) shall be paid by the claimant, but shall be reimbursed by the impounding agency if the claimant prevails. To the extent practicable, the civil and criminal cases shall be heard at the same time in an expedited, consolidated proceeding. A proceeding in the civil case is a limited civil case.

(5) The burden of proof in the civil case shall be on the prosecuting agency, by a preponderance of the evidence. All questions that may arise shall be decided and all other proceedings shall be conducted as in an ordinary civil action. A judgment of forfeiture does not require as a condition precedent the conviction of a defendant of an offense which made the vehicle subject to forfeiture. The filing of a claim within the time limits specified in paragraph (3) is considered a jurisdictional prerequisite for the availing of the action authorized by that paragraph.

(6) All right, title, and interest in the vehicle shall vest in the state upon commission of the act giving rise to the forfeiture.

(7) The filing fee in paragraph (4) shall be distributed as follows:

(A) To the county law library fund as provided in Section 6320 of the Business and Professions Code, the amount specified in Sections 6321 and 6322.1 of the Business and Professions Code.

(B) To the Trial Court Trust Fund, the remainder of the fee.

(f) Any vehicle impounded that is not redeemed pursuant to subdivision (d) and is subsequently forfeited pursuant to this section shall be sold once an order of forfeiture is issued by the district attorney of the county of the impounding agency or a court, as the case may be, pursuant to subdivision (e).

(g) Any legal owner who is a motor vehicle dealer, bank, credit union, acceptance corporation, or other licensed financial institution legally operating in this state, or the agent of that legal owner, may take possession and conduct the sale of the forfeited vehicle if the legal owner or agent notifies the agency impounding the vehicle of its intent to conduct the sale within 15 days of the mailing of the notice pursuant to subdivision (e). Sale of the vehicle after forfeiture pursuant to this subdivision may be conducted at the time, in the manner, and on the notice usually given for the sale of repossessed or surrendered vehicles. The proceeds of any sale conducted by or on behalf of the legal owner shall be disposed of as provided in subdivision (i). A notice pursuant to this subdivision may be presented in person, by certified mail, by facsimile transmission, or by electronic mail.

(h) If the legal owner or agent of the owner does not notify the agency impounding the vehicle of its intent to conduct the sale as provided in subdivision (g), the agency shall offer the forfeited vehicle for sale at public auction within 60 days of receiving title to the vehicle. Low value vehicles shall be disposed of pursuant to subdivision (k).

(i) The proceeds of a sale of a forfeited vehicle shall be disposed of in the following priority:

(1) To satisfy the towing and storage costs following impoundment, the costs of providing notice pursuant to subdivision (e), the costs of sale, and the unfunded costs of judicial proceedings, if any.

(2) To the legal owner in an amount to satisfy the indebtedness owed to the legal owner remaining as of the date of sale, including accrued interest or finance charges and delinquency charges, providing that the principal indebtedness was incurred prior to the date of impoundment.

(3) To the holder of any subordinate lien or encumbrance on the vehicle, other than a registered or legal owner, to satisfy any indebtedness so secured if written notification of demand is received before distribution of the proceeds is completed. The holder of a subordinate lien or encumbrance, if requested, shall furnish reasonable proof of its interest and, unless it does so upon request, is not entitled to distribution pursuant to this paragraph.

(4) To any other person, other than a registered or legal owner, who can reasonably establish an interest in the vehicle, including a community property interest, to the extent of his or her provable interest, if written notification is received before distribution of the proceeds is completed.

(5) Of the remaining proceeds, funds shall be made available to pay any local agency and court costs, that are reasonably related to the implementation of this section, that remain unsatisfied.

(6) Of the remaining proceeds, half shall be transferred to the Controller for deposit in the Vehicle Inspection and Repair Fund for the high-polluter repair assistance and removal program created by Article 9 (commencing with Section 44090) of Chapter 5 of Part 5 of Division 26 of the Health and Safety Code, and half shall be transferred to the general fund of the city or county of the impounding agency, or the city or county where the impoundment occurred. A portion of the local funds may be used to establish a reward fund for persons coming forward with information leading to the arrest and conviction of hit-and-run drivers and to publicize the availability of the reward fund.

(j) The person conducting the sale shall disburse the proceeds of the sale as provided in subdivision (i) and shall provide a written accounting regarding the disposition to the impounding agency and, on request, to any person entitled to or claiming a share of the proceeds, within 15 days after the sale is conducted.

(k) If the vehicle to be sold pursuant to this section is not of the type that can readily be sold to the public generally, the vehicle shall be conveyed to a licensed dismantler or donated to an eleemosynary institution. License plates shall be removed from any vehicle conveyed to a dismantler pursuant to this subdivision.

(*l*) No vehicle shall be sold pursuant to this section if the impounding agency determines the vehicle to have been stolen. In this event, the vehicle may be claimed by the registered owner at any time after impoundment, providing the vehicle registration is current and the registered owner has no outstanding traffic violations or parking penalties on his or her driving record or on the registration record of any vehicle registered to the person. If the identity of the legal and registered owners of the vehicle cannot be reasonably ascertained, the vehicle may be sold.

(m) Any owner of a vehicle who suffers any loss due to the impoundment or forfeiture of any vehicle pursuant to this section may recover the amount of the loss from the unlicensed, suspended, or revoked driver. If possession of a vehicle has been tendered to a business establishment in good faith, and an unlicensed driver employed or otherwise directed by the business establishment is the cause of the impoundment of the vehicle, a registered owner of the impounded vehicle may recover damages for the loss of use of the vehicle from the business establishment.

(n)(1) The impounding agency, if requested to do so not later than 10 days after the date the vehicle was impounded, shall provide the opportunity for a poststorage hearing to determine the validity of the storage to the persons who were the registered and legal owners of the vehicle at the time of impoundment, except that the hearing shall be requested within three days after the date the vehicle was impounded if personal service was provided to a registered owner pursuant to paragraph (2) of subdivision (e) and no mailed notice is required.

(2) The poststorage hearing shall be conducted not later than two days after the date it was requested. The impounding agency may authorize its own officer or employee to conduct the hearing if the hearing officer is not the same person who directed the storage of the vehicle. Failure of either the registered or legal owner to request a hearing as provided in paragraph (1) or to attend a scheduled hearing shall satisfy the poststorage hearing requirement.

(3) The agency employing the person who directed the storage is responsible for the costs incurred for towing and storage if it is determined that the driver at the time of impoundment had a valid driver's license.

(*o*) As used in this section, "days" means workdays not including weekends and holidays.

(p) Charges for towing and storage for any vehicle impounded pursuant to this section shall not exceed the normal towing and storage rates for other vehicle towing and storage conducted by the impounding agency in the normal course of business.

(q) The Judicial Council and the Department of Justice may prescribe standard forms and procedures for implementation of this section to be used by all jurisdictions throughout the state.

(r) The impounding agency may act as the agent of the state in carrying out this section.

(s) No vehicle shall be impounded pursuant to this section if the driver has a valid license but the license is for a class of vehicle other than the vehicle operated by the driver.

(t) This section does not apply to vehicles subject to Sections 14608 and 14609, if there has been compliance with the procedures in those sections.

(u) As used in this section, "district attorney" includes a city attorney charged with the duty of prosecuting misdemeanor offenses.

(v) The agent of a legal owner acting pursuant to subdivision (g) shall be licensed, or exempt from licensure, pursuant to Chapter 11 (commencing with Section 7500) of Division 3 of the Business and Professions Code. *(Added by Stats.1994, c. 1133 (A.B.3148), § 12. Amended by Stats.1995, c. 404 (S.B.240), § 4; Stats.1998, c. 582 (S.B.117), § 6; Stats.1998, c. 931 (S.B.2139), § 457, eff. Sept. 28, 1998; Stats.1998, c. 931 (S.B.2139), § 457.5, eff. Sept. 28, 1998, operative Jan. 1, 1999; Stats.2005, c. 75 (A.B.145), § 151, eff. July 19, 2005, operative Jan. 1, 2006.)*

Cross References

Burden of proof, generally, see Evidence Code § 500 et seq.
Deposit of fees or fines collected pursuant to this section in the Trial Court Trust Fund, effect of prior agreements or practices, long-term revenue allocation schedule proposal, see Government Code § 68085.5.
Maintenance of records, stipulated vehicle release agreements entered into pursuant to this section, see Vehicle Code § 1806.1
Misdemeanors, definition and penalties, see Penal Code §§ 17, 19 and 19.2.
Organization and government of courts, collection of fees and fines pursuant to this section, distributions, see Government Code § 68085.1.
State Controller, generally, see Government Code § 12402 et seq.
Title transfer fees for vehicles transferred pursuant to this section, see Vehicle Code § 9255.3.

Research References

West's California Judicial Council Forms MC–202, Petition for Forfeiture of Vehicle and Notice of Hearing.
3 Witkin, California Criminal Law 4th Punishment § 190 (2021), Noncriminal Actions.

3 Witkin, California Criminal Law 4th Punishment § 195 (2021), Impounding of Motor Vehicles.

§ 14607.8. Motor vehicles subject to forfeiture as a nuisance; first misdemeanor convictions

Upon a first misdemeanor conviction of a violation of subdivision (a) of Section 12500 or Section 14601, 14601.1, 14601.2, 14601.3, 14601.4, or 14601.5, the court shall inform the defendant that, pursuant to Section 14607.6, a motor vehicle is subject to forfeiture as a nuisance if it is driven on a highway in this state by a driver with a suspended or revoked license, or by an unlicensed driver, who is a registered owner of the vehicle and has a previous misdemeanor conviction for a violation of subdivision (a) of Section 12500 or Section 14601, 14601.1, 14601.2, 14601.3, 14601.4, or 14601.5. *(Added by Stats.1994, c. 1133 (A.B.3148), § 13.)*

Cross References

Misdemeanors, definition and penalties, see Penal Code §§ 17, 19 and 19.2.

§ 14608. Rental of vehicles; requirements; rental to blind or disabled persons who are nondrivers

(a) A person shall not rent a motor vehicle to another person unless both of the following requirements have been met:

(1) The person to whom the vehicle is rented is licensed under this code or is a nonresident who is licensed under the laws of the state or country of his or her residence.

(2) The person renting to another person has inspected the driver's license of the person to whom the vehicle is to be rented and compared either the signature thereon with that of the person to whom the vehicle is to be rented or the photograph thereon with the person to whom the vehicle is to be rented.

(b) This section does not prohibit a blind or disabled person who is a nondriver from renting a motor vehicle if both of the following conditions exist at the time of rental:

(1) The blind or disabled person either holds an identification card issued pursuant to this code or is not a resident of this state.

(2) The blind or disabled person has a driver present who is either licensed to drive a vehicle pursuant to this code or is a nonresident licensed to drive a vehicle pursuant to the laws of the state or country of the driver's residence. *(Stats.1959, c. 3, p. 1634, § 14608. Amended by Stats.1993, c. 1292 (S.B.274), § 11; Stats.2012, c. 406 (A.B.2659), § 2; Stats.2012, c. 862 (A.B.2189), § 4.)*

Cross References

Duties of persons renting automobiles to keep records, see Vehicle Code § 14609.
Issuance and contents of license, see Vehicle Code § 12811.
Nonresident defined, see Vehicle Code § 435.
Persons who must be licensed, see Vehicle Code § 12500 et seq.
Vehicle rental agreements, rental company not subject to requirements of this section, conditions, see Civil Code § 1939.37.

Research References

California Jury Instructions-Civil, 8th Edition 13.80, Negligent Entrustment of Vehicle—Special Findings.
2 Witkin, California Criminal Law 4th Crimes Against Public Peace and Welfare § 309 (2021), Permitting Unlicensed Person to Drive.

§ 14609. Records of rental

(a) Every person renting a motor vehicle to another person shall keep a record of the registration number of the motor vehicle rented, the name and address of the person to whom the vehicle is rented, his or her driver's license number, the jurisdiction that issued the driver's license, and the expiration date of the driver's license.

(b) If the person renting the vehicle is a nondriver pursuant to subdivision (c) of Section 14608, the record maintained pursuant to this section shall include the name and address of the person renting the vehicle and, if applicable, his or her identification card number, the jurisdiction that issued the identification card, and the expiration date of the identification card. The record shall also include the name and address of the licensed driver, his or her driver's license number, and the expiration date of his or her driver's license. *(Stats.1959, c. 3, p. 1634, § 14609. Amended by Stats.1975, c. 389, p. 867, § 6; Stats.1993, c. 1292 (S.B.274), § 12.)*

Research References

2 Witkin, California Criminal Law 4th Crimes Against Public Peace and Welfare § 309 (2021), Permitting Unlicensed Person to Drive.

§ 14610. Unlawful use of license; license defined

(a) It is unlawful for any person:

(1) To display or cause or permit to be displayed or have in his possession any canceled, revoked, suspended, fictitious, fraudulently altered, or fraudulently obtained driver's license.

(2) To lend his driver's license to any other person or knowingly permit the use thereof by another.

(3) To display or represent any driver's license not issued to him as being his license.

(4) To fail or refuse to surrender to the department upon its lawful demand any driver's license which has been suspended, revoked or canceled.

(5) To permit any unlawful use of a driver's license issued to him.

(6) To do any act forbidden or fail to perform any act required by this division.

(7) To photograph, photostat, duplicate, or in any way reproduce any driver's license or facsimile thereof in such a manner that it could be mistaken for a valid license, or to display or have in his possession any such photograph, photostat, duplicate, reproduction, or facsimile unless authorized by the provisions of this code.

(8) To alter any driver's license in any manner not authorized by this code.

(b) For purposes of this section, "driver's license" includes a temporary permit to operate a motor vehicle. *(Stats.1959, c. 3. p. 1634, § 14610. Amended by Stats.1967, c. 545, p. 1894, § 1; Stats.1971, c. 1174, p. 2240, § 4, operative May 3, 1972; Stats.1990, c. 44 (A.B.1648), § 5.)*

Cross References

Cancellation, suspension and revocation of license by department, see Vehicle Code § 13350 et seq.
Contents,
  Application for license, see Vehicle Code § 12800.
  License, see Vehicle Code § 12811.
Minor's use of fraudulent license for purpose of purchasing or leasing a vehicle, see Vehicle Code § 15501.
Permitting unlicensed person to drive, see Vehicle Code § 14606.
Person defined, see Vehicle Code § 470.
Procedure upon revocation, suspension or cancellation, see Vehicle Code § 13351.
Suspension or revocation of license by court, see Vehicle Code § 13200 et seq.
Violation a misdemeanor, see Vehicle Code § 40000.11.

Research References

2 Witkin, California Criminal Law 4th Crimes Against Property § 199 (2021), Motor Vehicle Items.
2 Witkin, California Criminal Law 4th Crimes Against Public Peace and Welfare § 310 (2021), Unlawful Use of License.

§ 14610.1. Manufacture or sale of similar identification document prohibited; penalties; other prosecution not precluded

(a) A person shall not manufacture or sell an identification document of a size and form substantially similar to, or that purports to confer the same privileges as, the drivers' licenses issued by the department.

(b) A violation of this section is a misdemeanor punishable as follows:

(1) The court shall impose a fine of not less than two hundred fifty dollars ($250) and not more than one thousand dollars ($1,000), and 24 hours of community service, to be served when the person is not employed or is not attending school. No part of the fine or community service shall be suspended or waived.

(2) In lieu of the penalties imposed under paragraph (1), the court, in its discretion, may impose a jail term of up to one year and a fine of up to one thousand dollars ($1,000). In exercising its discretion the court shall consider the extent of the defendant's commercial motivation for the offense.

(c) Prosecution under this section shall not preclude prosecution under any other applicable provision of law. *(Added by Stats.1990, c. 170 (S.B.1873), § 2. Amended by Stats.2007, c. 743 (A.B.1658), § 6; Stats.2010, c. 684 (A.B.2471), § 2.)*

Cross References

Identification cards, manufacture or sale of similar identification document prohibited, see Vehicle Code § 13004.1.
Misdemeanors, definition and penalties, see Penal Code §§ 17, 19 and 19.2.

§ 14610.5. Unlawful sale, offer to sell, distribution or use of crib sheet or cribbing device; unlawful impersonation; punishment

(a) It is unlawful for any person to do any of the following:

(1) Sell, offer for sale, distribute, or use any crib sheet or cribbing device that contains the answers to any examination administered by the department for any class of driver's license, permit, or certificate.

(2) Impersonate or allow the impersonation of an applicant for any class of driver's license, permit, or certificate for the purpose of fraudulently qualifying the applicant for any class of driver's license, permit, or certificate.

(b) A first conviction under this section is punishable as either an infraction or a misdemeanor; a second or subsequent conviction is punishable as a misdemeanor. *(Added by Stats.1986, c. 960, § 2. Amended by Stats.1995, c. 243 (S.B.307), § 1.)*

Cross References

Crib sheet or cribbing device defined, see Vehicle Code § 273.
License examination and driving test, see Vehicle Code §§ 12803, 12804.9.
Misdemeanors, definition and penalties, see Penal Code §§ 17, 19 and 19.2.

§ 14610.7. Assisting in obtaining a license or identification card for persons present in United States in violation of federal law

It is a misdemeanor for any person to knowingly assist in obtaining a driver's license or identification card for any person whose presence in the United States is not authorized under federal law. *(Added by Stats.1993, c. 820 (S.B.976), § 3.)*

Cross References

License requirements, authorized presence in United States under federal law, see Vehicle Code § 12801.5.
Misdemeanors, definition and penalties, see Penal Code §§ 17, 19 and 19.2.

§ 14611. Vehicles transporting highway route controlled quantity of Class 7 radioactive materials; directing operation of vehicle with driver not possessing training certificate and proper license; penalty

(a) A person shall not knowingly direct the operation of a vehicle transporting a highway route controlled quantity of Class 7 radioactive materials, as defined in Section 173.403 of Title 49 of the Code of Federal Regulations, by a person who does not possess a training certificate pursuant to Section 12524 and a valid driver's license of the appropriate class.

(b) A person convicted under this section shall be punished by a fine of not less than five thousand dollars ($5,000) nor more than ten thousand dollars ($10,000). *(Added by Stats.1983, c. 893, § 5, operative July 1, 1984. Amended by Stats.2010, c. 491 (S.B.1318), § 38; Stats.2017, c. 397 (S.B.810), § 5, eff. Jan. 1, 2018.)*

Cross References

Driver's license and certification for hauling fissile class III shipments or large quantity radioactive materials, see Vehicle Code § 12524.

Division 6.5

MOTOR VEHICLE TRANSACTIONS WITH MINORS

CHAPTER 1. DRIVER'S LICENSE REQUIREMENTS

§ 15500. Acquisition of vehicle by minor; driver's license required

It is unlawful for any minor who does not possess a valid driver's license issued under this code to order, purchase or lease, attempt to purchase or lease, contract to purchase or lease, accept, or otherwise obtain, any vehicle of a type subject to registration. *(Added by Stats.1968, c. 1020, p. 1972, § 1.)*

§ 15501. Unlawful for minor to present false driver's license

It is unlawful for any minor to present or offer to any person offering for sale or lease or to give or otherwise furnish thereto any motor vehicle of a type subject to registration, a driver's license which is false, fraudulent, or not actually his own for the purpose of ordering, purchasing or leasing, attempting to purchase or lease, contracting to purchase or lease, accepting, or otherwise obtaining such a vehicle. *(Added by Stats.1968, c. 1020, p. 1972, § 1.)*

Cross References

Unlawful use of driver's license, see Vehicle Code § 14610.
Violation a misdemeanor, see Vehicle Code § 40000.11.

Division 10

ACCIDENTS AND ACCIDENT REPORTS

CHAPTER 1. ACCIDENTS AND ACCIDENT REPORTS

§ 20000. Application of division

The provisions of this division apply upon highways and elsewhere throughout the State, unless expressly provided otherwise. *(Stats. 1959, c. 3, p. 1661, § 20000.)*

Cross References

Administration and enforcement, see Vehicle Code § 2800 et seq.
Highway defined, see Vehicle Code § 360.
Rules of the road, applicability to animals, see Vehicle Code § 21050.
Uniformity of code, see Vehicle Code § 21.

Research References

2 Witkin, California Criminal Law 4th Crimes Against Public Peace and Welfare § 311 (2021), In General.
2 Witkin, California Criminal Law 4th Crimes Against Public Peace and Welfare § 530 (2021), Bicycles.
2 Witkin, California Criminal Law 4th Crimes Against Public Peace and Welfare § 531 (2021), Low-Speed Vehicles and Motorized Scooters.

§ 20001. Duty to stop at scene of injury accident; penalties

(a) The driver of a vehicle involved in an accident resulting in injury to a person, other than himself or herself, or in the death of a person shall immediately stop the vehicle at the scene of the accident and shall fulfill the requirements of Sections 20003 and 20004.

(b)(1) Except as provided in paragraph (2), a person who violates subdivision (a) shall be punished by imprisonment in the state prison, or in a county jail for not more than one year, or by a fine of not less than one thousand dollars ($1,000) nor more than ten thousand dollars ($10,000), or by both that imprisonment and fine.

(2) If the accident described in subdivision (a) results in death or permanent, serious injury, a person who violates subdivision (a) shall be punished by imprisonment in the state prison for two, three, or four years, or in a county jail for not less than 90 days nor more than one year, or by a fine of not less than one thousand dollars ($1,000) nor more than ten thousand dollars ($10,000), or by both that imprisonment and fine. However, the court, in the interests of justice and for reasons stated in the record, may reduce or eliminate the minimum imprisonment required by this paragraph.

(3) In imposing the minimum fine required by this subdivision, the court shall take into consideration the defendant's ability to pay the fine and, in the interests of justice and for reasons stated in the record, may reduce the amount of that minimum fine to less than the amount otherwise required by this subdivision.

(c) A person who flees the scene of the crime after committing a violation of Section 191.5 of, or paragraph (1) of subdivision (c) of Section 192 of the Penal Code, upon conviction of any of those sections, in addition and consecutive to the punishment prescribed, shall be punished by an additional term of imprisonment of five years in the state prison. This additional term shall not be imposed unless the allegation is charged in the accusatory pleading and admitted by the defendant or found to be true by the trier of fact. The court shall not strike a finding that brings a person within the provisions of this subdivision or an allegation made pursuant to this subdivision.

(d) As used in this section, "permanent, serious injury" means the loss or permanent impairment of function of a bodily member or organ. *(Stats.1959, c. 3, p. 1661, § 20001. Amended by Stats.1967, c. 652, p. 2009, § 1; Stats.1976, c. 1139, p. 5171, § 337, operative July 1, 1977; Stats.1983, c. 1092, § 389, eff. Sept. 29, 1983, operative Jan. 1, 1984; Stats.1988, c. 1207, § 1; Stats.1992, c. 501 (S.B.143), § 1; Stats.1996, c. 645 (A.B.1985), § 4; Stats.1999, c. 854 (S.B.1282), § 1, eff. Oct. 10, 1999; Stats.2007, c. 747 (A.B.678), § 30.)*

Cross References

Accident report forms, see Vehicle Code § 2407.
Applicability of this section to trolley coaches, see Vehicle Code § 21051.
Conviction of a violation of this section as a ground for cancelling, suspending or revoking license to teach driving, see Vehicle Code § 11110.
Crime of violence, within act for indemnification of victims of crime, see Government Code § 13960.
Definitions,
Driver, see Vehicle Code § 305.
Negligent operator, see Vehicle Code § 12810.
Vehicle, see Vehicle Code § 670.
Department of the California highway patrol,
Accident report forms, see Vehicle Code § 2407.
Dissemination of traffic accident information, see Vehicle Code § 2408.
Investigation of accidents, see Vehicle Code § 2412.
Tabulation and analyzation of accident reports, see Vehicle Code § 2408.
Non-compliance with this section as a ground for revoking license, see Vehicle Code § 13350.
Number of convictions for prima facie presumption as negligent operator, see Vehicle Code § 12810.
Public offense defined, see Penal Code § 15.
Records to be kept by department of motor vehicles, see Vehicle Code § 1800.
Report of accident or conviction, see Vehicle Code § 1806.
Revocation of driver's license, juvenile offenders, see Vehicle Code § 13355.
Revocation or suspension of occupational licenses, see Vehicle Code § 11110.
Time of commencing criminal actions, tolling or extension of time periods, see Penal Code § 803.
Traffic violation point count, violation of this section, see Vehicle Code § 12810.
Traffic violator schools, suspension or revocation of license for violation of this section, see Vehicle Code § 11215.
Yellow alert, activation requirements, report, see Government Code § 8594.15.

Research References

California Jury Instructions - Criminal 1.21, "Knowingly"—Defined.
California Jury Instructions - Criminal 8.98, Felony Vehicular Manslaughter—Fleeing Scene Enhancement.
California Jury Instructions - Criminal 12.70, Felony Hit and Run.
California Jury Instructions - Criminal 17.01, Verdict May be Based on One of a Number of Unlawful Acts.
2 Witkin, California Criminal Law 4th Crimes Against Public Peace and Welfare § 311 (2021), In General.
2 Witkin, California Criminal Law 4th Crimes Against Public Peace and Welfare § 312 (2021), Accident Causing Injury or Death.
2 Witkin, California Criminal Law 4th Crimes Against Public Peace and Welfare § 313 (2021), Accident Causing Property Damage.
2 Witkin, California Criminal Law 4th Crimes Against Public Peace and Welfare § 314 (2021), Persons Subject to Prosecution.
2 Witkin, California Criminal Law 4th Crimes Against Public Peace and Welfare § 315 (2021), What Constitutes Involvement in Accident.
2 Witkin, California Criminal Law 4th Crimes Against Public Peace and Welfare § 316 (2021), Duty to Stop.
2 Witkin, California Criminal Law 4th Crimes Against Public Peace and Welfare § 317 (2021), Illustrations of Violation.
2 Witkin, California Criminal Law 4th Crimes Against Public Peace and Welfare § 319 (2021), Knowledge of Accident.
2 Witkin, California Criminal Law 4th Crimes Against Public Peace and Welfare § 530 (2021), Bicycles.
1 Witkin California Criminal Law 4th Crimes Against the Person § 262 (2021), In General.

1 Witkin California Criminal Law 4th Crimes Against the Person § 264 (2021), Liability of Passenger.
1 Witkin California Criminal Law 4th Crimes Against the Person § 269 (2021), Punishment.
1 Witkin California Criminal Law 4th Defenses § 258 (2021), In General.
1 Witkin California Criminal Law 4th Introduction to Crimes § 96 (2021), Different Treatment of Perpetrator and Abettor.
4 Witkin, California Criminal Law 4th Pretrial Proceedings § 208 (2021), Simplified Pleading.
3 Witkin, California Criminal Law 4th Punishment § 120 (2021), Damages Recoverable.
3 Witkin, California Criminal Law 4th Punishment § 279 (2021), Homicide and Other Crimes.
3 Witkin, California Criminal Law 4th Punishment § 350 (2021), General Provision.

§ 20002. Duty where property damaged

(a) The driver of any vehicle involved in an accident resulting only in damage to any property, including vehicles, shall immediately stop the vehicle at the nearest location that will not impede traffic or otherwise jeopardize the safety of other motorists. Moving the vehicle in accordance with this subdivision does not affect the question of fault. The driver shall also immediately do either of the following:

(1) Locate and notify the owner or person in charge of that property of the name and address of the driver and owner of the vehicle involved and, upon locating the driver of any other vehicle involved or the owner or person in charge of any damaged property, upon being requested, present his or her driver's license, and vehicle registration, to the other driver, property owner, or person in charge of that property. The information presented shall include the current residence address of the driver and of the registered owner. If the registered owner of an involved vehicle is present at the scene, he or she shall also, upon request, present his or her driver's license information, if available, or other valid identification to the other involved parties.

(2) Leave in a conspicuous place on the vehicle or other property damaged a written notice giving the name and address of the driver and of the owner of the vehicle involved and a statement of the circumstances thereof and shall without unnecessary delay notify the police department of the city wherein the collision occurred or, if the collision occurred in unincorporated territory, the local headquarters of the Department of the California Highway Patrol.

(b) Any person who parks a vehicle which, prior to the vehicle again being driven, becomes a runaway vehicle and is involved in an accident resulting in damage to any property, attended or unattended, shall comply with the requirements of this section relating to notification and reporting and shall, upon conviction thereof, be liable to the penalties of this section for failure to comply with the requirements.

(c) Any person failing to comply with all the requirements of this section is guilty of a misdemeanor and, upon conviction thereof, shall be punished by imprisonment in the county jail not exceeding six months, or by a fine not exceeding one thousand dollars ($1,000), or by both that imprisonment and fine. *(Formerly § 20007, enacted by Stats.1959, c. 3, p. 1662, § 20007. Amended by Stats.1963, c. 406, p. 1213, § 1. Renumbered § 20002 and amended by Stats.1965, c. 872, p. 2474, § 3. Amended by Stats.1967, c. 652, p. 2009, § 2; Stats.1980, c. 680, p. 2063, § 1; Stats.1983, c. 1092, § 390, eff. Sept. 27, 1983, operative Jan. 1, 1984; Stats.1991, c. 1103 (S.B.148), § 2; Stats.1992, c. 621 (A.B.2517), § 3; Stats.1999, c. 421 (S.B.681), § 1; Stats.2001, c. 825 (S.B.290), § 16.)*

Cross References

Applicability of this section to trolley coaches, see Vehicle Code § 21051.
Conviction of violation of this section as ground for cancelling, suspending or revoking license to teach driving, see Vehicle Code § 11110.
Conviction under this section counted as two convictions for prima facie presumption as negligent operator, see Vehicle Code § 12810.
Driver's license, suspension or revocation by department, see Vehicle Code § 13350.
Guilty plea, see Vehicle Code § 41610.
Impounding vehicles for investigations, see Vehicle Code § 22655.
Procedure on arrest for violation of this section, see Vehicle Code § 40303.
Revocation of driver's license, juvenile offenders, see Vehicle Code § 13355.
Suspension of driver's license, grounds, see Vehicle Code § 13361.
Suspension of license by court upon conviction for violating this section, see Vehicle Code § 13201.
Traffic violation point count, violation of this section, see Vehicle Code § 12810.
Traffic violator schools, suspension or revocation of license for violation of this section, see Vehicle Code § 11215.
Violation as misdemeanor, see Vehicle Code § 40000.13.

Research References

California Jury Instructions - Criminal 1.21, "Knowingly"—Defined.
California Jury Instructions - Criminal 12.70, Felony Hit and Run.
California Jury Instructions - Criminal 16.650, Misdemeanor Hit and Run.
2 Witkin, California Criminal Law 4th Crimes Against Governmental Authority § 26 (2021), Misdemeanor Hit-And-Run Violations.
2 Witkin, California Criminal Law 4th Crimes Against Public Peace and Welfare § 311 (2021), In General.
2 Witkin, California Criminal Law 4th Crimes Against Public Peace and Welfare § 313 (2021), Accident Causing Property Damage.
2 Witkin, California Criminal Law 4th Crimes Against Public Peace and Welfare § 315 (2021), What Constitutes Involvement in Accident.
3 Witkin, California Criminal Law 4th Punishment § 658 (2021), Condition is Proper When Related to Crime for Which Convicted.

§ 20003. Duty upon injury or death

(a) The driver of any vehicle involved in an accident resulting in injury to or death of any person shall also give his or her name, current residence address, the names and current residence addresses of any occupant of the driver's vehicle injured in the accident, the registration number of the vehicle he or she is driving, and the name and current residence address of the owner to the person struck or the driver or occupants of any vehicle collided with, and shall give the information to any traffic or police officer at the scene of the accident. The driver also shall render to any person injured in the accident reasonable assistance, including transporting, or making arrangements for transporting, any injured person to a physician, surgeon, or hospital for medical or surgical treatment if it is apparent that treatment is necessary or if that transportation is requested by any injured person.

(b) Any driver or injured occupant of a driver's vehicle subject to the provisions of subdivision (a) shall also, upon being requested, exhibit his or her driver's license, if available, or, in the case of an injured occupant, any other available identification, to the person struck or to the driver or occupants of any vehicle collided with, and to any traffic or police officer at the scene of the accident. *(Stats.1959, c. 3, p. 1661, § 20003. Amended by Stats.1980, c. 680, p. 2064, § 2; Stats.1991, c. 1103 (S.B.148), § 3; Stats.1992, c. 621 (A.B.2517), § 4; Stats.1994, c. 1247 (A.B.1926), § 9.)*

Cross References

Applicability of this section to trolley coaches, see Vehicle Code § 21051.
Conviction of a violation of this section as a ground for cancelling, suspending or revoking license to teach driving, see Vehicle Code § 11110.
Impounding vehicle for investigation on reasonable belief of failure of compliance with this section, see Vehicle Code § 22655.
Traffic violator schools, suspension or revocation of license for violation of this section, see Vehicle Code § 11215.
Violation as misdemeanor, see Vehicle Code § 40000.13.

Research References

California Jury Instructions - Criminal 1.21, "Knowingly"—Defined.
California Jury Instructions - Criminal 12.70, Felony Hit and Run.
2 Witkin, California Criminal Law 4th Crimes Against Public Peace and Welfare § 311 (2021), In General.
2 Witkin, California Criminal Law 4th Crimes Against Public Peace and Welfare § 312 (2021), Accident Causing Injury or Death.

2 Witkin, California Criminal Law 4th Crimes Against Public Peace and Welfare § 317 (2021), Illustrations of Violation.
2 Witkin, California Criminal Law 4th Crimes Against Public Peace and Welfare § 319 (2021), Knowledge of Accident.

§ 20004. Duty upon death

In the event of death of any person resulting from an accident, the driver of any vehicle involved after fulfilling the requirements of this division, and if there be no traffic or police officer at the scene of the accident to whom to give the information required by Section 20003, shall, without delay, report the accident to the nearest office of the Department of the California Highway Patrol or office of a duly authorized police authority and submit with the report the information required by Section 20003. *(Stats.1959, c. 3, p. 1661, § 20004.)*

Cross References

Applicability of this section to trolley coaches, see Vehicle Code § 21051.
Impounding vehicles for investigations, see Vehicle Code § 22655.
Revocation or suspension of occupational licenses, see Vehicle Code § 11110.
Traffic violator schools, suspension or revocation of license for violation of this section, see Vehicle Code § 11215.

Research References

California Jury Instructions - Criminal 1.21, "Knowingly"—Defined.
California Jury Instructions - Criminal 12.70, Felony Hit and Run.

§ 20006. Driver without license

If the driver does not have his driver's license in his possession, he shall exhibit other valid evidences of identification to the occupants of a vehicle with which he collided. *(Stats.1959, c. 3, p. 1662, § 20006.)*

Cross References

Applicability of this section to trolley coaches, see Vehicle Code § 21051.
Impounding vehicles for investigations, see Vehicle Code § 22655.
Revocation or suspension of occupational licenses, see Vehicle Code § 11110.
Traffic violator schools, suspension or revocation of license for violation of this section, see Vehicle Code § 11215.

Research References

2 Witkin, California Criminal Law 4th Crimes Against Public Peace and Welfare § 312 (2021), Accident Causing Injury or Death.

§ 20008. Duty to report accidents

(a) The driver of a vehicle, other than a common carrier vehicle, involved in any accident resulting in injuries to or death of any person shall within 24 hours after the accident make or cause to be made a written report of the accident to the Department of the California Highway Patrol or, if the accident occurred within a city, to either the Department of the California Highway Patrol or the police department of the city in which the accident occurred. If the agency which receives the report is not responsible for investigating the accident, it shall immediately forward the report to the law enforcement agency which is responsible for investigating the accident.

On or before the fifth day of each month, every police department which received a report during the previous calendar month of an accident which it is responsible for investigating shall forward the report or a copy thereof to the main office of the Department of the California Highway Patrol at Sacramento.

(b) The owner or driver of a common carrier vehicle involved in any such accident shall make a like report to the Department of California Highway Patrol on or before the 10th day of the month following the accident. *(Stats.1959, c. 3, § 20008. Amended by Stats.1970, c. 224, p. 474, § 1.)*

Cross References

Accident reports as evidence, see Vehicle Code § 20013.
Applicability of this section to trolley coaches, see Vehicle Code § 21051.
Confidential nature of report, see Vehicle Code § 20012.
Department of motor vehicles to prescribe forms, see Vehicle Code § 1652.
Department of the California Highway Patrol,
Accident report forms, duty to supply, see Vehicle Code § 2407.
Dissemination of traffic accident information, see Vehicle Code § 2408.
Investigation of accidents, see Vehicle Code § 2412.
Tabulation and analyzation of accident reports, see Vehicle Code § 2408.
Driving schools and driving instructors, revocation or suspension of license for violation of this section, see Vehicle Code § 11110.
Physical inability to report, see Vehicle Code § 20010.
Traffic violator schools, suspension or revocation of license for violation of this section, see Vehicle Code § 11215.

Research References

2 Witkin, California Criminal Law 4th Crimes Against Public Peace and Welfare § 312 (2021), Accident Causing Injury or Death.

§ 20009. Supplemental reports

The Department of the California Highway Patrol may require any driver, or the owner of a common carrier vehicle, involved in any accident of which a report must be made as provided in Section 20008 to file supplemental reports and may require witnesses of accidents to render reports to it whenever the original report is insufficient in the opinion of such department. *(Stats.1959, c. 3, p. 1663, § 20009.)*

Cross References

Accident reports as evidence, see Vehicle Code § 20013.
Applicability of this section to trolley coaches, see Vehicle Code § 21051.
Confidential nature of report, see Vehicle Code § 20012.
Department of California highway patrol,
Accident report forms, duty to supply, see Vehicle Code § 2407.
Dissemination of traffic accident information, see Vehicle Code § 2408.
Investigation of accidents, see Vehicle Code § 2412.
Tabulation and analyzation of accident reports, see Vehicle Code § 2408.
Department of motor vehicles to prescribe forms, see Vehicle Code § 1652.

Research References

2 Witkin, California Criminal Law 4th Crimes Against Public Peace and Welfare § 312 (2021), Accident Causing Injury or Death.

§ 20010. Driver unable to report

Whenever the driver of a vehicle is physically incapable of making a required accident report, any occupant in the vehicle at the time of the accident shall make the report or cause it to be made. *(Stats.1959, c. 3, p. 1663, § 20010.)*

Research References

2 Witkin, California Criminal Law 4th Crimes Against Public Peace and Welfare § 312 (2021), Accident Causing Injury or Death.

§ 20011. Coroner or medical examiner's report

A coroner or medical examiner shall on or before the 10th day of each month report in writing to the Department of the California Highway Patrol the death of any person during the preceding calendar month as the result of an accident involving a motor vehicle and the circumstances of the accident. Chemical test results, including blood alcohol content and blood drug concentrations, shall be reported in writing when available. *(Stats.1959, c. 3, p. 1663, § 20011. Amended by Stats.2022, c. 223 (S.B.925), § 2, eff. Jan. 1, 2023.)*

§ 20012. Reports confidential; exceptions; copies; fee

All required accident reports, and supplemental reports, shall be without prejudice to the individual so reporting and shall be for the confidential use of the Department of Motor Vehicles and the Department of the California Highway Patrol, except that the Department of the California Highway Patrol or the law enforcement agency to whom the accident was reported shall disclose the entire contents of the reports, including, but not limited to, the names and addresses of persons involved or injured in, or witnesses to, an accident, the registration numbers and descriptions of vehicles involved, the date, time and location of an accident, all diagrams, statements of the drivers involved or occupants injured in the accident and the statements of all witnesses, to any person who may have a proper interest therein, including, but not limited to, the driver or drivers involved, or the guardian or conservator thereof, the parent of a minor driver, the authorized representative of a driver, or to any named person injured therein, the owners of vehicles or property damaged thereby, persons who may incur civil liability, including liability based upon a breach of warranty arising out of the accident, and any attorney who declares under penalty of perjury that he or she represents any of the above persons.

A request for a copy of an accident report shall be accompanied by payment of a fee, provided such fee shall not exceed the actual cost of providing the copy. *(Stats.1959, c. 3, p. 1663, § 20012. Amended by Stats.1965, c. 1285, p. 3168, § 1; Stats.1969, c. 19, p. 80, § 1; Stats.1979, c. 730, p. 2521, § 115, operative Jan. 1, 1981; Stats.1979, c. 932, p. 3227, § 1; Stats.1979, c. 932, p. 3227, § 2, operative Jan. 1, 1981; Stats.1994, c. 1247 (A.B.1926), § 10.)*

Law Revision Commission Comments

Section 20012 is amended to add the reference to a conservator.

Cross References

Department of highway patrol to tabulate and analyze accident reports, see Vehicle Code § 2408.
Insurance Information and Privacy Protection Act, disclosure of personal or privileged information, see Insurance Code § 791.13.
Use of vehicle report information, see Vehicle Code § 1810.3.

Research References

1 Witkin California Criminal Law 4th Introduction to Crimes § 134 (2021), In General.

§ 20013. Reports as evidence

No such accident report shall be used as evidence in any trial, civil or criminal, arising out of an accident, except that the department shall furnish upon demand of any person who has, or claims to have, made such a report or upon demand of any court, a certificate showing that a specified accident report has or has not been made to the department solely to prove a compliance or failure to comply with the requirement that such a report be made to the department. *(Stats.1959, c. 3, p. 1663, § 20013. Amended by Stats.1959, c. 1996, p. 4629, § 22.)*

§ 20014. Use of reports

All required accident reports and supplemental reports and all reports made to the Department of the California Highway Patrol by any peace officer, member of the Department of the California Highway Patrol, or other employee of the Department of Motor Vehicles and the Department of the California Highway Patrol, shall be immediately available for the confidential use of any division in the department needing the same, for confidential use of the Department of Transportation, and, with respect to accidents occurring on highways other than state highways, for the confidential use of the local authority having jurisdiction over the highway. *(Stats. 1959, c. 3, p. 1663, § 20014. Amended by Stats.1959, c. 1627, p. 3999, § 2; Stats.1974, c. 545, p. 1314, § 167.)*

Cross References

Department of the highway patrol to tabulate and analyze accident reports, see Vehicle Code § 2408.
Use of vehicle report information, see Vehicle Code § 1810.3.

§ 20015. Counter report of a property-damage accident; exclusion of determination of fault; exceptions; definition

(a) No traffic or police officer shall include in any counter report of a property-damage accident, as defined in this section, any determination by the peace officer of fault of the reporting person, including, but not limited to, inattentiveness. This section does not apply to a determination which is the result of an examination of the physical evidence of the accident at the site of the accident by the traffic or police officer or the result of an express, knowing admission of the reporting person if the basis for the determination is also included in the report.

(b) As used in this section, "counter report of a property-damage accident" means any report of an accident involving one or more vehicles which meets the following criteria:

(1) The accident reported caused damage to property, but did not cause personal injury to or the death of any person.

(2) The report is prepared at an office of the California Highway Patrol or local law enforcement agency.

(3) The report is written or recorded by, or with the assistance of, a peace officer. *(Added by Stats.1984, c. 861, § 1.)*

§ 20016. Persons injured on highways

Any peace officer, any member of an organized fire department or fire protection district, any employee of the Department of Transportation assigned to maintenance operations, or any member of the California Highway Patrol may transport or arrange for the transportation of any person injured in an accident upon any highway to a physician and surgeon or hospital, if the injured person does not object to such transportation. Any officer, member, or employee exercising ordinary care and precaution shall not be liable for any damages due to any further injury or for any medical, ambulance, or hospital bills incurred in behalf of the injured party. *(Stats.1959, c. 3, p. 1664, § 20016. Amended by Stats.1967, c. 1000, p. 2592, § 1; Stats.1974, c. 545, p. 1314, § 168.)*

§ 20017. Spill or accidental release of pesticide

Any peace officer who knows, or has reasonable cause to believe, that a pesticide has been spilled or otherwise accidentally released, shall report the spill as required in Section 105215 of the Health and Safety Code. *(Added by Stats.1979, c. 935, p. 3235, § 5. Amended by Stats.1996, c. 1023 (S.B.1497), § 425, eff. Sept. 29, 1996.)*

§ 20018. Written policy for law enforcement officers providing assistance to disabled motorists

Every law enforcement agency having traffic law enforcement responsibility as specified in subdivision (a) of Section 830.1 and in subdivision (a) of Section 830.2 of the Penal Code may develop, adopt, and implement a written policy for its officers to provide assistance to disabled motorists on highways within its primary jurisdiction. A copy of the policy, if adopted, shall be available to the public upon request. *(Added by Stats.1985, c. 1203, § 1. Amended by Stats.1993, c. 59 (S.B.443), § 18, eff. June 30, 1993.)*

Division 11

RULES OF THE ROAD

CHAPTER 1. OBEDIENCE TO AND EFFECT OF TRAFFIC LAWS

ARTICLE 1. DEFINITIONS

§ 21000. Department

Wherever in this division "department" occurs, it means the Department of the California Highway Patrol. *(Stats.1959, c. 3, p. 1664, § 21000.)*

Cross References

Department defined, see Vehicle Code §§ 290, 2101, 24000.
Department of the California highway patrol, generally, see Vehicle Code § 2100 et seq.
Powers and duties of commissioner, see Vehicle Code § 2400 et seq.

Research References

2 Witkin, California Criminal Law 4th Crimes Against Public Peace and Welfare § 530 (2021), Bicycles.
2 Witkin, California Criminal Law 4th Crimes Against Public Peace and Welfare § 531 (2021), Low-Speed Vehicles and Motorized Scooters.
4 Witkin, California Criminal Law 4th Pretrial Proceedings § 60 (2021), Juvenile Offenses.
3 Witkin, California Criminal Law 4th Punishment § 220 (2021), Distinction: Investigation and Hearing.

§ 21001. Scope of division

The provisions of this division refer exclusively to the operation of vehicles upon the highways, unless a different place is specifically referred to. *(Stats.1959, c. 3, p. 1664, § 21001.)*

Cross References

Highway defined, see Vehicle Code § 360.
Vehicle defined, see Vehicle Code § 670.

ARTICLE 2. EFFECT OF TRAFFIC LAWS

§ 21050. Animals

Every person riding or driving an animal upon a highway has all of the rights and is subject to all of the duties applicable to the driver of a vehicle by this division and Division 10 (commencing with Section 20000), except those provisions which by their very nature can have no application. *(Stats.1959, c. 3, p. 1664, § 21050. Amended by Stats.1963, c. 479, p. 1337, § 1; Stats.1967, c. 586, p. 1931, § 2.)*

Cross References

Animals on highway, generally, see Food and Agricultural Code § 16902 et seq.
Animals prohibited on vehicular crossing, see Vehicle Code § 23330.
Caution required in passing animals, see Vehicle Code § 21759.

§ 21051. Trolley coaches

The following sections apply to trolley coaches:

(a) Sections 1800, 4000, 4001, 4002, 4003, 4006, 4009, 4150, 4151, 4152, 4153, 4155, 4156, 4158, 4166, 4300 to 4309, inclusive, 4450 to 4454, inclusive, 4457, 4458, 4459, 4460, 4600 to 4610, inclusive, 4750, 4751, 4850, 4851, 4852, 4853, 5000, 5200 to 5205, inclusive, 5904, 6052, 8801, 9254, and 40001 with respect to 4000, relating to original and renewal of registration.

(b) Sections 9250, 9265, 9400, 9406, 9407, 9408, 9550, 9552, 9553, 9554, 9800 to 9808, inclusive, 14901, 42230 to 42233, inclusive, relating to registration and other fees.

(c) Sections 2800, 10851, 10852, 10853, 20001 to 20009, inclusive, 21052, 21053, 21054, 21450 to 21457, inclusive, 21461, 21650, 21651, 21658, 21659, 21700, 21701, 21702, 21703, 21709, 21712, 21750, 21753, 21754, 21755, 21800, 21801, 21802, 21806, 21950, 21951, 22106, 22107, 22108, 22109, 22350, 22351, 22352, 22400, 22450 to 22453, inclusive, 23103, 23104, 23105, 23110, 23152, 23153, 40831, 42002 with respect to 10852 and 10853, and 42004, relating to traffic laws.

(d) Sections 26706, 26707, and 26708, relating to equipment.

(e) Sections 17301, 17302, 17303, 21461, 35000, 35100, 35101, 35105, 35106, 35111, 35550, 35551, 35750, 35751, 35753, 40000.1 to 40000.25, inclusive, 40001, 40003, and 42031, relating to the size, weight, and loading of vehicles. *(Stats.1959, c. 3, p. 1664, § 21051. Amended by Stats.1977, c. 579, p. 1917, § 186; Stats.1981, c. 714, p. 2799, § 445; Stats.1982, c. 53, p. 171, § 22, eff. Feb. 18, 1982; Stats.2000, c. 135 (A.B.2539), § 161; Stats.2007, c. 682 (A.B.430), § 15.)*

Cross References

Trolley coach defined, see Vehicle Code § 650.

§ 21052. Public officers and employees

The provisions of this code applicable to the drivers of vehicles upon the highways apply to the drivers of all vehicles while engaged in the course of employment by this State, any political subdivision thereof, any municipal corporation, or any district, including authorized emergency vehicles subject to those exemptions granted such authorized emergency vehicles in this code. *(Stats.1959, c. 3, p. 1665, § 21052.)*

Cross References

Applicability of this section to trolley coaches, see Vehicle Code § 21051.
Definitions,
Driver, see Vehicle Code § 305.
Emergency vehicle, see Vehicle Code §§ 165, 165.5.
Highway, see Vehicle Code §§ 360, 590.

Exemptions granted to drivers of authorized emergency vehicles, see Vehicle Code § 21055.

§ 21053. Public employees working on highway

This code, except Chapter 1 (commencing with Section 20000) of Division 10, Article 2 (commencing with Section 23152) of Chapter 12 of Division 11, and Sections 25268 and 25269, does not apply to public employees and publicly owned teams, motor vehicles, and other equipment while actually engaged in work upon the surface of a highway, or work of installation, removal, repairing, or maintaining official traffic control devices. This code does apply to those persons and vehicles when traveling to or from their work. *(Stats.1959, c. 3, p. 1665, § 21053. Amended by Stats.1961, c. 653, p. 1860, § 27, operative Jan. 1, 1962; Stats.1995, c. 766 (S.B.726), § 21; Stats.1998, c. 877 (A.B.2132), § 62.)*

Cross References

Applicability of this section to trolley coaches, see Vehicle Code § 21051.
Definitions,
Highway, see Vehicle Code §§ 360, 590.
Motor vehicle, see Vehicle Code § 415.
Official traffic control device, see Vehicle Code § 440.

§ 21054. Representative of public agency

The provisions of this division do not apply to the duly authorized representatives of any public agency while actually engaged in performing any of the work described in Section 21053 but apply to such persons when traveling to and from such work. *(Stats.1959, c. 3, p. 1665, § 21054.)*

Cross References

Applicability of this section to trolley coaches, see Vehicle Code § 21051.

§ 21055. Exemption of authorized emergency vehicles

The driver of an authorized emergency vehicle is exempt from Chapter 2 (commencing with Section 21350), Chapter 3 (commencing with Section 21650), Chapter 4 (commencing with Section 21800), Chapter 5 (commencing with Section 21950), Chapter 6 (commencing with 22100), Chapter 7 (commencing with Section 22348), Chapter 8 (commencing with Section 22450), Chapter 9 (commencing with Section 22500), and Chapter 10 (commencing with Section 22650) of this division, and Article 3 (commencing with Section 38305) and Article 4 (commencing with Section 38312) of Chapter 5 of Division 16.5, under all of the following conditions:

(a) If the vehicle is being driven in response to an emergency call or while engaged in rescue operations or is being used in the immediate pursuit of an actual or suspected violator of the law or is responding to, but not returning from, a fire alarm, except that fire department vehicles are exempt whether directly responding to an emergency call or operated from one place to another as rendered desirable or necessary by reason of an emergency call and operated to the scene of the emergency or operated from one fire station to another or to some other location by reason of the emergency call.

(b) If the driver of the vehicle sounds a siren as may be reasonably necessary and the vehicle displays a lighted red lamp visible from the front as a warning to other drivers and pedestrians.

A siren shall not be sounded by an authorized emergency vehicle except when required under this section. *(Stats.1959, c. 3, p. 1665, § 21055. Amended by Stats.1961, c. 524, p. 1627, § 1; Stats.1976, c. 1079, p. 4889, § 90; Stats.1977, c. 1017, p. 3050, § 2, eff. Sept. 23, 1977.)*

Cross References

Additional lights, see Vehicle Code § 25258.
Additional lights on emergency vehicles, see Vehicle Code §§ 25252, 25252.5.
Civil liability of owners and operators, see Vehicle Code § 17000 et seq.
Definitions,
Authorized emergency vehicle, see Vehicle Code §§ 165, 165.5.
Driver, see Vehicle Code § 305.
Highway, see Vehicle Code §§ 360, 590.
Exemption for physicians on emergency calls, see Vehicle Code § 21058.
Flashing headlamps, see Vehicle Code § 25252.5.
Following emergency vehicle, see Vehicle Code § 21706.
Highway patrol regulations, effect on compliance with this section, see Vehicle Code § 2512.
Obedience to traffic control signals, see Vehicle Code § 21462.
Police and traffic officer's use of siren and illegal speed in escorting vehicles, see Vehicle Code § 21057.
Right-of-way of authorized emergency vehicles, see Vehicle Code § 21806.
Traffic control signal changing devices, priority of emergency vehicle over bus, see Vehicle Code § 25352.
Use of sirens and Hi–Lo warning sounds, see Vehicle Code § 27002.

Research References

California Jury Instructions-Civil, 8th Edition 5.80, Authorized Emergency Vehicle Exemption.

§ 21056. Effect of exemption

Section 21055 does not relieve the driver of a vehicle from the duty to drive with due regard for the safety of all persons using the highway, nor protect him from the consequences of an arbitrary exercise of the privileges granted in that section. *(Stats.1959, c. 3, p. 1666, § 21056.)*

Cross References

Liability of operator of authorized emergency vehicles, see Vehicle Code § 17004.

Research References

California Jury Instructions-Civil, 8th Edition 5.80, Authorized Emergency Vehicle Exemption.

§ 21057. Sirens and illegal speed of escorts

Every police and traffic officer is hereby expressly prohibited from using a siren or driving at an illegal speed when serving as an escort of any vehicle, except when the escort or conveyance is furnished for the preservation of life or when expediting movements of supplies and personnel for any federal, state, or local governmental agency during a national emergency, or state of war emergency, or state of emergency, or local emergency as defined in Section 8558 of the Government Code. *(Stats.1959, c. 3, p. 1666, § 21057. Amended by Stats.1971, c. 131, p. 178, § 1, operative May 3, 1972.)*

Cross References

Speed laws, see Vehicle Code § 22349 et seq.

§ 21058. Vehicles owned by physicians

A physician traveling in response to an emergency call shall be exempt from the provisions of Sections 22351 and 22352 if the vehicle so used by him displays an insigne approved by the department indicating that the vehicle is owned by a licensed physician. The provisions of this section do not relieve the driver of the vehicle from the duty to drive with due regard for the safety of all persons using the highway, nor protect the driver from the consequences of an arbitrary exercise of the privileges of this section. *(Stats.1959, c. 3, p. 1666, § 21058. Amended by Stats.1959, c. 1996, p. 4629, § 23.)*

Research References

California Jury Instructions-Civil, 8th Edition 5.82, Licensed Physician Answering Emergency Call.

§ 21059. Rubbish and garbage vehicles

Sections 21211, 21650, 21660, 22502, 22504, and subdivision (h) of Section 22500 do not apply to the operation of a rubbish or garbage truck while actually engaged in the collection of rubbish or garbage within a business or residence district, if the front turn signal lamps at each side of the vehicle are being flashed simultaneously and the rear turn signal lamps at each side of the vehicle are being flashed simultaneously.

This provision does not apply when the vehicle is being driven to and from work, and it does not relieve the driver of the vehicle from the duty to drive with due regard for the safety of all persons using the highway or protect him or her from the consequences of an arbitrary exercise of the privilege granted. *(Added by Stats.1965, c. 490, p. 1800, § 1. Amended by Stats.1999, c. 1007 (S.B.532), § 20.)*

Research References

California Jury Instructions-Civil, 8th Edition 5.83, Exemption of Rubbish or Garbage Truck.

§ 21060. Streetsweeping and watering vehicles

Between the hours of 1 a.m. and 5 a.m., Sections 21650, 21660, 22502, 22504, and subdivision (h) of Section 22500 do not apply to the operation of a streetsweeper vehicle or watering vehicle, operated by a local authority, while the vehicle is actually sweeping streets or watering landscaping or vegetation within a business or residence district. The exemption is not applicable unless the turn signal lamps at each side of the front and rear of the streetsweeper vehicle or watering vehicle are being flashed simultaneously.

This provision shall not apply when the vehicle is being driven to and from such work, nor does it relieve the driver of such a vehicle from the duty to drive with due regard for the safety of all persons using the highway or protect the driver from the consequences of an arbitrary exercise of the privilege granted. *(Added by Stats.1979, c. 469, p. 1626, § 1.)*

§ 21061. Notice of reexamination; evidence of incapacity to operate vehicle

(a) In addition to any action prescribed in Division 17 (commencing with Section 40000.1), a traffic officer may issue a notice of reexamination to any person who violates any provision of this division and who, at the time of the violation, exhibits evidence of incapacity to the traffic officer which leads the traffic officer to reasonably believe that the person is incapable of operating a motor vehicle in a manner so as not to present a clear or potential danger of risk of injury to that person or others if that person is permitted to resume operation of a motor vehicle.

(b) For purposes of this section, "evidence of incapacity" means evidence, other than violations of this division, of serious physical injury or illness or mental impairment or disorientation which is apparent to the traffic officer and which presents a clear or potential danger or risk of injury to the person or others if that person is permitted to resume operation of a motor vehicle. *(Added by Stats.1986, c. 304, § 3, operative July 1, 1987.)*

Cross References

Reexamination pursuant to notice, see Vehicle Code § 12818.
Three-tier assessment system, pilot study, see Vehicle Code § 1659.9.

§ 21062. Copy of notice of reexamination to department; record of notice in driver's license record

The arresting officer shall, before the end of the next working day, transmit, or cause to be transmitted, a legible copy of the notice of reexamination to the Department of Motor Vehicles, and the department shall enter the record of the notice in the driver's license record maintained by electronic recording and storage media by the department within five working days of its receipt. *(Added by Stats.1986, c. 304, § 4, operative July 1, 1987.)*

§ 21070. Offense of unsafe operation of motor vehicle with bodily injury or great bodily injury; punishment

Notwithstanding any other provision of law, a driver who violates any provision of this division, that is punishable as an infraction, and as a result of that violation proximately causes bodily injury or great bodily injury, as defined in Section 12022.7 of the Penal Code, to another person is guilty of the public offense of unsafe operation of a motor vehicle with bodily injury or great bodily injury. That violation is punishable as an infraction pursuant to Section 42001.19. *(Added by Stats.2006, c. 898 (S.B.1021), § 3.)*

Cross References

Conviction under Vehicle Code § 21070, fines, see Vehicle Code § 42001.19.
Infractions, see Penal Code § 16.

ARTICLE 4. OPERATION OF BICYCLES

§ 21200.5. Riding under influence of alcohol and drugs; chemical tests; punishment

Notwithstanding Section 21200, it is unlawful for any person to ride a bicycle upon a highway while under the influence of an alcoholic beverage or any drug, or under the combined influence of an alcoholic beverage and any drug. Any person arrested for a violation of this section may request to have a chemical test made of the person's blood, breath, or urine for the purpose of determining the alcoholic or drug content of that person's blood pursuant to Section 23612, and, if so requested, the arresting officer shall have the test performed. A conviction of a violation of this section shall be punished by a fine of not more than two hundred fifty dollars ($250). Violations of this section are subject to Section 13202.5. *(Added by Stats.1985, c. 1013, § 3. Amended by Stats.1990, c. 1697 (S.B.2635), § 5; Stats.1998, c. 740 (S.B.1890), § 3; Stats.1999, c. 22 (S.B.24), § 17, eff. May 26, 1999.)*

Research References

2 Witkin, California Criminal Law 4th Crimes Against Public Peace and Welfare § 530 (2021), Bicycles.

ARTICLE 5. OPERATION OF MOTORIZED SCOOTERS

§ 21221.5. Driving under the influence

Notwithstanding Section 21221, it is unlawful for any person to operate a motorized scooter upon a highway while under the influence of an alcoholic beverage or any drug, or under the combined influence of an alcoholic beverage and any drug. Any person arrested for a violation of this section may request to have a chemical test made of the person's blood or breath for the purpose of determining the alcoholic or drug content of that person's blood pursuant to subdivision (d) of Section 23612, and, if so requested, the arresting officer shall have the test performed. A conviction of a violation of this section shall be punished by a fine of not more than two hundred fifty dollars ($250). *(Added by Stats.1999, c. 722 (S.B.441), § 5. Amended by Stats.2000, c. 287 (S.B.1955), § 25.)*

Research References

2 Witkin, California Criminal Law 4th Crimes Against Public Peace and Welfare § 531 (2021), Low-Speed Vehicles and Motorized Scooters.

ARTICLE 7. OPERATION OF ELECTRICALLY MOTORIZED BOARDS

§ 21290. Definitions

(a) For purposes of this article, "bikeway" is defined in Section 890.4 of the Streets and Highways Code.

(b) For purposes of this article, an "electrically motorized board" is defined in Section 313.5. *(Added by Stats.2015, c. 777 (A.B.604), § 3, eff. Jan. 1, 2016.)*

Research References

2 Witkin, California Criminal Law 4th Crimes Against Public Peace and Welfare § 322 (2021), Pedestrian's Rights and Duties.

§ 21291. Age of operation

An electrically motorized board shall be operated only by a person who is 16 years of age or older. *(Added by Stats.2015, c. 777 (A.B.604), § 3, eff. Jan. 1, 2016.)*

§ 21292. Use of bicycle helmet

A person shall not operate an electrically motorized board upon a highway, bikeway, or any other public bicycle path, sidewalk, or trail, unless that person is wearing a properly fitted and fastened bicycle helmet that meets the standards described in Section 21212. *(Added by Stats.2015, c. 777 (A.B.604), § 3, eff. Jan. 1, 2016.)*

§ 21293. Operation upon highway during darkness; necessary equipment

(a) Every electrically motorized board operated upon a highway during darkness shall be equipped with all of the following:

(1) Except as provided in subdivision (b), a lamp emitting a white light that, while the electrically motorized board is in motion, illuminates the highway in front of the operator and is visible from a distance of 300 feet in front of the electrically motorized board.

(2) Except as provided in subdivision (c), a red reflector on the rear that is visible from a distance of 500 feet to the rear when directly in front of lawful upper beams of headlamps on a motor vehicle.

(3) Except as provided in subdivision (d), a white or yellow reflector on each side that is visible from a distance of 200 feet from the sides of the electrically motorized board.

(b) A lamp or lamp combination, emitting a white light, attached to the operator and visible from a distance of 300 feet in front of the electrically motorized board, may be used in lieu of the lamp required by paragraph (1) of subdivision (a).

(c) A red reflector, or reflectorizing material meeting the requirements of Section 25500, attached to the operator and visible from a distance of 500 feet to the rear when directly in front of lawful upper beams of headlamps on a motor vehicle, may be used in lieu of the reflector required by paragraph (2) of subdivision (a).

(d) A white or yellow reflector, or reflectorizing material meeting the requirements of Section 25500, attached to the operator and visible from a distance of 200 feet from the sides of the electrically motorized board, may be used in lieu of the reflector required by paragraph (3) of subdivision (a). *(Added by Stats.2015, c. 777 (A.B.604), § 3, eff. Jan. 1, 2016.)*

§ 21294. Speed limit of highway that electrically motorized boards are allowed to operate on; maximum speed of operation

(a) An electrically motorized board shall only operate upon a highway designated with a speed limit of 35 miles per hour or less, unless the electrically motorized board is operated entirely within a designated Class II or Class IV bikeway.

(b) A person shall not operate an electrically motorized board upon a highway, bikeway, or any other public bicycle path, sidewalk, or trail, at a speed in excess of 15 miles per hour.

(c) Notwithstanding subdivision (b), a person shall not operate an electrically motorized board at a speed greater than is reasonable or prudent having due regard for weather, visibility, pedestrian and vehicular traffic, and the surface and width of the highway, bikeway, public bicycle path, sidewalk, or trail, and in no event at a speed that endangers the safety of any person or property. *(Added by Stats. 2015, c. 777 (A.B.604), § 3, eff. Jan. 1, 2016. Amended by Stats.2016, c. 86 (S.B.1171), § 302, eff. Jan. 1, 2017.)*

§ 21295. Submission of report to Legislature regarding effect of electrically motorized boards on traffic safety

The Commissioner of the California Highway Patrol shall submit a report to the Legislature, on or before January 1, 2021, to assist in determining the effect that the use of electrically motorized boards has on traffic safety. The report shall include detailed statewide traffic collision data involving electrically motorized boards, including property damage only, injury, and fatal traffic collisions. The report shall be submitted in compliance with Section 9795 of the Government Code. Pursuant to Section 10231.5 of the Government Code, this section is repealed on January 1, 2025. *(Added by Stats.2015, c. 777 (A.B.604), § 3, eff. Jan. 1, 2016.)*

Repeal

For repeal of this section, see its terms.

§ 21296. Operation under the influence; blood or breath test; punishment

(a) It is unlawful for a person to operate an electrically motorized board upon a highway while under the influence of an alcoholic beverage or any drug, or under the combined influence of an alcoholic beverage and any drug.

(b) A person arrested for a violation of this section may request to have a chemical test made of his or her blood or breath for the purpose of determining the alcoholic or drug content of that person's blood pursuant to subdivision (d) of Section 23612, and, if so requested, the arresting officer shall have the test performed.

(c) A conviction for a violation of this section shall be punished by a fine of not more than two hundred fifty dollars ($250). *(Added by Stats.2015, c. 777 (A.B.604), § 3, eff. Jan. 1, 2016.)*

ARTICLE 8. HORSEBACK RIDING

§ 21300. Riding equestrian animal upon paved highway; helmet and reflective gear requirements

(a) A person under 18 years of age shall not ride an equestrian animal upon a paved highway unless that person is wearing a properly fitted and fastened helmet that meets the standards of either the American Society for Testing and Materials or the United States Consumer Product Safety Commission, or standards subsequently established by those entities.

(b) A person riding an equestrian animal upon a paved highway during hours of darkness, as defined in Section 280, shall do one of the following:

(1) Wear reflective gear or have reflective gear on the equestrian animal that shall be visible from a distance of 500 feet on the rear and the sides when directly in front of the lawful upper beams of headlamps on a motor vehicle.

(2) Have a lamp emitting a white light attached to either the person or the equestrian animal that is visible from a distance of 300 feet in front of and from the sides of the equestrian animal.

(c) Notwithstanding subdivisions (a) and (b), a person is not required to wear a helmet or reflective gear while riding an equestrian animal when participating in a parade or festival, or while crossing a paved highway from an unpaved highway.

(d) In a civil action, a violation of subdivision (a) or (b) does not establish negligence as a matter of law or negligence per se for comparative fault purposes, but negligence may be proven as a fact without regard to the violation.

(e) A charge under this section shall be dismissed when the person charged alleges in court, under oath, that the charge against the person is the first charge against that person under this section, unless it is otherwise established in court that the charge is not the first charge against the person.

(f)(1) Except as provided in subdivision (e), a violation of this section is an infraction punishable by a fine of not more than twenty-five dollars ($25).

(2) The parent or legal guardian having control or custody of an unemancipated minor whose conduct violates this section shall be jointly and severally liable with the minor for the amount of the fine imposed pursuant to this subdivision. *(Added by Stats.2021, c. 175 (A.B.974), § 1, eff. Jan. 1, 2022.)*

CHAPTER 2. TRAFFIC SIGNS, SIGNALS, AND MARKINGS

ARTICLE 3. OFFENSES RELATING TO TRAFFIC DEVICES

§ 21450. Official traffic control signals

Text of section as amended by Stats.2005, c. 126 (A.B.56), § 1, eff. July 25, 2005.

Section 21450 was added by Stats.1959, c. 3, § 21450, amended by Stats.1981, c. 413, § 3; Stats.1999, c. 277 (A.B.134), § 1, and repealed by its own terms, operative Jan. 1, 2005. Therefore, this section was not in effect from Jan. 1, 2005 until July 25, 2005.

Stats.2005, c. 126 (A.B.56), § 1, might be given effect as a new addition of this section; but see Government Code § 9609.

Whenever traffic is controlled by official traffic control signals showing different colored lights, color-lighted arrows, or color-lighted bicycle symbols, successively, one at a time, or in combination, only the colors green, yellow, and red shall be used, except for pedestrian control signals, and those lights shall indicate and apply to drivers of vehicles, operators of bicycles, and pedestrians as provided in this chapter. *(Amended by Stats.2005, c. 126 (A.B.56), § 1, eff. July 25, 2005.)*

Cross References

Applicability of this section to trolley coaches, see Vehicle Code § 21051.
Disobedience to traffic laws as misdemeanor, see Vehicle Code §§ 40000.1 et seq., 42001.
Flashing signals, see Vehicle Code § 21457.
Illegal signs, signals and lights, see Vehicle Code §§ 21465 to 21467.
Obedience to official traffic signals, see Vehicle Code § 21462.
Obedience to peace officers, see Vehicle Code § 2800.
Official traffic control signal defined, see Vehicle Code § 445.
Pedestrian control signals, see Vehicle Code § 21456.
Right of way, see Vehicle Code § 21800 et seq.
Traffic defined, see Vehicle Code § 620.

Research References

2 Witkin, California Criminal Law 4th Crimes Against Public Peace and Welfare § 322 (2021), Pedestrian's Rights and Duties.
2 Witkin, California Criminal Law 4th Crimes Against Public Peace and Welfare § 327 (2021), Miscellaneous Regulations.

§ 21450.5. Traffic-actuated signal; detection of bicycle or motorcycle traffic; pedestrian signal and detector

(a) A traffic-actuated signal is an official traffic control signal, as specified in Section 445, that displays one or more of its indications in response to the presence of traffic detected by mechanical, visual, electrical, or other means.

(b) Upon the first placement of a traffic-actuated signal or replacement of the loop detector of a traffic-actuated signal, the traffic-actuated signal shall, to the extent feasible and in conformance with professional traffic engineering practice, be installed and maintained * * * to detect lawful bicycle or motorcycle traffic on the roadway.

(c) Cities, counties, and cities and counties shall not be required to comply with the provisions contained in subdivision (b) until the Department of Transportation, in consultation with these entities, has established uniform standards, specifications, and guidelines for the detection of bicycles and motorcycles by traffic-actuated signals and related signal timing.

(d)(1) Upon the first placement or replacement of a state-owned or operated traffic-actuated signal, a traffic-actuated signal shall be installed and maintained to have a leading pedestrian interval, and shall include the installation, activation, and maintenance of an accessible pedestrian signal and detector that complies with sections 4E.08 to 4E.13 of the California Manual on Uniform Traffic Control Devices in effect on December 31, 2022.

(2) An existing state-owned or operated traffic-actuated signal capable of being implemented with remote installation or in-person programming shall have a leading pedestrian interval programmed when maintenance work is done on the intersection in which the traffic-actuated signal is located, if the traffic-actuated signal is in any of the following areas:

(A) A residential district.

(B) A business district.

(C) A business activity district.

(D) A safety corridor.

(E) A school zone.

(F) An area with a high concentration of pedestrians and cyclists, as determined by the Department of Transportation pursuant to Section 22358.7.

(3) The requirements in paragraphs (1) and (2) do not apply when prohibited by the California Manual on Uniform Traffic Control Devices.

(4) As used in this subdivision, a "leading pedestrian interval" means an official traffic control signal that advances the "WALK" signal for three to seven seconds while the red signal halting traffic continues to be displayed on parallel through or turning traffic.

(5) As used in this subdivision, an "accessible pedestrian signal and detector" means an integrated device that communicates information about the "WALK" and "DON'T WALK" intervals at signalized intersections in nonvisual formats, including audible tones, speech messages, and vibrotactile surfaces, to pedestrians who are blind or have low vision. *(Added by Stats.2007, c. 337 (A.B.1581), § 2. Amended by Stats.2017, c. 432 (S.B.672), § 1, eff. Jan. 1, 2018; Stats.2022, c. 496 (A.B.2264), § 1, eff. Jan. 1, 2023.)*

§ 21451. Circular green signal; green arrow signal

(a) A driver facing a circular green signal shall proceed straight through or turn right or left or make a U-turn unless a sign prohibits a U-turn. Any driver, including one turning, shall yield the right-of-way to other traffic and to pedestrians lawfully within the intersection or an adjacent crosswalk.

(b) A driver facing a green arrow signal, shown alone or in combination with another indication, shall enter the intersection only to make the movement indicated by that green arrow or any other movement that is permitted by other indications shown at the same time. A driver facing a left green arrow may also make a U-turn unless prohibited by a sign. A driver shall yield the right-of-way to other traffic and to * * * a pedestrian lawfully within the intersection or an adjacent crosswalk.

(c) A pedestrian facing a circular green signal, unless prohibited by sign or otherwise directed by a pedestrian control signal as provided in Section 21456, may proceed across the roadway within any marked or unmarked crosswalk, but shall yield the right-of-way to vehicles lawfully within the intersection at the time that signal is first shown.

(d) A pedestrian facing a green arrow turn signal, unless otherwise directed by a pedestrian control signal as provided in Section 21456, shall not enter the roadway.

(e)(1) A peace officer, as defined in Chapter 4.5 (commencing with Section 830) of Title 3 of Part 2 of the Penal Code, shall not stop a pedestrian for a violation of subdivision (c) or (d) unless a reasonably careful person would realize there is an immediate danger of a collision with a moving vehicle or other device moving exclusively by human power.

(2) This subdivision does not relieve a pedestrian from the duty of using due care for their safety.

(3) This subdivision does not relieve a driver of a vehicle from the duty of exercising due care for the safety of any pedestrian within the roadway. *(Stats.1959, c. 3, p. 1674, § 21451. Amended by Stats.1959, c. 971, p. 3002, § 1; Stats.1973, c. 228, p. 612, § 1, operative July 1, 1974; Stats.1976, c. 394, p. 1043, § 1; Stats.1977, c. 1017, p. 3052, § 3, eff. Sept. 23, 1977; Stats.1981, c. 413, p. 1609, § 4; Stats.2022, c. 957 (A.B.2147), § 1, eff. Jan. 1, 2023.)*

Cross References

Applicability of this section to trolley coaches, see Vehicle Code § 21051.
Crossing between controlled intersections, see Vehicle Code § 21955.
Definitions,
Crosswalk, see Vehicle Code § 275.
Intersection, see Vehicle Code § 365.
Official traffic control signal, see Vehicle Code § 445.
Right-of-way, see Vehicle Code § 525.
Traffic, see Vehicle Code § 620.
Vehicle, see Vehicle Code § 670.
Violation as misdemeanor, punishment, see Vehicle Code §§ 40000.5 et seq., 42001.

Research References

California Jury Instructions-Civil, 8th Edition 5.54, Pedestrian—Change of Signal After Crossing Begun.
2 Witkin, California Criminal Law 4th Crimes Against Public Peace and Welfare § 327 (2021), Miscellaneous Regulations.

§ 21452. Steady circular yellow or yellow arrow signal

(a) A driver facing a steady circular yellow or yellow arrow signal is, by that signal, warned that the related green movement is ending or that a red indication will be shown immediately thereafter.

(b) A pedestrian facing a steady circular yellow or a yellow arrow signal, unless otherwise directed by a pedestrian control signal as provided in Section 21456, is, by that signal, warned that there is insufficient time to cross the roadway and shall not enter the roadway.

(c)(1) A peace officer, as defined in Chapter 4.5 (commencing with Section 830) of Title 3 of Part 2 of the Penal Code, shall not stop a pedestrian for a violation of subdivision (b) unless a reasonably careful person would realize there is an immediate danger of a collision with a moving vehicle or other device moving exclusively by human power.

(2) This subdivision does not relieve a pedestrian from the duty of using due care for their safety.

(3) This subdivision does not relieve a driver of a vehicle from the duty of exercising due care for the safety of any pedestrian within the roadway. *(Stats.1959, c. 3, p. 1675, § 21452. Amended by Stats.1981,*

c. 413, p. 1610, § 5; Stats.1986, c. 256, § 1; Stats.2022, c. 957 (A.B.2147), § 2, eff. Jan. 1, 2023.)

Cross References

Applicability of this section to trolley coaches, see Vehicle Code § 21051.
Definitions,
Official traffic control signal, see Vehicle Code § 445.
Roadway, see Vehicle Code § 530.
Traffic, see Vehicle Code § 620.
Violation as misdemeanor, punishment, see Vehicle Code §§ 40000.5 et seq., 42002.

Research References

California Jury Instructions-Civil, 8th Edition 5.54, Pedestrian—Change of Signal After Crossing Begun.
2 Witkin, California Criminal Law 4th Crimes Against Public Peace and Welfare § 327 (2021), Miscellaneous Regulations.

§ 21453. Steady circular red signal; steady red arrow signal

(a) A driver facing a steady circular red signal alone shall stop at a marked limit line, but if none, before entering the crosswalk on the near side of the intersection or, if none, then before entering the intersection, and shall remain stopped until an indication to proceed is shown, except as provided in subdivision (b).

(b) Except when a sign is in place prohibiting a turn, a driver, after stopping as required by subdivision (a), facing a steady circular red signal, may turn right, or turn left from a one-way street onto a one-way street. A driver making that turn shall yield the right-of-way to pedestrians lawfully within an adjacent crosswalk and to any vehicle that has approached or is approaching so closely as to constitute an immediate hazard to the driver, and shall continue to yield the right-of-way to that vehicle until the driver can proceed with reasonable safety.

(c) A driver facing a steady red arrow signal shall not enter the intersection to make the movement indicated by the arrow and, unless entering the intersection to make a movement permitted by another signal, shall stop at a clearly marked limit line, but if none, before entering the crosswalk on the near side of the intersection, or if none, then before entering the intersection, and shall remain stopped until an indication permitting movement is shown.

(d) Unless otherwise directed by a pedestrian control signal as provided in Section 21456, a pedestrian facing a steady circular red or red arrow signal shall not enter the roadway.

(e)(1) A peace officer, as defined in Chapter 4.5 (commencing with Section 830) of Title 3 of Part 2 of the Penal Code, shall not stop a pedestrian for a violation of subdivision (d) unless a reasonably careful person would realize there is an immediate danger of a collision with a moving vehicle or other device moving exclusively by human power.

(2) This subdivision does not relieve a pedestrian from the duty of using due care for their safety.

(3) This subdivision does not relieve a driver of a vehicle from the duty of exercising due care for the safety of any pedestrian within the roadway. *(Stats.1959, c. 3, p. 1675, § 21453. Amended by Stats.1969, c. 246, p. 595, § 1; Stats.1981, c. 413, p. 1610, § 6; Stats.1982, c. 741, p. 2944, § 1; Stats.2001, c. 14 (A.B.563), § 1; Stats.2022, c. 957 (A.B.2147), § 3, eff. Jan. 1, 2023.)*

Cross References

Applicability of this section to trolley coaches, see Vehicle Code § 21051.
Definitions,
Crosswalk, see Vehicle Code § 275.
Driver, see Vehicle Code § 305.
Intersection, see Vehicle Code § 365.
Local authorities, see Vehicle Code § 385.
Official traffic control signal, see Vehicle Code § 445.
Traffic, see Vehicle Code § 620.
Vehicle, see Vehicle Code § 670.
Local authorities, maintenance of traffic signs, signals and devices, see Vehicle Code § 21351.
Notice to appear, violation recorded by automated enforcement system, see Vehicle Code § 40518.
Violation as misdemeanor, punishment, see Vehicle Code §§ 40000.5 et seq., 42002.

Research References

California Jury Instructions-Civil, 8th Edition 5.54, Pedestrian—Change of Signal After Crossing Begun.
2 Witkin, California Criminal Law 4th Crimes Against Public Peace and Welfare § 327 (2021), Miscellaneous Regulations.

§ 21454. Lane use control signals placed over individual lanes

When lane use control signals are placed over individual lanes, those signals shall indicate and apply to drivers of vehicles as follows:

(a) Green indication: A driver may travel in any lane over which a green signal is shown.

(b) Steady yellow indication: A driver is thereby warned that a lane control change is being made.

(c) Steady red indication: A driver shall not enter or travel in any lane over which a red signal is shown.

(d) Flashing yellow indication: A driver may use the lane only for the purpose of making a left turn to or from the highway. *(Stats.1959, c. 3, p. 1675, § 21454. Amended by Stats.1959, c. 1342, p. 3615, § 1; Stats.1961, c. 1727, p. 3737, § 1; Stats.1965, c. 183, p. 1150, § 1; Stats.1973, c. 228, p. 612, § 2, operative July 1, 1974; Stats.1975, c. 529, p. 1095, § 1; Stats.1977, c. 1017, p. 3053, § 4, eff. Sept. 23, 1977; Stats.1981, c. 413, p. 1610, § 7.)*

Cross References

Applicability of this section to trolley coaches, see Vehicle Code § 21051.
Definitions,
Crosswalk, see Vehicle Code § 275.
Intersection, see Vehicle Code § 365.
Official traffic control signal, see Vehicle Code § 445.
Right-of-way, see Vehicle Code § 525.
Traffic, see Vehicle Code § 620.
Vehicle, see Vehicle Code § 670.
Violation as misdemeanor, punishment, see Vehicle Code §§ 40000.5 et seq., 42002.

Research References

2 Witkin, California Criminal Law 4th Crimes Against Public Peace and Welfare § 327 (2021), Miscellaneous Regulations.

§ 21455. Official traffic control signal at place other than intersection

If an official traffic control signal is erected and maintained at a place other than an intersection, including a freeway or highway on ramp, this article applies, except those provisions that by their nature can have no application. A stop required shall be made at a sign, crosswalk, or limit line indicating where the stop shall be made, but, in the absence of that sign or marking, the stop shall be made at the signal. *(Stats.1959, c. 3, p. 1676, § 21455. Amended by Stats.1981, c. 413, p. 1611, § 8; Stats.2017, c. 555 (A.B.1094), § 1, eff. Jan. 1, 2018.)*

Cross References

Applicability of this section to trolley coaches, see Vehicle Code § 21051.
Violation as misdemeanor, punishment, see Vehicle Code §§ 40000.5 et seq., 42002.

Research References

2 Witkin, California Criminal Law 4th Crimes Against Public Peace and Welfare § 327 (2021), Miscellaneous Regulations.

§ 21455.5. Automated traffic enforcement system; requirements; use of printed representation as evidence; confidentiality and retention of records; review of alleged violation by registered owner; manufacturers and suppliers; duties and contract limitations

(a) The limit line, the intersection, or a place designated in Section 21455, where a driver is required to stop, may be equipped with an automated traffic enforcement system if the governmental agency utilizing the system meets all of the following requirements:

(1) Identifies the system by signs posted within 200 feet of an intersection where a system is operating that clearly indicate the system's presence and are visible to traffic approaching from all directions in which the automated traffic enforcement system is being utilized to issue citations. A governmental agency utilizing this type of system does not need to post signs visible to traffic approaching the intersection from directions not subject to the automated traffic enforcement system. Automated traffic enforcement systems installed as of January 1, 2013, shall be identified no later than January 1, 2014.

(2) Locates the system at an intersection and ensures that the system meets the criteria specified in Section 21455.7.

(b) Prior to issuing citations under this section, a local jurisdiction utilizing an automated traffic enforcement system shall commence a program to issue only warning notices for 30 days. The local jurisdiction shall also make a public announcement of the automated traffic enforcement system at least 30 days prior to the commencement of the enforcement program.

(c) Only a governmental agency, in cooperation with a law enforcement agency, may operate an automated traffic enforcement system. A governmental agency that operates an automated traffic enforcement system shall do all of the following:

(1) Develop uniform guidelines for screening and issuing violations and for the processing and storage of confidential information, and establish procedures to ensure compliance with those guidelines. For systems installed as of January 1, 2013, a governmental agency that operates an automated traffic enforcement system shall establish those guidelines by January 1, 2014.

(2) Perform administrative functions and day-to-day functions, including, but not limited to, all of the following:

(A) Establishing guidelines for the selection of a location. Prior to installing an automated traffic enforcement system after January 1, 2013, the governmental agency shall make and adopt a finding of fact establishing that the system is needed at a specific location for reasons related to safety.

(B) Ensuring that the equipment is regularly inspected.

(C) Certifying that the equipment is properly installed and calibrated, and is operating properly.

(D) Regularly inspecting and maintaining warning signs placed under paragraph (1) of subdivision (a).

(E) Overseeing the establishment or change of signal phases and the timing thereof.

(F) Maintaining controls necessary to ensure that only those citations that have been reviewed and approved by law enforcement are delivered to violators.

(d) The activities listed in subdivision (c) that relate to the operation of the system may be contracted out by the governmental agency, if it maintains overall control and supervision of the system. However, the activities listed in paragraph (1) of, and subparagraphs (A), (D), (E), and (F) of paragraph (2) of, subdivision (c) shall not be contracted out to the manufacturer or supplier of the automated traffic enforcement system.

(e) The printed representation of computer-generated information, video, or photographic images stored by an automated traffic enforcement system does not constitute an out-of-court hearsay statement by a declarant under Division 10 (commencing with Section 1200) of the Evidence Code.

(f)(1) Notwithstanding Article 1 (commencing with Section 7922.500) and Article 2 (commencing with Section 7922.525) of Chapter 1 of Part 3 of Division 10 of Title 1 of the Government Code, or any other law, photographic records made by an automated traffic enforcement system shall be confidential, and shall be made available only to governmental agencies and law enforcement agencies and only for the purposes of this article.

(2) Confidential information obtained from the Department of Motor Vehicles for the administration or enforcement of this article shall be held confidential, and shall not be used for any other purpose.

(3) Except for court records described in Section 68152 of the Government Code, the confidential records and information described in paragraphs (1) and (2) may be retained for up to six months from the date the information was first obtained, or until final disposition of the citation, whichever date is later, after which time the information shall be destroyed in a manner that will preserve the confidentiality of any person included in the record or information.

(g) Notwithstanding subdivision (f), the registered owner or any individual identified by the registered owner as the driver of the vehicle at the time of the alleged violation shall be permitted to review the photographic evidence of the alleged violation.

(h)(1) A contract between a governmental agency and a manufacturer or supplier of automated traffic enforcement equipment shall not include provision for the payment or compensation to the manufacturer or supplier based on the number of citations generated, or as a percentage of the revenue generated, as a result of the use of the equipment authorized under this section.

(2) Paragraph (1) does not apply to a contract that was entered into by a governmental agency and a manufacturer or supplier of automated traffic enforcement equipment before January 1, 2004, unless that contract is renewed, extended, or amended on or after January 1, 2004.

(3) A governmental agency that proposes to install or operate an automated traffic enforcement system shall not consider revenue generation, beyond recovering its actual costs of operating the system, as a factor when considering whether or not to install or operate a system within its local jurisdiction.

(i) A manufacturer or supplier that operates an automated traffic enforcement system pursuant to this section shall, in cooperation with the governmental agency, submit an annual report to the Judicial Council that includes, but is not limited to, all of the following information if this information is in the possession of, or readily available to, the manufacturer or supplier:

(1) The number of alleged violations captured by the systems they operate.

(2) The number of citations issued by a law enforcement agency based on information collected from the automated traffic enforcement system.

(3) For citations identified in paragraph (2), the number of violations that involved traveling straight through the intersection, turning right, and turning left.

(4) The number and percentage of citations that are dismissed by the court.

(5) The number of traffic collisions at each intersection that occurred prior to, and after the installation of, the automated traffic enforcement system.

(j) If a governmental agency utilizing an automated traffic enforcement system has posted signs on or before January 1, 2013, that met the requirements of paragraph (1) of subdivision (a) of this section, as it read on January 1, 2012, the governmental agency shall not remove those signs until signs are posted that meet the requirements specified in this section, as it reads on January 1, 2013. *(Added by Stats.1995, c. 922 (S.B.833), § 4. Amended by Stats.1998, c. 54 (S.B.1136), § 3; Stats.2001, c. 496 (S.B.667), § 1; Stats.2003, c. 511 (A.B.1022), § 1; Stats.2010, c. 328 (S.B.1330), § 230; Stats.2012, c. 735 (S.B.1303), § 3; Stats.2021, c. 615 (A.B.474), § 426, eff. Jan. 1, 2022, operative Jan. 1, 2023.)*

Law Revision Commission Comments

Section 21455.5 is amended to reflect nonsubstantive recodification of the California Public Records Act. See California Public Records Act Clean-Up, 46 Cal. L. Revision Comm'n Reports 207 (2019).

The section is also amended to make a technical change. [46 Cal.L.Rev. Comm. Reports 563 (2019)].

Cross References

Inspection of public records, exemptions from disclosure, automated traffic enforcement system, photographic records, see Government Code § 6276.04.
Printed representation of computer-generated information, see Evidence Code § 1552.
Printed representation of video or digital images, see Evidence Code § 1553.
Procedure, certain violations recorded by automated traffic enforcement system, notice to appear, contents, notice of nonliability, form, dismissal, see Vehicle Code § 40518.

Research References

2 Witkin, California Criminal Law 4th Crimes Against Public Peace and Welfare § 327 (2021), Miscellaneous Regulations.

§ 21455.6. Automated enforcement system; public hearing; activities that can be contracted out; photo radar

(a) A city council or county board of supervisors shall conduct a public hearing on the proposed use of an automated enforcement system authorized under Section 21455.5 prior to authorizing the city or county to enter into a contract for the use of the system.

(b)(1) The activities listed in subdivision (c) of Section 21455.5 that relate to the operation of an automated enforcement system may be contracted out by the city or county, except that the activities listed in paragraph (1) of, and subparagraphs (A), (D), (E), or (F) of paragraph (2) of, subdivision (c) of Section 21455.5 may not be contracted out to the manufacturer or supplier of the automated enforcement system.

(2) Paragraph (1) does not apply to a contract that was entered into by a city or county and a manufacturer or supplier of automated enforcement equipment before January 1, 2004, unless that contract is renewed, extended, or amended on or after January 1, 2004.

(c) The authorization in Section 21455.5 to use automated enforcement systems does not authorize the use of photo radar for speed enforcement purposes by any jurisdiction. *(Added by Stats. 1998, c. 828 (S.B.1637), § 17. Amended by Stats.2000, c. 833 (A.B.2522), § 7; Stats.2000, c. 860 (A.B.2908), § 8; Stats.2003, c. 511 (A.B.1022), § 2.)*

§ 21455.7. Intersections with automated enforcement system; minimum yellow light change intervals

(a) At an intersection at which there is an automated enforcement system in operation, the minimum yellow light change interval shall be established in accordance with the California Manual on Uniform Traffic Control Devices.

(b) For purposes of subdivision (a), the minimum yellow light change intervals relating to designated approach speeds provided in the California Manual on Uniform Traffic Control Devices are mandatory minimum yellow light intervals.

(c) A yellow light change interval may exceed the minimum interval established pursuant to subdivision (a). *(Added by Stats. 2001, c. 496 (S.B.667), § 2. Amended by Stats.2003, c. 511 (A.B. 1022), § 3; Stats.2015, c. 451 (S.B.491), § 46, eff. Jan. 1, 2016.)*

§ 21456. Requirements for pedestrian traffic control signals

Section operative until Jan. 1, 2024. See, also, § 21456 operative Jan. 1, 2024.

(a) If a pedestrian control signal showing the words "WALK" or "WAIT" or "DON'T WALK" or other approved symbol is in place, the signal shall indicate as follows:

(1) A "WALK" or approved "Walking Person" symbol means a pedestrian facing the signal may proceed across the roadway in the direction of the signal, but shall yield the right-of-way to vehicles lawfully within the intersection at the time that signal is first shown.

(2) A flashing "DON'T WALK" or "WAIT" or approved "Upraised Hand" symbol with a "countdown" signal indicating the time remaining for a pedestrian to cross the roadway means a pedestrian facing the signal may start to cross the roadway in the direction of the signal, but must complete the crossing prior to the display of the steady "DON'T WALK" or "WAIT" or approved "Upraised Hand" symbol when the "countdown" ends.

(3) A steady "DON'T WALK" or "WAIT" or approved "Upraised Hand" symbol or a flashing "DON'T WALK" or "WAIT" or approved "Upraised Hand" without a "countdown" signal indicating the time remaining for a pedestrian to cross the roadway means a pedestrian facing the signal shall not start to cross the roadway in the direction of the signal, but any pedestrian who started the crossing during the display of the "WALK" or approved "Walking Person" symbol and who has partially completed crossing shall proceed to a sidewalk or safety zone or otherwise leave the roadway while the steady "WAIT" or "DON'T WALK" or approved "Upraised Hand" symbol is showing.

(b)(1) A peace officer, as defined in Chapter 4.5 (commencing with Section 830) of Title 3 of Part 2 of the Penal Code, shall not stop a pedestrian for a violation of this section unless a reasonably careful person would realize there is an immediate danger of a collision with a moving vehicle or other device moving exclusively by human power.

(2) This subdivision does not relieve a pedestrian from the duty of using due care for their safety.

(3) This subdivision does not relieve a driver of a vehicle from the duty of exercising due care for the safety of any pedestrian within the roadway.

(c) This section shall remain in effect only until January 1, 2024, and as of that date is repealed. *(Stats.1959, c. 3, p. 1676, § 21456. Amended by Stats.1981, c. 413, p. 1611, § 9; Stats.2017, c. 402 (A.B.390), § 1, eff. Jan. 1, 2018; Stats.2022, c. 343 (A.B.1909), § 2, eff. Jan. 1, 2023; Stats.2022, c. 957 (A.B.2147), § 4.5, eff. Jan. 1, 2023.)*

Repeal

For repeal of this section, see its terms.

Cross References

Applicability of this section to trolley coaches, see Vehicle Code § 21051.
Definitions,
Intersection, see Vehicle Code § 365.
Official traffic control signal, see Vehicle Code § 445.
Roadway, see Vehicle Code § 530.
Duty of driver to yield right-of-way to pedestrian at crosswalk, see Vehicle Code § 21950.
Violation as misdemeanor, punishment, see Vehicle Code §§ 40000.5 et seq., 42002.

Research References

California Jury Instructions-Civil, 8th Edition 5.54, Pedestrian—Change of Signal After Crossing Begun.
2 Witkin, California Criminal Law 4th Crimes Against Public Peace and Welfare § 327 (2021), Miscellaneous Regulations.

§ 21456. Requirements for pedestrian traffic control signals

Section operative Jan. 1, 2024. See, also, § 21456 operative until Jan. 1, 2024.

(a) If a pedestrian control signal showing the words "WALK" or "WAIT" or "DON'T WALK" or other approved symbol is in place, the signal shall indicate as follows:

(1) A "WALK" or approved "Walking Person" symbol means a pedestrian facing the signal may proceed across the roadway in the direction of the signal, but shall yield the right-of-way to vehicles

lawfully within the intersection at the time that signal is first shown. Except as otherwise directed by a bicycle control signal described in Section 21456.3, the operator of a bicycle facing a pedestrian control signal displaying a "WALK" or approved "Walking Person" symbol may proceed across the roadway in the direction of the signal, but shall yield the right-of-way to any vehicles or pedestrians lawfully within the intersection.

(2) A flashing "DON'T WALK" or "WAIT" or approved "Upraised Hand" symbol with a "countdown" signal indicating the time remaining for a pedestrian to cross the roadway means a pedestrian facing the signal may start to cross the roadway in the direction of the signal, but must complete the crossing prior to the display of the steady "DON'T WALK" or "WAIT" or approved "Upraised Hand" symbol when the "countdown" ends.

(3) A steady "DON'T WALK" or "WAIT" or approved "Upraised Hand" symbol or a flashing "DON'T WALK" or "WAIT" or approved "Upraised Hand" without a "countdown" signal indicating the time remaining for a pedestrian to cross the roadway means a pedestrian facing the signal shall not start to cross the roadway in the direction of the signal, but any pedestrian who started the crossing during the display of the "WALK" or approved "Walking Person" symbol and who has partially completed crossing shall proceed to a sidewalk or safety zone or otherwise leave the roadway while the steady "WAIT" or "DON'T WALK" or approved "Upraised Hand" symbol is showing.

(b)(1) A peace officer, as defined in Chapter 4.5 (commencing with Section 830) of Title 3 of Part 2 of the Penal Code, shall not stop a pedestrian for a violation of this section unless a reasonably careful person would realize there is an immediate danger of a collision with a moving vehicle or other device moving exclusively by human power.

(2) This subdivision does not relieve a pedestrian from the duty of using due care for their safety.

(3) This subdivision does not relieve a driver of a vehicle from the duty of exercising due care for the safety of any pedestrian within the roadway.

(c) This section shall become operative on January 1, 2024. *(Added by Stats.2022, c. 957 (A.B.2147), § 4.6, eff. Jan. 1, 2023, operative Jan. 1, 2024.)*

Cross References

Applicability of this section to trolley coaches, see Vehicle Code § 21051.
Definitions,
Intersection, see Vehicle Code § 365.
Official traffic control signal, see Vehicle Code § 445.
Roadway, see Vehicle Code § 530.
Duty of driver to yield right-of-way to pedestrian at crosswalk, see Vehicle Code § 21950.
Violation as misdemeanor, punishment, see Vehicle Code §§ 40000.5 et seq., 42002.

§ 21456.1. Pedestrian traffic control

Whenever an official traffic control signal exhibiting an approved "Walking Person" symbol, an approved "Upraised Hand" symbol, or the words "WALK" or "WAIT" or "DON'T WALK" is shown concurrently with official traffic control signals exhibiting the words "GO" or "CAUTION" or "STOP" or exhibiting different colored lights successively, one at a time or with arrows, a pedestrian facing those traffic control signals shall obey the "Walking Person," "Upraised Hand," "WALK" or "WAIT" or "DON'T WALK" control signal as provided in Section 21456. *(Added by Stats.1961, c. 810, p. 2089, § 1. Amended by Stats.1993, c. 272 (A.B.301), § 39, eff. Aug. 2, 1993.)*

Research References

California Jury Instructions-Civil, 8th Edition 5.54, Pedestrian—Change of Signal After Crossing Begun.
2 Witkin, California Criminal Law 4th Crimes Against Public Peace and Welfare § 327 (2021), Miscellaneous Regulations.

§ 21456.2. Bicycle operators; obeying provisions of this article; bicycle signals

Section operative until Jan. 1, 2024. See, also, § 21456.2 operative Jan. 1, 2024.

(a) Unless otherwise directed by a bicycle signal as provided in Section 21456.3, an operator of a bicycle shall obey the provisions of this article applicable to the driver of a vehicle.

(b) Whenever an official traffic control signal exhibiting different colored bicycle symbols is shown concurrently with official traffic control signals exhibiting different colored lights or arrows, an operator of a bicycle facing those traffic control signals shall obey the bicycle signals as provided in Section 21456.3.

(c) This section shall remain in effect only until January 1, 2024, and as of that date is repealed. *(Amended by Stats.2005, c. 126 (A.B.56), § 3, eff. July 25, 2005; Stats.2022, c. 343 (A.B.1909), § 4, eff. Jan. 1, 2023.)*

Repeal

For repeal of this section, see its terms.

Research References

2 Witkin, California Criminal Law 4th Crimes Against Public Peace and Welfare § 530 (2021), Bicycles.

§ 21456.2. Bicycle operators; obeying provisions of this article; bicycle signals

Section operative Jan. 1, 2024. See, also, § 21456.2 operative until Jan. 1, 2024.

(a) Unless otherwise directed by a bicycle signal as provided in Section 21456.3, or as otherwise provided in subdivision (a) of Section 21456, an operator of a bicycle shall obey the provisions of this article applicable to the driver of a vehicle.

(b) Whenever an official traffic control signal exhibiting different colored bicycle symbols is shown concurrently with official traffic control signals or pedestrian control signals exhibiting different colored lights or arrows, an operator of a bicycle facing those traffic control signals shall obey the bicycle signals as provided in Section 21456.3.

(c) This section shall become operative on January 1, 2024. *(Added by Stats.2022, c. 343 (A.B.1909), § 5, eff. Jan. 1, 2023, operative Jan. 1, 2024.)*

§ 21456.3. Bicycle signals

Text of section as amended by Stats.2005, c. 126 (A.B.56), § 4, eff. July 25, 2005.

Section 21456.3 was added by Stats.1999, c. 277 (A.B.134), § 3, and repealed by its own terms, operative Jan. 1, 2005. Therefore, this section was not in effect from Jan. 1, 2005 until July 25, 2005.

Stats.2005, c. 126 (A.B.56), § 4, might be given effect as a new addition of this section; but see Government Code § 9609.

(a) An operator of a bicycle facing a green bicycle signal shall proceed straight through or turn right or left or make a U-turn unless a sign prohibits a U-turn. An operator of a bicycle, including one turning, shall yield the right-of-way to other traffic and to pedestrians lawfully within the intersection or an adjacent crosswalk.

(b) An operator of a bicycle facing a steady yellow bicycle signal is, by that signal, warned that the related green movement is ending or that a red indication will be shown immediately thereafter.

(c) Except as provided in subdivision (d), an operator of a bicycle facing a steady red bicycle signal shall stop at a marked limit line, but if none, before entering the crosswalk on the near side of the intersection, or, if none, then before entering the intersection, and shall remain stopped until an indication to proceed is shown.

(d) Except when a sign is in place prohibiting a turn, an operator of a bicycle, after stopping as required by subdivision (c), facing a steady red bicycle signal, may turn right, or turn left from a one-way street onto a one-way street. An operator of a bicycle making a turn shall yield the right-of-way to pedestrians lawfully within an adjacent crosswalk and to traffic lawfully using the intersection.

(e) A bicycle signal may be used only at those locations that meet geometric standards or traffic volume standards, or both, as adopted by the Department of Transportation. *(Amended by Stats.2005, c. 126 (A.B.56), § 4, eff. July 25, 2005.)*

§ 21457. Illuminated flashing red or yellow lights used in traffic signal or with traffic sign

Whenever an illuminated flashing red or yellow light is used in a traffic signal or with a traffic sign, it shall require obedience by drivers as follows:

(a) Flashing red (stop signal): When a red lens is illuminated with rapid intermittent flashes, a driver shall stop at a clearly marked limit line, but if none, before entering the crosswalk on the near side of the intersection, or if none, then at the point nearest the intersecting roadway where the driver has a view of approaching traffic on the intersecting roadway before entering it, and the driver may proceed subject to the rules applicable after making a stop at a stop sign.

(b) Flashing yellow (caution signal): When a yellow lens is illuminated with rapid intermittent flashes, a driver may proceed through the intersection or past the signal only with caution. *(Stats.1959, c. 3, p. 1676, § 21457. Amended by Stats.1959, c. 975, p. 3004, § 1; Stats.1972, c. 46, p. 64, § 1; Stats.1981, c. 413, p. 1611, § 10.)*

Cross References

Applicability of this section to trolley coaches, see Vehicle Code § 21051.
Definitions,
Crosswalk, see Vehicle Code § 275.
Intersection, see Vehicle Code § 365.
Official traffic control device, see Vehicle Code § 440.
Traffic, see Vehicle Code § 620.
Right of way, see Vehicle Code § 21802.
Violation as misdemeanor, punishment, see Vehicle Code §§ 40000.5 et seq., 42002.

Research References

2 Witkin, California Criminal Law 4th Crimes Against Public Peace and Welfare § 327 (2021), Miscellaneous Regulations.

§ 21458. Curb markings

(a) Whenever local authorities enact local parking regulations and indicate them by the use of paint upon curbs, the following colors only shall be used, and the colors indicate as follows:

(1) Red indicates no stopping, standing, or parking, whether the vehicle is attended or unattended, except that a bus may stop in a red zone marked or signposted as a bus loading zone.

(2) Yellow indicates stopping only for the purpose of loading or unloading passengers or freight for the time as may be specified by local ordinance.

(3) White indicates stopping for either of the following purposes:

(A) Loading or unloading of passengers for the time as may be specified by local ordinance.

(B) Depositing mail in an adjacent mailbox.

(4) Green indicates time limit parking specified by local ordinance.

(5) Blue indicates parking limited exclusively to the vehicles of disabled persons and disabled veterans.

(b) Regulations adopted pursuant to subdivision (a) shall be effective on days and during hours or times as prescribed by local ordinances. *(Stats.1959, c. 3, p. 1676, § 21458. Amended by Stats.1975, c. 688, p. 1636, § 1; Stats.1985, c. 1041, § 4; Stats.1992, c. 1243 (A.B.3090), § 88, eff. Sept. 30, 1992.)*

Cross References

Local authorities defined, see Vehicle Code § 385.
Stopping, standing or parking, see Vehicle Code § 22500 et seq.
Violation as misdemeanor, punishment, see Vehicle Code §§ 40000.5 et seq., 42002.

Research References

2 Witkin, California Criminal Law 4th Crimes Against Public Peace and Welfare § 327 (2021), Miscellaneous Regulations.

§ 21459. Distinctive roadway markings

(a) The Department of Transportation in respect to state highways and a local authority with respect to highways under its jurisdiction, is authorized to place and maintain upon highways distinctive roadway markings as described and with the effect set forth in Section 21460.

(b) The distinctive roadway markings shall be employed to designate any portion of a highway where the volume of traffic or the vertical or other curvature of the roadway renders it hazardous to drive on the left side of the marking or to indicate no driving to the left as provided in Section 21460, and shall not be employed for any other purpose.

(c) Any pavement marking other than as described in this section placed by the Department of Transportation or any local authority shall not be effective to indicate no driving over or to the left of the marking. *(Stats.1959, c. 3, p. 1677, § 21459. Amended by Stats.1974, c. 545, p. 1318, § 185.)*

Cross References

Definitions,
Highway, see Vehicle Code § 360.
Local authorities, see Vehicle Code § 385.
Roadway, see Vehicle Code § 530.
Powers of local authorities, generally, see Vehicle Code § 21100 et seq.
Traffic signs, signals, and markings, maintenance and placing by State Department of Transportation and local authorities, see Vehicle Code §§ 21350, 21351.

Research References

2 Witkin, California Criminal Law 4th Crimes Against Public Peace and Welfare § 327 (2021), Miscellaneous Regulations.

§ 21460. Double lines

(a) If double parallel solid yellow lines are in place, a person driving a vehicle shall not drive to the left of the lines, except as permitted in this section.

(b) If double parallel solid white lines are in place, a person driving a vehicle shall not cross any part of those double solid white lines, except as permitted in this section or Section 21655.8.

(c) If the double parallel lines, one of which is broken, are in place, a person driving a vehicle shall not drive to the left of the lines, except as follows:

(1) If the driver is on the side of the roadway in which the broken line is in place, the driver may cross over the double lines or drive to the left of the double lines when overtaking or passing other vehicles.

(2) As provided in Section 21460.5.

(d) The markings as specified in subdivision (a), (b), or (c) do not prohibit a driver from crossing the marking if (1) turning to the left at an intersection or into or out of a driveway or private road, or (2) making a U–turn under the rules governing that turn, and the markings shall be disregarded when authorized signs have been erected designating offcenter traffic lanes as permitted pursuant to Section 21657.

(e) Raised pavement markers may be used to simulate painted lines described in this section if the markers are placed in accordance with standards established by the Department of Transportation. *(Stats.1959, c. 3, p. 1677, § 21460. Amended by Stats.1959, c. 255, p. 2157, § 1; Stats.1959, c. 1996, p. 4630, § 25; Stats.1961, c. 446, p. 1519, § 1; Stats.1968, c. 508, p. 1152, § 1; Stats.1971, c. 988, p. 1903, § 2, operative May 3, 1972; Stats.1974, c. 545, p. 1318, § 186; Stats.1976, c. 482, p. 1226, § 1; Stats.1984, c. 462, § 1; Stats.2011, c. 114 (A.B.1105), § 2.)*

Cross References

Definitions,
  Driver, see Vehicle Code § 305.
  Intersection, see Vehicle Code § 365.
  Roadway, see Vehicle Code § 530.
  Vehicle, see Vehicle Code § 670.
Violation as misdemeanor, punishment, see Vehicle Code §§ 40000.5 et seq., 42002.

Research References

California Jury Instructions-Civil, 8th Edition 11.59, Failure to Provide Regulatory Traffic Signs and Signals.
2 Witkin, California Criminal Law 4th Crimes Against Public Peace and Welfare § 327 (2021), Miscellaneous Regulations.

§ 21460.5. Two-way left-turn lanes

(a) The Department of Transportation and local authorities in their respective jurisdictions may designate a two-way left-turn lane on a highway. A two-way left-turn lane is a lane near the center of the highway set aside for use by vehicles making left turns in both directions from or into the highway.

(b) Two-way left-turn lanes shall be designated by distinctive roadway markings consisting of parallel double yellow lines, interior line dashed and exterior line solid, on each side of the lane. The Department of Transportation may determine and prescribe standards and specifications governing length, width, and positioning of the distinctive pavement markings. All pavement markings designating a two-way left-turn lane shall conform to the Department of Transportation's standards and specifications.

(c) A vehicle shall not be driven in a designated two-way left-turn lane except when preparing for or making a left turn from or into a highway or when preparing for or making a U-turn when otherwise permitted by law, and shall not be driven in that lane for more than 200 feet while preparing for and making the turn or while preparing to merge into the adjacent lanes of travel. A left turn or U-turn shall not be made from any other lane where a two-way left-turn lane has been designated.

(d) This section does not prohibit driving across a two-way left-turn lane.

(e) Raised pavement markers may be used to simulate the painted lines described in this section when those markers are placed in accordance with standards established by the Department of Transportation. *(Added by Stats.1976, c. 482, p. 1227, § 3, operative Jan. 1, 1980. Amended by Stats.1979, c. 364, p. 1229, § 1; Stats.1990, c. 232 (A.B.2769), § 1.)*

Research References

California Jury Instructions-Civil, 8th Edition 11.59, Failure to Provide Regulatory Traffic Signs and Signals.
2 Witkin, California Criminal Law 4th Crimes Against Public Peace and Welfare § 327 (2021), Miscellaneous Regulations.

§ 21461. Obedience by driver to official traffic control devices

(a) It is unlawful for a driver of a vehicle to fail to obey a sign or signal defined as regulatory in the federal Manual on Uniform Traffic Control Devices, or a Department of Transportation approved supplement to that manual of a regulatory nature erected or maintained to enhance traffic safety and operations or to indicate and carry out the provisions of this code or a local traffic ordinance or resolution adopted pursuant to a local traffic ordinance, or to fail to obey a device erected or maintained by lawful authority of a public body or official.

(b) Subdivision (a) does not apply to acts constituting violations under Chapter 9 (commencing with Section 22500) of this division or to acts constituting violations of a local traffic ordinance adopted pursuant to Chapter 9 (commencing with Section 22500). *(Stats. 1959, c. 3, p. 1677, § 21461. Amended by Stats.1970, c. 827, p. 1561, § 1; Stats.1981, c. 775, p. 3029, § 2; Stats.2004, c. 203 (A.B.1951), § 1.)*

Cross References

Applicability of this section to trolley coaches, see Vehicle Code § 21051.
Damage to highway, weight or size of vehicle, see Vehicle Code § 17302.
Highway signs, markers or warning notices, failure to observe, see Vehicle Code §§ 21367, 40000.14.
Official traffic control device defined, see Vehicle Code § 440.
Weight violations, penalty, see Vehicle Code § 42030 et seq.

Research References

2 Witkin, California Criminal Law 4th Crimes Against Public Peace and Welfare § 327 (2021), Miscellaneous Regulations.

§ 21461.5. Obedience by pedestrian to official traffic control devices; enforcement by peace officer

(a) It shall be unlawful for any pedestrian to fail to obey any sign or signal erected or maintained to indicate or carry out the provisions of this code or any local traffic ordinance or resolution adopted pursuant to a local traffic ordinance, or to fail to obey any device erected or maintained pursuant to Section 21352.

(b)(1) A peace officer, as defined in Chapter 4.5 (commencing with Section 830) of Title 3 of Part 2 of the Penal Code, shall not stop a pedestrian for a violation of subdivision (a) unless a reasonably careful person would realize there is an immediate danger of a collision with a moving vehicle or other device moving exclusively by human power.

(2) This subdivision does not relieve a pedestrian from the duty of using due care for their safety.

(3) This subdivision does not relieve a driver of a vehicle from the duty of exercising due care for the safety of any pedestrian within the roadway. *(Added by Stats.1970, c. 827, p. 1561, § 2. Amended by Stats.2022, c. 957 (A.B.2147), § 5, eff. Jan. 1, 2023.)*

§ 21462. Obedience to traffic control signals; enforcement by peace officer

(a) The driver of a vehicle, the person in charge of an animal, a pedestrian, and the motorist of a streetcar shall obey the instructions of an official traffic signal applicable to them and placed as provided by law, unless otherwise directed by a police or traffic officer or when it is necessary for the purpose of avoiding a collision or in case of other emergency, subject to the exemptions granted by Section 21055.

(b)(1) A peace officer, as defined in Chapter 4.5 (commencing with Section 830) of Title 3 of Part 2 of the Penal Code, shall not stop a pedestrian for a violation of subdivision (a) unless a reasonably careful person would realize there is an immediate danger of a collision with a moving vehicle or other device moving exclusively by human power.

(2) This subdivision does not relieve a pedestrian from the duty of using due care for their safety.

(3) This subdivision does not relieve a driver of a vehicle from the duty of exercising due care for the safety of any pedestrian within the

roadway. *(Stats.1959, c. 3, p. 1677, § 21462. Amended by Stats.2022, c. 957 (A.B.2147), § 6, eff. Jan. 1, 2023.)*

Cross References

Crossing between controlled intersections, see Vehicle Code § 21955.
Duration of prohibition against operation of commercial motor vehicle, see Vehicle Code § 15312.
Emergency vehicles, right-of-way, see Vehicle Code § 21806.
Exemption of authorized emergency vehicles, see Vehicle Code § 21055.
Obedience to peace officers, see Vehicle Code § 2800.
Official traffic control signal defined, see Vehicle Code § 445.
Violations, see Vehicle Code § 40000.1 et seq.

§ 21463. Illegal operation of signals

No person shall operate a manually or traffic actuated signal other than for the purpose of permitting a pedestrian or vehicle to cross a roadway. *(Stats.1959, c. 3, p. 1678, § 21463.)*

Cross References

Violations, see Vehicle Code § 40000.1 et seq.

§ 21464. Interference with traffic devices; limitations on use and purchase, possession, manufacture, sale, etc. of mobile infrared transmitters and related devices; penalties

(a) A person, without lawful authority, may not deface, injure, attach any material or substance to, knock down, or remove, nor may a person shoot at, any official traffic control device, traffic guidepost, traffic signpost, motorist callbox, or historical marker placed or erected as authorized or required by law, nor may a person without lawful authority deface, injure, attach any material or substance to, or remove, nor may a person shoot at, any inscription, shield, or insignia on any device, guide, or marker.

(b) A person may not use, and a vehicle, other than an authorized emergency vehicle or a public transit passenger vehicle, may not be equipped with, any device, including, but not limited to, a mobile infrared transmitter, that is capable of sending a signal that interrupts or changes the sequence patterns of an official traffic control signal unless that device or use is authorized by the Department of Transportation pursuant to Section 21350 or by local authorities pursuant to Section 21351.

(c) A person may not buy, possess, manufacture, install, sell, offer for sale, or otherwise distribute a device described in subdivision (b), including, but not limited to, a mobile infrared transmitter (MIRT), unless the purchase, possession, manufacture, installation, sale, offer for sale, or distribution is for the use of the device by a peace officer or other person authorized to operate an authorized emergency vehicle or a public transit passenger vehicle, in the scope of his or her duties.

(d) Any willful violation of subdivision (a), (b), or (c) that results in injury to, or the death of, a person is punishable by imprisonment pursuant to subdivision (h) of Section 1170 of the Penal Code, or by imprisonment in a county jail for a period of not more than six months, and by a fine of not less than five thousand dollars ($5,000) nor more than ten thousand dollars ($10,000).

(e) Any willful violation of subdivision (a), (b), or (c) that does not result in injury to, or the death of, a person is punishable by a fine of not more than five thousand dollars ($5,000).

(f) The court shall allow the offender to perform community service designated by the court in lieu of all or part of any fine imposed under this section. *(Stats.1959, c. 3, p. 1678, § 21464. Amended by Stats.1959, c. 1996, p. 4630, § 26; Stats.1963, c. 659, p. 1648, § 1; Stats.1970, c. 810, p. 1532, § 1; Stats.1976, c. 1139, p. 5172, § 338, operative July 1, 1977; Stats.1977, c. 805, p. 2457, § 1; Stats.1990, c. 447 (A.B.2723), § 1; Stats.1992, c. 1243 (A.B.3090), § 89, eff. Sept. 30, 1992; Stats.2004, c. 338 (A.B.340), § 1; Stats.2004, c. 391 (S.B.1085), § 1; Stats.2011, c. 15 (A.B.109), § 607, eff. April 4, 2011, operative Oct. 1, 2011.)*

Cross References

Highway signs, markers or warning notices, failure to observe, see Vehicle Code §§ 21367, 40000.14.
Illegal operation of signals, see Vehicle Code § 21463.
Official traffic control device, see Vehicle Code § 440.
Public offenses, infractions and special misdemeanors, see Vehicle Code § 42001.
Violations, see Vehicle Code § 40000.1 et seq.

Research References

2 Witkin, California Criminal Law 4th Crimes Against Property § 301 (2021), Acts Involving Roads, Highways, or Traffic Devices.

§ 21465. Unauthorized traffic devices

No person shall place, maintain, or display upon, or in view of, any highway any unofficial sign, signal, device, or marking, or any sign, signal, device, or marking which purports to be or is an imitation of, or resembles, an official traffic control device or which attempts to direct the movement of traffic or which hides from view any official traffic control device. *(Stats.1959, c. 3, p. 1678, § 21465. Amended by Stats.1967, c. 486, p. 1693, § 1.)*

Cross References

Definitions,
Highway, see Vehicle Code § 360.
Official traffic control device, see Vehicle Code § 440.
Traffic, see Vehicle Code § 620.
Highway signs, markers or warning notices, failure to observe, see Vehicle Code §§ 21367, 40000.14.
Violations, see Vehicle Code § 40000.1 et seq.

Research References

2 Witkin, California Criminal Law 4th Crimes Against Property § 301 (2021), Acts Involving Roads, Highways, or Traffic Devices.

§ 21466. Light preventing recognition of official traffic control device

No person shall place or maintain or display upon or in view of any highway any light in such position as to prevent the driver of a vehicle from readily recognizing any official traffic control device. *(Stats. 1959, c. 3, p. 1678, § 21466. Amended by Stats.1970, c. 968, p. 1736, § 2, eff. Sept. 14, 1970.)*

Cross References

Definitions,
Driver, see Vehicle Code § 305.
Highway, see Vehicle Code § 360.
Official traffic control device, see Vehicle Code § 440.
Vehicle, see Vehicle Code § 670.
Violations, see Vehicle Code § 40000.1 et seq.

§ 21466.5. Light impairing driver's vision

No person shall place or maintain or display, upon or in view of any highway, any light of any color of such brilliance as to impair the vision of drivers upon the highway. A light source shall be considered vision impairing when its brilliance exceeds the values listed below.

The brightness reading of an objectionable light source shall be measured with a 1½-degree photoelectric brightness meter placed at the driver's point of view. The maximum measured brightness of the light source within 10 degrees from the driver's normal line of sight shall not be more than 1,000 times the minimum measured brightness in the driver's field of view, except that when the minimum measured brightness in the field of view is 10 foot-lamberts or less, the measured brightness of the light source in foot-lambert shall not exceed 500 plus 100 times the angle, in degrees, between the driver's line of sight and the light source.

The provisions of this section shall not apply to railroads as defined in Section 229 of the Public Utilities Code. *(Added by Stats.1970, c. 968, p. 1736, § 3, eff. Sept. 14, 1970.)*

§ 21467. Prohibited signs and devices

Every prohibited sign, signal, device, or light is a public nuisance, and the Department of Transportation, members of the California Highway Patrol, and local authorities are hereby authorized and empowered without notice to remove the same, or cause the same to be removed, or the Director of Transportation, the commissioner, or local authorities may bring an action as provided by law to abate such nuisance. *(Stats.1959, c. 3, p. 1678, § 21467. Amended by Stats. 1974, c. 545, p. 1319, § 188.)*

Cross References

Abatement of public nuisance, see Civil Code § 3494; Code of Civil Procedure § 731.
Definition,
Commissioner, see Vehicle Code § 265.
Local authorities, see Vehicle Code § 385.

§ 21468. Public utilities

This division does not modify or limit the authority of the Public Utilities Commission to erect or maintain, or cause to be erected and maintained, signs, signals or other traffic control devices as authorized by law. *(Stats.1959, c. 3, p. 1678, § 21468.)*

Cross References

Official traffic control device defined, see Vehicle Code § 440.

CHAPTER 3. DRIVING, OVERTAKING, AND PASSING

ARTICLE 1. DRIVING ON RIGHT SIDE

§ 21650. Highways; vehicles required to drive on right side of roadway; exceptions

Upon all highways, a vehicle shall be driven upon the right half of the roadway, except as follows:

(a) When overtaking and passing another vehicle proceeding in the same direction under the rules governing that movement.

(b) When placing a vehicle in a lawful position for, and when the vehicle is lawfully making, a left turn.

(c) When the right half of a roadway is closed to traffic under construction or repair.

(d) Upon a roadway restricted to one-way traffic.

(e) When the roadway is not of sufficient width.

(f) When the vehicle is necessarily traveling so slowly as to impede the normal movement of traffic, that portion of the highway adjacent to the right edge of the roadway may be utilized temporarily when in a condition permitting safe operation.

(g) This section does not prohibit the operation of bicycles on any shoulder of a highway, on any sidewalk, on any bicycle path within a highway, or along any crosswalk or bicycle path crossing, where the operation is not otherwise prohibited by this code or local ordinance.

(h) This section does not prohibit the operation of a transit bus on the shoulder of a state highway in conjunction with the implementation of a program authorized pursuant to Section 148.1 of the Streets and Highways Code on state highways within the areas served by the transit services of the Monterey–Salinas Transit District or the Santa Cruz Metropolitan Transit District. *(Stats.1959, c. 3, p. 1678, § 21650. Amended by Stats.1961, c. 1185, p. 2919, § 1; Stats.1969, c. 136, p. 288, § 2; Stats.1988, c. 58, § 1; Stats.2009, c. 200 (S.B.734), § 10; Stats.2013, c. 426 (A.B.946), § 2.)*

Cross References

Applicability of this section to trolley coaches, see Vehicle Code § 21051.
Limitations on overtaking on left, see Vehicle Code §§ 21751, 21752.
Overtaking and passing of vehicles on right, see Vehicle Code §§ 21754, 21755.
Overtaking and passing on grades prohibited, see Vehicle Code § 21758.
Overtaking animals, caution required in, see Vehicle Code § 21759.
Passing of vehicles going in opposite directions, see Vehicle Code §§ 21660, 21661.
Roadways laned for traffic, regulations as to driving on, see Vehicle Code §§ 21658, 21659.
Rubbish or garbage trucks, exemption, see Vehicle Code § 21059.
Rules governing overtaking of vehicle on left, see Vehicle Code § 21750 et seq.
Rules of the road, exemption of authorized emergency vehicles, see Vehicle Code § 21054.
School bus, overtaking of, see Vehicle Code § 22454.

Research References

2 Witkin, California Criminal Law 4th Crimes Against Public Peace and Welfare § 327 (2021), Miscellaneous Regulations.

§ 21650.1. Bicycles; operation on roadway or shoulder; direction

A bicycle operated on a roadway, or the shoulder of a highway, shall be operated in the same direction as vehicles are required to be driven upon the roadway. *(Added by Stats.1988, c. 58, § 2.)*

Research References

2 Witkin, California Criminal Law 4th Crimes Against Public Peace and Welfare § 327 (2021), Miscellaneous Regulations.

§ 21651. Divided highways

(a) Whenever a highway has been divided into two or more roadways by means of intermittent barriers or by means of a dividing section of not less than two feet in width, either unpaved or delineated by curbs, double-parallel lines, or other markings on the roadway, it is unlawful to do either of the following:

(1) To drive any vehicle over, upon, or across the dividing section.

(2) To make any left, semicircular, or U-turn with the vehicle on the divided highway, except through an opening in the barrier designated and intended by public authorities for the use of vehicles or through a plainly marked opening in the dividing section.

(b) It is unlawful to drive any vehicle upon a highway, except to the right of an intermittent barrier or a dividing section which separates two or more opposing lanes of traffic. Except as otherwise provided in subdivision (c), a violation of this subdivision is a misdemeanor.

(c) Any willful violation of subdivision (b) which results in injury to, or death of, a person shall be punished by imprisonment pursuant to subdivision (h) of Section 1170 of the Penal Code, or imprisonment in a county jail for a period of not more than six months. *(Added by Stats.1982, c. 569, p. 2525, § 2. Amended by Stats.1986, c. 362, § 2; Stats.1988, c. 765, § 1; Stats.2011, c. 15 (A.B.109), § 608, eff. April 4, 2011, operative Oct. 1, 2011.)*

Cross References

Animals, caution in passing, see Vehicle Code § 21759.
Applicability of this section to trolley coaches, see Vehicle Code § 21051.
Overtaking and passing, see Vehicle Code § 21750 et seq.
Overtaking school bus, see Vehicle Code § 22454.
Passing on grades, see Vehicle Code § 21758.
Passing on the right, see Vehicle Code §§ 21754, 21755.
Traffic violation point count, violation of this section, see Vehicle Code § 12810.
Violation as misdemeanor, see Vehicle Code § 40000.13.

Research References

2 Witkin, California Criminal Law 4th Crimes Against Public Peace and Welfare § 327 (2021), Miscellaneous Regulations.

§ 21652. Entering or leaving public highway via service road

When any service road has been constructed on or along any public highway and the main thoroughfare of the highway has been separated from the service road, it is unlawful for any person to drive any vehicle into the main thoroughfare from the service road or from the main thoroughfare into the service road except through an opening in the dividing curb, section, separation, or line. *(Stats.1959, c. 3, p. 1679, § 21652. Amended by Stats.1959, c. 507, p. 2468, § 2; Stats.1963, c. 335, p. 1124, § 1.)*

Cross References

Highway defined, see Vehicle Code §§ 360, 590.

Research References

2 Witkin, California Criminal Law 4th Crimes Against Public Peace and Welfare § 327 (2021), Miscellaneous Regulations.

§ 21654. Slow-moving vehicles

(a) Notwithstanding the prima facie speed limits, any vehicle proceeding upon a highway at a speed less than the normal speed of traffic moving in the same direction at such time shall be driven in the right-hand lane for traffic or as close as practicable to the right-hand edge or curb, except when overtaking and passing another vehicle proceeding in the same direction or when preparing for a left turn at an intersection or into a private road or driveway.

(b) If a vehicle is being driven at a speed less than the normal speed of traffic moving in the same direction at such time, and is not being driven in the right-hand lane for traffic or as close as practicable to the right-hand edge or curb, it shall constitute prima facie evidence that the driver is operating the vehicle in violation of subdivision (a) of this section.

(c) The Department of Transportation, with respect to state highways, and local authorities, with respect to highways under their jurisdiction, may place and maintain upon highways official signs directing slow-moving traffic to use the right-hand traffic lane except when overtaking and passing another vehicle or preparing for a left turn. *(Stats.1959, c. 3, p. 1679, § 21654. Amended by Stats.1959, c. 1747, p. 4205, § 2, eff. July 13, 1959; Stats.1965, c. 448, p. 1758, § 1; Stats.1974, c. 545, p. 1319, § 189.)*

Cross References

Conditions for overtaking and passing vehicle on right, see Vehicle Code §§ 21754, 21755.
Highway defined, see Vehicle Code § 590.
Intersection defined, see Vehicle Code § 365.
Prima facie speed limits, see Vehicle Code § 22352.
Private road or driveway defined, see Vehicle Code § 490.
Speed laws generally, see Vehicle Code § 22349 et seq.

Research References

2 Witkin, California Criminal Law 4th Crimes Against Public Peace and Welfare § 327 (2021), Miscellaneous Regulations.

§ 21655. Designated lanes for certain vehicles

(a) Whenever the Department of Transportation or local authorities with respect to highways under their respective jurisdictions determines upon the basis of an engineering and traffic investigation that the designation of a specific lane or lanes for the travel of vehicles required to travel at reduced speeds would facilitate the safe and orderly movement of traffic, the department or local authority may designate a specific lane or lanes for the travel of vehicles which are subject to the provisions of Section 22406 and shall erect signs at reasonable intervals giving notice thereof.

(b) Any trailer bus, except as provided in Section 21655.5, and any vehicle subject to the provisions of Section 22406 shall be driven in the lane or lanes designated pursuant to subdivision (a) whenever signs have been erected giving notice of that designation. Except as otherwise provided in this subdivision, when a specific lane or lanes have not been so designated, any of those vehicles shall be driven in the right-hand lane for traffic or as close as practicable to the right edge or curb. If, however, a specific lane or lanes have not been designated on a divided highway having four or more clearly marked lanes for traffic in one direction, any of those vehicles may also be driven in the lane to the immediate left of that right-hand lane, unless otherwise prohibited under this code. When overtaking and passing another vehicle proceeding in the same direction, the driver shall use either the designated lane, the lane to the immediate left of the right-hand lane, or the right-hand lane for traffic as permitted under this code.

This subdivision does not apply to a driver who is preparing for a left- or right-hand turn or who is entering into or exiting from a highway or to a driver who must necessarily drive in a lane other than the right-hand lane to continue on his or her intended route. *(Stats.1959, c. 3, p. 1679, § 21655. Amended by Stats.1963, c. 323, p. 1110, § 1; Stats.1963, c. 1585, p. 3165, § 1; Stats.1965, c. 69, p. 949, § 1; Stats.1967, c. 78, p. 975, § 1; Stats.1970, c. 219, p. 471, § 1; Stats.1974, c. 545, p. 1320, § 190; Stats.1975, c. 542, p. 1109, § 1; Stats.1988, c. 843, § 4.)*

Cross References

Highway defined, see Vehicle Code §§ 360, 590.
Intersection defined, see Vehicle Code § 365.
Overtaking on right, when permitted, see Vehicle Code §§ 21754, 21755.
Private road or driveway defined, see Vehicle Code § 490.

Research References

2 Witkin, California Criminal Law 4th Crimes Against Public Peace and Welfare § 327 (2021), Miscellaneous Regulations.

§ 21655.1. Exclusive use of public transit buses

(a) A person shall not operate a motor vehicle on a portion of a highway that has been designated for the exclusive use of public transit buses, except in compliance with the directions of a peace officer or official traffic control device.

(b) This section does not apply to a driver who is required to enter a lane designated for the exclusive use of public transit buses in order to make a right turn or a left turn in a location where there is no left-turn lane for motorists, or who is entering into or exiting from a highway, unless there are signs prohibiting turns across the lane or the lane is delineated by a physical separation, including, but not limited to, a curb, fence, landscaping, or other barrier.

(c) A public transit agency, with the agreement of the agency with jurisdiction over the highway, shall place and maintain, or cause to be placed and maintained, signs and other official traffic control devices, as necessary, indicating that a portion of a highway is designated for the exclusive use of public transit buses and to advise motorists of the hours of operation of the lane as an exclusive public transit bus lane. *(Added by Stats.2016, c. 716 (S.B.998), § 1, eff. Jan. 1, 2017.)*

Research References

2 Witkin, California Criminal Law 4th Crimes Against Public Peace and Welfare § 327 (2021), Miscellaneous Regulations.

§ 21655.5. Exclusive or preferential use of highway lanes for high-occupancy vehicles; exceptions for motorcycles, mass transit vehicles, blood transport vehicles and paratransit vehicles

(a) The Department of Transportation and local authorities, with respect to highways under their respective jurisdictions, may authorize or permit exclusive or preferential use of highway lanes for high-occupancy vehicles. Prior to establishing the lanes, competent engineering estimates shall be made of the effect of the lanes on safety, congestion, and highway capacity.

(b) The Department of Transportation and local authorities, with respect to highways under their respective jurisdictions, shall place and maintain, or cause to be placed and maintained, signs and other official traffic control devices to designate the exclusive or preferential lanes, to advise motorists of the applicable vehicle occupancy levels, and, except where ramp metering and bypass lanes are regulated with the activation of traffic signals, to advise motorists of the hours of high-occupancy vehicle usage. A person shall not drive a vehicle upon those lanes except in conformity with the instructions imparted by the official traffic control devices. A motorcycle, a mass transit vehicle, a blood transport vehicle that is clearly and identifiably marked as such on all sides of the vehicle, or a paratransit vehicle that is clearly and identifiably marked on all sides of the vehicle with the name of the paratransit provider may be operated upon those exclusive or preferential use lanes unless specifically prohibited by a traffic control device.

(c) When responding to an existing emergency or breakdown in which a mass transit vehicle is blocking an exclusive or preferential use lane, a clearly marked mass transit vehicle, mass transit supervisor's vehicle, or mass transit maintenance vehicle that is responding to the emergency or breakdown may be operated in the segment of the exclusive or preferential use lane being blocked by the mass transit vehicle, regardless of the number of persons in the vehicle responding to the emergency or breakdown, if both vehicles are owned or operated by the same agency, and that agency provides public mass transit services.

(d) For purposes of this section, the following definitions apply:

(1) "Blood transport vehicle" means a vehicle owned and operated by the American Red Cross or a blood bank that is transporting blood between collection points and hospitals or storage centers.

(2) "Mass transit vehicle" means a transit bus regularly used to transport paying passengers in mass transit service.

(3) "Paratransit vehicle" as defined in Section 462.

(e) It is the intent of the Legislature, in amending this section, to stimulate and encourage the development of ways and means of relieving traffic congestion on California highways and, at the same time, to encourage individual citizens to pool their vehicular resources and thereby conserve fuel and lessen emission of air pollutants.

(f) The provisions of this section regarding mass transit vehicles and paratransit vehicles shall only apply if the Director of Transportation determines that the application will not subject the state to a reduction in the amount of federal aid for highways.

(g) The authority for a blood transport vehicle to use exclusive or preferential lanes in accordance with subdivision (b) shall only be operative under either of the following circumstances:

(1) The Director of Transportation determines that the use of those lanes by those vehicles will not cause a reduction of federal aid funds for highways or otherwise be inconsistent with federal law or regulations, or with any agreement between the state and a federal agency or department, and the director posts that determination on the Department of Transportation's Internet Web site.

(2) The Federal Highway Administration of the United States Department of Transportation, upon the request of the director, makes that determination and the director posts the determination on the Department of Transportation's Internet Web site. *(Added by Stats.1970, c. 1295, p. 2399, § 12. Amended by Stats.1974, c. 545, p. 1320, § 191; Stats.1974, c. 773, p. 1697, § 5; Stats.1982, c. 466, p. 2057, § 114; Stats.1984, c. 826, § 1, eff. Aug. 31, 1984; Stats.1991, c. 143 (A.B.340), § 1; Stats.1993, c. 133 (S.B.948), § 1; Stats.1997, c. 579 (S.B.236), § 1; Stats.2002, c. 277 (A.B.2582), § 1; Stats.2017, c. 392 (S.B.406), § 2, eff. Jan. 1, 2018.)*

Cross References

Administration of state highways, San Diego Association of Governments (SANDAG), value pricing and transit development demonstration program, see Streets and Highways Code § 149.4.
State highway administration, Santa Clara Valley Transportation Authority, value pricing program on high-occupancy vehicle lane systems, see Streets and Highways Code § 149.6.
State highway administration, Sunol Smart Carpool Lane Joint Powers Authority, value pricing high-occupancy vehicle program, see Streets and Highways Code § 149.5.
Value pricing and transit development program on State Highway Route 5 in managed lanes serving as high-occupancy vehicle expressway, single-occupant vehicles meeting specified requirements exempt from this section, see Streets and Highways Code § 149.10.
Value-pricing and transit development program involving high-occupancy toll lanes on State Highway Routes 10 and 110, operation by Los Angeles County Metropolitan Transportation Authority, exemptions from this section, see Streets and Highways Code § 149.9.

Research References

2 Witkin, California Criminal Law 4th Crimes Against Public Peace and Welfare § 327 (2021), Miscellaneous Regulations.

§ 21655.6. Highway lanes for high-occupancy vehicles; approval required

(a) Whenever the Department of Transportation authorizes or permits exclusive or preferential use of highway lanes for high-occupancy vehicles on any highway located within the territory of a transportation planning agency, as defined in Section 99214 of the Public Utilities Code, or a county transportation commission, the department shall obtain the approval of the transportation planning agency or county transportation commission prior to establishing the exclusive or preferential use of the highway lanes.

(b) If the department authorizes or permits additional exclusive or preferential use of highway lanes for high-occupancy vehicles on that portion of State Highway Route 101 located within the boundaries of the City of Los Angeles, the department shall obtain the approval of the Los Angeles County Transportation Commission by at least a two-thirds majority vote of the entire membership eligible to vote prior to establishing the additional exclusion or preferential use of the highway lanes.

(c) If the department restricts or requires the restriction of the use of any lane on any federal-aid highway in the unincorporated areas of Alameda County to high-occupancy vehicles, the Metropolitan Transportation Commission shall review the use patterns of those lanes and shall determine if congestion relief is being efficiently achieved by the creation of the high-occupancy vehicle lanes. The commission shall report its findings and recommendations in its HOV Master Plan Update for the San Francisco Bay area no later than two years after those high-occupancy vehicle lanes become operational. *(Added by Stats.1982, c. 588, p. 2548, § 1, eff. Aug. 25, 1982. Amended by Stats.1984, c. 25, § 1; Stats.1998, c. 653 (A.B. 1624), § 1.)*

Cross References

State highway administration, Santa Clara Valley Transportation Authority, value pricing program on high-occupancy vehicle lane systems, see Streets and Highways Code § 149.6.

State highway administration, Sunol Smart Carpool Lane Joint Powers Authority, value pricing high-occupancy vehicle program, see Streets and Highways Code § 149.5.

§ 21655.7. Public mass transit guideway; highway use; local permit

A local authority, with respect to any highway under its jurisdiction, may authorize or permit a portion of the highway to be used exclusively for a public mass transit guideway. *(Added by Stats.1981, c. 1055, p. 4079, § 12.)*

§ 21655.8. Exclusive or preferential use lanes for high-occupancy vehicles; entrance or exit

(a) Except as required under subdivision (b), when exclusive or preferential use lanes for high-occupancy vehicles are established pursuant to Section 21655.5 and double parallel solid lines are in place to the right thereof, no person driving a vehicle may cross over these double lines to enter into or exit from the exclusive or preferential use lanes, and entrance or exit may be made only in areas designated for these purposes or where a single broken line is in place to the right of the exclusive or preferential use lanes.

(b) Upon the approach of an authorized emergency vehicle displaying a red light or siren, as specified in Section 21806, a person driving a vehicle in an exclusive or preferential use lane shall exit that lane immediately upon determining that the exit can be accomplished with reasonable safety.

(c) Raised pavement markers may be used to simulate painted lines described in this section. *(Added by Stats.1988, c. 1054, § 2. Amended by Stats.1996, c. 1154 (A.B.3020), § 67, eff. Sept. 30, 1996.)*

§ 21655.9. Exclusive or preferential use of highway lanes or access ramps for vehicles with distinctive identifiers; report to Legislature on degradation status of high-occupancy vehicle lanes

(a)(1) Whenever the Department of Transportation or a local authority authorizes or permits exclusive or preferential use of highway lanes or highway access ramps for high-occupancy vehicles pursuant to Section 21655.5, the use of those lanes or ramps shall also be extended to vehicles that are issued distinctive decals, labels, or other identifiers pursuant to Section 5205.5 regardless of vehicle occupancy or ownership.

(2) A local authority during periods of peak congestion shall suspend for a lane the access privileges extended pursuant to paragraph (1) for those vehicles issued distinctive decals, labels, or other identifiers pursuant to Section 5205.5, if a periodic review of lane performance by that local authority discloses both of the following factors regarding the lane:

(A) The lane, or a portion of the lane, exceeds a level of service C, as described in subdivision (b) of Section 65089 of the Government Code.

(B) The operation or projected operation of vehicles in the lane, or a portion of the lane, will significantly increase congestion.

(b) A person shall not drive a vehicle described in subdivision (a) of Section 5205.5 with a single occupant upon a high-occupancy vehicle lane pursuant to this section unless the decal, label, or other identifier issued pursuant to Section 5205.5 is properly displayed on the vehicle, and the vehicle registration described in Section 5205.5 is with the vehicle.

(c) A person shall not operate or own a vehicle displaying a decal, label, or other identifier, as described in Section 5205.5, if that decal, label, or identifier was not issued for that vehicle pursuant to Section 5205.5. A violation of this subdivision is a misdemeanor.

(d) If the provisions in Section 5205.5 authorizing the department to issue decals, labels, or other identifiers to hybrid and alternative fuel vehicles become inoperative, vehicles displaying those decals, labels, or other identifiers shall not access high-occupancy vehicle lanes without meeting the occupancy requirements otherwise applicable to those lanes.

(e)(1) This section shall become inoperative on the date the federal authorization pursuant to Section 166 of Title 23 of the United States Code expires, or the date the Secretary of State receives the notice described in subdivision (i) of Section 5205.5, whichever occurs first.

(2) With respect to a vehicle described in subparagraph (B) of paragraph (1) of subdivision (a) of Section 5205.5, this section shall become inoperative on January 1, 2019.

(f)(1) The Department of Transportation shall prepare and submit a report to the Legislature on or before December 1, 2017, on the degradation status of high-occupancy vehicle lanes on the state highway system.

(2) The requirement that a report be submitted pursuant to paragraph (1) shall be inoperative on December 1, 2021, pursuant to Section 10231.5 of the Government Code.

(3) A report submitted pursuant to paragraph (1) shall be submitted in compliance with Section 9795 of the Government Code.

(g) This section is repealed as of September 30, 2025. *(Added by Stats.1999, c. 330 (A.B.71), § 3. Amended by Stats.2004, c. 725 (A.B.2628), § 2; Stats.2006, c. 606 (A.B.1407), § 4; Stats.2006, c. 614 (A.B.2600), § 4; Stats.2010, c. 37 (A.B.1500), § 2; Stats.2010, c. 215 (S.B.535), § 2; Stats.2013, c. 405 (A.B.266), § 3; Stats.2013, c. 414 (S.B.286), § 3.5; Stats.2016, c. 339 (S.B.838), § 17, eff. Sept. 13, 2016; Stats.2017, c. 630 (A.B.544), § 2, eff. Jan. 1, 2018; Stats.2018, c. 367 (S.B.957), § 2, eff. Jan. 1, 2019.)*

Repeal

For repeal of this section, see its terms.

Cross References

Violation of subd.(c) of this section considered as misdemeanor, see Vehicle Code § 40000.13.

Research References

2 Witkin, California Criminal Law 4th Crimes Against Property § 199 (2021), Motor Vehicle Items.

2 Witkin, California Criminal Law 4th Crimes Against Public Peace and Welfare § 327 (2021), Miscellaneous Regulations.

§ 21656. Vehicles proceeding at speed less than normal speed of traffic to turn off

On a two-lane highway where passing is unsafe because of traffic in the opposite direction or other conditions, any vehicle proceeding upon the highway at a speed less than the normal speed of traffic moving in the same direction at that time, behind which five or more vehicles are formed in line, shall turn off the roadway at the nearest place designated as a turnout by signs erected by the authority having jurisdiction over the highway, or wherever sufficient area for a safe turnout exists, in order to permit the vehicles following it to proceed. *(Stats.1959, c. 3, p. 1680, § 21656. Amended by Stats.1961, c. 528, p. 1631, § 1; Stats.1965, c. 448, p. 1759, § 2; Stats.2015, c. 265 (A.B.208), § 1, eff. Jan. 1, 2016.)*

Research References

2 Witkin, California Criminal Law 4th Crimes Against Public Peace and Welfare § 327 (2021), Miscellaneous Regulations.

§ 21657. Designated traffic direction

The authorities in charge of any highway may designate any highway, roadway, part of a roadway, or specific lanes upon which vehicular traffic shall proceed in one direction at all or such times as shall be indicated by official traffic control devices. When a roadway has been so designated, a vehicle shall be driven only in the direction designated at all or such times as shall be indicated by traffic control devices. *(Stats.1959, c. 3, p. 1680, § 21657. Amended by Stats.1969, c. 136, p. 288, § 4.)*

Cross References

Department of California highway patrol, generally, see Vehicle Code § 2100 et seq.
Driving on one-way street, see Vehicle Code § 21650.
Obedience to traffic signals, etc., see Vehicle Code §§ 21461, 21462.
Powers and duties of California highway patrol, see Vehicle Code § 2400 et seq.
Powers of local authorities with respect to regulating use of highways, see Vehicle Code §§ 21100, 21101.
Traffic signs, signals, and markings, generally, see Vehicle Code § 21350 et seq.
Violations, see Vehicle Code § 40000.1 et seq.

Research References

California Jury Instructions-Civil, 8th Edition 11.60, Failure to Provide Warning Signs Authorized by Vehicle Code.
2 Witkin, California Criminal Law 4th Crimes Against Public Peace and Welfare § 327 (2021), Miscellaneous Regulations.

§ 21658. Laned roadways

Whenever any roadway has been divided into two or more clearly marked lanes for traffic in one direction, the following rules apply:

(a) A vehicle shall be driven as nearly as practical entirely within a single lane and shall not be moved from the lane until such movement can be made with reasonable safety.

(b) Official signs may be erected directing slow-moving traffic to use a designated lane or allocating specified lanes to traffic moving in the same direction, and drivers of vehicles shall obey the directions of the traffic device. *(Stats.1959, c. 3, p. 1680, § 21658. Amended by Stats.1961, c. 528, p. 1632, § 2; Stats.1970, c. 405, p. 817, § 5; Stats.1973, c. 670, p. 1226, § 1; Stats.1975, c. 450, p. 948, § 1.)*

Cross References

Application of this section to trolley coaches, see Vehicle Code § 21051.
Driving on right side of roadway, exceptions to, see Vehicle Code § 21650.
Roadway defined, see Vehicle Code § 530.
Traffic signs and markings, generally, see Vehicle Code § 21350 et seq.
Violations, see Vehicle Code § 40000.1 et seq.

Research References

California Jury Instructions-Civil, 8th Edition 11.60, Failure to Provide Warning Signs Authorized by Vehicle Code.
2 Witkin, California Criminal Law 4th Crimes Against Public Peace and Welfare § 327 (2021), Miscellaneous Regulations.
3 Witkin, California Criminal Law 4th Punishment § 266 (2021), Infractions.

§ 21658.1. Lane splitting; development of guidelines to ensure safety of motorcyclists and surrounding vehicles

(a) For the purposes of this section, "lane splitting" means driving a motorcycle, as defined in Section 400, that has two wheels in contact with the ground, between rows of stopped or moving vehicles in the same lane, including on both divided and undivided streets, roads, or highways.

(b) The Department of the California Highway Patrol may develop educational guidelines relating to lane splitting in a manner that would ensure the safety of the motorcyclist and the drivers and passengers of the surrounding vehicles.

(c) In developing guidelines pursuant to this section, the department shall consult with agencies and organizations with an interest in road safety and motorcyclist behavior, including, but not limited to, all of the following:

(1) The Department of Motor Vehicles.

(2) The Department of Transportation.

(3) The Office of Traffic Safety.

(4) A motorcycle organization focused on motorcyclist safety. *(Added by Stats.2016, c. 141 (A.B.51), § 1, eff. Jan. 1, 2017.)*

§ 21659. Three-laned highways

Upon a roadway which is divided into three lanes a vehicle shall not be driven in the extreme left lane at any time, nor in the center lane except when overtaking and passing another vehicle where the roadway ahead is clearly visible and the center lane is clear of traffic within a safe distance, or in preparation for a left turn, or where the center lane is at the time allocated exclusively to traffic moving in the direction the vehicle is proceeding and is signposted to give notice of such allocation. This section does not apply upon a one-way roadway. *(Stats.1959, c. 3, p. 1680, § 21659.)*

Cross References

Application of this section to trolley coaches, see Vehicle Code § 21051.
Roadway defined, see Vehicle Code § 530.
Violations, see Vehicle Code § 40000.1 et seq.

§ 21660. Approaching vehicles

Drivers of vehicles proceeding in opposite directions shall pass each other to the right, and, except when a roadway has been divided into traffic lanes, each driver shall give to the other at least one-half of the main traveled portion of the roadway whenever possible. *(Stats.1959, c. 3, p. 1680, § 21660.)*

Cross References

Roadway defined, see Vehicle Code § 530.
Rubbish or garbage trucks, exemption, see Vehicle Code § 21059.
Violations, see Vehicle Code § 40000.1 et seq.

Research References

2 Witkin, California Criminal Law 4th Crimes Against Public Peace and Welfare § 327 (2021), Miscellaneous Regulations.

§ 21661. Narrow roadways

Whenever upon any grade the width of the roadway is insufficient to permit the passing of vehicles approaching from opposite directions at the point of meeting, the driver of the vehicle descending the grade shall yield the right-of-way to the vehicle ascending the grade and shall, if necessary, back his vehicle to a place in the highway where it is possible for the vehicles to pass. *(Stats.1959, c. 3, p. 1680, § 21661.)*

Cross References

Roadway defined, see Vehicle Code § 530.

Research References

2 Witkin, California Criminal Law 4th Crimes Against Public Peace and Welfare § 327 (2021), Miscellaneous Regulations.

§ 21662. Mountain driving

The driver of a motor vehicle traveling through defiles or canyons or upon mountain highways shall hold the motor vehicle under control at all times and shall do the following when applicable:

(a) If the roadway has no marked centerline, the driver shall drive as near the right-hand edge of the roadway as is reasonably possible.

(b) If the roadway has insufficient width to permit a motor vehicle to be driven entirely to the right of the center of the roadway, the driver shall give audible warning with the horn of the motor vehicle upon approaching any curve where the view is obstructed within a distance of 200 feet along the highway. *(Stats.1959, c. 3, p. 1681, § 21662. Amended by Stats.1959, c. 973, p. 3004, § 1; Stats.1984, c. 462, § 2.)*

Cross References

Driving on right side of highway, generally, see Vehicle Code § 21650.
Exemption of emergency vehicles from rules of the road, exceptions, see Vehicle Code § 21054.
Overtaking vehicles when approaching crest of grade or where view obstructed, see Vehicle Code § 21752.
Passing without sufficient clearance, see Vehicle Code § 21751.

Research References

2 Witkin, California Criminal Law 4th Crimes Against Public Peace and Welfare § 327 (2021), Miscellaneous Regulations.

§ 21663. Driving on sidewalk

Except as expressly permitted pursuant to this code, including Sections 21100.4 and 21114.5, no person shall operate or move a motor vehicle upon a sidewalk except as may be necessary to enter or leave adjacent property. *(Added by Stats.1965, c. 1343, p. 3230, § 1. Amended by Stats.1987, c. 600, § 2; Stats.1996, c. 124 (A.B.3470), § 126.)*

Cross References

Electric carts on sidewalks, local regulations, see Vehicle Code §§ 21100, 21114.5.

Research References

2 Witkin, California Criminal Law 4th Crimes Against Public Peace and Welfare § 327 (2021), Miscellaneous Regulations.

§ 21664. On-ramp exit

It is unlawful for the driver of any vehicle to enter or exit any freeway which has full control of access and no crossings at grade, except upon a designated on ramp with respect to entering the freeway or a designated off ramp with respect to exiting the freeway. *(Added by Stats.1965, c. 1100, p. 2747, § 1. Amended by Stats.1988, c. 765, § 2.)*

Research References

2 Witkin, California Criminal Law 4th Crimes Against Public Peace and Welfare § 327 (2021), Miscellaneous Regulations.

ARTICLE 2. ADDITIONAL DRIVING RULES

§ 21700. Obstruction to driving

No person shall drive a vehicle when it is so loaded, or when there are in the front seat such number of persons as to obstruct the view of the driver to the front or sides of the vehicle or as to interfere with the driver's control over the driving mechanism of the vehicle. *(Stats.1959, c. 3, p. 1681, § 21700. Amended by Stats.1965, c. 1500, p. 3523, § 7.)*

Cross References

Application of this section to trolley coaches, see Vehicle Code § 21051.

Research References

2 Witkin, California Criminal Law 4th Crimes Against Public Peace and Welfare § 327 (2021), Miscellaneous Regulations.

§ 21700.5. Buses transporting school pupils in City of San Diego

No person shall knowingly drive a bus within the City of San Diego which is transporting any public or private school pupil who is enrolled in kindergarten or any of grades 1 to 12, inclusive, to or from a public or private school, unless every such pupil is seated in a seat. *(Added by Stats.1972, c. 1124, p. 2161, § 1.)*

§ 21701. Interference with driver or mechanism

No person shall wilfully interfere with the driver of a vehicle or with the mechanism thereof in such manner as to affect the driver's control of the vehicle. The provisions of this section shall not apply to a drivers' license examiner or other employee of the Department of Motor Vehicles when conducting the road or driving test of an applicant for a driver's license nor to a person giving instruction as a part of a course in driver training conducted by a public school, educational institution or a driver training school licensed by the Department of Motor Vehicles. *(Stats.1959, c. 3, p. 1681, § 21701.)*

Cross References

Application of this section to trolley coaches, see Vehicle Code § 21051.
License examination and driving test, see Vehicle Code §§ 12803, 12804.9.
Violation of this section with intent to capture image, recording or impression for a commercial purpose, see Vehicle Code § 40008.

Research References

2 Witkin, California Criminal Law 4th Crimes Against Public Peace and Welfare § 327 (2021), Miscellaneous Regulations.

§ 21702. Limitation on driving hours

(a) No person shall drive upon any highway any vehicle designed or used for transporting persons for compensation for more than 10 consecutive hours nor for more than 10 hours spread over a total of

15 consecutive hours. Thereafter, such person shall not drive any such vehicle until eight consecutive hours have elapsed.

Regardless of aggregate driving time, no driver shall drive for more than 10 hours in any 24-hour period unless eight consecutive hours off duty have elapsed.

(b) No person shall drive upon any highway any vehicle designed or used for transporting merchandise, freight, materials or other property for more than 12 consecutive hours nor for more than 12 hours spread over a total of 15 consecutive hours. Thereafter, such person shall not drive any such vehicle until eight consecutive hours have elapsed.

Regardless of aggregate driving time, no driver shall drive for more than 12 hours in any 24-hour period unless eight consecutive hours off duty have elapsed.

(c) This section does not apply in any case of casualty or unavoidable accident or an act of God.

(d) In computing the number of hours under this section, any time spent by a person in driving such a vehicle outside this state shall, upon the vehicle entering this state, be included.

(e) Any person who violates any provision of this section is guilty of a misdemeanor and is punishable by a fine of not less than one hundred dollars ($100) nor more than one thousand dollars ($1,000) for each offense.

(f) This section shall not apply to the driver of a vehicle which is subject to the provisions of Section 34500. *(Stats.1959, c. 3, p. 1681, § 21702. Amended by Stats.1963, c. 2148, p. 4483, § 7; Stats.1967, c. 564, p. 1911, § 1; Stats.1983, c. 1092, § 391, eff. Sept. 27, 1983, operative Jan. 1, 1984.)*

Cross References

Application of this section to trolley coaches, see Vehicle Code § 21051.
Misdemeanor defined, see Penal Code § 17.
Uncertified highway carriers of persons, see Penal Code § 654.1 et seq.

Research References

2 Witkin, California Criminal Law 4th Crimes Against Public Peace and Welfare § 327 (2021), Miscellaneous Regulations.

§ 21703. Following too closely

The driver of a motor vehicle shall not follow another vehicle more closely than is reasonable and prudent, having due regard for the speed of such vehicle and the traffic upon, and the condition of, the roadway. *(Stats.1959, c. 3, p. 1682, § 21703.)*

Cross References

Application of this section to trolley coaches, see Vehicle Code § 21051.
Following emergency vehicle, see Vehicle Code § 21706.
Rules of the road, exemption of authorized emergency vehicles, see Vehicle Code § 21054.
Violation of this section with intent to capture image, recording or impression for a commercial purpose, see Vehicle Code § 40008.

Research References

2 Witkin, California Criminal Law 4th Crimes Against Public Peace and Welfare § 327 (2021), Miscellaneous Regulations.
6 Witkin, California Criminal Law 4th Criminal Appeal § 216 (2021), Reversal for Prosecutorial or Judicial Delay.

§ 21704. Distance between vehicles subject to special speed restrictions

(a) The driver of any motor vehicle subject to the speed restriction of Section 22406 that is operated outside of a business or residence district, shall keep the vehicle he is driving at a distance of not less than 300 feet to the rear of any other motor vehicle subject to such speed restriction which is preceding it.

(b) The provisions of this section shall not prevent overtaking and passing nor shall they apply upon a highway with two or more lanes for traffic in the direction of travel. *(Stats.1959, c. 3, p. 1682, § 21704. Amended by Stats.1967, c. 371, p. 1598, § 1; Stats.1969, c. 226, p. 558, § 1.)*

Cross References

Definitions,
Business district, see Vehicle Code § 235.
Driver, see Vehicle Code § 305.
Motor vehicle, see Vehicle Code § 415.
Residence district, see Vehicle Code § 515.
Rules of the road, exemption of authorized emergency vehicles, see Vehicle Code § 21054.
Speed laws generally, see Vehicle Code § 22349 et seq.

Research References

2 Witkin, California Criminal Law 4th Crimes Against Public Peace and Welfare § 327 (2021), Miscellaneous Regulations.

§ 21705. Caravans

Motor vehicles being driven outside of a business or residence district in a caravan or motorcade, whether or not towing other vehicles, shall be so operated as to allow sufficient space and in no event less than 100 feet between each vehicle or combination of vehicles so as to enable any other vehicle to overtake or pass. *(Stats.1959, c. 3, p. 1682, § 21705.)*

Cross References

Rules of the road, exemption of authorized emergency vehicles, see Vehicle Code § 21054.

Research References

2 Witkin, California Criminal Law 4th Crimes Against Public Peace and Welfare § 327 (2021), Miscellaneous Regulations.

§ 21706. Following emergency vehicle

No motor vehicle, except an authorized emergency vehicle, shall follow within 300 feet of any authorized emergency vehicle being operated under the provisions of Section 21055.

This section shall not apply to a police or traffic officer when serving as an escort within the purview of Section 21057. *(Stats.1959, c. 3, p. 1682, § 21706. Amended by Stats.1963, c. 564, p. 1444, § 1; Stats.1972, c. 46, p. 64, § 2.)*

Cross References

Authorized emergency vehicle defined, see Vehicle Code § 165.
Rules of the road, exemption of authorized emergency vehicles, see Vehicle Code § 21054.

Research References

2 Witkin, California Criminal Law 4th Crimes Against Public Peace and Welfare § 327 (2021), Miscellaneous Regulations.

§ 21706.5. Operation of vehicle in unsafe manner within emergency incident zone

(a) For purposes of this section, the following terms have the following meanings:

(1) "Emergency incident zone" means an area on a freeway that is within 500 feet of, and in the direction of travel of, a stationary authorized emergency vehicle that has its emergency lights activated. Traffic in the opposite lanes of the freeway is not in an "emergency incident zone."

(2) "Operate a vehicle in an unsafe manner" means operating a motor vehicle in violation of an act made unlawful under this division, except a violation of Section 21809.

(b) A person shall not operate a vehicle in an unsafe manner within an emergency incident zone. *(Added by Stats.2006, c. 375 (S.B.1610), § 1.)*

Research References

2 Witkin, California Criminal Law 4th Crimes Against Public Peace and Welfare § 327 (2021), Miscellaneous Regulations.

§ 21707. Fire areas

No motor vehicle, except an authorized emergency vehicle or a vehicle of a duly authorized member of a fire or police department, shall be operated within the block wherein an emergency situation responded to by any fire department vehicle exists, except that in the event the nearest intersection to the emergency is more than 300 feet therefrom, this section shall prohibit operation of vehicles only within 300 feet of the emergency, unless directed to do so by a member of the fire department or police department, sheriff, deputy sheriff, or member of the California Highway Patrol. The emergency shall be deemed to have ceased to exist when the official of the fire department in charge at the scene of the emergency shall so indicate. Officials of the fire department or police department or the Department of the California Highway Patrol who are present shall make every effort to prevent the closing off entirely of congested highway traffic passing the scene of any such emergency. *(Stats.1959, c. 3, p. 1682, § 21707.)*

Cross References

Authorized emergency vehicle defined, see Vehicle Code § 165.
California highway patrol, see Vehicle Code § 2100 et seq.
Emergency vehicles, suspension or revocation of permits, see Vehicle Code § 2417.
Exemptions of authorized emergency vehicles, see Vehicle Code §§ 21055, 21056.
Operation of fire department vehicles, see Vehicle Code § 21055.
Parking of utility vehicles, see Vehicle Code § 22512.
Rules of the road, exemption of authorized emergency vehicles, see Vehicle Code § 21054.

Research References

2 Witkin, California Criminal Law 4th Crimes Against Public Peace and Welfare § 327 (2021), Miscellaneous Regulations.

§ 21708. Fire hoses

No person shall drive or propel any vehicle or conveyance upon, over, or across, or in any manner damage any fire hose or chemical hose used by or under the supervision and control of any organized fire department. However, any vehicle may cross a hose provided suitable jumpers or other appliances are installed to protect the hose. *(Stats.1959, c. 3, p. 1683, § 21708.)*

Cross References

Parking of utility vehicles, see Vehicle Code § 22512.
Rules of the road, exemption of authorized emergency vehicles, see Vehicle Code § 21054.

Research References

2 Witkin, California Criminal Law 4th Crimes Against Public Peace and Welfare § 327 (2021), Miscellaneous Regulations.

§ 21709. Safety zones

No vehicle shall at any time be driven through or within a safety zone. *(Stats.1959, c. 3, p. 1683, § 21709.)*

Cross References

Application of this section to trolley coaches, see Vehicle Code § 21051.
Rules of the road, exemption of authorized emergency vehicles, see Vehicle Code § 21054.
Safety zone defined, see Vehicle Code § 540.
Stopping, standing or parking in safety zone prohibited, see Vehicle Code § 22500.
Vehicle defined, see Vehicle Code § 670.

Research References

2 Witkin, California Criminal Law 4th Crimes Against Public Peace and Welfare § 327 (2021), Miscellaneous Regulations.

§ 21710. Coasting prohibited

The driver of a motor vehicle when traveling on down grade upon any highway shall not coast with the gears of such vehicle in neutral. *(Stats.1959, c. 3, p. 1683, § 21710.)*

Research References

2 Witkin, California Criminal Law 4th Crimes Against Public Peace and Welfare § 327 (2021), Miscellaneous Regulations.

§ 21711. Towed vehicles swerving

No person shall operate a train of vehicles when any vehicle being towed whips or swerves from side to side or fails to follow substantially in the path of the towing vehicle. *(Stats.1959, c. 3, p. 1683, § 21711. Amended by Stats.1959, c. 44, p. 1902, § 3.)*

Cross References

Safety chains, see Vehicle Code § 29004.
Size of drawbar, see Vehicle Code § 29005.

Research References

2 Witkin, California Criminal Law 4th Crimes Against Public Peace and Welfare § 327 (2021), Miscellaneous Regulations.

§ 21712. Unlawful riding and towing

(a) A person driving a motor vehicle shall not knowingly permit a person to ride on a vehicle or upon a portion of a vehicle that is not designed or intended for the use of passengers.

(b) A person shall not ride on a vehicle or upon a portion of a vehicle that is not designed or intended for the use of passengers.

(c) A person driving a motor vehicle shall not knowingly permit a person to ride in the trunk of that motor vehicle.

(d) A person shall not ride in the trunk of a motor vehicle.

(e) A person violating subdivision (c) or (d) shall be punished as follows:

(1) By a fine of one hundred dollars ($100).

(2) For a second violation occurring within one year of a prior violation that resulted in a conviction, a fine of two hundred dollars ($200).

(3) For a third or a subsequent violation occurring within one year of two or more prior violations that resulted in convictions, a fine of two hundred fifty dollars ($250).

(f) Subdivisions (a) and (b) do not apply to an employee engaged in the necessary discharge of his or her duty or in the case of persons riding completely within or upon vehicle bodies in the space intended for a load on the vehicle.

(g) A person shall not drive a motor vehicle that is towing a trailer coach, camp trailer, or trailer carrying a vessel, containing a passenger, except when a trailer carrying or designed to carry a vessel is engaged in the launching or recovery of the vessel.

(h) A person shall not knowingly drive a motor vehicle that is towing a person riding upon a motorcycle, motorized bicycle, bicycle, coaster, roller skates, sled, skis, or toy vehicle.

(i) Subdivision (g) does not apply to a trailer coach that is towed with a fifth-wheel device if the trailer coach is equipped with safety glazing materials wherever glazing materials are used in windows or doors, with an audible or visual signaling device that a passenger inside the trailer coach can use to gain the attention of the motor vehicle driver, and with at least one unobstructed exit capable of being opened from both the interior and exterior of the trailer coach.

(Stats.1959, c. 3, p. 1683, § 21712. Amended by Stats.1961, c. 117, p. 1128, § 1; Stats.1965, c. 333, p. 1440, § 1; Stats.1971, c. 1536, p. 3043, § 2; Stats.1972, c. 262, p. 511, § 1; Stats.1972, c. 881, p. 1559, § 3; Stats.1974, c. 578, p. 1397, § 1; Stats.1981, c. 813, p. 3155, § 12; Stats.1992, c. 1243 (A.B.3090), § 90, eff. Sept. 30, 1992; Stats.2006, c. 900 (A.B.1850), § 2.)

Cross References

Application of this section to trolley coaches, see Vehicle Code § 21051.
Traffic violation point counts, allocation of points, see Vehicle Code § 12810.

Research References

2 Witkin, California Criminal Law 4th Crimes Against Public Peace and Welfare § 327 (2021), Miscellaneous Regulations.

§ 21713. Privately-owned armored cars

No person shall operate on any highway any privately owned armored car unless a license to operate such car has first been obtained from the commissioner in accordance with Chapter 2.5 (commencing with Section 2500) of Division 2.

Violation of this section is a misdemeanor and upon conviction is punishable by a fine not exceeding one thousand dollars ($1,000) or by imprisonment in the county jail for not to exceed six months or by both such fine and imprisonment. *(Stats.1959, c. 3, p. 1683, § 21713. Amended by Stats.1968, c. 1309, p. 2473, § 9, operative Jan. 1, 1969; Stats.1973, c. 89, p. 149, § 1; Stats.1983, c. 1092, § 392, eff. Sept. 27, 1983, operative Jan. 1, 1984.)*

Cross References

Armored car defined, see Vehicle Code § 115.
Misdemeanor defined, see Penal Code § 17.

Research References

2 Witkin, California Criminal Law 4th Crimes Against Public Peace and Welfare § 327 (2021), Miscellaneous Regulations.

§ 21714. Fully enclosed 3-wheeled motor vehicles of specified dimensions; operation of vehicles; prohibited areas

The driver of a vehicle described in subdivision (f) of Section 27803 shall not operate the vehicle in either of the following areas:

(a) On, or immediately adjacent to, the striping or other markers designating adjacent traffic lanes.

(b) Between two or more vehicles that are traveling in adjacent traffic lanes. *(Added by Stats.1997, c. 710 (A.B.1029), § 1. Amended by Stats.2008, c. 672 (A.B.2272), § 2.)*

§ 21715. Passenger vehicle combinations; number and weight limits

(a) No passenger vehicle regardless of weight, or any other motor vehicle under 4,000 pounds unladen, shall draw or tow more than one vehicle in combination, except that an auxiliary dolly or tow dolly may be used with the towed vehicle.

(b) No motor vehicle under 4,000 pounds unladen shall tow any vehicle weighing 6,000 pounds or more gross. *(Added by Stats.1961, c. 643, p. 1849, § 1. Amended by Stats.1963, c. 134, p. 807, § 1; Stats.1963, c. 850, p. 2074, § 1; Stats.1963, c. 2149, p. 4487, § 13.5; Stats.1977, c. 770, p. 2399, § 3; Stats.1983, c. 708, § 8.)*

Cross References

Almond trailers, see Vehicle Code § 36627.
Cotton trailers, see Vehicle Code § 36626.
Vehicle drawing or towing unladen implements of husbandry, see Vehicle Code § 36625.

Research References

2 Witkin, California Criminal Law 4th Crimes Against Public Peace and Welfare § 327 (2021), Miscellaneous Regulations.

§ 21716. Golf carts; operation

Except as provided in Section 21115.1 and Chapter 6 (commencing with Section 1950) of Division 2.5 of the Streets and Highways Code, no person shall operate a golf cart on any highway except in a speed zone of 25 miles per hour or less. *(Added by Stats.1968, c. 1303, p. 2457, § 4. Amended by Stats.1991, c. 192 (A.B.789), § 2; Stats.1992, c. 44 (A.B.1229), § 2; Stats.1994, c. 598 (S.B.2016), § 2; Stats.1995, c. 334 (A.B.110), § 12; Stats.1997, c. 536 (S.B.525), § 3; Stats.2000, c. 155 (A.B.2221), § 2.)*

Cross References

Golf cart defined, see Vehicle Code § 345.
Highway defined, see Vehicle Code § 360.

Research References

2 Witkin, California Criminal Law 4th Crimes Against Public Peace and Welfare § 327 (2021), Miscellaneous Regulations.

§ 21717. Turning across bicycle lanes

Whenever it is necessary for the driver of a motor vehicle to cross a bicycle lane that is adjacent to his lane of travel to make a turn, the driver shall drive the motor vehicle into the bicycle lane prior to making the turn and shall make the turn pursuant to Section 22100. *(Added by Stats.1976, c. 751, p. 1785, § 12.)*

Research References

2 Witkin, California Criminal Law 4th Crimes Against Public Peace and Welfare § 327 (2021), Miscellaneous Regulations.

§ 21718. Freeways; stopping, parking or leaving vehicles standing; exceptions to prohibition; violation; conviction

(a) No person shall stop, park, or leave standing any vehicle upon a freeway which has full control of access and no crossings at grade except:

(1) When necessary to avoid injury or damage to persons or property.

(2) When required by law or in obedience to a peace officer or official traffic control device.

(3) When any person is actually engaged in maintenance or construction on freeway property or any employee of a public agency is actually engaged in the performance of official duties.

(4) When any vehicle is so disabled that it is impossible to avoid temporarily stopping and another vehicle has been summoned to render assistance to the disabled vehicle or driver of the disabled vehicle. This paragraph applies when the vehicle summoned to render assistance is a vehicle owned by the donor of free emergency assistance that has been summoned by display upon or within a disabled vehicle of a placard or sign given to the driver of the disabled vehicle by the donor for the specific purpose of summoning assistance, other than towing service, from the donor.

(5) Where stopping, standing, or parking is specifically permitted. However, buses may not stop on freeways unless sidewalks are provided with shoulders of sufficient width to permit stopping without interfering with the normal movement of traffic and without the possibility of crossing over fast lanes to reach the bus stop.

(6) Where necessary for any person to report a traffic accident or other situation or incident to a peace officer or any person specified in paragraph (3), either directly or by means of an emergency telephone or similar device.

(7) When necessary for the purpose of rapid removal of impediments to traffic by the owner or operator of a tow truck operating under an agreement with the Department of the California Highway Patrol.

(b) A conviction of a violation of this section is a conviction involving the safe operation of a motor vehicle upon the highway if a notice to appear for the violation was issued by a peace officer described in Section 830.1 or 830.2 of the Penal Code. *(Added by Stats.1997, c. 945 (A.B.1561), § 17.)*

Cross References

Pilot program for issuance of wildlife salvage permits, see Fish and Game Code § 2000.6.

Research References

2 Witkin, California Criminal Law 4th Crimes Against Public Peace and Welfare § 324 (2021), Stopping and Standing.

§ 21719. Tow truck use of center median or right shoulder on roadway

(a) Notwithstanding any other law, in the event of an emergency occurring on a roadway that requires the rapid removal of impediments to traffic or the rendering of assistance to a disabled vehicle obstructing a roadway, a tow truck driver who is operating under an agreement with the law enforcement agency responsible for investigating traffic collisions on the roadway, summoned by the owner or operator of a vehicle involved in a collision or that is otherwise disabled on the roadway, or operating pursuant to subdivision (a) of Section 2430.1 may utilize the center median or right shoulder of a roadway if all of the following conditions are met:

(1) A peace officer employed by the investigating law enforcement agency is at the scene of the roadway obstruction and has determined that the obstruction has caused an unnecessary delay to motorists using the roadway.

(2) A peace officer employed by the investigating law enforcement agency has determined that a tow truck can provide emergency roadside assistance by removing the disabled vehicle and gives explicit permission to the tow truck driver allowing the utilization of the center median or right shoulder of the roadway.

(3) The tow truck is not operated on the center median or right shoulder at a speed greater than what is reasonable or prudent having due regard for weather, visibility, the traffic on, and the surface and width of, the roadway, and in no event at a speed that endangers the safety of persons or property.

(4) The tow truck displays flashing amber warning lamps to the front, rear, and both sides while driving in the center median or right shoulder of a roadway pursuant to this section.

(b) For purposes of this section, "utilize the center median" includes making a U-turn across the center median. *(Added by Stats.2015, c. 30 (A.B.198), § 1, eff. Jan. 1, 2016. Amended by Stats.2016, c. 208 (A.B.2906), § 14, eff. Jan. 1, 2017.)*

Research References

2 Witkin, California Criminal Law 4th Crimes Against Public Peace and Welfare § 323 (2021), Parking.

§ 21720. Pocket bikes; operation of vehicles; prohibited areas

A pocket bike shall not be operated on a sidewalk, roadway, or any other part of a highway, or on a bikeway, bicycle path or trail, equestrian trail, hiking or recreational trail, or on public lands open to off-highway motor vehicle use. *(Added by Stats.2005, c. 323 (A.B.1051), § 3.)*

Cross References

Pocket bike defined, see Vehicle Code § 473.

§ 21721. Pocket bikes; removal or seizure; costs associated with removal, seizure or storage; return of bike

(a) A peace officer, as defined in Chapter 4.5 (commencing with Section 830) of Title 3 of Part 2 of the Penal Code, may cause the removal and seizure of a pocket bike, upon the notice to appear for a violation of Section 21720. A pocket bike so seized shall be held for a minimum of 48 hours.

(b) A violator of this section shall be responsible for all costs associated with the removal, seizure, and storage of the pocket bike.

(c) A city, county, or city and county may adopt a regulation, ordinance, or resolution imposing charges equal to its administrative costs relating to the removal, seizure, and storage costs of a pocket bike. The charges shall not exceed the actual costs incurred for the expenses directly related to removing, seizing, and storing a pocket bike.

(d) An agency shall release a seized pocket bike to the owner, violator, or the violator's agent after 48 hours, if all of the following conditions are met:

(1) The violator or authorized agent's request is made during normal business hours.

(2) The applicable removal, seizure, and storage costs have been paid by the owner, or any other responsible party. *(Added by Stats.2005, c. 323 (A.B.1051), § 4.)*

Cross References

Pocket bike defined, see Vehicle Code § 473.

ARTICLE 3. OVERTAKING AND PASSING

Section

§ 21750. Overtake and pass to left

(a) The driver of a vehicle overtaking another vehicle proceeding in the same direction shall pass to the left at a safe distance without interfering with the safe operation of the overtaken vehicle, subject to the limitations and exceptions set forth in this article.

(b) This section shall become operative on September 16, 2014. *(Added by Stats.2013, c. 331 (A.B.1371), § 2, operative Sept. 16, 2014.)*

Cross References

Application of this section to trolley coaches, see Vehicle Code § 21051.
Rules of the road, exemption of authorized emergency vehicles, see Vehicle Code § 21055.

Research References

2 Witkin, California Criminal Law 4th Crimes Against Public Peace and Welfare § 327 (2021), Miscellaneous Regulations.

§ 21751. Passing without sufficient clearance

On a two-lane highway, no vehicle shall be driven to the left side of the center of the roadway in overtaking and passing another vehicle proceeding in the same direction unless the left side is clearly visible and free of oncoming traffic for a sufficient distance ahead to permit such overtaking and passing to be completely made without interfering with the safe operation of any vehicle approaching from the opposite direction. *(Stats.1959, c. 3, p. 1684, § 21751. Amended by Stats.1961, c. 577, p. 1718, § 2; Stats.1973, c. 50, p. 83, § 1.)*

Cross References

Overtaking and passing vehicles on left, see Vehicle Code § 21750.

Research References

2 Witkin, California Criminal Law 4th Crimes Against Public Peace and Welfare § 327 (2021), Miscellaneous Regulations.

§ 21752. When driving on left prohibited

No vehicle shall be driven to the left side of the roadway under the following conditions:

(a) When approaching or upon the crest of a grade or a curve in the highway where the driver's view is obstructed within such distance as to create a hazard in the event another vehicle might approach from the opposite direction.

(b) When the view is obstructed upon approaching within 100 feet of any bridge, viaduct, or tunnel.

(c) When approaching within 100 feet of or when traversing any railroad grade crossing.

(d) When approaching within 100 feet of or when traversing any intersection.

This section shall not apply upon a one-way roadway. *(Stats.1959, c. 3, p. 1684, § 21752. Amended by Stats.1969, c. 417, p. 948, § 1; Stats.2000, c. 596 (A.B.2909), § 7.)*

Cross References

Traffic school, rail transit safety film or fine, see Penal Code § 369b.

Research References

2 Witkin, California Criminal Law 4th Crimes Against Public Peace and Welfare § 327 (2021), Miscellaneous Regulations.

§ 21753. Yielding for passing

Except when passing on the right is permitted, the driver of an overtaken vehicle shall safely move to the right-hand side of the highway in favor of the overtaking vehicle after an audible signal or a momentary flash of headlights by the overtaking vehicle, and shall not increase the speed of his or her vehicle until completely passed by the overtaking vehicle. This section does not require the driver of an overtaken vehicle to drive on the shoulder of the highway in order to allow the overtaking vehicle to pass. *(Stats.1959, c. 3, p. 1684, § 21753. Amended by Stats.1996, c. 440 (S.B.1588), § 9; Stats.1999, c. 724 (A.B.1650), § 40.)*

Cross References

Application of this section to trolley coaches, see Vehicle Code § 21051.
Overtaking and passing vehicles on right, see Vehicle Code § 21755.

Research References

2 Witkin, California Criminal Law 4th Crimes Against Public Peace and Welfare § 327 (2021), Miscellaneous Regulations.

§ 21754. Passing on the right

The driver of a vehicle may overtake and pass to the right of another vehicle only under the following conditions:

(a) When the vehicle overtaken is making or about to make a left turn.

(b) Upon a highway within a business or residence district with unobstructed pavement of sufficient width for two or more lines of moving vehicles in the direction of travel.

(c) Upon any highway outside of a business or residence district with unobstructed pavement of sufficient width and clearly marked for two or more lines of moving traffic in the direction of travel.

(d) Upon a one-way street.

(e) Upon a highway divided into two roadways where traffic is restricted to one direction upon each of such roadways.

The provisions of this section shall not relieve the driver of a slow moving vehicle from the duty to drive as closely as practicable to the right hand edge of the roadway. *(Stats.1959, c. 3, p. 1684, § 21754. Amended by Stats.2010, c. 491 (S.B.1318), § 39.)*

Cross References

Application of this section to trolley coaches, see Vehicle Code § 21051.
Driving in right hand lane, slow-moving vehicles, see Vehicle Code § 21654.

Research References

2 Witkin, California Criminal Law 4th Crimes Against Public Peace and Welfare § 327 (2021), Miscellaneous Regulations.

§ 21755. Passing on the right safely; use of bicycle in bicycle lane or on shoulder not prohibited

(a) The driver of a vehicle may overtake and pass another vehicle upon the right only under conditions permitting that movement in safety. In no event shall that movement be made by driving off the paved or main-traveled portion of the roadway.

(b) This section does not prohibit the use of a bicycle in a bicycle lane or on a shoulder. *(Stats.1959, c. 3, p. 1684, § 21755. Amended by Stats.2010, c. 491 (S.B.1318), § 40.)*

Cross References

Application of this section to trolley coaches, see Vehicle Code § 21051.
Driving, overtaking or passing slow-moving vehicles, see Vehicle Code § 21654.

§ 21756. Passing standing streetcar, trolley coach, or bus

(a) The driver of a vehicle overtaking any interurban electric or streetcar stopped or about to stop for the purpose of receiving or discharging any passenger shall stop the vehicle to the rear of the nearest running board or door of such car and thereupon remain standing until all passengers have boarded the car or upon alighting have reached a place of safety, except as provided in subdivision (b) hereof.

(b) Where a safety zone has been established or at an intersection where traffic is controlled by an officer or a traffic control signal device, a vehicle need not be brought to a stop before passing any interurban electric or streetcar but may proceed past such car at a speed not greater than 10 miles per hour and with due caution for the safety of pedestrians.

(c) Whenever any trolley coach or bus has stopped at a safety zone to receive or discharge passengers, a vehicle may proceed past such trolley coach or bus at a speed not greater than 10 miles per hour. *(Stats.1959, c. 3, p. 1685, § 21756. Amended by Stats.1959, c. 969, p. 3001, § 1.)*

Cross References

Driving through safety zone prohibited, see Vehicle Code § 21709.
Intersection defined, see Vehicle Code § 365.
Pedestrians' rights and duties, see Vehicle Code § 21950 et seq.
Prima facie speed limits at intersections, see Vehicle Code § 22352.
Safety zone defined, see Vehicle Code § 540.
Stopping, standing or parking prohibited between safety zone and adjacent curb, see Vehicle Code § 22500.

Research References

2 Witkin, California Criminal Law 4th Crimes Against Public Peace and Welfare § 327 (2021), Miscellaneous Regulations.

§ 21757. Passing streetcar on left

The driver of a vehicle shall not overtake and pass upon the left, nor shall any driver of a vehicle drive upon the left side of, any interurban electric or street car proceeding in the same direction whether the street car is actually in motion or temporarily at rest, except:

(a) When so directed by a police or traffic officer.

(b) When upon a one-way street.

(c) When upon a street where the tracks are so located as to prevent compliance with this section. *(Stats.1959, c. 3, p. 1685, § 21757.)*

Cross References

Limitations on overtaking on left, see Vehicle Code §§ 21751, 21752.
Obedience to peace officers, see Vehicle Code § 2800.
Overtaking vehicles on left or right, generally, see Vehicle Code § 21750 et seq.
Passing school bus, see Vehicle Code § 22454.

Research References

2 Witkin, California Criminal Law 4th Crimes Against Public Peace and Welfare § 327 (2021), Miscellaneous Regulations.

§ 21758. Passing on grades

In the event any vehicle is being operated on any grade outside of a business or residence district at a speed of less than 20 miles per hour, no person operating any other motor vehicle shall attempt to overtake and pass such slow moving vehicle unless the overtaking vehicle is operated at a speed of at least 10 miles per hour in excess of the speed of the overtaken vehicle, nor unless the passing movement is completed within a total distance not greater than one-quarter of a mile. *(Stats.1959, c. 3, p. 1685, § 21758.)*

Research References

2 Witkin, California Criminal Law 4th Crimes Against Public Peace and Welfare § 327 (2021), Miscellaneous Regulations.

§ 21759. Caution in passing animals

The driver of any vehicle approaching any horse drawn vehicle, any ridden animal, or any livestock shall exercise proper control of his vehicle and shall reduce speed or stop as may appear necessary or as may be signalled or otherwise requested by any person driving, riding or in charge of the animal or livestock in order to avoid frightening and to safeguard the animal or livestock and to insure the safety of any person driving or riding the animal or in charge of the livestock. *(Stats.1959, c. 3, p. 1685, § 21759.)*

Cross References

Livestock on highways, duties of owners, see Food and Agricultural Code § 16902.
Open range country, warning against livestock on highway, see Vehicle Code § 21365.
Riding or driving animal on highway, effect of traffic laws, see Vehicle Code § 21050.
Signs at livestock crossing, erection, see Vehicle Code § 21364.

Research References

2 Witkin, California Criminal Law 4th Crimes Against Public Peace and Welfare § 327 (2021), Miscellaneous Regulations.

§ 21760. Three Feet for Safety Act; overtaking and passing bicycles; violations and penalties

(a) This section shall be known and may be cited as the Three Feet for Safety Act.

(b) The driver of a motor vehicle overtaking and passing a bicycle that is proceeding in the same direction on a highway shall pass in compliance with the requirements of this article applicable to overtaking and passing a vehicle, and shall do so at a safe distance that does not interfere with the safe operation of the overtaken bicycle, having due regard for the size and speed of the motor vehicle and the bicycle, traffic conditions, weather, visibility, and the surface and width of the highway.

(c) A driver of a motor vehicle shall not overtake or pass a bicycle proceeding in the same direction on a highway at a distance of less than three feet between any part of the motor vehicle and any part of the bicycle or its operator. The driver of a motor vehicle overtaking or passing a bicycle that is proceeding in the same direction and in the same lane of travel shall, if another lane of traffic proceeding in the same direction is available, make a lane change into another available lane with due regard for safety and traffic conditions, if practicable and not prohibited by law, before overtaking or passing the bicycle.

(d) If the driver of a motor vehicle is unable to comply with subdivision (c), due to traffic or roadway conditions, the driver shall slow to a speed that is reasonable and prudent, and may pass only when doing so would not endanger the safety of the operator of the bicycle, taking into account the size and speed of the motor vehicle and bicycle, traffic conditions, weather, visibility, and surface and width of the highway.

(e)(1) A violation of subdivision (b), (c), or (d) is an infraction punishable by a fine of thirty-five dollars ($35).

(2) If a collision occurs between a motor vehicle and a bicycle causing bodily injury to the operator of the bicycle, and the driver of the motor vehicle is found to be in violation of subdivision (b), (c), or (d), a two-hundred-twenty-dollar ($220) fine shall be imposed on that driver.

* * * *(Added by Stats.2013, c. 331 (A.B.1371), § 3, operative Sept. 16, 2014. Amended by Stats.2022, c. 343 (A.B.1909), § 6, eff. Jan. 1, 2023.)*

Cross References

Transportation network companies, requirements for participating drivers, see Public Utilities Code § 5445.3.

Research References

2 Witkin, California Criminal Law 4th Crimes Against Public Peace and Welfare § 327 (2021), Miscellaneous Regulations.

§ 21761. Passing waste service vehicle

(a) The driver of a vehicle on a public street or highway approaching and overtaking a stopped waste service vehicle shall make a lane change into an available lane adjacent to the waste service vehicle and shall pass at a safe distance without interfering with the safe operation of the waste service vehicle, with due regard for safety and traffic conditions, if practicable and not prohibited by law.

(b) If the maneuver described in subdivision (a) would be unsafe or impractical, a driver approaching and overtaking a stopped waste service vehicle shall slow to a reasonable and prudent speed that is safe for existing weather, road, and vehicular or pedestrian traffic conditions.

(c) For purposes of this section, "waste service vehicle" means a refuse collection vehicle, including a vehicle collecting recyclables or yard waste that is used for curbside collection, and sewer and catch basin maintenance vehicles.

(d) The requirements in subdivisions (a) and (b) apply when both of the following circumstances exist:

(1) The waste service vehicle is readily identifiable as a waste service vehicle based on the vehicle configuration or markings on the vehicle.

(2) The waste service vehicle displays flashing amber lights.

(e) Subdivisions (a) and (b) do not apply to a waste service vehicle that is located on a private driveway or highway, when the waste service vehicle is not adjacent to the street or highway, or is separated from the street or highway by a protective physical barrier.

(f) This section shall be operative on and after January 1, 2020. *(Added by Stats.2018, c. 710 (A.B.2115), § 1, eff. Jan. 1, 2019, operative Jan. 1, 2020.)*

Research References

2 Witkin, California Criminal Law 4th Crimes Against Public Peace and Welfare § 327 (2021), Miscellaneous Regulations.

CHAPTER 4. RIGHT–OF–WAY

§ 21800. Intersections without functioning traffic control signals or yield sign, or with all-direction stop signs, except left-turning vehicle with vehicle approaching from opposite direction

(a) The driver of a vehicle approaching an intersection shall yield the right-of-way to any vehicle which has entered the intersection from a different highway.

(b)(1) When two vehicles enter an intersection from different highways at the same time, the driver of the vehicle on the left shall yield the right-of-way to the vehicle on his or her immediate right, except that the driver of any vehicle on a terminating highway shall yield the right-of-way to any vehicle on the intersecting continuing highway.

(2) For the purposes of this section, "terminating highway" means a highway which intersects, but does not continue beyond the intersection, with another highway which does continue beyond the intersection.

(c) When two vehicles enter an intersection from different highways at the same time and the intersection is controlled from all directions by stop signs, the driver of the vehicle on the left shall yield the right-of-way to the vehicle on his or her immediate right.

(d)(1) The driver of any vehicle approaching an intersection which has official traffic control signals that are inoperative shall stop at the intersection, and may proceed with caution when it is safe to do so.

(2) When two vehicles enter an intersection from different highways at the same time, and the official traffic control signals for the intersection are inoperative, the driver of the vehicle on the left shall yield the right-of-way to the vehicle on his or her immediate right, except that the driver of any vehicle on a terminating highway shall yield the right-of-way to any vehicle on the intersecting continuing highway.

(e) This section does not apply to any of the following:

(1) Any intersection controlled by an official traffic control signal or yield right-of-way sign.

(2) Any intersection controlled by stop signs from less than all directions.

(3) When vehicles are approaching each other from opposite directions and the driver of one of the vehicles intends to make, or is making, a left turn. *(Stats.1959, c. 3, p. 1685, § 21800. Amended by Stats.1980, c. 195, p. 418, § 1; Stats.1982, c. 349, § 1; Stats.1987, c. 455, § 1; Stats.1988, c. 623, § 1; Stats.2001–2002, 2nd Ex.Sess., c. 6 (S.B.84), § 2, eff. Oct. 1, 2001; Stats.2009, c. 200 (S.B.734), § 11.)*

Cross References

Applicability of this section to trolley coaches, see Vehicle Code § 21051.
Intersection defined, see Vehicle Code § 365.
Local regulation of turning movements at intersection, see Vehicle Code § 22113.
Markings or signs for turning, see Vehicle Code § 22101.
Method of turning at intersections, see Vehicle Code § 22100.
Pedestrians, see Vehicle Code § 21950.
Program to provide battery backup power for official traffic control signals determined to be high priority, see Public Resources Code § 25403.8.
Right-of-way defined, see Vehicle Code § 525.
Rights and duties of pedestrians, see Vehicle Code § 21950 et seq.
Rules of the road, exemption of authorized emergency vehicles, see Vehicle Code § 21055.
Speed of vehicles at intersections, see Vehicle Code § 22352.
Turning signals, see Vehicle Code § 22110.
Vehicle entering through highway, stopping and yielding of right of way, see Vehicle Code § 21802.

Research References

2 Witkin, California Criminal Law 4th Crimes Against Public Peace and Welfare § 327 (2021), Miscellaneous Regulations.

§ 21801. Left turn or U–turn right of way

(a) The driver of a vehicle intending to turn to the left or to complete a U-turn upon a highway, or to turn left into public or private property, or an alley, shall yield the right-of-way to all vehicles approaching from the opposite direction which are close enough to constitute a hazard at any time during the turning movement, and shall continue to yield the right-of-way to the approaching vehicles until the left turn or U-turn can be made with reasonable safety.

(b) A driver having yielded as prescribed in subdivision (a), and having given a signal when and as required by this code, may turn left or complete a U-turn, and the drivers of vehicles approaching the intersection or the entrance to the property or alley from the opposite direction shall yield the right-of-way to the turning vehicle. *(Stats.1959, c. 3, p. 1686, § 21801. Amended by Stats.1963, c. 1844, p. 3793, § 1; Stats.1969, c. 312, p. 679, § 1; Stats.1988, c. 623, § 2; Stats.1993, c. 272 (A.B.301), § 40, eff. Aug. 2, 1993.)*

Cross References

Applicability of this section to trolley coaches, see Vehicle Code § 21051.
Intersection defined, see Vehicle Code § 365.
Markings or signs for turning, see Vehicle Code § 22101.
Signals on turning and stopping, see Vehicle Code § 22107 et seq.
Speed limit at intersection, see Vehicle Code § 22352.
Turning at intersections, required position and method of, see Vehicle Code § 22100.

Research References

California Jury Instructions-Civil, 8th Edition 5.20, Turning a Vehicle.
California Jury Instructions-Civil, 8th Edition 5.21, Left Turn—Vehicle Having Right of Way as a Hazard.
2 Witkin, California Criminal Law 4th Crimes Against Public Peace and Welfare § 327 (2021), Miscellaneous Regulations.

§ 21802. Approaching intersection entrance

(a) The driver of any vehicle approaching a stop sign at the entrance to, or within, an intersection shall stop as required by Section 22450. The driver shall then yield the right-of-way to any vehicles which have approached from another highway, or which are approaching so closely as to constitute an immediate hazard, and shall continue to yield the right-of-way to those vehicles until he or she can proceed with reasonable safety.

(b) A driver having yielded as prescribed in subdivision (a) may proceed to enter the intersection, and the drivers of all other approaching vehicles shall yield the right-of-way to the vehicle entering or crossing the intersection.

(c) This section does not apply where stop signs are erected upon all approaches to an intersection. *(Stats.1959, c. 3. p. 1686, § 21802. Amended by Stats.1959, c. 975, p. 3005, § 2; Stats.1963, c. 1844, p. 3793, § 2; Stats.1969, c. 1101, p. 2100, § 2; Stats.1988, c. 623, § 3.)*

Cross References

Applicability of this section to trolley coaches, see Vehicle Code § 21051.
Definitions,
Intersection, see Vehicle Code § 365.
Right-of-way, see Vehicle Code § 525.
Through highway, see Vehicle Code § 600.
Flashing signals at intersections, see Vehicle Code § 21457.
Markings or signs for turning at intersections, see Vehicle Code § 22101.
Speed limit at intersection, see Vehicle Code § 22352.
Stop signs at through highway, see Vehicle Code § 21352 et seq.
Turning at intersections, required position and method, see Vehicle Code § 22100.

Research References

California Jury Instructions-Civil, 8th Edition 5.12, Through Highway Intersection—Vehicle Having Right of Way as a Hazard.
2 Witkin, California Criminal Law 4th Crimes Against Public Peace and Welfare § 327 (2021), Miscellaneous Regulations.

§ 21803. Yield right-of-way

(a) The driver of any vehicle approaching any intersection which is controlled by a yield right-of-way sign shall, upon arriving at the sign, yield the right-of-way to any vehicles which have entered the intersection, or which are approaching on the intersecting highway close enough to constitute an immediate hazard, and shall continue to yield the right-of-way to those vehicles until he or she can proceed with reasonable safety.

(b) A driver having yielded as prescribed in subdivision (a) may proceed to enter the intersection, and the drivers of all other approaching vehicles shall yield the right-of-way to the vehicle entering or crossing the intersection. *(Stats.1959, c. 3, p. 1686, § 21803. Amended by Stats.1959, c. 255, p. 2158, § 2; Stats.1963, c. 1844, p. 3793, § 3; Stats.1967, c. 370, p. 1597, § 2; Stats.1969, c. 834, p. 1668, § 2, operative July 1, 1970; Stats.1988, c. 623, § 4.)*

Cross References

Definitions,
Intersection, see Vehicle Code § 365.
Right-of-way, see Vehicle Code § 525.
Official traffic control devices, see Vehicle Code §§ 21400, 21401.
Signs, see Vehicle Code § 21356.
Speed limits, yield right-of-way signs, see Vehicle Code § 22352.
Traffic signs, signals and markings, see Vehicle Code § 21350 et seq.

Research References

California Jury Instructions-Civil, 8th Edition 5.13, Yield Right of Way Intersection—Vehicle Having Right of Way as a Hazard.
2 Witkin, California Criminal Law 4th Crimes Against Public Peace and Welfare § 327 (2021), Miscellaneous Regulations.

§ 21804. Entry onto highway; yield to approaching traffic constituting immediate hazard; yield by approaching traffic

(a) The driver of any vehicle about to enter or cross a highway from any public or private property, or from an alley, shall yield the right-of-way to all traffic, as defined in Section 620, approaching on the highway close enough to constitute an immediate hazard, and shall continue to yield the right-of-way to that traffic until he or she can proceed with reasonable safety.

(b) A driver having yielded as prescribed in subdivision (a) may proceed to enter or cross the highway, and the drivers of all other vehicles approaching on the highway shall yield the right-of-way to the vehicle entering or crossing the intersection. *(Stats.1959, c. 3, p. 1686, § 21804. Amended by Stats.1959, c. 970, p. 3002, § 1; Stats.1963, c. 409, p. 1214, § 2; Stats.1963, c. 1844, p. 3794, § 4; Stats.1969, c. 312, p. 680, § 2; Stats.1976, c. 751, p. 1785, § 13; Stats.1978, c. 122, p. 291, § 1; Stats.1987, c. 284, § 1; Stats.1988, c. 623, § 5.)*

Cross References

Airports, see Vehicle Code § 21108.
Definitions,
Highway, see Vehicle Code §§ 360, 590, 591.
Private road or driveway, see Vehicle Code § 490.
Right-of-way, see Vehicle Code § 525.
Housing projects, see Vehicle Code § 21111.
Traffic control, see Vehicle Code § 21360.
Traffic control by local authorities, see Vehicle Code § 21107.

Research References

California Jury Instructions-Civil, 8th Edition 5.22, Entering Highway—Vehicle Having Right of Way as a Hazard.
2 Witkin, California Criminal Law 4th Crimes Against Public Peace and Welfare § 327 (2021), Miscellaneous Regulations.

§ 21805. Equestrian crossings

(a) The Department of Transportation, and local authorities with respect to highways under their jurisdiction, may designate any intersection of a highway as a bridle path or equestrian crossing by erecting appropriate signs. The signs shall be erected on the highway at or near the approach to the intersection, and shall be of a type approved by the Department of Transportation. The signs shall indicate the crossing and any crossmarks, safety devices, or signals the authorities deem necessary to safeguard vehicular and equestrian traffic at the intersection.

(b) The driver of any vehicle shall yield the right-of-way to any horseback rider who is crossing the highway at any designated equestrian crossing which is marked by signs as prescribed in subdivision (a).

(c) Subdivision (b) does not relieve any horseback rider from the duty of using due care for his or her own safety. No horseback rider shall leave a curb or other place of safety and proceed suddenly into the path of a vehicle which is close enough to constitute an immediate hazard. *(Stats.1959, c. 3, p. 1686, § 21805. Amended by Stats.1973, c. 495, p. 970, § 1; Stats.1988, c. 623, § 6.)*

Cross References

Highway signs, markers or warning notices, failure to observe, see Vehicle Code §§ 21367, 40000.14.
Intersection defined, see Vehicle Code § 365.
Livestock crossings, signs, see Vehicle Code § 21364.
Livestock on highways, see Food and Agricultural Code § 16902.
Rights and duties of persons riding or driving animals, see Vehicle Code § 21050.
Traffic signs, signals and markings, generally, see Vehicle Code § 21350 et seq.

Research References

California Jury Instructions-Civil, 8th Edition 11.60, Failure to Provide Warning Signs Authorized by Vehicle Code.
2 Witkin, California Criminal Law 4th Crimes Against Public Peace and Welfare § 327 (2021), Miscellaneous Regulations.

§ 21806. Authorized emergency vehicles

Upon the immediate approach of an authorized emergency vehicle which is sounding a siren and which has at least one lighted lamp exhibiting red light that is visible, under normal atmospheric conditions, from a distance of 1,000 feet to the front of the vehicle, the surrounding traffic shall, except as otherwise directed by a traffic officer, do the following:

(a)(1) Except as required under paragraph (2), the driver of every other vehicle shall yield the right-of-way and shall immediately drive to the right-hand edge or curb of the highway, clear of any intersection, and thereupon shall stop and remain stopped until the authorized emergency vehicle has passed.

(2) A person driving a vehicle in an exclusive or preferential use lane shall exit that lane immediately upon determining that the exit can be accomplished with reasonable safety.

(b) The operator of every street car shall immediately stop the street car, clear of any intersection, and remain stopped until the authorized emergency vehicle has passed.

(c) All pedestrians upon the highway shall proceed to the nearest curb or place of safety and remain there until the authorized emergency vehicle has passed. *(Stats.1959, c. 3, p. 1687, § 21806. Amended by Stats.1978, c. 252, p. 533, § 2, eff. June 16, 1978; Stats.1988, c. 623, § 7; Stats.1996, c. 1154 (A.B.3020), § 68, eff. Sept. 30, 1996.)*

Cross References

Applicability of this section to trolley coaches, see Vehicle Code § 21051.
Authorized emergency vehicles, see Vehicle Code § 165.
Coroner vehicles, see Vehicle Code § 25264.
Exemptions of authorized emergency vehicles, see Vehicle Code §§ 21055, 21056.
Punishment for violation of section, see Vehicle Code § 42001.12.
Right-of-way, definition, see Vehicle Code § 525.
Sirens, use of on authorized emergency vehicles, see Vehicle Code § 27002.
Utility vehicles, see Vehicle Code §§ 25260, 25260.1.

Research References

California Jury Instructions - Criminal 12.85, Flight from Pursuing Peace Officer—Reckless Driving.
2 Witkin, California Criminal Law 4th Crimes Against Public Peace and Welfare § 327 (2021), Miscellaneous Regulations.
2 Witkin, California Criminal Law 4th Crimes Against Public Peace and Welfare § 329 (2021), Flight from Pursuing Peace Officer.

§ 21807. Effect of exemption

The provisions of Section 21806 shall not operate to relieve the driver of an authorized emergency vehicle from the duty to drive with due regard for the safety of all persons and property. *(Added by Stats.1961, c. 653, p. 1861, § 28, operative Jan. 1, 1962.)*

§ 21809. Driving vehicle in lane immediately adjacent to stationary emergency vehicle, tow truck, or Department of Transportation vehicle; penalty; exceptions

(a) A person driving a vehicle on a highway approaching a stationary authorized emergency vehicle that is displaying emergency lights, a stationary tow truck that is displaying flashing amber warning lights, or a stationary marked Department of Transportation vehicle that is displaying flashing amber warning lights, shall approach with due caution and, before passing in a lane immediately adjacent to the authorized emergency vehicle, tow truck, or Department of Transportation vehicle, absent other direction by a peace officer, proceed to do one of the following:

(1) Make a lane change into an available lane not immediately adjacent to the authorized emergency vehicle, tow truck, or Department of Transportation vehicle, with due regard for safety and traffic conditions, if practicable and not prohibited by law.

(2) If the maneuver described in paragraph (1) would be unsafe or impracticable, slow to a reasonable and prudent speed that is safe for existing weather, road, and vehicular or pedestrian traffic conditions.

(b) A violation of subdivision (a) is an infraction, punishable by a fine of not more than fifty dollars ($50).

(c) The requirements of subdivision (a) do not apply if the stationary authorized emergency vehicle that is displaying emergency lights, the stationary tow truck that is displaying flashing amber warning lights, or the stationary marked Department of Transportation vehicle that is displaying flashing amber warning lights is not adjacent to the highway or is separated from the highway by a protective physical barrier. *(Added by Stats.2006, c. 375 (S.B.1610), § 2. Amended by Stats.2009, c. 33 (S.B.159), § 1; Stats.2009, c. 175 (S.B.240), § 1; Stats.2020, c. 100 (A.B.2285), § 3, eff. Jan. 1, 2021.)*

Cross References

Infractions, see Penal Code § 16.
Operation of vehicle in unsafe manner within emergency incident zone, see Vehicle Code § 21706.5.

Research References

2 Witkin, California Criminal Law 4th Crimes Against Public Peace and Welfare § 327 (2021), Miscellaneous Regulations.

CHAPTER 5. PEDESTRIANS' RIGHTS AND DUTIES

Section

§ 21949. Legislative findings and declarations; pedestrian travel and access

(a) The Legislature hereby finds and declares that it is the policy of the State of California that safe and convenient pedestrian travel and access, whether by foot, wheelchair, walker, or stroller, be provided to the residents of the state.

(b) In accordance with the policy declared under subdivision (a), it is the intent of the Legislature that all levels of government in the state, particularly the Department of Transportation, work to provide convenient and safe passage for pedestrians on and across all streets and highways, increase levels of walking and pedestrian travel, and reduce pedestrian fatalities and injuries. *(Added by Stats.2000, c. 833 (A.B.2522), § 6.)*

§ 21949.5. Report to Legislature on pedestrian-related traffic crash data and traffic safety; impact of changes regarding peace officer enforcement

(a) On or before January 1, 2028, the Commissioner of the California Highway Patrol, in consultation with the Institute of Transportation Studies at the University of California, shall submit a report to the Legislature regarding statewide pedestrian-related traffic crash data and any associated impacts to traffic safety,

Vehicle

including an evaluation of whether and how the changes made to this chapter and Article 3 (commencing with Section 21450) of Chapter 2 by the act that added this section [1] have impacted pedestrian safety.

(b)(1) A report to be submitted pursuant to subdivision (a) shall be submitted in compliance with Section 9795 of the Government Code.

(2) Pursuant to Section 10231.5 of the Government Code, this section is repealed on January 1, 2032. *(Added by Stats.2022, c. 957 (A.B.2147), § 7, eff. Jan. 1, 2023.)*

[1] Stats.2022, c. 957 (A.B.2147).

Repeal

For repeal of this section, see its terms.

§ 21950. Right-of-way at crosswalks

(a) The driver of a vehicle shall yield the right-of-way to a pedestrian crossing the roadway within any marked crosswalk or within any unmarked crosswalk at an intersection, except as otherwise provided in this chapter.

(b) This section does not relieve a pedestrian from the duty of using due care for * * * their safety. No pedestrian may suddenly leave a curb or other place of safety and walk or run into the path of a vehicle that is so close as to constitute an immediate hazard. No pedestrian may unnecessarily stop or delay traffic while in a marked or unmarked crosswalk.

(c) The driver of a vehicle approaching a pedestrian within any marked or unmarked crosswalk shall exercise all due care and shall reduce the speed of the vehicle or take any other action relating to the operation of the vehicle as necessary to safeguard the safety of the pedestrian.

(d) Subdivision (b) does not relieve a driver of a vehicle from the duty of exercising due care for the safety of any pedestrian within any marked crosswalk or within any unmarked crosswalk at an intersection.

(e)(1) A peace officer, as defined in Chapter 4.5 (commencing with Section 830) of Title 3 of Part 2 of the Penal Code, shall not stop a pedestrian for a violation of this section unless a reasonably careful person would realize there is an immediate danger of a collision with a moving vehicle or other device moving exclusively by human power.

(2) This subdivision does not relieve a pedestrian from the duty of using due care for their safety.

(3) This subdivision does not relieve a driver of a vehicle from the duty of exercising due care for the safety of any pedestrian within the roadway. *(Stats.1959, c. 3, p. 1687, § 21950. Amended by Stats.1965, c. 1265, p. 3140, § 1; Stats.1970, c. 1001, p. 1799, § 1; Stats.1982, c. 741, p. 2944, § 2; Stats.2000, c. 833 (A.B.2522), § 8; Stats.2022, c. 957 (A.B.2147), § 8, eff. Jan. 1, 2023.)*

Cross References

Applicability of this section to trolley coaches, see Vehicle Code § 21051.
Blind persons, right-of-way, see Vehicle Code § 21963 et seq.
Crossing at other than crosswalks, see Vehicle Code § 21954.
Crosswalks, establishment of, see Vehicle Code § 21106.
Definitions,
 Crosswalk, see Vehicle Code § 275.
 Driver, see Vehicle Code § 305.
 Intersection, see Vehicle Code § 365.
 Right-of-way, see Vehicle Code § 525.
 Roadway, see Vehicle Code § 530.
 Vehicle, see Vehicle Code § 670.
Emergency vehicles, right-of-way, see Vehicle Code § 21806.
Pedestrian at controlled intersections, see Vehicle Code § 21955.
Pedestrian right-of-way on sidewalk, see Vehicle Code § 21952.
Pedestrian traffic control, see Vehicle Code § 21456.1.
Pedestrian tunnel or overhead crossing, right-of-way, see Vehicle Code § 21953.
Rules of the road, exemption of authorized emergency vehicles, see Vehicle Code § 21055.
Violations, see Vehicle Code § 40000.1 et seq.

Research References

California Jury Instructions-Civil, 8th Edition 5.52.1, Pedestrian Crossing at Crosswalk.
California Jury Instructions-Civil, 8th Edition 5.53, Definition—Immediate Hazard to Pedestrian—Unmarked Crosswalk.
California Jury Instructions-Civil, 8th Edition 5.55, Roadway—Definition Of.
2 Witkin, California Criminal Law 4th Crimes Against Public Peace and Welfare § 322 (2021), Pedestrian's Rights and Duties.
1 Witkin California Criminal Law 4th Defenses § 130 (2021), Competency of Court and Jury.
1 Witkin California Criminal Law 4th Defenses § 193 (2021), Homicide and Other Crimes.

§ 21950.5. Removal of crosswalk; notice

(a) An existing marked crosswalk may not be removed unless notice and opportunity to be heard is provided to the public not less than 30 days prior to the scheduled date of removal. In addition to any other public notice requirements, the notice of proposed removal shall be posted at the crosswalk identified for removal.

(b) The notice required by subdivision (a) shall include, but is not limited to, notification to the public of both of the following:

(1) That the public may provide input relating to the scheduled removal.

(2) The form and method of providing the input authorized by paragraph (1). *(Added by Stats.2000, c. 833 (A.B.2522), § 9.)*

§ 21951. Vehicles stopped for pedestrians

Whenever any vehicle has stopped at a marked crosswalk or at any unmarked crosswalk at an intersection to permit a pedestrian to cross the roadway the driver of any other vehicle approaching from the rear shall not overtake and pass the stopped vehicle. *(Stats.1959, c. 3, p. 1687, § 21951.)*

Cross References

Applicability of this section to trolley coaches, see Vehicle Code § 21051.
Definitions,
 Crosswalk, see Vehicle Code § 275.
 Driver, see Vehicle Code § 305.
 Intersection, see Vehicle Code § 365.
 Right-of-way, see Vehicle Code § 525.
 Roadway, see Vehicle Code § 530.
 Vehicle, see Vehicle Code § 670.
Establishment of crosswalks, see Vehicle Code § 21106.
Violations, see Vehicle Code § 40000.1 et seq.

Research References

2 Witkin, California Criminal Law 4th Crimes Against Public Peace and Welfare § 322 (2021), Pedestrian's Rights and Duties.

§ 21952. Right-of-way on sidewalk

The driver of any motor vehicle, prior to driving over or upon any sidewalk, shall yield the right-of-way to any pedestrian approaching thereon. *(Stats.1959, c. 3, p. 1687, § 21952.)*

Cross References

Sidewalk defined, see Vehicle Code § 555.

Research References

2 Witkin, California Criminal Law 4th Crimes Against Public Peace and Welfare § 322 (2021), Pedestrian's Rights and Duties.

§ 21953. Tunnel or overhead crossing

(a) Whenever any pedestrian crosses a roadway other than by means of a pedestrian tunnel or overhead pedestrian crossing, if a pedestrian tunnel or overhead crossing serves the place where the pedestrian is crossing the roadway, such pedestrian shall yield the right-of-way to all vehicles on the highway so near as to constitute an immediate hazard.

(b) This section shall not be construed to mean that a marked crosswalk, with or without a signal device, cannot be installed where a pedestrian tunnel or overhead crossing exists.

(c)(1) A peace officer, as defined in Chapter 4.5 (commencing with Section 830) of Title 3 of Part 2 of the Penal Code, shall not stop a pedestrian for a violation of subdivision (a) unless a reasonably careful person would realize there is an immediate danger of a collision with a moving vehicle or other device moving exclusively by human power.

(2) This subdivision does not relieve a pedestrian from the duty of using due care for their safety.

(3) This subdivision does not relieve a driver of a vehicle from the duty of exercising due care for the safety of any pedestrian within the roadway. *(Stats.1959, c. 3, p. 1687, § 21953. Amended by Stats.1971, c. 1017, p. 1956, § 1, operative May 3, 1972; Stats.1972, c. 680, p. 1264, § 1; Stats.2022, c. 957 (A.B.2147), § 9, eff. Jan. 1, 2023.)*

Research References

2 Witkin, California Criminal Law 4th Crimes Against Public Peace and Welfare § 322 (2021), Pedestrian's Rights and Duties.

§ 21954. Pedestrians outside crosswalks

(a) Every pedestrian upon a roadway at any point other than within a marked crosswalk or within an unmarked crosswalk at an intersection shall yield the right-of-way to all vehicles upon the roadway so near as to constitute an immediate hazard.

(b) The provisions of this section shall not relieve the driver of a vehicle from the duty to exercise due care for the safety of any pedestrian upon a roadway.

(c)(1) A peace officer, as defined in Chapter 4.5 (commencing with Section 830) of Title 3 of Part 2 of the Penal Code, shall not stop a pedestrian for a violation of subdivision (a) unless a reasonably careful person would realize there is an immediate danger of a collision with a moving vehicle or other device moving exclusively by human power.

(2) This subdivision does not relieve a pedestrian from the duty of using due care for their safety.

(3) This subdivision does not relieve a driver of a vehicle from the duty of exercising due care for the safety of any pedestrian within the roadway. *(Stats.1959, c. 3, p. 1687, § 21954. Amended by Stats.1961, c. 1308, p. 3088, § 1; Stats.1971, c. 1015, p. 1955, § 1, operative May 3, 1972; Stats.2022, c. 957 (A.B.2147), § 10, eff. Jan. 1, 2023.)*

Cross References

Definitions,
  Crosswalk, see Vehicle Code § 275.
  Intersection, see Vehicle Code § 365.
  Roadway, see Vehicle Code § 530.
Local regulations prohibiting pedestrians from crossing at other than crosswalks, see Vehicle Code § 21961.
Right-of-way of pedestrians at crosswalk, see Vehicle Code § 21950.

Research References

California Jury Instructions-Civil, 8th Edition 5.52.2, Pedestrian on Roadway Outside Crosswalk.
California Jury Instructions-Civil, 8th Edition 5.53, Definition—Immediate Hazard to Pedestrian—Unmarked Crosswalk.
California Jury Instructions-Civil, 8th Edition 5.55, Roadway—Definition Of.
2 Witkin, California Criminal Law 4th Crimes Against Public Peace and Welfare § 322 (2021), Pedestrian's Rights and Duties.

4 Witkin, California Criminal Law 4th Illegally Obtained Evidence § 300 (2021), Illustrations: Detention was Unreasonable.

§ 21955. Crossing between controlled intersections

(a) Between adjacent intersections controlled by traffic control signal devices or by police officers, pedestrians shall not cross the roadway at any place except in a crosswalk.

(b)(1) A peace officer, as defined in Chapter 4.5 (commencing with Section 830) of Title 3 of Part 2 of the Penal Code, shall not stop a pedestrian for a violation of subdivision (a) unless a reasonably careful person would realize there is an immediate danger of a collision with a moving vehicle or other device moving exclusively by human power.

(2) This subdivision does not relieve a pedestrian from the duty of using due care for their safety.

(3) This subdivision does not relieve a driver of a vehicle from the duty of exercising due care for the safety of any pedestrian within the roadway. *(Stats.1959, c. 3, p. 1688, § 21955. Amended by Stats.2022, c. 957 (A.B.2147), § 11, eff. Jan. 1, 2023.)*

Cross References

Crosswalks defined, see Vehicle Code § 275.
Intersection defined, see Vehicle Code § 365.
Local regulation of pedestrians, see Vehicle Code § 21961.
Official traffic control devices, see Vehicle Code § 21350 et seq.
Official traffic signals, see Vehicle Code § 21450 et seq.
Pedestrians' right-of-way at crosswalks, see Vehicle Code § 21951.
Powers of local authorities on traffic regulations, see Vehicle Code § 21100 et seq.
Roadway defined, see Vehicle Code § 530.

Research References

2 Witkin, California Criminal Law 4th Crimes Against Public Peace and Welfare § 322 (2021), Pedestrian's Rights and Duties.

§ 21956. Pedestrian on roadway

(a) A pedestrian * * * shall not walk upon a roadway outside of a business or residence district otherwise than close to * * * the pedestrian's left-hand edge of the roadway.

(b) A pedestrian may walk close to * * * their right-hand edge of the roadway if a crosswalk or other means of safely crossing the roadway is not available or if existing traffic or other conditions would compromise the safety of a pedestrian attempting to cross the road.

(c)(1) A peace officer, as defined in Chapter 4.5 (commencing with Section 830) of Title 3 of Part 2 of the Penal Code, shall not stop a pedestrian for a violation of this section unless a reasonably careful person would realize there is an immediate danger of a collision with a moving vehicle or other device moving exclusively by human power.

(2) This subdivision does not relieve a pedestrian from the duty of using due care for their safety.

(3) This subdivision does not relieve a driver of a vehicle from the duty of exercising due care for the safety of any pedestrian within the roadway. *(Stats.1959, c. 3, p. 1688, § 21956. Amended by Stats.2000, c. 833 (A.B.2522), § 10; Stats.2022, c. 957 (A.B.2147), § 12, eff. Jan. 1, 2023.)*

Cross References

Business district defined, see Vehicle Code § 235.
Limitations in determining business and residence districts, see Vehicle Code § 240.
Residence district defined, see Vehicle Code § 515.

Research References

California Jury Instructions-Civil, 8th Edition 5.55, Roadway—Definition Of.
2 Witkin, California Criminal Law 4th Crimes Against Public Peace and Welfare § 322 (2021), Pedestrian's Rights and Duties.

4 Witkin, California Criminal Law 4th Illegally Obtained Evidence § 301 (2021), Stop Based on Mistake of Law.

§ 21957. Hitchhiking

No person shall stand in a roadway for the purpose of soliciting a ride from the driver of any vehicle. *(Stats.1959, c. 3, p. 1688, § 21957.)*

Cross References

Roadway defined, see Vehicle Code § 530.

Research References

2 Witkin, California Criminal Law 4th Crimes Against Public Peace and Welfare § 322 (2021), Pedestrian's Rights and Duties.

§ 21959. Skiing or tobogganing

It is unlawful for any person to ski or toboggan on or across any roadway in such a manner as to interfere with the movement of vehicles thereon. A person on skis proceeding on or across a highway at a pace no greater than a walk is not within the prohibition of this section and shall be considered to be a pedestrian with all the rights and duties thereof as prescribed in this code. *(Stats.1959, c. 3, p. 1688, § 21959. Amended by Stats.1972, c. 46, p. 64, § 3.)*

Research References

2 Witkin, California Criminal Law 4th Crimes Against Public Peace and Welfare § 322 (2021), Pedestrian's Rights and Duties.

§ 21960. Freeways and expressways

(a) The Department of Transportation and local authorities, by order, ordinance, or resolution, with respect to freeways, expressways, or designated portions thereof under their respective jurisdictions, to which vehicle access is completely or partially controlled, may prohibit or restrict the use of the freeways, expressways, or any portion thereof by pedestrians, bicycles or other nonmotorized traffic or by any person operating a motor-driven cycle, motorized bicycle, motorized scooter, or electrically motorized board. A prohibition or restriction pertaining to bicycles, motor-driven cycles, motorized scooters, or electrically motorized boards shall be deemed to include motorized bicycles. A person shall not operate a motorized bicycle wherever that prohibition or restriction is in force. Notwithstanding any order, ordinance, or resolution to the contrary, the driver or passengers of a disabled vehicle stopped on a freeway or expressway may walk to the nearest exit, in either direction, on that side of the freeway or expressway upon which the vehicle is disabled, from which telephone or motor vehicle repair services are available.

(b) The prohibitory regulation authorized by subdivision (a) shall be effective when appropriate signs giving notice thereof are erected upon any freeway or expressway and the approaches thereto. If any portion of a county freeway or expressway is contained within the limits of a city within the county, the county may erect signs on that portion as required under this subdivision if the ordinance has been approved by the city pursuant to subdivision (b) of Section 1730 of the Streets and Highways Code.

(c) No ordinance or resolution of local authorities shall apply to any state highway until the proposed ordinance or resolution has been presented to, and approved in writing by, the Department of Transportation.

(d) An ordinance or resolution adopted under this section on or after January 1, 2005, to prohibit pedestrian access to a county freeway or expressway shall not be effective unless it is supported by a finding by the local authority that the freeway or expressway does not have pedestrian facilities and pedestrian use would pose a safety risk to the pedestrian. *(Stats.1959, c. 3, p. 1688, § 21960. Amended by Stats.1972, c. 498, p. 869, § 1; Stats.1974, c. 545, p. 1321, § 192; Stats.1975, c. 987, p. 2331, § 7.5; Stats.1999, c. 722 (S.B.441), § 6; Stats.2004, c. 615 (S.B.1233), § 28; Stats.2015, c. 777 (A.B.604), § 4, eff. Jan. 1, 2016.)*

Cross References

Definition, see Vehicle Code § 332.
Exemption of emergency vehicles from rules of the road, exceptions, see Vehicle Code § 21055.
Local authorities defined, see Vehicle Code § 385.
Motor-driven cycle defined, see Vehicle Code § 405.
Motorized bicycle, see Vehicle Code § 406.
Powers of local authorities, see Vehicle Code § 21100 et seq.
Traffic signs, generally, see Vehicle Code § 21350 et seq.

Research References

2 Witkin, California Criminal Law 4th Crimes Against Public Peace and Welfare § 322 (2021), Pedestrian's Rights and Duties.

§ 21961. Local regulation of pedestrians; enforcement by peace officer

(a) This chapter does not prevent local authorities from adopting ordinances prohibiting pedestrians from crossing roadways at other than crosswalks.

(b)(1) A peace officer, as defined in Chapter 4.5 (commencing with Section 830) of Title 3 of Part 2 of the Penal Code, shall not stop a pedestrian for a violation of an ordinance adopted by a local authority pursuant to this section, unless a reasonably careful person would realize there is an immediate danger of a collision with a moving vehicle or other device moving exclusively by human power.

(2) This subdivision does not relieve a pedestrian from the duty of using due care for their safety.

(3) This subdivision does not relieve a driver of a vehicle from the duty of exercising due care for the safety of any pedestrian within the roadway. *(Stats.1959, c. 3, p. 1688, § 21961. Amended by Stats.2022, c. 957 (A.B.2147), § 13, eff. Jan. 1, 2023.)*

Cross References

Definitions,
  Crosswalk, see Vehicle Code § 275.
  Intersection, see Vehicle Code § 365.
  Local authorities, see Vehicle Code § 385.
  Roadway, see Vehicle Code § 530.
Establishment of crosswalks by local authorities, see Vehicle Code § 21106.
Exemption of emergency vehicles from rules of the road, exemptions, see Vehicle Code § 21055.
Local regulation of traffic, see Vehicle Code § 21100 et seq.
Pedestrian Mall Law of 1960, see Streets and Highways Code § 11000 et seq.
Pedestrians' right-of-way in crosswalks, see Vehicle Code § 21950.

Research References

2 Witkin, California Criminal Law 4th Crimes Against Public Peace and Welfare § 322 (2021), Pedestrian's Rights and Duties.

§ 21962. Pedestrian on bridge

Any peace officer having reasonable cause to believe that any pedestrian is stopped or standing on any bridge or overpass for the purpose of violating Section 23110, may lawfully order such person from the bridge or overpass. *(Added by Stats.1965, c. 1673, p. 3794, § 1.)*

§ 21963. Visually handicapped pedestrian

A totally or partially blind pedestrian who is carrying a predominantly white cane (with or without a red tip), or using a guide dog, shall have the right-of-way, and the driver of any vehicle approaching this pedestrian, who fails to yield the right-of-way, or to take all reasonably necessary precautions to avoid injury to this blind pedestrian, is guilty of a misdemeanor, punishable by imprisonment in the county jail not exceeding six months, or by a fine of not less than five hundred dollars ($500) nor more than one thousand dollars ($1,000), or both. This section shall not preclude prosecution under any other applicable provision of law. *(Added by Stats.1968, c. 461, p. 1094, § 7. Amended by Stats.1993, c. 1149 (A.B.1419), § 7.)*

Research References

2 Witkin, California Criminal Law 4th Crimes Against Public Peace and Welfare § 322 (2021), Pedestrian's Rights and Duties.

§ 21964. White canes

No person, other than those totally or partially blind, shall carry or use on any highway or in any public building, public facility, or other public place, a predominantly white cane (with or without a red tip). *(Added by Stats.1968, c. 461, p. 1094, § 8.)*

Research References

2 Witkin, California Criminal Law 4th Crimes Against Public Peace and Welfare § 322 (2021), Pedestrian's Rights and Duties.

§ 21965. Definitions

As used in Sections 21963 and 21964, "blind," "totally blind," and "partially blind," mean having central visual acuity not to exceed 20/200 in the better eye, with corrected lenses, as measured by the Snellen test, or visual acuity greater than 20/200, but with a limitation in the field of vision such that the widest diameter of the visual field subtends an angle not greater than 20 degrees. *(Added by Stats.1968, c. 461, p. 1094, § 9.)*

Research References

2 Witkin, California Criminal Law 4th Crimes Against Public Peace and Welfare § 322 (2021), Pedestrian's Rights and Duties.

§ 21966. Pedestrian in bicycle lane

* * * (a) A pedestrian shall not proceed along a bicycle path or lane where there is an adjacent adequate pedestrian facility.

(b)(1) A peace officer, as defined in Chapter 4.5 (commencing with Section 830) of Title 3 of Part 2 of the Penal Code, shall not stop a pedestrian for a violation of subdivision (a) unless a reasonably careful person would realize there is an immediate danger of a collision with a moving vehicle or other device moving exclusively by human power.

(2) This subdivision does not relieve a pedestrian from the duty of using due care for their safety.

(3) This subdivision does not relieve a bicyclist from the duty of exercising due care for the safety of any pedestrian within the roadway. *(Added by Stats.1976, c. 751, p. 1785, § 14. Amended by Stats.2022, c. 957 (A.B.2147), § 14, eff. Jan. 1, 2023.)*

Cross References

Electric personal assistive mobility devices, use by a pedestrian, authority to impose time, place or manner ordinances, see Vehicle Code § 21282.

Research References

2 Witkin, California Criminal Law 4th Crimes Against Public Peace and Welfare § 322 (2021), Pedestrian's Rights and Duties.

§ 21967. Skateboards or electrically motorized boards on highways, sidewalks, or roadways

Except as provided in Section 21968, a local authority may adopt rules and regulations by ordinance or resolution prohibiting or restricting persons from riding or propelling skateboards, or electrically motorized boards, on highways, sidewalks, or roadways. *(Formerly § 21114.6, added by Stats.1976, c. 1359, p. 6202, § 1. Renumbered § 21967 and amended by Stats.1977, c. 275, p. 1169, § 1, eff. July 8, 1977. Amended by Stats.1978, c. 380, p. 1203, § 144; Stats.1987, c. 1184, § 35; Stats.2015, c. 777 (A.B.604), § 5, eff. Jan. 1, 2016.)*

Research References

2 Witkin, California Criminal Law 4th Crimes Against Public Peace and Welfare § 322 (2021), Pedestrian's Rights and Duties.

§ 21968. Motorized skateboards; propulsion restrictions on sidewalks, roadways, bikeways, etc.

(a) A motorized skateboard shall not be propelled on any sidewalk, roadway, or any other part of a highway or on any bikeway, bicycle path or trail, equestrian trail, or hiking or recreational trail.

(b) For purposes of this section, an electrically motorized board, as defined in Section 313.5, is not a motorized skateboard. *(Added by Stats.1977, c. 275, p. 1169, § 2, eff. July 8, 1977. Amended by Stats.2015, c. 777 (A.B.604), § 6, eff. Jan. 1, 2016.)*

§ 21969. Roller skating on highways, sidewalks or roadways; adoption of rules and regulations by ordinance

A local authority may adopt rules and regulations by ordinance regulating persons engaged in roller skating on a highway, sidewalk, or roadway. *(Added by Stats.1981, c. 145, p. 944, § 1.)*

§ 21970. Vehicle blocking crosswalk or sidewalk; one-way streets

(a) No person may stop a vehicle unnecessarily in a manner that causes the vehicle to block a marked or unmarked crosswalk or sidewalk.

(b) Subdivision (a) does not preclude the driver of a vehicle facing a steady circular red light from turning right or turning left from a one-way street onto a one-way street pursuant to subdivision (b) of Section 21453. *(Added by Stats.2000, c. 833 (A.B.2522), § 11.)*

Research References

2 Witkin, California Criminal Law 4th Crimes Against Public Peace and Welfare § 322 (2021), Pedestrian's Rights and Duties.

§ 21971. Specified violations of sections 21451, 21453, 21950 or 21952 causing bodily injury; punishment

Notwithstanding any other provision of law, any person who violates subdivision (a) or (b) of Section 21451, subdivision (b) of Section 21453, subdivision (a) of Section 21950, or Section 21952, and causes the bodily injury of anyone other than the driver is guilty of an infraction punishable under Section 42001.18. *(Added by Stats.2000, c. 833 (A.B.2522), § 12.)*

Research References

2 Witkin, California Criminal Law 4th Crimes Against Public Peace and Welfare § 322 (2021), Pedestrian's Rights and Duties.

2 Witkin, California Criminal Law 4th Crimes Against Public Peace and Welfare § 327 (2021), Miscellaneous Regulations.

CHAPTER 6. TURNING AND STOPPING AND TURNING SIGNALS

Section

§ 22100. Turning upon a highway

Except as provided in Section 22100.5 or 22101, the driver of any vehicle intending to turn upon a highway shall do so as follows:

(a) Right Turns. Both the approach for a right-hand turn and a right-hand turn shall be made as close as practicable to the right-hand curb or edge of the roadway except:

(1) Upon a highway having three marked lanes for traffic moving in one direction that terminates at an intersecting highway accommodating traffic in both directions, the driver of a vehicle in the middle lane may turn right into any lane lawfully available to traffic moving in that direction upon the roadway being entered.

(2) If a right-hand turn is made from a one-way highway at an intersection, a driver shall approach the turn as provided in this subdivision and shall complete the turn in any lane lawfully available to traffic moving in that direction upon the roadway being entered.

(3) Upon a highway having an additional lane or lanes marked for a right turn by appropriate signs or markings, the driver of a vehicle may turn right from any lane designated and marked for that turning movement.

(b) Left Turns. The approach for a left turn shall be made as close as practicable to the left-hand edge of the extreme left-hand lane or portion of the roadway lawfully available to traffic moving in the direction of travel of the vehicle and, when turning at an intersection, the left turn shall not be made before entering the intersection. After entering the intersection, the left turn shall be made so as to leave the intersection in a lane lawfully available to traffic moving in that direction upon the roadway being entered, except that upon a highway having three marked lanes for traffic moving in one direction that terminates at an intersecting highway accommodating traffic in both directions, the driver of a vehicle in the middle lane may turn left into any lane lawfully available to traffic moving in that direction upon the roadway being entered. *(Added by Stats.1971, c. 286, p. 592, § 2, operative May 3, 1972. Amended by Stats.1972, c. 1060, p. 1970, § 1; Stats.1982, c. 741, p. 2944, § 3; Stats.2004, c. 183 (A.B.3082), § 353.)*

Cross References

Division of highways of state department of public works, see Streets and Highways Code §§ 50, 70 et seq.
Duration of signal, see Vehicle Code § 22108.
Highway signs, markers or warning notices, failure to observe, see Vehicle Code §§ 21367, 40000.14.
Intersection defined, see Vehicle Code § 365.
Means and method of giving signal, see Vehicle Code §§ 22110, 22111.
Regulations, state highways, see Vehicle Code § 21352.
Right-of-way, see Vehicle Code § 21800 et seq.
Rules of the road, exemption of authorized emergency vehicles, see Vehicle Code § 21055.
Signs reducing speed limits in exercise of authority to link districts, see Vehicle Code § 22360.
Streetcars, see Vehicle Code § 21455.
Traffic signs, signals and markings, see Vehicle Code § 21350 et seq.

Research References

2 Witkin, California Criminal Law 4th Crimes Against Public Peace and Welfare § 327 (2021), Miscellaneous Regulations.

§ 22100.5. U-turn at intersection controlled by traffic signals or devices

No driver shall make a U-turn at an intersection controlled by official traffic signals except as provided in Section 21451, and then only from the far lefthand lane that is lawfully available to traffic moving in the direction of travel from which the turn is commenced. No driver shall make a U-turn at an intersection controlled by official traffic control devices except from the far lefthand lane that is lawfully available to traffic moving in the direction of travel from which the turn is commenced. *(Added by Stats.1981, c. 413, p. 1611, § 11. Amended by Stats.1984, c. 700, § 2.)*

Research References

2 Witkin, California Criminal Law 4th Crimes Against Public Peace and Welfare § 327 (2021), Miscellaneous Regulations.

§ 22101. Regulation of turns at intersection

(a) The Department of Transportation or local authorities, in respect to highways under their respective jurisdictions, may cause official traffic control devices to be placed or erected within or adjacent to intersections to regulate or prohibit turning movements at such intersections.

(b) When turning movements are required at an intersection, notice of that requirement shall be given by erection of a sign, unless an additional clearly marked traffic lane is provided for the approach to the turning movement, in which event notice as applicable to that additional traffic lane shall be given by an official traffic control device.

(c) When right- or left-hand turns are prohibited at an intersection, notice of that prohibition shall be given by erection of a sign.

(d) When an official traffic control device is placed as required in subdivisions (b) or (c), it is unlawful for a driver of a vehicle to disobey the directions of the official traffic control device.

(e)(1) A person operating a bicycle may travel straight through a right- or left-hand turn only lane when an official traffic control device indicates that the movement is permitted.

(2) The Department of Transportation shall develop standards for lane striping, pavement markings, and appropriate regulatory signs to implement this subdivision. *(Stats.1959, c. 3, p. 1689, § 22101. Amended by Stats.1963, c. 481, p. 1339, § 1; Stats.1974, c. 545, p. 1321, § 193; Stats.2019, c. 221 (A.B.1266), § 1, eff. Jan. 1, 2020.)*

Cross References

Intersection defined, see Vehicle Code § 365.
Local authorities, regulation,
  Determination of speed limit in linking districts on local highways, see Vehicle Code § 22360.
  Pedestrians crossing roadways, see Vehicle Code § 21961.
  Traffic control devices, see Vehicle Code § 21100 et seq.
  Turning movements at intersections, see Vehicle Code § 22113.
Notice to appear, violation recorded by automated enforcement system, see Vehicle Code § 40518.
Street name signs, see Vehicle Code § 21366.
Traffic signs, signals and markings, see Vehicle Code § 21350 et seq.

Research References

2 Witkin, California Criminal Law 4th Crimes Against Public Peace and Welfare § 327 (2021), Miscellaneous Regulations.

§ 22102. U-turn in business district

No person in a business district shall make a U-turn, except at an intersection, or on a divided highway where an opening has been provided in accordance with Section 21651. This turning movement shall be made as close as practicable to the extreme left-hand edge of the lanes moving in the driver's direction of travel immediately prior to the initiation of the turning movement, when more than one lane in the direction of travel is present. *(Stats.1959, c. 3, p. 1689, § 22102. Amended by Stats.1961, c. 1312, p. 3091, § 1; Stats.1970, c. 620, p. 1231, § 2; Stats.1985, c. 47, § 1.)*

Cross References

Definitions,
  Business district, see Vehicle Code § 235.

Intersection, see Vehicle Code § 365.
Residence district, see Vehicle Code § 515.
Turning near fire stations or on curve or crest of grade prohibited, see Vehicle Code §§ 22104, 22105.

Research References

2 Witkin, California Criminal Law 4th Crimes Against Public Peace and Welfare § 327 (2021), Miscellaneous Regulations.

§ 22103. U-turn in residence district

No person in a residence district shall make a U-turn when any other vehicle is approaching from either direction within 200 feet, except at an intersection when the approaching vehicle is controlled by an official traffic control device. *(Stats.1959, c. 3, p. 1689, § 22103. Amended by Stats.1963, c. 255, p. 1016, § 1; Stats.1970, c. 620, p. 1231, § 3.)*

Cross References

Intersection defined, see Vehicle Code § 365.
Residence district defined, see Vehicle Code § 515.

Research References

2 Witkin, California Criminal Law 4th Crimes Against Public Peace and Welfare § 327 (2021), Miscellaneous Regulations.

§ 22104. U-turns near fire stations

No person shall make a U-turn in front of the driveway entrance or approaches to a fire station. No person shall use the driveway entrance or approaches to a fire station for the purpose of turning a vehicle so as to proceed in the opposite direction. *(Stats.1959, c. 3, p. 1689, § 22104. Amended by Stats.1970, c. 620, p. 1231, § 4.)*

Research References

2 Witkin, California Criminal Law 4th Crimes Against Public Peace and Welfare § 327 (2021), Miscellaneous Regulations.

§ 22105. Unobstructed view necessary for U-turn

No person shall make a U-turn upon any highway where the driver of such vehicle does not have an unobstructed view for 200 feet in both directions along the highway and of any traffic thereon. *(Stats.1959, c. 3, p. 1689, § 22105. Amended by Stats.1970, c. 620, p. 1231, § 5; Stats.1972, c. 64, p. 84, § 1.)*

Research References

2 Witkin, California Criminal Law 4th Crimes Against Public Peace and Welfare § 327 (2021), Miscellaneous Regulations.

§ 22106. Starting parked vehicles or backing

No person shall start a vehicle stopped, standing, or parked on a highway, nor shall any person back a vehicle on a highway until such movement can be made with reasonable safety. *(Stats.1959, c. 3, p. 1689, § 22106.)*

Cross References

Applicability of this section to trolley coaches, see Vehicle Code § 21051.
Parking regulations, see Vehicle Code § 22500 et seq.

Research References

2 Witkin, California Criminal Law 4th Crimes Against Public Peace and Welfare § 327 (2021), Miscellaneous Regulations.

§ 22107. Turning movements and required signals

No person shall turn a vehicle from a direct course or move right or left upon a roadway until such movement can be made with reasonable safety and then only after the giving of an appropriate signal in the manner provided in this chapter in the event any other vehicle may be affected by the movement. *(Stats.1959, c. 3, p. 1689, § 22107. Amended by Stats.1959, c. 1996, p. 4630, § 27.)*

Cross References

Applicability of this section to trolley coaches, see Vehicle Code § 21051.
Manner and method of giving signal, see Vehicle Code §§ 22110, 22111.
Position and method of turning at intersection, see Vehicle Code §§ 22100, 22101.
Restrictions on turning of vehicles, see Vehicle Code § 22102 et seq.

Research References

California Jury Instructions-Civil, 8th Edition 5.20, Turning a Vehicle.
2 Witkin, California Criminal Law 4th Crimes Against Public Peace and Welfare § 327 (2021), Miscellaneous Regulations.
4 Witkin, California Criminal Law 4th Illegally Obtained Evidence § 299 (2021), Illustrations: Detention was Reasonable.
4 Witkin, California Criminal Law 4th Illegally Obtained Evidence § 300 (2021), Illustrations: Detention was Unreasonable.

§ 22108. Duration of signal

Any signal of intention to turn right or left shall be given continuously during the last 100 feet traveled by the vehicle before turning. *(Stats.1959, c. 3, p. 1689, § 22108.)*

Cross References

Applicability of this section to trolley coaches, see Vehicle Code § 21051.

Research References

2 Witkin, California Criminal Law 4th Crimes Against Public Peace and Welfare § 327 (2021), Miscellaneous Regulations.
4 Witkin, California Criminal Law 4th Illegally Obtained Evidence § 300 (2021), Illustrations: Detention was Unreasonable.

§ 22109. Signal when stopping

No person shall stop or suddenly decrease the speed of a vehicle on a highway without first giving an appropriate signal in the manner provided in this chapter to the driver of any vehicle immediately to the rear when there is opportunity to give the signal. *(Stats.1959, c. 3, p. 1689, § 22109.)*

Cross References

Applicability of this section to trolley coaches, see Vehicle Code § 21051.

Research References

2 Witkin, California Criminal Law 4th Crimes Against Public Peace and Welfare § 327 (2021), Miscellaneous Regulations.

§ 22110. Method of signaling

(a) The signals required by this chapter shall be given by signal lamp, unless a vehicle is not required to be and is not equipped with turn signals. Drivers of vehicles not required to be and not equipped with turn signals shall give a hand and arm signal when required by this chapter.

(b) In the event the signal lamps become inoperable while driving, hand and arm signals shall be used in the manner required in this chapter. *(Stats.1959, c. 3, p. 1690, § 22110. Amended by Stats.1961, c. 118, p. 1128, § 1; Stats.1965, c. 1012, p. 2643, § 1; Stats.1967, c. 859, p. 2300, § 1; Stats.1999, c. 1008 (S.B.533), § 12.)*

Cross References

Approval of signal device, see Vehicle Code § 26100 et seq.
Unauthorized signals, see Vehicle Code § 21465.

Research References

2 Witkin, California Criminal Law 4th Crimes Against Public Peace and Welfare § 327 (2021), Miscellaneous Regulations.

§ 22111. Hand signals

All required signals given by hand and arm shall be given from the left side of a vehicle in the following manner:

(a) Left turn—hand and arm extended horizontally beyond the side of the vehicle.

(b) Right turn—hand and arm extended upward beyond the side of the vehicle, except that a bicyclist may extend the right hand and arm horizontally to the right side of the bicycle.

(c) Stop or sudden decrease of speed signal—hand and arm extended downward beyond the side of the vehicle. *(Stats.1959, c. 3, p. 1690, § 22111. Amended by Stats.1963, c. 153, p. 821, § 1; Stats.1976, c. 751, p. 1785, § 15.)*

Cross References

Means of giving signal, see Vehicle Code § 22110.

§ 22112. Operation of amber warning light system, flashing red signal lights and stop signal arm system; stopping to load or unload pupils

(a) On approach to a schoolbus stop where pupils are loading or unloading from a schoolbus, the schoolbus driver shall activate an approved amber warning light system, if the schoolbus is so equipped, beginning 200 feet before the schoolbus stop. The schoolbus driver shall deactivate the amber warning light system after reaching the schoolbus stop. The schoolbus driver shall operate the flashing red light signal system and stop signal arm, as required on the schoolbus, at all times when the schoolbus is stopped for the purpose of loading or unloading pupils. The flashing red light signal system, amber warning lights system, and stop signal arm shall not be operated at any place where traffic is controlled by a traffic officer or at any location identified in subdivision (e) of this section. The schoolbus flashing red light signal system, amber warning lights system, and stop signal arm shall not be operated at any other time.

(b) The schoolbus driver shall stop to load or unload pupils only at a schoolbus stop designated for pupils by the school district superintendent or the head or principal of a private school, or authorized by any of those individuals for school activity trips.

(c) When a schoolbus is stopped on a highway or private road for the purpose of loading or unloading pupils, at a location where traffic is not controlled by a traffic officer, the driver shall, before opening the door, ensure that the flashing red light signal system and stop signal arm are activated, and that it is safe to enter or exit the schoolbus.

(d) When a schoolbus is stopped on a highway or private road for the purpose of loading or unloading pupils, at a location where traffic is not controlled by a traffic officer or official traffic control signal, the schoolbus driver shall do all of the following:

(1) Escort all pupils in prekindergarten, kindergarten, or any of grades 1 to 8, inclusive, who need to cross the highway or private road upon which the schoolbus is stopped. The driver shall use an approved hand-held "STOP" sign while escorting all pupils.

(2) Require all pupils who need to cross the highway or private road upon which the schoolbus is stopped to walk in front of the bus as they cross.

(3) Ensure that all pupils who need to cross the highway or private road upon which the schoolbus is stopped have crossed safely, and that all other pupils and pedestrians are a safe distance from the schoolbus before setting the schoolbus in motion.

(e) Except at a location where pupils are loading or unloading from a schoolbus and must cross a highway or private road upon which the schoolbus is stopped, the schoolbus driver may not activate the amber warning light system, the flashing red light signal system and stop signal arm at any of the following locations:

(1) Schoolbus loading zones on or adjacent to school grounds or during an activity trip, if the schoolbus is lawfully stopped or parked.

(2) Where the schoolbus is disabled due to mechanical breakdown. The driver of a relief bus that arrives at the scene to transport pupils from the disabled schoolbus shall not activate the amber warning light system, the flashing red light system, and stop signal arm.

(3) Where a pupil requires physical assistance from the driver or authorized attendant to board or leave the schoolbus and providing the assistance extends the length of time the schoolbus is stopped beyond the time required to load or unload a pupil that does not require physical assistance.

(4) Where the roadway surface on which the bus is stopped is partially or completely covered by snow or ice and requiring traffic to stop would pose a safety hazard as determined by the schoolbus motor carrier.

(5) On a state highway with a posted speed limit of 55 miles per hour or higher where the schoolbus is completely off the main traveled portion of the highway.

(6) Any location determined by a school district or a private school, with the approval of the Department of the California Highway Patrol, to present a traffic or safety hazard.

(f) Notwithstanding subdivisions (a) to (d), inclusive, the Department of the California Highway Patrol may require the activation of an approved flashing amber warning light system, if the schoolbus is so equipped, or the flashing red light signal system and stop signal arm, as required on the schoolbus, at any location where the department determines that the activation is necessary for the safety of school pupils loading or unloading from a schoolbus. *(Stats.1959, c. 3, p. 1690, § 22112. Amended by Stats.1977, c. 553, p. 1778, § 1; Stats.1981, c. 813, p. 3156, § 13; Stats.1992, c. 624 (A.B.3144), § 4, eff. Sept. 14, 1992; Stats.1994, c. 831 (S.B.2019), § 2, eff. Sept. 27, 1994; Stats.1997, c. 739 (A.B.1297), § 3; Stats.1999, c. 647 (A.B. 1573), § 2, eff. Oct. 10, 1999; Stats.2002, c. 397 (S.B.1685), § 1; Stats.2012, c. 769 (A.B.2679), § 35.)*

Cross References

Crossing control arm, use of control arm by operator of a schoolbus, responsibility for safety of students, see Vehicle Code § 35400.
Display of signs, see Vehicle Code § 27906.
Duties of drivers, see Vehicle Code § 22454.
Schoolbus defined, see Vehicle Code § 545.
Signal equipment, see Vehicle Code § 25257.

Research References

2 Witkin, California Criminal Law 4th Crimes Against Public Peace and Welfare § 327 (2021), Miscellaneous Regulations.

§ 22113. Local authorities

This chapter does not prevent local authorities, by ordinance, from prohibiting the making of any turning movement by any vehicle at any intersection or between any designated intersections. *(Stats. 1959, c. 3, p. 1690, § 22113.)*

Cross References

Adoption of rules and regulations, see Vehicle Code § 21100 et seq.
Definitions,
  Intersection, see Vehicle Code § 365.
  Local authorities, see Vehicle Code § 385.
  Vehicle, see Vehicle Code § 670.
Exemption of emergency vehicles from rules of the road, exceptions, see Vehicle Code § 21055.
Traffic regulation, see Vehicle Code § 21100 et seq.

Research References

2 Witkin, California Criminal Law 4th Crimes Against Public Peace and Welfare § 327 (2021), Miscellaneous Regulations.

CHAPTER 7. SPEED LAWS

ARTICLE 1. GENERALLY

§ 22348. Exceeding the speed limit on highways; punishment for driving at a speed greater than 100 miles per hour; driving in designated lanes

(a) Notwithstanding subdivision (b) of Section 22351, a person shall not drive a vehicle upon a highway with a speed limit established pursuant to Section 22349 or 22356 at a speed greater than that speed limit.

(b) A person who drives a vehicle upon a highway at a speed greater than 100 miles per hour is guilty of an infraction punishable, as follows:

(1) Upon a first conviction of a violation of this subdivision, by a fine of not to exceed five hundred dollars ($500). The court may also suspend the privilege of the person to operate a motor vehicle for a period not to exceed 30 days pursuant to Section 13200.5.

(2) Upon a conviction under this subdivision of an offense that occurred within three years of a prior offense resulting in a conviction of an offense under this subdivision, by a fine of not to exceed seven hundred fifty dollars ($750). The person's privilege to operate a motor vehicle shall be suspended by the Department of Motor Vehicles pursuant to subdivision (a) of Section 13355.

(3) Upon a conviction under this subdivision of an offense that occurred within five years of two or more prior offenses resulting in convictions of offenses under this subdivision, by a fine of not to exceed one thousand dollars ($1,000). The person's privilege to operate a motor vehicle shall be suspended by the Department of Motor Vehicles pursuant to subdivision (b) of Section 13355.

(c) A vehicle subject to Section 22406 shall be driven in a lane designated pursuant to Section 21655, or if a lane has not been so designated, in the right-hand lane for traffic or as close as practicable to the right-hand edge or curb. When overtaking and passing another vehicle proceeding in the same direction, the driver shall use either the designated lane, the lane to the immediate left of the right-hand lane, or the right-hand lane for traffic as permitted under this code. If, however, specific lane or lanes have not been designated on a divided highway having four or more clearly marked lanes for traffic in one direction, a vehicle may also be driven in the lane to the immediate left of the right- hand lane, unless otherwise prohibited under this code. This subdivision does not apply to a driver who is preparing for a left- or right-hand turn or who is in the process of entering into or exiting from a highway or to a driver who is required necessarily to drive in a lane other than the right- hand lane to continue on his or her intended route. *(Added by Stats.1973, c. 1218, p. 2935, § 1, eff. Dec. 12, 1973, operative Jan. 1, 1974. Amended by Stats.1975, c. 153, p. 285, § 1, eff. June 28, 1975; Stats.1978, c. 217, p. 466, § 1, eff. June 8, 1978; Stats.1983, c. 980, § 3; Stats.1984, c. 276, § 3; Stats.1987, c. 25, § 1, eff. May 28, 1987; Stats.1987, c. 72, § 2, eff. June 30, 1987; Stats.2004, c. 300 (A.B.2237), § 1.)*

Cross References

Fine for violation of this section, see Vehicle Code § 42000.1.
Suspension of privilege to operate motor vehicle, violation of this section, see Vehicle Code §§ 13200.5, 13355.
Traffic violation point count, violation of this section, see Vehicle Code § 12810.

Research References

California Jury Instructions Civil, 8th Edition 5.31, The Prima Facie Speed Limits.
2 Witkin, California Criminal Law 4th Crimes Against Public Peace and Welfare § 320 (2021), In General.
2 Witkin, California Criminal Law 4th Crimes Against Public Peace and Welfare § 327 (2021), Miscellaneous Regulations.
3 Witkin, California Criminal Law 4th Punishment § 211 (2021), Discretionary Suspension.
3 Witkin, California Criminal Law 4th Punishment § 215 (2021), Excessive Speed.

§ 22349. Maximum speed limit

(a) Except as provided in Section 22356, no person may drive a vehicle upon a highway at a speed greater than 65 miles per hour.

(b) Notwithstanding any other provision of law, no person may drive a vehicle upon a two-lane, undivided highway at a speed greater than 55 miles per hour unless that highway, or portion thereof, has been posted for a higher speed by the Department of Transportation or appropriate local agency upon the basis of an engineering and traffic survey. For purposes of this subdivision, the following apply:

(1) A two-lane, undivided highway is a highway with not more than one through lane of travel in each direction.

(2) Passing lanes may not be considered when determining the number of through lanes.

(c) It is the intent of the Legislature that there be reasonable signing on affected two-lane, undivided highways described in subdivision (b) in continuing the 55 miles-per-hour speed limit, including placing signs at county boundaries to the extent possible, and at other appropriate locations. *(Added by Stats.1995, c. 766*

(S.B.726), § 23. Amended by Stats.1996, c. 20 (S.B.848), § 1, eff. March 29, 1996; Stats.1999, c. 724 (A.B.1650), § 41.)

Research References

California Jury Instructions - Criminal 8.97, Vehicular Manslaughter—Maximum Speed Law.
California Jury Instructions-Civil, 8th Edition 5.31, The Prima Facie Speed Limits.
California Jury Instructions-Civil, 8th Edition 5.32, The Maximum Speed Limit.
2 Witkin, California Criminal Law 4th Crimes Against Public Peace and Welfare § 320 (2021), In General.

§ 22350. Basic speed law

No person shall drive a vehicle upon a highway at a speed greater than is reasonable or prudent having due regard for weather, visibility, the traffic on, and the surface and width of, the highway, and in no event at a speed which endangers the safety of persons or property. *(Stats.1959, c. 3, p. 1690, § 22350. Amended by Stats.1963, c. 252, p. 1014, § 1.)*

Validity

This statute was held preempted by the Commercial Motor Vehicle Safety Act with respect to speed limits for commercial vehicles, in the decision of Weaver v. Chavez (App. 2 Dist. 2005) 35 Cal.Rptr.3d 514, 133 Cal.App.4th 1350, rehearing denied, review denied.

Cross References

Applicability of this section to trolley coaches, see Vehicle Code § 21051.
Buses, motor trucks or truck tractors, fine for violation of this section, see Vehicle Code § 42000.5.
Highway defined, see Vehicle Code § 590.
Other speed laws, see Vehicle Code § 22400 et seq.
Passing animals, see Vehicle Code § 21759.
Passing on grades, see Vehicle Code § 21758.
Passing streetcar or bus, see Vehicle Code § 21756.
Physicians and surgeons, vehicles, see Vehicle Code § 21058.
Police escorts, see Vehicle Code § 21057.
Reckless driving defined, see Vehicle Code §§ 23103, 23104.
Rules of the road, exemption of authorized emergency vehicles, see Vehicle Code § 21055.
Signs restricting speed, see Vehicle Code §§ 21357, 21359.
Speed contests, see Vehicle Code § 23109.
Speeding, suspension or revocation of license by court, see Vehicle Code § 13200.

Research References

California Jury Instructions - Criminal 8.95, Vehicular Manslaughter—Basic Speed Law.
California Jury Instructions-Civil, 8th Edition 3.45, Negligence Per Se—Violation of Statute, Ordinance, or Safety Order.
California Jury Instructions-Civil, 8th Edition 5.30, Basic Speed Law.
California Jury Instructions-Civil, 8th Edition 5.31, The Prima Facie Speed Limits.
2 Witkin, California Criminal Law 4th Crimes Against Public Peace and Welfare § 320 (2021), In General.
1 Witkin California Criminal Law 4th Crimes Against the Person § 220 (2021), In General.
5 Witkin, California Criminal Law 4th Criminal Trial § 707 (2021), Technical or Specialized Terms.

§ 22351. Speed law violations

(a) The speed of any vehicle upon a highway not in excess of the limits specified in Section 22352 or established as authorized in this code is lawful unless clearly proved to be in violation of the basic speed law.

(b) The speed of any vehicle upon a highway in excess of the prima facie speed limits in Section 22352 or established as authorized in this code is prima facie unlawful unless the defendant establishes by competent evidence that the speed in excess of said limits did not constitute a violation of the basic speed law at the time, place and under the conditions then existing. *(Stats.1959, c. 3, p. 1690, § 22351.)*

Cross References

Applicability of this section to trolley coaches, see Vehicle Code § 21051.
Definitions,
Business district, see Vehicle Code § 235.
Residence district, see Vehicle Code § 515.
Emergency call of physician, exemption from this section, see Vehicle Code § 21058.
Other speed laws, see Vehicle Code § 22400 et seq.
Presumption as to correctness of speed restriction signs, see Vehicle Code § 41100.
Prima facie speed limit,
Authority to alter, see Vehicle Code § 22354 et seq.
Necessity of alleging in notice, complaint, or information charging violation of speed laws, see Vehicle Code § 40503.
Proof of speed in excess of prima facie limit as not constituting negligence as matter of law, see Vehicle Code § 40831.

Research References

California Jury Instructions - Criminal 8.96, Vehicular Manslaughter—Prima Facie Speed Limits.
2 Witkin, California Criminal Law 4th Crimes Against Public Peace and Welfare § 320 (2021), In General.

§ 22352. Prima facie speed limits

The prima facie limits are as follows and shall be applicable unless changed as authorized in this code and, if so changed, only when signs have been erected giving notice thereof:

(a) Fifteen miles per hour:

(1) When traversing a railway grade crossing, if during the last 100 feet of the approach to the crossing the driver does not have a clear and unobstructed view of the crossing and of any traffic on the railway for a distance of 400 feet in both directions along the railway. This subdivision does not apply in the case of any railway grade crossing where a human flagperson is on duty or a clearly visible electrical or mechanical railway crossing signal device is installed but does not then indicate the immediate approach of a railway train or car.

(2) When traversing any intersection of highways if during the last 100 feet of the driver's approach to the intersection the driver does not have a clear and unobstructed view of the intersection and of any traffic upon all of the highways entering the intersection for a distance of 100 feet along all those highways, except at an intersection protected by stop signs or yield right-of-way signs or controlled by official traffic control signals.

(3) On any alley.

(b) Twenty-five miles per hour:

(1) On any highway, in any business or residence district unless a different speed is determined by local authority or the Department of Transportation under procedures set forth in this code.

(2) When approaching or passing a school building or the grounds thereof, contiguous to a highway and posted with a standard "SCHOOL" warning sign, while children are going to or leaving the school either during school hours or during the noon recess period. The prima facie limit shall also apply when approaching or passing any school grounds which are not separated from the highway by a fence, gate, or other physical barrier while the grounds are in use by children and the highway is posted with a standard "SCHOOL" warning sign. For purposes of this subparagraph, standard "SCHOOL" warning signs may be placed at any distance up to 500 feet away from school grounds.

(3) When passing a senior center or other facility primarily used by senior citizens, contiguous to a street other than a state highway and posted with a standard "SENIOR" warning sign. A local authority may erect a sign pursuant to this paragraph when the local agency makes a determination that the proposed signing should be

implemented. A local authority may request grant funding from the Active Transportation Program pursuant to Chapter 8 (commencing with Section 2380) of Division 3 of the Streets and Highways Code, or any other grant funding available to it, and use that grant funding to pay for the erection of those signs, or may utilize any other funds available to it to pay for the erection of those signs, including, but not limited to, donations from private sources. *(Added by Stats.1997, c. 421 (A.B.1209), § 2, operative March 1, 2001. Amended by Stats.2000, c. 521 (A.B.280), § 2, operative March 1, 2001; Stats.2013, c. 240 (A.B.707), § 1; Stats.2015, c. 12 (A.B.95), § 15, eff. June 24, 2015; Stats.2021, c. 690 (A.B.43), § 3, eff. Jan. 1, 2022.)*

Cross References

Applicability of this section to trolley coaches, see Vehicle Code § 21051.
Definitions,
Business district, see Vehicle Code § 235.
Residence district, see Vehicle Code § 515.
Emergency call of physician, exemption from this section, see Vehicle Code § 21058.
Multiple highways, prima facie speed limit, see Vehicle Code § 22361.
Route 184, school zone, see Streets and Highways Code § 484.1.
Speed in excess of prima facie limit not negligence as a matter of law, see Vehicle Code § 40831.
Speed signs for business or residence districts, see Vehicle Code § 21357.
Speed trap defined, see Vehicle Code § 40802.

Research References

California Jury Instructions - Criminal 8.96, Vehicular Manslaughter—Prima Facie Speed Limits.
California Jury Instructions-Civil, 8th Edition 5.31, The Prima Facie Speed Limits.
California Jury Instructions-Civil, 8th Edition 11.60, Failure to Provide Warning Signs Authorized by Vehicle Code.
2 Witkin, California Criminal Law 4th Crimes Against Public Peace and Welfare § 320 (2021), In General.

§ 22353. Equestrian safety; factors in engineering and traffic surveys

When conducting an engineering and traffic survey, the City of Norco, in addition to the factors set forth in Section 627, may also consider equestrian safety. *(Added by Stats.2002, c. 186 (A.B.2402), § 1.)*

§ 22353.2. City of Burbank; equestrian safety; factors in engineering and traffic surveys

The City of Burbank may also consider equestrian safety when conducting an engineering and traffic survey of the public streets within the boundaries of the Rancho Master Plan Area in the City of Burbank, as described in the City of Burbank's General Plan adopted on February 19, 2013, in addition to the factors set forth in Section 627. *(Added by Stats.2018, c. 398 (A.B.2955), § 1, eff. Jan. 1, 2019.)*

§ 22353.3. City of Glendale; equestrian safety; factors in engineering and traffic surveys

The City of Glendale may also consider equestrian safety when conducting an engineering and traffic survey of the public streets within the boundaries of the Horse Overlay Zone, commonly known as the Riverside Rancho Area, in the City of Glendale, as described in Chapter 30.21 of the Glendale Municipal Code, in addition to the factors set forth in Section 627. *(Added by Stats.2018, c. 398 (A.B.2955), § 2, eff. Jan. 1, 2019.)*

§ 22353.4. City of Los Angeles; equestrian safety; factors in engineering and traffic surveys

The City of Los Angeles may also consider equestrian safety when conducting an engineering and traffic survey of the public streets within the boundaries of the Sylmar Community Plan Area and the Sunland–Tujunga–Lake View Terrace–Shadow Hills–East La Tuna Canyon Community Plan Area in the City of Los Angeles, as described in the Sylmar Community Plan adopted on June 10, 2015, and the Sunland–Tujunga–Lake View Terrace–Shadow Hills–East La Tuna Canyon Community Plan Update adopted on November 18, 1997, respectively, in addition to the factors set forth in Section 627. *(Added by Stats.2018, c. 398 (A.B.2955), § 3, eff. Jan. 1, 2019.)*

§ 22353.5. Engineering and traffic surveys within Orange Park Acres; consideration of equestrian safety

When conducting an engineering and traffic survey of the public streets within the boundaries of the common interest development known as Orange Park Acres, in addition to the factors set forth in Section 627, the County of Orange may also consider equestrian safety. *(Added by Stats.2014, c. 282 (A.B.1669), § 1, eff. Jan. 1, 2015.)*

§ 22354. Decrease of state highway limits

(a) Whenever the Department of Transportation determines upon the basis of an engineering and traffic survey that the limit of 65 miles per hour is more than is reasonable or safe upon any portion of a state highway where the limit of 65 miles is applicable, the department may determine and declare a prima facie speed limit of 60, 55, 50, 45, 40, 35, 30, 25, 20, or 15 miles per hour, whichever is found most appropriate to facilitate the orderly movement of traffic and is reasonable and safe, which declared prima facie speed limit shall be effective when appropriate signs giving notice thereof are erected upon the highway.

(b) This section shall become operative on the date specified in subdivision (c) of Section 22366. *(Added by Stats.1995, c. 766 (S.B.726), § 25. Amended by Stats.2021, c. 690 (A.B.43), § 4, eff. Jan. 1, 2022.)*

Cross References

Department of Transportation,
Authority to install and maintain traffic control devices, see Vehicle Code §§ 21350 et seq., 21654, 21655, 23300, 23334.
Closing or restricting use of highways, see Streets and Highways Code §§ 124, 125.
Delegation of powers and jurisdiction to city, see Streets and Highways Code §§ 116, 676.
Determination of speed on bridges and structures, see Vehicle Code § 22402 et seq.
Publishing and distribution of copies of traffic rules, see Vehicle Code § 23335.
Multiple lane highways, see Vehicle Code § 22361.
Speed trap defined, see Vehicle Code § 40802.

Research References

2 Witkin, California Criminal Law 4th Crimes Against Public Peace and Welfare § 320 (2021), In General.

§ 22354.5. Increase or decrease of state highway limits

(a) Whenever the Department of Transportation determines, upon the basis of an engineering and traffic survey, to increase or decrease the existing speed limit on a particular portion of a state highway pursuant to Section 22354, it shall, prior to increasing or decreasing that speed limit, consult with, and take into consideration the recommendations of, the Department of the California Highway Patrol.

(b) The city council or board of supervisors of a city or county through which any portion of a state highway subject to subdivision (a) extends may conduct a public hearing on the proposed increase or decrease at a convenient location as near as possible to that portion of state highway. The Department of Transportation shall take into consideration the results of the public hearing in determining whether to increase or decrease the speed limit. *(Added by Stats.1991, c. 219 (A.B.289), § 1.)*

§ 22355. Variable speed limits

Whenever the Department of Transportation determines upon the basis of an engineering and traffic survey that the safe and orderly movement of traffic upon any state highway which is a freeway will be facilitated by the establishment of variable speed limits, the department may erect, regulate, and control signs upon the state highway which is a freeway, or any portion thereof, which signs shall be so designed as to permit display of different speed limits at various times of the day or night. Such signs need not conform to the standards and specifications established by regulations of the Department of Transportation pursuant to Section 21400, but shall be of sufficient size and clarity to give adequate notice of the applicable speed limit. The speed limit upon the freeway at a particular time and place shall be that which is then and there displayed upon such sign. *(Stats.1959, c. 3, p. 1692, § 22355. Amended by Stats.1959, c. 11, p. 1855, § 19, operative Jan. 1, 1960; Stats.1973, c. 78, p. 137, § 17.)*

Cross References

Department of Transportation,
  Authority to install and maintain traffic control devices, see Vehicle Code §§ 21350 et seq., 21654, 21655, 23300, 23334.
  Closing or restricting use of highways, see Streets and Highways Code §§ 124, 125.
  Delegation of powers and jurisdiction to city, see Streets and Highways Code §§ 116, 676.
  Determination of speed on bridges and structures, see Vehicle Code § 22402 et seq.
  Publishing and distribution of copies of traffic rules, see Vehicle Code § 23335.
Multiple lane highways, see Vehicle Code § 22361.

Research References

2 Witkin, California Criminal Law 4th Crimes Against Public Peace and Welfare § 320 (2021), In General.

§ 22356. Increase of highway speed limit

(a) Whenever the Department of Transportation, after consultation with the Department of the California Highway Patrol, determines upon the basis of an engineering and traffic survey on existing highway segments, or upon the basis of appropriate design standards and projected traffic volumes in the case of newly constructed highway segments, that a speed greater than 65 miles per hour would facilitate the orderly movement of vehicular traffic and would be reasonable and safe upon any state highway, or portion thereof, that is otherwise subject to a maximum speed limit of 65 miles per hour, the Department of Transportation, with the approval of the Department of the California Highway Patrol, may declare a higher maximum speed of 70 miles per hour for vehicles not subject to Section 22406, and shall cause appropriate signs to be erected giving notice thereof. The Department of Transportation shall only make a determination under this section that is fully consistent with, and in full compliance with, federal law.

(b) No person shall drive a vehicle upon that highway at a speed greater than 70 miles per hour, as posted.

(c) This section shall become operative on the date specified in subdivision (c) of Section 22366. *(Added by Stats.1995, c. 766 (S.B.726), § 27.)*

Research References

California Jury Instructions-Civil, 8th Edition 5.32, The Maximum Speed Limit.
2 Witkin, California Criminal Law 4th Crimes Against Public Peace and Welfare § 320 (2021), In General.

§ 22357. Increase of local limits

(a) Whenever a local authority determines upon the basis of an engineering and traffic survey that a speed greater than 25 miles per hour would facilitate the orderly movement of vehicular traffic and would be reasonable and safe upon any street other than a state highway otherwise subject to a prima facie limit of 25 miles per hour, the local authority may by ordinance determine and declare a prima facie speed limit of 30, 35, 40, 45, 50, 55, or 60 miles per hour or a maximum speed limit of 65 miles per hour, whichever is found most appropriate to facilitate the orderly movement of traffic and is reasonable and safe. The declared prima facie or maximum speed limit shall be effective when appropriate signs giving notice thereof are erected upon the street and shall not thereafter be revised except upon the basis of an engineering and traffic survey. This section does not apply to any 25–mile–per–hour prima facie limit which is applicable when passing a school building or the grounds thereof or when passing a senior center or other facility primarily used by senior citizens.

(b) This section shall become operative on the date specified in subdivision (c) of Section 22366. *(Added by Stats.1995, c. 766 (S.B.726), § 29.)*

Cross References

Delegation of powers to local authorities by Department of Transportation, see Streets and Highways Code §§ 116, 676.
Local authorities defined, see Vehicle Code § 385.
Powers of local authorities, see Vehicle Code § 21100 et seq.
Speed trap defined, see Vehicle Code § 40802.
Speed zoning on multiple lane highways, see Vehicle Code § 22361.

Research References

California Jury Instructions-Civil, 8th Edition 5.31, The Prima Facie Speed Limits.

§ 22357.1. Park playground; adjacent streets; 25 m.p.h. prima facie limit

Notwithstanding Section 22357, a local authority may, by ordinance or resolution, set a prima facie speed limit of 25 miles per hour on any street, other than a state highway, adjacent to any children's playground in a public park but only during particular hours or days when children are expected to use the facilities. The 25 mile per hour speed limit shall be effective when signs giving notice of the speed limit are posted. *(Added by Stats.1989, c. 508, § 1.)*

§ 22358. Decrease of local limits

(a) Whenever a local authority determines upon the basis of an engineering and traffic survey that the limit of 65 miles per hour is more than is reasonable or safe upon any portion of any street other than a state highway where the limit of 65 miles per hour is applicable, the local authority may by ordinance determine and declare a prima facie speed limit of 60, 55, 50, 45, 40, 35, 30, 25, 20, or 15 miles per hour, whichever is found most appropriate to facilitate the orderly movement of traffic and is reasonable and safe, which declared prima facie limit shall be effective when appropriate signs giving notice thereof are erected upon the street.

(b) This section shall become operative on the date specified in subdivision (c) of Section 22366. *(Added by Stats.1995, c. 766 (S.B.726), § 31. Amended by Stats.2021, c. 690 (A.B.43), § 5, eff. Jan. 1, 2022.)*

Cross References

Delegation of powers to local authorities by Department of Transportation, see Streets and Highways Code §§ 116, 676.
Local authorities,
  Definition, see Vehicle Code § 385.
  Powers, see Vehicle Code § 21100 et seq.
Speed trap defined, see Vehicle Code § 40802.
Speed zoning on multiple lane highways, see Vehicle Code § 22361.

§ 22358.3. Decrease on narrow street

Whenever a local authority determines upon the basis of an engineering and traffic survey that the prima facie speed limit of 25 miles per hour in a business or residence district or in a public park on any street having a roadway not exceeding 25 feet in width, other than a state highway, is more than is reasonable or safe, the local authority may, by ordinance or resolution, determine and declare a prima facie speed limit of 20 or 15 miles per hour, whichever is found most appropriate and is reasonable and safe. The declared prima facie limit shall be effective when appropriate signs giving notice thereof are erected upon the street. *(Added by Stats.1965, c. 1614, p. 3702, § 1. Amended by Stats.1972, c. 372, p. 692, § 1; Stats.1972, c. 1095, p. 2056, § 3.)*

Cross References

Speed trap defined, see Vehicle Code § 40802.

Research References

1 Witkin California Criminal Law 4th Introduction to Crimes § 68 (2021), In General.

§ 22358.4. Decrease of local limits near schools

(a)(1) Whenever a local authority determines upon the basis of an engineering and traffic survey that the prima facie speed limit of 25 miles per hour established by subdivision (b) of Section 22352 is more than is reasonable or safe, the local authority may, by ordinance or resolution, determine and declare a prima facie speed limit of 20 or 15 miles per hour, whichever is justified as the appropriate speed limit by that survey.

(2) An ordinance or resolution adopted under paragraph (1) shall not be effective until appropriate signs giving notice of the speed limit are erected upon the highway and, in the case of a state highway, until the ordinance is approved by the Department of Transportation and the appropriate signs are erected upon the highway.

(b)(1) Notwithstanding subdivision (a) or any other provision of law, a local authority may, by ordinance or resolution, determine and declare prima facie speed limits as follows:

(A) A 15 miles per hour prima facie limit in a residence district, on a highway with a posted speed limit of 30 miles per hour or slower, when approaching, at a distance of less than 500 feet from, or passing, a school building or the grounds of a school building, contiguous to a highway and posted with a school warning sign that indicates a speed limit of 15 miles per hour, while children are going to or leaving the school, either during school hours or during the noon recess period. The prima facie limit shall also apply when approaching, at a distance of less than 500 feet from, or passing, school grounds that are not separated from the highway by a fence, gate, or other physical barrier while the grounds are in use by children and the highway is posted with a school warning sign that indicates a speed limit of 15 miles per hour.

(B) A 25 miles per hour prima facie limit in a residence district, on a highway with a posted speed limit of 30 miles per hour or slower, when approaching, at a distance of 500 to 1,000 feet from, a school building or the grounds thereof, contiguous to a highway and posted with a school warning sign that indicates a speed limit of 25 miles per hour, while children are going to or leaving the school, either during school hours or during the noon recess period. The prima facie limit shall also apply when approaching, at a distance of 500 to 1,000 feet from, school grounds that are not separated from the highway by a fence, gate, or other physical barrier while the grounds are in use by children and the highway is posted with a school warning sign that indicates a speed limit of 25 miles per hour.

(2) The prima facie limits established under paragraph (1) apply only to highways that meet all of the following conditions:

(A) A maximum of two traffic lanes.

(B) A maximum posted 30 miles per hour prima facie speed limit immediately prior to and after the school zone.

(3) The prima facie limits established under paragraph (1) apply to all lanes of an affected highway, in both directions of travel.

(4) When determining the need to lower the prima facie speed limit, the local authority shall take the provisions of Section 627 into consideration.

(5)(A) An ordinance or resolution adopted under paragraph (1) shall not be effective until appropriate signs giving notice of the speed limit are erected upon the highway and, in the case of a state highway, until the ordinance is approved by the Department of Transportation and the appropriate signs are erected upon the highway.

(B) For purposes of subparagraph (A) of paragraph (1), school warning signs indicating a speed limit of 15 miles per hour may be placed at a distance up to 500 feet away from school grounds.

(C) For purposes of subparagraph (B) of paragraph (1), school warning signs indicating a speed limit of 25 miles per hour may be placed at any distance between 500 and 1,000 feet away from the school grounds.

(D) A local authority shall reimburse the Department of Transportation for all costs incurred by the department under this subdivision. *(Added by Stats.1974, c. 102, p. 217, § 1. Amended by Stats.1990, c. 441 (A.B.2883), § 3; Stats.1990, c. 542 (S.B.1860), § 3; Stats.2005, c. 279 (S.B.1107), § 23; Stats.2007, c. 384 (A.B.321), § 1; Stats.2016, c. 208 (A.B.2906), § 15, eff. Jan. 1, 2017.)*

§ 22358.5. Downward speed zoning

It is the intent of the Legislature that physical conditions such as width, curvature, grade and surface conditions, or any other condition readily apparent to a driver, in the absence of other factors, would not require special downward speed zoning, as the basic rule of section 22350 is sufficient regulation as to such conditions. *(Added by Stats.1959, c. 11, p. 1856, § 23, operative Jan. 1, 1960.)*

§ 22358.6. Authority to round speed limits to the nearest five miles per hour

(a) The Department of Transportation shall, in the next scheduled revision, revise and thereafter maintain the California Manual on Uniform Traffic Control Devices to require the Department of Transportation or a local authority to round speed limits to the nearest five miles per hour of the 85th percentile of the free-flowing traffic.

* * * (b) In cases in which the speed limit needs to be rounded down to the nearest five miles per hour increment of the 85th-percentile speed, the Department of Transportation or a local authority may lower the speed limit by five miles per hour from the nearest five mile per hour increment of the 85th-percentile speed, in compliance with Sections 627 and 22358.5 and the California Manual on Uniform Traffic Control Devices, as it read on March 30, 2021, if the reasons for the lower speed limit are documented in an engineering and traffic survey. The Department of Transportation or a local authority may also take into consideration Sections 22353, 22353.2, 22353.3, 22353.4, and 22353.5, if applicable.

(c) In cases in which the speed limit needs to be rounded up to the nearest five miles per hour increment of the 85th-percentile speed, the Department of Transportation or a local authority may decide to instead round down the speed limit to the lower five miles per hour increment. * * * If the speed limit is rounded down pursuant to this subdivision, the speed limit shall not be reduced any further pursuant to subdivision (b).

(d) In addition to subdivisions (b) and (c), a local authority may additionally lower the speed limit as provided in Section 22358.7.

(e) The total reduction in the speed limit pursuant to subdivisions (a) to (d), inclusive, shall not exceed 12.4 miles per hour from the 85th percentile speed.

(f) Notwithstanding subdivisions (a) to (e), inclusive, a local authority may retain the currently adopted speed limit as provided in Section 22358.8 without further reduction, or restore the immediately prior adopted speed limit as provided in Section 22358.8 without further reduction. *(Added by Stats.2021, c. 690 (A.B.43), § 6, eff. Jan. 1, 2022. Amended by Stats.2022, c. 406 (A.B.1938), § 2, eff. Jan. 1, 2023.)*

§ 22358.7. Reducing speed limit by ordinance; warning citations for violations of exceeding the speed limit

(a) If a local authority, after completing an engineering and traffic survey, finds that the speed limit is still more than is reasonable or safe, the local authority may, by ordinance, determine and declare a prima facie speed limit that has been reduced an additional five miles per hour for either of the following reasons:

(1) The portion of highway has been designated as a safety corridor. A local authority shall not deem more than one-fifth of their streets as safety corridors.

(2) The portion of highway is adjacent to any land or facility that generates high concentrations of bicyclists or pedestrians, especially those from vulnerable groups such as children, seniors, persons with disabilities, and the unhoused.

(b)(1) As used in this section, "safety corridor" shall be defined by the Department of Transportation in the next revision of the California Manual on Uniform Traffic Control Devices. In making this determination, the department shall consider highways that have the highest number of serious injuries and fatalities based on collision data that may be derived from, but not limited to, the Statewide Integrated Traffic Records System.

(2) The Department of Transportation shall, in the next revision of the California Manual on Uniform Traffic Control Devices, determine what constitutes land or facilities that generate high concentrations of bicyclists and pedestrians, as used in paragraph (2) of subdivision (a). In making this determination, the department shall consider density, road use type, and bicycle and pedestrian infrastructure present on a section of highway.

(c) A local authority may not lower a speed limit as authorized by this section until June 30, 2024, or until the Judicial Council has developed an online tool for adjudicating infraction violations statewide as specified in Article 7 (commencing with Section 68645) of Chapter 2 of Title 8 of the Government Code, whichever is sooner.

(d) A local authority shall issue only warning citations for violations of exceeding the speed limit by 10 miles per hour or less for the first 30 days that a lower speed limit is in effect as authorized by this section. *(Added by Stats.2021, c. 690 (A.B.43), § 7, eff. Jan. 1, 2022.)*

§ 22358.8. Retaining currently adopted speed limit or restoring immediately prior adopted speed limit if that speed limit was established with an engineering and traffic survey

(a) If a local authority, after completing an engineering and traffic survey, finds that the speed limit is still more than is reasonable or safe, the local authority may, by ordinance, retain the * * * currently adopted speed limit or restore the immediately prior adopted speed limit if that speed limit was established with an engineering and traffic survey and if a registered engineer has evaluated the section of highway and determined that no additional general purpose lanes have been added to the roadway since completion of the traffic survey that established * * * that speed limit.

(b) This section does not authorize a speed limit to be reduced by any more than five miles per hour from the * * * currently adopted speed limit nor below the immediately prior speed limit.

(c) A local authority shall issue only warning citations for violations of exceeding the speed limit by 10 miles per hour or less for the first 30 days that a lower speed limit is in effect as authorized by this section. *(Added by Stats.2021, c. 690 (A.B.43), § 8, eff. Jan. 1, 2022. Amended by Stats.2022, c. 406 (A.B.1938), § 3, eff. Jan. 1, 2023.)*

§ 22358.9. 25 or 20 miles per hour prima facie speed limit on a highway contiguous to a business activity district

(a)(1) Notwithstanding any other law, a local authority may, by ordinance, determine and declare a 25 or 20 miles per hour prima facie speed limit on a highway contiguous to a business activity district when posted with a sign that indicates a speed limit of 25 or 20 miles per hour.

(2) The prima facie limits established under paragraph (1) apply only to highways that meet all of the following conditions:

(A) A maximum of four traffic lanes.

(B) A maximum posted 30 miles per hour prima facie speed limit immediately prior to and after the business activity district, if establishing a 25 miles per hour speed limit.

(C) A maximum posted 25 miles per hour prima facie speed limit immediately prior to and after the business activity district, if establishing a 20 miles per hour speed limit.

(b) As used in this section, a "business activity district" is that portion of a highway and the property contiguous thereto that includes central or neighborhood downtowns, urban villages, or zoning designations that prioritize commercial land uses at the downtown or neighborhood scale and meets at least three of the following requirements in paragraphs (1) to (4), inclusive:

(1) No less than 50 percent of the contiguous property fronting the highway consists of retail or dining commercial uses, including outdoor dining, that open directly onto sidewalks adjacent to the highway.

(2) Parking, including parallel, diagonal, or perpendicular spaces located alongside the highway.

(3) Traffic control signals or stop signs regulating traffic flow on the highway, located at intervals of no more than 600 feet.

(4) Marked crosswalks not controlled by a traffic control device.

(c) A local authority shall not declare a prima facie speed limit under this section on a portion of a highway where the local authority has already lowered the speed limit as permitted under Section 22358.7 * * *, has retained the currently adopted speed limit under Section 22358.8, or has restored the immediately prior adopted speed limit under Section 22358.8.

(d) A local authority shall issue only warning citations for violations of exceeding the speed limit by 10 miles per hour or less for the first 30 days that a lower speed limit is in effect as authorized by this section. *(Added by Stats.2021, c. 690 (A.B.43), § 9, eff. Jan. 1, 2022. Amended by Stats.2022, c. 406 (A.B.1938), § 4, eff. Jan. 1, 2023.)*

§ 22359. Boundary line streets

With respect to boundary line streets and highways where portions thereof are within different jurisdictions, no ordinance adopted under Sections 22357 and 22358 shall be effective as to any such portion until all authorities having jurisdiction of the portions of the street concerned have approved the same. This section shall not apply in the case of boundary line streets consisting of separate roadways within different jurisdictions. *(Stats.1959, c. 3, p. 1693, § 22359. Amended by Stats.1963, c. 209, p. 949, § 8, eff. April 29, 1963.)*

Cross References

Boundary line streets and highways, traffic laws with respect to, see Vehicle Code § 21105.
Delegation of powers to local authorities by Department of Transportation, see Streets and Highways Code §§ 116, 676.
Local authorities,
Definition, see Vehicle Code § 385.
Powers, see Vehicle Code § 21100 et seq.
Speed zoning on multiple lane highways, see Vehicle Code § 22361.

§ 22360. Decrease of limit; portion of highway between districts

(a) Whenever a local authority determines upon the basis of an engineering and traffic survey that the limit of 65 miles per hour is more than is reasonable or safe upon any portion of a highway other than a state highway for a distance of not exceeding 2,000 feet in length between districts, either business or residence, the local authority may determine and declare a reasonable and safe prima facie limit thereon lower than 65 miles per hour, but not less than 25 miles per hour, which declared prima facie speed limit shall be effective when appropriate signs giving notice thereof are erected upon the street or highway.

(b) This section shall become operative on the date specified in subdivision (c) of Section 22366. *(Added by Stats.1995, c. 766 (S.B.726), § 33.)*

Cross References

Business district defined, see Vehicle Code § 235.
Department of Transportation to install and maintain traffic control devices, see Vehicle Code § 21350 et seq.
Local authorities,
Definition, see Vehicle Code § 385.
Powers, see Vehicle Code § 21100 et seq.
Residence district defined, see Vehicle Code § 515.
Speed zoning on multiple lane highways, see Vehicle Code § 22361.

§ 22361. Multiple-lane highways

On multiple-lane highways with two or more separate roadways different prima facie speed limits may be established for different roadways under any of the procedures specified in Sections 22354 to 22359, inclusive. *(Stats.1959, c. 3, p. 1693, § 22361. Amended by Stats.1963, c. 209, p. 949, § 9, eff. April 29, 1963.)*

Cross References

Freeway,
Defined, see Vehicle Code § 332.
Variable speed limits, see Vehicle Code § 22355.

§ 22362. Speed limit where persons at work

It is prima facie a violation of the basic speed law for any person to operate a vehicle in excess of the posted speed limit upon any portion of a highway where officers or employees of the agency having jurisdiction of the same, or any contractor of the agency or his employees, are at work on the roadway or within the right-of-way so close thereto as to be endangered by passing traffic. This section applies only when appropriate signs, indicating the limits of the restricted zone, and the speed limit applicable therein, are placed by such agency within 400 feet of each end of such zone. The signs shall display the figures indicating the applicable limit, which shall not be less than 25 miles per hour, and shall indicate the purpose of the speed restriction. Nothing in this section shall be deemed to relieve any operator of a vehicle from complying with the basic speed law. *(Stats.1959, c. 3, p. 1693, § 22362. Amended by Stats.1970, c. 515, p. 1001, § 1.)*

Cross References

Care and protection of state highways, see Streets and Highways Code § 660 et seq.
Speed signs for business or residence districts or special areas, see Vehicle Code §§ 21357, 21359.
Traffic signs, signals and markings, generally, see Vehicle Code § 21350 et seq.

Research References

2 Witkin, California Criminal Law 4th Crimes Against Public Peace and Welfare § 320 (2021), In General.

§ 22363. Restrictions because of snow or ice conditions

Notwithstanding any speed limit that may be in effect upon the highway, the Department of Transportation in respect to state highways, or a local authority with respect to highways under its jurisdiction, may determine and declare a prima facie speed limit of 40, 35, 30, or 25 miles per hour, whichever is found most appropriate and is reasonable and safe based on the prevailing snow or ice conditions upon such highway or any portion thereof. Signs may be placed and removed as snow or ice conditions vary. *(Stats.1959, c. 3, p. 1694, § 22363. Amended by Stats.1970, c. 515, p. 1001, § 2; Stats.1974, c. 545, p. 1322, § 196.)*

Cross References

Delegation of powers and jurisdiction to city, see Streets and Highways Code §§ 116, 676.
Department of Transportation to maintain and install official traffic control devices, see Vehicle Code § 21350 et seq.
Powers of local authorities to regulate traffic, see Vehicle Code § 21100 et seq.

§ 22364. Lane speed limits

Whenever the Department of Transportation determines, upon the basis of an engineering and traffic survey, that the safe and orderly movement of traffic upon any state highway will be facilitated by the establishment of different speed limits for the various lanes of traffic, the department may place signs upon the state highway, or any portion thereof. The signs shall designate the speed limits for each of the lanes of traffic. *(Added by Stats.1965, c. 1542, p. 3636, § 1. Amended by Stats.1974, c. 545, p. 1322, § 197; Stats.1982, c. 681, p. 2812, § 84.)*

§ 22365. South Coast Air Quality Management District; unpaved roads; ordinances to establish speed limits lower than limits otherwise permitted by code

Notwithstanding any other provision of law, any county or city, which is contained, in whole or in part, within the South Coast Air Quality Management District, may, if the county or city determines that it is necessary to achieve or maintain state or federal ambient air quality standards for particulate matter, determine and declare by ordinance a prima facie speed limit that is lower than that which the county or city is otherwise permitted by this code to establish, for any unpaved road under the jurisdiction of the county or city and within the district. That declared prima facie speed limit shall be effective when appropriate signs giving notice thereof are erected along the road. *(Added by Stats.1997, c. 16 (S.B.191), § 1, eff. May 30, 1997.)*

§ 22366. Highway speed limit of 65 miles per hour; date when state not subject to reduction in federal aid; notice

(a) Whenever the Director of Transportation determines the date upon which the state may establish a maximum speed limit of 65 miles per hour on highways without subjecting the state to a reduction in the amount of federal aid for highways, the director shall notify the Secretary of State of that determination.

(b) The notice required under subdivision (a) shall state that it is being made pursuant to this section.

(c) The notice shall specify a date which is either the date determined pursuant to subdivision (a), or a later date designated by the director.[1] *(Added by Stats.1995, c. 766 (S.B.726), § 34.)*

[1] The Secretary of State notified that the date was Jan. 3, 1996.

Research References

California Jury Instructions-Civil, 8th Edition 5.32, The Maximum Speed Limit.

ARTICLE 2. OTHER SPEED LAWS

§ 22400. Minimum speed law

(a) No person shall drive upon a highway at such a slow speed as to impede or block the normal and reasonable movement of traffic unless the reduced speed is necessary for safe operation, because of a grade, or in compliance with law.

No person shall bring a vehicle to a complete stop upon a highway so as to impede or block the normal and reasonable movement of traffic unless the stop is necessary for safe operation or in compliance with law.

(b) Whenever the Department of Transportation determines on the basis of an engineering and traffic survey that slow speeds on any part of a state highway consistently impede the normal and reasonable movement of traffic, the department may determine and declare a minimum speed limit below which no person shall drive a vehicle, except when necessary for safe operation or in compliance with law, when appropriate signs giving notice thereof are erected along the part of the highway for which a minimum speed limit is established.

Subdivision (b) of this section shall apply only to vehicles subject to registration. *(Stats.1959, c. 3, p. 1694, § 22400. Amended by Stats.1959, c. 1304, p. 3577, § 1; Stats.1974, c. 545, p. 1322, § 198; Stats.1979, c. 364, p. 1230, § 2.)*

Cross References

Application of this section to trolley coaches, see Vehicle Code § 21051.
Driving at reduced rate of speed, see Vehicle Code § 22350.
Motor truck defined, see Vehicle Code § 410.
Rules of the road, exemption of authorized emergency vehicles, see Vehicle Code § 21054.

Research References

2 Witkin, California Criminal Law 4th Crimes Against Public Peace and Welfare § 320 (2021), In General.
2 Witkin, California Criminal Law 4th Crimes Against Public Peace and Welfare § 324 (2021), Stopping and Standing.

§ 22401. Traffic signals

Local authorities in timing traffic signals may so regulate the timing thereof as to permit the movement of traffic in an orderly and safe manner at speeds slightly at variance from the speed otherwise applicable under this code. *(Stats.1959, c. 3, p. 1694, § 22401.)*

Cross References

Department of Transportation to maintain and install official traffic control devices, see Vehicle Code § 21350 et seq.
Local authorities defined, see Vehicle Code § 385.
Local regulation,
  Parking, see Vehicle Code § 22507.
  Pedestrians, see Vehicle Code § 21961.
  Turning movement, intersections, see Vehicle Code § 22113.
Power of local authorities to regulate traffic, see Vehicle Code § 21100 et seq.
Subways, tubes, tunnels, bridges or viaducts, local regulation of vehicular and pedestrian traffic, see Vehicle Code § 21109.
Traffic signs, signals and markings, generally, see Vehicle Code § 21350 et seq.

Research References

2 Witkin, California Criminal Law 4th Crimes Against Public Peace and Welfare § 320 (2021), In General.

§ 22402. Bridges and structures

The Department of Transportation may, in the manner provided in Section 22404 determine the maximum speed, not less than five miles per hour, which can be maintained with safety to any bridge, elevated structure, tube, or tunnel on a state highway. Said department may also make a determination with reference to any other highway upon receiving a request therefor from the board of supervisors or road commissioner of the county, the governing body of the local authority having jurisdiction over the bridge, elevated structure, tube, or tunnel. *(Stats.1959, c. 3, p. 1694, § 22402. Amended by Stats.1974, c. 545, p. 1323, § 199.)*

Cross References

Department of Transportation to maintain and install official traffic control devices, see Vehicle Code § 21350 et seq.
Powers and duties of director of Department of Transportation, see Government Code § 14005.

Research References

2 Witkin, California Criminal Law 4th Crimes Against Public Peace and Welfare § 320 (2021), In General.

§ 22403. Local bridges and structures

Any local authority may, in the manner provided in Section 22404, determine the maximum speed, not less than five miles per hour, which can be maintained with safety to any bridge, elevated structure, tube, or tunnel under its jurisdiction, or may request the Department of Transportation to make such determination. *(Stats.1959, c. 3, p. 1694, § 22403. Amended by Stats.1974, c. 545, p. 1323, § 200.)*

Cross References

Powers of local authorities, see Vehicle Code § 21109.

§ 22404. Revision of speed limit on bridges and structures

The Department of Transportation or local authority making a determination of the maximum safe speed upon a bridge, elevated structure, tube, or tunnel shall first make an engineering investigation and shall hold a public hearing.

Notice of the time and place of the public hearing shall be posted upon the bridge, elevated structure, tube, or tunnel at least five days before the date fixed for the hearing. Upon the basis of the investigation and all evidence presented at the hearing, the department or local authority shall determine by order in writing the maximum speed which can be maintained with safety to the bridge, elevated structure, tube or tunnel. Thereupon, the authority having jurisdiction over the bridge, elevated structure, tube, or tunnel shall erect and maintain suitable signs specifying the maximum speed so determined at a distance of not more than 500 feet from each end of the bridge, elevated structure, tube, tunnel, or any approach thereto. *(Stats.1959, c. 3, p. 1694, § 22404. Amended by Stats.1974, c. 545, p. 1323, § 201.)*

Cross References

Department of Transportation, see Government Code § 14000 et seq.
Powers of local authorities, see Vehicle Code § 21109.
Traffic signs, signals and markings, see Vehicle Code § 21350 et seq.

§ 22405. Violations on bridges and structures

(a) No person shall drive a vehicle on any bridge, elevated structure, tube, or tunnel constituting a part of a highway, at a speed which is greater than the maximum speed which can be maintained with safety to such structure.

(b) Upon the trial of any person charged with a violation of this section with respect to a sign erected under Section 22404, proof of the determination of the maximum speed by the Department of Transportation or local authority and the erection and maintenance of the speed signs shall constitute prima facie evidence of the maximum speed which can be maintained with safety to the bridge, elevated structure, tube, or tunnel. *(Stats.1959, c. 3, p. 1695, § 22405. Amended by Stats.1974, c. 545, p. 1323, § 202.)*

§ 22406. Maximum speed limit for certain vehicles

No person may drive any of the following vehicles on a highway at a speed in excess of 55 miles per hour:

(a) A motortruck or truck tractor having three or more axles or any motortruck or truck tractor drawing any other vehicle.

(b) A passenger vehicle or bus drawing any other vehicle.

(c) A schoolbus transporting any school pupil.

(d) A farm labor vehicle when transporting passengers.

(e) A vehicle transporting explosives.

(f) A trailer bus, as defined in Section 636. *(Added by Stats.1967, c. 78, p. 976, § 4. Amended by Stats.1980, c. 676, p. 2025, § 312; Stats.1988, c. 843, § 5; Stats.1999, c. 724 (A.B.1650), § 42; Stats. 2000, c. 787 (S.B.1404), § 22.)*

Cross References

Buses, motor trucks or truck tractors, fine for violation of this section, see Vehicle Code § 42000.5.
Definitions,
Motor truck, see Vehicle Code § 410.
Passenger vehicle, see Vehicle Code § 465.
Schoolbus, see Vehicle Code § 545; Education Code §§ 39830, 82321.
Trailer, see Vehicle Code § 630.
Truck tractor, see Vehicle Code § 655.
Distance between vehicles subject to speed limits of this section, see Vehicle Code § 21704.
Driving lanes, see Vehicle Code § 22348.
Lanes for vehicles described in this section, see Vehicle Code § 22348.
Liability for damage to highway or bridge as result of maximum weight, see Vehicle Code § 17301.
Maximum weights on bridges and other structures, see Vehicle Code § 35750 et seq.
Penalties for violating weight restrictions, see Vehicle Code § 42030 et seq.
Power of Department of Transportation to issue permits for increased size and weight, see Vehicle Code § 35780 et seq.
Power of local authorities to increase or decrease weight limits, see Vehicle Code § 35700 et seq.
Reduction of weights on secondary highways, see Vehicle Code § 35651 et seq.

Research References

California Jury Instructions-Civil, 8th Edition 5.31, The Prima Facie Speed Limits.
2 Witkin, California Criminal Law 4th Crimes Against Public Peace and Welfare § 320 (2021), In General.
1 Witkin California Criminal Law 4th Introduction to Crimes § 32 (2021), Illustrations.

§ 22406.1. Commercial motor vehicles; violations

(a) A person who operates a commercial motor vehicle, as defined in subdivision (b) of Section 15210, upon a highway at a speed exceeding a posted speed limit established under this code by 15 miles per hour or more, is guilty of a misdemeanor.

(b) A person who holds a commercial driver's license, as defined in subdivision (a) of Section 15210, and operates a noncommerical [1] motor vehicle upon a highway at a speed exceeding a posted speed limit established under this code by 15 miles per hour or more, is guilty of an infraction.

(c) A violation of either subdivision (a) or (b) is a "serious traffic violation," as defined in subdivision (p) of Section 15210, and is subject to the sanctions provided under Section 15306 or 15308, in addition to any other penalty provided by law.

(d) This section shall become operative on September 20, 2005. *(Added by Stats.2000, c. 787 (S.B.1404), § 23. Amended by Stats. 2004, c. 952 (A.B.3049), § 29, operative Sept. 20, 2005.)*

[1] So in chaptered law.

Research References

2 Witkin, California Criminal Law 4th Crimes Against Public Peace and Welfare § 320 (2021), In General.

§ 22406.5. Tank vehicles transporting flammable liquids

Any person who drives a tank vehicle subject to Division 14.7 (commencing with Section 34000) while transporting more than 500 gallons of flammable liquid at a speed greater than the applicable speed limit or in willful or wanton disregard for the safety of persons or property is, in addition to any other applicable penalty, subject to a fine of not less than five hundred dollars ($500) for a first offense and, for a second or subsequent offense within two years of a prior offense, to a fine of not less than two thousand dollars ($2,000) and a suspension of up to six months of a hazardous materials or cargo tank endorsement, or both. *(Added by Stats.1991, c. 1043 (S.B.123), § 1.)*

Research References

2 Witkin, California Criminal Law 4th Crimes Against Public Peace and Welfare § 271 (2021), Reckless Driving.
2 Witkin, California Criminal Law 4th Crimes Against Public Peace and Welfare § 320 (2021), In General.

§ 22407. Decreasing maximum speed law for certain vehicles

Whenever the Department of Transportation or local authority determines upon the basis of engineering studies and a traffic survey that the speed of 55 miles per hour is more than is reasonable or safe for vehicles mentioned in subdivision (a) of Section 22406, which have a manufacturer's gross vehicle weight rating of 10,000 pounds or more, in descending a grade upon any portion of a highway, the department or local authority, with respect to highways under their respective jurisdiction, may determine and declare a speed limit of 50, 45, 40, 35, 30, 25, or 20 miles per hour, whichever is found most appropriate to facilitate the orderly movement of traffic and is reasonable and safe, which declared speed limit shall be effective for such vehicles when appropriate signs giving notice thereof are erected upon the highway. *(Stats.1959, c. 3, p. 1695, § 22407. Amended by Stats.1965, c. 184, p. 1150, § 1; Stats.1965, c. 1210, p. 3031, § 1; Stats.1967, c. 78, p. 977, § 5; Stats.1973, c. 82, p. 143, § 1.)*

Cross References

Buses, motor trucks or truck tractors, fine for violation of this section, see Vehicle Code § 42000.5.

Research References

2 Witkin, California Criminal Law 4th Crimes Against Public Peace and Welfare § 320 (2021), In General.

§ 22409. Solid tire

No person shall operate any vehicle equipped with any solid tire when such vehicle has a gross weight as set forth in the following table at any speed in excess of the speed set forth opposite such gross weight:

When gross weight of vehicle and load is:	Maximum speed in miles per hour:
10,000 lbs. or more but less than 16,000 lbs.	25
16,000 lbs. or more but less than 22,000 lbs.	15
22,000 lbs. or more	12

(Stats.1959, c. 3, p. 1695, § 22409.)

Cross References

Restriction as to tire equipment, see Vehicle Code § 27450 et seq.
Solid tire defined, see Vehicle Code § 560.
Weight permitted per inch on certain tires, see Vehicle Code §§ 35600, 35601.

§ 22410. Metal tires

No person shall operate any vehicle equipped with any metal tire in contact with the surface of the highway at a speed in excess of six miles per hour. *(Stats.1959, c. 3, p. 1695, § 22410.)*

Cross References

Metal tire defined, see Vehicle Code § 395.

Restriction as to tire equipment, see Vehicle Code § 27450 et seq.
Weight permitted per inch on certain tires, see Vehicle Code §§ 35600, 35601.

§ 22411. Speed limit for motorized scooters

No person shall operate a motorized scooter at a speed in excess of 15 miles per hour. *(Added by Stats.1999, c. 722 (S.B.441), § 7.)*

Research References

2 Witkin, California Criminal Law 4th Crimes Against Public Peace and Welfare § 531 (2021), Low-Speed Vehicles and Motorized Scooters.

§ 22413. Decreasing speed limit on grades

Whenever a local authority determines upon the basis of an engineering and traffic survey that the prima facie limit of 25 miles per hour is more than is reasonable and safe on any portion of a street having a grade in excess of 10 percent, the local authority may by ordinance determine and declare a maximum limit of 20 or 15 miles per hour, whichever is found most appropriate and is reasonable and safe. The declared maximum speed shall be effective when appropriate signs giving notice thereof are erected upon the street. *(Added by Stats.1959, c. 318, p. 2245, § 2, eff. May 8, 1959.)*

CHAPTER 8. SPECIAL STOPS REQUIRED

§ 22450. Stop requirements

(a) The driver of any vehicle approaching a stop sign at the entrance to, or within, an intersection shall stop at a limit line, if marked, otherwise before entering the crosswalk on the near side of the intersection.

If there is no limit line or crosswalk, the driver shall stop at the entrance to the intersecting roadway.

(b) The driver of a vehicle approaching a stop sign at a railroad grade crossing shall stop at a limit line, if marked, otherwise before crossing the first track or entrance to the railroad grade crossing.

(c) Notwithstanding any other provision of law, a local authority may adopt rules and regulations by ordinance or resolution providing for the placement of a stop sign at any location on a highway under its jurisdiction where the stop sign would enhance traffic safety. *(Stats.1959, c. 3, p. 1696, § 22450. Amended by Stats.1969, c. 364, p. 890, § 1; Stats.1993, c. 272 (A.B.301), § 41, eff. Aug. 2, 1993; Stats.2007, c. 630 (A.B.1728), § 8.)*

Cross References

Application of this section to trolley coaches, see Vehicle Code § 21051.
Contributory negligence, see Civil Code § 1714.
Definitions,
 Crosswalk, see Vehicle Code § 275.
 Highway, see Vehicle Code §§ 360, 590, 592.
 Intersection, see Vehicle Code § 365.
 Roadway, see Vehicle Code § 530.
 Stop or stopping, see Vehicle Code §§ 587, 21453.
 Through highway, see Vehicle Code § 600.
Farm or private grade crossing of a railroad, see Public Utilities Code § 7538.
Obstructing railroad track, punishment, see Penal Code § 218.1.
Prohibition of stopping, see Vehicle Code § 22500.
Rail transit related traffic violations, county populations greater than 500,000, punishment, see Penal Code § 369b.
Railroad grade crossing violations, see Vehicle Code § 42001.16.
Regulations for intersections,
 Required position and method of turning, see Vehicle Code §§ 22100, 22101.
 Right-of-way, see Vehicle Code § 21800 et seq.
 Signals, see Vehicle Code § 22107 et seq.
Rules of the road, exemption of authorized emergency vehicles, see Vehicle Code § 21054.
Signs indicating railroad crossings, see Vehicle Code § 21362.
Stop signs indicating through highway, see Vehicle Code § 21352 et seq.
Traffic devices on private road or driveway, see Vehicle Code § 21360.
Vehicle entering through highway, see Vehicle Code § 21802.

Research References

California Jury Instructions-Civil, 8th Edition 6.40, Duty of One Crossing Tracks.
2 Witkin, California Criminal Law 4th Crimes Against Public Peace and Welfare § 327 (2021), Miscellaneous Regulations.

§ 22451. Train signals

(a) The driver of any vehicle or pedestrian approaching a railroad or rail transit grade crossing shall stop not less than 15 feet from the nearest rail and shall not proceed until he or she can do so safely, whenever the following conditions exist:

(1) A clearly visible electric or mechanical signal device or a flagman gives warning of the approach or passage of a train, car, or on-track equipment.

(2) An approaching train, car, or on-track equipment is plainly visible or is emitting an audible signal and, by reason of its speed or nearness, is an immediate hazard.

(b) No driver or pedestrian shall proceed through, around, or under any railroad or rail transit crossing gate while the gate is closed.

(c) Whenever a railroad or rail transit crossing is equipped with an automated enforcement system, a notice of a violation of this section is subject to the procedures provided in Section 40518.

(d) For purposes of this section, "on-track equipment" means any locomotive or any other car, rolling stock, equipment, or other device that, alone or coupled to others, is operated on stationary rails. *(Added by Stats.1967, c. 406, p. 1627, § 3. Amended by Stats.1970, c. 608, p. 1189, § 1; Stats.1994, c. 1216 (S.B.1802), § 5; Stats.1995, c. 922 (S.B.833), § 5; Stats.1998, c. 54 (S.B.1136), § 4; Stats.2000, c. 1035 (S.B.1403), § 27; Stats.2017, c. 110 (A.B.695), § 1, eff. Jan. 1, 2018.)*

Cross References

Application of this section to trolley coaches, see Vehicle Code § 21051.
Contributory negligence, see Civil Code § 1714.
Duration of prohibition against operation of commercial motor vehicle, see Vehicle Code § 15312.
Locomotive bell to be rung at intersections, see Public Utilities Code § 7604.
Rail transit related traffic violations, county populations greater than 500,000, punishment, see Penal Code § 369b.
Railroad warning approach signs, see Vehicle Code § 21362.
Regulation of railroad grade crossing, see Vehicle Code § 21110.
Requirement that certain vehicles stop at all railway crossings, see Vehicle Code §§ 22452, 22453.
Safety devices, authority of public utility commission to direct use, see Public Utilities Code § 768.
Speed limits and violations, see Vehicle Code §§ 22351, 22352.
Traffic school, rail transit safety film or fine, see Penal Code § 369b.

Research References

2 Witkin, California Criminal Law 4th Crimes Against Public Peace and Welfare § 322 (2021), Pedestrian's Rights and Duties.

2 Witkin, California Criminal Law 4th Crimes Against Public Peace and Welfare § 327 (2021), Miscellaneous Regulations.

§ 22452. Railroad crossings

(a) Subdivisions (b) and (d) apply to the operation of the following vehicles:

(1) A bus or farm labor vehicle carrying passengers.

(2) A motortruck transporting employees in addition to those riding in the cab.

(3) A schoolbus and a school pupil activity bus transporting school pupils, except as otherwise provided in paragraph (4) of subdivision (d).

(4) A commercial motor vehicle transporting any quantity of a Division 2.3 chlorine, as classified by Title 49 of the Code of Federal Regulations.

(5) A commercial motor vehicle that is required to be marked or placarded in accordance with the regulations of Title 49 of the Code of Federal Regulations with one of the following federal classifications:

(A) Division 1.1.

(B) Division 1.2, or Division 1.3.

(C) Division 2.3 Poison gas.

(D) Division 4.3.

(E) Class 7.

(F) Class 3 Flammable.

(G) Division 5.1.

(H) Division 2.2.

(I) Division 2.3 Chlorine.

(J) Division 6.1 Poison.

(K) Division 2.2 Oxygen.

(L) Division 2.1.

(M) Class 3 Combustible liquid.

(N) Division 4.1.

(O) Division 5.1.

(P) Division 5.2.

(Q) Class 8.

(R) Class Division 1.4.

(S) A cargo tank motor vehicle, whether loaded or empty, used for the transportation of a hazardous material, as defined in Parts 107 to 180, inclusive, of Title 49 of the Code of Federal Regulations.

(6) A cargo tank motor vehicle transporting a commodity that at the time of loading has a temperature above its flashpoint, as determined under Section 173.120 of Title 49 of the Code of Federal Regulations.

(7) A cargo tank motor vehicle, whether loaded or empty, transporting a commodity under exemption in accordance with Subpart B of Part 107 of Title 49 of the Code of Federal Regulations.

(b) Before traversing a railroad grade crossing, the driver of a vehicle described in subdivision (a) shall stop that vehicle not less than 15 nor more than 50 feet from the nearest rail of the track and while so stopped shall listen, and look in both directions along the track, for an approaching train or on-track equipment and for signals indicating the approach of a train or on-track equipment, and shall not proceed until he or she can do so safely. Upon proceeding, the gears shall not be shifted manually while crossing the tracks.

(c) The driver of a commercial motor vehicle, other than those listed in subdivision (a), upon approaching a railroad grade crossing, shall be driven at a rate of speed that allows the commercial vehicle to stop before reaching the nearest rail of that crossing, and shall not be driven upon, or over, the crossing until due caution is taken to ascertain that the course is clear.

(d) A stop need not be made at a crossing in the following circumstances:

(1) Of railroad tracks running along and upon the roadway within a business or residence district.

(2) Where a traffic officer or an official traffic control signal directs traffic to proceed.

(3) Where an exempt sign was authorized by the Public Utilities Commission prior to January 1, 1978.

(4) Where an official railroad crossing stop exempt sign in compliance with Section 21400 has been placed by the Department of Transportation or a local authority pursuant to Section 22452.5. This paragraph does not apply with respect to a schoolbus or to a school pupil activity bus transporting school pupils.

(e) For purposes of this section, "on-track equipment" means any locomotive or any other car, rolling stock, equipment, or other device that, alone or coupled to others, is operated on stationary rails. *(Stats.1959, c. 3, p. 1696, § 22452. Amended by Stats.1959, c. 1881, p. 4442, § 1; Stats.1963, c. 828, p. 2023, § 1; Stats.1967, c. 406, p. 1627, § 1; Stats.1969, c. 26, p. 129, § 9; Stats.1970, c. 608, p. 1189, § 2; Stats.1977, c. 1053, p. 3187, § 1; Stats.1981, c. 813, p. 3157, § 15; Stats.2001, c. 504 (A.B.1280), § 6; Stats.2006, c. 574 (A.B.2520), § 18; Stats.2007, c. 630 (A.B.1728), § 9; Stats.2010, c. 491 (S.B. 1318), § 41; Stats.2017, c. 110 (A.B.695), § 2, eff. Jan. 1, 2018.)*

Cross References

Application of this section to trolley coaches, see Vehicle Code § 21051.
Definitions,
  Bus, see Vehicle Code § 233.
  Business district, see Vehicle Code § 235.
  Liquefied petroleum gas, see Vehicle Code § 380.
  Motor truck, see Vehicle Code § 410.
  Residence district, see Vehicle Code § 515.
  Schoolbus, see Vehicle Code § 545.
Degree of care and skill required of carriers of persons for reward, see Civil Code § 2100.
Duration of prohibition against operation of commercial motor vehicle, see Vehicle Code § 15312.
Public utilities commission's power over state highways, see Streets and Highways Code § 661.
Rail transit related traffic violations, county populations greater than 500,000, punishment, see Penal Code § 369b.
Stopping at intersections signposted with stop sign, see Vehicle Code § 22450.
Suspension of license by court upon conviction for violating this section, see Vehicle Code § 13201.

Research References

California Jury Instructions-Civil, 8th Edition 6.40, Duty of One Crossing Tracks.
2 Witkin, California Criminal Law 4th Crimes Against Public Peace and Welfare § 327 (2021), Miscellaneous Regulations.

§ 22452.5. Railroad crossings; signs authorizing certain vehicles to traverse crossings without stopping

The Department of Transportation and local authorities, with respect to highways under their respective jurisdictions, may place signs at railroad grade crossings permitting any vehicle described in subdivision (a) of Section 22452 to traverse such crossings without stopping. Such signs shall be placed in accordance with criteria adopted by the Public Utilities Commission. Prior to placing such signs, the Department of Transportation or local authority shall consult with the Department of the California Highway Patrol, railroad corporations involved, and the operators involved and shall secure the permission of the Public Utilities Commission if a railroad corporation under the jurisdiction of the Public Utilities Commission is affected. Prior to permitting the placement of such signs, the Public Utilities Commission shall seek the concurrence of the

Department of the California Highway Patrol. *(Added by Stats.1977, c. 1053, p. 3188, § 2. Amended by Stats.1979, c. 373, p. 1383, § 324.)*

§ 22453. Effect of negligence on passengers

Failure of the driver of a motor vehicle carrying any passenger for hire to stop as required in Section 22452 shall not be imputed to any bona fide passenger for hire in such vehicle. *(Stats.1959, c. 3, p. 1697, § 22453.)*

§ 22454. Meeting or overtaking schoolbus stopped to load or unload pupils; stop requirement; violation; warning letter; form

(a) The driver of any vehicle, upon meeting or overtaking, from either direction, any schoolbus equipped with signs as required in this code, that is stopped for the purpose of loading or unloading any schoolchildren and displays a flashing red light signal and stop signal arm, as defined in paragraph (4) of subdivision (b) of Section 25257, if equipped with a stop signal arm, visible from front or rear, shall bring the vehicle to a stop immediately before passing the schoolbus and shall not proceed past the schoolbus until the flashing red light signal and stop signal arm, if equipped with a stop signal arm, cease operation.

(b)(1) The driver of a vehicle upon a divided highway or multiple-lane highway need not stop upon meeting or passing a schoolbus that is upon the other roadway.

(2) For the purposes of this subdivision, a multiple-lane highway is any highway that has two or more lanes of travel in each direction.

(c)(1) If a vehicle was observed overtaking a schoolbus in violation of subdivision (a), and the driver of the schoolbus witnessed the violation, the driver may, within 24 hours, report the violation and furnish the vehicle license plate number and description and the time and place of the violation to the local law enforcement agency having jurisdiction of the offense. That law enforcement agency shall issue a letter of warning prepared in accordance with paragraph (2) with respect to the alleged violation to the registered owner of the vehicle. The issuance of a warning letter under this paragraph shall not be entered on the driving record of the person to whom it is issued, but does not preclude the imposition of any other applicable penalty.

(2) The Attorney General shall prepare and furnish to every law enforcement agency in the state a form letter for purposes of paragraph (1), and the law enforcement agency may issue those letters in the exact form prepared by the Attorney General. The Attorney General may charge a fee to any law enforcement agency that requests a copy of the form letter to recover the costs of preparing and providing that copy.

(d) This section also applies to a roadway upon private property. *(Stats.1959, c. 3, p. 1697, § 22454. Amended by Stats.1971, c. 877, p. 1722, § 2, operative May 3, 1972; Stats.1981, c. 813, p. 3157, § 16; Stats.1990, c. 1296 (S.B.2061), § 1; Stats.1992, c. 624 (A.B.3144), § 5, eff. Sept. 14, 1992; Stats.1993, c. 589 (A.B.2211), § 18; Stats.1999, c. 647 (A.B.1573), § 3, eff. Oct. 10, 1999.)*

Cross References

Application of this section to trolley coaches, see Vehicle Code § 21051.
Authorized school bus stops, see Vehicle Code § 22504.
Intersection defined, see Vehicle Code § 365.
Operation of flashing red signal lamps by school bus driver, see Vehicle Code § 22112.
Roadway defined, see Vehicle Code § 530.
School bus stops, see Vehicle Code § 22500 et seq.
Schoolbus defined, see Vehicle Code § 545.
Transportation network companies, requirements for participating drivers, see Public Utilities Code § 5445.3.

Research References

2 Witkin, California Criminal Law 4th Crimes Against Public Peace and Welfare § 327 (2021), Miscellaneous Regulations.

§ 22454.5. Violations of § 22454; penalties

Notwithstanding Section 42001, a person convicted of a first violation of Section 22454 shall be punished by a fine of not less than one hundred fifty dollars ($150) or more than two hundred fifty dollars ($250). A person convicted of a second separate violation of Section 22454 shall be punished by a fine of not less than five hundred dollars ($500) or more than one thousand dollars ($1,000). If a person is convicted of a third or subsequent violation of Section 22454 and the offense occurred within three years of two or more separate violations of Section 22454, the Department of Motor Vehicles shall suspend the person's privilege to operate a motor vehicle for one year. *(Added by Stats.1986, c. 699, § 1. Amended by Stats.1990, c. 1296 (S.B.2061), § 2.)*

Research References

2 Witkin, California Criminal Law 4th Crimes Against Public Peace and Welfare § 327 (2021), Miscellaneous Regulations.

§ 22455. Street vendors; parking in residential districts; ordinances or resolutions

(a) The driver of any commercial vehicle engaged in vending upon a street may vend products on a street in a residence district only after bringing the vehicle to a complete stop and lawfully parking adjacent to the curb, consistent with the requirements of Chapter 9 (commencing with Section 22500) and local ordinances adopted pursuant thereto.

(b) Notwithstanding subdivision (a) of Section 114315 of the Health and Safety Code or any other provision of law, a local authority may, by ordinance or resolution, adopt additional requirements for the public safety regulating the type of vending and the time, place, and manner of vending from vehicles upon any street. *(Added by Stats.1984, c. 362, § 1. Amended by Stats.1985, c. 495, § 1; Stats.2008, c. 139 (A.B.2588), § 3.)*

Cross References

Food facilities, local regulations, see Health and Safety Code § 113709.

Research References

2 Witkin, California Criminal Law 4th Crimes Against Public Peace and Welfare § 327 (2021), Miscellaneous Regulations.

§ 22456. Destiny Nicole Stout Memorial Act; trucks vending ice cream and similar foods

(a) This section shall be known and may be cited as the Destiny Nicole Stout Memorial Act.

(b) The Legislature finds and declares that motor vehicles engaged in vending ice cream and similar food items in residential neighborhoods can increase the danger to children, and it is necessary that these vehicles are clearly seen and noticed by motorists and pedestrians to protect public safety.

(c) As used in this section, the term "ice cream truck" means a motor vehicle engaged in the curbside vending or sale of frozen or refrigerated desserts, confections, or novelties commonly known as ice cream, or prepackaged candies, prepackaged snack foods, or soft drinks, primarily intended for the sale to children under 12 years of age.

(d) Any ice cream truck shall be equipped at all times, while engaged in vending in a residential area, with signs mounted on both the front and the rear and clearly legible from a distance of 100 feet under daylight conditions, incorporating the words "WARNING" and "CHILDREN CROSSING." Each sign shall be at least 12 inches high by 48 inches wide, with letters of a dark color and at least four inches in height, a one-inch wide solid border, and a sharply contrasting background.

(e) A person may not vend from an ice cream truck that is stopped, parked, or standing on any public street, alley, or highway under any of the following conditions:

(1) On a street, alley, or highway with a posted speed limit greater than 25 miles per hour.

(2) If the street, alley, or highway is within 100 feet of an intersection with an opposing highway that has a posted speed limit greater than 25 miles per hour.

(3) If the vendor does not have an unobstructed view for 200 feet in both directions along the highway and of any traffic on the highway. *(Added by Stats.2000, c. 344 (S.B.2185), § 1.)*

Research References

2 Witkin, California Criminal Law 4th Crimes Against Public Peace and Welfare § 327 (2021), Miscellaneous Regulations.

CHAPTER 9. STOPPING, STANDING, AND PARKING

§ 22500. Prohibited stopping, standing, or parking

A person shall not stop, park, or leave standing any vehicle whether attended or unattended, except when necessary to avoid conflict with other traffic or in compliance with the directions of a peace officer or official traffic control device, in any of the following places:

(a) Within an intersection, except adjacent to curbs as may be permitted by local ordinance.

(b) On a crosswalk, except that a bus engaged as a common carrier or a taxicab may stop in an unmarked crosswalk to load or unload passengers when authorized by the legislative body of a city pursuant to an ordinance.

(c) Between a safety zone and the adjacent right-hand curb or within the area between the zone and the curb as may be indicated by a sign or red paint on the curb, which sign or paint was erected or placed by local authorities pursuant to an ordinance.

(d) Within 15 feet of the driveway entrance to a fire station. This subdivision does not apply to any vehicle owned or operated by a fire department and clearly marked as a fire department vehicle.

(e)(1) In front of a public or private driveway, except that a bus engaged as a common carrier, schoolbus, or a taxicab may stop to load or unload passengers when authorized by local authorities pursuant to an ordinance.

(2) In unincorporated territory, where the entrance of a private road or driveway is not delineated by an opening in a curb or by other curb construction, so much of the surface of the ground as is paved, surfaced, or otherwise plainly marked by vehicle use as a private road or driveway entrance, shall constitute a driveway.

(f) On a portion of a sidewalk, or with the body of the vehicle extending over a portion of a sidewalk, except electric carts when authorized by local ordinance, as specified in Section 21114.5. Lights, mirrors, or devices that are required to be mounted upon a vehicle under this code may extend from the body of the vehicle over the sidewalk to a distance of not more than 10 inches.

(g) Alongside or opposite a street or highway excavation or obstruction when stopping, standing, or parking would obstruct traffic.

(h) On the roadway side of a vehicle stopped, parked, or standing at the curb or edge of a highway, except for a schoolbus when stopped to load or unload pupils in a business or residence district where the speed limit is 25 miles per hour or less.

(i) Except as provided under Section 22500.5, alongside curb space authorized for the loading and unloading of passengers of a bus engaged as a common carrier in local transportation when indicated by a sign or red paint on the curb erected or painted by local authorities pursuant to an ordinance.

(j) In a tube or tunnel, except vehicles of the authorities in charge, being used in the repair, maintenance, or inspection of the facility.

(k) Upon a bridge, except vehicles of the authorities in charge, being used in the repair, maintenance, or inspection of the facility, and except that buses engaged as a common carrier in local transportation may stop to load or unload passengers upon a bridge where sidewalks are provided, when authorized by local authorities pursuant to an ordinance, and except that local authorities pursuant to an ordinance or the Department of Transportation pursuant to an order, within their respective jurisdictions, may permit parking on bridges having sidewalks and shoulders of sufficient width to permit parking without interfering with the normal movement of traffic on the roadway. Local authorities, by ordinance or resolution, may permit parking on these bridges on state highways in their respective jurisdictions if the ordinance or resolution is first approved in writing by the Department of Transportation. Parking shall not be permitted unless there are signs in place, as may be necessary, to indicate the provisions of local ordinances or the order of the Department of Transportation.

(*l*) In front of or upon that portion of a curb that has been cut down, lowered, or constructed to provide wheelchair accessibility to the sidewalk.

(m) In a portion of a highway that has been designated for the exclusive use of public transit buses. *(Stats.1959, c. 3, p. 1698, § 22500. Amended by Stats.1963, c. 1661, p. 3252, § 1; Stats.1965, c. 85, p. 1026, § 1; Stats.1965, c. 295, p. 1293, § 1; Stats.1965, c. 1092, p. 2736, § 1; Stats.1972, c. 490, p. 862, § 3; Stats.1974, c. 545, p. 1324, § 203; Stats.1982, c. 822, p. 3125, § 1; Stats.1984, c. 852, § 1; Stats.1992, c. 624 (A.B.3144), § 6, eff. Sept. 14, 1992; Stats.1998, c. 877 (A.B.2132), § 66; Stats.2002, c. 640 (A.B.1314), § 1; Stats.2016, c. 716 (S.B.998), § 2, eff. Jan. 1, 2017.)*

Cross References

Definitions,
  Bus, see Vehicle Code § 233.
  Crosswalk, see Vehicle Code § 275.
  Driving through safety zone prohibited, see Vehicle Code § 21709.
  Intersection, see Vehicle Code § 365.
  Local authorities, see Vehicle Code § 385.
  Park or parking, see Vehicle Code § 463.
  Private road or driveway, see Vehicle Code § 490.
  Roadway, see Vehicle Code § 530.
  Safety zone, see Vehicle Code § 540.
  Schoolbus, see Vehicle Code § 545.
  Sidewalk, see Vehicle Code § 555.
  Stop or stopping, see Vehicle Code § 587.
  Street or highway, see Vehicle Code §§ 360, 590, 592.
Local regulation of electric carts on sidewalks, see Vehicle Code § 21100.
Markings to indicate parking regulations, see Vehicle Code § 21458.
Moving vehicle from one place to another, see Vehicle Code § 22654.
Official traffic control devices, see Vehicle Code § 21350 et seq.
Parking on educational institution grounds, restrictions, see Vehicle Code § 21113.
Parking violations, see Vehicle Code § 40200 et seq.
Removal of parked vehicles, authorization, see Vehicle Code § 22654.
Report of convictions to department, exceptions, see Vehicle Code § 1803 et seq.
Rubbish or garbage trucks, exemption, see Vehicle Code § 21059.
Rules of the road, exemption of authorized emergency vehicles, see Vehicle Code § 21054.
Stopping,
  Standing or parking in unincorporated areas, see Vehicle Code § 22504.
  Standing or parking on vehicular crossing prohibited, see Vehicle Code § 23333.
Streetsweeping and watering vehicles, application of section, see Vehicle Code § 21060.
Warning devices on disabled or parked vehicles, see Vehicle Code §§ 25300, 25301, 25305.

Research References

2 Witkin, California Criminal Law 4th Crimes Against Public Peace and Welfare § 323 (2021), Parking.
2 Witkin, California Criminal Law 4th Crimes Against Public Peace and Welfare § 330 (2021), Financial Responsibility Law.

§ 22500.1. Fire lanes; parking violations; signs

In addition to Section 22500, no person shall stop, park, or leave standing any vehicle, whether attended or unattended, except when necessary to avoid conflict with other traffic or in compliance with the directions of a peace officer or official traffic control device along the edge of any highway, at any curb, or in any location in a publicly or privately owned or operated off-street parking facility, designated as a fire lane by the fire department or fire district with jurisdiction over the area in which the place is located.

The designation shall be indicated (1) by a sign posted immediately adjacent to, and visible from, the designated place clearly stating in letters not less than one inch in height that the place is a fire lane, (2) by outlining or painting the place in red and, in contrasting color, marking the place with the words "FIRE LANE", which are clearly visible from a vehicle, or (3) by a red curb or red paint on the edge of the roadway upon which is clearly marked the words "FIRE LANE". *(Added by Stats.1983, c. 328, § 1. Amended by Stats.1984, c. 129, § 1, eff. May 21, 1984.)*

Research References

2 Witkin, California Criminal Law 4th Crimes Against Public Peace and Welfare § 323 (2021), Parking.

§ 22500.2. Prohibited stopping, parking, or leaving standing within 15 feet of driveway used by emergency vehicle

(a) A local authority may, by ordinance, prohibit a person from stopping, parking, or leaving standing a vehicle, whether attended or unattended, except if necessary to avoid conflict with other traffic or in compliance with the directions of a peace officer or official traffic control device, within 15 feet of a driveway that is used by an emergency vehicle owned or operated by a police department, ambulance service care provider, or general acute care hospital, to enter or exit a police station, ambulance service provider facility, or general acute care hospital. This section does not apply to any vehicle owned or operated by a fire department, police department, ambulance service provider, or general acute care hospital, if the vehicle is clearly marked as a fire department vehicle, police department vehicle, ambulance, or general acute care hospital vehicle.

(b) A local authority that enacts an ordinance pursuant to subdivision (a) shall provide appropriate curb markings or "KEEP CLEAR" pavement markings and post signs that delineate the area specified in subdivision (a). *(Added by Stats.2016, c. 358 (A.B.2491), § 1, eff. Jan. 1, 2017.)*

Research References

2 Witkin, California Criminal Law 4th Crimes Against Public Peace and Welfare § 323 (2021), Parking.

§ 22500.5. Schoolbus stopping; local ordinance

Upon agreement between a transit system operating buses engaged as common carriers in local transportation and a public school district or private school, local authorities may, by ordinance, permit schoolbuses owned by, or operated under contract for, that public school district or private school to stop for the loading or unloading of passengers alongside any or all curb spaces designated for the loading or unloading of passengers of the transit system buses. *(Added by Stats.1982, c. 822, p. 3126, § 2. Amended by Stats.2012, c. 769 (A.B.2679), § 36.)*

§ 22501. Local regulation of state highways

No ordinance enacted by local authorities pursuant to subdivisions (e) and (k) of Section 22500 or Section 22507.2 shall become effective as to any state highway without prior submission to and approval by the Department of Transportation in the same manner as required by Section 21104. Nothing contained in this section and Section 22500 shall be construed as authorizing local authorities to enact legislation which is contrary to the provisions of Sections 22512 and 25301. *(Stats.1959, c. 3, p. 1698, § 22501. Amended by Stats.1965, c. 1500, p. 3524, § 8; Stats.1974, c. 545, p. 1325, § 204; Stats.1980, c. 158, p. 356, § 1, eff. June 11, 1980.)*

Cross References

Department of Transportation, see Streets and Highways Code § 90 et seq.
Local authorities defined, see Vehicle Code § 385.
Local regulation, see Vehicle Code § 21100 et seq.

Research References

2 Witkin, California Criminal Law 4th Crimes Against Public Peace and Welfare § 323 (2021), Parking.

§ 22502. Adjacent curbs or class IV bikeways; local ordinances; exception

(a) Except as otherwise provided in this chapter, a vehicle stopped or parked upon a roadway with adjacent curbs or class IV bikeways, as defined in Section 890.4 of the Streets and Highways Code, shall be stopped or parked with the right-hand wheels of the vehicle parallel to, and within 18 inches of, the right-hand curb or the right-hand edge of the class IV bikeway, except that a motorcycle shall be parked with at least one wheel or fender touching the right-hand curb or edge. If no curbs, barriers, or class IV bikeways bound a two-way roadway, right-hand parallel parking is required unless otherwise indicated.

(b)(1) The provisions of subdivision (a) or (e) do not apply to a commercial vehicle if a variation from the requirements of subdivision (a) or (e) is reasonably necessary to accomplish the loading or unloading of merchandise or passengers on, or from, a vehicle and while anything connected with the loading, or unloading, is being executed.

(2) This subdivision does not permit a vehicle to stop or park upon a roadway in a direction opposite to that in which traffic normally moves.

(c) Notwithstanding subdivision (b), a local authority may, by ordinance, prohibit a commercial vehicle from stopping, parking, or standing on one side of a roadway in a business district with the wheels of the vehicle more than 18 inches from the curb or the edge of a class IV bikeway. The ordinance shall be effective only if signs are placed clearly indicating the prohibition in the areas to which it applies.

(d) This section does not apply to vehicles of a public utility when the vehicles are being used in connection with the operation, maintenance, or repair of facilities of the public utility or are being used in connection with providing public utility service.

(e)(1) Upon a one-way roadway, a vehicle may be stopped or parked as provided in subdivision (a) or with the left-hand wheels parallel to, and within 18 inches of, the left-hand curb or left-hand edge of a class IV bikeway, except that a motorcycle, if parked on the left-hand side, shall have either one wheel or one fender touching the curb or edge. If no curb, barriers, or class IV bikeway bound a one-way roadway, parallel parking on either side is required unless otherwise indicated.

(2) This subdivision does not apply upon a roadway of a divided highway.

(f)(1) The City of Long Beach may, by ordinance or resolution, implement a pilot program to authorize vehicles to park on the left-hand side of the roadway parallel to and within 18 inches of the left-hand curb on two-way local residential streets that dead-end with no cul-de-sac or other designated area in which to turn around, if the City of Long Beach has first made a finding, supported by a professional engineering study, that the ordinance or resolution is justified by the need to facilitate the safe and orderly movement of vehicles on the roadways affected by the resolution or ordinance. The area covered by the ordinance or resolution shall be limited to the streets perpendicular to Ocean Boulevard beginning at Balboa Place and ending at 72nd Place, but shall not cover 62nd Place. The ordinance or resolution permitting that parking shall not apply until signs or markings giving adequate notice have been placed near the designated roadways. The city shall submit to the Legislature, two years from the date of the enactment of the ordinance or resolution that establishes the pilot program, a report that outlines the advantages and disadvantages of the pilot program. The report submitted pursuant to this subdivision shall be submitted in compliance with Section 9795 of the Government Code.

(2) The pilot program authorized under this subdivision shall terminate, and this subdivision shall become inoperative, three years from the date of enactment of the ordinance or resolution that establishes the pilot program. *(Stats.1959, c. 3, p. 1699, § 22502. Amended by Stats.1959, c. 978, p. 3006, § 1; Stats.1965, c. 308, p. 1404, § 1; Stats.1967, c. 767, p. 2155, § 1; Stats.1969, c. 777, p. 1555, § 1; Stats.1971, c. 448, p. 933, § 1, operative May 3, 1972; Stats.2010,*

c. 135 (A.B.2067), § 1; Stats.2016, c. 208 (A.B.2906), § 16, eff. Jan. 1, 2017.)

Cross References

Commercial vehicles defined, see Vehicle Code § 260.
Curb markings to indicate parking regulations, see Vehicle Code § 21458.
Local authorities defined, see Vehicle Code § 385.
Park or parking defined, see Vehicle Code § 463.
Report of convictions to department, exceptions, see Vehicle Code § 1803 et seq.
Rubbish or garbage trucks, exemptions, see Vehicle Code § 21059.
Stop or stopping defined, see Vehicle Code § 587.
Streetsweeping and watering vehicles, application of section, see Vehicle Code § 21060.

Research References

2 Witkin, California Criminal Law 4th Crimes Against Public Peace and Welfare § 323 (2021), Parking.

§ 22503. Local ordinance; angle parking

Local authorities may by ordinance permit angle parking on any roadway, or left-hand parking upon one-way roadways of divided highways, except that no ordinance is effective with respect to any state highway until the proposed ordinance has been submitted to and approved in writing by the Department of Transportation. *(Stats.1959, c. 3, p. 1699, § 22503. Amended by Stats.1971, c. 448, p. 933, § 2, operative May 3, 1972; Stats.1974, c. 545, p. 1325, § 205.)*

Cross References

Authority of Department of Transportation over local authorities in traffic rules, see Vehicle Code §§ 21104, 21350, 21353.
Highway defined, see Vehicle Code § 360.
Local authorities defined, see Vehicle Code § 385.
Report of convictions to department, exceptions, see Vehicle Code § 1803 et seq.
Roadway defined, see Vehicle Code § 530.

Research References

2 Witkin, California Criminal Law 4th Crimes Against Public Peace and Welfare § 323 (2021), Parking.

§ 22503.5. Two or three-wheeled motor vehicle parking regulations

Notwithstanding any other provision of this code, any local authority may, by ordinance or resolution, establish special parking regulations for two-wheeled or three-wheeled motor vehicles. *(Added by Stats.1965, c. 1131, p. 2777, § 1. Amended by Stats.1972, c. 1095, p. 2056, § 4.)*

Cross References

Motor vehicle defined, see Vehicle Code § 415.

Research References

2 Witkin, California Criminal Law 4th Crimes Against Public Peace and Welfare § 323 (2021), Parking.

§ 22504. Unincorporated area parking; exception; school bus stops

(a) Upon any highway in unincorporated areas, a person shall not stop, park, or leave standing any vehicle, whether attended or unattended, upon the roadway when it is practicable to stop, park, or leave the vehicle off such portion of the highway, but in every event an unobstructed width of the highway opposite a standing vehicle shall be left for the free passage of other vehicles and a clear view of the stopped vehicle shall be available from a distance of 200 feet in each direction upon the highway. This section shall not apply upon a highway where the roadway is bounded by adjacent curbs.

(b) This section does not apply to the driver of any vehicle which is disabled in such a manner and to such extent that it is impossible to avoid stopping and temporarily leaving the disabled vehicle on the roadway.

(c)(1) A schoolbus stop shall not be designated where there is not a clear view of a proposed or existing schoolbus stop from a distance of 200 feet in each direction along a highway, or upon the main traveled portion of a highway where there is not a clear view of the stop from 500 feet in each direction along the highway and the speed limit is more than 25 miles per hour, unless approved by the Department of the California Highway Patrol upon the request of the school district superintendent or the head or principal of a private school. If the schoolbus stop is approved by the Department of the California Highway Patrol, the Department of Transportation, in respect to state highways, and local authorities, in respect to highways under their jurisdiction, shall place sufficient signs along the highway to give adequate notice to motorists that they are approaching such bus stops.

(2) A school bus stop shall not be designated on any divided or multiple-lane highway where pupils must cross the highway to board or after exiting the bus, unless traffic is controlled by a traffic officer or official traffic control signal. For purposes of this section, a multiple- lane highway is defined as any highway having two or more lanes of travel in each direction. *(Stats.1959, c. 3, p. 1699, § 22504. Amended by Stats.1961, c. 1429, p. 3230, § 1; Stats.1974, c. 545, p. 1325, § 206; Stats.2012, c. 769 (A.B.2679), § 37.)*

Cross References

Curb markings indicating parking regulations, see Vehicle Code § 21458.
Definitions,
Roadway, see Vehicle Code § 530.
Street or highway, see Vehicle Code §§ 360, 590, 592.
Vehicle, see Vehicle Code § 670.
Display of warning devices when commercial vehicle disabled, see Vehicle Code § 25300.
Illegal parking, see Vehicle Code § 40200 et seq.
Impounding of vehicle by officer for inspection, see Vehicle Code § 22655.
Local parking regulations, see Vehicle Code § 22507.
Parking facility, use of street by, see Vehicle Code § 22951.
Removal of parked vehicles, authorization, see Vehicle Code § 22654.
Roadway with adjacent curbs, parking of vehicles upon, see Vehicle Code §§ 22502, 22508.
Rubbish or garbage trucks, exemption, see Vehicle Code § 21059.
Selling or vending from vehicle parked on highway, see Streets and Highways Code § 731.
Snow areas, parking in, see Vehicle Code § 22510.
Stopping, standing or parking prohibited in specified places, see Vehicle Code § 22500.
Stopping for school buses, see Vehicle Code § 22454.
Streetsweeping and watering vehicles, application of section, see Vehicle Code § 21060.
Tow cars, right to park to assist disabled vehicles, see Vehicle Code § 22513.
Utility vehicles, stopping, standing or parking of, see Vehicle Code §§ 22512, 25301.

Research References

2 Witkin, California Criminal Law 4th Crimes Against Public Peace and Welfare § 323 (2021), Parking.

§ 22505. Stopping, standing, or parking in certain areas

(a) The Department of Transportation with respect to highways under its jurisdiction may place signs or markings prohibiting or restricting the stopping, standing, or parking of vehicles, including, but not limited to, vehicles which are six feet or more in height (including any load thereon), in any of the following areas and under the following conditions:

(1) In areas where, in its opinion, stopping, standing, or parking is dangerous to those using the highway or where the stopping, standing, or parking of vehicles would unduly interfere with the free movement of traffic thereon.

(2) In areas within one-half mile of the boundary of any unit of the state park system which the Director of Conservation has determined are unusually high fire hazard areas, upon notification of the

Department of Transportation of such determination by the Director of Conservation.

(3) In areas within one-half mile of the boundary of any unit of the state park system which the county health officer has determined are areas where a substantial public health hazard would result if camping were allowed, upon notification of the Department of Transportation of such determination by the county health officer.

(b) No person shall stop, park, or leave standing any vehicle in violation of the restrictions stated on the signs or markings.

(c) This section does not apply to any of the following:

(1) Public utility vehicles while performing a work operation.

(2) The driver of any vehicle which is disabled in such a manner and to such an extent that it is impossible to avoid stopping, parking, or leaving the disabled vehicle standing on the roadway. *(Stats.1959, c. 3, p. 1699, § 22505. Amended by Stats.1963, c. 888, p. 2132, § 1; Stats.1970, c. 515, p. 1002, § 3; Stats.1974, c. 52, p. 115, § 1; Stats.1985, c. 912, § 1; Stats.1987, c. 455, § 2.)*

Cross References

Department of Transportation may close or restrict use of highway, see Streets and Highways Code § 124.
Official traffic control devices by Department of Transportation and by local authorities, see Vehicle Code §§ 21350, 21351.
Parking defined, see Vehicle Code § 463.
Stopping defined, see Vehicle Code § 587.

Research References

2 Witkin, California Criminal Law 4th Crimes Against Public Peace and Welfare § 323 (2021), Parking.

§ 22506. Local regulation of state highways

Local authorities may by ordinance or resolution prohibit or restrict the stopping, standing, or parking of vehicles on a state highway, in their respective jurisdictions, if the ordinance or resolution is first submitted to and approved in writing by the Department of Transportation, except that where maintenance of any state highway is delegated by the Department of Transportation to a city, the department may also delegate to the city the powers conferred on the department. *(Stats.1959, c. 3, p. 1699, § 22506. Amended by Stats.1974, c. 545, p. 1325, § 207; Stats.1987, c. 455, § 3.)*

Cross References

Delegation of powers to city by Department of Transportation, see Streets and Highways Code § 116.
Local authorities defined, see Vehicle Code § 385.
Parking defined, see Vehicle Code § 463.

Research References

2 Witkin, California Criminal Law 4th Crimes Against Public Peace and Welfare § 323 (2021), Parking.

§ 22507. Local regulation; preferential parking

(a) Local authorities may, by ordinance or resolution, prohibit or restrict the stopping, parking, or standing of vehicles, including, but not limited to, vehicles that are six feet or more in height (including any load thereon) within 100 feet of any intersection, on certain streets or highways, or portions thereof, during all or certain hours of the day. The ordinance or resolution may include a designation of certain streets upon which preferential parking privileges are given to residents and merchants adjacent to the streets for their use and the use of their guests, under which the residents and merchants may be issued a permit or permits that exempt them from the prohibition or restriction of the ordinance or resolution. With the exception of alleys, the ordinance or resolution shall not apply until signs or markings giving adequate notice thereof have been placed. A local ordinance or resolution adopted pursuant to this section may contain provisions that are reasonable and necessary to ensure the effectiveness of a preferential parking program.

(b) An ordinance or resolution adopted under this section may also authorize preferential parking permits for members of organizations, professions, or other designated groups, including, but not limited to, school personnel, to park on specified streets if the local authority determines that the use of the permits will not adversely affect parking conditions for residents and merchants in the area. *(Stats.1959, c. 3, p. 1700, § 22507. Amended by Stats.1963, c. 1070, p. 2530, § 1; Stats.1969, c. 541, p. 1168, § 1; Stats.1976, c. 1102, p. 4982, § 1; Stats.1980, c. 140, p. 334, § 1; Stats.1984, c. 181, § 2; Stats.1985, c. 912, § 2; Stats.1987, c. 455, § 4; Stats.1997, c. 343 (S.B.626), § 2; Stats.2001, c. 223 (S.B.779), § 1.)*

Cross References

Authority to remove vehicles, mobile advertising displays parked or left standing in violation of local resolution or ordinance, warning citations issued in lieu of posting signs giving notice of ordinance, see Vehicle Code § 22651.
Definitions,
 Alley, see Vehicle Code § 110.
 Highway, see Vehicle Code §§ 360, 592.
 Local authorities, see Vehicle Code § 385.
 Park or parking, see Vehicle Code § 463.
 Street, see Vehicle Code § 590.
 Vehicle, see Vehicle Code § 670.
Exemption of emergency vehicles from rules of the road, exceptions, see Vehicle Code § 21055.
Stopping, standing or parking, generally, see Vehicle Code § 22500 et seq.
Traffic regulation by local authorities, see Vehicle Code § 21100 et seq.
Utility vehicles, application of this section, see Vehicle Code § 22512.

Research References

2 Witkin, California Criminal Law 4th Crimes Against Public Peace and Welfare § 323 (2021), Parking.

§ 22507.1. Designation of streets or portions thereof for exclusive or nonexclusive parking privilege for participants in car share or ridesharing program

(a) A local authority may, by ordinance or resolution, designate certain streets or portions of streets for the exclusive or nonexclusive parking privilege of motor vehicles participating in a car share vehicle program or ridesharing program. The ordinance or resolution shall establish the criteria for a public or private company or organization to participate in the program, and may limit the types of motor vehicles that may be included in the program. Under the car share vehicle program, a car share vehicle or ridesharing vehicle shall be assigned a permit, if necessary, by the local authority that allows that vehicle to park in the exclusive or nonexclusive designated parking areas.

(b) If exclusive parking privilege is authorized, the ordinance or resolution described in subdivision (a) does not apply until signs or markings giving adequate notice thereof have been placed.

(c) A local ordinance or resolution adopted pursuant to subdivision (a) may contain provisions that are reasonable and necessary to ensure the effectiveness of a car share vehicle program or ridesharing program.

(d) For purposes of this section, a "car share vehicle" is a motor vehicle that is operated as part of a regional fleet by a public or private car sharing company or organization and provides hourly or daily service. *(Added by Stats.2006, c. 189 (A.B.2154), § 1. Amended by Stats.2015, c. 41 (A.B.1015), § 1, eff. Jan. 1, 2016; Stats.2016, c. 86 (S.B.1171), § 303, eff. Jan. 1, 2017.)*

§ 22507.2. Parking in front of private driveways; ordinance; permits

Notwithstanding subdivision (e) of Section 22500, a local authority may, by ordinance, authorize the owner or lessee of property to park a vehicle in front of the owner's or lessee's private driveway when the vehicle displays a permit issued pursuant to the ordinance authorizing such parking.

The local authority may charge a nonrefundable fee to defray the costs of issuing and administering the permits.

A local ordinance adopted pursuant to this section may not authorize parking on a sidewalk in violation of subdivision (f) of Section 22500. *(Added by Stats.1980, c. 158, p. 356, § 2, eff. June 11, 1980. Amended by Stats.1984, c. 219, § 1, eff. June 20, 1984; Stats.1985, c. 45, § 1.)*

Research References

2 Witkin, California Criminal Law 4th Crimes Against Public Peace and Welfare § 323 (2021), Parking.

§ 22507.5. Local regulation; overnight parking; commercial vehicles or trailer component thereof; vehicles transporting hazardous waste

(a) Notwithstanding Section 22507, local authorities may, by ordinance or resolution, prohibit or restrict the parking or standing of vehicles on certain streets or highways, or portions thereof, between the hours of 2 a.m. and 6 a.m., and may, by ordinance or resolution, prohibit or restrict the parking or standing, on any street, or portion thereof, in a residential district, of commercial vehicles having a manufacturer's gross vehicle weight rating of 10,000 pounds or more. The ordinance or resolution relating to parking between the hours of 2 a.m. and 6 a.m. may provide for a system of permits for the purpose of exempting from the prohibition or restriction of the ordinance or resolution, disabled persons, residents, and guests of residents of residential areas, including, but not limited to, high-density and multiple-family dwelling areas, lacking adequate offstreet parking facilities. The ordinance or resolution relating to the parking or standing of commercial vehicles in a residential district, however, shall not be effective with respect to any commercial vehicle, or trailer component thereof, making pickups or deliveries of goods, wares, and merchandise from or to any building or structure located on the restricted streets or highways or for the purpose of delivering materials to be used in the actual and bona fide repair, alteration, remodeling, or construction of any building or structure upon the restricted streets or highways for which a building permit has previously been obtained.

(b) Subdivision (a) of this section is applicable to vehicles specified in subdivision (a) of Section 31303, except that an ordinance or resolution adopted pursuant to subdivision (a) of this section shall not permit the parking of those vehicles which is otherwise prohibited under this code.

(c) For the purpose of implementing this section, each local authority may, by ordinance, define the term "residential district" in accordance with its zoning ordinance. The ordinance is not effective unless the legislative body of the local authority holds a public hearing on the proposed ordinance prior to its adoption, with notice of the public hearing given in accordance with Section 65090 of the Government Code. *(Added by Stats.1969, c. 541, p. 1168, § 2. Amended by Stats.1975, c. 1213, p. 3069, § 1; Stats.1976, c. 37, p. 64, § 1, eff. March 9, 1976; Stats.1987, c. 349, § 1; Stats.1989, c. 533, § 11; Stats.1996, c. 1156 (A.B.3157), § 1; Stats.2004, c. 404 (S.B. 1725), § 11; Stats.2004, c. 518 (A.B.2201), § 3.)*

Cross References

Definitions,
- Highway, see Vehicle Code §§ 360, 592.
- Local authorities, see Vehicle Code § 385.
- Parking, see Vehicle Code § 463.
- Street, see Vehicle Code § 590.
- Vehicle, see Vehicle Code § 670.

Research References

2 Witkin, California Criminal Law 4th Crimes Against Public Peace and Welfare § 323 (2021), Parking.

§ 22507.6. Local regulation; street sweeping; commercial vehicles; signs

Local authorities may, by ordinance or resolution, prohibit or restrict the parking or standing of vehicles on designated streets or highways, or portions thereof, for the purpose of street sweeping. No ordinance or resolution relating to the parking or standing of commercial vehicles in a residential district shall be effective with respect to any commercial vehicle making pickups or deliveries of goods, wares, or merchandise from or to any building or structure located on the restricted street or highway, or for the purpose of delivering materials to be used in the repair, alteration, remodeling, or reconstruction of any building or structure for which a building permit has previously been obtained. No such ordinance or resolution shall be effective until the street or highway, or portion thereof, has been sign-posted in accordance with the uniform standards and specifications of the Department of Transportation, or local authorities have caused to be posted in a conspicuous place at each entrance to the street a notice not less than 17 inches by 22 inches in size, with lettering not less than one inch in height, setting forth the day or days and hours parking is prohibited. As used in this section, "entrance" means the intersection of any street or streets comprising an area of restricted parking for street-sweeping purposes on the same day or days and hours with another street or highway not subject to such a parking restriction, or subject to parking restrictions on different days and hours. *(Added by Stats.1980, c. 391, p. 772, § 1. Amended by Stats.1981, c. 80, p. 196, § 1; Stats.1982, c. 466, p. 2058, § 115.)*

Cross References

Parking of utility vehicles, see Vehicle Code § 22512.

Research References

2 Witkin, California Criminal Law 4th Crimes Against Public Peace and Welfare § 323 (2021), Parking.

§ 22507.8. Disabled persons' and veterans' parking spaces; unauthorized parking or obstructing; offstreet parking facilities

(a) It is unlawful for any person to park or leave standing any vehicle in a stall or space designated for disabled persons and disabled veterans pursuant to Section 22511.7 or 22511.8 of this code or Section 14679 of the Government Code, unless the vehicle displays either a special identification license plate issued pursuant to Section 5007 or a distinguishing placard issued pursuant to Section 22511.55 or 22511.59.

(b) It is unlawful for any person to obstruct, block, or otherwise bar access to those parking stalls or spaces except as provided in subdivision (a).

(c) It is unlawful for any person to park or leave standing any vehicle, including a vehicle displaying a special identification license plate issued pursuant to Section 5007 or a distinguishing placard issued pursuant to Section 22511.55 or 22511.59, in either of the following places:

(1) On the lines marking the boundaries of a parking stall or space designated for disabled persons or disabled veterans.

(2) In any area of the pavement adjacent to a parking stall or space designated for disabled persons or disabled veterans that is marked by crosshatched lines and is thereby designated, pursuant to any local ordinance, for the loading and unloading of vehicles parked in the stall or space.

(d) Subdivisions (a), (b), and (c) apply to all offstreet parking facilities owned or operated by the state, and to all offstreet parking facilities owned or operated by a local authority. Subdivisions (a), (b), and (c) also apply to any privately owned and maintained offstreet parking facility. *(Added by Stats.1989, c. 338, § 2, eff. Sept. 11, 1989, operative Jan. 1, 1991. Amended by Stats.1990, c. 303 (A.B.3849), § 1; Stats.1994, c. 1149 (A.B.2878), § 4; Stats.1997, c. 945 (A.B.1561), § 18; Stats.2009, c. 200 (S.B.734), § 12.)*

Cross References

Authority of city or county to adopt an ordinance or resolution to assess an additional penalty relating to disabled parking violations, see Vehicle Code § 4461.3.

Fines and penalties, limits, see Vehicle Code § 40203.5.
Issuance and renewal of disabled parking placards, penalty printing requirements, see Vehicle Code §§ 22511.55 and 22511.59.
Parking penalties, additional assessments, see Vehicle Code § 40203.6.
Penalty for person convicted of infraction for violation of this section, see Vehicle Code § 42001.13.
Private parking facilities, see Vehicle Code § 21107.8.
Removal of unauthorized vehicle from physically handicapped parking space, see Vehicle Code § 22652.
Violation, punishment, see Vehicle Code § 42001.5.

Research References

2 Witkin, California Criminal Law 4th Crimes Against Public Peace and Welfare § 323 (2021), Parking.

§ 22507.9. Special enforcement units; handicapped parking enforcement; compensation and benefits; application of section

Local authorities may establish a special enforcement unit for the sole purpose of providing adequate enforcement of Section 22507.8 and local ordinances and resolutions adopted pursuant to Section 22511.7.

Local authorities may establish recruitment and employment guidelines that encourage and enable employment of qualified disabled persons in these special enforcement units.

Members of the special enforcement unit may issue notices of parking violation for violations of Section 22507.8 and local ordinances adopted pursuant to Section 22511.7. Members of the special enforcement unit shall not be peace officers and shall not make arrests in the course of their official duties, but shall wear distinctive uniforms and badges while on duty. A two-way radio unit, which may utilize police frequencies or citizens' band, may be issued by the local authority to each member of the special enforcement unit for use while on duty.

The local authority may pay the cost of uniforms and badges for the special enforcement unit, and may provide daily cleaning of the uniforms. Additionally, the local authority may provide motorized wheelchairs for use by members of the special unit while on duty, including batteries and necessary recharging thereof. Any motorized wheelchair used by a member of the special enforcement unit while on duty shall be equipped with a single headlamp in the front and a single stoplamp in the rear.

Members of the special enforcement unit may be paid an hourly wage without the compensatory benefits provided other permanent and temporary employees, but shall be entitled to applicable workers' compensation benefits as provided by law. Insurance provided by the local authority for disability or liability of a member of the special enforcement unit shall be the same as for other employees performing similar duties.

Nothing in this section precludes a local authority from using regular full-time employees to enforce this chapter and ordinances adopted pursuant thereto.

This section applies to all counties and cities, including every charter city and city and county. *(Added by Stats.1984, c. 1095, § 1. Amended by Stats.1996, c. 124 (A.B.3470), § 127.)*

§ 22508. Parking meter zones; fee rates; fee payment

(a) A local authority shall not establish parking meter zones or fix the rate of fees for those zones except by ordinance. The rate of fees may be variable, based upon criteria identified by the local authority in the ordinance. An ordinance establishing a parking meter zone shall describe the area that would be included within the zone.

(b) A local authority may by ordinance cause streets and highways to be marked with white lines designating parking spaces and require vehicles to park within the parking spaces.

(c) An ordinance adopted by a local authority pursuant to this section with respect to any state highway shall not become effective until the proposed ordinance has been submitted to and approved in writing by the Department of Transportation. The proposed ordinance shall be submitted to the department only by action of the local legislative body and the proposed ordinance shall be submitted in complete draft form.

(d) An ordinance adopted pursuant to this section establishing a parking meter zone or fixing rates of fees for that zone shall be subject to local referendum processes in the same manner as if the ordinance dealt with a matter of purely local concern.

(e) A local authority may accept but shall not require payment of parking meter fees by a mobile device. *(Stats.1959, c. 3, p. 1700, § 22508. Amended by Stats.1961, c. 2017, p. 4231, § 2; Stats.1974, c. 545, p. 1326, § 208; Stats.2012, c. 70 (S.B.1388), § 1.)*

Cross References

Colors used in curb markings, see Vehicle Code § 21458.
Definitions,
Highway, see Vehicle Code §§ 360, 591, 592.
Local authorities, see Vehicle Code § 385.
Park or parking, see Vehicle Code § 463.
Street, see Vehicle Code §§ 590, 591.
Local regulation of traffic matters, see Vehicle Code § 21100 et seq.
Referendum in municipalities, see Elections Code § 9235 et seq.
Report of previous convictions, see Vehicle Code § 1803.

Research References

2 Witkin, California Criminal Law 4th Crimes Against Public Peace and Welfare § 323 (2021), Parking.

§ 22508.5. Inoperable parking meter or payment center; prohibitions or restrictions

(a) A vehicle may park, for up to the posted time limit, in any parking space that is regulated by an inoperable parking meter or an inoperable parking payment center.

(b) A vehicle may park without time limit in any parking space that does not have a posted time limit and that is regulated by an inoperable parking meter or inoperable parking payment center, subject to any other applicable regulations regarding parking vehicles.

(c) A local authority may limit parking to four hours for a parking space that does not have a posted time limit and that is regulated by an inoperable parking meter or an inoperable parking payment center, if the local authority posts signs clearly providing notice of the time limitation applicable when that parking meter or parking payment center is inoperable.

(d) If a parking space is regulated by a parking meter or parking payment center that cannot physically accept payment, a local authority shall not issue a citation for nonpayment of parking fees notwithstanding the fact that the parking meter or parking payment center may accept payment by other nonphysical means.

(e) Except as provided in subdivision (c), a local authority shall not, by ordinance or resolution, prohibit or restrict the parking of vehicles in a space that is regulated by an inoperable parking meter or inoperable parking payment center.

(f) For purposes of this section:

(1) "Inoperable parking meter" means a meter located next to and designated for an individual parking space that has become inoperable and cannot accept payment in any form or cannot register that a payment in any form has been made.

(2) "Inoperable parking payment center" means an electronic parking meter or pay station serving one or more parking spaces that is closest to the space where a person has parked and that cannot accept payment in any form, cannot register that a payment in any form has been made, or cannot issue a receipt that is required to be displayed in a conspicuous location on or in the vehicle. *(Added by Stats.2012, c. 70 (S.B.1388), § 2. Amended by Stats.2013, c. 71*

(A.B.61), § 1; Stats.2017, c. 352 (A.B.1625), § 1, eff. Jan. 1, 2018; Stats.2018, c. 92 (S.B.1289), § 210, eff. Jan. 1, 2019.)

Research References

2 Witkin, California Criminal Law 4th Crimes Against Public Peace and Welfare § 323 (2021), Parking.

§ 22509. Parking on hills

Local authorities within the reasonable exercise of their police powers may adopt rules and regulations by ordinance or resolution providing that no person driving, or in control of, or in charge of, a motor vehicle shall permit it to stand on any highway unattended when upon any grade exceeding 3 percent within any business or residence district without blocking the wheels of the vehicle by turning them against the curb or by other means. *(Stats.1959, c. 3, p. 1700, § 22509.)*

Cross References

Business and residence districts defined, see Vehicle Code §§ 235, 515.
Exemption of emergency vehicles from rules of the road, exceptions, see Vehicle Code § 21055.
Local authorities defined, see Vehicle Code § 385.
Motor vehicle defined, see Vehicle Code § 415.
Utility vehicles, application of this section, see Vehicle Code § 22512.

Research References

2 Witkin, California Criminal Law 4th Crimes Against Public Peace and Welfare § 323 (2021), Parking.

§ 22510. Snow removal areas; parking restrictions; signs

(a) Local authorities may, by ordinance or resolution, prohibit or restrict the parking or standing of vehicles on designated streets or highways within their jurisdiction, or portions thereof, for the purpose of snow removal. The ordinance or resolution shall not be effective until the street or highway, or portion thereof, has been sign-posted in accordance with the uniform standards and specifications of the Department of Transportation, or until the local authorities have caused to be posted in a conspicuous place at each entrance to the street or highway, a notice not less than 17 inches by 22 inches in size, with lettering not less than one inch in height, setting forth the days parking is prohibited. The signs shall, at a minimum, be placed on each affected street or highway, at the boundary of the local authority, and at the beginning and end of each highway or highway segment included in that area. No person shall stop, park, or leave standing any vehicle, whether attended or unattended, within the area marked by signs, except when necessary to avoid conflict with other traffic or in compliance with the directions of a traffic or peace officer.

(b) No ordinance or resolution authorized by subdivision (a) which affects a state highway shall be effective until it is submitted to, and approved by, the Department of Transportation.

(c) The Department of Transportation, with respect to state highways, may restrict the parking or standing of vehicles for purposes of snow removal. The restrictions shall not be effective until the highway, or portion thereof, has been posted with signs in accordance with the uniform standards and specifications of the department. No person shall stop, park, or leave standing any vehicle, whether attended or unattended, within the area marked by parking restriction signs, except when necessary to avoid conflict with other traffic or in compliance with the directions of a traffic or peace officer. *(Added by Stats.1990, c. 692 (A.B.3398), § 3.)*

Cross References

Department of Transportation may close or restrict use of highway, see Streets and Highways Code § 124.
Local authorities defined, see Vehicle Code § 385.
Official traffic control device defined, see Vehicle Code § 440.
Traffic signs, signals and markings, generally, see Vehicle Code § 21350 et seq.

Research References

2 Witkin, California Criminal Law 4th Crimes Against Public Peace and Welfare § 323 (2021), Parking.

§ 22511. Electric vehicle parking stalls or spaces; removal of vehicles not connected for electric charging purposes; off-street parking facility posting and signage requirements; local ordinances

(a)(1) A local authority, by ordinance or resolution, and a person in lawful possession of an offstreet parking facility may designate stalls or spaces in an offstreet parking facility owned or operated by that local authority or person for the exclusive purpose of charging and parking a vehicle that is connected for electric charging purposes.

(2) A local authority, by ordinance or resolution, may designate stalls or spaces on a public street within its jurisdiction for the exclusive purpose of charging and parking a vehicle that is connected for electric charging purposes.

(b) If posted in accordance with subdivision (d) or (e), the owner or person in lawful possession of a privately owned or operated offstreet parking facility, after notifying the police or sheriff's department, may cause the removal of a vehicle from a stall or space designated pursuant to subdivision (a) in the facility to the nearest public garage if the vehicle is not connected for electric charging purposes.

(c)(1) If posted in accordance with paragraph (1) of subdivision (d), the local authority owning or operating an offstreet parking facility, after notifying the police or sheriff's department, may cause the removal of a vehicle from a stall or space designated pursuant to paragraph (1) of subdivision (a) in the facility to the nearest garage, as defined in Section 340, that is owned, leased, or approved for use by a public agency if the vehicle is not connected for electric charging purposes.

(2) If posted in accordance with paragraph (2) of subdivision (d), the local authority, after notifying the police or sheriff's department, may cause the removal of a vehicle from a stall or space designated pursuant to paragraph (2) of subdivision (a) to the nearest garage, as defined in Section 340, that is owned, leased, or approved for use by a public agency if the vehicle is not connected for electric charging purposes.

(d)(1) The posting required for an offstreet parking facility owned or operated either privately or by a local authority shall consist of a sign not less than 17 by 22 inches in size with lettering not less than one inch in height that clearly and conspicuously states the following: "Unauthorized vehicles not connected for electric charging purposes will be towed away at owner's expense. Towed vehicles may be reclaimed at

____________________________ or by telephoning
(Address)
____."
(Telephone number of local law enforcement agency)

The sign shall be posted in either of the following locations:

(A) Immediately adjacent to, and visible from, the stall or space.

(B) In a conspicuous place at each entrance to the offstreet parking facility.

(2) The posting required for stalls or spaces on a public street designated pursuant to paragraph (2) of subdivision (a) shall follow the California Manual of Uniform Traffic Control Devices.

(e) If the parking facility is privately owned and public parking is prohibited by the posting of a sign meeting the requirements of paragraph (1) of subdivision (a) of Section 22658, the requirements of subdivision (b) may be met by the posting of a sign immediately adjacent to, and visible from, each stall or space indicating that a vehicle not meeting the requirements of subdivision (a) will be removed at the owner's expense and containing the telephone number of the local traffic law enforcement agency.

(f) This section does not interfere with existing law governing the ability of local authorities to adopt ordinances related to parking programs within their jurisdiction, such as programs that provide free parking in metered areas or municipal garages for electric vehicles. *(Added by Stats.2002, c. 640 (A.B.1314), § 2. Amended by Stats.2011, c. 274 (A.B.475), § 1; Stats.2017, c. 635 (A.B.1452), § 1, eff. Jan. 1, 2018.)*

§ 22511.1. Electric vehicle parking stalls or spaces; unauthorized parking or obstructing

(a) A person shall not park or leave standing a vehicle in a stall or space designated pursuant to Section 22511 unless the vehicle is connected for electric charging purposes.

(b) A person shall not obstruct, block, or otherwise bar access to parking stalls or spaces described in subdivision (a) except as provided in subdivision (a). *(Added by Stats.2002, c. 640 (A.B.1314), § 3. Amended by Stats.2011, c. 274 (A.B.475), § 2.)*

Cross References

Punishment upon conviction, penalty amount, see Vehicle Code § 42001.6.

Research References

2 Witkin, California Criminal Law 4th Crimes Against Public Peace and Welfare § 323 (2021), Parking.

§ 22511.2. Electric vehicle parking stalls or spaces; local jurisdictions; counting of spaces with electric vehicle supply equipment or charging spaces toward minimum parking space requirements; definitions

(a) A parking space served by electric vehicle supply equipment or a parking space designated as a future electric vehicle charging space shall count as at least one standard automobile parking space for the purpose of complying with any applicable minimum parking space requirements established by a local jurisdiction.

(b) An accessible parking space with an access aisle served by electric vehicle supply equipment or an accessible parking space with an aisle designated as a future electric vehicle charging space shall count as at least two standard automobile parking spaces for the purpose of complying with any applicable minimum parking space requirements established by a local jurisdiction.

(c) This section does not modify the approval requirements for an electric vehicle charging station pursuant to Section 65850.7 of the Government Code.

(d) The following definitions apply for purposes of this section:

(1) "Electric vehicle supply equipment" has the same definition as that term is used in the latest published version of the California Electrical Code, that is in effect, and applies to any level or capacity of supply equipment installed specifically for the purpose of transferring energy between the premises wiring and the electric vehicle.

(2) "Electric vehicle charging space" means a space designated by a local jurisdiction for charging electric vehicles.

(3) "Local jurisdiction" means a city, including a charter city, county, or city and county. *(Added by Stats.2019, c. 819 (A.B.1100), § 2, eff. Jan. 1, 2020.)*

§ 22511.3. Veterans displaying special license plates; metered parking spaces; privileges

(a) A veteran displaying special license plates issued under Section 5101.3, 5101.4, 5101.5, 5101.6, or 5101.8 may park his or her motor vehicle, weighing not more than 6,000 pounds gross weight, without charge, in a metered parking space.

(b) Nothing in this section restricts the rights of a person displaying either a special identification license plate issued pursuant to Section 5007 or a distinguishing placard issued pursuant to Section 22511.55 or 22511.59.

(c)(1) This section does not exempt a vehicle displaying special license plates issued under Section 5101.3, 5101.4, 5101.5, 5101.6, or 5101.8 from compliance with any other state law or ordinance, including, but not limited to, vehicle height restrictions, zones that prohibit stopping, parking, or standing of all vehicles, parking time limitations, street sweeping, restrictions of the parking space to a particular type of vehicle, or the parking of a vehicle that is involved in the operation of a street vending business.

(2) This section does not authorize a vehicle displaying special license plates issued under Section 5101.3, 5101.4, 5101.5, 5101.6, or 5101.8 to park in a state parking facility that is designated only for state employees.

(3) This section does not authorize a vehicle displaying special license plates issued under Section 5101.3, 5101.4, 5101.5, 5101.6, or 5101.8 to park during time periods other than the normal business hours of, or the maximum time allotted by, a state or local authority parking facility.

(4) This section does not require the state or a local authority to designate specific parking spaces for vehicles displaying special license plates issued under Section 5101.3, 5101.4, 5101.5, 5101.6, or 5101.8.

(d) A local authority's compliance with subdivision (a) is solely contingent upon the approval of its governing body. *(Added by Stats.2008, c. 588 (A.B.190), § 1.)*

§ 22511.5. Disabled persons or disabled veterans; parking privileges

(a)(1) A disabled person or disabled veteran displaying special license plates issued under Section 5007 or a distinguishing placard issued under Section 22511.55 or 22511.59 is allowed to park for unlimited periods in any of the following zones:

(A) In any restricted zone described in paragraph (5) of subdivision (a) of Section 21458 or on streets upon which preferential parking privileges and height limits have been given pursuant to Section 22507.

(B) In any parking zone that is restricted as to the length of time parking is permitted as indicated by a sign erected pursuant to a local ordinance.

(2) A disabled person or disabled veteran is allowed to park in any metered parking space without being required to pay parking meter fees.

(3) This subdivision does not apply to a zone for which state law or ordinance absolutely prohibits stopping, parking, or standing of all vehicles, or which the law or ordinance reserves for special types of vehicles, or to the parking of a vehicle that is involved in the operation of a street vending business.

(b) A disabled person or disabled veteran is allowed to park a motor vehicle displaying a special disabled person license plate or placard issued by a foreign jurisdiction with the same parking privileges authorized in this code for any motor vehicle displaying a special license plate or a distinguishing placard issued by the Department of Motor Vehicles. *(Added by Stats.1978, c. 457, p. 1550, § 2. Amended by Stats.1980, c. 261, p. 533, § 1; Stats.1982, c. 974, p. 3487, § 2; Stats.1982, c. 975, p. 3494, § 6.5; Stats.1984, c. 510, § 1; Stats.1984, c. 1118, § 1; Stats.1985, c. 1041, § 7; Stats.1986, c. 351, § 3; Stats.1988, c. 115, § 1; Stats.1989, c. 554, § 3; Stats.1991, c. 893 (A.B.274), § 4; Stats.1992, c. 785 (A.B.2289), § 3; Stats.1992, c. 1241 (S.B.1615), § 21; Stats.1994, c. 1149 (A.B.2878), § 5; Stats. 2004, c. 404 (S.B.1725), § 12; Stats.2010, c. 478 (A.B.2777), § 11.)*

Cross References

Exemption of disabled person from weight fees, see Vehicle Code § 9410.
Parking facilities, state agencies, see Government Code § 14679.

Research References

2 Witkin, California Criminal Law 4th Crimes Against Public Peace and Welfare § 323 (2021), Parking.

§ 22511.55. Issuance and renewal of disabled parking placard; conditions; printing requirements

(a)(1) A disabled person or disabled veteran may apply to the department for the issuance of a distinguishing placard. The placard may be used in lieu of the special license plate or plates issued under Section 5007 for parking purposes described in Section 22511.5 when (A) suspended from the rearview mirror, (B) if there is no rearview mirror, when displayed on the dashboard of a vehicle, or (C) inserted in a clip designated for a distinguishing placard and installed by the manufacturer on the driver's side of the front window. It is the intent of the Legislature to encourage the use of distinguishing placards because they provide law enforcement officers with a more readily recognizable symbol for distinguishing vehicles qualified for the parking privilege. The placard shall be the size, shape, and color determined by the department and shall bear the International Symbol of Access adopted pursuant to Section 3 of Public Law 100–641,[1] commonly known as the "wheelchair symbol." The department shall incorporate instructions for the lawful use of a placard, and a summary of the penalties for the unlawful use of a placard, into the identification card issued to the placard owner.

(2)(A) The department may establish procedures for the issuance and renewal of the placards. The procedures shall include, but are not limited to, advising an applicant in writing on the application for a placard of the procedure to apply for a special license plate or plates, as described in Section 5007, and the fee exemptions established pursuant to Section 9105 and in subdivision (a) of Section 10783 of the Revenue and Taxation Code. The placards shall have a fixed expiration date of June 30 every two years. A portion of the placard shall be printed in a contrasting color that shall be changed every two years. The size and color of this contrasting portion of the placard shall be large and distinctive enough to be readily identifiable by a law enforcement officer in a passing vehicle.

(B) As used in this section, "year" means the period between the inclusive dates of July 1 through June 30.

(C) Prior to the end of each year, the department shall, for the most current three years available, compare its record of disability placards issued against the records of the Office of Vital Records of the State Department of Public Health, or its successor, and * * * a nationwide vital statistics clearinghouse, and withhold any renewal notices or placards that otherwise would have been sent for a placardholder identified as deceased.

(D) The department shall, six years after the first issuance of a placard and every six years thereafter, send the placardholder a renewal form * * * at least 90 days prior to the June 30 expiration date of the current placard. Certification of medical disability and proof of true full name is not required for the renewal. A placardholder who wishes to renew a placard shall fill out the form and submit it to the department * * * prior to expiration of the current placard.

(3) Except as provided in paragraph (4), a person shall not be eligible for more than one placard at a time.

(4) Organizations and agencies involved in the transportation of disabled persons or disabled veterans may apply for a placard for each vehicle used for the purpose of transporting disabled persons or disabled veterans.

(5) The department shall require a person who applies for a placard pursuant to this section to provide proof of the person's true full name and date of birth that shall be established by submitting one of the following to the department:

(A) A copy or facsimile of the applicant's state issued driver's license or identification card.

(B) A copy or facsimile of the document required for an applicant for a driver's license or identification card to establish the applicant's true full name.

(C) An applicant unable to establish legal presence in the United States may fulfill the true full name and date of birth requirement by providing the department a copy or facsimile of the documents used to establish identity pursuant to Section 12801.9.

(b)(1) Except as provided in paragraph (4), prior to issuing an original distinguishing placard to a disabled person or disabled veteran, the department shall require the submission of a certificate, in accordance with paragraph (2), signed by the physician and surgeon, or to the extent that it does not cause a reduction in the receipt of federal aid highway funds, by a nurse practitioner, certified nurse-midwife, or physician assistant, substantiating the disability, unless the applicant's disability is readily observable and uncontested. The disability of a person who has lost, or has lost use of, one or more lower extremities or one hand, for a disabled veteran, or both hands, for a disabled person, or who has significant limitation in the use of lower extremities, may also be certified by a licensed chiropractor. The disability of a person related to the foot or ankle may be certified by a licensed podiatrist. The blindness of an applicant shall be certified by a licensed physician and surgeon who specializes in diseases of the eye or a licensed optometrist. The physician and surgeon, nurse practitioner, certified nurse-midwife, physician assistant, chiropractor, or optometrist certifying the qualifying disability shall provide a full description of the illness or disability on the form submitted to the department.

(2) The physician and surgeon, nurse practitioner, certified nurse midwife, physician assistant, chiropractor, podiatrist, or optometrist who signs a certificate submitted under this subdivision shall retain information sufficient to substantiate that certificate and, upon request of the department, shall make that information available for inspection by the Medical Board of California or the appropriate regulatory board.

(3) The department shall maintain in its records all information on an applicant's certification of permanent disability and shall make that information available to eligible law enforcement or parking control agencies upon a request pursuant to Section 22511.58.

(4) For a disabled veteran, the department shall accept, in lieu of the certificate described in paragraph (1), a certificate from a county veterans service officer, the Department of Veterans Affairs, or the United States Department of Veterans Affairs that certifies that the applicant is a disabled veteran as described in Section 295.7.

(c) A person who is issued a distinguishing placard pursuant to subdivision (a) may apply to the department for a substitute placard without recertification of eligibility, if that placard is lost or stolen. The department shall not issue a substitute placard to a person more than four times in a two-year renewal period. A person who requires a substitute placard in excess of the four replacements authorized pursuant to this subdivision shall reapply to the department for a new placard and submit a new certificate of disability as described in subdivision (b).

(d) The distinguishing placard shall be returned to the department not later than 60 days after the death of the disabled person or disabled veteran to whom the placard was issued.

(e) The department shall print on any distinguishing placard issued on or after January 1, 2005, the maximum penalty that may be imposed for a violation of Section 4461. For purposes of this subdivision, the "maximum penalty" is the amount derived from adding all of the following:

(1) The maximum fine that may be imposed under Section 4461.

(2) The penalty required to be imposed under Section 70372 of the Government Code.

(3) The penalty required to be levied under Section 76000 of the Government Code.

(4) The penalty required to be levied under Section 1464 of the Penal Code.

(5) The surcharge required to be levied under Section 1465.7 of the Penal Code.

(6) The penalty authorized to be imposed under Section 4461.3. *(Added by Stats.1991, c. 893 (A.B.274), § 5. Amended by Stats.1991, c. 894 (S.B.234), § 3; Stats.1993, c. 1292 (S.B.274), § 13; Stats.1994, c. 1149 (A.B.2878), § 6; Stats.1996, c. 1033 (S.B.1498), § 1; Stats. 2000, c. 524 (A.B.1792), § 5; Stats.2001, c. 708 (A.B.677), § 3; Stats.2003, c. 555 (A.B.327), § 5; Stats.2004, c. 404 (S.B.1725), § 13; Stats.2006, c. 116 (A.B.2120), § 3; Stats.2010, c. 196 (A.B.1855), § 1; Stats.2010, c. 421 (A.B.1944), § 2; Stats.2010, c. 491 (S.B.1318), § 42.3; Stats.2017, c. 485 (S.B.611), § 19, eff. Jan. 1, 2018; Stats. 2020, c. 42 (A.B.408), § 2, eff. Jan. 1, 2021; Stats.2022, c. 71 (S.B.198), § 14, eff. June 30, 2022.)*

[1] For public law sections classified to the U.S.C.A., see USCA–Tables.

Cross References

Additional fines imposed for violation of disabled parking restrictions, see Penal Code § 1465.6.
Authority of city or county to adopt an ordinance or resolution to assess an additional penalty relating to disabled parking violations, see Vehicle Code § 4461.3.
Disabled person placards, annual random audits of applications, see Vehicle Code § 1825.
Fines and penalties, suspension, see Vehicle Code § 40203.5.
Fines imposed and collected for violation of disabled parking restrictions, see Penal Code § 1465.5.
Former prisoners of war, disabled veterans, or Congressional Medal of Honor recipients, exemptions from fees for certain plates, certificates, or cards, see Vehicle Code § 9105.
Mounting of plates, see Vehicle Code § 5201.
Parking facilities for physically handicapped persons and disabled veterans, display of distinguishing placard, see Government Code § 14679.

Research References

2 Witkin, California Criminal Law 4th Crimes Against Property § 199 (2021), Motor Vehicle Items.
2 Witkin, California Criminal Law 4th Crimes Against Public Peace and Welfare § 323 (2021), Parking.

§ 22511.56. Placard or specialty license plate; presentation of identification and evidence of issuance; failure to present; penalties for misuse; confiscation; cancellation

(a) A person using a distinguishing placard issued under Section 22511.55 or 22511.59, or a special license plate issued under Section 5007, for parking as permitted by Section 22511.5 shall, upon request of a peace officer or person authorized to enforce parking laws, ordinances, or regulations, present identification and evidence of the issuance of that placard or plate to that person, or that vehicle if the plate was issued pursuant to paragraph (3) of subdivision (a) of Section 5007.

(b) Failure to present the requested identification and evidence of the issuance of that placard or plate shall be a rebuttable presumption that the placard or plate is being misused and that the associated vehicle has been parked in violation of Section 22507.8, or has exercised a disabled person's parking privilege pursuant to Section 22511.5.

(c) In addition to any other applicable penalty for the misuse of a placard, the officer or parking enforcement person may confiscate a placard being used for parking purposes that benefit a person other than the person to whom the placard was issued by the Department of Motor Vehicles. A placard lawfully used by a person transporting a disabled person pursuant to subdivision (b) of Section 4461 may not be confiscated.

(d) In addition to any other applicable penalty for the misuse of a special license plate issued under Section 5007, a peace officer may confiscate the plate being used for parking purposes that benefit a person other than the person to whom the plate was issued by the Department of Motor Vehicles.

(e) After verification with the Department of Motor Vehicles that the user of the placard or plate is not the registered owner of the placard or plate, the appropriate agency that confiscated the placard or plate shall notify the department of the placard or plate number and the department shall cancel the placard or plate. A placard or plate canceled by the department pursuant to this subdivision may be destroyed by the agency that confiscated the placard or plate. *(Added by Stats.1991, c. 894 (S.B.234), § 4. Amended by Stats.1994, c. 1149 (A.B.2878), § 7; Stats.2000, c. 135 (A.B.2539), § 162; Stats.2004, c. 363 (A.B.1138), § 3; Stats.2006, c. 203 (A.B.1910), § 2.)*

§ 22511.57. Disabled person placards lost or stolen; owner of placard deceased; vehicle parking restrictions and prohibitions

A local authority may, by ordinance or resolution, prohibit or restrict the parking or standing of a vehicle on streets or highways or in a parking stall or space in a privately or publicly owned or operated offstreet parking facility within its jurisdiction when the vehicle displays, in order to obtain special parking privileges, a distinguishing placard or special license plate, issued pursuant to Section 5007, 22511.55, or 22511.59, and any of the following conditions are met:

(a) The records of the Department of Motor Vehicles for the identification number assigned to the placard or license plate indicate that the placard or license plate has been reported as lost, stolen, surrendered, canceled, revoked, or expired, or was issued to a person who has been reported as deceased for a period exceeding 60 days.

(b) The placard or license plate is displayed on a vehicle that is not being used to transport, and is not in the reasonable proximity of, the person to whom the license plate or placard was issued or a person who is authorized to be transported in the vehicle displaying that placard or license plate.

(c) The placard or license plate is counterfeit, forged, altered, or mutilated. *(Added by Stats.1994, c. 221 (S.B.1378), § 1, operative July 1, 1995. Amended by Stats.2004, c. 363 (A.B.1138), § 4; Stats.2004, c. 404 (S.B.1725), § 14; Stats.2009, c. 415 (A.B.144), § 4; Stats.2011, c. 341 (S.B.565), § 3.)*

Cross References

Fines and penalties, limits, see Vehicle Code § 40203.5.
Parking penalties, additional assessments, see Vehicle Code § 40203.6.

§ 22511.58. Physician's certificate information; release to specified local agencies; local review board

(a) Upon a request to the department by a local public law enforcement agency or local agency responsible for the administration or enforcement of parking regulations, the department shall make available to the requesting agency any information contained in a physician's certificate submitted to the department as part of the application for a disabled person's parking privileges, substantiating the disability of a person applying for or who has been issued a parking placard pursuant to Section 22511.55. The department shall not provide the information specified in this subdivision to any private or other third-party parking citation processing agency.

(b) Local authorities may establish a review board or panel, which shall include a qualified physician or medical authority, for purposes of reviewing information contained in the applications for special parking privileges and the certification of qualifying disabilities for persons residing within the jurisdiction of the local authority. Any findings or determinations by a review board or panel under this section indicating that an application or certification is fraudulent or lacks proper certification may be transmitted to the department or other appropriate authorities for further review and investigation. *(Added by Stats.1996, c. 1033 (S.B.1498), § 2.)*

§ 22511.59. Temporary distinguishing placard; renewal

(a) Upon the receipt of the applications and documents required by subdivision (b), (c), or (d), the department shall issue a temporary distinguishing placard bearing the International Symbol of Access adopted pursuant to Section 3 of Public Law 100–641,[1] commonly known as the "wheelchair symbol." During the period for which it is valid, the temporary distinguishing placard may be used for the parking purposes described in Section 22511.5 in the same manner as a distinguishing placard issued pursuant to Section 22511.55.

(b)(1) A person who is temporarily disabled for a period of not more than six months may apply to the department for the issuance of the temporary distinguishing placard described in subdivision (a).

(2) Prior to issuing a placard pursuant to this subdivision, the department shall require the submission of a certificate signed by a physician and surgeon, or to the extent that it does not cause a reduction in the receipt of federal aid highway funds, by a nurse practitioner, certified nurse midwife, physician assistant, chiropractor, podiatrist, or optometrist, as described in subdivision (b) of Section 22511.55, substantiating the temporary disability and stating the date upon which the disability is expected to terminate.

(3) The physician and surgeon, nurse practitioner, certified nurse midwife, physician assistant, chiropractor, podiatrist, or optometrist who signs a certificate submitted under this subdivision shall maintain information sufficient to substantiate that certificate and, upon request of the department, shall make that information available for inspection by the Medical Board of California or the appropriate regulatory board.

(4) A placard issued pursuant to this subdivision shall expire not later than 180 days from the date of issuance or upon the expected termination date of the disability, as stated on the certificate required by paragraph (2), whichever is less.

(5) The fee for a temporary placard issued pursuant to this subdivision shall be six dollars ($6).

(6) A placard issued pursuant to this subdivision shall be renewed a maximum of six times consecutively.

(c)(1) A permanently disabled person or disabled veteran who is not a resident of this state and plans to travel within the state may apply to the department for the issuance of the temporary distinguishing placard described in subdivision (a).

(2) Prior to issuing a placard pursuant to this subdivision, the department shall require certification of the disability, as described in subdivision (b) of Section 22511.55.

(3) The physician and surgeon, nurse practitioner, certified nurse midwife, physician assistant, chiropractor, podiatrist, or optometrist who signs a certificate submitted under this subdivision shall maintain information sufficient to substantiate that certificate and, upon request of the department, shall make that information available for inspection by the Medical Board of California or the appropriate regulatory board.

(4) A placard issued pursuant to this subdivision shall expire not later than 90 days from the date of issuance.

(5) The department shall not charge a fee for issuance of a placard under this subdivision.

(6) A placard issued pursuant to this subdivision shall be renewed a maximum of six times consecutively.

(d)(1) A permanently disabled person or disabled veteran who has been issued either a distinguishing placard pursuant to Section 22511.55 or special license plates pursuant to Section 5007, but not both, may apply to the department for the issuance of the temporary distinguishing placard described in subdivision (a) for the purpose of travel.

(2) Prior to issuing a placard pursuant to this subdivision, the department shall require the applicant to submit either the number identifying the distinguishing placard issued pursuant to Section 22511.55 or the number on the special license plates.

(3) A placard issued pursuant to this subdivision shall expire not later than 30 days from the date of issuance.

(4) The department shall not charge a fee for issuance of a placard under this subdivision.

(5) A placard issued pursuant to this subdivision shall be renewed a maximum of six times consecutively.

(e) The department shall print on a temporary distinguishing placard, the maximum penalty that may be imposed for a violation of Section 4461. For the purposes of this subdivision, the "maximum penalty" is the amount derived from adding all of the following:

(1) The maximum fine that may be imposed under Section 4461.

(2) The penalty required to be imposed under Section 70372 of the Government Code.

(3) The penalty required to be levied under Section 76000 of the Government Code.

(4) The penalty required to be levied under Section 1464 of the Penal Code.

(5) The surcharge required to be levied under Section 1465.7 of the Penal Code.

(6) The penalty authorized to be imposed under Section 4461.3.

(f) The department shall require a person who applies for a temporary placard pursuant to this section to provide proof of his or her true full name and date of birth that shall be established by submitting one of the following to the department:

(1) A copy or facsimile of the applicant's state issued driver's license or identification card.

(2) A copy or facsimile of the document required for an applicant for a driver's license or identification card to establish the applicant's true full name.

(3) An applicant unable to establish legal presence in the United States may fulfill the true full name and date of birth requirement by providing the department a copy or facsimile of the documents used to establish identity pursuant to Section 12801.9. *(Added by Stats. 1994, c. 1149 (A.B.2878), § 8. Amended by Stats.2000, c. 524 (A.B.1792), § 6; Stats.2001, c. 708 (A.B.677), § 4; Stats.2003, c. 555 (A.B.327), § 6; Stats.2004, c. 404 (S.B.1725), § 15; Stats.2006, c. 116 (A.B.2120), § 4; Stats.2007, c. 413 (A.B.1531), § 2; Stats.2017, c. 485 (S.B.611), § 20, eff. Jan. 1, 2018.)*

[1] For public law sections classified to the U.S.C.A., see USCA–Tables.

Cross References

Disabled person placards, annual random audits of applications, see Vehicle Code § 1825.
Fines and penalties, suspension, see Vehicle Code § 40203.5.
Parking facilities for physically handicapped persons and disabled veterans, display of distinguishing placard, see Government Code § 14679.

Research References

2 Witkin, California Criminal Law 4th Crimes Against Property § 199 (2021), Motor Vehicle Items.

§ 22511.6. Cancellation or revocation of distinguishing placards

(a) The Department of Motor Vehicles may cancel or revoke a distinguishing placard issued pursuant to Section 22511.55 or 22511.59 in any of the following events:

(1) When the department is satisfied that the placard was fraudulently obtained or erroneously issued.

(2) When the department determines that the required fee has not been paid and the fee is not paid upon reasonable notice and demand.

(3) When the placard could have been refused when last issued or renewed.

(4) When the department determines that the owner of the placard has committed any offense described in Section 4461 or 4463, involving the placard to be canceled or revoked.

(5) When the department determines that the owner of the placard is deceased.

(b) Whenever the Department of Motor Vehicles cancels or revokes a distinguishing placard, the owner or person in possession of the placard shall immediately return the placard to the department. *(Added by Stats.1984, c. 510, § 2; Stats.1984, c. 1118, § 2. Amended by Stats.1993, c. 1292 (S.B.274), § 14; Stats.1994, c. 1149 (A.B.2878), § 9.)*

§ 22511.7. Designation of parking for disabled persons and veterans

(a) In addition to Section 22511.8 for offstreet parking, a local authority may, by ordinance or resolution, designate onstreet parking spaces for the exclusive use of a vehicle that displays either a special identification license plate issued pursuant to Section 5007 or a distinguishing placard issued pursuant to Section 22511.55 or 22511.59.

(b)(1) Whenever a local authority so designates a parking space, it shall be indicated by blue paint on the curb or edge of the paved portion of the street adjacent to the space. In addition, the local authority shall post immediately adjacent to and visible from the space a sign consisting of a profile view of a wheelchair with occupant in white on a blue background.

(2) The sign required pursuant to paragraph (1) shall clearly and conspicuously state the following: "Minimum Fine $250." This paragraph applies only to signs for parking spaces constructed on or after July 1, 2008, and signs that are replaced on or after July 1, 2008.

(3) If the loading and unloading area of the pavement adjacent to a parking stall or space designated for disabled persons or disabled veterans is to be marked by a border and hatched lines, the border shall be painted blue and the hatched lines shall be painted a suitable contrasting color to the parking space. Blue or white paint is preferred. In addition, within the border the words "No Parking" shall be painted in white letters no less than 12 inches high. This paragraph applies only to parking spaces constructed on or after July 1, 2008, and painting that is done on or after July 1, 2008.

(c) This section does not restrict the privilege granted to disabled persons and disabled veterans by Section 22511.5. *(Added by Stats.1975, c. 688, p. 1636, § 2. Amended by Stats.1976, c. 1096, p. 4961, § 4; Stats.1983, c. 270, § 2, eff. July 15, 1983; Stats.1985, c. 1041, § 8; Stats.1987, c. 314, § 2; Stats.1989, c. 554, § 4; Stats.1990, c. 692 (A.B.3398), § 4; Stats.1994, c. 1149 (A.B.2878), § 10; Stats. 2007, c. 413 (A.B.1531), § 3; Stats.2009, c. 200 (S.B.734), § 13.)*

Cross References

Removal of unauthorized vehicle from physically handicapped parking space, see Vehicle Code § 22652.

Request by state agency for local agency to provide handicapped parking, see Government Code § 14679.

Research References

2 Witkin, California Criminal Law 4th Crimes Against Public Peace and Welfare § 323 (2021), Parking.

§ 22511.8. Offstreet parking; designation of parking for disabled persons and veterans; removal of unauthorized vehicles

(a) A local authority, by ordinance or resolution, and a person in lawful possession of an offstreet parking facility may designate stalls or spaces in an offstreet parking facility owned or operated by the local authority or person for the exclusive use of a vehicle that displays either a special license plate issued pursuant to Section 5007 or a distinguishing placard issued pursuant to Section 22511.55 or 22511.59. The designation shall be made by posting a sign as described in paragraph (1), and by either of the markings described in paragraph (2) or (3):

(1)(A) By posting immediately adjacent to, and visible from, each stall or space, a sign consisting of a profile view of a wheelchair with occupant in white on a blue background.

(B) The sign shall also clearly and conspicuously state the following: "Minimum Fine $250." This subparagraph applies only to signs for parking spaces constructed on or after July 1, 2008, and signs that are replaced on or after July 1, 2008, or as the State Architect deems necessary when renovations, structural repair, alterations, and additions occur to existing buildings and facilities on or after July 1, 2008.

(2)(A) By outlining or painting the stall or space in blue and outlining on the ground in the stall or space in white or suitable contrasting color a profile view depicting a wheelchair with occupant.

(B) The loading and unloading area of the pavement adjacent to a parking stall or space designated for disabled persons or disabled veterans shall be marked by a border and hatched lines. The border shall be painted blue and the hatched lines shall be painted a suitable contrasting color to the parking space. Blue or white paint is preferred. In addition, within the border the words "No Parking" shall be painted in white letters no less than 12 inches high. This subparagraph applies only to parking spaces constructed on or after July 1, 2008, and painting that is done on or after July 1, 2008, or as the State Architect deems necessary when renovations, structural repair, alterations, and additions occur to existing buildings and facilities on or after July 1, 2008.

(3) By outlining a profile view of a wheelchair with occupant in white on a blue background, of the same dimensions as in paragraph (2). The profile view shall be located so that it is visible to a traffic enforcement officer when a vehicle is properly parked in the space.

(b) The Department of General Services under the Division of the State Architect shall develop pursuant to Section 4450 of the Government Code, as appropriate, conforming regulations to ensure compliance with subparagraph (B) of paragraph (1) of subdivision (a) and subparagraph (B) of paragraph (2) of subdivision (a). Initial regulations to implement these provisions shall be adopted as emergency regulations. The adoption of these regulations shall be considered by the Department of General Services to be an emergency necessary for the immediate preservation of the public peace, health and safety, or general welfare.

(c) If posted in accordance with subdivision (e) or (f), the owner or person in lawful possession of a privately owned or operated offstreet parking facility, after notifying the police or sheriff's department, may cause the removal of a vehicle from a stall or space designated pursuant to subdivision (a) in the facility to the nearest public garage unless a special license plate issued pursuant to Section 5007 or distinguishing placard issued pursuant to Section 22511.55 or 22511.59 is displayed on the vehicle.

(d) If posted in accordance with subdivision (e), the local authority owning or operating an offstreet parking facility, after notifying the police or sheriff's department, may cause the removal of a vehicle from a stall or space designated pursuant to subdivision (a) in the facility to the nearest public garage unless a special license plate issued pursuant to Section 5007 or a distinguishing placard issued pursuant to Section 22511.55 or 22511.59 is displayed on the vehicle.

(e) Except as provided in Section 22511.9, the posting required for an offstreet parking facility owned or operated either privately or by a local authority shall consist of a sign not less than 17 by 22 inches in size with lettering not less than one inch in height which clearly and conspicuously states the following: "Unauthorized vehicles parked in designated accessible spaces not displaying distinguishing placards or special license plates issued for persons with disabilities will be towed away at the owner's expense. Towed vehicles may be reclaimed at: ______________________ or by telephoning

(Address)

______________________________."

(Telephone number of local law enforcement agency)

The sign shall be posted in either of the following locations:

(1) Immediately adjacent to, and visible from, the stall or space.

(2) In a conspicuous place at each entrance to the offstreet parking facility.

(f) If the parking facility is privately owned and public parking is prohibited by the posting of a sign meeting the requirements of paragraph (1) of subdivision (a) of Section 22658, the requirements of subdivision (c) may be met by the posting of a sign immediately adjacent to, and visible from, each stall or space indicating that a vehicle not meeting the requirements of subdivision (a) will be removed at the owner's expense and containing the telephone number of the local traffic law enforcement agency.

(g) This section does not restrict the privilege granted to disabled persons and disabled veterans by Section 22511.5. *(Added by Stats.1975, c. 688, p. 1636, § 3. Amended by Stats.1976, c. 1096, p. 4962, § 5; Stats.1982, c. 975, p. 3495, § 7; Stats.1983, c. 270, § 3, eff. July 15, 1983; Stats.1985, c. 312, § 1; Stats.1985, c. 1041, § 9; Stats.1987, c. 314, § 3; Stats.1989, c. 554, § 5; Stats.1990, c. 216 (S.B.2510), § 118; Stats.1991, c. 928 (A.B.1886), § 27, eff. Oct. 14, 1991; Stats.1994, c. 1149 (A.B.2878), § 11; Stats.2004, c. 404 (S.B.1725), § 16; Stats.2007, c. 413 (A.B.1531), § 4; Stats.2009, c. 200 (S.B.734), § 14.)*

Cross References

Immunity from liability removal of vehicle from handicapped parking, see Vehicle Code § 22652.5.
Private parking facilities, see Vehicle Code § 21107.8.
Removal of unauthorized vehicle from physically handicapped parking space, see Vehicle Code § 22652.

Research References

2 Witkin, California Criminal Law 4th Crimes Against Public Peace and Welfare § 323 (2021), Parking.

§ 22511.85. Public offstreet parking facilities; loading and unloading disabled persons; sufficient space

A vehicle, identified with a special license plate issued pursuant to Section 5007 or a distinguishing placard issued pursuant to Section 22511.55 or 22511.59, which is equipped with a lift, ramp, or assistive equipment that is used for the loading and unloading of a person with a disability may park in not more than two adjacent stalls or spaces on a street or highway or in a public or private off-street parking facility if the equipment has been or will be used for loading or unloading a person with a disability, and if there is no single parking space immediately available on the street or highway or within the facility that is suitable for that purpose, including, but not limited to, when there is not sufficient space to operate a vehicle lift, ramp, or assistive equipment, or there is not sufficient room for a person with a disability to exit the vehicle or maneuver once outside the vehicle. *(Added by Stats.2000, c. 215 (A.B.1276), § 3. Amended by Stats.2007, c. 387 (A.B.463), § 1; Stats.2008, c. 179 (S.B.1498), § 221.)*

Research References

2 Witkin, California Criminal Law 4th Crimes Against Public Peace and Welfare § 323 (2021), Parking.

§ 22511.9. Replacement signs relating to parking privileges for disabled persons; contents

Every new or replacement sign installed on or after January 1, 1992, relating to parking privileges for disabled persons shall refer to "disabled persons" rather than "physically handicapped persons" or any other similar term, whenever such a reference is required on a sign. *(Added by Stats.1991, c. 928 (A.B.1886), § 28, eff. Oct. 14, 1991.)*

§ 22511.95. New or replacement signs installed after July 1, 2008; content; parking privileges for disabled persons

All new or replacement signs installed on or after July 1, 2008, relating to parking privileges for disabled persons shall refer to "persons with disabilities" rather than "disabled persons" or any other similar term, whenever the reference is required on the sign. *(Added by Stats.2007, c. 413 (A.B.1531), § 5.)*

Research References

2 Witkin, California Criminal Law 4th Crimes Against Public Peace and Welfare § 323 (2021), Parking.

§ 22511.10. Legislative findings and declarations

The Legislature hereby finds and declares all of the following:

(a) Two and one-half million Californians suffer from some form of chronic obstructive pulmonary disease. Those persons who are not in wheelchairs have difficulty walking long distances.

(b) Encouraging those with physical disabilities to engage in activities outside of the home promotes better health and self-esteem, thereby lowering health costs.

(c) Placing disabled person parking spaces closest to the main entrances of buildings does not cost taxpayers, but provides accessibility to the physically disabled.

(d) It is the intent of the Legislature, in enacting Section 22511.11, to direct the Office of the State Architect to propose regulations that require disabled person parking spaces to be located on the shortest accessible route of travel to an accessible entrance or exit of a building or parking facility. *(Added by Stats.1992, c. 1187 (S.B.2043), § 1.)*

§ 22511.11. Office of State Architect; regulations; location of disabled person parking stalls or spaces

(a) The Office of the State Architect shall propose regulations specifying the location of disabled person parking stalls or spaces designated pursuant to Section 22511.8, for parking facilities constructed or reconstructed pursuant to a building permit issued on or after October 1, 1993. In specifying the placement of those stalls or spaces near buildings or facilities and within parking structures, consideration shall be given to the special access needs of disabled persons.

(b) The Office of the State Architect shall submit the regulations proposed pursuant to subdivision (a) to the State Building Standards Commission on or before July 1, 1993, for approval, adoption, and publication in Title 24 of the California Code of Regulations. *(Added by Stats.1992, c. 1187 (S.B.2043), § 2.)*

§ 22512. Driver or owner of utility service vehicle; exemption from provisions

Except as otherwise indicated in subdivision (b), none of the following provisions shall apply to the driver or owner of any service vehicle owned or operated by or for or operated under contract with a utility or public utility, whether privately, municipally, or publicly owned, used in the construction, operation, removal, or repair of utility or public utility property or facilities, if warning devices are displayed and when the vehicle is stopped, standing, or parked at the site of work involving the construction, operation, removal, or repair of the utility or public utility property or facilities upon, in, over, under, or adjacent to a highway, bicycle lane, bikeway, or bicycle path or trail, or of a vehicle, whether privately, municipally, or publicly owned, if warning devices are displayed and when the vehicle is engaged in authorized work on the highway, bicycle lane, bikeway, or bicycle path or trail:

(a) Sections 21112, 21211, 21707, 21708, 22507.6, 24605, 25253, 25300, 27700, and 27907.

(b) This chapter, except Sections 22507, 22509, 22515, and 22517.

(c) Chapter 10 (commencing with Section 22650). *(Stats.1959, c. 3, p. 1700, § 22512. Amended by Stats.1972, c. 618, p. 1150, § 146; Stats.1974, c. 545, p. 1327, § 210; Stats.1980, c. 391, p. 773, § 2; Stats.1987, c. 499, § 2; Stats.1996, c. 124 (A.B.3470), § 128.)*

Cross References

Off-highway vehicle exemption, see Vehicle Code § 38010.
Public utility defined, see Cal. Const. Art. 12, § 3; Public Utilities Code § 216.
Regulations governing color of lights on public utility repair vehicles, see Vehicle Code §§ 25260, 25260.1.
Speed limit on highways where persons are at work, see Vehicle Code § 22362.
Warning lights and devices on utility vehicles, see Vehicle Code § 25301.

Research References

2 Witkin, California Criminal Law 4th Crimes Against Public Peace and Welfare § 323 (2021), Parking.

§ 22513. Tow trucks; stopping at scene of accident or near disabled vehicle; soliciting an engagement for towing services or to remove vehicle; conditions; documentation and reporting requirements; fees; misdemeanors; exceptions

(a)(1) It is a misdemeanor for a towing company or the owner or operator of a tow truck to stop or cause a person to stop at the scene of an accident or near a disabled vehicle for the purpose of soliciting an engagement for towing services, either directly or indirectly, to furnish towing services, to move a vehicle from a highway, street, or public property when the vehicle has been left unattended or when there is an injury as the result of an accident, or to accrue charges for services furnished under those circumstances, unless requested to perform that service by a law enforcement officer or public agency pursuant to that agency's procedures, or unless summoned to the scene or requested to stop by the owner or operator of a disabled vehicle.

(2)(A) A towing company or the owner or operator of a tow truck summoned, or alleging it was summoned, to the scene by the owner or operator of a disabled vehicle shall possess all of the following information in writing prior to arriving at the scene:

(i) The first and last name and working telephone number of the person who summoned it to the scene.

(ii) The make, model, year, and license plate number of the disabled vehicle.

(iii) The date and time it was summoned to the scene.

(iv) The name of the person who obtained the information in clauses (i), (ii), and (iii).

(B) A towing company or the owner or operator of a tow truck summoned, or alleging it was summoned, to the scene by a motor club, as defined by Section 12142 of the Insurance Code, pursuant to the request of the owner or operator of a disabled vehicle is exempt from the requirements of subparagraph (A), provided it possesses all of the following information in writing prior to arriving at the scene:

(i) The business name of the motor club.

(ii) The identification number the motor club assigns to the referral.

(iii) The date and time it was summoned to the scene by the motor club.

(3) A towing company or the owner or operator of a tow truck requested, or alleging it was requested, to stop at the scene by the owner or operator of a disabled vehicle shall possess all of the following information in writing upon arriving at the scene:

(A) The first and last name and working telephone number of the person who requested the stop.

(B) The make, model, and license plate number, if one is displayed, of the disabled vehicle.

(C) The date and time it was requested to stop.

(D) The name of the person who obtained the information in subparagraphs (A), (B), and (C).

(4) A towing company or the owner or operator of a tow truck summoned or requested, or alleging it was summoned or requested, by a law enforcement officer or public agency pursuant to that agency's procedures to stop at the scene of an accident or near a disabled vehicle for the purpose of soliciting an engagement for towing services, either directly or indirectly, to furnish towing services, or that is expressly authorized to move a vehicle from a highway, street, or public property when the vehicle has been left unattended or when there is an injury as the result of an accident, shall possess all of the following in writing before leaving the scene:

(A) The identity of the law enforcement agency or public agency.

(B) The log number, call number, incident number, or dispatch number assigned to the incident by law enforcement or the public agency, or the surname and badge number of the law enforcement officer, or the surname and employee identification number of the public agency employee.

(C) The date and time of the summons, request, or express authorization.

(5) For purposes of this section, "writing" includes electronic records.

(b) The towing company or the owner or operator of a tow truck shall make the written information described in subdivision (a) available to law enforcement, upon request, from the time it appears at the scene until the time the vehicle is towed and released to a third party, and shall maintain that information for three years. The towing company or owner or operator of a tow truck shall make that information available for inspection and copying within 48 hours of a written request from any officer or agent of a police department, sheriff's department, the Department of the California Highway Patrol, the Attorney General's office, a district attorney's office, or a city attorney's office.

(c)(1) Prior to attaching a vehicle to the tow truck, if the vehicle owner or operator is present at the time and location of the anticipated tow, the towing company or the owner or operator of the tow truck shall furnish the vehicle's owner or operator with a written itemized estimate of all charges and services to be performed. The estimate shall include all of the following:

(A) The name, address, telephone number, and motor carrier permit number of the towing company.

(B) The license plate number of the tow truck performing the tow.

(C) The first and last name of the towing operator, and if different than the towing operator, the first and last name of the person from the towing company furnishing the estimate.

(D) A description and cost for all services, including, but not limited to, charges for labor, special equipment, mileage from dispatch to return, and storage fees, expressed as a 24–hour rate.

(2) The tow truck operator shall obtain the vehicle owner or operator's signature on the itemized estimate and shall furnish a copy to the person who signed the estimate.

(3) The requirements in paragraph (1) may be completed after the vehicle is attached and removed to the nearest safe shoulder or street if done at the request of law enforcement or a public agency, provided the estimate is furnished prior to the removal of the vehicle from the nearest safe shoulder or street.

(4) The towing company or the owner or operator of a tow truck shall maintain the written documents described in this subdivision for three years, and shall make them available for inspection and copying within 48 hours of a written request from any officer or agent of a

police department, sheriff's department, the Department of the California Highway Patrol, the Attorney General's office, a district attorney's office, or a city attorney's office.

(5) This subdivision does not apply to a towing company or the owner or operator of a tow truck summoned to the scene by a motor club, as defined by Section 12142 of the Insurance Code, pursuant to the request of the owner or operator of a disabled vehicle.

(6) This subdivision does not apply to a towing company or the owner or operator of a tow truck summoned to the scene by law enforcement or a public agency pursuant to that agency's procedures, and operating at the scene pursuant to a contract with that law enforcement agency or public agency.

(d)(1) Except as provided in paragraph (2), a towing company or the owner or operator of a tow truck shall not charge a fee for towing or storage, or both, of a vehicle in excess of the greater of the following:

(A) The fee that would have been charged for that towing or storage, or both, made at the request of a law enforcement agency under an agreement between a towing company and the law enforcement agency that exercises primary jurisdiction in the city in which the vehicle was, or was attempted to be, removed, or if not located within a city, the law enforcement agency that exercises primary jurisdiction in the county in which the vehicle was, or was attempted to be, removed.

(B) The fee that would have been charged for that towing or storage, or both, under the rate approved for that towing operator by the Department of the California Highway Patrol for the jurisdiction from which the vehicle was, or was attempted to be, removed.

(2) Paragraph (1) does not apply to the towing or transportation of a vehicle or temporary storage of a vehicle in transit, if the towing or transportation is performed with the prior consent of the owner or operator of the vehicle.

(3) No charge shall be made in excess of the estimated price without the prior consent of the vehicle owner or operator.

(4) All services rendered by a tow company or tow truck operator, including any warranty or zero cost services, shall be recorded on an invoice, as described in subdivision (e) of Section 22651.07. The towing company or the owner or operator of a tow truck shall maintain the written documents described in this subdivision for three years, and shall make the documents available for inspection and copying within 48 hours of a written request from any officer or agent of a police department, sheriff's department, the Department of the California Highway Patrol, the Attorney General's office, a district attorney's office, or a city attorney's office.

(e) A person who willfully violates subdivision (b), (c), or (d) is guilty of a misdemeanor, punishable by a fine of not more than two thousand five hundred dollars ($2,500), or by imprisonment in a county jail for not more than three months, or by both that fine and imprisonment.

(f) This section shall not apply to the following:

(1) A vehicle owned or operated by, or under contract to, a motor club, as defined by Section 12142 of the Insurance Code, which stops to provide services for which compensation is neither requested nor received, provided that those services may not include towing other than that which may be necessary to remove the vehicle to the nearest safe shoulder. The owner or operator of that vehicle may contact a law enforcement agency or other public agency on behalf of a motorist, but may not refer a motorist to a tow truck owner or operator, unless the motorist is a member of the motor club, the motorist is referred to a tow truck owner or operator under contract to the motor club, and, if there is a dispatch facility that services the area and is owned or operated by the motor club, the referral is made through that dispatch facility.

(2) A tow truck operator employed by a law enforcement agency or other public agency.

(3) A tow truck owner or operator acting under contract with a law enforcement or other public agency to abate abandoned vehicles, or to provide towing service or emergency road service to motorists while involved in freeway service patrol operations, to the extent authorized by law. *(Stats.1959, c. 3, p. 1701, § 22513. Amended by Stats.1967, c. 441, p. 1654, § 1; Stats.1988, c. 924, § 8; Stats.1991, c. 755 (S.B.600), § 1; Stats.1991, c. 1004 (S.B.887), § 3; Stats.2015, c. 309 (A.B.1222), § 1, eff. Jan. 1, 2016; Stats.2016, c. 518 (A.B.2167), § 1, eff. Jan. 1, 2017.)*

Cross References

Freeway defined, see Vehicle Code § 332.
Rear lighting equipment for tow trucks and towed vehicles, see Vehicle Code § 24605.
Tow truck defined, see Vehicle Code § 615.
Towing and loading equipment, see Vehicle Code § 29000 et seq.
Warning lights on tow trucks, see Vehicle Code § 25253.

Research References

2 Witkin, California Criminal Law 4th Crimes Against Public Peace and Welfare § 323 (2021), Parking.

§ 22513.1. Business that takes possession of vehicle from tow truck; documentation requirements; misdemeanor

(a)(1) A business taking possession of a vehicle from a tow truck during hours the business is open to the public shall document all of the following:

(A) The name, address, and telephone number of the towing company.

(B) The name and driver's license number, driver's identification number issued by a motor club, as defined in Section 12142 of the Insurance Code, or other government authorized unique identifier of the tow truck operator.

(C) The make, model, and license plate or vehicle identification number.

(D) The date and time that possession was taken of the vehicle.

(2) For purposes of subparagraph (B) of paragraph (1), if a tow truck operator refuses to provide information described in subparagraph (B) of paragraph (1) to a new motor vehicle dealer, as defined in Section 426, a new motor vehicle dealer is in compliance with this section if the new motor vehicle dealer documents the reasonable efforts made to obtain this information from the tow truck operator.

(b) A business taking possession of a vehicle from a tow truck when the business is closed to the public shall document all of the following:

(1) The make, model, and license plate or vehicle identification number.

(2) The date and time that the business first observed the vehicle on its property.

(3) The reasonable effort made by the business to contact the towing company, if identifying information was left with the vehicle, and the vehicle's owner or operator to obtain and document both of the following:

(A) The name, address, and telephone number of the towing company.

(B) The name and driver's license number, driver's identification number issued by a motor club, as defined in Section 12142 of the Insurance Code, or other government authorized unique identifier of the tow truck operator.

(c) The information required in this section shall be maintained for three years and shall be available for inspection and copying within 48 hours of a written request by any officer or agent of a police department, a sheriff's department, the Department of the California Highway Patrol, the Attorney General's office, the Bureau of

Automotive Repair, a district attorney's office, or a city attorney's office.

(d) For purposes of this section, a new motor vehicle dealer, as defined in Section 426, is not open to the public during hours its repair shop is closed to the public.

(e) A person who willfully violates this section is guilty of a misdemeanor, and that violation is punishable by a fine of not more than two thousand five hundred dollars ($2,500), or by imprisonment in a county jail for not more than three months, or by both that fine and imprisonment. *(Added by Stats.2015, c. 309 (A.B.1222), § 2, eff. Jan. 1, 2016. Amended by Stats.2016, c. 518 (A.B.2167), § 2, eff. Jan. 1, 2017; Stats.2017, c. 561 (A.B.1516), § 254, eff. Jan. 1, 2018.)*

§ 22514. Fire hydrants

No person shall stop, park, or leave standing any vehicle within 15 feet of a fire hydrant except as follows:

(a) If the vehicle is attended by a licensed driver who is seated in the front seat and who can immediately move such vehicle in case of necessity.

(b) If the local authority adopts an ordinance or resolution reducing that distance. If the distance is less than 10 feet total length when measured along the curb or edge of the street, the distance shall be indicated by signs or markings.

(c) If the vehicle is owned or operated by a fire department and is clearly marked as a fire department vehicle. *(Stats.1959, c. 3, p. 1701, § 22514. Amended by Stats.1961, c. 1615, p. 3458, § 35; Stats.1987, c. 488, § 1.)*

Cross References

Local authorities defined, see Vehicle Code § 385.
Park defined, see Vehicle Code § 463.
Report of convictions to department, exceptions, see Vehicle Code § 1803 et seq.
Stop or stopping defined, see Vehicle Code § 587.

Research References

2 Witkin, California Criminal Law 4th Crimes Against Public Peace and Welfare § 323 (2021), Parking.

§ 22515. Unattended vehicles

(a) No person driving, or in control of, or in charge of, a motor vehicle shall permit it to stand on any highway unattended without first effectively setting the brakes thereon and stopping the motor thereof.

(b) No person in control of, or in charge of, any vehicle, other than a motor vehicle, shall permit it to stand on any highway without first effectively setting the brakes thereon, or blocking the wheels thereof, to effectively prevent the movement of the vehicle. *(Stats. 1959, c. 3, p. 1701, § 22515. Amended by Stats.1986, c. 362, § 3.)*

Cross References

Exemption of emergency vehicles from rules of the road, exceptions, see Vehicle Code § 21055.
Utility vehicles, application of this section, see Vehicle Code § 22512.

Research References

2 Witkin, California Criminal Law 4th Crimes Against Public Peace and Welfare § 324 (2021), Stopping and Standing.

§ 22516. Locked vehicle

No person shall leave standing a locked vehicle in which there is any person who cannot readily escape therefrom. *(Stats.1959, c. 3, p. 1701, § 22516.)*

Research References

2 Witkin, California Criminal Law 4th Crimes Against Public Peace and Welfare § 324 (2021), Stopping and Standing.

1 Witkin California Criminal Law 4th Crimes Against the Person § 274 (2021), Similar Offenses.

§ 22517. Opening and closing doors

No person shall open the door of a vehicle on the side available to moving traffic unless it is reasonably safe to do so and can be done without interfering with the movement of such traffic, nor shall any person leave a door open on the side of a vehicle available to moving traffic for a period of time longer than necessary to load or unload passengers. *(Stats.1959, c. 3, p. 1701, § 22517. Amended by Stats.1963, c. 162, p. 895, § 1.)*

Cross References

Exemption of emergency vehicles from rules of the road, exceptions, see Vehicle Code § 21055.
Utility vehicles, application of this section, see Vehicle Code § 22512.
Vehicle defined, see Vehicle Code § 670.

Research References

2 Witkin, California Criminal Law 4th Crimes Against Public Peace and Welfare § 324 (2021), Stopping and Standing.

§ 22518. Fringe and transportation corridor parking facilities; authorized vehicles

(a) Fringe and transportation corridor parking facilities constructed, maintained, or operated by the Department of Transportation pursuant to Section 146.5 of the Streets and Highways Code shall be used only by persons using a bicycle or public transit, or engaged in ridesharing, including, but not limited to, carpools or vanpools. A person shall not park a vehicle 30 feet or more in length, engage in loitering or camping, or engage in vending or any other commercial activity on any fringe or transportation corridor parking facility.

(b) This section does not apply to alternatively fueled infrastructure programs in park-and-ride lots owned and operated by the Department of Transportation. *(Added by Stats.1992, c. 1243 (A.B.3090), § 91, eff. Sept. 30, 1992. Amended by Stats.2012, c. 676 (A.B.2583), § 3.)*

§ 22519. Regulation of offstreet parking

Local authorities may by ordinance or resolution prohibit, restrict or regulate the parking, stopping or standing of vehicles on any offstreet parking facility which it owns or operates. No such ordinance or resolution shall apply until signs giving notice thereof have been erected. *(Added by Stats.1959, c. 1486, p. 3778, § 1.)*

Cross References

Local authorities defined, see Vehicle Code § 385.

Research References

2 Witkin, California Criminal Law 4th Crimes Against Public Peace and Welfare § 323 (2021), Parking.

§ 22520.5. Vending merchandise or services near freeways; exceptions; violations; penalties

(a) No person shall solicit, display, sell, offer for sale, or otherwise vend or attempt to vend any merchandise or service while being wholly or partly within any of the following:

(1) The right-of-way of any freeway, including any on ramp, off ramp, or roadway shoulder which lies within the right-of-way of the freeway.

(2) Any roadway or adjacent shoulder within 500 feet of a freeway off ramp or on ramp.

(3) Any sidewalk within 500 feet of a freeway off ramp or on ramp, when vending or attempting to vend to vehicular traffic.

(b) Subdivision (a) does not apply to a roadside rest area or vista point located within a freeway right-of-way which is subject to Section 22520.6, to a tow truck or service vehicle rendering assistance to a disabled vehicle, or to a person issued a permit to vend upon the freeway pursuant to Section 670 of the Streets and Highways Code.

(c) A violation of this section is an infraction. A second or subsequent conviction of a violation of this section is a misdemeanor. *(Added by Stats.1981, c. 936, p. 3540, § 1. Amended by Stats.1983, c. 275, § 2, eff. July 15, 1983; Stats.1984, c. 487, § 1; Stats.1988, c. 924, § 10.)*

Cross References

Displaying, selling, or vending merchandise, foodstuffs, or services within vista points or safety roadside rest areas prohibited, exception, see Streets and Highways Code § 225.5.
Violation as misdemeanor, see Vehicle Code § 40000.13.

Research References

2 Witkin, California Criminal Law 4th Crimes Against Public Peace and Welfare § 324 (2021), Stopping and Standing.

§ 22520.6. Roadside rest areas or vista points; violations; penalties

(a) No person shall engage in any activity within a highway roadside rest area or vista point prohibited by rules and regulations adopted pursuant to Section 225 of the Streets and Highways Code.

(b) A violation of this section is an infraction. A second or subsequent conviction of a violation of this section is a misdemeanor. *(Added by Stats.1983, c. 275, § 3, eff. July 15, 1983.)*

Cross References

Displaying, selling, or vending merchandise, foodstuffs, or services within vista points or safety roadside rest areas prohibited, exception, see Streets and Highways Code § 225.5.
Violation as misdemeanor, see Vehicle Code § 40000.13.

§ 22521. Parking upon or near railroad track

No person shall park a vehicle upon any railroad track or within 7½ feet of the nearest rail. *(Added by Stats.1968, c. 625, p. 1309, § 1.)*

Research References

2 Witkin, California Criminal Law 4th Crimes Against Public Peace and Welfare § 323 (2021), Parking.

§ 22522. Parking near sidewalk access ramps

No person shall park a vehicle within three feet of any sidewalk access ramp constructed at, or adjacent to, a crosswalk or at any other location on a sidewalk so as to be accessible to and usable by the physically disabled, if the area adjoining the ramp is designated by either a sign or red paint. *(Added by Stats.1974, c. 760, p. 1675, § 1. Amended by Stats.1994, c. 221 (S.B.1378), § 2, operative July 1, 1995; Stats.1999, c. 1007 (S.B.532), § 22.)*

Cross References

Parking penalties, additional assessments, see Vehicle Code § 40203.6.

Research References

2 Witkin, California Criminal Law 4th Crimes Against Public Peace and Welfare § 323 (2021), Parking.

§ 22523. Abandonment; fine; liability for cost of removal and disposition; offense; liability for deficiency

(a) No person shall abandon a vehicle upon any highway.

(b) No person shall abandon a vehicle upon public or private property without the express or implied consent of the owner or person in lawful possession or control of the property.

(c) Any person convicted of a violation of this section shall be punished by a fine of not less than one hundred dollars ($100) and shall provide proof that the costs of removal and disposition of the vehicle have been paid. No part of any fine imposed shall be suspended. The fine may be paid in installments if the court determines that the defendant is unable to pay the entire amount in one payment.

(d) Proof that the costs of removal and disposition of the vehicle have been paid shall not be required if proof is provided to the court that the vehicle was stolen prior to abandonment. That proof may consist of a police report or other evidence acceptable to the court.

(e) The costs required to be paid for the removal and disposition of any vehicle determined to be abandoned pursuant to Section 22669 shall not exceed those for towing and seven days of storage. This subdivision does not apply if the registered owner or legal owner has completed and returned to the lienholder a "Declaration of Opposition" form within the time specified in Section 22851.8.

(f)(1) If a vehicle is abandoned in violation of subdivision (b) and is not redeemed after impound, the last registered owner is guilty of an infraction. In addition to any other penalty, the registered owner shall be liable for any deficiency remaining after disposal of the vehicle under Section 3071 or 3072 of the Civil Code or Section 22851.10 of this code.

(2) The filing of a report of sale or transfer of the vehicle pursuant to Section 5602, the filing of a vehicle theft report with a law enforcement agency, or the filing of a form or notice with the department pursuant to subdivision (b) of Section 4456 or Section 5900 or 5901 relieves the registered owner of liability under this subdivision. *(Added by Stats.1988, c. 1267, § 5, eff. Sept. 26, 1988, operative July 1, 1989. Amended by Stats.1990, c. 111 (S.B.2006), § 1; Stats.1996, c. 676 (S.B.1111), § 2.)*

Cross References

Highway defined, see Vehicle Code §§ 360, 591, 592.
Movement of abandoned vehicle standing on highway, authority of peace officer, see Vehicle Code § 22654.
Removal of abandoned vehicles, see Vehicle Code § 22669.
Report of vehicles stored in a garage, repair shop, parking lot or trailer park or public parking area for 30 days, see Vehicle Code § 10652.
Violation, punishment, see Vehicle Code § 42001.5.

§ 22524. Presumption; overcoming presumption

(a) The abandonment of any vehicle in a manner as provided in Section 22523 shall constitute a prima facie presumption that the last registered owner of record is responsible for the abandonment and is thereby liable for the cost of removal and disposition of the vehicle.

(b) An owner who has made a bona fide sale or transfer of a vehicle and has delivered possession of the vehicle to a purchaser may overcome the presumption prescribed in subdivision (a) by demonstrating that he or she has complied with Section 5900 or providing other proof satisfactory to the court.

(c) This section shall become operative on July 1, 1989. *(Added by Stats.1988, c. 1267, § 7, eff. Sept. 26, 1988, operative July 1, 1989.)*

Cross References

Presumptions, see Evidence Code § 600 et seq.

§ 22524.5. Automobile insurance; ordinary and reasonable towing and storage charges; accident or stolen recovery; discharge of obligation; unreasonable fees; agreement between law enforcement agency and towing company

(a) Any insurer that is responsible for coverage for ordinary and reasonable towing and storage charges under an automobile insurance policy to an insured or on behalf of an insured to a valid claimant, is liable for those charges to the person performing those services when a vehicle is towed and stored as a result of an accident or stolen recovery. The insurer may discharge the obligation by making payment to the person performing the towing and storage services or to the insured or on behalf of the insured to the claimant.

(b) Any insured or claimant who has received payment, which includes towing and storage charges, from an insurer for a loss relating to a vehicle is liable for those charges to the person performing those services.

(c)(1) All towing and storage fees charged when those services are performed as a result of an accident or recovery of a stolen vehicle shall be reasonable.

(2)(A) For purposes of this section, a towing and storage charge shall be deemed reasonable if it does not exceed those fees and rates charged for similar services provided in response to requests initiated by a public agency, including, but not limited to, the Department of the California Highway Patrol or local police department.

(B) A storage rate and fee shall also be deemed reasonable if it is comparable to storage-related rates and fees charged by other facilities in the same locale. This does not preclude a rate or fee that is higher or lower if it is otherwise reasonable.

(3) The following rates and fees are presumptively unreasonable:

(A) Administrative or filing fees, except those incurred related to documentation from the Department of Motor Vehicles and those related to the lien sale of a vehicle.

(B) Security fees.

(C) Dolly fees.

(D) Load and unload fees.

(E) Pull–out fees.

(F) Gate fees, except when the owner or insurer of the vehicle requests that the vehicle be released outside of regular business hours.

(d) Notwithstanding this section, an insurer shall comply with all of its obligations under Section 2695.8 of Chapter 5 of Title 10 of the California Code of Regulations.

(e) Nothing in paragraph (3) of subdivision (c) prohibits any fees authorized in an agreement between a law enforcement agency and a towing company, if the tow was initiated by the law enforcement agency. *(Added by Stats.1986, c. 1380, § 1. Amended by Stats.2018, c. 434 (A.B.2392), § 2, eff. Jan. 1, 2019.)*

Cross References

Charges for towing or storage, Towing and Storage Fees and Access Notice, rights of vehicle owner, payment by bank draft, penalties, exceptions, see Vehicle Code § 22651.07.
Motor vehicle storage fees, see Vehicle Code § 10652.5.

§ 22525. Vanpool vehicles; use of state highway bus stops; local ordinance or resolution

Local authorities may by ordinance or resolution authorize vanpool vehicles to utilize designated state highway bus stops.

The ordinance or resolution shall be submitted to the Department of Transportation for approval. No ordinance or resolution shall become effective until approved by the department. The department shall review the ordinance or resolution within 45 days after receipt. *(Added by Stats.1987, c. 262, § 1.)*

§ 22526. Anti–Gridlock Act of 1987; parking or stopping violation

(a) Notwithstanding any official traffic control signal indication to proceed, a driver of a vehicle shall not enter an intersection or marked crosswalk unless there is sufficient space on the other side of the intersection or marked crosswalk to accommodate the vehicle driven without obstructing the through passage of vehicles from either side.

(b) A driver of a vehicle which is making a turn at an intersection who is facing a steady circular yellow or yellow arrow signal shall not enter the intersection or marked crosswalk unless there is sufficient space on the other side of the intersection or marked crosswalk to accommodate the vehicle driven without obstructing the through passage of vehicles from either side.

(c) A driver of a vehicle shall not enter a railroad or rail transit crossing, notwithstanding any official traffic control device or signal indication to proceed, unless there is sufficient undercarriage clearance to cross the intersection without obstructing the through passage of a railway vehicle, including, but not limited to, a train, trolley, or city transit vehicle.

(d) A driver of a vehicle shall not enter a railroad or rail transit crossing, notwithstanding any official traffic control device or signal indication to proceed, unless there is sufficient space on the other side of the railroad or rail transit crossing to accommodate the vehicle driven and any railway vehicle, including, but not limited to, a train, trolley, or city transit vehicle.

(e) A local authority may post appropriate signs at the entrance to intersections indicating the prohibition in subdivisions (a), (b), and (c).

(f) A violation of this section is not a violation of a law relating to the safe operation of vehicles and is the following:

(1) A stopping violation when a notice to appear has been issued by a peace officer described in Section 830.1, 830.2, or 830.33 of the Penal Code.

(2) A parking violation when a notice of parking violation is issued by a person, other than a peace officer described in paragraph (1), who is authorized to enforce parking statutes and regulations.

(g) This section shall be known and may be cited as the Anti–Gridlock Act of 1987. *(Added by Stats.1987, c. 739, § 1. Amended by Stats.1993, c. 647 (S.B.952), § 2; Stats.1996, c. 116 (S.B.1527), § 2; Stats.2001, c. 504 (A.B.1280), § 7; Stats.2005, c. 716 (A.B.1067), § 6; Stats.2010, c. 216 (A.B.2144), § 11.)*

Cross References

Conviction of infraction for violation of section, see Vehicle Code § 42001.1.
Duration of prohibition against operation of commercial motor vehicle, see Vehicle Code § 15312.
Obstructing railroad track, punishment, see Penal Code § 218.1.
Rail transit related traffic violations, county populations greater than 500,000, punishment, see Penal Code § 369b.
Railroad grade crossing violations, see Vehicle Code § 42001.16.
Suspension or revocation of driver's license, conviction of a violation pursuant to this section, no violation point count, see Vehicle Code § 12810.4.

Research References

2 Witkin, California Criminal Law 4th Crimes Against Public Peace and Welfare § 324 (2021), Stopping and Standing.

CHAPTER 10. REMOVAL OF PARKED AND ABANDONED VEHICLES

ARTICLE 1. AUTHORITY TO REMOVE VEHICLES

§ 22650. Prohibition of removal; reasonable seizure; hearings concerning storage; court actions

(a) It is unlawful for a peace officer or an unauthorized person to remove an unattended vehicle from a highway to a garage or to any other place, except as provided in this code.

(b) Any removal of a vehicle is a seizure under the Fourth Amendment of the Constitution of the United States and Section 13 of Article I of the California Constitution, and shall be reasonable and subject to the limits set forth in Fourth Amendment jurisprudence. A removal pursuant to an authority, including, but not limited to, as provided in Section 22651, that is based on community caretaking, is only reasonable if the removal is necessary to achieve the community caretaking need, such as ensuring the safe flow of traffic or protecting property from theft or vandalism.

(c) Those law enforcement and other agencies identified in this chapter as having the authority to remove vehicles shall also have the authority to provide hearings in compliance with the provisions of Section 22852. During these hearings the storing agency shall have the burden of establishing the authority for, and the validity of, the removal.

(d) This section does not prevent a review or other action as may be permitted by the laws of this state by a court of competent jurisdiction. *(Stats.1959, c. 3, p. 1701, § 22650. Amended by Stats.1979, c. 1022, p. 3490, § 1; Stats.2018, c. 592 (A.B.2876), § 1, eff. Jan. 1, 2019.)*

Cross References

Abandoned vehicle, removal, see Vehicle Code § 22669.
Movement of vehicle standing on highway, authority of peace officer, see Vehicle Code § 22654.
Parking of utility vehicles, see Vehicle Code § 22512.
Peace officer defined, see Penal Code §§ 7, 830 et seq., 852.1.
Private property, removal of vehicles, see Vehicle Code § 22653.
Removal and seizure of vehicle, release of vehicle to registered owner, see Vehicle Code § 2480.
Rules of the road, exemption of authorized emergency vehicles, see Vehicle Code § 21055.

§ 22651. Circumstances permitting removal

A peace officer, as defined in Chapter 4.5 (commencing with Section 830) of Title 3 of Part 2 of the Penal Code, or a regularly employed and salaried employee, who is engaged in directing traffic or enforcing parking laws and regulations, of a city, county, or jurisdiction of a state agency in which a vehicle is located, may remove a vehicle located within the territorial limits in which the officer or employee may act, under the following circumstances:

(a) If a vehicle is left unattended upon a bridge, viaduct, or causeway or in a tube or tunnel where the vehicle constitutes an obstruction to traffic.

(b) If a vehicle is parked or left standing upon a highway in a position so as to obstruct the normal movement of traffic or in a condition so as to create a hazard to other traffic upon the highway.

(c) If a vehicle is found upon a highway or public land and a report has previously been made that the vehicle is stolen or a complaint has been filed and a warrant thereon is issued charging that the vehicle was embezzled.

(d) If a vehicle is illegally parked so as to block the entrance to a private driveway and it is impractical to move the vehicle from in front of the driveway to another point on the highway.

(e) If a vehicle is illegally parked so as to prevent access by firefighting equipment to a fire hydrant and it is impracticable to move the vehicle from in front of the fire hydrant to another point on the highway.

(f) If a vehicle, except highway maintenance or construction equipment, is stopped, parked, or left standing for more than four hours upon the right-of-way of a freeway that has full control of access and no crossings at grade and the driver, if present, cannot move the vehicle under its own power.

(g) If the person in charge of a vehicle upon a highway or public land is, by reason of physical injuries or illness, incapacitated to an extent so as to be unable to provide for its custody or removal.

(h)(1) If an officer arrests a person driving or in control of a vehicle for an alleged offense and the officer is, by this code or other law, required or permitted to take, and does take, the person into custody.

(2) If an officer serves a notice of an order of suspension or revocation pursuant to Section 13388 or 13389.

(i)(1) If a vehicle, other than a rented vehicle, is found upon a highway or public land, or is removed pursuant to this code, and it is known that the vehicle has been issued five or more notices of parking violations to which the owner or person in control of the vehicle has not responded within 21 calendar days of notice of citation issuance or citation issuance or 14 calendar days of the mailing of a notice of delinquent parking violation to the agency responsible for processing notices of parking violations, or the registered owner of the vehicle is known to have been issued five or more notices for failure to pay or failure to appear in court for traffic violations for which a certificate has not been issued by the magistrate or clerk of the court hearing the case showing that the case has been adjudicated or concerning which the registered owner's record has not been cleared pursuant to Chapter 6 (commencing with Section 41500) of Division 17, the vehicle may be impounded until that person furnishes to the impounding law enforcement agency all of the following:

(A) Evidence of his or her identity.

(B) An address within this state where he or she can be located.

(C) Satisfactory evidence that all parking penalties due for the vehicle and all other vehicles registered to the registered owner of the impounded vehicle, and all traffic violations of the registered owner, have been cleared.

(2) The requirements in subparagraph (C) of paragraph (1) shall be fully enforced by the impounding law enforcement agency on and after the time that the Department of Motor Vehicles is able to provide access to the necessary records.

(3) A notice of parking violation issued for an unlawfully parked vehicle shall be accompanied by a warning that repeated violations may result in the impounding of the vehicle. In lieu of furnishing satisfactory evidence that the full amount of parking penalties or bail has been deposited, that person may demand to be taken without unnecessary delay before a magistrate, for traffic offenses, or a hearing examiner, for parking offenses, within the county where the offenses charged are alleged to have been committed and who has jurisdiction of the offenses and is nearest or most accessible with reference to the place where the vehicle is impounded. Evidence of current registration shall be produced after a vehicle has been impounded, or, at the discretion of the impounding law enforcement agency, a notice to appear for violation of subdivision (a) of Section 4000 shall be issued to that person.

(4) A vehicle shall be released to the legal owner, as defined in Section 370, if the legal owner does all of the following:

(A) Pays the cost of towing and storing the vehicle.

(B) Submits evidence of payment of fees as provided in Section 9561.

(C) Completes an affidavit in a form acceptable to the impounding law enforcement agency stating that the vehicle was not in possession of the legal owner at the time of occurrence of the offenses relating to standing or parking. A vehicle released to a legal owner under this subdivision is a repossessed vehicle for purposes of disposition or sale. The impounding agency shall have a lien on any surplus that remains upon sale of the vehicle to which the registered owner is or may be entitled, as security for the full amount of the parking penalties for all notices of parking violations issued for the vehicle and for all local administrative charges imposed pursuant to Section 22850.5. The legal owner shall promptly remit to, and deposit with, the agency responsible for processing notices of parking violations from that surplus, on receipt of that surplus, the full amount of the parking penalties for all notices of parking violations issued for the vehicle and for all local administrative charges imposed pursuant to Section 22850.5.

(5) The impounding agency that has a lien on the surplus that remains upon the sale of a vehicle to which a registered owner is entitled pursuant to paragraph (4) has a deficiency claim against the registered owner for the full amount of the parking penalties for all notices of parking violations issued for the vehicle and for all local administrative charges imposed pursuant to Section 22850.5, less the amount received from the sale of the vehicle.

(j) If a vehicle is found illegally parked and there are no license plates or other evidence of registration displayed, the vehicle may be impounded until the owner or person in control of the vehicle furnishes the impounding law enforcement agency evidence of his or her identity and an address within this state where he or she can be located.

(k) If a vehicle is parked or left standing upon a highway for 72 or more consecutive hours in violation of a local ordinance authorizing removal.

(*l*) If a vehicle is illegally parked on a highway in violation of a local ordinance forbidding standing or parking and the use of a highway, or a portion thereof, is necessary for the cleaning, repair, or construction of the highway, or for the installation of underground utilities, and signs giving notice that the vehicle may be removed are erected or placed at least 24 hours prior to the removal by a local authority pursuant to the ordinance.

(m) If the use of the highway, or a portion of the highway, is authorized by a local authority for a purpose other than the normal flow of traffic or for the movement of equipment, articles, or structures of unusual size, and the parking of a vehicle would prohibit or interfere with that use or movement, and signs giving notice that the vehicle may be removed are erected or placed at least 24 hours prior to the removal by a local authority pursuant to the ordinance.

(n) Whenever a vehicle is parked or left standing where local authorities, by resolution or ordinance, have prohibited parking and have authorized the removal of vehicles. Except as provided in subdivisions (v) and (w), a vehicle shall not be removed unless signs are posted giving notice of the removal.

(*o*)(1) If a vehicle is found or operated upon a highway, public land, or an offstreet parking facility under any of the following circumstances:

(A) With a registration expiration date in excess of six months before the date it is found or operated on the highway, public lands, or the offstreet parking facility.

(B) Displaying in, or upon, the vehicle, a registration card, identification card, temporary receipt, license plate, special plate, registration sticker, device issued pursuant to Section 4853, or permit that was not issued for that vehicle, or is not otherwise lawfully used on that vehicle under this code.

(C) Displaying in, or upon, the vehicle, an altered, forged, counterfeit, or falsified registration card, identification card, temporary receipt, license plate, special plate, registration sticker, device issued pursuant to Section 4853, or permit.

(D)(i) The vehicle is operating using autonomous technology, without the registered owner or manufacturer of the vehicle having first applied for, and obtained, a valid permit that is required to operate the vehicle on public roads pursuant to Section 38750, and Article 3.7 (commencing with Section 227.00) and Article 3.8 (commencing with Section 228.00) of Title 13 of the California Code of Regulations.

(ii) The vehicle is operating using autonomous technology after the registered owner or person in control of the vehicle received notice that the vehicle's permit required for the operation of the vehicle pursuant to Section 38750, and Article 3.7 (commencing with Section 227.00) and Article 3.8 (commencing with Section 228.00) of

Title 13 of the California Code of Regulations is suspended, terminated, or revoked.

(iii) For purposes of this subdivision, the terms "autonomous technology" and "autonomous vehicle" have the same meanings as in Section 38750.

(iv) This subparagraph does not provide the authority for a peace officer to stop an autonomous vehicle solely for the purpose of determining whether the vehicle is operating using autonomous technology without a valid permit required to operate the autonomous vehicle on public roads pursuant to Section 38750, and Article 3.7 (commencing with Section 227.00) and Article 3.8 (commencing with Section 228.00) of Title 13 of the California Code of Regulations.

(2) If a vehicle described in paragraph (1) is occupied, only a peace officer, as defined in Chapter 4.5 (commencing with Section 830) of Title 3 of Part 2 of the Penal Code, may remove the vehicle.

(3) For the purposes of this subdivision, the vehicle shall be released under any of the following circumstances:

(A) If the vehicle has been removed pursuant to subparagraph (A), (B), or (C) of paragraph (1), to the registered owner of, or person in control of, the vehicle only after the owner or person furnishes the storing law enforcement agency with proof of current registration and a valid driver's license to operate the vehicle.

(B) If the vehicle has been removed pursuant to subparagraph (D) of paragraph (1), to the registered owner of, or person in control of, the autonomous vehicle, after the registered owner or person furnishes the storing law enforcement agency with proof of current registration and a valid driver's license, if required to operate the autonomous vehicle, and either of the following:

(i) Proof of a valid permit required to operate the autonomous vehicle using autonomous technology on public roads pursuant to Section 38750, and Article 3.7 (commencing with Section 227.00) and Article 3.8 (commencing with Section 228.00) of Title 13 of the California Code of Regulations.

(ii) A declaration or sworn statement to the Department of Motor Vehicles that states that the autonomous vehicle will not be operated using autonomous technology upon public roads without first obtaining a valid permit to operate the vehicle pursuant to Section 38750, and Article 3.7 (commencing with Section 227.00) and Article 3.8 (commencing with Section 228.00) of Title 13 of the California Code of Regulations.

(C) To the legal owner or the legal owner's agency, without payment of any fees, fines, or penalties for parking tickets or registration and without proof of current registration, if the vehicle will only be transported pursuant to the exemption specified in Section 4022 and if the legal owner does all of the following:

(i) Pays the cost of towing and storing the vehicle.

(ii) Completes an affidavit in a form acceptable to the impounding law enforcement agency stating that the vehicle was not in possession of the legal owner at the time of occurrence of an offense relating to standing or parking. A vehicle released to a legal owner under this subdivision is a repossessed vehicle for purposes of disposition or sale. The impounding agency has a lien on any surplus that remains upon sale of the vehicle to which the registered owner is or may be entitled, as security for the full amount of parking penalties for any notices of parking violations issued for the vehicle and for all local administrative charges imposed pursuant to Section 22850.5. Upon receipt of any surplus, the legal owner shall promptly remit to, and deposit with, the agency responsible for processing notices of parking violations from that surplus, the full amount of the parking penalties for all notices of parking violations issued for the vehicle and for all local administrative charges imposed pursuant to Section 22850.5.

(4) The impounding agency that has a lien on the surplus that remains upon the sale of a vehicle to which a registered owner is entitled has a deficiency claim against the registered owner for the full amount of parking penalties for any notices of parking violations issued for the vehicle and for all local administrative charges imposed pursuant to Section 22850.5, less the amount received from the sale of the vehicle.

(5) As used in this subdivision, "offstreet parking facility" means an offstreet facility held open for use by the public for parking vehicles and includes a publicly owned facility for offstreet parking, and a privately owned facility for offstreet parking if a fee is not charged for the privilege to park and it is held open for the common public use of retail customers.

(p) If the peace officer issues the driver of a vehicle a notice to appear for a violation of Section 12500, 14601, 14601.1, 14601.2, 14601.3, 14601.4, 14601.5, or 14604, and the vehicle is not impounded pursuant to Section 22655.5. A vehicle so removed from the highway or public land, or from private property after having been on a highway or public land, shall not be released to the registered owner or his or her agent, except upon presentation of the registered owner's or his or her agent's currently valid driver's license to operate the vehicle and proof of current vehicle registration, to the impounding law enforcement agency, or upon order of a court.

(q) If a vehicle is parked for more than 24 hours on a portion of highway that is located within the boundaries of a common interest development, as defined in Section 4100 or 6534 of the Civil Code, and signs, as required by paragraph (1) of subdivision (a) of Section 22658 of this code, have been posted on that portion of highway providing notice to drivers that vehicles parked thereon for more than 24 hours will be removed at the owner's expense, pursuant to a resolution or ordinance adopted by the local authority.

(r) If a vehicle is illegally parked and blocks the movement of a legally parked vehicle.

(s)(1) If a vehicle, except highway maintenance or construction equipment, an authorized emergency vehicle, or a vehicle that is properly permitted or otherwise authorized by the Department of Transportation, is stopped, parked, or left standing for more than eight hours within a roadside rest area or viewpoint.

(2) Notwithstanding paragraph (1), if a commercial motor vehicle, as defined in paragraph (1) of subdivision (b) of Section 15210, is stopped, parked, or left standing for more than 10 hours within a roadside rest area or viewpoint.

(3) For purposes of this subdivision, a roadside rest area or viewpoint is a publicly maintained vehicle parking area, adjacent to a highway, utilized for the convenient, safe stopping of a vehicle to enable motorists to rest or to view the scenery. If two or more roadside rest areas are located on opposite sides of the highway, or upon the center divider, within seven miles of each other, then that combination of rest areas is considered to be the same rest area.

(t) If a peace officer issues a notice to appear for a violation of Section 25279.

(u) If a peace officer issues a citation for a violation of Section 11700, and the vehicle is being offered for sale.

(v)(1) If a vehicle is a mobile billboard advertising display, as defined in Section 395.5, and is parked or left standing in violation of a local resolution or ordinance adopted pursuant to subdivision (m) of Section 21100, if the registered owner of the vehicle was previously issued a warning citation for the same offense, pursuant to paragraph (2).

(2) Notwithstanding subdivision (a) of Section 22507, a city or county, in lieu of posting signs noticing a local ordinance prohibiting mobile billboard advertising displays adopted pursuant to subdivision (m) of Section 21100, may provide notice by issuing a warning citation advising the registered owner of the vehicle that he or she may be subject to penalties upon a subsequent violation of the ordinance, that may include the removal of the vehicle as provided in paragraph (1). A city or county is not required to provide further

notice for a subsequent violation prior to the enforcement of penalties for a violation of the ordinance.

(w)(1) If a vehicle is parked or left standing in violation of a local ordinance or resolution adopted pursuant to subdivision (p) of Section 21100, if the registered owner of the vehicle was previously issued a warning citation for the same offense, pursuant to paragraph (2).

(2) Notwithstanding subdivision (a) of Section 22507, a city or county, in lieu of posting signs noticing a local ordinance regulating advertising signs adopted pursuant to subdivision (p) of Section 21100, may provide notice by issuing a warning citation advising the registered owner of the vehicle that he or she may be subject to penalties upon a subsequent violation of the ordinance that may include the removal of the vehicle as provided in paragraph (1). A city or county is not required to provide further notice for a subsequent violation prior to the enforcement of penalties for a violation of the ordinance. *(Stats.1959, c. 3, p. 1701, § 22651. Amended by Stats.1959, c. 972, p. 3003, § 1; Stats.1960, 1st Ex.Sess., c. 59, p. 408, § 3; Stats.1963, c. 1004, p. 2271, § 2; Stats.1967, c. 543, p. 1891, § 1; Stats.1968, c. 749, p. 1452, § 1; Stats.1969, c. 1116, p. 2177, § 1; Stats.1970, c. 886, p. 1620, § 1; Stats.1971, c. 130, p. 172, § 1, operative May 3, 1972; Stats.1974, c. 545, p. 1327, § 211; Stats.1977, c. 73, p. 477, § 1; Stats.1977, c. 486, p. 1605, § 2; Stats.1977, c. 1129, p. 3624, § 2; Stats.1979, c. 831, p. 2874, § 1; Stats.1979, c. 909, p. 3123, § 2.3; Stats.1980, c. 1340, p. 4735, § 31, eff. Sept. 30, 1980; Stats.1981, c. 343, p. 1501, § 1; Stats.1982, c. 344, p. 1647, § 1; Stats.1983, c. 816, § 1; Stats.1983, c. 1017, § 3; Stats.1985, c. 1007, § 1; Stats.1985, c. 1126, § 5, eff. Sept. 28, 1985; Stats.1985, c. 1126, § 6, eff. Sept. 28, 1985, operative April 1, 1986; Stats.1986, c. 328, § 2; Stats.1986, c. 1236, § 2; Stats.1986, c. 1262, § 1; Stats.1987, c. 521, § 1, eff. Sept. 11, 1987; Stats.1988, c. 619, § 1; Stats.1988, c. 1008, § 3; Stats.1989, c. 331, § 1; Stats.1991, c. 90 (A.B.1297), § 68, eff. June 30, 1991; Stats.1991, c. 189 (A.B.544), § 40, eff. July 29, 1991; Stats.1992, c. 633 (A.B.1067), § 3; Stats.1992, c. 1242 (S.B.602), § 3; Stats.1992, c. 1244 (A.B.408), § 5, operative July 1, 1993; Stats.1993, c. 272 (A.B.301), § 42, eff. Aug. 2, 1993; Stats.1993, c. 614 (A.B.481), § 1; Stats.1993, c. 1093 (A.B.780), § 1.5; Stats.1994, c. 268 (A.B.3017), § 2; Stats.1994, c. 938 (S.B.1295), § 12, eff. Sept. 28, 1994; Stats.1994, c. 1220 (A.B.3132), § 60, eff. Sept. 30, 1994; Stats.1994, c. 1221 (S.B.1758), § 17; Stats.1995, c. 734 (A.B.1228), § 1; Stats.1996, c. 10 (A.B.1869), § 16, eff. Feb. 9, 1996; Stats.1996, c. 1142 (S.B.1797), § 8, eff. Sept. 30, 1996; Stats.1996, c. 1154 (A.B.3020), § 69, eff. Sept. 30, 1996; Stats.1996, c. 1156 (A.B.3157), § 3.7; Stats.1998, c. 118 (S.B.1186), § 11.5, operative July 1, 1999; Stats.1999, c. 22 (S.B.24), § 17.5, eff. May 26, 1999, operative July 1, 1999; Stats.2007, c. 453 (A.B.1589), § 1; Stats.2007, c. 749 (A.B.1165), § 4.5, operative Jan. 1, 2009; Stats.2008, c. 460 (A.B. 2402), § 1; Stats.2008, c. 736 (A.B.2042), § 2; Stats.2009, c. 140 (A.B.1164), § 180; Stats.2010, c. 615 (A.B.2756), § 4; Stats.2011, c. 341 (S.B.565), § 4; Stats.2011, c. 538 (A.B.1298), § 4.5; Stats.2012, c. 181 (A.B.806), § 81, operative Jan. 1, 2014; Stats.2012, c. 769 (A.B.2679), § 38; Stats.2013, c. 605 (S.B.752), § 50; Stats.2018, c. 667 (A.B.87), § 1, eff. Jan. 1, 2019.)*

Law Revision Commission Comments

Subdivision (q) of Section 22651 is amended to correct a cross-reference to former Civil Code Section 1351(c). [40 Cal.L.Rev.Comm. Reports 235 (2010)].

Subdivision (q) of Section 22651 is amended to add a cross-reference to Civil Code Section 6534, reflecting the enactment of the Commercial and Industrial Common Interest Development Act (Civ. Code §§ 6500–6876). [42 Cal. L.Rev.Comm. Reports 1 (2012)].

Cross References

Abandoned vehicle, removal, see Vehicle Code § 22669.
Arrested person, taking before magistrate, see Vehicle Code §§ 40302, 40303.
Department of the California Highway Patrol, generally, see Vehicle Code § 2100 et seq.
Freeway defined, see Vehicle Code § 332.
Lien sales, impounded vehicles, see Vehicle Code § 22851.1.
Local regulations, see Vehicle Code § 21100 et seq.
Private property, removal of vehicles, see Vehicle Code § 22653.
Private road or driveway defined, see Vehicle Code § 490.
Registered owner, responsibility for unattended vehicle, see Vehicle Code § 40200 et seq.
Release of vehicle to registered owner or agent, see Vehicle Code § 14602.
Removal of unauthorized vehicle from physically handicapped parking space, see Vehicle Code § 22652.
Removing standing vehicle from highway by authorized peace officer, see Vehicle Code § 22654.
Snow areas, parking in, see Vehicle Code § 22510.
Stolen vehicles, reports, see Vehicle Code § 10500 et seq.
Storage of vehicles, see Vehicle Code § 22850 et seq.
Transportation of agricultural irrigation supplies, inspection of bills of lading, shipping, or delivery papers, care of apprehended supplies, see Vehicle Code § 2810.2.
Utility vehicles, stopping, standing or parking, see Vehicle Code §§ 22512, 25301.
Vehicle parked or placed on highway for purpose of selling articles, removal, see Streets and Highways Code § 731.

Research References

4 Witkin, California Criminal Law 4th Illegally Obtained Evidence § 203 (2021), In General.
4 Witkin, California Criminal Law 4th Illegally Obtained Evidence § 204 (2021), Inventory Search Under Standard Police Procedures.
4 Witkin, California Criminal Law 4th Illegally Obtained Evidence § 205 (2021), When Vehicle May be Impounded.
4 Witkin, California Criminal Law 4th Illegally Obtained Evidence § 299 (2021), Illustrations: Detention was Reasonable.
4 Witkin, California Criminal Law 4th Pretrial Proceedings § 45 (2021), In General.

§ 22651.05. Trained volunteers of state or local law enforcement agencies; requirements; circumstances permitting removal

(a) A trained volunteer of a state or local law enforcement agency, who is engaged in directing traffic or enforcing parking laws and regulations, of a city, county, or jurisdiction of a state agency in which a vehicle is located, may remove or authorize the removal of a vehicle located within the territorial limits in which an officer or employee of that agency may act, under any of the following circumstances:

(1) When a vehicle is parked or left standing upon a highway for 72 or more consecutive hours in violation of a local ordinance authorizing the removal.

(2) When a vehicle is illegally parked or left standing on a highway in violation of a local ordinance forbidding standing or parking and the use of a highway, or a portion thereof, is necessary for the cleaning, repair, or construction of the highway, or for the installation of underground utilities, and signs giving notice that the vehicle may be removed are erected or placed at least 24 hours prior to the removal by local authorities pursuant to the ordinance.

(3) Wherever the use of the highway, or a portion thereof, is authorized by local authorities for a purpose other than the normal flow of traffic or for the movement of equipment, articles, or structures of unusual size, and the parking of a vehicle would prohibit or interfere with that use or movement, and signs giving notice that the vehicle may be removed are erected or placed at least 24 hours prior to the removal by local authorities pursuant to the ordinance.

(4) Whenever a vehicle is parked or left standing where local authorities, by resolution or ordinance, have prohibited parking and have authorized the removal of vehicles. A vehicle may not be removed unless signs are posted giving notice of the removal.

(5) Whenever a vehicle is parked for more than 24 hours on a portion of highway that is located within the boundaries of a common interest development, as defined in Section 4100 or 6534 of the Civil Code, and signs, as required by Section 22658.2, have been posted on that portion of highway providing notice to drivers that vehicles parked thereon for more than 24 hours will be removed at the

owner's expense, pursuant to a resolution or ordinance adopted by the local authority.

(b) The provisions of this chapter that apply to a vehicle removed pursuant to Section 22651 apply to a vehicle removed pursuant to subdivision (a).

(c) For purposes of subdivision (a), a "trained volunteer" is a person who, of his or her own free will, provides services, without any financial gain, to a local or state law enforcement agency, and who is duly trained and certified to remove a vehicle by a local or state law enforcement agency. *(Added by Stats.2004, c. 371 (A.B.1847), § 1. Amended by Stats.2012, c. 181 (A.B.806), § 82, operative Jan. 1, 2014; Stats.2013, c. 605 (S.B.752), § 51.)*

Law Revision Commission Comments

Section 22651.05 is amended to correct a cross-reference to former Civil Code Section 1351(c). [40 Cal.L.Rev.Comm. Reports 235 (2010)].

Section 22651.05 is amended to add a cross-reference to Civil Code Section 6534, reflecting the enactment of the Commercial and Industrial Common Interest Development Act (Civ. Code §§ 6500–6876). [42 Cal.L.Rev.Comm. Reports 1 (2012)].

Cross References

Local regulations, see Vehicle Code § 21100 et seq.
Registered owner, responsibility for unattended vehicle, see Vehicle Code § 40200 et seq.
Snow areas, parking in, see Vehicle Code § 22510.
Utility vehicles, stopping, standing or parking, see Vehicle Code §§ 22512, 25301.
Vehicle parked or placed on highway for purpose of selling articles, removal, see Streets and Highways Code § 731.

§ 22651.07. Charges for towing or storage; Towing and Storage Fees and Access Notice; rights of vehicle owner; payment by bank draft; penalties; exceptions

(a) A person, including a law enforcement agency, city, county, city and county, the state, a tow yard, storage facility, or an impounding yard, that charges for towing or storage, or both, shall do all of the following:

(1)(A) Except as provided in subparagraph (B), post in the office area of the storage facility, in plain view of the public, the Towing and Storage Fees and Access Notice and have copies readily available to the public.

(B) An automotive repair dealer, registered pursuant to Article 3 (commencing with Section 9884) of Chapter 20.3 of Division 3 of the Business and Professions Code, that does not provide towing services is exempt from the requirements to post the Towing and Storage Fees and Access Notice in the office area.

(2) Provide, upon request, a copy of the Towing and Storage Fees and Access Notice to any owner or operator of a towed or stored vehicle.

(3) Provide a distinct notice on an itemized invoice for any towing or storage, or both, charges stating: "Upon request, you are entitled to receive a copy of the Towing and Storage Fees and Access Notice." This notice shall be contained within a bordered text box, printed in no less than 10–point type.

(b) Prior to receiving payment for any towing, recovery, or storage-related fees, a facility that charges for towing or storage, or both, shall provide an itemized invoice of actual charges to the vehicle owner or his or her agent. If an automotive repair dealer, registered pursuant to Article 3 (commencing with Section 9884) of Chapter 20.3 of Division 3 of the Business and Professions Code, did not provide the tow, and passes along, from the tower to the consumer, any of the information required on the itemized invoice, pursuant to subdivision (g) the automotive repair dealer shall not be responsible for the accuracy of those items of information that remain unaltered.

(c) Prior to paying any towing, recovery, or storage-related fees, a vehicle owner or his or her agent or a licensed repossessor shall, at any facility where the vehicle is being stored, have the right to all of the following:

(1) Receive his or her personal property, at no charge, during normal business hours. Normal business hours for releasing collateral and personal property are Monday through Friday from 8:00 a.m. to 5:00 p.m., inclusive, except state holidays.

(2) Retrieve his or her vehicle during the first 72 hours of storage and not pay a lien fee.

(3)(A) Inspect the vehicle without paying a fee.

(B) Have his or her insurer inspect the vehicle at the storage facility, at no charge, during normal business hours. However, the storage facility may limit the inspection to increments of 45 consecutive minutes in order to provide service to any other waiting customer, after which the insurer may resume the inspection for additional increments of 45 consecutive minutes, as necessary.

(4) Request a copy of the Towing and Storage Fees and Access Notice.

(5) Be permitted to pay by cash, insurer's check, or a valid bank credit card. Credit charges for towing and storage services shall comply with Section 1748.1 of the Civil Code. Law enforcement agencies may include the costs of providing for payment by credit when agreeing with a towing or storage provider on rates.

(d) A storage facility shall be open and accessible during normal business hours, as defined in subdivision (c). Outside of normal business hours, the facility shall provide a telephone number that permits the caller to leave a message. Calls to this number shall be returned no later than six business hours after a message has been left.

(e) The Towing and Storage Fees and Access Notice shall be a standardized document plainly printed in no less that 10–point type. A person may distribute the form using its own letterhead, but the language of the Towing and Storage Fees and Access Notice shall read as follows:

Towing and Storage Fees and Access Notice

Note: The following information is intended to serve as a general summary of some of the laws that provide vehicle owners certain rights when their vehicle is towed. It is not intended to summarize all of the laws that may be applicable nor is it intended to fully and completely state the entire law in any area listed. Please review the applicable California code for a definitive statement of the law in your particular situation.

How much can a towing company charge?

Rates for public tows and storage are generally established by an agreement between the law enforcement agency requesting the tow and the towing company (to confirm the approved rates, you may contact the law enforcement agency that initiated the tow; additionally, these rates are required to be posted at the storage facility).

Rates for private property tows and storage cannot exceed the approved rates for the law enforcement agency that has primary jurisdiction for the property from which the vehicle was removed or the towing company's approved CHP rate.

Rates for owner's request tows and storage are generally established by mutual agreement between the requestor and the towing company, but may be dictated by agreements established between the requestor's motor club and motor club service provider.

Where can you complain about a towing company?

For public tows: Contact the law enforcement agency initiating the tow.

Your rights if your vehicle is towed:

Generally, prior to paying any towing and storage-related fees you have the right to:

- Receive an itemized invoice of actual charges.
- Receive your personal property, at no charge, during normal business hours.
- Retrieve your vehicle during the first 72 hours of storage and not pay a lien fee.
- Request a copy of the Towing and Storage Fees and Access Notice.
- Pay by cash, valid bank credit card, or a check issued by your insurer.
- Inspect your vehicle.
- Have your insurer inspect your vehicle at the storage facility, at no charge, during normal business hours. However, the storage facility may limit the inspection to increments of 45 consecutive minutes in order to provide service to any other waiting customer, after which the insurer may resume the inspection for additional increments of 45 consecutive minutes, as necessary.

You and your insurance company or the insurance company representative have the right to have the vehicle released immediately upon (1) payment of all towing and storage-related fees, (2) presentation of a valid photo identification, (3) presentation of reliable documentation showing that you are the owner, insured, or insurer of the vehicle or that the owner has authorized you to take possession of the vehicle, and (4), if applicable, in the case of a fatality or crime, presentation of any required police or law enforcement release documents.

Prior to your vehicle being repaired:

- You have the right to choose the repair facility and to have no repairs made to your vehicle unless you authorize them in writing.
- Any authorization you sign for towing and any authorization you sign for repair must be on separate forms.

What if I do not pay the towing and storage-related fees or abandon my vehicle at the towing company?

Pursuant to Sections 3068.1 to 3074, inclusive, of the Civil Code, a towing company may sell your vehicle and any moneys received will be applied to towing and storage-related fees that have accumulated against your vehicle.

You are responsible for paying the towing company any outstanding balance due on any of these fees once the sale is complete.

Who is liable if my vehicle was damaged during towing or storage?

Generally the owner of a vehicle may recover for any damage to the vehicle resulting from any intentional or negligent act of a person causing the removal of, or removing, the vehicle.

What happens if a towing company violates the law?

If a tow company does not satisfactorily meet certain requirements detailed in this notice, you may bring a lawsuit in court, generally in small claims court. The tower may be civilly liable for damages up to two times the amount charged, not to exceed $500, and possibly more for certain violations.

(f) "Insurer," as used in this section, means either a first-party insurer or third-party insurer.

(g) "Itemized invoice," as used in this section, means a written document that contains the following information. Any document that substantially complies with this subdivision shall be deemed an "itemized invoice" for purposes of this section:

(1) The name, address, telephone number, and carrier identification number as required by subdivision (a) of Section 34507.5 of the person that is charging for towing and storage.

(2) If ascertainable, the registered owner or operator's name, address, and telephone number.

(3) The date service was initiated.

(4) The location of the vehicle at the time service was initiated, including either the address or nearest intersecting roadways.

(5) A vehicle description that includes, if ascertainable, the vehicle year, make, model, odometer reading, license plate number, or if a license plate number is unavailable, the vehicle identification number (VIN).

(6) The service dispatch time, the service arrival time of the tow truck, and the service completion time.

(7) A clear, itemized, and detailed explanation of any additional services that caused the total towing-related service time to exceed one hour between service dispatch time and service completion time.

(8) The hourly rate or per item rate used to calculate the total towing and recovery-related fees. These fees shall be listed as separate line items.

(9) If subject to storage fees, the daily storage rate and the total number of days stored. The storage fees shall be listed as a separate line item. Storage rates shall comply with the requirements of subdivision (c) of Section 22524.5.

(10) If subject to a gate fee, the date and time the vehicle was released after normal business hours. Normal business hours are Monday through Friday from 8:00 a.m. to 5:00 p.m., inclusive, except state holidays. A gate fee shall be listed as a separate line item. A gate fee shall comply with the requirements in subdivision (c) of Section 22524.5.

(11) A description of the method of towing.

(12) If the tow was not requested by the vehicle's owner or driver, the identity of the person or governmental agency that directed the tow. This paragraph shall not apply to information otherwise required to be redacted under Section 22658.

(13) A clear, itemized, and detailed explanation of any additional services or fees.

(h) "Person," as used in this section, includes those entities described in subdivision (a) and has the same meaning as described in Section 470.

(i) An insurer, insurer's agent, or tow hauler, shall be permitted to pay for towing and storage charges by a valid bank credit card, insurer's check, or bank draft.

(j) Except as otherwise exempted in this section, the requirements of this section apply to any facility that charges for the storage of a vehicle, including, but not limited to, a vehicle repair garage or service station, but not including a new motor vehicle dealer.

(k) A person who violates this section is civilly liable to a registered or legal owner of the vehicle, or a registered owner's insurer, for up to two times the amount charged. Liability in any action brought under this section shall not exceed five hundred dollars ($500) per vehicle.

(*l*) A suspected violation of this section may be reported by any person, including, without limitation, the legal or registered owner of a vehicle or his or her insurer.

(m) This section shall not apply to the towing or storage of a repossessed vehicle by any person subject to, or exempt from, the Collateral Recovery Act (Chapter 11 (commencing with Section 7500) of Division 3 of the Business and Professions Code).

(n) This section does not relieve a person from the obligation to comply with any other law.

(*o*) Notwithstanding this section, an insurer shall comply with all of its obligations under Section 2695.8 of Chapter 5 of Title 10 of the California Code of Regulations. *(Added by Stats.2010, c. 566 (A.B.519), § 2. Amended by Stats.2015, c. 740 (A.B.281), § 16, eff. Jan. 1, 2016; Stats.2018, c. 434 (A.B.2392), § 3, eff. Jan. 1, 2019.)*

§ 22651.1. Towing and service charges; credit card or cash payment

Persons operating or in charge of any storage facility where vehicles are stored pursuant to Section 22651 shall accept a valid bank credit card or cash for payment of towing and storage by the registered owner, legal owner, or the owner's agent claiming the vehicle. A credit card shall be in the name of the person presenting the card. "Credit card" means "credit card" as defined in subdivision (a) of Section 1747.02 of the Civil Code, except, for the purposes of this section, credit card does not include a credit card issued by a retail seller. A person operating or in charge of any storage facility who refuses to accept a valid bank credit card shall be liable to the owner of the vehicle or to the person who tendered the fees for four times the amount of the towing and storage charges, but not to exceed five hundred dollars ($500). In addition, persons operating or in charge of the storage facility shall have sufficient funds on the premises to accommodate and make change in a reasonable monetary transaction.

Credit charges for towing and storage services shall comply with Section 1748.1 of the Civil Code. Law enforcement agencies may include the costs of providing for payment by credit when agreeing with a towing or storage provider on rates. *(Added by Stats.1989, c. 502, § 1. Amended by Stats.1990, c. 309 (S.B.1763), § 2; Stats.1992, c. 246 (A.B.2895), § 1; Stats.2009, c. 322 (A.B.515), § 9.)*

§ 22651.2. Removal of vehicles from highways or public lands; conditions

(a) Any peace officer, as defined in Chapter 4.5 (commencing with Section 830) of Title 3 of Part 2 of the Penal Code, or any regularly employed and salaried employee, who is engaged in directing traffic or enforcing parking laws and regulations of a city, county, or jurisdiction of a state agency in which a vehicle is located, may remove a vehicle located within the territorial limits in which the officer or employee may act when the vehicle is found upon a highway or any public lands, and if all of the following requirements are satisfied:

(1) Because of the size and placement of signs or placards on the vehicle, it appears that the primary purpose of parking the vehicle at that location is to advertise to the public an event or function on private property or on public property hired for a private event or function to which the public is invited.

(2) The vehicle is known to have been previously issued a notice of parking violation that was accompanied by a notice warning that an additional parking violation may result in the impoundment of the vehicle.

(3) The registered owner of the vehicle has been mailed a notice advising of the existence of the parking violation and that an additional violation may result in the impoundment of the vehicle.

(b) Subdivision (a) does not apply to a vehicle bearing any sign or placard advertising any business or enterprise carried on by or through the use of that vehicle.

(c) Section 22852 applies to the removal of any vehicle pursuant to this section. *(Added by Stats.1990, c. 73 (S.B.819), § 1. Amended by Stats.1996, c. 1142 (S.B.1797), § 9, eff. Sept. 30, 1996; Stats.1997, c. 17 (S.B.947), § 144.)*

§ 22651.3. Offstreet parking facility; removal of vehicles without current registration or known to have been issued multiple notices of parking violations

(a) Any peace officer, as that term is defined in Chapter 4.5 (commencing with Section 830) of Title 3 of Part 2 of the Penal Code, or any regularly employed and salaried employee, who is engaged in directing traffic or enforcing parking laws and regulations, of a city, county, or jurisdiction of a state agency in which any vehicle, other than a rented vehicle, is located may remove the vehicle from an offstreet public parking facility located within the territorial limits in which the officer or employee may act when the vehicle is known to have been issued five or more notices of parking violation over a period of five or more days, to which the owner or person in control of the vehicle has not responded or when any vehicle is illegally parked so as to prevent the movement of a legally parked vehicle.

A notice of parking violation issued to a vehicle which is registered in a foreign jurisdiction or is without current California registration and is known to have been issued five or more notices of parking violation over a period of five or more days shall be accompanied by a warning that repeated violations may result in the impounding of the vehicle.

(b) The vehicle may be impounded until the owner or person in control of the vehicle furnishes to the impounding law enforcement agency evidence of his or her identity and an address within this state at which he or she can be located and furnishes satisfactory evidence that bail has been deposited for all notices of parking violation issued for the vehicle. In lieu of requiring satisfactory evidence that the bail has been deposited, the impounding law enforcement agency may, in its discretion, issue a notice to appear for the offenses charged, as provided in Article 2 (commencing with Section 40500) of Chapter 2 of Division 17. In lieu of either furnishing satisfactory evidence that the bail has been deposited or accepting the notice to appear, the owner or person in control of the vehicle may demand to be taken without unnecessary delay before a magistrate within the county in which the offenses charged are alleged to have been committed and who has jurisdiction of the offenses and is nearest or most accessible with reference to the place where the vehicle is impounded.

(c) Evidence of current registration shall be produced after a vehicle has been impounded. At the discretion of the impounding law enforcement agency, a notice to appear for violation of subdivision (a) of Section 4000 may be issued to the owner or person in control of the vehicle, if the two days immediately following the day of impoundment are weekend days or holidays. *(Added by Stats. 1985, c. 858, § 2. Amended by Stats.1988, c. 619, § 2; Stats.1994, c. 1220 (A.B.3132), § 61, eff. Sept. 30, 1994; Stats.1996, c. 1142 (S.B.1797), § 10, eff. Sept. 30, 1996.)*

§ 22651.4. Impounding or storing vehicle from another country

(a) A peace officer, as defined in Chapter 4.5 (commencing with Section 830) of Title 3 of Part 2 of the Penal Code, may impound a vehicle and its cargo pursuant to Section 34517.

(b) A member of the department may impound a vehicle and its cargo pursuant to Section 34518.

(c) A member of the department may store or impound a vehicle upon determination that the registrant of the vehicle or the driver of the vehicle has failed to pay registration, regulatory, fuel permit, or other fees, or has an outstanding warrant in a county in the state. The impoundment charges are the responsibility of the owner of the vehicle. The stored or impounded vehicle shall be released upon payment of those fees or fines or the posting of bail. The driver or owner of the vehicle may request a hearing to determine the validity of the seizure. *(Added by Stats.1991, c. 707 (A.B.1355), § 1. Amended by Stats.2006, c. 288 (A.B.3011), § 6.)*

§ 22651.5. Removal of vehicles with activated alarm devices or horns; report

(a) Any peace officer, as defined in Chapter 4.5 (commencing with Section 830) of Title 3 of Part 2 of the Penal Code, or any regularly employed and salaried employee who is engaged in directing traffic or enforcing parking laws or regulations, may, upon the complaint of any person, remove a vehicle parked within 500 feet of any occupied building of a school, community college, or university during normal hours of operation, or a vehicle parked within a residence or business district, from a highway or from public or private property, if an alarm device or horn has been activated within the vehicle, whether continuously activated or intermittently and repeatedly activated, the peace officer or designated employee is unable to locate the owner of the vehicle within 20 minutes from the time of arrival at the vehicle's location, and the alarm device or horn has not been completely silenced prior to removal.

(b) Upon removal of a vehicle from a highway or from public or private property pursuant to this section, the peace officer or designated employee ordering the removal shall immediately report the removal and the location to which the vehicle is removed to the Stolen Vehicle System of the Department of Justice. *(Added by Stats.1983, c. 1267, § 1. Amended by Stats.1991, c. 928 (A.B.1886), § 29, eff. Oct. 14, 1991; Stats.1993, c. 540 (A.B.1849), § 1; Stats.1997, c. 945 (A.B.1561), § 20.)*

§ 22651.6. Removal of vehicles used in motor vehicle speed contests

A peace officer or employee specified in Section 22651 may remove a vehicle located within the territorial limits in which the officer or employee may act when the vehicle was used by a person who was engaged in a motor vehicle speed contest, as described in subdivision (a) of Section 23109, and the person was arrested and taken into custody for that offense by a peace officer. *(Added by Stats.1996, c. 884 (A.B.2288), § 1.)*

Cross References

Release of vehicles removed and seized pursuant to this section, liability for towing and storage fees, see Vehicle Code § 23109.2.

Research References

2 Witkin, California Criminal Law 4th Crimes Against Public Peace and Welfare § 321 (2021), Speed Contests and Exhibitions.

3 Witkin, California Criminal Law 4th Punishment § 195 (2021), Impounding of Motor Vehicles.

§ 22651.7. Immobilization of certain vehicles on highway or public lands; five or more delinquent notices of parking violation

(a) In addition to, or as an alternative to, removal, a peace officer, as defined in Chapter 4.5 (commencing with Section 830) of Title 3 of Part 2 of the Penal Code, or a regularly employed and salaried employee who is engaged in directing traffic or enforcing parking laws and regulations, of a jurisdiction in which a vehicle is located may immobilize the vehicle with a device designed and manufactured for the immobilization of vehicles, on a highway or any public lands located within the territorial limits in which the officer or employee may act if the vehicle is found upon a highway or public lands and it is known to have been issued five or more notices of parking violations that are delinquent because the owner or person in control of the vehicle has not responded to the agency responsible for processing notices of parking violation within 21 calendar days of notice of citation issuance or citation issuance or 14 calendar days of the mailing of a notice of delinquent parking violation, or the registered owner of the vehicle is known to have been issued five or more notices for failure to pay or failure to appear in court for traffic violations for which no certificate has been issued by the magistrate or clerk of the court hearing the case showing that the case has been adjudicated or concerning which the registered owner's record has not been cleared pursuant to Chapter 6 (commencing with Section 41500) of Division 17. The vehicle may be immobilized until that person furnishes to the immobilizing law enforcement agency all of the following:

(1) Evidence of his or her identity.

(2) An address within this state at which he or she can be located.

(3) Satisfactory evidence that the full amount of parking penalties has been deposited for all notices of parking violation issued for the vehicle and any other vehicle registered to the registered owner of the immobilized vehicle and that bail has been deposited for all traffic violations of the registered owner that have not been cleared. The requirements in this paragraph shall be fully enforced by the immobilizing law enforcement agency on and after the time that the Department of Motor Vehicles is able to provide access to the necessary records. A notice of parking violation issued to the vehicle shall be accompanied by a warning that repeated violations may result in the impounding or immobilization of the vehicle. In lieu of furnishing satisfactory evidence that the full amount of parking penalties or bail, or both, have been deposited that person may demand to be taken without unnecessary delay before a magistrate, for traffic offenses, or a hearing examiner, for parking offenses, within the county in which the offenses charged are alleged to have been committed and who has jurisdiction of the offenses and is nearest or most accessible with reference to the place where the vehicle is immobilized. Evidence of current registration shall be produced after a vehicle has been immobilized or, at the discretion of the immobilizing law enforcement agency, a notice to appear for violation of subdivision (a) of Section 4000 shall be issued to that person.

(b) A person, other than a person authorized under subdivision (a), shall not immobilize a vehicle. *(Added by Stats.1986, c. 181, § 1, eff. June 23, 1986. Amended by Stats.1991, c. 90 (A.B.1297), § 69, eff. June 30, 1991; Stats.1991, c. 189 (A.B.544), § 41, eff. July 29, 1991; Stats.1992, c. 1244 (A.B.408), § 6, operative July 1, 1993; Stats.1993, c. 1093 (A.B.780), § 2; Stats.1994, c. 1220 (A.B.3132), § 62, eff. Sept. 30, 1994; Stats.1995, c. 734 (A.B.1228), § 2; Stats.1996, c. 1156 (A.B.3157), § 4; Stats.2006, c. 609 (A.B.2210), § 2.)*

§ 22651.8. Satisfactory evidence for payment of notices of parking violations defined

For purposes of paragraph (1) of subdivision (i) of Section 22651 and Section 22651.7, "satisfactory evidence" includes, but is not limited to, a copy of a receipt issued by the department pursuant to subdivision (a) of Section 4760 for the payment of notices of parking violations appearing on the department's records at the time of payment. The processing agency shall, within 72 hours of receiving that satisfactory evidence, update its records to reflect the payments made to the department. If the processing agency does not receive the amount of the parking penalties and administrative fees from the department within four months of the date of issuance of that satisfactory evidence, the processing agency may revise its records to reflect that no payments were received for the notices of parking violation. *(Added by Stats.1991, c. 587 (A.B.1126), § 2, operative July 1, 1992.)*

§ 22651.9. Vehicle removal; location; private sale advertisement

(a) Any peace officer, as defined in Chapter 4.5 (commencing with Section 830) of Title 3 of Part 2 of the Penal Code, or any regularly employed and salaried employee, who is engaged in directing traffic or enforcing parking laws and regulations, of a city, county, or city and county in which a vehicle is located, may remove a vehicle located within the territorial limits in which the officer or employee may act when the vehicle is found upon a street or any public lands, if all of the following requirements are satisfied:

(1) Because of a sign or placard on the vehicle, it appears that the primary purpose of parking the vehicle at that location is to advertise to the public the private sale of that vehicle.

(2) Within the past 30 days, the vehicle is known to have been previously issued a notice of parking violation, under local ordinance, which was accompanied by a notice containing all of the following:

(A) A warning that an additional parking violation may result in the impoundment of the vehicle.

(B) A warning that the vehicle may be impounded pursuant to this section, even if moved to another street, so long as the signs or placards offering the vehicle for sale remain on the vehicle.

(C) A listing of the streets or public lands subject to the resolution or ordinance adopted pursuant to paragraph (4), or if all streets are covered, a statement to that effect.

(3) The notice of parking violation was issued at least 24 hours prior to the removal of the vehicle.

(4) The local authority of the city, county, or city and county has, by resolution or ordinance, authorized the removal of vehicles pursuant to this section from the street or public lands on which the vehicle is located.

(b) Section 22852 applies to the removal of any vehicle pursuant to this section. *(Added by Stats.1993, c. 481 (A.B.1169), § 1, eff. Sept. 27, 1993.)*

§ 22652. Removal of unauthorized vehicle from physically handicapped person's parking space

(a) A peace officer, as defined in Chapter 4.5 (commencing with Section 830) of Title 3 of Part 2 of the Penal Code, or any regularly employed and salaried employee engaged in directing traffic or enforcing parking laws and regulations of a city, county, or jurisdiction of a state agency may remove any vehicle from a stall or space designated for physically disabled persons pursuant to Section 22511.7 or 22511.8, located within the jurisdictional limits in which the officer or employee is authorized to act, if the vehicle is parked in violation of Section 22507.8 and if the police or sheriff's department or the Department of the California Highway Patrol is notified.

(b) In a privately or publicly owned or operated offstreet parking facility, this section applies only to those stalls and spaces if the posting requirements under subdivisions (a) and (d) of Section 22511.8 have been complied with and if the stalls or spaces are clearly signed or marked. *(Added by Stats.1982, c. 975, p. 3497, § 9. Amended by Stats.1983, c. 270, § 4, eff. July 15, 1983; Stats.1985, c. 312, § 2; Stats.1985, c. 1041, § 11; Stats.1996, c. 1142 (S.B.1797), § 11, eff. Sept. 30, 1996; Stats.2004, c. 404 (S.B.1725), § 17.)*

§ 22652.5. Handicapped parking; vehicle removal; immunity from liability

The owner or person in lawful possession of an offstreet parking facility, or any local authority owning or operating an offstreet parking facility, who causes a vehicle to be removed from the parking facility pursuant to Section 22511.8, or any state, city, or county employee, is not civilly liable for the removal if the police or sheriff's department in whose jurisdiction the offstreet parking facility or the stall or space is located or the Department of the California Highway Patrol has been notified prior to the removal. *(Added by Stats.1983, c. 232, § 1, eff. July 14, 1983.)*

§ 22652.6. Disabled person placard; unlawful use; vehicle removal

Any peace officer, as defined in Chapter 4.5 (commencing with Section 830) of Title 3 of Part 2 of the Penal Code, or any regularly employed and salaried employee engaged in directing traffic or enforcing parking laws and regulations of a city or county, may remove any vehicle parked or standing on the streets or highways or from a stall or space of a privately or publicly owned or operated offstreet parking facility within the jurisdiction of the city or county when the vehicle is in violation of a local ordinance or resolution adopted pursuant to Section 22511.57. *(Added by Stats.1994, c. 221 (S.B.1378), § 3, operative July 1, 1995.)*

§ 22653. Removal from private property

(a) Any peace officer, as that term is defined in Chapter 4.5 (commencing with Section 830) of Title 3 of Part 2 of the Penal Code, other than an employee directing traffic or enforcing parking laws and regulations, may remove a vehicle from private property located within the territorial limits in which the officer is empowered to act, when a report has previously been made that the vehicle has been stolen or a complaint has been filed and a warrant thereon issued charging that the vehicle has been embezzled.

(b) Any peace officer, as that term is defined in Chapter 4.5 (commencing with Section 830) of Title 3 of Part 2 of the Penal Code, may, after a reasonable period of time, remove a vehicle from private property located within the territorial limits in which the officer is empowered to act, if the vehicle has been involved in, and left at the scene of, a traffic accident and no owner is available to grant permission to remove the vehicle. This subdivision does not authorize the removal of a vehicle where the owner has been contacted and has refused to grant permission to remove the vehicle.

(c) Any peace officer, as that term is defined in Chapter 4.5 (commencing with Section 830) of Title 3 of Part 2 of the Penal Code, may, at the request of the property owner or person in lawful possession of any private property, remove a vehicle from private property located within the territorial limits in which the officer is empowered to act when an officer arrests any person driving or in control of a vehicle for an alleged offense and the officer is, by this code or other law, required or authorized to take, and does take the person arrested before a magistrate without unnecessary delay. *(Stats.1959, c. 3, p. 1702, § 22653. Amended by Stats.1977, c. 73, p. 479, § 3; Stats.1978, c. 427, p. 1327, § 1; Stats.1980, c. 1340, p. 4737, § 32, eff. Sept. 30, 1980; Stats.1985, c. 912, § 3.)*

Cross References

Department of the California Highway Patrol, generally, see Vehicle Code § 2100 et seq.
Local authorities, powers, see Vehicle Code § 21100 et seq.
Obstructing traffic, removal of vehicle, see Vehicle Code § 22651.
Peace officer, definition, see Penal Code §§ 7, 830 et seq., 852.1.
Procedure to remove and store vehicles, see Vehicle Code § 22850 et seq.
Removal from private property, see Vehicle Code § 22658.
Removal of abandoned vehicles, see Vehicle Code § 22523 et seq.
Stolen vehicles, reports, see Vehicle Code § 10500 et seq.

§ 22654. Authorization for moving a vehicle

(a) Whenever any peace officer, as that term is defined in Chapter 4.5 (commencing with Section 830) of Title 3 of Part 2 of the Penal Code, or other employee directing traffic or enforcing parking laws and regulations, finds a vehicle standing upon a highway, located within the territorial limits in which the officer or employee is empowered to act, in violation of Sections 22500 and 22504, the officer or employee may move the vehicle or require the driver or other person in charge of the vehicle to move it to the nearest available position off the roadway or to the nearest parking location, or may remove and store the vehicle if moving it off the roadway to a parking location is impracticable.

(b) Whenever the officer or employee finds a vehicle standing upon a street, located within the territorial limits in which the officer or employee is empowered to act, in violation of a traffic ordinance enacted by local authorities to prevent flooding of adjacent property, he or she may move the vehicle or require the driver or person in charge of the vehicle to move it to the nearest available location in the vicinity where parking is permitted.

(c) Any state, county, or city authority charged with the maintenance of any highway may move any vehicle which is disabled or abandoned or which constitutes an obstruction to traffic from the place where it is located on a highway to the nearest available position on the same highway as may be necessary to keep the highway open or safe for public travel. In addition, employees of the Department of Transportation may remove any disabled vehicle which constitutes an obstruction to traffic on a freeway from the place where it is located to the nearest available location where parking is permitted; and, if the vehicle is unoccupied, the department shall comply with the notice requirements of subdivision (d).

(d) Any state, county, or city authority charged with the maintenance or operation of any highway, highway facility, or public works facility, in cases necessitating the prompt performance of any work on or service to the highway, highway facility, or public works facility, may move to the nearest available location where parking is permitted, any unattended vehicle which obstructs or interferes with the performance of the work or service or may remove and store the vehicle if moving it off the roadway to a location where parking is permitted would be impracticable. If the vehicle is moved to another location where it is not readily visible from its former parked location or it is stored, the person causing the movement or storage of the vehicle shall immediately, by the most expeditious means, notify the owner of the vehicle of its location. If for any reason the vehicle owner cannot be so notified, the person causing the vehicle to be moved or stored shall immediately, by the most expeditious means, notify the police department of the city in which the vehicle was parked, or, if the vehicle had been parked in an unincorporated area of a county, notify the sheriff's department and nearest office of the California Highway Patrol in that county. No vehicle may be removed and stored pursuant to this subdivision unless signs indicating that no person shall stop, park, or leave standing any vehicle within the areas marked by the signs because the work or service would be done, were placed at least 24 hours prior to the movement or removal and storage.

(e) Whenever any peace officer finds a vehicle parked or standing upon a highway in a manner so as to obstruct necessary emergency services, or the routing of traffic at the scene of a disaster, the officer may move the vehicle or require the driver or other person in charge of the vehicle to move it to the nearest available parking location. If the vehicle is unoccupied, and moving the vehicle to a parking location is impractical, the officer may store the vehicle pursuant to Sections 22850 and 22852 and subdivision (a) or (b) of Section 22853. If the vehicle so moved or stored was otherwise lawfully parked, no moving or storage charges shall be assessed against or collected from the driver or owner. *(Stats.1959, c. 3, p. 1702, § 22654. Amended by Stats.1969, c. 1229, p. 2382, § 1; Stats.1971, c. 874, p. 1719, § 1, operative May 3, 1972; Stats.1974, c. 545, p. 1328, § 212; Stats.1977, c. 73, p. 479, § 4; Stats.1980, c. 1340, p. 4737, § 33, eff. Sept. 30, 1980; Stats.1981, c. 281, p. 4737, § 1; Stats.1983, c. 913, § 2.)*

Cross References

Local impounding ordinances, see Vehicle Code § 22850 et seq.
Obstructing traffic, removal of vehicle, see Vehicle Code § 22651.
Peace officer, definition, see Penal Code §§ 7, 830 et seq., 852.1.
Private property, removal of vehicles, see Vehicle Code §§ 22653, 22658, 22852.
Procedure to remove and store vehicles, see Vehicle Code § 22850 et seq.
Removal of abandoned vehicles, see Vehicle Code § 22669.
Removal of vehicle parked or placed on highway for purpose of selling articles, see Streets and Highways Code § 731.

§ 22655. Vehicles involved in hit-and-run accidents; removal for inspection; release of vehicle; transfer of cargo

(a) When any peace officer, as that term is defined in Chapter 4.5 (commencing with Section 830) of Title 3 of Part 2 of the Penal Code or any regularly employed and salaried employee who is engaged in directing traffic or enforcing parking statutes and regulations, has reasonable cause to believe that a motor vehicle on a highway or on private property open to the general public onto which the public is explicitly or implicitly invited, located within the territorial limits in which the officer is empowered to act, has been involved in a hit-and-run accident, and the operator of the vehicle has failed to stop and comply with Sections 20002 to 20006, inclusive, the officer may remove the vehicle from the highway or from public or private property for the purpose of inspection.

(b) Unless sooner released, the vehicle shall be released upon the expiration of 48 hours after the removal from the highway or private property upon demand of the owner. When determining the 48–hour period, weekends, and holidays shall not be included.

(c) Notwithstanding subdivision (b), when a motor vehicle to be inspected pursuant to subdivision (a) is a commercial vehicle, any cargo within the vehicle may be removed or transferred to another vehicle.

This section shall not be construed to authorize the removal of any vehicle from an enclosed structure on private property that is not open to the general public. *(Stats.1959, c. 3, p. 1703, § 22655. Amended by Stats.1961, c. 1198, p. 2932, § 1; Stats.1963, c. 804, p. 1834, § 1; Stats.1967, c. 236, p. 1371, § 6; Stats.1967, c. 253, p. 1403, § 7; Stats.1969, c. 1116, p. 2178, § 2; Stats.1971, c. 130, p. 173, § 2, operative May 3, 1972; Stats.1974, c. 545, p. 1329, § 213; Stats.1975, c. 109, p. 181, § 1; Stats.1977, c. 486, p. 1606, § 3; Stats.1978, c. 505, p. 1650, § 1; Stats.1979, c. 791, p. 2693, § 1; Stats.1979, c. 831, p. 2878, § 2; Stats.1979, c. 909, p. 3126, § 3.2; Stats.1980, c. 1340, p. 4738, § 34, eff. Sept. 30, 1980; Stats.1997, c. 945 (A.B.1561), § 21.)*

Cross References

Department of the California Highway Patrol, generally, see Vehicle Code § 2100 et seq.
Peace officer, definition, see Penal Code §§ 7, 830 et seq., 852.1.

§ 22655.3. Impounding vehicle used to flee or evade peace officer

Any peace officer, as defined in Chapter 4.5 (commencing with Section 830) of Title 3 of Part 2 of the Penal Code, pursuing a fleeing or evading person in a motor vehicle may remove and store, or cause to be removed and stored, any vehicle used in violation of Section 2800.1 or 2800.2 from property other than that of the registered owner of the vehicle for the purposes of investigation, identification, or apprehension of the driver if the driver of the vehicle abandons the vehicle and leaves it unattended. All towing and storage fees for a vehicle removed under this section shall be paid by the owner, unless the vehicle was stolen or taken without permission.

No vehicle shall be impounded under this section if the driver is arrested before arrival of the towing equipment or if the registered owner is in the vehicle.

As used in this section, "remove and store a vehicle" means that the peace officer may cause the removal of a vehicle to, and storage of a vehicle in, a private lot where the vehicle may be secured by the owner of the facility or by the owner's representative.

This section is not intended to change current statute and case law governing searches and seizures. *(Formerly § 22651.7, added by*

Stats.1987, c. 279, § 1. Renumbered § 22655.3 and amended by Stats.1988, c. 160, § 181.)

§ 22655.5. Impoundment of motor vehicle by peace officer with probable cause to believe vehicle used as means to commit public offense or is evidence or contains evidence of crime

A peace officer, as defined in Chapter 4.5 (commencing with Section 830) of Title 3 of Part 2 of the Penal Code, may remove a motor vehicle from the highway or from public or private property within the territorial limits in which the officer may act under the following circumstances:

(a) When any vehicle is found upon a highway or public or private property and a peace officer has probable cause to believe that the vehicle was used as the means of committing a public offense.

(b) When any vehicle is found upon a highway or public or private property and a peace officer has probable cause to believe that the vehicle is itself evidence which tends to show that a crime has been committed or that the vehicle contains evidence, which cannot readily be removed, which tends to show that a crime has been committed.

(c) Notwithstanding Section 3068 of the Civil Code or Section 22851 of this code, no lien shall attach to a vehicle removed under this section unless the vehicle was used by the alleged perpetrator of the crime with the express or implied permission of the owner of the vehicle.

(d) In any prosecution of the crime for which a vehicle was impounded pursuant to this section, the prosecutor may request, and the court may order, the perpetrator of the crime, if convicted, to pay the costs of towing and storage of the vehicle, and any administrative charges imposed pursuant to Section 22850.5.

(e) This section shall become operative on January 1, 1993. *(Added by Stats.1990, c. 1515 (A.B.3410), § 2, operative Jan. 1, 1993. Amended by Stats.1993, c. 614 (A.B.481), § 2; Stats.1996, c. 1142 (S.B.1797), § 12, eff. Sept. 30, 1996.)*

Research References

4 Witkin, California Criminal Law 4th Pretrial Proceedings § 45 (2021), In General.

§ 22656. Removal from railroad, railway or light rail right of way

Any peace officer, as that term is defined in Chapter 4.5 (commencing with Section 830) of Title 3 of Part 2 of the Penal Code, may remove a vehicle from the right-of-way of a railroad, street railway, or light rail line located within the territorial limits in which the officer is empowered to act if the vehicle is parked or abandoned upon any track or within 7½ feet of the nearest rail. The officer may also remove a vehicle that is parked beyond 7½ feet of the nearest rail but within the right-of-way of a railroad, street railway, or light rail if signs are posted giving notice that vehicles may be removed. *(Added by Stats.1968, c. 625, p. 1310, § 2. Amended by Stats.1969, c. 1116, p. 2178, § 3; Stats.1971, c. 130, p. 174, § 3, operative May 3, 1972; Stats.1974, c. 545, p. 1330, § 214; Stats.1974, c. 797, p. 1745, § 1; Stats.1975, c. 110, p. 181, § 1; Stats.1977, c. 486, p. 1607, § 4; Stats.1978, c. 182, p. 412, § 1; Stats.1979, c. 831, p. 2881, § 3; Stats.1979, c. 909, p. 3129, § 4.5; Stats.1980, c. 1340, p. 4739, § 35, eff. Sept. 30, 1980; Stats.1988, c. 18, § 1; Stats.2002, c. 438 (A.B.3026), § 29.)*

Cross References

Department of the California Highway Patrol, generally, see Vehicle Code § 2100 et seq.

Unauthorized driving of vehicle on railroad track or right-of-way, see Penal Code § 369g.

§ 22658. Removal of vehicle from private property by property owner; towing companies and charges

(a) The owner or person in lawful possession of private property, including an association of a common interest development, as defined in Sections 4080 and 4100 or Sections 6528 and 6534 of the Civil Code, may cause the removal of a vehicle parked on the property to a storage facility that meets the requirements of subdivision (n) under any of the following circumstances:

(1) There is displayed, in plain view at all entrances to the property, a sign not less than 17 inches by 22 inches in size, with lettering not less than one inch in height, prohibiting public parking and indicating that vehicles will be removed at the owner's expense, and containing the telephone number of the local traffic law enforcement agency and the name and telephone number of each towing company that is a party to a written general towing authorization agreement with the owner or person in lawful possession of the property. The sign may also indicate that a citation may also be issued for the violation.

(2) The vehicle has been issued a notice of parking violation, and 96 hours have elapsed since the issuance of that notice.

(3) The vehicle is on private property and lacks an engine, transmission, wheels, tires, doors, windshield, or any other major part or equipment necessary to operate safely on the highways, the owner or person in lawful possession of the private property has notified the local traffic law enforcement agency, and 24 hours have elapsed since that notification.

(4) The lot or parcel upon which the vehicle is parked is improved with a single-family dwelling.

(b) The tow truck operator removing the vehicle, if the operator knows or is able to ascertain from the property owner, person in lawful possession of the property, or the registration records of the Department of Motor Vehicles the name and address of the registered and legal owner of the vehicle, shall immediately give, or cause to be given, notice in writing to the registered and legal owner of the fact of the removal, the grounds for the removal, and indicate the place to which the vehicle has been removed. If the vehicle is stored in a storage facility, a copy of the notice shall be given to the proprietor of the storage facility. The notice provided for in this section shall include the amount of mileage on the vehicle at the time of removal, if the vehicle has a visible odometer, and the time of the removal from the property. If the tow truck operator does not know and is not able to ascertain the name of the owner or for any other reason is unable to give the notice to the owner as provided in this section, the tow truck operator shall comply with the requirements of subdivision (c) of Section 22853 relating to notice in the same manner as applicable to an officer removing a vehicle from private property.

(c) This section does not limit or affect any right or remedy that the owner or person in lawful possession of private property may have by virtue of other provisions of law authorizing the removal of a vehicle parked upon private property.

(d) The owner of a vehicle removed from private property pursuant to subdivision (a) may recover for any damage to the vehicle resulting from any intentional or negligent act of a person causing the removal of, or removing, the vehicle.

(e)(1) An owner or person in lawful possession of private property, or an association of a common interest development, causing the removal of a vehicle parked on that property is liable for double the storage or towing charges whenever there has been a failure to comply with paragraph (1), (2), or (3) of subdivision (a) or to state the grounds for the removal of the vehicle if requested by the legal or registered owner of the vehicle as required by subdivision (f).

(2) A property owner or owner's agent or lessee who causes the removal of a vehicle parked on that property pursuant to the exemption set forth in subparagraph (A) of paragraph (1) of subdivision (*l*) and fails to comply with that subdivision is guilty of an infraction, punishable by a fine of one thousand dollars ($1,000).

(f) An owner or person in lawful possession of private property, or an association of a common interest development, causing the removal of a vehicle parked on that property shall notify by telephone or, if impractical, by the most expeditious means available, the local traffic law enforcement agency within one hour after authorizing the tow. An owner or person in lawful possession of private property, an association of a common interest development, causing the removal of a vehicle parked on that property, or the tow truck operator who removes the vehicle, shall state the grounds for the removal of the vehicle if requested by the legal or registered owner of that vehicle. A towing company that removes a vehicle from private property in compliance with subdivision (*l*) is not responsible in a situation relating to the validity of the removal. A towing company that removes the vehicle under this section shall be responsible for the following:

(1) Damage to the vehicle in the transit and subsequent storage of the vehicle.

(2) The removal of a vehicle other than the vehicle specified by the owner or other person in lawful possession of the private property.

(g)(1)(A) Possession of a vehicle under this section shall be deemed to arise when a vehicle is removed from private property and is in transit.

(B) Upon the request of the owner of the vehicle or that owner's agent, the towing company or its driver shall immediately and unconditionally release a vehicle that is not yet removed from the private property and in transit.

(C) A person failing to comply with subparagraph (B) is guilty of a misdemeanor.

(2) If a vehicle is released to a person in compliance with subparagraph (B) of paragraph (1), the vehicle owner or authorized agent shall immediately move that vehicle to a lawful location.

(h) A towing company may impose a charge of not more than one-half of the regular towing charge for the towing of a vehicle at the request of the owner, the owner's agent, or the person in lawful possession of the private property pursuant to this section if the owner of the vehicle or the vehicle owner's agent returns to the vehicle after the vehicle is coupled to the tow truck by means of a regular hitch, coupling device, drawbar, portable dolly, or is lifted off the ground by means of a conventional trailer, and before it is removed from the private property. The regular towing charge may only be imposed after the vehicle has been removed from the property and is in transit.

(i)(1)(A) A charge for towing or storage, or both, of a vehicle under this section is excessive if the charge exceeds the greater of the following:

(i) That which would have been charged for that towing or storage, or both, made at the request of a law enforcement agency under an agreement between a towing company and the law enforcement agency that exercises primary jurisdiction in the city in which is located the private property from which the vehicle was, or was attempted to be, removed, or if the private property is not located within a city, then the law enforcement agency that exercises primary jurisdiction in the county in which the private property is located.

(ii) That which would have been charged for that towing or storage, or both, under the rate approved for that towing operator by the Department of the California Highway Patrol for the jurisdiction in which the private property is located and from which the vehicle was, or was attempted to be, removed.

(B) A towing operator shall make available for inspection and copying * * * their rate approved by the Department of the California Highway Patrol, if any, within 24 hours of a request without a warrant to law enforcement, the Attorney General, district attorney, or city attorney.

(2) If a vehicle is released within 24 hours from the time the vehicle is brought into the storage facility, regardless of the calendar date, the storage charge shall be for only one day. Not more than one day's storage charge may be required for a vehicle released the same day that it is stored.

(3) If a request to release a vehicle is made and the appropriate fees are tendered and documentation establishing that the person requesting release is entitled to possession of the vehicle, or is the owner's insurance representative, is presented within the initial 24 hours of storage, and the storage facility fails to comply with the request to release the vehicle or is not open for business during normal business hours, then only one day's storage charge may be required to be paid until after the first business day. A business day is any day in which the lienholder is open for business to the public for at least eight hours. If a request is made more than 24 hours after the vehicle is placed in storage, charges may be imposed on a full calendar day basis for each day, or part thereof, that the vehicle is in storage.

(j)(1) A person who charges a vehicle owner a towing, service, or storage charge at an excessive rate, as described in subdivision (h) or (i), is civilly liable to the vehicle owner for four times the amount charged.

(2) A person who knowingly charges a vehicle owner a towing, service, or storage charge at an excessive rate, as described in subdivision (h) or (i), or who fails to make available * * * their rate as required in subparagraph (B) of paragraph (1) of subdivision (i), is guilty of a misdemeanor, punishable by a fine of not more than two thousand five hundred dollars ($2,500), or by imprisonment in a county jail for not more than three months, or by both that fine and imprisonment.

(k)(1) A person operating or in charge of a storage facility where vehicles are stored pursuant to this section shall accept a valid bank credit card or cash for payment of towing and storage by a registered owner, the legal owner, or the owner's agent claiming the vehicle. A credit card shall be in the name of the person presenting the card. "Credit card" means "credit card" as defined in subdivision (a) of Section 1747.02 of the Civil Code, except, for the purposes of this section, credit card does not include a credit card issued by a retail seller.

(2) A person described in paragraph (1) shall conspicuously display, in that portion of the storage facility office where business is conducted with the public, a notice advising that all valid credit cards and cash are acceptable means of payment.

(3) A person operating or in charge of a storage facility who refuses to accept a valid credit card or who fails to post the required notice under paragraph (2) is guilty of a misdemeanor, punishable by a fine of not more than two thousand five hundred dollars ($2,500), or by imprisonment in a county jail for not more than three months, or by both that fine and imprisonment.

(4) A person described in paragraph (1) who violates paragraph (1) or (2) is civilly liable to the registered owner of the vehicle or the person who tendered the fees for four times the amount of the towing and storage charges.

(5) A person operating or in charge of the storage facility shall have sufficient moneys on the premises of the primary storage facility during normal business hours to accommodate, and make change in, a reasonable monetary transaction.

(6) Credit charges for towing and storage services shall comply with Section 1748.1 of the Civil Code. Law enforcement agencies may include the costs of providing for payment by credit when making agreements with towing companies as described in subdivision (i).

(*l*)(1)(A) A towing company shall not remove or commence the removal of a vehicle from private property without first obtaining the written authorization from the property owner or lessee, including an association of a common interest development, or an employee or agent thereof, who shall be present at the time of removal and verify the alleged violation, except that presence and verification is not required if the person authorizing the tow is the property owner, or the owner's agent who is not a tow operator, of a residential rental property of 15 or fewer units that does not have an onsite owner, owner's agent or employee, and the tenant has verified the violation, requested the tow from that tenant's assigned parking space, and provided a signed request or * * * email, or has called and provides a signed request or * * * email within 24 hours, to the property owner or owner's agent, which the owner or agent shall provide to the towing company within 48 hours of authorizing the tow. The signed request or * * * email shall contain the name and address of the tenant, and the date and time the tenant requested the tow. A towing company shall obtain, within 48 hours of receiving the written authorization to tow, a copy of a tenant request required pursuant to this subparagraph. For the purpose of this subparagraph, a person providing the written authorization who is required to be present on the private property at the time of the tow does not have to be physically present at the specified location of where the vehicle to be removed is located on the private property.

(B) The written authorization under subparagraph (A) shall include all of the following:

(i) The make, model, vehicle identification number, and license plate number of the removed vehicle. If the vehicle is a shared mobility device or does not have an identifiable make, model, vehicle identification number, or license plate number, the authorization shall include any identification numbers on the vehicle, including, but not limited to, a quick response (QR) code or serial number.

(ii) The name, signature, job title, residential or business address, and working telephone number of the person, described in subparagraph (A), authorizing the removal of the vehicle.

(iii) The grounds for the removal of the vehicle.

(iv) The time when the vehicle was first observed parked at the private property.

(v) The time that authorization to tow the vehicle was given.

(C)(i) When the vehicle owner or * * * their agent claims the vehicle, the towing company prior to payment of a towing or storage charge shall provide a photocopy of the written authorization to the vehicle owner or the agent.

(ii) If the vehicle was towed from a residential property, the towing company shall redact the information specified in clause (ii) of subparagraph (B) in the photocopy of the written authorization provided to the vehicle owner or the agent pursuant to clause (i).

(iii) The towing company shall also provide to the vehicle owner or the agent a separate notice that provides the telephone number of the appropriate local law enforcement or prosecuting agency by stating "If you believe that you have been wrongfully towed, please contact the local law enforcement or prosecuting agency at [insert appropriate telephone number]." The notice shall be in English and in the most populous language, other than English, that is spoken in the jurisdiction.

(D) A towing company shall not remove or commence the removal of a vehicle from private property described in subdivision (a) of Section 22953 unless the towing company has made a good faith inquiry to determine that the owner or the property owner's agent complied with Section 22953.

(E)(i) General authorization to remove or commence removal of a vehicle at the towing company's discretion shall not be delegated to a towing company or its affiliates except in the case of a vehicle unlawfully parked within 15 feet of a fire hydrant or in a fire lane, or in a manner which interferes with an entrance to, or exit from, the private property.

(ii) In those cases in which general authorization is granted to a towing company or its affiliate to undertake the removal or commence the removal of a vehicle that is unlawfully parked within 15 feet of a fire hydrant or in a fire lane, or that interferes with an entrance to, or exit from, private property, the towing company and the property owner, or owner's agent, or person in lawful possession of the private property shall have a written agreement granting that general authorization.

(2) If a towing company removes a vehicle under a general authorization described in subparagraph (E) of paragraph (1) and that vehicle is unlawfully parked within 15 feet of a fire hydrant or in a fire lane, or in a manner that interferes with an entrance to, or exit from, the private property, the towing company shall take, prior to the removal of that vehicle, a photograph of the vehicle that clearly indicates that parking violation. Prior to accepting payment, the towing company shall keep one copy of the photograph taken pursuant to this paragraph, and shall present that photograph and provide, without charge, a photocopy to the owner or an agent of the owner, when that person claims the vehicle.

(3) A towing company shall maintain the original written authorization, or the general authorization described in subparagraph (E) of paragraph (1) and the photograph of the violation, required pursuant to this section, and any written requests from a tenant to the property owner or owner's agent required by subparagraph (A) of paragraph (1), for a period of three years and shall make them available for inspection and copying within 24 hours of a request without a warrant to law enforcement, the Attorney General, district attorney, or city attorney.

(4) A person who violates this subdivision is guilty of a misdemeanor, punishable by a fine of not more than two thousand five hundred dollars ($2,500), or by imprisonment in a county jail for not more than three months, or by both that fine and imprisonment.

(5) A person who violates this subdivision is civilly liable to the owner of the vehicle or * * * their agent for four times the amount of the towing and storage charges.

(m)(1) A towing company that removes a vehicle from private property under this section shall notify the local law enforcement agency of that tow after the vehicle is removed from the private property and is in transit.

(2) A towing company is guilty of a misdemeanor if the towing company fails to provide the notification required under paragraph (1) within 60 minutes after the vehicle is removed from the private property and is in transit or 15 minutes after arriving at the storage facility, whichever time is less.

(3) A towing company that does not provide the notification under paragraph (1) within 30 minutes after the vehicle is removed from the private property and is in transit is civilly liable to the registered owner of the vehicle, or the person who tenders the fees, for three times the amount of the towing and storage charges.

(4) If notification is impracticable, the times for notification, as required pursuant to paragraphs (2) and (3), shall be tolled for the time period that notification is impracticable. This paragraph is an affirmative defense.

(n) A vehicle removed from private property pursuant to this section shall be stored in a facility that meets all of the following requirements:

(1)(A) Is located within a 10–mile radius of the property from where the vehicle was removed.

(B) The 10–mile radius requirement of subparagraph (A) does not apply if a towing company has prior general written approval from the law enforcement agency that exercises primary jurisdiction in the city in which is located the private property from which the vehicle was removed, or if the private property is not located within a city, then the law enforcement agency that exercises primary jurisdiction in the county in which is located the private property.

(2)(A) Remains open during normal business hours and releases vehicles after normal business hours.

(B) A gate fee may be charged for releasing a vehicle after normal business hours, weekends, and state holidays. However, the maximum hourly charge for releasing a vehicle after normal business hours shall be one-half of the hourly tow rate charged for initially towing the vehicle, or less.

(C) Notwithstanding any other provision of law and for purposes of this paragraph, "normal business hours" are Monday to Friday, inclusive, from 8 a.m. to 5 p.m., inclusive, except state holidays.

(3) Has a public pay telephone in the office area that is open and accessible to the public.

(*o*)(1) It is the intent of the Legislature in the adoption of subdivision (k) to assist vehicle owners or their agents by, among other things, allowing payment by credit cards for towing and storage services, thereby expediting the recovery of towed vehicles and concurrently promoting the safety and welfare of the public.

(2) It is the intent of the Legislature in the adoption of subdivision (*l*) to further the safety of the general public by ensuring that a private property owner or lessee has provided * * * authorization for the removal of a vehicle from * * * their property, thereby promoting the safety of those persons involved in ordering the removal of the vehicle as well as those persons removing, towing, and storing the vehicle.

(3) It is the intent of the Legislature in the adoption of subdivision (g) to promote the safety of the general public by requiring towing companies to unconditionally release a vehicle that is not lawfully in their possession, thereby avoiding the likelihood of dangerous and violent confrontation and physical injury to vehicle owners and towing operators, the stranding of vehicle owners and their passengers at a dangerous time and location, and impeding expedited vehicle recovery, without wasting law enforcement's limited resources.

(p) The remedies, sanctions, restrictions, and procedures provided in this section are not exclusive and are in addition to other remedies, sanctions, restrictions, or procedures that may be provided in other provisions of law, including, but not limited to, those that are provided in Sections 12110 and 34660.

(q) A vehicle removed and stored pursuant to this section shall be released by the law enforcement agency, impounding agency, or person in possession of the vehicle, or any person acting on behalf of them, to the legal owner or the legal owner's agent upon presentation of the assignment, as defined in subdivision (b) of Section 7500.1 of the Business and Professions Code; a release from the one responsible governmental agency, only if required by the agency; a government-issued photographic identification card; and any one of the following as determined by the legal owner or the legal owner's agent: a certificate of repossession for the vehicle, a security agreement for the vehicle, or title, whether paper or electronic, showing proof of legal ownership for the vehicle. Any documents presented may be originals, photocopies, or facsimile copies, or may be transmitted electronically. The storage facility shall not require any documents to be notarized. The storage facility may require the agent of the legal owner to produce a photocopy or facsimile copy of its repossession agency license or registration issued pursuant to Chapter 11 (commencing with Section 7500) of Division 3 of the Business and Professions Code, or to demonstrate, to the satisfaction of the storage facility, that the agent is exempt from licensure pursuant to Section 7500.2 or 7500.3 of the Business and Professions Code. *(Added by Stats.1959, c. 963, p. 2994, § 1. Amended by Stats.1963, c. 639, p. 1632, § 1; Stats.1971, c. 1698, p. 3639, § 1, operative May 3, 1972; Stats.1979, c. 1022, p. 3491, § 2; Stats.1980, c. 308, p. 634, § 1; Stats.1982, c. 738, p. 2935, § 1; Stats.1983, c. 913, § 3; Stats.1984, c. 255, § 1; Stats.1984, c. 325, § 1; Stats.1984, c. 1334, § 2; Stats.1985, c. 312, § 3; Stats.1985, c. 1335, § 1; Stats. 1986, c. 1262, § 2; Stats.1987, c. 572, § 1; Stats.1990, c. 309 (S.B.1763), § 3; Stats.1990, c. 998 (A.B.2789), § 2; Stats.1991, c. 711 (A.B.1390), § 3; Stats.1991, c. 1004 (S.B.887), § 4; Stats.1992, c. 246 (A.B.2895), § 2; Stats.1992, c. 1220 (A.B.3424), § 7; Stats.1993, c. 272 (A.B.301), § 43, eff. Aug. 2, 1993; Stats.1994, c. 1220 (A.B.3132), § 63, eff. Sept. 30, 1994; Stats.1995, c. 404 (S.B.240), § 5; Stats.1999, c. 1007 (S.B.532), § 23; Stats.2003, c. 212 (A.B.792), § 1; Stats.2006, c. 609 (A.B.2210), § 3; Stats.2009, c. 322 (A.B.515), § 10; Stats.2012, c. 181 (A.B.806), § 83, operative Jan. 1, 2014; Stats.2013, c. 605 (S.B.752), § 52; Stats.2022, c. 206 (A.B.2174), § 2, eff. Jan. 1, 2023.)*

Law Revision Commission Comments

Subdivision (a) of Section 22658 is amended to correct a cross-reference to former Civil Code Section 1351(a), (c). [40 Cal.L.Rev.Comm. Reports 235 (2010)].

Subdivision (a) of Section 22658 is amended to add cross-references to Civil Code Section 6528 and 6534, reflecting the enactment of the Commercial and Industrial Common Interest Development Act (Civ. Code §§ 6500–6876). [42 Cal.L.Rev.Comm. Reports 1 (2012)].

Cross References

Disabled persons and veterans, designation of parking, removal of unauthorized vehicles from private parking facilities, see Vehicle Code § 22511.8.
Improperly causing vehicle to be towed or removed to create or acquire lien, forfeiture of claims and liability to owner or lessee, see Civil Code § 3070.
Liens on vehicles or vessels, enforcement, disposition of proceeds, see Business and Professions Code § 21702.5.
Mobilehome parks, removal of vehicles pursuant to this section, see Civil Code § 798.28.5.
Removal from private property, see Vehicle Code § 22653.

§ 22658.1. Damaging of fence while removing vehicle; location and notification of property owner by towing company

(a) Any towing company that, in removing a vehicle, cuts, removes, otherwise damages, or leaves open a fence without the prior approval of the property owner or the person in charge of the property shall then and there do either of the following:

(1) Locate and notify the owner or person in charge of the property of the damage or open condition of the fence, the name and address of the towing company, and the license, registration, or identification number of the vehicle being removed.

(2) Leave in a conspicuous place on the property the name and address of the towing company, and the license, registration, or identification number of the vehicle being removed, and shall without unnecessary delay, notify the police department of the city in which the property is located, or if the property is located in unincorporated territory, either the sheriff or the local headquarters of the Department of the California Highway Patrol, of that information and the location of the damaged or opened fence.

(b) Any person failing to comply with all the requirements of this section is guilty of an infraction. *(Added by Stats.1985, c. 608, § 1. Amended by Stats.2001, c. 854 (S.B.205), § 68.)*

§ 22659. State or district agricultural association property

Any peace officer of the Department of the California Highway Patrol or any person duly authorized by the state agency in possession of property owned by the state, or rented or leased from others by the state and any peace officer of the Department of the California Highway Patrol providing policing services to property of a district agricultural association may, subsequent to giving notice to the city police or county sheriff, whichever is appropriate, cause the removal of a vehicle from the property to the nearest public garage, under any of the following circumstances:

(a) When the vehicle is illegally parked in locations where signs are posted giving notice of violation and removal.

(b) When an officer arrests any person driving or in control of a vehicle for an alleged offense and the officer is by this code or other law required to take the person arrested before a magistrate without unnecessary delay.

(c) When any vehicle is found upon the property and report has previously been made that the vehicle has been stolen or complaint has been filed and a warrant thereon issued charging that the vehicle has been embezzled.

(d) When the person or persons in charge of a vehicle upon the property are by reason of physical injuries or illness incapacitated to that extent as to be unable to provide for its custody or removal.

The person causing removal of the vehicle shall comply with the requirements of Sections 22852 and 22853 relating to notice. *(Added by Stats.1981, c. 32, p. 76, § 4, eff. May 14, 1981. Amended by Gov.Reorg.Plan No. 1 of 1995, § 68, eff. July 12, 1995; Stats.1996, c. 305 (A.B.3103), § 70.)*

§ 22659.5. Vehicle used in commission of specified offenses; public nuisance; notice of impounding; poststorage hearing; release of vehicle; towing and storage charges

Notwithstanding any other provision of law, a city or a county may adopt an ordinance declaring a motor vehicle to be a public nuisance subject to seizure and an impoundment period of up to 30 days when the motor vehicle is used in the commission or attempted commission of an act that violates Section 266h or 266i of, subdivision (h) of Section 374.3 of, or subdivision (b) of Section 647 of, the Penal Code, if the owner or operator of the vehicle has had a prior conviction for the same offense within the past three years. An ordinance adopted pursuant to this section may incorporate any combination or all of these offenses. The vehicle may only be impounded pursuant to a valid arrest of the driver for a violation of one of these provisions. An ordinance adopted pursuant to this section shall, at a minimum, contain all of the following provisions:

(a) Within two working days after impoundment, the impounding agency shall send a notice by certified mail, return receipt requested, to the legal owner of the vehicle, at the address obtained from the department, informing the owner that the vehicle has been impounded. The notice shall also include notice of the opportunity for a poststorage hearing to determine the validity of the storage or to determine mitigating circumstances establishing that the vehicle should be released. The impounding agency shall be prohibited from charging for more than five days' storage if it fails to notify the legal owner within two working days after the impoundment when the legal owner redeems the impounded vehicle. The impounding agency shall maintain a published telephone number that provides information 24 hours a day regarding the impoundment of vehicles and the rights of a legal owner and a registered owner to request a hearing. The notice shall include all of the following information:

(1) The name, address, and telephone number of the agency providing the notice.

(2) The location of the place of storage and description of the vehicle, that shall include, if available, the model or make, the manufacturer, the license plate number, and the mileage.

(3) The authority and purpose for the removal of the vehicle.

(4) A statement that, in order to receive a poststorage hearing, the owners, or their agents, shall request the hearing in person, writing, or by telephone within 10 days of the date appearing on the notice.

(b) The poststorage hearing shall be conducted within 48 hours of the request, excluding weekends and holidays. The public agency may authorize one of its own officers or employees to conduct the hearing if that hearing officer is not the same person who directed the seizure of the vehicle.

(c) Failure of the legal and the registered owners, or their agents, to request or to attend a scheduled hearing shall satisfy the poststorage hearing requirement.

(d) The agency employing the person who directed the storage shall be responsible for the costs incurred for towing and storage if it is determined in the poststorage hearing that reasonable grounds for the storage are not established.

(e) Any period during which a vehicle is subjected to storage under an ordinance adopted pursuant to this section shall be included as part of the period of impoundment.

(f) The impounding agency shall release the vehicle to the registered owner or his or her agent prior to the end of the impoundment period under any of the following circumstances:

(1) The driver of the impounded vehicle was arrested without probable cause.

(2) The vehicle is a stolen vehicle.

(3) The vehicle is subject to bailment and was driven by an unlicensed employee of a business establishment, including a parking service or repair garage.

(4) The driver of the vehicle is not the sole registered owner of the vehicle and the vehicle is being released to another registered owner of the vehicle who agrees not to allow the driver to use the vehicle until after the end of the impoundment period.

(5) The registered owner of the vehicle was neither the driver nor a passenger of the vehicle at the time of the alleged violation, or was unaware that the driver was using the vehicle to engage in activities subject to Section 266h or 266i of, or subdivision (b) of Section 647 of, the Penal Code.

(6) A spouse, registered domestic partner, or other affected third party objects to the impoundment of the vehicle on the grounds that it would create a hardship if the subject vehicle is the sole vehicle in a household. The hearing officer shall release the vehicle where the hardship to a spouse, registered domestic partner, or other affected third party created by the impoundment of the subject vehicle, or the length of the impoundment, outweigh the seriousness and the severity of the act in which the vehicle was used.

(g) Notwithstanding any provision of law, if a motor vehicle is released prior to the conclusion of the impoundment period because the driver was arrested without probable cause, neither the arrested person nor the registered owner of the motor vehicle shall be responsible for the towing and storage charges.

(h) Except as provided in subdivision (g), the registered owner or his or her agent shall be responsible for all towing and storage charges related to the impoundment.

(i) A vehicle removed and seized under an ordinance adopted pursuant to this section shall be released to the legal owner of the vehicle or the legal owner's agent prior to the end of the impoundment period if both of the following conditions are met:

(1) The legal owner is a motor vehicle dealer, bank, credit union, acceptance corporation, or other licensed financial institution legally operating in this state, or is another person who is not the registered owner and holds a security interest in the vehicle.

(2) The legal owner or the legal owner's agent pays all towing and storage fees related to the seizure and impoundment of the vehicle.

(j)(1) No lien sale processing fees shall be charged to the legal owner who redeems the vehicle prior to the 15th day of the impoundment period. Neither the impounding authority nor any person having possession of the vehicle shall collect from the legal owner as described in paragraph (1) of subdivision (i), or the legal owner's agent, any administrative charges imposed pursuant to Section 22850.5, unless the legal owner voluntarily requested a poststorage hearing.

(2) A person operating or in charge of a storage facility where vehicles are stored pursuant to this section shall accept a valid bank credit card or cash for payment of towing, storage, and related fees by a legal or registered owner or the owner's agent claiming the vehicle. A credit card or debit card shall be in the name of the person presenting the card. For purposes of this section, "credit card" is as defined in subdivision (a) of Section 1747.02 of the Civil Code. Credit card does not include a credit card issued by a retail seller.

(3) A person operating or in charge of a storage facility described in paragraph (2) who violates paragraph (2) shall be civilly liable to the owner of the vehicle or the person who tendered the fees for four times the amount of the towing, storage, and related fees not to exceed five hundred dollars ($500).

(4) A person operating or in charge of the storage facility described in paragraph (2) shall have sufficient funds on the premises of the primary storage facility during normal business hours to accommodate, and make change for, a reasonable monetary transaction.

(5) Credit charges for towing and storage services shall comply with Section 1748.1 of the Civil Code. Law enforcement agencies may include the costs of providing for payment by credit when making agreements with towing companies on rates.

(6) A failure by a storage facility to comply with any applicable conditions set forth in this subdivision shall not affect the right of the legal owner or the legal owner's agent to retrieve the vehicle if all conditions required of the legal owner or legal owner's agent under this subdivision are satisfied.

(k)(1) The legal owner or the legal owner's agent shall present to the law enforcement agency, impounding agency, person in possession of the vehicle, or any person acting on behalf of those agencies, a copy of the assignment, as defined in subdivision (b) of Section 7500.1 of the Business and Professions Code, a release from the one responsible governmental agency, only if required by the agency, a government-issued photographic identification card, and any one of the following as determined by the legal owner or the legal owner's agent: a certificate of repossession for the vehicle, a security agreement for the vehicle, or title, whether or not paperless or electronic, showing proof of legal ownership for the vehicle. Any documents presented may be originals, photocopies, or facsimile copies, or may be transmitted electronically. The law enforcement agency, impounding agency, or other governmental agency, or any person acting on behalf of those agencies, shall not require any documents to be notarized. The law enforcement agency, impounding agency, or any person acting on behalf of those agencies may require the agent of the legal owner to produce a photocopy or facsimile copy of its repossession agency license or registration issued pursuant to Chapter 11 (commencing with Section 7500) of Division 3 of the Business and Professions Code, or to demonstrate, to the satisfaction of the law enforcement agency, impounding agency, or any person acting on behalf of those agencies that the agent is exempt from licensure pursuant to Section 7500.2 or 7500.3 of the Business and Professions Code.

(2) Administrative costs authorized under subdivision (a) of Section 22850.5 shall not be charged to the legal owner of the type specified in paragraph (1) of subdivision (i) who redeems the vehicle unless the legal owner voluntarily requests a poststorage hearing. A city, county, city and county, or state agency shall not require a legal owner or a legal owner's agent to request a poststorage hearing as a requirement for release of the vehicle to the legal owner or the legal owner's agent. The law enforcement agency, impounding agency, or other governmental agency, or any person acting on behalf of those agencies, shall not require any documents other than those specified in this paragraph. The legal owner or the legal owner's agent shall be given a copy of any documents he or she is required to sign, except for a vehicle evidentiary hold log book. The law enforcement agency, impounding agency, or any person acting on behalf of those agencies, or any person in possession of the vehicle, may photocopy and retain the copies of any documents presented by the legal owner or legal owner's agent. The legal owner shall indemnify and hold harmless a storage facility from any claims arising out of the release of the vehicle to the legal owner or the legal owner's agent and from any damage to the vehicle after its release, including the reasonable costs associated with defending any such claims.

(*l*) A legal owner, who meets the requirements for release of a vehicle pursuant to subdivision (i), or the legal owner's agent, shall not be required to request a poststorage hearing as a requirement for release of the vehicle to the legal owner or the legal owner's agent.

(m)(1) A legal owner, who meets the requirements for release of a vehicle pursuant to subdivision (i), or the legal owner's agent, shall not release the vehicle to the registered owner of the vehicle or an agent of the registered owner, unless the registered owner is a rental car agency, until after the termination of the impoundment period.

(2) Prior to relinquishing the vehicle, the legal owner may require the registered owner to pay all towing and storage charges related to the seizure and impoundment.

(n)(1) A vehicle removed and seized pursuant to an ordinance adopted pursuant to this section shall be released to a rental car agency prior to the end of the impoundment period if the agency is either the legal owner or registered owner of the vehicle and the agency pays all towing and storage fees related to the seizure and impoundment of the vehicle.

(2) The owner of a rental vehicle that was seized under an ordinance adopted pursuant to this section may continue to rent the vehicle upon recovery of the vehicle. However, the rental car agency shall not rent another vehicle to the driver of the vehicle that was seized until the impoundment period has expired.

(3) The rental car agency may require the person to whom the vehicle was rented to pay all towing and storage charges related to the seizure and impoundment. *(Added by Stats.2009, c. 210 (A.B.14), § 2.)*

Research References

1 Witkin California Criminal Law 4th Introduction to Crimes § 68 (2021), In General.

3 Witkin, California Criminal Law 4th Punishment § 195 (2021), Impounding of Motor Vehicles.

§ 22660. Local ordinances

Notwithstanding any other provision of law, a city, county, or city and county may adopt an ordinance establishing procedures for the abatement and removal, as public nuisances, of abandoned, wrecked, dismantled, or inoperative vehicles or parts thereof from private or public property, and for the recovery, pursuant to Section 25845 or 38773.5 of the Government Code, or assumption by the local authority, of costs of administration and the removal. *(Added by Stats.1967, c. 1055, p. 2660, § 1. Amended by Stats.1970, c. 427, p. 855, § 1; Stats.1971, c. 130, p. 174, § 3.5, operative May 3, 1972; Stats.1975, c. 627, p. 1358, § 1; Stats.1976, c. 29, p. 45, § 1; Stats.1988, c. 126, § 1.)*

Cross References

Automobile dismantler,
  Generally, see Vehicle Code § 11500 et seq.
  Defined, see Vehicle Code § 220.
Dealer,
  Generally, see Vehicle Code § 11700 et seq.
  Defined, see Vehicle Code § 285.
Equalized county assessment roll, see Revenue and Taxation Code § 2050 et seq.
Evidences of registration, see Vehicle Code § 4450 et seq.
Junkyards, see Business and Professions Code § 21600 et seq.
Public nuisances,
  Generally, see Penal Code § 370 et seq.
  Defined, see Civil Code § 3480.
  Remedies, see Civil Code § 3490 et seq.
Reimbursement of governmental or private agency for removal of abandoned vehicles, see Vehicle Code § 22710.
Service authority for abatement of abandoned vehicles, see Vehicle Code § 22710.

§ 22661. Contents of ordinance

Any ordinance establishing procedures for the removal of abandoned vehicles shall contain all of the following provisions:

(a) The requirement that notice be given to the Department of Motor Vehicles within five days after the date of removal, identifying the vehicle or part thereof and any evidence of registration available, including, but not limited to, the registration card, certificates of ownership, or license plates.

(b) Making the ordinance inapplicable to (1) a vehicle or part thereof that is completely enclosed within a building in a lawful manner where it is not visible from the street or other public or private property or (2) a vehicle or part thereof that is stored or parked in a lawful manner on private property in connection with the business of a licensed dismantler, licensed vehicle dealer, or a junkyard. This exception shall not, however, authorize the maintenance of a public or private nuisance as defined under provisions of law other than this chapter.

(c) The requirement that not less than a 10-day notice of intention to abate and remove the vehicle or part thereof as a public nuisance be issued, unless the property owner and the owner of the vehicle have signed releases authorizing removal and waiving further interest in the vehicle or part thereof. However, the notice of intention is not required for removal of a vehicle or part thereof that is inoperable due to the absence of a motor, transmission, or wheels and incapable of being towed, is valued at less than two hundred dollars ($200) by a person specified in Section 22855, and is determined by the local agency to be a public nuisance presenting an immediate threat to public health or safety, provided that the property owner has signed a release authorizing removal and waiving further interest in the vehicle or part thereof. Prior to final disposition under Section 22662 of such a low-valued vehicle or part for which evidence of registration was recovered pursuant to subdivision (a), the local agency shall provide notice to the registered and legal owners of intent to dispose of the vehicle or part, and if the vehicle or part is not claimed and removed within 12 days after the notice is mailed, from a location specified in Section 22662, final disposition may proceed. No local agency or contractor thereof shall be liable for damage caused to a vehicle or part thereof by removal pursuant to this section.

This subdivision applies only to inoperable vehicles located upon a parcel that is (1) zoned for agricultural use or (2) not improved with a residential structure containing one or more dwelling units.

(d) The 10-day notice of intention to abate and remove a vehicle or part thereof, when required by this section, shall contain a statement of the hearing rights of the owner of the property on which the vehicle is located and of the owner of the vehicle. The statement shall include notice to the property owner that he or she may appear in person at a hearing or may submit a sworn written statement denying responsibility for the presence of the vehicle on the land, with his or her reasons for such denial, in lieu of appearing. The notice of intention to abate shall be mailed, by registered or certified mail, to the owner of the land as shown on the last equalized assessment roll and to the last registered and legal owners of record unless the vehicle is in such condition that identification numbers are not available to determine ownership.

(e) The requirement that a public hearing be held before the governing body of the city, county, or city and county, or any other board, commissioner, or official of the city, county, or city and county as designated by the governing body, upon request for such a hearing by the owner of the vehicle or the owner of the land on which the vehicle is located. This request shall be made to the appropriate public body, agency, or officer within 10 days after the mailing of notice of intention to abate and remove the vehicle or at the time of signing a release pursuant to subdivision (c). If the owner of the land on which the vehicle is located submits a sworn written statement denying responsibility for the presence of the vehicle on his or her land within that time period, this statement shall be construed as a request for hearing that does not require the presence of the owner submitting the request. If the request is not received within that period, the appropriate public body, agency, or officer shall have the authority to remove the vehicle.

(f) The requirement that after a vehicle has been removed, it shall not be reconstructed or made operable, unless it is a vehicle that qualifies for either horseless carriage license plates or historical vehicle license plates, pursuant to Section 5004, in which case the vehicle may be reconstructed or made operable.

(g) A provision authorizing the owner of the land on which the vehicle is located to appear in person at the hearing or present a sworn written statement denying responsibility for the presence of the vehicle on the land, with his or her reasons for the denial. If it is determined at the hearing that the vehicle was placed on the land without the consent of the landowner and that he or she has not subsequently acquiesced to its presence, then the local authority shall not assess costs of administration or removal of the vehicle against the property upon which the vehicle is located or otherwise attempt to collect those costs from the owner. *(Added by Stats.1976, c. 29, p. 45, § 2. Amended by Stats.1983, c. 372, § 1; Stats.1993, c. 589 (A.B.2211), § 187.)*

§ 22662. Disposition of vehicle or parts

Vehicles or parts thereof may be disposed of by removal to a scrapyard, automobile dismantler's yard, or any suitable site operated by a local authority for processing as scrap, or other final disposition consistent with subdivision (e) of Section 22661. A local authority may operate such a disposal site when its governing body determines that commercial channels of disposition are not available or are inadequate, and it may make final disposition of such vehicles or parts, or the local agency may transfer such vehicle or parts to another, provided such disposal shall be only as scrap. *(Added by Stats.1976, c. 29, p. 46, § 3.)*

Cross References

Local authorities defined, see Vehicle Code § 385.

§ 22663. Administration of ordinance

Any ordinance adopted pursuant to Section 22660 shall provide for administration of the ordinance by regularly salaried full-time employees of the city, county, or city and county, except that the removal of vehicles or parts thereof from property may be by any other duly authorized person. Any such authorized person may enter upon private property for the purposes specified in the ordinance to examine a vehicle or parts thereof, obtain information as to the identity of a vehicle, and remove or cause the removal of a vehicle or part thereof declared to be a nuisance pursuant to the ordinance. *(Added by Stats.1976, c. 29, p. 46, § 4.)*

§ 22664. Waiver; reporting requirements and fees

Any licensed dismantler or commercial enterprise acquiring vehicles removed pursuant to such ordinance shall be excused from the reporting requirements of Section 11520; and any fees and penalties which would otherwise be due the Department of Motor Vehicles are hereby waived, provided that a copy of the resolution or order authorizing disposition of the vehicle is retained in the dismantler's or commercial enterprise's business records. *(Added by Stats.1976, c. 29, p. 46, § 5.)*

§ 22665. Administration of abandoned vehicle abatement and removal program

Notwithstanding Section 22710 or any other provision of law, the department may, at the request of a local authority, other than a service authority, administer on behalf of the authority its abandoned vehicle abatement and removal program established pursuant to Section 22660. *(Added by Stats.1976, c. 29, p. 47, § 6. Amended by Stats.1990, c. 1684 (A.B.4114), § 4.)*

Cross References

Local authorities defined, see Vehicle Code § 385.

§ 22666. Regulations of highway patrol

Whenever the department is administering a program pursuant to Section 22665, it shall by regulation establish procedures for the abatement and removal of vehicles that are identical to the requirements specified in Section 22661, except that the department shall provide by agreement with the requesting local authority for the conduct of a public hearing pursuant to subdivision (d) of Section 22661 by the local authority and for the reimbursement of the department for its costs of administration and removal which the local authority is authorized to recover from the property owner pursuant to Section 22660. Such regulations shall also provide for the administration of the regulations by regularly salaried, full-time personnel of the department, except that the removal of vehicles or parts thereof from property may be done by any other duly authorized person. Any such person may enter upon private property for the purposes specified in the regulations to examine a vehicle or parts thereof, obtain information as to the identity of a vehicle, and remove or cause the removal of a vehicle or part thereof declared to be a nuisance pursuant to the regulations.

The provisions of Sections 22662 and 22664 shall also apply to any vehicle removed by the department. *(Added by Stats.1976, c. 29, p. 47, § 7.)*

Cross References

Local authorities defined, see Vehicle Code § 385.

§ 22667. Abatement and removal; priorities

In establishing procedures for the abatement and removal of abandoned vehicles, the department shall give priority to the removal of abandoned vehicles from corridors of the state highway system, from public lands and parks, and from river and wildlife areas. *(Added by Stats.1976, c. 29, p. 47, § 8.)*

§ 22668. Abandoned Vehicle Trust Fund; prohibited disbursements

No local authority whose abandoned vehicle abatement and removal program is administered pursuant to Section 22665 shall be eligible for any disbursement from the Abandoned Vehicle Trust Fund pursuant to Section 22710. *(Added by Stats.1976, c. 29, p. 47, § 9.)*

Cross References

Local authorities defined, see Vehicle Code § 385.

§ 22669. Removal of abandoned vehicles

(a) Any peace officer, as that term is defined in Chapter 4.5 (commencing with Section 830) of Title 3 of Part 2 of the Penal Code, or any other employee of the state, county, or city designated by an agency or department of the state or the board of supervisors or city council to perform this function, in the territorial limits in which the officer or employee is authorized to act, who has reasonable grounds to believe that the vehicle has been abandoned, as determined pursuant to Section 22523, may remove the vehicle from a highway or from public or private property.

(b) Any person performing a franchise or contract awarded pursuant to subdivision (a) of Section 22710, may remove a vehicle from a highway or place to which it has been removed pursuant to subdivision (c) of Section 22654 or from public or private property, after a determination by a peace officer, as that term is defined in Chapter 4.5 (commencing with Section 830) of Title 3 of Part 2 of the Penal Code, or other designated employee of the state, county, or city in which the vehicle is located that the vehicle is abandoned, as determined pursuant to Section 22523.

(c) A state, county, or city employee, other than a peace officer or employee of a sheriff's department or a city police department, designated to remove vehicles pursuant to this section may do so only after he or she has mailed or personally delivered a written report identifying the vehicle and its location to the office of the Department of the California Highway Patrol located nearest to the vehicle.

(d) Motor vehicles which are parked, resting, or otherwise immobilized on any highway or public right-of-way and which lack an engine, transmission, wheels, tires, doors, windshield, or any other part or equipment necessary to operate safely on the highways of this state, are hereby declared a hazard to public health, safety, and welfare and may be removed immediately upon discovery by a peace officer or other designated employee of the state, county, or city. *(Formerly § 22702, added by Stats.1959, c. 3, p. 1703, § 22702. Amended by Stats.1960, 1st Ex.Sess., c. 57, p. 406, § 6; Stats.1965, c. 1135, p. 2789, § 9; Stats.1967, c. 1055, p. 2662, § 2; Stats.1969, c. 547, p. 1174, § 2; Stats.1969, c. 1116, p. 2180, § 7; Stats.1970, c. 1431, p. 2775, § 2; Stats.1971, c. 130, p. 176, § 4, operative May 3, 1972; Stats.1971, c. 1624, p. 3499, § 7, operative May 3, 1972; Stats.1973, c. 78, p. 138, § 18; Stats.1973, c. 49, p. 81, § 2, eff. May 15, 1973; Stats.1974, c. 797, p. 1746, § 3; Stats.1979, c. 831, p. 2883, § 4; Stats.1979, c. 909, p. 3131, § 5.5; Stats.1980, c. 1340, p. 4739, § 38, eff. Sept. 30, 1980. Renumbered § 22669 and amended by Stats.1980, c. 1111, p. 3569, § 22; Stats.1980, c. 1340, p. 4739, § 38.2, eff. Sept. 30, 1980, operative Jan. 1, 1981. Amended by Stats.1987, c. 1133, § 4.)*

Cross References

Department of the California Highway Patrol, generally, see Vehicle Code § 2100 et seq.
Peace officer, definition, see Penal Code §§ 7, 830 et seq., 852.1.
Private property, removal of vehicles, see Vehicle Code §§ 22653, 22658, 22852.
Report of abandoned or unlawfully stored vehicle, see Vehicle Code § 10652.
Storage of vehicles, see Vehicle Code § 22850.

§ 22670. Determination of estimated value of vehicle

(a) For lien sale purposes, the public agency causing the removal of the vehicle shall determine if the estimated value of the vehicle that has been ordered removed, towed, or stored is five hundred dollars ($ 500) or less, over five hundred dollars ($500) but four thousand dollars ($4,000) or less, or over four thousand dollars ($4,000).

(b) If the public agency fails or refuses to put a value on, or to estimate the value of, the vehicle within three days after the date of removal of the vehicle, the garage keeper specified in Section 22851 or the garage keeper's agent shall determine, under penalty of perjury, if the estimated value of the vehicle that has been ordered removed, towed, or stored, is five hundred dollars ($500) or less, over five hundred dollars ($500) but four thousand dollars ($4,000) or less, or over four thousand dollars ($4,000). *(Added by Stats.1980, c. 1111, p. 3568, § 18. Amended by Stats.1984, c. 73, § 4; Stats.1984, c. 1381, § 1; Stats.1987, c. 1091, § 5; Stats.1992, c. 1220 (A.B.3424), § 8; Stats.1998, c. 203 (S.B.1650), § 6; Stats.2004, c. 650 (A.B.3047), § 10.)*

Cross References

Disposal of low-valued vehicle, see Vehicle Code § 22851.10.
Lien sales, impounded vehicles, see Vehicle Code §§ 22851.4, 22851.6.
Satisfaction of lien, see Vehicle Code § 22851.4.

§ 22671. Local franchise or contract for removal

A local authority may either issue a franchise or execute a contract for the removal of abandoned vehicles in accordance with the provisions of this chapter. *(Formerly § 22706, added by Stats.1967, c. 1055, p. 2663, § 4. Renumbered § 22671 and amended by Stats.1980, c. 1111, p. 3570, § 26.)*

Cross References

Local authorities defined, see Vehicle Code § 385.

§ 22710. Service authority for abatement of abandoned vehicles

(a) A service authority for the abatement of abandoned vehicles may be established, and a one dollar ($1) vehicle registration fee imposed, in a county if the board of supervisors of the county, by a two-thirds vote, and a majority of the cities having a majority of the incorporated population within the county have adopted resolutions providing for the establishment of the authority and imposition of the fee. The membership of the authority shall be determined by concurrence of the board of supervisors and a majority vote of the majority of the cities within the county having a majority of the incorporated population.

(b) The authority may contract and may undertake any act convenient or necessary to carry out a law relating to the authority. The authority shall be staffed by existing personnel of the city, county, or county transportation commission.

(c)(1) Notwithstanding any other provision of law, a service authority may adopt an ordinance establishing procedures for the abatement, removal, and disposal, as a public nuisance, of an abandoned, wrecked, dismantled, or inoperative vehicle or part of the vehicle from private or public property; and for the recovery, pursuant to Section 25845 or 38773.5 of the Government Code, or assumption by the service authority, of costs associated with the enforcement of the ordinance. Cost recovery shall only be undertaken by an entity that may be a county or city or the department, pursuant to contract with the service authority as provided in this section.

(2)(A) The money received by an authority pursuant to Section 9250.7 and this section shall be used only for the abatement, removal, or the disposal as a public nuisance of any abandoned, wrecked, dismantled, or inoperative vehicle or part of the vehicle from private or public property. The money received shall not be used to offset the costs of vehicles towed under authorities other than an ordinance adopted pursuant to paragraph (1) or when costs are recovered under Section 22850.5.

(B) The money received by a service authority pursuant to Section 9250.7 and this section that are unexpended in a fiscal year may be carried forward by the service authority for the abandoned vehicle abatement program in the following fiscal year as agreed upon by the service authority and its member agencies.

(d)(1) An abandoned vehicle abatement program and plan of a service authority shall be implemented only with the approval of the county and a majority of the cities having a majority of the incorporated population.

(2)(A) The department shall provide guidelines for an abandoned vehicle abatement program. An authority's abandoned vehicle abatement plan and program shall be consistent with those guidelines, and shall provide for, but not be limited to, an estimate of the number of abandoned vehicles, a disposal and enforcement strategy including contractual agreements, and appropriate fiscal controls.

(B) The department's guidelines provided pursuant to this paragraph shall include, but not be limited to, requiring each service authority receiving funds from the Abandoned Vehicle Trust Fund to report to the Controller on an annual basis pursuant to subdivision (c) of Section 9250.7, in a manner prescribed by the department, and pursuant to an approved abandoned vehicle abatement program.

(C) A service authority may carry out an abandoned vehicle abatement from a public property after providing a notice as specified by the local ordinance adopted pursuant to Section 22660 of the jurisdiction in which the abandoned vehicle is located and that notice has expired.

(3) After a plan has been approved pursuant to paragraph (1), the service authority shall, not later than August 1 of the year in which the plan was approved, submit it to the department for review, and the department shall, not later than October 1 of that same year, either approve the plan as submitted or make recommendations for revision. After the plan has received the department's approval as being consistent with the department's guidelines, the service authority shall submit it to the Controller.

(4) Except as provided in subdivision (e), the Controller shall not make an allocation for a fiscal year, commencing on July 1 following the Controller's determination to suspend a service authority when a service authority has failed to comply with the provisions set forth in Section 9250.7.

(5) A governmental agency shall not receive funds from a service authority for the abatement of abandoned vehicles pursuant to an approved abandoned vehicle abatement program unless the governmental agency has submitted an annual report to the service authority stating the manner in which the funds were expended, and the number of vehicles abated. The governmental agency shall receive that percentage of the total funds collected by the service authority that is equal to its share of the formula calculated pursuant to paragraph (6).

(6) Each service authority shall calculate a formula for apportioning funds to each governmental agency that receives funds from the service authority and submit that formula to the Controller with the annual report required pursuant to paragraph (2). The formula shall apportion 50 percent of the funds received by the service authority to a governmental agency based on the percentage of vehicles abated by that governmental agency of the total number of abandoned vehicles abated by all member agencies, and 50 percent based on population and geographic area, as determined by the service authority. When the formula is first submitted to the Controller, and each time the formula is revised thereafter, the service authority shall include a detailed explanation of how the service authority determined the apportionment between per capita abatements and service area.

(7) Notwithstanding any other provision of this subdivision, the Controller may allocate to the service authority in the County of Humboldt the net amount of the abandoned vehicle abatement funds received from the fee imposed by that authority, as described in subdivision (b) of Section 9250.7, for calendar years 2000 and 2001.

(e) A plan that has been submitted to the Controller pursuant to subdivision (d) may be revised pursuant to the procedure prescribed in that subdivision, including compliance with any dates described therein for submission to the department and the Controller, respectively, in the year in which the revisions are proposed by the service authority. Compliance with that procedure shall only be required if the revisions are substantial.

(f) For purposes of this section, "abandoned vehicle abatement" means the removal of a vehicle from public or private property by towing or any other means after the vehicle has been marked as abandoned by an official of a governmental agency that is a member of the service authority.

(g) A service authority shall cease to exist on the date that all revenues received by the authority pursuant to this section and Section 9250.7 have been expended.

(h) In the event of a conflict with other provisions of law, this section shall govern the disbursement of money collected pursuant to this section and from the Abandoned Vehicle Trust Fund for the implementation of the abandoned vehicle abatement program. *(Added by Stats.1990, c. 1684 (A.B.4114), § 6. Amended by Stats. 1991, c. 928 (A.B.1886), § 30, eff. Oct. 14, 1991; Stats.1995, c. 819 (A.B.135), § 3; Stats.1997, c. 272 (S.B.112), § 2, eff. Aug. 15, 1997; Stats.2001, c. 175 (S.B.106), § 2; Stats.2002, c. 500 (S.B.1329), § 3; Stats.2004, c. 650 (A.B.3047), § 11; Stats.2007, c. 389 (A.B.468), § 2.)*

Cross References

Registration fee, service authority for abatement of abandoned vehicles, see Vehicle Code § 9250.7.

§ 22711. Transportation to and disposition of abandoned vehicle at institution under jurisdiction of director of corrections for restoration and rebuilding

Notwithstanding any other provision of law, the California Highway Patrol, any city, county, or city and county which has an abandoned vehicle abatement program, and any service authority established under Section 22710, upon satisfying all applicable reporting requirements provided in this chapter, may, with the consent of the Director of Corrections, transport any abandoned vehicle to, and dispose of any abandoned vehicle at, any institution under the jurisdiction of the director which has a program established pursuant to Section 2813.5 of the Penal Code. *(Added by Stats.1991, c. 1157 (A.B.2157), § 2.)*

ARTICLE 2. VEHICLE DISPOSITION

§ 22850. Storage of vehicle; mileage

Whenever an officer or employee removes a vehicle from a highway, or from public or private property, unless otherwise provided, he shall take the vehicle to the nearest garage or other place of safety or to a garage designated or maintained by the governmental agency of which the officer or employee is a member, where the vehicle shall be placed in storage.

At the time of such removal, the officer or employee shall determine the amount of mileage on the vehicle. *(Stats.1959, c. 3, p. 1705, § 22850. Amended by Stats.1960, 1st Ex.Sess., c. 57, p. 405, § 2; Stats.1968, c. 1070, p. 2077, § 3; Stats.1975, c. 239, p. 629, § 1.)*

Cross References

Individual violations of code governing repossessors, penalties, investigations and actions, see Business and Professions Code § 7502.1.
Liens on vehicles, see Civil Code § 3068 et seq.
Removal of abandoned vehicles, see Vehicle Code § 22669.
Removal of vehicles, see Vehicle Code § 22651.
Storage of unclaimed property, see Vehicle Code § 2414.
Unlawful use or tampering with vehicle by bailee, see Vehicle Code § 10854.

§ 22850.3. Release to owner or person in control on proof of current registration or on issuance of notice to appear for registration violation; posting of notice

(a) A vehicle placed in storage pursuant to Section 22850 shall be released to the owner or person in control of the vehicle only if the owner or person furnishes, to the law enforcement agency or employee who placed the vehicle in storage, satisfactory proof of current vehicle registration. The agency which caused the vehicle to be stored may, in its discretion, issue a notice to appear for the registration violation, if the two days immediately following the day of impoundment are weekend days or holidays.

(b) At every storage facility there shall be posted in a conspicuous place a notice to the effect that a vehicle placed in storage pursuant to Section 22850 may be released only on proof of current registration or, at the discretion of the impounding agency, upon the issuance of a notice to appear for the registration violation by the local agency which caused the vehicle to be stored, specifying the name and telephone number of that local agency. *(Added by Stats.1990, c. 1199 (A.B.4191), § 1. Amended by Stats.1994, c. 1220 (A.B.3132), § 64, eff. Sept. 30, 1994.)*

§ 22850.5. Impounded vehicles; release procedures; charges for administrative costs

(a) A city, county, or city and county, or a state agency may adopt a regulation, ordinance, or resolution establishing procedures for the release of properly impounded vehicles to the registered owner or the agent of the registered owner and for the imposition of a charge equal to its administrative costs relating to the removal, impound, storage, or release of the vehicles to the registered owner or to the agent of the registered owner. Those administrative costs may be waived by the local or state authority upon verifiable proof that the vehicle was reported stolen at the time the vehicle was removed.

(b) The following apply to any charges imposed for administrative costs pursuant to subdivision (a):

(1) The charges shall only be imposed on the registered owner or the agents of that owner and shall not include any vehicle towed under an abatement program or sold at a lien sale pursuant to Sections 3068.1 to 3074, inclusive, of, and Section 22851 of, the Civil Code unless the sale is sufficient in amount to pay the lienholder's total charges and proper administrative costs.

(2) Any charges shall be collected by the local or state authority only from the registered owner or an agent of the registered owner.

(3) The charges shall be in addition to any other charges authorized or imposed pursuant to this code.

(4) No charge may be imposed for any hearing or appeal relating to the removal, impound, storage, or release of a vehicle unless that hearing or appeal was requested in writing by the registered or legal owner of the vehicle or an agent of that registered or legal owner. In addition, the charge may be imposed only upon the person requesting that hearing or appeal.

No administrative costs authorized under subdivision (a) shall be charged to the legal owner who redeems the vehicle unless the legal owner voluntarily requests a poststorage hearing. No city, county, city and county, or state agency shall require a legal owner or a legal owner's agent to request a poststorage hearing as a requirement for release of the vehicle to the legal owner or the legal owner's agent. The impounding agency, or any person acting on behalf of the agency, shall not require the legal owner or the legal owner's agent to produce any documents other than those specified in paragraph (3) of subdivision (f) of Section 14602.6 or paragraph (3) of subdivision (e) of Section 14602.7. The impounding agency, or any person acting on behalf of the agency, shall not require any documents to be notarized. *(Added by Stats.1993, c. 614 (A.B.481), § 3. Amended by Stats.1996, c. 1142 (S.B.1797), § 13, eff. Sept. 30, 1996; Stats.1996, c. 1156 (A.B.3157), § 5.5; Stats.1998, c. 169 (A.B.1329), § 1; Stats. 1999, c. 456 (S.B.378), § 15; Stats.2001, c. 554 (A.B.783), § 4; Stats.2002, c. 402 (A.B.1883), § 9; Stats.2007, c. 192 (S.B.659), § 12, eff. Sept. 7, 2007; Stats.2015, c. 740 (A.B.281), § 17, eff. Jan. 1, 2016.)*

Cross References

Arrest of persons engaged in speed contests or reckless driving, removal and seizure of vehicles, see Vehicle Code § 23109.2.
Charter-party carrier buses, impoundment and storage, hearing, release of vehicle, see Vehicle Code § 14602.9.
Driving without a license, impounding vehicle, see Vehicle Code § 14602.6.
Fleeing or evading a peace officer, impounding vehicle, see Vehicle Code § 14602.7.
Immediate removal and seizure of vehicle driven by repeat offender, storage and impoundment, vehicle owner's rights and responsibilities, see Vehicle Code § 14602.8.
Removal and seizure of vehicle, release of vehicle to registered owner, see Vehicle Code § 2480.
Service authority for abatement of abandoned vehicles, see Vehicle Code § 22710.
Traffic laws, seizure and impoundment of vehicles, see Vehicle Code § 21100.4.
Vehicle used in commission of specified offenses, public nuisance, see Vehicle Code § 22659.5.
Vehicle used in violation of code governing repossessors, seizure, release and liability, including fees, see Vehicle Code § 23118.

§ 22851. Lien on stored vehicle

(a)(1) Whenever a vehicle has been removed to a garage under this chapter and the keeper of the garage has received the notice or notices as provided herein, the keeper shall have a lien dependent upon possession for his or her compensation for towage and for caring for and keeping safe the vehicle for a period not exceeding 60 days or, if an application for an authorization to conduct a lien sale has been filed pursuant to Section 3068. 1 of the Civil Code within 30 days after the removal of the vehicle to the garage, 120 days and, if the vehicle is not recovered by the owner within that period or the owner is unknown, the keeper of the garage may satisfy his or her lien in the manner prescribed in this article. The lien shall not be assigned. Possession of the vehicle is deemed to arise when a vehicle is removed and is in transit, or when vehicle recovery operations or load salvage operations that have been requested by a law enforcement agency have begun at the scene.

(2) Whenever a vehicle owner returns to a vehicle that is in possession of a towing company prior to the removal of the vehicle, the owner may regain possession of the vehicle from the towing company if the owner pays the towing company the towing charges.

(b) No lien shall attach to any personal property in or on the vehicle. The personal property in or on the vehicle shall be given to the current registered owner or the owner's authorized agent upon demand and without charge during normal business hours. Notwithstanding any other provision of law, normal business hours are Monday to Friday, inclusive, from 8 a.m. to 5 p.m., inclusive, except state holidays. A gate fee may be charged for returning property after normal business hours, weekends, and state holidays. The maximum hourly charge for nonbusiness hours releases shall be one-half the hourly tow rate charged for initially towing the vehicle, or less. The lienholder is not responsible for property after any vehicle has been disposed of pursuant to this chapter. *(Stats.1959, c. 3, p. 1705, § 22851. Amended by Stats.1959, c. 963, p. 2994, § 2; Stats.1965, c. 1135, p. 2790, § 15; Stats.1967, c. 993, p. 2587, § 1; Stats.1971, c. 510, p. 1005, § 3, operative May 3, 1972; Stats.1974, c. 1262, p. 2741, § 7, eff. Sept. 23, 1974, operative Nov. 1, 1974 to Dec. 31, 1976; Stats.1980, c. 1111, p. 3571, § 29; Stats.1989, c. 457, § 2; Stats.1995, c. 404 (S.B.240), § 6; Stats.2001, c. 127 (S.B.46), § 8, eff. July 30, 2001.)*

Cross References

Determination of estimated value of vehicle, duration of amendment, see Vehicle Code § 22670.
Garage defined, see Vehicle Code § 340.
Liens on vehicles, see Civil Code § 3068 et seq.
Method of giving notice, see Vehicle Code §§ 22 et seq., 29.
Removal of vessel from public waterways by peace officers, lifeguards, or marine safety officers, see Harbors and Navigation Code § 523.

§ 22851.1. Impounded vehicles; lien sales; priorities; defenses; bail

(a) If the vehicle is impounded pursuant to subdivision (i) of Section 22651 and not released as provided in that subdivision, the vehicle may be sold pursuant to this chapter to satisfy the liens specified in Section 22851 and in subdivision (b) of this section.

(b) A local authority impounding a vehicle pursuant to subdivision (i) of Section 22651 shall have a lien dependent upon possession by the keeper of the garage for satisfaction of bail for all outstanding notices of parking violation issued by the local authority for the vehicle, when the conditions specified in subdivision (c) have been met. This lien shall be subordinate in priority to the lien established by Section 22851, and the proceeds of any sale shall be applied accordingly. Consistent with this order of priority, the term "lien," as used in this article and in Chapter 6.5 (commencing with Section 3067) of Title 14 of Part 4 of Division 3 of the Civil Code, includes a lien imposed by this subdivision. In any action brought to perfect the lien, where required by subdivision (d) of Section 22851.8 of this code, or by subdivision (d) of Section 3071 or subdivision (d) of Section 3072 of the Civil Code, it shall be a defense to the recovery of bail that the owner of the vehicle at the time of impoundment was not the owner of the vehicle at the time of the parking offense.

(c) A lien shall exist for bail with respect to parking violations for which no person has answered the charge in the notice of parking violation given, or filed an affidavit of nonownership pursuant to and within the time specified in subdivision (b) of Section 41103. *(Added by Stats.1984, c. 138, § 1. Amended by Stats.1996, c. 124 (A.B.3470), § 129.)*

§ 22851.2. Disposition of low-valued vehicle

(a) Excepting a vehicle removed pursuant to Section 22669, if the vehicle is determined to have a value not exceeding five hundred dollars ($500) pursuant to Section 22670, the public agency that removed the vehicle shall do all of the following:

(1) Within 48 hours after removal of the vehicle, notify the Stolen Vehicle System of the Department of Justice in Sacramento of the removal.

(2) Prepare and give to the lienholder a report that includes all of the following:

(A) The value of the vehicle estimated pursuant to Section 22670.

(B) The identification of the estimator.

(C) The location of the vehicle.

(D) A description of the vehicle, including the make, year model, identification number, license number, state of registration, and, if a motorcycle, an engine number.

(E) The statutory authority for storage.

(b) If the vehicle is in a condition that there is no means of determining ownership, the public agency that removed the vehicle may give authorization to dispose of the vehicle. If authorization for disposal is not issued, a vehicle identification number shall be assigned prior to commencing the lien sale proceedings. *(Formerly § 22705, added by Stats.1965, c. 1135, p. 2789, § 13. Amended by Stats.1967, c. 1055, p. 2662, § 3; Stats.1970, c. 1431, p. 2776, § 3; Stats.1971, c. 510, p. 1004, § 2, operative May 3, 1972; Stats.1972, c.*

98, p. 135, § 6, eff. May 30, 1972, operative Oct. 1, 1972; Stats.1972, c. 791, p. 1407, § 4; Stats.1974, c. 1262, p. 2741, § 6, eff. Sept. 23, 1974, operative Nov. 1, 1974; Stats.1975, c. 1036, p. 2450, § 4, eff. Sept. 24, 1975; Stats.1977, c. 821, p. 2492, § 4; Stats.1978, c. 1005, p. 3091, § 12. Renumbered § 22851.2 and amended by Stats.1980, c. 1111, p. 3570, § 24. Amended by Stats.1983, c. 913, § 4; Stats.1986, c. 1059, § 1, eff. Sept. 24, 1986; Stats.1987, c. 530, § 1; Stats.1987, c. 1091, § 6; Stats.2004, c. 650 (A.B.3047), § 12.)

Cross References

Automobile dismantler,
  Generally, see Vehicle Code § 11500 et seq.
  Defined, see Vehicle Code § 220.
Evidences of registration, see Vehicle Code § 4450 et seq.

§ 22851.3. Disposal of low-value vehicle by public agency after removal of abandoned vehicle; procedure

Whenever a peace officer, as defined in Chapter 4.5 (commencing with Section 830) of Title 3 of Part 2 of the Penal Code, or any other employee of a public agency authorized pursuant to Section 22669, removes, or causes the removal of, a vehicle pursuant to Section 22669 and the public agency or, at the request of the public agency, the lienholder determines the estimated value of the vehicle is five hundred dollars ($500) or less, the public agency that removed, or caused the removal of, the vehicle shall cause the disposal of the vehicle under this section, subject to all of the following requirements:

(a) Not less than 72 hours before the vehicle is removed, the peace officer or the authorized public employee has securely attached to the vehicle a distinctive notice which states that the vehicle will be removed by the public agency. This subdivision does not apply to abandoned vehicles removed pursuant to subdivision (d) of Section 22669 which are determined by the public agency to have an estimated value of three hundred dollars ($300) or less.

(b) Immediately after removal of the vehicle, the public agency which removed, or caused the removal of, the vehicle shall notify the Stolen Vehicle System of the Department of Justice in Sacramento of the removal.

(c) The public agency that removed, or caused the removal of, the vehicle or, at the request of the public agency, the lienholder shall obtain a copy of the names and addresses of all persons having an interest in the vehicle, if any, from the Department of Motor Vehicles either directly or by use of the California Law Enforcement Telecommunications System. This subdivision does not require the public agency or lienholder to obtain a copy of the actual record on file at the Department of Motor Vehicles.

(d) Within 48 hours of the removal, excluding weekends and holidays, the public agency that removed, or caused the removal of, the vehicle or, at the request of the public agency, the lienholder shall send a notice to the registered and legal owners at their addresses of record with the Department of Motor Vehicles, and to any other person known to have an interest in the vehicle. A notice sent by the public agency shall be sent by certified or first-class mail, and a notice sent by the lienholder shall be sent by certified mail. The notice shall include all of the following information:

(1) The name, address, and telephone number of the public agency providing the notice.

(2) The location of the place of storage and description of the vehicle which shall include, if available, the vehicle make, license plate number, vehicle identification number, and mileage.

(3) The authority and purpose for the removal of the vehicle.

(4) A statement that the vehicle may be disposed of 15 days from the date of the notice.

(5) A statement that the owners and interested persons, or their agents, have the opportunity for a poststorage hearing before the public agency that removed, or caused the removal of, the vehicle to determine the validity of the storage if a request for a hearing is made in person, in writing, or by telephone within 10 days from the date of notice; that, if the owner or interested person, or his or her agent, disagrees with the decision of the public agency, the decision may be reviewed pursuant to Section 11523 of the Government Code; and that during the time of the initial hearing, or during the time the decision is being reviewed pursuant to Section 11523 of the Government Code, the vehicle in question may not be disposed of.

(e)(1) A requested hearing shall be conducted within 48 hours of the request, excluding weekends and holidays. The public agency that removed the vehicle may authorize its own officers to conduct the hearing if the hearing officer is not the same person who directed the storage of the vehicle.

(2) Failure of either the registered or legal owner or interested person, or his or her agent, to request or to attend a scheduled hearing shall satisfy the poststorage validity hearing requirement of this section.

(f) The public agency employing the person, or utilizing the services of a contractor or franchiser pursuant to subdivision (b) of Section 22669, that removed, or caused the removal of, the vehicle and that directed any towing or storage, is responsible for the costs incurred for towing and storage if it is determined in the hearing that reasonable grounds to believe that the vehicle was abandoned are not established.

(g) An authorization for disposal may not be issued by the public agency that removed, or caused the removal of, the vehicle to a lienholder who is storing the vehicle prior to the conclusion of a requested poststorage hearing or any judicial review of that hearing.

(h) If, after 15 days from the notification date, the vehicle remains unclaimed and the towing and storage fees have not been paid, and if no request for a poststorage hearing was requested or a poststorage hearing was not attended, the public agency that removed, or caused the removal of, the vehicle shall provide to the lienholder who is storing the vehicle, on a form approved by the Department of Motor Vehicles, authorization to dispose of the vehicle. The lienholder may request the public agency to provide the authorization to dispose of the vehicle.

(i) If the vehicle is claimed by the owner or his or her agent within 15 days of the notice date, the lienholder who is storing the vehicle may collect reasonable fees for services rendered, but may not collect lien sale fees as provided in Section 22851.12.

(j) Disposal of the vehicle by the lienholder who is storing the vehicle may only be to a licensed dismantler or scrap iron processor. A copy of the public agency's authorization for disposal shall be forwarded to the licensed dismantler within five days of disposal to a licensed dismantler. A copy of the public agency's authorization for disposal shall be retained by the lienholder who stored the vehicle for a period of 90 days if the vehicle is disposed of to a scrap iron processor.

(k) If the names and addresses of the registered and legal owners of the vehicle are not available from the records of the Department of Motor Vehicles, either directly or by use of the California Law Enforcement Telecommunications System, the public agency may issue to the lienholder who stored the vehicle an authorization for disposal at any time after the removal.

The lienholder may request the public agency to issue an authorization for disposal after the lienholder ascertains that the names and addresses of the registered and legal owners of the vehicle are not available from the records of the Department of Motor Vehicles either directly or by use of the California Law Enforcement Telecommunications System.

(*l*) A vehicle disposed of pursuant to this section may not be reconstructed or made operable, unless it is a vehicle that qualifies for either horseless carriage license plates or historical vehicle license plates, pursuant to Section 5004, in which case the vehicle may be reconstructed or made operable. *(Added by Stats.1986, c. 1059, § 2, eff. Sept. 24, 1986. Amended by Stats.1987, c. 530, § 2; Stats.1987, c. 1091, § 7; Stats.1987, c. 1133, § 5; Stats.2003, c. 67 (A.B.478), § 1.)*

Cross References

Failure of registered owner of mobilehome, manufactured home, or recreational vehicle to pay costs of remediation, warehouseman's lien, see Health and Safety Code § 25400.47.

§ 22851.4. Satisfaction of lien

If the vehicle is determined to have a value exceeding five hundred dollars ($500) pursuant to Section 22670, the lien shall be satisfied pursuant to Sections 3067 to 3074, inclusive, of the Civil Code. *(Added by Stats.1980, c. 1111, p. 3571, § 31. Amended by Stats.1984, c. 1381, § 2; Stats.1987, c. 1091, § 9; Stats.2004, c. 650 (A.B.3047), § 13.)*

§ 22851.6. Satisfaction of lien; low-valued vehicles; forms

(a) Lienholders who acquire a vehicle subject to Section 22851.2 shall satisfy their lien pursuant to Sections 22851.8 and 22851.10 if the vehicle has a value not exceeding five hundred dollars ($500), as determined pursuant to Section 22670.

(b) All forms required by Sections 22851.8 and 22851.10 shall be prescribed by the Department of Motor Vehicles. The language used in the notices and declarations shall be simple and nontechnical. *(Added by Stats.1980, c. 1111, p. 3571, § 32. Amended by Stats.1984, c. 1381, § 3; Stats.1986, c. 1059, § 3, eff. Sept. 24, 1986; Stats.1987, c. 530, § 3; Stats.1987, c. 1091, § 10; Stats.2004, c. 650 (A.B.3047), § 14.)*

§ 22851.8. Disposal of low-valued vehicle

(a) The lienholder shall, within 15 working days following the date of possession of the vehicle, make a request to the Department of Motor Vehicles for the names and addresses of all persons having an interest in the vehicle. A storage charge may not accrue beyond the 15–day period unless the lienholder has made a request to the Department of Motor Vehicles as provided for in this section.

(b) By certified mail with return receipt requested or by United States Postal Service Certificate of Mailing, the lienholder shall immediately, upon receipt of this information, send the following prescribed forms and enclosures to the registered owner and legal owner at their addresses of record with the Department of Motor Vehicles, and to any other person known to have an interest in the vehicle:

(1) A completed form entitled "Notice of Intent to Dispose of a Vehicle Valued at $500 or Less."

(2) A blank form entitled "Declaration of Opposition."

(3) A return envelope preaddressed to the lienholder.

(c) All notices to persons having an interest in the vehicle shall be signed under penalty of perjury and shall include all of the following:

(1) A description of the vehicle, including make, year, model, identification number, license number, and state of registration. For motorcycles, the engine number shall also be included.

(2) The names and addresses of the registered and legal owners of the vehicle and any other person known to have an interest in the vehicle.

(3) The following statements and information:

(A) The amount of the lien.

(B) The facts concerning the claim that gives rise to the lien.

(C) The person has a right to a hearing in court.

(D) If a hearing in court is desired, a Declaration of Opposition form shall be signed under penalty of perjury and returned to the lienholder within 10 days of the date the notice form specified in paragraph (1) of subdivision (b) was mailed.

(E) If the Declaration of Opposition form is signed and mailed, the lienholder shall be allowed to dispose of the vehicle only if the lienholder obtains a court judgment or a subsequent release from the declarant or if the declarant cannot be served as described in subdivision (e).

(F) If a court action is filed, the declarant shall be notified of the lawsuit at the address shown on the Declaration of Opposition form, and the declarant may appear to contest the claim.

(G) The declarant may be liable for court costs if a judgment is entered in favor of the lienholder.

(4) A statement that the lienholder may dispose of the vehicle to a licensed dismantler or scrap iron processor if it is not redeemed or if a Declaration of Opposition form is not signed and mailed to the lienholder within 10 days of the date the notice form specified in paragraph (1) of subdivision (b) was mailed.

(d) If the lienholder receives a completed Declaration of Opposition form within the time prescribed, the vehicle shall not be disposed of unless the lienholder files an action in court within 20 days of the date the notice form specified in paragraph (1) of subdivision (b) was mailed and a judgment is subsequently entered in favor of the lienholder or unless the declarant subsequently releases his or her interest in the vehicle. If a money judgment is entered in favor of the lienholder and the judgment is not paid within five days after becoming final, then the lienholder may dispose of the vehicle through a dismantler or scrap iron processor.

(e)(1) Service on the declarant in person or by certified mail, return receipt requested, signed by the addressee at the address shown on the Declaration of Opposition form, shall be effective for the serving of process.

(2) If the lienholder has served the declarant by certified mail, return receipt requested, at the address shown on the Declaration of Opposition form and the mail has been returned unclaimed, or if the lienholder has attempted to effect service on the declarant in person with a marshal, sheriff, or licensed process server and the marshal, sheriff, or licensed process server has been unable to effect service on the declarant, the lienholder may proceed with the judicial proceeding or proceed with the lien sale without a judicial proceeding. The lienholder shall notify the Department of Motor Vehicles of the inability to effect service on the declarant and shall provide the Department of Motor Vehicles with a copy of the documents with which service on the declarant was attempted. Upon receipt of the notification of unsuccessful service, the Department of Motor Vehicles shall send authorization of the sale to the lienholder and send notification of the authorization to the declarant. If service is effected on the declarant, the proof of service shall be submitted to the Department of Motor Vehicles with the documents specified in Section 22851.10. *(Added by Stats.1980, c. 1111, p. 3571, § 33. Amended by Stats.1987, c. 1091, § 11; Stats.1990, c. 1284 (A.B.3049), § 5; Stats.1992, c. 1220 (A.B.3424), § 9; Stats.1996, c. 676 (S.B. 1111), § 3; Stats.2004, c. 650 (A.B.3047), § 15.)*

Cross References

Failure of registered owner of mobilehome, manufactured home, or recreational vehicle to pay costs of remediation, warehouseman's lien, see Health and Safety Code § 25400.47.

§ 22851.10. Disposal of low-valued vehicle; dismantler or scrap iron processor; forms and information; reconstruction of vehicle

(a) A vehicle determined to have a value not exceeding five hundred dollars ($500) pursuant to Section 22670 that was stored pursuant to this chapter, and that remains unclaimed, or for which reasonable towing and storage charges remain unpaid, shall be disposed of only to a licensed dismantler or scrap iron processor not earlier than 15 days after the date the Notice of Intent to Dispose of a Vehicle Valued at $500 or Less form required pursuant to subdivision (b) of Section 22851.8 was mailed, unless a Declaration of Opposition form has been signed and returned to the lienholder.

(b) If the vehicle has been disposed of to a licensed dismantler or scrap iron processor, the lienholder shall forward the following forms and information to the licensed dismantler or scrap iron processor within five days:

(1) A statement, signed under penalty of perjury, that a properly executed Declaration of Opposition form was not received.

(2) A copy of the notice sent to all interested parties.

(3) A certification from the public agency that made the determination of value pursuant to Section 22670.

(4) The proof of service pursuant to subdivision (e) of Section 22851.8 or a copy of the court judgment, if any in favor of the lienholder entered pursuant to subdivision (d) of Section 22851.8.

(5) The name, address, and telephone number of the licensed dismantler or scrap iron processor who received the vehicle.

(6) The amount the lienholder received for the vehicle.

(c) A vehicle disposed of pursuant to this section shall not be reconstructed or made operable, unless it is a vehicle that qualifies for either horseless carriage license plates or historical vehicle license plates, pursuant to Section 5004, in which case the vehicle may be reconstructed or made operable. *(Added by Stats.1980, c. 1111, p. 3573, § 34. Amended by Stats.1982, c. 664, p. 2725, § 8; Stats.1987, c. 1091, § 12; Stats.1990, c. 1284 (A.B.3049), § 6; Stats.2004, c. 650 (A.B.3047), § 16.)*

§ 22851.12. Lien–sale preparations; fees

The lienholder may charge a fee for lien-sale preparations not to exceed seventy dollars ($70) in the case of a vehicle having a value determined to be four thousand dollars ($4,000) or less and not to exceed one hundred dollars ($100) in the case of a vehicle having a value determined to be greater than four thousand dollars ($4,000), from any person who redeems the vehicle prior to disposal or is sold through a lien sale pursuant to this chapter. These charges may commence and become part of the possessory lien when the lienholder requests the names and addresses of all persons having an interest in the vehicle from the department. Not more than 50 percent of the allowable fee may be charged until the lien sale notifications are mailed to all interested parties and the lienholder or the registration service agent has possession of the required lien processing documents. This charge shall not be made in the case of any vehicle redeemed prior to 72 hours from the initial storage. *(Added by Stats.1995, c. 404 (S.B.240), § 8. Amended by Stats.1996, c. 676 (S.B.1111), § 4; Stats.1998, c. 203 (S.B.1650), § 7.)*

§ 22852. Storage; notice; hearing; application of section

(a) Whenever an authorized member of a public agency directs the storage of a vehicle, as permitted by this chapter, or upon the storage of a vehicle as permitted under this section (except as provided in subdivision (f) or (g)), the agency or person directing the storage shall provide the vehicle's registered and legal owners of record, or their agents, with the opportunity for a poststorage hearing to determine the validity of the storage.

(b) A notice of the storage shall be mailed or personally delivered to the registered and legal owners within 48 hours, excluding weekends and holidays, and shall include all of the following information:

(1) The name, address, and telephone number of the agency providing the notice.

(2) The location of the place of storage and description of the vehicle, which shall include, if available, the name or make, the manufacturer, the license plate number, and the mileage.

(3) The authority and purpose for the removal of the vehicle.

(4) A statement that, in order to receive their poststorage hearing, the owners, or their agents, shall request the hearing in person, writing, or by telephone within 10 days of the date appearing on the notice.

(c) The poststorage hearing shall be conducted within 48 hours of the request, excluding weekends and holidays. The public agency may authorize its own officer or employee to conduct the hearing if the hearing officer is not the same person who directed the storage of the vehicle.

(d) Failure of either the registered or legal owner, or his or her agent, to request or to attend a scheduled hearing shall satisfy the poststorage hearing requirement.

(e) The agency employing the person who directed the storage shall be responsible for the costs incurred for towing and storage if it is determined in the poststorage hearing that reasonable grounds for the storage are not established.

(f) This section does not apply to vehicles abated under the Abandoned Vehicle Abatement Program pursuant to Sections 22660 to 22668, inclusive, and Section 22710, or to vehicles impounded for investigation pursuant to Section 22655, or to vehicles removed from private property pursuant to Section 22658.

(g) This section does not apply to abandoned vehicles removed pursuant to Section 22669 that are determined by the public agency to have an estimated value of five hundred dollars ($500) or less. *(Added by Stats.1979, c. 1022, p. 3491, § 4. Amended by Stats.1986, c. 1059, § 4, eff. Sept. 24, 1986; Stats.1987, c. 530, § 4; Stats.1987, c. 1091, § 14; Stats.2004, c. 650 (A.B.3047), § 17.)*

Cross References

Arrest of persons engaged in speed contests or reckless driving, removal and seizure of vehicles, see Vehicle Code § 23109.2.
Charter-party carrier buses, impoundment and storage, hearing, release of vehicle, see Vehicle Code § 14602.9.
Garage defined, see Vehicle Code § 340.
Legal owner defined, see Vehicle Code § 370.
Notice,
Illegal parking, see Vehicle Code § 40202 et seq.
Method of giving, see Vehicle Code §§ 22 et seq., 29.
Notifying National Law Enforcement Telecommunication System whenever officer or employee of public agency directs storage of vehicle, see Vehicle Code § 22854.5.
Registered owner defined, see Vehicle Code § 505.
Registration of vehicles, generally, see Vehicle Code § 4000 et seq.
Removal and seizure of vehicle, release of vehicle to registered owner, see Vehicle Code § 2480.

Research References

3 Witkin, California Criminal Law 4th Punishment § 195 (2021), Impounding of Motor Vehicles.

§ 22852.5. Loss of lien through trick, fraud, or device; revival of lien; misdemeanor

(a) Whenever the possessory lien upon any vehicle is lost through trick, fraud, or device, the repossession of the vehicle by the lienholder revives the possessory lien, but any lien so revived is subordinate to any right, title, or interest of any person under any sale, transfer, encumbrance, lien, or other interest acquired or secured in good faith and for value between the time of the loss of possession and the time of repossession.

(b) It is a misdemeanor for any person to obtain possession of any vehicle or any part thereof subject to a lien pursuant to the provisions of this chapter by trick, fraud, or device.

(c) It is a misdemeanor for any person claiming a lien on a vehicle to knowingly violate any provision of this chapter. *(Added by Stats.1980, c. 1111, p. 3573, § 36.)*

§ 22853. Notice to department of justice and proprietor of storage garage; reports; notice to owner

(a) Whenever an officer or an employee removing a California registered vehicle from a highway or from public property for storage under this chapter does not know and is not able to ascertain the name of the owner or for any other reason is unable to give notice to the owner as required by Section 22852, the officer or employee shall immediately notify, or cause to be notified, the Department of Justice, Stolen Vehicle System, of its removal. The officer or employee shall file a notice with the proprietor of any public garage in which the vehicle may be stored. The notice shall include a complete description of the vehicle, the date, time, and place from which removed, the amount of mileage on the vehicle at the time of removal, and the name of the garage or place where the vehicle is stored.

(b) Whenever an officer or an employee removing a vehicle not registered in California from a highway or from public property for storage under this chapter does not know and is not able to ascertain the owner or for any other reason is unable to give the notice to the owner as required by Section 22852, the officer or employee shall immediately notify, or cause to be notified, the Department of Justice, Stolen Vehicle System. If the vehicle is not returned to the owner within 120 hours, the officer or employee shall immediately send, or cause to be sent, a written report of the removal by mail to the Department of Justice at Sacramento and shall file a copy of the notice with the proprietor of any public garage in which the vehicle may be stored. The report shall be made on a form furnished by that department and shall include a complete description of the vehicle, the date, time, and place from which the vehicle was removed, the amount of mileage on the vehicle at the time of removal, the grounds for removal, and the name of the garage or place where the vehicle is stored.

(c) Whenever an officer or employee or private party removing a vehicle from private property for storage under this chapter does not know and is not able to ascertain the name of the owner or for any other reason is unable to give the notice to the owner as required by Section 22852 and if the vehicle is not returned to the owner within a period of 120 hours, the officer or employee or private party shall immediately send, or cause to be sent, a written report of the removal by mail to the Department of Justice at Sacramento and shall file a copy of the notice with the proprietor of any public garage in which the vehicle may be stored. The report shall be made on a form furnished by that department and shall include a complete description of the vehicle, the date, time, and place from which the vehicle was removed, the amount of mileage on the vehicle at the time of removal, the grounds for removal, and the name of the garage or place where the vehicle is stored. *(Added by Stats.1983, c. 913, § 6.)*

Cross References

Notifying National Law Enforcement Telecommunication System whenever officer or employee of public agency directs storage of vehicle, see Vehicle Code § 22854.5.
Removal of vehicle from private property, see Vehicle Code § 22658.

§ 22854. Notice to owner

The Department of Justice upon receiving notice under Section 22853 of the removal of a vehicle from a highway, or from public or private property, shall notify the registered and legal owner in writing at the addresses of such persons as shown by the records of the Department of Motor Vehicles, if the vehicle is registered in this state, of the removal of such vehicle, and give the name of the officer reporting such removal, the grounds upon which the removal was authorized and the location of the vehicle. If the vehicle is not registered in this state, the department shall make reasonable effort to notify the legal or registered owner of the removal and location of the vehicle. The notice to the registered or legal owner shall list the amount of mileage on the vehicle at the time of removal. *(Stats. 1959, c. 3, p. 1706, § 22854. Amended by Stats.1960, 1st Ex.Sess., c. 57, p. 406, § 5; Stats.1972, c. 98, p. 137, § 8, eff. May 30, 1972, operative Oct. 1, 1972; Stats.1975, c. 239, p. 630, § 4.)*

Cross References

Legal owner defined, see Vehicle Code § 370.
Registered owner defined, see Vehicle Code § 505.

§ 22854.5. Notifying National Law Enforcement Telecommunication System whenever officer or employee of public agency directs storage of vehicle under this chapter; means of notification

Whenever an officer or employee of a public agency directs the storage of a vehicle under this chapter, the officer, employee, or agency directing that storage may notify the National Law Enforcement Telecommunication System by transmitting by any means available, including, but not limited to, electronic means, the vehicle identification number, the information listed in paragraphs (1), (2), and (3) of subdivision (b) of Section 22852, and the information described under Section 22853. *(Added by Stats.2003, c. 622 (A.B.616), § 1.)*

§ 22855. Appraisers

The following persons shall have the authority to make appraisals of the value of vehicles for purposes of this chapter, subject to the conditions stated in this chapter:

(a) Any peace officer of the Department of the California Highway Patrol designated by the commissioner.

(b) Any regularly employed and salaried deputy sheriff, any reserve deputy sheriff listed under Section 830.6 of the Penal Code, or any other employee designated by the sheriff of any county.

(c) Any regularly employed and salaried police officer, any reserve police officer listed under Section 830.6 of the Penal Code, or any other employee designated by the chief of police of any city.

(d) Any officer or employee of the Department of Motor Vehicles designated by the director of that department.

(e) Any regularly employed and salaried police officer, or reserve police officer, or other employee of the University of California Police Department designated by the chief of the department.

(f) Any regularly salaried employee of a city, county, or city and county designated by a board of supervisors or a city council pursuant to subdivision (a) of Section 22669.

(g) Any regularly employed and salaried police officer, or reserve police officer, or other employee of the police department of a California State University designated by the chief thereof.

(h) Any regularly employed and salaried security officer or other employee of a transit district security force designated by the chief thereof.

(i) Any regularly employed and salaried peace officer, or reserve peace officer, or other employee of the Department of Parks and Recreation designated by the director of that department. *(Stats. 1959, c. 3, p. 1706, § 22855. Amended by Stats.1965, c. 1135, p. 2790, § 16; Stats.1967, c. 1055, p. 2663, § 6; Stats.1969, c. 1116, p. 2179, § 5; Stats.1970, c. 1431, p. 2777, § 5; Stats.1971, c. 130, p. 177, § 5, operative May 3, 1972; Stats.1974, c. 545, p. 1330, § 215; Stats.1974, c. 798, p. 1748, § 1; Stats.1979, c. 909, p. 3132, § 6; Stats.1983, c. 143, § 218; Stats.1986, c. 1019, § 68; Gov.Reorg.Plan No. 1 of 1995, § 69, eff. July 12, 1995; Stats.1996, c. 305 (A.B.3103), § 71; Stats.2003, c. 292 (A.B.1436), § 8.)*

Cross References

Criminal procedure, deputized or appointed peace officers, see Penal Code § 830.6.
Disposition of low-valued vehicles, see Vehicle Code §§ 22851.2, 22851.6 et seq.

Ordinance for removal of abandoned vehicles, contents, see Vehicle Code § 22661.

§ 22856. Despoliation of evidence; actions against towing companies

Notwithstanding any other provision of law, no cause of action for despoliation of evidence shall arise against any towing company that sells any vehicle at, or disposes of any vehicle after, a lien sale, unless the company knew, or should have known, that the vehicle will be needed as evidence in a legal action. *(Added by Stats.1989, c. 457, § 3.)*

CHAPTER 12. PUBLIC OFFENSES

ARTICLE 1. DRIVING OFFENSES

§ 23100. Application of chapter

The provisions of this chapter apply to vehicles upon the highways and elsewhere throughout the State unless expressly provided otherwise. *(Stats.1959, c. 3, p. 1707, § 23100.)*

Cross References

Definitions,
Highway, see Vehicle Code §§ 360, 591, 592.
Vehicle, see Vehicle Code § 670.

§ 23103. Reckless driving

(a) A person who drives a vehicle upon a highway in willful or wanton disregard for the safety of persons or property is guilty of reckless driving.

(b) A person who drives a vehicle in an offstreet parking facility, as defined in subdivision (c) of Section 12500, in willful or wanton disregard for the safety of persons or property is guilty of reckless driving.

(c) Except as otherwise provided in Section 40008, persons convicted of the offense of reckless driving shall be punished by imprisonment in a county jail for not less than five days nor more than 90 days or by a fine of not less than one hundred forty-five dollars ($145) nor more than one thousand dollars ($1,000), or by both that fine and imprisonment, except as provided in Section 23104 or 23105. *(Added by Stats.1978, c. 790, p. 2535, § 5.5, eff. Sept. 18, 1978, operative July 1, 1980. Amended by Stats.1980, c. 276, p. 552, § 8, eff. June 30, 1980; Stats.1980, c. 661, p. 1850, § 9; Stats.1981, c. 155, p. 960, § 1; Stats.1982, c. 331, p. 1472, § 2, eff. June 30, 1982; Stats.1983, c. 1092, § 393, eff. Sept. 27, 1983, operative Jan. 1, 1984; Stats.1985, c. 160, § 1; Stats.1991, c. 928 (A.B.1886), § 30.5, eff. Oct. 14, 1991; Stats.2001, c. 739 (A.B.1707), § 19; Stats.2007, c. 682 (A.B.430), § 16; Stats.2010, c. 685 (A.B.2479), § 2.)*

Cross References

Advisory statement to be given by court to person convicted of a violation of this section, see Vehicle Code § 23593.
Applicability of this section to trolley coaches, see Vehicle Code § 21051.
Arraignment or plea and sentencing in certain misdemeanors, presence of defendant, see Penal Code § 977.
Arrest of persons engaged in speed contests or reckless driving, removal and seizure of vehicles, see Vehicle Code § 23109.2.
Chemical blood, breath or urine tests, see Vehicle Code § 13353.
Conviction of violation of § 23152 within five years after two violations of §§ 23152, 23153 or 23103 as specified in § 23103.5, see Vehicle Code § 23546.
Conviction of violation of § 23152 within five years of three or more violations of §§ 23152, 23153 or 23103 as specified in § 23103.5, see Vehicle Code § 23550.
Conviction of violation of this section as a ground for cancelling, suspending or revoking license to teach driving, see Vehicle Code § 11110.
Deposit in special account for each conviction under this section, see Penal Code § 1463.14.
Driver's license, suspension or revocation,
Court, see Vehicle Code § 13200.
Department, see Vehicle Code §§ 13350, 13361.
Driving after suspension or revocation, see Vehicle Code § 14601.

Driving privileges, suspension or delay, restricted driving privileges imposed on showing of critical need to drive, see Vehicle Code § 13353.8.
Driving under influence of alcoholic beverages, see Vehicle Code §§ 23152, 23153.
Guilty plea, see Vehicle Code § 41610.
Immunity from criminal prosecution under specified minor consumption provisions, inapplicability to this section, see Business and Professions Code § 25667.
Investigation by the department, see Vehicle Code § 13800 et seq.
Medical assistance exception to controlled substance possession and related offenses, persons experiencing drug-related overdose, no exception to laws prohibiting actions made dangerous by controlled substance use, see Health and Safety Code § 11376.5.
Prior convictions under §§ 23103, 23152 or 23153, effect on sentencing and driving privileges, see Vehicle Code § 23622.
Procedure on arrest for violation of this section, see Vehicle Code § 40303.
Public offenses, State Amnesty Program, not applicable to parking violations and violations of this section, see Vehicle Code § 42008.7.
Records available to courts and law enforcement officials, incidents under certain DWI and homicide laws, period of time records must be available, see Vehicle Code § 1808.
Refusal to submit to alcohol testing under DUI laws, calculation of prior convictions, certain foreign convictions recognized, see Vehicle Code §§ 13353, 13353.1 and 13353.3.
Subsequent convictions, grounds for suspension of license, see Vehicle Code § 13361.
Suspension or revocation of driving privilege for a violation of this section, notice by personal service, see Vehicle Code § 13106.
Traffic violation point count, see Vehicle Code § 12810.
Traffic violator schools, suspension or revocation of license for violation of this section, see Vehicle Code § 11215.
Violation as misdemeanor, see Vehicle Code § 40000.15.
Violation of this section, relinquishment of motor vehicle to convicted minor, see Penal Code § 193.8.

Research References

California Jury Instructions - Criminal 12.82, Reckless Driving Causing Certain Injuries.
California Jury Instructions - Criminal 12.85, Flight from Pursuing Peace Officer—Reckless Driving.
California Jury Instructions - Criminal 16.840, Reckless Driving.
California Jury Instructions - Criminal 17.29, Willful Refusal to Take or Complete Tests Regarding Driving Under the Influence.
California Jury Instructions - Criminal 2200, Reckless Driving.
2 Witkin, California Criminal Law 4th Crimes Against Public Peace and Welfare § 269 (2021), Nonfelony Offenses of Persons in Custody.
2 Witkin, California Criminal Law 4th Crimes Against Public Peace and Welfare § 271 (2021), Reckless Driving.
2 Witkin, California Criminal Law 4th Crimes Against Public Peace and Welfare § 279 (2021), In General.
2 Witkin, California Criminal Law 4th Crimes Against Public Peace and Welfare § 290 (2021), Ignition Interlock Device.
2 Witkin, California Criminal Law 4th Crimes Against Public Peace and Welfare § 304 (2021), Relinquishing Possession of Vehicle to Intoxicated Minor.
2 Witkin, California Criminal Law 4th Crimes Against Public Peace and Welfare § 306 (2021), Reason for Suspension, Revocation, or Restriction.
2 Witkin, California Criminal Law 4th Crimes Against Public Peace and Welfare § 530 (2021), Bicycles.
5 Witkin, California Criminal Law 4th Criminal Trial § 480 (2021), Vehicle Code Convictions.
5 Witkin, California Criminal Law 4th Criminal Trial § 508 (2021), Misdemeanor Cases.
4 Witkin, California Criminal Law 4th Pretrial Proceedings § 254 (2021), Presence of Defendant.

§ 23103.5. Acceptance of guilty or nolo contendere plea to violation of § 23103 in place of charge for violation of § 23152; statement by prosecution; duty of court; violations; effect

Section operative until Jan. 1, 2026. See, also, § 23103.5 operative Jan. 1, 2026.

(a) If the prosecution agrees to a plea of guilty or nolo contendere to a charge of a violation of Section 23103 in satisfaction of, or as a substitute for, an original charge of a violation of Section 23152, the prosecution shall state for the record a factual basis for the satisfaction or substitution, including whether or not there had been consumption of an alcoholic beverage or ingestion or administration of a drug, or both, by the defendant in connection with the offense. The statement shall set forth the facts that show whether or not there was a consumption of an alcoholic beverage or the ingestion or administration of a drug by the defendant in connection with the offense.

(b) The court shall advise the defendant, prior to the acceptance of the plea offered pursuant to a factual statement pursuant to subdivision (a), of the consequences of a conviction of a violation of Section 23103 as set forth in subdivision (c).

(c) If the court accepts the defendant's plea of guilty or nolo contendere to a charge of a violation of Section 23103 and the prosecutor's statement under subdivision (a) states that there was consumption of an alcoholic beverage or the ingestion or administration of a drug by the defendant in connection with the offense, the resulting conviction shall be a prior offense for the purposes of Section 23540, 23546, 23550, 23560, 23566, or 23622, as specified in those sections.

(d) The court shall notify the Department of Motor Vehicles of each conviction of Section 23103 that is required under this section to be a prior offense for purposes of Section 23540, 23546, 23550, 23560, 23566, or 23622.

(e) Except as provided in paragraph (1) of subdivision (f), if the court places the defendant on probation for a conviction of Section 23103 that is required under this section to be a prior offense for purposes of Section 23540, 23546, 23550, 23560, 23566, or 23622, the court shall order the defendant to enroll in an alcohol and drug education program licensed under Chapter 9 (commencing with Section 11836) of Part 2 of Division 10.5 of the Health and Safety Code and complete, at a minimum, the educational component of that program, as a condition of probation. If compelling circumstances exist that mitigate against including the education component in the order, the court may make an affirmative finding to that effect. The court shall state the compelling circumstances and the affirmative finding on the record, and may, in these cases, exclude the educational component from the order.

(f)(1) If the court places on probation a defendant convicted of a violation of Section 23103 that is required under this section to be a prior offense for purposes of Section 23540, 23546, 23550, 23560, 23566, or 23622, and that offense occurred within 10 years of a separate conviction of a violation of Section 23103, as specified in this section, or within 10 years of a conviction of a violation of Section 23152 or 23153, the court shall order the defendant to participate for nine months or longer, as ordered by the court, in a program licensed under Chapter 9 (commencing with Section 11836) of Part 2 of Division 10.5 of the Health and Safety Code that consists of at least 60 hours of program activities, including education, group counseling, and individual interview sessions.

(2) The court shall revoke the person's probation, except for good cause shown, for the failure to enroll in, participate in, or complete a program specified in paragraph (1).

(g) Commencing January 1, 2019, the court may require a person convicted on or after January 1, 2019, of a violation of Section 23103, as described in this section, to install a functioning, certified ignition interlock device on any vehicle that the person operates and prohibit that person from operating a motor vehicle unless that vehicle is equipped with a functioning, certified ignition interlock device. If the court orders the ignition interlock device restriction, the term shall be determined by the court for a period of at least three months, but no longer than the term specified in Section 23575.3 that would have applied to the defendant had he or she instead been convicted of a violation of Section 23152, from the date of conviction. The court shall notify the Department of Motor Vehicles, as specified in subdivision (a) of Section 1803, of the terms of the restrictions in accordance with subdivision (a) of Section 1804. The Department of

Motor Vehicles shall place the restriction in the person's records in the Department of Motor Vehicles. A person who is required to install a functioning, certified ignition interlock device pursuant to this subdivision shall submit the "Verification of Installation" form described in paragraph (2) of subdivision (g) of Section 13386 and maintain the ignition interlock device as required under subdivision (f) of Section 23575.3. The department shall monitor the installation and maintenance of the ignition interlock device installed pursuant to this subdivision.

(h) The Department of Motor Vehicles shall include in its annual report to the Legislature under Section 1821 an evaluation of the effectiveness of the programs described in subdivisions (e) and (g) as to treating persons convicted of violating Section 23103.

(i) This section shall remain in effect only until January 1, 2026, and as of that date is repealed, unless a later enacted statute, that is enacted before January 1, 2026, deletes or extends that date. *(Added by Stats.1981, c. 941, p. 3587, § 5. Amended by Stats.1982, c. 53, p. 171, § 24, eff. Feb. 18, 1982; Stats.1988, c. 939, § 1, operative July 1, 1989; Stats.1988, c. 1273, § 2, operative July 1, 1989; Stats.1998, c. 118 (S.B.1186), § 11.9, operative July 1, 1999; Stats.1998, c. 487 (S.B.1176), § 3; Stats.1998, c. 487 (S.B.1176), § 4, operative July 1, 1999; Stats.2008, c. 103 (A.B.2802), § 2; Stats.2016, c. 783 (S.B. 1046), § 24, eff. Jan. 1, 2017.)*

Repeal

For repeal of this section, see its terms.

Cross References

Advisory statement to be given by court to person convicted of a violation of this section, see Vehicle Code § 23593.
Arraignment, presence of defendant, see Penal Code § 977.
Challenging constitutional validity of separate conviction, see Vehicle Code § 41403.
Chemical blood, breath or urine tests, see Vehicle Code § 13353.
Conviction of violation of § 23152 within five years after two violations of §§ 23152, 23153 or 23103 as specified in § 23103.5, see Vehicle Code § 23546.
Conviction of violation of § 23152 within five years of three or more violations of §§ 23152, 23153 or 23103 as specified in § 23103.5, see Vehicle Code § 23550.
Driving privileges, suspension or delay, restricted driving privileges imposed on showing of critical need to drive, see Vehicle Code § 13353.8.
Immunity from criminal prosecution under specified minor consumption provisions, inapplicability to this section, see Business and Professions Code § 25667.
Investigation for driver's license suspension or revocation, three convictions in three years under this or other specified sections, see Vehicle Code § 13800.
Investigations by the department, see Vehicle Code § 13800.
Mandatory participation in alcohol and drug problem assessment program for conviction of violation of this section, see Vehicle Code § 23647 et seq.
Medical assistance exception to controlled substance possession and related offenses, persons experiencing drug-related overdose, no exception to laws prohibiting actions made dangerous by controlled substance use, see Health and Safety Code § 11376.5.
Prior convictions under §§ 23103, 23152 or 23153, effect on sentencing and driving privileges, see Vehicle Code § 23622.
Refusal to submit to alcohol testing under DUI laws, calculation of prior convictions, certain foreign convictions recognized, see Vehicle Code §§ 13353, 13353.1 and 13353.3.

Research References

2 Witkin, California Criminal Law 4th Crimes Against Public Peace and Welfare § 271 (2021), Reckless Driving.
2 Witkin, California Criminal Law 4th Crimes Against Public Peace and Welfare § 281 (2021), One Separate Conviction of Related Offense.
2 Witkin, California Criminal Law 4th Crimes Against Public Peace and Welfare § 282 (2021), Two Separate Convictions of Related Offenses.
2 Witkin, California Criminal Law 4th Crimes Against Public Peace and Welfare § 283 (2021), Three or More Separate Convictions of Related Offenses.
2 Witkin, California Criminal Law 4th Crimes Against Public Peace and Welfare § 286 (2021), One Separate Conviction of Related Offense.
2 Witkin, California Criminal Law 4th Crimes Against Public Peace and Welfare § 287 (2021), Two or More Separate Convictions of Related Offenses.
2 Witkin, California Criminal Law 4th Crimes Against Public Peace and Welfare § 302 (2021), Administrative Sanctions.
2 Witkin, California Criminal Law 4th Crimes Against Public Peace and Welfare § 304 (2021), Relinquishing Possession of Vehicle to Intoxicated Minor.
2 Witkin, California Criminal Law 4th Crimes Against Public Peace and Welfare § 306 (2021), Reason for Suspension, Revocation, or Restriction.
1 Witkin California Criminal Law 4th Crimes Against the Person § 267 (2021), Vehicular Manslaughter While Intoxicated.
5 Witkin, California Criminal Law 4th Criminal Trial § 480 (2021), Vehicle Code Convictions.
5 Witkin, California Criminal Law 4th Criminal Trial § 508 (2021), Misdemeanor Cases.
4 Witkin, California Criminal Law 4th Pretrial Proceedings § 254 (2021), Presence of Defendant.

§ 23103.5. Acceptance of guilty or nolo contendere plea to violation of § 23103 in place of charge for violation of § 23152; statement by prosecution; duty of court; violations; effect

Section operative Jan. 1, 2026. See, also, § 23103.5 operative until Jan. 1, 2026.

(a) If the prosecution agrees to a plea of guilty or nolo contendere to a charge of a violation of Section 23103 in satisfaction of, or as a substitute for, an original charge of a violation of Section 23152, the prosecution shall state for the record a factual basis for the satisfaction or substitution, including whether or not there had been consumption of an alcoholic beverage or ingestion or administration of a drug, or both, by the defendant in connection with the offense. The statement shall set forth the facts that show whether or not there was a consumption of an alcoholic beverage or the ingestion or administration of a drug by the defendant in connection with the offense.

(b) The court shall advise the defendant, prior to the acceptance of the plea offered pursuant to a factual statement pursuant to subdivision (a), of the consequences of a conviction of a violation of Section 23103 as set forth in subdivision (c).

(c) If the court accepts the defendant's plea of guilty or nolo contendere to a charge of a violation of Section 23103 and the prosecutor's statement under subdivision (a) states that there was consumption of an alcoholic beverage or the ingestion or administration of a drug by the defendant in connection with the offense, the resulting conviction shall be a prior offense for the purposes of Section 23540, 23546, 23550, 23560, 23566, or 23622, as specified in those sections.

(d) The court shall notify the Department of Motor Vehicles of each conviction of Section 23103 that is required under this section to be a prior offense for purposes of Section 23540, 23546, 23550, 23560, 23566, or 23622.

(e) Except as provided in paragraph (1) of subdivision (f), if the court places the defendant on probation for a conviction of Section 23103 that is required under this section to be a prior offense for purposes of Section 23540, 23546, 23550, 23560, 23566, or 23622, the court shall order the defendant to enroll in an alcohol and drug education program licensed under Chapter 9 (commencing with Section 11836) of Part 2 of Division 10.5 of the Health and Safety Code and complete, at a minimum, the educational component of that program, as a condition of probation. If compelling circumstances exist that mitigate against including the education component in the order, the court may make an affirmative finding to that effect. The court shall state the compelling circumstances and the affirmative finding on the record, and may, in these cases, exclude the educational component from the order.

(f)(1) If the court places on probation a defendant convicted of a violation of Section 23103 that is required under this section to be a prior offense for purposes of Section 23540, 23546, 23550, 23560, 23566, or 23622, and that offense occurred within 10 years of a separate conviction of a violation of Section 23103, as specified in this section, or within 10 years of a conviction of a violation of Section 23152 or 23153, the court shall order the defendant to participate for nine months or longer, as ordered by the court, in a program licensed under Chapter 9 (commencing with Section 11836) of Part 2 of Division 10.5 of the Health and Safety Code that consists of at least 60 hours of program activities, including education, group counseling, and individual interview sessions.

(2) The court shall revoke the person's probation, except for good cause shown, for the failure to enroll in, participate in, or complete a program specified in paragraph (1).

(g) The Department of Motor Vehicles shall include in its annual report to the Legislature under Section 1821 an evaluation of the effectiveness of the programs described in subdivisions (e) and (f) as to treating persons convicted of violating Section 23103.

(h) This section shall become operative January 1, 2026. *(Added by Stats.2016, c. 783 (S.B.1046), § 25, eff. Jan. 1, 2017, operative Jan. 1, 2026.)*

Cross References

Advisory statement to be given by court to person convicted of a violation of this section, see Vehicle Code § 23593.
Arraignment, presence of defendant, see Penal Code § 977.
Challenging constitutional validity of separate conviction, see Vehicle Code § 41403.
Chemical blood, breath or urine tests, see Vehicle Code § 13353.
Conviction of violation of § 23152 within five years after two violations of §§ 23152, 23153 or 23103 as specified in § 23103.5, see Vehicle Code § 23546.
Conviction of violation of § 23152 within five years of three or more violations of §§ 23152, 23153 or 23103 as specified in § 23103.5, see Vehicle Code § 23550.
Driving privileges, suspension or delay, restricted driving privileges imposed on showing of critical need to drive, see Vehicle Code § 13353.8.
Immunity from criminal prosecution under specified minor consumption provisions, inapplicability to this section, see Business and Professions Code § 25667.
Investigation for driver's license suspension or revocation, three convictions in three years under this or other specified sections, see Vehicle Code § 13800.
Investigations by the department, see Vehicle Code § 13800.
Mandatory participation in alcohol and drug problem assessment program for conviction of violation of this section, see Vehicle Code § 23647 et seq.
Medical assistance exception to controlled substance possession and related offenses, persons experiencing drug-related overdose, no exception to laws prohibiting actions made dangerous by controlled substance use, see Health and Safety Code § 11376.5.
Prior convictions under §§ 23103, 23152 or 23153, effect on sentencing and driving privileges, see Vehicle Code § 23622.
Refusal to submit to alcohol testing under DUI laws, calculation of prior convictions, certain foreign convictions recognized, see Vehicle Code §§ 13353, 13353.1 and 13353.3.

Research References

2 Witkin, California Criminal Law 4th Crimes Against Public Peace and Welfare § 271 (2021), Reckless Driving.
2 Witkin, California Criminal Law 4th Crimes Against Public Peace and Welfare § 281 (2021), One Separate Conviction of Related Offense.
2 Witkin, California Criminal Law 4th Crimes Against Public Peace and Welfare § 282 (2021), Two Separate Convictions of Related Offenses.
2 Witkin, California Criminal Law 4th Crimes Against Public Peace and Welfare § 283 (2021), Three or More Separate Convictions of Related Offenses.
2 Witkin, California Criminal Law 4th Crimes Against Public Peace and Welfare § 286 (2021), One Separate Conviction of Related Offense.
2 Witkin, California Criminal Law 4th Crimes Against Public Peace and Welfare § 287 (2021), Two or More Separate Convictions of Related Offenses.
2 Witkin, California Criminal Law 4th Crimes Against Public Peace and Welfare § 302 (2021), Administrative Sanctions.
2 Witkin, California Criminal Law 4th Crimes Against Public Peace and Welfare § 304 (2021), Relinquishing Possession of Vehicle to Intoxicated Minor.
2 Witkin, California Criminal Law 4th Crimes Against Public Peace and Welfare § 306 (2021), Reason for Suspension, Revocation, or Restriction.
1 Witkin California Criminal Law 4th Crimes Against the Person § 267 (2021), Vehicular Manslaughter While Intoxicated.
5 Witkin, California Criminal Law 4th Criminal Trial § 480 (2021), Vehicle Code Convictions.
5 Witkin, California Criminal Law 4th Criminal Trial § 508 (2021), Misdemeanor Cases.
4 Witkin, California Criminal Law 4th Pretrial Proceedings § 254 (2021), Presence of Defendant.

§ 23104. Reckless driving; bodily injury; great bodily injury and prior conviction

(a) Except as provided in subdivision (b), whenever reckless driving of a vehicle proximately causes bodily injury to a person other than the driver, the person driving the vehicle shall, upon conviction thereof, be punished by imprisonment in the county jail for not less than 30 days nor more than six months or by a fine of not less than two hundred twenty dollars ($220) nor more than one thousand dollars ($1,000), or by both the fine and imprisonment.

(b) A person convicted of reckless driving that proximately causes great bodily injury, as defined in Section 12022.7 of the Penal Code, to a person other than the driver, who previously has been convicted of a violation of Section 23103, 23104, 23105, 23109, 23109.1, 23152, or 23153, shall be punished by imprisonment pursuant to subdivision (h) of Section 1170 of the Penal Code, by imprisonment in the county jail for not less than 30 days nor more than six months or by a fine of not less than two hundred twenty dollars ($220) nor more than one thousand dollars ($1,000) or by both the fine and imprisonment. *(Added by Stats.1978, c. 790, p. 2535, § 6.5, eff. Sept. 18, 1978, operative July 1, 1980. Amended by Stats.1980, c. 276, p. 553, § 10, eff. June 30, 1980; Stats.1980, c. 661, p. 1851, § 12; Stats.1981, c. 155, p. 960, § 3; Stats.1982, c. 331, p. 1632, § 3, eff. June 30, 1982; Stats.1983, c. 1092, § 394, eff. Sept. 27, 1983, operative Jan. 1, 1984; Stats.1983, c. 965, § 1; Stats.1984, c. 216, § 11; Stats.2007, c. 682 (A.B.430), § 17; Stats.2011, c. 15 (A.B.109), § 609, eff. April 4, 2011, operative Oct. 1, 2011.)*

Cross References

Applicability of this section to trolley coaches, see Vehicle Code § 21051.
Conviction of a violation of this section as a ground for cancelling, suspending or revoking license to teach driving, see Vehicle Code § 11110.
Deposit in special account for each conviction under this section, see Penal Code § 1463.14.
Driver's license, suspension or revocation,
By court, see Vehicle Code §§ 13200, 13201.
By department, see Vehicle Code §§ 13350, 13361.
Driving after suspension or revocation, see Vehicle Code § 14601.
Guilty plea, see Vehicle Code § 41610.
Investigation by the department, see Vehicle Code § 13800 et seq.
Manslaughter in driving of a vehicle, see Penal Code § 192.
Procedure on arrest for violation of this section, see Vehicle Code § 40303.
Public offenses, State Amnesty Program, not applicable to parking violations and violations of this section, see Vehicle Code § 42008.7.
Subsequent convictions, grounds for suspension of license, see Vehicle Code § 13361.
Suspension or revocation of driving privilege for a violation of this section, notice by personal service, see Vehicle Code § 13106.
Traffic violation point count, see Vehicle Code § 12810.
Traffic violators schools, suspension or revocation of license for violation of this section, see Vehicle Code § 11215.
Violation as misdemeanor, see Vehicle Code § 40000.15.

Research References

California Jury Instructions - Criminal 16.842, Reckless Driving Causing Bodily Injury to Person Other Than Driver.
2 Witkin, California Criminal Law 4th Crimes Against Public Peace and Welfare § 271 (2021), Reckless Driving.
1 Witkin California Criminal Law 4th Elements § 17 (2021), Assault.

1 Witkin California Criminal Law 4th Elements § 43 (2021), In General.
3 Witkin, California Criminal Law 4th Punishment § 211 (2021), Discretionary Suspension.

§ 23105. Conviction for reckless driving; injuries to another; penalties

(a) A person convicted of reckless driving in violation of Section 23103 that proximately causes one or more of the injuries specified in subdivision (b) to a person other than the driver, shall be punished by imprisonment pursuant to subdivision (h) of Section 1170 of the Penal Code, or by imprisonment in a county jail for not less than 30 days nor more than six months, or by a fine of not less than two hundred twenty dollars ($220) nor more than one thousand dollars ($1,000), or by both that fine and imprisonment.

(b) This section applies to all of the following injuries:

(1) A loss of consciousness.

(2) A concussion.

(3) A bone fracture.

(4) A protracted loss or impairment of function of a bodily member or organ.

(5) A wound requiring extensive suturing.

(6) A serious disfigurement.

(7) Brain injury.

(8) Paralysis.

(c) This section does not preclude or prohibit prosecution under any other provision of law. *(Added by Stats.2006, c. 432 (A.B.2190), § 1. Amended by Stats.2011, c. 15 (A.B.109), § 610, eff. April 4, 2011, operative Oct. 1, 2011.)*

Cross References

Applicability of this section to trolley coaches, see Vehicle Code § 21051.
Conviction of a violation of this section as a ground for cancelling, suspending or revoking license to teach driving, see Vehicle Code § 11110.
Motor vehicle speed contests, injuries to another, see Vehicle Code § 23109.1.
Public offenses, State Amnesty Program, not applicable to parking violations and violations of this section, see Vehicle Code § 42008.7.
Traffic violator schools, suspension or revocation of license for violation of this section, see Vehicle Code § 11215.

Research References

California Jury Instructions - Criminal 12.82, Reckless Driving Causing Certain Injuries.
2 Witkin, California Criminal Law 4th Crimes Against Public Peace and Welfare § 271 (2021), Reckless Driving.

§ 23109. Speed contests and exhibitions of speed

(a) A person shall not engage in a motor vehicle speed contest on a highway or in an offstreet parking facility. As used in this section, a motor vehicle speed contest includes a motor vehicle race against another vehicle, a clock, or other timing device. For purposes of this section, an event in which the time to cover a prescribed route of more than 20 miles is measured, but in which the vehicle does not exceed the speed limits, is not a speed contest.

(b) A person shall not aid or abet in any motor vehicle speed contest on a highway or in an offstreet parking facility.

(c) A person shall not engage in a motor vehicle exhibition of speed on a highway or in an offstreet parking facility, and a person shall not aid or abet in a motor vehicle exhibition of speed on any highway or in an offstreet parking facility.

(d) A person shall not, for the purpose of facilitating or aiding or as an incident to any motor vehicle speed contest or exhibition upon a highway or in an offstreet parking facility, in any manner obstruct or place a barricade or obstruction or assist or participate in placing a barricade or obstruction upon a highway or in an offstreet parking facility.

(e)(1) A person convicted of a violation of subdivision (a) shall be punished by imprisonment in a county jail for not less than 24 hours nor more than 90 days or by a fine of not less than three hundred fifty-five dollars ($355) nor more than one thousand dollars ($1,000), or by both that fine and imprisonment. That person shall also be required to perform 40 hours of community service. The court may order the privilege to operate a motor vehicle suspended for 90 days to six months, as provided in paragraph (8) of subdivision (a) of Section 13352. The person's privilege to operate a motor vehicle may be restricted for 90 days to six months to necessary travel to and from that person's place of employment and, if driving a motor vehicle is necessary to perform the duties of the person's employment, restricted to driving in that person's scope of employment. This subdivision does not interfere with the court's power to grant probation in a suitable case.

(2) If a person is convicted of a violation of subdivision (a) and that violation proximately causes bodily injury to a person other than the driver, the person convicted shall be punished by imprisonment in a county jail for not less than 30 days nor more than six months or by a fine of not less than five hundred dollars ($500) nor more than one thousand dollars ($1,000), or by both that fine and imprisonment.

(f)(1) If a person is convicted of a violation of subdivision (a) for an offense that occurred within five years of the date of a prior offense that resulted in a conviction of a violation of subdivision (a), that person shall be punished by imprisonment in a county jail for not less than four days nor more than six months, and by a fine of not less than five hundred dollars ($500) nor more than one thousand dollars ($1,000).

(2) If the perpetration of the most recent offense within the five-year period described in paragraph (1) proximately causes bodily injury to a person other than the driver, a person convicted of that second violation shall be imprisoned in a county jail for not less than 30 days nor more than six months and by a fine of not less than five hundred dollars ($500) nor more than one thousand dollars ($1,000).

(3) If the perpetration of the most recent offense within the five-year period described in paragraph (1) proximately causes serious bodily injury, as defined in paragraph (4) of subdivision (f) of Section 243 of the Penal Code, to a person other than the driver, a person convicted of that second violation shall be imprisoned in the state prison, or in a county jail for not less than 30 days nor more than one year, and by a fine of not less than five hundred dollars ($500) nor more than one thousand dollars ($1,000).

(4) The court shall order the privilege to operate a motor vehicle of a person convicted under paragraph (1), (2), or (3) suspended for a period of six months, as provided in paragraph (9) of subdivision (a) of Section 13352. In lieu of the suspension, the person's privilege to operate a motor vehicle may be restricted for six months to necessary travel to and from that person's place of employment and, if driving a motor vehicle is necessary to perform the duties of the person's employment, restricted to driving in that person's scope of employment.

(5) This subdivision does not interfere with the court's power to grant probation in a suitable case.

(g) If the court grants probation to a person subject to punishment under subdivision (f), in addition to subdivision (f) and any other terms and conditions imposed by the court, which may include a fine, the court shall impose as a condition of probation that the person be confined in a county jail for not less than 48 hours nor more than six months. The court shall order the person's privilege to operate a motor vehicle to be suspended for a period of six months, as provided in paragraph (9) of subdivision (a) of Section 13352 or restricted pursuant to subdivision (f).

(h) If a person is convicted of a violation of subdivision (a) and the vehicle used in the violation is registered to that person, the vehicle may be impounded at the registered owner's expense for not less than one day nor more than 30 days.

(i)(1) A person who violates subdivision (b), (c), or (d) shall upon conviction of that violation be punished by imprisonment in a county jail for not more than 90 days, by a fine of not more than five hundred dollars ($500), or by both that fine and imprisonment.

(2)(A) Commencing July 1, 2025, the court may order the privilege to operate a motor vehicle suspended for 90 days to six months for a person who violates subdivision (c), as provided in subparagraph (B) of paragraph (8) of subdivision (a) of Section 13352, only if the violation occurred as part of a sideshow. For purposes of this section, "sideshow" is defined as an event in which two or more persons block or impede traffic on a highway or in an offstreet parking facility, for the purpose of performing motor vehicle stunts, motor vehicle speed contests, motor vehicle exhibitions of speed, or reckless driving, for spectators.

(B) The person's privilege to operate a motor vehicle may be restricted for 90 days to six months to necessary travel to and from that person's place of employment and, if driving a motor vehicle is necessary to perform the duties of the person's employment, restricted to driving in that person's scope of employment.

(C) If the court is considering suspending or restricting the privilege to operate a motor vehicle pursuant to this paragraph, the court shall also consider whether a medical, personal, or family hardship exists that requires a person to have a driver's license for such limited purpose as the court deems necessary to address the hardship. This subdivision does not interfere with the court's power to grant probation in a suitable case.

(j) If a person's privilege to operate a motor vehicle is restricted by a court pursuant to this section, the court shall clearly mark the restriction and the dates of the restriction on that person's driver's license and promptly notify the Department of Motor Vehicles of the terms of the restriction in a manner prescribed by the department. The Department of Motor Vehicles shall place that restriction in the person's records in the Department of Motor Vehicles and enter the restriction on a license subsequently issued by the Department of Motor Vehicles to that person during the period of the restriction.

(k) The court may order that a person convicted under this section, who is to be punished by imprisonment in a county jail, be imprisoned on days other than days of regular employment of the person, as determined by the court.

(*l*) For purposes of this section, "offstreet parking facility" has the same meaning as in subdivision (c) of Section 12500.

(m) This section shall be known and may be cited as the Louis Friend Memorial Act. *(Stats.1959, c. 3, p. 1709, § 23109. Amended by Stats.1967, c. 607, p. 1956, § 1; Stats.1983, c. 935, § 1; Stats.1983, c. 1092, § 395, eff. Sept. 27, 1983, operative Jan. 1, 1984; Stats.1983, c. 953, § 2.5; Stats.1984, c. 216, § 12; Stats.2004, c. 595 (S.B.1541), § 2; Stats.2005, c. 475 (A.B.1325), § 1; Stats.2006, c. 538 (S.B.1852), § 661; Stats.2009, c. 193 (S.B.598), § 3, operative July 1, 2010; Stats.2010, c. 301 (A.B.1601), § 2; Stats.2011, c. 15 (A.B.109), § 611, eff. April 4, 2011, operative Oct. 1, 2011; Stats.2011, c. 39 (A.B.117), § 64, eff. June 30, 2011, operative Oct. 1, 2011; Stats.2021, c. 611 (A.B.3), § 3, eff. Jan. 1, 2022; Stats.2022, c. 436 (A.B.2000), § 1, eff. Jan. 1, 2023.)*

Cross References

Highway defined, see Vehicle Code §§ 360, 591, 592.
Influence of alcoholic beverage or drug, suspension or revocation of driving privileges, see Vehicle Code § 13352.
Manslaughter, voluntary, involuntary, and vehicular, see Penal Code § 192.
Private parking facilities, application of section, see Vehicle Code § 21107.8.
Procedure on arrest for violation of this section, see Vehicle Code § 40303.
Removal of vehicles used in motor vehicle speed contests in violation of this section, removal by peace officers or specified employees, see Vehicle Code § 22651.6.
Revocation or suspension of driver's license for speeding, see Vehicle Code § 13200.
Revocation or suspension of license for violation of this section, see Vehicle Code § 13352.
Speed laws, see Vehicle Code § 22349 et seq.
Supervised visitations, considerations by court, see Vehicle Code § 23517.
Testimony based on speed trap, applicability of provisions to violations of this section, see Vehicle Code § 40804.
Traffic violation point count, violation of this section, see Vehicle Code § 12810.
Uniform of traffic officer investigating violations of this section, see Vehicle Code § 40800.
Violation as misdemeanor, see Vehicle Code § 40000.15.

Research References

California Jury Instructions - Criminal 12.83, Speed Contest Causing Certain Injuries.
California Jury Instructions - Criminal 16.860, Speed Contest.
California Jury Instructions - Criminal 16.870, Exhibition of Speed.
2 Witkin, California Criminal Law 4th Crimes Against Public Peace and Welfare § 321 (2021), Speed Contests and Exhibitions.
1 Witkin California Criminal Law 4th Introduction to Crimes § 90 (2021), Misdemeanor-Infraction.
3 Witkin, California Criminal Law 4th Punishment § 215 (2021), Excessive Speed.

§ 23109.1. Motor vehicle speed contests; injuries to another; penalties

(a) A person convicted of engaging in a motor vehicle speed contest in violation of subdivision (a) of Section 23109 that proximately causes one or more of the injuries specified in subdivision (b) to a person other than the driver, shall be punished by imprisonment pursuant to subdivision (h) of Section 1170 of the Penal Code, or by imprisonment in a county jail for not less than 30 days nor more than six months, or by a fine of not less than five hundred dollars ($500) nor more than one thousand dollars ($1,000), or by both that fine and imprisonment.

(b) This section applies to all of the following injuries:

(1) A loss of consciousness.

(2) A concussion.

(3) A bone fracture.

(4) A protracted loss or impairment of function of a bodily member or organ.

(5) A wound requiring extensive suturing.

(6) A serious disfigurement.

(7) Brain injury.

(8) Paralysis.

(c) This section does not preclude or prohibit prosecution under any other provision of law. *(Added by Stats.2006, c. 432 (A.B.2190), § 2. Amended by Stats.2011, c. 15 (A.B.109), § 612, eff. April 4, 2011, operative Oct. 1, 2011.)*

Cross References

Conviction for reckless driving, injuries to another, see Vehicle Code § 23105.
Traffic violation point count, violation of this section, see Vehicle Code § 12810.

Research References

California Jury Instructions - Criminal 12.83, Speed Contest Causing Certain Injuries.
2 Witkin, California Criminal Law 4th Crimes Against Public Peace and Welfare § 321 (2021), Speed Contests and Exhibitions.

§ 23109.2. Arrest of persons engaged in speed contests or reckless driving; removal and seizure of vehicles; impoundment of vehicles; storage hearing; release of impounded vehicles; liability for towing and storage charges

(a)(1) Whenever a peace officer determines that a person was engaged in any of the activities set forth in paragraph (2), the peace officer may immediately arrest and take into custody that person and may cause the removal and seizure of the motor vehicle used in that offense in accordance with Chapter 10 (commencing with Section 22650). A motor vehicle so seized may be impounded for not more than 30 days.

(2)(A) A motor vehicle speed contest, as described in subdivision (a) of Section 23109.

(B) Reckless driving on a highway, as described in subdivision (a) of Section 23103.

(C) Reckless driving in an offstreet parking facility, as described in subdivision (b) of Section 23103.

(D) Exhibition of speed on a highway, as described in subdivision (c) of Section 23109.

(b) The registered and legal owner of a vehicle removed and seized under subdivision (a) or their agents shall be provided the opportunity for a storage hearing to determine the validity of the storage in accordance with Section 22852.

(c)(1) Notwithstanding Chapter 10 (commencing with Section 22650) or any other provision of law, an impounding agency shall release a motor vehicle to the registered owner or his or her agent prior to the conclusion of the impoundment period described in subdivision (a) under any of the following circumstances:

(A) If the vehicle is a stolen vehicle.

(B) If the person alleged to have been engaged in the motor vehicle speed contest, as described in subdivision (a), was not authorized by the registered owner of the motor vehicle to operate the motor vehicle at the time of the commission of the offense.

(C) If the registered owner of the vehicle was neither the driver nor a passenger of the vehicle at the time of the alleged violation pursuant to subdivision (a), or was unaware that the driver was using the vehicle to engage in any of the activities described in subdivision (a).

(D) If the legal owner or registered owner of the vehicle is a rental car agency.

(E) If, prior to the conclusion of the impoundment period, a citation or notice is dismissed under Section 40500, criminal charges are not filed by the district attorney because of a lack of evidence, or the charges are otherwise dismissed by the court.

(2) A vehicle shall be released pursuant to this subdivision only if the registered owner or his or her agent presents a currently valid driver's license to operate the vehicle and proof of current vehicle registration, or if ordered by a court.

(3) If, pursuant to subparagraph (E) of paragraph (1) a motor vehicle is released prior to the conclusion of the impoundment period, neither the person charged with a violation of subdivision (a) of Section 23109 nor the registered owner of the motor vehicle is responsible for towing and storage charges nor shall the motor vehicle be sold to satisfy those charges.

(d) A vehicle seized and removed under subdivision (a) shall be released to the legal owner of the vehicle, or the legal owner's agent, on or before the 30th day of impoundment if all of the following conditions are met:

(1) The legal owner is a motor vehicle dealer, bank, credit union, acceptance corporation, or other licensed financial institution legally operating in this state, or is another person, not the registered owner, holding a security interest in the vehicle.

(2) The legal owner or the legal owner's agent pays all towing and storage fees related to the impoundment of the vehicle. No lien sale processing fees shall be charged to a legal owner who redeems the vehicle on or before the 15th day of impoundment.

(3) The legal owner or the legal owner's agent presents foreclosure documents or an affidavit of repossession for the vehicle.

(e)(1) The registered owner or his or her agent is responsible for all towing and storage charges related to the impoundment, and any administrative charges authorized under Section 22850.5.

(2) Notwithstanding paragraph (1), if the person convicted of engaging in the activities set forth in paragraph (2) of subdivision (a) was not authorized by the registered owner of the motor vehicle to operate the motor vehicle at the time of the commission of the offense, the court shall order the convicted person to reimburse the registered owner for any towing and storage charges related to the impoundment, and any administrative charges authorized under Section 22850.5 incurred by the registered owner to obtain possession of the vehicle, unless the court finds that the person convicted does not have the ability to pay all or part of those charges.

(3) If the vehicle is a rental vehicle, the rental car agency may require the person to whom the vehicle was rented to pay all towing and storage charges related to the impoundment and any administrative charges authorized under Section 22850.5 incurred by the rental car agency in connection with obtaining possession of the vehicle.

(4) The owner is not liable for any towing and storage charges related to the impoundment if acquittal or dismissal occurs.

(5) The vehicle may not be sold prior to the defendant's conviction.

(6) The impounding agency is responsible for the actual costs incurred by the towing agency as a result of the impoundment should the registered owner be absolved of liability for those charges pursuant to paragraph (3) of subdivision (c). Notwithstanding this provision, nothing shall prohibit impounding agencies from making prior payment arrangements to satisfy this requirement.

(f) Any period when a vehicle is subjected to storage under this section shall be included as part of the period of impoundment ordered by the court under subdivision (h) of Section 23109. *(Added by Stats.2007, c. 727 (S.B.67), § 3, eff. Oct. 14, 2007.)*

Research References

2 Witkin, California Criminal Law 4th Crimes Against Public Peace and Welfare § 271 (2021), Reckless Driving.

2 Witkin, California Criminal Law 4th Crimes Against Public Peace and Welfare § 321 (2021), Speed Contests and Exhibitions.

§ 23109.5. Speed contests; prior offenses; effect on punishment

(a) In any case charging a violation of subdivision (a) of Section 23109 and where the offense occurs within five years of one or more prior offenses which resulted in conviction of violation of subdivision (a) of Section 23109, the court shall not strike any prior conviction of those offenses for purposes of sentencing in order to avoid imposing, as part of the sentence or term of probation, the minimum time of imprisonment, as provided in subdivision (f) of Section 23109, or for purposes of avoiding revocation, suspension, or restriction of the privilege to operate a motor vehicle, as provided in Section 13352 or 23109.

(b) In any case charging a violation of subdivision (a) of Section 23109, the court shall obtain a copy of the driving record of the person charged from the Department of Motor Vehicles and may obtain any records from the Department of Justice or any other source to determine if one or more prior convictions of the person for violation of subdivision (a) of Section 23109 have occurred within five years of the charged offense. *(Added by Stats.1983, c. 953, § 3.)*

Cross References

Destruction of court records, notice, retention periods, see Government Code § 68152.

Research References

2 Witkin, California Criminal Law 4th Crimes Against Public Peace and Welfare § 321 (2021), Speed Contests and Exhibitions.

§ 23110. Throwing substance at vehicles

(a) Any person who throws any substance at a vehicle or any occupant thereof on a highway is guilty of a misdemeanor.

(b) Any person who with intent to do great bodily injury maliciously and willfully throws or projects any rock, brick, bottle, metal or other missile, or projects any other substance capable of doing serious bodily harm at such vehicle or occupant thereof is guilty of a felony and upon conviction shall be punished by imprisonment in the state prison. *(Stats.1959, c. 3, p. 1709, § 23110. Amended by Stats.1976, c. 1139, p. 5173, § 341, operative July 1, 1977; Stats.1976, c. 1119, p. 5023, § 2; Stats.2011, c. 15 (A.B.109), § 613, eff. April 4, 2011, operative Oct. 1, 2011; Stats.2011, c. 39 (A.B.117), § 65, eff. June 30, 2011, operative Oct. 1, 2011.)*

Cross References

Applicability of this section to trolley coaches, see Vehicle Code § 21051.
Misdemeanor and felony defined, see Penal Code § 17.
Punishment for misdemeanors, see Vehicle Code § 42002.
Shooting on public highways, see Penal Code § 374c.
Throwing substances upon highway likely to injure persons, animals or vehicles, see Penal Code § 588a.
Violation as misdemeanor, see Vehicle Code § 40000.15.

Research References

2 Witkin, California Criminal Law 4th Crimes Against Property § 299 (2021), Acts Directed at Vehicles.
1 Witkin California Criminal Law 4th Crimes Against the Person § 27 (2021), In General.
1 Witkin California Criminal Law 4th Defenses § 195 (2021), Assault and Other Crimes.

§ 23111. Throwing substances on highways or adjoining areas

No person in any vehicle and no pedestrian shall throw or discharge from or upon any road or highway or adjoining area, public or private, any lighted or nonlighted cigarette, cigar, match, or any flaming or glowing substance. This section shall be known as the Paul Buzzo Act. *(Stats.1959, c. 3, p. 1709, § 23111. Amended by Stats.1963, c. 2038, p. 4267, § 30; Stats.1965, c. 474, p. 1778, § 1; Stats.1965, c. 1261, p. 3137, § 1; Stats.1970, c. 1548, p. 3151, § 8.)*

Cross References

Definitions,
Highway, see Vehicle Code §§ 360, 591, 592.
Private road or driveway, see Vehicle Code § 490.
Forfeiture of bail, see Vehicle Code § 40512.
Litter violations, disposition of fines and forfeitures, see Penal Code § 1463.9.
Littering or dumping on highways, see Penal Code § 374.3.
Optional bail forfeiture, see Vehicle Code § 40512.5.
Punishment for littering violations, see Vehicle Code § 42001.7.
Safety roadside rest, refuse disposal, see Streets and Highways Code § 224.
Similar provision, see Health and Safety Code § 13002.
Throwing substances upon highway likely to injure persons, animals or vehicles, see Penal Code § 588a.
Warning signs, see Streets and Highways Code § 101.6.

Research References

2 Witkin, California Criminal Law 4th Crimes Against Property § 301 (2021), Acts Involving Roads, Highways, or Traffic Devices.
2 Witkin, California Criminal Law 4th Crimes Against Public Peace and Welfare § 463 (2021), Fire.

§ 23112. Throwing, depositing, or dumping matter on highway

(a) No person shall throw or deposit, nor shall the registered owner or the driver, if such owner is not then present in the vehicle, aid or abet in the throwing or depositing upon any highway any bottle, can, garbage, glass, nail, offal, paper, wire, any substance likely to injure or damage traffic using the highway, or any noisome, nauseous, or offensive matter of any kind.

(b) No person shall place, deposit, or dump, or cause to be placed, deposited, or dumped, any rocks, refuse, garbage, or dirt in or upon any highway, including any portion of the right-of-way thereof, without the consent of the state or local agency having jurisdiction over the highway. *(Stats.1959, c. 3, p. 1709, § 23112. Amended by Stats.1959, c. 40, p. 1896, § 2; Stats.1965, c. 1261, p. 3137, § 2; Stats.1970, c. 62, p. 77, § 1; Stats.1976, c. 213, p. 399, § 2; Stats.1980, c. 74, p. 190, § 4.)*

Cross References

Forfeiture of bail, see Vehicle Code § 40512.
Highway defined, see Vehicle Code §§ 360, 591, 592.
Litter violations, disposition of fines and forfeitures, see Penal Code § 1463.9.
Littering or dumping on highways, see Penal Code § 374.3.
Optional bail forfeiture, see Vehicle Code § 40512.5.
Punishment for littering violations, see Vehicle Code § 42001.7.
Right-of-way defined, see Vehicle Code § 525.
Safety roadside rest, refuse disposal, see Streets and Highways Code § 224.
Throwing substances upon highway likely to injure persons, animals or vehicles, see Penal Code § 588a.

Research References

2 Witkin, California Criminal Law 4th Crimes Against Property § 301 (2021), Acts Involving Roads, Highways, or Traffic Devices.

§ 23112.5. Dumping, spilling, or releasing hazardous material or waste on highway; notification; penalty

(a) Any person who dumps, spills, or causes the release of hazardous material, as defined by Section 353, or hazardous waste, as defined by Section 25117 of the Health and Safety Code, upon any highway shall notify the Department of the California Highway Patrol or the agency having traffic jurisdiction for that highway of the dump, spill, or release, as soon as the person has knowledge of the dump, spill, or release and notification is possible. Upon receiving notification pursuant to this section, the Department of the California Highway Patrol shall, as soon as possible, notify the Office of Emergency Services of the dump, spill, or release, except for petroleum spills of less than 42 gallons from vehicular fuel tanks.

(b) Any person who is convicted of a violation of this section shall be punished by a mandatory fine of not less than two thousand dollars ($2,000). *(Added by Stats.1985, c. 646, § 1. Amended by Stats.1990, c. 429 (A.B.3904), § 1; Stats.1994, c. 1214 (A.B.3404), § 8; Stats.2010, c. 618 (A.B.2791), § 294; Stats.2013, c. 352 (A.B. 1317), § 525, eff. Sept. 26, 2013, operative July 1, 2013.)*

§ 23112.7. Illegal dumping of waste matter or harmful waste matter; impoundment; civil forfeiture

(a)(1) A motor vehicle used for illegal dumping of waste matter on public or private property is subject to impoundment pursuant to subdivision (c).

(2) A motor vehicle used for illegal dumping of harmful waste matter on public or private property is subject to impoundment and civil forfeiture pursuant to subdivision (d).

(b) For the purposes of this section, the following terms have the following meanings:

(1) "Illegal dumping" means the willful or intentional depositing, dropping, dumping, placing, or throwing of any waste matter onto public or private property that is not expressly designated for the purpose of disposal of waste matter. "Illegal dumping" does not include the discarding of small quantities of waste matter related to consumer goods and that are reasonably understood to be ordinarily carried on or about the body of a living person, including, but not limited to, beverage containers and closures, packaging, wrappers, wastepaper, newspaper, magazines, or other similar waste matter that escapes or is allowed to escape from a container, receptacle, or package.

(2) "Waste matter" means any form of tangible matter described by any of the following:

(A) All forms of garbage, refuse, rubbish, recyclable materials, and solid waste.

(B) Dirt, soil, rock, decomposed rock, gravel, sand, or other aggregate material dumped or deposited as refuse.

(C) Abandoned or discarded furniture; or commercial, industrial, or agricultural machinery, apparatus, structure, or other container; or a piece, portion, or part of these items.

(D) All forms of liquid waste not otherwise defined in or deemed to fall within the purview of Section 25117 of the Health and Safety Code, including, but not limited to, water-based or oil-based paints, chemical solutions, water contaminated with any substance rendering it unusable for irrigation or construction, oils, fuels, and other petroleum distillates or byproducts.

(E) Any form of biological waste not otherwise designated by law as hazardous waste, including, but not limited to, body parts, carcasses, and any associated container, enclosure, or wrapping material used to dispose these matters.

(F) A physical substance used as an ingredient in any process, now known or hereafter developed or devised, to manufacture a controlled substance specified in Section 11054, 11055, 11056, 11057, or 11058 of the Health and Safety Code, or that is a byproduct or result of the manufacturing process of the controlled substance.

(3) "Harmful waste matter" is a hazardous substance as defined in Section 374.8 of the Penal Code; a hazardous waste as defined in Section 25117 of the Health and Safety Code; waste that, pursuant to Division 30 (commencing with Section 40000) of the Public Resources Code, cannot be disposed in a municipal solid waste landfill without special handling, processing, or treatment; or waste matter in excess of one cubic yard.

(c)(1) Whenever a person, who has one or more prior convictions of Section 374.3 or 374.8 of the Penal Code that are not infractions, is convicted of a misdemeanor violation of Section 374.3 of the Penal Code, or of a violation of Section 374.8 of the Penal Code, for illegally dumping waste matter or harmful waste matter that is committed while driving a motor vehicle of which he or she is the registered owner of the vehicle, or is the registered owner's agent or employee, the court at the time of sentencing may order the motor vehicle impounded for a period of not more than six months.

(2) In determining the impoundment period imposed pursuant to paragraph (1), the court shall consider both of the following factors:

(A) The size and nature of the waste matter dumped.

(B) Whether the dumping occurred for a business purpose.

(3) The cost of keeping the vehicle is a lien on the vehicle pursuant to Chapter 6.5 (commencing with Section 3067) of Title 14 of Part 4 of Division 3 of the Civil Code.

(4) Notwithstanding paragraph (1), a vehicle impounded pursuant to this subdivision shall be released to the legal owner or his or her agent pursuant to subdivision (b) of Section 23592.

(5) The impounding agency shall not be liable to the registered owner for the release of the vehicle to the legal owner or his or her agent when made in compliance with paragraph (4).

(6) This subdivision does not apply if there is a community property interest in the vehicle that is owned by a person other than the defendant and the vehicle is the only vehicle available to the defendant's immediate family that may be operated on the highway with a class A, class B, or class C driver's license.

(d)(1) Notwithstanding Section 86 of the Code of Civil Procedure and any other provision of law otherwise prescribing the jurisdiction of the court based upon the value of the property involved, whenever a person, who has two or more prior convictions of Section 374.3 or 374.8 of the Penal Code that are not infractions, is charged with a misdemeanor violation of Section 374.3 of the Penal Code, or of a violation of Section 374.8 of the Penal Code, for illegally dumping harmful waste matter, the court with jurisdiction over the offense may, upon a motion of the prosecutor or the county counsel in a criminal action, declare a motor vehicle if used by the defendant in the commission of the violation, to be a nuisance, and upon conviction order the vehicle sold pursuant to Section 23596, if the person is the registered owner of the vehicle or the registered owner's employee or agent.

(2) The proceeds of the sale of the vehicle pursuant to this subdivision shall be distributed and used in decreasing order of priority, as follows:

(A) To satisfy all costs of the sale, including costs incurred with respect to the taking and keeping of the vehicle pending sale.

(B) To the legal owner in an amount to satisfy the indebtedness owed to the legal owner remaining as of the date of the sale, including accrued interest or finance charges and delinquency charges.

(C) To recover the costs made, incurred, or associated with the enforcement of this section, the abatement of waste matter, and the deterrence of illegal dumping.

(3) A vehicle shall not be sold pursuant to this subdivision in either of the following circumstances:

(A) The vehicle is owned by the employer or principal of the defendant and the use of the vehicle was made without the employer's or principal's knowledge and consent, and did not provide a direct benefit to the employer's or principal's business.

(B) There is a community property interest in the vehicle that is owned by a person other than the defendant and the vehicle is the only vehicle available to the defendant's immediate family that may be operated on the highway with a class A, class B, or class C driver's license. *(Added by Stats.2006, c. 765 (A.B.2253), § 1.)*

Cross References

Infractions, see Penal Code § 16.
Misdemeanor, definition and penalties, see Penal Code §§ 17, 19, 19.2.

Research References

2 Witkin, California Criminal Law 4th Crimes Against Public Peace and Welfare § 461 (2021), Dumping and Littering.

§ 23113. Removal of material from highway

(a) Any person who drops, dumps, deposits, places, or throws, or causes or permits to be dropped, dumped, deposited, placed, or thrown, upon any highway or street any material described in Section 23112 or in subdivision (d) of Section 23114 shall immediately remove the material or cause the material to be removed.

(b) If the person fails to comply with subdivision (a), the governmental agency responsible for the maintenance of the street or highway on which the material has been deposited may remove the material and collect, by civil action, if necessary, the actual cost of the removal operation in addition to any other damages authorized by law from the person made responsible under subdivision (a).

(c) A member of the Department of the California Highway Patrol may direct a responsible party to remove the aggregate material described in subdivision (d) of Section 23114 from a highway when that material has escaped or been released from a vehicle.

(d) Notwithstanding any other provision of law, a government agency described in subdivision (b), the Department of the California Highway Patrol, or the employees or officers of those agencies, may not be held liable for any damage to material, to cargo, or to personal property caused by a negligent act or omission of the employee or officer when the employee or officer is acting within the scope and purpose of subdivision (b) or (c). Nothing in this subdivision affects liability for purposes of establishing gross negligence or willful misconduct. This subdivision applies to the negligent performance of a ministerial act, and does not affect liability under any provision of law, including liability, if any, derived from the failure to preserve evidence in a civil or criminal action. *(Stats.1959, c. 3, p. 1709, § 23113. Amended by Stats.1963, c. 1668, p. 3257, § 1; Stats.1965, c. 552, p. 1879, § 1; Stats.1988, c. 1486, § 2; Stats.1989, c. 1360, § 158;*

Stats.1989, c. 125, § 1, eff. July 12, 1989; Stats.1999, c. 421 (S.B.681), § 2.)

Cross References

Forfeiture of bail, see Vehicle Code § 40512.
Highway defined, see Vehicle Code §§ 360, 591, 592.
Litter violations, disposition of fines and forfeitures, see Penal Code § 1463.9.
Optional bail forfeiture, see Vehicle Code § 40512.5.
Punishment for littering violations, see Vehicle Code § 42001.7.
Street defined, see Vehicle Code §§ 590, 591.

Research References

2 Witkin, California Criminal Law 4th Crimes Against Property § 301 (2021), Acts Involving Roads, Highways, or Traffic Devices.

§ 23114. Spilling loads on highway; cargo area; equipment; covering of transported material

(a) Except as provided in Subpart I (commencing with Section 393.100) of Title 49 of the Code of Federal Regulations related to hay and straw, a vehicle shall not be driven or moved on any highway unless the vehicle is so constructed, covered, or loaded as to prevent any of its contents or load other than clear water or feathers from live birds from dropping, sifting, leaking, blowing, spilling, or otherwise escaping from the vehicle.

(b)(1) Aggregate material shall only be carried in the cargo area of a vehicle. The cargo area shall not contain any holes, cracks, or openings through which that material may escape, regardless of the degree to which the vehicle is loaded, except as provided in paragraph (2).

(2) Every vehicle used to transport aggregate materials, regardless of the degree to which the vehicle is loaded, shall be equipped with all of the following:

(A) Properly functioning seals on any openings used to empty the load, including, but not limited to, bottom dump release gates and tailgates.

(B) Splash flaps behind every tire, or set of tires, regardless of the position on the truck, truck tractor, or trailer.

(C) Center flaps at a location to the rear of each bottom dump release gate as to trucks or trailers equipped with bottom dump release gates. The center flap may be positioned directly behind the bottom dump release gate and in front of the rear axle of the vehicle, or it may be positioned to the rear of the rear axle in line with the splash flaps required behind the tires. The width of the center flap may extend not more than one inch from one sidewall to the opposite sidewall of the inside tires and shall extend to within five inches of the pavement surface, and may be not less than 24 inches from the bottom edge to the top edge of that center flap.

(D) Fenders starting at the splash flap with the leading edge of the fenders extending forward at least six inches beyond the center of the axle that cover the tops of tires not already covered by the truck, truck tractor, or trailer body.

(E) Complete enclosures on all vertical sides of the cargo area, including, but not limited to, tailgates.

(F) Shed boards designed to prevent aggregate materials from being deposited on the vehicle body during top loading.

(c) Vehicles comprised of full rigid enclosures are exempt only from subparagraphs (C) and (F) of paragraph (2) of subdivision (b).

(d) For purposes of this section, "aggregate material" means rock fragments, pebbles, sand, dirt, gravel, cobbles, crushed base, asphalt, and other similar materials.

(e)(1) In addition to subdivisions (a) and (b), a vehicle may not transport any aggregate material upon a highway unless the material is covered.

(2) Vehicles transporting loads composed entirely of asphalt material are exempt only from the provisions of this section requiring that loads be covered.

(3) Vehicles transporting loads composed entirely of petroleum coke material are not required to cover their loads if they are loaded using safety procedures, specialized equipment, and a chemical surfactant designed to prevent materials from blowing, spilling, or otherwise escaping from the vehicle.

(4) Vehicles transporting loads of aggregate materials are not required to cover their loads if the load, where it contacts the sides, front, and back of the cargo container area, remains six inches from the upper edge of the container area, and if the load does not extend, at its peak, above any part of the upper edge of the cargo container area.

(f) A person who provides a location for vehicles to be loaded with an aggregate material or other material shall provide a location for vehicle operators to comply with this section before entering a highway.

(1) A person is exempt from the requirements of this subdivision if the location that he or she provides for vehicles to be loaded with the materials described in this subdivision has 100 yards or less between the scale houses where the trucks carrying aggregate material are weighed and the point of egress to a public road.

(2) A driver of a vehicle loaded with aggregate material leaving locations exempted from the requirements of this subdivision is authorized to operate on public roads only until that driver is able to safely cover the load at a site near the location's point of egress to the public road. Except as provided under paragraph (4) of subdivision (e), an uncovered vehicle described in this paragraph may not operate more than 200 yards from the point of egress to the public road. *(Stats.1959, c. 3, p. 1709, § 23114. Amended by Stats.1961, c. 713, p. 1953, § 1; Stats.1965, c. 455, p. 1765, § 1; Stats.1988, c. 1486, § 3; Stats.1989, c. 125, § 2, eff. July 12, 1989; Stats.1989, c. 533, § 12; Stats.2002, c. 673 (S.B.1530), § 1; Stats.2004, c. 518 (A.B.2201), § 4; Stats.2008, c. 250 (A.B.2714), § 1.)*

Cross References

Damage to highway, weight or size of vehicle, see Vehicle Code § 17302.

§ 23115. Rubbish vehicles

(a) No vehicle transporting garbage, swill, used cans or bottles, wastepapers, waste cardboard, ashes, refuse, trash, or rubbish, or any noisome, nauseous, or offensive matter, or anything being transported for disposal or recycling shall be driven or moved upon any highway unless the load is totally covered in a manner that will prevent the load or any part of the load from spilling or falling from the vehicle.

(b) Subdivision (a) does not prohibit a rubbish vehicle from being without cover while in the process of acquiring its load if no law, administrative regulation, or local ordinance requires that it be covered in those circumstances.

(c) Vehicles transporting wastepaper, waste cardboard, or used cans or bottles, are in compliance with subdivision (a) if appropriate binders including, but not limited to, bands, wires, straps, or netting are used to prevent the load, or any part of the load, from spilling or falling from the vehicle.

(d) This section does not apply to any vehicle engaged in transporting wet waste fruit or vegetable matter, or waste products to or from a food processing establishment. *(Stats.1959, c. 3, p. 1709, § 23115. Amended by Stats.1975, c. 1166, p. 2884, § 1; Stats.1988, c. 1486, § 4, operative Sept. 1, 1990; Stats.2001, c. 279 (S.B.624), § 1.)*

Cross References

Definitions,
Highway, see Vehicle Code §§ 360, 591, 592.
Vehicle, see Vehicle Code § 670.

§ 23116. Pickup or flatbed motor truck; transportation in back; section application

(a) No person driving a pickup truck or a flatbed motortruck on a highway shall transport any person in or on the back of the truck.

(b) No person shall ride in or on the back of a truck or flatbed motortruck being driven on a highway.

(c) Subdivisions (a) and (b) do not apply if the person in the back of the truck is secured with a restraint system. The restraint system shall meet or exceed the federal motor vehicle safety standards published in Sections 571.207, 571.209, and 571.210 of Title 49 of the Code of Federal Regulations.

(d) Subdivisions (a), (b), and (c) do not apply to any person transporting one or more persons in the back of a truck or flatbed motortruck owned by a farmer or rancher, if that vehicle is used exclusively within the boundaries of lands owned or managed by that farmer or rancher, including the incidental use of that vehicle on not more than one mile of highway between one part of the farm or ranch to another part of that farm or ranch.

(e) Subdivisions (a), (b), and (c) do not apply if the person in the back of the truck or the flatbed is being transported in an emergency response situation by a public agency or pursuant to the direction or authority of a public agency.

As used in this subdivision, "emergency response situation" means instances in which necessary measures are needed in order to prevent injury or death to persons or to prevent, confine, or mitigate damage or destruction to property.

(f) Subdivisions (a) and (b) do not apply if the person in the back of the truck or flatbed motortruck is being transported in a parade that is supervised by a law enforcement agency and the speed of the truck while in the parade does not exceed eight miles per hour. *(Added by Stats.1982, c. 1275, p. 4709, § 1. Amended by Stats.1984, c. 128, § 1; Stats.1993, c. 895 (A.B.153), § 1; Stats.1995, c. 766 (S.B.726), § 35; Stats.2000, c. 308 (A.B.602), § 2.)*

Research References

2 Witkin, California Criminal Law 4th Crimes Against Public Peace and Welfare § 477 (2021), Mandatory Use of Seat Belts.

§ 23117. Transportation of animals; enclosure or restraint requirements

(a) No person driving a motor vehicle shall transport any animal in the back of the vehicle in a space intended for any load on the vehicle on a highway unless the space is enclosed or has side and tail racks to a height of at least 46 inches extending vertically from the floor, the vehicle has installed means of preventing the animal from being discharged, or the animal is cross tethered to the vehicle, or is protected by a secured container or cage, in a manner which will prevent the animal from being thrown, falling, or jumping from the vehicle.

(b) This section does not apply to any of the following:

(1) The transportation of livestock.

(2) The transportation of a dog whose owner either owns or is employed by a ranching or farming operation who is traveling on a road in a rural area or who is traveling to and from a livestock auction.

(3) The transportation of a dog for purposes associated with ranching or farming. *(Added by Stats.1987, c. 224, § 1.)*

§ 23118. Vehicle used in violation of code governing repossessors; seizure; release; notice and hearing; liability

(a)(1) A magistrate presented with the affidavit of a peace officer establishing reasonable cause to believe that a vehicle, described by vehicle type and license number, is being used or operated in violation of Section 7502.1 of the Business and Professions Code shall issue a warrant or order authorizing any peace officer to immediately seize and cause the removal of the vehicle.

(2) The warrant or court order may be entered into a computerized database.

(3) Any vehicle so impounded may be impounded until such time as the owner of the property, or the person in possession of the property at the time of the impoundment, produces proof of licensure pursuant to Chapter 11 (commencing with Section 7500) of Division 3 of the Business and Professions Code, or proof of an exemption from licensure pursuant to Section 7500.2 or 7500.3 of the Business and Professions Code.

(4) The impounding agency, within two working days of impoundment, shall send a notice by certified mail, return receipt requested, to the legal owner of the vehicle, at an address obtained from the department, informing the owner that the vehicle has been impounded and providing the owner with a copy of the warrant or court order. Failure to notify the legal owner within two working days shall prohibit the impounding agency from charging for more than 15 days impoundment when a legal owner redeems the impounded vehicle. The law enforcement agency shall be open to issue a release to the registered owner or legal owner, or the agent of either, whenever the agency is open to serve the public for regular, nonemergency business.

(b)(1) An impounding agency shall release a vehicle to the registered owner or his or her agent prior to the end of the impoundment period and without the permission of the magistrate authorizing the vehicle's seizure under any of the following circumstances:

(A) When the vehicle is a stolen vehicle.

(B) When the vehicle was seized under this section for an offense that does not authorize the seizure of the vehicle.

(2) No vehicle may be released under this subdivision, except upon presentation of the registered owner's or agent's currently valid license to operate the vehicle, and proof of current vehicle registration, or upon order of the court.

(c)(1) Whenever a vehicle is impounded under this section, the magistrate ordering the storage shall provide the vehicle's registered and legal owners of record, or their agents, with the opportunity for a poststorage hearing to determine the validity of the storage.

(2) A notice of the storage shall be mailed or personally delivered to the registered and legal owners within 48 hours after issuance of the warrant or court order, excluding weekends and holidays, by the person or agency executing the warrant or court order, and shall include all of the following information:

(A) The name, address, and telephone number of the agency providing the notice.

(B) The location of the place of storage and a description of the vehicle, which shall include, if available, the name or make, the manufacturer, the license plate number, and the mileage of the vehicle.

(C) A copy of the warrant or court order and the peace officer's affidavit, as described in subdivision (a).

(D) A statement that, in order to receive their poststorage hearing, the owners, or their agents, are required to request the hearing from the magistrate issuing the warrant or court order in person, in writing, or by telephone, within 10 days of the date of the notice.

(3) The poststorage hearing shall be conducted within two court days after receipt of the request for the hearing.

(4) At the hearing, the magistrate may order the vehicle released if he or she finds any of the circumstances described in subdivision (b) or (e) that allow release of a vehicle by the impounding agency.

(5) Failure of either the registered or legal owner, or his or her agent, to request, or to attend, a scheduled hearing satisfies the poststorage hearing requirement.

(6) The agency employing the peace officer who caused the magistrate to issue the warrant or court order shall be responsible for the costs incurred for towing and storage if it is determined in the poststorage hearing that reasonable grounds for the storage are not established.

(d) The registered owner or his or her agent is responsible for all towing and storage charges related to the impoundment, and any administrative charges authorized under Section 22850.5.

(e) A vehicle removed and seized under subdivision (a) shall be released to the legal owner of the vehicle or the legal owner's agent prior to the end of the impoundment period and without the permission of the magistrate authorizing the seizure of the vehicle if all of the following conditions are met:

(1) The legal owner is a motor vehicle dealer, bank, credit union, acceptance corporation, or other licensed financial institution legally operating in this state or is another person, not the registered owner, holding a security interest in the vehicle.

(2)(A) The legal owner or the legal owner's agent pays all towing and storage fees related to the seizure of the vehicle. Except as specifically authorized by this subdivision, no other fees shall be charged to the legal owner or the agent of the legal owner. No lien sale processing fees shall be charged to the legal owner who redeems the vehicle prior to the 15th day of impoundment. Neither the impounding authority nor any person having possession of the vehicle shall collect from the legal owner of the type specified in paragraph (1), or the legal owner's agent any administrative charges imposed pursuant to Section 22850.5 unless the legal owner voluntarily requested a poststorage hearing.

(B) A person operating or in charge of a storage facility where vehicles are stored pursuant to this section shall accept a valid bank credit card or cash for payment of towing, storage, and related fees by a legal or registered owner or the owner's agent claiming the vehicle. A credit card shall be in the name of the person presenting the card. "Credit card" means "credit card" as defined in subdivision (a) of Section 1747.02 of the Civil Code, except, for the purposes of this section, credit card does not include a credit card issued by a retail seller.

(C) A person operating or in charge of a storage facility described in subparagraph (B) who violates subparagraph (B) shall be civilly liable to the owner of the vehicle or to the person who tendered the fees for four times the amount of the towing, storage, and related fees, but not to exceed five hundred dollars ($500).

(D) A person operating or in charge of the storage facility shall have sufficient funds on the premises of the primary storage facility during normal business hours to accommodate, and make change in, a reasonable monetary transaction.

(E) Credit charges for towing and storage services shall comply with Section 1748.1 of the Civil Code. Law enforcement agencies may include the costs of providing for payment by credit when making agreements with towing companies on rates.

(3)(A) The legal owner or the legal owner's agent presents to the law enforcement agency or impounding agency, or any person acting on behalf of those agencies, a copy of the assignment, as defined in subdivision (b) of Section 7500.1 of the Business and Professions Code; a release from the one responsible governmental agency, only if required by the agency; a government-issued photographic identification card; and any one of the following as determined by the legal owner or the legal owner's agent: a certificate of repossession for the vehicle, a security agreement for the vehicle, or title, whether paper or electronic, showing proof of legal ownership for the vehicle. The law enforcement agency, impounding agency, or any other governmental agency, or any person acting on behalf of those agencies, shall not require the presentation of any other documents.

(B) The legal owner or the legal owner's agent presents to the person in possession of the vehicle, or any person acting on behalf of the person in possession, a copy of the assignment, as defined in subdivision (b) of Section 7500.1 of the Business and Professions Code; a release from the one responsible governmental agency, only if required by the agency; a government-issued photographic identification card; and any one of the following as determined by the legal owner or the legal owner's agent: a certificate of repossession for the vehicle, a security agreement for the vehicle, or title, whether paper or electronic, showing proof of legal ownership for the vehicle. The person in possession of the vehicle, or any person acting on behalf of the person in possession, shall not require the presentation of any other documents.

(C) All presented documents may be originals, photocopies, or facsimile copies, or may be transmitted electronically. The law enforcement agency, impounding agency, or any person in possession of the vehicle, or anyone acting on behalf of them, shall not require a document to be notarized. The law enforcement agency, impounding agency, or any person acting on behalf of those agencies, may require the agent of the legal owner to produce a photocopy or facsimile copy of its repossession agency license or registration issued pursuant to Chapter 11 (commencing with Section 7500) of Division 3 of the Business and Professions Code, or to demonstrate, to the satisfaction of the law enforcement agency, impounding agency, or any person in possession of the vehicle, or anyone acting on behalf of them, that the agent is exempt from licensure pursuant to Section 7500.2 or 7500.3 of the Business and Professions Code.

(D) No administrative costs authorized under subdivision (a) of Section 22850.5 shall be charged to the legal owner of the type specified in paragraph (1), who redeems the vehicle unless the legal owner voluntarily requests a poststorage hearing. No city, county, city and county, or state agency shall require a legal owner or a legal owner's agent to request a poststorage hearing as a requirement for release of the vehicle to the legal owner or the legal owner's agent. The law enforcement agency, impounding agency, or any other governmental agency, or any person acting on behalf of those agencies, shall not require any documents other than those specified in this paragraph. The law enforcement agency, impounding agency, or other governmental agency, or any person acting on behalf of those agencies, may not require any documents to be notarized. The legal owner or the legal owner's agent shall be given a copy of any documents he or she is required to sign, except for a vehicle evidentiary hold logbook. The law enforcement agency, impounding agency, or any person acting on behalf of those agencies, or any person in possession of the vehicle, may photocopy and retain the copies of any documents presented by the legal owner or legal owner's agent.

(4) A failure by a storage facility to comply with any applicable conditions set forth in this subdivision shall not affect the right of the legal owner or the legal owner's agent to retrieve the vehicle, provided all conditions required of the legal owner or legal owner's agent under this subdivision are satisfied.

(f)(1) A legal owner or the legal owner's agent that obtains release of the vehicle pursuant to subdivision (e) shall not release the vehicle to the registered owner of the vehicle or the person who was listed as the registered owner when the vehicle was impounded or the person in possession of the vehicle at the time of the impound or any agents of the registered owner until the termination of the impoundment period.

(2) The legal owner or the legal owner's agent shall not relinquish the vehicle to the registered owner or the person who was listed as the registered owner when the vehicle was impounded until the registered owner or that owner's agent presents his or her valid driver's license or valid temporary driver's license to the legal owner or the legal owner's agent. The legal owner or the legal owner's

agent or the person in possession of the vehicle shall make every reasonable effort to ensure that the licenses presented are valid and possession of the vehicle will not be given to the driver who was involved in the original impound proceeding until the expiration of the impoundment period.

(3) Prior to relinquishing the vehicle, the legal owner may require the registered owner to pay all towing and storage charges related to the impoundment and the administrative charges authorized under Section 22850.5 that were incurred by the legal owner in connection with obtaining the custody of the vehicle.

(4) Any legal owner who knowingly releases or causes the release of a vehicle to a registered owner or the person in possession of the vehicle at the time of the impound or any agent of the registered owner in violation of this subdivision shall be guilty of a misdemeanor and subject to a fine in the amount of two thousand dollars ($2,000) in addition to any other penalties established by law.

(5) The legal owner, registered owner, or person in possession of the vehicle shall not change or attempt to change the name of the legal owner or the registered owner on the records of the department until the vehicle is released from the impound.

(g) Notwithstanding any other provision of this section, the registered owner and not the legal owner shall remain responsible for any towing and storage charges related to the impoundment and the administrative charges authorized under Section 22850.5 and any parking fines, penalties, and administrative fees incurred by the registered owner.

(h) The law enforcement agency and the impounding agency, including any storage facility acting on behalf of the law enforcement agency or impounding agency, shall comply with this section and shall not be liable to the registered owner for the improper release of the vehicle to the legal owner or the legal owner's agent provided the release complies with the provisions of this section. The legal owner shall indemnify and hold harmless a storage facility from any claims arising out of the release of the vehicle to the legal owner or the legal owner's agent and from any damage to the vehicle after its release, including the reasonable costs associated with defending any such claims. A law enforcement agency shall not refuse to issue a release to a legal owner or the agent of a legal owner on the grounds that it previously issued a release. *(Added by Stats.2009, c. 322 (A.B.515), § 11.)*

§ 23120. Temple width of glasses

No person shall operate a motor vehicle while wearing glasses having a temple width of one-half inch or more if any part of such temple extends below the horizontal center of the lens so as to interfere with lateral vision. *(Added by Stats.1959, c. 531, p. 2498, § 1.)*

§ 23123. Driving a motor vehicle while using a wireless telephone; penalty; exceptions

(a) A person shall not drive a motor vehicle while using a wireless telephone unless that telephone is specifically designed and configured to allow hands-free listening and talking, and is used in that manner while driving.

(b) A violation of this section is an infraction punishable by a base fine of twenty dollars ($20) for a first offense and fifty dollars ($50) for each subsequent offense.

(c) This section does not apply to a person using a wireless telephone for emergency purposes, including, but not limited to, an emergency call to a law enforcement agency, health care provider, fire department, or other emergency services agency or entity.

(d) This section does not apply to an emergency services professional using a wireless telephone while operating an authorized emergency vehicle, as defined in Section 165, in the course and scope of his or her duties.

(e) This section does not apply to a person driving a schoolbus or transit vehicle that is subject to Section 23125.

(f) This section does not apply to a person while driving a motor vehicle on private property.

(g) This section shall become operative on July 1, 2011. *(Added by Stats.2006, c. 290 (S.B.1613), § 5, operative July 1, 2011. Amended by Stats.2007, c. 214 (S.B.33), § 3, operative July 1, 2011.)*

Cross References

Conviction of violation of this section, giving of violation points, see Vehicle Code § 12810.3.

Suspension or revocation of license for driving under the influence or engaging in speed contests or exhibitions of speed, reinstatement conditions, see Vehicle Code § 13352.

Transportation network companies, requirements for participating drivers, see Public Utilities Code § 5445.3.

Research References

2 Witkin, California Criminal Law 4th Crimes Against Public Peace and Welfare § 326 (2021), Using Wireless Communication Devices.

§ 23123.5. Driving motor vehicle while holding and operating a handheld wireless telephone or electronic wireless communications device; prohibition; exceptions; penalty

(a) A person shall not drive a motor vehicle while holding and operating a handheld wireless telephone or an electronic wireless communications device unless the wireless telephone or electronic wireless communications device is specifically designed and configured to allow voice-operated and hands-free operation, and it is used in that manner while driving.

(b) This section shall not apply to manufacturer-installed systems that are embedded in the vehicle.

(c) A handheld wireless telephone or electronic wireless communications device may be operated in a manner requiring the use of the driver's hand while the driver is operating the vehicle only if both of the following conditions are satisfied:

(1) The handheld wireless telephone or electronic wireless communications device is mounted on a vehicle's windshield in the same manner a portable Global Positioning System (GPS) is mounted pursuant to paragraph (12) of subdivision (b) of Section 26708 or is mounted on or affixed to a vehicle's dashboard or center console in a manner that does not hinder the driver's view of the road.

(2) The driver's hand is used to activate or deactivate a feature or function of the handheld wireless telephone or wireless communications device with the motion of a single swipe or tap of the driver's finger.

(d) A violation of this section is an infraction punishable by a base fine of twenty dollars ($20) for a first offense and fifty dollars ($50) for each subsequent offense.

(e) This section does not apply to an emergency services professional using an electronic wireless communications device while operating an authorized emergency vehicle, as defined in Section 165, in the course and scope of his or her duties.

(f) For the purposes of this section, "electronic wireless communications device" includes, but is not limited to, a broadband personal communication device, a handheld device or laptop computer with mobile data access, or a pager. *(Added by Stats.2016, c. 660 (A.B.1785), § 2, eff. Jan. 1, 2017. Amended by Stats.2017, c. 297 (A.B.1222), § 1, eff. Jan. 1, 2018.)*

Cross References

Driving commercial motor vehicle while using electronic wireless communication device to write, send, or read text-based communications, defined as serious traffic violation, see Vehicle Code § 15210.

Transportation network companies, requirements for participating drivers, see Public Utilities Code § 5445.3.

Research References

2 Witkin, California Criminal Law 4th Crimes Against Public Peace and Welfare § 326 (2021), Using Wireless Communication Devices.
4 Witkin, California Criminal Law 4th Illegally Obtained Evidence § 299 (2021), Illustrations: Detention was Reasonable.

§ 23124. Driving motor vehicle while using wireless telephone or electronic wireless communications device; minor drivers; penalty; enforcement; exceptions

(a) This section applies to a person under the age of 18 years.

(b) Notwithstanding Sections 23123 and 23123.5, a person described in subdivision (a) shall not drive a motor vehicle while using a wireless telephone or an electronic wireless communications device, even if equipped with a hands-free device.

(c) A violation of this section is an infraction punishable by a base fine of twenty dollars ($20) for a first offense and fifty dollars ($50) for each subsequent offense.

(d) A law enforcement officer shall not stop a vehicle for the sole purpose of determining whether the driver is violating subdivision (b).

(e) Subdivision (d) does not prohibit a law enforcement officer from stopping a vehicle for a violation of Section 23123 or 23123.5.

(f) This section does not apply to a person using a wireless telephone or a mobile service device for emergency purposes, including, but not limited to, an emergency call to a law enforcement agency, health care provider, fire department, or other emergency services agency or entity.

(g) For the purposes of this section, "electronic wireless communications device" includes, but is not limited to, a broadband personal communication device, specialized mobile radio device, handheld device or laptop computer with mobile data access, pager, and two-way messaging device. *(Added by Stats.2007, c. 214 (S.B.33), § 4, operative July 1, 2008. Amended by Stats.2013, c. 754 (S.B.194), § 1.)*

Cross References

Issuance and renewal of licenses, violation points, see Vehicle Code § 12810.3.

Research References

2 Witkin, California Criminal Law 4th Crimes Against Public Peace and Welfare § 326 (2021), Using Wireless Communication Devices.

§ 23125. School bus or transit vehicles; prohibition upon use of wireless telephones during operation; exceptions

(a) A person may not drive a schoolbus or transit vehicle, as defined in subdivision (g) of Section 99247 of the Public Utilities Code, while using a wireless telephone.

(b) This section does not apply to a driver using a wireless telephone for work-related purposes, or for emergency purposes, including, but not limited to, an emergency call to a law enforcement agency, health care provider, fire department, or other emergency service agency or entity.

(c) Notwithstanding any other provision of law, a violation of subdivision (a) does not constitute a serious traffic violation within the meaning of subdivision (i) of Section 15210. *(Added by Stats.2004, c. 505 (A.B.2785), § 1.)*

Research References

2 Witkin, California Criminal Law 4th Crimes Against Public Peace and Welfare § 326 (2021), Using Wireless Communication Devices.

§ 23127. Trails and paths

No person shall operate an unauthorized motor vehicle on any state, county, city, private, or district hiking or horseback riding trail or bicycle path that is clearly marked by an authorized agent or owner with signs at all entrances and exits and at intervals of not more than one mile indicating no unauthorized motor vehicles are permitted on the hiking or horseback riding trail or bicycle path, except bicycle paths which are contiguous or adjacent to a roadway dedicated solely to motor vehicle use.

For the purpose of this section "unauthorized motor vehicle" means any motor vehicle that is driven upon a hiking or horseback riding trail or bicycle path without the written permission of an agent or the owner of the trail or path.

This section does not apply to the operation of an authorized emergency or maintenance vehicle on a hiking or horseback riding trail or bicycle path whenever necessary in furtherance of the purpose for which the vehicle has been classed as an authorized emergency vehicle. Any person who violates this section is guilty of a misdemeanor. *(Added by Stats.1965, c. 1559, p. 3650, § 1. Amended by Stats.1973, c. 951, p. 1790, § 1.)*

Cross References

Authorized emergency vehicle, see Vehicle Code § 165.
Motorized bicycles, prohibited operation, see Vehicle Code § 21207.5.
Punishment for violation of this section, see Vehicle Code § 42001.

Research References

2 Witkin, California Criminal Law 4th Crimes Against Public Peace and Welfare § 327 (2021), Miscellaneous Regulations.

§ 23128. Snowmobiles

It is unlawful for any person to operate a snowmobile in the following manner:

(a) On a highway except as provided in Section 38025.

(b) In a careless or negligent manner so as to endanger a person or property.

(c) For the purpose of pursuing deer or other game mammal with intent to harass such animals.

(d) For the purpose of violating Section 602 of the Penal Code. *(Formerly § 23337, added by Stats.1969, c. 1075, p. 2064, § 9. Renumbered § 23128 and amended by Stats.1971, c. 438, p. 909, § 194, operative May 3, 1972. Amended by Stats.1972, c. 973, p. 1759, § 17, eff. Aug. 16, 1972.)*

Cross References

Snowmobile defined, see Vehicle Code § 557.

§ 23129. Camper mounted on motor vehicle; exit requirements

No person shall drive a motor vehicle upon which is mounted a camper containing any passengers unless there is at least one unobstructed exit capable of being opened from both the interior and exterior of such camper. *(Added by Stats.1972, c. 432, p. 797, § 1.)*

Cross References

Camper defined, see Vehicle Code § 243.

§ 23135. Motorized bicycles; modifications

It is unlawful for any person to operate upon a highway any vehicle which was originally manufactured as a motorized bicycle, as defined in Section 406, and which has been modified in such a manner that it no longer conforms to the definition of a motorized bicycle. *(Added by Stats.1978, c. 421, p. 1320, § 3.)*

Cross References

Punishment for violations, see Vehicle Code § 42001.9.

ARTICLE 1.3. OFFENSES BY PERSONS UNDER 21 YEARS OF AGE INVOLVING ALCOHOL

§ 23136. Blood alcohol concentration of .01 or greater; implied consent to testing; failure to submit to or complete testing

(a) Notwithstanding Sections 23152 and 23153, it is unlawful for a person under the age of 21 years who has a blood-alcohol concentration of 0.01 percent or greater, as measured by a preliminary alcohol screening test or other chemical test, to drive a vehicle. However, this section shall not be a bar to prosecution under Section 23152 or 23153 or any other provision of law.

(b) A person shall be found to be in violation of subdivision (a) if the person was, at the time of driving, under the age of 21 years, and the trier of fact finds that the person had consumed an alcoholic beverage and was driving a vehicle with a blood-alcohol concentration of 0.01 percent or greater, as measured by a preliminary alcohol screening test or other chemical test.

(c)(1) Any person under the age of 21 years who drives a motor vehicle is deemed to have given his or her consent to a preliminary alcohol screening test or other chemical test for the purpose of determining the presence of alcohol in the person, if lawfully detained for an alleged violation of subdivision (a).

(2) The testing shall be incidental to a lawful detention and administered at the direction of a peace officer having reasonable cause to believe the person was driving a motor vehicle in violation of subdivision (a).

(3) The person shall be told that his or her failure to submit to, or the failure to complete, a preliminary alcohol screening test or other chemical test as requested will result in the suspension or revocation of the person's privilege to operate a motor vehicle for a period of one year to three years, as provided in Section 13353.1. *(Added by Stats.1993, c. 899 (S.B.689), § 11. Amended by Stats.1994, c. 938 (S.B.1295), § 13, eff. Sept. 28, 1994; Stats.1996, c. 10 (A.B.1869), § 18, eff. Feb. 9, 1996.)*

Cross References

Driving privileges, suspension or delay, restricted driving privileges imposed on showing of critical need to drive, see Vehicle Code § 13353.8.

Research References

2 Witkin, California Criminal Law 4th Crimes Against Public Peace and Welfare § 277 (2021), Driving With Unlawful Blood-Alcohol Level.
2 Witkin, California Criminal Law 4th Crimes Against Public Peace and Welfare § 293 (2021), Nature and Scope of Law.
2 Witkin, California Criminal Law 4th Crimes Against Public Peace and Welfare § 295 (2021), Test as Incidental to Lawful Arrest or Detention.
2 Witkin, California Criminal Law 4th Crimes Against Public Peace and Welfare § 297 (2021), Notice of Consequences of Refusal to Submit to Test.
2 Witkin, California Criminal Law 4th Crimes Against Public Peace and Welfare § 298 (2021), Administration of Test.
2 Witkin, California Criminal Law 4th Crimes Against Public Peace and Welfare § 302 (2021), Administrative Sanctions.

ARTICLE 1.5. JUVENILE OFFENSES INVOLVING ALCOHOL

§ 23140. Persons under 21 years of age; blood-alcohol concentration of .05 or more; driving vehicle prohibited; abstract of record

(a) It is unlawful for a person under the age of 21 years who has 0.05 percent or more, by weight, of alcohol in his or her blood to drive a vehicle.

(b) A person may be found to be in violation of subdivision (a) if the person was, at the time of driving, under the age of 21 years and under the influence of, or affected by, an alcoholic beverage regardless of whether a chemical test was made to determine that person's blood-alcohol concentration and if the trier of fact finds that the person had consumed an alcoholic beverage and was driving a vehicle while having a concentration of 0.05 percent or more, by weight, of alcohol in his or her blood.

(c) Notwithstanding any provision of law to the contrary, upon a finding that a person has violated this section, the clerk of the court shall prepare within 10 days after the finding and immediately forward to the department an abstract of the record of the court in which the finding is made. That abstract shall be a public record and available for public inspection in the same manner as other records reported under Section 1803. *(Added by Stats.1986, c. 1105, § 1. Amended by Stats.1989, c. 1465, § 5; Stats.1994, c. 938 (S.B.1295), § 16, eff. Sept. 28, 1994; Stats.2007, c. 263 (A.B.310), § 32.)*

Law Revision Commission Comments

Subdivision (c) of Section 23140 is amended to delete unnecessary language authorizing the judge to substitute for the clerk if there is no clerk. See Code Civ. Proc. § 167 (judge may perform any act court clerk may perform); Gov't Code §§ 69840–69848 (duties of clerk of superior court), 71620(b) (executive or administrative officer has authority of clerk of court). [35 Cal.L.Rev.Comm. Reports 219 (2007)].

Cross References

Driving privileges, suspension or delay, restricted driving privileges imposed on showing of critical need to drive, see Vehicle Code § 13353.8.
Gross vehicular manslaughter while intoxicated, see Penal Code § 191.5.
Immediate removal and seizure of vehicle driven by repeat offender, storage and impoundment, vehicle owner's rights and responsibilities, see Vehicle Code § 14602.8.
Juvenile offenders, programs of supervision, see Welfare and Institutions Code § 654.1.
Records available to courts and law enforcement officials, incidents under certain DWI and homicide laws, period of time records must be available, see Vehicle Code § 1808.
Refusal to submit to alcohol testing under DUI laws, calculation of prior convictions, certain foreign convictions recognized, see Vehicle Code §§ 13353, 13353.1 and 13353.3.
Search warrants, grounds for issuance, see Penal Code § 1524.
Violation of this section, relinquishment of motor vehicle to convicted minor, see Penal Code § 193.8.
Violations of this section, punishment, see Vehicle Code § 42001.25.

Research References

2 Witkin, California Criminal Law 4th Crimes Against Public Peace and Welfare § 277 (2021), Driving With Unlawful Blood-Alcohol Level.
2 Witkin, California Criminal Law 4th Crimes Against Public Peace and Welfare § 279 (2021), In General.
2 Witkin, California Criminal Law 4th Crimes Against Public Peace and Welfare § 293 (2021), Nature and Scope of Law.
2 Witkin, California Criminal Law 4th Crimes Against Public Peace and Welfare § 295 (2021), Test as Incidental to Lawful Arrest or Detention.
2 Witkin, California Criminal Law 4th Crimes Against Public Peace and Welfare § 296 (2021), Choice of Test.
2 Witkin, California Criminal Law 4th Crimes Against Public Peace and Welfare § 301 (2021), Notice of Suspension or Revocation of License.
2 Witkin, California Criminal Law 4th Crimes Against Public Peace and Welfare § 302 (2021), Administrative Sanctions.
2 Witkin, California Criminal Law 4th Crimes Against Public Peace and Welfare § 304 (2021), Relinquishing Possession of Vehicle to Intoxicated Minor.
1 Witkin California Criminal Law 4th Crimes Against the Person § 267 (2021), Vehicular Manslaughter While Intoxicated.
1 Witkin California Criminal Law 4th Crimes Against the Person § 268 (2021), In General.
4 Witkin, California Criminal Law 4th Illegally Obtained Evidence § 111 (2021), Statutory Grounds.

3 Witkin, California Criminal Law 4th Punishment § 214 (2021), Drunk Driving.

ARTICLE 2. OFFENSES INVOLVING ALCOHOL AND DRUGS

§ 23152. Driving under influence; blood alcohol percentage; presumptions

(a) It is unlawful for a person who is under the influence of any alcoholic beverage to drive a vehicle.

(b) It is unlawful for a person who has 0.08 percent or more, by weight, of alcohol in his or her blood to drive a vehicle.

For purposes of this article and Section 34501.16, percent, by weight, of alcohol in a person's blood is based upon grams of alcohol per 100 milliliters of blood or grams of alcohol per 210 liters of breath.

In any prosecution under this subdivision, it is a rebuttable presumption that the person had 0.08 percent or more, by weight, of alcohol in his or her blood at the time of driving the vehicle if the person had 0.08 percent or more, by weight, of alcohol in his or her blood at the time of the performance of a chemical test within three hours after the driving.

(c) It is unlawful for a person who is addicted to the use of any drug to drive a vehicle. This subdivision shall not apply to a person who is participating in a narcotic treatment program approved pursuant to Article 3 (commencing with Section 11875) of Chapter 1 of Part 3 of Division 10.5 of the Health and Safety Code.

(d) It is unlawful for a person who has 0.04 percent or more, by weight, of alcohol in his or her blood to drive a commercial motor vehicle, as defined in Section 15210. In a prosecution under this subdivision, it is a rebuttable presumption that the person had 0.04 percent or more, by weight, of alcohol in his or her blood at the time of driving the vehicle if the person had 0.04 percent or more, by weight, of alcohol in his or her blood at the time of the performance of a chemical test within three hours after the driving.

(e) Commencing July 1, 2018, it shall be unlawful for a person who has 0.04 percent or more, by weight, of alcohol in his or her blood to drive a motor vehicle when a passenger for hire is a passenger in the vehicle at the time of the offense. For purposes of this subdivision, "passenger for hire" means a passenger for whom consideration is contributed or expected as a condition of carriage in the vehicle, whether directly or indirectly flowing to the owner, operator, agent, or any other person having an interest in the vehicle. In a prosecution under this subdivision, it is a rebuttable presumption that the person had 0.04 percent or more, by weight, of alcohol in his or her blood at the time of driving the vehicle if the person had 0.04 percent or more, by weight, of alcohol in his or her blood at the time of the performance of a chemical test within three hours after the driving.

(f) It is unlawful for a person who is under the influence of any drug to drive a vehicle.

(g) It is unlawful for a person who is under the combined influence of any alcoholic beverage and drug to drive a vehicle. *(Added by Stats.1989, c. 1114, § 25, operative Jan. 1, 1992. Amended by Stats.1992, c. 974 (S.B.1600), § 16, eff. Sept. 28, 1992; Stats.1995, c. 455 (A.B.1113), § 31, eff. Sept. 5, 1995; Stats.2012, c. 753 (A.B.2552), § 2, operative Jan. 1, 2014; Stats.2016, c. 765 (A.B.2687), § 1, eff. Jan. 1, 2017.)*

Cross References

Advisory statement to be given by court to person convicted of a violation of this section, see Vehicle Code § 23593.
Alcohol and drug problem assessment program, violator participation, sentencing, and assessment upon fine, see Vehicle Code § 23646 et seq.
Alcoholic beverages in vehicles, see Vehicle Code § 23220 et seq.
Applicability of this section to trolley coaches, see Vehicle Code § 21051.
Arraignment or plea and sentencing in certain misdemeanors, presence of defendant, see Penal Code § 977.
Arrest without warrant, see Vehicle Code § 40300.5.
Board of Pilot Commissioners, participation in pull-notice system, purpose of participation, periodic reports from Department of Motor Vehicles, notification of termination of pilot's license, removal from training program, fee exemption, board action based on reports, see Harbors and Navigation Code § 1178.5.
Challenging constitutional validity of separate conviction, see Vehicle Code § 41403.
Chemical blood, breath or urine tests, see Vehicle Code § 13353.
Chemical tests as evidence, see Vehicle Code § 23610.
Commercial motor vehicles,
First time violations, see Vehicle Code § 15300.
Multiple violations, see Vehicle Code § 15302.
Conditions preventing deferral of sentencing from being offered, see Penal Code § 1001.98.
Coroner's inquiry into deaths, see Government Code § 27491.25.

County alcohol and drug problem assessment programs, mandatory participation for convicted violators of this section, see Vehicle Code §§ 23646, 23647.
Crime of violence, within act for indemnification of victims of crime, see Government Code § 13960.
Data and monitoring system, evaluation of intervention programs, recidivism tracking system, see Vehicle Code § 1821.
Defense of drug use to violations, see Vehicle Code § 23630.
Drivers license revocation, conviction of driver under eighteen, see Vehicle Code § 13352.3.
Driving privileges, suspension or delay, restricted driving privileges imposed on showing of critical need to drive, see Vehicle Code § 13353.8.
Driving school or instructor, revocation or suspension of license for violation of this section, see Vehicle Code § 11110.
Gross vehicular manslaughter while intoxicated, see Penal Code § 191.5.
Guilty plea, see Vehicle Code § 41610.
Immediate removal and seizure of vehicle driven by repeat offender, storage and impoundment, vehicle owner's rights and responsibilities, see Vehicle Code § 14602.8.
Immunity from criminal prosecution under specified minor consumption provisions, inapplicability to this section, see Business and Professions Code § 25667.
Impoundment of vehicle of registered owner convicted under this section, see Vehicle Code § 23594.
Influence of alcoholic beverage or drug, suspension or revocation of driving privileges, see Vehicle Code § 13352.
Investigations by the department, see Vehicle Code § 13800.
Juvenile offenders, programs of supervision, see Welfare and Institutions Code § 654.1.
Medical assistance exception to controlled substance possession and related offenses, persons experiencing drug-related overdose, no exception to laws prohibiting actions made dangerous by controlled substance use, see Health and Safety Code § 11376.5.
Military diversion program, application of provisions, pretrial diversion program, see Penal Code § 1001.80.
Persons certified as consenting to participation in programs, see Vehicle Code § 13352.5.
Persons certified or granted probation on conviction of driving under the influence of alcohol or drugs or combined influence on certain conditions, restriction, revocation or suspension of driving privilege, consent to participation in treatment program, see Vehicle Code § 13352.5.
Please Don't Drink and Drive memorial signs, requests for and duration of placement, exception for a party to an accident convicted or determined to be mentally incompetent under this section, see Streets and Highways Code § 101.10.
Presentence investigation and assessment, see Vehicle Code § 23655.
Presumptions, see Evidence Code § 600 et seq.
Prior convictions under §§ 23103, 23152 or 23153, effect on sentencing and driving privileges, see Vehicle Code § 23622.
Procedure on arrest for violation of this section, see Vehicle Code § 40302.
Public offenses, State Amnesty Program, not applicable to parking violations and violations of this section, see Vehicle Code § 42008.7.
Records available to courts and law enforcement officials, incidents under certain DWI and homicide laws, period of time records must be available, see Vehicle Code § 1808.
Refusal to submit to alcohol testing under DUI laws, calculation of prior convictions, certain foreign convictions recognized, see Vehicle Code §§ 13353, 13353.1 and 13353.3.
Restricted driver's license, application of this section, see Vehicle Code § 13352.2.
Search warrants, grounds for issuance, see Penal Code § 1524.
Surrender of driver's license to court, see Vehicle Code § 13550.
Suspension or revocation of driving privilege for a violation of this section, notice by personal service, see Vehicle Code § 13106.
Suspension or revocation of license,
  Generally, see Vehicle Code § 13352.
  Alcohol-related accident within five years of vehicular manslaughter, see Vehicle Code § 13954.
  Driver license compact, see Vehicle Code § 15000 et seq.
  Driving after suspension or revocation, see Vehicle Code § 14601.2.
  Investigation by department, three convictions in three years under this or other specified statutes, see Vehicle Code § 13800.
  Prior convictions, record, see Vehicle Code § 13209.
Traffic violation point count, violation of this section, see Vehicle Code § 12810.
Traffic violators schools, suspension or revocation of license for violation of this section, see Vehicle Code § 11215.
Vehicular homicide, see Penal Code § 192.
Violation as misdemeanor, see Vehicle Code § 40000.15.
Violation of this section, relinquishment of motor vehicle to convicted minor, see Penal Code § 193.8.
Youthful drunk driver visitation program, see Vehicle Code § 23509 et seq.

Research References

California Jury Instructions - Criminal 12.61, Driving Under the Influence—Inference of Intoxication.
California Jury Instructions - Criminal 12.61.1, Driving With [0.04] [0.08] Percent or More—Inference.
California Jury Instructions - Criminal 12.65, Driving Under the Influence, etc.—Felony Prosecutions.
California Jury Instructions - Criminal 12.66, Driving With 0.08 Percent Blood Alcohol—Felony Prosecutions.
California Jury Instructions - Criminal 16.830.01, Misdemeanor Driving Under the Influence of an Alcoholic Beverage.
California Jury Instructions - Criminal 16.830.1, Misdemeanor Driving With 0.08 Percent Alcohol.
California Jury Instructions - Criminal 16.830.02, Misdemeanor Driving Under the Influence of Any Drug.
California Jury Instructions - Criminal 16.830.03, Misdemeanor Driving Under the Combined Influence of Any Drug or Alcohol.
California Jury Instructions - Criminal 16.830.04, Misdemeanor Driving While Addicted.
California Jury Instructions - Criminal 16.830.05, Misdemeanor Driving With 0.04 Percent Blood Alcohol.
California Jury Instructions - Criminal 16.831.1, Driving Vehicle While Addicted—Addiction Defined.
California Jury Instructions - Criminal 16.832, Alcoholic or Drug Influenced Driving—Under the Influence Relates to Condition of Driver.
California Jury Instructions-Civil, 8th Edition 5.40, Influence of Alcoholic Beverage or Drug—Driver.
California Jury Instructions-Civil, 8th Edition 5.42, Influence of Alcoholic Beverage—Non-Driver.
2 Witkin, California Criminal Law 4th Crimes Against Public Peace and Welfare § 91C (2021), (New) Effect on Other Laws.
2 Witkin, California Criminal Law 4th Crimes Against Public Peace and Welfare § 269 (2021), Nonfelony Offenses of Persons in Custody.
2 Witkin, California Criminal Law 4th Crimes Against Public Peace and Welfare § 271 (2021), Reckless Driving.
2 Witkin, California Criminal Law 4th Crimes Against Public Peace and Welfare § 272 (2021), Statutory Framework.
2 Witkin, California Criminal Law 4th Crimes Against Public Peace and Welfare § 273 (2021), Misdemeanors.
2 Witkin, California Criminal Law 4th Crimes Against Public Peace and Welfare § 276 (2021), Driving Under the Influence.
2 Witkin, California Criminal Law 4th Crimes Against Public Peace and Welfare § 277 (2021), Driving With Unlawful Blood-Alcohol Level.
2 Witkin, California Criminal Law 4th Crimes Against Public Peace and Welfare § 278 (2021), Driving by Addict.
2 Witkin, California Criminal Law 4th Crimes Against Public Peace and Welfare § 279 (2021), In General.
2 Witkin, California Criminal Law 4th Crimes Against Public Peace and Welfare § 280 (2021), First Violation.
2 Witkin, California Criminal Law 4th Crimes Against Public Peace and Welfare § 281 (2021), One Separate Conviction of Related Offense.
2 Witkin, California Criminal Law 4th Crimes Against Public Peace and Welfare § 282 (2021), Two Separate Convictions of Related Offenses.
2 Witkin, California Criminal Law 4th Crimes Against Public Peace and Welfare § 283 (2021), Three or More Separate Convictions of Related Offenses.
2 Witkin, California Criminal Law 4th Crimes Against Public Peace and Welfare § 284 (2021), Enhanced Punishment Where Minor is Passenger.
2 Witkin, California Criminal Law 4th Crimes Against Public Peace and Welfare § 286 (2021), One Separate Conviction of Related Offense.
2 Witkin, California Criminal Law 4th Crimes Against Public Peace and Welfare § 287 (2021), Two or More Separate Convictions of Related Offenses.
2 Witkin, California Criminal Law 4th Crimes Against Public Peace and Welfare § 289 (2021), Prior Violation Punished as Felony.
2 Witkin, California Criminal Law 4th Crimes Against Public Peace and Welfare § 290 (2021), Ignition Interlock Device.
2 Witkin, California Criminal Law 4th Crimes Against Public Peace and Welfare § 291 (2021), Striking Separate Convictions.
2 Witkin, California Criminal Law 4th Crimes Against Public Peace and Welfare § 292 (2021), Time of Separate Convictions.

2 Witkin, California Criminal Law 4th Crimes Against Public Peace and Welfare § 293 (2021), Nature and Scope of Law.
2 Witkin, California Criminal Law 4th Crimes Against Public Peace and Welfare § 295 (2021), Test as Incidental to Lawful Arrest or Detention.
2 Witkin, California Criminal Law 4th Crimes Against Public Peace and Welfare § 297 (2021), Notice of Consequences of Refusal to Submit to Test.
2 Witkin, California Criminal Law 4th Crimes Against Public Peace and Welfare § 301 (2021), Notice of Suspension or Revocation of License.
2 Witkin, California Criminal Law 4th Crimes Against Public Peace and Welfare § 302 (2021), Administrative Sanctions.
2 Witkin, California Criminal Law 4th Crimes Against Public Peace and Welfare § 304 (2021), Relinquishing Possession of Vehicle to Intoxicated Minor.
2 Witkin, California Criminal Law 4th Crimes Against Public Peace and Welfare § 306 (2021), Reason for Suspension, Revocation, or Restriction.
1 Witkin California Criminal Law 4th Crimes Against the Person § 267 (2021), Vehicular Manslaughter While Intoxicated.
1 Witkin California Criminal Law 4th Crimes Against the Person § 268 (2021), In General.
1 Witkin California Criminal Law 4th Crimes Against the Person § 269 (2021), Punishment.
5 Witkin, California Criminal Law 4th Criminal Trial § 480 (2021), Vehicle Code Convictions.
5 Witkin, California Criminal Law 4th Criminal Trial § 482 (2021), Interplay Between Rules for Misdemeanors and Felonies.
5 Witkin, California Criminal Law 4th Criminal Trial § 508 (2021), Misdemeanor Cases.
5 Witkin, California Criminal Law 4th Criminal Trial § 630 (2021), Prohibition Against Conclusively Presuming Element of Crime.
5 Witkin, California Criminal Law 4th Criminal Trial § 668 (2021), Minor Vehicle Offenses.
1 Witkin California Criminal Law 4th Introduction to Crimes § 32 (2021), Illustrations.
4 Witkin, California Criminal Law 4th Pretrial Proceedings § 31 (2021), Intoxication and Motor Vehicles.
4 Witkin, California Criminal Law 4th Pretrial Proceedings § 48 (2021), Mandatory Requirements.
4 Witkin, California Criminal Law 4th Pretrial Proceedings § 53 (2021), Failure to Appear.
4 Witkin, California Criminal Law 4th Pretrial Proceedings § 254 (2021), Presence of Defendant.
4 Witkin, California Criminal Law 4th Pretrial Proceedings § 401 (2021), Other Programs.
3 Witkin, California Criminal Law 4th Punishment § 195 (2021), Impounding of Motor Vehicles.
3 Witkin, California Criminal Law 4th Punishment § 214 (2021), Drunk Driving.
3 Witkin, California Criminal Law 4th Punishment § 217 (2021), Other Serious Offenses.
3 Witkin, California Criminal Law 4th Punishment § 295 (2021), In General.
3 Witkin, California Criminal Law 4th Punishment § 298 (2021), Driving Under the Influence: Multiple Victims.
3 Witkin, California Criminal Law 4th Punishment § 345 (2021), Pleading and Proof.
3 Witkin, California Criminal Law 4th Punishment § 435 (2021), Dual Use of Prior Conviction.

§ 23152.5. Driving under the influence; research on impaired driving

Notwithstanding Section 23152, a person who is under the influence of a drug or the combined influence of an alcoholic beverage and drug who is under the supervision of, and on the property of, the Department of the California Highway Patrol may drive a vehicle for purposes of conducting research on impaired driving. *(Added by Stats.2019, c. 68 (A.B.127), § 1, eff. July 10, 2019.)*

§ 23153. Driving under the influence and causing bodily injury to another person; blood alcohol percentage; presumptions

(a) It is unlawful for a person, while under the influence of any alcoholic beverage, to drive a vehicle and concurrently do any act forbidden by law, or neglect any duty imposed by law in driving the vehicle, which act or neglect proximately causes bodily injury to any person other than the driver.

(b) It is unlawful for a person, while having 0.08 percent or more, by weight, of alcohol in his or her blood to drive a vehicle and concurrently do any act forbidden by law, or neglect any duty imposed by law in driving the vehicle, which act or neglect proximately causes bodily injury to any person other than the driver.

In any prosecution under this subdivision, it is a rebuttable presumption that the person had 0.08 percent or more, by weight, of alcohol in his or her blood at the time of driving the vehicle if the person had 0.08 percent or more, by weight, of alcohol in his or her blood at the time of the performance of a chemical test within three hours after driving.

(c) In proving the person neglected any duty imposed by law in driving the vehicle, it is not necessary to prove that any specific section of this code was violated.

(d) It is unlawful for a person, while having 0.04 percent or more, by weight, of alcohol in his or her blood to drive a commercial motor vehicle, as defined in Section 15210 and concurrently to do any act forbidden by law or neglect any duty imposed by law in driving the vehicle, which act or neglect proximately causes bodily injury to any person other than the driver. In a prosecution under this subdivision, it is a rebuttable presumption that the person had 0.04 percent or more, by weight, of alcohol in his or her blood at the time of driving the vehicle if the person had 0.04 percent or more, by weight, of alcohol in his or her blood at the time of performance of a chemical test within three hours after driving.

(e) Commencing July 1, 2018, it shall be unlawful for a person, while having 0.04 percent or more, by weight, of alcohol in his or her blood to drive a motor vehicle when a passenger for hire is a passenger in the vehicle at the time of the offense, and concurrently to do any act forbidden by law or neglect any duty imposed by law in driving the vehicle, which act or neglect proximately causes bodily injury to any person other than the driver. For purposes of this subdivision, "passenger for hire" means a passenger for whom consideration is contributed or expected as a condition of carriage in the vehicle, whether directly or indirectly flowing to the owner, operator, agent, or any other person having an interest in the vehicle. In a prosecution under this subdivision, it is a rebuttable presumption that the person had 0.04 percent or more, by weight, of alcohol in his or her blood at the time of driving the vehicle if the person had 0.04 percent or more, by weight, of alcohol in his or her blood at the time of performance of a chemical test within three hours after driving.

(f) It is unlawful for a person, while under the influence of any drug, to drive a vehicle and concurrently do any act forbidden by law, or neglect any duty imposed by law in driving the vehicle, which act or neglect proximately causes bodily injury to any person other than the driver.

(g) It is unlawful for a person, while under the combined influence of any alcoholic beverage and drug, to drive a vehicle and concurrently do any act forbidden by law, or neglect any duty imposed by law in driving the vehicle, which act or neglect proximately causes bodily injury to any person other than the driver. *(Added by Stats.1989, c. 1114, § 30, operative Jan. 1, 1992. Amended by Stats.1992, c. 974 (S.B.1600), § 18, eff. Sept. 28, 1992; Stats.2012, c. 753 (A.B.2552), § 5, operative Jan. 1, 2014; Stats.2016, c. 765 (A.B.2687), § 2, eff. Jan. 1, 2017.)*

Cross References

Advisory statement to be given by court to person convicted of a violation of this section, see Vehicle Code § 23593.
Alcohol and drug problem assessment program, violator participation, sentencing, and assessment upon fine, see Vehicle Code § 23646 et seq.
Alcoholic beverages in vehicles, see Vehicle Code § 23220 et seq.
Applicability of this section to trolley coaches, see Vehicle Code § 21051.
Arraignment or plea and sentencing in certain misdemeanors, presence of defendant, see Penal Code § 977.
Arrest without warrant, see Vehicle Code § 40300.5.

Board of Pilot Commissioners, participation in pull-notice system, purpose of participation, periodic reports from Department of Motor Vehicles, notification of termination of pilot's license, removal from training program, fee exemption, board action based on reports, see Harbors and Navigation Code § 1178.5.
Challenging constitutional validity of separate conviction, see Vehicle Code § 41403.
Chemical blood, breath or urine tests, see Vehicle Code § 13353.
Chemical tests as evidence, see Vehicle Code § 23610.
Commercial motor vehicles,
First time violations, see Vehicle Code § 15300.
Multiple violations, see Vehicle Code § 15302.
Conditions preventing deferral of sentencing from being offered, see Penal Code § 1001.98.
Conviction of vehicular manslaughter as conviction of violation of this section, see Vehicle Code § 13350.5.
Conviction of violation of specified subdivisions of Penal Code § 192 to be deemed conviction of violation of this section, see Vehicle Code § 13350.5.
Coroner's inquiry into deaths, see Government Code § 27491.25.
County alcohol and drug problem assessment programs, mandatory participation for convicted violators of this section, see Vehicle Code §§ 23646, 23647.
Crime of violence, within act for indemnification of victims of crime, see Government Code § 13960.
Data and monitoring system, evaluation of intervention programs, recidivism tracking system, see Vehicle Code § 1821.
Defense of drug use to violations, see Vehicle Code § 23630.
Deposit in special account for each conviction under this section, see Penal Code § 1463.14.
Drivers license revocation, conviction of driver under eighteen, see Vehicle Code § 13352.3.
Driving privileges, suspension or delay, restricted driving privileges imposed on showing of critical need to drive, see Vehicle Code § 13353.8.
Driving schools and driving instructors, revocation or suspension of license for violation of this section, see Vehicle Code § 11110.
Felony defined, see Penal Code § 17.
Gross vehicular manslaughter while intoxicated, see Penal Code § 191.5.
Guilty plea, see Vehicle Code § 41610.
Immediate removal and seizure of vehicle driven by repeat offender, storage and impoundment, vehicle owner's rights and responsibilities, see Vehicle Code § 14602.8.
Immunity from criminal prosecution under specified minor consumption provisions, inapplicability to this section, see Business and Professions Code § 25667.
Impoundment of vehicle of registered owner convicted under this section, see Vehicle Code § 23594.
Influence of alcoholic beverage or drug, suspension or revocation of driving privileges, see Vehicle Code § 13352.
Injury to guest by intoxicated driver, see Vehicle Code § 17158.
Investigations by the department, see Vehicle Code § 13800.
Manslaughter, negligent homicide by vehicle, see Penal Code § 192.
Medical assistance exception to controlled substance possession and related offenses, persons experiencing drug-related overdose, no exception to laws prohibiting actions made dangerous by controlled substance use, see Health and Safety Code § 11376.5.
Military diversion program, application of provisions, pretrial diversion program, see Penal Code § 1001.80.
Nuisance, sale or other disposition of motor vehicle driven by defendant, see Vehicle Code § 23596.
Please Don't Drink and Drive memorial signs, requests for and duration of placement, exception for a party to an accident convicted or determined to be mentally incompetent under this section, see Streets and Highways Code § 101.10.
Presentence investigation and assessment, see Vehicle Code § 23655.
Prior convictions under §§ 23103, 23152 or 23153, effect on sentencing and driving privileges, see Vehicle Code § 23622.
Public offenses, State Amnesty Program, not applicable to parking violations and violations of this section, see Vehicle Code § 42008.7.
Records available to courts and law enforcement officials, incidents under certain DWI and homicide laws, period of time records must be available, see Vehicle Code § 1808.
Refusal to submit to alcohol testing under DUI laws, calculation of prior convictions, certain foreign convictions recognized, see Vehicle Code §§ 13353, 13353.1 and 13353.3.
Release on own recognizance, report, violation of this section, see Penal Code § 1318.1.
Search warrants, grounds for issuance, see Penal Code § 1524.
Suspension or revocation of driving privilege for a violation of this section, notice by personal service, see Vehicle Code § 13106.
Suspension or revocation of license,
Generally, see Vehicle Code § 13350.
Alcohol-related accident within five years of vehicular manslaughter, see Vehicle Code § 13954.
Driver license compact, see Vehicle Code § 15000 et seq.
Driving after suspension or revocation, see Vehicle Code § 14601.2.
Driving under the influence or engaging in speed contests or exhibitions of speed, reinstatement conditions, see Vehicle Code § 13352.
Investigation by department, three convictions in three years under this or other specified sections, see Vehicle Code § 13800.
Prior convictions, record, see Vehicle Code § 13209.
Traffic violation point count, violation of this section, see Vehicle Code § 12810.
Traffic violators schools, suspension or revocation of license for violation of this section, see Vehicle Code § 11215.
Violation of this section, relinquishment of motor vehicle to convicted minor, see Penal Code § 193.8.

Research References

California Jury Instructions - Criminal 8.93, [Gross] Vehicular Manslaughter While Intoxicated.
California Jury Instructions - Criminal 12.60.01, Felony Driving Under the Influence of Any Alcoholic Beverage.
California Jury Instructions - Criminal 12.60.1, Felony Driving With 0.08 Percent.
California Jury Instructions - Criminal 12.60.02, Felony Driving Under the Influence of Any Drug.
California Jury Instructions - Criminal 12.60.03, Felony Driving Under the Combined Influence of Any Drug and Alcoholic Beverage.
California Jury Instructions - Criminal 12.60.05, Felony Driving Wwith 0.04 Percent Blood Alcohol.
California Jury Instructions - Criminal 12.61, Driving Under the Influence—Inference of Intoxication.
California Jury Instructions - Criminal 12.61.1, Driving With [0.04] [0.08] Percent or More—Inference.
California Jury Instructions - Criminal 12.67, Felony Driving Under the Influence—Priors.
California Jury Instructions - Criminal 12.68, Felony Driving With 0.08 Percent.
California Jury Instructions-Civil, 8th Edition 5.42, Influence of Alcoholic Beverage—Non-Driver.
2 Witkin, California Criminal Law 4th Crimes Against Public Peace and Welfare § 269 (2021), Nonfelony Offenses of Persons in Custody.
2 Witkin, California Criminal Law 4th Crimes Against Public Peace and Welfare § 271 (2021), Reckless Driving.
2 Witkin, California Criminal Law 4th Crimes Against Public Peace and Welfare § 274 (2021), Felonies.
2 Witkin, California Criminal Law 4th Crimes Against Public Peace and Welfare § 275 (2021), What Constitutes Driving.
2 Witkin, California Criminal Law 4th Crimes Against Public Peace and Welfare § 276 (2021), Driving Under the Influence.
2 Witkin, California Criminal Law 4th Crimes Against Public Peace and Welfare § 277 (2021), Driving With Unlawful Blood-Alcohol Level.
2 Witkin, California Criminal Law 4th Crimes Against Public Peace and Welfare § 279 (2021), In General.
2 Witkin, California Criminal Law 4th Crimes Against Public Peace and Welfare § 285 (2021), First Violation.
2 Witkin, California Criminal Law 4th Crimes Against Public Peace and Welfare § 286 (2021), One Separate Conviction of Related Offense.
2 Witkin, California Criminal Law 4th Crimes Against Public Peace and Welfare § 287 (2021), Two or More Separate Convictions of Related Offenses.
2 Witkin, California Criminal Law 4th Crimes Against Public Peace and Welfare § 288 (2021), Enhanced Punishment for Multiple Victims.
2 Witkin, California Criminal Law 4th Crimes Against Public Peace and Welfare § 289 (2021), Prior Violation Punished as Felony.
2 Witkin, California Criminal Law 4th Crimes Against Public Peace and Welfare § 290 (2021), Ignition Interlock Device.
2 Witkin, California Criminal Law 4th Crimes Against Public Peace and Welfare § 293 (2021), Nature and Scope of Law.
2 Witkin, California Criminal Law 4th Crimes Against Public Peace and Welfare § 297 (2021), Notice of Consequences of Refusal to Submit to Test.

2 Witkin, California Criminal Law 4th Crimes Against Public Peace and Welfare § 304 (2021), Relinquishing Possession of Vehicle to Intoxicated Minor.
2 Witkin, California Criminal Law 4th Crimes Against Public Peace and Welfare § 306 (2021), Reason for Suspension, Revocation, or Restriction.
1 Witkin California Criminal Law 4th Crimes Against the Person § 267 (2021), Vehicular Manslaughter While Intoxicated.
1 Witkin California Criminal Law 4th Crimes Against the Person § 268 (2021), In General.
1 Witkin California Criminal Law 4th Crimes Against the Person § 269 (2021), Punishment.
1 Witkin California Criminal Law 4th Crimes Against the Person § 271 (2021), Jury Instructions.
6 Witkin, California Criminal Law 4th Criminal Judgment § 74 (2021), Illustrations: Offenses Not Included.
5 Witkin, California Criminal Law 4th Criminal Trial § 508 (2021), Misdemeanor Cases.
1 Witkin California Criminal Law 4th Defenses § 193 (2021), Homicide and Other Crimes.
4 Witkin, California Criminal Law 4th Pretrial Proceedings § 53 (2021), Failure to Appear.
4 Witkin, California Criminal Law 4th Pretrial Proceedings § 135 (2021), In General.
4 Witkin, California Criminal Law 4th Pretrial Proceedings § 210 (2021), Statutory Language Not Sufficient.
4 Witkin, California Criminal Law 4th Pretrial Proceedings § 254 (2021), Presence of Defendant.
4 Witkin, California Criminal Law 4th Pretrial Proceedings § 401 (2021), Other Programs.
3 Witkin, California Criminal Law 4th Punishment § 214 (2021), Drunk Driving.
3 Witkin, California Criminal Law 4th Punishment § 216 (2021), Offenses Involving Injury.
3 Witkin, California Criminal Law 4th Punishment § 279 (2021), Homicide and Other Crimes.
3 Witkin, California Criminal Law 4th Punishment § 298 (2021), Driving Under the Influence: Multiple Victims.
3 Witkin, California Criminal Law 4th Punishment § 350 (2021), General Provision.

§ 23154. Persons on probation for driving under the influence; operation of motor vehicle with blood-alcohol percentage of .01 percent or greater prohibited; use of preliminary alcohol screening test

(a) It is unlawful for a person who is on probation for a violation of Section 23152 or 23153 to operate a motor vehicle at any time with a blood-alcohol concentration of 0.01 percent or greater, as measured by a preliminary alcohol screening test or other chemical test.

(b) A person may be found to be in violation of subdivision (a) if the person was, at the time of driving, on probation for a violation of Section 23152 or 23153, and the trier of fact finds that the person had consumed an alcoholic beverage and was driving a vehicle with a blood-alcohol concentration of 0.01 percent or greater, as measured by a preliminary alcohol screening test or other chemical test.

(c)(1) A person who is on probation for a violation of Section 23152 or 23153 who drives a motor vehicle is deemed to have given his or her consent to a preliminary alcohol screening test or other chemical test for the purpose of determining the presence of alcohol in the person, if lawfully detained for an alleged violation of subdivision (a).

(2) The testing shall be incidental to a lawful detention and administered at the direction of a peace officer having reasonable cause to believe the person is driving a motor vehicle in violation of subdivision (a).

(3) The person shall be told that his or her failure to submit to, or the failure to complete, a preliminary alcohol screening test or other chemical test as requested will result in the suspension or revocation of the person's privilege to operate a motor vehicle for a period of one year to three years, as provided in Section 13353.1. *(Added by Stats.2007, c. 749 (A.B.1165), § 5, operative Jan. 1, 2009.)*

Cross References

Drivers' licenses, review of suspension or revocation order, see Vehicle Code § 13557.

Research References

2 Witkin, California Criminal Law 4th Crimes Against Public Peace and Welfare § 277 (2021), Driving With Unlawful Blood-Alcohol Level.
2 Witkin, California Criminal Law 4th Crimes Against Public Peace and Welfare § 293 (2021), Nature and Scope of Law.
2 Witkin, California Criminal Law 4th Crimes Against Public Peace and Welfare § 297 (2021), Notice of Consequences of Refusal to Submit to Test.

§ 23155. Disposition report; driving under the influence; cannabis as sole drug

Beginning January 1, 2022, when a disposition described in Section 13151 of the Penal Code is a conviction for a violation of subdivision (f) of Section 23152 or subdivision (f) of Section 23153 for which cannabis was the sole drug, the disposition report shall state that the convicted offense was due to cannabis. *(Added by Stats.2019, c. 610 (A.B.397), § 1, eff. Jan. 1, 2020.)*

§ 23158. Administration of tests; additional tests by person tested; disclosure of results; immunity from liability of medical personnel

(a) Notwithstanding any other provision of law, only a licensed physician and surgeon, registered nurse, licensed vocational nurse, duly licensed clinical laboratory scientist or clinical laboratory bioanalyst, a person who has been issued a "certified phlebotomy technician" certificate pursuant to Section 1246 of the Business and Professions Code, unlicensed laboratory personnel regulated pursuant to Sections 1242, 1242.5, and 1246 of the Business and Professions Code, or certified paramedic acting at the request of a peace officer may withdraw blood for the purpose of determining the alcoholic content therein. This limitation does not apply to the taking of breath specimens. An emergency call for paramedic services takes precedence over a peace officer's request for a paramedic to withdraw blood for determining its alcoholic content. A certified paramedic shall not withdraw blood for this purpose unless authorized by his or her employer to do so.

(b) The person tested may, at his or her own expense, have a licensed physician and surgeon, registered nurse, licensed vocational nurse, duly licensed clinical laboratory scientist or clinical laboratory bioanalyst, person who has been issued a "certified phlebotomy technician" certificate pursuant to Section 1246 of the Business and Professions Code, unlicensed laboratory personnel regulated pursuant to Sections 1242, 1242.5, and 1246 of the Business and Professions Code, or any other person of his or her own choosing administer a test in addition to any test administered at the direction of a peace officer for the purpose of determining the amount of alcohol in the person's blood at the time alleged as shown by chemical analysis of his or her blood, breath, or urine. The failure or inability to obtain an additional test by a person does not preclude the admissibility in evidence of the test taken at the direction of a peace officer.

(c) Upon the request of the person tested, full information concerning the test taken at the direction of the peace officer shall be made available to the person or the person's attorney.

(d) Notwithstanding any other provision of law, no licensed physician and surgeon, registered nurse, licensed vocational nurse, duly licensed clinical laboratory scientist or clinical laboratory bioanalyst, person who has been issued a "certified phlebotomy technician" certificate pursuant to Section 1246 of the Business and Professions Code, unlicensed laboratory personnel regulated pursuant to Sections 1242, 1242.5, and 1246 of the Business and Professions Code, or certified paramedic, or hospital, laboratory, or clinic employing or utilizing the services of the licensed physician and surgeon, registered nurse, licensed vocational nurse, duly licensed clinical laboratory scientist or clinical laboratory bioanalyst, person who has been issued a "certified phlebotomy technician" certificate pursuant to Section 1246 of the Business and Professions Code, unlicensed laboratory personnel regulated pursuant to Sections 1242, 1242.5, and 1246 of the Business and Professions Code, or certified paramedic, owning or leasing the premises on which tests are performed, shall incur any civil or criminal liability as a result of the administering of a blood test in a reasonable manner in a hospital, clinical laboratory, medical clinic environment, jail, or law enforcement facility, according to accepted venipuncture practices, without violence by the person administering the test, and when requested in writing by a peace officer to administer the test.

(e) Notwithstanding any other provision of law, a person who has been issued a "certified phlebotomy technician" certificate pursuant to Section 1246 of the Business and Professions Code and who is authorized by this section to draw blood at the request and in the presence of a peace officer for purposes of determining its alcoholic content, may do so in a jail, law enforcement facility, or medical facility, with general supervision. The "certified phlebotomy technician" shall draw blood following the policies and procedures approved by a physician and surgeon licensed under Chapter 5 (commencing with Section 2000) of Division 2 of the Business and Professions Code, appropriate to the location where the blood is being drawn and in accordance with state regulations.

(f) The Certified Phlebotomy Technician I or II shall carry a current, valid identification card issued by the State Department of Health Services, attesting to the technician's name, certificate type, and effective dates of certification, when performing blood withdrawals.

(g) As used in this section, "general supervision" means that the supervisor of the technician is licensed under the Business and Professions Code as a physician and surgeon, physician assistant, clinical laboratory bioanalyst, registered nurse, or clinical laboratory scientist, and reviews the competency of the technician before the technician may perform blood withdrawals without direct supervision, and on an annual basis thereafter. The supervisor is also required to review the work of the technician at least once a month to ensure compliance with venipuncture policies, procedures, and regulations. The supervisor, or another person licensed as a physician and surgeon, physician assistant, clinical laboratory bioanalyst, registered nurse, or clinical laboratory scientist, shall be accessible to the location where the technician is working to provide onsite, telephone, or electronic consultation, within 30 minutes when needed.

(h) Nothing in this section shall be construed as requiring the certified phlebotomy technician who is authorized to withdraw blood by this section at the request and in the presence of a peace officer for purposes of determining alcoholic content to be associated with a clinical laboratory or to be directly supervised after competency has been established.

(i) If the test given under Section 23612 is a chemical test of urine, the person tested shall be given such privacy in the taking of the urine specimen as will ensure the accuracy of the specimen and, at the same time, maintain the dignity of the individual involved.

(j) The department, in cooperation with the State Department of Health Services or any other appropriate agency, shall adopt uniform standards for the withdrawal, handling, and preservation of blood samples prior to analysis.

(k) As used in this section, "certified paramedic" does not include any employee of a fire department.

(*l*) Consent, waiver of liability, or the offering to, acceptance by, or refusal of consent or waiver of liability by the person on whom a test is administered, is not an issue or relevant to the immunity from liability for medical or law enforcement personnel or other facilities designated under subdivision (d). *(Formerly § 13354, added by Stats.1972, c. 188 p. 406, § 2, operative July 1, 1973. Amended by Stats.1978, c. 554, p. 1728, § 1; Stats.1981, c. 939, p. 3558, § 8; Stats.1982, c. 1339, p. 4982, § 9, eff. Sept. 24, 1982. Renumbered § 23158 and amended by Stats.1985, c. 735, § 4. Amended by Stats.1989, c. 80, § 1; Stats.1998, c. 118 (S.B.1186), § 30, operative July 1, 1999; Stats.2004, c. 14 (A.B.371), § 2, eff. Feb. 11, 2004.)*

Research References

2 Witkin, California Criminal Law 4th Crimes Against Public Peace and Welfare § 298 (2021), Administration of Test.

2 Witkin, California Criminal Law 4th Crimes Against Public Peace and Welfare § 299 (2021), What Constitutes Refusal.

§ 23213. Social rehabilitation facility patient or resident; registered motor vehicle on or near premises

No patient or other person residing in a social rehabilitation facility licensed pursuant to Chapter 3 (commencing with Section 1500) of Division 2 of the Health and Safety Code for the rehabilitation of persons who have abused alcohol or drugs, shall have a motor vehicle registered in the name of that patient or person on or near the premises of that facility unless the patient or person has an operator's license issued pursuant to this code which is not suspended or revoked. *(Added by Stats.1982, c. 1339, p. 4993, § 30, eff. Sept. 24, 1982.)*

§ 23215. Departmental enforcement of § 23152 provisions

The department may, but shall not be required to, provide patrol or enforce the provisions of Section 23152 for offenses which occur other than upon a highway. *(Added by Stats.1981, c. 940, p. 3571, § 32.)*

§ 23216. Express application of provisions of §§ 2, 6, 7, and 10; references to renumbered sections; construction of other references; retroactive effect of section

(a) The provisions of Sections 2, 6, 7, and 10 expressly apply to the provisions of this article, and, further, for any recidivist or enhancement purpose, reference to an offense by section number is a reference to the provisions contained in that section, insofar as they were renumbered by Chapter 940 of the Statutes of 1981 without substantive change, and those provisions shall be construed as restatements and continuations thereof and not as new enactments.

(b) Any reference in the provisions of this code to a separate violation of Section 23152 shall include a separate offense under Section 23102 or 23105, as those sections read prior to January 1, 1982.

(c) Any reference in the provisions of the Vehicle Code to a separate violation of Section 23153 shall include a separate offense under Section 23101 or 23106 as those sections read prior to January 1, 1982.

(d) The provisions of this section are to be given retroactive effect. *(Added by Stats.1984, c. 1205, § 13.)*

§ 23217. Legislative findings and declarations; repeat offenders of prohibition against driving under influence of alcohol or drugs; sequence of convictions not to affect enhancement of punishment for prior offenses; application of section

The Legislature finds and declares that some repeat offenders of the prohibition against driving under the influence of alcohol or drugs, when they are addicted or when they have too much alcohol in their systems, may be escaping the intent of the Legislature to punish the offender with progressively greater severity if the offense is repeated one or more times within a 10–year period. This situation may occur when a conviction for a subsequent offense occurs before a conviction is obtained on an earlier offense.

The Legislature further finds and declares that the timing of court proceedings should not permit a person to avoid aggravated mandatory minimum penalties for multiple separate offenses occurring within a 10–year period. It is the intent of the Legislature to provide that a person be subject to enhanced mandatory minimum penalties for multiple offenses within a period of 10 years, regardless of whether the convictions are obtained in the same sequence as the offenses had been committed.

Nothing in this section requires consideration of judgment of conviction in a separate proceeding that is entered after the judgment in the present proceeding, except as it relates to violation of probation.

Nothing in this section or the amendments to Section 23540, 23546, 23550, 23560, 23566, 23622, or 23640 made by Chapter 1205 of the Statutes of 1984 affects the penalty for a violation of Section 23152 or 23153 occurring prior to January 1, 1985. *(Added by Stats.1984, c. 1205, § 14. Amended by Stats.1986, c. 1117, § 13; Stats.1998, c. 118 (S.B.1186), § 72.5, operative July 1, 1999; Stats. 2004, c. 550 (S.B.1694), § 11.)*

Research References

2 Witkin, California Criminal Law 4th Crimes Against Public Peace and Welfare § 292 (2021), Time of Separate Convictions.

§ 23220. Drinking alcoholic beverage or smoking or ingesting marijuana product in vehicle on lands

(a) A person shall not drink any alcoholic beverage or smoke or ingest marijuana or any marijuana product while driving a motor vehicle on any lands described in subdivision (c).

(b) A person shall not drink any alcoholic beverage or smoke or ingest marijuana or any marijuana product while riding as a passenger in any motor vehicle being driven on any lands described in subdivision (c).

(c) As used in this section, "lands" means those lands to which the Chappie–Z'berg Off–Highway Motor Vehicle Law of 1971 (Division 16.5 (commencing with Section 38000)) applies as to off-highway motor vehicles, as described in Section 38001.

(d) A violation of subdivision (a) or (b) shall be punished as an infraction. *(Formerly § 23121, added by Stats.1961, c. 1903, p. 4010, § 1. Amended by Stats.1979, c. 363, p. 1228, § 2. Renumbered § 23220 and amended by Stats.1981, c. 940, p. 3569, § 23. Amended by Stats.1998, c. 384 (S.B.1639), § 1, eff. Aug. 24, 1998; Stats.2017, c. 232 (S.B.65), § 1, eff. Jan. 1, 2018.)*

Cross References

Driving while under the influence of alcoholic beverage or drugs, see Vehicle Code §§ 23152, 23153.
Exceptions to application of this section, see Vehicle Code § 23229.
Person under the influence of intoxicating liquor, drug, controlled substance or toluene in public place as disorderly person, see Penal Code § 647.

Research References

2 Witkin, California Criminal Law 4th Crimes Against Public Peace and Welfare § 303 (2021), Drinking or Possessing Alcohol or Marijuana.

§ 23221. Drinking alcoholic beverage or smoking or ingesting marijuana product in motor vehicle upon highway

(a) A driver shall not drink any alcoholic beverage or smoke or ingest marijuana or any marijuana product while driving a motor vehicle upon a highway.

(b) A passenger shall not drink any alcoholic beverage or smoke or ingest marijuana or any marijuana product while in a motor vehicle being driven upon a highway.

(c) A violation of this section shall be punished as an infraction. *(Formerly § 23121.5, added by Stats.1979, c. 363, p. 1228, § 3. Renumbered § 23221 and amended by Stats.1981, c. 940, p. 3569, § 24. Amended by Stats.1999, c. 723 (A.B.194), § 2; Stats.2017, c. 232 (S.B.65), § 2, eff. Jan. 1, 2018.)*

Cross References

Driving while under the influence of alcohol or drugs, see Vehicle Code §§ 23152, 23153.
Exceptions to application of this section, see Vehicle Code § 23229.
Motor vehicle defined, see Vehicle Code § 415.
Person under the influence of intoxicating liquor, drug, controlled substance or toluene in public place as disorderly person, see Penal Code § 647.

Research References

2 Witkin, California Criminal Law 4th Crimes Against Public Peace and Welfare § 303 (2021), Drinking or Possessing Alcohol or Marijuana.

§ 23222. Possession of open container containing alcoholic beverage or cannabis while driving a motor vehicle; penalty; exceptions

(a) A person shall not have in their possession on their person, while driving a motor vehicle upon a highway or on lands, as described in subdivision (c) of Section 23220, a bottle, can, or other receptacle, containing an alcoholic beverage which has been opened, or a seal broken, or the contents of which have been partially removed.

(b)(1) Except as authorized by law, a person who has in their possession on their person, while driving a motor vehicle upon a highway or on lands, as described in subdivision (c) of Section 23220, a receptacle containing cannabis or cannabis products, as defined by Section 11018.1 of the Health and Safety Code, which has been opened or has a seal broken, or loose cannabis flower not in a container, is guilty of an infraction punishable by a fine of not more than one hundred dollars ($100).

(2) Paragraph (1) does not apply to a person who has a receptacle containing cannabis or cannabis products that has been opened, has a seal broken, or the contents of which have been partially removed, or to a person who has a loose cannabis flower not in a container, if the receptacle or loose cannabis flower not in a container is in the trunk of the vehicle.

(c) Subdivision (b) does not apply to a qualified patient or person with an identification card, as defined in Section 11362.7 of the Health and Safety Code, if both of the following apply:

(1) The person is carrying a current identification card or a physician's recommendation.

(2) The cannabis or cannabis product is contained in a container or receptacle that is either sealed, resealed, or closed. *(Formerly § 23122, added by Stats.1961, c. 1903, p. 4010, § 2. Amended by Stats.1968, c. 238, p. 549, § 1; Stats.1979, c. 363, p. 1228, § 4. Renumbered § 23222 and amended by Stats.1981, c. 940, p. 3569, § 25. Amended by Stats.1983, c. 1005, § 1; Stats.1998, c. 384 (S.B.1639), § 2, eff. Aug. 24, 1998; Stats.2010, c. 708 (S.B.1449), § 2; Stats.2017, c. 27 (S.B.94), § 174, eff. June 27, 2017; Stats.2019, c. 497 (A.B.991), § 274, eff. Jan. 1, 2020; Stats.2019, c. 610 (A.B.397), § 2, eff. Jan. 1, 2020.)*

Cross References

Alcoholic beverage defined, see Business and Professions Code § 23004.
Driving while under the influence of alcoholic beverages or drugs, see Vehicle Code §§ 23152, 23153.
Exceptions to application of this section, see Vehicle Code § 23229.
Investigation for driver's license suspension or revocation, three convictions in three years under this or other specified sections, see Vehicle Code § 13800.
Investigations by the department, see Vehicle Code § 13800.
Misdemeanor, marijuana possession, see Vehicle Code § 40000.15.
Motor vehicle defined, see Vehicle Code § 415.
Person under the influence of intoxicating liquor, drug, controlled substance or toluene in public place as disorderly person, see Penal Code § 647.

Special proceedings in narcotics and drug abuse cases, application to violation of this section, see Penal Code § 1000.

Research References

California Jury Instructions - Criminal 16.035, Marijuana—Gives Away or Transports Not More Than 28.5 Grams.
2 Witkin, California Criminal Law 4th Crimes Against Public Peace and Welfare § 149 (2021), Protection from Criminal Liability.
2 Witkin, California Criminal Law 4th Crimes Against Public Peace and Welfare § 303 (2021), Drinking or Possessing Alcohol or Marijuana.
4 Witkin, California Criminal Law 4th Pretrial Proceedings § 386 (2021), Offenses and Conditions.

§ 23223. Possession of opened container in a motor vehicle

(a) A driver shall not have in the driver's possession, while in a motor vehicle upon a highway or on lands, as described in subdivision (c) of Section 23220, any bottle, can, or other receptacle, containing any alcoholic beverage that has been opened, or a seal broken, or the contents of which have been partially removed.

(b) A passenger shall not have in the passenger's possession, while in a motor vehicle upon a highway or on lands, as described in subdivision (c) of Section 23220, any bottle, can, or other receptacle containing any alcoholic beverage that has been opened or a seal broken, or the contents of which have been partially removed. *(Formerly § 23122.5, added by Stats.1979, c. 363, p. 1228, § 5. Renumbered § 23223 and amended by Stats.1981, c. 940, p. 3569, § 26. Amended by Stats.1998, c. 384 (S.B.1639), § 3, eff. Aug. 24, 1998; Stats.1999, c. 723 (A.B.194), § 3; Stats.2019, c. 497 (A.B.991), § 275, eff. Jan. 1, 2020.)*

Cross References

Third or subsequent violations of provisions relating to storage and possession of open containers by driver operating under valid certificate or permit pursuant to Passenger Charter-party Carriers' Act, misdemeanor, see Vehicle Code § 40000.20.

Research References

2 Witkin, California Criminal Law 4th Crimes Against Public Peace and Welfare § 303 (2021), Drinking or Possessing Alcohol or Marijuana.

§ 23224. Possession of alcoholic beverage in vehicle; persons under 21; penalties

(a) No person under 21 years of age shall knowingly drive any motor vehicle carrying any alcoholic beverage, unless the person is accompanied by a parent, responsible adult relative, any other adult designated by the parent, or legal guardian for the purpose of transportation of an alcoholic beverage, or is employed by a licensee under the Alcoholic Beverage Control Act (Division 9 (commencing with Section 23000) of the Business and Professions Code), and is driving the motor vehicle during regular hours and in the course of the person's employment. If the driver was unaccompanied, they shall have a complete defense if they were following, in a timely manner, the reasonable instructions of a parent, legal guardian, responsible adult relative, or adult designee relating to disposition of the alcoholic beverage.

(b) No passenger in any motor vehicle who is under 21 years of age shall knowingly possess or have under that person's control any alcoholic beverage, unless the passenger is accompanied by a parent, legal guardian, responsible adult relative, any other adult designated by the parent, or legal guardian for the purpose of transportation of an alcoholic beverage, or is employed by a licensee under the Alcoholic Beverage Control Act (Division 9 (commencing with Section 23000) of the Business and Professions Code), and possession or control is during regular hours and in the course of the passenger's employment. If the passenger was unaccompanied, they shall have a complete defense if they were following, in a timely manner, the reasonable instructions of a parent, legal guardian, responsible adult relative or adult designee relating to disposition of the alcoholic beverage.

(c) If the vehicle used in any violation of subdivision (a) or (b) is registered to an offender who is under 21 years of age, the vehicle may be impounded at the owner's expense for not less than one day nor more than 30 days for each violation.

(d) Any person convicted for a violation of subdivision (a) or (b) is guilty of a misdemeanor and shall be punished upon conviction by a fine of not more than one thousand dollars ($1,000) or by imprisonment in the county jail for not more than six months, or by both that fine and imprisonment. *(Formerly § 23123.5, added by Stats.1965, c. 1662, p. 3772, § 2. Amended by Stats.1972, c. 881, p. 1559, § 2. Renumbered § 23224 and amended by Stats.1981, c. 940, p. 3569, § 28. Amended by Stats.1990, c. 1697 (S.B.2635), § 6; Stats.1996, c. 690 (A.B.2000), § 1; Stats.2019, c. 505 (S.B.485), § 14, eff. Jan. 1, 2020.)*

Cross References

Alcoholic beverage defined, see Business and Professions Code § 23004.
Driving while under the influence of alcoholic beverages or drugs, see Vehicle Code §§ 23152, 23153.
Investigation for driver's license suspension or revocation, three convictions in three years under this or other specified sections, see Vehicle Code § 13800.
Investigations by the department, see Vehicle Code § 13800.
Procedure to remove and store vehicles, see Vehicle Code § 22850 et seq.

Research References

2 Witkin, California Criminal Law 4th Crimes Against Public Peace and Welfare § 303 (2021), Drinking or Possessing Alcohol or Marijuana.
3 Witkin, California Criminal Law 4th Punishment § 195 (2021), Impounding of Motor Vehicles.

§ 23225. Storage of opened container

(a)(1) It is unlawful for the registered owner of any motor vehicle to keep in a motor vehicle, when the vehicle is upon any highway or on lands, as described in subdivision (c) of Section 23220, any bottle, can, or other receptacle containing any alcoholic beverage that has been opened, or a seal broken, or the contents of which have been partially removed, unless the container is kept in the trunk of the vehicle.

(2) If the vehicle is not equipped with a trunk and is not an off-highway motor vehicle subject to identification, as defined in Section 38012, the bottle, can, or other receptacle described in paragraph (1) shall be kept in some other area of the vehicle that is not normally occupied by the driver or passengers. For the purposes of this paragraph, a utility compartment or glove compartment shall be deemed to be within the area occupied by the driver and passengers.

(3) If the vehicle is not equipped with a trunk and is an off-highway motor vehicle subject to identification, as defined in subdivision (a) of Section 38012, the bottle, can, or other receptacle described in paragraph (1) shall be kept in a locked container. As used in this paragraph, "locked container" means a secure container that is fully enclosed and locked by a padlock, key lock, combination lock, or similar locking device.

(b) Subdivision (a) is also applicable to a driver of a motor vehicle if the registered owner is not present in the vehicle.

(c) This section shall not apply to the living quarters of a housecar or camper. *(Formerly § 23123, added by Stats.1961, c. 1903, p. 4010, § 3. Amended by Stats.1968, c. 238, p. 549, § 2. Renumbered § 23225 and amended by Stats.1981, c. 940, p. 3569, § 27. Amended by Stats.1998, c. 384 (S.B.1639), § 4, eff. Aug. 24, 1998; Stats.1999, c. 723 (A.B.194), § 4; Stats.2019, c. 497 (A.B.991), § 276, eff. Jan. 1, 2020.)*

Cross References

Alcoholic beverage defined, see Business and Professions Code § 23004.
Camper defined, see Vehicle Code § 243.
Driving while under the influence of alcoholic beverages or drugs, see Vehicle Code §§ 23152, 23153.

Exceptions to application of this section, see Vehicle Code § 23229.
House car defined, see Vehicle Code § 362.
Motor vehicle defined, see Vehicle Code § 415.
Third or subsequent violations of provisions relating to storage and possession of open containers by driver operating under valid certificate or permit pursuant to Passenger Charter-party Carriers' Act, misdemeanor, see Vehicle Code § 40000.20.
Violation of this section by driver of limousine or officer, agent or employee of charter-party carrier of passengers, penalties, see Public Utilities Code § 5384.5.

Research References

2 Witkin, California Criminal Law 4th Crimes Against Public Peace and Welfare § 303 (2021), Drinking or Possessing Alcohol or Marijuana.

§ 23226. Keeping open container in passenger compartment of motor vehicle; exceptions

(a) It is unlawful for any driver to keep in the passenger compartment of a motor vehicle, when the vehicle is upon any highway or on lands, as described in subdivision (c) of Section 23220, any bottle, can, or other receptacle containing any alcoholic beverage that has been opened, or a seal broken, or the contents of which have been partially removed.

(b) It is unlawful for any passenger to keep in the passenger compartment of a motor vehicle, when the vehicle is upon any highway or on lands, as described in subdivision (c) of Section 23220, any bottle, can, or other receptacle containing any alcoholic beverage that has been opened or a seal broken, or the contents of which have been partially removed.

(c) This section does not apply to the living quarters of a housecar or camper. *(Formerly § 23123.6, added by Stats.1979, c. 363, p. 1228, § 6. Renumbered § 23226 and amended by Stats.1981, c. 940, p. 3570, § 29. Amended by Stats.1998, c. 384 (S.B.1639), § 5, eff. Aug. 24, 1998; Stats.1999, c. 723 (A.B.194), § 5; Stats.2019, c. 497 (A.B.991), § 277, eff. Jan. 1, 2020.)*

Research References

2 Witkin, California Criminal Law 4th Crimes Against Public Peace and Welfare § 303 (2021), Drinking or Possessing Alcohol or Marijuana.

§ 23229. Possession of alcoholic beverage in for-hire vehicles; exceptions

(a) Except as provided in Section 23229.1, Section 23221, as it applies to an alcoholic beverage, and Section 23223 do not apply to passengers in any bus, taxicab, or limousine for hire licensed to transport passengers pursuant to the Public Utilities Code or proper local authority, the living quarters of a housecar or camper, or of a pedicab operated pursuant to Article 4.5 (commencing with Section 21215) of Chapter 1.

(b) Except as provided in Section 23229.1, Section 23225 does not apply to the driver or owner of a bus, taxicab, or limousine for hire licensed to transport passengers pursuant to the Public Utilities Code or proper local authority, or of a pedicab operated pursuant to Article 4.5 (commencing with Section 21215) of Chapter 1. *(Added by Stats.1988, c. 1105, § 7, operative July 1, 1989. Amended by Stats.2015, c. 496 (S.B.530), § 3, eff. Jan. 1, 2016; Stats.2019, c. 636 (A.B.1810), § 8, eff. Jan. 1, 2020.)*

Research References

2 Witkin, California Criminal Law 4th Crimes Against Public Peace and Welfare § 303 (2021), Drinking or Possessing Alcohol or Marijuana.

§ 23229.1. Application of prohibition against possession or storage of opened container to driver providing prearranged transportation services as a charter-party carrier of passengers while transporting passenger under 21; forwarding record of conviction to Public Utilities Commission

(a) Subject to subdivision (b), Sections 23223 and 23225 apply to any driver providing transportation services on a prearranged basis as a charter-party carrier of passengers, as defined in Section 5360 of the Public Utilities Code, when the driver of the vehicle transports any passenger under 21 years of age and fails to comply with the requirements of Section 5384.1 of the Public Utilities Code.

(b) For purposes of subdivision (a), it is not a violation of Section 23225 for any driver providing transportation services on a prearranged basis as a charter-party carrier of passengers that is licensed pursuant to the Public Utilities Code to keep any bottle, can, or other receptacle containing any alcoholic beverage in a locked utility compartment within the area occupied by the driver and passengers.

(c) In addition to the requirements of Section 1803, every clerk of a court in which any driver in subdivision (a) was convicted of a violation of Section 23225 shall prepare within 10 days after conviction, and immediately forward to the Public Utilities Commission at its office in San Francisco, an abstract of the record of the court covering the case in which the person was convicted. If sentencing is not pronounced in conjunction with the conviction, the abstract shall be forwarded to the commission within 10 days after sentencing, and the abstract shall be certified, by the person required to prepare it, to be true and correct. For the purposes of this subdivision, a forfeiture of bail is equivalent to a conviction. *(Added by Stats.1988, c. 1105, § 8, operative July 1, 1989. Amended by Stats.2007, c. 263 (A.B.310), § 33; Stats.2012, c. 461 (A.B.45), § 6.)*

Law Revision Commission Comments

Subdivision (c) of Section 23229.1 is amended to delete unnecessary language authorizing the judge to substitute for the clerk if there is no clerk. See Code Civ. Proc. § 167 (judge may perform any act court clerk may perform); Gov't Code §§ 69840–69848 (duties of clerk of superior court), 71620(b) (executive or administrative officer has authority of clerk of court).

Subdivision (c) is also amended to make a stylistic revision.

Subdivision (d) is deleted as obsolete. [35 Cal.L.Rev.Comm. Reports 219 (2007)].

Research References

2 Witkin, California Criminal Law 4th Crimes Against Public Peace and Welfare § 303 (2021), Drinking or Possessing Alcohol or Marijuana.

ARTICLE 4. IGNITION INTERLOCK DEVICE

Section

§ 23247. Prohibited activities regarding persons whose driving privileges have been restricted pursuant to Section 13352, 13352.1, 13353.6, 13353.75, 23575, 23575.3, or 23700; punishment

Section operative until Jan. 1, 2026. See, also, § 23247 operative Jan. 1, 2026.

(a) It is unlawful for a person to knowingly rent, lease, or lend a motor vehicle to another person known to have had his or her driving privilege restricted as provided in Section 13352, 13352.1, 13353.6, 13353.75, 23575, 23575.3, or 23700, unless the vehicle is equipped with a functioning, certified ignition interlock device. A person, whose driving privilege is restricted pursuant to Section 13352, 13352.1, 13353.6, 13353.75, 23575, 23575.3, or 23700 shall notify any other person who rents, leases, or loans a motor vehicle to him or her of the driving restriction imposed under that section.

(b) It is unlawful for any person whose driving privilege is restricted pursuant to Section 13352, 13352.1, 13353.6, 13353.75, 23575, 23575.3, or 23700 to request or solicit any other person to blow into an ignition interlock device or to start a motor vehicle equipped with the device for the purpose of providing the person so restricted with an operable motor vehicle.

(c) It is unlawful to blow into an ignition interlock device or to start a motor vehicle equipped with the device for the purpose of providing an operable motor vehicle to a person whose driving privilege is restricted pursuant to Section 13352, 13352.1, 13353.6, 13353.75, 23575, 23575.3, or 23700.

(d) It is unlawful to remove, bypass, or tamper with, an ignition interlock device.

(e) It is unlawful for any person whose driving privilege is restricted pursuant to Section 13352, 13352.1, 13353.6, 13353.75, 23575, 23575.3, or 23700 to operate any vehicle not equipped with a functioning ignition interlock device.

(f) Any person convicted of a violation of this section shall be punished by imprisonment in a county jail for not more than six months or by a fine of not more than five thousand dollars ($5,000), or by both that fine and imprisonment.

(g)(1) If any person whose driving privilege is restricted pursuant to Section 13352, 13352.1, 13353.6, or 13353.75 is convicted of a violation of subdivision (e), the court shall notify the Department of Motor Vehicles, which shall immediately terminate the restriction and shall suspend or revoke the person's driving privilege for the remaining period of the originating suspension or revocation and until all reinstatement requirements in Section 13352 or 13353.3 are met.

(2) If any person who is restricted pursuant to Section 23575.3, subdivision (a) or (i) of Section 23575, or Section 23700 is convicted of a violation of subdivision (e), the department shall suspend the person's driving privilege for one year from the date of the conviction.

(h) Notwithstanding any other law, if a vehicle in which a functioning, certified ignition interlock device has been installed is impounded, the manufacturer or installer of the device shall have the right to remove the device from the vehicle during normal business hours. No charge shall be imposed for the removal of the device nor shall the manufacturer or installer be liable for any removal, towing, impoundment, storage, release, or administrative costs or penalties associated with the impoundment. Upon request, the person seeking to remove the device shall present documentation to justify removal of the device from the vehicle. Any damage to the vehicle resulting from the removal of the device is the responsibility of the person removing it.

(i) This section shall become operative on January 1, 2019.

(j) This section shall remain in effect only until January 1, 2026, and as of that date is repealed, unless a later enacted statute, that is enacted before January 1, 2026, deletes or extends that date. *(Added by Stats.2016, c. 783 (S.B.1046), § 27, eff. Jan. 1, 2017, operative Jan. 1, 2019. Amended by Stats.2017, c. 485 (S.B.611), § 21, eff. Jan. 1, 2018, operative Jan. 1, 2019.)*

Repeal

For repeal of this section, see its terms.

Cross References

Out of state residents, expiration of suspension or revocation period, see Vehicle Code § 13353.5.

Research References

2 Witkin, California Criminal Law 4th Crimes Against Public Peace and Welfare § 290 (2021), Ignition Interlock Device.

§ 23247. Prohibited activities regarding persons whose driving privileges have been restricted pursuant to Section 13352, 23575, or 23700; punishment

Section operative Jan. 1, 2026. See, also, § 23247 operative until Jan. 1, 2026.

(a) It is unlawful for a person to knowingly rent, lease, or lend a motor vehicle to another person known to have had his or her driving privilege restricted as provided in Section 13352, 23575, or 23700, unless the vehicle is equipped with a functioning, certified ignition interlock device. A person, whose driving privilege is restricted pursuant to Section 13352, 23575, or 23700 shall notify any other person who rents, leases, or loans a motor vehicle to him or her of the driving restriction imposed under that section.

(b) It is unlawful for any person whose driving privilege is restricted pursuant to Section 13352, 23575, or 23700 to request or solicit any other person to blow into an ignition interlock device or to start a motor vehicle equipped with the device for the purpose of providing the person so restricted with an operable motor vehicle.

(c) It is unlawful to blow into an ignition interlock device or to start a motor vehicle equipped with the device for the purpose of providing an operable motor vehicle to a person whose driving privilege is restricted pursuant to Section 13352, 23575, or 23700.

(d) It is unlawful to remove, bypass, or tamper with, an ignition interlock device.

(e) It is unlawful for any person whose driving privilege is restricted pursuant to Section 13352, 23575, or 23700 to operate any vehicle not equipped with a functioning, certified ignition interlock device.

(f) Any person convicted of a violation of this section shall be punished by imprisonment in a county jail for not more than six months or by a fine of not more than five thousand dollars ($5,000), or by both that fine and imprisonment.

(g)(1) If any person whose driving privilege is restricted pursuant to Section 13352 is convicted of a violation of subdivision (e), the court shall notify the Department of Motor Vehicles, which shall immediately terminate the restriction and shall suspend or revoke the person's driving privilege for the remaining period of the originating suspension or revocation and until all reinstatement requirements in Section 13352 are met.

(2) If any person who is restricted pursuant to subdivision (a) or (*l*) of Section 23575 or Section 23700 is convicted of a violation of subdivision (e), the department shall suspend the person's driving privilege for one year from the date of the conviction.

(h) Notwithstanding any other law, if a vehicle in which a functioning, certified ignition interlock device has been installed is impounded, the manufacturer or installer of the device shall have the right to remove the device from the vehicle during normal business hours. No charge shall be imposed for the removal of the device nor shall the manufacturer or installer be liable for any removal, towing, impoundment, storage, release, or administrative costs or penalties associated with the impoundment. Upon request, the person seeking to remove the device shall present documentation to justify removal of the device from the vehicle. Any damage to the vehicle resulting from the removal of the device is the responsibility of the person removing it.

(i) This section shall become operative January 1, 2026. *(Added by Stats.2016, c. 783 (S.B.1046), § 28, eff. Jan. 1, 2017, operative Jan. 1, 2026.)*

Cross References

Out of state residents, expiration of suspension or revocation period, see Vehicle Code § 13353.5.

Research References

2 Witkin, California Criminal Law 4th Crimes Against Public Peace and Welfare § 290 (2021), Ignition Interlock Device.

ARTICLE 5. ALCOHOL AND DRUG PROBLEM ASSESSMENT PROGRAM

§ 23249.50. Legislative findings and intent

(a) The Legislature finds and declares all of the following:

(1) Driving under the influence of an alcoholic beverage or a drug is a serious problem, constituting the largest group of misdemeanor violations in many counties.

(2) Studies of first offenders have found that more than half of first offenders are alcoholics or problem drinkers. There are higher percentages of problem drinkers among second offenders than among first offenders.

(3) As the link between the health and legal aspects of the problem has become recognized, the courts have sought more information on a presentence basis in determining the appropriate sentence.

(4) Laws relating to driving under the influence of an alcoholic beverage or a drug allow the courts to order a presentence investigation to determine whether a person can benefit from an education, training, or treatment program. The Legislature thus finds that, to adequately assess whether an individual arrested for driving under the influence of an alcoholic beverage or a drug is chemically dependent, it is important to develop and implement screening programs in order to continue to address the problem of driving under the influence of alcoholic beverages or drugs in the state.

(b) It is therefore the intent of the Legislature to establish an additional procedure to assist the courts in the use of presentence investigations of individuals convicted of driving under the influence of an alcoholic beverage or a drug and to enable the courts to make appropriate dispositions in these cases. As part of this process, the courts should obtain and consider a presentence investigation report detailing the defendant's driving and criminal record, and, where possible, an alcohol or drug problem assessment report. In all cases, an alcohol or drug problem assessment report should be completed by qualified personnel prior to the determination of an education or treatment plan and subsequent sentencing by the courts. *(Added by Stats.1988, c. 160, § 183.)*

CHAPTER 13. VEHICULAR CROSSINGS AND TOLL HIGHWAYS

ARTICLE 1. GENERAL PROVISIONS

§ 23250. Application of chapter

All of the provisions of this code not inconsistent with the provisions of this chapter shall be applicable to vehicular crossings and toll highways. This chapter shall control over any provision of this code inconsistent with this chapter. *(Stats.1959, c. 3, p. 1710, § 23250. Amended by Stats.1996, c. 1154 (A.B.3020), § 72, eff. Sept. 30, 1996.)*

Cross References

Vehicular crossing defined, see Vehicle Code § 23254.

§ 23251. Authority of California Highway Patrol; temporary arrangements made by private operators of toll highways; reimbursement

(a) The Department of the California Highway Patrol shall provide for proper and adequate policing of all toll highways and all vehicular crossings to ensure the enforcement thereon of this code and of any other law relating to the use and operation of vehicles upon toll highways, highways or vehicular crossings, and of the rules and regulations of the Department of Transportation in respect thereto, and to cooperate with the Department of Transportation to the end that vehicular crossings be operated at all times in a manner as to carry traffic efficiently. The authority of the Department of the California Highway Patrol is exclusive except as to the authority conferred by law upon the Department of Transportation in respect to vehicular crossings.

(b) Notwithstanding subdivision (a), a private operator of a toll highway may make temporary arrangements, not to exceed 30 days, for traffic law enforcement services with an agency that employs peace officers as described in Section 830.1 of the Penal Code, if the Department of the California Highway Patrol cannot fulfill its responsibilities as described in this section, as determined by the Secretary of the Business, Transportation and Housing Agency.

(c) The services provided by the Department of the California Highway Patrol for all toll highways that are operated by a private entity shall be reimbursed pursuant to Section 30809.1 of the Streets and Highways Code. If the private operator of a toll highway and the Department of the California Highway Patrol reach an impasse in negotiating an agreement for reimbursement, the Secretary of the Business, Transportation and Housing Agency shall assist in resolving the impasse. *(Stats.1959, c. 3, p. 1710, § 23251. Amended by Stats.1974, c. 545, p. 1332, § 218; Stats.1992, c. 1241 (S.B.1615), § 23.)*

Cross References

Inspection of vehicles by highway patrol members, see Vehicle Code § 2804.
Powers of California Highway Patrol generally, see Vehicle Code § 2400 et seq.
Powers of Department of Transportation over use of highways, generally, see Streets and Highways Code § 92.

§ 23252. Authority of Department of Transportation personnel

The chief of toll services, captains, lieutenants, and sergeants employed by the Department of Transportation shall have the powers and authority of peace officers as listed in Section 830.4 of the Penal Code while so employed on any vehicular crossing or as may be necessary to the performance of their duties while not upon such vehicular crossing. Captains, lieutenants, and sergeants so employed shall wear, while on duty, a uniform which shall be distinctly different from that of the California Highway Patrol, to be specified by the Director of Transportation. *(Stats.1959, c. 3, p. 1710, § 23252. Amended by Stats.1968, c. 1222, p. 2330, § 75.5; Stats.1974, c. 545, p. 1332, § 219.)*

Cross References

Minimum standards for public officers or employees having powers of peace officers, see Government Code § 1031.
Peace officers, see Penal Code § 830.4.
Powers of Department of Transportation over use of highways generally, see Streets and Highways Code § 92.
Powers of peace officers, see Penal Code § 830 et seq.

§ 23253. Obedience to officers

All persons in, or upon, any toll highway or vehicular crossing shall at all times comply with any lawful order, signal, or direction by voice or hand of any member of the California Highway Patrol or an employee of the Department of Transportation who is a peace officer. *(Stats.1959, c. 3, p. 1710, § 23253. Amended by Stats.1974, c. 545, p. 1332, § 220; Stats.1992, c. 1241 (S.B.1615), § 24.)*

Cross References

Obedience to peace officers, see Vehicle Code § 2800.

Violation as misdemeanor, see Vehicle Code § 40000.15.

§ 23254. "Vehicular crossing" defined

A "vehicular crossing" is any toll bridge or toll highway crossing and the approaches thereto, constructed or acquired by the Department of Transportation under the provisions of the California Toll Bridge Authority Act.[1] *(Stats.1959, c. 3, p. 1710, § 23254. Amended by Stats.1974, c. 545, p. 1333, § 221.)*

[1] Streets and Highways Code § 30000 et seq.

Cross References

Policing of vehicular crossings, see Vehicle Code § 23251 et seq.
Right-of-way, see Vehicle Code § 21802.
Special traffic regulations pertaining to vehicular crossing, see Vehicle Code § 23330 et seq.
Tolls and other charges, see Vehicle Code § 23300 et seq.
Towing on vehicular crossings, see Vehicle Code § 23270 et seq.

§ 23255. "Approach" defined

An "approach" is that portion of a state highway leading to or from a toll bridge or toll highway crossing which lies between one end of the bridge or crossing and the nearest intersection of a highway with the state highway. A ramp or other structure designed exclusively for use in connection with a toll bridge or toll highway crossing shall not be deemed an intersecting highway but is a part of the approach. *(Stats.1959, c. 3, p. 1710, § 23255.)*

Cross References

Definitions,
  Highway, see Vehicle Code § 360.
  Intersection, see Vehicle Code § 365.
Tolls and other charges, see Vehicle Code § 23300 et seq.

ARTICLE 2. TOWING ON VEHICULAR CROSSINGS

§ 23270. Unauthorized towing; maximum towing fee; permits

(a) No person shall commence to tow any vehicle or other object on any vehicular crossing unless authorized to do so by the Department of Transportation and unless the towing is done by means of a tow truck as defined in Section 615. No person, other than a member of the California Highway Patrol or an employee of the Department of Transportation, shall, by means of pushing with another vehicle, propel any vehicle or object on a vehicular crossing. No person, other than an employee of the Department of Transportation, shall, on any vehicular crossing, tow any vehicle or other object except a vehicle or object constructed and designed to be towed by a vehicle of a type similar to that being used for this purpose.

(b) The California Transportation Commission shall, by regulation, establish the maximum towing fee which may be charged by any person authorized to tow a vehicle pursuant to subdivision (a). No authorized person shall charge a fee for towing a vehicle which is in excess of the maximum fee established by the California Transportation Commission.

(c) The Director of Transportation may grant a special permit to any person to tow any vehicle or object over and completely across any vehicular crossing when in his or her judgment the towing vehicle is so constructed and equipped that the vehicle or object can be towed across the vehicular crossing without endangering persons or property and without interrupting the orderly traffic across the vehicular crossing.

(d) The prohibitions of this section shall apply only on those vehicular crossings upon which a towing service is maintained by the Department of Transportation. *(Stats.1959, c. 3, p. 1711, § 23270. Amended by Stats.1969, c. 221, p. 551, § 1; Stats.1972, c. 510, p. 889, § 1; Stats.1974, c. 545, p. 1333, § 222; Stats.1980, c. 622, p. 1707, § 4; Stats.1990, c. 216 (S.B.2510), § 119.)*

Cross References

Tow truck requirements, see Vehicle Code §§ 22513, 23273, 24605, 25253, 27700, 27907.

§ 23271. Towing service; maintenance on each vehicular crossing; rates

A towing service may be maintained on each vehicular crossing by the Department of Transportation, and the department may furnish such service as is necessary to permit the orderly flow of traffic upon such crossing. The Department of Transportation may prescribe and collect reasonable rates for towing services furnished. *(Stats.1959, c. 3, p. 1711, § 23271. Amended by Stats.1974, c. 545, p. 1333, § 223; Stats.1974, c. 1053, p. 2271, § 1.)*

§ 23272. Disposition of towed vehicles; charges for fuel or tires

When any vehicle or object on any vehicular crossing, upon which towing service is maintained, is stopped for any reason and is obstructing or may obstruct traffic, the vehicle or object shall be towed by the towing service either to the nearest property of the Department of Transportation designated for the parking or storing of vehicles, or to a suitable parking location on a public street or highway and thereupon left in the custody of the owner or operator of the vehicle or object, or his agent, or, if no owner, operator, or agent is present, or if an owner, operator, or agent so requests, to a public garage or off-street parking facility. The department may prescribe the limits within which the towing service shall be operated.

Notwithstanding the foregoing provisions, the department may furnish and deliver fuel to vehicles, the supply of which is exhausted, or change tires, and may charge a reasonable sum for the services and materials furnished or, if the department deems it safe and advisable, and the owner or operator of the vehicle or object so requests, it may be towed from the vehicular crossing. *(Stats.1959, c. 3, p. 1711, § 23272. Amended by Stats.1974, c. 545, p. 1333, § 224; Stats.1980, c. 622, p. 1707, § 5; Stats.1982, c. 681, p. 2812, § 85.)*

§ 23273. Inapplicability of tow car requirements

Sections 24605, 25253, 27700, and 27907 do not apply to vehicles operated by the Department of Transportation pursuant to this article. *(Stats.1959, c. 3, p. 1712, § 23273. Amended by Stats.1961, c. 58, p. 1011, § 43, eff. March 31, 1961; Stats.1971, c. 438, p. 909, § 193, operative May 3, 1972; Stats.1974, c. 545, p. 1334, § 225.)*

Cross References

Rules of the road, exemption of authorized emergency vehicles, see Vehicle Code § 21055.

ARTICLE 3. TOLLS AND OTHER CHARGES

§ 23300. Signs

The Department of Transportation shall erect appropriate signs at each entrance to a vehicular crossing to notify traffic that it is entering upon a vehicular crossing. *(Stats.1959, c. 3, p. 1712, § 23300. Amended by Stats.1974, c. 545, p. 1334, § 226.)*

Cross References

Highway signs, markers or warning notices, failure to observe, misdemeanor, see Vehicle Code §§ 21367, 40000.14.
Vehicular crossing defined, see Vehicle Code § 23254.

§ 23301. Toll on crossings

Except as provided in * * * Sections 23301.3 and 23301.5, a vehicle that enters into or upon a vehicular crossing * * * is liable for those tolls and other charges * * * prescribed by the California Transportation Commission. *(Stats.1959, c. 3, p. 1712, § 23301. Amended by Stats.1980, c. 622, p. 1708, § 6; Stats.2009, c. 425 (A.B.254), § 1; Stats.2022, c. 871 (A.B.2949), § 1, eff. Jan. 1, 2023.)*

Cross References

Toll bridges, toll roads, and toll ferries, see Streets and Highways Code § 30800 et seq.

§ 23301.3. Vehicles exempted from tolls

(a) A vehicle described in subdivision (b) is exempt from a toll or other charge on a toll road, toll bridge, toll highway, vehicular crossing, or other toll facility.

(b) The exemption described in subdivision (a) applies only to a vehicle that meets all of the following criteria:

(1) The vehicle is registered to a veteran.

(2) The vehicle is displaying one of the following license plates:

(A) A license plate issued to a disabled veteran, pursuant to Section 5007.

(B) A license plate issued to a Pearl Harbor survivor, pursuant to Section 5101.3.

(C) A license plate issued to a recipient of the Army Medal of Honor, Navy Medal of Honor, Air Force Medal of Honor, Army Distinguished Service Cross, Navy Cross, or Air Force Cross, pursuant to Section 5101.4.

(D) A license plate issued to a former American prisoner of war, pursuant to Section 5101.5.

(E) A license plate issued to a recipient of the Congressional Medal of Honor, pursuant to Section 5101.6.

(F) A license plate issued to a recipient of the Purple Heart, pursuant to Section 5101.8.

(3) The vehicle is registered to a transponder or other electronic toll payment device account with an issuing agency as defined in Section 40250.

(c) This section does not exempt a vehicle described in subdivision (b) from a toll on a high-occupancy toll (HOT) lane.

(d) Sections 23302 and 23302.5 do not apply to a vehicle exempt pursuant to this section. *(Added by Stats.2022, c. 871 (A.B.2949), § 2, eff. Jan. 1, 2023.)*

§ 23301.5. Emergency vehicles; exemption from tolls

(a) An authorized emergency vehicle is exempt from any requirement to pay a toll or other charge on a vehicular crossing, toll highway, or high-occupancy toll (HOT) lane, including the requirements of Section 23301, if all of the following conditions are satisfied:

(1) The authorized emergency vehicle is properly displaying an exempt California license plate, and is properly identified or marked as an authorized emergency vehicle, including, but not limited to, displaying an external surface-mounted red warning light, blue warning light, or both, and displaying public agency identification, including, but not limited to, "Fire Department," "Sheriff," or "Police."

(2)(A) The vehicle is being driven while responding to or returning from an urgent or emergency call, engaged in an urgent or emergency response, or engaging in a fire station coverage assignment directly related to an emergency response.

(B) For purposes of this paragraph, an "urgent" response or call means an incident or circumstance that requires an immediate response to a public safety-related incident, but does not warrant the use of emergency warning lights. "Urgent" does not include any personal use, commuting, training, or administrative uses.

(C) Notwithstanding subparagraph (A), an authorized emergency vehicle, when returning from an urgent or emergency call, or from being engaged in an urgent or emergency response, or from engaging in a fire station coverage assignment directly related to an emergency response, shall not be exempt from any requirement to pay a toll or other charge imposed while traveling on a HOT lane.

(3) The driver of the vehicle determines that the use of the toll facility shall likely improve the availability or response and arrival time of the authorized emergency vehicle and its delivery of essential public safety services.

(b) If the operator of a toll facility elects to send a bill or invoice to the public agency for the use of the toll facility by an authorized emergency vehicle, exempt pursuant to subdivision (a), the fire chief, police chief, county sheriff, head of the public agency, or * * * their designee, is authorized to certify in writing that the authorized emergency vehicle was responding to or returning from an emergency call or response and is exempt from the payment of the toll or other charge in accordance with this section. The letter shall be accepted by the toll operator in lieu of payment and is a public document.

(c) An authorized emergency vehicle that does not comply with this section is not exempt from the requirement to pay a toll or other charge on a toll highway, vehicular crossing, or HOT lane. Upon information and belief of the toll operator that an authorized emergency vehicle is not in compliance with this section, the fire chief, police chief, county sheriff, head of the public agency, or * * * their designee, upon the written request of the owner or operator of the toll facility, shall provide or otherwise make accessible to the toll operator the dispatch records or log books relevant to the time period when the vehicle was in use on the toll highway, vehicular crossing, or HOT lane.

(d) * * * Upon the request of a local emergency service provider, an owner or operator of a toll facility * * * shall enter into an agreement to establish mutually agreed upon terms for the use of the toll facility by the emergency service provider. This section shall not prohibit the owner or operator of a toll facility from having a policy that meets or exceeds this section. If at any time an emergency service provider or the owner or operator of a toll facility opts to terminate an agreement regarding the payment and processing of tolls or other charges, this section shall apply to the emergency service provider and the toll facility. An agreement between an emergency service provider and the owner or operator of a toll facility does not exempt other emergency service providers not named in the original agreement and the toll facility from the requirements of this section when those other emergency service providers use a toll facility in the jurisdiction of the owner or operator of the toll facility.

(e) Sections 23302 and 23302.5 do not apply to authorized emergency vehicles exempt pursuant to this section.

(f) As used in this section, "toll facility" includes a toll road, HOT lane, toll bridge, toll highway, a vehicular crossing for which payment of a toll or charge is required, or any other toll facility. *(Added by Stats.2009, c. 425 (A.B.254), § 2. Amended by Stats.2017, c. 561 (A.B.1516), § 255, eff. Jan. 1, 2018; Stats.2022, c. 497 (A.B.2270), § 1, eff. Jan. 1, 2023.)*

§ 23301.8. Pay-by-plate toll payment; public information

Where an issuing agency permits pay-by-plate toll payment as described in subdivision (e) of Section 23302, it shall communicate, as practicable, the pay-by-plate toll amount in the same manner as it communicates other toll payment methods. The issuing agency shall provide publicly available information on how pay-by-plate toll payment works, including the toll amount, process for payment, and period of time a vehicle has to resolve the payment before an issuing agency may process the trip as a violation under Section 40255. Communication of this information may include the Department of Transportation's approved signage, posting of information on the issuing agency's Internet Web site, media advertising, public meeting or disclosure as required by the issuing agency's policies, or other methods of communication. Except where the issuing agency has an agreement with a vehicle owner that specifies in advance any administrative fees that will be imposed on the owner for pay-by-plate toll payment, administrative costs shall be incorporated into the pay-by-plate toll amount, and no additional administrative costs shall be added above the posted pay-by-plate toll amount. *(Added by Stats.2009, c. 459 (A.B.628), § 1.)*

§ 23302. Failure to pay tolls; transponder or other electronic toll payment device; prima facie evidence

(a)(1) It is unlawful for a driver to fail to pay tolls or other charges on any vehicular crossing or toll highway. Except as otherwise provided in subdivision (b), (c), or (d), it is prima facie evidence of a violation of this section for a person to drive a vehicle onto any vehicular crossing or toll highway without either lawful money of the United States in the driver's immediate possession in an amount sufficient to pay the prescribed tolls or other charges due from that driver or a transponder or other electronic toll payment device associated with a valid Automatic Vehicle Identification account with a balance sufficient to pay those tolls.

(2) Except as specified in paragraph (3), if a transponder or other electronic toll payment device is used to pay tolls or other charges due, the device shall be located in or on the vehicle in a location so as to be visible for the purpose of enforcement at all times when the vehicle is located on the vehicular crossing or toll highway. If required by the operator of a vehicular crossing or toll highway, this requirement applies even if the operator offers free travel or nontoll accounts to certain classes of users.

(3) If a motorcyclist uses a transponder or other electronic toll payment device to lawfully enter a vehicle crossing or toll highway, the motorcyclist shall use any one of the following methods as long as the transponder or device is able to be read by the toll operator's detection equipment:

(A) Place the transponder or other electronic toll payment device in the motorcyclist's pocket.

(B) Place the transponder or other electronic toll payment device inside a cycle net that drapes over the gas tank of the motorcycle.

(C) Mount the transponder or other electronic toll payment device on license plate devices provided by the toll operator, if the toll operator provides those devices.

(D) Keep the transponder or other electronic toll payment device in the glove or storage compartment of the motorcycle.

(E) Mount the transponder or other electronic toll payment device on the windshield of the motorcycle.

(b) For vehicular crossings and toll highways that use electronic toll collection as the only method of paying tolls or other charges, it is prima facie evidence of a violation of this section for a driver to drive a vehicle onto the vehicular crossing or toll highway without a transponder or other electronic toll payment device associated with a valid Automatic Vehicle Identification account with a balance sufficient to pay those tolls.

(c) For vehicular crossings and toll highways where the issuing agency, as defined in Section 40250, permits pay-by-plate payment of tolls and other charges, in accordance with policies adopted by the issuing agency, it is prima facie evidence of a violation of this section for a driver to drive a vehicle onto the vehicular crossing or toll highway without at least one of the following:

(1) Lawful money of the United States in the driver's immediate possession in an amount sufficient to pay the prescribed tolls or other charges due from that person.

(2) A transponder or other electronic toll payment device associated with a valid Automatic Vehicle Identification account with a balance sufficient to pay those tolls.

(3) Valid vehicle license plates, registered to a vehicle with an up-to-date vehicle registration address pursuant to Section 4159, properly attached pursuant to Section 4850.5 or 5200 to the vehicle in which that driver enters onto the vehicular crossing or toll highway.

(d) For vehicular crossings and toll highways where the issuing agency, as defined in Section 40250, permits pay-by-plate payment of tolls and other charges in accordance with policies adopted by the issuing agency, and where electronic toll collection is the only other method of paying tolls or other charges, it is prima facie evidence of a violation of this section for a driver to drive a vehicle onto the vehicular crossing or toll highway without either a transponder or other electronic toll payment device associated with a valid Automatic Vehicle Identification account with a balance sufficient to pay those tolls or valid vehicle license plates, registered to a vehicle with an up-to-date vehicle registration address pursuant to Section 4159, properly attached to the vehicle pursuant to Section 4850.5 or 5200 in which that driver enters onto the vehicular crossing or toll highway.

(e) As used in this article, "pay-by-plate toll payment" means an issuing agency's use of on-road vehicle license plate identification recognition technology to accept payment of tolls in accordance with policies adopted by the issuing agency.

(f) This section does not require an issuing agency to offer pay-by-plate toll processing as a method for paying tolls. *(Stats.1959, c. 3, p. 1712, § 23302. Amended by Stats.1993, c. 1292 (S.B.274), § 15; Stats.1995, c. 739 (A.B.1223), § 6; Stats.1996, c. 1154 (A.B.3020), § 73, eff. Sept. 30, 1996; Stats.2009, c. 459 (A.B.628), § 2; Stats.2012, c. 81 (A.B.1890), § 1; Stats.2022, c. 969 (A.B.2594), § 3, eff. Jan. 1, 2023.)*

Cross References

Electronic toll collection system, transportation agencies prohibited from using personally identifiable information obtained from nonsubscribers for marketing activities, exception for toll-related products or services contained in notice of toll evasion pursuant to this section, see Streets and Highways Code § 31490.

Statute making one fact prima facie evidence of another fact, see Evidence Code § 602.

Research References

2 Witkin, California Criminal Law 4th Crimes Against Public Peace and Welfare § 528 (2021), Streets and Highways.

§ 23302.5. Evasion of tolls

(a) No person shall evade or attempt to evade the payment of tolls or other charges on any vehicular crossing or toll highway.

(b) A violation of subdivision (a) is subject to civil penalties and is neither an infraction nor a public offense, as defined in Section 15 of the Penal Code. The enforcement of those civil penalties shall be governed by the civil administrative procedures set forth in Article 4 (commencing with Section 40250) of Chapter 1 of Division 17. *(Added by Stats.1995, c. 739 (A.B.1223), § 7.)*

Research References

2 Witkin, California Criminal Law 4th Crimes Against Public Peace and Welfare § 528 (2021), Streets and Highways.

§ 23303. Liens

The Department of Transportation shall have a lien and may enforce such lien, as provided in Chapter 6.5 (commencing with Section 3067) of Title 14 of Part 4 of Division 3 of the Civil Code, for all tolls and charges provided by this chapter. *(Stats.1959, c. 3, p. 1712, § 23303. Amended by Stats.1974, c. 545, p. 1334, § 227.)*

§ 23304. Invoice by mail for unpaid tolls; nonpayment

Section operative July 1, 2024.

(a) With respect to a toll bridge, an issuing agency that permits pay-by-plate toll payment as described in subdivision (e) of Section 23302 or that permits payment by a transponder or other electronic toll payment device shall send an invoice by mail for any unpaid toll to the registered vehicle owner. The invoice shall include a notice to the registered owner that, unless the registered owner pays the toll by the due date shown on the invoice, a toll evasion penalty will be assessed. The invoice due date shall not be less than 30 days from the invoice date.

(b) If a toll invoice is not paid by the due date shown on the invoice, the nonpayment shall be deemed an evasion of tolls and the issuing agency, or processing agency as the case may be, shall mail a notice of toll evasion violation to the registered owner pursuant to subdivision (a) of Section 40254.

(c) This section shall become operative on July 1, 2024. *(Added by Stats.2022, c. 969 (A.B.2594), § 4, eff. Jan. 1, 2023, operative July 1, 2024.)*

§ 23305. Registration of transponder or other electronic toll payment device account for drivers of rental cars; publication and notice of how to open an account or acquire a transponder or other electronic toll payment device

Section operative July 7, 2024.

(a) An issuing agency shall allow a driver of a rental vehicle to register the rental vehicle to a transponder or other electronic toll payment device account with the issuing agency prior to traveling on the issuing agency's toll facility for the purpose of paying all tolls with a credit or debit card. The issuing agency may require the use of a transponder for this purpose.

(b) The public entities operating or planning to implement a toll facility in this state shall cooperate to publish an internet website at which the public and rental car agencies can view and download, or that provides direct links to, information about how to open an account or acquire a transponder or other electronic toll payment device, for use of each issuing agency's toll facility. The rental car agency shall provide the customer with a written or electronic notice, including the electronic link for the internet website. The notice shall be separate from the rental contract and, if an electronic notice, emailed to the rental customer.

(c) This section shall become operative on July 1, 2024. *(Added by Stats.2022, c. 969 (A.B.2594), § 5, eff. Jan. 1, 2023, operative July 1, 2024.)*

§ 23306. Availability and acquisition of transponder or other electronic toll payment device; price

Section operative July 1, 2024.

(a)(1) An issuing agency that operates an electronic toll collection system that permits payment by a transponder or other electronic toll payment device shall, directly or through a third-party vendor, make the transponder or other electronic toll payment device available for acquisition online, by mail, and in person at a retail outlet, the office of an issuing agency or processing agency, as defined in Section 40253, or customer service center.

(2) At least one retail outlet, kiosk, or customer service center that offers the transponder or other electronic toll payment device associated with the issuing agency shall be located within the jurisdiction of the issuing agency.

(3) The issuing agency shall post on an internet website related to its electronic toll collection system locations where tolls may be paid with cash, and locations at which a transponder or other electronic toll payment device may be acquired.

(b) The price of the transponder or other electronic toll payment device shall not exceed the reasonable cost to the issuing agency based on the estimated cost to procure and distribute the device.

(c) As used in this article, "retail outlet" includes a store managed by the issuing agency, a cash payment location, or other locations not managed by the issuing agency.

(d) This section shall become operative on July 1, 2024. *(Added by Stats.2022, c. 969 (A.B.2594), § 6, eff. Jan. 1, 2023, operative July 1, 2024.)*

§ 23307. Use of cash, credit card or debit card to acquire transponder or other electronic toll payment device; transaction fees

Section operative July 1, 2024.

(a) If an issuing agency offers a transponder or other electronic toll payment device, a person shall be allowed to acquire a transponder or other electronic toll payment device with cash, or with a credit or debit card, and shall be allowed to load a minimum of one hundred dollars ($100) onto the associated account with cash or with a credit or debit card.

(b) Except as otherwise provided in subdivision (b) of Section 23306, there shall be no additional transaction fee charged to acquire the transponder or other electronic toll payment device.

(c) An issuing agency shall not assess any additional transaction fee to the amount a person is charged by a cash payment network company to load funds to an account using cash through a cash payment network.

(d) This section shall become operative on July 1, 2024. *(Added by Stats.2022, c. 969 (A.B.2594), § 7, eff. Jan. 1, 2023, operative July 1, 2024.)*

§ 23308. Customer service centers; hours of operation; transactions to be conducted; transaction fees for cash payments; location and number of physical locations

Section operative July 1, 2024.

(a) Subject to extenuating circumstances and holidays, the hours during which one of the issuing or processing agency's offices or customer service centers are open to the public to provide customer service related to electronic toll collection shall include at least five hours per week between the hours of 6 a.m. to 8 a.m. or 5 p.m. to 7 p.m., or on a Saturday.

(b) A person shall be able to conduct all of the following transactions at either the issuing agency's office or customer service center:

(1) Acquire the issuing agency's transponder or other electronic toll payment device.

(2) Load money onto an account with the issuing agency.

(3) Pay a toll notice, including fines and penalties.

(4) Register or remove a license plate to or from a transponder or other electronic toll payment device account with the issuing agency for payment of tolls.

(c) Except as otherwise provided in subdivision (b) of Section 23306, the issuing agency shall not charge persons paying cash an additional transaction fee for any transaction listed in paragraphs (1) to (3), inclusive, of subdivision (b) that are conducted at the issuing or processing agency's office, or customer service center. There shall be at least one issuing or processing agency's office or customer service center within the issuing agency's jurisdiction.

(d) The issuing agency shall have two or more physical locations within each county in which a toll facility operated by the issuing agency is located for purposes of conducting the transactions set forth in paragraphs (2) and (3) of subdivision (b).

(e) This section shall become operative on July 1, 2024. *(Added by Stats.2022, c. 969 (A.B.2594), § 8, eff. Jan. 1, 2023, operative July 1, 2024.)*

§ 23309. Customer service telephone line; hours of operation; assistive services

Section operative July 1, 2024.

(a) Subject to extenuating circumstances and holidays, the issuing agency, directly or through a third-party vendor, shall maintain a customer service telephone line that shall be operated by a live person for at least 35 hours per week between the hours of 8 a.m. to 5 p.m. and an additional 5 hours per week between the hours of 6 a.m. to 8 a.m., from 5 p.m. to 7 p.m., or on a Saturday. The customer service telephone line shall be available to address questions related to acquiring a transponder or other electronic toll payment device, paying toll notices, disputing tolls and penalties, setting up payment plans, and registering the license plate of a vehicle to a transponder or other electronic toll payment device account.

(b) The customer service telephone line shall provide language interpreter services and assistance for deaf or hard-of-hearing individuals.

(c) This section shall become operative on July 1, 2024. *(Added by Stats.2022, c. 969 (A.B.2594), § 9, eff. Jan. 1, 2023, operative July 1, 2024.)*

ARTICLE 4. SPECIAL TRAFFIC REGULATIONS

Section

§ 23330. Animals and vehicles

Except where a special permit has been obtained from the Department of Transportation under the provisions of Article 6 (commencing with Section 35780) of Chapter 5 of Division 15, none of the following shall be permitted on any vehicular crossing:

(a) Animals while being led or driven, even though tethered or harnessed.

(b) Bicycles, motorized bicycles, or motorized scooters, unless the department by signs indicates that bicycles, motorized bicycles, or motorized scooters, or any combination thereof, are permitted upon all or any portion of the vehicular crossing.

(c) Vehicles having a total width of vehicle or load exceeding 102 inches.

(d) Vehicles carrying items prohibited by regulations promulgated by the Department of Transportation. *(Stats.1959, c. 3, p. 1712, § 23330. Amended by Stats.1972, c. 437, p. 802, § 1; Stats.1974, c. 545, p. 1334, § 228; Stats.1975, c. 987, p. 2331, § 8; Stats.1978, c. 611, p. 2050, § 1; Stats.1999, c. 722 (S.B.441), § 8.)*

Cross References

Bicycle defined, see Vehicle Code § 231.
Motorized bicycle, see Vehicle Code §§ 406, 4020.
Transportation of explosives, see Vehicle Code § 31600 et seq.

§ 23331. Pedestrians

Pedestrians shall not be permitted upon any vehicular crossing, unless unobstructed sidewalks of more than three feet in width are constructed and maintained and signs indicating that pedestrians are permitted are in place. *(Stats.1959, c. 3, p. 1712, § 23331.)*

Cross References

Pedestrian defined, see Vehicle Code § 467.
Sidewalk defined, see Vehicle Code § 555.

§ 23332. Trespass prohibited

It is unlawful for any person to be upon any portion of a vehicular crossing which is not intended for public use without the permission of the Department of Transportation. This section does not apply to a person engaged in the operation, maintenance, or repair of a vehicular crossing or any facility thereon nor to any person attempting to effect a rescue. *(Stats.1959, c. 3, p. 1712, § 23332. Amended by Stats.1974, c. 545, p. 1334, § 229.)*

Cross References

Procedure on arrest for violation of this section, see Vehicle Code § 40303.
Violation as misdemeanor, punishment, see Vehicle Code §§ 40000.15, 42001.

§ 23333. Stopping and parking

No vehicle shall stop, stand, or be parked in or upon any vehicular crossing except:

(a) When necessary to avoid injury or damage to persons or property.

(b) When necessary for the repair, maintenance or operation of a publicly owned toll bridge.

(c) In compliance with the direction of a member of the California Highway Patrol or an employee of the Department of Transportation who is a peace officer or with the direction of a sign or signal.

(d) In such places as may be designated by the Director of Transportation. *(Stats.1959, c. 3, p. 1713, § 23333. Amended by Stats.1974, c. 545, p. 1335, § 230.)*

Cross References

Stopping, standing or parking, generally, see Vehicle Code § 22500 et seq.

§ 23334. Adoption of traffic rules

The Department of Transportation may adopt rules and regulations not inconsistent with this chapter for the control of traffic on any vehicular crossing to aid and insure the safe and orderly flow of traffic, and shall, so far as practicable, notify the public of the rules and regulations by signs on the vehicular crossing. *(Stats.1959, c. 3, p. 1713, § 23334. Amended by Stats.1974, c. 545, p. 1335, § 231.)*

§ 23335. Publication of traffic rules

The Department of Transportation shall cause to be published and made available to the public at the tollgates of each vehicular crossing copies of those traffic laws and rules and regulations particularly applicable thereto. *(Stats.1959, c. 3, p. 1713, § 23335. Amended by Stats.1974, c. 545, p. 1335, § 232.)*

§ 23336. Violation of rules and regulations

It is unlawful to violate any rules or regulations adopted under Section 23334, notice of which has been given either by a sign on a vehicular crossing or by publication as provided in Section 23335. *(Stats.1959, c. 3, p. 1713, § 23336.)*

Cross References

Violations, punishment, see Vehicle Code § 42001 et seq.

Division 11.5

SENTENCING FOR DRIVING WHILE UNDER THE INFLUENCE

CHAPTER 1. COURT–IMPOSED PENALTIES: PERSONS LESS THAN 21 YEARS OF AGE

ARTICLE 1. GENERAL PROVISIONS

§ 23500. Application of chapter

This chapter applies to the imposition of penalties and sanctions by the courts on persons who were less than 21 years of age at the time of the commission of the driving while under the influence offenses described in Chapter 12 (commencing with Section 23100) of Division 11. *(Added by Stats.1998, c. 118 (S.B.1186), § 84, operative July 1, 1999.)*

Research References

4 Witkin, California Criminal Law 4th Pretrial Proceedings § 60 (2021), Juvenile Offenses.

ARTICLE 2. PENALTIES FOR A VIOLATION OF SECTION 23140

§ 23502. Driving-under-the-influence program; required attendance

(a) Notwithstanding any other provision of law, if a person who is at least 18 years of age is convicted of a first violation of Section 23140, in addition to any penalties, the court shall order the person to attend a program licensed under Section 11836 of the Health and Safety Code, subject to a fee schedule developed under paragraph (2) of subdivision (b) of Section 11837.4 of the Health and Safety Code.

(b) The attendance in a licensed driving-under-the-influence program required under subdivision (a) shall be as follows:

(1) If, within 10 years of the current violation of Section 23140, the person has not been convicted of a separate violation of Section 23140, 23152, or 23153, or of Section 23103, with a plea of guilty under Section 23103.5, or of Section 655 of the Harbors and Navigation Code, or of Section 191.5 of, or subdivision (a) of Section 192.5 of, the Penal Code, the person shall complete, at a minimum, the education component of that licensed driving-under-the-influence program.

(2) If the person does not meet the requirements of paragraph (1), the person shall complete, at a minimum, the program described in paragraph (1) of subdivision (c) of Section 11837 of the Health and Safety Code.

(c) The person's privilege to operate a motor vehicle shall be suspended by the department as required under Section 13352.6, and the court shall require the person to surrender his or her driver's license to the court in accordance with Section 13550.

(d) The court shall advise the person at the time of sentencing that the driving privilege will not be restored until the person has provided the department with proof satisfactory to the department that the person has successfully completed the driving-under-the-influence program required under this section. *(Added by Stats.2000, c. 1063 (A.B.803), § 4. Amended by Stats.2004, c. 550 (S.B.1694), § 12; Stats.2007, c. 747 (A.B.678), § 32.)*

Research References

2 Witkin, California Criminal Law 4th Crimes Against Public Peace and Welfare § 279 (2021), In General.

2 Witkin, California Criminal Law 4th Crimes Against Public Peace and Welfare § 527 (2021), Operation While Under the Influence or Addicted.

ARTICLE 3. YOUTHFUL DRUNK DRIVER VISITATION PROGRAM

§ 23509. Short title of article

This article shall be known and may be cited as the "Youthful Drunk Driver Visitation Program Act." *(Added by Stats.1998, c. 118 (S.B.1186), § 84, operative July 1, 1999.)*

Research References

2 Witkin, California Criminal Law 4th Crimes Against Public Peace and Welfare § 76 (2021), In General.

2 Witkin, California Criminal Law 4th Crimes Against Public Peace and Welfare § 279 (2021), In General.

2 Witkin, California Criminal Law 4th Crimes Against Public Peace and Welfare § 365 (2021), Purchase of Liquor by Minors.

§ 23510. Legislative findings and declarations

The Legislature finds and declares all of the following:

(a) Young drivers often do not realize the consequences of drinking alcohol or ingesting any other drugs, whether legal or not, and driving a motor vehicle while their physical capabilities to drive safely are impaired by those substances.

(b) Young drivers who use alcohol or other drugs are likely to become dependent on those substances and prompt intervention is needed to protect other persons, as well as the young driver, from death or serious injury.

(c) The conviction of a young driver for driving under the influence of an alcoholic beverage, a drug, or both, identifies that person as a risk to the health and safety of others, as well as that young driver, because of the young driver's inability to control his or her conduct.

(d) It has been demonstrated that close observation of the effects on others of alcohol and other drugs, both chronic and acute, by a young driver convicted of driving under the influence has a marked effect on recidivism and should therefore be encouraged by the courts, prehospital emergency medical care personnel, and other officials charged with cleaning up the carnage and wreckage caused by drunk drivers.

(e) The program prescribed in this article provides guidelines for the operation of an intensive program to discourage recidivism by convicted young drunk drivers. *(Added by Stats.1998, c. 118 (S.B. 1186), § 84, operative July 1, 1999.)*

Research References

3 Witkin, California Criminal Law 4th Punishment § 664 (2021), Counseling, Treatment, and Education.

§ 23512. "Program" defined

For the purposes of this article, "program" means the Youthful Drunk Driver Visitation Program prescribed in this article. *(Added by Stats.1998, c. 118 (S.B.1186), § 84, operative July 1, 1999.)*

§ 23514. Violation of specified alcohol related offenses; participation in program as term and condition of probation; age preference; abstinence requirement

(a) If a person is found to be in violation of Section 23140, is convicted of, or is adjudged a ward of the juvenile court for, a violation of Section 21200.5, 23140, or 23152 punishable under Section 23536, or Section 23220, 23221, or 23222, subdivision (a) or (b) of Section 23224, or Section 23225 or 23226, and is granted probation, the court may order, with the consent of the defendant or ward, as a term and condition of probation in addition to any other term and condition required or authorized by law, that the defendant or ward participate in the program.

(b) The court shall give preference for participation in the program to defendants or wards who were less than 21 years of age at the time of the offense if the facilities of the program in the jurisdiction are limited to fewer than the number of defendants or wards eligible and consenting to participate.

(c) The court shall require that the defendant or ward not drink any alcoholic beverage at all before reaching the age of 21 years and not use illegal drugs. *(Added by Stats.1998, c. 118 (S.B.1186), § 84, operative July 1, 1999.)*

§ 23516. Suitability of defendant or ward; appropriateness of program

The court shall investigate and consult with the defendant or ward, defendant's or ward's counsel, if any, and any proposed supervisor of a visitation under the program, and the court may consult with any other person whom the court finds may be of value, including, but not limited to, the defendant's or ward's parents or other family members, in order to ascertain that the defendant or ward is suitable for the program, that the visitation will be educational and meaningful to the defendant or ward, and that there are no physical, emotional, or mental reasons to believe the program would not be appropriate or would cause any injury to the defendant or ward. *(Added by Stats.1998, c. 118 (S.B.1186), § 84, operative July 1, 1999.)*

§ 23517. Supervised visitations; places to visit; coordination through substance abuse counselors; counseling sessions; termination; considerations by court

(a) To the extent that personnel and facilities are made available to the court, the court may include a requirement for supervised visitation by the defendant or ward to all, or any, of the following:

(1) A trauma facility, as defined in Section 1798.160 of the Health and Safety Code, a base hospital designated pursuant to Section 1798.100 or 1798.101 of the Health and Safety Code, or a general acute care hospital having a basic emergency medical services special permit issued pursuant to subdivision (c) of Section 1277 of the Health and Safety Code that regularly receives victims of vehicle crashes, between the hours of 10 p.m. and 2 a.m. on a Friday or Saturday night to observe appropriate victims of vehicle crashes involving drinking drivers, under the supervision of any of the following:

(A) A registered nurse trained in providing emergency trauma care or prehospital advanced life support.

(B) An emergency room physician.

(C) An emergency medical technician-paramedic or an emergency medical technician II.

* * *

(2) If approved by the county coroner, the county coroner's office or the county morgue to observe appropriate victims of vehicle crashes involving drinking drivers, under the supervision of the coroner or a deputy coroner.

(b) As used in this section, "appropriate victims" means victims whose condition is determined by the visitation supervisor to demonstrate the results of crashes involving drinking drivers without being excessively gruesome or traumatic to the probationer.

(c) If persons trained in counseling or substance abuse are made available to the court, the court may coordinate the visitation program or the visitations at any facility designated in subdivision (a) through those persons.

(d) Any visitation shall include, before any observation of victims or disabled persons by the probationer, a comprehensive counseling session with the visitation supervisor at which the supervisor shall explain and discuss the experiences that may be encountered during the visitation in order to ascertain whether the visitation is appropriate for the probationer.

(e) If at any time, whether before or during a visitation, the supervisor of the probationer determines that the visitation may be or is traumatic or otherwise inappropriate for the probationer, or is uncertain whether the visitation may be traumatic or inappropriate, the visitation shall be terminated without prejudice to the probationer.

(f) Prior to the court including a requirement for supervised visitation, pursuant to subdivision (a), the court shall consider the speed of the vehicle, the severity of any injuries sustained as a result of the violation, and whether the defendant or ward was engaged in a speed competition, as defined in Section 23109. *(Added by Stats. 1998, c. 118 (S.B.1186), § 84, operative July 1, 1999. Amended by Stats.2022, c. 81 (A.B.2198), § 5, eff. Jan. 1, 2023.)*

§ 23518. Personal conference or written report or letter after visitation

(a) The program may include a personal conference after the visitations described in Section 23517 between the sentencing judge or judicial officer or the person responsible for coordinating the program for the judicial district and the probationer, his or her counsel, and, if available, the probationer's parents to discuss the experiences of the visitation and how those experiences may impact the probationer's future conduct.

(b) If a personal conference described in subdivision (a) is not practicable, because of the probationer's absence from the jurisdiction, conflicting time schedules, or other reasons, the program should provide for a written report or letter by the probationer to the court discussing the experiences and their impact on the probationer. *(Added by Stats.1998, c. 118 (S.B.1186), § 84, operative July 1, 1999.)*

§ 23518.5. Civil immunity

The county, a court, any facility visited pursuant to the program, the agents, employees, or independent contractors of the court, county, or facility visited pursuant to the program, and any person supervising a probationer during the visitation, is not liable for any civil damages resulting from injury to the probationer, or civil damages caused by the probationer, during, or from any activities relating to, the visitation, except for willful or grossly negligent acts intended to, or reasonably expected to result in, that injury or damage and except for workers' compensation for the probationer as prescribed by law if the probationer performs community service at the facility as an additional term or condition of probation. *(Added by Stats.1998, c. 118 (S.B.1186), § 84, operative July 1, 1999.)*

ARTICLE 4. PENALTIES FOR A VIOLATION OF SECTION 23152 OR 23153

Section

§ 23520. Juvenile offenders; first drug or alcohol offense; alcohol or drug education program requirement; expenses and fees; waiver; application of section

(a) Whenever, in any county specified in subdivision (b), a judge of a juvenile court, a juvenile hearing officer, or referee of a juvenile court finds that a person has committed a first violation of Section 23152 or 23153, the person shall be required to participate in and successfully complete an alcohol or drug education program, or both of those programs, as designated by the court. The expense of the person's attendance in the program shall be paid by the person's parents or guardian so long as the person is under the age of 18 years, and shall be paid by the person thereafter. However, in approving the program, each county shall require the program to provide for the payment of the fee for the program in installments by any person who cannot afford to pay the full fee at the commencement of the program and shall require the program to provide for the waiver of the fee for any person who is indigent, as determined by criteria for indigency established by the board of supervisors. Whenever it can be done without substantial additional cost, each county shall require that the program be provided for juveniles at a separate location from, or at a different time of day than, alcohol and drug education programs for adults.

(b) This section applies only in those counties that have one or more alcohol or drug education programs certified by the county alcohol program administrator and approved by the board of supervisors. *(Added by Stats.1998, c. 118 (S.B.1186), § 84, operative July 1, 1999. Amended by Stats.2003, c. 149 (S.B.79), § 85.)*

Law Revision Commission Comments

Subdivision (a) of Section 23520 is amended to reflect the redesignation of traffic hearing officers as juvenile hearing officers. See 1997 Cal. Stat. ch. 679. [33 Cal.L.Rev.Comm. Reports 259 (2003)].

Research References

2 Witkin, California Criminal Law 4th Crimes Against Public Peace and Welfare § 279 (2021), In General.

§ 23521. Finding of another jurisdiction as conviction of violation of §§ 23152 and 23153

(a) Any finding of a juvenile court judge, juvenile hearing officer, or referee of a juvenile court of a commission of an offense in any state, territory, possession of the United States, the District of Columbia, the Commonwealth of Puerto Rico, or the Dominion of Canada that, if committed in this state, would be a violation of Section 23152, is a conviction of a violation of Section 23152 for the purposes of Sections 13352, 13352.3, 13352.4, and 13352.5, and the finding of a juvenile court judge, juvenile hearing officer, or referee of a juvenile court of a commission of an offense that, if committed in this state, would be a violation of Section 23153 is a conviction of a violation of Section 23153 for the purposes of Sections 13352 and 13352.3.

(b) This section shall become operative on September 20, 2005. *(Added by Stats.1998, c. 118 (S.B.1186), § 84, operative July 1, 1999. Amended by Stats.2002, c. 545 (S.B.1852), § 18; Stats.2003, c. 149 (S.B.79), § 86; Stats.2004, c. 551 (S.B.1697), § 14, operative Sept. 20, 2005.)*

Law Revision Commission Comments

Section 23521 is amended to reflect the redesignation of traffic hearing officers as juvenile hearing officers. See 1997 Cal. Stat. ch. 679. [33 Cal.L.Rev. Comm. Reports 259 (2003)].

Research References

2 Witkin, California Criminal Law 4th Crimes Against Public Peace and Welfare § 279 (2021), In General.

CHAPTER 2. COURT PENALTIES

ARTICLE 1. GENERAL PROVISIONS

Section

§ 23530. Application of chapter

This chapter applies to the imposition of penalties, sanctions, and probation upon persons convicted of violating driving while under the influence offenses that are set forth in Chapter 12 (commencing with Section 23100) of Division 11. *(Added by Stats.1998, c. 118 (S.B.1186), § 84, operative July 1, 1999.)*

ARTICLE 2. PENALTIES FOR A VIOLATION OF SECTION 23152

Section

§ 23536. Conviction of first violation of § 23152; punishment

(a) If a person is convicted of a first violation of Section 23152, that person shall be punished by imprisonment in the county jail for not less than 96 hours, at least 48 hours of which shall be continuous, nor more than six months, and by a fine of not less than three hundred ninety dollars ($390), nor more than one thousand dollars ($1,000).

(b) The court shall order that a person punished under subdivision (a), who is to be punished by imprisonment in the county jail, be imprisoned on days other than days of regular employment of the person, as determined by the court. If the court determines that 48 hours of continuous imprisonment would interfere with the person's work schedule, the court shall allow the person to serve the imprisonment whenever the person is normally scheduled for time off from work. The court may make this determination based upon a representation from the defendant's attorney or upon an affidavit or testimony from the defendant.

(c) The person's privilege to operate a motor vehicle shall be suspended by the department under paragraph (1) of subdivision (a) of Section 13352 or Section 13352.1. The court shall require the person to surrender the driver's license to the court in accordance with Section 13550.

(d) Whenever, when considering the circumstances taken as a whole, the court determines that the person punished under this section would present a traffic safety or public safety risk if authorized to operate a motor vehicle during the period of suspension imposed under paragraph (1) of subdivision (a) of Section 13352 or Section 13352.1, the court may disallow the issuance of a restricted driver's license required under Section 13352.4. *(Formerly § 23160, added by Stats.1981, c. 940, p. 3571, § 32. Amended by Stats.1982, c. 53, p. 174, § 29, eff. Feb. 18, 1982; Stats.1982, c. 331, p. 1632, § 4, eff. June 30, 1982; Stats.1982, c. 1339, § 15, eff. Sept. 24, 1982; Stats.1984, c. 216, § 13; Stats.1990, c. 286 (A.B.3009), § 1; Stats.1998, c. 756 (A.B.762), § 11, operative July 1, 1999. Renumbered § 23536 and amended by Stats.1999, c. 22 (S.B.24), § 19, eff. May 26, 1999, operative July 1, 1999. Amended by Stats.2002, c. 545 (S.B.1852), § 19; Stats.2004, c. 551 (S.B.1697), § 15, operative Sept. 20, 2005; Stats.2006, c. 692 (S.B.1756), § 5.)*

Cross References

Alcohol and drug problem assessment program, violator participation, sentencing, and assessment upon fine, see Vehicle Code § 23646 et seq.
Alcoholic beverages in vehicles, see Vehicle Code § 23220 et seq.
Applicability of this section to trolley coaches, see Vehicle Code § 21051.
Arrest without warrant, see Vehicle Code § 40300.5.
Challenging constitutional validity of separate conviction, see Vehicle Code § 41403.
Chemical blood, breath or urine tests, see Vehicle Code § 13353.
Chemical tests as evidence, see Vehicle Code § 23610.
Conviction of violation of specified subdivisions of Penal Code § 192 to be deemed conviction of violation of specified DUI provisions, see Vehicle Code § 13350.5.
Coroner's inquiry into deaths, see Government Code § 27491.25.
County alcohol and drug problem assessment programs, mandatory participation for convicted violators of this section, see Vehicle Code §§ 23646, 23647.
Crime of violence, within act for indemnification of victims of crime, see Government Code § 13960.
Defense of drug use to violations, see Vehicle Code § 23630.
Deposit in special account for each conviction under DUI provisions, see Penal Code § 1463.14.
Drivers license revocation, conviction of driver under eighteen, see Vehicle Code § 13352.3.
Driving school or instructor, revocation or suspension of license for violation of this section, see Vehicle Code § 11110.
Gross vehicular manslaughter while intoxicated, see Penal Code § 191.5.
Guilty plea, see Vehicle Code § 41610.
Impoundment of vehicle of registered owner convicted under this section, see Vehicle Code § 23594.
Influence of alcoholic beverage or drug, suspension or revocation of driving privileges, see Vehicle Code § 13352.
Injury to guest by intoxicated driver, see Vehicle Code § 17158.
Juvenile offenders, programs of supervision, see Welfare and Institutions Code § 654.1.
Manslaughter, negligent homicide by vehicle, see Penal Code § 192.
Nuisance, sale or other disposition of motor vehicle driven by defendant, see Vehicle Code § 23596.
Persons certified or granted probation on conviction of driving under the influence of alcohol or drugs or combined influence on certain conditions, restriction, revocation or suspension of driving privilege, consent to participation in treatment program, see Vehicle Code § 13352.5.
Please Don't Drink and Drive memorial signs, requests for and duration of placement, exception for a party to an accident convicted or determined to be mentally incompetent under this section, see Streets and Highways Code § 101.10.
Presentence investigation and assessment, see Vehicle Code § 23655.
Presumptions, see Evidence Code § 600 et seq.
Prior convictions under sections 23103, 23152 or 23153, effect on sentencing and driving privileges, see Vehicle Code § 23622.
Procedure on arrest for violation of this section, see Vehicle Code § 40302.
Records available to courts and law enforcement officials, incidents under certain DWI and homicide laws, period of time records must be available, see Vehicle Code § 1808.
Refusal to submit to alcohol testing under DUI laws, calculation of prior convictions, certain foreign convictions recognized, see Vehicle Code §§ 13353, 13353.1 and 13353.3.
Surrender of driver's license to court, see Vehicle Code § 13550.
Suspension or revocation of driving privilege for a violation of this section, notice by personal service, see Vehicle Code § 13106.
Suspension or revocation of license,
  Generally, see Vehicle Code § 13352.
  Alcohol-related accident within five years of vehicular manslaughter, see Vehicle Code § 13954.
  Driver license compact, see Vehicle Code § 15000 et seq.
  Driving after suspension or revocation, see Vehicle Code § 14601.2.
  Investigation by department, three convictions in three years under this or other specified statutes, see Vehicle Code § 13800.
  Prior convictions, record, see Vehicle Code § 13209.
Traffic violation point count, violation of this section, see Vehicle Code § 12810.
Traffic violators schools, suspension or revocation of license for violation of this section, see Vehicle Code § 11215.
Vehicular homicide, see Penal Code § 192.
Violation as misdemeanor, see Vehicle Code § 40000.15.
Violation of this section, relinquishment of motor vehicle to convicted minor, see Penal Code § 193.8.
Youthful drunk driver visitation program, see Vehicle Code § 23509 et seq.

Research References

2 Witkin, California Criminal Law 4th Crimes Against Public Peace and Welfare § 280 (2021), First Violation.

§ 23538. Conditions of probation for first time offense

(a)(1) If the court grants probation to person punished under Section 23536, in addition to the provisions of Section 23600 and any other terms and conditions imposed by the court, the court shall impose as a condition of probation that the person pay a fine of at least three hundred ninety dollars ($390), but not more than one thousand dollars ($1,000). The court may also impose, as a condition of probation, that the person be confined in a county jail for at least 48 hours, but not more than six months.

(2) The person's privilege to operate a motor vehicle shall be suspended by the department under paragraph (1) of subdivision (a) of Section 13352 or Section 13352.1. The court shall require the person to surrender the driver's license to the court in accordance with Section 13550.

(3) Whenever, when considering the circumstances taken as a whole, the court determines that the person punished under this section would present a traffic safety or public safety risk if authorized to operate a motor vehicle during the period of suspension imposed under paragraph (1) of subdivision (a) of Section 13352

or Section 13352.1, the court may disallow the issuance of a restricted driver's license required under Section 13352.4.

(b) In any county where the board of supervisors has approved, and the State Department of Health Care Services has licensed, a program or programs described in Section 11837.3 of the Health and Safety Code, the court shall also impose as a condition of probation that the driver shall enroll and participate in, and successfully complete a driving-under-the- influence program, licensed pursuant to Section 11836 of the Health and Safety Code, in the driver's county of residence or employment, as designated by the court. For the purposes of this subdivision, enrollment in, participation in, and completion of an approved program shall be subsequent to the date of the current violation. Credit may not be given for any program activities completed prior to the date of the current violation.

(1) The court shall refer a first offender whose blood-alcohol concentration was less than 0.20 percent, by weight, to participate for at least three months or longer, as ordered by the court, in a licensed program that consists of at least 30 hours of program activities, including those education, group counseling, and individual interview sessions described in Chapter 9 (commencing with Section 11836) of Part 2 of Division 10.5 of the Health and Safety Code.

(2) The court shall refer a first offender whose blood-alcohol concentration was 0.20 percent or more, by weight, or who refused to take a chemical test, to participate for at least nine months or longer, as ordered by the court, in a licensed program that consists of at least 60 hours of program activities, including those education, group counseling, and individual interview sessions described in Chapter 9 (commencing with Section 11836) of Part 2 of Division 10.5 of the Health and Safety Code.

(3) The court shall advise the person at the time of sentencing that the driving privilege shall not be restored until proof satisfactory to the department of successful completion of a driving-under-the-influence program of the length required under this code that is licensed pursuant to Section 11836 of the Health and Safety Code has been received in the department's headquarters.

(c)(1) The court shall revoke the person's probation pursuant to Section 23602, except for good cause shown, for the failure to enroll in, participate in, or complete a program specified in subdivision (b).

(2) The court, in establishing reporting requirements, shall consult with the county alcohol program administrator. The county alcohol program administrator shall coordinate the reporting requirements with the department and with the State Department of Health Care Services. That reporting shall ensure that all persons who, after being ordered to attend and complete a program, may be identified for either (A) failure to enroll in, or failure to successfully complete, the program, or (B) successful completion of the program as ordered. *(Added by Stats.2004, c. 551 (S.B.1697), § 16.5, operative Sept. 20, 2005. Amended by Stats.2005, c. 164 (A.B.1353), § 3; Stats.2006, c. 692 (S.B.1756), § 6; Stats.2013, c. 22 (A.B.75), § 87, eff. June 27, 2013, operative July 1, 2013.)*

Cross References

County alcohol and drug problem assessment programs, mandatory participation for convicted violators of this section, see Vehicle Code § 23646.
Drug treatment programs, referral of first offenders, see Health and Safety Code § 11837.
Influence of alcoholic beverage or drug, suspension or revocation of driving privileges, see Vehicle Code § 13352.
Presentence investigation, see Vehicle Code § 23655.

Research References

2 Witkin, California Criminal Law 4th Crimes Against Public Peace and Welfare § 280 (2021), First Violation.
3 Witkin, California Criminal Law 4th Punishment § 666 (2021), Other Express Conditions.

§ 23540. Second offense; punishment

(a) If a person is convicted of a violation of Section 23152 and the offense occurred within 10 years of a separate violation of Section 23103, as specified in Section 23103.5, 23152, or 23153, that resulted in a conviction, that person shall be punished by imprisonment in the county jail for not less than 90 days nor more than one year and by a fine of not less than three hundred ninety dollars ($390) nor more than one thousand dollars ($1,000). The person's privilege to operate a motor vehicle shall be suspended by the department pursuant to paragraph (3) of subdivision (a) of Section 13352. The court shall require the person to surrender the driver's license to the court in accordance with Section 13550.

(b) Whenever, when considering the circumstances taken as a whole, the court determines that the person punished under this section would present a traffic safety or public safety risk if authorized to operate a motor vehicle during the period of suspension imposed under paragraph (3) of subdivision (a) of Section 13352, the court may disallow the issuance of a restricted driver's license required under Section 13352.5.

(c) This section shall become operative on September 20, 2005. *(Added by Stats.2004, c. 551 (S.B.1697), § 17.5, operative Sept. 20, 2005.)*

Cross References

Alcohol and drug problem assessment program, violator participation, sentencing, and assessment upon fine, see Vehicle Code § 23646 et seq.
Alcoholic beverages in vehicles, see Vehicle Code § 23220 et seq.
Applicability of this section to trolley coaches, see Vehicle Code § 21051.
Arrest without warrant, see Vehicle Code § 40300.5.
Challenging constitutional validity of separate conviction, see Vehicle Code § 41403.
Chemical blood, breath or urine tests, see Vehicle Code § 13353.
Chemical tests as evidence, see Vehicle Code § 23610.
Conviction of violation of specified subdivisions of Penal Code § 192 to be deemed conviction of violation of specified DUI provisions, see Vehicle Code § 13350.5.
Coroner's inquiry into deaths, see Government Code § 27491.25.
County alcohol and drug problem assessment programs, mandatory participation for convicted violators of this section, see Vehicle Code §§ 23646, 23647.
Crime of violence, within act for indemnification of victims of crime, see Government Code § 13960.
Defense of drug use to violations, see Vehicle Code § 23630.
Deposit in special account for each conviction under DUI provisions, see Penal Code § 1463.14.
Drivers license revocation, conviction of driver under eighteen, see Vehicle Code § 13352.3.
Driving school or instructor, revocation or suspension of license for violation of this section, see Vehicle Code § 11110.
Gross vehicular manslaughter while intoxicated, see Penal Code § 191.5.
Guilty plea, see Vehicle Code § 41610.
Impoundment of vehicle of registered owner convicted under this section, see Vehicle Code § 23594.
Influence of alcoholic beverage or drug, suspension or revocation of driving privileges, see Vehicle Code § 13352.
Injury to guest by intoxicated driver, see Vehicle Code § 17158.
Juvenile offenders, programs of supervision, see Welfare and Institutions Code § 654.1.
Manslaughter, negligent homicide by vehicle, see Penal Code § 192.
Nuisance, sale or other disposition of motor vehicle driven by defendant, see Vehicle Code § 23596.
Persons certified or granted probation on conviction of driving under the influence of alcohol or drugs or combined influence on certain conditions, restriction, revocation or suspension of driving privilege, consent to participation in treatment program, see Vehicle Code § 13352.5.
Please Don't Drink and Drive memorial signs, requests for and duration of placement, exception for a party to an accident convicted or determined to be mentally incompetent under this section, see Streets and Highways Code § 101.10.
Presentence investigation and assessment, see Vehicle Code § 23655.

Presumptions, see Evidence Code § 600 et seq.
Prior convictions under sections 23103, 23152 or 23153, effect on sentencing and driving privileges, see Vehicle Code § 23622.
Procedure on arrest for violation of this section, see Vehicle Code § 40302.
Records available to courts and law enforcement officials, incidents under certain DWI and homicide laws, period of time records must be available, see Vehicle Code § 1808.
Refusal to submit to alcohol testing under DUI laws, calculation of prior convictions, certain foreign convictions recognized, see Vehicle Code §§ 13353, 13353.1 and 13353.3.
Restricted driver's license, application of this section, see Vehicle Code § 13352.2.
Surrender of driver's license to court, see Vehicle Code § 13550.
Suspension or revocation of driving privilege for a violation of this section, notice by personal service, see Vehicle Code § 13106.
Suspension or revocation of license,
Generally, see Vehicle Code § 13352.
Alcohol-related accident within five years of vehicular manslaughter, see Vehicle Code § 13954.
Driver license compact, see Vehicle Code § 15000 et seq.
Driving after suspension or revocation, see Vehicle Code § 14601.2.
Investigation by department, three convictions in three years under this or other specified statutes, see Vehicle Code § 13800.
Prior convictions, record, see Vehicle Code § 13209.
Traffic violation point count, violation of this section, see Vehicle Code § 12810.
Traffic violators schools, suspension or revocation of license for violation of this section, see Vehicle Code § 11215.
Vehicular homicide, see Penal Code § 192.
Violation as misdemeanor, see Vehicle Code § 40000.15.
Violation of this section, relinquishment of motor vehicle to convicted minor, see Penal Code § 193.8.
Youthful drunk driver visitation program, see Vehicle Code § 23509 et seq.

Research References

2 Witkin, California Criminal Law 4th Crimes Against Public Peace and Welfare § 281 (2021), One Separate Conviction of Related Offense.
1 Witkin California Criminal Law 4th Crimes Against the Person § 269 (2021), Punishment.
1 Witkin California Criminal Law 4th Introduction to Crimes § 21 (2021), Recidivist Statutes.
3 Witkin, California Criminal Law 4th Punishment § 214 (2021), Drunk Driving.

§ 23542. Conditions of probation for second offense

(a)(1) If the court grants probation to a person punished under Section 23540, in addition to the provisions of Section 23600 and any other terms and conditions imposed by the court, the court shall impose as conditions of probation that the person be confined in county jail and fined under either of the following:

(A) For at least 10 days, but not more than one year, and pay a fine of at least three hundred ninety dollars ($390), but not more than one thousand dollars ($1,000).

(B) For at least 96 hours, but not more than one year, and pay a fine of at least three hundred ninety dollars ($390), but not more than one thousand dollars ($1,000). A sentence of 96 hours of confinement shall be served in two increments consisting of a continuous 48 hours each. The two 48–hour increments may be served nonconsecutively.

(2) The person's privilege to operate a motor vehicle shall be suspended by the department under paragraph (3) of subdivision (a) of Section 13352. The court shall require the person to surrender the driver's license to the court in accordance with Section 13550.

(b) In addition to the conditions specified in subdivision (a), the court shall require the person to do either of the following:

(1) Enroll and participate, for at least 18 months subsequent to the date of the underlying violation and in a manner satisfactory to the court, in a driving-under-the-influence program licensed pursuant to Section 11836 of the Health and Safety Code, as designated by the court. The person shall complete the entire program subsequent to, and shall not be given any credit for any program activities completed prior to, the date of the current violation. The program shall provide for persons who cannot afford the program fee pursuant to paragraph (2) of subdivision (b) of Section 11837.4 of the Health and Safety Code in order to enable those persons to participate.

(2) Enroll and participate, for at least 30 months subsequent to the date of the underlying violation and in a manner satisfactory to the court, in a driving-under-the-influence program licensed pursuant to Section 11836 of the Health and Safety Code. The person shall complete the entire program subsequent to, and shall not be given any credit for any program activities completed prior to, the date of the current violation.

(c) The court shall advise the person at the time of sentencing that the driving privilege shall not be restored until proof satisfactory to the Department of Motor Vehicles of successful completion of a driving-under-the-influence program of the length required under this code licensed pursuant to Section 11836 of the Health and Safety Code has been received in the department's headquarters.

(d) Whenever, when considering the circumstances taken as a whole, the court determines that the person punished under this section would present a traffic safety or public safety risk if authorized to operate a motor vehicle during the period of suspension imposed under paragraph (3) of subdivision (a) of Section 13352, the court may disallow the issuance of a restricted driver's license required under Section 13352.5.

(e) This section shall become operative on September 20, 2005. *(Added by Stats.2004, c. 551 (S.B.1697), § 18.5, operative Sept. 20, 2005.)*

Cross References

Persons certified or granted probation on conviction or driving under the influence of alcohol or drugs or combined influence on certain conditions, restriction, revocation or suspension of driving privilege, consent to participation in treatment program, see Vehicle Code § 13352.5.
Presentence investigation, see Vehicle Code § 23655.
Restricted driver's license, application of this section, see Vehicle Code § 13352.2.

Research References

2 Witkin, California Criminal Law 4th Crimes Against Public Peace and Welfare § 281 (2021), One Separate Conviction of Related Offense.
3 Witkin, California Criminal Law 4th Punishment § 218 (2021), Effect of Criminal Proceedings.

§ 23546. Third offense; punishment

(a) If a person is convicted of a violation of Section 23152 and the offense occurred within 10 years of two separate violations of Section 23103, as specified in Section 23103.5, 23152, or 23153, or any combination thereof, that resulted in convictions, that person shall be punished by imprisonment in the county jail for not less than 120 days nor more than one year and by a fine of not less than three hundred ninety dollars ($390) nor more than one thousand dollars ($1,000). The person's privilege to operate a motor vehicle shall be revoked by the Department of Motor Vehicles as required in paragraph (5) of subdivision (a) of Section 13352. The court shall require the person to surrender his or her driver's license to the court in accordance with Section 13550.

(b) A person convicted of a violation of Section 23152 punishable under this section shall be designated as a habitual traffic offender for a period of three years, subsequent to the conviction. The person shall be advised of this designation pursuant to subdivision (b) of Section 13350. *(Added by Stats.1998, c. 118 (S.B.1186), § 84, operative July 1, 1999. Amended by Stats.1999, c. 22 (S.B.24), § 34, eff. May 26, 1999, operative July 1, 1999; Stats.2002, c. 545 (S.B.1852), § 23; Stats.2004, c. 550 (S.B.1694), § 14.)*

Cross References

Alcohol and drug problem assessment program, violator participation, sentencing, and assessment upon fine, see Vehicle Code § 23646 et seq.

Alcoholic beverages in vehicles, see Vehicle Code § 23220 et seq.
Applicability of this section to trolley coaches, see Vehicle Code § 21051.
Arrest without warrant, see Vehicle Code § 40300.5.
Challenging constitutional validity of separate conviction, see Vehicle Code § 41403.
Chemical blood, breath or urine tests, see Vehicle Code § 13353.
Chemical tests as evidence, see Vehicle Code § 23610.
Conviction of violation of specified subdivisions of Penal Code § 192 to be deemed conviction of violation of specified DUI provisions, see Vehicle Code § 13350.5.
Coroner's inquiry into deaths, see Government Code § 27491.25.
County alcohol and drug problem assessment programs, mandatory participation for convicted violators of this section, see Vehicle Code §§ 23646, 23647.
Crime of violence, within act for indemnification of victims of crime, see Government Code § 13960.
Defense of drug use to violations, see Vehicle Code § 23630.
Deposit in special account for each conviction under DUI provisions, see Penal Code § 1463.14.
Drivers license revocation, conviction of driver under eighteen, see Vehicle Code § 13352.3.
Driving school or instructor, revocation or suspension of license for violation of this section, see Vehicle Code § 11110.
Gross vehicular manslaughter while intoxicated, see Penal Code § 191.5.
Guilty plea, see Vehicle Code § 41610.
Impoundment of vehicle of registered owner convicted under this section, see Vehicle Code § 23594.
Influence of alcoholic beverage or drug, suspension or revocation of driving privileges, see Vehicle Code § 13352.
Injury to guest by intoxicated driver, see Vehicle Code § 17158.
Juvenile offenders, programs of supervision, see Welfare and Institutions Code § 654.1.
Manslaughter, negligent homicide by vehicle, see Penal Code § 192.
Nuisance, sale or other disposition of motor vehicle driven by defendant, see Vehicle Code § 23596.
Persons certified or granted probation on conviction of driving under the influence of alcohol or drugs or combined influence on certain conditions, restriction, revocation or suspension of driving privilege, consent to participation in treatment program, see Vehicle Code § 13352.5.
Please Don't Drink and Drive memorial signs, requests for and duration of placement, exception for a party to an accident convicted or determined to be mentally incompetent under this section, see Streets and Highways Code § 101.10.
Presentence investigation and assessment, see Vehicle Code § 23655.
Presumptions, see Evidence Code § 600 et seq.
Prior convictions under sections 23103, 23152 or 23153, effect on sentencing and driving privileges, see Vehicle Code § 23622.
Procedure on arrest for violation of this section, see Vehicle Code § 40302.
Records available to courts and law enforcement officials, incidents under certain DWI and homicide laws, period of time records must be available, see Vehicle Code § 1808.
Refusal to submit to alcohol testing under DUI laws, calculation of prior convictions, certain foreign convictions recognized, see Vehicle Code §§ 13353, 13353.1 and 13353.3.
Surrender of driver's license to court, see Vehicle Code § 13550.
Suspension or revocation of driving privilege for a violation of this section, notice by personal service, see Vehicle Code § 13106.
Suspension or revocation of license,
  Generally, see Vehicle Code § 13352.
  Alcohol-related accident within five years of vehicular manslaughter, see Vehicle Code § 13954.
  Driver license compact, see Vehicle Code § 15000 et seq.
  Driving after suspension or revocation, see Vehicle Code § 14601.2.
  Investigation by department, three convictions in three years under this or other specified statutes, see Vehicle Code § 13800.
  Prior convictions, record, see Vehicle Code § 13209.
Traffic violation point count, violation of this section, see Vehicle Code § 12810.
Traffic violators schools, suspension or revocation of license for violation of this section, see Vehicle Code § 11215.
Vehicular homicide, see Penal Code § 192.
Violation as misdemeanor, see Vehicle Code § 40000.15.
Violation of this section, relinquishment of motor vehicle to convicted minor, see Penal Code § 193.8.
Youthful drunk driver visitation program, see Vehicle Code § 23509 et seq.

Research References

2 Witkin, California Criminal Law 4th Crimes Against Public Peace and Welfare § 279 (2021), In General.
2 Witkin, California Criminal Law 4th Crimes Against Public Peace and Welfare § 282 (2021), Two Separate Convictions of Related Offenses.
3 Witkin, California Criminal Law 4th Punishment § 214 (2021), Drunk Driving.

§ 23548. Conditions of probation for third offense

(a)(1) If the court grants probation to any person punished under Section 23546, in addition to the provisions of Section 23600 and any other terms and conditions imposed by the court, the court shall impose as conditions of probation that the person be confined in the county jail for at least 120 days but not more than one year and pay a fine of at least three hundred ninety dollars ($390) but not more than one thousand dollars ($1,000).

(2) The person's privilege to operate a motor vehicle shall be revoked by the department under paragraph (5) of subdivision (a) of Section 13352. The court shall require the person to surrender the driver's license to the court in accordance with Section 13550.

(b) In addition to subdivision (a), if the court grants probation to any person punished under Section 23546, the court may order as a condition of probation that the person participate, for at least 30 months subsequent to the underlying conviction and in a manner satisfactory to the court, in a driving-under-the-influence program licensed pursuant to Section 11836 of the Health and Safety Code. In lieu of the minimum term of imprisonment specified in subdivision (a), the court shall impose as a condition of probation under this subdivision that the person be confined in the county jail for at least 30 days but not more than one year. The court shall not order the treatment prescribed by this subdivision unless the person makes a specific request and shows good cause for the order, whether or not the person has previously completed a treatment program pursuant to paragraph (4) of subdivision (b) of Section 23542 or paragraph (4) of subdivision (b) of Section 23562. In order to enable all required persons to participate, each person shall pay the program costs commensurate with the person's ability to pay as determined pursuant to Section 11837.4 of the Health and Safety Code. No condition of probation required pursuant to this subdivision is a basis for reducing any other probation requirement in this section or Section 23600 or for avoiding the mandatory license revocation provisions of paragraph (5) of subdivision (a) of Section 13352.

(c) In addition to the provisions of Section 23600 and subdivision (a), if the court grants probation to any person punished under Section 23546 who has not previously completed a treatment program pursuant to paragraph (4) of subdivision (b) of Section 23542 or paragraph (4) of subdivision (b) of Section 23562, and unless the person is ordered to participate in and complete a driving-under-the-influence program under subdivision (b), the court shall impose as a condition of probation that the person, subsequent to the date of the current violation, enroll and participate, for at least 18 months and in a manner satisfactory to the court, in a driving-under-the-influence program licensed pursuant to Section 11836 of the Health and Safety Code, as designated by the court. The person shall complete the entire program subsequent to, and shall not be given any credit for program activities completed prior to, the date of the current violation. Any person who has previously completed a 12–month or 18–month program licensed pursuant to Section 11836 of the Health and Safety Code shall not be eligible for referral pursuant to this subdivision unless a 30–month licensed driving-under-the-influence program is not available for referral in the county of the person's residence or employment. The program shall provide for persons who cannot afford the program fee pursuant to paragraph (2) of subdivision (b) of Section 11837.4 of the Health and Safety Code in order to enable those persons to participate. No condition of probation required pursuant to this subdivision is a basis for reducing any other probation requirement in this section or Section 23600 or for avoiding the mandatory license revocation provisions of paragraph (5) of subdivision (a) of Section 13352.

(d) The court shall advise the person at the time of sentencing that the driving privilege may not be restored until the person provides proof satisfactory to the department of successful completion of a driving-under-the-influence program of the length required under this code that is licensed pursuant to Section 11836 of the Health and Safety Code.

(e) This section shall become operative on September 20, 2005. *(Added by Stats.1998, c. 118 (S.B.1186), § 84, operative July 1, 1999. Amended by Stats.2002, c. 545 (S.B.1852), § 24; Stats.2004, c. 551 (S.B.1697), § 19, operative Sept. 20, 2005.)*

Cross References

Conviction for driving under the influence or engaging in speed contests or exhibitions of speed, suspension or revocation of license, eligibility for restricted license, reinstatement conditions, see Vehicle Code § 13352.

Research References

2 Witkin, California Criminal Law 4th Crimes Against Public Peace and Welfare § 282 (2021), Two Separate Convictions of Related Offenses.

§ 23550. Multiple offenses within 10 years; punishment; habitual traffic offender designation

(a) If a person is convicted of a violation of Section 23152 and the offense occurred within 10 years of three or more separate violations of Section 23103, as specified in Section 23103.5, or Section 23152 or 23153, or any combination thereof, that resulted in convictions, that person shall be punished by imprisonment pursuant to subdivision (h) of Section 1170 of the Penal Code, or in a county jail for not less than 180 days nor more than one year, and by a fine of not less than three hundred ninety dollars ($390) nor more than one thousand dollars ($1,000). The person's privilege to operate a motor vehicle shall be revoked by the Department of Motor Vehicles pursuant to paragraph (7) of subdivision (a) of Section 13352. The court shall require the person to surrender the driver's license to the court in accordance with Section 13550.

(b) A person convicted of a violation of Section 23152 punishable under this section shall be designated as a habitual traffic offender for a period of three years, subsequent to the conviction. The person shall be advised of this designation pursuant to subdivision (b) of Section 13350. *(Added by Stats.1998, c. 118 (S.B.1186), § 84, operative July 1, 1999. Amended by Stats.1999, c. 22 (S.B.24), § 34.2, eff. May 26, 1999, operative July 1, 1999; Stats.2002, c. 545 (S.B.1852), § 25; Stats.2004, c. 550 (S.B.1694), § 15; Stats.2009, c. 193 (S.B.598), § 4, operative July 1, 2010; Stats.2010, c. 301 (A.B.1601), § 3; Stats.2011, c. 15 (A.B.109), § 614, eff. April 4, 2011, operative Oct. 1, 2011.)*

Cross References

Alcohol and drug problem assessment program, violator participation, sentencing, and assessment upon fine, see Vehicle Code § 23646 et seq.
Alcoholic beverages in vehicles, see Vehicle Code § 23220 et seq.
Applicability of this section to trolley coaches, see Vehicle Code § 21051.
Arrest without warrant, see Vehicle Code § 40300.5.
Challenging constitutional validity of separate conviction, see Vehicle Code § 41403.
Chemical blood, breath or urine tests, see Vehicle Code § 13353.
Chemical tests as evidence, see Vehicle Code § 23610.
Conviction of violation of specified subdivisions of Penal Code § 192 to be deemed conviction of violation of specified DUI provisions, see Vehicle Code § 13350.5.
Coroner's inquiry into deaths, see Government Code § 27491.25.
County alcohol and drug problem assessment programs, mandatory participation for convicted violators of this section, see Vehicle Code §§ 23646, 23647.
Crime of violence, within act for indemnification of victims of crime, see Government Code § 13960.
Defense of drug use to violations, see Vehicle Code § 23630.
Deposit in special account for each conviction under DUI provisions, see Penal Code § 1463.14.
Drivers license revocation, conviction of driver under eighteen, see Vehicle Code § 13352.3.
Driving school or instructor, revocation or suspension of license for violation of this section, see Vehicle Code § 11110.
Gross vehicular manslaughter while intoxicated, see Penal Code § 191.5.
Guilty plea, see Vehicle Code § 41610.
Impoundment of vehicle of registered owner convicted under this section, see Vehicle Code § 23594.
Influence of alcoholic beverage or drug, suspension or revocation of driving privileges, see Vehicle Code § 13352.
Injury to guest by intoxicated driver, see Vehicle Code § 17158.
Juvenile offenders, programs of supervision, see Welfare and Institutions Code § 654.1.
Manslaughter, negligent homicide by vehicle, see Penal Code § 192.
Nuisance, sale or other disposition of motor vehicle driven by defendant, see Vehicle Code § 23596.
Persons certified or granted probation on conviction of driving under the influence of alcohol or drugs or combined influence on certain conditions, restriction, revocation or suspension of driving privilege, consent to participation in treatment program, see Vehicle Code § 13352.5.
Please Don't Drink and Drive memorial signs, requests for and duration of placement, exception for a party to an accident convicted or determined to be mentally incompetent under this section, see Streets and Highways Code § 101.10.
Presentence investigation and assessment, see Vehicle Code § 23655.
Presumptions, see Evidence Code § 600 et seq.
Prior convictions under sections 23103, 23152 or 23153, effect on sentencing and driving privileges, see Vehicle Code § 23622.
Procedure on arrest for violation of this section, see Vehicle Code § 40302.
Records available to courts and law enforcement officials, incidents under certain DWI and homicide laws, period of time records must be available, see Vehicle Code § 1808.
Refusal to submit to alcohol testing under DUI laws, calculation of prior convictions, certain foreign convictions recognized, see Vehicle Code §§ 13353, 13353.1 and 13353.3.
Surrender of driver's license to court, see Vehicle Code § 13550.
Suspension or revocation of driving privilege for a violation of this section, notice by personal service, see Vehicle Code § 13106.
Suspension or revocation of license,
  Generally, see Vehicle Code § 13352.
  Alcohol-related accident within five years of vehicular manslaughter, see Vehicle Code § 13954.
  Driver license compact, see Vehicle Code § 15000 et seq.
  Driving after suspension or revocation, see Vehicle Code § 14601.2.
  Investigation by department, three convictions in three years under this or other specified statutes, see Vehicle Code § 13800.
  Prior convictions, record, see Vehicle Code § 13209.
Traffic violation point count, violation of this section, see Vehicle Code § 12810.
Traffic violators schools, suspension or revocation of license for violation of this section, see Vehicle Code § 11215.
Vehicular homicide, see Penal Code § 192.
Violation as misdemeanor, see Vehicle Code § 40000.15.
Violation of this section, relinquishment of motor vehicle to convicted minor, see Penal Code § 193.8.
Youthful drunk driver visitation program, see Vehicle Code § 23509 et seq.

Research References

California Jury Instructions - Criminal 12.65, Driving Under the Influence, etc.—Felony Prosecutions.
California Jury Instructions - Criminal 12.66, Driving With 0.08 Percent Blood Alcohol—Felony Prosecutions.
2 Witkin, California Criminal Law 4th Crimes Against Public Peace and Welfare § 283 (2021), Three or More Separate Convictions of Related Offenses.
2 Witkin, California Criminal Law 4th Crimes Against Public Peace and Welfare § 287 (2021), Two or More Separate Convictions of Related Offenses.
2 Witkin, California Criminal Law 4th Crimes Against Public Peace and Welfare § 289 (2021), Prior Violation Punished as Felony.
2 Witkin, California Criminal Law 4th Crimes Against Public Peace and Welfare § 292 (2021), Time of Separate Convictions.
1 Witkin California Criminal Law 4th Introduction to Crimes § 21 (2021), Recidivist Statutes.

1 Witkin California Criminal Law 4th Introduction to Crimes § 77 (2021), Illustrations: Special Statute is Not Controlling.

4 Witkin, California Criminal Law 4th Pretrial Proceedings § 247 (2021), In General.

3 Witkin, California Criminal Law 4th Punishment § 214 (2021), Drunk Driving.

§ 23550.5. Additional public offense for multiple driving under the influence violations within 10 years; punishment; habitual traffic offender designation

(a) A person is guilty of a public offense, punishable by imprisonment in the state prison or confinement in a county jail for not more than one year and by a fine of not less than three hundred ninety dollars ($390) nor more than one thousand dollars ($1,000) if that person is convicted of a violation of Section 23152 or 23153, and the offense occurred within 10 years of any of the following:

(1) A separate violation of Section 23152 that was punished as a felony under Section 23550 or this section, or both, or under former Section 23175 or former Section 23175.5, or both.

(2) A separate violation of Section 23153 that was punished as a felony.

(3) A separate violation of paragraph (1) of subdivision (c) of Section 192 of the Penal Code that was punished as a felony.

(b) Each person who, having previously been convicted of a violation of subdivision (a) of Section 191.5 of the Penal Code, a felony violation of subdivision (b) of Section 191.5, or a violation of subdivision (a) of Section 192.5 of the Penal Code, is subsequently convicted of a violation of Section 23152 or 23153 is guilty of a public offense punishable by imprisonment in the state prison or confinement in a county jail for not more than one year and by a fine of not less than three hundred ninety dollars ($390) nor more than one thousand dollars ($1,000).

(c) The privilege to operate a motor vehicle of a person convicted of a violation that is punishable under subdivision (a) or (b) shall be revoked by the department pursuant to paragraph (7) of subdivision (a) of Section 13352, unless paragraph (6) of subdivision (a) of Section 13352 is also applicable, in which case the privilege shall be revoked under that provision. The court shall require the person to surrender the driver's license to the court in accordance with Section 13550.

(d) A person convicted of a violation of Section 23152 or 23153 that is punishable under this section shall be designated as a habitual traffic offender for a period of three years, subsequent to the conviction. The person shall be advised of this designation under subdivision (b) of Section 13350. *(Added by Stats.1998, c. 118 (S.B.1186), § 84, operative July 1, 1999. Amended by Stats.1999, c. 22 (S.B.24), § 34.6, eff. May 26, 1999, operative July 1, 1999; Stats.1999, c. 706 (A.B.1236), § 14, eff. Oct. 10, 1999; Stats.2001, c. 849 (A.B.1078), § 1; Stats.2002, c. 545 (S.B.1852), § 26; Stats.2007, c. 747 (A.B.678), § 33; Stats.2009, c. 193 (S.B.598), § 5, operative July 1, 2010; Stats.2010, c. 301 (A.B.1601), § 4; Stats.2014, c. 509 (A.B. 2690), § 1, eff. Jan. 1, 2015.)*

Cross References

Alcohol and drug problem assessment program, violator participation, sentencing, and assessment upon fine, see Vehicle Code § 23646 et seq.

Alcoholic beverages in vehicles, see Vehicle Code § 23220 et seq.

Applicability of this section to trolley coaches, see Vehicle Code § 21051.

Arrest without warrant, see Vehicle Code § 40300.5.

Challenging constitutional validity of separate conviction, see Vehicle Code § 41403.

Chemical blood, breath or urine tests, see Vehicle Code § 13353.

Chemical tests as evidence, see Vehicle Code § 23610.

Conviction of violation of specified subdivisions of Penal Code § 192 to be deemed conviction of violation of specified DUI provisions, see Vehicle Code § 13350.5.

Coroner's inquiry into deaths, see Government Code § 27491.25.

County alcohol and drug problem assessment programs, mandatory participation for convicted violators of this section, see Vehicle Code §§ 23646, 23647.

Crime of violence, within act for indemnification of victims of crime, see Government Code § 13960.

Defense of drug use to violations, see Vehicle Code § 23630.

Deposit in special account for each conviction under DUI provisions, see Penal Code § 1463.14.

Drivers license revocation, conviction of driver under eighteen, see Vehicle Code § 13352.3.

Driving school or instructor, revocation or suspension of license for violation of this section, see Vehicle Code § 11110.

Gross vehicular manslaughter while intoxicated, see Penal Code § 191.5.

Guilty plea, see Vehicle Code § 41610.

Impoundment of vehicle of registered owner convicted under this section, see Vehicle Code § 23594.

Influence of alcoholic beverage or drug, suspension or revocation of driving privileges, see Vehicle Code § 13352.

Injury to guest by intoxicated driver, see Vehicle Code § 17158.

Juvenile offenders, programs of supervision, see Welfare and Institutions Code § 654.1.

Manslaughter, negligent homicide by vehicle, see Penal Code § 192.

Nuisance, sale or other disposition of motor vehicle driven by defendant, see Vehicle Code § 23596.

Persons certified or granted probation on conviction of driving under the influence of alcohol or drugs or combined influence on certain conditions, restriction, revocation or suspension of driving privilege, consent to participation in treatment program, see Vehicle Code § 13352.5.

Please Don't Drink and Drive memorial signs, requests for and duration of placement, exception for a party to an accident convicted or determined to be mentally incompetent under this section, see Streets and Highways Code § 101.10.

Presentence investigation and assessment, see Vehicle Code § 23655.

Presumptions, see Evidence Code § 600 et seq.

Prior convictions under sections 23103, 23152 or 23153, effect on sentencing and driving privileges, see Vehicle Code § 23622.

Procedure on arrest for violation of this section, see Vehicle Code § 40302.

Records available to courts and law enforcement officials, incidents under certain DWI and homicide laws, period of time records must be available, see Vehicle Code § 1808.

Records open to public inspection, criminal records, see Vehicle Code § 1808.

Refusal to submit to alcohol testing under DUI laws, calculation of prior convictions, certain foreign convictions recognized, see Vehicle Code §§ 13353, 13353.1 and 13353.3.

Surrender of driver's license to court, see Vehicle Code § 13550.

Suspension or revocation of driving privilege for a violation of this section, notice by personal service, see Vehicle Code § 13106.

Suspension or revocation of license,

Generally, see Vehicle Code § 13352.

Alcohol-related accident within five years of vehicular manslaughter, see Vehicle Code § 13954.

Driver license compact, see Vehicle Code § 15000 et seq.

Driving after suspension or revocation, see Vehicle Code § 14601.2.

Investigation by department, three convictions in three years under this or other specified statutes, see Vehicle Code § 13800.

Prior convictions, record, see Vehicle Code § 13209.

Traffic violation point count, violation of this section, see Vehicle Code § 12810.

Traffic violators schools, suspension or revocation of license for violation of this section, see Vehicle Code § 11215.

Vehicular homicide, see Penal Code § 192.

Violation as misdemeanor, see Vehicle Code § 40000.15.

Violation of this section, relinquishment of motor vehicle to convicted minor, see Penal Code § 193.8.

Youthful drunk driver visitation program, see Vehicle Code § 23509 et seq.

Research References

California Jury Instructions - Criminal 12.65, Driving Under the Influence, etc.—Felony Prosecutions.

California Jury Instructions - Criminal 12.66, Driving With 0.08 Percent Blood Alcohol—Felony Prosecutions.

California Jury Instructions - Criminal 12.67, Felony Driving Under the Influence—Priors.

California Jury Instructions - Criminal 12.68, Felony Driving With 0.08 Percent.

2 Witkin, California Criminal Law 4th Crimes Against Public Peace and Welfare § 279 (2021), In General.

2 Witkin, California Criminal Law 4th Crimes Against Public Peace and Welfare § 283 (2021), Three or More Separate Convictions of Related Offenses.
2 Witkin, California Criminal Law 4th Crimes Against Public Peace and Welfare § 287 (2021), Two or More Separate Convictions of Related Offenses.
2 Witkin, California Criminal Law 4th Crimes Against Public Peace and Welfare § 289 (2021), Prior Violation Punished as Felony.
3 Witkin, California Criminal Law 4th Punishment § 214 (2021), Drunk Driving.
3 Witkin, California Criminal Law 4th Punishment § 435 (2021), Dual Use of Prior Conviction.

§ 23552. Additional conditions of probation for multiple offenses; condition upon restoration of driving privilege

(a)(1) If the court grants probation to a person punished under Section 23550, in addition to the provisions of Section 23600 and any other terms and conditions imposed by the court, the court shall impose as conditions of probation that the person be confined in a county jail for at least 180 days but not more than one year and pay a fine of at least three hundred ninety dollars ($390) but not more than one thousand dollars ($1,000).

(2) The person's privilege to operate a motor vehicle shall be revoked by the department under paragraph (7) of subdivision (a) of Section 13352. The court shall require the person to surrender the driver's license to the court in accordance with Section 13550.

(b) In addition to subdivision (a), if the court grants probation to any person punished under Section 23550, the court may order as a condition of probation that the person participate, for at least 30 months subsequent to the underlying conviction and in a manner satisfactory to the court, in a driving-under-the-influence program licensed pursuant to Section 11836 of the Health and Safety Code. In lieu of the minimum term of imprisonment in subdivision (a), the court shall impose as a condition of probation under this subdivision that the person be confined in the county jail for at least 30 days but not more than one year. The court shall not order the treatment prescribed by this subdivision unless the person makes a specific request and shows good cause for the order, whether or not the person has previously completed a treatment program pursuant to subdivision (b) of Section 23542 or paragraph (4) of subdivision (b) of Section 23562. In order to enable all required persons to participate, each person shall pay the program costs commensurate with the person's ability to pay as determined pursuant to Section 11837.4 of the Health and Safety Code. No condition of probation required pursuant to this subdivision is a basis for reducing any other probation requirement in this section or Section 23600 or for avoiding the mandatory license revocation provisions of paragraph (7) of subdivision (a) of Section 13352.

(c) In addition to Section 23600 and subdivision (a), if the court grants probation to any person punished under Section 23550 who has not previously completed a treatment program pursuant to subdivision (b) of Section 23542 or paragraph (4) of subdivision (b) of Section 23562, and unless the person is ordered to participate in, and complete, a program under subdivision (b), the court shall impose as a condition of probation that the person, subsequent to the date of the current violation, enroll in and participate, for at least 18 months and in a manner satisfactory to the court, in a driving-under-the- influence program licensed pursuant to Section 11836 of the Health and Safety Code, as designated by the court. The person shall complete the entire program subsequent to, and shall not be given any credit for program activities completed prior to, the date of the current violation. A person who has previously completed a 12–month or 18–month driving-under-the- influence program licensed pursuant to Section 11836 of the Health and Safety Code shall not be eligible for referral pursuant to this subdivision unless a 30–month driving-under-the-influence program licensed pursuant to Section 11836 of the Health and Safety Code is not available for referral in the county of the person's residence or employment. A condition of probation required pursuant to this subdivision is not a basis for reducing any other probation requirement in this section or Section 23600 or for avoiding the mandatory license revocation provisions of paragraph (7) of subdivision (a) of Section 13352.

(d) The court shall advise the person at the time of sentencing that the driving privilege may not be restored until the person provides proof satisfactory to the department of successful completion of a driving-under-the-influence program of the length required under this code that is licensed pursuant to Section 11836 of the Health and Safety Code. *(Added by Stats.1998, c. 118 (S.B.1186), § 84, operative July 1, 1999. Amended by Stats.1999, c. 22 (S.B.24), § 35.7, eff. May 26, 1999, operative July 1, 1999; Stats.2002, c. 545 (S.B.1852), § 27; Stats.2004, c. 551 (S.B.1697), § 20, operative Sept. 20, 2005; Stats. 2009, c. 193 (S.B.598), § 6, operative July 1, 2010; Stats.2010, c. 301 (A.B.1601), § 5.)*

Research References

2 Witkin, California Criminal Law 4th Crimes Against Public Peace and Welfare § 283 (2021), Three or More Separate Convictions of Related Offenses.

ARTICLE 3. PENALTIES FOR A VIOLATION OF SECTION 23153

§ 23554. First offense; punishment

If any person is convicted of a first violation of Section 23153, that person shall be punished by imprisonment in the state prison, or in a county jail for not less than 90 days nor more than one year, and by a fine of not less than three hundred ninety dollars ($390) nor more than one thousand dollars ($1,000). The person's privilege to operate a motor vehicle shall be suspended by the Department of Motor Vehicles pursuant to paragraph (2) of subdivision (a) of Section 13352. The court shall require the person to surrender the driver's license to the court in accordance with Section 13550. *(Added by Stats.1998, c. 118 (S.B.1186), § 84, operative July 1, 1999. Amended by Stats.2002, c. 545 (S.B.1852), § 28.)*

Cross References

Alcohol and drug problem assessment program, violator participation, sentencing, and assessment upon fine, see Vehicle Code § 23646 et seq.
Alcoholic beverages in vehicles, see Vehicle Code § 23220 et seq.
Applicability of this section to trolley coaches, see Vehicle Code § 21051.
Arrest without warrant, see Vehicle Code § 40300.5.
Challenging constitutional validity of separate conviction, see Vehicle Code § 41403.
Chemical blood, breath or urine tests, see Vehicle Code § 13353.
Chemical tests as evidence, see Vehicle Code § 23610.
Conviction of violation of specified subdivisions of Penal Code § 192 to be deemed conviction of violation of specified DUI provisions, see Vehicle Code § 13350.5.
Coroner's inquiry into deaths, see Government Code § 27491.25.
County alcohol and drug problem assessment programs, mandatory participation for convicted violators of this section, see Vehicle Code §§ 23646, 23647.
Crime of violence, within act for indemnification of victims of crime, see Government Code § 13960.
Defense of drug use to violations, see Vehicle Code § 23630.

Deposit in special account for each conviction under DUI provisions, see Penal Code § 1463.14.
Drivers license revocation, conviction of driver under eighteen, see Vehicle Code § 13352.3.
Driving school or instructor, revocation or suspension of license for violation of this section, see Vehicle Code § 11110.
Gross vehicular manslaughter while intoxicated, see Penal Code § 191.5.
Guilty plea, see Vehicle Code § 41610.
Impoundment of vehicle of registered owner convicted under this section, see Vehicle Code § 23594.
Influence of alcoholic beverage or drug, suspension or revocation of driving privileges, see Vehicle Code § 13352.
Injury to guest by intoxicated driver, see Vehicle Code § 17158.
Juvenile offenders, programs of supervision, see Welfare and Institutions Code § 654.1.
Manslaughter, negligent homicide by vehicle, see Penal Code § 192.
Nuisance, sale or other disposition of motor vehicle driven by defendant, see Vehicle Code § 23596.
Persons certified or granted probation on conviction of driving under the influence of alcohol or drugs or combined influence on certain conditions, restriction, revocation or suspension of driving privilege, consent to participation in treatment program, see Vehicle Code § 13352.5.
Please Don't Drink and Drive memorial signs, requests for and duration of placement, exception for a party to an accident convicted or determined to be mentally incompetent under this section, see Streets and Highways Code § 101.10.
Presentence investigation and assessment, see Vehicle Code § 23655.
Presumptions, see Evidence Code § 600 et seq.
Prior convictions under sections 23103, 23152 or 23153, effect on sentencing and driving privileges, see Vehicle Code § 23622.
Procedure on arrest for violation of this section, see Vehicle Code § 40302.
Records available to courts and law enforcement officials, incidents under certain DWI and homicide laws, period of time records must be available, see Vehicle Code § 1808.
Refusal to submit to alcohol testing under DUI laws, calculation of prior convictions, certain foreign convictions recognized, see Vehicle Code §§ 13353, 13353.1 and 13353.3.
Surrender of driver's license to court, see Vehicle Code § 13550.
Suspension or revocation of driving privilege for a violation of this section, notice by personal service, see Vehicle Code § 13106.
Suspension or revocation of license,
 Generally, see Vehicle Code § 13352.
 Alcohol-related accident within five years of vehicular manslaughter, see Vehicle Code § 13954.
 Driver license compact, see Vehicle Code § 15000 et seq.
 Driving after suspension or revocation, see Vehicle Code § 14601.2.
 Investigation by department, three convictions in three years under this or other specified statutes, see Vehicle Code § 13800.
 Prior convictions, record, see Vehicle Code § 13209.
Traffic violation point count, violation of this section, see Vehicle Code § 12810.
Traffic violators schools, suspension or revocation of license for violation of this section, see Vehicle Code § 11215.
Vehicular homicide, see Penal Code § 192.
Violation as misdemeanor, see Vehicle Code § 40000.15.
Violation of this section, relinquishment of motor vehicle to convicted minor, see Penal Code § 193.8.
Youthful drunk driver visitation program, see Vehicle Code § 23509 et seq.

Research References

2 Witkin, California Criminal Law 4th Crimes Against Public Peace and Welfare § 285 (2021), First Violation.

§ 23556. Conditions of probation for first offense

(a)(1) If the court grants probation to any person punished under Section 23554, in addition to the provisions of Section 23600 and any other terms and conditions imposed by the court, the court shall impose as a condition of probation that the person be confined in the county jail for at least five days but not more than one year and pay a fine of at least three hundred ninety dollars ($390) but not more than one thousand dollars ($1,000).

(2) The person's privilege to operate a motor vehicle shall be suspended by the department under paragraph (2) of subdivision (a) of Section 13352. The court shall require the person to surrender the driver's license to the court in accordance with Section 13550.

(b)(1) In a county where the county alcohol program administrator has certified, and the board of supervisors has approved, a program or programs, the court shall also impose as a condition of probation that the driver shall participate in, and successfully complete, an alcohol and other drug education and counseling program, established pursuant to Section 11837.3 of the Health and Safety Code, as designated by the court.

(2) In any county where the board of supervisors has approved and the State Department of Health Care Services has licensed an alcohol and other drug education and counseling program, the court shall also impose as a condition of probation that the driver enroll in, participate in, and successfully complete, a driving-under-the-influence program licensed pursuant to Section 11836 of the Health and Safety Code, in the driver's county of residence or employment, as designated by the court. For the purposes of this paragraph, enrollment in, participation in, and completion of, an approved program shall be subsequent to the date of the current violation. Credit may not be given to any program activities completed prior to the date of the current violation.

(3) The court shall refer a first offender whose blood-alcohol concentration was less than 0.20 percent, by weight, to participate for three months or longer, as ordered by the court, in a licensed program that consists of at least 30 hours of program activities, including those education, group counseling, and individual interview sessions described in Chapter 9 (commencing with Section 11836) of Part 2 of Division 10.5 of the Health and Safety Code.

(4) The court shall refer a first offender whose blood-alcohol concentration was 0.20 percent or more, by weight, or who refused to take a chemical test, to participate for nine months or longer, as ordered by the court, in a licensed program that consists of at least 60 hours of program activities, including those education, group counseling, and individual interview sessions described in Chapter 9 (commencing with Section 11836) of Part 2 of Division 10.5 of the Health and Safety Code.

(c)(1) The court shall revoke the person's probation pursuant to Section 23602, except for good cause shown, for the failure to enroll in, participate in, or complete a program specified in subdivision (b).

(2) The court, in establishing reporting requirements, shall consult with the county alcohol program administrator. The county alcohol program administrator shall coordinate the reporting requirements with the department and with the State Department of Health Care Services. That reporting shall ensure that all persons who, after being ordered to attend and complete a program, may be identified for either (A) failure to enroll in, or failure to successfully complete, the program, or (B) successful completion of the program as ordered.

(d) The court shall advise the person at the time of sentencing that the driving privilege shall not be restored until the person has provided proof satisfactory to the department of successful completion of a driving-under-the-influence program of the length required under this code that is licensed pursuant to Section 11836 of the Health and Safety Code.

(e) This section shall become operative on September 20, 2005.

(Added by Stats.1998, c. 118 (S.B.1186), § 84, operative July 1, 1999. Amended by Stats.2002, c. 545 (S.B.1852), § 29; Stats.2004, c. 551 (S.B.1697), § 21, operative Sept. 20, 2005; Stats.2005, c. 164 (A.B. 1353), § 4; Stats.2013, c. 22 (A.B.75), § 88, eff. June 27, 2013, operative July 1, 2013.)

Cross References

County alcohol and drug problem assessment programs, mandatory participation for convicted violators of this section, see Vehicle Code § 23646.

Research References

2 Witkin, California Criminal Law 4th Crimes Against Public Peace and Welfare § 285 (2021), First Violation.

§ 23558. Causing bodily injury or death to more than one victim while driving in violation of specified sections; felony convictions; enhancement of punishment

A person who proximately causes bodily injury or death to more than one victim in any one instance of driving in violation of Section

23153 of this code or in violation of Section 191.5 of, or subdivision (a) of Section 192.5 of, the Penal Code, shall, upon a felony conviction, and notwithstanding subdivision (g) of Section 1170.1 of the Penal Code, receive an enhancement of one year in the state prison for each additional injured victim. The enhanced sentence provided for in this section shall not be imposed unless the fact of the bodily injury to each additional victim is charged in the accusatory pleading and admitted or found to be true by the trier of fact. The maximum number of one year enhancements that may be imposed pursuant to this section is three.

Notwithstanding any other provision of law, the court may strike the enhancements provided in this section if it determines that there are circumstances in mitigation of the additional punishment and states on the record its reasons for striking the additional punishment. *(Added by Stats.1998, c. 118 (S.B.1186), § 84, operative July 1, 1999. Amended by Stats.1999, c. 706 (A.B.1236), § 15, eff. Oct. 10, 1999; Stats.2007, c. 747 (A.B.678), § 34.)*

Research References

2 Witkin, California Criminal Law 4th Crimes Against Public Peace and Welfare § 285 (2021), First Violation.
2 Witkin, California Criminal Law 4th Crimes Against Public Peace and Welfare § 286 (2021), One Separate Conviction of Related Offense.
2 Witkin, California Criminal Law 4th Crimes Against Public Peace and Welfare § 287 (2021), Two or More Separate Convictions of Related Offenses.
2 Witkin, California Criminal Law 4th Crimes Against Public Peace and Welfare § 288 (2021), Enhanced Punishment for Multiple Victims.
1 Witkin California Criminal Law 4th Crimes Against the Person § 267 (2021), Vehicular Manslaughter While Intoxicated.
1 Witkin California Criminal Law 4th Crimes Against the Person § 268 (2021), In General.
1 Witkin California Criminal Law 4th Introduction to Crimes § 77 (2021), Illustrations: Special Statute is Not Controlling.
3 Witkin, California Criminal Law 4th Punishment § 118 (2021), Definition of Victim.
3 Witkin, California Criminal Law 4th Punishment § 255 (2021), In General.
3 Witkin, California Criminal Law 4th Punishment § 350 (2021), General Provision.

§ 23560. Second offense; punishment

If a person is convicted of a violation of Section 23153 and the offense occurred within 10 years of a separate violation of Section 23103, as specified in Section 23103.5, 23152, or 23153 that resulted in a conviction, that person shall be punished by imprisonment in the state prison, or in a county jail for not less than 120 days nor more than one year, and by a fine of not less than three hundred ninety dollars ($390) nor more than five thousand dollars ($5,000). The person's privilege to operate a motor vehicle shall be revoked by the Department of Motor Vehicles pursuant to paragraph (4) of subdivision (a) of Section 13352. The court shall require the person to surrender the driver's license to the court in accordance with Section 13550. *(Added by Stats.1998, c. 118 (S.B.1186), § 84, operative July 1, 1999. Amended by Stats.2002, c. 545 (S.B.1852), § 30; Stats.2004, c. 550 (S.B.1694), § 16.)*

Cross References

Alcohol and drug problem assessment program, violator participation, sentencing, and assessment upon fine, see Vehicle Code § 23646 et seq.
Alcoholic beverages in vehicles, see Vehicle Code § 23220 et seq.
Applicability of this section to trolley coaches, see Vehicle Code § 21051.
Arrest without warrant, see Vehicle Code § 40300.5.
Challenging constitutional validity of separate conviction, see Vehicle Code § 41403.
Chemical blood, breath or urine tests, see Vehicle Code § 13353.
Chemical tests as evidence, see Vehicle Code § 23610.
Conviction of violation of specified subdivisions of Penal Code § 192 to be deemed conviction of violation of specified DUI provisions, see Vehicle Code § 13350.5.
Coroner's inquiry into deaths, see Government Code § 27491.25.
County alcohol and drug problem assessment programs, mandatory participation for convicted violators of this section, see Vehicle Code §§ 23646, 23647.
Crime of violence, within act for indemnification of victims of crime, see Government Code § 13960.
Defense of drug use to violations, see Vehicle Code § 23630.
Deposit in special account for each conviction under DUI provisions, see Penal Code § 1463.14.
Drivers license revocation, conviction of driver under eighteen, see Vehicle Code § 13352.3.
Driving school or instructor, revocation or suspension of license for violation of this section, see Vehicle Code § 11110.
Gross vehicular manslaughter while intoxicated, see Penal Code § 191.5.
Guilty plea, see Vehicle Code § 41610.
Impoundment of vehicle of registered owner convicted under this section, see Vehicle Code § 23594.
Influence of alcoholic beverage or drug, suspension or revocation of driving privileges, see Vehicle Code § 13352.
Injury to guest by intoxicated driver, see Vehicle Code § 17158.
Juvenile offenders, programs of supervision, see Welfare and Institutions Code § 654.1.
Manslaughter, negligent homicide by vehicle, see Penal Code § 192.
Nuisance, sale or other disposition of motor vehicle driven by defendant, see Vehicle Code § 23596.
Persons certified or granted probation on conviction of driving under the influence of alcohol or drugs or combined influence on certain conditions, restriction, revocation or suspension of driving privilege, consent to participation in treatment program, see Vehicle Code § 13352.5.
Please Don't Drink and Drive memorial signs, requests for and duration of placement, exception for a party to an accident convicted or determined to be mentally incompetent under this section, see Streets and Highways Code § 101.10.
Presentence investigation and assessment, see Vehicle Code § 23655.
Presumptions, see Evidence Code § 600 et seq.
Prior convictions under sections 23103, 23152 or 23153, effect on sentencing and driving privileges, see Vehicle Code § 23622.
Procedure on arrest for violation of this section, see Vehicle Code § 40302.
Records available to courts and law enforcement officials, incidents under certain DWI and homicide laws, period of time records must be available, see Vehicle Code § 1808.
Refusal to submit to alcohol testing under DUI laws, calculation of prior convictions, certain foreign convictions recognized, see Vehicle Code §§ 13353, 13353.1 and 13353.3.
Surrender of driver's license to court, see Vehicle Code § 13550.
Suspension or revocation of driving privilege for a violation of this section, notice by personal service, see Vehicle Code § 13106.
Suspension or revocation of license,
  Generally, see Vehicle Code § 13352.
  Alcohol-related accident within five years of vehicular manslaughter, see Vehicle Code § 13954.
  Driver license compact, see Vehicle Code § 15000 et seq.
  Driving after suspension or revocation, see Vehicle Code § 14601.2.
  Investigation by department, three convictions in three years under this or other specified statutes, see Vehicle Code § 13800.
  Prior convictions, record, see Vehicle Code § 13209.
Traffic violation point count, violation of this section, see Vehicle Code § 12810.
Traffic violators schools, suspension or revocation of license for violation of this section, see Vehicle Code § 11215.
Vehicular homicide, see Penal Code § 192.
Violation as misdemeanor, see Vehicle Code § 40000.15.
Violation of this section, relinquishment of motor vehicle to convicted minor, see Penal Code § 193.8.
Youthful drunk driver visitation program, see Vehicle Code § 23509 et seq.

Research References

2 Witkin, California Criminal Law 4th Crimes Against Public Peace and Welfare § 286 (2021), One Separate Conviction of Related Offense.
3 Witkin, California Criminal Law 4th Punishment § 214 (2021), Drunk Driving.

§ 23562. Conditions of probation for second offense

If the court grants probation to a person punished under Section 23560, in addition to the provisions of Section 23600 and any other terms and conditions imposed by the court, the court shall impose as conditions of probation that the person be subject to either subdivision (a) or (b), as follows:

(a) Be confined in the county jail for at least 120 days and pay a fine of at least three hundred ninety dollars ($390), but not more than five thousand dollars ($5,000). The person's privilege to operate a motor vehicle shall be revoked by the department under paragraph (4) of subdivision (a) of Section 13352. The court shall require the person to surrender the driver's license to the court in accordance with Section 13550.

(b) All of the following apply:

(1) Be confined in the county jail for at least 30 days, but not more than one year.

(2) Pay a fine of at least three hundred ninety dollars ($390), but not more than one thousand dollars ($1,000).

(3) The privilege to operate a motor vehicle shall be revoked by the department under paragraph (4) of subdivision (a) of Section 13352. The court shall require the person to surrender the driver's license to the court in accordance with Section 13550.

(4) Either of the following:

(A) Enroll and participate, for at least 18 months subsequent to the date of the underlying violation and in a manner satisfactory to the court, in a driving-under-the-influence program licensed pursuant to Section 11836 of the Health and Safety Code, if available in the county of the person's residence or employment, as designated by the court. The person shall complete the entire program subsequent to, and shall not be given any credit for program activities completed prior to, the date of the current violation. The program shall provide for persons who cannot afford the program fee pursuant to paragraph (2) of subdivision (b) of Section 11837.4 of the Health and Safety Code in order to enable those persons to participate.

(B) Enroll and participate, for at least 30 months subsequent to the date of the underlying violation and in a manner satisfactory to the court, in a driving-under-the-influence program licensed pursuant to Section 11836 of the Health and Safety Code, if available in the county of the person's residence or employment. The person shall complete the entire program subsequent to, and shall not be given any credit for program activities completed prior to, the date of the current violation.

(c) The court shall advise the person at the time of sentencing that the driving privilege shall not be restored until the person has provided proof satisfactory to the department of successful completion of a driving-under-the-influence program of the length required under this code that is licensed pursuant to Section 11836 of the Health and Safety Code.

(d) This section shall become operative on September 20, 2005. *(Formerly § 23186, added by Stats.1981, c. 940, p. 3571, § 32. Amended by Stats.1982, c. 53, p. 177, § 38, eff. Feb. 18, 1982; Stats.1982, c. 1338, p. 4972, § 11, operative July 1, 1983; Stats.1982, c. 1339, p. 4990, § 25, eff. Sept. 24, 1982; Stats.1982, c. 1339, p. 4991, § 26, eff. Sept. 24, 1982, operative July 1, 1983; Stats.1984, c. 667, p. 3, § 17, operative July 1, 1985; Stats.1987, c. 214, § 4; Stats.1989, c. 803, § 8; Stats.1991, c. 990 (S.B.713), § 4, eff. Oct. 14, 1991; Stats.1992, c. 974 (S.B.1600), § 23, eff. Sept. 28, 1992; Stats.1993, c. 272 (A.B.301), § 48, eff. Aug. 2, 1993; Stats.1997, c. 493 (S.B.1177), § 4; Stats.1998, c. 756 (A.B.762), § 15, operative July 1, 1999. Renumbered § 23562 and amended by Stats.1999, c.22 (S.B.24), § 22, eff. May 26, 1999, operative July 1, 1999. Amended by Stats.2002, c. 545 (S.B.1852), § 31; Stats.2004, c. 551 (S.B.1697), § 22, operative Sept. 20, 2005.)*

Cross References

Conviction for driving under the influence or engaging in speed contests or exhibitions of speed, suspension or revocation of license, eligibility for restricted license, reinstatement conditions, see Vehicle Code § 13352.

Persons certified or granted probation on conviction or driving under the influence of alcohol or drugs or combined influence on certain conditions, restriction, revocation or suspension of driving privilege, consent to participation in treatment program, see Vehicle Code § 13352.5.

Presentence investigation, see Vehicle Code § 23655.

Research References

2 Witkin, California Criminal Law 4th Crimes Against Public Peace and Welfare § 286 (2021), One Separate Conviction of Related Offense.

§ 23566. Three or more convictions; punishment; habitual traffic offender designation; order for participation in alcohol or drug program

(a) If a person is convicted of a violation of Section 23153 and the offense occurred within 10 years of two or more separate violations of Section 23103, as specified in Section 23103.5, or Section 23152 or 23153, or any combination of these violations, that resulted in convictions, that person shall be punished by imprisonment in the state prison for a term of two, three, or four years and by a fine of not less than one thousand fifteen dollars ($1,015) nor more than five thousand dollars ($5,000). The person's privilege to operate a motor vehicle shall be revoked by the Department of Motor Vehicles pursuant to paragraph (6) of subdivision (a) of Section 13352. The court shall require the person to surrender the driver's license to the court in accordance with Section 13550.

(b) If a person is convicted of a violation of Section 23153, and the act or neglect proximately causes great bodily injury, as defined in Section 12022.7 of the Penal Code, to any person other than the driver, and the offense occurred within 10 years of two or more separate violations of Section 23103, as specified in Section 23103.5, or Section 23152 or 23153, or any combination of these violations, that resulted in convictions, that person shall be punished by imprisonment in the state prison for a term of two, three, or four years and by a fine of not less than one thousand fifteen dollars ($1,015) nor more than five thousand dollars ($5,000). The person's privilege to operate a motor vehicle shall be revoked by the Department of Motor Vehicles pursuant to paragraph (6) of subdivision (a) of Section 13352. The court shall require the person to surrender the driver's license to the court in accordance with Section 13550.

(c) If a person is convicted under subdivision (b), and the offense for which the person is convicted occurred within 10 years of four or more separate violations of Section 23103, as specified in Section 23103.5, or Section 23152 or 23153, or any combination of these violations, that resulted in convictions, that person shall, in addition and consecutive to the sentences imposed under subdivision (b), be punished by an additional term of imprisonment in the state prison for three years.

The enhancement allegation provided in this subdivision shall be pleaded and proved as provided by law.

(d) A person convicted of Section 23153 punishable under this section shall be designated as a habitual traffic offender for a period of three years, subsequent to the conviction. The person shall be advised of this designation pursuant to subdivision (b) of Section 13350.

(e) A person confined in state prison under this section shall be ordered by the court to participate in an alcohol or drug program, or both, that is available at the prison during the person's confinement. Completion of an alcohol or drug program under this section does not meet the program completion requirement of paragraph (6) of subdivision (a) of Section 13352, unless the drug or alcohol program is licensed under Section 11836 of the Health and Safety Code, or is a program specified in Section 8001 of the Penal Code. *(Added by Stats.1998, c. 118 (S.B.1186), § 84, operative July 1, 1999. Amended by Stats.1999, c. 22 (S.B.24), § 36, eff. May 26, 1999, operative July 1, 1999; Stats.2002, c. 545 (S.B.1852), § 32; Stats.2004, c. 550 (S.B.*

1694), § 17; Stats.2009, c. 193 (S.B.598), § 7, operative July 1, 2010; Stats.2010, c. 301 (A.B.1601), § 6.)

Cross References

Suspension or revocation of license for driving under the influence or engaging in speed contests or exhibitions of speed, reinstatement conditions, see Vehicle Code § 13352.

Research References

California Jury Instructions - Criminal 12.67, Felony Driving Under the Influence—Priors.

California Jury Instructions - Criminal 12.68, Felony Driving With 0.08 Percent.

2 Witkin, California Criminal Law 4th Crimes Against Public Peace and Welfare § 283 (2021), Three or More Separate Convictions of Related Offenses.

2 Witkin, California Criminal Law 4th Crimes Against Public Peace and Welfare § 287 (2021), Two or More Separate Convictions of Related Offenses.

2 Witkin, California Criminal Law 4th Crimes Against Public Peace and Welfare § 289 (2021), Prior Violation Punished as Felony.

2 Witkin, California Criminal Law 4th Crimes Against Public Peace and Welfare § 292 (2021), Time of Separate Convictions.

1 Witkin California Criminal Law 4th Introduction to Crimes § 77 (2021), Illustrations: Special Statute is Not Controlling.

3 Witkin, California Criminal Law 4th Punishment § 214 (2021), Drunk Driving.

3 Witkin, California Criminal Law 4th Punishment § 350 (2021), General Provision.

§ 23568. Additional conditions of probation for persons punished under § 23566

(a) If the court grants probation to a person punished under Section 23566, in addition to the provisions of Section 23600 and any other terms and conditions imposed by the court, the court shall impose as conditions of probation that the person be confined in the county jail for at least one year, that the person pay a fine of at least three hundred ninety dollars ($390) but not more than five thousand dollars ($5,000), and that the person make restitution or reparation pursuant to Section 1203.1 of the Penal Code. The person's privilege to operate a motor vehicle shall be revoked by the department under paragraph (6) of subdivision (a) of Section 13352. The court shall require the person to surrender the driver's license to the court in accordance with Section 13550.

(b) In addition to Section 23600 and subdivision (a), if the court grants probation to a person punished under Section 23566, the court shall impose as a condition of probation that the person enroll in and complete, subsequent to the date of the underlying violation and in a manner satisfactory to the court, an 18–month driving-under-the-influence program licensed pursuant to Section 11836 of the Health and Safety Code or, if available in the county of the person's residence or employment, a 30–month driving-under-the-influence program licensed pursuant to Section 11836 of the Health and Safety Code, as designated by the court. The person shall complete the entire program subsequent to, and shall not be given any credit for program activities completed prior to, the date of the current violation. In lieu of the minimum term of imprisonment in subdivision (a), the court shall impose as a minimum condition of probation under this subdivision that the person be confined in the county jail for at least 30 days but not more than one year. Except as provided in this subdivision, if the court grants probation under this section, the court shall order the treatment prescribed by this subdivision, whether or not the person has previously completed a treatment program pursuant to subdivision (b) of Section 23542 or paragraph (4) of subdivision (b) of Section 23562. In order to enable all required persons to participate, each person shall pay the program costs commensurate with the person's ability to pay as determined pursuant to Section 11837.4 of the Health and Safety Code. No condition of probation required pursuant to this subdivision is a basis for reducing any other probation requirement in this section or Section 23600 or for avoiding the mandatory license revocation provisions of paragraph (6) of subdivision (a) of Section 13352.

(c) The court shall advise the person at the time of sentencing that the driving privilege may not be restored until the person provides proof satisfactory to the department of successful completion of a driving-under-the-influence program of the length required under this code that is licensed pursuant to Section 11836 of the Health and Safety Code. *(Added by Stats.1998, c. 118 (S.B.1186), § 84, operative July 1, 1999. Amended by Stats.1999, c. 22 (S.B.24), § 37, eff. May 26, 1999, operative July 1, 1999; Stats.2002, c. 545 (S.B.1852), § 33; Stats.2004, c. 551 (S.B.1697), § 23, operative Sept. 20, 2005; Stats. 2009, c. 193 (S.B.598), § 8, operative July 1, 2010; Stats.2010, c. 301 (A.B.1601), § 7.)*

Cross References

Suspension or revocation of license for driving under the influence or engaging in speed contests or exhibitions of speed, reinstatement conditions, see Vehicle Code § 13352.

Research References

2 Witkin, California Criminal Law 4th Crimes Against Public Peace and Welfare § 287 (2021), Two or More Separate Convictions of Related Offenses.

3 Witkin, California Criminal Law 4th Punishment § 656 (2021), Particular Statutes.

ARTICLE 4. ADDITIONAL PUNISHMENTS

Section

§ 23572. Conviction of violation of § 23152; minor in vehicle; enhanced punishment

(a) If any person is convicted of a violation of Section 23152 and a minor under 14 years of age was a passenger in the vehicle at the time of the offense, the court shall impose the following penalties in addition to any other penalty prescribed:

(1) If the person is convicted of a violation of Section 23152 punishable under Section 23536, the punishment shall be enhanced by an imprisonment of 48 continuous hours in the county jail, whether or not probation is granted, no part of which shall be stayed.

(2) If a person is convicted of a violation of Section 23152 punishable under Section 23540, the punishment shall be enhanced by an imprisonment of 10 days in the county jail, whether or not probation is granted, no part of which may be stayed.

(3) If a person is convicted of a violation of Section 23152 punishable under Section 23546, the punishment shall be enhanced by an imprisonment of 30 days in the county jail, whether or not probation is granted, no part of which may be stayed.

(4) If a person is convicted of a violation of Section 23152 which is punished as a misdemeanor under Section 23550, the punishment shall be enhanced by an imprisonment of 90 days in the county jail, whether or not probation is granted, no part of which may be stayed.

(b) The driving of a vehicle in which a minor under 14 years of age was a passenger shall be pled and proven.

(c) No punishment enhancement shall be imposed pursuant to this section if the person is also convicted of a violation of Section 273a of the Penal Code arising out of the same facts and incident. *(Added by Stats.1998, c. 118 (S.B.1186), § 84, operative July 1, 1999. Amended by Stats.1999, c. 22 (S.B.24), § 38, eff. May 26, 1999, operative July 1, 1999.)*

Cross References

Alcohol and drug problem assessment program, violator participation, sentencing, and assessment upon fine, see Vehicle Code § 23646 et seq.

Alcoholic beverages in vehicles, see Vehicle Code § 23220 et seq.
Applicability of this section to trolley coaches, see Vehicle Code § 21051.
Arrest without warrant, see Vehicle Code § 40300.5.
Challenging constitutional validity of separate conviction, see Vehicle Code § 41403.
Chemical blood, breath or urine tests, see Vehicle Code § 13353.
Chemical tests as evidence, see Vehicle Code § 23610.
Conviction of violation of specified subdivisions of Penal Code § 192 to be deemed conviction of violation of specified DUI provisions, see Vehicle Code § 13350.5.
Coroner's inquiry into deaths, see Government Code § 27491.25.
County alcohol and drug problem assessment programs, mandatory participation for convicted violators of this section, see Vehicle Code §§ 23646, 23647.
Crime of violence, within act for indemnification of victims of crime, see Government Code § 13960.
Defense of drug use to violations, see Vehicle Code § 23630.
Deposit in special account for each conviction under DUI provisions, see Penal Code § 1463.14.
Drivers license revocation, conviction of driver under eighteen, see Vehicle Code § 13352.3.
Driving school or instructor, revocation or suspension of license for violation of this section, see Vehicle Code § 11110.
Gross vehicular manslaughter while intoxicated, see Penal Code § 191.5.
Guilty plea, see Vehicle Code § 41610.
Impoundment of vehicle of registered owner convicted under this section, see Vehicle Code § 23594.
Influence of alcoholic beverage or drug, suspension or revocation of driving privileges, see Vehicle Code § 13352.
Injury to guest by intoxicated driver, see Vehicle Code § 17158.
Juvenile offenders, programs of supervision, see Welfare and Institutions Code § 654.1.
Manslaughter, negligent homicide by vehicle, see Penal Code § 192.
Nuisance, sale or other disposition of motor vehicle driven by defendant, see Vehicle Code § 23596.
Persons certified or granted probation on conviction of driving under the influence of alcohol or drugs or combined influence on certain conditions, restriction, revocation or suspension of driving privilege, consent to participation in treatment program, see Vehicle Code § 13352.5.
Please Don't Drink and Drive memorial signs, requests for and duration of placement, exception for a party to an accident convicted or determined to be mentally incompetent under this section, see Streets and Highways Code § 101.10.
Presentence investigation and assessment, see Vehicle Code § 23655.
Presumptions, see Evidence Code § 600 et seq.
Prior convictions under sections 23103, 23152 or 23153, effect on sentencing and driving privileges, see Vehicle Code § 23622.
Procedure on arrest for violation of this section, see Vehicle Code § 40302.
Records available to courts and law enforcement officials, incidents under certain DWI and homicide laws, period of time records must be available, see Vehicle Code § 1808.
Refusal to submit to alcohol testing under DUI laws, calculation of prior convictions, certain foreign convictions recognized, see Vehicle Code §§ 13353, 13353.1 and 13353.3.
Surrender of driver's license to court, see Vehicle Code § 13550.
Suspension or revocation of driving privilege for a violation of this section, notice by personal service, see Vehicle Code § 13106.
Suspension or revocation of license,
 Generally, see Vehicle Code § 13352.
 Alcohol-related accident within five years of vehicular manslaughter, see Vehicle Code § 13954.
 Driver license compact, see Vehicle Code § 15000 et seq.
 Driving after suspension or revocation, see Vehicle Code § 14601.2.
 Investigation by department, three convictions in three years under this or other specified statutes, see Vehicle Code § 13800.
 Prior convictions, record, see Vehicle Code § 13209.
Traffic violation point count, violation of this section, see Vehicle Code § 12810.
Traffic violators schools, suspension or revocation of license for violation of this section, see Vehicle Code § 11215.
Vehicular homicide, see Penal Code § 192.
Violation as misdemeanor, see Vehicle Code § 40000.15.
Violation of this section, relinquishment of motor vehicle to convicted minor, see Penal Code § 193.8.
Youthful drunk driver visitation program, see Vehicle Code § 23509 et seq.

Research References

2 Witkin, California Criminal Law 4th Crimes Against Public Peace and Welfare § 284 (2021), Enhanced Punishment Where Minor is Passenger.

ARTICLE 5. ADDITIONAL PENALTIES AND SANCTIONS

Section

§ 23573. Violations necessitating functioning, certified ignition interlock device; installation and maintenance; license restriction; exemptions; failure to comply

Section operative until Jan. 1, 2026. See, also, § 23573 operative Jan. 1, 2026.

(a) The Department of Motor Vehicles, upon receipt of the court's abstract of conviction for a violation listed in subdivision (j), shall inform the convicted person of the requirements of this section and the term for which the person is required to have a functioning, certified ignition interlock device installed. The records of the department shall reflect the mandatory use of the device for the term required and the time when the device is required to be installed pursuant to this code.

(b) The department shall advise the person that installation of a functioning, certified ignition interlock device on a vehicle does not allow the person to drive without a valid driver's license.

(c) A person who is notified by the department pursuant to subdivision (a) shall, within 30 days of notification, complete all of the following:

(1) Arrange for each vehicle operated by the person to be fitted with a functioning, certified ignition interlock device by a certified ignition interlock device provider under Section 13386.

(2) Notify the department and provide to the department proof of installation by submitting the "Verification of Installation" form described in paragraph (2) of subdivision (g) of Section 13386.

(3) Pay to the department a fee sufficient to cover the costs of administration of this section, including startup costs, as determined by the department.

(d) The department shall place a restriction on the driver's license record of the convicted person that states the driver is restricted to driving only vehicles equipped with a functioning, certified ignition interlock device.

(e)(1) A person who is notified by the department pursuant to subdivision (a) shall arrange for each vehicle with an ignition interlock device to be serviced by the installer at least once every 60 days in order for the installer to recalibrate and monitor the operation of the device.

(2) The installer shall notify the department if the device is removed or indicates that the person has attempted to remove, bypass, or tamper with the device, or if the person fails three or more times to comply with any requirement for the maintenance or calibration of the ignition interlock device.

(f) The department shall monitor the installation and maintenance of the functioning, certified ignition interlock device installed pursuant to subdivision (a).

(g)(1) A person who is notified by the department, pursuant to subdivision (a), is exempt from the requirements of subdivision (c) if all of the following circumstances occur:

(A) Within 30 days of the notification, the person certifies to the department all of the following:

(i) The person does not own a vehicle.

(ii) The person does not have access to a vehicle at his or her residence.

(iii) The person no longer has access to the vehicle being driven by the person when he or she was arrested for a violation that subsequently resulted in a conviction for a violation listed in subdivision (j).

(iv) The person acknowledges that he or she is only allowed to drive a vehicle that is fitted with a functioning, certified ignition interlock device and that he or she is required to have a valid driver's license before he or she can drive.

(v) The person is subject to the requirements of this section when he or she purchases or has access to a vehicle.

(B) The person's driver's license record has been restricted pursuant to subdivision (d).

(C) The person complies with this section immediately upon commencing operation of a vehicle subject to the required installation of a functioning, certified ignition interlock device.

(2) A person who has been granted an exemption pursuant to this subdivision and who subsequently drives a vehicle in violation of the exemption is subject to the penalties of subdivision (i) in addition to any other applicable penalties in law.

(h) This section does not permit a person to drive without a valid driver's license.

(i) A person who is required under subdivision (c) to install a functioning, certified ignition interlock device who willfully fails to install the ignition interlock device within the time period required under subdivision (c) is guilty of a misdemeanor and shall be punished by imprisonment in a county jail for not more than six months or by a fine of not more than five thousand dollars ($5,000), or by both that fine and imprisonment.

(j) In addition to all other requirements of this code, a person convicted of any of the following violations shall be punished as follows:

(1) Upon a conviction of a violation of Section 14601.2, 14601.4, or 14601.5 subsequent to one prior conviction of a violation of Section 23103.5, 23152, or 23153, within a 10–year period, the person shall immediately install a functioning, certified ignition interlock device, pursuant to this section, in all vehicles operated by that person for a term of one year.

(2) Upon a conviction of a violation of Section 14601.2, 14601.4, or 14601.5 subsequent to two prior convictions of a violation of Section 23103.5, 23152, or 23153, within a 10–year period, or one prior conviction of Section 14601.2, 14601.4, or 14601.5, within a 10–year period, the person shall immediately install a functioning, certified ignition interlock device, pursuant to this section, in all vehicles operated by that person for a term of two years.

(3) Upon a conviction of a violation of Section 14601.2, 14601.4, or 14601.5 subsequent to three or more prior convictions of a violation of Section 23103.5, 23152, or 23153, within a 10–year period, or two or more prior convictions of Section 14601.2, 14601.4, or 14601.5, within a 10–year period, the person shall immediately install a functioning, certified ignition interlock device, pursuant to this section, in all vehicles operated by that person for a term of three years.

(k) The department shall notify the court if a person subject to this section has failed to show proof of installation within 30 days of the department informing the person he or she is required to install a functioning, certified ignition interlock device.

(*l*) Subdivisions (g), (h), (j), (k), and (*l*) of Section 23575 apply to this section.

(m) The requirements of this section are in addition to any other requirements of law.

(n) This section shall become operative on January 1, 2019.

(*o*) This section shall remain in effect only until January 1, 2026, and as of that date is repealed, unless a later enacted statute, that is enacted before January 1, 2026, deletes or extends that date. *(Added by Stats.2016, c. 783 (S.B.1046), § 30, eff. Jan. 1, 2017, operative Jan. 1, 2019. Amended by Stats.2017, c. 485 (S.B.611), § 23, eff. Jan. 1, 2018, operative Jan. 1, 2019.)*

Repeal

For repeal of this section, see its terms.

Research References

2 Witkin, California Criminal Law 4th Crimes Against Public Peace and Welfare § 290 (2021), Ignition Interlock Device.

2 Witkin, California Criminal Law 4th Crimes Against Public Peace and Welfare § 306 (2021), Reason for Suspension, Revocation, or Restriction.

§ 23573. Violations necessitating functioning, certified ignition interlock device; installation and maintenance; license restriction; exemptions; failure to comply

Section operative Jan. 1, 2026. See, also, § 23573 operative until Jan. 1, 2026.

(a) The Department of Motor Vehicles, upon receipt of the court's abstract of conviction for a violation listed in subdivision (j), shall inform the convicted person of the requirements of this section and the term for which the person is required to have a functioning, certified ignition interlock device installed. The records of the department shall reflect the mandatory use of the device for the term required and the time when the device is required to be installed pursuant to this code.

(b) The department shall advise the person that installation of a functioning, certified ignition interlock device on a vehicle does not allow the person to drive without a valid driver's license.

(c) A person who is notified by the department pursuant to subdivision (a) shall, within 30 days of notification, complete all of the following:

(1) Arrange for each vehicle operated by the person to be fitted with a functioning, certified ignition interlock device by a certified ignition interlock device provider under Section 13386.

(2) Notify the department and provide to the department proof of installation by submitting the "Verification of Installation" form described in paragraph (2) of subdivision (g) of Section 13386.

(3) Pay to the department a fee sufficient to cover the costs of administration of this section, including startup costs, as determined by the department.

(d) The department shall place a restriction on the driver's license record of the convicted person that states the driver is restricted to driving only vehicles equipped with a functioning, certified ignition interlock device.

(e)(1) A person who is notified by the department pursuant to subdivision (a) shall arrange for each vehicle with an ignition interlock device to be serviced by the installer at least once every 60 days in order for the installer to recalibrate and monitor the operation of the device.

(2) The installer shall notify the department if the device is removed or indicates that the person has attempted to remove, bypass, or tamper with the device, or if the person fails three or more times to comply with any requirement for the maintenance or calibration of the ignition interlock device.

(f) The department shall monitor the installation and maintenance of the ignition interlock device installed pursuant to subdivision (a).

(g)(1) A person who is notified by the department, pursuant to subdivision (a), is exempt from the requirements of subdivision (c) if all of the following circumstances occur:

(A) Within 30 days of the notification, the person certifies to the department all of the following:

(i) The person does not own a vehicle.

(ii) The person does not have access to a vehicle at his or her residence.

(iii) The person no longer has access to the vehicle being driven by the person when he or she was arrested for a violation that subsequently resulted in a conviction for a violation listed in subdivision (j).

(iv) The person acknowledges that he or she is only allowed to drive a vehicle that is fitted with a functioning, certified ignition interlock device and that he or she is required to have a valid driver's license before he or she can drive.

(v) The person is subject to the requirements of this section when he or she purchases or has access to a vehicle.

(B) The person's driver's license record has been restricted pursuant to subdivision (d).

(C) The person complies with this section immediately upon commencing operation of a vehicle subject to the required installation of a functioning, certified ignition interlock device.

(2) A person who has been granted an exemption pursuant to this subdivision and who subsequently drives a vehicle in violation of the exemption is subject to the penalties of subdivision (i) in addition to any other applicable penalties in law.

(h) This section does not permit a person to drive without a valid driver's license.

(i) A person who is required under subdivision (c) to install a functioning, certified ignition interlock device who willfully fails to install the ignition interlock device within the time period required under subdivision (c) is guilty of a misdemeanor and shall be punished by imprisonment in a county jail for not more than six months or by a fine of not more than five thousand dollars ($5,000), or by both that fine and imprisonment.

(j) In addition to all other requirements of this code, a person convicted of any of the following violations shall be punished as follows:

(1) Upon a conviction of a violation of Section 14601.2, 14601.4, or 14601.5 subsequent to one prior conviction of a violation of Section 23103.5, 23152, or 23153, within a 10–year period, the person shall immediately install a functioning, certified ignition interlock device, pursuant to this section, in all vehicles operated by that person for a term of one year.

(2) Upon a conviction of a violation of Section 14601.2, 14601.4, or 14601.5 subsequent to two prior convictions of a violation of Section 23103.5, 23152, or 23153, within a 10–year period, or one prior conviction of Section 14601.2, 14601.4, or 14601.5, within a 10–year period, the person shall immediately install a functioning, certified ignition interlock device, pursuant to this section, in all vehicles operated by that person for a term of two years.

(3) Upon a conviction of a violation of Section 14601.2, 14601.4, or 14601.5 subsequent to three or more prior convictions of a violation of Section 23103.5, 23152, or 23153, within a 10–year period, or two or more prior convictions of Section 14601.2, 14601.4, or 14601.5, within a 10–year period, the person shall immediately install a functioning, certified ignition interlock device, pursuant to this section, in all vehicles operated by that person for a term of three years.

(k) The department shall notify the court if a person subject to this section has failed to show proof of installation within 30 days of the department informing the person he or she is required to install a functioning, certified ignition interlock device.

(*l*) Subdivisions (j), (k), (m), (n), and (*o*) of Section 23575 apply to this section.

(m) The requirements of this section are in addition to any other requirements of law.

(n) This section shall become operative January 1, 2026. *(Added by Stats.2016, c. 783 (S.B.1046), § 31, eff. Jan. 1, 2017, operative Jan. 1, 2026. Amended by Stats.2017, c. 485 (S.B.611), § 24, eff. Jan. 1, 2018, operative Jan. 1, 2026.)*

Research References

2 Witkin, California Criminal Law 4th Crimes Against Public Peace and Welfare § 290 (2021), Ignition Interlock Device.
2 Witkin, California Criminal Law 4th Crimes Against Public Peace and Welfare § 306 (2021), Reason for Suspension, Revocation, or Restriction.

§ 23575. Court-mandated use of functioning, certified ignition interlock device

Section operative until Jan. 1, 2026. See, also, § 23575 operative Jan. 1, 2026.

(a) The court shall require a person convicted of a violation of Section 14601.2 to install a functioning, certified ignition interlock device on any vehicle that the person operates and prohibit the person from operating a motor vehicle unless the vehicle is equipped with a functioning, certified ignition interlock device. The term of the restriction shall be determined by the court for a period not to exceed three years from the date of conviction. The court shall notify the Department of Motor Vehicles, as specified in subdivision (a) of Section 1803, of the terms of the restrictions in accordance with subdivision (a) of Section 1804. The Department of Motor Vehicles shall place the restriction in the person's records in the Department of Motor Vehicles.

(b) The court shall include on the abstract of conviction or violation submitted to the Department of Motor Vehicles under Section 1803 or 1816 the requirement and term for the use of a functioning, certified ignition interlock device. The records of the department shall reflect mandatory use of the device for the term ordered by the court.

(c) The court shall advise the person that installation of an ignition interlock device on a vehicle does not allow the person to drive without a valid driver's license.

(d) A person whose driving privilege is restricted by the court pursuant to this section shall arrange for each vehicle with a functioning, certified ignition interlock device to be serviced by the installer at least once every 60 days in order for the installer to recalibrate and monitor the operation of the device. The installer shall notify the court if the device is removed or indicates that the person has attempted to remove, bypass, or tamper with the device, or if the person fails three or more times to comply with any requirement for the maintenance or calibration of the ignition interlock device. There is no obligation for the installer to notify the court if the person has complied with all of the requirements of this article.

(e) The court shall monitor the installation and maintenance of a functioning, certified ignition interlock device restriction ordered pursuant to subdivision (a) or (i). If a person fails to comply with the court order, the court shall give notice of the fact to the department pursuant to Section 40509.1.

(f) Nothing in this section permits a person to drive without a valid driver's license.

(g) Pursuant to this section, an out-of-state resident who otherwise would qualify for an ignition interlock device restricted license in California shall be prohibited from operating a motor vehicle in California unless that vehicle is equipped with a functioning, certified ignition interlock device. An ignition interlock device is not required to be installed on any vehicle owned by the defendant that is not driven in California.

(h) If a medical problem does not permit a person to breathe with sufficient strength to activate the device, that person shall only have the suspension option.

(i) This section does not restrict a court from requiring installation of a functioning, certified ignition interlock device and prohibiting operation of a motor vehicle unless that vehicle is equipped with a functioning, certified ignition interlock device for a person to whom subdivision (a) does not apply. The term of the restriction shall be determined by the court for a period not to exceed three years from the date of conviction. The court shall notify the Department of Motor Vehicles, as specified in subdivision (a) of Section 1803, of the terms of the restrictions in accordance with subdivision (a) of Section 1804. The Department of Motor Vehicles shall place the restriction in the person's records in the Department of Motor Vehicles.

(j) For the purposes of this section, "vehicle" does not include a motorcycle until the state certifies an ignition interlock device that can be installed on a motorcycle. Any person subject to an ignition interlock device restriction shall not operate a motorcycle for the duration of the ignition interlock device restriction period.

(k)(1) For the purposes of this section, "owned" means solely owned or owned in conjunction with another person or legal entity.

(2) For purposes of this section, "operates" includes operating a vehicle that is not owned by the person subject to this section.

(*l*) For the purposes of this section, "bypass" means either of the following:

(1) Failure to take any random retest.

(2) Failure to pass any random retest with a breath alcohol concentration not exceeding 0.03 percent breath alcohol concentration.

(m) The department shall adopt regulations specifying the intervals between random retests.

(n) For purposes of this section, "random retest" means a breath test performed by the driver upon a certified ignition interlock device at random intervals after the initial engine startup breath test and while the vehicle's motor is running.

(*o*) This section shall become operative on January 1, 2019.

(p) This section shall remain in effect only until January 1, 2026, and as of that date is repealed, unless a later enacted statute, that is enacted before January 1, 2026, deletes or extends that date. *(Added by Stats.2016, c. 783 (S.B.1046), § 33, eff. Jan. 1, 2017, operative Jan. 1, 2019. Amended by Stats.2017, c. 485 (S.B.611), § 26, eff. Jan. 1, 2018, operative Jan. 1, 2019.)*

Repeal

For repeal of this section, see its terms.

Cross References

Out of state residents, expiration of suspension or revocation period, see Vehicle Code § 13353.5.

Research References

West's California Judicial Council Forms CR–221, Order to Install Ignition Interlock Device.
West's California Judicial Council Forms CR–222, Ignition Interlock Installation Verification.
West's California Judicial Council Forms CR–223, Ignition Interlock Calibration Verification.
West's California Judicial Council Forms CR–224, Ignition Interlock Noncompliance Report.
West's California Judicial Council Forms CR–225, Ignition Interlock Removal and Modification to Probation Order.
West's California Judicial Council Forms CR–226, Notice to Employers of Ignition Interlock Restriction.
2 Witkin, California Criminal Law 4th Crimes Against Public Peace and Welfare § 279 (2021), In General.
2 Witkin, California Criminal Law 4th Crimes Against Public Peace and Welfare § 290 (2021), Ignition Interlock Device.
2 Witkin, California Criminal Law 4th Crimes Against Public Peace and Welfare § 306 (2021), Reason for Suspension, Revocation, or Restriction.

§ 23575. Court-mandated use of functioning, certified ignition interlock device

Section operative Jan. 1, 2026. See, also, § 23575 operative until Jan. 1, 2026.

(a)(1) In addition to any other law, the court may require that a person convicted of a first offense violation of Section 23152 or 23153 install a functioning, certified ignition interlock device on any vehicle that the person operates and prohibit that person from operating a motor vehicle unless that vehicle is equipped with a functioning, certified ignition interlock device. The court shall give heightened consideration to applying this sanction to a first offense violator with 0.15 percent or more, by weight, of alcohol in his or her blood at arrest, or with two or more prior moving traffic violations, or to persons who refused the chemical tests at arrest. If the court orders the ignition interlock device restriction, the term shall be determined by the court for a period not to exceed three years from the date of conviction. The court shall notify the Department of Motor Vehicles, as specified in subdivision (a) of Section 1803, of the terms of the restrictions in accordance with subdivision (a) of Section 1804. The Department of Motor Vehicles shall place the restriction in the person's records in the Department of Motor Vehicles.

(2) The court shall require a person convicted of a violation of Section 14601.2 to install a functioning, certified ignition interlock device on any vehicle that the person operates and prohibit the person from operating a motor vehicle unless the vehicle is equipped with a functioning, certified ignition interlock device. The term of the restriction shall be determined by the court for a period not to exceed three years from the date of conviction. The court shall notify the Department of Motor Vehicles, as specified in subdivision (a) of Section 1803, of the terms of the restrictions in accordance with subdivision (a) of Section 1804. The Department of Motor

Vehicles shall place the restriction in the person's records in the Department of Motor Vehicles.

(b) The court shall include on the abstract of conviction or violation submitted to the Department of Motor Vehicles under Section 1803 or 1816 the requirement and term for the use of a functioning, certified ignition interlock device. The records of the department shall reflect mandatory use of the device for the term ordered by the court.

(c) The court shall advise the person that installation of a functioning, certified ignition interlock device on a vehicle does not allow the person to drive without a valid driver's license.

(d) A person whose driving privilege is restricted by the court pursuant to this section shall arrange for each vehicle with a functioning, certified ignition interlock device to be serviced by the installer at least once every 60 days in order for the installer to recalibrate and monitor the operation of the device. The installer shall notify the court if the device is removed or indicates that the person has attempted to remove, bypass, or tamper with the device, or if the person fails three or more times to comply with any requirement for the maintenance or calibration of the ignition interlock device. There is no obligation for the installer to notify the court if the person has complied with all of the requirements of this article.

(e) The court shall monitor the installation and maintenance of a functioning, certified ignition interlock device restriction ordered pursuant to subdivision (a) or (*l*). If a person fails to comply with the court order, the court shall give notice of the fact to the department pursuant to Section 40509.1.

(f)(1) If a person is convicted of a violation of Section 23152 or 23153 and the offense occurred within 10 years of one or more separate violations of Section 23152 or 23153 that resulted in a conviction, or if a person is convicted of a violation of Section 23103, as specified in Section 23103.5, and is suspended for one year under Section 13353.3, the person may apply to the Department of Motor Vehicles for a restricted driver's license pursuant to Section 13352 or 13353.3 that prohibits the person from operating a motor vehicle unless that vehicle is equipped with a functioning, certified ignition interlock device, certified pursuant to Section 13386. The restriction shall remain in effect for at least the remaining period of the original suspension or revocation and until all reinstatement requirements in Section 13352 or 13353.4 are met.

(2) Pursuant to subdivision (g), the Department of Motor Vehicles shall immediately terminate the restriction issued pursuant to Section 13352 or 13353.3 and shall immediately suspend or revoke the privilege to operate a motor vehicle of a person who attempts to remove, bypass, or tamper with the device, who has the device removed prior to the termination date of the restriction, or who fails three or more times to comply with any requirement for the maintenance or calibration of the ignition interlock device ordered pursuant to Section 13352 or 13353.3. The privilege shall remain suspended or revoked for the remaining period of the originating suspension or revocation and until all reinstatement requirements in Section 13352 or 13353.4 are met, except that if the person provides proof to the satisfaction of the department that he or she is in compliance with the restriction issued pursuant to this section, the department may, in its discretion, restore the privilege to operate a motor vehicle and reimpose the remaining term of the restriction.

(g) A person whose driving privilege is restricted by the Department of Motor Vehicles pursuant to Section 13352 or 13353.3 shall arrange for each vehicle with a functioning, certified ignition interlock device to be serviced by the installer at least once every 60 days in order for the installer to recalibrate the device and monitor the operation of the device. The installer shall notify the Department of Motor Vehicles if the device is removed or indicates that the person has attempted to remove, bypass, or tamper with the device, or if the person fails three or more times to comply with any requirement for the maintenance or calibration of the ignition interlock device. There is no obligation on the part of the installer to notify the department or the court if the person has complied with all of the requirements of this section.

(h) This section does not permit a person to drive without a valid driver's license.

(i) The Department of Motor Vehicles shall include information along with the order of suspension or revocation for repeat offenders informing them that after a specified period of suspension or revocation has been completed, the person may either install a functioning, certified ignition interlock device on any vehicle that the person operates or remain with a suspended or revoked driver's license.

(j) Pursuant to this section, an out-of-state resident who otherwise would qualify for a functioning, certified ignition interlock device restricted license in California shall be prohibited from operating a motor vehicle in California unless that vehicle is equipped with a functioning, certified ignition interlock device. An ignition interlock device is not required to be installed on any vehicle owned by the defendant that is not driven in California.

(k) If a medical problem does not permit a person to breathe with sufficient strength to activate the device, that person shall only have the suspension option.

(*l*) This section does not restrict a court from requiring installation of a functioning, certified ignition interlock device and prohibiting operation of a motor vehicle unless that vehicle is equipped with a functioning, certified ignition interlock device for a person to whom subdivision (a) or (b) does not apply. The term of the restriction shall be determined by the court for a period not to exceed three years from the date of conviction. The court shall notify the Department of Motor Vehicles, as specified in subdivision (a) of Section 1803, of the terms of the restrictions in accordance with subdivision (a) of Section 1804. The Department of Motor Vehicles shall place the restriction in the person's records in the Department of Motor Vehicles.

(m) For the purposes of this section, "vehicle" does not include a motorcycle until the state certifies an ignition interlock device that can be installed on a motorcycle. Any person subject to an ignition interlock device restriction shall not operate a motorcycle for the duration of the ignition interlock device restriction period.

(n)(1) For the purposes of this section, "owned" means solely owned or owned in conjunction with another person or legal entity.

(2) For purposes of this section, "operates" includes operating a vehicle that is not owned by the person subject to this section.

(*o*) For the purposes of this section, "bypass" means either of the following:

(1) Failure to take any random retest.

(2) Failure to pass a random retest with a breath alcohol concentration not exceeding 0.03 percent breath alcohol concentration.

(p) For purposes of this section, "random retest" means a breath test performed by the driver upon a certified ignition interlock device at random intervals after the initial engine startup breath test and while the vehicle's motor is running.

(q) This section shall become operative January 1, 2026. *(Added by Stats.2016, c. 783 (S.B.1046), § 34, eff. Jan. 1, 2017, operative Jan. 1, 2026. Amended by Stats.2017, c. 485 (S.B.611), § 27, eff. Jan. 1, 2018, operative Jan. 1, 2026.)*

Cross References

Out of state residents, expiration of suspension or revocation period, see Vehicle Code § 13353.5.

Research References

West's California Judicial Council Forms CR–221, Order to Install Ignition Interlock Device.
West's California Judicial Council Forms CR–222, Ignition Interlock Installation Verification.
West's California Judicial Council Forms CR–223, Ignition Interlock Calibration Verification.
West's California Judicial Council Forms CR–224, Ignition Interlock Noncompliance Report.
West's California Judicial Council Forms CR–225, Ignition Interlock Removal and Modification to Probation Order.
West's California Judicial Council Forms CR–226, Notice to Employers of Ignition Interlock Restriction.
2 Witkin, California Criminal Law 4th Crimes Against Public Peace and Welfare § 279 (2021), In General.
2 Witkin, California Criminal Law 4th Crimes Against Public Peace and Welfare § 290 (2021), Ignition Interlock Device.
2 Witkin, California Criminal Law 4th Crimes Against Public Peace and Welfare § 306 (2021), Reason for Suspension, Revocation, or Restriction.

§ 23575.1. Ignition interlock devices; effectiveness study and report

The department may undertake a study and report its findings of that study to the Legislature on or before January 1, 2013, regarding the overall effectiveness of the use of ignition interlock devices (IID) to reduce the recidivism rate of first-time violators of Section 23152 or 23153. If the department exercises this authority, the study shall focus on those drivers who actually have an IID installed in their vehicles rather than on those who are subject to a judicial order to have an IID installed. *(Added by Stats.2008, c. 392 (S.B.1190), § 2.)*

§ 23575.3. Notice of requirement to install functioning, certified ignition interlock device; monitoring of installation and maintenance; term of requirement; fee schedule

(a) In addition to any other requirement imposed by law, a court shall notify a person convicted of a violation listed in subdivision (h) that he or she is required to install a functioning, certified ignition interlock device on any vehicle that the person operates and that he or she is prohibited from operating a motor vehicle unless that vehicle is equipped with a functioning, certified ignition interlock device in accordance with this section.

(b) The Department of Motor Vehicles, upon receipt of the court's abstract of conviction for a violation listed in subdivision (h), shall inform the convicted person of the requirements of this section, including the term for which the person is required to have a certified ignition interlock device installed. The records of the department shall reflect the mandatory use of the device for the term required and the time when the device is required to be installed by this code.

(c) The department shall advise the person that installation of a functioning, certified ignition interlock device on a vehicle does not allow the person to drive without a valid driver's license.

(d)(1) A person who is notified by the department pursuant to subdivision (b) shall do all of the following:

(A) Arrange for each vehicle operated by the person to be equipped with a functioning, certified ignition interlock device by a certified ignition interlock device provider under Section 13386.

(B) Provide to the department proof of installation by submitting the "Verification of Installation" form described in paragraph (2) of subdivision (g) of Section 13386.

(C) Pay a fee, determined by the department, that is sufficient to cover the costs of administration of this section.

(2) A person who is notified by the department pursuant to subdivision (b), is exempt from the requirements of this subdivision until the time he or she purchases or has access to a vehicle if, within 30 days of the notification, the person certifies to the department all of the following:

(A) The person does not own a vehicle.

(B) The person does not have access to a vehicle at his or her residence.

(C) The person no longer has access to the vehicle he or she was driving at the time he or she was arrested for a violation that subsequently resulted in a conviction for a violation listed in subdivision (h).

(D) The person acknowledges that he or she is only allowed to drive a vehicle that is equipped with a functioning, certified ignition interlock device.

(E) The person acknowledges that he or she is required to have a valid driver's license before he or she can drive.

(F) The person acknowledges that he or she is subject to the requirements of this section when he or she purchases or has access to a vehicle.

(e) In addition to any other restrictions the department places on the driver's license record of the convicted person when the person is issued a restricted driver's license pursuant to Section 13352 or 13352.4, the department shall place a restriction on the driver's license record of the person that states the driver is restricted to driving only vehicles equipped with a functioning, certified ignition interlock device for the applicable term.

(f)(1) A person who is notified by the department pursuant to subdivision (b) shall arrange for each vehicle with a functioning, certified ignition interlock device to be serviced by the installer at least once every 60 days in order for the installer to recalibrate and monitor the operation of the device.

(2) The installer shall notify the department if the device is removed or indicates that the person has attempted to remove, bypass, or tamper with the device, or if the person fails three or more times to comply with any requirement for the maintenance or calibration of the ignition interlock device.

(g) The department shall monitor the installation and maintenance of the ignition interlock device installed pursuant to subdivision (d).

(h) A person is required to install a functioning, certified ignition interlock device pursuant to this section for the applicable term, as follows:

(1) A person convicted of a violation of subdivision (a), (b), (d), (e), or (g) of Section 23152 shall be required to do the following, as applicable:

(A) Upon a conviction with no priors, punishable under Section 23536, only one of the following may occur:

(i) The court may order installation of a functioning, certified ignition interlock device on any vehicle that the person operates and prohibit that person from operating a motor vehicle unless that vehicle is equipped with a functioning, certified ignition interlock device. If the court orders the ignition interlock device restriction, the term shall be determined by the court for a period not to exceed six months from the date of conviction. The court shall notify the department of the conviction as specified in subdivision (a) of Section 1803 or Section 1816, and shall specify the terms of the ignition interlock device restriction in accordance with subdivision (a) of Section 1804. The department shall place the restriction on the driver's license record of the person that states the driver is restricted to driving only vehicles equipped with a functioning, certified ignition interlock device for the applicable term.

(ii) The person may apply to the department for a restriction of the driving privilege under Section 13352.4.

(iii) The person may apply to the department for a restriction of the driving privilege under paragraph (1) of subdivision (a) of Section 13352 or subdivision (c) of Section 13352.1.

(B) Upon a conviction with one prior, punishable under Section 23540, the person shall install a functioning, certified ignition interlock device in the vehicle, as ordered by the court, that is operated by that person for a mandatory term of 12 months.

(C) Upon a conviction with two priors, punishable under Section 23546, the person shall install a functioning, certified ignition interlock device in the vehicle, as ordered by the court, that is operated by that person for a mandatory term of 24 months.

(D) Upon a conviction with three or more priors punishable under Section 23550, or a conviction punishable under Section 23550.5, the person shall install a functioning, certified ignition interlock device in the vehicle, as ordered by the court, that is operated by that person for a mandatory term of 36 months.

(2) A person convicted of a violation of subdivision (a), (b), (d), (e), or (g) of Section 23153 shall install a functioning, certified ignition interlock device, as follows:

(A) Upon a conviction with no priors, punishable under Section 23554, the person shall install a functioning, certified ignition interlock device in the vehicle, as ordered by the court, that is operated by that person for a mandatory term of 12 months.

(B) Upon a conviction with one prior, punishable under Section 23560, the person shall install a functioning, certified ignition interlock device in the vehicle, as ordered by the court, that is operated by that person for a mandatory term of 24 months.

(C) Upon a conviction with two priors, punishable under Section 23550 or 23566, the person shall install a functioning, certified ignition interlock device in the vehicle, as ordered by the court, that is operated by that person for a mandatory term of 36 months.

(D) Upon a conviction with one prior punishable under Section 23550.5, the person shall install a functioning, certified ignition interlock device in the vehicle, as ordered by the court, that is operated by that person for a mandatory term of 48 months.

(3) For the purposes of paragraphs (1) and (2), "prior" means a conviction for a separate violation of Section 23103, as specified in Section 23103.5, or Section 23152 or 23153, subdivision (a) or (b) of Section 191.5 of, or subdivision (a) of Section 192.5 of, the Penal Code, or subdivision (b), (c), (d), (e), or (f) of Section 655 of the Harbors and Navigation Code, that occurred within 10 years of the current violation.

(4) The terms prescribed in this subdivision shall begin once a person has complied with subparagraph (B) of paragraph (1) of subdivision (d) and either upon the reinstatement of the privilege to drive pursuant to Section 13352 or the issuance of a restricted driver's license pursuant to Section 13352. A person shall receive credit for any period in which he or she had a restricted driver's license issued pursuant to Section 13353.6 or 13353.75.

(i) Subdivisions (g), (h), (j), and (k) of Section 23575 apply to this section.

(j) If a person fails to comply with any of the requirements regarding ignition interlock devices, the period in which the person was not in compliance shall not be credited towards the mandatory term for which the ignition interlock device is required to be installed.

(k)(1) Every manufacturer and manufacturer's agent certified by the department to provide ignition interlock devices, under Section 13386, shall adopt the following fee schedule that provides for the payment of the costs of the certified ignition interlock device by offenders subject to this chapter in amounts commensurate with that person's income relative to the federal poverty level, as defined in Section 127400 of the Health and Safety Code:

(A) A person with an income at 100 percent of the federal poverty level or below and who provides income verification pursuant to paragraph (2) is responsible for 10 percent of the cost of the manufacturer's standard ignition interlock device program costs, and any additional costs accrued by the person for noncompliance with program requirements.

(B) A person with an income at 101 to 200 percent of the federal poverty level and who provides income verification pursuant to paragraph (2) is responsible for 25 percent of the cost of the manufacturer's standard ignition interlock device program costs, and any additional costs accrued by the person for noncompliance with program requirements.

(C) A person with an income at 201 to 300 percent of the federal poverty level and who provides income verification pursuant to paragraph (2) is responsible for 50 percent of the cost of the manufacturer's standard ignition interlock device program costs, and any additional costs accrued by the person for noncompliance with program requirements.

(D) A person who is receiving CalFresh benefits and who provides proof of those benefits to the manufacturer or manufacturer's agent or authorized installer is responsible for 50 percent of the cost of the manufacturer's standard ignition interlock device program costs, and any additional costs accrued by the person for noncompliance with program requirements.

(E) A person with an income at 301 to 400 percent of the federal poverty level and who provides income verification pursuant to paragraph (2) is responsible for 90 percent of the cost of the manufacturer's standard ignition interlock device program costs, and any additional costs accrued by the person for noncompliance with program requirements.

(F) All other offenders are responsible for 100 percent of the cost of the ignition interlock device.

(G) The manufacturer is responsible for the percentage of costs that the offender is not responsible for pursuant to subparagraphs (A) to (E), inclusive.

(2) The ignition interlock device provider shall verify the offender's income to determine the cost of the ignition interlock device pursuant to this subdivision by verifying one of the following documents from the offender:

(A) The previous year's federal income tax return.

(B) The previous three months of weekly or monthly income statements.

(C) Employment Development Department verification of unemployment benefits.

(*l*) The Department of Consumer Affairs may impose a civil assessment not to exceed one thousand dollars ($1,000) upon a manufacturer or manufacturer's agent certified to provide ignition interlock devices who fails to inform an offender subject to this chapter of the provisions of subdivision (k), or who fails to comply with the provisions of subdivision (k).

(m) This section does not permit a person to drive without a valid driver's license.

(n) The requirements of this section are in addition to any other requirements of law.

(*o*) For the purposes of this section, the following definitions apply:

(1) "Bypass" means either of the following:

(A) Failure to take any random retest.

(B) Failure to pass a random retest with a breath alcohol concentration not exceeding 0.03 percent, by weight of alcohol, in the person's blood.

(2) "Operates" includes operating a vehicle that is not owned by the person subject to this section.

(3) "Owned" means solely owned or owned in conjunction with another person or legal entity.

(4) "Random retest" means a breath test performed by the driver upon a certified ignition interlock device at random intervals after the initial engine startup breath test and while the vehicle's motor is running.

(5) "Vehicle" does not include a motorcycle until the state certifies an ignition interlock device that can be installed on a motorcycle. A person subject to an ignition interlock device restriction shall not operate a motorcycle for the duration of the ignition interlock device restriction period.

(p) The requirements of this section shall apply only to a person who is convicted for a violation of Section 23152 or 23153 that occurred on or after January 1, 2019.

(q) This section shall become operative on January 1, 2019.

(r) This section shall remain in effect only until January 1, 2026, and as of that date is repealed, unless a later enacted statute, that is enacted before January 1, 2026, deletes or extends that date. *(Added by Stats.2016, c. 783 (S.B.1046), § 35, eff. Jan. 1, 2017, operative Jan. 1, 2019. Amended by Stats.2017, c. 485 (S.B.611), § 28, eff. Jan. 1, 2018, operative Jan. 1, 2019.)*

Repeal

For repeal of this section, see its terms.

Cross References

Automotive repair, installation, calibration, service, etc. of certified ignition interlock devices, compliance with fee provisions of this section, see Business and Professions Code § 9882.14.
Proceedings to contest citation for violation of this section, conduct, see Business and Professions Code § 9848.
Service dealers, installation, calibration, service, etc. of certified ignition interlock devices, compliance with fee provisions of this section, see Business and Professions Code § 9807.

Research References

2 Witkin, California Criminal Law 4th Crimes Against Public Peace and Welfare § 280 (2021), First Violation.
2 Witkin, California Criminal Law 4th Crimes Against Public Peace and Welfare § 281 (2021), One Separate Conviction of Related Offense.
2 Witkin, California Criminal Law 4th Crimes Against Public Peace and Welfare § 282 (2021), Two Separate Convictions of Related Offenses.
2 Witkin, California Criminal Law 4th Crimes Against Public Peace and Welfare § 283 (2021), Three or More Separate Convictions of Related Offenses.
2 Witkin, California Criminal Law 4th Crimes Against Public Peace and Welfare § 285 (2021), First Violation.
2 Witkin, California Criminal Law 4th Crimes Against Public Peace and Welfare § 286 (2021), One Separate Conviction of Related Offense.
2 Witkin, California Criminal Law 4th Crimes Against Public Peace and Welfare § 287 (2021), Two or More Separate Convictions of Related Offenses.
2 Witkin, California Criminal Law 4th Crimes Against Public Peace and Welfare § 290 (2021), Ignition Interlock Device.
3 Witkin, California Criminal Law 4th Punishment § 214 (2021), Drunk Driving.

§ 23575.5. Reporting of data regarding implementation and efficacy of ignition interlock program; contract for analysis of data; assessment and report to Legislature

(a) On or before March 1, 2024, the Department of Motor Vehicles shall report data to the Transportation Agency regarding the implementation and efficacy of the program enacted by the act that added this section.

(b) The data described in subdivision (a) shall, at a minimum, include all of the following:

(1) The number of individuals who were required to have a functioning, certified ignition interlock device installed as a result of the program who killed or injured anyone in * * * a crash while * * * they were operating a vehicle under the influence of alcohol.

(2) The number of individuals who were required to have a functioning, certified ignition interlock device installed as a result of the program who were convicted of an alcohol-related violation of Section 23103, as specified in Section 23103.5, or Section 23140, 23152, or 23153, or Section 191.5 or subdivision (a) of Section 192.5 of the Penal Code during the term in which the person was required to have the ignition interlock device installed.

(3) The number of injuries and deaths resulting from alcohol-related motor vehicle crashes between January 1, 2019, and January 1, 2024, inclusive, and during periods of similar duration prior to the implementation of the program.

(4) The number of individuals who have been convicted more than one time for driving under the influence of alcohol between January 1, 2019, and January 1, 2024, inclusive, and periods of similar duration prior to the implementation of the program.

(5) Any other information requested by the Transportation Agency to assess the effectiveness of the statewide ignition interlock device requirement in reducing recidivism for driving-under-the-influence violations.

(c) The Transportation Agency may contract with educational institutions to obtain and analyze the data required by this section.

(d) The Transportation Agency shall assess the program based on the data provided pursuant to subdivision (b) and shall report to the Legislature on the outcomes of the program no later than January 1, 2025.

(e) The report described in subdivision (a) shall be submitted in compliance with Section 9795 of the Government Code.

(f)(1) This section shall become operative on January 1, 2019.

(2) This section is repealed as of January 1, 2029, unless a later enacted statute, that becomes operative on or before January 1, 2029, deletes or extends the dates on which it becomes inoperative and is repealed. *(Added by Stats.2016, c. 783 (S.B.1046), § 36, eff. Jan. 1, 2017, operative Jan. 1, 2019. Amended by Stats.2022, c. 81 (A.B.2198), § 6, eff. Jan. 1, 2023.)*

Repeal

For repeal of this section, see its terms.

§ 23576. Motor vehicle owned by employer; installation of ignition interlock device; exemption

Section operative until Jan. 1, 2026. See, also, § 23576 operative Jan. 1, 2026.

(a) Notwithstanding Sections 13352, 13352.1, 13353.6, 13353.75, 23573, 23575, 23575.3, and 23700, if a person is required to operate a motor vehicle in the course and scope of his or her employment and if the vehicle is owned by the employer, the person may operate that vehicle without installation of a functioning, certified approved ignition interlock device if the employer has been notified by the person that the person's driving privilege has been restricted pursuant to Section 13352, 13352.1, 13353.6, 13353.75, 23573, 23575, 23575.3, or 23700 and if the person has proof of that notification in his or her possession, or if the notice, or a facsimile copy thereof, is with the vehicle.

(b) A motor vehicle owned by a business entity that is all or partly owned or controlled by a person otherwise subject to Section 13352, 13352.1, 13353.6, 13353.75, 23573, 23575, 23575.3, or 23700, is not a motor vehicle owned by the employer subject to the exemption in subdivision (a).

(c) This section shall become operative on January 1, 2019.

(d) This section shall remain in effect only until January 1, 2026, and as of that date is repealed, unless a later enacted statute, that is enacted before January 1, 2026, deletes or extends that date. *(Added by Stats.2016, c. 783 (S.B.1046), § 38, eff. Jan. 1, 2017, operative Jan. 1, 2019. Amended by Stats.2017, c. 485 (S.B.611), § 29, eff. Jan. 1, 2018, operative Jan. 1, 2019.)*

Repeal

For repeal of this section, see its terms.

Research References

West's California Judicial Council Forms CR–221, Order to Install Ignition Interlock Device.
West's California Judicial Council Forms CR–224, Ignition Interlock Noncompliance Report.
West's California Judicial Council Forms CR–225, Ignition Interlock Removal and Modification to Probation Order.
West's California Judicial Council Forms CR–226, Notice to Employers of Ignition Interlock Restriction.
2 Witkin, California Criminal Law 4th Crimes Against Public Peace and Welfare § 290 (2021), Ignition Interlock Device.

§ 23576. Motor vehicle owned by employer; installation of ignition interlock device; exemption

Section operative Jan. 1, 2026. See, also, § 23576 operative until Jan. 1, 2026.

(a) Notwithstanding Sections 23575 and 23700, if a person is required to operate a motor vehicle in the course and scope of his or her employment and if the vehicle is owned by the employer, the person may operate that vehicle without installation of a functioning, certified ignition interlock device if the employer has been notified by the person that the person's driving privilege has been restricted pursuant to Section 23575 or 23700 and if the person has proof of that notification in his or her possession, or if the notice, or a facsimile copy thereof, is with the vehicle.

(b) A motor vehicle owned by a business entity that is all or partly owned or controlled by a person otherwise subject to Section 23575 or 23700 is not a motor vehicle owned by the employer subject to the exemption in subdivision (a).

(c) This section shall become operative January 1, 2026. *(Added by Stats.2016, c. 783 (S.B.1046), § 39, eff. Jan. 1, 2017, operative Jan. 1, 2026.)*

Research References

West's California Judicial Council Forms CR–221, Order to Install Ignition Interlock Device.
West's California Judicial Council Forms CR–224, Ignition Interlock Noncompliance Report.
West's California Judicial Council Forms CR–225, Ignition Interlock Removal and Modification to Probation Order.
West's California Judicial Council Forms CR–226, Notice to Employers of Ignition Interlock Restriction.
2 Witkin, California Criminal Law 4th Crimes Against Public Peace and Welfare § 290 (2021), Ignition Interlock Device.

§ 23577. Additional penalties for willful refusal to submit to or willful failure to complete breath or urine test at time of arrest

(a) If a person is convicted of a violation of Section 23152 or 23153, and at the time of the arrest leading to that conviction that person willfully refused a peace officer's request to submit to, or willfully failed to complete, the breath or urine tests pursuant to Section 23612, the court shall impose the following penalties:

(1) If the person is convicted of a first violation of Section 23152, notwithstanding any other provision of subdivision (a) of Section 23538, the terms and conditions of probation shall include the conditions in paragraph (1) of subdivision (a) of Section 23538.

(2) If the person is convicted of a first violation of Section 23153, the punishment shall be enhanced by an imprisonment of 48 continuous hours in the county jail, whether or not probation is granted and no part of which may be stayed, unless the person is sentenced to, and incarcerated in, the state prison and the execution of that sentence is not stayed.

(3) If the person is convicted of a second violation of Section 23152, punishable under Section 23540, or a second violation of Section 23153, punishable under Section 23560, the punishment shall be enhanced by an imprisonment of 96 hours in the county jail, whether or not probation is granted and no part of which may be stayed, unless the person is sentenced to, and incarcerated in, the state prison and execution of that sentence is not stayed.

(4) If the person is convicted of a third violation of Section 23152, punishable under Section 23546, the punishment shall be enhanced by an imprisonment of 10 days in the county jail, whether or not probation is granted and no part of which may be stayed.

(5) If the person is convicted of a fourth or subsequent violation of Section 23152, punishable under Section 23550 or 23550.5, the punishment shall be enhanced by imprisonment of 18 days in the county jail, whether or not probation is granted and no part of which may be stayed.

(b) The willful refusal or failure to complete the breath or urine test required pursuant to Section 23612 shall be pled and proven.

(c) The penalties in this section do not apply to a person who refused to submit to or complete a blood test pursuant to Section 23612. This section does not prohibit imposition of administrative actions involving driving privileges. *(Added by Stats.1998, c. 118 (S.B.1186), § 84, operative July 1, 1999. Amended by Stats.1999, c. 22 (S.B.24), § 39, eff. May 26, 1999, operative July 1, 1999; Stats.2018, c. 177 (A.B.2717), § 1, eff. Jan. 1, 2019.)*

Research References

California Jury Instructions - Criminal 17.29, Willful Refusal to Take or Complete Tests Regarding Driving Under the Influence.
California Jury Instructions - Criminal 17.29.1, Implied Consent—Choice of Tests.
2 Witkin, California Criminal Law 4th Crimes Against Public Peace and Welfare § 279 (2021), In General.
2 Witkin, California Criminal Law 4th Crimes Against Public Peace and Welfare § 280 (2021), First Violation.
2 Witkin, California Criminal Law 4th Crimes Against Public Peace and Welfare § 281 (2021), One Separate Conviction of Related Offense.
2 Witkin, California Criminal Law 4th Crimes Against Public Peace and Welfare § 282 (2021), Two Separate Convictions of Related Offenses.
2 Witkin, California Criminal Law 4th Crimes Against Public Peace and Welfare § 283 (2021), Three or More Separate Convictions of Related Offenses.
2 Witkin, California Criminal Law 4th Crimes Against Public Peace and Welfare § 285 (2021), First Violation.
2 Witkin, California Criminal Law 4th Crimes Against Public Peace and Welfare § 286 (2021), One Separate Conviction of Related Offense.
4 Witkin, California Criminal Law 4th Illegally Obtained Evidence § 193A (2021), (New) Body Search for Blood Alcohol Level.

§ 23578. Special factors for enhancement of sentencing or probation; blood alcohol concentration of 0.15 percent or greater; refusal to take breath or urine test

In addition to any other provision of this code, if a person is convicted of a violation of Section 23152 or 23153, the court shall consider a concentration of alcohol in the person's blood of 0.15 percent or more, by weight, or the refusal of the person to take a breath or urine test, as a special factor that may justify enhancing the penalties in sentencing, in determining whether to grant probation, and, if probation is granted, in determining additional or enhanced terms and conditions of probation. *(Added by Stats.1998, c. 118 (S.B.1186), § 84, operative July 1, 1999. Amended by Stats.2005, c. 89 (A.B.571), § 1; Stats.2018, c. 177 (A.B.2717), § 2, eff. Jan. 1, 2019.)*

Cross References

Alcohol and drug problem assessment program, violator participation, sentencing, and assessment upon fine, see Vehicle Code § 23646 et seq.
Alcoholic beverages in vehicles, see Vehicle Code § 23220 et seq.

Applicability of this section to trolley coaches, see Vehicle Code § 21051.
Arrest without warrant, see Vehicle Code § 40300.5.
Challenging constitutional validity of separate conviction, see Vehicle Code § 41403.
Chemical blood, breath or urine tests, see Vehicle Code § 13353.
Chemical tests as evidence, see Vehicle Code § 23610.
Conviction of violation of specified subdivisions of Penal Code § 192 to be deemed conviction of violation of specified DUI provisions, see Vehicle Code § 13350.5.
Coroner's inquiry into deaths, see Government Code § 27491.25.
County alcohol and drug problem assessment programs, mandatory participation for convicted violators of this section, see Vehicle Code §§ 23646, 23647.
Crime of violence, within act for indemnification of victims of crime, see Government Code § 13960.
Defense of drug use to violations, see Vehicle Code § 23630.
Deposit in special account for each conviction under DUI provisions, see Penal Code § 1463.14.
Drivers license revocation, conviction of driver under eighteen, see Vehicle Code § 13352.3.
Driving school or instructor, revocation or suspension of license for violation of this section, see Vehicle Code § 11110.
Gross vehicular manslaughter while intoxicated, see Penal Code § 191.5.
Guilty plea, see Vehicle Code § 41610.
Impoundment of vehicle of registered owner convicted under this section, see Vehicle Code § 23594.
Influence of alcoholic beverage or drug, suspension or revocation of driving privileges, see Vehicle Code § 13352.
Injury to guest by intoxicated driver, see Vehicle Code § 17158.
Juvenile offenders, programs of supervision, see Welfare and Institutions Code § 654.1.
Manslaughter, negligent homicide by vehicle, see Penal Code § 192.
Nuisance, sale or other disposition of motor vehicle driven by defendant, see Vehicle Code § 23596.
Persons certified or granted probation on conviction of driving under the influence of alcohol or drugs or combined influence on certain conditions, restriction, revocation or suspension of driving privilege, consent to participation in treatment program, see Vehicle Code § 13352.5.
Please Don't Drink and Drive memorial signs, requests for and duration of placement, exception for a party to an accident convicted or determined to be mentally incompetent under this section, see Streets and Highways Code § 101.10.
Presentence investigation and assessment, see Vehicle Code § 23655.
Presumptions, see Evidence Code § 600 et seq.
Prior convictions under sections 23103, 23152 or 23153, effect on sentencing and driving privileges, see Vehicle Code § 23622.
Procedure on arrest for violation of this section, see Vehicle Code § 40302.
Records available to courts and law enforcement officials, incidents under certain DWI and homicide laws, period of time records must be available, see Vehicle Code § 1808.
Refusal to submit to alcohol testing under DUI laws, calculation of prior convictions, certain foreign convictions recognized, see Vehicle Code §§ 13353, 13353.1 and 13353.3.
Surrender of driver's license to court, see Vehicle Code § 13550.
Suspension or revocation of driving privilege for a violation of this section, notice by personal service, see Vehicle Code § 13106.
Suspension or revocation of license,
  Generally, see Vehicle Code § 13352.
  Alcohol-related accident within five years of vehicular manslaughter, see Vehicle Code § 13954.
  Driver license compact, see Vehicle Code § 15000 et seq.
  Driving after suspension or revocation, see Vehicle Code § 14601.2.
  Investigation by department, three convictions in three years under this or other specified statutes, see Vehicle Code § 13800.
  Prior convictions, record, see Vehicle Code § 13209.
Traffic violation point count, violation of this section, see Vehicle Code § 12810.
Traffic violators schools, suspension or revocation of license for violation of this section, see Vehicle Code § 11215.
Vehicular homicide, see Penal Code § 192.
Violation as misdemeanor, see Vehicle Code § 40000.15.
Violation of this section, relinquishment of motor vehicle to convicted minor, see Penal Code § 193.8.
Youthful drunk driver visitation program, see Vehicle Code § 23509 et seq.

Research References

2 Witkin, California Criminal Law 4th Crimes Against Public Peace and Welfare § 279 (2021), In General.
2 Witkin, California Criminal Law 4th Crimes Against Public Peace and Welfare § 281 (2021), One Separate Conviction of Related Offense.
2 Witkin, California Criminal Law 4th Crimes Against Public Peace and Welfare § 282 (2021), Two Separate Convictions of Related Offenses.
2 Witkin, California Criminal Law 4th Crimes Against Public Peace and Welfare § 283 (2021), Three or More Separate Convictions of Related Offenses.
2 Witkin, California Criminal Law 4th Crimes Against Public Peace and Welfare § 285 (2021), First Violation.
2 Witkin, California Criminal Law 4th Crimes Against Public Peace and Welfare § 286 (2021), One Separate Conviction of Related Offense.

§ 23580. Second or subsequent offense involving alcohol or drugs; minimum confinement

(a) If any person is convicted of a violation of Section 23152 or 23153 and the offense was a second or subsequent offense punishable under Section 23540, 23546, 23550, 23550.5, 23560, or 23566, the court shall require that any term of imprisonment that is imposed include at least one period of not less than 48 consecutive hours of imprisonment or, in the alternative and notwithstanding Section 4024.2 of the Penal Code, that the person serve not less than 10 days of community service.

(b) Notwithstanding any other provision of law, except Section 2900.5 of the Penal Code, unless the court expressly finds in the circumstances that the punishment inflicted would be cruel or unusual punishment prohibited by Section 17 of Article I of the California Constitution, no court or person to whom a person is remanded for execution of sentence shall release, or permit the release of, a person from the requirements of subdivision (a), including, but not limited to, any work-release program, weekend service of sentence program, diversion or treatment program, or otherwise.

(c) For the purposes of this section, "imprisonment" means confinement in a jail, in a minimum security facility, or in an inpatient rehabilitation facility, as provided in Part 1309 (commencing with Section 1309.1) of Title 23 of the Code of Federal Regulations. *(Added by Stats.1998, c. 118 (S.B.1186), § 84, operative July 1, 1999. Amended by Stats.2002, c. 664 (A.B.3034), § 223.)*

Cross References

Alcohol and drug problem assessment program, violator participation, sentencing, and assessment upon fine, see Vehicle Code § 23646 et seq.
Alcoholic beverages in vehicles, see Vehicle Code § 23220 et seq.
Applicability of this section to trolley coaches, see Vehicle Code § 21051.
Arrest without warrant, see Vehicle Code § 40300.5.
Challenging constitutional validity of separate conviction, see Vehicle Code § 41403.
Chemical blood, breath or urine tests, see Vehicle Code § 13353.
Chemical tests as evidence, see Vehicle Code § 23610.
Conviction of violation of specified subdivisions of Penal Code § 192 to be deemed conviction of violation of specified DUI provisions, see Vehicle Code § 13350.5.
Coroner's inquiry into deaths, see Government Code § 27491.25.
County alcohol and drug problem assessment programs, mandatory participation for convicted violators of this section, see Vehicle Code §§ 23646, 23647.
Crime of violence, within act for indemnification of victims of crime, see Government Code § 13960.
Defense of drug use to violations, see Vehicle Code § 23630.
Deposit in special account for each conviction under DUI provisions, see Penal Code § 1463.14.
Drivers license revocation, conviction of driver under eighteen, see Vehicle Code § 13352.3.
Driving school or instructor, revocation or suspension of license for violation of this section, see Vehicle Code § 11110.
Gross vehicular manslaughter while intoxicated, see Penal Code § 191.5.
Guilty plea, see Vehicle Code § 41610.

Impoundment of vehicle of registered owner convicted under this section, see Vehicle Code § 23594.
Influence of alcoholic beverage or drug, suspension or revocation of driving privileges, see Vehicle Code § 13352.
Injury to guest by intoxicated driver, see Vehicle Code § 17158.
Juvenile offenders, programs of supervision, see Welfare and Institutions Code § 654.1.
Manslaughter, negligent homicide by vehicle, see Penal Code § 192.
Nuisance, sale or other disposition of motor vehicle driven by defendant, see Vehicle Code § 23596.
Persons certified or granted probation on conviction of driving under the influence of alcohol or drugs or combined influence on certain conditions, restriction, revocation or suspension of driving privilege, consent to participation in treatment program, see Vehicle Code § 13352.5.
Please Don't Drink and Drive memorial signs, requests for and duration of placement, exception for a party to an accident convicted or determined to be mentally incompetent under this section, see Streets and Highways Code § 101.10.
Presentence investigation and assessment, see Vehicle Code § 23655.
Presumptions, see Evidence Code § 600 et seq.
Prior convictions under sections 23103, 23152 or 23153, effect on sentencing and driving privileges, see Vehicle Code § 23622.
Procedure on arrest for violation of this section, see Vehicle Code § 40302.
Records available to courts and law enforcement officials, incidents under certain DWI and homicide laws, period of time records must be available, see Vehicle Code § 1808.
Refusal to submit to alcohol testing under DUI laws, calculation of prior convictions, certain foreign convictions recognized, see Vehicle Code §§ 13353, 13353.1 and 13353.3.
Surrender of driver's license to court, see Vehicle Code § 13550.
Suspension or revocation of driving privilege for a violation of this section, notice by personal service, see Vehicle Code § 13106.
Suspension or revocation of license,
  Generally, see Vehicle Code § 13352.
  Alcohol-related accident within five years of vehicular manslaughter, see Vehicle Code § 13954.
  Driver license compact, see Vehicle Code § 15000 et seq.
  Driving after suspension or revocation, see Vehicle Code § 14601.2.
  Investigation by department, three convictions in three years under this or other specified statutes, see Vehicle Code § 13800.
  Prior convictions, record, see Vehicle Code § 13209.
Traffic violation point count, violation of this section, see Vehicle Code § 12810.
Traffic violators schools, suspension or revocation of license for violation of this section, see Vehicle Code § 11215.
Vehicular homicide, see Penal Code § 192.
Violation as misdemeanor, see Vehicle Code § 40000.15.
Violation of this section, relinquishment of motor vehicle to convicted minor, see Penal Code § 193.8.
Youthful drunk driver visitation program, see Vehicle Code § 23509 et seq.

§ 23582. Driving under the influence; additional penalty for excessive speed and reckless driving during commission of offense

(a) Any person who drives a vehicle 30 or more miles per hour over the maximum, prima facie, or posted speed limit on a freeway, or 20 or more miles per hour over the maximum, prima facie, or posted speed limit on any other street or highway, and in a manner prohibited by Section 23103 during the commission of a violation of Section 23152 or 23153 shall, in addition to the punishment prescribed for that person upon conviction of a violation of Section 23152 or 23153, be punished by an additional and consecutive term of 60 days in the county jail.

(b) If the court grants probation or suspends the execution of sentence, it shall require as a condition of probation or suspension that the defendant serve 60 days in the county jail, in addition and consecutive to any other sentence prescribed by this chapter.

(c) On a first conviction under this section, the court shall order the driver to participate in, and successfully complete, an alcohol or drug education and counseling program, or both an alcohol and a drug education and counseling program. Except in unusual cases where the interests of justice would be served, a finding making this section applicable to a defendant shall not be stricken pursuant to Section 1385 of the Penal Code or any other provision of law. If the court decides not to impose the additional and consecutive term, it shall specify on the court record the reasons for that order.

(d) The additional term provided in this section shall not be imposed unless the facts of driving in a manner prohibited by Section 23103 and driving the vehicle 30 or more miles per hour over the maximum, prima facie, or posted speed limit on a freeway, or 20 or more miles per hour over the maximum, prima facie, or posted speed limit on any other street or highway, are charged in the accusatory pleading and admitted or found to be true by the trier of fact. A finding of driving in that manner shall be based on facts in addition to the fact that the defendant was driving while under the influence of alcohol, any drug, or both, or with a specified percentage of alcohol in the blood. *(Added by Stats.1998, c. 118 (S.B.1186), § 84, operative July 1, 1999.)*

Research References

2 Witkin, California Criminal Law 4th Crimes Against Public Peace and Welfare § 279 (2021), In General.

ARTICLE 6. ADDITIONAL COURT–IMPOSED ORDERS AND DIRECTIONS

Section

§ 23592. Impoundment of vehicle; specified offenses

(a)(1) Whenever a person is convicted of any of the following offenses committed while driving a motor vehicle of which he or she is the owner, the court, at the time sentence is imposed on the person, may order the motor vehicle impounded for a period of not more than six months for a first conviction, and not more than 12 months for a second or subsequent conviction:

(A) Driving with a suspended or revoked driver's license.

(B) A violation of Section 2800.2 resulting in an accident or Section 2800.3, if either violation occurred within seven years of one or more separate convictions for a violation of any of the following:

(i) Section 23103, if the vehicle involved in the violation was driven at a speed of 100 or more miles per hour.

(ii) Section 23152.

(iii) Section 23153.

(iv) Subdivisions (a) and (b) of Section 191.5 of the Penal Code.

(v) Subdivision (c) of Section 192 of the Penal Code.

(vi) Subdivision (a) of Section 192.5 of the Penal Code.

(2) The cost of keeping the vehicle is a lien on the vehicle pursuant to Chapter 6.5 (commencing with Section 3067) of Title 14 of Part 4 of Division 3 of the Civil Code.

(b) Notwithstanding subdivision (a), a motor vehicle impounded pursuant to this section that is subject to a chattel mortgage, conditional sale contract, or lease contract shall be released by the court to the legal owner upon the filing of an affidavit by the legal owner that the chattel mortgage, conditional sale contract, or lease contract is in default and shall be delivered to the legal owner upon payment of the accrued cost of keeping the vehicle. *(Added by Stats.1998, c. 118 (S.B.1186), § 84, operative July 1, 1999. Amended by Stats.2007, c. 747 (A.B.678), § 35.)*

Cross References

Illegal dumping of waste matter, impoundment, see Vehicle Code § 23112.7.

Research References

3 Witkin, California Criminal Law 4th Punishment § 195 (2021), Impounding of Motor Vehicles.

§ 23593. Advisory statement to be given by court to person convicted of violation of specified sections

(a) The court shall advise a person convicted of a violation of Section 23103, as specified in Section 23103.5, or a violation of Section 23152 or 23153, as follows:

"You are hereby advised that being under the influence of alcohol or drugs, or both, impairs your ability to safely operate a motor vehicle. Therefore, it is extremely dangerous to human life to drive while under the influence of alcohol or drugs, or both. If you continue to drive while under the influence of alcohol or drugs, or both, and, as a result of that driving, someone is killed, you can be charged with murder."

(b) The advisory statement may be included in a plea form, if used, or the fact that the advice was given may be specified on the record.

(c) The court shall include on the abstract of the conviction or violation submitted to the department under Section 1803 or 1816, the fact that the person has been advised as required under subdivision (a). *(Added by Stats.2004, c. 502 (A.B.2173), § 1. Amended by Stats.2005, c. 22 (S.B.1108), § 203; Stats.2005, c. 279 (S.B.1107), § 24.)*

Research References

1 Witkin California Criminal Law 4th Crimes Against the Person § 220 (2021), In General.

§ 23594. Impoundment of vehicle of registered owner convicted of violation of § 23152 or § 23153; prior offenses; considerations; exemption

(a) Except as provided in subdivision (b), the interest of any registered owner of a motor vehicle that has been used in the commission of a violation of Section 23152 or 23153 for which the owner was convicted, is subject to impoundment as provided in this section. Upon conviction, the court may order the vehicle impounded at the registered owner's expense for not less than one nor more than 30 days.

If the offense occurred within five years of a prior offense which resulted in conviction of a violation of Section 23152 or 23153, the prior conviction shall also be charged in the accusatory pleading and if admitted or found to be true by the jury upon a jury trial or by the court upon a court trial, the court shall, except in an unusual case where the interests of justice would best be served by not ordering impoundment, order the vehicle impounded at the registered owner's expense for not less than one nor more than 30 days.

If the offense occurred within five years of two or more prior offenses which resulted in convictions of violations of Section 23152 or 23153, the prior convictions shall also be charged in the accusatory pleading and if admitted or found to be true by the jury upon a jury trial or by the court upon a court trial, the court shall, except in an unusual case where the interests of justice would best be served by not ordering impoundment, order the vehicle impounded at the registered owner's expense for not less than one nor more than 90 days.

For the purposes of this section, the court may consider in the interests of justice factors such as whether impoundment of the vehicle would result in a loss of employment of the offender or the offender's family, impair the ability of the offender or the offender's family to attend school or obtain medical care, result in the loss of the vehicle because of inability to pay impoundment fees, or unfairly infringe upon community property rights or any other facts the court finds relevant. When no impoundment is ordered in an unusual case pursuant to this section, the court shall specify on the record and shall enter in the minutes the circumstances indicating that the interests of justice would best be served by that disposition.

(b) No vehicle which may be lawfully driven on the highway with a class C or class M driver's license, as specified in Section 12804.9, is subject to impoundment under this section if there is a community property interest in the vehicle owned by a person other than the defendant and the vehicle is the sole vehicle available to the defendant's immediate family which may be operated on the highway with a class C or class M driver's license. *(Added by Stats.1998, c. 118 (S.B.1186), § 84, operative July 1, 1999.)*

Cross References

Immediate removal and seizure of vehicle driven by repeat offender, storage and impoundment, vehicle owner's rights and responsibilities, see Vehicle Code § 14602.8.

Research References

2 Witkin, California Criminal Law 4th Crimes Against Public Peace and Welfare § 279 (2021), In General.

3 Witkin, California Criminal Law 4th Punishment § 195 (2021), Impounding of Motor Vehicles.

§ 23596. Motor vehicle as nuisance; sale of vehicle

(a)(1) Upon its own motion or upon motion of the prosecutor in a criminal action for a violation of any of the following offenses, the court with jurisdiction over the offense, notwithstanding Section 86 of the Code of Civil Procedure and any other provision of law otherwise prescribing the jurisdiction of the court based upon the value of the property involved, may declare the motor vehicle driven by the defendant to be a nuisance if the defendant is the registered owner of the vehicle:

(A) A violation of Section 191.5 of, or subdivision (a) of Section 192.5 of, the Penal Code.

(B) A violation of Section 23152 that occurred within seven years of two or more separate offenses of Section 191.5 of, or subdivision (a) of Section 192.5 of, the Penal Code, or Section 23152 or 23153, or any combination thereof, that resulted in convictions.

(C) A violation of Section 23153 that occurred within seven years of one or more separate offenses of Section 191.5 of, or subdivision (a) of Section 192.5 of, the Penal Code, or Section 23152 or 23153, that resulted in convictions.

(2) The court or the prosecutor shall give notice of the motion to the defendant, and the court shall hold a hearing before a motor vehicle may be declared a nuisance under this section.

(b) Except as provided in subdivision (g), upon the conviction of the defendant and at the time of pronouncement of sentence, the court with jurisdiction over the offense shall order a vehicle declared to be a nuisance pursuant to subdivision (a) to be sold. A vehicle ordered to be sold pursuant to this subdivision shall be surrendered to the sheriff of the county or the chief of police of the city in which the violation occurred. The officer to whom the vehicle is surrendered shall promptly ascertain from the department the names and addresses of all legal and registered owners of the vehicle and, within five days of receiving that information, shall send by certified mail a notice to all legal and registered owners of the vehicle other than the defendant, at the addresses obtained from the department, informing them that the vehicle has been declared a nuisance and will be sold or otherwise disposed of pursuant to this section and of the approximate date and location of the sale or other disposition. The notice shall

Vehicle

also inform a legal owner of its right to conduct the sale pursuant to subdivision (c).

(c) The legal owner who is a motor vehicle dealer, bank, credit union, acceptance corporation, or other licensed finance institution legally operating in this state, or the agent of that legal owner, may take possession and conduct the sale of the vehicle declared to be a nuisance if it notifies the officer to whom the vehicle is surrendered of its intent to conduct the sale within 15 days of the mailing of the notice pursuant to subdivision (b). Sale of the vehicle pursuant to this subdivision may be conducted at the time, in the manner, and on the notice usually given for the sale of repossessed or surrendered vehicles. The proceeds of a sale conducted by the legal owner shall be disposed of as provided in subdivision (e). A notice pursuant to this subdivision may be presented in person, by certified mail, by facsimile transmission, or by electronic mail. The agent of a legal owner acting pursuant to this subdivision shall be licensed, or exempt from licensure, pursuant to Chapter 11 (commencing with Section 7500) of Division 3 of the Business and Professions Code.

(d) If the legal owner or the agent of the legal owner does not notify the officer to whom the vehicle is surrendered of its intent to conduct the sale as provided in subdivision (c), the officer shall offer the vehicle for sale at public auction within 60 days of receiving the vehicle. At least 10 days but not more than 20 days prior to the sale, not counting the day of the sale, the officer shall give notice of the sale by advertising once in a newspaper of general circulation published in the city or county, as the case may be, in which the vehicle is located, that notice shall contain a description of the make, year, model, identification number, and license number of the vehicle and the date, time, and location of the sale. For motorcycles, the engine number shall also be included. If there is no newspaper of general circulation published in the county, notice shall be given by posting a notice of sale containing the information required by this subdivision in three of the most public places in the city or county in which the vehicle is located, and at the place where the vehicle is to be sold, for 10 consecutive days prior to and including the day of the sale.

(e) The proceeds of a sale conducted pursuant to this section shall be disposed of in the following priority:

(1) To satisfy the costs of the sale, including costs incurred with respect to the taking and keeping of the vehicle pending sale.

(2) To the legal owner in an amount to satisfy the indebtedness owed to the legal owner remaining as of the date of the sale, including accrued interest or finance charges and delinquency charges.

(3) To the holder of a subordinate lien or encumbrance on the vehicle to satisfy any indebtedness so secured if written notification of demand is received before distribution of the proceeds is completed. The holder of a subordinate lien or encumbrance, if requested, shall reasonably furnish reasonable proof of its interest and, unless it does so on request, is not entitled to distribution pursuant to this paragraph.

(4) To any other person who can establish an interest in the vehicle, including a community property interest, to the extent of his or her provable interest.

(5) If the vehicle was forfeited as a result of a felony violation of subdivision (a) of Section 191.5 of, or subdivision (a) of Section 192.5 of, the Penal Code, or of Section 23153 that resulted in serious bodily injury to a person other than the defendant, the balance, if any, to the city or county in which the violation occurred, to be deposited in its general fund.

(6) Except as provided in paragraph (5), the balance, if any, to the city or county in which the violation occurred, to be expended for community-based adolescent substance abuse treatment services.

The person conducting the sale shall disburse the proceeds of the sale as provided in this subdivision, and provide a written accounting regarding the disposition to all persons entitled to or claiming a share of the proceeds, within 15 days after the sale is conducted.

(f) If the vehicle to be sold under this section is not of the type that can readily be sold to the public generally, the vehicle shall be destroyed or donated to an eleemosynary institution.

(g) No vehicle shall be sold pursuant to this section in either of the following circumstances:

(1) The vehicle is stolen, unless the identity of the legal and registered owners of the vehicle cannot be reasonably ascertained.

(2) The vehicle is owned by another, or there is a community property interest in the vehicle owned by a person other than the defendant and the vehicle is the only vehicle available to the defendant's immediate family that may be operated on the highway with a class 3 or class 4 driver's license.

(h) The Legislature finds and declares it to be the public policy of this state that no policy of insurance shall afford benefits that would alleviate the financial detriment suffered by a person as a direct or indirect result of a confiscation of a vehicle pursuant to this section.

(Added by Stats.1999, c. 22 (S.B.24), § 40.4, eff. May 26, 1999, operative July 1, 1999. Amended by Stats.2007, c. 747 (A.B.678), § 36.)

Cross References

Illegal dumping of harmful waste matter, impoundment and civil forfeiture, see Vehicle Code § 23112.7.

Research References

2 Witkin, California Criminal Law 4th Crimes Against Public Peace and Welfare § 279 (2021), In General.

§ 23597. Ten-year revocation for person convicted of three or more separate driving under the influence offenses; application for reinstatement; conditions

Section operative until Jan. 1, 2026. See, also, § 23597 operative Jan. 1, 2026.

(a) Notwithstanding Sections 13202.5, 13203, and 13352, a court may order a 10–year revocation of the driver's license of a person who has been convicted of three or more separate violations of Section 23152 or 23153, the last of which is punishable under Section 23546, 23550, 23550.5, or 23566. When making this order, the court shall consider all of the following:

(1) The person's level of remorse for the acts.

(2) The period of time that has elapsed since the person's previous convictions.

(3) The person's blood-alcohol level at the time of the violation.

(4) The person's participation in an alcohol treatment program.

(5) The person's risk to traffic or public safety.

(6) The person's ability to install a functioning, certified ignition interlock device in each motor vehicle that he or she operates.

(b) Upon receipt of a duly certified abstract of the record of the court showing the court has ordered a 10–year revocation of a driver's license pursuant to this section, the department shall revoke the person's driver's license for 10 years, except as provided in subdivision (c).

(c)(1) Five years from the date of the last conviction of a violation of Section 23152 or 23153, a person whose license was revoked pursuant to subdivision (a) may apply to the department to have his or her privilege to operate a motor vehicle reinstated, subject to the condition that the person submits the "Verification of Installation" form described in paragraph (2) of subdivision (g) of Section 13386 and agrees to maintain a functioning, certified ignition interlock device as required under subdivision (f) of Section 23575.3. Notwithstanding Chapter 5 (commencing with Section 23700) or Section 23575.3, the ignition interlock device shall remain on the person's motor vehicle for two years following the reinstatement of the person's driving privilege pursuant to this section.

(2) The department shall reinstate the person's license pursuant to paragraph (1), if the person satisfies all of the following conditions:

(A) The person was not convicted of any drug- or alcohol-related offenses, under state law, during the driver's license revocation period.

(B) The person successfully completed a driving-under-the-influence program, licensed pursuant to Section 11836 of the Health and Safety Code, following the date of the last conviction of a violation of Section 23152 or 23153 of this code.

(C) The person was not convicted of violating Section 14601, 14601.1, 14601.2, 14601.4, or 14601.5 during the driver's license revocation period.

(3) The department shall immediately revoke the privilege to operate a motor vehicle of a person who attempts to remove, bypass, or tamper with the device, who has the device removed prior to the termination date of the restriction, or who fails three or more times to comply with any requirement for the maintenance or calibration of the ignition interlock device. The privilege shall remain revoked for the remaining period of the original revocation and until all reinstatement requirements are met, provided, however, that if the person provides proof to the satisfaction of the department that the person is in compliance with the restriction issued pursuant to this section, the department may, in its discretion, restore the privilege to operate a motor vehicle and reimpose the remaining term of the restriction.

(d) This section shall become operative on January 1, 2019.

(e) This section shall remain in effect only until January 1, 2026, and as of that date is repealed, unless a later enacted statute, that is enacted before January 1, 2026, deletes or extends that date. *(Added by Stats.2016, c. 783 (S.B.1046), § 41, eff. Jan. 1, 2017, operative Jan. 1, 2019. Amended by Stats.2017, c. 485 (S.B.611), § 30, eff. Jan. 1, 2018, operative Jan. 1, 2019.)*

Repeal

For repeal of this section, see its terms.

Research References

2 Witkin, California Criminal Law 4th Crimes Against Public Peace and Welfare § 283 (2021), Three or More Separate Convictions of Related Offenses.

2 Witkin, California Criminal Law 4th Crimes Against Public Peace and Welfare § 287 (2021), Two or More Separate Convictions of Related Offenses.

2 Witkin, California Criminal Law 4th Crimes Against Public Peace and Welfare § 289 (2021), Prior Violation Punished as Felony.

3 Witkin, California Criminal Law 4th Punishment § 214 (2021), Drunk Driving.

§ 23597. Ten-year revocation for person convicted of three or more separate driving under the influence offenses; application for reinstatement; conditions

Section operative Jan. 1, 2026. See, also, § 23597 operative until Jan. 1, 2026.

(a) Notwithstanding Sections 13202.5, 13203, and 13352, a court may order a 10–year revocation of the driver's license of a person who has been convicted of three or more separate violations of Section 23152 or 23153, the last of which is punishable under Section 23546, 23550, 23550.5, or 23566. When making this order, the court shall consider all of the following:

(1) The person's level of remorse for the acts.

(2) The period of time that has elapsed since the person's previous convictions.

(3) The person's blood-alcohol level at the time of the violation.

(4) The person's participation in an alcohol treatment program.

(5) The person's risk to traffic or public safety.

(6) The person's ability to install a certified ignition interlock device in each motor vehicle that he or she owns or operates.

(b) Upon receipt of a duly certified abstract of the record of the court showing the court has ordered a 10–year revocation of a driver's license pursuant to this section, the department shall revoke the person's driver's license for 10 years, except as provided in subdivision (c).

(c)(1) Five years from the date of the last conviction of a violation of Section 23152 or 23153, a person whose license was revoked pursuant to subdivision (a) may apply to the department to have his or her privilege to operate a motor vehicle reinstated, subject to the condition that the person submits the "Verification of Installation" form described in paragraph (2) of subdivision (g) of Section 13386 and agrees to maintain the ignition interlock device as required under subdivision (g) of Section 23575. Notwithstanding Chapter 5 (commencing with Section 23700) or subdivision (f) of Section 23575, the ignition interlock device shall remain on the person's motor vehicle for two years following the reinstatement of the person's driving privilege pursuant to this section.

(2) The department shall reinstate the person's license pursuant to paragraph (1), if the person satisfies all of the following conditions:

(A) The person was not convicted of any drug- or alcohol-related offenses, under state law, during the driver's license revocation period.

(B) The person successfully completed a driving-under-the-influence program, licensed pursuant to Section 11836 of the Health and Safety Code, following the date of the last conviction of a violation of Section 23152 or 23153.

(C) The person was not convicted of violating Section 14601, 14601.1, 14601.2, 14601.4, or 14601.5 during the driver's license revocation period.

(3) The department shall immediately terminate the restriction issued pursuant to this section and shall immediately revoke the privilege to operate a motor vehicle of a person who attempts to remove, bypass, or tamper with the device, who has the device removed prior to the termination date of the restriction, or who fails three or more times to comply with any requirement for the maintenance or calibration of the ignition interlock device. The privilege shall remain revoked for the remaining period of the original revocation and until all reinstatement requirements are met.

(d) This section shall become operative January 1, 2026. *(Added by Stats.2016, c. 783 (S.B.1046), § 42, eff. Jan. 1, 2017, operative Jan. 1, 2026.)*

Research References

2 Witkin, California Criminal Law 4th Crimes Against Public Peace and Welfare § 283 (2021), Three or More Separate Convictions of Related Offenses.

2 Witkin, California Criminal Law 4th Crimes Against Public Peace and Welfare § 287 (2021), Two or More Separate Convictions of Related Offenses.

2 Witkin, California Criminal Law 4th Crimes Against Public Peace and Welfare § 289 (2021), Prior Violation Punished as Felony.

3 Witkin, California Criminal Law 4th Punishment § 214 (2021), Drunk Driving.

ARTICLE 7. ALTERNATIVE TO ALCOHOL OR DRUG EDUCATION PROGRAM

Section

§ 23598. Live-in alternative to incarceration rehabilitation programs

In lieu of the alcohol or drug education program prescribed by Section 23538, 23542, 23548, 23552, 23556, 23562, or 23568, a court may impose, as a condition of probation, that the person complete, subsequent to the underlying conviction, a program specified in Section 8001 of the Penal Code, if the person consents and has been accepted into that program. Acceptance into that program shall be verified by a certification, under penalty of perjury, by the director of the program. *(Added by Stats.1998, c. 118 (S.B.1186), § 84, operative July 1, 1999.)*

Research References

2 Witkin, California Criminal Law 4th Crimes Against Public Peace and Welfare § 279 (2021), In General.
2 Witkin, California Criminal Law 4th Crimes Against Public Peace and Welfare § 280 (2021), First Violation.
2 Witkin, California Criminal Law 4th Crimes Against Public Peace and Welfare § 282 (2021), Two Separate Convictions of Related Offenses.
2 Witkin, California Criminal Law 4th Crimes Against Public Peace and Welfare § 283 (2021), Three or More Separate Convictions of Related Offenses.
2 Witkin, California Criminal Law 4th Crimes Against Public Peace and Welfare § 285 (2021), First Violation.
2 Witkin, California Criminal Law 4th Crimes Against Public Peace and Welfare § 286 (2021), One Separate Conviction of Related Offense.
2 Witkin, California Criminal Law 4th Crimes Against Public Peace and Welfare § 287 (2021), Two or More Separate Convictions of Related Offenses.
3 Witkin, California Criminal Law 4th Punishment § 664 (2021), Counseling, Treatment, and Education.

CHAPTER 3. PROBATION

§ 23600. Conviction and pronouncement of sentence for violations of Section 23152 or 23153; probation; minimum confinement or fine; violation of probation

(a) If any person is convicted of a violation of Section 23152 or 23153, the court shall not stay or suspend pronouncement of sentencing, and shall pronounce sentence in conjunction with the conviction in a reasonable time, including time for receipt of any presentence investigation report ordered pursuant to Section 23655.

(b) If any person is convicted of a violation of Section 23152 or 23153 and is granted probation, the terms and conditions of probation shall include, but not be limited to, the following:

(1) Notwithstanding Section 1203a of the Penal Code, a period of probation not less than three nor more than five years; provided, however, that if the maximum sentence provided for the offense may exceed five years in the state prison, the period during which the sentence may be suspended and terms of probation enforced may be for a longer period than three years but may not exceed the maximum time for which sentence of imprisonment may be pronounced.

(2) A requirement that the person shall not drive a vehicle with any measurable amount of alcohol in his or her blood.

(3) A requirement that the person, if arrested for a violation of Section 23152 or 23153, shall not refuse to submit to a chemical test of his or her blood, breath, or urine, pursuant to Section 23612, for the purpose of determining the alcoholic content of his or her blood.

(4) A requirement that the person shall not commit any criminal offense.

(c) The court shall not absolve a person who is convicted of a violation of Section 23152 or 23153 from the obligation of spending the minimum time in confinement, if any, or of paying the minimum fine imposed by law.

(d) In addition to any other provision of law, if any person violates paragraph (2) or (3) of subdivision (b) and the person had a blood alcohol concentration of over 0.04 percent as determined by a chemical test, the court shall revoke or terminate the person's probation as provided by Section 23602, regardless of any other proceeding, and shall only grant a new term of probation of not more than five years on the added condition that the person be confined in the county jail for not less than 48 hours for each of these violations of probation, except in unusual cases where the interests of justice would best be served if this additional condition were not imposed. *(Added by Stats.1998, c. 118 (S.B.1186), § 84, operative July 1, 1999. Amended by Stats.1999, c. 22 (S.B.24), § 40.6, eff. May 26, 1999, operative July 1, 1999.)*

Research References

2 Witkin, California Criminal Law 4th Crimes Against Public Peace and Welfare § 279 (2021), In General.
2 Witkin, California Criminal Law 4th Crimes Against Public Peace and Welfare § 280 (2021), First Violation.
2 Witkin, California Criminal Law 4th Crimes Against Public Peace and Welfare § 281 (2021), One Separate Conviction of Related Offense.
2 Witkin, California Criminal Law 4th Crimes Against Public Peace and Welfare § 282 (2021), Two Separate Convictions of Related Offenses.
2 Witkin, California Criminal Law 4th Crimes Against Public Peace and Welfare § 283 (2021), Three or More Separate Convictions of Related Offenses.
2 Witkin, California Criminal Law 4th Crimes Against Public Peace and Welfare § 285 (2021), First Violation.
2 Witkin, California Criminal Law 4th Crimes Against Public Peace and Welfare § 286 (2021), One Separate Conviction of Related Offense.
2 Witkin, California Criminal Law 4th Crimes Against Public Peace and Welfare § 287 (2021), Two or More Separate Convictions of Related Offenses.

§ 23601. Convictions under Section 23152 or 23153; fine, restitution, or assessment; enforcement

(a) Except as provided in subdivision (c), an order to pay any fine, restitution, or assessment, imposed as a condition of the grant of probation or as part of a judgment of conditional sentence for a violation of Section 23152 or 23153, may be enforced in the same manner provided for the enforcement of money judgments.

(b) A willful failure to pay any fine, restitution, or assessment during the term of probation is a violation of the terms and conditions of probation.

(c) If an order to pay a fine as a condition of probation is stayed, a writ of execution shall not be issued, and any failure to pay the fine is not willful, until the stay is removed. *(Added by Stats.1998, c. 118 (S.B.1186), § 84, operative July 1, 1999.)*

Research References

2 Witkin, California Criminal Law 4th Crimes Against Public Peace and Welfare § 279 (2021), In General.

§ 23602. Suspended sentence and probation; violation of probation; procedure for revocation

Except as otherwise expressly provided in this code, if a person has been convicted of a violation of Section 23152 or 23153 and the court has suspended execution of the sentence for that conviction and has granted probation, and during the time of that probation, the person is found by the court to have violated a required term or condition of that probation, the court shall revoke the suspension of sentence, revoke or terminate probation, and shall proceed in the manner provided in subdivision (c) of Section 1203.2 of the Penal Code.

(Added by Stats.1998, c. 118 (S.B.1186), § 84, operative July 1, 1999. Amended by Stats.1999, c. 22 (S.B.24), § 41, eff. May 26, 1999, operative July 1, 1999.)

Research References

2 Witkin, California Criminal Law 4th Crimes Against Public Peace and Welfare § 279 (2021), In General.
2 Witkin, California Criminal Law 4th Crimes Against Public Peace and Welfare § 280 (2021), First Violation.
2 Witkin, California Criminal Law 4th Crimes Against Public Peace and Welfare § 281 (2021), One Separate Conviction of Related Offense.
2 Witkin, California Criminal Law 4th Crimes Against Public Peace and Welfare § 282 (2021), Two Separate Convictions of Related Offenses.
2 Witkin, California Criminal Law 4th Crimes Against Public Peace and Welfare § 283 (2021), Three or More Separate Convictions of Related Offenses.
2 Witkin, California Criminal Law 4th Crimes Against Public Peace and Welfare § 285 (2021), First Violation.
2 Witkin, California Criminal Law 4th Crimes Against Public Peace and Welfare § 286 (2021), One Separate Conviction of Related Offense.
2 Witkin, California Criminal Law 4th Crimes Against Public Peace and Welfare § 287 (2021), Two or More Separate Convictions of Related Offenses.

CHAPTER 4. PROCEDURES

ARTICLE 1. GENERAL PROVISIONS

Section

§ 23610. Blood alcohol percentages; presumptions; other evidence

(a) Upon the trial of any criminal action, or preliminary proceeding in a criminal action, arising out of acts alleged to have been committed by any person while driving a vehicle while under the influence of an alcoholic beverage in violation of subdivision (a) of Section 23152 or subdivision (a) of Section 23153, the amount of alcohol in the person's blood at the time of the test as shown by chemical analysis of that person's blood, breath, or urine shall give rise to the following presumptions affecting the burden of proof:

(1) If there was at that time less than 0.05 percent, by weight, of alcohol in the person's blood, it shall be presumed that the person was not under the influence of an alcoholic beverage at the time of the alleged offense.

(2) If there was at that time 0.05 percent or more but less than 0.08 percent, by weight, of alcohol in the person's blood, that fact shall not give rise to any presumption that the person was or was not under the influence of an alcoholic beverage, but the fact may be considered with other competent evidence in determining whether the person was under the influence of an alcoholic beverage at the time of the alleged offense.

(3) If there was at that time 0.08 percent or more, by weight, of alcohol in the person's blood, it shall be presumed that the person was under the influence of an alcoholic beverage at the time of the alleged offense.

(b) Percent, by weight, of alcohol in the person's blood shall be based upon grams of alcohol per 100 milliliters of blood or grams of alcohol per 210 liters of breath.

(c) This section shall not be construed as limiting the introduction of any other competent evidence bearing upon the question of whether the person ingested any alcoholic beverage or was under the influence of an alcoholic beverage at the time of the alleged offense.
(Added by Stats.1998, c. 118 (S.B.1186), § 84, operative July 1, 1999.)

Research References

California Jury Instructions - Criminal 12.61, Driving Under the Influence—Inference of Intoxication.
2 Witkin, California Criminal Law 4th Crimes Against Public Peace and Welfare § 276 (2021), Driving Under the Influence.

§ 23612. Chemical, blood, breath, or urine tests

(a)(1)(A) A person who drives a motor vehicle is deemed to have given his or her consent to chemical testing of his or her blood or breath for the purpose of determining the alcoholic content of his or her blood, if lawfully arrested for an offense allegedly committed in violation of Section 23140, 23152, or 23153. If a blood or breath test, or both, are unavailable, then paragraph (2) of subdivision (d) applies.

(B) A person who drives a motor vehicle is deemed to have given his or her consent to chemical testing of his or her blood for the purpose of determining the drug content of his or her blood, if lawfully arrested for an offense allegedly committed in violation of Section 23140, 23152, or 23153. If a blood test is unavailable, the person shall be deemed to have given his or her consent to chemical testing of his or her urine and shall submit to a urine test.

(C) The testing shall be incidental to a lawful arrest and administered at the direction of a peace officer having reasonable cause to believe the person was driving a motor vehicle in violation of Section 23140, 23152, or 23153.

(D) The person shall be told that his or her failure to submit to, or the failure to complete, the required breath or urine testing will result in a fine and mandatory imprisonment if the person is convicted of a violation of Section 23152 or 23153. The person shall also be told that his or her failure to submit to, or the failure to complete, the required breath, blood, or urine tests will result in (i) the administrative suspension by the department of the person's privilege to operate a motor vehicle for a period of one year, (ii) the administrative revocation by the department of the person's privilege to operate a motor vehicle for a period of two years if the refusal occurs within 10 years of a separate violation of Section 23103 as specified in Section 23103.5, or of Section 23140, 23152, or 23153 of this code, or of Section 191.5 or subdivision (a) of Section 192.5 of the Penal Code that resulted in a conviction, or if the person's privilege to operate a motor vehicle has been suspended or revoked pursuant to Section 13353, 13353.1, or 13353.2 for an offense that occurred on a separate occasion, or (iii) the administrative revocation by the department of the person's privilege to operate a motor vehicle for a period of three years if the refusal occurs within 10 years of two or more separate violations of Section 23103 as specified in Section 23103.5, or of Section 23140, 23152, or 23153 of this code, or of Section 191.5 or subdivision (a) of Section 192.5 of the Penal Code, or any combination thereof, that resulted in convictions, or if the person's privilege to operate a motor vehicle has been suspended or revoked two or more times pursuant to Section 13353, 13353.1, or 13353.2 for offenses that occurred on separate occasions, or if there is any combination of those convictions, administrative suspensions, or revocations.

(2)(A) If the person is lawfully arrested for driving under the influence of an alcoholic beverage, the person has the choice of whether the test shall be of his or her blood or breath and the officer shall advise the person that he or she has that choice. If the person arrested either is incapable, or states that he or she is incapable, of completing the chosen test, the person shall submit to the remaining test. If a blood or breath test, or both, are unavailable, then paragraph (2) of subdivision (d) applies.

(B) If the person is lawfully arrested for driving under the influence of any drug or the combined influence of an alcoholic beverage and any drug, the person has the choice of whether the test shall be of his or her blood or breath, and the officer shall advise the person that he or she has that choice.

(C) A person who chooses to submit to a breath test may also be requested to submit to a blood test if the officer has reasonable cause to believe that the person was driving under the influence of a drug or the combined influence of an alcoholic beverage and a drug and if the officer has reasonable cause to believe that a blood test will reveal evidence of the person being under the influence. The officer shall state in his or her report the facts upon which those beliefs are based. The officer shall advise the person that he or she is required to submit to an additional test. The person shall submit to and complete a blood test. If the person arrested is incapable of completing the blood test, the person shall submit to and complete a urine test.

(3) If the person is lawfully arrested for an offense allegedly committed in violation of Section 23140, 23152, or 23153, and, because of the need for medical treatment, the person is first transported to a medical facility where it is not feasible to administer a particular test of, or to obtain a particular sample of, the person's blood or breath, the person has the choice of those tests, including a urine test, that are available at the facility to which that person has been transported. In that case, the officer shall advise the person of those tests that are available at the medical facility and that the person's choice is limited to those tests that are available.

(4) The officer shall also advise the person that he or she does not have the right to have an attorney present before stating whether he or she will submit to a test or tests, before deciding which test or tests to take, or during administration of the test or tests chosen, and that, in the event of refusal to submit to a test or tests, the refusal may be used against him or her in a court of law.

(5) A person who is unconscious or otherwise in a condition rendering him or her incapable of refusal is deemed not to have withdrawn his or her consent and a test or tests may be administered whether or not the person is told that his or her failure to submit to, or the noncompletion of, the test or tests will result in the suspension or revocation of his or her privilege to operate a motor vehicle. A person who is dead is deemed not to have withdrawn his or her consent and a test or tests may be administered at the direction of a peace officer.

(b) A person who is afflicted with hemophilia is exempt from the blood test required by this section, but shall submit to, and complete, a urine test.

(c) A person who is afflicted with a heart condition and is using an anticoagulant under the direction of a licensed physician and surgeon is exempt from the blood test required by this section, but shall submit to, and complete, a urine test.

(d)(1) A person lawfully arrested for an offense allegedly committed while the person was driving a motor vehicle in violation of Section 23140, 23152, or 23153 may request the arresting officer to have a chemical test made of the arrested person's blood or breath for the purpose of determining the alcoholic content of that person's blood, and, if so requested, the arresting officer shall have the test performed.

(2) If a blood or breath test is not available under subparagraph (A) of paragraph (1) of subdivision (a), or under subparagraph (A) of paragraph (2) of subdivision (a), or under paragraph (1) of this subdivision, the person shall submit to the remaining test in order to determine the percent, by weight, of alcohol in the person's blood. If both the blood and breath tests are unavailable, the person shall be deemed to have given his or her consent to chemical testing of his or her urine and shall submit to a urine test.

(e) If the person, who has been arrested for a violation of Section 23140, 23152, or 23153, refuses or fails to complete a chemical test or tests, or requests that a blood or urine test be taken, the peace officer, acting on behalf of the department, shall serve the notice of the order of suspension or revocation of the person's privilege to operate a motor vehicle personally on the arrested person. The notice shall be on a form provided by the department.

(f) If the peace officer serves the notice of the order of suspension or revocation of the person's privilege to operate a motor vehicle, the peace officer shall take possession of all driver's licenses issued by this state that are held by the person. The temporary driver's license shall be an endorsement on the notice of the order of suspension and shall be valid for 30 days from the date of arrest.

(g)(1) The peace officer shall immediately forward a copy of the completed notice of suspension or revocation form and any driver's license taken into possession under subdivision (f), with the report required by Section 13380, to the department. If the person submitted to a blood or urine test, the peace officer shall forward the results immediately to the appropriate forensic laboratory. The forensic laboratory shall forward the results of the chemical tests to the department within 15 calendar days of the date of the arrest.

(2)(A) Notwithstanding any other law, a document containing data prepared and maintained in the governmental forensic laboratory computerized database system that is electronically transmitted or retrieved through public or private computer networks to or by the department is the best available evidence of the chemical test results in all administrative proceedings conducted by the department. In addition, any other official record that is maintained in the governmental forensic laboratory, relates to a chemical test analysis prepared and maintained in the governmental forensic laboratory computerized database system, and is electronically transmitted and retrieved through a public or private computer network to or by the department is admissible as evidence in the department's administrative proceedings. In order to be admissible as evidence in administrative proceedings, a document described in this subparagraph shall bear a certification by the employee of the department who retrieved the document certifying that the information was received or retrieved directly from the computerized database system of a governmental forensic laboratory and that the document accurately reflects the data received or retrieved.

(B) Notwithstanding any other law, the failure of an employee of the department to certify under subparagraph (A) is not a public offense.

(h) A preliminary alcohol screening test that indicates the presence or concentration of alcohol based on a breath sample in order to establish reasonable cause to believe the person was driving a vehicle in violation of Section 23140, 23152, or 23153 is a field sobriety test and may be used by an officer as a further investigative tool.

(i) If the officer decides to use a preliminary alcohol screening test, the officer shall advise the person that he or she is requesting that person to take a preliminary alcohol screening test to assist the officer in determining if that person is under the influence of alcohol or drugs, or a combination of alcohol and drugs. The person's obligation to submit to a blood, breath, or urine test, as required by this section, for the purpose of determining the alcohol or drug content of that person's blood, is not satisfied by the person submitting to a preliminary alcohol screening test. The officer shall advise the person of that fact and of the person's right to refuse to take the preliminary alcohol screening test. *(Formerly § 23157, added by Stats.1992, c. 1281 (A.B.3580), § 9.7, operative July 1, 1993. Amended by Stats.1993, c. 272 (A.B.301), § 44.5, eff. Aug. 2, 1993; Stats.1993, c. 1244 (S.B.126), § 16; Stats.1994, c. 938 (S.B.1295), § 17, eff. Sept. 28, 1994; Stats.1996, c. 1154 (A.B.3020), § 70, eff. Sept. 30, 1996; Stats.1998, c. 740 (S.B.1890), § 4. Renumbered § 23612 and amended by Stats.1999, c. 22 (S.B.24), § 18.4, eff. May 26, 1999, operative July 1, 1999. Amended by Stats.1999, c. 853 (S.B.832), § 17; Stats.1999, c. 854 (S.B.1282), § 2, eff. Oct. 10, 1999; Stats.2000, c. 287 (S.B.1955), § 26; Stats.2003, c. 254 (S.B.408), § 2; Stats.2004, c. 550 (S.B.1694), § 19; Stats.2007, c. 747 (A.B.678), § 37; Stats.2012, c. 196 (A.B.2020), § 1; Stats.2013, c. 76 (A.B.383), § 196; Stats.2018, c. 177 (A.B.2717), § 3, eff. Jan. 1, 2019.)*

Cross References

Commercial motor vehicles, first time violations, see Vehicle Code § 15300.
Commercial motor vehicles, multiple violations, see Vehicle Code § 15302.
Search warrants, grounds for issuance, see Penal Code § 1524.

Research References

California Jury Instructions - Criminal 16.835, Liquor Influenced Driving—Refusal to Take Sobriety Test—Consciousness of Guilt.
California Jury Instructions - Criminal 17.29, Willful Refusal to Take or Complete Tests Regarding Driving Under the Influence.
California Jury Instructions - Criminal 17.29.1, Implied Consent—Choice of Tests.
2 Witkin, California Criminal Law 4th Crimes Against Public Peace and Welfare § 276 (2021), Driving Under the Influence.
2 Witkin, California Criminal Law 4th Crimes Against Public Peace and Welfare § 277 (2021), Driving With Unlawful Blood-Alcohol Level.
2 Witkin, California Criminal Law 4th Crimes Against Public Peace and Welfare § 279 (2021), In General.
2 Witkin, California Criminal Law 4th Crimes Against Public Peace and Welfare § 280 (2021), First Violation.
2 Witkin, California Criminal Law 4th Crimes Against Public Peace and Welfare § 281 (2021), One Separate Conviction of Related Offense.
2 Witkin, California Criminal Law 4th Crimes Against Public Peace and Welfare § 282 (2021), Two Separate Convictions of Related Offenses.
2 Witkin, California Criminal Law 4th Crimes Against Public Peace and Welfare § 283 (2021), Three or More Separate Convictions of Related Offenses.
2 Witkin, California Criminal Law 4th Crimes Against Public Peace and Welfare § 285 (2021), First Violation.
2 Witkin, California Criminal Law 4th Crimes Against Public Peace and Welfare § 286 (2021), One Separate Conviction of Related Offense.
2 Witkin, California Criminal Law 4th Crimes Against Public Peace and Welfare § 293 (2021), Nature and Scope of Law.
2 Witkin, California Criminal Law 4th Crimes Against Public Peace and Welfare § 295 (2021), Test as Incidental to Lawful Arrest or Detention.
2 Witkin, California Criminal Law 4th Crimes Against Public Peace and Welfare § 296 (2021), Choice of Test.
2 Witkin, California Criminal Law 4th Crimes Against Public Peace and Welfare § 297 (2021), Notice of Consequences of Refusal to Submit to Test.
2 Witkin, California Criminal Law 4th Crimes Against Public Peace and Welfare § 298 (2021), Administration of Test.
2 Witkin, California Criminal Law 4th Crimes Against Public Peace and Welfare § 300 (2021), Lack of Capacity to Refuse Test.
2 Witkin, California Criminal Law 4th Crimes Against Public Peace and Welfare § 302 (2021), Administrative Sanctions.
2 Witkin, California Criminal Law 4th Crimes Against Public Peace and Welfare § 530 (2021), Bicycles.
2 Witkin, California Criminal Law 4th Crimes Against Public Peace and Welfare § 531 (2021), Low-Speed Vehicles and Motorized Scooters.
4 Witkin, California Criminal Law 4th Illegally Obtained Evidence § 62A (2021), (New) Consent Under Implied Consent Law.
4 Witkin, California Criminal Law 4th Illegally Obtained Evidence § 111 (2021), Statutory Grounds.
4 Witkin, California Criminal Law 4th Pretrial Proceedings § 31 (2021), Intoxication and Motor Vehicles.

§ 23614. Chemical blood, breath, or urine tests; advising persons submitting to breath tests; admissibility of evidence

(a) In addition to the requirements of Section 23612, a person who chooses to submit to a breath test shall be advised before or after the test that the breath-testing equipment does not retain any sample of the breath and that no breath sample will be available after the test which could be analyzed later by that person or any other person.

(b) The person shall also be advised that, because no breath sample is retained, the person will be given an opportunity to provide a blood or urine sample that will be retained at no cost to the person so that there will be something retained that may be subsequently analyzed for the alcoholic content of the person's blood. If the person completes a breath test and wishes to provide a blood or urine sample to be retained, the sample shall be collected and retained in the same manner as if the person had chosen a blood or urine test initially.

(c) The person shall also be advised that the blood or urine sample may be tested by either party in any criminal prosecution. The failure of either party to perform this test shall place neither a duty upon the opposing party to perform the test nor affect the admissibility of any other evidence of the alcoholic content of the blood of the person arrested.

(d) No failure or omission to advise pursuant to this section shall affect the admissibility of any evidence of the alcoholic content of the blood of the person arrested. *(Added by Stats.1998, c. 118 (S.B. 1186), § 84, operative July 1, 1999.)*

Research References

2 Witkin, California Criminal Law 4th Crimes Against Public Peace and Welfare § 298 (2021), Administration of Test.

ARTICLE 2. PRIOR AND SEPARATE OFFENSES

Section

§ 23620. Separate offenses

(a) For the purposes of this division, Section 13352, and Chapter 12 (commencing with Section 23100) of Division 11, a separate offense that resulted in a conviction of a violation of subdivision (f) of Section 655 of the Harbors and Navigation Code or of Section 191.5 of, or subdivision (a) of Section 192.5 of, the Penal Code is a separate offense of a violation of Section 23153.

(b) For the purposes of this division and Chapter 12 (commencing with Section 23100) of Division 11, and Section 13352, a separate offense that resulted in a conviction of a violation of subdivision (b), (c), (d), or (e) of Section 655 of the Harbors and Navigation Code is a separate violation of Section 23152. *(Added by Stats.1998, c. 118 (S.B.1186), § 84, operative July 1, 1999. Amended by Stats.1999, c. 724 (A.B.1650), § 43; Stats.2007, c. 747 (A.B.678), § 38.)*

Research References

2 Witkin, California Criminal Law 4th Crimes Against Public Peace and Welfare § 279 (2021), In General.

§ 23622. Violations of Section 23152 or 23153 within 10 years of specified offenses; effect upon sentencing

(a) In any case charging a violation of Section 23152 or 23153 and the offense occurred within 10 years of one or more separate violations of Section 23103, as specified in Section 23103.5, that occurred on or after January 1, 1982, 23152, or 23153, or any combination thereof, that resulted in convictions, the court shall not strike any separate conviction of those offenses for purposes of sentencing in order to avoid imposing, as part of the sentence or term of probation, the minimum time of imprisonment and the minimum fine, as provided in this chapter, or for purposes of avoiding revocation, suspension, or restriction of the privilege to operate a motor vehicle, as provided in this code.

(b) In any case charging a violation of Section 23152 or 23153, the court shall obtain a copy of the driving record of the person charged from the Department of Motor Vehicles and may obtain any records from the Department of Justice or any other source to determine if one or more separate violations of Section 23103, as specified in Section 23103.5, that occurred on or after January 1, 1982, 23152, or 23153, or any combination thereof, that resulted in convictions, have occurred within 10 years of the charged offense. The court may obtain, and accept as rebuttable evidence, a printout from the Department of Motor Vehicles of the driving record of the person charged, maintained by electronic and storage media pursuant to Section 1801 for the purpose of proving those separate violations.

(c) If any separate convictions of violations of Section 23152 or 23153 are reported to have occurred within 10 years of the charged offense, the court shall notify each court where any of the separate convictions occurred for the purpose of enforcing terms and conditions of probation pursuant to Section 23602. *(Added by Stats.1998, c. 118 (S.B.1186), § 84, operative July 1, 1999. Amended by Stats. 2004, c. 550 (S.B.1694), § 20.)*

Research References

2 Witkin, California Criminal Law 4th Crimes Against Public Peace and Welfare § 279 (2021), In General.
2 Witkin, California Criminal Law 4th Crimes Against Public Peace and Welfare § 281 (2021), One Separate Conviction of Related Offense.
2 Witkin, California Criminal Law 4th Crimes Against Public Peace and Welfare § 282 (2021), Two Separate Convictions of Related Offenses.
2 Witkin, California Criminal Law 4th Crimes Against Public Peace and Welfare § 283 (2021), Three or More Separate Convictions of Related Offenses.
2 Witkin, California Criminal Law 4th Crimes Against Public Peace and Welfare § 286 (2021), One Separate Conviction of Related Offense.
2 Witkin, California Criminal Law 4th Crimes Against Public Peace and Welfare § 287 (2021), Two or More Separate Convictions of Related Offenses.
2 Witkin, California Criminal Law 4th Crimes Against Public Peace and Welfare § 291 (2021), Striking Separate Convictions.

§ 23624. Separate conviction; challenge to constitutional validity; use in judicial or administrative proceedings

Only one challenge shall be permitted to the constitutionality of a separate conviction of a violation of Section 14601, 14601.2, 23152, or 23153, which was entered in a separate proceeding. When a proceeding to declare a separate judgment of conviction constitutionally invalid has been held, a determination by the court that the separate conviction is constitutional precludes any subsequent attack on constitutional grounds in a subsequent prosecution in which the same separate conviction is charged. In addition, any determination that a separate conviction is unconstitutional precludes any allegation or use of that separate conviction in any judicial or administrative proceeding, and the department shall strike that separate conviction from its records. Pursuant to Section 1803, the court shall report to the Department of Motor Vehicles any determination upholding a conviction on constitutional grounds and any determination that a conviction is unconstitutional.

This section shall not preclude a subsequent challenge to a conviction if, at a later time, a subsequent statute or appellate court decision having retroactive application affords any new basis to challenge the constitutionality of the conviction. *(Added by Stats. 1998, c. 118 (S.B.1186), § 84, operative July 1, 1999.)*

Research References

5 Witkin, California Criminal Law 4th Criminal Trial § 480 (2021), Vehicle Code Convictions.

§ 23626. Effect of convictions in other jurisdictions

A conviction of an offense in any state, territory, or possession of the United States, the District of Columbia, the Commonwealth of Puerto Rico, or the Dominion of Canada that, if committed in this state, would be a violation of Section 23152 or 23153 of this code, or Section 191.5 of, or subdivision (a) of Section 192.5 of, the Penal Code, is a conviction of Section 23152 or 23153 of this code, or Section 191.5 of, or subdivision (a) of Section 192.5 of, the Penal Code for the purposes of this code. *(Added by Stats.1998, c. 118 (S.B.1186), § 84, operative July 1, 1999. Amended by Stats.2007, c. 747 (A.B.678), § 39.)*

Research References

2 Witkin, California Criminal Law 4th Crimes Against Public Peace and Welfare § 279 (2021), In General.
1 Witkin California Criminal Law 4th Crimes Against the Person § 267 (2021), Vehicular Manslaughter While Intoxicated.
1 Witkin California Criminal Law 4th Crimes Against the Person § 268 (2021), In General.

ARTICLE 3. DEFENSES

§ 23630. Legality of drug use as defense to violations

The fact that any person charged with driving under the influence of any drug or the combined influence of alcoholic beverages and any drug in violation of Section 23152 or 23153 is, or has been entitled to use, the drug under the laws of this state shall not constitute a defense against any violation of the sections. *(Added by Stats.1998, c. 118 (S.B.1186), § 84, operative July 1, 1999.)*

Research References

2 Witkin, California Criminal Law 4th Crimes Against Public Peace and Welfare § 276 (2021), Driving Under the Influence.

ARTICLE 4. DISMISSAL ON THE RECORD

§ 23635. Dismissal of allegation of violation of Section 23152, substitution of lesser offense, or dismissal or striking of allegation of separate conviction; reasons by court and prosecution

When an allegation of a violation of Section 23152 is dismissed by the court, an allegation of a different or lesser offense is substituted for an allegation of a violation of Section 23152, or an allegation of a separate conviction is dismissed or stricken, the court shall specify on the record its reason or reasons for the order. The court shall also specify on the record whether the dismissal, substitution, or striking was requested by the prosecution and whether the prosecution concurred in or opposed the dismissal, substitution, or striking.

When the prosecution makes a motion for a dismissal or substitution, or for the striking of a separate conviction, the prosecution shall submit a written statement which shall become part of the court record and which gives the reasons for the motion. The reasons shall include, but need not be limited to, problems of proof, the interests of justice, why another offense is more properly charged, if applicable, and any other pertinent reasons. If the reasons include the "interests of justice," the written statement shall specify all of the factors which contributed to this conclusion. *(Added by Stats.1998, c. 118 (S.B.1186), § 84, operative July 1, 1999.)*

Research References

2 Witkin, California Criminal Law 4th Crimes Against Public Peace and Welfare § 291 (2021), Striking Separate Convictions.
4 Witkin, California Criminal Law 4th Pretrial Proceedings § 361 (2021), In General.

ARTICLE 5. COURT RESTRICTIONS

§ 23640. Participation in driver improvement or treatment programs; no suspension or stay of proceedings prior to acquittal or conviction of violation of Section 23152 or 23153; effect after conviction and sentencing

(a) In any case in which a person is charged with a violation of Section 23152 or 23153, prior to acquittal or conviction, the court shall neither suspend nor stay the proceedings for the purpose of allowing the accused person to attend or participate, nor shall the court consider dismissal of or entertain a motion to dismiss the proceedings because the accused person attends or participates during that suspension, in any one or more education, training, or treatment programs, including, but not limited to, a driver improvement program, a treatment program for persons who are habitual users of alcohol or other alcoholism program, a program designed to offer alcohol services to problem drinkers, an alcohol or drug education program, or a treatment program for persons who are habitual users of drugs or other drug-related program.

(b) This section shall not apply to any attendance or participation in any education, training, or treatment programs after conviction and sentencing, including attendance or participation in any of those programs as a condition of probation granted after conviction when permitted. *(Added by Stats.1998, c. 118 (S.B.1186), § 84, operative July 1, 1999. Amended by Stats.1999, c. 22 (S.B.24), § 42, eff. May 26, 1999, operative July 1, 1999.)*

Cross References

Military diversion program, application of provisions, pretrial diversion program, see Penal Code § 1001.80.

Research References

2 Witkin, California Criminal Law 4th Crimes Against Public Peace and Welfare § 279 (2021), In General.

4 Witkin, California Criminal Law 4th Pretrial Proceedings § 401 (2021), Other Programs.

ARTICLE 6. ALCOHOL ASSESSMENT

§ 23645. Alcohol abuse education and prevention penalty assessment; determination of ability to pay; annual evaluation of primary prevention programs

(a) Except as otherwise provided in subdivision (c), any person convicted of a violation of Section 23152 or 23153 shall, in addition to any other fine, assessment, or imprisonment imposed pursuant to law, pay an alcohol abuse education and prevention penalty assessment in an amount not to exceed fifty dollars ($50) for deposit and distribution pursuant to Section 1463.25 of the Penal Code.

(b) The payment of the penalty assessment under this section shall be ordered upon conviction of a person of a violation of Section 23152 or 23153 irrespective of any other proceeding and, if probation is granted, the payment of the penalty assessment shall also be ordered as a condition of probation, except in unusual cases that are subject to subdivision (d) of Section 1464 of the Penal Code.

(c) The court shall determine if the defendant has the ability to pay a penalty assessment. If the court determines that the defendant has the ability to pay a penalty assessment, the court may set the amount to be paid and order the defendant to pay that sum to the county in the manner in which the court believes reasonable and compatible with the defendant's financial ability. In making a determination of whether a defendant has the ability to pay, the court shall take into account the amount of any fine imposed upon the defendant and any amount the defendant has been ordered to pay in restitution. If the court determines that the defendant does not have the ability to pay a penalty assessment, the defendant shall not be required to pay a penalty assessment.

(d) Five percent of the funds allocated to primary prevention programs to the school and the communities pursuant to subdivision (a) of Section 11802 of the Health and Safety Code shall be used to conduct an annual evaluation. The annual evaluation shall be conducted by the office of the county superintendent of schools in counties where the program is operating in a single county or in the office of the county superintendent of schools in the county designated as the lead county in counties where the program is operating as a consortium of counties. The evaluation shall contain the following:

(1) A needs assessment evaluation that provides specific data regarding the problem to be resolved.

(2) A written report of the planning process outlining the deliberations, considerations, and conclusions following a review of the needs assessment.

(3) An end of fiscal year accountability evaluation that will indicate the program's continuing ability to reach appropriate program beneficiaries, deliver the appropriate benefits, and use funds appropriately.

(4) An impact evaluation charged with the task of assessing the effectiveness of the program. Guidelines for the evaluation report format and the timeliness for the submission of the report shall be developed by the State Department of Education. Each county shall submit an evaluation report annually to the State Department of Education and the State Department of Education shall write and submit a report to the Legislature and Governor. *(Added by Stats.1998, c. 118 (S.B.1186), § 84, operative July 1, 1999.)*

§ 23646. County alcohol and drug problem assessment program

(a) Each county alcohol program administrator or the administrator's designee shall develop, implement, operate, and administer an alcohol and drug problem assessment program pursuant to this article for each person described in subdivision (b). The alcohol and drug problem assessment program may include a referral and client tracking component.

(b)(1) The court shall order a person to participate in an alcohol and drug problem assessment program pursuant to this section and Sections 23647 to 23649, inclusive, and the related regulations of the State Department of Health Care Services, if the person was convicted of a violation of Section 23152 or 23153 that occurred within 10 years of a separate violation of Section 23152 or 23153 that resulted in a conviction.

(2) A court may order a person convicted of a violation of Section 23152 or 23153 to attend an alcohol and drug problem assessment program pursuant to this article.

(3) The court shall order a person convicted of a violation of Section 23152 or 23153 who has previously been convicted of a violation of Section 23152 or 23153 that occurred more than 10 years ago, or has been previously convicted of a violation of subdivision (f) of Section 647 of the Penal Code, to attend and complete an alcohol and drug problem assessment program under this article. In order to determine whether a previous conviction for a violation occurring more than 10 years ago exists, the court shall rely on state summary

criminal history information, local summary history information, or records made available to the judge through the district attorney.

(c) The State Department of Health Care Services shall establish minimum specifications for alcohol and other drug problem assessments and reports. *(Formerly § 23249.52, added by Stats.1988, c. 160, § 183. Amended by Stats.1998, c. 656 (A.B.1916), § 4. Renumbered § 23646 and amended by Stats.1999, c. 22 (S.B.24), § 29, eff. May 26, 1999, operative July 1, 1999. Amended by Stats.2000, c. 1064 (A.B.2227), § 12, eff. Sept. 30, 2000; Stats.2004, c. 550 (S.B.1694), § 21; Stats.2013, c. 22 (A.B.75), § 89, eff. June 27, 2013, operative July 1, 2013; Stats.2017, c. 485 (S.B.611), § 31, eff. Jan. 1, 2018.)*

§ 23647. Alcohol-related or drug-related driving offenses; participation in program

(a) Any person convicted of a violation of Section 23152 or 23153 who is required to participate in a county alcohol and drug problem assessment program shall participate in that program.

(b) Any person convicted of a violation of Section 23103, as specified in Section 23103.5, in a judicial district that participates in a county alcohol and drug problem assessment program pursuant to this article, may be ordered to participate in the program. *(Formerly § 23249.53, added by Stats.1988, c. 160, § 183. Amended by Stats. 1991, c. 1175 (A.B.2091), § 1; Stats.1998, c. 656 (A.B.1916), § 5. Renumbered § 23647 and amended by Stats.1999, c. 22 (S.B.24), § 30, eff. May 26, 1999, operative July 1, 1999.)*

§ 23648. Assessment report

(a) Each county shall prepare, or contract to be prepared, an alcohol and drug problem assessment report on each person described in subdivision (b) of Section 23646.

(b) The assessment report shall include, if applicable, a recommendation for any additional treatment and the duration of the treatment. The treatment shall be in addition to the education and counseling program required under Section 11837 of the Health and Safety Code. The assessment report shall be submitted to the court not more than 14 days after the date the assessment was conducted.

(c) Within 30 days of the receipt of the report, the court shall order the person to complete the recommendations set forth in the report in satisfaction of, and consistent with, the terms and conditions of probation. If the court elects not to order the completion of the recommended plan, the court shall specify on the record its reason for not adopting these recommendations.

(d) This section shall become operative on January 1, 2000. *(Formerly § 23249.54, added by Stats.1998, c. 656 (A.B.1916), § 7, operative Jan. 1, 2000. Renumbered § 23648 and amended by Stats.1999, c. 22 (S.B.24), § 32, eff. May 26, 1999, operative Jan. 1, 2000.)*

§ 23649. Fine or penalty assessment; use of moneys

(a) Notwithstanding any other provision of law, in addition to any other fine or penalty assessment, there shall be levied an assessment of not more than one hundred dollars ($100) upon every fine, penalty, or forfeiture imposed and collected by the courts for a violation of Section 23152 or 23153 in any judicial district that participates in a county alcohol and drug problem assessment program. An assessment of not more than one hundred dollars ($100) shall be imposed and collected by the courts from each person convicted of a violation of Section 23103, as specified in Section 23103.5, who is ordered to participate in a county alcohol and drug problem assessment program pursuant to Section 23647.

(b) The court shall determine if the defendant has the ability to pay the assessment. If the court determines that the defendant has the ability to pay the assessment then the court may set the amount to be reimbursed and order the defendant to pay that sum to the county in the manner that the court determines is reasonable and compatible with the defendant's financial ability. In making a determination of whether a defendant has the ability to pay, the court shall take into account the amount of any fine imposed upon the defendant and any amount the defendant has been ordered to pay in restitution.

(c) Notwithstanding Section 1463 or 1464 of the Penal Code or any other provision of law, all moneys collected pursuant to this section shall be deposited in a special account in the county treasury and shall be used exclusively by the county alcohol program administrator or the administrator's designee to pay for the costs of developing, implementing, operating, maintaining, and evaluating alcohol and drug problem assessment programs.

(d) On January 15 of each year, the treasurer of each county that administers an alcohol and drug problem assessment program shall determine those moneys in the special account that were not expended during the preceding fiscal year, and shall transfer those moneys to the general fund of the county.

(e) Any moneys remaining in the special account, if and when the alcohol and drug problem assessment program is terminated, shall be transferred to the general fund of the county.

(f) The county treasurer shall annually transfer an amount of money equal to the county's administrative cost incurred pursuant to this section, as he or she shall determine, from the special account to the general fund of the county. *(Formerly § 23249.55, added by Stats.1988, c. 160, § 183. Amended by Stats.1991, c. 1175 (A.B.2091), § 3; Stats.1998, c. 656 (A.B.1916), § 8. Renumbered § 23649 and amended by Stats.1999, c. 22 (S.B.24), § 33, eff. May 26, 1999, operative July 1, 1999. Amended by Stats.2000, c. 1064 (A.B.2227), § 13, eff. Sept. 30, 2000.)*

§ 23650. Rules and guidelines

The Office of Traffic Safety shall adopt rules and guidelines to implement Sections 23646 to 23649, inclusive. *(Added by Stats.1998, c. 118 (S.B.1186), § 84, operative July 1, 1999. Amended by Stats. 1999, c. 22 (S.B.24), § 43, eff. May 26, 1999, operative July 1, 1999.)*

§ 23651. Editorial Note

Stats.1998, c. 118 (S.B.1186), provided for repeal of § 23249.58 and addition of this similar section. Stats.1998, c. 656 (A.B.1916), § 10 amended § 23249.58. Section affected by two or more acts at the same session of the legislature, see Government Code § 9605.

ARTICLE 7. PRESENTENCE INVESTIGATION

Section

§ 23655. Convictions of Section 23152 or 23153; determination of benefit of education, training, or treatment programs; conditions of probation; standard form

(a) Upon any conviction of a violation of Section 23152 or 23153, any judge of the court may order a presentence investigation to determine whether a person convicted of the violation would benefit from one or more education, training, or treatment programs, and the court may order suitable education, training, or treatment for the person, in addition to imposing any penalties required by this code.

(b) In determining whether to require, as a condition of probation, the participation in a program pursuant to subdivision (b) of Section 23538, subdivision (b) of Section 23542, subdivision (b) of Section 23548, subdivision (b) of Section 23552, subdivision (b) of Section

23556, subdivision (b) of Section 23562, or subdivision (b) of Section 23568, the court may consider any relevant information about the person made available pursuant to a presentence investigation, which is permitted but not required by subdivision (a), or other screening procedure. That information shall not be furnished to the court by any person who also provides services in a privately operated, approved program or who has any direct interest in a privately operated, approved program. In addition, the court shall obtain from the Department of Motor Vehicles a copy of the person's driving record to determine whether the person is eligible to participate in an approved program.

(c) The Judicial Council shall adopt a standard form for use by all courts, defendants, and alcohol or drug education programs in certifying to the court that the person has achieved both of the following:

(1) Enrolled within the specified time period.

(2) Successfully completed any program required by Section 23538 or 23556. *(Added by Stats.1998, c. 118 (S.B.1186), § 84, operative July 1, 1999. Amended by Stats.1999, c. 22 (S.B.24), § 44, eff. May 26, 1999, operative July 1, 1999.)*

Research References

West's California Judicial Council Forms CR–220, Proof of Enrollment or Completion (Alcohol or Drug Program).
2 Witkin, California Criminal Law 4th Crimes Against Public Peace and Welfare § 279 (2021), In General.
6 Witkin, California Criminal Law 4th Criminal Judgment § 161 (2021), In General.

ARTICLE 8. SURRENDER AND NOTIFICATION OF LICENSE RESTRICTION

§ 23660. Suspension or revocation of privilege to operate motor vehicle; surrender of license; application of section

(a) If a person's privilege to operate a motor vehicle is required to be suspended or revoked by the department under other provisions of this code upon the conviction of an offense described in Article 2 (commencing with Section 23152) of Chapter 12 of Division 11, that person shall surrender each and every operator's license of that person to the court upon conviction. The court shall transmit the license or licenses required to be suspended or revoked to the department under Section 13550, and the court shall notify the department.

(b) This section does not apply to an administrative proceeding by the department to suspend or revoke the driving privilege of any person pursuant to other provisions of law.

(c) This section shall become operative on September 20, 2005. *(Formerly § 23204, added by Stats.1981, c. 940, p. 3571, § 32. Amended by Stats.1984, c. 1205, § 8; Stats.1986, c. 1117, § 11; Stats.1998, c. 756 (A.B.762), § 18, operative July 1, 1999. Renumbered § 23660 and amended by Stats.1999, c. 22 (S.B.24), § 24, eff. May 26, 1999, operative July 1, 1999. Amended by Stats.2004, c. 551 (S.B. 1697), § 24, operative Sept. 20, 2005.)*

Research References

2 Witkin, California Criminal Law 4th Crimes Against Public Peace and Welfare § 279 (2021), In General.

§ 23662. Department of Motor Vehicles notified of probation

If a person is placed on probation, the court shall promptly notify the Department of Motor Vehicles of the probation and probationary term and conditions in a manner prescribed by the department. The department shall place the fact of probation and the probationary term and conditions on the person's records in the department. *(Formerly § 23203, added by Stats.1981, c. 940, p. 3571, § 32. Amended by Stats.1984, c. 1417, § 3, operative July 1, 1985; Stats.1996, c. 124 (A.B.3470), § 131; Stats.1998, c. 756 (A.B.762), § 17, operative July 1, 1999. Renumbered § 23662 and amended by Stats.1999, c. 22 (S.B.24), § 23, eff. May 26, 1999, operative July 1, 1999.)*

ARTICLE 9. DELAYED SUSPENSIONS AND REVOCATIONS

§ 23665. Driving under the influence; bodily injury to person other than driver; jail sentence; postponement of revocation or suspension

(a) If a person is convicted of a violation of Section 20001, or of Section 23152 or 23153 and is sentenced to one year in a county jail or more than one year in the state prison under Section 23540, 23542, 23546, 23548, 23550, 23550.5, 23552, 23554, 23556, 23558, 23560, 23562, 23566, or 23568, the court may postpone the revocation or suspension of the person's driving privilege until the term of imprisonment is served.

(b) This section shall become operative on September 20, 2005. *(Added by Stats.1998, c. 118 (S.B.1186), § 84, operative July 1, 1999. Amended by Stats.1999, c. 22 (S.B.24), § 45, eff. May 26, 1999, operative July 1, 1999; Stats.2004, c. 551 (S.B.1697), § 25, operative Sept. 20, 2005.)*

ARTICLE 10. CONFLICT OF INTEREST

§ 23670. Referral to program in which employee of court has economic interest

A court shall not order or refer any person to any program, including an alcohol and other drug education program or a program licensed pursuant to Chapter 9 (commencing with Section 11836) of Part 2 of Division 10.5 of the Health and Safety Code, or to a provider of a program, in which any employee of the court has a direct or indirect economic interest. *(Added by Stats.1998, c. 118 (S.B.1186), § 84, operative July 1, 1999.)*

ARTICLE 11. OPERATIVE DATE

§ 23675. Operative date of Division

This division shall become operative on July 1, 1999. *(Added by Stats.1998, c. 118 (S.B.1186), § 84, operative July 1, 1999.)*

Division 12

EQUIPMENT OF VEHICLES

CHAPTER 5. OTHER EQUIPMENT

ARTICLE 3. SAFETY BELTS AND INFLATABLE RESTRAINT SYSTEMS

§ 27315. Motor Vehicle Safety Act; mandatory use of seatbelts; violations; penalties; application; partial conditional inoperation

(a) The Legislature finds that a mandatory seatbelt law will contribute to reducing highway deaths and injuries by encouraging greater usage of existing manual seatbelts, that automatic crash protection systems that require no action by vehicle occupants offer the best hope of reducing deaths and injuries, and that encouraging the use of manual safety belts is only a partial remedy for addressing this major cause of death and injury. The Legislature declares that the enactment of this section is intended to be compatible with support for federal motor vehicle safety standards requiring automatic crash protection systems and should not be used in any manner to rescind federal requirements for installation of automatic restraints in new cars.

(b) This section shall be known and may be cited as the Motor Vehicle Safety Act.

(c)(1) As used in this section, "motor vehicle" means a passenger vehicle, a motortruck, or a truck tractor, but does not include a motorcycle.

(2) For purposes of this section, a "motor vehicle" also means a farm labor vehicle, regardless of the date of certification under Section 31401.

(d)(1) A person shall not operate a motor vehicle on a highway unless that person and all passengers 16 years of age or over are properly restrained by a safety belt. This paragraph does not apply to the operator of a taxicab, as defined in Section 27908, when the taxicab is driven on a city street and is engaged in the transportation of a fare-paying passenger. The safety belt requirement established by this paragraph is the minimum safety standard applicable to employees being transported in a motor vehicle. This paragraph does not preempt more stringent or restrictive standards imposed by the Labor Code or another state or federal regulation regarding the transportation of employees in a motor vehicle.

(2) For purposes of this section the phrase, "properly restrained by a safety belt" means that the lower (lap) portion of the belt crosses the hips or upper thighs of the occupant and the upper (shoulder) portion of the belt, if present, crosses the chest in front of the occupant.

(3) The operator of a limousine for hire or the operator of an authorized emergency vehicle, as defined in subdivision (a) of Section 165, shall not operate the limousine for hire or authorized emergency vehicle unless the operator and any passengers eight years of age or over in the front seat, are properly restrained by a safety belt.

(4) The operator of a taxicab shall not operate the taxicab unless any passengers eight years of age or over in the front seat, are properly restrained by a safety belt.

(e) A person 16 years of age or over shall not be a passenger in a motor vehicle on a highway unless that person is properly restrained by a safety belt. This subdivision does not apply to a passenger in a sleeper berth, as defined in subdivision (x) of Section 1201 of Title 13 of the California Code of Regulations.

(f) An owner of a motor vehicle, including an owner or operator of a taxicab, as defined in Section 27908, or a limousine for hire, operated on a highway shall maintain safety belts in good working order for the use of the occupants of the vehicle. The safety belts shall conform to motor vehicle safety standards established by the United States Department of Transportation. This subdivision, however, does not require installation or maintenance of safety belts if it is not required by the laws of the United States applicable to the vehicle at the time of its initial sale.

(g) This section does not apply to a passenger or operator with a physically disabling condition or medical condition that would prevent appropriate restraint in a safety belt, if the condition is duly certified by a licensed physician and surgeon or by a licensed chiropractor who shall state the nature of the condition, as well as the reason the restraint is inappropriate. This section also does not apply to a public employee, if the public employee is in an authorized emergency vehicle as defined in paragraph (1) of subdivision (b) of Section 165, or to a passenger in a seat behind the front seat of an authorized emergency vehicle as defined in paragraph (1) of subdivision (b) of Section 165 operated by the public employee, unless required by the agency employing the public employee.

(h) Notwithstanding subdivision (a) of Section 42001, a violation of subdivision (d), (e), or (f) is an infraction punishable by a fine of not more than twenty dollars ($20) for a first offense, and a fine of not more than fifty dollars ($50) for each subsequent offense. In lieu of the fine and any penalty assessment or court costs, the court, pursuant to Section 42005, may order that a person convicted of a first offense attend a school for traffic violators or another court-approved program in which the proper use of safety belts is demonstrated.

(i) In a civil action, a violation of subdivision (d), (e), or (f), or information of a violation of subdivision (h), does not establish negligence as a matter of law or negligence per se for comparative fault purposes, but negligence may be proven as a fact without regard to the violation.

(j) If the United States Secretary of Transportation fails to adopt safety standards for manual safety belt systems by September 1, 1989, a motor vehicle manufactured after that date for sale or sold in this state shall not be registered unless it contains a manual safety belt system that meets the performance standards applicable to automatic crash protection devices adopted by the United States Secretary of Transportation pursuant to Federal Motor Vehicle Safety Standard No. 208 (49 C.F.R. 571.208) as in effect on January 1, 1985.

(k) A motor vehicle offered for original sale in this state that has been manufactured on or after September 1, 1989, shall comply with the automatic restraint requirements of Section S4.1.2.1 of Federal Motor Vehicle Safety Standard No. 208 (49 C.F.R. 571.208), as published in Volume 49 of the Federal Register, No. 138, page 29009. An automobile manufacturer that sells or delivers a motor vehicle subject to this subdivision, and fails to comply with this subdivision, shall be punished by a fine of not more than five hundred dollars ($500) for each sale or delivery of a noncomplying motor vehicle.

(*l*) Compliance with subdivision (j) or (k) by a manufacturer shall be made by self-certification in the same manner as self-certification is accomplished under federal law.

(m) This section does not apply to a person actually engaged in delivery of newspapers to customers along the person's route if the person is properly restrained by a safety belt prior to commencing and subsequent to completing delivery on the route.

(n) This section does not apply to a person actually engaged in collection and delivery activities as a rural delivery carrier for the United States Postal Service if the person is properly restrained by a safety belt prior to stopping at the first box and subsequent to stopping at the last box on the route.

(*o*) This section does not apply to a driver actually engaged in the collection of solid waste or recyclable materials along that driver's collection route if the driver is properly restrained by a safety belt prior to commencing and subsequent to completing the collection route.

(p) Subdivisions (d), (e), (f), (g), and (h) shall become inoperative immediately upon the date that the United States Secretary of Transportation, or his or her delegate, determines to rescind the portion of the Federal Motor Vehicle Safety Standard No. 208 (49 C.F.R. 571.208) that requires the installation of automatic restraints in new motor vehicles, except that those subdivisions shall not become inoperative if the secretary's decision to rescind that Standard No. 208 is not based, in any respect, on the enactment or continued operation of those subdivisions. *(Added by Stats.1992, c. 122 (A.B.338), § 2, operative Jan. 1, 1996. Amended by Stats.1994, c. 1101 (S.B.2004), § 2, operative Jan. 1, 1996; Stats.1995, c. 365 (A.B.1400), § 1, operative Jan. 1, 1996; Stats.1996, c. 1154 (A.B.3020), § 78, eff. Sept. 30, 1996; Stats.1997, c. 153 (A.B.1278), § 1; Stats. 1998, c. 471 (A.B.2062), § 1; Stats.1998, c. 877 (A.B.2132), § 67.5; Stats.1999, c. 557 (A.B.1165), § 3, eff. Sept. 29, 1999; Stats.2003, c. 521 (A.B.1625), § 1; Stats.2004, c. 420 (A.B.2139), § 1; Stats.2008, c. 179 (S.B.1498), § 223; Stats.2011, c. 474 (S.B.929), § 1.)*

Cross References

Children under eight years of age, obligation of parent, legal guardian, or driver not to transport in motor vehicle unless secured in rear seat child passenger restraint system, see Vehicle Code § 27360.

Traffic violation point count, convictions under this section, see Vehicle Code § 12810.2.

Research References

California Jury Instructions-Civil, 8th Edition 5.90, Seat Belt Defense.

California Jury Instructions-Civil, 8th Edition 5.91, Passenger in Truck Sleeping Berth—Seat Belt Available.

California Jury Instructions-Civil, 8th Edition 712, Affirmative Defense—Failure to Wear a Seat Belt.

2 Witkin, California Criminal Law 4th Crimes Against Public Peace and Welfare § 476 (2021), Equipment Requirements.

2 Witkin, California Criminal Law 4th Crimes Against Public Peace and Welfare § 477 (2021), Mandatory Use of Seat Belts.

1 Witkin California Criminal Law 4th Crimes Against the Person § 270 (2021), Gross Negligence.

§ 27318. Bus passengers; mandatory use of safety belts or appropriate child passenger restraint systems; penalty for violation

(a) A passenger who is 16 years of age or older in a bus shall be properly restrained by a safety belt.

(b) A parent, legal guardian, or chartering party shall not transport on a bus, or permit to be transported on a bus, a child, ward, or passenger who is eight years of age or older, but under 16 years of age, unless he or she is properly restrained by a safety belt.

(c) Except as provided in subdivision (d), a parent, legal guardian, or chartering party shall not transport on a bus, or permit to be transported on a bus, a child, ward, or passenger who is under eight years of age and under four feet nine inches in height, unless he or she is acceptably restrained by a safety belt.

(d) If it is not possible to ensure a child, ward, or passenger who is under eight years of age and under four feet nine inches in height is acceptably restrained by a safety belt because of his or her size, a parent, legal guardian, or chartering party shall either secure him or her in an appropriate child passenger restraint system that meets applicable federal motor vehicle safety standards, or if the child, ward, or passenger is under two years of age, may authorize a parent, legal guardian, or chartering party to hold him or her.

(e)(1) For purposes of this section, "acceptably restrained by a safety belt" means all of the following:

(A) The latch plate is securely fastened in the buckle.

(B) The lap belt shall be adjusted to fit low and tight across the hips or upper thighs, not the stomach area.

(C) The shoulder belt shall be adjusted snugly across the chest and the middle of the shoulder, away from the neck.

(D) The shoulder belt shall not be placed behind the back or under the arm.

(2) For purposes of this section, "properly restrained by a safety belt" means that the lap belt crosses the hips or upper thighs of the occupant and the shoulder belt, if present, crosses the chest in front of the occupant.

(3) For purposes of this section, "bus" means a bus that is equipped with safety belts, including a bus that is required to be equipped with a seatbelt assembly pursuant to Federal Motor Vehicle Safety Standard No. 208 (49 C.F.R. 571.208).

(f) Subdivisions (a), (b), (c), and (d) do not apply to a passenger that is leaving, has left, or is returning from his or her seat to use an onboard bathroom.

(g) If the bus is equipped with safety belts, the motor carrier shall maintain safety belts in good working order for the use of passengers of the vehicle.

(h) A motor carrier operating a bus equipped with safety belts shall do one of the following:

(1) Require the bus driver, before departure of a bus carrying passengers, to inform passengers of the requirement to wear the seatbelt under California law and inform passengers that not wearing a seatbelt is punishable by a fine.

(2) Post, or allow to be posted, signs or placards that inform passengers of the requirement to wear a seatbelt under California law and that not wearing a seatbelt is punishable by a fine. The signs or placards shall be in a font type and font size that is reasonably easy to read and shall be affixed to a bus in multiple, conspicuous locations.

(i) Notwithstanding subdivision (a) of Section 42001, a violation of subdivision (a), (b), (c), or (d) is an infraction punishable by a fine of not more than twenty dollars ($20) for a first offense, and a fine of not more than fifty dollars ($50) for each subsequent offense.

(j) This section does not apply to a schoolbus described in Section 27316 or a school pupil activity bus described in Section 27316.5.

(k) This section shall be operative July 1, 2018. *(Added by Stats.2017, c. 593 (S.B.20), § 2, eff. Jan. 1, 2018, operative July 1, 2018.)*

Research References

2 Witkin, California Criminal Law 4th Crimes Against Public Peace and Welfare § 477 (2021), Mandatory Use of Seat Belts.

§ 27319. Bus drivers; mandatory use of safety belts; penalty for violation

(a) If a bus is equipped with a driver safety belt, the driver of the bus shall not operate the vehicle unless he or she is properly restrained by the safety belt.

(b) If a bus is equipped with a driver safety belt, the motor carrier shall maintain the safety belt in good working order for the use of the driver.

(c) Notwithstanding subdivision (a) of Section 42001, a violation of this section is an infraction punishable by a fine of not more than twenty dollars ($20) for a first offense and a fine of not more than fifty dollars ($50) for each subsequent offense.

(d) The requirements of this section are intended to satisfy the requirements of Section 392.16 of Title 49 of the Code of Federal Regulations, or any similar federal law or regulation, but shall remain in effect in the absence of those laws.

(e) This section shall be operative July 1, 2018. *(Added by Stats.2017, c. 593 (S.B.20), § 3, eff. Jan. 1, 2018, operative July 1, 2018.)*

Research References

2 Witkin, California Criminal Law 4th Crimes Against Public Peace and Welfare § 477 (2021), Mandatory Use of Seat Belts.

ARTICLE 3.3. CHILD SAFETY BELT AND PASSENGER RESTRAINT REQUIREMENTS

§ 27360. Child safety seats; obligation of parent, legal guardian or driver; transporting children under eight years of age; transporting children under two years of age; exception for driver if parent or legal guardian is present and not driving

(a) Except as provided in Section 27363, a parent, legal guardian, or driver who transports a child under eight years of age on a highway in a motor vehicle, as defined in paragraph (1) of subdivision (c) of Section 27315, shall properly secure that child in a rear seat in an appropriate child passenger restraint system meeting applicable federal motor vehicle safety standards.

(b) Except as provided in Section 27363, a parent, legal guardian, or driver who transports a child under two years of age on a highway in a motor vehicle, as defined in paragraph (1) of subdivision (c) of Section 27315, shall properly secure the child in a rear-facing child passenger restraint system that meets applicable federal motor vehicle safety standards, unless the child weighs 40 or more pounds or is 40 or more inches tall. The child shall be secured in a manner that complies with the height and weight limits specified by the manufacturer of the child passenger restraint system.

(c) This section does not apply to a driver if the parent or legal guardian of the child is a passenger in the motor vehicle.

(d) This section shall become operative January 1, 2017. *(Added by Stats.2015, c. 292 (A.B.53), § 2, eff. Jan. 1, 2016, operative Jan. 1, 2017.)*

Cross References

Traffic violation point counts, allocation of points, see Vehicle Code § 12810.

Research References

2 Witkin, California Criminal Law 4th Crimes Against Public Peace and Welfare § 478 (2021), Children Under Age 8.

§ 27360.5. Children eight years of age but under sixteen years of age; obligation of parent, legal guardian, or driver not to transport in motor vehicle unless secured in child passenger restraint system or safety belt; exception for driver if parent or legal guardian is present and not driving

(a) A parent, legal guardian, or driver shall not transport on a highway in a motor vehicle, as defined in paragraph (1) of subdivision (c) of Section 27315, a child or ward who is eight years of age or older, but less than 16 years of age, without properly securing that child or ward in an appropriate child passenger restraint system or safety belt meeting applicable federal motor vehicle safety standards.

(b) Subdivision (a) does not apply to a driver if the parent or legal guardian of the child is also present in the motor vehicle and is not the driver. *(Added by Stats.2011, c. 474 (S.B.929), § 6.)*

Cross References

Signs posted at day care centers, contents, requirements concerning child passenger restraint system under this section, see Health and Safety Code § 1596.95.

Traffic violation point counts, allocation of points, see Vehicle Code § 12810.

Research References

2 Witkin, California Criminal Law 4th Crimes Against Public Peace and Welfare § 479 (2021), Children Ages 8 to 16.

§ 27360.6. Conviction under Section 27360 or 27360.5; penalties for first offense; penalties for second or subsequent conviction; allocation of fines collected

(a)(1) For a conviction under Section 27360 or 27360.5, a first offense is punishable by a fine of one hundred dollars ($100), except that the court may reduce or waive the fine if the defendant establishes to the satisfaction of the court that he or she is economically disadvantaged, and the court, instead, refers the defendant to a community education program that includes, but is not limited to, education on the proper installation and use of a child passenger restraint system for children of all ages, and provides certification to the court of completion of that program. Upon completion of the program, the defendant shall provide proof of participation in the program. If an education program on the proper installation and use of a child passenger restraint system is not available within 50 miles of the residence of the defendant, the requirement to participate in that program shall be waived. If the fine is paid, waived, or reduced, the court shall report the conviction to the department pursuant to Section 1803.

(2) The court may require a defendant described under paragraph (1) to attend an education program that includes demonstration of proper installation and use of a child passenger restraint system and provides certification to the court that the defendant has presented for inspection a child passenger restraint system that meets applicable federal safety standards.

(b)(1) A second or subsequent conviction under Section 27360 or 27360.5 is punishable by a fine of two hundred fifty dollars ($250), no part of which may be waived by the court, except that the court may reduce or waive the fine if the defendant establishes to the satisfaction of the court that he or she is economically disadvantaged, and the court, instead refers the defendant to a community education program that includes, but is not limited to, education on the proper installation and use of child passenger restraint systems for children of all ages, and provides certification to the court of completion of that program. Upon completion of the program, the defendant shall provide proof of participation in the program. If an education program on the proper installation and use of a child passenger restraint system is not available within 50 miles of the residence of the defendant, the requirement to participate in that program shall be waived. If the fine is paid, waived, or reduced, the court shall report the conviction to the department pursuant to Section 1803.

(2) The court may require a defendant described under paragraph (1) to attend an education program that includes demonstration of proper installation and use of a child passenger restraint system and provides certification to the court that the defendant has presented for inspection a child passenger restraint system that meets applicable federal safety standards.

(c) Notwithstanding any other law, the fines collected under this section shall be allocated as follows:

(1)(A) Sixty percent to health departments of local jurisdictions where the violation occurred, to be used for a community education and assistance program that includes, but is not limited to, demonstration of the proper installation and use of child passenger restraint systems for children of all ages and assistance to economically disadvantaged families in obtaining a restraint system through a low-cost purchase or loan. The county or city health department shall designate a coordinator to facilitate the creation of a special account and to develop a relationship with the court system to facilitate the transfer of funds to the program. The county or city may contract for the implementation of the program. Prior to obtaining possession of a child passenger restraint system pursuant to this subdivision, a person shall attend an education program that includes demonstration of proper installation and use of a child passenger restraint system.

(B) As the proceeds from fines become available, county or city health departments shall prepare and maintain a listing of all child passenger restraint low-cost purchase or loaner programs in their counties, including a semiannual verification that all programs listed are in existence. Each county or city shall forward the listing to the Office of Traffic Safety in the Business, Transportation and Housing Agency and the courts, birthing centers, community child health and disability prevention programs, county clinics, prenatal clinics, women, infants, and children programs, and county hospitals in that county, who shall make the listing available to the public. The Office of Traffic Safety shall maintain a listing of all of the programs in the state.

(2) Twenty-five percent to the county or city for the administration of the community education program.

(3) Fifteen percent to the city, to be deposited in its general fund except that, if the violation occurred in an unincorporated area, this amount shall be allocated to the county for purposes of paragraph (1). *(Added by Stats.2011, c. 474 (S.B.929), § 7.)*

Research References

2 Witkin, California Criminal Law 4th Crimes Against Public Peace and Welfare § 478 (2021), Children Under Age 8.
2 Witkin, California Criminal Law 4th Crimes Against Public Peace and Welfare § 479 (2021), Children Ages 8 to 16.

§ 27361. Stopping of vehicles believed to be in violation; notice to appear

A law enforcement officer reasonably suspecting a violation of Section 27360 or 27360.5, or both of those sections, may stop a vehicle transporting a child appearing to the officer to be within the age specified in Section 27360 or 27360.5. The officer may issue a notice to appear for a violation of Section 27360 or 27360.5. *(Added by Stats.1982, c. 839, p. 3165, § 2. Amended by Stats.2000, c. 675 (S.B.567), § 7; Stats.2004, c. 420 (A.B.2139), § 4; Stats.2011, c. 474 (S.B.929), § 8.)*

Research References

2 Witkin, California Criminal Law 4th Crimes Against Public Peace and Welfare § 478 (2021), Children Under Age 8.
2 Witkin, California Criminal Law 4th Crimes Against Public Peace and Welfare § 479 (2021), Children Ages 8 to 16.

§ 27368. Child passengers; three-wheeled motor vehicles; vehicle length, height, and weight restrictions

This article applies to child passengers in a fully enclosed three-wheeled motor vehicle that is not less than seven feet in length and not less than four feet in width, and has an unladen weight of 900 pounds or more. *(Added by Stats.1997, c. 710 (A.B.1029), § 3.)*

Research References

2 Witkin, California Criminal Law 4th Crimes Against Public Peace and Welfare § 480 (2021), Other Requirements.

Division 17

OFFENSES AND PROSECUTION

CHAPTER 1. OFFENSES

ARTICLE 1. VIOLATION OF CODE

§ 40000.1. Infractions

Except as otherwise provided in this article, it is unlawful and constitutes an infraction for any person to violate, or fail to comply with any provision of this code, or any local ordinance adopted pursuant to this code. *(Added by Stats.1971, c. 1178, p. 2245, § 3, operative May 3, 1972.)*

Cross References

Drivers' licenses, financial compensation prohibited for filling out original driver's license application for another person, this section not applicable, see Vehicle Code § 12801.2.
Infractions, see Penal Code § 19.6 et seq.
Leaving a child unsupervised inside a motor vehicle, prosecution, see Vehicle Code § 15620.
Person defined, see Vehicle Code § 470.

Research References

2 Witkin, California Criminal Law 4th Crimes Against Public Peace and Welfare § 266 (2021), Infractions.
2 Witkin, California Criminal Law 4th Crimes Against Public Peace and Welfare § 423 (2021), Manufacturers, Transporters, and Dealers.
2 Witkin, California Criminal Law 4th Crimes Against Public Peace and Welfare § 454 (2021), Vehicular Pollution Control.
2 Witkin, California Criminal Law 4th Crimes Against Public Peace and Welfare § 475 (2021), General Equipment Requirements.
2 Witkin, California Criminal Law 4th Crimes Against Public Peace and Welfare § 530 (2021), Bicycles.
2 Witkin, California Criminal Law 4th Crimes Against Public Peace and Welfare § 531 (2021), Low-Speed Vehicles and Motorized Scooters.
1 Witkin California Criminal Law 4th Introduction to Crimes § 86 (2021), In General.

§ 40000.3. Felonies and offenses punishable either as felonies or misdemeanor violation of court order punishable as contempt

A violation expressly declared to be a felony, or a public offense which is punishable, in the discretion of the court, either as a felony or misdemeanor, or a willful violation of a court order which is punishable as contempt pursuant to subdivision (a) of Section 42003, is not an infraction. *(Added by Stats.1971, c. 1178, p. 2245, § 4, operative May 3, 1972. Amended by Stats.1973, c. 1162, p. 2419, § 1.5.)*

Research References

2 Witkin, California Criminal Law 4th Crimes Against Public Peace and Welfare § 266 (2021), Infractions.

§ 40000.5. Misdemeanors

A violation of any of the following provisions shall constitute a misdemeanor, and not an infraction:

Section 20, relating to false statements.

Section 27, relating to impersonating a member of the California Highway Patrol.

Section 31, relating to giving false information.

Paragraph (3) of subdivision (a), or subdivision (b), or both, of Section 221, relating to proper evidence of clearance for dismantling. *(Added by Stats.1971, c. 1178, p. 2245, § 5, operative May 3, 1972. Amended by Stats.1976, c. 937, p. 2146, § 3; Stats.1999, c. 316 (A.B.342), § 3.)*

Research References

2 Witkin, California Criminal Law 4th Crimes Against Governmental Authority § 167 (2021), Misleading Motor Vehicle Authorities or Probation Officers.
2 Witkin, California Criminal Law 4th Crimes Against Public Peace and Welfare § 266 (2021), Infractions.
2 Witkin, California Criminal Law 4th Crimes Against Public Peace and Welfare § 267 (2021), Misdemeanors.

§ 40000.6. Misdemeanor

A violation of any of the following is a misdemeanor and not an infraction:

(a) Subdivision (b) of Section 1808.1, relating to enrollment in the pull notice system.

(b) Subdivision (f) of Section 1808.1, relating to employment of disqualified drivers. *(Added by Stats.1986, c. 1306, § 20. Amended by Stats.1987, c. 726, § 9, operative July 1, 1988; Stats.1988, c. 1586, § 10, operative Jan. 1, 1990; Stats.1991, c. 928 (A.B.1886), § 37, eff. Oct. 14, 1991.)*

§ 40000.61. Misdemeanor; unauthorized disclosure of department records

A violation of Section 1808.45, relating to unauthorized disclosure of department records, is a misdemeanor, and not an infraction. *(Added by Stats.1989, c. 1213, § 18.)*

§ 40000.65. Misdemeanors; emergency road service

A violation of Section 2430.5 or 2432, relating to emergency road service, is a misdemeanor and not an infraction. *(Added by Stats.1991, c. 488 (A.B.123), § 9.)*

§ 40000.7. Misdemeanors

(a) A violation of any of the following provisions is a misdemeanor, and not an infraction:

(1) Section 2416, relating to regulations for emergency vehicles.

(2) Section 2800, relating to failure to obey an officer's lawful order or submit to a lawful inspection.

(3) Section 2800.1, relating to fleeing from a peace officer.

(4) Section 2801, relating to failure to obey a firefighter's lawful order.

(5) Section 2803, relating to unlawful vehicle or load.

(6) Section 2813, relating to stopping for inspection.

(7) Subdivisions (b), (c), and (d) of Section 4461 and subdivisions (b) and (c) of Section 4463, relating to disabled person placards and disabled person and disabled veteran license plates.

(8) Section 4462.5, relating to deceptive or false evidence of vehicle registration.

(9) Section 4463.5, relating to deceptive or facsimile license plates.

(10) Section 5500, relating to the surrender of registration documents and license plates before dismantling may begin.

(11) Section 5506, relating to the sale of a total loss salvage vehicle, or of a vehicle reported for dismantling by a salvage vehicle rebuilder.

(12) Section 5753, relating to delivery of certificates of ownership and registration when committed by a dealer or any person while a dealer within the preceding 12 months.

(13) Section 5901, relating to dealers and lessor-retailers giving notice.

(14) Section 5901.1, relating to lessors giving notice and failure to pay fee.

(15) Section 8802, relating to the return of canceled, suspended, or revoked certificates of ownership, registration cards, or license plates, when committed by any person with intent to defraud.

(16) Section 8803, relating to return of canceled, suspended, or revoked documents and license plates of a dealer, manufacturer, remanufacturer, transporter, dismantler, or salesman.

(b) This section shall become operative on January 1, 2001. *(Added by Stats.1996, c. 697 (A.B.2852), § 4, operative Jan. 1, 2001. Amended by Stats.2002, c. 670 (S.B.1331), § 10; Stats.2010, c. 709 (S.B.1062), § 26.)*

Cross References

Infractions, see Penal Code § 19.6 et seq.
Misdemeanor, see Penal Code §§ 19, 19.2.

§ 40000.70. Notification of on-highway hazardous spill

A violation of Section 23112.5, relating to notification of an on-highway hazardous material or hazardous waste spill, is a misdemeanor and not an infraction. *(Added by Stats.1990, c. 429 (A.B.3904), § 10.)*

§ 40000.77. Misdemeanors; transportation of pupils

A violation of Article 7 (commencing with Section 2570) of Chapter 2.5 of Division 2, relating to transportation of school pupils, is a misdemeanor, and not an infraction. *(Added by Stats.1990, c. 1563 (A.B.3243), § 62.)*

§ 40000.8. Misdemeanors; vessels

A violation of any of the following provisions is a misdemeanor, and not an infraction:

Section 9872, relating to the registration of vessels.

Section 9872.1, relating to unidentified vessels. *(Added by Stats. 1972, c. 618, p. 1151, § 152. Amended by Stats.1991, c. 922 (A.B.1201), § 7.)*

Cross References

Infractions, see Penal Code § 19.6 et seq.
Misdemeanor, see Penal Code §§ 19, 19.2.

§ 40000.9. Misdemeanors

A violation of any of the following provisions shall constitute a misdemeanor, and not an infraction:

Section 10501, relating to false report of vehicle theft.

Sections 10750 and 10751, relating to altered or defaced vehicle identifying numbers.

Section 10851.5, relating to theft of binder chains.

Sections 10852 and 10853, relating to injuring or tampering with a vehicle.

Section 10854, relating to unlawful use of stored vehicle. *(Added by Stats.1971, c. 1178, p. 2246, § 7, operative May 3, 1972.)*

Cross References

Infractions, see Penal Code § 19.6 et seq.
Misdemeanor, see Penal Code §§ 19, 19.2.

Research References

2 Witkin, California Criminal Law 4th Crimes Against Property § 265 (2021), Miscellaneous Frauds.

§ 40000.10. Fines; misdemeanor or infraction; unlicensed drivers

A violation of subdivision (a) of Section 12500 shall be punished as follows:

(a) Except as provided in subdivision (b), as an infraction by a fine of one hundred dollars ($100) for a first or second violation.

(b) As a misdemeanor or an infraction as prescribed by Section 19.8 of the Penal Code if a person has a prior driver's license suspension or revocation for a violation of subdivision (c) of Section 192 of the Penal Code, subdivision (e) of Section 12809, or of Section 13353, 13353.1, 13353.2, 23103, 23104, 23105, 23109, 23152, 23153, or 23154.

(c) As a misdemeanor or an infraction as prescribed by Section 19.8 of the Penal Code for a third or subsequent violation. *(Added by Stats.2022, c. 800 (A.B.2746), § 20, eff. Jan. 1, 2023.)*

§ 40000.11. Misdemeanors

A violation of any of the following provisions is a misdemeanor, and not an infraction:

(a) Division 5 (commencing with Section 11100), relating to occupational licensing and business regulations.

* * *

(b) Section 12515, subdivision (b), relating to persons under 21 years of age driving, and the employment of those persons to drive, vehicles engaged in interstate commerce or transporting hazardous substances or wastes.

(c) Section 12517, relating to a special driver's certificate to operate a schoolbus or school pupil activity bus.

(d) Section 12517.45, relating to a special driver's certificate and vehicle inspection for the transportation of pupils to or from school-related activities by a passenger charter-party carrier as defined in subdivision (k) of Section 545.

(e) Section 12519, subdivision (a), relating to a special driver's certificate to operate a farm labor vehicle.

(f) Section 12520, relating to a special driver's certificate to operate a tow truck.

(g) Section 12804, subdivision (d), relating to medical certificates.

(h) Section 12951, subdivision (b), relating to refusal to display license.

(i) Section 13004, relating to unlawful use of an identification card.

(j) Section 13004.1, relating to identification documents.

(k) Sections 14601, 14601.1, 14601.2, and 14601.5, relating to driving with a suspended or revoked driver's license.

(*l*) Section 14604, relating to unlawful use of a vehicle.

(m) Section 14610, relating to unlawful use of a driver's license.

(n) Section 14610.1, relating to identification documents.

(o) Section 15501, relating to use of false or fraudulent license by a minor. *(Added by Stats.1971, c. 1178, p. 2246, § 8, operative May 3, 1972. Amended by Stats.1981, c. 940, p. 3581, § 43; Stats.1982, c. 1233, p. 4547, § 3; Stats.1984, c. 779, § 5; Stats.1990, c. 170 (S.B.1873), § 3; Stats.1991, c. 488 (A.B.123), § 8; Stats.1994, c. 1221 (S.B.1758), § 22; Stats.1995, c. 101 (S.B.317), § 5; Stats.1995, c. 922 (S.B.833), § 7; Stats.2008, c. 649 (A.B.830), § 5; Stats.2022, c. 800 (A.B.2746), § 21, eff. Jan. 1, 2023.)*

Cross References

Infractions, see Penal Code § 19.6 et seq.
Misdemeanor, see Penal Code §§ 19, 19.2.
Unlawful to drive unless licensed, see Vehicle Code § 12500.
Violation of license provisions, see Vehicle Code § 14600 et seq.

Research References

California Jury Instructions - Criminal 16.632, Failure to Present License Upon Demand.
2 Witkin, California Criminal Law 4th Crimes Against Public Peace and Welfare § 422 (2021), In General.
2 Witkin, California Criminal Law 4th Crimes Against Public Peace and Welfare § 423 (2021), Manufacturers, Transporters, and Dealers.

§ 40000.13. Misdemeanors

Section operative until the date that the Secretary of State receives notice from the Director of Transportation as described in § 5205.5. See, also, section operative on the date such notice is received.

A violation of any of the following provisions is a misdemeanor, and not an infraction:

(a) Section 16560, relating to interstate highway carriers.

(b) Sections 20002 and 20003, relating to duties at accidents.

(c) Section 21200.5, relating to riding a bicycle while under the influence of an alcoholic beverage or any drug.

(d) Subdivision (b) of Section 21651, relating to wrong-way driving on divided highways.

(e) Subdivision (c) of Section 21655.9, relating to illegal use of decals, labels, or other identifiers.

(f) Section 22520.5, a second or subsequent conviction of an offense relating to vending on or near freeways.

(g) Section 22520.6, a second or subsequent conviction of an offense relating to roadside rest areas and vista points.

(h) This section shall remain in effect only until the date that the Secretary of State receives the notice from the Director of Transportation as described in Section 5205.5, and as of that date is repealed. *(Added by Stats.1971, c. 1178, p. 2246, § 9, operative May 3, 1972. Amended by Stats.1980, c. 680, p. 2064, § 3; Stats.1981, c. 936, p. 3540, § 2; Stats.1981, c. 937, p. 3541, § 3; Stats.1983, c. 275, § 4, eff. July 15, 1983; Stats.1984, c. 487, § 2; Stats.1985, c. 1013, § 4; Stats.1988, c. 765, § 3; Stats.1999, c. 330 (A.B.71), § 4; Stats.2006, c. 614 (A.B.2600), § 5; Stats.2010, c. 37 (A.B.1500), § 3; Stats.2010, c. 215 (S.B.535), § 3.)*

Repeal

For repeal of this section, see its terms.

Cross References

Infractions, see Penal Code § 19.6 et seq.
Misdemeanor, see Penal Code §§ 19, 19.2.

§ 40000.13. Misdemeanors

Section operative on the date that the Secretary of State receives notice from the Director of Transportation as described in § 5205.5. See, also, section operative until the date such notice is received.

A violation of any of the following provisions is a misdemeanor, and not an infraction:

(a) Section 16560, relating to interstate highway carriers.

(b) Scctions 20002 and 20003, relating to duties at accidents.

(c) Section 21200.5, relating to riding a bicycle while under the influence of an alcoholic beverage or any drug.

(d) Subdivision (b) of Section 21651, relating to wrong- way driving on divided highways.

(e) Section 22520.5, a second or subsequent conviction of an offense relating to vending on or near freeways.

(f) Section 22520.6, a second or subsequent conviction of an offense relating to roadside rest areas and vista points.

(g) This section shall become operative on the date that the Secretary of State receives the notice from the Director of Transportation as described in Section 5205.5. *(Added by Stats.1999, c. 330 (A.B.71), § 5, operative Jan. 1, 2008. Amended by Stats.2006, c. 614 (A.B.2600), § 6, operative Jan. 1, 2011; Stats.2010, c. 215 (S.B.535), § 4, operative contingent.)*

§ 40000.14. Failure to obey person or control devices at site of construction, maintenance or repair; penalties

A violation of subdivision (b) or (c) of Section 21367 is an infraction, except as follows:

(a) A willful violation is a misdemeanor.

(b) A willful violation committed in a manner exhibiting a wanton disregard for the safety of persons is a misdemeanor punishable by imprisonment in the county jail for not more than one year. *(Added by Stats.1986, c. 748, § 3.)*

§ 40000.15. Misdemeanors

A violation of any of the following provisions shall constitute a misdemeanor, and not an infraction:

Subdivision (g), (j), (k), (*l*), or (m) of Section 22658, relating to unlawfully towed or stored vehicles.

Sections 23103 and 23104, relating to reckless driving.

Section 23109, relating to speed contests or exhibitions.

Subdivision (a) of Section 23110, relating to throwing at vehicles.

Section 23152, relating to driving under the influence.

Subdivision (b) of Section 23222, relating to possession of marijuana.

Subdivision (a) or (b) of Section 23224, relating to persons under 21 years of age knowingly driving, or being a passenger in, a motor vehicle carrying any alcoholic beverage.

Section 23253, relating to directions on toll highways or vehicular crossings.

Section 23332, relating to trespassing.

Section 24002.5, relating to unlawful operation of a farm vehicle.

Section 24011.3, relating to vehicle bumper strength notices.

Section 27150.1, relating to sale of exhaust systems.

Section 27362, relating to child passenger seat restraints.

Section 28050, relating to true mileage driven.

Section 28050.5, relating to nonfunctional odometers.

Section 28051, relating to resetting odometers.

Section 28051.5, relating to devices to reset odometers.

Subdivision (d) of Section 28150, relating to possessing four or more jamming devices. *(Added by Stats.1971, c. 1178, p. 2246, § 10, operative May 3, 1972. Amended by Stats.1973, c. 610, p. 1131, § 2; Stats.1973, c. 1162, p. 2420, § 6; Stats.1980, c. 313, p. 644, § 1; Stats.1981, c. 939, p. 3560, § 12; Stats.1981, c. 940, p. 3582, § 44; Stats.1983, c. 1005, § 2; Stats.1986, c. 1108, § 6; Stats.1983, c. 1005, § 2, operative Jan. 1, 1990; Stats.1990, c. 33 (S.B.1372), § 8, eff. March 26, 1990; Stats.1990, c. 1403 (A.B.2040), § 7, eff. Sept. 28, 1990; Stats.1991, c. 1219 (S.B.265), § 2; Stats.1996, c. 690 (A.B. 2000), § 2; Stats.1998, c. 493 (S.B.1964), § 2; Stats.1999, c. 83 (S.B.966), § 190; Stats.2000, c. 873 (A.B.2086), § 6; Stats.2006, c. 609 (A.B.2210), § 6.)*

Cross References

Infractions, see Penal Code § 19.6 et seq.

Misdemeanor, definition and penalties, see Penal Code §§ 17, 19, 19.2.

§ 40000.16. Escape of materials from vehicle; offense

A second or subsequent violation of Section 23114, relating to preventing the escape of materials from vehicles, occurring within two years of a prior violation of that section is a misdemeanor, and not an infraction. *(Added by Stats.1988, c. 1486, § 5. Amended by Stats.1997, c. 945 (A.B.1561), § 32.)*

§ 40000.18. Misdemeanors

A violation of subdivision (b) of Section 31401 or Section 31402 or 31403, relating to farm labor vehicles, is a misdemeanor and not an infraction. *(Added by Stats.1988, c. 613, § 2.)*

§ 40000.19. Misdemeanors

A violation of any of the following provisions is a misdemeanor, and not an infraction:

(a) Section 31303, relating to transportation of hazardous waste.

(b) Division 14 (commencing with Section 31600), relating to transportation of explosives.

(c) Division 14.1 (commencing with Section 32000), relating to the transportation of hazardous material.

(d) Division 14.3 (commencing with Section 32100), relating to transportation of inhalation hazards.

(e) Division 14.5 (commencing with Section 33000), relating to transportation of radioactive materials.

(f) Division 14.7 (commencing with Section 34001), relating to flammable liquids. *(Added by Stats.1971, c. 1178, p. 2247, § 11, operative May 3, 1972. Amended by Stats.1981, c. 860, p. 3298, § 14; Stats.1984, c. 1683, § 3; Stats.1988, c. 1384, § 6.)*

Cross References

Infractions, see Penal Code § 19.6 et seq.
Misdemeanor, see Penal Code §§ 19, 19.2.

§ 40000.20. Third or subsequent violations of provisions relating to storage and possession of open containers by driver operating under valid certificate or permit pursuant to Passenger Charter-party Carriers' Act; misdemeanor

A third or subsequent violation of Section 23225, relating to the storage of an opened container of an alcoholic beverage, or Section 23223, relating to the possession of an open container of an alcoholic beverage, by a driver of a vehicle used to provide transportation services on a prearranged basis, operating under a valid certificate or permit pursuant to the Passenger Charter-party Carriers' Act (Chapter 8 (commencing with Section 5351) of Division 2 of the Public Utilities Code), is a misdemeanor. *(Added by Stats.2012, c. 461 (A.B.45), § 7. Amended by Stats.2013, c. 76 (A.B.383), § 198.)*

Research References

2 Witkin, California Criminal Law 4th Crimes Against Public Peace and Welfare § 303 (2021), Drinking or Possessing Alcohol or Marijuana.

§ 40000.21. Misdemeanors

A violation of any of the following provisions is a misdemeanor, and not an infraction:

(a) Subdivision (a) of Section 34506, relating to the hours of service of drivers.

(b) Subdivision (b) of Section 34506, relating to the transportation of hazardous materials.

(c) Subdivision (c) of Section 34506, relating to schoolbuses.

(d) Subdivision (d) of Section 34506, relating to youth buses.

(e) Section 34505 or subdivision (e) of Section 34506, relating to tour buses.

(f) Section 34505.5 or subdivision (f) of Section 34506, relating to vehicles described in subdivisions (a) to (g), inclusive, of Section 34500.

(g) Subdivision (a) of Section 34501.3, relating to unlawful scheduling of runs by motor carriers.

(h) Subdivision (g) of Section 34506, relating to school pupil activity buses.

(i) Subparagraph (D) of paragraph (4) of subdivision (a) of Section 34505.9, relating to intermodal chassis. *(Added by Stats. 1971, c. 1178, p. 2247, § 12, operative May 3, 1972. Amended by Stats.1977, c. 406, p. 1418, § 14, eff. Aug. 27, 1977; Stats.1982, c. 383, p. 1714, § 9, eff. July 4, 1982; Stats.1986, c. 1306, § 21; Stats.1988, c. 1586, § 11; Stats.1990, c. 429 (A.B.3904), § 9; Stats.1991, c. 928 (A.B.1886), § 38, eff. Oct. 14, 1991; Stats.1994, c. 58 (A.B.1633), § 6, eff. April 26, 1994; Stats.1998, c. 340 (A.B.346), § 4, eff. Aug. 24, 1998.)*

Cross References

Infractions, see Penal Code § 19.6 et seq.
Misdemeanor, see Penal Code §§ 19, 19.2.

§ 40000.22. Misdemeanors; inspections; violations of Motor Carriers of Property Permit Act

(a) A violation of subdivision (e) of Section 34501, subdivision (b) or (d) of Section 34501.12, or subdivision (c) of Section 34501.14, relating to applications for inspections, is a misdemeanor and not an infraction.

(b) A violation of Division 14.85 (commencing with Section 34600), relating to motor carriers of property, is a misdemeanor and not an infraction.

(c) This section shall become operative on January 1, 2016. *(Added by Stats.2013, c. 500 (A.B.529), § 20, operative Jan. 1, 2016.)*

Research References

2 Witkin, California Criminal Law 4th Crimes Against Public Peace and Welfare § 532 (2021), Public Utilities.

§ 40000.23. Misdemeanors

A violation of any of the following provisions is a misdemeanor, and not an infraction:

(a) Paragraph (1) of subdivision (c) of Section 35784, relating to special permit violations.

(b) Subdivision (a) of Section 35784.5 relating to extralegal loads and operation of vehicles without a special permit.

(c) Other provisions of Chapter 5 (commencing with Section 35550) of Division 15, which relate to weight restrictions, except in cases of weight violations where the amount of excess weight is less than 4,501 pounds. *(Added by Stats.1971, c. 1178, p. 2247, § 13, operative May 3, 1972. Amended by Stats.1984, c. 542, § 9.)*

Cross References

Infractions, see Penal Code § 19.6 et seq.
Misdemeanor, see Penal Code §§ 19, 19.2.

§ 40000.24. Misdemeanors

A violation of any of the following provisions shall constitute a misdemeanor and not an infraction:

(a) Subdivision (c) of Section 38301.5, relating to unauthorized operation of a vehicle within a mountain fire district.

(b) Section 38316, relating to reckless driving.

(c) Section 38317, relating to reckless driving with injury.

(d) Subdivision (a) of Section 38318 or subdivision (a) of Section 38318.5, relating to off-highway vehicles.

(e) Section 38319, relating to protection of the environment.

(f) Section 38320, relating to the depositing of matter. *(Added by Stats.1976, c. 1093, p. 4953, § 29. Amended by Stats.1984, c. 729, § 3; Stats.1984, c. 1015, § 3.)*

§ 40000.25. Misdemeanors

A violation of any of the following provisions shall constitute a misdemeanor, and not an infraction:

Section 40005, relating to owner's responsibility.

Section 40504, relating to false signatures.

Section 40508, relating to failure to appear or to pay fine.

Section 40519, relating to failure to appear.

Section 40614, relating to use of a fictitious name.

Section 40616, relating to a willful violation of a notice to correct.

Section 42005, relating to failure to attend traffic school. *(Added by Stats.1971, c. 1178, p. 2247, § 14, operative May 3, 1972. Amended by Stats.1973, c. 1162, p. 2419, § 3; Stats.1978, c. 1350, p. 4478, § 1, operative July 1, 1979.)*

Cross References

Infractions, see Penal Code § 19.6 et seq.
Misdemeanor, see Penal Code §§ 19, 19.2.

§ 40000.26. Misdemeanors; failure to submit to inspection

A violation of subdivision (g) of Section 34501.12 or subdivision (d) of Section 34501.14, relating to inspections, is a misdemeanor and not an infraction. *(Added by Stats.1988, c. 1586, § 13.5, operative Jan. 1, 1992. Amended by Stats.1992, c. 724 (A.B.2326), § 3; Stats.1992, c. 1243 (A.B.3090), § 107, eff. Sept. 30, 1992; Stats.1992, c. 1243 (A.B.3090), § 107.1, eff. Sept. 30, 1992, operative Jan. 1, 1993.)*

§ 40000.28. Misdemeanor; three or more violations

Any offense which would otherwise be an infraction is a misdemeanor if a defendant has been convicted of three or more violations of this code or any local ordinance adopted pursuant to this code within the 12-month period immediately preceding the commission of the offense and such prior convictions are admitted by the defendant or alleged in the accusatory pleading. For this purpose, a bail forfeiture shall be deemed to be a conviction of the offense charged.

This section shall have no application to violations by pedestrians. *(Added by Stats.1973, c. 1162, p. 2419, § 4. Amended by Stats.1975, c. 635, p. 1379, § 1.)*

Research References

2 Witkin, California Criminal Law 4th Crimes Against Public Peace and Welfare § 267 (2021), Misdemeanors.

§ 40001. Owner, lessee, or any other person; codefendant; rebuttable presumption

(a) It is unlawful for the owner, or any other person, employing or otherwise directing the driver of any vehicle to cause the operation of the vehicle upon a highway in any manner contrary to law.

(b) It is unlawful for an owner to request, cause, or permit the operation of any vehicle that is any of the following:

(1) Not registered or for which any fee has not been paid under this code.

(2) Not equipped as required in this code.

(3) Not in compliance with the size, weight, or load provisions of this code.

(4) Not in compliance with the regulations promulgated pursuant to this code, or with applicable city or county ordinances adopted pursuant to this code.

(5) Not in compliance with the provisions of Part 5 (commencing with Section 43000) of Division 26 of the Health and Safety Code and the rules and regulations of the State Air Resources Board.

(c) Any employer who violates an out-of-service order, that complies with Section 396.9 of Title 49 of the Code of Federal Regulations, or who knowingly requires or permits a driver to violate or fail to comply with that out-of-service order, is guilty of a misdemeanor.

(d) An employer who is convicted of allowing, permitting, requiring, or authorizing a driver to operate a commercial motor vehicle in violation of any statute or regulation pertaining to a railroad-highway grade crossing is subject to a fine of not more than ten thousand dollars ($10,000).

(e) Whenever a violation is chargeable to the owner or lessee of a vehicle pursuant to subdivision (a) or (b), the driver shall not be arrested or cited for the violation unless the vehicle is registered in a state or country other than California, or unless the violation is for an offense that is clearly within the responsibility of the driver.

(f) Whenever the owner, or lessee, or any other person is prosecuted for a violation pursuant to this section, the court may, on the request of the defendant, take appropriate steps to make the driver of the vehicle, or any other person who directs the loading, maintenance, or operation of the vehicle, a codefendant. However, the court may make the driver a codefendant only if the driver is the owner or lessee of the vehicle, or the driver is an employee or a contractor of the defendant who requested the court to make the driver a codefendant. If the codefendant is held solely responsible and found guilty, the court may dismiss the charge against the defendant.

(g) In any prosecution under this section, it is a rebuttable presumption that any person who gives false or erroneous information in a written certification of actual gross cargo weight has directed, requested, caused, or permitted the operation of a vehicle in a manner contrary to law in violation of subdivision (a) or (b), or both. *(Stats.1959, c. 3, p. 1773, § 40001. Amended by Stats.1961, c. 58, p. 1015, § 66.6; Stats.1963, c. 1322, p. 2843, § 1; Stats.1965, c. 2031, p. 4616, § 16, eff. July 23, 1965; Stats.1965, c. 2032, p. 4617, § 1; Stats.1968, c. 49, p. 197, § 15, eff. April 25, 1968; Stats.1979, c. 373, p. 1384, § 328; Stats.1984, c. 981, § 2, operative July 1, 1985; Stats.1989, c. 533, § 15; Stats.1993, c. 647 (S.B.952), § 3; Stats.1993, c. 757 (S.B.619), § 5; Stats.1999, c. 724 (A.B.1650), § 51; Stats.2001, c. 504 (A.B.1280), § 10; Stats.2004, c. 193 (S.B.111), § 200.)*

Law Revision Commission Comments

Section 40001 is amended to delete reference to an obsolete reporting requirement. The required report was to be completed by January 1, 1988. [33 Cal.L.Rev.Comm. Reports 498 (2004)].

Cross References

Applicability of this section to trolley coaches, see Vehicle Code § 21051.
Driving while under the influence of alcohol or drugs as felony or misdemeanor, see Vehicle Code §§ 23152, 23153.
Equipment testing, see Vehicle Code § 26100 et seq.
Highway defined, see Vehicle Code § 360.
Limitation on driving hours, see Vehicle Code § 21702.
Miscellaneous rules as to traffic laws, generally, see Vehicle Code § 21000 et seq.
Notice of offense under this section, time notice complete, see Vehicle Code § 23.
Parking violations, see Vehicle Code § 40200 et seq.
Reckless driving, punishment for, see Vehicle Code §§ 23103, 23104.
Registration indices and records, generally, see Vehicle Code § 1800 et seq.
Speed laws in general, limitations with respect to, see Vehicle Code § 22349 et seq.
Theft of vehicles, see Vehicle Code § 10851.
Traffic violation point count and negligent operation defined, see Vehicle Code § 12810.
Vehicular homicide, see Penal Code § 192.

Violations of,
Additional and accessory equipment regulations, see Vehicle Code § 27000 et seq.
Traffic laws, see Vehicle Code § 21000 et seq.
Vehicular crossing regulations, see Vehicle Code § 23250 et seq.
Weight violations, penalty, see Vehicle Code § 42030 et seq.

Research References

2 Witkin, California Criminal Law 4th Crimes Against Public Peace and Welfare § 270 (2021), Responsibilities of Owner, Operator, Employer, and Employee.

§ 40002. Prosecution of persons owning or controlling vehicles

(a)(1) If there is a violation of Section 40001, an owner or any other person subject to Section 40001, who was not driving the vehicle involved in the violation, may be mailed a written notice to appear. An exact and legible duplicate copy of that notice when filed with the court, in lieu of a verified complaint, is a complaint to which the defendant may plead "guilty."

(2) If, however, the defendant fails to appear in court or does not deposit lawful bail, or pleads other than "guilty" of the offense charged, a verified complaint shall be filed which shall be deemed to be an original complaint, and thereafter proceedings shall be had as provided by law, except that a defendant may, by an agreement in writing, subscribed by the defendant and filed with the court, waive the filing of a verified complaint and elect that the prosecution may proceed upon a written notice to appear.

(3) A verified complaint pursuant to paragraph (2) shall include a paragraph that informs the person that unless he or she appears in the court designated in the complaint within 21 days after being given the complaint and answers the charge, renewal of registration of the vehicle involved in the offense may be precluded by the department, or a warrant of arrest may be issued against him or her.

(b)(1) If a person mailed a notice to appear pursuant to paragraph (1) of subdivision (a) fails to appear in court or deposit bail, a warrant of arrest shall not be issued based on the notice to appear, even if that notice is verified. An arrest warrant may be issued only after a verified complaint pursuant to paragraph (2) of subdivision (a) is given the person and the person fails to appear in court to answer that complaint.

(2) If a person mailed a notice to appear pursuant to paragraph (1) of subdivision (a) fails to appear in court or deposit bail, the court may give by mail to the person a notice of noncompliance. A notice of noncompliance shall include a paragraph that informs the person that unless he or she appears in the court designated in the notice to appear within 21 days after being given by mail the notice of noncompliance and answers the charge on the notice to appear, or pays the applicable fine and penalties if an appearance is not required, renewal of registration of the vehicle involved in the offense may be precluded by the department.

(c) A verified complaint filed pursuant to this section shall conform to Chapter 2 (commencing with Section 948) of Title 5 of Part 2 of the Penal Code.

(d)(1) The giving by mail of a notice to appear pursuant to paragraph (1) of subdivision (a) or a notice of noncompliance pursuant to paragraph (2) of subdivision (b) shall be done in a manner prescribed by Section 22.

(2) The verified complaint pursuant to paragraph (2) of subdivision (a) shall be given in a manner prescribed by Section 22. *(Added by Stats.2007, c. 452 (A.B.1464), § 3. Amended by Stats.2008, c. 179 (S.B.1498), § 224; Stats.2008, c. 699 (S.B.1241), § 26; Stats.2010, c. 328 (S.B.1330), § 232.)*

Cross References

Execution of warrants on behalf of local peace officers by highway patrol, expenses of, see Vehicle Code § 40516.
Service of warrants, authority of members of highway patrol with respect to, see Vehicle Code § 2411.

§ 40002.1. Notice of noncompliance or subsequent adjudication; transmittal to department; warrant of arrest

(a) Whenever a person has failed to appear in the court designated in the notice to appear or a verified complaint specified in Section 40002, following personal service of the notice of noncompliance or deposit in the mail pursuant to Section 22, the magistrate or clerk of the court may give notice of that fact to the department.

(b) Whenever the matter is adjudicated, including a dismissal of the charges upon forfeiture of bail or otherwise, the magistrate or clerk of the court hearing the matter shall immediately do all of the following:

(1) Endorse a certificate to that effect.

(2) Provide the person or the person's attorney with a copy of the certificate.

(3) Transmit a copy of the certificate to the department.

(c) A notice of noncompliance shall not be transmitted to the department pursuant to subdivision (a) if a warrant of arrest has been issued on the same offense pursuant to subdivision (b) of Section 40002. A warrant of arrest shall not be issued pursuant to subdivision (b) of Section 40002 if a notice of noncompliance has been transmitted to the department on the same offense pursuant to this section, except that, when a notice has been received by the court pursuant to subdivision (c) of Section 4766 or recalled by motion of the court, a warrant may then be issued. *(Added by Stats.1984, c. 981, § 4, operative July 1, 1985. Amended by Stats.1998, c. 877 (A.B.2132), § 75; Stats.2007, c. 452 (A.B.1464), § 4.)*

§ 40003. Prosecution of employees

Whenever an employee is prosecuted for a violation of any provision of this code, or regulations promulgated pursuant to this code, relating to the size, weight, registration, equipment, or loading of a vehicle while operating a vehicle he was employed to operate, and which is owned by his employer, the court shall on the request of the employee take appropriate proceedings to make the owner of the vehicle a codefendant. In the event it is found that the employee had reasonable grounds to believe that the vehicle operated by him as an employee did not violate such provisions, and in the event the owner is found guilty under the provisions of Section 40001, the court may dismiss the charges against the employee.

In those cases in which the charges against the employee are dismissed, the abstract of the record of the court required by Section 1803 shall clearly indicate that such charges were dismissed and that the owner of the vehicle was found guilty under Section 40001. *(Stats.1959, c. 3, p. 1773, § 40003. Amended by Stats.1963, c. 950, p. 2205, § 1; Stats.1967, c. 819, p. 2245, § 1.)*

Cross References

Applicability of this section to trolley coaches, see Vehicle Code § 21051.

Research References

2 Witkin, California Criminal Law 4th Crimes Against Public Peace and Welfare § 270 (2021), Responsibilities of Owner, Operator, Employer, and Employee.

§ 40004. Period for commencement of criminal actions

(a) The period for commencing criminal action against any person having filed or caused to be filed any false, fictitious, altered, forged or counterfeit document with the Department of Motor Vehicles or the Department of the California Highway Patrol shall, if the offense is a misdemeanor, expire one year from time of discovery of such act.

(b) The period for commencing criminal action against any person having filed or caused to be filed any false, fictitious, altered, forged or counterfeit document with the Department of Motor Vehicles or the Department of the California Highway Patrol shall, if the offense is a felony, expire three years from time of discovery of such act.

(c) The time allowed for commencing criminal proceedings as provided in subdivisions (a) and (b) of this section shall not extend beyond five years from the date of commission of the act. *(Added by Stats.1968, c. 1192, p. 2262, § 12, operative Jan. 1, 1969.)*

Research References

1 Witkin California Criminal Law 4th Defenses § 252 (2021), Discovery of Crime: Statutory Provisions.

§ 40005. Employer's failure

Whenever a driver is cited for a violation of any provision of this code, or regulations promulgated pursuant to this code, relating to the size, weight, equipment, registration, fees, or loading of a vehicle, while operating a vehicle he was employed or otherwise directed to operate, and which is not owned by him, and the driver gives the citation to the owner or any other person referred to in Section 40001, if the owner or other person undertakes to answer the charge or otherwise to cause its disposition without any further action by the driver and then fails to act in accordance with the undertaking as a consequence of which a warrant is issued for the arrest of the driver, the owner or other person is guilty of a misdemeanor. *(Added by Stats.1965, c. 294, p. 1292, § 1.)*

Cross References

Violation a misdemeanor, see Vehicle Code § 40000.25.

Research References

2 Witkin, California Criminal Law 4th Crimes Against Public Peace and Welfare § 270 (2021), Responsibilities of Owner, Operator, Employer, and Employee.

4 Witkin, California Criminal Law 4th Pretrial Proceedings § 53 (2021), Failure to Appear.

§ 40006. Towing unregistered disabled vehicle; infraction

Whenever a disabled vehicle, being taken to a repair shop, garage, or other place of storage, is being towed upon a highway by a tow car and the vehicle is determined to be in violation of subdivision (a) of Section 4000, the violation shall be charged as prescribed in Section 40001. *(Added by Stats.1979, c. 152, p. 349, § 1.)*

§ 40007. Application of other statutory provisions applicable to acts violating Division 5

Division 5 (commencing with Section 11100) does not preclude the application of any other statutory provision which is applicable to any act violating any provision of Division 5. *(Added by Stats.1985, c. 93, § 1.)*

§ 40008. Intent to capture image, recording or impression for a commercial purpose; endangerment of minor

(a) Notwithstanding any other provision of law, except as otherwise provided in subdivision (c), any person who violates Section 21701, 21703, or 23103, with the intent to capture any type of visual image, sound recording, or other physical impression of another person for a commercial purpose, is guilty of a misdemeanor and not an infraction and shall be punished by imprisonment in a county jail for not more than six months and by a fine of not more than two thousand five hundred dollars ($2,500).

(b) Notwithstanding any other provision of law, except as otherwise provided in subdivision (c), any person who violates Section 21701, 21703, or 23103, with the intent to capture any type of visual image, sound recording, or other physical impression of another person for a commercial purpose and who causes a minor child or children to be placed in a situation in which the child's person or health is endangered, is guilty of a misdemeanor and not an infraction and shall be punished by imprisonment in a county jail for not more than one year and by a fine of not more than five thousand dollars ($5,000).

(c) Pursuant to Section 654 of the Penal Code, an act or omission described in subdivision (a) or (b) that is punishable in different ways by different provisions of law shall be punished under the provision that provides for the longest potential term of imprisonment, but in no case shall the act or omission be punished under more than one provision. An acquittal or conviction and sentence under any one provision bars a prosecution for the same act or omission under any other provision. *(Added by Stats.2010, c. 685 (A.B.2479), § 3.)*

Research References

2 Witkin, California Criminal Law 4th Crimes Against Public Peace and Welfare § 271 (2021), Reckless Driving.

ARTICLE 3. PROCEDURE ON PARKING VIOLATIONS

§ 40200. Application of article

(a) Any violation of any regulation that is not a misdemeanor governing the standing or parking of a vehicle under this code, under any federal statute or regulation, or under any ordinance enacted by local authorities is subject to a civil penalty. The enforcement of those civil penalties shall be governed by the civil administrative procedures set forth in this article.

(b) Except as provided in Section 40209, the registered owner and driver, rentee, or lessee of a vehicle cited for any violation of any regulation governing the parking of a vehicle under this code, under any federal statute or regulation, or under any ordinance enacted by a local authority shall be jointly liable for parking penalties imposed under this article, unless the owner can show that the vehicle was used without consent of that person, express or implied. An owner who pays any parking penalty, civil judgment, costs, or administrative fees pursuant to this article shall have the right to recover the same from the driver, rentee, or lessee.

(c) The driver of a vehicle who is not the owner thereof but who uses or operates the vehicle with the express or implied permission of the owner shall be considered the agent of the owner to receive notices of parking violations served in accordance with this article and may contest the notice of violation. *(Added by Stats.1986, c. 939, § 15. Amended by Stats.1992, c. 1244 (A.B.408), § 7, operative July 1, 1993; Stats.1993, c. 1093 (A.B.780), § 3.)*

Cross References

Emergency Medical Air Transportation Act, penalty assessment, exclusion for violations under this Article, see Government Code § 76000.10.

Research References

2 Witkin, California Criminal Law 4th Crimes Against Public Peace and Welfare § 323 (2021), Parking.
2 Witkin, California Criminal Law 4th Crimes Against Public Peace and Welfare § 325 (2021), Civil Enforcement.
1 Witkin California Criminal Law 4th Introduction to Crimes § 86 (2021), In General.
4 Witkin, California Criminal Law 4th Pretrial Proceedings § 51 (2021), Citation, Promise, and Release.
3 Witkin, California Criminal Law 4th Punishment § 103 (2021), State and County Assessments and Surcharges.

§ 40200.1. Notice of parking violation and notice to appear for same violation

A person shall not be subject to both a notice of parking violation and a notice to appear for the same violation. *(Added by Stats.2009, c. 415 (A.B.144), § 5.)*

§ 40200.3. Deposit and transfer of amounts collected by processing agency; report; public record

(a) All parking penalties collected by the processing agency, which may be the issuing agency, including process service fees and fees and collection costs related to civil debt collection, shall be deposited to the account of the issuing agency, except that those sums attributable to the issuance of a notice of parking violation by a peace officer of the Department of the California Highway Patrol shall be deposited in the account in the jurisdiction where the violation occurred, and except those sums payable to a county pursuant to Chapter 12 (commencing with Section 76000) of Title 8 of the Government Code and that portion of any parking penalty which is attributable to an increase in the parking bail amount effective between September 16, 1988, and July 1, 1992, inclusive, pursuant to Section 1463.28 of the Penal Code. Those funds attributable to this increase in bail shall be transferred to the county treasurer and deposited in the general fund. Any increase in parking penalties effective after July 1, 1992, shall accrue to the benefit of the issuing agency.

(b) The processing agency shall prepare a report at the end of each fiscal year setting forth the number of cases processed, and all sums received and distributed, together with any other information that may be required by the issuing agency or the Controller. This report is a public record and shall be delivered to each issuing agency. Copies shall be made available, upon request, to the county auditor, the Controller, and the grand jury. *(Added by Stats.1992, c. 1244 (A.B.408), § 10.2, operative July 1, 1993. Amended by Stats. 1993, c. 1093 (A.B.780), § 4; Gov.Reorg.Plan No. 1 of 1995, § 70, eff. July 12, 1995; Stats.1995, c. 734 (A.B.1228), § 3; Stats.1996, c. 305 (A.B.3103), § 72.)*

§ 40200.4. Deposit of sums due county; transfer of processing function; counties with contracts to process violations; law governing; prohibition on termination of court employees

(a) The processing agency shall deposit with the county treasurer all sums due the county as the result of processing a parking violation not later than 45 calendar days after the last day of the month in which the parking penalty was received.

(b) Except as provided in subdivisions (c) and (d), if a court within a county has been processing notices of parking violations and notices of delinquent parking violations for a city, a district, or any other issuing agency, the issuing agency and the county shall provide in an agreement for the orderly transfer of the processing activity as soon as possible but not later than January 1, 1994. The agreement shall permit the court to phase out, and the issuing agency to phase in, or transfer, personnel, equipment, and facilities that may have been acquired or need to be acquired in contemplation of a long-term commitment to processing of notices of parking violations and notices of delinquent parking violations for the issuing agency under this article. The court shall transfer the processing function for parking citations issued by the Department of the California Highway Patrol to the processing agency in the city or county where the violation occurred.

(c) If Contra Costa County or San Mateo County, or a court in either county, had a contract in effect on January 1, 1992, to process notices of parking violations and notices of delinquent parking violations for a city, district, or other issuing agency within the particular county or counties, the county may continue to provide those services to the issuing agencies pursuant to the terms of the contract and any amendments thereto, to and including June 30, 1996, after which Section 40200.5 shall govern any contracts entered into for these services.

(d) San Francisco Municipal Court employees engaged in processing notices of parking violations and the positions of those employees shall be transferred to equivalent civil service positions in the City and County of San Francisco.

(e) No court employee shall be terminated or otherwise released from employment as a result of the transfer of processing notices of parking violations and notices of delinquent parking violations from the courts to the issuing agencies.

(f) As used in this article, "parking penalty" includes the fine authorized by law, including assessments authorized by this article, any late payment penalty, and costs of collection as provided by law. *(Added by Stats.1986, c. 939, § 15. Amended by Stats.1992, c. 1244 (A.B.408), § 11, operative July 1, 1993; Stats.1993, c. 1093 (A.B.780), § 5; Gov.Reorg.Plan No. 1 of 1995, § 71, eff. July 12, 1995; Stats.1995, c. 734 (A.B.1228), § 4; Stats.1996, c. 305 (A.B.3103), § 73.)*

§ 40200.5. Contract for processing notices of violations; minority business participation; distribution of amounts collected; provision of qualified examiners or administrative hearing providers

(a) Except as provided in subdivision (c) of Section 40200.4, an issuing agency may elect to contract with the county, with a private vendor, or with any other city or county processing agency, other than the Department of the California Highway Patrol or other state law enforcement agency, within the county, with the consent of that other entity, for the processing of notices of parking violations and notices of delinquent parking violations, prior to filing with the court pursuant to Section 40230.

If an issuing agency contracts with a private vendor for processing services, it shall give special consideration to minority business enterprise participation in providing those services. For purposes of this subdivision, "special consideration" has the same meaning as specified in subdivision (c) of Section 14838 of the Government Code, as it relates to small business preference.

(b) A contract entered pursuant to subdivision (a) shall provide for monthly distribution of amounts collected between the parties, except those amounts payable to a county pursuant to Chapter 12 (commencing with Section 76000) of Title 8 of the Government Code and amounts payable to the Department of Motor Vehicles pursuant to Section 4763 of this code.

(c) If a contract entered into pursuant to subdivision (a) includes the provision of qualified examiners or administrative hearing providers, the contract shall be based on either a fixed monthly rate or on the number of notices processed and shall not include incentives for the processing entity based on the number of notices upheld or denied or the amount of fines collected. *(Added by Stats.1986, c. 939, § 15. Amended by Stats.1992, c. 1244 (A.B.408), § 12, operative July 15, 1993; Stats.1993, c. 1093 (A.B.780), § 6; Gov.Reorg.Plan No. 1 of 1995, § 72, eff. July 12, 1995; Stats.1996, c. 305 (A.B.3103), § 74; Stats.2008, c. 13 (A.B.602), § 1.)*

§ 40200.6. Processing agency; contracts for processing notices of violations; policies and procedures; oversight; complaint resolution

(a) If a contract is entered into pursuant to Section 40200.5, for the purposes of this article, "processing agency" means the contracting party responsible for the processing of the notices of parking violations and notices of delinquent parking violations.

(b) The governing body of the issuing agency shall establish written policies and procedures pursuant to which the contracting party shall provide services.

(c) The issuing agency shall be responsible for all actions taken by contracting parties and shall exercise effective oversight over the parties. "Effective oversight" includes, at a minimum, an annual review of the services of the processing agency and a review of complaints made by motorists using the services of the processing agency. The issuing agency shall establish procedures to investigate and resolve complaints by motorists about any processing agency.

(d) Subdivision (c) does not apply to an issuing agency that is a law enforcement agency if the issuing agency does not also act as the processing agency. *(Added by Stats.1986, c. 939, § 15. Amended by Stats.1995, c. 734 (A.B.1228), § 5.)*

§ 40200.8. Parking citations; recall of hold on vehicle registration; notice to department

The parking processing agency shall notify the department and recall any hold on the registration of a vehicle that it filed with the department in connection with a parking citation if the processing agency is awarded a civil judgment for the citation pursuant to subdivision (b) or (c) of Section 40220, or if the processing agency has granted a review of the issuance of the citation pursuant to Section 40200.7 or Section 40215. *(Added by Stats.1995, c. 766 (S.B.726), § 41.)*

§ 40202. Notice of violation attached to vehicle; contents; filing; alteration or destruction prior to filing; cancellation of violation; corrections

(a) If a vehicle is unattended during the time of the violation, the peace officer or person authorized to enforce parking laws and regulations shall securely attach to the vehicle a notice of parking violation setting forth the violation, including reference to the section of this code or of the Public Resources Code, the local ordinance, or the federal statute or regulation so violated; the date; the approximate time thereof; the location where the violation occurred; a statement printed on the notice indicating that the date of payment is required to be made not later than 21 calendar days from the date of citation issuance; and the procedure for the registered owner, lessee, or rentee to deposit the parking penalty or, pursuant to Section 40215, contest the citation. The notice of parking violation shall also set forth the vehicle license number and registration expiration date if they are visible, the last four digits of the vehicle identification number, if that number is readable through the windshield, the color of the vehicle, and, if possible, the make of the vehicle. The notice of parking violation, or copy thereof, shall be considered a record kept in the ordinary course of business of the issuing agency and the processing agency and shall be prima facie evidence of the facts contained therein.

(b) The notice of parking violation shall be served by attaching it to the vehicle either under the windshield wiper or in another conspicuous place upon the vehicle so as to be easily observed by the person in charge of the vehicle upon the return of that person.

(c) Once the issuing officer has prepared the notice of parking violation and has attached it to the vehicle as provided in subdivisions (a) and (b), the officer shall file the notice with the processing agency. Any person, including the issuing officer and any member of the officer's department or agency, or any peace officer who alters, conceals, modifies, nullifies, or destroys, or causes to be altered, concealed, modified, nullified, or destroyed the face of the remaining original or any copy of a citation that was retained by the officer, for any reason, before it is filed with the processing agency or with a person authorized to receive the deposit of the parking penalty, is guilty of a misdemeanor.

(d) If, during the issuance of a notice of parking violation, without regard to whether the vehicle was initially attended or unattended, the vehicle is driven away prior to attaching the notice to the vehicle, the issuing officer shall file the notice with the processing agency. The processing agency shall mail, within 15 calendar days of issuance of the notice of parking violation, a copy of the notice of parking violation or transmit an electronic facsimile of the notice to the registered owner.

(e) If, within 21 days after the notice of parking violation is attached to the vehicle, the issuing officer or the issuing agency determines that, in the interest of justice, the notice of parking violation should be canceled, the issuing agency, pursuant to subdivision (a) of Section 40215, shall cancel the notice of parking violation or, if the issuing agency has contracted with a processing agency, shall notify the processing agency to cancel the notice of parking violation pursuant to subdivision (a) of Section 40215. The reason for the cancellation shall be set forth in writing.

If, after a copy of the notice of parking violation is attached to the vehicle, the issuing officer determines that there is incorrect data on the notice, including, but not limited to, the date or time, the issuing officer may indicate in writing, on a form attached to the original notice, the necessary correction to allow for the timely entry of the notice on the processing agency's data system. A copy of the correction shall be mailed to the registered owner of the vehicle.

(f) Under no circumstances shall a personal relationship with any officer, public official, or law enforcement agency be grounds for cancellation. *(Added by Stats.1986, c. 939, § 15. Amended by Stats.1987, c. 72, § 3, eff. June 30, 1987; Stats.1990, c. 1004 (A.B.3261), § 1; Stats.1992, c. 1243 (A.B.3090), § 108, eff. Sept. 30, 1992; Stats.1992, c. 1244 (A.B.408), § 15, operative July 1, 1993; Stats.1993, c. 1093 (A.B.780), § 8; Stats.1993, c. 1292 (S.B.274), § 17; Stats.1995, c. 734 (A.B.1228), § 7; Stats.1996, c. 1156 (A.B.3157), § 6; Stats.1998, c. 885 (A.B.1730), § 3.)*

Cross References

Trial by written declaration, see Vehicle Code § 40902.

Research References

2 Witkin, California Criminal Law 4th Crimes Against Public Peace and Welfare § 325 (2021), Civil Enforcement.
4 Witkin, California Criminal Law 4th Illegally Obtained Evidence § 298 (2021), In General.

§ 40203. Notice of amount of parking penalty; payment by mail; procedures to contest notice of violation

The notice of parking violation shall be accompanied by a written notice of the amount of the parking penalty due for that violation, the address of the person authorized to receive a deposit of the parking penalty, a statement in bold print that payments of the parking penalty for the parking violation may be sent through the mail, and instructions on obtaining information on the procedures to contest the notice of parking violation. *(Added by Stats.1986, c. 939, § 15. Amended by Stats.1995, c. 734 (A.B.1228), § 8.)*

Research References

2 Witkin, California Criminal Law 4th Crimes Against Public Peace and Welfare § 325 (2021), Civil Enforcement.

§ 40203.5. Parking penalties; late payment penalties; minimum and maximum penalties; suspension of penalty; installment payments

(a) The schedule of parking penalties for parking violations and late payment penalties shall be established by the governing body of the jurisdiction where the notice of violation is issued. To the extent possible, issuing agencies within the same county shall standardize parking penalties.

(b) Parking penalties under this article shall be collected as civil penalties.

(c)(1) Notwithstanding subdivision (a) the penalty for a violation of Section 22507.8 or an ordinance or resolution adopted pursuant to Section 22511.57 shall be not less than two hundred fifty dollars ($250) and not more than one thousand dollars ($1,000).

(2) The issuing agency may suspend the imposition of the penalty in paragraph (1), if the violator, at the time of the offense, possesses but failed to display a valid special identification license plate issued pursuant to Section 5007 or a distinguishing placard issued pursuant to Section 22511.55 or 22511.59.

(3) A penalty imposed pursuant to this subdivision may be paid in installments if the issuing agency determines that the violator is unable to pay the entire amount in one payment. *(Added by Stats.1986, c. 939, § 15. Amended by Stats.1990, c. 203 (S.B.1944), § 1; Stats.1991, c. 329 (A.B.2170), § 1; Stats.1992, c. 1244 (A.B.408), § 16, operative July 1, 1993; Stats.1995, c. 734 (A.B.1228), § 9; Stats.2009, c. 415 (A.B.144), § 6.)*

§ 40203.6. Additional assessments

(a) In addition to an assessment levied pursuant to any other law, an additional assessment equal to 10 percent of the penalty established pursuant to Section 40203.5 shall be imposed by the governing body of the jurisdiction where the notice of parking violation is issued for a civil violation of any of the following:

(1) Subdivisions (b), (c), and (d) of Section 4461.

(2) Subdivision (c) of Section 4463.

(3) Section 22507.8.

(4) An ordinance or resolution adopted pursuant to Section 22511.57.

(5) Section 22522.

(b) An assessment imposed pursuant to this section shall be deposited with the city or county where the violation occurred. *(Added by Stats.2009, c. 415 (A.B.144), § 7.)*

§ 40204. Termination of proceedings on receipt of penalty by authorized person; installment payments

(a) If the parking penalty is received by the person authorized to receive the deposit of the parking penalty and there is no contest as to that parking violation, the proceedings under this article shall terminate.

(b) The issuing agency may, consistent with the written guidelines established by the agency, allow payment of the parking penalty in installments if the violator provides evidence satisfactory to the issuing agency of an inability to pay the parking penalty in full. *(Added by Stats.1986, c. 939, § 15. Amended by Stats.1992, c. 1244 (A.B.408), § 17, operative July 1, 1993; Stats.2015, c. 112 (A.B.1151), § 1, eff. Jan. 1, 2016.)*

§ 40205. Contest of parking violation; procedure of processing agency

If a person contests the parking violation, the processing agency shall proceed in accordance with Section 40215. *(Added by Stats. 1986, c. 939, § 15. Amended by Stats.1992, c. 1244 (A.B.408), § 18, operative July 1, 1993.)*

§ 40206. Service or mailing of notice of delinquent violation

(a) If the payment of the parking penalty is not received by the person authorized to receive a deposit of the parking penalty by the date fixed on the notice of parking violation under Section 40202, the processing agency shall deliver to the registered owner a notice of delinquent parking violation.

(b) Delivery of a notice of delinquent parking violation under this section may be made by personal service or by first-class mail addressed to the registered owner, as shown on records of the Department of Motor Vehicles. *(Added by Stats.1986, c. 939, § 15. Amended by Stats.1992, c. 1244 (A.B.408), § 19, operative July 1, 1993.)*

Cross References

Trial by written declaration, see Vehicle Code § 40902.

Research References

2 Witkin, California Criminal Law 4th Crimes Against Public Peace and Welfare § 325 (2021), Civil Enforcement.

§ 40206.5. Copy of original notice of violation; fee; cancellation upon failure of vehicle to match description

(a) Within 15 days of a request, by mail or in person, the processing agency shall mail or otherwise provide to any person who has received a notice of delinquent parking violation, or his or her agent, a photostatic copy of the original notice of parking violation or an electronically produced facsimile of the original notice of parking violation. The issuing agency may charge a fee sufficient to recover the actual cost of providing the copy, not to exceed two dollars ($2). Until the issuing agency complies with a request for a copy of the original notice of parking violation, the processing agency may not proceed pursuant to subdivision (i) of Section 22651, Section 22651.7, or Section 40220.

(b) If the description of the vehicle on the notice of parking violation does not substantially match the corresponding information on the registration card for that vehicle and the processing agency is satisfied that the vehicle has not been incorrectly described due to the intentional switching of license plates, the processing agency shall, on written request of the person cancel the notice of parking violation without the necessity of an appearance by that person.

(c) For purposes of this section, a copy of the notice of parking violation may be a photostatic copy or an electronically produced facsimile. *(Added by Stats.1986, c. 939, § 15. Amended by Stats. 1989, c. 502, § 2; Stats.1992, c. 1244 (A.B.408), § 20, operative July 1, 1993; Stats.1993, c. 1093 (A.B.780), § 9.)*

§ 40207. Contents of notice of delinquent violation

(a) The notice of delinquent parking violation shall contain the information specified in subdivision (a) of Section 40202 or subdivision (a) of Section 40248, as applicable, and Section 40203, and, additionally shall contain a notice to the registered owner that, unless the registered owner pays the parking penalty or contests the citation within 21 calendar days from the date of issuance of the citation or 14 calendar days after the mailing of the notice of delinquent parking violation or completes and files an affidavit of nonliability that complies with Section 40208 or 40209, the renewal of the vehicle registration shall be contingent upon compliance with the notice of delinquent parking violation. If the registered owner, by appearance or by mail, makes payment to the processing agency within 21 calendar days from the date of issuance of the citation or 14 calendar days after the mailing of the notice of delinquent parking violation, the parking penalty shall consist solely of the amount of the original penalty. Additional fees, assessments, or other charges shall not be added.

(b) This section shall become operative on January 1, 2016. *(Added by Stats.2007, c. 377 (A.B.101), § 2, operative Jan. 1, 2012. Amended by Stats.2010, c. 471 (A.B.2567), § 2, operative Jan. 1, 2012; Stats.2011, c. 325 (A.B.1041), § 2, operative Jan. 1, 2016.)*

§ 40208. Affidavit of nonliability; information and instructions

The notice of delinquent parking violation shall contain, or be accompanied with, an affidavit of nonliability and information of what constitutes nonliability, information as to the effect of executing the affidavit, and instructions for returning the affidavit to the issuing agency. *(Added by Stats.1986, c. 939, § 15.)*

§ 40209. Affidavit of nonliability; proof of written lease or rental of vehicle; notice of delinquent violation; proceedings against rentee or lessee

If the affidavit of nonliability is returned to the processing agency within 30 calendar days of the mailing of the notice of delinquent parking violation together with the proof of a written lease or rental agreement between a bona fide rental or leasing company, and its customer which identifies the rentee or lessee and provides the driver's license number, name, and address of the rentee or lessee, the processing agency shall serve or mail to the rentee or lessee identified in the affidavit of nonliability a notice of delinquent parking violation. If payment is not received within 21 calendar days from the date of issuance of the citation or 14 calendar days after the mailing of the notice of delinquent parking violation, the processing agency may proceed against the rentee or lessee pursuant to Section 40220. *(Added by Stats.1986, c. 939, § 15. Amended by Stats.1989, c. 750, § 3; Stats.1992, c. 1244 (A.B.408), § 22, operative July 1, 1993; Stats.1995, c. 734 (A.B.1228), § 11; Stats.1996, c. 1156 (A.B.3157), § 8.)*

Research References

2 Witkin, California Criminal Law 4th Crimes Against Public Peace and Welfare § 325 (2021), Civil Enforcement.

§ 40210. Affidavit of nonliability; evidence of prior sale or transfer and delivery of vehicle to purchaser; cancellation of notice of delinquent violation; proceedings against owner; collection of penalties from person having ownership on date of alleged violation

(a) If the affidavit of nonliability is returned and indicates that the registered owner served has made a bona fide sale or transfer of the vehicle and has delivered possession of the vehicle to the purchaser prior to the date of the alleged violation, the processing agency shall obtain verification from the department that the registered owner has complied with Section 5602.

(b) If the registered owner has complied with Section 5602, the processing agency shall cancel the notice of delinquent parking violation or violations with respect to the registered owner.

(c) If the registered owner has not complied with Section 5602, the processing agency shall inform the registered owner that the citation shall be paid in full or contested pursuant to Section 40215 unless the registered owner delivers evidence within 15 days of the notice that establishes that the transfer of ownership and possession of the vehicle occurred prior to the date of the alleged violation. If the registered owner does not comply with this notice, the processing agency shall proceed pursuant to Section 40220. If the registered owner delivers the evidence within 15 days of the notice, the processing agency shall cancel the notice of delinquent parking violation or violations with respect to the registered owner.

(d) For purposes of subdivision (c), evidence sufficient to establish that the transfer of ownership and possession occurred prior to the date of the alleged violation or violations shall include, but is not limited to, a copy of the executed agreement showing the date of the transfer of vehicle ownership.

(e) This section does not limit or impair the ability or the right of the processing agency to pursue the collection of delinquent parking penalties from the person having ownership and possession of the vehicle on the date the alleged violation occurred. *(Added by Stats.1986, c. 939, § 15. Amended by Stats.1992, c. 1244 (A.B.408), § 23, operative July 1, 1993; Stats.1995, c. 734 (A.B.1228), § 12; Stats.2008, c. 741 (A.B.2401), § 3.)*

Research References

2 Witkin, California Criminal Law 4th Crimes Against Public Peace and Welfare § 325 (2021), Civil Enforcement.

§ 40211. Deposit of penalty with authorized person; processing agency procedures; termination of proceedings

(a) If the registered owner, or an agent of the registered owner, or a rentee or lessee who was served with the notice of delinquent parking violation pursuant to Section 40206 or Section 40209, or any other person who presents the notice of parking violation or notice of delinquent parking violation after the notice of delinquent parking violation has been issued for delivery under Section 40206, deposits the parking penalty with a person authorized to receive it, the processing agency shall do both of the following:

(1) Deliver a copy of one of the following: the notice of delinquent parking violation issued under Section 40206; a true and correct abstract containing the information set forth in the notice of parking violation if the citation was issued electronically; or an electronically reproduced listing of the citation information presented in a notice of delinquent parking violation to the person and

record the name, address, and driver's license number of the person actually given the copy in the records of the issuing agency.

For the purposes of this paragraph, a copy of the notice of delinquent parking violation may be a photostatic copy.

(2) Determine whether the notice of delinquent parking violation has been filed with the department pursuant to subdivision (b) of Section 40220 or a civil judgment has been entered pursuant to Section 40220.

(b) If the notice of delinquent parking violation has not been filed with the department or judgment entered and payment of the parking penalty, including any applicable assessments, is received, the proceedings under this article shall terminate.

(c) If the notice of delinquent parking violation has been filed with the department, has been returned under subdivision (b) or (c) of Section 4760 or Section 4764, and payment of the parking penalty together with the administrative service fee of the processing agency for costs of service and any applicable assessments is received, the proceedings under this article shall terminate.

(d) If the notice of delinquent parking violation has been filed with the department and has not been returned under Section 4760, 4762, and 4764, and payment of the parking penalty for, and any applicable costs of, service in connection with civil debt collection, is received by the processing agency, the processing agency shall do all of the following:

(1) Deliver a certificate of payment to the registered owner, the agent, the lessee, or the rentee or other person making the payment.

(2) Immediately transmit the payment information to the department in the manner prescribed by the department.

(3) Terminate proceedings on the notice of delinquent parking violation.

(4) Transmit for deposit all parking penalties and assessments in accordance with law. *(Added by Stats.1986, c. 939, § 15. Amended by Stats.1989, c. 750, § 4; Stats.1992, c. 1244 (A.B.408), § 24, operative July 1, 1993; Stats.1995, c. 734 (A.B.1228), § 13.)*

Research References

2 Witkin, California Criminal Law 4th Crimes Against Public Peace and Welfare § 325 (2021), Civil Enforcement.

§ 40215. Review of notice of parking violation; initial review by issuing agency; administrative hearing; process; application of section to certain agencies

(a) For a period of 21 calendar days from the issuance of a notice of parking violation or 14 calendar days from the mailing of a notice of delinquent parking violation, exclusive of any days from the day the processing agency receives a request for a copy or facsimile of the original notice of parking violation pursuant to Section 40206.5 and the day the processing agency complies with the request, a person may request an initial review of the notice by the issuing agency. The request may be made by telephone, in writing, or in person. There shall not be a charge for this review. If, following the initial review, the issuing agency is satisfied that the violation did not occur, that the registered owner was not responsible for the violation, or that extenuating circumstances make dismissal of the citation appropriate in the interest of justice, the issuing agency shall cancel the notice of parking violation or notice of delinquent parking violation. The issuing agency shall advise the processing agency, if any, of the cancellation. The issuing agency or the processing agency shall mail the results of the initial review to the person contesting the notice, and, if following that review, cancellation of the notice does not occur, include a reason for that denial, notification of the ability to request an administrative hearing, and notice of the procedure adopted pursuant to subdivision (b) for waiving prepayment of the parking penalty based upon an inability to pay.

(b) If the person is dissatisfied with the results of the initial review, the person may request an administrative hearing of the violation no later than 21 calendar days following the mailing of the results of the issuing agency's initial review. The request may be made by telephone, in writing, or in person. The person requesting an administrative hearing shall deposit the amount of the parking penalty with the processing agency. The issuing agency shall adopt a written procedure to allow a person who is indigent, as defined in Section 40220, to request an administrative hearing without payment of the parking penalty upon satisfactory proof of an inability to pay the amount due. An administrative hearing shall be held within 90 calendar days following the receipt of a request for an administrative hearing, excluding time tolled pursuant to this article. The person requesting the hearing may request one continuance, not to exceed 21 calendar days.

(c) The administrative hearing process shall include all of the following:

(1) The person requesting a hearing shall have the choice of a hearing by mail or in person. An in-person hearing shall be conducted within the jurisdiction of the issuing agency. If an issuing agency contracts with an administrative provider, hearings shall be held within the jurisdiction of the issuing agency or within the county of the issuing agency.

(2) If the person requesting a hearing is a minor, that person shall be permitted to appear at a hearing or admit responsibility for the parking violation without the necessity of the appointment of a guardian. The processing agency may proceed against the minor in the same manner as against an adult.

(3) The administrative hearing shall be conducted in accordance with written procedures established by the issuing agency and approved by the governing body or chief executive officer of the issuing agency. The hearing shall provide an independent, objective, fair, and impartial review of contested parking violations.

(4)(A) The issuing agency's governing body or chief executive officer shall appoint or contract with qualified examiners or administrative hearing providers that employ qualified examiners to conduct the administrative hearings. Examiners shall demonstrate those qualifications, training, and objectivity necessary to conduct a fair and impartial review. An examiner shall not be employed, managed, or controlled by a person whose primary duties are parking enforcement or parking citation, processing, collection, or issuance. The examiner shall be separate and independent from the citation, collection, or processing function. An examiner's continued employment, performance evaluation, compensation, and benefits shall not, directly or indirectly, be linked to the amount of fines collected by the examiner.

(B)(i) Examiners shall have a minimum of 20 hours of training. The examiner is responsible for the costs of the training. The issuing agency may reimburse the examiner for those costs.

(ii) Training may be provided through any of the following:

(I) An accredited college or university.

(II) A program conducted by the Commission on Peace Officer Standards and Training.

(III) American Arbitration Association or a similar established organization.

(IV) Through a program approved by the governing board of the issuing agency, including a program developed and provided by, or for, the issuing agency.

(iii) Training programs may include topics relevant to the administrative hearing, including, but not limited to, applicable laws and regulations, parking enforcement procedures, due process, evaluation of evidence, hearing procedures, and effective oral and written communication.

(iv) Upon the approval of the governing board of the issuing agency, up to 12 hours of relevant experience may be substituted for up to 12 hours of training. In addition, up to eight hours of the training requirements described in clause (i) may be credited to an individual, at the discretion of the governing board of the issuing agency, based upon training programs or courses described in clause (ii) that the individual attended within the last five years.

(5) The officer or person who issues a notice of parking violation shall not be required to participate in an administrative hearing. The issuing agency shall not be required to produce any evidence other than the notice of parking violation or copy of the notice and information received from the Department of Motor Vehicles identifying the registered owner of the vehicle. The documentation in proper form shall be prima facie evidence of the violation.

(6) The examiner's decision following the administrative hearing may be personally delivered to the person by the examiner or sent by first-class mail, and, if the notice is not cancelled, include a written reason for that denial.

(7) The examiner or the issuing agency may, at any stage of the initial review or the administrative hearing process, and consistent with the written guidelines established by the issuing agency, allow payment of the parking penalty in installments, or the issuing agency may allow for deferred payment, if the person provides evidence satisfactory to the examiner or the issuing agency, as the case may be, of an inability to pay the parking penalty in full. If authorized by the governing board of the issuing agency, the examiner may permit the performance of community service in lieu of payment of a parking penalty.

(d) The provisions of this section relating to the administrative appeal process do not apply to an issuing agency that is a law enforcement agency if the issuing agency does not also act as the processing agency. *(Added by Stats.1995, c. 734 (A.B.1228), § 15. Amended by Stats.2002, c. 640 (A.B.1314), § 4; Stats.2008, c. 13 (A.B.602), § 2; Stats.2009, c. 200 (S.B.734), § 16; Stats.2015, c. 112 (A.B.1151), § 2, eff. Jan. 1, 2016; Stats.2016, c. 86 (S.B.1171), § 304, eff. Jan. 1, 2017; Stats.2017, c. 741 (A.B.503), § 5, eff. Jan. 1, 2018.)*

Cross References

Notice of parking violation, contents, procedure to contest, see Vehicle Code § 40248.

Private parking facilities, parking fees, necessary provisions, see Vehicle Code § 21107.8.

Research References

2 Witkin, California Criminal Law 4th Crimes Against Public Peace and Welfare § 325 (2021), Civil Enforcement.

§ 40220. Collection of unpaid parking penalty and related service fees; options of processing agency; payment plan for indigent persons; application

(a) Except as otherwise provided in Sections 40220.5, 40221, and 40222, the processing agency may proceed under one of the following options in order to collect an unpaid parking penalty and related service fees:

(1)(A) File an itemization of unpaid parking penalties and related service fees with the department for collection with the registration of the vehicle pursuant to Section 4760. For unpaid parking penalties issued on and after July 1, 2018, and related service fees, the processing agency shall not file an itemization with the department unless all of the following conditions have been satisfied:

(i) The processing agency provides a payment plan option for indigent persons that, at a minimum, does all of the following:

(I) Allows payment of unpaid parking penalties and related service fees in monthly installments of no more than twenty-five dollars ($25) for total amounts due that are five hundred dollars ($500) or less. The amount of late fees and penalty assessments waived pursuant to subclause (II) shall not be counted in calculating that total amount of five hundred dollars ($500) or less. Unpaid parking penalties and fees shall be paid off within 24 months. There shall be no prepayment penalty for paying off the balance prior to the payment period expiring.

(II) Waives all late fees and penalty assessments, exclusive of any state surcharges described in Sections 70372, 76000, and 76000.3 of the Government Code, if an indigent person enrolls in the payment plan. Waived late fees and penalty assessments may be reinstated if the person falls out of compliance with the payment plan.

(III) Limits the processing fee to participate in a payment plan to five dollars ($5) or less for indigent persons. The processing fee for an indigent person may be added to the payment plan amount, at the discretion of the indigent person. If a processing agency offers a payment plan option to persons who are not indigent, limits the processing fee to participate in the payment plan to twenty-five dollars ($25) or less.

(IV) Allows a person a period of 120 calendar days from the issuance of a notice of parking violation or 10 days after the administrative hearing determination, whichever is later, to file a request to participate in a payment plan.

(ii) The processing agency includes the information described in subclauses (I) and (II) in the notice of parking violation, and includes both in the notice of parking violation and on its public internet website, a web page link and telephone number to more information on the payment program. Each processing agency shall ensure that the linked internet web page is readily accessible in a prominent location on the parking citation payment section of the agency's internet website and includes all of the following information:

(I) The availability of an installment payment plan and the timeframe in which to apply.

(II) The person's right to request an indigency determination and the timeframe in which the person must apply.

(III) Clear language about how the person can request an indigency determination and what that determination will entail.

(IV) Documents needed by the processing agency to make an indigency determination.

(iii) The person fails to enroll in the payment plan within the time specified in the notice or is not eligible for the payment plan because the person is not indigent.

(B) The processing agency shall allow a person who falls out of compliance with the payment plan a one-time extension of 45 calendar days from the date the payment plan becomes delinquent to resume payments before the processing agency files an itemization of unpaid parking penalties and related service fees with the department pursuant to subparagraph (A).

(C) The processing agency shall rescind the filing of an itemization of unpaid parking penalties and related service fees with the department for an indigent person, for one time only, if the registered owner or lessee enrolls in a payment plan and pays a late fee of no more than five dollars ($5).

(D)(i) Each California State University and community college district governing board shall adopt a parking citation payment plan for persons with multiple unpaid parking citations. A parking citation payment policy adopted under this subparagraph shall include, but not be limited to, all of the following requirements:

(I) Late fees shall be placed in abeyance while the payment plan is in place and the person adheres to its terms, and shall be waived once the payment plan is completed.

(II) Once the payment plan is in place and the person adheres to its terms, an itemization of unpaid parking penalties and service fees as described in subparagraph (A) shall not be filed with the department.

(III) Each California State University and community college district campus shall post the parking citation payment policy on its internet website for students' awareness and access.

(ii) A California State University or community college district governing board that fails to implement a parking citation payment plan pursuant to clause (i) shall implement the payment plan as provided in subparagraphs (A) to (C), inclusive, and subdivision (c).

(2)(A) If more than four hundred dollars ($400) in unpaid penalties and fees have been accrued by a person or registered owner, proof thereof may be filed with the court and shall have the same effect as a civil judgment. Execution may be levied and other measures may be taken for the collection of the judgment as are authorized for the collection of an unpaid civil judgment entered against a defendant in an action on a debtor. The court may assess costs against a judgment debtor to be paid upon satisfaction of the judgment. The processing agency shall send a notice by first-class mail to the person or registered owner indicating that a judgment shall be entered for the unpaid penalties, fees, and costs and that, after 21 calendar days from the date of the mailing of the notice, the judgment shall have the same effect as an entry of judgment against a judgment debtor. The person or registered owner shall also be notified at that time that execution may be levied against their assets, liens may be placed against their property, their wages may be garnished, and other steps may be taken to satisfy the judgment. If a judgment is rendered for the processing agency, the processing agency may contract with a collection agency to collect the amount of the judgment.

(B) Notwithstanding any other law, the processing agency shall pay the established first paper civil filing fee at the time an entry of civil judgment is requested.

(3) If the registration of the vehicle has not been renewed for 60 days beyond the renewal date, and the citation has not been collected by the department pursuant to Section 4760, file proof of unpaid penalties and fees with the court with the same effect as a civil judgment as provided in paragraph (2).

(b) This section does not apply to a registered owner of a vehicle if the citation was issued prior to the registered owner taking possession of the vehicle, and the department has notified the processing agency pursuant to Section 4764.

(c)(1) For purposes of paragraph (1) of subdivision (a), a person is "indigent" if any of the following conditions is met:

(A) The person meets the income criteria set forth in subdivision (b) of Section 68632 of the Government Code.

(B) The person receives public benefits from a program listed in subdivision (a) of Section 68632 of the Government Code.

(2) The person may demonstrate that the person is indigent by providing either of the following information, as applicable:

(A) Proof of income from a pay stub or another form of proof of earnings, such as a bank statement, that shows that the person meets the income criteria set forth in subdivision (b) of Section 68632 of the Government Code, subject to review and approval by the processing agency or its designee. The processing agency or its designee shall not unreasonably withhold its approval.

(B) Proof of receipt of benefits under the programs described in subparagraph (B) of paragraph (1), including, but not limited to, an electronic benefits transfer card or another card, subject to review and approval by the processing agency. The processing agency or its designee shall not unreasonably withhold its approval.

(3) If a defendant's indigent status is found to have been willfully fraudulent, the defendant's penalties and fees reduction shall be overturned and the full amount of penalties and fees shall be restored. *(Added by Stats.1986, c. 939, § 15. Amended by Stats.1987, c. 852, § 5; Stats.1991, c. 329 (A.B.2170), § 2; Stats.1992, c. 1244 (A.B.408), § 27, operative July 1, 1993; Stats.1995, c. 734 (A.B.1228), § 16; Stats.2008, c. 741 (A.B.2401), § 4; Stats.2017, c. 741 (A.B.503), § 6, eff. Jan. 1, 2018; Stats.2018, c. 494 (A.B.2544), § 1, eff. Sept. 18, 2018; Stats.2019, c. 495 (A.B.833), § 1, eff. Oct. 3, 2019; Stats.2020, c. 55 (A.B.3277), § 1, eff. Jan. 1, 2021.)*

Research References

2 Witkin, California Criminal Law 4th Crimes Against Public Peace and Welfare § 325 (2021), Civil Enforcement.

§ 40220.5. Processing agencies; collection of unpaid parking penalties issued before July 1, 2018; provision of payment plans for indigent persons; notice of ability to request indigency determination; payment plan requirements

(a)(1) A processing agency may only use the process set forth in Section 4760 to collect unpaid parking penalties that were issued before July 1, 2018, and related service fees, if the processing agency provides indigent persons with the payment plan program described in this section.

(2) A processing agency shall not be required to comply with this section to collect unpaid parking penalties that were issued before July 1, 2018, and related service fees, pursuant to the process set forth in Section 4760 for a person who does not file an application for an indigency determination, a person who falls out of compliance with a payment plan, except as set forth in subdivision (d), or a person who the processing agency has determined is not an indigent person.

(b) A processing agency shall provide notice on its internet website of a person's ability to request an indigency determination to qualify for a payment plan pursuant to this section. The notice shall include all of the following information:

(1) The availability of a payment plan for indigent persons to pay parking penalties that were issued before July 1, 2018, and related service fees.

(2) Clear language about how a person can request an indigency determination and what that determination will entail.

(3) Documents needed by the processing agency to make an indigency determination.

(c) A processing agency shall provide an indigent person an opportunity to pay unpaid parking penalties that were issued before July 1, 2018, and related service fees, pursuant to a payment plan that, at a minimum, does all of the following:

(1) Allows payment of unpaid parking penalties that were issued before July 1, 2018, and related service fees, in monthly installments of no more than twenty-five dollars ($25) for total amounts due that are three hundred dollars ($300) or less. The amount of late fees and penalty assessments waived pursuant to paragraph (2) shall not be counted in calculating that total amount of three hundred dollars ($300) or less. Unpaid parking penalties and related service fees shall be paid off within 18 months. There shall be no prepayment penalty for paying off the balance prior to the payment period expiring.

(2) Waives all late fees and penalty assessments, exclusive of any state surcharges described in Sections 70372, 76000, and 76000.3 of the Government Code. Waived late fees and penalty assessments may be reinstated if the indigent person falls out of compliance with the payment plan.

(3) Limits the processing fee to participate in a payment plan to five dollars ($5) or less. The processing fee may be added to the payment plan amount, at the discretion of the indigent person.

(d) A processing agency shall allow an indigent person who falls out of compliance with the payment plan a one-time extension of 45 calendar days from the date the payment plan became delinquent to resume payment.

(e) A processing agency shall rescind the collection of unpaid parking penalties that were issued before July 1, 2018, and related service fees, with the department pursuant to the process set forth in

Section 4760 for an indigent person, if the indigent person enrolls in a payment plan pursuant to this section.

(f) "Indigent" shall have the same meaning as set forth in subdivision (c) of Section 40220.

(g) This section shall remain in effect until January 1, 2027, and as of that date is repealed. *(Added by Stats.2018, c. 494 (A.B.2544), § 2, eff. Sept. 18, 2018. Amended by Stats.2019, c. 495 (A.B.833), § 2, eff. Oct. 3, 2019.)*

Repeal

For repeal of this section, see its terms.

§ 40221. Civil judgment; filing; prerequisites

The processing agency shall not file a civil judgment with the court relating to a parking violation which has been filed with the department unless the processing agency has determined that the registration of the vehicle has not been renewed for 60 days beyond the renewal date and the citation has not been collected by the department pursuant to Section 4760. *(Added by Stats.1986, c. 939, § 15. Amended by Stats.1992, c. 1244 (A.B.408), § 28, operative July 1, 1993.)*

§ 40222. Termination of processing agency proceedings on notice of delinquent violation

The processing agency shall terminate proceedings on a notice of a delinquent parking violation or violations in all of the following cases:

(a) Upon receipt of collected penalties and administrative fees remitted by the department under Section 4762 for that notice of delinquent parking violation or violations. The termination under this subdivision is by satisfaction of the parking penalty or penalties.

(b) If the notice of a delinquent parking violation or violations was returned to the processing agency pursuant to Section 4764 and five years have elapsed since the date of the last violation. The termination under this subdivision is by the running of a statute of limitation of proceedings.

(c) The processing agency receives information, that it shall verify with the department, that the penalty or penalties have been paid to the department pursuant to Section 4762.

(d)(1) If the registered owner of the vehicle provides proof to the processing agency that he or she was not the registered owner on the date of the violation.

(2) This subdivision does not limit or impair the ability or the right of the processing agency to pursue the collection of a delinquent parking violation or violations from the person who was the registered owner or lessee of the vehicle on the date of the violation. *(Added by Stats.1986, c. 939, § 15. Amended by Stats.2008, c. 741 (A.B.2401), § 5.)*

§ 40224. Limitation of actions; tolling until return or recall of notice of delinquent violation

The time limitation provided by law for commencement of a civil action for a violation specified in Section 40200 shall be tolled from and after the date a notice of delinquent parking violation is filed with the department pursuant to subdivision (b) of Section 40220 until the notice is returned to the processing agency under subdivision (b) of Section 4760 or Section 4762 or 4764 or is recalled by the processing agency pursuant to subdivision (d) of Section 40211. *(Added by Stats.1986, c. 939, § 15. Amended by Stats.1992, c. 1244 (A.B.408), § 29, operative July 1, 1993; Stats.1995, c. 734 (A.B.1228), § 17.)*

§ 40225. Equipment violation; entry on notice of parking violation; civil penalty; allocation

(a) An equipment violation entered on the notice of parking violation attached to the vehicle under Section 40203 shall be processed in accordance with this article. All of the violations entered on the notice of parking violation shall be noticed in the notice of delinquent parking violation delivered pursuant to Section 40206, together with the amount of civil penalty.

(b) Whether or not a vehicle is in violation of any regulation governing the standing or parking of a vehicle but is in violation of subdivision (a) of Section 5204, a person authorized to enforce parking laws and regulations shall verify, using available Department of Motor Vehicle records, that no current registration exists for that vehicle. A citation shall not be issued for failure to comply with subdivision (a) of Section 5204 against any vehicle that has a current registration on file with the department. If the person authorized to enforce parking laws and regulations does not have immediate access to those records, a citation shall not be issued for failure to comply with subdivision (a) of Section 5204. A person authorized to enforce parking laws and regulations shall issue a written notice of parking violation for a vehicle that does not have a tab or a verified current registration, setting forth the alleged violation. The violation shall be processed pursuant to this section.

(c) The civil penalty for each equipment violation, including failure to properly display a license plate, is the amount established for the violation in the Uniform Bail and Penalty Schedule, as adopted by the Judicial Council, except that upon proof of the correction to the processing agency, the penalty shall be reduced to ten dollars ($10). The reduction provided for in this subdivision involving failure to properly display license plates shall only apply if, at the time of the violation, valid license plates were issued for that vehicle in accordance with this code. The civil penalty for each violation of Section 5204 is the amount established for the violation in the Uniform Bail and Penalty Schedule, as adopted by the Judicial Council, except that upon proof of the correction to the processing agency, the penalty shall be reduced to ten dollars ($10).

(d) Fifty percent of any penalty collected pursuant to this section for registration or equipment violations by a processing agency shall be paid to the county for remittance to the State Treasurer and the remaining 50 percent shall be retained by the issuing agency and processing agency subject to the terms of the contract described in Section 40200.5.

(e) Subdivisions (a) and (b) do not preclude the recording of a violation of subdivision (a) or (b) of Section 4000 on a notice of parking violation or the adjudication of that violation under the civil process set forth in this article. *(Added by Stats.1986, c. 939, § 15. Amended by Stats.1989, c. 729, § 2, operative July 1, 1990; Stats.1992, c. 1244 (A.B.408), § 30, operative July 1, 1993; Stats.1993, c. 1093 (A.B.780), § 12; Stats.1996, c. 1154 (A.B.3020), § 84, eff. Sept. 30, 1996; Stats.1998, c. 885 (A.B.1730), § 4; Stats.2022, c. 306 (S.B. 1359), § 2, eff. Jan. 1, 2023.)*

Research References

2 Witkin, California Criminal Law 4th Crimes Against Public Peace and Welfare § 325 (2021), Civil Enforcement.

§ 40226. Cancellation of citation for failure to display a disabled placard; fees

An issuing agency may, in lieu of collecting a fine for a citation for failure to display a disabled placard, charge an administrative fee not to exceed twenty-five dollars ($25) to process cancellation of a citation in any case where the individual who received the citation can show proof that he or she had been issued a valid placard at the time the citation was received. *(Added by Stats.2002, c. 640 (A.B.1314), § 5.)*

§ 40230. Review; filing of appeal; notice; evidence; fee

(a) Within 30 calendar days after the mailing or personal delivery of the final decision described in subdivision (b) of Section 40215, the contestant may seek review by filing an appeal to be heard by the superior court where the same shall be heard de novo, except that the contents of the processing agency's file in the case shall be received in evidence. A copy of the notice of parking violation or, if the citation was issued electronically, a true and correct abstract containing the information set forth in the notice of parking violation shall be admitted into evidence as prima facie evidence of the facts stated therein. A copy of the notice of appeal shall be served in person or by first-class mail upon the processing agency by the contestant. For purposes of computing the 30-calendar-day period, Section 1013 of the Code of Civil Procedure shall be applicable. A proceeding under this subdivision is a limited civil case.

(b) The fee for filing the notice of appeal is as provided in Section 70615 of the Government Code. The court shall request that the processing agency's file on the case be forwarded to the court, to be received within 15 calendar days of the request. The court shall notify the contestant of the appearance date by mail or personal delivery. The court shall retain the fee under Section 70615 of the Government Code regardless of the outcome of the appeal. If the court finds in favor of the contestant, the amount of the fee shall be reimbursed to the contestant by the processing agency. Any deposit of parking penalty shall be refunded by the processing agency in accordance with the judgment of the court.

(c) The conduct of the appeal under this section is a subordinate judicial duty that may be performed by traffic trial commissioners and other subordinate judicial officials at the direction of the presiding judge of the court.

(d) If no notice of appeal of the processing agency's decision is filed within the period set forth in subdivision (a), the decision shall be deemed final.

(e) If the parking penalty has not been deposited and the decision is against the contestant, the processing agency shall, after the decision becomes final, proceed to collect the penalty pursuant to Section 40220. *(Added by Stats.1992, c. 1244 (A.B.408), § 33, operative July 1, 1993. Amended by Stats.1993, c. 1093 (A.B.780), § 13; Stats.1995, c. 734 (A.B.1228), § 18; Stats.1998, c. 931 (S.B. 2139), § 459, eff. Sept. 28, 1998; Stats.2005, c. 75 (A.B.145), § 152, eff. July 19, 2005, operative Jan. 1, 2006; Stats.2007, c. 738 (A.B.1248), § 43.)*

Law Revision Commission Comments

Section 40230 is amended to accommodate unification of the municipal and superior courts in a county. Cal. Const. art. VI, § 5(e). The section is also amended to reflect elimination of the justice court. Cal. Const. art. VI, §§ 1, 5(b).

A limited civil case is within the original jurisdiction of the municipal court or of the superior court in a county in which there is no municipal court. Cal. Const. art. VI, 10 (superior court jurisdiction); Code Civ. Proc. §§ 85, 85.1 (limited civil cases). See also Code Civ. Proc. §§ 91, 904.2, 1085 (trial procedures and writ and appellate jurisdiction for limited civil cases). [28 Cal.L.Rev.Comm. Reports 51 (1998)].

Cross References

Notice of parking violation, contents, procedure for court review, see Vehicle Code § 40248.

Organization and government of courts, collection of fees and fines pursuant to this section, deposits, see Government Code § 68085.1.

Research References

2 Witkin, California Criminal Law 4th Crimes Against Public Peace and Welfare § 325 (2021), Civil Enforcement.

ARTICLE 3.5. PROCEDURE ON VIDEO IMAGING OF PARKING VIOLATIONS OCCURRING IN TRANSIT–ONLY LANES

§ 40240. Automated forward facing parking control devices; video imaging of parking violations

Section operative until Jan. 1, 2027. See, also, § 40240 operative Jan. 1, 2027.

(a) A public transit operator, as defined in Section 99210 of the Public Utilities Code, may install automated forward facing parking control devices on city-owned or district-owned public transit vehicles, as defined by Section 99211 of the Public Utilities Code, for the purpose of video imaging of parking violations occurring in transit-only traffic lanes and at transit stops. Citations shall be issued only for violations captured during the posted hours of operation for a transit-only traffic lane or during the scheduled operating hours at transit stops. The devices shall be angled and focused so as to capture video images of parking violations and not unnecessarily capture identifying images of other drivers, vehicles, and pedestrians. The devices shall record the date and time of the violation at the same time as the video images are captured. Transit agencies may share the relevant data, video, and images of parking violations collected by automated forward facing parking control devices with the local parking enforcement entity and local agency in the jurisdiction where the violation occurred. A transit operator, including the City and County of San Francisco and the Alameda-Contra Costa Transit District, may only install forward facing cameras pursuant to this section if the examiner or issuing agency, as described in Section 40215, includes options to reduce or waive the payment of a parking penalty if the examiner or issuing agency determines that the person is an indigent person as defined in Section 40220.

(b) Prior to issuing notices of parking violations pursuant to subdivision (a) of Section 40241, a public transit operator, in partnership with a city, county, city and county, or local enforcement authority, shall commence a program to issue only warning notices for 60 days and shall also make a public announcement of the program and provide the public with information about the enforcement program, existing parking regulations, and the payment options available for low-income persons at least 60 days prior to commencement of issuing notices of parking violations.

(c) A designated employee of a city, county, city and county, or a contracted law enforcement agency for a special transit district, who is qualified by a city, county, city and county, or district to issue parking citations, shall review video image recordings for the purpose of determining whether a parking violation occurred in a transit-only traffic lane or at a transit stop. A violation of a statute, regulation, or ordinance governing vehicle parking under this code, under a federal or state statute or regulation, or under an ordinance enacted by a city, county, city and county, or special transit district occurring in a transit-only traffic lane or at a transit stop observed by the designated employee in the recordings is subject to a civil penalty.

(d) The registered owner shall be permitted to review the video image evidence of the alleged violation during normal business hours at no cost.

(e)(1) Except as it may be included in court records described in Section 68152 of the Government Code, or as provided in paragraph (2), the video image evidence may be retained for up to six months from the date the information was first obtained, or 60 days after final disposition of the citation, whichever date is later, after which time the information shall be destroyed.

(2) Notwithstanding Section 26202.6 of the Government Code, video image evidence from forward facing automated enforcement devices that does not contain evidence of a parking violation occurring in a transit-only traffic lane or at a transit stop shall be destroyed within 15 days after the information was first obtained. Video image data and records collected pursuant to this section shall not be used or processed by an automated license plate recognition system, as defined in Section 1798.90.5 of the Civil Code, unless the public transit operator, city, county, city and county, or local enforcement authority meets the requirements in this paragraph and paragraph (1), the requirements of subdivision (f), and the requirements of subdivision (e) of Section 40241.

(f) Notwithstanding Article 1 (commencing with Section * * * 7922.500) and Article 2 (commencing with Section 7922.525) of Chapter 1 of Part 3 of Division 10 of Title 1 of the Government Code, or any other law, the video image records are confidential. Public agencies shall use and allow access to these records only for the purposes authorized by this article.

(g) The following definitions shall apply for purposes of this article:

(1) "Local agency" means a public transit operator as defined in Section 99210 of the Public Utilities Code or a local city, county, or city and county parking enforcement authority.

(2) "Transit-only traffic lane" means any designated transit-only lane on which use is restricted to mass transit vehicles, or other designated vehicles including taxis and vanpools, during posted times.

(h) This section shall remain in effect only until January 1, 2027, and as of that date is repealed. *(Added by Stats.2007, c. 377 (A.B.101), § 3. Amended by Stats.2008, c. 179 (S.B.1498), § 225; Stats.2011, c. 325 (A.B.1041), § 3; Stats.2012, c. 162 (S.B.1171), § 183; Stats.2016, c. 427 (S.B.1051), § 1, eff. Jan. 1, 2017; Stats.2021, c. 615 (A.B.474), § 427, eff. Jan. 1, 2022, operative Jan. 1, 2023; Stats.2021, c. 709 (A.B.917), § 1, eff. Jan. 1, 2022; Stats.2022, c. 28 (S.B.1380), § 155, eff. Jan. 1, 2023.)*

Repeal

For repeal of this section, see its terms.

Cross References

Inspection of public records, exemptions from disclosure, automated forward facing parking control devices, video imaging records, see Government Code § 6276.04.

§ 40240. Automated forward facing parking control devices; video imaging of parking violations

Section operative Jan. 1, 2027. See, also, § 40240 operative until Jan. 1, 2027.

(a) The City and County of San Francisco may install automated forward facing parking control devices on city-owned or district-owned public transit vehicles, as defined in Section 99211 of the Public Utilities Code, for the purpose of video imaging of parking violations occurring in transit-only traffic lanes and at transit stops. Citations shall be issued only for violations captured during the posted hours of operation for a transit-only traffic lane or during the scheduled operating hours at transit stops. The devices shall be angled and focused so as to capture video images of parking violations and not unnecessarily capture identifying images of other drivers, vehicles, and pedestrians. The devices shall record the date and time of the violation at the same time as the video images are captured. Transit agencies may share the relevant data, video, and images of parking violations collected by automated forward facing parking control devices with the local parking enforcement entity and local agency in the jurisdiction where the violation occurred. The City and County of San Francisco may only install forward facing cameras pursuant to this section if the examiner or issuing agency, as described in Section 40215, includes options to reduce or waive the payment of a parking penalty if the examiner or issuing agency determines that the person is an indigent person as defined in Section 40220.

(b) Prior to issuing notices of parking violations pursuant to subdivision (a) of Section 40241, the City and County of San Francisco shall commence a program to issue only warning notices for 60 days and shall also make a public announcement of the program and provide the public with information about the enforcement program, existing parking regulations, and the payment options available for low-income persons at least 60 days prior to commencement of issuing notices of parking violations.

(c) A designated employee of the City and County of San Francisco who is qualified to issue parking citations shall review video image recordings for the purpose of determining whether a parking violation occurred in a transit-only traffic lane or at a transit stop. A violation of a statute, regulation, or ordinance governing vehicle parking under this code, under a federal or state statute or regulation, or under an ordinance enacted by the City and County of San Francisco occurring in a transit-only traffic lane or at a transit stop observed by the designated employee in the recordings is subject to a civil penalty.

(d) The registered owner shall be permitted to review the video image evidence of the alleged violation during normal business hours at no cost.

(e)(1) Except as it may be included in court records described in Section 68152 of the Government Code, or as provided in paragraph (2), the video image evidence may be retained for up to six months from the date the information was first obtained, or 60 days after final disposition of the citation, whichever date is later, after which time the information shall be destroyed.

(2) Notwithstanding Section 26202.6 of the Government Code, video image evidence from forward facing automated enforcement devices that does not contain evidence of a parking violation occurring in a transit-only traffic lane or at a transit stop shall be destroyed within 15 days after the information was first obtained. Video image data and records collected pursuant to this section shall not be used or processed by an automated license plate recognition system, as defined in Section 1798.90.5 of the Civil Code, unless the public transit operator, city, county, city and county, or local enforcement authority meets the requirements of this paragraph and paragraph (1), the requirements of subdivision (f), and the requirements of subdivision (e) of Section 40241.

(f) Notwithstanding Article 1 (commencing with Section * * * 7922.500) and Article 2 (commencing with Section 7922.525) of Chapter 1 of Part 3 of Division 10 of Title 1 of the Government Code or any other law, the video image records are confidential. Public agencies shall use and allow access to these records only for the purposes authorized by this article.

(g) For purposes of this article, "transit-only traffic lane" means any designated transit-only lane on which use is restricted to mass transit vehicles or other designated vehicles, including taxis and vanpools, during posted times.

(h) This section shall become operative on January 1, 2027. *(Added by Stats.2021, c. 709 (A.B.917), § 2, eff. Jan. 1, 2022, operative Jan. 1, 2027. Amended by Stats.2022, c. 28 (S.B.1380), § 156, eff. Jan. 1, 2023, operative Jan. 1, 2027.)*

Law Revision Commission Comments

Section 40240 (as added by 2021 Cal. Stat. ch. 709, § 2) is amended to reflect nonsubstantive recodification of the California Public Records Act. See California Public Records Act Clean-Up, 46 Cal. L. Revision Comm'n Reports 207 (2019). [49 Cal.L.Rev.Comm. Reports __ (2022) [2022-23 AR Appx. 4]].

Cross References

Inspection of public records, exemptions from disclosure, automated forward facing parking control devices, video imaging records, see Government Code § 6276.04.

§ 40240.5. Automated enforcement system; report to Legislature

(a) A public transit operator, including the Alameda-Contra Costa Transit District, that implements an automated enforcement system to enforce parking violations occurring in transit-only traffic lanes and at transit stops pursuant to this article, shall provide to the transportation, privacy, and judiciary committees of the Legislature an evaluation report of the enforcement system's effectiveness, impact on privacy, impact on traffic outcomes, cost to implement, change in citations issued, and generation of revenue, no later than January 1, 2025. This section shall not apply to the City and County of San Francisco.

(b) A report submitted pursuant to this section shall be submitted in compliance with Section 9795 of the Government Code. *(Added by Stats.2021, c. 709 (A.B.917), § 4, eff. Jan. 1, 2022.)*

§ 40241. Notice of parking violation

Section operative until Jan. 1, 2027. See, also, § 40241 operative Jan. 1, 2027.

(a) A designated employee of the local agency, including a contracted law enforcement agency, shall issue a notice of parking violation to the registered owner of a vehicle within 15 calendar days of the date of the violation. A designated employee or contracted law enforcement agency may decline to issue a ticket based on the evidence in the video illustrating hardship. The notice of parking violation shall set forth the violation of a statute, regulation, or ordinance governing vehicle parking under this code, under a federal or state statute or regulation, or under an ordinance enacted by the local agency occurring in a transit-only traffic lane or at a transit stop, a statement indicating that payment is required within 21 calendar days from the date of citation issuance, and the procedure for the registered owner, lessee, or rentee to deposit the parking penalty or contest the citation pursuant to Section 40215. The notice of parking violation shall also set forth the date, time, and location of the violation, the vehicle license number, registration expiration date, if visible, the color of the vehicle, and, if possible, the make of the vehicle. The notice of parking violation, or copy of the notice, shall be considered a record kept in the ordinary course of business of the local agency and shall be prima facie evidence of the facts contained in the notice. The local agency shall send information regarding the process for requesting review of the video image evidence along with the notice of parking violation.

(b) The notice of parking violation shall be served by depositing the notice in the United States mail to the registered owner's last known address listed with the Department of Motor Vehicles. Proof of mailing demonstrating that the notice of parking violation was mailed to that address shall be maintained by the local agency. If the registered owner, by appearance or by mail, makes payment to the processing agency or contests the violation within either 21 calendar days from the date of mailing of the citation, or 14 calendar days after the mailing of the notice of delinquent parking violation, the parking penalty shall consist solely of the amount of the original penalty.

(c) If, within 21 days after the notice of parking violation is issued, the local agency determines that, in the interest of justice, the notice of parking violation should be canceled, the local agency shall cancel the notice of parking violation pursuant to subdivision (a) of Section 40215. The reason for the cancellation shall be set forth in writing.

(d) Following an initial review by the local agency, and an administrative hearing, pursuant to Section 40215, a contestant may seek court review by filing an appeal pursuant to Section 40230.

(e) A local agency or a contracted law enforcement agency, may contract with a private vendor for the processing of notices of parking violations and notices of delinquent violations. The local agency shall maintain overall control and supervision of the program.

(f) This section shall remain in effect only until January 1, 2027, and as of that date is repealed. *(Added by Stats.2007, c. 377 (A.B.101), § 3. Amended by Stats.2016, c. 427 (S.B.1051), § 3, eff. Jan. 1, 2017; Stats.2021, c. 709 (A.B.917), § 5, eff. Jan. 1, 2022.)*

Repeal

For repeal of this section, see its terms.

§ 40241. Notice of parking violation

Section operative Jan. 1, 2027. See, also, § 40241 operative until Jan. 1, 2027.

(a) A designated employee of the City and County of San Francisco, including a contracted law enforcement agency, shall issue a notice of parking violation to the registered owner of a vehicle within 15 calendar days of the date of the violation. A designated employee or contracted law enforcement agency may decline to issue a ticket based on the evidence in the video illustrating hardship. The notice of parking violation shall set forth the violation of a statute, regulation, or ordinance governing vehicle parking under this code, under a federal or state statute or regulation, or under an ordinance enacted by the City and County of San Francisco occurring in a transit-only traffic lane or at a transit stop, a statement indicating that payment is required within 21 calendar days from the date of citation issuance, and the procedure for the registered owner, lessee, or rentee to deposit the parking penalty or contest the citation pursuant to Section 40215. The notice of parking violation shall also set forth the date, time, and location of the violation, the vehicle license number, registration expiration date, if visible, the color of the vehicle, and, if possible, the make of the vehicle. The notice of parking violation, or copy of the notice, shall be considered a record kept in the ordinary course of business of the City and County of San Francisco and shall be prima facie evidence of the facts contained in the notice. The City and County of San Francisco shall send information regarding the process for requesting review of the video image evidence along with the notice of parking violation.

(b) The notice of parking violation shall be served by depositing the notice in the United States mail to the registered owner's last known address listed with the Department of Motor Vehicles. Proof of mailing demonstrating that the notice of parking violation was mailed to that address shall be maintained by the City and County of San Francisco. If the registered owner, by appearance or by mail, makes payment to the processing agency or contests the violation within either 21 calendar days from the date of mailing of the citation, or 14 calendar days after the mailing of the notice of delinquent parking violation, the parking penalty shall consist solely of the amount of the original penalty.

(c) If, within 21 days after the notice of parking violation is issued, the City and County of San Francisco determines that, in the interest of justice, the notice of parking violation should be canceled, the City and County of San Francisco shall cancel the notice of parking violation pursuant to subdivision (a) of Section 40215. The reason for the cancellation shall be set forth in writing.

(d) Following an initial review by the City and County of San Francisco and an administrative hearing pursuant to Section 40215, a contestant may seek court review by filing an appeal pursuant to Section 40230.

(e) The City and County of San Francisco or a contracted law enforcement agency may contract with a private vendor for the processing of notices of parking violations and notices of delinquent violations. The City and County of San Francisco shall maintain overall control and supervision of the program.

(f) This section shall become operative on January 1, 2027. *(Added by Stats.2021, c. 709 (A.B.917), § 6, eff. Jan. 1, 2022, operative Jan. 1, 2027.)*

ARTICLE 4. PROCEDURE ON TOLL EVASION VIOLATIONS

§ 40250. Civil penalties; parties liable; application of article; definitions

(a) Except where otherwise specifically provided, a violation of a statute, regulation, or ordinance governing the evasion of tolls on toll facilities under this code, under a federal or state statute or regulation, or under an ordinance enacted by a local authority including a joint powers authority, or a district organized pursuant to Part 3 (commencing with Section 27000) of Division 16 of the Streets and Highways Code is subject to a civil penalty. The enforcement of a civil penalty is governed by the civil administrative procedures set forth in this article.

(b) Except as provided in Section 40264, the registered owner, driver, rentee, or lessee of a vehicle cited for a toll evasion violation of a toll facility, under an applicable statute, regulation, or ordinance shall be jointly and severally liable for the toll evasion penalty imposed under this article, unless the owner can show that the vehicle was used without the express or implied consent of that person. A person who pays a toll evasion penalty, a civil judgment, costs, or administrative fees pursuant to this article has the right to recover the same from the driver, rentee, or lessee.

(c) The driver of a vehicle who is not the vehicle owner but who uses or operates the vehicle with the express or implied permission of the owner is the agent of the owner to receive a notice of a toll evasion violation served in accordance with this article and may contest the notice of violation.

(d) If the driver of the vehicle is in violation of a statute, regulation, or ordinance governing toll evasion violations, and if the driver is arrested pursuant to Article 1 (commencing with Section 40300) of Chapter 2, this article does not apply.

(e) For the purposes of this article, the following definitions apply:

(1) "Issuing agency" is an entity, public or private, authorized to collect tolls.

(2) "Registered owner" is either of the following:

(A) A person described in Section 505.

(B) A person registered as the owner of the vehicle by the appropriate agency or authority of another state, the District of Columbia, or a territory or possession of the United States. *(Added by Stats.1995, c. 739 (A.B.1223), § 8. Amended by Stats.2007, c. 150 (S.B.124), § 1, eff. July 27, 2007.)*

§ 40251. Deposit of toll evasion penalties and fees

All toll evasion penalties collected by the processing agency, as defined in Section 40253, including all administrative fees, process service fees, and fees and collection costs related to civil debt collection, shall be deposited to the account of the issuing agency, except that those sums attributable to the issuance of a toll evasion violation by a member of the California Highway Patrol shall be deposited in accordance with Article 1 (commencing with Section 42200) of Chapter 2 of Division 18 in the city or county where the violation occurred. At the end of each fiscal year, the issuing agencies of facilities which have been developed pursuant to Section 143 of the Streets and Highways Code shall deposit in the State Highway Account in the State Transportation Fund any amounts collected under Section 40253 in excess of the sum of the unpaid toll, administrative fees, other costs incurred by the issuing agency that are related to toll evasion, process service fees, and fees and collection costs related to civil debt collection. *(Added by Stats.1995, c. 739 (A.B.1223), § 8.)*

§ 40252. Issuing agencies may contract for processing of notices of toll evasion violations

(a) An issuing agency may elect to contract with the state, the county, a local authority, or a district organized pursuant to Part 3 (commencing with Section 27000) of Division 16 of the Streets and Highways Code, or with a private vendor, for the processing of notices of toll evasion violations and notices of delinquent toll evasion violations, prior to filing with the court pursuant to Section 40256.

(b) As used in this article, "toll evasion penalty" includes, but is not limited to, any late payment penalty, administrative fee, fine, assessment, and costs of collection as provided by law. *(Added by Stats.1995, c. 739 (A.B.1223), § 8.)*

§ 40253. Processing agencies

If a contract is entered into pursuant to Section 40252, for the purpose of this article, "processing agency" means the party responsible for the processing of the notices of toll evasions and notices of delinquent toll evasions. Absent such contract, "processing agency" shall be synonymous with "issuing agency." *(Added by Stats.1995, c. 739 (A.B.1223), § 8.)*

§ 40254. Notice of toll evasion violations; timeliness; repeat violators; contents

(a) If a vehicle is found, by automated devices, visual observation, or otherwise, to have evaded tolls on a toll road or toll bridge, and subdivision (d) of Section 40250 does not apply, an issuing agency or a processing agency, as the case may be, shall, within 21 days of the violation, forward to the registered owner a notice of toll evasion violation setting forth the violation, including reference to the section violated, the approximate time thereof, and the location where the violation occurred. If accurate information concerning the identity and address of the registered owner is not available to the processing agency within 21 days of the violation, the processing agency shall have an additional 45 calendar days to obtain such information and forward the notice of toll evasion violation. If the registered owner is a repeat violator, the processing agency shall forward the notice of toll evasion violation within 90 calendar days of the violation. "Repeat violator" means any registered owner for whom more than five violations have been issued pursuant to this section in any calendar month within the preceding 12–month period. The notice of toll evasion violation shall also set forth, if applicable, all of the following:

(1) The vehicle license plate number.

(2) If practicable, the registration expiration date and the make of the vehicle.

(3) If a vehicle is found, by automated devices, to have evaded the toll through failure to meet occupancy requirements in a high-occupancy toll lane, a copy of photographic evidence on which the determination was based.

(4) A clear and concise explanation of the procedures for contesting the violation and appealing an adverse decision pursuant to Sections 40255 and 40256.

(b) After the authorized person has notified the processing agency of a toll evasion violation, the processing agency shall prepare and forward the notice of violation to the registered owner of the vehicle cited for the violation. Any person, including the authorized person and any member of the person's department or agency, or any peace officer who, with intent to prejudice, damage, or defraud, is found guilty of altering, concealing, modifying, nullifying, or destroying, or causing to be altered, concealed, modified, nullified, or destroyed, the face of the original or any copy of a notice that was retained by the authorized person before it is filed with the processing agency or with a person authorized to receive the deposit of the toll evasion violation is guilty of a misdemeanor.

(c) If, after a copy of the notice of toll evasion violation has been sent to the registered owner, the issuing person determines that, due to a failure of proof of apparent violation, the notice of toll evasion violation should be dismissed, the issuing agency may recommend, in writing, that the charges be dismissed. The recommendation shall cite the reasons for the recommendation and shall be filed with the processing agency.

(d) If the processing agency makes a finding that there are grounds for dismissal, the notice of toll evasion violation shall be canceled pursuant to Section 40255.

(e) A personal relationship with any law enforcement officer, public official, law enforcement agency, processing agency, or toll operating agency or entity shall not be grounds for dismissal of the violation.

(f) The processing agency shall use its best efforts to obtain accurate information concerning the identity and address of the registered owner for the purpose of forwarding a notice of toll evasion violation pursuant to subdivision (a). *(Added by Stats.1995, c. 739 (A.B.1223), § 8. Amended by Stats.1996, c. 1154 (A.B.3020), § 85, eff. Sept. 30, 1996; Stats.2002, c. 184 (A.B.2299), § 1; Stats. 2018, c. 435 (A.B.2535), § 1, eff. Jan. 1, 2019; Stats.2019, c. 497 (A.B.991), § 278, eff. Jan. 1, 2020.)*

§ 40255. Right to contest notice; administrative procedures

Section operative until July 1, 2024. See, also, § 40255 operative July 1, 2024.

(a) Within 21 days from the issuance of the notice of toll evasion violation, or within 15 days from the mailing of the notice of delinquent toll evasion, whichever occurs later, a person may contest a notice of toll evasion violation or a notice of delinquent toll evasion. In that case, the processing agency shall do the following:

(1) The processing agency shall either investigate with its own records and staff or request that the issuing agency investigate the circumstances of the notice with respect to the contestant's written explanation of reasons for contesting the toll evasion violation. If, based upon the results of that investigation, the processing agency is satisfied that the violation did not occur or that the registered owner was not responsible for the violation, the processing agency shall cancel the notice of toll evasion violation and make an adequate record of the reasons for canceling the notice. The processing agency shall mail the results of the investigation to the person who contested the notice of toll evasion violation or the notice of delinquent toll evasion violation.

(2) If the person contesting a notice of toll evasion violation or notice of delinquent toll evasion violation is not satisfied with the results of the investigation provided for in paragraph (1), the person may, within 15 days of the mailing of the results of the investigation, deposit the amount of the toll evasion penalty and request an administrative review. After January 1, 1996, an administrative hearing shall be held within 90 calendar days following the receipt of a request for an administrative hearing, excluding any time tolled pursuant to this article. The person requesting the hearing may request one continuance, not to exceed 21 calendar days.

(b) The administrative review procedure shall consist of the following:

(1) The person requesting an administrative review shall indicate to the processing agency * * * their election for a review by mail or personal conference.

(2) If the person requesting an administrative review is a minor, that person shall be permitted to appear at an administrative review or admit responsibility for a toll evasion violation without the necessity of the appointment of a guardian. The processing agency may proceed against that person in the same manner as if that person were an adult.

(3)(A) The administrative review shall be conducted before a reviewer designated to conduct the review by the issuing agency's governing body or chief executive officer. In the case of violations on facilities developed pursuant to Section 143 of the Streets and Highways Code, the processing agency shall contract with a public agency or a private entity that has no financial interest in the facility for the provision of administrative review services pursuant to this subdivision. The costs of those administrative review services shall be included in the administrative fees authorized by this article.

(B) In addition to any other requirements of employment, a reviewer shall demonstrate those qualifications, training, and objectivity prescribed by the issuing agency's governing body or chief executive as are necessary and which are consistent with the duties and responsibilities set forth in this article.

(C) The examiner's continued employment, performance evaluation, compensation, and benefits shall not be directly or indirectly linked to the amount of fines collected by the examiner.

(4) The officer or person authorized to issue a notice of toll evasion violation shall not be required to participate in an adminis-

trative review. The issuing agency shall not be required to produce any evidence other than the notice of toll evasion violation or copy thereof, information received from the department identifying the registered owner of the vehicle, and a statement under penalty of perjury from the person reporting the violation. The documentation in proper form shall be considered prima facie evidence of the violation.

(5) For a toll evasion violation that occurs on a vehicular crossing or toll highway where the issuing agency allows pay-by-plate toll payment, as defined in subdivision (e) of Section 23302, the officer or person authorized to issue a notice of toll evasion violation shall not be required to participate in an administrative review. The issuing agency shall not be required to produce any evidence other than the notice of toll evasion violation or copy thereof, information received from the department identifying the registered owner of the vehicle, and a statement from the officer or person authorized to issue a notice of toll evasion that the tolls or other charges and any applicable fee was not paid in accordance with the issuing agency's policies for pay-by-plate toll payment. Any officer or person who knowingly provides false information pursuant to this paragraph shall be subject to a civil penalty for each violation in the minimum amount of two hundred fifty dollars ($250) up to a maximum amount of two thousand five hundred dollars ($2,500). An action for a civil penalty may be brought by any public prosecutor in the name of the people of the State of California. The documentation in proper form shall be considered prima facie evidence of the violation.

(6) The review shall be conducted in accordance with the written procedure established by the processing agency which shall ensure fair and impartial review of contested toll evasion violations. The agency's final decision may be delivered personally or by first-class mail.

(c) This section shall become inoperative on July 1, 2024, and, as of January 1, 2025, is repealed. *(Added by Stats.1995, c. 739 (A.B.1223), § 8. Amended by Stats.2009, c. 459 (A.B.628), § 3; Stats.2022, c. 969 (A.B.2594), § 10, eff. Jan. 1, 2023.)*

Inoperative Date and Repeal

For inoperative date and repeal of this section, see its terms.

Cross References

Pay-by-plate toll payments, grace periods, public information, see Vehicle Code § 23301.8.

§ 40255. Right to contest notice; administrative procedures

Section operative July 1, 2024. See, also, § 40255 operative until July 1, 2024.

(a) Within 21 days from the issuance of the notice of toll evasion violation, or within 30 days from the mailing of the notice of delinquent toll evasion, whichever occurs later, a person may contest a notice of toll evasion violation or a notice of delinquent toll evasion, without having to deposit the outstanding toll or toll evasion penalty. In that case, the processing agency shall do the following:

(1) The processing agency shall either investigate with its own records and staff or request that the issuing agency investigate the circumstances of the notice with respect to the contestant's written explanation of reasons for contesting the toll evasion violation. At a minimum, the processing agency or issuing agency shall review the evidence on which the alleged violation was based, including any photographs of the alleged violation, the department's registered owner information, and confirmation that a full and complete payment was not made. If, based upon the results of that investigation, the processing agency is satisfied that the violation did not occur or that the registered owner was not responsible for the violation, the processing agency shall cancel the notice of toll evasion violation and make an adequate record of the reasons for canceling the notice. The processing agency shall mail the results of the investigation to the person who contested the notice of toll evasion violation or the notice of delinquent toll evasion violation, or may email the results if the person contesting the notice requests email notification in lieu of mail and provides an email address.

(2) If the person contesting a notice of toll evasion violation or notice of delinquent toll evasion violation is not satisfied with the results of the investigation provided for in paragraph (1), the person may, within 15 days of the mailing or emailing of the results of the investigation, deposit the amount of the toll evasion penalty and request an administrative review. If the person meets the income criteria in subdivision (a) of Section 40269.5, as verified by the issuing or processing agency or their designee, the person shall only be required to deposit the amount of the toll, and not the amount of the toll evasion penalty. After January 1, 1996, an administrative hearing shall be held within 90 calendar days following the receipt of a request for an administrative hearing, excluding any time tolled pursuant to this article. The person requesting the hearing may request one continuance, not to exceed 21 calendar days.

(b) The administrative review procedure shall consist of the following:

(1) The person requesting an administrative review shall indicate to the processing agency their election for a review by mail or personal conference.

(2) If the person requesting an administrative review is a minor, that person shall be permitted to appear at an administrative review or admit responsibility for a toll evasion violation without the necessity of the appointment of a guardian. The processing agency may proceed against that person in the same manner as if that person were an adult.

(3)(A) The administrative review shall be conducted before a reviewer designated to conduct the review by the issuing agency's governing body or chief executive officer. In the case of violations on facilities developed pursuant to Section 143 of the Streets and Highways Code, the processing agency shall contract with a public agency or a private entity that has no financial interest in the facility for the provision of administrative review services pursuant to this subdivision. The costs of those administrative review services shall be included in the administrative fees authorized by this article.

(B) In addition to any other requirements of employment, a reviewer shall demonstrate those qualifications, training, and objectivity prescribed by the issuing agency's governing body or chief executive as are necessary and which are consistent with the duties and responsibilities set forth in this article.

(C) The examiner's continued employment, performance evaluation, compensation, and benefits shall not be directly or indirectly linked to the amount of fines collected by the examiner.

(4) The officer or person authorized to issue a notice of toll evasion violation shall not be required to participate in an administrative review. The issuing agency shall not be required to produce any evidence other than the notice of toll evasion violation or copy thereof, information received from the department identifying the registered owner of the vehicle, and a statement under penalty of perjury from the person reporting the violation. The documentation in proper form shall be considered prima facie evidence of the violation.

(5) For a toll evasion violation that occurs on a vehicular crossing or toll highway where the issuing agency allows pay-by-plate toll payment, as defined in subdivision (e) of Section 23302, the officer or person authorized to issue a notice of toll evasion violation shall not be required to participate in an administrative review. The issuing agency shall not be required to produce any evidence other than the notice of toll evasion violation or copy thereof, information received from the department identifying the registered owner of the vehicle, and a statement from the officer or person authorized to issue a notice of toll evasion that the tolls or other charges and any applicable fee was not paid in accordance with the issuing agency's

policies for pay-by-plate toll payment. Any officer or person who knowingly provides false information pursuant to this paragraph shall be subject to a civil penalty for each violation in the minimum amount of two hundred fifty dollars ($250) up to a maximum amount of two thousand five hundred dollars ($2,500). An action for a civil penalty may be brought by any public prosecutor in the name of the people of the State of California. The documentation in proper form shall be considered prima facie evidence of the violation.

(6) The review shall be conducted in accordance with the written procedure established by the processing agency which shall ensure fair and impartial review of contested toll evasion violations. The agency's final decision may be delivered personally or by first-class mail.

(c) This section shall become operative on July 1, 2024. *(Added by Stats.2022, c. 969 (A.B.2594), § 11, eff. Jan. 1, 2023, operative July 1, 2024.)*

Cross References

Pay-by-plate toll payments, grace periods, public information, see Vehicle Code § 23301.8.

§ 40256. Appeals

(a) Within 20 days after the mailing of the final decision described in subdivision (b) of Section 40255, the contestant may seek review by filing an appeal to the superior court, where the same shall be heard de novo, except that the contents of the processing agency's file in the case on appeal shall be received in evidence. A copy of the notice of toll evasion violation shall be admitted into evidence as prima facie evidence of the facts stated therein. A copy of the notice of appeal shall be served in person or by first-class mail upon the processing agency by the contestant. For purposes of computing the 20-day period, Section 1013 of the Code of Civil Procedure shall be applicable. A proceeding under this subdivision is a limited civil case.

(b) Notwithstanding Section 72055 of the Government Code, the fee for filing the notice of appeal shall be twenty-five dollars ($25). If the appellant prevails, this fee, together with any deposit of toll evasion penalty, shall be promptly refunded by the processing agency in accordance with the judgment of the court.

(c) The conduct of the hearing on appeal under this section is a subordinate judicial duty which may be performed by commissioners and other subordinate judicial officials at the direction of the presiding judge of the court.

(d) If no notice of appeal of the processing agency's decision is filed within the period set forth in subdivision (a), the decision shall be deemed final.

(e) If the toll evasion penalty has not been deposited and the decision is adverse to the contestant, the processing agency may, promptly after the decision becomes final, proceed to collect the penalty under Section 40267. *(Added by Stats.1995, c. 739 (A.B. 1223), § 8. Amended by Stats.1998, c. 931 (S.B.2139), § 460, eff. Sept. 28, 1998; Stats.2002, c. 784 (S.B.1316), § 602.)*

Law Revision Commission Comments

Section 40256 is amended to accommodate unification of the municipal and superior courts in a county. Cal. Const. art. VI, § 5(e). The section is also amended to reflect elimination of the justice court. Cal. Const. art. VI, §§ 1, 5(b).

A limited civil case is within the original jurisdiction of the municipal court or of the superior court in a county in which there is no municipal court. Cal. Const. art. VI, 10 (superior court jurisdiction); Code Civ. Proc. §§ 85, 85.1 (limited civil cases). See also Code Civ. Proc. §§ 91, 904.2, 1085 (trial procedures and writ and appellate jurisdiction for limited civil cases). [28 Cal.L.Rev.Comm. Reports 51 (1998)].

Subdivision (a) of Section 40256 is amended to reflect unification of the municipal and superior courts pursuant to Article VI, Section 5(e), of the California Constitution.

Subdivision (b) is amended to make clear that the fee for seeking review pursuant to this section is the amount specified in this section ($25), not the usual fee for filing the first paper in a limited civil case. [32 Cal.L.Rev.Comm. Reports 543 (2002)].

§ 40257. Accompanying notice of penalty; contents; payment by mail

The notice of toll evasion violation shall be accompanied by a written notice of the toll evasion penalty due for that violation and the address of the person authorized to receive a deposit of the toll evasion penalty, to whom payments may be sent, and a statement in bold print that payments of the toll evasion penalty for the toll evasion violation may be sent through the mail. *(Added by Stats. 1995, c. 739 (A.B.1223), § 8.)*

§ 40258. Penalty schedule

Section operative until July 1, 2024. See, also, § 40258 operative July 1, 2024.

(a) The schedule of toll evasion penalties for toll evasion violations shall be limited to one hundred dollars ($100) for the first violation, two hundred fifty dollars ($250) for a second violation within one year, and five hundred dollars ($500) for each additional violation within one year.

(b) Toll evasion penalties under this article shall be collected as civil penalties.

(c) This section shall become inoperative on July 1, 2024, and, as of January 1, 2025, is repealed. *(Added by Stats.1995, c. 739 (A.B.1223), § 8. Amended by Stats.2022, c. 969 (A.B.2594), § 12, eff. Jan. 1, 2023.)*

Inoperative Date and Repeal

For inoperative date and repeal of this section, see its terms.

§ 40258. Penalty schedule

Section operative July 1, 2024. See, also, § 40258 operative until July 1, 2024.

(a)(1) The schedule of toll evasion penalties for a toll evasion violation on a toll bridge shall not exceed twenty-five dollars ($25) for the notice of toll evasion violation, and shall not exceed fifty dollars ($50) for the notice of delinquent toll evasion violation for a cumulative total of fifty dollars ($50) for each individual toll evasion violation.

(2) Notwithstanding paragraph (1), the schedule of toll evasion penalties may include any administrative fee, fine, or assessment imposed by the state after enactment of this chapter in addition to the cumulative fifty-dollar ($50) limit per each individual toll evasion violation.

(b) If the registered owner, by appearance or by mail, makes payment to the processing agency within 15 days of the mailing of the notice of toll evasion violation issued pursuant to subdivision (a) of Section 40254 for a bridge toll evasion, the amount owed shall consist of the amount of the toll without any additional penalties, administrative fees, or charges.

(c) The maximum penalty for each toll evasion violation included in a notice of toll evasion for either a toll highway, toll road, or express lane shall be sixty dollars ($60). The maximum cumulative toll evasion penalty shall not exceed one hundred dollars ($100) for each individual toll evasion violation.

(d) Toll evasion penalties under this article shall be collected as civil penalties.

(e) The amounts specified in this section may be adjusted periodically by an issuing agency at a rate not to exceed any increase in the California Consumer Price Index as compiled and reported by the Department of Industrial Relations.

(f) An issuing agency shall waive the toll evasion penalty for a first violation with the issuing agency if the person contacts, as applicable, the issuing or processing agency customer service center within 21 days from the mailing of the notice of toll evasion violation, and the person is not currently an accountholder with the issuing agency, signs up for an account, and pays the outstanding toll.

(g) This section shall become operative on July 1, 2024. *(Added by Stats.2022, c. 969 (A.B.2594), § 13, eff. Jan. 1, 2023, operative July 1, 2024.)*

§ 40259. Termination of proceedings after payment

If the toll evasion penalty is received by the person authorized to receive the deposit of the toll evasion penalty and there is no contest as to that toll evasion violation, the proceedings under this article shall terminate. *(Added by Stats.1995, c. 739 (A.B.1223), § 8.)*

§ 40260. Delivery of notice of delinquent violation after failure to pay penalty

(a) If the payment of the toll evasion penalty is not received by the person authorized to receive a deposit of the toll evasion penalty by the time and date fixed for appearance on the notice of toll evasion violation under Section 40254, the processing agency shall serve or mail to the registered owner a notice of delinquent toll evasion violation.

(b) Delivery of a notice of delinquent toll evasion violation under this section may be made by personal service or by first-class mail addressed to the registered owner. *(Added by Stats.1995, c. 739 (A.B.1223), § 8.)*

§ 40261. Request for photostatic copy or electronically produced facsimile of original notice; cancellation of notice when vehicle description inconsistent with registration records

(a) Within 10 days from the mailing of a notice of delinquent toll evasion violation, any person or his or her agent, may request by mail or in person a photostatic copy or an electronically produced facsimile of the original notice of toll evasion violation. The issuing agency may charge a fee sufficient to recover the actual cost of providing the copy, not to exceed two dollars ($2). Within 15 days of the request, the processing agency shall mail or otherwise provide the copy. Until the issuing agency complies with a request for a copy of the original notice of toll evasion violation, the processing agency may not proceed pursuant to subdivision (i) of Section 22651, or Section 22651.7 or 40267.

(b) If the description of the vehicle on the notice of toll evasion violation does not match the department's corresponding vehicle registration record, the processing agency may, on written request of the person, cancel the notice of toll evasion violation without the necessity of an appearance by that person. *(Added by Stats.1995, c. 739 (A.B.1223), § 8.)*

§ 40262. Information required in notice of delinquent violation

Section operative until July 1, 2024. See, also, § 40262 operative July 1, 2024.

(a) The notice of delinquent toll evasion violation shall contain the information specified in Section 40254 and, additionally shall contain a notice to the registered owner that, unless the registered owner pays the toll evasion penalty or contests the notice within 15 days after mailing of the notice of delinquent toll evasion violation or completes and files an affidavit of nonliability which complies with Section 40263 or 40264, the renewal of the vehicle registration shall be contingent upon compliance with the notice of delinquent toll evasion violation. If the registered owner, by appearance or by mail, makes payment to the processing agency within 15 days of the mailing of the notice of delinquent toll evasion violation, the toll evasion penalty shall consist of the amount of the original penalty without any additional administrative fees or charges.

(b) This section shall become inoperative on July 1, 2024, and, as of January 1, 2025, is repealed. *(Added by Stats.1995, c. 739 (A.B.1223), § 8. Amended by Stats.2022, c. 969 (A.B.2594), § 14, eff. Jan. 1, 2023.)*

Inoperative Date and Repeal

For inoperative date and repeal of this section, see its terms.

§ 40262. Information required in notice of delinquent violation; administrative fees or charges

Section operative July 1, 2024. See, also, § 40262 operative until July 1, 2024.

(a)(1) The notice of delinquent toll evasion violation shall contain the information specified in Section 40254 and, additionally shall contain a notice to the registered owner that, unless the registered owner pays the toll evasion penalty or contests the notice within 30 days after mailing of the notice of delinquent toll evasion violation or completes and files an affidavit of nonliability that complies with Section 40263 or 40264, the renewal of the vehicle registration shall be contingent upon compliance with the notice of delinquent toll evasion violation.

(2) If the toll evasion penalty is not paid as specified in the notice of delinquent toll evasion violation, the issuing agency may notify the department and the department shall refuse to renew that person's vehicle registration pursuant to Section 4770. If the registered owner pays the toll, toll evasion penalty, and all related fees, or enters into a payment plan pursuant to Section 40269.5 and makes the first payment, the issuing or processing agency shall notify the department electronically, and the department shall not refuse renewal of the person's vehicle registration. If the issuing agency subsequently notifies the department electronically that the registered owner is delinquent under the payment plan for more than 10 business days, the department shall refuse to renew the vehicle registration until the registered owner has fully satisfied the terms of the payment plan and the issuing agency has notified the department electronically.

(3) Notwithstanding paragraph (2), if a registered owner pays the toll, toll evasion penalty, and all related fees, or has entered into a payment plan authorized pursuant to subdivision (e) of Section 40269.5, and meets the agency's requirements for that payment plan, the issuing or processing agency shall notify the department electronically, and the department shall not refuse renewal of the person's vehicle registration. If the registered owner is delinquent under the payment plan for more than 10 business days and the issuing agency or processing agency subsequently notifies the department electronically, the department shall refuse to renew the vehicle registration until the registered owner has fully satisfied the terms of the payment plan and the issuing agency and the issuing agency has notified the department electronically.

(b) If the registered owner, by appearance or by mail, makes payment to the processing agency within 15 days of the mailing of the notice of delinquent toll evasion violation, the toll evasion penalty shall consist of the amount of the original penalty without any additional administrative fees or charges.

(c) This section shall become operative on July 1, 2024. *(Added by Stats.2022, c. 969 (A.B.2594), § 15, eff. Jan. 1, 2023, operative July 1, 2024.)*

§ 40262.5. Failure to pay penalty; liability of registered owner

If the registered owner fails to pay the toll evasion penalty, as required in Section 40262, or fails to contest the violation, as provided in Section 40255, the registered owner shall be deemed liable for the violation by operation of law, and the toll evasion penalty and any administrative fees or charges shall be considered a debt due and owing the issuing agency by the registered owner. *(Added by Stats.1995, c. 739 (A.B.1223), § 8.)*

§ 40263. Affidavit of nonliability

The notice of delinquent toll evasion violation shall contain, or be accompanied with, an affidavit of nonliability and information of what constitutes nonliability, information as to the effect of executing the affidavit, and instructions for returning the affidavit to the issuing agency. *(Added by Stats.1995, c. 739 (A.B.1223), § 8.)*

§ 40264. Return of affidavit; rental agreement or lease

If the affidavit of nonliability is returned to the agency within 30 days of the mailing of the notice of toll evasion violation together with the proof of a written rental agreement or lease between a bona fide renting or leasing company and its customer which identifies the rentee or lessee and provides the driver's license number, name, and address of the rentee or lessee, the processing agency shall serve or mail to the rentee or lessee identified in the affidavit of nonliability a notice of delinquent toll evasion violation. If payment is not received within 15 days of the mailing of the notice of delinquent toll evasion violation, the processing agency may proceed against the rentee or lessee pursuant to Section 40267. *(Added by Stats.1995, c. 739 (A.B.1223), § 8.)*

Cross References

Toll evasion violations, civil penalties and parties liable, see Vehicle Code § 40250.

§ 40265. Return of affidavit; sale or transfer of vehicle; evidence of transfer

(a) If the affidavit of nonliability is returned and indicates that the registered owner served has made a bona fide sale or transfer of the vehicle and has delivered possession of the vehicle to the purchaser prior to the date of the alleged violation, the processing agency shall obtain verification from the department that the registered owner has complied with subdivision (b) of Section 5602.

(b) If the registered owner has complied with subdivision (b) of Section 5602, the processing agency shall cancel the notice of toll evasion violation with respect to the registered owner.

(c) If the registered owner has not complied with subdivision (b) of Section 5602, the processing agency shall inform the registered owner that the notice shall be paid in full or contested pursuant to Section 40255 unless the registered owner delivers evidence within 15 days of the notice that establishes that the transfer of ownership and possession of the vehicle occurred prior to the date of the alleged violation. If the registered owner does not comply with this notice, the processing agency shall proceed pursuant to Section 40220. If the registered owner delivers the evidence within 15 days of the notice, the processing agency shall cancel the notice of delinquent toll evasion violation or violations with respect to the registered owner.

(d) For purposes of subdivision (c), evidence sufficient to establish that the transfer of ownership and possession occurred prior to the date of the alleged violation or violations shall include, but is not limited to, a copy of the executed agreement showing the date of the transfer of vehicle ownership.

(e) This section does not limit or impair the ability or the right of the processing agency to pursue the collection of delinquent toll evasion penalties from the person having ownership and possession of the vehicle on the date the alleged violation occurred. *(Added by Stats.1995, c. 739 (A.B.1223), § 8. Amended by Stats.2008, c. 741 (A.B.2401), § 6.)*

§ 40266. Processing of payment of penalties

(a) If the registered owner, or an agent of the registered owner, or a rentee or lessee who was served with the notice of delinquent toll evasion violation pursuant to Section 40260 or 40264, or any other person who presents the notice of toll evasion violation or notice of delinquent toll evasion violation after the notice of delinquent toll evasion violation has been issued for delivery under Section 40260, deposits that toll evasion violation penalty with a person authorized to receive it, the processing agency shall do both of the following:

(1) Deliver a copy of the notice of delinquent toll evasion violation issued under Section 40260, or a listing of the notice information presented in a notice of delinquent toll evasion violation to the person and record the name, address, and driver's license number of the person actually given the copy in the records of the issuing agency.

For the purposes of this paragraph, a copy of the notice of delinquent toll evasion violation may be a photostatic copy.

(2) Determine whether the notice of delinquent toll evasion violation has been filed with the department pursuant to subdivision (b) of Section 40267 or a civil judgment has been entered pursuant to Section 40267.

(b) If the notice of delinquent toll evasion violation has not been filed with the department or judgment entered and payment of the toll evasion penalty and any applicable assessments is received, the proceedings under this article shall terminate.

(c) If the notice of delinquent toll evasion violation has been filed with the department, has been returned to the processing agency pursuant to subdivision (b) or (c) of Section 4770 or pursuant to Section 4774, and payment of the toll evasion penalty together with the administrative service fee of the processing agency for costs of service and any applicable assessment is received, the proceedings under this article shall terminate.

(d) If the notice of delinquent toll evasion violation has been filed with the department and has not been returned to the processing agency pursuant to Section 4770, 4772, or 4774, and payment of the toll evasion penalty together with the administrative fee of the department established under Section 4773, and administrative service fee of the issuing agency for costs of service, and any applicable assessments is received by the processing agency, the processing agency shall do all of the following:

(1) Immediately transmit the payment information to the department in the manner prescribed by the department.

(2) Terminate proceedings on the notice of delinquent toll evasion violation.

(3) Transmit for deposit all toll evasion penalties and assessments in accordance with law. *(Added by Stats.1995, c. 739 (A.B.1223), § 8.)*

§ 40267. Unpaid toll evasion penalties; collection options

Except as otherwise provided in Sections 40268 and 40269, the processing agency shall proceed under one or more of the following options to collect an unpaid toll evasion penalty:

(a) The processing agency may file an itemization of unpaid toll evasion penalties and administrative and service fees with the department for collection with the registration of the vehicle pursuant to Section 4770.

(b)(1) If more than four hundred dollars ($400) in unpaid penalties and fees have been accrued by a person or registered owner, the processing agency may file proof of that fact with the court with the same effect as a civil judgment. Execution may be levied and other measures may be taken for the collection of the judgment as are authorized for the collection of an unpaid civil judgment entered against a defendant in an action on a debt. The court may assess costs against a judgment debtor to be paid upon satisfaction of the judgment. The processing agency shall send a notice by first-class mail to the person or registered owner indicating that a judgment shall be entered for the unpaid penalties, fees, and costs and that, after 30 days from the date of the mailing of the notice, the judgment shall have the same effect as an entry of judgment against a judgment debtor. The person or registered owner shall also be notified at that time that execution may be levied against his or her assets, liens may be placed against his or her property, his or her wages may be garnished, and other steps may be taken to satisfy the judgment. The filing fee plus any costs of collection shall be added to the judgment amount.

(2) Notwithstanding any other provision of law, the processing agency shall pay the established first paper civil filing fee, if required by law, at the time an entry of civil judgment is requested.

(c) If the registration of the vehicle has not been renewed for 60 days beyond the renewal date, and the notice has not been collected by the department pursuant to Section 4770, the processing agency may file proof of unpaid penalties and fees with the court with the same effect as a civil judgment as provided in subdivision (b), except that if the amount of the unpaid penalties and fees is not more than four hundred dollars ($400), the filing fee shall be collectible by the court from the debtor.

(d) The issuing agency may contract with a collection agency to collect unpaid toll evasion penalties, fees, and charges.

(e) This section does not apply to the registered owner of a vehicle if the toll evasion violation occurred prior to the registered owner taking possession of the vehicle and the department has notified the processing agency pursuant to Section 4774. *(Added by Stats.1995, c. 739 (A.B.1223), § 8. Amended by Stats.2008, c. 741 (A.B.2401), § 7.)*

§ 40268. Filing of civil judgment

The processing agency shall not file a civil judgment with the court relating to a toll evasion violation which has been filed with the department unless the processing agency has determined that the registration of the vehicle has not been renewed for 60 days beyond the renewal date and the notice has not been collected by the department pursuant to Section 4770. *(Added by Stats.1995, c. 739 (A.B.1223), § 8.)*

§ 40269. Termination of proceedings by processing agency

(a) The processing agency shall terminate proceedings on the notice of a delinquent toll evasion violation in any of the following cases:

(1) Upon receipt of collected penalties and administrative fees remitted by the department under Section 4772 for that notice of delinquent toll evasion violation. The termination under this subdivision is by satisfaction of the toll evasion penalty.

(2) If the notice of delinquent toll evasion violation was returned to the processing agency pursuant to Section 4774 and five years have elapsed since the date of the violation. The termination under this subdivision is by the running of a statute of limitation of proceedings.

(3) The processing agency receives information, which it shall verify with the department, that the penalty has been paid to the department pursuant to Section 4772.

(4) If the registered owner of the vehicle provides proof to the processing agency that he or she was not the registered owner on the date of the toll evasion violation.

(b) This section does not limit or impair the ability or the right of the processing agency to pursue the collection of delinquent toll evasion penalties from the person who was the registered owner or lessee of the vehicle on the date of the alleged toll evasion violation. *(Added by Stats.1995, c. 739 (A.B.1223), § 8. Amended by Stats.2008, c. 741 (A.B.2401), § 8.)*

§ 40269.5. Availability of payment plans; terms; publication of policy; concurrent or subsequent payment plans

Section operative July 1, 2023 for toll bridges, and operative July 1, 2024 for toll highways, toll roads, and express lanes.

(a)(1) An issuing agency shall make a payment plan option available to a person whose monthly income is 200 percent of the current poverty guidelines, or less, as updated periodically in the Federal Register by the United States Department of Health and Human Services under the authority of paragraph (2) of Section 9902 of Title 42 of the United States Code, as determined by the issuing agency or processing agency or their designee.

(2) For purposes of verifying a person's eligibility an issuing agency or processing agency or their designee shall accept all of the following: (A) unexpired proof of enrollment of participation in the CalFresh program established pursuant to (Chapter 10 (commencing with Section 18900) of Part 6 of Division 9 of the Welfare and Institutions Code), Medi-Cal, or another low-income program with the same or more exacting low-income requirement; or (B) an unexpired county benefit eligibility letter. Other evidence of the persons' income may also be accepted, as determined to be sufficient by the issuing agency or processing agency or their designee.

(b) The payment plan option for qualifying individuals shall do all of the following:

(1) Apply to toll evasion penalties in excess of one hundred dollars ($100).

(2) Require payment of no more than twenty-five dollars ($25) per month for total outstanding toll evasion penalties of six hundred dollars ($600) or less.

(3) Include no prepayment penalty for paying off the balance prior to the payment period expiring.

(4) Include a process for removal of any registration hold placed pursuant to Section 4770.

(c) Information regarding the issuing agency's payment plan policy shall be posted on an internet website related to the issuing agency's electronic toll collection system.

(d) Notwithstanding subdivision (a), the issuing agency shall not be required to offer more than one payment plan to a person at any given time. The issuing agency shall not be required to offer a person more than two payment plans in a six-year period. The issuing agency shall not be required to offer a payment plan if the person has more than two thousand five hundred dollars ($2,500) in outstanding toll evasion penalties.

(e) The requirements of subdivisions (a) and (b) are minimum standards only, and shall not limit the discretion of the issuing agency to establish or provide payment plan options that exceed the minimum requirements in those subdivisions, including, but not limited to, allowing payment plans for a person who owes less than the amount specified in paragraph (1) of subdivision (b), and making a payment plan available to more individuals than those who meet the economic criteria in subdivision (a). For those individuals who exceed the income criteria set forth in subdivision (a), the issuing agency may set payment plan requirements that differ from those established in subdivision (a) or (b), such as requiring higher monthly payments than those specified in paragraph (2) of subdivision (b), or similar requirements.

(f) This section shall become operative on July 1, 2023, for toll bridges. With respect to toll highways, toll roads, and express lanes, this section shall become operative on July 1, 2024. *(Added by Stats.2022, c. 969 (A.B.2594), § 16, eff. Jan. 1, 2023, operative July 1, 2023.)*

§ 40269.6. Waiver of outstanding toll evasion penalties; eligibility; publication of program information

(a) Commencing July 1, 2023, an issuing agency shall provide a one-time waiver of outstanding toll evasion penalties for toll evasion violations on a toll bridge occurring from March 20, 2020, to January 1, 2023, inclusive. The waiver program shall be available, upon request, to individuals whose monthly income is 200 percent of the current poverty guidelines, or less, as updated periodically in the Federal Register by the United States Department of Health and Human Services under the authority of paragraph (2) of Section 9902 of Title 42 of the United States Code, as determined by the issuing agency or processing agency or their designee. For purposes of verifying an individual's eligibility, an issuing agency, processing agency, or their designee shall accept the evidence of income specified in paragraph (2) of subdivision (a) of Section 40269.5.

(b) Commencing July 1, 2023, in addition to meeting the income criteria described in subdivision (a), an eligible individual who applies for a waiver under this section shall satisfy both of the following conditions:

(1) The applicant shall pay the total amount of all outstanding tolls subject to the penalty waiver, and any related fees, fines, or assessments imposed by the department, not using the payment plan option established pursuant to Section 40269.5.

(2) The issuing agency may require, as a condition of the waiver, that applicant open an account and acquire a transponder or other electronic toll payment device. This paragraph applies only with respect to vehicles registered in California.

(c) Commencing January 1, 2023, an issuing agency, processing agency, or their designee shall do both of the following with respect to the one-time waiver program established pursuant to this section:

(1) Include information about the availability of the one-time waiver program on an internet website related to the issuing agency's electronic toll collection system.

(2) Direct its customer service center representatives to inform the public about the availability of the program when responding to inquiries about toll evasion violations incurred from March 20, 2020, to January 1, 2023, inclusive.

(d) This section shall become inoperative on September 30, 2024, and, as of January 1, 2025, is repealed. *(Added by Stats.2022, c. 969 (A.B.2594), § 17, eff. Jan. 1, 2023.)*

Inoperative Date and Repeal

For inoperative date and repeal of this section, see its terms.

§ 40270. Notice of noncollection; cancellation of notice of delinquency

If the notice of delinquent toll evasion violation is filed with the department pursuant to subdivision (b) of Section 40267 and the department returns the notice of delinquent toll evasion violation by notice of noncollection pursuant to subdivision (b) of Section 4770 or Section 4774, the processing agency may cancel the notice of delinquent toll evasion violation. *(Added by Stats.1995, c. 739 (A.B.1223), § 8.)*

§ 40271. Commencement of civil action; limitations period; tolling

The time limitation provided by law for commencement of a civil action for a violation specified in Section 40250 shall be tolled from and after the date a notice of delinquent toll evasion violation is filed with the department pursuant to subdivision (b) of Section 40267 until the notice is returned to the processing agency under subdivision (b) of Section 4770, or Section 4772 or 4774, or is recalled by the processing agency pursuant to subdivision (b) of Section 40255. *(Added by Stats.1995, c. 739 (A.B.1223), § 8.)*

§ 40272. Civil liability under § 23302.5 not a conviction or part of driving record or insurance coverage

Notwithstanding any other provision of law, an imposition of civil liability for a violation of Section 23302.5 shall not be deemed a conviction of a driver, rentee, lessee, or registered owner and shall not be made part of the driving record of the person upon whom that liability is imposed, nor shall it be used for insurance purposes in connection with the provision of motor vehicle insurance coverage. *(Added by Stats.1995, c. 739 (A.B.1223), § 8.)*

§ 40273. Confidentiality of information obtained from automated devices

Any information obtained pursuant to this article through the use of automated devices shall not be used for any purpose other than to identify, and obtain the mailing address information of, either of the following:

(a) Toll evasion violators, to facilitate the serving of notices of toll evasion violations and notices of delinquent toll evasion violations.

(b) Persons entering a vehicular crossing and toll highway where pay-by-plate toll payment, as defined in Section 23302, is permitted by the toll operator to facilitate the collection of tolls. *(Added by Stats.1995, c. 739 (A.B.1223), § 8. Amended by Stats.2009, c. 459 (A.B.628), § 4.)*

CHAPTER 2. PROCEDURE ON ARRESTS

ARTICLE 1. ARRESTS

§ 40300. Application of chapter

The provisions of this chapter shall govern all peace officers in making arrests for violations of this code without a warrant for offenses committed in their presence, but the procedure prescribed herein shall not otherwise be exclusive of any other method prescribed by law for the arrest and prosecution of a person for an offense of like grade. *(Stats.1959, c. 3, p. 1774, § 40300.)*

Cross References

Arrest without warrant by peace officer, see Penal Code §§ 836, 849.
Powers and duties of peace officers generally, see Penal Code § 830 et seq.

Research References

4 Witkin, California Criminal Law 4th Pretrial Proceedings § 45 (2021), In General.
4 Witkin, California Criminal Law 4th Pretrial Proceedings § 46 (2021), Without Warrant.

§ 40300.2. Commercial motor vehicles; indication on complaints or notices

Whenever a person is arrested for a violation of this code, or a violation of any other statute required to be reported under Section 1803, the written complaint, notice to appear in court, or other notice of violation, shall indicate whether the vehicle involved in the offense is a commercial motor vehicle, as defined in subdivision (b) of Section 15210. *(Added by Stats.1988, c. 1509, § 10.)*

§ 40300.5. Arrest without warrant

In addition to the authority to make an arrest without a warrant pursuant to paragraph (1) of subdivision (a) of Section 836 of the Penal Code, a peace officer may, without a warrant, arrest a person when the officer has reasonable cause to believe that the person had been driving while under the influence of an alcoholic beverage or any drug, or under the combined influence of an alcoholic beverage and any drug when any of the following exists:

(a) The person is involved in a traffic crash.

(b) The person is observed in or about a vehicle that is obstructing a roadway.

(c) The person will not be apprehended unless immediately arrested.

(d) The person may cause injury to themselves or * * * damage property unless immediately arrested.

(e) The person may destroy or conceal evidence of the crime unless immediately arrested. *(Added by Stats.1969, c. 956, p. 1904, § 1. Amended by Stats.1977, c. 16, p. 28, § 1; Stats.1982, c. 53, p. 179, § 42, eff. Feb. 18, 1982; Stats.1984, c. 722, § 1; Stats.1996, c. 1078 (S.B.1379), § 6; Stats.2022, c. 81 (A.B.2198), § 7, eff. Jan. 1, 2023.)*

Cross References

Driving while under the influence of alcohol or drugs, see Vehicle Code §§ 23152, 23153.
Peace officers, arrest without warrant, see Penal Code § 836.

Research References

California Jury Instructions - Criminal 8.81.8, Special Circumstances—Peace Officer Victim—"Performance of Official Duties"—Defined.
California Jury Instructions - Criminal 9.24.1, Lawful Arrest by Peace Officer—Driving Under the Influence.
4 Witkin, California Criminal Law 4th Pretrial Proceedings § 31 (2021), Intoxication and Motor Vehicles.
4 Witkin, California Criminal Law 4th Pretrial Proceedings § 46 (2021), Without Warrant.

§ 40300.6. Liberal interpretation of § 40300.5 required

Section 40300.5 shall be liberally interpreted to further safe roads and the control of driving while under the influence of an alcoholic beverage or any drug in order to permit arrests to be made pursuant to that section within a reasonable time and distance away from the scene of a traffic crash.

The enactment of this section during the 1985–86 Regular Session of the Legislature does not constitute a change in, but is declaratory of, the existing law. *(Added by Stats.1986, c. 584, § 1. Amended by Stats.2022, c. 81 (A.B.2198), § 8, eff. Jan. 1, 2023.)*

Research References

4 Witkin, California Criminal Law 4th Pretrial Proceedings § 46 (2021), Without Warrant.

§ 40301. Procedure

Except as provided in this chapter, whenever a person is arrested for any violation of this code declared to be a felony, he shall be dealt with in like manner as upon arrest for the commission of any other felony. *(Stats.1959, c. 3, p. 1774, § 40301.)*

Cross References

Driving offenses, see Vehicle Code § 23103 et seq.
Felony defined, see Penal Code § 17.

Research References

4 Witkin, California Criminal Law 4th Pretrial Proceedings § 45 (2021), In General.
4 Witkin, California Criminal Law 4th Pretrial Proceedings § 48 (2021), Mandatory Requirements.

§ 40302. Mandatory appearance

Whenever any person is arrested for any violation of this code, not declared to be a felony, the arrested person shall be taken without unnecessary delay before a magistrate within the county in which the offense charged is alleged to have been committed and who has jurisdiction of the offense and is nearest or most accessible with reference to the place where the arrest is made in any of the following cases:

(a) When the person arrested fails to present both his or her driver's license or other satisfactory evidence of his or her identity and an unobstructed view of his or her full face for examination.

(b) When the person arrested refuses to give his or her written promise to appear in court.

(c) When the person arrested demands an immediate appearance before a magistrate.

(d) When the person arrested is charged with violating Section 23152. *(Stats.1959, c. 3, p. 1774, § 40302. Amended by Stats.1963, c. 1341, p. 2864, § 1; Stats.1968, c. 647, p. 1332, § 1; Stats.1971, c. 1530, p. 3028, § 21, operative May 3, 1972; Stats.1982, c. 53, p. 179, § 43, eff. Feb. 18, 1982; Stats.2015, c. 82 (A.B.346), § 1, eff. Jan. 1, 2016.)*

Cross References

Acceptance of bail by magistrate's clerk or officer in charge of jail, see Vehicle Code § 40307.
Driving offenses, see Vehicle Code § 23103 et seq.
Infractions, release procedures, see Penal Code § 853.5.
Option of arresting officer to take person immediately before magistrate, see Vehicle Code § 40303.
Reasons for nonrelease after arrest, see Penal Code § 853.6.

Research References

2 Witkin, California Criminal Law 4th Crimes Against Governmental Authority § 19 (2021), Verbal Interference.
4 Witkin, California Criminal Law 4th Pretrial Proceedings § 48 (2021), Mandatory Requirements.
4 Witkin, California Criminal Law 4th Pretrial Proceedings § 49 (2021), Arresting Officer's Discretion.
4 Witkin, California Criminal Law 4th Pretrial Proceedings § 50 (2021), Procedure Before Magistrate.
4 Witkin, California Criminal Law 4th Pretrial Proceedings § 61 (2021), Reasons for Nonrelease.

§ 40302.5. Traffic infraction cases; custody of person under age 18

Whenever any person under the age of 18 years is taken into custody in connection with any traffic infraction case, and he is not taken directly before a magistrate, he shall be delivered to the custody of the probation officer. Unless sooner released, the probation officer shall keep the minor in the juvenile hall pending his appearance before a magistrate. When a minor is cited for an offense not involving the driving of a motor vehicle, the minor shall not be taken into custody pursuant to subdivision (a) of Section 40302 solely for failure to present a driver's license. *(Added by Stats.1980, c. 1299, p. 4389, § 2.)*

Research References

4 Witkin, California Criminal Law 4th Pretrial Proceedings § 48 (2021), Mandatory Requirements.

§ 40303. Optional appearance before a magistrate; procedure for contesting charge on basis that person charged is other than person issued notice to appear

(a) Whenever a person is arrested for any of the offenses listed in subdivision (b) and the arresting officer is not required to take the person without unnecessary delay before a magistrate, the arrested person shall, in the judgment of the arresting officer, either be given a 10 days' notice to appear, or be taken without unnecessary delay before a magistrate within the county in which the offense charged is alleged to have been committed and who has jurisdiction of the offense and is nearest or most accessible with reference to the place where the arrest is made. The officer may require that the arrested person, if he or she does not have satisfactory identification, place a right thumbprint, or a left thumbprint or fingerprint if the person has a missing or disfigured right thumb, on the 10 days' notice to appear when a 10 days' notice is provided. Except for law enforcement purposes relating to the identity of the arrestee, a person or entity shall not sell, give away, allow the distribution of, include in a database, or create a database with, this print.

(b) Subdivision (a) applies to the following offenses:

(1) Section 10852 or 10853, relating to injuring or tampering with a vehicle.

(2) Section 23103 or 23104, relating to reckless driving.

(3) Subdivision (a) of Section 2800, insofar as it relates to a failure or refusal of the driver of a vehicle to stop and submit to an inspection or test of the lights upon the vehicle pursuant to Section 2804, that is punishable as a misdemeanor.

(4) Subdivision (a) of Section 2800, insofar as it relates to a failure or refusal of the driver of a vehicle to stop and submit to a brake test that is punishable as a misdemeanor.

(5) Subdivision (a) of Section 2800, relating to the refusal to submit vehicle and load to an inspection, measurement, or weighing as prescribed in Section 2802 or a refusal to adjust the load or obtain a permit as prescribed in Section 2803.

(6) Subdivision (a) of Section 2800, insofar as it relates to a driver who continues to drive after being lawfully ordered not to drive by a member of the Department of the California Highway Patrol for violating the driver's hours of service or driver's log regulations adopted pursuant to subdivision (a) of Section 34501.

(7) Subdivision (b), (c), or (d) of Section 2800, relating to a failure or refusal to comply with a lawful out-of-service order.

(8) Section 20002 or 20003, relating to duties in the event of an accident.

(9) Section 23109, relating to participating in a speed contest or exhibition of speed.

(10) Section 14601, 14601.1, 14601.2, or 14601.5, relating to driving while the privilege to operate a motor vehicle is suspended or revoked.

(11) When the person arrested has attempted to evade arrest.

(12) Section 23332, relating to persons upon vehicular crossings.

(13) Section 2813, relating to the refusal to stop and submit a vehicle to an inspection of its size, weight, and equipment.

(14) Section 21461.5, insofar as it relates to a pedestrian who, after being cited for a violation of Section 21461.5, is, within 24 hours, again found upon the freeway in violation of Section 21461.5 and thereafter refuses to leave the freeway after being lawfully ordered to do so by a peace officer and after having been informed that his or her failure to leave could result in his or her arrest.

(15) Subdivision (a) of Section 2800, insofar as it relates to a pedestrian who, after having been cited for a violation of subdivision (a) of Section 2800 for failure to obey a lawful order of a peace officer issued pursuant to Section 21962, is within 24 hours again found upon the bridge or overpass and thereafter refuses to leave after being lawfully ordered to do so by a peace officer and after having been informed that his or her failure to leave could result in his or her arrest.

(16) Section 21200.5, relating to riding a bicycle while under the influence of an alcoholic beverage or a drug.

(17) Section 21221.5, relating to operating a motorized scooter while under the influence of an alcoholic beverage or a drug.

(c)(1) A person contesting a charge by claiming under penalty of perjury not to be the person issued the notice to appear may choose to submit a right thumbprint, or a left thumbprint if the person has a missing or disfigured right thumb, to the issuing court through his or her local law enforcement agency for comparison with the one placed on the notice to appear. A local law enforcement agency providing this service may charge the requester no more than the actual costs. The issuing court may refer the thumbprint submitted and the notice to appear to the prosecuting attorney for comparison of the thumbprints. When there is no thumbprint or fingerprint on the notice to appear, or when the comparison of thumbprints is inconclusive, the court shall refer the notice to appear or copy thereof back to the issuing agency for further investigation, unless the court finds that referral is not in the interest of justice.

(2) Upon initiation of the investigation or comparison process by referral of the court, the court shall continue the case and the speedy trial period shall be tolled for 45 days.

(3) Upon receipt of the issuing agency's or prosecuting attorney's response, the court may make a finding of factual innocence pursuant to Section 530.6 of the Penal Code if the court determines that there is insufficient evidence that the person cited is the person charged and shall immediately notify the Department of Motor Vehicles of its determination. If the Department of Motor Vehicles determines the citation or citations in question formed the basis of a suspension or revocation of the person's driving privilege, the department shall immediately set aside the action.

(4) If the prosecuting attorney or issuing agency fails to respond to a court referral within 45 days, the court shall make a finding of factual innocence pursuant to Section 530.6 of the Penal Code, unless the court finds that a finding of factual innocence is not in the interest of justice.

(5) The citation or notice to appear may be held by the prosecuting attorney or issuing agency for future adjudication should the arrestee who received the citation or notice to appear be found. *(Stats.1959, c. 3, p. 1775, § 40303. Amended by Stats.1959, c. 1996, p. 4639, § 48.5; Stats.1961, c. 63, p. 1034, § 1; Stats.1967, c. 236, p. 1372, § 7; Stats.1967, c. 253, p. 1403, § 8; Stats.1967, c. 607, p. 1957, § 2; Stats.1968, c. 1195, p. 2270, § 6; Stats.1969, c. 517, p. 1126, § 1; Stats.1975, c. 759, p. 1770, § 1; Stats.1976, c. 1082, p. 4905, § 1; Stats.1980, c. 680, p. 2064, § 4; Stats.1981, c. 675, p. 2470, § 3; Stats.1982, c. 53, p. 179, § 44, eff. Feb. 18, 1982; Stats.1985, c. 1013, § 5; Stats.1992, c. 468 (A.B.2617), § 2; Stats.1999, c. 724 (A.B.1650), § 52; Stats.2000, c. 860 (A.B.2908), § 14; Stats.2003, c. 467 (S.B. 752), § 4; Stats.2006, c. 288 (A.B.3011), § 19.)*

Cross References

Acceptance of bail by magistrate's clerk or officer in charge of jail, see Vehicle Code § 40307.

Infractions, release procedures, see Penal Code § 853.5.

Reasons for nonrelease after arrest, see Penal Code § 853.6.

Research References

4 Witkin, California Criminal Law 4th Pretrial Proceedings § 49 (2021), Arresting Officer's Discretion.
4 Witkin, California Criminal Law 4th Pretrial Proceedings § 51 (2021), Citation, Promise, and Release.

§ 40303.5. Notice to correct violations; offenses; conditions

An arresting officer shall permit a person arrested for any of the following offenses to execute a notice containing a promise to correct the violation in accordance with the provisions of Section 40610 unless the arresting officer finds that any of the disqualifying conditions specified in subdivision (b) of Section 40610 exist:

(a) A registration infraction set forth in Division 3 (commencing with Section 4000).

(b) A driver's license infraction set forth in Division 6 (commencing with Section 12500), and subdivision (a) of Section 12951, relating to possession of a driver's license.

(c) Section 21201, relating to bicycle equipment.

(d) Subdivision (a) of Section 21212.

(e) An infraction involving equipment set forth in Division 12 (commencing with Section 24000), Division 13 (commencing with Section 29000), Division 14.8 (commencing with Section 34500), Division 16 (commencing with Section 36000), Division 16.5 (commencing with Section 38000), and Division 16.7 (commencing with Section 39000).

(f) Section 2482, relating to registration decals for vehicles transporting inedible kitchen grease.

(g) Section 9850, relating to expired vessel registration.

(h) Section 9853.2, relating to the display of vessel identification numbers.

(i) Section 678.11 of the Harbors and Navigation Code, relating to possessing a vessel operator card.

(j) Subparagraph (a) or (c) of Section 190.00 of Title 13 of the California Code of Regulations, relating to the display of vessel identification numbers.

(k) Section 190.01 of Title 13 of the California Code of Regulations, relating to vessel registration stickers.

(*l*) Section 6565.8 of Title 14 of the California Code of Regulations, relating to personal floatation devices on vessels.

(m) Section 6569 of Title 14 of the California Code of Regulations, relating to serviceable fire extinguishers on vessels.

(n) Section 6572 of Title 14 of the California Code of Regulations, relating to markings on fire extinguishers on vessels. *(Added by Stats.1978, c. 1350, p. 4479, § 2, operative July 1, 1979. Amended by Stats.1979, c. 71, p. 173, § 1, eff. May 19, 1979; Stats.1981, c. 774, p. 3026, § 13; Stats.1984, c. 915, § 1, operative July 1, 1985; Stats.1989, c. 729, § 3, operative July 1, 1990; Stats.1992, c. 258 (S.B.133), § 4; Stats.2014, c. 595 (A.B.1566), § 20, eff. Jan. 1, 2015; Stats.2015, c. 303 (A.B.731), § 543, eff. Jan. 1, 2016; Stats.2018, c. 502 (A.B.3077), § 2, eff. Jan. 1, 2019; Stats.2021, c. 57 (A.B.591), § 1, eff. Jan. 1, 2022.)*

Cross References

Dismissal of charge on proof of correction, see Vehicle Code § 40522.
Nonresident defined, see Vehicle Code § 435.
Notice to appear, dismissal upon proof of correction, see Vehicle Code § 40522.
Vehicle sale reporting system, required steps, wholesale vehicle auctions, operation without license plate, see Vehicle Code § 4456.

Research References

4 Witkin, California Criminal Law 4th Pretrial Proceedings § 54 (2021), Promise to Correct Violation.

§ 40304. Discretionary procedure

Whenever any person is arrested by any member of the California Highway Patrol for any violation of any state law regulating the operation of vehicles or the use of the highways declared to be a misdemeanor but which offense is not specified in this code, he shall, in the judgment of the arresting officer, either be given a 10-day notice to appear in the manner provided in this chapter or be taken without unnecessary delay before a magistrate within the county in which the offense charged is alleged to have been committed and who has jurisdiction of the offense and is nearest or most accessible with reference to the place where the arrest is made, or, upon demand of the person arrested, before a magistrate in the judicial district in which the offense is alleged to have been committed. *(Stats.1959, c. 3, p. 1775, § 40304.)*

Cross References

Misdemeanor defined, see Penal Code § 17.

Research References

4 Witkin, California Criminal Law 4th Pretrial Proceedings § 49 (2021), Arresting Officer's Discretion.

§ 40304.5. Failure to appear on citation for parking offense or traffic infraction; deposit of bail; booking, photographing, fingerprinting and arrest record; requirements

Notwithstanding any other provision of law, whenever any person is taken into custody for bail to be collected on two or fewer outstanding warrants for failure to appear on a citation for a parking offense or a traffic infraction, the person shall be provided the opportunity immediately to post bail, and shall not be booked, photographed, or fingerprinted, nor shall an arrest record be made, when the amount of bail required to be paid on the warrant may be ascertained by reference to the face thereof or to a fixed schedule of bail, unless and until all of the following requirements have been exhausted:

(a) If the person has sufficient cash in his or her possession, that person shall be given the opportunity immediately to post bail with the person in charge of the jail or his or her designee.

(b) If the person does not have sufficient cash in his or her possession, that person shall be informed of his or her rights and given the opportunity to do all of the following:

(1) Make not less than three completed telephone calls to obtain bail. The person shall be permitted the use of the police or sheriff's department telephone to make not less than three completed local or collect long-distance telephone calls to obtain bail.

(2) Have not less than three hours in which to arrange for the deposit of bail. *(Added by Stats.1984, c. 35, § 3, eff. March 8, 1984, operative March 31, 1984.)*

Research References

4 Witkin, California Criminal Law 4th Pretrial Proceedings § 53 (2021), Failure to Appear.

§ 40305. Offense by nonresident; procedure where charge is contested on basis that charged person is other than person issued notice to appear

(a) Whenever a nonresident is arrested for violating any section of this code while driving a motor vehicle and does not furnish satisfactory evidence of identity and an address within this state at which he or she can be located, he or she may, in the discretion of the arresting officer, be taken immediately before a magistrate within the county where the offense charged is alleged to have been committed, and who has jurisdiction over the offense and is nearest or most accessible with reference to the place where the arrest is made. If the magistrate is not available at the time of the arrest and the arrested person is not taken before any other person authorized to receive a deposit of bail, and if the arresting officer does not have the authority or is not required to take the arrested person before a magistrate or other person authorized to receive a deposit of bail by some other provision of law, the officer may require the arrested person, if he or she has no satisfactory identification, to place a right thumbprint, or a left thumbprint or fingerprint if the person has a missing or disfigured right thumb, on the notice to appear as provided in Article 2 (commencing with Section 40500).

Except for law enforcement purposes relating to the identity of the arrestee, no person or entity may sell, give away, allow the distribution of, include in a database, or create a database with, this print.

(b)(1) A person contesting a charge by claiming under penalty of perjury not to be the person issued the notice to appear may choose to submit a right thumbprint, or a left thumbprint if the person has a missing or disfigured right thumb, to the issuing court through his or her local law enforcement agency for comparison with the one placed on the notice to appear. A local law enforcement agency providing this service may charge the requester no more than the actual costs. The issuing court may refer the thumbprint submitted and the notice to appear to the prosecuting attorney for comparison of the thumbprints. When there is no thumbprint or fingerprint on the notice to appear, or when the comparison of thumbprints is inconclusive, the court shall refer the notice to appear or copy thereof back to the issuing agency for further investigation, unless the court finds that referral is not in the interest of justice.

(2) Upon initiation of the investigation or comparison process by referral of the court, the court shall continue the case and the speedy trial period shall be tolled for 45 days.

(3) Upon receipt of the issuing agency's or prosecuting attorney's response, the court may make a finding of factual innocence pursuant to Section 530.6 of the Penal Code if the court determines that there is insufficient evidence that the person cited is the person charged and shall immediately notify the Department of Motor Vehicles of its determination. If the Department of Motor Vehicles determines the citation or citations in question formed the basis of a suspension or revocation of the person's driving privilege, the department shall immediately set aside the action.

(4) If the prosecuting attorney or issuing agency fails to respond to a court referral within 45 days, the court shall make a finding of factual innocence pursuant to Section 530.6 of the Penal Code, unless the court determines that a finding of factual innocence is not in the interest of justice.

(5) The citation or notice to appear may be held by the prosecuting attorney or issuing agency for future adjudication should the arrestee who received the citation or notice to appear be found. *(Stats.1959, c. 3, p. 1776, § 40305. Amended by Stats.1961, c. 314, p. 1357, § 1; Stats.2003, c. 467 (S.B.752), § 5.)*

Cross References

Bail, generally, see Penal Code § 1268 et seq.
Infractions, release procedures, see Penal Code § 853.5.
Nonresident defined, see Vehicle Code § 435.

Research References

4 Witkin, California Criminal Law 4th Pretrial Proceedings § 49 (2021), Arresting Officer's Discretion.

§ 40305.5. Nonresidents; offenses while driving commercially registered motor vehicles; guaranteed traffic arrest bail bond certificate in lieu of proceedings; contents; procedures where charge is contested by charged person claiming to be other than person issued notice to appear

(a) If a nonresident is arrested for violating this code while driving a commercially registered motor vehicle, excluding house cars, with an unladen weight of 7,000 pounds or more, and does not furnish satisfactory evidence of identity and an address within this state at which he or she can be located, the arresting officer may, in lieu of the procedures set forth in Section 40305, accept a guaranteed traffic arrest bail bond certificate, and the nonresident shall be released from custody upon giving a written promise to appear as provided in Article 2 (commencing with Section 40500). The officer may require the arrested person, if he or she has no satisfactory identification, to place a right thumbprint, or a left thumbprint or fingerprint if the person has a missing or disfigured right thumb, on the notice to appear as provided in Article 2 (commencing with Section 45000). Except for law enforcement purposes relating to the identity of the arrestee, a person or entity shall not sell, give away, allow the distribution of, include in a database, or create a database with, this print.

(b) Every guaranteed traffic arrest bail bond certificate shall contain all of the following information:

(1) The name and address of the surety and of the issuer, if other than the surety.

(2) The name, address, driver's license number and signature of the individual covered by the certificate.

(3) The maximum amount guaranteed.

(4) Exclusions from coverage.

(5) A statement that the issuing company guarantees the appearance of a person to whom a guaranteed traffic arrest bail bond certificate is issued and, in the event of the failure of the person to appear in court at the time of trial, the issuing company shall pay any fine or forfeiture imposed on the person, not to exceed the amount stated on the certificate.

(6) The expiration date of the certificate.

(c) A guaranteed traffic arrest bail bond certificate may be issued by a surety admitted in this state. The certificate may also be issued by an association of motor carriers if all of the following conditions are met:

(1) The association is incorporated, or authorized to do business, in this state.

(2) The association is covered by a guaranteed traffic arrest bail bond issued by a surety admitted in this state.

(3) The association agrees to pay fines or bail assessed against the guaranteed traffic arrest bail bond certificate.

(4) The surety guarantees payment of fines or bail assessed against the guaranteed traffic arrest bail bond certificates issued by the association.

(d) The arresting officer shall file the guaranteed traffic arrest bail bond certificate with the notice to appear required to be filed by Section 40506.

(e) A "guaranteed traffic arrest bail bond certificate" is a document that guarantees the payment of fines or bail assessed against an individual for violation of this code, except driving while under the influence of alcohol or drugs, driving without a license or driving with a suspended or revoked license, operating a motor vehicle without the permission of the owner, or any violation punishable as a felony.

(f) A "guaranteed traffic arrest bail bond" is a bond issued by a surety guaranteeing the obligations of the issuer of guaranteed traffic arrest bail bond certificates. The bond shall be in the amount of fifty thousand dollars ($50,000) and shall be filed with the Secretary of State. Any court in this state may assess against the surety the amount of covered fines or bail that the issuer of a guaranteed traffic arrest bail bond certificate fails to pay.

(g)(1) A person contesting a charge by claiming under penalty of perjury not to be the person issued the notice to appear may choose to submit a right thumbprint, or a left thumbprint if the person has a missing or disfigured right thumb, to the issuing court through his or her local law enforcement agency for comparison with the one placed on the notice to appear. A local law enforcement agency providing this service may charge the requester no more than the actual costs. The issuing court may refer the thumbprint submitted and the notice to appear to the prosecuting attorney for comparison of the thumbprints. If there is no thumbprint or fingerprint on the notice to appear or the comparison of thumbprints is inconclusive, the court shall refer the notice to appear or copy of the notice to appear back to the issuing agency for further investigation, unless the court finds that referral is not in the interest of justice.

(2) Upon initiation of the investigation or comparison process by referral of the court, the court shall continue the case and the speedy trial period shall be tolled for 45 days.

(3) Upon receipt of the issuing agency's or prosecuting attorney's response, the court may make a finding of factual innocence pursuant to Section 530.6 of the Penal Code if the court determines that there is insufficient evidence that the person cited is the person charged and shall immediately notify the Department of Motor Vehicles of its determination. If the Department of Motor Vehicles determines the citation or citations in question formed the basis of a suspension or revocation of the person's driving privilege, the department shall immediately set aside the action.

(4) If the prosecuting attorney or issuing agency fails to respond to a court referral within 45 days, the court shall make a finding of factual innocence pursuant to Section 530.6 of the Penal Code, unless the court determines that a finding of factual innocence is not in the interest of justice.

(5) The citation or notice to appear may be held by the prosecuting attorney or issuing agency for future adjudication should the arrestee who received the citation or notice to appear be found. *(Added by Stats.1982, c. 1394, p. 5309, § 3. Amended by Stats.2003, c. 467 (S.B.752), § 6; Stats.2011, c. 296 (A.B.1023), § 310.)*

Cross References

Infractions, release procedures, see Penal Code § 853.5.

Research References

4 Witkin, California Criminal Law 4th Pretrial Proceedings § 49 (2021), Arresting Officer's Discretion.

§ 40306. Misdemeanor and infraction procedure before magistrate

(a) Whenever a person is arrested for a misdemeanor or an infraction and is taken before a magistrate, the arresting officer shall file with the magistrate a complaint stating the offense with which the person is charged.

(b) The person taken before a magistrate shall be entitled to at least five days continuance of his case in which to plead and prepare for trial and the person shall not be required to plead or be tried within the five days unless he waives such time in writing or in open court.

(c) The person taken before a magistrate shall thereupon be released from custody upon his own recognizance or upon such bail as the magistrate may fix. *(Stats.1959, c. 3, p. 1776, § 40306. Amended by Stats.1968, c. 1192, p. 2262, § 13, operative Jan. 1, 1969.)*

Research References

5 Witkin, California Criminal Law 4th Criminal Trial § 401 (2021), Motion for Continuance.

4 Witkin, California Criminal Law 4th Pretrial Proceedings § 50 (2021), Procedure Before Magistrate.

§ 40307. Magistrate unavailable

(a) When an arresting officer attempts to take a person arrested for a misdemeanor or infraction of this code before a magistrate and the magistrate or person authorized to act for him or her is not available, the arresting officer shall take the person arrested, without unnecessary delay, before one of the following:

(1) The clerk of the magistrate, who shall admit the person to bail for the full amount set for the offense in a schedule fixed as provided in Section 1269b of the Penal Code.

(2) The officer in charge of the most accessible county or city jail or other place of detention within the county, who shall admit the person to bail for the full amount set for the offense in a schedule fixed as provided in Section 1269b of the Penal Code or may, in lieu of bail, release the person on his or her written promise to appear as provided in subdivisions (a) to (f), inclusive, of Section 853.6 of the Penal Code.

(b) Whenever a person is taken into custody pursuant to subdivision (a) of Section 40302 and is arrested for a misdemeanor or infraction of this code pertaining to the operation of a motor vehicle, the officer in charge of the most accessible county or city jail or other place of detention within the county may detain the person arrested for a reasonable period of time, not to exceed two hours, in order to verify his or her identity. *(Stats.1959, c. 3, p. 1776, § 40307. Amended by Stats.1968, c. 1192, p. 2262, § 14, operative Jan. 1, 1969; Stats.1970, c. 753, p. 1433, § 1; Stats.1971, c. 1528, p. 3019, § 1, operative May 3, 1972; Stats.1974, c. 593, p. 1419, § 1; Stats.2007, c. 738 (A.B.1248), § 44.)*

Cross References

Bail, generally, see Penal Code § 1268 et seq.

Research References

4 Witkin, California Criminal Law 4th Illegally Obtained Evidence § 202 (2021), Specific Searches.

4 Witkin, California Criminal Law 4th Pretrial Proceedings § 50 (2021), Procedure Before Magistrate.

§ 40309. Mailing of parking penalty payment

Whenever a notice of parking violation is issued in accordance with Sections 40202 and 40203, or a notice of delinquent parking violation is issued pursuant to Section 40206, the amount fixed as a parking penalty for the violation charged may be forwarded by United States mail to the person authorized to receive a deposit of the parking penalty. Payment of a parking penalty forwarded by mail is effective only when actually received, and the presumption that a letter duly directed and mailed was received does not apply. Section 40512 is applicable to a parking penalty posted pursuant to this section. *(Added by Stats.1960, 1st Ex.Sess., c. 40, p. 384, § 1. Amended by Stats.1986, c. 939, § 16.)*

§ 40310. Adoption of uniform traffic penalty schedule; maximum penalty; notice of assessment; payment

The Judicial Council shall annually adopt a uniform traffic penalty schedule which shall be applicable to all nonparking infractions specified in this code, unless in a particular case before the court the judge or authorized hearing officer specifies a different penalty. No penalty shall be established for any infraction in an amount, exclusive of any additional penalty levied pursuant to Section 1464 of the Penal Code, in excess of the amount of the maximum fine pursuant to Section 42001 or 42001.5, and penalties shall be set without regard to residence. In case a traffic penalty is not paid within 20 days following mailing of a notice that the penalty has been assessed, a late charge shall be due in the amount of 50 percent of total initial penalty.

In establishing a uniform traffic penalty schedule, the Judicial Council shall classify the offenses into four or fewer penalty categories, according to the severity of offenses, so as to permit convenient notice and payment of the scheduled penalty. *(Added by Stats.1980, c. 618, p. 1702, § 2. Amended by Stats.1986, c. 953, § 13; Stats.1992, c. 696 (A.B.1344), § 93, eff. Sept. 15, 1992.)*

Research References

2 Witkin, California Criminal Law 4th Crimes Against Public Peace and Welfare § 265 (2021), In General.

2 Witkin, California Criminal Law 4th Crimes Against Public Peace and Welfare § 266 (2021), Infractions.
5 Witkin, California Criminal Law 4th Criminal Trial § 668 (2021), Minor Vehicle Offenses.
4 Witkin, California Criminal Law 4th Pretrial Proceedings § 94 (2021), On Arrest.

§ 40311. Arraignment for other violations

Whenever a person is arrested under authority of a warrant, the court to which such person is taken shall, with his consent, have jurisdiction to arraign him at that time for any other alleged violation of this code or an ordinance relating to traffic offenses for which he has been issued a written notice to appear in court, notwithstanding the fact that the time for appearance specified in such notice has not yet arrived. *(Added by Stats.1959, c. 977, p. 3006, § 1.)*

Research References

4 Witkin, California Criminal Law 4th Pretrial Proceedings § 50 (2021), Procedure Before Magistrate.

§ 40312. Payment of fines; receipts; arrest for outstanding warrants prohibited

A peace officer shall not arrest, on the basis of an outstanding warrant arising from a violation of this code, any person who presents to the peace officer a receipt, from a proper official of the court, indicating that the person has paid the fine for the violation that caused the warrant to be issued. The receipt shall contain sufficient information to identify the name and number of the court issuing the receipt, the date the case was adjudicated or the fine was paid, the case number or docket number, and the violations disposed of. *(Added by Stats.1982, c. 290, p. 930, § 1.)*

Research References

4 Witkin, California Criminal Law 4th Pretrial Proceedings § 50 (2021), Procedure Before Magistrate.

§ 40313. Notice of reexamination issued arrested person; notation and record

If a notice of reexamination was issued pursuant to Section 21061, the record of arrest for the traffic violation, or any notice to appear issued under this article, or both, shall include a notation indicating that the notice of reexamination was issued to the arrested person and the driver's license record maintained by the department shall contain a record of the notice of reexamination. The record of the notice of reexamination shall be considered confidential by the department pursuant to Section 1808.5. *(Added by Stats.1986, c. 304, § 5, operative July 1, 1987.)*

ARTICLE 2. RELEASE UPON PROMISE TO APPEAR

Section

§ 40500. Notice to appear; form; bail; delivery; alteration or destruction of notice before filing; arresting agency recommendation that case be dismissed; contest of charge by charged person claiming to be other than person issued notice to appear

(a) Whenever a person is arrested for any violation of this code not declared to be a felony, or for a violation of an ordinance of a city or county relating to traffic offenses and he or she is not immediately taken before a magistrate, as provided in this chapter, the arresting officer shall prepare in triplicate a written notice to appear in court or before a person authorized to receive a deposit of bail, containing the name and address of the person, the license number of his or her vehicle, if any, the name and address, when available, of the registered owner or lessee of the vehicle, the offense charged and the time and place when and where he or she shall appear. If the arrestee does not have a driver's license or other satisfactory evidence of identity in his or her possession, the officer may require the arrestee to place a right thumbprint, or a left thumbprint or fingerprint if the person has a missing or disfigured right thumb, on the notice to appear. Except for law enforcement purposes relating to the identity of the arrestee, no person or entity may sell, give away, allow the distribution of, include in a database, or create a database with, this print.

(b) The Judicial Council shall prescribe the form of the notice to appear.

(c) Nothing in this section requires the law enforcement agency or the arresting officer issuing the notice to appear to inform any person arrested pursuant to this section of the amount of bail required to be deposited for the offense charged.

(d) Once the arresting officer has prepared the written notice to appear, and has delivered a copy to the arrested person, the officer shall deliver the remaining original and all copies of the notice to appear as provided by Section 40506.

Any person, including the arresting officer and any member of the officer's department or agency, or any peace officer, who alters, conceals, modifies, nullifies, or destroys, or causes to be altered, concealed, modified, nullified, or destroyed, the face side of the remaining original or any copy of a citation that was retained by the officer, for any reason, before it is filed with the magistrate or with a person authorized by the magistrate or judge to receive a deposit of bail, is guilty of a misdemeanor.

If, after an arrested person has signed and received a copy of a notice to appear, the arresting officer or other officer of the issuing agency, determines that, in the interest of justice, the citation or notice should be dismissed, the arresting agency may recommend, in writing, to the magistrate or judge that the case be dismissed. The recommendation shall cite the reasons for the recommendation and be filed with the court.

If the magistrate or judge makes a finding that there are grounds for dismissal, the finding shall be entered on the record and the infraction or misdemeanor dismissed.

Under no circumstances shall a personal relationship with any officer, public official, or law enforcement agency be grounds for dismissal.

(e)(1) A person contesting a charge by claiming under penalty of perjury not to be the person issued the notice to appear may choose to submit a right thumbprint, or a left thumbprint if the person has a missing or disfigured right thumb, to the issuing court through his or her local law enforcement agency for comparison with the one placed on the notice to appear. A local law enforcement agency providing this service may charge the requester no more than the actual costs. The issuing court may refer the thumbprint submitted and the notice to appear to the prosecuting attorney for comparison of the thumbprints. When there is no thumbprint or fingerprint on the notice to appear, or when the comparison of thumbprints is inconclusive, the court shall refer the notice to appear or copy thereof back to the issuing agency for further investigation, unless the court determines that referral is not in the interest of justice.

(2) Upon initiation of the investigation or comparison process by referral of the court, the court shall continue the case and the speedy trial period shall be tolled for 45 days.

(3) Upon receipt of the issuing agency's or prosecuting attorney's response, the court may make a finding of factual innocence pursuant to Section 530.6 of the Penal Code if the court determines that there is insufficient evidence that the person cited is the person charged and shall immediately notify the Department of Motor Vehicles of its determination. If the Department of Motor Vehicles determines the citation or citations in question formed the basis of a suspension or revocation of the person's driving privilege, the department shall immediately set aside the action.

(4) If the prosecuting attorney or issuing agency fails to respond to a court referral within 45 days, the court shall make a finding of factual innocence pursuant to Section 530.6 of the Penal Code, unless the court determines that a finding of factual innocence is not in the interest of justice.

(5) The citation or notice to appear may be held by the prosecuting attorney or issuing agency for future adjudication should the arrestee who received the citation or notice to appear be found. *(Stats.1959, c. 3, p. 1777, § 40500. Amended by Stats.1961, c. 58, p. 1016, § 68; Stats.1965, c. 1052, p. 2691, § 1, operative July 1, 1966; Stats.1975, c. 1257, p. 3295, § 1; Stats.1987, c. 72, § 4, eff. June 30, 1987; Stats.1995, c. 93 (A.B.219), § 3; Stats.2003, c. 467 (S.B.752), § 7.)*

Cross References

Acceptance by municipal court commissioner or traffic referee, see Government Code § 72304.
Arrest of persons engaged in speed contests or reckless driving, removal and seizure of vehicles, see Vehicle Code § 23109.2.
Bail, generally, see Penal Code § 1268 et seq.
Inapplicability of forfeiture of bail provisions of Penal Code to cases arising under this section, see Penal Code § 1306.1.
Online trials offered through online tool, evidence, applicable rules, see Vehicle Code § 40287.
Procedure for bail of nonresidents, see Vehicle Code § 40305.
Procedure on equipment violations, see Vehicle Code § 40150 et seq.
Removal and seizure of vehicle, release of vehicle to registered owner, see Vehicle Code § 2480.
Trials, documentary evidence of infractions, see Vehicle Code § 40901.
Trials by written declaration, see Vehicle Code § 40902.

Research References

West's California Judicial Council Forms TR–106, Continuation of Notice to Appear.
West's California Judicial Council Forms TR–108, Continuation of Citation.
West's California Judicial Council Forms TR–130, Traffic/Nontraffic Notice to Appear.
West's California Judicial Council Forms TR–135, Electronic Traffic/Nontraffic Notice to Appear (4 Format).
West's California Judicial Council Forms TR–145, Electronic Traffic/Nontraffic Notice to Appear (3 Format).
5 Witkin, California Criminal Law 4th Criminal Trial § 668 (2021), Minor Vehicle Offenses.
4 Witkin, California Criminal Law 4th Illegally Obtained Evidence § 336 (2021), Detention for Warrant Check.
4 Witkin, California Criminal Law 4th Pretrial Proceedings § 23 (2021), Other Process Distinguished.
4 Witkin, California Criminal Law 4th Pretrial Proceedings § 49 (2021), Arresting Officer's Discretion.
4 Witkin, California Criminal Law 4th Pretrial Proceedings § 51 (2021), Citation, Promise, and Release.
4 Witkin, California Criminal Law 4th Pretrial Proceedings § 300 (2021), Plea Options for Infractions.

§ 40501. Time to appear

(a) The time specified in the notice to appear shall be a specific date which is at least 21 days after the arrest, except that the court having jurisdiction over the offense charged may authorize the arresting officer to specify on the notice that an appearance may be made before the time specified.

(b) In the case of juveniles, the court having jurisdiction over the offense charged may require the arresting officer to indicate on the notice "to be notified" rather than specifying a specific date pursuant to subdivision (a). *(Stats.1959, c. 3, p. 1777, § 40501. Amended by Stats.1985, c. 1289, § 2; Stats.1986, c. 557, § 1, eff. Aug. 22, 1986.)*

Research References

4 Witkin, California Criminal Law 4th Pretrial Proceedings § 51 (2021), Citation, Promise, and Release.

§ 40502. Place to appear

The place specified in the notice to appear shall be any of the following:

(a) Before a magistrate within the county in which the offense charged is alleged to have been committed and who has jurisdiction of the offense and is nearest or most accessible with reference to the place where the arrest is made.

(b) Upon demand of the person arrested, before a judge or other magistrate having jurisdiction of the offense at the county seat of the county in which the offense is alleged to have been committed. This subdivision applies only if the person arrested resides, or the person's principal place of employment is located, closer to the county seat than to the magistrate nearest or most accessible to the place where the arrest is made.

(c) Before a person authorized to receive a deposit of bail.

The clerk and deputy clerks of the superior court are persons authorized to receive bail in accordance with a schedule of bail approved by the judges of that court.

(d) Before the juvenile court, a juvenile court referee, or a juvenile hearing officer within the county in which the offense charged is alleged to have been committed, if the person arrested appears to be under the age of 18 years. The juvenile court shall by order designate the proper person before whom the appearance is to be made.

In a county that has implemented the provisions of Section 603.5 of the Welfare and Institutions Code, if the offense alleged to have been committed by a minor is classified as an infraction under this code, or is a violation of a local ordinance involving the driving, parking, or operation of a motor vehicle, the citation shall be issued as provided in subdivision (a), (b), or (c); provided, however, that if the citation combines an infraction and a misdemeanor, the place specified shall be as provided in subdivision (d).

If the place specified in the notice to appear is within a county where a department of the superior court is to hold a night session within a period of not more than 10 days after the arrest, the notice to appear shall contain, in addition to the above, a statement notifying the person arrested that the person may appear before a night session of the court. *(Stats.1959, c. 3, p. 1777, § 40502. Amended by Stats.1961, c. 1616, p. 3508, § 6; Stats.1965, c. 1704, p. 3837, § 2; Stats.1965, c. 1705, p. 3838, § 2; Stats.1980, c. 1299, p. 4390, § 3; Stats.1984, c. 400, § 1; Stats.1998, c. 931 (S.B.2139), § 461, eff. Sept. 28, 1998; Stats.2002, c. 784 (S.B.1316), § 603; Stats.2003, c. 149 (S.B.79), § 87.)*

Law Revision Commission Comments

Section 40502 is amended to accommodate unification of the municipal and superior courts in a county. Cal. Const. art. VI, § 5(e). *Cf.* Penal Code § 808 (magistrates). In a county in which there is no municipal court, the relevant geographical unit is the county rather than judicial district. *Cf.* Code Civ. Proc. § 38 & Comment ("judicial district" defined). The section is also amended to reflect elimination of the justice court. Cal. Const. art. VI, §§ 1, 5(b). [28 Cal.L.Rev.Comm. Reports 51 (1998)].

Section 40502 is amended to reflect unification of the municipal and superior courts pursuant to Article VI, Section 5(e), of the California Constitution. *Cf.* Code Civ. Proc. § 38 (judicial district). [32 Cal.L.Rev.Comm. Reports 544 (2002)].

Subdivision (b) of Section 40502 is amended to reflect unification of the municipal and superior courts pursuant to former Section 5(e) of Article VI of the California Constitution.

Subdivision (d) is amended to reflect the redesignation of traffic hearing officers as juvenile hearing officers. See 1997 Cal. Stat. ch. 679. [33 Cal.L.Rev. Comm. Reports 261 (2003)].

Cross References

Minors charged with traffic offense, conduct of hearing on written notice to appear, see Welfare and Institutions Code § 257.
Municipal court commissioner or traffic referee, power to fix bail and endorse it on notice for appearance, see Government Code § 72304.
Renewal of license, refusal for failure to appear in court, see Vehicle Code § 12808.

Research References

4 Witkin, California Criminal Law 4th Jurisdiction and Venue § 63 (2021), Other Offenses.
4 Witkin, California Criminal Law 4th Pretrial Proceedings § 51 (2021), Citation, Promise, and Release.

§ 40503. Speed charge

Every notice to appear or notice of violation and every complaint or information charging a violation of any provision of this code regulating the speed of vehicles upon a highway shall specify the approximate speed at which the defendant is alleged to have driven and exactly the prima facie or maximum speed limit applicable to the highway at the time and place of the alleged offense and shall state any other speed limit alleged to have been exceeded if applicable to the particular type of vehicle or combination of vehicles operated by the defendant. *(Stats.1959, c. 3, p. 1777, § 40503. Amended by Stats.1961, c. 917, p. 2544, § 1; Stats.1969, c. 1056, p. 2039, § 1.)*

Cross References

Speed laws in general, see Vehicle Code § 22349 et seq.

Research References

4 Witkin, California Criminal Law 4th Pretrial Proceedings § 51 (2021), Citation, Promise, and Release.

§ 40504. Delivery of notice; promise to appear; evidence of identification; use of false or fictitious name; procedure for contest of charge where charged person claims to be other than person issued notice to appear

(a) The officer shall deliver one copy of the notice to appear to the arrested person and the arrested person in order to secure release must give his or her written promise to appear in court or before a person authorized to receive a deposit of bail by signing two copies of the notice which shall be retained by the officer, and the officer may require the arrested person, if this person has no satisfactory identification, to place a right thumbprint, or a left thumbprint or fingerprint if the person has a missing or disfigured right thumb, on the notice to appear. Thereupon, the arresting officer shall forthwith release the person arrested from custody. Except for law enforcement purposes relating to the identity of the arrestee, no person or entity may sell, give away, allow the distribution of, include in a database, or create a database with, this print.

(b) Any person who signs a written promise to appear with a false or fictitious name is guilty of a misdemeanor regardless of the disposition of the charge upon which he or she was originally arrested.

(c)(1) A person contesting a charge by claiming under penalty of perjury not to be the person issued the notice to appear may choose to submit a right thumbprint, or a left thumbprint if the person has a missing or disfigured right thumb, to the issuing court through his or her local law enforcement agency for comparison with the one placed on the notice to appear. A local law enforcement agency providing this service may charge the requester no more than the actual costs. The issuing court may refer the thumbprint submitted and the notice to appear to the prosecuting attorney for comparison of the thumbprints. When there is no thumbprint or fingerprint on the notice to appear, or when the comparison of thumbprints is inconclusive, the court shall refer the notice to appear or copy thereof back to the issuing agency for further investigation, unless the court finds that referral is not in the interest of justice.

(2) Upon initiation of the investigation or comparison process by referral of the court, the court shall continue the case and the speedy trial period shall be tolled for 45 days.

(3) Upon receipt of the issuing agency's or prosecuting attorney's response, the court may make a finding of factual innocence pursuant to Section 530.6 of the Penal Code if the court determines that there is insufficient evidence that the person cited is the person charged and shall immediately notify the Department of Motor Vehicles of its determination. If the Department of Motor Vehicles determines the citation or citations in question formed the basis of a suspension or revocation of the person's driving privilege, the department shall immediately set aside the action.

(4) If the prosecuting attorney or issuing agency fails to respond to a court referral within 45 days, the court shall make a finding of factual innocence pursuant to Section 530.6 of the Penal Code, unless the court finds that a finding of factual innocence is not in the interest of justice.

(5) The citation or notice to appear may be held by the prosecuting attorney or issuing agency for future adjudication should the arrestee who received the citation or notice to appear be found. *(Stats.1959, c. 3, p. 1777, § 40504. Amended by Stats.1963, c. 802, p. 1833, § 1; Stats.1995, c. 93 (A.B.219), § 4; Stats.2003, c. 467 (S.B.752), § 8.)*

Cross References

Violation a misdemeanor, see Vehicle Code § 40000.25.

Research References

4 Witkin, California Criminal Law 4th Illegally Obtained Evidence § 277 (2021), Search for Identification.
1 Witkin California Criminal Law 4th Introduction to Crimes § 76 (2021), Illustrations: Special Statute is Controlling.
1 Witkin California Criminal Law 4th Introduction to Crimes § 77 (2021), Illustrations: Special Statute is Not Controlling.
4 Witkin, California Criminal Law 4th Pretrial Proceedings § 51 (2021), Citation, Promise, and Release.

§ 40505. Copy of notice

Whenever any traffic or police officer delivers a notice to appear or notice of violation charging an offense under this code to any person, it shall include all information set forth upon the copy of the notice filed with a magistrate and no traffic or police officer shall set forth on any notice filed with a magistrate or attach thereto or accompany the notice with any written statement giving information or containing allegations which have not been delivered to the person receiving the notice to appear or notice of violation. *(Stats.1959, c. 3, p. 1778, § 40505. Amended by Stats.1969, c. 1056, p. 2039, § 2.)*

Cross References

Misdemeanor defined, see Penal Code § 17.

Research References

4 Witkin, California Criminal Law 4th Pretrial Proceedings § 51 (2021), Citation, Promise, and Release.

§ 40506. Filing copies

The officer shall, as soon as practicable, file a copy of the notice with the magistrate or before a person authorized by the magistrate or judge to receive a deposit of bail specified therein, and a copy with the commissioner, chief of police, sheriff or other superior officer of the arresting officer. *(Stats.1959, c. 3, p. 1778, § 40506.)*

Cross References

Nonresidents, offenses while driving commercially registered motor vehicles, guaranteed traffic arrest bail bond certificate in lieu of proceedings, see Vehicle Code § 40305.5.

Research References

4 Witkin, California Criminal Law 4th Pretrial Proceedings § 51 (2021), Citation, Promise, and Release.

§ 40506.5. Request for continuance; authorization

Prior to the date upon which the defendant promised to appear and without depositing bail, the defendant may request a continuance of the written promise to appear. A judge of the superior court may authorize the clerk to grant the continuance. *(Added by Stats.1979, c. 235, p. 489, § 1. Amended by Stats.1998, c. 931 (S.B.2139), § 462, eff. Sept. 28, 1998; Stats.2002, c. 784 (S.B.1316), § 604.)*

Law Revision Commission Comments

Section 40506.5 is amended to accommodate unification of the municipal and superior courts in a county. Cal. Const. art. VI, § 5(e). The section is also amended to reflect elimination of the justice court. Cal. Const. art. VI, 1, 5(b). [28 Cal.L.Rev.Comm. Reports 51 (1998)].

Section 40506.5 is amended to reflect unification of the municipal and superior courts pursuant to Article VI, Section 5(e), of the California Constitution. [32 Cal.L.Rev.Comm. Reports 545 (2002)].

Research References

5 Witkin, California Criminal Law 4th Criminal Trial § 401 (2021), Motion for Continuance.

§ 40507. Appearance by counsel

A written promise to appear in court may be complied with by an appearance by counsel. *(Stats.1959, c. 3, p. 1778, § 40507.)*

Cross References

Appearance defined, see Code of Civil Procedure § 1014.

Research References

4 Witkin, California Criminal Law 4th Pretrial Proceedings § 52 (2021), Appearance, Bail Forfeiture, or Trial.

§ 40508. Promise to appear; fine payment; court order condition; violations; driver's license impoundment

(a) A person willfully violating his or her written promise to appear or a lawfully granted continuance of his or her promise to appear in court or before a person authorized to receive a deposit of bail is guilty of a misdemeanor regardless of the disposition of the charge upon which he or she was originally arrested.

(b) A person willfully failing to pay bail in installments as agreed to under Section 40510.5 or a lawfully imposed fine for a violation of a provision of this code or a local ordinance adopted pursuant to this code within the time authorized by the court and without lawful excuse having been presented to the court on or before the date the bail or fine is due is guilty of a misdemeanor regardless of the full payment of the bail or fine after that time.

(c) A person willfully failing to comply with a condition of a court order for a violation of this code, other than for failure to appear or failure to pay a fine, is guilty of a misdemeanor, regardless of his or her subsequent compliance with the order.

(d) If a person convicted of an infraction fails to pay bail in installments as agreed to under Section 40510.5, or a fine or an installment thereof, within the time authorized by the court, the court may, except as otherwise provided in this subdivision, impound the person's driver's license and order the person not to drive for a period not to exceed 30 days. Before returning the license to the person, the court shall endorse on the reverse side of the license that the person was ordered not to drive, the period for which that order was made, and the name of the court making the order. If a defendant with a class C or M driver's license satisfies the court that impounding his or her driver's license and ordering the defendant not to drive will affect his or her livelihood, the court shall order that the person limit his or her driving for a period not to exceed 30 days to driving that is essential in the court's determination to the person's employment, including the person's driving to and from his or her place of employment if other means of transportation are not reasonably available. The court shall provide for the endorsement of the limitation on the person's license. The impounding of the license and ordering the person not to drive or the order limiting the person's driving does not constitute a suspension of the license, but a violation of the order constitutes contempt of court. *(Stats.1959, c. 3, p. 1778, § 40508. Amended by Stats.1961, c. 1653, p. 3608, § 2; Stats.1968, c. 1192, p. 2262, § 15, operative Jan. 1, 1969; Stats.1979, c. 235, p. 489, § 2; Stats.1987, c. 726, § 10, operative July 1, 1988; Stats.1993, c. 272 (A.B.301), § 56, eff. Aug. 2, 1993; Stats.1993, c. 909 (S.B.15), § 16; Stats.2003, c. 451 (A.B.1718), § 21; Stats.2007, c. 738 (A.B.1248), § 45.)*

Cross References

Bail, payment and forfeiture, see Vehicle Code § 40510.5.
Continuance, see Vehicle Code § 40506.5.
Misdemeanor defined, see Penal Code § 17.
One-time infraction amnesty program, eligibility, see Vehicle Code § 42008.8.
Public offenses, State Amnesty Program, eligible violations of this section, see Vehicle Code § 42008.7.

Refusal to appear, denial of license for, see Vehicle Code § 12807.
Renewal of license, checking record for failure to appear in court, see Vehicle Code § 12808.
Suspension of driver's license for violation of section, see Vehicle Code § 13365.
Violation a misdemeanor, see Vehicle Code § 40000.25.

Research References

California Jury Instructions - Criminal 16.880, Violation of Promise to Appear.
2 Witkin, California Criminal Law 4th Crimes Against Public Peace and Welfare § 265 (2021), In General.
6 Witkin, California Criminal Law 4th Criminal Judgment § 176 (2021), Fines and Fees.
5 Witkin, California Criminal Law 4th Criminal Trial § 512 (2021), In General.
1 Witkin California Criminal Law 4th Introduction to Crimes § 90 (2021), Misdemeanor-Infraction.
4 Witkin, California Criminal Law 4th Pretrial Proceedings § 53 (2021), Failure to Appear.
3 Witkin, California Criminal Law 4th Punishment § 108 (2021), Enforcement.
3 Witkin, California Criminal Law 4th Punishment § 213 (2021), In General.

§ 40508.6. Administrative assessments for costs

The superior court in any county may establish administrative assessments, not to exceed ten dollars ($10), for clerical and administrative costs incurred for * * * recording and maintaining a record of the defendant's prior convictions for violations of this code. The assessment shall be payable at the time of payment of a fine or when bail is forfeited for any subsequent violations of this code other than parking, pedestrian, or bicycle violations.

* * * *(Added by Stats.1991, c. 651 (S.B.757), § 3. Amended by Stats.1998, c. 931 (S.B.2139), § 463, eff. Sept. 28, 1998; Stats.2002, c. 784 (S.B.1316), § 604.5; Stats.2022, c. 800 (A.B.2746), § 22, eff. Jan. 1, 2023.)*

Law Revision Commission Comments

Section 40508.6 is amended to reflect elimination of the justice court. Cal. Const. art. VI, §§ 1, 5(b). [28 Cal.L.Rev.Comm. Reports 51 (1998)].

Section 40508.6 is amended to reflect unification of the municipal and superior courts pursuant to Article VI, Section 5(e), of the California Constitution.

The section is also amended to reflect enactment of the Trial Court Funding Act. See Gov't Code § 77001 (local trial court management).

Cross References

Carry over of unexpended funds by trial courts, funds excluded from calculation of amount authorized to be carried over commencing June 30, 2014, see Government Code § 77203.

§ 40509.1. Notice of willful failure to comply with certain court orders

If any person has willfully failed to comply with a court order, except a failure to appear, to pay a fine, or to attend traffic violator school, which was issued for a violation of this code, the magistrate or clerk of the court may give notice of the fact to the department. *(Added by Stats.1993, c. 158 (A.B.392), § 22.5, eff. July 21, 1993. Amended by Stats.1998, c. 877 (A.B.2132), § 77.)*

§ 40510. Deposit of bail or parking penalty; payment by personal check; agency policy

(a) Prior to the date upon which a defendant promised to appear, or prior to the expiration of any lawful continuance of that date, or upon receipt of information that an action has been filed and prior to the scheduled court date, the defendant may deposit bail with the magistrate or the person authorized to receive a deposit of bail.

(b) For any offense which is not declared to be a felony, a deposit of bail or a penalty may be by a personal check meeting the criteria established in accordance with subdivision (c).

(c) Each court, sheriff, or other agency which regularly accepts deposits of bail or penalties, shall adopt a written policy governing the acceptance of personal checks in payment of bail or penalty deposits. The policy shall permit clerks and other appropriate officers to accept personal checks under conditions which tend to assure the validity of the checks.

(d) The written policy governing the acceptance of personal checks adopted pursuant to subdivision (c) shall provide that the payee of the deposit made by personal check shall be the agency accepting the deposit. *(Stats.1959, c. 3, p. 1778, § 40510. Amended by Stats.1970, c. 299, p. 572, § 1; Stats.1979, c. 235, p. 490, § 4; Stats.1979, c. 951, p. 3278, § 1; Stats.1981, c. 775, p. 3029, § 3; Stats.1984, c. 481, § 4; Stats.1986, c. 939, § 18; Stats.1992, c. 1244 (A.B.408), § 34, operative July 1, 1993.)*

Research References

4 Witkin, California Criminal Law 4th Pretrial Proceedings § 52 (2021), Appearance, Bail Forfeiture, or Trial.
4 Witkin, California Criminal Law 4th Pretrial Proceedings § 105 (2021), Deposit of Cash, Check, or Money Order.

§ 40510.5. Payment and forfeiture of bail; circumstances

(a) The clerk of the court may accept a payment and forfeiture of at least 10 percent of the total bail amount for each infraction violation of this code prior to the date on which the defendant promised to appear, or prior to the expiration of any lawful continuance of that date, or upon receipt of information that an action has been filed and prior to the scheduled court date, if all of the following circumstances exist:

(1) The defendant is charged with an infraction violation of this code or an infraction violation of an ordinance adopted pursuant to this code.

(2) The defendant submits proof of correction, when proof of correction is mandatory for a correctable offense.

(3) The offense does not require an appearance in court.

(4) The defendant signs a written agreement to pay and forfeit the remainder of the required bail according to an installment schedule as agreed upon with the court. The Judicial Council shall prescribe the form of the agreement for payment and forfeiture of bail in installments for infraction violations.

(b) When a clerk accepts an agreement for payment and forfeiture of bail in installments, the clerk shall continue the appearance date of the defendant to the date to complete payment and forfeiture of bail in the agreement.

(c) Except for subdivisions (b) and (c) of Section 1269b and Section 1305.1, the provisions of Chapter 1 (commencing with Section 1268) of Title 10 of Part 2 of the Penal Code do not apply to an agreement to pay and forfeit bail in installments under this section.

(d) For the purposes of reporting violations of this code to the department under Section 1803, the date that the defendant signs an agreement to pay and forfeit bail in installments shall be reported as the date of conviction.

(e) When the defendant fails to make an installment payment according to an agreement under subdivision (a) above, the court may charge a failure to appear or pay under Section 40508 and impose a civil assessment as provided in Section 1214.1 of the Penal Code or issue an arrest warrant for a failure to appear.

(f) Payment of a bail amount under this section is forfeited when collected and shall be distributed by the court in the same manner as other fines, penalties, and forfeitures collected for infractions.

(g) This section shall become operative on January 1, 2022. *(Added by Stats.2021, c. 257 (A.B.177), § 44, eff. Sept. 23, 2021, operative Jan. 1, 2022.)*

Cross References

Development of online tool for adjudicating infraction violations, available requests, recommended payments, see Vehicle Code § 40282.

Research References

West's California Judicial Council Forms TR–300, Agreement to Pay and Forfeit Bail in Installments.
2 Witkin, California Criminal Law 4th Crimes Against Public Peace and Welfare § 265 (2021), In General.
4 Witkin, California Criminal Law 4th Pretrial Proceedings § 52 (2021), Appearance, Bail Forfeiture, or Trial.

§ 40511. Fixing bail

If bail has not been previously fixed and approved by the judges of the court in accordance with a schedule of bail, the magistrate shall fix the amount of bail which in his judgment, in accordance with Section 1275 of the Penal Code, will be reasonable and sufficient for the appearance of the defendant and shall endorse upon the notice a statement signed by him in the form set forth in Section 815a of the Penal Code. *(Stats.1959, c. 3, p. 1778, § 40511.)*

Cross References

Authority of municipal court commissioner or traffic referee to accept bail, see Government Code § 72304.

Research References

4 Witkin, California Criminal Law 4th Pretrial Proceedings § 88 (2021), Purpose of Bail.

§ 40512. Forfeiture of bail; guaranteed traffic arrest bail bond certificates

(a)(1) Except as specified in paragraph (2) and subdivision (b), if at the time the case is called for arraignment before the magistrate the defendant does not appear, either in person or by counsel, the magistrate may declare the bail forfeited and may, in his or her discretion, order that no further proceedings be had in the case, unless the defendant has been charged with a violation of Section 23111 or 23112, or subdivision (a) of Section 23113, and he or she has been previously convicted of the same offense, except if the magistrate finds that undue hardship will be imposed upon the defendant by requiring him or her to appear, the magistrate may declare the bail forfeited and order that no further proceedings shall be had in the case.

(2) If the defendant has posted surety bail and the magistrate has ordered the bail forfeited and that no further proceedings shall be had in the case, the bail retains the right to obtain relief from the forfeiture as provided in Section 1305 of the Penal Code if the amount of the bond, money, or property deposited exceeds seven hundred dollars ($700).

(b)(1) If, at the time the case is called for a compliance appearance before the magistrate, the defendant has entered into a bail installment agreement pursuant to Section 40510.5 but has not made an installment payment as agreed and does not appear, either in person or by counsel, the court may continue the arraignment to a date beyond the last agreed upon installment payment, issue a warrant of arrest, or impose a civil assessment as provided in Section 1214.1 of the Penal Code for the failure to appear.

(2) If, at the time the case is called for a compliance appearance before the magistrate, the defendant has paid all required bail funds and the defendant does not appear, either in person or by counsel, the court may order that no further proceedings shall be had in the case, unless the defendant has been charged with a violation of Section 23111 or 23112, or subdivision (a) of Section 23113, and he or she has been previously convicted of the same offense, except that if the magistrate finds that undue hardship will be imposed upon the defendant by requiring him or her to appear, the magistrate may order that no further proceedings shall be had in the case.

(c) Upon the making of the order that no further proceedings shall be had, all sums deposited as bail shall be paid into the city or county treasury, as the case may be.

(d) If a guaranteed traffic arrest bail bond certificate has been filed, the clerk of the court shall bill the issuer for the amount of bail fixed by the uniform countywide schedule of bail required under subdivision (c) of Section 1269b of the Penal Code.

(e) Upon presentation by a court of the bill for a fine or bail assessed against an individual covered by a guaranteed traffic arrest bail bond certificate, the issuer shall pay to the court the amount of the fine or forfeited bail that is within the maximum amount guaranteed by the terms of the certificate.

(f) The court shall return the guaranteed traffic arrest bail bond certificate to the issuer upon receipt of payment in accordance with subdivision (d). *(Stats.1959, c. 3, p. 1778, § 40512. Amended by Stats.1970, c. 1548, p. 3151, § 9; Stats.1982, c. 1394, p. 5310, § 4; Stats.1993, c. 524 (A.B.734), § 6; Stats.2006, c. 538 (S.B.1852), § 666; Stats.2007, c. 738 (A.B.1248), § 49.)*

Cross References

Equivalent of conviction, see Vehicle Code §§ 1803, 13103.
Inapplicability of forfeiture of bail provisions of Penal Code to cases arising under § 40500, see Penal Code § 1306.1.

Research References

4 Witkin, California Criminal Law 4th Pretrial Proceedings § 52 (2021), Appearance, Bail Forfeiture, or Trial.

§ 40512.5. Optional bail forfeiture

(a) Except as specified in subdivision (b), if at the time the case is called for trial the defendant does not appear, either in person or by counsel, and has not requested in writing that the trial proceed in his or her absence, the court may declare the bail forfeited and may, in its discretion, order that no further proceedings be had in the case, or the court may act pursuant to Section 1043 of the Penal Code. However, if the defendant has been charged with a violation of Section 23111 or 23112, or subdivision (a) of Section 23113, and he or she has been previously convicted of a violation of the same section, the court may declare the bail forfeited, but shall issue a bench warrant for the arrest of the person charged, except if the magistrate finds that undue hardship will be imposed upon the defendant by requiring him or her to appear, the magistrate may declare the bail forfeited and order that no further proceedings shall be had in the case.

(b) If the defendant has posted surety bail and the magistrate has ordered the bail forfeited and that no further proceedings shall be had in the case, the bail retains the right to obtain relief from the forfeiture as provided in Section 1305 of the Penal Code if the amount of the bond, money, or property deposited exceeds seven hundred dollars ($700). *(Added by Stats.1968, c. 1109, p. 2123, § 1. Amended by Stats.1970, c. 1548, p. 3151, § 10; Stats.1993, c. 524 (A.B.734), § 7.)*

Research References

4 Witkin, California Criminal Law 4th Pretrial Proceedings § 52 (2021), Appearance, Bail Forfeiture, or Trial.

§ 40512.6. Failure to submit proof of completion of traffic violators school; forfeiture of bail

(a) If a defendant who elects or is ordered to attend a traffic violator school in accordance with Section 42005 and has paid the full traffic violator school bail amount required under Section 42007 fails to successfully complete the program within the time ordered by the court or any extension thereof, the court may, following notice to the defendant, order that the fee paid by the defendant be converted to bail and declare the bail forfeited. The bail forfeiture under this section shall be distributed as provided by Section 42007. Upon forfeiture of the bail, the court may order that no further proceedings shall be had in the case.

(b) This section shall become operative on July 1, 2011. *(Added by Stats.2010, c. 599 (A.B.2499), § 11.5, operative July 1, 2011.)*

Cross References

State surcharge on state penalty imposed on fines, penalties, or forfeitures imposed and collected by the courts for offenses involving Vehicle Code violations, exceptions, see Penal Code § 1465.7.

§ 40513. Filing of notice in lieu of complaint

(a) Whenever written notice to appear has been prepared, delivered, and filed with the court, an exact and legible duplicate copy of the notice when filed with the magistrate, in lieu of a verified complaint, shall constitute a complaint to which the defendant may plead "guilty" or "nolo contendere."

If, however, the defendant violates his or her promise to appear in court or does not deposit lawful bail, or pleads other than "guilty" or "nolo contendere" to the offense charged, a complaint shall be filed that shall conform to Chapter 2 (commencing with Section 948) of Title 5 of Part 2 of the Penal Code, which shall be deemed to be an original complaint, and thereafter proceedings shall be had as provided by law, except that a defendant may, by an agreement in writing, subscribed by him or her and filed with the court, waive the filing of a verified complaint and elect that the prosecution may proceed upon a written notice to appear.

(b) Notwithstanding subdivision (a), whenever the written notice to appear has been prepared on a form approved by the Judicial Council, an exact and legible duplicate copy of the notice when filed with the magistrate shall constitute a complaint to which the defendant may enter a plea and, if the notice to appear is verified, upon which a warrant may be issued. If the notice to appear is not verified, the defendant may, at the time of arraignment, request that a verified complaint be filed. In the case of an infraction violation in which the defendant is a minor, the defendant may enter a plea at the arraignment upon a written notice to appear. Notwithstanding any other provision of law, in the case of an infraction violation, no consent of the minor is required prior to conducting the hearing upon a written notice to appear. *(Stats.1959, c. 3, p. 1778, § 40513. Amended by Stats.1959, c. 606, p. 2591, § 6; Stats.1963, c. 325, p. 1111, § 1; Stats.1965, c. 1190, p. 3006, § 1; Stats.1968, c. 906, p. 1697, § 2; Stats.1996, c. 124 (A.B.3470), § 143; Stats.1997, c. 17 (S.B.947), § 145; Stats.2001, c. 830 (S.B.940), § 1.)*

Research References

West's California Judicial Council Forms TR–106, Continuation of Notice to Appear.
West's California Judicial Council Forms TR–108, Continuation of Citation.
West's California Judicial Council Forms TR–130, Traffic/Nontraffic Notice to Appear.
West's California Judicial Council Forms TR–135, Electronic Traffic/Nontraffic Notice to Appear (4 Format).
West's California Judicial Council Forms TR–145, Electronic Traffic/Nontraffic Notice to Appear (3 Format).
1 Witkin California Criminal Law 4th Defenses § 130 (2021), Competency of Court and Jury.
4 Witkin, California Criminal Law 4th Pretrial Proceedings § 52 (2021), Appearance, Bail Forfeiture, or Trial.
4 Witkin, California Criminal Law 4th Pretrial Proceedings § 53 (2021), Failure to Appear.

§ 40514. Issuance of warrant

No warrant shall issue on the charge for the arrest of a person who has given his written promise to appear in court or before a person authorized to receive a deposit of bail, unless he has violated the promise, the lawfully granted continuance of his promise, or has failed to deposit bail, to appear for arraignment, trial or judgment, or to comply with the terms and provisions of the judgment, as required by law. *(Stats.1959, c. 3, p. 1779, § 40514. Amended by Stats.1979, c. 235, p. 491, § 5.)*

Cross References

Arrest on failure to post bond, see Vehicle Code § 40515.

Research References

4 Witkin, California Criminal Law 4th Pretrial Proceedings § 53 (2021), Failure to Appear.

§ 40515. Issuance of warrant for violation of promise to appear or continuance of promise to appear

(a) When a person signs a written promise to appear or is granted a continuance of his or her promise to appear at the time and place specified in the written promise to appear or the continuance thereof, and has not posted full bail or has failed to pay an installment of bail as agreed to under Section 40510.5, the magistrate may issue and have delivered for execution a warrant for his or her arrest within 20 days after his or her failure to appear before the magistrate or pay an installment of bail as agreed, or if the person promises to appear before an officer authorized to accept bail other than a magistrate and fails to do so on or before the date on which he or she promised to appear, then, within 20 days after the delivery of the written promise to appear by the officer to a magistrate having jurisdiction over the offense.

(b) When the person violates his or her promise to appear before an officer authorized to receive bail other than a magistrate, the officer shall immediately deliver to a magistrate having jurisdiction over the offense charged the written promise to appear and the complaint, if any, filed by the arresting officer. *(Stats.1959, c. 3, p. 1779, § 40515. Amended by Stats.1968, c. 831, p. 1603, § 1; Stats.1971, c. 1042, p. 1998, § 1, operative May 3, 1972; Stats.1979, c. 235, p. 491, § 6; Stats.2007, c. 738 (A.B.1248), § 51.)*

Cross References

Bail, generally, see Penal Code § 1268 et seq.

Research References

4 Witkin, California Criminal Law 4th Pretrial Proceedings § 53 (2021), Failure to Appear.

§ 40516. Expense to departments

(a) The expenses incurred by the Department of the California Highway Patrol and the Department of Motor Vehicles in executing any warrant issued as a result of a notice to appear issued by a member of the California Highway Patrol shall be a legal charge against the city or county in which jurisdiction the warrant was issued except where the commissioner authorizes the acceptance of a warrant for execution within 30 days of the date of its issuance.

(b) The commissioner or director shall certify to the Controller the cost of executing warrants on behalf of each city or county under this section. The departments shall be reimbursed for costs as provided in Section 11004.5 of the Revenue and Taxation Code.

(c) The peace officer to whom a warrant has been delivered for execution, upon demand, shall transfer the warrant, if it has not been executed within 30 days of the date of its issuance, to any member of the California Highway Patrol or to the Department of Motor Vehicles for execution. *(Stats.1959, c. 3, p. 1779, § 40516. Amended by Stats.1959, c. 1996, p. 4640, § 52.)*

Cross References

County charges, generally, see Government Code § 29600 et seq.
Deduction from allocations of amounts chargeable to each city and county under this section, see Revenue and Taxation Code § 11004.5.
Police authority of members of highway patrol, see Vehicle Code § 2409.

Service of warrants by highway patrol, see Vehicle Code § 2411.

§ 40518. Certain violations recorded by automated traffic enforcement system; notice to appear; contents; notice of nonliability; form; dismissal

(a) Whenever a written notice to appear has been issued by a peace officer or by a qualified employee of a law enforcement agency on a form approved by the Judicial Council for an alleged violation of Section 22451, or, based on an alleged violation of Section 21453, 21455, or 22101 recorded by an automated traffic enforcement system pursuant to Section 21455.5 or 22451, and delivered by mail within 15 days of the alleged violation to the current address of the registered owner of the vehicle on file with the department, with a certificate of mailing obtained as evidence of service, an exact and legible duplicate copy of the notice when filed with the magistrate shall constitute a complaint to which the defendant may enter a plea. Preparation and delivery of a notice to appear pursuant to this section is not an arrest.

(b)(1) A notice to appear shall contain the name and address of the person, the license plate number of the person's vehicle, the violation charged, including a description of the offense, and the time and place when, and where, the person may appear in court or before a person authorized to receive a deposit of bail. The time specified shall be at least 10 days after the notice to appear is delivered. If, after the notice to appear has been issued, the citing peace officer or qualified employee of a law enforcement agency determines that, in the interest of justice, the citation or notice should be dismissed, the citing agency may recommend, in writing, to the magistrate or the judge that the case be dismissed. The recommendation shall cite the reasons for the recommendation and be filed with the court. If the magistrate or judge makes a finding that there are grounds for dismissal, the finding shall be entered on the record and the infraction dismissed.

(2) A notice to appear shall also contain all of the following information:

(A) The methods by which the registered owner of the vehicle or the alleged violator may view and discuss with the issuing agency, both by telephone and in person, the evidence used to substantiate the violation.

(B) The contact information of the issuing agency.

(c)(1) This section and Section 40520 do not preclude the issuing agency or the manufacturer or supplier of the automated traffic enforcement system from mailing a notice of nonliability to the registered owner of the vehicle or the alleged violator prior to issuing a notice to appear. The notice of nonliability shall be substantively identical to the following form:

COURTESY NOTICE: THIS IS NOT A TICKET

[insert name of jurisdiction]
PHOTO ENFORCEMENT PROGRAM
Agency Address:

<Name>
<Address>
<City State, Zip>

VIOLATION #						
ADDRESS			CITY		STATE	ZIP
COLOR	YEAR	MAKE	MODEL	STYLE	LICENSE PLATE	STATE
MONTH	DAY	YEAR	TIME			
LOCATION			VEHICLE SPEED		POSTED SPEED	
Statute			**Violation Description**			
Officer's Name			**Badge #**			

SCENE A	SCENE B
ZOOM FACE	ZOOM PLATE

Certificate of Mailing

I, (name_of_mailer), of____________________________________, do certify that I am over 18 years old and not a party to the above entitled case. On (Print_Date) I placed this Notice in an envelope addressed to the registered owner or lessee as shown above, sealed it and deposited the envelope in a United States Postal Service receptacle located in (city, state). In the ordinary course of business, the envelope is sealed, affixed with proper postage and mailed. I declare under the penalty of perjury under the laws of the State of California that the foregoing is true and correct.

Dated:

Signature of Mailer

(Code of Civil Procedure 1013a [3], 2015.5)

COURTESY NOTICE: THIS IS NOT A TICKET

[Insert agency name]

INSTRUCTION PAGE

The Reason You Received This Notice:
A vehicle registered in your name was photographed failing to stop for an official red light traffic control signal. This is a violation of the State of California Vehicle Code Section 21453(a) or (c) pursuant to Section 21455 5

You are encouraged to view the video of this violation and to respond to this notice. You may make an appointment to view the evidence by calling the [insert agency name] at (000) 000-0000. During this viewing, an officer or qualified employee will show you a high quality video and still images depicting the violation in greater detail than the printed photos in this notice.

You can also view the video online at www 0000000000.

The video is available online for 60 days from the date of violation. After 60 days an appointment must be made with [insert agency name].

DO NOT CALL THE COURT REGARDING THIS NOTICE. For additional questions contact the Photo Enforcement Program at (000) 000-0000.

Tear Here Tear Here Tear Here

NOTICE OF NON-LIABILITY

IF YOU WERE NOT THE DRIVER/OWNER
Violation #: <<Enter #>>

Last Issued To: <<Enter Name>>

[Insert agency name]

CHECK ONE:
☐ **The person named below was the driver of the vehicle.**
☐ **I sold the vehicle prior to the violation date to the person named below.**
☐ **I have never owned this vehicle or license plate.**

CHECK ONE:
☐ **I am an individual.**
☐ **I am a car rental or leasing company.**

Print Actual Driver/New Owner's Name: ____________ **Driver's License/ID No.:** ____________

Address: ____________ **Issued in the State of:** ____________

City, State, ZIP Code: ____________ **Date of Birth:** ____________

Gender: ______ **Hair Color:** ______ **Eye Color:** ______ **Height:** ______ **Weight:** ______

DECLARATION
I CERTIFY THAT THE FOREGOING IS TRUE AND CORRECT

Signature ____________ **Print Name** ____________

Your Telephone Number (   ) ____ - ____ **Date** ____________

(2) The form specified in paragraph (1) may be translated to other languages.

(d) A manufacturer or supplier of an automated traffic enforcement system or the governmental agency operating the system shall not alter the notice to appear or any other form approved by the Judicial Council. If a form is found to have been materially altered, the citation based on the altered form may be dismissed. *(Added by Stats.1994, c. 1216 (S.B.1802), § 7. Amended by Stats.1995, c. 922 (S.B.833), § 8; Stats.1998, c. 54 (S.B.1136), § 6; Stats.2012, c. 735 (S.B.1303), § 4.)*

Cross References

Evidence,
Printed representation of computer-generated information, see Evidence Code § 1552.
Printed representation of video or digital images, see Evidence Code § 1553.
Offenses, automated traffic enforcement system, requirements, use of printed representation as evidence, confidentiality and retention of records, review of alleged violation by registered owner, manufacturers and suppliers, duties and contract limitations, see Vehicle Code § 21455.5.

Research References

West's California Judicial Council Forms TR–115, Automated Traffic Enforcement System Notice to Appear.

§ 40519. Trial scheduling; written not guilty plea

(a) Any person who has received a written notice to appear for an infraction may, prior to the time at which the person is required to appear, make a deposit and declare the intention to plead not guilty to the clerk of the court named in the notice to appear. The deposit shall be in the amount of bail established pursuant to Section 1269b of the Penal Code, together with any assessment required by Section 42006 of this code or Section 1464 of the Penal Code, for the offense charged, and shall be used for the purpose of guaranteeing the appearance of the defendant at the time and place scheduled by the clerk for arraignment and for trial, and to apply toward the payment of any fine or assessment prescribed by the court in the event of conviction. The case shall thereupon be set for arraignment and trial on the same date, unless the defendant requests separate arraignment. A deposit of bail under this section does not constitute entry of a plea or a court appearance. A plea of not guilty under this section must be made in court at the arraignment.

(b) Any person who has received a written notice to appear may, prior to the time at which the person is required to appear, plead not guilty in writing in lieu of appearing in person. The written plea shall be directed to the court named in the notice to appear and, if mailed, shall be sent by certified or registered mail postmarked not later than five days prior to the day upon which appearance is required. The written plea and request to the court or city agency shall be accompanied by a deposit consisting of the amount of bail established pursuant to Section 1269b of the Penal Code, together with any assessment required by Section 42006 of this code or Section 1464 of the Penal Code, for that offense, which amount shall be used for the purpose of guaranteeing the appearance of the defendant at the time and place set by the court for trial and to apply toward the payment of any fine or assessment prescribed by the court in the event of conviction. Upon receipt of the plea and deposit, the case shall be set for arraignment and trial on the same date, unless the defendant requests separate arraignment. Thereafter, the case shall be conducted in the same manner as if the defendant had appeared in person, had made his or her plea in open court, and had deposited that sum as bail. The court or the clerk of the court shall notify the accused of the time and place of trial by first-class mail postmarked at least 10 days prior to the time set for the trial. Any person using this procedure shall be deemed to have waived the right to be tried within the statutory period.

(c) Any person using the procedure set forth in subdivision (a) or (b) shall be deemed to have given a written promise to appear at the time designated by the court for trial, and failure to appear at the trial shall constitute a misdemeanor. *(Added by Stats.1975, c. 1257, p. 3296, § 3. Amended by Stats.1983, c. 210, § 1; Stats.1986, c. 631, § 1; Stats.1986, c. 953, § 15.5; Stats.1987, c. 852, § 7; Stats.1992, c. 1244 (A.B.408), § 35, operative July 1, 1993; Stats.2009, c. 35 (S.B.174), § 30.)*

Cross References

Violation a misdemeanor, see Vehicle Code § 40000.25.

Research References

West's California Judicial Council Forms TR–505, Notice and Waiver of Rights and Request for Remote Video Arraignment and Trial.
4 Witkin, California Criminal Law 4th Pretrial Proceedings § 300 (2021), Plea Options for Infractions.

§ 40520. Automatic enforcement system violation; notice to appear; affidavit of nonliability

(a) A notice to appear issued pursuant to Section 40518 for an alleged violation recorded by an automatic enforcement system shall contain, or be accompanied by, an affidavit of nonliability and information as to what constitutes nonliability, information as to the effect of executing the affidavit, and instructions for returning the affidavit to the issuing agency.

(b)(1) If a notice to appear is sent to a car rental or leasing company, as the registered owner of the vehicle, the company may return the notice of nonliability pursuant to paragraph (2), if the violation occurred when the vehicle was either leased or rented and operated by a person other than an employee of the rental or leasing company.

(2) If the affidavit of nonliability is returned to the issuing agency by the registered owner within 30 days of the mailing of the notice to appear together with the proof of a written rental agreement or lease between a bona fide renting or leasing company and its customer and that agreement identifies the renter or lessee and provides the driver's license number, name, and address of the renter or lessee, the agency shall cancel the notice for the registered owner to appear and shall, instead, issue a notice to appear to the renter or lessee identified in the affidavit of nonliability.

(c) Nothing in this section precludes an issuing agency from establishing a procedure whereby registered owners, other than bona fide renting and leasing companies, may execute an affidavit of nonliability if the registered owner identifies the person who was the driver of the vehicle at the time of the alleged violation and whereby the issuing agency issues a notice to appear to that person. *(Added by Stats.1998, c. 828 (S.B.1637), § 26.)*

§ 40521. Forfeiture of bail; payment of assessments

(a) Except when personal appearance is required by the bail schedule established under Section 1269b of the Penal Code, a person to whom a notice to appear has been issued under Section 40500, who intends to forfeit bail and to pay any assessment may forward by United States mail the full amount fixed as bail, together with the appropriate amount of any assessment, to the person authorized to receive a deposit of bail. The amounts may be paid in the form of a personal check which meets the criteria established pursuant to subdivision (c) of Section 40510, or a bank cashier's check or a money order. Bail and any assessment shall be paid not later than the day of appearance set forth in the notice to appear or prior to the expiration of any lawful continuance of that date.

(b) Bail forwarded by mail is effective only when the funds are actually received.

(c) Paragraph (1) of subdivision (a) of Section 40512 is applicable to bail paid pursuant to this section. Upon the making of the order pursuant to Section 40512 that no further proceedings be had, the amount paid as bail shall be paid into the city or county treasury, as the case may be, and the assessment shall be transmitted to the State Treasury in the manner provided in Section 1464 of the Penal Code. *(Added by Stats.1976, c. 127, p. 204, § 1, operative Jan. 1, 1978. Amended by Stats.1980, c. 561, p. 1548, § 7; Stats.1981, c. 775, p. 3029, § 4; Stats.1986, c. 939, § 19; Stats.1986, c. 953, § 16; Stats.1992, c. 1244 (A.B.408), § 36, operative July 1, 1993; Stats.2007, c. 738 (A.B.1248), § 52.)*

Research References

4 Witkin, California Criminal Law 4th Pretrial Proceedings § 105 (2021), Deposit of Cash, Check, or Money Order.
4 Witkin, California Criminal Law 4th Pretrial Proceedings § 300 (2021), Plea Options for Infractions.

§ 40522. Notice; registration, license or mechanical violations; dismissal on proof of correction

Whenever a person is arrested for violations specified in Section 40303.5 and none of the disqualifying conditions set forth in subdivision (b) of Section 40610 exist, and the officer issues a notice to appear, the notice shall specify the offense charged and note in a form approved by the Judicial Council that the charge shall be dismissed on proof of correction. If the arrested person presents, by mail or in person, proof of correction, as prescribed in Section 40616, on or before the date on which the person promised to appear, the court shall dismiss the violation or violations charged pursuant to Section 40303.5. *(Added by Stats.1979, c. 71, p. 173, § 3, eff. May 19, 1979. Amended by Stats.1979, c. 874, p. 3045, § 1, eff. Sept. 22, 1979; Stats.1984, c. 915, § 2, operative July 1, 1985; Stats.1985, c. 898, § 1; Stats.1989, c. 729, § 4, operative July 1, 1990; Stats.1991, c. 1168 (A.B.2142), § 8, eff. Oct. 14, 1991; Stats.1992, c. 258 (S.B.133), § 5.)*

Research References

West's California Judicial Council Forms TR–106, Continuation of Notice to Appear.
West's California Judicial Council Forms TR–108, Continuation of Citation.
West's California Judicial Council Forms TR–130, Traffic/Nontraffic Notice to Appear.
West's California Judicial Council Forms TR–135, Electronic Traffic/Nontraffic Notice to Appear (4 Format).
West's California Judicial Council Forms TR–145, Electronic Traffic/Nontraffic Notice to Appear (3 Format).

4 Witkin, California Criminal Law 4th Pretrial Proceedings § 54 (2021), Promise to Correct Violation.

ARTICLE 3. NOTICE OF VIOLATION

§ 40600. Notice to appear; reasonable cause for issuance

(a) Notwithstanding any other provision of law, a peace officer who has successfully completed a course or courses of instruction, approved by the Commission on Peace Officer Standards and Training, in the investigation of traffic accidents may prepare, in triplicate, on a form approved by the Judicial Council, a written notice to appear when the peace officer has reasonable cause to believe that any person involved in a traffic accident has violated a provision of this code not declared to be a felony or a local ordinance and the violation was a factor in the occurrence of the traffic accident.

(b) A notice to appear shall contain the name and address of the person, the license number of the person's vehicle, if any, the name and address, when available, of the registered owner or lessee of the vehicle, the offense charged, and the time and place when and where the person may appear in court or before a person authorized to receive a deposit of bail. The time specified shall be at least 10 days after the notice to appear is delivered.

(c) The preparation and delivery of a notice to appear pursuant to this section is not an arrest.

(d) For purposes of this article, a peace officer has reasonable cause to issue a written notice to appear if, as a result of the officer's investigation, the officer has evidence, either testimonial or real, or a combination of testimonial and real, that would be sufficient to issue a written notice to appear if the officer had personally witnessed the events investigated.

(e) As used in this section, "peace officer" means any person specified under Section 830.1 or 830.2 of the Penal Code, or any reserve police officer or reserve deputy sheriff listed in Section 830.6 of the Penal Code, with the exception of members of the California National Guard.

(f) A written notice to appear prepared on a form approved by the Judicial Council and issued pursuant to this section shall be accepted by any court. *(Added by Stats.1974, c. 794, p. 1737, § 2. Amended by Stats.1975, c. 525, p. 1091, § 1; Stats.1978, c. 722, p. 2253, § 2; Stats.1979, c. 229, p. 483, § 4; Stats.1987, c. 191, § 1; Stats.1992, c. 1242 (S.B.602), § 5; Stats.1996, c. 1155 (S.B.1587), § 8; Stats.2003, c. 292 (A.B.1436), § 12.)*

Cross References

Criminal procedure, deputized or appointed peace officers, see Penal Code § 830.6.

Research References

West's California Judicial Council Forms TR–106, Continuation of Notice to Appear.
West's California Judicial Council Forms TR–130, Traffic/Nontraffic Notice to Appear.
West's California Judicial Council Forms TR–135, Electronic Traffic/Non-traffic Notice to Appear (4 Format).
West's California Judicial Council Forms TR–145, Electronic Traffic/Non-traffic Notice to Appear (3 Format).
4 Witkin, California Criminal Law 4th Pretrial Proceedings § 55 (2021), Notice of Violation in Traffic Accident.

§ 40604. Issuance of warrant

(a) If the person charged with the offense has not signed a promise to appear, no warrant for arrest may be issued following the filing of the written notice to appear issued pursuant to Section 40600, until 15 days after a notice of the filing has been served upon the person by personal delivery or by mail, addressed to the person at the address shown in the accident report.

(b) The notice shall contain the name and address of the person, the license number of the vehicle involved, the name and address, when available, of the registered owner or lessee of the vehicle, the offense shown on the written notice to appear, and the approximate time of the commission of the offense. The notice shall inform the person that, unless he or she appears in the court designated in the notice within 10 days after the service of the notice and answers the charges, a warrant will be issued for his or her arrest.

(c) Proof of service shall be made by the affidavit of any person over 18 years of age making the service showing the time, place, and manner of service and facts showing that the service was made in accordance with this section. If service is made by mail, no warrant for arrest may be issued until 14 days after the deposit of the notice of filing in the mail. *(Added by Stats.1974, c. 794, p. 1738, § 4. Amended by Stats.1992, c. 1242 (S.B.602), § 9; Stats.1992, c. 1243 (A.B.3090), § 107.7, eff. Sept. 30, 1992, operative Jan. 1, 1993.)*

Research References

4 Witkin, California Criminal Law 4th Pretrial Proceedings § 55 (2021), Notice of Violation in Traffic Accident.

ARTICLE 4. NOTICE TO CORRECT VIOLATION

§ 40610. Registration, license, safety certificate, or mechanical violations; conditions for use; proof of corrections

Section operative until Jan. 1, 2027. See, also, § 40610 operative Jan. 1, 2027.

(a)(1) Except as provided in paragraph (2), if, after an arrest, crash investigation, or other law enforcement action, it appears that a violation has occurred involving a registration, license, all-terrain vehicle safety certificate, or mechanical requirement of this code, and none of the disqualifying conditions set forth in subdivision (b) exist and the investigating officer decides to take enforcement action, the officer shall prepare, in triplicate, and the violator shall sign, a written notice containing the violator's promise to correct the alleged violation and to deliver proof of correction of the violation to the issuing agency.

(2) If a person is arrested for a violation of Section 4454, and none of the disqualifying conditions set forth in subdivision (b) exist, the arresting officer shall prepare, in triplicate, and the violator shall sign, a written notice containing the violator's promise to correct the alleged violation and to deliver proof of correction of the violation to the issuing agency. In lieu of issuing a notice to correct violation pursuant to this section, the officer may issue a notice to appear, as specified in Section 40522.

(b) Pursuant to subdivision (a), a notice to correct violation shall be issued as provided in this section or a notice to appear shall be issued as provided in Section 40522, unless the officer finds any of the following:

(1) Evidence of fraud or persistent neglect.

(2) The violation presents an immediate safety hazard.

(3) The violator does not agree to, or cannot, promptly correct the violation.

(4) The violation cited is of subdivision (a) of Section 27151 for a motorcycle.

(c) If any of the conditions set forth in subdivision (b) exist, the procedures specified in this section or Section 40522 are inapplicable, and the officer may take other appropriate enforcement action.

(d) Except as otherwise provided in subdivision (a), the notice to correct violation shall be on a form approved by the Judicial Council and, in addition to the owner's or operator's address and identifying information, shall contain an estimate of the reasonable time required for correction and proof of correction of the particular defect, not to exceed 30 days, or 90 days for the all-terrain vehicle safety certificate.

(e) This section shall remain in effect only until January 1, 2027, and as of that date is repealed. *(Added by Stats.1978, c. 1350, p. 4479, § 3, operative July 1, 1979. Amended by Stats.1979, c. 71, p. 173, § 2, eff. May 19, 1979; Stats.1980, c. 399, p. 785, § 9, eff. July 11, 1980; Stats.1982, c. 466, p. 2059, § 119; Stats.1982, c. 402, p. 1739, § 2; Stats.1984, c. 915, § 3, operative July 1, 1985; Stats.1985, c. 898, § 2; Stats.1989, c. 729, § 5, operative July 1, 1990; Stats.1991, c. 90 (A.B.1297), § 71, eff. June 30, 1991; Stats.1992, c. 258 (S.B.133), § 6; Stats.2004, c. 908 (A.B.2666), § 27; Stats.2018, c. 38 (A.B.1824), § 4, eff. June 27, 2018; Stats.2019, c. 364 (S.B.112), § 19, eff. Sept. 27, 2019; Stats.2022, c. 595 (A.B.2496), § 4, eff. Jan. 1, 2023.)*

Repeal

For repeal of this section, see its terms.

Cross References

Arrest for certain offenses, notice to correct, see Vehicle Code § 40303.5.
Dismissal of charge on proof of correction, see Vehicle Code § 40522.
Exhaust products, heavy-duty vehicles, correctable violation, see Vehicle Code § 27153.
Heavy-duty vehicle, malfunction indicator light (MIL) displaying engine symbol F01, mechanical violation, correction, see Vehicle Code § 24019.
Notice to appear, dismissal upon proof of correction, see Vehicle Code § 40522.

Research References

4 Witkin, California Criminal Law 4th Pretrial Proceedings § 54 (2021), Promise to Correct Violation.

§ 40610. Registration, license, safety certificate, or mechanical violations; conditions for use; proof of corrections

Section operative Jan. 1, 2027. See, also, § 40610 operative until Jan. 1, 2027.

(a)(1) Except as provided in paragraph (2), if, after an arrest, crash investigation, or other law enforcement action, it appears that a violation has occurred involving a registration, license, all-terrain vehicle safety certificate, or mechanical requirement of this code, and none of the disqualifying conditions set forth in subdivision (b) exist and the investigating officer decides to take enforcement action, the officer shall prepare, in triplicate, and the violator shall sign, a written notice containing the violator's promise to correct the alleged violation and to deliver proof of correction of the violation to the issuing agency.

(2) If a person is arrested for a violation of Section 4454, and none of the disqualifying conditions set forth in subdivision (b) exist, the arresting officer shall prepare, in triplicate, and the violator shall sign, a written notice containing the violator's promise to correct the alleged violation and to deliver proof of correction of the violation to the issuing agency. In lieu of issuing a notice to correct violation pursuant to this section, the officer may issue a notice to appear, as specified in Section 40522.

(b) Pursuant to subdivision (a), a notice to correct violation shall be issued as provided in this section or a notice to appear shall be issued as provided in Section 40522, unless the officer finds any of the following:

(1) Evidence of fraud or persistent neglect.

(2) The violation presents an immediate safety hazard.

(3) The violator does not agree to, or cannot, promptly correct the violation.

(c) If any of the conditions set forth in subdivision (b) exist, the procedures specified in this section or Section 40522 are inapplicable, and the officer may take other appropriate enforcement action.

(d) Except as otherwise provided in subdivision (a), the notice to correct violation shall be on a form approved by the Judicial Council and, in addition to the owner's or operator's address and identifying information, shall contain an estimate of the reasonable time required for correction and proof of correction of the particular defect, not to exceed 30 days, or 90 days for the all-terrain vehicle safety certificate.

(e) This section shall become operative on January 1, 2027. *(Added by Stats.2022, c. 595 (A.B.2496), § 5, eff. Jan. 1, 2023, operative Jan. 1, 2027.)*

Cross References

Arrest for certain offenses, notice to correct, see Vehicle Code § 40303.5.
Dismissal of charge on proof of correction, see Vehicle Code § 40522.
Exhaust products, heavy-duty vehicles, correctable violation, see Vehicle Code § 27153.
Heavy-duty vehicle, malfunction indicator light (MIL) displaying engine symbol F01, mechanical violation, correction, see Vehicle Code § 24019.
Notice to appear, dismissal upon proof of correction, see Vehicle Code § 40522.

§ 40611. Transaction fee upon proof of correction of alleged violation

(a) Upon proof of correction of an alleged violation of Section 12500 or 12951, or any violation cited pursuant to Section 40610, or upon submission of evidence of financial responsibility pursuant to subdivision (e) of Section 16028, the clerk shall collect a twenty-five-dollar ($25) transaction fee for each violation. The fees shall be deposited by the clerk in accordance with Section 68084 of the Government Code.

(b)(1) For each citation, ten dollars ($10) shall be allocated monthly as follows:

(A) Thirty-three percent shall be transferred to the local governmental entity in whose jurisdiction the citation was issued for deposit in the general fund of the entity.

(B) Thirty-four percent shall be transferred to the State Treasury for deposit in the State Penalty Fund established by Section 1464 of the Penal Code.

(C) Thirty-three percent shall be deposited in the county general fund.

(2) The remainder of the fees collected on each citation shall be deposited in the State Court Facilities Construction Fund, established in Section 70371 of the Government Code.

(c) No fee shall be imposed pursuant to this section if the violation notice is processed only by the issuing agency and no record of the action is transmitted to the court. *(Added by Stats.1991, c. 90 (A.B.1297), § 72, eff. June 30, 1991. Amended by Stats.1991, c. 189 (A.B.544), § 42, eff. July 29, 1991; Stats.1991, c. 613 (A.B.195), § 11; Stats.1992, c. 427 (A.B.3355), § 168; Stats.1994, c. 704 (S.B.1699), § 23; Stats.1996, c. 1126 (A.B.650), § 16, operative Jan. 1, 1997; Stats.1999, c. 880 (S.B.652), § 21; Stats.2008, c. 311 (S.B.1407), § 30; Stats.2021, c. 79 (A.B.143), § 37, eff. July 16, 2021.)*

Cross References

Bicycle helmets required for persons under 18 to operate a bicycle, nonmotorized scooter, skateboard, or in-line or roller skates, passenger requirements, helmet conformity to safety standards, sales of helmet, violations, allocation of fines collected, see Vehicle Code § 21212.

§ 40612. Copies; delivery to violators

An exact, legible copy of the notice to correct shall be delivered to the alleged violator at the time he or she signs such notice. *(Added by Stats.1978, c. 1350, p. 4479, § 3, operative July 1, 1979.)*

§ 40614. False or fictitious names; signatures; misdemeanor

Any person who signs a notice to correct or a certificate of correction with a false or fictitious name is guilty of a misdemeanor. *(Added by Stats.1978, c. 1350, p. 4479, § 3, operative July 1, 1979.)*

Cross References

Violation as misdemeanor, see Vehicle Code § 40000.25.

Research References

4 Witkin, California Criminal Law 4th Pretrial Proceedings § 54 (2021), Promise to Correct Violation.

§ 40616. Failure to correct; proof of correction; misdemeanor

Any person willfully violating a written promise to correct or willfully failing to deliver proof of correction of violation is guilty of a misdemeanor. Proof of correction may consist of a certification by an authorized representative of one of the following agencies that the alleged violation has been corrected:

(a) Brake, lamp, smog device, or muffler violations may be certified as corrected by any station licensed to inspect and certify for the violation pursuant to Article 8 (commencing with Section 9889.15) of Chapter 20.3 of Division 3 of the Business and Professions Code and Section 27150.2.

(b) Driver license and registration violations may be certified as corrected by the Department of Motor Vehicles or by any clerk or deputy clerk of a court.

(c) Any violation may be certified as corrected by a police department, the California Highway Patrol, sheriff, marshal, or other law enforcement agency regularly engaged in enforcement of the Vehicle Code. *(Added by Stats.1978, c. 1350, p. 4479, § 3, operative July 1, 1979. Amended by Stats.1983, c. 361, § 1.)*

Cross References

Dismissal of charge on proof of correction, see Vehicle Code § 40522.
Notice to appear, dismissal upon proof of correction, see Vehicle Code § 40522.
Violation as misdemeanor, see Vehicle Code § 40000.25.

Research References

4 Witkin, California Criminal Law 4th Pretrial Proceedings § 54 (2021), Promise to Correct Violation.

§ 40618. Failure to receive proof of correction; delivery of signed promise; certification; complaint; warrant

Whenever proof of correction of violation is not received by the issuing agency in accordance with Section 40610, the issuing agency may deliver the signed promise to the court having jurisdiction of the violation with a certification that no proof of correction has been received. If prepared on a form approved by the Judicial Council, the promise under Section 40610, together with the certification under this section, shall constitute a complaint to which the defendant may enter a plea, and upon which a warrant may be issued if the complaint is verified. *(Added by Stats.1978, c. 1350, p. 4479, § 3, operative July 1, 1979.)*

Research References

4 Witkin, California Criminal Law 4th Pretrial Proceedings § 54 (2021), Promise to Correct Violation.

CHAPTER 3. ILLEGAL EVIDENCE

ARTICLE 1. PROSECUTIONS UNDER CODE

Section

§ 40800. Vehicle and uniform used by officers

(a) A traffic officer on duty for the exclusive or main purpose of enforcing the provisions of Division 10 (commencing with Section 20000) or Division 11 (commencing with Section 21000) shall wear a full distinctive uniform, and if the officer while on duty uses a motor vehicle, it shall be a distinctive color specified by the commissioner.

(b) This section does not apply to an officer assigned exclusively to the duty of investigating and securing evidence in reference to the theft of a vehicle, failure of a person to stop in the event of an accident, violation of Section 23109 or 23109.1, in reference to a felony charge, or to an officer engaged in serving a warrant when the officer is not engaged in patrolling the highways for the purpose of enforcing the traffic laws. *(Stats.1959, c. 3, p. 1780, § 40800. Amended by Stats.1961, c. 202, p. 1212, § 2; Stats.2007, c. 682 (A.B.430), § 18; Stats.2016, c. 59 (S.B.1474), § 9, eff. Jan. 1, 2017.)*

Cross References

Officers as witnesses, competency, see Vehicle Code § 40804.
Powers and duties of director, generally, see Vehicle Code § 1650 et seq.
Prohibited ownership of vehicle painted as law enforcement vehicle, see Vehicle Code § 27605.
Repainting on sale of law enforcement vehicles, see Vehicle Code § 27604.
Unauthorized wearing of uniforms, misdemeanor, see Military and Veterans Code § 422.
Wearing of uniforms, see Vehicle Code § 2261.

Research References

West's California Judicial Council Forms TR–108, Continuation of Citation.
4 Witkin, California Criminal Law 4th Illegally Obtained Evidence § 2 (2021), Types of Excludable Evidence.
4 Witkin, California Criminal Law 4th Pretrial Proceedings § 47 (2021), Speed Traps.

§ 40801. Speed trap prohibition

No peace officer or other person shall use a speed trap in arresting, or participating or assisting in the arrest of, any person for any alleged violation of this code nor shall any speed trap be used in securing evidence as to the speed of any vehicle for the purpose of an arrest or prosecution under this code. *(Stats.1959, c. 3, p. 1780, § 40801.)*

§ 40802. "Speed trap" defined

(a) A "speed trap" is either of the following:

(1) A particular section of a highway measured as to distance and with boundaries marked, designated, or otherwise determined in order that the speed of a vehicle may be calculated by securing the time it takes the vehicle to travel the known distance.

(2) A particular section of a highway with a prima facie speed limit that is provided by this code or by local ordinance under paragraph (1) of subdivision (b) of Section 22352, or established under Section 22354, 22357, 22358, or 22358.3, if that prima facie speed limit is not justified by an engineering and traffic survey conducted within five years prior to the date of the alleged violation, and enforcement of the speed limit involves the use of radar or any other electronic device that measures the speed of moving objects. This paragraph does not apply to a local street, road, school zone, senior zone, * * * business activity district, or speed limit adopted under Section 22358.7 or 22358.8.

(b)(1) For purposes of this section, a local street or road is one that is functionally classified as "local" on the "California Road System Maps," that are approved by the Federal Highway Administration and maintained by the Department of Transportation. It may also be defined as a "local street or road" if it primarily provides access to abutting residential property and meets the following three conditions:

(A) Roadway width of not more than 40 feet.

(B) Not more than one-half of a mile of uninterrupted length. Interruptions shall include official traffic control signals as defined in Section 445.

(C) Not more than one traffic lane in each direction.

(2) For purposes of this section, "school zone" means that area approaching or passing a school building or the grounds thereof that is contiguous to a highway and on which is posted a standard "SCHOOL" warning sign, while children are going to or leaving the school either during school hours or during the noon recess period. "School zone" also includes the area approaching or passing any school grounds that are not separated from the highway by a fence, gate, or other physical barrier while the grounds are in use by children if that highway is posted with a standard "SCHOOL" warning sign.

(3) For purposes of this section, "senior zone" means that area approaching or passing a senior center building or other facility primarily used by senior citizens, or the grounds thereof that is contiguous to a highway and on which is posted a standard "SENIOR" warning sign, pursuant to Section 22352.

(4) For purposes of this section, "business activity district" means a section of highway described in subdivision (b) of Section 22358.9 in which a standard 25 miles per hour or 20 miles per hour speed limit sign has been posted pursuant to paragraph (1) of subdivision (a) of that section.

(c)(1) When all of the following criteria are met, paragraph (2) of this subdivision shall be applicable and subdivision (a) shall not be applicable:

(A) When radar is used, the arresting officer has successfully completed a radar operator course of not less than 24 hours on the use of police traffic radar, and the course was approved and certified by the Commission on Peace Officer Standards and Training.

(B) When laser or any other electronic device is used to measure the speed of moving objects, the arresting officer has successfully completed the training required in subparagraph (A) and an additional training course of not less than two hours approved and certified by the Commission on Peace Officer Standards and Training.

(C)(i) The prosecution proved that the arresting officer complied with subparagraphs (A) and (B) and that an engineering and traffic survey has been conducted in accordance with subparagraph (B) of paragraph (2). The prosecution proved that, prior to the officer issuing the notice to appear, the arresting officer established that the radar, laser, or other electronic device conformed to the requirements of subparagraph (D).

(ii) The prosecution proved the speed of the accused was unsafe for the conditions present at the time of alleged violation unless the citation was for a violation of Section 22349, 22356, or 22406.

(D) The radar, laser, or other electronic device used to measure the speed of the accused meets or exceeds the minimal operational standards of the National Highway Traffic Safety Administration, and has been calibrated within the three years prior to the date of the alleged violation by an independent certified laser or radar repair and testing or calibration facility.

(2) A "speed trap" is either of the following:

(A) A particular section of a highway measured as to distance and with boundaries marked, designated, or otherwise determined in order that the speed of a vehicle may be calculated by securing the time it takes the vehicle to travel the known distance.

(B)(i) A particular section of a highway or state highway with a prima facie speed limit that is provided by this code or by local ordinance under paragraph (1) of subdivision (b) of Section 22352, or established under Section 22354, 22357, 22358, or 22358.3, if that prima facie speed limit is not justified by an engineering and traffic survey conducted within one of the following time periods, prior to the date of the alleged violation, and enforcement of the speed limit involves the use of radar or any other electronic device that measures the speed of moving objects:

(I) Except as specified in subclause (II), seven years.

(II) If an engineering and traffic survey was conducted more than seven years prior to the date of the alleged violation, and a registered engineer evaluates the section of the highway and determines that no significant changes in roadway or traffic conditions have occurred, including, but not limited to, changes in adjoining property or land use, roadway width, or traffic volume, 14 years.

(ii) This subparagraph does not apply to a local street, road, or school zone, senior zone, * * * business activity district, or speed limit adopted under Section 22358.7 or 22358.8. *(Added by Stats. 1995, c. 315 (S.B.574), § 2, operative Jan. 1, 1999. Amended by Stats.1996, c. 124 (A.B.3470), § 145, operative Jan. 1, 1999; Stats. 1996, c. 104 (S.B.2006), § 2, operative Jan. 1, 1999; Stats.1998, c. 1037 (A.B.2222), § 1; Stats.1999, c. 1008 (S.B.533), § 18; Stats.2000, c. 521 (A.B.280), § 3; Stats.2010, c. 491 (S.B.1318), § 49; Stats.2016, c. 208 (A.B.2906), § 26, eff. Jan. 1, 2017; Stats.2017, c. 397 (S.B.810), § 9, eff. Jan. 1, 2018; Stats.2021, c. 690 (A.B.43), § 10, eff. Jan. 1, 2022; Stats.2022, c. 406 (A.B.1938), § 5, eff. Jan. 1, 2023.)*

Research References

4 Witkin, California Criminal Law 4th Pretrial Proceedings § 47 (2021), Speed Traps.

§ 40803. Speed trap evidence

(a) No evidence as to the speed of a vehicle upon a highway shall be admitted in any court upon the trial of any person in any prosecution under this code upon a charge involving the speed of a vehicle when the evidence is based upon or obtained from or by the maintenance or use of a speedtrap.

(b) In any prosecution under this code of a charge involving the speed of a vehicle, where enforcement involves the use of radar or other electronic devices which measure the speed of moving objects, the prosecution shall establish, as part of its prima facie case, that the evidence or testimony presented is not based upon a speedtrap as defined in paragraph (2) of subdivision (a) of Section 40802.

(c) When a traffic and engineering survey is required pursuant to paragraph (2) of subdivision (a) of Section 40802, evidence that a traffic and engineering survey has been conducted within five years of the date of the alleged violation or evidence that the offense was committed on a local street or road as defined in paragraph (2) of subdivision (a) of Section 40802 shall constitute a prima facie case that the evidence or testimony is not based upon a speedtrap as defined in paragraph (2) of subdivision (a) of Section 40802.

(Stats.1959, c. 3, p. 1781, § 40803. Amended by Stats.1981, c. 357, p. 1530, § 3; Stats.1991, c. 459 (S.B.733), § 3; Stats.1992, c. 538, (A.B.3659), § 1; Stats.1996, c. 124 (A.B.3470), § 147.)

Research References

4 Witkin, California Criminal Law 4th Pretrial Proceedings § 47 (2021), Speed Traps.

§ 40804. Testimony based on speed trap

(a) In any prosecution under this code upon a charge involving the speed of a vehicle, an officer or other person shall be incompetent as a witness if the testimony is based upon or obtained from or by the maintenance or use of a speed trap.

(b) An officer arresting, or participating or assisting in the arrest of, a person so charged while on duty for the exclusive or main purpose of enforcing the provisions of Divisions 10 (commencing with Section 20000) and 11 (commencing with Section 21000) is incompetent as a witness if at the time of that arrest he was not wearing a distinctive uniform, or was using a motor vehicle not painted the distinctive color specified by the commissioner.

(c) This section does not apply to an officer assigned exclusively to the duty of investigating and securing evidence in reference to the theft of a vehicle or failure of a person to stop in the event of an accident or violation of Section 23109 or 23109.1 or in reference to a felony charge or to an officer engaged in serving a warrant when the officer is not engaged in patrolling the highways for the purpose of enforcing the traffic laws. *(Stats.1959, c. 3, p. 1781, § 40804. Amended by Stats.1961, c. 58, p. 1016, § 69, eff. March 31, 1961; Stats.1978, c. 84, p. 219, § 1; Stats.2007, c. 682 (A.B.430), § 19.)*

Cross References

Color of vehicles and uniform used by enforcement officers, see Vehicle Code § 40800.
Speed trap prohibited, see Vehicle Code § 40801.

§ 40805. Admission of speed trap evidence

Every court shall be without jurisdiction to render a judgment of conviction against any person for a violation of this code involving the speed of a vehicle if the court admits any evidence or testimony secured in violation of, or which is inadmissible under this article. *(Stats.1959, c. 3, p. 1781, § 40805.)*

Research References

4 Witkin, California Criminal Law 4th Pretrial Proceedings § 47 (2021), Speed Traps.

§ 40806. Police reports

In the event a defendant charged with an offense under this code pleads guilty, the trial court shall not at any time prior to pronouncing sentence receive or consider any report, verbal or written, of any police or traffic officer or witness of the offense without fully informing the defendant of all statements in the report or statement of witnesses, or without giving the defendant an opportunity to make answer thereto or to produce witnesses in rebuttal, and for such purpose the court shall grant a continuance before pronouncing sentence if requested by the defendant. *(Stats.1959, c. 3, p. 1781, § 40806.)*

§ 40807. Use of evidence regarding departmental action

No record of any action taken by the department against a person's privilege to operate a motor vehicle, nor any testimony regarding the proceedings at, or concerning, or produced at, any hearing held in connection with such action, shall be admissible as evidence in any court in any criminal action.

No provision of this section shall in any way limit the admissibility of such records or testimony as is necessary to enforce the provisions of this code relating to operating a motor vehicle without a valid driver's license or when the driving privilege is suspended or revoked, the admissibility of such records or testimony in any prosecution for failure to disclose any matter at such a hearing when required by law to do so, or the admissibility of such records and testimony when introduced solely for the purpose of impeaching the credibility of a witness. *(Added by Stats.1977, c. 804, p. 2454, § 4.)*

§ 40808. Effect of constitutional right to truth-in-evidence provision

Subdivision (d) of Section 28 of Article I of the California Constitution shall not be construed as abrogating the evidentiary provisions of this article. *(Added by Stats.1992, c. 538, (A.B.3659), § 2.)*

Research References

4 Witkin, California Criminal Law 4th Pretrial Proceedings § 47 (2021), Speed Traps.

ARTICLE 2. CIVIL ACTIONS

Section

§ 40830. Effect of convictions

In either of the following circumstances a violation of any provision of this code does not establish negligence as a matter of law, but in any civil action under either of the circumstances negligence must be proved as a fact without regard to the violation. The circumstances under which this section applies are either:

(a) Where violation of the provision was required by a law of the federal government or by any rule, regulation, directive or order of any agency of the federal government, the violation of which is subject to penalty under an act of Congress or by any valid order of military authority.

(b) Where violation of the provision was required in order to comply with any regulation, directive, or order of the Governor promulgated under the California Emergency Services Act. *(Stats. 1959, c. 3, p. 1781, § 40830. Amended by Stats.1971, c. 438, p. 909, § 195, operative May 3, 1972.)*

§ 40831. Effect of speed conviction

In any civil action proof of speed in excess of any prima facie limit declared in Section 22352 at a particular time and place does not establish negligence as a matter of law but in all such actions it shall be necessary to establish as a fact that the operation of a vehicle at the excess speed constituted negligence. *(Stats.1959, c. 3, p. 1782, § 40831.)*

Cross References

Applicability of this section to trolley coaches, see Vehicle Code § 21051.
Negligent operator defined, see Vehicle Code § 12810.
Rules of the road, exemption of authorized emergency vehicles, see Vehicle Code § 21055.
Speed charge to be specified, see Vehicle Code § 40503.
Speed laws, see Vehicle Code § 22349 et seq.

Research References

California Jury Instructions-Civil, 8th Edition 5.31, The Prima Facie Speed Limits.

§ 40832. Suspension or revocation of driving privilege

No record of the suspension or revocation of the privilege to operate a motor vehicle by the department, nor any testimony of or concerning or produced at the hearing terminating in the suspension or revocation, shall be admissible as evidence in any court in any civil action. *(Stats.1959, c. 3, p. 1782, § 40832.)*

Cross References

Revocation and suspension of license by a court, see Vehicle Code § 13200 et seq.

§ 40833. Report or action of department as evidence

Neither the report required by Sections 16000, 16001, 16002, or 16003, the action taken by the department pursuant to Chapter 1 of Division 7 (commencing at Section 16000), the findings, if any, of the department upon which action is based, nor the security filed as provided in that chapter shall be referred to in any way, or be any evidence of the negligence or due care of any party, at the trial of any action at law to recover damages. *(Stats.1959, c. 3, p. 1782, § 40833.)*

§ 40834. Effect of conviction

A judgment of conviction for any violation of this code or of any local ordinance relating to the operation of a motor vehicle or a finding reported under Section 1816 shall not be res judicata or constitute a collateral estoppel of any issue determined therein in any subsequent civil action. *(Added by Stats.1963, c. 1530, p. 3116, § 1.)*

CHAPTER 3.5. EVIDENCE

§ 40900. Electronic verification of vehicle ownership

Notwithstanding any other provision of law, a verification by telegraph, teletype, facsimile transmission, or any other electronic device, from the department, of ownership of a vehicle registered pursuant to this code, is admissible in evidence as proof of ownership of the vehicle in any proceeding involving a parking violation of this code, or any local parking ordinance adopted pursuant to this code. *(Added by Stats.1973, c. 616, p. 1141, § 1. Amended by Stats.1991, c. 13 (A.B.37), § 65, eff. Feb. 13, 1991.)*

§ 40901. Trials; infractions; rules

(a) A court, pursuant to this section, may by rule provide for the trial of any alleged infraction involving a violation of this code or any local ordinance adopted pursuant to this code.

(b) The rules governing the trials may provide for testimony and other relevant evidence to be introduced in the form of a notice to appear issued pursuant to Section 40500 and, notwithstanding Division 10 (commencing with Section 1200) of the Evidence Code, a business record or receipt.

(c) Prior to the entry of a waiver of constitutional right pursuant to any rules adopted under this section, the court shall inform the defendant in writing of the nature of the proceedings and of his or her right to confront and cross-examine witnesses, to subpoena witnesses on his or her behalf, and to hire counsel at his or her own expense. The court shall ascertain that the defendant knowingly and voluntarily waives his or her right to be confronted by the witnesses against him or her, to subpoena witnesses in his or her behalf, and to hire counsel on his or her behalf before proceeding.

(d) In any jurisdiction with a non-English speaking population exceeding 5 percent of the total population of the jurisdiction in any one language, a written explanation of the procedures and rights under this section shall be available in that language.

(e) Except as set forth above, nothing contained herein shall be interpreted to permit the submission of evidence other than in accordance with the law, nor to prevent courts from adopting other rules to provide for trials in accordance with the law. *(Added by Stats.1976, c. 1232, p. 5549, § 1. Amended by Stats.1996, c. 124 (A.B.3470), § 148.)*

Research References

West's California Judicial Council Forms TR–505, Notice and Waiver of Rights and Request for Remote Video Arraignment and Trial.
West's California Judicial Council Forms TR–510, Notice and Waiver of Rights and Request for Remote Video Proceeding.
5 Witkin, California Criminal Law 4th Criminal Trial § 668 (2021), Minor Vehicle Offenses.

§ 40902. Trial by written declaration; adoption of rules and forms; introduction of evidence; trial de novo

(a)(1) The court, pursuant to this section, shall, by rule, provide that the defendant may elect to have a trial by written declaration upon any alleged infraction, as charged by the citing officer, involving a violation of this code or any local ordinance adopted pursuant to this code, other than an infraction cited pursuant to Article 2 (commencing with Section 23152) of Chapter 12 of Division 11.

(2) The Judicial Council may adopt rules and forms governing trials by declaration in accordance with this section. Any rule or form adopted by the Judicial Council pursuant to this paragraph shall supersede any local rule of a court adopted pursuant to paragraph (1).

(b) If the defendant elects to have a trial by written declaration, the defendant shall, at the time of submitting that declaration, submit bail in the amount established in the uniform traffic penalty schedule pursuant to Section 40310. If the defendant is found not guilty or if the charges are otherwise dismissed, the amount of the bail shall be promptly refunded to the defendant.

(c) Notwithstanding Division 10 (commencing with Section 1200) of the Evidence Code, the rules governing trials by written declaration may provide for testimony and other relevant evidence to be introduced in the form of a notice to appear issued pursuant to Section 40500, a business record or receipt, a sworn declaration of the arresting officer, or a written statement or letter signed by the defendant.

(d) If the defendant is dissatisfied with a decision of the court in a proceeding pursuant to this section, the defendant shall be granted a trial de novo. *(Added by Stats.1978, c. 1282, p. 4187, § 1. Amended by Stats.1983, c. 345, § 1; Stats.1988, c. 91, § 1; Stats.1993, c. 488 (A.B.1398), § 1; Stats.1998, c. 265 (S.B.1813), § 1.)*

Cross References

Offer of online trials for infractions where personal appearance not required, requirements, see Government Code § 68645.4.

Research References

West's California Judicial Council Forms TR–200, Instructions to Defendant.
West's California Judicial Council Forms TR–205, Request for Trial by Written Declaration.
West's California Judicial Council Forms TR–210, Notice and Instructions to Arresting Officer.
West's California Judicial Council Forms TR–215, Decision and Notice of Decision.
West's California Judicial Council Forms TR–220, Request for New Trial (Trial De Novo).
West's California Judicial Council Forms TR–225, Order and Notice to Defendant of New Trial (Trial De Novo).
West's California Judicial Council Forms TR–235, Officer's Declaration.
5 Witkin, California Criminal Law 4th Criminal Trial § 668 (2021), Minor Vehicle Offenses.

§ 40903. Failure to appear; evidence

(a) Any person who fails to appear as provided by law may be deemed to have elected to have a trial by written declaration upon any alleged infraction, as charged by the citing officer, involving a violation of this code or any local ordinance adopted pursuant to this code.

(b) Notwithstanding Division 10 (commencing with Section 1200) of the Evidence Code, testimony and other relevant evidence may be introduced in the form of a notice to appear issued pursuant to Section 40500, a notice of parking violation issued pursuant to Section 40202, a notice of delinquent parking violation issued pursuant to Section 40206, a business record or receipt, a sworn declaration of the arresting officer, or a written statement or letter signed by the defendant. *(Added by Stats.1992, c. 696 (A.B.1344), § 95, eff. Sept. 15, 1992.)*

Research References

5 Witkin, California Criminal Law 4th Criminal Trial § 668 (2021), Minor Vehicle Offenses.

CHAPTER 4. PRESUMPTIONS

§ 41100. Speed restriction signs

In any action involving the question of unlawful speed of a vehicle upon a highway which has been signposted with speed restriction signs of a type complying with the requirements of this code, it shall be presumed that existing facts authorize the erection of the signs and that the prima facie speed limit on the highway is the limit stated on the signs. This presumption may be rebutted. *(Stats.1959, c. 3, p. 1782, § 41100.)*

Cross References

Business and residential areas defined, see Vehicle Code §§ 235, 515.
Presumptions and inferences,
  Generally, see Evidence Code § 600 et seq.
  Burden of producing evidence, see Evidence Code § 630 et seq.
  Burden of proof, see Evidence Code § 660 et seq.
Signs restricting speed, see Vehicle Code §§ 21357, 21359.
Speed laws generally, see Vehicle Code § 22349 et seq.
Statute making one fact prima facie evidence of another, see Evidence Code § 602.

§ 41101. Official signs and traffic control devices

(a) Whenever a traffic sign or traffic control device is placed in a position approximately conforming to the requirements of this code, it shall be presumed to have been placed by the official act or direction of lawful authority, unless the contrary is established by competent evidence.

(b) Any sign or traffic control device placed pursuant to this code and purporting to conform to the lawful requirements pertaining to it shall be presumed to comply with the requirements of this code unless the contrary is established by competent evidence. *(Stats. 1959, c. 3, p. 1782, § 41101.)*

Cross References

Presumption of regular performance of official duty, see Evidence Code § 664.
Traffic signs, signals, and markings, see Vehicle Code § 21350 et seq.

§ 41104. Train of vehicles

In any case, involving an accident or otherwise, where any rear component of a train of vehicles fails to follow substantially in the path of the towing vehicle while moving upon a highway, the vehicle shall be presumed to have been operated in violation of Section 21711. *(Added by Stats.1959, c. 44, p. 1902, § 4.)*

CHAPTER 5. DEFENSES

§ 41400. Prior conviction or acquittal

Whenever any person is charged with a violation of this code, it is a sufficient defense to such charge if it appears that in a criminal prosecution in another state or by the Federal Government, founded upon the act or omission in respect to which he is on trial, he has been convicted or acquitted. *(Stats.1959, c. 3, p. 1783, § 41400.)*

Cross References

Double jeopardy, prohibition against, see Cal. Const. Art. 1, § 15; Penal Code §§ 687, 1023.
Foreign conviction or acquittal, defense, see Penal Code § 656.

Research References

1 Witkin California Criminal Law 4th Defenses § 184 (2021), California Rule.

§ 41401. Federal law

No person shall be prosecuted for a violation of any provision of this code if the violation was required by a law of the federal government, by any rule, regulation, directive or order of any agency of the federal government, the violation of which is subject to penalty under an act of Congress, or by any valid order of military authority. *(Stats.1959, c. 3, p. 1784, § 41401. Amended by Stats.1973, c. 78, p. 140, § 24.)*

Research References

1 Witkin California Criminal Law 4th Defenses § 279 (2021), Vehicle Offenses.

§ 41402. Emergency Services Act

No person shall be prosecuted for a violation of any provision of this code when violation of such provision is required in order to comply with any regulation, directive, or order of the Governor promulgated under the California Emergency Services Act. *(Stats. 1959, c. 3, p. 1784, § 41402. Amended by Stats.1971, c. 438, p. 909, § 196, operative May 3, 1972.)*

Cross References

California Emergency Service Act, see Government Code § 8550 et seq.

Research References

1 Witkin California Criminal Law 4th Defenses § 279 (2021), Vehicle Offenses.

§ 41403. Challenging constitutional validity of separate convictions; procedure; burden of proof; hearing at time of sentencing

(a) In any proceedings to have a judgment of conviction of a violation of Section 14601, 14601.1, 14601.2, 23152, or 23153, or Section 23103 as specified in Section 23103.5, which was entered in a separate proceeding, declared invalid on constitutional grounds, the defendant shall state in writing and with specificity wherein the defendant was deprived of the defendant's constitutional rights, which statement shall be filed with the clerk of the court and a copy served on the court that rendered that judgment and on the prosecuting attorney in the present proceedings at least five court days prior to the hearing thereon.

(b) Except as provided in subdivision (c), the court shall, prior to the trial of any pending criminal action against the defendant wherein the separate conviction is charged as such, hold a hearing, outside of the presence of the jury, in order to determine the constitutional validity of the charged separate conviction issue. At the hearing the procedure, the burden of proof, and the burden of producing evidence shall be as follows:

(1) The prosecution shall initially have the burden of producing evidence of the separate conviction sufficient to justify a finding that the defendant has suffered that separate conviction.

(2) After the production of evidence required by paragraph (1), the defendant then has the burden of proof by a preponderance of the evidence that the defendant's constitutional rights were infringed in the separate proceeding at issue. If the separate conviction sought to be invalidated is based upon a plea of guilty or nolo contendere, the defendant shall provide the court with evidence of the prior plea, including the court docket, written waivers of constitutional rights executed by the defendant, and transcripts of the relevant court proceedings at the time of the entry of the defendant's plea. These records shall be provided to the defendant without cost to him or her, when the defendant is represented by the public defender or counsel appointed pursuant to Section 987.2 of the Penal Code.

(3) If the defendant bears this burden successfully, the prosecution shall have the right to produce evidence in rebuttal.

(4) The court shall make a finding on the basis of the evidence thus produced and shall strike from the accusatory pleading any separate conviction found to be constitutionally invalid.

(c) If the defendant fails to comply with the notice requirement of subdivision (a) or fails to produce the evidence required by paragraph (2) of subdivision (b), the court shall hear the motion at the time of sentencing in lieu of continuing the trial, unless good cause is shown for failure to provide notice pursuant to subdivision (a) or produce the evidence required by paragraph (2) of subdivision (b), in which case the court shall grant a continuance of the trial for a reasonable period. The procedure, burden of proof, and burden of producing evidence as provided in subdivision (b) shall apply regardless of when the motion is heard. *(Formerly § 23102.2, added by Stats.1973, c. 1128, p. 2296, § 4. Amended by Stats.1977, c. 186, p. 705, § 1. Renumbered § 23208 and amended by Stats.1981, c. 940, p. 3567, § 15. Amended by Stats.1984, c. 1205, § 10. Renumbered § 41403 and amended by Stats.1984, c. 1585, § 2. Amended by Stats.1995, c. 83 (A.B.232), § 1.)*

Research References

2 Witkin, California Criminal Law 4th Crimes Against Public Peace and Welfare § 279 (2021), In General.
5 Witkin, California Criminal Law 4th Criminal Trial § 480 (2021), Vehicle Code Convictions.
4 Witkin, California Criminal Law 4th Pretrial Proceedings § 175 (2021), In General.

CHAPTER 6. NONPROSECUTION OF VIOLATIONS

§ 41500. Nonfelony offenses of persons in custody

(a) A person shall not be subject to prosecution for a nonfelony offense arising out of the operation of a motor vehicle or violation of this code as a pedestrian that is pending against * * * them at the time of * * * their commitment to the custody of the Secretary of the Department of Corrections and Rehabilitation, the Division of Juvenile Justice in the Department of Corrections and Rehabilitation, or to a county jail pursuant to subdivision (h) of Section 1170 of the Penal Code.

(b) Notwithstanding any other law, a driver's license shall not be suspended or revoked, and the issuance or renewal of a license shall not be refused as a result of a pending nonfelony offense occurring prior to the time a person was committed to the custody of the Secretary of the Department of Corrections and Rehabilitation, the Division of Juvenile Justice of the Department of Corrections and Rehabilitation, or a county jail pursuant to subdivision (h) of Section 1170 of the Penal Code, or as a result of a notice received by the department pursuant to subdivision (a) of former Section 40509 when the offense that gave rise to the notice occurred prior to the time a person was committed to the custody of the Secretary of the Department of Corrections and Rehabilitation or the Division of Juvenile Justice of the Department of Corrections and Rehabilitation.

(c) The department shall remove from its records notice received by it pursuant to subdivision (a) of former Section 40509 upon receipt of satisfactory evidence that a person was committed to the custody of the Secretary of the Department of Corrections and Rehabilitation, the Division of Juvenile Justice of the Department of Corrections and Rehabilitation, or a county jail pursuant to subdivision (h) of Section 1170 of the Penal Code, after the offense that gave rise to the notice occurred.

(d) The provisions of this section shall not apply to a nonfelony offense if the department is required by this code to immediately revoke or suspend the privilege of a person to drive a motor vehicle upon receipt of a duly certified abstract of the record of a court showing that the person has been convicted of that nonfelony offense.

(e) The provisions of subdivisions (a), (b), and (c) do not apply to an offense committed by a person while * * * that person is temporarily released from custody pursuant to law or while * * * they are on parole or postrelease community supervision.

(f) The provisions of subdivisions (a), (b), and (c) do not apply if the pending offense is a violation of Section 23103, 23152, or 23153. *(Added by Stats.1970, c. 1163, p. 2066, § 2. Amended by Stats.1972, c. 1073, p. 2009, § 1; Stats.1975, c. 545, p. 1111, § 1; Stats.1992, c. 950 (A.B.3569), § 1; Stats.2015, c. 378 (A.B.1156), § 12, eff. Jan. 1, 2016; Stats.2022, c. 800 (A.B.2746), § 25, eff. Jan. 1, 2023.)*

Cross References

Director of Corrections, see Penal Code § 5050 et seq.
Record of license applicant for conviction of traffic violations and traffic accidents, see Vehicle Code § 12808.
Youth Authority, see Welfare and Institutions Code § 1700 et seq.

Research References

2 Witkin, California Criminal Law 4th Crimes Against Public Peace and Welfare § 269 (2021), Nonfelony Offenses of Persons in Custody.

§ 41501. Continuance; attendance at licensed school for traffic violators, licensed driving school, or court approved program of driving instruction; conviction held confidential

(a) After a deposit of bail and bail forfeiture, a plea of guilty or no contest, or a conviction, the court may order a continuance of a proceeding against a person, who receives a notice to appear in court for a violation of a statute relating to the safe operation of a vehicle, in consideration for successful completion of a course of instruction at a licensed school for traffic violators and pursuant to Section 1803.5 or 42005, the court may order that the conviction be held confidential by the department in accordance with Section 1808.7. The court shall notify a person that only one conviction within 18 months will be held confidential.

(b) Subdivision (a) does not apply to a person who receives a notice to appear as to, or is otherwise charged with, a violation of an offense described in subdivisions (a) to (e), inclusive, of Section 12810.

(c) This section shall become operative on July 1, 2011. *(Added by Stats.2010, c. 599 (A.B.2499), § 12.5, operative July 1, 2011. Amended by Stats.2011, c. 296 (A.B.1023), § 311.)*

Cross References

Additional fee imposed for maintenance of funding for court security upon conviction for criminal offense involving violations of Vehicle Code, exceptions, see Penal Code § 1465.8.

Occupational licensing, traffic violator schools, duties of Judicial Council, see Vehicle Code § 11205.4.

CHAPTER 7. ARREST QUOTAS

§ 41600. "Arrest quota" defined

For purposes of this chapter, "arrest quota" means any requirement regarding the number of arrests made, or the number of citations issued, by a peace officer, or parking enforcement employee, or the proportion of those arrests made and citations issued by a peace officer or parking enforcement employee, relative to the arrests made and citations issued by another peace officer or parking enforcement employee, or group of officers or employees. *(Added by Stats.1976, c. 1111, p. 5001, § 1. Amended by Stats.2002, c. 105 (S.B.2069), § 1.)*

§ 41601. "Citation" defined

For purposes of this chapter, "citation" means a notice to appear, notice of violation, or notice of parking violation. *(Added by Stats.1976, c. 1111, p. 5001, § 1.)*

§ 41601.5. "Agency" defined

For purposes of this chapter, "agency" includes the Regents of the University of California. *(Added by Stats.2002, c. 105 (S.B.2069), § 2.)*

§ 41602. Arrest quota prohibited

No state or local agency employing peace officers or parking enforcement employees engaged in the enforcement of this code or any local ordinance adopted pursuant to this code, may establish any policy requiring any peace officer or parking enforcement employees to meet an arrest quota. *(Added by Stats.1976, c. 1111, p. 5001, § 1. Amended by Stats.2002, c. 105 (S.B.2069), § 3.)*

§ 41603. Evaluation of peace officer's or parking enforcement officer's performance

No state or local agency employing peace officers or parking enforcement employees engaged in the enforcement of this code shall use the number of arrests or citations issued by a peace officer or parking enforcement employees as the sole criterion for promotion, demotion, dismissal, or the earning of any benefit provided by the agency. Those arrests or citations, and their ultimate dispositions, may only be considered in evaluating the overall performance of a peace officer or parking enforcement employees. An evaluation may include, but shall not be limited to, criteria such as attendance, punctuality, work safety, complaints by civilians, commendations, demeanor, formal training, and professional judgment. *(Added by Stats.1976, c. 1111, p. 5001, § 1. Amended by Stats.1977, c. 579, p. 1920, § 189; Stats.1979, c. 373, p. 1385, § 329; Stats.2002, c. 105 (S.B.2069), § 4; Stats.2016, c. 99 (A.B.1953), § 7, eff. Jan. 1, 2017.)*

CHAPTER 8. CONSOLIDATED DISPOSITION

§ 41610. Guilty plea to traffic infraction or misdemeanor; election to enter guilty plea for consolidated disposition of other charged offenses; procedure; exceptions

(a) Whenever a person who is in custody enters a guilty plea to an infraction or misdemeanor under this code and there is outstanding any warrant of arrest for a violation of this code or a local ordinance adopted pursuant to this code that is filed in any court within the same county, the defendant may elect to enter a guilty plea to any of these charged offenses of which the court has a record, except offenses specified in subdivision (b). The court shall sentence the defendant for each of the offenses for which a guilty plea has been entered pursuant to this section, and shall notify the appropriate court or department in each affected judicial district of the disposition. After receiving that notice of disposition, the court in which each complaint was filed shall prepare and transmit to the department any certification required by applicable provisions of <u>former</u> Section 40509 as if the court had heard the case.

(b) Subdivision (a) does not authorize entry of a guilty plea as specified in that subdivision to an offense for which a notice of parking violation has been issued, nor to any offense specified in Section 14601.2, 14601.3, 20002, 23103, 23104, 23105, 23152, or 23153, subdivision (a) of Section 14601, or subdivision (a) of Section 14601.1. *(Added by Stats.1983, c. 989, § 1. Amended by Stats.2007, c. 682 (A.B.430), § 20; Stats.2022, c. 800 (A.B.2746), § 26, eff. Jan. 1, 2023.)*

Research References

4 Witkin, California Criminal Law 4th Pretrial Proceedings § 299 (2021), Consolidated Pleas.

Division 18

PENALTIES AND DISPOSITION OF FEES, FINES, AND FORFEITURES

CHAPTER 1. PENALTIES

ARTICLE 1. PUBLIC OFFENSES

§ 42000. Felony

Unless a different penalty is expressly provided by this code, every person convicted of a felony for a violation of any provision of this code shall be punished by a fine of not less than one thousand dollars ($1,000) or more than ten thousand dollars ($10,000), or by imprisonment pursuant to subdivision (h) of Section 1170 of the Penal Code, or by both such fine and imprisonment. *(Stats.1959, c. 3, p. 1784, § 42000. Amended by Stats.1976, c. 1139, p. 5173, § 342, operative July 1, 1977; Stats.1983, c. 1092, § 401, eff. Sept. 27, 1983, operative Jan. 1, 1984; Stats.2011, c. 15 (A.B.109), § 615, eff. April 4, 2011, operative Oct. 1, 2011.)*

Cross References

Felony defined, see Penal Code § 17.
Punishment for felony, see Penal Code § 18.

Research References

2 Witkin, California Criminal Law 4th Crimes Against Public Peace and Welfare § 268 (2021), Felonies.
2 Witkin, California Criminal Law 4th Crimes Against Public Peace and Welfare § 530 (2021), Bicycles.
2 Witkin, California Criminal Law 4th Crimes Against Public Peace and Welfare § 531 (2021), Low-Speed Vehicles and Motorized Scooters.

§ 42000.1. Speeding in excess of 100 miles per hour; fine

Notwithstanding Section 42001, every person convicted of an infraction for a violation described in subdivision (b) of Section 22348 shall be punished by a fine not exceeding five hundred dollars ($500). *(Added by Stats.1983, c. 980, § 4.)*

Research References

2 Witkin, California Criminal Law 4th Crimes Against Public Peace and Welfare § 266 (2021), Infractions.

§ 42000.5. Buses, motor trucks or truck tractors; speed limit violations

Every person convicted of an infraction for a violation of Section 22350, 22406, or 22407 while operating a bus, motor truck, or truck tractor having three or more axles, or any motor truck or truck tractor drawing any other vehicle, shall be punished by a fine not exceeding one hundred dollars ($100) for a first conviction, except that if the person has exceeded the specified speed limit by 10 miles per hour or more, the fine shall not exceed two hundred dollars ($200) for a first conviction, and not exceeding three hundred dollars ($300) for a second or subsequent conviction. *(Added by Stats.1987, c. 1170, § 1. Amended by Stats.1989, c. 980, § 1.)*

Research References

2 Witkin, California Criminal Law 4th Crimes Against Public Peace and Welfare § 266 (2021), Infractions.

§ 42001. Fines for violation of code or local ordinance; infractions committed by bicyclists

(a) Except as provided in this code, a person convicted of an infraction for a violation of this code or of a local ordinance adopted pursuant to this code shall be punished as follows:

(1) By a fine not exceeding one hundred dollars ($100).

(2) For a second infraction occurring within one year of a prior infraction that resulted in a conviction, a fine not exceeding two hundred dollars ($200).

(3) For a third or subsequent infraction occurring within one year of two or more prior infractions that resulted in convictions, a fine not exceeding two hundred fifty dollars ($250).

(b) A pedestrian convicted of an infraction for a violation of this code or any local ordinance adopted pursuant to this code shall be punished by a fine not exceeding fifty dollars ($50).

(c) A person convicted of a violation of subdivision (a) or (b) of Section 27150.3 shall be punished by a fine of two hundred fifty dollars ($250), and a person convicted of a violation of subdivision (c) of Section 27150.3 shall be punished by a fine of one thousand dollars ($1,000).

(d) Notwithstanding any other provision of law, a local public entity that employs peace officers, as designated under Chapter 4.5 (commencing with Section 830) of Title 3 of Part 2 of the Penal Code, the California State University, and the University of California may, by ordinance or resolution, establish a schedule of fines applicable to infractions committed by bicyclists within its jurisdiction. A fine, including all penalty assessments and court costs, established pursuant to this subdivision shall not exceed the maximum fine, including penalty assessment and court costs, otherwise authorized by this code for that violation. If a bicycle fine schedule is adopted, it shall be used by the courts having jurisdiction over the area within which the ordinance or resolution is applicable instead of the fines, including penalty assessments and court costs, otherwise applicable under this code. *(Stats.1959, c. 3, p. 1784, § 42001. Amended by Stats.1961, c. 1974, p. 4164, § 1; Stats.1965, c. 1123, p. 2771, § 1; Stats.1968, c. 1192, p. 2264, § 16, operative Jan. 1, 1969; Stats.1970, c. 1431, p. 2778, § 7; Stats.1973, c. 1162, p. 2420, § 5; Stats.1975, c. 635, p. 1379, § 2; Stats.1977, c. 1104, p. 3527, § 2; Stats.1978, c. 421, p. 1321, § 7; Stats.1978, c. 626, p. 2078, § 3; Stats.1979, c. 373, p. 1385, § 330; Stats.1983, c. 1092, § 402, eff. Sept. 27, 1983, operative Jan. 1, 1984; Stats.1983, c. 619, § 1; Stats.1984, c. 69, § 2, eff. April 5, 1984; Stats.1984, c. 396, § 1; Stats.1984, c. 508, § 2; Stats.1985, c. 1126, § 7, eff. Sept. 28, 1985, operative April 1, 1986; Stats.1987, c. 1170, § 2; Stats.1988, c. 504, § 5, eff. Aug. 22, 1988; Stats.1988, c. 1054, § 4; Stats.1988, c. 1544, § 62; Stats.1991, c. 13 (A.B.37), § 66, eff. Feb. 13, 1991; Stats.1993, c. 307 (A.B.669), § 1; Stats.1997, c. 852 (A.B.1191), § 3; Stats.1999, c. 841 (A.B.923), § 4; Stats.2000, c. 833 (A.B.2522), § 13; Stats.2003, c. 432 (A.B.377), § 2; Stats.2003, c. 555 (A.B.327), § 7.5; Stats.2004, c. 338 (A.B.340), § 2; Stats.2004, c. 391 (S.B.1085), § 2; Stats.2005, c. 166 (A.B.1637), § 3; Stats.2006, c. 538 (S.B.1852), § 667; Stats.2006, c. 898 (S.B.1021), § 4; Stats.2006, c. 899 (A.B.2752), § 2; Stats.2006, c. 900 (A.B.1850), § 3.)*

Cross References

Family day care homes, licensees to sign statement showing no conviction of crimes other than traffic infractions under this section, see Health and Safety Code § 1597.59.
Infractions under automotive repair act, application of this section, see Business and Professions Code § 9889.21.
Maximum penalty for infractions, residence, see Vehicle Code § 40310.
Misdemeanor defined, see Penal Code § 17.
Punishments,
Infractions, see Penal Code § 19.6.
Misdemeanors, see Penal Code §§ 19.2, 19.4.
School safety patrol traffic signals, disregarding, see Education Code § 49307.
Traffic referees, powers and duties, see Government Code § 72401.

Research References

2 Witkin, California Criminal Law 4th Crimes Against Public Peace and Welfare § 266 (2021), Infractions.
2 Witkin, California Criminal Law 4th Crimes Against Public Peace and Welfare § 322 (2021), Pedestrian's Rights and Duties.
2 Witkin, California Criminal Law 4th Crimes Against Public Peace and Welfare § 424 (2021), Automotive Repair Dealers.
4 Witkin, California Criminal Law 4th Introduction to Criminal Procedure § 48 (2021), Traffic Referee.

§ 42001.1. Conviction of infraction for violation of §§ 2815, 22526; punishment

(a) Every person convicted of an infraction for a violation of Section 2815 or a violation of subdivision (a) or (b) of Section 22526 at an intersection posted pursuant to subdivision (d) of Section 22526 shall be punished as follows:

(1) For a first conviction, a fine of not less than fifty dollars ($50) nor more than one hundred dollars ($100).

(2) For a second conviction within a period of one year, a fine of not less than one hundred dollars ($100) nor more than two hundred dollars ($200).

(3) For a third or any subsequent conviction within a period of two years, a fine of not less than two hundred fifty dollars ($250) nor more than five hundred dollars ($500).

(b) In addition to the fine specified in subdivision (a), the court may order the department to suspend the driver's license for up to 30 days of any person convicted of a third or any subsequent conviction of Section 2815 within a period of two years, and the department shall suspend the license for the period of time so ordered. *(Added by Stats.1984, c. 69, § 4, eff. April 5, 1984. Amended by Stats.1987, c. 739, § 2; Stats.1999, c. 724 (A.B.1650), § 53; Stats.2005, c. 716 (A.B.1067), § 7.)*

Cross References

Anti–Gridlock Act of 1987, see Vehicle Code § 22526.
Obstructing railroad track, punishment, see Penal Code § 218.1.
Rail transit related traffic violations, county populations greater than 500,000, punishment, see Penal Code § 369b.

Research References

2 Witkin, California Criminal Law 4th Crimes Against Public Peace and Welfare § 266 (2021), Infractions.

§ 42001.2. Violations of § 27153.5; subsequent violations of § 27153

(a) A person convicted of an infraction for a violation of Section 27153.5 with a motor vehicle having a manufacturer's maximum gross vehicle weight rating of 6,001 or more pounds is punishable by a fine for the first offense of not less than two hundred fifty dollars ($250) and not more than two thousand five hundred dollars ($2,500), and for a second or subsequent offense within one year of not less than five hundred dollars ($500) and not more than five thousand dollars ($5,000).

(b) A person convicted of an infraction for a second or subsequent violation of Section 27153, or a second or subsequent violation of 27153.5, with a motor vehicle having a manufacturer's maximum gross vehicle weight rating of less than 6,001 pounds, is punishable by a fine of not less than one hundred thirty-five dollars ($135) nor more than two hundred eighty-five dollars ($285).

(c) Notwithstanding Section 40616, the penalties in subdivision (b) apply when a person is guilty of willfully violating a written promise to correct, or willfully failing to deliver proof of correction, as prescribed in Section 40616, when an offense described in subdivision (b) was the violation for which the notice to correct was issued and the person was previously convicted of the same offense, except that costs of repair shall be limited to those specified in Section 44017 of the Health and Safety Code.

(d) Notwithstanding any other provision of law and subject to Section 1463.15 of the Penal Code, revenues collected from fines and forfeitures imposed under this section shall be allocated as follows: 15 percent to the county in which the prosecution is conducted, 10 percent to the prosecuting agency, 25 percent to the enforcement agency, except the Department of the California Highway Patrol, and 50 percent to the air quality management district or air pollution control district in which the infraction occurred, to be used for programs to regulate or control emissions from vehicular sources of air pollution. If the enforcement agency is the Department of the California Highway Patrol, the revenues shall be allocated 25 percent to the county in which the prosecution is conducted, 25 percent to the prosecuting agency, and 50 percent to the air quality management district or air pollution control district in which the infraction occurred. If no prosecuting agency is involved, the revenues that would otherwise be allocated to the prosecuting agency shall instead be allocated to the air quality management district or air pollution control district in which the infraction occurred.

(e) For the purposes of subdivisions (a), (b), and (c), a second or subsequent offense does not include an offense involving a different motor vehicle. *(Added by Stats.1988, c. 1544, § 63. Amended by Stats.1990, c. 367 (A.B.911), § 1; Stats.1991, c. 928 (A.B.1886), § 39, eff. Oct. 14, 1991; Stats.1992, c. 1243 (A.B.3090), § 110, eff. Sept. 30, 1992; Stats.2003, c. 482 (S.B.708), § 4.)*

§ 42001.3. Maintenance of driving logs; violations of truck and school bus safety regulations; punishment

(a) Violations of Section 34506.3, with respect to any regulation adopted under Section 34501 relative to the maintenance of driving logs, shall be punishable by a fine of not more than five hundred dollars ($500).

(b) Violations of subdivision (a) of Section 34506, with respect to any regulation adopted under Section 34501 relative to drivers' hours of service, shall be punishable by a fine of not less than five hundred dollars ($500) nor more than one thousand dollars ($1,000). In addition, the violations may be punishable by imprisonment in the county jail for not more than six months. *(Added by Stats.1983, c. 619, § 2. Amended by Stats.1988, c. 631, § 1.)*

§ 42001.4. Transportation of animals; failure to enclose or restrain

Every person convicted of an infraction for violation of Section 23117 shall be punished as follows:

(a) By a fine of not less than fifty dollars ($50) nor more than one hundred dollars ($100).

(b) For a second infraction occurring within one year of a prior infraction which resulted in a conviction, a fine of not less than seventy-five dollars ($75) nor more than two hundred dollars ($200).

(c) For a third or any subsequent infraction occurring within one year of two or more prior infractions which resulted in convictions, a fine of not less than one hundred dollars ($100) nor more than two hundred fifty dollars ($250). *(Added by Stats.1987, c. 224, § 2.)*

§ 42001.5. Parking in disabled person's space or sidewalk access area

(a) A person convicted of an infraction for a violation of subdivision (i) or (*l*) of Section 22500, or of Section 22522, shall be punished by a fine of not less than two hundred fifty dollars ($250).

(b) No part of any fine imposed under this section may be suspended, except the court may suspend that portion of the fine above one hundred dollars ($100).

(c) A fine imposed under this section may be paid in installments if the court determines that the defendant is unable to pay the entire amount in one payment. *(Added by Stats.1970, c. 1431, p. 2778, § 8. Amended by Stats.1977, c. 590, p. 1956, § 2; Stats.1982, c. 975, p. 3497, § 11; Stats.1986, c. 328, § 3; Stats.1988, c. 1008, § 5; Stats.1991, c. 630 (A.B.1346), § 2; Stats.1992, c. 785 (A.B.2289), § 4; Stats.1992, c. 1243 (A.B.3090), § 111, eff. Sept. 30, 1992; Stats.1992, c. 1243 (A.B.3090), § 111.1, eff. Sept. 30, 1992, operative Jan. 1, 1993; Stats.1994, c. 221 (S.B.1378), § 4, operative July 1, 1995; Stats.1994, c. 1149 (A.B.2878), § 12; Stats.2003, c. 555 (A.B.327), § 8.)*

Cross References

Disposition of fines, see Penal Code § 1463.20.
Maximum penalty for infractions, residence, see Vehicle Code § 40310.

§ 42001.6. Parking in zero-emission vehicle (ZEV) space

Every person convicted of an infraction for a violation of Section 22511.1 is punishable by a fine of one hundred dollars ($100).

No part of any fine imposed shall be suspended, except the court may suspend that portion of the fine above twenty-five dollars ($25) for a violation of Section 22511.1 if the person convicted possessed at the time of the offense, but failed to display, a valid zero-emission vehicle decal identification issued pursuant to subdivision (a) of Section 5205.5. The fine may be paid in installments if the court determines that the defendant is unable to pay the entire amount in one payment. *(Added by Stats.2002, c. 640 (A.B.1314), § 6. Amended by Stats.2013, c. 414 (S.B.286), § 4.)*

§ 42001.7. Littering

(a) Every person convicted of a violation of Section 23111 or 23112, or subdivision (a) of Section 23113, shall be punished by a mandatory fine of not less than one hundred dollars ($100) nor more than one thousand dollars ($1,000) upon a first conviction, by a mandatory fine of not less than five hundred dollars ($500) nor more than one thousand dollars ($1,000) upon a second conviction, and by a mandatory fine of not less than seven hundred fifty dollars ($750) nor more than one thousand dollars ($1,000) upon a third or subsequent conviction.

In no case may the court order imprisonment in the county jail for a violation punishable under this subdivision, unless imprisonment is ordered pursuant to Section 166 of the Penal Code.

(b) The court shall, in addition to the fines imposed pursuant to subdivision (a), order the offender to pick up litter or clean up graffiti at a time and place within the jurisdiction of the court as follows:

(1) For a first conviction punished pursuant to subdivision (a), the court shall require the offender to pick up litter or clean up graffiti for not less than eight hours.

(2) For a second conviction punished pursuant to subdivision (a), the court shall require the offender to pick up litter or clean up graffiti for not less than 16 hours.

(3) For a third or subsequent conviction punished pursuant to subdivision (a), the court shall require the offender to pick up litter or clean up graffiti for not less than 24 hours.

(c) It is the intent of the Legislature that persons convicted of highway littering be required to bear the penalty for their actions. Therefore, the court may not suspend the mandatory fines required by subdivision (a) except in unusual cases where the interest of justice would best be served by suspension of the fine. If the court suspends imposition of any fine required by subdivision (a), it shall, as a condition of that suspension, require the offender to pick up litter or clean up graffiti at a time and place within the jurisdiction of the court for not less than eight hours for every one hundred dollars ($100) of fine suspended. The court may not suspend the order to pick up litter or clean up graffiti required by this subdivision or subdivision (b) except in unusual cases where the interest of justice would best be served by suspension of that order. *(Added by Stats.1970, c. 1548, p. 3152, § 11. Amended by Stats.1983, c. 1092, § 403, eff. Sept. 27, 1983, operative Jan. 1, 1984; Stats.1987, c. 133, § 6; Stats.1990, c. 982 (A.B.4229), § 1.)*

Research References

2 Witkin, California Criminal Law 4th Crimes Against Property § 301 (2021), Acts Involving Roads, Highways, or Traffic Devices.

§ 42001.8. Vehicle registration offenses

Every person convicted of an infraction for a violation of Section 4000 shall be punished by a fine of not less than fifty dollars ($50) and not more than two hundred fifty dollars ($250). *(Added by Stats.1985, c. 1126, § 8, eff. Sept. 28, 1985, operative April 1, 1986.)*

§ 42001.9. Violations of section 23135

Every person convicted of an infraction for a violation of Section 23135 shall be punished by a fine of fifty dollars ($50). *(Added by Stats.1978, c. 421, p. 1321, § 8.)*

§ 42001.10. Violations of § 38020

Every person convicted for a violation of Section 38020 shall be punished by a fine of not less than fifty dollars ($50) for a first offense, and not more than two hundred fifty dollars ($250) for every subsequent offense. *(Formerly § 42001.9, added by Stats.1986, c. 1009, § 6. Amended by Stats.1987, c. 56, § 175; Stats.1987, c. 1027, § 29. Renumbered § 42001.10 by Stats.1988, c. 160, § 184.)*

§ 42001.11. Violations of sections 21655.5 or 21655.8

Every person convicted of an infraction for a violation of Section 21655.5 or 21655.8 shall be punished as follows:

(a) For a first conviction, a fine of not less than one hundred dollars ($100), nor more than one hundred fifty dollars ($150).

(b) For a second conviction within a period of one year, a fine of not less than one hundred fifty dollars ($150), nor more than two hundred dollars ($200).

(c) For a third or any subsequent conviction within a period of two years, a fine of not less than two hundred fifty dollars ($250), nor more than five hundred dollars ($500). *(Added by Stats.1988, c. 1054, § 5.)*

§ 42001.12. Failure to yield right-of-way to emergency vehicles; punishment

Every person convicted of an infraction for a violation of Section 21806 shall be punished as follows:

(a) For a first conviction, by a fine of not less than one hundred dollars ($100) nor more than two hundred fifty dollars ($250).

(b) For a second conviction within one year, by a fine of not less than one hundred fifty dollars ($150) nor more than five hundred dollars ($500).

(c) For a third or any subsequent conviction within three years, by a fine of not less than two hundred fifty dollars ($250) nor more than five hundred dollars ($500). *(Added by Stats.1991, c. 13 (A.B.37), § 67, eff. Feb. 13, 1991.)*

Cross References

Failure to yield right-of-way to emergency vehicles, see Vehicle Code § 21806.

§ 42001.13. Penalty for person convicted of infraction for violation of § 22507.8; suspension of penalty; payment of fine

(a) A person who commits a violation of Section 22507.8 is subject to either a civil notice of parking violation pursuant to Article 3 (commencing with Section 40200) of Chapter 1 of Division 17 or a criminal notice to appear.

(b) If a notice to appear is issued and upon conviction of an infraction for a violation of Section 22507.8, a person shall be punished as follows:

(1) A fine of not less than two hundred fifty dollars ($250) and not more than five hundred dollars ($500) for the first offense.

(2) A fine of not less than five hundred dollars ($500) and not more than seven hundred fifty dollars ($750) for the second offense.

(3) A fine of not less than seven hundred fifty dollars ($750) and not more than one thousand dollars ($1,000) for three or more offenses.

(c) The court may suspend the imposition of the fine if the person convicted possessed at the time of the offense, but failed to display, a valid special identification license plate issued pursuant to Section 5007 or a distinguishing placard issued pursuant to Section 22511.55 or 22511.59.

(d) A fine imposed under this section may be paid in installments if the court determines that the defendant is unable to pay the entire amount in one payment. *(Added by Stats.2003, c. 555 (A.B.327), § 9. Amended by Stats.2007, c. 413 (A.B.1531), § 6; Stats.2009, c. 415 (A.B.144), § 8; Stats.2010, c. 328 (S.B.1330), § 233.)*

Cross References

Additional fines imposed for violation of disabled parking restrictions, see Penal Code § 1465.6.

Designation of parking for disabled persons and veterans, display of fine on parking space sign, see Vehicle Code § 22511.7.

Fines imposed and collected for violation of disabled parking restrictions, see Penal Code § 1465.5.

Issuance and renewal of disabled parking placards, penalty printing requirements, see Vehicle Code §§ 22511.55 and 22511.59.

Offstreet parking, designation of parking for disabled persons and veterans, display of fine on parking space sign, see Vehicle Code § 22511.8.

Parking facilities for physically handicapped persons and disabled veterans, display of fine on parking space sign, see Government Code § 14679.

Parking violations, additional assessments equal to 10 percent, see Vehicle Code § 40203.6.

Parking violations, authority of city or county to assess an additional penalty, see Vehicle Code § 4461.3.

Penalties for infractions and special misdemeanors, application of this section, see Vehicle Code § 42001.

Research References

2 Witkin, California Criminal Law 4th Crimes Against Public Peace and Welfare § 323 (2021), Parking.

§ 42001.14. Disconnecting, modifying, or altering required pollution control devices; punishment

(a) Every person convicted of an infraction for the offense of disconnecting, modifying, or altering a required pollution control device in violation of Section 27156 shall be punished as follows:

(1) For a first conviction, by a fine of not less than fifty dollars ($50), nor more than one hundred dollars ($100).

(2) For a second or subsequent conviction, by a fine of not less than one hundred dollars ($100), nor more than two hundred fifty dollars ($250).

(b)(1) The fines collected under subdivision (a) shall be allocated pursuant to subdivision (d) of Section 42001.2.

(2) The amounts allocated pursuant to paragraph (1) to the air pollution control district or air quality management district in which the infraction occurred shall first be allocated to the State Air Resources Board and the Bureau of Automotive Repair to pay the costs of the state board and the bureau under Article 8 (commencing with Section 44080) of Chapter 5 of Part 5 of Division 26 of the Health and Safety Code.

(3) The funds collected under subdivision (a) which are not required for purposes of paragraph (2) shall be used for the enforcement of Section 27156 or for the implementation of Article 8 (commencing with Section 44080) of Chapter 5 of Part 5 of Division 26 of the Health and Safety Code. *(Added by Stats.1992, c. 972 (S.B.1404), § 3.)*

§ 42001.15. Violations of sections relating to steady red circular or arrow signals; lane use control signals; illuminated flashing red traffic signal; fines

Every person convicted of an infraction for a violation of subdivision (a) or (c) of Section 21453, subdivision (c) of Section 21454, or subdivision (a) of Section 21457 shall be punished by a fine of one hundred dollars ($100). *(Added by Stats.1997, c. 852 (A.B.1191), § 4.)*

§ 42001.16. Railroad grade crossing violations

(a) Every person convicted of an infraction for a violation of subdivision (c) of Section 21752, subdivision (c) of Section 22526, or Section 22450, involving railroad grade crossings, or Section 22451 or 22452 shall be punished as follows:

(1) For the first infraction, by a fine of one hundred dollars ($100).

(2) For a second infraction of any of the offenses described in this subdivision occurring within one year of a prior infraction that resulted in a conviction, by a fine not exceeding two hundred dollars ($200).

(3) For a third or any subsequent infraction of any of the offenses described in this subdivision occurring within one year of two or more prior infractions that resulted in convictions, by a fine not exceeding two hundred fifty dollars ($250).

(b) In addition to the fine imposed pursuant to subdivision (a), a court, in a county in which Section 369b of the Penal Code applies, may require the person to attend a traffic school as described in Section 369b of the Penal Code. *(Added by Stats.1999, c. 841 (A.B.923), § 5. Amended by Stats.2005, c. 716 (A.B.1067), § 8.)*

Cross References

Obstructing railroad track, punishment, see Penal Code § 218.1.
Rail transit related traffic violations, county populations greater than 500,000, punishment, see Penal Code § 369b.

§ 42001.17. Conviction under § 21951; fines

Notwithstanding any other provision of law, every person convicted of an infraction for a violation of Section 21951 shall be punished as follows:

(a) For the first infraction, by a fine of one hundred dollars ($100).

(b) For a second infraction for a violation of Section 21951 occurring within one year of a prior infraction of violating of that section that resulted in a conviction, by a fine not exceeding two hundred dollars ($200), as provided in paragraph (2) of subdivision (a) of Section 42001.

(c) For a third or any subsequent infraction for a violation of Section 21951 occurring within one year of two or more prior infractions of violating that section that resulted in convictions, by a fine not exceeding two hundred fifty dollars ($250), as provided in paragraph (3) of subdivision (a) of Section 42001. *(Added by Stats.2000, c. 833 (A.B.2522), § 14.)*

Research References

2 Witkin, California Criminal Law 4th Crimes Against Public Peace and Welfare § 322 (2021), Pedestrian's Rights and Duties.

§ 42001.18. Conviction under § 21971; fines

Notwithstanding any other provision of law, every person convicted of an infraction for a violation of Section 21971 shall be punished as follows:

(a) For the first infraction, by a fine of two hundred twenty dollars ($220).

(b) For a second infraction for a violation of Section 21971 occurring within one year of a prior violation of that section that resulted in a conviction, by a fine of three hundred twenty dollars ($320).

(c) For a third or any subsequent infraction for a violation of Section 21971 occurring within one year of two or more prior infractions of violating that section that resulted in convictions by a fine of three hundred seventy dollars ($370). *(Added by Stats.2000, c. 833 (A.B.2522), § 15.)*

§ 42001.19. Conviction under § 21070; fines

Notwithstanding any other provision of law, a person convicted of a violation of Section 21070 is punishable, as follows:

(a) For a violation involving bodily injury, by a fine of seventy dollars ($70).

(b) For a violation involving great bodily injury, as defined in Section 12022.7 of the Penal Code, by a fine of ninety-five dollars ($95). *(Added by Stats.2006, c. 898 (S.B.1021), § 5.)*

Cross References

Traffic laws, unsafe operation of motor vehicle with bodily injury or great bodily injury, see Vehicle Code § 21070.

§ 42001.20. Violation of section relating to warning devices on certain refuse or garbage trucks

Notwithstanding any other provision of law, a person who violates subdivision (b) or (c) of Section 27000 is punishable as follows:

(a) By a fine of one hundred fifty dollars ($150).

(b) For a second infraction occurring within one year of a prior infraction that resulted in a conviction, a fine not exceeding two hundred dollars ($200).

(c) For a third or any subsequent infraction occurring within one year of two or more prior infractions that resulted in convictions, a fine, not exceeding two hundred fifty dollars ($250). *(Added by Stats.2005, c. 166 (A.B.1637), § 4.)*

§ 42001.25. Violations of § 23140

Notwithstanding any other provision of law, a person who violates Section 23140 is punishable as follows:

(a) By a fine of one hundred dollars ($100).

(b) For a second infraction occurring within one year of a prior infraction that resulted in a conviction, a fine of two hundred dollars ($200).

(c) For a third or any subsequent infraction occurring within one year of two or more prior infractions that resulted in convictions, a fine of three hundred dollars ($300). *(Added by Stats.2006, c. 899 (A.B.2752), § 3.)*

Research References

2 Witkin, California Criminal Law 4th Crimes Against Public Peace and Welfare § 279 (2021), In General.

§ 42002. General misdemeanors

Unless a different penalty is expressly provided by this code, every person convicted of a misdemeanor for a violation of any of the provisions of this code shall be punished by a fine of not exceeding one thousand dollars ($1,000) or by imprisonment in the county jail for not exceeding six months, or by both such fine and imprisonment. *(Stats.1959, c. 3, p. 1785, § 42002. Amended by Stats.1983, c. 1092, § 404, eff. Sept. 27, 1983, operative Jan. 1, 1984.)*

Cross References

Applicability of this section to trolley coaches, see Vehicle Code § 21051.
Fines, disabled parking restrictions, see Penal Code § 1465.6.
Parking lots, failure to post charges and closing hour, see Vehicle Code § 22950.
Safety roadside rests, refuse disposal violations, see Streets and Highways Code § 224.
Unauthorized wearing of uniforms of California Highway Patrol, see Vehicle Code § 2261.

Research References

2 Witkin, California Criminal Law 4th Crimes Against Public Peace and Welfare § 267 (2021), Misdemeanors.

3 Witkin, California Criminal Law 4th Punishment § 306 (2021), Where Punishment is Not Specified.

§ 42002.1. Failure to stop and submit to inspection of equipment or an unsafe condition endangering a person; punishment

A person convicted of a misdemeanor violation of Section 2800, 2801, or 2803, insofar as it affects a failure to stop and submit to inspection of equipment or for an unsafe condition endangering a person, shall be punished as follows:

(a) By a fine not exceeding fifty dollars ($50) or imprisonment in the county jail not exceeding five days.

(b) For a second conviction within a period of one year, a fine not exceeding one hundred dollars ($100) or imprisonment in the county jail not exceeding 10 days, or both that fine and imprisonment.

(c) For a third or a subsequent conviction within a period of one year, a fine not exceeding five hundred dollars ($500) or imprisonment in the county jail not exceeding six months, or both that fine and imprisonment. *(Added by Stats.2006, c. 898 (S.B.1021), § 6.)*

Cross References

Fulfillment of conditions of probation for the entire period of probation, dismissal of charges, see Penal Code § 1203.4.
Misdemeanor, definition, penalties, see Penal Code §§ 17, 19 and 19.2.

Research References

2 Witkin, California Criminal Law 4th Crimes Against Public Peace and Welfare § 267 (2021), Misdemeanors.
3 Witkin, California Criminal Law 4th Punishment § 716 (2021), Exceptions.
3 Witkin, California Criminal Law 4th Punishment § 720 (2021), Without Probation.

§ 42002.4. Purchase, sale, receipt or possession of vehicles or components with removed or altered serial or identification numbers; punishment

A violation of Section 10751 shall be punished by imprisonment in the county jail not exceeding six months if the value of the property does not exceed nine hundred fifty dollars ($950), and by imprisonment in the county jail not exceeding one year if the value of the property is more than nine hundred fifty dollars ($950). *(Added by Stats.1990, c. 408 (A.B.3483), § 2. Amended by Stats.2009–2010, 3rd Ex.Sess., c. 28 (S.B.18), § 55, eff. Jan. 25, 2010.)*

Research References

2 Witkin, California Criminal Law 4th Crimes Against Property § 308 (2021), Tampering or Injuring.
2 Witkin, California Criminal Law 4th Crimes Against Public Peace and Welfare § 267 (2021), Misdemeanors.

§ 42002.5. Violations of §§ 10852 or 10853 involving vehicle modified for use of disabled person; penalties

Notwithstanding Section 42002, every person convicted of a violation of Section 10852 or 10853 involving a vehicle that has been modified for the use of a disabled veteran or any other disabled person and that displays a special identification license plate issued pursuant to Section 5007 or a distinguishing placard issued pursuant to Section 22511.55 or 22511.59, if those facts are known or should reasonably have been known to the person, shall be punished by a fine of not more than two thousand dollars ($2,000) or by imprisonment in the county jail for not more than one year, or by both the fine and imprisonment. *(Added by Stats.1986, c. 1214, § 2. Amended by Stats.1994, c. 1149 (A.B.2878), § 13.)*

Research References

2 Witkin, California Criminal Law 4th Crimes Against Public Peace and Welfare § 267 (2021), Misdemeanors.

§ 42003. Payment of fines and costs

(a) A judgment that a person convicted of an infraction be punished by a fine may also provide for the payment to be made within a specified time or in specified installments. A judgment granting a defendant time to pay the fine shall order that if the defendant fails to pay the fine or any installment thereof on the date that it is due, he or she shall appear in court on that date for further proceedings. Willful violation of the order is punishable as contempt.

(b) A judgment that a person convicted of any other violation of this code be punished by a fine may also order, adjudge, and decree that the person be imprisoned until the fine is satisfied. In all of these cases, the judgment shall specify the extent of the imprisonment which shall not exceed one day for every thirty dollars ($30) of the fine, nor extend in this case beyond the term for which the defendant might be sentenced to imprisonment for the offense of which he or she was convicted.

(c) In any case when a person appears before a traffic referee or judge of the superior court for adjudication of a violation of this code, the court, upon request of the defendant, shall consider the defendant's ability to pay. Consideration of a defendant's ability to pay may include his or her future earning capacity. A defendant shall bear the burden of demonstrating lack of his or her ability to pay. Express findings by the court as to the factors bearing on the amount of the fine shall not be required. The reasonable cost of these services and of probation shall not exceed the amount determined to be the actual average cost thereof. The court shall order the defendant to appear before a county officer designated by the court to make an inquiry into the ability of the defendant to pay all or a portion of those costs or the court or traffic referee may make this determination at a hearing. At that hearing, the defendant shall be entitled to have, but shall not be limited to, the opportunity to be heard in person, to present witnesses and other documentary evidence, to confront and cross-examine adverse witnesses, to disclosure of the evidence against him or her, and to a written statement of the findings of the court or the county officer. If the court determines that the defendant has the ability to pay all or part of the costs, the court shall set the amount to be reimbursed and order the defendant to pay that sum to the county in the manner in which the court believes reasonable and compatible with the defendant's financial ability; or, with the consent of a defendant who is placed on probation, the court shall order the probation officer to set the amount of payment, which shall not exceed the maximum amount set by the court, and the manner in which the payment shall be made to the county. In making a determination of whether a defendant has the ability to pay, the court shall take into account the amount of any fine imposed upon the defendant and any amount the defendant has been ordered to pay in restitution.

The court may hold additional hearings during the probationary period. If practicable, the court or the probation officer shall order payments to be made on a monthly basis. Execution may be issued on the order in the same manner as a judgment in a civil action. The order to pay all or part of the costs shall not be enforced by contempt.

A payment schedule for reimbursement of the costs of presentence investigation based on income shall be developed by the probation department of each county and approved by the presiding judge of the superior court.

(d) The term "ability to pay" means the overall capability of the defendant to reimburse the costs, or a portion of the costs, of conducting the presentence investigation, preparing the presentence report, and probation, and includes, but is not limited to, all of the following regarding the defendant:

(1) Present financial position.

(2) Reasonably discernible future financial position. In no event shall the court consider a period of more than six months from the date of the hearing for purposes of determining reasonably discernible future financial position.

(3) Likelihood that the defendant will be able to obtain employment within the six-month period from the date of the hearing.

(4) Any other factors that may bear upon the defendant's financial capability to reimburse the county for the costs.

(e) At any time during the pendency of the judgment rendered according to the terms of this section, a defendant against whom a judgment has been rendered may petition the rendering court to modify or vacate its previous judgment on the grounds of a change of circumstances with regard to the defendant's ability to pay the judgment. The court shall advise the defendant of this right at the time of rendering of the judgment. *(Stats.1959, c. 3, p. 1785, § 42003. Amended by Stats.1968, c. 1192, p. 2264, § 17, operative Jan. 1, 1969; Stats.1971, c. 1532, p. 3037, § 4, operative May 3, 1972; Stats.1976, c. 1045, p. 4666, § 4; Stats.1993, c. 674 (A.B.708), § 1; Stats.1996, c. 124 (A.B.3470), § 149; Stats.1996, c. 1077 (A.B.2898), § 30; Stats.2002, c. 784 (S.B.1316), § 605.)*

Law Revision Commission Comments

Subdivision (c) of Section 42003 is amended to reflect unification of the municipal and superior courts pursuant to Article VI, Section 5(e), of the California Constitution. [32 Cal.L.Rev.Comm. Reports 546 (2002)].

Cross References

Deposit of bail, parking violations, see Vehicle Code § 40509.
Felonies and offenses punishable either as felonies or misdemeanor violation of court order punishable as contempt, see Vehicle Code § 40000.3.
Notice of violations to department, courtesy warning notice, criteria for arrest warrant issuance, see Vehicle Code § 40509.5.
Suspension of driver's license for violation of section, see Vehicle Code § 13365.
Violation a misdemeanor, see Vehicle Code § 40000.25.

Research References

West's California Judicial Council Forms CR–320, Can't Afford to Pay Fine: Traffic and Other Infractions.
West's California Judicial Council Forms CR–321, Can't Afford to Pay Fine: Traffic and Other Infractions (Court Order).
West's California Judicial Council Forms TR–320, Can't Afford to Pay Fine: Traffic and Other Infractions.
West's California Judicial Council Forms TR–321, Can't Afford to Pay Fine: Traffic and Other Infractions (Court Order).
2 Witkin, California Criminal Law 4th Crimes Against Public Peace and Welfare § 265 (2021), In General.
6 Witkin, California Criminal Law 4th Criminal Judgment § 176 (2021), Fines and Fees.
3 Witkin, California Criminal Law 4th Punishment § 105 (2021), General Rule.

§ 42004. Determination of penalty

For the purpose of determining the penalty to be imposed pursuant to this code, the court may consider a written report from the Department of Motor Vehicles containing information from its records showing prior convictions; and the communication is prima facie evidence of such convictions, if the defendant admits them, regardless of whether or not the complaint commencing the proceedings has alleged prior convictions.

For the purpose of this chapter a prior bail forfeiture shall be deemed to be a conviction of the offense charged. *(Added by Stats.1968, c. 1192, p. 2265, § 19, operative Jan. 1, 1969.)*

Cross References

Forfeiture of bail, see Penal Code §§ 1269b, 1305 et seq.
Report of accident or conviction, see Vehicle Code § 1806.
Report of court action, see Vehicle Code § 1803.

Research References

2 Witkin, California Criminal Law 4th Crimes Against Public Peace and Welfare § 265 (2021), In General.

§ 42004.5. 24-hour suspension of sentence

Upon conviction of any violation of any provision of this code, other than a felony violation and except this section, execution of sentence of imprisonment in the county jail shall be suspended, at the request of the convicted person, for a period of 24 hours, unless the judge determines that the person would not return. If, prior to the end of such period, the person does not deliver himself into custody for commencement of the execution of such sentence, his failure to appear shall constitute a misdemeanor. *(Added by Stats.1973, c. 1184, p. 2470, § 1.)*

Research References

2 Witkin, California Criminal Law 4th Crimes Against Public Peace and Welfare § 265 (2021), In General.
6 Witkin, California Criminal Law 4th Criminal Judgment § 174 (2021), Jail Sentence.

§ 42005. Traffic violator schools; courts may permit or require attendance; conviction records not confidential; convictions not added to violation point counts; commercial motor vehicle drivers ineligible; other violations rendering operators ineligible; choice of school; failure to attend as misdemeanor

(a) Except as otherwise provided in this section, after a deposit of the fee under Section 42007 or bail, a plea of guilty or no contest, or a conviction, a court may order or permit a person who holds a noncommercial class C, class M1, or class M2 driver's license who pleads guilty or who pleads no contest or who is convicted of a traffic offense to attend a traffic violator school licensed pursuant to Chapter 1.5 (commencing with Section 11200) of Division 5.

(b) To the extent the court is in conformance with Title 49 of the Code of Federal Regulations, and except as otherwise provided in this section, the court may, after deposit of the fee under Section 42007 or bail, order or permit a person who holds a class A, class B, or commercial class C driver's license, who pleads guilty or no contest or is convicted of a traffic offense, to complete a course of instruction at a licensed traffic violator school if the person was operating a vehicle requiring only a class C license, or a class M license. The court may not order that the record of conviction be kept confidential. However, the conviction shall not be added to a violation point count for purposes of determining whether a driver is presumed to be a negligent operator under Section 12810.5.

(c) The court shall not order that a conviction of an offense be kept confidential according to Section 1808.7, order or permit avoidance of consideration of violation point counts under subdivision (b), or permit a person, regardless of the driver's license class, to complete a program at a licensed traffic violator school in lieu of adjudicating an offense if any of the following applies to the offense:

(1) It occurred in a commercial motor vehicle, as defined in subdivision (b) of Section 15210.

(2) Is a violation of Section 20001, 20002, 23103, 23104, 23105, 23140, 23152, or 23153, or of Section 23103, as specified in Section 23103.5.

(3) It is a violation described in subdivision (d) or (e) of Section 12810.

(d) A person ordered to attend a traffic violator school pursuant to subdivision (a) or (b) may choose the traffic violator school the person will attend. The court shall provide to each person subject to that order or referral the department's current list of licensed traffic violator schools.

(e) A person who willfully fails to comply with a court order to attend traffic violator school is guilty of a misdemeanor. *(Added by Stats.2010, c. 599 (A.B.2499), § 13.5, operative July 1, 2011. Amended by Stats.2012, c. 302 (A.B.1888), § 2.)*

Cross References

Ability-to-pay determination, impact on eligibility to attend traffic violator school, see Government Code § 68645.15.
Additional fee imposed for maintenance of funding for court security upon conviction for criminal offense involving violations of Vehicle Code, exceptions, see Penal Code § 1465.8.

Child passenger restraint violators, see Vehicle Code § 27360 et seq.
General misdemeanors, see Vehicle Code § 42002.
Occupational licensing, traffic violator schools, duties of Judicial Council, see Vehicle Code § 11205.4.
Traffic violator school defined, see Vehicle Code § 626.
Violation a misdemeanor, see Vehicle Code § 40000.25

Research References

2 Witkin, California Criminal Law 4th Crimes Against Public Peace and Welfare § 265 (2021), In General.
1 Witkin California Criminal Law 4th Introduction to Crimes § 90 (2021), Misdemeanor-Infraction.

§ 42005.1. Participation in study of traffic violator schools in lieu of attendance

The court may order a person designated to attend a traffic violator school to instead participate in a study of traffic violator schools licensed pursuant to Chapter 1.5 (commencing with Section 11200) of Division 5. The person's participation in that study constitutes attending a licensed traffic violator school program. *(Added by Stats.1990, c. 1354 (A.B.2999), § 1. Amended by Stats. 2010, c. 599 (A.B.2499), § 13.7.)*

§ 42005.3. Driver awareness or education program participation; traffic violations; application of section to diversion programs

(a) A local authority shall not allow a person who is alleged to have committed a traffic offense in violation of this code, or an ordinance or resolution adopted under this code, to participate in a driver awareness or education program or in any other diversion program as an alternative to the procedure required to be followed under this code for alleged violations of this code.

(b) This section does not apply to a diversion program sanctioned by local law enforcement for a person who committed an infraction not involving a motor vehicle. *(Added by Stats.1992, c. 1199 (A.B.2409), § 13, eff. Sept. 30, 1992. Amended by Stats.2015, c. 306 (A.B.902), § 1, eff. Jan. 1, 2016.)*

Research References

2 Witkin, California Criminal Law 4th Crimes Against Public Peace and Welfare § 265 (2021), In General.

§ 42005.5. Attendance at school for traffic violators; computation of average daily attendance

Notwithstanding Section 46300 or 84500 of the Education Code or any other provision of law, on and after September 1, 1985, attendance at a school for traffic violators permitted or ordered pursuant to Section 41501 or 42005 shall not be included in computing the average daily attendance of any school district, community college district, or other public educational institution for purposes of allocation of state funds. *(Added by Stats.1985, c. 959, § 1. Amended by Stats.2010, c. 599 (A.B.2499), § 15.)*

§ 42006. Night court assessment

(a) Except as provided in subdivision (c), there may be levied a special assessment in an amount equal to one dollar ($1) for every fine, forfeiture, and traffic violator school fee imposed and collected by any court that conducts a night or weekend session of the court, on all offenses involving a violation of a section of this code or any local ordinance adopted pursuant to this code, except offenses relating to parking.

(b) When a person makes a deposit of bail for an offense to which this section applies, in a case in which the person is required to appear in a court that conducts a night or weekend session, the person making the deposit shall also deposit a sufficient amount to include the assessment prescribed in this section for forfeited bail. If bail is forfeited, the amount of the assessment shall be transmitted by the clerk of the court to the county treasury for disposition as prescribed by subdivision (d).

(c) If a court conducts night or weekend sessions at two or more locations, the court may do either of the following:

(1) Levy assessments only on those persons who are required to appear at the location where night or weekend sessions are held.

(2) Levy assessments on persons who have the option to appear at a location where night or weekend court sessions are held and that is within 25 miles of the location of the court where the person is otherwise required to appear.

(d) After a determination by the court of the amount of the assessment due, the clerk of the court shall collect the amount and transmit it as provided in subdivision (g).

(e) In any case where a person convicted of any offense to which this section applies is imprisoned until the fine is satisfied, the court shall waive the penalty assessment.

(f) As used in subdivisions (g) and (h), the following terms have the following meanings:

(1) "Court Facilities Trust Fund" means the fund established by Section 70352 of the Government Code.

(2) "Location" means a court facility holding night or weekend sessions under this section.

(3) "Transfer of responsibility" means the transfer of responsibility for court facilities from the counties to the state pursuant to Chapter 5.7 (commencing with Section 70301) of Title 8 of the Government Code.

(g)(1) If transfer of responsibility for a location has occurred, the clerk shall collect any assessment imposed pursuant to subdivision (c) and transmit it to the Court Facilities Trust Fund. Moneys deposited pursuant to this subdivision shall be used for any purpose provided by subdivision (b) of Section 70352 of the Government Code.

(2) If transfer of responsibility for a location has not occurred, the clerk shall collect any assessment imposed pursuant to subdivision (c) and transmit it to the county treasury to be deposited in the night court session fund, and the moneys in the fund shall be expended by the county for maintaining courts for which transfer of responsibility has not occurred and that have night or weekend sessions for traffic offenses.

(h)(1) The county treasurer of each county shall transfer from the night court session fund to the Court Facilities Trust Fund an amount that is the same percentage of the night court session fund as of January 1, 2009, as the square footage of locations for which transfer of responsibility has occurred on or before January 1, 2009, is to the total square footage of locations.

(2) For locations for which transfer of responsibility occurs after January 1, 2009, the county treasurer shall, at the time of transfer of any location, transfer from the night court session fund to the Court Facilities Trust Fund an amount that is the same percentage of the night court session fund as the square footage of the location for which transfer of responsibility is occurring is to the sum of the square footage of locations for which transfer of responsibility has not occurred and the square footage of the location being transferred.

(3) Upon the transfer of responsibility for all locations, the county treasurer shall transfer to the Court Facilities Trust Fund any amount remaining in the night court session fund.

(4) Any expenditures made from the fund for a purpose other than those specified in paragraph (2) of subdivision (g) shall be repaid to the state for deposit in the Court Facilities Trust Fund. *(Added by Stats.1965, c. 1705, p. 3839, § 3. Amended by Stats.1970, c. 1009, p. 1816, § 3; Stats.1973, c. 739, p. 1332, § 1; Stats.1974, c. 181, p. 367, § 4; Stats.1974, c. 1265, p. 2745, § 1; Stats.1981, c. 362, p. 1539, § 4; Stats.1982, c. 900, p. 3329, § 1; Stats.1991, c. 613 (A.B.195), § 12; Stats.2007, c. 738 (A.B.1248), § 53; Stats.2008, c. 218 (A.B.1949), § 7.)*

Cross References

Trial scheduling, written not guilty pleas, see Vehicle Code § 40519.

Research References

4 Witkin, California Criminal Law 4th Pretrial Proceedings § 300 (2021), Plea Options for Infractions.

§ 42007. Uniform fee for traffic violator school

(a)(1) The clerk of the court shall collect a fee from every person who is ordered or permitted to attend a traffic violator school pursuant to Section 41501 or 42005 in an amount equal to the total bail set forth for the eligible offense on the uniform countywide bail schedule. As used in this subdivision, "total bail" means the amount established pursuant to Section 1269b of the Penal Code in accordance with the Uniform Bail and Penalty Schedule adopted by the Judicial Council, including all assessments, surcharges, and penalty amounts. Where multiple offenses are charged in a single notice to appear, the "total bail" is the amount applicable for the greater of the qualifying offenses. However, the court may determine a lesser fee under this subdivision upon a showing that the defendant is unable to pay the full amount.

The fee shall not include the cost, or any part thereof, of traffic safety instruction offered by a traffic violator school.

(2) The clerk may accept from a defendant who is ordered or permitted to attend traffic violator school a payment of at least 10 percent of the fee required by paragraph (1) upon filing a written agreement by the defendant to pay the remainder of the fee according to an installment payment schedule of no more than 90 days as agreed upon with the court. The Judicial Council shall prescribe the form of the agreement for payment of the fee in installments. When the defendant signs the Judicial Council form for payment of the fee in installments, the court shall continue the case to the date in the agreement to complete payment of the fee and submit the certificate of completion of traffic violator school to the court. The clerk shall collect a fee of up to thirty-five dollars ($35) to cover administrative and clerical costs for processing an installment payment of the traffic violator school fee under this paragraph.

(3) If a defendant fails to make an installment payment of the fee according to an installment agreement, the court may convert the fee to bail, declare it forfeited, and report the forfeiture as a conviction under Section 1803. The court may also charge a failure to pay under Section 40508 and impose a civil assessment as provided in Section 1214.1 of the Penal Code or issue an arrest warrant for a failure to pay. For the purposes of reporting a conviction under this subdivision to the department under Section 1803, the date that the court declares the bail forfeited shall be reported as the date of conviction.

(b) Revenues derived from the fee collected under this section shall be deposited in accordance with Section 68084 of the Government Code in the general fund of the county and, as may be applicable, distributed as follows:

(1) In any county in which a fund is established pursuant to Section 76100 or 76101 of the Government Code, the sum of one dollar ($1) for each fund so established shall be deposited with the county treasurer and placed in that fund.

(2) In any county that has established a Maddy Emergency Medical Services Fund pursuant to Section 1797.98a of the Health and Safety Code, an amount equal to the sum of each two dollars ($2) for every seven dollars ($7) that would have been collected pursuant to Section 76000 of the Government Code and, commencing January 1, 2009, an amount equal to the sum of each two dollars ($2) for every ten dollars ($10) that would have been collected pursuant to Section 76000.5 of the Government Code with respect to those counties to which that section is applicable shall be deposited in that fund. Nothing in the act that added this paragraph shall be interpreted in a manner that would result in either of the following:

(A) The utilization of penalty assessment funds that had been set aside, on or before January 1, 2000, to finance debt service on a capital facility that existed before January 1, 2000.

(B) The reduction of the availability of penalty assessment revenues that had been pledged, on or before January 1, 2000, as a means of financing a facility which was approved by a county board of supervisors, but on January 1, 2000, is not under construction.

(3) The amount of the fee that is attributable to Section 70372 of the Government Code shall be transferred pursuant to subdivision (f) of that section.

(c) For fees resulting from city arrests, an amount equal to the amount of base fines that would have been deposited in the treasury of the appropriate city pursuant to paragraph (3) of subdivision (b) of Section 1463.001 of the Penal Code shall be deposited in the treasury of the appropriate city.

(d) The clerk of the court, in a county that offers traffic school shall include in any courtesy notice mailed to a defendant for an offense that qualifies for traffic school attendance the following statement:

NOTICE: If you are eligible and decide not to attend traffic school your automobile insurance may be adversely affected. For drivers with a noncommercial driver's license, one conviction in any 18–month period will be held confidential and not show on your driving record if you complete a traffic violator school program. For drivers with a commercial driver's license, one conviction in any 18–month period will show on your driving record without a violation point if you complete a traffic violator school program.

(e) Notwithstanding any other provision of law, a county that has established a Maddy Emergency Medical Services Fund pursuant to Section 1797. 98a of the Health and Safety Code shall not be held liable for having deposited into the fund, prior to January 1, 2009, an amount equal to two dollars ($2) for every ten dollars ($10) that would have been collected pursuant to Section 76000.5 of the Government Code from revenues derived from traffic violator school fees collected pursuant to this section. *(Added by Stats.1976, c. 1205, p. 5487, § 1. Amended by Stats.1981, c. 362, p. 1539, § 5; Stats.1985, c. 396, § 24, eff. July 30, 1985; Stats.1985, c. 1289, § 4; Stats.1987, c. 775, § 1; Stats.1990, c. 1354 (A.B.2999), § 4; Stats.1991, c. 90 (A.B.1297), § 73, eff. June 30, 1991; Stats.1991, c. 189 (A.B.544), § 43, eff. July 29, 1991; Stats.1991, c. 1168 (A.B.2142), § 9, eff. Oct. 14, 1991; Stats.1997, c. 850 (A.B.233), § 59; Stats.1999, c. 679 (S.B.623), § 2; Stats.2003, c. 592 (S.B.256), § 26; Stats.2004, c. 193 (S.B.111), § 201; Stats.2007, c. 738 (A.B.1248), § 54; Stats.2008, c. 511 (A.B.3076), § 1, eff. Sept. 28, 2008; Stats.2010, c. 599 (A.B.2499), § 16; Stats.2010, c. 720 (S.B.857), § 37, eff. Oct. 19, 2010; Stats.2011, c. 341 (S.B.565), § 6; Stats.2013, c. 523 (S.B.788), § 31.)*

Cross References

Additional fee imposed for maintenance of funding for court security upon conviction for criminal offense involving violations of Vehicle Code, exceptions, see Penal Code § 1465.8.

Court facility funding, assessments on criminal convictions, see Government Code § 1463.

Maddy Emergency Medical Services Fund, report to Legislature on implementation and status, see Health and Safety Code § 1797.98b.

Occupational licensing, traffic violator schools, duties of Judicial Council, see Vehicle Code § 11205.4.

State surcharge on state penalty imposed on fines, penalties, or forfeitures imposed and collected by the courts for offenses involving Vehicle Code violations, exceptions, see Penal Code § 1465.7.

Research References

West's California Judicial Council Forms TR–310, Agreement to Pay Traffic Violator School Fees in Installments.

2 Witkin, California Criminal Law 4th Crimes Against Public Peace and Welfare § 265 (2021), In General.

§ 42007.1. Amount of fee collected pursuant to subd. (a) of § 42007; allocation of fees assessed pursuant to subd. (c) of § 11208

(a) The amount collected by the clerk pursuant to subdivision (a) of Section 42007 shall be in an amount equal to the total bail set forth for the eligible offense on the uniform countywide bail schedule plus a forty-nine-dollar ($49) fee, and a fee determined by the department to be sufficient to defray the cost of routine monitoring of traffic violator school instruction pursuant to subdivision (c) of Section 11208, and a fee, if any, established by the court pursuant to subdivision (c) of Section 11205.2 to defray the costs incurred by a traffic assistance program.

(b) Notwithstanding subdivision (b) of Section 42007, the revenue from the forty-nine-dollar ($49) fee collected under this section shall be deposited in the county general fund. Fifty–one percent of the amount collected under this section and deposited into the county general fund shall be transmitted therefrom monthly to the Controller for deposit in the State Court Facilities Construction Fund, established in Section 70371 of the Government Code.

(c) The fee assessed pursuant to subdivision (c) of Section 11208 shall be allocated to the department to defray the costs of monitoring traffic violator school instruction. *(Added by Stats.1997, c. 850 (A.B.233), § 60. Amended by Stats.2008, c. 311 (S.B.1407), § 31; Stats.2010, c. 599 (A.B.2499), § 17; Stats.2021, c. 79 (A.B.143), § 38, eff. July 16, 2021.)*

§ 42007.3. Traffic violator school for infraction violations relating to steady red circular or arrow signal; lane use control signals; illuminated flashing red traffic signal; allocation of fees

(a) Notwithstanding Section 42007, revenues derived from fees collected under Section 42007 from each person required or permitted to attend traffic violator school pursuant to Section 41501 or 42005 as a result of a violation of subdivision (a) or (c) of Section 21453, subdivision (c) of Section 21454, or subdivision (a) of Section 21457 shall be allocated as follows:

(1) The first 30 percent of the amount collected shall be allocated to the general fund of the city or county in which the offense occurred.

(2) The balance of the amount collected shall be deposited by the county treasurer under Section 42007.

(b) This section does not apply to the additional forty-nine-dollar ($49) court administrative fee assessed pursuant to subdivision (c) of Section 11208 collected under subdivision (a) of Section 42007.1. *(Added by Stats.1997, c. 852 (A.B.1191), § 5. Amended by Stats.2010, c. 599 (A.B.2499), § 18.)*

§ 42007.4. Use of fees collected from persons attending traffic violator school as a result of railroad grade crossing violations

(a) Notwithstanding Section 42007, revenues derived from fees collected under Section 42007 from each person required or permitted to attend traffic violator school pursuant to Section 369b of the Penal Code as a result of a violation of subdivision (c) of Section 21752, involving railroad grade crossings, or Section 22451 or 22452 shall be allocated as follows:

(1) If the offense occurred in an area where a transit district or transportation commission established under Division 12 (commencing with Section 130000) of the Public Utilities Code provides rail transportation, the first 30 percent of the amount collected shall be allocated to the general fund of that transit district or transportation commission to be used only for public safety and public education purposes relating to railroad grade crossings.

(2) If there is no transit district or transportation commission providing rail transportation in the area where the offense occurred, the first 30 percent of the amount collected shall be allocated to the general fund of the county in which the offense occurred, to be used only for public safety and public education purposes relating to railroad grade crossings.

(3) The balance of the amount collected shall be deposited by the county treasurer under Section 1463 of the Penal Code.

(4) A transit district, transportation commission, or a county that is allocated funds pursuant to paragraph (1) or (2) shall provide public safety and public education relating to railroad grade crossings only to the extent that those purposes are funded by the allocations provided pursuant to paragraph (1) or (2).

(b) This section does not apply to the additional forty-nine-dollar ($49) court administrative fee assessed pursuant to subdivision (c) of Section 11208 collected under subdivision (a) of Section 42007.1. *(Added by Stats.1999, c. 841 (A.B.923), § 6. Amended by Stats.2010, c. 599 (A.B.2499), § 19.)*

§ 42008. County amnesty program for delinquent fines and bail; implementation and application; amount; effect of payment under program; deposit of funds

(a) Any county may operate an amnesty program for delinquent fines and bail imposed for an infraction or misdemeanor violation of the Vehicle Code, except parking violations of the Vehicle Code and violations of Section 23103, 23104, 23152, or 23153. The program shall be implemented by the courts in accordance with Judicial Council guidelines, and shall apply to infraction or misdemeanor violations of the Vehicle Code, except parking violations, upon which a fine or bail was delinquent on or before April 1, 1991.

(b) Under the amnesty program, any person owing a fine or bail due on or before April 1, 1991, that was imposed for an infraction or misdemeanor violation of the Vehicle Code, except violations of Section 23103, 23104, 23152, or 23153 or parking violations, may pay to the superior court the amount scheduled by the court, which shall be either (1) 70 percent of the total fine or bail or (2) the amount of one hundred dollars ($100) for an infraction or five hundred dollars ($500) for a misdemeanor. This amount shall be accepted by the court in full satisfaction of the delinquent fine or bail.

(c) No criminal action shall be brought against any person for a delinquent fine or bail paid under this amnesty program and no other additional penalties shall be assessed for the late payment of the fine or bail made under the amnesty program.

(d) Notwithstanding Section 1463 of the Penal Code, the total amount of funds collected by the courts pursuant to the amnesty program created by this section shall be deposited in the county treasury. *(Added by Stats.1991, c. 90 (A.B.1297), § 74, eff. June 30, 1991. Amended by Stats.1991, c. 189 (A.B.544), § 44, eff. July 29, 1991; Stats.1991, c. 1168 (A.B.2142), § 10, eff. Oct. 14, 1991; Stats.1992, c. 696 (A.B.1344), § 96, eff. Sept. 15, 1992; Stats.1998, c. 931 (S.B.2139), § 464, eff. Sept. 28, 1998; Stats.2002, c. 784 (S.B. 1316), § 606.)*

Law Revision Commission Comments

Section 42008 is amended to accommodate unification of the municipal and superior courts in a county. Cal. Const. art. VI, § 5(e). The section is also amended to reflect elimination of the justice court. Cal. Const. art. VI, §§ 1, 5(b).

The phrase "of the Penal Code" was inadvertently omitted from subdivision (d) when originally enacted. [28 Cal.L.Rev.Comm. Reports 51 (1998)].

Subdivision (b) of Section 42008 is amended to reflect unification of the municipal and superior courts pursuant to Article VI, Section 5(e), of the California Constitution. [32 Cal.L.Rev.Comm. Reports 548 (2002)].

§ 42008.5. County one-time amnesty program

(a) A county may establish a one-time amnesty program for fines and bail that have been delinquent for not less than six months as of the date upon which the program commences and were imposed for an infraction or misdemeanor violation of this code, except parking violations of this code and violations of Section 23103, 23104, 23105, 23152, or 23153.

(b) A person owing a fine or bail that is eligible for amnesty under the program may pay to the superior or juvenile court the amount scheduled by the court, that shall be accepted by the court in full satisfaction of the delinquent fine or bail and shall be either of the following:

(1) Seventy percent of the total fine or bail.

(2) The amount of one hundred dollars ($100) for an infraction or five hundred dollars ($500) for a misdemeanor.

(c) The amnesty program shall be implemented by the courts of the county on a one-time basis and conducted in accordance with Judicial Council guidelines for a period of not less than 120 days. The program shall operate not longer than six months from the date the court initiates the program.

(d) No criminal action shall be brought against a person for a delinquent fine or bail paid under the amnesty program and no other additional penalties, except as provided in Section 1214.1 of the Penal Code, shall be assessed for the late payment of the fine or bail made under the amnesty program.

(e) Notwithstanding Section 1463 of the Penal Code, the total amount of funds collected by the courts pursuant to the amnesty program shall be deposited in the county treasury until 150 percent of the cost of operating the program, excluding capital expenditures, have been so deposited. Thereafter, 37 percent of the amount of the delinquent fines and bail deposited in the county treasury shall be distributed by the county pursuant to Section 1464 of the Penal Code, 26 percent of the amount deposited shall be distributed by the county pursuant to Article 2 (commencing with Section 76100) of Chapter 12 of Title 8 of the Government Code, and the remaining 37 percent of the amount deposited shall be retained by the county.

(f) The deposit of fines and bails in the county treasury as described in subdivision (e) is limited to the amnesty program described in this section, and it is the intent of the Legislature that it shall not be considered a precedent with respect to affecting programs that receive funding pursuant to Section 1463 of the Penal Code.

(g) Each county participating in the program shall file, not later than six months after the termination of the program, a written report with the Assembly Committee on Judiciary and the Senate Committee on Judiciary. The report shall summarize the amount of money collected, operating costs of the program, distribution of funds collected, and when possible, how the funds were expended. *(Added by Stats.1996, c. 742 (A.B.3095), § 1, eff. Sept. 23, 1996. Amended by Stats.2002, c. 784 (S.B.1316), § 607; Stats.2007, c. 682 (A.B.430), § 21.)*

Law Revision Commission Comments

Subdivision (b) of Section 42008.5 is amended to reflect unification of the municipal and superior courts pursuant to Article VI, Section 5(e), of the California Constitution. [32 Cal.L.Rev.Comm. Reports 549 (2002)].

§ 42008.7. State amnesty program

(a) The State of California continues to face a fiscal and economic crisis affecting the State Budget and the overall state economy. In light of this crisis, a one-time infraction amnesty program would do the following:

(1) Provide relief to individuals who have found themselves in violation of a court-ordered obligation because they are financially unable to pay traffic bail or fines.

(2) Provide increased revenue at a time when revenue is scarce by encouraging payment of old fines that have remained unpaid.

(3) Allow courts and counties to resolve older delinquent cases and focus limited resources on collecting on more recent cases.

(b) A one-time amnesty program for fines and bail meeting the eligibility requirements set forth in subdivision (e) shall be established in each county. Unless agreed otherwise by the court and the county in writing, the government entities that are responsible for the collection of delinquent court-ordered debt shall be responsible for implementation of the amnesty program as to that debt, maintaining the same division of responsibility in place with respect to the collection of court-ordered debt under subdivision (b) of Section 1463.010 of the Penal Code.

(c) As used in this section, the term "fine" or "bail" refers to the total amounts due in connection with a specific violation, which include, but are not limited to, the following:

(1) Base fine or bail, as established by court order, by statute, or by the court's bail schedule.

(2) Penalty assessments imposed pursuant to Section 1464 of the Penal Code and Sections 70372, 76000, 76000.5, 76104.6, and 76104.7 of the Government Code.

(3) Civil assessment imposed pursuant to Section 1214.1 of the Penal Code.

(4) State surcharge imposed pursuant to Section 1465.7 of the Penal Code.

(5) Court security fee imposed pursuant to Section 1465.8 of the Penal Code.

(d) In addition to and at the same time as the mandatory one-time amnesty program is established pursuant to subdivision (b), the court and the county may jointly agree to extend that amnesty program to fines and bail imposed for a misdemeanor violation of this code and a violation of Section 853.7 of the Penal Code added to the misdemeanor case otherwise subject to the amnesty. The amnesty program authorized pursuant to this subdivision shall not apply to parking violations and violations of Section 23103, 23104, 23105, 23152, or 23153 of this code.

(e) Violations are only eligible for amnesty if paragraph (1), (2), or (3) applies and the requirements of paragraphs (4), (5), and (6) are met:

(1) The violation is an infraction violation filed with the court.

(2) It is a violation of subdivision (a) or (b) of Section 40508, or a violation of Section 853.7 of the Penal Code added to the case subject to paragraph (1).

(3) The violation is a misdemeanor violation filed with the court to which subdivision (d) applies.

(4) The due date for payment of the fine or bail was on or before January 1, 2009.

(5) The defendant does not owe victim restitution on any case within the county.

(6) There are no outstanding misdemeanor or felony warrants for the defendant within the county, except for misdemeanor warrants for misdemeanor violations authorized by the court and the county pursuant to subdivision (d).

(f) Each amnesty program shall accept, in full satisfaction of any eligible fine or bail, 50 percent of the fine or bail amount, as defined in subdivision (c) of this section. Payment of a fine or bail under an amnesty program implemented pursuant to this section shall be accepted beginning January 1, 2012, and ending June 30, 2012. The Judicial Council shall adopt guidelines for the amnesty program no later than November 1, 2011, and each program shall be conducted in accordance with Judicial Council guidelines.

(g) No criminal action shall be brought against a person for a delinquent fine or bail paid under the amnesty program.

(h) The total amount of funds collected under the amnesty program shall as soon as practical after receipt thereof be deposited in the county treasury or the account established under Section 77009 of the Government Code. Any unreimbursed costs of operating the amnesty program, excluding capital expenditures, may be deducted from the revenues collected under the amnesty program by the court or the county that incurred the expense of operating the program. Notwithstanding Section 1203.1d of the Penal Code, the remaining revenues collected under the amnesty program shall be distributed on a pro rata basis in the same manner as a partial payment distributed pursuant to Section 1462.5 of the Penal Code.

(i) Each court or county implementing an amnesty program shall file, not later than September 30, 2012, a written report with the Judicial Council, on a form approved by the Judicial Council. The report shall include information about the number of cases resolved, the amount of money collected, and the operating costs of the amnesty program. Notwithstanding Section 10231.5 of the Government Code, on or before December 31, 2012, the Judicial Council shall submit a report to the Legislature summarizing the information provided by each court or county. *(Added by Stats.2010, c. 720 (S.B.857), § 38, eff. Oct. 19, 2010. Amended by Stats.2011, c. 662 (A.B.1358), § 1.)*

§ 42008.8. One-time infraction amnesty program; eligibility

(a) The Legislature finds and declares that a one-time infraction amnesty program would do all of the following:

(1) Provide relief to individuals who have found themselves in violation of a court-ordered obligation because they have unpaid traffic bail or fines.

(2) Provide relief to individuals who have found themselves in violation of a court-ordered obligation or who have had their driving privileges suspended pursuant to Section 13365.

(3) Provide increased revenue at a time when revenue is scarce by encouraging payment of old fines that have remained unpaid.

(4) Allow courts and counties to resolve older delinquent cases and focus limited resources on collections for more recent cases.

(b) A one-time amnesty program for unpaid fines and bail meeting the eligibility requirements set forth in subdivision (g) shall be established in each county. Unless agreed otherwise by the court and the county in writing, the government entities that are responsible for the collection of delinquent court-ordered debt shall be responsible for implementation of the amnesty program as to that debt, maintaining the same division of responsibility in place with respect to the collection of court-ordered debt under subdivision (b) of Section 1463.010 of the Penal Code.

(c) As used in this section, the term "fine" or "bail" refers to the total amounts due in connection with a specific violation, including, but not limited to, all of the following:

(1) Base fine or bail, as established by court order, by statute, or by the court's bail schedule.

(2) Penalty assessments imposed pursuant to Section 1464 of the Penal Code, and Sections 70372, 76000, 76000.5, 76104.6, and 76104.7 of, and paragraph (1) of subdivision (c) of Section 76000.10 of, the Government Code, and Section 42006 of this code.

(3) State surcharges imposed pursuant to Section 1465.7 of the Penal Code.

(4) Court operations assessments imposed pursuant to Section 1465.8 of the Penal Code.

(5) Criminal conviction assessments pursuant to Section 70373 of the Government Code.

(d) Notwithstanding subdivision (c), any civil assessment imposed pursuant to Section 1214.1 of the Penal Code shall not be collected, nor shall the payment of that assessment be a requirement of participation in the amnesty program.

(e) Concurrent with the amnesty program established pursuant to subdivision (b), between October 1, 2015, to March 31, 2017, inclusive, the following shall apply:

(1) The court shall, within 90 days, issue and file the appropriate certificate pursuant to subdivisions (a) and (b) of Section 40509 for any participant of the one-time amnesty program established pursuant to subdivision (b) demonstrating that the participant has appeared in court, paid the fine, or otherwise satisfied the court, if the driving privilege of that participant was suspended pursuant to Section 13365 in connection with a specific violation described in paragraph (1), (2), or (3) of subdivision (g). For applications submitted prior to January 1, 2017, that remain outstanding as of that date, the court shall issue and file the certificate no later than March 31, 2017. For applications submitted on or before March 31, 2017, all terms and procedures related to the participant's payment plans shall remain in effect after March 31, 2017.

(2) The court shall, within 90 days, issue and file with the department the appropriate certificate pursuant to subdivisions (a) and (b) of Section 40509 for any person in good standing in a comprehensive collection program pursuant to subdivision (c) of Section 1463.007 of the Penal Code demonstrating that the person has appeared in court, paid the fine, or otherwise satisfied the court, if the driving privilege was suspended pursuant to Section 13365 in connection with a specific violation described in paragraph (1), (2), or (3) of subdivision (g). For applications submitted prior to January 1, 2017, that remain outstanding as of that date, the court shall issue and file the certificate no later than March 31, 2017. For applications submitted on or before March 31, 2017, all terms and procedures related to the participant's payment plans shall remain in effect after March 31, 2017.

(3) Any person who is eligible for a driver's license pursuant to Section 12801, 12801.5, or 12801.9 shall be eligible for the amnesty program established pursuant to subdivision (b) for any specific violation described in subdivision (g). The department shall issue a driver's license to any person who is eligible pursuant to Section 12801, 12801.5, or 12801.9 if the person is participating in the amnesty program and is otherwise eligible for the driver's license but for the fines or bail to be collected through the program.

(4) The Department of Motor Vehicles shall not deny reinstating the driving privilege of any person who participates in the amnesty program established pursuant to subdivision (b) for any fines or bail in connection with the specific violation that is the basis for participation in the amnesty program.

(f) In addition to, and at the same time as, the mandatory one-time amnesty program is established pursuant to subdivision (b), the court and the county may jointly agree to extend that amnesty program to fines and bail imposed for a misdemeanor violation of this code and a violation of Section 853.7 of the Penal Code that was added to the misdemeanor case otherwise subject to the amnesty. The amnesty program authorized pursuant to this subdivision shall not apply to parking violations and violations of Sections 23103, 23104, 23105, 23152, and 23153.

(g) A violation is only eligible for amnesty if paragraph (1), (2), or (3) applies, and the requirements of paragraphs (4) to (8), inclusive, are met:

(1) The violation is an infraction violation filed with the court.

(2) It is a violation of subdivision (a) or (b) of Section 40508, or a violation of Section 853.7 of the Penal Code that was added to the case subject to paragraph (1).

(3) The violation is a misdemeanor violation filed with the court to which subdivision (f) applies.

(4) The initial due date for payment of the fine or bail was on or before January 1, 2013.

(5) There are no outstanding misdemeanor or felony warrants for the defendant within the county, except for misdemeanor warrants for misdemeanor violations subject to this section.

(6) The person does not owe victim restitution on any case within the county.

(7) The person has not made any payments for the violation after September 30, 2015, to a comprehensive collection program in the county pursuant to subdivision (c) of Section 1463.007 of the Penal Code.

(8) The person filed a request with the court on or before March 31, 2017.

(h)(1) Except as provided in paragraph (2), each amnesty program shall accept, in full satisfaction of any eligible fine or bail, 50 percent of the fine or bail amount, as defined in subdivision (c).

(2) If the participant certifies under penalty of perjury that he or she receives any of the public benefits listed in subdivision (a) of Section 68632 of the Government Code or is within the conditions described in subdivision (b) of Section 68632 of the Government Code, the amnesty program shall accept, in full satisfaction of any eligible fine or bail, 20 percent of the fine or bail amount, as defined in subdivision (c).

(i) The Judicial Council, in consultation with the California State Association of Counties, shall adopt guidelines for the amnesty program no later than October 1, 2015, and each program shall be conducted in accordance with the Judicial Council's guidelines. As part of its guidelines, the Judicial Council shall include all of the following:

(1) Each court or county responsible for implementation of the amnesty program pursuant to subdivision (b) shall recover costs pursuant to subdivision (a) of Section 1463.007 of the Penal Code and may charge an amnesty program fee of fifty dollars ($50) that may be collected with the receipt of the first payment of a participant.

(2) A payment plan option created pursuant to Judicial Council guidelines in which a monthly payment is equal to the amount that an eligible participant can afford to pay per month consistent with Sections 68633 and 68634 of the Government Code. If a participant chooses the payment plan option, the county or court shall collect all relevant information to allow for collection by the Franchise Tax Board pursuant to existing protocols prescribed by the Franchise Tax Board to collect delinquent debts of any amount in which a participant is delinquent or otherwise in default under his or her amnesty payment plan.

(3) If a participant does not comply with the terms of his or her payment plan under the amnesty program, including failing to make one or more payments, the appropriate agency shall send a notice to the participant that he or she has failed to make one or more payments and that the participant has 30 days to either resume making payments or to request that the agency change the payment amount. If the participant fails to respond to the notice within 30 days, the appropriate agency may refer the participant to the Franchise Tax Board for collection of any remaining balance owed, including an amount equal to the reasonable administrative costs incurred by the Franchise Tax Board to collect the delinquent amount owed. The Franchise Tax Board shall collect any delinquent amounts owed pursuant to existing protocols prescribed by the Franchise Tax Board. The comprehensive collection program may also utilize additional collection efforts pursuant to Section 1463.007 of the Penal Code, except for subparagraph (C) of paragraph (4) of subdivision (c) of that section.

(4) A plan for outreach that will, at a minimum, make available via an Internet Web site relevant information regarding the amnesty program, including how an individual may participate in the amnesty program.

(5) The Judicial Council shall reimburse costs incurred by the Department of Motor Vehicles up to an amount not to exceed two hundred fifty thousand dollars ($250,000), including all of the following:

(A) Providing on a separate insert with each motor vehicle registration renewal notice a summary of the amnesty program established pursuant to this section that is compliant with Section 7292 of the Government Code.

(B) Posting on the department's Internet Web site information regarding the amnesty program.

(C) Personnel costs associated with the amnesty program.

(j) The Judicial Council, in consultation with the department, may, within its existing resources, consider, adopt, or develop recommendations for an appropriate mechanism or mechanisms to allow reinstatement of the driving privilege of any person who otherwise meets the criteria for amnesty but who has violations in more than one county.

(k) A criminal action shall not be brought against a person for a delinquent fine or bail paid under the amnesty program.

(*l*)(1) The total amount of funds collected under the amnesty program shall, as soon as practical after receipt thereof, be deposited in the county treasury or the account established under Section 77009 of the Government Code. After acceptance of the amount specified in subdivision (h), notwithstanding Section 1203.1d of the Penal Code, the remaining revenues collected under the amnesty program shall be distributed on a pro rata basis in the same manner as a partial payment distributed pursuant to Section 1462.5 of the Penal Code.

(2) Notwithstanding Section 1464 of the Penal Code, the amount of funds collected pursuant to this section that would be available for distribution pursuant to subdivision (f) of Section 1464 of the Penal Code shall instead be distributed as follows:

(A) The first two hundred fifty thousand dollars ($250,000) received shall be transferred to the Judicial Council.

(B) Following the transfer of the funds described in subparagraph (A), once a month, both of the following transfers shall occur:

(i) An amount equal to 82.20 percent of the amount of funds collected pursuant to this section during the preceding month shall be transferred into the Peace Officers' Training Fund.

(ii) An amount equal to 17.80 percent of the amount of funds collected pursuant to this section during the preceding month shall be transferred into the Corrections Training Fund.

(m) Each court or county implementing an amnesty program shall file, not later than May 31, 2017, a written report with the Judicial Council, on a form approved by the Judicial Council. The report shall include information about the number of cases resolved, the amount of money collected, and the operating costs of the amnesty program. Notwithstanding Section 10231.5 of the Government Code, on or before August 31, 2017, the Judicial Council shall submit a report to the Legislature summarizing the information provided by each court or county. *(Added by Stats.2015, c. 26 (S.B.85), § 42, eff. June 24, 2015. Amended by Stats.2015, c. 385 (S.B.405), § 2, eff. Sept. 30, 2015; Stats.2016, c. 779 (S.B.881), § 1, eff. Jan. 1, 2017.)*

§ 42009. Violations within highway construction or maintenance area

(a) For an offense specified in subdivision (b), committed by the driver of a vehicle within a highway construction or maintenance area, during any time when traffic is regulated or restricted through or around that area pursuant to Section 21367, or when the highway construction or maintenance is actually being performed in the area by workers acting in their official capacity, the fine, in a misdemeanor case, shall be double the amount otherwise prescribed. In an infraction case, the fine shall be one category higher than the penalty otherwise prescribed by the uniform traffic penalty schedule established pursuant to Section 40310.

(b) A violation of the following is an offense that is subject to subdivision (a):

(1) Section 21367, relating to regulation of traffic at a construction site.

(2) Article 3 (commencing with Section 21450) of Chapter 2 of Division 11, relating to obedience to traffic devices.

(3) Chapter 3 (commencing with Section 21650) of Division 11, relating to driving, overtaking, and passing.

(4) Chapter 4 (commencing with Section 21800) of Division 11, relating to yielding the right-of-way.

(5) Chapter 6 (commencing with Section 22100) of Division 11, relating to turning and stopping and turn signals.

(6) Chapter 7 (commencing with Section 22348) of Division 11, relating to speed limits.

(7) Chapter 8 (commencing with Section 22450) of Division 11, relating to special traffic stops.

(8) Section 23103, relating to reckless driving.

(9) Section 23104 or 23105, relating to reckless driving which results in bodily injury to another.

(10) Section 23109 or 23109.1, relating to speed contests.

(11) Section 23152, relating to driving under the influence of alcohol or a controlled substance, or a violation of Section 23103, as specified in Section 23103.5, relating to alcohol-related reckless driving.

(12) Section 23153, relating to driving under the influence of alcohol or a controlled substance, which results in bodily injury to another.

(13) Section 23154, relating to convicted drunk drivers operating a motor vehicle with a blood-alcohol concentration of 0.01 percent or greater.

(14) Section 23220, relating to drinking while driving.

(15) Section 23221, relating to drinking in a motor vehicle while on the highway.

(16) Section 23222, relating to driving while possessing an open alcoholic beverage container.

(17) Section 23223, relating to being in a vehicle on the highway while possessing an open alcoholic beverage container.

(18) Section 23224, relating to being a driver or passenger under the age of 21 possessing an open alcoholic beverage container.

(19) Section 23225, relating to being the owner or driver of a vehicle in which there is an open alcoholic beverage container.

(20) Section 23226, relating to being a passenger in a vehicle in which there is an open alcoholic beverage container.

(c) This section applies only when construction or maintenance work is actually being performed by workers, and there are work zone traffic control devices, traffic controls or warning signs, or any combination of those, to notify motorists and pedestrians of construction or maintenance workers in the area. *(Added by Stats.1993, c. 674 (A.B.708), § 2. Amended by Stats.2007, c. 682 (A.B.430), § 22; Stats.2007, c. 749 (A.B.1165), § 6.5, operative Jan. 1, 2009.)*

Research References

2 Witkin, California Criminal Law 4th Crimes Against Public Peace and Welfare § 265 (2021), In General.

§ 42010. Offenses committed within Safety Enhancement–Double Fine Zones

(a) For an offense specified in subdivision (b) that is committed by the driver of a vehicle within an area that has been designated as a Safety Enhancement–Double Fine Zone pursuant to Section 97 and following of the Streets and Highways Code, the fine, in a misdemeanor case, shall be double the amount otherwise prescribed, and, in an infraction case, the fine shall be one category higher than the penalty otherwise prescribed by the uniform traffic penalty schedule established pursuant to Section 40310.

(b) A violation of the following is an offense that is subject to subdivision (a):

(1) Chapter 3 (commencing with Section 21650) of Division 11, relating to driving, overtaking, and passing.

(2) Chapter 7 (commencing with Section 22348) of Division 11, relating to speed limits.

(3) Section 23103, relating to reckless driving.

(4) Section 23104 or 23105, relating to reckless driving that results in bodily injury to another.

(5) Section 23109 or 23109.1, relating to speed contests.

(6) Section 23152, relating to driving under the influence of alcohol or a controlled substance, or a violation of Section 23103, as specified in Section 23103.5, relating to alcohol-related reckless driving.

(7) Section 23153, relating to driving under the influence of alcohol or a controlled substance, which results in bodily injury to another.

(8) Section 23154, relating to convicted drunk drivers operating a motor vehicle with a blood-alcohol concentration of 0.01 percent or greater.

(9) Section 23220, relating to drinking while driving.

(10) Section 23221, relating to drinking in a motor vehicle while on the highway.

(11) Section 23222, relating to driving while possessing an open alcoholic beverage container.

(12) Section 23223, relating to being in a vehicle on the highway while possessing an open alcoholic beverage container.

(13) Section 23224, relating to being a driver or passenger under 21 years of age possessing an open alcoholic beverage container.

(14) Section 23225, relating to being the owner or driver of a vehicle in which there is an open alcoholic beverage container.

(15) Section 23226, relating to being a passenger in a vehicle in which there is an open alcoholic beverage container.

(c) This section applies only when traffic controls or warning signs have been placed pursuant to Section 97 or 97.1 of the Streets and Highways Code.

(d)(1) Notwithstanding any other provision of law, the enhanced fine imposed pursuant to this section shall be based only on the base fine imposed for the underlying offense and shall not include any other enhancements imposed pursuant to law.

(2) Notwithstanding any other provision of law, any additional penalty, forfeiture, or assessment imposed by any other statute shall be based on the amount of the base fine before enhancement or doubling and shall not be based on the amount of the enhanced fine imposed pursuant to this section. *(Added by Stats.2006, c. 179 (S.B.3), § 3. Amended by Stats.2007, c. 682 (A.B.430), § 23; Stats.2007, c. 749 (A.B.1165), § 7.5, operative Jan. 1, 2009.)*

Cross References

Designation of Safety Enhancement-Double Fine Zones, see Streets and Highways Code § 97.

Vasco Road Safety Enhancement–Double Fine Zone, requirements, limitation of liability, see Streets and Highways Code § 97.4.

Research References

2 Witkin, California Criminal Law 4th Crimes Against Public Peace and Welfare § 265 (2021), In General.

ARTICLE 2. WEIGHT VIOLATIONS

§ 42030. Penalties for violations of weight limitation provisions

(a) Every person convicted of a violation of any weight limitation provision of Division 15 (commencing with Section 35000), and every person convicted of a violation of Section 21461 with respect to signs provided pursuant to Section 35654 or 35752, and every person convicted of a violation of Section 40001 for requiring the operation of a vehicle upon a highway in violation of any provision referred to in this section shall be punished by a fine which equals the amounts specified in the following table:

Pounds of excess weight	Fine
0 - 1,000	$ 20
1,001- 1,500	30
1,501- 2,000	40
2,001- 2,500	55
2,501- 3,000	85
3,001- 3,500	105
3,501- 4,000	125
4,001- 4,500	145
4,501- 5,000	175
5,001- 6,000	.04 each lb.
6,001- 7,000	.06 each lb.
7,001- 8,000	.08 each lb.
8,001-10,000	.15 each lb.
10,001 and over	.20 each lb.

(b) No part of the penalties prescribed by this section shall be suspended for a conviction of any of the following:

(1) Section 40001 for requiring operation of a vehicle upon a highway in violation of any provision referred to in this section.

(2) Any provision referred to in this section when the amount of the weight exceeds 4,000 pounds.

(3) Any provision referred to in this section when a second or subsequent conviction of a violation thereof occurs within three years immediately preceding the violation charged.

(c) However, notwithstanding any other provision of this section, the court shall exercise discretion with respect to the imposition of the fine under this section for excess weight not exceeding 1,000 pounds if the load of the vehicle cited consisted entirely of field-loaded, unprocessed bulk agricultural or forest products or livestock being transported from the field to the first point of processing or handling.

(d) Notwithstanding any other provision of this section, the court may exercise discretion with respect to the imposition of the fine under this section if any applicable local permit was obtained prior to the court hearing and, at the time of issuance of the notice to appear, the motor carrier was transporting construction equipment or materials and a valid extra-legal load permit from the Department of Transportation was in effect. *(Stats.1959, c. 3, p. 1785, § 42030. Amended by Stats.1971, c. 259, p. 415, § 2, operative May 3, 1972; Stats.1983, c. 145, § 19, eff. June 28, 1983; Stats.1984, c. 542, § 10; Stats.1996, c. 456 (A.B.2345), § 1.)*

Cross References

Axle weight limits, see Vehicle Code § 35550.
Computation of allowable gross weight, see Vehicle Code § 35551.
State Route 2 from La Canada Flintridge to Los Angeles County, vehicle weight restriction, see Vehicle Code § 35655.6.
Vehicles transporting logs, see Vehicle Code § 35552.
Violation of decreased restrictions, see Vehicle Code § 35753.
Violation of special permit, see Vehicle Code § 35784.

Research References

2 Witkin, California Criminal Law 4th Crimes Against Public Peace and Welfare § 266 (2021), Infractions.

§ 42030.1. Penalties for violations of declared gross vehicle weight limitation provisions

(a) Every person convicted of a violation of any declared gross vehicle weight limitation provision of this code, shall be punished by a fine that equals the amounts specified in the following table:

Pounds in Excess of the Declared Gross Vehicle Weight	Fine
1,001–1,500	$ 250
1,501–2,000	300
2,001–2,500	350
2,501–3,000	400
3,001–3,500	450
3,501–4,000	500
4,001–4,500	550
4,501–5,000	600
5,001–6,000	700
6,001–7,000	800
7,001–8,000	900
8,001–10,000	1,000
10,001 and over	2,000

(b) No part of the penalties prescribed by this section shall be suspended for a conviction of any of the following:

(1) Section 40001 for requiring operation of a vehicle upon a highway in violation of any provision referred to in this section.

(2) Any provision referred to in this section when a second or subsequent conviction of a violation thereof occurs within three years immediately preceding the violation charged. *(Added by Stats.2000, c. 861 (S.B.2084), § 58, eff. Sept. 29, 2000.)*

Research References

2 Witkin, California Criminal Law 4th Crimes Against Public Peace and Welfare § 327 (2021), Miscellaneous Regulations.

§ 42031. Weight and axle or wheel weight

Whenever the gross weight and any axle or wheel weight of a vehicle are in excess of the limits prescribed in this code, the excess weights shall be deemed one offense in violation of this code. *(Stats.1959, c. 3, p. 1786, § 42031.)*

Cross References

Applicability of this section to trolley coaches, see Vehicle Code § 21051.
Axle weight limits, see Vehicle Code § 35550.

§ 42032. Excessive weight violation convictions; ownership or operation of vehicles used for collection of garbage, etc.; penalties

(a) In addition to any other fines and penalties, any local public agency which owns or operates vehicles used for the collection of garbage, refuse, or rubbish and which has, within any 90-day period, been convicted an excessive number of times for operating those vehicles in violation of any of the weight limitations set forth in Chapter 5 (commencing with Section 35550) of Division 15, taking into consideration the total number of trip routes for those vehicles which are normally scheduled in the same 90-day period, may be assessed a civil penalty not to exceed two thousand five hundred dollars ($2,500) for each violation. Nothing in this section affects the legal standards, proof requirements, or penalty provisions of any other provision of the law.

(b) The penalties imposed by this section shall be assessed and recovered in a civil action brought by the Attorney General or by any district attorney or city attorney. Prior to undertaking a civil action, a reasonable effort for informal resolution of the problem of excessive violations shall be made by the applicable attorney. Penalties recovered shall be paid to the Treasurer for deposit in the State Highway Account in the State Transportation Fund and used, upon appropriation, for purposes of highway maintenance. *(Added by Stats.1990, c. 88 (A.B.776), § 1.)*

CHAPTER 2. DISPOSITION OF FEES, FINES, AND FORFEITURES

ARTICLE 1. FINES AND FORFEITURES

Section

§ 42200. Disposition by cities

(a) Of the total amount of fines and forfeitures received by a city under Section 1463 of the Penal Code that proportion which is represented by fines and forfeitures collected from any person charged with a misdemeanor under this code following arrest by an officer employed by a city, shall be paid into the treasury of the city and deposited in a special fund to be known as the "Traffic Safety Fund," and shall be used exclusively for official traffic control devices, the maintenance thereof, equipment and supplies for traffic law enforcement and traffic accident prevention, and for the maintenance, improvement, or construction of public streets, bridges, and culverts within the city, but the fund shall not be used to pay the compensation of traffic or other police officers. The fund may be used to pay the compensation of school crossing guards who are not regular full-time members of the police department of the city.

(b) For purposes of this section, "city" includes any city, city and county, district, including any enterprise special district, community service district, or county service area engaged in police protection activities as reported to the Controller for inclusion in the 1989–90 edition of the Financial Transactions Report Concerning Special Districts under the heading of Police Protection and Public Safety, authority, or other local agency (other than a county) which employs persons authorized to make arrests or to issue notices to appear or notices of violation which may be filed in court. *(Stats.1959, c. 3, p. 1787, § 42200. Amended by Stats.1995, c. 285 (A.B.433), § 2.)*

Cross References

Misdemeanor defined, see Penal Code § 17.
Reimbursement of school districts employing school crossing guards from funds collected pursuant to this section, see Education Code § 45451.

§ 42201. Disposition by county

(a) Of the total amount of fines and forfeitures received by a county under Section 1463.001 of the Penal Code, fines and forfeitures collected from any person charged with a misdemeanor under this code following arrest by any officer employed by the state or by the county shall be paid into the general fund of the county. However, the board of supervisors of the county may, by resolution, provide that a portion thereof be transferred into the road fund of the county.

(b) The board of supervisors of a county may enter into a contract with the Department of the California Highway Patrol for the purpose of providing adequate protection for school pupils who are required to cross heavily traveled streets, highways, and roadways in the unincorporated areas of the county. When requested, the Department of the California Highway Patrol may provide such service and the county shall reimburse the state for salaries and wages of crossing guards furnished by the Department of the California Highway Patrol pursuant to such contract, including any necessary retirement and general administrative costs and expenses in connection therewith, and may pay the costs thereof from amounts deposited in the road fund pursuant to this section.

(c) Fines and forfeitures received by a county under Section 1463.001 of the Penal Code may be used to pay the compensation of school crossing guards and necessary equipment costs and administrative costs.

(d) When requested by any county which had in effect on June 30, 1979, a contract with the Department of the California Highway Patrol, to provide protection for school pupils at school crossings, the department upon request of a county shall continue to administer such school crossing program until June 30, 1980. The county shall reimburse the Department of the California Highway Patrol for general administrative costs and expenses in connection therewith, except that, effective January 1, 1980, the crossing guards shall be furnished to the California Highway Patrol and such crossing guards shall be employees of the county, the county superintendent of schools, the affected school districts, or both the superintendent and the affected school districts, at the option of the board of supervisors of the county. Any salaries and wages of crossing guards, including necessary retirement and equipment costs and any administrative costs shall be paid or reimbursed by the county from amounts deposited in the road fund pursuant to this section.

(e) The board of supervisors may adopt standards for the provision of school crossing guards. The board has final authority over the total cost of the school crossing guard program of any agency to be paid or reimbursed from amounts deposited in the road fund pursuant to this section. The board of supervisors may specify that a designated county officer, employee, or commissioner is to hire school crossing guards, or, in the alternative, the board may specify that any school district crossing guard program in unincorporated areas shall be maintained by the school districts desiring the program. *(Stats.1959, c. 3, p. 1788, § 42201. Amended by Stats.1961, c. 801, p. 2066, § 15; Stats.1965, c. 60, p. 941, § 1, eff. April 9, 1965; Stats.1968, c. 538, p. 1199, § 2; Stats.1970, c. 1248, p. 2241, § 1, eff. Sept. 16, 1970; Stats.1978, c. 295, p. 619, § 3, eff. June 27, 1978; Stats.1979, c. 1039, p. 3617, § 1, eff. Sept. 26, 1979; Stats.1994, c. 308 (A.B.2544), § 34, eff. July 21, 1994.)*

Cross References

Highway funds, generally, see Streets and Highways Code §§ 1580, 2150.
Reimbursement of school districts employing school crossing guards from funds collected pursuant to this section, see Education Code § 45451.
Road fund, see Streets and Highways Code § 1622.

§ 42201.1. Reimbursement to state for construction of platform scales and vehicle inspection facilities

Fines and forfeitures received by a county under Section 1463 of the Penal Code may be used to reimburse the state for the construction of platform scales and vehicle inspection facilities in the county. *(Added by Stats.1985, c. 407, § 1, eff. July 30, 1985.)*

§ 42201.5. Disposition of infraction fines and forfeitures

Fines, forfeitures, and deposits of bail collected as a result of a charge or conviction of an infraction shall be deposited and distributed in the same manner as fines, forfeitures, and deposits of bail collected from a person charged with or convicted of a misdemeanor. *(Added by Stats.1968, c. 1192, p. 2265, § 22, operative Jan. 1, 1969.)*

§ 42201.6. Refund of bail deposits; multiple or duplicate deposits; interest

(a) A deposit of bail received with respect to an infraction violation of this code, or any local ordinance adopted pursuant to this code, including, but not limited to, a violation involving the standing or parking of a vehicle, shall be refunded by the agency which issued the notice of violation or the court within 30 days of a cancellation, dismissal, or finding of not guilty of the offense charged.

(b) Multiple or duplicate deposits of bail or parking penalty shall be identified by the court or agency and refunded within 30 days of identification.

(c) Any amount to be refunded in accordance with subdivision (a) or (b) shall accrue interest, at the rate specified in Section 3289 of the Civil Code, on and after the 60th day of a cancellation, dismissal, or finding of not guilty or identification of multiple or duplicate deposits, and shall be refunded as soon as possible thereafter along with accrued interest. *(Added by Stats.1985, c. 1289, § 5. Amended by Stats.1989, c. 290, § 1.)*

§ 42202. Disobedience by officials

Failure, refusal, or neglect on the part of any judicial or other officer or employee receiving or having custody of any fine or forfeiture mentioned in this article either before or after deposit in the respective fund to comply with the foregoing provisions of this article is misconduct in office and ground for removal therefrom. *(Stats.1959, c. 3, p. 1788, § 42202.)*

§ 42203. Disposition of fines and forfeitures for violations on certain county owned premises

Notwithstanding Section 42201 or 42201.5, 50 percent of all fines and forfeitures collected in a superior court upon conviction or upon the forfeiture of bail for violations of any provisions of the Vehicle Code, or of any local ordinance or resolution, relating to stopping, standing, or parking a vehicle, that have occurred upon the premises of facilities physically located in such county, but which are owned by another county, which other county furnishes law enforcement personnel for the premises, shall be transmitted pursuant to this section to the county which owns the facilities upon which the violations occurred. The court receiving such moneys shall, once each month, transmit such moneys received in the preceding month to the county treasurer of the county in which the court is located. Once each month in which the county treasurer receives such moneys, the county treasurer shall transmit to the county which owns such facilities an amount equal to 50 percent thereof. The county owning such facilities shall, upon receipt of such moneys from the superior court of the county in which the facilities are physically located, deposit such moneys in its county treasury for use solely in meeting traffic control and law enforcement expenses on the premises upon which the violations occurred.

This section shall not apply when the county in which such facilities are located performs all law enforcement functions with respect to such facilities. *(Added by Stats.1970, c. 449, p. 898, § 3. Amended by Stats.1998, c. 931 (S.B.2139), § 465, eff. Sept. 28, 1998; Stats.2002, c. 784 (S.B.1316), § 608.)*

Law Revision Commission Comments

Section 42203 is amended to accommodate unification of the municipal and superior courts in a county. Cal. Const. art. VI, § 5(e). The section is also amended to reflect elimination of the justice court. Cal. Const. art. VI, 1, 5(b). [28 Cal.L.Rev.Comm. Reports 51 (1998)].

Section 42203 is amended to reflect unification of the municipal and superior courts pursuant to Article VI, Section 5(e), of the California Constitution. [32 Cal.L.Rev.Comm. Reports 550 (2002)].

§ 42204. Disposition of off-highway vehicle fines and forfeitures

Notwithstanding any other provisions of law, all fines and forfeitures collected for violations of Division 16.5 (commencing with Section 38000) shall be deposited in the appropriate fund in the county where the violation occurred and distributed in the same manner as specified in Section 42201.5, and shall be used for enforcing laws related to the operation of off-highway motor vehicles. *(Added by Stats.1971, c. 1816, p. 3936, § 10, eff. Dec. 22, 1971, operative July 1, 1972. Amended by Stats.1973, c. 974, p. 1874, § 6; Stats.1978, c. 380, p. 1205, § 147; Stats.1982, c. 994, p. 3626, § 16; Stats.2002, c. 563 (A.B.2274), § 46.)*

§ 42205. Disposition of weight fees for commercial vehicles

(a) Notwithstanding Chapter 3 (commencing with Section 42270), the department shall file, at least monthly with the Controller, a report of money received by the department pursuant to Section 9400 for the previous month and shall, at the same time, remit all money so reported to the Treasurer. On order of the Controller, the Treasurer shall deposit all money so remitted into the State Highway Account in the State Transportation Fund, or directly into the Transportation Debt Service Fund as provided in paragraph (2) of subdivision (c) of Section 9400.4, as applicable.

(b) The Legislature shall appropriate from the State Highway Account in the State Transportation Fund to the department and the Franchise Tax Board amounts equal to the costs incurred by each in performing their duties pursuant to Article 3 (commencing with Section 9400) of Chapter 6 of Division 3. The applicable amounts shall be determined so that the appropriate costs for registration and weight fee collection activities are appropriated between the recipients of revenues in proportion to the revenues that would have been received individually by those recipients if the total fee imposed under the Vehicle License Fee Law (Part 5 (commencing with Section 10701) of Division 2 of the Revenue and Taxation Code) was 2 percent of the market value of a vehicle. The remainder of the funds collected under Section 9400 and deposited in the account, other than the direct deposits to the Transportation Debt Service Fund referenced in subdivision (a), may be appropriated to the Department of Transportation, the Department of the California Highway Patrol, and the Department of Motor Vehicles for the purposes authorized under Section 3 of Article XIX of the California Constitution. *(Added by Stats.1981, c. 541, p. 2185, § 38, eff. Sept. 17, 1981, operative Jan. 1, 1982. Amended by Stats.1984, c. 123, § 2; Stats.1994, c. 1243 (S.B.1805), § 77.5, eff. Sept. 30, 1994, operative Jan. 1, 1994; Stats.1996, c. 10 (A.B.1869), § 23, eff. Feb. 9, 1996; Stats.1999, c. 85 (A.B.1660), § 2; Stats.2004, c. 211 (S.B.1096), § 42, eff. Aug. 5, 2004; Stats.2013, c. 35 (S.B.85), § 15, eff. June 27, 2013.)*

Cross References

State Highway Account revenues derived from weight fees, use of revenues to make remaining authorized bond debt service reimbursement and loans to the General Fund, see Streets and Highways Code § 2103.

Transportation Debt Service Fund, creation, use of moneys, Transportation Bond Direct Payment Account, state covenant regarding alteration, amendment, or restriction of specified provisions relating to transfer of weight fees, transfers to General Fund, see Government Code § 16965.

ARTICLE 2. REFUND OF FEES AND PENALTIES

Section

§ 42230. Return after rejection of application

Whenever any application made under this code is accompanied by any fee, except an application for an occupational license accompanied by a fee as specified in Section 9262, 9262.5, 11309, or 11820, or an application for a duplicate driver's license, as required by law, and the application is refused or rejected, the fees shall be returned to the applicant, except that, whenever any application is made for the first set of special plates under subdivision (a) of Section 9262 and the application is refused or rejected, the fee for the special plates only shall be returned to the applicant or, when application is made for the first set of special plates under subdivision (1) of Section 9264 and the application is refused or rejected, the fee for the special plates shall be returned to the applicant. *(Stats.1959, c. 3, p. 1788, § 42230. Amended by Stats.1959, c. 1015, p. 3037, § 1; Stats.1961, c. 1615, p. 3458, § 36; Stats.1963, c. 142, p. 814, § 1; Stats.1967, c. 1064, p. 2694, § 4; Stats.1980, c. 608, p. 1680, § 10; Stats.1996, c. 124 (A.B.3470), § 150.)*

Cross References

Applicability of this section to trolley coaches, see Vehicle Code § 21051.
Department of California Highway Patrol, see Vehicle Code § 2100 et seq.
Grounds for refusal of license, see Vehicle Code § 12805 et seq.
Procedure for refund, see Vehicle Code § 42231 et seq.
Similar provision, see Revenue and Taxation Code § 10901.

§ 42231. Erroneous collection of fees

Whenever any application is made under this code and the application is accompanied by any fee which is excessive or not legally due, or whenever the department in consequence of any error either of fact or of law as to the proper amount of any fee or any penalty thereon or as to the necessity of obtaining any privilege under this code collects any fee or penalty which is excessive, erroneous, or not legally due, the person who has paid the erroneous or excessive fee or penalty, or his agent on his behalf, may apply for and receive a refund of the amount thereof as provided in this article, or the department may refund the same within three years after the date of the payment or collection. *(Stats.1959, c. 3, p. 1788, § 42231. Amended by Stats.1961, c. 20, p. 579, § 2.)*

Cross References

Applicability of this section to trolley coaches, see Vehicle Code § 21051.
Disposition of overpayments of fees less than $10, see Government Code § 16302.1.

§ 42232. Application for refund

The application for refund shall be presented to the department in a format prescribed by the department within three years from the date of payment of the erroneous or excessive fee or penalty and shall identify the payment made and state the grounds upon which it is claimed that the payment was excessive or erroneous. *(Stats.1959, c. 3, p. 1778, § 42232. Amended by Stats.1961, c. 20, p. 579, § 3; Stats.2000, c. 787 (S.B.1404), § 26.)*

Cross References

Applicability of this section to trolley coaches, see Vehicle Code § 21051.

§ 42233. Refund procedures

(a) Whenever any fee or penalty subject to refund under Section 42231 after application therefor has not been paid into the State Treasury, the department shall refund the fee or penalty.

(b) Whenever any fee or penalty subject to refund under Section 42231 after application therefor or Section 10901 of the Revenue and Taxation Code has been paid into the State Treasury to the credit, in whole or in part, of the Motor Vehicle License Fee Account in the Transportation Tax Fund (hereafter referred to in this section as the Motor Vehicle License Fee Account), or to the credit, in whole or in part, of the Motor Vehicle Account in the State Transportation Fund (hereafter referred to in this section as the Motor Vehicle Account), the department shall prepare a claim setting forth the facts pertaining to the fee or penalty sought to be refunded, and the State Controller shall draw his warrant upon the account or accounts to which the fee or penalty was credited. In lieu of filing claims for refund against both the Motor Vehicle Account and the Motor Vehicle License Fee Account when an amount has been determined to be due from both accounts, the director may file a single claim with the State Controller, drawn against the Motor Vehicle Account covering the amount of both refunds, and the State Controller shall thereupon draw his warrant on the Motor Vehicle Account. At least quarterly, the director shall certify to the State Controller the amounts paid from the Motor Vehicle Account which are properly chargeable to the Motor Vehicle License Fee Account supported by such detail as the State Controller may require. Upon order of the State Controller, the amounts so required shall be transferred from the Motor Vehicle License Fee Account to the credit of the Motor Vehicle Account.

(c) This section is an appropriation of any and all amounts necessary to refund and repay any excessive or erroneous fees and penalties collected under this code, and the procedure prescribed in this article for refunds shall be deemed a compliance with the requirements of the Government Code relating to the refund of excessive or erroneous fees or penalties. *(Stats.1959, c. 3, p. 1789, § 42233. Amended by Stats.1974, c. 545, p. 1346, § 268; Stats.1978, c. 669, p. 2158, § 10.)*

Cross References

Applicability of this section to trolley coaches, see Vehicle Code § 21051.
Disposition of overpayments of $10 or less by state agencies, see Government Code § 16302.1.
Refunds in general, see Government Code § 13140 et seq.

§ 42235. Late application for refund

Whenever the department collects any fee which is excessive or not legally due and application for the refund of the fee is not filed within the time prescribed by law because the applicant failed to receive from the department a certificate of registration for the vehicle upon which the refund of fee is sought, the director shall have the power to authorize the payment of a refund in such a case upon a proper showing by the applicant that the delay in applying for the refund was due to the failure to receive the certificate of registration within the statutory period allowed for making application for refund of fees. *(Stats.1959, c. 3, p. 1789, § 42235.)*

ARTICLE 3. UNCOLLECTIBLE COSTS

Section

§ 42240. Unpaid balances of court-imposed costs; unenforceable and uncollectible; vacation of judgment

On and after January 1, 2022, the unpaid balance of any court-imposed costs pursuant to Section 40508.5 and subdivision (g) of Section 40510.5, as those sections read on December 31, 2021, shall be unenforceable and uncollectible and any portion of a judgment imposing those costs shall be vacated. *(Added by Stats.2021, c. 257 (A.B.177), § 45, eff. Sept. 23, 2021.)*

WELFARE AND INSTITUTIONS CODE

Division 2

CHILDREN

Part 1

DELINQUENTS AND WARDS OF THE JUVENILE COURT

CHAPTER 1. COURT–APPOINTED SPECIAL ADVOCATES

§ 100. Program guidelines; funding

(a) The Judicial Council shall establish a planning and advisory group consisting of appropriate professional and program specialists to recommend on the development of program guidelines and funding procedures consistent with this chapter. At a minimum, the council shall adopt program guidelines consistent with the guidelines established by the National Court Appointed Special Advocate Association, and with California law, but the council may require additional or more stringent standards. State funding shall be contingent on a program adopting and adhering to the program guidelines adopted by the council.

(b) The program guidelines adopted by the council shall be adopted and incorporated into local rules of court by each participating superior court as a prerequisite to funding pursuant to this chapter.

(c) The council shall adopt program guidelines and criteria for funding that encourage multicounty CASA programs where appropriate, and shall not provide for funding more than one program per county.

(d) The council shall establish, in a timely fashion, a request-for-proposal process to establish, maintain, or expand local CASA programs and may require local matching funds or in-kind funds not to exceed the proposal request. The maximum state grant per county program per year shall not exceed seventy thousand dollars ($70,000) in counties in which the population is less than 700,000 and shall not exceed one hundred thousand dollars ($100,000) in counties in which the population is 700,000 or more, according to the annual population report provided by the Department of Finance. *(Added by Stats.1988, c. 723, § 5. Amended by Stats.1998, c. 406 (A.B.1590), § 8, eff. Aug. 26, 1998; Stats.2000, c. 447 (S.B.1533), § 12; Stats.2001, c. 824 (A.B.1700), § 37; Stats.2020, c. 36 (A.B.3364), § 45, eff. Jan. 1, 2021.)*

Cross References

CASA defined for purposes of this Chapter, see Welfare and Institutions Code § 101.

Department of Finance, generally, see Government Code § 13000 et seq.

Research References

3 Witkin, California Criminal Law 4th Punishment § 38A (2021), (New) Private Prisons.

§ 101. Definitions

As used in this chapter, the following definitions shall apply:

(a) "Adult" means a person 18 years of age or older.

(b) "Child or minor" means a person under the jurisdiction of the juvenile court pursuant to Section 300, 601, or 602.

(c) "CASA" means a Court–Appointed Special Advocate. "CASA" also refers to a Court Designated Child Advocate in programs that have utilized that title. A CASA has the duties and responsibilities described in this chapter and shall be trained by and function under the auspices of a Court–Appointed Special Advocate program as set forth in this chapter.

(d) "Court" means the superior court, including the juvenile court.

(e) "Dependent" means a person described in Section 300.

(f) "Nonminor dependent" means a person as described in subdivision (v) of Section 11400.

(g) "Ward" means a person described in Section 601 or 602. *(Added by Stats.1988, c. 723, § 5. Amended by Stats.2012, c. 846 (A.B.1712), § 8; Stats.2015, c. 71 (A.B.424), § 1, eff. Jan. 1, 2016.)*

Cross References

Child Abuse and Neglect Reporting Act, notice to child protection agencies or district attorneys, availability of information, see Penal Code § 1170.

Research References

West's California Judicial Council Forms JV–474, Nonminor Dependent—Consent to Copy and Inspect Nonminor Dependent Court File.

§ 102. Staff; appointment of CASAs; duties

(a) Each CASA program shall, if feasible, be staffed by a minimum of one paid administrator. The staff shall be directly accountable to the presiding juvenile court judge and the CASA program board of directors, as applicable.

(b) The program shall provide for volunteers to serve as CASAs. A CASA may be appointed to any dependent, nonminor dependent, or ward who is subject to the jurisdiction of the juvenile court.

(c) Each CASA shall serve at the pleasure of the court having jurisdiction over the proceedings in which a CASA has been appointed and that appointment may continue after the child attains his or her age of majority, with the consent of the nonminor dependent. A CASA shall do all of the following:

(1) Provide independent, factual information to the court regarding the cases to which he or she is appointed.

(2) Represent the best interests of the child involved, and consider the best interests of the family, in the cases to which he or she is appointed.

(3) At the request of the judge, monitor cases to which he or she has been appointed to ensure that the court's orders have been fulfilled.

(d) The Judicial Council, through its rules and regulations, shall require an initial and ongoing training program consistent with this chapter for all persons acting as a CASA, including, but not limited to, each of the following:

(1) Dynamics of child abuse and neglect.

(2) Court structure, including juvenile court laws.

(3) Social service systems.

(4) Child development.

(5) Cultural competency and sensitivity relating to, and best practices for, providing adequate care to lesbian, gay, bisexual, and transgender youth.

(6) Interviewing techniques.

(7) Report writing.

(8) Roles and responsibilities of a CASA.

(9) Rules of evidence and discovery procedures.

(10) Problems associated with verifying reports.

(e) The Judicial Council, through its CASA Advisory Committee, shall adopt guidelines for the screening of CASA volunteers, which shall include personal interviews, reference checks, checks for records of sex offenses and other criminal records, information from the Department of Motor Vehicles, and other information that the Judicial Council deems appropriate. *(Added by Stats.1988, c. 723, § 5. Amended by Stats.2012, c. 846 (A.B.1712), § 9; Stats.2013, c. 300 (A.B.868), § 2; Stats.2015, c. 71 (A.B.424), § 2, eff. Jan. 1, 2016.)*

Cross References

CASA defined for purposes of this Chapter, see Welfare and Institutions Code § 101.
Child or minor defined for purposes of this Chapter, see Welfare and Institutions Code § 101.
Court defined for purposes of this Chapter, see Welfare and Institutions Code § 101.

Research References

West's California Judicial Council Forms JV–474, Nonminor Dependent—Consent to Copy and Inspect Nonminor Dependent Court File.

§ 103. Qualifications; training; investigative authority

(a) Persons acting as a CASA shall be individuals who have demonstrated an interest in children and their welfare. Each CASA shall participate in a training course conducted under the rules and regulations adopted by the Judicial Council and in ongoing training and supervision throughout his or her involvement in the program. Each CASA shall be evaluated before and after initial training to determine his or her fitness for these responsibilities. Ongoing training shall be provided at least monthly.

(b) Each CASA shall commit a minimum of one year of service to a child until a permanent placement is achieved for the child or until relieved by the court, whichever is first. At the end of each year of service, the CASA, with the approval of the court, may recommit for an additional year.

(c) A CASA shall have no associations that create a conflict of interest with his or her duties as a CASA.

(d) An adult otherwise qualified to act as a CASA shall not be discriminated against based upon marital status, socioeconomic factors, or because of any characteristic listed or defined in Section 11135 of the Government Code.

(e) Each CASA is an officer of the court, with the relevant rights and responsibilities that pertain to that role and shall act consistently with the local rules of court pertaining to CASAs.

(f) Each CASA shall be sworn in by a superior court judge or commissioner before beginning his or her duties.

(g) A judge may appoint a CASA when, in the opinion of the judge, a child requires services which can be provided by the CASA, consistent with the local rules of court.

(h) To accomplish the appointment of a CASA, the judge making the appointment shall sign an order, which may grant the CASA the authority to review specific relevant documents and interview parties involved in the case, as well as other persons having significant information relating to the child, to the same extent as any other officer of the court appointed to investigate proceedings on behalf of the court.

(i) Each CASA shall be considered court personnel for purposes of subdivision (a) of Section 827. *(Added by Stats.1988, c. 723, § 5. Amended by Stats.2008, c. 682 (A.B.2654), § 10; Stats.2015, c. 71 (A.B.424), § 3, eff. Jan. 1, 2016.)*

Cross References

Adult defined for purposes of this Chapter, see Welfare and Institutions Code § 101.
CASA defined for purposes of this Chapter, see Welfare and Institutions Code § 101.
Child or minor defined for purposes of this Chapter, see Welfare and Institutions Code § 101.
Court defined for purposes of this Chapter, see Welfare and Institutions Code § 101.

§ 104. Extent of duties; investigations

(a) The court shall determine the extent of the CASA's duties in each case. These duties may include an independent investigation of the circumstances surrounding a case to which he or she has been appointed, interviewing and observing the child and other appropriate individuals, and the reviewing of appropriate records and reports.

(b) The CASA shall report the results of the investigation to the court.

(c) The CASA shall follow the direction and orders of the court and shall provide information specifically requested by the court. *(Added by Stats.1988, c. 723, § 5.)*

Cross References

CASA defined for purposes of this Chapter, see Welfare and Institutions Code § 101.
Child or minor defined for purposes of this Chapter, see Welfare and Institutions Code § 101.
Court defined for purposes of this Chapter, see Welfare and Institutions Code § 101.

§ 105. Confidentiality of records and information

All otherwise confidential records and information acquired or reviewed by a CASA during the course of his or her duties shall remain confidential and shall be disclosed only pursuant to a court order. *(Added by Stats.1988, c. 723, § 5.)*

Cross References

CASA defined for purposes of this Chapter, see Welfare and Institutions Code § 101.
Court defined for purposes of this Chapter, see Welfare and Institutions Code § 101.
Inspection of public records, other exemptions from disclosure, "Conservatee" to "Customer list of telephone answering service", see Government Code § 6276.12.

§ 106. Notice of hearings and proceedings

The CASA shall be notified of hearings and other proceedings concerning the case to which he or she has been appointed. *(Added by Stats.1988, c. 723, § 5.)*

Cross References

CASA defined for purposes of this Chapter, see Welfare and Institutions Code § 101.

Court defined for purposes of this Chapter, see Welfare and Institutions Code § 101.

§ 107. Inspection of records; copies; nonminor dependents

(a) Except as provided in subdivision (b), upon presentation of the order of his or her appointment by the CASA, and upon specific court order and consistent with the rules of evidence, any agency, hospital, school, organization, division or department of the state, physician and surgeon, nurse, other health care provider, psychologist, psychiatrist, police department, or mental health clinic shall permit the CASA to inspect and copy any records relating to the child involved in the case of appointment without the consent of the child or parents.

(b) Subdivision (a) does not apply to the records of or pertaining to a nonminor dependent. The CASA may have access to those records only with the explicit written and informed consent of the nonminor dependent. *(Added by Stats.1988, c. 723, § 5. Amended by Stats.2012, c. 846 (A.B.1712), § 10.)*

Cross References

CASA defined for purposes of this Chapter, see Welfare and Institutions Code § 101.
Child or minor defined for purposes of this Chapter, see Welfare and Institutions Code § 101.
Court defined for purposes of this Chapter, see Welfare and Institutions Code § 101.

§ 108. Report to Legislature

The Judicial Council shall report to the Legislature on the implementation of the program, and shall include recommendations on the continued funding and expansion of the program, as appropriate. *(Added by Stats.1988, c. 723, § 5.)*

§ 109. Participation in certain proceedings

(a) Except as provided in subdivisions (b) and (c), nothing in this chapter permits a person acting as a CASA to participate or appear in criminal proceedings or in proceedings to declare a person a ward of the juvenile court pursuant to Section 601 or 602.

(b) A person acting as a CASA may participate in determinations made pursuant to Section 241.1, and in all delinquency proceedings after adjudication of delinquency.

(c) This section does not apply to a person acting as a CASA when that person is acting solely as a support person to the child or who is in court on behalf of a child who is the victim of a crime. *(Added by Stats.1988, c. 723, § 5. Amended by Stats.2015, c. 71 (A.B.424), § 4, eff. Jan. 1, 2016.)*

Cross References

CASA defined for purposes of this Chapter, see Welfare and Institutions Code § 101.

CHAPTER 2. JUVENILE COURT LAW

ARTICLE 1. GENERAL PROVISIONS

§ 200. Title of chapter

This chapter shall be known and may be cited as the "Arnold–Kennick Juvenile Court Law." *(Added by Stats.1976, c. 1068, p. 4741, § 1.5.)*

Cross References

Liability of public entities and public employees, juvenile court and child protection workers, exceptions to immunity, see Government Code § 820.21.
Minors, incompetent persons or persons for whom conservator appointed, appearance by guardian, waiver of juvenile law rights, see Code of Criminal Procedure § 372.
Privileges,
Privilege for confidential marital communications, juvenile court proceedings, see Evidence Code § 986.
Privilege not to testify against spouse, exceptions to privilege, see Evidence Code § 972.
Probation officers, officers appointed under juvenile court law as ex officio adult probation officers, exception, see Penal Code § 1203.
State School Fund, school districts with change in number of units of average daily attendance at necessary small high school, see Education Code § 41601.7.

§ 201. Construction

The provisions of this chapter, insofar as they are substantially the same as existing statutory provisions relating to the same subject matter, shall be construed as restatements and continuations thereof, and not as new enactments. *(Added by Stats.1976, c. 1068, p. 4741, § 1.5.)*

§ 202. Purpose; protective services; reunification with family; guidance for delinquents; accountability for objectives and results; punishment defined

(a) The purpose of this chapter is to provide for the protection and safety of the public and each minor under the jurisdiction of the juvenile court and to preserve and strengthen the minor's family ties whenever possible, removing the minor from the custody of his or her parents only when necessary for his or her welfare or for the safety and protection of the public. If removal of a minor is determined by the juvenile court to be necessary, reunification of the minor with his or her family shall be a primary objective. If the minor is removed from his or her own family, it is the purpose of this chapter to secure for the minor custody, care, and discipline as nearly as possible equivalent to that which should have been given by his or her parents. This chapter shall be liberally construed to carry out these purposes.

(b) Minors under the jurisdiction of the juvenile court who are in need of protective services shall receive care, treatment, and guidance consistent with their best interest and the best interest of the public. Minors under the jurisdiction of the juvenile court as a consequence of delinquent conduct shall, in conformity with the interests of public safety and protection, receive care, treatment, and guidance that is consistent with their best interest, that holds them accountable for their behavior, and that is appropriate for their circumstances. This guidance may include punishment that is consistent with the rehabilitative objectives of this chapter. If a minor has been removed from the custody of his or her parents, family preservation and family reunification are appropriate goals for the juvenile court to consider when determining the disposition of a minor under the jurisdiction of the juvenile court as a consequence of delinquent conduct when those goals are consistent with his or her best interests and the best interests of the public. When the minor is no longer a ward of the juvenile court, the guidance he or she received should enable him or her to be a law-abiding and productive member of his or her family and the community.

(c) It is also the purpose of this chapter to reaffirm that the duty of a parent to support and maintain a minor child continues, subject to the financial ability of the parent to pay, during any period in which the minor may be declared a ward of the court and removed from the custody of the parent.

(d) Juvenile courts and other public agencies charged with enforcing, interpreting, and administering the juvenile court law shall consider the safety and protection of the public, the importance of redressing injuries to victims, and the best interests of the minor in all deliberations pursuant to this chapter. Participants in the juvenile justice system shall hold themselves accountable for its results. They shall act in conformity with a comprehensive set of objectives established to improve system performance in a vigorous and ongoing manner. In working to improve system performance, the presiding judge of the juvenile court and other juvenile court judges designated by the presiding judge of the juvenile court shall take into consideration the recommendations contained in subdivision (e) of Standard 5.40 of Title 5 of the California Standards of Judicial Administration, contained in the California Rules of Court.

(e) As used in this chapter, "punishment" means the imposition of sanctions. It does not include retribution and shall not include a court order to place a child in foster care as defined by Section 727.3. Permissible sanctions may include any of the following:

(1) Payment of a fine by the minor.

(2) Rendering of compulsory service without compensation performed for the benefit of the community by the minor.

(3) Limitations on the minor's liberty imposed as a condition of probation or parole.

(4) Commitment of the minor to a local detention or treatment facility, such as a juvenile hall, camp, or ranch.

(5) Commitment of the minor to the Division of Juvenile Facilities, Department of Corrections and Rehabilitation.

(f) In addition to the actions authorized by subdivision (e), the juvenile court may, as appropriate, direct the offender to complete a victim impact class, participate in victim offender conferencing subject to the victim's consent, pay restitution to the victim or victims, and make a contribution to the victim restitution fund after all victim restitution orders and fines have been satisfied, in order to hold the offender accountable or restore the victim or community. *(Added by Stats.1984, c. 756, § 2. Amended by Stats.1989, c. 569, § 1, eff. Sept. 21, 1989; Stats.1998, c. 761 (S.B.2074), § 1; Stats.1999, c. 997 (A.B.575), § 1; Stats.2001, c. 830 (S.B.940), § 2; Stats.2007, c. 130 (A.B.299), § 242.)*

Cross References

Attorney notification regarding agency placement decision on dependent child, see Welfare and Institutions Code § 16010.6.
Construction of provisions governing,
Aid and medical assistance, see Welfare and Institutions Code § 11000.
Persons subject to judicial commitment, see Welfare and Institutions Code § 6250.
Department of Corrections, generally, see Penal Code § 5000 et seq.
Statutory construction,
Amended statutes, see Government Code § 9605.
Amendment of repealed statutes, see Government Code § 9609.
Court's duties, see Code of Civil Procedure § 1858.
Intention of Legislature, see Code of Civil Procedure § 1859.
Natural rights preferred, see Code of Civil Procedure § 1866.
Repeal of repealing statutes, see Government Code § 9607.
Temporary suspension of law, see Government Code § 9611.

§ 202.5. Probation officers' duties deemed social service; governing authority

The duties of the probation officer, as described in this chapter with respect to minors alleged or adjudged to be described by Section 300, whether or not delegated pursuant to Section 272, shall be deemed to be social service as defined by Section 10051, and subject to the administration, supervision and regulations of the State Department of Social Services. *(Added by Stats.1982, c. 978, § 3, eff. Sept. 13, 1982, operative July 1, 1982.)*

Cross References

Probation officer or social worker defined for purposes of this Chapter, see Welfare and Institutions Code § 215.

§ 203. Order adjudging minor ward of juvenile court; effect; proceedings

An order adjudging a minor to be a ward of the juvenile court shall not be deemed a conviction of a crime for any purpose, nor shall a proceeding in the juvenile court be deemed a criminal proceeding. *(Added by Stats.1976, c. 1068, p. 4741, § 1.5.)*

Research References

3 Witkin, California Criminal Law 4th Punishment § 86 (2021), Youth Authority Act.
3 Witkin, California Criminal Law 4th Punishment § 421B (2021), (New) in General.

§ 204. Information available for juvenile court proceedings regarding best interest of child; confidentiality

Notwithstanding any other provision of law, except provisions of law governing the retention and storage of data, a family law court and a court hearing a probate guardianship matter shall, upon request from the juvenile court in any county, provide to the court all available information the court deems necessary to make a determination regarding the best interest of a child, as described in Section 202, who is the subject of a proceeding before the juvenile court pursuant to this division. The information shall also be released to a child protective services worker or juvenile probation officer acting within the scope of his or her duties in that proceeding. Any information released pursuant to this section that is confidential pursuant to any other provision of law shall remain confidential and may not be released, except to the extent necessary to comply with this section. No records shared pursuant to this section may be disclosed to any party in a case unless the party requests the agency or court that originates the record to release these records and the request is granted. In counties that provide confidential family law mediation, or confidential dependency mediation, those mediations are not covered by this section. *(Added by Stats.2004, c. 574 (A.B.2228), § 3.)*

Cross References

Child custody evaluations, availability of report, see Family Code § 3111.
Information available for probate guardianship proceeding and guardianship investigator regarding best interest of child, confidentiality, see Probate Code § 1514.5.
Probation officer or social worker defined for purposes of this Chapter, see Welfare and Institutions Code § 215.

§ 204.5. Disclosure of minor's name

Notwithstanding any other provision of law, the name of a minor may be disclosed to the public if the minor is 14 years of age or older and found by the juvenile court to be a person described in Section 602 as a result of a sustained petition for the commission of any of the offenses listed in Section 667.5 of the Penal Code, or in subdivision (c) of Section 1192.7 of the Penal Code. *(Added by Stats.1994, c. 1019 (A.B.3309), § 1.)*

§ 205. Commitments; religious beliefs

All commitments to institutions or for placement in family homes under this chapter shall be, so far as practicable, either to institutions or for placement in family homes of the same religious belief as that of the person so committed or of his parents or to institutions affording opportunity for instruction in such religious belief. *(Added by Stats.1976, c. 1068, p. 4741, § 1.5.)*

Cross References

Commitments to Youth Authority, generally, see Welfare and Institutions Code § 1730 et seq.
Institutions for delinquents, generally, see Welfare and Institutions Code § 1000 et seq.

§ 206. Separate segregated facilities for habitual delinquents or truants; secure and nonsecure facilities; temporary custody; arrest record

Persons taken into custody and persons alleged to be within the description of Section 300, or persons adjudged to be such and made dependent children of the court pursuant to this chapter solely upon that ground, shall be provided by the board of supervisors with separate facilities segregated from persons either alleged or adjudged to come within the description of Section 601 or 602 except as provided in Section 16514. Separate segregated facilities may be provided in the juvenile hall or elsewhere.

The facilities required by this section shall, with regard to minors alleged or adjudged to come within Section 300, be nonsecure.

For the purposes of this section, the term "secure facility" means a facility which is designed and operated so as to insure that all entrances to, and exits from, the facility are under the exclusive control of the staff of the facility, whether or not the person being detained has freedom of movement within the perimeters of the facility, or which relies on locked rooms and buildings, fences, or physical restraints in order to control behavior of its residents. The term "nonsecure facility" means a facility that is not characterized by the use of physically restricting construction, hardware, and procedures and which provides its residents access to the surrounding community with minimal supervision. A facility shall not be deemed secure due solely to any of the following conditions: (1) the existence within the facility of a small room for the protection of individual residents from themselves or others; (2) the adoption of regulations establishing reasonable hours for residents to come and go from the facility based upon a sensible and fair balance between allowing residents free access to the community and providing the staff with sufficient authority to maintain order, limit unreasonable actions by residents, and to ensure that minors placed in their care do not come and go at all hours of the day and night or absent themselves at will for days at a time; and (3) staff control over ingress and egress no greater than that exercised by a prudent parent. The State Department of Social Services may adopt regulations governing the use of small rooms pursuant to this section.

No minor described in this section may be held in temporary custody in any building that contains a jail or lockup for the confinement of adults, unless, while in the building, the minor is under continuous supervision and is not permitted to come into or remain in contact with adults in custody in the building. In addition, no minor who is alleged to be within the description of Section 300 may be held in temporary custody in a building that contains a jail or lockup for the confinement of adults, unless the minor is under the direct and continuous supervision of a peace officer or other child protective agency worker, as specified in Section 11165.9 of the Penal Code, until temporary custody and detention of the minor is assumed pursuant to Section 309. However, if a child protective agency worker is not available to supervise the minor as certified by the law enforcement agency which has custody of the minor, a trained volunteer may be directed to supervise the minor. The volunteer shall be trained and function under the auspices of the agency which utilizes the volunteer. The minor may not remain under the supervision of the volunteer for more than three hours. A county which elects to utilize trained volunteers for the temporary supervision of minors shall adopt guidelines for the training of the volunteers which guidelines shall be approved by the State Department of Social Services. Each county which elects to utilize trained volunteers for the temporary supervision of minors shall report annually to the department on the number of volunteers utilized, the number of minors under their supervision, and the circumstances under which volunteers were utilized.

No record of the detention of such a person shall be made or kept by any law enforcement agency or the Department of Justice as a record of arrest. *(Added by Stats.1982, c. 978, § 3.8, eff. Sept. 13, 1982, operative July 1, 1982. Amended by Stats.1986, c. 1271, § 1; Stats.1987, c. 1485, § 1.5; Stats.1989, c. 913, § 2.)*

Cross References

Jail defined for purposes of this Chapter, see Welfare and Institutions Code § 207.1.
Juvenile court, jurisdiction to adjudge,
Destitute minor, minor in need of effective parental care, minor who is physically dangerous, minor whose home is unfit, and minor who has been freed for adoption, a dependent child, see Welfare and Institutions Code § 300.
Habitually disobedient or truant, a ward of the court, see Welfare and Institutions Code § 601.
Minor who violates laws, a ward of the court, see Welfare and Institutions Code § 602.
Lockup defined for purposes of this Chapter, see Welfare and Institutions Code § 207.1.
Transfer for study, diagnosis and treatment, see Welfare and Institutions Code § 1755.5.

§ 207. Place of detention; contact with other detainees; records; reports; disclosure

(a) A minor shall not be detained in any jail, lockup, juvenile hall, or other secure facility if the minor is taken into custody solely upon the ground that the minor is a person described by Section 213.3, or described by Section 601 or adjudged to be such or made a ward of the juvenile court solely upon that ground, except as provided in subdivision (b). If any such minor, other than a minor described in subdivision (b), is detained, the minor shall be detained in a sheltered-care facility or crisis resolution home as provided for in Section 654, or in a nonsecure facility provided for in subdivision (a), (b), (c), or (d) of Section 727.

(b) A minor taken into custody upon the ground that the minor is a person described in Section 601, or adjudged to be a ward of the juvenile court solely upon that ground, may be held in a secure facility, other than a facility in which adults are held in secure custody, in any of the following circumstances:

(1) For up to 12 hours after having been taken into custody for the purpose of determining if there are any outstanding wants, warrants, or holds against the minor in cases where the arresting officer or probation officer has cause to believe that the wants, warrants, or holds exist.

(2) For up to 24 hours after having been taken into custody, in order to locate the minor's parent or guardian as soon as possible and to arrange the return of the minor to the minor's parent or guardian, with the exception of an out-of-state runaway who is being held pursuant to the Interstate Compact for Juveniles.[1]

(c) Any minor detained in juvenile hall pursuant to subdivision (b) shall not be permitted to come or remain in contact with any person detained on the basis that the minor has been taken into custody upon the ground that the minor is a person described in Section 602 or adjudged to be such or made a ward of the juvenile court upon that ground.

(d) Minors detained in juvenile hall pursuant to Sections 601 and 602 may be held in the same facility provided they are not permitted to come or remain in contact within that facility.

(e) Every county shall keep a record of each minor detained under subdivision (b), the place and length of time of the detention, and the reasons why the detention was necessary. Every county shall report this information to the Board of State and Community Corrections on a monthly basis, on forms to be provided by that agency.

The board shall not disclose the name of the detainee, or any personally identifying information contained in reports sent to the Division of Juvenile Justice under this subdivision. *(Added by Stats.1976, c. 1068, p. 4741, § 1.5. Amended by Stats.1977, c. 910, p. 2782, § 2; Stats.1977, c. 1241, p. 4180, § 1, eff. Oct. 1, 1977; Stats.1978, c. 1061, p. 3271, § 1, eff. Sept. 25, 1978; Stats.1979, c. 373, p. 1387, § 347; Stats.1986, c. 1271, § 2; Stats.1996, c. 12 (A.B.1397), § 2, eff. Feb. 14, 1996; Stats.2010, c. 96 (A.B.2350), § 1; Stats.2014, c. 70 (S.B.1296), § 2, eff. Jan. 1, 2015; Stats.2019, c. 497 (A.B.991), § 289, eff. Jan. 1, 2020.)*

[1] See Welfare and Institutions Code § 1400.

Cross References

Felony defined, see Penal Code § 17.
Jail defined for purposes of this Chapter, see Welfare and Institutions Code § 207.1.
Lockup defined for purposes of this Chapter, see Welfare and Institutions Code § 207.1.
Probation officer or social worker defined for purposes of this Chapter, see Welfare and Institutions Code § 215.

Research References

3 Witkin, California Criminal Law 4th Punishment § 18 (2021), Nature of Confinement.

§ 207.1. Detention of minor in jail or lockup; conditions; implementation assistance; compliance exemptions; extensions; special purpose juvenile halls; evaluation and testing

(a) A court, judge, referee, peace officer, or employee of a detention facility shall not knowingly detain any minor in a jail or lockup, unless otherwise permitted by any other law.

(b)(1) A minor 14 years of age or older who is taken into temporary custody by a peace officer on the basis of being a person described by Section 602, and who, in the reasonable belief of the peace officer, presents a serious security risk of harm to self or others, may be securely detained in a law enforcement facility that contains a lockup for adults, if all of the following conditions are met:

(A) The minor is held in temporary custody for the purpose of investigating the case, facilitating release of the minor to a parent or guardian, or arranging transfer of the minor to an appropriate juvenile facility.

(B) The minor is detained in the law enforcement facility for a period that does not exceed six hours except as provided in subdivision (d).

(C) The minor is informed at the time the minor is securely detained of the purpose of the secure detention, of the length of time the secure detention is expected to last, and of the maximum six-hour period the secure detention is authorized to last. In the event an extension is granted pursuant to subdivision (d), the minor shall be informed of the length of time the extension is expected to last.

(D) Contact between the minor and adults confined in the facility is restricted in accordance with Section 208.

(E) The minor is adequately supervised.

(F) A log or other written record is maintained by the law enforcement agency showing the offense that is the basis for the secure detention of the minor in the facility, the reasons and circumstances forming the basis for the decision to place the minor in secure detention, and the length of time the minor was securely detained.

(2) Any other minor, other than a minor to which paragraph (1) applies, who is taken into temporary custody by a peace officer on the basis that the minor is a person described by Section 602 may be taken to a law enforcement facility that contains a lockup for adults and may be held in temporary custody in the facility for the purposes of investigating the case, facilitating the release of the minor to a parent or guardian, or arranging for the transfer of the minor to an appropriate juvenile facility. While in the law enforcement facility, the minor may not be securely detained and shall be supervised in a manner so as to ensure that there will be no contact with adults in custody in the facility. If the minor is held in temporary, nonsecure custody within the facility, the peace officer shall exercise one of the dispositional options authorized by Sections 626 and 626.5 without unnecessary delay and, in every case, within six hours.

(3) "Law enforcement facility," as used in this subdivision, includes a police station or a sheriff's station, but does not include a jail, as defined in subdivision (g).

(c) The Board of State and Community Corrections shall assist law enforcement agencies, probation departments, and courts with the implementation of this section by doing all of the following:

(1) The board shall advise each law enforcement agency, probation department, and court affected by this section as to its existence and effect.

(2) The board shall make available and, upon request, shall provide, technical assistance to each governmental agency that reported the confinement of a minor in a jail or lockup in calendar year 1984 or 1985. The purpose of this technical assistance is to develop alternatives to the use of jails or lockups for the confinement of minors. These alternatives may include secure or nonsecure facilities located apart from an existing jail or lockup, improved transportation or access to juvenile halls or other juvenile facilities, and other programmatic alternatives recommended by the board. The technical assistance shall take any form the board deems appropriate for effective compliance with this section.

(d)(1)(A) Under the limited conditions of inclement weather, acts of God, or natural disasters that result in the temporary unavailability of transportation, an extension of the six-hour maximum period of detention set forth in paragraph (2) of subdivision (b) may be granted to a county by the Board of Corrections. The extension may be granted only by the board, on an individual, case-by-case basis. If the extension is granted, the detention of minors under those conditions shall not exceed the duration of the special conditions, plus a period reasonably necessary to accomplish transportation of the minor to a suitable juvenile facility, not to exceed six hours after the restoration of available transportation.

(B) A county that receives an extension under this paragraph shall comply with the requirements set forth in subdivision (b). The county also shall provide a written report to the board that specifies when the inclement weather, act of God, or natural disaster ceased to exist, when transportation availability was restored, and when the minor was delivered to a suitable juvenile facility. If the minor was detained in excess of 24 hours, the board shall verify the information contained in the report.

(2) Under the limited condition of temporary unavailability of transportation, an extension of the six-hour maximum period of detention set forth in paragraph (2) of subdivision (b) may be granted by the board to an offshore law enforcement facility. The extension may be granted only by the board, on an individual, case-by-case basis. If the extension is granted, the detention of minors under those conditions shall extend only until the next available mode of transportation can be arranged.

An offshore law enforcement facility that receives an extension under this paragraph shall comply with the requirements set forth in subdivision (b). The facility also shall provide a written report to the board that specifies when the next mode of transportation became available, and when the minor was delivered to a suitable juvenile facility. If the minor was detained in excess of 24 hours, the board shall verify the information contained in the report.

(3) At least annually, the board shall review and report on extensions sought and granted under this subdivision. If, upon that review, the board determines that a county has sought one or more extensions resulting in the excessive confinement of minors in adult facilities, or that a county is engaged in a pattern and practice of seeking extensions, it shall require the county to submit a detailed explanation of the reasons for the extensions sought and an assessment of the need for a conveniently located and suitable juvenile facility. Upon receiving this information, the board shall make available, and the county shall accept, technical assistance for the purpose of developing suitable alternatives to the confinement of minors in adult lockups.

(e) Any county that did not have a juvenile hall on January 1, 1987, may establish a special purpose juvenile hall, as defined by the Board of Corrections, for the detention of minors for a period not to exceed 96 hours. Any county that had a juvenile hall on January 1, 1987, also may establish, in addition to the juvenile hall, a special purpose juvenile hall. The board shall prescribe minimum standards for that type of facility.

(f) No part of a building or a building complex that contains a jail may be converted or utilized as a secure juvenile facility unless all of the following criteria are met:

(1) The juvenile facility is physically, or architecturally, separate and apart from the jail or lockup such that there could be no contact between juveniles and incarcerated adults.

(2) Sharing of nonresidential program areas only occurs where there are written policies and procedures that assure that there is time-phased use of those areas that prevents contact between juveniles and incarcerated adults.

(3) The juvenile facility has a dedicated and separate staff from the jail or lockup, including management, security, and direct care staff. Staff who provide specialized services such as food, laundry, maintenance, engineering, or medical services, who are not normally in contact with detainees, or whose infrequent contacts occur under conditions of separation of juveniles and adults, may serve both populations.

(4) The juvenile facility complies with all applicable state and local statutory, licensing, and regulatory requirements for juvenile facilities of its type.

(g)(1) "Jail," as used in this chapter, means a locked facility administered by a law enforcement or governmental agency, the purpose of which is to detain adults who have been charged with violations of criminal law and are pending trial, or to hold convicted adult criminal offenders sentenced for less than one year.

(2) "Lockup," as used in this chapter, means any locked room or secure enclosure under the control of a sheriff or other peace officer that is primarily for the temporary confinement of adults upon arrest.

(3) "Offshore law enforcement facility," as used in this section, means a sheriff's station containing a lockup for adults that is located on an island located at least 22 miles from the California coastline.

(h) This section shall not be deemed to prevent a peace officer or employee of an adult detention facility or jail from escorting a minor into the detention facility or jail for the purpose of administering an evaluation, test, or chemical test pursuant to Section 23157 of the Vehicle Code, if all of the following conditions are met:

(1) The minor is taken into custody by a peace officer on the basis of being a person described by Section 602 and there is no equipment for the administration of the evaluation, test, or chemical test located at a juvenile facility within a reasonable distance of the point where the minor was taken into custody.

(2) The minor is not locked in a cell or room within the adult detention facility or jail, is under the continuous, personal supervision of a peace officer or employee of the detention facility or jail, and is not permitted to come in contact or remain in contact with in-custody adults.

(3) The evaluation, test, or chemical test administered pursuant to Section 23157 of the Vehicle Code is performed as expeditiously as possible, so that the minor is not delayed unnecessarily within the adult detention facility or jail. Upon completion of the evaluation, test, or chemical test, the minor shall be removed from the detention facility or jail as soon as reasonably possible. A minor shall not be held in custody in an adult detention facility or jail under the authority of this paragraph in excess of two hours. *(Added by Stats.1995, c. 304 (A.B.904), § 2, eff. Aug. 3, 1995. Amended by Stats.1996, c. 12 (A.B.1397), § 3, eff. Feb. 14, 1996; Stats.1997, c. 17 (S.B.947), § 147; Stats.1998, c. 694 (S.B.2147), § 1; Stats.2019, c. 497 (A.B.991), § 290, eff. Jan. 1, 2020; Stats.2020, c. 337 (S.B.823), § 16, eff. Sept. 30, 2020.)*

Research References

West's California Judicial Council Forms JV–710, Order to Transfer Juvenile to Criminal Court Jurisdiction (Welfare and Institutions Code, §707) (Also Available in Spanish).

§ 207.2. Temporary custody

A minor who is held in temporary custody in a law enforcement facility that contains a lockup for adults pursuant to subdivision (b) of Section 207.1 may be released to a parent, guardian, or responsible relative by the law enforcement agency operating the facility, or may at the discretion of the law enforcement agency be released into their own custody, provided that a minor released into their own custody is furnished, upon request, with transportation to their home or to the place where the minor was taken into custody. *(Added by Stats.1992, c. 429 (S.B.1274), § 2, eff. Aug. 3, 1992. Amended by Stats.2017, c. 678 (S.B.190), § 5, eff. Jan. 1, 2018; Stats.2020, c. 337 (S.B.823), § 17, eff. Sept. 30, 2020.)*

§ 207.5. Misrepresentation or false identification to secure admission to facility; misdemeanor

Every person who misrepresents or falsely identifies himself or herself either verbally or by presenting any fraudulent written instrument to any probation officer, or to any superintendent, director, counselor, or employee of a juvenile hall, ranch, or camp for the purpose of securing admission to the premises or grounds of any juvenile hall, ranch, or camp, or to gain access to any minor detained therein, and who would not otherwise qualify for admission or access thereto, is guilty of a misdemeanor. *(Added by Stats.1981, c. 697, p. 2517, § 1. Amended by Stats.1998, c. 694 (S.B.2147), § 2.)*

Cross References

Misdemeanor, definition, penalties, see Penal Code §§ 17, 19 and 19.2.
Probation officer or social worker defined for purposes of this Chapter, see Welfare and Institutions Code § 215.

Research References

2 Witkin, California Criminal Law 4th Crimes Against Governmental Authority § 167 (2021), Misleading Motor Vehicle Authorities or Probation Officers.

§ 208. Detention or sentence to adult facility; contact with adults; adults committed for sex offenses

(a) When any person under 18 years of age is detained in or sentenced to an adult facility, including a jail or other facility established for the purpose of confinement of adults, it shall be unlawful to permit that person to come or remain in contact with adults confined there.

(b) A person who is a ward or dependent child of the juvenile court who is detained in or committed to any state hospital or other state facility shall not be permitted to come or remain in contact with any adult person who has been committed to any state hospital or other state facility as a mentally disordered sex offender under the provisions of Article 1 (commencing with Section 6300) of Chapter 2 of Part 2 of Division 6, or with any adult person who has been charged in an accusatory pleading with the commission of any sex offense for which registration of the convicted offender is required under Section 290 of the Penal Code and who has been committed to any state hospital or other state facility pursuant to Section 1026 or 1370 of the Penal Code.

(c) As used in this section, "contact" does not include participation in supervised group therapy or other supervised treatment activities, participation in work furlough programs, or participation in hospital recreational activities which are directly supervised by employees of the hospital, so long as living arrangements are strictly segregated and all precautions are taken to prevent unauthorized associations.

(d) This section shall be operative January 1, 1998. *(Added by Stats.1993–94, 1st Ex.Sess., c. 23 (A.B.45), § 2, eff. Nov. 30, 1994, operative Jan. 1, 1998. Amended by Stats.2021, c. 18 (S.B.92), § 2, eff. May 14, 2021.)*

§ 208.1. Voice communication services

(a) A county or city youth residential placement or detention center shall provide persons in their custody with accessible, functional voice communication services free of charge to the person initiating and the person receiving the communication.

(b) A county or city agency shall not receive revenue from the provision of voice communication services or any other communication services to any person confined in a county or city youth residential placement or detention center. *(Added by Stats.2022, c. 827 (S.B.1008), § 4, eff. Jan. 1, 2023.)*

§ 208.3. Placement of minor or ward in room confinement; guidelines; length of confinement; exceptions

(a) For purposes of this section, the following definitions apply:

(1) "Juvenile facility" includes any of the following:

(A) A juvenile hall, as described in Section 850.

(B) A juvenile camp or ranch, as described in Article 24 (commencing with Section 880).

(C) A facility of the Department of Corrections and Rehabilitation, Division of Juvenile Justice.

(D) A regional youth educational facility, as described in Section 894.

(E) A youth correctional center, as described in Article 9 (commencing with Section 1850) of Chapter 1 of Division 2.5.

(F) A juvenile regional facility as described in Section 5695.

(G) Any other local or state facility used for the confinement of minors or wards.

(2) "Minor" means a person who is any of the following:

(A) A person under 18 years of age.

(B) A person under the maximum age of juvenile court jurisdiction who is confined in a juvenile facility.

(C) A person under the jurisdiction of the Department of Corrections and Rehabilitation, Division of Juvenile Justice.

(3) "Room confinement" means the placement of a minor or ward in a locked sleeping room or cell with minimal or no contact with persons other than correctional facility staff and attorneys. Room confinement does not include confinement of a minor or ward in a locked single-person room or cell for a brief * * * period lasting no longer than two hours when it is necessary for required institutional operations.

(4) "Ward" means a person who has been declared a ward of the court pursuant to Section 602.

(b) The placement of a minor or ward in room confinement shall be accomplished in accordance with the following guidelines:

(1) Room confinement shall not be used before other less restrictive options have been attempted and exhausted, unless attempting those options poses a threat to the safety or security of any minor, ward, or staff.

(2) Room confinement shall not be used for the purposes of punishment, coercion, convenience, or retaliation by staff.

(3) Room confinement shall not be used to the extent that it compromises the mental and physical health of the minor or ward.

(c) A minor or ward may be held up to four hours in room confinement. After the minor or ward has been held in room confinement for a period of four hours, staff shall do one or more of the following:

(1) Return the minor or ward to general population.

(2) Consult with mental health or medical staff.

(3) Develop an individualized plan that includes the goals and objectives to be met in order to reintegrate the minor or ward to general population.

(d) If room confinement must be extended beyond four hours, staff shall do the following:

(1) Document the reason for room confinement and the basis for the extension, the date and time the minor or ward was first placed in room confinement, and when * * * the minor or ward is eventually released from room confinement.

(2) Develop an individualized plan that includes the goals and objectives to be met in order to reintegrate the minor or ward to general population.

(3) Obtain documented authorization by the facility superintendent or * * * their designee every four hours thereafter.

(e) This section is not intended to limit the use of single-person rooms or cells for the housing of minors or wards in juvenile facilities and, except as provided in subdivision (f), does not apply to normal sleeping hours.

(f) Minors and wards who are confined shall be provided reasonable access to toilets at all hours, including during normal sleeping hours.

(g) This section does not apply to minors or wards in court holding facilities or adult facilities.

(h) This section shall not be construed to conflict with any law providing greater or additional protections to minors or wards.

(i) This section does not apply during an extraordinary, emergency circumstance that requires a significant departure from normal institutional operations, including a natural disaster or facilitywide threat that poses an imminent and substantial risk of harm to multiple staff, minors, or wards. This exception shall apply for the shortest amount of time needed to address the imminent and substantial risk of harm.

(j) This section does not apply when a minor or ward is placed in a locked cell or sleeping room to treat and protect against the spread of a communicable disease for the shortest amount of time required to reduce the risk of infection, with the written approval of a licensed physician or nurse practitioner, when the minor or ward is not required to be in an infirmary for an illness. Additionally, this section does not apply when a minor or ward is placed in a locked cell or sleeping room for required extended care after medical treatment with the written approval of a licensed physician or nurse practitioner, when the minor or ward is not required to be in an infirmary for illness.

* * * *(Added by Stats.2016, c. 726 (S.B.1143), § 1, eff. Jan. 1, 2017, operative Jan. 1, 2018. Amended by Stats.2017, c. 561 (A.B. 1516), § 263, eff. Jan. 1, 2018; Stats.2022, c. 781 (A.B.2321), § 1, eff. Jan. 1, 2023.)*

Cross References

Donation of unused medications, requirements, direct delivery and central storage, see Health and Safety Code § 150202.

§ 208.5. Persons whose case originated in juvenile court; continued housing in county juvenile facility until age 25; petition to house persons age 19 years or older in adult facility; hearing

(a) Notwithstanding any other law, any person whose case originated in juvenile court shall remain, if the person is held in secure detention, in a county juvenile facility until the person attains 25 years of age, except as provided in subdivisions (b) and (c) of this section and Section 731. A person whose case originated in juvenile court but who was sentenced in criminal court shall not serve their sentence in a juvenile facility, but if not otherwise excluded, may remain in the juvenile facility until transferred to serve their sentence in an adult facility. This section is not intended to authorize confinement in a juvenile facility where authority would not otherwise exist.

(b) The probation department may petition the court to house a person who is 19 years of age or older in an adult facility, including a jail or other facility established for the purpose of confinement of adults.

(c) Upon receipt of a petition to house a person who is 19 years of age or older in an adult facility, the court shall hold a hearing. There shall be a rebuttable presumption that the person will be retained in a juvenile facility. At the hearing, the court shall determine whether the person will be moved to an adult facility, and make written findings of its decision based on the totality of the following criteria:

(1) The impact of being held in an adult facility on the physical and mental health and well-being of the person.

(2) The benefits of continued programming at the juvenile facility and whether required education and other services called for in any juvenile court disposition or otherwise required by law or court order can be provided in the adult facility.

(3) The capacity of the adult facility to separate younger and older people as needed and to provide them with safe and age-appropriate housing and program opportunities.

(4) The capacity of the juvenile facility to provide needed separation of older from younger people given the youth currently housed in the facility.

(5) Evidence demonstrating that the juvenile facility is unable to currently manage the person's needs without posing a significant danger to staff or other youth in the facility.

(d) If a person who is 19 to 24 years of age, inclusive, is removed from a juvenile facility pursuant to this section, upon the motion of any party and a showing of changed circumstances, the court shall consider the criteria in subdivision (c) and determine whether the person should be housed at a juvenile facility.

(e) A person who is 19 years of age or older and who has been committed to a county juvenile facility or a facility of a contracted entity shall remain in the facility and shall not be subject to a petition for transfer to an adult facility. This section is not intended to authorize or extend confinement in a juvenile facility where authority would not otherwise exist. *(Added by Stats.2020, c. 337 (S.B.823), § 20, eff. Sept. 30, 2020. Amended by Stats.2021, c. 18 (S.B.92), § 3, eff. May 14, 2021.)*

Cross References

Jail defined for purposes of this Chapter, see Welfare and Institutions Code § 207.1.
Powers and duties of Youth Authority, modification of conditions of supervision, return to custody, see Welfare and Institutions Code § 1767.35.
Probation officer or social worker defined for purposes of this Chapter, see Welfare and Institutions Code § 215.

§ 209. Inspection of juvenile detention facilities for suitability; minimum standards

(a)(1) The judge of the juvenile court of a county, or, if there is more than one judge, any of the judges of the juvenile court shall, at least annually, inspect any jail, juvenile hall, or special purpose juvenile hall that, in the preceding calendar year, was used for confinement, for more than 24 hours, of any minor.

(2) The judge shall promptly notify the operator of the jail, juvenile hall, or special purpose juvenile hall of any observed noncompliance with minimum standards for juvenile facilities adopted by the Board of State and Community Corrections under Section 210. Based on the facility's subsequent compliance with the provisions of subdivisions (d) and (e), the judge shall thereafter make a finding whether the facility is a suitable place for the confinement of minors and shall note the finding in the minutes of the court.

(3)(A) The Board of State and Community Corrections shall conduct a biennial inspection of each jail, juvenile hall, lockup, or special purpose juvenile hall situated in this state that, during the preceding calendar year, was used for confinement, for more than 24 hours, of any minor. The board shall promptly notify the operator of any jail, juvenile hall, lockup, or special purpose juvenile hall of any noncompliance found, upon inspection, with any of the minimum standards for juvenile facilities adopted by the Board of State and Community Corrections under Section 210 or 210.2.

(B) Any duly authorized officer, employee, or agent of the board may, upon presentation of proper identification, enter and inspect any area of a local detention facility, without notice, to conduct an inspection required by this paragraph.

(4) If either a judge of the juvenile court or the board, after inspection of a jail, juvenile hall, special purpose juvenile hall, or lockup, finds that it is not being operated and maintained as a suitable place for the confinement of minors, the juvenile court or the board shall give notice of its finding to all persons having authority to confine minors pursuant to this chapter and commencing 60 days thereafter the facility shall not be used for confinement of minors until the time the judge or board, as the case may be, finds, after reinspection of the facility that the conditions that rendered the facility unsuitable have been remedied, and the facility is a suitable place for confinement of minors.

(5) The custodian of each jail, juvenile hall, special purpose juvenile hall, and lockup shall make any reports as may be requested by the board or the juvenile court to effectuate the purposes of this section.

(b)(1) The Board of State and Community Corrections may inspect any law enforcement facility that contains a lockup for adults and that it has reason to believe may not be in compliance with the requirements of subdivision (b) of Section 207.1 or with the certification requirements or standards adopted under Section 210.2. A judge of the juvenile court shall conduct an annual inspection, either in person or through a delegated member of the appropriate county or regional juvenile justice commission, of any law enforcement facility that contains a lockup for adults which, in the preceding year, was used for the secure detention of any minor. If the law enforcement facility is observed, upon inspection, to be out of compliance with the requirements of subdivision (b) of Section 207.1, or with any standard adopted under Section 210.2, the board or the judge shall promptly notify the operator of the law enforcement facility of the specific points of noncompliance.

(2) If either the judge or the board finds after inspection that the facility is not being operated and maintained in conformity with the requirements of subdivision (b) of Section 207.1 or with the certification requirements or standards adopted under Section 210.2, the juvenile court or the board shall give notice of its finding to all persons having authority to securely detain minors in the facility, and, commencing 60 days thereafter, the facility shall not be used for the secure detention of a minor until the time the judge or the board, as the case may be, finds, after reinspection, that the conditions that rendered the facility unsuitable have been remedied, and the facility is a suitable place for the confinement of minors in conformity with all requirements of law.

(3) The custodian of each law enforcement facility that contains a lockup for adults shall make any report as may be requested by the board or by the juvenile court to effectuate the purposes of this subdivision.

(c) The board shall collect biennial data on the number, place, and duration of confinements of minors in jails and lockups, as defined in subdivision (g) of Section 207.1, and shall publish biennially this information in the form as it deems appropriate for the purpose of providing public information on continuing compliance with the requirements of Section 207.1.

(d) Except as provided in subdivision (e), a juvenile hall, special purpose juvenile hall, law enforcement facility, or jail shall be unsuitable for the confinement of minors if it is not in compliance with one or more of the minimum standards for juvenile facilities adopted by the Board of State and Community Corrections under Section 210 or 210.2, and if, within 60 days of having received notice of noncompliance from the board or the judge of the juvenile court, the juvenile hall, special purpose juvenile hall, law enforcement facility, or jail has failed to file an approved corrective action plan with the Board of State and Community Corrections to correct the condition or conditions of noncompliance of which it has been notified. The corrective action plan shall outline how the juvenile hall, special purpose juvenile hall, law enforcement facility, or jail plans to correct the issue of noncompliance and give a reasonable timeframe, not to exceed 90 days, for resolution, that the board shall either approve or deny. In the event the juvenile hall, special purpose juvenile hall, law enforcement facility, or jail fails to meet its commitment to resolve noncompliance issues outlined in its corrective action plan, the board shall make a determination of suitability at its next scheduled meeting.

(e) If a juvenile hall is not in compliance with one or more of the minimum standards for juvenile facilities adopted by the Board of State and Community Corrections under Section 210, and where the noncompliance arises from sustained occupancy levels that are above the population capacity permitted by applicable minimum standards, the juvenile hall shall be unsuitable for the confinement of minors if the board or the judge of the juvenile court determines that conditions in the facility pose a serious risk to the health, safety, or welfare of minors confined in the facility. In making its determination of suitability, the board or the judge of the juvenile court shall consider, in addition to the noncompliance with minimum standards, the totality of conditions in the juvenile hall, including the extent and duration of overpopulation as well as staffing, program, physical plant, and medical and mental health care conditions in the facility. The Board of State and Community Corrections may develop guidelines and procedures for its determination of suitability in accordance with this subdivision and to assist counties in bringing their juvenile halls into full compliance with applicable minimum standards. This subdivision shall not be interpreted to exempt a juvenile hall from having to correct, in accordance with subdivision (d), any minimum standard violations that are not directly related to overpopulation of the facility.

(f) In accordance with the federal Juvenile Justice and Delinquency Prevention Act of 2002 (42 U.S.C. Sec. 5601 et seq.), the Corrections Standards Authority shall inspect and collect relevant data from any facility that may be used for the secure detention of minors.

(g) All reports and notices of findings prepared by the Board of State and Community Corrections pursuant to this section shall be posted on the Board of State and Community Corrections' internet website in a manner in which they are accessible to the public. *(Added by Stats.1992, c. 695 (S.B.97), § 27, eff. Sept. 15, 1992, operative July 1, 1995. Amended by Stats.1993, c. 59 (S.B.443), § 20, eff. June 30, 1993, operative July 1, 1995; Stats.1995, c. 304 (A.B.904), § 3, eff. Aug. 3, 1995; Stats.1996, c. 805 (A.B.1325), § 8; Stats.1998, c. 694 (S.B.2147), § 3; Stats.2010, c. 157 (S.B.1447), § 1; Stats.2017, c. 17 (A.B.103), § 55, eff. June 27, 2017; Stats.2020, c. 337 (S.B.823), § 21, eff. Sept. 30, 2020; Stats.2021, c. 80 (A.B.145), § 26, eff. July 16, 2021.)*

§ 210. Standards for juvenile halls

The Board of Corrections shall adopt minimum standards for the operation and maintenance of juvenile halls for the confinement of minors. *(Added by Stats.1976, c. 1068, p. 4741, § 1.5. Amended by Stats.1996, c. 12 (A.B.1397), § 5, eff. Feb. 14, 1996; Stats.1998, c. 694 (S.B.2147), § 4.)*

Cross References

Reimbursement of county detention facilities for Youth Authority parole violators, see Welfare and Institutions Code § 1776.

§ 210.1. Guidelines for operation and maintenance of nonsecure placement facilities

The Board of Corrections shall develop guidelines for the operation and maintenance of nonsecure placement facilities for persons alleged or found to be persons coming within the terms of Section 601 or 602. *(Added by Stats.1978, c. 1157, p. 3553, § 1, eff. Sept. 26, 1978. Amended by Stats.1996, c. 12 (A.B.1397), § 6, eff. Feb. 14, 1996.)*

§ 210.2. Standards for facilities containing adult lockups; certification

(a) The Board of Corrections shall adopt regulations establishing standards for law enforcement facilities which contain lockups for adults and which are used for the temporary, secure detention of minors upon arrest under subdivision (b) of Section 207.1. The standards shall identify appropriate conditions of confinement for minors in law enforcement facilities, including standards for places within a police station or sheriff's station where minors may be securely detained; standards regulating contact between minors and adults in custody in lockup, booking, or common areas; standards for the supervision of minors securely detained in these facilities; and any other related standard as the board deems appropriate to effectuate compliance with subdivision (b) of Section 207.1.

(b) Every person in charge of a law enforcement facility which contains a lockup for adults and which is used in any calendar year for the secure detention of any minor shall certify annually that the facility is in conformity with the regulations adopted by the board under subdivision (a). The certification shall be endorsed by the sheriff or chief of police of the jurisdiction in which the facility is located and shall be forwarded to and maintained by the board. The board may provide forms and instructions to local jurisdictions to facilitate compliance with this requirement. *(Added by Stats.1986, c. 1271, § 5. Amended by Stats.1996, c. 12 (A.B.1397), § 7, eff. Feb. 14, 1996; Stats.2020, c. 337 (S.B.823), § 22, eff. Sept. 30, 2020.)*

§ 210.5. Tulare County Juvenile Facility; construction and operation; staffing ratios and housing capacity; review

The Legislature finds and declares that it is in the best public interest to encourage innovations in staffing ratios, maximization of housing unit size, and experimentation with innovative architectural designs and program components, designs, or operations in the operation and maintenance of new juvenile detention facilities. Therefore, to these ends, Tulare County, as a demonstration project, may undertake the construction and operation of a juvenile detention facility, to be known as the "Tulare County Juvenile Facility," that shall not be subject to laws or regulations governing staffing ratios and housing capacity for juvenile facilities except as provided in this section. Before the county proceeds with the construction and operation of the Tulare County Juvenile Facility, the schematics and the proposed staffing patterns of this project shall be subject to review and approval by the Board of Corrections, which shall consider the proposed regulations, applicable current case law, and appropriate juvenile correctional practices in order to determine the merits of the proposal and to ensure the safety and security of wards and the staff. Any review conducted by the Board of Corrections pursuant to this section shall consider community, inmate, and staff safety, and the extent to which the project makes the most efficient use of resources. In addition, progress reports and evaluative data regarding the success of the demonstration project shall be provided to the Board of Corrections by the county.

Nothing contained in this section shall affect the applicability of the provisions of the Labor Code. *(Added by Stats.1996, c. 100 (A.B.2189), § 1, eff. July 1, 1996.)*

§ 210.6. Mechanical restraints

(a)(1) Mechanical restraints, including, but not limited to, handcuffs, chains, irons, straitjackets or cloth or leather restraints, or other similar items, may be used on a juvenile detained in or committed to a local secure juvenile facility, camp, ranch, or forestry camp, as established pursuant to Sections 850 and 881, during transportation outside of the facility only upon a determination made by the probation department, in consultation with the transporting agency, that the mechanical restraints are necessary to prevent physical harm to the juvenile or another person or due to a substantial risk of flight.

(2) If a determination is made that mechanical restraints are necessary, the least restrictive form of restraint shall be used consistent with the legitimate security needs of each juvenile.

(3) A county probation department that chooses to use mechanical restraints other than handcuffs on juveniles shall establish procedures for the documentation of their use, including the reasons for the use of those mechanical restraints.

(4) This subdivision does not apply to mechanical restraints used by medical care providers in the course of medical care or transportation.

(b)(1) Mechanical restraints may only be used during a juvenile court proceeding if the court determines that the individual juvenile's behavior in custody or in court establishes a manifest need to use mechanical restraints to prevent physical harm to the juvenile or another person or due to a substantial risk of flight.

(2) The burden to establish the need for mechanical restraints pursuant to paragraph (1) is on the prosecution.

(3) If the court determines that mechanical restraints are necessary, the least restrictive form of restraint shall be used and the reasons for the use of mechanical restraints shall be documented in the record. *(Added by Stats.2017, c. 660 (A.B.878), § 1, eff. Jan. 1, 2018.)*

§ 211. Commitment to correctional facilities

(a) A person under the age of 14 years shall not be committed to a state prison or be transferred thereto from any other institution.

(b) Notwithstanding any other law, a person under the age of 16 years shall not be housed in any facility under the jurisdiction of the Department of Corrections and Rehabilitation. *(Added by Stats. 1976, c. 1068, p. 4741, § 1.5. Amended by Stats.1994, c. 453 (A.B.560), § 2.7; Stats.2019, c. 497 (A.B.991), § 291, eff. Jan. 1, 2020.)*

Cross References

Department of Corrections, generally, see Penal Code § 5000 et seq.
Transfer for study, diagnosis and treatment, see Welfare and Institutions Code § 1755.5.

Research References

3 Witkin, California Criminal Law 4th Punishment § 93 (2021), Institutions and Facilities.

§ 212. Fees; expenses

There shall be no fee for filing a petition under this chapter nor shall any fees be charged by any public officer for his services in filing or serving papers or for the performance of any duty enjoined upon him by this chapter, except where the sheriff transports a person to a state institution. If the judge of the juvenile court orders that a ward or dependent child go to a state institution without being accompanied by an officer or that a ward or dependent child be taken to an institution by the probation officer of the county or parole officer of the institution or by some other suitable person, all expenses necessarily incurred therefor shall be allowed and paid in the same manner and from the same funds as such expenses would be allowed and paid were such transportation effected by the sheriff. *(Added by Stats.1976, c. 1068, p. 4741, § 1.5.)*

Cross References

Petition, see Welfare and Institutions Code § 650.
Probation officer or social worker defined for purposes of this Chapter, see Welfare and Institutions Code § 215.
Transportation,
County ambulance service, see Health and Safety Code § 1444.
Indigent nonresidents, see Welfare and Institutions Code § 17004.
Juvenile court wards, nonresidents of state, see Welfare and Institutions Code § 738.
Needy sick and indigents, see Health and Safety Code § 1443.
Nonresidents confined in state hospitals, see Welfare and Institutions Code § 4119 et seq.
Youth Authority, nonresident persons committed to, see Welfare and Institutions Code § 1009.

§ 212.5. Electronic filing and service; conditions

(a) Unless otherwise provided by law, a document in a juvenile court matter may be filed and served electronically, as prescribed by Section 1010.6 of the Code of Civil Procedure, under the following conditions:

(1) Electronic service is authorized only if the county and the court permit electronic service.

(2)(A) On or before December 31, 2018, electronic service on a party or other person is permitted only if the party or other person has consented to accept electronic service in that specific action. A party or other person may subsequently withdraw its consent to electronic service.

(B) On or after January 1, 2019, electronic service on a party or other person is permitted only if the party or other person has expressly consented, as provided in Section 1010.6 of the Code of Civil Procedure. A party or other person may subsequently withdraw its consent to electronic service by completing the appropriate Judicial Council form.

(3) Consent, or the withdrawal of consent, to receive electronic service may be completed by a party or other person entitled to service, or that person's attorney.

(4) Electronic service shall be provided in the following manner:

(A) Electronic service is not permitted on any party or person who is under 10 years of age.

(B) Electronic service is not permitted on any party or person who is between 10 years of age and 15 years of age without the express consent of the minor and the minor's attorney.

(C) Electronic service shall be permitted on any party or person who is 16 to 18 years of age, inclusive, only if the minor, after consultation with his or her attorney, consents. By January 1, 2019, the Judicial Council shall develop a rule of court on the duties of the minor's attorney during the required consultation.

(D) Electronic service of psychological or medical documentation related to a minor shall not be permitted, other than the summary required pursuant to Section 16010 when included as part of a required report to the court.

(5) In the following matters, the party or other person shall be served by both electronic means and by other means specified by law if the document to be served is one of the following:

(A) A notice of hearing or an appellate advisement issued pursuant to subparagraph (A) of paragraph (3) of subdivision (*l*) of Section 366.26 for a hearing at which a social worker is recommending the termination of parental rights.

(B) A citation issued pursuant to Section 661.

(C) A notice of hearing pursuant to subdivision (d) of Section 777.

(6) If it is known or there is reason to know that the child is an Indian child, as defined by Section 224.1, and the hearing may culminate in an order for foster care placement, termination of parental rights, preadoptive placement, or adoptive placement as described in paragraph (1) of subdivision (d) of Section 224.1, service shall be made pursuant to Section 224.3.

(7) Electronic service and electronic filing shall be conducted in a manner that preserves and ensures the confidentiality of records by encryption.

(8) The requirements of this section shall be consistent with Section 1010.6 of the Code of Civil Procedure and rules of court adopted by the Judicial Council pursuant to that section.

(b) This section does not preclude the use of electronic means to send information regarding the date, time, and place of a juvenile court hearing, without the need to comply with paragraphs (1) to (4), inclusive, of subdivision (a), provided that the requirement of paragraph (7) of subdivision (a) is met. However, information shared, as described in this subdivision, shall only be in addition to, and not in lieu of, any required service or notification made in accordance with any other law governing how that service or notification is provided. *(Added by Stats.2017, c. 319 (A.B.976), § 108, eff. Jan. 1, 2018. Amended by Stats.2018, c. 833 (A.B.3176), § 1, eff. Jan. 1, 2019; Stats.2018, c. 910 (A.B.1930), § 21.5, eff. Jan. 1, 2019.)*

§ 213. Contempt of court

Any willful disobedience or interference with any lawful order of the juvenile court or of a judge or referee thereof constitutes a contempt of court. *(Added by Stats.1976, c. 1068, p. 4741, § 1.5.)*

Cross References

Contempt of court, generally, see Code of Civil Procedure § 1209 et seq.
Inducing persons under eighteen years of age to refuse to conform to court order, punishment, see Penal Code § 272.
Judgments and orders, wards, see Welfare and Institutions Code § 725 et seq.

§ 213.3. Willful disobedience or interference with juvenile court order; detainment prohibited; orders to ensure school attendance

A person under 18 years of age shall not be detained in a secure facility, as defined in Section 206, solely upon the ground that he or she is in willful disobedience or interference with any lawful order of the juvenile court, if the basis of an order of contempt is the failure to comply with a court order pursuant to subdivision (b) of Section 601. Upon a finding of contempt of court, the court may issue any other lawful order, as necessary, to ensure the minor's school attendance. *(Added by Stats.2014, c. 70 (S.B.1296), § 3, eff. Jan. 1, 2015.)*

§ 213.5. Proceedings to declare a minor child a dependent child; ex parte orders

(a) After a petition has been filed pursuant to Section 311 to declare a child a dependent child of the juvenile court, and until the time that the petition is dismissed or dependency is terminated, upon application in the manner provided by Section 527 of the Code of Civil Procedure or in the manner provided by Section 6300 of the Family Code, if related to domestic violence, the juvenile court has exclusive jurisdiction to issue ex parte orders (1) enjoining a person from molesting, attacking, striking, stalking, threatening, sexually assaulting, battering, harassing, telephoning, including, but not limited to, making annoying telephone calls as described in Section 653m of the Penal Code, destroying the personal property, contacting, either directly or indirectly, by mail or otherwise, coming within a specified distance of, or disturbing the peace of the child or any other child in the household; and (2) excluding a person from the dwelling of the person who has care, custody, and control of the child. A court may also issue an ex parte order enjoining a person from molesting, attacking, striking, stalking, threatening, sexually assaulting, battering, harassing, telephoning, including, but not limited to, making annoying telephone calls as described in Section 653m of the Penal Code, destroying the personal property, contacting, either directly or indirectly, by mail or otherwise, coming within a specified distance of, or disturbing the peace of any parent, legal guardian, or current caretaker of the child, regardless of whether the child resides with that parent, legal guardian, or current caretaker, upon application in the manner provided by Section 527 of the Code of Civil Procedure or, if related to domestic violence, in the manner provided by Section 6300 of the Family Code. A court may also issue an ex parte order enjoining a person from molesting, attacking, striking, stalking, threatening, sexually assaulting, battering, harassing, telephoning, including, but not limited to, making annoying telephone calls as described in Section 653m of the Penal Code, destroying the personal property, contacting, either directly or indirectly, by mail or otherwise, coming within a specified distance of, or disturbing the peace of the child's current or former social worker or court appointed special advocate, upon application in the manner provided by Section 527 of the Code of Civil Procedure. On a showing of good cause, in an ex parte order issued pursuant to this subdivision in connection with an animal owned, possessed, leased, kept, or held by a person protected by the restraining order, or residing in the residence or household of a person protected by the restraining order, the court may do either or both of the following:

(1) Grant the applicant exclusive care, possession, or control of the animal.

(2) Order the restrained person to stay away from the animal and refrain from taking, transferring, encumbering, concealing, molesting, attacking, striking, threatening, harming, or otherwise disposing of the animal.

(b) After a petition has been filed pursuant to Section 601 or 602 to declare a child a ward of the juvenile court, and until the time that the petition is dismissed or wardship is terminated, upon application in the manner provided by Section 527 of the Code of Civil Procedure or, if related to domestic violence, in the manner provided by Section 6300 of the Family Code, the juvenile court may issue ex parte orders (1) enjoining a person from molesting, attacking, striking, stalking, threatening, sexually assaulting, battering, harassing, telephoning, including, but not limited to, making annoying telephone calls as described in Section 653m of the Penal Code, destroying the personal property, contacting, either directly or indirectly, by mail or otherwise, coming within a specified distance of, or disturbing the peace of the child or any other child in the household; (2) excluding a person from the dwelling of the person who has care, custody, and control of the child; or (3) enjoining the child from contacting, threatening, stalking, or disturbing the peace of a person the court finds to be at risk from the conduct of the child, or with whom association would be detrimental to the child. A court may also issue an ex parte order enjoining a person from molesting, attacking, striking, stalking, threatening, sexually assaulting, battering, harassing, telephoning, including, but not limited to, making annoying telephone calls as described in Section 653m of the Penal Code, destroying the personal property, contacting, either directly or indirectly, by mail or otherwise, coming within a specified distance of, or disturbing the peace of any parent, legal guardian, or current caretaker of the child, regardless of whether the child resides with that parent, legal guardian, or current caretaker, upon application in the manner provided by Section 527 of the Code of Civil Procedure or, if related to domestic violence, in the manner provided by Section 6300 of the Family Code. A court may also issue an ex parte order enjoining a person from molesting, attacking, striking, stalking, threatening, sexually assaulting, battering, harassing, telephoning, including, but not limited to, making annoying telephone calls as described in Section 653m of the Penal Code, destroying the personal property, contacting, either directly or indirectly, by mail or otherwise, coming within a specified distance of, or disturbing the peace of the child's current or former probation officer or court appointed special advocate, upon application in the manner provided by Section 527 of the Code of Civil Procedure. On a showing of good cause, in an ex parte order issued pursuant to this subdivision in connection with an animal owned, possessed, leased, kept, or held by a person protected by the restraining order, or residing in the residence or household of a person protected by the restraining order, the court may do either or both of the following:

(1) Grant the applicant exclusive care, possession, or control of the animal.

(2) Order the respondent to stay away from the animal and refrain from taking, transferring, encumbering, concealing, molesting, attacking, striking, threatening, harming, or otherwise disposing of the animal.

(c)(1) If a temporary restraining order is granted without notice, the matter shall be made returnable on an order requiring cause to be shown why the order should not be granted, on the earliest day that the business of the court will permit, but not later than 21 days or, if good cause appears to the court, 25 days from the date the temporary restraining order is granted. The court may, on the motion of the person seeking the restraining order, or on its own motion, shorten the time for the service of the order to show cause on the person to be restrained.

(2) The respondent shall be entitled, as a matter of course, to one continuance, for a reasonable period, to respond to the petition.

(3) Either party may request a continuance of the hearing, which the court shall grant on a showing of good cause. The request may be made in writing before or at the hearing or orally at the hearing. The court may also grant a continuance on its own motion.

(4) If the court grants a continuance, a temporary restraining order that has been issued shall remain in effect until the end of the continued hearing, unless otherwise ordered by the court. In granting a continuance, the court may modify or terminate a temporary restraining order.

(5) A hearing pursuant to this section may be held simultaneously with any regularly scheduled hearings held in proceedings to declare a child a dependent child or ward of the juvenile court pursuant to Section 300, 601, or 602, or subsequent hearings regarding the dependent child or ward.

(d)(1) The juvenile court may issue, upon notice and a hearing, any of the orders set forth in subdivisions (a), (b), and (c). A restraining order granted pursuant to this subdivision shall remain in effect, in the discretion of the court, no more than three years, unless otherwise terminated by the court, extended by mutual consent of all parties to the restraining order, or extended by further order of the court on the motion of any party to the restraining order.

(2) If an action is filed for the purpose of terminating or modifying a protective order prior to the expiration date specified in the order by a party other than the protected party, the party who is protected by the order shall be given notice, pursuant to subdivision (b) of Section 1005 of the Code of Civil Procedure, of the proceeding by personal service or, if the protected party has satisfied the requirements of Chapter 3.1 (commencing with Section 6205) of Division 7 of Title 1 of the Government Code, by service on the Secretary of State. If the party who is protected by the order cannot be notified prior to the hearing for modification or termination of the protective order, the juvenile court shall deny the motion to modify or terminate the order without prejudice or continue the hearing until the party who is protected can be properly noticed and may, upon a showing of good cause, specify another method for service of process that is reasonably designed to afford actual notice to the protected party. The protected party may waive the right to notice if the party is physically present and does not challenge the sufficiency of the notice.

(e)(1) The juvenile court may issue an order made pursuant to subdivision (a), (b), or (d) excluding a person from a residence or dwelling. This order may be issued for the time and on the conditions that the court determines, regardless of which party holds legal or equitable title or is the lessee of the residence or dwelling.

(2) The court may issue an order under paragraph (1) only on a showing of all of the following:

(A) Facts sufficient for the court to ascertain that the party who will stay in the dwelling has a right under color of law to possession of the premises.

(B) That the party to be excluded has assaulted or threatens to assault the other party or any other person under the care, custody, and control of the other party, or a minor child of the parties or of the other party.

(C) That physical or emotional harm would otherwise result to the other party, to a person under the care, custody, and control of the other party, or to a minor child of the parties or of the other party.

(f) An order issued pursuant to subdivision (a), (b), (c), or (d) shall state on its face the date of expiration of the order.

(g)(1) In a case where a court issues a protective order pursuant to subdivision (a), (b), (c), or (d), Section 6389 of the Family Code shall apply. In accordance with that section, the court shall make a determination as to whether the restrained person is in possession or control of a firearm or ammunition, as provided in Section 6322.5 of the Family Code.

(2) Subdivision (m) of Section 6389 of the Family Code does not apply if the restrained person is a child under the jurisdiction of the juvenile court pursuant to Section 601 or 602.

(h) All data with respect to a juvenile court protective order, or extension, modification, or termination thereof, granted pursuant to subdivision (a), (b), (c), or (d), shall be transmitted by the court or its designee, within one business day, to law enforcement personnel by either one of the following methods:

(1) Transmitting a physical copy of the order to a local law enforcement agency authorized by the Department of Justice to enter orders into the California Law Enforcement Telecommunications System (CLETS).

(2) With the approval of the Department of Justice, entering the order into CLETS directly.

(i) A willful and knowing violation of an order granted pursuant to subdivision (a), (b), (c), or (d) shall be a misdemeanor punishable under Section 273.65 of the Penal Code.

(j) A juvenile court restraining order related to domestic violence issued by a court pursuant to this section shall be issued on forms adopted by the Judicial Council and that have been approved by the Department of Justice pursuant to subdivision (i) of Section 6380 of the Family Code. However, the fact that an order issued by a court pursuant to this section was not issued on forms adopted by the Judicial Council and approved by the Department of Justice shall not, in and of itself, make the order unenforceable.

(k)(1) Prior to a hearing on the issuance or denial of an order under this part, a search shall be conducted as described in subdivision (a) of Section 6306 of the Family Code.

(2) Prior to deciding whether to issue an order under this part, the court shall consider the following information obtained pursuant to a search conducted under paragraph (1): a conviction for a violent felony specified in Section 667.5 of the Penal Code or a serious felony specified in Section 1192.7 of the Penal Code; a misdemeanor conviction involving domestic violence, weapons, or other violence; an outstanding warrant; parole or probation status; a prior restraining order; and a violation of a prior restraining order.

(3)(A) If the results of the search conducted pursuant to paragraph (1) indicate that an outstanding warrant exists against the subject of the search, the court shall order the clerk of the court to immediately notify, by the most effective means available, appropriate law enforcement officials of information obtained through the search that the court determines is appropriate. The law enforcement officials notified shall take all actions necessary to execute outstanding warrants or any other actions, as appropriate and as soon as practicable.

(B) If the results of the search conducted pursuant to paragraph (1) indicate that the subject of the search is currently on parole or probation, the court shall order the clerk of the court to immediately notify, by the most effective means available, the appropriate parole or probation officer of information obtained through the search that the court determines is appropriate. The parole or probation officer notified shall take all actions necessary to revoke parole or probation, or any other actions, with respect to the subject person, as appropriate and as soon as practicable.

(*l*) Upon making any order for custody or visitation pursuant to this section, the court shall follow the procedures specified in subdivisions (c) and (d) of Section 6323 of the Family Code. *(Added by Stats.1989, c. 1409, § 2. Amended by Stats.1996, c. 1138 (A.B. 2154), § 1; Stats.1996, c. 1139 (A.B.2647), § 3.5; Stats.1998, c. 390 (S.B.2017), § 1; Stats.1999, c. 661 (A.B.825), § 13; Stats.1999, c. 980 (A.B.1671), § 19.5; Stats.2001, c. 572 (S.B.66), § 5; Stats.2001, c. 713 (A.B.1129), § 1.5; Stats.2002, c. 664 (A.B.3034), § 229; Stats.2002, c. 1008 (A.B.3028), § 30; Stats.2003, c. 365 (A.B.1710), § 6; Stats.2005, c. 634 (A.B.519), § 1; Stats.2010, c. 572 (A.B.1596), § 25, operative Jan. 1, 2012; Stats.2011, c. 101 (A.B.454), § 5; Stats.2014, c. 54 (S.B.1461), § 17, eff. Jan. 1, 2015; Stats.2015, c. 303 (A.B.731), § 564, eff. Jan. 1, 2016; Stats.2015, c. 401 (A.B.494), § 2, eff. Jan. 1, 2016; Stats.2015, c. 411 (A.B.1081), § 7.5, eff. Jan. 1, 2016; Stats.2021, c. 685 (S.B.320), § 14, eff. Jan. 1, 2022.)*

Cross References

Arrest with and without warrant, citizen's arrest by domestic victim, concealed weapon offense, see Penal Code § 836.
Emancipation of minors, notice of declaration proceedings, warning that court may void or rescind declaration and parents may become liable for support and medical insurance coverage, see Family Code § 7121.
Felonies, definition and penalties, see Penal Code §§ 17, 18.
Lease not to be terminated based on domestic or sexual assault against tenant, landlord's liability for compliance, form for affirmative defense to unlawful detainer action, see Code of Civil Procedure § 1161.3.
Misdemeanors, definition and penalties, see Penal Code §§ 17, 19 and 19.2.
Prevention of domestic violence,
Issuance and effect of emergency protective order, application for restraining orders under this section, see Family Code § 6257.

Issuance and effect of emergency protective order, contents of orders, see Family Code § 6253.
Issuance and effect of emergency protective order, inclusion of other orders, see Family Code § 6252.
Probation officer or social worker defined for purposes of this Chapter, see Welfare and Institutions Code § 215.
Tenant protected by restraining order against another tenant, change of locks on dwelling unit, definitions, see Civil Code § 1941.6.
Tenant protected by restraining order against non-tenant, change of locks on dwelling unit, definitions, see Civil Code § 1941.5.
Victims of domestic violence, sexual assault, or stalking, written notice to terminate tenancy, requirements, see Civil Code § 1946.7.

Research References

West's California Judicial Council Forms JV–245, Request for Restraining Order—Juvenile (Also Available in Chinese, Korean, Spanish, and Vietnamese).
West's California Judicial Council Forms JV–250, Notice of Hearing and Temporary Restraining Order—Juvenile (Also Available in Chinese, Korean, Spanish, and Vietnamese).
West's California Judicial Council Forms JV–251, Request and Order to Continue Hearing (Also Available in Chinese, Korean, Spanish, and Vietnamese).
West's California Judicial Council Forms JV–255, Restraining Order—Juvenile (Clets—Juv) (Also Available in Chinese, Korean, Spanish, and Vietnamese).
West's California Judicial Council Forms JV–257, Change to Restraining Order After Hearing (Also Available in Chinese, Korean, Spanish, and Vietnamese).
2 Witkin, California Criminal Law 4th Crimes Against Governmental Authority § 10 (2021), Orders, Protocol, and Sanctions.
4 Witkin, California Criminal Law 4th Pretrial Proceedings § 32 (2021), Domestic Violence.

§ 213.6. Subsequent restraining orders or protective orders based upon prior temporary restraining order or emergency protective order; service of subsequent orders; statement regarding service in judicial forms

(a) If a person named in a temporary restraining order or emergency protective order issued under this part is personally served with the order and notice of hearing with respect to a subsequent restraining order or protective order based thereon, but the person does not appear at the hearing either in person or by counsel, and the terms and conditions of the restraining order or protective order are identical to those of the prior temporary restraining order, except for the duration of the order, the subsequent restraining order or protective order may be served on the person by first-class mail sent to that person at the most current address for the person available to the court.

(b) The judicial forms for temporary restraining orders or emergency protective orders issued under this part shall contain a statement in substantially the following form:

"If you have been personally served with a temporary restraining order or emergency protective order and notice of hearing, but you do not appear at the hearing either in person or by counsel, and a restraining order or protective order is issued at the hearing that does not differ from the prior temporary restraining order or protective order except with respect to the duration of the order, a copy of the order will be served upon you by mail at the following address: ________. If that address is not correct or if you wish to verify that the temporary order was made permanent without substantive change, call the clerk of the court at ________." *(Added by Stats.2003, c. 365 (A.B.1710), § 7.)*

§ 213.7. Addresses or locations of persons protected under court order; prohibition upon certain enjoined parties from acting to obtain such information

(a) The court shall order that any party enjoined pursuant to Section 213.5, 304, 362.4, or 726.5 be prohibited from taking any action to obtain the address or location of a protected party or a protected party's family members, caretakers, or guardian, unless there is good cause not to make that order.

(b) The Judicial Council shall promulgate forms necessary to effectuate this section. *(Added by Stats.2005, c. 472 (A.B.978), § 6.)*

Research References

West's California Judicial Council Forms JV–245, Request for Restraining Order—Juvenile (Also Available in Chinese, Korean, Spanish, and Vietnamese).
West's California Judicial Council Forms JV–250, Notice of Hearing and Temporary Restraining Order—Juvenile (Also Available in Chinese, Korean, Spanish, and Vietnamese).
West's California Judicial Council Forms JV–255, Restraining Order—Juvenile (Clets—Juv) (Also Available in Chinese, Korean, Spanish, and Vietnamese).

§ 214. Written promise to appear; failure to perform; misdemeanor

In each instance in which a provision of this chapter authorizes the execution by any person of a written promise to appear or to have any other person appear before the probation officer or before the juvenile court, any willful failure of such promissor to perform as promised constitutes a misdemeanor and is punishable as such if at the time of the execution of such written promise the promissor is given a copy of such written promise upon which it is clearly written that failure to appear or to have any other person appear as promised is punishable as a misdemeanor. *(Added by Stats.1976, c. 1068, p. 4741, § 1.5.)*

Cross References

Misdemeanors, definition and penalties, see Penal Code §§ 17, 19 and 19.2.
Probation officer or social worker defined for purposes of this Chapter, see Welfare and Institutions Code § 215.
Promise to appear, violation, see Vehicle Code § 40508.
Promise to appear of juvenile or parent, see Welfare and Institutions Code § 629.

§ 215. Probation officer or social worker; department of probation

As used in this chapter, unless otherwise specifically provided, the term "probation officer" or "social worker" shall include the juvenile probation officer or the person who is both the juvenile probation officer and the adult probation officer, and any social worker in a county welfare department or any social worker in a California Indian tribe or any out-of-state Indian tribe that has reservation land that extends into the state that has authority, pursuant to an agreement with the department concerning child welfare services or foster care payments under the Aid to Families with Dependent Children program when supervising dependent children of the juvenile court pursuant to Section 272 by order of the court under Section 300, and the term "department of probation" shall mean the department of juvenile probation or the department wherein the services of juvenile and adult probation are both performed. *(Added by Stats.1976, c. 1068, p. 4741, § 1.5. Amended by Stats.1995, c. 724 (A.B.1525), § 1.5; Stats.1998, c. 1054 (A.B.1091), § 1.)*

Cross References

Child or nonminor whose jurisdiction is modified pursuant to subd. (d) of § 241.1, supervision, see Welfare and Institutions Code § 300.3.
Indian, Indian child, Indian child's tribe, Indian custodian, Indian tribe, reservation, and tribal court defined for purposes of this Division, see Welfare and Institutions Code § 224.1.
Probation officer, assistant and deputy for each county, see Welfare and Institutions Code § 270.

§ 216. Application of chapter to fugitive under 18

This chapter shall not apply:

(a) To any person who violates any law of this state defining a crime, and is at the time of such violation under the age of 18 years, if such person thereafter flees from this state. Any such person may be proceeded against in the manner otherwise provided by law for proceeding against persons accused of crime. Upon the return of such person to this state by extradition or otherwise, proceedings shall be commenced in the manner provided for in this chapter.

(b) To any person who violates any law of another state defining a crime, and is at the time of such violation under the age of 18 years, if such person thereafter flees from that state into this state. Any such person may be proceeded against as an adult in the manner provided in Chapter 4 (commencing with Section 1547) of Title 12 of Part 2 of the Penal Code. The magistrate shall, for purposes of detention, detain such person in juvenile hall if space is available. If no space is available in juvenile hall, the magistrate may detain such person in the county jail. *(Added by Stats.1976, c. 1068, p. 4741, § 1.5.)*

Cross References

Jail defined for purposes of this Chapter, see Welfare and Institutions Code § 207.1.

§ 217. Unclaimed personal property; use in programs designed to prevent delinquency; notification to owner

(a) The board of supervisors of any county or the governing body of any city may by ordinance provide that any personal property with a value of not more than five hundred dollars ($500) in the possession of the sheriff of the county or in the possession of the police department of the city which have been unclaimed for a period of at least 90 days may, instead of being sold at public auction to the highest bidder pursuant to the provisions of Section 2080.5 of the Civil Code, be turned over to the probation officer, to the welfare department of the county, or to any charitable or nonprofit organization which is authorized under its articles of incorporation to participate in a program or activity designed to prevent juvenile delinquency and which is exempt from income taxation under federal or state law, or both, for use in any program or activity designed to prevent juvenile delinquency.

(b) Before any property subject to this section is turned over to the probation officer, to the welfare department of the county, or to any charitable or nonprofit organization, the police department or sheriff's department shall notify the owner, if his or her identity is known or can be reasonably ascertained, that it possesses the property, and where the property may be claimed. The owner may be notified by mail, telephone, or by means of a notice published in a newspaper of general circulation which it determines is most likely to give notice to the owner of the property. *(Added by Stats.1976, c. 1068, p. 4741, § 1.5. Amended by Stats.1986, c. 865, § 1; Stats.1999, c. 233 (A.B.191), § 1.)*

Cross References

Probation officer or social worker defined for purposes of this Chapter, see Welfare and Institutions Code § 215.
Sale of property stolen or embezzled and unclaimed by owner, see Penal Code § 1411.

§ 218. Counsel; compensation and expenses

In any case in which, pursuant to this chapter, the court appoints counsel to represent any person who desires but is unable to employ counsel, counsel shall receive a reasonable sum for compensation and for necessary expenses, the amount of which shall be determined by the court, to be paid out of the general fund of the county. *(Added by Stats.1976, c. 1068, p. 4741, § 1.5.)*

Cross References

Juvenile offender, appointment of counsel, see Welfare and Institutions Code §§ 317, 634.

§ 218.5. Domestic violence training programs; participation by counsel; requirements

All counsel performing duties under this chapter, including, but not limited to, county counsel, court appointed counsel, or volunteer counsel, shall participate in mandatory training on domestic violence where available through existing programs at no additional cost to the county. The training shall meet the requirements of Section 16206. *(Added by Stats.1996, c. 1139 (A.B.2647), § 4.)*

§ 219. Workers' compensation for ward injured while doing rehabilitative work

The board of supervisors of a county may provide a ward of the juvenile court engaged in rehabilitative work without pay, under an assignment by order of the juvenile court to a work project in a county department, with workers' compensation benefits for injuries sustained while performing such rehabilitative work, in accordance with Section 3364.55 of the Labor Code. *(Added by Stats.1976, c. 1068, p. 4741, § 1.5.)*

Cross References

Workers' compensation, see Labor Code § 3200 et seq.

§ 219.5. Work providing access to personal information pertaining to private individuals; ineligibility of certain juvenile offenders

(a) No ward of the juvenile court or Department of Youth and Community Restoration, shall perform any function that provides access to personal information of private individuals, including, but not limited to: addresses; telephone numbers; health insurance, taxpayer, school, or employee identification numbers; mothers' maiden names; demand deposit account, debit card, credit card, savings or checking account numbers, PINs, or passwords; social security numbers; places of employment; dates of birth; state or government issued driver's license or identification numbers; United States Citizenship and Immigration Services-assigned numbers; government passport numbers; unique biometric data, such as fingerprints, facial scan identifiers, voice prints, retina or iris images, or other similar identifiers; unique electronic identification numbers; address or routing codes; and telecommunication identifying information or access devices.

(b) Subdivision (a) shall apply to a person who has been adjudicated to have committed an offense described by any of the following categories:

(1) An offense involving forgery or fraud.

(2) An offense involving misuse of a computer.

(3) An offense for which the person is required to register as a sex offender pursuant to Section 290 of the Penal Code.

(4) An offense involving any misuse of the personal or financial information of another person.

(c) If asked, any person who is a ward of the juvenile court or the Department of Youth and Community Restoration, and who has access to any personal information, shall disclose that the person is a ward of the juvenile court or the Department of the Youth Authority before taking any personal information from anyone.

(d) Any program involving the taking of personal information over the telephone by a person who is a ward of the juvenile court or the Department of Youth and Community Restoration, shall be subject to random monitoring of those telephone calls.

(e) Any program involving the taking of personal information by a person who is a ward of the juvenile court or the Department of Youth and Community Restoration, shall provide supervision at all times of the ward's activities.

(f) This section shall not apply to wards in employment programs or public service facilities where incidental contact with personal information may occur. *(Added by Stats.1998, c. 551 (A.B.2649), § 3. Amended by Stats.2002, c. 196 (A.B.2456), § 3; Stats.2021, c. 296 (A.B.1096), § 62, eff. Jan. 1, 2022.)*

Research References

3 Witkin, California Criminal Law 4th Punishment § 82 (2021), Particular Employments.

§ 220. Abortions; conditions and restrictions; eligibility

No condition or restriction upon the obtaining of an abortion by a female detained in any local juvenile facility, pursuant to the Therapeutic Abortion Act (Article 2 (commencing with Section 123400) of Chapter 2 of Part 2 of Division 106 of the Health and Safety Code), other than those contained in that act, shall be imposed. Females found to be pregnant and desiring abortions, shall be permitted to determine their eligibility for an abortion pursuant to law, and if determined to be eligible, shall be permitted to obtain an abortion.

For the purposes of this section, "local juvenile facility" means any city, county, or regional facility used for the confinement of female juveniles for more than 24 hours.

The rights provided for females by this section shall be posted in at least one conspicuous place to which all females have access. *(Added by Stats.1976, c. 1068, p. 4741, § 1.5. Amended by Stats.1996, c. 1023 (S.B.1497), § 455, eff. Sept. 29, 1996.)*

Research References

3 Witkin, California Criminal Law 4th Punishment § 83 (2021), Special Requirements for Women Prisoners.

§ 221. Female in state or local juvenile facility; use of materials for personal hygiene or birth control measures; family planning services; furnishing; operative date

(a) Any female confined in a state or local juvenile facility shall upon her request be allowed to continue to use materials necessary for (1) personal hygiene with regard to her menstrual cycle and reproductive system and (2) birth control measures as prescribed by her physician.

(b) Any female confined in a state or local juvenile facility shall upon her request be furnished by the confining state or local agency with information and education regarding prescription birth control measures.

(c) Family planning services shall be offered to each and every woman inmate at least 60 days prior to a scheduled release date. Upon request any woman inmate shall be furnished by the confining state or local agency with the services of a licensed physician, or she shall be furnished by the confining state or local agency or by any other agency which contracts with the confining state or local agency, with services necessary to meet her family planning needs at the time of her release.

(d) For the purposes of this section, "local juvenile facility" means any city, county, or regional facility used for the confinement of juveniles for more than 24 hours.

This section shall become operative on January 1, 1988. *(Added by Stats.1981, c. 618, p. 2367, § 2, operative Jan. 1, 1988.)*

Research References

3 Witkin, California Criminal Law 4th Punishment § 22 (2021), Special Provisions for Women.

§ 222. Pregnancy; determination; right of choice and services of any physician or surgeon

(a) A female in the custody of a local juvenile facility shall have the right to summon and receive the services of a physician and surgeon of her choice in order to determine whether she is pregnant. If she is found to be pregnant, she is entitled to a determination of the extent of the medical services needed by her and to the receipt of those services from the physician and surgeon of her choice. Expenses occasioned by the services of a physician and surgeon whose services are not provided by the facility shall be borne by the female.

(b) A ward who is known to be pregnant or in recovery from delivery shall not be restrained except as provided in Section 3407 of the Penal Code.

(c) For purposes of this section, "local juvenile facility" means a city, county, or regional facility used for the confinement of juveniles for more than 24 hours.

(d) The rights provided to females by this section shall be posted in at least one conspicuous place to which all female wards have access. *(Added by Stats.1976, c. 1068, p. 4741, § 1.5. Amended by Stats.2005, c. 608 (A.B.478), § 6; Stats.2012, c. 726 (A.B.2530), § 4.)*

Cross References

Community treatment programs, notice and written application forms to pregnant inmate, see Penal Code § 3419.
Community treatment programs, prenatal health care, pregnant inmates, see Penal Code § 3424.
Corrections Standards Authority, pregnant inmates, see Penal Code § 6030.
Transfer of pregnant inmate to hospital, charges for care, see Penal Code § 3423.
Transfer of pregnant inmate to hospital, shackles, see Penal Code § 5007.7.
Youth Authority, right of pregnant female committed to Youth Authority to choice and services of physician and surgeon, see Welfare and Institutions Code § 1774.

Research References

3 Witkin, California Criminal Law 4th Punishment § 83 (2021), Special Requirements for Women Prisoners.

§ 223. Notice to parent or guardian of serious injury or offense committed against minor in state or county custody

(a)(1) The parents or guardians of any minor in the custody of the state or the county, if they can reasonably be located, shall be notified within 24 hours by the public officer responsible for the well-being of that minor, of any serious injury or serious offense committed against the minor, upon reasonable substantiation that a serious injury or offense has occurred.

(2) This section shall not apply if the minor requests that his or her parents or guardians not be informed and the chief probation officer or the Director of the Youth Authority, as appropriate, determines it would be in the best interest of the minor not to inform the parents or guardians.

(b) For purposes of this section, "serious offense" means any offense that is chargeable as a felony and that involves violence against another person. "Serious injury" means, for purposes of this section, any illness or injury that requires hospitalization, is potentially life threatening, or that potentially will permanently impair the use of a major body organ, appendage, or limb. *(Added by Stats.1998, c. 496 (S.B.2081), § 2.)*

Cross References

Felonies, definition and penalties, see Penal Code §§ 17, 18.
Probation officer or social worker defined for purposes of this Chapter, see Welfare and Institutions Code § 215.

§ 223.1. Suicide attempt by or serious injury to person in custody of Division of Juvenile Facilities; notice to appropriate party; information for ward's record

(a)(1) At least one individual who is a parent, guardian, or designated emergency contact of a person in the custody of the Division of Juvenile Facilities, if the individual can reasonably be located, shall be successfully notified within 24 hours by the public officer responsible for the well-being of that person, of any suicide attempt by the person, or any serious injury or serious offense committed against the person. In consultation with division staff, as appropriate, and with concurrence of the public officer responsible for the well-being of that person, the person may designate other persons who should be notified in addition to, or in lieu of, parents or guardians, of any suicide attempt by the person, or any serious injury or serious offense committed against the person.

(2) This section shall not apply if either of the following conditions is met:

(A) A minor requests that his or her parents, guardians, or other persons not be notified, and the director of the division facility, as appropriate, determines it would be in the best interest of the minor not to notify the parents, guardians, or other persons.

(B) A person 18 years of age or older does not consent to the notification.

(b) Upon intake of a person into a division facility, and again upon attaining 18 years of age while in the custody of the division, an appropriate staff person shall explain, using language clearly understandable to the person, all of the provisions of this section, including that the person has the right to (1) request that the information described in paragraph (1) of subdivision (a) not be provided to a parent or guardian, and (2) request that another person or persons in addition to, or in lieu of, a parent or guardian be notified. The division shall provide the person with forms and any information necessary to provide informed consent as to who shall be notified. Any designation made pursuant to paragraph (1) of subdivision (a), the consent to notify parents, guardians, or other persons, and the withholding of that consent, may be amended or revoked by the person, and shall be transferable among facilities.

(c) Staff of the division shall enter the following information into the ward's record, as appropriate, upon its occurrence:

(1) A minor's request that his or her parents, guardians, or other persons not be notified of an emergency pursuant to this section, and the determination of the relevant public officer on that request.

(2) The designation of persons who are emergency contacts, in lieu of parents or guardians, who may be notified pursuant to this section.

(3) The revocation or amendment of a designation or consent made pursuant to this section.

(4) A person's consent, or withholding thereof, to notify parents, guardians, or other persons pursuant to this section.

(d) For purposes of this section, the following terms have the following meanings:

(1) "Serious offense" means any offense that is chargeable as a felony and that involves violence against another person.

(2) "Serious injury" means any illness or injury that requires hospitalization, requires an evaluation for involuntary treatment for a mental health disorder or grave disability under the Lanterman–Petris–Short Act (Part 1 (commencing with Section 5000) of Division 5), is potentially life threatening, or that potentially will permanently impair the use of a major body organ, appendage, or limb.

(3) "Suicide attempt" means a self-inflicted destructive act committed with explicit or inferred intent to die. *(Added by Stats.2008, c. 522 (S.B.1250), § 1. Amended by Stats.2009, c. 140 (A.B.1164), § 185.)*

§ 223.2. Unpaid outstanding balances of county-assessed or court-ordered costs; minors

(a) The unpaid outstanding balance of any county-assessed or court-ordered costs imposed before January 1, 2018, pursuant to Section 207.2, 903, or 903.1, former Section 903.15, or Section 903.2, 903.25, 903.4, or 903.5 against the parent, guardian, or other person liable for the support of a minor is vacated and shall be unenforceable and uncollectable if the minor was adjudged to be a ward of the juvenile court, was on probation pursuant to Section 725, was the subject of a petition filed to adjudge the minor a ward, or was the subject of a program of supervision undertaken pursuant to Section 654. This subdivision applies to dual status children for purposes of delinquency jurisdiction.

(b) The unpaid outstanding balance of any county-assessed or court-ordered costs imposed before January 1, 2018, pursuant to Section 729.9 against a minor is vacated and shall be unenforceable and uncollectable. This subdivision applies to dual status children for purposes of delinquency jurisdiction.

(c) The unpaid outstanding balance of any county-assessed or court-ordered costs imposed before January 1, 2018, pursuant to Sections 1203.016, 1203.1ab, and 1208.2 of the Penal Code against adults who at the time were not adults who were over 21 years of age and were under the jurisdiction of the criminal court is vacated and shall be unenforceable and uncollectable. *(Added by Stats.2020, c. 340 (S.B.1290), § 1, eff. Jan. 1, 2021.)*

§ 224. Legislative findings and declarations; Indian child custody proceedings

(a) The Legislature finds and declares the following:

(1) There is no resource that is more vital to the continued existence and integrity of Indian tribes than their children, and the State of California has an interest in protecting Indian children who are members or citizens of, or are eligible for membership or citizenship in, an Indian tribe. The state is committed to protecting the essential tribal relations and best interest of an Indian child by promoting practices, in accordance with the federal Indian Child Welfare Act of 1978 (25 U.S.C. Sec. 1901 et seq.) and other applicable state and federal law, designed to prevent the child's involuntary out-of-home placement and, whenever that placement is necessary or ordered, by placing the child, whenever possible, in a placement that reflects the unique values of the child's tribal culture and is best able to assist the child in establishing, developing, and maintaining a political, cultural, and social relationship with the child's tribe and tribal community.

(2) It is in the interest of an Indian child that the child's membership or citizenship in the child's Indian tribe and connection to the tribal community be encouraged and protected, regardless of whether the child is in the physical custody of an Indian parent or Indian custodian at the commencement of an Indian child custody proceeding, the parental rights of the child's parents have been terminated, or where the child has resided or been domiciled.

(b) In all Indian child custody proceedings, as defined in the federal Indian Child Welfare Act the court shall consider all of the findings contained in subdivision (a), strive to promote the stability and security of Indian tribes and families, comply with the federal Indian Child Welfare Act of 1978 and other applicable federal law, and seek to protect the best interest of the child. Whenever an Indian child is removed from a foster care home or institution, guardianship, or adoptive placement for the purpose of further foster care, guardianship, or adoptive placement, placement of the child shall be in accordance with the federal Indian Child Welfare Act of 1978 and other applicable state and federal law.

(c) A determination by an Indian tribe that an unmarried person, who is under the age of 18 years, is either (1) a member or citizen of an Indian tribe or (2) eligible for membership or citizenship in an Indian tribe and a biological child of a member or citizen of an Indian tribe shall constitute a significant political affiliation with the tribe and shall require the application of the federal Indian Child Welfare Act of 1978 and other applicable state and federal law to the proceedings.

(d) In any case in which this code or other applicable state or federal law provides a higher standard of protection to the rights of the parent or Indian custodian of an Indian child, or the Indian child's tribe, than the rights provided under the federal Indian Child Welfare Act of 1978, the court shall apply the higher standard.

(e) Any Indian child, the Indian child's tribe, or the parent or Indian custodian from whose custody the child has been removed, may petition the court to invalidate an action in an Indian child custody proceeding for foster care or guardianship placement or termination of parental rights if the action violated Section 1911, 1912, or 1913 of the federal Indian Child Welfare Act of 1978. *(Added by Stats.2006, c. 838 (S.B.678), § 29. Amended by Stats.2018, c. 833 (A.B.3176), § 2, eff. Jan. 1, 2019.)*

Cross References

Indian, Indian child, Indian child's tribe, Indian custodian, Indian tribe, reservation, and tribal court defined for purposes of this Division, see Welfare and Institutions Code § 224.1.

Indian child custody proceeding defined for purposes of this Division, see Welfare and Institutions Code § 224.1.

§ 224.1. Definitions

(a) As used in this division, unless the context requires otherwise, the terms "Indian," "Indian child," "Indian custodian," "Indian tribe," "reservation," and "tribal court" shall be defined as provided in Section 1903 of the federal Indian Child Welfare Act (25 U.S.C. Sec. 1901 et seq.).

(b) As used in connection with an Indian child custody proceeding, the term "Indian child" also means an unmarried person who is 18 years of age or over, but under 21 years of age, who is a member of an Indian tribe or eligible for membership in an Indian tribe and is the biological child of a member of an Indian tribe, and who is under the jurisdiction of the dependency court, unless that person or their attorney elects not to be considered an Indian child for purposes of the Indian child custody proceeding. All Indian child custody proceedings involving persons 18 years of age and older shall be conducted in a manner that respects the person's status as a legal adult.

(c) As used in connection with an Indian child custody proceeding, the terms "extended family member" and "parent" shall be defined as provided in Section 1903 of the federal Indian Child Welfare Act.

(d)(1) "Indian child custody proceeding" means a hearing during a juvenile court proceeding brought under this code, or a proceeding under the Probate Code or the Family Code, involving an Indian child, other than an emergency proceeding under Section 319, that may culminate in one of the following outcomes:

(A) Foster care placement, which includes removal of an Indian child from their parent, parents, or Indian custodian for placement in a foster home, institution, or the home of a guardian or conservator, in which the parent or Indian custodian may not have the child returned upon demand, but in which parental rights have not been terminated. Foster care placement does not include an emergency placement of an Indian child pursuant to Section 309, as long as the emergency proceeding requirements set forth in Section 319 are met.

(B) Termination of parental rights, which includes any action involving an Indian child resulting in the termination of the parent-child relationship.

(C) Preadoptive placement, which includes the temporary placement of an Indian child in a foster home or institution after the termination of parental rights, but prior to, or in lieu of, adoptive placement.

(D) Adoptive placement, which includes the permanent placement of an Indian child for adoption, including any action resulting in a final decree of adoption.

(E) If a child is placed in foster care or another out-of-home placement as a result of a status offense, that status offense proceeding is considered an Indian child custody proceeding.

(2) "Indian child custody proceeding" does not include a voluntary foster care or guardianship placement if the parent or Indian custodian retains the right to have the child returned upon demand.

(e)(1) "Indian child's tribe" means the Indian tribe in which an Indian child is a member or citizen or eligible for membership or citizenship, or in the case of an Indian child who is a member or citizen of, or eligible for membership or citizenship in, more than one tribe, the Indian tribe with which the Indian child has the more significant contacts.

(2) In the case of an Indian child who meets the definition of "Indian child" through more than one tribe, deference should be given to the tribe of which the Indian child is already a member or citizen, unless otherwise agreed to by the tribes.

(3) If an Indian child meets the definition of "Indian child" through more than one tribe because the child is a member or citizen of more than one tribe or the child is not a member or citizen but is eligible for membership or citizenship in more than one tribe, the court shall provide the tribes the opportunity to determine which tribe shall be designated as the Indian child's tribe.

(4) If the tribes are able to reach an agreement, the agreed-upon tribe shall be designated as the Indian child's tribe.

(5) If the tribes are unable to reach an agreement, the court shall designate as the Indian child's tribe, the tribe with which the Indian child has the more significant contacts, taking into consideration all of the following:

(A) Preference of the parents for membership of the child.

(B) Length of past domicile or residence on or near the reservation of each tribe.

(C) Tribal membership of the child's custodial parent or Indian custodian.

(D) Interest asserted by each tribe in the child custody proceeding.

(E) Whether there has been a previous adjudication with respect to the child by a court of one of the tribes.

(F) Self–identification by the child, if the child is of sufficient age and capacity to meaningfully self-identify.

(6) If an Indian child becomes a member of a tribe other than the one designated by the court as the Indian child's tribe under paragraph (5), actions taken based on the court's determination prior to the child's becoming a tribal member continue to be valid.

(7) A determination of the Indian child's tribe for purposes of the federal Indian Child Welfare Act does not constitute a determination for any other purpose.

(f) "Active efforts" means affirmative, active, thorough, and timely efforts intended primarily to maintain or reunite an Indian child with their family. If an agency is involved in an Indian child custody proceeding, active efforts shall involve assisting the parent, parents, or Indian custodian through the steps of a case plan and with accessing or developing the resources necessary to satisfy the case plan. To the maximum extent possible, active efforts shall be provided in a manner consistent with the prevailing social and cultural conditions and way of life of the Indian child's tribe and shall be conducted in partnership with the Indian child and the Indian child's parents, extended family members, Indian custodians, and tribe. Active efforts shall be tailored to the facts and circumstances of the case and may include, but are not limited to, any of the following:

(1) Conducting a comprehensive assessment of the circumstances of the Indian child's family, with a focus on safe reunification as the most desirable goal.

(2) Identifying appropriate services and helping the parents overcome barriers, including actively assisting the parents in obtaining those services.

(3) Identifying, notifying, and inviting representatives of the Indian child's tribe to participate in providing support and services to the Indian child's family and in family team meetings, permanency planning, and resolution of placement issues.

(4) Conducting or causing to be conducted a diligent search for the Indian child's extended family members, and contacting and

consulting with extended family members to provide family structure and support for the Indian child and the Indian child's parents.

(5) Offering and employing all available and culturally appropriate family preservation strategies and facilitating the use of remedial and rehabilitative services provided by the child's tribe.

(6) Taking steps to keep siblings together whenever possible.

(7) Supporting regular visits with parents or Indian custodians in the most natural setting possible, as well as trial home visits of the Indian child during any period of removal, consistent with the need to ensure the health, safety, and welfare of the child.

(8) Identifying community resources, including housing, financial assistance, transportation, mental health and substance abuse services, and peer support services, and actively assisting the Indian child's parents or, when appropriate, the child's family, in utilizing and accessing those resources.

(9) Monitoring progress and participation in services.

(10) Considering alternative ways to address the needs of the Indian child's parents and, where appropriate, the family, if the optimum services do not exist or are not available.

(11) Providing postreunification services and monitoring.

(g) "Assistant Secretary" means the Assistant Secretary of the Bureau of Indian Affairs.

(h) "Bureau of Indian Affairs" means the Bureau of Indian Affairs of the Department of the Interior.

(i) "Continued custody" means physical custody or legal custody or both, under any applicable tribal law or tribal custom or state law, that a parent or Indian custodian already has or had at any time in the past. The biological mother of an Indian child is deemed to have had custody of the Indian child.

(j) "Custody" means physical custody or legal custody or both, under any applicable tribal law or tribal custom or state law.

(k) "Domicile" means either of the following:

(1) For a parent, Indian custodian, or legal guardian, the place that a person has been physically present and that the person regards as home. This includes a person's true, fixed, principal, and permanent home, to which that person intends to return and remain indefinitely even though the person may be currently residing elsewhere.

(2) For an Indian child, the domicile of the Indian child's parents, Indian custodian, or legal guardian. In the case of an Indian child whose parents are not married to each other, the domicile of the Indian child means the domicile of the Indian child's custodial parent.

(*l*) "Emergency proceeding" for purposes of juvenile dependency proceedings is the initial petition hearing held pursuant to Section 319.

(m) "Indian foster home" means a foster home where one or more of the licensed or approved foster parents is an Indian as defined in Section 3 of the federal Indian Child Welfare Act of 1978.

(n) "Involuntary proceeding" means an Indian child custody proceeding in which the parent does not consent of their free will to the foster care, preadoptive, or adoptive placement, or termination of parental rights. "Involuntary proceeding" also means an Indian child custody proceeding in which the parent consents to the foster care, preadoptive, or adoptive placement, under threat of removal of the child by a state court or agency.

(*o*) "Status offense" means an offense that would not be considered criminal if committed by an adult, including, but not limited to, school truancy and incorrigibility.

(p) "Upon demand" means, in the case of an Indian child, the parent or Indian custodian may regain physical custody during a voluntary proceeding simply upon verbal request, without any delay, formalities, or contingencies.

(q) "Voluntary proceeding" means an Indian child custody proceeding that is not an involuntary proceeding, including, but not limited to, a proceeding for foster care, preadoptive or adoptive placement that either parent, both parents, or the Indian custodian has, of their free will, without a threat of removal by a state agency, consented to for the Indian child, or a proceeding for voluntary termination of parental rights.

(r) "Tribally approved home" means a home that has been licensed or approved by an Indian child's tribe, or a tribe or tribal organization designated by the Indian child's tribe, for foster care or adoptive placement of an Indian child using standards established by the child's tribe pursuant to Section 1915 of the federal Indian Child Welfare Act (25 U.S.C. Sec. 1901 et seq.). A tribally approved home is not required to be licensed or approved by the state or county and is equivalent to a state-licensed or county-licensed or approved home, including an approved resource family home. Background check requirements for foster care or adoptive placement as required by Sections 1522 and 1522.1 of the Health and Safety Code shall apply to a tribally approved home. *(Added by Stats.2006, c. 838 (S.B.678), § 30. Amended by Stats.2010, c. 468 (A.B.2418), § 1; Stats.2018, c. 833 (A.B.3176), § 3, eff. Jan. 1, 2019; Stats.2019, c. 27 (S.B.80), § 17, eff. June 27, 2019.)*

Cross References

Resource family applicant of foster family agency, reference check, see Health and Safety Code § 1517.2.

Writing defined, see Welfare and Institutions Code § 8.

Research References

West's California Judicial Council Forms JV–421, Dispositional Attachment: Removal from Custodial Parent—Placement With Nonparent (Welf. & Inst. Code, §§361, 361.2).

West's California Judicial Council Forms JV–461, Findings and Orders After Nonminor Disposition Hearing.

West's California Judicial Council Forms JV–461(A), Dispositional Attachment: Nonminor Dependent.

West's California Judicial Council Forms JV–462, Findings and Orders After Nonminor Dependent Status Review Hearing.

West's California Judicial Council Forms JV–463, Nonminor's Informed Consent to Hold Disposition Hearing.

West's California Judicial Council Forms JV–464–INFO, How to Ask to Return to Juvenile Court Jurisdiction and Foster Care (Also Available in Chinese, Korean, Spanish, and Vietnamese).

West's California Judicial Council Forms JV–466, Request to Return to Juvenile Court Jurisdiction and Foster Care.

West's California Judicial Council Forms JV–468, Confidential Information—Request to Return to Juvenile Court Jurisdiction and Foster Care.

§ 224.2. Determination whether child is an Indian child; considerations; scope of inquiry; membership status

(a) The court, county welfare department, and the probation department have an affirmative and continuing duty to inquire whether a child for whom a petition under Section 300, 601, or 602 may be or has been filed, is or may be an Indian child. The duty to inquire begins with the initial contact, including, but not limited to, asking the party reporting child abuse or neglect whether the party has any information that the child may be an Indian child.

(b) If a child is placed into the temporary custody of a county welfare department pursuant to Section 306 or county probation department pursuant to Section 307, the county welfare department or county probation department has a duty to inquire whether that child is an Indian child. Inquiry includes, but is not limited to, asking the child, parents, legal guardian, Indian custodian, extended family members, others who have an interest in the child, and the party reporting child abuse or neglect, whether the child is, or may be, an Indian child and where the child, the parents, or Indian custodian is domiciled.

(c) At the first appearance in court of each party, the court shall ask each participant present in the hearing whether the participant knows or has reason to know that the child is an Indian child. The court shall instruct the parties to inform the court if they subsequently receive information that provides reason to know the child is an Indian child.

(d) There is reason to know a child involved in a proceeding is an Indian child under any of the following circumstances:

(1) A person having an interest in the child, including the child, an officer of the court, a tribe, an Indian organization, a public or private agency, or a member of the child's extended family informs the court that the child is an Indian child.

(2) The residence or domicile of the child, the child's parents, or Indian custodian is on a reservation or in an Alaska Native village.

(3) Any participant in the proceeding, officer of the court, Indian tribe, Indian organization, or agency informs the court that it has discovered information indicating that the child is an Indian child.

(4) The child who is the subject of the proceeding gives the court reason to know that the child is an Indian child.

(5) The court is informed that the child is or has been a ward of a tribal court.

(6) The court is informed that either parent or the child possess an identification card indicating membership or citizenship in an Indian tribe.

(e) If the court, social worker, or probation officer has reason to believe that an Indian child is involved in a proceeding, but does not have sufficient information to determine that there is reason to know that the child is an Indian child, the court, social worker, or probation officer shall make further inquiry regarding the possible Indian status of the child, and shall make that inquiry as soon as practicable.

(1) There is reason to believe a child involved in a proceeding is an Indian child whenever the court, social worker, or probation officer has information suggesting that either the parent of the child or the child is a member or may be eligible for membership in an Indian tribe. Information suggesting membership or eligibility for membership includes, but is not limited to, information that indicates, but does not establish, the existence of one or more of the grounds for reason to know enumerated in paragraphs (1) to (6), inclusive, of subdivision (d).

(2) When there is reason to believe the child is an Indian child, further inquiry is necessary to help the court, social worker, or probation officer determine whether there is reason to know a child is an Indian child. Further inquiry includes, but is not limited to, all of the following:

(A) Interviewing the parents, Indian custodian, and extended family members to gather the information required in paragraph (5) of subdivision (a) of Section 224.3.

(B) Contacting the Bureau of Indian Affairs and the State Department of Social Services for assistance in identifying the names and contact information of the tribes in which the child may be a member, or eligible for membership in, and contacting the tribes and any other person that may reasonably be expected to have information regarding the child's membership status or eligibility.

(C) Contacting the tribe or tribes and any other person that may reasonably be expected to have information regarding the child's membership, citizenship status, or eligibility. Contact with a tribe shall, at a minimum, include telephone, facsimile, or electronic mail contact to each tribe's designated agent for receipt of notices under the federal Indian Child Welfare Act of 1978 (25 U.S.C. Sec. 1901 et seq.). Contact with a tribe shall include sharing information identified by the tribe as necessary for the tribe to make a membership or eligibility determination, as well as information on the current status of the child and the case.

(f) If there is reason to know, as set forth in subdivision (d), that the child is an Indian child, the party seeking foster care placement shall provide notice in accordance with paragraph (5) of subdivision (a) of Section 224.3.

(g) If there is reason to know the child is an Indian child, but the court does not have sufficient evidence to determine that the child is or is not an Indian child, the court shall confirm, by way of a report, declaration, or testimony included in the record that the agency or other party used due diligence to identify and work with all of the tribes of which there is reason to know the child may be a member, or eligible for membership, to verify whether the child is in fact a member or whether a biological parent is a member and the child is eligible for membership.

(h) A determination by an Indian tribe that a child is or is not a member of, or eligible for membership in, that tribe, or testimony attesting to that status by a person authorized by the tribe to provide that determination, shall be conclusive. Information that the child is not enrolled, or is not eligible for enrollment in, the tribe is not determinative of the child's membership status unless the tribe also confirms in writing that enrollment is a prerequisite for membership under tribal law or custom.

(i)(1) When there is reason to know that the child is an Indian child, the court shall treat the child as an Indian child unless and until the court determines on the record and after review of the report of due diligence as described in subdivision (g), and a review of the copies of notice, return receipts, and tribal responses required pursuant to Section 224.3, that the child does not meet the definition of an Indian child as used in Section 224.1 and the federal Indian Child Welfare Act of 1978 (25 U.S.C. Sec. 1901 et seq.).

(2) If the court makes a finding that proper and adequate further inquiry and due diligence as required in this section have been conducted and there is no reason to know whether the child is an Indian child, the court may make a finding that the federal Indian Child Welfare Act of 1978 (25 U.S.C. Sec. 1901 et seq.) does not apply to the proceedings, subject to reversal based on sufficiency of the evidence. The court shall reverse its determination if it subsequently receives information providing reason to believe that the child is an Indian child and order the social worker or probation officer to conduct further inquiry pursuant to Section 224.3.

(j) Notwithstanding a determination that the federal Indian Child Welfare Act of 1978 does not apply to the proceedings, if the court, social worker, or probation officer subsequently receives any information required by Section 224.3 that was not previously available or included in the notice issued under Section 224.3, the party seeking placement shall provide the additional information to any tribes entitled to notice under Section 224.3 and to the Secretary of the Interior's designated agent.

(k) * * * Notwithstanding any other provision, an Indian child's tribe may participate by telephone, or other remote appearance options * * *, in proceedings * * * in which the federal Indian Child Welfare Act of 1978 (25 U.S.C. Sec. 1901 et seq.) may apply. * * * The method of appearance may be determined by the court consistent with court capacity and contractual obligations, and taking into account the capacity of the tribe, as long as a method of effective remote appearance and participation sufficient to allow the tribe to fully exercise its rights is provided. Fees shall not be charged for court appearances established under this subdivision * * * conducted in whole or in part by remote means. *(Added by Stats.2018, c. 833 (A.B.3176), § 5, eff. Jan. 1, 2019. Amended by Stats.2019, c. 434 (A.B.686), § 2, eff. Jan. 1, 2020; Stats.2020, c. 104 (A.B.2944), § 15, eff. Sept. 18, 2020; Stats.2022, c. 420 (A.B.2960), § 43, eff. Jan. 1, 2023.)*

Cross References

Indian, Indian child, Indian child's tribe, Indian custodian, Indian tribe, reservation, and tribal court defined for purposes of this Division, see Welfare and Institutions Code § 224.1.

Probation officer or social worker defined for purposes of this Chapter, see Welfare and Institutions Code § 215.
Writing defined, see Welfare and Institutions Code § 8.

Research References

West's California Judicial Council Forms ICWA–020, Parental Notification of Indian Status (Also Available in Spanish).
West's California Judicial Council Forms ICWA–030, Notice of Child Custody Proceeding for Indian Child (Also Available in Spanish).
West's California Judicial Council Forms ICWA–030(A), Attachment to Notice of Child Custody Proceeding for Indian Child (Also Available in Spanish).

§ 224.3. Matters involving an Indian child; notice to interested parties; time to notify; proof

(a) If the court, a social worker, or probation officer knows or has reason to know, as described in subdivision (d) of Section 224.2, that an Indian child is involved, notice pursuant to Section 1912 of the federal Indian Child Welfare Act of 1978 (25 U.S.C. Sec. 1901 et seq.) shall be provided for hearings that may culminate in an order for foster care placement, termination of parental rights, preadoptive placement, or adoptive placement, as described in paragraph (1) of subdivision (d) of Section 224.1. The notice shall be sent to the minor's parents or legal guardian, Indian custodian, if any, and the child's tribe. Copies of all notices sent shall be served on all parties to the dependency proceeding and their attorneys. Notice shall comply with all of the following requirements:

(1) Notice shall be sent by registered or certified mail with return receipt requested. Additional notice by first-class mail is recommended, but not required.

(2) Notice to the tribe shall be to the tribal chairperson, unless the tribe has designated another agent for service.

(3) Notice of all Indian child custody hearings shall be sent by the party seeking placement of the child to all of the following:

(A) All tribes of which the child may be a member or citizen, or eligible for membership or citizenship, unless either of the following occur:

(i) A tribe has made a determination that the child is not a member or citizen, or eligible for membership or citizenship.

(ii) The court makes a determination as to which tribe is the child's tribe in accordance with subdivision (e) of Section 224.1, after which notice need only be sent to the Indian child's tribe.

(B) The child's parents.

(C) The child's Indian custodian.

(4) Notice, to the extent required by federal law, shall be sent to the Secretary of the Interior's designated agent.

(5) In addition to the information specified in other sections of this article, notice shall include all of the following information:

(A) The name, birth date, and birthplace of the Indian child, if known.

(B) The name of the Indian tribe in which the child is a member, or may be eligible for membership, if known.

(C) All names known of the Indian child's biological parents, grandparents, and great-grandparents, or Indian custodians, including maiden, married, and former names or aliases, as well as their current and former addresses, birth dates, places of birth and death, tribal enrollment information of other direct lineal ancestors of the child, and any other identifying information, if known.

(D) A copy of the petition by which the proceeding was initiated.

(E) A copy of the child's birth certificate, if available.

(F) The location, mailing address, and telephone number of the court and all parties notified pursuant to this section.

(G) The information regarding the time, date, and any location of any scheduled hearings.

(H) A statement of all of the following:

(i) The name of the petitioner and the name and address of the petitioner's attorney.

(ii) The absolute right of the child's parents, Indian custodians, and tribe to intervene in the proceeding.

(iii) The right of the child's parents, Indian custodians, and tribe to petition the court to transfer the proceeding to the tribal court of the Indian child's tribe, absent objection by either parent and subject to declination by the tribal court.

(iv) The right of the child's parents, Indian custodians, and tribe to, upon request, be granted up to an additional 20 days from the receipt of the notice to prepare for the proceeding.

(v) The potential legal consequences of the proceedings on the future custodial and parental rights of the child's parents or Indian custodians.

(vi) That if the parents or Indian custodians are unable to afford counsel, counsel will be appointed to represent the parents or Indian custodians pursuant to Section 1912 of the federal Indian Child Welfare Act of 1978.

(vii) In accordance with Section 827, the information contained in the notice, petition, pleading, and other court documents is confidential. Any person or entity notified shall maintain the confidentiality of the information contained in the notice concerning the particular proceeding and not reveal that information to anyone who does not need the information in order to exercise the tribe's rights under the federal Indian Child Welfare Act of 1978.

(b) Notice shall be sent whenever it is known or there is reason to know that an Indian child is involved, and for every hearing that may culminate in an order for foster care placement, termination of parental rights, preadoptive placement, or adoptive placement, as described in paragraph (1) of subdivision (d) of Section 224.1, unless it is determined that the federal Indian Child Welfare Act of 1978 does not apply to the case in accordance with Section 224.2. After a tribe acknowledges that the child is a member of, or eligible for membership in, that tribe, or after a tribe intervenes in a proceeding, the information set out in subparagraphs (C), (D), (E), and (H) of paragraph (5) of subdivision (a) need not be included with the notice.

(c) Proof of the notice, including copies of notices sent and all return receipts and responses received, shall be filed with the court in advance of the hearing, except as permitted under subdivision (d).

(d) A proceeding shall not be held until at least 10 days after receipt of notice by the parent, Indian custodian, the tribe, or the Bureau of Indian Affairs, except for a hearing held pursuant to Section 319, provided that notice of the hearing held pursuant to Section 319 shall be given as soon as possible after the filing of the petition to declare the Indian child a dependent child. Notice to tribes of the hearing pursuant to Section 319 shall be consistent with the requirements for notice to parents set forth in Sections 290.1 and 290.2. With the exception of the hearing held pursuant to Section 319, the parent, Indian custodian, or tribe shall, upon request, be granted up to 20 additional days to prepare for that proceeding. This subdivision does not limit the rights of the parent, Indian custodian, or tribe to more than 10 days' notice when a lengthier notice period is required by law.

(e) With respect to giving notice to Indian tribes, a party is subject to court sanctions if that person knowingly and willfully falsifies or conceals a material fact concerning whether the child is an Indian child, or counsels a party to do so.

(f) The inclusion of contact information of any adult or child that would otherwise be required to be included in the notification pursuant to this section shall not be required if that person is at risk of harm as a result of domestic violence, child abuse, sexual abuse, or stalking.

(g) For any hearing that does not meet the definition of an Indian child custody proceeding set forth in Section 224.1, or is not an emergency proceeding, notice to the child's parents, Indian custodian, and tribe shall be sent in accordance with Sections 292, 293, and 295. *(Added by Stats.2018, c. 833 (A.B.3176), § 7, eff. Jan. 1, 2019.)*

Cross References

Juvenile court law, electronic filing and service, conditions, see Welfare and Institutions Code § 212.5.
Notice of subsequent petitions, supplemental petitions, petitions for modification, see Welfare and Institutions Code § 297.
Probation officer or social worker defined for purposes of this Chapter, see Welfare and Institutions Code § 215.
Writing defined, see Welfare and Institutions Code § 8.

Research References

West's California Judicial Council Forms ICWA–030, Notice of Child Custody Proceeding for Indian Child (Also Available in Spanish).
West's California Judicial Council Forms ICWA–030(A), Attachment to Notice of Child Custody Proceeding for Indian Child (Also Available in Spanish).

§ 224.4. Intervention in proceedings by tribe

The Indian child's tribe and Indian custodian have the right to intervene at any point in an Indian child custody proceeding. *(Added by Stats.2006, c. 838 (S.B.678), § 33.)*

Cross References

Indian, Indian child, Indian child's tribe, Indian custodian, Indian tribe, reservation, and tribal court defined for purposes of this Division, see Welfare and Institutions Code § 224.1.
Indian child custody proceeding defined for purposes of this Division, see Welfare and Institutions Code § 224.1.

Research References

West's California Judicial Council Forms ICWA–040, Notice of Designation of Tribal Representative in a Court Proceeding Involving an Indian Child.

§ 224.5. Full faith and credit to tribal proceedings and records

In an Indian child custody proceeding, the court shall give full faith and credit to the public acts, records, judicial proceedings, and judgments of any Indian tribe applicable to the proceeding to the same extent that such entities give full faith and credit to the public acts, records, judicial proceedings, and judgments of any other entity. *(Added by Stats.2006, c. 838 (S.B.678), § 34.)*

Cross References

Indian, Indian child, Indian child's tribe, Indian custodian, Indian tribe, reservation, and tribal court defined for purposes of this Division, see Welfare and Institutions Code § 224.1.
Indian child custody proceeding defined for purposes of this Division, see Welfare and Institutions Code § 224.1.
Parent and child relationship, freedom from parental custody and control, declaration that Indian child is free from custody or control of parent, see Family Code § 7892.5.

§ 224.6. Testimony of qualified expert witnesses; qualifications; participation at hearings; written reports and recommendations

(a) When testimony of a "qualified expert witness" is required in an Indian child custody proceeding, a "qualified expert witness" shall be qualified to testify regarding whether continued custody of the child by the parent or Indian custodian is likely to result in serious emotional or physical damage to the child and shall be qualified to testify to the prevailing social and cultural standards of the Indian child's tribe. A person may be designated by the child's tribe as qualified to testify to the prevailing social and cultural standards of the Indian child's tribe. The individual may not be an employee of the person or agency recommending foster care placement or termination of parental rights.

(b) In considering whether to remove an Indian child from the custody of a parent or Indian custodian or to terminate the parental rights of the parent of an Indian child, the court shall do both of the following:

(1) Require that a qualified expert witness testify regarding whether continued custody of the child by the parent or Indian custodian is likely to result in serious emotional or physical damage to the child.

(2) Consider evidence concerning the prevailing social and cultural standards of the Indian child's tribe, including that tribe's family organization and child-rearing practices.

(c) Persons with the following characteristics are most likely to meet the requirements for a qualified expert witness for purposes of Indian child custody proceedings:

(1) A person designated by the Indian child's tribe as being qualified to testify to the prevailing social and cultural standards of the Indian child's tribe.

(2) A member or citizen of the Indian child's tribe who is recognized by the tribal community as knowledgeable in tribal customs as they pertain to family organization and child-rearing practices.

(3) An expert witness having substantial experience in the delivery of child and family services to Indians, and extensive knowledge of prevailing social and cultural standards and child-rearing practices within the Indian child's tribe.

(d) The court or any party may request the assistance of the Indian child's tribe or Bureau of Indian Affairs agency serving the Indian child's tribe in locating persons qualified to serve as expert witnesses.

(e) The court may accept a declaration or affidavit from a qualified expert witness in lieu of testimony only if the parties have so stipulated in writing and the court is satisfied the stipulation is made knowingly, intelligently, and voluntarily. *(Added by Stats.2006, c. 838 (S.B.678), § 35. Amended by Stats.2018, c. 833 (A.B.3176), § 8, eff. Jan. 1, 2019.)*

Cross References

Custody of minor child, matters to be considered in granting custody, custody award to nonparent, see Family Code § 3041.
Indian, Indian child, Indian child's tribe, Indian custodian, Indian tribe, reservation, and tribal court defined for purposes of this Division, see Welfare and Institutions Code § 224.1.
Indian child custody proceeding defined for purposes of this Division, see Welfare and Institutions Code § 224.1.
Probation officer or social worker defined for purposes of this Chapter, see Welfare and Institutions Code § 215.
Termination of parental rights or permanent foster care placement, children of Indian ancestry, standards for termination, see Welfare and Institutions Code § 361.7.
Writing defined, see Welfare and Institutions Code § 8.

ARTICLE 1.5. YOUTH BILL OF RIGHTS

Section

§ 224.70. Definitions

For the purposes of this article:

* * *

(a) "Extended family member" means any adult related to the youth by blood, adoption, or marriage, and any adult who has an established familial or mentoring relationship with the youth, including, but not limited to, godparents, clergy, teachers, neighbors, and family friends.

(b) "* * * Juvenile facility" means a place of confinement that is operated by, or contracted for, the * * * county probation department or juvenile court for the purpose of the * * * confinement of youth who are taken into custody and alleged to be within the description of Section 601 or 602 * * * who are adjudged to be a ward of the court.

(c) "Youth" means any person detained in a * * * juvenile facility. *(Added by Stats.2007, c. 649 (S.B.518), § 2. Amended by Stats.2022, c. 786 (A.B.2417), § 1, eff. Jan. 1, 2023.)*

Cross References

Department of Corrections, generally, see Penal Code § 5000 et seq.

§ 224.71. Rights of youth confined in a juvenile facility

It is the policy of the state that all youth confined in a juvenile facility * * * shall have the following rights, which are established by existing law and regulation:

(a) To live in a safe, healthy, and clean environment conducive to treatment, positive youth development, and healing and where they are treated with dignity and respect.

(b) To be free from physical, sexual, emotional, or other abuse, or corporal punishment.

(c) To receive adequate and healthy meals and snacks, clean water at any time, timely access to toilets, access to daily showers, sufficient personal hygiene items, clean bedding, and clean clothing in good repair, including clean undergarments on a daily basis, and new underwear that * * * fits. Clothing, grooming, and hygiene products shall be adequate and * * * respect the child's culture, ethnicity, and gender identity and expression.

(d) To receive adequate, appropriate, and timely medical, reproductive, dental, vision, and mental health services provided by qualified professionals and consistent with current professional standards of care.

(e) To refuse the administration of psychotropic and other medications consistent with applicable law or unless immediately necessary for the preservation of life or the prevention of serious bodily harm.

(f) To not be searched for the purpose of harassment or humiliation * * *, a form of discipline or punishment, or to verify the youth's gender. To searches that preserve the privacy and dignity of the person and to have access to a written search policy at any time, including the policy on who may perform searches.

(g) To maintain frequent and continuing contact with parents, guardians, siblings, children, and extended family members, through visits, telephone calls, and mail. Youth may be provided with access to computer technology and the internet for maintaining relationships with family as an alternative, but not as a replacement for, in-person visiting.

(h) To make and receive confidential telephone calls, send and receive confidential mail, and have confidential visits with attorneys and their authorized representatives, ombudspersons, including the Division of the Ombudsperson of the Office of Youth and Community Restoration, and other advocates, holders of public office, state and federal court personnel, and legal service organizations.

(i) To have fair and equal access to all available services, housing, care, treatment, and benefits, and to not be subjected to discrimination or harassment on the basis of actual or perceived race, * * * ethnicity, ancestry, national origin, language, color, religion, sex, sexual orientation, gender identity, gender expression, mental or physical disability, immigration status, or HIV status.

(j) To have * * * daily opportunities for age-appropriate physical exercise and recreation, including time spent outdoors and access to leisure reading, letter writing, and entertainment.

(k) To contact attorneys, ombudspersons, including the Division of the Ombudsperson of the Office of Youth and Community Restoration, and other advocates, and representatives of state or local agencies, regarding conditions of confinement or violations of rights, and to be free from retaliation for making these contacts or complaints.

(*l*) To exercise the religious or spiritual practice of their choice and to participate in or refuse to participate in religious services and activities * * *.

(m) To not be deprived of any of the following as a disciplinary measure: food, contact with parents, guardians, family, or attorneys, sleep, exercise, education, bedding, clothing, access to religious services, a daily shower, * * * clean water, a toilet, hygiene products, medical services, reading material, or the right to send and receive mail; to not be subject to room confinement as a disciplinary measure; to access written disciplinary policies, including the right to be informed of accusations against them, have an opportunity to be heard, present evidence and testimony, and their right to appeal disciplinary decisions.

(n) To receive a rigorous, quality education that complies with state law, and the abilities of students and prepares them for high school graduation, career entry, and postsecondary education; to attend * * * appropriate level school classes and vocational training * * *; to have access to postsecondary academic and career technical education courses and programs; to have access to computer technology and the internet for the purposes of education and to continue to receive educational services while on disciplinary or medical status; and to have access to information about the educational options available to youth.

(*o*) To information about their rights as parents, including available parental support, reunification advocacy, and opportunities to maintain or develop a connection with their children; to access educational information or programming about pregnancy, infant care, parenting, and breast-feeding, and childhood development; to proper prenatal care, diet, vitamins, nutrition, and medical treatment; to counseling for pregnant and post partum youth; to not be restrained by the use of leg irons, waist chains, or handcuffs behind the body while pregnant or in recovery after delivery; to not be restrained during a medical emergency, labor, delivery, or recovery unless deemed necessary for their safety and security, and to have restraints removed when a medical professional determines removal is medically necessary; and to access written policies about pregnant, post partum, and lactating youth.

(p) To attend all court hearings pertaining to them.

(q) To have counsel and a prompt probable cause hearing when detained on probation * * * violations.

(r) To make at least two free telephone calls within an hour after initially being placed in a juvenile facility * * * following an arrest. *(Added by Stats.2007, c. 649 (S.B.518), § 2. Amended by Stats.2022, c. 786 (A.B.2417), § 2, eff. Jan. 1, 2023.)*

Cross References

Detained defined for purposes of this Article, see Welfare and Institutions Code § 224.70.

Extended family member defined for purposes of this Article, see Welfare and Institutions Code § 224.70.

Facility of the Division of Juvenile Facilities defined for purposes of this Article, see Welfare and Institutions Code § 224.70.

Punishment defined for purposes of this Chapter, see Welfare and Institutions Code § 202.

Youth defined for purposes of this Article, see Welfare and Institutions Code § 224.70.

§ 224.72. Juvenile facilities; developmentally appropriate orientation; posting and copy of rights

(a) Every juvenile facility * * * shall provide each youth who is placed in the facility with an age and developmentally appropriate orientation that includes an explanation and a copy of the rights and responsibilities of the youth, as specified in Section 224.71, and that addresses the youth's questions and concerns.

(b) Each juvenile facility * * * shall post a listing of the rights provided by Section 224.71 in a conspicuous location * * *, including classrooms and living units.

* * *

(c) A copy of the rights of the youth shall be included in orientation packets provided to parents or guardians of wards. Copies of the rights of youth in English, Spanish, and other languages shall also be made available in the visiting areas of * * * juvenile justice facilities and, upon request, to parents or guardians. *(Added by Stats.2007, c. 649 (S.B.518), § 2. Amended by Stats.2008, c. 522 (S.B.1250), § 2; Stats.2022, c. 786 (A.B.2417), § 3, eff. Jan. 1, 2023.)*

Cross References

Facility of the Division of Juvenile Facilities defined for purposes of this Article, see Welfare and Institutions Code § 224.70.
Youth defined for purposes of this Article, see Welfare and Institutions Code § 224.70.

§ 224.73. Juvenile facilities; youth safety, dignity, and care; nondiscrimination

All juvenile facilities * * * shall ensure the safety and dignity of all youth in their care and shall * * * not discriminate against any youth * * * on the basis of actual or perceived race, * * * ethnicity, ancestry, national origin, color, religion, gender, sexual orientation, gender identity, gender expression, mental or physical disability, immigration status, or HIV status. *(Added by Stats.2007, c. 649 (S.B.518), § 2. Amended by Stats.2022, c. 786 (A.B.2417), § 4, eff. Jan. 1, 2023.)*

Cross References

Facility of the Division of Juvenile Facilities defined for purposes of this Article, see Welfare and Institutions Code § 224.70.
Youth defined for purposes of this Article, see Welfare and Institutions Code § 224.70.

§ 224.74. Office of Youth and Community Restoration; development of standardized information explaining rights

* * * The Office of * * * Youth and Community Restoration, in consultation with youth, youth advocate and support groups, and groups representing children, families, children's facilities, and other interested parties, shall develop, no later than July 1, 2023, standardized information explaining the rights specified in Section 224.71. The information developed shall be age-appropriate.

* * * *(Added by Stats.2007, c. 649 (S.B.518), § 2. Amended by Stats.2022, c. 786 (A.B.2417), § 5, eff. Jan. 1, 2023.)*

Cross References

Writing defined, see Welfare and Institutions Code § 8.
Youth defined for purposes of this Article, see Welfare and Institutions Code § 224.70.

ARTICLE 2. COMMISSIONS AND COMMITTEES

Section

§ 225. County juvenile justice commission; membership; term of office; vacancies

In each county there shall be a juvenile justice commission consisting of not less than 7 and no more than 15 citizens. Two or more of the members shall be persons who are between 14 and 21 years of age, provided there are available persons between 14 and 21 years of age who are able to carry out the duties of a commission member in a manner satisfactory to the appointing authority. Each person serving as a member of a probation committee immediately prior to September 15, 1961, shall be a member of the juvenile justice commission and shall continue to serve as such until such time as his or her term of appointment as a member of the probation committee would have expired under any prior provision of law. Upon a vacancy occurring in the membership of the commission and upon the expiration of the term of office of any member, a successor shall be appointed by the presiding judge of the superior court with the concurrence of the judge of the juvenile court or, in a county having more than one judge of the juvenile court, with the concurrence of the presiding judge of the juvenile court for a term of four years. When a vacancy occurs for any reason other than the expiration of a term of office, the appointee to fill such vacancy shall hold office for the unexpired term of his or her predecessor.

Appointments may be made by the presiding judge of the superior court, in the same manner designated in this section for the filling of vacancies, to increase the membership of a commission to the maximum of 15 in any county which has a commission with a membership of less than 15 members.

In any county in which the membership of the commission, on the effective date of amendments to this section enacted at the 1971 Regular Session of the Legislature, exceeds the maximum number permitted by this section, no additional appointments shall be made until the number of commissioners is less than the maximum number permitted by this section. In any case, such county's commission membership shall, on or after January 1, 1974, be no greater than the maximum permitted by this section. *(Added by Stats.1976, c. 1068, p. 4746, § 2. Amended by Stats.1980, c. 751, p. 2252, § 1.)*

Cross References

Probation commission in lieu of county juvenile justice commission in certain counties, see Welfare and Institutions Code § 240.

§ 226. Regional juvenile justice commission; membership; term of office; vacancies

In lieu of county juvenile justice commissions, the boards of supervisors of two or more adjacent counties may agree to establish a regional juvenile justice commission consisting of not less than eight citizens, and having a sufficient number of members so that their appointment may be equally apportioned between the participating counties. Two or more of the members shall be persons who are between 14 and 21 years of age, provided there are available persons between 14 and 21 years of age who are able to carry out the duties of a commission member in a manner satisfactory to the appointing authority. The presiding judge of the superior court with the concurrence of the judge of the juvenile court or, in a county having more than one judge of the juvenile court, with the concurrence of the presiding judge of the juvenile court of each of the participating counties shall appoint an equal number of members to the regional justice commission and they shall hold office for a term of four years. Of those first appointed, however, if the number appointed be an even number, half shall serve for a term of two years and half shall serve for a term of four years and if the number of members first appointed be an odd number, the greater number nearest half shall serve for a term of two years and the remainder shall serve for a term of four years. The respective terms of the members first appointed shall be determined by lot as soon as possible after their appointment. Upon a vacancy occurring in the membership of the commission and upon the expiration of the term of office of any member, a successor shall be appointed by the presiding judge of the superior court with the concurrence of the judge of the juvenile court or, in a county having more than one judge of the juvenile court, with the concurrence of the presiding judge of the juvenile court of the county which originally appointed such vacating or retiring member. When a vacancy occurs for any reason other than the expiration of a term of office, the appointee shall hold office for the unexpired term of his or her predecessor. *(Added by Stats.1976, c. 1068, p. 4746, § 2. Amended by Stats.1980, c. 751, p. 2253, § 2.)*

§ 227. Qualification of members; oath; record

The clerk of the court of the appointing judge shall immediately notify each person appointed a member of a county or regional juvenile justice commission and thereupon such person shall appear before the appointing judge and qualify by taking an oath faithfully to perform the duties of a member of the juvenile justice commission. The qualification of each member shall be entered in the juvenile court record. *(Added by Stats.1976, c. 1068, p. 4746, § 2.)*

Cross References

Oath of office, generally, see Const. Art. 20, § 3; Government Code § 1360 et seq.

§ 228. Chairman and vice chairman

A juvenile justice commission shall elect a chairman and vice chairman annually. *(Added by Stats.1976, c. 1068, p. 4746, § 2.)*

§ 229. Duty of commission; access to publicly administered institutions; subpoenas; inspection of jail; report

It shall be the duty of a juvenile justice commission to inquire into the administration of the juvenile court law in the county or region in which the commission serves. For this purpose the commission shall have access to all publicly administered institutions authorized or whose use is authorized by this chapter situated in the county or region, shall inspect such institutions no less frequently than once a year, and may hold hearings. A judge of the juvenile court shall have the power to issue subpoenas requiring attendance and testimony of witnesses and production of papers at hearings of the commission.

A juvenile justice commission shall annually inspect any jail or lockup within the county which in the preceding calendar year was used for confinement for more than 24 hours of any minor. It shall report the results of such inspection together with its recommendations based thereon, in writing, to the juvenile court and to the Board of Corrections. *(Added by Stats.1976, c.1068, p. 4746, § 2. Amended by Stats.1996, c. 12 (A.B.1397), § 8, eff. Feb. 14, 1996.)*

Cross References

Inspection of jails, juvenile halls, or lockups by judge or board of corrections, see Welfare and Institutions Code § 209.

Jail defined for purposes of this Chapter, see Welfare and Institutions Code § 207.1.

Lockup defined for purposes of this Chapter, see Welfare and Institutions Code § 207.1.

Nomination of probation officers by commission, see Welfare and Institutions Code § 270.

Subpoena, see Code of Civil Procedure § 1985 et seq.

§ 229.5. Juvenile justice commissions; inquiries into group home operations; notice of visits; findings

(a) Notwithstanding any other provision of law, a juvenile justice commission may inquire into the operation of any group home that serves wards or dependent children of the juvenile court and is located in the county or region the commission serves. The commission may review the safety and well-being of wards or dependent children placed in the group home and the program and services provided in relation to the home's published program statement.

(b) In conducting its review, the commission shall respect the confidentiality of minors' records and other information protected under other provisions of law. It may review court or case records of a child provided it keeps the identities of minors named in those records confidential, and may review the financial records of a group home. However, the commission may not review the personnel records of employees or the records of donors to the group home.

(c) The commission shall give the group home manager at least 24 hours' advance notice of a visit to a group home. If the commission believes that there is a serious violation of applicable licensing laws or regulations or that residents of a group home are in danger of physical or mental abuse, abandonment or other substantial threat to their health and safety, the commission shall notify the Community Care Licensing Division of the State Department of Social Services for appropriate action, shall consult with the presiding judge of the juvenile court and chief probation officer as to whether or not a visit is appropriate, and shall notify other juvenile justice commissions of its actions, as appropriate.

(d) Upon the completion of a visit, if the commission finds any condition in the group home that poses a danger to its residents or otherwise violates any applicable law, ordinance, or regulation, the commission shall verbally advise the group home manager of its findings, unless it determines that the advisement could be detrimental to the children placed there, and shall send written confirmation of its findings to the group home manager within 14 days. The commission may also report its findings to the presiding judge of the juvenile court, chief probation officer, State Department of Social Services, or other juvenile justice commissions as appropriate. A group home manager may meet with the juvenile justice commission, chief probation officer, county welfare director, juvenile court, or the State Department of Social Services to resolve any problem or to submit a plan of correction. *(Added by Stats.1987, c. 228, § 1. Amended by Stats.1994, c. 358 (A.B.2592), § 1; Stats.2000, c. 908 (S.B.1611), § 1.)*

Cross References

Probation officer or social worker defined for purposes of this Chapter, see Welfare and Institutions Code § 215.

§ 230. Recommendations; publication

A juvenile justice commission may recommend to any person charged with the administration of any of the provisions of this chapter such changes as it has concluded, after investigation, will be beneficial. A commission may publicize its recommendations. *(Added by Stats.1976, c. 1068, p. 4746, § 2.)*

§ 231. Necessary expenses; reimbursement

Members of a juvenile justice commission shall be reimbursed for their actual and necessary expenses incurred in the performance of their duties. Such reimbursement shall be made by the county of appointment or, in lieu of such actual and necessary expenses the board of supervisors may provide that the members of the commission shall be paid not to exceed the sum of twenty-five dollars ($25) per meeting not exceeding two meetings per month. In the case of a regional justice commission, the duty of reimbursement shall be divided among the participating counties in the manner prescribed by agreement of the boards of supervisors. *(Added by Stats.1976, c. 1068, p. 4746, § 2.)*

§ 232. County agency or department; coordination of activities

The board of supervisors may by ordinance provide for the establishment, support, and maintenance of one or more agencies or departments to cooperate with and assist in coordinating on a countywide basis the work of those community agencies engaged in activities designed to prevent juvenile and adult delinquency; and such agencies or departments may cooperate with any such public or community committees, agencies, or councils at their invitation. *(Added by Stats.1976, c. 1068, p. 4746, § 2.)*

§ 233. Delinquency prevention commission

The board of supervisors may by ordinance provide for the establishment, support, and maintenance of a delinquency prevention commission, composed of not fewer than seven citizens, to coordinate on a countywide basis the work of those governmental and nongovernmental organizations engaged in activities designed to prevent juvenile delinquency. If the board so elects, it may designate the juvenile justice commission, or any other committee or council appointed pursuant to Section 232 or 235, to serve in such capacity.

The commission may receive funds from governmental and nongovernmental sources to hire an executive secretary and necessary staff and to defray needed administrative expenses. The board of supervisors may direct any county department to provide necessary staff service to the commission. The commission may expend its funds on specific projects designed to accomplish its objectives.

Members of the delinquency prevention commission shall be appointed by the board of supervisors to serve a term of four years, and they shall be reimbursed for their actual and necessary expenses incurred in the performance of their duties. Upon a vacancy occurring in the membership in the commission and upon the expiration in the term of office of any member, a successor shall be appointed by the board of supervisors. When a vacancy occurs for any reason other than the expiration of a term of office, the appointee to fill such vacancy shall hold office for the unexpired term of his or her predecessor.

The board of supervisors may appoint initial members to any delinquency prevention commission created after the effective date of the amendment made to this section at the 1973–74 Regular Session of the Legislature to hold office for the following terms: one-half of the membership of an even-numbered commission for a term of two years and one-half plus one of the membership of an odd-numbered commission for a term of two years. The remaining initial members and the term of office of each successor appointed to fill a vacancy occurring on the expiration of a term thereafter shall be four years.

For a delinquency prevention commission existing on the effective date of the amendment made to this section at the 1973–74 Regular Session of the Legislature the board of supervisors may at any time upon the expiration of all the members' terms of office appoint members to hold office for the following terms: one-half of the membership of an even-numbered commission for a term of two years and one-half plus one of the membership of an odd-numbered commission for a term of two years. The remaining members and the term of office of each successor appointed to fill a vacancy occurring on the expiration of a term thereafter shall be four years.

Notwithstanding the preceding provisions of this section, the board of supervisors shall appoint two or more persons who are between 14 and 21 years of age to membership on a delinquency prevention commission, provided there are available persons between 14 and 21 years of age who are able to carry out the duties of a commission member in a manner satisfactory to the appointing authority. *(Added by Stats.1976, c. 1068, p. 4746, § 2. Amended by Stats.1980, c. 751, p. 2254, § 3.)*

§ 233.5. Indecent or pornographic materials; assistance and advice concerning publication and distribution

In a county having a population of over 6,000,000, the board of supervisors may assign the responsibility for assisting and advising the board and other county officers concerning the publication and distribution of allegedly indecent or pornographic materials and such other related duties as the board may determine proper to the delinquency prevention commission established pursuant to Section 233. *(Added by Stats.1979, c. 431, p. 1550, § 1.)*

§ 234. Delinquency prevention agency or department

The board of supervisors may by ordinance provide for the establishment, support, and maintenance of a delinquency prevention agency or department, or may assign delinquency prevention duties to any existing county agency, or department. Any such agency or department may engage in activities designed to prevent juvenile and adult delinquency, including rendering direct and indirect services to persons in the community, and may cooperate with any other agency of government in carrying out its purposes. *(Added by Stats.1976, c. 1068, p. 4746, § 2.)*

§ 235. Public councils or committees; establishment

The juvenile court and the probation department of any county may establish, or assist in the establishment of, any public council or committee having as its object the prevention of juvenile delinquency and may cooperate with, or participate in, the work of any such councils or committees for the purpose of preventing or decreasing juvenile delinquency, including the improving of recreational, health, and other conditions in the community affecting juvenile welfare. *(Added by Stats.1976, c. 1068, p. 4746, § 2.)*

§ 236. Probation departments; juvenile delinquency prevention services

Notwithstanding any other law, probation departments may engage in activities designed to prevent juvenile delinquency. These activities include rendering direct and indirect services to persons in the community. Probation departments shall not be limited to providing services only to those persons on probation being supervised under Section 330 or 654, but may provide services to any juveniles in the community. Services or programs offered to minors or minors' parents or guardians who are not on probation are voluntary and shall not include probation conditions or consequences as a result of not engaging in or completing those programs or services. For minors not on probation, the provision of services or programs under this section shall not be construed to allow probation departments to maintain a formal or informal caseload, establish formal or informal contracts with minors or minors' parents or guardians, or create mandated-probation conditions. *(Added by Stats.1976, c. 1068, p. 4746, § 2. Amended by Stats.2020, c. 323 (A.B.901), § 6, eff. Jan. 1, 2021.)*

ARTICLE 3. PROBATION COMMISSION

Section

§ 240. Counties in excess of 6,000,000 population; membership; appointments

In counties having a population in excess of 6,000,000 in lieu of a county juvenile justice commission, there shall be a probation commission consisting of not less than seven members who shall be appointed by the same authority as that authorized to appoint the probation officer in that county. *(Added by Stats.1976, c. 1068, p. 4750, § 3. Amended by Stats.1980, c. 190, p. 411, § 1; Stats.1980, c. 1117, p. 3607, § 23.5; Stats.1987, c. 228, § 3.)*

Cross References

County juvenile justice commission, see Welfare and Institutions Code § 225.
Probation officer or social worker defined for purposes of this Chapter, see Welfare and Institutions Code § 215.

§ 241. Appointments prior to effective date of article; continuance in office

The members of a probation commission appointed and holding office under prior provisions of law on January 1, 1977, shall continue in office and shall be members of the probation commission created hereby for the same term as that for which they were appointed. *(Added by Stats.1976, c. 1068, p. 4750, § 3. Amended by Stats.1987, c. 228, § 4.)*

§ 241.1. Minor who appears to be dependent child and ward of court; initial determination of status; dual status children; creation of protocol; modification of jurisdiction

(a) Whenever a minor appears to come within the description of both Section 300 and Section 601 or 602, the county probation department and the child welfare services department shall, pursuant to a jointly developed written protocol described in subdivision (b), initially determine which status will serve the best interests of the minor and the protection of society. The recommendations of both departments shall be presented to the juvenile court with the petition that is filed on behalf of the minor, and the court shall determine which status is appropriate for the minor. Any other juvenile court having jurisdiction over the minor shall receive notice from the court, within five calendar days, of the presentation of the recommendations of the departments. The notice shall include the name of the judge to whom, or the courtroom to which, the recommendations were presented.

(b)(1) The probation department and the child welfare services department in each county shall jointly develop a written protocol to ensure appropriate local coordination in the assessment of a minor described in subdivision (a), and the development of recommendations by these departments for consideration by the juvenile court.

(2) These protocols shall require, but not be limited to, consideration of the nature of the referral, the age of the minor, the prior record of the minor's parents for child abuse, the prior record of the minor for out-of-control or delinquent behavior, the parents' cooperation with the minor's school, the minor's functioning at school, the nature of the minor's home environment, and the records of other agencies that have been involved with the minor and his or her family. The protocols also shall contain provisions for resolution of disagreements between the probation and child welfare services departments regarding the need for dependency or ward status and provisions for determining the circumstances under which filing a new petition is required to change the minor's status.

(3)(A) These protocols may also require immediate notification of the child welfare services department and the minor's dependency attorney upon referral of a dependent minor to probation, procedures for release to, and placement by, the child welfare services department pending resolution of the determination pursuant to this section, timelines for dependents in secure custody to ensure timely resolution of the determination pursuant to this section for detained dependents, and nondiscrimination provisions to ensure that dependents are provided with any option that would otherwise be available to a nondependent minor.

(B) If the alleged conduct that appears to bring a dependent minor within the description of Section 601 or 602 occurs in, or under the supervision of, a foster home, group home, or other licensed facility that provides residential care for minors, the county probation department and the child welfare services department may consider whether the alleged conduct was within the scope of behaviors to be managed or treated by the foster home or facility, as identified in the minor's case plan, needs and services plan, placement agreement, facility plan of operation, or facility emergency intervention plan, in determining which status will serve the best interests of the minor and the protection of society pursuant to subdivision (a).

(4) The protocols shall contain the following processes:

(A) A process for determining which agency and court shall supervise a child whose jurisdiction is modified from delinquency jurisdiction to dependency jurisdiction pursuant to paragraph (2) of subdivision (b) of Section 607.2 or subdivision (i) of Section 727.2.

(B) A process for determining which agency and court shall supervise a nonminor dependent under the transition jurisdiction of the juvenile court.

(C) A process that specifically addresses the manner in which supervision responsibility is determined when a nonminor dependent becomes subject to adult probation supervision.

(c) Whenever a minor who is under the jurisdiction of the juvenile court of a county pursuant to Section 300, 601, or 602 is alleged to come within the description of Section 300, 601, or 602 by another county, the county probation department or child welfare services department in the county that has jurisdiction under Section 300, 601, or 602 and the county probation department or child welfare services department of the county alleging the minor to be within one of those sections shall initially determine which status will best serve the best interests of the minor and the protection of society. The recommendations of both departments shall be presented to the juvenile court in which the petition is filed on behalf of the minor, and the court shall determine which status is appropriate for the minor. In making their recommendation to the juvenile court, the departments shall conduct an assessment consistent with the requirements of subdivision (b). Any other juvenile court having jurisdiction over the minor shall receive notice from the court in which the petition is filed within five calendar days of the presentation of the recommendations of the departments. The notice shall include the name of the judge to whom, or the courtroom to which, the recommendations were presented.

(d) Except as provided in subdivision (e), this section shall not authorize the filing of a petition or petitions, or the entry of an order by the juvenile court, to make a minor simultaneously both a dependent child and a ward of the court.

(e) Notwithstanding subdivision (d), the probation department and the child welfare services department, in consultation with the presiding judge of the juvenile court, in any county may create a jointly written protocol to allow the county probation department and the child welfare services department to jointly assess and produce a recommendation that the child be designated as a dual status child, allowing the child to be simultaneously a dependent child and a ward of the court. This protocol shall be signed by the chief probation officer, the director of the county social services agency, and the presiding judge of the juvenile court prior to its implementation. A juvenile court shall not order that a child is simultaneously a dependent child and a ward of the court pursuant to this subdivision unless and until the required protocol has been created and entered into. This protocol shall include all of the following:

(1) A description of the process to be used to determine whether the child is eligible to be designated as a dual status child.

(2) A description of the procedure by which the probation department and the child welfare services department will assess the necessity for dual status for specified children and the process to make joint recommendations for the court's consideration prior to making a determination under this section. These recommendations shall ensure a seamless transition from wardship to dependency jurisdiction, as appropriate, so that services to the child are not disrupted upon termination of the wardship.

(3) A provision for ensuring communication between the judges who hear petitions concerning children for whom dependency jurisdiction has been suspended while they are within the jurisdiction of the juvenile court pursuant to Section 601 or 602. A judge may communicate by providing a copy of any reports filed pursuant to Section 727.2 concerning a ward to a court that has jurisdiction over dependency proceedings concerning the child.

(4) A plan to collect data in order to evaluate the protocol pursuant to Section 241.2.

(5) Counties that exercise the option provided for in this subdivision shall adopt either an "on-hold" system as described in subparagraph (A) or a "lead court/lead agency" system as described in subparagraph (B). There shall not be any simultaneous or duplicative case management or services provided by both the county probation department and the child welfare services department. It is the intent of the Legislature that judges, in cases in which more than one judge is involved, shall not issue conflicting orders.

(A) In counties in which an on-hold system is adopted, the dependency jurisdiction shall be suspended or put on hold while the child is subject to jurisdiction as a ward of the court. When it appears that termination of the court's jurisdiction, as established pursuant to Section 601 or 602, is likely and that reunification of the child with his or her parent or guardian would be detrimental to the child, the county probation department and the child welfare services department shall jointly assess and produce a recommendation for the court regarding whether the court's dependency jurisdiction shall be resumed.

(B) In counties in which a lead court/lead agency system is adopted, the protocol shall include a method for identifying which court or agency will be the lead court/lead agency. That court or agency shall be responsible for case management, conducting statutorily mandated court hearings, and submitting court reports.

(f) Whenever the court determines pursuant to this section or Section 607.2 or 727.2 that it is necessary to modify the court's jurisdiction over a dependent or ward who was removed from his or her parent or guardian and placed in foster care, the court shall ensure that all of the following conditions are met:

(1) The petition under which jurisdiction was taken at the time the dependent or ward was originally removed is not dismissed until the new petition has been sustained.

(2) The order modifying the court's jurisdiction contains all of the following provisions:

(A) Reference to the original removal findings and a statement that findings that continuation in the home is contrary to the child's welfare, and that reasonable efforts were made to prevent removal, remain in effect.

(B) A statement that the child continues to be removed from the parent or guardian from whom the child was removed under the original petition.

(C) Identification of the agency that is responsible for placement and care of the child based upon the modification of jurisdiction.

(Added by Stats.1989, c. 1441, § 1. Amended by Stats.1998, c. 390 (S.B.2017), § 2; Stats.2001, c. 830 (S.B.940), § 3; Stats.2004, c. 468 (A.B.129), § 1; Stats.2006, c. 538 (S.B.1852), § 684; Stats.2006, c. 901 (S.B.1422), § 13; Stats.2009, c. 140 (A.B.1164), § 186; Stats. 2010, c. 559 (A.B.12), § 5.5; Stats.2011, c. 459 (A.B.212), § 5, eff. Oct. 4, 2011; Stats.2014, c. 760 (A.B.388), § 4, eff. Jan. 1, 2015.)

Cross References

Child or nonminor whose jurisdiction is modified pursuant to subd. (d) of this section, supervision, see Welfare and Institutions Code § 300.3.
Court–Appointed Special Advocates, participation in status determination, see Welfare and Institutions Code § 109.
Modification of juvenile court judgments and orders, petitions, see Welfare and Institutions Code § 388.
Modification of order of jurisdiction and assumption of transition jurisdiction as alternative to termination of jurisdiction, management of case, supervision, appointment of counsel, see Welfare and Institutions Code § 451.
Probation officer or social worker defined for purposes of this Chapter, see Welfare and Institutions Code § 215.
Restitution for economic losses, see Welfare and Institutions Code § 730.6.
Reunification of minor in foster care with family or establishment of alternative permanent plan, ongoing review of status of minor, see Welfare and Institutions Code § 727.2.
Termination of jurisdiction over ward satisfying specified criteria, hearing, see Welfare and Institutions Code § 607.2.
Wards of juvenile court, petition for order to terminate jurisdiction of juvenile court, notice and hearing, see Welfare and Institutions Code § 785.

§ 241.2. Committee to develop and report recommendations to facilitate and enhance comprehensive data and outcome tracking for youth involved in both child welfare system and juvenile justice system; implementation of system for tracking youth

(a) The Judicial Council shall convene a committee comprised of stakeholders involved in serving the needs of dependents or wards of the juvenile court, including, but not limited to, judges, probation officers, social workers, youth involved in both the child welfare system and the juvenile justice system, child welfare and juvenile justice attorneys, child welfare and juvenile justice advocates, education officials, and representatives from the State Department of Social Services, county child welfare agencies, and county probation departments. By January 1, 2018, the committee shall develop and report to the Legislature, pursuant to Section 9795 of the Government Code, its recommendations to facilitate and enhance comprehensive data and outcome tracking for the state's youth involved in both the child welfare system and the juvenile justice system. The committee's recommendations shall include, but not be limited to, all of the following:

(1) A common identifier for counties to use to reconcile data across child welfare and juvenile justice systems statewide.

(2) Standardized definitions for terms related to the populations of youth involved in both the child welfare system and the juvenile justice system.

(3) Identified and defined outcomes for counties to track youth involved in both the child welfare system and the juvenile justice system, including, but not limited to, outcomes related to recidivism, health, pregnancy, homelessness, employment, and education.

(4) Established baselines and goals for the identified and defined outcomes specified in paragraph (3).

(5) An assessment as to the costs and benefits associated with requiring all counties to implement the committee's recommendations.

(6) An assessment of whether a single technology system, including, but not limited to, the State Department of Social Services' Child Welfare Services/Case Management System (CWS/CMS) or the Child Welfare Services–New System (CWS–NS), is needed to track youth in the child welfare system and the juvenile justice system.

(b) The State Department of Social Services shall, on or before January 1, 2019, implement a function within the applicable case management system that will enable county child welfare agencies and county probation departments to identify youth involved in both the child welfare system and the juvenile justice system who are within their counties and shall issue instructions to all counties on how to completely and consistently track the involvement of these youth in both the child welfare system and the juvenile justice system. *(Added by Stats.2016, c. 637 (A.B.1911), § 2, eff. Jan. 1, 2017.)*

§ 242. Terms of office; vacancies

The members of the probation commission shall hold office for four years and until their successors are appointed and qualify. Of those first appointed, however, one shall hold office for one year, two for two years, two for three years, and two for four years; and the respective terms of the members first appointed shall be determined by lot as soon as possible after their appointment. When a vacancy occurs in a probation commission by expiration of the term of office of any member thereof, his or her successor shall be appointed to hold office for the term of four years. When a vacancy occurs for any other reason the appointee shall hold office for the unexpired term of his or her predecessor. *(Added by Stats.1976, c. 1068, p. 4750, § 3. Amended by Stats.1987, c. 228, § 5.)*

Cross References

Oath of office, generally, see Government Code § 1360 et seq.
Vacancies in office, see Government Code § 1770 et seq.

§ 243. Advisory capacity

The probation commission shall function in an advisory capacity to the probation officer. *(Added by Stats.1976, c. 1068, p. 4750, § 3. Amended by Stats.1987, c. 228, § 6.)*

Cross References

Probation officer defined, see Welfare and Institutions Code § 215.
Probation officers, see Welfare and Institutions Code § 270 et seq.

ARTICLE 4. THE JUVENILE COURT

§ 245. Jurisdiction; name

Each superior court shall exercise the jurisdiction conferred by this chapter, and while sitting in the exercise of such jurisdiction, shall be known and referred to as the juvenile court. Appealable orders and judgments of the juvenile court are subject to the appellate jurisdiction of the court of appeal. *(Added by Stats.1976, c. 1068, p. 4751, § 4. Amended by Stats.1998, c. 931 (S.B.2139), § 468, eff. Sept. 28, 1998.)*

Law Revision Commission Comments

Section 245 makes clear that the court of appeal is the proper appellate court to review appealable orders and judgments of the juvenile court. See Welf. & Inst. Code §§ 395, 800 (appealable orders and judgments of the juvenile court). The Judicial Council already has enacted rules of practice and procedure governing juvenile court appeals. See Rules of Court, Rules 39, 39.1, 39.1A, 39.1B, 1435, 1436, 1436.5. [28 Cal.L.Rev.Comm. Reports 51 (1998)].

Cross References

Jurisdiction of juvenile court, see Welfare and Institutions Code § 300 et seq.
Superior court, jurisdiction, see Const. Art. 6, §§ 10, 11; Code of Civil Procedure § 77.

Research References

West's California Judicial Council Forms JV–462, Findings and Orders After Nonminor Dependent Status Review Hearing.

§ 245.5. Direction of orders to parents or guardians

In addition to all other powers granted by law, the juvenile court may direct all such orders to the parent, parents, or guardian of a minor who is subject to any proceedings under this chapter as the court deems necessary and proper for the best interests of or for the rehabilitation of the minor. These orders may concern the care, supervision, custody, conduct, maintenance, and support of the minor, including education and medical treatment. *(Added by Stats.1978, c. 282, p. 568, § 1. Amended by Stats.1990, c. 182 (A.B.1528), § 6.)*

§ 246. Designation of judge

The presiding judge of the superior court shall annually, in the month of January, designate one or more judges of the court to hear all cases under this chapter during the ensuing year, and shall, from time to time, designate such additional judges as may be necessary for the prompt disposition of the judicial business before the juvenile court.

In all counties where more than one judge is designated as a judge of the juvenile court, the presiding judge of the superior court shall also designate one such judge as presiding judge of the juvenile court. *(Added by Stats.1976, c. 1068, p. 4751, § 4. Amended by Stats.2002, c. 784 (S.B.1316), § 609.)*

Law Revision Commission Comments

Section 246 is amended to reflect the fact that every superior court has at least two judgeships as a result of trial court unification. See Gov't Code § 69580 *et seq.* (number of judges). Where a court has only one judge due to a vacancy or otherwise, a reference to the "presiding judge" means the sole judge of the court. See Gov't Code § 69508.5 (presiding judge).

The section is also amended to delete language referring to the senior judge. Every superior court has a presiding judge. See Gov't Code §§ 69508, 69508.5. [32 Cal.L.Rev.Comm. Reports 551 (2002)].

Cross References

Session in judicial district in which juvenile hall located, see Code of Civil Procedure § 73e.
Session of superior court, see Government Code § 69740 et seq.
Special or separate session, see Welfare and Institutions Code § 675.

§ 247.5. Disqualification of referee; reassignment of matter

The provisions of Sections 170 and 170.6 of the Code of Civil Procedure shall apply to a referee, provided, that the presiding judge of the juvenile court shall if the motion is granted reassign the matter to another referee or to a judge of the juvenile court. *(Formerly § 553.2, added by Stats.1976, c. 1071, p. 4818, § 10. Renumbered § 247.5 and amended by Stats.1977, c. 910, p. 2783, § 7.)*

§ 248. Hearing assigned cases; findings and order; right of review; service

(a) A referee shall hear those cases that are assigned to him or her by the presiding judge of the juvenile court, with the same powers as a judge of the juvenile court, except that a referee shall not conduct any hearing to which the state or federal constitutional prohibitions against double jeopardy apply unless all of the parties thereto stipulate in writing that the referee may act in the capacity of a temporary judge. A referee shall promptly furnish to the presiding judge of the juvenile court and the minor, if the minor is 14 or more years of age or if younger has so requested, and shall serve upon the minor's attorney of record and the minor's parent or guardian or adult relative and the attorney of record for the minor's parent or guardian or adult relative a written copy of his or her findings and order and shall also furnish to the minor, if the minor is 14 or more years of age or if younger has so requested, and to the parent or guardian or adult relative, with the findings and order, a written explanation of the right of those persons to seek review of the order by the juvenile court.

(b) Service, as provided in this section, shall be made as follows:

(1) If a minor, parent, or guardian is present in court at the time the findings and order are made, then the findings and order may be served in court on any minor, parent, or guardian who is present in court on that date and a written explanation of the right to seek review of the order as required pursuant to subdivision (a) shall be furnished at that time.

(2) If paragraph (1) is not applicable, service shall be made by mail or electronic service pursuant to Section 212.5, within the time period specified in Section 248.5, to the last known address of those persons or to the address designated by those persons appearing at the hearing before the referee and the documents served shall include, if applicable, the written explanation of the right to seek review of the order. If the parent or guardian does not have a last known address or electronic service address designated, service shall be to that party in care of his or her counsel. *(Added by Stats.1976, c. 1068, p. 4751, § 4. Amended by Stats.1980, c. 532, p. 1483, § 1; Stats.2010, c. 66 (S.B.179), § 1; Stats.2017, c. 319 (A.B.976), § 109, eff. Jan. 1, 2018.)*

Cross References

References and trials by referees, see Code of Civil Procedure § 638 et seq.
Writing defined, see Welfare and Institutions Code § 8.

Research References

4 Witkin, California Criminal Law 4th Introduction to Criminal Procedure § 49 (2021), Court Commissioner as Temporary Judge.

§ 248.5. Findings and orders; service

All written findings and orders of the court shall be served by the clerk of the court personally, by first-class mail, or by electronic service pursuant to Section 212.5, within three judicial days of their issuance on the petitioner, the minor or the minor's counsel, the parent or the parent's counsel, and the guardian or the guardian's counsel. *(Added by Stats.1990, c. 1530 (S.B.2232), § 2. Amended by Stats.2017, c. 319 (A.B.976), § 110, eff. Jan. 1, 2018.)*

§ 249. Order removing minor from home; approval

No order of a referee removing a minor from his home shall become effective until expressly approved by a judge of the juvenile court. *(Added by Stats.1976, c. 1068, p. 4751, § 4.)*

§ 250. Orders of referee; force and effect; finality

Except as provided in Section 251, all orders of a referee other than those specified in Section 249 shall become immediately effective, subject also to the right of review as hereinafter provided, and shall continue in full force and effect until vacated or modified upon rehearing by order of the judge of the juvenile court. In a case in which an order of a referee becomes effective without approval of a judge of the juvenile court, it becomes final on the expiration of the time allowed by Section 252 for application for rehearing, if application therefor is not made within such time and if the judge of the juvenile court has not within such time ordered a rehearing pursuant to Section 253.

Where a referee sits as a temporary judge, his or her orders become final in the same manner as orders made by a judge. *(Added by Stats.1976, c. 1068, p. 4751, § 4. Amended by Stats.1980, c. 532, p. 1484, § 2.)*

Cross References

Appeals, see Welfare and Institutions Code § 800.
Modification of judgments and orders, see Welfare and Institutions Code § 775 et seq.

§ 251. Orders of referee; court approval

The judge of the juvenile court, or in counties having more than one judge of the juvenile court, the presiding judge of the juvenile court may establish requirements that any or all orders of referees shall be expressly approved by a judge of the juvenile court before becoming effective. *(Added by Stats.1976, c. 1068, p. 4751, § 4.)*

§ 252. Rehearing; application

At any time prior to the expiration of 10 days after service of a written copy of the order and findings of a referee, a minor or his or her parent or guardian or, in cases brought pursuant to Section 300, the county welfare department may apply to the juvenile court for a rehearing. That application may be directed to all or to any specified part of the order or findings, and shall contain a statement of the reasons the rehearing is requested. If all of the proceedings before the referee have been taken down by an official reporter, the judge of the juvenile court may, after reading the transcript of those proceedings, grant or deny the application. If proceedings before the referee have not been taken down by an official reporter, the application shall be granted as of right. If an application for rehearing is not granted, denied, or extended within 20 days following the date of its receipt, it shall be deemed granted. However, the court, for good cause, may extend the period beyond 20 days, but not in any event beyond 45 days, following the date of receipt of the application, at which time the application for rehearing shall be deemed granted unless it is denied within that period. All decisions to grant or deny the application, or to extend the period, shall be expressly made in a written minute order with copies provided to the minor or his or her parent or guardian, and to the attorneys of record. *(Added by Stats.1976, c. 1068, p. 4751, § 4. Amended by Stats.1979, c. 596, p. 1858, § 1; Stats.1997, c. 510 (A.B.329), § 2.)*

§ 253. Order for rehearing; motion of court

A judge of the juvenile court may, on his own motion made within 20 judicial days of the hearing before a referee, order a rehearing of any matter heard before a referee. *(Added by Stats.1976, c. 1068, p. 4751, § 4.)*

§ 254. Conduct of rehearing

All rehearings of matters heard before a referee shall be before a judge of the juvenile court and shall be conducted de novo. *(Added by Stats.1976, c. 1068, p. 4751, § 4.)*

§ 255. Juvenile hearing officers; appointment; designation of court

The court may appoint as subordinate judicial officers one or more persons of suitable experience, who may be a probation officer or assistant or deputy probation officers, to serve as juvenile hearing officers on a full-time or part-time basis. A hearing officer shall serve at the pleasure of the court, and unless the court makes an order terminating the appointment of a hearing officer, the hearing officer shall continue to serve until the appointment of his or her successor. The court shall determine whether any compensation shall be paid to hearing officers, not otherwise employed by a public agency or holding another public office, and shall establish the amounts and rates thereof. An appointment of a probation officer, assistant probation officer, or deputy probation officer as a juvenile hearing officer may be made only with the consent of the probation officer. A juvenile court shall be known as the Informal Juvenile and Traffic Court when a hearing officer appointed pursuant to this section hears a case specified in Section 256. *(Added by Stats.1976, c. 1068, p. 4751, § 4. Amended by Stats.1997, c. 679 (A.B.1105), § 1; Stats.1998, c. 931 (S.B.2139), § 469, eff. Sept. 28, 1998; Stats.2002, c. 784 (S.B.1316), § 610.)*

Law Revision Commission Comments

Section 255 is amended to accommodate unification of the municipal and superior courts in a county. Cal. Const. art. VI, § 5(e). [28 Cal.L.Rev.Comm. Reports 51 (1998)].

Section 255 is amended to reflect unification of the municipal and superior courts pursuant to Article VI, Section 5(e), of the California Constitution.

The section is also amended to reflect enactment of the Trial Court Funding Act. See Gov't Code §§ 77001 (local trial court management), 77200 (state funding of trial court operations).

The section is also amended to reflect enactment of the Trial Court Employment Protection and Governance Act. See Gov't Code § 71622(a) (each trial court may appoint subordinate judicial officers as deemed necessary, subject to Judicial Council approval).

The section is also amended to delete language referring to the senior judge. Every juvenile court with more than one juvenile court judge has a presiding judge. See Section 246 (appointment of presiding judge). [32 Cal.L.Rev. Comm. Reports 552 (2002)].

Cross References

Probation officer or social worker defined for purposes of this Chapter, see Welfare and Institutions Code § 215.

§ 256. Powers of juvenile hearing officers

Subject to the orders of the juvenile court, a juvenile hearing officer may hear and dispose of any case in which a minor under the age of 18 years as of the date of the alleged offense is charged with (1) any violation of the Vehicle Code, except Section 23136, 23140, 23152, or 23153 of that code, not declared to be a felony, (2) a violation of subdivision (m) of Section 602 of the Penal Code, (3) a violation of the Fish and Game Code not declared to be a felony, (4) a violation of any of the equipment provisions of the Harbors and Navigation Code or the vessel registration provisions of the Vehicle Code, (5) a violation of any provision of state or local law relating to traffic offenses, loitering or curfew, or evasion of fares on a public transportation system, as defined by Section 99211 of the Public Utilities Code, (6) a violation of Section 27176 of the Streets and Highways Code, (7) a violation of Section 640 or 640a of the Penal Code, (8) a violation of the rules and regulations established pursuant to Sections 5003 and 5008 of the Public Resources Code, (9) a violation of Section 33211.6 of the Public Resources Code, (10) a violation of Section 25658, 25658.5, 25661, or 25662 of the Business and Professions Code, (11) a violation of subdivision (f) of Section 647 of the Penal Code, (12) a misdemeanor violation of Section 594 of the Penal Code, involving defacing property with paint or any other liquid, (13) a violation of subdivision (b), (d), or (e) of Section 594.1 of the Penal Code, (14) a violation of subdivision (b) of Section 11357 of the Health and Safety Code, (15) any infraction, (16) any misdemeanor for which the minor is cited to appear by a probation officer pursuant to subdivision (f) of Section 660.5, or (17) a violation of subdivision (b) of Section 601 that is due to having four or more truancies, as described in Section 48260 of the Education Code, within one school year. *(Added by Stats.1976, c. 1068, p. 4751, § 4. Amended by Stats.1982, c. 1235, § 4; Stats.1983, c. 22, § 2; Stats. 1988, c. 1454, § 1; Stats.1989, c. 1244, § 1; Stats.1990, c. 1697 (S.B.2635), § 7; Stats.1991, c. 493 (S.B.65), § 1; Stats.1991, c. 1202 (S.B.377), § 8; Stats.1993, c. 90 (A.B.612), § 1; Stats.1995, c. 55 (A.B.1445), § 1; Stats.1997, c. 666 (S.B.810), § 6; Stats.1997, c. 679 (A.B.1105), § 2.5; Stats.2000, c. 228 (A.B.2744), § 1; Stats.2014, c. 898 (A.B.2195), § 1, eff. Jan. 1, 2015.)*

Cross References

Department of Motor Vehicles, records open to public inspection, driver's license suspension actions, see Vehicle Code § 1808.
Expedited Youth Accountability Program, citations, notice and time to appear, see Welfare and Institutions Code § 660.5.
Felonies, definition and penalties, see Penal Code §§ 17, 18.
Misdemeanors, definition and penalties, see Penal Code §§ 17, 19 and 19.2.
Notice to appear for violations listed in this section, see Penal Code § 853.6a.
Probation officer or social worker defined for purposes of this Chapter, see Welfare and Institutions Code § 215.
Procedure on arrests,
  Release upon promise to appear, notice of violations, see Vehicle Code § 40509.
  Release upon promise to appear, notice of violations, criteria for arrest warrants, see Vehicle Code § 40509.5.

Research References

4 Witkin, California Criminal Law 4th Pretrial Proceedings § 60 (2021), Juvenile Offenses.

§ 256.5. Arrest warrant for failure to appear; issuance

A juvenile hearing officer may request the juvenile court judge or referee to issue a warrant of arrest against a minor who is issued and signs a written notice to appear for any violation listed in Section 256 and who fails to appear at the time and place designated in the notice. The juvenile court judge or referee may issue and have delivered for execution a warrant of arrest against a minor within 20 days after the minor's failure to appear as promised or within 20 days after the minor's failure to appear after a lawfully granted continuance of his or her promise to appear. A juvenile hearing officer who is also a referee or juvenile court judge may personally issue the warrant of arrest. *(Added by Stats.1991, c. 1202 (S.B.377), § 9. Amended by Stats.1997, c. 679 (A.B.1105), § 3.)*

§ 257. Conduct of hearing upon copy of notice to appear in lieu of petition

(a)(1) Except in the case of infraction violations, with the consent of the minor, a hearing before a juvenile hearing officer, or a hearing before a referee or a judge of the juvenile court, when the minor is charged with an offense as specified in this section, may be conducted upon an exact legible copy of a written notice given pursuant to Article 2 (commencing with Section 40500) of Chapter 2 of Division 17 or Section 41103 of the Vehicle Code, or an exact legible copy of a written notice given pursuant to Chapter 5C (commencing with Section 853.5) of Title 3 of Part 2 of the Penal Code when the offense charged is a violation listed in Section 256, or an exact legible copy of a citation as set forth in subdivision (e) of Section 660.5, or an exact legible copy of the notice given pursuant to subdivision (d) of Section 601 when the minor is within the jurisdiction of the juvenile court pursuant to subdivision (b) of Section 601, in lieu of a petition as provided in Article 16 (commencing with Section 650).

(2) Notwithstanding any other law, in the case of infraction violations, consent of the minor is not required prior to conducting a hearing upon written notice to appear.

(b) Prior to the hearing, the judge, referee, or juvenile hearing officer may request the probation officer to commence a proceeding, as provided in Article 16 (commencing with Section 650), in lieu of a hearing in Informal Juvenile and Traffic Court. *(Added by Stats. 1976, c. 1068, p. 4751, § 4. Amended by Stats.1982, c. 1235, § 5; Stats.1983, c. 22, § 3; Stats.1988, c. 1454, § 2; Stats.1989, c. 1244, § 2; Stats.1990, c. 1697 (S.B.2635), § 8; Stats.1991, c. 493 (S.B.65), § 2; Stats.1991, c. 1202 (S.B.377), § 10; Stats.1997, c. 679 (A.B. 1105), § 4; Stats.2001, c. 830 (S.B.940), § 4; Stats.2014, c. 898 (A.B.2195), § 2, eff. Jan. 1, 2015.)*

Cross References

Citation directing appearance at hearing, see Welfare and Institutions Code § 338.
Citation to appear at hearing, see Welfare and Institutions Code § 661.
Probation officer or social worker defined for purposes of this Chapter, see Welfare and Institutions Code § 215.
Proceedings in misdemeanor and infraction cases, distribution of fines and forfeitures imposed and collected for crimes, see Penal Code § 1463.
Vehicle Code violations by minor, place to appear for hearing, see Vehicle Code § 40502.

§ 258. Disposition of traffic violation or truancy hearing; orders; jurisdiction

(a) Upon a hearing conducted in accordance with Section 257, and upon either an admission by the minor of the commission of a violation charged, or a finding that the minor did in fact commit the violation, the judge, referee, or juvenile hearing officer may do any of the following:

(1) Reprimand the minor and take no further action.

(2) Direct that the probation officer undertake a program of supervision of the minor for a period not to exceed six months, in addition to or in place of the following orders.

(3) Order that the minor pay a fine up to the amount that an adult would pay for the same violation, unless the violation is otherwise specified within this section, in which case the fine shall not exceed two hundred fifty dollars ($250). This fine may be levied in addition to or in place of the following orders and the court may waive any or all of this fine, if the minor is unable to pay. In determining the minor's ability to pay, the court shall not consider the ability of the minor's family to pay.

(4) Subject to the minor's right to a restitution hearing, order that the minor pay restitution to the victim, in lieu of all or a portion of the fine specified in paragraph (3). The total dollar amount of the fine, restitution, and any program fees ordered pursuant to paragraph (9) shall not exceed the maximum amount which may be ordered pursuant to paragraph (3). This paragraph shall not be construed to limit the right to recover damages, less any amount actually paid in restitution, in a civil action.

(5) Order that the driving privileges of the minor be suspended or restricted as provided in the Vehicle Code or, notwithstanding Section 13203 of the Vehicle Code or any other provision of law, when the Vehicle Code does not provide for the suspension or restriction of driving privileges, that, in addition to any other order, the driving privileges of the minor be suspended or restricted for a period of not to exceed 30 days.

(6) In the case of a traffic related offense, order the minor to attend a licensed traffic school, or other court approved program of traffic school instruction pursuant to Chapter 1.5 (commencing with Section 11200) of Division 5 of the Vehicle Code, to be completed by the juvenile within 60 days of the court order.

(7) Order that the minor produce satisfactory evidence that the vehicle or its equipment has been made to conform with the requirements of the Vehicle Code pursuant to Section 40150 of the Vehicle Code if the violation involved an equipment violation.

(8) Order that the minor perform community service work in a public entity or any private nonprofit entity, for not more than 50 hours over a period of 60 days, during times other than his or her hours of school attendance or employment. Work performed pursuant to this paragraph shall not exceed 30 hours during any 30-day period. The timeframes established by this paragraph shall not be modified except in unusual cases where the interests of justice would best be served. When the order to work is made by a referee or a juvenile hearing officer, it shall be approved by a judge of the juvenile court.

For purposes of this paragraph, a judge, referee, or juvenile hearing officer shall not, without the consent of the minor, order the minor to perform work with a private nonprofit entity that is affiliated with any religion.

(9) In the case of a misdemeanor, order that the minor participate in and complete a counseling or educational program, or, if the offense involved a violation of a controlled substance law, a drug treatment program, if those programs are available. Fees for participation shall be subject to the right to a hearing as the minor's ability to pay and shall not, together with any fine or restitution order, exceed the maximum amount that may be ordered pursuant to paragraph (3).

(10) Require that the minor attend a school program without unexcused absence.

(11) If the offense is a misdemeanor committed between 10 p.m. and 6 a.m., require that the minor be at his or her legal residence at hours to be specified by the juvenile hearing officer between the hours of 10 p.m. and 6 a.m., except for a medical or other emergency, unless the minor is accompanied by his or her parent, guardian, or other person in charge of the minor. The maximum length of an order made pursuant to this paragraph shall be six months from the effective date of the order.

(12) Make any or all of the following orders with respect to a violation of the Fish and Game Code which is not charged as a felony:

(A) That the fishing or hunting license involved be suspended or restricted.

(B) That the minor work in a park or conservation area for a total of not to exceed 20 hours over a period not to exceed 30 days, during times other than his or her hours of school attendance or employment.

(C) That the minor forfeit, pursuant to Section 12157 of the Fish and Game Code, any device or apparatus designed to be, and capable of being, used to take birds, mammals, fish, reptiles, or amphibia and that was used in committing the violation charged. The judge, referee, or juvenile hearing officer shall, if the minor committed an offense that is punishable under Section 12008 or 12008.1 of the Fish and Game Code, order the device or apparatus forfeited pursuant to Section 12157 of the Fish and Game Code.

(13) If the violation charged is of an ordinance of a city, county, or local agency relating to loitering, curfew, or fare evasion on a public transportation system, as defined by Section 99211 of the Public Utilities Code, or is a violation of Section 640 or 640a of the Penal Code, make the order that the minor shall perform community service for a total time not to exceed 20 hours over a period not to exceed 30 days, during times other than his or her hours of school attendance or employment.

(b) If the minor is before the court on the basis of truancy, as described in subdivision (b) of Section 601, all of the following procedures and limitations shall apply:

(1) The judge, referee, or juvenile hearing officer shall not proceed with a hearing unless both of the following have been provided to the court:

(A) Evidence that the minor's school has undertaken the actions specified in subdivisions (a), (b), and (c) of Section 48264.5 of the Education Code. If the school district does not have an attendance review board, as described in Section 48321 of the Education Code, the minor's school is not required to provide evidence to the court of any actions the school has undertaken that demonstrate the intervention of a school attendance review board.

(B) The available record of previous attempts to address the minor's truancy.

(2) The court is encouraged to set the hearing outside of school hours, so as to avoid causing the minor to miss additional school time.

(3) Pursuant to paragraph (1) of subdivision (a) of Section 257, the minor and his or her parents shall be advised of the minor's right to refuse consent to a hearing conducted upon a written notice to appear.

(4) The minor's parents shall be permitted to participate in the hearing.

(5) The judge, referee, or juvenile hearing officer may continue the hearing to allow the minor the opportunity to demonstrate improved attendance before imposing any of the orders specified in paragraph (6). Upon demonstration of improved attendance, the court may dismiss the case.

(6) Upon a finding that the minor violated subdivision (b) of Section 601, the judge, referee, or juvenile hearing officer shall direct his or her orders at improving the minor's school attendance. The judge, referee, or juvenile hearing officer may do any of the following:

(A) Order the minor to perform community service work, as described in Section 48264.5 of the Education Code, which may be performed at the minor's school.

(B) Order the payment of a fine by the minor of not more than fifty dollars ($50), for which a parent or legal guardian of the minor may be jointly liable. The fine described in this subparagraph shall not be subject to Section 1464 of the Penal Code or additional penalty pursuant to any other law. The minor, at his or her discretion, may perform community service, as described in subparagraph (A), in lieu of any fine imposed under this subparagraph.

(C) Order a combination of community service work described in subparagraph (A) and payment of a portion of the fine described in subparagraph (B).

(D) Restrict driving privileges in the manner set forth in paragraph (5) of subdivision (a). The minor may request removal of the driving restrictions if he or she provides proof of school attendance, high school graduation, GED completion, or enrollment in adult education, a community college, or a trade program. Any driving restriction shall be removed at the time the minor attains 18 years of age.

(c)(1) The judge, referee, or juvenile hearing officer shall retain jurisdiction of the case until all orders made under this section have been fully complied with.

(2) If a minor is before the judge, referee, or juvenile hearing officer on the basis of truancy, jurisdiction shall be terminated upon the minor attaining 18 years of age. *(Added by Stats.1976, c. 1068, p. 4751, § 4. Amended by Stats.1980, c. 530, p. 1480, § 12; Stats.1981, c. 166, p. 972, § 15, eff. July 12, 1981; Stats.1982, c. 73, § 1; Stats.1988, c. 1454, § 3; Stats.1990, c. 292 (A.B.3325), § 1; Stats. 1991, c. 1202 (S.B.377), § 11; Stats.1997, c. 679 (A.B.1105), § 5; Stats.2003, c. 149 (S.B.79), § 89; Stats.2014, c. 898 (A.B.2195), § 3, eff. Jan. 1, 2015; Stats.2015, c. 303 (A.B.731), § 565, eff. Jan. 1, 2016; Stats.2016, c. 340 (S.B.839), § 49, eff. Sept. 13, 2016.)*

Law Revision Commission Comments

Subdivision (a)(8) of Section 258 is amended to reflect the redesignation of traffic hearing officers as juvenile hearing officers. See 1997 Cal. Stat. ch. 679. [33 Cal.L.Rev.Comm. Reports 265 (2003)].

Cross References

Cattle protection, forfeiture of property, wrongful taking or killing of cattle, see Food and Agricultural Code § 21856.
Felonies, definition and penalties, see Penal Code §§ 17, 18.
Misdemeanors, definition and penalties, see Penal Code §§ 17, 19, 19.2.
Probation officer or social worker defined for purposes of this Chapter, see Welfare and Institutions Code § 215.

Research References

6 Witkin, California Criminal Law 4th Criminal Judgment § 161 (2021), In General.
1 Witkin California Criminal Law 4th Introduction to Crimes § 36 (2021), Rule of Expressio Unius Est Exclusio Alterius.

§ 260. Written report of findings; transmittal of abstract

A juvenile hearing officer shall promptly furnish a written report of his or her findings and orders to the clerk of the juvenile court. The clerk of the juvenile court shall promptly transmit an abstract of those findings and orders to the Department of Motor Vehicles. *(Added by Stats.1976, c. 1068, p. 4751, § 4. Amended by Stats.1997, c. 679 (A.B.1105), § 6.)*

§ 261. Immediate effect of orders

Subject to the provisions of Section 262, all orders of a juvenile hearing officer shall be immediately effective. *(Added by Stats.1976, c. 1068, p. 4751, § 4. Amended by Stats.1997, c. 679 (A.B.1105), § 7.)*

§ 262. Setting aside or modifying orders

Upon motion of the minor or his or her parent or guardian for good cause, or upon his or her own motion, a judge of the juvenile court may set aside or modify any order of a juvenile hearing officer, or may order or himself or herself conduct a rehearing. If the minor or parent or guardian has made a motion that the judge set aside or modify the order or has applied for a rehearing, and the judge has not set aside or modified the order or ordered or conducted a rehearing within 10 days after the date of the order, the motion or application shall be deemed denied as of the expiration of that period. *(Added by Stats.1976, c. 1068, p. 4751, § 4. Amended by Stats.1997, c. 679 (A.B.1105), § 8.)*

§ 263. Transfer of case to county of minor's residence; motion

At any time prior to the final disposition of a hearing pursuant to Section 257, the judge, referee, or juvenile hearing officer may, on motion of the minor, his or her parent, or guardian, or on its own motion, transfer the case to the county of the minor's residence for further proceedings pursuant to Sections 258, 260, 261, and 262. *(Added by Stats.1976, c. 1068, p. 4751, § 4. Amended by Stats.1997, c. 679 (A.B.1105), § 9.)*

Cross References

Determination of residence of minor, see Welfare and Institutions Code § 17.1.
Transfer of cases between counties, see Welfare and Institutions Code § 750 et seq.

§ 264. Statewide regional conferences

At the direction and under the supervision of the Judicial Council, judges of the juvenile courts and juvenile court referees shall meet from time to time in statewide or regional conferences, to discuss problems arising in the course of administration of this chapter, for the purpose of improving the administration of justice in the juvenile courts. Actual and necessary expenses incurred by a judge or referee in attending any such conference shall be a charge upon the county. *(Added by Stats.1976, c. 1068, p. 4751, § 4.)*

§ 265. Rules governing practice and procedure

The Judicial Council shall establish rules governing practice and procedure in the juvenile court not inconsistent with law. *(Added by Stats.1976, c. 1068, p. 4751, § 4.)*

ARTICLE 5. PROBATION OFFICERS

§ 270. Appointment and compensation of chief probation officer

The chief probation officer shall be appointed and compensation for the position shall be determined as provided in Chapter 16 (commencing with Section 27770) of Part 3 of Division 2 of Title 3 of the Government Code. *(Added by Stats.2017, c. 17 (A.B.103), § 57, eff. June 27, 2017.)*

Cross References

Adult probation officers, see Penal Code § 1203.5; Government Code §§ 27770, 27772.
Conferences with director of youth authority, see Welfare and Institutions Code § 1752.95.
Delegation of powers and duties, see Welfare and Institutions Code § 7.
Existing probation officers, assistants and deputies, continuance in office, see Welfare and Institutions Code § 286.
Mendocino County, ordinance establishing offices of assistant and deputy probation officer, see Government Code § 69906.5.
Peace officers, authority, see Penal Code § 830.31.
Probation officer defined, see Welfare and Institutions Code § 215.

§ 271. County charter provisions

In counties having charters that provide a method of appointment and tenure of office for the superintendent, matron, and other employees of the juvenile hall, the charter provisions shall control as to those matters and, in counties that have established or hereafter establish merit or civil service systems governing the methods of appointment and the tenure of office for the superintendent, matrons, and other employees of the juvenile hall, the provisions of the merit or civil service systems shall control as to those matters. In all other counties, these matters shall be controlled exclusively by the provisions of this code. *(Added by Stats.2017, c. 17 (A.B.103), § 59, eff. June 27, 2017.)*

Cross References

County civil service, see Government Code § 31100 et seq.
Probation officer or social worker defined for purposes of this Chapter, see Welfare and Institutions Code § 215.

§ 272. Delegation of probation officer's duties; Indian tribes; probation officer's right of access to state summary criminal history information

(a)(1) The board of supervisors may delegate to the county welfare department all or part of the duties of the probation officer concerning dependent children described in Section 300.

(2) The State Department of Social Services may delegate child welfare service or AFDC–FC foster care payment duties, or both, concerning dependent children described in Section 300 to any Indian tribe that has entered into an agreement pursuant to Section 10553.1.

(b) The board of supervisors may also delegate to those persons within the county welfare department and to any Indian tribe that has entered into an agreement pursuant to Section 10553.1 performing child welfare services the probation officer's right of access to state summary criminal history information pursuant to Section 11105 of the Penal Code as is necessary to carry out its duties concerning children reasonably believed to be described by Section 300. The information shall include any current incarceration, the location of any current probation or parole, any current requirement that the individual register pursuant to Section 290 or 457.1 of the Penal Code, or pursuant to Section 11140 or 11590 of the Health and Safety Code, and any history of offenses involving abuse or neglect of, or violence against, a child, or convictions of any offenses involving violence, sexual offenses, the abuse or illegal possession, manufacture, or sale of alcohol or controlled substances, and any arrest for which the person is released on bail or on his or her own recognizance.

(c) Notwithstanding subdivision (a), a social worker in a county welfare department or an Indian tribe that has entered into an agreement pursuant to Section 10553.1 may perform the duties specified by Section 306. *(Added by Stats.1976, c. 1068, p. 4755, § 5. Amended by Stats.1989, c. 408, § 1; Stats.1990, c. 1530 (S.B.2232), § 3; Stats.1995, c. 724 (A.B.1525), § 2.)*

Cross References

Child or nonminor whose jurisdiction is modified pursuant to subd. (d) of § 241.1, supervision, see Welfare and Institutions Code § 300.3.
Indian, Indian child, Indian child's tribe, Indian custodian, Indian tribe, reservation, and tribal court defined for purposes of this Division, see Welfare and Institutions Code § 224.1.
Local summary criminal history information, furnishing to authorized persons, see Penal Code § 13300.
Probation officer, definition to include social worker in county welfare department when supervising dependent children of the juvenile court pursuant to this section, see Welfare and Institutions Code § 215.
Temporary custody, see Welfare and Institutions Code § 306.

§ 273. Employment of psychiatrists, psychologists and other clinical experts

The probation officer may, within budgetary limitations established by the board of supervisors, employ such psychiatrists, psychologists, and other clinical experts as are required to assist in determining appropriate treatment of minors within the jurisdiction of the juvenile court and in the implementation of such treatment. *(Added by Stats.1976, c. 1068, p. 4755, § 5.)*

Cross References

Probation officer or social worker defined for purposes of this Chapter, see Welfare and Institutions Code § 215.

§ 274. Bonds

Each probation officer and each assistant and deputy probation officer receiving an official salary shall furnish a bond in the sum of not more than two thousand dollars ($2,000) and approved by the judge of the juvenile court, conditioned for the faithful discharge of the duties of his office. If such bonds, or any of them, are furnished by a surety company licensed to transact business in the state, the premium thereon shall be paid out of the county treasury. In the event the probation officer, assistants and deputies are included as covered employees in a master bond pursuant to Sections 1481 and 1481.1 of the Government Code, the individual bonds prescribed above shall not be required. *(Added by Stats.1976, c. 1068, p. 4755, § 5.)*

Cross References

Official bonds, generally, see Government Code § 1450 et seq.
Probation officer or social worker defined for purposes of this Chapter, see Welfare and Institutions Code § 215.

§ 275. Books and accounts; receipts and vouchers; annual audit

(a) For the purpose of handling the reimbursement and other payments provided for in this chapter, the probation officer or other county officer designated by the board of supervisors of the county shall keep suitable books and accounts and shall give and keep suitable receipts and vouchers.

(b) The auditor of the county shall audit these books and accounts annually, or at least biennially if so ordered by the board of supervisors upon the recommendation of the county auditor, on a fiscal year basis ending June 30 and shall make a report thereon to the judge of the court and to the supervisors of the county prior to the 31st day of the next succeeding month of January. This subdivision shall become inoperative on July 1, 1993, and shall remain inoperative until July 1, 1994, on which date this section shall become operative. *(Added by Stats.1976, c. 1068, p. 4755, § 5. Amended by Stats.1993, c. 60 (S.B.452), § 12, eff. June 30, 1993.)*

Cross References

County auditor, see Government Code § 26900 et seq.
County financial evaluation officer, see Government Code § 27750 et seq.
Probation officer functions, see Government Code § 27751.
Probation officer or social worker defined for purposes of this Chapter, see Welfare and Institutions Code § 215.

§ 276. Additional power of officer; receipt, deposit and disbursement of money

In addition to the powers and duties of the probation officer elsewhere prescribed in this chapter, the probation officer is authorized to receive money, give his or her receipt therefor, deposit or invest such money as soon as practicable in the county treasury, in a commercial bank account designated and approved for such a purpose by the board of supervisors, or in investment certificates or share accounts issued by a savings and loan association doing business in this state, insured by the Federal Savings and Loan Insurance Corporation and designated and approved for such purpose by the board of supervisors, and direct the disbursement thereof, in any of the following instances:

(a) Money payable to spouse or child in an action for divorce, separate maintenance, or similar action, together with court costs, upon order of a court of competent jurisdiction. Instead of designating the probation officer to act as court trustee for the receipt and disbursement of money payable to a spouse or child under this subdivision, the court may designate in its order a bonded employee of the court to act as court trustee for that purpose.

(b) Money payable to or on behalf of a ward or dependent child of the juvenile court or a person concerning whom a petition has been filed in the juvenile court. The probation officer may petition the court for approval of any past or prospective disbursement.

(c) Money payable to, by, or on behalf of probationers under the supervision of the probation officer. The probation officer may petition the court for approval of any past or prospective disbursement.

(d) Money payable to a child, wife, or indigent parent when it has been alleged or claimed that there has been a violation of either Section 270, 270a, or 270c of the Penal Code and the matter has been referred to the probation officer by the district attorney.

(e) Gifts of money made to the county to assist in the prevention or correction of delinquency or crime when the donor requests the probation officer to disburse such funds for such purposes and the board of supervisors accepts the gift upon such conditions.

(f) Other similar cases.

In addition to the foregoing, the probation officer is authorized to receive money payable to the county when ordered to do so by a court of competent jurisdiction. Such money shall be deposited or invested in the same manner as the other items set forth in this section.

If a bank account or savings and loan association investment certificate or share account is authorized pursuant to this section, the probation officer shall pay into the county treasury all money collected by him or under his or her control during the preceding month that is payable into the treasury in conformity with Section 24353 of the Government Code. *(Added by Stats.1976, c. 1068, p. 4755, § 5. Amended by Stats.1992, c. 848 (S.B.1614), § 13, eff. Sept. 22, 1992.)*

Cross References

County financial evaluation officer, see Government Code § 27750 et seq.
Probation officer functions, see Government Code § 27751.
Probation officer or social worker defined for purposes of this Chapter, see Welfare and Institutions Code § 215.

§ 277. Authorizing sale of probationers' handiwork

The probation officer may authorize the sale of articles of handiwork made by wards under the jurisdiction of the probation officer to the public at probation institutions, in public buildings, at fairs, or on property operated by nonprofit associations. The cost of any county materials or other property consumed in the manufacture of articles shall be paid for out of funds received from the sale of the articles. The remainder of any funds received from the sale of the articles shall be placed in the ward's trust account pursuant to subdivision (b) of Section 276. *(Added by Stats.1976, c. 1068, p. 4755, § 5.)*

Cross References

Probation officer or social worker defined for purposes of this Chapter, see Welfare and Institutions Code § 215.

§ 278. Delegation of certain functions of probation officer to county auditor or other officer

The board of supervisors may delegate to the auditor or other county officer any of the functions of the probation officer authorized by Section 276 and required by Sections 1685 to 1687, inclusive, of the Code of Civil Procedure. *(Added by Stats.1976, c. 1068, p. 4755, § 5.)*

Cross References

Probation officer or social worker defined for purposes of this Chapter, see Welfare and Institutions Code § 215.

§ 279. Imposition of service charge in relation to payments under section 276

The board of supervisors may impose a service charge at a uniform rate sufficient to defray the cost of services of the probation officer or other officer designated to act as trustee, not exceeding 2 percent of the amount collected, in addition to the payments made under subdivision (a), (c), (d), or (f) of Section 276. However, a service charge may not be imposed for services relating to child support.

The service charge imposed in relation to payments under subdivision (c) of Section 276 shall be imposed only for payments made by probationers, and the service charge imposed in relation to payments made under subdivision (f) of Section 276 shall be imposed only for cases similar to those listed in subdivision (a), (c), or (d) of that section.

When the payments are ordered by the court, the payment of the service charge shall be included in the order. All proceeds shall be deposited in the general fund of the county. *(Added by Stats.1976, c. 1068, p. 4755, § 5. Amended by Stats.1992, c. 848 (S.B.1614), § 14, eff. Sept. 22, 1992.)*

Cross References

Child support order, provision for service charge, see Family Code § 4203.
Probation officer or social worker defined for purposes of this Chapter, see Welfare and Institutions Code § 215.
Spousal support, payment to court-designated officer and enforcement by district attorney, expenses and charges, see Family Code § 4352.
Spousal support payments to court or to county officer, see Family Code § 4350.

§ 280. Duties of officers in court; social study of minor; contents

Except where waived by the probation officer, judge, or referee and the minor, the probation officer shall be present in court to represent the interests of each person who is the subject of a petition to declare that person to be a ward or dependent child upon all hearings or rehearings of his or her case, and shall furnish to the court such information and assistance as the court may require. If so ordered, the probation officer shall take charge of that person before and after any hearing or rehearing.

It shall be the duty of the probation officer to prepare for every hearing on the disposition of a case as provided by Section 356, 358, 358.1, 361.5, 364, 366, 366.2, or 366.21 as is appropriate for the specific hearing, or, for a hearing as provided by Section 702, a social study of the minor, containing such matters as may be relevant to a proper disposition of the case. The social study shall include a recommendation for the disposition of the case. *(Added by Stats. 1976, c. 1068, p. 4755, § 5. Amended by Stats.1987, c. 1485, § 2.)*

Cross References

Control and conduct of proceedings, see Welfare and Institutions Code § 680.
Hearings, see Welfare and Institutions Code § 675 et seq.
Probation officer or social worker defined for purposes of this Chapter, see Welfare and Institutions Code § 215.
Securing witnesses to prove allegations of petition, see Welfare and Institutions Code § 701.
Social study, reception at hearing, see Welfare and Institutions Code § 706.

§ 281. Investigation; reports

The probation officer shall upon order of any court in any matter involving the custody, status, or welfare of a minor or minors, make an investigation of appropriate facts and circumstances and prepare and file with the court written reports and written recommendations in reference to such matters. The court is authorized to receive and consider the reports and recommendations of the probation officer in determining any such matter. *(Added by Stats.1976, c. 1068, p. 4755, § 5.)*

Cross References

Probation investigation and report, see Penal Code § 1203.10.
Probation officer or social worker defined for purposes of this Chapter, see Welfare and Institutions Code § 215.
Social study, reception at hearing, see Welfare and Institutions Code § 706.
Supervising conciliation counsel's authority to make investigations, reports, and recommendations as provided in this section, see Family Code § 1814.

§ 281.5. Removal of minor from custody of parent or guardian; placement with relative of minor; recommendation

If a probation officer determines to recommend to the court that a minor alleged to come within Section 300, 601, or 602, or adjudged to come within Section 300, 601, or 602 should be removed from the physical custody of his parent or guardian, the probation officer shall give primary consideration to recommending to the court that the minor be placed with a relative of the minor, if such placement is in the best interests of the minor and will be conducive to reunification of the family. *(Added by Stats.1977, c. 236, p. 1080, § 1.)*

Cross References

Probation officer or social worker defined for purposes of this Chapter, see Welfare and Institutions Code § 215.

§ 282. Examination of institutions; reports

At any time the judge of the juvenile court may, and upon the request of the county board of supervisors shall, require the probation officer to examine into and report to the court upon the qualifications and management of any society, association, or corporation, other than a state institution, which applies for or receives custody of any ward or dependent child of the juvenile court. No probation officer, however, shall, under authority of this section, enter any institution without its consent. If such consent is refused, commitments to that institution shall not be made. *(Added by Stats.1976, c. 1068, p. 4755, § 5.)*

Cross References

Probation officer or social worker defined for purposes of this Chapter, see Welfare and Institutions Code § 215.

§ 283. Powers of peace officer

Every probation officer, assistant probation officer, and deputy probation officer shall have the powers and authority conferred by law upon peace officers listed in Section 830.5 of the Penal Code. *(Added by Stats.1976, c. 1068, p. 4755, § 5.)*

Cross References

Authority of peace officer to arrest, see Penal Code § 836.
Minimum standards for public officers or employees having powers of peace officers, see Government Code § 1031.
Peace officer defined, see Penal Code §§ 7, 830 et seq.
Probation officer or social worker defined for purposes of this Chapter, see Welfare and Institutions Code § 215.
Temporary custody and detention of wards, authority of peace officer, see Welfare and Institutions Code § 625 et seq.

§ 284. Reports to Youth Authority

All probation officers shall make such special and periodic reports to the Youth Authority as the authority may require and upon forms furnished by the authority. *(Added by Stats.1976, c. 1068, p. 4755, § 5.)*

Cross References

Conferences with director of Youth Authority, see Welfare and Institutions Code § 1752.95.
Information furnished to Youth Authority, see Welfare and Institutions Code § 1741.
Probation officer or social worker defined for purposes of this Chapter, see Welfare and Institutions Code § 215.
Youth Authority, generally, see Welfare and Institutions Code § 1700 et seq.

§ 285. Reports to Attorney General

All probation officers shall make periodic reports to the Attorney General at those times and in the manner prescribed by the Attorney General, provided that no names or social security numbers shall be transmitted regarding any proceeding under Section 300 or 601. *(Added by Stats.1976, c. 1068, p. 4755, § 5. Amended by Stats.1977, c. 884, p. 2653, § 1; Stats.1979, c. 610, p. 1906, § 1; Stats.2004, c. 405 (S.B.1796), § 25.)*

Cross References

Attorney General, generally, see Government Code §§ 12500 et seq.
Department of criminal statistics, see Penal Code § 13010 et seq.

Probation officer or social worker defined for purposes of this Chapter, see Welfare and Institutions Code § 215.

§ 286. Appointments prior to effective date of section; continuance in office

Any person lawfully appointed to serve as a probation officer or assistant or deputy probation officer prior to the effective date of this section shall continue in his office or employment as if appointed in the manner prescribed by this article. *(Added by Stats.1976, c. 1068, p. 4755, § 5.)*

Cross References

Probation officer or social worker defined for purposes of this Chapter, see Welfare and Institutions Code § 215.

ARTICLE 13.6. SERIOUS HABITUAL OFFENDERS

§ 500. Legislative findings

The Legislature hereby finds that a substantial and disproportionate amount of serious crime is committed by a relatively small number of chronic juvenile offenders commonly known as serious habitual offenders. In enacting this article, the Legislature intends to support increased efforts by the juvenile justice system comprised of law enforcement, district attorneys, probation departments, juvenile courts, and schools to identify these offenders early in their careers, and to work cooperatively together to investigate and record their activities, prosecute them aggressively by using vertical prosecution techniques, sentence them appropriately, and to supervise them intensively in institutions and in the community. The Legislature further supports increased interagency efforts to gather comprehensive data and actively disseminate it to the agencies in the juvenile justice system, to produce more informed decisions by all agencies in that system, through organizational and operational techniques that have already proven their effectiveness in selected counties in this and other states. *(Added by Stats.1986, c. 1441, § 1.)*

Cross References

Public defender, duties, see Government Code § 27706.

§ 501. Establishment of program; administration of funds appropriated; allocation and awarding of funds; application for funds; information gathering and analysis unit

(a) There is hereby established in the Office of Criminal Justice Planning a program of financial assistance for law enforcement, district attorneys, probation departments, juvenile courts, and schools, designated the Serious Habitual Offender Program. All funds appropriated to the Office of Criminal Justice Planning for the purposes of this article shall be administered and disbursed by the executive director of that office, and shall, to the greatest extent feasible, be coordinated or consolidated with federal funds that may be made available for these purposes.

(b) From moneys appropriated therefor, the Executive Director of the Office of Criminal Justice Planning may allocate and award funds to agencies in which programs are established in substantial compliance with the policies and criteria set forth in this article. Awards made to individual agencies shall not exceed three years in duration. An agency receiving an award shall provide matching funds at an increasing rate each year; the rate shall be as determined by the Office of Criminal Justice Planning for that agency.

(c) Allocation and award of funds for the purposes of this article shall be made upon application by a district attorney, a local law enforcement agency, a probation department, or a school district, that has been approved by the appropriate governing board of the particular agency. The applicant agency shall use the funds to create an information gathering and analysis unit responsible for the identification of serious habitual offenders and for the dissemination of information about the activities of those offenders to the juvenile justice system. This unit shall participate in the planning, support, and assistance of activities required in Sections 503 to 506, inclusive. Funds disbursed under this article shall not supplant local funds that would, in absence of the program established by this article, be made available to support the juvenile justice system. Local grant awards made under the program shall not be subject to review as specified in Section 14780 of the Government Code. *(Added by Stats.1986, c. 1441, § 1. Amended by Stats.1989, c. 1356, § 1.)*

§ 502. Program participation; selection criteria; arrests; limitations

(a) An individual shall be the subject of the efforts of programs established pursuant to this article who has been previously adjudged a ward pursuant to Section 602 and is described in any of the following paragraphs:

(1) Has accumulated five total arrests, three arrests for crimes chargeable as felonies and three arrests within the preceding 12 months.

(2) Has accumulated 10 total arrests, two arrests for crimes chargeable as felonies and three arrests within the preceding 12 months.

(3) Has been arrested once for three or more burglaries, robberies, or sexual assaults within the preceding 12 months.

(4) Has accumulated 10 total arrests, eight or more arrests for misdemeanor crimes of theft, assault, battery, narcotics or controlled substance possession, substance abuse, or use or possession of weapons, and has three arrests within the preceding 12 months.

(b) Arrests for infractions or conduct described in Section 601 shall not be utilized in determining whether an individual is described in subdivision (a). All arrests used in determining eligibility for selection for program participation that did not result in a sustained petition shall be certified by the prosecutor as having been provable.

(c) In applying the selection criteria set forth above, a program may elect to limit its efforts to persons described in one or more of the categories listed in subdivision (a), or specified felonies, if crime statistics demonstrate that the persons so identified present a particularly serious problem in the county, or that the incidence of the felonies so specified present a particularly serious problem in the county. *(Added by Stats.1986, c. 1441, § 1.)*

Cross References

Felonies, definition and penalties, see Penal Code §§ 17, 18.
Misdemeanors, definition and penalties, see Penal Code §§ 17, 19 and 19.2.

§ 503. Policies for programs

Programs funded under this article shall adopt and pursue the following policies:

(a) Each participating law enforcement agency shall do all of the following:

(1) Gather data on identified serious habitual offenders.

(2) Compile data into a usable format for law enforcement, prosecutors, probation officers, schools, and courts pursuant to an interagency agreement.

(3) Regularly update data and disseminate data to juvenile justice system agencies, as needed.

(4) Establish local policies in cooperation with the prosecutor, the probation officer, schools, and the juvenile court regarding data collection, arrest, and detention of serious habitual offenders.

(5) Provide support and assistance to other agencies engaged in the program.

(b) Each participating district attorney's office shall do all of the following:

(1) File petitions based on the most serious provable offenses of each arrest of a serious habitual offender.

(2) Use all reasonable prosecutorial efforts to resist the release, where appropriate, of the serious habitual offender at all stages of the prosecution.

(3) Seek an admission of guilt on all offenses charged in the petition against the offender. The only cases in which the prosecutor may request the court to reduce or dismiss the charges shall be cases in which the prosecutor decides there is insufficient evidence to prove the people's case, the testimony of a material witness cannot be obtained or a reduction or dismissal will not result in a substantial change in sentence. In those cases, the prosecutor shall file a written declaration with the court stating the specific factual and legal basis for such a reduction or dismissal and the court shall make specific findings on the record of its ruling and the reasons therefor.

(4) Vertically prosecute all cases involving serious habitual offenders, whereby the prosecutor who makes the initial filing decision or appearance on such a case shall perform all subsequent court appearances on that case through its conclusion, including the disposition phase.

(5) Make all reasonable prosecutorial efforts to persuade the court to impose the most appropriate sentence upon such an offender at the time of disposition. As used in this paragraph, "most appropriate sentence" means any disposition available to the juvenile court.

(6) Make all reasonable prosecutorial efforts to reduce the time between arrest and disposition of the charge.

(7) Act as liaison with the court and other criminal justice agencies to establish local policies regarding the program and to ensure interagency cooperation in the planning and implementation of the program.

(8) Provide support and assistance to other agencies engaged in the program.

(c) Each participating probation department shall do all of the following:

(1) Cooperate in gathering data for use by all participating agencies pursuant to interagency agreement.

(2) Detain minors in custody who meet the detention criteria set forth in Section 628.

(3) Consider the data relating to serious habitual offenders when making all decisions regarding the identified individual and include relevant data in written reports to the court.

(4) Use all reasonable efforts to file violations of probation pursuant to Section 777 in a timely manner.

(5) Establish local policies in cooperation with law enforcement, the district attorney, schools, and the juvenile court regarding the program and provide support and assistance to other agencies engaged in the program.

(d) Each participating school district shall do all of the following:

(1) Cooperate in gathering data for use by all participating agencies pursuant to interagency agreement. School district access to records and data shall be limited to that information that is otherwise authorized by law.

(2) Report all crimes that are committed on campus by serious habitual offenders to law enforcement.

(3) Report all violations of probation committed on campus by serious habitual offenders to the probation officer or his or her designee.

(4) Provide educational supervision and services appropriate to serious habitual offenders attending schools.

(5) Establish local policies in cooperation with law enforcement, the district attorney, probation and the juvenile court regarding the program and provide support and assistance to other agencies engaged in the program. *(Added by Stats.1986, c. 1441, § 1. Amended by Stats.2004, c. 193 (S.B.111), § 207.)*

Law Revision Commission Comments

Section 503 is amended to delete reference to an obsolete reporting requirement. The required report was to be completed by March 1, 1988. [33 Cal.L.Rev.Comm. Reports 505 (2004)].

Cross References

Probation officer or social worker defined for purposes of this Chapter, see Welfare and Institutions Code § 215.

§ 504. Inspection of records by agency charged with compilation of data

The judge of the juvenile court shall authorize the inspection of juvenile court records, probation and protective services records, district attorney records, school records, and law enforcement records by the participating law enforcement agency charged with the compilation of the data relating to serious habitual offenders into the format used by all participating agencies. *(Added by Stats.1986, c. 1441, § 1.)*

§ 505. Interagency agreement; execution by participating agencies; contents; meetings to plan, implement and refine operation of program

Within three months of implementation of the program, all participating agencies in a county shall execute a written interagency agreement outlining their role in the program, including the duties they will perform, the duties other agencies will perform for and with them, and the categories of information to be collected and the plan for its distribution and use. All participating agencies will meet no less than once each month to plan, implement, and refine the operation of the program and to exchange information about individuals subject to the program or other related topics. *(Added by Stats.1986, c. 1441, § 1. Amended by Stats.1989, c. 1356, § 2.)*

§ 506. Juvenile criminal history; procedures requiring check of history of adults presented to district attorney's office for filing; charge, plea, and sentence

Law enforcement agencies and district attorneys participating in programs funded pursuant to this article shall adopt procedures to require a check of juvenile criminal history of all adults whose cases are presented to the district attorney's office for filing. The juvenile criminal history shall be considered by the district attorney in the charging decision and establishing the district attorney's position on the appropriate plea and sentence. *(Added by Stats.1986, c. 1441, § 1.)*

ARTICLE 14. WARDS—JURISDICTION

§ 601. Minors habitually disobedient or truant; contact with minor in truancy program; notice to appear

(a) Any minor between 12 years of age and 17 years of age, inclusive, who persistently or habitually refuses to obey the reasonable and proper orders or directions of the minor's parents, guardian, or custodian, or who is beyond the control of that person, or who is a minor between 12 years of age and 17 years of age, inclusive, when the minor violated any ordinance of any city or county of this state establishing a curfew based solely on age is within the jurisdiction of the juvenile court which may adjudge the minor to be a ward of the court.

(b) If a minor between 12 years of age and 17 years of age, inclusive, has four or more truancies within one school year as defined in Section 48260 of the Education Code or a school attendance review board or probation officer determines that the available public and private services are insufficient or inappropriate to correct the habitual truancy of the minor, or if the minor fails to respond to directives of a school attendance review board or probation officer or to services provided, the minor is then within the jurisdiction of the juvenile court which may adjudge the minor to be a ward of the court pursuant to this section. However, it is the intent of the Legislature that a minor who is described in this subdivision, adjudged a ward of the court pursuant solely to this subdivision, or found in contempt of court for failure to comply with a court order pursuant to this subdivision, shall not be held in a secure facility and shall not be removed from the custody of the parent or guardian except for the purposes of school attendance.

(c) To the extent practically feasible, a minor who is adjudged a ward of the court pursuant to this section shall not be permitted to come into or remain in contact with any minor ordered to participate in a truancy program, or the equivalent thereof, pursuant to Section 602.

(d) Any peace officer may issue a notice to appear to a minor who is within the jurisdiction of the juvenile court pursuant to this section. Before issuing a notice to appear under this subdivision, a peace officer shall refer a minor who is within the jurisdiction of this section to a community-based resource, the probation department, a health agency, a local educational agency, or other governmental entities that may provide services. *(Added by Stats.1961, c. 1616, p. 3471, § 2. Amended by Stats.1971, c. 1748, p. 3766, § 65; Stats.1974, c. 1215, p. 2629, § 8; Stats.1975, c. 192, p. 550, § 1; Stats.1975, c. 1183, p. 2917, § 2, eff. Sept. 30, 1975; Stats.1976, c. 1071, p. 4818, § 11; Stats.1994, c. 1023 (S.B.1728), § 6; Stats.1994, c. 1024 (A.B.2658), § 4.2; Stats.2014, c. 70 (S.B.1296), § 4, eff. Jan. 1, 2015; Stats.2018, c. 1006 (S.B.439), § 1, eff. Jan. 1, 2019; Stats.2020, c. 323 (A.B.901), § 7, eff. Jan. 1, 2021.)*

Cross References

Adjudication as ward of court or probation, see Welfare and Institutions Code § 725.
Affidavit to commence proceedings, see Welfare and Institutions Code § 653.
Annoying or molesting child under fourteen, see Penal Code § 647.6.
Annual calculation of county local control funding formula, see Education Code § 2574.
Appeal from judgment declaring minor who habitually refuses to obey parents a ward of court, see Welfare and Institutions Code § 800.
Application or petition for change of name, venue, contents, petitions for minors, see Code of Civil Procedure § 1276.
Causing or encouraging persons under age of 18 years to come within provisions of this section, see Penal Code § 272.
Child or nonminor dependents placed in Group Home for Children with Special Health Care Needs, condition, assessment, persons included in individual health care plan team, see Welfare and Institutions Code § 4684.76.
Child welfare, family reunification and maintenance pilot program, see Welfare and Institutions Code § 16500.5 et seq.
Child welfare services, psychotropic medications, training, see Welfare and Institutions Code § 16501.4.
Child welfare services, reunification of family, hearing, findings by court, incarcerated parents, adoption assessment, see Welfare and Institutions Code § 361.5.
Children of minor or nonminor dependent parents, considerations regarding risk of abuse or neglect, right to legal consultation, see Welfare and Institutions Code § 361.8.
Commitment of minor who habitually refuses to obey parents to juvenile home, ranch or camp, see Welfare and Institutions Code § 730.
Community service, persons described in this section, see Welfare and Institutions Code § 727.5.
Compulsory Education Law, violations, notice of outcome of each truancy-related referral, see Education Code § 48297.
Conduct of hearing upon copy of notice to appear in lieu of petition, see Welfare and Institutions Code § 257.
Contract with county for temporary emergency detention facilities, see Welfare and Institutions Code § 1752.15.
Contributing to delinquency of persons under 18 years, persuading, luring, or transporting minors 12 years of age or younger, see Penal Code § 272.
Conviction for sex offense, AIDS testing, see Penal Code § 1202.1.
County community schools, enrollment of pupils, see Education Code § 1981.
County jails, strip and body cavity searches, see Penal Code § 4030.
County-sponsored charter school, average daily attendance rate, funding, see Education Code § 47631.
Court orders, welfare of ward, parent counseling or education programs, see Welfare and Institutions Code § 727.
Court–Appointed Special Advocate (CASA) program, see Welfare and Institutions Code § 101 et seq.
Criminal subpoenas, service upon designated agent of minors, see Penal Code § 1328.

Criteria for apportionments, juvenile court and community school account, see Education Code § 42238.18.
Description of minor as person habitually refusing to obey parents, reception of evidence at hearing, see Welfare and Institutions Code § 701.
Destruction of records, notice, retention period, see Government Code § 68152.
Detention of minors taken into custody solely on grounds described in this section, see Welfare and Institutions Code § 207.
Determination whether child is an Indian child, considerations, see Welfare and Institutions Code § 224.2.
Disclosure of minor's medical information, mental health condition, see Civil Code § 56.103.
Disorderly conduct, see Penal Code § 647.
Disposition of traffic violation or truancy hearing, orders, jurisdiction, see Welfare and Institutions Code § 258.
Duties of appointed counsel, see Welfare and Institutions Code § 634.3.
Education-based foster youth services program, applications to Superintendent of Public Instruction, see Education Code § 42921.
Eligibility for AFDC–FC aid, conditions, see Welfare and Institutions Code § 11401.
Failure of person in charge of minor to respond to directives of school attendance review board, referral to probation department, see Welfare and Institutions Code § 601.2.
Family preservation programs, Solano and Alameda counties, expanded services, see Welfare and Institutions Code § 16500.51.
Family reunification services with respect to children separated from parents because of abuse, neglect or exploitation, see Welfare and Institutions Code § 16507.
Finding as to whether minor is within this section, see Welfare and Institutions Code § 702.
First through fourth truancies, penalties, see Education Code § 48264.5.
Guidelines for operation and maintenance of nonsecure placement facilities for persons coming within the terms of this section or § 602, see Welfare and Institutions Code § 210.1.
Habitual truants, see Education Code §§ 48262, 48613.
Hearings, see Welfare and Institutions Code § 675 et seq.
Homeless youth emergency service pilot projects, see Welfare and Institutions Code § 13701 et seq.
Imprisonment to compel performance of acts, exemptions, definitions, see Code of Civil Procedure § 1219.
Incompetency of minor within jurisdiction of court pursuant to this section, suspension of juvenile proceedings, see Welfare and Institutions Code § 709.
Interagency responsibilities for providing services to children with disabilities, surrogate parent, see Government Code § 7579.5.
Juvenile traffic offender, see Vehicle Code § 1816.
Kin–GAP for children, eligibility requirements, see Welfare and Institutions Code § 11386.
Kin–GAP for children, payment by county having jurisdiction, see Welfare and Institutions Code § 11390.
Licensure of enhanced behavioral supports home as adult residential facility or a group home, placement of dual agency clients, see Health and Safety Code § 1567.62.
Minor in foster care adjudged ward of the court,
Considerations and procedures at a permanency planning hearing, see Welfare and Institutions Code § 727.3.
Procedure for reunification of minor with family, instances where reunification not warranted, see Welfare and Institutions Code § 727.2.
Minor who appears to be dependent child and ward of court, initial determination of status pursuant to jointly developed written protocol, dual status children, creation of protocol, see Welfare and Institutions Code § 241.1.
Modification of juvenile court judgments and orders, petitions, see Welfare and Institutions Code § 388.
Notice, compulsory school attendance violations, issuance and service of citations, see Welfare and Institutions Code § 661.
Open hearing, choice and disqualification of judge, see Welfare and Institutions Code § 700.2.
Order adjudging minor ward of juvenile court, see Welfare and Institutions Code § 203.
Order for removal from custody and placement in foster home or institution, hearing upon supplemental petition, see Welfare and Institutions Code § 387.
Order to show cause, recovery of moneys or incurred costs for support of juveniles, see Welfare and Institutions Code § 903.4.
Paternity issue raised during a hearing pursuant to this section, inquiry to district attorney concerning superior court order addressing the issue, see Welfare and Institutions Code § 903.41.
Petition, notice and hearing, see Welfare and Institutions Code § 656.
Probation officer or social worker defined for purposes of this Chapter, see Welfare and Institutions Code § 215.
Probation officer's investigation to determine whether proceedings should be commenced, see Welfare and Institutions Code § 652.
Programs of supervision in lieu of filing petition to declare minor a ward of court under this section, see Welfare and Institutions Code § 654.
Proper court, see Welfare and Institutions Code § 651.
Prosecution for contributing to delinquency of minor coming within this section, see Welfare and Institutions Code § 11481.
Protection and safety of public and minors under jurisdiction of the juvenile court, see Welfare and Institutions Code § 202.
Pupils with exceptional needs placed in group homes, invitation for group home representative to attend individualized education program team meeting, see Education Code § 56341.2.
Purposes for which emancipated minors are considered an adult, see Family Code § 7050.
Release or destruction of juvenile court records, see Welfare and Institutions Code § 826.6.
Removal of minor from custody of parent or guardian, recommendation by probation officer of placement with relative of minor, see Welfare and Institutions Code § 281.5.
Rights of minors and nonminors in foster care, see Welfare and Institutions Code § 16001.9.
Segregation of dependent minors from habitual delinquents or truants, see Welfare and Institutions Code § 206.
Self-incrimination and confrontation of witnesses, see Welfare and Institutions Code § 702.5.
Sex offender registrants who have committed offense against minor, prohibited from residing, working, or volunteering in specified children's facilities, see Penal Code § 3003.6.
Sex offenders, required AIDS testing, see Penal Code § 1202.1.
Subpoena, notice to produce party or agent, method of service, see Code of Civil Procedure § 1987.
Supplemental petition to change custody of ward of court, see Welfare and Institutions Code § 777.
Surrender of custody of minor, authorization by parent, legal custodian, or related caregiver, see Health and Safety Code § 1283.
Temporary custody of minor who habitually refuses to obey parents, see Welfare and Institutions Code § 625.
Truancy mediation program, see Welfare and Institutions Code § 601.3.
Use of juvenile probation funds for specified children, see Welfare and Institutions Code § 18221.
Wards, judgment and orders, psychotropic medications, see Welfare and Institutions Code § 739.5.
Warrant of arrest against minor, see Welfare and Institutions Code § 663.
Willful disobedience or interference with juvenile court order, detainment prohibited, see Welfare and Institutions Code § 213.3.
Youth Bill of Rights, purpose of article, see Welfare and Institutions Code § 224.70.

Research References

West's California Judicial Council Forms JV–548, Motion for Transfer Out.
West's California Judicial Council Forms JV–550, Juvenile Court Transfer—Out Orders (Also Available in Spanish).
West's California Judicial Council Forms JV–600, Juvenile Wardship Petition (Also Available in Spanish).
West's California Judicial Council Forms JV–610, Child Habitually Disobedient §601(A) (Also Available in Spanish).
West's California Judicial Council Forms JV–611, Child Habitually Truant §601(B) (Also Available in Spanish).
California Jury Instructions - Criminal 16.162, Contributing to Delinquency of Minor—"Delinquent Child"—Defined.
2 Witkin, California Criminal Law 4th Crimes Against Public Peace and Welfare § 243 (2021), Minors.
2 Witkin, California Criminal Law 4th Crimes Against Public Peace and Welfare § 524 (2021), Students.
4 Witkin, California Criminal Law 4th Illegally Obtained Evidence § 202 (2021), Specific Searches.
3 Witkin, California Criminal Law 4th Punishment § 211 (2021), Discretionary Suspension.
2 Witkin, California Criminal Law 4th Sex Offenses and Crimes Against Decency § 154 (2021), In General.

2 Witkin, California Criminal Law 4th Sex Offenses and Crimes Against Decency § 156 (2021), Relationship to Other Offenses.

§ 601.2. Failure of parent, guardian, or person in charge of minor to respond to directives of school attendance review board; disposition of minor

In the event that a parent or guardian or person in charge of a minor described in Section 48264.5 of the Education Code fails to respond to directives of the school attendance review board or to services offered on behalf of the minor, the school attendance review board shall direct that the minor be referred to the probation department or to the county welfare department under Section 300, and the school attendance review board may require the school district to file a complaint against the parent, guardian, or other person in charge of such minor as provided in Section 48291 or Section 48454 of the Education Code. *(Added by Stats.1974, c. 1215, p. 2629, § 10. Amended by Stats.1976, c. 1068, p. 4782, § 21; Stats.1978, c. 380, p. 1208, § 154; Stats.1994, c. 1023 (S.B.1728), § 8.)*

§ 601.3. Truancy mediation program

(a) If the district attorney or the probation officer receives notice from the school district pursuant to subdivision (b) of Section 48260.6 of the Education Code that a minor continues to be classified as a truant after the parents or guardians have been notified pursuant to subdivision (a) of Section 48260.5 of the Education Code, or if the district attorney or the probation officer receives notice from the school attendance review board, or the district attorney receives notice from the probation officer, pursuant to subdivision (a) of Section 48263.5 of the Education Code that a minor continues to be classified as a truant after review and counseling by the school attendance review board or probation officer, the district attorney or the probation officer, or both, may request the parents or guardians and the child to attend a meeting in the district attorney's office or at the probation department to discuss the possible legal consequences of the minor's truancy.

(b) Notice of a meeting to be held pursuant to this section shall contain all of the following:

(1) The name and address of the person to whom the notice is directed.

(2) The date, time, and place of the meeting.

(3) The name of the minor classified as a truant.

(4) The section pursuant to which the meeting is requested.

(5) Notice that the district attorney may file a criminal complaint against the parents or guardians pursuant to Section 48293 of the Education Code for failure to compel the attendance of the minor at school.

(c) Notice of a meeting to be held pursuant to this section shall be served at least five days prior to the meeting on each person required to attend the meeting. Service shall be made personally or by certified mail with return receipt requested.

(d) At the commencement of the meeting authorized by this section, the district attorney or the probation officer shall advise the parents or guardians and the child that any statements they make could be used against them in subsequent court proceedings.

(e) Upon completion of the meeting authorized by this section, the probation officer or the district attorney, after consultation with the probation officer, may file a petition pursuant to Section 601 if the district attorney or the probation officer determines that available community resources cannot resolve the truancy problem, or if the pupil or the parents or guardians of the pupil, or both, have failed to respond to services provided or to the directives of the school, the school attendance review board, the probation officer, or the district attorney.

(f) The truancy mediation program authorized by this section may be established by the district attorney or by the probation officer. The district attorney and the probation officer shall coordinate their efforts and shall cooperate in determining whether another public agency, a community-based organization, the probation department, or the district attorney is best able to operate a truancy mediation program in their county pursuant to this section. *(Added by Stats.1984, c. 754, § 5. Amended by Stats.1991, c. 1202 (S.B.377), § 14; Stats.1992, c. 427 (A.B.3355), § 175; Stats.1994, c. 1024 (A.B.2658), § 6; Stats.2020, c. 323 (A.B.901), § 8, eff. Jan. 1, 2021.)*

Cross References

Access to pupil records by persons without written parental consent or under judicial order, see Education Code § 49076.
Admission of public and persons having interest in case, see Welfare and Institutions Code § 676.
Attendance review board or probation officer, notice meeting to discuss consequences of failure to compel attendance, see Education Code § 48263.5.
Counties not having school attendance review board, notice meeting to discuss consequences of failure to compel attendance, see Education Code § 48260.6.
Felonies prosecuted by indictment or information, see Penal Code § 737.
First through fourth truancies, penalties, see Education Code § 48264.5.
Probation officer or social worker defined for purposes of this Chapter, see Welfare and Institutions Code § 215.
Special or separate session hearings, see Welfare and Institutions Code § 675.

§ 601.4. Compulsory education violations; jurisdiction; prosecution; coordinating actions

(a) The juvenile court judge may be assigned to sit as a superior court judge to hear any complaint alleging that a parent, guardian, or other person having control or charge of a minor has violated Section 48293 of the Education Code. The jurisdiction of the juvenile court granted by this section shall not be exclusive and the charge may be prosecuted instead in a superior court. However, upon motion, that action shall be transferred to the juvenile court.

(b) Notwithstanding Section 737 of the Penal Code, a violation of Section 48293 of the Education Code may be prosecuted pursuant to subdivision (a), by written complaint filed in the same manner as an infraction may be prosecuted. The juvenile court judge, sitting as a superior court judge, may coordinate the action involving the minor with any action involving the parent, guardian, or other person having control or charge of the minor. Both matters may be heard and decided at the same time unless the parent, guardian, other person having control or charge of the minor, or any member of the press or public objects to a closed hearing of the proceedings charging violation of Section 48293 of the Education Code. *(Added by Stats.1985, c. 120, § 2. Amended by Stats.1989, c. 1117, § 5; Stats.1998, c. 931 (S.B.2139), § 470, eff. Sept. 28, 1998; Stats.2002, c. 784 (S.B.1316), § 612.)*

Law Revision Commission Comments

Section 601.4 is amended to accommodate unification of the municipal and superior courts in a county. Cal. Const. art. VI, § 5(e). The jurisdictional and procedural distinctions between a judge sitting as a juvenile court judge and sitting as a superior court judge are significant and are preserved in this amendment. The section is also amended to reflect elimination of the justice court. Cal. Const. art. VI, §§ 1, 5(b). [28 Cal.L.Rev.Comm. Reports 51 (1998)].

Section 601.4 is amended to reflect unification of the municipal and superior courts pursuant to Article VI, Section 5(e), of the California Constitution. [32 Cal.L.Rev.Comm. Reports 553 (2002)].

Cross References

Compulsory education, jurisdiction, see Education Code § 48295.
Penalties against parents for truancy, see Education Code § 48293.

§ 601.5. At–Risk Youth Early Intervention Program; establishment; Youth Referral Centers

(a) Any county may, upon adoption of a resolution by the board of supervisors, establish an At–Risk Youth Early Intervention Program designed to assess and serve families with children who have chronic behavioral problems that place the child at risk of becoming a ward of the juvenile court under Section 601 or 602. The purpose of the program is to provide a swift and local service response to youth behavior problems so that future involvement with the justice system may be avoided.

(b) The At–Risk Youth Early Intervention Program shall be designed and developed by a collaborative group which shall include representatives of the juvenile court, the probation department, the district attorney, the public defender, the county department of social services, the county education department, county health and mental health agencies, and local and community-based youth and family service providers.

(c) The At–Risk Youth Early Intervention Program shall include one or more neighborhood-based Youth Referral Centers for at-risk youth and their families. These Youth Referral Centers shall be flexibly designed by each participating county to serve the local at-risk youth population with family assessments, onsite services, and referrals to offsite services. The operator of a Youth Referral Center may be a private nonprofit community-based agency or a public agency, or both. A center shall be staffed by youth and family service counselors who may be public or private employees and who shall be experienced in dealing with at-risk youth who are eligible for the program, as described in subdivision (d). The center may also be staffed as a collaborative service model involving onsite youth and family counselors, probation officers, school representatives, health and mental health practitioners, or other service providers. A center shall be located at one or more community sites that are generally accessible to at-risk youth and families and shall be open during daytime, evening, and weekend hours, as appropriate, based upon local service demand and resources available to the program.

(d) A minor may be referred to a Youth Referral Center by a parent or guardian, a law enforcement officer, a probation officer, a child welfare agency, or a school, or a minor may self-refer. A minor may be referred to the program if the minor is at least 10 years of age and is believed by the referring source to be at risk of justice system involvement due to chronic disobedience to parents, curfew violations, repeat truancy, incidents of running away from home, experimentation with drugs or alcohol, or other serious behavior problems. Whenever a minor is referred to the program, the Youth Referral Center shall make an initial determination as to whether the minor is engaged in a pattern of at-risk behavior likely to result in future justice system involvement, and, if satisfied that the minor is significantly at risk, the center shall initiate a family assessment. The family assessment shall identify the minor's behavioral problem, the family's circumstances and relationship to the problem, and the needs of the minor or the family in relation to the behavioral problem. The assessment shall be performed using a risk and needs assessment instrument, based on national models of successful youth risk and needs assessment instruments and utilizing objective assessment criteria, as appropriate for the clientele served by the program. At a minimum, the assessment shall include information drawn from interviews with the minor and with the parents or other adults having custody of the minor, and it shall include information on the minor's probation, school, health, and mental health status to the extent such information may be available and accessible.

(e) If the Youth Referral Center confirms upon assessment that the minor is at significant risk of future justice system involvement and that the minor may benefit from referral to services, the Youth Referral Center staff shall work with the minor and the parents to produce a written service plan to be implemented over a period of up to six months. The plan shall identify specific programs or services that are recommended by the center and are locally available to the minor and the family as a means of addressing the behavior problems that led to the referral. The plan may include a requirement that the minor obey reasonable rules of conduct at home or in school including reasonable home curfew and school attendance rules, while the service plan is being implemented. The plan may also require, as a condition of further participation in the program, that a parent or other family member engage in counseling, parenting classes, or other relevant activities. To the extent possible given available resources, the staff at the Youth Referral Center shall facilitate compliance with the service plan by assisting the minor and the family in making appointments with service providers, by responding to requests for help by the minor or the parent as they seek to comply with the plan, and by monitoring compliance until the plan is completed.

(f)(1) The caseworker at the Youth Referral Center shall explain the service plan to the minor and the parents and, prior to any referral to services, the minor and the parents shall agree to the plan. The minor and the parents shall be informed that the minor's failure to accept or to cooperate with the service plan may result in the filing of a petition and a finding of wardship under Section 601.

(2) With the cooperation of the collaborative group described in subdivision (b), the Youth Referral Center shall review youth and family services offered within its local service area and shall identify providers, programs, and services that are available for referral of minors and parents under this section. Providers to which minors and parents may be referred under this section may be public or private agencies or individuals offering counseling, health, educational, parenting, mentoring, community service, skill-building, and other relevant services that are considered likely to resolve the behavioral problems that are referred to the center.

(g)(1) Unless the probation department is directly operating and staffing the Youth Referral Center, the probation department shall designate one or more probation officers to serve as liaison to a Youth Referral Center for the purpose of facilitating and monitoring compliance with service plans established in individual cases by the center.

(2) If, upon consultation with the minor's parents and with providers designated in the service plan, the supervising caseworker at the center and the liaison probation officer agree that the minor has willfully, significantly, and repeatedly failed to cooperate with the service plan, the minor shall be referred to the probation department which shall verify the failure and, upon verification, shall file a petition seeking to declare the minor a ward of the juvenile court under subdivision (a) of Section 601. No minor shall be referred to the probation department for the filing of a petition under this subdivision until at least 90 days have elapsed after the first attempt to implement the service plan. No minor shall be subject to filing of a petition under this subdivision for a failure to complete the service plan which is due principally to an inability of the minor or the family to pay for services listed in the service plan.

(3) If, within 180 days of the start of the service plan, the minor and the family have substantially completed the service plan and the minor's behavior problem appears to have been resolved, the center shall notify the probation department that the plan has been successfully completed.

(h) If a petition to declare the minor a ward of the juvenile court under subdivision (a) of Section 601 has been filed by the probation officer under this section, the court shall review the petition and any other facts which the court deems appropriate in relation to the minor's alleged failure to comply with the service plan described in subdivision (e). Based upon this review, the court may continue any hearing on the petition for up to six months so that the minor and the minor's parents may renew their efforts to comply with the service plan under court supervision. During the period in which the hearing is continued, the court may order that the minor and the parent cooperate with the service plan designed by the Youth Referral Center, or the court may modify the service plan or may impose additional conditions upon the minor or the parents as may be appropriate to encourage resolution of the behavior problems that led to the filing of the petition. The court shall, during the period of continuance, periodically review compliance with the extended service plan through reports from the probation officer or by calling the parties back into court, based upon a review schedule deemed appropriate by the court.

(i) The juvenile court of any county participating in the At–Risk Youth Early Intervention Program shall designate a judicial officer to serve as a liaison to the program in order to participate in the development of the program and to coordinate program operations with the juvenile court. The liaison judicial officer may be designated by the juvenile court as the principal judicial officer assigned to review and hear petitions filed under this section, or if the court does not elect to designate a principal judicial officer to hear these cases, the juvenile court shall take steps to train or familiarize other judicial officers reviewing or hearing these cases as to the operations, procedures, and services of the At–Risk Youth Early Intervention Program. *(Added by Stats.1997, c. 909 (S.B.1050), § 1.)*

Cross References

Probation officer or social worker defined for purposes of this Chapter, see Welfare and Institutions Code § 215.

§ 602. Minors violating laws defining crime; ward of court

(a) Except as provided in Section 707, any minor who is between 12 years of age and 17 years of age, inclusive, when he or she violates any law of this state or of the United States or any ordinance of any city or county of this state defining crime other than an ordinance establishing a curfew based solely on age, is within the jurisdiction of the juvenile court, which may adjudge the minor to be a ward of the court.

(b) Any minor who is under 12 years of age when he or she is alleged to have committed any of the following offenses is within the jurisdiction of the juvenile court, which may adjudge the minor to be a ward of the court:

(1) Murder.

(2) Rape by force, violence, duress, menace, or fear of immediate and unlawful bodily injury.

(3) Sodomy by force, violence, duress, menace, or fear of immediate and unlawful bodily injury.

(4) Oral copulation by force, violence, duress, menace, or fear of immediate and unlawful bodily injury.

(5) Sexual penetration by force, violence, duress, menace, or fear of immediate and unlawful bodily injury. *(Added by Stats.1961, c. 1616, p. 3472, § 2. Amended by Stats.1971, c. 1748, p. 3766, § 66; Stats.1972, c. 84, p. 109, § 1, eff. May 19, 1972; Stats.1976, c. 1071, p. 4819, § 12; Stats.1999, c. 996 (S.B.334), § 12.2; Initiative Measure (Prop. 21, § 18, approved March 7, 2000, eff. March 8, 2000); Stats.2001, c. 854 (S.B.205), § 72; Stats.2014, c. 54 (S.B.1461), § 18, eff. Jan. 1, 2015; Initiative Measure (Prop. 57, § 4.1, approved Nov. 8, 2016, eff. Nov. 9, 2016); Stats.2018, c. 1006 (S.B.439), § 2, eff. Jan. 1, 2019.)*

Cross References

Adjudication as ward of court or probation, see Welfare and Institutions Code § 725.
Adult inducing minor to violate provisions relating to controlled substances, see Health and Safety Code § 11353.
Affidavit to commence proceedings, see Welfare and Institutions Code § 653.
Annual calculation of county local control funding formula, see Education Code § 2574.
Antigang violence parenting classes for parents or guardians of minors who are first-time offenders of a gang-related offense, curriculum, liability for cost of classes, see Welfare and Institutions Code § 727.7.
Appeal from judgment declaring person who violates laws a ward of court, see Welfare and Institutions Code § 800.
Applicability of chapter to persons under age eighteen who violate laws defining crime and who flee state, see Welfare and Institutions Code § 216.
Application or petition for change of name, venue, contents, petitions for minors, see Code of Civil Procedure § 1276.
Arrest for or conviction of nonviolent offense committed while victim of intimate partner violence or sexual violence, petition for vacatur relief, hearing, order, see Penal Code § 236.15.
Child Abuse and Neglect Reporting Act, confidentiality of identity of persons reporting, see Penal Code § 11167.
Child or nonminor dependents placed in Group Home for Children with Special Health Care Needs, condition, assessment, persons included in individual health care plan team, see Welfare and Institutions Code § 4684.76.
Child welfare, family reunification and maintenance pilot program, see Welfare and Institutions Code § 16500.5 et seq.
Child welfare services, psychotropic medications, training, see Welfare and Institutions Code § 16501.4.
Child welfare services, reunification of family, hearing, findings by court, incarcerated parents, adoption assessment, see Welfare and Institutions Code § 361.5.
Children of minor or nonminor dependent parents, considerations regarding risk of abuse or neglect, right to legal consultation, see Welfare and Institutions Code § 361.8.
Children's Mental Health Services Act, see Welfare and Institutions Code § 5850 et seq.
Coercion to commit offense as direct result of being victim of intimate partner violence or sexual violence, affirmative defense to charge of a crime, see Penal Code § 236.24.
Collection of replacement specimen found spoiled or unusable, collection of specimen from sex offense registrants and outstate transferees, see Penal Code § 296.2.
Commitment of person who violates laws to Youth Authority, see Welfare and Institutions Code § 731.
Commitment of ward who is 14 years of age or older to secure youth treatment facility, maximum term of confinement, see Welfare and Institutions Code § 875.
Commitment to youth correctional centers as condition of probation, see Welfare and Institutions Code § 1853.
Contact or association with dependent minors, separate and segregated facilities, see Welfare and Institutions Code § 206.
Contempt, disobedience of order of juvenile court, see Welfare and Institutions Code § 213.
Contracts to furnish housing to ward whose commitment has been recalled, minor not adjudged to be a ward of the court pursuant to this section, see Welfare and Institutions Code § 1752.16.
Contributing to delinquency of persons under 18 years, persuading, luring, or transporting minors 12 years of age or younger, see Penal Code § 272.
Conviction for sex offense, AIDS testing, see Penal Code § 1202.1.
County community schools, enrollment of pupils, see Education Code § 1981.
County jails, strip and body cavity searches, see Penal Code § 4030.
County-sponsored charter school, average daily attendance rate, funding, see Education Code § 47631.
Court orders, welfare of ward, parent counseling or education programs, see Welfare and Institutions Code § 727.
Court–Appointed Special Advocate (CASA) program, see Welfare and Institutions Code § 101 et seq.
Criminal subpoenas, service upon designated agent of minors, see Penal Code § 1328.
Custodial interrogation of person who is or may be adjudged ward of juvenile court, see Welfare and Institutions Code § 626.8.
Deceased minor victims of criminal acts, sealing of autopsy report and associated evidence, see Code of Civil Procedure § 130.
Delinquent juveniles within interstate compact, see Welfare and Institutions Code § 1400.
Description of minor as person violating laws, reception of evidence at hearing, see Welfare and Institutions Code § 701.
Destruction of records, notice, retention period, see Government Code § 68152.
Determination of offense as misdemeanor in juvenile court proceedings under this section, see Welfare and Institutions Code § 700.3.
Determination whether child is an Indian child, considerations, see Welfare and Institutions Code § 224.2.
Discharge from Youth Authority, see Welfare and Institutions Code § 1769.
Disclosure of minor's name to the public, see Welfare and Institutions Code § 204.5.
Discovery, minors alleged to be wards of court in juvenile proceedings, mental state placed in issue and mental health expert examinations, see Penal Code § 1054.3.

DNA and Forensic Identification Database and Data Bank Act,
Findings and intent, administration and implementation of chapter, responsibility for collection of specimens, samples and imprints, costs and funds, see Penal Code § 295.
Offenders subject to collection of specimens, samples and print impressions, see Penal Code § 296.
Duties of appointed counsel, see Welfare and Institutions Code § 634.3.
Educational liaisons, continuation in school of origin, transfer to new school, see Education Code § 48853.5.
Education-based foster youth services program, applications to Superintendent of Public Instruction, see Education Code § 42921.
Elementary and secondary education, required courses of study, pupil in foster care defined, see Education Code § 51225.2.
Family preservation programs, Solano and Alameda counties, expanded services, see Welfare and Institutions Code § 16500.51.
Finding as to whether minor is within this section, see Welfare and Institutions Code § 702.
Forfeiture of property used in committing telecommunications or computer crimes, application to minors, see Penal Code § 502.01.
Foster care pupils, effect of absences due to change of placement or court-ordered activity on grades, see Education Code § 49069.5.
Graffiti abatement, liability for expense, report of names and addresses of persons with custody or control of minors to local government officials, see Government Code § 38772.
Guidelines for operation and maintenance of nonsecure placement facilities for persons coming within § 601 or this section, see Welfare and Institutions Code § 210.1.
Hearings, see Welfare and Institutions Code § 675 et seq.
Hearings for release on parole of persons committed to Youth Authority, see Welfare and Institutions Code § 1767.
Incidents involving contact with law enforcement, reports to Community Care Licensing Division, amount of reports triggering inspection, inspection reports, see Health and Safety Code § 1538.7.
Incompetency of minor within jurisdiction of court pursuant to this section, suspension of juvenile proceedings, see Welfare and Institutions Code § 709.
Individuals subject to gang violence prosecution efforts, see Penal Code § 13826.3.
Interagency responsibilities for providing services to children with disabilities, surrogate parent, see Government Code § 7579.5.
Involuntary transfer of pupils, adoption of policies and procedures, see Education Code § 48662.
Juvenile court law,
Arrest and remand to county of residence, return to placement county, see Welfare and Institutions Code § 740.1.
Insanity plea joined with general denial, see Welfare and Institutions Code § 702.3.
Juvenile court wards, see Welfare and Institutions Code § 6550 et seq.
Juvenile delinquency proceedings, mental health and developmental disability issues, see Government Code § 68553.5.
Juvenile homes, ranches and camps, commitment to, see Welfare and Institutions Code § 880 et seq.
Juvenile traffic offender, see Vehicle Code § 1816.
Juveniles adjudicated a ward of the juvenile court for specified sex offenses and sent to the Division of Juvenile Justice, or equivalent thereof, duty to register, see Penal Code § 290.008.
Kin–GAP for children, eligibility requirements, see Welfare and Institutions Code § 11386.
Kin–GAP for children, payment by county having jurisdiction, see Welfare and Institutions Code § 11390.
Licensure of enhanced behavioral supports home as adult residential facility or a group home, placement of dual agency clients, see Health and Safety Code § 1567.62.
Marijuana, adults employing or selling to minors, see Health and Safety Code § 11361.
Material witnesses, order for written undertaking, commitment for refusal to comply, see Penal Code § 1332.
Mental health evaluations, recommendations, and dispositional procedures for minors, see Welfare and Institutions Code § 710 et seq.
Minor in foster care adjudged ward of the court,
Considerations and procedures at a permanency planning hearing, see Welfare and Institutions Code § 727.3.
Procedure for reunification of minor with family, instances where reunification not warranted, see Welfare and Institutions Code § 727.2.
Minor who appears to be dependent child and ward of court, initial determination of status pursuant to jointly developed written protocol, dual status children, creation of protocol, see Welfare and Institutions Code § 241.1.
Minors adjudged ward of court on basis on being person described in this section, conditions allowing placement other than in county of residence, see Welfare and Institutions Code § 740.
Modification of juvenile court judgments and orders, petitions, see Welfare and Institutions Code § 388.
Order adjudging minor ward of juvenile court, see Welfare and Institutions Code § 203.
Order for removal from custody and placement in foster home or institution, hearing upon supplemental petition, see Welfare and Institutions Code § 387.
Order to show cause, recovery of moneys or incurred costs for support of juveniles, see Welfare and Institutions Code § 903.4.
Out-of-county placements, notice to probation officer, see Health and Safety Code § 1567.3.
Paternity issue raised during a hearing pursuant to this section, inquiry to district attorney concerning superior court order addressing the issue, see Welfare and Institutions Code § 903.41.
Petition for dismissal or recall of sentence arising from violation of Section 647f, credit for time served, resentencing, see Penal Code § 1170.22.
Probation, chief probation officer, duties and obligations, see Government Code § 27771.
Probation officer's investigation to determine whether proceedings should be commenced, see Welfare and Institutions Code § 652.
Procedures for requiring HIV testing,
Failure to submit to tests, grounds for revocation of release, probation, or other sentence, see Penal Code § 7519.
Reports by law enforcement personnel of contacts with bodily fluids of inmates, etc., see Penal Code § 7510.
Programs of supervision in lieu of requesting that petition be filed by prosecuting attorney to declare minor a ward of court under this section, see Welfare and Institutions Code § 654.
Prohibited commitments to Corrections and Rehabilitation, Division of Juvenile Justice, see Welfare and Institutions Code § 733.1.
Proper court, see Welfare and Institutions Code § 651.
Property of minors, forfeiture procedures applicable, see Health and Safety Code § 11470.3.
Prosecution for contributing to delinquency of minor coming within this section, see Welfare and Institutions Code § 11481.
Protection and safety of public and minors under jurisdiction of the juvenile court, see Welfare and Institutions Code § 202.
Pupils with exceptional needs placed in group homes, invitation for group home representative to attend individualized education program team meeting, see Education Code § 56341.2.
Release or destruction of juvenile records, see Welfare and Institutions Code § 826.6.
Removal of minor from custody of parent or guardian, recommendation by probation officer of placement with relative of minor, see Welfare and Institutions Code § 281.5.
Repair, removal or replacement of defaced public or privately owned property, see Government Code § 53069.3.
Rights of minors and nonminors in foster care, see Welfare and Institutions Code § 16001.9.
Sealing of record, application of section, scope of authority to seal record, see Penal Code § 1203.47.
Segregation of dependent minors from habitual delinquents or truants, see Welfare and Institutions Code § 206.
Self-incrimination and confrontation of witnesses, see Welfare and Institutions Code § 702.5.
Sex offender registrants who have committed offense against minor, prohibited from residing, working, or volunteering in specified children's facilities, see Penal Code § 3003.6.
Sex offenders, required AIDS testing, see Penal Code § 1202.1.
Subpoena, notice to produce party or agent, method of service, see Code of Civil Procedure § 1987.
Supplemental petition to change custody of ward of court, see Welfare and Institutions Code § 777.
Surrender of custody of minor, authorization by parent, legal custodian, or related caregiver, see Health and Safety Code § 1283.
Temporary custody of person who violates laws, see Welfare and Institutions Code § 625.
Transitional housing placement program, eligibility, youth on psychotropic medication, see Welfare and Institutions Code § 16522.1.

Unlawful carrying and possession of weapons, specified convictions, narcotic addiction, see Penal Code § 12021.
Use of juvenile probation funds for specified children, see Welfare and Institutions Code § 18221.
Wards, judgment and orders, psychotropic medications, see Welfare and Institutions Code § 739.5.
Warrant of arrest against minor, see Welfare and Institutions Code § 663.
Youth Authority, discharge of persons convicted of felony, discharge of specified persons on or after July 1, 2012, see Welfare and Institutions Code § 1771.
Youth Bill of Rights, see Welfare and Institutions Code § 224.70 et seq.

Research References

West's California Judicial Council Forms JV–548, Motion for Transfer Out.
West's California Judicial Council Forms JV–550, Juvenile Court Transfer—Out Orders (Also Available in Spanish).
2 Witkin, California Criminal Law 4th Crimes Against Public Peace and Welfare § 15 (2021), Violation of Curfew.
2 Witkin, California Criminal Law 4th Crimes Against Public Peace and Welfare § 163A (2021), (New) Resentencing or Dismissal of Marijuana Conviction.
2 Witkin, California Criminal Law 4th Crimes Against Public Peace and Welfare § 241 (2021), Juvenile Offenders.
1 Witkin California Criminal Law 4th Crimes Against the Person § 25 (2021), Hospital.
1 Witkin California Criminal Law 4th Crimes Against the Person § 278 (2021), Human Trafficking.
1 Witkin California Criminal Law 4th Defenses § 181 (2021), California Decisions.
1 Witkin California Criminal Law 4th Defenses § 243 (2021), Statutory Provision.
4 Witkin, California Criminal Law 4th Illegally Obtained Evidence § 28 (2021), Juvenile Court Proceedings.
4 Witkin, California Criminal Law 4th Illegally Obtained Evidence § 202 (2021), Specific Searches.
4 Witkin, California Criminal Law 4th Illegally Obtained Evidence § 324 (2021), Detention of Student on School Grounds.
1 Witkin California Criminal Law 4th Introduction to Crimes § 18 (2021), Changes Involving Parole and Probation.
1 Witkin California Criminal Law 4th Introduction to Crimes § 140 (2021), Gang Violence and Juvenile Crime Prevention Act (Proposition 21).
4 Witkin, California Criminal Law 4th Introduction to Criminal Procedure § 56 (2021), Persons Required to Provide Forensic Material.
3 Witkin, California Criminal Law 4th Punishment § 86 (2021), Youth Authority Act.
3 Witkin, California Criminal Law 4th Punishment § 88 (2021), Persons Ineligible for Commitment.
3 Witkin, California Criminal Law 4th Punishment § 91 (2021), Commitment Procedure.
3 Witkin, California Criminal Law 4th Punishment § 95 (2021), In General.
3 Witkin, California Criminal Law 4th Punishment § 154 (2021), Definitions.
3 Witkin, California Criminal Law 4th Punishment § 308–I (2021), (New) Application to Juveniles.
3 Witkin, California Criminal Law 4th Punishment § 427 (2021), Juvenile Adjudication.
3 Witkin, California Criminal Law 4th Punishment § 536B (2021), (New) in General.
3 Witkin, California Criminal Law 4th Punishment § 679 (2021), Other Invalid Conditions.
2 Witkin, California Criminal Law 4th Sex Offenses and Crimes Against Decency § 154 (2021), In General.
2 Witkin, California Criminal Law 4th Sex Offenses and Crimes Against Decency § 156 (2021), Relationship to Other Offenses.

§ 602.1. Legislative intent; least restrictive alternatives; release of minor to parent, guardian, or caregiver

(a) In order to ensure the safety and well-being of minors who are under 12 years of age and whose behavior would otherwise bring them within the jurisdiction of the juvenile court pursuant to Section 601 or 602, it is the intent of the Legislature that counties pursue appropriate measures to serve and protect a child only as needed, avoiding any intervention whenever possible, and using the least restrictive alternatives through available school-, health-, and community-based services. It is the intent of the Legislature that counties use existing funding for behavioral health, mental health, or other available existing funding sources to provide the alternative services required by this section.

(b) Except as provided in subdivision (b) of Section 602, when a minor under 12 years of age comes to the attention of law enforcement because his or her behavior or actions are as described in Section 601 or 602, the response of the county shall be to release the minor to his or her parent, guardian, or caregiver. Counties shall develop a process for determining the least restrictive responses that may be used instead of, or in addition to, the release of the minor to his or her parent, guardian, or caregiver.

(c) This section shall become operative on January 1, 2020. *(Added by Stats.2018, c. 1006 (S.B.439), § 3, eff. Jan. 1, 2019, operative Jan. 1, 2020.)*

Research References

3 Witkin, California Criminal Law 4th Punishment § 86 (2021), Youth Authority Act.

§ 602.3. Personal use of firearm in the commission of a violent felony; placement order

(a) Notwithstanding any other law and pursuant to the provisions of this section, the juvenile court shall commit any minor adjudicated to be a ward of the court for the personal use of a firearm in the commission of a violent felony, as defined in subdivision (c) of Section 667.5 of the Penal Code, to placement in a juvenile hall, ranch, camp, or with the Department of the Youth Authority.

(b) A court may impose a treatment-based alternative placement order on any minor subject to this section if the court finds the minor has a mental disorder requiring intensive treatment. Any alternative placement order under this subdivision shall be made on the record, in writing, and in accordance with Article 3 (commencing with Section 6550) of Chapter 2 of Part 2 of Division 6. *(Formerly § 602.5, added by Stats.1999, c. 996 (S.B.334), § 13. Renumbered § 602.3 and amended by Stats.2001, c. 854 (S.B.205), § 73.)*

Cross References

Writing defined, see Welfare and Institutions Code § 8.

§ 602.5. Minor's criminal history; report

The juvenile court shall report the complete criminal history of any minor found to be a person adjudged to be a ward of the court under Section 602 because of the commission of any felony offense to the Department of Justice. The Department of Justice shall retain this information and make it available in the same manner as information gathered pursuant to Chapter 2 (commencing with Section 13100) of Title 3 of Part 4 of the Penal Code. *(Added by Initiative Measure (Prop. 21, § 19, approved March 7, 2000, eff. March 8, 2000).)*

Cross References

Criminal statistics, juvenile justice system, use and purpose of data collection, see Penal Code § 13010.5.
Department of Justice, criminal statistics, statewide information in annual report, see Penal Code § 13012.5.
Felonies, definition and penalties, see Penal Code §§ 17, 18.

Research References

4 Witkin, California Criminal Law 4th Introduction to Criminal Procedure § 51 (2021), In General.

§ 603. Preliminary examination; trying case upon accusatory pleading

(a) No court shall have jurisdiction to conduct a preliminary examination or to try the case of any person upon an accusatory pleading charging that person with the commission of a public offense or crime when the person was under the age of 18 years at the time of the alleged commission thereof unless the matter has first been submitted to the juvenile court by petition as provided in Article

7 (commencing with Section 650), and the juvenile court has made an order directing that the person be prosecuted under the general law.

(b) This section shall not apply in any case involving a minor against whom a complaint may be filed directly in a court of criminal jurisdiction pursuant to Section 707.01. *(Added by Stats.1961, c. 1616, p. 3472, § 2. Amended by Stats.1996, c. 481 (S.B.1377), § 1.)*

Cross References

Fitness hearing, see Welfare and Institutions Code § 707.

§ 603.5. Vehicle Code infractions or violations of local ordinances involving motor vehicles; jurisdiction; referral to juvenile court; application of section

(a) Notwithstanding any other provision of law, in a county that adopts the provisions of this section, jurisdiction over the case of a minor alleged to have committed only a violation of the Vehicle Code classified as an infraction or a violation of a local ordinance involving the driving, parking, or operation of a motor vehicle, is with the superior court, except that the court may refer to the juvenile court for adjudication, cases involving a minor who has been adjudicated a ward of the juvenile court, or who has other matters pending in the juvenile court.

(b) The cases specified in subdivision (a) shall not be governed by the procedures set forth in the juvenile court law.

(c) Any provisions of juvenile court law requiring that confidentiality be observed as to cases and proceedings, prohibiting or restricting the disclosure of juvenile court records, or restricting attendance by the public at juvenile court proceedings shall not apply. The procedures for bail specified in Chapter 1 (commencing with Section 1268) of Title 10 of Part 2 of the Penal Code shall apply.

(d) The provisions of this section shall apply in a county in which the trial courts make the section applicable as to any matters to be heard and the court has determined that there is available funding for any increased costs. *(Added by Stats.1980, c. 1299, p. 4390, § 4. Amended by Stats.1993, c. 1151 (A.B.1436), § 1; Stats.1994, c. 478 (A.B.3115), § 1, eff. Sept. 12, 1994; Stats.1996, c. 93 (A.B.2686), § 1; Stats.1998, c. 931 (S.B.2139), § 471, eff. Sept. 28, 1998; Stats.2001, c. 824 (A.B.1700), § 38; Stats.2008, c. 56 (S.B.1182), § 11.)*

Law Revision Commission Comments

Section 603.5 is amended to accommodate unification of the municipal and superior courts in a county. Cal. Const. art. VI, § 5(e). [28 Cal.L.Rev.Comm. Reports 51 (1998)].

Subdivision (a) of Section 603.5 is amended to reflect unification of the municipal and superior courts pursuant to former Section 5(e) of Article VI of the California Constitution.

Subdivision (a) is further amended to make stylistic revisions. [37 Cal. L.Rev.Comm. Reports 171 (2007)].

Cross References

Procedure on arrests, place to appear, see Vehicle Code § 40502.

Research References

4 Witkin, California Criminal Law 4th Pretrial Proceedings § 51 (2021), Citation, Promise, and Release.

§ 604. Proceedings; suspension, resumption, new proceedings; certification to juvenile court; pleadings

(a) Whenever a case is before any court upon an accusatory pleading and it is suggested or appears to the judge before whom the person is brought that the person charged was, at the date the offense is alleged to have been committed, under the age of 18 years, the judge shall immediately suspend all proceedings against the person on the charge. The judge shall examine into the age of the person, and if, from the examination, it appears to his or her satisfaction that the person was at the date the offense is alleged to have been committed under the age of 18 years, he or she shall immediately certify all of the following to the juvenile court of the county:

(1) That the person (naming him or her) is charged with a crime (briefly stating its nature).

(2) That the person appears to have been under the age of 18 years at the date the offense is alleged to have been committed, giving the date of birth of the person when known.

(3) That proceedings have been suspended against the person on the charge by reason of his or her age, with the date of the suspension.

The judge shall attach a copy of the accusatory pleading to the certification.

(b) When a court certifies a case to the juvenile court pursuant to subdivision (a), it shall be deemed that jeopardy has not attached by reason of the proceedings prior to certification, but the court may not resume proceedings in the case, nor may a new proceeding under the general law be commenced in any court with respect to the same matter unless the juvenile court has found that the minor is not a fit subject for consideration under the juvenile court law and has ordered that proceedings under the general law resume or be commenced.

(c) The certification and accusatory pleading shall be promptly transmitted to the clerk of the juvenile court. Upon receipt thereof, the clerk of the juvenile court shall immediately notify the probation officer who shall immediately proceed in accordance with Article 16 (commencing with Section 650).

(d) This section does not apply to any minor who may have a complaint filed directly against him or her in a court of criminal jurisdiction pursuant to Section 707.01. *(Added by Stats.1982, c. 1088, § 3. Amended by Stats.1984, c. 1412, § 1; Stats.1996, c. 481 (S.B.1377), § 2.)*

Cross References

Declaring minor a ward of the court through Juvenile court proceedings, see Welfare and Institutions Code § 650.
Fitness hearing, see Welfare and Institutions Code § 707.
Probation officer or social worker defined for purposes of this Chapter, see Welfare and Institutions Code § 215.
Prosecution under criminal statute or ordinance, see Welfare and Institutions Code § 606.

§ 605. Statute of limitations; suspension

Whenever a petition is filed in a juvenile court alleging that a minor is a person within the description of Section 602, and while the case is before the juvenile court, the statute of limitations applicable under the general law to the offense alleged to bring the minor within such description is suspended. *(Added by Stats.1961, c. 1616, p. 3473, § 2.)*

Cross References

Computation of time, exclusions, see Penal Code § 802.
Effect of honorable discharge from control by Youth Authority Board parole board, see Welfare and Institutions Code § 1772.
Hearing to determine fitness for juvenile court, see Welfare and Institutions Code § 707.
Petition, see Welfare and Institutions Code § 650 et seq.
Statutes of limitations, generally, see Penal Code § 799 et seq.

Research References

1 Witkin California Criminal Law 4th Defenses § 258 (2021), In General.

§ 606. Subjecting minor to criminal prosecution

When a petition has been filed in a juvenile court, the minor who is the subject of the petition shall not thereafter be subject to criminal prosecution based on the facts giving rise to the petition unless the juvenile court finds that the minor is not a fit and proper subject to be dealt with under this chapter and orders that criminal proceedings be resumed or instituted against him, or the petition is transferred to a court of criminal jurisdiction pursuant to subdivision (b) of Section

707.01. *(Added by Stats.1961, c. 1616, p. 3473, § 2. Amended by Stats.1999, c. 996 (S.B.334), § 14.)*

Cross References

Hearing to determine fitness for juvenile court, see Welfare and Institutions Code § 707.
Petition, see Welfare and Institutions Code § 650 et seq.

§ 607. Retention of, and discharge from, jurisdiction

(a) The court may retain jurisdiction over a person who is found to be a ward or dependent child of the juvenile court until the ward or dependent child attains 21 years of age, except as provided in subdivisions (b), (c), (d), and (e).

(b) The court may retain jurisdiction over a person who is found to be a person described in Section 602 by reason of the commission of an offense listed in subdivision (b) of Section 707, until that person attains 23 years of age, or two years from the date of commitment to a secure youth treatment facility pursuant to Section 875, whichever occurs later, subject to the provisions of subdivision (c).

(c) The court may retain jurisdiction over a person who is found to be a person described in Section 602 by reason of the commission of an offense listed in subdivision (b) of Section 707 until that person attains 25 years of age, or two years from the date of commitment to a secure youth treatment facility pursuant to Section 875, whichever occurs later, if the person, at the time of adjudication of a crime or crimes, would, in criminal court, have faced an aggregate sentence of seven years or more.

(d) The court shall not discharge a person from its jurisdiction who has been committed to the Department of Corrections and Rehabilitation, Division of Juvenile Justice while the person remains under the jurisdiction of the Department of Corrections and Rehabilitation, Division of Juvenile Justice, including periods of extended control ordered pursuant to Section 1800.

(e) The court may retain jurisdiction over a person described in Section 602 by reason of the commission of an offense listed in subdivision (b) of Section 707, who has been confined in a state hospital or other appropriate public or private mental health facility pursuant to Section 702.3 until that person attains 25 years of age, unless the court that committed the person finds, after notice and hearing, that the person's sanity has been restored.

(f) The court may retain jurisdiction over a person while that person is the subject of a warrant for arrest issued pursuant to Section 663.

(g) Notwithstanding subdivisions (b), (c), and (e), a person who is committed by the juvenile court to the Department of Corrections and Rehabilitation, Division of Juvenile Justice on or after July 1, 2012, but before July 1, 2018, and who is found to be a person described in Section 602 by reason of the commission of an offense listed in subdivision (b) of Section 707 shall be discharged upon the expiration of a two-year period of control, or when the person attains 23 years of age, whichever occurs later, unless an order for further detention has been made by the committing court pursuant to Article 6 (commencing with Section 1800) of Chapter 1 of Division 2.5. This subdivision does not apply to a person who is committed to the Department of Corrections and Rehabilitation, Division of Juvenile Justice, or to a person who is confined in a state hospital or other appropriate public or private mental health facility, by a court prior to July 1, 2012, pursuant to subdivisions (b), (c), and (e).

(h)(1) Notwithstanding subdivision (g), a person who is committed by the juvenile court to the Department of Corrections and Rehabilitation, Division of Juvenile Justice, on or after July 1, 2018, and who is found to be a person described in Section 602 by reason of the commission of an offense listed in subdivision (c) of Section 290.008 of the Penal Code or subdivision (b) of Section 707 of this code, shall be discharged upon the expiration of a two-year period of control, or when the person attains 23 years of age, whichever occurs later, unless an order for further detention has been made by the committing court pursuant to Article 6 (commencing with Section 1800) of Chapter 1 of Division 2.5.

(2) A person who, at the time of adjudication of a crime or crimes, would, in criminal court, have faced an aggregate sentence of seven years or more, shall be discharged upon the expiration of a two-year period of control, or when the person attains 25 years of age, whichever occurs later, unless an order for further detention has been made by the committing court pursuant to Article 6 (commencing with Section 1800) of Chapter 1 of Division 2.5.

(3) This subdivision does not apply to a person who is committed to the Department of Corrections and Rehabilitation, Division of Juvenile Justice, or to a person who is confined in a state hospital or other appropriate public or private mental health facility, by a court prior to July 1, 2018, as described in subdivision (g).

(i) The amendments to this section made by Chapter 342 of the Statutes of 2012 apply retroactively.

(j) This section does not change the period of juvenile court jurisdiction for a person committed to the Division of Juvenile Justice prior to July 1, 2018.

(k) This section shall become operative July 1, 2021. *(Added by Stats.2020, c. 337 (S.B.823), § 24, eff. Sept. 30, 2020, operative July 1, 2021. Amended by Stats.2021, c. 18 (S.B.92), § 4, eff. May 14, 2021, operative July 1, 2021; Stats.2022, c. 58 (A.B.200), § 38, eff. June 30, 2022.)*

Cross References

Children subject to juvenile court's jurisdiction, see Welfare and Institutions Code § 300 et seq.
Closure of Division of Juvenile Justice, continuation of services for state hospital patients referred by division, see Welfare and Institutions Code § 1732.10.
Insanity plea joined with general denial by a minor, see Welfare and Institutions Code § 702.3.
Jurisdiction of juvenile court, see Welfare and Institutions Code § 601.
Parole and discharge of minors, see Welfare and Institutions Code § 1176 et seq.
Release or destruction of juvenile court records, see Welfare and Institutions Code § 826.6.
Termination of jurisdiction over ward satisfying specified criteria, hearing, see Welfare and Institutions Code § 607.2.

§ 607.1. Retention of jurisdiction; criteria

(a) This section shall become operative on the 90th day after the enactment of the act adding this section.[1]

(b)(1) Notwithstanding Section 607, the court shall retain jurisdiction as described in paragraph (2) over any person who meets both of the following criteria:

(A) The person has been discharged from the physical custody of a facility of the Department of Corrections and Rehabilitation, Division of Juvenile Facilities.

(B) The person is subject to subdivision (b) of Section 1766 or subdivision (c) of Section 1766.01.

(2) The court shall retain jurisdiction over a person who is described in paragraph (1) until one of the following applies:

(A) The person attains the age of 25 years.

(B) The court terminates jurisdiction pursuant to Section 778 or 779, or any other applicable law.

(C) Jurisdiction is terminated by operation of any other applicable law. *(Added by Stats.2010, c. 729 (A.B.1628), § 10, eff. Oct. 19, 2010, operative Jan. 17, 2011.)*

[1] Stats.2010, c. 729 (A.B.1628), eff. Oct. 19, 2010.

Welf. & Inst.

Cross References

Minors violating laws defining crime and adjudged ward of court, committing court's jurisdiction after discharge, see Welfare and Institutions Code § 731.

§ 607.2. Termination of jurisdiction over ward satisfying specified criteria; hearing

(a)(1) On and after January 1, 2012, the court shall hold a hearing prior to terminating jurisdiction over a ward who satisfies any of the following criteria:

(A) Is a minor subject to an order for foster care placement described in Section 11402 as a ward who has not previously been subject to the jurisdiction of the court as a result of a petition filed pursuant to Section 325.

(B) Is a nonminor who was subject to an order for foster care placement described in Section 11402 as a ward on the day he or she attained 18 years of age.

(C) Is a ward who was subject to an order for foster care placement described in Section 11402 as a dependent of the court at the time the court adjudged the child to be a ward of the court under Section 725.

(2) The notice of hearing under this subdivision may be served electronically pursuant to Section 212.5.

(b) At a hearing during which termination of jurisdiction over a ward described in subdivision (a) is being considered, the court shall take one of the following actions:

(1) Modify its jurisdiction from delinquency jurisdiction to transition jurisdiction, if the court finds the ward is a person described in Section 450.

(2)(A) For a ward who was not previously subject to the jurisdiction of the court as a result of a petition filed pursuant to Section 325, order the probation department or the ward's attorney to submit an application to the child welfare services department pursuant to Section 329 to declare the minor a dependent of the court and modify the court's jurisdiction from delinquency jurisdiction to dependency jurisdiction, if the court finds all of the following:

(i) The ward is a minor.

(ii) The ward does not come within the description in Section 450, but jurisdiction as a ward may no longer be required.

(iii) The ward appears to come within the description of Section 300 and cannot be returned home safely.

(B) The court shall set a hearing within 20 judicial days of the date of the order described in subparagraph (A) to review the child welfare services department's decision and may either affirm its decision not to file a petition pursuant to Section 300 or order the child welfare services department to file a petition pursuant to Section 300. The notice of hearing under this subparagraph may be served electronically pursuant to Section 212.5.

(3) Vacate the order terminating jurisdiction over the minor as a dependent of the court, resume jurisdiction pursuant to Section 300 based on the prior petition filed pursuant to Section 325, and terminate the court's jurisdiction over the minor as a ward, if the minor was subject to an order for foster care placement described in Section 11402 as a dependent of the court at the time the court adjudged the minor to be a ward and assumed jurisdiction over the minor under Section 725.

(4) Continue its delinquency jurisdiction over a ward pursuant to Section 303 as a nonminor dependent, as defined in subdivision (v) of Section 11400, who is eligible to remain in foster care pursuant to Section 11403, if the ward is a nonminor and the court did not modify its jurisdiction as described in Section 450, unless the court finds that after reasonable and documented efforts, the ward cannot be located or does not wish to become a nonminor dependent. In making this finding and prior to entering an order terminating its delinquency jurisdiction, the court shall ensure that the ward has had an opportunity to confer with his or her counsel and has been informed of his or her options, including the right to reenter foster care placement by completing a voluntary reentry agreement as described in subdivision (z) of Section 11400 and to file a petition pursuant to subdivision (e) of Section 388 for the court to assume or resume transition jurisdiction over him or her pursuant to Section 450. The fact that a ward declines to be a nonminor dependent does not restrict the authority of the court to maintain delinquency jurisdiction pursuant to Section 607.

(5) Continue its delinquency jurisdiction.

(6) Terminate its delinquency jurisdiction if the ward does not come within the provisions of paragraphs (1) to (4), inclusive.

(c) If the court modifies jurisdiction, its order shall comply with the requirements of subdivision (f) of Section 241.1.

(d) This section shall not be construed as changing the requirements of Section 727.2 or 727.3 with respect to reunification of minors with their families or the establishment of an alternative permanent plan for minors for whom reunification is not pursued. *(Added by Stats.2011, c. 459 (A.B.212), § 15, eff. Oct. 4, 2011. Amended by Stats.2017, c. 319 (A.B.976), § 136, eff. Jan. 1, 2018.)*

Cross References

Minor who appears to be dependent child and ward of court, initial determination of status pursuant to jointly developed written protocol, creation of protocol, modification of juristic over dependent or ward placed in foster care, see Welfare and Institutions Code § 241.1.

Petition for hearing to resume dependency jurisdiction over former dependent or to assume or resume transition jurisdiction over former delinquent ward, see Welfare and Institutions Code § 388.

Supervision of child or nonminor whose jurisdiction is modified pursuant to this section and placed in foster care, see Welfare and Institutions Code § 300.3.

Research References

West's California Judicial Council Forms JV–361, First Review Hearing After Youth Turns 16 Years of Age—Information, Documents, and Services.

West's California Judicial Council Forms JV–362, Review Hearing for Youth Approaching 18 Years of Age—Information, Documents, and Services.

West's California Judicial Council Forms JV–363, Review Hearing for Youth 18 Years of Age or Older—Information, Documents, and Services.

West's California Judicial Council Forms JV–365, Termination of Juvenile Court Jurisdiction—Nonminor (Also Available in Spanish).

West's California Judicial Council Forms JV–367, Findings and Orders After Hearing to Consider Termination of Juvenile Court Jurisdiction Over a Nonminor.

West's California Judicial Council Forms JV–680, Findings and Orders for Child Approaching Majority—Delinquency.

West's California Judicial Council Forms JV–681, Attachment: Hearing for Dismissal—Additional Findings and Orders—Foster Care Placement—Delinquency.

§ 607.3. Hearing for termination of jurisdiction over ward satisfying specified criteria; duties of probation department

On and after January 1, 2012, at the hearing required under Section 607.2 for a ward who is 18 years of age or older and subject to an order for foster care placement as described in Section 11402, the probation department shall complete all of the following actions:

(a) Ensure that the nonminor has been informed of his or her options, including the right to reenter foster care placement by completing a voluntary reentry agreement as described in subdivision (z) of Section 11400 and the right to file a petition pursuant to subdivision (e) of Section 388 for the court to resume transition jurisdiction pursuant to Section 450.

(b) Ensure that the ward has had an opportunity to confer with his or her counsel.

(c) Ensure that the ward is present in court for the hearing, unless the ward has waived his or her right to appear in court and elects to appear by a telephone instead, or document the efforts it made to locate the ward when the ward is not available to appear at the hearing.

(d) Submit a report to the court describing all of the following:

(1) Whether it is in the ward's best interest for a court to assume or continue transition jurisdiction over the ward as a nonminor dependent pursuant to Section 450.

(2) Whether the ward has indicated that he or she does not want juvenile court jurisdiction to continue.

(3) Whether the ward has been informed of his or her right to reenter foster care by completing the voluntary reentry agreement as described in subdivision (z) of Section 11400.

(e) Submit to the court the completed 90–day transition plan.

(f) Submit to the court written verification that the information, documents, and services set forth in paragraphs (1) to (8), inclusive, of subdivision (e) of Section 391 have been provided to the ward.

(g) Submit to the court written verification that the requirements set forth in Section 607.5 have been completed. *(Added by Stats. 2011, c. 459 (A.B.212), § 16, eff. Oct. 4, 2011.)*

Research References

West's California Judicial Council Forms JV–361, First Review Hearing After Youth Turns 16 Years of Age—Information, Documents, and Services.
West's California Judicial Council Forms JV–362, Review Hearing for Youth Approaching 18 Years of Age—Information, Documents, and Services.
West's California Judicial Council Forms JV–363, Review Hearing for Youth 18 Years of Age or Older—Information, Documents, and Services.
West's California Judicial Council Forms JV–365, Termination of Juvenile Court Jurisdiction—Nonminor (Also Available in Spanish).
West's California Judicial Council Forms JV–367, Findings and Orders After Hearing to Consider Termination of Juvenile Court Jurisdiction Over a Nonminor.

§ 607.5. Termination of jurisdiction over ward designated dependent of court, or release of ward from facility that is not a foster care facility; information to be provided to person

(a) Notwithstanding any other provision of law, whenever the juvenile court terminates jurisdiction over a ward who has also been designated a dependent of the court, or upon release of a ward from a facility that is not a foster care facility, a probation officer or parole officer shall provide the person with, at a minimum, all of the following:

(1) A written notice stating that the person is a former foster child and may be eligible for the services and benefits that are available to a former foster child through public and private programs, including, but not limited to, any independent living program for former foster children. Providing the proof of dependency and wardship document described in All–County Letter 07–33 and Section 31–525.6 of Chapter 31–500 of Division 31 of the State Department of Social Services Manual of Policies and Procedures, as it existed on January 1, 2010, shall satisfy this requirement.

(2) Existing information described in Section 31–525.61 of Chapter 31–500 of Division 31 of the State Department of Social Services Manual of Policies and Procedures, as it existed on January 1, 2010, that informs the person of the availability of assistance to enable the person to apply for, and gain acceptance into, federal and state programs that provide benefits to former foster children, including, but not limited to, financial assistance, housing, and educational resources for which he or she may be eligible.

(3) Existing information described in Section 31–525.61 of Chapter 31–500 of Division 31 of the State Department of Social Services Manual of Policies and Procedures, as it existed on January 1, 2010, that informs the person of the availability of assistance to enable the person to apply for, and gain acceptance into, federal and state programs that provide independent living services to youth 16 years of age and over who may be eligible for services.

(b) This section shall apply to any ward who was previously adjudged a dependent child of the court pursuant to Section 300 or a child who at any time has been placed in foster care pursuant to Section 727.

(c) Nothing in this section shall be interpreted to alter or amend the obligations of probation officers under current law. *(Added by Stats.2010, c. 631 (S.B.945), § 2.)*

Cross References

Termination of transition jurisdiction over nonminor dependent, hearing, duties of supervising agency, general jurisdiction, see Welfare and Institutions Code § 452.

§ 608. Age of person at issue; method of examination to determine by scientific or medical test

In any case in which a person is alleged to be a person described in Section 601 or 602, or subdivision (a) of Section 604, and the age of the person is at issue and the court finds that a scientific or medical test would be of assistance in determining the age of the person, the court may consider ordering an examination of the minor using the method described in "The Permanent Mandibular Third Molar" from the Journal of Forensic Odonto-Stomatology, Vol. 1: No. 1: January–June 1983. *(Added by Stats.1990, c. 749 (A.B.3877), § 1.)*

ARTICLE 15. WARDS—TEMPORARY CUSTODY AND DETENTION

Section

§ 625. Temporary custody; peace officer; warrant

A peace officer may, without a warrant, take into temporary custody a minor:

(a) Who is under the age of 18 years when such officer has reasonable cause for believing that such minor is a person described in Section 601 or 602, or

(b) Who is a ward of the juvenile court or concerning whom an order has been made under Section 636 or 702, when such officer has reasonable cause for believing that person has violated an order of the juvenile court or has escaped from any commitment ordered by the juvenile court, or

(c) Who is under the age of 18 years and who is found in any street or public place suffering from any sickness or injury which requires care, medical treatment, hospitalization, or other remedial care.

In any case where a minor is taken into temporary custody on the ground that there is reasonable cause for believing that such minor is a person described in Section 601 or 602, or that he has violated an order of the juvenile court or escaped from any commitment ordered by the juvenile court, the officer shall advise such minor that anything he says can be used against him and shall advise him of his constitutional rights, including his right to remain silent, his right to have counsel present during any interrogation, and his right to have counsel appointed if he is unable to afford counsel. *(Added by Stats.1961, c. 1616, p. 3473, § 2. Amended by Stats.1967, c. 1355, p. 3192, § 1; Stats.1971, c. 1730, p. 3681, § 1; Stats.1971, c. 1748, p. 3767, § 69; Stats.1976, c. 1068, p. 4782, § 24.)*

Cross References

Citations for misdemeanors, minors under 18, see Penal Code § 853.6a.
Costs of support of a minor, liability, see Welfare and Institutions Code § 903.
Detention of minors, see Welfare and Institutions Code § 206 et seq.
Detention of minors taken into custody solely on grounds described in this section, see Welfare and Institutions Code § 207.
Petition to seal court records by person arrested for misdemeanor while a minor, see Penal Code § 851.7.
Probation officers as peace officers, see Welfare and Institutions Code § 283.
Temporary custody of dependent children, see Welfare and Institutions Code § 305.

Research References

4 Witkin, California Criminal Law 4th Pretrial Proceedings § 60 (2021), Juvenile Offenses.
3 Witkin, California Criminal Law 4th Punishment § 725 (2021), Where Minor was Not Convicted.

§ 625.1. Temporary custody; voluntary chemical testing

Any minor who is taken into temporary custody pursuant to subdivision (a) of Section 625, when the peace officer has reasonable cause for believing the minor is a person described in Section 602, or pursuant to subdivision (b) or (c) of Section 625, may be requested to submit to voluntary chemical testing of his or her urine for the purpose of determining the presence of alcohol or illegal drugs. The peace officer shall inform the minor that the chemical test is voluntary. The results of this test may be considered by the court in determining the disposition of the minor pursuant to Section 706 or 777. Unless otherwise provided by law, the results of such a test shall not be the basis of a petition filed by the prosecuting attorney to declare the minor a person described in Section 602, nor shall it be the basis for such a finding by a court pursuant to Section 702. *(Added by Stats.1989, c. 1117, § 6.)*

§ 625.2. Admonition preceding voluntary chemical testing

(a) Before administering the chemical test pursuant to Section 625.1, the peace officer shall give the following admonition: "I am asking you to take a voluntary urine test to test for the presence of drugs or alcohol in your body. You have the right to refuse to take this test. If you do take the test, it cannot be used as the basis for filing any additional charges against you. It can be used by a court for the purpose of sentencing. You have the right to telephone your parent or guardian before you decide whether or not to take this test."

(b) The admonition in subdivision (a) shall not be given when a chemical test is administered pursuant to Section 23612 of the Vehicle Code. *(Added by Stats.1989, c. 1117, § 7. Amended by Stats.2019, c. 497 (A.B.991), § 294, eff. Jan. 1, 2020.)*

§ 625.3. Release of minor who used firearm in committing a felony

Notwithstanding Section 625, a minor who is 14 years of age or older and who is taken into custody by a peace officer for the personal use of a firearm in the commission or attempted commission of a felony or any offense listed in subdivision (b) of Section 707 shall not be released until that minor is brought before a judicial officer. *(Added by Stats.1996, c. 843 (S.B.2165), § 1. Amended by Stats.1999, c. 996 (S.B.334), § 15; Initiative Measure (Prop. 21, § 20, approved March 7, 2000, eff. March 8, 2000).)*

Cross References

Felonies, definition and penalties, see Penal Code §§ 17, 18.

Research References

1 Witkin California Criminal Law 4th Introduction to Crimes § 140 (2021), Gang Violence and Juvenile Crime Prevention Act (Proposition 21).

§ 625.4. Law enforcement request for voluntary DNA reference sample from minor; conditions; detention for purpose of requesting sample; retention and expungement of sample; use and analysis of sample; civil liability to minor for violations of section; scope and application of section

(a) A law enforcement officer, employee of a law enforcement agency, or any agent thereof, shall not request that a voluntary DNA reference sample be collected directly from the person of a minor unless all of the following conditions are met:

(1) The minor consents in writing, after being verbally informed of the purpose and manner of the collection, the right to refuse consent, the right to sample expungement, and the right to consult with an attorney, parent, or legal guardian prior to providing consent.

(2) A specific parent or legal guardian identified by the minor, or an attorney representing the minor, is contacted, is provided the information specified in paragraph (1), is allowed to privately consult by telephone or in person with the minor, and, after that consultation, concurs with the minor's decision to consent.

(3) Local law enforcement provides the minor with a form for requesting expungement of the voluntary DNA buccal swab sample, if a sample is consented to and collected pursuant to this section.

(b) Nothing in subdivision (a) is intended to create a right to the appointment of counsel.

(c) The detention of a minor that occurs for the purpose of requesting a voluntary DNA reference sample directly from the person of that minor pursuant to this section shall not be unreasonably extended solely for the purpose of contacting a parent, legal guardian, or attorney pursuant to paragraph (2) of subdivision (a), if a parent, legal guardian, or attorney cannot be reached after reasonable attempts have been made.

(d) The court shall, in adjudicating the admissibility of a voluntary DNA reference sample taken directly from a minor pursuant to this section, consider the effect of any failure to comply with this section.

(e) The law enforcement agency obtaining a voluntary DNA reference sample directly from the person of a minor pursuant to this section shall determine within two years whether the person remains a suspect in a criminal investigation. If, within two years, the voluntary DNA reference sample that is collected pursuant to this section is not found to implicate the minor as a suspect in a criminal offense, the local law enforcement agency shall promptly expunge the sample and the DNA profile information from that voluntary DNA reference sample from the databases or data banks into which they have been entered.

(f) If the minor requests expungement of a voluntary DNA reference sample collected directly from the person of a minor pursuant to this section, the local law enforcement agency shall make reasonable efforts to promptly expunge the sample and the DNA profile information from that voluntary DNA reference sample from all DNA databases or data banks unless the voluntary DNA reference sample has implicated the minor as a suspect in a criminal investigation. If expungement occurs, law enforcement shall make reasonable efforts to notify the minor when the minor's DNA sample and DNA profile information have been expunged.

(g) A voluntary DNA reference sample taken directly from the person of a minor pursuant to this section and the DNA profile information from that voluntary DNA reference sample shall not be searched, analyzed, or compared to DNA samples or profiles in the investigation of crimes other than the investigation or investigations for which it was taken, unless that additional use is permitted by a court order.

(h) Any local law enforcement agency that is found by clear and convincing evidence to maintain a pattern and practice of collecting voluntary DNA reference samples directly from the person of a minor in violation of this section after January 1, 2019, shall be liable to each minor whose sample was inappropriately collected in the amount of five thousand dollars ($5,000) for each violation, plus attorney's fees and costs.

(i) The scope of this section is limited to the collection of voluntary DNA reference samples directly from the person of minors, and, as such, subdivisions (a) to (h), inclusive have no application to the collection and use of DNA under other circumstances, including, but not limited to, any of the following:

(1) The sample collection or use is expressly authorized pursuant to the state's DNA Act as set forth in the DNA and Forensic Identification Database and Data Bank Act of 1998, as amended, (Chapter 6 (commencing with Section 295) of Title 9 of Part 1 of the Penal Code.

(2) A DNA reference sample collection and analysis that occurs pursuant to a valid search warrant or court order or exigent circumstances.

(3) A DNA reference sample collection that occurs in the investigation or identification of a missing or abducted minor.

(4) Any DNA reference sample collected from a juvenile victim or suspected perpetrator of a sexual assault or other crime as authorized by law.

(5) Any DNA sample that is collected as evidence in a criminal investigation, such as evidence from a crime scene or an abandoned sample. *(Added by Stats.2018, c. 745 (A.B.1584), § 1, eff. Jan. 1, 2019.)*

Research References

4 Witkin, California Criminal Law 4th Introduction to Criminal Procedure § 58A (2021), (New) Voluntary DNA Reference Sample from Minor.

§ 625.5. Curfew ordinance violations; transport of minor to residence; warning citation; parental notification; collection of actual costs; fee waivers

(a) It is the intent of the Legislature in enacting this section to accomplish the following purposes:

(1) To safeguard the fiscal integrity of cities and counties by enabling them to recoup the law enforcement costs of identifying, detaining, and transporting minors who violate curfew ordinances to their places of residence.

(2) To encourage parents and legal guardians to exercise reasonable care, supervision, and control over their minor children so as to prevent them from committing unlawful acts.

(3) To help eradicate criminal street gang activity.

(b) This section shall only apply to a city, county, or city and county in which the governing body of the city, county, or city and county has enacted an ordinance prohibiting minors from remaining in or upon the public streets unsupervised after hours and has adopted a resolution to implement this section.

(c) Except as provided in subdivision (d), law enforcement personnel are authorized to temporarily detain any minor upon a reasonable suspicion based on articulable facts that the minor is in violation of the ordinance described in subdivision (b) and to transport that minor to his or her place of permanent or temporary residence within the state, whether the place of residence is located within or without the jurisdiction of the governing body, or to the custody of his or her parents or legal guardian. A law enforcement officer may decide not to temporarily detain and transport a minor if he or she determines that the minor has a legitimate reason based on extenuating circumstances for violating the ordinance.

(d) Upon the first violation of the ordinance described in subdivision (b), the law enforcement officer shall issue to the minor a warning citation regarding the consequences of a second violation of the ordinance. A designated representative of the governmental entity issuing the citation shall mail to the parents of the minor or legal guardian a notification that states that upon a second violation, the parents or legal guardian may be held liable for actual administrative and transportation costs, and that requires the parents or legal guardian to sign and return the notification. This notification shall include a space for the explanation of any circumstances relevant to an applicable exemption from the fee as provided by subdivision (e). This explanation shall be reviewed by a designated representative of the governmental entity that issued the citation and notification. If the explanation is found to be insufficient, the representative may request a consultation with the parents or legal guardian for the purpose of discussing the circumstances claimed to be relevant to an applicable exemption.

(e) A fee for the actual costs of administrative and transportation services for the return of the minor to his or her place of residence, or to the custody of his or her parents or legal guardian, may be charged jointly or severally to the minor, his or her parents, or legal guardian, in an amount not to exceed those actual costs. Upon petition of the person required to pay the fee, the governmental entity issuing the citation shall conduct a hearing as to the validity of the fees charged, and may waive payment of the fee by the minor, his or her parents, or legal guardian, upon a finding of good cause. If authorized by the governing body, the city, county, or city and county may charge this fee, in which case the city, county, or city and county may (1) provide for waiver of the payment of the fee by the parents or legal guardian upon a determination that the person has made reasonable efforts to exercise supervision and control over the minor, (2) provide for a determination of the ability to pay the fee and provide that the fee may be waived if neither the minor nor the parents or legal guardian has the ability to pay the fee, (3) provide for the performance of community service in lieu of imposition of the fee, and (4) provide for waiver of the payment of the fee by the parents or legal guardian upon a determination that the parents or legal guardian has limited physical or legal custody and control of the minor.

(f) In a civil action commenced by a city, county, or city and county to collect the fee, a court may waive payment of the fee by the minor, his or her parents, or legal guardian, upon a finding of good cause. *(Added by Stats.1994, c. 810 (A.B.3797), § 1.)*

Cross References

Hearing defined for purposes of this Article, see Welfare and Institutions Code § 727.4.
Reasonable efforts defined for purposes of this Article, see Welfare and Institutions Code § 727.4.

Research References

4 Witkin, California Criminal Law 4th Pretrial Proceedings § 2 (2021), Distinction: Temporary Detention.

§ 625.6. Custodial interrogation; consultation with legal counsel; application of section; effect on probation officers

(a) Prior to a custodial interrogation, and before the waiver of any Miranda rights, a youth 17 years of age or younger shall consult with legal counsel in person, by telephone, or by video conference. The consultation may not be waived.

(b) The court shall, in adjudicating the admissibility of statements of a youth 17 years of age or younger made during or after a custodial interrogation, consider the effect of failure to comply with subdivision (a) and, additionally, shall consider any willful violation of subdivision (a) in determining the credibility of a law enforcement officer under Section 780 of the Evidence Code.

(c) This section does not apply to the admissibility of statements of a youth 17 years of age or younger if both of the following criteria are met:

(1) The officer who questioned the youth reasonably believed the information the officer sought was necessary to protect life or property from an imminent threat.

(2) The officer's questions were limited to those questions that were reasonably necessary to obtain that information.

(d) This section does not require a probation officer to comply with subdivision (a) in the normal performance of the probation officer's duties under Section 625, 627.5, or 628. *(Added by Stats.2017, c. 681 (S.B.395), § 2, eff. Jan. 1, 2018. Amended by Stats.2020, c. 335 (S.B.203), § 2, eff. Jan. 1, 2021.)*

§ 625.7. Custodial interrogation; prohibition on use of threats, physical harm, deception, or psychologically manipulative interrogation tactics by law enforcement officers; criteria; lie detector test

Section operative July 1, 2024.

(a) During a custodial interrogation of a person 17 years of age or younger relating to the commission of a misdemeanor or felony, a law enforcement officer shall not employ threats, physical harm, deception, or psychologically manipulative interrogation tactics.

(b) As used in this section, the following terms have the following meanings:

(1) "Deception," includes, but is not limited to, the knowing communication of false facts about evidence, misrepresenting the accuracy of the facts, or false statements regarding leniency.

(2) "Psychologically manipulative interrogation tactics" include, but are not limited to the following:

(A) Maximization and minimization and other interrogation practices that rely on a presumption of guilt or deceit.

(i) Under this section, maximization includes techniques to scare or intimidate the person by repetitively asserting the person is guilty despite their denials, or exaggerating the magnitude of the charges or the strength of the evidence, including suggesting the existence of evidence that does not exist.

(ii) Under this section, minimization involves minimizing the moral seriousness of the offense, a tactic that falsely communicates that the conduct is justified, excusable, or accidental.

(B) Making direct or indirect promises of leniency, such as indicating the person will be released if the person cooperates.

(C) Employing the "false" or "forced" choice strategy, where the person is encouraged to select one of two options, both incriminatory, but one is characterized as morally or legally justified or excusable.

(c) Subdivision (a) does not apply to interrogations of a person 17 years of age or younger if both of the following criteria are met:

(1) The law enforcement officer who questioned the person reasonably believed the information the officer sought was necessary to protect life or property from an imminent threat.

(2) The questions by law enforcement officers were limited to those questions that were reasonably necessary to obtain information related to the imminent threat.

(d) This section does not prevent an officer from using a lie detector test as long it is voluntary and was not obtained through the use of threats, physical harm, deception, or psychologically manipulative interrogation tactics as defined herein, and the officer does not suggest that the lie detector results are admissible in court or misrepresent the lie detector results to the person.

(e) This section shall become operative on July 1, 2024.

(f) For the purposes of this section, "custodial interrogation" shall have the same meaning as defined in Section 859.5 of the Penal Code. *(Added by Stats.2022, c. 289 (A.B.2644), § 1, eff. Jan. 1, 2023, operative July 1, 2024.)*

§ 626. Temporary custody; alternative dispositions

An officer who takes a minor into temporary custody under the provisions of Section 625 may do any of the following:

(a) Release the minor.

(b) Deliver or refer the minor to a public or private agency with which the city or county has an agreement or plan to provide shelter care, counseling, or diversion services to minors so delivered. A placement of a child in a community care facility as specified in Section 1530.8 of the Health and Safety Code shall be made in accordance with Section 319.2 or 319. 3, as applicable, and with paragraph (8) or (9) of subdivision (e) of Section 361.2, as applicable.

(c) Prepare in duplicate a written notice to appear before the probation officer of the county in which the minor was taken into custody at a time and place specified in the notice. The notice shall also contain a concise statement of the reasons the minor was taken into custody. The officer shall deliver one copy of the notice to the minor or to a parent, guardian, or responsible relative of the minor and may require the minor or the minor's parent, guardian, or relative, or both, to sign a written promise to appear at the time and place designated in the notice. Upon the execution of the promise to appear, the officer shall immediately release the minor. The officer shall, as soon as practicable, file one copy of the notice with the probation officer. The written notice to appear may require that the minor be fingerprinted, photographed, or both, upon the minor's appearance before the probation officer, if the minor is a person described in Section 602 and he or she was taken into custody upon reasonable cause for the commission of a felony.

(d) Take the minor without unnecessary delay before the probation officer of the county in which the minor was taken into custody, or in which the minor resides, or in which the acts take place or the circumstances exist which are alleged to bring the minor within the provisions of Section 601 or 602, and deliver the custody of the minor to the probation officer. The peace officer shall prepare a concise written statement of the probable cause for taking the minor into temporary custody and the reasons the minor was taken into custody and shall provide the statement to the probation officer at the time the minor is delivered to the probation officer. In no case shall the officer delay the delivery of the minor to the probation officer for more than 24 hours if the minor has been taken into custody without a warrant on the belief that the minor has committed a misdemeanor.

In determining which disposition of the minor to make, the officer shall prefer the alternative which least restricts the minor's freedom of movement, provided that alternative is compatible with the best interests of the minor and the community. *(Added by Stats.1961, c. 1616, p. 3474, § 2. Amended by Stats.1963, c. 1486, p. 3052, § 1; Stats.1976, c. 1068, p. 4783, § 26; Stats.1978, c. 1372, p. 4552, § 2; Stats.1982, c. 461, § 3; Stats.1982, c. 1091, § 1; Stats.1984, c. 260, § 4; Stats.1989, c. 878, § 1; Stats.2001, c. 334 (A.B.701), § 1; Stats.2013, c. 21 (A.B.74), § 10, eff. June 27, 2013.)*

Cross References

Dependent children, similar provision, see Welfare and Institutions Code § 307.
Failure to perform written promise to appear as misdemeanor, see Welfare and Institutions Code § 214.
Felonies, definition and penalties, see Penal Code §§ 17, 18.
Investigation and report, minors delivered to public or private agencies, see Welfare and Institutions Code § 652.5.
Juvenile court and case records, petition for sealing and destruction of records, information on eligibility and procedures, see Welfare and Institutions Code § 781.
Misdemeanors, definition and penalties, see Penal Code §§ 17, 19 and 19.2.
Probation officer or social worker defined for purposes of this Chapter, see Welfare and Institutions Code § 215.
Relative defined for purposes of this Article, see Welfare and Institutions Code § 727.4.
Release by,
Court, see Welfare and Institutions Code § 635.
Probation officer, see Welfare and Institutions Code § 628.
Temporary custody of minor in county other than county in which minor comes with juvenile court jurisdiction, see Welfare and Institutions Code § 641.
Transfer of cases between counties, see Welfare and Institutions Code § 750 et seq.

Research References

4 Witkin, California Criminal Law 4th Illegally Obtained Evidence § 335 (2021), Transport to Police Station.

§ 626.5. Minors brought before juvenile court; alternative actions

If an officer who takes a minor into temporary custody under the provisions of Section 625 determines that the minor should be brought to the attention of the juvenile court, he or she shall thereafter take one of the following actions:

(a) He or she may prepare in duplicate a written notice to appear before the probation officer of the county in which the minor was taken in custody at a time and place specified in the notice. The notice shall also contain a concise statement of the reasons the minor was taken into custody. The officer shall deliver one copy of the notice to the minor or to a parent, guardian, or responsible relative of the minor and may require the minor or his or her parent, guardian, or relative, or both, to sign a written promise that either or both will appear at the time and place designated in the notice. Upon the execution of the promise to appear, the officer shall immediately release the minor. The officer shall, as soon as practicable, file one copy of the notice with the probation officer.

(b) He or she may take the minor without unnecessary delay before the probation officer of the county in which the minor was taken into custody, or in which the minor resides, or in which the acts took place or the circumstances exist which are alleged to bring the minor within the provisions of Section 601 or 602, and deliver the custody of the minor to the probation officer. The peace officer shall prepare a concise written statement of the probable cause for taking the minor into temporary custody and the reasons the minor was taken into custody and shall provide that statement to the probation officer at the time the minor is delivered to the probation officer. In no case shall he or she delay the delivery of the minor to the probation officer for more than 24 hours if the minor has been taken into custody without a warrant on the belief that he or she has committed a misdemeanor.

In determining which disposition of the minor he or she will make, the officer shall prefer the alternative which least restricts the minor's freedom of movement, provided that alternative is compatible with the best interests of the minor and the community. *(Added by Stats.1982, c. 1091, § 3. Amended by Stats.1989, c. 878, § 2.)*

Cross References

Misdemeanors, definition and penalties, see Penal Code §§ 17, 19 and 19.2.
Programs of supervision, see Welfare and Institutions Code § 654.

§ 626.6. Delivery of custody of minor to probation officer

Notwithstanding Section 626.5, any peace officer who takes a minor who is 14 years of age or older into temporary custody under Section 625.3 shall take the minor without unnecessary delay before the probation officer of the county in which the minor was taken into custody, or in which the minor resides, or in which the acts took place or the circumstances exist which are alleged to bring the minor within the provisions of Section 602, and deliver the custody of the minor to the probation officer. The peace officer shall prepare a concise written statement of the probable cause for taking the minor into temporary custody and the reasons the minor was taken into custody and shall provide that statement to the probation officer at the time the minor is delivered to the probation officer. *(Added by Stats.1996, c. 843 (S.B.2165), § 2.)*

Cross References

Probation officer or social worker defined for purposes of this Chapter, see Welfare and Institutions Code § 215.

§ 626.8. Custodial interrogation of person who is or may be adjudged ward of juvenile court; electronic recording or other record

(a) Subdivisions (a) to (d), inclusive, paragraphs (1) and (2) of subdivision (e) and subdivision (g) of Section 859.5 of the Penal Code shall apply to any custodial interrogation of a person who is or who may be adjudged a ward of the juvenile court pursuant to Section 602 related to murder, as listed in paragraph (1) of subdivision (b) of Section 707.

(b)(1) Except as otherwise provided in paragraph (2), Article 22 (commencing with Section 825) shall apply to any electronic recording or other record made pursuant to this section.

(2) The interrogating entity shall maintain an original or exact copy of any electronic recording made of a custodial interrogation until the person is no longer subject to the jurisdiction of the juvenile court, unless the person is transferred to a court of criminal jurisdiction. If the person is transferred to a court of criminal jurisdiction, subdivision (f) of Section 859.5 of the Penal Code shall apply. The interrogating entity may make one or more true, accurate, and complete copies of the electronic recording in a different format. *(Added by Stats.2013, c. 799 (S.B.569), § 3.)*

Research References

5 Witkin, California Criminal Law 4th Criminal Trial § 170A (2021), (New) Interrogation of Murder Suspect.

§ 627. Notice to parent or guardian; right to make telephone calls; notice to public defender

(a) When an officer takes a minor before a probation officer at a juvenile hall or to any other place of confinement pursuant to this article, * * * the officer shall take immediate steps to notify the minor's parent, guardian, or a responsible relative that such minor is in custody and the place where * * * the minor is being held.

(b) Immediately after being taken to a place of confinement pursuant to this article and, except where physically impossible, no later than one hour after * * * the minor has been taken into custody, the minor shall be advised and has the right to make at least two telephone calls from the place where * * * the minor is being held, one call completed to * * * the minor's parent or guardian, a responsible relative, or their employer, and another call completed to an attorney. The calls shall be at public expense, if the calls are completed to telephone numbers within the local calling area, and in the presence of a public officer or employee. Any public officer or employee who willfully deprives a minor taken into custody of their right to make such telephone calls is guilty of a misdemeanor.

(c) Immediately after being taken to a place of confinement pursuant to this article, and no later than two hours after a minor has been taken into custody, the probation officer shall immediately notify the public defender or if there is no public defender, the indigent defense provider for the county, that the minor has been taken into custody. *(Added by Stats.1961, c. 1616, p. 3474, § 2. Amended by Stats.1971, c. 1030, p. 1977, § 1; Stats.1980, c. 1092, p. 3505, § 2; Stats.2022, c. 289 (A.B.2644), § 2, eff. Jan. 1, 2023.)*

Cross References

Misdemeanors, definition and penalties, see Penal Code §§ 17, 19 and 19.2.
Probation officer or social worker defined for purposes of this Chapter, see Welfare and Institutions Code § 215.
Relative defined for purposes of this Article, see Welfare and Institutions Code § 727.4.

§ 627.5. Advice as to constitutional rights

In any case where a minor is taken before a probation officer pursuant to the provisions of Section 626 and it is alleged that such minor is a person described in Section 601 or 602, the probation officer shall immediately advise the minor and his parent or guardian that anything the minor says can be used against him and shall advise them of the minor's constitutional rights, including his right to remain silent, his right to have counsel present during any interrogation, and his right to have counsel appointed if he is unable to afford counsel. If the minor or his parent or guardian requests counsel, the probation officer shall notify the judge of the juvenile court of such request and counsel for the minor shall be appointed pursuant to Section 634. *(Added by Stats.1967, c. 1355, p. 3193, § 2.)*

Cross References

Probation officer or social worker defined for purposes of this Chapter, see Welfare and Institutions Code § 215.

§ 628. Investigation; release of minor; intent of Legislature; compliance with federal law; identification of adult relatives; notice of removal

(a)(1) Upon delivery to the probation officer of a minor who has been taken into temporary custody under the provisions of this article, the probation officer shall immediately investigate the circumstances of the minor and the facts surrounding * * * their being taken into custody and shall immediately release the minor to the custody of * * * their parent, legal guardian, or responsible relative unless it can be demonstrated upon the evidence before the court that continuance in the home is contrary to the minor's welfare and one or more of the following conditions exist:

(A) Continued detention of the minor is a matter of immediate and urgent necessity for the protection of the minor or reasonable necessity for the protection of the person or property of another.

(B) The minor is likely to flee the jurisdiction of the court.

(C) The minor has violated an order of the juvenile court.

(2) The probation officer's decision to detain a minor who is currently a dependent of the juvenile court pursuant to Section 300 or the subject of a petition to declare * * * the minor a dependent of the juvenile court pursuant to Section 300 and who has been removed from the custody of * * * their parent or guardian by the juvenile court shall not be based on any of the following:

(A) The minor's status as a dependent of the juvenile court or as the subject of a petition to declare * * * the minor a dependent of the juvenile court.

(B) A determination that continuance in the minor's current placement is contrary to the minor's welfare.

(C) The child welfare services department's inability to provide a placement for the minor.

(3) The probation officer shall immediately release a minor described in paragraph (2) to the custody of the child welfare services department or * * * the minor's current foster parent or other caregiver unless the probation officer determines that one or more of the conditions in paragraph (1) exist.

(4) This section does not limit a probation officer's authority to refer a minor to child welfare services.

(b) If the probation officer has reason to believe that the minor is at risk of entering foster care placement, as defined in paragraphs (1) and (2) of subdivision (d) of Section 727.4, the probation officer shall, as part of the investigation undertaken pursuant to subdivision (a), make reasonable efforts, as described in paragraph (5) of subdivision (d) of Section 727.4, to prevent or eliminate the need for removal of the minor from * * * their home.

(c) In any case in which there is reasonable cause for believing that a minor who is under the care of a physician or surgeon or a hospital, clinic, or other medical facility and cannot be immediately moved is a person described in subdivision (d) of Section 300, the minor shall be deemed to have been taken into temporary custody and delivered to the probation officer for the purposes of this chapter while * * * the minor is at the office of the physician or surgeon or that medical facility.

(d)(1) It is the intent of the Legislature that this subdivision shall comply with paragraph (29) of subsection (a) of Section 671 of Title 42 of the United States Code as added by the Fostering Connections to Success and Increasing Adoptions Act of 2008 (Public Law 110–351).[1] It is further the intent of the Legislature that the identification and notification of relatives shall be made as early as possible after the removal of a youth who is at risk of entering foster care placement.

(2) If the minor is detained and the probation officer has reason to believe that the minor is at risk of entering foster care placement, as defined in paragraphs (1) and (2) of subdivision (d) of Section 727.4, then the probation officer shall conduct, within 30 days, an investigation in order to identify and locate all grandparents, adult siblings, and other relatives of the child, as defined in paragraph (2) of subdivision (f) of Section 319, including any other adult relatives suggested by the parents. The probation officer shall provide to all adult relatives who are located, except when that relative's history of family or domestic violence makes notification inappropriate, within 30 days of the date on which the child is detained, written notification and shall also, whenever appropriate, provide oral notification, in person or by telephone, of all the following information:

(A) The child has been removed from the custody of * * * the child's parent or parents, or * * * guardians.

(B) An explanation of the various options to participate in the care and placement of the child and support for the child's family, including any options that may be lost by failing to respond. The notice shall provide information about providing care for the child, how to become a foster family home, approved relative or nonrelative extended family member, as defined in Section 362.7, or resource family home, and additional services and support that are available in out-of-home placements. The notice shall also include information regarding the Kin-GAP Program (Article 4.5 (commencing with Section 11360) of Chapter 2 of Part 3 of Division 9), the CalWORKs program for approved relative caregivers (Chapter 2 (commencing with Section 11200) of Part 3 of Division 9), adoption and adoption assistance (Chapter 2.1 (commencing with Section 16115) of Part 4 of Division 9), as well as other options for contact with the child, including, but not limited to, visitation. When oral notification is provided, the probation officer is not required to provide detailed information about the various options to help with the care and placement of the child.

(3)(A) The probation officer shall use due diligence in investigating the names and locations of the relatives, including any parent and alleged parent, pursuant to paragraph (2), including, but not limited to, asking the child in an age-appropriate manner about any parent, alleged parent, and relatives important to the child, consistent with the child's best interest, and obtaining information regarding the location of the child's parents, alleged parents, and adult relatives. Each county probation department shall do both of the following:

(i) Create and make public a procedure by which a parent and relatives of a child who has been removed from their parents or guardians may identify themselves to the county probation department and be provided with the notices required by paragraphs (1) and (2).

(ii) Notify the State Department of Social Services, on or before January 1, 2024, in an email or other correspondence, whether it has adopted one of the suggested practices for family finding described in All-County Letter 18–42 and, generally, whether the practice has been implemented through training, memoranda, manuals, or comparable documents. If a county probation department has not adopted one of the suggested practices for family finding described in All-County Letter 18–42, the county probation department shall provide a copy to the State Department of Social Services of its existing family finding policies and practices, as reflected in memoranda, handbooks, manuals, training manuals, or any other document, that are in existence prior to January 1, 2022.

(B) The due diligence required under subparagraph (A) shall include family finding. For purposes of this section, "family finding" means conducting an investigation, including, but not limited to, through a computer-based search engine, to identify relatives and kin and to connect a child or youth, who may be disconnected from their parents, with those relatives and kin in an effort to provide family support and possible placement. If it is known or there is reason to know that the child is an Indian child, as defined by Section 224.1, "family finding" also includes contacting the Indian child's tribe to identify relatives and kin.

(4) To the extent allowed by federal law as a condition of receiving funding under Title IV–E of the federal Social Security Act (42 U.S.C. Sec. 670 et seq.), if the probation officer did not conduct the identification and notification of relatives, as required in paragraph (2), but the court orders foster care placement, the probation officer shall conduct the investigation to find and notify relatives within 30 days of the placement order. Nothing in this section shall be construed to delay foster care placement for an individual child. *(Stats.1961, c. 1616, p. 3474, § 2. Amended by Stats.1967, c. 1356, p. 3196, § 1; Stats.1971, c. 1389, p. 2742, § 2; Stats.1971, c. 1729, p. 3677, § 2.5; Stats.1976, c. 1068, p. 4783, § 27; Stats.1976, c. 1071, p. 4819, § 15; Stats.1977, c. 579, p. 1921, § 195; Stats.1999, c. 997 (A.B.575), § 4; Stats.2001, c. 831 (A.B.1696), § 1; Stats.2009, c. 261 (A.B.938), § 2; Stats.2016, c. 646 (A.B.2813), § 1, eff. Jan. 1, 2017; Stats.2017, c. 732 (A.B.404), § 53, eff. Jan. 1, 2018; Stats.2022, c. 811 (S.B.384), § 2, eff. Jan. 1, 2023.)*

[1] For public law sections classified to the U.S.C.A., see USCA–Tables.

Cross References

Child support enforcement, California Parent Locator Service and Central Registry, California Child Support Automation System, see Family Code § 17506.

Probation officer or social worker defined for purposes of this Chapter, see Welfare and Institutions Code § 215.

Release by,
Arresting officer, see Welfare and Institutions Code § 626.
Court, see Welfare and Institutions Code § 635.

§ 628.1. Release of minor to home supervision

If the minor meets one or more of the criteria for detention under Section 628, but the probation officer believes that 24–hour secure detention is not necessary in order to protect the minor or the person or property of another, or to ensure that the minor does not flee the jurisdiction of the court, the probation officer shall proceed according to this section.

Unless one of the conditions described in paragraph (1), (2), or (3) of subdivision (a) of Section 628 exists, the probation officer shall release such minor to his or her parent, guardian, or responsible relative on home supervision. As a condition for such release, the probation officer shall require the minor to sign a written promise that he or she understands and will observe the specific conditions of home supervision release. As an additional condition for release, the probation officer also shall require the minor's parent, guardian, or responsible relative to sign a written promise, translated into a language the parent understands, if necessary, that he or she understands the specific conditions of home supervision release. These conditions may include curfew and school attendance requirements related to the protection of the minor or the person or property of another, or to the minor's appearances at court hearings. A minor who violates a specific condition of home supervision release which he or she has promised in writing to obey may be taken into custody and placed in secure detention, subject to court review at a detention hearing.

A minor on home supervision shall be entitled to the same legal protections as a minor in secure detention, including a detention hearing. *(Added by Stats.1976, c. 1071, p. 4820, § 16. Amended by Stats.1999, c. 996 (S.B.334), § 16.)*

Cross References

Hearing defined for purposes of this Article, see Welfare and Institutions Code § 727.4.

Home supervision defined, see Welfare and Institutions Code § 840 et seq.

Nonqualification as peace officer, see Welfare and Institutions Code § 842.

Placement of minor on home supervision, finding that criteria of this section are applicable, see Welfare and Institutions Code § 636.

Probation officer or social worker defined for purposes of this Chapter, see Welfare and Institutions Code § 215.

Programs of supervision, see Welfare and Institutions Code § 654.
Relative defined for purposes of this Article, see Welfare and Institutions Code § 727.4.
Writing defined, see Welfare and Institutions Code § 8.

Research References

West's California Judicial Council Forms JV–624, Terms and Conditions.

§ 628.2. Electronic monitoring device; minor; credit against maximum term of confinement

(a) As used in this section, the following definitions shall apply:

(1) "Minor" means a person under the jurisdiction of the juvenile court pursuant to Section 602.

(2) "Electronic monitoring" means technology used to identify, track, record, or otherwise monitor a minor's location or movement through electronic means.

(b) Electronic monitoring devices shall not be used to converse with a minor or to eavesdrop or record any conversation.

(c) A minor shall be entitled to have one day credited against the minor's maximum term of confinement for each day, or fraction thereof, that the minor serves on electronic monitoring. The provision of custody credits pursuant to this subdivision shall apply to custody credits earned beginning January 1, 2023.

(d) If electronic monitoring is imposed for a period greater than 30 days, the court shall hold a hearing every 30 days to ensure that the minor does not remain on electronic monitoring for an unreasonable length of time. In determining whether a length of time is unreasonable, the court shall consider whether there are less restrictive conditions of release that would achieve the rehabilitative purpose of the juvenile court. If less restrictive conditions of release are warranted, the court shall order removal of the electronic monitor or modify the terms of the electronic monitoring order to achieve the less restrictive alternative.

(e) The Department of Justice shall collect data regarding the use of electronic monitoring, as specified in Section 13012.4 of the Penal Code. *(Added by Stats.2022, c. 796 (A.B.2658), § 3, eff. Jan. 1, 2023.)*

§ 629. Written promise to appear

(a) As a condition for the release of a minor pursuant to Section 628.1 and subject to Sections 631 and 632, the probation officer shall require the minor to sign, and may also require his or her parent, guardian, or relative to sign, a written promise to appear before the probation officer at the juvenile hall or other suitable place designated by the probation officer at a specified time.

(b) A minor who is 14 years of age or older who is taken into custody by a peace officer for the commission or attempted commission of a felony offense shall not be released until the minor has signed a written promise to appear before the probation officer at the juvenile hall or other suitable place designated by the peace officer, or has been given an order to appear at the juvenile court on a date certain. The peace officer may also require the minor's parent, guardian, or relative to sign a written promise to appear at the same place designated for the minor. *(Added by Stats.1961, c. 1616, p. 3474, § 2. Amended by Stats.1999, c. 996 (S.B.334), § 17; Initiative Measure (Prop. 21, § 21, approved March 7, 2000, eff. March 8, 2000); Stats.2000, c. 663 (S.B.1603), § 1.)*

Cross References

Breach of promise to appear, see Welfare and Institutions Code § 214.
Felonies, definition and penalties, see Penal Code §§ 17, 18.
Probation officer or social worker defined for purposes of this Chapter, see Welfare and Institutions Code § 215.
Relative defined for purposes of this Article, see Welfare and Institutions Code § 727.4.
Written promise to appear before the probation officer, see Welfare and Institutions Code § 310.

Research References

West's California Judicial Council Forms JV–635, Promise to Appear—Juvenile Delinquency (Juvenile 14 Years or Older) (Also Available in Spanish).

§ 629.1. Retention of specified minors in custody until brought before judicial officer

Notwithstanding Section 628 or 628.1, whenever a minor who is 14 years of age or older is delivered to the custody of the probation officer pursuant to Section 626.6, the probation officer shall retain the minor in custody until such time that the minor can be brought before a judicial officer of the juvenile court pursuant to Section 632. *(Added by Stats.1996, c. 843 (S.B.2165), § 3.)*

Cross References

Probation officer or social worker defined for purposes of this Chapter, see Welfare and Institutions Code § 215.

§ 630. Filing petition; notice of hearing; privileges and rights of minor

(a) If the probation officer determines that the minor shall be retained in custody, he or she shall immediately proceed in accordance with Article 16 (commencing with Section 650) to cause the filing of a petition pursuant to Section 656 with the clerk of the juvenile court who shall set the matter for hearing on the detention calendar. Immediately upon filing the petition with the clerk of the juvenile court, if the minor is alleged to be a person described in Section 601 or 602, the probation officer or the prosecuting attorney shall serve the minor with a copy of the petition and notify him or her of the time and place of the detention hearing. The probation officer or the prosecuting attorney shall notify each parent or each guardian of the minor of the time and place of the hearing if the whereabouts of each parent or guardian can be ascertained by due diligence. Notice pursuant to this subdivision may be given orally and shall not be delivered electronically.

(b) In a hearing conducted pursuant to this section, the minor has a privilege against self-incrimination and has a right to confrontation by, and cross-examination of, any person examined by the court as provided in Section 635. *(Added by Stats.1961, c. 1616, p. 3474, § 2. Amended by Stats.1967, c. 1355, p. 3193, § 3; Stats.1968, c. 536, p. 1188, § 1; Stats.1972, c. 906, p. 1610, § 2; Stats.1975, c. 82, p. 150, § 1; Stats.1976, c. 1068, p. 4784, § 28; Stats.1977, c. 1241, p. 4181, § 2, eff. Oct. 1, 1977; Stats.2017, c. 319 (A.B.976), § 137, eff. Jan. 1, 2018.)*

Cross References

Filing petition, see Welfare and Institutions Code § 650.
Hearing defined for purposes of this Article, see Welfare and Institutions Code § 727.4.
Probation officer or social worker defined for purposes of this Chapter, see Welfare and Institutions Code § 215.
Rehearing for want of notice, see Welfare and Institutions Code § 637.

Research References

West's California Judicial Council Forms JV–625, Notice of Hearing—Juvenile Delinquency Proceeding (Also Available in Spanish).

§ 630.1. Notice of hearings

Upon reasonable notification by counsel representing the minor, his parents or guardian, the clerk of the court shall notify such counsel of the hearings in the manner provided for notice to the parent or guardian of the minor under this chapter. *(Added by Stats.1967, c. 507, p. 1852, § 1.)*

Cross References

Hearing defined for purposes of this Article, see Welfare and Institutions Code § 727.4.

Research References

West's California Judicial Council Forms JV–625, Notice of Hearing—Juvenile Delinquency Proceeding (Also Available in Spanish).

§ 631. Maximum time of detention of minor in absence of petition or criminal complaint; exceptions; review and approval of decision to detain

(a) Except as provided in subdivision (b), whenever a minor is taken into custody by a peace officer or probation officer, except when the minor willfully misrepresents himself or herself as 18 or more years of age, the minor shall be released within 48 hours after having been taken into custody, excluding nonjudicial days, unless within that period of time a petition to declare the minor a ward has been filed pursuant to this chapter or a criminal complaint against the minor has been filed in a court of competent jurisdiction.

(b) Except when the minor represents himself or herself as 18 or more years of age, whenever a minor is taken into custody by a peace officer or probation officer without a warrant on the belief that the minor has committed a misdemeanor that does not involve violence, the threat of violence, or possession or use of a weapon, and if the minor is not currently on probation or parole, the minor shall be released within 48 hours after having been taken into custody, excluding nonjudicial days, unless a petition has been filed to declare the minor to be a ward of the court and the minor has been ordered detained by a judge or referee of the juvenile court pursuant to Section 635. In all cases involving the detention of a minor pursuant to this subdivision, any decision to detain the minor more than 24 hours shall be subject to written review and approval by a probation officer who is a supervisor as soon as possible after it is known that the minor will be detained more than 24 hours. However, if the initial decision to detain the minor more than 24 hours is made by a probation officer who is a supervisor, the decision shall not be subject to review and approval.

(c) Whenever a minor who has been held in custody for more than 24 hours by the probation officer is subsequently released and no petition is filed, the probation officer shall prepare a written explanation of why the minor was held in custody for more than 24 hours. The written explanation shall be prepared within 72 hours after the minor is released from custody and filed in the record of the case. A copy of the written explanation shall be sent to the parents, guardian, or other person having care or custody of the minor. *(Added by Stats.1961, c. 1616, p. 3475, § 2. Amended by Stats.1969, c. 1008, p. 1979, § 1; Stats.1971, c. 1543, p. 3051, § 1; Stats.1972, c. 579, p. 1018, § 53; Stats.1976, c. 1068, p. 4784, § 29; Stats.1978, c. 1372, p. 4553, § 3; Stats.1985, c. 291, § 1; Stats.1989, c. 686, § 1.)*

Cross References

Courts closed for transaction of judicial business, conditions, see Government Code § 68106.
Misdemeanors, definition and penalties, see Penal Code §§ 17, 19 and 19.2.
Petition,
 Failure to file, see Welfare and Institutions Code § 655.
 Filing, see Welfare and Institutions Code § 650.
Probation officer or social worker defined for purposes of this Chapter, see Welfare and Institutions Code § 215.
Public calamities, destruction of court building, influx of criminal cases, emergency conditions, orderly operation of court, alternate judicial processes, see Government Code § 68115.

Research References

4 Witkin, California Criminal Law 4th Pretrial Proceedings § 71 (2021), Distinction: Detention of Juveniles.

§ 631.1. Misrepresentation of age

When a minor willfully misrepresents himself to be 18 or more years of age when taken into custody by a peace officer or probation officer, and this misrepresentation effects a material delay in investigation which prevents the filing of a petition pursuant to the provisions of this chapter or the filing of a criminal complaint against him in a court of competent jurisdiction within 48 hours, such petition or complaint shall be filed within 48 hours from the time his true age is determined, excluding nonjudicial days. If, in such cases, the petition or complaint is not filed within the time prescribed by this section, the minor shall be immediately released from custody. *(Added by Stats.1969, c. 1008, p. 1972, § 2. Amended by Stats.1972, c. 579, p. 1018, § 54.)*

Cross References

Probation officer or social worker defined for purposes of this Chapter, see Welfare and Institutions Code § 215.

§ 632. Detention hearing; exception; review and approval of decision not to bring minor before judge or referee within 24 hours

(a) Except as provided in subdivision (b), unless sooner released, a minor taken into custody under the provisions of this article shall, as soon as possible but in any event before the expiration of the next judicial day after a petition to declare the minor a ward or dependent child has been filed, be brought before a judge or referee of the juvenile court for a hearing to determine whether the minor shall be further detained. Such a hearing shall be referred to as a "detention hearing."

(b) Whenever a minor is taken into custody without a warrant on the belief that he or she has committed a misdemeanor not involving violence, a threat of violence, or possession or use of weapons, if the minor is not currently on probation or parole, he or she shall be brought before a judge or referee of the juvenile court for a detention hearing as soon as possible, but no later than 48 hours after having been taken into custody, excluding nonjudicial days, after a petition to declare the minor a ward has been filed. In all cases involving the detention of a minor pursuant to this subdivision where the minor will not be brought before the judge or referee of the juvenile court within 24 hours, the decision not to bring the minor before the judge or referee within 24 hours shall be subject to written review and approval by a probation officer who is a supervisor as soon as possible after it is known that the minor will not be brought before the judge or referee within 24 hours. However, if the decision not to bring the minor before the judge or referee within 24 hours is made by a probation officer who is a supervisor, the decision shall not be subject to review and approval.

(c) If the minor is not brought before a judge or referee of the juvenile court within the period prescribed by this section, he or she shall be released from custody. *(Added by Stats.1961, c. 1616, p. 3475, § 2. Amended by Stats.1963, c. 917, p. 2166, § 5; Stats.1978, c. 1372, p. 4553, § 4; Stats.1985, c. 291, § 2; Stats.1989, c. 686, § 2.)*

Cross References

Arrest warrants, see Penal Code § 813 et seq.
Courts closed for transaction of judicial business, conditions, see Government Code § 68106.
Hearing defined for purposes of this Article, see Welfare and Institutions Code § 727.4.
Hearings, wards, see Welfare and Institutions Code § 675 et seq.
Misdemeanors, definition and penalties, see Penal Code §§ 17, 19 and 19.2.
Nonsecure detention facilities, housing in secure facility pending detention hearing pursuant to this section for leaving nonsecure facility without permission, see Welfare and Institutions Code § 636.2.
Notice to parent, see Welfare and Institutions Code § 630.
Probation officer or social worker defined for purposes of this Chapter, see Welfare and Institutions Code § 215.

Public calamities, destruction of or danger to court building, influx of criminal cases, alternate judicial processes, see Government Code § 68115.

Research References

4 Witkin, California Criminal Law 4th Pretrial Proceedings § 71 (2021), Distinction: Detention of Juveniles.

§ 633. Informing minor as to reasons for custody; nature of proceedings; right to counsel

Upon his appearance before the court at the detention hearing, such minor and his parent or guardian, if present, shall first be informed of the reasons why the minor was taken into custody, the nature of the juvenile court proceedings, and the right of such minor and his parent or guardian to be represented at every stage of the proceedings by counsel. *(Added by Stats.1961, c. 1616, p. 3475, § 2.)*

Cross References

Appointment of counsel, see Welfare and Institutions Code §§ 317, 353, 700.
Hearing defined for purposes of this Article, see Welfare and Institutions Code § 727.4.
Information as to right to counsel, see Welfare and Institutions Code §§ 353, 700.
Notice relating to right to counsel, see Welfare and Institutions Code § 659.
Persons entitled to counsel, see Welfare and Institutions Code §§ 349, 679.

Research References

West's California Judicial Council Forms JV–642, Initial Appearance Hearing—Juvenile Delinquency.

§ 634. Appointment of counsel

When it appears to the court that the minor or his or her parent or guardian desires counsel but is unable to afford and cannot for that reason employ counsel, the court may appoint counsel. In a case in which the minor is alleged to be a person described in Section 601 or 602, the court shall appoint counsel for the minor if he or she appears at the hearing without counsel, whether he or she is unable to afford counsel or not, unless there is an intelligent waiver of the right of counsel by the minor. In any case in which it appears to the court that there is such a conflict of interest between a parent or guardian and child that one attorney could not properly represent both, the court shall appoint counsel, in addition to counsel already employed by a parent or guardian or appointed by the court to represent the minor or parent or guardian. In a county where there is no public defender, the court may fix the compensation to be paid by the county for service of that appointed counsel. *(Added by Stats.1961, c. 1616, p. 3475, § 2. Amended by Stats.1963, c. 2136, p. 4445, § 1; Stats.1967, c. 1355, p. 3193, § 4; Stats.1968, c. 1223, p. 2332, § 1; Stats.1970, c. 625, p. 1241, § 1; Stats.1971, c. 667, p. 1322, § 2; Stats.2017, c. 678 (S.B.190), § 7, eff. Jan. 1, 2018.)*

Cross References

Appointment of counsel, see Welfare and Institutions Code §§ 353, 700.
Compensation and expenses of court appointed counsel, see Welfare and Institutions Code § 218.
Hearing defined for purposes of this Article, see Welfare and Institutions Code § 727.4.
Liability for cost of legal services for a minor, see Welfare and Institutions Code § 903.1.
Modification of order of jurisdiction and assumption of transition jurisdiction as alternative to termination of jurisdiction, management of case, supervision, appointment of counsel, see Welfare and Institutions Code § 451.
Notice of right to counsel, see Welfare and Institutions Code §§ 316, 353, 633, 659, 700.
Persons entitled to counsel, see Welfare and Institutions Code §§ 316, 349, 679.
Primary responsibilities, representation of indigents, assistance and training for public defender offices, see Government Code § 15420.

Support and maintenance of ward or dependent child of the juvenile court, see Welfare and Institutions Code § 900 et seq.

Research References

5 Witkin, California Criminal Law 4th Criminal Trial § 178 (2021), When Counsel is Required.

§ 634.3. Duties of appointed counsel; adoption of rules of court

(a) Counsel appointed pursuant to Section 634 to represent youth in proceedings under Sections 601 and 602 shall do all of the following:

(1) Provide effective, competent, diligent, and conscientious advocacy and make rational and informed decisions founded on adequate investigation and preparation.

(2) Provide legal representation based on the client's expressed interests, and maintain a confidential relationship with the minor.

(3) Confer with the minor prior to each court hearing, and have sufficient contact with the minor to establish and maintain a meaningful and professional attorney-client relationship, including in the postdispositional phase.

(4) When appropriate, delinquency attorneys should consult with social workers, mental health professionals, educators, and other experts reasonably necessary for the preparation of the minor's case, and, when appropriate, seek appointment of those experts pursuant to Sections 730 and 952 of the Evidence Code.

(5) Nothing in this subdivision shall be construed to modify the role of counsel pursuant to subdivision (b) of Section 657.

(b) By July 1, 2016, the Judicial Council, in consultation and collaboration with delinquency defense attorneys, judges, and other justice partners including child development experts, shall adopt rules of court to do all of the following:

(1) Establish minimum hours of training and education, or sufficient recent experience in delinquency proceedings in which the attorney has demonstrated competence, necessary in order to be appointed as counsel in delinquency proceedings. Training hours that the State Bar has approved for Minimum Continuing Legal Education (MCLE) credit shall be counted toward the MCLE hours required of all attorneys by the State Bar.

(2) Establish required training areas that may include, but are not limited to, an overview of juvenile delinquency law and procedure, child and adolescent development, special education, competence and mental health issues, counsel's ethical duties, advocacy in the postdispositional phase, appellate issues, direct and collateral consequences of court involvement for a minor, and securing effective rehabilitative resources.

(3) Encourage public defender offices and agencies that provide representation in proceedings under Sections 601 and 602 to provide training on juvenile delinquency issues that the State Bar has approved for MCLE credit.

(4) Provide that attorneys practicing in juvenile delinquency courts shall be solely responsible for compliance with the training and education requirements adopted pursuant to this section. *(Added by Stats.2015, c. 369 (A.B.703), § 2, eff. Jan. 1, 2016.)*

Cross References

Primary responsibilities, representation of indigents, assistance and training for public defender offices, see Government Code § 15420.

Research References

West's California Judicial Council Forms JV–700, Declaration of Eligibility for Appointment to Represent Youth in Delinquency Court.

§ 634.6. Counsel; appearance on behalf of minor; continuity in representation

Any counsel upon entering an appearance on behalf of a minor shall continue to represent that minor unless relieved by the court upon the substitution of other counsel or for cause. *(Added by Stats.1975, c. 205, p. 578, § 2.)*

Cross References

Primary responsibilities, representation of indigents, assistance and training for public defender offices, see Government Code § 15420.

§ 635. Examination by court; order releasing minor from custody; factors in determination; written report by probation officer

(a) The court will examine the minor, his or her parent, legal guardian, or other person having relevant knowledge, hear relevant evidence the minor, his or her parent, legal guardian, or counsel desires to present, and, unless it appears that the minor has violated an order of the juvenile court or has escaped from the commitment of the juvenile court or that it is a matter of immediate and urgent necessity for the protection of the minor or reasonably necessary for the protection of the person or property of another that he or she be detained or that the minor is likely to flee to avoid the jurisdiction of the court, the court shall make its order releasing the minor from custody.

(b)(1) The circumstances and gravity of the alleged offense may be considered, in conjunction with other factors, to determine whether it is a matter of immediate and urgent necessity for the protection of the minor or reasonably necessary for the protection of the person or property of another that the minor be detained.

(2) If a minor is a dependent of the court pursuant to Section 300, the court's decision to detain shall not be based on the minor's status as a dependent of the court or the child welfare services department's inability to provide a placement for the minor.

(c)(1) The court shall order release of the minor from custody unless a prima facie showing has been made that the minor is a person described in Section 601 or 602.

(2) If the court orders release of a minor who is a dependent of the court pursuant to Section 300, the court shall order the child welfare services department either to ensure that the minor's current foster parent or other caregiver takes physical custody of the minor or to take physical custody of the minor and place the minor in a licensed or approved placement.

(d) If the probation officer has reason to believe that the minor is at risk of entering foster care placement as described in Section 11402, then the probation officer shall submit a written report to the court containing all of the following:

(1) The reasons why the minor has been removed from the parent's custody.

(2) Any prior referrals for abuse or neglect of the minor or any prior filings regarding the minor pursuant to Section 300.

(3) The need, if any, for continued detention.

(4) The available services that could facilitate the return of the minor to the custody of the minor's parents or guardians.

(5) Whether there are any relatives who are able and willing to provide effective care and control over the minor. *(Added by Stats.1961, c. 1616, p. 3475, § 2. Amended by Stats.1976, c. 1070, p. 4809, § 1.5, eff. Sept. 21, 1976; Stats.1976, c. 1071, p. 4831, § 36; Stats.1977, c. 1241, p. 4182, § 3, eff. Oct. 1, 1977; Stats.1999, c. 997 (A.B.575), § 5; Stats.2014, c. 760 (A.B.388), § 5, eff. Jan. 1, 2015.)*

Cross References

At risk of entering foster care defined for purposes of this Article, see Welfare and Institutions Code § 727.4.
Continuance, see Welfare and Institutions Code §§ 322, 638.
Foster care defined for purposes of this Article, see Welfare and Institutions Code § 727.4.
Hearings, see Welfare and Institutions Code §§ 345 et seq., 675 et seq.
Judicial findings and order on detention or placement of child, see Welfare and Institutions Code § 319.
Order for,
Detention, see Welfare and Institutions Code § 636.
Reappearance, see Welfare and Institutions Code §§ 323, 639.
Probation officer or social worker defined for purposes of this Chapter, see Welfare and Institutions Code § 215.
Rehearing, see Welfare and Institutions Code §§ 321, 637.
Relative defined for purposes of this Article, see Welfare and Institutions Code § 727.4.
Release by,
Arresting officer, see Welfare and Institutions Code §§ 307, 626.
Probation officer, see Welfare and Institutions Code §§ 309, 628.

Research References

West's California Judicial Council Forms JV–642, Initial Appearance Hearing—Juvenile Delinquency.

§ 635.1. Minors in need of specialized mental health treatment; notification of county mental health department

When the court finds a minor to be a person described by Section 602 and believes the minor may need specialized mental health treatment while the minor is unable to reside in his or her natural home, the court shall notify the director of the county mental health department in the county where the minor resides. The county mental health department shall perform the duties required under Section 5697.5 for all those minors.

Nothing in this section shall restrict the provision of emergency psychiatric services to those minors who have not yet reached the point of adjudication or disposition, nor shall it operate to restrict evaluations at an earlier stage of the proceedings or to restrict the use of Sections 4011.6 and 4011.8 of the Penal Code. *(Added by Stats.1985, c. 1286, § 2, eff. Sept. 30, 1985. Amended by Stats.2001, c. 854 (S.B.205), § 74.)*

Cross References

Detention or sentence to adult institutions for adults who committed sex offenses, see Welfare and Institutions Code § 208.
Mental health evaluations, recommendations, and dispositional procedures for minors, see Welfare and Institutions Code § 710 et seq.
Petition by juvenile court to petition services of psychiatrists for treatment of a minor, see Welfare and Institutions Code § 741.

§ 636. Order detaining minor in juvenile hall or on home supervision; documentation supporting detention recommendation; criteria; findings; parental cooperation

(a) If it appears upon the hearing that the minor has violated an order of the juvenile court or has escaped from a commitment of the juvenile court or that it is a matter of immediate and urgent necessity for the protection of the minor or reasonably necessary for the protection of the person or property of another that the minor be detained or that the minor is likely to flee to avoid the jurisdiction of the court, and that continuance in the home is contrary to the minor's welfare, the court may make its order that the minor be detained in the juvenile hall or other suitable place designated by the juvenile court for a period not to exceed 15 judicial days and shall enter the order together with its findings of fact in support thereof in the records of the court. The circumstances and gravity of the alleged offense may be considered, in conjunction with other factors, to determine whether it is a matter of immediate and urgent necessity for the protection of the minor or the person or property of another that the minor be detained. If a minor is a dependent of the court pursuant to Section 300, the court's decision to detain shall not be based on the minor's status as a dependent of the court or the child welfare services department's inability to provide a placement for the minor.

(b) If the court finds that the criteria of Section 628.1 are applicable, the court shall place the minor on home supervision for a period not to exceed 15 judicial days, and shall enter the order together with its findings of fact in support thereof in the records of the court. If the court releases the minor on home supervision, the court may continue, modify, or augment any conditions of release previously imposed by the probation officer, or may impose new conditions on a minor released for the first time. If there are new or modified conditions, the minor shall be required to sign a written promise to obey those conditions pursuant to Section 628.1.

(c) If the probation officer is recommending that the minor be detained, the probation officer shall submit to the court documentation, as follows:

(1) Documentation that continuance in the home is contrary to the minor's welfare shall be submitted to the court as part of the detention report prepared pursuant to Section 635.

(2) Documentation that reasonable efforts were made to prevent or eliminate the need for removal of the minor from the home and documentation of the nature and results of the services provided shall be submitted to the court either as part of the detention report prepared pursuant to Section 635, or as part of a case plan prepared pursuant to Section 636.1, but in no case later than 60 days from the date of detention.

(d) Except as provided in subdivision (e), before detaining the minor, the court shall determine whether continuance in the home is contrary to the minor's welfare and whether there are available services that would prevent the need for further detention. The court shall make that determination on a case-by-case basis and shall make reference to the documentation provided by the probation officer or other evidence relied upon in reaching its decision.

(1) If the minor can be returned to the custody of the minor's parent or legal guardian at the detention hearing, through the provision of services to prevent removal, the court shall release the minor to the physical custody of the minor's parent or legal guardian and order that those services be provided.

(2) If the minor cannot be returned to the custody of the minor's parent or legal guardian at the detention hearing, the court shall state the facts upon which the detention is based. The court shall make the following findings on the record and reference the probation officer's report or other evidence relied upon to make its setting determinations:

(A) Whether continuance in the home of the parent or legal guardian is contrary to the minor's welfare.

(B) Whether reasonable efforts have been made to safely maintain the minor in the home of the minor's parent or legal guardian and to prevent or eliminate the need for removal of the minor from the minor's home. This finding shall be made at the detention hearing if possible, but in no case later than 60 days following the minor's removal from the home.

(3) If the minor cannot be returned to the custody of the minor's parent or legal guardian at the detention hearing, the court shall make the following orders:

(A) The probation officer shall provide services as soon as possible to enable the minor's parent or legal guardian to obtain any assistance as may be needed to enable the parent or guardian to effectively provide the care and control necessary for the minor to return to the home.

(B) The minor's placement and care shall be the responsibility of the probation department pending disposition or further order of the court.

(4) If the matter is set for rehearing pursuant to Section 637, or continued pursuant to Section 638, or continued for any other reason, the court shall find that the continuance of the minor in the parent's or guardian's home is contrary to the minor's welfare at the initial petition hearing or order the release of the minor from custody.

(e) For a minor who is a dependent of the court pursuant to Section 300, the court's decision to detain the minor shall not be based on a finding that continuance in the minor's current placement is contrary to the minor's welfare. If the court determines that continuance in the minor's current placement is contrary to the minor's welfare, the court shall order the child welfare services department to place the minor in another licensed or approved placement.

(f) For a placement made on or after October 1, 2021, each placement of the minor in a short-term residential therapeutic program shall comply with the requirements of Section 4096 and be reviewed by the court pursuant to Section 727.12.

(g) For a placement made on or after July 1, 2022, each placement of the minor in a community treatment facility shall comply with the requirements of Section 4096 and be reviewed by the court pursuant to Section 727.12.

(h) Whether the minor is returned home or detained, the court shall order the minor's parent or guardian to cooperate with the probation officer in obtaining those services described in paragraph (1) of, or in subparagraph (A) of paragraph (3) of, subdivision (d). *(Added by Stats.1961, c. 1616, p. 3476, § 2. Amended by Stats.1976, c. 1070, p. 4810, § 2, eff. Sept. 21, 1976; Stats.1976, c. 1071, p. 4831, § 37; Stats.1999, c. 997 (A.B.575), § 6; Stats.2001, c. 831 (A.B.1696), § 2; Stats.2004, c. 332 (A.B.2795), § 1; Stats.2005, c. 22 (S.B.1108), § 216; Stats.2014, c. 760 (A.B.388), § 6, eff. Jan. 1, 2015; Stats.2021, c. 86 (A.B.153), § 25, eff. July 16, 2021; Stats.2022, c. 50 (S.B.187), § 23, eff. June 30, 2022.)*

Cross References

Continuance, see Welfare and Institutions Code §§ 322, 638.
Establishment of home supervision program in each county for minors by probation department, see Welfare and Institutions Code § 840 et seq.
Hearing defined for purposes of this Article, see Welfare and Institutions Code § 727.4.
Judgments and orders, see Welfare and Institutions Code §§ 360 et seq., 725 et seq.
Probation officer or social worker defined for purposes of this Chapter, see Welfare and Institutions Code § 215.
Reasonable efforts defined for purposes of this Article, see Welfare and Institutions Code § 727.4.
Rehearing, see Welfare and Institutions Code §§ 321, 637.
Temporary custody of minor violating court order, see Welfare and Institutions Code § 625.

Research References

West's California Judicial Council Forms JV–642, Initial Appearance Hearing—Juvenile Delinquency.

§ 636.1. Case plans for detained minors; requirements

(a) When a minor is detained pursuant to Section 636 following a finding by the court that continuance in the home is contrary to the minor's welfare and the minor is at risk of entering foster care, the probation officer shall, within 60 calendar days of initial removal, or by the date of the disposition hearing, whichever occurs first, complete a case plan.

(b) If the probation officer believes that reasonable efforts by the minor, his or her parent or legal guardian, and the probation officer will enable the minor to safely return home, the case plan shall focus on those issues and activities associated with those efforts, including a description of the strengths and needs of the minor and his or her family and identification of the services that will be provided to the minor and his or her family in order to reduce or eliminate the need for the minor to be placed in foster care and make it possible for the minor to safely return to his or her home.

(c) If, based on the information available to the probation officer, the probation officer believes that foster care placement is the most appropriate disposition, the case plan shall include all the information required by Section 706.6. *(Added by Stats.1999, c. 997 (A.B.575), § 7. Amended by Stats.2001, c. 831 (A.B.1696), § 3; Stats.2004, c. 332 (A.B.2795), § 2.)*

Cross References

At risk of entering foster care defined for purposes of this Article, see Welfare and Institutions Code § 727.4.
Foster care defined for purposes of this Article, see Welfare and Institutions Code § 727.4.
Hearing defined for purposes of this Article, see Welfare and Institutions Code § 727.4.
Probation officer or social worker defined for purposes of this Chapter, see Welfare and Institutions Code § 215.
Reasonable efforts defined for purposes of this Article, see Welfare and Institutions Code § 727.4.

§ 636.2. Nonsecure detention facilities; operation; criteria for detention therein

The probation officer may operate and maintain nonsecure detention facilities, or may contract with public or private agencies offering such services, for those minors who are not considered escape risks and are not considered a danger to themselves or to the person or property of another. Criteria to be considered for detention in such facilities shall include, but not be limited to: (a) the nature of the offense, (b) the minor's previous record including escapes from secure detention facilities, (c) lack of criminal sophistication, and (d) the age of the minor. A minor detained in such facilities who leaves the same without permission may be housed in a secure facility following his apprehension, pending a detention hearing pursuant to Section 632. *(Added by Stats.1976, c. 1071, p. 4832, § 19. Amended by Stats.1977, c. 1241, p. 4182, § 3.5, eff. Oct. 1, 1977.)*

Cross References

Hearing defined for purposes of this Article, see Welfare and Institutions Code § 727.4.
Probation officer or social worker defined for purposes of this Chapter, see Welfare and Institutions Code § 215.

§ 637. Rehearing; continuance

When a hearing is held under the provisions of this article and no parent or guardian of such minor is present and no parent or guardian has had actual notice of the hearing, a parent or guardian of such minor may file his affidavit setting forth such facts with the clerk of the juvenile court and the clerk shall immediately set the matter for rehearing at a time within 24 hours, excluding Sundays and nonjudicial days from the filing of the affidavit. Upon the rehearing, the court shall proceed in the same manner as upon the original hearing.

If the minor or, if the minor is represented by an attorney, the minor's attorney, requests evidence of the prima facie case, a rehearing shall be held within three judicial days to consider evidence of the prima facie case. If the prima facie case is not established, the minor shall be released from detention.

When the court ascertains that the rehearing cannot be held within three judicial days because of the unavailability of a witness, a reasonable continuance may be granted for a period not to exceed five judicial days. *(Added by Stats.1961, c. 1616, p. 3476, § 2. Amended by Stats.1975, c. 1266, p. 3324, § 1.)*

Cross References

Continuance, see Welfare and Institutions Code §§ 322, 638.
Courts closed for transaction of judicial business, conditions, see Government Code § 68106.
Examination of minor, see Welfare and Institutions Code §§ 319, 635.
Hearing defined for purposes of this Article, see Welfare and Institutions Code § 727.4.
Notice, duty of probation officer, see Welfare and Institutions Code § 630.
Public calamities, destruction of or danger to court building, influx of criminal cases, alternate judicial processes, see Government Code § 68115.

§ 638. Continuance; motion

Upon motion of the minor or a parent or guardian of such minor, the court shall continue any hearing or rehearing held under the provisions of this article for one day, excluding Sundays and nonjudicial days. *(Added by Stats.1961, c. 1616, p. 3476, § 2.)*

Cross References

Examination, see Welfare and Institutions Code §§ 319, 635.
Hearing defined for purposes of this Article, see Welfare and Institutions Code § 727.4.
Rehearing, see Welfare and Institutions Code § 321.

Research References

West's California Judicial Council Forms JV–688, Continuance—Juvenile Delinquency.

§ 639. Order requiring reappearance of minor, parent or guardian

Upon any hearing or rehearing under the provisions of this article, the court may order such minor or any parent or guardian of such minor who is present in court to again appear before the court or the probation officer or the county financial evaluation officer at a time and place specified in said order. *(Added by Stats.1961, c. 1616, p. 3476, § 2. Amended by Stats.1985, c. 1485, § 11.)*

Cross References

Examination, see Welfare and Institutions Code §§ 319, 635.
Hearing defined for purposes of this Article, see Welfare and Institutions Code § 727.4.
Judgments and orders, see Welfare and Institutions Code §§ 360 et seq., 725 et seq.
Probation officer or social worker defined for purposes of this Chapter, see Welfare and Institutions Code § 215.

Research References

West's California Judicial Council Forms JV–625, Notice of Hearing—Juvenile Delinquency Proceeding (Also Available in Spanish).

§ 641. County of custody; petition and warrant of requesting county

Whenever any minor is taken into temporary custody under the provisions of this article in any county other than the county in which the minor is alleged to be within or to come within the jurisdiction of the juvenile court, which county is referred to herein as the requesting county, the officer who has taken the minor into temporary custody may notify the law enforcement agency in the requesting county of the fact that the minor is in custody. When a law enforcement officer, of such requesting county files a petition pursuant to Section 656 with the clerk of the juvenile court of his respective county and secures a warrant therefrom, he shall forward said warrant, or a telegraphic copy thereof to the officer who has the minor in temporary custody as soon as possible within 48 hours, excluding Sundays and nonjudicial days, from the time said juvenile was taken into temporary custody. Thereafter an officer from said requesting county shall take custody of the minor within five days, in the county in which the minor is in temporary custody, and shall take the minor before the juvenile court judge who issued the warrant, or before some other juvenile court of the same county without unnecessary delay. If the minor is not brought before a judge of the juvenile court within the period prescribed by this section, he must be released from custody. *(Added by Stats.1961, c. 1616, p. 3476, § 2.)*

Cross References

Warrant of arrest against,
Minor, see Welfare and Institutions Code §§ 340, 663.
Parent or guardian, see Welfare and Institutions Code §§ 339, 662.

ARTICLE 16. WARDS—COMMENCEMENT OF PROCEEDINGS

Section

§ 650. Commencement of proceedings

(a) Juvenile court proceedings to declare a minor a ward of the court pursuant to Section 601 are commenced by the filing of a petition by the probation officer except as specified in subdivision (b).

(b) Juvenile court proceedings to declare a minor a ward of the court pursuant to subdivision (e) of Section 601.3 may be commenced by the filing of a petition by the probation officer or the district attorney after consultation with the probation officer.

(c) Juvenile court proceedings to declare a minor a ward of the court pursuant to Section 602 are commenced by the filing of a petition by the prosecuting attorney. *(Added by Stats.1982, c. 1088, § 6. Amended by Stats.1984, c. 1412, § 3; Stats.1991, c. 1202 (S.B.377), § 15.)*

Cross References

Certification to juvenile court of persons under eighteen years of age, see Welfare and Institutions Code § 604.
Commitment of mentally disordered persons, see Welfare and Institutions Code § 5000 et seq.
Compliance with this section before trial on an accusatory pleading, see Welfare and Institutions Code § 603.
Contents of petition, see Welfare and Institutions Code § 656.
Effect of filing on criminal prosecution, see Welfare and Institutions Code § 606.
Jurisdiction of juvenile court, wards, see Welfare and Institutions Code § 601.
Non-criminal nature of proceedings, see Welfare and Institutions Code § 203.
Petition for detention, see Welfare and Institutions Code § 630.
Probation officer or social worker defined for purposes of this Chapter, see Welfare and Institutions Code § 215.
Refusal to commence proceedings, review, see Welfare and Institutions Code § 655.
Suspension of limitations, see Welfare and Institutions Code § 605.
Traffic charge, notice in lieu of petition, see Welfare and Institutions Code § 257.

Research References

West's California Judicial Council Forms JV–640, Delinquency Court Proceeding Findings and Orders.

§ 651. Venue

Proceedings under this chapter may be commenced either in the juvenile court for the county in which a minor resides, or in which a minor is found, or in which the circumstances exist or acts take place to bring a minor within the provisions of Section 601 or Section 602. *(Added by Stats.1982, c. 1088, § 9. Amended by Stats.1984, c. 260, § 6; Stats.1984, c. 1412, § 5.)*

Cross References

Petition to free minor from parental control, see Family Code § 7845.
Residence of minor, see Welfare and Institutions Code § 17.1.
Return of nonresident minors to legal residence, see Welfare and Institutions Code § 738.
Transfer of cases, see Welfare and Institutions Code § 750 et seq.

§ 651.5. "Community-based organization" defined

For purposes of this article, "community-based organization" means a public or private nonprofit organization of demonstrated effectiveness that is representative of a community or significant segments of a community and provides educational, physical, or mental health, recreational, arts, and other youth development or related services to individuals in the community. *(Added by Stats. 2020, c. 323 (A.B.901), § 9, eff. Jan. 1, 2021.)*

§ 652. Reasonable cause; investigation

Whenever the probation officer has cause to believe that there was or is within the county, or residing therein, a person within the provisions of Section 601 or 602, the probation officer shall immediately make an investigation he or she deems necessary to determine whether proceedings in the juvenile court should be commenced, including whether reasonable efforts, as described in paragraph (5) of subdivision (d) of Section 727.4, have been made to prevent or eliminate the need for removal of the minor from his or her home. However, this section does not require an investigation by the probation officer with respect to a minor delivered or referred to an agency pursuant to subdivision (b) of Section 626. *(Added by Stats.1961, c. 1616, p. 3477, § 2. Amended by Stats.1976, c. 1068, p. 4785, § 35; Stats.1982, c. 1091, § 2; Stats.1984, c. 260, § 7; Stats.1984, c. 1227, § 3; Stats.1999, c. 997 (A.B.575), § 8.)*

Cross References

Investigation by probation officer, see Welfare and Institutions Code §§ 281, 628, 653, 654.
Probation officer or social worker defined for purposes of this Chapter, see Welfare and Institutions Code § 215.

Probation officers, see Welfare and Institutions Code § 270 et seq.

§ 652.5. Agency receiving minor referred or delivered by officers; investigation; service program; notification of referring officer

(a) Whenever an officer refers or delivers a minor pursuant to subdivision (b) of Section 626, the agency to which the minor is referred or delivered shall immediately make such investigation as that agency deems necessary to determine what disposition of the minor that agency shall make and shall initiate a service program for the minor when appropriate.

(b) The service program for any minor referred or delivered to the agency for any act described in Section 602 shall include constructive assignments that will help the minor learn to be responsible for his or her actions. The assignments may include, but not be limited to, requiring the minor to repair damaged property or to make other appropriate restitution, or requiring the minor to participate in an educational or counseling program.

(c) If the referral agency does not initiate a service program on behalf of a minor referred to the agency within 20 calendar days, or initiate a service program on behalf of a minor delivered to the agency within 10 days, that agency shall immediately notify the referring officer of that decision in writing. The referral agency shall retain a copy of that written notification for 30 days. *(Added by Stats.1984, c. 1227, § 4. Amended by Stats.1990, c. 258 (A.B.3741), § 1; Stats.2017, c. 678 (S.B.190), § 8, eff. Jan. 1, 2018.)*

§ 653. Application to commence proceedings; form; contents; investigation

Whenever any person applies to the probation officer or the district attorney in accordance with subdivision (e) of Section 601.3, to commence proceedings in the juvenile court, the application shall be in the form of an affidavit alleging that there was or is within the county, or residing therein, a minor within the provisions of Section 601 and setting forth facts in support thereof. The probation officer or the district attorney, in consultation with the probation officer, shall immediately make any investigation he or she deems necessary to determine whether proceedings in the juvenile court should be commenced. *(Added by Stats.1982, c. 1088, § 12. Amended by Stats.1984, c. 1412, § 7; Stats.1991, c. 1202 (S.B.377), § 16; Stats. 1992, c. 427 (A.B.3355), § 176; Stats.1993, c. 59 (S.B.443), § 21, eff. June 30, 1993; Stats.1994, c. 450 (A.B.1180), § 1.)*

Cross References

Investigation by probation officer, see Welfare and Institutions Code §§ 281, 628, 652.
Petition, see Welfare and Institutions Code § 656.
Probation officer or social worker defined for purposes of this Chapter, see Welfare and Institutions Code § 215.
Review of failure to file petition, see Welfare and Institutions Code § 655.
Traffic charge, notice in lieu of petition, see Welfare and Institutions Code § 257.

§ 653.1. Alleged commission of serious crime by minor 14 years of age or older; submission of affidavit to prosecuting attorney

Notwithstanding Section 653, in the case of an affidavit alleging that the minor is a person described in Section 602, the probation officer shall cause the affidavit to be immediately taken to the prosecuting attorney if it appears to the probation officer that the minor has been referred to the probation officer for any violation of an offense listed in subdivision (b) of Section 707 and that offense was allegedly committed when the minor was 14 years of age or older. If the prosecuting attorney decides not to file a petition, he or she may return the affidavit to the probation officer for any other appropriate action. *(Added by Stats.1987, c. 1499, § 4. Amended by Stats.1994, c. 453 (A.B.560), § 4; Stats.2018, c. 423 (S.B.1494), § 124, eff. Jan. 1, 2019.)*

Cross References

Probation officer or social worker defined for purposes of this Chapter, see Welfare and Institutions Code § 215.

§ 653.5. Application to commence proceedings; affidavits

(a) Whenever any person applies to the probation officer to commence proceedings in the juvenile court, the application shall be in the form of an affidavit alleging that there was or is within the county, or residing therein, a minor within the provisions of Section 602, or that a minor committed an offense described in Section 602 within the county, and setting forth facts in support thereof. The probation officer shall immediately make any investigation the probation officer deems necessary to determine whether proceedings in the juvenile court shall be commenced. If the probation officer determines that it is appropriate to recommend services to the family to prevent or eliminate the need for removal of the minor from the minor's home, the probation officer shall make a referral to those services. The probation officer shall refer the youth to services provided by a health agency, community-based organization, local educational agency, an appropriate non-law-enforcement agency, or the probation department.

(b) Except as provided in subdivision (c), if the probation officer determines that proceedings pursuant to Section 650 should be commenced to declare a person to be a ward of the juvenile court on the basis that the minor is a person described in Section 602, the probation officer shall cause the affidavit to be taken to the prosecuting attorney.

(c) Notwithstanding subdivision (b), the probation officer shall cause the affidavit to be taken within 48 hours to the prosecuting attorney in all of the following cases:

(1) If it appears to the probation officer that the minor has been referred to the probation officer for any violation of an offense listed in subdivision (b), paragraph (2) of subdivision (d), or subdivision (e) of Section 707.

(2) If it appears to the probation officer that the minor is under 14 years of age at the date of the offense and that the offense constitutes a second felony referral to the probation officer.

(3) If it appears to the probation officer that the minor was 14 years of age or older at the date of the offense and that the offense constitutes a felony referral to the probation officer.

(4) If it appears to the probation officer that the minor has been referred to the probation officer for the sale or possession for sale of a controlled substance as defined in Chapter 2 (commencing with Section 11053) of Division 10 of the Health and Safety Code.

(5) If it appears to the probation officer that the minor has been referred to the probation officer for a violation of Section 11350 or 11377 of the Health and Safety Code where the violation takes place at a public or private elementary, vocational, junior high school, or high school, or a violation of Section 245.5, 626.9, or 626.10 of the Penal Code.

(6) If it appears to the probation officer that the minor has been referred to the probation officer for a violation of Section 186.22 of the Penal Code.

(7) If it appears to the probation officer that the minor has committed an offense in which the restitution owed to the victim exceeds one thousand dollars ($1,000). For purposes of this paragraph, the definition of "victim" in paragraph (1) of subdivision (a) of Section 730.6 and "restitution" in subdivision (h) of Section 730.6 shall apply.

Except for offenses listed in paragraph (5), subdivision (c) shall not apply to a narcotics and drug offense set forth in Section 1000 of the Penal Code.

The prosecuting attorney shall within their discretionary power institute proceedings in accordance with their role as public prosecutor pursuant to subdivision (b) of Section 650 and Section 26500 of the Government Code. However, if it appears to the prosecuting attorney that the affidavit was not properly referred, that the offense for which the minor was referred should be charged as a misdemeanor, or that the minor may benefit from a program of informal supervision, they shall refer the matter to the probation officer for whatever action the probation officer may deem appropriate.

(d) In all matters where the minor is not in custody and is already a ward of the court or a probationer under Section 602, the prosecuting attorney, within five judicial days of receipt of the affidavit from the probation officer, shall institute proceedings in accordance with their role as public prosecutor pursuant to subdivision (b) of Section 650 of this code and Section 26500 of the Government Code, unless it appears to the prosecuting attorney that the affidavit was not properly referred or that the offense for which the minor was referred requires additional substantiating information, in which case they shall immediately notify the probation officer of what further action they are taking.

(e) This section shall become operative on January 1, 1997. *(Added by Stats.1993, c. 1125 (A.B.1630), § 16, eff. Oct. 11, 1993, operative Jan. 1, 1997. Amended by Stats.1994, c. 450 (A.B.1180), § 3, operative Jan. 1, 1997; Stats.1994, c. 453 (A.B.560), § 6.5, operative Jan. 1, 1997; Stats.1996, c. 1077 (A.B.2898), § 31, operative Jan. 1, 1997; Stats.1999, c. 997 (A.B.575), § 9; Stats.2020, c. 323 (A.B.901), § 10, eff. Jan. 1, 2021.)*

Cross References

Felonies, definition and penalties, see Penal Code §§ 17, 18.
Misdemeanors, definition and penalties, see Penal Code §§ 17, 19, 19.2.
Probation officer or social worker defined for purposes of this Chapter, see Welfare and Institutions Code § 215.
Special proceedings in narcotics and drug abuse cases, see Penal Code § 1000 et seq.

§ 653.7. Decision not to proceed

If the probation officer does not take action under Section 654 and does not file a petition in juvenile court within 21 court days after the application, or in the case of an affidavit alleging that a minor committed an offense described in Section 602 or alleging that a minor is within Section 602, does not cause the affidavit to be taken to the prosecuting attorney within 21 court days after the application, he or she shall endorse upon the affidavit of the applicant the decision not to proceed further and the reasons therefor and shall immediately notify the applicant of the action taken or the decision rendered by him or her under this section. The probation officer shall retain the affidavit and the endorsement thereon for a period of 30 court days after the notice to the applicant. *(Added by Stats.1982, c. 1088, § 15. Amended by Stats.1984, c. 1412, § 10.)*

Cross References

Probation officer or social worker defined for purposes of this Chapter, see Welfare and Institutions Code § 215.

§ 654. Programs of supervision

(a) In any case in which a probation officer, after investigation of an application for a petition or any other investigation the probation officer is authorized to make, concludes that a minor is within the jurisdiction of the juvenile court, or would come within the jurisdiction of the court if a petition were filed, the probation officer may, in lieu of filing a petition to declare a minor a ward of the court under Section 601 or requesting that a petition be filed by the prosecuting attorney to declare a minor a ward of the court under subdivision (e) of Section 601.3 or Section 602 and with consent of the minor and the minor's parent or guardian, refer the minor to services provided by a health agency, community-based organization, local educational agency, an appropriate non-law-enforcement agency, or the probation department. If the services are provided by the probation department, the probation officer may delineate specific programs of supervision for the minor, not to exceed six months, and attempt thereby to adjust the situation that brings the minor within the jurisdiction of the court. This section does not prevent the probation officer from requesting the prosecuting attorney to file a petition at any time within the six-month period or a 90–day period thereafter. If the probation officer determines that the minor has not participated in the specific programs within 60 days, the probation officer may file a petition or request that a petition be filed by the prosecuting attorney. However, when in the judgment of the probation officer the interest of the minor and the community can be protected, the probation officer shall make a diligent effort to proceed under this section.

(b) The program of supervision of the minor undertaken pursuant to this section may call for the minor to obtain care and treatment for the misuse of, or addiction to, controlled substances from a county mental health service or other appropriate community agency.

(c) The program of supervision shall encourage the parents or guardians of the minor to participate with the minor in counseling or education programs, including, but not limited to, parent education and parenting programs operated by community colleges, school districts, or other appropriate agencies designated by the court if the program of supervision is pursuant to the procedure prescribed in Section 654.2.

(d) Further, a probation officer with consent of the minor and the minor's parent or guardian may provide the following services in lieu of filing a petition:

(1) Maintain and operate sheltered-care facilities, or contract with private or public agencies to provide these services. The placement shall be limited to a maximum of 90 days. Counseling services shall be extended to the sheltered minor and the minor's family during this period of diversion services. Referrals for sheltered-care diversion may be made by the minor, the minor's family, schools, any law enforcement agency, or any other private or public social service agency.

(2) Maintain and operate crisis resolution homes, or contract with private or public agencies offering these services. Residence at these facilities shall be limited to 20 days during which period individual and family counseling shall be extended to the minor and the minor's family. Failure to resolve the crisis within the 20–day period may result in the minor's referral to a sheltered-care facility for a period not to exceed 90 days. Referrals shall be accepted from the minor, the minor's family, schools, law enforcement, or any other private or public social service agency.

(3) Maintain and operate counseling and educational centers, or contract with community-based organizations or public agencies to provide vocational training or skills, counseling and mental health resources, educational supports, and arts, recreation, and other youth development services. These services may be provided separately or in conjunction with crisis resolution homes to be operated by the probation officer. The probation officer shall be authorized to make referrals to those organizations when available.

At the conclusion of the program of supervision undertaken pursuant to this section, the probation officer shall prepare and maintain a followup report of the actual program measures taken. *(Added by Stats.1982, c. 1088, § 18, operative Jan. 1, 1985. Amended by Stats.1984, c. 1635, § 95; Stats.1989, c. 1117, § 10; Stats.1991, c. 1202 (S.B.377), § 17; Stats.2017, c. 678 (S.B.190), § 9, eff. Jan. 1, 2018; Stats.2020, c. 323 (A.B.901), § 11, eff. Jan. 1, 2021.)*

Cross References

Alternative dispositions of a minor, see Welfare and Institutions Code §§ 626, 626.5.
Annual calculation of county local control funding formula, see Education Code § 2574.
County-sponsored charter school, average daily attendance rate, funding, see Education Code § 47631.
Home supervision, or electronic surveillance of a minor, liability for cost, see Welfare and Institutions Code § 903.2.

Juvenile court school pupils, criteria for apportionments, see Education Code § 42238.18.
Juvenile delinquency prevention services in probation departments, see Welfare and Institutions Code § 236.
Minors in need of specialized mental health treatment, see Welfare and Institutions Code § 635.1.
Narcotic drug defined, see Health and Safety Code § 11019.
Order directing payment of support and maintenance expenses for minor subject to program of supervision, see Welfare and Institutions Code § 900.
Petition, see Welfare and Institutions Code § 656.
Petition to declare a person free from custody and control of parents, see Family Code § 7840 et seq.
Placing the minor on probation under supervision of a probation officer, see Welfare and Institutions Code § 725.
Probation officer or social worker defined for purposes of this Chapter, see Welfare and Institutions Code § 215.
Release of minor to home supervision, see Welfare and Institutions Code § 628.1.
Unlawful possession of a controlled substance, see Health and Safety Code § 11377 et seq.

§ 654.1. Programs of supervision; violation of Section 23140 or 23152 of Vehicle Code

(a) Notwithstanding Section 654 or any other provision of law, in any case in which a minor has been charged with a violation of Section 23140 or 23152 of the Vehicle Code, the probation officer may, in lieu of requesting that a petition be filed by the prosecuting attorney to declare the minor a ward of the court under Section 602, proceed in accordance with Section 654 and delineate a program of supervision for the minor. However, the probation officer shall cause the citation for a violation of Section 23140 or 23152 of the Vehicle Code to be heard and disposed of by the judge, referee, or juvenile hearing officer pursuant to Sections 257 and 258 as a condition of any program of supervision.

(b) This section may not be construed to prevent the probation officer from requesting the prosecuting attorney to file a petition to declare the minor a ward of the court under Section 602 for a violation of Section 23140 or 23152 of the Vehicle Code. However, if in the judgment of the probation officer, the interest of the minor and the community can be protected by adjudication of a violation of Section 23140 or 23152 of the Vehicle Code in accordance with subdivision (a), the probation officer shall proceed under subdivision (a). *(Added by Stats.1988, c. 1258, § 1. Amended by Stats.2003, c. 149 (S.B.79), § 90.)*

Law Revision Commission Comments

Subdivision (a) of Section 654.1 is amended to reflect the redesignation of traffic hearing officers as juvenile hearing officers. See 1997 Cal. Stat. ch. 679. [33 Cal.L.Rev.Comm. Reports 266 (2003)].

Cross References

Hearing defined for purposes of this Article, see Welfare and Institutions Code § 727.4.
Probation officer or social worker defined for purposes of this Chapter, see Welfare and Institutions Code § 215.

§ 654.2. Continuance of hearing; successful completion of program of supervision

(a) If a petition has been filed by the prosecuting attorney to declare a minor a ward of the court under Section 602, the court may, without adjudging the minor a ward of the court and with the consent of the minor and the minor's parents or guardian, continue any hearing on a petition for six months and order the minor to participate in a program of supervision as set forth in Section 654. If the probation officer recommends additional time to enable the minor to complete the program, the court at its discretion may order an extension. Fifteen days prior to the final conclusion of the program of supervision undertaken pursuant to this section, the probation officer shall submit to the court a followup report of the minor's participation in the program. The minor and the minor's parents or guardian shall be ordered to appear at the conclusion of the six-month period and at the conclusion of each additional three-month period. If the minor successfully completes the program of supervision, the court shall order the petition be dismissed. If the minor has not successfully completed the program of supervision, proceedings on the petition shall proceed no later than 12 months from the date the petition was filed.

(b) If the minor is eligible for Section 654 supervision, and the probation officer believes the minor would benefit from a program of supervision pursuant to this section, the probation officer may, in referring the affidavit described in Section 653.5 to the prosecuting attorney, recommend informal supervision as provided in this section. *(Added by Stats.1989, c. 1117, § 11. Amended by Stats.1994, c. 213 (A.B.3691), § 1.)*

Cross References

Completion of supervision program or probation, dismissal of petition, sealing records, see Welfare and Institutions Code § 786.
Hearing defined for purposes of this Article, see Welfare and Institutions Code § 727.4.
Probation officer or social worker defined for purposes of this Chapter, see Welfare and Institutions Code § 215.

Research References

West's California Judicial Council Forms JV–624, Terms and Conditions.

§ 654.3. Eligibility for program of supervision

(a) A minor shall not be eligible for the program of supervision set forth in Section 654 or 654.2 in the following cases, except where the interests of justice would best be served and the court specifies on the record the reasons for its decision:

(1) A petition alleges that the minor has violated Section 245.5, 626.9, or 626.10 of the Penal Code.

(2) A petition alleges that the minor has violated Section 186.22 of the Penal Code.

(3) The minor has previously participated in a program of supervision pursuant to Section 654.

(4) The minor has previously been adjudged a ward of the court pursuant to Section 602.

(5)(A) A petition alleges that the minor has violated an offense in which the restitution owed to the victim exceeds one thousand dollars ($1,000). However, a minor's inability to pay restitution due to the minor's indigence shall not be grounds for finding a minor ineligible for the program of supervision or a finding that the minor has failed to comply with the terms of the program of supervision.

(B) For purposes of this paragraph, the definition of "victim" in paragraph (1) of subdivision (a) of Section 730.6 and "restitution" in subdivision (h) of Section 730.6 shall apply.

(b) A minor shall not be eligible for the program of supervision set forth in Section 654 or 654.2 in the case of a petition alleging that the minor has violated an offense listed in subdivision (b) of Section 707, except in unusual cases where the court determines the interests of justice would be best served and the court specified on the record the reason for its decision. *(Added by Stats.1989, c. 1117, § 12. Amended by Stats.1994, c. 453 (A.B.560), § 7; Stats.1996, c. 1077 (A.B.2898), § 32; Initiative Measure (Prop. 21, § 22, approved March 7, 2000, eff. March 8, 2000); Stats.2021, c. 603 (S.B.383), § 1, eff. Jan. 1, 2022.)*

Research References

1 Witkin California Criminal Law 4th Introduction to Crimes § 140 (2021), Gang Violence and Juvenile Crime Prevention Act (Proposition 21).

§ 654.4. Completion of alcohol or drug education program; controlled substance offenders; program of supervision

Any minor who is placed in a program of supervision set forth in Section 654 or 654.2 for a violation of an offense involving the unlawful possession, use, sale, or other furnishing of a controlled substance, as defined in Chapter 2 (commencing with Section 11053) of Division 10 of the Health and Safety Code, or for violating subdivision (f) of Section 647 of the Penal Code or Section 23140 or 23152 of the Vehicle Code, shall be required to participate in and successfully complete an alcohol or drug education program from a county mental health agency or other appropriate community program. *(Added by Stats.1989, c. 1117, § 13.)*

§ 654.6. Constructive assignments

A program of supervision pursuant to Section 654 or 654.2 for any minor described in Section 602 shall include constructive assignments that will help the minor learn to be responsible for his or her actions. The assignments may include, but not be limited to, requiring the minor to perform at least 10 hours of community service, requiring the minor to repair damaged property or to make other appropriate restitution, or requiring the minor to participate in an educational or counseling program. *(Added by Stats.1990, c. 258 (A.B.3741), § 2. Amended by Stats.2017, c. 678 (S.B.190), § 10, eff. Jan. 1, 2018.)*

§ 655. Failure of probation officer or district attorney to commence proceedings; review

(a) When any person has applied to the probation officer, pursuant to Section 653, to request commencement of juvenile court proceedings to declare a minor a ward of the court under Section 602 and the probation officer does not cause the affidavit to be taken to the prosecuting attorney pursuant to Section 653 within 21 court days after such application, the applicant may, within 10 court days after receiving notice of the probation officer's decision not to file a petition, apply to the prosecuting attorney to review the decision of the probation officer, and the prosecuting attorney may either affirm the decision of the probation officer or commence juvenile court proceedings.

(b) When any person has applied to the probation officer or the district attorney, pursuant to Section 653, to commence juvenile court proceedings to declare a minor a dependent child of the court or a ward of the court under Section 601 and the probation officer or district attorney fails to file a petition within 21 court days after making such application, the applicant may, within 10 court days after receiving notice of the probation officer's or district attorney's decision not to file a petition, apply to the juvenile court to review the decision of the probation officer or district attorney, and the court may either affirm the decision of the probation officer or district attorney or order him or her to commence juvenile court proceedings.

(c) Nothing in subdivision (b) shall be construed so as to allow district attorneys to file a petition to make a minor a ward of the court under Section 601, except as specifically allowed by Section 653 in accordance with subdivision (e) of Section 601.3. *(Added by Stats.1961, c. 1616, p. 3478, § 2. Amended by Stats.1963, c. 1880, p. 3865, § 1; Stats.1976, c. 1071, p. 4823, § 23; Stats.1977, c. 1241, p. 4184, § 6, eff. Oct. 1, 1977; Stats.1980, c. 670, p. 1864, § 1; Stats.1991, c. 1202 (S.B.377), § 18.)*

Cross References

Probation officer or social worker defined for purposes of this Chapter, see Welfare and Institutions Code § 215.

§ 655.5. Taking minor to community service program for abused or neglected children; decision not to initiate service program; application of referring agency for review

When an officer has referred or delivered a minor pursuant to subdivision (b) of Section 626, and the referral agency does not initiate a service program for the minor within the time periods required by Section 652.5, the referring agency may within 10 court days following receipt of the notification by the referral agency, apply to the probation officer for a review of that decision. *(Added by Stats.1984, c. 260, § 9.)*

Cross References

Probation officer or social worker defined for purposes of this Chapter, see Welfare and Institutions Code § 215.

§ 656. Petition; verification; contents

A petition to commence proceedings in the juvenile court to declare a minor a ward of the court shall be verified and shall contain all of the following:

(a) The name of the court to which it is addressed.

(b) The title of the proceeding.

(c) The code section and subdivision under which the proceedings are instituted.

(d) The name, age, and address, if any, of the minor upon whose behalf the petition is brought.

(e) The names and residence addresses, if known to the petitioner, of both of the parents and any guardian of the minor. If there is no parent or guardian residing within the state, or if his or her place of residence is not known to the petitioner, the petition shall also contain the name and residence address, if known, of any adult relative residing within the county, or, if there are none, the adult relative residing nearest to the location of the court.

(f) A concise statement of facts, separately stated, to support the conclusion that the minor upon whose behalf the petition is being brought is a person within the definition of each of the sections and subdivisions under which the proceedings are being instituted.

(g) The fact that the minor upon whose behalf the petition is brought is detained in custody or is not detained in custody, and if he or she is detained in custody, the date and the precise time the minor was taken into custody.

(h) In a proceeding alleging that the minor comes within Section 601, notice to the parent, guardian, or other person having control or charge of the minor that failure to comply with the compulsory school attendance laws is an infraction, which may be charged and prosecuted before the juvenile court judge sitting as a superior court judge. In those cases, the petition shall also include notice that the parent, guardian, or other person having control or charge of the minor has the right to a hearing on the infraction before a judge different than the judge who has heard or is to hear the proceeding pursuant to Section 601. The notice shall explain the provisions of Section 170.6 of the Code of Civil Procedure.

(i) If a proceeding is pending against a minor child for a violation of Section 594.2, 640.5, 640.6, or 640.7 of the Penal Code, a notice to the parent or legal guardian of the minor that if the minor is found to have violated either or both of these provisions that (1) any community service that may be required of the minor may be performed in the presence, and under the direct supervision, of the parent or legal guardian pursuant to either or both of these provisions, and (2) if the minor is personally unable to pay any fine levied for the violation of either or both of these provisions, that the parent or legal guardian of the minor shall be liable for payment of the fine pursuant to those sections.

(j) A notice to the parent or guardian of the minor that if the minor is ordered to make restitution to the victim pursuant to Section 729.6, as operative on or before August 2, 1995, Section 731.1, as operative on or before August 2, 1995, or Section 730.6, or to pay fines or penalty assessments, the parent or guardian may be liable for the payment of restitution, fines, or penalty assessments. *(Added by Stats.1961, c. 1616, p. 3478, § 2. Amended by Stats.1963, c. 917, p. 2166, § 6; Stats.1963, c. 1761, p. 3514, § 3; Stats.1976, c. 1068, p. 4786, § 37; Stats.1982, c. 1276, § 4, eff. Sept. 22, 1982; Stats.1985, c. 120, § 3; Stats.1990, c. 1530 (S.B.2232), § 10; Stats.1994, c. 575 (A.B.2595), § 2; Stats.1994, c. 836 (A.B.1629), § 1; Stats.1995, c. 42 (A.B.1837), § 2; Stats.1995, c. 313 (A.B.817), § 17, eff. Aug. 3, 1995; Stats.1995, c. 935 (S.B.816), § 6; Stats.1996, c. 1077 (A.B.2898), § 33; Stats.1998, c. 931 (S.B.2139), § 472, eff. Sept. 28, 1998; Stats.2002, c.*

784 (S.B.1316), § 613; Stats.2017, c. 678 (S.B.190), § 11, eff. Jan. 1, 2018.)

Law Revision Commission Comments

Section 656(i) is amended to accommodate unification of the municipal and superior courts in a county. Cal. Const. art. VI, § 5(e). See Section 85 (limited civil cases) & Comment. The jurisdictional and procedural distinctions between a judge sitting as a juvenile court judge and sitting as a superior court judge are significant and are preserved in this amendment. [28 Cal.L.Rev.Comm. Reports 51 (1998)].

Subdivision (i) of Section 656 is amended to reflect unification of the municipal and superior courts pursuant to Article VI, Section 5(e), of the California Constitution. [32 Cal.L.Rev.Comm. Reports 554 (2002)].

Cross References

Applicability of Code of Civil Procedure for variance and amendment of pleadings, see Welfare and Institutions Code § 678.
Authority of county superintendent of schools to file petition in juvenile court for habitual truancy or insubordination, see Education Code § 48403.
Exemption from criminal prosecution, exception, see Welfare and Institutions Code § 606.
Hearing defined for purposes of this Article, see Welfare and Institutions Code § 727.4.
Non-criminal nature of proceedings, see Welfare and Institutions Code § 203.
Petition to declare person free from custody and control of parents, see Family Code § 7840 et seq.
Probation officer or social worker defined for purposes of this Chapter, see Welfare and Institutions Code § 215.
Probation officer's duty to file under this section on determining that minor be detained, see Welfare and Institutions Code § 630.
Relative defined for purposes of this Article, see Welfare and Institutions Code § 727.4.
Traffic charge, notice in lieu of petition, see Welfare and Institutions Code § 257.
Variance, mistakes in pleadings and amendments, see Code of Civil Procedure § 469 et seq.
Verification of pleadings, generally, see Code of Civil Procedure § 446.

Research References

West's California Judicial Council Forms JV–640, Delinquency Court Proceeding Findings and Orders.

§ 656.1. Specification of crime in petition

Any petition alleging that the minor is a person described by Section 602 shall specify as to each count whether the crime charged is a felony or a misdemeanor. *(Added by Stats.1976, c. 1071, p. 4824, § 24.5.)*

Cross References

Felonies, definition and penalties, see Penal Code §§ 17, 18.
Misdemeanors, definition and penalties, see Penal Code §§ 17, 19, 19.2.

§ 656.2. Hearings concerning petitions filed pursuant to Section 602 alleging commission of criminal offense; victim impact statement; information to victim concerning rights; disclosure of information related to minors

(a)(1) Notwithstanding any other law, a victim shall have the right to present a victim impact statement in all juvenile court hearings concerning petitions filed pursuant to Section 602 alleging the commission of any criminal offense. In any case in which a minor is alleged to have committed a criminal offense, the probation officer shall inform the victim of the rights of victims to submit a victim impact statement. If the victim exercises the right to submit a victim impact statement to the probation officer, the probation officer is encouraged to include the statement in his or her social study submitted to the court pursuant to Section 706 and, if applicable, in his or her report submitted to the court pursuant to Section 707. The probation officer also shall advise those persons as to the time and place of the disposition hearing to be conducted pursuant to Sections 702 and 706; any fitness hearing to be conducted pursuant to Section 707, and any other judicial proceeding concerning the case.

(2) The officer shall also provide the victim with information concerning the victim's right to an action for civil damages against the minor and his or her parents and the victim's opportunity to be compensated from the restitution fund. The information shall be in the form of written material prepared by the Judicial Council and shall be provided to each victim for whom the probation officer has a current mailing address.

(b) Notwithstanding any other law, the persons from whom the probation officer is required to solicit a statement pursuant to subdivision (a) shall have the right to attend the disposition hearing conducted pursuant to Section 702 and to express their views concerning the offense and disposition of the case pursuant to Section 706, to attend any fitness hearing conducted pursuant to Section 707, and to be present during juvenile proceedings as provided in Section 676.5.

(c)(1) Notwithstanding any other law, in any case in which a minor is alleged to have committed an act subject to a fitness hearing under Section 707, the victim shall have the right to be informed of all court dates and continuances pertaining to the case, and shall further have the right to obtain copies of the charging petition, the minutes of the proceedings, and orders of adjudications and disposition of the court that are contained in the court file. The arresting agency shall notify the victim in a timely manner of the address and telephone number of the juvenile branch of the district attorney's office that will be responsible for the case and for informing the victim of the victim's right to attend hearings and obtain documents as provided in this section. The district attorney shall, upon request, inform the victim of the date of the fitness hearing, the date of the disposition hearing, and the dates for any continuances of those hearings, and shall inform the court if the victim seeks to exercise his or her right to obtain copies of the documents described in this subdivision.

(2) Where the proceeding against the minor is based on a felony that is not listed in Section 676, a victim who obtains information about the minor under this subdivision shall not disclose or disseminate this information beyond his or her immediate family or support persons authorized by Section 676, unless authorized to do so by a judge of the juvenile court, and the judge may suspend or terminate the right of the victim to access to information under this subdivision if the information is improperly disclosed or disseminated by the victim or any members of his or her immediate family. The intentional dissemination of documents in violation of this subdivision is a misdemeanor and shall be punished by a fine of not more than five hundred dollars ($500). Documents released by the court to a victim pursuant to this section shall be stamped as confidential and with a statement that the unlawful dissemination of the documents is a misdemeanor punishable by a fine of not more than five hundred dollars ($500).

(d) Upon application of the district attorney for good cause and a showing of potential danger to the public, the court may redact any information contained in any documents released by the court to a victim pursuant to this section.

(e) For purposes of this section, "victim" means the victim, the parent or guardian of the victim if the victim is a minor, or, if the victim has died, the victim's next of kin. *(Added by Stats.1989, c. 569, § 3, eff. Sept. 21, 1989. Amended by Stats.1995, c. 234 (A.B.889), § 2; Stats.1997, c. 910 (S.B.1195), § 1; Stats.1999, c. 996 (S.B.334), § 17.5; Stats.2013, c. 28 (S.B.71), § 91, eff. June 27, 2013.)*

Cross References

Felonies, definition and penalties, see Penal Code §§ 17, 18.
Hearing defined for purposes of this Article, see Welfare and Institutions Code § 727.4.
Misdemeanors, definition and penalties, see Penal Code §§ 17, 19, 19.2.
Probation officer or social worker defined for purposes of this Chapter, see Welfare and Institutions Code § 215.

Statutory rights of victims and witnesses of crimes, see Penal Code § 679.02.

§ 656.5. Unverified petition; dismissal without prejudice

Any petition filed in juvenile court to commence proceedings pursuant to this chapter that is not verified may be dismissed without prejudice by such court. *(Added by Stats.1972, c. 897, p. 1594, § 1.)*

§ 657. Time for hearing; waiver of jurisdictional hearing

(a) Upon the filing of the petition, the clerk of the juvenile court shall set the same for hearing within 30 days, except as follows:

(1) In the case of a minor detained in custody at the time of the filing of the petition, the petition must be set for hearing within 15 judicial days from the date of the order of the court directing such detention.

(2) In the case of a minor not before the juvenile court at the time of the filing of the petition and for whom a warrant of arrest has been issued pursuant to Section 663, the hearing on the petition shall be stayed until the minor is brought before the juvenile court on the warrant of arrest. The clerk of the juvenile court shall set the petition for hearing within 30 days of the minor's initial appearance in juvenile court on the petition, except that in the case of a minor detained in custody, the petition shall be set for hearing within 15 judicial days from the date of the order of the court directing such detention.

(b) At the detention hearing, or any time thereafter, a minor who is alleged to come within the provisions of Section 601 or 602, may, with the consent of counsel, admit in court the allegations of the petition and waive the jurisdictional hearing. *(Added by Stats.1961, c. 1616, p. 3478, § 2. Amended by Stats.1971, c. 1389, p. 2743, § 4; Stats.1984, c. 158, § 1.)*

Cross References

Continuance of hearing, see Welfare and Institutions Code § 702.
Courts closed for transaction of judicial business, conditions, see Government Code § 68106.
Duties of appointed counsel, see Welfare and Institutions Code § 634.3.
Hearing defined for purposes of this Article, see Welfare and Institutions Code § 727.4.
Public calamities, destruction of or danger to court building, influx of criminal cases, alternate judicial processes, see Government Code § 68115.
Subjecting minor to criminal prosecution, see Welfare and Institutions Code § 606.

§ 658. Notice of hearing on filing of petition or supplemental petition

(a) Except as provided in subdivision (b), upon the filing of the petition, the clerk of the juvenile court shall issue a notice, to which shall be attached a copy of the petition, and he or she shall cause the same to be served upon the minor, if the minor is eight or more years of age, and upon each of the persons described in subdivision (e) of Section 656 whose residence addresses are set forth in the petition and thereafter before the hearing upon all persons whose residence addresses become known to the clerk. If the court has ordered the care, custody, and control of the minor to be under the supervision of the probation officer for foster care placement pursuant to subdivision (a) of Section 727, the clerk shall also issue a copy of that notice to any foster parents, preadoptive parents, legal guardians, or relatives providing care to the minor. The clerk shall issue a copy of the petition, to the minor's attorney and to the district attorney, if the district attorney has notified the clerk of the court that he or she wishes to receive the petition, containing the time, date, and place of the hearing. Service under this subdivision may be by electronic service pursuant to Section 212.5, except that electronic service is not authorized if the minor is detained and those persons entitled to notice are not present at the initial detention hearing.

(b) Upon the filing of a supplemental petition where the minor has been declared a ward of the court or a probationer under Section 602 in the original matter, the clerk of the juvenile court shall issue a notice, to which shall be attached a copy of the petition, and he or she shall cause the notice to be served upon the minor, if the minor is eight or more years of age, and upon each of the persons described in subdivision (e) of Section 656 whose residence addresses are set forth in the supplemental petition and thereafter known to the clerk. The clerk shall issue a copy of the supplemental petition to the minor's attorney, and to the district attorney if the probation officer is the petitioner, or, to the probation officer if the district attorney is the petitioner, containing the time, date, and place of the hearing. If the court has ordered the care, custody, and control of the minor to be under the supervision of the probation officer for foster care placement pursuant to subdivision (a) of Section 727, the clerk shall also issue a copy of that notice to any foster parents, preadoptive parents, legal guardians, or relatives providing care to the minor. Service under this subdivision may be by electronic service pursuant to Section 212.5. *(Added by Stats.1961, c. 1616, p. 3479, § 2. Amended by Stats.1963, c. 917, p. 2167, § 7; Stats.1965, c. 393, p. 1699, § 2; Stats.1967, c. 506, p. 1852, § 1; Stats.1967, c. 1355, p. 3194, § 5; Stats.1972, c. 906, p. 1610, § 3; Stats.1976, c. 1068, p. 4786, § 38; Stats.1986, c. 757, § 4; Stats.1999, c. 997 (A.B.575), § 10; Stats.2001, c. 831 (A.B.1696), § 4; Stats.2017, c. 319 (A.B.976), § 138, eff. Jan. 1, 2018.)*

Cross References

Citation, see Welfare and Institutions Code § 661.
Contents of notice, see Welfare and Institutions Code § 659.
Foster care defined for purposes of this Article, see Welfare and Institutions Code § 727.4.
Hearing defined for purposes of this Article, see Welfare and Institutions Code § 727.4.
Modification of order by removing minor from custody of parents and directing placement in foster home, notice of hearing, see Welfare and Institutions Code § 777.
Notice of,
Application for modification of judgment or order, see Welfare and Institutions Code § 776.
Confinement of minor, see Welfare and Institutions Code § 627.
Detention hearing, see Welfare and Institutions Code § 630.
Medical, surgical or dental care, see Welfare and Institutions Code § 739.
Persons entitled to notice, right to attend hearing, see Welfare and Institutions Code § 679.
Preadoptive parent defined for purposes of this Article, see Welfare and Institutions Code § 727.4.
Probation officer or social worker defined for purposes of this Chapter, see Welfare and Institutions Code § 215.
Relative defined for purposes of this Article, see Welfare and Institutions Code § 727.4.
Removal of minor from physical custody of parent, see Welfare and Institutions Code § 777.
Service of notice, generally, see Welfare and Institutions Code § 660.
Traffic charge notice, see Welfare and Institutions Code § 270; Vehicle Code § 40500 et seq.

Research References

West's California Judicial Council Forms JV–625, Notice of Hearing—Juvenile Delinquency Proceeding (Also Available in Spanish).

§ 659. Contents of notice

The notice shall contain all of the following:

(a) The name and address of the person to whom the notice is directed.

(b) The date, time, and place of the hearing on the petition.

(c) The name of the minor upon whose behalf the petition has been brought.

(d) Each section and subdivision under which the proceeding has been instituted.

(e) A statement that the minor and his or her parent or guardian or adult relative, as the case may be, to whom notice is required to be given, are entitled to have an attorney present at the hearing on the petition, and that, if the parent or guardian or the adult relative is indigent and cannot afford an attorney, and the minor or his or her parent or guardian or the adult relative desires to be represented by an attorney, the parent or guardian or adult relative shall promptly notify the clerk of the juvenile court, and that in the event counsel or legal assistance is furnished by the court, the parent or guardian or adult relative shall be liable to the county, to the extent of his, her, or their financial ability, for all or a portion of the cost thereof, but he or shall not be liable for the cost of counsel or legal assistance furnished by the court for purposes of representing the minor.

(f) A statement that the parent or guardian of the minor may be liable for the payment of restitution, fines, or penalty assessments if the minor is ordered to make restitution to the victim or to pay fines or penalty assessments. *(Added by Stats.1961, c. 1616, p. 3479, § 2. Amended by Stats.1963, c. 917, p. 2167, § 8; Stats.1985, c. 1485, § 12; Stats.1994, c. 836 (A.B.1629), § 2; Stats.1995, c. 313 (A.B.817), § 18, eff. Aug. 3, 1995; Stats.2017, c. 678 (S.B.190), § 12, eff. Jan. 1, 2018.)*

Cross References

Appointment of counsel, see Welfare and Institutions Code §§ 634, 700.
Hearing defined for purposes of this Article, see Welfare and Institutions Code § 727.4.
Information as to right to counsel, see Welfare and Institutions Code §§ 633, 700.
Persons entitled to counsel, see Welfare and Institutions Code §§ 633, 679.
Relative defined for purposes of this Article, see Welfare and Institutions Code § 727.4.
Supplemental petition to change custody of ward of court, service of notice of hearing, see Welfare and Institutions Code § 777.
Traffic charge notice, see Welfare and Institutions Code § 257; Vehicle Code § 40500 et seq.

Research References

West's California Judicial Council Forms JV–625, Notice of Hearing—Juvenile Delinquency Proceeding (Also Available in Spanish).

§ 660. Service of notice and petition

(a) Except as provided in subdivision (b), if the minor is detained, the clerk of the juvenile court shall cause the notice and copy of the petition to be served on all persons required to receive that notice and copy of the petition pursuant to subdivision (e) of Section 656 and Section 658, either personally or by certified mail with request for return receipt, as soon as possible after filing of the petition and at least five days before the time set for hearing, unless the hearing is set less than five days from the filing of the petition, in which case, the notice and copy of the petition shall be served at least 24 hours before the time set for hearing. Service under this subdivision shall not be made by electronic service.

(b) If the minor is detained, and all persons entitled to notice pursuant to subdivision (e) of Section 656 and Section 658 were present at the detention hearing, the clerk of the juvenile court shall cause the notice and copy of the petition to be served on all persons required to receive the notice and copy of the petition, by personal service, by first-class mail, or by electronic service pursuant to Section 212.5, as soon as possible after the filing of the petition and at least five days before the time set for hearing, unless the hearing is set less than five days from the filing of the petition, in which case the notice and copy of the petition shall be served at least 24 hours before the time set for the hearing. Service under this subdivision may be by electronic service pursuant to Section 212.5 except that electronic service is not authorized if the minor is detained and those persons entitled to notice are not present at the detention hearing.

(c) If the minor is not detained, the clerk of the juvenile court shall cause the notice and copy of the petition to be served on all persons required to receive the notice and copy of the petition, by personal service, by first-class mail, or by electronic service pursuant to Section 212.5 at least 10 days before the time set for hearing. If that person is known to reside outside of the county, the clerk of the juvenile court shall serve the notice and copy of the petition, by first-class mail or by electronic service pursuant to Section 212.5, to that person, as soon as possible after the filing of the petition and at least 10 days before the time set for hearing. Failure to respond to the notice shall in no way result in arrest or detention. In the instance of failure to appear after notice by first-class mail or by electronic service pursuant to Section 212.5, the court shall direct that the notice and copy of the petition is to be personally served on all persons required to receive the notice and a copy of the petition. However, if the whereabouts of the minor are unknown, personal service of the notice and a copy of the petition is not required and a warrant for the arrest of the minor may be issued pursuant to Section 663. Personal service of the notice and copy of the petition outside of the county at least 10 days before the time set for hearing is equivalent to service by first-class mail or electronic service. Service may be waived by any person by a voluntary appearance entered in the minutes of the court or by a written waiver of service filed with the clerk of the court at or prior to the hearing.

(d) For purposes of this section, service on the minor's attorney shall constitute service on the minor's parent or legal guardian. *(Added by Stats.1967, c. 1355, p. 3194, § 7. Amended by Stats.1969, c. 664, p. 1329, § 1; Stats.1972, c. 906, p. 1611, § 4; Stats.1974, c. 726, p. 1611, § 1; Stats.1976, c. 1068, p. 4786, § 39; Stats.1984, c. 481, § 6; Stats.1997, c. 447 (A.B.1325), § 1; Stats.1999, c. 997 (A.B.575), § 11; Initiative Measure (Prop. 21, § 23, approved March 7, 2000, eff. March 8, 2000); Stats.2017, c. 319 (A.B.976), § 139, eff. Jan. 1, 2018.)*

Cross References

Contents of petition, see Welfare and Institutions Code § 656.
Hearing defined for purposes of this Article, see Welfare and Institutions Code § 727.4.
Supplemental petition to change custody of ward of court, service of notice of hearing, see Welfare and Institutions Code § 777.

Research References

West's California Judicial Council Forms JV–625, Notice of Hearing—Juvenile Delinquency Proceeding (Also Available in Spanish).

§ 660.5. Expedited Youth Accountability Program

(a) This section shall be known as the Expedited Youth Accountability Program. It shall be operative in the superior court in Los Angeles County. It shall also be operative in any other county in which a committee consisting of the sheriff, the chief probation officer, the district attorney, the public defender, and the presiding judge of the superior court votes to participate in the program, upon approval by the board of supervisors.

(b) It is the intent of the Legislature to hold nondetained, delinquent youth accountable for their crimes in a swift and certain manner.

(c) Each county participating in the Expedited Youth Accountability Program shall establish agreed upon time deadlines for law enforcement, probation, district attorney, and court functions which shall assure that a case which is to proceed pursuant to this section shall be ready to be heard within 60 calendar days after the minor is cited to the court.

(d)(1) Notwithstanding Sections 658, 659, and 660, if a minor is not detained for any misdemeanor or felony offense and is not cited to Informal Juvenile and Traffic Court pursuant to paragraphs (1) to (15), inclusive, of Section 256 and Section 853.6a of the Penal Code, the peace officer or probation officer releasing the minor shall issue a citation and obtain a written promise to appear in juvenile court, or record the minor's refusal to sign the promise to appear and serve a notice to appear in juvenile court. The appearance shall not be set for more than 60 calendar days nor less than 10 calendar days from the issuance of the citation. If the 60th day falls on a court holiday, the appearance date shall be on the next date that the court is in session. The date set for the appearance of the minor shall allow for sufficient time for the probation department to evaluate eligible minors for informal handling under Section 654 or any other disposition provided by law. However, nothing in this section shall be construed to limit or conflict with Sections 653.1 and 653.5.

(2) Upon receipt of the citation and petition, but in no event less than 72 hours, excluding nonjudicial days and holidays prior to the hearing, the clerk of the juvenile court shall issue a copy of the citation and petition to the public defender or the minor's attorney of record. If a copy of the citation and petition is not provided at least 72 hours, excluding nonjudicial days and holidays prior to the hearing, it shall be grounds to request a continuance pursuant to Sections 682 and 700. At a hearing conducted under Section 700, the minor and minor's parent or guardian shall be furnished a copy of the petition and any other material required to be provided under Section 659.

(3) The original citation and promise or notice to appear shall be retained by the court if a petition is filed. In addition, there shall be three copies of the citation and promise or notice to appear, which shall be distributed as follows:

(A) One copy shall be provided to the person to whom the citation is issued.

(B) One copy shall be provided to the probation department.

(C) If a petition is requested, the second copy of the citation shall go to the district attorney along with the petition request, and the third copy shall be retained by the agency issuing the citation.

(4) The original citation shall include a copy of all police reports relating to the citation and a petition request. The citation shall contain the following information:

(A) Date, time, and location of the issuance of the citation.

(B) The name, address, telephone number if known, driver's license number, age, date of birth, sex, race, height, weight, hair color, and color of eyes of the person to whom the citation is issued.

(C) A list of the offenses and the location where the offense or offenses were committed.

(D) Date and time of the required court appearance.

(E) Address of the juvenile court where the person to whom the citation is issued is to appear.

(F) A preprinted promise to appear which is signed by the person to whom the citation is issued, or where the person refused to sign the written promise, the notice to appear.

(G) A preprinted declaration under penalty of perjury that the above information is true and correct, signed by the peace officer or probation officer issuing the citation.

(H) A statement that the failure to appear is punishable as a misdemeanor.

(e) The minor's parent or guardian shall be issued a citation in the same manner as described in subdivision (b).

(f) The willful failure to appear in court pursuant to a citation or notice issued as required pursuant to this section is a misdemeanor.

(g)(1) Notwithstanding Section 662, if a parent or guardian to whom a citation has been issued pursuant to this section fails to appear, a warrant of arrest may issue for that person. A warrant of arrest may also issue for a parent or guardian who is not personally served where efforts to effect personal service have been unsuccessful, upon an affidavit, under penalty of perjury, signed by a peace officer stating facts sufficient to establish that all reasonable efforts to locate the person have failed or that the person has willfully evaded service of process.

(2) Notwithstanding Section 663, if a minor to whom a citation has been issued pursuant to this section fails to appear, and the minor's parent or guardian has either appeared or the prerequisite conditions for issuing a warrant against the minor's parent or guardian under paragraph (1) have been met, a warrant of arrest may issue for the minor.

(3) A warrant of arrest may also issue for a minor who is not personally served where each of the following occur:

(A) Efforts to effect personal service have been unsuccessful.

(B) An affidavit is submitted under penalty of perjury, signed by a peace officer, stating facts sufficient to establish that all reasonable efforts to locate the minor have failed or that minor has willfully evaded service of process.

(C) The minor's parent or guardian has either appeared or the prerequisite conditions for issuing a warrant against the minor's parent or guardian under paragraph (1) have been met.

(h)(1) Notwithstanding Section 654 or any other provision of law, a probation officer in a county in which this subdivision is applicable may, in lieu of filing a petition or proceeding under Section 654, issue a citation in the form described in subdivision (d) to the Informal Juvenile and Traffic Court pursuant to Section 256 for any misdemeanor except the following:

(A) Any crime involving a firearm.

(B) Any crime involving violence.

(C) Any crime involving a sex-related offense.

(D) Any minor who has previously been declared a ward of the court.

(E) Any minor who has previously been referred to juvenile traffic court pursuant to this section.

(2) This subdivision shall apply only if the case will be heard by a juvenile hearing officer who meets the minimum qualifications of a juvenile court referee and only in those counties in which a committee consisting of the sheriff, the chief probation officer, the district attorney, the public defender, and the presiding judge of the superior court vote for this subdivision to apply and then only upon approval of the board of supervisors. This approval shall be required in Los Angeles and all other counties participating in the program, and shall be in addition to that required by subdivision (a) for participation in the Expedited Youth Accountability Program.

(3) In counties in which this subdivision is applicable, the probation department shall conduct a risk and needs assessment for each minor eligible for citation to the Informal Juvenile and Traffic Court pursuant to paragraph (1). The risk and needs assessment shall consider the best interest of the minor and the protection of the community. It shall also include an assessment of whether the child has any significant problems in the home, school, or community, whether the matter appears to have arisen from a temporary problem within the family which has been or can be resolved, and whether any agency or other resource in the community is better suited to serve the needs of the child, the parent or guardian, or both.

(i) In the event that the probation officer places a minor on informal probation or cites the minor to Informal Juvenile and Traffic Court, or elects some other lawful disposition not requiring the hearing set forth in subdivision (b), the probation officer shall so inform the minor and his or her parent or guardian no later than 72 hours, excluding nonjudicial days and holidays, prior to the hearing, that a court appearance is not required.

(j) Except as modified by this section, the requirements of this chapter shall remain in full force and effect.

(k) This section shall be operative on January 1, 1998, and shall be implemented in all branches of the juvenile court in Los Angeles County on or before July 1, 1998.

(*l*) It is the intent of the Legislature that an interim hearing be conducted by appropriate policy committees in the Legislature prior to January 1, 2002, to examine the success of the program in expediting punishment for juvenile offenses, reducing delinquent behavior, and promoting greater accountability on the part of juvenile offenders. *(Added by Stats.1997, c. 679 (A.B.1105), § 10, operative Jan. 1, 1998. Amended by Stats.2002, c. 110 (A.B.2154), § 1.)*

Cross References

Citations for misdemeanors, minors under 18, see Penal Code § 853.6a.
Felonies, definition and penalties, see Penal Code §§ 17, 18.
Hearing defined for purposes of this Article, see Welfare and Institutions Code § 727.4.
Misdemeanors, definition and penalties, see Penal Code §§ 17, 19, 19.2.
Probation officer or social worker defined for purposes of this Chapter, see Welfare and Institutions Code § 215.
Punishment defined for purposes of this Chapter, see Welfare and Institutions Code § 202.
Reasonable efforts defined for purposes of this Article, see Welfare and Institutions Code § 727.4.

Research References

4 Witkin, California Criminal Law 4th Pretrial Proceedings § 60 (2021), Juvenile Offenses.

§ 661. Notice; citation; compulsory school attendance infractions; issuance and service of citations

(a) In addition to the notice provided in Sections 658 and 659, the juvenile court may issue a citation directing any parent, guardian, or foster parent of the person concerning whom a petition has been filed to appear at the time and place set for any hearing or financial evaluation under the provisions of this chapter, including a hearing under the provisions of Section 257, and directing any person having custody or control of the minor concerning whom the petition has been filed to bring the minor with him or her.

(b) The notice shall in addition state that a parent, guardian, or foster parent may be required to participate in a counseling or education program with the minor concerning whom the petition has been filed.

(c) If the proceeding is one alleging that the minor comes within the provisions of Section 601, the notice shall in addition contain notice to the parent, guardian, or other person having control or charge of the minor that failure to comply with the compulsory school attendance laws is an infraction, which may be charged and prosecuted before the juvenile court judge sitting as a superior court judge. In those cases, the notice shall also include notice that the parent, guardian, or other person having control or charge of the minor has the right to a hearing on the infraction before a judge different than the judge who has heard or is to hear the proceeding pursuant to Section 601. The notice shall also explain the provisions of Section 170.6 of the Code of Civil Procedure.

(d) Personal service of the citation shall be made at least 24 hours before the time stated therein for the appearance. The citation may also be electronically served pursuant to Section 212.5, but only in addition to service by other forms of service required by law. *(Added by Stats.1961, c. 1616, p. 3479, § 2. Amended by Stats.1975, c. 1266, p. 3324, § 2; Stats.1976, c. 1068, p. 4787, § 40; Stats.1984, c. 162, § 3; Stats.1985, c. 120, § 4; Stats.1985, c. 1485, § 14; Stats.1998, c. 931 (S.B.2139), § 473, eff. Sept. 28, 1998; Stats.2002, c. 784 (S.B. 1316), § 614; Stats.2017, c. 319 (A.B.976), § 140, eff. Jan. 1, 2018.)*

Law Revision Commission Comments

Section 661 is amended to accommodate unification of the municipal and superior courts in a county. Cal. Const. art. VI, § 5(e). See Section 85 (limited civil cases) & Comment. The jurisdictional and procedural distinctions between a judge sitting as a juvenile court judge and sitting as a superior court judge are significant and are preserved in this amendment. [28 Cal.L.Rev.Comm. Reports 51 (1998)].

Section 661 is amended to reflect unification of the municipal and superior courts pursuant to Article VI, Section 5(e), of the California Constitution. [32 Cal.L.Rev.Comm. Reports 556 (2002)].

Cross References

Hearing defined for purposes of this Article, see Welfare and Institutions Code § 727.4.

§ 662. Warrant of arrest against parent or guardian

In case such citation cannot be served, or the person served fails to obey it, or in any case in which it appears to the court that the citation will probably be ineffective, a warrant of arrest may issue on the order of the court either against the parent, or guardian, or the person having the custody of the minor, or with whom the minor is. *(Added by Stats.1961, c. 1616, p. 3480, § 2.)*

Cross References

Attachment for contempt, see Code of Civil Procedure § 1212 et seq.
Disobedience of order as contempt, see Welfare and Institutions Code § 213.
Non-criminal nature of proceedings, see Welfare and Institutions Code § 203.
Warrant of arrest generally, see Penal Code § 813 et seq.

§ 663. Warrant of arrest against minor

(a) Whenever a petition has been filed in the juvenile court alleging that a minor comes within the provisions of Section 601 or 602 of this code and praying for a hearing thereon, or whenever any subsequent petition has been filed praying for a hearing in the matter of the minor, a warrant of arrest may be issued immediately for the minor upon a showing that any one of the following conditions are satisfied:

(1) It appears to the court that the conduct and behavior of the minor may endanger the health, person, welfare, or property of himself or herself, or others, or that the circumstances of his or her home environment may endanger the health, person, welfare, or property of the minor.

(2) It appears to the court that either personal service upon the minor has been unsuccessful, or the whereabouts of the minor are unknown.

(3) It appears to the court that the minor has willfully evaded service of process.

(b) Nothing in this section shall be construed to limit the right of parents or guardians to receive the notice and a copy of the petition pursuant to Section 660. *(Added by Stats.1961, c. 1616, p. 3480, § 2. Amended by Stats.1963, c. 1761, p. 3514, § 4; Stats.1976, c. 1068, p. 4787, § 41; Stats.1997, c. 447 (A.B.1325), § 2; Initiative Measure (Prop. 21, § 24, approved March 7, 2000, eff. March 8, 2000).)*

Cross References

Hearing defined for purposes of this Article, see Welfare and Institutions Code § 727.4.
Non-criminal nature of proceedings, see Welfare and Institutions Code § 203.
Warrant for minor in another county, see Welfare and Institutions Code § 641.
Warrant of arrest generally, see Penal Code § 813 et seq.

§ 664. Subpoenas

(a) The district attorney or the attorney of record for the minor may issue, and upon request of the probation officer, the minor, or the minor's parent, guardian, or custodian, the court or the clerk of the court shall issue, and, on the court's own motion, the court may issue, subpoenas requiring attendance and testimony of witnesses and production of papers at any hearing regarding a minor who is alleged or determined by the court to be a person described by Section 601 or 602.

(b) When a person attends a juvenile court hearing as a witness upon a subpoena, in its discretion, the court may by an order on its minutes, direct the county auditor to draw his or her warrant upon the county treasurer in favor of the witness for witness fees in the amount and manner prescribed by Section 68093 of the Government Code. The fees are county charges.

(c)(1) The court shall use whatever means are appropriate, including, but not limited to, the issuance of a subpoena, if appropriate, to require the presence of the parent, parents, or guardian of a child at the detention, jurisdictional, and disposition hearings regarding a minor who is alleged or determined by the court to be a person described by Section 601 or 602 unless the court determines that it would be in the best interests of the child for the parent to not attend or the court finds that it would impose a hardship upon the parent or guardian to attend. Any parent or guardian who does not attend a hearing pursuant to a subpoena under this section is guilty of contempt unless the court excuses, for good cause, the parent or guardian from attending the hearing or the court finds that the parent or guardian has a satisfactory excuse for not attending.

(2) For purposes of this subdivision, the term "parent" includes a foster parent. *(Added by Stats.1961, c. 1616, p. 3480, § 2. Amended by Stats.1967, c. 507, p. 1852, § 2; Stats.1996, c. 90 (A.B.2007), § 2; Stats.1997, c. 903 (A.B.761), § 1.)*

Cross References

Hearing defined for purposes of this Article, see Welfare and Institutions Code § 727.4.
Probation officer or social worker defined for purposes of this Chapter, see Welfare and Institutions Code § 215.

ARTICLE 17. WARDS—HEARINGS

§ 675. Special or separate session; presence of persons on trial or awaiting trial; hearings

(a) All cases under the provisions of this chapter shall be heard at a special or separate session of the court, and no other matter shall be heard at that session. Except as provided in subdivision (b), no person on trial, awaiting trial, or under accusation of crime, other than a parent, guardian, or relative of the minor, shall be permitted to be present at any such session, except as a witness.

(b) Hearings for two or more minors may be heard upon the same rules of joinder, consolidation, and severance as apply to trials in a court of criminal jurisdiction. *(Added by Stats.1961, c. 1616, p. 3480, § 2. Amended by Stats.1969, c. 185, p. 465, § 1; Stats.1976, c. 1068, p. 4788, § 43; Stats.1983, c. 390, § 1.)*

Cross References

Exclusion of public, see Welfare and Institutions Code § 676.
Hearing defined for purposes of this Article, see Welfare and Institutions Code § 727.4.
Hearing on traffic charge, see Welfare and Institutions Code §§ 257, 258.
Non-criminal nature of proceedings, see Welfare and Institutions Code § 203.
Official reporter, presence, see Welfare and Institutions Code § 677.
Persons entitled to be declared free from parental custody and control, see Family Code § 7820 et seq.
Persons entitled to be present, see Welfare and Institutions Code § 679.
Persons subject to jurisdiction, see Welfare and Institutions Code § 300 et seq.
Presence of probation officer, see Welfare and Institutions Code § 280.
Relative defined for purposes of this Article, see Welfare and Institutions Code § 727.4.

§ 676. Admission of public and persons having interest in case; exceptions; confidentiality of name; disclosure of court documents

(a) Unless requested by the minor concerning whom the petition has been filed and any parent or guardian present, the public shall not be admitted to a juvenile court hearing. Nothing in this section shall preclude the attendance of up to two family members of a prosecuting witness for the support of that witness, as authorized by Section 868.5 of the Penal Code. The judge or referee may nevertheless admit those persons he or she deems to have a direct

Welf. & Inst.

and legitimate interest in the particular case or the work of the court. However, except as provided in subdivision (b), members of the public shall be admitted, on the same basis as they may be admitted to trials in a court of criminal jurisdiction, to hearings concerning petitions filed pursuant to Section 602 alleging that a minor is a person described in Section 602 by reason of the violation of any one of the following offenses:

(1) Murder.

(2) Arson of an inhabited building.

(3) Robbery while armed with a dangerous or deadly weapon.

(4) Rape with force or violence, threat of great bodily harm, or when the person is prevented from resisting due to being rendered unconscious by any intoxicating, anesthetizing, or controlled substance, or when the victim is at the time incapable, because of a disability, of giving consent, and this is known or reasonably should be known to the person committing the offense.

(5) Sodomy by force, violence, duress, menace, threat of great bodily harm, or when the person is prevented from resisting due to being rendered unconscious by any intoxicating, anesthetizing, or controlled substance, or when the victim is at the time incapable, because of a disability, of giving consent, and this is known or reasonably should be known to the person committing the offense.

(6) Oral copulation by force, violence, duress, menace, threat of great bodily harm, or when the person is prevented from resisting due to being rendered unconscious by any intoxicating, anesthetizing, or controlled substance, or when the victim is at the time incapable, because of a disability, of giving consent, and this is known or reasonably should be known to the person committing the offense.

(7) Any offense specified in subdivision (a) or (e) of Section 289 of the Penal Code.

(8) Kidnapping for ransom.

(9) Kidnapping for purpose of robbery.

(10) Kidnapping with bodily harm.

(11) Assault with intent to murder or attempted murder.

(12) Assault with a firearm or destructive device.

(13) Assault by any means of force likely to produce great bodily injury.

(14) Discharge of a firearm into an inhabited dwelling or occupied building.

(15) Any offense described in Section 1203.09 of the Penal Code.

(16) Any offense described in Section 12022.5 or 12022.53 of the Penal Code.

(17) Any felony offense in which a minor personally used a weapon described in any provision listed in Section 16590 of the Penal Code.

(18) Burglary of an inhabited dwelling house or trailer coach, as defined in Section 635 of the Vehicle Code, or the inhabited portion of any other building, if the minor previously has been adjudged a ward of the court by reason of the commission of any offense listed in this section, including an offense listed in this paragraph.

(19) Any felony offense described in Section 136.1 or 137 of the Penal Code.

(20) Any offense as specified in Sections 11351, 11351.5, 11352, 11378, 11378.5, 11379, and 11379.5 of the Health and Safety Code.

(21) Criminal street gang activity which constitutes a felony pursuant to Section 186.22 of the Penal Code.

(22) Manslaughter as specified in Section 192 of the Penal Code.

(23) Driveby shooting or discharge of a weapon from or at a motor vehicle as specified in Sections 246, 247, and 26100 of the Penal Code.

(24) Any crime committed with an assault weapon, as defined in Section 30510 of the Penal Code, including possession of an assault weapon as specified in Section 30605 of the Penal Code.

(25) Carjacking, while armed with a dangerous or deadly weapon.

(26) Kidnapping, in violation of Section 209.5 of the Penal Code.

(27) Torture, as described in Sections 206 and 206.1 of the Penal Code.

(28) Aggravated mayhem, in violation of Section 205 of the Penal Code.

(b) Where the petition filed alleges that the minor is a person described in Section 602 by reason of the commission of rape with force or violence or great bodily harm; sodomy by force, violence, duress, menace, threat of great bodily harm, or when the person is prevented from resisting by any intoxicating, anesthetizing, or controlled substance, or when the victim is at the time incapable, because of mental disorder or developmental or physical disability, of giving consent, and this is known or reasonably should be known to the person committing the offense; oral copulation by force, violence, duress, menace, threat of great bodily harm, or when the person is prevented from resisting by any intoxicating, anesthetizing, or controlled substance, or when the victim is at the time incapable, because of mental disorder or developmental or physical disability, of giving consent, and this is known or reasonably should be known to the person committing the offense; any offense specified in Section 289 of the Penal Code, members of the public shall not be admitted to the hearing in either of the following instances:

(1) Upon a motion for a closed hearing by the district attorney, who shall make the motion if so requested by the victim.

(2) During the victim's testimony, if, at the time of the offense the victim was under 16 years of age.

(c) The name of a minor found to have committed one of the offenses listed in subdivision (a) shall not be confidential, unless the court, for good cause, so orders. As used in this subdivision, "good cause" shall be limited to protecting the personal safety of the minor, a victim, or a member of the public. The court shall make a written finding, on the record, explaining why good cause exists to make the name of the minor confidential.

(d) Notwithstanding Sections 827 and 828 and subject to subdivisions (e) and (f), when a petition is sustained for any offense listed in subdivision (a), the charging petition, the minutes of the proceeding, and the orders of adjudication and disposition of the court that are contained in the court file shall be available for public inspection. Nothing in this subdivision shall be construed to authorize public access to any other documents in the court file.

(e) The probation officer or any party may petition the juvenile court to prohibit disclosure to the public of any file or record. The juvenile court shall prohibit the disclosure if it appears that the harm to the minor, victims, witnesses, or public from the public disclosure outweighs the benefit of public knowledge. However, the court shall not prohibit disclosure for the benefit of the minor unless the court makes a written finding that the reason for the prohibition is to protect the safety of the minor.

(f) Nothing in this section shall be applied to limit the disclosure of information as otherwise provided for by law.

(g) The juvenile court shall for each day that the court is in session, post in a conspicuous place which is accessible to the general public, a written list of hearings that are open to the general public pursuant to this section, the location of those hearings, and the time when the hearings will be held. *(Added by Stats.1961, c. 1616, p. 3480, § 2. Amended by Stats.1980, c. 322, p. 662, § 1; Stats.1981, c. 140, p. 922, § 1; Stats.1982, c. 283, § 1, eff. June 21, 1982; Stats.1982, c. 1295, § 1; Stats.1984, c. 398, § 1; Stats.1987, c. 828, § 169; Stats.1987, c. 704, § 2; Stats.1990, c. 246 (A.B.2638), § 2; Stats.1993, c. 610 (A.B.6), § 29, eff. Oct. 1, 1993; Stats.1993, c. 611 (S.B.60), § 33, eff. Oct. 1, 1993; Stats.1994, c. 453 (A.B.560), § 8; Stats.1998, c.*

925 (A.B.1290), § 6; Stats.1998, c. 936 (A.B.105), § 20, eff. Sept. 28, 1998; Stats.1998, c. 936 (A.B.105), § 20.5, eff. Sept. 28, 1998, operative Jan. 1, 1999; Stats.1999, c. 996 (S.B.334), § 18; Initiative Measure (Prop. 21, § 25, approved March 7, 2000, eff. March 8, 2000); Stats.2010, c. 178 (S.B.1115), § 96, operative Jan. 1, 2012; Stats.2014, c. 919 (S.B.838), § 2, eff. Jan. 1, 2015.)

Law Revision Commission Comments

Subdivision (a) of Section 676 is amended to reflect nonsubstantive reorganization of the statutes governing control of deadly weapons. [38 Cal.L.Rev.Comm. Reports 217 (2009)].

Cross References

Denial of probation and suspension of sentence for crimes against persons 60 years of age or older, blind persons, paraplegics or quadriplegics, see Penal Code § 1203.09.
Felonies, definition and penalties, see Penal Code §§ 17, 18.
Hearing defined for purposes of this Article, see Welfare and Institutions Code § 727.4.
Non-criminal nature of proceedings, see Welfare and Institutions Code § 203.
Official reporter, presence, see Welfare and Institutions Code § 677.
Persons entitled to be present, see Welfare and Institutions Code §§ 675, 679.
Probation officer, presence, see Welfare and Institutions Code § 280.
Probation officer or social worker defined for purposes of this Chapter, see Welfare and Institutions Code § 215.

Research References

West's California Judicial Council Forms JV–640, Delinquency Court Proceeding Findings and Orders.

§ 676.5. Victims; right to presence at proceedings; exclusion criteria

For Executive Order N–49–20 (2019 CA EO 49-20), relating to changes in the discharge and re-entry process at the Division of Juvenile Justice due to the COVID-19 pandemic, see Historical and Statutory Notes under Welfare and Institutions Code § 1766.

The right of victims of juvenile offenses to be present during juvenile proceedings, as specified in subdivision (a), shall be secured as follows:

(a) Notwithstanding any other law, and except as provided in subdivision (d), a victim and up to two support persons of the victim's choosing shall be entitled to be admitted, on the same basis as he or she may be admitted to trials in a court of criminal jurisdiction, to juvenile court hearings concerning petitions filed pursuant to Section 602 alleging the commission of any criminal offense, and shall be so notified by the probation officer in person or by registered mail, return receipt requested, together with a notice explaining all other rights and services available to the victim with respect to the case.

(b) A victim or his or her support person may be excluded from a juvenile court hearing described in subdivision (a) only if each of the following criteria are met:

(1) Any movant, including the minor defendant, who seeks to exclude the victim or his or her support person from a hearing demonstrates that there is a substantial probability that overriding interests will be prejudiced by the presence of the victim or his or her support person.

(2) The court considers reasonable alternatives to exclusion of the victim or his or her support person from the hearing.

(3) The exclusion of the victim or his or her support person from a hearing, or any limitation on his or her presence at a hearing, is narrowly tailored to serve the overriding interests identified by the movant.

(4) Following a hearing at which any person who is to be excluded from a juvenile court hearing is afforded an opportunity to be heard, the court makes specific factual findings that support the exclusion of the victim or his or her support person from, or any limitation on his or her presence at, the juvenile court hearing.

(c) As used in this section, "victim" means (1) the alleged victim of the offense and one person of his or her choosing or however many more the court may allow under the particular circumstances surrounding the proceeding, (2) in the event that the victim is unable to attend the proceeding, two persons designated by the victim or however many more the court may allow under the particular circumstances surrounding the proceeding, or (3) if the victim is no longer living, two members of the victim's immediate family or however many more the court may allow under the particular circumstances surrounding the proceeding.

(d) Nothing in this section shall prevent a court from excluding a victim or his or her support person from a hearing, pursuant to Section 777 of the Evidence Code, when the victim is subpoenaed as a witness. An order of exclusion shall be consistent with the objectives of paragraphs (1) to (4), inclusive, of subdivision (b) to allow the victim to be present, whenever possible, at all hearings. *(Added by Stats.1995, c. 332 (A.B.149), § 4. Amended by Stats.1999, c. 996 (S.B.334), § 19.)*

Cross References

Hearing defined for purposes of this Article, see Welfare and Institutions Code § 727.4.
Probation officer or social worker defined for purposes of this Chapter, see Welfare and Institutions Code § 215.

§ 677. Court reporter; writing out and transcribing notes; costs

At any juvenile court hearing conducted by a juvenile court judge, an official court reporter shall, and at any such hearing conducted by a juvenile court referee, the official reporter, as directed by the court, may take down in shorthand all the testimony and all of the statements and remarks of the judge and all persons appearing at the hearing; and, if directed by the judge, or requested by the person on whose behalf the petition was brought, or by his parent or legal guardian, or the attorneys of such persons, he must, within such reasonable time after the hearing of the petition as the court may designate, write out the same or such specific portions thereof as may be requested in plain and legible longhand or by typewriter or other printing machine and certify to the same as being correctly reported and transcribed, and when directed by the court, file the same with the clerk of the court. Unless otherwise directed by the judge, the costs of writing out and transcribing all or any portion of the reporter's shorthand notes shall be paid in advance at the rates fixed for transcriptions in a civil action by the person requesting the same. *(Added by Stats.1961, c. 1616, p. 3480, § 2.)*

Cross References

Continuance of hearing considering the minor's interests, see Welfare and Institutions Code § 352.
Court reporters, duties, see Code of Civil Procedure § 269.
Hearing defined for purposes of this Article, see Welfare and Institutions Code § 727.4.
Writing defined, see Welfare and Institutions Code § 8.

§ 678. Variance and amendment of pleadings; applicability of Code of Civil Procedure

The provisions of Chapter 8 (commencing with Section 469) of Title 6 of Part 2 of the Code of Civil Procedure relating to variance and amendment of pleadings in civil actions shall apply to petitions and proceedings under this chapter, to the same extent and with the same effect as if proceedings under this chapter were civil actions. *(Added by Stats.1961, c. 1616, p. 3481, § 2.)*

Cross References

Contents of petition, see Welfare and Institutions Code § 656.

§ 679. Presence of minor and person entitled to notice; right to counsel

A minor who is the subject of a juvenile court hearing and any person entitled to notice of the hearing under the provisions of

Section 658, is entitled to be present at such hearing. Any such minor and any such person has the right to be represented at such hearing by counsel of his own choice or, if unable to afford counsel, has the right to be represented by counsel appointed by the court. *(Added by Stats.1961, c. 1616, p. 3481, § 2. Amended by Stats.1967, c. 1355, p. 3195, § 8; Stats.1976, c. 1068, p. 4788, § 44.)*

Cross References

Appointment of counsel, see Welfare and Institutions Code §§ 634, 700.
Hearing defined for purposes of this Article, see Welfare and Institutions Code § 727.4.
Information as to right to counsel, see Welfare and Institutions Code §§ 633, 700.
Notice relating to right to counsel, see Welfare and Institutions Code §§ 633, 659.

Research References

West's California Judicial Council Forms JV–625, Notice of Hearing—Juvenile Delinquency Proceeding (Also Available in Spanish).
5 Witkin, California Criminal Law 4th Criminal Trial § 178 (2021), When Counsel is Required.

§ 680. Control and conduct of proceedings

The judge of the juvenile court shall control all proceedings during the hearings with a view to the expeditious and effective ascertainment of the jurisdictional facts and the ascertainment of all information relative to the present condition and future welfare of the person upon whose behalf the petition is brought. Except where there is a contested issue of fact or law, the proceedings shall be conducted in an informal nonadversary atmosphere with a view to obtaining the maximum co-operation of the minor upon whose behalf the petition is brought and all persons interested in his welfare with such provisions as the court may make for the disposition and care of such minor. *(Added by Stats.1961, c. 1616, p. 3481, § 2.)*

Cross References

Duties of probation officer in court, see Welfare and Institutions Code § 280.
Hearing defined for purposes of this Article, see Welfare and Institutions Code § 727.4.
Hearing on traffic charge, see Welfare and Institutions Code §§ 257, 258.
Non-criminal nature of proceedings, see Welfare and Institutions Code § 203.
Traffic hearing officers, see Welfare and Institutions Code §§ 255, 256.

§ 681. Appearance by district attorney; consent of court

(a) In a juvenile court hearing which is based upon a petition that alleges that the minor upon whose behalf the petition is being brought is a person within the description of Section 602, the prosecuting attorney shall appear on behalf of the people of the State of California.

(b) In a juvenile court hearing which is based upon a petition that alleges that the minor upon whose behalf the petition is being brought is a person within the description of Section 601 and the minor who is the subject of the hearing is represented by counsel, the prosecuting attorney may, with the consent or at the request of the juvenile court judge, or at the request of the probation officer with the consent of the juvenile court judge, appear and participate in the hearing to assist in the ascertaining and presenting of the evidence. Where the petition in a juvenile court proceeding alleges that a minor is a person described in subdivision (a), (b), or (d) of Section 300, and either of the parents, or the guardian, or other person having care or custody of the minor, or who resides in the home of the minor, is charged in a pending criminal prosecution based upon unlawful acts committed against the minor, the prosecuting attorney shall, with the consent or at the request of the juvenile court judge, represent the minor in the interest of the state at the juvenile court proceeding. The terms and conditions of such representation shall be with the consent or approval of the judge of the juvenile court. *(Added by Stats.1976, c. 1071, p. 4824, § 26. Amended by Stats.1978, c. 380, p. 1210, § 157.)*

Cross References

Access to pupil records by persons without written parental consent or under judicial order, see Education Code § 49076.
Hearing defined for purposes of this Article, see Welfare and Institutions Code § 727.4.
Probation officer or social worker defined for purposes of this Chapter, see Welfare and Institutions Code § 215.

§ 681.5. Representation of minor in criminal hearing; dependency proceedings

If a prosecuting attorney has appeared on behalf of the people of the State of California in any juvenile court hearing which is based upon a petition that alleges that a minor is a person within the description of Section 602, neither that prosecuting attorney nor any attorney from the office of that prosecuting attorney shall represent the minor in a juvenile court proceeding alleging that a minor is a person described in Section 300. *(Formerly § 618.5, added by Stats.1992, c. 1327 (A.B.3663), § 2. Renumbered § 681.5 and amended by Stats.2009, c. 140 (A.B.1164), § 188.)*

Cross References

Hearing defined for purposes of this Article, see Welfare and Institutions Code § 727.4.

§ 682. Continuance of hearings relating to proceedings under § 601 or 602

(a) To continue any hearing relating to proceedings pursuant to Section 601 or 602, regardless of the custody status of the minor, beyond the time limit within which the hearing is otherwise required to be heard, a written notice shall be filed and served on all parties to the proceeding at least two court days before the hearing sought to be continued, together with affidavits or declarations detailing specific facts showing good cause for the continuance.

(b) A continuance shall be granted only upon a showing of good cause and only for that period of time shown to be necessary by the moving party at the hearing on the motion. Neither stipulation of the parties nor convenience of the parties is, in and of itself, good cause. Whenever any continuance is granted, the facts which require the continuance shall be entered into the minutes.

(c) Notwithstanding subdivision (a), a party may make a motion for a continuance without complying with the requirements of that subdivision. However, unless the moving party shows good cause for failure to comply with those requirements, the court shall deny the motion.

(d) In any case in which the minor is represented by counsel and no objection is made to an order continuing any such hearing beyond the time limit within which the hearing is otherwise required to be held, the absence of such an objection shall be deemed a consent to the continuance.

(e) When any hearing is continued pursuant to this section, the hearing shall commence on the date to which it was continued or within seven days thereafter whenever the court is satisfied that good cause exists and the moving party will be prepared to proceed within that time. *(Added by Stats.1971, c. 698, p. 1356, § 3. Amended by Stats.1990, c. 1508 (A.B.3216), § 1; Stats.1992, c. 126 (A.B.2073), § 1, eff. July 7, 1992.)*

Cross References

Continuance in referring minor to juvenile justice community resource program, see Welfare and Institutions Code § 702.
Detention recommendation, see Welfare and Institutions Code § 636.
Factors in determination for order releasing minor from custody, see Welfare and Institutions Code § 635.

Hearing defined for purposes of this Article, see Welfare and Institutions Code § 727.4.

Research References

West's California Judicial Council Forms JV–688, Continuance—Juvenile Delinquency.

§ 700. Reading of petition; advice regarding counsel and restitution; continuance

At the beginning of the hearing on a petition filed pursuant to Article 16 (commencing with Section 650) of this chapter, the judge or clerk shall first read the petition to those present and upon request of the minor upon whose behalf the petition has been brought or upon the request of any parent, relative or guardian, the judge shall explain any term of allegation contained therein and the nature of the hearing, its procedures, and possible consequences. The judge shall advise those present that if the petition or petitions are sustained and the minor is ordered to make restitution to the victim, or to pay fines or penalty assessments, the parent or guardian may be liable for the payment of restitution, fines, or penalty assessments. The judge shall ascertain whether the minor and his or her parent or guardian or adult relative, as the case may be, has been informed of the right of the minor to be represented by counsel, and if not, the judge shall advise the minor and that person, if present, of the right to have counsel present and where applicable, of the right to appointed counsel. The court shall appoint counsel to represent the minor if he or she appears at the hearing without counsel, whether he or she is unable to afford counsel or not, unless there is an intelligent waiver of the right of counsel by the minor * * *. The court shall continue the hearing for not to exceed seven days, as necessary to make an appointment of counsel, or to enable counsel to acquaint himself or herself with the case, and shall continue the hearing as necessary to provide reasonable opportunity for the minor and the parent or guardian or adult relative to prepare for the hearing. *(Added by Stats.1961, c. 1616, p. 3481, § 2. Amended by Stats.1963, c. 917, p. 2167, § 9; Stats.1967, c. 1355, p. 3195, § 10; Stats.1968, c. 1223, p. 2333, § 2; Stats.1970, c. 625, p. 1242, § 2; Stats.1976, c. 1068, p. 4788, § 46; Stats.1994, c. 836 (A.B.1629), § 3; Stats.1995, c. 313 (A.B.817), § 19, eff. Aug. 3, 1995; Stats.2017, c. 678 (S.B.190), § 13, eff. Jan. 1, 2018.)*

Cross References

Appointment of counsel, see Welfare and Institutions Code § 634.
County financial evaluation officer, see Government Code § 27750 et seq.
Hearing defined for purposes of this Article, see Welfare and Institutions Code § 727.4.
Information as to right to counsel, see Welfare and Institutions Code §§ 633, 659.
Persons entitled to counsel, see Welfare and Institutions Code §§ 633, 679.
Probation officer, attendance to represent interests of minor, see Welfare and Institutions Code § 280.
Public defender, duty to represent juvenile upon order of court, see Government Code § 27706.
Relative defined for purposes of this Article, see Welfare and Institutions Code § 727.4.

Research References

West's California Judicial Council Forms JV–642, Initial Appearance Hearing—Juvenile Delinquency.
West's California Judicial Council Forms JV–644, Jurisdiction Hearing—Juvenile Delinquency.
5 Witkin, California Criminal Law 4th Criminal Trial § 178 (2021), When Counsel is Required.

§ 700.1. Motion to suppress evidence resulting from search and seizure; time of hearing; judgment of dismissal

Any motion to suppress as evidence any tangible or intangible thing obtained as a result of an unlawful search or seizure shall be heard prior to the attachment of jeopardy and shall be heard at least five judicial days after receipt of notice by the people unless the people are willing to waive a portion of this time.

If the court grants a motion to suppress prior to the attachment of jeopardy over the objection of the people, the court shall enter a judgment of dismissal as to all counts of the petition except those counts on which the prosecuting attorney elects to proceed pursuant to Section 701.

If, prior to the attachment of jeopardy, opportunity for this motion did not exist or the person alleged to come within the provisions of the juvenile court law was not aware of the grounds for the motion, that person shall have the right to make this motion during the course of the proceeding under Section 701. *(Added by Stats.1980, c. 1095, p. 3511, § 2.)*

Cross References

Ruling on motion to suppress, appeal, see Welfare and Institutions Code § 800.

Research References

4 Witkin, California Criminal Law 4th Illegally Obtained Evidence § 443 (2021), Nature of Statute.

§ 700.2. Compulsory education violations; open hearing; choice and disqualification of judge

Upon his or her appearance before the juvenile court on a complaint charging violation of Section 48293 of the Education Code, the juvenile court shall inform the parent, guardian, or other person having control or charge of the minor of the right to an open hearing and of the right to have a hearing on the complaint before a judge different than the judge who has heard or is to hear the proceeding pursuant to Section 601. The provisions of Section 170.6 of the Code of Civil Procedure shall be explained to the parent, guardian, or other person having control or charge of the minor. *(Added by Stats.1985, c. 120, § 6.)*

Cross References

Hearing defined for purposes of this Article, see Welfare and Institutions Code § 727.4.

§ 700.3. Determination of offense as misdemeanor in juvenile court proceedings under Section 602

If a petition filed in the juvenile court alleging that a minor comes within the provisions of Section 602 alleges that a minor has committed an offense that would, in the case of an adult, be punishable alternatively as a felony or a misdemeanor, the court, subject to a hearing, at any stage of a proceeding under Section 602, may determine that the offense is a misdemeanor, in which event the case shall proceed as if the minor had been brought before the court on a misdemeanor petition. *(Added by Stats.2022, c. 197 (S.B.1493), § 37, eff. Jan. 1, 2023.)*

§ 701. Description of minor; reception of evidence; extrajudicial admissions or confessions; objections to evidence

At the hearing, the court shall first consider only the question whether the minor is a person described by Section 300, 601, or 602. The admission and exclusion of evidence shall be pursuant to the rules of evidence established by the Evidence Code and by judicial decision. Proof beyond a reasonable doubt supported by evidence, legally admissible in the trial of criminal cases, must be adduced to support a finding that the minor is a person described by Section 602, and a preponderance of evidence, legally admissible in the trial of civil cases must be adduced to support a finding that the minor is a person described by Section 300 or 601. When it appears that the minor has made an extrajudicial admission or confession and denies the same at the hearing, the court may continue the hearing for not to exceed seven days to enable the prosecuting attorney to subpoena witnesses to attend the hearing to prove the allegations of the petition. If the minor is not represented by counsel at the hearing, it shall be deemed that objections that could have been made to the evidence were made. *(Added by Stats.1961, c. 1616, p. 3482, § 2.*

Amended by Stats.1971, c. 934, p. 1833, § 1; Stats.1976, c. 1068, p. 4789, § 48; Stats.1976, c. 1071, p. 4825, § 27; Stats.1977, c. 579, p. 1922, § 196.)

Cross References

Access to pupil records by persons without written parental consent or under judicial order, see Education Code § 49076.
Attendance of witness required by subpoena, see Code of Civil Procedure §§ 1985, 1985.5, 1986.
Duties of probation officer in court, see Welfare and Institutions Code § 280.
Entry of findings and orders, see Welfare and Institutions Code § 825.
Explanation of petition, see Welfare and Institutions Code § 700.
Findings, orders and judgment, see Welfare and Institutions Code §§ 702 et seq., 725 et seq.
Hearing defined for purposes of this Article, see Welfare and Institutions Code § 727.4.
Right to counsel, see Welfare and Institutions Code §§ 633, 634, 659, 679, 700.
Self-incrimination and confrontation of witnesses, see Welfare and Institutions Code § 702.5.

Research References

West's California Judicial Council Forms JV–644, Jurisdiction Hearing—Juvenile Delinquency.

§ 701.1. Motion to dismiss at close of petitioner's evidence

At the hearing, the court, on motion of the minor or on its own motion, shall order that the petition be dismissed and that the minor be discharged from any detention or restriction therefore ordered, after the presentation of evidence on behalf of the petitioner has been closed, if the court, upon weighing the evidence then before it, finds that the minor is not a person described by Section 601 or 602. If such a motion at the close of evidence offered by the petitioner is not granted, the minor may offer evidence without first having reserved that right. *(Added by Stats.1980, c. 266, p. 539, § 2.)*

Cross References

Hearing defined for purposes of this Article, see Welfare and Institutions Code § 727.4.

§ 702. Finding and order; dismissal; discharge; continuance to refer minor to juvenile justice community resource program and receive social study or other evidence; detention order

After hearing the evidence, the court shall make a finding, noted in the minutes of the court, whether or not the minor is a person described by Section 300, 601, or 602. If it finds that the minor is not such a person, it shall order that the petition be dismissed and the minor be discharged from any detention or restriction theretofore ordered. If the court finds that the minor is such a person, it shall make and enter its findings and order accordingly, and shall then proceed to hear evidence on the question of the proper disposition to be made of the minor. Prior to doing so, it may continue the hearing, if necessary, to receive the social study of the probation officer, to refer the minor to a juvenile justice community resource program as defined in Article 5.2 (commencing with Section 1784) of Chapter 1 of Division 2.5, or to receive other evidence on its own motion or the motion of a parent or guardian for not to exceed 10 judicial days if the minor is detained during the continuance. If the minor is not detained, it may continue the hearing to a date not later than 30 days after the date of filing of the petition. The court may, for good cause shown continue the hearing for an additional 15 days, if the minor is not detained. The court may make such order for detention of the minor or his or her release from detention, during the period of the continuance, as is appropriate.

If the minor is found to have committed an offense which would in the case of an adult be punishable alternatively as a felony or a misdemeanor, the court shall declare the offense to be a misdemeanor or felony. *(Added by Stats.1961, c. 1616, p. 3482, § 2. Amended by Stats.1963, c. 917, p. 2167, § 10; Stats.1968, c. 536, p. 1188, § 2; Stats.1976, c. 1068, p. 4789, § 49; Stats.1976, c. 1071, p. 4825, § 28; Stats.1977, c. 579, p. 1923, § 203; Stats.1984, c. 1752, § 1.)*

Cross References

California Community Care Facilities Act, residence in facility within one mile of elementary school by person convicted of sex offense against minor prohibited, see Health and Safety Code § 1564.
Community colleges, provisions applying to all employees, "ex offense", see Education Code § 87010.
Courts closed for transaction of judicial business, conditions, see Government Code § 68106.
Dismissal of petition in the interests of justice and welfare of minor, see Welfare and Institutions Code § 782.
Entry of findings and orders, see Welfare and Institutions Code § 825.
Felonies, definition and penalties, see Penal Code §§ 17, 18.
First pleading by people in superior court, see Penal Code § 949.
Hearing defined for purposes of this Article, see Welfare and Institutions Code § 727.4.
Hearing on traffic charge, see Welfare and Institutions Code §§ 257, 258.
Judgments and orders, see Welfare and Institutions Code § 725 et seq.
Misdemeanors, definition and penalties, see Penal Code §§ 17, 19, 19.2.
Modification of Juvenile Court Judgments and Orders, see Welfare and Institutions Code § 775 et seq.
Order adjudging minor ward of juvenile court, see Welfare and Institutions Code § 203.
Probation officer or social worker defined for purposes of this Chapter, see Welfare and Institutions Code § 215.
Rights of minor in releasing or destruction of juvenile court records, see Welfare and Institutions Code § 826.6.
Self-incrimination and confrontation of witnesses, see Welfare and Institutions Code § 702.5.
Social study of minor, preparation by probation officer for disposition of case, see Welfare and Institutions Code § 280.
Statement of court that social study was read and considered, see Welfare and Institutions Code § 706.
Temporary custody of minors violating court order, see Welfare and Institutions Code § 625.

Research References

West's California Judicial Council Forms JV–644, Jurisdiction Hearing—Juvenile Delinquency.
West's California Judicial Council Forms JV–665, Disposition—Juvenile Delinquency.
West's California Judicial Council Forms JV–667, Custodial and Out-Of-Home Placement Disposition Attachment.

§ 702.3. Insanity plea joined with general denial; hearings; treatment; period of commitment

Notwithstanding any other provision of law:

(a) When a minor denies, by a plea of not guilty by reason of insanity, the allegations of a petition filed pursuant to Section 602 of the Welfare and Institutions Code, and also joins with that denial a general denial of the conduct alleged in the petition, he or she shall first be subject to a hearing as if he or she had made no allegation of insanity. If the petition is sustained or if the minor denies the allegations only by reason of insanity, then a hearing shall be held on the question of whether the minor was insane at the time the offense was committed.

(b) If the court finds that the minor was insane at the time the offense was committed, the court, unless it appears to the court that the minor has fully recovered his or her sanity, shall direct that the minor be confined in a state hospital for the care and treatment of the mentally disordered or any other appropriate public or private mental health facility approved by the community program director, or the court may order the minor to undergo outpatient treatment as specified in Title 15 (commencing with Section 1600) of Part 2 of the Penal Code. The court shall transmit a copy of its order to the community program director or his or her designee. If the allegations of the petition specifying any felony are found to be true, the court shall direct that the minor be confined in a state hospital or other public or private mental health facility approved by the community program director for a minimum of 180 days, before the minor may be released on outpatient treatment. Prior to making the order directing that the minor be confined in a state hospital or other facility or ordered to undergo outpatient treatment, the court shall order the community program director or his or her designee to evaluate the minor and to submit to the court within 15 judicial days of the order his or her written recommendation as to whether the minor should be required to undergo outpatient treatment or committed to a state hospital or another mental health facility. If, however, it shall appear to the court that the minor has fully recovered his or her sanity the minor shall be remanded to the custody of the probation department until his or her sanity shall have been finally determined in the manner prescribed by law. A minor committed to a state hospital or other facility or ordered to undergo outpatient treatment shall not be released from confinement or the required outpatient treatment unless and until the court which committed him or her shall, after notice and hearing, in the manner provided in Section 1026.2 of the Penal Code, find and determine that his or her sanity has been restored.

(c) When the court, after considering the placement recommendation for the community program director required in subdivision (b), orders that the minor be confined in a state hospital or other public or private mental health facility, the court shall provide copies of the following documents which shall be taken with the minor to the state hospital or other treatment facility where the minor is to be confined:

(1) The commitment order, including a specification of the charges.

(2) The computation or statement setting forth the maximum time of commitment in accordance with Section 1026.5 and subdivision (e).

(3) A computation or statement setting forth the amount of credit, if any, to be deducted from the maximum term of commitment.

(4) State Summary Criminal History information.

(5) Any arrest or detention reports prepared by the police department or other law enforcement agency.

(6) Any court-ordered psychiatric examination or evaluation reports.

(7) The community program director's placement recommendation report.

(d) The procedures set forth in Sections 1026, 1026.1, 1026.2, 1026.3, 1026.4, 1026.5, and 1027 of the Penal Code, and in Title 15 (commencing with Section 1600) of Part 2 of the Penal Code, shall be applicable to minors pursuant to this section, except that, in cases involving minors, the probation department rather than the sheriff, shall have jurisdiction over the minor.

(e) No minor may be committed pursuant to this section for a period longer than the jurisdictional limits of the juvenile court, pursuant to Section 607, unless, at the conclusion of the commitment, by reason of a mental disease, defect, or disorder, he or she represents a substantial danger of physical harm to others, in which case the commitment for care and treatment beyond the jurisdictional age may be extended by proceedings in superior court in accordance with and under the circumstances specified in subdivision (b) of Section 1026.5 of the Penal Code.

(f) The provision of a jury trial in superior court on the issue of extension of commitment shall not be construed to authorize the determination of any issue in juvenile court proceedings to be made by a jury. *(Added by Stats.1978, c. 867, p. 2729, § 1. Amended by Stats.1984, c. 1415, § 3; Stats.1984, c. 1488, § 14.5; Stats.1989, c. 625, § 3.)*

Cross References

Detention or sentence of minor to adult institutions for sex offenses unlawful, see Welfare and Institutions Code § 208.

Hearing defined for purposes of this Article, see Welfare and Institutions Code § 727.4.

Research References

1 Witkin California Criminal Law 4th Introduction to Crimes § 11 (2021), Nature of Protection.

§ 702.5. Privilege against self-incrimination; confrontation by and cross-examination of witnesses

In any hearing conducted pursuant to Section 701 or 702 to determine whether a minor is a person described in Section 601 or 602, the minor has a privilege against self-incrimination and has a right to confrontation by, and cross-examination of, witnesses. *(Added by Stats.1967, c. 1355, p. 3196, § 11.)*

Cross References

Hearing defined for purposes of this Article, see Welfare and Institutions Code § 727.4.

Privilege against self-incrimination, see Const. Art. 1, § 15, cl. 6.

§ 705. Holding minor in psychopathic ward of county hospital

Whenever the court, before or during the hearing on the petition, is of the opinion that the minor is mentally disordered or if the court is in doubt concerning the mental health of any such person, the court may proceed as provided in Section 6550 of this code or Section 4011.6 of the Penal Code. *(Added by Stats.1961, c. 1616, p. 3484, § 2. Amended by Stats.1967, c. 1267, p. 3072, § 1; Stats.1976, c. 445, p. 1178, § 3, eff. July 10, 1976.)*

Cross References

Detention or sentence of minor to adult institutions for sex offenses unlawful, see Welfare and Institutions Code § 208.

Hearing defined for purposes of this Article, see Welfare and Institutions Code § 727.4.

§ 706. Evidence as to proper disposition of minor; social study; victims' statements; other evidence; risk assessment score if registration as sex offender recommended

After finding that a minor is a person described in Section 601 or 602, the court shall hear evidence on the question of the proper disposition to be made of the minor. The court shall receive in evidence the social study of the minor made by the probation officer and any other relevant and material evidence that may be offered, including any written or oral statement offered by the victim, the parent or guardian of the victim if the victim is a minor, or if the victim has died or is incapacitated, the victim's next of kin, as authorized by subdivision (b) of Section 656.2. In addition, if the probation officer has recommended that the minor be transferred to the Department of Corrections and Rehabilitation, Division of Juvenile Justice pursuant to an adjudication for an offense requiring him or her to register as a sex offender pursuant to Section 290.008 of the Penal Code, the SARATSO selected pursuant to subdivision (d) of Section 290.04 of the Penal Code shall be used to assess the minor, and the court shall receive that risk assessment score into evidence. In any judgment and order of disposition, the court shall state that the social study made by the probation officer has been read and that the social study and any statement has been considered by the court. *(Added by Stats.1961, c. 1616, p. 3485, § 2. Amended by Stats.1976, c. 1068, p. 4790, § 50; Stats.1995, c. 234 (A.B.889), § 3; Stats.2009, c. 582 (S.B.325), § 6.)*

Cross References

Continuance to receive social study, see Welfare and Institutions Code § 702.

Duty of probation officer to prepare social study, see Welfare and Institutions Code § 280.

Mental health evaluations, recommendations, and dispositional procedures for minors, see Welfare and Institutions Code § 710 et seq.

Probation officer or social worker defined for purposes of this Chapter, see Welfare and Institutions Code § 215.

Reasonable cause for probation officer to make an investigation, see Welfare and Institutions Code § 652.
Rights of minor in releasing or destruction of juvenile court records, see Welfare and Institutions Code § 826.6.
Sex offenders, access to records by persons authorized to administer SARATSO or authorized to train, monitor, or review scoring, see Penal Code § 290.07.
Sex offenders, administration of SARATSO, immunity from liability for good faith conduct, see Penal Code § 290.06.

§ 706.5. Contents and scope of social study

(a) If placement in foster care is recommended by the probation officer, or where the minor is already in foster care placement or pending placement pursuant to an earlier order, the social study prepared by the probation officer that is received into evidence at disposition pursuant to Section 706 shall include a case plan, as described in Section 706.6. If the court elects to hold the first status review at the disposition hearing, the social study shall also include, but not be limited to, the factual material described in subdivision (c).

(b) If placement in foster care is not recommended by the probation officer prior to disposition, but the court orders foster care placement, the court shall order the probation officer to prepare a case plan, as described in Section 706.6, within 30 days of the placement order. The case plan shall be filed with the court.

(c) At each status review hearing, the social study shall include, but not be limited to, an updated case plan as described in Section 706.6 and the following information:

(1)(A) The continuing necessity for and appropriateness of the placement.

(B) On and after October 1, 2021, for the minor or nonminor dependent whose placement in a short-term residential therapeutic program has been reviewed and approved, and, on and after July 1, 2022, for the minor or nonminor dependent whose placement in a community treatment facility has been reviewed and approved, pursuant to Section 727.12, the social study shall include evidence of each of the following:

(i) Ongoing assessment of the strengths and needs of the minor or nonminor dependent continues to support the determination that the needs of the minor or nonminor dependent cannot be met by family members or in another family-based setting, placement in a short-term residential therapeutic program or community treatment facility, as applicable, continues to provide the most effective and appropriate level of care in the least restrictive environment, and the placement is consistent with the short- and long-term mental and behavioral health goals and permanency plan for the minor or nonminor dependent.

(ii) Documentation of the minor or nonminor dependent's specific treatment or service needs that will be met in the placement, and the length of time the minor or nonminor dependent is expected to need the treatment or services. For a Medi-Cal beneficiary, the determination of services and expected length of time for those services funded by Medi-Cal shall be based upon medical necessity and on all other state and federal Medi-Cal requirements, and shall be reflected in the documentation.

(iii) Documentation of the intensive and ongoing efforts made by the probation department, consistent with the minor or nonminor dependent's permanency plan, to prepare the minor or nonminor dependent to return home or to be placed with a fit and willing relative, a legal guardian, an adoptive parent, in a resource family home, tribally approved home, or in another appropriate family-based setting, or, in the case of a nonminor dependent, in a supervised independent living setting.

(2) The extent of the probation department's compliance with the case plan in making reasonable efforts to safely return the minor to the minor's home or to complete whatever steps are necessary to finalize the permanent placement of the minor.

(3) The extent of progress that has been made by the minor and parent or guardian toward alleviating or mitigating the causes necessitating placement in foster care.

(4) If the first permanency planning hearing has not yet occurred, the social study shall include the likely date by which the minor may be returned to and safely maintained in the home or placed for adoption, appointed a legal guardian, permanently placed with a fit and willing relative, or referred to another planned permanent living arrangement.

(5) Whether the minor has been or will be referred to educational services and what services the minor is receiving, including special education and related services if the minor has exceptional needs as described in Part 30 (commencing with Section 56000) of Division 4 of Title 2 of the Education Code or accommodations if the child has disabilities as described in Chapter 16 (commencing with Section 701) of Title 29 of the United States Code Annotated. The probation officer or child advocate shall solicit comments from the appropriate local education agency prior to completion of the social study.

(6) If the parent or guardian is unwilling or unable to participate in making an educational or developmental services decision for their child, or if other circumstances exist that compromise the ability of the parent or guardian to make educational or developmental services decisions for the child, the probation department shall consider whether the right of the parent or guardian to make educational or developmental services decisions for the minor should be limited. If the study makes that recommendation, it shall identify whether there is a responsible adult available to make educational or developmental services decisions for the minor pursuant to Section 726.

(7) When the minor is 16 years of age or older and in another planned permanent living arrangement, the social study shall include a description of all of the following:

(A) The intensive and ongoing efforts to return the minor to the home of the parent, place the minor for adoption, or establish a legal guardianship, as appropriate.

(B) The steps taken to do both of the following:

(i) Ensure that the minor's care provider is following the reasonable and prudent parent standard.

(ii) Determine whether the minor has regular, ongoing opportunities to engage in age or developmentally appropriate activities, including consulting with the minor about opportunities for the minor to participate in the activities.

(8) When the minor is under 16 years of age and has a permanent plan of return home, adoption, legal guardianship, or placement with a fit and willing relative, the social study shall include a description of any barriers to achieving the permanent plan and the efforts made by the agency to address those barriers.

(9)(A) For a child who is 10 years of age or older and has been declared a ward of the juvenile court pursuant to Section 601 or 602 for a year or longer, the information in subparagraph (B) of paragraph (1) of subdivision (h) of Section 366.1.

(B) For a child who is 10 years of age or older, whether the probation officer has informed the minor or nonminor dependent of the information in paragraph (2) of subdivision (h) of Section 366.1.

(C) This paragraph does not affect any applicable confidentiality law.

(10) For a child who is 16 years of age or older or for a nonminor dependent, whether the probation officer has, pursuant to the requirements of paragraph (22) of subdivision (g) of Section 16501.1, identified the person or persons who shall be responsible for assisting the child or nonminor dependent with applications for postsecondary education and related financial aid, or that the child or nonminor

dependent stated that they do not want to pursue postsecondary education, including career or technical education.

(d) At each permanency planning hearing, the social study shall include, but not be limited to, an updated case plan as described in Section 706.6, the factual material described in subdivision (c) of this section, and a recommended permanent plan for the minor. *(Added by Stats.2001, c. 831 (A.B.1696), § 6. Amended by Stats.2002, c. 785 (S.B.1677), § 6; Stats.2011, c. 471 (S.B.368), § 3; Stats.2015, c. 425 (S.B.794), § 16, eff. Jan. 1, 2016; Stats.2021, c. 86 (A.B.153), § 26, eff. July 16, 2021; Stats.2022, c. 50 (S.B.187), § 24, eff. June 30, 2022.)*

Cross References

Foster care defined for purposes of this Article, see Welfare and Institutions Code § 727.4.
Hearing defined for purposes of this Article, see Welfare and Institutions Code § 727.4.
Minor in foster care adjudged ward of the court, considerations and procedures at a permanency planning hearing, see Welfare and Institutions Code § 727.3.
Minor in foster care adjudged ward of the court, procedure for reunification of minor with family, see Welfare and Institutions Code § 727.2.
Probation officer or social worker defined for purposes of this Chapter, see Welfare and Institutions Code § 215.
Reasonable efforts defined for purposes of this Article, see Welfare and Institutions Code § 727.4.
Relative defined for purposes of this Article, see Welfare and Institutions Code § 727.4.

§ 706.6. Information required in case plan where foster care is being considered

(a) Services to minors are best provided in a framework that integrates service planning and delivery among multiple service systems, including the mental health system, using a team-based approach, such as a child and family team. A child and family team brings together individuals that engage with the child or youth and family in assessing, planning, and delivering services. Use of a team approach increases efficiency, and thus reduces cost, by increasing coordination of formal services and integrating the natural and informal supports available to the child or youth and family.

(b)(1) For the purposes of this section, "child and family team" has the same meaning as in paragraph (4) of subdivision (a) of Section 16501.

(2) In its development of the case plan, the probation agency shall consider and document any recommendations of the child and family team, as defined in paragraph (4) of subdivision (a) of Section 16501. The agency shall document the rationale for any inconsistencies between the case plan and the child and family team recommendations.

(c) A case plan prepared as required by Section 706.5 shall be submitted to the court. It shall either be attached to the social study or incorporated as a separate section within the social study. The case plan shall include, but not be limited to, the following information:

(1) A description of the circumstances that resulted in the minor being placed under the supervision of the probation department and in foster care.

(2) Documentation of the preplacement assessment of the minor's and family's strengths and service needs showing that preventive services have been provided, and that reasonable efforts to prevent out-of-home placement have been made. The assessment shall include the type of placement best equipped to meet those needs.

(3)(A) A description of the type of home or institution in which the minor is to be placed, and the reasons for that placement decision, including a discussion of the safety and appropriateness of the placement, including the recommendations of the child and family team, if available.

(B) An appropriate placement is a placement in the least restrictive, most family-like environment that promotes normal childhood experiences, in closest proximity to the minor's home, that meets the minor's best interests and special needs.

(d) The following shall apply:

(1) The agency selecting a placement shall consider, in order of priority:

(A) Placement with relatives, nonrelated extended family members, and tribal members.

(B) Foster family homes and certified homes or resource families of foster family agencies.

(C) Treatment and intensive treatment certified homes or resource families of foster family agencies, or multidimensional treatment foster homes or therapeutic foster care homes.

(D) Group care placements in the following order:

(i) Short-term residential therapeutic programs.

(ii) Group homes vendored by a regional center.

(iii) Community treatment facilities.

(iv) Out-of-state residential facilities as authorized by subdivision (b) of Section 727.1.

(2) Although the placement options shall be considered in the preferential order specified in paragraph (1), the placement of a child may be with any of these placement settings in order to ensure the selection of a safe placement setting that is in the child's best interests and meets the child's special needs.

(3)(A) A minor may be placed into a community care facility licensed as a short-term residential therapeutic program, as defined in subdivision (ad) of Section 11400, provided the case plan indicates that the placement is for the purposes of providing short-term, specialized, intensive, and trauma-informed treatment for the minor, the case plan specifies the need for, nature of, and anticipated duration of this treatment, and the case plan includes transitioning the minor to a less restrictive environment and the projected timeline by which the minor will be transitioned to a less restrictive environment.

(B) On and after October 1, 2021, within 30 days of the minor's placement in a short-term residential therapeutic program, and, on and after July 1, 2022, within 30 days of the minor's placement in a community treatment facility, the case plan shall document all of the following:

(i) The reasonable and good faith effort by the probation officer to identify and include all required individuals in the child and family team.

(ii) All contact information for members of the child and family team, as well as contact information for other relatives and nonrelative extended family members who are not part of the child and family team.

(iii) Evidence that meetings of the child and family team, including the meetings related to the determination required under Section 4096, are held at a time and place convenient for the family.

(iv) If reunification is the goal, evidence that the parent from whom the minor or nonminor dependent was removed provided input on the members of the child and family team.

(v) Evidence that the determination required under Section 4096 was conducted in conjunction with the child and family team.

(vi) The placement preferences of the minor or nonminor dependent and the child and family team relative to the determination and, if the placement preferences of the minor or nonminor dependent or the child and family team are not the placement setting recommended by the qualified individual conducting the determination, the reasons why the preferences of the team or minor or nonminor dependent were not recommended.

(C) Following the court review required pursuant to Section 727.12, the case plan shall document the court's approval or disapproval of the placement.

(D) When the minor or nonminor dependent has been placed in a short-term residential therapeutic program or a community treatment facility for more than 12 consecutive months or 18 nonconsecutive months, or, in the case of a minor who has not attained 13 years of age, for more than six consecutive or nonconsecutive months, the case plan shall include both of the following:

(i) Documentation of the information submitted to the court pursuant to subparagraph (B) of paragraph (1) of subdivision (c) of Section 706.5.

(ii) Documentation that the chief probation officer of the county probation department, or their designee, has approved the continued placement of the minor or nonminor dependent in the setting.

(E)(i) On and after October 1, 2021, prior to discharge from a short-term residential therapeutic program, and, on and after July 1, 2022, prior to discharge from a community treatment facility, the case plan shall include a description of the type of in-home or institution-based services to encourage the safety, stability, and appropriateness of the next placement, including the recommendations of the child and family team, if available.

(ii) A plan, developed in collaboration with the short-term residential therapeutic program or community treatment facility, as applicable, for the provision of discharge planning and family-based aftercare support pursuant to Section 4096.6.

(e) Effective January 1, 2010, a case plan shall ensure the educational stability of the child while in foster care and shall include both of the following:

(1) Assurances that the placement takes into account the appropriateness of the current educational setting and the proximity to the school in which the child is enrolled at the time of placement.

(2) An assurance that the placement agency has coordinated with appropriate local educational agencies to ensure that the child remains in the school in which the child is enrolled at the time of placement, or, if remaining in that school is not in the best interests of the child, assurances by the placement agency and the local educational agency to provide immediate and appropriate enrollment in a new school and to provide all of the child's educational records to the new school.

(f) Specific time-limited goals and related activities designed to enable the safe return of the minor to the minor's home, or in the event that return to the minor's home is not possible, activities designed to result in permanent placement or emancipation. Specific responsibility for carrying out the planned activities shall be assigned to one or more of the following:

(1) The probation department.

(2) The minor's parent or parents or legal guardian or guardians, as applicable.

(3) The minor.

(4) The foster parents or licensed agency providing foster care.

(g) The projected date of completion of the case plan objectives and the date services will be terminated.

(h)(1) Scheduled visits between the minor and the minor's family and an explanation if no visits are made.

(2) Whether the child has other siblings, and, if any siblings exist, all of the following:

(A) The nature of the relationship between the child and the child's siblings.

(B) The appropriateness of developing or maintaining the sibling relationships pursuant to Section 16002.

(C) If the siblings are not placed together in the same home, why the siblings are not placed together and what efforts are being made to place the siblings together, or why those efforts are not appropriate.

(D) If the siblings are not placed together, all of the following:

(i) The frequency and nature of the visits between the siblings.

(ii) If there are visits between the siblings, whether the visits are supervised or unsupervised. If the visits are supervised, a discussion of the reasons why the visits are supervised, and what needs to be accomplished in order for the visits to be unsupervised.

(iii) If there are visits between the siblings, a description of the location and length of the visits.

(iv) Any plan to increase visitation between the siblings.

(E) The impact of the sibling relationships on the child's placement and planning for legal permanence.

(F) The continuing need to suspend sibling interaction, if applicable, pursuant to subdivision (c) of Section 16002.

(3) The factors the court may consider in making a determination regarding the nature of the child's sibling relationships may include, but are not limited to, whether the siblings were raised together in the same home, whether the siblings have shared significant common experiences or have existing close and strong bonds, whether either sibling expresses a desire to visit or live with the child's sibling, as applicable, and whether ongoing contact is in the child's best emotional interests.

(i)(1) When placement is made in a resource family home, short-term residential therapeutic program, or other children's residential facility that is either a substantial distance from the home of the minor's parent or legal guardian or out of state, the case plan shall specify the reasons why the placement is the most appropriate and is in the best interest of the minor.

(2) When an out-of-state residential facility placement is recommended or made, the case plan shall comply with Section 727.1 of this code and Section 7911.1 of the Family Code. In addition, the case plan shall include documentation that the county placing agency has satisfied Section 16010.9. The case plan shall also address what in-state services or facilities were used or considered and why they were not recommended.

(j) If applicable, efforts to make it possible to place siblings together, unless it has been determined that placement together is not in the best interest of one or more siblings.

(k) A schedule of visits between the minor and the probation officer, including a monthly visitation schedule for those children placed in group short-term residential therapeutic programs or out-of-state residential facilities, as defined in subdivision (b) of Section 7910 of the Family Code.

(*l*) Health and education information about the minor, school records, immunizations, known medical problems, and any known medications the minor may be taking, names and addresses of the minor's health and educational providers; the minor's grade level performance; assurances that the minor's placement in foster care takes into account proximity to the school in which the minor was enrolled at the time of placement; and other relevant health and educational information.

(m) When out-of-home services are used and the goal is reunification, the case plan shall describe the services that were provided to prevent removal of the minor from the home, those services to be provided to assist in reunification and the services to be provided concurrently to achieve legal permanency if efforts to reunify fail.

(n)(1) The updated case plan prepared for a permanency planning hearing shall include a recommendation for a permanent plan for the minor. The identified permanent plan for a minor under 16 years of age shall be return home, adoption, legal guardianship, or placement with a fit and willing relative. The case plan shall identify any barriers to achieving legal permanence and the steps the agency will take to address those barriers.

(2) If, after considering reunification, adoptive placement, legal guardianship, or permanent placement with a fit and willing relative the probation officer recommends placement in a planned permanent living arrangement for a minor 16 years of age or older, the case plan shall include documentation of a compelling reason or reasons why termination of parental rights is not in the minor's best interest. For purposes of this subdivision, a "compelling reason" shall have the same meaning as in subdivision (c) of Section 727.3. The case plan shall also identify the intensive and ongoing efforts to return the minor to the home of the parent, place the minor for adoption, establish a legal guardianship, or place the minor with a fit and willing relative, as appropriate. Efforts shall include the use of technology, including social media, to find biological family members of the minor.

(*o*) Each updated case plan shall include a description of the services that have been provided to the minor under the plan and an evaluation of the appropriateness and effectiveness of those services.

(p) A statement that the parent or legal guardian, and the minor have had an opportunity to participate in the development of the case plan, to review the case plan, to sign the case plan, and to receive a copy of the plan, or an explanation about why the parent, legal guardian, or minor was not able to participate or sign the case plan.

(q) For a minor in out-of-home care who is 16 years of age or older, a written description of the programs and services, which will help the minor prepare for the transition from foster care to successful adulthood. *(Added by Stats.1999, c. 997 (A.B.575), § 13. Amended by Stats.2001, c. 831 (A.B.1696), § 7; Stats.2009–2010, 4th Ex.Sess., c. 4 (A.B.4), § 8, eff. July 28, 2009; Stats.2014, c. 773 (S.B.1099), § 8, eff. Jan. 1, 2015; Stats.2015, c. 425 (S.B.794), § 17, eff. Jan. 1, 2016; Stats.2015, c. 773 (A.B.403), § 49.5, eff. Jan. 1, 2016; Stats.2016, c. 612 (A.B.1997), § 76, eff. Jan. 1, 2017; Stats.2021, c. 86 (A.B.153), § 27, eff. July 16, 2021; Stats.2022, c. 50 (S.B.187), § 25, eff. June 30, 2022.)*

Cross References

Case plans for detained minors, recommendation of foster care placement, see Welfare and Institutions Code § 636.1.
Foster care defined for purposes of this Article, see Welfare and Institutions Code § 727.4.
Hearing defined for purposes of this Article, see Welfare and Institutions Code § 727.4.
Probation officer or social worker defined for purposes of this Chapter, see Welfare and Institutions Code § 215.
Relative defined for purposes of this Article, see Welfare and Institutions Code § 727.4.
Termination of parental rights, minor ward of the state and in foster care fifteen of twenty-two months, see Welfare and Institutions Code § 727.32.

Research References

West's California Judicial Council Forms JV–665, Disposition—Juvenile Delinquency.
West's California Judicial Council Forms JV–667, Custodial and Out-Of-Home Placement Disposition Attachment.

§ 707. Fitness hearing

(a)(1) In any case in which a minor is alleged to be a person described in Section 602 by reason of the violation, when * * * the minor was 16 years of age or older, of any offense listed in subdivision (b) or any other felony criminal statute, the district attorney or other appropriate prosecuting officer may make a motion to transfer the minor from juvenile court to a court of criminal jurisdiction. The motion shall be made prior to the attachment of jeopardy. Upon the motion, the juvenile court shall order the probation officer to submit a report on the behavioral patterns and social history of the minor. The report shall include any written or oral statement offered by the victim pursuant to Section 656.2.

(2) In any case in which an individual is alleged to be a person described in Section 602 by reason of the violation, when * * * the individual was 14 or 15 years of age, of any offense listed in subdivision (b), but was not apprehended prior to the end of juvenile court jurisdiction, the district attorney or other appropriate prosecuting officer may make a motion to transfer the individual from juvenile court to a court of criminal jurisdiction. The motion shall be made prior to the attachment of jeopardy. Upon the motion, the juvenile court shall order the probation officer to submit a report on the behavioral patterns and social history of the individual. The report shall include any written or oral statement offered by the victim pursuant to Section 656.2.

(3) Following submission and consideration of the report, and of any other relevant evidence that the petitioner or the minor may wish to submit, the juvenile court shall decide whether the minor should be transferred to a court of criminal jurisdiction. In order to find that the minor should be transferred to a court of criminal jurisdiction, the court shall find by clear and convincing evidence that the minor is not amenable to rehabilitation while under the jurisdiction of the juvenile court. In making its decision, the court shall consider the criteria specified in subparagraphs (A) to (E), inclusive. If the court orders a transfer of jurisdiction, the court shall recite the basis for its decision in an order entered upon the minutes, which shall include the reasons supporting the court's finding that the minor is not amenable to rehabilitation while under the jurisdiction of the juvenile court. In any case in which a hearing has been noticed pursuant to this section, the court shall postpone the taking of a plea to the petition until the conclusion of the transfer hearing, and a plea that has been entered already shall not constitute evidence at the hearing.

(A)(i) The degree of criminal sophistication exhibited by the minor.

(ii) When evaluating the criterion specified in clause (i), the juvenile court may give weight to any relevant factor, including, but not limited to, the minor's age, maturity, intellectual capacity, and physical, mental, and emotional health at the time of the alleged offense, the minor's impetuosity or failure to appreciate risks and consequences of criminal behavior, the effect of familial, adult, or peer pressure on the minor's actions, and the effect of the minor's family and community environment and childhood trauma on the minor's criminal sophistication.

(B)(i) Whether the minor can be rehabilitated prior to the expiration of the juvenile court's jurisdiction.

(ii) When evaluating the criterion specified in clause (i), the juvenile court may give weight to any relevant factor, including, but not limited to, the minor's potential to grow and mature.

(C)(i) The minor's previous delinquent history.

(ii) When evaluating the criterion specified in clause (i), the juvenile court may give weight to any relevant factor, including, but not limited to, the seriousness of the minor's previous delinquent history and the effect of the minor's family and community environment and childhood trauma on the minor's previous delinquent behavior.

(D)(i) Success of previous attempts by the juvenile court to rehabilitate the minor.

(ii) When evaluating the criterion specified in clause (i), the juvenile court may give weight to any relevant factor, including, but not limited to, the adequacy of the services previously provided to address the minor's needs.

(E)(i) The circumstances and gravity of the offense alleged in the petition to have been committed by the minor.

(ii) When evaluating the criterion specified in clause (i), the juvenile court may give weight to any relevant factor, including, but not limited to, the actual behavior of the person, the mental state of the person, the person's degree of involvement in the crime, the level of harm actually caused by the person, and the person's mental and emotional development.

(b) This subdivision is applicable to any case in which a minor is alleged to be a person described in Section 602 by reason of the violation of one of the following offenses:

(1) Murder.

(2) Arson, as provided in subdivision (a) or (b) of Section 451 of the Penal Code.

(3) Robbery.

(4) Rape with force, violence, or threat of great bodily harm.

(5) Sodomy by force, violence, duress, menace, or threat of great bodily harm.

(6) A lewd or lascivious act as provided in subdivision (b) of Section 288 of the Penal Code.

(7) Oral copulation by force, violence, duress, menace, or threat of great bodily harm.

(8) An offense specified in subdivision (a) of Section 289 of the Penal Code.

(9) Kidnapping for ransom.

(10) Kidnapping for purposes of robbery.

(11) Kidnapping with bodily harm.

(12) Attempted murder.

(13) Assault with a firearm or destructive device.

(14) Assault by any means of force likely to produce great bodily injury.

(15) Discharge of a firearm into an inhabited or occupied building.

(16) An offense described in Section 1203.09 of the Penal Code.

(17) An offense described in Section 12022.5 or 12022.53 of the Penal Code.

(18) A felony offense in which the minor personally used a weapon described in any provision listed in Section 16590 of the Penal Code.

(19) A felony offense described in Section 136.1 or 137 of the Penal Code.

(20) Manufacturing, compounding, or selling one-half ounce or more of a salt or solution of a controlled substance specified in subdivision (e) of Section 11055 of the Health and Safety Code.

(21) A violent felony, as defined in subdivision (c) of Section 667.5 of the Penal Code, which also would constitute a felony violation of subdivision (b) of Section 186.22 of the Penal Code.

(22) Escape, by the use of force or violence, from a county juvenile hall, home, ranch, camp, or forestry camp in violation of subdivision (b) of Section 871 if great bodily injury is intentionally inflicted upon an employee of the juvenile facility during the commission of the escape.

(23) Torture as described in Sections 206 and 206.1 of the Penal Code.

(24) Aggravated mayhem, as described in Section 205 of the Penal Code.

(25) Carjacking, as described in Section 215 of the Penal Code, while armed with a dangerous or deadly weapon.

(26) Kidnapping for purposes of sexual assault, as punishable in subdivision (b) of Section 209 of the Penal Code.

(27) Kidnapping as punishable in Section 209.5 of the Penal Code.

(28) The offense described in subdivision (c) of Section 26100 of the Penal Code.

(29) The offense described in Section 18745 of the Penal Code.

(30) Voluntary manslaughter, as described in subdivision (a) of Section 192 of the Penal Code. *(Added by Stats.1975, c. 1266, p. 3325, § 4. Amended by Stats.1976, c. 1071, p. 4825, § 28.5; Stats. 1977, c. 1150, p. 3693, § 2; Stats.1979, c. 944, p. 3263, § 19; Stats.1979, c. 1177, p. 4600, § 2; Stats.1982, c. 283, § 2, eff. June 21, 1982; Stats.1982, c. 1094, § 2; Stats.1982, c. 1282, § 4.5; Stats.1983, c. 390, § 2; Stats.1986, c. 676, § 2; Stats.1989, c. 820, § 1; Stats.1990, c. 249 (A.B.2601), § 1; Stats.1991, c. 303 (A.B.1780), § 1; Stats.1993, c. 610 (A.B.6), § 30, eff. Oct. 1, 1993; Stats.1993, c. 611 (S.B.60), § 34, eff. Oct. 1, 1993; Stats.1994, c. 448 (A.B.1948), § 3; Stats.1994, c. 453 (A.B.560), § 9.5; Stats.1997, c. 910 (S.B.1195), § 2; Stats.1998, c. 925 (A.B.1290), § 7; Stats.1998, c. 936 (A.B.105), § 21, eff. Sept. 28, 1998; Stats.1998, c. 936 (A.B.105), § 21.5, eff. Sept. 28, 1998, operative Jan. 1, 1999; Initiative Measure (Prop. 21, § 26, approved March 7, 2000, eff. March 8, 2000); Stats.2007, c. 137 (A.B.686), § 1; Stats.2008, c. 179 (S.B.1498), § 236; Stats.2010, c. 178 (S.B.1115), § 97, operative Jan. 1, 2012; Stats.2015, c. 234 (S.B.382), § 2, eff. Jan. 1, 2016; Initiative Measure (Prop. 57, § 4.2, approved Nov. 8, 2016, eff. Nov. 9, 2016); Stats.2018, c. 1012 (S.B.1391), § 1, eff. Jan. 1, 2019; Stats.2022, c. 330 (A.B.2361), § 1, eff. Jan. 1, 2023.)*

Law Revision Commission Comments

Subdivision (b) of Section 707 is amended to reflect nonsubstantive reorganization of the statutes governing control of deadly weapons. [38 Cal.L.Rev.Comm. Reports 217 (2009)].

Cross References

Affidavit alleging violation of offense listed in subdivision (b) of this section committed by minor age sixteen or older, submission by probation officer to prosecuting attorney, see Welfare and Institutions Code §§ 653.1, 653.5.

Commitment of ward who is 14 years of age or older to secure youth treatment facility criteria, baseline and maximum terms of confinement, individual rehabilitation plans, progress review hearings, transfer to less restrictive program, see Welfare and Institutions Code § 875.

Commitments to youth authority, pilot program for transition-aged youth, see Welfare and Institutions Code § 1731.7.

Completion of supervision program or probation, dismissal of petition, sealing records, see Welfare and Institutions Code § 786.

Contracts to furnish housing to ward whose commitment has been recalled, minor not adjudged to be a ward of the court for commission of certain offenses under this section, see Welfare and Institutions Code § 1752.16.

Criminal prosecution prevented after filing of petition, see Welfare and Institutions Code § 606.

Custodial interrogation of a minor, electronic recording requirement, see Penal Code § 859.5.

Custodial interrogation of person who is or may be adjudged ward of juvenile court, see Welfare and Institutions Code § 626.8.

Department of Justice, criminal statistics, statewide information in annual report, see Penal Code § 13012.5.

Detention of minor in jail or lockup, see Welfare and Institutions Code § 207.1.

Discharge from Youth Authority, see Welfare and Institutions Code § 1769.

Failure to petition for hearing, commencement of prosecution for offenses punishable by death or life imprisonment, or for embezzlement of public money, see Penal Code § 799.

Firearms, unlawful carrying and possession of weapons, prohibited ownership or possession of firearms upon prior conviction of certain violent offenses, see Penal Code § 29800.

Hearing defined for purposes of this Article, see Welfare and Institutions Code § 727.4.

Honorable discharge by Youthful Offender Parole Board, admissibility of conviction of offense listed in this section in subsequent proceedings, see Welfare and Institutions Code § 1772.

Influencing testimony or information given to a law enforcement official, see Penal Code § 137.

Intimidation of witnesses and victims from attending or giving testimony at any trial, see Penal Code § 136.1.

Juvenile Justice Realignment Block Grant, realignment target population, see Welfare and Institutions Code § 1990.

Notice of hearing by Youthful Offender Parole Board, see Welfare and Institutions Code § 1767.1.

Powers and duties of Board of Parole Hearings when a person has been committed to Department of Corrections and Rehabilitation, Division of Juvenile Facilities, provisions applicable to wards eligible for release on parole on or after Sept. 1, 2007, see Welfare and Institutions Code § 1766.
Prior felony conviction, see Penal Code § 1170.12.
Prohibited commitments to Corrections and Rehabilitation, Division of Juvenile Justice, see Welfare and Institutions Code § 733.1.
Prosecuting violent sex crimes under statutes that provide sentencing under a "one strike," "three strikes" or habitual sex offender statute, see Penal Code § 1192.7.
Return to custody of parolee under the jurisdiction of the Division of Juvenile Parole Operations, see Welfare and Institutions Code § 1767.35.
Statute of limitations suspended by filing of petition, see Welfare and Institutions Code § 605.
Time of commencing criminal actions, offenses punishable by death or life imprisonment, application to minors, see Penal Code § 799.

Research References

West's California Judicial Council Forms JV–710, Order to Transfer Juvenile to Criminal Court Jurisdiction (Welfare and Institutions Code, §707) (Also Available in Spanish).
2 Witkin, California Criminal Law 4th Crimes Against Public Peace and Welfare § 241 (2021), Juvenile Offenders.
5 Witkin, California Criminal Law 4th Criminal Trial § 170A (2021), (New) Interrogation of Murder Suspect.
1 Witkin California Criminal Law 4th Defenses § 4 (2021), Children.
1 Witkin California Criminal Law 4th Defenses § 240 (2021), Capital Crimes, Embezzlement of Public Money, and Felonies.
1 Witkin California Criminal Law 4th Introduction to Crimes § 140 (2021), Gang Violence and Juvenile Crime Prevention Act (Proposition 21).
4 Witkin, California Criminal Law 4th Pretrial Proceedings § 199 (2021), Nature and Requisites.
3 Witkin, California Criminal Law 4th Punishment § 87 (2021), Persons Eligible for Commitment.
3 Witkin, California Criminal Law 4th Punishment § 88 (2021), Persons Ineligible for Commitment.
3 Witkin, California Criminal Law 4th Punishment § 91 (2021), Commitment Procedure.
3 Witkin, California Criminal Law 4th Punishment § 95 (2021), In General.
3 Witkin, California Criminal Law 4th Punishment § 99 (2021), Probation and Parole.
3 Witkin, California Criminal Law 4th Punishment § 308–I (2021), (New) Application to Juveniles.
3 Witkin, California Criminal Law 4th Punishment § 427 (2021), Juvenile Adjudication.

§ 707.01. Minor found unfit subject for juvenile court law pursuant to § 707; previous juvenile court adjudications; transfers to court of criminal jurisdiction; appeal of finding of fitness

(a) If a minor is found an unfit subject to be dealt with under the juvenile court law pursuant to Section 707, then the following shall apply:

(1) The jurisdiction of the juvenile court with respect to any previous adjudication resulting in the minor being made a ward of the juvenile court that did not result in the minor's commitment to the Youth Authority shall not terminate, unless a hearing is held pursuant to Section 785 and the jurisdiction of the juvenile court over the minor is terminated.

(2) The jurisdiction of the juvenile court and the Youth Authority with respect to any previous adjudication resulting in the minor being made a ward of the juvenile court that resulted in the minor's commitment to the Youth Authority shall not terminate.

(3) All petitions pending against the minor shall be transferred to the court of criminal jurisdiction where one of the following applies:

(A) Jeopardy has not attached and the minor was 16 years of age or older at the time he or she is alleged to have violated the criminal statute or ordinance.

(B) Jeopardy has not attached and the minor is alleged to have violated a criminal statute for which he or she may be presumed or may be found to be not a fit and proper subject to be dealt with under the juvenile court law.

(4) All petitions pending against the minor shall be disposed of in the juvenile court pursuant to the juvenile court law, where one of the following applies:

(A) Jeopardy has attached.

(B) The minor was under 16 years of age at the time he or she is alleged to have violated a criminal statute for which he or she may not be presumed or may not be found to be not a fit and proper subject to be dealt with under the juvenile court law.

(5) If, subsequent to a finding that a minor is an unfit subject to be dealt with under the juvenile court law, the minor is convicted of the violations which were the subject of the proceeding that resulted in a finding of unfitness, a new petition or petitions alleging the violation of any law or ordinance defining crime which would otherwise cause the minor to be a person described in Section 602 committed by the minor prior to or after the finding of unfitness need not be filed in the juvenile court if one of the following applies:

(A) The minor was 16 years of age or older at the time he or she is alleged to have violated a criminal statute or ordinance.

(B) The minor is alleged to have violated a criminal statute for which he or she may be presumed or may be found to be not a fit and proper subject to be dealt with under the juvenile court law.

(6) Subsequent to a finding that a minor is an unfit subject to be dealt with under the juvenile court law, which finding was based solely on either or both the minor's previous delinquent history or a lack of success of previous attempts by the juvenile court to rehabilitate the minor, and the minor was not convicted of the offense, a new petition or petitions alleging the violation of any law or ordinance defining crime which would otherwise cause the minor to be a person described in Section 602 committed by the minor prior to or after the finding of unfitness need not be filed in the juvenile court if one of the following applies:

(A) The minor was 16 years of age or older at the time he or she is alleged to have violated a criminal statute or ordinance.

(B) The minor is alleged to have violated a criminal statute for which he or she may be presumed or may be found to be not a fit and proper subject to be dealt with under the juvenile court law.

(7) If, subsequent to a finding that a minor is an unfit subject to be dealt with under the juvenile court law, the minor is not convicted of the violations which were the subject of the proceeding that resulted in a finding of unfitness and the finding of unfitness was not based solely on either or both the minor's previous delinquent history or a lack of success of previous attempts by the juvenile court to rehabilitate the minor, a new petition or petitions alleging the violation of any law or ordinance defining a crime which would otherwise cause the minor to be a person described in Section 602 committed by the minor prior to or after the finding of unfitness shall be first filed in the juvenile court. This paragraph does not preclude the prosecuting attorney from seeking to find the minor unfit in a subsequent petition.

(b) As to a violation referred to in paragraph (5) or (6) of subdivision (a), if a petition based on those violations has already been filed in the juvenile court, it shall be transferred to the court of criminal jurisdiction without any further proceedings.

(c) The probation officer shall not be required to investigate or submit a report regarding the fitness of a minor for any charge specified in paragraph (5) or (6) of subdivision (a) which is refiled in the juvenile court.

(d) This section shall not be construed to affect the right to appellate review of a finding of unfitness or the duration of the jurisdiction of the juvenile court as specified in Section 607. *(Added by Stats.1994, c. 453 (A.B.560), § 10.8.)*

Cross References

Hearing defined for purposes of this Article, see Welfare and Institutions Code § 727.4.

Probation officer or social worker defined for purposes of this Chapter, see Welfare and Institutions Code § 215.

§ 707.1. Minor's case transferred from juvenile court; criminal prosecution; release

(a) If, pursuant to a transfer hearing, the minor's case is transferred from juvenile court to a court of criminal jurisdiction, the district attorney or other appropriate prosecuting officer may file an accusatory pleading against the minor in a court of criminal jurisdiction. The case shall proceed from that point according to the laws applicable to a criminal case. If a prosecution has been commenced in another court but has been suspended while juvenile court proceedings are being held, it shall be ordered that the proceedings upon that prosecution shall resume.

(b) A minor whose case is transferred to a court of criminal jurisdiction shall, upon the conclusion of the transfer hearing, be entitled to release on bail or on their own recognizance on the same circumstances, terms, and conditions as an adult alleged to have committed the same offense. *(Added by Stats.1975, c. 1266, p. 3325, § 5. Amended by Stats.1979, c. 539, p. 1740, § 1; Stats.1983, c. 204, § 1; Stats.1986, c. 1271, § 6; Stats.1994, c. 448 (A.B.1948), § 4; Stats.1994, c. 453 (A.B.560), § 11.5; Stats.1995, c. 61 (S.B.7), § 1; Stats.2020, c. 337 (S.B.823), § 25, eff. Sept. 30, 2020.)*

Cross References

Hearing defined for purposes of this Article, see Welfare and Institutions Code § 727.4.

§ 707.4. Report; failure to convict in criminal court; disposition of records

In any case arising under this article in which there is no conviction in the criminal court, the clerk of the criminal court shall report such disposition to the juvenile court, to the probation department, to the law enforcement agency which arrested the minor for the offense which resulted in his remand to criminal court, and to the Department of Justice. Unless the minor has had a prior conviction in a criminal court, the clerk of the criminal court shall deliver to the clerk of the juvenile court all copies of the minor's record in criminal court and shall obliterate the minor's name from any index or minute book maintained in the criminal court. The clerk of the juvenile court shall maintain the minor's criminal court record as provided by Article 22 (commencing with Section 825) of this chapter until such time as the juvenile court may issue an order that they be sealed pursuant to Section 781. *(Added by Stats.1975, c. 1266, p. 3326, § 8. Amended by Stats.1976, c. 1069, p. 4808, § 3; Stats.1978, c. 380, p. 1212, § 164.)*

§ 707.5. Cases transferred to court of criminal jurisdiction; return to juvenile court for disposition

(a) In any case in which a person is transferred from juvenile court to a court of criminal jurisdiction pursuant to Section 707, upon conviction or entry of a plea, the person may, under the circumstances described in subdivision (b), request the criminal court to return the case to the juvenile court for disposition.

(b) Upon motion by the person, the criminal court shall have the authority to return the case to juvenile court for disposition in the following circumstances:

(1) If the person is convicted at trial in criminal court solely of a misdemeanor or misdemeanors, upon request by the defense, the case shall be returned to juvenile court, as provided in subdivisions (d) and (e).

(2) If any of the allegations in the juvenile court petition that were the basis for transfer involved an offense listed in subdivision (b) of Section 707, and the person is convicted at trial in criminal court only of felony offenses that are not listed in subdivision (b) of Section 707, or a combination of such felony offenses and misdemeanors, upon request by the defense, the court shall have the discretion to return the case to juvenile court for further proceedings pursuant to subdivision (c).

(3) If the allegations in the juvenile court petition that were the basis for transfer involved only offenses not listed in subdivision (b) of Section 707, and pursuant to a plea agreement the person pleads guilty only to a misdemeanor or misdemeanors, or if any of the allegations in the juvenile court petition that were the basis for transfer involved an offense listed in subdivision (b) of Section 707, and pursuant to a plea agreement the person pleads guilty only to a misdemeanor or misdemeanors, felony offenses that are not listed in subdivision (b) of Section 707, or a combination of such felony offenses and misdemeanors, upon agreement and request of the parties, and subject to the approval of the court, the case shall be returned to juvenile court for further proceedings pursuant to subdivision (c).

(c) In determining whether the case should be returned to juvenile court pursuant to paragraph (2) of subdivision (b), or in determining whether to approve the agreement pursuant to paragraph (3) of subdivision (b), the court shall make a finding by a preponderance of the evidence that a juvenile disposition is in the interests of justice and the welfare of the person, and shall so state on the minute order with the specific reasons for making that finding. In making the determination, the court shall consider the transcript and minute order of the transfer hearing, the time that the person has served in custody, the dispositions and services available to the person in the juvenile court, and any relevant evidence submitted by either party. A case that is ordered returned to juvenile court shall comply with subdivisions (d) and (e).

(d) Upon determining that the case shall be returned to the juvenile court, the court shall return the entire case to the juvenile court and the matter shall be calendared within two court days.

(e) The juvenile court shall order the probation department to prepare a social study on the questions of the proper disposition, and the case shall proceed to disposition as set forth in Sections 702, 706, 706.5, and 730, and Article 18 (commencing with Section 725), as applicable. A conviction or guilty plea that is returned to juvenile court shall be considered an adjudication or admission before the juvenile court for all purposes.

(f) The clerk of the criminal court shall report the return to juvenile court to the probation department, the law enforcement agency that arrested the minor for the offense, and the Department of Justice. The clerk of the criminal court shall deliver to the clerk of the juvenile court all copies of the minor's record in criminal court and shall obliterate the person's name for any index maintained in the criminal court. The clerk of the juvenile court shall maintain the criminal court records as provided by Article 22 (commencing with Section 825) until such time as the juvenile court may issue an order that the records be sealed. *(Added by Stats.2019, c. 583 (A.B.1423), § 1, eff. Jan. 1, 2020.)*

§ 708. Minor using controlled substances; continuance of hearing; 72–hour treatment and evaluation; report; disposition; reimbursement of expenditure

(a) Whenever a minor who appears to be a danger to himself or herself or others as a result of the use of controlled substances (as defined in Division 10 (commencing with Section 11000) of the Health and Safety Code), is brought before any judge of the juvenile court, the judge may continue the hearing and proceed pursuant to this section. The court may order the minor taken to a facility designated by the county and approved by the State Department of Health Care Services as a facility for 72–hour treatment and evaluation. Thereupon the provisions of Section 5343 shall apply, except that the professional person in charge of the facility shall make a written report to the court concerning the results of the evaluation of the minor.

(b) If the professional person in charge of the facility for 72-hour evaluation and treatment reports to the juvenile court that the minor is not a danger to himself or herself or others as a result of the use of controlled substances or that the minor does not require 14-day intensive treatment, or if the minor has been certified for not more than 14 days of intensive treatment and the certification is terminated, the minor shall be released if the juvenile court proceedings have been dismissed; referred for further care and treatment on a voluntary basis, subject to the disposition of the juvenile court proceedings; or returned to the juvenile court, in which event the court shall proceed with the case pursuant to this chapter.

(c) Any expenditure for the evaluation or intensive treatment of a minor under this section shall be considered an expenditure made under Part 2 (commencing with Section 5600) of Division 5, and shall be reimbursed by the state as are other local expenditures pursuant to that part. *(Added by Stats.1970, c. 1129, p. 2005, § 1. Amended by Stats.1981, c. 714, p. 2806, § 462; Stats.1984, c. 1635, § 96; Stats. 2012, c. 34 (S.B.1009), § 41, eff. June 27, 2012; Stats.2013, c. 23 (A.B.82), § 28, eff. June 27, 2013.)*

Cross References

Community controlled substances treatment services, see Welfare and Institutions Code § 5340 et seq.

Counseling or education programs for people convicted of an offense involving substance abuse, see Health and Safety Code § 11376.

Courts closed for transaction of judicial business, conditions, see Government Code § 68106.

Hearing defined for purposes of this Article, see Welfare and Institutions Code § 727.4.

§ 709. Incompetency; suspension of proceedings; stipulation, or submission by the parties to finding that minor lacks competency or court appoints expert to evaluate minor; experts qualifications and duties; evidentiary hearing, stipulation, or submission by the parties to findings of expert; procedures if minor is found competent or incompetent

(a)(1) If the court has a doubt that a minor who is subject to any juvenile proceedings is competent, the court shall suspend all proceedings and proceed pursuant to this section.

(2) A minor is incompetent for purposes of this section if the minor lacks sufficient present ability to consult with counsel and assist in preparing the minor's defense with a reasonable degree of rational understanding, or lacks a rational as well as factual understanding of the nature of the charges or proceedings against them. Incompetency may result from the presence of any condition or conditions, including, but not limited to, mental illness, mental disorder, developmental disability, or developmental immaturity. Except as specifically provided otherwise, this section applies to a minor who is alleged to come within the jurisdiction of the court pursuant to Section 601 or 602.

(3) Notwithstanding paragraph (1), during the pendency of any juvenile proceeding, the court may receive information from any source regarding the minor's ability to understand the proceedings. The minor's counsel or the court may express a doubt as to the minor's competency. If the court finds substantial evidence that raises a doubt as to the minor's competency, the proceedings shall be suspended.

(b)(1) Unless the parties stipulate to a finding that the minor lacks competency, or the parties are willing to submit on the issue of the minor's lack of competency, the court shall appoint an expert to evaluate the minor and determine whether the minor suffers from a mental illness, mental disorder, developmental disability, developmental immaturity, or other condition affecting competency and, if so, whether the minor is incompetent as defined in paragraph (2) of subdivision (a).

(2) The expert shall have expertise in child and adolescent development and forensic evaluation of juveniles for purposes of adjudicating competency, shall be familiar with competency standards and accepted criteria used in evaluating juvenile competency, shall have received training in conducting juvenile competency evaluations, and shall be familiar with competency remediation for the condition or conditions affecting competence in the particular case.

(3) The expert shall personally interview the minor and review all of the available records provided, including, but not limited to, medical, education, special education, probation, child welfare, mental health, regional center, and court records, and any other relevant information that is available. The expert shall consult with the minor's counsel and any other person who has provided information to the court regarding the minor's lack of competency. The expert shall gather a developmental history of the minor. If any information is unavailable to the expert, the expert shall note in the report the efforts to obtain that information. The expert shall administer age-appropriate testing specific to the issue of competency unless the facts of the particular case render testing unnecessary or inappropriate. The expert shall be proficient in the language preferred by the minor, or, if that is not feasible, the expert shall employ the services of a certified interpreter and use assessment tools that are linguistically and culturally appropriate for the minor. In a written report, the expert shall opine whether the minor has the sufficient present ability to consult with the minor's counsel with a reasonable degree of rational understanding and whether the minor has a rational and factual understanding of the proceedings against them. The expert shall also state the basis for these conclusions. If the expert concludes that the minor lacks competency, the expert shall give their opinion on whether the minor is likely to attain competency in the foreseeable future, and, if so, make recommendations regarding the type of remediation services that would be effective in assisting the minor in attaining competency.

(4) The Judicial Council, in conjunction with groups or individuals representing judges, defense counsel, district attorneys, chief probation officers, counties, advocates for people with developmental and mental disabilities, experts in special education testing, psychologists and psychiatrists specializing in adolescents, professional associations and accredited bodies for psychologists and psychiatrists, and other interested stakeholders, shall adopt a rule of court identifying the training and experience needed for an expert to be competent in forensic evaluations of juveniles. The Judicial Council shall develop and adopt rules for the implementation of the other requirements in this subdivision.

(5) Statements made to the appointed expert during the minor's competency evaluation and statements made by the minor to mental health professionals during the remediation proceedings, and any fruits of these statements, shall not be used in any other hearing against the minor in either juvenile or adult court.

(6) The district attorney or minor's counsel may retain or seek the appointment of additional qualified experts who may testify during the competency hearing. The expert's report and qualifications shall be disclosed to the opposing party within a reasonable time before, but no later than five court days before, the hearing. If disclosure is not made in accordance with this paragraph, the court may make any order necessary to enforce the provisions of this paragraph, including, but not limited to, immediate disclosure, contempt proceedings, delaying or prohibiting the testimony of the expert or consideration of the expert's report upon a showing of good cause, or any other lawful order. If, after disclosure of the report, the opposing party requests a continuance in order to further prepare for the hearing and shows good cause for the continuance, the court shall grant a continuance for a reasonable period of time. This paragraph does not allow a qualified expert retained or appointed by the district attorney to perform a competency evaluation on a minor without an order from the juvenile court after petitioning the court for an order pursuant to the Civil Discovery Act (Title 4 (commencing with Section 2016.010) of Part 4 of the Code of Civil Procedure).

(7) If the expert believes the minor is developmentally disabled, the court shall appoint the director of a regional center for developmentally disabled individuals described in Article 1 (commencing with Section 4620) of Chapter 5 of Division 4.5, or the director's designee, to evaluate the minor. The director of the regional center, or the director's designee, shall determine whether the minor is eligible for services under the Lanterman Developmental Disabilities Services Act (Division 4.5 (commencing with Section 4500)), and shall provide the court with a written report informing the court of his or her determination. The court's appointment of the director of the regional center for determination of eligibility for services shall not delay the court's proceedings for determination of competency.

(8) An expert's opinion that a minor is developmentally disabled does not supersede an independent determination by the regional center whether the minor is eligible for services under the Lanterman Developmental Disabilities Services Act (Division 4.5 (commencing with Section 4500)).

(9) This section does not authorize or require determinations regarding the competency of a minor by the director of the regional center or the director's designee.

(c) The question of the minor's competency shall be determined at an evidentiary hearing unless there is a stipulation or submission by the parties on the findings of the expert that the minor is incompetent. It shall be presumed that the minor is mentally competent, unless it is proven by a preponderance of the evidence that the minor is mentally incompetent. With respect to a minor under 14 years of age at the time of the commission of the alleged offense, the court shall make a determination as to the minor's capacity pursuant to Section 26 of the Penal Code prior to deciding the issue of competency.

(d) If the court finds the minor to be competent, the court shall reinstate proceedings and proceed commensurate with the court's jurisdiction.

(e) If the court finds, by a preponderance of evidence, that the minor is incompetent, all proceedings shall remain suspended for a period of time that is no longer than reasonably necessary to determine whether there is a substantial probability that the minor will attain competency in the foreseeable future, or the court no longer retains jurisdiction and the case must be dismissed. Prior to a dismissal, the court may make orders that it deems appropriate for services. Further, the court may rule on motions that do not require the participation of the minor in the preparation of the motions. These motions include, but are not limited to, all of the following:

(1) Motions to dismiss.

(2) Motions regarding a change in the placement of the minor.

(3) Detention hearings.

(4) Demurrers.

(f) If the minor is found to be incompetent and the petition contains only misdemeanor offenses, the petition shall be dismissed.

(g)(1) Upon a finding of incompetency, the court shall refer the minor to services designed to help the minor attain competency, unless the court finds that competency cannot be achieved within the foreseeable future. The court may also refer the minor to treatment services to assist in remediation that may include, but are not limited to, mental health services, treatment for trauma, medically supervised medication, behavioral counseling, curriculum-based legal education, or training in socialization skills, consistent with any laws requiring consent. Service providers and evaluators shall adhere to the standards stated in this section and the California Rules of Court. Services shall be provided in the least restrictive environment consistent with public safety, as determined by the court. A finding of incompetency alone shall not be the basis for secure confinement. The minor shall be returned to court at the earliest possible date. The court shall review remediation services at least every 30 calendar days for minors in custody and every 45 calendar days for minors out of custody prior to the expiration of the total remediation period specified in paragraph (3) of subdivision (h). If the minor is in custody, the county mental health department shall provide the court with suitable alternatives for the continued delivery of remediation services upon release from custody as part of the court's review of remediation services. The court shall consider appropriate alternatives to juvenile hall confinement, including, but not limited to, all of the following:

(A) Placement through regional centers.

(B) Short–term residential therapeutic programs.

(C) Crisis residential programs.

(D) Civil commitment.

(E) Foster care, relative placement, or other nonsecure placement.

(F) Other residential treatment programs.

(2) The court may make any orders necessary to assist with the delivery of remediation services in an alternative setting to secure confinement.

(h)(1) Within six months of the initial receipt of a recommendation by the designated person or entity, the court shall hold an evidentiary hearing on whether the minor is remediated or is able to be remediated unless the parties stipulate to, or agree to the recommendation of, the remediation program. If the recommendation is that the minor has attained competency, and if the minor disputes that recommendation, the burden is on the minor to prove by a preponderance of evidence that he or she remains incompetent. If the recommendation is that the minor is unable to be remediated and if the prosecutor disputes that recommendation, the burden is on the prosecutor to prove by a preponderance of evidence that the minor is remediable. If the prosecution contests the evaluation of continued incompetence, the minor shall be presumed incompetent and the prosecution shall have the burden to prove by a preponderance of evidence that the minor is competent. The provisions of subdivision (c) shall apply at this stage of the proceedings.

(2) If the court finds that the minor has been remediated, the court shall reinstate the proceedings.

(3) If the court finds that the minor has not yet been remediated, but is likely to be remediated within six months, the court shall order the minor to return to the remediation program. However, the total remediation period shall not exceed one year from the finding of incompetency and secure confinement shall not exceed the limit specified in subparagraph (A) of paragraph (5).

(4) If the court finds that the minor will not achieve competency within six months, the court shall dismiss the petition. The court may invite persons and agencies with information about the minor, including, but not limited to, the minor and the minor's attorney, the probation department, parents, guardians, or relative caregivers, mental health treatment professionals, the public guardian, educational rights holders, education providers, and social services agencies, to the dismissal hearing to discuss any services that may be available to the minor after jurisdiction is terminated. If appropriate, the court shall refer the minor for evaluation pursuant to Article 6 (commencing with Section 5300) of Chapter 2 of Part 1 of Division 5 or Article 3 (commencing with Section 6550) of Chapter 2 of Part 2 of Division 6.

(5)(A) Secure confinement shall not extend beyond six months from the finding of incompetence, except as provided in this section. In making that determination, the court shall consider all of the following:

(i) Where the minor will have the best chance of obtaining competence.

(ii) Whether the placement is the least restrictive setting appropriate for the minor.

(iii) Whether alternatives to secure confinement have been identified and pursued and why alternatives are not available or appropriate.

(iv) Whether the placement is necessary for the safety of the minor or others.

(B) If the court determines, upon consideration of these factors, that it is in the best interests of the minor and the public's safety for the minor to remain in secure confinement, the court shall state the reasons on the record.

(C) Only in cases where the petition involves an offense listed in subdivision (b) of Section 707 may the court consider whether it is necessary and in the best interests of the minor and the public's safety to order secure confinement of a minor for up to an additional year, not to exceed 18 months from the finding of incompetence.

(i) The presiding judge of the juvenile court, the probation department, the county mental health department, the public defender and any other entity that provides representation for minors, the district attorney, the regional center, if appropriate, and any other participants that the presiding judge shall designate, shall develop a written protocol describing the competency process and a program to ensure that minors who are found incompetent receive appropriate remediation services. *(Added by Stats.2018, c. 991 (A.B.1214), § 2, eff. Jan. 1, 2019. Amended by Stats.2019, c. 161 (A.B.439), § 1, eff. July 31, 2019.)*

Cross References

Eligibility for admission to developmental center, see Welfare and Institutions Code § 7505.

§ 710. Mental health services recommendations; application of §§ 711 to 713

(a) Sections 711, 712, and 713 shall not be applicable in a county unless the application of those sections in the county has been approved by a resolution adopted by the board of supervisors. A county may establish a program pursuant to Section 711, 712, or 713, or pursuant to two or all three of those sections, on a permanent basis, or it may establish the program on a limited duration basis for a specific number of years. Moneys from a grant from the Mental Health Services Act [1] used to fund a program pursuant to Section 711, 712, or 713 may be used only for services related to mental health assessment, treatment, and evaluation.

(b) It is the intent of the Legislature that in a county where funding exists through the Mental Health Services Act, and the board of supervisors has adopted a resolution pursuant to subdivision (a), the courts may, under the guidelines established in Section 711, make available the evaluation described in Section 712, and receive treatment and placement recommendations from the multidisciplinary assessment team as described in Section 713. *(Added by Stats.2005, c. 265 (S.B.570), § 3.)*

[1] Children's Mental Health Services Act, see Welfare and Institutions Code § 5850 et seq.

Cross References

Judiciary training, juvenile proceedings, mental health and developmental disability issues, see Government Code § 68553.5.

§ 711. Referral for mental health evaluation

(a) When it appears to the court, or upon request of the prosecutor or counsel for the minor, at any time, that a minor who is alleged to come within the jurisdiction of the court under Section 602, may have a serious mental disorder, is seriously emotionally disturbed, or has a developmental disability, the court may order that the minor be referred for evaluation, as described in Section 712.

(b) A minor, with the approval of his or her counsel, may decline the referral for mental health evaluation described in Section 712 or the multidisciplinary team review described in Section 713, in which case the matter shall proceed without the application of Sections 712 and 713, and in accordance with all other applicable provisions of law. *(Added by Stats.2005, c. 265 (S.B.570), § 4.)*

Cross References

Children's Mental Health Services Act, see Welfare and Institutions Code § 5850 et seq.

Judiciary training, juvenile proceedings, mental health and developmental disability issues, see Government Code § 68553.5.

§ 712. Evaluation by director of regional center or designee or mental health professional; examination; report

(a) The evaluation ordered by the court under Section 711 shall be made, in accordance with the provisions of Section 741 and Division 4.5 (commencing with Section 4500), by either of the following, as applicable:

(1) For minors suspected to be developmentally disabled, by the director of a regional center or his or her designee, pursuant to paragraph (7) of subdivision (b) of Section 709.

(2) For all other minors, by an appropriate and licensed mental health professional who meets one or more of the following criteria:

(A) The person is licensed to practice medicine in the State of California and is trained and actively engaged in the practice of psychiatry.

(B) The person is licensed as a psychologist under Chapter 6.6 (commencing with Section 2900) of Division 2 of the Business and Professions Code.

(b) The evaluator selected by the court shall personally examine the minor, conduct appropriate psychological or mental health screening, assessment, or testing, according to a uniform protocol developed by the county mental health department, and prepare and submit to the court a written report indicating his or her findings and recommendations to guide the court in determining whether the minor has a serious mental disorder or is seriously emotionally disturbed, as described in Section 5600.3. If the minor is detained, the examination shall occur within three court days of the court's order of referral for evaluation, and the evaluator's report shall be submitted to the court not later than five court days after the evaluator has personally examined the minor, unless the submission date is extended by the court for good cause shown.

(c) Based on the written report by the evaluator or the regional center, the court shall determine whether the minor has a serious mental disorder or is seriously emotionally disturbed, as described in Section 5600.3, or has a developmental disability, as defined in Section 4512. If the court determines that the minor has a serious mental disorder, is seriously emotionally disturbed, or has a developmental disability, the case shall proceed as described in Section 713. If the court determines that the minor does not have a serious mental disorder, is not seriously emotionally disturbed, or does not have a developmental disability, the matter shall proceed without the application of Section 713 and in accordance with all other applicable provisions of law.

(d) This section shall not be construed to interfere with the legal authority of the juvenile court or of any other public or private agency or individual to refer a minor for mental health evaluation or treatment as provided in Section 370, 635.1, 704, 741, 5150, 5694.7, 5699.2, 5867.5, or 6551 of this code, or in Section 4011.6 of the Penal Code. *(Added by Stats.2005, c. 265 (S.B.570), § 5. Amended by Stats.2011, c. 37 (A.B.104), § 4, eff. June 30, 2011; Stats.2012, c. 162 (S.B.1171), § 191; Stats.2018, c. 991 (A.B.1214), § 3, eff. Jan. 1, 2019.)*

Cross References

Children's Mental Health Services Act, see Welfare and Institutions Code § 5850 et seq.

Judiciary training, juvenile proceedings, mental health and developmental disability issues, see Government Code § 68553.5.

§ 713. Dispositional procedures

(a) For any minor described in Section 711 who is determined by the court under Section 712 to be seriously emotionally disturbed, have a serious mental disorder, or have a developmental disability, and who is adjudicated a ward of the court under Section 602, the dispositional procedures set forth in this section shall apply.

(b) Prior to the preparation of the social study required under Section 706, 706.5, or 706.6, the minor shall be referred to a multidisciplinary team for dispositional review and recommendation. The multidisciplinary team shall consist of qualified persons who are collectively able to evaluate the minor's full range of treatment needs and may include representatives from local probation, mental health, regional centers, regional resource development projects, child welfare, education, community-based youth services, and other agencies or service providers. The multidisciplinary team shall include at least one licensed mental health professional as described in subdivision (a) of Section 712. If the minor has been determined to have both a mental disorder and a developmental disorder, the multidisciplinary team may include both an appropriate mental health agency and a regional center.

(c) The multidisciplinary team shall review the nature and circumstances of the case, including the minor's family circumstances, as well as the minor's relevant tests, evaluations, records, medical and psychiatric history, and any existing individual education plan or individual program plans. The multidisciplinary team shall provide for the involvement of the minor's available parent, guardian, or primary caretaker in its review, including any direct participation in multidisciplinary team proceedings as may be helpful or appropriate for development of a treatment plan in the case. The team shall identify the mental health or other treatment services, including in-home and community-based services that are available and appropriate for the minor, including services that may be available to the minor under federal and state programs and initiatives, such as wraparound service programs. At the conclusion of its review, the team shall then produce a recommended disposition and written treatment plan for the minor, to be appended to, or incorporated into, the probation social study presented to the court.

(d) The court shall review the treatment plan and the dispositional recommendations prepared by the multidisciplinary team and shall take them into account when making the dispositional order in the case. The dispositional order in the case shall be consistent with the protection of the public and the primary treatment needs of the minor as identified in the report of the multidisciplinary team. The minor's disposition order shall incorporate, to the extent feasible, the treatment plan submitted by the multidisciplinary team, with any adjustments deemed appropriate by the court.

(e) The dispositional order in the case shall authorize placement of the minor in the least restrictive setting that is consistent with the protection of the public and the minor's treatment needs, and with the treatment plan approved by the court. The court shall, in making the dispositional order, give preferential consideration to the return of the minor to the home of his or her family, guardian, or responsible relative with appropriate in-home, outpatient, or wraparound services, unless that action would be, in the reasonable judgment of the court, inconsistent with the need to protect the public or the minor, or with the minor's treatment needs.

(f) Whenever a minor is recommended for placement at a state developmental center, the regional center director or designee shall submit a report to the Director of the Department of Developmental Services or his or her designee. The regional center report shall include the assessments, individual program plan, and a statement describing the necessity for a developmental center placement. The Director of Developmental Services or his or her designee may, within 60 days of receiving the regional center report, submit to the court a written report evaluating the ability of an alternative community option or a developmental center to achieve the purposes of treatment for the minor and whether a developmental center placement can adequately provide the security measures or systems required to protect the public health and safety from the potential dangers posed by the minor's known behaviors. *(Added by Stats. 2005, c. 265 (S.B.570), § 6.)*

Cross References

Children's Mental Health Services Act, see Welfare and Institutions Code § 5850 et seq.
Department of Developmental Services, see Welfare and Institutions Code § 4400 et seq.
Judiciary training, juvenile proceedings, mental health and developmental disability issues, see Government Code § 68553.5.
Relative defined for purposes of this Article, see Welfare and Institutions Code § 727.4.

§ 714. Assessment or services to minors by regional centers

A regional center, as described in Chapter 5 (commencing with Section 4620) of Division 4.5, shall not be required to provide assessments or services to minors pursuant to Section 711, 712, or 713 solely on the basis of a finding by the court under subdivision (c) of Section 712 that the minor is developmentally disabled. Regional center representatives may, at their option and on a case-by-case basis, participate in the multidisciplinary teams described in Section 713. However, any assessment provided by or through a regional center to a minor determined by the court to be developmentally disabled under subdivision (c) of Section 712 shall be provided in accordance with the provisions and procedures in Chapter 5 (commencing with Section 4620) of Division 4.5 that relate to regional centers. *(Added by Stats.2005, c. 265 (S.B.570), § 7.)*

Cross References

Children's Mental Health Services Act, see Welfare and Institutions Code § 5850 et seq.
Judiciary training, juvenile proceedings, mental health and developmental disability issues, see Government Code § 68553.5.

ARTICLE 18. WARDS—JUDGMENTS AND ORDERS

Section

§ 725. Judgment; placing minor on probation; adjudging minor ward of court

After receiving and considering the evidence on the proper disposition of the case, the court may enter judgment as follows:

(a) If the court has found that the minor is a person described by Section 601 or 602, by reason of the commission of an offense other than any of the offenses set forth in Section 654.3, it may, without adjudging the minor a ward of the court, place the minor on probation, under the supervision of the probation officer, for a period not to exceed six months. The minor's probation shall include the conditions required in Section 729.2 except in any case in which the court makes a finding and states on the record its reasons that any of those conditions would be inappropriate. If the offense involved the unlawful possession, use, or furnishing of a controlled substance, as defined in Chapter 2 (commencing with Section 11053) of Division 10 of the Health and Safety Code, a violation of subdivision (f) of Section 647 of the Penal Code, or a violation of Section 25662 of the Business and Professions Code, the minor's probation shall include the conditions required by Section 729.10. If the minor fails to comply with the conditions of probation imposed, the court may order and adjudge the minor to be a ward of the court.

(b) If the court has found that the minor is a person described by Section 601 or 602, it may order and adjudge the minor to be a ward of the court. *(Added by Stats.1961, c. 1616, p. 3485, § 2. Amended by Stats.1963, c. 1761, p. 3514, § 5; Stats.1976, c. 1068, p. 4790, § 52; Stats.1989, c. 936, § 2; Stats.1989, c. 1117, § 14.)*

Cross References

Appealable orders, rulings, and judgments, see Welfare and Institutions Code § 800.
Completion of supervision program or probation, dismissal of petition, sealing records, see Welfare and Institutions Code § 786.
Discharge and continuance to refer minor to juvenile justice community resource program and receive social study, see Welfare and Institutions Code § 702.
Enrollment of pupils, see Education Code § 1981.
General effect of judgments and orders, see Code of Civil Procedure § 1908 et seq.
Inducing disobedience to juvenile court order, see Penal Code § 272.
Juvenile court record, see Welfare and Institutions Code § 825.
Minor or nonminor within transition jurisdiction of juvenile court, criteria, see Welfare and Institutions Code § 450.
Modification of orders, see Welfare and Institutions Code § 775 et seq.
Non-criminal nature of proceedings, see Welfare and Institutions Code § 203.
Probation officer or social worker defined for purposes of this Chapter, see Welfare and Institutions Code § 215.
Retention of jurisdiction, see Welfare and Institutions Code § 607.
Rights of minor in releasing or destruction of juvenile court records, see Welfare and Institutions Code § 826.6.
Sex offenders, required AIDS testing, see Penal Code § 1202.1.
Termination of jurisdiction over ward satisfying specified criteria, hearing, see Welfare and Institutions Code § 607.2.
Willful disobedience or interference with juvenile court order as contempt, see Welfare and Institutions Code § 213.
Workers' compensation and insurance, employees, juvenile traffic offenders or probationers engaged in rehabilitative work on public property, see Labor Code § 3364.6.

Research References

West's California Judicial Council Forms JV–624, Terms and Conditions.
West's California Judicial Council Forms JV–665, Disposition—Juvenile Delinquency.
West's California Judicial Council Forms JV–667, Custodial and Out-Of-Home Placement Disposition Attachment.

§ 725.5. Evidence to be considered

In determining the judgment and order to be made in any case in which the minor is found to be a person described in Section 602, the court shall consider, in addition to other relevant and material evidence, (1) the age of the minor, (2) the circumstances and gravity of the offense committed by the minor, and (3) the minor's previous delinquent history. *(Added by Stats.1982, c. 1090, § 1.)*

§ 726. Limitations on parental or guardian control; removal from physical custody; limitation on right to make educational or developmental services decisions; appointment of responsible adult; conflicts of interest; appointment of developmental services decisionmaker; physical confinement of minor; jurisdiction

(a) In all cases in which a minor is adjudged a ward or dependent child of the court, the court may limit the control to be exercised over the ward or dependent child by any parent or guardian and shall, in its order, clearly and specifically set forth all those limitations, but no ward or dependent child shall be taken from the physical custody of a parent or guardian, unless upon the hearing the court finds one of the following facts:

(1) That the parent or guardian is incapable of providing or has failed or neglected to provide proper maintenance, training, and education for the minor.

(2) That the minor has been tried on probation while in custody and has failed to reform.

(3) That the welfare of the minor requires that custody be taken from the minor's parent or guardian.

(b) Whenever the court specifically limits the right of the parent or guardian to make educational or developmental services decisions for the minor, the court shall at the same time appoint a responsible adult to make educational or developmental services decisions for the child until one of the following occurs:

(1) The minor reaches 18 years of age, unless the child chooses not to make educational or developmental services decisions for themselves, or is deemed by the court to be incompetent.

(2) Another responsible adult is appointed to make educational or developmental services decisions for the minor pursuant to this section.

(3) The right of the parent or guardian to make educational or developmental services decisions for the minor is fully restored.

(4) A successor guardian or conservator is appointed.

(5) The child is placed into a planned permanent living arrangement pursuant to paragraph (5) or (6) of subdivision (b) of Section 727.3, at which time, for educational decisionmaking, the foster parent, relative caretaker, or nonrelative extended family member, as defined in Section 362.7, has the right to represent the child in educational matters pursuant to Section 56055 of the Education Code, and for decisions relating to developmental services, unless the court specifies otherwise, the foster parent, relative caregiver, or nonrelative extended family member of the planned permanent living arrangement has the right to represent the child in matters related to developmental services.

(c) An individual who would have a conflict of interest in representing the child, as specified under federal regulations, may not be appointed to make educational decisions. The limitations applicable to conflicts of interest for educational rights holders shall also apply to authorized representatives for developmental services decisions pursuant to subdivision (b) of Section 4701.6. For purposes of this section, "an individual who would have a conflict of interest" means a person having any interests that might restrict or bias their ability to make educational or developmental services decisions, including, but not limited to, those conflicts of interest prohibited by Section 1126 of the Government Code, and the receipt of compensation or attorneys' fees for the provision of services pursuant to this section. A foster parent may not be deemed to have a conflict of interest solely because the foster parent receives compensation for the provision of services pursuant to this section.

(1) If the court limits the parent's educational rights pursuant to subdivision (a), the court shall determine whether there is a responsible adult who is a relative, nonrelative extended family member, or other adult known to the child and who is available and willing to serve as the child's educational representative before appointing an educational representative or surrogate who is not known to the child.

If the court cannot identify a responsible adult who is known to the child and available to make educational decisions for the child and paragraphs (1) to (5), inclusive, of subdivision (b) do not apply, and the child has either been referred to the local educational agency for special education and related services or has a valid individualized education program, the court shall refer the child to the local educational agency for appointment of a surrogate parent pursuant to Section 7579.5 of the Government Code.

(2) All educational and school placement decisions shall seek to ensure that the child is in the least restrictive educational programs and has access to the academic resources, services, and extracurricular and enrichment activities that are available to all pupils. In all instances, educational and school placement decisions shall be based on the best interests of the child. If an educational representative or surrogate is appointed for the child, the representative or surrogate shall meet with the child, shall investigate the child's educational needs and whether those needs are being met, and shall, before each review hearing held under Article 10 (commencing with Section 360), provide information and recommendations concerning the child's educational needs to the child's social worker, make written recommendations to the court, or attend the hearing and participate in those portions of the hearing that concern the child's education.

(3) Nothing in this section in any way removes the obligation to appoint surrogate parents for students with disabilities who are without parental representation in special education procedures as required by state and federal law, including Section 1415(b)(2) of Title 20 of the United States Code, Section 56050 of the Education Code, Section 7579.5 of the Government Code, and Rule 5.650 of the California Rules of Court.

If the court appoints a developmental services decisionmaker pursuant to this section, they shall have the authority to access the child's information and records pursuant to subdivision (u) of Section 4514 and subdivision (y) of Section 5328, and to act on the child's behalf for the purposes of the individual program plan process pursuant to Sections 4646, 4646.5, and 4648 and the fair hearing process pursuant to Chapter 7 (commencing with Section 4700) of Division 4.5, and as set forth in the court order.

(d)(1) If the minor is removed from the physical custody of the minor's parent or guardian as the result of an order of wardship made pursuant to Section 602, the order shall specify that the minor may not be held in physical confinement for a period in excess of the middle term of imprisonment which could be imposed upon an adult convicted of the offense or offenses which brought or continued the minor under the jurisdiction of the juvenile court.

(2) As used in this section and in Section 731, "maximum term of imprisonment" means the middle of the three time periods set forth in paragraph (3) of subdivision (a) of Section 1170 of the Penal Code, but without the need to follow the provisions of subdivision (b) of Section 1170 of the Penal Code or to consider time for good behavior or participation pursuant to Sections 2930, 2931, and 2932 of the Penal Code, plus enhancements which must be proven if pled.

(3) If the court elects to aggregate the period of physical confinement on multiple counts or multiple petitions, including previously sustained petitions adjudging the minor a ward within Section 602, the "maximum term of imprisonment" shall be the aggregate term of imprisonment specified in subdivision (a) of Section 1170.1 of the Penal Code, which includes any additional term imposed pursuant to Section 667, 667.5, 667.6, or 12022.1 of the Penal Code, and Section 11370.2 of the Health and Safety Code.

(4) If the charged offense is a misdemeanor or a felony not included within the scope of Section 1170 of the Penal Code, the "maximum term of imprisonment" is the middle term of imprisonment prescribed by law.

(5) "Physical confinement" means placement in a juvenile hall, ranch, camp, forestry camp or secure juvenile home pursuant to Section 730, or in a secure youth treatment facility pursuant to Section 875, or in any institution operated by the Department of Corrections and Rehabilitation, Division of Juvenile Justice.

(6) This section does not limit the power of the court to retain jurisdiction over a minor and to make appropriate orders pursuant to Section 727 for the period permitted by Section 607. *(Added by Stats.1961, c. 1616, p. 3486, § 2. Amended by Stats.1976, c. 1068, p. 4790, § 53; Stats.1976, c. 1071, p. 4827, § 29; Stats.1977, c. 1238, p. 4158, § 1, eff. Oct. 1, 1977; Stats.1994, c. 181 (A.B.1146), § 1; Stats.2002, c. 180 (A.B.886), § 3; Stats.2003, c. 862 (A.B.490), § 12; Stats.2011, c. 471 (S.B.368), § 5; Stats.2012, c. 176 (A.B.2060), § 3; Stats.2013, c. 59 (S.B.514), § 12; Stats.2014, c. 71 (S.B.1304), § 183, eff. Jan. 1, 2015; Stats.2021, c. 18 (S.B.92), § 7, eff. May 14, 2021; Stats.2022, c. 58 (A.B.200), § 39, eff. June 30, 2022.)*

Cross References

Adoption of child declared free from custody and control of parents, see Family Code § 8606.
Appealable orders, rulings, and judgments, see Welfare and Institutions Code § 800.
Child welfare, family reunification and maintenance pilot program, see Welfare and Institutions Code § 16500.5 et seq.
Commitment of ward who is 14 years of age or older to secure youth treatment facility, maximum term of confinement, see Welfare and Institutions Code § 875.
Dependent children, persons appointed to make educational decisions for, see Welfare and Institutions Code § 361.
Educational placement of pupils residing in licensed children's institutions, placement in regular public school, child's best interests, see Education Code § 48853.
Elementary and secondary education, educational placement of pupils residing in licensed children's institutions, educational liaisons, see Education Code § 48853.5.
Family preservation programs, Solano and Alameda counties, expanded services, see Welfare and Institutions Code § 16500.51.
Felonies, definition and penalties, see Penal Code §§ 17, 18.
Foster family agencies, short-term residential treatment program staff, and and caregivers, access to enrolled or former pupil records, purpose, communications, see Education Code § 49069.3.
Freedom from parental custody and control, see Family Code § 7802 et seq.
Hearing defined for purposes of this Article, see Welfare and Institutions Code § 727.4.
Minor wards or conservatees, appointment of responsible adult to make educational decisions for, see Probate Code § 2662.
Misdemeanors, definition and penalties, see Penal Code §§ 17, 19, 19.2.
Parents' entitlement to custody, see Family Code § 3010.
Person identified to act as parent of child to make educational decisions by judicial decree or order also deemed parent for purposes of this section, see Education Code § 56028.
Regional centers for persons with developmental disabilities, transition of services for transferred consumers, procedure and court appointments pursuant to this section, see Welfare and Institutions Code § 4643.5.
Relative defined for purposes of this Article, see Welfare and Institutions Code § 727.4.
Removal from parent's custody and commitment to foster homes, institutions, or Youth Authority, see Welfare and Institutions Code § 777.
Services for developmentally disabled, access to records by developmental services decisionmaker, see Welfare and Institutions Code § 4726.
Services for developmentally disabled, planning team defined to include minor's, dependent's, or ward's court-appointed developmental services decisionmaker, see Welfare and Institutions Code § 4512.
Wards, judgment and orders, psychotropic medications, see Welfare and Institutions Code § 739.5.

Research References

West's California Judicial Council Forms JV–250, Notice of Hearing and Temporary Restraining Order—Juvenile (Also Available in Chinese, Korean, Spanish, and Vietnamese).
West's California Judicial Council Forms JV–535, Order Designating Educational Rights Holder (Also Available in Spanish).
West's California Judicial Council Forms JV–535(A), Attachment to Order Designating Educational Rights Holder (Also Available in Spanish).
West's California Judicial Council Forms JV–535–INFO, Information on Educational Rights Holders.
1 Witkin California Criminal Law 4th Introduction to Crimes § 11 (2021), Nature of Protection.
3 Witkin, California Criminal Law 4th Punishment § 96 (2021), Constitutional Limitations.
3 Witkin, California Criminal Law 4th Punishment § 251 (2021), Scope of Prohibition: Particular Commitments.
3 Witkin, California Criminal Law 4th Punishment § 308–I (2021), (New) Application to Juveniles.

3 Witkin, California Criminal Law 4th Punishment § 536B (2021), (New) in General.

§ 726.4. Disposition hearing; parentage inquiries; notice to alleged fathers; proceedings

(a) At the disposition hearing, in any case where the court orders the care, custody, and control of the minor to be under the supervision of the probation officer for foster care placement pursuant to subdivision (a) of Section 727, the court shall inquire of the mother and any other appropriate person as to the identity and address of all presumed or alleged fathers. The presence at the hearing of a man claiming to be the father shall not relieve the court of its duty of inquiry. The inquiry may include all of the following:

(1) Whether a judgment of paternity already exists.

(2) Whether the mother was married or believed she was married at the time of conception of the child or at any time thereafter.

(3) Whether the mother was cohabiting with a man at the time of conception or birth of the child.

(4) Whether the mother has received support payments or promises of support with respect to the child or in connection with her pregnancy.

(5) Whether any man has formally or informally acknowledged or declared his possible paternity of the child.

(6) Whether paternity tests have been administered and the results, if any.

(b) If, after the court inquiry, one or more men are identified as an alleged father, each alleged father shall be provided notice at his last and usual place of abode by certified mail return receipt requested alleging that he is or could be the father of the child. The notice shall state that the child is the subject of proceedings under Section 602 and that the proceedings could result in the termination of parental rights and adoption of the child. Nothing in this section shall preclude a court from terminating a father's parental rights even if he appears at the hearing and files an action under Section 7630 or 7631 of the Family Code.

(c) The court may determine that the failure of an alleged father to return the certified mail receipt is not good cause to continue a hearing pursuant to Section 682.

(d) If a man appears in the delinquency action and files an action under Section 7630 or 7631 of the Family Code, the court shall determine if he is the father.

(e) After a petition has been filed to declare a minor a ward of the court, and until the time that the petition is dismissed, wardship is terminated, or parental rights are terminated pursuant to Section 727.31, the juvenile court which has jurisdiction of the wardship action shall have exclusive jurisdiction to hear an action filed under Section 7630 or 7631 of the Family Code. *(Added by Stats.1999, c. 997 (A.B.575), § 14.)*

Cross References

Foster care defined for purposes of this Article, see Welfare and Institutions Code § 727.4.

Hearing defined for purposes of this Article, see Welfare and Institutions Code § 727.4.

Probation officer or social worker defined for purposes of this Chapter, see Welfare and Institutions Code § 215.

§ 726.5. Protective order; parentage, custody, or visitation order

(a) At any time when (1) the minor is a ward of the juvenile court under Section 725, or the court terminates wardship while the minor remains under the age of 18 years, and (2) proceedings for dissolution of marriage, for nullity of marriage, or for legal separation of the minor's parents, proceedings to determine custody of the child, or to establish paternity of the minor under the Uniform Parentage Act, Part 3 (commencing with Section 7600) of Division 12 of the Family Code are pending in the superior court of any county, or an order has been entered with regard to the custody of the minor, the juvenile court may issue a protective order as provided in Section 213.5 or as defined in Section 6218 of the Family Code and may issue an order determining parentage, custody of, or visitation with, the minor.

A custody or visitation order issued by the juvenile court pursuant to this subdivision shall be made in accordance with the procedures and criteria of Part 2 (commencing with Section 3020) of Division 8 of the Family Code. An order determining parentage issued by the juvenile court pursuant to this subdivision shall be made in accordance with the procedures and presumptions of the Uniform Parentage Act, Part 3 (commencing with Section 7600) of Division 12 of the Family Code.

(b) If the juvenile court decides to issue an order pursuant to subdivision (a), the juvenile court shall provide notice of that decision to the superior court in which the proceeding to decide parentage, custody of, or visitation with, the minor is pending. The clerk of the superior court, upon receipt of the notice, shall file the notice with other documents and records of the pending proceeding and send by first-class mail a copy of the notice to all parties of record in that proceeding.

(c) Any order issued under this section shall continue until modified or terminated by a subsequent order of the juvenile court. The order of the juvenile court shall be filed in the proceeding for nullity, dissolution, or legal separation, or in the proceeding to determine custody or to establish paternity, if that proceeding is pending at the time the juvenile court terminates its jurisdiction over the minor. The order shall then become a part of that proceeding and may be terminated or modified as the court in that proceeding deems appropriate.

(d) If no action is filed or pending relating to the custody of the minor in the superior court of any county at the time the juvenile court terminates its jurisdiction over the minor, the juvenile court order entered pursuant to subdivision (a) may be used as the sole basis for opening a file in the superior court of the county in which the parent who has been awarded physical custody resides. The clerk of the juvenile court shall transmit the order to the clerk of the superior court of the county in which the order is to be filed. The clerk of the superior court shall, upon receipt, open a file, without a filing fee, and assign a case number.

(e) The clerk of the superior court shall, upon the filing of any juvenile court order pursuant to subdivision (d), send by first-class mail a copy of the order with the case number, to the juvenile court and to the parents at the address listed on the order.

(f) The Judicial Council shall adopt forms for orders issued under this section. These orders shall not be confidential. *(Added by Stats.1998, c. 390 (S.B.2017), § 3.)*

Research References

West's California Judicial Council Forms JV–200, Custody Order—Juvenile—Final Judgment (Also Available in Spanish).

West's California Judicial Council Forms JV–205, Visitation Order—Juvenile (Also Available in Spanish).

West's California Judicial Council Forms JV–206, Reasons for No or Supervised Visitation—Juvenile (Also Available in Spanish).

West's California Judicial Council Forms JV–245, Request for Restraining Order—Juvenile (Also Available in Chinese, Korean, Spanish, and Vietnamese).

West's California Judicial Council Forms JV–250, Notice of Hearing and Temporary Restraining Order—Juvenile (Also Available in Chinese, Korean, Spanish, and Vietnamese).

West's California Judicial Council Forms JV–255, Restraining Order—Juvenile (Clets—Juv) (Also Available in Chinese, Korean, Spanish, and Vietnamese).

§ 727. Order for care, supervision, custody, conduct, maintenance and support of ward; proceedings joined by court; parent counseling or education programs; court orders

(a)(1) If a minor or nonminor is adjudged a ward of the court on the ground that the minor or nonminor is a person described by Section 601 or 602, the court may make any reasonable orders for the care, supervision, custody, conduct, maintenance, and support of the minor or nonminor, including medical treatment, subject to further order of the court.

(2) In the discretion of the court, a ward may be ordered to be on probation without supervision of the probation officer. The court, in so ordering, may impose on the ward any and all reasonable conditions of behavior as may be appropriate under this disposition. A minor or nonminor who has been adjudged a ward of the court on the basis of the commission of any of the offenses described in subdivision (b) or paragraph (2) of subdivision (d) of Section 707, Section 459 of the Penal Code, or subdivision (a) of Section 11350 of the Health and Safety Code, shall not be eligible for probation without supervision of the probation officer. A minor or nonminor who has been adjudged a ward of the court on the basis of the commission of an offense involving the sale or possession for sale of a controlled substance, except misdemeanor offenses involving marijuana, as specified in Chapter 2 (commencing with Section 11053) of Division 10 of the Health and Safety Code, or of an offense in violation of Section 32625 of the Penal Code, shall be eligible for probation without supervision of the probation officer only if the court determines that the interests of justice would best be served and states reasons on the record for that determination.

(3) In all other cases, the court shall order the care, custody, and control of the minor or nonminor to be under the supervision of the probation officer.

(4) It is the responsibility, pursuant to Section 672(a)(2)(B) of Title 42 of the United States Code, of the probation agency to determine the appropriate placement for the ward once the court issues a placement order. In determination of the appropriate placement for the ward, the probation officer shall consider any recommendations of the child and family. The probation agency may place the minor or nonminor in any of the following:

(A) The approved home of a relative or the approved home of a nonrelative, extended family member, as defined in Section 362.7. If a decision has been made to place the minor in the home of a relative, the court may authorize the relative to give legal consent for the minor's medical, surgical, and dental care and education as if the relative caregiver were the custodial parent of the minor.

(B) A foster home, the approved home of a resource family, as defined in Section 16519.5, or a home or facility in accordance with the federal Indian Child Welfare Act (25 U.S.C. Sec. 1901 et seq.).

(C) A suitable licensed community care facility, as identified by the probation officer, except a youth homelessness prevention center licensed by the State Department of Social Services pursuant to Section 1502.35 of the Health and Safety Code.

(D) A foster family agency, as defined in subdivision (g) of Section 11400 and paragraph (4) of subdivision (a) of Section 1502 of the Health and Safety Code, in a suitable certified family home or with a resource family.

(E) A minor or nonminor dependent may be placed in a group home vendored by a regional center pursuant to Section 56004 of Title 17 of the California Code of Regulations or a short-term residential therapeutic program, as defined in subdivision (ad) of Section 11400 and paragraph (18) of subdivision (a) of Section 1502 of the Health and Safety Code. The placing agency shall also comply with requirements set forth in paragraph (9) of subdivision (e) of Section 361.2, that includes, but is not limited to, authorization, limitation on length of stay, extensions, and additional requirements related to minors. For youth 13 years of age and older, the chief probation officer of the county probation department, or their designee, shall approve the placement if it is longer than 12 months, and no less frequently than every 12 months thereafter.

(F)(i) A minor adjudged a ward of the juvenile court shall be entitled to participate in age-appropriate extracurricular, enrichment, and social activities. A state or local regulation or policy shall not prevent, or create barriers to, participation in those activities. Each state and local entity shall ensure that private agencies that provide foster care services to wards have policies consistent with this section and that those agencies promote and protect the ability of wards to participate in age-appropriate extracurricular, enrichment, and social activities. A short-term residential therapeutic program or a group home administrator, a facility manager, or their responsible designee, and a caregiver, as defined in paragraph (1) of subdivision (a) of Section 362.04, shall use a reasonable and prudent parent standard, as defined in paragraph (2) of subdivision (a) of Section 362.04, in determining whether to give permission for a minor residing in foster care to participate in extracurricular, enrichment, and social activities. A short-term residential therapeutic program or a group home administrator, a facility manager, or their responsible designee, and a caregiver shall take reasonable steps to determine the appropriateness of the activity taking into consideration the minor's age, maturity, and developmental level. For every minor placed in a setting described in subparagraphs (A) through (E), inclusive, age-appropriate extracurricular, enrichment, and social activities shall include access to computer technology and the internet.

(ii) A short-term residential therapeutic program or a group home administrator, facility manager, or their responsible designee, is encouraged to consult with social work or treatment staff members who are most familiar with the minor at the group home or short-term residential therapeutic program in applying and using the reasonable and prudent parent standard.

(G) For nonminors, an approved supervised independent living setting, as defined in Section 11400, including a residential housing unit certified by a licensed transitional housing placement provider.

(5) The minor or nonminor shall be released from juvenile detention upon an order being entered under paragraph (3), unless the court determines that a delay in the release from detention is reasonable pursuant to Section 737.

(b)(1) To facilitate coordination and cooperation among agencies, the court may, at any time after a petition has been filed, after giving notice and an opportunity to be heard, join in the juvenile court proceedings any agency that the court determines has failed to meet a legal obligation to provide services to a minor, for whom a petition has been filed under Section 601 or 602, to a nonminor, as described in Section 303, or to a nonminor dependent, as defined in subdivision (v) of Section 11400. In any proceeding in which an agency is joined, the court shall not impose duties upon the agency beyond those mandated by law. The purpose of joinder under this section is to ensure the delivery and coordination of legally mandated services to the minor. The joinder shall not be maintained for any other purpose. Nothing in this section shall prohibit agencies that have received notice of the hearing on joinder from meeting prior to the hearing to coordinate services.

(2) The court has no authority to order services unless it has been determined through the administrative process of an agency that has been joined as a party, that the minor, nonminor, or nonminor dependent is eligible for those services. With respect to mental health assessment, treatment, and case management services pursuant to an individualized education program developed pursuant to Article 2 (commencing with Section 56320) of Chapter 4 of Part 30 of Division 4 of Title 2 of the Education Code, the court's determination shall be limited to whether the agency has complied with that chapter.

(3) For the purposes of this subdivision, "agency" means any governmental agency or any private service provider or individual that receives federal, state, or local governmental funding or

reimbursement for providing services directly to a child, nonminor, or nonminor dependent.

(c) If a minor has been adjudged a ward of the court on the ground that the minor is a person described in Section 601 or 602, and the court finds that notice has been given in accordance with Section 661, and if the court orders that a parent or guardian shall retain custody of that minor either subject to or without the supervision of the probation officer, the parent or guardian may be required to participate with that minor in a counseling or education program, including, but not limited to, parent education and parenting programs operated by community colleges, school districts, or other appropriate agencies designated by the court.

(d)(1) The juvenile court may direct any reasonable orders to the parents and guardians of the minor who is the subject of any proceedings under this chapter as the court deems necessary and proper to carry out subdivisions (a), (b), and (c), including orders to appear before a county financial evaluation officer, to ensure the minor's regular school attendance, and to make reasonable efforts to obtain appropriate educational services necessary to meet the needs of the minor.

(2) If counseling or other treatment services are ordered for the minor, the parent, guardian, or foster parent shall be ordered to participate in those services, unless participation by the parent, guardian, or foster parent is deemed by the court to be inappropriate or potentially detrimental to the minor.

(e) The court may, after receipt of relevant testimony and other evidence from the parties, affirm or reject the placement determination. If the court rejects the placement determination, the court may instruct the probation department to determine an alternative placement for the ward, or the court may modify the placement order to an alternative placement recommended by a party to the case after the court has received the probation department's assessment of that recommendation and other relevant evidence from the parties. *(Added by Stats.1961, c. 1616, p. 3486, § 2. Amended by Stats.1963, c. 1761, p. 3515, § 6; Stats.1968, c. 218, p. 524, § 1; Stats.1971, c. 1593, p. 3322, § 324, operative July 1, 1973; Stats.1971, c. 1729, p. 3678, § 4; Stats.1973, c. 1212, p. 2836, § 325; Stats.1975, c. 678, p. 1501, § 73; Stats.1975, c. 1266, p. 3327, § 9; Stats.1976, c. 1068, p. 4791, § 54; Stats.1976, c. 1070, p. 4812, § 3, eff. Sept. 21, 1976, operative Jan. 1, 1977; Stats.1976, c. 1079, p. 4890, § 95; Stats.1976, c. 1071, p. 4832, § 38; Stats.1977, c. 1252, p. 4479, § 479, operative July 1, 1978; Stats.1977, c. 579, p. 1924, § 204; Stats.1978, c. 429, p. 1438, § 177.5, eff. July 17, 1978, operative July 1, 1978; Stats.1978, c. 432, p. 1498, § 8.7, eff. July 17, 1978, operative July 1, 1978; Stats.1980, c. 626, p. 1712, § 1; Stats.1980, c. 991, p. 3136, § 1; Stats.1982, c. 978, § 28, eff. Sept. 13, 1982, operative July 1, 1982; Stats.1984, c. 162, § 4; Stats.1984, c. 867, § 4; Stats.1985, c. 1485, § 15; Stats.1986, c. 1120, § 12, eff. Sept. 24, 1986; Stats.1987, c. 1022, § 9; Stats.1988, c. 99, § 1; Stats.1989, c. 936, § 3; Stats.1992, c. 1307 (A.B.3553), § 2; Stats.1993, c. 1089 (A.B.2129), § 7; Stats.1994, c. 453 (A.B.560), § 12; Stats.2000, c. 911 (A.B.686), § 4; Stats.2001, c. 653 (A.B.1695), § 13, eff. Oct. 10, 2001; Stats.2008, c. 483 (A.B.2096), § 2; Stats.2010, c. 178 (S.B.1115), § 98, operative Jan. 1, 2012; Stats.2012, c. 130 (S.B.1048), § 2; Stats.2013, c. 21 (A.B.74), § 11, eff. June 27, 2013; Stats.2013, c. 485 (A.B.346), § 6; Stats.2013, c. 487 (A.B.787), § 4.5; Stats.2014, c. 615 (A.B.2607), § 1, eff. Jan. 1, 2015; Stats.2014, c. 772 (S.B.1460), § 13.5, eff. Jan. 1, 2015; Stats.2015, c. 773 (A.B.403), § 50, eff. Jan. 1, 2016; Stats.2016, c. 612 (A.B.1997), § 77, eff. Jan. 1, 2017; Stats.2017, c. 561 (A.B.1516), § 266, eff. Jan. 1, 2018; Stats. 2017, c. 732 (A.B.404), § 54, eff. Jan. 1, 2018; Stats.2018, c. 92 (S.B.1289), § 220, eff. Jan. 1, 2019; Stats.2018, c. 997 (A.B.2448), § 2, eff. Jan. 1, 2019; Stats.2019, c. 341 (A.B.1235), § 15, eff. Jan. 1, 2020; Stats.2021, c. 76 (A.B.136), § 15, eff. July 16, 2021.)*

Law Revision Commission Comments

Subdivision (a) of Section 727 is amended to reflect nonsubstantive reorganization of the statutes governing control of deadly weapons. [38 Cal.L.Rev.Comm. Reports 217 (2009)].

Cross References

Acceptance of person committed, see Welfare and Institutions Code § 736.
Adjustment school commitment, see Welfare and Institutions Code § 976.
Appealable orders, rulings and judgments, see Welfare and Institutions Code § 800.
California Community Care Facilities Act, exempt facilities and arrangements, see Health and Safety Code § 1505.
Child welfare, family reunification and maintenance pilot program, see Welfare and Institutions Code § 16500.5 et seq.
Commitment of ward who is 14 years of age or older to secure youth treatment facility criteria, baseline and maximum terms of confinement, individual rehabilitation plans, progress review hearings, transfer to less restrictive program, see Welfare and Institutions Code § 875.
County financial evaluation officer, see Government Code § 27750 et seq.
Detention until execution of commitment order, see Welfare and Institutions Code § 737.
Educational placement of pupils residing in licensed children's institutions, placement in regular public school, child's best interests, see Education Code § 48853.
Family preservation programs, Solano and Alameda counties, expanded services, see Welfare and Institutions Code § 16500.51.
Foster care placement, prevention of unnecessary or abrupt placement changes, see Welfare and Institutions Code § 16010.7.
Hearing defined for purposes of this Article, see Welfare and Institutions Code § 727.4.
Imprisonment to compel performance of acts, exemptions, definitions, see Code of Civil Procedure § 1219.
Institutions for delinquents, generally, see Welfare and Institutions Code § 1000 et seq.
Juvenile court school pupils, criteria for apportionments, see Education Code §§ 42238.18, 48645.1.
Juvenile court schools, generally, see Education Code § 48645.
Juvenile court schools, cost of providing onsite school structures, see Education Code § 48645.6.
Minor law violator, availability of treatment prescribed by this section, see Welfare and Institutions Code § 731.
Misdemeanors, definition and penalties, see Penal Code §§ 17, 19, 19.2.
Probation officer or social worker defined for purposes of this Chapter, see Welfare and Institutions Code § 215.
Reasonable efforts defined for purposes of this Article, see Welfare and Institutions Code § 727.4.
Relative defined for purposes of this Article, see Welfare and Institutions Code § 727.4.
Retention of jurisdiction, nonminor dependent remaining under delinquency jurisdiction and under foster care placement order, see Welfare and Institutions Code § 303.
Youth Authority, generally, see Welfare and Institutions Code § 1700 et seq.

Research References

West's California Judicial Council Forms JV–540, Notice of Hearing on Joinder—Juvenile (Also Available in Spanish).
West's California Judicial Council Forms JV–665, Disposition—Juvenile Delinquency.
West's California Judicial Council Forms JV–667, Custodial and Out-Of-Home Placement Disposition Attachment.

§ 727.05. Emergency placement with relative or nonrelative extended family member; duties of agency; criminal records check

(a) Notwithstanding paragraph (4) of subdivision (a) of Section 727, the probation agency may make an emergency placement of a minor ordered into its care, custody, and control with a relative or nonrelative extended family member.

(b) Prior to making the emergency placement, the probation agency shall do all of the following:

(1) Conduct an in-home inspection to assess the safety of the home and the ability of the relative or nonrelative extended family member to care for the minor's needs.

(2) Ensure that a state-level criminal records check is conducted by an appropriate government agency through the California Law Enforcement Telecommunications System (CLETS) pursuant to Section 16504.5 for all of the following:

(A) Any person over 18 years of age living in the home of the relative or nonrelative extended family member who seeks emergency placement of the minor, excluding any person who is a nonminor dependent, as defined in subdivision (v) of Section 11400.

(B) At the discretion of the probation agency, any person over 18 years of age known to the agency to be regularly present in the home, other than any professional providing professional services to the minor.

(C) At the discretion of the agency, any person over 14 years of age living in the home who the agency believes may have a criminal record, excluding any child who is under the jurisdiction of the juvenile court.

(3) Conduct a check of allegations of prior child abuse or neglect concerning the relative or nonrelative extended family member and other adults in the home.

(c)(1) If the CLETS information that is obtained pursuant to paragraph (2) of subdivision (b) indicates that a person has no criminal record, the probation agency may place the minor in the home on an emergency basis.

(2) If the CLETS information obtained pursuant to paragraph (2) of subdivision (b) indicates that a person has been convicted of an offense described in subparagraph (B) or (D) of paragraph (2) of subdivision (g) of Section 1522 of the Health and Safety Code, the minor shall not be placed in the home unless a criminal records exemption has been granted using the exemption criteria specified in paragraph (2) of subdivision (g) of Section 1522 of the Health and Safety Code.

(3) Notwithstanding paragraph (2), a minor may be placed on an emergency basis if the CLETS information obtained pursuant to paragraph (2) of subdivision (b) indicates that the person has been convicted of an offense not described in subclause (II) of clause (i) of subparagraph (B) of paragraph (2) of subdivision (g) of Section 1522 of the Health and Safety Code, pending a criminal records exemption decision based on live scan fingerprint results if all of the following conditions are met:

(A) The conviction does not involve an offense against a child.

(B) The chief probation officer, or their designee, determines that the placement is in the best interests of the minor.

(C) No party to the case objects to the placement.

(4) If the CLETS information obtained pursuant to paragraph (2) of subdivision (b) indicates that the person has been arrested for any offense described in paragraph (2) of subdivision (e) of Section 1522 of the Health and Safety Code, the minor shall not be placed on an emergency basis in the home until the investigation required by paragraph (1) of subdivision (e) of Section 1522 of the Health and Safety Code has been completed and the chief probation officer, or their designee, and the court have considered the investigation results when determining whether the placement is in the best interests of the child.

(5) If the CLETS information obtained pursuant to paragraph (2) of subdivision (b) indicates that the person has been convicted of an offense described in subparagraph (A) of paragraph (2) of subdivision (g) of Section 1522 of the Health and Safety Code, the minor shall not be placed in the home on an emergency basis.

(6) Notwithstanding paragraphs (2) and (5), or the placement recommendation of the county probation agency, the court may authorize the placement of a child on an emergency basis in the home of a relative, regardless of the status of any criminal record exemption or resource family approval, if the court finds that the placement does not pose a risk to the health and safety of the child.

(d) If the relative or nonrelative extended family member has not submitted an application for approval as a resource family at the time of the emergency placement, the probation agency shall require the relative or nonrelative extended family member to submit the application and initiate the home environment assessment no later than five business days after the emergency placement.

(e) Unless the fingerprint clearance check has already been initiated, the probation agency shall ensure that, within five days of the emergency placement, a fingerprint clearance check of the relative or nonrelative extended family member and any other person whose criminal record was obtained pursuant to this section is initiated through the Department of Justice to ensure the accuracy of the criminal records check conducted through the CLETS and to ensure criminal record clearance of the relative or nonrelative extended family member and all adults in the home pursuant to subparagraph (A) of paragraph (2) of subdivision (d) of Section 16519.5 and any associated written directives or regulations.

(f) An identification card from a foreign consulate or foreign passport shall be considered a valid form of identification for conducting a criminal records check pursuant to this section. *(Added by Stats.2019, c. 777 (A.B.819), § 19, eff. Jan. 1, 2020. Amended by Stats.2021, c. 687 (S.B.354), § 10, eff. Jan. 1, 2022.)*

Cross References

Interim support for emergency caregivers with pending applications under the Resource Family Approval Program, criteria, funding, see Welfare and Institutions Code § 11461.36.

Resource family approval process, see Welfare and Institutions Code § 16519.5.

§ 727.1. Placement of minor under supervision of probation officer; placement of minor adjudged a ward of the court; considerations; periodic review; public funds

(a) If the court orders the care, custody, and control of the minor to be under the supervision of the probation officer for foster care placement pursuant to subdivision (a) of Section 727, the decision regarding choice of placement, pursuant to Section 706.6, shall be based upon selection of a safe setting that is the least restrictive or most family-like, and the most appropriate setting that meets the individual needs of the minor and is available, in proximity to the parent's home, consistent with the selection of the environment best suited to meet the minor's special needs and best interests. The selection shall consider, in order of priority, placement with relatives, tribal members, and foster family, group care, and residential treatment pursuant to Section 7950 of the Family Code.

(b) Unless otherwise authorized by law, the court shall not order the placement of a minor who is adjudged a ward of the court on the basis that the ward is a person described by either Section 601 or 602 in an out-of-state residential facility, as defined in subdivision (b) of Section 7910 of the Family Code, unless the court finds, in its order of placement and based on evidence presented by the county probation department, that all of the following conditions are met:

(1) The out-of-state residential facility is licensed or certified for the placement of children by an agency of the state in which the ward will be placed.

(2) The out-of-state residential facility has been certified by the State Department of Social Services or is exempt from that certification, pursuant to Section 7911.1 of the Family Code.

(3) On and after July 1, 2021, the county probation department has fulfilled its responsibilities as set forth in Sections 4096 and 16010.9.

(4) The court has reviewed the documentation of any required assessment, technical assistance efforts, or recommendations and finds that in-state facilities or programs are unavailable or inadequate to meet the needs of the ward.

(c) If, upon inspection, the probation officer of the county in which the minor is adjudged a ward of the court determines that the out-of-state facility or program is not in compliance with the standards required under paragraph (2) of subdivision (b) or has an adverse impact on the health and safety of the minor, the probation officer may temporarily remove the minor from the facility or program. The probation officer shall promptly inform the court of the minor's removal, and shall return the minor to the court for a hearing to review the suitability of continued out-of-state placement. The probation officer shall, within one business day of removing the minor, notify the State Department of Social Services' Compact Administrator, and, within five working days, submit a written report of the findings and actions taken.

(d) The court shall review each of these placements for compliance with the requirements of subdivision (b) at least once every six months.

(e) The county shall not be entitled to receive or expend any public funds for the placement of a minor in an out-of-state group home or short-term residential therapeutic program, unless the conditions of subdivisions (b) and (d) are met.

(f) Notwithstanding any other law, on and after July 1, 2022, the court shall not order or approve any new placement of a minor by a county probation department in an out-of-state residential facility, as defined in subdivision (b) of Section 7910 of the Family Code, except for placements described in subdivision (h) of Section 7911.1 of the Family Code.

(g) Notwithstanding any other law, the court shall order any minor placed out of state by a county probation department in an out-of-state residential facility, as defined in subdivision (b) of Section 7910 of the Family Code, to be returned to California no later than January 1, 2023, except for placements described in subdivision (h) of Section 7911.1 of the Family Code. *(Added by Stats.1986, c. 798, § 1. Amended by Stats.1994, c. 1128 (A.B.1892), § 3; Stats.1996, c. 12 (A.B.1397), § 9, eff. Feb. 14, 1996; Stats.1998, c. 311 (S.B.933), § 54, eff. Aug. 19, 1998; Stats.1999, c. 881 (A.B.1659), § 7, eff. Oct. 10, 1999; Stats.2001, c. 831 (A.B.1696), § 8; Stats.2015, c. 773 (A.B.403), § 51, eff. Jan. 1, 2016; Stats.2016, c. 612 (A.B.1997), § 78, eff. Jan. 1, 2017; Stats.2017, c. 561 (A.B.1516), § 267, eff. Jan. 1, 2018; Stats. 2021, c. 86 (A.B.153), § 28, eff. July 16, 2021.)*

Cross References

Foster care defined for purposes of this Article, see Welfare and Institutions Code § 727.4.
Hearing defined for purposes of this Article, see Welfare and Institutions Code § 727.4.
Probation officer or social worker defined for purposes of this Chapter, see Welfare and Institutions Code § 215.
Relative defined for purposes of this Article, see Welfare and Institutions Code § 727.4.

§ 727.12. Review of placement in short-term residential therapeutic program

(a)(1) For a placement made on and after October 1, 2021, each placement of the minor or nonminor dependent in a short-term residential therapeutic program, including the initial placement and each subsequent placement into a short-term residential therapeutic program, shall be reviewed by the court within 45 days of the start of placement in accordance with this section. In no event shall the court grant a continuance pursuant to Section 682 that would cause the review to be completed more than 60 days after the start of the placement.

(2) For a placement made on and after July 1, 2022, each placement of the minor or nonminor dependent in a community treatment facility, including the initial placement and each subsequent placement into a community treatment facility, shall be reviewed by the court within 45 days of the start of placement in accordance with this section. In no event shall the court grant a continuance pursuant to Section 682 that would cause the review to be completed more than 60 days after the start of the placement.

(b)(1) * * * At any time after the decision to place a minor or nonminor dependent into a short-term residential therapeutic program or a community treatment facility has been made, but no later than five calendar days following each placement, the probation officer shall request the juvenile court to schedule a hearing to review the placement.

(2) The probation officer shall serve a copy of the request on all parties to the delinquency proceeding, the minor's court-appointed special advocate, if applicable, and the minor's tribe in the case of an Indian child to whom subparagraph (E) of paragraph (1) of subdivision (d) of Section 224.1 applies.

(c)(1) The probation officer shall prepare and submit a report that shall include all of the following:

(A) A copy of the assessment, determination, and documentation prepared by the qualified individual pursuant to subdivision (g) of Section 4096.

(B) The case plan documentation required pursuant to subparagraph (B) of paragraph (3) of subdivision (d) of Section 706.6.

(C) In the case of an Indian child, a statement regarding whether the minor's tribe had an opportunity to confer regarding the departure from the placement preferences described in Section 361.31, and the active efforts made prior to placement in a short-term therapeutic program or community treatment facility to satisfy subdivision (f) of Section 224.1.

(D) A statement regarding whether the minor or nonminor dependent or any party to the proceeding, or minor's tribe in the case of an Indian child to whom subparagraph (E) of paragraph (1) of subdivision (d) of Section 224.1 applies, objects to the placement of the minor or nonminor dependent in the short-term residential therapeutic program or community treatment facility.

(2) The probation officer shall serve a copy of the report on all parties to the proceeding no later than seven calendar days before the hearing.

(d) Within five calendar days of the request described in subdivision (b), the court shall set a hearing to be held within 45 days after the start of the placement and give notice of the hearing to all parties to the proceeding, and the minor's tribe in the case of an Indian child to whom subparagraph (E) of paragraph (1) of subdivision (d) of Section 224.1 applies.

(e) When reviewing each placement of the minor or nonminor dependent in a short-term residential therapeutic program or community treatment facility, the court shall do all of the following:

(1) Consider the information specified in subdivision (c).

(2) Determine whether the needs of the minor or nonminor dependent can be met through placement in a family-based setting, or, if not, whether placement in a short-term residential therapeutic program or community treatment facility, as applicable, provides the most effective and appropriate care setting for the minor or nonminor dependent in the least restrictive environment. A shortage or lack of resource family homes shall not be an acceptable reason for determining that the needs of the minor or nonminor dependent cannot be met in a family-based setting.

(3) Determine whether the short-term residential therapeutic program or community treatment facility level of care, as applicable, is consistent with the short- and long-term mental and behavioral health goals and permanency plan for the minor or nonminor dependent.

(4) In the case of an Indian child, determine whether there is good cause to depart from the placement preferences set forth in Section 361.31.

(5) Approve or disapprove the placement.

(6) Make a finding, either in writing or on the record, of the basis for its determinations pursuant to this subdivision.

(f) If the court disapproves the placement, the court shall order the probation officer to transition the minor or nonminor dependent to a placement setting that is consistent with the determinations made pursuant to subdivision (e) within 30 days of the disapproval.

(g) This section does not prohibit the court from reviewing the placement of a minor or nonminor dependent in a short-term residential therapeutic program or community treatment facility pursuant to subdivision (a) at a regularly scheduled hearing if that hearing is held within 60 days of the placement and the information described in subdivision (c) has been presented to the court.

(h)(1) On or before October 1, 2021, for placements into a short-term residential therapeutic program, the Judicial Council shall amend or adopt rules of court and shall develop or amend appropriate forms, as necessary, to implement this section, including developing a procedure to enable the court to review the placement without a hearing.

(2) On or before October 1, 2022, for placements into a community treatment facility, the Judicial Council shall amend or adopt rules of court and shall develop or amend appropriate forms, as necessary, to implement this section, including developing a procedure to enable the court to review the placement without a hearing. *(Added by Stats.2021, c. 86 (A.B.153), § 29, eff. July 16, 2021. Amended by Stats.2022, c. 50 (S.B.187), § 26, eff. June 30, 2022.)*

Research References

West's California Judicial Council Forms JV–235, Placing Agency's Request for Review of Placement in Short-Term Residential Therapeutic Program.
West's California Judicial Council Forms JV–236, Input on Placement in Short-Term Residential Therapeutic Program.
West's California Judicial Council Forms JV–237, Proof of Service—Short-Term Residential Therapeutic Program Placement.
West's California Judicial Council Forms JV–238, Notice of Hearing on Placement in Short-Term Residential Therapeutic Program.
West's California Judicial Council Forms JV–239, Order on Placement in Short-Term Residential Therapeutic Program.

§ 727.13. Voluntary admission into a psychiatric residential treatment facility for a minor or nonminor dependent pursuant to Section 601 or 602; ex parte application for an order authorizing voluntary admission; hearing; determination of clear and convincing evidence; content and filing of application; review hearings; procedure upon discharge; review of probation department plan; protection of privileged or confidential information; application to foster children after reaching age of majority

(a)(1) Whenever voluntary admission into a psychiatric residential treatment facility is sought for a minor or nonminor dependent who is subject to a petition pursuant to Section 601 or 602, the court shall review the application for a voluntary admission as described in this section. A minor may not be admitted for inpatient treatment prior to court authorization unless the minor is subject to an involuntary hold pursuant to Chapter 2 (commencing with Section 5585.50) of Part 1.5 of Division 5.

(2) For purposes of this section, "voluntary admission" for a child within the custody of a parent, guardian, or Indian custodian refers to the parent, guardian, or Indian custodian's voluntary decision to have the child admitted to a psychiatric residential treatment facility. "Voluntary admission" for a child not within the custody of a parent, guardian, or Indian custodian refers to the child's decision to voluntarily admit themselves pursuant to Section 6552. "Voluntary admission" for a nonminor dependent refers to the nonminor dependent's decision to voluntarily admit themselves.

(b)(1) When a parent, guardian, or Indian custodian who retains physical custody of a minor under the jurisdiction of the juvenile court pursuant to Section 601 or 602 seeks to have a minor admitted to a psychiatric residential treatment facility, or when a minor who is the subject of a petition pursuant to Section 601 or 602 seeks to make a voluntary admission to a psychiatric residential treatment facility, the probation officer shall file an ex parte application for an order authorizing the voluntary admission pursuant to Section 6552 within 48 hours of being informed of the request or, if the courts are closed for more than 48 hours after being informed of the request, on the first judicial day after being informed of the request. The application shall satisfy the requirements of Title 3 of the California Rules of Court, and include all of the following:

(A) A brief description of the minor mental disorder.

(B) The name of the psychiatric residential treatment facility proposed for treatment.

(C) A brief description of how the mental disorder may reasonably be expected to be cured or ameliorated by the course of treatment offered by the psychiatric residential treatment facility.

(D) A brief description of why the facility is the least restrictive setting for care and why there are no other available hospitals, programs, or facilities which might better serve the minor's medical needs and best interest.

(E) A copy of the plan required by subdivisions (c) and (d) of Section 16010.10.

(F)(i) If the parent, guardian, or Indian custodian is seeking the minor's admission to the facility, the basis of their belief that the minor's admission to a psychiatric residential treatment facility is necessary.

(ii) If the minor is seeking admission, whether the parent, guardian, or Indian custodian agrees with the minor request for admission.

(G) A description of any mental health services, including community-based mental health services, that were offered or provided and an explanation for why those services were not sufficient, or an explanation for why no such services were offered or provided.

(H) A statement describing how the minor was given the opportunity to confer privately with their counsel regarding the application.

(I) A brief description of whether any member of the minor's child and family team, if applicable, objects to the admission, and the reasons for the objection, if any.

(J) The information required by this paragraph shall be sufficient to satisfy the applicant's initial burden of establishing the need for an ex parte hearing required by subdivision (c) of Rule 3.1202 of the California Rules of Court.

(2) Upon receipt of an ex parte application pursuant to paragraph (1), the juvenile court shall schedule a hearing for the next judicial day. The court clerk shall immediately notify the probation officer and the minor's counsel of the date, time, and place for the hearing.

(3) The probation officer shall provide notice of the hearing in accordance with Title 3 of the California Rules of Court to the minor and their counsel of record, the minor's parents or guardian, the minor's tribe in the case of an Indian child, and any person designated as the minor's educational or developmental representative pursuant to subdivision (b) of Section 726. The provisions in subdivision (c) of Section 527 of the Code of Civil Procedure shall apply to notice of the hearing. The probation officer shall make arrangements for the minor to be transported to the hearing.

(b)(1)[1] At the hearing, the court shall consider evidence in the form of oral testimony under oath, affidavit, or declaration, or other admissible evidence, including a probation department court report, as to all of the following:

(A) Whether the minor suffers from a mental disorder which may reasonably be expected to be cured or ameliorated by a course of treatment offered by the psychiatric residential treatment facility in which the minor wishes to be placed.

(B) Whether the psychiatric residential treatment facility is the least restrictive setting for care.

(C) Whether there is any other available hospital, program, or facility which might better serve the minor's medical needs and best interest, including less restrictive facilities or community-based care.

(D) Whether and how the minor, parent, or legal guardian, as appropriate, has been advised of the nature of inpatient psychiatric services, patient's rights as identified in Section 6006, and their right to contact a patients' rights advocate.

(E) Whether and how the probation officer addressed the possible voluntary admission with the minor's attorney.

(F) Whether the minor was given the opportunity to confer privately with their attorney while considering a voluntary admission.

(G) Whether and how the possible voluntary admission was addressed with the child and family team, whether any member of the team objects to voluntary admission, and the reasons for the objection.

(H) The probation department's plan for the minor, as described in Section 16010.10.

(I) A brief description of any community-based mental health services that were offered or provided, or an explanation for why no such services were offered or provided.

(2)(A) If the minor's parent, guardian, or Indian custodian seeks to give voluntary consent to the child's admission, the court shall inquire about the child's position on the admission.

(B) If the minor seeks to give voluntary consent to admission, the court shall inquire of the minor whether they knowingly and intelligently consent to admission into the psychiatric residential treatment facility, and whether they are giving consent without fear or threat of detention or initiation of conservatorship proceedings.

(3) The court shall not continue the hearing unless the minor consents to the continuance and the court determines that additional evidence is necessary to support the findings required by subdivision (c). Any continuance shall be for only such period of time as is necessary to obtain the evidence and only if it is not detrimental to the minor's health condition.

(d)(1) The court may grant a parent, guardian, or Indian custodian's request to have a child admitted, or authorize the minor's voluntary consent to admission, into a psychiatric residential treatment facility only if it finds, by clear and convincing evidence, all of the following:

(A) That the minor suffers from a mental disorder which may reasonably be expected to be cured or ameliorated by a course of treatment offered by the hospital, facility, or program in which the minor wishes to be placed.

(B) That the psychiatric residential treatment facility is the least restrictive setting to treat the child's mental disorder.

(C) That there is no other available hospital, program, facility, or community-based care which might better serve the minor's medical needs and best interest.

(D) That the minor has given knowing and intelligent consent to admission to the facility and that the consent was not made under fear or threat of detention or initiation of conservatorship proceedings.

(E) That the minor and, where appropriate, the parent or guardian have been advised of the nature of inpatient psychiatric, patient's rights as identified in Section 6006, and their right to contact a patients' rights advocate.

(2)(A) When authorizing a parent's or guardian's consent to admission or the minor's voluntary consent, the court may make any orders necessary to ensure that the child welfare services agency promptly makes all necessary arrangements to ensure that the minor is discharged in a timely manner and with all services and supports in place as necessary for a successful transition into a less restrictive setting.

(B) The court's order authorizing the admission to a psychiatric residential treatment facility shall be effective until the first of the following events occurs: (1) the parent, guardian, or Indian custodian, or the child if admission was granted pursuant to Section 6552, withdraws consent for the child to be present in the psychiatric residential treatment facility, (2) the court finds that the child no longer suffers from a mental disorder that may reasonably expected to be ameliorated by the treatment offered by the facility or that the psychiatric residential treatment facility is no longer the least restrictive setting for the treatment of the child's mental health needs, or (3) the court makes a superseding order.

(3) For minors who were in the custody of their parent, legal guardian or Indian custodian at the time of the authorization of admission, and based on the evidence presented during the ex parte hearing, the court shall consider whether the parent's, legal guardian's or Indian custodian's conduct contributed to the deterioration of the minor's mental disorder. If the court determines that the parent's, legal guardian's, or Indian custodian's conduct may have contributed to the deterioration, it shall direct the county probation department to investigate whether the child may be safely returned to the custody of the parent, legal guardian or Indian custodian upon their discharge from the psychiatric residential treatment facility and to take appropriate action, including, but not limited to, assessing the minor pursuant to Section 241.1, making a report to the county child welfare services agency's suspected child abuse and neglect hotline, or proceeding to modify court orders pursuant to Article 20 (commencing with Section 775).

(e)(1) Whenever a nonminor dependent under the supervision of a county juvenile probation department seeks to voluntarily consent to admission to a psychiatric residential treatment facility, the probation officer shall file an ex parte application within 48 hours of the request or, if the courts are closed for more than 48 hours after being informed of the request, on the first judicial day after being informed of the request, for a hearing to address whether the nonminor dependent has been advised of the nature of inpatient psychiatric services, patient's rights as identified in Section 6006, and their right to contact a patients' rights advocate, and gives informed voluntary consent to admission. The application shall satisfy the requirements of Title 3 of the California Rules of Court, and include all of the following:

(A) A brief description of the medical necessity for admission into a psychiatric residential treatment facility.

(B) The name of the psychiatric residential treatment facility proposed for treatment.

(C) A copy of the probation department's plan developed pursuant to subdivisions (c) and (d) of Section 16010.10.

(D) A description of any mental health services, including community-based mental health services, that were offered or provided to the nonminor dependent and an explanation for why those services were not sufficient, or an explanation for why no such services were offered or provided.

(E) A brief description of whether the nonminor dependent believes admission to a less restrictive facility would not adequately address their mental disorder.

(F) A statement describing how the nonminor dependent was given the opportunity to confer privately with their counsel regarding the application.

(G) The information required by this paragraph shall be considered sufficient to satisfy the applicant's initial burden of establishing the need for an ex parte hearing required by subdivision (c) of Rule 3.1202 of the California Rules of Court.

(2) Upon receipt of an ex parte application pursuant to paragraph (1), the juvenile court shall schedule a hearing for the next judicial

day. The court clerk shall immediately notify the probation officer and the nonminor dependent's counsel of the date, time, and place for the hearing.

(3) The probation officer shall provide notice of the hearing in accordance with Title 3 of the California Rules of Court to all parties to the proceeding and their counsel of record, the nonminor dependent's tribe, if applicable, the nonminor dependent's court-appointed special advocate, if applicable, and any person designated as the nonminor dependent's educational or developmental representative pursuant to subdivision (b) of Section 726. The provisions in subdivision (c) of Section 527 of the Code of Civil Procedure shall apply to notice of the hearing. The probation officer shall make arrangements for the nonminor dependent to be present for the hearing.

(4) At the hearing, the court shall consider evidence in the form of oral testimony under oath, affidavit, or declaration, or other admissible evidence, as to all of the following:

(A) Whether the nonminor dependent's receipt of treatment in the psychiatric residential treatment facility is medically necessary.

(B) Whether there is an available less restrictive setting sufficient to meet the nonminor dependent's needs, including a less restrictive facility or community-based care.

(C) Whether and how the nonminor dependent has been advised of the nature of inpatient psychiatric services, patient's rights as identified in Section 6006, and their right to contact a patients' rights advocate.

(D) Whether and how the probation officer addressed the voluntary admission with the nonminor dependent's attorney, including whether the nonminor dependent was given the opportunity to confer privately with their attorney about a voluntary admission.

(E) Whether and how the possible voluntary admission was addressed with the child and family team, whether any member of the team objects to voluntary admission, and the reasons for the objection.

(F) The probation department's plan for the nonminor dependent, as described in Section 16010.10.

(5)(A) The court shall make a finding whether the nonminor dependent has given knowing and intelligent consent to admission. If the court finds that the nonminor dependent has not given knowing and intelligent consent, it shall direct the probation officer to convey its finding to the facility and direct the facility to discharge the nonminor dependent. If the court finds that the nonminor dependent has given knowing and intelligent consent, nothing in this section requires a court order to discharge the nonminor if the nonminor dependent subsequently withdraws their consent.

(B) The court may make any orders necessary to ensure that the probation department promptly makes all necessary arrangements to ensure that the nonminor dependent is discharged in a timely manner and with all services and supports in place as necessary for a successful transition into a less restrictive setting.

(6) The judicial proceedings described in this subdivision shall not delay a nonminor dependent's access to medically necessary services as defined in Section 14059.5 and Section 1396d(r) of Title 42 of the United States Code, which may include voluntary admission to a psychiatric residential treatment facility for inpatient psychiatric services, while the judicial proceedings are ongoing.

(f)(1)(A) No later than 60 days following the admission of a minor to a psychiatric residential treatment facility, and every 30 days thereafter, the court shall hold a review hearing on the minor's placement in the facility and the medical necessity of the placement.

(B) If the hearing described in subparagraph (A) coincides with the date for a review hearing pursuant to Section 727.2, the court may hold the hearing simultaneously with the status review hearing.

(C) At the hearing described in subparagraph (A), the court shall consider all of the following:

(i) Whether the minor, or parent or guardian, continues to consent to the voluntary admission made pursuant to this section.

(ii) Whether the minor continues to suffer from a mental disorder which may reasonably be expected to be cured or ameliorated by a course of treatment offered by the facility.

(iii) Whether there continues to be no other available hospital, program, facility, or community-based mental health service which might better serve the minor's medical needs and best interest.

(iv) Whether the psychiatric residential treatment facility, which is licensed pursuant to Section 4081, continues to meet its legal obligation to provide services to the minor.

(v) The county probation department's plan as described in subdivisions (c) and (d) of Section 16010.10, and the department's actions to implement that plan.

(D) If the court finds that the minor or their parent or guardian continues to give voluntary consent to admission, that the minor continues to suffer from a mental disorder which may reasonably be expected to be cured or ameliorated by a course of treatment offered by the facility, and that there continues to be no other available hospital, program, facility, or community-based mental health service which might better serve the minor's medical need and best interest, the court may authorize continued inpatient psychiatric services for the minor in a psychiatric residential treatment facility. If the child has been in the facility for over 30 days, there shall be a rebuttable presumption that the facility is not the least restrictive alternative to serve the child's medical need and best interest.

(E)(i) If the court finds that the minor or their parent or guardian no longer consents to the minor's admission, the court shall direct the probation officer to work immediately with the facility for discharge to a different setting with the appropriate and necessary services and supports in place. A statement from the minor's attorney that the minor no longer gives voluntary consent to the admission to the facility may be sufficient to support a finding that the minor no longer gives voluntary consent. The court shall set a hearing no later than 30 days to verify that the minor has been discharged. If the minor has not been discharged by the time of the hearing, the court shall issue any and all orders to effectuate the child's immediate discharge, including exercising its powers under subdivision (b) of Section 727. This paragraph does not preclude involuntary detention of the minor pursuant to the requirements of the Children's Civil Commitment and Mental Health Treatment Act of 1988 or Lanterman-Petris-Short Act if the minor withdraws voluntary consent. This paragraph does not preclude a parent, guardian, Indian custodian, or the minor's probation officer or attorney from arranging the minor's discharge from the facility without a court order.

(ii) If the court's determination under clause (i) includes a determination that the minor should receive treatment through another hospital, program, facility, or community-based mental health service, the court shall hold a hearing no later than 60 days from the child's discharge to ensure that the other services have been provided.

(F) If the court determines the psychiatric residential treatment facility, which is licensed pursuant to Section 4081, failed to meet its legal obligation to provide services to the minor, it may direct the social worker to engage with the facility to ensure the minor is receiving all necessary services. If necessary, the court may exercise its powers under subdivision (b) of Section 727.

(G) The court may make any orders necessary to ensure that the county probation department makes all necessary arrangements for the minor's discharge promptly and that all services and supports are in place for the minor's successful transition to a different setting. The court may direct the social worker to work with the facility on the child's aftercare plans as appropriate based on the child's progress.

(2)(A) No later than 60 days following the admission of a nonminor dependent to a psychiatric residential treatment facility, and every 30 days thereafter, the court shall hold a review hearing on the child or nonminor dependent's placement in the facility and the medical necessity of that placement.

(B) If the hearing described in subparagraph (A) coincides with the date for a hearing pursuant to Sections 366.31 and 727.25, the court may hold the hearing simultaneously with the status review hearing.

(C) At the hearing in subparagraph (A), the court shall consider all of the following:

(i) Whether the nonminor dependent continues to consent to the voluntary admission made pursuant to this section.

(ii) Whether there is an available less restrictive setting sufficient to meet the nonminor dependent's needs, including a less restrictive facility or community-based care.

(iii) Whether the nonminor dependent continues to meet medical necessity for care and treatment in the psychiatric residential treatment facility.

(iv) Whether the psychiatric residential treatment facility, which is licensed pursuant to Section 4081, continues to meet its legal obligation to provide services to the nonminor dependent.

(v) The county child welfare agency's plan as described in subdivisions (c) and (d) of Section 16010.10, and the agency's actions to implement that plan.

(D) If the court finds at any review hearing that the nonminor dependent continues to voluntarily consent to admission and that the evidence supports the nonminor dependent's need for care and treatment in the psychiatric residential treatment facility, the court shall enter these findings in the record and direct the probation officer to transmit them to the facility or interdisciplinary team. If the nonminor dependent continues to voluntarily consent to admission, the court may direct the probation officer to work with the facility on the nonminor dependent's aftercare plans as appropriate based on the nonminor dependent's needs to achieve independence.

(E)(i) If the court finds that the nonminor dependent no longer voluntarily consents, the court shall direct the probation officer to notify the facility and immediately work with the nonminor dependent and the facility for discharge to a less restrictive setting with the appropriate and necessary services and supports in place. A statement from the nonminor dependent's attorney that the nonminor dependent no longer gives voluntary consent to the admission to the facility may be sufficient to support a finding that the nonminor dependent no longer gives voluntary consent. The court shall set a hearing no later than 30 days to verify that the nonminor dependent has been discharged. If the nonminor dependent has not been discharged by the time of the hearing, the court shall issue any and all orders to effectuate the nonminor dependents's immediate discharge, including exercising its powers under subdivision (b) of Section 727. This paragraph does not preclude involuntary detention of the nonminor dependent pursuant to the requirements of the Lanterman-Petris-Short Act if the nonminor dependent withdraws voluntary consent. This paragraph does not preclude the nonminor dependent from arranging their own discharge from the facility without a court order.

(ii) If the court's determination under clause (i) includes a determination that the nonminor dependent should receive treatment through another hospital, program, facility, or community-based mental health service, the court shall hold a hearing no later than 60 days from the nonminor dependent's discharge to ensure that the other services have been provided.

(F) This paragraph does not prevent the court from holding review hearings more frequently at its discretion.

(g)(1) The court's order authorizing a request for admission to a psychiatric residential treatment facility shall be effective until the first of the following events occurs: (1) the parent, guardian, or Indian custodian, or minor if admission was granted pursuant to Section 6552, or nonminor dependent withdraws consent for the minor or nonminor dependent to be present in the psychiatric residential treatment facility, (2) the court finds that the minor or nonminor dependent no longer suffers from a mental disorder that may reasonably expected to be ameliorated by the treatment offered by the facility or that the psychiatric residential treatment facility is no longer the least restrictive setting for the treatment of the minor's mental health needs, or (3) the court makes a superseding order. This section does not require a court order to discharge a patient if the parent, guardian, Indian custodian, minor, or nonminor dependent withdraw their consent for admission.

(2) Whenever a minor or nonminor dependent is discharged due to revocation of consent to admission, the county probation department shall, within two court days of being notified of the revocation of consent, file a petition pursuant to Section 778 requesting an order vacating the court's authorization of the minor's or nonminor dependent's admission to the facility. This subdivision does not require a court order for the discharge of a minor arranged for by the child's probation officer or attorney or nonminor dependent when consent to admission has been withdrawn.

(h) At any review hearing pursuant to Section 366.31, 727.2, or 727.25, if a minor or nonminor dependent has been admitted to a psychiatric residential treatment facility, as defined in Section 1250.10, pursuant to the consent of a conservator, the court shall review the probation department's plan developed pursuant to subdivisions (c) and (d) of Section 16010.10. The court may make any orders necessary to ensure that the probation department promptly makes all necessary arrangements to ensure that the minor or nonminor dependent is discharged in a timely manner and with all services and supports in place as necessary for a successful transition to a less restrictive setting. The court may direct the probation officer to work with the facility or, where appropriate, the minor's or nonminor dependent's court-appointed conservator to ensure the minor or nonminor dependent is receiving all necessary child welfare services and to develop the minor's or nonminor dependent's aftercare plan as appropriate based on the evidence of the minor's or nonminor dependent's progress.

(i) The documentation required by this section shall not contain information that is privileged or confidential under existing state or federal law or regulation without the appropriate wavier or consent.

(j) For purposes of this section, a "psychiatric residential treatment facility" refers to a psychiatric residential treatment facility defined in Section 1250.10 of the Health and Safety Code.

(k) All provisions in this section that apply to nonminor dependents shall apply equally to foster children who remain under juvenile court jurisdiction pursuant to subdivision (a) of Section 303 after reaching the age of majority even if they do not meet the definition of "nonminor dependent" contained in subdivision (v) of Section 11400. *(Added by Stats.2022, c. 589 (A.B.2317), § 7, eff. Jan. 1, 2023.)*

1 No subd. (c) in enrolled bill.

§ 727.2. Reunification of minor in foster care with family or establishment of alternative permanent plan; reunification services; ongoing review of status of minor

The purpose of this section is to provide a means to monitor the safety and well-being of every minor in foster care who has been declared a ward of the juvenile court pursuant to Section 601 or 602 and to ensure that everything reasonably possible is done to facilitate the safe and early return of the minor to the minor's home or to establish an alternative permanent plan for the minor.

(a) If the court orders the care, custody, and control of the minor to be under the supervision of the probation officer for placement pursuant to subdivision (a) of Section 727, the juvenile court shall order the probation department to ensure the provision of reunification services to facilitate the safe return of the minor to the minor's home or the permanent placement of the minor, and to address the needs of the minor while in foster care, except as provided in subdivision (b).

(b)(1) Reunification services need not be provided to a parent or legal guardian if the court finds by clear and convincing evidence that one or more of the following is true:

(A) Reunification services were previously terminated for that parent or guardian, pursuant to Section 366.21, 366.22, or 366.25, or not offered, pursuant to subdivision (b) of Section 361.5, in reference to the same minor.

(B) The parent has been convicted of any of the following:

(i) Murder of another child of the parent.

(ii) Voluntary manslaughter of another child of the parent.

(iii) Aiding or abetting, attempting, conspiring, or soliciting to commit that murder or manslaughter described in clause (i) or (ii).

(iv) A felony assault that results in serious bodily injury to the minor or another child of the parent.

(C) The parental rights of the parent with respect to a sibling have been terminated involuntarily, and it is not in the best interest of the minor to reunify with the minor's parent or legal guardian.

(2) If no reunification services are offered to the parent or guardian, the permanency planning hearing, as described in Section 727.3, shall occur within 30 days of the date of the hearing at which the decision is made not to offer services.

(c) The status of every minor declared a ward and ordered to be placed in foster care shall be reviewed by the court no less frequently than once every six months. The six-month time periods shall be calculated from the date the minor entered foster care, as defined in paragraph (4) of subdivision (d) of Section 727.4. If the court so elects, the court may declare the hearing at which the court orders the care, custody, and control of the minor to be under the supervision of the probation officer for foster care placement pursuant to subdivision (a) of Section 727 at the first status review hearing. It shall be the duty of the probation officer to prepare a written social study report pursuant to subdivision (c) of Section 706.5, including an updated case plan, as described in Section 706.6, and submit the report to the court prior to each status review hearing, pursuant to subdivision (b) of Section 727.4. The social study report shall include all reports the probation officer relied upon in making their recommendations.

(d) Prior to any status review hearing involving a minor in the physical custody of a community care facility or foster family agency, the facility or agency may provide the probation officer with a report containing its recommendations. Prior to any status review hearing involving the physical custody of a foster parent, relative caregiver, preadoptive parent, or legal guardian, that person may present to the court a report containing the person's recommendations. The court shall consider all reports and recommendations filed pursuant to subdivision (c) and pursuant to this subdivision.

(e) At any status review hearing prior to the first permanency planning hearing, the court shall consider the safety of the minor and make findings and orders which determine the following:

(1) The continuing necessity for and appropriateness of the placement. If the minor or nonminor dependent is placed in a short-term residential therapeutic program on or after October 1, 2021, or a community treatment facility on or after July 1, 2022, the court shall consider the evidence and documentation submitted in the social study pursuant to subparagraph (B) of paragraph (1) of subdivision (c) of Section 706.5 in making this determination.

(2) The extent of the probation department's compliance with the case plan in making reasonable efforts, or in the case of a child 16 years of age or older with another planned permanent living arrangement, the ongoing and intensive efforts to safely return the minor to the minor's home or to complete whatever steps are necessary to finalize the permanent placement of the minor.

(3) Whether there should be any limitation on the right of the parent or guardian to make educational decisions for the minor. That limitation shall be specifically addressed in the court order and may not exceed what is necessary to protect the minor. If the court specifically limits the right of the parent or guardian to make educational decisions for the minor, the court shall at the same time appoint a responsible adult to make educational decisions for the minor pursuant to Section 726.

(4) The extent of progress that has been made by the minor and parent or guardian toward alleviating or mitigating the causes necessitating placement in foster care.

(5) The likely date by which the minor may be returned to and safely maintained in the home or placed for adoption, appointed a legal guardian, permanently placed with a fit and willing relative, or, if the minor is 16 years of age or older, referred to another planned permanent living arrangement.

(6)(A) In the case of a minor who has reached 16 years of age, the court shall, in addition, determine the services needed to assist the minor to make the transition from foster care to successful adulthood.

(B) The court shall make these determinations on a case-by-case basis and reference in its written findings the probation officer's report and any other evidence relied upon in reaching its decision.

(7)(A) For a child who is 10 years of age or older, is in junior high, middle, or high school, and has been declared a ward of the juvenile court pursuant to Section 601 or 602 for a year or longer whether the probation officer has taken the actions described in subparagraph (F) of paragraph (1) of subdivision (a) of Section 366.

(B) On or before January 1, 2023, the Judicial Council shall amend and adopt rules of court and develop appropriate forms for the implementation of this paragraph.

(8) For a child who is 16 years of age or older or for a nonminor dependent, whether the probation officer has, pursuant to the requirements of paragraph (22) of subdivision (g) of Section 16501.1, identified the person or persons who shall be responsible for assisting the child or nonminor dependent with applications for postsecondary education and related financial aid, or that the child or nonminor dependent stated that they do not want to pursue postsecondary education, including career or technical education.

(f) At any status review hearing prior to the first permanency hearing, after considering the admissible and relevant evidence, the court shall order return of the minor to the physical custody of the minor's parent or legal guardian unless the court finds, by a preponderance of evidence, that the return of the minor to the minor's parent or legal guardian would create a substantial risk of detriment to the safety, protection, or physical or emotional well-being of the minor. The probation department shall have the burden of establishing that detriment. In making its determination, the court shall review and consider the social study report, recommendations, and the case plan pursuant to subdivision (b) of Section 706.5, the report and recommendations of any child advocate appointed for the minor in the case, and any other reports submitted to the court pursuant to subdivision (d), and shall consider the efforts or progress, or both, demonstrated by the minor and family and the extent to which the minor availed themselves of the services provided.

(g) At all status review hearings subsequent to the first permanency planning hearing, the court shall consider the safety of the minor and make the findings and orders as described in paragraphs (1) to (4), inclusive, and (6) of subdivision (e). The court shall either make a finding that the previously ordered permanent plan continues to be appropriate or shall order that a new permanent plan be adopted pursuant to subdivision (b) of Section 727.3. However, the court shall not order a permanent plan of "return to the physical custody of the parent or legal guardian after further reunification services are offered," as described in paragraph (2) of subdivision (b) of Section 727.3.

(h) The status review hearings required by subdivision (c) may be heard by an administrative review panel, provided that the administrative panel meets all of the requirements listed in subparagraph (B) of paragraph (7) of subdivision (d) of Section 727.4.

(i)(1) At any status review hearing at which a recommendation to terminate delinquency jurisdiction is being considered, or at the status review hearing held closest to the ward attaining 18 years of age, but no fewer than 90 days before the ward's 18th birthday, the court shall consider whether to modify its jurisdiction pursuant to Section 601 or 602 and assume transition jurisdiction over the minor pursuant to Section 450. The probation department shall address this issue in its report to the court and make a recommendation as to whether transition jurisdiction is appropriate for the minor.

(2) The court shall order the probation department or the minor's attorney to submit an application to the child welfare services department pursuant to Section 329 to declare the minor a dependent of the court and modify its jurisdiction from delinquency to dependency jurisdiction if it finds both of the following:

(A) The ward does not come within the description set forth in Section 450, but jurisdiction as a ward may no longer be required.

(B) The ward appears to come within the description of Section 300 and cannot be returned home safely.

(3) The court shall set a hearing within 20 judicial days of the date of its order issued pursuant to paragraph (2) to review the decision of the child welfare services department and may either affirm the decision not to file a petition pursuant to Section 300 or order the child welfare services department to file a petition pursuant to Section 300.

(j) If a review hearing pursuant to this section is the last review hearing to be held before the minor attains 18 years of age, the court shall ensure that the minor's transitional independent living case plan includes a plan for the minor to meet one or more of the criteria in paragraphs (1) to (5), inclusive, of subdivision (b) of Section 11403, so that the minor can become a nonminor dependent, and that the minor has been informed of the minor's right to decline to become a nonminor dependent and to seek termination of the court's jurisdiction pursuant to Section 607.2. *(Added by Stats.2001, c. 831 (A.B.1696), § 10. Amended by Stats.2002, c. 785 (S.B.1677), § 7; Stats.2003, c. 862 (A.B.490), § 13; Stats.2010, c. 559 (A.B.12), § 29; Stats.2011, c. 459 (A.B.212), § 17, eff. Oct. 4, 2011; Stats.2012, c. 208 (A.B.2292), § 4; Stats.2015, c. 425 (S.B.794), § 18, eff. Jan. 1, 2016; Stats.2021, c. 86 (A.B.153), § 30, eff. July 16, 2021; Stats.2022, c. 50 (S.B.187), § 27, eff. June 30, 2022.)*

Cross References

Felonies, definition and penalties, see Penal Code §§ 17, 18.

Minor who appears to be dependent child and ward of court, initial determination of status pursuant to jointly developed written protocol, creation of protocol, modification of juristic over dependent or ward placed in foster care, see Welfare and Institutions Code § 241.1.

Order for removal from custody and placement in foster home or institution, hearing upon supplemental petition, see Welfare and Institutions Code § 387.

Probation officer or social worker defined for purposes of this Chapter, see Welfare and Institutions Code § 215.

Supervision of child or nonminor whose jurisdiction is modified pursuant to this section and placed in foster care, see Welfare and Institutions Code § 300.3.

Research References

West's California Judicial Council Forms JV–280, Notice of Review Hearing (Also Available in Spanish).

West's California Judicial Council Forms JV–665, Disposition—Juvenile Delinquency.

West's California Judicial Council Forms JV–667, Custodial and Out-Of-Home Placement Disposition Attachment.

West's California Judicial Council Forms JV–672, Findings and Orders After Six-Month Prepermanency Hearing—Delinquency.

West's California Judicial Council Forms JV–680, Findings and Orders for Child Approaching Majority—Delinquency.

West's California Judicial Council Forms JV–681, Attachment: Hearing for Dismissal—Additional Findings and Orders—Foster Care Placement—Delinquency.

§ 727.25. Nonminor dependents; continuation of court-ordered family reunification services

(a) Notwithstanding any other law, the court may order family reunification services to continue for a nonminor dependent, as defined in subdivision (v) of Section 11400, if all parties are in agreement that the continued provision of court-ordered family reunification services is in the best interests of the nonminor dependent, and there is a substantial probability that the nonminor dependent will be able to safely reside in the home of the parent or guardian by the next review hearing. The continuation of court-ordered family reunification services shall not exceed the timeframes in Section 727.3.

(b) If all parties are not in agreement or the court finds there is not a substantial probability that the nonminor will be able to return and safely reside in the home of the parent or guardian, the court shall terminate reunification services to the parents or guardian.

(c) The continuation of court-ordered family reunification services under this section does not affect the nonminor's eligibility for extended foster care benefits as a nonminor dependent as defined in subdivision (v) of Section 11400. The reviews conducted for any nonminor dependent shall be pursuant to Section 366.31.

(d) The extension of reunification services only applies to youth under the delinquency jurisdiction of the court. *(Added by Stats. 2012, c. 846 (A.B.1712), § 31.)*

§ 727.3. Minor in foster care adjudged ward of the court; permanency planning hearing and plan; considerations; termination of parental rights

The purpose of this section is to provide a means to monitor the safety and well-being of every minor in foster care who has been declared a ward of the juvenile court pursuant to Section 601 or 602 and to ensure that everything reasonably possible is done to facilitate the safe and early return of the minor to his or her own home or to establish an alternative permanent plan for the minor.

(a)(1) For every minor declared a ward and ordered to be placed in foster care, a permanency planning hearing shall be conducted within 12 months of the date the minor entered foster care, as defined in paragraph (4) of subdivision (d) of Section 727.4. Subsequent permanency planning hearings shall be conducted periodically, but no less frequently than once every 12 months thereafter during the period of placement. It shall be the duty of the probation officer to prepare a written social study report including an updated case plan and a recommendation for a permanent plan, pursuant to subdivision (c) of Section 706.5, and submit the report to the court prior to each permanency planning hearing, pursuant to subdivision (b) of Section 727.4.

(2) Prior to any permanency planning hearing involving a minor in the physical custody of a community care facility or foster family agency, the facility or agency may file with the court a report containing its recommendations, in addition to the probation officer's social study. Prior to any permanency planning hearing involving the physical custody of a foster parent, relative caregiver, preadoptive parent, or legal guardian, that person may present to the court a report containing his or her recommendations. The court shall consider all reports and recommendations filed pursuant to this subdivision.

(3) If the minor has a continuing involvement with his or her parents or legal guardians, the parents or legal guardians shall be involved in the planning for a permanent placement. The court order placing the minor in a permanent placement shall include a specification of the nature and frequency of visiting arrangements with the parents or legal guardians and, if any, the siblings.

(4) At each permanency planning hearing, the court shall order a permanent plan for the minor, as described in subdivision (b). The court shall also make findings, as described in subdivision (e) of Section 727.2. In the case of a minor who has reached 16 years of age or older, the court shall, in addition, determine the services needed to assist the minor to make the transition from foster care to successful adulthood. The court shall make all of these determinations on a case-by-case basis and make reference to the probation officer's report, the case plan, or other evidence relied upon in making its decisions.

(5) When the minor is 16 years of age or older, and is in another planned permanent living arrangement, the court, at each permanency planning hearing, shall do all of the following:

(A) Ask the minor about his or her desired permanency outcome.

(B) Make a judicial determination explaining why, as of the hearing date, another planned permanent living arrangement is the best permanency plan for the minor.

(C) State for the record the compelling reason or reasons why it continues not to be in the best interest of the minor to return home, be placed for adoption, be placed with a legal guardian, or be placed with a fit and willing relative.

(b) At all permanency planning hearings, the court shall determine the permanent plan for the minor. The court shall order one of the following permanent plans, in order of priority:

(1) Return of the minor to the physical custody of the parent or legal guardian. After considering the admissible and relevant evidence, the court shall order the return of the minor to the physical custody of his or her parent or legal guardian unless:

(A) Reunification services were not offered, pursuant to subdivision (b) of Section 727.2.

(B) The court finds, by a preponderance of the evidence, that the return of the minor to his or her parent or legal guardian would create a substantial risk of detriment to the safety, protection, or physical or emotional well-being of the minor. The probation department shall have the burden of establishing that detriment. In making its determination, the court shall review and consider the social study report and recommendations pursuant to Section 706.5, the report and recommendations of any child advocate appointed for the minor in the case, and any other reports submitted pursuant to paragraph (2) of subdivision (a), and shall consider the efforts or progress, or both, demonstrated by the minor and family and the extent to which the minor availed himself or herself of the services provided.

(2) Order that the permanent plan for the minor will be to return the minor to the physical custody of the parent or legal guardian, order further reunification services to be provided to the minor and his or her parent or legal guardian for a period not to exceed six months and continue the case for up to six months for a subsequent permanency planning hearing, provided that the subsequent hearing shall occur within 18 months of the date the minor was originally taken from the physical custody of his or her parent or legal guardian. The court shall continue the case only if it finds that there is a substantial probability that the minor will be returned to the physical custody of his or her parent or legal guardian and safely maintained in the home within the extended period of time or that reasonable services have not been provided to the parent or guardian. For purposes of this section, in order to find that there is a substantial probability that the minor will be returned to the physical custody of his or her parent or legal guardian, the court shall be required to find that the minor and his or her parent or legal guardian have demonstrated the capacity and ability to complete the objectives of the case plan.

The court shall inform the parent or legal guardian that if the minor cannot be returned home by the next permanency planning hearing, a proceeding pursuant to Section 727.31 may be initiated.

The court shall not continue the case for further reunification services if it has been 18 months or more since the date the minor was originally taken from the physical custody of his or her parent or legal guardian.

(3) Identify adoption as the permanent plan and order that a hearing be held within 120 days, pursuant to the procedures described in Section 727.31. The court shall only set a hearing pursuant to Section 727.31 if there is clear and convincing evidence that reasonable services have been provided or offered to the parents. When the court sets a hearing pursuant to Section 727.31, it shall order that an adoption assessment report be prepared, pursuant to subdivision (b) of Section 727.31.

(4) Order a legal guardianship, pursuant to procedures described in subdivisions (c) to (f), inclusive, of Section 728.

(5) Place the minor with a fit and willing relative. "Placement with a fit and willing relative" means placing the minor with an appropriate approved relative who is willing to provide a permanent and stable home for the minor, but is unable or unwilling to become the legal guardian. When a minor is placed with a fit and willing relative, the court may authorize the relative to provide the same legal consent for the minor's medical, surgical, and dental care, and education as the custodial parent of the minor.

(6)(A) If he or she is 16 years of age or older, place the minor in another planned permanent living arrangement. For purposes of this section, "planned permanent living arrangement" means any permanent living arrangement described in Section 11402 that is ordered by the court for a minor 16 years of age or older when there is a compelling reason or reasons to determine that it is not in the best interest of the minor to have any permanent plan listed in paragraphs (1) to (5), inclusive. These plans include, but are not limited to, placement in a specific, identified foster home, program, or facility on a permanent basis, or placement with a transitional housing placement provider. When the court places a minor in a planned permanent living arrangement, the court shall specify the goal of the placement, which may include, but shall not be limited to, return home, emancipation, guardianship, or permanent placement with a relative.

The court shall only order that the minor remain in a planned permanent living arrangement if the court finds by clear and convincing evidence, based upon the evidence already presented to it, that there is a compelling reason, as defined in subdivision (c), for determining that a plan of termination of parental rights and adoption is not in the best interest of the minor.

(B) If the minor is under 16 years of age and the court finds by clear and convincing evidence, based upon the evidence already presented to it, that there is a compelling reason, as defined in subdivision (c), for determining that a plan of termination of parental rights and adoption is not in the best interest of the minor as of the hearing date, the court shall order the minor to remain in a foster care placement with a permanent plan of return home, adoption, legal guardianship, or placement with a fit and willing relative, as appropriate. The court shall make factual findings identifying any barriers to achieving the permanent plan as of the hearing date.

(c) A compelling reason for determining that a plan of termination of parental rights and adoption is not in the best interest of the minor is any of the following:

(1) Documentation by the probation department that adoption is not in the best interest of the minor and is not an appropriate

permanency goal. That documentation may include, but is not limited to, documentation that:

(A) The minor is 12 years of age or older and objects to termination of parental rights.

(B) The minor is 17 years of age or older and specifically requests that transition to independent living with the identification of a caring adult to serve as a lifelong connection be established as his or her permanent plan. On and after January 1, 2012, this includes a minor who requests that his or her transitional independent living case plan include modification of his or her jurisdiction to that of dependency jurisdiction pursuant to subdivision (b) of Section 607.2 or subdivision (i) of Section 727.2, or to that of transition jurisdiction pursuant to Section 450, in order to be eligible as a nonminor dependent for the extended benefits pursuant to Section 11403.

(C) The parent or guardian and the minor have a significant bond, but the parent or guardian is unable to care for the minor because of an emotional or physical disability, and the minor's caregiver has committed to raising the minor to the age of majority and facilitating visitation with the disabled parent or guardian.

(D) The minor agrees to continued placement in a residential treatment facility that provides services specifically designed to address the minor's treatment needs, and the minor's needs could not be served by a less restrictive placement.

The probation department's recommendation that adoption is not in the best interest of the minor shall be based on the present family circumstances of the minor and shall not preclude a different recommendation at a later date if the minor's family circumstances change.

(2) Documentation by the probation department that no grounds exist to file for termination of parental rights.

(3) Documentation by the probation department that the minor is an unaccompanied refugee minor, or there are international legal obligations or foreign policy reasons that would preclude terminating parental rights.

(4) A finding by the court that the probation department was required to make reasonable efforts to reunify the minor with the family pursuant to subdivision (a) of Section 727.2, and did not make those efforts.

(5) Documentation by the probation department that the minor is living with a relative who is unable or unwilling to adopt the minor because of exceptional circumstances that do not include an unwillingness to accept legal or financial responsibility for the minor, but who is willing to provide, and capable of providing, the minor with a stable and permanent home environment, and the removal of the minor from the physical custody of his or her relative would be detrimental to the minor's emotional well-being.

(d) Nothing in this section shall be construed to limit the ability of a parent to voluntarily relinquish his or her child to the State Department of Social Services when it is acting as an adoption agency or to a county adoption agency at any time while the minor is a ward of the juvenile court if the department or county adoption agency is willing to accept the relinquishment.

(e) Any change in the permanent plan of a minor placed with a fit and willing relative or in a planned permanent living arrangement shall be made only by order of the court pursuant to a petition filed in accordance with Section 778 or at a regularly scheduled and noticed status review hearing or permanency planning hearing. Any change in the permanent plan of a minor placed in a guardianship shall be made only by order of the court pursuant to a motion filed in accordance with Section 728. *(Added by Stats.2001, c. 831 (A.B. 1696), § 12. Amended by Stats.2011, c. 459 (A.B.212), § 18, eff. Oct. 4, 2011; Stats.2012, c. 35 (S.B.1013), § 62, eff. June 27, 2012; Stats.2012, c. 208 (A.B.2292), § 5; Stats.2015, c. 425 (S.B.794), § 19, eff. Jan. 1, 2016; Stats.2016, c. 719 (S.B.1060), § 3, eff. Jan. 1, 2017; Stats.2017, c. 731 (S.B.612), § 6, eff. Jan. 1, 2018.)*

Cross References

Elementary and secondary education, special education programs, rights of foster parents pertaining to foster child's education, see Education Code § 56055.

Probation officer or social worker defined for purposes of this Chapter, see Welfare and Institutions Code § 215.

Research References

West's California Judicial Council Forms JV–280, Notice of Review Hearing (Also Available in Spanish).

West's California Judicial Council Forms JV–300, Notice of Hearing on Selection of a Permanent Plan (Also Available in Spanish).

West's California Judicial Council Forms JV–320, Orders Under Welfare and Institutions Code Sections 366.24, 366.26, 727.3, 727.31.

West's California Judicial Council Forms JV–674, Findings and Orders After Permanency Hearing—Delinquency.

West's California Judicial Council Forms JV–678, Findings and Orders After Postpermanency Hearing—Delinquency.

§ 727.31. Termination of parental rights; proceedings; representation of minor; pre-hearing assessment; legal guardianship or adoption; Kin–GAP aid; responsibility for adoption-related decisions; judgment

(a) This section applies to all minors placed in out-of-home care pursuant to Section 727.2 or 727.3 and for whom the juvenile court orders a hearing to consider permanently terminating parental rights to free the minor for adoption.

Except for subdivision (j) of Section 366.26, the procedures for permanently terminating parental rights for minors described by this section shall proceed exclusively pursuant to Section 366.26.

At the beginning of any proceeding pursuant to this section, if the minor is not being represented by previously retained or appointed counsel, the court shall appoint counsel to represent the minor, and the minor shall be present in court unless the minor or the minor's counsel so requests and the court so orders. If a parent appears without counsel and is unable to afford counsel, the court shall appoint counsel for the parent, unless this representation is knowingly and intelligently waived. The same counsel shall not be appointed to represent both the minor and the parent. Private counsel appointed under this section shall receive a reasonable sum for compensation and expenses as specified in subdivision (f) of paragraph (3) of Section 366.26.

(b) Whenever the court orders that a hearing pursuant to this section shall be held, it shall direct the agency supervising the minor and the county adoption agency, or the State Department of Social Services when it is acting as an adoption agency, to prepare an assessment that shall include all of the following:

(1) Current search efforts for an absent parent or parents.

(2) A review of the amount and nature of any contact between the minor and his or her parents and other members of his or her extended family since the time of placement. Although the extended family of each minor shall be reviewed on a case-by-case basis, "extended family" for the purpose of the paragraph shall include, but not be limited to, the minor's siblings, grandparents, aunts, and uncles.

(3) An evaluation of the minor's medical, developmental, scholastic, mental, and emotional status.

(4) A preliminary assessment of the eligibility and commitment of any identified prospective adoptive parent or guardian, particularly the caretaker, to include a social history, including screening for criminal records and prior referrals for child abuse or neglect, the capability to meet the minor's needs, and the understanding of the legal and financial rights and responsibilities of adoption and guardianship. If a proposed guardian is a relative of the minor, the assessment shall also consider, but need not be limited to, all of the factors specified in subdivision (a) of Section 361.3 and Section 361.4.

(5) The relationship of the minor to any identified prospective adoptive parent or guardian, the duration and character of the relationship, the degree of attachment of the child to the prospective relative guardian or adoptive parent, the relative's or adoptive parent's strong commitment to caring permanently for the child, the motivation for seeking adoption or guardianship, a statement from the minor concerning placement and the adoption or guardianship, and whether the minor, if over 12 years of age, has been consulted about the proposed relative guardianship arrangements, unless the minor's age or physical, emotional, or other condition precludes his or her meaningful response, and if so, a description of the condition.

(6) An analysis of the likelihood that the minor will be adopted if parental rights are terminated.

(c) A relative caregiver's preference for legal guardianship over adoption, if it is due to circumstances that do not include an unwillingness to accept legal or financial responsibility for the child, shall not constitute the sole basis for recommending removal of the child from the relative caregiver for purposes of adoptive placement. A relative caregiver shall be given information regarding the permanency options of guardianship and adoption, including the long-term benefits and consequences of each option, prior to establishing legal guardianship or pursuing adoption.

(d) If at any hearing held pursuant to Section 366.26, a legal guardianship is established for the minor with an approved relative caregiver and juvenile court dependency is subsequently dismissed, the minor shall be eligible for aid under the Kin–GAP Program, as provided for in Article 4.5 (commencing with Section 11360) or Article 4.7 (commencing with Section 11385), as applicable, of Chapter 2 of Part 3 of Division 9.

(e) For purposes of this section, "relative" means an adult who is related to the child by blood, adoption, or affinity within the fifth degree of kinship, including stepparents, stepsiblings, and all relatives whose status is preceded by the words "great," "great-great," or "grand," or the spouse of any of those persons, even if the marriage was terminated by death or dissolution.

(f) Whenever the court orders that a hearing pursuant to procedures described in this section be held, it shall order that the county adoption agency, or the State Department of Social Services when it is acting as an adoption agency, has exclusive responsibility for determining the adoptive placement and making all adoption-related decisions.

(g) If the court, by order of judgment declares the minor free from the custody and control of both parents, or one parent if the other does not have custody and control, the court shall at the same time order the minor referred to the State Department of Social Services when it is acting as an adoption agency or a county adoption agency for adoptive placement by the agency. The order shall state that responsibility for custody of the minor shall be held jointly by the probation department and the State Department of Social Services when it is acting as an adoption agency or the county adoption agency. The order shall also state that the State Department of Social Services when it is acting as an adoption agency or the county adoption agency has exclusive responsibility for determining the adoptive placement and for making all adoption-related decisions. However, no petition for adoption may be granted until the appellate rights of the natural parents have been exhausted.

(h) The notice procedures for terminating parental rights for minors described by this section shall proceed exclusively pursuant to Section 366.23. *(Added by Stats.1999, c. 997 (A.B.575), § 17. Amended by Stats.2000, c. 135 (A.B.2539), § 167; Stats.2001, c. 831 (A.B.1696), § 13; Stats.2011, c. 459 (A.B.212), § 19, eff. Oct. 4, 2011; Stats.2012, c. 35 (S.B.1013), § 63, eff. June 27, 2012.)*

Cross References

Foster care defined for purposes of this Article, see Welfare and Institutions Code § 727.4.

Hearing defined for purposes of this Article, see Welfare and Institutions Code § 727.4.

Notices in dependent child proceedings, selection and implementation hearings, see Welfare and Institutions Code § 294.

Relative defined for purposes of this Article, see Welfare and Institutions Code § 727.4.

Research References

West's California Judicial Council Forms JV–320, Orders Under Welfare and Institutions Code Sections 366.24, 366.26, 727.3, 727.31.

§ 727.32. Termination of parental rights where minor declared ward of juvenile court and in foster care 15 of most recent 22 months

(a) In any case where a minor has been declared a ward of the juvenile court and has been in foster care for 15 of the most recent 22 months, the probation department shall follow the procedures described in Section 727.31 to terminate the parental rights of the minor's parents, unless the probation department has documented in the probation department file a compelling reason for determining that termination of the parental rights would not be in the minor's best interests, or the probation department has not provided the family with reasonable efforts necessary to achieve reunification. For purposes of this section, compelling reasons for not terminating parental rights are those described in subdivision (c) of Section 727.3.

(b) For the purposes of this section, 15 out of the 22 months shall be calculated from the "date entered foster care," as defined in paragraph (4) of subdivision (d) of Section 727.4. When a minor experiences multiple exits from and entries into foster care during the 22–month period, the 15 months shall be calculated by adding together the total number of months the minor spent in foster care in the past 22 months. However, trial home visits and runaway episodes should not be included in calculating 15 months in foster care.

(c) If the probation department documented a compelling reason at the time of the permanency planning hearing, pursuant to subdivision (n) of Section 706.6, the probation department need not provide any additional documentation to comply with the requirements of this section.

(d) When the probation department sets a hearing pursuant to Section 727.31, it shall concurrently make efforts to identify an approved family for adoption, and follow the procedures described in subdivision (b) of Section 727.31. *(Added by Stats.2001, c. 830 (S.B.940), § 6; Stats.2001, c. 831 (A.B.1696), § 14. Amended by Stats.2019, c. 497 (A.B.991), § 295, eff. Jan. 1, 2020.)*

§ 727.4. Notice of hearings; filing and copy of social study report; definitions

(a)(1) Notice of any hearing pursuant to Section 727, 727.2, or 727.3 shall be served by the probation officer to the minor, the minor's parent or guardian, any adult provider of care to the minor including, but not limited to, foster parents, relative caregivers, preadoptive parents, resource family, community care facility, or foster family agency, and to the counsel of record if the counsel of record was not present at the time that the hearing was set by the court, by first-class mail addressed to the last known address of the person to be notified, by personal service on those persons, or by electronic service pursuant to Section 212.5, not earlier than 30 days nor later than 15 days preceding the date of the hearing. The notice shall contain a statement regarding the nature of the status review or permanency planning hearing and any change in the custody or status of the minor being recommended by the probation department. The notice shall also include a statement informing the foster parents, relative caregivers, or preadoptive parents that he or she may attend all hearings or may submit any information he or she deems relevant to the court in writing. The foster parents, relative caregiver, and preadoptive parents are entitled to notice and opportunity to be heard but need not be made parties to the proceedings. Proof of notice shall be filed with the court.

(2) If the court or probation officer knows or has reason to know that the minor is or may be an Indian child, any notice sent under this section shall comply with the requirements of Section 224.2.

(b) At least 10 calendar days before each status review and permanency planning hearing, after the hearing during which the court orders that the care, custody, and control of the minor to be under the supervision of the probation officer for placement pursuant to subdivision (a) of Section 727, the probation officer shall file a social study report with the court, pursuant to the requirements listed in Section 706.5.

(c) The probation department shall inform the minor, the minor's parent or guardian, and all counsel of record that a copy of the social study prepared for the hearing will be available 10 days before the hearing and may be obtained from the probation officer.

(d) As used in Article 15 (commencing with Section 625) to Article 18 (commencing with Section 725), inclusive:

(1) "Foster care" means residential care provided in any of the settings described in Section 11402 or 11402.01.

(2) "At risk of entering foster care" means that conditions within a minor's family may necessitate his or her entry into foster care unless those conditions are resolved.

(3) "Preadoptive parent" means a licensed foster parent who has been approved for adoption by the State Department of Social Services when it is acting as an adoption agency or by a licensed adoption agency.

(4) "Date of entry into foster care" means the date that is 60 days after the date on which the minor was removed from his or her home, unless one of the exceptions below applies:

(A) If the minor is detained pending foster care placement, and remains detained for more than 60 days, then the date of entry into foster care means the date the court adjudges the minor a ward and orders the minor placed in foster care under the supervision of the probation officer.

(B) If, before the minor is placed in foster care, the minor is committed to a ranch, camp, school, or other institution pending placement, and remains in that facility for more than 60 days, then the "date of entry into foster care" is the date the minor is physically placed in foster care.

(C) If at the time the wardship petition was filed, the minor was a dependent of the juvenile court and in out-of-home placement, then the "date of entry into foster care" is the earlier of the date the juvenile court made a finding of abuse or neglect, or 60 days after the date on which the child was removed from his or her home.

(5) "Reasonable efforts" means:

(A) Efforts made to prevent or eliminate the need for removing the minor from the minor's home.

(B) Efforts to make it possible for the minor to return home, including, but not limited to, case management, counseling, parenting training, mentoring programs, vocational training, educational services, substance abuse treatment, transportation, and therapeutic day services.

(C) Efforts to complete whatever steps are necessary to finalize a permanent plan for the minor.

(D) In child custody proceedings involving an Indian child, "reasonable efforts" shall also include "active efforts" as defined in Section 361.7.

(6) "Relative" means an adult who is related to the minor by blood, adoption, or affinity within the fifth degree of kinship including stepparents, stepsiblings, and all relatives whose status is preceded by the words "great," "great-great," "grand," or the spouse of any of these persons even if the marriage was terminated by death or dissolution. "Relative" shall also include an "extended family member" as defined in the federal Indian Child Welfare Act (25 U.S.C. Sec. 1903(2)).

(7) "Hearing" means a noticed proceeding with findings and orders that are made on a case-by-case basis, heard by either of the following:

(A) A judicial officer, in a courtroom, recorded by a court reporter.

(B) An administrative panel, provided that the hearing is a status review hearing and that the administrative panel meets the following conditions:

(i) The administrative review shall be open to participation by the minor and parents or legal guardians and all those persons entitled to notice under subdivision (a).

(ii) The minor and his or her parents or legal guardians receive proper notice as required in subdivision (a).

(iii) The administrative review panel is composed of persons appointed by the presiding judge of the juvenile court, the membership of which shall include at least one person who is not responsible for the case management of, or delivery of services to, the minor or the parents who are the subjects of the review.

(iv) The findings of the administrative review panel shall be submitted to the juvenile court for the court's approval and shall become part of the official court record. *(Added by Stats.1999, c. 997 (A.B.575), § 18. Amended by Stats.2000, c. 287 (S.B.1955), § 28; Stats.2001, c. 831 (A.B.1696), § 15; Stats.2002, c. 664 (A.B.3034), § 230; Stats.2006, c. 838 (S.B.678), § 53; Stats.2016, c. 612 (A.B. 1997), § 79, eff. Jan. 1, 2017; Stats.2017, c. 319 (A.B.976), § 141, eff. Jan. 1, 2018.)*

Cross References

Indian, Indian child, Indian child's tribe, Indian custodian, Indian tribe, reservation, and tribal court defined for purposes of this Division, see Welfare and Institutions Code § 224.1.
Minor taken into temporary custody and at risk of entering foster care placement, probation officer obligations, see Welfare and Institutions Code § 628.
Probation officer or social worker defined for purposes of this Chapter, see Welfare and Institutions Code § 215.
Wards, judgment and orders, psychotropic medications, see Welfare and Institutions Code § 739.5.
Writing defined, see Welfare and Institutions Code § 8.

Research References

West's California Judicial Council Forms JV–300, Notice of Hearing on Selection of a Permanent Plan (Also Available in Spanish).
West's California Judicial Council Forms JV–320, Orders Under Welfare and Institutions Code Sections 366.24, 366.26, 727.3, 727.31.
West's California Judicial Council Forms JV–625, Notice of Hearing—Juvenile Delinquency Proceeding (Also Available in Spanish).

§ 727.5. Community service; habitually disobedient or truant minors

If a minor is found to be a person described in Section 601, the court may order the minor to perform community service, including, but not limited to, graffiti cleanup, for a total time not to exceed 20 hours over a period not to exceed 30 days, during a time other than his or her hours of school attendance or employment. *(Added by Stats.1991, c. 1202 (S.B.377), § 19.)*

§ 727.6. Minor who has committed sexually violent offense; sexual offender treatment

Where any minor has been adjudged a ward of the court for the commission of a "sexually violent offense," as defined in Section 6600, and committed to the Department of the Youth Authority, the ward shall be given sexual offender treatment consistent with protocols for that treatment developed or implemented by the Department of the Youth Authority. *(Formerly § 727.2, added by*

Stats.1999, c. 995 (S.B.746), § 1. Renumbered § 727.6 and amended by Stats.2000, c. 287 (S.B.1955), § 27.)

§ 727.7. Antigang violence parenting classes for parent or guardian of certain first-time minor offenders; curriculum; liability for cost of classes

(a) If a minor is found to be a person described in Section 601 or 602 and the court finds that the minor is a first-time offender and orders that a parent or guardian retain custody of that minor, the court may order the parent or guardian to attend antigang violence parenting classes if the court finds the presence of significant risk factors for gang involvement on the part of the minor.

(b) The Department of Justice shall establish curriculum for the antigang violence parenting classes required pursuant to this section, including, but not limited to, all of the following criteria:

(1) A meeting in which the families of innocent victims of gang violence share their experience.

(2) A meeting in which the surviving parents of a deceased gang member share their experience.

(3) How to identify gang and drug activity in children.

(4) How to communicate effectively with adolescents.

(5) An overview of pertinent support agencies and organizations for intervention, education, job training, and positive recreational activities, including telephone numbers, locations, and contact names of those agencies and organizations.

(6) The potential fines and periods of incarceration for the commission of additional gang-related offenses.

(7) The potential penalties that may be imposed upon parents for aiding and abetting crimes committed by their children.

(c) For purposes of this section, "gang-related" means that the minor was an active participant in a criminal street gang, as specified in subdivision (a) of Section 186.22 of the Penal Code, or committed an offense for the benefit of, or at the direction of, a criminal street gang, as specified in subdivision (b) or (d) of Section 186.22 of the Penal Code.

(d) The father, mother, spouse, or other person liable for the support of the minor, the estate of that person, and the estate of the minor shall be liable for the cost of classes ordered pursuant to this section, unless the court finds that the person or estate does not have the financial ability to pay. In evaluating financial ability to pay, the court shall take into consideration the combined household income, the necessary obligations of the household, the number of persons dependent upon this income, and whether reduced monthly payments would obviate the need to waive liability for the full costs. *(Added by Stats.2007, c. 457 (A.B.1291), § 1. Amended by Stats.2011, c. 258 (A.B.177), § 1.)*

§ 728. Termination or modification of guardianship under the Probate Code; recommendations; motion; hearing

(a) The juvenile court may terminate or modify a guardianship of the person of a minor previously established under the Probate Code, or appoint a coguardian or successor guardian of the person of the minor, if the minor is the subject of a petition filed under Section 300, 601, or 602. If the probation officer supervising the minor provides information to the court regarding the minor's present circumstances and makes a recommendation to the court regarding a motion to terminate or modify a guardianship established in any county under the Probate Code, or to appoint a coguardian or successor guardian, of the person of a minor who is before the juvenile court under a petition filed under Section 300, 601, or 602, the court shall order the appropriate county department, or the district attorney or county counsel, to file the recommended motion. The motion may also be made by the guardian or the minor's attorney. The hearing on the motion may be held simultaneously with any regularly scheduled hearing held in proceedings to declare the minor a dependent child or ward of the court, or at any subsequent hearing concerning the dependent child or ward. Notice requirements of Section 294 shall apply to the proceedings in juvenile court under this subdivision.

(b) If the juvenile court decides to terminate or modify a guardianship previously established under the Probate Code pursuant to subdivision (a), the juvenile court shall provide notice of that decision to the court in which the guardianship was originally established. The clerk of the superior court, upon receipt of the notice, shall file the notice with other documents and records of the pending proceeding and deliver by first-class mail or by electronic service pursuant to Section 1215 of the Probate Code a copy of the notice to all parties of record in the superior court.

(c) If, at any time during the period a minor under the age of 18 years is a ward of the juvenile court, the probation officer supervising the minor recommends to the court that the court establish a guardianship of the person of the minor and appoint a specific adult to act as guardian, or on the motion of the minor's attorney, or on the order of the court that a guardianship shall be established as the minor's permanent plan pursuant to paragraph (4) of subdivision (b) of Section 727.3, the court shall set a hearing to consider the recommendation or motion and shall order the clerk to notice the minor's parents and relatives as required in Section 294. If the motion is not made by the minor's attorney, the court may appoint the district attorney or county counsel to prosecute the action.

(d) The procedures for appointment of a guardian shall be conducted exclusively pursuant to Section 366.26, except that subdivision (j) of Section 366.26 shall not apply.

(e) Upon the appointment of a guardian pursuant to subdivision (d), the court may continue wardship and conditions of probation, or may terminate the wardship of the minor.

(f) Notwithstanding Section 1601 of the Probate Code, the proceedings to modify or terminate a guardianship granted under this section shall be held in the juvenile court unless the termination is due to the emancipation or adoption of the minor.

(g) The Judicial Council shall develop rules of court and adopt appropriate forms for the findings and orders under this section. *(Added by Stats.1998, c. 390 (S.B.2017), § 4. Amended by Stats.2001, c. 831 (A.B.1696), § 16; Stats.2011, c. 459 (A.B.212), § 20, eff. Oct. 4, 2011; Stats.2017, c. 319 (A.B.976), § 142, eff. Jan. 1, 2018.)*

Cross References

Hearing defined for purposes of this Article, see Welfare and Institutions Code § 727.4.

Kin–GAP for children, eligibility requirements, see Welfare and Institutions Code § 11386.

Kinship Guardianship Assistance Payment Program, kinship guardianship assistance agreement, payment rates, see Welfare and Institutions Code § 11364.

Kinship Guardianship Assistance Payments for Children, kinship guardianship assistance agreement, payment rates, see Welfare and Institutions Code § 11387.

Minor or nonminor within transition jurisdiction of juvenile court, criteria, see Welfare and Institutions Code § 450.

Probation officer or social worker defined for purposes of this Chapter, see Welfare and Institutions Code § 215.

Relative defined for purposes of this Article, see Welfare and Institutions Code § 727.4.

Research References

West's California Judicial Council Forms JV–320, Orders Under Welfare and Institutions Code Sections 366.24, 366.26, 727.3, 727.31.

West's California Judicial Council Forms JV–330, Letters of Guardianship (Juvenile) (Also Available in Chinese, Korean, Spanish, Vietnamese).

§ 729. Battery committed under Penal Code § 243.5; ward of court; custody of parent or guardian; restitution or community service as condition of probation

If a minor is found to be a person described in Section 602 by reason of the commission of a battery on school property as described in Penal Code Section 243.5, and the court does not remove the minor from the physical custody of the parent or guardian, the court as a condition of probation, except in any case in which the court makes a finding and states on the record its reasons that the condition would be inappropriate, shall require the minor to make restitution to the victim of the battery. If restitution is found to be inappropriate, the court, except in any case in which the court makes a finding and states on the record its reasons that the condition would be inappropriate, shall require the minor to perform specified community service. Nothing in this section shall be construed to limit the authority of a juvenile court to provide conditions of probation. *(Added by Stats.1981, c. 566, p. 2223, § 2. Amended by Stats.1994, c. 146 (A.B.3601), § 223.)*

Cross References

Department of Developmental Services, see Welfare and Institutions Code § 4400 et seq.

§ 729.1. Offenses against persons on public transit vehicles; conditions of probation

(a)(1) If a minor is found to be a person described in Section 602 by reason of the commission of a crime which takes place on a public transit vehicle, and the court does not remove the minor from the physical custody of the parent or guardian, the court as a condition of probation, except in any case in which the court makes a finding and states on the record its reasons that the condition would be inappropriate, shall require the minor to wash, paint, repair or replace the damaged or destroyed property, or otherwise make restitution to the property owner. If restitution is found to be inappropriate, the court, except in any case in which the court makes a finding and states on the record its reasons that the condition would be inappropriate, shall require the minor to perform specified community service. Nothing in this section shall be construed to limit the authority of a juvenile court to provide conditions of probation.

(2) In lieu of the community service required pursuant to paragraph (1), the court may, if a jurisdiction has adopted a graffiti abatement program as defined in subdivision (f) of Section 594 of the Penal Code, order the defendant, and his or her parents or guardians, as a condition of probation, to keep a specified property in the community free of graffiti for 90 days. Participation of a parent or guardian is not required under this paragraph if the court deems this participation to be detrimental to the defendant, or if the parent or guardian is a single parent who must care for young children.

(b) As used in subdivision (a), "public transit vehicle" means any motor vehicle, street car, trackless trolley, bus, shuttle, light rail system, rapid transit system, subway, train, taxi cab, or jitney, which transports members of the public for hire.

(c) The court may order any person ordered to perform community service or graffiti removal pursuant to subdivision (a) to undergo counseling. *(Formerly § 729, added by Stats.1982, c. 297, § 2. Renumbered § 729.1 and amended by Stats.1986, c. 248, § 247. Amended by Stats.1996, c. 600 (A.B.2295), § 10.)*

§ 729.2. Minors not removed from physical custody of parent or guardian; conditions of probation

If a minor is found to be a person described in Section 601 or 602 and the court does not remove the minor from the physical custody of the parent or guardian, the court as a condition of probation, except in any case in which the court makes a finding and states on the record its reasons that that condition would be inappropriate, shall:

(a) Require the minor to attend a school program approved by the probation officer without absence.

(b) Require the parents or guardian of the minor to participate with the minor in a counseling or education program, including, but not limited to, parent education and parenting programs operated by community colleges, school districts, or other appropriate agencies designated by the court or the probation department, unless the minor has been declared a dependent child of the court pursuant to Section 300 or a petition to declare the minor a dependent child of the court pursuant to Section 300 is pending.

(c) Require the minor to be at his or her legal residence between the hours of 10:00 p.m. and 6:00 a.m. unless the minor is accompanied by his or her parent or parents, legal guardian or other adult person having the legal care or custody of the minor. *(Added by Stats.1989, c. 1117, § 15.)*

Cross References

Probation officer or social worker defined for purposes of this Chapter, see Welfare and Institutions Code § 215.

Research References

West's California Judicial Council Forms JV–624, Terms and Conditions.

§ 729.3. Urine testing; condition of probation; minors not removed from custody of parent or guardian

If a minor is found to be a person described in Section 601 or 602 and the court does not remove the minor from the physical custody of his or her parent or guardian, the court, as a condition of probation, may require the minor to submit to urine testing upon the request of a peace officer or probation officer for the purpose of determining the presence of alcohol or drugs. *(Added by Stats.1989, c. 1117, § 16.)*

Cross References

Probation officer or social worker defined for purposes of this Chapter, see Welfare and Institutions Code § 215.

§ 729.5. Criminal violation by minor; restitution hearing; citation ordering appearance by parents or guardians; liability; execution of restitution order; petition to modify or vacate order; insurer's liability

(a) If a petition alleges that a minor is a person described by Section 602 and the petition is sustained, the court, in addition to the notice required by any other provision of law, may issue a citation to the minor's parents or guardians, ordering them to appear in the court at the time and date stated for a hearing to impose a restitution fine pursuant to Section 730.6.

(b) The citation shall notify the parent or guardian that, at the hearing, the parent or guardian may be held liable for the payment of restitution if the minor is ordered to make restitution to the victim. The citation shall contain a warning that the failure to appear at the time and date stated may result in an order that the parent or guardian pay restitution up to the limits provided for in Sections 1714.1 and 1714.3 of the Civil Code.

(c) The hearing described in subdivision (b) may be held immediately following the disposition hearing or at a later date, at the option of the court.

(d) If the parent or guardian fails to appear pursuant to this section, the court may hold the parent or guardian jointly and severally liable with the minor for restitution, subject to the limitations contained in subdivision (b).

(e) Execution may be issued on an order holding a parent or guardian jointly or severally liable with the minor for restitution in the same manner as on a judgment in a civil action, including any balance unpaid at the termination of the court's jurisdiction over the minor.

(f) At any time prior to the full payment of restitution ordered pursuant to this section, a person held liable for payment of restitution may petition the court to modify or vacate the order based on a showing of change in circumstances.

(g) Service of the citation shall be made on all parents or guardians of the minor whose names and addresses are known to the petitioner.

(h) Service of the citation shall be made at least 10 days prior to the time and date stated therein for appearance, in the manner provided by law for the service of a summons in a civil action, other than by publication.

(i) This section shall not apply to any case where a citation has been issued pursuant to Section 742.18.

(j) Nothing in this section shall be interpreted to make an insurer liable for a loss caused by the willful act of the insured or the insured's dependents within the meaning of Section 533 of the Insurance Code.

(k) This section does not apply to foster parents. *(Added by Stats.1995, c. 268 (A.B.989), § 1. Amended by Stats.1996, c. 520 (A.B.3050), § 1.)*

Cross References

Hearing defined for purposes of this Article, see Welfare and Institutions Code § 727.4.

§ 729.6. Minors violating criminal law; court order to attend counseling as condition of punishment; expense of parents

If a minor is found to be a person described in Section 602 by reason of the commission of an offense described in Section 241.2 or 243.2 of the Penal Code, the court shall, in addition to any other fine, sentence, or as a condition of probation, order the minor to attend counseling at the expense of the minor's parents. The court shall take into consideration the ability of the minor's parents consistent with Section 730.7 to pay, however, no minor shall be relieved of attending counseling because of the minor's parents' inability to pay for the counseling imposed by this section. *(Added by Stats.2001, c. 484 (A.B.653), § 4.)*

Research References

1 Witkin California Criminal Law 4th Crimes Against the Person § 24 (2021), School or Park.

1 Witkin California Criminal Law 4th Crimes Against the Person § 25 (2021), Hospital.

§ 729.7. Mediation of service contract; restitution paid by performance of services; condition of probation

At the request of the victim, the probation officer shall assist in mediating a service contract between the victim and the minor under which the amount of restitution owed to the victim by the minor pursuant to Section 729.6, as operative on or before August 2, 1995, or Section 730.6 may be paid by performance of specified services. If the court approves of the contract, the court may make performance of services under the terms of the contract a condition of probation. Successful performance of service shall be credited as payment of restitution in accordance with the terms of the contract approved by the court. *(Added by Stats.1983, c. 939, § 2. Amended by Stats.1996, c. 1077 (A.B.2898), § 34.)*

Cross References

Probation officer or social worker defined for purposes of this Chapter, see Welfare and Institutions Code § 215.

§ 729.8. Community service requirement; minors committing offense involving possession, use, sale or other furnishing of controlled substance

(a) If a minor is found to be a person described in Section 602 by reason of the unlawful possession, use, sale, or other furnishing of a controlled substance, as defined in Chapter 2 (commencing with Section 11053) of the Health and Safety Code, an imitation controlled substance, as defined in Section 109550 of the Health and Safety Code, or toluene or a toxic, as described in Section 381 of the Penal Code, upon the grounds of any school providing instruction in kindergarten, or any of grades 1 to 12, inclusive, or any church or synagogue, playground, public or private youth center, child day care facility, or public swimming pool, during hours in which these facilities are open for business, classes, or school-related activities or programs, or at any time when minors are using the facility, the court, as a condition of probation, except in any case in which the court makes a finding and states on the record its reasons that the condition would be inappropriate, shall require the minor to perform not more than 100 hours of community service.

(b) The definitions contained in subdivision (e) of Section 11353.1 shall apply to this section.

(c) As used in this section, "community service" means any of the following:

(1) Picking up litter along public streets or highways.

(2) Cleaning up graffiti on school grounds or any public property.

(3) Performing services in a drug rehabilitation center. *(Added by Stats.1983, c. 736, § 1. Amended by Stats.1990, c. 1664 (A.B.2645), § 8; Stats.1993, c. 589 (A.B.2211), § 191; Stats.1993, c. 556 (A.B. 312), § 4; Stats.1996, c. 1023 (S.B.1497), § 456, eff. Sept. 29, 1996.)*

§ 729.9. Minor committing offense involving unlawful possession, use, sale or other furnishing of controlled substance; condition of probation; prohibition of use or being under influence of controlled substance; submission to tests

If a minor is found to be a person described in Section 602 by reason of the commission of an offense involving the unlawful possession, use, sale, or other furnishing of a controlled substance, as defined in Chapter 2 (commencing with Section 11053) of Division 10 of the Health and Safety Code, and, unless it makes a finding that this condition would not serve the interests of justice, the court, when recommended by the probation officer, shall require, as a condition of probation, in addition to any other disposition authorized by law, that the minor shall not use or be under the influence of any controlled substance and shall submit to drug and substance abuse testing as directed by the probation officer. *(Added by Stats.1987, c. 879, § 2. Amended by Stats.2017, c. 678 (S.B.190), § 14, eff. Jan. 1, 2018.)*

Cross References

Probation officer or social worker defined for purposes of this Chapter, see Welfare and Institutions Code § 215.

§ 729.10. Alcohol or drug education programs; attendance by minors convicted of controlled substance offenses

(a) Whenever, in any county specified in subdivision (b), a judge of a juvenile court or referee of a juvenile court finds a minor to be a person described in Section 602 by reason of the commission of an offense involving the unlawful possession, use, sale, or other furnishing of a controlled substance, as defined in Chapter 2 (commencing with Section 11053) of Division 10 of the Health and Safety Code, or for violating subdivision (f) of Section 647 of the Penal Code, or Section 25662 of the Business and Professions Code, the minor shall be required to participate in, and successfully complete, an alcohol or drug education program, or both of those programs, as designated by the court. Whenever it can be done without substantial additional cost, each county shall require that the program be provided for juveniles at a separate location from, or at a different time of day than, alcohol and drug education programs for adults.

(b) This section applies only in those counties that have one or more alcohol or drug education programs certified by the county alcohol program administrator and approved by the board of supervisors. *(Added by Stats.1989, c. 1117, § 17. Amended by Stats.2017, c. 678 (S.B.190), § 15, eff. Jan. 1, 2018.)*

§ 729.12. Assessment, Orientation, and Volunteer Mentor Pilot Program

(a) It is the intent of the Legislature to authorize an Assessment, Orientation, and Volunteer Mentor Pilot Program in San Diego County. The pilot project will operate under the authority of the county behavioral health director in conjunction with the San Diego Juvenile Court and the County of San Diego Probation Department.

(b) Whenever a judge of the San Diego County Juvenile Court or a referee of the San Diego Juvenile Court finds a minor to be a person described in Section 601 or 602 for any reason, the minor may be assessed and screened for drug and alcohol use and abuse; and if the assessment and screening determines the need for drug and alcohol education and intervention, the minor may be required to participate in, and successfully complete, an alcohol and drug orientation, and to participate in, and successfully complete, an alcohol or drug program with a local community-based service provider, as designated by the court.

(c) The Assessment, Orientation, and Volunteer Mentor Pilot Program may operate for a minimum of three years and may screen and assess for drug and alcohol problems, minors who are declared wards of San Diego Juvenile Court.

(d) Drug and alcohol assessments may be conducted utilizing a standardized instrument that shall be approved by the county behavioral health director in conjunction with San Diego Juvenile Court and the San Diego County Probation Department.

(e) Those minors who are determined to have drug and alcohol problems, may be required to participate in, and successfully complete, a drug and alcohol orientation. The orientation may provide drug and alcohol education and intervention, referral to community resources for followup education and intervention and arrange for volunteers to serve as mentors to assist each minor in addressing their drug and alcohol problem. Parents or guardians of minors will have the opportunity to participate in the orientation program in order to help juveniles address drug and alcohol use or abuse problems.

(f) As a condition of probation, each minor may be required to submit to drug testing. Drug testing may be conducted on a random basis by a qualified drug and alcohol service provider in coordination with the county probation department. All contested drug tests may be confirmed by a National Institute for Drug Abuse certified drug laboratory and the findings may be reported to the probation officer for appropriate action. The drug testing protocol may be approved by the county behavioral health director in conjunction with San Diego Juvenile Court and the County of San Diego Probation Department.

(g) An evaluation of the pilot program shall be conducted and results of the program shall be submitted to state alcohol and drug programs and to the Legislature at the conclusion of the pilot program. The evaluation shall include, but not be limited to, all of the following:

(1) The number and percentage of juveniles screened.

(2) The number and percentage of juveniles given followup education and intervention.

(3) The number of mentors recruited and trained.

(4) The number and percentage of juveniles assigned to a mentor.

(5) The length of time in an education and intervention program.

(6) The program completion rates.

(7) The number of subsequent violations.

(8) The number of re-arrests.

(9) The urine test results.

(10) The subsequent drug or alcohol use.

(11) The participant's perceptions of program utility.

(12) The provider's perceptions of program utility.

(13) The mentor's perceptions of program utility. *(Added by Stats.1996, c. 733 (A.B.2564), § 1. Amended by Stats.2015, c. 455 (S.B.804), § 12, eff. Jan. 1, 2016.)*

Cross References

Probation officer or social worker defined for purposes of this Chapter, see Welfare and Institutions Code § 215.

§ 729.13. Exemplary Californians; recognition awards; outstanding achievements

(a) The Department of the Youth Authority shall recognize, on an annual basis, exemplary Californians who do any of the following:

(1) Voluntarily participate in a youth mentoring program in their communities.

(2) Perform special acts or special services that promote youth mentoring programs in their communities.

(3) By their superior accomplishments, make exceptional contributions to creating, maintaining, or fostering volunteer youth mentoring programs in California.

(b) The Department of the Youth Authority shall recognize, on an annual basis, the outstanding achievements of present and former wards of the juvenile court, whether committed to state institutions or community-based programs.

(c) Recognition awards shall be made in accordance with procedures and standards established by the department.

(d) Any expenditures made or costs incurred for the purposes of this section may be paid from funds appropriated for the support of the department that are otherwise unencumbered.

(e) As used in subdivision (a), "youth mentoring programs" means programs designed to foster positive, role-model relationships between adult community volunteers and minors who are living in conditions that place them at risk for delinquent or criminal conduct. *(Added by Stats.1997, c. 281 (S.B.1204), § 1.)*

§ 730. Minor violating criminal law; ward of court; court orders; probation conditions; sex offender treatment

(a)(1) When a minor is adjudged a ward of the court on the ground that they are a person described by Section 602, the court may order any of the types of treatment referred to in Section 727, and as an additional alternative, may commit the minor to a juvenile home, ranch, camp, or forestry camp. If there is no county juvenile home, ranch, camp, or forestry camp within the county, the court may commit the minor to the county juvenile hall. In addition, the court may also make any of the following orders:

(A) Order the ward to make restitution, to pay a fine up to two hundred fifty dollars ($250) for deposit in the county treasury if the court finds that the minor has the financial ability to pay the fine, or to participate in uncompensated work programs.

(B) Commit the ward to a sheltered-care facility.

(C) Order that the ward and the ward's family or guardian participate in a program of professional counseling as arranged and directed by the probation officer as a condition of continued custody of the ward.

(D) Order placement of the ward at the Pine Grove Youth Conservation Camp if the ward meets the placement criteria, the county has entered into a contract with the Department of * * * Corrections and Rehabilitation, either directly or through another county, the department has found the ward amenable, and there is space and resources available for the placement. The county probation department shall receive approval from the department prior to transporting the ward to the camp. The * * * department shall immediately notify the county probation department if the ward is no longer amenable for continued camp placement and coordinate the immediate return of the ward to the county of jurisdiction.

(2) A court shall not commit a juvenile to any juvenile facility for a period that exceeds the middle term of imprisonment that could be imposed upon an adult convicted of the same offense.

(b) When a ward described in subdivision (a) is placed under the supervision of the probation officer or committed to the care, custody, and control of the probation officer, the court may make any and all reasonable orders for the conduct of the ward including the requirement that the ward go to work and earn money for the support of the ward's dependents or to effect reparation and in either case that the ward keep an account of the ward's earnings and report the same to the probation officer and apply these earnings as directed by the court. The court may impose and require any and all reasonable conditions that it may determine fitting and proper to the end that justice may be done and the reformation and rehabilitation of the ward enhanced.

(c) When a ward described in subdivision (a) is placed under the supervision of the probation officer or committed to the care, custody, and control of the probation officer, and is required as a condition of probation to participate in community service or graffiti cleanup, the court may impose a condition that if the minor unreasonably fails to attend or unreasonably leaves prior to completing the assigned daily hours of community service or graffiti cleanup, a law enforcement officer may take the minor into custody for the purpose of returning the minor to the site of the community service or graffiti cleanup.

(d) When a minor is adjudged or continued as a ward of the court on the ground that the ward is a person described by Section 602 by reason of the commission of rape, sodomy, oral copulation, or an act of sexual penetration specified in Section 289 of the Penal Code, the court shall order the minor to complete a sex offender treatment program, if the court determines, in consultation with the county probation officer, that suitable programs are available. In determining what type of treatment is appropriate, the court shall consider all of the following: the seriousness and circumstances of the offense, the vulnerability of the victim, the minor's criminal history and prior attempts at rehabilitation, the sophistication of the minor, the threat to public safety, the minor's likelihood of reoffending, and any other relevant information presented. If ordered by the court to complete a sex offender treatment program, the minor shall pay all or a portion of the reasonable costs of the sex offender treatment program after a determination is made of the ability of the minor to pay.

(e) This section shall become operative July 1, 2021. *(Added by Stats.2020, c. 337 (S.B.823), § 27, eff. Sept. 30, 2020, operative July 1, 2021. Amended by Stats.2021, c. 80 (A.B.145), § 27, eff. July 16, 2021; Stats.2022, c. 58 (A.B.200), § 40, eff. June 30, 2022.)*

Cross References

Appealable orders, rulings and judgments, see Welfare and Institutions Code § 800.

Probation officer or social worker defined for purposes of this Chapter, see Welfare and Institutions Code § 215.

§ 730.5. Fines

When a minor is adjudged a ward of the court on the ground that he or she is a person described in Section 602, in addition to any of the orders authorized by Section 726, 727, 730, or 731, the court may levy a fine against the minor up to the amount that could be imposed on an adult for the same offense, if the court finds that the minor has the financial ability to pay the fine. Section 1464 of the Penal Code applies to fines levied pursuant to this section. *(Added by Stats.1980, c. 991, p. 3137, § 2. Amended by Stats.1981, c. 727, p. 2879, § 2; Stats.1988, c. 99, § 2.)*

§ 730.6. Restitution for economic loss

(a)(1) It is the intent of the Legislature that a victim of conduct for which a minor is found to be a person described in Section 602 who incurs an economic loss as a result of the minor's conduct shall receive restitution directly from that minor.

(2) Upon a minor being found to be a person described in Section 602, the court shall consider levying a fine in accordance with Section 730.5. In addition, the court shall order the minor to pay, in addition to any other penalty provided or imposed under the law, both of the following:

(A) A restitution fine in accordance with subdivision (b).

(B) Restitution to the victim or victims, if any, in accordance with subdivision (h).

(b) If a minor is found to be a person described in Section 602, the court shall impose a separate and additional restitution fine. The restitution fine shall be set at the discretion of the court and commensurate with the seriousness of the offense as follows:

(1) If the minor is found to be a person described in Section 602 by reason of the commission of one or more felony offenses, the restitution fine shall not be less than one hundred dollars ($100) and not more than one thousand dollars ($1,000). A separate hearing for the fine shall not be required.

(2) If the minor is found to be a person described in Section 602 by reason of the commission of one or more misdemeanor offenses, the restitution fine shall not exceed one hundred dollars ($100). A separate hearing for the fine shall not be required.

(c) The restitution fine shall be in addition to any other disposition or fine imposed and shall be imposed regardless of the minor's inability to pay. This fine shall be deposited in the Restitution Fund.

(d)(1) In setting the amount of the fine pursuant to subparagraph (A) of paragraph (2) of subdivision (a), the court shall consider any relevant factors including, but not limited to, the minor's ability to pay, the seriousness and gravity of the offense and the circumstances of its commission, any economic gain derived by the minor as a result of the offense, and the extent to which others suffered losses as a result of the offense. The losses may include pecuniary losses to the victim or his or her dependents as well as intangible losses such as psychological harm caused by the offense.

(2) The consideration of a minor's ability to pay may include his or her future earning capacity. A minor shall bear the burden of demonstrating a lack of his or her ability to pay.

(e) Express findings of the court as to the factors bearing on the amount of the fine shall not be required.

(f) Except as provided in subdivision (g), under no circumstances shall the court fail to impose the separate and additional restitution fine required by subparagraph (A) of paragraph (2) of subdivision (a). This fine shall not be subject to penalty assessments pursuant to Section 1464 of the Penal Code.

(g)(1) In a case in which the minor is a person described in Section 602 by reason of having committed a felony offense, if the court finds that there are compelling and extraordinary reasons, the court may waive imposition of the restitution fine required by subparagraph (A) of paragraph (2) of subdivision (a). If a waiver is granted, the court shall state on the record all reasons supporting the waiver.

(2) If the minor is a person described in subdivision (a) of Section 241.1, the court shall waive imposition of the restitution fine required by subparagraph (A) of paragraph (2) of subdivision (a).

(h)(1) Restitution ordered pursuant to subparagraph (B) of paragraph (2) of subdivision (a) shall be imposed in the amount of the losses, as determined. If the amount of loss cannot be ascertained at the time of sentencing, the restitution order shall include a provision that the amount shall be determined at the direction of the court at any time during the term of the commitment or probation. The court shall order full restitution unless it finds compelling and extraordinary reasons for not doing so, and states them on the record. A minor's inability to pay shall not be considered a compelling or extraordinary reason not to impose a restitution order, nor shall inability to pay be a consideration in determining the amount of the restitution order. A restitution order pursuant to subparagraph (B) of paragraph (2) of subdivision (a), to the extent possible, shall identify each victim, unless the court for good cause finds that the order should not identify a victim or victims, and the amount of each victim's loss to which it pertains, and shall be of a dollar amount sufficient to fully reimburse the victim or victims for all determined economic losses incurred as the result of the minor's conduct for which the minor was found to be a person described in Section 602, including all of the following:

(A) Full or partial payment for the value of stolen or damaged property. The value of stolen or damaged property shall be the replacement cost of like property, or the actual cost of repairing the property when repair is possible.

(B) Medical expenses.

(C) Wages or profits lost due to injury incurred by the victim, and if the victim is a minor, wages or profits lost by the minor's parent, parents, guardian, or guardians, while caring for the injured minor. Lost wages shall include any commission income as well as any base wages. Commission income shall be established by evidence of commission income during the 12–month period prior to the date of the crime for which restitution is being ordered, unless good cause for a shorter time period is shown.

(D) Wages or profits lost by the victim, and if the victim is a minor, wages or profits lost by the minor's parent, parents, guardian, or guardians, due to time spent as a witness or in assisting the police or prosecution. Lost wages shall include any commission income as well as any base wages. Commission income shall be established by evidence of commission income during the 12–month period prior to the date of the crime for which restitution is being ordered, unless good cause for a shorter time period is shown.

(2) A minor shall have the right to a hearing before a judge to dispute the determination of the amount of restitution. The court may modify the amount on its own motion or on the motion of the district attorney, the victim or victims, or the minor. If a motion is made for modification of a restitution order, the victim shall be notified of that motion at least 10 days prior to the hearing on the motion. If the amount of victim restitution is not known at the time of disposition, the court order shall identify the victim or victims, unless the court finds for good cause that the order should not identify a victim or victims, and state that the amount of restitution for each victim is to be determined. If feasible, the court shall also identify on the court order, any co-offenders who are jointly and severally liable for victim restitution.

(i) A restitution order imposed pursuant to subparagraph (B) of paragraph (2) of subdivision (a) shall identify the losses to which it pertains, and shall be enforceable as a civil judgment pursuant to subdivision (r). The making of a restitution order pursuant to this subdivision shall not affect the right of a victim to recovery from the Restitution Fund in the manner provided elsewhere, except to the extent that restitution is actually collected pursuant to the order. Restitution collected pursuant to this subdivision shall be credited to any other judgments for the same losses obtained against the minor or the minor's parent or guardian arising out of the offense for which the minor was found to be a person described in Section 602. Restitution imposed shall be ordered to be made to the Restitution Fund to the extent that the victim, as defined in subdivision (j), has received assistance from the Victims of Crime Program pursuant to Article 5 (commencing with Section 13959) of Chapter 5 of Part 4 of Division 3 of Title 2 of the Government Code.

(j) For purposes of this section, "victim" shall include:

(1) The immediate surviving family of the actual victim.

(2) A governmental entity that is responsible for repairing, replacing, or restoring public or privately owned property that has been defaced with graffiti or other inscribed material, as defined in subdivision (e) of Section 594 of the Penal Code, and that has sustained an economic loss as the result of a violation of Section 594, 594.3, 594.4, 640.5, 640.6, or 640.7 of the Penal Code.

(3) A corporation, business trust, estate, trust, partnership, association, joint venture, government, governmental subdivision, agency, or instrumentality, or any other legal or commercial entity when that entity is a direct victim of a crime.

(4) A person who has sustained economic loss as the result of a crime and who satisfies any of the following conditions:

(A) At the time of the crime was the parent, grandparent, sibling, spouse, child, or grandchild of the victim.

(B) At the time of the crime was living in the household of the victim.

(C) At the time of the crime was a person who had previously lived in the household of the victim for a period of not less than two years in a relationship substantially similar to a relationship listed in subparagraph (A).

(D) Is another family member of the victim, including, but not limited to, the victim's fiancé or fiancée, and who witnessed the crime.

(E) Is the primary caretaker of a minor victim.

(k) If the direct victim of an offense is a group home or other facility licensed to provide residential care in which the minor was placed as a dependent or ward of the court, or an employee thereof, restitution shall be limited to out-of-pocket expenses that are not covered by insurance and that are paid by the facility or employee.

(*l*) Upon a minor being found to be a person described in Section 602, the court shall require, as a condition of probation, the payment of restitution fines and orders imposed under this section. Any portion of a restitution order that remains unsatisfied after a minor is no longer on probation shall continue to be enforceable by a victim pursuant to subdivision (r) until the obligation is satisfied in full.

(m) Probation shall not be revoked for failure of a person to make restitution pursuant to this section as a condition of probation unless the court determines that the person has willfully failed to pay or failed to make sufficient bona fide efforts to legally acquire the resources to pay.

(n) If the court finds and states on the record compelling and extraordinary reasons why restitution should not be required as provided in paragraph (2) of subdivision (a), the court shall order, as a condition of probation, that the minor perform specified community service.

(*o*) The court may avoid ordering community service as a condition of probation only if it finds and states on the record compelling and extraordinary reasons not to order community service in addition to the finding that restitution pursuant to paragraph (2) of subdivision (a) should not be required.

(p) If a minor is committed to the Division of Juvenile Facilities, Department of Corrections and Rehabilitation, the court shall order restitution to be paid to the victim or victims, if any. Payment of restitution to the victim or victims pursuant to this subdivision shall take priority in time over payment of any other restitution fine imposed pursuant to this section.

(q) At its discretion, the board of supervisors of any county may impose a fee to cover the actual administrative cost of collecting the restitution fine, not to exceed 10 percent of the amount ordered to be paid, to be added to the restitution fine and included in the order of the court, the proceeds of which shall be deposited in the general fund of the county.

(r) If the judgment is for a restitution fine ordered pursuant to subparagraph (A) of paragraph (2) of subdivision (a), or a restitution order imposed pursuant to subparagraph (B) of paragraph (2) of subdivision (a), the judgment may be enforced in the manner provided in Section 1214 of the Penal Code. *(Added by Stats.1994, c. 1106 (A.B.3169), § 7, eff. Sept. 29, 1994. Amended by Stats.1995, c. 313 (A.B.817), § 21, eff. Aug. 3, 1995; Stats.1996, c. 1077 (A.B.2898), § 35; Stats.1998, c. 451 (S.B.2021), § 3, eff. Sept. 14, 1998; Stats. 2000, c. 481 (S.B.1943), § 2; Stats.2000, c. 1016 (A.B.2491), § 12.5; Stats.2005, c. 238 (S.B.972), § 5; Stats.2009, c. 454 (A.B.576), § 2; Stats.2014, c. 760 (A.B.388), § 7, eff. Jan. 1, 2015; Stats.2015, c. 131 (S.B.651), § 1, eff. Jan. 1, 2016.)*

Cross References

Administration of state prisons, crime victim restitution fine or order, deduction from wages and trust account deposits, see Penal Code § 2085.5.
California Victim Compensation and Government Claims Board, indemnification of victims of crime, lien and action or claim by recipient, see Government Code § 13963.
Deduction of restitution fine from wages of persons committed to or housed in a Youth Authority facility, see Welfare and Institutions Code § 1752.82.
Deduction of restitution fines or restitution orders from trust account deposits and compensatory or punitive damage awards and settlements of wards committed to the Youth Authority, see Welfare and Institutions Code § 1752.81.
Felonies, definition and penalties, see Penal Code §§ 17, 18.
Hearing defined for purposes of this Article, see Welfare and Institutions Code § 727.4.
Misdemeanors, definition and penalties, see Penal Code §§ 17, 19, 19.2.
Payment of restitution fine as condition of liberty from Youth Authority, see Welfare and Institutions Code § 1766.1.
Restitution fines, property defaced by graffiti, see Penal Code § 1202.4.

Research References

West's California Judicial Council Forms CR–110, Order for Victim Restitution.
West's California Judicial Council Forms CR–111, Abstract of Judgment—Restitution.
West's California Judicial Council Forms JV–790, Order for Victim Restitution.
West's California Judicial Council Forms JV–791, Abstract of Judgment—Restitution.
3 Witkin, California Criminal Law 4th Punishment § 109 (2021), In General.
3 Witkin, California Criminal Law 4th Punishment § 121 (2021), In General.
3 Witkin, California Criminal Law 4th Punishment § 123 (2021), Effect of Insurance or Other Third-Party Payment.

§ 730.7. Restitution, fine, or penalty assessment order; liability of parent or guardian; ability to pay; notice to victim

(a) In a case in which a minor is ordered to make restitution to the victim or victims, or the minor is ordered to pay fines and penalty assessments under any provision of this code, a parent or guardian who has joint or sole legal and physical custody and control of the minor shall be rebuttably presumed to be jointly and severally liable with the minor in accordance with Sections 1714.1 and 1714.3 of the Civil Code for the amount of restitution, fines, and penalty assessments so ordered, up to the limits provided in those sections, subject to the court's consideration of the parent's or guardian's inability to pay. When considering the parent's or guardian's inability to pay, the court may consider future earning capacity, present income, the number of persons dependent on that income, and the necessary obligations of the family, including, but not limited to, rent or mortgage payments, food, children's school tuition, children's clothing, medical bills, and health insurance. The parent or guardian shall have the burden of showing an inability to pay. The parent or guardian shall also have the burden of showing by a preponderance of the evidence that the parent or guardian was either not given notice of potential liability for payment of restitution, fines, and penalty assessments prior to the petition being sustained by an admission or adjudication, or that he or she was not present during the proceedings wherein the petition was sustained either by admission or adjudication and any hearing thereafter related to restitution, fines, or penalty assessments.

(b) In cases in which the court orders restitution to the victim or victims of the offense, each victim in whose favor the restitution order has been made shall be notified within 60 days after restitution has been ordered of the following:

(1) The name and address of the minor ordered to make restitution.

(2) The amount and any terms or conditions of restitution.

(3) The offense or offenses that were sustained.

(4) The name and address of the parent or guardian of the minor.

(5) The rebuttable presumption that the parent or guardian is jointly and severally liable with the minor for the amount of restitution so ordered in accordance with Sections 1714.1 and 1714.3 of the Civil Code, up to the limits provided in those sections, and that the parent or guardian has the burden of showing by a preponderance of the evidence that the parent or guardian was either not given notice of potential liability for payment of restitution prior to the petition being sustained by an admission or adjudication, or that he or she was not present during the proceedings wherein the petition was sustained by an admission or adjudication and any hearings thereafter related to restitution.

(6) Whether the notice and presence requirements of paragraph (5) were met.

(7) The victim's rights to a certified copy of the order reflecting the information specified in this subdivision.

(c) The victim has a right, upon request, to a certified copy of the order reflecting the information specified in subdivision (b).

(d) This section does not apply to foster parents.

(e) Nothing in this section shall be construed to make an insurer liable for a loss caused by the willful act of the insured or the dependents of the insured pursuant to Section 533 of the Insurance Code. *(Added by Stats.1995, c. 313 (A.B.817), § 22, eff. Aug. 3, 1995. Amended by Stats.1996, c. 520 (A.B.3050), § 2; Stats.1998, c. 451 (S.B.2021), § 4, eff. Sept. 14, 1998.)*

Cross References

Hearing defined for purposes of this Article, see Welfare and Institutions Code § 727.4.

§ 730.8. Minors ordered to pay restitution; community service; compliance

(a) Except as provided in subdivision (b), the court shall require any minor who is ordered to pay restitution pursuant to Section 730.6, or to perform community service, to report to the court on his or her compliance with the court's restitution order or order for community service, or both, no less than annually until the order is fulfilled.

(b) For any minor committed to the Department of the Youth Authority, the department shall monitor the compliance with any order of the court that requires the minor to pay restitution. Upon the minor's discharge from the Department of the Youth Authority, the department shall notify the court regarding the minor's compliance with an order to pay restitution. *(Formerly § 730.7, added by Stats.1999, c. 996 (S.B.334), § 21. Renumbered § 730.8 and amended by Stats.2001, c. 854 (S.B.205), § 75.)*

Cross References

Juvenile court law, judgments and order, counseling, see Welfare and Institutions Code § 729.6.

§ 731. Commitment of ward of the court to Division of Juvenile Justice; term of confinement

(a) If a minor is adjudged a ward of the court on the grounds that the minor is a person described by Section 602, the court may commit the ward to the Department of Corrections and Rehabilitation, Division of Juvenile Justice if the ward has committed an offense described in subdivision (b) of Section 707 or subdivision (c) of Section 290.008 of the Penal Code, and has been the subject of a motion filed to transfer the ward to the jurisdiction of the criminal court as provided in subdivision (c) of Section 736.5 and is not otherwise ineligible for commitment to the division under Section 733.

(b) A ward committed to the Division of Juvenile Justice shall not be confined in excess of the term of confinement set by the committing court. The court shall set a maximum term based upon the facts and circumstances of the matter or matters that brought or continued the ward under the jurisdiction of the court and as deemed appropriate to achieve rehabilitation. The court shall not commit a ward to the Division of Juvenile Justice for a period that exceeds the middle term of imprisonment that could be imposed upon an adult convicted of the same offense. This subdivision does not limit the power of the Board of Juvenile Hearings to discharge a ward committed to the Division of Juvenile Justice pursuant to Sections 1719 and 1769. Upon discharge, the committing court may retain jurisdiction of the ward pursuant to Section 607.1 and establish the conditions of supervision pursuant to subdivision (b) of Section 1766.

(c) This section shall become operative on July 1, 2021, and shall remain in effect until the final closure of the Division of Juvenile Justice. *(Added by Stats.2021, c. 18 (S.B.92), § 8, eff. May 14, 2021, operative July 1, 2021.)*

Research References

West's California Judicial Council Forms JV–732, Commitment to the California Department of Corrections and Rehabilitation, Division of Juvenile Facilities (Also Available in Spanish).
1 Witkin California Criminal Law 4th Introduction to Crimes § 12 (2021), Increase in Punishment.
3 Witkin, California Criminal Law 4th Punishment § 86 (2021), Youth Authority Act.
3 Witkin, California Criminal Law 4th Punishment § 94 (2021), Treatment and Work.
3 Witkin, California Criminal Law 4th Punishment § 96 (2021), Constitutional Limitations.

§ 731.1. Recall of the commitment of a ward

(a) Notwithstanding any other law, the court committing a ward to the Department of Corrections and Rehabilitation, Division of Juvenile Facilities, upon the recommendation of the chief probation officer of the county, may recall that commitment in the case of any ward confined in an institution operated by the division. Upon recall of the ward, the court shall set and convene a recall disposition hearing for the purpose of ordering an alternative disposition for the ward that is appropriate under all of the circumstances prevailing in the case. The court shall provide to the division no less than 15 days advance notice of the recall hearing date, and the division shall transport and deliver the ward to the custody of the probation department of the committing county no less than five days prior to the scheduled date of the recall hearing. Pending the recall disposition hearing, the ward shall be supervised, detained, or housed in the manner and place, consistent with the requirements of law, as may be directed by the court in its order of recall. The timing and procedure of the recall disposition hearing shall be consistent with the rules, rights, and procedures applicable to delinquency disposition hearings, as described in Article 17 (commencing with Section 675).

(b) A court may also convene a recall disposition hearing, as specified in subdivision (a), regarding any ward who remains under parole supervision by the Division of Juvenile Parole Operations. *(Added by Stats.2007, c. 175 (S.B.81), § 20, eff. Aug. 24, 2007, operative Sept. 1, 2007. Amended by Stats.2007, c. 257 (A.B.191), § 3, eff. Sept. 29, 2007; Stats.2008, c. 699 (S.B.1241), § 27; Stats.2010, c. 729 (A.B.1628), § 11, eff. Oct. 19, 2010; Stats.2011, c. 36 (S.B.92), § 75, eff. June 30, 2011, operative Dec. 13, 2011.)*

Cross References

Department of Corrections, generally, see Penal Code § 5000 et seq.
Hearing defined for purposes of this Article, see Welfare and Institutions Code § 727.4.
Local Revenue Fund 2011, creation of fund, accounts, and subaccounts, use of moneys in Youthful Offender Block Grant Subaccount, see Government Code § 30025.
Probation officer or social worker defined for purposes of this Chapter, see Welfare and Institutions Code § 215.
Youthful Offender Block Grant Fund, allocation to eligible county for offenders subject to this section, determination, see Welfare and Institutions Code § 1956.

§ 731.2. Juvenile boot camp; pilot program; Fresno County

(a) The Department of the Youth Authority and Fresno County may enter into a partnership for the establishment and maintenance of a pilot program juvenile boot camp similar to the program described in Section 731.6, but developed primarily by the county with the Department of the Youth Authority and the county sharing the costs equally, except as specified in subdivision (b).

(b) Under the partnership, the Department of the Youth Authority shall bear all the costs of retrofitting a facility, which is to be provided by the county at county expense.

(c) The implementation of this pilot program shall be contingent upon the appropriation of funds to the Department of the Youth Authority for the pilot program in either the Budget Act of 1996 or subsequent legislation. *(Added by Stats.1994, c. 1055 (A.B.3246), § 1.)*

§ 731.5. Minor violating Section 490.5 of Penal Code; public services

In addition to the provisions of Section 731, if a minor's conduct constitutes a violation of Section 490.5 of the Penal Code, the court may require the minor to perform public services designated by the court. *(Added by Stats.1976, c. 1131, p. 5049, § 2.)*

§ 732. Conveyance to state or county institution

Before a minor is conveyed to any state or county institution pursuant to this article, it shall be ascertained from the superintendent thereof that such person can be received. *(Added by Stats.1961, c. 1616, p. 3487, § 2.)*

§ 733. Prohibited commitments to juvenile facilities division of Department of Corrections and Rehabilitation

A ward of the juvenile court who meets any condition described below shall not be committed to the Department of Corrections and Rehabilitation, Division of Juvenile Facilities:

(a) The ward is under 11 years of age.

(b) The ward is suffering from any contagious, infectious, or other disease that would probably endanger the lives or health of the other inmates of any facility.

(c) The ward has been or is adjudged a ward of the court pursuant to Section 602, and the most recent offense alleged in any petition and admitted or found to be true by the court is not described in subdivision (b) of Section 707 or subdivision (c) of Section 290.008 of the Penal Code. This subdivision shall be effective on and after September 1, 2007. *(Added by Stats.2007, c. 175 (S.B.81), § 22, eff. Aug. 24, 2007, operative Sept. 1, 2007. Amended by Stats.2008, c. 699 (S.B.1241), § 28; Stats.2012, c. 7 (A.B.324), § 2, eff. Feb. 29, 2012.)*

Cross References

Department of Corrections, generally, see Penal Code § 5000 et seq.
Local Revenue Fund 2011, creation of fund, accounts, and subaccounts, use of moneys in Youthful Offender Block Grant Subaccount, see Government Code § 30025.
Youthful Offender Block Grant Fund, allocation to each county for offenders subject to this section, distribution, see Welfare and Institutions Code § 1955.

§ 733.1. Prohibited commitments to Corrections and Rehabilitation, Division of Juvenile Justice

(a) Notwithstanding any other law, except as otherwise provided in this section, a ward of the juvenile court shall not be committed to the Department of Corrections and Rehabilitation, Division of Juvenile Justice on or after July 1, 2021.

(b) A court may commit a ward to the Department of Corrections and Rehabilitation, Division of Juvenile Justice as authorized in subdivision (c) of Section 736.5.

(c) Effective July 1, 2021, a person adjudged a ward of the court pursuant to Section 602, shall not be committed to the Department of Corrections and Rehabilitation, Division of Juvenile Justice, as long as allocations required by Section 1991 are authorized in statute and disbursed by September 1, 2021, and September 1 annually thereafter. To the extent that the allocations required by Section 1991 are not authorized in statute and disbursed annually thereafter, it is the intent of this section that wards adjudged wards of the court pursuant to Section 602 for an offense described in subdivision (b) of Section 707 of this code or subdivision (c) of Section 290.008 of the Penal Code may be committed to the Division of Juvenile Justice or, upon the final closure of the Division of Juvenile Justice, another state-funded facility, if the ward could have been committed to the Division of Juvenile Justice pursuant to Section 731, as that section read on January 1, 2021, and Sections 733, 734, and 736.5. For the purpose of determining the state's compliance with this subdivision, the presumption shall be that the state is meeting its commitment in Section 1991 if that section is not materially changed from the law in effect on the operative date of this section. *(Added by Stats.2020, c. 337 (S.B.823), § 29, eff. Sept. 30, 2020. Amended by Stats.2021, c. 18 (S.B.92), § 9, eff. May 14, 2021.)*

§ 734. Conditions of commitment to Youth Authority

No ward of the juvenile court shall be committed to the Youth Authority unless the judge of the court is fully satisfied that the mental and physical condition and qualifications of the ward are such as to render it probable that he will be benefited by the reformatory educational discipline or other treatment provided by the Youth Authority. *(Added by Stats.1961, c. 1616, p. 3487, § 2.)*

Cross References

Changing, modifying or setting aside order of commitment to Youth Authority, authority of court, see Welfare and Institutions Code § 779.

Return of minor from Youth Authority to committing court, see Welfare and Institutions Code § 780.

Youth Authority, generally, see Welfare and Institutions Code § 1700 et seq.

§ 735. Summary of facts accompanying commitment papers

Accompanying the commitment papers, the court shall send to the Director of the Youth Authority a summary of all the facts in the possession of the court, covering the history of the ward committed and a statement of the mental and physical condition of the ward. *(Added by Stats.1961, c. 1616, p. 3488, § 2.)*

Cross References

Case histories furnished to Youth Authority, see Welfare and Institutions Code § 1741.

§ 736. Acceptance of ward committed; determination of individuals best served by Division of Juvenile Facilities

(a) Except as provided in Section 733, the Department of Corrections and Rehabilitation, Division of Juvenile Facilities, shall accept a ward committed to it pursuant to this article if the Director of the Division of Juvenile Justice believes that the ward can be materially benefited by the division's reformatory and educational discipline, and if the division has adequate facilities, staff, and programs to provide that care. A ward subject to this section shall not be transported to any facility under the jurisdiction of the division until the superintendent of the facility has notified the committing court of the place to which that ward is to be transported and the time at which he or she can be received.

(b) To determine who is best served by the Division of Juvenile Facilities, and who would be better served by the State Department of State Hospitals, the Director of the Division of Juvenile Justice and the Director of State Hospitals shall, at least annually, confer and establish policy with respect to the types of cases that should be the responsibility of each department. *(Added by Stats.1961, c. 1616, p. 3488, § 2. Amended by Stats.1981, c. 714, p. 2807, § 463; Stats.2006, c. 257 (S.B.1742), § 1; Stats.2007, c. 175 (S.B.81), § 23, eff. Aug. 24, 2007, operative Sept. 1, 2007; Stats.2012, c. 24 (A.B.1470), § 60, eff. June 27, 2012; Stats.2012, c. 41 (S.B.1021), § 88, eff. June 27, 2012; Stats.2014, c. 442 (S.B.1465), § 13, eff. Sept. 18, 2014.)*

Cross References

Department of Corrections, generally, see Penal Code § 5000 et seq.

Order for care, supervision, custody, maintenance and support of dependent child, see Welfare and Institutions Code § 727.

§ 736.5. Closure of Division of Juvenile Justice within Department of Corrections and Rehabilitation; commitment of wards

(a) It is the intent of the Legislature to close the Division of Juvenile Justice within the Department of Corrections and Rehabilitation, through shifting responsibility for all youth adjudged a ward of the court, commencing July 1, 2021, to county governments and providing annual funding for county governments to fulfill this new responsibility.

(b) Beginning July 1, 2021, a ward shall not be committed to the Department of Corrections and Rehabilitation, Division of Juvenile Justice, except as described in subdivision (c).

(c) Pending the final closure of the Department of Corrections and Rehabilitation, Division of Juvenile Justice, a court may commit a ward who is otherwise eligible to be committed under existing law and in whose case a motion to transfer the minor from juvenile court to a court of criminal jurisdiction was filed. The court shall consider, as an alternative to commitment to the Division of Juvenile Justice, placement in local programs, including those established as a result of the implementation of Chapter 337 of the Statutes of 2020.

(d) All wards committed to the Department of Corrections and Rehabilitation, Division of Juvenile Justice prior to July 1, 2021 or pursuant to (c), shall remain within its custody until the ward is discharged, released or otherwise moved pursuant to law, or until final closure of the Division of Juvenile Justice.

(e) The Division of Juvenile Justice within the Department of Corrections and Rehabilitation shall close on June 30, 2023.

(f) The Director of the Division of Juvenile Justice shall develop a plan, by January 1, 2022, for the transfer of jurisdiction of youth remaining at the Division of Juvenile Justice who are unable to discharge or otherwise move pursuant to law prior to final closure on June 30, 2023. *(Added by Stats.2020, c. 337 (S.B.823), § 30, eff. Sept. 30, 2020. Amended by Stats.2021, c. 18 (S.B.92), § 10, eff. May 14, 2021.)*

Research References

1 Witkin California Criminal Law 4th Crimes Against the Person § 57 (2021), Assault or Battery Against Nonprisoner.

1 Witkin California Criminal Law 4th Crimes Against the Person § 63 (2021), Confined in State Prison.

4 Witkin, California Criminal Law 4th Introduction to Criminal Procedure § 50 (2021), Comprehensive Planning Agencies.

3 Witkin, California Criminal Law 4th Punishment § 6 (2021), Department of Corrections and Rehabilitation.

3 Witkin, California Criminal Law 4th Punishment § 8 (2021), Division of Juvenile Justice.

3 Witkin, California Criminal Law 4th Punishment § 13 (2021), Inspector General.

3 Witkin, California Criminal Law 4th Punishment § 86 (2021), Youth Authority Act.

3 Witkin, California Criminal Law 4th Punishment § 87 (2021), Persons Eligible for Commitment.
3 Witkin, California Criminal Law 4th Punishment § 88 (2021), Persons Ineligible for Commitment.
3 Witkin, California Criminal Law 4th Punishment § 89 (2021), Trial Court's Discretion.
3 Witkin, California Criminal Law 4th Punishment § 90 (2021), Factors to be Considered.
3 Witkin, California Criminal Law 4th Punishment § 92 (2021), Division's Acceptance of Commitment.
3 Witkin, California Criminal Law 4th Punishment § 93 (2021), Institutions and Facilities.
3 Witkin, California Criminal Law 4th Punishment § 96 (2021), Constitutional Limitations.
3 Witkin, California Criminal Law 4th Punishment § 97 (2021), Extended Detention.
3 Witkin, California Criminal Law 4th Punishment § 99 (2021), Probation and Parole.
3 Witkin, California Criminal Law 4th Punishment § 137 (2021), In General.
3 Witkin, California Criminal Law 4th Punishment § 151 (2021), Other Means of Disclosure.
3 Witkin, California Criminal Law 4th Punishment § 251 (2021), Scope of Prohibition: Particular Commitments.
3 Witkin, California Criminal Law 4th Punishment § 311 (2021), Commitment to Juvenile Facility.
3 Witkin, California Criminal Law 4th Punishment § 341 (2021), When Statement is Required.
3 Witkin, California Criminal Law 4th Punishment § 342 (2021), When Statement is Not Required.
3 Witkin, California Criminal Law 4th Punishment § 483 (2021), Juveniles and Youthful Offenders.

§ 737. Detention until execution of commitment order; review of detention of minor; reasonable delay

(a) Whenever a person has been adjudged a ward of the juvenile court and has been committed or otherwise disposed of as provided in this chapter for the care of wards of the juvenile court, the court may order that the ward be detained until the execution of the order of commitment or of other disposition.

(b) In any case in which a minor or nonminor is detained for more than 15 days pending the execution of the order of commitment or of any other disposition, the court shall periodically review the case to determine whether the delay is reasonable. These periodic reviews shall occur at a hearing held at least every 15 days, commencing from the time the minor or nonminor was initially detained pending the execution of the order of commitment or of any other disposition. Prior to the hearing, the probation officer shall contact appropriate placements in order to identify specific, appropriate, and available placements for the minor or nonminor. During the course of each review, the court shall inquire regarding the action taken by the probation department to carry out its order, the reasons for the delay, and the effect of the delay upon the minor or nonminor. The probation department shall explain to the court what steps have been taken to identify an appropriate placement for the minor or nonminor.

(c)(1) A court shall not consider any of the following to be a reasonable delay:

(A) The probation officer's inability to identify a specific, appropriate, and available placement for the minor or nonminor when the court finds that the probation officer has not made reasonable efforts to identify a specific, appropriate, and available placement for the minor or nonminor.

(B) A delay caused by administrative processes, including, but not limited to, the workload of county personnel, transfer or reassignment of a case, or the availability of reports or records.

(C) A delay in convening any meetings between agencies. For purposes of this paragraph, "agency" has the same meaning as defined in Section 727.

(2) This subdivision does not preclude the court from determining that any other delay is not reasonable, including, but not limited to, in the case of a minor or nonminor who was previously adjudged to be a dependent child of the court and was in foster care at the time the petition was filed pursuant to Section 601 or 602, if the probation officer does not identify a specific, appropriate, and available placement for the minor or nonminor in the case plan described in Section 706.6 upon the court issuing its orders pursuant to paragraph (3) of subdivision (a) of Section 727, unless the probation officer provides documentation that his or her efforts to find an appropriate placement were reasonable.

(d)(1) If the court finds the delay to be unreasonable, the court shall order the probation officer to assess the availability of any suitable temporary placements or other alternatives to continued detention of the minor or nonminor in a secure setting. The court may order that the minor or nonminor be placed in a suitable and available temporary nonsecure placement or alternative to continued detention after consultation with all interested parties present at the hearing, including the probation officer, the minor or nonminor, the family of the minor or nonminor, and other providers of services. In addition to the orders authorized by this subdivision, the court may issue any other orders or relief pursuant to its authority under paragraph (1) of subdivision (a) of Section 727.

(2) The court shall continue to periodically review the case, pursuant to subdivision (b), until the execution of the order of commitment or of other disposition.

(e) It is the intent of the Legislature, in amending this section in the 2013–14 Regular Session, that minors and nonminors are to be released to their court-ordered dispositions expeditiously, and that any unreasonable periods of detention must be eliminated because they are not in the best interests of the minor or nonminor. *(Added by Stats.1961, c. 1616, p. 3488, § 2. Amended by Stats.1971, c. 1543, p. 3051, § 2; Stats.1976, c. 1068, p. 4792, § 61; Stats.1983, c. 101, § 164; Stats.2014, c. 615 (A.B.2607), § 2, eff. Jan. 1, 2015.)*

Cross References

Detention home as meaning juvenile hall, see Welfare and Institutions Code § 850.
Jail defined for purposes of this Chapter, see Welfare and Institutions Code § 207.1.
Order for care, supervision, custody, maintenance and support of dependent child, see Welfare and Institutions Code § 727.

§ 738. Nonresident wards of the juvenile court

In a case where the residence of a minor placed on probation under the provisions of Section 725 or of a ward of the juvenile court is out of the state and in another state or foreign country, or in a case where such minor is a resident of this state but his parents, relatives, guardian, or person charged with his custody is in another state, the court may order such minor sent to his parents, relatives, or guardian, or to the person charged with his custody, or, if the minor is a resident of a foreign country, to an official of a juvenile court of such foreign country or an agency of such country authorized to accept the minor, and in such case may order transportation and accommodation furnished, with or without an attendant, as the court deems necessary. If the court deems an attendant necessary, the court may order the probation officer or other suitable person to serve as such attendant. The probation officer shall authorize the necessary expenses of such minor and of the attendant and claims therefor shall be audited, allowed and paid in the same manner as other county claims. *(Added by Stats.1961, c. 1616, p. 3488, § 2. Amended by Stats.1976, c. 1068, p. 4792, § 62.)*

Cross References

County claims, generally, see Government Code § 29700 et seq.
Determination of minor's residence, see Welfare and Institutions Code § 17.1; Government Code § 244.
Probation officer or social worker defined for purposes of this Chapter, see Welfare and Institutions Code § 215.
Relative defined for purposes of this Article, see Welfare and Institutions Code § 727.4.

Residence as determining court's jurisdiction, see Welfare and Institutions Code §§ 651, 652.

§ 739. Medical, surgical or dental care; recommendation of physician and surgeon; court order; release of information; right to refuse care

(a) Upon referral to the probation officer of a minor who has been taken into temporary custody under Section 625, the probation officer may authorize a medical examination that complies with regulations adopted by the Corrections Standards Authority. If the minor is retained in custody by the probation officer, and prior to the court detention hearing required under Section 632, the probation officer may authorize medical or dental treatment or care based on the written recommendation of the examining physician and considered necessary for the health of the minor. No treatment or care under this subdivision may be authorized by the probation officer unless the probation officer has made a reasonable effort to notify and to obtain the consent of the parent, guardian, or person standing in loco parentis for the minor, and, if the parent, guardian, or person standing in loco parentis objects, the treatment or care shall be given only upon order of the court in the exercise of its discretion. The probation officer shall document the efforts made to notify and obtain parental consent under this subdivision and shall enter this information into the case file for the minor.

(b) Whenever it appears to the juvenile court that any person concerning whom a petition has been filed with the court is in need of medical, surgical, dental, or other remedial care, and that there is no parent, guardian, or person standing in loco parentis capable of authorizing or willing to authorize the remedial care or treatment for that person, the court, upon the written recommendation of a licensed physician and surgeon or, if the person needs dental care, a licensed dentist, and after due notice to the parent, guardian, or person standing in loco parentis, if any, may make an order authorizing the performance of the necessary medical, surgical, dental, or other remedial care for that person.

(c) Whenever a person is placed by order of the juvenile court within the care and custody or under the supervision of the probation officer of the county in which the person resides and it appears to the court that there is no parent, guardian, or person standing in loco parentis capable of authorizing or willing to authorize medical, surgical, dental, or other remedial care or treatment for the person, the court may, after due notice to the parent, guardian, or person standing in loco parentis, if any, order that the probation officer may authorize the medical, surgical, dental, or other remedial care for the person by licensed practitioners, as may from time to time appear necessary.

(d)(1) Whenever it appears that a minor otherwise within subdivision (a), (b), or (c) requires immediate emergency medical, surgical, or other remedial care in an emergency situation, that care may be provided by a licensed physician and surgeon or, if the minor needs dental care in an emergency situation, by a licensed dentist, without a court order and upon authorization of a probation officer. If the minor needs foot or ankle care within the scope of practice of podiatric medicine, as defined in Section 2472 of the Business and Professions Code, a probation officer may authorize the care to be provided by a podiatrist after obtaining the advice and concurrence of a physician and surgeon. The probation officer shall make reasonable efforts to obtain the consent of, or to notify, the parent, guardian, or person standing in loco parentis prior to authorizing emergency medical, surgical, dental, or other remedial care.

(2) For purposes of this subdivision, "emergency situation" means a minor requires immediate treatment for the alleviation of severe pain or an immediate diagnosis and treatment of an unforeseeable medical, surgical, dental, or other remedial condition or contagious disease that, if not immediately diagnosed and treated, would lead to serious disability or death. An emergency situation also includes known conditions or illnesses that, during any period of secure detention of the minor by the probation officer, require immediate laboratory testing, medication, or treatment to prevent an imminent and severe or life- threatening risk to the health of the minor.

(e) In any case in which the court orders the performance of any medical, surgical, dental, or other remedial care pursuant to this section, the court may also make an order authorizing the release of information concerning that care to probation officers, parole officers, or any other qualified individuals or agencies caring for or acting in the interest and welfare of the minor under order, commitment, or approval of the court.

(f) Nothing in this section shall be construed as limiting the right of a parent, guardian, or person standing in loco parentis, who has not been deprived of the custody or control of the minor by order of the court, in providing any medical, surgical, dental, or other remedial treatment recognized or permitted under the laws of this state.

(g) The parent of any person described in this section may authorize the performance of medical, surgical, dental, or other remedial care provided for in this section notwithstanding his or her age or marital status. In nonemergency situations the parent authorizing the care shall notify the other parent prior to the administration of the care.

(h) Nothing in this section shall be construed to interfere with a minor's right to authorize or refuse medical, surgical, dental, or other care when the minor's consent for care is sufficient or specifically required pursuant to existing law, or to interfere with a minor's right to refuse, verbally or in writing, nonemergency medical and mental health care. *(Added by Stats.1961, c. 1616, p. 3489, § 2. Amended by Stats.1968, c. 629, p. 1313, § 1; Stats.1971, c. 640, p. 1259, § 5; Stats.1972, c. 1021, p. 1892, § 1; Stats.1974, c. 745, p. 1652, § 1; Stats.1975, c. 1129, p. 2773, § 2; Stats.1976, c. 654, p. 1619, § 1; Stats.1976, c. 1068, p. 4792, § 63; Stats.1990, c. 566 (A.B.2193), § 2; Stats.1992, c. 981 (S.B.1968), § 10; Stats.2011, c. 256 (S.B.913), § 1.)*

Cross References

Expense of support of wards and dependent children, see Welfare and Institutions Code § 900 et seq.

Probation officer or social worker defined for purposes of this Chapter, see Welfare and Institutions Code § 215.

Reasonable efforts defined for purposes of this Article, see Welfare and Institutions Code § 727.4.

§ 739.5. Psychotropic medications; authorization based on physician request; adoption of rules and forms for implementation of section; agency completion of request; time for decision on request

(a)(1) If a minor who has been adjudged a ward of the court under Section 601 or 602 is removed from the physical custody of the parent under Section 726 and placed into foster care, as defined in Section 727.4, only a juvenile court judicial officer shall have authority to make orders regarding the administration of psychotropic medications for that minor. The juvenile court may issue a specific order delegating this authority to a parent upon making findings on the record that the parent poses no danger to the minor and has the capacity to authorize psychotropic medications. Court authorization for the administration of psychotropic medication shall be based on a request from a physician, indicating the reasons for the request, a description of the minor's diagnosis and behavior, the expected results of the medication, and a description of any side effects of the medication.

(2)(A) The Judicial Council shall amend and adopt rules of court and develop appropriate forms for the implementation of this section, in consultation with the State Department of Social Services, the State Department of Health Care Services, and stakeholders, including, but not limited to, the County Welfare Directors Association of California, the County Behavioral Health Directors Association of California, the Chief Probation Officers of California, associations representing current and former foster children, caregivers, and minor's attorneys. This effort shall be undertaken in coordination with the updates required under paragraph (2) of subdivision (a) of Section 369.5.

(B) The rules of court and forms developed pursuant to subparagraph (A) shall address all of the following:

(i) The minor and the minor's caregiver and court-appointed special advocate, if any, have an opportunity to provide input on the medications being prescribed.

(ii) Information regarding the minor's overall mental health assessment and treatment plan is provided to the court.

(iii) Information regarding the rationale for the proposed medication, provided in the context of past and current treatment efforts, is provided to the court. This information shall include, but not be limited to, information on other pharmacological and nonpharmacological treatments that have been utilized and the minor's response to those treatments, a discussion of symptoms not alleviated or ameliorated by other current or past treatment efforts, and an explanation of how the psychotropic medication being prescribed is expected to improve the minor's symptoms.

(iv) Guidance is provided to the court on how to evaluate the request for authorization, including how to proceed if information, otherwise required to be included in a request for authorization under this section, is not included in a request for authorization submitted to the court.

(C) The rules of court and forms developed pursuant to subparagraph (A) shall include a process for periodic oversight by the court of orders regarding the administration of psychotropic medications that includes the caregiver's and minor's observations regarding the effectiveness of the medication and side effects, information on medication management appointments and other followup appointments with medical practitioners, and information on the delivery of other mental health treatments that are a part of the minor's overall treatment plan. This oversight process shall be conducted in conjunction with other regularly scheduled court hearings and reports provided to the court by the county probation agency.

(D)(i) By September 1, 2020, the forms developed pursuant to subparagraph (A) shall include a request for authorization by the minor or the minor's attorney to release the minor's medical information to the Medical Board of California in order to ascertain whether there is excessive prescribing of psychotropic medication that is inconsistent with the standard of care described in Section 2245 of the Business and Professions Code. The authorization shall be limited to medical information relevant to the investigation of the prescription of psychotropic medication, and the information may only be used for the purpose set forth in this subparagraph and Section 2245 of the Business and Professions Code.

(ii) The Medical Board of California or its representative shall request the medical information obtained pursuant to this section to be sealed if the medical information is admitted as an exhibit in an administrative hearing pursuant to Chapter 5 (commencing with Section 11500) of Part 1 of Division 3 of Title 2 of the Government Code.

(b)(1) The agency that completes the request for authorization for the administration of psychotropic medication is encouraged to complete the request within three business days of receipt from the physician of the information necessary to fully complete the request.

(2) Nothing in this subdivision is intended to change current local practice or local court rules with respect to the preparation and submission of requests for authorization for the administration of psychotropic medication.

(c)(1) Within seven court days from receipt by the court of a completed request, the juvenile court judicial officer shall either approve or deny in writing a request for authorization for the administration of psychotropic medication to the minor, or shall, upon a request by the parent, the legal guardian, or the minor's attorney, or upon its own motion, set the matter for hearing.

(2)(A) Notwithstanding Section 827 or any other law, upon the approval or denial by the juvenile court judicial officer of a request for authorization for the administration of psychotropic medication, the county probation agency or other person or entity who submitted the request shall provide a copy of the court order approving or denying the request to the minor's caregiver.

(B) If the court approves the request, the copy of the order shall include the last two pages of form JV–220(A) or the last two pages of JV–220(B) and all medication information sheets that were attached to form JV–220(A) or form JV–220(B), which are all referenced in Rule 5.640 of the California Rules of Court.

(C) If the child changes placement, the social worker or probation officer shall provide the new caregiver with a copy of the order, including the last two pages of form JV–220(A) or the last two pages of JV–220(B), and the medication information sheets that were attached to form JV–220(A) or form JV–220(B), which are all referenced in Rule 5.640 of the California Rules of Court.

(d) Psychotropic medication or psychotropic drugs are those medications administered for the purpose of affecting the central nervous system to treat psychiatric disorders or illnesses. These medications include, but are not limited to, anxiolytic agents, antidepressants, mood stabilizers, antipsychotic medications, anti-Parkinson agents, hypnotics, medications for dementia, and psychostimulants.

(e) Nothing in this section is intended to supersede local court rules regarding a minor's right to participate in mental health decisions.

(f) This section does not apply to nonminor dependents, as defined in subdivision (v) of Section 11400. *(Added by Stats.2007, c. 120 (A.B.1514), § 1. Amended by Stats.2015, c. 534 (S.B.238), § 6, eff. Jan. 1, 2016; Stats.2019, c. 547 (S.B.377), § 2, eff. Jan. 1, 2020; Stats.2022, c. 812 (S.B.528), § 2, eff. Jan. 1, 2023.)*

Cross References

Children in group home, use of psychotropic medicines as authorized pursuant to this section, see Health and Safety Code § 1507.6.

Writing defined, see Welfare and Institutions Code § 8.

Research References

West's California Judicial Council Forms JV–216, Order Delegating Judicial Authority Over Over Psychotropic Medication.

West's California Judicial Council Forms JV–217–INFO, Guide to Psychotropic Medication Forms (Also Available in Spanish).

West's California Judicial Council Forms JV–220, Application for Psychotropic Medication.

West's California Judicial Council Forms JV–220(A), Physician'S Statement—Attachment.

West's California Judicial Council Forms JV–220(B), Physician's Request to Continue Medication--Attachment.

West's California Judicial Council Forms JV–223, Order on Application for Psychotropic Medication (Also Available in Spanish).

West's California Judicial Council Forms JV–224, County Report on Psychotropic Medication.

West's California Judicial Council Forms JV–228, Position on Release of Information to Medical Board of California.

West's California Judicial Council Forms JV–228–INFO, Background on Release of Information to Medical Board of California.

West's California Judicial Council Forms JV–229, Withdrawal of Release of Information to Medical Board of California.

§ 739.6. Psychotropic medications; record review for all authorization requests

(a)(1) The State Department of Social Services, in consultation with the State Department of Health Care Services, shall contract for child psychiatry services to complete a record review for all authorization requests for psychotropic medications for which a second opinion review is requested by a county. The second opinion review shall occur within three business days of the county request and shall include discussion of the psychosocial interventions that have been or will be offered to the child and caretaker, if appropriate, to address the behavioral health needs of the child.

(2)(A) Recommended indicators for identifying those requests for authorizations of psychotropic medications for which a county may request a second opinion record review may include, but are not limited to, prescriptions for concurrent psychotropic medications, dosages that exceed recommended guidelines for use in children, off-label prescribing, and requests for psychotropic medication usage without any other concurrent psychosocial services.

(B) The State Department of Social Services shall, by July 1, 2018, issue guidance regarding the second opinion review process and may periodically revise that guidance following consultation with counties, other state departments, advocates for children and youth, and other stakeholders.

(3) The child psychiatry services contracted for by the State Department of Social Services shall be available to provide second opinion reviews to those counties that do not have a second opinion review program. This section does not prohibit a county from operating its own second opinion review program and does not supersede any county-operated second opinion review program.

(4) This section does not prevent the administration of medication in an emergency, as otherwise authorized or required by law or regulation.

(b) The State Department of Health Care Services shall seek any necessary federal approvals to obtain federal financial participation for the second opinion review service pursuant to this section, including any approvals necessary to obtain enhanced federal financial participation as applicable. Notwithstanding any other law, this section shall be implemented only if, and to the extent that, any necessary federal approvals are obtained by the department and federal financial participation is available and is not otherwise jeopardized. *(Added by Stats.2017, c. 24 (S.B.89), § 12, eff. June 27, 2017.)*

§ 740. Minors adjudged ward of court on basis of being person described in § 602 and placed in community care facility; conditions allowing placement other than in county of residence; notice and documentation requirements; plan of supervision and visitation; formal agreements; disclosure of felony offenses of minor; review of placement decisions; payment of costs

(a) Any minor adjudged to be a ward of the court on the basis that he or she is a person described in Section 602 and who is placed in a community care facility shall be placed in a community care facility within his or her county of residence, unless both of the following apply:

(1) He or she has identifiable needs requiring specialized care that cannot be provided in a local facility or his or her needs dictate physical separation from his or her family.

(2) The county of residence agrees to pay the placement county the costs of providing services to the minor, pursuant to Section 1566.25 of the Health and Safety Code.

(b)(1) Before the placement of a minor adjudged to be a ward of the court on the basis that he or she is a person described in Section 602 in any community care facility outside the ward's county of residence, the probation officer of the county making the placement, or in the case of a ward of the Department of Corrections and Rehabilitation, Division of Juvenile Facilities, the parole officer in charge of his or her case, shall send, via mail, delivery, fax, or electronically, written notice of the placement, including the name of the ward, the juvenile record of the ward (including any known prior offenses), and the ward's county of residence, to the probation officer of the county in which the community care facility is located. It is the intention of the Legislature, in regard to this requirement, that the probation officer of the county making the placement, or in the case of a ward of the Department of Corrections and Rehabilitation, Division of Juvenile Facilities, the parole officer in charge of his or her case, shall make his or her best efforts to send, via mail, fax, or electronically, or to hand deliver, the notice at least 24 hours prior to the time the placement is made. When that placement is terminated, the probation officer of the county making the placement, or in the case of a ward of the Department of Corrections and Rehabilitation, Division of Juvenile Facilities, the parole officer in charge of his or her case, shall send notice thereof to any person or agency receiving notification of the placement.

(2) When it has been determined that it is necessary for a ward whose board and care is funded through the Aid to Families with Dependent Children–Foster Care program to be placed in a county other than the ward's parents' or guardians' county of residence, the specific reason the out-of-county placement is necessary shall be documented in the ward's case plan. If the reason is lack of resources in the sending county to meet the specific needs of the ward, those specific resources needs shall be documented in the case plan.

(3) When it has been determined that a ward whose board and care is funded through the Aid to Families with Dependent Children–Foster Care program is to be placed out-of-county and that the sending county is to maintain responsibility for supervision and visitation of the ward, the sending county shall develop a plan of supervision and visitation activities to be performed, and shall specify that the sending county is responsible for performing those activities. In addition to the plan of supervision and visitation, the sending county shall document information regarding known or suspected gang affiliation or dangerous behavior of the ward that indicates the ward may pose a safety concern in the receiving county. The sending county shall send to the receiving county a copy of the plan of supervision and visitation, in addition to the notice of placement required in paragraph (1), prior to placement of the ward. If placement occurs on a holiday or weekend, the plan of supervision and visitation and the notice of placement shall be provided to the receiving county on or before the end of the next business day.

(4) When it has been determined that a ward whose placement is funded through the Aid to Families with Dependent Children–Foster Care program is to be placed out-of-county and the sending county plans that the receiving county shall be responsible for the supervision and visitation of the ward, the sending county shall develop a formal agreement between the sending and receiving counties. The formal agreement shall specify the supervision and visitation to be provided the ward, and shall specify that the receiving county is responsible for providing the supervision and visitation. The formal agreement shall be approved and signed by the sending and receiving counties prior to placement of the ward in the receiving county. Additionally, the notice of placement required by paragraph (1) shall be provided to the receiving county prior to placement of the ward in that county. Upon completion of the case plan, the sending county shall provide a copy of the completed case plan to the receiving county. The case plan shall include information regarding known or suspected gang affiliation or dangerous behavior of the ward that indicates the ward may pose a safety concern for the receiving county.

(5) The probation department of a receiving county that has a group home in which a minor is placed by the probation department of another county, after adjudication of the minor for any felony offense, may disclose to the sheriff of the receiving county or to the municipal police department of the city in which the group home is located, the name of the minor, the felony offense or offenses for which the minor has been adjudicated, and the address of the group home. This information shall be utilized only for law enforcement purposes and may not be utilized in a manner that is inconsistent with the rehabilitative program in which the minor has been placed or with the progress the minor may be making in the placement program. Notwithstanding any other law, the information provided by the probation department to a law enforcement agency under this

paragraph may be provided to other law enforcement personnel for the limited law enforcement purposes described in this paragraph, but shall otherwise remain confidential.

(c) Notwithstanding subdivision (e) of Section 1538.5 of the Health and Safety Code, at the request of the probation department of the county in which the group home facility is located, the group home shall notify a probation official designated by the probation department to receive notifications pursuant to this subdivision, of unusual incidents concerning a ward placed by the sending county that involved a response by local law enforcement or emergency services personnel, including runaway incidents. The notification shall include identifying information about the ward. A group home facility shall notify the designated probation official of a requesting probation department of an unusual incident no later than the applicable deadline imposed by law or department regulation for a group home facility to notify the licensing agency of the unusual incident. The requesting probation department shall maintain the confidentiality of any identifying information about the ward contained in the notification and shall not share, transfer, or otherwise release the identifying information to a third party unless otherwise authorized by state or federal law.

(d) A minor, the parent or guardian of a minor, and counsel representing a minor or the parent or guardian of a minor may petition the juvenile court for the review of a placement decision concerning the minor made by the probation officer pursuant to subdivision (a). The petition shall state the petitioner's relationship to the minor and shall set forth in concise language the grounds on which the review is sought. The court shall order that a hearing shall be held on the petition and shall give prior notice, or cause prior notice to be given, to the persons and by the means prescribed by Section 776, and, in instances in which the means of giving notice is not prescribed by that section, then by any means as the court prescribes.

(e) If a minor is placed in a community care facility out of his or her county of residence and is then arrested and placed in juvenile hall pending a jurisdictional hearing, the county of residence shall pay to the probation department of the county of placement all reasonable costs resulting directly from the minor's stay in the juvenile hall, provided that these costs exceed one hundred dollars ($100).

(f) If, as a result of the hearing in subdivision (d), the minor is remanded back to his or her county of residence, the county of residence shall pay to the probation department of the county of placement, in addition to any payment made pursuant to subdivision (e), all reasonable costs resulting directly from transporting the minor to the county of residency, provided that these costs exceed one hundred dollars ($100).

(g) Claims made by the probation department in the county of placement to the county of residence, pursuant to subdivisions (e) and (f), shall be paid within 30 days of the submission of these claims and the probation department in the county of placement shall bear the remaining expense.

(h) As used in this section:

(1) "Community care facility" shall be defined as provided in Section 1502 of the Health and Safety Code.

(2) "Gang affiliation" shall have the same meaning as defined for data entry into the CalGang system.

(3) "Group home" has the same meaning as provided in paragraph (1) of subdivision (g) of Section 80001 of Title 22 of the California Code of Regulations. *(Added by Stats.1984, c. 821, § 3. Amended by Stats.1991, c. 1202 (S.B.377), § 20; Stats.1992, c. 427 (A.B.3355), § 177; Stats.1992, c. 1153 (S.B.1573), § 6; Stats.1993, c. 1089 (A.B.2129), § 8; Stats.2004, c. 375 (A.B.1948), § 1; Stats.2005, c. 22 (S.B.1108), § 217; Stats.2009, c. 46 (S.B.352), § 4.)*

Cross References

California Community Care Facilities Act, community care facilities for wards of the juvenile court, out-of-county placements, see Health and Safety Code § 1567.3.

Felonies, definition and penalties, see Penal Code §§ 17, 18.

Foster care defined for purposes of this Article, see Welfare and Institutions Code § 727.4.

Hearing defined for purposes of this Article, see Welfare and Institutions Code § 727.4.

Probation officer or social worker defined for purposes of this Chapter, see Welfare and Institutions Code § 215.

§ 740.1. Arrest and remand to county of residence; return to placement county

(a) Any minor adjudged to be a ward of the court on the basis that he or she is a person described in Section 602 of the Welfare and Institutions Code and who is placed in a community care facility outside his or her county of residence who is then arrested and after receiving a jurisdictional hearing is remanded back to his or her county of residence shall not be placed back into the placement county without the testimony and documentation or request, if any, from the placement county pursuant to subdivision (b).

(b) The placement county may provide to the juvenile court relevant testimony and documentation pertaining to the ward's conduct while residing in the placement county, and may request that the ward not be returned to the placement county.

(c) "Community care facility," as used in this section, shall be defined as provided in Section 1502 of the Health and Safety Code. *(Added by Stats.1992, c. 1153 (S.B.1573), § 7.)*

Cross References

Hearing defined for purposes of this Article, see Welfare and Institutions Code § 727.4.

§ 741. Services of psychiatrists, psychologists, and other medical and clinical experts; costs for diagnosis or treatment due to, or related to, drug or alcohol use

The juvenile court may, in any case before it in which a petition has been filed as provided in Article 16 (commencing with Section 650), order that the probation officer obtain the services of such psychiatrists, psychologists, physicians and surgeons, dentists, optometrists, audiologists, or other clinical experts as may be required to assist in determining the appropriate treatment of the minor and as may be required in the conduct or implementation of the treatment. Payment for the services shall be a charge against the county.

Whenever diagnosis or treatment pursuant to this section is due to, or related to, drug or alcohol use, the cost thereof shall be considered for the use of funds made available to the county from state or federal sources for the purpose of providing care and treatment for drug- and alcohol-related illness or for drug or alcohol abuse. *(Added by Stats.1961, c. 1616, p. 3489, § 2. Amended by Stats.1976, c. 1068, p. 4794, § 64; Stats.1985, c. 101, § 1; Stats.1991, c. 482 (A.B.124), § 3, eff. Oct. 4, 1991.)*

Cross References

Mental health evaluations, recommendations, and dispositional procedures for minors, see Welfare and Institutions Code § 710 et seq.

Probation officer or social worker defined for purposes of this Chapter, see Welfare and Institutions Code § 215.

§ 742. Informing alleged victim of crime of final disposition upon request; restitution; victim impact programs

(a) Upon the request of an alleged victim of a crime, the probation officer shall, within 60 days of the final disposition of a case within which a petition has been filed pursuant to Section 602, inform that person by letter of the final disposition of the case. "Final disposition" means dismissal, acquittal, or findings made pursuant to this article. If the court orders that restitution shall be made to the victim of a crime, the amount, terms, and conditions thereof shall be included in the information provided pursuant to this section.

(b) In any case in which a petition has been filed pursuant to Section 602, the probation officer shall inform the victim of the offense, if any, of any victim-offender conferencing program or victim impact class available in the county, and of his or her right pursuant to subdivision (a) to be informed of the final disposition of the case, including his or her right, if any, to victim restitution, as permitted by law. *(Added by Stats.1976, c. 1070, p. 4813, § 4. Amended by Stats.1981, c. 447, p. 1696, § 1; Stats.1998, c. 761 (S.B.2074), § 2.)*

Cross References

Probation officer or social worker defined for purposes of this Chapter, see Welfare and Institutions Code § 215.

ARTICLE 18.5. GRAFFITI REMOVAL AND DAMAGE RECOVERY PROGRAM

Section

§ 742.10. Legislative intent

It is the intent of the Legislature in enacting this article to accomplish the following purposes:

(a) To assist public and private owners and possessors of property defaced by minors with graffiti or other inscribed material to recover their full damages.

(b) To safeguard the fiscal integrity of cities and counties that expend public funds to remove graffiti and other material inscribed by minors from public or private property, or to repair or replace public or private property defaced by minors with graffiti or other inscribed material, by enabling those cities and counties to recoup the full costs of that removal, repair, and replacement.

(c) To safeguard the fiscal integrity of cities and counties by enabling them to recoup the law enforcement costs of identifying and apprehending minors who deface the property of others with graffiti or other inscribed material.

(d) To minimize the costs of collecting those costs and damages.

(e) To discourage the inscription of graffiti and other material by minors by requiring the offending minors, and their parents who have the financial ability to do so, to bear the costs associated with the unlawful defacement of property with graffiti or other inscribed material.

(f) To retain in the juvenile court the discretion needed to accomplish the goal of rehabilitating minors. *(Added by Stats.1994, c. 909 (S.B.1779), § 11.)*

Cross References

Graffiti or other inscribed material defined for purposes of this Article, see Welfare and Institutions Code § 742.12.

§ 742.12. Definitions

(a) As used in this article, the term "graffiti or other inscribed material" includes any unauthorized inscription, word, figure, mark, or design that is written, marked, etched, scratched, drawn, or painted on real or personal property.

(b) As used in subdivision (d) of Section 742.16, the word "custody" means either legal custody or physical custody of a minor. *(Added by Stats.1994, c. 909 (S.B.1779), § 11.)*

§ 742.14. Recoupment of defacement costs by probation officer; ordinance

(a) A city, county, or city and county may elect, by ordinance, to have the probation officer of the county recoup for it, through juvenile court proceedings in accordance with Section 742.16, its costs associated with defacement by minors of its property and the property of others by graffiti or other inscribed material. That ordinance shall include the cost finding or findings specified in subdivision (b), and if the city, county, or city and county enacts an ordinance pursuant to Section 53069.3 of the Government Code, the cost findings specified in subdivision (c). These cost findings shall be reviewed at least once every three years, at which time the city, county, or city and county, by resolution, shall adopt updated cost findings in accordance with subdivisions (b) and (c). A city, county, or city and county may rescind, by ordinance, its election to have the probation officer recoup its costs pursuant to this section. Immediately after adoption, the city or county shall cause a certified copy of an ordinance adopted pursuant to this subdivision and any resolution containing updated cost findings to be forwarded to the clerk of the juvenile court in the county and to the probation officer of the county.

(b) A city, county, or city and county that adopts an ordinance pursuant to subdivision (a) shall include therein a finding or findings, to be reviewed at least once every three years, of the average costs per unit of measure incurred by the law enforcement agency with primary jurisdiction in the city, county, or city and county in identifying and apprehending a person subsequently convicted of violation of Section 594, 594.3, 594.4, 640.5, 640.6, or 640.7 of the Penal Code or a minor subsequently found to be a person described in Section 602 by reason of the commission of an act prohibited by Section 594, 594.3, 594.4, 640.5, 640.6, or 640.7 of the Penal Code. A city, county, or city and county that does not adopt an ordinance pursuant to subdivision (a) may adopt an ordinance containing the cost finding or findings described in this subdivision. Findings of costs per unit of measure may include, but are not limited to, findings of the hourly costs of employee time and of the costs per mile of operating patrol vehicles.

(c) If a city, county, or city and county enacts an ordinance pursuant to Section 53069.3 of the Government Code and enacts an ordinance pursuant to subdivision (a), the ordinance enacted pursuant to subdivision (a) shall contain findings, to be reviewed at least once every three years, of the average cost to the city, county, or city and county per unit of measure of removing graffiti and other inscribed material, and of repairing and replacing property of the types frequently defaced with graffiti or other inscribed material that cannot be removed cost effectively. A city, county, or city and county that does not adopt an ordinance pursuant to subdivision (a) may adopt an ordinance containing the cost findings described in this subdivision. Findings of costs per unit of measure may include, but are not limited to, findings of the costs per square inch of removing painted graffiti or of the costs per item of replacing items that have been etched.

(d) A school district, district, or other local public agency may elect, by formal action of its governing body, to have the probation officer of the county recoup for it, through juvenile court proceedings in accordance with Section 742.16, its costs associated with the defacement by minors of property it owns or possesses by graffiti or other inscribed material. Upon election, the school district, district, or other local public agency shall make the cost findings described in subdivision (c). These cost findings shall be reviewed at least once every three years, at which time the school district, district, or other local public agency, by formal action of its governing body, shall adopt updated cost findings in accordance with subdivision (c). A school district, district, or other local public agency may rescind, by resolution, its election to have the probation officer recoup its costs pursuant to this section. Immediately after making the election described in this subdivision and adopting initial or updated cost findings, and immediately after rescinding said election, the school district, district, or other local public agency shall cause a certified copy of a document memorializing the election, rescission, or cost findings to be forwarded to the clerk of the juvenile court in the county and to the probation officer of the county. A school district, district, or other local public agency that does not elect to have the probation officer of the county recoup its costs pursuant to Section 742.16 may adopt the cost findings described in this subdivision.

(e) A city, county, or city and county that has elected to have the probation officer of the county recoup its costs pursuant to Section 742.16 shall transmit to the probation officer, forthwith, data about its expenditure of resources in identifying and apprehending any minor about whom a petition is filed alleging that the minor is a person described by Section 602 by reason of the commission of an act prohibited by Section 594, 594.3, 594.4, 640.5, 640.6, or 640.7 of the Penal Code. That data shall be sufficient to enable the probation officer and the juvenile court to calculate the costs to the city, county, or city and county in identifying and apprehending the minor.

(f) A city, county, or other public agency that has elected to have the probation officer of the county recoup its costs pursuant to Section 742.16 and that has made cost findings pursuant to subdivisions (c) or (d) shall transmit to the probation officer, forthwith, data about its expenditure of resources to remove graffiti or other material inscribed by, or to repair or replace property defaced by, any minor about whom a petition is filed alleging that the minor is a person described by Section 602 by reason of the commission of an act prohibited by Section 594, 594.3, 594.4, 640.5, 640.6, or 640.7 of the Penal Code. That data shall be sufficient to enable the probation officer and the juvenile court to calculate the costs to the city, county, or other local agency for that removal, repair, or replacement.

(g) The probation officer of a county may establish procedures for collecting the data described in subdivision (e) and (f). These procedures may include a provision that the juvenile court may not award and the probation officer may refuse to collect costs described in this section unless the data required to be provided to the probation officer pursuant to subdivisions (e) and (f) is provided to him or her within a time certain after he or she makes a demand therefor. *(Added by Stats.1994, c. 909 (S.B.1779), § 11.)*

Cross References

Graffiti or other inscribed material defined for purposes of this Article, see Welfare and Institutions Code § 742.12.

Probation officer or social worker defined for purposes of this Chapter, see Welfare and Institutions Code § 215.

§ 742.16. Clean up, repair or replacement of property; condition of probation; restitution

(a) If a minor is found to be a person described in Section 602 of this code by reason of the commission of an act prohibited by Section 594, 594.3, 594.4, 640.5, 640.6, or 640.7 of the Penal Code, and the court does not remove the minor from the physical custody of the parent or guardian, the court as a condition of probation, except in any case in which the court makes a finding and states on the record its reasons why that condition would be inappropriate, shall require the minor to wash, paint, repair, or replace the property defaced, damaged, or destroyed by the minor or otherwise pay restitution to the probation officer of the county for disbursement to the owner or possessor of the property or both. In any case in which the minor is not granted probation or in which the minor's cleanup, repair, or replacement of the property will not return the property to its condition before it was defaced, damaged, or destroyed, the court shall make a finding of the amount of restitution that would be required to fully compensate the owner and possessor of the property for their damages. The court shall order the minor or the minor's estate to pay that restitution to the probation officer of the county for disbursement to the owner or possessor of the property or both, to the extent the court determines that the minor or the minor's estate have the ability to do so, except in any case in which the court makes a finding and states on the record its reasons why full restitution would be inappropriate. If full restitution is found to be inappropriate, the court shall require the minor to perform specified community service, except in any case in which the court makes a finding and states on the record its reasons why that condition would be inappropriate.

(b) If a minor is found to be a person described in Section 602 of this code by reason of the commission of an act prohibited by Section 594, 594.3, 594.4, 640.5, 640.6, or 640.7 of the Penal Code, and the graffiti or other material inscribed by the minor has been removed, or the property defaced by the minor has been repaired or replaced by a public entity that has elected, pursuant to Section 742.14, to have the probation officer of the county recoup its costs through proceedings in accordance with this section and has made cost findings in accordance with subdivision (c) or (d) of Section 742.14, the court shall determine the total cost incurred by the public entity for said removal, repair, or replacement, using, if applicable, the cost findings most recently adopted by the public entity pursuant to subdivision (c) or (d) of Section 742.14. The court shall order the minor or the minor's estate to pay those costs to the probation officer of the county to the extent the court determines that the minor or the minor's estate have the ability to do so.

(c) If the minor is found to be a person described in Section 602 of this code by reason of the commission of an act prohibited by Section 594, 594.3, 594.4, 640.5, 640.6, or 640.7 of the Penal Code, and the minor was identified or apprehended by the law enforcement agency of a city or county that has elected, pursuant to Section 742.14, to have the probation officer of the county recoup its costs through proceedings in accordance with this section, the court shall determine the cost of identifying or apprehending the minor, or both, using, if applicable, the cost findings adopted by the city or county pursuant to subdivision (b) of Section 742.14. The court shall order the minor or the minor's estate to pay those costs to the probation officer of the county to the extent the court determines that the minor or the minor's estate has the ability to do so.

(d) If the court determines that the minor or the minor's estate is unable to pay in full the costs and damages determined pursuant to subdivisions (a), (b), and (c), and if the minor's parent or parents have been cited into court pursuant to Section 742.18, the court shall hold a hearing to determine the liability of the minor's parent or parents pursuant to Section 1714.1 of the Civil Code for those costs and damages. Except when the court makes a finding setting forth unusual circumstances in which parental liability would not serve the interests of justice, the court shall order the minor's parent or parents to pay those costs and damages to the probation officer of the county to the extent the court determines that the parent or parents have the ability to pay, if the minor was in the custody or control of the parent or parents at the time he or she committed the act that forms the basis for the finding that the minor is a person described in Section 602. In evaluating the parent's or parents' ability to pay, the court shall take into consideration the family income, the necessary obligations of the family, and the number of persons dependent upon this income.

(e) The hearing described in subdivision (d) may be held immediately following the disposition hearing or at a later date, at the option of the court.

(f) If the amount of costs and damages sought to be recovered in the hearing pursuant to subdivision (d) is five thousand dollars ($5,000) or less, the parent or parents may not be represented by counsel and the probation officer of the county shall be represented by his or her nonattorney designee. The court shall conduct that hearing in accordance with Sections 116.510 and 116.520 of the Code of Civil Procedure. Notwithstanding the foregoing, if the court determines that a parent cannot properly present his or her defense, the court may, in its discretion, allow another individual to assist that parent. In addition, a spouse may appear and participate in the hearing on behalf of his or her spouse if the representative's spouse has given his or her consent and the court determines that the interest of justice would be served thereby.

(g) If the amount of costs and damages sought to be recovered in the hearing pursuant to subdivision (d) exceeds five thousand dollars ($5,000), the parent or parents may be represented by counsel of his or her or their own choosing, and the probation officer of the county shall be represented by the district attorney or an attorney or nonattorney designee of the probation officer. The parent or parents shall not be entitled to court-appointed counsel or to counsel compensated at public expense.

(h) At the hearing conducted pursuant to subdivision (d), there shall be a presumption affecting the burden of proof that the findings of the court made pursuant to subdivisions (a), (b), and (c) represent the actual damages and costs attributable to the act of the minor that forms the basis of the finding that the minor is a person described in Section 602.

(i) If the parent or parents, after having been cited to appear pursuant to Section 742.18, fail to appear as ordered, the court shall order the parent or parents to pay the full amount of the costs and damages determined by the court pursuant to subdivisions (a), (b), and (c).

(j) Execution may be issued on an order issued by the court pursuant to this section in the same manner as on a judgment in a civil action, including any balance unpaid at the termination of the court's jurisdiction over the minor.

(k) At any time prior to the satisfaction of a judgment entered pursuant to this section, a person against whom the judgment was entered may petition the rendering court to modify or vacate the judgment on the showing of a change in circumstances relating to his or her ability to pay the judgment.

(*l*) For purposes of a hearing conducted pursuant to subdivision (d), the judge of the juvenile court shall have the jurisdiction of a judge of the superior court in a limited civil case, and if the amount of the demand is within the jurisdictional limits stated in Sections 116.220 and 116.221 of the Code of Civil Procedure, the judge of the juvenile court shall have the powers of a judge presiding over the small claims court.

(m) Nothing in this section shall be construed to limit the authority of a juvenile court to provide conditions of probation.

(n) The options available to the court pursuant to subdivisions (a), (b), (c), (d), and (k), to order payment by the minor and his or her parent or parents of less than the full costs described in subdivisions (a), (b), and (c), on grounds of financial inability or for reasons of justice, shall not be available to a superior court in an ordinary civil proceeding pursuant to subdivision (b) of Section 1714.1 of the Civil Code, except that in any proceeding pursuant to either subdivision (b) of Section 1714.1 of the Civil Code or this section, the maximum amount that a parent or a minor may be ordered to pay shall not exceed twenty thousand dollars ($20,000) for each tort of the minor. *(Added by Stats.1994, c. 909 (S.B.1779), § 11. Amended by Stats. 1998, c. 931 (S.B.2139), § 474, eff. Sept. 28, 1998; Stats.2002, c. 784 (S.B.1316), § 615; Stats.2006, c. 167 (A.B.2618), § 10; Stats.2016, c. 50 (S.B.1005), § 120, eff. Jan. 1, 2017.)*

Law Revision Commission Comments

Section 742.16 is amended to accommodate unification of the municipal and superior courts in a county. Cal. Const. art. VI, § 5(e).

When the juvenile court judge sits to determine the liability of parents or guardians the judge has the jurisdiction of a municipal court judge. See subdivision (*l*). The amount in controversy cannot exceed $25,000. See subdivision (d), referring to Civ. Code § 1714.1. *Cf.* Code Civ. Proc. § 85 (limited civil cases). [28 Cal.L.Rev.Comm. Reports 51 (1998)].

Subdivisions (*l*) and (n) of Section 742.16 are amended to reflect unification of the municipal and superior courts pursuant to Article VI, Section 5(e), of the California Constitution. [32 Cal.L.Rev.Comm. Reports 557 (2002)].

Cross References

Burden of proof, generally, see Evidence Code § 500 et seq.
Custody defined for purposes of subdivision (d) of this section, see Welfare and Institutions Code § 742.12.
Probation officer or social worker defined for purposes of this Chapter, see Welfare and Institutions Code § 215.

Research References

3 Witkin, California Criminal Law 4th Punishment § 656 (2021), Particular Statutes.

§ 742.18. Citation to parent or legal guardian; restitution

(a) If the petition alleges that the minor is the person described by Section 602 by reason of the commission of an act prohibited by Section 594, 594.3, 594.4, 640.5, 640.6, or 640.7 of the Penal Code, and the petition is sustained, the court, in addition to the notice provided in Sections 658 and 659, shall issue a citation to the minor's parent or legal guardian, ordering them to appear in the court at the time and date stated for a hearing pursuant to subdivision (d) of Section 742.16.

(b) The citation shall notify the parent or legal guardian that at the hearing, he, she, or they may be ordered to pay restitution sufficient to fully compensate the owner and possessor of the property defaced by the minor for the damage caused by that defacement, the law enforcement costs of identifying and apprehending the minor, if applicable, and the costs incurred by a public entity to remove graffiti or other material inscribed by the minor, or to repair or replace the property defaced by the minor, if applicable. The citation shall set forth the provisions of Section 742.16 and shall advise the parent or parents that he, she, or they may be ordered to pay an amount not exceeding twenty thousand dollars ($20,000) for the above-referenced damages and costs. The citation shall contain a warning to the parent or parents that if he, she, or they fail to appear at the time and date stated, the court will order him, her, or them to pay in full the costs and damages caused by the act of the minor.

(c) Service of the citation shall be made on all parents or legal guardians of the minor whose names and addresses are known to the petitioner.

(d) Service of the citation shall be made at least 10 days prior to the time and date stated therein for appearance, in the manner provided by law for the service of a summons in a civil action, other than by publication. *(Added by Stats.1994, c. 909 (S.B.1779), § 11.)*

§ 742.20. Distribution of moneys collected; priority

Any moneys collected by the probation officer of the county pursuant to an order rendered pursuant to Section 742.16 shall be distributed by the county to the following persons and entities in the following priority:

(a) Restitution to the owner and possessor of the property defaced by the minor, in the amount determined by the court.

(b) After the restitution described in subdivision (a) has been paid in full, or if restitution was not ordered, the costs of removing graffiti or other material inscribed by the minor and of repairing or replacing property defaced by the minor, to the city, county, or other local public agency that incurred those costs, except that the county may deduct and retain 15 percent of the amount collected for the removal, repair, or replacement costs, or an amount equivalent to its actual costs of collection, whichever is less.

(c) After the costs and damages described in subdivisions (a) and (b) have been paid in full, or if there are no costs or damages, the law enforcement costs of identifying and apprehending the minor, to the city or county that incurred those costs, except that the county may deduct and retain 15 percent of the amount collected for those law enforcement costs, or an amount equivalent to its actual costs of collection, whichever is less. *(Added by Stats.1994, c. 909 (S.B.1779), § 11.)*

Cross References

Probation officer or social worker defined for purposes of this Chapter, see Welfare and Institutions Code § 215.

§ 742.22. Severability

If any provision or clause of this article or the application thereof to any person or circumstances is held invalid, the invalidity shall not affect other provisions or applications of this article which can be given effect without the invalid provision or application, and to this end the provisions of this article are severable. *(Added by Stats.1994, c. 909 (S.B.1779), § 11.)*

ARTICLE 18.6. REPEAT OFFENDER PREVENTION PROJECT

Section

§ 743. Establishment

Contingent upon the appropriation of funds therefor, there is hereby established a three-year pilot project which shall be known as the "Repeat Offender Prevention Project." This project shall operate in the Counties of Fresno, Humboldt, Los Angeles, Orange, San Diego, San Mateo, and Solano, and the City and County of San Francisco, unless the board of supervisors of one or more of these counties adopts a resolution to the effect it will not participate in the project, each of which shall either design, establish, implement, and evaluate a model program to meet the needs of a juvenile offender population identified as having the potential to become repeat serious offenders utilizing the findings of exploratory studies conducted in Orange County between 1989 and 1993 by the research staff of the Orange County Probation Department and which identified certain minors who were designated as the "8 percent" population. The main goal of this program is to develop and implement a cost-effective multiagency, multidisciplinary program which targets youth displaying behavior that may lead to delinquency and recidivism. *(Added by Stats.1994, c. 730 (A.B.3220), § 1. Amended by Stats.1996, c. 1049 (A.B.2447), § 1; Stats.1998, c. 327 (A.B.2594), § 1.)*

§ 744. Administration

(a) The Repeat Offender Prevention Project shall be administered by the Board of Corrections and each program shall be under the onsite administration of the chief probation officer in the county selected for participation in the project or under a consortium of chief probation officers representing each participating county.

(b) Pursuant to this article, a chief probation officer or the regional consortium, with the approval of the appropriate board or boards of supervisors, may apply to the Board of Corrections for funding to implement a program meeting the criteria specified in subdivision (b) of Section 745. The goal of each program shall be to develop and demonstrate intervention strategies which will end each participating minor's escalating pattern of criminal and antisocial behavior, a pattern that leads to chronic delinquency and, potentially, to adult criminal careers. These strategies shall be provided within the parameters of community protection and offender accountability. Application for program funding shall be made in accordance with written guidelines established by the Board of Corrections in consultation with chief probation officers throughout the state. *(Added by Stats.1994, c. 730 (A.B.3220), § 1. Amended by Stats.1998, c. 327 (A.B.2594), § 2.)*

Cross References

Probation officer or social worker defined for purposes of this Chapter, see Welfare and Institutions Code § 215.

§ 745. Selection of counties and regions; criteria; goals and deadlines; schedules

The Board of Corrections shall establish goals and deadlines against which the success or failure of the program demonstration projects may be measured. The board shall also develop selection criteria and funding schedules for participating counties which shall take into consideration, but not be limited to, all of the following:

(1) Size of the eligible target population as defined in Section 746.

(2) Demonstrated ability to administer the program.

(3) Identification of service delivery area.

(4) Demonstrated ability to provide or develop the key intervention strategies described in Section 748 to the eligible target population and their families.

(5) A formal research component utilizing an experimental research design and random assignment to the program. *(Added by Stats.1994, c. 730 (A.B.3220), § 1. Amended by Stats.1996, c. 1049 (A.B.2447), § 2; Stats.1998, c. 327 (A.B.2594), § 3.)*

§ 746. Minors; selection for participation in program; factors

A minor shall be selected for participation in a program established pursuant to this article based upon the following factors:

(a) The minor is 15½ years of age or younger, has been declared a ward of the juvenile court for the first time and is to be supervised by a probation department selected for participation in this project.

(b) The minor has been evaluated and found to have at least three of the following factors, that place the minor at a significantly greater risk of becoming a chronic juvenile or adult offender:

(1) School behavior and performance problems. This shall include at least one of the following: attendance problems; school suspension or expulsion; or failure in two or more academic classes during the previous six months or comparable academic period.

(2) Family problems. These shall include at least one of the following: poor parental supervision or control; documented circumstances of domestic violence; child abuse or neglect; or family members who have engaged in criminal activities.

(3) Substance abuse. This shall include any regular use of alcohol or drugs by the minor, other than experimentation.

(4) High-risk predelinquent behavior. This shall include at least one of the following: a pattern of stealing; chronic running away from home; or gang membership or association.

(5) The minor matches the at-risk profile for becoming a chronic and repeat juvenile offender according to the criteria developed by the Multi–Agency At–Risk Youth Committee (MAARYC). *(Added by Stats.1994, c. 730 (A.B.3220), § 1. Amended by Stats.1996, c. 1049 (A.B.2447), § 3; Stats.1998, c. 327 (A.B.2594), § 4.)*

§ 747. Minimum standards for project implementation, operation, and evaluation; written commitment by county or region to certain objectives

The Board of Corrections shall adopt written minimum standards for project implementation, operation, and evaluation which shall include a written commitment by a county or region to the following objectives:

(a) Teamwork on the part of all treatment and intervention agents involved in the project including the family, the professionals, and any community volunteers.

(b) Empowerment of the family to recognize and, ultimately, to solve the problems related to their minor's delinquent behavior and their involvement as an integral part of the treatment team and process.

(c) Creation of a multiagency, multidisciplinary, and culturally competent team so that the program can effectively draw on the professional knowledge, skill, and experience of many treatment disciplines in areas including, but not limited to, the following: education; job preparation and search; job skills and vocational training; life skills; psychological counseling; mental health services; drug and alcohol treatment; health care; parenting skills; community service opportunities; building self-esteem and self-confidence; mentoring programs; restitution programs; gang intervention; crime prevention; recreational, social, and cultural activities; and transportation and child care as needed. *(Added by Stats.1994, c. 730 (A.B.3220), § 1. Amended by Stats.1996, c. 1049 (A.B.2447), § 4; Stats.1998, c. 327 (A.B.2594), § 5.)*

§ 748. Intervention strategies; goals

Each county or region shall, in implementing their respective programs, provide the following key intervention strategies to ensure the following:

(a) Adequate levels of supervision, structure, and support to minors and their families both during and after the intervention and treatment process, in order to accomplish the following:

(1) Ensure protection of the community, the minor, and his or her family.

(2) Facilitate the development of new patterns of thinking and behavior.

(3) Eliminate any obvious stumbling blocks to the family's progress.

(4) Facilitate the development of enhanced parenting skills and parent-child relationships.

(b) Accountability on the part of the minor for his or her actions and assistance to the minor in developing a greater awareness and sensitivity to the impact of his or her actions on both people and situations.

(c) Assistance to families in their efforts to ensure that minors are attending school regularly.

(d) Assistance to the minor in developing strategies for attaining and reinforcing educational success.

(e) Promotion and development of positive social values, behavior, and relationships by providing opportunities for the minor to directly help people; to improve his or her community; to participate in positive leisure-time activities specially chosen to match his or her individual interests, skills, and abilities; and to have greater access and exposure to positive adult and juvenile role models.

(f) Promotion of partnerships between public and private agencies to develop individualized intervention strategies which shall include, but not be limited to, the following:

(1) Delivery of services in close proximity to the minor's or the minor's family's home.

(2) Community case advocates to assist in building bridges of trust, communication, and understanding between the minor, the family, and all treatment and intervention agents.

(g) Provision of a continuum of care with strong followup services that continue to be available to the minor and family as long as needed, not just on a crisis basis. *(Added by Stats.1994, c. 730 (A.B.3220), § 1. Amended by Stats.1996, c. 1049 (A.B.2447), § 5; Stats.1998, c. 327 (A.B.2594), § 6.)*

§ 749. Monitoring of project implementation; reports; measurement of success; criteria; eligibility for funding; program implementation and termination date; administrative expenses

(a) The Board of Corrections shall be responsible for monitoring demonstration project and expansion program implementations in accordance with an annual program plan submitted by the participating counties or regions. Written progress and evaluation reports shall be required of all participating counties pursuant to a schedule and guidelines developed by the Board of Corrections.

(b) The success of each funded demonstration project shall be determined, at a minimum, by comparing a control group, consisting of juvenile offenders who were not selected for participation in the project, to an experimental group, consisting of juvenile offenders who have participated in the project. Juveniles in each group shall be evaluated at 6–, 12–, 18–, and 24–month intervals, according to the following criteria:

(1) The number of subsequent petitions to declare the minor a ward of the juvenile court, pursuant to Section 602, and the subject matter and disposition of each of those petitions.

(2) The number of days served in any local or state correctional facilities.

(3) The number of days of school attendance during the current or most recent semester.

(4) The minor's grade point average for the most recently completed school semester.

(c) The Board of Corrections, based on reports provided pursuant to subdivision (a), shall report upon request to the Legislature on the effectiveness of these programs in achieving the demonstration project and program goals described in this article.

(d) The Board of Corrections shall determine county or regional eligibility for funding and, from money appropriated therefor, the board shall allocate and award funds to those counties or regions applying and eligible therefor and selected for project participation.

(e) The Repeat Offender Prevention Project shall be implemented within six months of the appropriation of funds therefor and shall terminate at the end of three years from that appropriation.

(f) Five percent of the funds allocated each fiscal year for the Repeat Offender Prevention Project shall be set aside for the administrative expenses of the Board of Corrections. *(Added by Stats.1994, c. 730 (A.B.3220), § 1. Amended by Stats.1998, c. 327 (A.B.2594), § 7.)*

ARTICLE 18.7. JUVENILE CRIME ENFORCEMENT AND ACCOUNTABILITY CHALLENGE GRANT PROGRAM

Section

§ 749.2. Short title

This article shall be known and may be cited as the Juvenile Crime Enforcement and Accountability Challenge Grant Program. *(Added by Stats.1996, c. 133 (S.B.1760), § 3, eff. July 10, 1996.)*

§ 749.21. Administration; award of grants

The Juvenile Crime Enforcement and Accountability Challenge Grant Program shall be administered by the Board of Corrections for the purpose of reducing juvenile crime and delinquency. This program shall award grants on a competitive basis following request-for-proposal evaluation standards and guidelines developed by the Board of Corrections, as authorized by this article, to counties that (a) develop and implement a comprehensive, multiagency local action plan that provides for a continuum of responses to juvenile crime and delinquency, including collaborative ways to address local problems of juvenile crime; and (b) demonstrate a collaborative and integrated approach for implementing a system of swift, certain, graduated responses, and appropriate sanctions for at-risk youth and juvenile offenders. *(Added by Stats.1996, c. 133 (S.B.1760), § 3, eff. July 10, 1996. Amended by Stats.1998, c. 325 (A.B.2261), § 1, eff. Aug. 21, 1998.)*

§ 749.22. County juvenile justice coordinating councils; membership; comprehensive plans; community punishment plans

To be eligible for this grant, each county shall be required to establish a multiagency juvenile justice coordinating council that shall develop and implement a continuum of county-based responses to juvenile crime. The coordinating councils shall, at a minimum, include the chief probation officer, as chair, and one representative each from the district attorney's office, the public defender's office, the sheriff's department, the board of supervisors, the department of social services, the department of mental health, a community-based drug and alcohol program, a city police department, the county office of education or a school district, and an at-large community representative. In order to carry out its duties pursuant to this section, a coordinating council shall also include representatives from nonprofit community-based organizations providing services to minors. The board of supervisors shall be informed of community-based organizations participating on a coordinating council. The coordinating councils shall develop a comprehensive, multiagency plan that identifies the resources and strategies for providing an effective continuum of responses for the prevention, intervention, supervision, treatment, and incarceration of male and female juvenile offenders, including strategies to develop and implement locally based or regionally based out-of-home placement options for youths who are persons described in Section 602. Counties may utilize community punishment plans developed pursuant to grants awarded from funds included in the 1995 Budget Act to the extent the plans address juvenile crime and the juvenile justice system or local action plans previously developed for this program. The plan shall include, but not be limited to, the following components:

(a) An assessment of existing law enforcement, probation, education, mental health, health, social services, drug and alcohol and youth services resources which specifically target at-risk juveniles, juvenile offenders, and their families.

(b) An identification and prioritization of the neighborhoods, schools, and other areas in the community that face a significant public safety risk from juvenile crime, such as gang activity, daylight burglary, late-night robbery, vandalism, truancy, controlled substance sales, firearm-related violence, and juvenile alcohol use within the council's jurisdiction.

(c) A local action plan (LAP) for improving and marshaling the resources set forth in subdivision (a) to reduce the incidence of juvenile crime and delinquency in the areas targeted pursuant to subdivision (b) and the greater community. The councils shall prepare their plans to maximize the provision of collaborative and integrated services of all the resources set forth in subdivision (a), and shall provide specified strategies for all elements of response, including prevention, intervention, suppression, and incapacitation, to provide a continuum for addressing the identified male and female juvenile crime problem, and strategies to develop and implement locally based or regionally based out-of-home placement options for youths who are persons described in Section 602.

(d) Develop information and intelligence-sharing systems to ensure that county actions are fully coordinated, and to provide data for measuring the success of the grantee in achieving its goals. The plan shall develop goals related to the outcome measures that shall be used to determine the effectiveness of the program.

(e) Identify outcome measures which shall include, but not be limited to, the following:

(1) The rate of juvenile arrests.

(2) The rate of successful completion of probation.

(3) The rate of successful completion of restitution and court-ordered community service responsibilities. *(Added by Stats.1996, c. 133 (S.B.1760), § 3, eff. July 10, 1996. Amended by Stats.1998, c. 325 (A.B.2261), § 2, eff. Aug. 21, 1998; Stats.1998, c. 500 (S.B.491), § 6, eff. Sept. 15, 1998.)*

Cross References

Plan for rehabilitation and supervision services, creation of subcommittee and composition, see Welfare and Institutions Code § 1995.
Probation officer or social worker defined for purposes of this Chapter, see Welfare and Institutions Code § 215.
Punishment defined for purposes of this Chapter, see Welfare and Institutions Code § 202.
Supplemental local law enforcement funding, establishment of fund and allocations, see Government Code § 30061.

§ 749.23. Grants to supplement existing programs

The Board of Corrections shall award grants that provide funding for three years. Funding shall be used to supplement, rather than supplant, existing programs and grants may be awarded to any county including those counties currently receiving funds pursuant to this article. Grant funds shall be used for programs that are identified in the local action plan as part of a continuum of responses to reduce juvenile crime and delinquency. No grant shall be awarded unless the applicant makes available resources in an amount equal to at least 25 percent of the amount of the grant. Resources may include in-kind contributions from participating agencies. In awarding grants, priority shall be given to those proposals which include additional funding that exceeds 25 percent of the amount of the grant. In awarding grants, priority shall also be given to programs in counties where the population exceeds 500,000 and the rate of violent crime exceeds the state average. *(Added by Stats.1996, c. 133 (S.B.1760), § 3, eff. July 10, 1996. Amended by Stats.1998, c. 325 (A.B.2261), § 3, eff. Aug. 21, 1998.)*

§ 749.24. Grant awards; minimum standards, funding schedules and procedures; criteria

The Board of Corrections shall establish minimum standards, funding schedules, and procedures for awarding grants, which shall take into consideration, but not be limited to, all of the following:

(a) Size of the eligible high-risk youth population.

(b) Demonstrated ability to administer the program.

(c) Demonstrated ability to provide and develop a continuum of responses to juvenile crime and delinquency that includes prevention, intervention, diversion, suppression, and incapacitation.

(d) Demonstrated ability to implement a plan that provides a collaborative and integrated approach to juvenile crime and delinquency.

(e) Demonstrated history of maximizing federal, state, local, and private funding sources.

(f) Demonstrated efforts to implement a multicounty juvenile justice program.

(g) Likelihood that the program will continue to operate after state grant funding ends. *(Added by Stats.1996, c. 133 (S.B.1760), § 3, eff. July 10, 1996.)*

§ 749.25. Assistance grants

The Board of Corrections may award up to a total of two million dollars ($2,000,000) statewide, in individual grants not exceeding one hundred and fifty thousand dollars ($150,000), on a competitive basis to counties to assist in establishing a multiagency coordinating group or developing a local action plan. *(Added by Stats.1996, c. 133 (S.B.1760), § 3, eff. July 10, 1996.)*

§ 749.26. Evaluation of program; reports

The Board of Corrections shall create an evaluation design for the Juvenile Crime Enforcement and Accountability Challenge Grant Program that will assess the effectiveness of the program. For grants awarded before July 1, 1998, the board shall develop an interim report to be submitted to the Legislature on or before March 1, 1999, and a final analysis of the grant program in a report to be submitted to the Legislature on or before March 1, 2001. For grants awarded after July 1, 1998, the board shall develop an interim report to be submitted to the Legislature on or before March 1, 2001, and a final analysis of the grant program in a report to be submitted to the Legislature on or before March 1, 2003. *(Added by Stats.1996, c. 133 (S.B.1760), § 3, eff. July 10, 1996. Amended by Stats.1998, c. 325 (A.B.2261), § 4, eff. Aug. 21, 1998.)*

§ 749.27. Appropriations

Funding for the Juvenile Crime Enforcement and Accountability Challenge Grant Program for grant awards made before July 1, 1998, shall be provided from the amount appropriated in Item 5430–101–0001 of the Budget Act of 1996. Up to 5 percent of the amount appropriated in Item 5430–101–0001 of the Budget Act of 1996 shall be transferred upon the approval of the Director of Finance, to Item 5430–001–0001 for expenditure as necessary for the board to administer this program, including technical assistance to counties and the development of an evaluation component. *(Added by Stats.1996, c. 133 (S.B.1760), § 3, eff. July 10, 1996. Amended by Stats.1998, c. 325 (A.B.2261), § 5, eff. Aug. 21, 1998.)*

ARTICLE 18.8. COUNTY JUVENILE CORRECTIONAL FACILITIES ACT

Section

§ 749.3. Short title

This title shall be known and may be cited as the County Juvenile Correctional Facilities Act. *(Added by Stats.1998, c. 499 (A.B.2796), § 1, eff. Sept. 15, 1998.)*

§ 749.31. Legislative findings

The Legislature finds and declares all of the following:

(a) While the County Correctional Capital Expenditure Bond Act of 1986 and the County Correctional Facility Capital Expenditure and Youth Facility Bond Act of 1988 have provided ninety million dollars ($90,000,000) for county juvenile facilities for remodeling to help ensure health and safety requirements, many problems remain.

(b) Numerous county juvenile facilities throughout California are dilapidated and overcrowded and do not meet standards. Over 40 percent or 4,335 facility beds are in need of renovation, reconstruction, construction, and deferred maintenance.

(c) Capital improvements are necessary to protect the life and safety of the persons confined or employed in juvenile facilities and to upgrade the health and sanitary conditions of those facilities.

(d) Over two hundred twenty million dollars ($220,000,000) is needed to remodel, upgrade, or replace 4,335 beds by the year 2000.

(e) Due to fiscal constraints associated with the loss of local property tax revenues, counties are unable to finance the construction of adequate juvenile facilities.

(f) Local juvenile facilities are operating over capacity or must implement emergency release procedures, and the population of these facilities is still increasing. It is essential to the public safety that construction proceed as expeditiously as possible to relieve overcrowding and to maintain public safety and security.

(g) County juvenile facilities are threatened with closure or the imposition of court ordered sanctions if health and safety deficiencies are not corrected immediately. *(Added by Stats.1998, c. 499 (A.B. 2796), § 1, eff. Sept. 15, 1998.)*

Cross References

County juvenile facilities defined for purposes of this Article, see Welfare and Institutions Code § 749.32.

§ 749.32. Definitions

As used in this article, the following terms have the following meanings:

(a) "County juvenile facilities" means county juvenile halls or camps.

(b) "Board" means the Board of Corrections. *(Added by Stats. 1998, c. 499 (A.B.2796), § 1, eff. Sept. 15, 1998.)*

§ 749.33. County juvenile facility renovation, construction or replacement; competitive grant awards; application and qualification

(a) Upon appropriation by the Legislature, moneys may be available to the board for the purpose of awarding grants on a competitive basis to counties for the renovation, reconstruction, construction, completion of construction, and replacement of county juvenile facilities, and the performance of deferred maintenance on county juvenile facilities. However, deferred maintenance for facilities shall only include items with a useful life of at least 10 years. Up to 1½ percent of these moneys may be used by the board for administration of this article.

(b) No grant shall be awarded pursuant to this article unless the applicant makes available resources in an amount equal to at least 25 percent of the amount of the grant. Resources may include in-kind contributions from participating agencies, but in no event shall the applicant's cash contribution be less than 10 percent of the grant.

(c) An application for funds shall be in the manner and form prescribed by the board and pursuant to recommendations of an allocation advisory committee appointed by the board. From these recommendations, an allocation plan shall be developed and adopted by the board. The allocation advisory committee shall convene upon notification by the board.

(d) Any application for funds shall include, but not be limited to, all of the following:

(1) Documentation of need for the project or projects.

(2) Adoption of a formal county plan to finance construction of the proposed project or projects.

(3) Submittal of a preliminary staffing plan for the project or projects.

(4) Submittal of architectural drawings, which shall be approved by the board for compliance with minimum juvenile detention facility standards and which shall also be approved by the State Fire Marshal for compliance with fire and life safety requirements.

(5) Documentation that the facilities will be safely staffed and operated in compliance with law, including applicable regulations of the board.

(e) The board shall not be deemed a responsible agency, as defined in Section 21069 of the Public Resources Code, or otherwise be subject to the California Environmental Quality Act (Division 13 (commencing with Section 21000) of the Public Resources Code) for any activities undertaken or funded pursuant to this title. This subdivision does not exempt any local agency from the requirements of the California Environmental Quality Act. *(Added by Stats.1998, c. 499 (A.B.2796), § 1, eff. Sept. 15, 1998.)*

Cross References

Board defined for purposes of this Article, see Welfare and Institutions Code § 749.32.
County juvenile facilities defined for purposes of this Article, see Welfare and Institutions Code § 749.32.

ARTICLE 18.9. JUVENILE JUSTICE COMMUNITY REENTRY CHALLENGE GRANT PROGRAM

§ 749.5. Title and citation of article

This article shall be known and may be cited as the Juvenile Justice Community Reentry Challenge Grant Program. *(Added by Stats. 2006, c. 69 (A.B.1806), § 35, eff. July 12, 2006.)*

§ 749.6. Legislative intent regarding improvement in youthful offender rehabilitation outcomes and reduction in recidivism

It is the intent of the Legislature to support the systematic and cultural transformation of the Division of Juvenile Justice into a rehabilitative model that improves youthful offender outcomes and reduces recidivism. As a key component of meeting these goals, it is further the intent of the Legislature to support the development of local infrastructure that provides comprehensive reentry services for juvenile parolees. These services shall be complementary to, and consistent with, the long-term objective of providing a continuum of state and local responses to juvenile delinquency that enhance public safety and improve offender outcomes. *(Added by Stats.2006, c. 69 (A.B.1806), § 35, eff. July 12, 2006.)*

§ 749.7. Administration of grant program; criteria for awarding grants; applicant eligibility

(a) The Juvenile Justice Community Reentry Challenge Grant Program shall be administered by the Division of Juvenile Justice, in consultation with the Corrections Standards Authority, for the purpose of improving the performance and cost-effectiveness of postcustodial reentry supervision of juvenile parolees, reducing the recidivism rates of juvenile offenders, and piloting innovative reentry programs consistent with the division's focus on a rehabilitative treatment model.

(b) This program shall award grants on a competitive basis to applicants that demonstrate a collaborative and comprehensive approach to the successful community reintegration of juvenile parolees, through the provision of wrap-around services that may include, but are not limited to, the following:

(1) Transitional or step-down housing, including, but not limited to, group homes subject to Section 18987.62.

(2) Occupational development and job placement.

(3) Outpatient mental health services.

(4) Substance abuse treatment services.

(5) Education.

(6) Life skills counseling.

(7) Restitution and community service.

(8) Case management.

(9) Intermediate sanctions for technical violations of conditions of parole.

(c) To be eligible for consideration, applicants shall submit a program plan that includes, but is not limited to, the following:

(1) The target population.

(2) The type of housing and wrap-around services provided.

(3) A parole and community reentry plan for each parolee.

(4) Potential sanctions for a parolee's failure to observe the conditions of the program.

(5) Coordination with local probation and other law enforcement agencies.

(6) Coordination with other service providers and community partners. *(Added by Stats.2006, c. 69 (A.B.1806), § 35, eff. July 12, 2006.)*

§ 749.8. Awarding of grants to counties and nonprofit organizations; use of grant awards; case supervision plans

(a) The Division of Juvenile Justice, in consultation with the Corrections Standards Authority, shall award grants that provide funding for three years on a competitive basis to counties and nonprofit organizations.

(b) A minimum of 75 percent of the grant award shall be for providing program services to individuals on parole from the Division of Juvenile Justice. The remainder of the grant award may additionally be used for providing program services to youthful offenders under the jurisdiction of the county or local juvenile court who are transitioning from out-of-home placements back into the community.

(c) The division shall award grants in a manner that maximizes the development of meaningful and innovative local programs to provide comprehensive reentry services for juvenile parolees.

(d) For any grant award, the division shall work with the juvenile court and the probation department of the county or counties in the grant service area to identify state and local case supervision responsibilities that are appropriate for the effective operation and management of the reentry programs supported by the grant. These responsibilities shall be incorporated into a case supervision plan for the grant that shall describe the role of local courts and probation departments in facilitating individual reentry plans, in assigning or removing parolees from grant-funded programs, and in meeting evaluation criteria for the grant. *(Added by Stats.2006, c. 69 (A.B.1806), § 35, eff. July 12, 2006.)*

§ 749.9. Establishment of minimum standards, funding schedules, and procedures for awarding grants

The Division of Juvenile Justice, in consultation with the Corrections Standards Authority, the Chief Probation Officers of California, and experts in the field of California juvenile justice programs, shall establish minimum standards, funding schedules, and procedures for awarding grants, which shall take into consideration, but not be limited to, all of the following:

(a) The size of the eligible population.

(b) A demonstrated ability to administer the program.

(c) A demonstrated ability to develop and provide a collaborative approach to improving parolee success rates that includes the participation of nonprofit and community partners.

(d) A demonstrated ability to provide comprehensive services to support improved parolee outcomes, including housing, training, and treatment.

(e) A demonstrated ability to provide effective oversight and management of youthful offenders or young adults who have been committed to a detention facility, and parolees that require reentry supervision and control.

(f) A demonstrated history of maximizing federal, state, local, and private funding sources. *(Added by Stats.2006, c. 69 (A.B.1806), § 35, eff. July 12, 2006.)*

Cross References

Probation officer or social worker defined for purposes of this Chapter, see Welfare and Institutions Code § 215.

§ 749.95. Establishment and tracking of outcome measures by grant recipients; creation of evaluation design; report to Legislature

(a) Each grant recipient shall be required to establish and track outcome measures, including, but not limited to:

(1) Annual recidivism rates, including technical parole violations and new offenses.

(2) The number and percent of participants successfully completing parole.

(3) The number and percent of participants engaged in part-time or full-time employment, enrolled in higher education or vocational training, receiving drug and substance abuse treatment, or receiving mental health treatment.

(4) The number and percent of participants that obtain stable housing, including the type of housing.

(b) The Division of Juvenile Justice, in consultation with the Corrections Standards Authority, the Chief Probation Officers of California, and experts in the field of California juvenile justice programs, shall create an evaluation design for the Juvenile Justice Community Reentry Challenge Grant Program that will assess the effectiveness of the program. The division shall develop an interim report to be submitted to the Legislature on or before March 1, 2009, and a final analysis of the grant program in a report to be submitted to the Legislature on or before March 1, 2011. *(Added by Stats.2006, c. 69 (A.B.1806), § 35, eff. July 12, 2006.)*

Cross References

Probation officer or social worker defined for purposes of this Chapter, see Welfare and Institutions Code § 215.

ARTICLE 19. WARDS—TRANSFER OF CASES BETWEEN COUNTIES

§ 750. Petition; conditions for transfer

Whenever a petition is filed in the juvenile court of a county other than the residence of the person named in the petition, or whenever, subsequent to the filing of a petition in the juvenile court of the county where such minor resides, the residence of the person who would be legally entitled to the custody of such minor were it not for the existence of a court order issued pursuant to this chapter is changed to another county, the entire case may be transferred to the juvenile court of the county wherein such person then resides at any time after the court has made a finding of the facts upon which it has exercised its jurisdiction over such minor, and the juvenile court of the county wherein such person then resides shall take jurisdiction of the case upon the receipt and filing with it of such finding of the facts and an order transferring the case. *(Added by Stats.1961, c. 1616, p. 3490, § 2. Amended by Stats.1968, c. 1082, p. 2037, § 1; Stats.1971, c. 606, p. 1210, § 1.)*

Cross References

Dismissal of petition, grounds, see Welfare and Institutions Code § 782.
Juvenile court proceedings, see Welfare and Institutions Code § 650 et seq.
Minor's residence, place of, see Welfare and Institutions Code § 17.1.
Persons entitled to be declared free from parental custody and control, see Family Code § 7820 et seq.
Residence, determination of place of, see Government Code § 244.
Transfer of cases generally, see Code of Civil Procedure § 396 et seq.
Transfer of traffic cases, see Welfare and Institutions Code § 263.
Venue, see Welfare and Institutions Code § 651.

Research References

West's California Judicial Council Forms JV–548, Motion for Transfer Out.
West's California Judicial Council Forms JV–550, Juvenile Court Transfer—Out Orders (Also Available in Spanish).

§ 751. Expenses

The expense of the transfer and all expenses in connection with the transfer and for the support and maintenance of such person shall be paid from the county treasury of the court ordering the transfer until the receipt and filing of the finding and order of transfer in the juvenile court of the transferee county.

The judge shall inquire into the financial condition of such person and of the parent, parents, guardian, or other person charged with his support and maintenance, and if he finds such person, parent, parents, guardian, or other person able, in whole or in part, to pay the expense of such transfer, he shall make a further order requiring such person, parent, parents, guardian, or other person to repay to the county such part, or all, of such expense of transfer as, in the opinion of the court, is proper. Such repayment shall be made to the probation officer who shall keep suitable accounts of such expenses and repayments and shall deposit all such collections in the county treasury. *(Added by Stats.1961, c. 1616, p. 3490, § 2. Amended by Stats.1971, c. 606, p. 1210, § 2.)*

Cross References

County financial evaluation officer, see Government Code § 27750 et seq.
Probation officer or social worker defined for purposes of this Chapter, see Welfare and Institutions Code § 215.

§ 752. Certified copy of file; disposition; contents; maintenance of original court file

Whenever a case is transferred as provided in Section 750, a certified copy of the file may be made and forwarded to the county where the person resides and shall include the name and address of the legal residence of the parent or guardian of the minor. A certified copy shall be deemed to be the same as the original. The original court file may be kept in the files of the transferring county. *(Added by Stats.1961, c. 1616, p. 3490, § 2. Amended by Stats.1965, c. 912, p. 2522, § 1; Stats.1971, c. 606, p. 1211, § 3; Stats.1983, c. 939, § 3; Stats.1984, c. 205, § 1.)*

§ 753. Procedure on transfer

Whenever an order of transfer from another county is filed with the clerk of any juvenile court, the clerk shall place the transfer order on the calendar of the court, and it shall have precedence over all actions and civil proceedings not specifically given precedence by other provisions of law and shall be heard by the court at the earliest possible moment following the filing of the order. *(Added by Stats.1961, c. 1616, p. 3490, § 2.)*

Cross References

Transfer of traffic cases, see Welfare and Institutions Code § 263.

§ 754. County appeal from residence order

In any action under the provisions of this article in which the residence of a minor person is determined, both the county in which the court is situated and any other county which, as a result of the determination of residence, might be determined to be the county of residence of the minor person, shall be considered to be parties in the action and shall have the right to appeal any order by which residence of the minor person is determined. *(Added by Stats.1961, c. 1616, p. 3491, § 2.)*

Cross References

Appeals, see Welfare and Institutions Code § 800.
Minor's residence, place of, see Welfare and Institutions Code § 17.1.

§ 755. Order permitting residence in different county

Any person placed on probation by the juvenile court or adjudged to be a ward of the juvenile court may be permitted by order of the court to reside in a county other than the county of his legal residence, and the court shall retain jurisdiction over such person.

Whenever a ward of the juvenile court is permitted to reside in a county other than the county of his legal residence, he may be placed under the supervision of the probation officer of the county of actual residence, with the consent of such probation officer. The ward shall comply with the instructions of such probation officer and upon failure to do so shall be returned to the county of his legal residence for further hearing and order of the court. *(Added by Stats.1961, c. 1616, p. 3491, § 2. Amended by Stats.1976, c. 1068, p. 4794, § 66; Stats.1978, c. 380, p. 1213, § 166.)*

Cross References

Probation officer or social worker defined for purposes of this Chapter, see Welfare and Institutions Code § 215.
Residence,
Determination of minor's, see Welfare and Institutions Code § 17.1.
Determination of place of, generally, see Government Code § 244.

ARTICLE 20. WARDS—MODIFICATION OF JUVENILE COURT JUDGMENTS AND ORDERS

Section

§ 775. Changing, modifying or setting aside orders; procedural requirements

Any order made by the court in the case of any person subject to its jurisdiction may at any time be changed, modified, or set aside, as the judge deems meet and proper, subject to such procedural requirements as are imposed by this article. *(Added by Stats.1961, c. 1616, p. 3491, § 2.)*

Cross References

Judgments taken by mistake, relief from, see Code of Civil Procedure § 473.
State institutions for the mentally disordered, generally, see Welfare and Institutions Code § 4100 et seq.
Youth Authority, powers and duties, see Welfare and Institutions Code § 1750 et seq.

§ 776. Notice of application

No order changing, modifying, or setting aside a previous order of the juvenile court shall be made either in chambers, or otherwise, unless prior notice of the application therefor has been given by the judge or the clerk of the court to the probation officer and prosecuting attorney and to the minor's counsel of record, or, if there is no counsel of record, to the minor and his parent or guardian. *(Added by Stats.1961, c. 1616, p. 3491, § 2. Amended by Stats.1977, c. 1241, p. 4184, § 8, eff. Oct. 1, 1977.)*

Cross References

Powers of judges at chambers, see Code of Civil Procedure § 166.
Probation officer or social worker defined for purposes of this Chapter, see Welfare and Institutions Code § 215.

§ 777. Removal of minor from physical custody of parent, guardian, relative, or friend; placement or commitment; noticed hearing

An order changing or modifying a previous order by removing a minor from the physical custody of a parent, guardian, relative, or friend and directing placement in a foster home, or commitment to a private institution or commitment to a county institution, or an order changing or modifying a previous order by directing commitment to the Youth Authority shall be made only after a noticed hearing.

(a) The notice shall be made as follows:

(1) By the probation officer where a minor has been declared a ward of the court or a probationer under Section 601 in the original matter and shall contain a concise statement of facts sufficient to support the conclusion that the minor has violated an order of the court.

(2) By the probation officer or the prosecuting attorney if the minor is a court ward or probationer under Section 602 in the original matter and the notice alleges a violation of a condition of probation not amounting to a crime. The notice shall contain a concise statement of facts sufficient to support this conclusion.

(3) Where the probation officer is the petitioner pursuant to paragraph (2), prior to the attachment of jeopardy at the time of the jurisdictional hearing, the prosecuting attorney may make a motion to dismiss the notice and may request that the matter be referred to the probation officer for whatever action the prosecuting or probation officer may deem appropriate.

(b) Upon the filing of such notice, the clerk of the juvenile court shall immediately set the same for hearing within 30 days, and the probation officer shall cause notice of it to be served upon the persons and in the manner prescribed by Sections 658 and 660. Service under this subdivision may be by electronic service pursuant to Section 212.5.

(c) The facts alleged in the notice shall be established by a preponderance of the evidence at a hearing to change, modify, or set aside a previous order. The court may admit and consider reliable hearsay evidence at the hearing to the same extent that such evidence would be admissible in an adult probation revocation hearing, pursuant to the decision in People v. Brown, 215 Cal.App.3d (1989) and any other relevant provision of law.

(d) An order for the detention of the minor pending adjudication of the alleged violation may be made only after a hearing is conducted pursuant to Article 15 (commencing with Section 625) of this chapter. Service under this subdivision may be by electronic service pursuant to Section 212.5, but only in addition to other forms of service required by law. *(Added by Stats.1961, c. 1616, p. 3491, § 2. Amended by Stats.1971, c. 641, p. 1263, § 6; Stats.1976, c. 1068, p. 4795, § 68; Stats.1977, c. 1241, p. 4184, § 9, eff. Oct. 1, 1977; Stats.1979, c. 540, p. 1740, § 1; Stats.1981, c. 839, p. 3226, § 1; Stats.1981, c. 1142, p. 4536, § 9; Stats.1985, c. 1187, § 1; Stats.1986, c. 757, § 5; Stats.1989, c. 1117, § 18; Initiative Measure (Prop. 21, § 27, approved March 7, 2000, eff. March 8, 2000); Stats.2017, c. 319 (A.B.976), § 143, eff. Jan. 1, 2018.)*

Cross References

Commitment of wards to Youth Authority, see Welfare and Institutions Code § 730.
Courts closed for transaction of judicial business, conditions, see Government Code § 68106.
Hearsay evidence, see Evidence Code § 1200 et seq.
Order made after judgment, appeal, see Welfare and Institutions Code § 800.
Removal from parental custody, see Welfare and Institutions Code § 726; Family Code §§ 7802, 7807, 7808, 7820 et seq.

Research References

1 Witkin California Criminal Law 4th Introduction to Crimes § 13 (2021), Conviction on Lesser Evidence.
1 Witkin California Criminal Law 4th Introduction to Crimes § 18 (2021), Changes Involving Parole and Probation.
3 Witkin, California Criminal Law 4th Punishment § 697 (2021), Hearsay.

§ 778. Petition to change, modify or set aside order or terminate jurisdiction of court; hearing; petition to assert relationship as a sibling; visitation; appointment of guardian ad litem

(a)(1) Any parent or other person having an interest in a child who is a ward of the juvenile court or the child himself or herself through a properly appointed guardian may, upon grounds of change of circumstance or new evidence, petition the court in the same action in which the child was found to be a ward of the juvenile court for a hearing to change, modify, or set aside any order of court previously made or to terminate the jurisdiction of the court. The petition shall be verified and, if made by a person other than the child, shall state the petitioner's relationship to or interest in the child and shall set forth in concise language any change of circumstance or new evidence which are alleged to require such change of order or termination of jurisdiction.

(2) If it appears that the best interests of the child may be promoted by the proposed change of order or termination of jurisdiction, the court shall order that a hearing be held and shall give prior notice, or cause prior notice to be given, to such persons and by such means as prescribed by Sections 776 and 779, by electronic service pursuant to Section 212.5, and, in such instances as the means of giving notice is not prescribed by such sections, then by such means as the court prescribes.

(b)(1) Any person, including a ward, a transition dependent, or a nonminor dependent of the juvenile court, may petition the court to assert a relationship as a sibling related by blood, adoption, or affinity through a common legal or biological parent to a child who is, or is the subject of a petition for adjudication as, a ward of the juvenile court, and may request visitation with the ward, placement with or near the ward, or consideration when determining or implementing a case plan or permanent plan for the ward.

(2) A ward, transition dependent, or nonminor dependent of the juvenile court may petition the court to assert a relationship as a sibling related by blood, adoption, or affinity through a common legal or biological parent to a child who is in the physical custody of a common legal or biological parent, and may request visitation with the nondependent sibling in parental custody.

(3) Pursuant to subdivision (b) of Section 16002, a request for sibling visitation may be granted unless it is determined by the court that sibling visitation is contrary to the safety and well-being of any of the siblings.

(4) The court may appoint a guardian ad litem to file the petition for a ward asserting a sibling relationship pursuant to this subdivision if the court determines that the appointment is necessary for the best interests of the ward. The petition shall be verified and shall set forth the following:

(A) Through which parent he or she is related to the sibling.

(B) Whether he or she is related to the sibling by blood, adoption, or affinity.

(C) The request or order that the petitioner is seeking.

(D) Why that request or order is in the best interest of the ward. *(Added by Stats.1961, c. 1616, p. 3492, § 2. Amended by Stats.1963, c. 917, p. 2168, § 11; Stats.1976, c. 1068, p. 4795, § 69; Stats.2014, c. 773 (S.B.1099), § 9, eff. Jan. 1, 2015; Stats.2017, c. 319 (A.B.976), § 144, eff. Jan. 1, 2018.)*

Research References

West's California Judicial Council Forms JV–680, Findings and Orders for Child Approaching Majority—Delinquency.

West's California Judicial Council Forms JV–681, Attachment: Hearing for Dismissal—Additional Findings and Orders—Foster Care Placement—Delinquency.

§ 779. Changing, modifying or setting aside order of commitment to Youth Authority; notice; judicial considerations; application of chapter and section; transfers to a state hospital

The court committing a ward to the Youth Authority may thereafter change, modify, or set aside the order of commitment. Ten days' notice of the hearing of the application therefor shall be served upon the Director of the Youth Authority. In changing, modifying, or setting aside the order of commitment, the court shall give due consideration to the effect thereof upon the discipline and parole system of the Youth Authority or of the correctional school in which the ward may have been placed by the Youth Authority. Except as provided in this section, nothing in this chapter shall be deemed to interfere with the system of parole and discharge now or hereafter established by law, or by rule of the Youth Authority, for the parole and discharge of wards of the juvenile court committed to the Youth Authority, or with the management of any school, institution, or facility under the jurisdiction of the Youth Authority. Except as provided in this section, this chapter does not interfere with the system of transfer between institutions and facilities under the jurisdiction of the Youth Authority. This section does not limit the authority of the court to change, modify, or set aside an order of commitment after a noticed hearing and upon a showing of good cause that the Youth Authority is unable to, or failing to, provide treatment consistent with Section 734.

However, before any inmate of a correctional school may be transferred to a state hospital, he or she shall first be returned to a court of competent jurisdiction and, after hearing, may be committed to a state hospital for the insane in accordance with law. *(Added by Stats.1961, c. 1616, p. 3492, § 2. Amended by Stats.2003, c. 4 (S.B.459), § 2, eff. April 8, 2003, operative Jan. 1, 2004; Stats.2004, c. 183 (A.B.3082), § 371; Stats.2017, c. 319 (A.B.976), § 145, eff. Jan. 1, 2018.)*

Cross References

Powers and duties of Youth Authority, generally, see Welfare and Institutions Code § 1750 et seq.

Recall of commitment resentencing to Youth Authority, see Welfare and Institutions Code § 1737.

§ 779.5. Application to modify or set aside order of commitment of ward to secure youth treatment facility; failure or inability to provide ward with treatment, programming, and education consistent with individual rehabilitation plan; hearing

The court committing a ward to a secure youth treatment facility as provided in Section 875 may thereafter modify or set aside the order of commitment upon the written application of the ward or the probation department and upon a showing of good cause that the county or the commitment facility has failed, or is unable to, provide the ward with treatment, programming, and education that are consistent with the individual rehabilitation plan described in subdivision (d) of Section 875, that the conditions under which the ward is confined are harmful to the ward, or that the juvenile justice goals of rehabilitation and community safety are no longer served by continued confinement of the ward in a secure youth treatment facility. The court shall notice a hearing in which it shall hear any evidence from the ward, the probation department, and any behavioral health or other specialists having information relevant to consideration of the request to modify or set aside the order of commitment. The court shall, at the conclusion of the hearing, make its findings on the record, including findings as to the custodial and supervision status of the ward, based on the evidence presented. *(Added by Stats.2021, c. 18 (S.B.92), § 11, eff. May 14, 2021.)*

§ 780. Return of person to committing court; responsibilities of Department of Youth Authority; payment for transportation

If any person who has been committed to the Youth Authority appears to be an improper person to be received by or retained in any institution or facility under the jurisdiction of the Department of the Youth Authority or to be so incorrigible or so incapable of reformation under the discipline of any institution or facility under the jurisdiction of the department as to render his or her retention detrimental to the interests of the department, the department may order the return of that person to the committing court. However, the return of any person to the committing court does not relieve the department of any of its duties or responsibilities under the original commitment, and that commitment continues in full force and effect until it is vacated, modified, or set aside by order of the court.

If any person is returned to the committing court, his or her transportation shall be made, and the compensation therefor paid, as provided for the order of commitment. *(Added by Stats.1961, c. 1616, p. 3492, § 2. Amended by Stats.1979, c. 860, p. 2972, § 8; Stats.2003, c. 4 (S.B.459), § 3, eff. April 8, 2003, operative Jan. 1, 2004.)*

Cross References

Authority of court to order commitment to Youth Authority, see Welfare and Institutions Code § 731.

Commitment to Youth Authority, conditions of, see Welfare and Institutions Code § 734.

Return of person to committing court, see Welfare and Institutions Code § 1737.1.

Youth Authority, powers and duties in general, see Welfare and Institutions Code § 1750 et seq.

§ 781. Petition for sealing records; notice; hearing; grounds for and effect of order; inspection and destruction of records; access to sealed file to verify prior jurisdictional status; requirement to provide information on eligibility and procedures and petition form

(a)(1)(A) If a petition has been filed with a juvenile court to commence proceedings to adjudge a person a ward of the court, if a person is cited to appear before a probation officer or is taken before a probation officer pursuant to Section 626, or if a minor is taken before any officer of a law enforcement agency, the person or the county probation officer may, five years or more after the jurisdiction of the juvenile court has terminated as to the person, or, if a petition is not filed, five years or more after the person was cited to appear before a probation officer or was taken before a probation officer pursuant to Section 626 or was taken before any officer of a law enforcement agency, or, in any case at any time after the person has reached 18 years of age, petition the court for sealing of the records, including records of arrest, relating to the person's case, in the custody of the juvenile court and probation officer and any other agencies, including law enforcement agencies, entities, and public officials as the petitioner alleges, in the petition, to have custody of the records. The court shall notify the district attorney of the county and the county probation officer, if they are not the petitioner, and the district attorney or probation officer or any of their deputies or any other person having relevant evidence may testify at the hearing on the petition. If, after hearing, the court finds that since the termination of jurisdiction or action pursuant to Section 626, as the case may be, the person has not been convicted of a felony or of any misdemeanor involving moral turpitude and that rehabilitation has been attained to the satisfaction of the court, it shall order all records, papers, and exhibits in the person's case in the custody of the juvenile court sealed, including the juvenile court record, minute book entries, and entries on dockets, and any other records relating to the case in the custody of the other agencies, entities, and officials as are named in the order. Once the court has ordered the person's records sealed, the proceedings in the case shall be deemed never to have occurred, and the person may properly reply accordingly to any inquiry about the events, the records of which are ordered sealed.

(B) The court shall send a copy of the order to each agency, entity, and official named in the order, directing the agency or entity to seal its records. Each agency, entity, and official shall seal the records in its custody as directed by the order, shall advise the court of its compliance, and thereupon shall seal the copy of the court's order for sealing of records that the agency, entity, or official received.

(C) If a ward of the juvenile court is subject to the registration requirements set forth in Section 290 of the Penal Code, a court, in ordering the sealing of the juvenile records of the person, shall also provide in the order that the person is relieved from the registration requirement and for the destruction of all registration information in the custody of the Department of Justice and other agencies, entities, and officials.

(D)(i) A petition to seal the record or records relating to an offense listed in subdivision (b) of Section 707 that was committed after attaining 14 years of age and resulted in the adjudication of wardship by the juvenile court may only be filed or considered by the court pursuant to this section under the following circumstances:

(I) The person was committed to the Department of Corrections and Rehabilitation, Division of Juvenile Facilities, has attained 21 years of age, and has completed their period of probation supervision after release from the division.

(II) The person was not committed to the Department of Corrections and Rehabilitation, Division of Juvenile Facilities, has attained 18 years of age, and has completed any period of probation supervision related to that offense imposed by the court.

(ii) A record relating to an offense listed in subdivision (b) of Section 707 that was committed after attaining 14 years of age that has been sealed pursuant to this section may be accessed, inspected, or utilized in a subsequent proceeding against the person under any of the following circumstances:

(I) By the prosecuting attorney, as necessary, to make appropriate charging decisions or to initiate prosecution in a court of criminal jurisdiction for a subsequent felony offense, or by the prosecuting attorney or the court to determine the appropriate sentencing for a subsequent felony offense.

(II) By the prosecuting attorney, as necessary, to initiate a juvenile court proceeding to determine whether a minor shall be transferred from the juvenile court to a court of criminal jurisdiction pursuant to Section 707, and by the juvenile court to make that determination.

(III) By the prosecuting attorney, the probation department, or the juvenile court upon a subsequent finding by the juvenile court that the minor has committed a felony offense, for the purpose of determining an appropriate disposition of the case.

(IV) By the prosecuting attorney, or a court of criminal jurisdiction, for the purpose of proving a prior serious or violent felony conviction, and determining the appropriate sentence pursuant to Section 667 of the Penal Code.

(iii)(I) A record relating to an offense listed in subdivision (b) of Section 707 that was committed after attaining 14 years of age that has been sealed pursuant to this section may be accessed, inspected, or utilized by the prosecuting attorney in order to meet a statutory or constitutional obligation to disclose favorable or exculpatory evidence to a defendant in a criminal case in which the prosecuting attorney has reason to believe that access to the record is necessary to meet the disclosure obligation. A request to access information in the sealed record for this purpose, including the prosecutor's rationale for believing that access to the information in the record may be necessary to meet the disclosure obligation and the date by which the records are needed, shall be submitted by the prosecuting attorney to the juvenile court. The juvenile court shall approve the prosecutor's request to the extent that the court has, upon review of the relevant records, determined that access to a specific sealed record or portion of a sealed record is necessary to enable the prosecuting attorney to comply with the disclosure obligation. If the juvenile court approves the prosecuting attorney's request, the court shall state on the record appropriate limits on the access, inspection, and utilization of the sealed record information in order to protect the confidentiality of the person whose sealed record is accessed pursuant to this clause. A ruling allowing disclosure of information pursuant to this subdivision does not affect whether the information is admissible in a criminal or juvenile proceeding. This clause does not impose any discovery obligations on a prosecuting attorney that do not already exist.

(II) A record that was sealed pursuant to this section that was generated in connection with the investigation, prosecution, or adjudication of a qualifying offense as defined in subdivision (c) of Section 679.10 of the Penal Code may be accessed by a judge or prosecutor for the limited purpose of processing a request of a victim or victim's family member to certify victim helpfulness on the Form I–918 Supplement B certification or Form I–914 Supplement B declaration. The information obtained pursuant to this subclause shall not be disseminated to other agencies or individuals, except as necessary to certify victim helpfulness on the Form I–918 Supplement B certification or Form I–914 Supplement B declaration, and under no circumstances shall it be used to support the imposition of penalties, detention, or other sanctions upon an individual.

(III) This clause shall not apply to juvenile case files pertaining to matters within the jurisdiction of the juvenile court pursuant to Section 300.

(iv) A sealed record that is accessed, inspected, or utilized pursuant to clause (ii) or (iii) shall be accessed, inspected, or utilized only for the purposes described therein, and the information contained in the sealed record shall otherwise remain confidential and shall not be further disseminated. The access, inspection, or utilization of a sealed record pursuant to clause (ii) or (iii) shall not be deemed an unsealing of the record and shall not require notice to any other entity.

(E) Subparagraph (D) does not apply in cases in which the offense listed in subdivision (b) of Section 707 that was committed after attaining 14 years of age was dismissed or reduced to a misdemeanor by the court. In those cases, the person may petition the court to have the record sealed, and the court may order the sealing of the record in the same manner and with the same effect as otherwise provided in this section for records that do not relate to an offense listed in subdivision (b) of Section 707 that was committed after the person had attained 14 years of age.

(F) Notwithstanding subparagraphs (D) and (E), a record relating to an offense listed in subdivision (b) of Section 707 that was committed after attaining 14 years of age for which the person is required to register pursuant to Section 290.008 of the Penal Code shall not be sealed.

(2) An unfulfilled order of restitution that has been converted to a civil judgment pursuant to Section 730.6 shall not be a bar to sealing a record pursuant to this subdivision.

(3) Outstanding restitution fines and court-ordered fees shall not be considered when assessing whether a petitioner's rehabilitation has been attained to the satisfaction of the court and shall not be a bar to sealing a record pursuant to this subdivision.

(4) The person who is the subject of records sealed pursuant to this section may petition the superior court to permit inspection of the records by persons named in the petition, and the superior court may order the inspection of the records. Except as provided in subdivision (b), the records shall not be open to inspection.

(b) In any action or proceeding based upon defamation, a court, upon a showing of good cause, may order any records sealed under this section to be opened and admitted into evidence. The records shall be confidential and shall be available for inspection only by the court, jury, parties, counsel for the parties, and any other person who is authorized by the court to inspect them. Upon the judgment in the action or proceeding becoming final, the court shall order the records sealed.

(c)(1) Subdivision (a) does not apply to Department of Motor Vehicles records of any convictions for offenses under the Vehicle Code or any local ordinance relating to the operation, stopping and standing, or parking of a vehicle where the record of any such conviction would be a public record under Section 1808 of the Vehicle Code. However, if a court orders a case record containing any such conviction to be sealed under this section, and if the Department of Motor Vehicles maintains a public record of such a conviction, the court shall notify the Department of Motor Vehicles of the sealing and the department shall advise the court of its receipt of the notice.

(2) Notwithstanding any other law, subsequent to the notification, the Department of Motor Vehicles shall allow access to its record of convictions only to the subject of the record and to insurers which have been granted requestor code numbers by the department. Any insurer to which a record of conviction is disclosed, when the conviction record has otherwise been sealed under this section, shall be given notice of the sealing when the record is disclosed to the insurer. The insurer may use the information contained in the record for purposes of determining eligibility for insurance and insurance rates for the subject of the record, and the information shall not be used for any other purpose nor shall it be disclosed by an insurer to any person or party not having access to the record.

(3) This subdivision does not prevent the sealing of any record which is maintained by any agency or party other than the Department of Motor Vehicles.

(4) This subdivision does not affect the procedures or authority of the Department of Motor Vehicles for purging department records.

(d) Unless for good cause the court determines that the juvenile court record shall be retained, the court shall order the destruction of a person's juvenile court records that are sealed pursuant to this section as follows: five years after the record was ordered sealed, if the person who is the subject of the record was alleged or adjudged to be a person described by Section 601; or when the person who is the subject of the record reaches 38 years of age if the person was alleged or adjudged to be a person described by Section 602, except that if the subject of the record was found to be a person described in Section 602 because of the commission of an offense listed in subdivision (b) of Section 707 when the person was 14 years of age or older, the record shall not be destroyed. Any other agency in possession of sealed records may destroy its records five years after the record was ordered sealed.

(e) The court may access a file that has been sealed pursuant to this section for the limited purpose of verifying the prior jurisdictional status of a ward who is petitioning the court to resume its jurisdiction pursuant to subdivision (e) of Section 388. This access shall not be deemed an unsealing of the record and shall not require notice to any other entity.

(f) This section shall not permit the sealing of a person's juvenile court records for an offense where the person is convicted of that offense in a criminal court pursuant to the provisions of Section 707.1. This subdivision is declaratory of existing law.

(g)(1) This section does not prohibit a court from enforcing a civil judgment for an unfulfilled order of restitution obtained pursuant to Section 730.6. A minor is not relieved from the obligation to pay victim restitution, restitution fines, and court-ordered fines and fees because the minor's records are sealed.

(2) A victim or a local collection program may continue to enforce victim restitution orders, restitution fines, and court-ordered fines and fees after a record is sealed. The juvenile court shall have access to any records sealed pursuant to this section for the limited purposes of enforcing a civil judgment or restitution order.

(h)(1) On and after January 1, 2015, each court and probation department shall ensure that information regarding the eligibility for and the procedures to request the sealing and destruction of records pursuant to this section shall be provided to each person who is either of the following:

(A) A person for whom a petition has been filed on or after January 1, 2015, to adjudge the person a ward of the juvenile court.

(B) A person who is brought before a probation officer pursuant to Section 626.

(2) The Judicial Council shall, on or before January 1, 2015, develop informational materials for purposes of paragraph (1) and shall develop a form to petition the court for the sealing and destruction of records pursuant to this section. The informational materials and the form shall be provided to each person described in paragraph (1) when jurisdiction is terminated or when the case is dismissed. *(Added by Stats.1961, c. 1616, p. 3493, § 2. Amended by Stats.1961, c. 1673, p. 3640, § 2; Stats.1963, c. 1761, p. 3515, § 8; Stats.1965, c. 1413, p. 3330, § 1; Stats.1967, c. 1649, p. 3951, § 1; Stats.1967, c. 1650, p. 3952, § 1; Stats.1970, c. 497, p. 980, § 3; Stats.1972, c. 579, p. 1018, § 54.5; Stats.1976, c. 1068, p. 4795, § 70; Stats.1980, c. 1104, p. 3548, § 2; Stats.1980, c. 1319, p. 4573, § 2; Stats.1981, c. 488, p. 1836, § 1; Stats.1984, c. 1429, § 1; Stats.1985, c. 1474, § 4; Stats.1986, c. 277, § 1; Stats.1994, c. 453 (A.B.560), § 13; Stats.1994, c. 835 (A.B.234), § 1.2; Stats.1996, c. 745 (A.B.3294), § 1; Stats.1998, c. 374 (S.B.1387), § 1; Stats.1999, c. 83 (S.B.966), § 194; Initiative Measure (Prop. 21, § 28, approved March 7, 2000, eff. March 8, 2000); Stats.2011, c. 459 (A.B.212), § 21, eff. Oct. 4, 2011; Stats.2013, c. 269 (A.B.1006), § 1; Stats.2015, c. 388 (S.B.504), § 2, eff. Jan. 1, 2016; Stats.2017, c. 679 (S.B.312), § 1, eff. Jan. 1, 2018; Stats.2018, c. 423 (S.B.1494), § 125, eff. Jan. 1, 2019; Stats.2019, c. 50 (A.B.1537), § 2, eff. Jan. 1, 2020; Stats.2020, c. 329 (A.B.2321), § 1, eff. Jan. 1, 2021.)*

Cross References

Arson and attempted arson, persons convicted of arson, registration while residing California, see Penal Code § 457.1.

Disclosure of juvenile police records, see Welfare and Institutions Code § 827.9.

Felonies, definition and penalties, see Penal Code §§ 17, 18.

Inspection of public records, other exemptions from disclosure, see Government Code § 6276.48.

Management of trial court records, destruction of records, notice and retention periods, see Government Code § 68152.

Misdemeanors, definition and penalties, see Penal Code §§ 17, 19, 19.2.

Petition to seal court records by person arrested for misdemeanor while a minor, see Penal Code § 851.7.

Probation officer or social worker defined for purposes of this Chapter, see Welfare and Institutions Code § 215.

Sealing of record, application of section, scope of authority to seal record, see Penal Code § 1203.47.

Sex offenders, juveniles adjudicated a ward of the juvenile court for specified sex offenses and sent to the Division of Juvenile Justice, or equivalent thereof, duty to register, see Penal Code § 290.008.

Research References

West's California Judicial Council Forms JV–590, Order to Seal Juvenile Records—Welfare and Institutions Code Section 781 (Also Available in Spanish).

West's California Judicial Council Forms JV–591, Acknowledgment of Juvenile Record Sealed.

West's California Judicial Council Forms JV–592, Prosecutor Request for Access to Sealed Juvenile Case File.

West's California Judicial Council Forms JV–595, Request to Seal Juvenile Records.

West's California Judicial Council Forms JV–599, Order on Prosecutor Request for Access to Sealed File.
West's California Judicial Council Forms JV–710, Order to Transfer Juvenile to Criminal Court Jurisdiction (Welfare and Institutions Code, §707) (Also Available in Spanish).
West's California Judicial Council Forms JV–755, Deferred Entry of Judgment—Dismissal and Sealing of Juvenile Records (Also Available in Spanish).
1 Witkin California Criminal Law 4th Introduction to Crimes § 140 (2021), Gang Violence and Juvenile Crime Prevention Act (Proposition 21).
4 Witkin, California Criminal Law 4th Pretrial Proceedings § 86 (2021), Sealing of Records of Minors.
3 Witkin, California Criminal Law 4th Punishment § 156 (2021), In General.
3 Witkin, California Criminal Law 4th Punishment § 186 (2021), Arson Offenders.
3 Witkin, California Criminal Law 4th Punishment § 716 (2021), Exceptions.
3 Witkin, California Criminal Law 4th Punishment § 725 (2021), Where Minor was Not Convicted.
3 Witkin, California Criminal Law 4th Punishment § 725A (2021), (New) Minor Declared Ward for Commission of Prostitution Offenses.

§ 781.1. No fee to file a petition to seal records

A superior court or probation department shall not charge an applicant a fee for filing a petition to seal records under Section 781.
(Added by Stats.2019, c. 582 (A.B.1394), § 1, eff. Jan. 1, 2020.)

§ 781.5. Sealing and destruction of records; factually innocent minors

(a) Notwithstanding Section 781, in any case where a minor has been cited to appear before a probation officer, has been taken before a probation officer pursuant to Section 626, or has been taken before any officer of a law enforcement agency, and no accusatory pleading or petition to adjudge the minor a ward of the court has been filed, the minor may request in writing that the law enforcement agency and probation officer having jurisdiction over the offense destroy their records of the arrest or citation. A copy of the request shall be served upon the district attorney of the county having jurisdiction over the offense. The law enforcement agency and probation officer having jurisdiction over the offense, upon a determination that the minor is factually innocent, shall, with the concurrence of the district attorney, seal their records with respect to the minor and the request for relief under this section for three years from the date of the arrest or citation and thereafter destroy the records and the request. A determination of factual innocence shall not be made pursuant to this subdivision unless the law enforcement agency and probation officer, with the concurrence of the district attorney, determine that no reasonable cause exists to believe that the minor committed the offense for which the arrest was made or the citation was issued. The law enforcement agency and probation officer having jurisdiction over the offense shall notify the Department of Justice, and any other law enforcement agency or probation officer that arrested or cited the minor or participated in the arrest or citing of the minor for an offense for which the minor has been found factually innocent under this subdivision, of the sealing of the minor's records and the reason therefor. The Department of Justice and any law enforcement agency or probation officer so notified shall forthwith seal its records of the arrest or citation and the notice of sealing for three years from the date of the arrest or citation, and thereafter destroy those records and the notice of sealing. The law enforcement agency and probation officer having jurisdiction over the offense and the Department of Justice shall request the destruction of any records of the arrest or citation that they have given to any local, state, or federal agency or to any other person or entity. Each agency, person, or entity within the State of California receiving that request shall destroy its records of the arrest or citation and that request, unless otherwise provided in this section.

(b) If, after receipt by the law enforcement agency, probation officer, and the district attorney of a request for relief under subdivision (a), the law enforcement agency, probation officer, and district attorney do not respond to the request by accepting or denying the request within 60 days after the running of the statute of limitations for the offense for which the minor was cited or arrested or within 60 days after receipt of the petition in cases where the statute of limitations has previously lapsed, then the request shall be deemed to be denied. In any case where the request of a minor to the law enforcement agency and probation officer to have a record destroyed is denied, petition may be made to the juvenile court that would have had jurisdiction over the matter. A copy of the petition shall be served on the district attorney of the county having jurisdiction over the offense at least 10 days prior to the hearing thereon. The district attorney may present evidence to the court at the hearing. Notwithstanding any other provision of law, any judicial determination of factual innocence made pursuant to this subdivision may be heard and determined upon declarations, affidavits, police reports, or any other evidence submitted by the parties that is material, relevant, and reliable. A finding of factual innocence and an order for the sealing and destruction of records pursuant to this subdivision or subdivision (d) shall not be made unless the court finds that no reasonable cause exists to believe that the minor committed the offense for which the arrest was made or the citation was issued. In any court hearing to determine the factual innocence of a minor, the initial burden of proof shall rest with the minor to show that no reasonable cause exists to believe that the minor committed the offense for which the arrest was made or the citation was issued. If the court finds that this showing of no reasonable cause has been made by the minor, then the burden of proof shall shift to the respondent to show that a reasonable cause exists to believe that the minor committed the offense for which the arrest was made or the citation was issued.

(c) If the court finds the minor to be factually innocent of the charges for which the arrest was made or the citation was issued, then the court shall order the law enforcement agency and probation officer having jurisdiction over the offense, the Department of Justice, and any law enforcement agency or probation officer that arrested or cited the minor or participated in the arrest or citation of the minor for an offense for which the minor has been found factually innocent under this section, to seal their records relating to the minor and the court order to seal and destroy those records, for three years from the date of the arrest or citation and thereafter to destroy those records and the court order to seal and destroy those records. The court shall also order the law enforcement agency and probation officer having jurisdiction over the offense and the Department of Justice to request the destruction of any records of the arrest that they have given to any local, state, or federal agency, person or entity. Each state or local agency, person or entity within the State of California receiving that request shall destroy its records of the arrest or citation and the request to destroy those records, unless otherwise provided in this section. The court shall give to the minor a copy of any court order concerning the destruction of the arrest or citation records.

(d) Notwithstanding Section 781, in any case where a minor has been arrested or a citation has been issued, and an accusatory pleading or petition to adjudge the minor a ward of the court has been filed, but not sustained, the minor may, at any time after dismissal of the proceeding, request in writing from the court that dismissed the proceeding a finding that the minor is factually innocent of the charges for which the arrest was made or the citation was issued. A copy of the request shall be served on the district attorney of the county in which the accusatory pleading or petition was filed at least 10 days prior to the hearing on the minor's factual innocence. The district attorney may present evidence to the court at the hearing. The hearing shall be conducted as provided in subdivision (b). If the court finds the petitioner to be factually innocent of the charges for which the arrest was made or the citation was issued, then the court shall grant the relief as provided in subdivision (c).

(e) Notwithstanding Section 781, in any case where a minor has been arrested or cited and an accusatory pleading or petition to adjudge the minor a ward of the court has been filed, but not sustained, and it appears to the judge presiding at the proceeding that the minor was factually innocent of the offense, the court, upon the written or oral motion of any party in the case or on the court's own motion, may grant the relief provided in subdivision (c). If the district attorney objects to the court granting that relief, the district attorney may request a hearing as to the minor's factual innocence. This hearing shall be conducted as provided in subdivision (b).

(f) In any case where a minor who has been arrested or cited is granted relief pursuant to this section, the law enforcement agency and probation officer having jurisdiction over the offense or the court shall issue a written declaration to the minor stating that it is the determination of the law enforcement agency and probation officer having jurisdiction over the offense or the court that the minor is factually innocent of the charges for which the minor was arrested or cited and that the minor is thereby exonerated. Thereafter, the arrest or citation shall be deemed not to have occurred and the minor may answer accordingly any question relating to its occurrence.

(g) The Department of Justice shall furnish forms to be utilized by minors requesting the destruction of their arrest or citation records and for the written declaration that a minor was found factually innocent under this section.

(h) Documentation of arrest or citation records that are destroyed pursuant to this section that are contained in investigative police reports shall bear the notation "Exonerated" whenever reference is made to the minor. The minor shall be notified in writing by the law enforcement agency and probation officer having jurisdiction over the offense of the sealing and destruction of the arrest and citation records pursuant to this section.

(i) Any finding that a minor is factually innocent pursuant to this section shall not be admissible as evidence in any action.

(j) Destruction of records of arrest or citation pursuant to this section shall be accomplished by permanent obliteration of all entries or notations upon those records pertaining to the arrest or citation, and the record shall be prepared again so that it appears that the arrest or citation never occurred. However, where the only entries on the record pertain to the arrest or citation and the record can be destroyed without necessarily effecting the destruction of other records, then the document constituting the record shall be physically destroyed.

(k) No records shall be destroyed pursuant to this section if the minor or another individual arrested or cited for the same offense has filed a civil action against the peace officers, law enforcement agency, or probation officer that made the arrest, issued the citation, or commenced the proceedings and if the agency or officer that is the custodian of those records has received a certified copy of the complaint in the civil action, until the civil action has been resolved. Any records sealed pursuant to this section by the court in the civil action, upon a showing of good cause, may be opened and submitted into evidence. The records shall be confidential and shall be available for inspection only by the court, jury, parties, counsel for the parties, and any other person authorized by the court. Immediately following the final resolution of the civil action, records subject to this section shall be sealed and destroyed pursuant to this section.

(*l*) Any relief that is available to a minor under this section for an arrest or citation shall also be available for a minor who is taken into temporary custody and then released pursuant to Sections 625 and 626.

(m) This section shall not apply to any offense that is classified as an infraction.

(n)(1) This section shall be repealed on the effective date of a final judgment based on a claim under the California or United States Constitution holding that evidence that is relevant, reliable, and material may not be considered for purposes of a judicial determination of factual innocence under this section. For purposes of this subdivision, a judgment by the appellate division of a superior court is a final judgment if it is published and if it is not reviewed on appeal by a court of appeal. A judgment of a court of appeal is a final judgment if it is published and if it is not reviewed by the California Supreme Court.

(2) Any decision referred to in this subdivision shall be stayed pending appeal.

(3) If not otherwise appealed by a party to the action, any decision referred to in this subdivision that is a judgment by the appellate division of the superior court, shall be appealed by the Attorney General. *(Added by Stats.1999, c. 167 (A.B.744), § 1.)*

Repeal

This section is repealed by its own terms on the date of a judgment described in the section.

Cross References

Attorney General, generally, see Government Code § 12500 et seq.
Burden of proof, generally, see Evidence Code § 500 et seq.
DNA and Forensic Identification Database and Data Bank Act, reversal, dismissal or acquittal, request for expungement of information, specimens from persons no longer considered suspects, see Penal Code § 299.
Probation officer or social worker defined for purposes of this Chapter, see Welfare and Institutions Code § 215.

§ 782. Dismissal of petition; grounds; court authority; sealing of records; restitution

(a)(1) A judge of the juvenile court in which a petition was filed or that has taken jurisdiction of a case pursuant to Section 750 may dismiss the petition, or may set aside the findings and dismiss the petition, if the court finds that the interests of justice and the welfare of the person who is the subject of the petition require that dismissal, or if it finds that * * * they are not in need of treatment or rehabilitation. The court has jurisdiction to order dismissal or setting aside of the findings and dismissal regardless of whether the person who is the subject of the petition is, at the time of the order, a ward or dependent child of the court. Nothing in this section shall be interpreted to require the court to maintain jurisdiction over a person who is the subject of a petition between the time the court's jurisdiction over that person terminates and the point at which * * * their petition is dismissed.

(2)(A) When exercising its discretion under paragraph (1) at the time the court terminates jurisdiction or at any time thereafter, the court shall consider and afford great weight to evidence offered by a person to prove mitigating circumstances are present, including, but not limited to, satisfactory completion of a term of probation, that rehabilitation has been attained to the satisfaction of the court, that dismissal of the petition would not endanger public safety, or that the underlying offense is connected to mental illness, prior victimization, or childhood trauma. Proof of the presence of one or more mitigating circumstances weighs greatly in favor of dismissing the petition.

(B) "Satisfactory completion of a term of probation" shall be interpreted consistent with subdivision (a) of Section 786.

(C) "Rehabilitation has been attained to the satisfaction of the court" shall be interpreted consistent with subparagraph (A) of paragraph (1) of subdivision (a) of Section 781.

(D) "Mental illness," "childhood trauma," "prior victimization," and "endanger public safety" have the same meanings as defined in Section 1385 of the Penal Code.

(E) The great weight standard set forth in this paragraph shall not be applicable in cases where an individual has been convicted in criminal court of a serious or violent felony.

(F) For the purposes of subparagraph (E), a "serious or violent felony" means any offense defined in subdivision (c) of Section 667.5, or in subdivision (c) of Section 1192.7, of the Penal Code.

(G) The absence of the great weight standard under the circumstances described in this paragraph shall not affect the court's authority under paragraph (1).

(b) The reasons for a decision under this section shall be stated orally on the record. The court shall also set forth the reasons in an order entered upon the minutes if requested by either party or in any case in which the proceedings are not being recorded electronically or reported by a court reporter.

(c) The court has authority to exercise discretion pursuant to subdivision (a) at any time after the filing of the petition.

(d) The court has authority to exercise discretion pursuant to subdivision (a) regardless of whether a petition was sustained at trial, by admission or plea agreement.

(e) Dismissal of a petition, or setting aside of the findings and dismissal of a petition, pursuant to this section, after the person was declared a ward, does not alone constitute a sealing of records as defined in Section 781 or 786. Any unsealed records pertaining to the dismissed petition may be accessed, inspected, or used by the court, the probation department, the prosecuting attorney, or counsel for the minor in juvenile court proceedings commenced by the filing of a new petition alleging the person is a person described by Section 602.

(f) Dismissal of the petition, or setting aside the findings and dismissal of the petition, pursuant to this section does not relieve a person from the obligation to pay unfulfilled victim restitution ordered pursuant a civil judgment under Section 730.6. *(Added by Stats.1971, c. 607, p. 1211, § 1. Amended by Stats.2014, c. 249 (S.B.1038), § 1, eff. Jan. 1, 2015; Stats.2022, c. 197 (S.B.1493), § 38, eff. Jan. 1, 2023; Stats.2022, c. 970 (A.B.2629), § 1, eff. Jan. 1, 2023.)*

Research References

3 Witkin, California Criminal Law 4th Punishment § 398 (2021), What Constitutes Prior Conviction.
3 Witkin, California Criminal Law 4th Punishment § 427 (2021), Juvenile Adjudication.

§ 783. Adjudication of violation of Vehicle Code § 13202.5, subd. (d), by minor; report to Department of Motor Vehicles

An adjudication that a minor violated any of the provisions enumerated in subdivision (d) of Section 13202.5 of the Vehicle Code shall be reported to the Department of Motor Vehicles at its office in Sacramento within 10 days of the adjudication pursuant to Section 1803 of the Vehicle Code. *(Added by Stats.1983, c. 934, § 3. Amended by Stats.1988, c. 1254, § 5.)*

§ 784. Violations for which report required under Vehicle Code § 1803; abstract of record

Notwithstanding any other provision of law, upon any adjudication that a minor violated any provision of law for which a report would be required under Section 1803 of the Vehicle Code, including any determination that because of the act the minor is a person described in Section 601 or 602 or that a program of supervision should be instituted for the minor, the clerk shall, not more than 30 days after the violation and in no case later than 10 days after the adjudication, prepare an abstract of the record, certify the abstract to be true and correct, and immediately forward the abstract to the Department of Motor Vehicles. The record shall be a public record subject to disclosure in the same manner as reports made under Section 1803 of the Vehicle Code. *(Added by Stats.1989, c. 1465, § 6.)*

Cross References

Insurance, reduction and control of insurance rates, good driver discount policy, see Insurance Code § 1861.025.

§ 785. Wards of juvenile court; petition for order to terminate or modify jurisdiction of juvenile court; notice and hearing

(a) Where a minor is a ward of the juvenile court, the wardship did not result in the minor's commitment to the Youth Authority, and the minor is found not to be a fit and proper subject to be dealt with under the juvenile court law with respect to a subsequent allegation of criminal conduct, any parent or other person having an interest in the minor, or the minor, through a properly appointed guardian, the prosecuting attorney, or probation officer, may petition the court in the same action in which the minor was found to be a ward of the juvenile court for a hearing for an order to terminate or modify the jurisdiction of the juvenile court. The court shall order that a hearing be held and shall give prior notice, or cause prior notice to be given, to those persons and by the means prescribed by Sections 776 and 779, by electronic service pursuant to Section 212.5, or where the means of giving notice is not prescribed by those sections, then by such means as the court prescribes.

(b) The petition shall be verified and shall state why jurisdiction should be terminated or modified in concise language.

(c) In determining whether or not the wardship shall terminate or be modified, the court shall be guided by the policies set forth in Section 202.

(d) In addition to its authority under this chapter, the Judicial Council shall adopt rules providing criteria for the consideration of the juvenile court in determining whether or not to terminate or modify jurisdiction pursuant to this section. *(Added by Stats.1994, c. 448 (A.B.1948), § 6. Amended by Stats.2010, c. 559 (A.B.12), § 29.5; Stats.2011, c. 459 (A.B.212), § 22, eff. Oct. 4, 2011; Stats.2017, c. 319 (A.B.976), § 146, eff. Jan. 1, 2018.)*

Cross References

Modification of juvenile court judgments and orders, petitions, see Welfare and Institutions Code § 388.
Probation officer or social worker defined for purposes of this Chapter, see Welfare and Institutions Code § 215.
Reunification of minor in foster care with family or establishment of alternative permanent plan, ongoing review of status of minor, see Welfare and Institutions Code § 727.2.

§ 786. Completion of supervision program or probation; dismissal of petition; sealing of records; exception; access to records

(a) If a person who has been alleged or found to be a ward of the juvenile court satisfactorily completes (1) an informal program of supervision pursuant to Section 654.2, (2) probation under Section 725, or (3) a term of probation for any offense, the court shall order the petition dismissed. The court shall order sealed all records pertaining to the dismissed petition in the custody of the juvenile court, and in the custody of law enforcement agencies, the probation department, or the Department of Justice. The court shall send a copy of the order to each agency and official named in the order, direct the agency or official to seal its records, and specify a date by which the sealed records shall be destroyed. If a record contains a sustained petition rendering the person ineligible to own or possess a firearm until 30 years of age pursuant to Section 29820 of the Penal Code, then the date the sealed records shall be destroyed is the date upon which the person turns 33 years of age. Each agency and official named in the order shall seal the records in its custody as directed by the order, shall advise the court of its compliance, and, after advising the court, shall seal the copy of the court's order that was received. The court shall also provide notice to the person and the person's counsel that it has ordered the petition dismissed and the records sealed in the case. The notice shall include an advisement of the person's right to nondisclosure of the arrest and proceedings, as specified in subdivision (b).

(b) Upon the court's order of dismissal of the petition, the arrest and other proceedings in the case shall be deemed not to have occurred and the person who was the subject of the petition may reply accordingly to an inquiry by employers, educational institutions, or other persons or entities regarding the arrest and proceedings in the case.

(c)(1) For purposes of this section, satisfactory completion of an informal program of supervision or another term of probation described in subdivision (a) shall be deemed to have occurred if the person has no new findings of wardship or conviction for a felony offense or a misdemeanor involving moral turpitude during the period of supervision or probation and if the person has not failed to substantially comply with the reasonable orders of supervision or probation that are within their capacity to perform. The period of supervision or probation shall not be extended solely for the purpose of deferring or delaying eligibility for dismissal of the petition and sealing of the records under this section.

(2) An unfulfilled order or condition of restitution, including a restitution fine that can be converted to a civil judgment under Section 730.6 or an unpaid restitution fee shall not be deemed to constitute unsatisfactory completion of supervision or probation under this section.

(d) A court shall not seal a record or dismiss a petition pursuant to this section if the petition was sustained based on the commission of an offense listed in subdivision (b) of Section 707 that was committed when the individual was 14 years of age or older unless the finding on that offense was dismissed or was reduced to a misdemeanor or to a lesser offense that is not listed in subdivision (b) of Section 707.

(e) If a person who has been alleged to be a ward of the juvenile court has their petition dismissed by the court, whether on the motion of the prosecution or on the court's own motion, or if the petition is not sustained by the court after an adjudication hearing, the court shall order sealed all records pertaining to the dismissed petition in the custody of the juvenile court, and in the custody of law enforcement agencies, the probation department, or the Department of Justice. The court shall send a copy of the order to each agency and official named in the order, direct the agency or official to seal its records, and specify a date by which the sealed records shall be destroyed. Each agency and official named in the order shall seal the records in its custody as directed by the order, shall advise the court of its compliance, and, after advising the court, shall seal the copy of the court's order that was received. The court shall also provide notice to the person and the person's counsel that it has ordered the petition dismissed and the records sealed in the case. The notice shall include an advisement of the person's right to nondisclosure of the arrest and proceedings, as specified in subdivision (b).

(f)(1) The court may, in making its order to seal the record and dismiss the instant petition pursuant to this section, include an order to seal a record relating to, or to dismiss, any prior petition or petitions that have been filed or sustained against the individual and that appear to the satisfaction of the court to meet the sealing and dismissal criteria otherwise described in this section.

(2) An individual who has a record that is eligible to be sealed under this section may ask the court to order the sealing of a record pertaining to the case that is in the custody of a public agency other than a law enforcement agency, the probation department, or the Department of Justice, and the court may grant the request and order that the public agency record be sealed if the court determines that sealing the additional record will promote the successful reentry and rehabilitation of the individual.

(g)(1) A record that has been ordered sealed by the court under this section may be accessed, inspected, or utilized only under any of the following circumstances:

(A) By the prosecuting attorney, the probation department, or the court for the limited purpose of determining whether the minor is eligible and suitable for deferred entry of judgment pursuant to Section 790 or is ineligible for a program of supervision as defined in Section 654.3.

(B) By the court for the limited purpose of verifying the prior jurisdictional status of a ward who is petitioning the court to resume its jurisdiction pursuant to subdivision (e) of Section 388.

(C) If a new petition has been filed against the minor for a felony offense, by the probation department for the limited purpose of identifying the minor's previous court-ordered programs or placements, and in that event solely to determine the individual's eligibility or suitability for remedial programs or services. The information obtained pursuant to this subparagraph shall not be disseminated to other agencies or individuals, except as necessary to implement a referral to a remedial program or service, and shall not be used to support the imposition of penalties, detention, or other sanctions upon the minor.

(D) Upon a subsequent adjudication of a minor whose record has been sealed under this section and a finding that the minor is a person described by Section 602 based on the commission of a felony offense, by the probation department, the prosecuting attorney, counsel for the minor, or the court for the limited purpose of determining an appropriate juvenile court disposition. Access, inspection, or use of a sealed record as provided under this subparagraph shall not be construed as a reversal or modification of the court's order dismissing the petition and sealing the record in the prior case.

(E) Upon the prosecuting attorney's motion, made in accordance with Section 707, to initiate court proceedings to determine whether the case should be transferred to a court of criminal jurisdiction, by the probation department, the prosecuting attorney, counsel for the minor, or the court for the limited purpose of evaluating and determining if such a transfer is appropriate. Access, inspection, or use of a sealed record as provided under this subparagraph shall not be construed as a reversal or modification of the court's order dismissing the petition and sealing the record in the prior case.

(F) By the person whose record has been sealed, upon their request and petition to the court to permit inspection of the records.

(G) By the probation department of any county to access the records for the limited purpose of meeting federal Title IV–B and Title IV–E compliance.

(H) The child welfare agency of a county responsible for the supervision and placement of a minor or nonminor dependent may access a record that has been ordered sealed by the court under this section for the limited purpose of determining an appropriate placement or service that has been ordered for the minor or nonminor dependent by the court. The information contained in the sealed record and accessed by the child welfare worker or agency under this subparagraph may be shared with the court but shall in all other respects remain confidential and shall not be disseminated to any other person or agency. Access to the sealed record under this subparagraph shall not be construed as a modification of the court's order dismissing the petition and sealing the record in the case.

(I) By the prosecuting attorney for the evaluation of charges and prosecution of offenses pursuant to Section 29820 of the Penal Code.

(J) By the Department of Justice for the purpose of determining if the person is suitable to purchase, own, or possess a firearm, consistent with Section 29820 of the Penal Code.

(K)(i) A record that has been sealed pursuant to this section may be accessed, inspected, or utilized by the prosecuting attorney in order to meet a statutory or constitutional obligation to disclose favorable or exculpatory evidence to a defendant in a criminal case in which the prosecuting attorney has reason to believe that access to the record is necessary to meet the disclosure obligation. A request to access information in the sealed record for this purpose, including the prosecutor's rationale for believing that access to the information in the record may be necessary to meet the disclosure obligation and the date by which the records are needed, shall be submitted by the prosecuting attorney to the juvenile court. The juvenile court shall notify the person having the sealed record, including the person's attorney of record, that the court is considering the prosecutor's request to access the record, and the court shall provide that person with the opportunity to respond, in writing or by appearance, to the request prior to making its determination. The juvenile court shall review the case file and records that have been referenced by the prosecutor as necessary to meet the disclosure obligation and any response submitted by the person having the sealed record. The court shall approve the prosecutor's request to the extent that the court has, upon review of the relevant records, determined that access to a specific sealed record or portion of a sealed record is necessary to enable the prosecuting attorney to comply with the disclosure obligation. If the juvenile court approves the prosecuting attorney's request, the court shall state on the record appropriate limits on the access, inspection, and utilization of the sealed record information in order to protect the confidentiality of the person whose sealed record is accessed pursuant to this subparagraph. A ruling allowing disclosure of information pursuant to this subdivision does not affect whether the information is admissible in a criminal or juvenile proceeding. This subparagraph does not impose any discovery obligations on a prosecuting attorney that do not already exist.

(ii) This subparagraph shall not apply to juvenile case files pertaining to matters within the jurisdiction of the juvenile court pursuant to Section 300.

(L) If a new petition has been filed against the minor in juvenile court and the issue of competency is raised, by the probation department, the prosecuting attorney, counsel for the minor, and the court for the purpose of assessing the minor's competency in the proceedings on the new petition. Access, inspection, or utilization of the sealed records is limited to any prior competency evaluations submitted to the court, whether ordered by the court or not, all reports concerning remediation efforts and success, all court findings and orders relating to the minor's competency, and any other evidence submitted to the court for consideration in determining the minor's competency, including, but not limited to, school records and other test results. The information obtained pursuant to this subparagraph shall not be disseminated to any other person or agency except as necessary to evaluate the minor's competency or provide remediation services, and shall not be used to support the imposition of penalties, detention, or other sanctions on the minor. Access to the sealed record under this subparagraph shall not be construed as a modification of the court's order dismissing the petition and sealing the record in the case.

(M) A record that was sealed pursuant to this section that was generated in connection with the investigation, prosecution, or adjudication of a qualifying offense as defined in subdivision (c) of Section 679.10 of the Penal Code may be accessed by a judge or prosecutor for the limited purpose of processing a request of a victim or victim's family member to certify victim helpfulness on the Form I–918 Supplement B certification or Form I–914 Supplement B declaration. The information obtained pursuant to this subparagraph shall not be disseminated to other agencies or individuals, except as necessary to certify victim helpfulness on the Form I–918 Supplement B certification or Form I–914 Supplement B declaration, and under no circumstances shall it be used to support the imposition of penalties, detention, or other sanctions upon an individual.

(2) When a record has been sealed by the court based on a dismissed petition pursuant to subdivision (e), the prosecutor, within six months of the date of dismissal, may petition the court to access, inspect, or utilize the sealed record for the limited purpose of refiling the dismissed petition based on new circumstances, including, but not limited to, new evidence or witness availability. The court shall determine whether the new circumstances alleged by the prosecutor provide sufficient justification for accessing, inspecting, or utilizing the sealed record in order to refile the dismissed petition.

(3) Access to, or inspection of, a sealed record authorized by paragraphs (1) and (2) shall not be deemed an unsealing of the record and shall not require notice to any other agency.

(h)(1) This section does not prohibit a court from enforcing a civil judgment for an unfulfilled order of restitution ordered pursuant to Section 730.6. A minor is not relieved from the obligation to pay victim restitution, restitution fines, and court-ordered fines and fees because the minor's records are sealed.

(2) A victim or a local collection program may continue to enforce victim restitution orders, restitution fines, and court-ordered fines and fees after a record is sealed. The juvenile court shall have access to records sealed pursuant to this section for the limited purpose of enforcing a civil judgment or restitution order.

(i) This section does not prohibit the State Department of Social Services from meeting its obligations to monitor and conduct periodic evaluations of, and provide reports on, the programs carried under federal Title IV–B and Title IV–E as required by Sections 622, 629 et seq., and 671(a)(7) and (22) of Title 42 of the United States Code, as implemented by federal regulation and state statute.

(j) The Judicial Council shall adopt rules of court, and shall make available appropriate forms, providing for the standardized implementation of this section by the juvenile courts. *(Added by Stats. 2014, c. 249 (S.B.1038), § 2, eff. Jan. 1, 2015. Amended by Stats.2015, c. 368 (A.B.666), § 1, eff. Jan. 1, 2016; Stats.2015, c. 375 (A.B.989), § 1.5, eff. Jan. 1, 2016; Stats.2016, c. 86 (S.B.1171), § 312, eff. Jan. 1, 2017; Stats.2016, c. 858 (A.B.1945), § 1, eff. Jan. 1, 2017; Stats.2017, c. 679 (S.B.312), § 2, eff. Jan. 1, 2018; Stats.2017, c. 685 (A.B.529), § 1.5, eff. Jan. 1, 2018; Stats.2018, c. 793 (S.B.1281), § 1, eff. Jan. 1, 2019; Stats.2018, c. 1002 (A.B.2952), § 1.5, eff. Jan. 1, 2019; Stats.2019, c. 50 (A.B.1537), § 3, eff. Jan. 1, 2020; Stats.2020, c. 329 (A.B.2321), § 2, eff. Jan. 1, 2021; Stats.2020, c. 338 (S.B.1126), § 1.5, eff. Jan. 1, 2021.)*

Cross References

Coercion to commit offense as direct result of being victim of intimate partner violence or sexual violence, affirmative defense to charge of a crime, see Penal Code § 236.24.

Research References

West's California Judicial Council Forms JV–591, Acknowledgment of Juvenile Record Sealed.
West's California Judicial Council Forms JV–592, Prosecutor Request for Access to Sealed Juvenile Case File.
West's California Judicial Council Forms JV–593, Notice of Prosecutor Request for Access to Sealed Juvenile Case File.
West's California Judicial Council Forms JV–594, Response to Prosecutor Request for Access to Sealed Juvenile Case File.
West's California Judicial Council Forms JV–596, Dismissal and Sealing of Records—Welfare and Institutions Code Section 786.
West's California Judicial Council Forms JV–596–INFO, Sealing of Records for Satisfactory Completion of Probation (Also Available in Spanish).
West's California Judicial Council Forms JV–599, Order on Prosecutor Request for Access to Sealed File.
2 Witkin, California Criminal Law 4th Crimes Against Public Peace and Welfare § 241 (2021), Juvenile Offenders.

§ 786.5. Sealing of juvenile arrest records after completion of diversion or supervision program; notification

(a) Notwithstanding any other law, the probation department shall seal the arrest and other records in its custody relating to a juvenile's arrest and referral and participation in a diversion or supervision program under both of the following circumstances:

(1) Upon satisfactory completion of a program of diversion or supervision to which a juvenile is referred by the probation officer in lieu of the filing of a petition to adjudge the juvenile a ward of the juvenile court, including a program of informal supervision pursuant to Section 654.

(2) Upon satisfactory completion of a program of diversion or supervision to which a juvenile is referred by the prosecutor in lieu of the filing of a petition to adjudge the juvenile a ward of the juvenile court, including a program of informal supervision pursuant to Section 654.

(b) The probation department shall notify the arresting law enforcement agency to seal the arrest records described in subdivision (a), and the arresting law enforcement agency shall seal the records in its custody relating to the arrest no later than 60 days from the date of notification by the probation department. Upon sealing, the arresting law enforcement agency shall notify the probation department that the records have been sealed. Within 30 days from receipt of notification by the arresting law enforcement agency that the records have been sealed pursuant to this section, the probation department shall notify the minor in writing that their record has been sealed pursuant to this section. If records have not been sealed pursuant this section, the written notice from the probation department shall inform the minor of their ability to petition the court directly to seal their arrest and other related records.

(c) Upon sealing of the records pursuant to this section, the arrest or offense giving rise to any of the circumstances specified in subdivision (a) shall be deemed not to have occurred and the individual may respond accordingly to any inquiry, application, or process in which disclosure of this information is requested or sought.

(d)(1) For the records relating to the circumstances described in subdivision (a), the probation department shall issue notice as follows:

(A) The probation department shall notify a public or private agency operating a diversion program to which the juvenile has been referred under these circumstances to seal records in the program operator's custody relating to the arrest or referral and the participation of the juvenile in the diversion or supervision program, and the operator of the program shall seal the records in its custody relating to the juvenile's arrest or referral and participation in the program no later than 60 days from the date of notification by the probation department. Upon sealing, the public or private agency operating a diversion program shall notify the probation department that the records have been sealed.

(B) The probation department shall notify the participant in the supervision or diversion program in writing that their record has been sealed pursuant to the provisions of this section based on their satisfactory completion of the program. If the record is not sealed, the probation department shall notify the participant in writing of the reason or reasons for not sealing the record.

(2) An individual who receives notice from the probation department that the individual has not satisfactorily completed the diversion program and that the record has not been sealed pursuant to this section may petition the juvenile court for review of the decision in a hearing in which the program participant may seek to demonstrate, and the court may determine, that the individual has met the satisfactory completion requirement and is eligible for the sealing of the record by the probation department, the arresting law enforcement agency, and the program operator under the provisions of this section.

(e) Satisfactory completion of the program of supervision or diversion shall be defined for purposes of this section as substantial compliance by the participant with the reasonable terms of program participation that are within the capacity of the participant to perform. A determination of satisfactory or unsatisfactory completion shall be made by the probation department within 60 days of completion of the program by the juvenile, or, if the juvenile does not complete the program, within 60 days of determining that the program has not been completed by the juvenile.

(f)(1) Notwithstanding subdivision (a), the probation department of a county responsible for the supervision of a person may access a record sealed by a probation department pursuant to this section for the sole purpose of complying with subdivision (e) of Section 654.3. The information contained in the sealed record and accessed by the probation department under this paragraph shall in all other respects remain confidential and shall not be disseminated to any other person or agency. Access to, or inspection of, a sealed record authorized by this paragraph shall not be deemed an unsealing of the record and shall not require notice to any other agency.

(2)(A) Any record, that has been sealed pursuant to this section may be accessed, inspected, or utilized by the prosecuting attorney in order to meet a statutory or constitutional obligation to disclose favorable or exculpatory evidence to a defendant in a criminal case in which the prosecuting attorney has reason to believe that access to the record is necessary to meet the disclosure obligation.

(B)(i) A prosecuting attorney shall not use information contained in a record sealed pursuant to this section for any purpose other than those provided in subparagraph (A).

(ii) Once the case referenced in subparagraph (A) has been closed and is no longer subject to review on appeal, the prosecuting attorney shall destroy any records obtained pursuant to this subparagraph. *(Added by Stats.2017, c. 685 (A.B.529), § 2, eff. Jan. 1, 2018. Amended by Stats.2020, c. 330 (A.B.2425), § 1, eff. Jan. 1, 2021.)*

Research References

West's California Judicial Council Forms JV-589, Acknowledgment of Juvenile Diversion Record Sealed (Welf. & Inst. Code, §786.5).

West's California Judicial Council Forms JV-597, Probation Department Notice on Sealing of Records After Diversion Program.

3 Witkin, California Criminal Law 4th Punishment § 721 (2021), In General.

§ 787. Access to sealed records

(a) Notwithstanding any other law, a record sealed pursuant to Section 781, 786, or 786.5 may be accessed by a law enforcement agency, probation department, court, the Department of Justice, or other state or local agency that has custody of the sealed record for the limited purpose of complying with data collection or data reporting requirements that are imposed by other provisions of law. However, no personally identifying information from a sealed record accessed under this subdivision may be released, disseminated, or published by or through an agency, department, court, or individual that has accessed or obtained information from the sealed record.

(b) Notwithstanding any other law, a court may authorize a researcher or research organization to access information contained in records that have been sealed pursuant to Section 781, 786, or 786.5 for the purpose of conducting research on juvenile justice populations, practices, policies, or trends, if both of the following are true:

(1) The court is satisfied that the research project or study includes a methodology for the appropriate protection of the confidentiality of an individual whose sealed record is accessed pursuant to this subdivision.

(2) Personally identifying information relating to the individual whose sealed record is accessed pursuant to this subdivision is not further released, disseminated, or published by or through the researcher or research organization.

(c) For the purposes of this section "personally identifying information" has the same meaning as in Section 1798.79.8 of the Civil Code. *(Added by Stats.2015, c. 368 (A.B.666), § 2, eff. Jan. 1, 2016. Amended by Stats.2018, c. 1002 (A.B.2952), § 2, eff. Jan. 1, 2019.)*

ARTICLE 20.5. DEFERRED ENTRY OF JUDGMENT

Section

§ 790. Application of article; determination by prosecuting attorney; filing of declaration of eligibility; deferred entry of judgment

(a) Notwithstanding Section 654 or 654.2, or any other provision of law, this article shall apply whenever a case is before the juvenile court for a determination of whether a minor is a person described in Section 602 because of the commission of a felony offense, if all of the following circumstances apply:

(1) The minor has not previously been declared to be a ward of the court for the commission of a felony offense.

(2) The offense charged is not one of the offenses enumerated in subdivision (b) of Section 707.

(3) The minor has not previously been committed to the custody of the Department of Corrections and Rehabilitation, Division of Juvenile Facilities.

(4) The minor's record does not indicate that probation has ever been revoked without being completed.

(5) The minor is at least 14 years of age at the time of the hearing.

(6) The minor is eligible for probation pursuant to Section 1203.06 of the Penal Code.

(7) The offense charged is not rape, sodomy, oral copulation, or an act of sexual penetration specified in Section 289 of the Penal Code when the victim was prevented from resisting due to being rendered unconscious by any intoxicating, anesthetizing, or controlled substance, or when the victim was at the time incapable, because of mental disorder or developmental or physical disability, of giving consent, and that was known or reasonably should have been known to the minor at the time of the offense.

(b) The prosecuting attorney shall review their file to determine whether or not paragraphs (1) to (7), inclusive, of subdivision (a) apply. If the minor is found eligible for deferred entry of judgment, the prosecuting attorney shall file a declaration in writing with the court or state for the record the grounds upon which the determination is based, and shall make this information available to the minor and their attorney. Upon a finding that the minor is also suitable for deferred entry of judgment and would benefit from education, treatment, and rehabilitation efforts, the court may grant deferred entry of judgment. Under this procedure, the court may set the hearing for deferred entry of judgment at the initial appearance under Section 657. The court shall make findings on the record that a minor is appropriate for deferred entry of judgment pursuant to this article in any case where deferred entry of judgment is granted.

(c)(1) If a minor is eligible for deferred entry of judgment, but the minor resides in a different county and the case will be transferred, as described in Section 750, the court may adjudicate the case without determining the minor's suitability for deferred entry of judgment to enable the court in the minor's county of residence to make that determination.

(2) If a minor is eligible for deferred entry of judgment, but the court did not determine the minor's suitability for deferred entry of judgment pursuant to paragraph (1), upon transfer of the case to the minor's county of residence, the receiving court may, prior to determining the disposition of the case, determine the minor's suitability for deferred entry of judgment and modify the transferring court's finding accordingly. *(Added by Initiative Measure (Prop. 21, § 29, approved March 7, 2000, eff. March 8, 2000). Amended by Stats.2006, c. 675 (S.B.1626), § 1; Stats.2014, c. 919 (S.B.838), § 4, eff. Jan. 1, 2015; Stats.2021, c. 603 (S.B.383), § 2, eff. Jan. 1, 2022.)*

Cross References

Completion of supervision program or probation, dismissal of petition, sealing records, see Welfare and Institutions Code § 786.
Felonies, definition and penalties, see Penal Code §§ 17, 18.
Writing defined, see Welfare and Institutions Code § 8.

Research References

West's California Judicial Council Forms JV–750, Determination of Eligibility—Deferred Entry of Judgment— Juvenile (Also Available in Spanish).
West's California Judicial Council Forms JV–751, Citation and Written Notification for Deferred Entry of Judgment—Juvenile.
West's California Judicial Council Forms JV–760, Deferred Entry of Judgment Order.
1 Witkin California Criminal Law 4th Introduction to Crimes § 140 (2021), Gang Violence and Juvenile Crime Prevention Act (Proposition 21).

§ 791. Written notification to minor; contents; consent by minor; procedure; deferred entry of judgment

(a) The prosecuting attorney's written notification to the minor shall also include all of the following:

(1) A full description of the procedures for deferred entry of judgment.

(2) A general explanation of the roles and authorities of the probation department, the prosecuting attorney, the program, and the court in that process.

(3) A clear statement that, in lieu of jurisdictional and disposition hearings, the court may grant a deferred entry of judgment with respect to any offense charged in the petition, provided that the minor admits each allegation contained in the petition and waives time for the pronouncement of judgment, and that upon the successful completion of the terms of probation, as defined in Section 794, the positive recommendation of the probation department, and the motion of the prosecuting attorney, but no sooner that 12 months and no later than 36 months from the date of the minor's referral to the program, the court shall dismiss the charge or charges against the minor.

(4) A clear statement that upon any failure of the minor to comply with the terms of probation, including the rules of any program the minor is directed to attend, or any circumstances specified in Section 793, the prosecuting attorney or the probation department, or the court on its own, may make a motion to the court for entry of judgment and the court shall render a finding that the minor is a ward of the court pursuant to Section 602 for the offenses specified in the original petition and shall schedule a dispositional hearing.

(5) An explanation of record retention and disposition resulting from participation in the deferred entry of judgment program and the minor's rights relative to answering questions about their arrest and deferred entry of judgment following successful completion of the program.

(b) If the minor consents and waives their right to a speedy jurisdictional hearing, the court may refer the case to the probation department or the court may summarily grant deferred entry of judgment if the minor admits the charges in the petition and waives time for the pronouncement of judgment. When directed by the court, the probation department shall make an investigation and take into consideration the defendant's age, maturity, educational background, family relationships, demonstrable motivation, treatment history, if any, and other mitigating and aggravating factors in determining whether the minor is a person who would be benefited by education, treatment, or rehabilitation. The probation department shall also determine which programs would accept the minor. The probation department shall report its findings and recommendations to the court. The court shall make the final determination regarding education, treatment, and rehabilitation of the minor.

(c) If a minor is eligible for deferred entry of judgment, but the court did not determine the minor's suitability for deferred entry of judgment pursuant to paragraph (1) of subdivision (c) of Section 790, when the case is transferred, the receiving court may, prior to determining the disposition of the case, order the probation department to make an investigation and report pursuant to subdivision (b) to determine the minor's suitability for deferred entry of judgment.

(d) A minor's admission of the charges contained in the petition pursuant to this chapter shall not constitute a finding that a petition has been sustained for any purpose, unless a judgment is entered pursuant to subdivision (b) of Section 793. *(Added by Initiative Measure (Prop. 21, § 29, approved March 7, 2000, eff. March 8, 2000). Amended by Stats.2021, c. 603 (S.B.383), § 3, eff. Jan. 1, 2022.)*

Cross References

Enrollment of pupils, see Education Code § 1981.
Felonies, definition and penalties, see Penal Code §§ 17, 18.

Research References

West's California Judicial Council Forms JV–750, Determination of Eligibility—Deferred Entry of Judgment— Juvenile (Also Available in Spanish).
West's California Judicial Council Forms JV–751, Citation and Written Notification for Deferred Entry of Judgment—Juvenile.

§ 792. Parent or guardian; notice to appear

The judge shall issue a citation directing any custodial parent, guardian, or foster parent of the minor to appear at the time and place set for the hearing, and directing any person having custody or control of the minor concerning whom the petition has been filed to bring the minor with him or her. The notice shall in addition state that a parent, guardian, or foster parent may be required to participate in a counseling or education program with the minor concerning whom the petition has been filed. The notice shall explain the provisions of Section 170.6 of the Code of Civil Procedure. Personal service shall be made at least 24 hours before the time stated for the appearance. *(Added by Initiative Measure (Prop. 21, § 29, approved March 7, 2000, eff. March 8, 2000).)*

§ 793. Lifting of deferral and scheduling of dispositional hearing upon unsatisfactory performance; dismissal of charges upon satisfactory performance; access to sealed records

(a) If it appears to the prosecuting attorney, the court, or the probation department that the minor is not performing satisfactorily in the assigned program or is not complying with the terms of the minor's probation, or that the minor is not benefiting from education, treatment, or rehabilitation, the court shall lift the deferred entry of judgment and schedule a dispositional hearing. If after accepting deferred entry of judgment and during the period in which deferred entry of judgment was granted, the minor is convicted of, or declared to be a person described in Section 602 for the commission of, any felony offense or of any two misdemeanor offenses committed on separate occasions, the judge shall enter judgment and schedule a dispositional hearing. If the minor is convicted of, or found to be a person described in Section 602, because of the commission of one misdemeanor offense, or multiple misdemeanor offenses committed during a single occasion, the court may enter judgment and schedule a dispositional hearing.

(b) If the judgment previously deferred is imposed and a dispositional hearing scheduled pursuant to subdivision (a), the juvenile court shall report the complete criminal history of the minor to the Department of Justice, pursuant to Section 602.5.

(c) If the minor has performed satisfactorily during the period in which deferred entry of judgment was granted, at the end of that period the charge or charges in the wardship petition shall be dismissed and the arrest upon which the judgment was deferred shall be deemed never to have occurred and any records in the possession of the juvenile court shall be sealed, except that the prosecuting attorney and the probation department of any county shall have access to these records after they are sealed for the limited purpose of determining whether a minor is eligible for deferred entry of judgment pursuant to Section 790 and as described in subdivision (d).

(d)(1) A record that has been sealed pursuant to this section may be accessed, inspected, or utilized by the prosecuting attorney in order to meet a statutory or constitutional obligation to disclose favorable or exculpatory evidence to a defendant in a criminal case in which the prosecuting attorney has reason to believe that access to the record is necessary to meet the disclosure obligation. A request to access information in the sealed record for this purpose, including the prosecutor's rationale for believing that access to the information in the record may be necessary to meet the disclosure obligation and the date by which the records are needed, shall be submitted by the prosecuting attorney to the juvenile court. The juvenile court shall review the case file and records that have been referenced by the prosecutor as necessary to meet the disclosure obligation and any response submitted by the person having the sealed record. The court shall approve the prosecutor's request to the extent that the court has, upon review of the relevant records, determined that access to a specific sealed record or portion of a sealed record is necessary to enable the prosecuting attorney to comply with the disclosure obligation. If the juvenile court approves the prosecuting attorney's request, the court shall state on the record appropriate limits on the access, inspection, and utilization of the sealed record information in order to protect the confidentiality of the person whose sealed record is accessed pursuant to this subdivision. A ruling allowing disclosure of information pursuant to this subdivision does not affect whether the information is admissible in a criminal or juvenile proceeding. This subdivision does not impose any discovery obligations on a prosecuting attorney that do not already exist.

(2) This subdivision shall not apply to juvenile case files pertaining to matters within the jurisdiction of the juvenile court pursuant to Section 300. *(Added by Initiative Measure (Prop. 21, § 29, approved March 7, 2000, eff. March 8, 2000). Amended by Stats.2019, c. 50 (A.B.1537), § 4, eff. Jan. 1, 2020.)*

Cross References

Felonies, definition and penalties, see Penal Code §§ 17, 18.
Misdemeanors, definition and penalties, see Penal Code §§ 17, 19 and 19.2.

Research References

West's California Judicial Council Forms JV–592, Prosecutor Request for Access to Sealed Juvenile Case File.
West's California Judicial Council Forms JV–599, Order on Prosecutor Request for Access to Sealed File.
West's California Judicial Council Forms JV–615, Deferred Entry of Judgment Notice of Noncompliance (Also Available in Spanish).
West's California Judicial Council Forms JV–755, Deferred Entry of Judgment—Dismissal and Sealing of Juvenile Records (Also Available in Spanish).

§ 794. Terms and conditions of deferred entry of judgment participation

When a minor is permitted to participate in a deferred entry of judgment procedure, the judge shall impose, as a condition of probation, the requirement that the minor be subject to warrantless searches of his or her person, residence, or property under his or her control, upon the request of a probation officer or peace officer. The court shall also consider whether imposing random drug or alcohol testing, or both, including urinalysis, would be an appropriate condition of probation. The judge shall also, when appropriate, require the minor to periodically establish compliance with curfew and school attendance requirements. The court may, in consultation with the probation department, impose any other term of probation authorized by this code that the judge believes would assist in the education, treatment, and rehabilitation of the minor and the prevention of criminal activity. The minor may also be required to pay restitution to the victim or victims pursuant to the provisions of this code. *(Added by Initiative Measure (Prop. 21, § 29, approved March 7, 2000, eff. March 8, 2000).)*

Cross References

Probation officer or social worker defined for purposes of this Chapter, see Welfare and Institutions Code § 215.

Research References

West's California Judicial Council Forms JV–760, Deferred Entry of Judgment Order.

§ 795. Program administrator

The county probation officer or a person designated by the county probation officer shall serve in each county as the program administrator for juveniles granted deferred entry of judgment and shall be responsible for developing, supervising, and monitoring treatment programs and otherwise overseeing the placement and supervision of minors granted probation pursuant to the provisions of this chapter. *(Added by Initiative Measure (Prop. 21, § 29, approved March 7, 2000, eff. March 8, 2000).)*

Cross References

Probation officer or social worker defined for purposes of this Chapter, see Welfare and Institutions Code § 215.

ARTICLE 21. WARDS—APPEALS

§ 800. Appealable orders, rulings and judgments

(a) A judgment in a proceeding under Section 601 or 602 may be appealed from, by the minor, in the same manner as any final judgment, and any subsequent order may be appealed from, by the minor, as from an order after judgment. Pending appeal of the order or judgment, the granting or refusal to order release shall rest in the discretion of the juvenile court. The appeal shall have precedence over all other cases in the court to which the appeal is taken.

A ruling on a motion to suppress pursuant to Section 700.1 shall be reviewed on appeal even if the judgment is predicated upon an admission of the allegations of the petition.

A judgment or subsequent order entered by a referee shall become appealable whenever proceedings pursuant to Section 252, 253, or 254 have become completed or, if proceedings pursuant to Section 252, 253, or 254 are not initiated, when the time for initiating the proceedings has expired.

(b) An appeal may be taken by the people from any of the following:

(1) A ruling on a motion to suppress pursuant to Section 700.1 even if the judgment is a dismissal of the petition or any count or counts of the petition. However, no appeal by the people shall lie as to any count which, if the people are successful, will be the basis for further proceedings subjecting any person to double jeopardy.

(2) An order made after judgment entered pursuant to Section 777 or 785.

(3) An order modifying the jurisdictional finding by reducing the degree of the offense or modifying the offense to a lesser offense.

(4) An order or judgment dismissing or otherwise terminating the action before the minor has been placed in jeopardy, or where the minor has waived jeopardy. If, pursuant to this paragraph, the people prosecute an appeal of the decision or any review of that decision, it shall be binding upon the people and they shall be prohibited from refiling the case which was appealed.

(5) The imposition of an unlawful order at a dispositional hearing, whether or not the court suspends the execution of the disposition.

(c) Nothing contained in this section shall be construed to authorize an appeal from an order granting probation. Instead, the people may seek appellate review of any grant of probation, whether or not the court imposes disposition, by means of a petition for a writ of mandate or prohibition which is filed within 60 days after probation is granted. The review of any grant of probation shall include review of any order underlying the grant of probation.

(d) An appellant unable to afford counsel, shall be provided a free copy of the transcript in any appeal.

(e) The record shall be prepared and transmitted immediately after filing of the notice of appeal, without advance payment of fees. If the appellant is able to afford counsel, the county may seek reimbursement for the cost of the transcripts under subdivision (c) of Section 68511.3 of the Government Code as though the appellant had been granted permission to proceed in forma pauperis.

(f) All appeals shall be initiated by the filing of notice of appeal in conformity with the requirements of Section 1240.1 of the Penal Code. *(Added by Stats.1980, c. 1092, p. 3506, § 4. Amended by Stats.1980, c. 1095, p. 3512, § 4; Stats.1982, c. 454, § 189; Stats.1986, c. 823, § 5; Stats.1990, c. 482 (S.B.1849), § 1; Stats.1991, c. 649 (S.B.1137), § 1; Stats.1994, c. 448 (A.B.1948), § 7.)*

Cross References

Appealable orders and judgments, dependent persons, see Welfare and Institutions Code § 395.
Appeals in civil actions, see Code of Civil Procedure § 901 et seq.
Effect of order, see Welfare and Institutions Code § 203.
Judgments and orders, see Welfare and Institutions Code § 725 et seq.
Mandamus, purpose of writ of mandate, courts which may issue writ and parties to whom issued, see Code of Civil Procedure § 1085.
Stay of proceedings, see Code of Civil Procedure § 916 et seq.

Research References

West's California Judicial Council Forms JV–291–INFO, Information on Requesting Access to Records for Persons With a Limited Right to Appeal.
West's California Judicial Council Forms JV–800, Notice of Appeal—Juvenile.
West's California Judicial Council Forms JV–805–INFO, Information Regarding Appeal Rights.

§ 801. Immediate appeal of order transferring minor to court of criminal jurisdiction; stay of proceeding

(a) An order transferring a minor from the juvenile court to a court of criminal jurisdiction shall be subject to immediate appellate review if a notice of appeal is filed within 30 days of the order transferring the minor to a court of criminal jurisdiction. An order transferring the minor from the juvenile court to a court of criminal jurisdiction may not be heard on appeal from the judgment of conviction.

(b) Upon request of the minor, the superior court shall issue a stay of the criminal court proceedings until a final determination of the appeal. The superior court shall retain jurisdiction to modify or lift the stay upon request of the minor.

(c) The appeal shall have precedence in the court to which the appeal is taken and shall be determined as soon as practicable after the notice of appeal is filed.

(d) The Judicial Council shall adopt rules of court to ensure all of the following:

(1) The juvenile court shall advise the minor of the right to appeal, of the necessary steps and time for taking an appeal, and of the right to the appointment of counsel if the minor is unable to retain counsel.

(2) Following the timely filing of a notice of appeal, the prompt preparation and transmittal of the record from the superior court to the appellate court.

(3) Adequate time requirements for counsel and court personnel shall exist to implement the objectives of this section.

(e) It is the intent of the Legislature that this section provides for an expedited review on the merits by the appellate court of an order transferring the minor from the juvenile court to a court of criminal jurisdiction. *(Added by Stats.2021, c. 195 (A.B.624), § 1, eff. Jan. 1, 2022.)*

ARTICLE 22. WARDS AND DEPENDENT CHILDREN—RECORDS

Section

Section

§ 825. Juvenile court record

The order and findings of the superior court in each case under the provisions of this chapter shall be entered in a suitable book or other form of written record which shall be kept for that purpose and known as the "juvenile court record." *(Added by Stats.1961, c. 1616, p. 3494, § 2.)*

Cross References

Juvenile Reentry Grant for the reentry of persons discharged from the Division of Juvenile Facilities, annual reports not considered record information within meaning of this section, see Welfare and Institutions Code § 1982.

Research References

5 Witkin, California Criminal Law 4th Criminal Trial § 170A (2021), (New) Interrogation of Murder Suspect.

§ 825.5. Child of minor dependent parent or nonminor dependent parent who is subject of dependency petition; maintenance of court files and records

(a) The clerk of the superior court shall maintain court files and records concerning a minor dependent parent or a nonminor dependent parent of a child who is the subject of a dependency petition separate from court files and records concerning the child.

(b)(1) Dependency court records concerning a minor dependent parent or a nonminor dependent parent may be disclosed to the county and the court in the child's dependency proceedings; however, information from the records shall only be admitted as evidence in the child's dependency proceedings pursuant to a court order finding that the information is materially relevant to the case, subject to the provisions of subdivision (a) of Section 361.8.

(2) Any party to the child's dependency proceedings may request the admittance of the records described in paragraph (1) as evidence at any stage of the child's dependency proceedings. *(Added by Stats.2015, c. 511 (A.B.260), § 2, eff. Jan. 1, 2016.)*

§ 826. Release or destruction of court record; reproduction

(a) After five years from the date on which the jurisdiction of the juvenile court over a minor is terminated, the probation officer may destroy all records and papers in the proceedings concerning the minor.

The juvenile court record, which includes all records and papers, any minute book entries, dockets and judgment dockets, shall be destroyed by order of the court as follows: when the person who is the subject of the record reaches the age of 28 years, if the person was alleged or adjudged to be a person described by Section 300, when the person who is the subject of the record reaches the age of 21 years, if the person was alleged or adjudged to be a person described by Section 601, or when the person reaches the age of 38 years if the person was alleged or adjudged to be a person described by Section 602, unless for good cause the court determines that the juvenile record shall be retained, or unless the juvenile court record is released to the person who is the subject of the record pursuant to this section. However, a juvenile court record which is not permitted to be sealed pursuant to subdivision (f) of Section 781 shall not be destroyed pursuant to this section.

Any person who is the subject of a juvenile court record may by written notice request the juvenile court to release the court record to his or her custody. Wherever possible, the written notice shall include the person's full name, the person's date of birth, and the juvenile court case number. Any juvenile court receiving the written notice shall release the court record to the person who is the subject of the record five years after the jurisdiction of the juvenile court over the person has terminated, if the person was alleged or adjudged to be a person described by Section 300, or when the person reaches the age of 21 years, if the person was alleged or adjudged to be a person described by Section 601, unless for good cause the court determines that the record shall be retained. Exhibits shall be destroyed as provided under Section 1417 of the Penal Code. For the purpose of this section "destroy" means destroy or dispose of for the purpose of destruction. The proceedings in any case in which the juvenile court record is destroyed or released to the person who is the subject of the record pursuant to this section shall be deemed never to have occurred, and the person may reply accordingly to any inquiry about the events in the case.

(b) If an individual whose juvenile court record has been destroyed or released under subdivision (a) discovers that any other agency still retains a record, the individual may file a petition with the court requesting that the records be destroyed. The petition will include the name of the agency and the type of record to be destroyed. The court shall order that such records also be destroyed unless for good cause the court determines to the contrary. The court shall send a copy of the order to each agency and each agency shall destroy records in its custody as directed by the order, and shall advise the court of its compliance. The court shall then destroy the copy of the petition, the order, and the notice of compliance from each agency. Thereafter, the proceedings in such case shall be deemed never to have occurred.

(c) Juvenile court records in juvenile traffic matters, which include all records and papers, any minute book entries, dockets and judgment dockets, may be destroyed after five years from the date on which the jurisdiction of the juvenile court over a minor is terminated, or when the minor reaches the age of 21 years, if the person was alleged or adjudged to be a person described by Section 601. Prior to such destruction the original record may be microfilmed or photocopied. Every such reproduction shall be deemed and considered an original; and a transcript, exemplification or certified copy of any such reproduction shall be deemed and considered a transcript, exemplification or certified copy, as the case may be, of the original. *(Added by Stats.1980, c. 1104, p. 3551, § 4. Amended by Stats.1981, c. 488, p. 1835, § 2; Stats.1990, c. 698 (A.B.3466), § 1; Stats.1994, c. 835 (A.B.234), § 2; Stats.2011, c. 459 (A.B.212), § 23, eff. Oct. 4, 2011.)*

Cross References

Destruction of public records, see Government Code § 26201 et seq.
Destruction of public social services records, see Welfare and Institutions Code § 10851.
Management of trial court records, destruction of records, notice and retention periods, see Government Code § 68152.
Microfilmed and photographically reproduced records, see Government Code § 12276.
Probation officer or social worker defined for purposes of this Chapter, see Welfare and Institutions Code § 215.

§ 826.5. Destruction of records; papers and exhibits; microfilm or photocopies; reproductions as originals

(a) Notwithstanding the provisions of Section 826, at any time before a person reaches the age when his or her records are required to be destroyed, the judge or clerk of the juvenile court or the probation officer may destroy all records and papers, the juvenile court record, any minute book entries, dockets, and judgment dockets in the proceedings concerning the person as a minor if the records and papers, juvenile court record, any minute book entries, dockets, and judgment dockets are microfilmed or photocopied prior to destruction. Exhibits shall be destroyed as provided under Sections 1418, 1418.5, and 1419 of the Penal Code.

(b) Every reproduction shall be deemed and considered an original. A transcript, exemplification, or certified copy of any reproduction shall be deemed and considered a transcript, exemplification, or certified copy, as the case may be, of the original. *(Added by Stats.1980, c. 1104, p. 3552, § 6. Amended by Stats.1981, c. 488, p. 1836, § 3.)*

Cross References

Destruction of duplicate records, see Government Code § 26201 et seq.
Microfilmed and photographically reproduced records, see Government Code § 12276.
Probation officer or social worker defined for purposes of this Chapter, see Welfare and Institutions Code § 215.

§ 826.6. Release or destruction of records; notice of rights; form

(a) Any minor who is the subject of a petition that has been filed in juvenile court to adjudge the minor a dependent child or a ward of the court shall be given written notice by the clerk of the court upon disposition of the petition or the termination of jurisdiction of the juvenile court of all of the following:

(1) The statutory right of any person who has been the subject of juvenile court proceedings to petition for sealing of the case records.

(2) The statutory provisions regarding the destruction of juvenile court records and records of juvenile court proceedings retained by state or local agencies.

(3) The statutory right of any person who has been the subject of juvenile court proceedings to have his or her juvenile court record released to him or her in lieu of its destruction.

(b) In any juvenile case where a local welfare department, probation department, or district attorney is responsible for notifying the minor of the dismissal, release, or termination of the case, the agency shall provide written notice to the minor of the information specified in subdivision (a) upon the dismissal, release, or termination of the case.

(c) A written form providing the information described in this section shall be prepared by the clerk of the court and shall be made available to juvenile court clerks, probation departments, welfare departments, and district attorneys. *(Added by Stats.1980, c. 1104, p. 3552, § 7. Amended by Stats.1981, c. 488, p. 1836, § 4.)*

§ 826.7. Child who died as result of abuse or neglect; release of juvenile case files

Juvenile case files that pertain to a child who died as the result of abuse or neglect shall be released by the custodian of records of the county welfare department or agency to the public pursuant to Section 10850.4 or an order issued pursuant to paragraph (2) of subdivision (a) of Section 827. *(Added by Stats.2007, c. 468 (S.B.39), § 2.)*

§ 826.8. Proof of dependency or wardship

Notwithstanding Section 827 and in order to assist with establishing eligibility for programs or services, the State Department of Social Services may provide to a person who was previously adjudged a dependent or ward of the juvenile court, was placed in foster care, and whose dependency or wardship has been dismissed, upon request by that person, the information included in the proof of dependency or wardship document described in subparagraph (E) of paragraph (2) of subdivision (e) of Section 391, or any information necessary to provide verification that the person was formerly a dependent or ward of the juvenile court and placed in foster care. *(Added by Stats.2015, c. 215 (A.B.592), § 1, eff. Aug. 17, 2015.)*

§ 827. Juvenile case file inspection; confidentiality; release; probation reports; destruction of records; liability

(a)(1) Except as provided in Section 828, a case file may be inspected only by the following:

(A) Court personnel.

(B) The district attorney, a city attorney, or city prosecutor authorized to prosecute criminal or juvenile cases under state law.

(C) The minor who is the subject of the proceeding.

(D) The minor's parent or guardian.

(E) The attorneys for the parties, judges, referees, other hearing officers, probation officers, and law enforcement officers who are actively participating in criminal or juvenile proceedings involving the minor.

(F) The county counsel, city attorney, or any other attorney representing the petitioning agency in a dependency action.

(G) The superintendent or designee of the school district where the minor is enrolled or attending school.

(H) Members of the child protective agencies as described in Section 11165.9 of the Penal Code.

(I) The State Department of Social Services, to carry out its duties pursuant to Division 9 (commencing with Section 10000) of this code and Part 5 (commencing with Section 7900) of Division 12 of the Family Code to oversee and monitor county child welfare agencies, children in foster care or receiving foster care assistance, and out-of-state placements, Section 10850.4, and paragraph (2).

(J)(i) Authorized staff who are employed by, or authorized staff of entities who are licensed by, the State Department of Social Services, as necessary to the performance of their duties related to resource family approval, and authorized staff who are employed by the State Department of Social Services as necessary to inspect, approve, or license, and monitor or investigate community care facilities or resource families, and to ensure that the standards of care and services provided in those facilities are adequate and appropriate, and to ascertain compliance with the rules and regulations to which the facilities are subject.

(ii) The confidential information shall remain confidential except for purposes of inspection, approval or licensing, or monitoring or investigation pursuant to Chapter 3 (commencing with Section 1500) and Chapter 3.4 (commencing with Section 1596.70) of Division 2 of the Health and Safety Code and Article 2 (commencing with Section 16519.5) of Chapter 5 of Part 4 of Division 9. The confidential information may also be used by the State Department of Social Services in a criminal, civil, or administrative proceeding. The confidential information shall be available only to the judge or hearing officer and to the parties to the case. Names that are confidential shall be listed in attachments separate to the general pleadings. The confidential information shall be sealed after the conclusion of the criminal, civil, or administrative hearings, and may not subsequently be released except in accordance with this subdivision. If the confidential information does not result in a criminal, civil, or administrative proceeding, it shall be sealed after the State Department of Social Services determines that no further action will be taken in the matter. Except as otherwise provided in this subdivision, confidential information shall not contain the name of the minor.

(K) Members of children's multidisciplinary teams, persons, or agencies providing treatment or supervision of the minor.

(L) A judge, commissioner, or other hearing officer assigned to a family law case with issues concerning custody or visitation, or both, involving the minor, and the following persons, if actively participating in the family law case: a family court mediator assigned to a case involving the minor pursuant to Article 1 (commencing with Section 3160) of Chapter 11 of Part 2 of Division 8 of the Family Code, a court-appointed evaluator or a person conducting a court-connected child custody evaluation, investigation, or assessment pursuant to Section 3111 or 3118 of the Family Code, and counsel appointed for the minor in the family law case pursuant to Section 3150 of the Family Code. Prior to allowing counsel appointed for the minor in the family law case to inspect the file, the court clerk may require counsel to provide a certified copy of the court order appointing the minor's counsel.

(M) When acting within the scope of investigative duties of an active case, a statutorily authorized or court-appointed investigator who is conducting an investigation pursuant to Section 7663, 7851, or 9001 of the Family Code, or who is actively participating in a guardianship case involving a minor pursuant to Part 2 (commencing with Section 1500) of Division 4 of the Probate Code and acting within the scope of the investigator's duties in that case.

(N) A local child support agency for the purpose of establishing paternity and establishing and enforcing child support orders.

(O) Juvenile justice commissions as established under Section 225. The confidentiality provisions of Section 10850 shall apply to a juvenile justice commission and its members.

(P) The Department of Justice, to carry out its duties pursuant to Sections 290.008 and 290.08 of the Penal Code as the repository for sex offender registration and notification in California.

(Q) Any other person who may be designated by court order of the judge of the juvenile court upon filing a petition.

(R) A probation officer who is preparing a report pursuant to Section 1178 on behalf of a person who was in the custody of the Department of Corrections and Rehabilitation, Division of Juvenile Justice and who has petitioned the Board of Juvenile Hearings for an honorable discharge.

(S)(i) The attorneys in an administrative hearing involving the minor or nonminor only as necessary to meet the requirements of Sections 10952 and 10952.5.

(ii) The confidential information shall remain confidential for purposes of the administrative proceeding. The confidential information shall be available only to the judge or hearing officer and to the parties to the case. The confidential information shall be sealed after the conclusion of the administrative hearing, and shall not subsequently be released except in accordance with this subdivision.

(T) Personnel of the State Department of Social Services, to carry out the duties of the department pursuant to paragraph (1) of subdivision (c) of Section 9100 of the Family Code or paragraph (3) of subdivision (e) of Section 366.26.

(2)(A) Notwithstanding any other law and subject to subparagraph (A) of paragraph (3), juvenile case files, except those relating to matters within the jurisdiction of the court pursuant to Section 601 or 602, that pertain to a deceased child who was within the jurisdiction of the juvenile court pursuant to Section 300, shall be released to the public pursuant to an order by the juvenile court after a petition has been filed and interested parties have been afforded an opportunity to file an objection. Any information relating to another child or that could identify another child, except for information about the deceased, shall be redacted from the juvenile case file prior to release, unless a specific order is made by the juvenile court to the contrary. Except as provided in this paragraph, the presiding judge of the juvenile court may issue an order prohibiting or limiting access to the juvenile case file, or any portion thereof, of a deceased child only upon a showing by a preponderance of evidence that release of the juvenile case file or any portion thereof is detrimental to the safety, protection, or physical or emotional well-being of another child who is directly or indirectly connected to the juvenile case that is the subject of the petition.

(B) This paragraph represents a presumption in favor of the release of documents when a child is deceased unless the statutory reasons for confidentiality are shown to exist.

(C) If a child whose records are sought has died, and documents are sought pursuant to this paragraph, no weighing or balancing of the interests of those other than a child is permitted.

(D) A petition filed under this paragraph shall be served on interested parties by the petitioner, if the petitioner is in possession of their identity and address, and on the custodian of records. Upon receiving a petition, the custodian of records shall serve a copy of the request upon all interested parties that have not been served by the petitioner or on the interested parties served by the petitioner if the custodian of records possesses information, such as a more recent address, indicating that the service by the petitioner may have been ineffective.

(E) The custodian of records shall serve the petition within 10 calendar days of receipt. If an interested party, including the custodian of records, objects to the petition, the party shall file and serve the objection on the petitioning party no later than 15 calendar days after service of the petition.

(F) The petitioning party shall have 10 calendar days to file a reply. The juvenile court shall set the matter for hearing no more than 60 calendar days from the date the petition is served on the custodian of records. The court shall render its decision within 30 days of the hearing. The matter shall be decided solely upon the basis of the petition and supporting exhibits and declarations, if any, the objection and any supporting exhibits or declarations, if any, and the reply and any supporting declarations or exhibits thereto, and argument at hearing. The court may, solely upon its own motion, order the appearance of witnesses. If an objection is not filed to the petition, the court shall review the petition and issue its decision within 10 calendar days of the final day for filing the objection. An order of the court shall be immediately reviewable by petition to the appellate court for the issuance of an extraordinary writ.

(3) Access to juvenile case files pertaining to matters within the jurisdiction of the juvenile court pursuant to Section 300 shall be limited as follows:

(A) If a juvenile case file, or any portion thereof, is privileged or confidential pursuant to any other state law or federal law or regulation, the requirements of that state law or federal law or regulation prohibiting or limiting release of the juvenile case file or any portions thereof shall prevail. Unless a person is listed in subparagraphs (A) to (P), inclusive, of paragraph (1) and is entitled to access under the other state law or federal law or regulation without a court order, all those seeking access, pursuant to other authorization, to portions of, or information relating to the contents of, juvenile case files protected under another state law or federal law or regulation, shall petition the juvenile court. The juvenile court may only release the portion of, or information relating to the contents of, juvenile case files protected by another state law or federal law or regulation if disclosure is not detrimental to the safety, protection, or physical or emotional well-being of a child who is directly or indirectly connected to the juvenile case that is the subject of the petition. This paragraph does not limit the ability of the juvenile court to carry out its duties in conducting juvenile court proceedings.

(B) Prior to the release of the juvenile case file or any portion thereof, the court shall afford due process, including a notice of, and an opportunity to file an objection to, the release of the record or report to all interested parties.

(4) A juvenile case file, any portion thereof, and information relating to the content of the juvenile case file, may not be disseminated by the receiving agencies to a person or agency, other than a person or agency authorized to receive documents pursuant to this section. Further, a juvenile case file, any portion thereof, and information relating to the content of the juvenile case file, may not be made as an attachment to any other documents without the prior approval of the presiding judge of the juvenile court, unless it is used in connection with, and in the course of, a criminal investigation or a proceeding brought to declare a person a dependent child or ward of the juvenile court.

(5) Individuals listed in subparagraphs (A), (B), (C), (D), (E), (F), (H), (I), (J), * * * (P), (S), and (T) of paragraph (1) may also receive copies of the case file. For authorized staff of entities who are licensed by the State Department of Social Services, the confidential information shall be obtained through a child protective agency, as defined in subparagraph (H) of paragraph (1). In these circumstances, the requirements of paragraph (4) shall continue to apply to the information received.

(6) An individual other than a person described in subparagraphs (A) to (P), inclusive, of paragraph (1) who files a notice of appeal or petition for writ challenging a juvenile court order, or who is a respondent in that appeal or real party in interest in that writ proceeding, may, for purposes of that appeal or writ proceeding, inspect and copy any records in a juvenile case file to which the individual was previously granted access by the juvenile court pursuant to subparagraph (Q) of paragraph (1), including any records or portions thereof that are made a part of the appellate record. The requirements of paragraph (3) shall continue to apply to any other record, or a portion thereof, in the juvenile case file or made a part of the appellate record. The requirements of paragraph (4) shall continue to apply to files received pursuant to this paragraph. The Judicial Council shall adopt rules to implement this paragraph.

(b)(1) While the Legislature reaffirms its belief that juvenile court records, in general, should be confidential, it is the intent of the Legislature in enacting this subdivision to provide for a limited exception to juvenile court record confidentiality to promote more effective communication among juvenile courts, family courts, law enforcement agencies, and schools to ensure the rehabilitation of juvenile criminal offenders as well as to lessen the potential for drug use, violence, other forms of delinquency, and child abuse.

(2)(A) Notwithstanding subdivision (a), written notice that a minor enrolled in a public school, kindergarten to grade 12, inclusive, has been found by a court of competent jurisdiction to have committed a felony or misdemeanor involving curfew, gambling, alcohol, drugs, tobacco products, carrying of weapons, a sex offense listed in Section 290 of the Penal Code, assault or battery, larceny, vandalism, or graffiti shall be provided by the court, within seven days, to the superintendent of the school district of attendance. Written notice shall include only the offense found to have been committed by the minor and the disposition of the minor's case. This notice shall be expeditiously transmitted by the district superintendent to the principal at the school of attendance. The principal shall expeditiously disseminate the information to those counselors directly supervising or reporting on the behavior or progress of the minor. In addition, the principal shall disseminate the information to any teacher or administrator directly supervising or reporting on the behavior or progress of the minor whom the principal believes needs the information to work with the pupil in an appropriate fashion to avoid being needlessly vulnerable or to protect other persons from needless vulnerability.

(B) Any information received by a teacher, counselor, or administrator under this subdivision shall be received in confidence for the limited purpose of rehabilitating the minor and protecting students and staff, and shall not be further disseminated by the teacher, counselor, or administrator, except insofar as communication with the juvenile, the juvenile's parents or guardians, law enforcement personnel, and the juvenile's probation officer is necessary to effectuate the juvenile's rehabilitation or to protect students and staff.

(C) An intentional violation of the confidentiality provisions of this paragraph is a misdemeanor punishable by a fine not to exceed five hundred dollars ($500).

(3) If a minor is removed from public school as a result of the court's finding described in subdivision (b), the superintendent shall maintain the information in a confidential file and shall defer transmittal of the information received from the court until the minor is returned to public school. If the minor is returned to a school district other than the one from which the minor came, the parole or probation officer having jurisdiction over the minor shall so notify the

superintendent of the last district of attendance, who shall transmit the notice received from the court to the superintendent of the new district of attendance.

(c) Each probation report filed with the court concerning a minor whose record is subject to dissemination pursuant to subdivision (b) shall include on the face sheet the school at which the minor is currently enrolled. The county superintendent shall provide the court with a listing of all of the schools within each school district, within the county, along with the name and mailing address of each district superintendent.

(d)(1) Each notice sent by the court pursuant to subdivision (b) shall be stamped with the instruction: "Unlawful Dissemination Of This Information Is A Misdemeanor." Any information received from the court shall be kept in a separate confidential file at the school of attendance and shall be transferred to the minor's subsequent schools of attendance and maintained until the minor graduates from high school, is released from juvenile court jurisdiction, or reaches 18 years of age, whichever occurs first. After that time the confidential record shall be destroyed. At any time after the date by which a record required to be destroyed by this section should have been destroyed, the minor or the minor's parent or guardian shall have the right to make a written request to the principal of the school that the minor's school records be reviewed to ensure that the record has been destroyed. Upon completion of the requested review and no later than 30 days after the request for the review was received, the principal or a designee shall respond in writing to the written request and either shall confirm that the record has been destroyed or, if the record has not been destroyed, shall explain why destruction has not yet occurred.

(2) Except as provided in paragraph (2) of subdivision (b), liability shall not attach to a person who transmits or fails to transmit notice or information required under subdivision (b).

(e) For purposes of this section, a "juvenile case file" means a petition filed in a juvenile court proceeding, reports of the probation officer, and all other documents filed in that case or made available to the probation officer in making the probation officer's report, or to the judge, referee, or other hearing officer, and thereafter retained by the probation officer, judge, referee, or other hearing officer.

(f) The persons described in subparagraphs (A), (E), (F), (H), (K), (L), (M), and (N) of paragraph (1) of subdivision (a) include persons serving in a similar capacity for an Indian tribe, reservation, or tribal court when the case file involves a child who is a member of, or who is eligible for membership in, that tribe.

(g) Any portion of a case file that is covered by, or included in, an order of the court sealing a record pursuant to Section 781 or 786, or that is covered by a record sealing requirement pursuant to Section 786.5 or 827.95, may not be inspected, except as specified by those sections. *(Added by Stats.1961, c. 1616, p. 3494, § 2. Amended by Stats.1967, c. 315, p. 1501, § 1; Stats.1968, c. 344, p. 728, § 1; Stats.1970, c. 1236, p. 2224, § 1; Stats.1972, c. 1139, p. 2206, § 1; Stats.1982, c. 1103, § 4; Stats.1984, c. 1011, § 3; Stats.1984, c. 1370, § 3; Stats.1984, c. 1423, § 11, eff. Sept. 26, 1984; Stats.1990, c. 246 (A.B.2638), § 3; Stats.1991, c. 1202 (S.B.377), § 21; Stats.1992, c. 148, (A.B.2581), § 1; Stats.1993, c. 589 (A.B.2211), § 193; Stats. 1994, c. 453 (A.B.560), § 14; Stats.1994, c. 1018 (A.B.3053), § 1; Stats.1994, c. 1019 (A.B.3309), § 4; Stats.1995, c. 71 (S.B.1092), § 1, eff. July 6, 1995; Stats.1996, c. 599 (S.B.1938), § 1; Stats.1998, c. 311 (S.B.933), § 55, eff. Aug. 19, 1998; Stats.1999, c. 984 (S.B.199), § 1; Stats.1999, c. 985 (S.B.792), § 3; Stats.1999, c. 996 (S.B.334), § 22.3; Stats.2000, c. 135 (A.B.2539), § 168; Stats.2000, c. 908 (S.B.1611), § 3; Stats.2000, c. 926 (S.B.1716), § 8; Stats.2001, c. 754 (A.B.1697), § 6; Stats.2002, c. 305 (S.B.1704), § 2; Stats.2004, c. 339 (A.B.1704), § 12; Stats.2004, c. 574 (A.B.2228), § 4.5; Stats.2005, c. 22 (S.B. 1108), § 218; Stats.2007, c. 468 (S.B.39), § 3; Stats.2014, c. 57 (A.B.1618), § 1, eff. Jan. 1, 2015; Stats.2016, c. 702 (A.B.2872), § 3, eff. Jan. 1, 2017; Stats.2016, c. 858 (A.B.1945), § 2.5, eff. Jan. 1, 2017; Stats.2017, c. 269 (S.B.811), § 12, eff. Jan. 1, 2018; Stats.2017, c. 683 (S.B.625), § 1, eff. Jan. 1, 2018; Stats.2017, c. 732 (A.B.404), § 55.3, eff. Jan. 1, 2018; Stats.2018, c. 992 (A.B.1617), § 1, eff. Sept. 19, 2018; Stats.2019, c. 256 (S.B.781), § 14, eff. Jan. 1, 2020; Stats.2020, c. 330 (A.B.2425), § 2, eff. Jan. 1, 2021; Stats.2022, c. 613 (S.B.1071), § 1, eff. Jan. 1, 2023; Stats.2022, c. 870 (A.B.2711), § 3.5, eff. Jan. 1, 2023.)*

Cross References

California Community Care Facilities Act, suspension and revocation, confidentiality of proceedings, see Health and Safety Code § 1551.3.

California Victim Compensation and Government Claims Board, verification of claims, training sessions for center personnel, see Government Code § 13954.

Child abuse multidisciplinary personnel teams, investigation of reports of suspected child abuse or neglect, disclosure and exchange of information, see Welfare and Institutions Code § 18961.7.

Court–Appointed Special Advocate (CASA) considered court personnel, see Welfare and Institutions Code § 103.

Domestic violence, interagency death review teams, reporting procedures, see Penal Code § 11163.3.

Elementary and secondary education, suspension or expulsion, notice to superintendent of drug or poison use, assault, homicide, or rape, see Education Code § 48909.

Elementary and secondary education, teacher credentialing, presentation of allegations that may be grounds for denial, suspension or revocation of credential, see Education Code § 44242.5.

Felonies, definition and penalties, see Penal Code §§ 17, 18.

Health and education records, disclosure of records to prospective caretakers, see Welfare and Institutions Code § 16010.

Inclusion of juvenile case file information with position statement, availability, hearing postponement, see Welfare and Institutions Code § 10952.5.

Inspection of public records, disclosure of name, date of birth, and date of death of foster child to county child welfare agency, see Government Code § 6252.6.

Inspection of public records, other exemptions from disclosure, inspection of juvenile court documents, see Government Code § 6276.46.

Misdemeanors, definition and penalties, see Penal Code §§ 17, 19, 19.2.

Nonminor dependents, opening of separate court file, access to file, see Welfare and Institutions Code § 362.5.

Office of the State Foster Care Ombudsperson, establishment, see Welfare and Institutions Code § 16161.

Probation officer or social worker defined for purposes of this Chapter, see Welfare and Institutions Code § 215.

Public records, inspection of, see Government Code § 6250 et seq.

Termination of jurisdiction, continued jurisdiction, see Welfare and Institutions Code § 391.

Research References

West's California Judicial Council Forms JV–291–INFO, Information on Requesting Access to Records for Persons With a Limited Right to Appeal.

West's California Judicial Council Forms JV–569, Proof of Service—Petition for Access to Juvenile Case File.

West's California Judicial Council Forms JV–570, Petition for Access to Juvenile Case File (Also Available in Spanish).

West's California Judicial Council Forms JV–571, Notice of Petition for Access to Juvenile Case File.

West's California Judicial Council Forms JV–572, Objection to Release of Juvenile Case File.

West's California Judicial Council Forms JV–573, Order on Petition for Access to Juvenile Case File.

West's California Judicial Council Forms JV–574, Order After Judicial Review on Petition for Access to Juvenile Case File.

West's California Judicial Council Forms JV–690, School Notification of Court Adjudication (Welf. & Inst. Code Section 827(B)).

5 Witkin, California Criminal Law 4th Criminal Trial § 49 (2021), Witness's "Rap Sheet.".

§ 827.1. Computerized data base system; authorized access; security procedures

(a) Notwithstanding any other provision of law, a city, county, or city and county may establish a computerized data base system within that city, county, or city and county that permits the probation department, law enforcement agencies, and school districts to access probation department, law enforcement, school district, and juvenile court information and records which are nonprivileged and where release is authorized under state or federal law or regulation, regarding minors under the jurisdiction of the juvenile court pursuant to Section 602 or for whom a program of supervision has been undertaken where a petition could otherwise be filed pursuant to Section 602.

(b) Each city, county, or city and county permitting computer access to these agencies shall develop security procedures by which unauthorized personnel cannot access data contained in the system as well as procedures or devices to secure data from unauthorized access or disclosure. The right of access granted shall not include the right to add, delete, or alter data without the written permission of the agency holding the data. *(Added by Stats.1996, c. 343 (A.B.2617), § 2.)*

§ 827.10. Disclosure of juvenile case file and records when child is subject of family law or probate guardianship case; persons who may inspect or receive copies of records; subordination to other state and federal law; testimony of social worker; confidentiality of information or records obtained

(a) Notwithstanding Section 827, the child welfare agency is authorized to permit its files and records relating to a minor, who is the subject of either a family law or a probate guardianship case involving custody or visitation issues, or both, to be inspected by, and to provide copies to, the following persons, if these persons are actively participating in the family law or probate case:

(1) The judge, commissioner, or other hearing officer assigned to the family law or probate case.

(2) The parent or guardian of the minor.

(3) An attorney for a party to the family law or probate case.

(4) A family court mediator assigned to a case involving the minor pursuant to Article 1 (commencing with Section 3160) of Chapter 11 of Part 2 of Division 8 of the Family Code.

(5) A court-appointed investigator, evaluator, or a person conducting a court-connected child custody evaluation, investigation, or assessment pursuant to Section 3111 or 3118 of the Family Code or Part 2 (commencing with Section 1500) of Division 4 of the Probate Code.

(6) Counsel appointed for the minor in the family law case pursuant to Section 3150 of the Family Code. Prior to allowing counsel appointed for the minor in the family law case to inspect the file, the court clerk may require counsel to provide a certified copy of the court order appointing him or her as the counsel for the minor.

(b) If the child welfare agency files or records, or any portions thereof, are privileged or confidential pursuant to any other state law, except Section 827, or federal law or regulation, the requirements of that state law or federal law or regulation prohibiting or limiting release of the child welfare agency files or records, or any portions thereof, shall prevail.

(c) A social worker may testify in any family or probate proceeding with regard to any information that may be disclosed under this section.

(d) Any records or information obtained pursuant to this section, including the testimony of a social worker, shall be maintained solely in the confidential portion of the family law or probate file. *(Added by Stats.2010, c. 352 (A.B.939), § 21.)*

Research References

West's California Judicial Council Forms JV–573, Order on Petition for Access to Juvenile Case File.

West's California Judicial Council Forms JV–574, Order After Judicial Review on Petition for Access to Juvenile Case File.

§ 827.11. Information sharing; legislative findings and declarations

(a) The Legislature finds and declares all of the following:

(1) It is the intent of the Legislature to ensure quality care for children and youth who are placed in the continuum of foster care settings.

(2) Attracting and retaining quality caregivers is critical to achieving positive outcomes for children, youth, and families, and to ensuring the success of child welfare improvement efforts.

(3) Quality caregivers strengthen foster care by ensuring that a foster or relative family caring for a child provides the loving, committed, and skilled care that the child needs, while working effectively with the child welfare system to reach the child's goals.

(4) Caregivers who are informed of the child's educational, medical, dental, and mental health history and current needs are better able to meet those needs and address the effects of trauma, increasing placement stability and improving permanency outcomes.

(5) Sharing necessary information with the caregiver is a critical component of effective service delivery for children and youth in foster care.

(b) Therefore, consistent with state and federal law, information shall be provided to a caregiver regarding the child's or youth's educational, medical, dental, and mental health history and current needs.

(c) This section is declaratory of existing law and is not intended to impose a new program or higher level of service upon any local agency. It is intended, however, that this restatement of existing law should engender a renewed sense of commitment to engaging foster parents in order to provide quality care to children and youth in foster care.

(d) No later than January 1, 2017, the department shall consult with representatives of the County Counsels' Association of California, County Welfare Directors Association of California, and stakeholders to develop regulations or identify policy changes necessary to allow for the sharing of information as described in this section. *(Added by Stats.2015, c. 773 (A.B.403), § 52, eff. Jan. 1, 2016.)*

§ 827.12. Persons who may access juvenile delinquency case file; release of records for human subject research; disclosure of any dependency information prohibited

(a)(1) Records contained in a juvenile delinquency case file may be accessed by a law enforcement agency, probation department, court, the Department of Justice, or other state or local agency that has custody of the case file and juvenile record for the limited purpose of complying with data collection or data reporting requirements that are imposed under the terms of a grant or by another state or federal law. However, personally identifying information contained in a juvenile delinquency case file accessed under this subdivision shall not be released, disseminated, or published by or through an agency, department, court, or individual that has accessed or obtained information from the juvenile delinquency case file.

(2) Upon request of the chief probation officer, the juvenile court may authorize a probation department to access and provide data contained in juvenile delinquency case files and related juvenile records in the possession of the probation department for the purpose of data sharing or conducting or facilitating research on juvenile justice populations, practices, policies, or trends, if both of the following requirements are met:

(A) The court is satisfied that the research, evaluation, or study includes a sound methodology for the appropriate protection of the confidentiality of an individual whose juvenile delinquency case file is accessed pursuant to this subdivision.

(B) Personally identifying information relating to the individual whose juvenile delinquency case file is accessed pursuant to this subdivision is not further released, disseminated, or published by the probation department or by or through a program evaluator, researcher, or research organization that is retained by the department for research or evaluation purposes.

(3) For the purposes of this subdivision, "personally identifying information" has the same meaning as specified in subdivision (b) of Section 1798.79.8 of the Civil Code.

(b)(1) If information from a juvenile delinquency case record is being released for the purposes of human subject research, as defined in Part 46 of Title 45 of the Code of Federal Regulations, the probation department shall, after receiving authorization from the court but prior to the release of any information, enter into a formal agreement with the entity or entities conducting the research or evaluation that specifies what may and may not be done with the information disclosed.

(2) All human subject research governed by Part 46 of Title 45 of the Code of Federal Regulations shall be conducted in compliance with the protections set forth therein.

(c) The probation department shall not disclose any dependency information contained in a juvenile delinquency case record that pertains to a child who is currently receiving, or has previously received, public social services administered by the State Department of Social Services unless it has complied with the requirements for disclosure of that information set forth in Section 10850. *(Added by Stats.2017, c. 462 (S.B.462), § 1, eff. Jan. 1, 2018.)*

§ 827.15. Transfer of child custody proceeding to jurisdiction of tribal court; transfer of child case file

(a) Notwithstanding Section 827, whenever the juvenile court of a county has made a determination pursuant to subdivision (a), (b), or (f) of Section 305.5 that a child custody proceeding of an Indian child is to be transferred to the jurisdiction of a tribal court the child case file shall be transferred to the tribe.

(b) If an Indian child is under the jurisdiction of a Title IV–E tribe or a Tribal Title IV–E agency, federal law requires the safeguarding of information as set forth in 45 C.F.R 205.50.

(c) In all other transfers, the juvenile court shall order the release of the child's case file provided that the tribe agrees to maintain the documentation confidential consistent with state and federal law.

(d) As used in this section, a "child case file" means information including the juvenile case file retained by the juvenile court and the child welfare agency files or records retained by the county. For Title IV–E tribes or a Tribal Tile IV–E agency that information includes, but need not be limited to, the documentation set forth in 45 C.F.R. 1356.67. *(Added by Stats.2014, c. 772 (S.B.1460), § 14, eff. Jan. 1, 2015.)*

Cross References

Dependent children, temporary custody and detention, transfer of proceedings to tribal court, see Welfare and Institutions Code § 305.5.

§ 827.2. Commission of felony; notice; disclosure of information

(a) Notwithstanding Section 827 or any other provision of law, written notice that a minor has been found by a court of competent jurisdiction to have committed any felony pursuant to Section 602 shall be provided by the court within seven days to the sheriff of the county in which the offense was committed and to the sheriff of the county in which the minor resides. Written notice shall include only that information regarding the felony offense found to have been committed by the minor and the disposition of the minor's case. If at any time thereafter the court modifies the disposition of the minor's case, it shall also notify the sheriff as provided above. The sheriff may disseminate the information to other law enforcement personnel upon request, provided that he or she reasonably believes that the release of this information is generally relevant to the prevention or control of juvenile crime.

(b) Any information received pursuant to this section shall be received in confidence for the limited law enforcement purpose for which it was provided and shall not be further disseminated except as provided in this section. An intentional violation of the confidentiality provisions of this section is a misdemeanor punishable by a fine not to exceed five hundred dollars ($500).

(c) Notwithstanding subdivision (a) or (b), a law enforcement agency may disclose to the public or to any interested person the information received pursuant to subdivision (a) regarding a minor 14 years of age or older who was found by the court to have committed any felony enumerated in subdivision (b) of Section 707. The law enforcement agency shall not release this information if the court for good cause, with a written statement of reasons, so orders. *(Formerly § 827.1, added by Stats.1996, c. 422 (A.B.3224), § 1. Renumbered § 827.2 and amended by Initiative Measure (Prop. 21, § 30, approved March 7, 2000, eff. March 8, 2000).)*

Cross References

Felonies, definition and penalties, see Penal Code §§ 17, 18.
Misdemeanors, definition and penalties, see Penal Code §§ 17, 19, 19.2.

Research References

West's California Judicial Council Forms JV–692, Notification to Sheriff of Juvenile Delinquency Felony Adjudication (Welf. & Inst. Code Section 827.2).
1 Witkin California Criminal Law 4th Introduction to Crimes § 140 (2021), Gang Violence and Juvenile Crime Prevention Act (Proposition 21).

§ 827.5. Commission of serious felony; minor in custody; hearing commenced; disclosure of name

Notwithstanding any other provision of law except Sections 389 and 781 of this code and Section 1203.45 of the Penal Code, a law enforcement agency may disclose the name of any minor 14 years of age or older taken into custody for the commission of any serious felony, as defined in subdivision (c) of Section 1192.7 of the Penal Code, and the offenses allegedly committed, upon the request of interested persons, following the minor's arrest for that offense. *(Added by Stats.1993–94, 1st Ex.Sess., c. 37 (S.B.31), § 1, eff. Nov. 30, 1994. Amended by Stats.1999, c. 996 (S.B.334), § 24; Initiative Measure (Prop. 21, § 31, approved March 7, 2000, eff. March 8, 2000).)*

Cross References

Felonies, definition and penalties, see Penal Code §§ 17, 18.

§ 827.6. Commission of violent offense; release of information

A law enforcement agency may release the name, description, and the alleged offense of any minor alleged to have committed a violent offense, as defined in subdivision (c) of Section 667.5 of the Penal Code, and against whom an arrest warrant is outstanding, if the release of this information would assist in the apprehension of the minor or the protection of public safety. Neither the agency nor the city, county, or city and county in which the agency is located shall be liable for civil damages resulting from release of this information. *(Added by Stats.1999, c. 996 (S.B.334), § 26. Amended by Initiative Measure (Prop. 21, § 32, approved March 7, 2000, eff. March 8, 2000).)*

§ 827.7. Commission of felony; disposition of case; notice to sheriff; dissemination of information; penalties; disclosure of information

(a) Notwithstanding Section 827 or any other provision of law, written notice that a minor has been found by a court of competent jurisdiction to have committed any felony pursuant to Section 602 shall be provided by the court within seven days to the sheriff of the county in which the offense was committed and to the sheriff of the county in which the minor resides. Written notice shall include only that information regarding the felony offense found to have been committed by the minor and the disposition of the minor's case. If at any time thereafter the court modifies the disposition of the minor's case, it shall also notify the sheriff as provided above. The sheriff may disseminate the information to other law enforcement personnel upon request, provided that he or she reasonably believes that the release of this information is generally relevant to the prevention or control of juvenile crime.

Any information received pursuant to this section shall be received in confidence for the limited law enforcement purpose for which it was provided and shall not be further disseminated except as provided in this section. An intentional violation of the confidentiality provisions of this section is a misdemeanor punishable by a fine not to exceed five hundred dollars ($500).

(b) In the written notice provided pursuant to this section, a court may authorize a sheriff who receives information under this section to disclose this information where the release of the information is imperative for the protection of the public and the offense is a violent felony, as defined in subdivision (c) of Section 667.5 of the Penal Code. *(Formerly § 827.1, added by Stats.1996, c. 422 (A.B.3224), § 1. Renumbered § 827.7 and amended by Stats.1999, c. 996 (S.B.334), § 23.)*

Cross References

Felonies, definition and penalties, see Penal Code §§ 17, 18.
Misdemeanors, definition and penalties, see Penal Code §§ 17, 19, 19.2.

§ 827.9. Disclosure of juvenile police records

(a) It is the intent of the Legislature to reaffirm its belief that records or information gathered by law enforcement agencies relating to the taking of a minor into custody, temporary custody, or detention (juvenile police records) should be confidential. Confidentiality is necessary to protect those persons from being denied various opportunities, to further the rehabilitative efforts of the juvenile justice system, and to prevent the lifelong stigma that results from having a juvenile police record. Although these records generally should remain confidential, the Legislature recognizes that certain circumstances require the release of juvenile police records to specified persons and entities. The purpose of this section is to clarify the persons and entities entitled to receive a complete copy of a juvenile police record, to specify the persons or entities entitled to receive copies of juvenile police records with certain identifying information about other minors removed from the record, and to provide procedures for others to request a copy of a juvenile police record. This section does not govern the release of police records involving a minor who is the witness to or victim of a crime who is protected by other laws including, but not limited to, Section 841.5 of the Penal Code, Section 11167 et seq. of the Penal Code, and the provisions listed in Section 7920.505 of the Government Code.

(b) Except as provided in Sections 389, 781, and 786 of this code or Section 1203.45 of the Penal Code, a law enforcement agency shall release, upon request, a complete copy of a juvenile police record, as defined in subdivision (m), without notice or consent from the person who is the subject of the juvenile police record to the following persons or entities:

(1) Other law enforcement agencies including the office of the Attorney General of California, any district attorney, the Department of Corrections and Rehabilitation, including the Division of Juvenile Justice, and any peace officer as specified in subdivision (a) of Section 830.1 of the Penal Code.

(2) School district police.

(3) Child protective agencies as defined in Section 11165.9 of the Penal Code.

(4) The attorney representing the juvenile who is the subject of the juvenile police record in a criminal or juvenile proceeding.

(5) The Department of Motor Vehicles.

(c) Except as provided in Sections 389, 781, and 786 of this code or Section 1203.45 of the Penal Code, law enforcement agencies shall release, upon request, a copy of a juvenile police record to the following persons and entities only if identifying information pertaining to any other juvenile, within the meaning of subdivision (n), has been removed from the record:

(1) The person who is the subject of the juvenile police record.

(2) The parents or guardian of a minor who is the subject of the juvenile police record.

(3) An attorney for a parent or guardian of a minor who is the subject of the juvenile police record.

(d)(1)(A) If a person or entity listed in subdivision (c) seeks to obtain a complete copy of a juvenile police record that contains identifying information concerning the taking into custody or detention of any other juvenile, within the meaning of subdivision (n), who is not a dependent child or a ward of the juvenile court, that person or entity shall submit a completed Petition to Obtain Report of Law Enforcement Agency, as developed pursuant to subdivision (i), to the appropriate law enforcement agency. The law enforcement agency shall send a notice to the following persons that a Petition to Obtain Report of Law Enforcement Agency has been submitted to the agency:

(i) The juvenile about whom information is sought.

(ii) The parents or guardian of any minor described in clause (i). The law enforcement agency shall make reasonable efforts to obtain the address of the parents or guardian.

(B) For purposes of responding to a request submitted pursuant to this subdivision, a law enforcement agency may check the Juvenile Automated Index or may contact the juvenile court to determine whether a person is a dependent child or a ward of the juvenile court and whether parental rights have been terminated or the juvenile has been emancipated.

(C) The notice sent pursuant to this subdivision shall include the following information:

(i) The identity of the person or entity requesting a copy of the juvenile police record.

(ii) A copy of the completed Petition to Obtain Report of Law Enforcement Agency.

(iii) The time period for submitting an objection to the law enforcement agency, which shall be 20 days if notice is provided by mail or confirmed fax, or 15 days if notice is provided by personal service.

(iv) The means to submit an objection.

A law enforcement agency shall issue notice pursuant to this section within 20 days of the request. If no objections are filed, the law enforcement agency shall release the juvenile police record within 15 days of the expiration of the objection period.

(D) If any objections to the disclosure of the other juvenile's information are submitted to the law enforcement agency, the law enforcement agency shall send the completed Petition to Obtain Report of Law Enforcement Agency, the objections, and a copy of the requested juvenile police record to the presiding judge of the juvenile court or, in counties with no presiding judge of the juvenile court, the judge of the juvenile court or the judge's designee, to obtain authorization from the court to release a complete copy of the juvenile police record.

(2) If a person or entity listed in subdivision (c) seeks to obtain a complete copy of a juvenile police record that contains identifying information concerning the taking into custody or detention of any other juvenile, within the meaning of subdivision (n), who is a dependent child or a ward of the juvenile court, that person or entity shall submit a Petition to Obtain Report of Law Enforcement Agency, as developed pursuant to subdivision (i), to the appropriate law enforcement agency. The law enforcement agency shall send that Petition to Obtain Report of Law Enforcement Agency and a completed petition for authorization to release the information to that person or entity along with a complete copy of the requested juvenile police record to the presiding judge of the juvenile court, or, in counties with no presiding judge of the juvenile court, the judge of the juvenile court or the judge's designees. The juvenile court shall

provide notice of the petition for authorization to the following persons:

(A) If the person who would be identified if the information is released is a minor who is a dependent child of the juvenile court, notice of the petition shall be provided to the following persons:

(i) The minor.

(ii) The attorney of record for the minor.

(iii) The parents or guardian of the minor, unless parental rights have been terminated.

(iv) The child protective agency responsible for the minor.

(v) The attorney representing the child protective agency responsible for the minor.

(B) If the person who would be identified if the information is released is a ward of the juvenile court, notice of the petition shall be provided to the following:

(i) The ward.

(ii) The attorney of record for the ward.

(iii) The parents or guardian of the ward if the ward is under 18 years of age, unless parental rights have been terminated.

(iv) The district attorney.

(v) The probation department.

(e) Except as otherwise provided in this section or in Sections 389, 781, and 786 of this code or Section 1203.45 of the Penal Code, law enforcement agencies shall release copies of juvenile police records to any other person designated by court order upon the filing of a Petition to Obtain Report of Law Enforcement Agency with the juvenile court. The petition shall be filed with the presiding judge of the juvenile court, or, in counties with no presiding judge of the juvenile court, the judge of the juvenile court or the judge's designee, in the county where the juvenile police record is maintained.

(f)(1) After considering the petition and any objections submitted to the juvenile court pursuant to paragraph (1) or (2) of subdivision (d), the court shall determine whether the law enforcement agency may release a complete copy of the juvenile police record to the person or entity that submitted the request.

(2) In determining whether to authorize the release of a juvenile police record, the court shall balance the interests of the juvenile who is the subject of the record, the petitioner, and the public. The juvenile court may issue orders prohibiting or limiting the release of information contained in the juvenile police record. The court may also deny the existence of a juvenile police record where the record is properly sealed or the juvenile who is the subject of the record has properly denied its existence.

(3) Prior to authorizing the release of any juvenile police record, the juvenile court shall ensure that notice and an opportunity to file an objection to the release of the record has been provided to the juvenile who is the subject of the record or who would be identified if the information is released, that person's parents or guardian if the person is under 18 years of age, and any additional person or entity described in subdivision (d), as applicable. The period for filing an objection shall be 20 days from the date notice is given if notice is provided by mail or confirmed fax and 15 days from the date notice is given if notice is provided by personal service. If review of the petition is urgent, the petitioner may file a motion with the presiding judge of the juvenile court showing good cause why the objection period should be shortened. The court shall issue a ruling on the completed petition within 15 days of the expiration of the objection period.

(g) Any out-of-state entity comparable to the California entities listed in paragraphs (1) to (5), inclusive, of subdivision (b) shall file a petition with the presiding judge of the juvenile court in the county where the juvenile police record is maintained in order to receive a copy of a juvenile police record. A petition from that entity may be granted on an ex parte basis.

(h) Nothing in this section shall require the release of confidential victim or witness information protected by other laws including, but not limited to, Section 841.5 of the Penal Code, Section 11167 et seq. of the Penal Code, and the provisions listed in Section 7920.505 of the Government Code.

(i) The Judicial Council, in consultation with the California Law Enforcement Association of Record Supervisors (CLEARS), shall develop forms for distribution by law enforcement agencies to the public to implement this section. Those forms shall include, but are not limited to, the Petition to Obtain Report of Law Enforcement Agency. The material for the public shall include information about the persons who are entitled to a copy of the juvenile police record and the specific procedures for requesting a copy of the record if a petition is necessary. The Judicial Council shall provide law enforcement agencies with suggested forms for compliance with the notice provisions set forth in subdivision (d).

(j) Any information received pursuant to subdivisions (a) to (e), inclusive, and (g) of this section shall be received in confidence for the limited purpose for which it was provided and shall not be further disseminated. An intentional violation of the confidentiality provisions of this section is a misdemeanor, punishable by a fine not to exceed five hundred dollars ($500).

(k) A court shall consider any information relating to the taking of a minor into custody, if the information is not contained in a record that has been sealed, for purposes of determining whether an adjudication of the commission of a crime as a minor warrants a finding that there are circumstances in aggravation pursuant to Section 1170 of the Penal Code or to deny probation.

(*l*) When a law enforcement agency has been notified pursuant to Section 1155 that a minor has escaped from a secure detention facility, the law enforcement agency shall release the name of, and any descriptive information about, the minor to a person who specifically requests this information. The law enforcement agency may release the information on the minor without a request to do so if it finds that release of the information would be necessary to assist in recapturing the minor or that it would be necessary to protect the public from substantial physical harm.

(m) For purposes of this section, a "juvenile police record" refers to records or information relating to the taking of a minor into custody, temporary custody, or detention.

(n) For purposes of this section, with respect to a juvenile police record, "any other juvenile" refers to additional minors who were taken into custody or temporary custody, or detained and who also could be considered a subject of the juvenile police record.

(*o*) An evaluation of the efficacy of the procedures for the release of police records containing information about minors as described in this section shall be conducted by the juvenile court and law enforcement in Los Angeles County and the results of that evaluation shall be reported to the Legislature on or before December 31, 2006.

(p) This section shall only apply to Los Angeles County. *(Added by Stats.2001, c. 830 (S.B.940), § 7. Amended by Stats.2002, c. 545 (S.B.1852), § 34; Stats.2009, c. 35 (S.B.174), § 31; Stats.2016, c. 858 (A.B.1945), § 3, eff. Jan. 1, 2017; Stats.2021, c. 615 (A.B.474), § 433, eff. Jan. 1, 2022, operative Jan. 1, 2023.)*

Law Revision Commission Comments

Section 827.9 is amended to reflect nonsubstantive recodification of the California Public Records Act. See California Public Records Act Clean-Up, 46 Cal. L. Revision Comm'n Reports 207 (2019).

The section is also amended to eliminate gendered pronouns. [46 Cal. L.Rev.Comm. Reports 563 (2019)].

Cross References

Attorney General, generally, see Government Code § 12500 et seq.

Department of Corrections, generally, see Penal Code § 5000 et seq.
Misdemeanors, definition and penalties, see Penal Code §§ 17, 19, 19.2.

Research References

West's California Judicial Council Forms JV–575, Petition to Obtain Report of Law Enforcement Agency (Also Available in Spanish).

§ 827.95. Juvenile police records; disclosure; sealing of record; definitions; forms

(a)(1) Notwithstanding Section 827.9, a law enforcement agency in this state shall not release a copy of a juvenile police record if the subject of the juvenile police record is any of the following:

(A) A minor who has been diverted by police officers from arrest, citation, detention, or referral to probation or any district attorney, and who is currently participating in a diversion program or has satisfactorily completed a diversion program.

(B) A minor who has been counseled and released by police officers without an arrest, citation, detention, or referral to probation or any district attorney, and for whom no referral to probation has been made within 60 days of the release.

(C) A minor who does not fall within the jurisdiction of the juvenile delinquency court under current state law.

(2) A law enforcement agency shall release, upon request, a copy of a juvenile police record described in paragraph (1) to the minor who is the subject of the juvenile police record and their parent or guardian only if identifying information pertaining to any other juvenile, within the meaning of subdivision (d), has been removed from the record.

(b)(1) The law enforcement agency in possession of the juvenile police record described in subdivision (a) shall seal the applicable juvenile police record and all other records in its custody relating to the minor's law enforcement contact or referral and participation in a diversion program as follows:

(A) Any juvenile police record created following a law enforcement contact with a minor described in subparagraph (A) of paragraph (1) of subdivision (a) shall be considered confidential and deemed not to exist while the minor is completing a diversion program, except to the law enforcement agency, the service provider, the minor who is the subject of the police record, and their parent or guardian. The diversion service provider shall notify the referring law enforcement agency of a minor's satisfactory completion of a diversion program within 30 days of the minor's satisfactory completion. The law enforcement agency shall seal the juvenile police record no later than 30 days from the date of notification by the diversion service provider of the minor's satisfactory completion of a diversion program.

(B) Any juvenile police record created following a law enforcement contact with a minor described in subparagraph (B) of paragraph (1) of subdivision (a) shall be sealed no later than 60 days from the date of verification that the minor has not been referred to probation or any district attorney. Verification shall be completed within six months of the decision to counsel and release the minor.

(C) Any juvenile police record created following a law enforcement contact with a minor described in subparagraph (C) of paragraph (1) of subdivision (a) shall be sealed immediately upon verification that the minor does not fall within the jurisdiction of the juvenile delinquency court under current state law.

(D) Upon sealing of the records under this subdivision, the offense giving rise to the police record shall be deemed to not have occurred and the individual may respond accordingly to any inquiry, application, or process in which disclosure of this information is requested or sought.

(2) A law enforcement agency that seals a juvenile police record pursuant to subparagraph (A) of paragraph (1) shall notify the applicable diversion service provider immediately upon sealing of the record. Any records in the diversion service provider's custody relating to the minor's law enforcement contact or referral and participation in the program shall not be inspected by anyone other than the service provider, and shall be released only to the minor who is the subject of the record and their parent or guardian, as described in subdivision (c).

(3) If the minor is a dependent of the juvenile court, the law enforcement agency shall notify the minor's social worker that the juvenile police records have been sealed and that any such records in the social worker's custody relating to the minor's law enforcement contact or referral and participation in a diversion program shall also be sealed.

(4)(A) A law enforcement agency shall notify a minor in writing that their police record has been sealed pursuant to paragraph (1). If the law enforcement agency determines that a minor's juvenile police record is not eligible for sealing pursuant to paragraph (1), the law enforcement agency shall notify the minor in writing of its determination.

(B) An individual who receives notice from a law enforcement agency that they are not eligible for sealing under paragraph (1) may request reconsideration of the law enforcement agency's determination by submitting to the law enforcement agency a petition to seal a report of a law enforcement agency and any documentation supporting their eligibility for sealing under paragraph (1). For purposes of this subparagraph, a sworn statement by the petitioner shall qualify as supporting documentation.

(5) Police records sealed under paragraph (1) shall not be considered part of the "juvenile case file," as defined in subdivision (e) of Section 827.

(6)(A) Any police record that has been sealed pursuant to this section may be accessed, inspected, or utilized by the prosecuting attorney in order to meet a statutory or constitutional obligation to disclose favorable or exculpatory evidence to a defendant in a criminal case in which the prosecuting attorney has reason to believe that access to the record is necessary to meet the disclosure obligation.

(B)(i) A prosecuting attorney shall not use information contained in a record sealed pursuant to this section for any purpose other than those provided in subparagraph (A).

(ii) Once the case referenced in subparagraph (A) has been closed and is no longer subject to review on appeal, the prosecuting attorney shall destroy any records obtained pursuant to this subparagraph.

(c)(1) Diversion service provider records related to the provision of diversion services to a minor described in subparagraph (A) of paragraph (1) of subdivision (a) shall not be considered part of a "juvenile case file," as defined in subdivision (e) of Section 827, and shall be kept confidential except to the minor who is the subject of the record or information and their parent or guardian. This section does not require the release of confidential records created, collected, or maintained by diversion service providers in the course of diversion service delivery.

(2)(A) If any other state or federal law or regulation grants access to portions of, or information relating to, the contents of a diversion service provider record related to diversion, the requirements of that state or federal law or regulation governing access to the record or portions thereof shall prevail.

(B) The release of any diversion service provider records related to diversion by any party with access under applicable California state or federal laws shall be governed by those applicable state or federal laws, and shall otherwise be prohibited.

(3) Diversion service providers shall release diversion service provider records to the minor who is the subject of the record, or their parent or guardian, upon receiving a signature authorization by the minor, parent, or guardian and using existing internal confidentiality procedures of the service provider.

(d) For purposes of this section, the following definitions apply:

(1) "Juvenile police record" refers to records or information relating to the taking of a minor into custody, temporary custody, or detention.

(2) With respect to a juvenile police record, "any other juvenile" refers to additional minors who were taken into custody or temporary custody, or detained and who also could be considered a subject of the juvenile police record.

(3) "Diversion" refers to an intervention that redirects youth away from formal processing in the juvenile justice system, including, but not limited to, counsel and release or a referral to a diversion program as defined in Section 1457.

(4) "Diversion service provider" refers to an agency or organization providing diversion services to a minor.

(5) "Diversion service provider record" refers to any records or information collected, created, or maintained by the service provider in connection to providing diversion program services to the minor.

(6) "Satisfactory completion" refers to substantial compliance by the participant with the reasonable terms of program participation that are within the capacity of the participant to perform, as determined by the service provider.

(e) On or before January 1, 2022, the Judicial Council, in consultation with the California Law Enforcement Association of Record Supervisors (CLEARS), shall develop forms for distribution by law enforcement agencies to the public to implement this section. Those forms shall include, but are not limited to, the Petition to Seal Report of Law Enforcement Agency. The material for the public shall include information about the persons who are entitled to a copy of the juvenile police record described in subdivision (a) and the specific procedures for requesting a copy of the record if a petition is necessary. *(Added by Stats.2020, c. 330 (A.B.2425), § 3, eff. Jan. 1, 2021.)*

Research References

West's California Judicial Council Forms JV–581, Law Enforcement Notice on Sealing of Records (Welf. & Inst. Code, §827.95).

West's California Judicial Council Forms JV–582, Petition to Seal Juvenile Police Records.

§ 828. Disclosure of information gathered by law enforcement agency; release of descriptive information about minor escapees

(a)(1) Except as provided in Sections 389, 781, 786, 827.9, and 827.95 of this code or Section 1203.45 of the Penal Code, any information gathered by a law enforcement agency, including the Department of Justice, relating to the taking of a minor into custody may be disclosed to another law enforcement agency, including a school district police or security department, or to any person or agency that has a legitimate need for the information for purposes of official disposition of a case. When the disposition of a taking into custody is available, it shall be included with any information disclosed.

(2) A court shall consider any information relating to the taking of a minor into custody, if the information is not contained in a record that has been sealed, for purposes of determining whether adjudications of commission of crimes as a juvenile warrant a finding that there are circumstances in aggravation pursuant to Section 1170 of the Penal Code or to deny probation.

(b) When a law enforcement agency has been notified pursuant to Section 1155 that a minor has escaped from a secure detention facility, the law enforcement agency shall release the name of, and any descriptive information about, the minor to a person who specifically requests this information. The law enforcement agency may release the information on the minor without a request to do so if it finds that release of the information would be necessary to assist in recapturing the minor or that it would be necessary to protect the public from substantial physical harm. *(Added by Stats.1972, c. 1139, p. 2206, § 2. Amended by Stats.1976, c. 1068, p. 4797, § 73; Stats.1981, c. 1076, p. 4143, § 3; Stats.1984, c. 1420, § 2, eff. Sept. 26, 1984; Stats.1986, c. 359, § 2; Stats.1990, c. 776 (S.B.1429), § 1; Stats.2001, c. 830 (S.B.940), § 8; Stats.2003, c. 124 (S.B.873), § 4; Stats.2016, c. 858 (A.B.1945), § 4, eff. Jan. 1, 2017; Stats.2020, c. 330 (A.B.2425), § 4, eff. Jan. 1, 2021.)*

Cross References

Inspection of public records, other exemptions from disclosure, see Government Code § 6276.48.

Judgment, probation, probation officer investigation, report, and recommendations, see Penal Code § 1203.

Research References

West's California Judicial Council Forms JV–573, Order on Petition for Access to Juvenile Case File.

West's California Judicial Council Forms JV–574, Order After Judicial Review on Petition for Access to Juvenile Case File.

West's California Judicial Council Forms JV–575, Petition to Obtain Report of Law Enforcement Agency (Also Available in Spanish).

§ 828.1. School district police or security department; disclosure of juvenile criminal records; protection of vulnerable school staff and other students

(a) While the Legislature reaffirms its belief that juvenile criminal records, in general, should be confidential, it is the intent of the Legislature in enacting this section to provide for a limited exception to that confidentiality in cases involving serious acts of violence. Further, it is the intent of the Legislature that even in these selected cases the dissemination of juvenile criminal records be as limited as possible, consistent with the need to work with a student in an appropriate fashion, and the need to protect potentially vulnerable school staff and other students over whom the school staff exercises direct supervision and responsibility.

(b) Notwithstanding subdivision (a) of Section 828, a school district police or security department may provide written notice to the superintendent of the school district that a minor enrolled in a public school maintained by that school district, in kindergarten or any of grades 1 to 12, inclusive, has been found by a court of competent jurisdiction to have illegally used, sold, or possessed a controlled substance as defined in Section 11007 of the Health and Safety Code or to have committed any crime listed in paragraphs (1) to (15), inclusive, or paragraphs (17) to (19), inclusive, or paragraphs (25) to (28), inclusive, of subdivision (b) of, or in paragraph (2) of subdivision (d) of, or subdivision (e) of, Section 707. The information may be expeditiously transmitted to any teacher, counselor, or administrator with direct supervisorial or disciplinary responsibility over the minor, who the superintendent or his or her designee, after consultation with the principal at the school of attendance, believes needs this information to work with the student in an appropriate fashion, to avoid being needlessly vulnerable or to protect other persons from needless vulnerability.

(c) Any information received by a teacher, counselor, or administrator pursuant to this section shall be received in confidence for the limited purpose for which it was provided and shall not be further disseminated by the teacher, counselor, or administrator. An intentional violation of the confidentiality provisions of this section is a misdemeanor, punishable by a fine not to exceed five hundred dollars ($500). *(Added by Stats.1990, c. 776, (S.B.1429), § 2. Amended by Stats.1994, c. 453 (A.B.560), § 15; Stats.1998, c. 925 (A.B.1290), § 8.)*

Cross References

Inspection of public records, other exemptions from disclosure, see Government Code § 6276.28.

Misdemeanors, definition and penalties, see Penal Code §§ 17, 19, 19.2.

§ 828.3. Crimes against property, students, or personnel of school; juvenile custody or commission; information sharing

Notwithstanding any other provision of law, information relating to the taking of a minor into custody on the basis that he or she has committed a crime against the property, students, or personnel of a school district or a finding by the juvenile court that the minor has committed such a crime may be exchanged between law enforcement personnel, the school district superintendent, and the principal of a public school in which the minor is enrolled as a student if the offense was against the property, students, or personnel of that school. *(Added by Stats.1994, c. 215 (A.B.3786), § 1.)*

§ 829. Review of juvenile court records; suitability for release

Notwithstanding any other provision of law, the Board of Prison Terms, in order to evaluate the suitability for release of a person before the board, shall be entitled to review juvenile court records which have not been sealed, concerning the person before the board, if those records relate to a case in which the person was found to have committed an offense which brought the person within the jurisdiction of the juvenile court pursuant to Section 602. *(Added by Stats.1983, c. 241, § 1.)*

§ 830. Child abuse or neglect; disclosure of information and writings among members of multidisciplinary personnel team; definitions

(a) Notwithstanding any other provision of law, members of a multidisciplinary personnel team engaged in the prevention, identification, management, or treatment of child abuse or neglect may disclose and exchange information and writings to and with one another relating to any incidents of child abuse that may also be a part of a juvenile court record or otherwise designated as confidential under state law if the member of the team having that information or writing reasonably believes it is generally relevant to the prevention, identification, management, or treatment of child abuse, or the provision of child welfare services. All discussions relative to the disclosure or exchange of any such information or writings during team meetings are confidential unless disclosure is required by law. Notwithstanding any other provision of law, testimony concerning any such discussion is not admissible in any criminal, civil, or juvenile court proceeding.

(b) As used in this section:

(1) "Child abuse" has the same meaning as defined in Section 18951.

(2) "Multidisciplinary personnel" means a team as specified in Section 18951.

(3) "Child welfare services" means those services that are directed at preventing child abuse or neglect. *(Added by Stats.1987, c. 353, § 1. Amended by Stats.1989, c. 86, § 1; Stats.2010, c. 551 (A.B.2322), § 1, eff. Sept. 29, 2010.)*

Cross References

Inspection of public records, other exemptions from disclosure, see Government Code § 6276 et seq.
Writing defined, see Welfare and Institutions Code § 8.

§ 830.1. Nonprivileged information and writings; disclosure among members of juvenile justice multidisciplinary team

Notwithstanding any other provision of law, members of a juvenile justice multidisciplinary team engaged in the prevention, identification, and control of crime, including, but not limited to, criminal street gang activity, may disclose and exchange nonprivileged information and writings to and with one another relating to any incidents of juvenile crime, including criminal street gang activity, that may also be part of a juvenile court record or otherwise designated as confidential under state law if the member of the team having that information or writing reasonably believes it is generally relevant to the prevention, identification, or control of juvenile crime or criminal street gang activity. Every member of a juvenile justice multidisciplinary team who receives such information or writings shall be under the same privacy and confidentiality obligations and subject to the same penalties for violating those obligations as the person disclosing or providing the information or writings. The information obtained shall be maintained in a manner which ensures the protection of confidentiality.

As used in this section, "nonprivileged information" means any information not subject to a privilege pursuant to Division 8 (commencing with Section 900) of the Evidence Code.

As used in this section, "criminal street gang" has the same meaning as defined in Section 186.22 of the Penal Code.

As used in this section, "multidisciplinary team" means any team of three or more persons, the members of which are trained in the prevention, identification, and control of juvenile crime, including, but not limited to, criminal street gang activity, and are qualified to provide a broad range of services related to the problems posed by juvenile crime and criminal street gangs. The team may include, but is not limited to:

(a) Police officers or other law enforcement agents.

(b) Prosecutors.

(c) Probation officers.

(d) School district personnel with experience or training in juvenile crime or criminal street gang control.

(e) Counseling personnel with experience or training in juvenile crime or criminal street gang control.

(f) State, county, city, or special district recreation specialists with experience or training in juvenile crime or criminal street gang control. *(Added by Stats.1993–94, 1st Ex.Sess., c. 24 (A.B.67), § 1, eff. Nov. 30, 1994.)*

Cross References

Probation officer or social worker defined for purposes of this Chapter, see Welfare and Institutions Code § 215.

§ 831. Confidentiality of juvenile court records regardless of immigration status; disclosure

(a) It is the intent of the Legislature in enacting this section to clarify that juvenile court records should remain confidential regardless of the juvenile's immigration status. Confidentiality is integral to the operation of the juvenile justice system in order to avoid stigma and promote rehabilitation for all youth, regardless of immigration status.

(b) Nothing in this article authorizes the disclosure of juvenile information to federal officials absent a court order of the judge of the juvenile court upon filing a petition as provided by subparagraph (P) of paragraph (1) of subdivision (a) of Section 827.

(c) Nothing in this article authorizes the dissemination of juvenile information to, or by, federal officials absent a court order of the judge of the juvenile court upon filing a petition as provided by subparagraph (P) of paragraph (1) and paragraph (4) of subdivision (a) of Section 827.

(d) Nothing in this article authorizes the attachment of juvenile information to any other documents given to, or provided by, federal officials absent prior approval of the presiding judge of the juvenile court as provided by paragraph (4) of subdivision (a) of Section 827.

(e) For purposes of this section, "juvenile information" includes the "juvenile case file," as defined in subdivision (e) of Section 827, and information related to the juvenile, including, but not limited to, name, date or place of birth, and the immigration status of the juvenile that is obtained or created independent of, or in connection with, juvenile court proceedings about the juvenile and maintained by any government agency, including, but not limited to, a court, probation office, child welfare agency, or law enforcement agency.

(f) Nothing in this section shall be construed as authorizing any disclosure that would otherwise violate this article.

(g) The Legislature finds and declares that this section is declaratory of existing law. *(Added by Stats.2015, c. 267 (A.B.899), § 2, eff. Jan. 1, 2016.)*

§ 832. Disclosure of information by members of child and family team; authorization; confidentiality

(a)(1) To promote more effective communication needed for the development of a plan to address the needs of the child or youth and family, a person designated as a member of a child and family team as defined in paragraph (4) of subdivision (a) of Section 16501 may receive and disclose relevant information and records, subject to the confidentiality provisions of state and federal law.

(2) Information exchanged among the team shall be received in confidence for the limited purpose of providing necessary services and supports to the child or youth and family and shall not be further disclosed except to the juvenile court with jurisdiction over the child, subject to the privileges and confidentiality requirements of state and federal law, or as otherwise required by law. Civil and criminal penalties may apply to the inappropriate disclosure of information held by the team.

(b)(1) Each participant in the child and family team with legal power to consent shall sign an authorization to release information to team members. In the event that a child or youth who is a dependent or ward of the juvenile court does not have the legal power to consent to the release of information, the child's attorney or other authorized individual may consent on behalf of the child.

(2) Authorization to release information shall be in writing and shall comply with all other applicable state law governing release of medical, mental health, social service, and educational records, and that covers identified team members, including service providers, in order to permit the release of records to the team.

(3) This authorization shall not include release of adoption records.

(4) The knowing and informed consent to release information given pursuant to this section shall only be in force for the time that the child or youth, or family, or nonminor dependent, is participating in the child and family team.

(c) Upon obtaining the authorization to release information as described in subdivision (b), relevant information and records may be shared with members of the team. If the team determines that the disclosure of information would present a reasonable risk of a significant adverse or detrimental effect on the child's or youth's psychological or physical safety, the information shall not be released.

(d) Information and records communicated or provided to the team, by all providers, programs, and agencies, as well as information and records created by the team in the course of serving its children, youth, and their families, shall be deemed private and confidential and shall be protected from discovery and disclosure by all applicable statutory and common law. Nothing in this section shall be construed to affect the authority of a health care provider to disclose medical information pursuant to paragraph (1) of subdivision (c) of Section 56.10 of the Civil Code.

(e) If the child welfare agency files or records, or any portions thereof, are privileged or confidential, pursuant to any other state law, except Section 827, or federal law or regulation, the requirements of that state law or federal law or regulation prohibiting or limiting release of the child welfare agency files or records, or any portions thereof, shall prevail.

(f) All discussions during team meetings are confidential unless disclosure is required by law. Notwithstanding any other law, testimony concerning any team meeting discussion is not admissible in any criminal or civil proceeding except as provided in paragraph (2) of subdivision (a).

(g) Notwithstanding the rulemaking provisions of the Administrative Procedure Act (Chapter 3.5 (commencing with Section 11340) of Part 1 of Division 3 of Title 2 of the Government Code), the department shall, by July 1, 2021, issue written instructions to counties that describe all protections provided by statute for the confidentiality of mental health, reproductive and sexual health, and minor drug treatment information concerning minors and nonminor dependents for whom a child and family team meeting is held, including, but not limited to, the duties of therapists not to disclose confidential information, as described in Sections 123115 and 123116 of the Health and Safety Code and Section 1015 of the Evidence Code.

(h) Any request to sign an authorization for the release of information described in subdivision (g) provided to minors or nonminor dependents shall incorporate all statutory protections for the confidentiality of the information, including, but not limited to, their right to consult with an attorney before signing the release of information.

(i) As used in this section, "privileged information" means any information subject to a privilege pursuant to Division 8 (commencing with Section 900) of the Evidence Code. Disclosure of otherwise privileged information to team members shall not be construed to waive the privilege. *(Added by Stats.2015, c. 773 (A.B.403), § 53, eff. Jan. 1, 2016. Amended by Stats.2019, c. 780 (A.B.1068), § 3, eff. Jan. 1, 2020.)*

ARTICLE 22.5. HOME SUPERVISION

§ 840. Establishment of program in each county; home supervision defined

There shall be in each county probation department a program of home supervision to which minors described by Section 628.1 shall be referred. Home supervision is a program in which persons who would otherwise be detained in the juvenile hall are permitted to remain in their homes pending court disposition of their cases, under the supervision of a deputy probation officer, probation aide, or probation volunteer. *(Added by Stats.1976, c. 1071, p. 4829, § 32. Amended by Stats.1977, c. 1241, p. 4185, § 9.5, eff. Oct. 1, 1977.)*

Cross References

Probation officer or social worker defined for purposes of this Chapter, see Welfare and Institutions Code § 215.

Probation volunteer defined, see Welfare and Institutions Code § 842.

§ 841. Deputy probation officer, aide, community worker or volunteer; duties; assignment of minors

The duties of a deputy probation officer, or a probation aide, a community worker or a volunteer under the supervision of a deputy probation officer, assigned to home supervision are to assure the minor's appearance at probation officer interviews and court hearings and to assure that the minor obeys the conditions of his or her release and commits no public offenses pending final disposition of his or her case. A deputy probation officer, probation aide, or community worker assigned to home supervision shall have a caseload of no more than 10 minors. However, if the county probation department employs a method of home supervision which includes electronic surveillance, the caseload shall be no more than 15 minors. Whenever possible, a minor shall be assigned to a deputy probation officer, probation aide, community worker, or volunteer who resides in the same community as the minor. *(Added by Stats.1976, c. 1071, p. 4829, § 32. Amended by Stats.1978, c. 1157, p. 3553, § 2, eff. Sept. 26, 1978; Stats.1979, c. 291, p. 1072, § 1; Stats.1991, c. 155 (A.B.1037), § 1.)*

Cross References

Home supervision defined, see Welfare and Institutions Code § 840.
Probation officer or social worker defined for purposes of this Chapter, see Welfare and Institutions Code § 215.

§ 842. Volunteer, aide and community worker defined; nonqualification as peace officer

A probation volunteer is a person who donates personal services to the probation department and probationers without compensation. A probation aide or a community worker may receive compensation for such services. Probation aides, community workers, and volunteers shall not qualify for peace officer status pursuant to Section 830.5 of the Penal Code. *(Added by Stats.1978, c. 1157, p. 3553, § 3, eff. Sept. 26, 1978. Amended by Stats.1979, c. 291, p. 1072, § 2.)*

ARTICLE 23. WARDS AND DEPENDENT CHILDREN—JUVENILE HALLS

Section

§ 850. Establishment; maintenance; designation

The board of supervisors in every county shall provide and maintain, at the expense of the county, in a location approved by the judge of the juvenile court or in counties having more than one judge of the juvenile court, by the presiding judge of the juvenile court, a suitable house or place for the detention of wards and dependent children of the juvenile court and of persons alleged to come within the jurisdiction of the juvenile court. Such house or place shall be known as the "juvenile hall" of the county. Wherever, in any provision of law, reference is made to detention homes for juveniles, such reference shall be deemed and construed to refer to the juvenile halls provided for in this article. *(Added by Stats.1961, c. 1616, p. 3494, § 2.)*

Cross References

Establishment of standards, see Welfare and Institutions Code § 1760.7.
Expense for support and maintenance defined as value of support of ward or dependent child at juvenile hall, see Welfare and Institutions Code § 914.
Jail or lockup, inspection of, see Welfare and Institutions Code § 209.
Joint juvenile halls, see Welfare and Institutions Code § 870.
Juvenile court session when juvenile court not in county, holding of, see Code of Civil Procedure § 73e.
Juvenile homes, ranches and camps, see Welfare and Institutions Code § 880 et seq.
Segregated facilities, see Welfare and Institutions Code § 206.
Twenty-four hour schools, establishment, maintenance, purpose, see Welfare and Institutions Code § 940 et seq.

§ 851. Nature and environment of juvenile hall

Except as provided in Section 207.1, the juvenile hall shall not be in, or connected with, any jail or prison, and shall not be deemed to be, nor be treated as, a penal institution. It shall be a safe and supportive homelike environment. *(Added by Stats.1961, c. 1616, p. 3494, § 2. Amended by Stats.1998, c. 694 (S.B.2147), § 5.)*

Cross References

Separate facilities, when required, see Welfare and Institutions Code § 206.

§ 851.1. Access to computer technology and the Internet for educational purposes; denial of access

(a)(1) Minors detained in or committed to a juvenile hall shall be provided with access to computer technology and the Internet for the purposes of education.

(2) Minors detained in or committed to a juvenile hall may be provided with access to computer technology and the Internet for maintaining relationships with family.

(b) This section does not limit the authority of the chief probation officer, or his or her designee, to limit or deny access to computer technology or the Internet for safety and security or staffing reasons. *(Added by Stats.2018, c. 997 (A.B.2448), § 3, eff. Jan. 1, 2019.)*

§ 852. Management and control

The juvenile hall shall be under the management and control of the probation officer. *(Added by Stats.1961, c. 1616, p. 3494, § 2.)*

Cross References

Government of counties, chief probation officer, duties and obligations, see Government Code § 27771.
Probation commission, generally, see Welfare and Institutions Code § 240 et seq.
Probation officer or social worker defined for purposes of this Chapter, see Welfare and Institutions Code § 215.
Probation officers, generally, see Welfare and Institutions Code § 270 et seq.

§ 853. Superintendent; employees; salaries

The board of supervisors shall provide for a suitable superintendent to have charge of the juvenile hall, and for such other employees as may be needed for its efficient management, and shall provide for payment, out of the general fund of the county, of suitable salaries for such superintendent and other employees. *(Added by Stats.1961, c. 1616, p. 3494, § 2.)*

Cross References

County general fund, see Government Code § 29301.

§ 854. Appointment; removal

The superintendent and other employees of the juvenile hall shall be appointed by the probation officer, pursuant to a civil service or merit system, and may be removed, for cause, pursuant to such system. *(Added by Stats.1961, c. 1616, p. 3495, § 2.)*

Cross References

Probation officer or social worker defined for purposes of this Chapter, see Welfare and Institutions Code § 215.

§ 855. List of expenses

The probation officer shall keep a classified list of expenses for the operation of the juvenile hall and shall file a duplicate copy with the county board of supervisors. *(Added by Stats.1961, c. 1616, p. 3495, § 2.)*

Cross References

Probation officer or social worker defined for purposes of this Chapter, see Welfare and Institutions Code § 215.

§ 856. Establishment of schools; school facilities

The board of supervisors may provide for the establishment of a public elementary school and of a public secondary school in connection with any juvenile hall, juvenile house, day center, juvenile ranch, or juvenile camp, or residential or nonresidential boot camp for the education of the children in those facilities. *(Added by Stats.1961, c. 1616, p. 3495, § 2. Amended by Stats.1977, c. 430, p. 1448, § 2; Stats.1995, c. 72 (S.B.604), § 5.)*

Cross References

Juvenile court schools, see Education Code § 48645 et seq.
Juvenile offender local prevention and corrections program, coordination of state and local efforts to discipline and treat juvenile offenders and to provide partnership funding for juvenile camps, see Welfare and Institutions Code § 1805.

§ 857. Incarcerated minors; notice to Department of Social Services

Whenever a minor is incarcerated in a juvenile hall or other county juvenile facility for a period of at least 30 consecutive days, the facility may inform the State Department of Social Services of the name, date of birth, and social security number of the incarcerated person. *(Added by Stats.1994, c. 1042 (A.B.2844), § 1.)*

§ 858. Juveniles with high school diploma or California high school equivalency certificate; access to postsecondary education programs

(a) It is the intent of the Legislature that juveniles with a high school diploma or California high school equivalency certificate who are detained in, or committed to, a juvenile hall shall have access to rigorous postsecondary academic and career technical education programs that fulfill the requirements for transfer to the University of California and the California State University and prepare them for career entry, respectively.

(b)(1) A county probation department shall ensure that juveniles with a high school diploma or California high school equivalency certificate who are detained in, or committed to, a juvenile hall have access to, and can choose to participate in, public postsecondary academic and career technical courses and programs offered online, and for which they are eligible based on eligibility criteria and course schedules of the public postsecondary education campus providing the course or program. County probation departments, in coordination with county offices of education, may use juvenile court school classrooms and computers, in accordance with agreements entered into pursuant to Section 48646 of the Education Code, for the purpose of implementing this section. County probation departments are also encouraged to develop other educational partnerships with local public postsecondary campuses, as is feasible, to provide programs on campus and onsite at the juvenile hall.

(2) These programs shall be considered part of the current responsibilities of the county probation department to provide and coordinate services for juveniles that enable the juveniles to be law-abiding and productive members of their families and communities.

(c) For purposes of this section, "juvenile" means any person detained in, or committed to, a juvenile hall.

(d) This section does not preclude juvenile court school pupils who have not yet completed their high school graduation requirements from concurrently participating in postsecondary academic and career technical education programs. *(Added by Stats.2019, c. 857 (S.B.716), § 1, eff. Jan. 1, 2020.)*

§ 862. Federal custody; reception and detention by probation officer; time; reimbursement of costs

In addition to those juveniles specified in Section 850, the probation officer may receive and detain in the county juvenile hall any juvenile committed thereto by process or order issued under the authority of the United States until such juvenile is discharged according to law as if he had been committed under process issued under the authority of this state, provided, that, in the absence of a valid detention order issued by a federal court, such detention shall not exceed three judicial days. Juveniles detained pursuant to this section shall have all the rights, powers, privileges, and duties, and shall receive the same treatment, afforded juveniles detained pursuant to the laws of this state. The board of supervisors of a county may contract with the United States for reimbursement of the county's cost incurred in the support of such juvenile. *(Added by Stats.1976, c. 250, p. 520, § 1, eff. June 21, 1976.)*

Cross References

Probation officer or social worker defined for purposes of this Chapter, see Welfare and Institutions Code § 215.

§ 870. Joint juvenile hall

Two or more counties may, pursuant to Article 1 (commencing with Section 6500) of Chapter 5 of Division 7 of Title 1 of the Government Code, establish and operate a joint juvenile hall. A joint juvenile hall shall be under the management and control of the probation officers of the participating counties, acting jointly, or of one of such probation officers, as provided by the agreement among the counties, and shall be in the charge of a superintendent selected pursuant to a civil service or merit system. A joint juvenile hall shall be operated in the manner prescribed by this chapter for juvenile halls.

A county participating in the maintenance of a joint juvenile hall pursuant to this section need not maintain a separate juvenile hall. *(Added by Stats.1961, c. 1616, p. 3496, § 2.)*

Cross References

Juvenile facilities, construction of, see Public Contract Code § 20141.
Juvenile halls, see Welfare and Institutions Code § 850 et seq.
Probation officer or social worker defined for purposes of this Chapter, see Welfare and Institutions Code § 215.

§ 871. Minor under custody or commitment; escape; misdemeanor

(a) Any person under the custody of a probation officer or any peace officer in a county juvenile hall, or committed to a county juvenile ranch, camp, forestry camp, or regional facility, who escapes or attempts to escape from the institution or facility in which he or she is confined, who escapes or attempts to escape while being conveyed to or from such an institution or facility, or who escapes or attempts to escape while outside or away from such an institution or facility while under the custody of a probation officer or any peace officer, is guilty of a misdemeanor, punishable by imprisonment in a county jail not exceeding one year.

(b) Any person who commits any of the acts described in subdivision (a) by use of force or violence shall be punished by imprisonment in a county jail for not more than one year or by imprisonment in the state prison.

(c) The willful failure of a person under the custody of a probation officer or any peace officer in a county juvenile hall, or committed to a county juvenile ranch, camp, or forestry camp, to return to the county juvenile hall, ranch, camp, or forestry camp at the prescribed time while outside or away from the county facility on furlough or temporary release constitutes an escape punishable as provided in subdivision (a). However, a willful failure to return at the prescribed time shall not be considered an escape if the failure to return was reasonable under the circumstances.

(d) A minor who, while under the supervision of a probation officer, removes his or her electronic monitor without authority and who, for more than 48 hours, violates the terms and conditions of his or her probation relating to the proper use of the electronic monitor shall be guilty of a misdemeanor. If an electronic monitor is damaged or discarded while in the possession of the minor, restitution for the cost of replacing the unit may be ordered as part of the punishment.

(e) The liability established by this section shall be limited by the financial ability of the person or persons ordered to pay restitution under this section, who shall be entitled to an evaluation and determination of ability to pay under Section 903.45.

(f) For purposes of this section, "regional facility" means any facility used by one or more public entities for the confinement of juveniles for more than 24 hours. *(Added by Stats.1968, c. 536, p. 1188, § 3. Amended by Stats.1985, c. 1283, § 1; Stats.1993, c. 918 (A.B.2087), § 1; Stats.1997, c. 267 (A.B.1152), § 1; Stats.1998, c. 694 (S.B.2147), § 6; Stats.2003, c. 263 (A.B.355), § 1; Stats.2017, c. 678 (S.B.190), § 16, eff. Jan. 1, 2018.)*

Cross References

Escape from institutions under jurisdiction of youth authority, see Welfare and Institutions Code §§ 1152, 1154.
Escapes or aiding escapes, offenses, see Penal Code §§ 107 et seq., 2042, 4530 et seq.
Jail defined for purposes of this Chapter, see Welfare and Institutions Code § 207.1.
Misdemeanors, see Penal Code §§ 17, 19, 19.2.
Probation officer or social worker defined for purposes of this Chapter, see Welfare and Institutions Code § 215.
Punishment defined for purposes of this Chapter, see Welfare and Institutions Code § 202.

Research References

2 Witkin, California Criminal Law 4th Crimes Against Governmental Authority § 101 (2021), Escape from Juvenile Hall or Camp.
2 Witkin, California Criminal Law 4th Crimes Against Governmental Authority § 103 (2021), Assisting Escape.
1 Witkin California Criminal Law 4th Introduction to Crimes § 22 (2021), In General.
1 Witkin California Criminal Law 4th Introduction to Crimes § 76 (2021), Illustrations: Special Statute is Controlling.
1 Witkin California Criminal Law 4th Introduction to Crimes § 140 (2021), Gang Violence and Juvenile Crime Prevention Act (Proposition 21).

§ 871.5. Bringing or sending contraband into or possession within juvenile facility; posting of penalties

(a) Except as authorized by law, or when authorized by the person in charge of any county juvenile hall, ranch, camp, or forestry camp, or by an officer of any juvenile hall or camp empowered by the person in charge to give that authorization, any person who knowingly brings or sends into, or who knowingly assists in bringing into, or sending into, any county juvenile hall, ranch, camp, or forestry camp, or any person who while confined in any of those institutions possesses therein, any controlled substance, the possession of which is prohibited by Division 10 (commencing with Section 11000) of the Health and Safety Code, any firearm, weapon, or explosive of any kind, or any tear gas or tear gas weapon shall be punished by imprisonment in a county jail for not more than one year or by imprisonment pursuant to subdivision (h) of Section 1170 of the Penal Code.

(b) Except as otherwise authorized in the manner provided in subdivision (a), any person who knowingly uses tear gas or uses a tear gas weapon in an institution or camp specified in subdivision (a) is guilty of a felony.

(c) A sign shall be posted at the entrance of each county juvenile hall, ranch, camp, or forestry camp specifying the conduct prohibited by this section and the penalties therefor.

(d) Except as otherwise authorized in the manner provided in subdivision (a), any person who knowingly brings or sends into, or who knowingly assists in bringing into, or sending into, any county juvenile hall, ranch, camp, or forestry camp, or any person who while confined in such an institution knowingly possesses therein, any alcoholic beverage shall be guilty of a misdemeanor.

(e) This section shall not be construed to preclude or in any way limit the applicability of any other law proscribing a course of conduct also proscribed by this section. *(Added by Stats.1981, c. 988, p. 3829, § 1. Amended by Stats.1985, c. 515, § 1; Stats.1998, c. 694 (S.B.2147), § 7; Stats.2011, c. 15 (A.B.109), § 617, eff. April 4, 2011, operative Oct. 1, 2011.)*

Cross References

Felonies, definition and penalties, see Penal Code §§ 17, 18.
Jail defined for purposes of this Chapter, see Welfare and Institutions Code § 207.1.
Misdemeanors, definition and penalties, see Penal Code §§ 17, 19, 19.2.

Research References

2 Witkin, California Criminal Law 4th Crimes Against Public Peace and Welfare § 161 (2021), Bringing Controlled Substances to Prisoners.

§ 872. Designation of another county's hall for detention; costs and liability; reimbursement

Where there is no juvenile hall in the county of residence of minors, or when the juvenile hall becomes unfit or unsafe for detention of minors, the presiding or sole juvenile court judge may, with the recommendation of the probation officer of the sending county and the consent of the probation officer of the receiving county, by written order filed with the clerk of the court, designate the juvenile hall of any county in the state for the detention of an individual minor for a period not to exceed 60 days. The court may, at any time, modify or vacate the order and shall require notice of the transfer to be given to the parent or guardian. The county of residence of a minor so transferred shall reimburse the receiving county for costs and liability as agreed upon by the two counties in connection with the order.

As used in this section, the terms "unfit" and "unsafe" shall include a condition in which a juvenile hall is considered by the juvenile court judge, the probation officer of that county, or the Board of State and Community Corrections to be too crowded for the proper and safe detention of minors. *(Added by Stats.1995, c. 304 (A.B.904), § 5, eff. Aug. 3, 1995. Amended by Stats.1996, c. 12 (A.B.1397), § 10, eff. Feb. 14, 1996; Stats.2002, c. 784 (S.B.1316), § 616; Stats.2019, c. 497 (A.B.991), § 296, eff. Jan. 1, 2020.)*

Law Revision Commission Comments

Section 872 is amended to reflect elimination of the county clerk's role as ex officio clerk of the superior court. See former Gov't Code § 26800 (county clerk acting as clerk of superior court). The powers, duties, and responsibilities formerly exercised by the county clerk as ex officio clerk of the court are delegated to the court administrative or executive officer, and the county clerk is relieved of those powers, duties, and responsibilities. See Gov't Code §§ 69840 (powers, duties, and responsibilities of clerk of court and deputy clerk of court), 71620 (trial court personnel). [32 Cal.L.Rev.Comm. Reports 561 (2002)].

Cross References

Probation officer or social worker defined for purposes of this Chapter, see Welfare and Institutions Code § 215.

§ 873. Store; establishment and operation; Ward Welfare Fund; expenditures

(a) Upon approval of the board of supervisors of a county, the chief probation officer of the county may establish, maintain, and operate a store in connection with the juvenile hall or other county juvenile facilities and for this purpose may purchase goods, articles and supplies, including, but not limited to, confectionery, snack foods and beverages, postage and writing materials, and toilet articles and supplies, and may sell these goods, articles, and supplies for cash to wards and detainees confined in the juvenile hall or other county juvenile facilities.

(b) The sale prices of the articles offered for sale at the store shall be fixed by the chief probation officer. Any profit shall be deposited in a Ward Welfare Fund which shall be established in the treasury of the county, if a store is established pursuant to subdivision (a).

(c) There shall also be deposited in the Ward Welfare Fund, if any, 10 percent of all gross sales of confined minor hobbycraft.

(d) There shall be deposited in the Ward Welfare Fund, if any, any money, refund, rebate, or commission received from a telephone company or pay telephone provider when the money, refund, rebate, or commission is attributable to the use of pay telephones which are primarily used by confined wards or detainees while incarcerated.

(e) The money and property deposited in the Ward Welfare Fund shall be expended by the chief probation officer primarily for the benefit, education, and welfare of the wards and detainees confined within the juvenile hall or other county juvenile facilities. Any funds that are not needed for the welfare of the confined wards and detainees may be expended by the chief probation officer at his or her sole discretion for the maintenance of county juvenile facilities. Maintenance of the juvenile hall or other county juvenile facilities may include, but is not limited to, the salary and benefits of personnel used in the programs to benefit the confined wards and detainees including, but not limited to, education, drug and alcohol treatment, welfare, library, accounting, and other programs deemed appropriate by the chief probation officer.

(f) The operation of a store within any other county juvenile detention facility which is not under the jurisdiction of the chief probation officer shall be governed by the provisions of this section, except that the board of supervisors shall designate the proper county official to exercise the duties otherwise allocated in this section to the chief probation officer.

(g) The treasurer may, pursuant to Article 1 (commencing with Section 53600), or Article 2 (commencing with Section 53630), of Chapter 4 of Part 1 of Division 2 of Title 5 of the Government Code, deposit, invest, or reinvest any part of the Ward Welfare Fund, in excess of that which the treasurer deems necessary for immediate use. The interest or increment accruing on these funds shall be deposited in the Ward Welfare Fund.

(h) The chief probation officer may expend money from the Ward Welfare Fund to provide indigent wards and detainees, prior to release from the juvenile hall, any county juvenile facility, or other juvenile detention facility under the jurisdiction of the chief probation officer, with essential clothing and transportation expenses within the county or, at the discretion of the chief probation officer, transportation to the minor's county of residence, if the county is within the state or 500 miles from the county of incarceration. This subdivision does not authorize expenditure of money from the Ward Welfare Fund for the transfer of any ward or detainees to the custody of any other law enforcement official or jurisdiction. *(Added by Stats.1997, c. 125 (S.B.590), § 1.)*

Cross References

Probation officer or social worker defined for purposes of this Chapter, see Welfare and Institutions Code § 215.
Writing defined, see Welfare and Institutions Code § 8.

ARTICLE 23.5. SECURE YOUTH TREATMENT FACILITIES

§ 875. Commitment of ward who is 14 years of age or older to secure youth treatment facility; criteria; baseline and maximum terms of confinement; individual rehabilitation plans; progress review hearings; transfer to less restrictive program

(a) In addition to the types of treatment specified in Sections 727 and 730, commencing July 1, 2021, the court may order that a ward who is 14 years of age or older * * * be committed to a secure youth treatment facility for a period of confinement described in subdivision (b) if the ward meets all of the following criteria:

(1) The juvenile is adjudicated and found to be a ward of the court based on an offense listed in subdivision (b) of Section 707 that was committed when the juvenile was 14 years of age or older.

(2) The adjudication described in paragraph (1) is the most recent offense for which the juvenile has been adjudicated.

(3) The court has made a finding on the record that a less restrictive, alternative disposition for the ward is unsuitable. In determining this, the court shall consider all relevant and material evidence, including the recommendations of counsel, the probation department, and any other agency or individual designated by the court to advise on the appropriate disposition of the case. The court shall additionally make its determination based on all of the following criteria:

(A) The severity of the offense or offenses for which the ward has been most recently adjudicated, including the ward's role in the offense, the ward's behavior, and harm done to victims.

(B) The ward's previous delinquent history, including the adequacy and success of previous attempts by the juvenile court to rehabilitate the ward.

(C) Whether the programming, treatment, and education offered and provided in a secure youth treatment facility is appropriate to meet the treatment and security needs of the ward.

(D) Whether the goals of rehabilitation and community safety can be met by assigning the ward to an alternative, less restrictive disposition that is available to the court.

(E) The ward's age, developmental maturity, mental and emotional health, sexual orientation, gender identity and expression, and any disabilities or special needs affecting the safety or suitability of committing the ward to a term of confinement in a secure youth treatment facility.

(b) In making its order of commitment for a ward, the court shall set a baseline term of confinement for the ward that is based on the most serious recent offense for which the ward has been adjudicated. The baseline term of confinement shall represent the time in custody necessary to meet the developmental and treatment needs of the ward and to prepare the ward for discharge to a period of probation supervision in the community. The baseline term of confinement for the ward shall be determined according to offense-based classifications that are approved by the Judicial Council, as described in subdivision (h). Pending the development and adoption of offense-based classifications by the Judicial Council, the court shall set a baseline term of confinement for the ward utilizing the discharge consideration date guidelines applied by the Department of Corrections and Rehabilitation, Division of Juvenile Justice prior to its closure and as set forth in Sections 30807 to 30813, inclusive, of Title 9 of the California Code of Regulations. These guidelines shall be used only to determine a baseline confinement time for the ward and shall not be used or relied on to modify the ward's confinement time in any manner other than as provided in this section. The court may, pending the adoption of Judicial Council guidelines, modify the initial baseline term with a deviation of plus or minus six months. The baseline term shall also be subject to modification in progress review hearings as described in subdivision (e).

(c)(1) In making its order of commitment, the court shall additionally set a maximum term of confinement for the ward * * * based upon the facts and circumstances of the matter or matters that brought or continued the ward under the jurisdiction of the court and as deemed appropriate to achieve rehabilitation. The maximum term of confinement shall represent the longest term of confinement in a facility that the ward may serve subject to the following:

(A) A ward committed to a secure youth treatment facility under this section shall not be held in secure confinement beyond 23 years of age, or two years from the date of the commitment, whichever occurs later. However, if the ward has been committed to a secure youth treatment facility based on adjudication for an offense or offenses for which the ward, if convicted in adult criminal court, would face an aggregate sentence of seven or more years, the * * * ward shall not * * * be held in secure confinement beyond 25 years of age, or two years from the date of * * * commitment, whichever occurs later.

(B) The maximum term of confinement shall not exceed the middle term of imprisonment that can be imposed upon an adult convicted of the same offense or offenses. If the court elects to aggregate the period of physical confinement on multiple counts or multiple petitions, including previously sustained petitions adjudging the minor a ward within Section 602, the maximum term of confinement shall be the aggregate term of imprisonment specified in subdivision (a) of Section 1170.1 of the Penal Code, which includes any additional term imposed pursuant to Section 667, 667.5, 667.6, or 12022.1 of the Penal Code, and Section 11370.2 of the Health and Safety Code.

(C) Precommitment credits for time served must be applied against the maximum term of confinement as set pursuant to this subdivision.

(2) For purposes of this section, "maximum term of confinement" has the same meaning as "maximum term of imprisonment," as defined in paragraph (2) of subdivision (d) of Section 726.

(d)(1) Within 30 judicial days of making an order of commitment to a secure youth treatment facility, the court shall receive, review, and approve an individual rehabilitation plan that meets the requirements of paragraph (2) for the ward that has been submitted to the court by the probation department and any other agencies or individuals the court deems necessary for the development of the plan. The plan may be developed in consultation with a multidisciplinary team of youth service, mental and behavioral health, education, and other treatment providers who are convened to advise the court for this purpose. The prosecutor and the counsel for the ward may provide input in the development of the rehabilitation plan prior to the court's approval of the plan. The plan may be modified by the court based on all of the information provided.

(2) An individual rehabilitation plan shall do all of the following:

(A) Identify the ward's needs in relation to treatment, education, and development, including any special needs the ward may have in relation to health, mental or emotional health, disabilities, or gender-related or other special needs.

(B) Describe the programming, treatment, and education to be provided to the ward in relation to the identified needs during the commitment period.

(C) Reflect, and be consistent with, the principles of trauma-informed, evidence-based, and culturally responsive care.

(D) The ward and their family shall be given the opportunity to provide input regarding the needs of the ward during the identification process stated in subparagraph (A), and the opinions of the ward and the ward's family shall be included in the rehabilitation plan report to the court.

(e)(1) The court shall, during the term of commitment, schedule and hold a progress review hearing for the ward not less frequently than once every six months. In the review hearing, the court shall evaluate the ward's progress in relation to the rehabilitation plan and shall determine whether the baseline term of confinement is to be modified. The court shall consider the recommendations of counsel, the probation department and any behavioral, educational, or other specialists having information relevant to the ward's progress. At the conclusion of each review hearing, upon making a finding on the record, the court may order that the ward remain in custody for the remainder of the baseline term or may order that the ward's baseline term or previously modified baseline term be modified downward by a reduction of confinement time not to exceed six months for each review hearing. The court may additionally order that the ward be assigned to a less restrictive program, as provided in subdivision (f).

(2) The ward's confinement time, including time spent in a less restrictive program described in subdivision (f), shall not be extended beyond the baseline confinement term, or beyond a modified baseline term, for disciplinary infractions or other in-custody behaviors. Any infractions or behaviors shall be addressed by alternative means, which may include a system of graduated sanctions for disciplinary infractions adopted by the operator of a secure youth treatment facility and subject to any relevant state standards or regulations that apply to juvenile facilities generally.

(3) The court shall, at the conclusion of the baseline confinement term, including any modified baseline term, hold a probation discharge hearing for the ward. For a ward who has been placed in a less restrictive program described in subdivision (f), the probation discharge hearing shall occur at the end of the period, or modified period, of placement that has been ordered by the court. At the discharge hearing, the court shall review the ward's progress toward meeting the goals of the individual rehabilitation plan and the recommendations of counsel, the probation department, and any other agencies or individuals having information the court deems necessary. At the conclusion of the hearing, the court shall order that the ward be discharged to a period of probation supervision in the community under conditions approved by the court, unless the court finds that the ward constitutes a substantial risk of imminent harm to others in the community if released from custody. If the court so finds, the ward may be retained in custody in a secure youth treatment facility for up to one additional year of confinement, subject to the review hearing and probation discharge hearing provisions of this subdivision and subject to the maximum confinement provisions of subdivision (c).

(4) If the ward is discharged to probation supervision, the court shall determine the reasonable conditions of probation that are suitable to meet the developmental needs and circumstances of the ward and to facilitate the ward's successful reentry into the community. The court shall periodically review the ward's progress under probation supervision and shall make any additional orders deemed necessary to modify the program of supervision in order to facilitate the provision of services or to otherwise support the ward's successful reentry into the community. If the court finds that the ward has failed materially to comply with the reasonable orders of probation

imposed by the court, the court may order that the ward be returned to a juvenile facility or to a placement described in subdivision (f) for a period not to exceed either the remainder of the baseline term, including any court-ordered modifications, or six months, whichever is longer, and in any case not to exceed the maximum confinement limits of subdivision (c).

(f)(1) Upon a motion from the probation department or the ward, the court may order that the ward be transferred from a secure youth treatment facility to less restrictive program, such as a halfway house, a camp or ranch, or a community residential or nonresidential service program. The purpose of a less restrictive program is to facilitate the safe and successful reintegration of the ward into the community. The court shall consider the transfer request at the next scheduled treatment review hearing or at a separately scheduled hearing. The court shall consider the recommendations of the probation department on the proposed change in placement. Approval of the request for a less restrictive program shall be made only upon the court's determination that the ward has made substantial progress toward the goals of the individual rehabilitation plan described in subdivision (d) and that placement is consistent with the goals of youth rehabilitation and community safety. In making its determination, the court shall consider both of the following factors:

(A) The ward's overall progress in relation to the rehabilitation plan during the period of confinement in a secure youth treatment facility.

(B) The programming and community transition services to be provided, or coordinated by the less restrictive program, including, but not limited to, any educational, vocational, counseling, housing, or other services made available through the program.

(2) In any order transferring the ward from a secure youth treatment facility to a less restrictive program, the court may require the ward to observe any conditions of performance or compliance with the program that are reasonable and appropriate in the individual case and that are within the capacity of the ward to perform. The court shall set the length of time the ward is to remain in a less restrictive program, not to exceed the remainder of the baseline or modified baseline term, prior to a probation discharge hearing described in subdivision (e). If, after placement in a less restrictive program, the court determines that the ward has materially failed to comply with the court-ordered conditions of placement in the program, the court may modify the terms and conditions of placement in the program or may order the ward to be returned to a secure youth treatment facility for the remainder of the baseline term, or modified baseline term, and subject to further periodic review hearings, as provided in subdivision (e) and to the maximum confinement provisions of subdivision (c). If the ward is returned to the secure youth treatment facility under the provisions of this paragraph, the ward's baseline or modified baseline term shall be adjusted to include credit for the time served by the ward in the less restrictive program.

(g) A secure youth treatment facility, as described in this section, shall meet the following criteria:

(1) The facility shall be a secure facility that is operated, utilized, or accessed by the county of commitment to provide appropriate programming, treatment, and education for wards having been adjudicated for the offenses specified in subdivision (a).

(2) The facility may be a stand-alone facility, such as a probation camp or other facility operated under contract with the county, or with another county, or may be a unit or portion of an existing county juvenile facility, including a juvenile hall or probation camp, that is configured and programmed to serve the population described in subdivision (a) and is in compliance with the standards described in paragraph (3).

(3) The Board of State and Community Corrections shall by July 1, 2023, review existing juvenile facility standards and modify or add standards for the establishment, design, security, programming and education, and staffing of any facility that is utilized or accessed by the court as a secure youth treatment facility under the provisions of this section. The standards shall be developed by the board with the coordination and concurrence of the Office of Youth and Community Restoration established by Section 2200. The standards shall specify how the facility may be used to serve or to separate juveniles, other than juveniles described in subdivision (a) serving baseline confinement terms, who may also be detained in or committed to the facility or to some portion of the facility. Pending the final adoption of these modified standards, a secure youth treatment facility shall comply with applicable minimum standards for juvenile facilities in Title 15 and Title 24 of the California Code of Regulations.

(4) A county proposing to establish a secure youth treatment facility for wards described in subdivision (a) shall notify the Board of State and Community Corrections of the operation of the facility and shall submit a description of the facility to the board in a format designated by the board. Commencing July 1, 2022, the Board of State and Community Corrections shall conduct a biennial inspection of each secure youth treatment facility that was used for the confinement of juveniles placed pursuant to subdivision (a) during the preceding calendar year. To the extent new standards are not yet in place, the board shall utilize the standards in existing regulations.

(5) In lieu of establishing its own secure youth treatment facility, a county may contract with another county having a secure youth treatment facility to accept commitments of wards described in subdivision (a).

(6) A county may establish a secure youth treatment facility to serve as a regional center for commitment of juveniles by one or more other counties on a contract payment basis.

(h)(1) By July 1, 2023, the Judicial Council shall develop and adopt a matrix of offense-based classifications to be applied by the juvenile courts in all counties in setting the baseline confinement terms described in subdivision (b). Each classification level or category shall specify a set of offenses within the level or category that is linked to a standard baseline term of years to be assigned to youth, based on their most serious recent adjudicated offense, who are committed to a secure youth treatment facility as provided in this section. The individual baseline term of years to be assigned in each case may be derived from a standard range of years for each offense level or category as designated by the Judicial Council. The classification matrix may provide for upward or downward deviations from the baseline term and may also provide for a system of positive incentives or credits for time served. In developing the matrix, the Judicial Council shall be advised by a working group of stakeholders, which shall include representatives from prosecution, defense, probation, behavioral health, youth service providers, youth formerly incarcerated in the Division of Juvenile Justice, and youth advocacy and other stakeholders and organizations having relevant expertise or information on dispositions and sentencing of youth in the juvenile justice system. In the development process, the Judicial Council shall also examine and take into account youth sentencing and length-of-stay guidelines or practices adopted by other states or recommended by organizations, academic institutions, or individuals having expertise or having conducted relevant research on dispositions and sentencing of youth in the juvenile justice system.

(2) Upon final adoption by the Judicial Council, the matrix of offense-based classifications shall be applied in a standardized manner by juvenile courts in each county in cases where the court is required to set a baseline confinement term under subdivision (b) for wards who are committed to a secure youth treatment facility. The discharge consideration date guidelines of the Division of Juvenile Justice that were applied on an interim basis, as provided in subdivision (b), shall not thereafter be utilized to determine baseline confinement terms for wards who are committed to a secure youth treatment facility under the provisions of this section.

(i) A court shall not commit a juvenile to any juvenile facility, including a secure youth treatment facility as defined in this section, for a period that exceeds the middle term of imprisonment that could be imposed upon an adult convicted of the same offense or offenses. *(Added by Stats.2021, c. 18 (S.B.92), § 12, eff. May 14, 2021. Amended by Stats.2022, c. 58 (A.B.200), § 41, eff. June 30, 2022.)*

Cross References

Application to modify or set aside order of commitment of ward to secure youth treatment facility, failure or inability to provide ward with treatment, programming, and education consistent with individual rehabilitation plan, hearing, see Welfare and Institutions Code § 779.5.

§ 875.5. Legislative intent; detention of persons physically dangerous to the public

(a) It is the intent of the Legislature to apply Article 6 (commencing with Section 1800) of Chapter 1 of Division 2.5, governing extended detention of persons physically dangerous to the public who are served by the Division of Juvenile Justice, to persons physically dangerous to the public who are committed to a secure treatment facility pursuant to Section 875, pending development of a specific commitment process for realigned persons pursuant to subdivision (b).

(b) The Governor and the Legislature shall work with stakeholders, including, but not limited to, the Division of Juvenile Justice, the State Department of State Hospitals, the Chief Probation Officers of California, the California State Association of Counties, advocacy organizations representing youth, and the Judicial Council to develop language by July 1, 2021, to replace the procedures specified in Section 876 with a commitment process that ensures the treatment capacity, legal protections, and court procedures are appropriate to successfully serve persons realigned from the Division of Juvenile Justice to the counties by Senate Bill 823 (Chapter 337, Statutes of 2020).

(c) It is the intent of the Legislature to enact legislation that would, effective July 1, 2022, extend detention of persons physically dangerous to the public who are in a secure youth treatment facility pursuant to the commitment process developed in subdivision (b). *(Added by Stats.2021, c. 18 (S.B.92), § 12, eff. May 14, 2021.)*

§ 876. Continuing confinement of persons who are physically dangerous to the public; petition by prosecuting attorney; hearing and trial

(a) If a probation department determines that the discharge of a person confined in a secure youth treatment facility from the control of the court at the time required by Section 875 would be physically dangerous to the public because of the person's mental or physical condition, disorder, or other problem that causes the person to have serious difficulty controlling their dangerous behavior, the department shall request the prosecuting attorney to petition the committing court for an order directing that the person remain subject to the control of the department beyond that time. The petition shall be filed at least 90 days before the time of discharge otherwise required. The petition shall be accompanied by a written statement of the facts upon which the department bases its opinion that discharge at the time stated would be physically dangerous to the public, but the petition may not be dismissed and an order may not be denied merely because of technical defects in the application.

(b) The prosecuting attorney shall promptly notify the probation department of a decision not to file a petition.

(c) If a petition is filed with the court and, upon review, the court determines that the petition, on its face, supports a finding of probable cause, the court shall order that a hearing be held. The court shall provide notification of the hearing to the person whose liberty is involved and, if the person is a minor, the minor's parent or guardian, if the minor's parent or guardian can be reached, and, if not, the court shall appoint a person to act in the place of the parent or guardian and shall afford the person an opportunity to appear at the hearing with the aid of counsel and the right to cross-examine experts or other witnesses upon whose information, opinion, or testimony the petition is based. The court shall inform the person named in the petition of their right of process to compel attendance of relevant witnesses and the production of relevant evidence. When the person is unable to provide their own counsel, the court shall appoint counsel to represent them. The probable cause hearing shall be held within 10 calendar days after the date the order is issued pursuant to this subdivision unless the person named in the petition waives this time.

(d) At the probable cause hearing, the court shall receive evidence and determine whether there is probable cause to believe that discharge of the person would be physically dangerous to the public because of the person's mental or physical condition, disorder, or other problem that causes the person to have serious difficulty controlling dangerous behavior. If the court determines there is not probable cause, the court shall dismiss the petition and the person shall be discharged from the control of a secure youth treatment facility at the time required by Section 875, as applicable. If the court determines there is probable cause, the court shall order that a trial be conducted to determine whether the person is physically dangerous to the public because of their mental or physical condition, disorder, or other problem.

(e) If a trial is ordered, the trial shall be by jury unless the right to a jury trial is personally waived by the person, after the person has been fully advised of the constitutional rights being waived, and by the prosecuting attorney, in which case trial shall be by the court. If the jury is not waived, the court shall cause a jury to be summoned and to be in attendance at a date stated, not less than 4 days nor more than 30 days from the date of the order for trial, unless the person named in the petition waives time. The court shall submit to the jury, or, at a court trial, the court shall answer, the following question: Is the person physically dangerous to the public because of a mental or physical condition, disorder, or other problem that causes the person to have serious difficulty controlling their dangerous behavior? The court's previous order entered pursuant to this section shall not be read to the jury, nor alluded to in the trial. The person shall be entitled to all rights guaranteed under the federal and state constitutions in criminal proceedings. A unanimous jury verdict shall be required in any jury trial. As to either a court or a jury trial, the standard of proof shall be that of proof beyond a reasonable doubt.

(f) If an order for continued detention is made pursuant to this section, the control of the department over the person shall continue, subject to the provisions of this article, but, unless the person is previously discharged as provided in Section 875, the department shall, within two years after the date of that order in the case of persons committed by the juvenile court, or within two years after the date of that order in the case of persons committed after conviction in criminal proceedings, file a new application for continued detention in accordance with the provisions of this section if continued detention is deemed necessary. These applications may be repeated at intervals as often as in the opinion of the department may be necessary for the protection of the public, except that the court shall have the power, in order to protect other persons in the custody of probation to refer the person for evaluation for civil commitment or to transfer the custody of any person over 25 years of age to the county adult probation authorities for placement in an appropriate institution. Each person shall be discharged from the control of the probation department at the termination of the period stated in this section unless the probation department has filed a new application and the court has made a new order for continued detention as provided above in this section.

(g) An order of the committing court made pursuant to this section is appealable by the person whose liberty is involved in the same manner as a judgment in a criminal case. The appellate court may affirm the order of the lower court, or modify it, or reverse it and order the appellant to be discharged. Pending appeal, the appellant shall remain under the control of the probation department. *(Added by Stats.2021, c. 18 (S.B.92), § 12, eff. May 14, 2021.)*

ARTICLE 24. WARDS AND DEPENDENT CHILDREN—JUVENILE HOMES, RANCHES AND CAMPS

§ 880. Purposes of establishment

In order to provide appropriate facilities for the housing of wards of the juvenile court in the counties of their residence or in adjacent counties so that those wards may be kept under direct supervision of the court, and in order to more advantageously apply the salutary effect of a safe and supportive home and family environment upon them, and also in order to secure a better classification and segregation of those wards according to their capacities, interests, and responsiveness to control and responsibility, and to give better opportunity for reform and encouragement of self-discipline in those wards, juvenile ranches or camps may be established, as provided in this article. *(Added by Stats.1961, c. 1616, p. 3496, § 2. Amended by Stats.1998, c. 694 (S.B.2147), § 8.)*

Cross References

Expense for support and maintenance defined as value of support of ward at forestry camp, juvenile home, ranch or camp, see Welfare and Institutions Code § 914.
Government of counties, chief probation officer, duties and obligations, see Government Code § 27771.
Juvenile facilities, construction of, see Public Contract Code § 20141.
Juvenile halls, see Welfare and Institutions Code § 850 et seq.
Local Agency Public Construction Act, counties of 500,000 or less population, exemptions, see Public Contract Code § 20150.14.

§ 881. Establishment; commitment; operation and administration

The board of supervisors of any county may, by ordinance, establish juvenile ranches, camps, or forestry camps, within or without the county, to which persons made wards of the court on the ground of fitting the description in Section 602 may be committed. As far as possible, the provisions of this chapter relating to commitments to the probation officer shall apply to commitments to those juvenile facilities, except that where any ward proves to be unfit to remain in any facility, in the opinion of the superintendent or director thereof, the superintendent or director shall make a recommendation to the probation department for consideration for other commitment. Complete operation and authority for the administration shall be vested in the county. *(Added by Stats.1961, c. 1616, p. 3496, § 2. Amended by Stats.1976, c. 1071, p. 4830, § 32.5; Stats.1998, c. 694 (S.B.2147), § 9.)*

Cross References

Juvenile facilities, construction of, see Public Contract Code § 20141.
Ordinance relating to feasibility of operation of ordinance, termination of operativeness, see Welfare and Institutions Code § 925.
Probation officer or social worker defined for purposes of this Chapter, see Welfare and Institutions Code § 215.

§ 881.5. Reduction in capacity of county juvenile facilities; increased commitments to Department of Youth Authority; county contribution; exceptions; increased rate of commitments; notification to controller

(a)(1) If a county receives funds pursuant to Section 17602, the county reduces the capacity of its juvenile ranches, camps, or forestry camps below the capacity for those facilities during the 1990–91 fiscal year, and if during the 12–month period subsequent to the month of reduction, there is an increase in the rate of commitments from the county's juvenile court to the Department of the Youth Authority above the commitments per 100,000 of the county's juvenile population, aged 12 to 17 years, during the 1990–91 fiscal year, the county shall contribute to the Department of the Youth Authority an amount equivalent to the actual cost, as determined by the Department of the Youth Authority.

(2) Paragraph (1) shall not apply to a county of the fifth class, for reductions in the capacity of its juvenile ranches, camps, or forestry camps that were made prior to January 1, 1993, if the reductions were due to fiscal constraints.

(b) Any county that provides juvenile ranch or camp space to another county pursuant to contract shall contribute to the Department of the Youth Authority an amount equivalent to the actual costs associated with any increase in the rate of commitments to which subdivision (a) applies, per 100,000, by the county's juvenile court to the Department of the Youth Authority above the rate of commitments during the 1991–92 fiscal year that are not attributable to a reduced capacity in juvenile ranches, camps, or forestry camps.

(c) The Department of the Youth Authority may notify the Controller of any county or counties that have experienced an increase in the rate of commitments for purposes of recovering the costs associated with that increase. Upon receiving this notice, the Controller shall redirect, from the funds that are provided to that county or counties pursuant to Section 17602, an amount equal to the costs associated with the increased commitments. Within 30 days of the notification of the Controller the Department of the Youth Authority shall also notify each county from which they are seeking reimbursement pursuant to subdivision (b). *(Added by Stats.1991, c. 91 (A.B.948), § 12, eff. June 30, 1991. Amended by Stats.1992, c. 1311 (S.B.1834), § 1, eff. Sept. 30, 1992; Stats.1993, c. 970 (A.B.1166), § 1, eff. Oct. 11, 1993; Stats.1998, c. 694 (S.B.2147), § 10.)*

Cross References

State Controller, generally, see Government Code § 12402 et seq.

§ 883. Work, studies and activities of committed wards; fire suppression, conditions

The wards committed to ranches, camps, or forestry camps may be required to labor on the buildings and grounds thereof, on the making of forest roads for fire prevention or firefighting, on forestation or reforestation of public lands, or on the making of firetrails or firebreaks, or to perform any other work or engage in any studies or activities on or off of the grounds of those ranches, camps, or forestry camps prescribed by the probation department, subject to such approval as the county board of supervisors by ordinance requires.

Wards may not be required to labor in fire suppression when under the age of 16 years.

Wards between the ages of 16 years and 18 years may be required to labor in fire suppression if all of the following conditions are met:

(a) The parent or guardian of the ward has given permission for that labor by the ward.

(b) The ward has completed 80 hours of training in forest firefighting and fire safety, including, but not limited to, the handling of equipment and chemicals, survival techniques, and first aid.

Whenever any ward committed to a camp is engaged in fire prevention work or the suppression of existing fires, he or she shall be subject to worker's compensation benefits to the same extent as a county employee, and the board of supervisors shall provide and cover any ward committed to a camp while performing that service, with accident, death and compensation insurance as is otherwise regularly provided for employees of the county. *(Added by Stats. 1961, c. 1616, p. 3497, § 2. Amended by Stats.1969, c. 590, p. 1223, § 1; Stats.1975, c. 1129, p. 2774, § 3; Stats.1998, c. 694 (S.B.2147), § 12.)*

Cross References

Courses of instruction, see Education Code § 33033.
Elementary and secondary education, juvenile court schools, minimum school-day and course of study, see Education Code § 48645.3.
Employment defined, and services regarding employment for public entities or Indian tribes, see Unemployment Insurance Code § 634.5.
Work furloughs, see Welfare and Institutions Code § 925 et seq.

§ 884. Wages

The board of supervisors may provide for the payment of wages and pay such wages from the treasury of such county to the wards for the work they do, the sums earned to be paid in reparation, or to the parents or dependents of the ward, or to the ward himself, in such manner and in such proportions as the court directs. *(Added by Stats.1961, c. 1616, p. 3497, § 2.)*

Cross References

Employment defined, and services regarding employment for public entities or Indian tribes, see Unemployment Insurance Code § 634.5.

§ 885. Standards; adoption; certification of conformity; reports

(a) The Board of State and Community Corrections shall adopt and prescribe the minimum standards of construction, operation, programs of education and training, and qualifications of personnel for juvenile ranches, camps, or forestry camps established under Section 881.

(b) The Board of State and Community Corrections shall conduct a biennial inspection of each juvenile ranch, camp, or forestry camp situated in this state that, during the preceding calendar year, was used for confinement of any minor for more than 24 hours.

(c) The custodian of each juvenile ranch, camp, or forestry camp shall make any reports that may be required by the board to effectuate the purposes of this section. *(Added by Stats.1995, c. 304 (A.B.904), § 7, eff. Aug. 3, 1995. Amended by Stats.1996, c. 12 (A.B.1397), § 12, eff. Feb. 14, 1996; Stats.1996, c. 805 (A.B.1325), § 9; Stats.1998, c. 694 (S.B.2147), § 13; Stats.2019, c. 497 (A.B.991), § 297, eff. Jan. 1, 2020.)*

Cross References

Youth Authority,
Generally, see Welfare and Institutions Code § 1700 et seq.
Succession to certain powers and duties by youthful offender parole board, see Welfare and Institutions Code § 1725.

§ 886. Maximum number of children

Except as provided in Section 886.5, no juvenile home, ranch, camp, or forestry camp established pursuant to the provisions of this article shall receive or contain more than 100 children at any one time. *(Added by Stats.1961, c. 1616, p. 3497, § 2. Amended by Stats.1981, c. 988, p. 3829, § 2; Stats.1998, c. 375 (S.B.1422), § 1.)*

§ 886.5. Expanded capacity; certificate of compliance; exceptions

(a) A juvenile home, ranch, camp, or forestry camp may receive or contain a maximum of 125 children at any one time if the county has determined that there is a consistent need for juvenile home, ranch, camp, or forestry camp placements which exceeds the beds available in the county. Any county desiring to expand the capacity of a juvenile home, ranch, camp, or forestry camp pursuant to this section shall certify to the Board of Corrections that the facility to be expanded will continue to meet the minimum standards adopted and prescribed pursuant to Section 885 during the period of expanded capacity.

(b)(1) The Legislature reaffirms its belief that juvenile ranches, camps, forestry camps, and other residential treatment facilities should be small enough to provide individualized guidance and treatment for juvenile offenders which enables them to return to their families and communities as productive and law abiding citizens. Consistent with this principle and upon demonstration of exceptional need, a juvenile ranch, camp, or forestry camp may receive or contain a maximum population in excess of 125 children at any one time if the Board of Corrections has approved that expanded capacity pursuant to the following procedure:

(A) The county shall submit an application to the Board of Corrections, endorsed by the board of supervisors, identifying the capacity requested and the reasons why the additional capacity is needed. The application shall include the county's plan to ensure that the facility will, with the additional capacity, comply with applicable minimum standards and maintain adequate levels of onsite staffing, program, and other services for children in the facility.

(B) The Board of Corrections shall review any application received under this subdivision and shall approve or deny the application based on a determination whether the county has demonstrated its ability to comply with minimum standards and maintain adequate staffing, program, and service levels for children in the expanded facility. In its review, the board shall consider any public comment that may be submitted while the application is pending. The board may approve an application with conditions, including a capacity below the requested number, remodeling or expansion of units or living quarters, staffing ratios in excess of those required by minimum standards, or other adjustments of program or procedure deemed appropriate by the board for a facility operating with a capacity in excess of 125 children. The board shall ensure that the staffing, program, and service levels are increased commensurate with the increased risks to residents and the staff that are a result of the expanded capacity.

(2) Notwithstanding the inspection schedule set forth in Section 885, the board shall conduct an annual inspection of any facility whose application for expanded capacity under this subdivision is approved. The approval to operate at a capacity above 125 children shall terminate, and the facility shall not thereafter receive or contain more than 125 children, if the board determines after any annual inspection that the facility is not in compliance with minimum standards, that program, staffing, or service levels for children in the expanded facility have not been maintained, or that the county has failed substantially to comply with a condition that was attached to the board's approval of the expanded capacity.

(c) The board may provide forms and instructions to local jurisdictions to facilitate compliance with this section. *(Added by*

Stats.1995, c. 304 (A.B.904), § 9, eff. Aug. 3, 1995. Amended by Stats.1996, c. 12 (A.B.1397), § 13, eff. Feb. 14, 1996; Stats.1998, c. 375 (S.B.1422), § 2.)

§ 888. Agreements with other counties

Any county establishing a juvenile ranch or camp under the provisions of this article may, by mutual agreement, accept children committed to that ranch or camp by the juvenile court of another county in the state. Two or more counties may, by mutual agreement, establish juvenile ranches or camps, and the rights granted and duties imposed by this article shall devolve upon those counties acting jointly. The provisions of this article shall not apply to any juvenile hall. *(Added by Stats.1961, c. 1616, p. 3498, § 2. Amended by Stats.1972, c. 886, p. 1568, § 1; Stats.1978, c. 461, p. 1557, § 3, eff. July 18, 1978, operative July 1, 1978; Stats.1978, c. 464, p. 1574, § 2, eff. July 18, 1978; Stats.1983, c. 288, § 2, eff. July 15, 1983; Stats.1998, c. 694 (S.B.2147), § 14.)*

§ 889. Administration and operation of public schools

The board of education shall provide for the administration and operation of public schools in any juvenile hall, day center, ranch, camp, regional youth educational facility, or Orange County youth correctional center in existence and providing services prior to the effective date of the amendments to this section made by the Statutes of 1989, established pursuant to Article 2.5 (commencing with Section 48645) of Chapter 4 of Part 27 of the Education Code, or Article 9 (commencing with Section 1850) of Chapter 1 of Division 2.5 of the Welfare and Institutions Code. *(Added by Stats.1977, c. 430, p. 1448, § 9. Amended by Stats.1984, c. 1455, § 5, eff. Sept. 26, 1984; Stats.1989, c. 929, § 3; Stats.1998, c. 694 (S.B.2147), § 15.)*

Cross References

Allowances to county school service funds for schools maintained in juvenile halls, homes and camps, see Education Code §§ 14057, 14058.
Courses of instruction, see Education Code § 33033.

§ 889.1. Access to computer technology and the Internet for educational purposes; denial of access

(a)(1) Minors detained in or committed to a juvenile ranch, camp, or forestry camp shall be provided with access to computer technology and the Internet for the purposes of education.

(2) Minors detained in or committed to a juvenile ranch, camp, or forestry camp may be provided with access to computer technology and the Internet for maintaining relationships with family.

(b) This section does not limit the authority of the chief probation officer, or his or her designee, to limit or deny access to computer technology or the Internet for safety and security or staffing reasons. *(Added by Stats.2018, c. 997 (A.B.2448), § 4, eff. Jan. 1, 2019.)*

§ 889.2. Juveniles with high school diploma or California high school equivalency certificate; access to postsecondary education programs

(a) It is the intent of the Legislature that juveniles with a high school diploma or California high school equivalency certificate who are detained in, or committed to, a juvenile ranch, camp, or forestry camp shall have access to rigorous postsecondary academic and career technical education programs that fulfill the requirements for transfer to the University of California and the California State University and prepare them for career entry, respectively.

(b)(1) A county probation department shall ensure that juveniles with a high school diploma or California high school equivalency certificate who are detained in, or committed to, a juvenile ranch, camp, or forestry camp have access to, and can choose to participate in, public postsecondary academic and career technical courses and programs offered online, and for which they are eligible based on eligibility criteria and course schedules of the public postsecondary education campus providing the course or program. County probation departments, in coordination with county offices of education, may use juvenile court school classrooms and computers, in accordance with agreements entered into pursuant to Section 48646 of the Education Code, for the purpose of implementing this section. County probation departments are also encouraged to develop other educational partnerships with local public postsecondary campuses, as is feasible, to provide programs on campus and onsite at the juvenile ranch, camp, or forestry camp.

(2) These programs shall be considered part of the current responsibilities of the county probation department to provide and coordinate services for juveniles that enable the juveniles to be law-abiding and productive members of their families and communities.

(c) For purposes of this section, "juvenile" means any person detained in, or committed to, a juvenile ranch, camp, or forestry camp.

(d) This section does not preclude juvenile court school pupils who have not yet completed their high school graduation requirements from concurrently participating in postsecondary academic and career technical education programs. *(Added by Stats.2019, c. 857 (S.B.716), § 2, eff. Jan. 1, 2020.)*

§ 891. Share of cost of construction; construction defined; limitation on amount of state assistance; application

(a) From any state moneys made available to it for that purpose, the Youth Authority shall share in the cost pursuant to this article of the construction of juvenile ranch camps or forestry camps established after July 1, 1957, and for construction at existing juvenile ranches, camps, or forestry camps, by counties that apply therefor.

(b) "Construction," as used in this section, includes construction of new buildings and acquisition of existing buildings and initial equipment of any of those buildings; and, to the extent provided for in regulations adopted by the Department of the Youth Authority, remodeling of existing buildings owned by the county, to serve the purposes of a juvenile ranch camp or forestry camp, and initial equipment thereof. "Construction" also includes payments made by a county under any lease-purchase agreement or similar arrangement authorized by law and payments for the necessary repair or improvements of property which is leased from the federal government or other public entity without cost to the county for a term of not less than 10 years. It does not include architects' fees or the cost of land acquisition.

(c) The amount of state assistance that shall be provided to any county shall not exceed 50 percent of the project cost approved by the Youth Authority, and, in no event shall it exceed three thousand dollars ($3,000) per bed unit of the new juvenile ranch, camp, or forestry camp or per bed unit added to an existing juvenile ranch camp, or forestry camp, as the case may be. The construction project shall be deemed to have as many bed units as the number of persons it is designed to accommodate, not exceeding 100 bed units for any one project.

(d) Application for state assistance for construction funds under this article shall be made to the Youth Authority in the manner and form prescribed by the Youth Authority. The Youth Authority shall prescribe the time and manner of payment of state assistance, if granted. *(Added by Stats.1978, c. 464, p. 1574, § 4, eff. July 18, 1978. Amended by Stats.1998, c. 694 (S.B.2147), § 16.)*

Cross References

Powers and duties of Youth Authority, see Welfare and Institutions Code § 1750 et seq.

§ 892. Cities; construction of border check station facilities; state aid

(a) From any state moneys made available to it for that purpose, the Youth Authority shall provide state assistance pursuant to this section to defray, in whole or part, the cost of construction of border check station facilities by any city which applies therefor.

"City" as used in this section means any city with a population in excess of 500,000 as determined by the last decennial census, all or part of the boundaries of which are contiguous with the boundaries of a foreign country adjoining this state.

(b) "Construction," as used in this section, includes construction of new buildings and acquisition of existing buildings and initial equipment of any such buildings to serve as a border check station facility. It does not include the cost of land acquisition.

(c) The amount of state assistance which shall be provided to any city shall not exceed 100 percent of the project cost approved by the Youth Authority, and, in no event shall it exceed one hundred thousand dollars ($100,000) for any one project.

(d) Application for state assistance for construction funds under this section shall be made to the Youth Authority in the manner and form prescribed by the Youth Authority. The Youth Authority shall prescribe the time and manner of payment of state assistance, if granted.

(e) The Youth Authority shall adopt and prescribe the minimum standards of construction for such border check station facility. No city shall be entitled to receive any state funds provided for in this section unless and until the minimum standards and qualifications referred to in this section are complied with by such city. Type and standards of construction shall be approved by the city architect's office, city department of public works, or such city department having jurisdiction over public construction. *(Added by Stats.1968, c. 1249, p. 2355, § 1.)*

Cross References

City census, see Government Code § 40200 et seq.
Powers and duties of youth authority, see Welfare and Institutions Code § 1750 et seq.

§ 893. Counties over 5,000,000; contracts with private organizations; certification of employees; enrollment; computation of allowance

(a) The board of supervisors of any county with a population of five million or more may provide and maintain a school or schools at a juvenile ranch or camp or residential or nonresidential boot camp under the control of the probation officer for the purpose of meeting the special educational needs of wards and dependent children of the juvenile court. The school or schools shall be conducted in a manner and under conditions that will minister to the specific individualized educational and training needs of each ward and dependent child in furtherance of the objective of assisting each of them, as much as possible, to fulfill his or her potential to be a contributing, law-abiding member of society. If the board of supervisors determines that this objective may be promoted as well as or better by provision of educational and training services by a qualified private organization, the board of supervisors on behalf of the county may enter into annual contracts, with or without options to renew, for the provision of those services by that organization.

(b) The Legislature hereby finds and determines that there are persons whose educational and vocational backgrounds and personal leadership qualities peculiarly fit them to instruct and train wards of the court in promotion of the aforesaid objective, but who lack certification qualifications. Accordingly, the probation officer is hereby authorized to certify to the county board of education and the Superintendent of Public Instruction that a person employed or to be employed by the probation officer or by an organization retained by contract to provide vocational training or vocational training courses at or in connection with the school or schools is peculiarly fit to provide wards of the court that vocational training in promotion of the aforesaid objective.

The certification shall specify the type or types of service the person is qualified to provide. Upon filing of that certification, the person shall be deemed to be a certificated employee for purposes of authorizing him or her to provide the services described in the certificate and for apportionment purposes.

(c) The individual school or schools shall have a maximum enrollment of 100 students.

(d) The county superintendent of schools shall report on behalf of the county the average daily attendance for the schools and classes maintained by the county in the school or schools in the manner provided in Sections 41601 and 84701 of the Education Code and other provisions of law.

(e) The Superintendent of Public Instruction shall compute the amount of allowance to be made to the county by reasons of the average daily attendance at the school or schools by multiplying the average daily attendance by the foundation program amount for a high school district that has an average daily attendance of 301 or more during the fiscal year, and shall make allowances based thereon and shall apportion to the county, the allowances so computed in the same manner and at the same times as would be done with respect to allowances and apportionments to the county school service fund. *(Added by Stats.1974, c. 1151, p. 2440, § 1, eff. Sept. 23, 1974. Amended by Stats.1976, c. 451, p. 1186, § 1, eff. July 12, 1976; Stats.1977, c. 312, p. 1250, § 1; Stats.1978, c. 380, p. 1213, § 167; Stats.1995, c. 72 (S.B.604), § 6; Stats.1998, c. 694 (S.B.2147), § 17.)*

Cross References

Average daily attendance, computation, see Education Code § 46300 et seq.
County boards of education, see Const. Art. 9, §§ 3.3, 7; Education Code § 1000 et seq.
County school service fund, see Education Code § 1600 et seq.
Population of counties, see Government Code § 28020.
Probation officer or social worker defined for purposes of this Chapter, see Welfare and Institutions Code § 215.
Superintendent of public instruction, see Const. Art. 9, § 2; Education Code § 33100 et seq.

ARTICLE 24.5. REGIONAL YOUTH EDUCATIONAL FACILITIES

Section

§ 894. Establishment of pilot regional youth educational facilities; participating minors; program provisions

In order to provide a sentencing alternative for the juvenile courts, one or more pilot regional youth educational facilities shall be established as short-term intensive residential programs to which primarily 16- and 17-year-old minor juvenile court wards not committed to the Youth Authority who fit the description in Section 602 may be committed. Participating minors shall be those who are awaiting out-of-home placement in county juvenile halls, educationally behind in school, educable, able to participate in vocational activities, and able to participate in work projects. Each facility shall provide a short-term intensive educational experience, including program elements such as competency-based education services, assessment for learning disabilities including visual perceptual screening and treatment, remedial individual educational plans for diagnosed learning disabilities, electronic and computer education, physical education, vocational and industrial arts and training, job training and experience, character education, victim awareness, and restitution. Wards who complete the short-term intensive program who need continuing services shall be transferred to local facilities for up to 60 days of additional education and training. Following institutional placement, all wards in the program shall receive intensive supervision by a probation officer in their county of residence for a minimum of 120 days. Intensive supervision means a 10 to 15 person caseload per deputy probation officer. *(Added by Stats.1984, c. 1455, § 6, eff. Sept. 26, 1984.)*

Cross References

Probation officer or social worker defined for purposes of this Chapter, see Welfare and Institutions Code § 215.

§ 895. Establishment of facilities by counties with assistance of Youth Authority; operation; contracting for services; selection criteria for participating counties

(a) From any state moneys made available to it for that purpose, the Youth Authority shall assist counties in the establishment of pilot regional youth educational facilities. Interested counties that agree to provide matching funds or resources, in compliance with standards established by the department, may enter agreements with the Youth Authority to establish these facilities. The facilities shall be operated by participating counties, either solely or under a joint powers agreement. The counties may contract with private agencies to provide job training consultation or other services.

(b) The Youth Authority shall develop selection criteria for participating counties to include, but not be limited to, all of the following factors:

(1) Eligible target population.

(2) Demonstrated ability to administer the program.

(3) Facility capability.

(4) Financial ability to provide matching funds or resources.

(5) Demonstrated need for the program.

(6) Ability to meet regional needs.

(7) Ability to provide specified program elements. *(Added by Stats.1984, c. 1455, § 6, eff. Sept. 26, 1984.)*

§ 896. Performance standards and personnel qualifications; certification of compliance; reports

(a) The Board of State and Community Corrections shall establish minimum performance standards for programs of education and training and for qualifications of personnel for all youth educational facilities in the program, including local continuation and intensive supervision components. These standards and qualifications shall be designed to achieve program goals such as an increase in the educational level of participants, better community protection and offender accountability, and preparation of participants to return to the community as responsible and productive members.

(b) Every person in charge of a regional youth educational facility, which, in the preceding calendar year, was used for confinement, for more than 24 hours, of any minor, shall certify annually to the board that the facility is in conformity with the standards adopted by the board under subdivision (a). The board may provide forms and instructions to local jurisdictions to facilitate compliance with this subdivision.

(c) The custodian of each regional youth educational facility shall make any reports as may be required by the board to effectuate the purposes of this section. *(Added by Stats.1995, c. 304 (A.B.904), § 11, eff. Aug. 3, 1995. Amended by Stats.1996, c. 12 (A.B.1397), § 14, eff. Feb. 14, 1996; Stats.2019, c. 497 (A.B.991), § 298, eff. Jan. 1, 2020.)*

§ 897. Capacity of facilities

The capacity of each regional youth educational facility shall be established pursuant to Sections 886 and 886.5. *(Added by Stats. 1984, c. 1455, § 6, eff. Sept. 26, 1984.)*

§ 898. Citizens advisory committee

The participating counties shall appoint a citizens advisory committee with a membership drawn from law enforcement, judiciary, probation, education, corrections, business, and the general public, whose function is to review the goals, objectives, and programs of each youth educational facility and provide input to the facility. *(Added by Stats.1984, c. 1455, § 6, eff. Sept. 26, 1984.)*

ARTICLE 25. SUPPORT OF WARDS AND DEPENDENT CHILDREN

Section

§ 900. Order directing payment

(a) If it is necessary that provision be made for the expense of support and maintenance of a dependent child of the juvenile court or of a minor person concerning whom a petition has been filed to declare the person a dependent child of the juvenile court in accordance with this chapter, the order providing for the care and custody of the dependent child or other minor person shall direct that the whole expense of support and maintenance of the dependent child or other minor person, up to the amount of twenty dollars ($20) per month, be paid from the county treasury and may direct that an amount up to any maximum amount per month established by the board of supervisors of the county be paid. The board of supervisors of each county is hereby authorized to establish, either generally or for individual dependent children or according to classes or groups of dependent children, a maximum amount that the court may order the county to pay for the support and maintenance. All orders made pursuant to this subdivision shall state the amounts to be paid from the county treasury, and those amounts shall constitute legal charges against the county.

(b) If it is necessary that provision be made for the expense of support and maintenance of a ward of the juvenile court or of a minor person concerning whom a petition has been filed to declare the person a ward of the juvenile court in accordance with this chapter, the order providing for the care and custody of the ward or other minor person shall direct that the whole expense of support and maintenance of the ward or other minor person be paid from the county treasury. All orders made pursuant to this subdivision shall state the amounts to be paid from the county treasury, and those amounts shall constitute legal charges against the county.

(c) This section is applicable to a minor who is the subject of a program of supervision undertaken by the probation department pursuant to Section 330 or 654 and who is temporarily placed out of his home by the probation department, with the approval of the court and the minor's parent or guardian, for a period not to exceed seven days. *(Added by Stats.1961, c. 1616, p. 3499, § 2. Amended by Stats.1972, c. 924, p. 1651, § 1; Stats.1976, c. 1068, p. 4798, § 77; Stats.1978, c. 380, p. 1214, § 168; Stats.2017, c. 678 (S.B.190), § 17, eff. Jan. 1, 2018.)*

Cross References

Claims against county, see Government Code § 29700 et seq.
County charges, generally, see Government Code § 29600 et seq.
Expense for support and maintenance defined, see Welfare and Institutions Code § 914.
Medical, surgical or dental care of minor, see Welfare and Institutions Code § 739.
Support of minor committed to adjustment school, see Welfare and Institutions Code § 983.

§ 901. Maximum amount

No order for payment shall be made in a sum in excess of the actual cost of supporting and maintaining the ward, dependent child or other minor person. *(Added by Stats.1961, c. 1616, p. 3499, § 2.)*

§ 902. Order for additional amount

(a) If it is found that the maximum amount established by the board of supervisors of the county is insufficient to pay the whole expense of support and maintenance of a dependent child or other minor person, the court may order and direct that the additional amount as is necessary shall be paid out of the earnings, property, or estate of the dependent child or other minor person, or by the parents or guardian of the dependent child or other minor person, or by any other person liable for his or her support and maintenance, to the county officers designated by the board of supervisors, who shall in turn pay it to the person, association, or institution that, under court order, is caring for and maintaining the dependent child or other minor person.

(b)(1) This section does not apply to a minor who is adjudged a ward of the juvenile court, who is placed on probation pursuant to Section 725, who is the subject of a petition that has been filed to adjudge the minor a ward of the juvenile court, or who is the subject of a program of supervision undertaken pursuant to Section 654.

(2) Notwithstanding paragraph (1), this section applies to a minor who is designated as a dual status child pursuant to Section 241.1, for purposes of the dependency jurisdiction only and not for purposes of the delinquency jurisdiction. *(Added by Stats.1961, c. 1616, p. 3499, § 2. Amended by Stats.1969, c. 437, p. 966, § 1; Stats.2017, c. 678 (S.B.190), § 18, eff. Jan. 1, 2018.)*

§ 903. Liability for costs of support

(a) The father, mother, spouse, or other person liable for the support of a minor, the estate of that person, and the estate of the minor, shall be liable for the reasonable costs of support of the minor while the minor is placed, or detained in, or committed to, any institution or other place pursuant to Section 625 or pursuant to an order of the juvenile court. However, a county shall not levy charges for the costs of support of a minor detained pursuant to Section 625 unless, at the detention hearing, the juvenile court determines that detention of the minor should be continued. The liability of these persons and estates shall be a joint and several liability.

(b) The county shall limit the charges it seeks to impose to the reasonable costs of support of the minor and shall exclude any costs of treatment or supervision for the protection of society and the minor and the rehabilitation of the minor. In the event that court-ordered child support paid to the county pursuant to subdivision (a) exceeds the amount of the costs authorized by this subdivision and subdivision (a), the county shall either hold the excess in trust for the minor's future needs pursuant to Section 302.52 of Title 45 of the Code of Federal Regulations or, with the approval of the minor's caseworker, pay the excess directly to the minor.

(c) It is the intent of the Legislature in enacting this subdivision to protect the fiscal integrity of the county, to protect persons against whom the county seeks to impose liability from excessive charges, to ensure reasonable uniformity throughout the state in the level of liability being imposed, and to ensure that liability is imposed only on persons with the ability to pay. In evaluating a family's financial ability to pay under this section, the county shall take into consideration the family's income, the necessary obligations of the family, and the number of persons dependent upon this income. Except as provided in paragraphs (1), (2), (3), and (4), "costs of support" as used in this section means only actual costs incurred by the county for food and food preparation, clothing, personal supplies, and medical expenses, not to exceed a combined maximum cost of thirty dollars ($30) per day, except that:

(1) The maximum cost of thirty dollars ($30) per day shall be adjusted every third year beginning January 1, 2012, to reflect the percentage change in the calendar year annual average of the California Consumer Price Index, All Urban Consumers, published by the Department of Industrial Relations, for the three-year period.

(2) No cost for medical expenses shall be imposed by the county until the county has first exhausted any eligibility the minor may have under private insurance coverage, standard or medically indigent Medi–Cal coverage, and the Robert W. Crown California Children's Services Act (Article 5 (commencing with Section 123800) of Chapter 3 of Part 2 of Division 106 of the Health and Safety Code).

(3) In calculating the cost of medical expenses, the county shall not charge in excess of 100 percent of the AFDC fee-for-service average Medi–Cal payment for that county for that fiscal year as calculated by the State Department of Health Services; however, if a minor has extraordinary medical or dental costs that are not met under any of the coverages listed in paragraph (2), the county may impose these additional costs.

(4) For those placements of a minor subject to this section in which an AFDC–FC grant is made, the local child support agency shall, subject to Sections 17550 and 17552 of the Family Code, seek an order pursuant to Section 17400 of the Family Code and the statewide child support guideline in effect in Article 2 (commencing with Section 4050) of Chapter 2 of Part 2 of Division 9 of the Family Code. For purposes of determining the correct amount of support of a minor subject to this section, the rebuttable presumption set forth in Section 4057 of the Family Code is applicable. This paragraph shall be implemented consistent with subdivision (a) of Section 17415 of the Family Code.

(d) Notwithstanding subdivision (a), the father, mother, spouse, or other person liable for the support of the minor, the estate of that person, or the estate of the minor, shall not be liable for the costs described in this section if a petition to declare the minor a dependent child of the court pursuant to Section 300 is dismissed at or before the jurisdictional hearing.

(e)(1) This section does not apply to a minor who is adjudged a ward of the juvenile court, who is placed on probation pursuant to Section 725, who is the subject of a petition that has been filed to adjudge the minor a ward of the juvenile court, or who is the subject of a program of supervision undertaken pursuant to Section 654.

(2) Notwithstanding paragraph (1), this section applies to a minor who is designated as a dual status child pursuant to Section 241.1, for purposes of the dependency jurisdiction only and not for purposes of the delinquency jurisdiction. *(Added by Stats.1983, c. 1135, § 3, eff. Sept. 28, 1983. Amended by Stats.1984, c. 485, § 1; Stats.1991, c. 110 (S.B.101), § 19; Stats.1991, c. 137 (A.B.2235), § 1; Stats.1992, c. 50 (A.B.1394), § 3, eff. May 11, 1992; Stats.1993, c. 219 (A.B.1500), § 228; Stats.1993, c. 876 (S.B.1068), § 31, eff. Oct. 6, 1993; Stats. 1994, c. 882 (A.B.1327), § 3; Stats.1994, c. 1269 (A.B.2208), § 62.1; Stats.1996, c. 1023 (S.B.1497), § 457, eff. Sept. 29, 1996; Stats.1996, c. 508 (A.B.1348), § 1; Stats.1997, c. 478 (S.B.238), § 1, eff. Sept. 25, 1997; Stats.2001, c. 463 (A.B.1449), § 4; Stats.2009, c. 606 (S.B.676), § 11; Stats.2017, c. 678 (S.B.190), § 19, eff. Jan. 1, 2018.)*

Law Revision Commission Comments

Section 903 is amended to omit a references to former Civil Code sections. This is a technical, nonsubstantive change. [24 Cal.L.Rev.Comm.Reports 547 (1994)].

Cross References

County financial evaluation officer, see Government Code § 27750 et seq.
Department of Health Care Services, generally, see Health and Safety Code § 100100 et seq.
Duty of parents to support and maintain children, see Family Code § 3900 et seq.
Liability, see Welfare and Institutions Code § 332.
Petition to commence proceedings in juvenile court to declare minor a ward of court, notice of liability under this section, see Welfare and Institutions Code § 656.
Probation officer or social worker defined for purposes of this Chapter, see Welfare and Institutions Code § 215.
Work furlough earnings of minors, see Welfare and Institutions Code §§ 929, 1834.

§ 903.1. Liability for cost of legal services; transmittal and deposit of fees

(a)(1)(A) The father, mother, spouse, or other person liable for the support of a minor, the estate of that person, and the estate of the minor, shall be liable for the cost to the county or the court, whichever entity incurred the expenses, of legal services rendered to the minor by an attorney pursuant to an order of the juvenile court.

(B)(i) This paragraph does not apply to a minor who is adjudged a ward of the juvenile court, who is placed on probation pursuant to Section 725, who is the subject of a petition that has been filed to adjudge the minor a ward of the juvenile court, or who is the subject of a program of supervision undertaken pursuant to Section 654.

(ii) Notwithstanding clause (i), this paragraph applies to a minor who is designated as a dual status child pursuant to Section 241.1, for purposes of the dependency jurisdiction only and not for purposes of the delinquency jurisdiction.

(2) The father, mother, spouse, or other person liable for the support of a minor and the estate of that person shall also be liable for any cost to the county or the court of legal services rendered directly to the father, mother, or spouse, of the minor or any other person liable for the support of the minor, in a dependency proceeding by an attorney appointed pursuant to an order of the juvenile court. The liability of those persons (in this article called relatives) and estates shall be a joint and several liability.

(b) Notwithstanding subdivision (a), the father, mother, spouse, or other person liable for the support of the minor, the estate of that person, or the estate of the minor, shall not be liable for the costs of any of the legal services provided to any person described in this section if a petition to declare the minor a dependent child of the court pursuant to Section 300 is dismissed at or before the jurisdictional hearing.

(c) Fees received pursuant to this section shall be transmitted to the Administrative Office of the Courts in the same manner as prescribed in Section 68085.1 of the Government Code. The Administrative Office of the Courts shall deposit the fees received pursuant to this section into the Trial Court Trust Fund. *(Added by Stats.1965, c. 2006, p. 4535, § 1. Amended by Stats.1981, c. 188, p. 1113, § 1; Stats.1992, c. 433 (A.B.2448), § 2; Stats.1996, c. 508 (A.B.1348), § 2; Stats.2009, c. 140 (A.B.1164), § 189; Stats.2009, c. 413 (A.B.131), § 1; Stats.2017, c. 678 (S.B.190), § 20, eff. Jan. 1, 2018.)*

Cross References

Collection of amounts due pursuant to this section by the Franchise Tax Board, see Revenue and Taxation Code § 19280.
County financial evaluation officer, see Government Code § 27750 et seq.
County financial evaluation officer, juveniles, powers of financial evaluation officer, see Government Code § 27757.
County financial evaluation officer, parental liability for costs of juveniles, see Government Code § 27756.
Liability, see Welfare and Institutions Code § 332.
Petition to commence proceedings in juvenile court to declare minor a ward of court, notice of liability under this section, see Welfare and Institutions Code § 656.
Public defender, see Government Code § 27700 et seq.
Right to counsel, see Penal Code § 686.

Research References

West's California Judicial Council Forms JV–130–INFO, Paying for Lawyers in Dependency Court—Information for Parents and Guardians (Also Available in Spanish).
West's California Judicial Council Forms JV–131, Order to Appear for Financial Evaluation.
West's California Judicial Council Forms JV–132, Financial Declaration—Juvenile Dependency.
West's California Judicial Council Forms JV–133, Recommendation Regarding Ability to Repay Cost of Legal Services.
West's California Judicial Council Forms JV–134, Response to Recommendation Regarding Ability to Repay Cost of Legal Services.
West's California Judicial Council Forms JV–135, Order for Repayment of Cost of Legal Services.
West's California Judicial Council Forms JV–136, Juvenile Dependency—Cost of Appointed Counsel: Repayment Recommendation/Response/Order.

§ 903.2. Home supervision; liability for cost

(a) The juvenile court may require that the father, mother, spouse, or other person liable for the support of a minor, the estate of that person, and the estate of the minor shall be liable for the cost to the county of the home supervision of the minor, pursuant to the order of the juvenile court, by the probation officer or social worker. The liability of these persons (in this article called relatives) and estates shall be a joint and several liability.

(b) Liability shall be imposed on a person pursuant to this section only if he or she has the financial ability to pay. In evaluating a family's financial ability to pay under this section, the county shall take into consideration the family income, the necessary obligations of the family, and the number of persons dependent upon this income.

(c)(1) This section does not apply to a minor who is adjudged a ward of the juvenile court, who is placed on probation pursuant to Section 725, who is the subject of a petition that has been filed to adjudge the minor a ward of the juvenile court, or who is the subject of a program of supervision undertaken pursuant to Section 654.

(2) Notwithstanding paragraph (1), this section applies to a minor who is designated as a dual status child pursuant to Section 241.1, for purposes of the dependency jurisdiction only and not for purposes of the delinquency jurisdiction. *(Added by Stats.1968, c. 1225, p. 2334, § 1. Amended by Stats.1996, c. 355 (S.B.1734), § 1; Stats.2017, c. 678 (S.B.190), § 22, eff. Jan. 1, 2018.)*

Cross References

County financial evaluation officer, see Government Code § 27750 et seq.
Liability, see Welfare and Institutions Code § 332.
Petition to commence proceedings in juvenile court to declare minor a ward of court, notice of liability under this section, see Welfare and Institutions Code § 656.
Probation officer or social worker defined for purposes of this Chapter, see Welfare and Institutions Code § 215.
Probation officers generally, see Welfare and Institutions Code § 270 et seq.

§ 903.25. Juveniles in custody of probation department or placed in children's receiving home, foster care home or facility; liability for costs

(a) In addition to the liability established by any other law, a parent or guardian of a minor who has been delivered to the custody of the probation department, or who has been placed into a children's receiving home, a foster care home or facility, shall be liable for the reasonable costs of food, shelter, and care of the minor while in the custody of the probation department when all of the following circumstances are applicable:

(1) The parent or guardian receives actual notice by telephone or by written communication from the probation officer that the minor is scheduled for release from custody and that the parent or guardian, in person or through a responsible relative, is requested to take delivery of the minor. The notice shall inform the parent or guardian of the financial liability created by this section.

(2) It is reasonably possible for the parent or guardian to take delivery of the minor, in person or through a responsible relative, at the place designated by the probation officer within 12 hours from the time notice of release was received, or within 48 hours from the time notice of release is received in any case where a petition to declare the minor a dependent child of the court pursuant to Section 300 was dismissed at or before the jurisdictional hearing.

(3) The parent states a refusal to take delivery of the minor or fails to make a reasonable effort to take delivery of the minor, in person or through a responsible relative, within 12 hours from the time of actual receipt of the notice, or within 48 hours from the time of actual receipt of the notice in any case where a petition to declare the minor a dependent child of the court pursuant to Section 300 was dismissed at or before the jurisdictional hearing.

(b) The liability established by this section, when combined with any liability arising under Section 903, shall not exceed one hundred dollars ($100) for each 24–hour period, beginning when notice of release was actually received, or beginning 48 hours after notice of release was actually received in any case where a petition to declare the minor a dependent child of the court pursuant to Section 300 was dismissed at or before the jurisdictional hearing, in which a notified parent or guardian has failed to make a reasonable effort to take delivery of the minor, in person or through a responsible relative, in accordance with the request and instructions of the probation officer.

(c) The liability established by this section shall be limited by the financial ability of the parents, guardians, or other persons to pay. Any parent, guardian, or other person who is assessed under this section shall, upon request, be entitled to an evaluation and determination of ability to pay under the provisions of Section 903.45. Any parent, guardian, or other person who is assessed under this section shall also be entitled, upon petition, to a hearing and determination by the juvenile court on the issues of liability and ability to pay.

(d)(1) This section does not apply to a minor who is adjudged a ward of the juvenile court, who is placed on probation pursuant to Section 725, who is the subject of a petition that has been filed to adjudge the minor a ward of the juvenile court, or who is the subject of a program of supervision undertaken pursuant to Section 654.

(2) Notwithstanding paragraph (1), this section applies to a minor who is designated as a dual status child pursuant to Section 241.1, for purposes of the dependency jurisdiction only and not for purposes of the delinquency jurisdiction. *(Added by Stats.1992, c. 429 (S.B.1274), § 6, eff. Aug. 3, 1992. Amended by Stats.1996, c. 508 (A.B.1348), § 3; Stats.2017, c. 678 (S.B.190), § 23, eff. Jan. 1, 2018.)*

Cross References

Probation officer or social worker defined for purposes of this Chapter, see Welfare and Institutions Code § 215.

§ 903.4. Legislative findings; recovery of moneys or incurred costs for support of juveniles; order to show cause

(a)(1) The Legislature finds that even though Section 903 establishes parental liability for the cost of the care, support, and maintenance of a child in a county institution or other place in which the child is placed, detained, or committed pursuant to an order of the juvenile court, the collection of child support for juveniles who have been placed in out-of-home care as dependents of the juvenile court under Section 300 has not been pursued routinely and effectively.

(2) It is the purpose of this section to substantially increase income to the state and to counties through court-ordered parental reimbursement for the support of juveniles who are in out-of-home placement. In this regard, the Legislature finds that the costs of collection will be offset by the additional income derived from the increased effectiveness of the parental support program.

(b) In any case in which a child is or has been declared a dependent child of the court pursuant to Section 300, the juvenile court shall order any agency that has expended moneys or incurred costs on behalf of the child pursuant to a detention or placement order of the juvenile court, to submit to the local child support agency, within 30 days, in the form of a declaration, a statement of its costs and expenses for the benefit, support, and maintenance of the child.

(c)(1)(A) The local child support agency may petition the superior court to issue an order to show cause why an order should not be entered for continuing support and reimbursement of the costs of the support of any minor described in Section 903.

(B) Any order entered as a result of the order to show cause shall be enforceable in the same manner as any other support order entered by the courts of this state at the time it becomes due and payable.

(C) In any case in which the local child support agency has received a declaration of costs or expenses from any agency, the declaration shall be deemed an application for assistance pursuant to Section 17400 of the Family Code.

(2) The order to show cause shall inform the parent of all of the following facts:

(A) He or she has been sued.

(B) If he or she wishes to seek the advice of an attorney in this matter, it should be done promptly so that his or her financial declaration and written response, if any, will be filed on time.

(C) He or she has a right to appear personally and present evidence in his or her behalf.

(D) His or her failure to appear at the order to show cause hearing, personally or through his or her attorney, may result in an order being entered against him or her for the relief requested in the petition.

(E) Any order entered could result in the garnishment of wages, taking of money or property to enforce the order, or being held in contempt of court.

(F) Any party has a right to request a modification of any order issued by the superior court in the event of a change in circumstances.

(3) Any existing support order shall remain in full force and effect unless the superior court modifies that order pursuant to subdivision (f).

(4) The local child support agency shall not be required to petition the court for an order for continuing support and reimbursement if, in the opinion of the local child support agency, it would not be appropriate to secure that order. The local child support agency shall not be required to continue collection efforts for any order if, in the opinion of the local child support agency, it would not be appropriate or cost effective to enforce the order pursuant to Section 17552 of the Family Code.

(d)(1) In any case in which an order to show cause has been issued and served upon a parent for continuing support and reimbursement of costs, a completed income and expense declaration shall be filed with the court by the parent; a copy of it shall be delivered to the local child support agency at least five days prior to the hearing on the order to show cause.

(2) Any person authorized by law to receive a parent's financial declaration or information obtained therefrom, who knowingly furnishes the declaration or information to a person not authorized by law to receive it, is guilty of a misdemeanor.

(e)(1) If a parent has been personally served with the order to show cause and no appearance is made by the parent, or an attorney in his or her behalf, at the hearing on the order to show cause, the court may enter an order for the principal amount and continuing support in the amount demanded in the petition.

(2) If the parent appears at the hearing on the order to show cause, the court may enter an order for the amount the court determines the parent is financially able to pay.

(f) The court shall have continuing jurisdiction to modify any order for continuing support entered pursuant to this section.

(g) As used in this section, "parent" includes any person specified in Section 903, the estate of that person, and the estate of the minor person. "Parent" does not include a minor or nonminor dependent whose minor child receives aid under Section 11401.4.

(h) The local child support agency may contract with another county agency for the performance of any of the duties required by this section.

(i)(1) This section does not apply to a minor who is adjudged a ward of the juvenile court, who is placed on probation pursuant to Section 725, who is the subject of a petition that has been filed to adjudge the minor a ward of the juvenile court, or who is the subject of a program of supervision undertaken pursuant to Section 654.

(2) Notwithstanding paragraph (1), this section applies to a minor who is designated as a dual status child pursuant to Section 241.1, for purposes of the dependency jurisdiction only and not for purposes of the delinquency jurisdiction. *(Added by Stats.1982, c. 1276, § 5, eff. Sept. 22, 1982. Amended by Stats.1984, c. 1720, § 1; Stats.2000, c. 808 (A.B.1358), § 118, eff. Sept. 28, 2000; Stats.2012, c. 846 (A.B. 1712), § 32; Stats.2017, c. 678 (S.B.190), § 24, eff. Jan. 1, 2018.)*

Cross References

County financial evaluation officer, parental liability for costs of juveniles, see Government Code § 27756.
District attorney, duties of, see Government Code § 26500 et seq.
Misdemeanors, definition and penalties, see Penal Code §§ 17, 19, 19.2.

§ 903.41. Parentage determinations; family law and juvenile departments; exchange of documents

(a) It is the intention of the Legislature that the family law departments and juvenile departments of each superior court coordinate determinations of parentage and the setting of support to ensure that the State of California remains in compliance with federal regulations for child support guidelines. The Legislature therefore enacts this section for the purpose of ensuring a document exchange between the family law departments and juvenile departments of each superior court as necessary to administer the public social services administered or supervised by the State Department of Social Services.

(b) If the issue of paternity is raised during any hearings pursuant to Section 300, 601, or 602, the court clerk shall notify the local child support agency for an inquiry concerning any superior court order or judgment which addresses the issue.

(1) If the local child support agency determines that a judgment for parentage already exists, the local child support agency shall obtain and forward certified copies of the judgment to the juvenile court and the court shall take judicial notice thereof.

(2) If the local child support agency determines that the issue of parentage has not been determined, the juvenile court may determine the issue of parentage and, if it does so, shall give notice to the local child support agency.

(c) If the court establishes paternity of a minor child, the court clerk shall forward the order on a form to be adopted by the Judicial Council to the local child support agency.

(d) If a child is receiving public assistance under the CalWORKs program, or if it appears to the court that the child may receive assistance under CalWORKs, the court shall direct the clerk of the court to advise the local child support agency.

(e) The court shall advise the parent of the minor of the possibility that the local child support agency may file an action for support if the child receives CalWORKs, pursuant to Section 17402 of the Family Code. *(Added by Stats.1994, c. 1269 (A.B.2208), § 62.2. Amended by Stats.2000, c. 808 (A.B.1358), § 119, eff. Sept. 28, 2000.)*

§ 903.45. Financial evaluation of liability; order to appear; citation; petition for order to pay; considerations; hearing; notice; agreement on terms; dispute; petition to modify or vacate judgment; execution of order

(a) The board of supervisors may designate a county financial evaluation officer pursuant to Section 27750 of the Government Code to make financial evaluations of liability for reimbursement pursuant to Sections 903, 903.1, 903.2, 903.25, 903.3, and 903.5, and other reimbursable costs allowed by law, as set forth in this section.

(b)(1)(A) In a county where a board of supervisors has designated a county financial evaluation officer, the juvenile court shall, at the close of the disposition hearing, order any person liable for the cost of support, pursuant to Section 903, the cost of legal services as provided for in Section 903.1, supervision costs as provided for in Section 903.2, or any other reimbursable costs allowed under this code, to appear before the county financial evaluation officer for a financial evaluation of his or her ability to pay those costs. If the responsible person is not present at the disposition hearing, the court shall cite him or her to appear for a financial evaluation. In the case of a parent, guardian, or other person assessed for the costs of transport, food, shelter, or care of a minor under Section 903.25, the juvenile court shall, upon request of the county probation department, order the appearance of the parent, guardian, or other person before the county financial evaluation officer for a financial evaluation of his or her ability to pay the costs assessed.

(B)(i) This paragraph does not apply to costs described in this paragraph for purposes of a minor who is adjudged a ward of the juvenile court, who is placed on probation pursuant to Section 725, who is the subject of a petition that has been filed to adjudge the minor a ward of the juvenile court, or who is the subject of a program of supervision undertaken pursuant to Section 654.

(ii) Notwithstanding clause (i), this paragraph applies to a minor who is designated as a dual status child pursuant to Section 241.1, for purposes of the dependency jurisdiction only and not for purposes of the delinquency jurisdiction.

(2) If the county financial evaluation officer determines that a person so responsible has the ability to pay all or part of the costs, the county financial evaluation officer shall petition the court for an order requiring the person to pay that sum to the county or court, depending on which entity incurred the expense. If the parent or guardian is liable for costs for legal services pursuant to Section 903.1, the parent or guardian has been reunified with the child pursuant to a court order, and the county financial evaluation officer determines that repayment of the costs would harm the ability of the parent or guardian to support the child, then the county financial evaluation officer shall not petition the court for an order of repayment, and the court shall not make that order. In addition, if the parent or guardian is currently receiving reunification services, and the court finds, or the county financial officer determines, that repayment by the parent or guardian will pose a barrier to reunification with the child because it will limit the ability of the parent or guardian to comply with the requirements of the reunification plan or compromise the parent's or guardian's current or future ability to meet the financial needs of the child, or in any case in which the court finds that the repayment would be unjust under the circumstances of the case, then the county financial evaluation officer shall not petition the court for an order of repayment, and the court shall not order repayment by the parent or guardian. In evaluating a person's ability to pay under this section, the county financial evaluation officer and the court shall take into consideration the family's income, the necessary obligations of the family, and the number of persons dependent upon this income. A person appearing for a financial evaluation has the right to dispute the county financial evaluation officer's determination, in which case he or she is entitled to a hearing before the juvenile court. The county financial evaluation officer, at the time of the financial evaluation, shall advise the person of his or her right to a hearing and of his or her rights pursuant to subdivision (c).

(3) At the hearing, a person responsible for costs is entitled to have, but shall not be limited to, the opportunity to be heard in person, to present witnesses and other documentary evidence, to confront and cross-examine adverse witnesses, to disclosure of the evidence against him or her, and to receive a written statement of the findings of the court. The person has the right to be represented by counsel, and, if the person is unable to afford counsel, the right to appointed counsel. If the court determines that the person has the ability to pay all or part of the costs, including the costs of any counsel appointed to represent the person at the hearing, the court shall set the amount to be reimbursed and order him or her to pay that sum to the county or court, depending on which entity incurred the expense, in a manner in which the court believes reasonable and compatible with the person's financial ability.

(4) If the person, after having been ordered to appear before the county financial evaluation officer, has been given proper notice and fails to appear as ordered, the county financial evaluation officer shall recommend to the court that the person be ordered to pay the full amount of the costs. Proper notice to the person shall contain all of the following:

(A) That the person has a right to a statement of the costs as soon as it is available.

(B) The person's procedural rights under Section 27755 of the Government Code.

(C) The time limit within which the person's appearance is required.

(D) A warning that if the person fails to appear before the county financial evaluation officer, the officer will recommend that the court order the person to pay the costs in full.

(5) If the county financial evaluation officer determines that the person has the ability to pay all or a portion of these costs, with or without terms, and the person concurs in this determination and agrees to the terms of payment, the county financial evaluation officer, upon his or her written evaluation and the person's written agreement, shall petition the court for an order requiring the person to pay that sum to the county or the court in a manner that is reasonable and compatible with the person's financial ability. This order may be granted without further notice to the person, provided that a copy of the order is served on the person by mail or by electronic means pursuant to Section 212.5.

(6) However, if the county financial evaluation officer cannot reach an agreement with the person with respect to either the liability for the costs, the amount of the costs, the person's ability to pay the costs, or the terms of payment, the matter shall be deemed in dispute and referred by the county financial evaluation officer back to the court for a hearing.

(c) At any time prior to the satisfaction of a judgment entered pursuant to this section, a person against whom the judgment was entered may petition the rendering court to modify or vacate the judgment on the basis of a change in circumstances relating to his or her ability to pay the judgment.

(d) Execution may be issued on the order in the same manner as on a judgment in a civil action, including any balance remaining unpaid at the termination of the court's jurisdiction over the minor. *(Added by Stats.1984, c. 1720, § 2. Amended by Stats.1985, c. 1485, § 15.1; Stats.1992, c. 429 (S.B.1274), § 7, eff. Aug. 3, 1992; Stats. 2001, c. 755 (S.B.943), § 23, eff. Oct. 12, 2001; Stats.2009, c. 413 (A.B.131), § 2; Stats.2013, c. 31 (S.B.75), § 26, eff. June 27, 2013; Stats.2017, c. 319 (A.B.976), § 147, eff. Jan. 1, 2018; Stats.2017, c. 678 (S.B.190), § 25.5, eff. Jan. 1, 2018.)*

Research References

West's California Judicial Council Forms JV–130–INFO, Paying for Lawyers in Dependency Court—Information for Parents and Guardians (Also Available in Spanish).

West's California Judicial Council Forms JV–131, Order to Appear for Financial Evaluation.

West's California Judicial Council Forms JV–132, Financial Declaration—Juvenile Dependency.

West's California Judicial Council Forms JV–133, Recommendation Regarding Ability to Repay Cost of Legal Services.

West's California Judicial Council Forms JV–134, Response to Recommendation Regarding Ability to Repay Cost of Legal Services.

West's California Judicial Council Forms JV–135, Order for Repayment of Cost of Legal Services.

West's California Judicial Council Forms JV–136, Juvenile Dependency—Cost of Appointed Counsel: Repayment Recommendation/Response/Order.

§ 903.47. Costs of counsel appointed to represent parents or minors in dependency proceedings; reimbursements program; financial evaluation officers; procedures

(a) The Judicial Council shall establish a program to collect reimbursements from the person liable for the costs of counsel appointed to represent parents or minors pursuant to Section 903.1 in dependency proceedings.

(1) As part of the program, the Judicial Council shall:

(A) Adopt a statewide standard for determining the ability to pay reimbursements for counsel, which shall at a minimum include the family's income, their necessary obligations, the number of individuals dependent on this income, and the cost-effectiveness of the program.

(B) Adopt policies and procedures allowing a court to recover from the money collected the costs associated with implementing the reimbursements program. The policies and procedures shall at a minimum limit the amount of money a court may recover to a reasonable proportion of the reimbursements collected and provide the terms and conditions under which a court may use a third party to collect reimbursements. For the purposes of this subparagraph, "costs associated with implementing the reimbursements program" means the court costs of assessing a parent's ability to pay for court-appointed counsel and the costs to collect delinquent reimbursements.

(2) The money collected shall be deposited as required by Section 68085.1 of the Government Code. Except as otherwise authorized by law, the money collected under this program shall be utilized to reduce caseloads, for attorneys appointed by the court, to the caseload standard approved by the Judicial Council. Priority shall be given to those courts with the highest attorney caseloads that also demonstrate the ability to immediately improve outcomes for parents and children as a result of lower attorney caseloads.

(b) The court may do either of the following:

(1) Designate a court financial evaluation officer to make financial evaluations of liability for reimbursement pursuant to Section 903.1.

(2) With the consent of the county and pursuant to the terms and conditions agreed upon by the court and county, designate a county financial evaluation officer to make financial evaluations of liability for reimbursement pursuant to Section 903.1.

(c) In handling reimbursement of payments pursuant to Section 903.1, the court financial evaluation officer and the county financial evaluation officer shall follow the procedures set forth for county financial evaluation officers in subdivisions (b), (c), and (d) of Section 903.45. *(Added by Stats.2009, c. 413 (A.B.131), § 3. Amended by Stats.2010, c. 569 (A.B.1229), § 1; Stats.2011, c. 308 (S.B.647), § 13.)*

Research References

West's California Judicial Council Forms JV–130–INFO, Paying for Lawyers in Dependency Court—Information for Parents and Guardians (Also Available in Spanish).
West's California Judicial Council Forms JV–131, Order to Appear for Financial Evaluation.
West's California Judicial Council Forms JV–132, Financial Declaration—Juvenile Dependency.
West's California Judicial Council Forms JV–133, Recommendation Regarding Ability to Repay Cost of Legal Services.
West's California Judicial Council Forms JV–134, Response to Recommendation Regarding Ability to Repay Cost of Legal Services.
West's California Judicial Council Forms JV–135, Order for Repayment of Cost of Legal Services.
West's California Judicial Council Forms JV–136, Juvenile Dependency—Cost of Appointed Counsel: Repayment Recommendation/Response/Order.

§ 903.5. Voluntary placement of minor in out-of-home care; liability for support

(a) In addition to the requirements of Section 903.4, and notwithstanding any other law, the parent or other person legally liable for the support of a minor, who voluntarily places the minor in 24–hour out-of-home care, shall be liable for the cost of the minor's care, support, and maintenance when the minor receives Aid to Families with Dependent Children–Foster Care (AFDC–FC), Supplemental Security Income–State Supplementary Program (SSI–SSP), or county-only funds. As used in this section, "parent" includes any person specified in Section 903. As used in this section, "parent" does not include a minor or nonminor dependent whose minor child receives aid under Section 11401.4. Whenever the county welfare department or the placing agency determines that a court order would be advisable and effective, pursuant to Section 17552 of the Family Code, the department or the agency shall notify the local child support agency, or the financial evaluation officer designated pursuant to Section 903.45, who shall proceed pursuant to Section 903.4 or 903.45.

(b)(1) This section does not apply to a minor who is adjudged a ward of the juvenile court, who is placed on probation pursuant to Section 725, who is the subject of a petition that has been filed to adjudge the minor a ward of the juvenile court, or who is the subject of a program of supervision undertaken pursuant to Section 654.

(2) Notwithstanding paragraph (1), this section applies to a minor who is designated as a dual status child pursuant to Section 241.1, for purposes of the dependency jurisdiction only and not for purposes of the delinquency jurisdiction. *(Added by Stats.1982, c. 1276, § 6, eff. Sept. 22, 1982. Amended by Stats.1993, c. 876 (S.B.1068), § 32, eff. Oct. 6, 1993; Stats.2000, c. 808 (A.B.1358), § 120, eff. Sept. 28, 2000; Stats.2001, c. 755 (S.B.943), § 24, eff. Oct. 12, 2001; Stats.2002, c. 664 (A.B.3034), § 231; Stats.2012, c. 846 (A.B.1712), § 33; Stats.2017, c. 678 (S.B.190), § 26, eff. Jan. 1, 2018.)*

§ 903.6. Distribution of funds collected

Funds collected pursuant to Sections 903, 903.4, and 903.5 shall be distributed in the following manner:

(a) If the program through which the minor is placed is a county-funded program, the county shall retain 100 percent of the funds collected. For the purposes of this subdivision, programs funded in whole or part with county justices system subvention program funds shall be considered to be 100 percent county funded.

(b) If the program through which the minor is placed is funded partially with state or federal funds, the amounts collected shall be distributed by the State Department of Social Services pursuant to Section 11457 and incentives shall be paid pursuant to Sections 15200.1, 15200.2, and 15200.3. *(Added by Stats.1982, c. 1276, § 7, eff. Sept. 22, 1982.)*

§ 903.7. Foster Children and Parent Training Fund; use of moneys; allocation

(a) There is in the State Treasury the Foster Children and Parent Training Fund. The moneys contained in the fund shall be used exclusively for the purposes set forth in this section.

(b) For each fiscal year beginning with the 1981–82 fiscal year, except as provided in Sections 15200.1, 15200.2, 15200.3, 15200.8, and 15200.81, and Section 17704 of the Family Code, the Department of Child Support Services shall determine the amount equivalent to the net state share of foster care collections attributable to the enforcement of parental fiscal liability pursuant to Sections 903, 903.4, and 903.5. On July 1, 1982, and every three months thereafter, the department shall notify the Chancellor of the Community Colleges, the Department of Finance, and the Superintendent of Public Instruction of the above-specified amount. The Department of Child Support Services shall authorize the quarterly transfer of any portion of this amount for any particular fiscal year exceeding three million seven hundred fifty thousand dollars ($3,750,000) of the net state share of foster care collections to the Treasurer for deposit in the Foster Children and Parent Training Fund, except that, commencing with the 2002–03 fiscal year, a total of not more than three million dollars ($3,000,000) may be transferred to the fund in any fiscal year.

(c)(1) If sufficient moneys are available in the Foster Children and Parent Training Fund, up to three million dollars ($3,000,000) shall be allocated for the support of foster parent training programs conducted in community colleges. The maximum amount authorized to be allocated pursuant to this subdivision shall be adjusted annually by a cost-of-living increase each year based on the percentage given to discretionary education programs. Funds for the training program shall be provided in a separate budget item in that portion of the Budget Act pertaining to the Chancellor of the

California Community Colleges, to be deposited in a separate bank account by the Chancellor of the California Community Colleges.

(2) The chancellor shall use these funds exclusively for foster parent training, as specified by the chancellor in consultation with the California State Foster Parents Association and the State Department of Social Services.

(3) The plans for each foster parent training program shall include the provision of training to facilitate the development of foster family homes and small family homes to care for no more than six children who have special mental, emotional, developmental, or physical needs.

(4) The State Department of Social Services shall facilitate the participation of county welfare departments in the foster parent training program. The California State Foster Parents Association, or the local chapters thereof, and the State Department of Social Services shall identify training participants and shall advise the chancellor on the form, content, and methodology of the training program. Funds shall be paid monthly to the foster parent training program until the maximum amount of funds authorized to be expended for that program is expended. No more than 10 percent or seventy-five thousand dollars ($75,000) of these moneys, whichever is greater, shall be used for administrative purposes; of the 10 percent or seventy-five thousand dollars ($75,000), no more than ten thousand dollars ($10,000) shall be expended to reimburse the State Department of Social Services for its services pursuant to this paragraph.

(d) Beginning with the 1983–84 fiscal year, and each fiscal year thereafter, after all allocations for foster parent training in community colleges have been made, any moneys remaining in the Foster Children and Parent Training Fund may be allocated for foster children services programs pursuant to Chapter 11.3 (commencing with Section 42920) of Part 24 of the Education Code.

(e)(1) The Controller shall transfer moneys from the Foster Children and Parent Training Fund to the Chancellor of the California Community Colleges and the Superintendent of Public Instruction as necessary to fulfill the requirements of subdivisions (c) and (d).

(2) After the maximum amount authorized in any fiscal year has been transferred to the Chancellor of the California Community Colleges and the Superintendent of Public Instruction, the Controller shall transfer any remaining funds to the General Fund for expenditure for any public purpose.

(f) This section shall be operative until June 30, 2005, and thereafter is operative only if specified in the annual Budget Act or in another statute. *(Added by Stats.1982, c. 1276, § 8, eff. Sept. 22, 1982. Amended by Stats.1983, c. 543, § 9, eff. July 28, 1983; Stats.1984, c. 1597, § 4; Stats.2000, c. 108 (A.B.2876), § 22, eff. July 10, 2000; Stats.2001, c. 755 (S.B.943), § 25, eff. Oct. 12, 2001; Stats.2002, c. 1022 (A.B.444), § 21, eff. Sept. 28, 2002; Stats.2005, c. 73 (S.B.63), § 26, eff. July 19, 2005.)*

Operative Effect

For operative effect of this section, see its terms.

Cross References

Department of Finance, generally, see Government Code § 13000 et seq.
State Controller, generally, see Government Code § 12402 et seq.

§ 903.8. Enhanced statewide basic foster parent training program; legislative intent

(a) Beginning January 1, 1994, the State Department of Social Services shall develop and implement an enhanced statewide basic foster parent training program. It is the intent of the Legislature to fund this program by allocating unexpended child welfare services funds from the 1992–93 fiscal year to support a two and one-half year training curricula development.

(b) During this two and one-half year period, the State Department of Social Services shall do all of the following, in cooperation with foster parents and representatives from county placement agencies and other foster care providers:

(1) Complete a comprehensive survey of existing foster parent training curricula and resources, evaluate the existing foster parent training delivery system and explore alternative delivery models, complete a needs assessment of foster parents, and develop and implement a statewide core curriculum.

(2) Develop and implement curricula for, teenage pregnancy prevention and other special needs topics, as identified in the needs assessment, to supplement the core curriculum. The teenage pregnancy prevention topics shall be based upon public health fact-based materials and programs. Curricula for teenage pregnancy prevention shall emphasize that abstinence from sexual intercourse is the only protection that is 100 percent effective against unwanted teenage pregnancy, sexually transmitted diseases, and acquired immune deficiency syndrome (AIDS) when transmitted sexually, and that all other methods of contraception carry a risk of failure in preventing unwanted teenage pregnancy. The curricula shall:

(A) Include statistics based on the latest medical information citing the failure and success rates of condoms and other contraceptives in preventing pregnancy.

(B) Stress that sexually transmitted diseases are serious possible hazards of sexual intercourse, and shall include statistics based on the latest medical information citing the failure and success rates of condoms in preventing AIDS and other sexually transmitted diseases.

(C) Include a discussion of the possible emotional and psychological consequences of preadolescent and adolescent sexual intercourse outside of marriage and the consequences of unwanted adolescent pregnancy.

(3) Evaluate the current foster parent training funding formula and explore funding alternatives to ensure that a permanent and adequate funding source is available.

(4) Evaluate current recruitment strategies and facilitate the expansion of recruitment activities, especially targeting minority families for the promotion of the placement of minority youth with trained and culturally competent families of the same ethnicity and cultural background.

(5) In its foster parent recruitment and training effort, place special emphasis on the recruitment of prospective foster parents willing to accept sibling placements and the training of foster parents to ensure they are able and ready to care for a sibling group.

(c) It is not the intent of the Legislature and nothing in this section shall be construed as requiring foster parents to participate in this training program in whole or in part. *(Added by Stats.1993, c. 1089 (A.B.2129), § 9. Amended by Stats.1995, c. 281 (S.B.1045), § 1.)*

§ 904. Determination of costs

(a) The monthly or daily charge, not to exceed cost, for care, support, and maintenance of minor persons placed or detained in or committed to any institution by order of a juvenile court, the cost of supervision referred to by Section 903.2, and the cost of sealing records in county or local agency custody referred to by Section 903.3 shall be determined by the board of supervisors. The cost of dependency-related legal services referred to by Section 903.1 and the cost of sealing records in court custody referred to by Section 903.3 shall be determined by the court. Any determination made by a court under this section shall be valid only if either (1) made under procedures adopted by the Judicial Council or (2) approved by the Judicial Council.

(b)(1) This section does not apply to a minor who is adjudged a ward of the juvenile court, who is placed on probation pursuant to Section 725, who is the subject of a petition that has been filed to adjudge the minor a ward of the juvenile court, or who is the subject of a program of supervision undertaken pursuant to Section 654.

(2) Notwithstanding paragraph (1), this section applies to a minor who is designated as a dual status child pursuant to Section 241.1, for purposes of the dependency jurisdiction only and not for purposes of the delinquency jurisdiction. *(Added by Stats.1961, c. 1616, p. 3500, § 2. Amended by Stats.1965, c. 336, p. 1442, § 1; Stats.1965, c. 2006, p. 4535, § 2; Stats.1968, c. 1225, p. 2334, § 2; Stats.1979, c. 978, p. 3348, § 2; Stats.1983, c. 1135, § 4, eff. Sept. 28, 1983; Stats.2001, c. 824 (A.B.1700), § 40; Stats.2017, c. 678 (S.B.190), § 27, eff. Jan. 1, 2018.)*

Cross References

Financial ability to contribute to support relative's responsibility, see Welfare and Institutions Code § 17300 et seq.
Relief Law of 1945, see Welfare and Institutions Code § 18511.

§ 911. Duration of order for payment; reimbursement of homes

No order for payment from the county treasury of the expense of support and maintenance of a ward or dependent child of the juvenile court shall be effective for more than 12 months, and no order for payment from the county treasury of the expense of support and maintenance of a minor person concerning whom a verified petition has been filed in accordance with the provision of this chapter, other than a ward or dependent child of the court, shall be effective for more than one month. Upon all hearings of the case of any ward or dependent child of the juvenile court, the case shall be continued on the calendar, but in no instance to exceed 12 months.

When any ward of the juvenile court is, with the consent of the juvenile court of the county committing him and the officer in charge of the state school to which he was committed or in which he is confined, placed in a boarding home, foster home, or work home, but continues to be under the supervision of such state school, the county may reimburse the boarding home, foster home, or work home in an amount adequate for the maintenance of the ward, but not to exceed twenty-five dollars ($25) per month. *(Added by Stats.1961, c. 1616, p. 3502, § 2.)*

§ 912. County payment to state; presentation and payment of claims; collection and maintenance of data about the movement of juvenile offenders

(a) A county from which a person is committed to the Department of Corrections and Rehabilitation, Division of Juvenile Facilities, shall pay to the state an annual rate of twenty-four thousand dollars ($24,000) while the person remains in an institution under the direct supervision of the division, or in an institution, boarding home, foster home, or other private or public institution in which the person is placed by the division, and cared for and supported at the expense of the division, as provided in this subdivision. This subdivision applies to a person who is committed to the division by a juvenile court on or after July 1, 2012.

The Department of Corrections and Rehabilitation, Division of Juvenile Facilities, shall present to the county, not more frequently than monthly, a claim for the amount due to the state under this subdivision, which the county shall process and pay pursuant to Chapter 4 (commencing with Section 29700) of Division 3 of Title 3 of the Government Code.

(b) A county from which a person is committed to the Department of Corrections and Rehabilitation, Division of Juvenile Facilities, on or after July 1, 2018, shall pay to the state an annual rate of twenty-four thousand dollars ($24,000) for the time the person remains in an institution under the direct supervision of the division, or in an institution, boarding home, foster home, or other private or public institution in which the person is placed by the division, and cared for and supported at the expense of the division, as provided in this subdivision. A county shall not pay the annual rate of twenty-four thousand dollars ($24,000) for a person who is 23 years of age or older. This subdivision applies to a person committed to the division by a juvenile court on or after July 1, 2018.

(c) A county from which a person is committed to the Department of Corrections and Rehabilitation, Division of Juvenile Justice, on or after July 1, 2021, shall pay to the state an annual rate of one-hundred and twenty-five thousand dollars ($125,000) for the time the person remains in an institution under the direct supervision of the division, or in an institution, boarding home, foster home, or other private or public institution in which the person is placed by the division, and cared for and supported at the expense of the division, as provided in this subdivision. A county shall not pay the annual rate of one-hundred and twenty-five thousand dollars ($125,000) for a person who is 23 years of age or older. This subdivision applies to a person committed to the division by a juvenile court on or after July 1, 2021.

(d) Consistent with Article 1 (commencing with Section 6024) of Chapter 5 of Title 7 of Part 3 of the Penal Code, the Board of State and Community Corrections shall collect and maintain available information and data about the movement of juvenile offenders committed by a juvenile court and placed in any institution, boarding home, foster home, or other private or public institution in which they are cared for, supervised, or both, by the division or the county while they are on parole, probation, or otherwise. *(Added by Stats.2011, c. 36 (S.B.92), § 77, eff. June 30, 2011, operative Dec. 13, 2011. Amended by Stats.2012, c. 162 (S.B.1171), § 192; Stats.2012, c. 41 (S.B.1021), § 89, eff. June 27, 2012; Stats.2018, c. 36 (A.B.1812), § 31, eff. June 27, 2018; Stats.2020, c. 337 (S.B.823), § 31, eff. Sept. 30, 2020.)*

§ 913. Contracts with custodian

When any person has been adjudged to be a ward or dependent child of the juvenile court, and the court has made an order committing such person to the care of any association, society, or corporation, embracing within its objects the purpose of caring for or obtaining homes for such persons, the county in which such person has been committed may contract with such custodian, for the supervision, investigation, and rehabilitation of such person by such custodian, and may, pursuant to such contract, pay to it an amount determined by mutual agreement, not to exceed the cost to such custodian of such service. *(Added by Stats.1961, c. 1616, p. 3503, § 2.)*

§ 914. Expense for support and maintenance

As used in this article, "expense for support and maintenance" includes the reasonable value of any medical services furnished to the ward or dependent child at the county hospital or at any other county institution, or at any private hospital or by any private physician with the approval of the juvenile court of the county concerned, and the reasonable value of the support of the ward or dependent child at any juvenile hall established pursuant to the provisions of Article 23 (commencing with Section 850) of this chapter or the reasonable value of the ward's support at any forestry camp, juvenile home, ranch, or camp established within or without the county pursuant to the provisions of Article 24 (commencing with Section 880) of this chapter. *(Added by Stats.1961, c. 1616, p. 3503, § 2. Amended by Stats.1976, c. 1068, p. 4798, § 78.)*

ARTICLE 26. WORK FURLOUGHS

Section

§ 925. Counties where article operative; termination

The provisions of this article shall be operative in any county in which the board of supervisors by ordinance finds, on the basis of employment conditions, the state of juvenile detention facilities, and other pertinent circumstances, that the operation of this article in that county is feasible. In such ordinance the board shall prescribe whether the probation officer or any official in charge of a county juvenile detention facility shall perform the functions of the juvenile work furlough administrator. The board of supervisors may also terminate the operativeness of this article in the county if it finds by ordinance that, because of changed circumstances, the operation of this article in that county is no longer feasible. *(Added by Stats.1967, c. 1070, p. 2701, § 1.)*

Cross References

Administration of juvenile homes, ranches, and camps, see Welfare and Institutions Code § 881.
County boards of supervisors generally, see Government Code §§ 25000, 25003 et seq.
Probation officer or social worker defined for purposes of this Chapter, see Welfare and Institutions Code § 215.

§ 926. Continuation of employment; new employment; conditions

When a minor is adjudged a ward of the juvenile court and committed to a county juvenile home, ranch, camp, or forestry camp, the juvenile work furlough administrator may, if he concludes that such person is a fit subject therefor, direct that such person be permitted to continue in his regular employment, if that is compatible with the requirements of Section 928, or may authorize the person to secure employment for himself in the county, unless the court at the time of commitment has ordered that such person not be granted work furloughs. *(Added by Stats.1967, c. 1070, p. 2701, § 1.)*

Cross References

Work provisions relating to wards generally, see Welfare and Institutions Code § 883.

§ 927. Arrangement for and nature of employment; wage rate; labor dispute

(a) If the juvenile work furlough administrator so directs that the minor be permitted to continue in his or her regular employment, the administrator shall arrange for a continuation of that employment when possible without interruption. If the minor does not have regular employment, and the administrator has authorized the minor to secure employment for himself or herself, the minor may do so, and the administrator may assist the minor in doing so. Any employment so secured must be suitable for the minor and must be at a wage at least as high as the prevailing wage for similar work in the area where the work is performed and in accordance with the prevailing working conditions in the area. In no event may any employment be permitted where there is a labor dispute in the establishment in which the minor is, or is to be, employed.

(b) If the minor does not have regular employment, the juvenile work furlough administrator may authorize the minor to apply for placement in a local job training program, and the administrator may assist him or her in doing so. The program may include, but shall not be limited to, job training assistance as provided through the Job Training Partnership Act (Public Law 97–300; 29 U.S.C.A. Sec. 1501 et seq.). *(Added by Stats.1967, c. 1070, p. 2701, § 1. Amended by Stats.1989, c. 48, § 2.)*

Cross References

Employment of minors generally, see Labor Code § 1285 et seq.
Minimum wages, general welfare of employees, see Const. Art. 14, § 1.
Payment of less than minimum wage unlawful, see Labor Code § 1197.

§ 928. Confinement periods

Whenever the minor is not employed and between the hours or periods of employment, he shall be confined in a juvenile detention facility unless the court or administrator directs otherwise. *(Added by Stats.1967, c. 1070, p. 2701, § 1.)*

§ 929. Earnings

The earnings of the minor shall be collected by the juvenile work furlough administrator, and it shall be the duty of the minor's employer to transmit such wages to the administrator at the latter's request. Earnings levied upon pursuant to Chapter 5 (commencing with Section 706.010) of Division 2 of Title 9 of Part 2 of the Code of Civil Procedure shall not be transmitted to the administrator. If the administrator has requested transmittal of earnings prior to levy, such request shall have priority. When an employer transmits such earnings to the administrator pursuant to this section the employer shall have no liability to the minor for such earnings. From such earnings the administrator shall pay the minor's board and personal expenses, both inside and outside the juvenile detention facility, and shall deduct so much of the costs of administration of this article as is allocable to such minor. If sufficient funds are available after making the foregoing payments, the administrator may, with the consent of the minor, pay, in whole or in part, the preexisting debts of the minor. Any balance shall be retained until the minor's discharge and thereupon shall be paid to the minor. *(Added by Stats.1967, c. 1070, p. 2701, § 1. Amended by Stats.1968, c. 218, p. 524, § 2; Stats.1982, c. 497, § 181, operative July 1, 1983.)*

Law Revision Commission Comments

Section 929 is amended to supply a cross-reference to the provisions governing wage garnishment which are the exclusive provisions governing the levy on earnings. The reference to attachment is deleted because wages may not be levied upon before judgment. See Code Civ.Proc. § 487.020(c) [16 Cal.L.Rev. Comm. Reports 1001].

Cross References

Payment of wages generally, see Labor Code § 200 et seq.
Probation officers, receipt, deposit and disbursement of monies, see Welfare and Institutions Code § 276.
Support of wards and dependent children generally, see Welfare and Institutions Code § 900 et seq.

§ 930. Violations; termination of work furlough

In the event the minor violates the conditions laid down for his conduct, custody, or employment, the juvenile work furlough administrator may order termination of work furloughs for such minor. *(Added by Stats.1967, c. 1070, p. 2701, § 1.)*

ARTICLE 27. 24–HOUR SCHOOLS

§ 940. Establishment and maintenance; purpose; costs

The board of supervisors in every county may provide and maintain, at the expense of the county, in a location approved by the judge of the juvenile court, or in counties having more than one judge of the juvenile court, by the presiding judge of the juvenile court, a 24–hour school or a nonresidential boot camp school program operated by the probation officer. The school shall be established to provide education and training for minors in accordance with the provisions of Article 1 (commencing with Section 48600) of Chapter 4 of Part 27 of the Education Code. The cost of providing education and training for the students shall be computed pursuant to the provisions of Section 893. *(Added by Stats.1967, c. 1542, p. 3675, § 18. Amended by Stats.1978, c. 380, p. 1214, § 169; Stats.1995, c. 72 (S.B.604), § 7.)*

Cross References

Probation officer or social worker defined for purposes of this Chapter, see Welfare and Institutions Code § 215.

§ 941. Management and control

The 24–hour school or a nonresidential boot camp school program shall be under the management and control of the probation officer. *(Added by Stats.1967, c. 1542, p. 3675, § 18. Amended by Stats.1995, c. 72 (S.B.604), § 8.)*

Cross References

Probation officer or social worker defined for purposes of this Chapter, see Welfare and Institutions Code § 215.

Probation officers generally, see Welfare and Institutions Code § 270 et seq.

§ 942. Superintendent and employees; employment; salaries

The board of supervisors shall provide for a suitable superintendent to have charge of the 24-hour school, and for such other employees as may be needed for its efficient management, and shall provide for payment, out of the general fund of the county, of suitable salaries for such superintendent and other employees. *(Added by Stats.1967, c. 1542, p. 3675, § 18.)*

Cross References

Employment of personnel, twenty-four hour elementary schools, see Education Code § 48603.

Twenty-four hour elementary schools, residence of superintendent and employment of personnel, see Education Code § 48604.

§ 943. Appointment and removal of superintendent and employees

The superintendent and other employees of the 24-hour school shall be appointed by the probation officer, pursuant to a civil service or merit system, and may be removed, for cause, pursuant to such system. *(Added by Stats.1967, c. 1542, p. 3675, § 18.)*

Cross References

Probation officer or social worker defined for purposes of this Chapter, see Welfare and Institutions Code § 215.

§ 944. Classified list of expenses, filing

The probation officer shall keep a classified list of expenses for the operation of the 24-hour school and shall file a duplicate copy with the county board of supervisors. *(Added by Stats.1967, c. 1542, p. 3675, § 18.)*

Cross References

Probation officer or social worker defined for purposes of this Chapter, see Welfare and Institutions Code § 215.

§ 945. Licensing of 24-hour schools

A 24-hour school shall be considered a children's institution for licensing purposes and shall be licensed by the department of social welfare of the county in which the 24-hour school is located. *(Added by Stats.1967, c. 1542, p. 3675, § 18.)*

ARTICLE 28. ADJUSTMENT SCHOOLS

Section

§ 960. Construction of article; powers of governing board

This article shall be construed in conformity with the intent as well as the expressed provisions thereof, and the governing board of any adjustment school may do all those lawful acts that it deems necessary to promote the prosperity of the adjustment school, or to promote the well-being and education of all minors entrusted to its charge. *(Added by Stats.1987, c. 1452, § 534.)*

§ 961. Statutes governing proceedings

The terms and provisions of Article 25 (commencing with Section 900) of Chapter 2 of Part 1 of Division 2 and Section 579 shall, so far as applicable, govern and control proceedings under this article. *(Added by Stats.1987, c. 1452, § 534.)*

§ 962. Establishment; ages; purpose

The boards of supervisors or other governing bodies of counties and cities and counties may organize, establish, equip, and maintain, including the purchase of suitable sites and the construction of suitable buildings, adjustment schools in each county or city and county for the purpose of furnishing to minors under the age of 18 years pursuant to this article, care, custody, education, training, and adjustment to good citizenship, which shall be continuous and uninterrupted during the period the minors remain in school. *(Added by Stats.1987, c. 1452, § 534.)*

§ 963. Joint establishment by two or more counties

The boards of supervisors of two or more counties may by regularly adopted resolutions or ordinances duly entered on the minutes or proceedings of their respective boards, unite in the organization, establishment, equipment, and maintenance of adjustment schools for the respective counties. In that event, the schools shall be located in one or more of the counties as shall be mutually agreed upon and designated in the resolutions or ordinances. *(Added by Stats.1987, c. 1452, § 534.)*

§ 964. Governing board; school organized by one county or city and county

If adjustment schools are organized by only one county or city and county, the government and management shall be vested in a governing board which shall be either the board of education, or similar school governing body, or the county probation committee of the juvenile court, or a board of trustees composed of seven members selected from both the board of education and the probation committee, as may be determined or chosen in the exercise of sound discretion by the board of supervisors or other governing body of the county or city and county. *(Added by Stats.1987, c. 1452, § 534.)*

§ 965. Governing board; school organized by two or more counties

If the adjustment schools are organized by the joint action of two or more counties, the boards of supervisors of the counties may by concerted action by duly adopted resolutions entrust the government and management to a governing board, which shall be any of the following:

(a) The board of education of the county in which at least one adjustment school is located.

(b) The probation committee of the juvenile court of the county in which at least one adjustment school is located.

(c) A board of trustees composed of seven members who shall represent all of the counties and each of whom may be selected from either the county board of education or the probation committee of the juvenile court of his or her respective county as shall be determined in the joint resolutions of the boards of supervisors. *(Added by Stats.1987, c. 1452, § 534.)*

§ 966. Term of office of trustees

If a board of trustees is chosen to govern and manage the adjustment school the term of office of the trustees shall be six years, except that of the seven trustees first selected, two shall hold office for two years, two shall hold office for four years, and three shall hold office for six years. Each of the two-, four-, and six-year terms shall be assigned by lot to each of the seven trustees. *(Added by Stats.1987, c. 1452, § 534.)*

§ 967. Rules and regulations; governing board duties

The governing board shall make all needful rules and regulations for the transaction of business and for the management and government of the adjustment school under its jurisdiction, and it shall see that proper care, custody, education, and training are provided for the minors under its care, to the end that the minors shall be adjusted to good citizenship and prepared to become honorable, self-supporting members of society. *(Added by Stats. 1987, c. 1452, § 534.)*

§ 968. Contracts; appropriation limits

The governing board shall make all contracts for the organization, establishment, including the purchase of a suitable site and the construction of suitable buildings, equipment, operation, and maintenance of the adjustment school that may be necessary or advisable. In no event shall the amount of money appropriated for any such purpose or other limitation prescribed by law or by order of the governing board, be exceeded or violated. *(Added by Stats.1987, c. 1452, § 534.)*

§ 969. Personal interest in contract

No member of the governing board, nor officer, nor employee of any adjustment school shall be interested, personally, directly, or indirectly, in any contract, purchase, or sale made, or in any business carried on in behalf of the school. Any money paid on the contracts or sales may be recovered by a civil suit, and the governing board upon the proof of such interest shall remove from office immediately the member, officer, or employee. *(Added by Stats.1987, c. 1452, § 534.)*

§ 970. Superintendent; appointment; qualifications; tenure

The governing board of the adjustment school shall appoint a superintendent, not of its own number, who shall be a person qualified by training and experience for the character of work to be performed at the adjustment school, and who shall hold office at the pleasure of the governing board. *(Added by Stats.1987, c. 1452, § 534.)*

§ 971. Officers and employees; salaries

The governing board shall determine the number, title, duties, and terms of office of all other officers and employees and shall fix their salaries, and that of the superintendent. *(Added by Stats.1987, c. 1452, § 534.)*

§ 972. Superintendent; oath; bond

The superintendent of the adjustment school shall, before entering upon the discharge of his or her duties, make and file with the governing board an oath that he or she will faithfully and impartially discharge his or her duties. The superintendent shall also file with the governing board a bond, running to the State of California in a sum the board may determine, and with sureties to be approved by the board, conditioned upon the faithful performance of his or her duties. The premium of the bond shall be a part of the cost of maintaining the adjustment school. *(Added by Stats.1987, c. 1452, § 534.)*

§ 973. Superintendent; custody of property; accounting

The superintendent, after making and filing the bond, shall, subject to the direction of the governing board, be invested with the custody of the lands, buildings, and all other property pertaining to or under the control of the adjustment school. The superintendent shall account to the governing board in the manner it may require for all property entrusted to the superintendent and for all money received by him or her as superintendent of the adjustment school, or for any of the minors entrusted to its care. *(Added by Stats.1987, c. 1452, § 534.)*

§ 974. Superintendent; appointment and supervision of officers and employees

The superintendent shall also, subject to the direction of the governing board, appoint all officers and employees of the adjustment school, who shall hold office at the pleasure of the superintendent. The superintendent shall exercise the supervisory, executive, and managing powers that are conferred upon him or her by the governing board. *(Added by Stats.1987, c. 1452, § 534.)*

§ 975. Residence of superintendent and other officers and employees

The superintendent shall reside in the adjustment school or one of the adjustment schools under his or her jurisdiction and shall be furnished suitable quarters, furniture, food supplies, and laundry for himself or herself and his or her family. The governing board may make similar provision for other officers and employees that the interests of the adjustment school may in its judgment require to reside on the premises. *(Added by Stats.1987, c. 1452, § 534.)*

§ 976. Commitment of minors by court order

The adjustment school shall receive into its care, custody, and control all boys and girls under 18 years of age who are committed to it by order of the juvenile court of the county or city and county maintaining or contributing to the maintenance of the adjustment school. *(Added by Stats.1987, c. 1452, § 534.)*

§ 977. Duration of custody

Any minor who has been committed to the care, custody, and control of any adjustment school shall remain in the school for the duration of the period provided in the order of commitment, or until further order of the juvenile court. *(Added by Stats.1987, c. 1452, § 534.)*

§ 978. Review of commitment order

The juvenile court shall review the order of commitment at least once each year, and upon review the court may continue, terminate, or modify the order of commitment. *(Added by Stats.1987, c. 1452, § 534.)*

§ 979. Revocation of commitment and return of minor to court

If at any time in the opinion of the superintendent of the adjustment school the further detention of the minor is detrimental to the interests of the school, the minor may immediately, upon order of the superintendent, be returned to the committing court, and the court may revoke its previous order, and proceedings may be resumed where they were suspended when the commitment was made. *(Added by Stats.1987, c. 1452, § 534.)*

§ 980. Conduct of school

The governing board of any adjustment school shall cause the school to be conducted as may seem best calculated to carry out the intentions of this article. *(Added by Stats.1987, c. 1452, § 534.)*

§ 981. Course of study

There shall be organized a course of study, corresponding as far as practicable with the course of study in the public schools of the state. *(Added by Stats.1987, c. 1452, § 534.)*

§ 982. Vocational and trade training

There shall be provided in the adjustment school the proper facilities and equipment for vocational and trade training, in addition to other public school education or training that may be determined upon by the governing board. Vocational or trade training education shall be given to each minor while under the care of the adjustment school, to the end that he or she may upon discharge be qualified for honorable and self-supporting employment. *(Added by Stats.1987, c. 1452, § 534.)*

§ 983. Order for support and maintenance of minor

Any order of the juvenile court committing a minor to the care, custody, and control of an adjustment school may provide the expense of his or her support and maintenance by directing that the expense be paid in whole or in part by his or her parent, guardian, or other person liable for his or her support and maintenance. *(Added by Stats.1987, c. 1452, § 534.)*

§ 984. Expense; school organized by one county or city and county

If the adjustment school is organized, established, equipped, and maintained by only one county or city and county, the entire expense of the school shall be borne by the county or city and county, and the board of supervisors, or other governing body of the county or city and county shall make due and annual provision therefor. The necessary items of expense shall be set forth in the annual budget of the county or city and county. *(Added by Stats.1987, c. 1452, § 534.)*

§ 985. Initial expense; school organized by two or more counties

If an adjustment school is organized, established, equipped, and maintained by two or more counties, the initial expense of organizing, establishing, and equipping the school shall be apportioned between each of the counties on a pro rata basis in the ratio that the number of children of school age residing in each county bears to the number of children of school age residing in all of the counties. *(Added by Stats.1987, c. 1452, § 534.)*

§ 986. Maintenance expense; school organized by two or more counties

The annual expense of maintaining the school by two or more counties, shall be apportioned between the counties on a pro rata basis in the ratio that the average daily enrollment of minors placed in the school from each county during the preceding year bears to the total average daily enrollment in the school from all of the counties during the year. *(Added by Stats.1987, c. 1452, § 534.)*

§ 987. Bond of officers

The governing board shall require any officer entrusted with money belonging to an adjustment school or to any of the minors entrusted to its care, or any officer placed in a position of trust and responsibility in the custody of property or in the handling of supplies belonging to the school, to file with the board a bond with sureties approved by the board and in a sum that it may determine, conditioned upon the faithful performance of the duties required, and upon the faithful accounting of all money and property coming into his or her hands or under his or her control by virtue of his or her office. The premiums on the bonds shall be a part of the cost of maintaining the adjustment school. *(Added by Stats.1987, c. 1452, § 534.)*

CHAPTER 3. INSTITUTIONS FOR DELINQUENTS

ARTICLE 1. ESTABLISHMENT AND GENERAL GOVERNMENT

Section

§ 1000. Jurisdiction

Commencing July 1, 2005, any reference to the Department of the Youth Authority refers to the Department of Corrections and Rehabilitation, Division of Juvenile Facilities, which has jurisdiction over all educational training and treatment institutions now or hereafter established and maintained in the state as correctional schools for the reception of wards of the juvenile court and other persons committed to the department. *(Stats.1937, c. 369, p. 1056, § 1000. Amended by Stats.1943, c. 481, p. 2021, § 26; Stats.1957, c. 311, p. 955, § 1; Gov.Reorg.Plan No. 1 of 2005, § 69, eff. May 5, 2005, operative July 1, 2005; Stats.2005, c. 10 (S.B.737), § 72, eff. May 10, 2005, operative July 1, 2005.)*

Cross References

Department of Corrections, generally, see Penal Code § 5000 et seq.
Department of Corrections and Rehabilitation, see Government Code § 12838 et seq.
Youth Authority, powers and duties, etc., see Welfare and Institutions Code §§ 1710 et seq., 1750 et seq.

§ 1000.1. Regional centers; development; programs and services provided; joint development

In order to provide counties with alternative placement options, the Department of the Youth Authority is authorized to establish, maintain, or facilitate the development of regional centers, which may be available on a contract basis to counties for the placement of wards. The regional centers, depending on the services needed, may provide, but are not limited to, the following: mental health programs, short-term incarceration and treatment services, and boot camp programs. This section shall not be interpreted to prohibit counties from jointly developing regional centers. *(Added by Stats. 1994, c. 452 (S.B.1539), § 1.)*

§ 1000.5. Whittier State School renamed

Where in any law of this State the name "Whittier State School" appears it shall hereafter be understood to mean and shall be construed to refer to Fred C. Nelles School for Boys. *(Formerly § 155.5, added by Stats.1941, c. 1266, p. 3212, § 1. Renumbered § 1000.5 and amended by Stats.1943, c. 481, p. 2021, § 27.)*

§ 1000.7. "Youth Authority", "authority", "the authority" and "board" defined

As used in this chapter, "Youth Authority," "authority," and "the authority" mean and refer to the Department of the Youth Authority, and "board" means and refers to the Youth Authority Board. *(Added by Stats.1945, c. 639, p. 1183, § 20. Amended by Stats.1979, c. 860, p. 2973, § 9; Stats.2003, c. 4 (S.B.459), § 4, eff. April 8, 2003, operative Jan. 1, 2004; Stats.2004, c. 183 (A.B.3082), § 372.)*

Cross References

Authority of court to order commitment to Youth Authority, see Welfare and Institutions Code § 731.
Changing, modifying or setting aside order of commitment to Youth Authority, authority of court, see Welfare and Institutions Code § 779.
Youth Authority, generally, see Welfare and Institutions Code § 1700 et seq.
Youth Authority Board, composition and appointment, see Welfare and Institutions Code § 1716.

§ 1001. Government and supervision

The general government and supervision of each such institution is vested in the Youth Authority. *(Stats.1937, c. 369, p. 1056, § 1001. Amended by Stats.1943, c. 481, p. 2021, § 28.)*

Cross References

"Youth Authority", "authority", and "the authority" as meaning and referring to the Department of the Youth Authority, see Welfare and Institutions Code § 1000.7.
Youth Authority, powers of, see Welfare and Institutions Code § 1750 et seq.

§ 1001.5. Bringing or sending contraband into grounds of or possession in Youth Authority institutions; punishment

(a) Except when authorized by law, or when authorized by the person in charge of an institution or camp administered by the Youth Authority, or by an officer of the institution or camp empowered by the person in charge of the institution or camp to give that authorization, any person who knowingly brings or sends into, or who knowingly assists in bringing into, or sending into, any institution or camp, or the grounds belonging to any institution or camp, administered by the Youth Authority, or any person who, while confined in the institution or camp knowingly possesses therein, any controlled substance, the possession of which is prohibited by Division 10 (commencing with Section 11000) of the Health and Safety Code; any alcoholic beverage; any firearm, weapon or explosive of any kind; or any tear gas or tear gas weapon shall be punished by imprisonment in a county jail for not more than one year or by imprisonment pursuant to subdivision (h) of Section 1170 of the Penal Code.

(b) Except as otherwise authorized in the manner provided in subdivision (a), any person who knowingly uses tear gas or uses a tear gas weapon in any institution or camp specified in subdivision (a) is guilty of a felony.

(c) This section shall not be construed to preclude or in any way limit the applicability of any other law proscribing a course of conduct also proscribed by this section. *(Added by Stats.1972, c. 497, p. 868, § 3. Amended by Stats.1976, c. 1139, p. 5173, § 343, operative July 1, 1977; Stats.1984, c. 1635, § 97; Stats.1985, c. 515, § 2; Stats.2011, c. 15 (A.B.109), § 618, eff. April 4, 2011, operative Oct. 1, 2011.)*

Cross References

Felonies, definition and penalties, see Penal Code §§ 17, 18.
"Youth Authority", "authority", and "the authority" as meaning and referring to the Department of the Youth Authority, see Welfare and Institutions Code § 1000.7.

Research References

2 Witkin, California Criminal Law 4th Crimes Against Public Peace and Welfare § 161 (2021), Bringing Controlled Substances to Prisoners.
2 Witkin, California Criminal Law 4th Crimes Against Public Peace and Welfare § 362 (2021), Furnishing Liquor to Specified Persons.

§ 1001.7. Youth Authority institutions; ex-convicts coming upon or near grounds in nighttime; refusal to leave

Every person who, having been previously convicted of a felony and confined in any state prison in this state, without the consent of the officer in charge of any California Youth Authority institution comes upon the grounds of any such institution, or lands belonging or adjacent thereto, in the nighttime, and who refuses or fails to leave upon being requested to do so by an employee of the institution, is guilty of a misdemeanor. *(Added by Stats.1972, c. 497, p. 869, § 4.)*

Cross References

Felony, misdemeanor, definitions and classification, see Penal Code § 17.
"Youth Authority", "authority", and "the authority" as meaning and referring to the Department of the Youth Authority, see Welfare and Institutions Code § 1000.7.

Research References

3 Witkin, California Criminal Law 4th Punishment § 93 (2021), Institutions and Facilities.

§ 1002. Powers of authority

The Youth Authority may do all lawful acts which it deems necessary to effectuate the purposes for which such schools are established, and to promote the well-being, education and reformation of the inmates thereof; but the authority shall not incur any indebtedness in excess of the moneys appropriated or otherwise made available for the use of such schools. *(Stats.1937, c. 369, p. 1056, § 1002. Amended by Stats.1943, c. 481, p. 2021, § 29.)*

Cross References

"Youth Authority", "authority", and "the authority" as meaning and referring to the Department of the Youth Authority, see Welfare and Institutions Code § 1000.7.
Youth Authority, powers of, see Welfare and Institutions Code § 1750 et seq.

§ 1003. Control of property

The authority shall have charge of the land, buildings, apparatus, tools, stock, provisions and other property belonging to each such institution. *(Stats.1937, c. 369, p. 1056, § 1003. Amended by Stats.1943, c. 481, p. 2021, § 30.)*

Cross References

"Youth Authority", "authority", and "the authority" as meaning and referring to the Department of the Youth Authority, see Welfare and Institutions Code § 1000.7.

§ 1004. Custody of persons committed

The authority shall have charge of the persons committed to or confined in each such institution, and shall provide for their care, supervision, education, training, employment, discipline, and government. It shall exercise its powers toward the correction of their faults, the development of their characters, and the promotion of their welfare. *(Stats.1937, c. 369, p. 1056, § 1004. Amended by Stats.1943, c. 481, p. 2021, § 31.)*

Cross References

"Youth Authority", "authority", and "the authority" as meaning and referring to the Department of the Youth Authority, see Welfare and Institutions Code § 1000.7.

Research References

3 Witkin, California Criminal Law 4th Punishment § 243 (2021), Corporal Punishment and Discipline.

§ 1006. Land for Preston School of Industry

The land purchased for the site of Preston School of Industry shall be used exclusively for the occupancy and purposes of the school. *(Stats.1937, c. 369, p. 1056, § 1006.)*

Cross References

Preston School of Industry,
Game refuge, see Fish and Game Code § 10841.
Inmates as road laborers, see Welfare and Institutions Code § 1125.5.

§ 1009. Return of nonresidents to state of residence

The Department of the Youth Authority may order the return of nonresident persons committed to the department or confined in institutions or facilities subject to the jurisdiction of the department to the states in which they have legal residence. Whenever any public officer, other than an officer or employee of the department, receives from any private source any moneys to defray the cost of that transportation, he or she shall immediately transmit the moneys to the department. All moneys, together with any moneys received directly by the department from private sources for transportation of nonresidents, shall be deposited by the department in the State Treasury, in augmentation of the current appropriation for the support of the department. *(Added by Stats.1943, c. 481, p. 2022, § 35. Amended by Stats.1945, c. 1280, p. 2406, § 1; Stats.1979, c. 860, p. 2973, § 10; Stats.2003, c. 4 (S.B.459), § 5, eff. April 8, 2003, operative Jan. 1, 2004.)*

Cross References

Interstate compact on juveniles, see Welfare and Institutions Code § 1400 et seq.
Residence, determination of place of, see Government Code § 244.
Return of nonresidents by Department of Mental Health, see Welfare and Institutions Code § 4119.

§ 1009.1. Refund of money not used to return nonresidents to other states

When, pursuant to Section 1009, money is received by the Department of the Youth Authority from private sources to defray the cost of transportation for the return of a nonresident committed to it and the nonresident is not returned or the money received exceeds the cost of such transportation, the department shall refund to such private sources such money or such excess money, as the case may be. *(Added by Stats.1968, c. 60, p. 207, § 1, eff. April 30, 1968.)*

§ 1009.2. Payment of refund; conditions

The fiscal officer of the Department of the Youth Authority shall make payment of any refund pursuant to Section 1009.1 if the Director of the Youth Authority prepares a voucher which sets forth the facts which pertain to the refund and authorizes its payment. *(Added by Stats.1968, c. 60, p. 207, § 2, eff. April 30, 1968.)*

§ 1009.3. Refund of moneys deposited in State Treasury

If any money which is to be refunded has been deposited in the State Treasury, the State Controller, upon receipt of a claim which is filed by the Department of the Youth Authority, shall draw his warrant for the payment of the refund from the fund to which the money was credited. *(Added by Stats.1968, c. 60, p. 207, § 3, eff. April 30, 1968.)*

Cross References

State Controller, generally, see Government Code § 12402 et seq.
Warrants, form, procedure, see Government Code § 17000 et seq.

§ 1009.4. Sums less than $3; retention; refund on demand

If the Director of the Youth Authority finds that the amount of any refund is less than three dollars ($3), he may retain such amount, unless demand for the payment of such refund is made within six months after the determination that a refund is due. If such demand is made, the refund shall be paid. *(Added by Stats.1968, c. 60, p. 207, § 4, eff. April 30, 1968.)*

Cross References

"Youth Authority", "authority", and "the authority" as meaning and referring to the Department of the Youth Authority, see Welfare and Institutions Code § 1000.7.

§ 1010. Determination of residence

In determining residence for purposes of transportation, a person who has lived continuously in this State for a period of one year and who has not acquired a residence in another State by living continuously therein for at least one year subsequent to his residence in this State shall be deemed to be a resident of this State. Time spent in a public institution or on parole therefrom shall not be counted in determining the matter of residence in this or another State. In determining the residence of a ward of the juvenile court committed to the Youth Authority or confined in any institution under its jurisdiction, due consideration shall be given to the residence of the parents of such ward, and if either one or both parents of the ward are residents of this State the ward shall also be deemed a resident of this State. *(Added by Stats.1943, c. 481, p. 2022, § 36.)*

Cross References

Interstate compact on juveniles, see Welfare and Institutions Code § 1400 et seq.
Paroles and dismissals, generally, see Welfare and Institutions Code § 1176 et seq.
Residence,
Determination of place of, see Government Code § 244.
Minors, ward or conservatee, see Welfare and Institutions Code § 17.1; Family Code § 7501; Probate Code §§ 2351.5, 2352.
"Youth Authority", "authority", and "the authority" as meaning and referring to the Department of the Youth Authority, see Welfare and Institutions Code § 1000.7.

§ 1011. Expenses of returning wards to and from state

All expenses incurred in returning these persons to other states shall be paid by this state, but the expense of returning residents of this state shall be borne by the states making the returns.

The cost and expense incurred in effecting the transportation of these persons shall be paid from the funds appropriated for that purpose, or, if necessary, from the money appropriated for the care of these persons. *(Added by Stats.1943, c. 481, p. 2022, § 37. Amended by Stats.1996, c. 320 (A.B.2160), § 42.)*

Cross References

California Victim Compensation and Government Claims Board, see Government Code § 13900 et seq.
Interstate compact on juveniles, see Welfare and Institutions Code § 1400 et seq.

§ 1015. Disposition of unclaimed personal property; death

Whenever any person confined in any state institution subject to the jurisdiction of the Youth Authority dies, and any personal funds or property of such person remains in the hands of the Director of the Youth Authority, and no demand is made upon said director by the owner of the funds or property or his legally appointed representative, all money and other personal property of such decedent remaining in the custody or possession of the Director of the Youth Authority shall be held by him for a period of one year from the date of death of the decedent, for the benefit of the heirs, legatees, or successors in interest of such decedent.

Upon the expiration of said one-year period, any money remaining unclaimed in the custody or possession of the director shall be delivered by him to the State Treasurer for deposit in the Unclaimed Property Fund under the provisions of Article 1 of Chapter 6 of Title 10 of Part 3 of the Code of Civil Procedure.[1]

Upon the expiration of said one-year period, all personal property and documents of the decedent, other than cash, remaining unclaimed in the custody or possession of the director shall be disposed of as follows:

(a) All deeds, contracts or assignments shall be filed by the director with the public administrator of the county of commitment of the decedent;

(b) All other personal property shall be sold by the director at public auction, or upon a sealed-bid basis, and the proceeds of the sale delivered by him to the State Treasurer in the same manner as is herein provided with respect to unclaimed money of the decedent. If he deems it expedient to do so, the director may accumulate the property of several decedents and sell the property in such lots as he may determine, provided that he makes a determination as to each decedent's share of the proceeds;

(c) If any personal property of the decedent is not salable at public auction, or upon a sealed-bid basis, or if it has no intrinsic value, or if its value is not sufficient to justify the deposit of such property in the State Treasury, the director may order it destroyed;

(d) All other unclaimed personal property of the decedent not disposed of as provided in paragraphs (a), (b), or (c) hereof, shall be delivered by the director to the State Controller for deposit in the State Treasury under the provisions of Article 1 of Chapter 6 of Title 10 of Part 3 of the Code of Civil Procedure. *(Added by Stats.1943, c. 481, p. 2023, § 39. Amended by Stats.1945, c. 639, p. 1183, § 22; Stats.1951, c. 1708, p. 3980, § 51; Stats.1955, c. 192, p. 661, § 4; Stats.1961, c. 1962, p. 4135, § 6.)*

[1] Code of Civil Procedure § 1440 et seq.

Cross References

Deceased prisoner, property deemed delivered under unclaimed property law, see Code of Civil Procedure § 1448.
Establishing fact of death, see Probate Code § 200 et seq.
Notice of disposition, see Welfare and Institutions Code § 1017.
Persons entitled to distribution, determination of, see Probate Code § 11700.
Property of inmates, lien for safekeeping after death, escape, discharge, or parole, see Government Code § 6600 et seq.
Schedule of property, see Welfare and Institutions Code § 1018.
State Controller, generally, see Government Code § 12402 et seq.
State Treasurer, generally, see Government Code § 12302 et seq.
Succession, generally, see Probate Code § 6400 et seq.
Suits against state for destroyed property, see Welfare and Institutions Code § 1019.
Unclaimed property, see Code of Civil Procedure §§ 1300, 1500 et seq.; Government Code § 13470; Penal Code § 5061 et seq.; Probate Code §§ 6800 et seq., 7643, 11428, 11854; Welfare and Institutions Code § 4126 et seq.
"Youth Authority", "authority", and "the authority" as meaning and referring to the Department of the Youth Authority, see Welfare and Institutions Code § 1000.7.

§ 1016. Disposition of unclaimed personal property; escape, discharge, or parole

(a) Whenever a person confined in a state institution subject to the jurisdiction of the Department of Corrections and Rehabilitation, Division of Juvenile Facilities, escapes, or is discharged or paroled from the institution, and any personal funds or property of that person remains in the hands of the Director of the Division of Juvenile Justice in the Department of Corrections and Rehabilitation, and no demand is made upon the director by the owner of the funds or property or his or her legally appointed representative, all money and other intangible personal property of that person, other than deeds, contracts, or assignments, remaining in the custody or possession of the director shall be held by him or her for a period of three years from the date of that escape, discharge, or parole, for the benefit of the person or his or her successors in interest. However, unclaimed personal funds or property of paroled minors may be exempted from the provisions of this section during the period of their minority and for a period of one year thereafter, at the discretion of the director.

(b) Upon the expiration of this three-year period, any money and other intangible personal property, other than deeds, contracts or assignments, remaining unclaimed in the custody or possession of the director shall be subject to the provisions of Chapter 7 (commencing with Section 1500) of Title 10 of Part 3 of the Code of Civil Procedure.

(c) Upon the expiration of one year from the date of the escape, discharge, or parole:

(1) All deeds, contracts, or assignments shall be filed by the director with the public administrator of the county of commitment of that person.

(2) All tangible personal property other than money, remaining unclaimed in his or her custody or possession, shall be sold by the director at public auction, or upon a sealed-bid basis, and the proceeds of the sale shall be held by him or her subject to the provisions of Section 1752.8 of this code, and subject to the provisions of Chapter 7 (commencing with Section 1500) of Title 10 of Part 3 of the Code of Civil Procedure. If he or she deems it expedient to do so, the director may accumulate the property of several inmates and may sell the property in lots as he or she may determine, provided that he or she makes a determination as to each inmate's share of the proceeds.

(d) If any tangible personal property covered by this section is not salable at public auction or upon a sealed-bid basis, or if it has no intrinsic value, or if its value is not sufficient to justify its retention by the director to be offered for sale at public auction or upon a sealed-bid basis at a later date, the director may order it destroyed. *(Added by Stats.1951, c. 1708, p. 3981, § 52. Amended by Stats.1955, c. 192, p. 662, § 5; Stats.1961, c. 1962, p. 4136, § 7; Stats.2008, c. 88 (A.B.1864), § 1; Stats.2012, c. 41 (S.B.1021), § 90, eff. June 27, 2012.)*

Cross References

Establishing fact of death, see Probate Code § 200 et seq.
Notice of disposition, see Welfare and Institutions Code § 1017.
Paroles and dismissals, see Welfare and Institutions Code § 1176 et seq.
Persons entitled to distribution, determination of, see Probate Code § 11700.
Schedule of property, see Welfare and Institutions Code § 1018.
Succession, generally, see Probate Code § 6400 et seq.
"Youth Authority", "authority", and "the authority" as meaning and referring to the Department of the Youth Authority, see Welfare and Institutions Code § 1000.7.

§ 1017. Notice of disposition

Before any money or other personal property or documents are delivered to the State Treasurer, State Controller, or public administrator, or sold at auction or upon a sealed-bid basis, or destroyed, under the provisions of Section 1015, and before any personal property or documents are delivered to the public administrator, or sold at auction or upon a sealed-bid basis, or destroyed, under the provisions of Section 1016, of this code, notice of said intended disposition shall be posted at least 30 days prior to the disposition, in a public place at the institution where the disposition is to be made, and a copy of such notice shall be mailed to the last known address of the owner or deceased owner, at least 30 days prior to such disposition. The notice prescribed by this section need not specifically describe each item of property to be disposed of. *(Added by Stats.1951, c. 1708, p. 3982, § 53. Amended by Stats.1955, c. 192, p. 663, § 6; Stats.1961, c. 1962, p. 4137, § 8.)*

Cross References

State Controller, generally, see Government Code § 12402 et seq.
State Treasurer, generally, see Government Code § 12302 et seq.

§ 1018. Schedule of property

At the time of delivering any money or other personal property to the State Treasurer or State Controller under the provisions of Section 1015 or of Chapter 7 of Title 10 of Part 3 of the Code of Civil Procedure,[1] the director shall deliver to the State Controller a schedule setting forth a statement and description of all money and other personal property delivered, and the name and last known address of the owner or deceased owner. *(Added by Stats.1951, c. 1708, p. 3983, § 54. Amended by Stats.1955, c. 192, p. 663, § 6.5; Stats.1961, c. 1962, p. 4137, § 9.)*

[1] Code of Civil Procedure § 1500 et seq.

Cross References

State Controller, generally, see Government Code § 12402 et seq.
State Treasurer, generally, see Government Code § 12302 et seq.
Unclaimed Property Law, see Code of Civil Procedure § 1500 et seq.

§ 1019. Limitation of actions for destroyed property

When any personal property has been destroyed as provided in Section 1015 or 1016, no suit shall thereafter be maintained by any person against the State or any officer thereof for or on account of such property. *(Added by Stats.1951, c. 1708, p. 3983, § 55.)*

Cross References

Claims against state, generally, see Government Code § 810 et seq.

§ 1020. Retroactive application

Notwithstanding any other provision of law, the provisions of Sections 1015 and 1016 shall apply (1) to all money and other personal property delivered to the State Treasurer or State Controller prior to the effective date of said sections, which would have been subject to the provisions thereof if they had been in effect on the date of such delivery; and (2) to all money and personal property delivered to the State Treasurer or State Controller prior to the effective date of the 1961 amendments to said sections, as said provisions would have applied on the date of such delivery if, on said date of delivery, the provisions of Chapter 1809, Statutes of 1959, had not been in effect. *(Added by Stats.1951, c. 1708, pp. 3933, 3983, § 56. Amended by Stats.1961, c. 1962, p. 4137, § 10.)*

Cross References

State Controller, generally, see Government Code § 12402 et seq.
State Treasurer, generally, see Government Code § 12302 et seq.

ARTICLE 3. SUPERINTENDENTS

§ 1049. Appointment, duties, compensation

Subject to the provisions of law relating to the State civil service, the Youth Authority may appoint, define the duties, and fix the salary of the superintendent or executive officer of each institution under this chapter. *(Added by Stats.1943, c. 481, p. 2024, § 41.)*

Cross References

Appointment of officers and employees, see Welfare and Institutions Code § 1254.
Employment and discharge, see Welfare and Institutions Code § 1752.
Requirements for filling a vacancy for superintendent, see Penal Code § 6126.6.
State civil service, generally, see Government Code § 18500.
"Youth Authority", "authority", and "the authority" as meaning and referring to the Department of the Youth Authority, see Welfare and Institutions Code § 1000.7.
Youth Authority, powers and duties, see Welfare and Institutions Code § 1750 et seq.

§ 1050. Qualifications

The superintendent of the institutions under this chapter shall be persons of high moral character, specially qualified for the position. *(Stats.1937, c. 369, p. 1057, § 1050. Amended by Stats.1943, c. 481, p. 2024, § 42; Stats.1975, c. 1129, p. 2775, § 4.)*

ARTICLE 4. EMPLOYEES

§ 1075. Appointment; compensation

The Youth Authority shall, in accordance with law, appoint all officers and employees required at the institutions under this chapter, and shall fix their remuneration. *(Stats.1937, c. 369, p. 1058, § 1075. Amended by Stats.1943, c. 481, p. 2024, § 43.)*

Cross References

Employment and discharge of personnel, see Welfare and Institutions Code § 1752.
"Youth Authority", "authority", and "the authority" as meaning and referring to the Department of the Youth Authority, see Welfare and Institutions Code § 1000.7.
Youth Authority, powers and duties generally, see Welfare and Institutions Code § 1750 et seq.

§ 1076. Powers of peace officer

The superintendent, assistant superintendent, supervisor, or any employee having custody of wards, of each institution of the Department of the Youth Authority, and any transportation officer of the Department of the Youth Authority, shall have the powers and authority of peace officers listed in Section 830.5 of the Penal Code. *(Stats.1937, c. 369, p. 1058, § 1076. Amended by Stats.1943, c. 481, p. 2024, § 44; Stats.1968, c. 1222, p. 2331, § 77; Stats.1969, c. 645, p. 1297, § 2.)*

Cross References

Arrest, see Penal Code § 833 et seq.
Duties of officer, see Penal Code §§ 818, 821, 822.

Escape, force to prevent, see Penal Code § 835a.
Peace officer, definition, see Penal Code §§ 7, 830 et seq., 852.1.

Research References

4 Witkin, California Criminal Law 4th Pretrial Proceedings § 7 (2021), Other Peace Officers.

§ 1077. Psychologist; license; requirements

(a) Any psychologist employed by or who contracts with the Department of the Youth Authority to provide services to wards under the jurisdiction of the department shall be licensed to practice in this state.

(b) Any psychologist employed by the department on July 1, 1999, shall be exempt from the requirements of subdivision (a), as long as he or she continues employment with the department in the same class.

(c) The requirements of subdivision (a) may be waived in order for a person to gain qualifying expertise for licensure as a psychologist in this state in accordance with Section 1277 of the Health and Safety Code. *(Added by Stats.2000, c. 659 (S.B.2098), § 1.)*

§ 1078. Mental health training; treatment; funding

To the extent that funding is available, the department, in consultation with the State Department of State Hospitals, shall develop training in the treatment of children and adolescents for mental health disorders and shall provide training to all appropriate mental health professionals. *(Added by Stats.2000, c. 659 (S.B.2098), § 2. Amended by Stats.2012, c. 440 (A.B.1488), § 58, eff. Sept. 22, 2012.)*

ARTICLE 6. CONDUCT, EDUCATION, AND DISCIPLINE

§ 1120. Legislative intent; annual assessment of each ward; courses of instruction

(a) It is the intent of the Legislature to insure an appropriate educational program for wards committed to the Department of the Youth Authority. The objective of the program shall be to improve the academic, vocational, and life survival skills of each ward so as to enable these wards to return to the community as productive citizens.

(b) The department shall assess the educational needs of each ward upon commitment and at least annually thereafter until released on parole. The initial assessment shall include a projection of the academic, vocational, and psychological needs of the ward and shall be used both in making a determination as to the appropriate educational program for the ward and as a measure of progress in subsequent assessments of the educational development of the ward.

The educational program of the department shall be responsive to the needs of all wards, including those who are educationally handicapped or limited-English-speaking wards.

(c) The statewide educational program of the department shall include, but shall not be limited to, all of the following courses of instruction:

(1) Academic preparation in the areas of verbal communication skills, reading, writing, and arithmetic.

(2) Vocational preparation including vocational counseling, training in marketable skills, and job placement assistance.

(3) Life survival skills, including preparation in the areas of consumer economics, family life, and personal and social adjustment.

All of the aforementioned courses of instruction shall be offered at each institution within the jurisdiction of the department except camps and those institutions whose primary function is the initial reception and classification of wards. At such camps and institutions the educational program shall take into consideration the purpose and function of the camp and institutional program. *(Added by Stats.1979, c. 981, p. 3353, § 2. Amended by Stats.2004, c. 193 (S.B.111), § 209.)*

Law Revision Commission Comments

Section 1120 is amended to delete reference to an obsolete reporting requirement. The required report was to be completed by February 1, 1980. [33 Cal.L.Rev.Comm. Reports 509 (2004)].

Cross References

Writing defined, see Welfare and Institutions Code § 8.

§ 1120.1. Value-based character education; Superintendent of Education

(a) In furtherance of the purpose of the Department of the Youth Authority to protect society from the consequences of criminal activity, the department's educational programs shall focus on value-based character education, emphasizing curriculum leading to a crime-free lifestyle. In furtherance of this goal, the department shall establish the office of the Superintendent of Education. The Superintendent of Education shall oversee educational programs under the jurisdiction of the department.

(b) The department shall ensure that each ward who has not attained a high school diploma or equivalent shall be enrolled in an appropriate educational program as deemed necessary by the department.

(c) The department shall develop a high school graduation plan for every ward identified pursuant to subdivision (b). *(Added by Stats.1995, c. 317 (S.B.775), § 3. Amended by Stats.1999, c. 996 (S.B.334), § 27.)*

§ 1120.2. Correctional education authority; course of study; standards of proficiency; diplomas; funding

(a) There is in the Department of the Youth Authority a correctional education authority for the purpose of carrying out the education and training of wards committed to the youth authority.

(b) The course of study for wards attending any of grades 7 to 12, inclusive, shall include those courses specified in Article 3 (commencing with Section 51220) of Chapter 2 of Part 28 of the Education Code. The course of study shall meet the model curriculum standards adopted by the Superintendent of Public Instruction pursuant to Section 51226 of the Education Code.

(c)(1) The correctional education authority shall adopt standards of proficiency in basic skills for wards attending a course of study for any of grades 7 to 12, inclusive.

(2) Differential standards and assessment procedures may be adopted for wards for whom an individualized education program has been developed and for whom the regular instructional program has been modified or for wards who have been diagnosed with a learning handicap or disability.

(d) The correctional education authority may issue diplomas of graduation from high school to wards who have completed the required course of study and meet the standards of proficiency in basic skills adopted by the correctional education authority. The authority may also administer to wards the general educational development tests that have been approved by the State Board of Education.

(e) For purposes of receiving federal funds, the correctional education authority shall be deemed a local educational agency.

(f) For purposes of receiving state funds pursuant to subdivision (b) of Section 8 of Article XVI of the California Constitution in accordance with the definitions set forth in Section 41202 of the Education Code, the correctional education authority shall be deemed a state agency and shall only be entitled to state funding for direct instructional services provided to wards attending a course of study. The correctional education authority may not receive state funds unless the funds are specifically appropriated to the Department of the Youth Authority for direct instructional services, and may not receive additional funds from the State Department of Education under any other program. *(Added by Stats.1996, c. 280 (A.B.2131), § 1. Amended by Stats.1999, c. 78 (A.B.1115), § 59, eff. July 7, 1999.)*

§ 1120.5. Division of instruction

At each institution under this chapter the Youth Authority shall organize and maintain a division of instruction and such other divisions as it deems necessary and advisable in the conduct of the school. *(Formerly § 1120, enacted by Stats.1937, c. 369, p. 1058, § 1120. Amended by Stats.1943, c. 481, p. 2024, § 47; Stats.1963, c. 183, p. 922, § 1. Renumbered § 1120.5 and amended by Stats.1979, c. 981, p. 3353, § 1.)*

Cross References

Adjustment schools, see Welfare and Institutions Code § 960 et seq.
State Board of Education, see Education Code § 33000 et seq.
"Youth Authority", "authority", and "the authority" as meaning and referring to the Department of the Youth Authority, see Welfare and Institutions Code § 1000.7.
Youth Authority, powers and duties in general, see Welfare and Institutions Code § 1750 et seq.

§ 1121. Chief of division; training

The chief of each such division of instruction shall be well trained in modern school administration. *(Stats.1937, c. 369, p. 1058, § 1121. Amended by Stats.1963, c. 183, p. 922, § 2.)*

§ 1122. Courses of instruction

Such divisions of instruction shall have jurisdiction over all courses of instruction. Such courses shall include academic and vocational training, and shall be subject to the approval of the State Superintendent of Public Instruction. *(Stats.1937, c. 369, p. 1058, § 1122. Amended by Stats.1963, c. 183, p. 922, § 3; Stats.1965, c. 1634, p. 3729, § 1.)*

Cross References

State Superintendent of Public Instruction, generally, see Education Code §§ 33100, 59203.

§ 1123. Distribution of AIDS and HIV information to inmates

Subject to the availability of adequate state funding for these purposes, the Director of the Youth Authority shall provide all wards at each penal institution within the jurisdiction of the department, including camps, with information about behavior that places a person at high risk for contracting the human immunodeficiency virus (HIV), and about the prevention of transmission of acquired immune deficiency syndrome (AIDS). The director shall provide all wards, who are within one month of release or being placed on parole, with information about agencies and facilities that provide testing, counseling, medical, and support services for AIDS victims. Information about AIDS prevention shall be solicited by the director from the State Department of Health Services, the county health officer, or local agencies providing services to persons with AIDS. The Director of Health Services, or his or her designee, shall approve protocols pertaining to the information to be disseminated, and the training to be provided, under this section. *(Added by Stats.1988, c. 1301, § 3.)*

Cross References

Department of Health Care Services, generally, see Health and Safety Code § 100100 et seq.
"Youth Authority", "authority", and "the authority" as meaning and referring to the Department of the Youth Authority, see Welfare and Institutions Code § 1000.7.

§ 1124. Purpose of instruction

Each institution under this chapter may manufacture, repair, and assemble products or may raise produce, for use in the institution or in any other State institution or for sale to or pursuant to contract with the public. The primary purpose of all instruction, discipline and industries shall be to benefit the inmates of the several schools and to qualify them for honorable employment and good citizenship. Moneys received from sales or contracts made or entered into under this section shall be used first to defray the expenses of the industry, including wages paid to the wards working in the industry. The wages shall be set by the director. Moneys in excess of those used to support the industry shall be deposited in the "Benefit Fund" as defined in Section 1752.5. *(Stats.1937, c. 369, p. 1059, § 1124. Amended by Stats.1943, c. 481, p. 2025, § 48; Stats.1981, c. 540, p. 2155, § 7, eff. Sept. 17, 1981.)*

§ 1125. Retention by inmate of articles of handiwork

Each inmate of an institution under this chapter shall be permitted to keep for his own use all articles of handiwork and other finished products suitable primarily for personal use, as determined by the director, which have been fabricated by the inmate. *(Added by Stats.1959, c. 78, p. 1937, § 1.)*

§ 1125.5. Road labor; inmates of Preston School of Industry

When any public road is a principal means of access to the Preston School of Industry the Department of the Youth Authority, with the consent of the Department of Finance, may arrange with the California Highway Commission or the board of supervisors of the county in which the road is located for the employment of the inmates of the school in the improvement or maintenance of the road, under supervision of the officers of the school and without compensation to the inmates so employed. *(Added by Stats.1955, c. 58, p. 498, § 1.)*

Cross References

Department of Finance, generally, see Government Code § 13000 et seq.
Preston School of Industry,
Game refuge, see Fish and Game Code § 10841.
Land use, see Welfare and Institutions Code § 1006.

ARTICLE 7. ESCAPES

§ 1152. Aiding or attempting to aid escape; penalty

(a) Any person who without the use of force or violence willfully assists any parolee of the Department of the Youth Authority whose parole has been revoked, any escapee, any ward confined to a Department of the Youth Authority institution or facility, or who is being transported to or from that institution or facility, or any person in the lawful custody of any officer or person to escape or in an attempt to escape from a Department of the Youth Authority institution or facility, or custody, is guilty of a misdemeanor.

(b) Any person who with the use of force or violence willfully assists any parolee of the Department of the Youth Authority whose parole has been revoked, any escapee, any ward confined to a Department of the Youth Authority institution or facility, or who is being transported to or from that institution or facility, or any person in the lawful custody of any officer or person to escape or in an attempt to escape from a Department of the Youth Authority institution or facility, or custody, is punishable by imprisonment in the state prison for a term of 16 months, two, or three years or in the county jail for a term not exceeding one year. *(Stats.1937, c. 369, p. 1060, § 1152. Amended by Stats.1943, c. 481, p. 2025, § 53; Stats.1953, c. 897, p. 2255, § 1; Stats.1991, c. 687 (S.B.1040), § 1.)*

Cross References

Escapes or aiding escapes, see Penal Code §§ 107 et seq., 2042, 4530 et seq.
Minor under custody or commitment, escape, misdemeanor, see Welfare and Institutions Code § 871.
Misdemeanor defined, see Penal Code § 17.

Research References

4 Witkin, California Criminal Law 4th Pretrial Proceedings § 212 (2021), Designation of Statute by Number.

§ 1154. Expense of returning escaped person

Whenever any person who has escaped from any institution or facility under the jurisdiction of the Youth Authority is returned by a sheriff or probation officer, the sheriff or probation officer shall be paid the same fees and expenses as are allowed such officers by law for the transportation of persons to institutions or facilities under the jurisdiction of the Youth Authority. *(Added by Stats.1945, c. 783, p. 1471, § 1.)*

Cross References

Fee or reward to peace officer for surrender of fugitive, prohibited, see Penal Code § 1558.
Sheriff's expenses for transporting prisoners, see Government Code § 26749.
"Youth Authority", "authority", and "the authority" as meaning and referring to the Department of the Youth Authority, see Welfare and Institutions Code § 1000.7.

§ 1155. Notification of chief of police or sheriff of escape of minor from secure detention facility; release of descriptive information

The person in charge of any secure detention facility, including, but not limited to, a prison, a juvenile hall, a county jail, or any institution under the jurisdiction of the California Youth Authority, shall promptly notify the chief of police of the city in which the facility is located, or the sheriff of the county if the facility is located in an unincorporated area, of an escape by a person in its custody. The person in charge of any secure detention facility under the jurisdiction of the Department of Corrections or the Youth Authority shall release the name of, and any descriptive information about, any person who has escaped from custody to other law enforcement agencies or to other persons if the release of the information would be necessary to assist in recapturing the person or would be necessary to protect the public from substantial physical harm. *(Added by Stats.1984, c. 1420, § 3, eff. Sept. 26, 1984. Amended by Stats.1986, c. 359, § 3.)*

Cross References

Department of Corrections, generally, see Penal Code § 5000 et seq.
"Youth Authority", "authority", and "the authority" as meaning and referring to the Department of the Youth Authority, see Welfare and Institutions Code § 1000.7.

ARTICLE 8. PAROLES AND DISMISSALS

§ 1176. Conditions of parole

When, in the opinion of the Youth Authority Board, any person committed to or confined in any such school deserves parole according to regulations established for the purpose, and it will be to his or her advantage to be paroled, the board may grant parole under conditions it deems best. A reputable home or place of employment shall be provided for each person so paroled. *(Stats.1937, c. 369, p. 1060, § 1176. Amended by Stats.1943, c. 481, p. 2026, § 56; Stats.1979, c. 860, p. 2973, § 11; Stats.2003, c. 4 (S.B.459), § 6, eff. April 8, 2003, operative Jan. 1, 2004.)*

Cross References

"Youth Authority", "authority", and "the authority" as meaning and referring to the Department of the Youth Authority, see Welfare and Institutions Code § 1000.7.
Youth Authority Board, composition and appointment, see Welfare and Institutions Code § 1716.

§ 1177. Honorable discharge; purpose; considerations

(a) Pursuant to Section 1178, if a person discharged from the Department of Corrections and Rehabilitation, Division of Juvenile Facilities by the Board of Juvenile Hearings has proven that person's ability to desist from criminal behavior and to initiate a successful transition into adulthood, the board may grant that person an honorable discharge.

(b) The purposes of an honorable discharge are to recognize and reward youth who have avoided reoffending and have pursued productive and engaged roles as members of society; to remove barriers to a youth's successful integration into society and to enable the pursuit of greater opportunities; to serve as an incentive for youth to participate in treatment and training while placed in the Division of Juvenile Facilities; to connect youth with resources and opportunities upon their reentry into the community; and to inspire and motivate youth committed to the Division of Juvenile Facilities to plan and pursue a positive life.

(c) When determining whether to grant an honorable discharge to a person who petitions the board pursuant to Section 1178, the board shall consider, but is not limited to, both of the following:

(1) The petitioner's offense history, if any, while the petitioner was under the jurisdiction of the Division of Juvenile Facilities, or during or after completion of local probation supervision.

(2) Efforts made by the petitioner toward successful community reintegration, including employment history, educational achievements or progress toward obtaining a degree, vocational training, volunteer work, community engagement, positive peer and familial relationships, and any other relevant indicators of successful reentry and rehabilitation.

(d) The board shall promulgate regulations setting forth the criteria for the award of an honorable discharge.

(e) The board shall promote the purposes of an honorable discharge designation and communicate the success of recipients of honorable discharge to youth currently committed to the Department of Corrections and Rehabilitation, Division of Juvenile Facilities.

(f) The board shall inform youth about the opportunity to earn an honorable discharge at initial case reviews, annual reviews, and discharge consideration hearings.

(g) The board may collaborate with public, private, and nonprofit organizations to assist youth in the fulfillment of the criteria described in subdivision (d) and in the completion of a petition for an honorable discharge. *(Added by Stats.2017, c. 683 (S.B.625), § 3, eff. Jan. 1, 2018.)*

Cross References

"Youth Authority", "authority", and "the authority" as meaning and referring to the Department of the Youth Authority, see Welfare and Institutions Code § 1000.7.

Youth Authority Board, composition and appointment, see Welfare and Institutions Code § 1716.

Research References

3 Witkin, California Criminal Law 4th Punishment § 100 (2021), Discharge.

§ 1178. Honorable discharge; time; information to be provided to youth under supervision; request for summary report

(a) A person previously committed to the Department of Corrections and Rehabilitation, Division of Juvenile Facilities may petition the Board of Juvenile Hearings for an honorable discharge upon his or her completion of local probation supervision following discharge, but not sooner than 18 months following the date of discharge, by the board.

(b) Commencing on or after July 1, 2018, a person housed at the Division of Juvenile Facilities pursuant to paragraph (3) of subdivision (c) of Section 1731.5 or Section 1731.7 may petition the Board of Juvenile Hearings for an honorable discharge upon his or her completion of parole or local probation supervision following release, but not sooner than 18 months following the date of release.

(c)(1) The county of commitment shall inform youth currently or previously under its supervision, who were previously under the jurisdiction of the division, about the opportunity and process of petitioning the board for an honorable discharge.

(2) The county of commitment shall send a letter regarding the opportunity and process of petitioning the board for an honorable discharge to the last known residence of a person previously under the supervision of the county of commitment.

(d) Upon receiving a petition for an honorable discharge, the board shall request of the county of commitment, and the county of commitment shall provide, a summary report of the petitioner's performance while on probation after release from the Division of Juvenile Facilities.

(e) The Division of Juvenile Facilities shall promulgate regulations to implement this section. *(Added by Stats.2017, c. 683 (S.B.625), § 5, eff. Jan. 1, 2018. Amended by Stats.2018, c. 36 (A.B.1812), § 32, eff. June 27, 2018.)*

§ 1179. Release from penalties or disabilities for persons honorably discharged by Board of Juvenile Hearings; employment as peace officer; certification of discharge

(a) Each person honorably discharged by the Board of Juvenile Hearings shall thereafter be released from all penalties or disabilities resulting from the offenses for which the person was committed, including, but not limited to, penalties or disabilities that affect access to education, employment, or occupational licenses. However, a release from all penalties and disabilities shall not affect a person's duty to register pursuant to Section 290.008 of the Penal Code. A person in receipt of an honorable discharge is not eligible for appointment as a peace officer employed by any public agency if that person's appointment is otherwise prohibited by Section 1029 of the Government Code.

(b) Persons who receive an honorable discharge and who petition the court for relief otherwise provided for by law may cite and the court shall recognize receipt of an honorable discharge as evidence of rehabilitation.

(c) Notwithstanding subdivision (a), a person may be appointed and employed as a peace officer by the Department of Corrections and Rehabilitation, Division of Juvenile Facilities if (1) at least five years have passed since that person's honorable discharge, and the person has had no misdemeanor or felony convictions except for traffic misdemeanors since the person was honorably discharged by the board, or (2) the person was employed as a peace officer by the department on or before January 1, 1983. A person who is under the jurisdiction of the Division of Juvenile Facilities or a county probation department shall not be admitted to an examination for a peace officer position with the Division of Juvenile Facilities unless and until the person has been honorably discharged from the jurisdiction of the Division of Juvenile Facilities pursuant to Sections 1177 and 1719.

(d) In the case of a person granted an honorable discharge, the Department of Corrections and Rehabilitation, Division of Juvenile Facilities shall immediately certify the discharge or dismissal in writing, and shall transmit the certificate to the committing court and the Department of Justice. The court shall thereupon dismiss the accusation and the action pending against that person. *(Stats.1937, c. 369, p. 1060, § 1179. Amended by Stats.1943, c. 481, p. 2026, § 59; Stats.1976, c. 1272, p. 5627, § 1; Stats.1982, c. 778, § 1; Stats.2003, c. 4 (S.B.459), § 9, eff. April 8, 2003, operative Jan. 1, 2004; Stats.2017, c. 683 (S.B.625), § 6, eff. Jan. 1, 2018.)*

Cross References

Civil rights of prisoners, see Penal Code §§ 2600, 2601.

Discharged probationer, release from penalties and disabilities, see Penal Code § 1203.4.

Felonies, definition and penalties, see Penal Code §§ 17, 18.

Honorable discharge, effect of, see Welfare and Institutions Code § 1772.

Misdemeanors, definition and penalties, see Penal Code §§ 17, 19, 19.2.

Restoration of rights, pardon, see Penal Code § 4852.01 et seq.

Revoked or suspended motor vehicle license, effect on, see Vehicle Code § 13555.

Writing defined, see Welfare and Institutions Code § 8.

Youth Authority Board, composition and appointment, see Welfare and Institutions Code § 1716.

§ 1180. Furnishing information concerning parolees to local authorities

The Department of the Youth Authority shall provide, within 10 days, upon request to the chief of police of a city or the sheriff of a county information available to the department, including actual, glossy photographs, no smaller than 3⅛ × 3⅛ inches in size, and, in conjunction with the Department of Justice, fingerprints concerning persons then on parole who are or may be residing or temporarily domiciled in that city or county. *(Added by Stats.1981, c. 1111, p. 4340, § 6. Amended by Stats.1983, c. 196, § 10; Stats.1986, c. 600, § 6.)*

Cross References

Similar provisions, adult offenders, see Penal Code § 3058.5.

ARTICLE 9. FINANCES

Section

§ 1200. Warrants; payment

The Controller of the State shall, on requisition of any of the institutions under this chapter, duly audited by him, draw his warrant on the State Treasurer for any moneys duly appropriated to pay for the necessary expenditures in the establishment and maintenance of such school, and the State Treasurer shall pay the same from the appropriations provided therefor. *(Stats.1937, c. 369, p. 1061, § 1200. Amended by Stats.1943, c. 481, p. 2026, § 60.)*

Cross References

State Treasurer, duties, see Government Code § 12320 et seq.
Warrants, see Government Code § 17000 et seq.

§ 1201. County payments to state

For each person committed to any state school the county from which he was committed shall make payments to the state as provided in Section 911 of this code. *(Stats.1937, c. 369, p. 1061, § 1201. Amended by Stats.1965, c. 605, p. 1940, § 2.)*

Cross References

Payment by county, see Welfare and Institutions Code § 10604.
Payments to state, see Welfare and Institutions Code § 912.

ARTICLE 10. THE CALIFORNIA YOUTH TRAINING SCHOOL

Section

§ 1250. Establishment

There is hereby established an institution for the confinement of males under the custody of the Director of Corrections and the Youth Authority to be known as the Heman G. Stark Youth Training School. *(Added by Stats.1949, c. 303, p. 591, § 1. Amended by Stats.1989, c. 555, § 1.)*

Cross References

Adult residential facilities for persons with special health care needs, pilot program, see Welfare and Institutions Code § 4684.50 et seq.
Director of Corrections, generally, see Penal Code § 5050 et seq.
Order of commitment, mentally retarded persons, placement in developmental center, see Welfare and Institutions Code § 6509.
"Youth Authority", "authority", and "the authority" as meaning and referring to the Department of the Youth Authority, see Welfare and Institutions Code § 1000.7.
Youth Authority, generally, see Welfare and Institutions Code § 1700 et seq.

§ 1251. Nature; purpose

The Heman G. Stark Youth Training School shall be an intermediate security type institution. Its primary purpose shall be to provide custody, care, industrial, vocational and other training, guidance and reformatory help for young men, too mature to be benefited by the programs of correctional schools for juveniles and too immature in crime for confinement in prisons. *(Added by Stats.1949, c. 303, p. 591, § 1. Amended by Stats.1989, c. 555, § 2.)*

§ 1252. Persons subject to confinement

There may be transferred to and confined in the Heman G. Stark Youth Training School any male subject to the custody, control and discipline of the Youth Authority, whom the Youth Authority believes will be benefited by confinement in such an institution. Whenever by reason of any law governing the commitment of a person to the Youth Authority or to an institution under the jurisdiction of the Youth Authority such a person is deemed not to be a person convicted of a crime, the transfer or placement of such a person in the Heman G. Stark Youth Training School shall not affect the status or rights of the person and shall not be deemed to constitute a conviction of a crime. *(Added by Stats.1949, c. 303, p. 591, § 1. Amended by Stats.1983, c. 229, § 3; Stats.1989, c. 555, § 3.)*

Cross References

Board of Prison Terms, generally, see Penal Code § 5075 et seq.
Director of Corrections, generally, see Penal Code § 5050 et seq.
Jurisdiction over correctional schools, see Welfare and Institutions Code § 1000.
"Youth Authority", "authority", and "the authority" as meaning and referring to the Department of the Youth Authority, see Welfare and Institutions Code § 1000.7.
Youth Authority, generally, see Welfare and Institutions Code § 1700 et seq.

§ 1253. Rules and regulations

The Youth Authority shall make rules and regulations for the government of the Heman G. Stark Youth Training School and the management of its affairs. *(Added by Stats.1949, c. 303, p. 591, § 1. Amended by Stats.1989, c. 555, § 4.)*

Cross References

Administrative Procedure Act, see Government Code § 11370 et seq.
Power of Department of Youth Authority to make rules and regulations, see Welfare and Institutions Code § 1712.
"Youth Authority", "authority", and "the authority" as meaning and referring to the Department of the Youth Authority, see Welfare and Institutions Code § 1000.7.

§ 1254. Officers and employees

The Youth Authority shall appoint, subject to civil service, a superintendent for the Heman G. Stark Youth Training School, and such officers and employees as may be necessary, and shall fix their compensation. *(Added by Stats.1949, c. 303, p. 591, § 1. Amended by Stats.1989, c. 555, § 5.)*

Cross References

Civil service appointments, see Government Code § 19050 et seq.
Personnel, employment and discharge, see Welfare and Institutions Code § 1752.
Superintendent and executive officers, appointment, see Welfare and Institutions Code § 1049.
"Youth Authority", "authority", and "the authority" as meaning and referring to the Department of the Youth Authority, see Welfare and Institutions Code § 1000.7.

§ 1255. Buildings and facilities

The Youth Authority shall construct and equip, in accordance with law, suitable buildings, structures, and facilities for the Heman G. Stark Youth Training School. *(Added by Stats.1949, c. 303, p. 591, § 1. Amended by Stats.1989, c. 555, § 6.)*

Cross References

"Youth Authority", "authority", and "the authority" as meaning and referring to the Department of the Youth Authority, see Welfare and Institutions Code § 1000.7.

§ 1256. Powers and duties of Youth Authority

The Youth Authority shall have the same powers, duties, and responsibilities in respect to the Heman G. Stark Youth Training School and the persons confined therein that the Youth Authority has in respect to institutions established for persons committed to the Youth Authority under Division 2.5 of this code [1] and in respect to such persons, except that the Youth Authority shall have no power to parole, discharge, grant leave of absence to, or otherwise release from the Heman G. Stark Youth Training School any person under the custody of the Director of Corrections and transferred to and confined in the Heman G. Stark Youth Training School, or to transfer any such person from the Heman G. Stark Youth Training School to any other institution whatever, except to return him to the custody of the Director of Corrections.

Except as otherwise provided in this article, the provisions of Part 3 of the Penal Code [2] continue to apply to all persons in the custody of the Director of Corrections who are transferred by the Adult Authority to the Heman G. Stark Youth Training School, so far as such provisions may be applicable. *(Added by Stats.1949, c. 303, p. 591, § 1. Amended by Stats.1989, c. 555, § 7.)*

[1] Welfare and Institutions Code § 1700 et seq.

[2] Penal Code § 2000 et seq.

Cross References

"Youth Authority", "authority", and "the authority" as meaning and referring to the Department of the Youth Authority, see Welfare and Institutions Code § 1000.7.

§ 1258. Construction of movable houses; sale to public; size

The Director of the Youth Authority, in connection with industrial training at the Heman G. Stark Youth Training School, Chino, California, may provide suitable materials and facilities for use by persons confined in the school in the construction of houses which can be moved which, upon their completion, shall be sold to the public upon competitive bids. Proceeds derived from the sale of any such house shall be deposited in the General Fund. Construction shall be limited to not more than one each calendar year and the size shall not exceed one thousand two hundred fifty (1,250) square feet. *(Added by Stats.1963, c. 1424, p. 2967, § 1. Amended by Stats.1989, c. 555, § 8.)*

Cross References

General Fund, see Government Code § 16300 et seq.
"Youth Authority", "authority", and "the authority" as meaning and referring to the Department of the Youth Authority, see Welfare and Institutions Code § 1000.7.

CHAPTER 4. THE INTERSTATE COMPACT FOR JUVENILES

Section

§ 1400. Compact text

THE INTERSTATE COMPACT FOR JUVENILES

ARTICLE I

PURPOSE

The compacting states to this Interstate Compact recognize that each state is responsible for the proper supervision or return of juveniles, delinquents, and status offenders who are on probation or parole and who have absconded, escaped, or run away from supervision and control and in so doing have endangered their own safety and the safety of others. The compacting states also recognize that each state is responsible for the safe return of juveniles who have run away from home and in doing so have left their state of residence. The compacting states also recognize that Congress, by enacting the Crime Control Act (4 U.S.C. Sec. 112), has authorized and encouraged compacts for cooperative efforts and mutual assistance in the prevention of crime.

It is the purpose of this compact, through means of joint and cooperative action among the compacting states to: (a) ensure that the adjudicated juveniles and status offenders subject to this compact are provided adequate supervision and services in the receiving state as ordered by the adjudicating judge or parole authority in the sending state; (b) ensure that the public safety interests of the citizens, including the victims of juvenile offenders, in both the sending and receiving states are adequately protected; (c) return juveniles who have run away, absconded, or escaped from supervision or control or have been accused of an offense to the state requesting their return; (d) make contracts for the cooperative institutionalization in public facilities in member states for delinquent youth needing special services; (e) provide for the effective tracking and supervision of juveniles; (f) equitably allocate the costs, benefits, and obligations of the compacting states; (g) establish procedures to manage the movement between states of juvenile offenders released to the community under the jurisdiction of courts, juvenile departments, or any other criminal or juvenile justice agency which has jurisdiction over juvenile offenders; (h) insure immediate notice to jurisdictions where defined offenders are authorized to travel or to relocate across state lines; (i) establish procedures to resolve pending charges (detainers) against juvenile offenders prior to transfer or release to the community under the terms of this compact; (j) establish a system of uniform data collection on information pertaining to juveniles subject to this compact that allows access by authorized juvenile justice and criminal justice officials, and regular reporting of compact activities to heads of state executive, judicial, and legislative branches and juvenile and criminal justice administrators; (k) monitor compliance with rules governing interstate movement of juveniles and initiate interventions to address and correct noncompliance; (*l*) coordinate training and education regarding the regulation of interstate movement of juveniles for officials involved in such activity; and (m) coordinate the implementation and operation of the compact with the Interstate Compact for the Placement of Children, the Interstate Compact for Adult Offender Supervision, and other compacts affecting juveniles particularly in those cases where concurrent or overlapping supervision issues arise. It is the policy of the compacting states that the activities conducted by the Interstate Commission created herein are the formation of public policies and therefore are public business. Furthermore, the compacting states shall cooperate and observe their individual and collective duties and responsibilities for the prompt return and acceptance of juveniles subject to the provisions of this compact. The provisions of this compact shall be reasonably and liberally construed to accomplish the purposes and policies of the compact.

ARTICLE II

DEFINITIONS

As used in this compact, unless the context clearly requires a different construction:

(a) "Bylaws" means those bylaws established by the Interstate Commission for its governance, or for directing or controlling its actions or conduct.

(b) "Compact Administrator" means the individual in each compacting state appointed pursuant to the terms of this compact, responsible for the administration and management of the state's supervision and transfer of juveniles subject to the terms of this compact, the rules adopted by the Interstate Commission, and policies adopted by the State Council for Interstate Juvenile Supervision under this compact.

(c) "Compacting state" means any state which has enacted the enabling legislation for this compact.

(d) "Commissioner" means the voting representative of each compacting state appointed pursuant to Article III of this compact.

(e) "Court" means any court having jurisdiction over delinquent, neglected, or dependent children.

(f) "Deputy Compact Administrator" means the individual, if any, in each compacting state appointed to act on behalf of a Compact Administrator pursuant to the terms of this compact responsible for the administration and management of the state's supervision and transfer of juveniles subject to the terms of this compact, the rules adopted by the Interstate Commission and policies adopted by the State Council under this compact.

(g) "Interstate Commission" means the Interstate Commission for Juveniles created by Article III of this compact.

(h) "Juvenile" means any person defined as a juvenile in any member state or by the rules of the Interstate Commission, including:

(1) "Accused delinquent" means a person charged with an offense that, if committed by an adult, would be a criminal offense;

(2) "Adjudicated delinquent" means a person found to have committed an offense that, if committed by an adult, would be a criminal offense;

(3) "Accused status offender" means a person charged with an offense that would not be a criminal offense if committed by an adult;

(4) "Adjudicated status offender" means a person found to have committed an offense that would not be a criminal offense if committed by an adult; and

(5) "Non-offender" means a person in need of supervision who has not been accused or adjudicated a status offender or delinquent.

(i) "Noncompacting state" means any state which has not enacted the enabling legislation for this compact.

(j) "Probation or parole" means any kind of supervision or conditional release of juveniles authorized under the laws of the compacting states.

(k) "Rule" means a written statement by the Interstate Commission promulgated pursuant to Article VI of this compact that is of general applicability, implements, interprets or prescribes a policy or provision of the compact, or an organizational, procedural, or practice requirement of the commission, and has the force and effect of statutory law in a compacting state, and includes the amendment, repeal, or suspension of an existing rule.

(*l*) "State" means a state of the United States, the District of Columbia (or its designee), the Commonwealth of Puerto Rico, the United States Virgin Islands, Guam, American Samoa, and the Northern Marianas Islands.

ARTICLE III

INTERSTATE COMMISSION FOR JUVENILES

(a) The compacting states hereby create the "Interstate Commission for Juveniles." The commission shall be a body corporate and joint agency of the compacting states. The commission shall have all the responsibilities, powers, and duties set forth herein, and such additional powers as may be conferred upon it by subsequent action of the respective legislatures of the compacting states in accordance with the terms of this compact.

(b) The Interstate Commission shall consist of commissioners appointed by the appropriate appointing authority in each state pursuant to the rules and requirements of each compacting state and in consultation with the State Council for Interstate Juvenile Supervision created hereunder. The commissioner shall be the compact administrator, deputy compact administrator, or designee from that state who shall serve on the Interstate Commission in such capacity under or pursuant to the applicable law of the compacting state.

(c) In addition to the commissioners who are the voting representatives of each state, the Interstate Commission shall include individuals who are not commissioners, but who are members of interested organizations. Such noncommissioner members must include a member of the national organizations of governors, legislators, state chief justices, attorneys general, Interstate Compact for Adult Offender Supervision, Interstate Compact for the Placement of Children, juvenile justice and juvenile corrections officials, and crime victims. All noncommissioner members of the Interstate Commission shall be ex officio (nonvoting) members. The Interstate Commission may provide in its bylaws for such additional ex officio (nonvoting) members, including members of other national organizations, in such numbers as shall be determined by the commission.

(d) Each compacting state represented at any meeting of the commission is entitled to one vote. A majority of the compacting states shall constitute a quorum for the transaction of business, unless a larger quorum is required by the bylaws of the Interstate Commission.

(e) The commission shall meet at least once each calendar year. The chairperson may call additional meetings and, upon the request of a simple majority of the compacting states, shall call additional meetings. Public notice shall be given of all meetings and meetings shall be open to the public.

(f) The Interstate Commission shall establish an executive committee, which shall include commission officers, members, and others as determined by the bylaws. The executive committee shall have the power to act on behalf of the Interstate Commission during periods when the Interstate Commission is not in session, with the exception of rulemaking or amendment to the compact. The executive committee shall oversee the day-to-day activities of the administration of the compact managed by an executive director and Interstate Commission staff, and the committee shall administer enforcement and compliance with the provisions of the compact, its bylaws and rules, and perform such other duties as directed by the Interstate Commission or set forth in the bylaws.

(g) Each member of the Interstate Commission shall have the right and power to cast a vote to which that compacting state is entitled and to participate in the business and affairs of the Interstate Commission. A member shall vote in person and shall not delegate a vote to another compacting state. However, a commissioner, in consultation with the state council, shall appoint another authorized representative, in the absence of the commissioner from that state, to cast a vote on behalf of the compacting state at a specified meeting. The bylaws may provide for members' participation in meetings by telephone or other means of telecommunication or electronic communication.

(h) The Interstate Commission's bylaws shall establish conditions and procedures under which the Interstate Commission shall make its information and official records available to the public for inspection or copying. The Interstate Commission may exempt from disclosure any information or official records to the extent they would adversely affect personal privacy rights or proprietary interests.

(i) Public notice shall be given of all meetings and all meetings shall be open to the public, except as set forth in the rules or as otherwise provided in the compact. The Interstate Commission and any of its committees may close a meeting to the public where it determines by two-thirds vote that an open meeting would be likely to:

(1) Relate solely to the Interstate Commission's internal personnel practices and procedures.

(2) Disclose matters specifically exempted from disclosure by statute.

(3) Disclose trade secrets or commercial or financial information which is privileged or confidential.

(4) Involve accusing any person of a crime, or formally censuring any person.

(5) Disclose information of a personal nature where disclosure would constitute a clearly unwarranted invasion of personal privacy.

(6) Disclose investigative records compiled for law enforcement purposes.

(7) Disclose information contained in or related to examination, operating or condition reports prepared by, or on behalf of or for the use of, the Interstate Commission with respect to a regulated person or entity for the purpose of regulation or supervision of such person or entity.

(8) Disclose information, the premature disclosure of which would significantly endanger the stability of a regulated person or entity.

(9) Specifically relate to the Interstate Commission's issuance of a subpoena, or its participation in a civil action or other legal proceeding.

(j) For every meeting closed pursuant to this provision, the Interstate Commission's legal counsel shall publicly certify that, in the legal counsel's opinion, the meeting may be closed to the public, and shall reference each relevant exemptive provision. The Interstate Commission shall keep minutes which shall fully and clearly describe all matters discussed in any meeting and shall provide a full and accurate summary of any actions taken, and the reasons therefore, including a description of each of the views expressed on any item and the record of any roll call vote (reflected in the vote of each member on the question). All documents considered in connection with any action shall be identified in such minutes.

(k) The Interstate Commission shall collect standardized data concerning the interstate movement of juveniles as directed through its rules which shall specify the data to be collected, the means of collection and data exchange and reporting requirements. Such methods of data collection, exchange and reporting shall insofar as is reasonably possible conform to up-to-date technology and coordinate its information functions with the appropriate repository of records.

ARTICLE IV

POWERS AND DUTIES OF THE INTERSTATE COMMISSION

The commission shall have the following powers and duties:

(a) To provide for dispute resolution among compacting states.

(b) To promulgate rules to effect the purposes and obligations as enumerated in this compact, which shall have the force and effect of statutory law and shall be binding in the compacting states to the extent and in the manner provided in this compact.

(c) To oversee, supervise, and coordinate the interstate movement of juveniles subject to the terms of this compact and any bylaws adopted and rules promulgated by the Interstate Commission.

(d) To enforce compliance with the compact provisions, the rules promulgated by the Interstate Commission, and the bylaws, using all necessary and proper means, including but not limited to the use of judicial process.

(e) To establish and maintain offices which shall be located within one or more of the compacting states.

(f) To purchase and maintain insurance and bonds.

(g) To borrow, accept, hire, or contract for services of personnel.

(h) To establish and appoint committees and hire staff which it deems necessary for the carrying out of its functions including, but not limited to, an executive committee as required by Article III which shall have the power to act on behalf of the Interstate Commission in carrying out its powers and duties hereunder.

(i) To elect or appoint such officers, attorneys, employees, agents, or consultants, and to fix their compensation, define their duties and determine their qualifications, and to establish the Interstate Commission's personnel policies and programs relating to, inter alia, conflicts of interest, rates of compensation, and qualifications of personnel.

(j) To accept any and all donations and grants of money, equipment, supplies, materials, and services, and to receive, utilize, and dispose of it.

(k) To lease, purchase, accept contributions or donations of, or otherwise to own, hold, improve or use any property, real, personal, or mixed.

(*l*) To sell, convey, mortgage, pledge, lease, exchange, abandon, or otherwise dispose of any property, real, personal or mixed.

(m) To establish a budget and make expenditures and levy dues as provided in Article VIII of this compact.

(n) To sue and be sued.

(*o*) To adopt a seal and bylaws governing the management and operation of the Interstate Commission.

(p) To perform such functions as may be necessary or appropriate to achieve the purposes of this compact.

(q) To report annually to the legislatures, governors, judiciary, and state councils of the compacting states concerning the activities of the Interstate Commission during the preceding year. Such reports shall also include any recommendations that may have been adopted by the Interstate Commission.

(r) To coordinate education, training, and public awareness regarding the interstate movement of juveniles for officials involved in such activity.

(s) To establish uniform standards of the reporting, collecting, and exchanging of data.

(t) The Interstate Commission shall maintain its corporate books and records in accordance with the bylaws.

ARTICLE V

ORGANIZATION AND OPERATION OF THE INTERSTATE COMMISSION

(a) Section A. Bylaws. The Interstate Commission shall, by a majority of the members present and voting, within 12 months after the first Interstate Commission meeting, adopt bylaws to govern its conduct as may be necessary or appropriate to carry out the purposes of the compact, including, but not limited to:

(1) Establishing the fiscal year of the Interstate Commission.

(2) Establishing an executive committee and such other committees as may be necessary.

(3) Provide for the establishment of committees governing any general or specific delegation of any authority or function of the Interstate Commission.

(4) Providing reasonable procedures for calling and conducting meetings of the Interstate Commission, and ensuring reasonable notice of each such meeting.

(5) Establishing the titles and responsibilities of the officers of the Interstate Commission.

(6) Providing a mechanism for concluding the operations of the Interstate Commission and the return of any surplus funds that may exist upon the termination of the compact after the payment or reserving of all of its debts and obligations.

(7) Providing "start-up" rules for initial administration of the compact.

(8) Establishing standards and procedures for compliance and technical assistance in carrying out the compact.

(b) Section B. Officers and Staff

(1) The Interstate Commission shall, by a majority of the members, elect annually from among its members a chairperson and a vice chairperson, each of whom shall have such authority and duties as may be specified in the bylaws. The chairperson or, in the chairperson's absence or disability, the vice-chairperson shall preside

at all meetings of the Interstate Commission. The officers so elected shall serve without compensation or remuneration from the Interstate Commission; provided that, subject to the availability of budgeted funds, the officers shall be reimbursed for any ordinary and necessary costs and expenses incurred by them in the performance of their duties and responsibilities as officers of the Interstate Commission.

(2) The Interstate Commission shall, through its executive committee, appoint or retain an executive director for such period, upon such terms and conditions and for such compensation as the Interstate Commission may deem appropriate. The executive director shall serve as secretary to the Interstate Commission, but shall not be a member and shall hire and supervise such other staff as may be authorized by the Interstate Commission.

(c) Section C. Qualified Immunity, Defense, and Indemnification

(1) The commission's executive director and employees shall be immune from suit and liability, either personally or in their official capacity, for any claim for damage to or loss of property or personal injury or other civil liability caused or arising out of or relating to any actual or alleged act, error, or omission that occurred, or that such person had a reasonable basis for believing occurred within the scope of commission employment, duties, or responsibilities, provided, that any such person shall not be protected from suit or liability for any damage, loss, injury, or liability caused by the intentional or willful and wanton misconduct of any such person.

(2) The liability of any commissioner, or the employee or agent of a commissioner, acting within the scope of such person's employment or duties for acts, errors, or omissions occurring within such person's state may not exceed the limits of liability set forth under the United States Constitution and laws of that state for state officials, employees, and agents. Nothing in this paragraph shall be construed to protect any such person from suit or liability for any damage, loss, injury, or liability caused by the intentional or willful and wanton misconduct of any such person.

(3) The Interstate Commission shall defend the executive director or the employees or representatives of the Interstate Commission and, subject to the approval of the Attorney General of the state represented by any commissioner of a compacting state, shall defend such commissioner or the commissioner's representatives or employees in any civil action seeking to impose liability arising out of any actual or alleged act, error or omission that occurred within the scope of Interstate Commission employment, duties or responsibilities, or that the defendant had a reasonable basis for believing occurred within the scope of Interstate Commission employment, duties, or responsibilities, provided that the actual or alleged act, error, or omission did not result from intentional or willful and wanton misconduct on the part of such person.

(4) The Interstate Commission shall indemnify and hold the commissioner of a compacting state, or the commissioner's representatives or employees, or the Interstate Commission's representatives or employees, harmless in the amount of any settlement or judgment obtained against such persons arising out of any actual or alleged act, error, or omission that occurred within the scope of Interstate Commission employment, duties, or responsibilities, or that such persons had a reasonable basis for believing occurred within the scope of Interstate Commission employment, duties, or responsibilities, provided that the actual or alleged act, error, or omission did not result from intentional or willful and wanton misconduct on the part of such persons.

ARTICLE VI

RULEMAKING FUNCTIONS OF THE INTERSTATE COMMISSION

(a) The Interstate Commission shall promulgate and publish rules in order to effectively and efficiently achieve the purposes of the compact.

(b) Rulemaking shall occur pursuant to the criteria set forth in this article and the bylaws and rules adopted pursuant thereto. Such rulemaking shall substantially conform to the principles of the "Model State Administrative Procedures Act," 1981 Act, Uniform Laws Annotated, Vol. 15, p.1 (2000), or such other administrative procedures act, as the Interstate Commission deems appropriate consistent with the due process requirements under the United States Constitution as now or hereafter interpreted by the United States Supreme Court. All rules and amendments shall become binding as of the date specified, as published with the final version of the rule as approved by the commission.

(c) When promulgating a rule, the Interstate Commission shall, at a minimum:

(1) Publish the proposed rule's entire text stating the reason(s) for that proposed rule.

(2) Allow and invite any and all persons to submit written data, facts, opinions and arguments, which information shall be added to the record, and be made publicly available.

(3) Provide an opportunity for an informal hearing if petitioned by 10 or more persons.

(4) Promulgate a final rule and its effective date, if appropriate, based on input from state or local officials, or interested parties.

(d) Allow, not later than sixty days after a rule is promulgated, any interested person to file a petition in the United States District Court for the District of Columbia or in the Federal District Court where the Interstate Commission's principal office is located for judicial review of such rule. If the court finds that the Interstate Commission's action is not supported by substantial evidence in the rulemaking record, the court shall hold the rule unlawful and set it aside. For purposes of this subdivision, evidence is substantial if it would be considered substantial evidence under the Model State Administrative Procedures Act.

(e) If a majority of the Legislatures of the compacting states rejects a rule, those states may, by enactment of a statute or resolution in the same manner used to adopt the compact, cause that such rule shall have no further force and effect in any compacting state.

(f) The existing rules governing the operation of the Interstate Compact on Juveniles superceded by this act shall be null and void 12 months after the first meeting of the Interstate Commission created hereunder.

(g) Upon determination by the Interstate Commission that a state of emergency exists, it may promulgate an emergency rule which shall become effective immediately upon adoption, provided that the usual rulemaking procedures provided hereunder shall be retroactively applied to said rule as soon as reasonably possible, but no later than 90 days after the effective date of the emergency rule.

ARTICLE VII

OVERSIGHT, ENFORCEMENT, AND DISPUTE RESOLUTION BY THE INTERSTATE COMMISSION

(a) Section A. Oversight

(1) The Interstate Commission shall oversee the administration and operations of the interstate movement of juveniles subject to this compact in the compacting states and shall monitor such activities being administered in noncompacting states which may significantly affect compacting states.

(2) The courts and executive agencies in each compacting state shall enforce this compact and shall take all actions necessary and appropriate to effectuate the compact's purposes and intent. The provisions of this compact and the rules promulgated hereunder shall be received by all the judges, public officers, commissions, and departments of the state government as evidence of the authorized

statute and administrative rules. All courts shall take judicial notice of the compact and the rules. In any judicial or administrative proceeding in a compacting state pertaining to the subject matter of this compact which may affect the powers, responsibilities or actions of the Interstate Commission, it shall be entitled to receive all service of process in any such proceeding, and shall have standing to intervene in the proceeding for all purposes.

(b) Section B. Dispute Resolution

(1) The compacting states shall report to the Interstate Commission on all issues and activities necessary for the administration of the compact as well as issues and activities pertaining to compliance with the provisions of the compact and its bylaws and rules.

(2) The Interstate Commission shall attempt, upon the request of a compacting state, to resolve any disputes or other issues which are subject to the compact and which may arise among compacting states and between compacting and noncompacting states. The commission shall promulgate a rule providing for both mediation and binding dispute resolution for disputes among the compacting states.

(3) The Interstate Commission, in the reasonable exercise of its discretion, shall enforce the provisions and rules of this compact using any or all means set forth in Article XI of this compact.

ARTICLE VIII

FINANCE

(a) The Interstate Commission shall pay or provide for the payment of the reasonable expenses of its establishment, organization, and ongoing activities.

(b) The Interstate Commission shall levy on and collect an annual assessment from each compacting state to cover the cost of the internal operations and activities of the Interstate Commission and its staff which must be in a total amount sufficient to cover the Interstate Commission's annual budget as approved each year. The aggregate annual assessment amount shall be allocated based upon a formula to be determined by the Interstate Commission, taking into consideration the population of each compacting state and the volume of interstate movement of juveniles in each compacting state and shall promulgate a rule binding upon all compacting states which governs said assessment.

(c) The Interstate Commission shall not incur any obligations of any kind prior to securing the funds adequate to meet the same, nor shall the Interstate Commission pledge the credit of any of the compacting states, except by and with the authority of the compacting state.

(d) The Interstate Commission shall keep accurate accounts of all receipts and disbursements. The receipts and disbursements of the Interstate Commission shall be subject to the audit and accounting procedures established under its bylaws. However, all receipts and disbursements of funds handled by the Interstate Commission shall be audited yearly by a certified or licensed public accountant and the report of the audit shall be included in and become part of the annual report of the Interstate Commission.

ARTICLE IX

THE STATE COUNCIL

Each member state shall create a State Council for Interstate Juvenile Supervision. While each state may determine the membership of its own state council, its membership must include at least one representative from the legislative, judicial, and executive branches of government, victims groups, and the compact administrator, deputy compact administrator or designee. Each compacting state retains the right to determine the qualifications of the compact administrator or deputy compact administrator. Each state council will advise and may exercise oversight and advocacy concerning that state's participation in Interstate Commission activities and other duties as may be determined by that state, including, but not limited to, development of policy concerning operations and procedures of the compact within that state.

ARTICLE X

COMPACTING STATES, EFFECTIVE DATE, AND AMENDMENT

(a) Any state, the District of Columbia (or its designee), the Commonwealth of Puerto Rico, the United States Virgin Islands, Guam, American Samoa, and the Northern Marianas Islands as defined in Article II of this compact is eligible to become a compacting state.

(b) The compact shall become effective and binding upon legislative enactment of the compact into law by no less than 35 of the states. The initial effective date shall be the later of July 1, 2004, or upon enactment into law by the 35th jurisdiction. Thereafter it shall become effective and binding as to any other compacting state upon enactment of the compact into law by that state. The governors of nonmember states or their designees shall be invited to participate in the activities of the Interstate Commission on a nonvoting basis prior to adoption of the compact by all states and territories of the United States.

(c) The Interstate Commission may propose amendments to the compact for enactment by the compacting states. No amendment shall become effective and binding upon the Interstate Commission and the compacting states unless and until it is enacted into law by unanimous consent of the compacting states.

ARTICLE XI

WITHDRAWAL, DEFAULT, TERMINATION, AND JUDICIAL ENFORCEMENT

(a) Section A. Withdrawal

(1) Once effective, the compact shall continue in force and remain binding upon each and every compacting state; provided that a compacting state may withdraw from the compact by specifically repealing the statute which enacted the compact into law.

(2) The effective date of withdrawal is the effective date of the repeal.

(3) The withdrawing state shall immediately notify the chairperson of the Interstate Commission in writing upon the introduction of legislation repealing this compact in the withdrawing state. The Interstate Commission shall notify the other compacting states of the withdrawing state's intent to withdraw within sixty days of its receipt thereof.

(4) The withdrawing state is responsible for all assessments, obligations, and liabilities incurred through the effective date of withdrawal, including any obligations, the performance of which extend beyond the effective date of withdrawal.

(5) Reinstatement following withdrawal of any compacting state shall occur upon the withdrawing state reenacting the compact or upon such later date as determined by the Interstate Commission

(b) Section B. Technical Assistance, Fines, Suspension, Termination, and Default

(1) If the Interstate Commission determines that any compacting state has at any time defaulted in the performance of any of its obligations or responsibilities under this compact, or the bylaws, or duly promulgated rules, the Interstate Commission may impose any or all of the following penalties:

(A) Remedial training and technical assistance as directed by the Interstate Commission.

(B) Alternative dispute resolution.

(C) Fines, fees, and costs in such amounts as are deemed to be reasonable as fixed by the Interstate Commission.

(D) Suspension or termination of membership in the compact, which shall be imposed only after all other reasonable means of securing compliance under the bylaws and rules have been exhausted and the Interstate Commission has therefore determined that the offending state is in default. Immediate notice of suspension shall be given by the Interstate Commission to the Governor, the Chief Justice or the Chief Judicial Officer of the state, the majority and minority leaders of the defaulting state's legislature, and the state council. The grounds for default include, but are not limited to, failure of a compacting state to perform such obligations or responsibilities imposed upon it by this compact, the bylaws, or duly promulgated rules and any other grounds designated in commission bylaws and rules. The Interstate Commission shall immediately notify the defaulting state in writing of the penalty imposed by the Interstate Commission and of the default pending a cure of the default. The commission shall stipulate the conditions and the time period within which the defaulting state must cure its default. If the defaulting state fails to cure the default within the time period specified by the commission, the defaulting state shall be terminated from the compact upon an affirmative vote of a majority of the compacting states and all rights, privileges, and benefits conferred by this compact shall be terminated from the effective date of termination.

(2) Within 60 days of the effective date of termination of a defaulting state, the commission shall notify the Governor, the Chief Justice or Chief Judicial Officer, the majority and minority leaders of the defaulting state's legislature, and the state council of such termination.

(3) The defaulting state is responsible for all assessments, obligations, and liabilities incurred through the effective date of termination including any obligations, the performance of which extends beyond the effective date of termination.

(4) The Interstate Commission shall not bear any costs relating to the defaulting state unless otherwise mutually agreed upon in writing between the Interstate Commission and the defaulting state.

(5) Reinstatement following termination of any compacting state requires both a reenactment of the compact by the defaulting state and the approval of the Interstate Commission pursuant to the rules.

(c) Section C. Judicial Enforcement

The Interstate Commission may, by majority vote of the members, initiate legal action in the United States District Court for the District of Columbia or, at the discretion of the Interstate Commission, in the federal district where the Interstate Commission has its offices, to enforce compliance with the provisions of the compact, its duly promulgated rules, and bylaws, against any compacting state in default. In the event judicial enforcement is necessary the prevailing party shall be awarded all costs of such litigation including reasonable attorney's fees.

(d) Section D. Dissolution of Compact

(1) The compact dissolves effective upon the date of the withdrawal or default of the compacting state, which reduces membership in the compact to one compacting state.

(2) Upon the dissolution of this compact, the compact becomes null and void and shall be of no further force or effect, and the business and affairs of the Interstate Commission shall be concluded and any surplus funds shall be distributed in accordance with the bylaws.

ARTICLE XII

SEVERABILITY AND CONSTRUCTION

(a) The provisions of this compact shall be severable, and if any phrase, clause, sentence, or provision is deemed unenforceable, the remaining provisions of the compact shall be enforceable.

(b) The provisions of this compact shall be liberally construed to effectuate its purposes.

ARTICLE XIII

BINDING EFFECT OF COMPACT AND OTHER LAWS

(a) Section A. Other Laws

(1) Nothing herein prevents the enforcement of any other law of a compacting state that is not inconsistent with this compact.

(2) All compacting states' laws other than state constitutions and other interstate compacts conflicting with this compact are superseded to the extent of the conflict.

(b) Section B. Binding Effect of the Compact

(1) All lawful actions of the Interstate Commission, including all rules and bylaws promulgated by the Interstate Commission, are binding upon the compacting states.

(2) All agreements between the Interstate Commission and the compacting states are binding in accordance with their terms.

(3) Upon the request of a party to a conflict over meaning or interpretation of Interstate Commission actions, and upon a majority vote of the compacting states, the Interstate Commission may issue advisory opinions regarding such meaning or interpretation.

(4) In the event any provision of this compact exceeds the constitutional limits imposed on the legislature of any compacting state, the obligations, duties, powers, or jurisdiction sought to be conferred by such provision upon the Interstate Commission shall be ineffective and such obligations, duties, powers, or jurisdiction shall remain in the compacting state and shall be exercised by the agency thereof to which such obligations, duties, powers, or jurisdiction are delegated by law in effect at the time this compact becomes effective. *(Added by Stats.2009, c. 268 (A.B.1053), § 2.)*

§ 1401. Secretary of the Department of Corrections and Rehabilitation

The compact administrator shall be the Secretary of the Department of Corrections and Rehabilitation, or his or her designee. *(Added by Stats.2009, c. 268 (A.B.1053), § 2. Amended by Stats.2014, c. 54 (S.B.1461), § 19, eff. Jan. 1, 2015.)*

§ 1402. Executive steering committee; review and recommendations; report

The executive director of the Corrections Standards Authority shall convene an executive steering committee to review and make recommendations regarding the Interstate Compact for Juveniles and whether permanent membership in the compact would be the most effective and prudent means by which California can achieve the purpose set forth in Section 1400 compared to other alternatives. The Corrections Standards Authority shall present the executive steering committee's final report, including recommendations for legislative action, if necessary, to the appropriate committees of the Legislature by January 1, 2011. The report shall be concise and may be produced and submitted solely in electronic format. *(Added by Stats.2009, c. 268 (A.B.1053), § 2.)*

CHAPTER 5. YOUTH REINVESTMENT GRANT PROGRAM

ARTICLE 1. GENERAL PROVISIONS

Section

§ 1450. Establishment of program; use of funds; administrative costs

(a) There is hereby established the Youth Reinvestment Grant Program within the Board of State and Community Corrections to grant funds pursuant to this chapter, upon an appropriation of funds for the purposes described in this chapter.

(b)(1) Notwithstanding any other law, the board may use any funds that were appropriated to the board in the Budget Act of 2018, but that have not been allocated as of January 1, 2020, for grants, as prescribed in Article 4 (commencing with Section 1456).

(2) Funds appropriated to the board in the Budget Act of 2019 for purposes of the Youth Reinvestment Fund grant program shall be used for grants, as prescribed in Article 4 (commencing with Section 1456).

(3) Funds appropriated to the board in the Budget Act of 2019 for purposes of the Tribal Youth Diversion grant program shall be used for grants, as prescribed in Article 2 (commencing with Section 1452).

(c) Three percent of the funds in the Youth Reinvestment Grant Program shall be used for administrative costs to the board resulting from the implementation of this chapter. *(Added by Stats.2018, c. 36 (A.B.1812), § 33, eff. June 27, 2018. Amended by Stats.2019, c. 584 (A.B.1454), § 1, eff. Jan. 1, 2020.)*

Cross References

Trauma-informed diversion programs for youth, allocation of funds, see Welfare and Institutions Code § 1458.

Trauma-informed diversion programs for youth, duties of Board of State and Community Corrections, see Welfare and Institutions Code § 1459.

§ 1451. Definitions

For purposes of Article 3 (commencing with Section 1454), the following definitions apply:

(a) "Board" means the Board of State and Community Corrections.

(b) "High rate" means a rate that exceeds the state average.

(c) "Trauma-informed" means an approach that involves an understanding of adverse childhood experiences and responding to symptoms of chronic interpersonal trauma and traumatic stress across the lifespan of an individual. *(Added by Stats.2018, c. 36 (A.B.1812), § 33, eff. June 27, 2018. Amended by Stats.2019, c. 584 (A.B.1454), § 2, eff. Jan. 1, 2020.)*

ARTICLE 2. TRAUMA–INFORMED DIVERSION PROGRAMS FOR INDIAN CHILDREN

§ 1452. "Indian child" and "Indian tribe" defined

For purposes of this article, "Indian child" and "Indian tribe" shall have the same meaning as provided in Section 224.1. *(Added by Stats.2018, c. 36 (A.B.1812), § 33, eff. June 27, 2018.)*

§ 1453. Allocation of funds to Indian tribes; funding priorities; application on regional efforts basis

(a) The board shall allocate 3 percent of funds for the Youth Reinvestment Grant Program, upon appropriation of funds pursuant to Section 1450, to Indian tribes through an application process for the purpose of implementing diversion programs for Indian children that use trauma-informed, community-based, and health-based interventions.

(b) Funding priority shall be given to diversion programs that address the needs of Indian children who experience the following:

(1) High rates of juvenile arrests.

(2) High rates of suicide.

(3) High rates of alcohol and substance abuse.

(4) Average high school graduation rates that are lower than 75 percent.

(c) Indian tribes may apply for funding under this article on a regional efforts basis and receive the aggregate amount of funds that they would have received if awarded as independent jurisdictions. *(Added by Stats.2018, c. 36 (A.B.1812), § 33, eff. June 27, 2018.)*

ARTICLE 3. TRAUMA–INFORMED DIVERSION PROGRAMS FOR MINORS

§ 1454. Allocation of funds for purpose of implementing trauma-informed diversion programs for minors; conditions for distribution of grants; application on regional efforts basis

(a) The board shall allocate 94 percent of funds for the Youth Reinvestment Grant Program, upon appropriation of funds pursuant to Section 1450, to local jurisdictions, including a county, city, or city and county, through a competitive grant process for the purpose of implementing trauma-informed diversion programs for minors.

(b) The board shall distribute a grant under this article pursuant to all of the following conditions:

(1) A local jurisdiction shall be awarded no less than fifty thousand dollars ($50,000) and no more than one million dollars ($1,000,000).

(2)(A) A local jurisdiction shall provide at least a 25–percent match to the grant that it receives pursuant to this article. Funds used to provide the 25–percent match amount may include a combination of federal, other state, local, or private funds.

(B) Notwithstanding subparagraph (A), a local jurisdiction may provide less than a 25–percent match, but at least a 10–percent match, to the grant if the local jurisdiction is identified by the board as high need with low or no local infrastructure for diversion programming.

(3)(A) Ten percent of the funds shall be distributed to a lead public agency to coordinate with local law enforcement agencies, social services agencies, and nonprofit organizations on implementation of diversion programs and alternatives to incarceration and involvement with the juvenile justice system.

(B) Ninety percent of the funds shall pass through the lead public agency to community-based organizations, that are nongovernmental and not local law enforcement agencies, to deliver services in underserved communities with high rates of juvenile arrests.

(4) Highest need is identified based on both of the following:

(A) Jurisdictions with high rates of juvenile arrests for misdemeanors and status offenses.

(B) Jurisdictions with racial or ethnic disparities on the basis of disproportionately high rates of juvenile arrests.

(5)(A) Services shall be community based, located in communities of local jurisdictions with the highest need.

(B) Services shall be evidence based or research supported, trauma informed, culturally relevant, and developmentally appropriate.

(C) Direct service providers who receive funding from a grant pursuant to this article shall be nongovernmental and not law enforcement or probation entities.

(D) Direct service providers shall have experience effectively serving at-risk youth populations.

(E) Services shall include all of the following:

(i) Diversion programs and alternatives to arrest, incarceration, and formal involvement with the juvenile justice system.

(ii) Educational services, including academic and vocational services.

(iii) Mentoring services.

(iv) Behavioral health services.

(v) Mental health services.

(c) Local jurisdictions may apply for funding under this article on a regional efforts basis and receive the aggregate amount of funds that they would have received if awarded as independent jurisdictions. *(Added by Stats.2018, c. 36 (A.B.1812), § 33, eff. June 27, 2018. Amended by Stats.2019, c. 497 (A.B.991), § 299, eff. Jan. 1, 2020.)*

§ 1455. Duties and responsibilities of board

(a) The board shall be responsible for administration oversight and accountability of the grant program under this article, in coordination with the California Health and Human Services Agency and the State Department of Education.

(b) The board, in collaboration with partner agencies, shall perform all of the following duties:

(1) Provide guidance to applicant and recipient local jurisdictions, including guidance regarding available federal, state, and local funds for the purposes of braiding and matching funds.

(2) Support data collection and analysis to identify and target jurisdictions with the highest need and to measure program outcomes and impacts.

(3) Track funding allocations and disbursements in accordance with the applicant's proposed plans.

(4)(A) Secure or set aside sufficient funds to contract with a research firm or university to conduct a statewide evaluation of the grant program and its outcomes over a three-year grant period.

(B) The board shall make available on its Internet Web site a report of grantees, projects, and outcomes at the state and local levels upon completion of the three-year period.

(C) The board and collaborating agencies shall assist the research firm or university by providing relevant, existing data for the purposes of tracking outcomes. Measures may include, but are not limited to, any of the following:

(i) Reductions in law enforcement responses to minors for low-level offenses, court caseloads and processing, days the minors spend in detention, placement of minors in congregate care, school and placement disruptions, and facility staff turnover.

(ii) Improvement in the health and well-being of the minors, school and community stability, educational attainment, and employment opportunities.

(iii) Projected state and local cost savings as a result of the diversion programming. *(Added by Stats.2018, c. 36 (A.B.1812), § 33, eff. June 27, 2018.)*

ARTICLE 4. TRAUMA-INFORMED DIVERSION PROGRAMS FOR YOUTH

Section

§ 1456. Application of article

Notwithstanding any other law, and except for grants provided to Indian tribes under Article 2 (commencing with Section 1452), commencing with the 2019–20 fiscal year and each fiscal year thereafter, this article shall apply to grants provided under the Youth Reinvestment Grant Program. *(Added by Stats.2019, c. 584 (A.B. 1454), § 3, eff. Jan. 1, 2020.)*

§ 1457. Definitions

For purposes of this article, the following definitions apply:

(a) "Applicant" means a nonprofit organization or local governmental entity.

(b) "Area of high need" means either of the following:

(1) A city or a ZIP Code with rates of youth arrests that are higher than the county average, based on available arrest data, as described by the applicant.

(2) A city or a ZIP Code with racial or ethnic disparities in youth arrests that are higher than their representation in the county population, as described by the applicant.

(c) "Board" means the Board of State and Community Corrections.

(d) "Diversion program" means a program that promotes positive youth development by relying on responses that prevent a young person's involvement or further involvement in the justice system. Diversion programs, which may follow a variety of different models, aim to divert youth from justice system engagement at the earliest possible point. Departments or agencies that may refer youth to diversion programs include, but are not limited to, schools, service organizations, police, probation, or prosecutors.

(e) "Local governmental entity" means a local government agency, including, but not limited to, a county child welfare agency, county probation department, county behavioral health department, county public health department, school district, or county office of education.

(f) "Nonprofit organization" means a private, community-based organization that is exempt from taxation pursuant to Section 501(c)(3) or 501(c)(4) of the Internal Revenue Code,[1] and that is nongovernmental and does not carry out any law enforcement duties. *(Added by Stats.2019, c. 584 (A.B.1454), § 3, eff. Jan. 1, 2020.)*

[1] Internal Revenue Code sections are in Title 26 of the U.S.C.A.

Cross References

Juvenile police records, disclosure, sealing of record, definitions, forms, see Welfare and Institutions Code § 827.95.

§ 1458. Allocation of funds; conditions for receipt of grant; multiple applicants

(a) The board shall allocate funds appropriated pursuant to Section 1450 through a competitive grant process for the purpose of implementing trauma-informed diversion programs for youth.

(b) The board shall distribute a grant under this article pursuant to all of the following conditions:

(1) A local governmental entity or nonprofit organization shall be awarded no less than fifty thousand dollars ($50,000) and no more than two million dollars ($2,000,000).

(2)(A) An applicant shall provide at least a 25–percent cash or in-kind match to the grant that it receives pursuant to this article. Funds used to provide the 25–percent match amount may include a combination of federal, other state, local, or private funds.

(B) Notwithstanding subparagraph (A), an applicant entity may provide less than a 25–percent match, but at least a 10–percent cash or in-kind match, to the grant if the applicant identifies the service area as high need with low or no local infrastructure for diversion programming.

(3) Ninety percent of the funds awarded to a local government entity shall pass through to community-based organizations to deliver services in underserved communities with high rates of youth arrests, as described by the applicant.

(4)(A) Services shall be community based, located in communities of local jurisdictions with high needs.

(B) Services shall be evidence based or research supported, trauma informed, culturally relevant, and developmentally appropriate.

(C) Direct service providers who receive funding from a grant pursuant to this article shall be nongovernmental and not law enforcement or probation entities.

(D) Direct service providers shall have experience effectively serving at-risk youth populations.

(E) Diversion programs shall include alternatives to arrest, incarceration, and formal involvement with the juvenile justice system. Diversion programs shall also include one or more of the following:

(i) Educational services, including academic and vocational services.

(ii) Mentoring services.

(iii) Behavioral health services.

(iv) Mental health services.

(c) Multiple applicants may apply for funding under this article on a regional basis in a single application and receive the aggregate amount of funds that they would have received if awarded as independent applicants. *(Added by Stats.2019, c. 584 (A.B.1454), § 3, eff. Jan. 1, 2020.)*

§ 1459. Duties of board

The board shall be responsible for administration oversight and accountability of the grant program under this article and shall perform both of the following duties:

(a) Support grantee data collection and analysis and require grantees to provide outcomes of the funded programs.

(b)(1) Set aside up to two hundred fifty thousand dollars ($250,-000) of funds appropriated for purposes of the grant program, exclusive of the funds set aside for administrative costs to the board pursuant to subdivision (c) of Section 1450, to contract with a research firm or university to conduct a statewide evaluation of the grant program and its outcomes over a three-year grant period.

(2) The board shall make available on its internet website a report of grantees, projects, and outcomes at the state and local levels within 180 days of completion of the grant cycle.

(3) The board shall assist the research firm or university by providing relevant, existing data for the purposes of tracking outcomes. Measures may include, but are not limited to, any of the following:

(A) Reductions in law enforcement responses to youth for low-level offenses, court caseloads and processing, days the youth spend in detention, placement of youth in congregate care, school and placement disruptions, and facility staff turnover.

(B) Improvement in the health and well-being of the youth, school and community stability, educational attainment, and employment opportunities.

(C) Projected state and local cost savings as a result of the diversion programming. *(Added by Stats.2019, c. 584 (A.B.1454), § 3, eff. Jan. 1, 2020.)*

Division 2.5

YOUTHS

CHAPTER 1. THE YOUTH AUTHORITY

ARTICLE 1. GENERAL PROVISIONS AND DEFINITIONS

§ 1700. Purpose of chapter

The purpose of this chapter is to protect society from the consequences of criminal activity and to that purpose community restoration, victim restoration, and offender training and treatment shall be substituted for retributive punishment and shall be directed toward the rehabilitation of young persons who have committed public offenses. *(Added by Stats.1981, c. 115, p. 849, § 2. Amended by Stats.1999, c. 333 (A.B.637), § 1; Stats.2019, c. 25 (S.B.94), § 54, eff. June 27, 2019.)*

Cross References

General powers of Youth Authority Board over persons committed, see Welfare and Institutions Code § 1766.
Purpose of code, see Welfare and Institutions Code § 19.
Statutory construction,
Amended statutes, see Government Code § 9605.
Court's duties, see Code of Civil Procedure § 1858.
General rules, see Code of Civil Procedure § 1858 et seq.; Government Code § 9603.
Giving effect to all provisions, see Code of Civil Procedure § 1858.
Intention of legislature, see Code of Civil Procedure § 1859.

Research References

3 Witkin, California Criminal Law 4th Punishment § 1 (2021), General Principles.
3 Witkin, California Criminal Law 4th Punishment § 86 (2021), Youth Authority Act.

§ 1701. Title of chapter

This chapter may be cited as the Youth Authority Act. *(Added by Stats.1941, c. 937, p. 2522, § 1. Amended by Stats.1943, c. 690, p. 2442, § 2.)*

§ 1702. Public offenses

This chapter shall apply only to public offenses committed subsequently to the date upon which it becomes effective. *(Added by Stats.1941, c. 937, p. 2523, § 1.)*

§ 1703. Definitions

As used in this chapter the following terms have the following meanings:

(a) "Public offenses" means public offenses as that term is defined in the Penal Code.

(b) "Court" includes any official authorized to impose sentence for a public offense.

(c) "Youth Authority," "Authority," "authority," or "division" means the Department of Corrections and Rehabilitation, Division of Juvenile Facilities.

(d) "Board" or "board" means the Board of Parole Hearings, until January 1, 2007, at which time "board" shall refer to the body created to hear juvenile parole matters under the jurisdiction of the Director of the Division of Juvenile Justice in the Department of Corrections and Rehabilitation.

(e) The masculine pronoun includes the feminine. *(Added by Stats.2020, c. 337 (S.B.823), § 33, eff. Sept. 30, 2020.)*

Cross References

Department of Corrections and Rehabilitation, see Government Code § 12838 et seq.
Department of Youth Authority, generally, see Welfare and Institutions Code § 1710 et seq.
Public offense definition, see Penal Code § 15.
Youth Authority Board, generally, see Welfare and Institutions Code § 1716 et seq.

Research References

3 Witkin, California Criminal Law 4th Punishment § 8 (2021), Division of Juvenile Justice.
3 Witkin, California Criminal Law 4th Punishment § 86 (2021), Youth Authority Act.
3 Witkin, California Criminal Law 4th Punishment § 87 (2021), Persons Eligible for Commitment.
3 Witkin, California Criminal Law 4th Punishment § 88 (2021), Persons Ineligible for Commitment.
3 Witkin, California Criminal Law 4th Punishment § 89 (2021), Trial Court's Discretion.
3 Witkin, California Criminal Law 4th Punishment § 90 (2021), Factors to be Considered.
3 Witkin, California Criminal Law 4th Punishment § 94 (2021), Treatment and Work.
3 Witkin, California Criminal Law 4th Punishment § 96 (2021), Constitutional Limitations.
3 Witkin, California Criminal Law 4th Punishment § 97 (2021), Extended Detention.
3 Witkin, California Criminal Law 4th Punishment § 98 (2021), Return of Incorrigible Person.
3 Witkin, California Criminal Law 4th Punishment § 251 (2021), Scope of Prohibition: Particular Commitments.
3 Witkin, California Criminal Law 4th Punishment § 448 (2021), In General.
3 Witkin, California Criminal Law 4th Punishment § 483 (2021), Juveniles and Youthful Offenders.
3 Witkin, California Criminal Law 4th Punishment § 719 (2021), Remaining Effects of Conviction.

§ 1704. Jurisdiction of juvenile court

Nothing in this chapter shall be deemed to interfere with or limit the jurisdiction of the juvenile court. *(Added by Stats.1941, c. 937, p. 2523, § 1.)*

Cross References

Juvenile court, jurisdiction, see Welfare and Institutions Code § 601.

§ 1705. Religious freedom

It is the intention of the Legislature that all persons in the custody of an institution under the supervision of the Department of the Youth Authority shall be afforded reasonable opportunities to exercise religious freedom. *(Added by Stats.1972, c. 1349, p. 2680, § 3.)*

Research References

3 Witkin, California Criminal Law 4th Punishment § 61 (2021), Freedom of Religion.

ARTICLE 2. DEPARTMENT OF THE YOUTH AUTHORITY

§ 1710. References to Department of Corrections and Rehabilitation, Division of Juvenile Justice; legislative findings and declarations

(a) Any reference to the Department of the Youth Authority in this code or any other code refers to the Department of Corrections and Rehabilitation, Division of Juvenile Justice.

(b) The Legislature finds and declares the following:

(1) The purpose of the Division of Juvenile Justice within the Department of Corrections and Rehabilitation is to protect society from the consequences of criminal activity by providing for the secure placement of youth, and to effectively and efficiently operate and manage facilities housing youthful offenders under the jurisdiction of the department, consistent with the purposes set forth in Section 1700.

(2) The purpose of the Division of Juvenile Programs within the Department of Corrections and Rehabilitation is to provide comprehensive education, training, treatment, and rehabilitative services to youthful offenders under the jurisdiction of the department, that are designed to promote community restoration, family ties, and victim restoration, and to produce youth who become law-abiding and productive members of society, consistent with the purposes set forth in Section 202.

(3) The purpose of the Division of Juvenile Parole Operations within the Department of Corrections and Rehabilitation is to monitor and supervise the reentry into society of youthful offenders under the jurisdiction of the department, and to promote the successful reintegration of youthful offenders into society, in order to reduce the rate of recidivism, thereby increasing public safety. *(Added by Stats.2020, c. 337 (S.B.823), § 35, eff. Sept. 30, 2020.)*

Cross References

Department of Corrections and Rehabilitation, see Government Code § 12838 et seq.
Institutions established for juvenile court wards committed to Youth Authority, see Welfare and Institutions Code § 1000 et seq.

Mission and strategies of Department of Youth and Community Restoration staff, training standards and requirements, see Government Code § 12836.
Powers and duties of Youth Authority, see Welfare and Institutions Code § 1752 et seq.
Youth Authority, see Penal Code § 6001.

Research References

3 Witkin, California Criminal Law 4th Punishment § 8 (2021), Division of Juvenile Justice.
3 Witkin, California Criminal Law 4th Punishment § 86 (2021), Youth Authority Act.

§ 1711. References to Director of the Division of Juvenile Justice in the Department of Corrections and Rehabilitation

Any reference to the Director of the Youth Authority shall be to the Director of the Division of Juvenile Justice in the Department of Corrections and Rehabilitation, unless otherwise expressly provided. *(Added by Stats.2020, c. 337 (S.B.823), § 37, eff. Sept. 30, 2020.)*

Cross References

Department of Corrections and Rehabilitation, see Government Code § 12838 et seq.

Research References

3 Witkin, California Criminal Law 4th Punishment § 8 (2021), Division of Juvenile Justice.

§ 1712. Powers, duties, and authority of Secretary of the Department of Corrections and Rehabilitation; promulgation, enforcement, and publication of rules

(a) All powers, duties, and functions pertaining to the care and treatment of wards provided by any provision of law and not specifically and expressly assigned to the Juvenile Justice branch of the Department of Corrections and Rehabilitation, or to the Board of Parole Hearings, shall be exercised and performed by the Secretary of the Department of Corrections and Rehabilitation. The secretary shall be the appointing authority for all civil service positions of employment in the department. The secretary may delegate the powers and duties vested in the secretary by law, in accordance with Section 7.

(b) Commencing July 1, 2005, the secretary is authorized to make and enforce all rules appropriate to the proper accomplishment of the functions of the Division of Juvenile Facilities, Division of Juvenile Programs, and Division of Juvenile Parole Operations. The rules shall be promulgated and filed pursuant to Chapter 3.5 (commencing with Section 11340) of Part 1 of Division 3 of Title 2 of the Government Code, and shall, to the extent practical, be stated in language that is easily understood by the general public.

(c) The secretary shall maintain, publish, and make available to the general public, a compendium of rules and regulations promulgated by the department pursuant to this section.

(d) The following exceptions to the procedures specified in this section shall apply to the department:

(1) The department may specify an effective date that is any time more than 30 days after the rule or regulation is filed with the Secretary of State; provided that no less than 20 days prior to that effective date, copies of the rule or regulation shall be posted in conspicuous places throughout each institution and shall be mailed to all persons or organizations who request them.

(2) The department may rely upon a summary of the information compiled by a hearing officer; provided that the summary and the testimony taken regarding the proposed action shall be retained as part of the public record for at least one year after the adoption, amendment, or repeal. *(Added by Stats.2020, c. 337 (S.B.823), § 39, eff. Sept. 30, 2020.)*

Cross References

Delegation of powers, see Welfare and Institutions Code § 1723.
Department of Corrections and Rehabilitation, see Government Code § 12838 et seq.
Minimum standards, see Welfare and Institutions Code § 885.
Powers and duties of authority, see Welfare and Institutions Code § 1750 et seq.
Rules and regulations, generally, see Government Code § 11340 et seq.

Research References

3 Witkin, California Criminal Law 4th Punishment § 8 (2021), Division of Juvenile Justice.

§ 1712.1. Family and community communication; telephone calls; suspension of visitation rights; toll-free telephone number

(a) A ward confined in a facility of the Department of Corrections and Rehabilitation, Division of Juvenile Facilities, shall be encouraged to communicate with family members, clergy, and others, and to participate in programs that will facilitate his or her education, rehabilitation, and accountability to victims, and that may help the ward become a law-abiding and productive member of society. If the division or a facility requires a ward to provide a list of allowed visitors, calls, or correspondents, that list shall be transferable from facility to facility, so that the transfer of the ward does not unduly interrupt family and community communication.

(b) A ward shall be allowed a minimum of four telephone calls to his or her family per month. A restriction or reduction of the minimum amount of telephone calls allowed to a ward shall not be imposed as a disciplinary measure. If calls conflict with institutional operations, supervision, or security, telephone usage may be temporarily restricted to the extent reasonably necessary for the continued operation and security of the facility. When speaking by telephone with a family member, clergy, or counsel, a ward may use his or her native language or the native language of the person to whom he or she is speaking.

(c)(1) If a ward's visitation rights are suspended, division or facility staff shall be prepared to inform one or more persons on the list of those persons allowed to visit the ward, if any of those persons should call to ask.

(2) The division or facility shall maintain a toll-free telephone number that families and others may call to confirm visiting times, and to provide timely updates on interruptions and rescheduling of visiting days, times, and conditions.

(3)(A) The division shall encourage correspondence with family or clergy by providing blank paper, envelopes, pencils, and postage. Materials shall be provided in a manner that protects institutional and public safety.

(B) When corresponding with a family member, clergy, or counsel in writing, the ward may use his or her native language or the native language of the person to whom he or she is writing.

(C) Blank paper, envelopes, and pencils shall not be deemed contraband nor seized except in cases where the staff determines that these items would likely be used to cause bodily harm, injury, or death to the ward or other persons, or, based on specific history of property damage by the individual ward, would likely be used to cause destruction of state property. If the staff asserts that it is necessary to seize materials normally used for correspondence, the reasons for the seizure shall be entered in writing in the ward's file or records. *(Added by Stats.2007, c. 458 (A.B.1300), § 3. Amended by Stats.2008, c. 522 (S.B.1250), § 3.)*

§ 1712.5. Possession or use of tobacco products by wards or inmates in institutions and camps under jurisdiction of Department of Youth Authority; use of tobacco products by others on grounds

(a) The possession or use of tobacco products by wards and inmates in all institutions and camps under the jurisdiction of the

Department of the Youth Authority is prohibited. The Director of the Youth Authority shall adopt regulations to implement this prohibition, which shall include an exemption for departmentally approved religious ceremonies.

(b) The use of tobacco products by any person not included in subdivision (a) on the grounds of any institution or facility under the jurisdiction of the Department of the Youth Authority is prohibited, with the exception of residential staff housing where inmates or wards are not present. *(Added by Stats.2004, c. 798 (A.B.384), § 7, operative July 1, 2005.)*

Cross References

Possession or use of tobacco products by inmates or others on grounds of any institution or facility under jurisdiction of Department of Corrections, see Penal Code § 5030.1.

Research References

3 Witkin, California Criminal Law 4th Punishment § 94 (2021), Treatment and Work.

§ 1713. Director of the Division of Juvenile Justice in the Department of Corrections and Rehabilitation; qualifications; recruitment and selection; appointments

(a) The Director of the Division of Juvenile Justice in the Department of Corrections and Rehabilitation shall have wide and successful administrative experience in youth or adult correctional programs embodying rehabilitative or delinquency prevention concepts.

(b) The Governor may request the State Personnel Board to use extensive recruitment and merit selection techniques and procedures to provide a list of persons qualified for appointment as that subordinate officer. The Governor may appoint any person from such list of qualified persons or may reject all names and appoint another person who meets the requirements of this section. *(Added by Stats.1979, c. 860, c. 2974, § 16. Amended by Gov.Reorg.Plan No. 1 of 2005, § 74, eff. May 5, 2005, operative July 1, 2005; Stats.2005, c. 10 (S.B.737), § 77, eff. May 10, 2005, operative July 1, 2005; Stats.2012, c. 41 (S.B.1021), § 93, eff. June 27, 2012.)*

Cross References

Department of Corrections and Rehabilitation, see Government Code § 12838 et seq.
State personnel board, generally, see Government Code § 18650 et seq.

§ 1714. Authority to transfer persons

The Secretary of the Department of Corrections and Rehabilitation may transfer persons confined in one institution or facility of the Division of Juvenile Justice to another. Proximity to family shall be one consideration in placement. *(Added by Stats.2020, c. 337 (S.B.823), § 41, eff. Sept. 30, 2020.)*

Cross References

Department of Corrections and Rehabilitation, see Government Code § 12838 et seq.

§ 1715. Radiologic technologists; reimbursement of fees for certification

From funds available for the support of the Youth Authority, the director may reimburse persons employed by the authority and certified as radiologic technologists pursuant to the Radiologic Technology Act (subdivision (f) of Section 27 of the Health and Safety Code) for the fees incurred both in connection with the obtaining of the certification since July 1, 1971, and with regard to the renewal thereof. *(Added by Stats.1979, c. 860, p. 2974, § 16. Amended by Stats.1996, c. 1023 (S.B.1497), § 458, eff. Sept. 29, 1996.)*

ARTICLE 2.5. BOARD OF JUVENILE HEARINGS

Section

§ 1716. References to Youth Authority Board; abolishment

Commencing July 1, 2016, any reference to the Youth Authority Board refers to the Board of Juvenile Hearings. *(Added by Stats.1979, c. 860, p. 2976, § 17. Amended by Stats.1982, c. 624, § 19; Stats.2003, c. 4 (S.B.459), § 13, eff. April 8, 2003, operative Jan. 1, 2004; Gov.Reorg.Plan No. 1 of 2005, § 76, eff. May 5, 2005, operative July 1, 2005; Stats.2005, c. 10 (S.B.737), § 79, eff. May 10, 2005, operative July 1, 2005; Stats.2016, c. 33 (S.B.843), § 40, eff. June 27, 2016.)*

Cross References

Department of Corrections and Rehabilitation, see Government Code § 12838 et seq.
Public officers and employees, generally, see Government Code § 1000 et seq.
Senate concurrence in nomination by governor, see Government Code § 1321.
Vacancies in office, see Government Code § 1770 et seq.

Research References

3 Witkin, California Criminal Law 4th Punishment § 8 (2021), Division of Juvenile Justice.
3 Witkin, California Criminal Law 4th Punishment § 86 (2021), Youth Authority Act.

§ 1718. Appointment of Board members

(a) The Governor shall appoint three commissioners, subject to Senate confirmation, to the Board of Juvenile Hearings. These commissioners shall be appointed and trained to hear only juvenile matters. The term of appointment for each commissioner shall be five years, and each term shall commence on the expiration of the predecessor. Each commissioner currently serving on the Board of Parole Hearings to hear only juvenile matters shall continue to serve as a commissioner of the Board of Juvenile Hearings until his or her current term expires. The Governor shall stagger the remaining vacancies as follows: one commissioner term to expire on July 1, 2018, and one commissioner term to expire on July 1, 2019. Any appointment to a vacancy that occurs for any reason other than expiration of the term shall be for the remainder of the unexpired term. Commissioners are eligible for reappointment. The selection of persons and their appointment by the Governor and confirmation by the Senate shall reflect as nearly as possible a cross section of the racial, sexual, economic, and geographic features of the population of the state.

(b) The Chair of the Board of Juvenile Hearings shall be designated by the Governor periodically. The Governor may appoint an executive officer of the board, subject to Senate confirmation, who shall hold office at the pleasure of the Governor. The executive officer shall be the administrative head of the board and shall exercise all duties and functions necessary to ensure that the responsibilities of the board are successfully discharged. The Director of the Division of Juvenile Facilities shall be the hiring authority for all civil service positions of employment with the board.

(c) Each commissioner shall participate in hearings, including discharge consideration hearings, initial case reviews, and annual reviews. *(Added by Stats.2016, c. 33 (S.B.843), § 41, eff. June 27, 2016.)*

Research References

3 Witkin, California Criminal Law 4th Punishment § 86 (2021), Youth Authority Act.

§ 1719. Powers and duties of Board; powers and duties of Division; promulgation of policies and regulations for addressing ward disciplinary matters; graduated sanctions

(a) The following powers and duties shall be exercised and performed by the Board of Juvenile Hearings: discharges of commitment, orders for discharge from the jurisdiction of the Division of Juvenile Facilities to the jurisdiction of the committing court, honorable discharge determinations, initial case reviews, and annual reviews.

(b) Any ward may appeal a decision by the Board of Juvenile Hearings to deny discharge to a panel comprised of at least two commissioners.

(c) The following powers and duties shall be exercised and performed by the Division of Juvenile Facilities: return of persons to the court of commitment for redisposition by the court or a reentry disposition, determination of offense category, setting of discharge consideration dates, developing and updating individualized treatment plans, institution placements, furlough placements, return of nonresident persons to the jurisdiction of the state of legal residence, disciplinary decisionmaking, and referrals pursuant to Section 1800.

(d) The department shall promulgate policies and regulations implementing a departmentwide system of graduated sanctions for addressing ward disciplinary matters. The disciplinary decisionmaking system shall be employed as the disciplinary system in facilities under the jurisdiction of the Division of Juvenile Facilities, and shall provide a framework for handling disciplinary matters in a manner that is consistent, timely, proportionate, and ensures the due process rights of wards. The department shall develop and implement a system of graduated sanctions that distinguishes between minor, intermediate, and serious misconduct. The department may not extend a ward's discharge consideration date. The department also may promulgate regulations to establish a process for granting wards who have successfully responded to disciplinary sanctions a reduction of any time acquired for disciplinary matters. *(Added by Stats.2010, c. 729 (A.B.1628), § 13, eff. Oct. 19, 2010, operative July 1, 2014. Amended by Stats.2012, c. 41 (S.B.1021), § 95, eff. June 27, 2012, operative Jan. 1, 2013; Stats.2012, c. 342 (A.B.1481), § 5, eff. Sept. 17, 2012, operative Jan. 1, 2013; Stats.2016, c. 33 (S.B.843), § 42, eff. June 27, 2016; Stats.2017, c. 683 (S.B.625), § 7, eff. Jan. 1, 2018.)*

Cross References

Department of Corrections and Rehabilitation, see Government Code § 12838 et seq.

General powers of Youth Authority Board over persons committed, see Welfare and Institutions Code § 1766.

Research References

3 Witkin, California Criminal Law 4th Punishment § 7 (2021), Board of Parole Hearings.

3 Witkin, California Criminal Law 4th Punishment § 86 (2021), Youth Authority Act.

3 Witkin, California Criminal Law 4th Punishment § 96 (2021), Constitutional Limitations.

§ 1720. Review of cases of wards

(a) The case of each ward shall be reviewed by the Board of Juvenile Hearings within 45 days of arrival at the department, and at other times as is necessary to meet the powers or duties of the board.

(b) The Board of Juvenile Hearings shall periodically review the case of each ward. These reviews shall be made as frequently as the Board of Juvenile Hearings considers desirable and shall be made with respect to each ward at intervals not exceeding one year.

(c) The ward shall be entitled to notice if his or her annual review is delayed beyond one year after the previous annual review hearing. The ward shall be informed of the reason for the delay and of the date the review hearing is to be held.

(d) Failure of the board to review the case of a ward within 15 months of a previous review shall not of itself entitle the ward to discharge from the control of the division but shall entitle him or her to petition the superior court of the county from which he or she was committed for an order of discharge, and the court shall discharge him or her unless the court is satisfied as to the need for further control.

(e) Reviews conducted by the board pursuant to this section shall be written and shall include, but not be limited to, the following: verification of the treatment or program goals and orders for the ward to ensure the ward is receiving treatment and programming that is narrowly tailored to address the correctional treatment needs of the ward and is being provided in a timely manner that is designed to meet the discharge consideration date set for the ward; an assessment of the ward's adjustment and responsiveness to treatment, programming, and custody; a review of the ward's disciplinary history and response to disciplinary sanctions; and a review of any additional information relevant to the ward's progress.

(f) The division shall provide copies of the reviews prepared pursuant to this section to the court and the probation department of the committing county. *(Added by Stats.1979, c. 860, p. 2976, § 17. Amended by Stats.1984, c. 680, § 1; Stats.2003, c. 4 (S.B.459), § 17, eff. April 8, 2003, operative Jan. 1, 2004; Gov.Reorg.Plan No. 1 of 2005, § 80, eff. May 5, 2005, operative July 1, 2005; Stats.2005, c. 10 (S.B.737), § 83, eff. May 10, 2005, operative July 1, 2005; Stats.2016, c. 33 (S.B.843), § 43, eff. June 27, 2016.)*

Cross References

Department of Corrections and Rehabilitation, see Government Code § 12838 et seq.

Juvenile court, discharge of persons committed by, see Welfare and Institutions Code § 1769.

Misdemeanor, discharge of persons convicted of, see Welfare and Institutions Code § 1770.

Powers and duties of Board of Parole Hearings when a person has been committed to Department of Corrections and Rehabilitation, Division of Juvenile Facilities, provisions applicable to wards eligible for release on parole on or after Sept. 1, 2007, see Welfare and Institutions Code § 1766.

Research References

3 Witkin, California Criminal Law 4th Punishment § 94 (2021), Treatment and Work.

§ 1721. Board of Juvenile Hearings meetings; time and place; hearings and decisions; powers and duties

(a) The Board of Juvenile Hearings shall meet at each of the facilities under the jurisdiction of the Division of Juvenile Facilities. Meetings shall be held at whatever times may be necessary for a full and complete study of the cases of all wards whose matters are considered. Other times and places of meeting may also be designated by the board, including, but not limited to, prisons or state facilities housing wards under the jurisdiction of the Division of Juvenile Facilities. Each commissioner of the board shall receive his or her actual necessary traveling expenses incurred in the performance of his or her official duties. If the board performs its functions by meeting en banc in either public or executive sessions to decide matters of general policy, no action shall be valid unless it is concurred in by a majority vote of those present.

(b) The Board of Juvenile Hearings may utilize board representatives to whom it may assign appropriate duties, including hearing cases and making decisions. Those decisions shall be made in accordance with policies approved by a majority of the total membership of the board. When determining whether commissioners or board representatives shall hear matters pursuant to subdivision (a) of Section 1719, or any other matter submitted to the board involving wards under the jurisdiction of the Division of Juvenile Facilities, the chair shall take into account the degree of complexity of the issues presented by the case.

(c) The board shall exercise the powers and duties specified in subdivision (a) of Section 1719 in accordance with rules and regulations adopted by the board. The board may conduct discharge hearings in panels. Each panel shall consist of two or more persons, at least one of whom shall be a commissioner. No panel action shall be valid unless concurred in by a majority vote of the persons present; in the event of a tie vote, the matter shall be referred to and heard by the board en banc. *(Added by Stats.2016, c. 33 (S.B.843), § 44, eff. June 27, 2016.)*

§ 1722. Procedures regarding rules and regulations promulgated by the Board

(a) Any rules and regulations, including any resolutions and policy statements, promulgated by the Board of Juvenile Hearings shall be promulgated and filed pursuant to Chapter 3.5 (commencing with Section 11340) of Part 1 of Division 3 of Title 2 of the Government Code, and shall, to the extent practical, be stated in language that is easily understood by the general public.

(b) The Board of Juvenile Hearings shall maintain, publish, and make available to the general public a compendium of its rules and regulations, including any resolutions and policy statements, promulgated pursuant to this section.

(c) Notwithstanding subdivisions (a) and (b), the chairperson may specify an effective date that is any time more than 30 days after the rule or regulation is filed with the Secretary of State. However, no less than 20 days prior to that effective date, copies of the rule or regulation shall be posted in conspicuous places throughout each institution and shall be mailed to all persons or organizations who request them. *(Added by Stats.2016, c. 33 (S.B.843), § 45, eff. June 27, 2016.)*

§ 1723. Powers and duties to be exercised and performed by board, its designee, subordinates, or division

(a) The powers and duties of the board described in subdivision (a) of Section 1719 shall be exercised and performed by the board or its designee, as authorized by this article.

(b) All other powers conferred to the board concerning wards under the jurisdiction of the division may be exercised through subordinates or delegated to the division under rules established by the board. Any person subjected to an order of those subordinates or of the division pursuant to that delegation may petition the board for review. The board may review those orders under appropriate rules and regulations.

(c) All board designees shall be subject to the training required pursuant to Section 1724. *(Added by Stats.1979, c. 860, p. 2976, § 17. Amended by Stats.2003, c. 4 (S.B.459), § 20, eff. April 8, 2003, operative Jan. 1, 2004; Gov.Reorg.Plan No. 1 of 2005, § 83, eff. May 5, 2005, operative July 1, 2005; Stats.2005, c. 10 (S.B.737), § 86, eff. May 10, 2005, operative July 1, 2005; Stats.2016, c. 33 (S.B.843), § 46, eff. June 27, 2016.)*

Cross References

Delegation of powers and duties, see Welfare and Institutions Code § 7.
Department of Corrections and Rehabilitation, see Government Code § 12838 et seq.

Research References

3 Witkin, California Criminal Law 4th Punishment § 99 (2021), Probation and Parole.
3 Witkin, California Criminal Law 4th Punishment § 100 (2021), Discharge.

§ 1724. Background and interests of commissioners and board representatives; training

(a) Commissioners and board representatives hearing matters pursuant to subdivision (a) of Section 1719 or any other matter involving wards under the jurisdiction of the Division of Juvenile Facilities shall have a broad background in, and ability to perform or understand, appraisal of youthful offenders and delinquents, the circumstances of delinquency for which those persons are committed, and the evaluation of an individual's progress toward reformation. Insofar as practicable, commissioners and board representatives selected to hear these matters also shall have a varied and sympathetic interest in juvenile justice and shall have experience or education in the fields of juvenile justice, sociology, law, law enforcement, mental health, medicine, drug treatment, or education.

(b) Within 60 days of appointment and annually thereafter, commissioners and board representatives described in subdivision (a) shall undergo a minimum of 40 hours of training in the following areas:

(1) Adolescent brain development, the principles of cognitive behavioral therapy, and evidence-based treatment and recidivism-reduction models.

(2) Treatment and training programs provided to wards at the Division of Juvenile Facilities, including, but not limited to, educational, vocational, mental health, medical, substance abuse, psychotherapeutic counseling, and sex offender treatment programs.

(3) Current national research on effective interventions with juvenile offenders and how they compare to division program and treatment services.

(4) Commissioner duties and responsibilities.

(5) Knowledge of laws and regulations applicable to conducting initial case reviews, annual reviews, and discharge hearings, including the rights of victims, witnesses, and wards.

(6) Factors influencing ward lengths of stay and ward recidivism rates and their relationship to one another. *(Added by Stats.2016, c. 33 (S.B.843), § 47, eff. June 27, 2016.)*

Research References

3 Witkin, California Criminal Law 4th Punishment § 100 (2021), Discharge.

§ 1725. Powers and duties to be exercised by Board of Juvenile Hearings; abolishment of Youthful Offender Parole Board and Youth Authority Board; transfer of commissioners

(a) Commencing July 1, 2016, the Board of Juvenile Hearings shall succeed, and shall exercise and perform all powers and duties previously granted to, exercised by, and imposed upon the Youthful Offender Parole Board and Youth Authority Board, as authorized by this article. The Youthful Offender Parole Board and Youth Authority Board are abolished.

(b) Commencing January 1, 2007, all commissioners appointed and trained to hear juvenile parole matters, together with their duties prescribed by law as functions of the Board of Parole Hearings concerning wards under the jurisdiction of the Department of Corrections and Rehabilitation, are transferred to the Director of the

Division of Juvenile Justice. *(Added by Stats.1979, c. 860, p. 2976, § 17. Amended by Stats.2003, c. 4 (S.B.459), § 22, eff. April 8, 2003, operative Jan. 1, 2004; Gov.Reorg.Plan No. 1 of 2005, § 84, eff. May 5, 2005, operative July 1, 2005; Stats.2005, c. 10 (S.B.737), § 87, eff. May 10, 2005, operative July 1, 2005; Stats.2012, c. 41 (S.B.1021), § 97, eff. June 27, 2012; Stats.2016, c. 33 (S.B.843), § 48, eff. June 27, 2016.)*

Cross References

Department of Corrections and Rehabilitation, see Government Code § 12838 et seq.

§ 1726. Employees; selection and appointment; transfers from Youthful Offender Parole Board to Department of Youth Authority; retention

(a) Employees of the Department of the Youth Authority who are needed to support the functions of the Youth Authority Board shall be selected and appointed pursuant to the State Civil Service Act.

(b) All officers and employees of the Youthful Offender Parole Board who on January 1, 2004, are serving in the state civil service, other than as temporary employees, as part of the direct staff of the Youthful Offender Parole Board shall be transferred to the Department of the Youth Authority and subject to retention pursuant to Section 19050.9 of the Government Code. *(Added by Stats.1979, c. 860, p. 2976, § 17. Amended by Stats.2003, c. 4 (S.B.459), § 23, eff. April 8, 2003, operative Jan. 1, 2004.)*

Cross References

Civil service, generally, see Government Code § 18500 et seq.
Discharge of personnel, director's authority, see Welfare and Institutions Code § 1752.

§ 1728. Removal of Board members

The Governor may remove any member of the Board of Juvenile Hearings for misconduct, incompetency, or neglect of duty after a full hearing by the Board of State and Community Corrections. *(Added by Stats.2016, c. 33 (S.B.843), § 49, eff. June 27, 2016.)*

Research References

3 Witkin, California Criminal Law 4th Punishment § 100 (2021), Discharge.

ARTICLE 3. COMMITMENTS TO YOUTH AUTHORITY

Section

Section

§ 1730. Certification to governor

(a) No person may be committed to the Authority until the Authority has certified in writing to the Governor that it has approved or established places of preliminary detention and places for examination and study of persons committed, and has other facilities and personnel sufficient for the proper discharge of its duties and functions.

(b) Before certification to the Governor as provided in subsection (a), a court shall, upon conviction of a person under 21 years of age at the time of his apprehension, deal with him without regard to the provisions of this chapter. *(Added by Stats.1941, c. 937, p. 2525, § 1. Amended by Stats.1944, 3d Ex.Sess., c. 2, p. 22, § 3.)*

Cross References

Confinement of addicted persons over eighteen years of age in controlled substance abuse treatment-control unit, see Health and Safety Code § 11562.
Entry of judgment placing minor on probation or adjudging minor ward or dependent child of court, see Welfare and Institutions Code § 725.

Research References

West's California Judicial Council Forms JV–732, Commitment to the California Department of Corrections and Rehabilitation, Division of Juvenile Facilities (Also Available in Spanish).

§ 1731. Determination of age; commitment of adult to Youth Authority

(a) When in any criminal proceeding in a court of this State a person has been convicted of a public offense and the person was a minor when he or she committed the offense, the court shall determine whether the person was less than 21 years of age at the time of the apprehension from which the criminal proceeding resulted. Proceedings in a juvenile court in respect to a juvenile are not criminal proceedings as that phrase is used in this chapter.

(b) Notwithstanding any other provision of law, no court shall have the power to order an adult convicted of a public offense in a court of criminal jurisdiction to be committed to the Youth Authority. This subdivision shall not apply to a transfer pursuant to Section 1731.5. *(Added by Stats.1941, c. 937, p. 2526, § 1. Amended by Stats.1944, 3d Ex.Sess., c. 2, p. 22, § 4; Stats.1994, c. 452 (S.B.1539), § 2.)*

Cross References

Jurisdiction of juvenile court, see Welfare and Institutions Code § 300 et seq.

Research References

3 Witkin, California Criminal Law 4th Punishment § 87 (2021), Persons Eligible for Commitment.
3 Witkin, California Criminal Law 4th Punishment § 88 (2021), Persons Ineligible for Commitment.

§ 1731.5. Commitment to the Division of Juvenile Justice; criteria; transfer

(a) After certification to the Governor as provided in this article, a court may, until July 1, 2021, commit to the Division of Juvenile Justice any person who meets all of the following:

(1) Is convicted of an offense described in subdivision (b) of Section 707 or subdivision (c) of Section 290.008 of the Penal Code.

(2) Is found to be less than 21 years of age at the time of apprehension.

(3) Is not sentenced to death, imprisonment for life, with or without the possibility of parole, whether or not pursuant to Section 190 of the Penal Code, imprisonment for 90 days or less, or the payment of a fine, or after having been directed to pay a fine, defaults in the payment thereof, and is subject to imprisonment for more than 90 days under the judgment.

(4) Is not granted probation, or was granted probation and that probation is revoked and terminated.

(b) The Division of Juvenile Justice shall accept a person committed to it prior to July 1,2021,[1] pursuant to this article if it believes that the person can be materially benefited by its reformatory and educational discipline, and if it has adequate facilities to provide that care.

(c) A person under 18 years of age who is not committed to the division pursuant to this section may be transferred to the division by the Secretary of the Department of Corrections and Rehabilitation with the approval of the Director of the Division of Juvenile Justice. In sentencing a person under 18 years of age, the court may, until July 1, 2021, order that the person be transferred to the custody of the Division of Juvenile Justice pursuant to this subdivision. If the court makes this order and the division fails to accept custody of the person, the person shall be returned to court for resentencing. The transfer shall be solely for the purposes of housing the inmate, allowing participation in the programs available at the institution by the inmate, and allowing division parole supervision of the inmate, who, in all other aspects shall be deemed to be committed to the Department of Corrections and Rehabilitation and shall remain subject to the jurisdiction of the Secretary of the Department of Corrections and Rehabilitation and the Board of Parole Hearings. Notwithstanding subdivision (b) of Section 2900 of the Penal Code, the secretary, with the concurrence of the director, may designate a facility under the jurisdiction of the director as a place of reception for a person described in this subdivision. The director has the same powers with respect to an inmate transferred pursuant to this subdivision as if the inmate had been committed or transferred to the Division of Juvenile Justice either under the Arnold–Kennick Juvenile Court Law or subdivision (a). The duration of the transfer shall extend until any of the following occurs:

(1) The director orders the inmate returned to the Department of Corrections and Rehabilitation.

(2) The inmate is ordered discharged by the Board of Parole Hearings.

(3) The inmate reaches 18 years of age. However, if the inmate's period of incarceration would be completed on or before the inmate's 25th birthday, the director may continue to house the inmate until the period of incarceration is completed or until final closure of the Division of Juvenile Justice.

(d) The amendments to subdivision (c), as that subdivision reads on July 1, 2018, made by the act adding this subdivision, apply retroactively. *(Added by Stats.2020, c. 337 (S.B.823), § 43, eff. Sept. 30, 2020. Amended by Stats.2021, c. 18 (S.B.92), § 13, eff. May 14, 2021.)*

[1] So in enrolled bill.

Cross References

Daily rate paid to county for convicted individuals under 18 years of age, see Welfare and Institutions Code § 1955.2.
Institutions for delinquents, paroles and dismissals, honorable discharge, see Welfare and Institutions Code § 1178.
Transfer of persons for study, diagnosis and treatment, see Welfare and Institutions Code § 1755.5.
Transfers of person from one institution to another, see Welfare and Institutions Code § 1714.

Research References

1 Witkin California Criminal Law 4th Introduction to Crimes § 32 (2021), Illustrations.
3 Witkin, California Criminal Law 4th Punishment § 87 (2021), Persons Eligible for Commitment.
3 Witkin, California Criminal Law 4th Punishment § 88 (2021), Persons Ineligible for Commitment.
3 Witkin, California Criminal Law 4th Punishment § 89 (2021), Trial Court's Discretion.
3 Witkin, California Criminal Law 4th Punishment § 90 (2021), Factors to be Considered.
3 Witkin, California Criminal Law 4th Punishment § 92 (2021), Division's Acceptance of Commitment.
3 Witkin, California Criminal Law 4th Punishment § 94 (2021), Treatment and Work.
3 Witkin, California Criminal Law 4th Punishment § 96 (2021), Constitutional Limitations.
3 Witkin, California Criminal Law 4th Punishment § 251 (2021), Scope of Prohibition: Particular Commitments.
3 Witkin, California Criminal Law 4th Punishment § 311 (2021), Commitment to Juvenile Facility.
3 Witkin, California Criminal Law 4th Punishment § 483 (2021), Juveniles and Youthful Offenders.

§ 1731.6. Temporary placement in center; diagnosis and recommendation; acceptance; costs

(a) In any county in which there is in effect a contract made pursuant to Section 1752.1, if a court has determined that a person comes within the provisions of Section 1731.5 and concludes that a proper disposition of the case requires such observation and diagnosis as can be made at a diagnostic and treatment center of the Division of Juvenile Justice, the court may continue the hearing and, until July 1, 2021, order that the person be placed temporarily in such a center for a period not to exceed 90 days, with the further provision in such order that the Director of the Division of Juvenile Justice report to the court its diagnosis and recommendations concerning the person within the 90–day period.

(b) The Director of the Division of Juvenile Justice shall, within the 90 days, cause the person to be observed and examined and shall forward to the court the diagnosis and recommendation concerning the person's future care, supervision, and treatment.

(c) The Division of Juvenile Justice shall accept that person if it believes that the person can be materially benefited by such diagnostic and treatment services and if the Director of the Division of Juvenile Justice certifies that staff and institutions are available. A person shall not be transported to any facility under the jurisdiction of the Division of Juvenile Justice until the director has notified the referring court of the place to which the person is to be transported and the time at which the person can be received.

(d) Notwithstanding subdivision (c), the Division of Juvenile Justice shall accept without cost to the county any persons remanded pursuant to Section 707.2.

(e) The sheriff of the county in which an order is made placing a person in a diagnostic and treatment center pursuant to this section, or any other peace officer designated by the court, shall execute the order placing the person in the center or returning them therefrom to the court. The expense of the sheriff or other peace officer incurred in executing that order is a charge upon the county in which the court is situated. *(Added by Stats.1976, c. 299, p. 607, § 1. Amended by Stats.2021, c. 18 (S.B.92), § 14, eff. May 14, 2021.)*

§ 1731.7. Pilot program for transition-aged youth

(a) The Department of Corrections and Rehabilitation, Division of Juvenile Justice, shall establish and operate a seven-year pilot program for transition-aged youth. Commencing on or after January 1, 2019, the program shall divert a limited number of transition-aged youth from adult prison to a juvenile facility in order to provide developmentally appropriate, rehabilitative programming designed for transition-aged youth with the goal of improving their outcomes and reducing recidivism.

(b) The department may develop criteria for placement in this program, initially targeting youth sentenced by a superior court who committed an offense described in subdivision (b) of Section 707 prior to 18 years of age. Youth with a period of incarceration that cannot be completed on or before their 25th birthday are ineligible for placement in the transition-aged youth program. The department may consider the availability of program credit earning opportunities that lower the total length of time a youth serves in determining eligibility.

(c) Notwithstanding any other law, following sentencing, an individual who is 18 years of age or older at the time of sentencing and who has been convicted of an offense described in subdivision (b) of Section 707 that occurred prior to 18 years of age shall remain in local detention pending a determination of acceptance or rejection by the Division of Juvenile Justice. The Division of Juvenile Justice shall notify the local detention authority upon determination of acceptance or rejection of an individual pursuant to this subdivision.

(d) An eligible person may be transferred to the Division of Juvenile Justice by the Secretary of the Department of Corrections and Rehabilitation with the approval of the Director of the Division of Juvenile Justice. Notwithstanding subdivision (b) of Section 2900 of the Penal Code, the secretary, with the concurrence of the director, may designate a facility under the jurisdiction of the Division of Juvenile Justice as a place of reception for a person described in this section.

(e) The duration of the transfer shall extend until either of the following occurs:

(1) The director orders the youth returned to the Department of Corrections and Rehabilitation.

(2) The youth's period of incarceration is completed.

(f) The Division of Juvenile Justice shall produce and submit a report to the Legislature on January 1, 2020, to assess the program. At a minimum, the report shall include all of the following:

(1) Criteria used to determine placement in the program.

(2) Guidelines for satisfactory completion of the program.

(3) Demographic data of eligible and selected participants, including, but not limited to, county of conviction, race, gender, sexual orientation, and gender identity and expression.

(4) Disciplinary infractions incurred by participants.

(5) Good conduct, milestone completion, rehabilitative achievement, and educational merit credits earned in custody.

(6) Quantitative and qualitative measures of progress in programming.

(7) Rates of attrition of program participants.

(g) The Division of Juvenile Justice shall contract with one or more independent universities or outside research organizations to evaluate the effects of participation in the program established by this section. This evaluation shall include, at a minimum, an evaluation of cost-effectiveness, recidivism data, consistency with evidence-based principles, and program fidelity. If sufficient data is available, the evaluation may also compare participant outcomes with a like group of similarly situated transition aged youth retained in the counties or incarcerated in adult institutions.

(h) The Division of Juvenile Justice shall promulgate regulations to implement this section.

(i) Effective July 1, 2020, the pilot program operated pursuant to this section shall be suspended. Any pilot program participants who were diverted from an adult prison pursuant to this section and who were housed at the Division of Juvenile Justice prior to January 1, 2020, may remain at the Division of Juvenile Justice pursuant to subdivision (e). *(Added by Stats.2018, c. 36 (A.B.1812), § 35, eff. June 27, 2018. Amended by Stats.2019, c. 497 (A.B.991), § 300, eff. Jan. 1, 2020; Stats.2019, c. 25 (S.B.94), § 67, eff. June 27, 2019; Stats.2020, c. 29 (S.B.118), § 42, eff. Aug. 6, 2020; Stats.2021, c. 18 (S.B.92), § 15, eff. May 14, 2021.)*

Cross References

Institutions for delinquents, paroles and dismissals, honorable discharge, see Welfare and Institutions Code § 1178.

§ 1731.8. Setting of initial parole consideration date; notice; guidelines

Notwithstanding any other provision of law, within 60 days of the commitment of a ward to the Department of the Youth Authority, the department shall set an initial parole consideration date for the ward and shall notify the probation department and the committing juvenile court of that date. The department shall use the category offense guidelines contained in Sections 4951 to 4957, inclusive, of, and the deviation guidelines contained in subdivision (i) of Section 4945 of, Title 15 of the California Code of Regulations, that were in effect on January 1, 2003, in setting an initial parole consideration date. *(Added by Stats.2003, c. 4 (S.B.459), § 25, eff. April 8, 2003, operative Jan. 1, 2004.)*

Research References

3 Witkin, California Criminal Law 4th Punishment § 95 (2021), In General.

§ 1732. Commitment to Department of Corrections and Rehabilitation, Division of Juvenile Facilities of 18-year-old sex offender with prior sex offense; prohibition

No person convicted of violating Section 261, 262, or 264.1 of, subdivision (b) of Section 288 of, Section 289 of, or of sodomy or oral copulation by force, violence, duress, menace or threat of great bodily harm as provided in Section 286 or 287 of, or former Section 288a of, the Penal Code committed when that person was 18 years of age who has previously been convicted of any such felony shall be committed to the Department of Corrections and Rehabilitation, Division of Juvenile Facilities. This section does not prohibit the adjournment of criminal proceedings pursuant to Division 3 (commencing with Section 3000) or Division 6 (commencing with Section 6000) of the Welfare and Institutions Code. *(Added by Stats.1979, c. 944, p. 3265, § 20. Amended by Stats.1989, c. 555, § 9; Stats.1996, c. 1075 (S.B.1444), § 17; Stats.2018, c. 423 (S.B.1494), § 126, eff. Jan. 1, 2019.)*

Research References

3 Witkin, California Criminal Law 4th Punishment § 88 (2021), Persons Ineligible for Commitment.

§ 1732.5. Serious felony; commission by person 18 or older; no commitment to Youth Authority; amendment of section

Notwithstanding any other provision of law, no person convicted of murder, rape or any other serious felony, as defined in Section 1192.7

of the Penal Code, committed when he or she was 18 years of age or older shall be committed to Youth Authority.

The provisions of this section shall not be amended by the Legislature except by statute passed in each house by rollcall vote entered in the journal, two-thirds of the membership concurring, or by a statute that becomes effective only when approved by the electors. *(Added by Initiative Measure, approved by the people, June 8, 1982.)*

Research References

1 Witkin California Criminal Law 4th Introduction to Crimes § 124 (2021), Constitutional Provisions and Statutes.
3 Witkin, California Criminal Law 4th Punishment § 88 (2021), Persons Ineligible for Commitment.
3 Witkin, California Criminal Law 4th Punishment § 234 (2021), Equal Protection Analysis.

§ 1732.6. Minors convicted of specific offenses; life sentence or other lengthy sentence; commitment to Youth Authority prohibited

(a) No minor shall be committed to the Youth Authority when he or she is convicted in a criminal action for an offense described in subdivision (c) of Section 667.5 or subdivision (c) of Section 1192.7 of the Penal Code and is sentenced to incarceration for life, an indeterminate period to life, or a determinate period of years such that the maximum number of years of potential confinement when added to the minor's age would exceed 25 years. Except as specified in subdivision (b), in all other cases in which the minor has been convicted in a criminal action, the court shall retain discretion to sentence the minor to the Department of Corrections or to commit the minor to the Youth Authority.

(b) No minor shall be committed to the Youth Authority when he or she is convicted in a criminal action for:

(1) An offense described in subdivision (b) of Section 602, or

(2) An offense described in paragraphs (1), (2), or (3) of subdivision (d) of Section 707, if the circumstances enumerated in those paragraphs are found to be true by the trier of fact.

(3) An offense described in subdivision (b) of Section 707, if the minor had attained the age of 16 years of age or older at the time of commission of the offense.

(c) Notwithstanding any other provision of law, no person under the age of 16 years shall be housed in any facility under the jurisdiction of the Department of Corrections. *(Added by Stats. 1993–94, 1st Ex.Sess., c. 15 (S.B.23), § 1. Amended by Initiative Measure (Prop. 21, § 34, approved March 7, 2000, eff. March 8, 2000); Stats.2002, c. 787 (S.B.1798), § 36.)*

Research References

1 Witkin California Criminal Law 4th Introduction to Crimes § 140 (2021), Gang Violence and Juvenile Crime Prevention Act (Proposition 21).
3 Witkin, California Criminal Law 4th Punishment § 87 (2021), Persons Eligible for Commitment.
3 Witkin, California Criminal Law 4th Punishment § 88 (2021), Persons Ineligible for Commitment.

§ 1732.7. Commitment to authority for minor offenses

A person who is convicted of a public offense for which the maximum penalty provided by law is imprisonment for not more than 90 days, and who is found to be less than 21 years of age at the time of his apprehension, may be committed to the Authority only if it is brought to the court's knowledge that the person has been previously convicted of a public offense or has been a ward of the juvenile court by reason of a public offense and the court is satisfied that society will best be protected by commitment to the Authority. *(Added by Stats.1941, c. 937, p. 2526, § 1. Amended by Stats.1944, 3d Ex.Sess., c. 2, p. 23, § 8.)*

Cross References

Public offense, definition, see Welfare and Institutions Code § 1703; Penal Code § 15.

Research References

3 Witkin, California Criminal Law 4th Punishment § 88 (2021), Persons Ineligible for Commitment.

§ 1732.8. Transfer and confinement of persons 18 years of age or older to Director of Corrections; consent requirements; educational or vocational programs

(a) Notwithstanding any other law and subject to the provisions of this section, the Director of the Youth Authority may transfer to and cause to be confined within the custody of the Director of Corrections any person 18 years of age or older who is subject to the custody, control, and discipline of the Department of the Youth Authority and who is scheduled to be returned, or has been returned, to the Department of the Youth Authority from the Department of Corrections after serving a sentence imposed pursuant to Section 1170 of the Penal Code for a felony that was committed while he or she was in the custody of the Department of the Youth Authority.

(b) No person shall be transferred pursuant to this section until and unless the person voluntarily, intelligently, and knowingly executes a written consent to the transfer, which shall be irrevocable.

(c) Prior to being returned to the Youth Authority, a person in the custody of the Department of Corrections who is scheduled to be returned to the Department of the Youth Authority shall meet personally with a Youth Authority parole agent or other appropriate Department of the Youth Authority staff member. The parole agent or staff member shall explain, using language clearly understandable to the person, all of the following matters:

(1) What will be expected from the person when he or she returns to a Youth Authority institution in terms of cooperative daily living conduct and participation in applicable counseling, academic, vocational, work experience, or specialized programming.

(2) The conditions of parole applicable to the person, and how those conditions will be monitored and enforced while the person is in the custody of the Youth Authority.

(3) The person's right under this section to voluntarily and irrevocably consent to continue to be housed in an institution under the jurisdiction of the Department of Corrections instead of being returned to the Youth Authority.

(d) A person who has been returned to the Youth Authority after serving a sentence described in subdivision (a) may be transferred to the custody of the Department of Corrections if the person consents to the transfer after having been provided with the explanations described in subdivision (c).

(e) If a Youth Authority person consents to being housed in an institution under the jurisdiction of the Department of Corrections pursuant to this section, he or she shall be subject to the general rules and regulations of the Department of Corrections. The Youth Authority Board shall continue to determine the person's eligibility for parole at the same intervals, in the same manner, and under the same standards and criteria that would be applicable if the person were confined in the Department of the Youth Authority. However, the board shall not order or recommend any treatment, education, or other programming that is unavailable in the institution where the person is housed, and shall not deny parole to a person housed in the institution based solely on the person's failure to participate in programs unavailable to the person.

(f) Any person housed in an institution under the jurisdiction of the Department of Corrections pursuant to this section who has not attained a high school diploma or its equivalent shall participate in educational or vocational programs, to the extent the appropriate programs are available.

(g) Upon notification by the Director of Corrections that the person should be no longer be housed in an institution under its jurisdiction, the Department of the Youth Authority shall immediately send for, take, and receive the person back into an institution under its jurisdiction. *(Added by Stats.2001, c. 476 (S.B.768), § 1. Amended by Stats.2003, c. 4 (S.B.459), § 26, eff. April 8, 2003, operative Jan. 1, 2004.)*

§ 1732.9. Closure of Division of Juvenile Justice; transfer of persons 18 years of age or older to institution under jurisdiction of Department of Corrections and Rehabilitation; consent requirements

(a) Notwithstanding any other law, immediately prior to closure of the Division of Juvenile Justice, a person 18 years of age or older who is subject to the custody, control, and discipline of the division and who has been sentenced to state prison pursuant to Section 1170 of the Penal Code for a felony committed while the person was in the custody of the division may voluntarily remain in an institution under the jurisdiction of the Department of Corrections and Rehabilitation to complete the remaining juvenile court commitment, subject to the provisions of this section, or may be returned to the county of commitment.

(b) Notwithstanding any other law, immediately prior to closure of the division, a person 18 years of age or older in the custody of the Department of Corrections and Rehabilitation pursuant to Section 1732.8 may voluntarily remain in an institution under the jurisdiction of the Department of Corrections and Rehabilitation to complete the person's juvenile court commitment, subject to the provisions of this section.

(c) As soon as possible, the Director of the Division shall notify the juvenile court of commitment, juvenile counsel of record, and the county probation agency of a person in the custody of the Department of Corrections and Rehabilitation pursuant to Section 1732.8 of this code or Section 1170 of the Penal Code for a felony committed while in the custody of the division, that the person has remaining juvenile court commitment time that can be voluntarily served at an institution under the jurisdiction of the Department of Corrections and Rehabilitation, subject to the provisions of the section. The division shall also notify the juvenile court of commitment of the youth's most recent projected board hearing date for court consideration.

(d) Prior to deciding whether to serve the remaining commitment time in the state prison or be returned to the county of commitment, a person in the custody of the Department of Corrections and Rehabilitation pursuant to Section 1732.8 who is scheduled to be returned to the county shall meet personally with a probation officer from the county of commitment and be advised by juvenile counsel of record. The probation officer shall explain, using language clearly understandable to the person, all of the following matters:

(1) What will be expected from the person when the person returns to county jurisdiction, in terms of cooperative daily living conduct and participation in applicable counseling, academic, vocational, work experience, or specialized programming.

(2) The conditions of probation applicable to the person, if set by the court, and how those conditions will be monitored and enforced.

(3) The person's right, under this section, to voluntarily and irrevocably consent to continue to be housed in an institution under the jurisdiction of the Department of Corrections and Rehabilitation instead of being returned to county custody.

(e) A person shall not be retained at the Department of Corrections and Rehabilitation pursuant to this section until and unless the person voluntarily, intelligently, and knowingly executes a written consent to the placement, which shall be irrevocable. This consent shall be irrevocable unless the youth can demonstrate that they are in danger of suffering great bodily harm. A youth returned to the county under this subdivision shall not be subsequently returned to the Department of Corrections and Rehabilitation.

(f) Notwithstanding any other law, a person who has been returned to the county after serving a sentence imposed pursuant to Section 1170 of the Penal Code for a felony committed while the person was in the custody of the division, may be transferred to the custody of the Department of Corrections and Rehabilitation if the person consents to the transfer after having been provided with the explanations described in subdivision (d), and after consulting with the juvenile counsel of record.

(g) If a person consents to being housed in an institution under the jurisdiction of the Department of Corrections and Rehabilitation pursuant to this section, the person shall be subject to the general rules and regulations of the department. The juvenile court of commitment shall continue to have jurisdiction over the juvenile case while the individual is in an institution under the jurisdiction of the Department of Corrections and Rehabilitation. The county probation department shall, with the assistance of the Department of Corrections and Rehabilitation, provide semiannual status reports to the court that summarize the person's progress in the department's care. However, the court shall not order or recommend any treatment, education, or other programming that is unavailable in the institution where the person is housed, and shall not deny release to a person housed in the institution based solely on the person's failure to participate in programs that were unavailable to the person.

(h) A person housed in an institution under the jurisdiction of the Department of Corrections and Rehabilitation pursuant to this section who has not attained a high school diploma or its equivalent shall participate in educational or vocational programs, to the extent the appropriate programs are available.

(i) Upon notification by the Secretary of the Department of Corrections and Rehabilitation that the person has completed the juvenile court commitment and should no longer be housed in an institution under its jurisdiction, the court of commitment shall immediately send for, take, and receive the person back into the county's jurisdiction.

(j) The county of commitment shall not be charged by the state for a person in custody of the Department of Corrections and Rehabilitation pursuant to this section while serving the person's juvenile court commitment.

(k) This section shall only apply to a person described in subdivision (a) or (b) who is in the custody of the Department of Corrections and Rehabilitation when the division closes. Additional persons shall not be subject to this section.

(*l*) This section shall remain in effect only until January 1, 2031, and as of that date is repealed. *(Added by Stats.2022, c. 58 (A.B.200), § 42, eff. June 30, 2022.)*

Repeal

For repeal of this section, see its terms.

Cross References

Arson and attempted arson, persons convicted of arson, registration while residing California, see Penal Code § 457.1.

Juveniles adjudicated a ward of the juvenile court for specified sex offenses and sent to the Division of Juvenile Justice, or equivalent thereof, duty to register, see Penal Code § 290.008.

§ 1732.10. Closure of Division of Juvenile Justice; continuation of services for state hospital patients referred by division

(a) Notwithstanding any other law, unless the committing court orders an alternative placement, upon closure of the Division of Juvenile Justice, the State Department of State Hospitals shall continue to provide evaluation, care, and treatment of state hospital patients referred by the division pursuant to Section 1756 and Interagency Agreement 21–00189, or a predecessor agreement, until clinical discharge, as defined in paragraph (9) of subdivision (b) is recommended by the State Department of State Hospitals, or until the patient referred by the division reaches the hospitalization release date in subdivision (e). When discharge is clinically indicated, the State Department of State Hospitals shall notify the juvenile court of commitment, juvenile counsel of record, the probation department, and the behavioral health department. The State Department of State Hospitals shall collaborate with county probation and behavioral health to ensure continuity of care. The division shall provide contact information for the committing court, juvenile counsel of record, and related probation department for all patients in the custody of the State Department of State Hospitals upon enactment of this section and any youth placed at the State Department of State Hospitals prior to closure of the division.

(b) Notwithstanding the confidentiality provision for information and records set forth under Section 5328, for any youth referred by the division who remains a patient after closure of the division, the State Department of State Hospitals shall do the following:

(1) Collaborate with the county probation department and behavioral health department prior to the expected discharge from the state hospital to assist the county in determining the least restrictive legal alternative placement for the youth.

(2) Provide the court, juvenile counsel of record, and county probation department, upon closure of the division and annually thereafter, a copy of the finalized treatment plan specifying the youth's goals of hospitalization, assessed needs, and how the staff will assist the youth to achieve the goals and objectives.

(3) Notify the juvenile court of commitment, juvenile counsel of record, and county probation as soon as safely possible, but no later than 24 hours following any of the following:

(A) A suicide or serious attempted suicide.

(B) A serious injury or battery, with or without a weapon.

(C) An alleged sexual assault.

(D) An escape or attempted escape.

(4) Provide county probation, biannually, a synopsis of behavioral incidences, including, but not limited to, self-harm, assault, contraband, and property damage.

(5) Notify the committing court, juvenile counsel of record, and the county probation department if a youth refuses to consent to clinically necessary medication treatment and provide the court with the clinical records and testimony necessary for the court to consider an order for involuntary medication administration. Notwithstanding any other law, the State Department of State Hospitals shall utilize the process outlined in Section 4210 of Title 9 of the California Code of Regulations and In re Qawi (2004) 32.Cal.4th.1 to obtain involuntary medication orders.

(6) Notify individuals covered by a youth's medical release of information, the juvenile counsel of record, the juvenile committing court, and the county probation department within 24 hours of the youth being hospitalized for a serious medical condition.

(7) Notify the youth's next of kin on record, juvenile counsel of record, the juvenile committing court, and the county probation department of the county of commitment within 24 hours, and the local county coroner and local law enforcement agencies within two hours, of the discovery of death when a youth dies during hospitalization at a state hospital, or if the death occurred immediately following transfer from a state hospital to a community medical facility.

(8) Notify the juvenile committing court, the juvenile counsel of record, and probation department if it believes the youth requires conservatorship upon discharge. For continuity of care, the State Department of State Hospitals shall accommodate any necessary access to the youth or medical records as needed for arranging conservatorship.

(9) Notify the juvenile court of commitment, juvenile counsel of record, and the county probation department when the youth is ready to discharge to the county based on the following:

(A) When the youth has improved to a degree that further hospitalization is unnecessary, or the primary illness or problem for which hospitalization was required is in substantial remission, and the remaining symptoms are those of a disorder for which hospitalization in a state hospital is not clinically necessary.

(B) When further hospitalization is unnecessary, not clinically appropriate, and will provide no further benefit.

(C) When a court has ordered an alternative placement.

(D) When the youth has reached the hospitalization release date described in subdivision (e).

(10) Provide a written discharge summary and all other pertinent medical and mental health data to the receiving juvenile court of commitment, juvenile counsel of record, and county probation department.

(c) For a youth remaining a patient in a state hospital pursuant to this section, the probation department shall do all of the following:

(1) Upon notification of discharge criteria having been met from the State Department of State Hospitals, find a placement for the patient within 45 days.

(2) Provide transportation to court appearances and from the state hospital to the county designated placement within 7 calendar days of the discharge date.

(3) Reimburse the State Department of State Hospitals for any off-site medical or surgical health care expense, if services could not be provided by the State Department of State Hospitals and prior approval was received from the county, except in cases of emergency.

(d) The county of commitment shall not be charged by the state for a person placed in a state hospital by the division prior to closure pursuant to Section 1756 or Interagency Agreement 21–00189 or a predecessor agreement, during this placement.

(e) A person in a state hospital under the provisions of Section 1756 or this section shall be released and discharged to the county of commitment no later than the person's maximum juvenile confinement time, as determined by Section 607 and all other provisions of law.

(f) Immediately prior to closure, the division shall notify the juvenile court of commitment and the juvenile counsel of record of the youth's most recent projected board hearing date for court consideration.

(g) This section shall only apply to the youth referred by the division prior to closure who remain a patient in a state hospital after closure of the division. Additional youth shall not be subject to this section.

(h) This section shall remain in effect only until January 1, 2031, and as of that date is repealed. *(Added by Stats.2022, c. 58 (A.B.200), § 43, eff. June 30, 2022. Amended by Stats.2022, c. 771 (A.B.160), § 22, eff. Sept. 29, 2022.)*

Repeal

For repeal of this section, see its terms.

Cross References

Arson and attempted arson, persons convicted of arson, registration while residing California, see Penal Code § 457.1.

Juveniles adjudicated a ward of the juvenile court for specified sex offenses and sent to the Division of Juvenile Justice, or equivalent thereof, duty to register, see Penal Code § 290.008.

§ 1733. Revocation or suspension of license

Nothing in this chapter prevents a court from revoking or suspending any license issued to the defendant under any law of this

State where such revocation or suspension is otherwise provided for. *(Added by Stats.1941, c. 937, p. 2627, § 1.)*

§ 1735. Unpaid fine; remittance; commitment to confinement

If the court sentences a person under 21 years of age at the time of his apprehension to the payment of a fine and the fine is not paid, the court may either remit the fine in whole or in part, or commit him to confinement for a length of time permitted by the statutes relating to imprisonment for failure to pay fines. But such confinement may be only in a place approved by the Authority. *(Added by Stats.1941, c. 937, p. 2527, § 1. Amended by Stats.1944, 3d Ex.Sess., c. 2, p. 23, § 9.)*

Cross References

Fine, imprisonment until payment, see Penal Code § 1205.
Misdemeanor punishment for offense with no punishment prescribed, see Penal Code § 19.4.

Research References

3 Witkin, California Criminal Law 4th Punishment § 88 (2021), Persons Ineligible for Commitment.
3 Witkin, California Criminal Law 4th Punishment § 105 (2021), General Rule.

§ 1736. Commitments by juvenile court

The juvenile court may in its discretion commit persons subject to its jurisdiction to the Authority, and the Authority may in its discretion accept such commitments. *(Added by Stats.1941, c. 937, p. 2527, § 1.)*

Cross References

Adjudging minor a ward or dependent child of court, see Welfare and Institutions Code § 725.
Discharge of persons committed to Youth Authority, see Welfare and Institutions Code § 1769.
Jurisdiction of juvenile court, see Welfare and Institutions Code § 300.
Religious beliefs, see Welfare and Institutions Code § 205.

Research References

3 Witkin, California Criminal Law 4th Punishment § 86 (2021), Youth Authority Act.

§ 1737. Recall of commitment and resentencing; credit for time served

When a person has been committed to the custody of the authority, if it is deemed warranted by a diagnostic study and recommendation approved by the director, the judge who ordered the commitment or, if the judge is not available, the presiding judge of the court, within 120 days of the date of commitment on his or her own motion, or the court, at any time thereafter upon recommendation of the director, may recall the commitment previously ordered and resentence the person as if he or she had not previously been sentenced. The time served while in custody of the authority shall be credited toward the term of any person resentenced pursuant to this section.

As used in this section, "time served while in custody of the authority" means the period of time during which the person was physically confined in a state institution by order of the Department of the Youth Authority or the Youth Authority Board. *(Added by Stats.1941, c. 937, p. 2527, § 1. Amended by Stats.1945, c. 779, p. 1466, § 3; Stats.1963, c. 443, p. 1277, § 3, eff. May 17, 1963; Stats.1975, c. 1103, p. 2676, § 1; Stats.1983, c. 221, § 1; Stats.2002, c. 784 (S.B.1316), § 617; Stats.2003, c. 4 (S.B.459), § 27, eff. April 8, 2003, operative Jan. 1, 2004.)*

Law Revision Commission Comments

Section 1737 is amended to delete language referring to the sole judge. Every superior court has at least two judgeships as a result of trial court unification. See Gov't Code § 69580 *et seq.* (number of judges). Where a court has only one judge due to a vacancy or otherwise, the reference to the "presiding judge" means the sole judge of the court. See Gov't Code § 69508.5 (presiding judge). [32 Cal.L.Rev.Comm. Reports 561 (2002)].

Research References

3 Witkin, California Criminal Law 4th Punishment § 91 (2021), Commitment Procedure.

§ 1737.1. Return of person to committing court

Whenever any person who has been convicted of a public offense in adult court and committed to and accepted by the Department of the Youth Authority appears to be an improper person to be retained by the department, or to be so incorrigible or so incapable of reformation under the discipline of the department as to render his or her detention detrimental to the interests of the department and the other persons committed thereto, the department may order the return of that person to the committing court. The court may then commit the person to a state prison or sentence him or her to a county jail as provided by law for punishment of the offense of which he or she was convicted. The maximum term of imprisonment for a person committed to a state prison under this section shall be a period equal to the maximum term prescribed by law for the offense of which he or she was convicted less the period during which he or she was under the control of the department. This section shall not apply to commitments from juvenile court.

As used in this section "period during which he or she was under the control of the department" means the period of time during which he or she was physically confined in a state institution by order of the department or the Youth Authority Board. *(Added by Stats.1945, c. 781, p. 1470, § 1. Amended by Stats.1969, c. 924, p. 1853, § 1; Stats.1976, c. 1071, p. 4830, § 33; Stats.1979, c. 860, p. 2979, § 18; Stats.1983, c. 221, § 2; Stats.2003, c. 4 (S.B.459), § 28, eff. April 8, 2003, operative Jan. 1, 2004.)*

Cross References

Commitment to state prison after expiration of control, see Welfare and Institutions Code § 1780 et seq.
Public offense, definition, see Welfare and Institutions Code § 1703; Penal Code § 15.
Return of minor to committing court, see Welfare and Institutions Code § 780.

Research References

3 Witkin, California Criminal Law 4th Punishment § 98 (2021), Return of Incorrigible Person.
3 Witkin, California Criminal Law 4th Punishment § 483 (2021), Juveniles and Youthful Offenders.

§ 1737.5. Effect of commitment

A commitment to the Authority is a judgment within the meaning of Chapter 1 of Title 8 of Part 2 of the Penal Code,[1] and is appealable. *(Added by Stats.1943, c. 898, p. 2746, § 1.)*

[1] Penal Code § 1191 et seq.

Cross References

Appeals in criminal cases, see Penal Code §§ 1235 et seq., 1466 et seq.
Crime as misdemeanor on commitment to Youth Authority, see Penal Code § 17.
Insanity as cause against pronouncement of judgment, see Penal Code § 1201.

Research References

6 Witkin, California Criminal Law 4th Criminal Appeal § 56 (2021), In General.
3 Witkin, California Criminal Law 4th Punishment § 91 (2021), Commitment Procedure.

§ 1738. Disposition of person after commitment

When the court commits a person to the authority the court may order him conveyed to some place of detention approved or established by the authority or may direct that he be left at liberty until otherwise ordered by the authority under such conditions as in the court's opinion will insure his submission to any orders which the authority may issue. No such person shall be transported to any facility under the jurisdiction of the Youth Authority until the director has notified the sheriff of the county of the committing court of the place to which said person is to be transported and the time at which he can be received. *(Added by Stats.1941, c. 937, p. 2527, § 1. Amended by Stats.1969, c. 1197, p. 2332, § 1.)*

Cross References

Judgment in criminal cases, generally, see Penal Code § 1191 et seq.
Orders adjudging minor a ward or dependent child of the court, see Welfare and Institutions Code § 725.

Research References

3 Witkin, California Criminal Law 4th Punishment § 91 (2021), Commitment Procedure.

§ 1739. Appeal

(a) The right of a person who has been convicted of a public offense to a new trial or to an appeal from the judgment of conviction shall not be affected by anything in this chapter.

(b) When a person who has been convicted and committed to the Authority appeals from the conviction, the execution of the commitment to the Authority shall not be stayed by the taking of the appeal except as provided in subsection (c). The person so committed shall remain subject to the control of the Authority, until final disposition of the appeal.

(c) A person convicted and committed to the Authority may be admitted to bail under the provisions of Section 1272 of the Penal Code, or in the discretion of the court, may be left at liberty, under such conditions as in the court's opinion will insure his cooperation in reasonable expedition of the appellate proceedings and his submission to the control of the Authority at the proper time. *(Added by Stats.1941, c. 937, p. 2527, § 1.)*

Cross References

Appeals in criminal cases, see Penal Code §§ 1235 et seq., 1466 et seq.
New trial, ordering of an appeal, see Penal Code §§ 1179 et seq., 1260, 1261.
Public offense, definition, see Welfare and Institutions Code § 1703; Penal Code § 15.
Stay of execution by appeal, see Penal Code § 1242 et seq.

Research References

6 Witkin, California Criminal Law 4th Criminal Appeal § 56 (2021), In General.
6 Witkin, California Criminal Law 4th Criminal Appeal § 108 (2021), Power and Procedure.
3 Witkin, California Criminal Law 4th Punishment § 91 (2021), Commitment Procedure.

§ 1740. Certified copy of commitment order

When a court commits a person to the Authority such court shall at once forward to the Authority a certified copy of the order of commitment. *(Added by Stats.1941, c. 937, p. 2528, § 1.)*

Cross References

Probation officers' reports, see Welfare and Institutions Code § 285.

Research References

3 Witkin, California Criminal Law 4th Punishment § 91 (2021), Commitment Procedure.

§ 1741. Case history reports to authority

The judge before whom the person was tried and committed, the district attorney or other official who conducted the prosecution, and the probation officer of the county, shall obtain and with the order of commitment furnish to the authority, in writing, all information that can be given in regard to the career, habits, degree of education, age, nationality, parentage and previous occupations of such person, together with a statement to the best of their knowledge as to whether such person was industrious, and of good character, the nature of his associates and his disposition.

The reports required by this section shall be made upon forms furnished by the authority or according to an outline furnished by it.

When a person has been committed to the authority, the court and the prosecuting and police authorities and other public officials shall make available to the authority all pertinent data in their possession in respect to the case. *(Added by Stats.1941, c. 937, p. 2527, § 1. Amended by Stats.1945, c. 782, p. 1471, § 1; Stats.1961, c. 79, p. 1060, § 3.)*

Cross References

Probation, investigation and reports on, see Welfare and Institutions Code § 1760.7.
Probation officer's reports and investigations, see Welfare and Institutions Code § 628.
Probation officer's reports to authority, see Welfare and Institutions Code § 284.

Research References

3 Witkin, California Criminal Law 4th Punishment § 91 (2021), Commitment Procedure.

§ 1742. Exceptional needs individual; transfer of previously prepared individualized education program

When the juvenile court commits to the Youth Authority a person identified as an individual with exceptional needs, as defined by Section 56026 of the Education Code, the juvenile court, subject to the requirements of subdivision (a) of Section 727 and subdivision (b) of Section 737, shall not order the juvenile conveyed to the physical custody of the Youth Authority until the juvenile's individualized education program previously developed pursuant to Article 3 (commencing with Section 56340) of Chapter 4 of Part 30 of Division 4 of Title 2 of the Education Code for the individual with exceptional needs, has been furnished to the Department of the Youth Authority.

To facilitate this process the juvenile court shall assure that the probation officer communicates with appropriate staff at the juvenile court school, county office of education, or special education local planning area. *(Added by Stats.1993, c. 175 (A.B.820), § 1.)*

ARTICLE 4. POWERS AND DUTIES OF YOUTH AUTHORITY

§ 1750. Expenditures

The Authority is limited in its expenditures to funds specifically made available for its use. *(Added by Stats.1941, c. 937, p. 2528, § 1.)*

Cross References

Confinement of addicted persons over eighteen years of age in controlled substance abuse treatment-control unit, see Health and Safety Code § 11562.
Delegation of powers, see Welfare and Institutions Code §§ 1712, 1719.
Exercise of powers and duties, see Penal Code § 6001 et seq.
Expenditures, limitations on, see Welfare and Institutions Code § 1002.

§ 1752. Powers of director

Section amended by Stats.1972, c. 1365, § 2. See, also, section amended by Stats.1981, c. 453, § 7, operative contingent under the terms of § 8 of that chapter.

To the extent that necessary funds are available for the purposes, the director may

(a) Establish and operate a treatment and training service and such other services as are proper for the discharge of his duties;

(b) Create administrative districts suitable to the performance of his duties;

(c) Employ and discharge all such persons as may be needed for the proper execution of the duties of the authority. Such employment and discharge shall be in accord with the civil service laws of this state.

Notwithstanding Section 18932 of the Government Code, the maximum age shall be 35 years for any open examination for the position of parole agent I, group supervisor, youth counselor, and other custodial and parole positions which normally afford entry into the Youth Authority service, unless the applicant is already a "state safety" member for the purposes of retirement and disability benefits. *(Added by Stats.1941, c. 937, p. 2528, § 1. Amended by Stats.1945, c. 639, p. 1179, § 7; Stats.1970, c. 1600, p. 3360, § 13, operative July 1, 1971; Stats.1972, c. 1365, p. 2717, § 2.)*

§ 1752. Powers of director

Section amended by Stats.1981, c. 453, § 7, operation contingent under the terms of § 8 of that chapter. See, also, section amended by Stats.1972, c. 1365, § 2.

To the extent that necessary funds are available for the purposes the director may:

(a) Establish and operate a treatment and training service and such other services as are proper for the discharge of his duties;

(b) Create administrative districts suitable to the performance of his duties;

(c) Employ and discharge all such persons as may be needed for the proper execution of the duties of the authority. Such employment and discharge shall be in accord with the civil service laws of this state.

Any open examination for the position of parole agent I, group supervisor, youth counselor, and other custodial and parole positions which normally afford entry into the Youth Authority service shall require the demonstration of the physical ability to effectively carry out the duties and responsibilities of the position in a manner which would not inordinately endanger the health or safety of a custodial person or a parolee or the health and safety of others. *(Added by Stats.1941, c. 937, p. 2528, § 1. Amended by Stats.1945, c. 639, p. 1179, § 7; Stats.1970, c. 1600, p. 3360, § 13, operative July 1, 1971; Stats.1972, c. 1365, p. 2717, § 2; Stats.1981, c. 453, p. 1705, § 7.)*

Cross References

Age limitations, see Government Code § 18932.
California Career Resource Network, composition, see Education Code § 53086.
Civil service,
  Appointments, see Government Code § 19050.
  Separations, see Government Code § 19996 et seq.
Director of Youth Authority, see Welfare and Institutions Code § 1711.
Institution employees, see Welfare and Institutions Code § 1075 et seq.
Personnel and employees, selection and appointment, see Welfare and Institutions Code § 1726.
Powers and duties of board and director, see Welfare and Institutions Code §§ 1712, 1719, 1720.
Superintendents of institutions, appointment of, see Welfare and Institutions Code § 1049.

§ 1752.05. Disciplinary matrix of offenses and punishments; code of conduct for employees; notification of availability of services; posting of code of conduct and transmission by electronic mail

(a) The director shall provide for the development and implementation of a disciplinary matrix with offenses and associated punishments applicable to all department employees, in order to ensure notice and consistency statewide. The disciplinary matrix shall take into account aggravating and mitigating factors for establishing a just and proper penalty for the charged misconduct, as required by the California Supreme Court in Skelly v. State Personnel Board (1975) 15 Cal.3d 194. The presence of aggravating or mitigating factors may result in the imposition of a greater or a lesser penalty than might otherwise be mandated by the disciplinary matrix.

(b) The director shall adopt a code of conduct for all employees of the department.

(c) The director shall ensure that employees who have reported improper governmental activities and who request services from the department are informed of the services available to them.

(d) The department shall post the code of conduct in locations where employee notices are maintained. On July 1, 2005, and annually thereafter, the department shall send by electronic mail to its employees who have authorized access to electronic mail, the following:

(1) Information regarding the code of conduct.

(2) The duty to report misconduct.

(3) How to report misconduct.

(4) The duty to fully cooperate during investigations.

(5) Assurances against retaliation. *(Added by Stats.2004, c. 738 (S.B.1431), § 3.)*

Cross References

Director of Corrections, disciplinary matrix of offenses and punishments, code of conduct for employees, see Penal Code § 5058.4.

Research References

3 Witkin, California Criminal Law 4th Punishment § 8 (2021), Division of Juvenile Justice.

§ 1752.1. Contracts for use of diagnosis and treatment services by counties; payment of costs; end date for acceptance of new cases

(a) The director may enter into contracts with the approval of the Director of Finance with any county of this state, upon request of the board of supervisors thereof, wherein the Division of Juvenile Justice agrees to furnish diagnosis and treatment services and temporary detention during a period of study to the county for selected cases of persons eligible for commitment to the Division of Juvenile Justice. The county shall reimburse the state for the cost of those services, the cost to be determined by the Director of the Division of Juvenile Justice.

(b) The Division of Juvenile Justice shall present to the county, not more frequently than monthly, a claim for the amount due the state under this section which the county shall process and pay pursuant to the provisions of Chapter 4 (commencing with Section 29700) of Division 3 of Title 3 of the Government Code.

(c) The Division of Juvenile Justice shall not accept new cases from the counties pursuant to this section on and after July 1, 2021. *(Added by Stats.1957, c. 1016, p. 2251, § 1. Amended by Stats.1963, c. 1786, p. 3594, § 74; Stats.1965, c. 263, p. 1259, § 17; Stats.1976, c. 299, p. 608, § 2; Stats.2021, c. 18 (S.B.92), § 17, eff. May 14, 2021.)*

Cross References

Department of finance,
Approval of Transactions, see Government Code § 13325.
Powers and duties, see Government Code §§ 13070, 13073 et seq.
Director of finance, powers and duties, see Government Code § 13004.
State controller, duties, see Government Code § 12410 et seq.
Temporary placement in diagnostic and treatment center, see Welfare and Institutions Code § 1731.6.

§ 1752.15. Contract with county for temporary emergency detention facilities; consultation between minor and attorney; visitation by parents; county reimbursement of costs; end date for acceptance of new cases

(a) The director may enter into contracts, with the approval of the Director of Finance, with any county of this state upon request of the board of supervisors thereof, wherein the Division of Juvenile Justice agrees to furnish temporary emergency detention facilities and necessary services incident thereto, for persons under the age of 18 years who are in the custody of the county probation officer pursuant to provisions of Chapter 2 (commencing with Section 200) of Part 1 of Division 2. Facilities of the department may be used only on a temporary basis when existing county juvenile facilities are rendered unsafe or inadequate because of a natural or manmade disaster, or when the continued presence of the minor or minors in the county juvenile facilities would, in the opinion of the judge of the juvenile court having jurisdiction over the minor, of the chief probation officer of the county, and of the director, present a significant risk of violence or escape. They may not be used for the detention of a person who is alleged to be or has been adjudged to be a person described by Section 300 or Section 601.

(b) Whenever any person is detained in a Division of Juvenile Justice facility located in a county other than the county which has contracted for services pursuant to this section, the county shall provide for adequate consultation between the minor and the minor's attorney; and, if the minor's parent or guardian lacks adequate private means of transportation, and if the minor has been detained in the facility for more than 10 days, the county shall make reasonable efforts to provide for visitation between the minor and the minor's parents or guardian.

(c) The county shall reimburse the state for the cost of these services, the cost to be determined by the director. The department shall present to the county, not more than once a month, a claim for the amount due the state under this section which the county shall process and pay pursuant to the provisions of Chapter 4 (commencing with Section 29700) of Division 3 of Title 3 of the Government Code.

(d) The Division of Juvenile Justice shall not accept new cases from the counties pursuant to this section on and after July 1, 2021. *(Added by Stats.1976, c. 1239, p. 5562, § 1, eff. Sept. 27, 1976. Amended by Stats.1978, c. 380, p. 1215, § 170; Stats.1991, c. 721 (A.B.1656), § 3; Stats.2021, c. 18 (S.B.92), § 18, eff. May 14, 2021.)*

Cross References

Department of finance,
Approval of transactions, see Government Code § 13325.
Powers and duties, see Government Code §§ 13070, 13073 et seq.
Director of finance, powers and duties, see Government Code § 13004.

§ 1752.16. Contracts to furnish housing to ward whose commitment has been recalled; legislative intent; reimbursement

(a) The chief of the Division of Juvenile Facilities, with approval of the Director of Finance, may enter into contracts with any county of this state for the Division of Juvenile Facilities to furnish housing to a ward who was in the custody of the Division of Juvenile Facilities on December 12, 2011, and whose commitment was recalled based on both of the following:

(1) The ward was committed to the Division of Juvenile Facilities for the commission of an offense described in subdivision (c) of Section 290.008 of the Penal Code.

(2) The ward has not been adjudged a ward of the court pursuant to Section 602 for commission of an offense described in subdivision (b) of Section 707.

(b) It is the intent of the Legislature in enacting this act to address the California Supreme Court's ruling in In re C.H. (2011) 53 Cal.4th 94 [1].

(c) Notwithstanding Sections 11010 and 11270 of the Government Code, any county entering into a contract pursuant to this section shall not be required to reimburse the state. *(Added by Stats.2012, c. 7 (A.B.324), § 3, eff. Feb. 29, 2012. Amended by Stats.2012, c. 41 (S.B.1021), § 99, eff. June 27, 2012.)*

1 133 Cal.Rptr.3d 573

§ 1752.2. Establishment of precorps transitional training program within the Division of Juvenile Justice; partnership with California Conservation Corps

(a) The Division of Juvenile Justice, in partnership with the California Conservation Corps and participating certified local conservation corps, shall develop and establish a precorps transitional training program within the Division of Juvenile Justice. This program shall operate within a facility identified by the Division of Juvenile Justice, with partnering state and local conservation corps responsible for program content, delivery, and administration. This program shall provide participating Division of Juvenile Justice corps members with a training and development program to approximate the experience of serving in a conservation corps, and include opportunities for skill building, job readiness training, community service, and conservation activities. Training shall include, but is not limited to, transferable professional skills known as "soft skills," social emotional learning, transitional life skills, and conservation jobs skills. Division of Juvenile Justice participants who successfully complete program curriculum shall qualify for a paid full-time placement within a local community corps program, and may be considered for a placement in the California Conservation Corps. This program shall be considered for expansion to additional Division of Juvenile Justice facilities if effective at reducing recidivism among participants.

(b) The Division of Juvenile Justice and the California Conservation Corps shall enter into an interagency agreement to implement this section. The agreement shall include input from participating certified local conservation corps. *(Added by Stats.2020, c. 337 (S.B.823), § 45, eff. Sept. 30, 2020.)*

§ 1752.3. Allocation of funds to local governmental and nongovernmental agencies to share in costs of local correctional programs

The director may, from any moneys made available for such purposes, allocate funds to local governmental and nongovernmental agencies to share in the cost of local correctional programs which are partially financed by federal grants. *(Added by Stats.1970, c. 816, p. 1546, § 1.)*

§ 1752.5. Canteen; Benefit Fund

The director may establish and maintain at any institution or camp under his jurisdiction a canteen for the sale to persons confined therein of candy, nutritional snacks, toilet articles, sundries, and other articles. The canteen shall operate on a nonprofit basis. However, if sales should exceed costs, the surplus shall be deposited in a special fund, to be designated "Benefit Fund." Any moneys contained in such fund shall be used for the benefit of the wards resident at the institution or camp. *(Added by Stats.1979, c. 110, p. 247, § 1. Amended by Stats.2004, c. 798 (A.B.384), § 8, operative July 1, 2005.)*

Cross References

Possession or use of tobacco products by inmates or others on grounds of any institution or facility under jurisdiction of Department of Corrections, see Penal Code § 5030.1.

§ 1752.6. Contracts for research and training

The director may, with the approval of the Director of General Services, enter into contracts with colleges, universities, and other organizations for the purposes of research in the field of delinquency and crime prevention and of training special workers, including teachers, institution employees, probation and parole officers, social workers and others engaged, whether as volunteers or for compensation, and whether part time or full time, in the fields of education, recreation, mental health, and treatment and prevention of delinquency. *(Added by Stats.1943, c. 675, p. 2431, § 1. Amended by Stats.1945, c. 639, p. 1180, § 9; Stats.1965, c. 371, p. 1600, § 302; Stats.2014, c. 144 (A.B.1847), § 57, eff. Jan. 1, 2015.)*

Cross References

Department of finance, powers and duties, see Government Code §§ 13070, 13073 et seq.
Department of General Services, see Government Code § 14600 et seq.
Director of finance, powers and duties, see Government Code § 13004.

§ 1752.7. Collection of statistics on juvenile delinquency

The director may collect statistics and information regarding juvenile delinquency, crimes reported and discovered, arrests made, complaints, informations, and indictments filed and the disposition made thereof, pleas, convictions, acquittals, probations granted or denied, commitments to and transfers and discharges from places of incarceration, and other data and information useful in determining the cause and amount of crime in this State, or in carrying out the powers and duties of the Authority.

All officers and employees of the State and of every county and city shall furnish to the director upon request such statistics and other information within their knowledge and control as the director deems necessary or proper to be collected pursuant to the provisions of this section. *(Added by Stats.1943, c. 291, p. 1275, § 1. Amended by Stats.1945, c. 639, p. 1180, § 10.)*

§ 1752.8. Deposit and investment of ward's funds

The Director of the Youth Authority may deposit any funds of wards committed to the authority in the director's possession in trust with the Treasurer pursuant to Section 16305.3 of the Government Code or in trust in insured bank, savings and loan, or state or federal credit union accounts bearing interest at rates up to the maximum permitted by law, and for the purpose of deposit only, may mingle the funds of any ward with the funds of other wards.

Such funds together with the interest paid thereon may be paid over to the ward upon his or her request, and shall be paid over to the ward upon his or her discharge from the Youth Authority.

Notwithstanding the provisions of this section and Section 1752.81, the Youth Authority may assess a ward's trust fund for actual costs for the ward's support, maintenance, training and treatment. *(Added by Stats.1949, c. 234, p. 458, § 1. Amended by Stats.1957, c. 1640, p. 3010, § 1; Stats.1965, c. 371, p. 1601, § 303; Stats.1969, c. 1272, p. 2484, § 1; Stats.1974, c. 466, p. 1091, § 1, eff. July 11, 1974; Stats.1974, c. 1221, p. 2654, § 48; Stats.1975, c. 437, p. 933, § 1, eff. Aug. 29, 1975; Stats.1983, c. 715, § 3.)*

Cross References

Department of General Services, see Government Code § 14600 et seq.

§ 1752.81. Release of funds; authorization by ward; exception; restitution fines and orders

(a) Whenever the Director of the Division of Juvenile Justice has in his or her possession in trust funds of a ward committed to the division, the funds may be released for any purpose when authorized by the ward. When the sum held in trust for any ward by the director exceeds five hundred dollars ($500), the amount in excess of five hundred dollars ($500) may be expended by the director pursuant to a lawful order of a court directing payment of the funds, without the authorization of the ward thereto.

(b) Whenever an adult or minor is committed to or housed in a Division of Juvenile Facilities facility and he or she owes a restitution fine imposed pursuant to Section 13967 of the Government Code, as operative on or before September 28, 1994, or Section 1202.4 or 1203.04 of the Penal Code, as operative on or before August 2, 1995, or pursuant to Section 729.6, 730.6 or 731.1, as operative on or before August 2, 1995, the director shall deduct the balance owing on the fine amount from the trust account deposits of a ward, up to a maximum of 50 percent of the total amount held in trust, unless prohibited by federal law. The director shall transfer that amount to the California Victim Compensation Board for deposit in the Restitution Fund in the State Treasury. Any amount so deducted shall be credited against the amount owing on the fine. The sentencing court shall be provided a record of the payments.

(c) Whenever an adult or minor is committed to, or housed in, a Division of Juvenile Facilities facility and he or she owes restitution to a victim imposed pursuant to Section 13967 of the Government Code, as operative on or before September 28, 1994, or Section 1202.4 or 1203.04 of the Penal Code, as operative on or before August 2, 1995, or pursuant to Section 729.6, 730.6, or 731.1, as operative on or before August 2, 1995, the director shall deduct the balance owing on the order amount from the trust account deposits of a ward, up to a maximum of 50 percent of the total amount held in trust, unless prohibited by federal law. The director shall transfer that amount directly to the victim. If the restitution is owed to a person who has filed an application with the Victims of Crime Program, the director shall transfer that amount to the California Victim Compensation Board for direct payment to the victim or payment shall be made to the Restitution Fund to the extent that the victim has received assistance pursuant to that program. The sentencing court shall be provided a record of the payments made to victims and of the payments deposited to the Restitution Fund pursuant to this subdivision.

(d) Any compensatory or punitive damages awarded by trial or settlement to a minor or adult committed to the Division of Juvenile Facilities in connection with a civil action brought against any federal, state, or local jail or correctional facility, or any official or agent thereof, shall be paid directly, after payment of reasonable attorney's fees and litigation costs approved by the court, to satisfy any outstanding restitution orders or restitution fines against the minor or adult. The balance of any award shall be forwarded to the minor or adult committed to the Division of Juvenile Facilities after full payment of all outstanding restitution orders and restitution fines subject to subdivision (e). The Division of Juvenile Facilities shall make all reasonable efforts to notify the victims of the crime for which the minor or adult was committed concerning the pending payment of any compensatory or punitive damages. This subdivision shall apply to cases settled or awarded on or after April 26, 1996, pursuant to Sections 807 and 808 of Title VIII of the federal Prison Litigation Reform Act of 1995 (P.L. 104–134;[1] 18 U.S.C. Sec. 3626 (Historical and Statutory Notes)).

(e) The director shall deduct and retain from the trust account deposits of a ward, unless prohibited by federal law, an administrative fee that totals 10 percent of any amount transferred pursuant to subdivision (b) and (c), or 5 percent of any amount transferred pursuant to subdivision (d). The director shall deposit the administrative fee moneys in a special deposit account for reimbursing administrative and support costs of the restitution and victims program of the Division of Juvenile Facilities. The director, at his or her discretion, may retain any excess funds in the special deposit account for future reimbursement of the division's administrative and support costs for the restitution and victims program or may transfer all or part of the excess funds for deposit in the Restitution Fund.

(f) When a ward has both a restitution fine and a restitution order from the sentencing court, the Division of Juvenile Facilities shall collect the restitution order first pursuant to subdivision (c).

(g) Notwithstanding subdivisions (a), (b), and (c), whenever the director holds in trust a ward's funds in excess of five dollars ($5) and the ward cannot be located, after one year from the date of discharge, absconding from the Division of Juvenile Facilities supervision, or escape, the Division of Juvenile Facilities shall apply the trust account balance to any unsatisfied victim restitution order or fine owed by that ward. If the victim restitution order or fine has been satisfied, the remainder of the ward's trust account balance, if any, shall be transferred to the Benefit Fund to be expended pursuant to Section 1752.5. If the victim to whom a particular ward owes restitution cannot be located, the moneys shall be transferred to the Benefit Fund to be expended pursuant to Section 1752.5. *(Added by Stats.1975, c. 353, p. 799, § 1. Amended by Stats.1997, c. 266 (A.B.1132), § 2; Stats.2000, c. 481 (S.B.1943), § 4; Stats.2006, c. 538 (S.B.1852), § 686; Stats.2012, c. 41 (S.B.1021), § 100, eff. June 27, 2012; Stats.2016, c. 31 (S.B.836), § 279, eff. June 27, 2016.)*

1 For public law sections classified to the U.S.C.A., see USCA-Tables.

Cross References

California Victim Compensation and Government Claims Board (formerly State Control Board), see Government Code § 13900 et seq.

§ 1752.82. Deduction from wages for payment of restitution to a victim or a restitution fine

(a) Whenever an adult or minor is committed to or housed in a Youth Authority facility and he or she owes restitution to a victim or a restitution fine imposed pursuant to Section 13967, as operative on or before September 28, 1994, of the Government Code, or Section 1202.4 of the Penal Code, or Section 1203.04, as operative on or before August 2, 1994, of the Penal Code, or pursuant to Section 729.6, as operative on or before August 2, 1995, Section 730.6 or 731.1, as operative on or before August 2, 1995, the director may deduct a reasonable amount not to exceed 50 percent from the wages of that adult or minor and the amount so deducted, exclusive of the costs of administering this section, which shall be retained by the director, shall be transferred to the California Victim Compensation Board for deposit in the Restitution Fund in the State Treasury in the case of a restitution fine, or, in the case of a restitution order, and upon the request of the victim, shall be paid directly to the victim. Any amount so deducted shall be credited against the amount owing on the fine or to the victim. The committing court shall be provided a record of any payments.

(b) A victim who has requested that restitution payments be paid directly to him or her pursuant to subdivision (a) shall provide a current address to the Youth Authority to enable the Youth Authority to send restitution payments collected on the victim's behalf to the victim.

(c) In the case of a restitution order, whenever the victim has died, cannot be located, or has not requested the restitution payment, the director may deduct a reasonable amount not to exceed 50 percent of the wages of that adult or minor and the amount so deducted, exclusive of the costs of administering this section, which shall be retained by the director, shall be transferred to the California Victim Compensation Board, pursuant to subdivision (d), after one year has elapsed from the time the ward is discharged by the Youth Authority Board. Any amount so deducted shall be credited against the amount owing to the victim. The funds so transferred shall be deposited in the Restitution Fund.

(d) If the Youth Authority has collected restitution payments on behalf of a victim, the victim shall request those payments no later than one year after the ward has been discharged by the Youth Authority Board. Any victim who fails to request those payments within that time period shall have relinquished all rights to the payments, unless he or she can show reasonable cause for failure to request those payments within that time period.

(e) The director shall transfer to the California Victim Compensation Board all restitution payments collected prior to the effective date of this section on behalf of victims who have died, cannot be located, or have not requested restitution payments. The California Victim Compensation Board shall deposit these amounts in the Restitution Fund.

(f) For purposes of this section, "victim" includes a victim's immediate surviving family member, on whose behalf restitution has been ordered. *(Added by Stats.1983, c. 954, § 5. Amended by Stats.1987, c. 511, § 1; Stats.1988, c. 181, § 2; Stats.1992, c. 682, (S.B.1444), § 10, eff. Sept. 14, 1992; Stats.1995, c. 336 (A.B.774), § 1; Stats.1996, c. 1077 (A.B.2898), § 36; Stats.2003, c. 4 (S.B.459), § 29, eff. April 8, 2003, operative Jan. 1, 2004; Stats.2016, c. 31 (S.B.836), § 280, eff. June 27, 2016.)*

§ 1752.83. Wards confined in Youth Authority facilities; destruction of public property; deduction from trust fund

(a) It is the intent of the Legislature that wards of the Youth Authority be held accountable for intentional damage and destruction of public property committed while they are confined in Youth Authority facilities. To that end, and notwithstanding the provisions of Sections 1752.8 and 1752.81, the Youth Authority may deduct from a ward's trust fund any amounts that are necessary to pay for intentional damage to public property caused by the ward while confined within an institution or other facility of the Youth Authority.

(b) The Youth Authority shall utilize the procedures in its regulations for disciplinary actions to determine whether the damage or destruction was intentionally caused by the ward and, if so, to determine the amount to be deducted to pay for the damage or destruction.

(c) Funds that are deducted shall remain with the Youth Authority and shall be used to repair or replace the public property damaged or destroyed as provided for in the Budget Act for that fiscal year. *(Formerly § 1752.82, added by Stats.1984, c. 494, § 1. Renumbered § 1752.83 and amended by Stats.1986, c. 248, § 248.)*

§ 1752.85. Sale of articles of handiwork; payment of costs; deposit of excess in ward's trust account

The Director of the Youth Authority may authorize the sale of articles of handiwork made by wards under the jurisdiction of the authority to the public at Youth Authority institutions, in public buildings, at fairs, or on property operated by nonprofit associations. The cost of any state property used for the manufacture of articles shall be paid for out of funds received from the sale of the articles. The remainder of any funds received from the sale of the articles shall be placed in the ward's trust account pursuant to Section 1752.8 of the Welfare and Institutions Code. *(Added by Stats.1969, c. 803, p. 1624, § 1.)*

§ 1752.9. Lease of land; terms

The Department of the Youth Authority, with the approval of the Director of General Services, may lease land at any institution under its jurisdiction, at a nominal rental, to any nonprofit or eleemosynary corporation. The terms of the lease shall require the corporation to construct a house of worship on such land, and to maintain and operate the same primarily for the use of Youth Authority wards and staff. All work as an employee on such house of worship performed under contract or by day labor shall be subject to the provisions of Division 2, Part 7, of the Labor Code. *(Added by Stats.1957, c. 1859, p. 3262, § 1. Amended by Stats.1965, c. 371, p. 1601, § 304.)*

Cross References

Approval of state agencies transactions, see Government Code § 13325.
Department of General Services, see Government Code § 14600 et seq.

§ 1752.95. Conferences with probation officers; expenses

The director may, from time to time, and as often as occasion may require, but not to exceed two meetings in any one calendar year call into conference the probation officers of the several counties, or such of them as he may deem advisable, for the purpose of discussing the duties of their offices.

The actual and necessary expenses of the probation officer incurred while traveling to and from and while attending the conferences shall be a county charge; provided, prior approval of the board of supervisors has been obtained. *(Added by Stats.1957, c. 1597, p. 2948, § 1.)*

Cross References

County charges, see Government Code § 29600 et seq.
County claims, filing and approval, see Government Code § 29700 et seq.

§ 1753. Use of other facilities, institutions, and agencies; agreements with public officials

For the purpose of carrying out its duties, the department is authorized to make use of law enforcement, detention, probation, parole, medical, educational, correctional, segregative and other facilities, institutions and agencies, whether public or private, within the state. The director may enter into agreements with the appropriate public officials for separate care and special treatment in existing institutions of persons subject to the control of the department. *(Added by Stats.1941, c. 937, p. 2529, § 1. Amended by Stats.1945, c. 639, p. 1180, § 11; Stats.1979, c. 860, p. 2980, § 20.)*

§ 1753.1. Agreements with federal agencies; use of facilities and services; costs; return to referring agency

(a) The Director of the Youth Authority may enter into agreements with any federal agency authorizing the use of the Youth Authority's facilities and services for the confinement, care and treatment of persons otherwise not under its jurisdiction when suitable facilities and services are available. The costs of the services provided by the Youth Authority shall be borne by the agency referring the person to the Director of the Youth Authority. The Director of the Youth Authority may order the person returned to the agency referring him when suitable facilities or services are not available. Any such person referred to the Youth Authority pursuant to this section shall be subject to its rules and regulations.

(b) As used in this section, "person" means any person under the age of 26 years who is under the jurisdiction of a Federal Correctional Agency pursuant to federal law. *(Added by Stats.1972, c. 772, p. 1384, § 1, eff. Aug. 11, 1972.)*

§ 1753.3. Transfer of wards to local correctional facilities; agreements; costs

(a) The Director of the Youth Authority may enter into an agreement with a city, county, or city and county, to permit transfer of wards in the custody of the Director of the Youth Authority to an appropriate facility of the city, county, or city and county, if the official having jurisdiction over the facility has consented. The agreement shall provide for contributions to the city, county, or city and county toward payment of costs incurred with reference to the transferred wards.

(b) When an agreement entered into pursuant to subdivision (a) is in effect with respect to a particular local facility, the Director of the Youth Authority may transfer wards and parole violators to the facility.

(c) Notwithstanding subdivision (b), the Director of the Youth Authority may deny placement in a local facility to a parole violator who was committed to the Youth Authority for the commission of any offense set forth in subdivision (b), paragraph (2) of subdivision (d), or subdivision (e) of Section 707.

(d) Wards transferred to those facilities are subject to the rules and regulations of the facility in which they are confined, but remain under the legal custody of the Department of the Youth Authority. *(Added by Stats.1987, c. 1450, § 11. Amended by Stats.1988, c. 1608, § 6; Stats.1994, c. 453 (A.B.560), § 17.)*

Cross References

Bid requirements in contracts awarded pursuant to this section, see Public Contract Code §§ 20134, 20168.5.
City contracts with state for correctional programs pursuant to this section, consultation with county, see Penal Code § 2913.
Minority business participation goals, contracts awarded pursuant to this section, see Public Contract Code § 10471.

§ 1753.4. Long-term agreements for placement of parole violators; reimbursement rate; site selection

(a) Pursuant to Section 1753.3 the Director of the Youth Authority may enter into a long-term agreement not to exceed 20 years with a city, county, or city and county to place parole violators in a facility which is specially designed and built for the incarceration of parole violators and state youth authority wards.

(b) The agreement shall provide that persons providing security at the facilities shall be peace officers who have completed the minimum standards for the training of local correctional peace officers established under Section 6035 of the Penal Code.

(c) In determining the reimbursement rate pursuant to an agreement entered into pursuant to subdivision (a), the director shall take into consideration the costs incurred by the city, county, or city and county for services and facilities provided, and any other factors which are necessary and appropriate to fix the obligations, responsibilities, and rights of the respective parties.

(d) The Director of the Youth Authority, to the extent possible, shall select city, county, or city and county facilities in areas where medical, food, and other support services are available from nearby existing prison facilities.

(e) The Director of the Youth Authority, with the approval of the Department of General Services, may enter into an agreement to lease state property for a period not in excess of 20 years to be used as the site for a facility operated by a city, county, or city and county authorized by this section.

(f) No agreement may be entered into under this section unless the cost per ward in the facility is no greater than the average costs of keeping a ward in a comparable Youth Authority facility, as determined by the Director of the Youth Authority. *(Added by Stats.1987, c. 1450, § 12.)*

§ 1753.6. Delivery of child of ward in county hospital; payment of expenses

In any case in which a ward of the Youth Authority is temporarily released from actual confinement in an institution of the authority and placed in a county hospital for purposes of delivery of her child, the authority may reimburse the county for the actual cost of services rendered by the county hospital to the newborn infant of the ward. *(Added by Stats.1965, c. 1912, p. 4424, § 1.)*

§ 1753.7. Confined females; use of materials for personal hygiene and birth control measures; family planning services

(a) Any female confined in a Department of the Youth Authority facility shall, upon her request, be allowed to continue to use materials necessary for (1) personal hygiene with regard to her menstrual cycle and reproductive system and (2) birth control measures as prescribed by her physician.

(b) Any female confined in a Department of the Youth Authority facility shall upon her request be furnished by the department with information and education regarding prescription birth control measures.

(c) Family planning services shall be offered to each and every female confined in a Department of Youth Authority facility at least 60 days prior to a scheduled release date. Upon request any such female shall be furnished by the department with the services of a licensed physician or she shall be furnished by the department or by any other agency which contracts with the department with services necessary to meet her family planning needs at the time of her release. *(Added by Stats.1972, c. 1104, p. 2113, § 4. Amended by Stats.1975, c. 1146, p. 2832, § 4.)*

Cross References

Minors consent to pregnancy related treatments, see Family Code § 6925.
Sterilization operations, see Health and Safety Code §§ 1232, 1258, 1459, 32128.10.

Research References

3 Witkin, California Criminal Law 4th Punishment § 94 (2021), Treatment and Work.

§ 1754. Limitations on use

Nothing in this chapter shall be taken to give the Youth Authority Board or the director control over existing facilities, institutions or agencies; or to require them to serve the board or the director inconsistently with their functions, or with the authority of their officers, or with the laws and regulations governing their activities; or to give the board or the director power to make use of any private institution or agency without its consent; or to pay a private institution or agency for services which a public institution or agency is willing and able to perform. *(Added by Stats.1941, c. 937, p. 2529, § 1. Amended by Stats.1945, c. 639, p. 1180, § 12; Stats.1979, c. 860, p. 2980, § 21; Stats.2003, c. 4 (S.B.459), § 30, eff. April 8, 2003, operative Jan. 1, 2004.)*

Cross References

Public social services, see Welfare and Institutions Code § 10000 et seq.

§ 1755. Duties of public institutions and agencies to accept persons referred by authority

Public institutions and agencies are hereby required to accept and care for persons sent to them by the Authority in the same manner as they would be required to do had such persons been committed by a court of criminal jurisdiction. *(Added by Stats.1941, c. 937, p. 2529, § 1.)*

Research References

3 Witkin, California Criminal Law 4th Punishment § 93 (2021), Institutions and Facilities.

§ 1755.3. Medical, surgical, and dental service

Whenever any person under the jurisdiction of the Youth Authority, or any minor under the jurisdiction of the Department of Corrections, is in need of medical, surgical, or dental care, the Youth Authority or the Department of Corrections, as applicable, may authorize, upon the recommendation of the attending physician or dentist, as applicable, the performance of that necessary medical, surgical, or dental service. *(Added by Stats.1951, c. 1611, p. 3623, § 1. Amended by Stats.1998, c. 496 (S.B.2081), § 1.)*

Cross References

Clinical laboratory technology, inapplicability of chapter, see Business and Professions Code § 1241.

Research References

West's California Judicial Council Forms JV–732, Commitment to the California Department of Corrections and Rehabilitation, Division of Juvenile Facilities (Also Available in Spanish).
3 Witkin, California Criminal Law 4th Punishment § 94 (2021), Treatment and Work.

§ 1755.4. Psychotropic medications; standards and guidelines

The Department of the Youth Authority, in consultation with the State Department of Mental Health shall establish, by regulations adopted at the earliest possible date, but no later than December 31, 2001, standards and guidelines for the administration of psychotropic medications to any person under the jurisdiction of the Department of the Youth Authority, in a manner that protects the health and short- and long-term well-being of those persons. The standards and guidelines adopted pursuant to this section shall be consistent with the due process requirements set forth in Section 2600 of the Penal Code. *(Added by Stats.2000, c. 659 (S.B.2098), § 3.)*

Research References

West's California Judicial Council Forms JV–732, Commitment to the California Department of Corrections and Rehabilitation, Division of Juvenile Facilities (Also Available in Spanish).

§ 1755.5. Transfer of persons for study, diagnosis, and treatment

The Department of the Youth Authority may transfer to and cause to be confined in the medical facility, the Correctional Training Facility at Soledad, the California Institution for Women at Corona, the Medical Correctional Institution, the California Institution for Men, the Richard J. Donovan Correctional Facility at Rock Mountain, or the California Men's Colony under the jurisdiction of the Department of Corrections for general study, diagnosis, and treatment, or any of them, any person over the age of 18 years who is subject to the custody, control, and discipline of the Department of the Youth Authority who was committed to the Department of the Youth Authority under Section 1731.5. The Director of Corrections may receive and keep in any institution specified in this section any person so transferred to that institution by the Department of the Youth Authority, with the same powers as if the person had been placed therein or transferred thereto pursuant to the Penal Code.

The Department of the Youth Authority may transfer to and cause to be confined in the California Rehabilitation Center for general study, diagnosis, and treatment, or any of them, any person over the age of 18 years who is subject to the custody, control and discipline of the Department of the Youth Authority. The Director of Corrections may receive and keep in the California Rehabilitation Center any person so transferred thereto by the Department of the Youth Authority, with the same powers as if the person had been placed therein or transferred thereto pursuant to Division 3 (commencing with Section 3000) of this code.

Part 3 (commencing with Section 2000) of the Penal Code, so far as those provisions may be applicable, applies to persons so transferred to and confined in any institution specified in this section, except that, whenever by reason of any law governing the commitment of a person to the Department of the Youth Authority the person is deemed not to be a person convicted of a crime, the transfer or placement of the person in the California Rehabilitation Center shall not affect the status or rights of the person and shall not be deemed to constitute a conviction of a crime. *(Added by Stats.1949, c. 302, p. 590, § 1. Amended by Stats.1957, c. 1598, p. 2948, § 1; Stats.1961, c. 850, p. 2228, § 4; Stats.1963, c. 866, p. 2102, § 3; Stats.1963, c. 1243, p. 2768, § 2; Stats.1975, c. 370, p. 820, § 3; Stats.1992, c. 209 (A.B.2403), § 1.)*

Research References

3 Witkin, California Criminal Law 4th Punishment § 93 (2021), Institutions and Facilities.

§ 1756. Persons with mental health disorder or developmental disability; transfer from state correctional schools to state hospitals

Notwithstanding any other law, if, in the opinion of the Chief Deputy Secretary for the Division of Juvenile Justice, the rehabilitation of a person with a mental health disorder or a developmental disability who is confined in a state correctional school may be expedited by treatment at one of the state hospitals under the jurisdiction of the State Department of State Hospitals or the State Department of Developmental Services, the Chief Deputy Secretary for the Division of Juvenile Justice shall certify that fact to the director of the appropriate department who may authorize receipt of the person at one of the hospitals for care and treatment. Upon notification from the director that the person will no longer benefit from further care and treatment in the state hospital, the Chief Deputy Secretary for the Division of Juvenile Justice shall immediately send for, take, and receive the person back into a state correctional school. A person placed in a state hospital under this section who is committed to the authority shall be released from the hospital upon termination of his or her commitment unless a petition for detention of that person is filed under the provisions of Part 1 (commencing with Section 5000) of Division 5. *(Added by Stats.1970, c. 937, p. 1696, § 4. Amended by Stats.1977, c. 1252, p. 4480, § 480, operative July 1, 1978; Stats.1978, c. 429, p. 1439, § 178, eff. July 17, 1978, operative July 1, 1978; Stats.1981, c. 714, p. 2808, § 464; Stats.2012, c. 24 (A.B.1470), § 61, eff. June 27, 2012; Stats.2014, c. 144 (A.B.1847), § 58, eff. Jan. 1, 2015.)*

Cross References

Closure of Division of Juvenile Justice, continuation of services for state hospital patients referred by division, see Welfare and Institutions Code § 1732.10.
Developmental disabilities state plan, see Welfare and Institutions Code § 4560 et seq.
Lanterman–Petris–Short Act on community mental health services, see Welfare and Institutions Code § 5000 et seq.
Mentally retarded persons, see Welfare and Institutions Code §§ 4119, 6500 et seq., 6715 et seq., 6740, 6741.
Regulations concerning patients' rights, see Welfare and Institutions Code § 4027.
State department of developmental services, see Welfare and Institutions Code § 4400 et seq.
State department of mental health, see Welfare and Institutions Code § 4000 et seq.

Research References

3 Witkin, California Criminal Law 4th Punishment § 93 (2021), Institutions and Facilities.

§ 1757. Inspection of institutions and agencies

The director may inspect all public institutions and agencies whose facilities he or she is authorized to utilize and all private institutions and agencies whose facilities he or she is using. Every institution or agency, whether public or private, is required to afford the director reasonable opportunity to examine or consult with persons committed to the Youth Authority who are for the time being in the custody of the institution or agency. *(Added by Stats.1941, c. 937, p. 2529, § 1. Amended by Stats.1945, c. 639, p. 1180, § 13; Stats.1979, c. 860, p. 2980, § 22; Stats.2003, c. 4 (S.B.459), § 31, eff. April 8, 2003, operative Jan. 1, 2004.)*

Cross References

Investigations of committed persons, see Welfare and Institutions Code § 1761.

§ 1758. Control of persons placed in other institutions or agencies

Placement of a person by the Authority in any institution or agency not operated by the Authority, or the discharge of such person by such an institution or agency, shall not terminate the control of the Authority over such person. *(Added by Stats.1941, c. 937, p. 2529, § 1.)*

Cross References

Discharge, see Welfare and Institutions Code § 1769.
Extent of control over committed persons, see Welfare and Institutions Code § 1765.

§ 1759. Approval of release of person by institution or agency

No person placed in such an institution or under such an agency may be released by the institution or agency until after approval of the release by the Authority, unless the institution or agency would have power under the law to release at its own discretion persons committed to it by order of a court. In the latter case, it may not release a person placed by the Authority until a reasonable time after it has notified the Authority of its intention to release him. *(Added by Stats.1941, c. 937, p. 2529, § 1.)*

§ 1760. Authority to establish and operate enumerated places, agencies and facilities

The director is hereby authorized when necessary and when funds are available for these purposes to establish and operate any of the following:

(a) Places for the detention, prior to examination and study, of all persons committed to the Youth Authority.

(b) Places for examination and study of persons committed to the Youth Authority.

(c) Places of confinement, educational institutions, hospitals and other correctional or segregative facilities, institutions and agencies, for the proper execution of the duties of the Youth Authority.

(d) Agencies and facilities for the supervision, training, and control of persons who have not been placed in confinement or who have been released from confinement by the Youth Authority Board upon conditions, and for aiding those persons to find employment and assistance.

(e) Agencies and facilities designed to aid persons who have been discharged by the Youth Authority Board in finding employment and in leading a law-abiding existence. *(Added by Stats.1941, c. 937, p. 2530, § 1. Amended by Stats.1945, c. 639, p. 1181, § 14; Stats.1979, c. 860, p. 2980, § 23; Stats.2003, c. 4 (S.B.459), § 32, eff. April 8, 2003, operative Jan. 1, 2004.)*

Research References

3 Witkin, California Criminal Law 4th Punishment § 93 (2021), Institutions and Facilities.

§ 1760.4. Wards in forestry camps, labor; fire suppression

(a) The wards housed in forestry camps established by the Department of the Youth Authority may be required to labor on the buildings and grounds of the camp, on the making of forest roads for fire prevention or firefighting, on forestation or reforestation of public lands, or on the making of firetrails and firebreaks, or to perform any other work or engage in any studies or activities prescribed or permitted by the department or any officer designated by it.

(b) The wards may be required to labor in fire suppression if all of the following conditions are met:

(1) The ward is under the age of 18 years and the parent or guardian of the ward has given permission for that labor by the ward, or the ward is 18 years of age or over.

(2) The ward has received not less than 16 hours of training in forest firefighting and fire safety.

The department may, during declared fire emergencies, allow the Director of the Department of Forestry and Fire Protection to use the wards for fire suppression efforts outside of the boundaries of

California, not to exceed a distance in excess of 25 miles from the California border, along the borders of Oregon, Nevada, or Arizona.

(c) The department may provide, in cooperation with the Department of Parks and Recreation and the Department of Conservation or otherwise, for the payment of wages to the wards for work they do while housed on the camps, the sums earned to be paid in reparation, or to the parents or dependents of the ward, or to the ward in any manner and in any proportions as the Department of the Youth Authority directs. *(Added by Stats.1961, c. 705, p. 1947, § 2. Amended by Stats.1963, c. 443, p. 1277, § 4, eff. May 17, 1963; Stats.1969, c. 590, p. 1224, § 2; Stats.1975, c. 1129, p. 2775, § 7; Stats.1989, c. 419, § 2.)*

Cross References

Department of conservation, see Public Resources Code § 600 et seq.
Department of parks and recreation, see Public Resources Code § 500 et seq.
Juvenile homes, ranches and camps, see Welfare and Institutions Code § 880 et seq.

Research References

3 Witkin, California Criminal Law 4th Punishment § 94 (2021), Treatment and Work.

§ 1760.45. Pine Grove Youth Conservation Camp

The Department of Corrections and Rehabilitation * * * is hereby authorized to enter into contracts with counties to meet the intent of the Legislature expressed in Senate Bill 823 (Chapter 337 of the Statutes of 2020) and Assembly Bill 145 (Chapter 80 of the Statutes of 2021) that the Pine Grove Youth Conservation Camp remain open through a state-local partnership, or other management arrangement, to train justice-involved youth in wildland firefighting skills.

(a) The department may contract with one or more counties to furnish training and rehabilitation programs, and necessary services incident thereto, at Pine Grove, for persons 18 years of age and older who are under the jurisdiction of the juvenile court and supervision of a county probation department following adjudication under Section 602 for a felony offense.

(b) Youth placed at Pine Grove pursuant to this section shall be required to comply with * * * rules and regulations * * * consistent with * * * the contracts entered into by the department and participating counties.

(c) Placement of a youth at Pine Grove shall not be considered a commitment to the Division of Juvenile Justice.

(d) The department shall establish camp eligibility criteria and assess individual amenability for the initial and continued placement at Pine Grove. *(Added by Stats.2021, c. 80 (A.B.145), § 28, eff. July 16, 2021. Amended by Stats.2022, c. 58 (A.B.200), § 44, eff. June 30, 2022.)*

§ 1760.5. Performance of conservation work by persons committed to authority; wages

The director may require persons committed to the authority to perform work necessary and proper to be done by the Department of Forestry and Fire Protection, the Department of Water Resources, the Department of Parks and Recreation, and the Department of Fish and Game, by the Division of State Lands, by the United States Department of Agriculture, and by the federal officials and departments in charge of national forests and parks within this state. For the purposes of this section, the director, with the approval of the Department of General Services, may enter into contracts with federal and state officials and departments. All moneys received by the director pursuant to any of those contracts shall be paid into the State Treasury to the credit and in augmentation of the current appropriation for the support of the authority. The director may provide, from those moneys, for the payment of wages to the wards for work they do pursuant to any of those contracts, the wages to be paid into the Indemnity Fund created pursuant to Section 13967 of the Government Code, or to the parents or dependents of the ward, or to the ward in the manner and in those proportions as the Department of the Youth Authority directs. *(Added by Stats.1943, c. 30, p. 159, § 1. Amended by Stats.1945, c. 639, p. 1181, § 15; Stats.1963, c. 443, p. 1277, § 5; Stats.1963, c. 1786, p. 3595, § 75, operative Oct. 1, 1963; Stats.1976, c. 1050, p. 4675, § 1; Stats.1981, c. 714, p. 2808, § 465; Stats.1983, c. 627, § 1; Stats.1992, c. 427 (A.B.3355), § 178.)*

Cross References

Work furloughs, see Welfare and Institutions Code § 1830 et seq.

§ 1760.6. Payment of wages for work by wards

The department may provide for the payment of wages to wards for work performed pursuant to Section 2816 of the Penal Code, the sums earned to be paid in reparation, or to the parents or dependents of the ward, or to the ward, in any manner and in any proportions that the department directs. *(Added by Stats.2008, c. 116 (S.B.1261), § 5.)*

§ 1760.7. Standards; probation; juvenile halls

The director shall investigate, examine, and make reports upon adult and juvenile probation.

The director may establish standards for the performance of probation duties, and upon request consult with and make investigations and recommendations to probation officers, probation committees, juvenile justice commissions, and to judges of the superior courts, including such judges as are designated juvenile court judges of any county.

The director may also, upon request, consult with, make investigations for, and recommendations to probation officers, probation committees, juvenile justice commissions, and to judges of the superior courts, including such judges as are designated juvenile court judges of any county, to aid them in the operation and maintenance of their juvenile halls. *(Added by Stats.1943, c. 397, p. 1917, § 1. Amended by Stats.1945, c. 639, p. 1182, § 17; Stats.1951, c. 325, p. 580, § 1; Stats.1955, c. 1500, p. 2742, § 1; Stats.1963, c. 866, p. 2103, § 5; Stats.1965, c. 605, p. 1940, § 3; Stats.1970, c. 530, p. 1027, § 3.)*

Cross References

Delegation of powers and duties of authority, see Welfare and Institutions Code §§ 1712, 1719, 1720.
Persons committed to Youth Authority, report on, see Welfare and Institutions Code § 1741.

§ 1760.8. Population management and facilities master plan; construction and renovation projects; contracts for services; decision–making authority; delegation

(a) The Department of the Youth Authority shall annually develop a population management and facilities master plan presenting projected population and strategies for treatment and housing of wards for the succeeding five-year period. This plan shall set forth the department's strategy for bridging the gap between available bedspace and the projected ward population.

(b) The Department of the Youth Authority may contract with the Department of Corrections or the Office of Project Development and Management within the Department of General Services for professional and construction services related to the construction of facilities or renovation projects included in the Department of the Youth Authority's 1994–99 master plan for which funds are appropriated by the Legislature. The Department of the Youth Authority shall be responsible for program planning and all design decisions. The Department of Corrections or the Department of General Services shall, in consultation with the Department of the Youth Authority, ensure that all facilities are designed and constructed specifically for the needs of the youthful offender population. The Department of the Youth Authority also shall ensure that the design and construction of any facilities are consistent with the mission of the Department of the Youth Authority, which emphasizes the protection of the public from criminal activity and the rehabilitation of youthful offenders by providing education, training, and treatment services for those offenders committed by the courts. Any power, function, or jurisdiction for planning, design, and construction of facilities or renovation projects pursuant to the 1994–99 master plan that is conferred upon the Department of General Services shall be deemed to be conferred upon the Department of Corrections for purposes of this section. The Director of the Department of General Services may, upon the request of the Director of the Department of Corrections, delegate to the Department of Corrections any power, function, or jurisdiction for planning, design, and construction of any additional projects included within subsequent Department of the Youth Authority master plans. *(Added by Stats.1994, c. 905 (S.B.1763), § 1. Amended by Stats.2012, c. 728 (S.B.71), § 188.)*

§ 1761. Case histories

The Youth Authority shall establish policies for a background assessment of all persons committed to the Youth Authority in order to supplement the case history provided by the county which committed the person to it. *(Added by Stats.1988, c. 612, § 2.)*

Cross References

Examination or consultation with persons committed to other institutions or agencies, see Welfare and Institutions Code § 1757.

Reports to be furnished authority on persons committed, see Welfare and Institutions Code § 1741.

Review of case history, see Welfare and Institutions Code § 1714.

Research References

3 Witkin, California Criminal Law 4th Punishment § 94 (2021), Treatment and Work.

§ 1762. Youth with high school diploma or California high school equivalency certificate; access to postsecondary education programs

(a) It is the intent of the Legislature that youth with a high school diploma or California high school equivalency certificate who are detained in, or committed to, a Division of Juvenile Justice facility shall have access to rigorous postsecondary academic and career technical education programs that fulfill the requirements for transfer to the University of California and the California State University and prepare them for career entry, respectively.

(b)(1) The Division of Juvenile Justice shall, to the extent feasible using available resources, ensure that youth with a high school diploma or California high school equivalency certificate who are detained in, or committed to, a Division of Juvenile Justice facility have access to, and can choose to participate in, public postsecondary academic and career technical courses and programs offered online, and for which they are eligible based on eligibility criteria and course schedules of the public postsecondary education campus providing the course or program. The division is also encouraged to develop other educational partnerships with local public postsecondary campuses, as is feasible, to provide programs on campus and onsite at the Division of Juvenile Justice facility.

(2) These programs shall be considered part of the current responsibilities of the Division of Juvenile Justice to provide and coordinate services for youth that enable the youth to be law-abiding and productive members of their families and communities.

(c) For purposes of this section, "youth" means any person detained in, or committed to, a Division of Juvenile Justice facility.

(d) This section does not preclude youth who have not yet completed their high school graduation requirements from concurrently participating in postsecondary academic and career technical education programs. *(Added by Stats.2020, c. 337 (S.B.823), § 47, eff. Sept. 30, 2020.)*

§ 1763. Records

The authority shall keep written records of all examinations and of the conclusions predicated thereon and of all orders concerning the disposition or treatment of every person subject to its control. After five years from the date on which the jurisdiction of the authority over a ward is terminated the authority may destroy such records. For the purposes of this section "destroy" means destroy or dispose of for the purpose of destruction. *(Added by Stats.1941, c. 937, p. 2530, § 1. Amended by Stats.1961, c. 250, p. 1278, § 1.)*

Research References

3 Witkin, California Criminal Law 4th Punishment § 94 (2021), Treatment and Work.

§ 1764. Records; disclosure

(a) Notwithstanding any other provision of law, any of the following information in the possession of the Youth Authority regarding persons 16 years of age or older who were committed to the Youth Authority by a court of criminal jurisdiction, or who were committed to the Department of Corrections and were subsequently transferred to the Youth Authority, shall be disclosed to any member of the public, upon request, by the director or the director's designee:

(1) The name and age of the person.

(2) The court of commitment and the offense that was the basis of commitment.

(3) The date of commitment.

(4) Any institution where the person is or was confined.

(5) The actions taken by any paroling authority regarding the person, which relate to parole dates.

(6) The date the person is scheduled to be released to the community, including release to a reentry work furlough program.

(7) The date the person was placed on parole.

(8) The date the person was discharged from the jurisdiction of the Youth Authority and the basis for the discharge.

(9) In any case where the person has escaped from any institution under the jurisdiction of the Youth Authority, a physical description of the person and the circumstances of the escape.

(b) The provisions of this section shall not be construed to authorize the release of any information that could place any individual in personal peril; that could threaten Youth Authority security; or that is exempt from disclosure pursuant to the California Public Records Act (Division 10 (commencing with Section 7920.000) of Title 1 of the Government Code). *(Added by Stats.1983, c. 1028, § 1. Amended by Stats.1989, c. 624, § 3.5; Stats.1989, c. 1048, § 1; Stats.2021, c. 615 (A.B.474), § 434, eff. Jan. 1, 2022, operative Jan. 1, 2023.)*

Law Revision Commission Comments

Section 1764 is amended to reflect nonsubstantive recodification of the California Public Records Act. See California Public Records Act Clean-Up, 46 Cal. L. Revision Comm'n Reports 207 (2019).

The section is also amended to make grammatical corrections, eliminate gendered pronouns, and use conventional subdivision and paragraph labels. [46 Cal.L.Rev.Comm. Reports 563 (2019)].

§ 1764.1. Release of information in possession of youth authority for offenses under § 676

Notwithstanding any other provision of law, the director or his or her designee may release the information described in Section 1764 regarding a person committed to the Youth Authority by a juvenile court for an offense described in subdivision (a) of Section 676, to any member of the public who requests the information, unless the court has ordered confidentiality under subdivision (c) of Section 676. *(Added by Stats.1986, c. 359, § 4. Amended by Stats.1989, c. 624, § 4; Stats.1989, c. 1048, § 2.)*

§ 1764.2. Release of information to victim or next of kin

(a) Notwithstanding any other provision of law, the Director of the Division of Juvenile Justice or the director's designee shall release the information described in Section 1764 regarding a person committed to the Division of Juvenile Facilities, to the victim of the offense, the next of kin of the victim, or his or her representative as designated by the victim or next of kin pursuant to Section 1767, upon request, unless the court has ordered confidentiality under subdivision (c) of Section 676. The victim or the next of kin shall be identified by the court or the probation department in the offender's commitment documents before the director is required to disclose this information.

(b) The Director of the Division of Juvenile Justice or the director's designee shall, with respect to persons committed to the Division of Juvenile Facilities, including persons committed to the Department of Corrections and Rehabilitation who have been transferred to the Division of Juvenile Facilities, inform each victim of that offense, the victim's next of kin, or his or her representative as designated by the victim or next of kin pursuant to Section 1767, of his or her right to request and receive information pursuant to subdivision (a) and Section 1767. *(Added by Stats.1989, c. 1048, § 3. Amended by Stats.1993, c. 560 (A.B.935), § 1; Stats.2000, c. 481 (S.B.1943), § 5; Stats.2008, c. 154 (A.B.2289), § 1; Stats.2012, c. 41 (S.B.1021), § 101, eff. June 27, 2012.)*

§ 1764.3. Notice of release of violent offenders under jurisdiction of Youth Authority

(a) Whenever a person is committed to the Youth Authority by a court of criminal jurisdiction, or is committed to the Department of Corrections and subsequently transferred to the Youth Authority, for a conviction of a violent felony listed in subdivision (c) of Section 667.5 of the Penal Code, the director or his or her designee shall, with respect to that person, provide all notices that would be required to be provided by the Board of Prison Terms or the Department of Corrections pursuant to Sections 3058.6 and 3058.8 of the Penal Code, if that person were confined in their respective institutions.

(b) In order to be entitled to receive from the department, pursuant to subdivision (a), the notice set forth in Section 3058.8 of the Penal Code, the requesting party shall keep the department informed of his or her current mailing address.

(c) The notice required under this section shall be provided within 10 days of release with respect to persons committed to the Youth Authority by a court of criminal jurisdiction. *(Added by Stats.1989, c. 624, § 6.)*

§ 1764.5. Incarcerated minors; notification of Department of Social Services

Whenever a minor is incarcerated in a Youth Authority facility for a period of at least 30 consecutive days, the Youth Authority shall inform the State Department of Social Services of the name, date of birth, social security number, and county of residence of the incarcerated person. *(Added by Stats.1994, c. 1042 (A.B.2844), § 2.)*

§ 1765. Continuous study of persons committed; discharge

(a) Except as otherwise provided in this chapter, the Department of the Youth Authority and the Youth Authority Board shall keep under continued study a person in their control and shall retain him or her, subject to the limitations of this chapter, under supervision and control so long as in their judgment that control is necessary for the protection of the public.

(b) The board shall discharge that person as soon as in its opinion there is reasonable probability that he or she can be given full liberty without danger to the public. *(Added by Stats.1941, c. 937, p. 2530, § 1. Amended by Stats.1979, c. 860, p. 2981, § 26; Stats.2003, c. 4 (S.B.459), § 33, eff. April 8, 2003, operative Jan. 1, 2004.)*

Cross References

Commitment to state prison following expiration of control, see Welfare and Institutions Code § 1780 et seq.
Control after discharge, see Welfare and Institutions Code § 1758.
Discharge of persons committed to authority by juvenile court, see Welfare and Institutions Code § 1769.

Research References

3 Witkin, California Criminal Law 4th Punishment § 95 (2021), In General.
3 Witkin, California Criminal Law 4th Punishment § 100 (2021), Discharge.

§ 1766. Powers and duties of Board of Juvenile Hearings when a person has been committed to Department of Corrections and Rehabilitation, Division of Juvenile Facilities; procedures regarding wards; information to be collected and shared with public; "ward case review" defined

For Executive Order N-49-20 (2019 CA EO 49-20), relating to changes in the discharge and re-entry process at the Division of Juvenile Justice due to the COVID-19 pandemic, see Historical and Statutory Notes under this section.

(a) Subject to Sections 733 and 1767.35, and subdivision (b) of this section, if a person has been committed to the Department of Corrections and Rehabilitation, Division of Juvenile Facilities, the Board of Juvenile Hearings, according to standardized review and appeal procedures established by the board in policy and regulation and subject to the powers and duties enumerated in subdivision (a) of Section 1719, may do any of the following:

(1) Set a date on which the ward shall be discharged from the jurisdiction of the Division of Juvenile Facilities and permitted his or her liberty under supervision of probation and subject to the jurisdiction of the committing court pursuant to subdivision (b).

(2) Deny discharge, except that a person committed to the division pursuant to Section 731 or 1731.5 shall not be held in physical confinement for a total period of time in excess of the maximum periods of time set forth in Section 731.

(b) The following provisions shall apply to any ward eligible for discharge from that ward's commitment to the custody of the Department of Corrections and Rehabilitation, Division of Juvenile Facilities. Any order entered by the court pursuant to this subdivision shall be consistent with evidence-based practices and the interest of public safety.

(1) The county of commitment shall supervise the reentry of any ward still subject to the court's jurisdiction and discharged from the jurisdiction of the Division of Juvenile Facilities. The conditions of the ward's supervision shall be established by the court pursuant to the provisions of this section.

(2) Not less than 60 days prior to the scheduled discharge consideration hearing of a ward described in this subdivision, the division shall provide to the probation department and the court of the committing county, and the ward's counsel, if known, the most recent written review prepared pursuant to Section 1720, along with notice of the discharge consideration hearing date.

(3)(A) Not less than 30 days prior to the scheduled discharge consideration hearing, the division shall notify the ward of the date and location of the discharge consideration hearing. A ward shall have the right to contact the ward's parent or guardian, if he or she can reasonably be located, to inform the parent or guardian of the date and location of the discharge consideration hearing. The division shall also allow the ward to inform other persons identified by the ward, if they can reasonably be located, and who are considered by the division as likely to contribute to a ward's preparation for the discharge consideration hearing or the ward's postrelease success.

(B) This paragraph shall not apply if either of the following conditions is met:

(i) A minor chooses not to contact the minor's parents, guardians, or other persons and the director of the division facility determines it would be in the best interest of the minor not to contact the parents, guardians, or other persons.

(ii) A person 18 years of age or older does not consent to the contact.

(C) Upon intake of a ward committed to a division facility, and again upon attaining 18 years of age while serving the ward's commitment in the custody of the division, an appropriate staff person shall explain the provisions of subparagraphs (A) and (B), using language clearly understandable to the ward.

(D) Nothing in this paragraph shall be construed to limit the right of a ward to an attorney under any other law.

(4) Not less than 30 days prior to the scheduled discharge consideration hearing of a ward described in this subdivision, the probation department of the committing county may provide the division with its written plan for the reentry supervision of the ward. At the discharge consideration hearing, the Board of Juvenile Hearings shall, in determining whether the ward is to be released, consider a reentry supervision plan submitted by the county.

(5) If the Board of Juvenile Hearings determines that a ward is ready for discharge to county supervision pursuant to subdivision (a), the board shall do both of the following:

(A) Set a date for discharge from the jurisdiction of the Division of Juvenile Facilities no less than 14 days after the date of such determination. The board shall also record any postrelease recommendations for the ward. These recommendations will be sent to the committing court responsible for setting the ward's conditions of supervision no later than seven days from the date of such determination.

(B) Notify the ward that he or she may petition the board for an honorable discharge after 18 months following his or her discharge by the board, provided that he or she is not on probation.

(6) No more than four days but no less than one day prior to the scheduled date of the reentry disposition hearing before the committing court, the Division of Juvenile Facilities shall transport and deliver the ward to the custody of the probation department of the committing county. On or prior to a ward's date of discharge from the Division of Juvenile Facilities, the committing court shall convene a reentry disposition hearing for the ward. The purpose of the hearing shall be for the court to identify those conditions of supervision that are appropriate under all the circumstances of the case and consistent with evidence-based practices. The court shall, to the extent it deems appropriate, incorporate postrelease recommendations made by the board as well as any reentry plan submitted by the county probation department and reviewed by the board into its disposition order. At the hearing the ward shall be fully informed of the terms and conditions of any order entered by the court, including the consequences for any violation thereof. The procedure of the reentry disposition hearing shall otherwise be consistent with the rules, rights, and procedures applicable to delinquency disposition hearings as described in Article 17 (commencing with Section 675) of Chapter 2 of Part 1 of Division 2.

(7) The Department of Corrections and Rehabilitation shall have no further jurisdiction over a ward who is discharged by the Board of Juvenile Hearings, except that the board shall make honorable discharge determinations.

(8) Notwithstanding any other law or any other provision of this section, commencing January 1, 2013, all wards who remain on parole under the jurisdiction of the Division of Juvenile Facilities shall be discharged, except for wards who are in custody pending revocation proceedings or serving a term of revocation. A ward that is pending revocation proceedings or serving a term of revocation shall be discharged after serving the ward's revocation term, including any revocation extensions, or when any allegations of violating the terms and conditions of the ward's parole are not sustained.

(c) Within 60 days of intake, the Division of Juvenile Facilities shall provide the court and the probation department with a treatment plan for the ward.

(d) Commencing January 1, 2013, and annually thereafter, for the preceding fiscal year, the department shall collect and make available to the public the following information:

(1) The total number of ward case reviews conducted by the division and the board, categorized by guideline category.

(2) The number of discharge consideration dates for each category set at guideline, above guideline, and below guideline.

(3) The number of ward case reviews resulting in a change to a discharge consideration date, including the category assigned to the ward and the specific reason for the change.

(4) The percentage of wards who have had a discharge consideration date changed to a later date, the percentage of wards who have had a discharge consideration date changed to an earlier date, and the average annual time added or subtracted per case.

(5) The number and percentage of wards who, while confined or on parole, are charged with a new misdemeanor or felony criminal offense.

(6) Any additional data or information identified by the department as relevant.

(e) As used in subdivision (d), the term "ward case review" means any review of a ward that changes, maintains, or appreciably affects the programs, treatment, or placement of a ward. *(Added by Stats.2010, c. 729 (A.B.1628), § 16, eff. Oct. 19, 2010, operative July 1, 2014. Amended by Stats.2011, c. 36 (S.B.92), § 80, eff. June 30, 2011, operative July 1, 2014; Stats.2012, c. 41 (S.B.1021), § 103, eff. June 27, 2012, operative Jan. 1, 2013; Stats.2016, c. 33 (S.B.843), § 50, eff. June 27, 2016; Stats.2017, c. 683 (S.B.625), § 8, eff. Jan. 1, 2018.)*

Cross References

Department of Corrections and Rehabilitation, see Government Code § 12838 et seq.

Disposition of person after commitment, see Welfare and Institutions Code §§ 1738, 1780.

Government of counties, chief probation officer, duties and obligations, see Government Code § 27771.

Local Revenue Fund 2011, creation of fund, accounts, and subaccounts, use of moneys in Youthful Offender Block Grant Subaccount, see Government Code § 30025.

Minors violating laws defining crime and adjudged ward of court, committing court's power to establish conditions of supervision, see Welfare and Institutions Code § 731.

Places for detention, examination, confinement, etc., authority to establish and operate, see Welfare and Institutions Code § 1760.

Powers and duties of authority, see Welfare and Institutions Code §§ 1712, 1719, 1720.

Youthful Offender Block Grant Fund, allocation to each county for offenders subject to this section, distribution, see Welfare and Institutions Code § 1955.

Research References

3 Witkin, California Criminal Law 4th Punishment § 94 (2021), Treatment and Work.

3 Witkin, California Criminal Law 4th Punishment § 96 (2021), Constitutional Limitations.

3 Witkin, California Criminal Law 4th Punishment § 99 (2021), Probation and Parole.

3 Witkin, California Criminal Law 4th Punishment § 100 (2021), Discharge.

§ 1766.1. Payment of restitution fine or restitution ordered as condition of release

When permitting an adult or minor committed to the Department of the Youth Authority his or her liberty pursuant to subdivision (a) of Section 1766, the Youth Authority Board shall impose as a condition thereof that the adult or minor pay in full any restitution fine or restitution order imposed pursuant to Section 13967, as operative on or before September 28, 1994, of the Government Code, or Section 1202.4 of the Penal Code, or Section 1203.4, as operative on or before August 2, 1994, of the Penal Code, or Section 730.6 or 731.1, as operative on or before August 2, 1995. Payment shall be in installments set in an amount consistent with the adult's or minor's ability to pay. *(Added by Stats.1983, c. 940, § 5. Amended by Stats.1987, c. 511, § 2; Stats.1988, c. 181, § 3; Stats.1996, c. 1077 (A.B.2898), § 37; Stats.2003, c. 4 (S.B.459), § 35, eff. April 8, 2003, operative Jan. 1, 2004.)*

§ 1766.2. Supervised parole; revocation

(a) Except as provided in subdivision (b), all applicable wards shall be placed on supervised parole within the period of 120 to 90 days prior to the date of release from custody from a Division of Juvenile Facilities institution pursuant to the discharge provisions of Section 1769, 1770, or 1771, or within the period of 120 to 90 days prior to completion of the maximum period of confinement pursuant to Section 731, whichever comes first.

(b) Subdivision (a) shall not apply when a petition or order for further detention of a juvenile has been requested by the Division of Juvenile Facilities or the Juvenile Parole Board pursuant to Section 1800.

(c) A ward who has been released under the provisions of subdivision (a) shall be subject to revocation of parole for alleged violations committed during the period of release. Any term of reconfinement under these circumstances shall remain subject to the limits of Section 731, 1769, 1770, or 1771, as applicable in each case. Any such revocation proceedings shall be in accordance with the procedures and due process protections for parolees under current law.

(d) For the purposes of this section, "applicable ward" means a person who is confined in a facility or institution operated by the Division of Juvenile Facilities 120 days prior to his or her discharge date under Section 1769, 1770, or 1771, or 120 days prior to completion of the maximum period of confinement under Section 731. *(Added by Stats.2009, c. 268 (A.B.1053), § 3.)*

§ 1766.5. Grievances; system for resolution; requirements

The director shall establish and maintain a fair, simple, and expeditious system for resolution of grievances of all persons committed to the Youth Authority regarding the substance or application of any written or unwritten policy, rule, regulation, or practice of the department or of an agent or contractor of the department or any decision, behavior, or action by an employee, agent, contractor, or other person confined within the institutions or camps of the Youth Authority which is directed toward the grievant, other than matters involving individual discipline. The system shall do all of the following:

(a) Provide for the participation of employees of the department and of persons committed to the Youth Authority on as equal a basis and at the most decentralized level reasonably possible and feasible in the design, implementation, and operation of the system.

(b) Provide, to the extent reasonably possible, for the selection by their peers of persons committed to the Youth Authority as participants in the design, implementation, and operation of the system.

(c) Provide, within specific time limits, for written responses with written reasons in support of them to all grievances at all decision levels within the system.

(d) Provide for priority processing of grievances which are of an emergency nature which would, by passage of time required for normal processing, subject the grievant to substantial risk of personal injury or other damage.

(e) Provide for the right of grievants to be represented by another person committed to the Youth Authority who is confined within the institutions or camps of the Youth Authority, by an employee, or by any other person, including a volunteer, who is a regular participant in departmental operations.

(f) Provide for safeguards against reprisals against any grievant or participant in the resolution of a grievance.

(g) Provide, at one or more decision levels of the process, for a full hearing of the grievance at which all parties to the controversy and their representatives shall have the opportunity to be present and to present evidence and contentions regarding the grievance,[1]

(h) Provide a method of appeal of grievance decisions available to all parties to the grievance, including, but not limited to, final right of appeal to advisory arbitration of the grievance by a neutral person not employed by the department, the decision of the arbitrator to be adopted by the department unless the decision is in violation of law, would result in physical danger to any persons, would require expenditure of funds not reasonably available for that purpose to the department, or, in the personal judgment of the director, would be detrimental to the public or to the proper and effective accomplishment of the duties of the department.

(i) Provide for the monitoring of the system by the department and also, pursuant to contract or other appropriate means, for a biennial evaluation of the system by a public or private agency independent of the department to the extent necessary to ascertain whether the requirements of this section are being met. The results of which evaluation shall be filed with the department, the Legislature, the Attorney General, and the State Public Defender. *(Added by Stats.1976, c. 710, p. 1726, § 1. Amended by Stats.1983, c. 636, § 1.)*

[1] So in enrolled bill.

Research References

3 Witkin, California Criminal Law 4th Punishment § 94 (2021), Treatment and Work.

§ 1767. Release on parole; notice to victim or next of kin; request; appearance and statement; duty of board; amendment of section

For Executive Order N–49–20 (2019 CA EO 49-20), relating to changes in the discharge and re-entry process at the Division of Juvenile Justice due to the COVID-19 pandemic, see Historical and Statutory Notes under Welfare and Institutions Code § 1766.

(a) Upon request, written notice of any hearing to consider the release on parole of any person under the control of the Youth Authority for the commission of a crime or committed to the authority as a person described in Section 602 shall be sent by the Department of the Youth Authority at least 30 days before the hearing to any victim of a crime committed by the person, or to the next of kin of the victim if the victim has died or is a minor. The requesting party shall keep the board apprised of his or her current mailing address.

(b) Any one of the following persons may appear, personally or by counsel, at the hearing:

(1) The victim of the offense and one support person of his or her choosing.

(2) In the event that the victim is unable to attend the proceeding, two support persons designated by the victim may attend to provide information about the impact of the crime on the victim.

(3) If the victim is no longer living, two members of the victim's immediate family may attend.

(4) If none of those persons appear personally at the hearing, any one of them may submit a statement recorded on videotape for the board's consideration at the hearing. Those persons shall also have

the right to submit a written statement to the board at least 10 days prior to the scheduled hearing for the board's consideration at the hearing.

(c) The board, in deciding whether to release the person on parole, shall consider the statements of victims, next of kin, or statements made on their behalf pursuant to this section and shall include in its report a statement of whether the person would pose a threat to public safety if released on parole.

(d) A representative designated by the victim or the victim's next of kin shall be either that person's legal counsel or a family or household member of the victim, for the purposes of this section.

(e) Support persons may only provide information about the impact of the crime on the victim and provide physical and emotional support to the victim or the victim's family.

(f) This section does not prevent the board from excluding a victim or his or her support person or persons from a hearing. The board may allow the presence of other support persons under particular circumstances surrounding the proceeding.

(g) The provisions of this section shall not be amended by the Legislature except by statute passed in each house by rollcall vote entered in the journal, two-thirds of the membership concurring, or by a statute that becomes effective only when approved by the electors. *(Added by Initiative Measure, approved by the people, June 8, 1982. Amended by Stats.1993, c. 560 (A.B.935), § 2; Stats.2000, c. 481 (S.B.1943), § 6; Stats.2015, c. 303 (A.B.731), § 570, eff. Jan. 1, 2016.)*

Cross References

Statutory rights of victims of crimes, parole eligibility hearing, see Penal Code § 679.02.

Research References

1 Witkin California Criminal Law 4th Introduction to Crimes § 124 (2021), Constitutional Provisions and Statutes.
3 Witkin, California Criminal Law 4th Punishment § 99 (2021), Probation and Parole.

§ 1767.1. Parole hearings; specified offenses; notices; statements; findings and reasons

At least 30 days before the Youth Authority Board meets to review or consider the parole of any person who has been committed to the control of the Department of the Youth Authority for the commission of any offense described in subdivision (b), paragraph (2) of subdivision (d), or subdivision (e) of Section 707, or for the commission of an offense in violation of paragraph (2) of subdivision (a) of Section 262 or paragraph (3) of subdivision (a) of Section 261 of the Penal Code, the board shall send written notice of the hearing to each of the following persons: the judge of the court that committed the person to the authority, the attorney for the person, the district attorney of the county from which the person was committed, the law enforcement agency that investigated the case, and the victim pursuant to Section 1767. The board shall also send a progress report regarding the ward to the judge of the court that committed the person at the same time it sends the written notice to the judge.

Each of the persons so notified shall have the right to submit a written statement to the board at least 10 days prior to the decision for the board's consideration. Nothing in this subdivision shall be construed to permit any person so notified to attend the hearing. With respect to the parole of any person over the age of 18 years, the presiding officer of the board shall state findings and supporting reasons for the decision of the board. The findings and reasons shall be reduced to writing, and shall be made available for inspection by members of the public no later than 30 days from the date of the decision. *(Added by Stats.1981, c. 645, p. 2415, § 1. Amended by Stats.1993, c. 560 (A.B.935), § 3; Stats.1994, c. 452 (S.B.1539), § 3; Stats.1994, c. 453 (A.B.560), § 18; Stats.1995, c. 61 (S.B.7), § 2; Stats.1996, c. 1075 (S.B.1444), § 18; Stats.2003, c. 4 (S.B.459), § 36, eff. April 8, 2003, operative Jan. 1, 2004.)*

Research References

3 Witkin, California Criminal Law 4th Punishment § 99 (2021), Probation and Parole.

§ 1767.2. Condition of probation or parole

Every order granting probation or parole to any person under the control of the authority who has been convicted of any of the offenses enumerated in Section 290 of the Penal Code shall require as a condition of such probation or parole that such person totally abstain from the use of alcoholic liquor or beverages. *(Added by Stats.1950, 1st Ex.Sess., c. 25, p. 467, § 3.)*

Research References

3 Witkin, California Criminal Law 4th Punishment § 99 (2021), Probation and Parole.

§ 1767.3. Written order of Director sufficient warrant to return to custody

(a) The written order of the Director of the Division of Juvenile Justice is a sufficient warrant for any peace officer to return to custody any person who has escaped from the custody of the Division of Juvenile Facilities or from any institution or facility in which he or she has been placed by the division.

(b) All peace officers shall execute the orders in like manner as a felony warrant. *(Added by Stats.1943, c. 238, p. 1149, § 1. Amended by Stats.1979, c. 860, p. 2982, § 29; Stats.1985, c. 496, § 1; Stats.1987, c. 354, § 2, eff. Aug. 28, 1987; Stats.1988, c. 160, § 186; Stats.2003, c. 4 (S.B.459), § 37, eff. April 8, 2003, operative Jan. 1, 2004; Stats.2007, c. 175 (S.B.81), § 26, eff. Aug. 24, 2007, operative Sept. 1, 2007; Stats.2012, c. 41 (S.B.1021), § 105, eff. June 27, 2012; Stats.2016, c. 33 (S.B.843), § 51, eff. June 27, 2016.)*

Cross References

Confinement of addicted persons over eighteen years of age in controlled substance treatment-control unit, see Health and Safety Code § 11562.
Peace officer, definition, see Penal Code §§ 7, 830 et seq., 852.1.
Sex offenders, failure to register with local enforcement agency, revocation of parole or probation, see Penal Code § 290.

Research References

3 Witkin, California Criminal Law 4th Punishment § 99 (2021), Probation and Parole.

§ 1767.35. Modification of conditions of supervision; hearing; return to custody

(a) For a ward discharged from the Division of Juvenile Justice to the jurisdiction of the committing court, that person may be detained by probation, for the purpose of initiating proceedings to modify the ward's conditions of supervision entered pursuant to paragraph (6) of subdivision (b) of Section 1766 if there is probable cause to believe that the ward has violated any of the court-ordered conditions of supervision. Within 15 days of detention, the committing court shall conduct a modification hearing for the ward. Pending the hearing, the ward may be detained by probation. At the hearing authorized by this subdivision, at which the ward shall be entitled to representation by counsel, the court shall consider the alleged violation of conditions of supervision, the risks and needs presented by the ward, and the supervision programs and sanctions that are available for the ward. Modification may include, as a sanction for a finding of a serious violation or a series of repeated violations of the conditions of supervision, an order for the reconfinement of a ward under 18 years of age in a juvenile facility, or for the reconfinement of a ward 18 years of age or older in a juvenile facility as authorized by Section 208.5, or for the reconfinement of a ward 18 years of age or older in a local adult facility as authorized by subdivision (b), or, until July 1, 2021, the Division of Juvenile Justice as authorized by subdivision (c).

The ward shall be fully informed by the court of the terms, conditions, responsibilities, and sanctions that are relevant to the order that is adopted by the court. The procedure of the supervision modification hearing, including the detention status of the ward in the event continuances are ordered by the court, shall be consistent with the rules, rights, and procedures applicable to delinquency disposition hearings, as described in Article 17 (commencing with Section 675) of Chapter 2 of Part 1 of Division 2.

(b) Notwithstanding any other law, subject to Chapter 1.6.[1] (commencing with Section 1980), and consistent with the maximum periods of time set forth in Section 731, in any case in which a person who was committed to and discharged from the Department of Corrections and Rehabilitation, Division of Juvenile Justice to the jurisdiction of the committing court attains 18 years of age prior to being discharged from the division or during the period of supervision by the committing court, the court may, upon a finding that the ward violated their conditions of supervision and after consideration of the recommendation of the probation officer and pursuant to a hearing conducted according to the provisions of subdivision (a), order that the person be delivered to the custody of the sheriff for a period not to exceed a total of 90 days, as a custodial sanction consistent with the reentry goals and requirements imposed by the court pursuant to paragraph (6) of subdivision (b) of Section 1766. Notwithstanding any other law, the sheriff may allow the person to come into and remain in contact with other adults in the county jail or in any other county correctional facility in which the person is housed.

(c) Notwithstanding any other law and subject to Chapter 1.6 (commencing with Section 1980), in any case in which a person who was committed to and discharged from the Department of Corrections and Rehabilitation, Division of Juvenile Justice, to the jurisdiction of the committing court, the juvenile court may, upon a finding that the ward violated their conditions of supervision and after consideration of the recommendation of the probation officer and pursuant to a hearing conducted according to the provisions of subdivision (a), order that the person be returned to the custody of the Department of Corrections and Rehabilitation, Division of Juvenile Justice, for a specified amount of time no shorter than 90 days and no longer than one year. This return shall be a sanction consistent with the reentry goals and requirements imposed by the court pursuant to paragraph (6) of subdivision (b) of Section 1766. A decision to return a ward to the custody of the Division of Juvenile Justice can only be made prior to July 1, 2021, and pursuant to the court making the following findings: (1) that appropriate local options and programs have been exhausted, and (2) that the ward has available confinement time that is greater than or equal to the length of the return.

(d) Upon ordering a ward to the custody of the Division of Juvenile Justice, the court shall send to the Division of Juvenile Justice a copy of its order along with a copy of the ward's probation plans and history while under the supervision of the county. *(Added by Stats.2010, c. 729 (A.B.1628), § 19, eff. Oct. 19, 2010, operative July 1, 2014. Amended by Stats.2012, c. 41 (S.B.1021), § 107, eff. June 27, 2012, operative Jan. 1, 2013; Stats.2021, c. 18 (S.B.92), § 19, eff. May 14, 2021.)*

[1] So in enrolled bill.

Cross References

Local Revenue Fund 2011, creation of fund, accounts, and subaccounts, use of moneys in Youthful Offender Block Grant Subaccount, see Government Code § 30025.

Youthful Offender Block Grant Fund, allocation to each county for offenders subject to this section, distribution, see Welfare and Institutions Code § 1955.

§ 1767.4. Expense of return to custody

Whenever any person paroled by the Youth Authority Board is returned to the department upon the order of the director by a peace officer or probation officer, the officer shall be paid the same fees and expenses as are allowed those officers by law for the transportation of persons to institutions or facilities under the jurisdiction of the department. *(Added by Stats.1947, c. 362, p. 926, § 1. Amended by Stats.1979, c. 860, p. 2982, § 30; Stats.2003, c. 4 (S.B.459), § 38, eff. April 8, 2003, operative Jan. 1, 2004.)*

Cross References

Peace officer defined, see Penal Code §§ 7, 830 et seq., 852.1.

§ 1767.5. Payment to private homes for care of paroled persons

The authority may pay any private home for the care of any person committed to the authority and paroled by the Youth Authority Board to the custody of the private home (including both persons committed to the authority under this chapter and persons committed to it by the juvenile court) at a rate to be approved by the Department of Finance. Payments for the care of paroled persons may be made from funds available to the authority for that purpose, or for the support of the institution or facility under the jurisdiction of the authority from which the person has been paroled. *(Added by Stats.1945, c. 780, p. 1469, § 1. Amended by Stats.1949, c. 970, p. 1760, § 1; Stats.1953, c. 1120, p. 2616, § 1; Stats.1957, c. 333, p. 971, § 1; Stats.1979, c. 860, p. 2982, § 31; Stats.2003, c. 4 (S.B.459), § 39, eff. April 8, 2003, operative Jan. 1, 2004.)*

Cross References

Approval of contracts and transactions, see Government Code § 13325.

§ 1767.6. Parole revocation proceedings; copies of police, arrest and crime reports; confidentiality

In parole revocation proceedings, a parolee or his attorney shall receive a copy of any police, arrest, and crime reports pertaining to such proceedings. Portions of such reports containing confidential information need not be disclosed if the parolee or his attorney has been notified that confidential information has not been disclosed. *(Added by Stats.1978, c. 856, p. 2716, § 4, eff. Sept. 19, 1978.)*

§ 1767.7. Revolving fund

A sum may be withdrawn by the authority from the funds available for the support of the authority without at the time furnishing vouchers and itemized statements. This sum shall be used as a revolving fund for payments for the care of persons paroled to private homes as provided in Section 1767.5. At the close of each fiscal year, or at any other time, upon demand of the Department of Finance the money so drawn shall be accounted for and substantiated by vouchers and itemized statements submitted to and audited by the State Controller. *(Added by Stats.1949, c. 262, p. 482, § 1. Amended by Stats.1979, c. 214, p. 459, § 1.)*

Cross References

Department of finance, see Government Code § 13000 et seq.
State controller, see Government Code § 12400 et seq.

§ 1767.9. Order of persons appearing or speaking at the hearing; rebuttal statements

Any person authorized to appear at a parole hearing pursuant to Section 1767 shall have the right to speak last before the board in regard to those persons appearing and speaking before the board at a parole hearing. Nothing in this section shall prohibit the person presiding at the hearing from taking any steps he or she deems appropriate to ensure that only accurate and relevant statements are considered in determining parole suitability as provided in law, including, but not limited to, the rebuttal of inaccurate statements made by any party. *(Added by Stats.2004, c. 1 (A.B.2), § 5, eff. Jan. 21, 2004.)*

§ 1768. Correctional activities

As a means of correcting the socially harmful tendencies of a person committed to the authority, the director may

(a) Require participation by him in vocational, physical, educational and corrective training and activities;

(b) Require such conduct and modes of life as seem best adapted to fit him for return to full liberty without danger to the public welfare;

(c) Make use of other methods of treatment conducive to the correction of the person and to the prevention of future public offenses by him;

(d) Provide useful work projects or work assignments for which such persons may qualify and be paid wages for such work from any moneys made available to the director for this purpose. *(Added by Stats.1941, c. 937, p. 2531, § 1. Amended by Stats.1945, c. 639, p. 1182, § 18; Stats.1969, c. 1023, p. 1990, § 1.)*

Cross References

Employment defined, and services regarding employment for public entities or Indian tribes, see Unemployment Insurance Code § 634.5.
Public offense definition, see Penal Code § 15.

Research References

3 Witkin, California Criminal Law 4th Punishment § 94 (2021), Treatment and Work.

§ 1768.1. Prohibition of employment or limitation of hours of work for replacement of employees on strike or subject to lockout

No contract shall be executed with an employer that will initiate employment by persons committed to the authority in the same job classification as other employees of the same employer who, at the time of execution of the contract, are on strike, as defined in Section 1132.6 of the Labor Code, or who are then subject to lockout, as defined in Section 1132.8 of the Labor Code. The total daily hours worked by persons committed to the authority and employed in the same job classification as other employees of the same employer who, subsequent to the employer's hiring of persons committed to the authority, go on strike, as defined in Section 1132.6 of the Labor Code, or are subjected to a lockout, as defined in Section 1132.8 of the Labor Code, shall not exceed, for the duration of the strike or lockout, the average daily hours worked for the preceding six months, or, if the authority's contract with the employer has been in operation for less than six months, the average for the period of operation. *(Added by Stats.1991, c. 739 (A.B.1787), § 2.)*

§ 1768.7. Escape or attempt to escape; punishment

(a) Any person committed to the authority who escapes or attempts to escape from the institution or facility in which he or she is confined, who escapes or attempts to escape while being conveyed to or from such an institution or facility, who escapes or attempts to escape while outside or away from such an institution or facility under custody of Youth Authority officials, officers, or employees, or who, with intent to abscond from the custody of the Youth Authority, fails to return to such an institution or facility at the prescribed time while outside or away from the institution or facility on furlough or temporary release, is guilty of a felony.

(b) Any offense set forth in subdivision (a) which is accomplished by force or violence is punishable by imprisonment in the state prison for a term of two, four, or six years. Any offense set forth in subdivision (a) which is accomplished without force or violence is punishable by imprisonment pursuant to subdivision (h) of Section 1170 of the Penal Code for a term of 16 months, two or three years or in the county jail not exceeding one year.

(c) For purposes of this section, "committed to the authority" means a commitment to the Youth Authority pursuant to Section 731 or 1731.5; a remand to the custody of the Youth Authority pursuant to Section 707.2; a placement at the Youth Authority pursuant to Section 704, 1731.6, or 1753.1; or a transfer to the custody of the Youth Authority pursuant to subdivision (c) of Section 1731.5. *(Added by Stats.1945, c. 781, p. 1470, § 2. Amended by Stats.1982, c. 1104, § 4; Stats.1985, c. 1283, § 2; Stats.2011, c. 15 (A.B.109), § 621, eff. April 4, 2011, operative Oct. 1, 2011.)*

Cross References

Escapes,
  Aiding or abetting, see Welfare and Institutions Code § 1152; Penal Code §§ 109, 4534.
  Attempts, see Penal Code §§ 4530, 4532.
  Industrial farm, see Penal Code § 4532.
  Prison, punishment, see Welfare and Institutions Code § 1252; Penal Code § 667.5.
  Public training schools, see Penal Code §§ 107, 109.
Felony,
  Definition, see Penal Code § 17.
  Punishment for felony not otherwise prescribed, see Penal Code § 18.

Research References

California Jury Instructions - Criminal 7.30, Escape Without Force or Violence—Defined.
2 Witkin, California Criminal Law 4th Crimes Against Governmental Authority § 102 (2021), Escape from Other Institutions.

§ 1768.8. Assault or battery on persons not confined; punishment

(a) An assault or battery by any person confined in an institution under the jurisdiction of the Department of the Youth Authority upon the person of any individual who is not confined therein shall be punishable by a fine not exceeding two thousand dollars ($2,000), or by imprisonment in the county jail not exceeding one year, or by both a fine and imprisonment.

(b) An assault by any person confined in an institution under the jurisdiction of the Department of the Youth Authority upon the person of any individual who is not confined therein, with a deadly weapon or instrument, or by any means of force likely to produce great bodily injury, is a felony punishable by imprisonment in the state prison for two, four, or six years. *(Added by Stats.1984, c. 709, § 1. Amended by Stats.1989, c. 995, § 1; Stats.1993, c. 165 (A.B.294), § 1.)*

Research References

1 Witkin California Criminal Law 4th Crimes Against the Person § 22 (2021), Offenses by Division of Juvenile Facilities Inmate.
1 Witkin California Criminal Law 4th Crimes Against the Person § 57 (2021), Assault or Battery Against Nonprisoner.

§ 1768.85. Battery by gassing of peace officer or institution employee; investigation; prosecution

(a) Every person confined under the jurisdiction of the Department of the Youth Authority who commits a battery by gassing upon the person of any peace officer, as defined in Chapter 4.5 (commencing with Section 830) of Title 3 of Part 2, or employee of the institution is guilty of aggravated battery and shall be punished by imprisonment in a county jail or by imprisonment pursuant to subdivision (h) of Section 1170 of the Penal Code for two, three, or four years.

(b) For purposes of this section, "gassing" means intentionally placing or throwing, or causing to be placed or thrown, upon the person of another, any human excrement or other bodily fluids or bodily substances or any mixture containing human excrement or other bodily fluids or bodily substances that results in actual contact with the person's skin or membranes.

(c) The person in charge of the institution under the jurisdiction of the Department of the Youth Authority shall use every available means to immediately investigate all reported or suspected violations of subdivision (a), including, but not limited to, the use of forensically acceptable means of preserving and testing the suspected gassing substance to confirm the presence of human excrement or other bodily fluids or bodily substances. If there is probable cause to believe that a ward has violated subdivision (a), the chief medical officer of the institution under the jurisdiction of the Department of the Youth Authority, or his or her designee, may, when he or she deems it medically necessary to protect the health of an officer or employee who may have been subject to a violation of this section, order the ward to receive an examination or test for hepatitis or tuberculosis or both hepatitis and tuberculosis on either a voluntary or involuntary basis immediately after the event, and periodically thereafter as determined to be necessary by the medical officer in order to ensure that further hepatitis or tuberculosis transmission does not occur. These decisions shall be consistent with an occupational exposure as defined by the Center for Disease Control and Prevention. The results of any examination or test shall be provided to the officer or employee who has been subject to a reported or suspected violation of this section. Nothing in this subdivision shall be construed to otherwise supersede the operation of Title 8 (commencing with Section 7500). Any person performing tests, transmitting test results, or disclosing information pursuant to this section shall be immune from civil liability for any action taken in accordance with this section.

(d) The person in charge of the institution under the jurisdiction of the Department of the Youth Authority shall refer all reports for which there is probable cause to believe that the inmate has violated subdivision (a) to the local district attorney for prosecution.

(e) The Department of the Youth Authority shall report to the Legislature, by January 1, 2003, its findings and recommendations on gassing incidents at the department's facilities and the medical testing authorized by this section. The report shall include, but not be limited to, all of the following:

(1) The total number of gassing incidents at each youth correctional facility up to the date of the report.

(2) The disposition of each gassing incident, including the administrative penalties imposed, the number of incidents that are prosecuted, and the results of those prosecutions, including any penalties imposed.

(3) A profile of the wards who commit the batteries by gassing, including the number of wards who have one or more prior serious or violent felony convictions.

(4) Efforts that the department has taken to limit these incidents, including staff training and the use of protective clothing and goggles.

(5) The results and costs of the medical testing authorized by this section.

(f) Nothing in this section shall preclude prosecution under both this section and any other provision of law. *(Added by Stats.2000, c. 627 (A.B.1449), § 3. Amended by Stats.2011, c. 15 (A.B.109), § 622, eff. April 4, 2011, operative Oct. 1, 2011.)*

Research References

1 Witkin California Criminal Law 4th Crimes Against the Person § 62 (2021), Battery by Gassing.

§ 1768.9. AIDS testing; required submission; pretest counseling; test procedures; notification; medical services; housing facilities; disclosure

(a) Notwithstanding any other provision of law, a person under the jurisdiction or control of the Department of the Youth Authority is obligated to submit to a test for the probable causative agent of AIDS upon a determination of the chief medical officer of the facility that clinical symptoms of AIDS or AIDS-related complex, as recognized by the Centers for Disease Control, is present in the person. In the event that the subject of the test refuses to submit to such a test, the department may seek a court order to require him or her to submit to the test.

(b) Prior to ordering a test pursuant to subdivision (a), the chief medical officer shall ensure that the subject of the test receives pretest counseling. The counseling shall include:

(1) Testing procedures, effectiveness, reliability, and confidentiality.

(2) The mode of transmission of HIV.

(3) Symptoms of AIDS and AIDS-related complex.

(4) Precautions to avoid exposure and transmission.

The chief medical officer shall also encourage the subject of the test to undergo voluntary testing prior to ordering a test. The chief medical officer shall also ensure that the subject of the test receives posttest counseling.

(c) The following procedures shall apply to testing conducted under this section:

(1) The withdrawal of blood shall be performed in a medically approved manner. Only a physician, registered nurse, licensed vocational nurse, licensed medical technician, or licensed phlebotomist may withdraw blood specimens for the purposes of this section.

(2) The chief medical officer shall order that the blood specimens be transmitted to a licensed medical laboratory which has been approved by the State Department of Health Services for the conducting of AIDS testing, and that tests, including all readily available confirmatory tests, be conducted thereon for medically accepted indications of exposure to or infection with HIV.

(3) The subject of the test shall be notified face-to-face as to the results of the test.

(d) All counseling and notification of test results shall be conducted by one of the following:

(1) A physician and surgeon who has received training in the subjects described in subdivision (b).

(2) A registered nurse who has received training in the subjects described in subdivision (b).

(3) A psychologist who has received training in the subjects described in subdivision (b) and who is under the purview of either a registered nurse or physician and surgeon who has received training in the subjects described in subdivision (b).

(4) A licensed social worker who has received training in the subjects described in subdivision (b) and who is under the purview of either a registered nurse or physician and surgeon who has received training in the subjects described in subdivision (b).

(5) A trained volunteer counselor who has received training in the subjects described in subdivision (b) and who is under the supervision of either a registered nurse or physician and surgeon who has received training in the subjects described in subdivision (b).

(e) The Department of the Youth Authority shall provide medical services appropriate for the diagnosis and treatment of those infected with HIV.

(f) The Department of the Youth Authority may operate separate housing facilities for wards and inmates who have tested positive for HIV infection and who continue to engage in activities which transmit HIV. These facilities shall be comparable to those of other wards and inmates with access to recreational and educational facilities, commensurate with the facilities available in the institution.

(g) Notwithstanding any other provision of law, the chief medical officer of a facility of the Department of the Youth Authority may do all of the following:

(1) Disclose results of a test for the probable causative agent of AIDS to the superintendent or administrator of the facility where the test subject is confined.

(2) When test results are positive, inform the test subject's known sexual partners or needle contacts in a Department of the Youth Authority facility of the positive results, provided that the test

subject's identity is kept confidential. All wards and inmates who are provided with this information shall be provided with the counseling described in subdivision (b).

(3) Include the test results in the subject's confidential medical record which is to be maintained separate from other case files and records.

(h) Actions taken pursuant to this section shall not be subject to subdivisions (a) to (c), inclusive, of Section 120980 of the Health and Safety Code. In addition, the requirements of subdivision (a) of Section 120990 of the Health and Safety Code shall not apply to testing performed pursuant to this section. *(Added by Stats.1989, c. 765, § 4. Amended by Stats.1996, c. 1023 (S.B.1497), § 459, eff. Sept. 29, 1996.)*

Research References

3 Witkin, California Criminal Law 4th Punishment § 42 (2021), Detection and Treatment of Communicable Diseases.

§ 1768.10. Tuberculosis examination or test requirement

Notwithstanding any other law, the Youth Authority Board may require a person under its jurisdiction or control to submit to an examination or test for tuberculosis when the board reasonably suspects that the parolee has, has had, or has been exposed to, tuberculosis in an infectious stage. For purposes of this section, an "examination or test for tuberculosis" means testing and followup examinations or treatment according to the Centers for Disease Control and the American Thoracic Society recommendations in effect at the time of the initial examination. *(Added by Stats.1992, c. 1263 (A.B.3467), § 6. Amended by Stats.2003, c. 4 (S.B.459), § 40, eff. April 8, 2003, operative Jan. 1, 2004.)*

§ 1769. Discharge of persons committed by juvenile court

(a) A person who is committed to the Department of Corrections and Rehabilitation, Division of Juvenile Facilities, by a juvenile court shall, except as provided in subdivision (b), be discharged upon the expiration of a two-year period of control or when he or she attains 21 years of age, whichever occurs later, unless an order for further detention has been made by the committing court pursuant to Article 6 (commencing with Section 1800).

(b) A person who is committed to the Department of Corrections and Rehabilitation, Division of Juvenile Facilities, by a juvenile court and who has been found to be a person described in Section 602 by reason of the commission of an offense listed in subdivision (b) of Section 707, shall be discharged upon the expiration of a two-year period of control or when he or she attains 25 years of age, whichever occurs later, unless an order for further detention has been made by the committing court pursuant to Article 6 (commencing with Section 1800).

(c) Notwithstanding subdivision (b), a person who is committed by a juvenile court to the Department of Corrections and Rehabilitation, Division of Juvenile Facilities, on or after July 1, 2012, who is found to be a person described in Section 602 by reason of the commission of an offense listed in subdivision (b) of Section 707, shall be discharged upon the expiration of a two-year period of control, or when he or she attains 23 years of age, whichever occurs later, unless an order for further detention has been made by the committing court pursuant to Article 6 (commencing with Section 1800). This subdivision does not apply to persons committed to the Department of Corrections and Rehabilitation, Division of Juvenile Facilities, by a juvenile court prior to July 1, 2012, pursuant to subdivision (b).

(d)(1) A person committed by a juvenile court to the Department of Corrections and Rehabilitation, Division of Juvenile Facilities, on or after July 1, 2018, who is found to be a person described in Section 602 by reason of the commission of an offense listed in subdivision (c) of Section 290.008 of the Penal Code or subdivision (b) of Section 707, shall be discharged upon the expiration of a two-year period of control, of when he or she attains 23 years of age, whichever occurs later, unless an order for further detention has been made by the committing court pursuant to Article 6 (commencing with Section 1800). This subdivision does not apply to a person who is committed to the Department of Corrections and Rehabilitation, Division of Juvenile Facilities, a state hospital, or another appropriate public or private mental health facility, by a juvenile court prior to July 1, 2018, pursuant to subdivision (b) or (c).

(2) A person who at the time of adjudication of a crime or crimes would, in criminal court, have faced an aggregate sentence of seven years or more, shall be discharged upon the expiration of a two-year period of control, or when the person attains 25 years of age, whichever occurs later, unless an order for further detention has been made by the committing court pursuant to Article 6 (commencing with Section 1800) of Chapter 1 of Division 2.5.

(3) This subdivision does not apply to a person who is committed to the Department of Corrections and Rehabilitation, Division of Juvenile Facilities, or to a person who is confined in a state hospital or other appropriate public or private mental health facility, by a court prior to July 1, 2018, as described in subdivision (b).

(e) The amendments to this section made by Chapter 342 of the Statutes of 2012 apply retroactively. *(Added by Stats.1941, c. 937, p. 2531, § 1. Amended by Stats.1963, c. 1693, p. 3322, § 1; Stats.1976, c. 1071, p. 4831, § 34; Stats.1982, c. 1102, § 2; Stats.1994, c. 452 (S.B.1539), § 4; Stats.1994, c. 453 (A.B.560), § 19; Stats.2012, c. 41 (S.B.1021), § 109, eff. June 27, 2012; Stats.2012, c. 342 (A.B.1481), § 7, eff. Sept. 17, 2012; Stats.2018, c. 36 (A.B.1812), § 36, eff. June 27, 2018.)*

Cross References

Commitment to prison upon expiration of Youth Authority's control, see Welfare and Institutions Code § 1780 et seq.

Discharge of commitment, see Welfare and Institutions Code §§ 1719, 1720.

Honorable discharge, see Welfare and Institutions Code § 1178.

Supervised parole prior to release from a Division of Juvenile Facilities institution and reconfinement, see Welfare and Institutions Code § 1766.2.

Research References

1 Witkin California Criminal Law 4th Introduction to Crimes § 11 (2021), Nature of Protection.

3 Witkin, California Criminal Law 4th Punishment § 95 (2021), In General.

3 Witkin, California Criminal Law 4th Punishment § 96 (2021), Constitutional Limitations.

§ 1770. Discharge of persons convicted of misdemeanor

Every person convicted of a misdemeanor and committed to the authority shall be discharged upon the expiration of a two-year period of control or when the person reaches his 23d birthday, whichever occurs later, unless an order for further detention has been made by the committing court pursuant to Article 6 (commencing with Section 1800). *(Added by Stats.1941, c. 937, p. 2531, § 1. Amended by Stats.1963, c. 1693, p. 3322, § 2.)*

Cross References

Misdemeanor, definition, see Penal Code § 17.

Supervised parole prior to release from a Division of Juvenile Facilities institution and reconfinement, see Welfare and Institutions Code § 1766.2.

Research References

3 Witkin, California Criminal Law 4th Punishment § 95 (2021), In General.

3 Witkin, California Criminal Law 4th Punishment § 96 (2021), Constitutional Limitations.

3 Witkin, California Criminal Law 4th Punishment § 100 (2021), Discharge.

§ 1771. Discharge of persons convicted of felony; discharge of specified persons committed on or after July 1, 2012; discharge of specified persons committed on or after July 1, 2018

(a) A person who is convicted of a felony and committed to the Department of Corrections and Rehabilitation, Division of Juvenile Facilities, shall be discharged when he or she attains 25 years of age, unless an order for further detention has been made by the committing court pursuant to Article 6 (commencing with Section 1800) or unless a petition is filed under Article 5 (commencing with Section 1780). If a petition under Article 5 (commencing with Section 1780) is filed, the division shall retain control until the final disposition of the proceeding under Article 5 (commencing with Section 1780).

(b) Notwithstanding subdivision (a), a person who is committed by a juvenile court to the Department of Corrections and Rehabilitation, Division of Juvenile Facilities, on or after July 1, 2012, and who is found to be a person described in Section 602 by reason of the commission of an offense listed in subdivision (b) of Section 707, shall be discharged upon the expiration of a two-year period of control, or when the person attains 23 years of age, whichever occurs later, unless an order for further detention has been made by the committing court pursuant to Article 6 (commencing with Section 1800). This subdivision does not apply to a person who is committed to the Department of Corrections and Rehabilitation, Division of Juvenile Facilities, by a juvenile court prior to July 1, 2012, pursuant to subdivision (a).

(c)(1) Notwithstanding subdivisions (a) or (b), a person who is committed by the juvenile court to the Department of Corrections and Rehabilitation, Division of Juvenile Facilities, on or after July 1, 2018, and who is found to be a person described in Section 602 by reason of the commission of an offense listed in subdivision (c) of Section 290.008 of the Penal Code or subdivision (b) of Section 707 of this code, shall be discharged upon the expiration of a two-year period of control, or when the person attains 23 years of age, whichever occurs later, unless an order for further detention has been made by the committing court pursuant to Article 6 (commencing with Section 1800) of Chapter 1 of Division 2.5.

(2) A person who at the time of adjudication of a crime or crimes would, in criminal court, have faced an aggregate sentence of seven years or more, shall be discharged upon the expiration of a two-year period of control, or when the person attains 25 years of age, whichever occurs later, unless an order for further detention has been made by the committing court pursuant to Article 6 (commencing with Section 1800) of Chapter 1 of Division 2.5.

(3) This subdivision does not apply to a person who is committed to the Department of Corrections and Rehabilitation, Division of Juvenile Facilities, or to a person who is confined in a state hospital or other appropriate public or private mental health facility by a court prior to July 1, 2018, pursuant to subdivision (a).

(d) The amendments to this section made by Chapter 342 of the Statutes of 2012 shall apply retroactively. *(Added by Stats.1941, c. 937, p. 2532, § 1. Amended by Stats.1963, c. 1693, p. 3322, § 3; Stats.2012, c. 41 (S.B.1021), § 110, eff. June 27, 2012; Stats.2012, c. 342 (A.B.1481), § 8, eff. Sept. 17, 2012; Stats.2018, c. 36 (A.B.1812), § 37, eff. June 27, 2018.)*

Cross References

Felony, definition, see Penal Code § 17.

Supervised parole prior to release from a Division of Juvenile Facilities institution and reconfinement, see Welfare and Institutions Code § 1766.2.

Research References

3 Witkin, California Criminal Law 4th Punishment § 95 (2021), In General.

§ 1772. Honorable discharge; release from penalties and disabilities; court petitions setting aside guilty verdict and dismissing accusation or information; remaining penalties and disabilities, including eligibility for appointment as peace officer

(a) Subject to subdivision (b), every person discharged by the Board of Juvenile Hearings may petition the court that committed him or her, and the court may upon that petition set aside the verdict of guilty and dismiss the accusation or information against the petitioner who shall thereafter be released from all penalties and disabilities resulting from the offense or crime for which he or she was committed, including, but not limited to, penalties or disabilities that affect access to education, employment, or occupational licenses.

(b) Notwithstanding subdivision (a), all of the following shall apply to a person described in subdivision (a) or a person honorably discharged by the Board of Juvenile Hearings:

(1) The person shall not be eligible for appointment as a peace officer employed by any public agency if that person's appointment would otherwise be prohibited by Section 1029 of the Government Code. However, that person may be appointed and employed as a peace officer by the Department of Corrections and Rehabilitation, Division of Juvenile Facilities if (A) at least five years have passed since the person's honorable discharge, and the person has had no misdemeanor or felony convictions except for traffic misdemeanors since he or she was honorably discharged by the Board of Juvenile Hearings, or (B) the person was employed as a peace officer by the Division of Juvenile Facilities on or before January 1, 1983. A person who is under the jurisdiction of the Division of Juvenile Facilities or a county probation department shall not be admitted to an examination for a peace officer position with the Division of Juvenile Facilities unless and until the person has been honorably discharged from the jurisdiction of the Board of Juvenile Hearings pursuant to Sections 1177 and 1719.

(2) The person is subject to Chapter 2 (commencing with Section 29800) and Chapter 3 (commencing with Section 29900) of Division 9 of Title 4 of Part 6 of the Penal Code.

(3) The conviction of the person for an offense listed in subdivision (b) of Section 707 is admissible in a subsequent criminal, juvenile, or civil proceeding if otherwise admissible, if all of the following are true:

(A) The person was 16 years of age or older at the time he or she committed the offense.

(B) The person was found unfit to be dealt with under the juvenile court law pursuant to Section 707 because he or she was alleged to have committed an offense listed in subdivision (b) of Section 707.

(C) The person was tried as an adult and convicted of an offense listed in subdivision (b) of Section 707.

(D) The person was committed to the Department of Corrections and Rehabilitation, Division of Juvenile Facilities for the offense referred to in subparagraph (C).

(4) The conviction of the person may be used to enhance the punishment for a subsequent offense.

(5) The conviction of a person who is 18 years of age or older at the time he or she committed the offense is admissible in a subsequent civil, criminal, or juvenile proceeding, if otherwise admissible pursuant to law.

(c) Every person discharged from control by the Board of Juvenile Hearings shall be informed of the provisions of this section in writing at the time of discharge.

(d) "Honorably discharged" as used in this section means and includes every person who was granted an honorable discharge by the Board of Juvenile Hearings pursuant to Sections 1177 and 1719.

(Added by Stats.1941, c. 937, p. 2532, § 1. Amended by Stats.1949, c. 235, p. 459, § 1; Stats.1976, c. 1272, p. 5627, § 2; Stats.1979, c. 860, p. 2982, § 32; Stats.1982, c. 778, § 2; Stats.1994, c. 453 (A.B.560), § 20; Stats.2003, c. 4 (S.B.459), § 41, eff. April 8, 2003, operative Jan. 1, 2004; Stats.2010, c. 178 (S.B.1115), § 99, operative Jan. 1, 2012; Stats.2017, c. 683 (S.B.625), § 9, eff. Jan. 1, 2018.)

Law Revision Commission Comments

Subdivision (b) of Section 1772 is amended to reflect nonsubstantive reorganization of the statutes governing control of deadly weapons. [38 Cal.L.Rev.Comm. Reports 217 (2009)].

Cross References

Civil rights of prisoners, see Penal Code § 2600 et seq.
Commitment to state prison after expiration of control, see Welfare and Institutions Code § 1780 et seq.
Completion of probation, withdrawal of plea and dismissal of accusations, see Penal Code § 1203.4.
Paroles, see Penal Code § 3040 et seq.
Penalties and disabilities, release upon discharge, see Welfare and Institutions Code § 1179.

Research References

2 Witkin, California Criminal Law 4th Crimes Against Public Peace and Welfare § 177 (2021), In General.
2 Witkin, California Criminal Law 4th Crimes Against Public Peace and Welfare § 233 (2021), Prohibitions.
3 Witkin, California Criminal Law 4th Punishment § 100 (2021), Discharge.
3 Witkin, California Criminal Law 4th Punishment § 398 (2021), What Constitutes Prior Conviction.
3 Witkin, California Criminal Law 4th Punishment § 425 (2021), Violent or Serious Felony.
3 Witkin, California Criminal Law 4th Punishment § 719 (2021), Remaining Effects of Conviction.
3 Witkin, California Criminal Law 4th Punishment § 723 (2021), Power to Seal is Statutory.

§ 1773. Abortions; conditions and restrictions; eligibility

(a) No condition or restriction upon the obtaining of an abortion by a female committed to the Division of Juvenile Facilities, pursuant to the Therapeutic Abortion Act (Article 2 (commencing with Section 123400) of Chapter 2 of Part 2 of Division 106 of the Health and Safety Code), other than those contained in that act, shall be imposed. Females found to be pregnant and desiring abortions shall be permitted to determine their eligibility for an abortion pursuant to law, and if determined to be eligible, shall be permitted to obtain an abortion.

(b) The rights provided for females by this section shall be posted in at least one conspicuous place to which all females have access. *(Added by Stats.1972, c. 1363, p. 2713, § 4. Amended by Stats.1996, c. 1023 (S.B.1497), § 460, eff. Sept. 29, 1996; Stats.2006, c. 538 (S.B.1852), § 687.)*

Cross References

Advertisements relating to abortion, see Business and Professions Code § 601.
Minor's consent to pregnancy related treatment and care, see Family Code § 6925.

Research References

3 Witkin, California Criminal Law 4th Punishment § 83 (2021), Special Requirements for Women Prisoners.

§ 1774. Pregnancy; determination; right to choice and services of any licensed physician and surgeon

(a) A female who has been committed to the Division of Juvenile Facilities shall have the right to summon and receive the services of a physician and surgeon of her choice in order to determine whether she is pregnant. The director may adopt reasonable rules and regulations with regard to the conduct of examinations to effectuate that determination.

(b) If she is found to be pregnant, she is entitled to a determination of the extent of the medical services needed by her and to the receipt of those services from the physician and surgeon of her choice. Expenses occasioned by the services of a physician and surgeon whose services are not provided by the facility shall be borne by the female.

(c) A ward who gives birth while under the jurisdiction of the Department of Corrections and Rehabilitation, Division of Juvenile Facilities, or a community treatment program has the right to the following services:

(1) Prenatal care.

(2) Access to prenatal vitamins.

(3) Childbirth education.

(d) A ward who is known to be pregnant or in recovery after delivery shall not be restrained except as provided by Section 3407 of the Penal Code.

(e) A physician providing services pursuant to this section shall possess a current, valid, and unrevoked certificate to engage in the practice of medicine issued pursuant to Chapter 5 (commencing with Section 2000) of Division 2 of the Business and Professions Code.

(f) The rights provided to females by this section shall be posted in at least one conspicuous place to which all female wards have access. *(Added by Stats.1972, c. 1362, p. 2712, § 4. Amended by Stats.2005, c. 608 (A.B.478), § 7; Stats.2012, c. 726 (A.B.2530), § 5.)*

Cross References

Community treatment programs, notice and written application forms to pregnant inmate, see Penal Code § 3419.
Community treatment programs, prenatal health care, pregnant inmates, see Penal Code § 3424.
Corrections Standards Authority, pregnant inmates, see Penal Code § 6030.
Juvenile Court, right of pregnant female in custody of local juvenile facility to choice and services of physician or surgeon, see Welfare and Institutions Code § 222.
Minor's consent to pregnancy related treatment and care, see Family Code § 6925.
Therapeutic Abortion Act, see Health and Safety Code § 123400 et seq.
Transfer of pregnant inmate to hospital, charges for care, see Penal Code § 3423.
Transfer of pregnant inmate to hospital, shackles, see Penal Code § 5007.7.

Research References

3 Witkin, California Criminal Law 4th Punishment § 83 (2021), Special Requirements for Women Prisoners.

§ 1776. Parole violators; county detention facilities; reimbursement

Whenever an alleged parole violator is detained in a county detention facility pursuant to a valid exercise of the powers of the Department of Corrections and Rehabilitation as specified in Sections 1753, 1755, and 1767.3 and when such detention is initiated by the Department of Corrections and Rehabilitation and is related solely to a violation of the conditions of parole and is not related to a new criminal charge, the county shall be reimbursed for the costs of such detention by the Department of the Department of Corrections and Rehabilitation. Such reimbursement shall be expended for maintenance, upkeep, and improvement of juvenile hall and jail conditions, facilities, and services. Before the county is reimbursed by the department, the total amount of all charges against that county authorized by law for services rendered by the department shall be first deducted from the gross amount of the reimbursement authorized by this section. Such net reimbursement shall be calculated and paid monthly by the department. The department shall withhold all or part of such net reimbursement to a county whose juvenile hall or jail facility or facilities do not conform to minimum standards for local detention facilities as authorized by Section 6030 of the Penal Code or Section 210 of this code.

"Costs of such detention," as used in this section, shall include the same cost factors as are utilized by the Department of Corrections and Rehabilitation in determining the cost of prisoner care in state correctional facilities.

No city, county, or other jurisdiction may file, and the state may not reimburse, a claim pursuant to this section that is presented to the Department of Corrections and Rehabilitation or to any other agency or department of the state more than six months after the close of the month in which the costs were incurred. *(Added by Stats.1977, c. 1157, p. 3744, § 1, eff. Sept. 30, 1977. Amended by Stats.1979, c. 373, p. 1389, § 350; Stats.1979, c. 860, p. 2983, § 33; Stats.1979, c. 1136, p. 4145, § 3, eff. Sept. 29, 1979; Stats.1980, c. 676, p. 2030, § 325; Stats.2007, c. 175 (S.B.81), § 28, eff. Aug. 24, 2007.)*

§ 1777. Federal Social Security Act moneys received by an incarcerated ward; liability for costs of support and maintenance

Any moneys received pursuant to the Federal Social Security Act by a ward who is incarcerated by the Youth Authority are liable for the reasonable costs of the ward's support and maintenance. *(Added by Stats.1983, c. 936, § 2.)*

§ 1778. Applicable law

Notwithstanding Section 11425.10 of the Government Code, Chapter 4.5 (commencing with Section 11400) of Part 1 of Division 3 of Title 2 of the Government Code does not apply to a parole hearing or other adjudication concerning rights of a person committed to the control of the Youth Authority conducted by the Department of the Youth Authority or the Youth Authority Board. *(Added by Stats. 1995, c. 938 (S.B.523), § 92, operative July 1, 1997. Amended by Stats.2003, c. 4 (S.B.459), § 42, eff. April 8, 2003, operative Jan. 1, 2004.)*

Law Revision Commission Comments

Section 1778 makes the general administrative adjudication provisions of the Administrative Procedure Act inapplicable to a parole hearing or other adjudication of rights of a ward conducted by the Youth Authority or the Youthful Offender Parole Board. Exemption of the agency's hearings from the Administrative Procedure Act does not exempt the hearings from the language assistance requirements of that act. Gov't Code § 11435.15(d).

Although Section 1778 is silent on the question, the formal hearing provisions of the Administrative Procedure Act (Chapter 5 (commencing with Section 11500) of Part 1 of Division 3 of Title 2 of the Government Code) do not apply to a parole hearing or other adjudication of rights of a ward conducted by the Youth Authority or the Youthful Offender Parole Board. *Cf.* Gov't Code § 11501 (application of chapter).

Nothing in Section 1778 excuses compliance with procedural protections required by due process of law. [25 Cal.L.Rev.Comm. Reports 55 (1995)].

ARTICLE 5. COMMITMENT TO STATE PRISON AFTER EXPIRATION OF CONTROL

§ 1780. Petition for commitment

If the date of discharge occurs before the expiration of a period of control equal to the maximum term prescribed by law for the offense of which he or she was convicted, and if the Department of the Youth Authority believes that unrestrained freedom for that person would be dangerous to the public, the Department of the Youth Authority shall petition the court by which the commitment was made.

The petition shall be accompanied by a written statement of the facts upon which the department bases its opinion that discharge from its control at the time stated would be dangerous to the public, but a petition may not be dismissed merely because of its form or an asserted insufficiency of its allegations; every order shall be reviewed upon its merits. *(Added by Stats.1941, c. 937, p. 2532, § 1. Amended by Stats.1979, c. 860, p. 2984, § 34; Stats.2003, c. 4 (S.B.459), § 43, eff. April 8, 2003, operative Jan. 1, 2004.)*

Cross References

Discharge of committed persons, see Welfare and Institutions Code § 1769 et seq.
Protection of public, see Welfare and Institutions Code § 1765.

Research References

3 Witkin, California Criminal Law 4th Punishment § 101 (2021), Imprisonment for Balance of Term.

§ 1781. Notice of petition and hearing; counsel

Upon the filing of a petition under this article, the court shall notify the person whose liberty is involved, and if he or she is a minor, his or her parent or guardian if practicable, of the application and shall afford him or her an opportunity to appear in court with the aid of counsel and of process to compel attendance of witnesses and production of evidence. When he or she is unable to provide his or her own counsel, the court shall appoint counsel to represent him or her.

In the case of any person who is the subject of such a petition and who is under the control of the Youth Authority for the commission of any offense of rape in violation of paragraph (1) or (2) of subdivision (a) of Section 262 or subdivision (2) or subdivision (3) of Section 261 of the Penal Code, or murder, the Department of the Youth Authority shall send written notice of the petition and of any hearing set for the petition to each of the following persons: the attorney for the person who is the subject of the petition, the district attorney of the county from which the person was committed, and the law enforcement agency that investigated the case. The department shall also send written notice to the victim of the rape or the next of kin of the person murdered if he or she requests notice from the department and keeps it apprised of his or her current mailing address. Notice shall be sent at least 30 days before the hearing. *(Added by Stats.1941, c. 937, p. 2532, § 1. Amended by Stats.1981, c. 588, p. 2301, § 3; Stats.1996, c. 1075 (S.B.1444), § 19; Stats.2003, c. 4 (S.B.459), § 44, eff. April 8, 2003, operative Jan. 1, 2004.)*

Cross References

Burden of producing evidence, see Evidence Code §§ 500, 550.
Informing defendant of charge and right to counsel, see Penal Code §§ 858, 859.
Minors,
  Definition, see Family Code § 6500.
  Enforcement of rights by guardian, see Family Code § 6601.
Right to counsel, see Const. Art. 1, § 14; Penal Code § 686.
Witnesses,
  Generally, see Code of Civil Procedure § 1878; Evidence Code § 700 et seq.
  Accused's right to compel attendance, see Const. Art. 1, § 15.
  Criminal actions, see Penal Code § 1321 et seq.
  Definition, see Code of Civil Procedure § 1878.

Research References

3 Witkin, California Criminal Law 4th Punishment § 101 (2021), Imprisonment for Balance of Term.

§ 1782. Authority of court; maximum term of imprisonment; time reductions

Such committing court may thereupon discharge the person, admit him or her to probation or may commit him or her to the state prison. The maximum term of imprisonment for a person committed to a state prison under this section shall be a period equal to the maximum term prescribed by law for the offense of which he or she was convicted less the period during which he or she was under the control of the Youth Authority. *(Added by Stats.1941, c. 937, p. 2532,*

§ 1. *Amended by Stats.1957, c. 2256, p. 3942, § 95; Stats.1979, c. 860, p. 2984, § 35.)*

Cross References

Board of prison terms, see Penal Code § 5075 et seq.
Execution of sentences of imprisonment, see Penal Code § 2900 et seq.

Research References

3 Witkin, California Criminal Law 4th Punishment § 101 (2021), Imprisonment for Balance of Term.

§ 1783. Appeal

An appeal may be taken from the order of the court committing a person to the State prison under this chapter in the same manner as appeals are taken from convictions in the criminal cases under the Penal Code. *(Added by Stats.1941, c. 937, p. 2533, § 1.)*

Cross References

Appeals in criminal cases, see Penal Code §§ 1235 et seq., 1466 et seq.

Research References

3 Witkin, California Criminal Law 4th Punishment § 101 (2021), Imprisonment for Balance of Term.

ARTICLE 5.2. JUVENILE JUSTICE COMMUNITY RESOURCE PROGRAMS

Section

§ 1784. Legislative findings and declaration

The Legislature finds and declares all of the following:

(a) That the mobilization of community resources to assist in providing youthful offenders with necessary educational, psychological, medical, and other services which relate to root causes of delinquency is vital.

(b) That due to increased and heavy caseloads, probation officers cannot be expected to assume the full burden of providing necessary services to youthful offenders.

(c) That addressing the root causes of delinquent behavior in a cost-effective manner yields enormous societal benefits in the prevention of future criminality and the integration of the offender into productive society.

(d) That by encouraging community participation, programs such as the Juvenile Justice Connection Project in Los Angeles County have achieved great success in providing services to young people at a substantial savings to the taxpayer.

(e) That efforts to implement similar projects throughout the state should be encouraged and supported. *(Added by Stats.1984, c. 1752, § 2.)*

§ 1784.1. Technical assistance; juvenile justice community resource program defined; youthful offender

(a) The Director of the Youth Authority shall, upon request, provide technical assistance to judges, probation officers, law enforcement officials, school administrators, welfare administrators, and other public and private organizations and citizen groups concerning the development and implementation of juvenile justice community resource programs.

(b) As used in this article, "juvenile justice community resource program" means a program which does both of the following:

(1) Develops a directory or bank of public and private agencies, practitioners, and other community resources to offer services that are needed by youthful offenders, including, but not limited to, medical, psychological, educational, recreational, and vocational services.

(2) Provides diagnostic screening for youthful offenders referred to the program and matches the offender with a provider of services.

(c) As used in this article, "youthful offender" means a person described by Section 601 or 602. *(Added by Stats.1984, c. 1752, § 2.)*

§ 1784.2. Grants; application for funding; organizational and program grants; factors considered in selecting applicants; time for initial evaluation, selection, and funding

(a) The Director of the Youth Authority shall provide grants from funds made available for this purpose, for the development, implementation, and support of juvenile justice community resource programs.

(b) Any public or private nonprofit agency that does not directly deliver services may apply to the director for funding as a juvenile justice community resource program pursuant to this article.

(c) Funding may consist of organizational and program grants.

(1) As used in this article, "organizational grants" means grants for the purpose of funding community organization efforts in order to develop a bank of public and private agencies, and other community resources, to provide services needed by youthful offenders and to provide financial support to the referral program. An applicant may receive only one organizational grant, which may not exceed thirty thousand dollars ($30,000).

(2) As used in this article, "program grants" means grants to support the operating costs of the referral programs. A program grant may not exceed fifty thousand dollars ($50,000) per applicant per year. As a further limitation, beginning in the second year of the program grant, the amount of the program grant may not exceed a prescribed percentage of the referral program's operating budget, as follows: 50 percent in the second year of the program grant, 33 percent in the third year, 25 percent in the fourth year, and 20 percent in the fifth and subsequent years of the program grant.

(d) The director shall consider all of the following factors, together with any other circumstances he or she deems appropriate, in selecting applicants to receive funds pursuant to this article.

(1) The stated goals of applicants.

(2) The number of youthful offenders to be served and the needs of the community.

(3) Evidence of community support, including, but not limited to, business, labor, professional, educational, charitable, and social service groups.

(e) In addition to the factors specified in subdivision (d), in selecting applicants to receive program grants, the director shall also consider all of the following:

(1) Description of the number and type of service providers available.

(2) Existence of support and involvement by participants in the local juvenile justice system, including law enforcement, probation, prosecution, and the judiciary.

(3) The organizational structure of the agency which will operate the program.

(4) Specific plans for meeting the percentage of local funding of operating costs as specified in paragraph (2) of subdivision (c).

(f) After consultation with the advisory committee, and upon evaluation of all applicants pursuant to the above criteria and any other criteria established by the advisory committee, the director shall select the public or private nonprofit agencies which he or she deems qualified to receive funds for the establishment and operation of the programs.

(g) The initial evaluation, selection, and funding of applicants shall take place prior to January 1, 1986. *(Added by Stats.1984, c. 1752, § 2. Amended by Stats.1992, c. 711 (A.B.2874), § 139, eff. Sept. 15, 1992.)*

§ 1784.3. Advisory committee on community resource referral programs; membership; expenses

The Director of the Youth Authority shall appoint an eight-member advisory committee on community resource referral programs to advise him or her on matters relating to this article. Committee members shall include representatives of business, labor, professional, charitable, educational, and social service groups, as well as those working within the juvenile justice system. The members of the committee shall be entitled to their reasonable expenses, including travel expenses, incurred in the discharge of their duties. *(Added by Stats.1984, c. 1752, § 2.)*

§ 1784.4. Acceptance of funds and grants

The director may accept funds and grants from any source, public or private, to assist in accomplishing the purposes of this article. *(Added by Stats.1984, c. 1752, § 2.)*

ARTICLE 5.3. RUNAWAY AND HOMELESS YOUTH

Section

§ 1785. State advisory groups; staff services

The state advisory group established pursuant to the Juvenile Justice and Delinquency Prevention Act of 1974 (42 U.S.C. 5601 et seq.) shall perform the duties imposed by this article.

Staff services shall be provided to the advisory group for the purposes of this article by the Youth Authority, the Office of Criminal Justice Planning, and the California Child, Youth and Family Coalition, an association of community-based agencies. *(Added by Stats.1984, c. 1612, § 1.)*

§ 1786. Duties; report; funding

The advisory group shall do all of the following:

(a) Identify existing programs dealing with runaway and homeless youth.

(b) Develop a directory of service providers.

(c) Study the feasibility of the establishment of a statewide referral system (a "hotline") for runaway and homeless youth.

(d) Compile statistics on runaway and homeless youth.

(e) Identify existing and potential funding sources for services to runaway and homeless youth.

(f) Coordinate and provide advice to administrators of programs relating to runaway and homeless youth on issues relating to federal funding of those programs.

The advisory group shall report to the Governor and the Legislature annually.

The staff provided to the advisory group for the purpose of this article shall seek funding for the activities specified in this section from existing agencies, both federal and state, as well as from private funding sources. *(Added by Stats.1984, c. 1612, § 1.)*

ARTICLE 5.4. RUNAWAY YOUTH AND FAMILIES IN CRISIS PROJECT

Section

§ 1787. Legislative findings and declaration

The Legislature finds and declares all of the following:

(a) A tremendous percentage of juveniles who commit status offenses including, but not limited to, running away, school truancy and incorrigibility, ultimately enter the juvenile justice system for subsequently engaging in delinquent, otherwise criminal behavior.

(b) In 1990, it was estimated that 48,629 youths ran away from their homes in California.

(c) In 1989, 776 runaway youths served by 33 nonprofit youth-runaway shelters in California, surveyed during a one-month period, identified one or more of the following as a problem:

(1) Family crisis 73%
(2) School problems 63%
(3) Victims of crime/abuse 57%
(4) Homeless/runaway 55%
(5) Substance abuse 43%
(6) Delinquent behavior 26%
(7) Other 9%

(d) It is estimated that 43 emergency shelters presently serve runaway youths as well as homeless youths and adults in California.

(e) It is estimated that 10 transitional living facilities are operated presently in California to provide youths with independent living skills, employment skills, and home responsibilities.

(f) It is conservatively projected that by the year 2000 there will be a deficit of 1,222 emergency shelter beds and 930 long-term beds statewide.

(g) Resources for runaway, homeless, and at-risk youth and their families are severely inadequate to meet their needs.

(h) The Counties of Fresno, Sacramento, San Bernardino, and Solano either (1) do not provide temporary or long-term shelter services or family crises services to runaway, homeless, and nonrunaway youth, or (2) do provide such services but at levels which substantially fail to meet the need.

The purpose of this chapter, therefore, is to establish three-year pilot projects in San Joaquin Central Valley, in the northern region of California, and in the southern region of California, whereby each project will provide temporary shelter services, transitional living shelter services, and low-cost family crisis resolution services based on a sliding fee scale to runaway youth, nonrunaway youth, and their working families. It is the intent of this chapter that services will be provided to prevent at-risk youth from engaging in delinquent and criminal behavior and to reduce the numbers of at-risk families from engaging in neglectful, abusive, and criminal behavior. *(Formerly § 1790, added by Stats.1998, c. 1065 (A.B.2495), § 2. Renumbered § 1787 and amended by Stats.1999, c. 83 (S.B.966), § 195.)*

§ 1788. Services to be provided by projects

Each Runaway Youth and Families in Crisis Project established under this article shall provide services which shall include, but not be limited to, all of the following:

(a) Temporary shelter and related services to runaway youth. The services shall include:

(1) Food and access to overnight shelter for no more than 14 days.

(2) Counseling and referrals to services which address immediate emotional needs or problems.

(3) Screening for basic health needs and referral to public and private health providers for health care. Shelters that are not equipped to house a youth with substance abuse problems shall refer that youth to an appropriate clinic or facility. The shelter shall monitor the youth's progress and assist the youth with services upon his or her release from the substance abuse facility.

(4) Long–term planning so that the youth may be returned to the home of the parent or guardian under conditions which favor long-term reunification with the family, or so the youth can be suitably placed in a situation outside of the parental or guardian home when such reunification is not possible.

(5) Outreach services and activities to locate runaway youth and to link them with project services.

(b) Family crisis resolution services to runaway and nonrunaway youth and their families which shall include:

(1) Parent training.

(2) Family counseling.

(3) Services designed to reunify youth and their families.

(4) Referral to other services offered in the community by public and private agencies.

(5) Long–term planning so that the youth may be returned to the home of the parent or guardian under conditions which favor long-term reunification with the family, or so the youth can be suitably placed in a situation outside of the parental or guardian home when such reunification is not possible.

(6) Followup services to ensure that the return to the parent or guardian or the placement outside of the parental or guardian home is stable.

(7) Outreach services and activities to locate runaway and nonrunaway youth and to link them with project services.

(c) Transitional living services shall include:

(1) Long–term shelter.

(2) Independent living skill services.

(3) Preemployment and employment skills training.

(4) Home responsibilities training.

(d) Where appropriate and necessary, some of the services identified under this section must also be provided in the local community and in the home of project clients. Projects shall notify parents that their children are staying at a project site consistent with state and federal parent notification requirements. *(Formerly § 1791, added by Stats.1998, c. 1065 (A.B.2495), § 2. Renumbered § 1788 and amended by Stats.1999, c. 83 (S.B.966), § 196. Amended by Stats.2000, c. 135 (A.B.2539), § 169.)*

§ 1789. Locations and sites; applications; eligibility

(a) A Runaway Youth and Families in Crisis Project shall be established in one or more counties in the San Joaquin Central Valley, in one or more counties in the northern region of California, and in one or more counties in the southern region of California. Each project may have one central location, or more than one site, in order to effectively serve the target population.

(b) The Office of Emergency Services shall prepare and disseminate a request for proposals to prospective grantees under this chapter within four months after this chapter has been approved and enacted by the Legislature. The Office of Emergency Services shall enter into grant award agreements for a period of no less than three years, and the operation of projects shall begin no later than four months after grant award agreements are entered into between the agency and the grantee. Grants shall be awarded based on the quality of the proposal, the documented need for services in regard to runaway youth, and to organizations, as specified in subdivision (d) of this section, in localities that receive a disproportionately low share of existing federal and state support for youth shelter programs.

(c) The Office of Emergency Services shall require applicants to identify, in their applications, measurable outcomes by which the agency will measure the success of the applicant's project. These measurable outcomes shall include, but not be limited to, the number of clients served and the percentage of clients who are successfully returned to the home of a parent or guardian or to an alternate living condition when reunification is not possible.

(d) Only private, nonprofit organizations shall be eligible to apply for funds under this chapter to operate a Runaway Youth and Families in Crisis Project, and these organizations shall be required to annually contribute a local match of at least 15 percent in cash or in-kind contribution to the project during the term of the grant award agreement. Preference shall be given to organizations that demonstrate a record of providing effective services to runaway youth or families in crisis for at least three years, successfully operating a youth shelter for runaway and homeless youth, or successfully operating a transitional living facility for runaway and homeless youth who do not receive transitional living services through the juvenile justice system. Additional weight shall also be given to those organizations that demonstrate a history of collaborating with other agencies and individuals in providing such services. Priority shall be given to organizations with existing facilities. Preference shall also be given to organizations that demonstrate the ability to progressively decrease their reliance on resources provided under this chapter and to operate this project beyond the period that the organization receives funds under this chapter. *(Formerly § 1792, added by Stats.1998, c. 1065 (A.B.2495), § 2. Renumbered § 1789 and amended by Stats.1999, c. 83 (S.B.966), § 197. Amended by Stats.2010, c. 618 (A.B.2791), § 304; Stats.2013, c. 352 (A.B.1317), § 535, eff. Sept. 26, 2013, operative July 1, 2013.)*

ARTICLE 5.5. CRIME AND DELINQUENCY PREVENTION

Section

§ 1790. Purpose

The purpose of this article is to reduce crime and delinquency by assisting the development, establishment and operation of comprehensive public and private community based programs for crime and delinquency prevention. *(Added by Stats.1974, c. 1401, p. 3066, § 2.)*

§ 1791. Department of youth authority; leadership; cooperation by state agencies

The Department of the Youth Authority shall exercise leadership on behalf of the state in order to accomplish the purpose of this article. All state agencies shall cooperate with the Department of the Youth Authority in order to bring about a statewide program for the reduction and prevention of crime and delinquency. *(Added by Stats.1974, c. 1401, p. 3066, § 2.)*

§ 1792. Funds for public or private agencies engaging in crime and delinquency prevention programs

The Director of the Youth Authority may provide funds for financial support, in amounts determined by him, from funds available for such purposes, to public or private agencies engaging in crime and delinquency prevention programs. No public or private organization may receive such support unless it complies with the standards developed pursuant to Section 1793. *(Added by Stats.1974, c. 1401, p. 3066, § 2.)*

§ 1792.1. County delinquency prevention commissions; administrative expenses; state aid

The director shall make annual allocations from funds made available to him for such purposes for administrative expenses to county delinquency prevention commissions established pursuant to Sections 233 and 235 not to exceed one thousand dollars ($1,000) per year for each commission. *(Added by Stats.1974, c. 1401, p. 3067, § 2. Amended by Stats.1978, c. 380, p. 1215, § 171.)*

§ 1792.2. Additional matching allocations to county commissions for delinquency prevention projects under operation of local governmental or nongovernmental organizations

The director may make additional matching allocations from funds available to him for such purposes, in amounts determined by him, to county delinquency prevention commissions for the development and operation of delinquency prevention projects or programs administered and operated by local governmental or nongovernmental organizations under the general supervision of the county delinquency prevention commission. *(Added by Stats.1974, c. 1401, p. 3067, § 2.)*

§ 1793. Standards for programs

The Director of the Youth Authority shall develop standards for the operation of programs funded under Sections 1792, 1792.1 and 1792.2. He shall seek advice from interested citizens, appropriate representatives of public and private agencies and youth groups in developing such standards. *(Added by Stats.1974, c. 1401, p. 3067, § 2.)*

§ 1794. Application for funds; payments

Application for funds under Sections 1792, 1792.1, and 1792.2 shall be made to the Director of the Youth Authority in the manner and form prescribed by the department. The department shall prescribe the amounts, time, and manner of payments of assistance if granted. *(Added by Stats.1974, c. 1401, p. 3067, § 2.)*

§ 1795. Assistance to local persons or groups

To help communities develop effective local programs, the Director of the Youth Authority may, upon request, provide technical assistance to judges, probation officers, law enforcement officials, school administrators, welfare administrators, and other public and private organizations, and citizen groups. The assistance may include studies and surveys to identify problems, development of written instructional or information materials, preparation of policy statements and procedural guides, field consultation with appropriate persons in the community, and other assistance as appears appropriate. *(Added by Stats.1974, c. 1401, p. 3067, § 2.)*

§ 1796. Funds for demonstration or experimental projects

The Director of the Youth Authority may from funds available to him for such purposes provide funds for demonstration or experimental projects designed to test the validity of new methods or strategies in delinquency prevention programs. *(Added by Stats.1974, c. 1401, p. 3067, § 2.)*

§ 1797. Assistance in establishment of and participation in work of public committees

The director may assist in the establishment of public committees having as their object the prevention or decrease of crime and delinquency among youth, and the director may participate in the work of any such existing or established committees. *(Added by Stats.1974, c. 1401, p. 3067, § 2.)*

§ 1798. Abolishment of State Commission on Juvenile Justice, Crime and Delinquency Prevention

As of July 1, 2005, the State Commission on Juvenile Justice, Crime and Delinquency Prevention is abolished. *(Added by Stats.1974, c. 1401, p. 3067, § 2. Amended by Stats.1984, c. 1479, § 1; Gov.Reorg.Plan No. 1 of 2005, § 86, eff. May 5, 2005, operative July 1, 2005; Stats.2005, c. 10 (S.B.737), § 89, eff. May 10, 2005, operative July 1, 2005.)*

Cross References

Department of Corrections and Rehabilitation, see Government Code § 12838 et seq.
State boards and commissions, expenses, see Government Code § 11009.
State officers and employees, traveling expenses, see Government Code § 11030 et seq.

§ 1799. Contracts

The director may, with the approval of the Director of General Services, enter into contracts with the federal government, other state governments, counties, cities, private foundations, private organizations, or any other group to accomplish the purposes of this article. *(Added by Stats.1974, c. 1401, p. 3068, § 2.)*

Cross References

Department of General Services, powers and duties, see Government Code §§ 14650, 14651, 14654 et seq.

ARTICLE 6. EXTENDED DETENTION OF DANGEROUS PERSONS

Section

§ 1800. Petition for order for further detention; timing; statement of facts; technical defects; notice of decision not to file petition

(a) Whenever the Division of Juvenile Facilities determines that the discharge of a person from the control of the division at the time required by Section 1766, 1769, 1770, or 1771, as applicable, would be physically dangerous to the public because of the person's mental or physical deficiency, disorder, or abnormality that causes the person to have serious difficulty controlling his or her dangerous behavior, the division, through the Director of the Division of Juvenile Justice, shall request the prosecuting attorney to petition the committing court for an order directing that the person remain subject to the control of the division beyond that time. The petition shall be filed at least 90 days before the time of discharge otherwise required. The petition shall be accompanied by a written statement of the facts upon which the division bases its opinion that discharge from control of the division at the time stated would be physically dangerous to the public, but the petition may not be dismissed and an order may not be denied merely because of technical defects in the application.

(b) The prosecuting attorney shall promptly notify the Division of Juvenile Facilities of a decision not to file a petition. *(Added by Stats.1963, c. 1693, p. 3323, § 4. Amended by Stats.1970, c. 371, p. 788, § 2; Stats.1979, c. 860, p. 2984, § 36; Stats.1984, c. 546, § 1; Stats.2003, c. 4 (S.B.459), § 45, eff. April 8, 2003, operative Jan. 1, 2004; Stats.2005, c. 110 (S.B.447), § 1, eff. July 21, 2005; Stats.2006, c. 538 (S.B.1852), § 688; Stats.2012, c. 41 (S.B.1021), § 111, eff. June 27, 2012.)*

Validity

A prior version of this statutory scheme, providing for juvenile extended detention (Welfare and Institutions Code § 1800 et seq.), required construction to preserve its constitutionality, in the decision of In re Howard N. (2005) 24 Cal.Rptr.3d 866, 35 Cal.4th 117, 106 P.3d 305.

Cross References

Protection of public, see Welfare and Institutions Code §§ 1765, 1780.

Research References

California Jury Instructions - Criminal 4.18, Commitment of Youth Authority for Further Detention.
5 Witkin, California Criminal Law 4th Criminal Trial § 816 (2021), Nature of Proceedings.
1 Witkin California Criminal Law 4th Defenses § 116 (2021), Nature and Elements of Defense.
3 Witkin, California Criminal Law 4th Punishment § 97 (2021), Extended Detention.

§ 1800.5. Review of cases by director where the Division of Juvenile Facilities has not made request for further detention; review by mental health professional; further petitions to court; supporting documents; time line

Notwithstanding any other provision of law, the Board of Parole Hearings may request the Director of the Division of Juvenile Justice to review any case in which the Division of Juvenile Facilities has not made a request to the prosecuting attorney pursuant to Section 1800 and the board finds that the ward would be physically dangerous to the public because of the ward's mental or physical deficiency, disorder, or abnormality that causes the person to have serious difficulty controlling his or her dangerous behavior. Upon the board's request, a mental health professional designated by the director shall review the case and thereafter may affirm the finding or order additional assessment of the ward. If, after review, the mental health designee affirms the initial finding, concludes that a subsequent assessment does not demonstrate that a ward is subject to extended detention pursuant to Section 1800, or fails to respond to a request from the board within the timeframe mandated by this section, the board thereafter may request the prosecuting attorney to petition the committing court for an order directing that the person remain subject to the control of the division pursuant to Section 1800 if the board continues to find that the ward would be physically dangerous to the public because of the ward's mental or physical deficiency, disorder, or abnormality that causes the person to have serious difficulty controlling his or her dangerous behavior. The board's request to the prosecuting attorney shall be accompanied by a copy of the ward's file and any documentation upon which the board bases its opinion, and shall include any documentation of the division's review and recommendations made pursuant to this section. Any request for review pursuant to this section shall be submitted to the director not less than 120 days before the date of final discharge, and the review shall be completed and transmitted to the board not more than 15 days after the request has been received. *(Added by Stats.2003, c. 4 (S.B.459), § 46, eff. April 8, 2003, operative Jan. 1, 2004. Amended by Stats.2005, c. 110 (S.B.447), § 2, eff. July 21, 2005; Stats.2006, c. 538 (S.B.1852), § 689; Stats.2012, c. 41 (S.B.1021), § 112, eff. June 27, 2012.)*

Validity

A prior version of this statutory scheme, providing for juvenile extended detention (Welfare and Institutions Code § 1800 et seq.), required construction to preserve its constitutionality, in the decision of In re Howard N. (2005) 24 Cal.Rptr.3d 866, 35 Cal.4th 117, 106 P.3d 305.

Research References

3 Witkin, California Criminal Law 4th Punishment § 97 (2021), Extended Detention.

§ 1801. Notice to person detained and parent or guardian; probable cause hearing; order for trial or discharge

(a) If a petition is filed with the court for an order as provided in Section 1800 and, upon review, the court determines that the petition, on its face, supports a finding of probable cause, the court shall order that a hearing be held pursuant to subdivision (b). The court shall notify the person whose liberty is involved and, if the person is a minor, his or her parent or guardian (if that person can be reached, and, if not, the court shall appoint a person to act in the place of the parent or guardian) of the hearing, and shall afford the person an opportunity to appear at the hearing with the aid of counsel and the right to cross-examine experts or other witnesses upon whose information, opinion, or testimony the petition is based. The court shall inform the person named in the petition of his or her right of process to compel attendance of relevant witnesses and the production of relevant evidence. When the person is unable to provide his or her own counsel, the court shall appoint counsel to represent him or her.

The probable cause hearing shall be held within 10 calendar days after the date the order is issued pursuant to this subdivision unless the person named in the petition waives this time.

(b) At the probable cause hearing, the court shall receive evidence and determine whether there is probable cause to believe that discharge of the person would be physically dangerous to the public because of his or her mental or physical deficiency, disorder, or abnormality which causes the person to have serious difficulty controlling his or her dangerous behavior. If the court determines there is not probable cause, the court shall dismiss the petition and the person shall be discharged from the control of the authority at the time required by Section 1766, 1769, 1770, 1770.1, or 1771, as applicable. If the court determines there is probable cause, the court shall order that a trial be conducted to determine whether the person is physically dangerous to the public because of his or her mental or physical deficiency, disorder, or abnormality. *(Added by Stats.1963, c. 1693, p. 3323, § 4. Amended by Stats.1984, c. 546, § 2; Stats.1998, c. 267 (S.B.2187), § 1; Stats.1999, c. 83 (S.B.966), § 199; Stats.2005, c. 110 (S.B.447), § 3, eff. July 21, 2005.)*

Validity

A prior version of this statutory scheme, providing for juvenile extended detention (Welfare and Institutions Code § 1800 et seq.), required construction to preserve its constitutionality, in the decision of In re Howard N. (2005) 24 Cal.Rptr.3d 866, 35 Cal.4th 117, 106 P.3d 305.

Cross References

Burden of producing evidence, see Evidence Code §§ 500, 550.
Informing defendant of charge and right to counsel, see Penal Code §§ 858, 859.
Right to counsel, see Const. Art. 1, §§ 14, 15; Penal Code § 686.
Witnesses,
Generally, see Evidence Code § 700 et seq.
Accused's right to compel attendance, see Const. Art. 1, § 15.
Criminal actions, see Penal Code § 1321 et seq.

Research References

3 Witkin, California Criminal Law 4th Punishment § 97 (2021), Extended Detention.

§ 1801.5. Trial of question whether person detained is physically dangerous to the public; jury; waiver

If a trial is ordered pursuant to Section 1801, the trial shall be by jury unless the right to a jury trial is personally waived by the person, after he or she has been fully advised of the constitutional rights being waived, and by the prosecuting attorney, in which case trial shall be by the court. If the jury is not waived, the court shall cause a jury to be summoned and to be in attendance at a date stated, not less than four days nor more than 30 days from the date of the order for trial, unless the person named in the petition waives time. The court shall submit to the jury, or, at a court trial, the court shall answer, the question: Is the person physically dangerous to the public because of his or her mental or physical deficiency, disorder, or abnormality which causes the person to have serious difficulty controlling his or her dangerous behavior? The court's previous order entered pursuant to Section 1801 shall not be read to the jury, nor alluded to in the trial. The person shall be entitled to all rights guaranteed under the federal and state constitutions in criminal proceedings. A unanimous jury verdict shall be required in any jury trial. As to either a court or a jury trial, the standard of proof shall be that of proof beyond a reasonable doubt. *(Added by Stats.1971, c. 1337, p. 2641, § 1; Stats.1971, c. 1389, p. 2744, § 5; Stats.1971, c. 1680, p. 3606, § 1. Amended by Stats.1984, c. 546, § 3; Stats.1998, c. 267 (S.B.2187), § 2; Stats.2005, c. 110 (S.B.447), § 4, eff. July 21, 2005.)*

Validity

A prior version of this statutory scheme, providing for juvenile extended detention (Welfare and Institutions Code § 1800 et seq.), required construction to preserve its constitutionality, in the decision of In re Howard N. (2005) 24 Cal.Rptr.3d 866, 35 Cal.4th 117, 106 P.3d 305.

Cross References

Constitutional provision for jury trial, see Const. Art. 1, § 16.
Jury trial, generally, see Code of Civil Procedure § 607 et seq.

Research References

California Jury Instructions - Criminal 4.18, Commitment of Youth Authority for Further Detention.
1 Witkin California Criminal Law 4th Defenses § 116 (2021), Nature and Elements of Defense.
3 Witkin, California Criminal Law 4th Punishment § 97 (2021), Extended Detention.

§ 1801.6. Change of venue; costs

When the venue of a proceeding under this chapter is changed, costs of the proceeding are chargeable as provided in Section 1037 of the Penal Code. *(Added by Stats.1988, c. 235, § 2.)*

Validity

A prior version of this statutory scheme, providing for juvenile extended detention (Welfare and Institutions Code § 1800 et seq.), required construction to preserve its constitutionality, in the decision of In re Howard N. (2005) 24 Cal.Rptr.3d 866, 35 Cal.4th 117, 106 P.3d 305.

§ 1802. Continuation of control over person detained; new application for continued detention

When an order for continued detention is made as provided in Section 1801, the control of the authority over the person shall continue, subject to the provisions of this chapter, but, unless the person is previously discharged as provided in Section 1766, the authority shall, within two years after the date of that order in the case of persons committed by the juvenile court, or within two years after the date of that order in the case of persons committed after conviction in criminal proceedings, file a new application for continued detention in accordance with the provisions of Section 1800 if continued detention is deemed necessary. These applications may be repeated at intervals as often as in the opinion of the authority may be necessary for the protection of the public, except that the department shall have the power, in order to protect other persons in the custody of the department to transfer the custody of any person over 21 years of age to the Director of Corrections for placement in the appropriate institution.

Each person shall be discharged from the control of the authority at the termination of the period stated in this section unless the authority has filed a new application and the court has made a new order for continued detention as provided above in this section. *(Added by Stats.1963, c. 1693, p. 3323, § 4. Amended by Stats.1979, c. 860, p. 2985, § 37; Stats.1980, c. 1117, p. 3607, § 25; Stats.2003, c. 4 (S.B.459), § 47, eff. April 8, 2003, operative Jan. 1, 2004.)*

Validity

A prior version of this statutory scheme, providing for juvenile extended detention (Welfare and Institutions Code § 1800 et seq.), required construction to preserve its constitutionality, in the decision of In re Howard N. (2005) 24 Cal.Rptr.3d 866, 35 Cal.4th 117, 106 P.3d 305.

Cross References

Protection of public, see Welfare and Institutions Code § 1765.

Research References

3 Witkin, California Criminal Law 4th Punishment § 97 (2021), Extended Detention.

§ 1803. Appeal

An order of the committing court made pursuant to this article is appealable by the person whose liberty is involved in the same manner as a judgment in a criminal case. The appellate court may affirm the order of the lower court, or modify it, or reverse it and order the appellant to be discharged. Pending appeal, the appellant shall remain under the control of the authority. *(Added by Stats. 1963, c. 1693, p. 3323, § 4.)*

Validity

A prior version of this statutory scheme, providing for juvenile extended detention (Welfare and Institutions Code § 1800 et seq.), required construction to preserve its constitutionality, in the decision of In re Howard N. (2005) 24 Cal.Rptr.3d 866, 35 Cal.4th 117, 106 P.3d 305.

Cross References

Appeals in criminal cases, see Penal Code §§ 1235 et seq., 1466 et seq.

Research References

3 Witkin, California Criminal Law 4th Punishment § 97 (2021), Extended Detention.

ARTICLE 7. COUNTY JUSTICE SYSTEM SUBVENTION PROGRAM

Section

§ 1805. Legislative intent

It is the intent of the Legislature in enacting this article to protect society from crime and delinquency by helping counties maintain and improve local correctional systems and crime and delinquency prevention programs by encouraging the continued availability of county operated juvenile correctional facilities, and by providing funding for services required or authorized by Chapter 1071 of the Statutes of 1976. It is also the intent of the Legislature to reduce the administrative costs of justice system programs, to provide maximum flexibility in meeting local needs in the delivery of services, and to enhance justice system planning and coordination efforts at the state and local levels. *(Added by Stats.1983, c. 288, § 5, eff. July 15, 1983.)*

§ 1806. Funds to counties; purposes; limitations on use

(a) From any state moneys made available to it for the program, commencing with fiscal year 1983–84, the Department of the Youth Authority shall provide funds to counties for the following purposes:

(1) To develop and maintain local programs for minors and adults who are eligible for commitment to the Department of Corrections or to the Department of the Youth Authority or who are considered to be at a high risk of becoming eligible for commitment.

(2) To maintain local programs for minors who have been found to be persons described by Section 602 and who are committed to a juvenile hall or to a juvenile home, ranch, camp, or forestry camp established pursuant to Sections 850 and 880.

(3) To develop and maintain programs to prevent crime and delinquency by persons who are not wards of the juvenile court or under court ordered probation supervision or serving a sentence as a result of a conviction in a court of criminal jurisdiction.

(4) To maintain programs or services required or authorized by Chapter 1071 of the Statutes of 1976.

(5) To provide funding for necessary county administrative expenses for the county justice system block grant program.

(b) In utilizing funds for the purposes set forth in subdivision (a), counties shall give primary consideration to programs which are local alternatives to the commitment of minors and adults to the Department of Corrections or the Department of the Youth Authority.

(c) Funds granted to counties under this article shall not be used for capital construction; for travel outside of the State of California; for law enforcement investigation or apprehension purposes; for the expense of prosecution or defense, except to the extent required by Chapter 1071 of the Statutes of 1976; or for the costs of confinement or detention in a jail, juvenile hall, or other secure lockup prior to sentencing or disposition by the court. *(Added by Stats.1983, c. 288, § 5, eff. July 15, 1983. Amended by Stats.1984, c. 1353, § 1, eff. Sept. 26, 1984; Stats.1991, c. 611 (A.B.1491), § 8, eff. Oct. 7, 1991.)*

ARTICLE 7.5. JUVENILE OFFENDER LOCAL PREVENTION AND CORRECTIONS ACT

§ 1820. Short title

This article shall be known and may be cited as the Juvenile Offender Local Prevention and Corrections Act. *(Added by Stats. 1993, c. 157 (A.B.799), § 2, eff. July 21, 1993.)*

§ 1820.05. Partnership funds

For purposes of this article, "partnership funds" means the state's share of funding for county juvenile ranches, camps, and forestry camps. *(Added by Stats.1993, c. 157 (A.B.799), § 2, eff. July 21, 1993.)*

§ 1820.1. Use of partnership funds

Partnership funds shall be used only for the purpose of confinement, discipline, and treatment of juvenile offenders in county juvenile ranches, camps, or forestry camps. *(Added by Stats.1993, c. 157 (A.B.799), § 2, eff. July 21, 1993.)*

§ 1820.15. Juvenile offender local prevention and corrections program; establishment and implementation; purpose

(a) The Department of the Youth Authority shall establish and implement the Juvenile Offender Local Prevention and Corrections Program.

(b) The purpose of the program required by subdivision (a) shall be to coordinate state and local efforts to confine, discipline, treat, and prevent juvenile offenders and to provide partnership funding for county juvenile ranches, camps, and forestry camps established pursuant to Section 880. *(Added by Stats.1993, c. 157 (A.B.799), § 2, eff. July 21, 1993.)*

§ 1820.2. Departmental duties

The Department of the Youth Authority shall, in the implementation of this article, do all of the following:

(a) Determine county eligibility for partnership funding.

(b) Distribute partnership funds to qualified counties quarterly based on the average daily population of the county's juvenile ranches, camps, and forestry camps for the previous fiscal quarter.

(c) Monitor county compliance with eligibility requirements.

(d) Provide technical assistance to counties to prevent unnecessary commitments to the Department of the Youth Authority and to expand the capacity of the counties to confine, discipline, and treat juvenile offenders in a manner consistent with public safety. *(Added by Stats.1993, c. 157 (A.B.799), § 2, eff. July 21, 1993.)*

§ 1820.25. Applications to receive partnership funds; procedures

A county may apply to receive partnership funds under this article by submitting an application to the department in a manner and at a time determined by the department. *(Added by Stats.1993, c. 157 (A.B.799), § 2, eff. July 21, 1993.)*

§ 1820.3. Eligibility for receipt of partnership fund; conditions

A county shall be eligible for the receipt of partnership funds under this article only if the county meets all of the following conditions:

(a) The county administers one or more juvenile ranches, camps, or forestry camps.

(b) The county's juvenile ranches, camps, or forestry camps possess, at a minimum, all of the following:

(1) A residential treatment program.

(2) A structured and disciplined program for each resident.

(3) Individual counseling.

(4) Physical fitness training.

(5) Social alternatives to gangs, drugs, and alcohol, including gang intervention programs where appropriate.

(6) Work experience and vocational training through work crew assignments.

(7) Access to certified, accredited courses in language arts, mathematics, science, social studies, computer laboratories, and basic reading and writing skills, with an emphasis on remedial education.

(8) Coordination with parents or guardians in preparation for family reunification.

However, the Director of Youth Authority, upon request of a county, may waive services required in paragraphs (3), (6), and (7), as appropriate, if the provision of those services is not feasible or necessary, as demonstrated by the county.

(c) The county program does all of the following:

(1) It provides a positive reinforcing environment that redirects physical, social, and emotional energies into constructive channels.

(2) It emphasizes responsibility for one's actions.

(3) It employs goal-setting methods to maximize self-discipline, self-confidence, and sense of pride.

(d) The county maintains at least the same number of beds as were available on June 30, 1993. The director, upon request of a county, may waive this requirement if the county demonstrates it is unable to comply due to unforeseen circumstances. *(Added by Stats.1993, c. 157 (A.B.799), § 2, eff. July 21, 1993.)*

§ 1820.4. Legislative intent; operation of juvenile camps or ranches

It is the intent of the Legislature that counties that do not operate juvenile camps or ranches, but instead contract for beds with counties that do, shall benefit from partnership funding via reduced contract costs, based on the host county's cost of providing the bed, excluding the state contribution. *(Added by Stats.1993, c. 157 (A.B.799), § 2, eff. July 21, 1993.)*

§ 1820.45. Coordination of state and local efforts; development of boot camp programs; legislative intent

(a)(1) The Department of the Youth Authority shall work with counties to develop boot camp programs, either separately or as part of existing ranches, camps, and forestry camps.

(2) Boot camps shall provide the same services as juvenile ranches, camps, and forestry camps but shall be conducted in a highly structured, military style environment.

(3) Boot camps shall include greater emphasis on physical conditioning, athletics, and team building than county juvenile ranches, camps, or forestry camps.

(b) It is the intent of the Legislature that the Department of the Youth Authority and participating counties shall develop a comprehensive boot camp program that incorporates the relevant design features of the federal juvenile boot camp pilot project. It is also the intent of the Legislature that the comprehensive boot camp program should include diagnostic assessment, community-based aftercare, and accountability. *(Added by Stats.1993, c. 157 (A.B.799), § 2, eff. July 21, 1993.)*

§ 1820.47. Boot camp programs for young, first-time, nonviolent offenders; contracts with military; services; costs

In order to develop, establish, and operate residential and nonresidential boot camp and similar programs for young, first-time offenders and nonserious and nonviolent offenders, a county may contract with the Military Department for the provision of the following services:

(a) Program planning assistance for counties contemplating the development of residential and nonresidential boot camp and similar programs.

(b) Training of personnel for residential and nonresidential boot camp and similar programs.

(c) Technical assistance for existing boot camp and similar programs.

(d) Assistance in establishing cooperative innovative military projects and career training (IMPACT) programs.

A county that contracts with the Military Department for any of these services shall be reimbursed for its costs to the extent that funds are made available in the annual Budget Act for these purposes. *(Added by Stats.1994, c. 1256 (A.B.3731), § 2. Amended by Stats. 1995, c. 72 (S.B.604), § 9.)*

§ 1820.5. Funding sources; amount of funds

(a) It is the intent of the Legislature that, commencing with the 1994–95 fiscal year, this article shall be funded by the federal government, the state, and eligible counties.

(b) It is the intent of the Legislature that the amount of funding from each source identified in paragraph (1) shall be determined in the Budget Act of 1994. *(Added by Stats.1993, c. 157 (A.B.799), § 2, eff. July 21, 1993.)*

§ 1820.55. Emergency regulations; adoption

The Department of the Youth Authority shall adopt emergency regulations for implementation of this article. *(Added by Stats.1993, c. 157 (A.B.799), § 2, eff. July 21, 1993.)*

ARTICLE 8. WORK FURLOUGHS

Section

§ 1830. Participation in program under Penal Code or this article; designation of administrator

The Director of the Youth Authority may participate in a local work furlough program established pursuant to subdivision (a) of Section 1208 of the Penal Code, or conduct or discontinue a work furlough rehabilitation program, in accordance with the provisions of this article, for appropriate classes of wards at one or more Youth Authority institutions. He or she may designate any officer or employee of the department to be the Youth Authority work furlough administrator and may assign personnel to assist the administrator. *(Added by Stats.1967, c. 1070, p. 2702, § 2. Amended by Stats.1969, c. 585, p. 1215, § 1; Stats.1979, c. 860, p. 2985, § 38; Stats.2003, c. 4 (S.B.459), § 48, eff. April 8, 2003, operative Jan. 1, 2004.)*

§ 1831. Continuation of employment; new employment; conditions

When a person is committed to a facility under the jurisdiction of the Youth Authority, the Youth Authority work furlough administrator may, if he concludes that such person is a fit subject therefor, direct that such person be permitted to continue in his regular employment, if that is compatible with the requirements of Section 1833, or may authorize the person to secure employment for himself in the county, unless the court at the time of commitment has ordered that such person not be granted work furloughs. *(Added by Stats.1967, c. 1070, p. 2702, § 2.)*

§ 1832. Arrangement for and nature of employment; wage rate; labor dispute

If the Youth Authority work furlough administrator so directs that the ward be permitted to continue in his regular employment, the administrator shall arrange for a continuation of such employment so far as possible without interruption. If the ward does not have regular employment, and the administrator has authorized the ward to secure employment for himself, the ward may do so, and the administrator may assist him in doing so. Any employment so secured must be suitable for the ward. Such employment must be at a wage at least as high as the prevailing wage for similar work in the area where the work is performed and in accordance with the prevailing working conditions in such area. In no event may any such employment be permitted where there is a labor dispute in the establishment in which the ward is, or is to be, employed. *(Added by Stats.1967, c. 1070, p. 2702, § 2.)*

§ 1833. Confinement periods

Whenever the ward is not employed and between the hours or periods of employment, he shall be confined in a detention facility unless the court or administrator directs otherwise. *(Added by Stats.1967, c. 1070, p. 2702, § 2.)*

§ 1834. Earnings

The earnings of the ward shall be collected by the Youth Authority work furlough administrator, and it shall be the duty of the ward's employer to transmit such wages to the administrator at the latter's request. Earnings levied upon pursuant to writ of execution or in other lawful manner shall not be transmitted to the administrator. If the administrator has requested transmittal of earnings prior to levy, such request shall have priority. When an employer transmits such earnings to the administrator pursuant to this section he shall have no liability to the ward for such earnings. From such earnings the administrator shall pay the ward's board and personal expenses, both inside and outside the detention facility, and shall deduct so much of the costs of administration of this article as is allocable to such ward. If sufficient funds are available after making the foregoing payments, the administrator may, with the consent of the ward, pay, in whole or in part, the preexisting debts of the ward. Any balance shall be retained until the ward's discharge and thereupon shall be paid to him. *(Added by Stats.1967, c. 1070, p. 2702, § 2. Amended by Stats.1968, c. 218, p. 525, § 3; Stats.1974, c. 1516, p. 3394, § 46, operative Jan. 1, 1977.)*

Law Revision Commission Comments

Section 1834 is amended to delete the reference to attachment of the earnings of a ward. Earnings of an employee are exempt from attachment. See Code Civ.Proc. § 487.020. See also Code Civ.Proc. §§ 483.010, 487.010. [13 Cal.L.Rev. Comm. Reports 1 (1975)].

§ 1835. Violations; termination of work furlough

In the event the ward violates the conditions laid down for his conduct, custody, or employment, the Youth Authority work furlough administrator may order termination of work furloughs for such minor. *(Added by Stats.1967, c. 1070, p. 2702, § 2.)*

ARTICLE 9. YOUTH CORRECTIONAL CENTERS

Section

§ 1850. Purpose; liberal interpretation

The purpose of this article is to protect society more effectively by providing a system of flexible constraints and controls that utilize short-term confinement for selected youthful offenders, followed by intensive probation supervision. To this end it is the intent of the Legislature that this article be liberally interpreted in conformity with its declared purpose. *(Added by Stats.1969, c. 1193, p. 2323, § 1.)*

§ 1851. Establishment of centers in community

In order to provide appropriate facilities for the rehabilitative treatment of young offenders who otherwise may be committed to the Department of the Youth Authority or the Department of Corrections, and in order to provide this treatment in the community where family and personal relationships can be strengthened rather than severed, and in order to provide a range of alternative dispositions to the courts before whom young offenders appear, and in order to provide opportunities for private citizens to contribute actively to the rehabilitation of offenders in their own neighborhood, youth correctional centers may be established by ordinance by boards of supervisors of any county, as provided in this article. *(Added by Stats.1969, c. 1193, p. 2323, § 1.)*

Cross References

Department of corrections, see Penal Code § 5000 et seq.

§ 1852. Operation and administration by county

Complete operation and authority for administration of the youth correctional center shall be vested in the county. The board of supervisors shall place responsibility for internal management with the chief probation officer. *(Added by Stats.1969, c. 1193, p. 2323, § 1.)*

§ 1853. Commitment to centers as condition of probation

Juvenile court wards and criminal offenders eligible for probation may be committed to youth correctional centers as a condition of probation, provided they come within all of the following descriptions:

(1) Who have not, at the time of commitment, reached the age of 25 years.

(2) Who have not been found guilty of a capital offense in a criminal proceeding.

(3) Who have been declared a ward of the juvenile court pursuant to Section 602, Welfare and Institutions Code, or who have been found guilty in a criminal proceeding of one or more public offenses

where the maximum term of confinement is not less than six months if the sentences run consecutively.

(4) Whose rehabilitation and reformation requires short-term confinement followed by intensive probation supervision.

The juvenile court may in its discretion commit any eligible ward of the juvenile court to the youth correctional center program and any criminal court may in its discretion commit any eligible offender to the youth correctional center program as a condition of probation, except that no commitment shall be placed into effect until the chief probation officer has certified to the committing court that the youth correctional center has adequate facilities to provide rehabilitative treatment for the offender. *(Added by Stats.1969, c. 1193, p. 2323, § 1.)*

§ 1854. Control of offender while under commitment

While under commitment to the youth correctional center, the offender is subject to the control of the chief probation officer. The offender may be confined to the center at all times; he may be released for brief periods to work, attend school, or engage in educational or recreational pursuits; or he may be allowed to live in the community and return to the center for specific services as directed by the chief probation officer. *(Added by Stats.1969, c. 1193, p. 2324, § 1.)*

§ 1855. Earnings of offenders

Earnings of offenders who reside in the center and work in the community shall be collected by the chief probation officer. From such earnings the chief probation officer may pay the offender's board and personal expenses and such administrative costs as are allocable to him. Any balance may be paid periodically to the offender as deemed appropriate by the chief probation officer. Upon the offender's release from juvenile court wardship or termination of his probation, all funds credited to his account shall be paid to him. *(Added by Stats.1969, c. 1193, p. 2324, § 1.)*

§ 1856. Unamenable offenders; alternative disposition

When in the opinion of the chief probation officer an offender appears to be unamenable to the program of the youth correctional center, he shall be returned to the committing court for further disposition. The court shall then make an alternative disposition. *(Added by Stats.1969, c. 1193, p. 2324, § 1.)*

§ 1857. Minimum standards and qualifications; receipt of state funds

The Board of Corrections shall adopt and prescribe the minimum standards of construction, operation, programs of education or rehabilitative training or treatment, and qualifications of personnel for youth correctional centers established pursuant to this article. No county establishing or conducting such a youth correctional center shall be entitled to receive any state funds provided for in this article unless and until the minimum standards and qualifications referred to in this section are complied with by such county. *(Added by Stats.1969, c. 1193, p. 2324, § 1. Amended by Stats.1996, c. 12 (A.B.1397), § 15, eff. Feb. 14, 1996.)*

§ 1858. Capacity

No youth correctional center established pursuant to this article shall be planned to accommodate more than 350 youths under supervision at any one time. Any youth correctional center that consistently exceeds this capacity shall be ineligible to receive subsidy funds. *(Added by Stats.1969, c. 1193, p. 2324, § 1.)*

§ 1859. Reimbursement to county

Where any such youth correctional center is established, and where the minimum standards and qualifications provided for in Section 1857 have been complied with by the county, the State of California through the Youth Authority, out of any money appropriated for this purpose, shall reimburse the county at the rate of two hundred dollars ($200) per month per person being supervised by the youth correctional center during the first six months of such person's first-time participation in the center program. This amount shall be adjusted annually, upward or downward, by the Director of Finance in accordance with the proportionate increase or decrease in per capita costs for supervising Youth Authority wards in institutions and on parole.

Whenever a claim made by a county pursuant to this section covering a prior fiscal year is found to have been in error, adjustment may be made on a current claim without necessity of applying the adjustment to the appropriation for the prior fiscal year. *(Added by Stats.1969, c. 1193, p. 2325, § 1.)*

§ 1860. Sharing cost of construction

(a) From any state moneys made available to it for that purpose, the Youth Authority shall share in the cost pursuant to this article of the construction of youth correctional centers established by counties which apply therefor.

(b) "Construction" as used in this section includes construction of new buildings and acquisition of existing buildings and initial equipment of any such buildings, and, to the extent provided for in regulations adopted by the Department of the Youth Authority, remodeling of existing buildings owned by the county, to serve as a youth correctional center, and initial equipment thereof. "Construction" also includes payments made by a county under any lease-purchase agreement or similar arrangement authorized by law and payments for the necessary repair or improvements of property which is leased from the federal government or other public entity without cost to the county for a term of not less than 10 years. It does not include architects' fees or the cost of land acquisition.

(c) The amount of state assistance which shall be provided to any county shall not exceed 50 percent of the project cost approved by the Youth Authority and in no event shall it exceed three thousand dollars ($3,000) per offender the program is designed to accommodate.

(d) Application for state assistance for construction funds under this article shall be made to the Youth Authority in the manner and form prescribed by the Youth Authority, and the Youth Authority shall prescribe the time and manner of payment of state assistance, if granted. *(Added by Stats.1969, c. 1193, p. 2325, § 1. Amended by Stats.1970, c. 1053, p. 1881, § 2; Stats.1971, c. 1411, p. 2814, § 2.)*

§ 1861. Report to Legislature

The Department of the Youth Authority shall report to the Legislature no later than the fifth legislative day of the 1974 Regular Session on the experiences and the results under the provisions of this article. Pending review by the Legislature of such report, the state shall not participate financially in the establishment of more than four youth correctional centers. *(Added by Stats.1969, c. 1193, p. 2325, § 1.)*

Division 3

NARCOTIC ADDICTS

CHAPTER 2. CALIFORNIA REHABILITATION CENTER

§ 3300. Establishment; branches

There is hereby established an institution and branches, under the jurisdiction of the Department of Corrections and Rehabilitation, to be known as the California Rehabilitation Center. Branches may be established in existing institutions of the Department of Corrections and Rehabilitation, Division of Adult Operations, in halfway houses as described in Section 3153, in such other facilities as may be made available on the grounds of other state institutions, and in city and county correctional facilities where treatment facilities are available. Branches shall not be established on the grounds of such other institutions in any manner which will result in the placement of patients of such institutions into inferior facilities. Branches placed in a facility of the State Department of State Hospitals shall have prior approval of the Director of State Hospitals, and branches placed in a facility of the State Department of Developmental Services shall have the prior approval of the Director of Developmental Services. Commencing July 1, 2005, the branches in the Department of Corrections and Rehabilitation, Division of Juvenile Facilities shall be established by order of the secretary, and shall be subject to his or her administrative direction. Branches placed in city or county facilities shall have prior approval of the legislative body of the city or county.

Persons confined pursuant to this section in branches established in city and county correctional facilities shall be housed separately from the prisoners therein, and shall be entitled to receive treatment substantially equal to that which would be afforded those persons if confined in the main institution of the California Rehabilitation Center. *(Added by Stats.1965, c. 1226, p. 3072, § 2. Amended by Stats.1968, c. 1310, p. 2476, § 1, eff. Aug. 13, 1968; Stats.1969, c. 138, p. 376, § 297, eff. Sept. 11, 1969; Stats.1971, c. 939, p. 1841, § 1; Stats.1971, c. 1593, p. 3322, § 327, operative July 1, 1973; Stats.1971, c. 939, p. 1842, § 2, operative July 1, 1973; Stats.1977, c. 1252, p. 4431, § 482, operative July 1, 1978; Stats.1982, c. 624, § 21; Gov.Reorg.Plan No. 1 of 2005, § 92, eff. May 5, 2005, operative July 1, 2005; Stats.2005, c. 10 (S.B.737), § 96, eff. May 10, 2005, operative July 1, 2005; Stats.2012, c. 24 (A.B.1470), § 62, eff. June 27, 2012.)*

Cross References

Department of Corrections, see Penal Code § 5000 et seq.
Department of Corrections and Rehabilitation, see Government Code § 12838 et seq.
Department of Youth Authority, see Welfare and Institutions Code § 1710 et seq.

Research References

2 Witkin, California Criminal Law 4th Crimes Against Public Peace and Welfare § 176 (2021), In General.
3 Witkin, California Criminal Law 4th Punishment § 14 (2021), Other State Agencies.

§ 3301. Purpose

The principal purpose of the California Rehabilitation Center shall be the receiving, control, confinement, employment, education, treatment and rehabilitation of persons under the custody of the Department of Corrections or any agency thereof who are addicted to the use of narcotics or are in imminent danger of becoming so addicted. *(Added by Stats.1965, c. 1226, p. 3072, § 2.)*

Research References

3 Witkin, California Criminal Law 4th Punishment § 14 (2021), Other State Agencies.

§ 3302. Buildings, structures and facilities

The Director of Corrections shall acquire, or construct, and equip, in accordance with law, suitable buildings, structures and facilities for the California Rehabilitation Center. *(Added by Stats.1965, c. 1226, p. 3072, § 2.)*

§ 3303. Rules and regulations

(a) The Director of Corrections may prescribe and amend rules and regulations for the administration of the California Rehabilitation Center. These rules and regulations shall be promulgated and filed pursuant to Chapter 3.5 (commencing with Section 11340) of Part 1 of Division 3 of Title 2 of the Government Code, and shall, to the extent practical, be stated in language that is easily understood by the general public.

(b) The director shall maintain, publish, and make available to the general public, a compendium of the rules and regulations promulgated by the director pursuant to this section.

(c) The following exceptions to the procedures specified in this section apply to the rules and regulations made by the director for the California Rehabilitation Center:

(1) The director may specify an effective date that is any time more than 30 days after the rule or regulation is filed with the Secretary of State; provided that no less than 20 days prior to that effective date, copies of the rule or regulation shall be posted in conspicuous places throughout each institution and shall be mailed to all persons or organizations who request them.

(2) The director may rely upon a summary of the information compiled by a hearing officer; provided that the summary and the testimony taken regarding the proposed action shall be retained as part of the public record for at least one year after the adoption, amendment, or repeal. *(Added by Stats.1965, c. 1226, p. 3072, § 2. Amended by Stats.1978, c. 774, p. 2408, § 6; Stats.1985, c. 106, § 172.)*

Cross References

Director of corrections, see Penal Code § 5050 et seq.

§ 3304. Warden; officers and employees; appointment

A warden shall be appointed for the California Rehabilitation Center pursuant to Section 6050 of the Penal Code, and the Director of Corrections shall appoint, subject to civil service, such other officers and employees as may be necessary. *(Added by Stats.1965, c. 1226, p. 3072, § 2. Amended by Stats.1989, c. 1420, § 25.)*

Cross References

Director of corrections, see Penal Code § 5050 et seq.

§ 3305. Supervision, management and control; applicability of provisions of Part 3 of Penal Code

The supervision, management and control of the California Rehabilitation Center and the responsibility for the care, custody, training, discipline, employment, and treatment of the persons confined in the center are vested in the Director of Corrections. Part 3 (commencing with Section 1999) of the Penal Code applies to the institution as a prison under the jurisdiction of the Department of Corrections and to the persons confined in the institution insofar as those provisions may be applicable. *(Added by Stats.1965, c. 1226, p. 3072, § 2. Amended by Stats.1985, c. 106, § 173.)*

Cross References

Department of corrections, see Penal Code § 5000 et seq.
Department of General Services, see Government Code § 14600 et seq.
Director of corrections, see Penal Code § 5050 et seq.

§ 3306. Temporary removal from center or branch; custody; time; expenses; conservation camp programs

The Director of Corrections may authorize the temporary removal from the California Rehabilitation Center or any of its branches under the jurisdiction of the Department of Corrections of any person confined therein. The director may require that such temporary removal be under custody. Unless the person is removed for medical treatment, the removal shall not be for a period longer than three days. The director may require the person to reimburse the state, in whole or in part, for expenses incurred by the state in connection with such temporary removal other than for medical treatment.

Under specific regulations established by the director for the selection of confined persons, the director may authorize assignment to conservation camp programs. *(Added by Stats.1969, c. 1425, p. 2925, § 1. Amended by Stats.1971, c. 1124, p. 2138, § 1, operative Jan. 1, 1972.)*

Cross References

Department of corrections, see Penal Code § 5000 et seq.
Director of corrections, see Penal Code § 5050 et seq.

Research References

2 Witkin, California Criminal Law 4th Crimes Against Governmental Authority § 92 (2021), Offenses.
2 Witkin, California Criminal Law 4th Crimes Against Governmental Authority § 102 (2021), Escape from Other Institutions.

§ 3307. Community correctional centers; establishment and operation

The Director of Corrections may establish and operate facilities to be known as community correctional centers. *(Added by Stats.1971, c. 1124, p. 2138, § 2, operative Jan. 1, 1972.)*

§ 3308. Purpose

The primary purpose of such facilities is to provide housing, supervision, counseling, and other correctional programs for persons committed to the Director of Corrections. *(Added by Stats.1971, c. 1124, p. 2138, § 3.)*

§ 3309. Rules and regulations

Commencing July 1, 2005, the Secretary of the Department of Corrections and Rehabilitation shall make rules and regulations for the government of the community correctional centers in the management of their affairs. *(Added by Stats.1971, c. 1124, p. 2138, § 4, operative Jan. 1, 1972. Amended by Gov.Reorg.Plan No. 1 of 2005, § 93, eff. May 5, 2005, operative July 1, 2005; Stats.2005, c. 10 (S.B.737), § 97, eff. May 10, 2005, operative July 1, 2005.)*

Cross References

Department of Corrections and Rehabilitation, see Government Code § 12838 et seq.

§ 3310. Transfer from center or branches; outpatient status

The Director of Corrections may transfer persons confined in the California Rehabilitation Center, or branches thereof, to community correctional centers and place persons on outpatient status in community correctional centers. *(Added by Stats.1971, c. 1124, p. 2318, § 5, operative Jan. 1, 1972.)*

§ 3311. Furloughs

The Director of Corrections may grant furloughs to residents of community correctional centers for the purpose of employment, education, including vocational training, or arranging a suitable employment and residence program. *(Added by Stats.1971, c. 1124, p. 2138, § 6, operative Jan. 1, 1972.)*

§ 3313. Comprehensive state prison system plan; report

(a) The Department of Finance and the Department of Corrections and Rehabilitation shall release a report that provides an updated comprehensive plan for the state prison system, including a permanent solution to the decaying infrastructure of the California Rehabilitation Center. The report shall be submitted with the Governor's 2016–17 Budget to the Assembly Committee on Appropriations, the Assembly Committee on Budget, the Senate Committee on Appropriations, the Senate Committee on Budget and Fiscal Review, and the Joint Legislative Budget Committee.

(b) The Legislature finds and declares that given the reduction in the prison population, further investment in building additional prisons is unnecessary at this time, and that the California Rehabilitation Center may be closed without jeopardizing the court-ordered prison population cap. *(Added by Stats.2015, c. 26 (S.B.85), § 43, eff. June 24, 2015.)*

Division 5

COMMUNITY MENTAL HEALTH SERVICES

Part 1

THE LANTERMAN–PETRIS–SHORT ACT

CHAPTER 1. GENERAL PROVISIONS

§ 5000. Short title

This part shall be known and may be cited as the Lanterman–Petris–Short Act. *(Added by Stats.1967, c. 1667, p. 4074, § 36, operative July 1, 1969.)*

Cross References

Detention, care and services for returned state resident who was confined in public institution in other state, see Welfare and Institutions Code § 4119.
Initial 72 hours of mental health evaluation and treatment provided to minor, see Welfare and Institutions Code § 5585.20.
Suspension of criminal charges until defendant becomes mentally competent, see Penal Code § 1370.

Research References

6 Witkin, California Criminal Law 4th Criminal Appeal § 47 (2021), Proceedings Where Rule is Not Applicable.
5 Witkin, California Criminal Law 4th Criminal Trial § 801 (2021), Where Defendant Has Recovered.
5 Witkin, California Criminal Law 4th Criminal Trial § 805 (2021), Custody and Treatment Pending Hearing.
5 Witkin, California Criminal Law 4th Criminal Trial § 817 (2021), Petition.
5 Witkin, California Criminal Law 4th Criminal Trial § 819 (2021), Hearing and Disposition.
5 Witkin, California Criminal Law 4th Criminal Trial § 821 (2021), Constitutional Requirements.
5 Witkin, California Criminal Law 4th Criminal Trial § 822 (2021), Statutory Requirements.
5 Witkin, California Criminal Law 4th Criminal Trial § 843 (2021), In General.
5 Witkin, California Criminal Law 4th Criminal Trial § 847 (2021), Disposition on Return.
5 Witkin, California Criminal Law 4th Criminal Trial § 848 (2021), Developmental Disability.
3 Witkin, California Criminal Law 4th Punishment § 176 (2021), California Cases.
3 Witkin, California Criminal Law 4th Punishment § 771 (2021), Petition Filed After Commitment Has Expired.
3 Witkin, California Criminal Law 4th Punishment § 775 (2021), Right to Refuse Antipsychotic Medication.
2 Witkin, California Criminal Law 4th Sex Offenses and Crimes Against Decency § 33 (2021), Victim Disabled.
2 Witkin, California Criminal Law 4th Sex Offenses and Crimes Against Decency § 39 (2021), Condition of Victim.
2 Witkin, California Criminal Law 4th Sex Offenses and Crimes Against Decency § 61 (2021), Victim Disabled.

§ 5001. Legislative intent

The provisions of this part and Part 1.5 (commencing with Section 5585) shall be construed to promote the legislative intent as follows:

(a) To end the inappropriate, indefinite, and involuntary commitment of persons with mental health disorders, developmental disabilities, and chronic alcoholism, and to eliminate legal disabilities.

(b) To provide prompt evaluation and treatment of persons with mental health disorders or impaired by chronic alcoholism.

(c) To guarantee and protect public safety.

(d) To safeguard individual rights through judicial review.

(e) To provide individualized treatment, supervision, and placement services by a conservatorship program for persons who are gravely disabled.

(f) To encourage the full use of all existing agencies, professional personnel, and public funds to accomplish these objectives and to prevent duplication of services and unnecessary expenditures.

(g) To protect persons with mental health disorders and developmental disabilities from criminal acts.

(h) To provide consistent standards for protection of the personal rights of persons receiving services under this part and under Part 1.5 (commencing with Section 5585).

(i) To provide services in the least restrictive setting appropriate to the needs of each person receiving services under this part and under Part 1.5 (commencing with Section 5585). *(Added by Stats. 1967, c. 1667, p. 4074, § 36, operative July 1, 1969. Amended by Stats.1977, c. 1167, p. 3824, § 1; Stats.2013, c. 567 (S.B.364), § 1.)*

Cross References

Evaluation defined for purposes of this Part, see Welfare and Institutions Code § 5008.
Report of operation of division, see Welfare and Institutions Code § 5402.

§ 5002. Persons who may not be judicially committed; receipt of services

(a) Persons with mental health disorders and persons impaired by chronic alcoholism may no longer be judicially committed.

(b) Persons with mental health disorders shall receive services pursuant to this part. Persons impaired by chronic alcoholism may receive services pursuant to this part if they elect to do so pursuant to Article 3 (commencing with Section 5225) of Chapter 2.

(c) Persons with epilepsy may no longer be judicially committed.

(d) This part shall not be construed to repeal or modify laws relating to the commitment of mentally disordered sex offenders, persons with an intellectual disability, and mentally disordered criminal offenders, except as specifically provided in Section 4011.6 of the Penal Code, or as specifically provided in other statutes. *(Added by Stats.1967, c. 1667, p. 4074, § 36, operative July 1, 1969. Amended by Stats.1970, c. 516, p. 1003, § 4; Stats.1971, c. 1459, p. 2875, § 1; Stats.2012, c. 448 (A.B.2370), § 50; Stats.2012, c. 457 (S.B.1381), § 50; Stats.2014, c. 144 (A.B.1847), § 84, eff. Jan. 1, 2015.)*

Cross References

Court ordered evaluations,
Mentally disordered persons, see Welfare and Institutions Code § 5200 et seq.
Persons impaired by chronic alcoholism or drug abuse, see Welfare and Institutions Code § 5225 et seq.
Judicially committed defined for purposes of this Division, see Welfare and Institutions Code § 5008.1.
Juvenile court wards, judicial commitment, see Welfare and Institutions Code § 6550 et seq.
Mentally retarded persons, judicial commitment, see Welfare and Institutions Code § 6500 et seq.
Nonresidents, return to states of legal residence, see Welfare and Institutions Code § 4119.
Statutory construction,
Amendment of repealed statutes, see Government Code § 9609.
Court's duties, see Code of Civil Procedure § 1858; Evidence Code § 310.
Intention of Legislature, see Code of Civil Procedure § 1859.
Natural rights preferred, see Code of Civil Procedure § 1866.
Repeal of repealing statutes, see Government Code § 9607.
Temporary suspension of law, see Government Code § 9611.

§ 5003. Voluntary applications for mental health services

Nothing in this part shall be construed in any way as limiting the right of any person to make voluntary application at any time to any public or private agency or practitioner for mental health services, either by direct application in person, or by referral from any other public or private agency or practitioner. *(Added by Stats.1967, c. 1667, p. 4074, § 36, operative July 1, 1969.)*

Cross References

Referral defined for purposes of this Part, see Welfare and Institutions Code § 5008.
Voluntary application for mental health services, by minors under juvenile court jurisdiction, see Welfare and Institutions Code § 6552.

§ 5004. Protection from criminal acts

Persons with mental health disorders and persons with developmental disabilities shall receive protection from criminal acts equal to that provided any other resident in this state. *(Added by Stats.1977, c. 1167, p. 3825, § 2. Amended by Stats.2014, c. 144 (A.B.1847), § 85, eff. Jan. 1, 2015.)*

§ 5004.5. Reports of crime; complaints

(a) Notwithstanding any other law, a legal guardian, conservator, or other person who reasonably believes a person with a mental health disorder or developmental disability is the victim of a crime may file a report with an appropriate law enforcement agency. The report shall specify the nature of the alleged offense and any pertinent evidence. Notwithstanding any other law, the information in that report shall not be deemed confidential in any manner. No person shall incur any civil or criminal liability as a result of making a report authorized by this section unless it can be shown that a false report was made and the person knew or should have known that the report was false.

(b) Where the district attorney of the county in which the alleged offense occurred finds, based upon the evidence contained in the report and any other evidence obtained through regular investigatory procedures, that a reasonable probability exists that a crime or public offense has been committed and that the person with the mental health disorder or developmental disability is the victim, the district attorney may file a complaint verified on information and belief.

(c) The filing of a report by a legal guardian, conservator, or any other person pursuant to this section shall not constitute evidence that a crime or public offense has been committed and shall not be considered in any manner by the trier of fact. *(Added by Stats.1977, c. 1167, p. 3825, § 3. Amended by Stats.2014, c. 144 (A.B.1847), § 86, eff. Jan. 1, 2015.)*

§ 5005. Rights of person complained against

Unless specifically stated, a person complained against in any petition or proceeding initiated by virtue of the provisions of this part shall not forfeit any legal right or suffer legal disability by reason of the provisions of this part. *(Added by Stats.1967, c. 1667, p. 4074, § 36, operative July 1, 1969.)*

Cross References

Effect of evaluation on competency, see Welfare and Institutions Code § 5331.
Persons involuntarily detained, legal and civil rights, see Welfare and Institutions Code § 5325 et seq.

§ 5006. Prayer treatment

The provisions of this part shall not be construed to deny treatment by spiritual means through prayer in accordance with the tenets and practices of a recognized church or denomination for any person detained for evaluation or treatment who desires such treatment, or to a minor if his parent, guardian, or conservator desires such treatment. *(Added by Stats.1967, c. 1667, p. 4074, § 36, operative July 1, 1969.)*

Cross References

Evaluation defined for purposes of this Part, see Welfare and Institutions Code § 5008.
Reliance on faith healing, exemption from medical or psychiatric treatment, see Welfare and Institutions Code § 7104.

§ 5007. Prospective application

Unless otherwise indicated, the provisions of this part shall not be construed to apply retroactively to terminate court commitments of mentally ill persons or inebriates under preexisting law. *(Added by Stats.1967, c. 1667, p. 4074, § 36, operative July 1, 1969.)*

Cross References

Court defined for purposes of this Part, see Welfare and Institutions Code § 5008.

§ 5008. Definitions

Unless the context otherwise requires, the following definitions shall govern the construction of this part:

(a) "Evaluation" consists of multidisciplinary professional analyses of a person's medical, psychological, educational, social, financial, and legal conditions as may appear to constitute a problem. Persons providing evaluation services shall be properly qualified professionals and may be full-time employees of an agency providing face-to-face, which includes telehealth, evaluation services or may be part-time employees or may be employed on a contractual basis.

(b) "Court–ordered evaluation" means an evaluation ordered by a superior court pursuant to Article 2 (commencing with Section 5200) or by a superior court pursuant to Article 3 (commencing with Section 5225) of Chapter 2.

(c) "Intensive treatment" consists of such hospital and other services as may be indicated. Intensive treatment shall be provided by properly qualified professionals and carried out in facilities qualifying for reimbursement under the California Medical Assistance Program (Medi–Cal) set forth in Chapter 7 (commencing with Section 14000) of Part 3 of Division 9, or under Title XVIII of the federal Social Security Act and regulations thereunder. Intensive treatment may be provided in hospitals of the United States government by properly qualified professionals. This part does not prohibit an intensive treatment facility from also providing 72–hour evaluation and treatment.

(d) "Referral" is referral of persons by each agency or facility providing assessment, evaluation, crisis intervention, or treatment services to other agencies or individuals. The purpose of referral shall be to provide for continuity of care, and may include, but need not be limited to, informing the person of available services, making appointments on the person's behalf, discussing the person's problem with the agency or individual to which the person has been referred, appraising the outcome of referrals, and arranging for personal escort and transportation when necessary. Referral shall be considered complete when the agency or individual to whom the person has been referred accepts responsibility for providing the necessary services. All persons shall be advised of available precare services that prevent initial recourse to hospital treatment or aftercare services that support adjustment to community living following hospital treatment. These services may be provided through county or city mental health departments, state hospitals under the jurisdiction of the State Department of State Hospitals, regional centers under contract with the State Department of Developmental Services, or other public or private entities.

Each agency or facility providing evaluation services shall maintain a current and comprehensive file of all community services, both public and private. These files shall contain current agreements with agencies or individuals accepting referrals, as well as appraisals of the results of past referrals.

(e) "Crisis intervention" consists of an interview or series of interviews within a brief period of time, conducted by qualified professionals, and designed to alleviate personal or family situations which present a serious and imminent threat to the health or stability of the person or the family. The interview or interviews may be conducted in the home of the person or family, or on an inpatient or outpatient basis with such therapy, or other services, as may be appropriate. The interview or interviews may include family members, significant support persons, providers, or other entities or individuals, as appropriate and as authorized by law. Crisis intervention may, as appropriate, include suicide prevention, psychiatric, welfare, psychological, legal, or other social services.

(f) "Prepetition screening" is a screening of all petitions for court-ordered evaluation as provided in Article 2 (commencing with Section 5200) of Chapter 2, consisting of a professional review of all petitions; an interview with the petitioner and, whenever possible, the person alleged, as a result of a mental health disorder, to be a danger to others, or to himself or herself, or to be gravely disabled, to assess the problem and explain the petition; when indicated, efforts to persuade the person to receive, on a voluntary basis, comprehensive evaluation, crisis intervention, referral, and other services specified in this part.

(g) "Conservatorship investigation" means investigation by an agency appointed or designated by the governing body of cases in which conservatorship is recommended pursuant to Chapter 3 (commencing with Section 5350).

(h)(1) For purposes of Article 1 (commencing with Section 5150), Article 2 (commencing with Section 5200), and Article 4 (commencing with Section 5250) of Chapter 2, and for the purposes of Chapter 3 (commencing with Section 5350), "gravely disabled" means either of the following:

(A) A condition in which a person, as a result of a mental health disorder, is unable to provide for his or her basic personal needs for food, clothing, or shelter.

(B) A condition in which a person, has been found mentally incompetent under Section 1370 of the Penal Code and all of the following facts exist:

(i) The complaint, indictment, or information pending against the person at the time of commitment charges a felony involving death, great bodily harm, or a serious threat to the physical well-being of another person.

(ii) There has been a finding of probable cause on a complaint pursuant to paragraph (2) of subdivision (a) of Section 1368.1 of the Penal Code, a preliminary examination pursuant to Section 859b of the Penal Code, or a grand jury indictment, and the complaint, indictment, or information has not been dismissed.

(iii) As a result of a mental health disorder, the person is unable to understand the nature and purpose of the proceedings taken against him or her and to assist counsel in the conduct of his or her defense in a rational manner.

(iv) The person represents a substantial danger of physical harm to others by reason of a mental disease, defect, or disorder.

(2) For purposes of Article 3 (commencing with Section 5225) and Article 4 (commencing with Section 5250), of Chapter 2, and for the purposes of Chapter 3 (commencing with Section 5350), "gravely disabled" means a condition in which a person, as a result of impairment by chronic alcoholism, is unable to provide for his or her basic personal needs for food, clothing, or shelter.

(3) The term "gravely disabled" does not include persons with intellectual disabilities by reason of that disability alone.

(i) "Peace officer" means a duly sworn peace officer as that term is defined in Chapter 4.5 (commencing with Section 830) of Title 3 of Part 2 of the Penal Code who has completed the basic training course established by the Commission on Peace Officer Standards and Training, or any parole officer or probation officer specified in Section 830.5 of the Penal Code when acting in relation to cases for which he or she has a legally mandated responsibility.

(j) "Postcertification treatment" means an additional period of treatment pursuant to Article 6 (commencing with Section 5300) of Chapter 2.

(k) "Court," unless otherwise specified, means a court of record.

(*l*) "Antipsychotic medication" means any medication customarily prescribed for the treatment of symptoms of psychoses and other severe mental and emotional disorders.

(m) "Emergency" means a situation in which action to impose treatment over the person's objection is immediately necessary for the preservation of life or the prevention of serious bodily harm to the patient or others, and it is impracticable to first gain consent. It is not necessary for harm to take place or become unavoidable prior to treatment.

(n) "Designated facility" or "facility designated by the county for evaluation and treatment" means a facility that is licensed or certified as a mental health treatment facility or a hospital, as defined in subdivision (a) or (b) of Section 1250 of the Health and Safety Code, by the State Department of Public Health, and may include, but is not limited to, a licensed psychiatric hospital, a licensed psychiatric health facility, and a certified crisis stabilization unit. *(Added by Stats.1967, c. 1667, p. 4074, § 36, operative July 1, 1969. Amended by Stats.1968, c. 1374, p. 2640, § 14, operative July 1, 1969; Stats.1969, c. 722, p. 1419, § 3, eff. Aug. 8, 1969, operative July 1, 1969; Stats.1970, c. 516, p. 1003, § 5; Stats.1971, c. 1593, p. 3335, § 366, operative July 1, 1973; Stats.1974, c. 1511, p. 3321, § 12, eff. Sept. 27, 1974; Stats.1977, c. 1252, p. 4564, § 551, operative July 1, 1978; Stats.1978, c. 429, p. 1450, § 202, eff. July 17, 1978, operative July 1, 1978; Stats.1978, c. 1294, p. 4241, § 1; Stats.1980, c. 77, p. 194, § 1; Stats.1980, c. 1215, p. 4123, § 2; Stats.1980, c. 1340, p. 4740, § 38.5, eff. Sept. 30, 1980; Stats.1988, c. 1202, § 1; Stats.1990, c. 216 (S.B.2510), § 124; Stats.1991, c. 681 (S.B.665), § 1; Stats.2012, c. 448 (A.B.2370), § 51; Stats.2012, c. 457 (S.B.1381), § 51; Stats.2012, c. 24 (A.B.1470), § 123, eff. June 27, 2012; Stats.2013, c. 76 (A.B.383), § 208; Stats.2013, c. 567 (S.B.364), § 2; Stats.2017, c. 246 (S.B.684), § 3, eff. Jan. 1, 2018.)*

Cross References

Administration of antipsychotic medication to persons subject to detention, see Welfare and Institutions Code § 5332.

Competence of defendant, criminal process, treatment order and antipsychotic medications, see Penal Code § 1370.01.

Competency of defendant, procedure after commitment, dismissal, see Penal Code § 1370.

Effect of mental competency finding on criminal process, options upon finding defendant mentally incompetent, see Penal Code § 1370.01.

Felonies, definition and penalties, see Penal Code §§ 17, 18.
Notice of certification, contents, allegation of grave disability, see Welfare and Institutions Code § 5252.
Reevaluation of incompetent to stand trial (IST) defendants, use of telehealth evaluations, goals of program, procedures, see Welfare and Institutions Code § 4335.2.
Trial of issue of mental competence, psychiatric evaluations, see Penal Code § 1369.

Research References

5 Witkin, California Criminal Law 4th Criminal Trial § 833 (2021), What Proceedings Are Not Suspended.
5 Witkin, California Criminal Law 4th Criminal Trial § 846 (2021), Return to Court.

§ 5008.1. "Judicially committed" defined

As used in this division and in Division 4 (commencing with Section 4000), Division 4.1 (commencing with Section 4400), Division 6 (commencing with Section 6000), Division 7 (commencing with Section 7100), and Division 8 (commencing with Section 8000), the term "judicially committed" means all of the following:

(a) Persons who are mentally disordered sex offenders placed in a state hospital or institutional unit for observation or committed to the State Department of State Hospitals pursuant to Article 1 (commencing with Section 6300) of Chapter 2 of Part 2 of Division 6.

(b) Developmentally disabled persons who are admitted to a state hospital upon application or who are committed to the State Department of Developmental Services by court order pursuant to Article 2 (commencing with Section 6500) of Chapter 2 of Part 2 of Division 6.

(c) Persons committed to the State Department of State Hospitals or a state hospital pursuant to the Penal Code. *(Added by Stats.1969, c. 722, p. 1421, § 4, eff. Aug. 8, 1969, operative July 1, 1969. Amended by Stats.1971, c. 1593, p. 3337, § 367, operative July 1, 1973; Stats.1977, c. 1252, p. 4566, § 552, operative July 1, 1978; Stats.1978, c. 429, p. 1451, § 203, eff. July 17, 1978, operative July 1, 1978; Stats.1979, c. 373, p. 1393, § 359; Stats.2012, c. 24 (A.B.1470), § 124, eff. June 27, 2012.)*

Cross References

Court defined for purposes of this Part, see Welfare and Institutions Code § 5008.
Department of Developmental Services, see Welfare and Institutions Code § 4400 et seq.

§ 5008.2. Applying definition of mental disorder; consideration of historical course of disorder

(a) When applying the definition of mental disorder for the purposes of Articles 2 (commencing with Section 5200), 4 (commencing with Section 5250), and 5 (commencing with Section 5275) of Chapter 2 and Chapter 3 (commencing with Section 5350), the historical course of the person's mental disorder, as determined by available relevant information about the course of the person's mental disorder, shall be considered when it has a direct bearing on the determination of whether the person is a danger to others, or to himself or herself, or is gravely disabled, as a result of a mental disorder. The historical course shall include, but is not limited to, evidence presented by persons who have provided, or are providing, mental health or related support services to the patient, the patient's medical records as presented to the court, including psychiatric records, or evidence voluntarily presented by family members, the patient, or any other person designated by the patient. Facilities shall make every reasonable effort to make information provided by the patient's family available to the court. The hearing officer, court, or jury shall exclude from consideration evidence it determines to be irrelevant because of remoteness of time or dissimilarity of circumstances.

(b) This section shall not be applied to limit the application of Section 5328 or to limit existing rights of a patient to respond to evidence presented to the court. *(Added by Stats.1986, c. 872, § 1. Amended by Stats.2001, c. 506 (A.B.1424), § 5.)*

Cross References

Court defined for purposes of this Part, see Welfare and Institutions Code § 5008.

§ 5009. Choice of physician

Persons receiving evaluation or treatment under this part shall be given a choice of physician or other professional person providing such services, in accordance with the policies of each agency providing services, and within the limits of available staff in the agency. *(Added by Stats.1967, c. 1667, p. 4074, § 36, operative July 1, 1969.)*

Cross References

Evaluation defined for purposes of this Part, see Welfare and Institutions Code § 5008.

§ 5010. Agency administering federal Developmental Disabilities Act; access to records

The agency established in this state to fulfill the requirements and assurances of Section 142 of the federal Developmental Disabilities Act of 1984 for a system to protect and advocate the rights of persons with developmental disabilities, as that term is defined by Section 102(7) of the federal act, shall have access to the records of a person with developmental disabilities who resides in a facility for persons with developmental disabilities when both of the following conditions apply:

(1) The agency has received a complaint from or on behalf of the person and the person consents to the disclosure of the records to the extent of his or her capabilities.

(2) The person does not have a parent, guardian or conservator, or the state or the designee of the state is the person's guardian or conservator. *(Added by Stats.1985, c. 1121, § 2.)*

§ 5012. Determining eligibility for payment or reimbursement for mental health or other health care services; persons taken into custody under this part

The fact that a person has been taken into custody under this part may not be used in the determination of that person's eligibility for payment or reimbursement for mental health or other health care services for which he or she has applied or received under the Medi–Cal program, any health care service plan licensed under the Knox-Keene Health Care Service Plan Act of 1975 (Chapter 2.2 (commencing with Section 1340) of Division 2 of the Health and Safety Code), or any insurer providing health coverage doing business in the state. *(Added by Stats.2001, c. 506 (A.B.1424), § 6.)*

§ 5013. Referrals between facilities, providers, and other organizations; legislative intent

(a) It is the intent of the Legislature that referrals between facilities, providers, and other organizations shall be facilitated by the sharing of information and records in accordance with Section 5328 and applicable federal and state laws.

(b) Each city or county mental health department is encouraged to include on its Internet Web site a current list of ambulatory services and other resources for persons with mental health disorders and substance use disorders in the city or county that may be accessed by providers and consumers of mental health services. The list of services on the Internet Web site should be updated at least annually by the city or county mental health department. *(Added by Stats.2013, c. 567 (S.B.364), § 3.)*

§ 5014. Funding; severability

(a) To the extent otherwise permitted under state and federal law and consistent with the Mental Health Services Act, both of the following apply for purposes of Article 1 (commencing with Section 5150) and Article 4 (commencing with Section 5250) of Chapter 2 and Chapter 3 (commencing with Section 5350):

(1) Counties may pay for the provision of services using funds distributed to the counties from the Mental Health Subaccount, the Mental Health Equity Subaccount, and the Vehicle License Collection Account of the Local Revenue Fund, funds from the Mental Health Account and the Behavioral Health Subaccount within the Support Services Account of the Local Revenue Fund 2011, funds from the Mental Health Services Fund when included in county plans pursuant to Section 5847, and any other funds from which the Controller makes distributions to the counties for those purposes.

(2) A person shall not be denied access to services funded by the Mental Health Services Fund based solely on the person's voluntary or involuntary legal status.

(b) The provisions of this section are severable. If any provision of this section or its application is held invalid, that invalidity shall not affect other provisions or applications that can be given effect without the invalid provision or application. *(Added by Stats.2022, c. 867 (A.B.2242), § 1, eff. Jan. 1, 2023.)*

§ 5020.1. Mentally ill minor; release from state hospital; aftercare plan for educational and training needs

A mentally ill minor, between the ages of 3 and 18, upon being considered for release from a state hospital shall have an aftercare plan developed. Such plan shall include educational or training needs, provided these are necessary for the patient's well-being. *(Added by Stats.1973, c. 1161, p. 2418, § 2.)*

§ 5110. Proceedings in superior court; costs

Whenever a proceeding is held in a superior court under Article 5 (commencing with Section 5275) or Article 6 (commencing with Section 5300) of this chapter or Chapter 3 (commencing with Section 5350) of this part involving a person who has been placed in a facility located outside the county of residence of the person, the provisions of this section shall apply. The appropriate financial officer or other designated official of the county in which the proceeding is held shall make out a statement of all of the costs incurred by the county for the investigation, preparation, and conduct of the proceedings, and the costs of appeal, if any. The statement shall be certified by a judge of the superior court of the county. The statement shall then be sent to the county of residence of the person, which shall reimburse the county providing the services. If it is not possible to determine the actual county of residence of the person, the statement shall be sent to the county in which the person was originally detained, which shall reimburse the county providing the services. *(Added by Stats.1968, c. 1374, p. 2643, § 15.5, operative July 1, 1969. Amended by Stats.1969, c. 722, p. 1422, § 5, eff. Aug. 8, 1969, operative July 1, 1969; Stats.1970, c. 1627, p. 3440, § 5; Stats.2002, c. 221 (S.B.1019), § 208.)*

Cross References

Construction of amended statutes, see Government Code § 9605.
Court defined for purposes of this Part, see Welfare and Institutions Code § 5008.
Payment of costs of proceedings, exception where this section applies, see Welfare and Institutions Code § 4117.

§ 5111. Compensation of appointed counsel

Any county without a public defender is authorized to compensate the attorneys appointed for persons entitled to be represented by counsel in proceedings under this part. *(Added by Stats.1970, c. 1627, p. 3441, § 6.)*

§ 5113. Exemptions from liability

Except as provided in Sections 5154, 5173, 5259.3, 5267, and 5306, the facility providing treatment pursuant to Article 1 (commencing with Section 5150), Article 1.5 (commencing with Section 5170), Article 4 (commencing with Section 5250), Article 4.5 (commencing with Section 5260) or Article 6 (commencing with Section 5300), the superintendent of the facility, the professional person in charge of the facility and his or her designee, or the peace officer responsible for the detainment of the person shall not be civilly or criminally liable for any action by a person released at or before the end of the period for which he or she was admitted pursuant to the provisions of the appropriate article. *(Added by Stats.1970, c. 1627, p. 3441, § 7. Amended by Stats.1985, c. 1288, § 1, eff. Sept. 30, 1985.)*

Cross References

Peace officer defined for purposes of this Part, see Welfare and Institutions Code § 5008.
Similar provisions, see Welfare and Institutions Code §§ 5154, 5173, 5259.3, 5267, 5278, 5306.

§ 5114. Proceedings by district attorney or county counsel

At any judicial proceeding under the provisions of this division, allegations that the person is a danger to others, or to himself, or gravely disabled as a result of mental disorder or impairment by chronic alcoholism, shall be presented by the district attorney for the county, unless the board of supervisors, by ordinance or resolution, delegates such duty to the county counsel. *(Added by Stats.1970, c. 1627, p. 3441, § 8.)*

Cross References

Copies of requests for outpatient status revocation, see Welfare and Institutions Code § 5306.5.
County counsel, duties, in mental health proceedings, see Government Code § 27646.
District attorney, see Government Code § 26500 et seq.
Duties of district attorney in mental health proceedings, see Government Code § 26530.
Evidence and continuance, hearing or trial in proceeding on petition for additional treatment of a dangerous person, see Welfare and Institutions Code § 5301.
Petition for determination whether outpatient should be continued on such status, see Welfare and Institutions Code § 5307.
Proceeding on request for revocation of outpatient status, documents, supplying to public officer and outpatient's counsel, see Welfare and Institutions Code § 5308.
Release prior to expiration of commitment period, notice, see Welfare and Institutions Code § 5309.
Remand for additional treatment, imminently dangerous persons, see Welfare and Institutions Code § 5304.
Reports as to status and progress of persons on outpatient status, see Welfare and Institutions Code § 5305.

§ 5115. Legislative findings and declarations

The Legislature hereby finds and declares:

(a) It is the policy of this state, as declared and established in this section and in the Lanterman Developmental Disabilities Services Act, Division 4.5 (commencing with Section 4500), that persons with mental health disorders or physical disabilities are entitled to live in normal residential surroundings and should not be excluded therefrom because of their disability.

(b) In order to achieve uniform statewide implementation of the policies of this section and those of the Lanterman Developmental Disabilities Services Act, it is necessary to establish the statewide policy that the use of property for the care of six or fewer persons with mental health disorders or other disabilities is a residential use of the property for the purposes of zoning. *(Added by Stats.1970, c. 1219, p. 2136, § 1. Amended by Stats.1978, c. 891, p. 2803, § 4, eff. Sept. 19, 1978; Stats.2014, c. 144 (A.B.1847), § 87, eff. Jan. 1, 2015.)*

§ 5116. Family care home, foster home, or group home serving six or fewer persons with mental health disorders; residential property for zoning purposes

(a) Pursuant to the policy stated in Section 5115, a state-authorized, certified, or licensed family care home, foster home, or group home serving six or fewer persons with mental health disorders or other disabilities or dependent and neglected children, shall be considered a residential use of property for the purposes of zoning if the homes provide care on a 24–hour–a–day basis.

(b) These homes shall be a permitted use in all residential zones, including, but not limited to, residential zones for single-family dwellings. *(Added by Stats.1970, c. 1219, p. 2136, § 2. Amended by Stats.1971, c. 1163, p. 2223, § 1; Stats.1972, c. 1127, p. 2167, § 1; Stats.1978, c. 891, p. 2803, § 5, eff. Sept. 19, 1978; Stats.2014, c. 144 (A.B.1847), § 88, eff. Jan. 1, 2015.)*

§ 5117. Plan for consolidation of facilities standard setting, licensure and ratesetting functions of departments

In order to further facilitate achieving the purposes of this act and the Lanterman Mental Retardation Act of 1969,[1] it is desirable that there be a consolidation of the facilities standard setting, licensure and ratesetting functions of the various state departments under the jurisdiction of the Health and Welfare Agency. *(Added by Stats. 1970, c. 1219, p. 2137, § 3. Amended by Stats.1979, c. 373, p. 1393, § 360.)*

1 See Lanterman Developmental Disabilities Services Act, Welfare and Institutions Code § 4500 et seq.

§ 5118. Hearings; time and place; conduct; public

(a) For the purpose of conducting hearings under this part, the court in and for the county where the petition is filed may be convened at any time and place within or outside the county suitable to the mental and physical health of the patient, and receive evidence both oral and written, and render decisions, except that the time and place for hearing shall not be different from the time and place for the trial of civil actions for such court if any party to the proceeding, prior to the hearing, objects to the different time or place.

(b) Hearings conducted at a state hospital or a mental health facility designated by a county as a treatment facility under this part or any facility referred to in Section 5358 or Division 7 (commencing with Section 7100), within or outside the county, shall be deemed to be hearings held in a place for the trial of civil actions and in a regular courtroom of the court.

(c)(1) Notwithstanding any other law, and except as otherwise provided in this subdivision, a hearing held under this part is presumptively closed to the public if that hearing involves the disclosure of confidential information.

(2) The individual who is the subject of the proceeding may demand that the hearing be public, and be held in a place suitable for attendance by the public.

(3) The individual who is the subject of the proceeding may also request the presence of any family member or friend without waiving the right to keep the hearing closed to the rest of the public.

(4) A request by any other party to the proceeding to make the hearing public may be granted if the judge, hearing officer, or other person conducting the hearing finds that the public interest in an open hearing clearly outweighs the individual's interest in privacy.

(5) Before commencing a hearing, the judge, hearing officer, or other person conducting the hearing shall inform the individual who is the subject of the proceeding of their rights under this section.

(d) As used in this section, "hearing" means any proceeding conducted under this part, including, but not limited to, conservatorship and other hearings held pursuant to Chapter 3 (commencing with Section 5350), certification review hearings, and jury trials. *(Added by Stats.1971, c. 1162, p. 2220, § 1. Amended by Stats.1979, c. 373, p. 1393, § 361; Stats.2021, c. 389 (S.B.578), § 1, eff. Jan. 1, 2022.)*

Cross References

Court defined for purposes of this Part, see Welfare and Institutions Code § 5008.

§ 5119. Employment of state employees in county mental health program; retention of benefits; retraining programs

On and after July 1, 1972, when a person who is an employee of the State Department of Mental Health at the time of employment by a county in a county mental health program or on and after July 1, 1972, when a person has been an employee of the State Department of Mental Health within the 12-month period prior to his employment by a county in a county mental health program, the board of supervisors may, to the extent feasible, allow such person to retain as a county employee, those employee benefits to which he was entitled or had accumulated as an employee of the State Department of Mental Health or provide such employee with comparable benefits provided for other county employees whose service as county employees is equal to the state service of the former employee of the State Department of Mental Health. Such benefits include, but are not limited to, retirement benefits, seniority rights under civil service, accumulated vacation and sick leave.

The county may on and after July 1, 1972, establish retraining programs for the State Department of Mental Health employees transferring to county mental health programs provided such programs are financed entirely with state and federal funds made available for that purpose.

For the purpose of this section "employee of the Department of Mental Health" means an employee of such department who performs functions which, prior to July 1, 1973, were vested in the Department of Mental Hygiene. *(Added by Stats.1972, c. 1228, p. 2369, § 6, eff. Dec. 11, 1972. Amended by Stats.1973, c. 142, p. 416, § 68, eff. June 30, 1973, operative July 1, 1973; Stats.1977, c. 1252, p. 4567, § 553, operative July 1, 1978.)*

Cross References

Resolution of conflicts between retirement systems applicable to state hospital employees transferred to county or local mental health programs, see Government Code § 20135.

§ 5120. State policy; care and treatment of patients in local community; discrimination in zoning; prohibition

It is the policy of this state as declared and established in this act and in the Lanterman–Petris–Short Act that the care and treatment of mental patients be provided in the local community. In order to achieve uniform statewide implementation of the policies of this act, it is necessary to establish the statewide policy that, notwithstanding any other provision of law, no city or county shall discriminate in the enactment, enforcement, or administration of any zoning laws, ordinances, or rules and regulations between the use of property for the treatment of general hospital or nursing home patients and the use of property for the psychiatric care and treatment of patients, both inpatient and outpatient.

Health facilities for inpatient and outpatient psychiatric care and treatment shall be permitted in any area zoned for hospitals or nursing homes, or in which hospitals and nursing homes are permitted by conditional use permit. *(Added by Stats.1971, c. 815, p. 1573, § 1. Amended by Stats.1972, c. 559, p. 961, § 1, eff. Aug. 4, 1972.)*

§ 5121. County behavioral health director; training procedures; professionals taking dangerous or gravely disabled persons into custody

(a) The county behavioral health director may develop procedures for the county's designation and training of professionals who will be designated to perform functions under Section 5150. These procedures may include, but are not limited to, the following:

(1) The license types, practice disciplines, and clinical experience of professionals eligible to be designated by the county.

(2) The initial and ongoing training and testing requirements for professionals eligible to be designated by the county.

(3) The application and approval processes for professionals seeking to be designated by the county, including the timeframe for initial designation and procedures for renewal of the designation.

(4) The county's process for monitoring and reviewing professionals designated by the county to ensure appropriate compliance with state law, regulations, and county procedures.

(b) A county behavioral health director may develop a training for the procedures for designation developed pursuant to subdivision (a).

(c) If a county behavioral health director denies or revokes an individual's designation, the county behavioral health director shall, in writing, notify the person who made the request for designation of the individual and the individual who is the subject of the request for designation describing the reasons for denial or revocation.

(d) Designated members of a mobile crisis team and designated professional persons shall not be prohibited from transporting a person taken into custody pursuant to Section 5150.

(e) If the county behavioral health director of the County of Sacramento develops procedures pursuant to subdivision (a), the county behavioral health director of the County of Sacramento shall, by April 1, 2022, issue a written policy regarding the procedures developed pursuant to subdivision (a). The policy shall address, at a minimum, the topics identified in paragraphs (1) to (4), inclusive, of subdivision (a). The policy shall require the county behavioral health director of the County of Sacramento to designate individuals employed by the City of Sacramento who are also members of a mobile crisis team or who are also professional persons if all of the following are true:

(1) The City of Sacramento submits a written request to the county behavioral health director.

(2) The individuals meet the requirements for designation included in the policy.

(3) If the county behavioral health director of the County of Sacramento has developed a training pursuant to subdivision (b), the individuals have completed that training. *(Added by Stats.2013, c. 567 (S.B.364), § 4. Amended by Stats.2015, c. 455 (S.B.804), § 17, eff. Jan. 1, 2016; Stats.2021, c. 399 (A.B.1443), § 1, eff. Jan. 1, 2022.)*

CHAPTER 2. INVOLUNTARY TREATMENT

ARTICLE 1. DETENTION OF MENTALLY DISORDERED PERSONS FOR EVALUATION AND TREATMENT

§ 5150. Dangerous or gravely disabled person; taking into custody; procedures

(a) When a person, as a result of a mental health disorder, is a danger to others, or to * * * themselves, or gravely disabled, a peace officer, professional person in charge of a facility designated by the county for evaluation and treatment, member of the attending staff, as defined by regulation, of a facility designated by the county for evaluation and treatment, designated members of a mobile crisis team, or professional person designated by the county may, upon probable cause, take, or cause to be taken, the person into custody for a period of up to 72 hours for assessment, evaluation, and crisis intervention, or placement for evaluation and treatment in a facility designated by the county for evaluation and treatment and approved by the State Department of Health Care Services. The 72–hour period begins at the time when the person is first detained. At a minimum, assessment, as defined in Section 5150.4, and evaluation, as defined in subdivision (a) of Section 5008, shall be conducted and provided on an ongoing basis. Crisis intervention, as defined in subdivision (e) of Section 5008, may be provided concurrently with assessment, evaluation, or any other service.

(b) When determining if a person should be taken into custody pursuant to subdivision (a), the individual making that determination shall apply the provisions of Section 5150.05, and shall not be limited to consideration of the danger of imminent harm.

(c) The professional person in charge of a facility designated by the county for evaluation and treatment, member of the attending staff, or professional person designated by the county shall assess the person to determine whether * * * the person can be properly served without being detained. If, in the judgment of the professional person in charge of the facility designated by the county for evaluation and treatment, member of the attending staff, or professional person designated by the county, the person can be properly served without being detained, * * * the person shall be provided evaluation, crisis intervention, or other inpatient or outpatient services on a voluntary basis. * * * This subdivision * * * does not prevent a peace officer from delivering * * * an individual to a designated facility for assessment under this section. Furthermore, the assessment requirement of this subdivision does not * * * require a peace officer to perform any additional duties other than those specified in Sections 5150.1 and 5150.2.

(d) If a person is evaluated by a professional person in charge of a facility designated by the county for evaluation or treatment, member of the attending staff, or professional person designated by the county and is found to be in need of mental health services, but is not admitted to the facility, all available alternative services provided pursuant to subdivision (c) shall be offered, as determined by the county mental health director.

(e) If, in the judgment of the professional person in charge of the facility designated by the county for evaluation and treatment, member of the attending staff, or the professional person designated by the county, the person cannot be properly served without being detained, the admitting facility shall require an application in writing stating the circumstances under which the person's condition was called to the attention of the peace officer, professional person in charge of the facility designated by the county for evaluation and treatment, member of the attending staff, or professional person designated by the county, and stating that the peace officer, professional person in charge of the facility designated by the county for evaluation and treatment, member of the attending staff, or professional person designated by the county has probable cause to believe that the person is, as a result of a mental health disorder, a danger to others, or to * * * themselves, or gravely disabled. The application shall also record whether the historical course of the person's mental disorder was considered in the determination, pursuant to Section 5150.05. If the probable cause is based on the statement of a person other than the peace officer, professional person in charge of the facility designated by the county for evaluation and treatment, member of the attending staff, or professional person designated by the county, the person shall be liable in a civil action for intentionally giving a statement that * * * the person knows to be false. A copy of the application shall be treated as the original.

(f) At the time a person is taken into custody for evaluation, or within a reasonable time thereafter, unless a responsible relative or the guardian or conservator of the person is in possession of the person's personal property, the person taking * * * them into custody shall take reasonable precautions to preserve and safeguard the personal property in the possession of or on the premises occupied by the person. The person taking * * * them into custody shall then furnish to the court a report generally describing the person's property so preserved and safeguarded and its disposition, in substantially the form set forth in Section 5211, except that if a responsible relative or the guardian or conservator of the person is in possession of the person's property, the report shall include only the name of the relative or guardian or conservator and the location of the property, whereupon responsibility of the person taking * * * them into custody for that property shall terminate. As used in this section, "responsible relative" includes the spouse, parent, adult child, domestic partner, grandparent, grandchild, or adult brother or sister of the person.

(g)(1) Each person, at the time * * * the person is first taken into custody under this section, shall be provided, by the person who takes * * * them into custody, the following information orally in a language or modality accessible to the person. If the person cannot understand an oral advisement, the information shall be provided in writing. The information shall be in substantially the following form:

My name is ____________________________.
I am a ____________________________.
(peace officer/mental health professional)
with ____________________________.
(name of agency)
You are not under criminal arrest, but I am taking you for an examination by mental health professionals at ____________________________.
____
(name of facility)
You will be told your rights by the mental health staff.

(2) If taken into custody at * * * the person's own residence, the person shall also be provided the following information:

You may bring a few personal items with you, which I will have to approve. Please inform me if you need assistance turning off any appliance or water. You may make a phone call and leave a note to tell your friends or family where you have been taken.

(h) The designated facility shall keep, for each patient evaluated, a record of the advisement given pursuant to subdivision (g) which shall include all of the following:

(1) The name of the person detained for evaluation.

(2) The name and position of the peace officer or mental health professional taking the person into custody.

(3) The date the advisement was completed.

(4) Whether the advisement was completed.

(5) The language or modality used to give the advisement.

(6) If the advisement was not completed, a statement of good cause, as defined by regulations of the State Department of Health Care Services.

(i)(1) Each person admitted to a facility designated by the county for evaluation and treatment shall be given the following information by admission staff of the facility. The information shall be given orally and in writing and in a language or modality accessible to the person. The written information shall be available to the person in English and in the language that is the person's primary means of communication. Accommodations for other disabilities that may affect communication shall also be provided. The information shall be in substantially the following form:

My name is ____________________________.
My position here is ____________________________.
You are being placed into this psychiatric facility because it is our professional opinion that, as a result of a mental health disorder, you are likely to (check applicable):

☐ Harm yourself.
☐ Harm someone else.
☐ Be unable to take care of your own food, clothing, and housing needs.

We believe this is true because
____
(list of the facts upon which the allegation of dangerous or gravely disabled due to mental health disorder is based, including pertinent facts arising from the admission interview).

You will be held for a period up to 72 hours. During the 72 hours you may also be transferred to another facility. You may request to be evaluated or treated at a facility of your choice. You may request to be evaluated or treated by a mental health professional of your choice. We cannot guarantee the facility or mental health professional you choose will be available, but we will honor your choice if we can.

During these 72 hours you will be evaluated by the facility staff, and you may be given treatment, including medications. It is possible for you to be released before the end of the 72 hours. But if the staff decides that you need continued treatment you can be held for a longer period of time. If you are held longer than 72 hours, you have the right to a lawyer and a qualified interpreter and a hearing before a judge. If you are unable to pay for the lawyer, then one will be provided to you free of charge.

If you have questions about your legal rights, you may contact the county Patients' Rights Advocate at ______________________________ (phone number for the county Patients' Rights ______________________________. Advocacy office)

Your 72–hour period began ______________________________. (date/time)

(2) If the notice is given in a county where weekends and holidays are excluded from the 72–hour period, the person shall be informed of this fact.

(j) For each person admitted for evaluation and treatment, the facility shall keep with the person's medical record a record of the advisement given pursuant to subdivision (i), which shall include all of the following:

(1) The name of the person performing the advisement.

(2) The date of the advisement.

(3) Whether the advisement was completed.

(4) The language or modality used to communicate the advisement.

(5) If the advisement was not completed, a statement of good cause.

(k) A facility to which a person who is involuntarily detained pursuant to this section is transported shall notify the county patients' rights advocate, as defined in Section 5500, if a person has not been released within 72 hours of the involuntary detention. *(Added by Stats.1967, c. 1667, p. 4074, § 36, operative July 1, 1969. Amended by Stats.1968, c. 1374, p. 2643, § 16, operative July 1, 1969; Stats.1970, c. 516, p. 1005, § 7; Stats.1971, c. 1593, p. 3337, § 368, operative July 1, 1973; Stats.1975, c. 960, p. 2243, § 2; Stats.1977, c. 1252, p. 4567, § 554, operative July 1, 1978; Stats.1980, c. 968, p. 3064, § 1; Stats.2012, c. 34 (S.B.1009), § 79, eff. June 27, 2012; Stats.2013, c. 23 (A.B.82), § 31, eff. June 27, 2013; Stats.2013, c. 567 (S.B.364), § 5; Stats.2015, c. 455 (S.B.804), § 18, eff. Jan. 1, 2016; Stats.2015, c. 570 (A.B.1194), § 1, eff. Jan. 1, 2016; Stats.2018, c. 258 (A.B.2099), § 1, eff. Jan. 1, 2019; Stats.2022, c. 960 (A.B.2275), § 1, eff. Jan. 1, 2023.)*

Cross References

Administration of antipsychotic medication to persons subject to detention, see Welfare and Institutions Code § 5332.
Adult persons who may file a petition to initiate CARE process, see Welfare and Institutions Code § 5974.
Assisted outpatient treatment, involuntary detention for mental health examination, see Welfare and Institutions Code § 5346.
Commitment of juvenile court wards, see Welfare and Institutions Code § 6551.
County mental health director, training procedures, see Welfare and Institutions Code § 5121.
Court defined for purposes of this Part, see Welfare and Institutions Code § 5008.
Emergency services, discrimination, liability of facility or health care personnel, see Health and Safety Code § 1317.
Evaluation defined for purposes of this Part, see Welfare and Institutions Code § 5008.
Evaluation of persons detained under prior court commitment, see Welfare and Institutions Code § 5366.1.
Examination of prisoner by physician, see Penal Code § 4011.6.
Federal investigators and officers assisting state peace officers in emergencies, exercise of powers under this section, see Penal Code § 830.8.
General acute care hospitals or acute psychiatric hospitals, detention or release, persons exhibiting mental disorders, see Health and Safety Code § 1799.111.
Gravely disabled defined for purposes of this Part, see Welfare and Institutions Code § 5008.
Gun violence restraining orders, policies and standards, see Penal Code § 18108.
Mental health evaluations, recommendations, and dispositional procedures for minors, see Welfare and Institutions Code § 710 et seq.
Notice,
  Disappearance of patient, see Welfare and Institutions Code § 5328.3.
  Unconditional release from intensive treatment, see Welfare and Institutions Code § 5250.1.
Peace officer defined for purposes of this Part, see Welfare and Institutions Code § 5008.
Preparation of forms by department of mental health, see Welfare and Institutions Code § 5325.
Procedure for confinement of outpatient pending proceeding for revocation of outpatient status as not preventing hospitalization under other sections, see Welfare and Institutions Code § 5308.
Report of operation of division, see Welfare and Institutions Code § 5402.
Total period of detention, see Welfare and Institutions Code § 5258.

Research References

2 Witkin, California Criminal Law 4th Crimes Against Public Peace and Welfare § 247 (2021), Confiscation of Firearm or Weapon.
6 Witkin, California Criminal Law 4th Criminal Judgment § 180 (2021), Sentence Other Than Death.
4 Witkin, California Criminal Law 4th Pretrial Proceedings § 9 (2021), Federal Officers.
4 Witkin, California Criminal Law 4th Pretrial Proceedings § 321 (2021), Withdrawal of Insanity Plea.

§ 5150.05. Determination of probable cause to take person into custody or cause person to be taken into custody

(a) When determining if probable cause exists to take a person into custody, or cause a person to be taken into custody, pursuant to Section 5150, any person who is authorized to take that person, or cause that person to be taken, into custody pursuant to that section shall consider available relevant information about the historical course of the person's mental disorder if the authorized person determines that the information has a reasonable bearing on the determination as to whether the person is a danger to others, or to himself or herself, or is gravely disabled as a result of the mental disorder.

(b) For purposes of this section, "information about the historical course of the person's mental disorder" includes evidence presented by the person who has provided or is providing mental health or related support services to the person subject to a determination described in subdivision (a), evidence presented by one or more members of the family of that person, and evidence presented by the person subject to a determination described in subdivision (a) or anyone designated by that person.

(c) If the probable cause in subdivision (a) is based on the statement of a person other than the one authorized to take the person into custody pursuant to Section 5150, a member of the attending staff, or a professional person, the person making the statement shall be liable in a civil action for intentionally giving any statement that he or she knows to be false.

(d) This section shall not be applied to limit the application of Section 5328. *(Added by Stats.2001, c. 506 (A.B.1424), § 7.)*

Cross References

Emergency services, discrimination, liability of facility or health care personnel, see Health and Safety Code § 1317.

Gravely disabled defined for purposes of this Part, see Welfare and Institutions Code § 5008.

§ 5150.1. Peace officer transporting person to designated facilities; prohibited activities by employees of facilities

No peace officer seeking to transport, or having transported, a person to a designated facility for assessment under Section 5150, shall be instructed by mental health personnel to take the person to, or keep the person at, a jail solely because of the unavailability of an acute bed, nor shall the peace officer be forbidden to transport the person directly to the designated facility. No mental health employee from any county, state, city, or any private agency providing Short–Doyle psychiatric emergency services shall interfere with a peace officer performing duties under Section 5150 by preventing the peace officer from entering a designated facility with the person to be assessed, nor shall any employee of such an agency require the peace officer to remove the person without assessment as a condition of allowing the peace officer to depart.

"Peace officer" for the purposes of this section also means a jailer seeking to transport or transporting a person in custody to a designated facility for assessment consistent with Section 4011.6 or 4011.8 of the Penal Code and Section 5150. *(Added by Stats.1985, c. 1286, § 6.2, eff. Sept. 30, 1985.)*

Cross References

Emergency defined for purposes of this Part, see Welfare and Institutions Code § 5008.
Peace officer defined for purposes of this Part, see Welfare and Institutions Code § 5008.

§ 5150.2. Detaining peace officer; documentation; disposition procedures and guidelines for persons not admitted

In each county whenever a peace officer has transported a person to a designated facility for assessment under Section 5150, that officer shall be detained no longer than the time necessary to complete documentation of the factual basis of the detention under Section 5150 and a safe and orderly transfer of physical custody of the person. The documentation shall include detailed information regarding the factual circumstances and observations constituting probable cause for the peace officer to believe that the individual required psychiatric evaluation under the standards of Section 5105.

Each county shall establish disposition procedures and guidelines with local law enforcement agencies as necessary to relate to persons not admitted for evaluation and treatment and who decline alternative mental health services and to relate to the safe and orderly transfer of physical custody of persons under Section 5150, including those who have a criminal detention pending. *(Added by Stats.1985, c. 1286, § 6.4, eff. Sept. 30, 1985.)*

Cross References

Evaluation defined for purposes of this Part, see Welfare and Institutions Code § 5008.
Peace officer defined for purposes of this Part, see Welfare and Institutions Code § 5008.

§ 5150.4. "Assessment" defined

"Assessment" for the purposes of this article, means the determination of whether a person shall be evaluated and treated pursuant to Section 5150. *(Added by Stats.1985, c. 1286, § 6.7, eff. Sept. 30, 1985.)*

§ 5150.5. Telehealth

(a) An examination or assessment pursuant to Section 5150 or 5151 may be conducted using telehealth. An examination or assessment provided pursuant to Section 5150 or 5151 shall be consistent with the county's authority to designate facilities for evaluation and treatment, pursuant to Sections 5150 and 5404.

(b) For the purposes of this section and Section 5151, "telehealth" means the mode of delivering health care services and public health via information and communication technologies, as defined in Section 2290.5 of the Business and Professions Code. *(Added by Stats.2020, c. 149 (A.B.3242), § 2, eff. Jan. 1, 2021.)*

§ 5151. Detention for evaluation; individual assessments prior to admission to determine appropriateness of detention; services provided

(a) If the facility designated by the county for evaluation and treatment admits the person, it may detain the person for evaluation and treatment for a period not to exceed 72 hours from the time that the person was first detained pursuant to Section 5150. Saturdays, Sundays, and holidays may be excluded from the period if the State Department of Health Care Services certifies for each facility that evaluation and treatment services cannot reasonably be made available on those days. The certification by the department is subject to renewal every two years. The department shall adopt regulations defining criteria for determining whether a facility can reasonably be expected to make evaluation and treatment services available on Saturdays, Sundays, and holidays.

(b) Prior to admitting a person to the facility for treatment and evaluation pursuant to Section 5150, the professional person in charge of the facility or a designee shall assess the individual to determine the appropriateness of the involuntary detention. This assessment shall be made face-to-face either in person or by synchronous interaction through a mode of telehealth that utilizes both audio and visual components. *(Added by Stats.1967, c. 1667, p. 4074, § 36, operative July 1, 1969. Amended by Stats.1978, c. 1294, p. 4243, § 2; Stats.1986, c. 323, § 1; Stats.2012, c. 34 (S.B.1009), § 80, eff. June 27, 2012; Stats.2013, c. 23 (A.B.82), § 32, eff. June 27, 2013; Stats.2013, c. 567 (S.B.364), § 7; Stats.2020, c. 149 (A.B.3242), § 3, eff. Jan. 1, 2021; Stats.2022, c. 960 (A.B.2275), § 2, eff. Jan. 1, 2023.)*

Cross References

Crisis intervention defined for purposes of this Part, see Welfare and Institutions Code § 5008.
Evaluation defined for purposes of this Part, see Welfare and Institutions Code § 5008.
Peace officer defined for purposes of this Part, see Welfare and Institutions Code § 5008.
Report of operation of division, see Welfare and Institutions Code § 5402.

Research References

2 Witkin, California Criminal Law 4th Crimes Against Public Peace and Welfare § 247 (2021), Confiscation of Firearm or Weapon.

§ 5152. Evaluation; treatment and care; care coordination plan; written and oral information on effects of medication; release or other disposition

(a) A person admitted to a facility for 72–hour treatment and evaluation under the provisions of this article shall receive an evaluation as soon as possible after * * * the person is admitted and shall receive whatever treatment and care * * * the person's condition requires for the full period that * * * they are held. The person shall be released before 72 hours have elapsed only if the psychiatrist directly responsible for the person's treatment believes, as a result of the psychiatrist's personal observations, that the person no longer requires evaluation or treatment. However, in those situations in which both a psychiatrist and psychologist have personally evaluated or examined a person who is placed under a 72–hour hold and there is a collaborative treatment relationship between the psychiatrist and psychologist, either the psychiatrist or psychologist may authorize the release of the person from the hold, but only after they have consulted with one another. In the event of a clinical or professional disagreement regarding the early release of a person who has been placed under a 72–hour hold, the hold shall be maintained unless the facility's medical director overrules the decision of the psychiatrist or psychologist opposing the release. Both the psychiatrist and psychologist shall enter their findings, concerns, or objections into the person's medical record. If any other professional person who is authorized to release the person believes the person should be released before 72 hours have elapsed, and the psychiatrist directly responsible for the person's treatment objects, the matter shall be referred to the medical director of the facility for the final decision. However, if the medical director is not a psychiatrist, * * * the medical director shall appoint a designee who is a psychiatrist. If the matter is referred, the person shall be released before 72 hours have elapsed only if the psychiatrist making the final decision believes, as a result of the psychiatrist's personal observations, that the person no longer requires evaluation or treatment.

(b) A person who has been detained for evaluation and treatment shall be released, referred for further care and treatment on a voluntary basis, or certified for intensive treatment, or a conservator or temporary conservator shall be appointed pursuant to this part as required.

(c)(1) A person who has been detained for evaluation and treatment and subsequently released with referral for further care and treatment on a voluntary basis, shall receive, prior to release, a care coordination plan developed by, at a minimum, the individual, the county behavioral health department, the health care payer, if different from the county, and any other individuals designated by the person as appropriate, with input and recommendations from the facility. The care coordination plan shall include a first followup appointment with an appropriate behavioral health professional. The appointment information shall be provided to the person before their release. In no event may the person be detained based on the requirements of this subdivision beyond when they would otherwise qualify for release. All care and treatment after release shall be voluntary.

(2) The requirement to develop a care coordination plan under this subdivision shall take effect immediately, without waiting for the department to create a model care coordination plan, as required pursuant to Section 5402.5.

(d) For purposes of care coordination and to schedule a followup appointment, the health plan, mental health plan, primary care provider, or other appropriate provider to whom the person has been referred pursuant to subdivision (c) shall make a good faith effort to contact the referred individual no fewer than three times, either by email, telephone, mail, or in-person outreach, whichever method or methods is most likely to reach the individual.

(e) A person designated by the mental health facility shall give to any person who has been detained at that facility for evaluation and treatment and who is receiving medication as a result of * * * their mental illness, as soon as possible after detention, written and oral information about the probable effects and possible side effects of the medication. The State Department of Health Care Services shall develop and promulgate written materials on the effects of medications, for use by county mental health programs as disseminated or as modified by the county mental health program, addressing the probable effects and the possible side effects of the medication. The following information shall be given orally to the patient:

(1) The nature of the mental illness, or behavior, that is the reason the medication is being given or recommended.

(2) The likelihood of improving or not improving without the medication.

(3) Reasonable alternative treatments available.

(4)(A) The name and type, frequency, amount, and method of dispensing the medication, and the probable length of time the medication will be taken.

(B) The fact that the information has or has not been given shall be indicated in the patient's chart. If the information has not been given, the designated person shall document in the patient's chart the justification for not providing the information. A failure to give information about the probable effects and possible side effects of the medication shall not constitute new grounds for release.

(f) The amendments to this section made by Assembly Bill 348 of the 2003–04 Regular Session [1] shall not be construed to revise or expand the scope of practice of psychologists, as defined in Chapter 6.6 (commencing with Section 2900) of Division 2 of the Business and Professions Code. *(Added by Stats.1967, c. 1667, p. 4074, § 36, operative July 1, 1969. Amended by Stats.1968, c. 1374, p. 2644, § 18, operative July 1, 1969; Stats.1970, c. 1627, p. 3441, § 9; Stats.1985, c. 1288, § 2, eff. Sept. 30, 1985; Stats.1986, c. 872, § 1.5; Stats.2003, c. 94 (A.B.348), § 1; Stats.2012, c. 34 (S.B.1009), § 81, eff. June 27, 2012; Stats.2022, c. 867 (A.B.2242), § 2, eff. Jan. 1, 2023.)*

[1] See Stats.2003, c. 94 (A.B.348), § 1.

Cross References

Evaluation defined for purposes of this Part, see Welfare and Institutions Code § 5008.
Intensive treatment defined for purposes of this Part, see Welfare and Institutions Code § 5008.
Suicidal persons, confinement for further intensive treatment, see Welfare and Institutions Code § 5260.

§ 5152.1. Notification to county behavioral health director, peace officer, or person designated by law enforcement agency employing peace officer; conditions

The professional person in charge of the facility providing 72–hour evaluation and treatment, or his or her designee, shall notify the county behavioral health director or the director's designee and the peace officer who makes the written application pursuant to Section 5150 or a person who is designated by the law enforcement agency that employs the peace officer, when the person has been released after 72–hour detention, when the person is not detained, or when the person is released before the full period of allowable 72–hour detention if all of the following conditions apply:

(a) The peace officer requests such notification at the time he or she makes the application and the peace officer certifies at that time in writing that the person has been referred to the facility under circumstances which, based upon an allegation of facts regarding actions witnessed by the officer or another person, would support the filing of a criminal complaint.

(b) The notice is limited to the person's name, address, date of admission for 72–hour evaluation and treatment, and date of release.

If a police officer, law enforcement agency, or designee of the law enforcement agency, possesses any record of information obtained pursuant to the notification requirements of this section, the officer, agency, or designee shall destroy that record two years after receipt of notification. *(Added by Stats.1975, c. 960, p. 2643, § 3. Amended by Stats.1983, c. 755, § 1; Stats.2015, c. 455 (S.B.804), § 19, eff. Jan. 1, 2016.)*

Cross References

Evaluation defined for purposes of this Part, see Welfare and Institutions Code § 5008.
Peace officer defined for purposes of this Part, see Welfare and Institutions Code § 5008.

§ 5152.2. Methods for prompt notification to peace officers

Each law enforcement agency within a county shall arrange with the county behavioral health director a method for giving prompt notification to peace officers pursuant to Section 5152.1. *(Added by Stats.1975, c. 960, p. 2643, § 4. Amended by Stats.2015, c. 455 (S.B.804), § 20, eff. Jan. 1, 2016.)*

Cross References

Peace officer defined for purposes of this Part, see Welfare and Institutions Code § 5008.

§ 5153. Plain clothes officers; vehicles

Whenever possible, officers charged with apprehension of persons pursuant to this article shall dress in plain clothes and travel in unmarked vehicles. *(Added by Stats.1967, c. 1667, p. 4074, § 36, operative July 1, 1969. Amended by Stats.1969, c. 722, p. 1422, § 6, eff. Aug. 8, 1969, operative July 1, 1969.)*

§ 5154. Exemption from liability

(a) Notwithstanding Section 5113, if the provisions of Section 5152 have been met, the professional person in charge of the facility providing 72–hour treatment and evaluation, their designee, the medical director of the facility or their designee described in Section 5152, the psychiatrist directly responsible for the person's treatment, or the psychologist shall not be held civilly or criminally liable for any action by a person released before the end of 72 hours pursuant to this article.

(b) The professional person in charge of the facility providing 72–hour treatment and evaluation, their designee, the medical director of the facility or their designee described in Section 5152, the psychiatrist directly responsible for the person's treatment, or the psychologist shall not be held civilly or criminally liable for any action by a person released at the end of the 72 hours pursuant to this article.

(c) The peace officer responsible for the detainment of the person shall not be civilly or criminally liable for any action by a person released at or before the end of the 72 hours pursuant to this article.

(d) A member of a mobile crisis team or a professional person who has been designated by the county pursuant to Section 5121 and who detains or transports a person pursuant to Section 5150 shall not, as a result of detaining or transporting the person, be civilly or criminally liable for any action by the person if the person is released at or before the end of the 72 hours pursuant to this article.

(e) The amendments to this section made by Assembly Bill 348 of the 2003–04 Regular Session [1] shall not be construed to revise or expand the scope of practice of psychologists, as defined in Chapter 6.6 (commencing with Section 2900) of Division 2 of the Business and Professions Code. *(Added by Stats.1967, c. 1667, p. 4074, § 36, operative July 1, 1969. Amended by Stats.1968, c. 1374, p. 2644, § 19, operative July 1, 1969; Stats.1985, c. 1288, § 3, eff. Sept. 30, 1985; Stats.2003, c. 94 (A.B.348), § 2; Stats.2021, c. 399 (A.B.1443), § 2, eff. Jan. 1, 2022.)*

[1] See Stats.2003, c. 94 (A.B.348), § 2.

Cross References

Determinations according to law, public employees' exemption from liability, see Government Code § 856.
Evaluation defined for purposes of this Part, see Welfare and Institutions Code § 5008.
Liability for excessive detention, see Welfare and Institutions Code §§ 5259.1, 5265.
Liability for false application, see Welfare and Institutions Code § 5203.
Peace officer defined for purposes of this Part, see Welfare and Institutions Code § 5008.
Similar provisions, see Welfare and Institutions Code §§ 5113, 5173, 5259.3, 5267, 5278, 5306.

§ 5155. Supplementary licenses; issuance by local entities

Nothing in this part shall be construed as granting authority to local entities to issue licenses supplementary to existing state and local licensing laws. *(Added by Stats.1968, c. 1374, p. 2645, § 20, operative July 1, 1969.)*

ARTICLE 1.5. DETENTION OF INEBRIATES FOR EVALUATION AND TREATMENT

Section

§ 5170. Dangerous or gravely disabled person; taking into civil protective custody

When any person is a danger to others, or to himself, or gravely disabled as a result of inebriation, a peace officer, member of the attending staff, as defined by regulation, of an evaluation facility designated by the county, or other person designated by the county may, upon reasonable cause, take, or cause to be taken, the person into civil protective custody and place him in a facility designated by the county and approved by the State Department of Alcohol and Drug Abuse as a facility for 72-hour treatment and evaluation of inebriates. *(Added by Stats.1969, c. 1472, p. 3015, § 2. Amended by Stats.1970, c. 516, p. 1006, § 8; Stats.1970, c. 1627, p. 3441, § 11; Stats.1971, c. 1593, p. 3338, § 369; Stats.1971, c. 1581, p. 3189, § 2; Stats.1973, c. 142, p. 416, § 69, eff. June 30, 1973, operative July 1, 1973; Stats.1977, c. 1252, p. 4568, § 555, operative July 1, 1978; Stats.1978, c. 429, p. 1453, § 204, eff. July 17, 1978, operative July 1, 1978.)*

Cross References

Evaluation defined for purposes of this Part, see Welfare and Institutions Code § 5008.
Peace officer defined, see Penal Code §§ 7, 830 et seq.
Peace officer defined for purposes of this Part, see Welfare and Institutions Code § 5008.

Research References

2 Witkin, California Criminal Law 4th Crimes Against Public Peace and Welfare § 79 (2021), Placement in Civil Protective Custody.

§ 5170.1. Treatment and evaluation facilities; inclusions

A 72-hour treatment and evaluation facility shall include one or more of the following:

(1) A screening, evaluation, and referral facility which may be accomplished by a mobile crisis unit, first aid station or ambulatory detoxification unit;

(2) A detoxification facility for alcoholic and acutely intoxicated persons.

(3) An alcohol recovery house. *(Added by Stats.1974, c. 1024, p. 2222, § 1, eff. Sept. 23, 1974.)*

Cross References

Evaluation defined for purposes of this Part, see Welfare and Institutions Code § 5008.

Referral defined for purposes of this Part, see Welfare and Institutions Code § 5008.

§ 5170.3. Evaluation facility; application

Such evaluation facility shall require an application in writing stating the circumstances under which the person's condition was called to the attention of the officer, member of the attending staff, or other designated person, and stating that the officer, member of the attending staff, or other designated person believes as a result of his personal observations that the person is, as a result of inebriation, a danger to others, or to himself, or gravely disabled or has violated subdivision (f) of Section 647 of the Penal Code. *(Added by Stats.1971, c. 1581, p. 3189, § 3.)*

Cross References

Evaluation defined for purposes of this Part, see Welfare and Institutions Code § 5008.

§ 5170.5. Right to make telephone calls

Any person placed in an evaluation facility has, immediately after he is taken to an evaluation facility and except where physically impossible, no later than three hours after he is placed in such facility or taken to such unit, the right to make, at his own expense, at least two completed telephone calls. If the person placed in the evaluation facility does not have money upon him with which to make such calls, he shall be allowed free at least two completed local toll free or collect telephone calls. *(Added by Stats.1971, c. 1581, p. 3189, § 4. Amended by Stats.1974, c. 1024, p. 2223, § 2, eff. Sept. 23, 1974.)*

Cross References

Evaluation defined for purposes of this Part, see Welfare and Institutions Code § 5008.

§ 5170.7. Release upon request; determination

A person who requests to be released from the facility before 72 hours have elapsed shall be released only if the psychiatrist directly responsible for the person's treatment believes, as a result of his or her personal observations, that the person is not a danger to others, or to himself or herself. If any other professional person who is authorized to release the person, believes the person should be released before 72 hours have elapsed, and the psychiatrist directly responsible for the person's treatment objects, the matter shall be referred to the medical director of the facility for the final decision. However, if the medical director is not a psychiatrist, he or she shall appoint a designee who is a psychiatrist. If the matter is referred, the person shall be released before 72 hours have elapsed only if the psychiatrist making the final decision believes, as a result of his or her personal observations, that the person is not a danger to others, or to himself or herself. *(Added by Stats.1971, c. 1581, p. 3190, § 5. Amended by Stats.1985, c. 1288, § 4, eff. Sept. 30, 1985.)*

§ 5171. Detention for evaluation; services provided

If the facility for 72-hour treatment and evaluation of inebriates admits the person, it may detain him for evaluation and detoxification treatment, and such other treatment as may be indicated, for a period not to exceed 72 hours. Saturdays, Sundays and holidays shall be included for the purpose of calculating the 72-hour period. However, a person may voluntarily remain in such facility for more than 72 hours if the professional person in charge of the facility determines the person is in need of and may benefit from further treatment and care, provided any person who is taken or caused to be taken to the facility shall have priority for available treatment and care over a person who has voluntarily remained in a facility for more than 72 hours.

If in the judgment of the professional person in charge of the facility providing evaluation and treatment, the person can be properly served without being detained, he shall be provided evaluation, detoxification treatment or other treatment, crisis intervention, or other inpatient or outpatient services on a voluntary basis. *(Added by Stats.1969, c. 1472, p. 3016, § 2. Amended by Stats.1971, c. 1581, p. 3190, § 6.)*

Cross References

Crisis intervention defined for purposes of this Part, see Welfare and Institutions Code § 5008.
Evaluation defined for purposes of this Part, see Welfare and Institutions Code § 5008.

§ 5172. Evaluation; treatment and care; release or other disposition

Each person admitted to a facility for 72-hour treatment and evaluation under the provisions of this article shall receive an evaluation as soon after he or she is admitted as possible and shall receive whatever treatment and care his or her condition requires for the full period that he or she is held. The person shall be released before 72 hours have elapsed only if, the psychiatrist directly responsible for the person's treatment believes, as a result of his or her personal observations, that the person no longer requires evaluation or treatment. If any other professional person who is authorized to release the person, believes the person should be released before 72 hours have elapsed, and the psychiatrist directly responsible for the person's treatment objects, the matter shall be referred to the medical director of the facility for the final decision. However, if the medical director is not a psychiatrist, he or she shall appoint a designee who is a psychiatrist. If the matter is referred, the person shall be released before 72 hours have elapsed only if the psychiatrist making the final decision believes, as a result of his or her personal observations, that the person no longer requires evaluation or treatment.

Persons who have been detained for evaluation and treatment shall be released, referred for further care and treatment on a voluntary basis, or, if the person, as a result of impairment by chronic alcoholism, is a danger to others or to himself or herself, or gravely disabled, he or she may be certified for intensive treatment, or a conservator or temporary conservator shall be appointed for him or her pursuant to this part as required. *(Added by Stats.1969, c. 1472, p. 3016, § 2. Amended by Stats.1971, c. 1443, p. 2848, § 1; Stats.1985, c. 1288, § 5, eff. Sept. 30, 1985.)*

Cross References

Evaluation defined for purposes of this Part, see Welfare and Institutions Code § 5008.
Intensive treatment defined for purposes of this Part, see Welfare and Institutions Code § 5008.

§ 5172.1. Voluntary application by inebriate for admission

Any person who is a danger to others, or to himself, or gravely disabled as a result of inebriation, may voluntarily apply for admission to a 72-hour evaluation and detoxification treatment facility for inebriates. *(Added by Stats.1971, c. 1581, p. 3190, § 7.)*

Cross References

Evaluation defined for purposes of this Part, see Welfare and Institutions Code § 5008.

§ 5173. Exemption from liability

(a) Notwithstanding Section 5113, if the provisions of Section 5170.7 or 5172 have been met, the professional person in charge of the facility providing 72-hour treatment and evaluation, the medical director of the facility or his or her designee described in Sections 5170.7 and 5172, and the psychiatrist directly responsible for the person's treatment shall not be held civilly or criminally liable for any action by a person released before the end of 72 hours pursuant to this article.

(b) The professional person in charge of the facility providing 72-hour treatment and evaluation, the medical director of the facility or his or her designee described in Sections 5170.7 and 5172, and the psychiatrist directly responsible for the person's treatment shall not be held civilly or criminally liable for any action by a person released at the end of the 72 hours pursuant to this article.

(c) The peace officer responsible for the detainment of the person shall not be civilly or criminally liable for any action by a person released at or before the end of the 72 hours pursuant to this article. *(Added by Stats.1969, c. 1472, p. 3016, § 2. Amended by Stats.1985, c. 1288, § 6, eff. Sept. 30, 1985.)*

Cross References

Determinations according to law, public employees' exemption from liability, see Government Code § 856.
Evaluation defined for purposes of this Part, see Welfare and Institutions Code § 5008.
Liability for excessive detention, see Welfare and Institutions Code §§ 5259.1, 5265.
Liability for false application, see Welfare and Institutions Code § 5203.
Peace officer defined for purposes of this Part, see Welfare and Institutions Code § 5008.
Similar provisions, see Welfare and Institutions Code §§ 5113, 5154, 5259.3, 5267, 5278, 5306.

§ 5174. Funding

It is the intent of the Legislature (a) that facilities for 72-hour treatment and evaluation of inebriates be subject to state funding under Part 2 (commencing with Section 5600) of this division only if they provide screening, evaluation and referral services and have available medical services in the facility or by referral agreement with an appropriate medical facility, and would normally be considered an integral part of a community health program; (b) that state reimbursement under Part 2 (commencing with Section 5600) for such 72-hour facilities and intensive treatment facilities, under this article shall not be included as priority funding as are reimbursements for other county expenditures under this part for involuntary treatment services, but may be provided on the basis of new and expanded services if funds for new and expanded services are available; that while facilities receiving funds from other sources may, if eligible for funding under this division, be designated as 72-hour facilities, or intensive treatment facilities for the purposes of this article, funding of such facilities under this division shall not be substituted for such previous funding.

No 72-hour facility, or intensive treatment facility for the purposes of this article shall be eligible for funding under Part 2 (commencing with Section 5600) of this division until approved by the Director of Alcohol and Drug Abuse in accordance with standards established by the State Department of Alcohol and Drug Abuse in regulations adopted pursuant to this part. To the maximum extent possible, each county shall utilize services provided for inebriates and persons impaired by chronic alcoholism by federal and other funds presently used for such services, including federal and other funds made available to the State Department of Rehabilitation and the State Department of Alcohol and Drug Abuse. McAteer funds shall not be utilized for the purposes of the 72-hour involuntary holding program as outlined in this chapter. *(Added by Stats.1969, c. 1472, p. 3016, § 2. Amended by Stats.1971, c. 1443, p. 2848, § 2; Stats.1971, c. 1593, p. 3338, § 370; Stats.1971, c. 1581, p. 3190, § 8; Stats.1973, c. 142, p. 416, § 70, eff. June 30, 1973, operative July 1, 1973; Stats.1973, c. 1212, p. 2836, § 326; Stats.1974, c. 1024, p. 2223, § 3, eff. Sept. 23, 1974; Stats.1977, c. 1252, p. 4568, § 556, operative July 1, 1978; Stats.1978, c. 429, p. 1453, § 205, eff. July 17, 1978, operative July 1, 1978.)*

Cross References

Evaluation defined for purposes of this Part, see Welfare and Institutions Code § 5008.
Intensive treatment defined for purposes of this Part, see Welfare and Institutions Code § 5008.
Referral defined for purposes of this Part, see Welfare and Institutions Code § 5008.

§ 5175. Evaluation and treatment of other persons

Nothing in this article shall be construed to prevent a facility designated as a facility for 72-hour evaluation and treatment of inebriates from also being designated as a facility for 72-hour evaluation and treatment of other persons subject to this part, including persons impaired by chronic alcoholism. *(Added by Stats.1969, c. 1472, p. 3016, § 2.)*

Cross References

Evaluation defined for purposes of this Part, see Welfare and Institutions Code § 5008.

§ 5176. Counties to which article applicable; designation of facilities and capacities

This article shall apply only to those counties wherein the board of supervisors has adopted a resolution stating that suitable facilities exist within the county for the care and treatment of inebriates and persons impaired by chronic alcoholism, designating the facilities to be used as facilities for 72-hour treatment and evaluation of inebriates and for the extensive treatment of persons impaired by chronic alcoholism, and otherwise adopting the provisions of this article.

Each county Short–Doyle plan for a county to which this article is made applicable shall designate the specific facility or facilities for 72-hour evaluation and detoxification treatment of inebriates and for intensive treatment of persons impaired by chronic alcoholism and for the treatment of such persons on a voluntary basis under this article, and shall specify the maximum number of patients that can be served at any one time by each such facility. *(Added by Stats.1969, c. 1472, p. 3016, § 2. Amended by Stats.1971, c. 1443, p. 2849, § 3; Stats.1974, c. 1024, p. 2223, § 4, eff. Sept. 23, 1974.)*

Cross References

Evaluation defined for purposes of this Part, see Welfare and Institutions Code § 5008.
Intensive treatment defined for purposes of this Part, see Welfare and Institutions Code § 5008.

ARTICLE 2. COURT–ORDERED EVALUATION FOR MENTALLY DISORDERED PERSONS

§ 5200. Persons who may be given evaluation; consideration of privacy and dignity

Any person alleged, as a result of mental disorder, to be a danger to others, or to himself, or to be gravely disabled, may be given an evaluation of his condition under a superior court order pursuant to this article. The provisions of this article shall be carried out with the utmost consideration for the privacy and dignity of the person for whom a court-ordered evaluation is requested. *(Added by Stats.1967, c. 1667, p. 4074, § 36, operative July 1, 1969.)*

Cross References

Court defined for purposes of this Part, see Welfare and Institutions Code § 5008.
Court-ordered evaluation defined for purposes of this Part, see Welfare and Institutions Code § 5008.
Evaluation defined for purposes of this Part, see Welfare and Institutions Code § 5008.
Examination of prisoner by physician, see Penal Code § 4011.6.
Gravely disabled defined for purposes of this Part, see Welfare and Institutions Code § 5008.
Investigation of alternatives to conservatorship, recommendations of conservatorship, report of investigation, service of report, see Welfare and Institutions Code § 5354.
Judicial commitment of mentally disordered persons prohibited, see Welfare and Institutions Code § 5002.
Procedures for handling mentally disordered persons charged with crime, see Welfare and Institutions Code § 6825; Penal Code §§ 1026 et seq., 1367 et seq.

§ 5201. Petition by individual

Any individual may apply to the person or agency designated by the county for a petition alleging that there is in the county a person who is, as a result of mental disorder a danger to others, or to himself, or is gravely disabled, and requesting that an evaluation of the person's condition be made. *(Added by Stats.1967, c. 1667, p. 4074, § 36, operative July 1, 1969.)*

Cross References

Evaluation defined for purposes of this Part, see Welfare and Institutions Code § 5008.
Gravely disabled defined for purposes of this Part, see Welfare and Institutions Code § 5008.

§ 5202. Pre-petition screening; report of findings

The person or agency designated by the county shall prepare the petition and all other forms required in the proceeding, and shall be responsible for filing the petition. Before filing the petition, the person or agency designated by the county shall request the person or agency designated by the county and approved by the State Department of Health Care Services to provide prepetition screening to determine whether there is probable cause to believe the allegations. The person or agency providing prepetition screening shall conduct a reasonable investigation of the allegations and make a reasonable effort to personally interview the subject of the petition. The screening shall also determine whether the person will agree voluntarily to receive crisis intervention services or an evaluation in his own home or in a facility designated by the county and approved by the State Department of Health Care Services. Following prepetition screening, the person or agency designated by the county shall file the petition if satisfied that there is probable cause to believe that the person is, as a result of mental disorder, a danger to others, or to himself or herself, or gravely disabled, and that the person will not voluntarily receive evaluation or crisis intervention.

If the petition is filed, it shall be accompanied by a report containing the findings of the person or agency designated by the county to provide prepetition screening. The prepetition screening report submitted to the superior court shall be confidential and shall be subject to the provisions of Section 5328. *(Added by Stats.1967, c. 1667, p. 4074, § 36, operative July 1, 1969. Amended by Stats.1968, c. 1374, p. 2645, § 22, operative July 1, 1969; Stats.1971, c. 1593, p. 3339, § 371, operative July 1, 1973; Stats.1977, c. 1252, p. 4569, § 557, operative July 1, 1978; Stats.1980, c. 1169, p. 3935, § 1; Stats.2012, c. 34 (S.B.1009), § 83, eff. June 27, 2012; Stats.2013, c. 23 (A.B.82), § 34, eff. June 27, 2013.)*

Cross References

Court defined for purposes of this Part, see Welfare and Institutions Code § 5008.
Crisis intervention defined for purposes of this Part, see Welfare and Institutions Code § 5008.
Evaluation defined for purposes of this Part, see Welfare and Institutions Code § 5008.
Gravely disabled defined for purposes of this Part, see Welfare and Institutions Code § 5008.
Inspection of public records, other exemptions from disclosure, see Government Code § 6276.30.
Prepetition screening defined for purposes of this Part, see Welfare and Institutions Code § 5008.

§ 5203. False application for petition; offense; civil liability

Any individual who seeks a petition for court-ordered evaluation knowing that the person for whom the petition is sought is not, as a result of mental disorder, a danger to himself, or to others, or gravely disabled is guilty of a misdemeanor, and may be held liable in civil damages by the person against whom the petition was sought. *(Added by Stats.1967, c. 1667, p. 4074, § 36, operative July 1, 1969. Amended by Stats.1969, c. 722, p. 1423, § 7, eff. Aug. 8, 1969, operative July 1, 1969.)*

Cross References

Court defined for purposes of this Part, see Welfare and Institutions Code § 5008.
Court-ordered evaluation defined for purposes of this Part, see Welfare and Institutions Code § 5008.
Evaluation defined for purposes of this Part, see Welfare and Institutions Code § 5008.
Exemption from liability, see Welfare and Institutions Code §§ 5154, 5173, 5259.3, 5267, 5278, 5306.
Gravely disabled defined for purposes of this Part, see Welfare and Institutions Code § 5008.
Immunity of public employee making a statutory determination, see Government Code § 856.
Liability for excessive detention, see Welfare and Institutions Code §§ 5259.1, 5265.
Misdemeanors, definition and penalties, see Penal Code §§ 17, 19 and 19.2.

§ 5204. Petition; contents

The petition for a court-ordered evaluation shall contain the following:

(a) The name and address of the petitioner and his interest in the case.

(b) The name of the person alleged, as a result of mental disorder, to be a danger to others, or to himself, or to be gravely disabled, and, if known to the petitioner, the address, age, sex, marital status, and occupation of the person.

(c) The facts upon which the allegations of the petition are based.

(d) The name of, as a respondent thereto, every person known or believed by the petitioner to be legally responsible for the care, support, and maintenance of the person alleged, as a result of mental disorder, to be a danger to others, or to himself, or to be gravely disabled, and the address of each such person, if known to the petitioner.

(e) Such other information as the court may require. *(Added by Stats.1967, c. 1667, p. 4074, § 36, operative July 1, 1969.)*

Cross References

Court defined for purposes of this Part, see Welfare and Institutions Code § 5008.
Court-ordered evaluation defined for purposes of this Part, see Welfare and Institutions Code § 5008.

Evaluation defined for purposes of this Part, see Welfare and Institutions Code § 5008.
Gravely disabled defined for purposes of this Part, see Welfare and Institutions Code § 5008.

§ 5205. Petition; form

The petition shall be in substantially the following form:

In the Superior Court of the State of California
for the County of ______

______

The People of the State of California Concerning ______ and ______ Respondents | No. ______ Petition for Evaluation

______

______, residing at ______ (tel. ______), being duly sworn, alleges: That there is now in the county, in the City or Town of ______, a person named ______, who resides at ______, and who is, as a result of mental disorder:

(1) A danger to others.
(2) A danger to himself or herself.
(3) Gravely disabled as defined in subdivision (h) of Section 5008 of the Welfare and Institutions Code (Strike out all inapplicable classifications).

That the person is ____ years of age; that __ the person is ____ (sex); and that __ the person is ____ (single, married, widowed, or divorced); and that ______ occupation is ______.

That the facts upon which the allegations of the petition are based are as follows: That __ the person, at ______ in the county, on the ____ day of ______, 20__, ______
______
______

That petitioner's interest in the case is ______
______

That the person responsible for the care, support, and maintenance of the person, and their relationship to the person are, so far as known to the petitioner, as follows: (Give names, addresses, and relationship of persons named as respondents)

Wherefore, petitioner prays that evaluation be made to determine the condition of ______, alleged, as a result of mental disorder, to be a danger to others, or to himself or herself, or to be gravely disabled.

______
Petitioner

Subscribed and sworn to before me this ____ day of ______ 20__.

______,
Clerk of the Court
By ______ Deputy

(Added by Stats.1967, c. 1667, p. 4074, § 36, operative July 1, 1969. Amended by Stats.1968, c. 1374, p. 2645, § 23, operative July 1, 1969; Stats.2002, c. 784 (S.B.1316), § 618; Stats.2003, c. 62 (S.B.600), § 325.)

Law Revision Commission Comments

Section 5205 is amended to reflect elimination of the county clerk's role as ex officio clerk of the superior court. See former Gov't Code § 26800 (county clerk acting as clerk of superior court). The powers, duties, and responsibilities formerly exercised by the county clerk as ex officio clerk of the court are delegated to the court administrative or executive officer, and the county clerk is relieved of those powers, duties, and responsibilities. See Gov't Code §§ 69840 (powers, duties, and responsibilities of clerk of court and deputy clerk of court), 71620 (trial court personnel). [32 Cal.L.Rev.Comm. Reports 562 (2002)].

Cross References

Court defined for purposes of this Part, see Welfare and Institutions Code § 5008.
Evaluation defined for purposes of this Part, see Welfare and Institutions Code § 5008.
Gravely disabled defined for purposes of this Part, see Welfare and Institutions Code § 5008.

§ 5206. Order for evaluation; issuance; service; presence of advisors; procedure on non-appearance; release or other disposition

Whenever it appears, by petition pursuant to this article, to the satisfaction of a judge of a superior court that a person is, as a result of mental disorder, a danger to others, or to himself, or gravely disabled, and the person has refused or failed to accept evaluation voluntarily, the judge shall issue an order notifying the person to submit to an evaluation at such time and place as designated by the judge. The order for an evaluation shall be served as provided in Section 5208 by a peace officer, counselor in mental health, or a court-appointed official. The person shall be permitted to remain in his home or other place of his choosing prior to the time of evaluation, and shall be permitted to be accompanied by one or more of his relatives, friends, an attorney, a personal physician, or other professional or religious advisor to the place of evaluation. If the person to receive evaluation so requests, the individual or individuals who accompany him may be present during the evaluation.

If the person refuses or fails to appear for evaluation after having been properly notified, a peace officer, counselor in mental health, or a court-appointed official shall take the person into custody and place him in a facility designated by the county as a facility for treatment and evaluation. The person shall be evaluated as promptly as possible, and shall in no event be detained longer than 72 hours under the court order, excluding Saturdays, Sundays, and holidays if treatment and evaluation services are not available on those days.

Persons who have been detained for evaluation shall be released, referred for care and treatment on a voluntary basis, certified for intensive treatment, or recommended for conservatorship pursuant to this part, as required. *(Added by Stats.1967, c. 1667, p. 4074, § 36, operative July 1, 1969.)*

Cross References

Court defined for purposes of this Part, see Welfare and Institutions Code § 5008.
Evaluation defined for purposes of this Part, see Welfare and Institutions Code § 5008.
Gravely disabled defined for purposes of this Part, see Welfare and Institutions Code § 5008.
Intensive treatment defined for purposes of this Part, see Welfare and Institutions Code § 5008.
Peace officer defined for purposes of this Part, see Welfare and Institutions Code § 5008.

§ 5207. Order for evaluation; form

The order for evaluation shall be in substantially the following form:

In the Superior Court of the State of California
for the County of ....

______

The People of the State of California Concerning .... and .... Respondents | No. .... Order for Evaluation or Detention

______

The People of the State of California to ....
....:

(Peace officer, counselor in mental health, or other official appointed by the court)

The petition of .... has been presented this day to me, a Judge of the Superior Court for the County of ...., State of California, from which it appears that there is now in this county, at ...., a person by the name of ...., who is, as a result of mental disorder, a danger to others, or to himself, or gravely disabled.

Now, therefore, you are directed to notify .... to submit to an evaluation at .... on the .... day of ...., 19..., at ... o'clock ...m.

.... shall be permitted to be accompanied by one or more of his relatives, friends, an attorney, a personal physician, or other professional or religious advisor.

The individual or individuals who accompany .... may be present during the evaluation if so requested by ....

* Provision for Detention for Evaluation

If the person fails or refuses to appear for evaluation when notified by order of this court, you are hereby directed to detain said .... or cause him to be detained at .... for a period no longer than 72 hours, excluding Saturdays, Sundays, and holidays if evaluation services are not available on those days, for the purposes of evaluation.

I hereby direct that a copy of this order together with a copy of the petition be delivered to said person and his representative, if any, at the time of his notification; and I further authorize the service of this order at any hour of the day or night.

Witness my hand, this .... day of ...., 19....

....
Judge of the Superior Court

*This paragraph is applicable only if the person to be evaluated fails or refuses to appear for evaluation after having been properly notified.

Return of Order

I hereby certify that I received the above order for the evaluation of .... and on the .... day of ...., 19..., personally served a copy of the order and of the petition on .... and the professional person in charge of the ...., a facility for treatment and evaluation, or his designee.

Dated: ...., 19....

....
Signature and Title

(Added by Stats.1967, c. 1667, p. 4074, § 36, operative July 1, 1969.)

Cross References

Court defined for purposes of this Part, see Welfare and Institutions Code § 5008.
Evaluation defined for purposes of this Part, see Welfare and Institutions Code § 5008.
Gravely disabled defined for purposes of this Part, see Welfare and Institutions Code § 5008.
Peace officer defined for purposes of this Part, see Welfare and Institutions Code § 5008.

§ 5208. Service of petition and order; notice of failure to appear

As promptly as possible, a copy of the petition and the order for evaluation shall be personally served on the person to be evaluated and the professional person in charge of the facility for treatment and evaluation named in the order, or his designee.

If the person to be evaluated fails to appear for an evaluation at the time designated in the order, the professional person in charge, or his designee, shall notify the person who served the order to have the person to be evaluated detained pursuant to the order. *(Added by Stats.1967, c. 1667, p. 4074, § 36, operative July 1, 1969.)*

Cross References

Evaluation defined for purposes of this Part, see Welfare and Institutions Code § 5008.

§ 5210. Precautions to preserve and safeguard personal property of patient; property report; responsible relative

At the time a person is taken into custody for evaluation, or within a reasonable time thereafter, unless a responsible relative or the guardian or conservator of the person is in possession of the person's personal property, the person taking him into custody shall take reasonable precautions to preserve and safeguard the personal property in the possession of or on the premises occupied by the person. The person taking him into custody shall then furnish to the court a report generally describing the person's property so preserved and safeguarded and its disposition, in substantially the form set forth in Section 5211; except that if a responsible relative or the guardian or conservator of the person is in possession of the person's property, the report shall include only the name of the relative or guardian or conservator and the location of the property, whereupon responsibility of the person taking him into custody for such property shall terminate.

As used in this section, "responsible relative" includes the spouse, parent, adult child, or adult brother or sister of the person, except that it does not include the person who applied for the petition under this article. *(Added by Stats.1967, c. 1667, p. 4074, § 36, operative July 1, 1969.)*

Cross References

Court defined for purposes of this Part, see Welfare and Institutions Code § 5008.
Evaluation defined for purposes of this Part, see Welfare and Institutions Code § 5008.

§ 5211. Property report; form

The report of a patient's property required by Section 5210 to be made by the person taking him into custody for evaluation shall be in substantially the following form:

Report of Officer

I hereby report to the Superior Court for the County of .... that the personal property of the person apprehended, described generally as .... was preserved and safeguarded by .... (Insert name of person taking him into custody, responsible relative, guardian, or conservator).

That property is now located at ....

Dated: .... 19....

....
Signature and Title

(Added by Stats.1967, c. 1667, p. 4074, § 36, operative July 1, 1969.)

Cross References

Court defined for purposes of this Part, see Welfare and Institutions Code § 5008.
Dangerous or gravely disabled person, taking into custody, procedures, see Welfare and Institutions Code § 5150.
Evaluation defined for purposes of this Part, see Welfare and Institutions Code § 5008.

Precautions to preserve patient's property, see Welfare and Institutions Code § 5229.

§ 5212. Plain clothes officers; vehicles

Whenever possible, persons charged with service of orders and apprehension of persons pursuant to this article shall dress in plain clothes and travel in unmarked vehicles. *(Added by Stats.1967, c. 1667, p. 4074, § 36, operative July 1, 1969. Amended by Stats.1969, c. 722, p. 1423, § 8, eff. Aug. 8, 1969, operative July 1, 1969.)*

§ 5213. Detention for treatment; duration; written and oral information on effects of medication

(a) If, upon evaluation, the person is found to be in need of treatment because the person is, as a result of a mental health disorder, a danger to self or others, or is gravely disabled, the person may be detained for treatment in a facility for 72–hour treatment and evaluation. Saturdays, Sundays, and holidays may be excluded from the 72–hour period if the State Department of Social Services certifies for each facility that evaluation and treatment services may not reasonably be made available on those days. The certification by the department is subject to renewal every two years. The department shall adopt regulations defining criteria for determining whether a facility may reasonably be expected to make evaluation and treatment services available on Saturdays, Sundays, and holidays.

(b) Persons who have been detained for evaluation and treatment, who are receiving medications as a result of their mental illness, shall be given, as soon as possible after detention, written and oral information about the probable effects and possible side effects of the medication, by a person designated by the mental health facility where the person is detained. The State Department of Social Services shall develop and promulgate written materials on the effects of medications, for use by county mental health programs as disseminated or as modified by the county mental health program, addressing the probable effects and the possible side effects of the medication. The following information shall be given orally to the patient:

(1) The nature of the mental illness, or behavior, that is the reason the medication is being given or recommended.

(2) The likelihood of improving or not improving without the medications.

(3) Reasonable alternative treatments available.

(4) The name and type, frequency, amount, and method of dispensing the medications, and the probable length of time that the medications will be taken.

(c) The fact that the information has or has not been given shall be indicated in the patient's chart. If the information has not been given, the designated person shall document in the patient's chart the justification for not providing the information. A failure to give information about the probable effects and possible side effects of the medication does not constitute new grounds for release. *(Added by Stats.1967, c. 1667, p. 4074, § 36, operative July 1, 1969. Amended by Stats.1986, c. 872, § 2; Stats.2012, c. 438 (A.B.1468), § 10, eff. Sept. 22, 2012; Stats.2019, c. 9 (A.B.46), § 21, eff. Jan. 1, 2020.)*

Cross References

Evaluation defined for purposes of this Part, see Welfare and Institutions Code § 5008.
Gravely disabled defined for purposes of this Part, see Welfare and Institutions Code § 5008.

ARTICLE 3. COURT–ORDERED EVALUATION FOR PERSONS IMPAIRED BY CHRONIC ALCOHOLISM OR DRUG ABUSE

§ 5225. Order for evaluation; transfer from justice court

Whenever a criminal defendant who appears, as a result of chronic alcoholism or the use of narcotics or restricted dangerous drugs, to be a danger to others, to himself, or to be gravely disabled, is brought before any judge, the judge may order the defendant's evaluation under conditions set forth in this article, provided evaluation services designated in the county plan pursuant to Section 5654 are available. *(Added by Stats.1967, c. 1667, p. 4074, § 36, operative July 1, 1969. Amended by Stats.1968, c. 1374, p. 2646, § 24, operative July 1, 1969; Stats.1969, c. 722, p. 1423, § 9, eff. Aug. 8, 1969, operative July 1, 1969; Stats.1970, c. 1129, p. 2007, § 4; Stats.1977, c. 1257, p. 4788, § 128, eff. Oct. 3, 1977; Stats.1979, c. 373, p. 1396, § 363.)*

Cross References

Evaluation defined for purposes of this Part, see Welfare and Institutions Code § 5008.
Gravely disabled defined for purposes of this Part, see Welfare and Institutions Code § 5008.
Narcotics and restricted dangerous drugs, construction of terms, see Health and Safety Code § 11032.

§ 5226. Advice as to rights and consequences; right of counsel

Such a criminal defendant must be advised of his right to immediately continue with the criminal proceeding, and it is the duty of the judge to apprise the defendant fully of his option and of the consequences which will occur if the defendant chooses the evaluation procedures. The defendant shall have a right to legal counsel at the proceedings at which the choice is made. *(Added by Stats.1967, c. 1667, p. 4074, § 36, operative July 1, 1969.)*

Cross References

Advice as to right of counsel, see Welfare and Institutions Code §§ 5254.1, 5276, 5302.
Appointment of public defender or other attorney, see Welfare and Institutions Code §§ 5276, 5302, 5365.
Evaluation defined for purposes of this Part, see Welfare and Institutions Code § 5008.
Right to counsel in criminal cases, see Const. Art. 1, § 15; Penal Code § 686.

§ 5226.1. Dismissal or suspension of proceedings on order for evaluation; resumption or dismissal of criminal proceedings; conservatorship

If a judge issues an order for evaluation under conditions set forth in this article, proceedings on the criminal charge then pending in the court from which the order for evaluation issued shall be dismissed or suspended until such time as the evaluation of the defendant and the subsequent detention of the defendant for involuntary treatment, if any, are completed. Upon completion of such evaluation and detention, if any, the defendant shall, if such criminal charge has not been dismissed, be returned by the sheriff of the county in which the order of evaluation was made, from the evaluation or intensive treatment facility to the custody of the sheriff who shall return the defendant to the court where the order for evaluation was made, and proceedings on the criminal charge shall be resumed or dismissed. If, during evaluation or detention for involuntary treatment, the defendant is recommended for conservatorship, and if the criminal charge has not previously been dismissed, the defendant shall be returned by the sheriff to the court in which such charge is pending for the disposition of the criminal charge prior to the initiation of the conservatorship proceedings. The judge of such court may order such defendant to be detained in the evaluation or treatment facility until the day set for the resumption of the proceedings on the criminal charge. *(Added by Stats.1968, c. 1199, p. 2274, § 1, operative July 1, 1969. Amended by Stats.1969, c. 722, p. 1423, § 10, eff. Aug. 8, 1969, operative July 1, 1969.)*

Cross References

Court defined for purposes of this Part, see Welfare and Institutions Code § 5008.
Evaluation defined for purposes of this Part, see Welfare and Institutions Code § 5008.
Intensive treatment defined for purposes of this Part, see Welfare and Institutions Code § 5008.
Release of involuntary patients, exceptions, see Welfare and Institutions Code §§ 5257, 5264.
Release of suicidal persons, exception for persons to whom this section applies, see Welfare and Institutions Code § 5264.
Release to sheriff after detention for treatment, see Welfare and Institutions Code § 5230.

§ 5227. Order for evaluation; form

The order for evaluation shall be in substantially the following form:

In the .... Court of the State of California for the County of ....

The People of the State of California Concerning .... and .... Respondents	No. .... Order for Evaluation

The People of the State of California to ....:

(Professional person in charge of the facility providing evaluation) .... has appeared before me and appears to be, as a result of .... (chronic alcoholism, the use of narcotics, or the use of restricted dangerous drugs), a danger to himself, or others, or gravely disabled.

Now, therefore, you are directed to evaluate .... at .... on the ...... day of ...., 19..., at ... o'clock ...m.

Witness my hand, this .... day of ...., 19....

....
Judge of the .... Court

Return of Order

I hereby certify that I received the above order for the evaluation of .... and on the .... day of ...., 19..., personally served a copy of the order and of the petition on the professional person in charge of the ...., a facility for treatment and evaluation, or his designee.

Dated: ...., 19....

....
Signature and title

(Added by Stats.1967, c. 1667, p. 4074, § 36, operative July 1, 1969. Amended by Stats.1968, c. 1374, p. 2647, § 25, operative July 1, 1969; Stats.1970, c. 1129, p. 2007, § 5.)

Cross References

Court defined for purposes of this Part, see Welfare and Institutions Code § 5008.
Evaluation defined for purposes of this Part, see Welfare and Institutions Code § 5008.
Gravely disabled defined for purposes of this Part, see Welfare and Institutions Code § 5008.

§ 5228. Order of evaluation; service of copy

As promptly as possible, a copy of the order for evaluation shall be personally served on the person to be evaluated and the professional person in charge of the facility for treatment and evaluation named in the order, or his designee. *(Added by Stats.1967, c. 1667, p. 4074, § 36, operative July 1, 1969.)*

Cross References

Evaluation defined for purposes of this Part, see Welfare and Institutions Code § 5008.

§ 5229. Precautions to preserve and safeguard personal property of patient; property report; responsible relative

At the time a person is ordered to undergo evaluation, or within a reasonable time thereafter, unless a responsible relative or the guardian or conservator of the person is in possession of the person's personal property, the person shall take reasonable precautions to preserve and safeguard the personal property in the possession of or on the premises occupied by the person. The person responsible for taking him to the evaluation facility shall then furnish to the court a report generally describing the person's property so preserved and safeguarded and its disposition, in substantially the form set forth in Section 5211; except that if a responsible relative or the guardian or conservator of the person is in possession of the person's property, the report shall include only the name of the relative or guardian or conservator and the location of the property, whereupon responsibility of the person responsible for taking him to the evaluation facility for such property shall terminate.

As used in this section, "responsible relative" includes the spouse, parent, adult child, or adult brother or sister of the person. *(Added by Stats.1967, c. 1667, p. 4074, § 36, operative July 1, 1969.)*

Cross References

Court defined for purposes of this Part, see Welfare and Institutions Code § 5008.
Evaluation defined for purposes of this Part, see Welfare and Institutions Code § 5008.

§ 5230. Detention for treatment

If, upon evaluation, the person is found to be in need of treatment because he is, as a result of impairment by chronic alcoholism or the use of narcotics or restricted dangerous drugs, a danger to others, or to himself, or is gravely disabled, he may be detained for treatment in a facility for 72-hour treatment and evaluation. Except as provided in this section, he shall in no event be detained longer than 72 hours from the time of evaluation or detention for evaluation, excluding Saturdays, Sundays and holidays if treatment services are not available on those days.

Persons who have been detained for evaluation and treatment shall be released if the criminal charge has been dismissed; released to the custody of the sheriff or continue to be detained pursuant to court order under Section 5226.1; referred for further care and treatment on a voluntary basis, subject to the disposition of the criminal action; certified for intensive treatment; or recommended for conservatorship pursuant to this part, subject to the disposition of the criminal charge; as required. *(Formerly § 5231, added by Stats.1967, c. 1667, p. 4085, § 36, operative July 1, 1969. Renumbered § 5230 and amended by Stats.1968, c. 1374, p. 2647, § 27, operative July 1, 1969. Amended by Stats.1969, c. 722, p. 1424, § 11, eff. Aug. 8, 1969, operative July 1, 1969; Stats.1970, c. 1129, p. 2008, § 6.)*

Cross References

Court defined for purposes of this Part, see Welfare and Institutions Code § 5008.
Evaluation defined for purposes of this Part, see Welfare and Institutions Code § 5008.
Gravely disabled defined for purposes of this Part, see Welfare and Institutions Code § 5008.
Intensive treatment defined for purposes of this Part, see Welfare and Institutions Code § 5008.
Liability for excessive detention, see Welfare and Institutions Code §§ 5259.1, 5265.

ARTICLE 4. CERTIFICATION FOR INTENSIVE TREATMENT

§ 5250. Time limitation on certification for intensive treatment; grounds for certification

If a person is detained for 72 hours under the provisions of Article 1 (commencing with Section 5150), or under court order for evaluation pursuant to Article 2 (commencing with Section 5200) or Article 3 (commencing with Section 5225) and has received an evaluation, he or she may be certified for not more than 14 days of intensive treatment related to the mental health disorder or impairment by chronic alcoholism, under the following conditions:

(a) The professional staff of the agency or facility providing evaluation services has analyzed the person's condition and has found the person is, as a result of a mental health disorder or impairment by chronic alcoholism, a danger to others, or to himself or herself, or gravely disabled.

(b) The facility providing intensive treatment is designated by the county to provide intensive treatment, and agrees to admit the person. No facility shall be designated to provide intensive treatment unless it complies with the certification review hearing required by this article. The procedures shall be described in the county Short–Doyle plan as required by Section 5651.3.

(c) The person has been advised of the need for, but has not been willing or able to accept, treatment on a voluntary basis.

(d)(1) Notwithstanding paragraph (1) of subdivision (h) of Section 5008, a person is not "gravely disabled" if that person can survive safely without involuntary detention with the help of responsible family, friends, or others who are both willing and able to help provide for the person's basic personal needs for food, clothing, or shelter.

(2) However, unless they specifically indicate in writing their willingness and ability to help, family, friends, or others shall not be considered willing or able to provide this help.

(3) The purpose of this subdivision is to avoid the necessity for, and the harmful effects of, requiring family, friends, and others to publicly state, and requiring the certification review officer to publicly find, that no one is willing or able to assist a person with a mental health disorder in providing for the person's basic needs for food, clothing, or shelter. *(Added by Stats.1982, c. 1598, § 4. Amended by Stats.1989, c. 999, § 1; Stats.2014, c. 144 (A.B.1847), § 89, eff. Jan. 1, 2015.)*

Cross References

Administration of antipsychotic medication to persons subject to detention, see Welfare and Institutions Code § 5332.
Adult persons who may file a petition to initiate CARE process, see Welfare and Institutions Code § 5974.
Commitment of juvenile court wards, see Welfare and Institutions Code § 6551.
Consumers placed on involuntary psychiatric hold or Lanterman–Petris–Short conservatorship, notification to clients' rights advocate, see Welfare and Institutions Code § 4696.3.
Court defined for purposes of this Part, see Welfare and Institutions Code § 5008.
Evaluation defined for purposes of this Part, see Welfare and Institutions Code § 5008.
Gravely disabled defined for purposes of this Part, see Welfare and Institutions Code § 5008.
Intensive treatment defined for purposes of this Part, see Welfare and Institutions Code § 5008.
Procedure for confinement of outpatient pending proceeding for revocation of outpatient status as not preventing hospitalization under other sections, see Welfare and Institutions Code § 5308.
Submission of copy of certification to superior court, see Welfare and Institutions Code § 5256.7.

§ 5250.1. Unconditional release from intensive treatment; notice; destruction of records

The professional person in charge of a facility providing intensive treatment, pursuant to Section 5250 or 5270.15, or that person's designee, shall notify the county behavioral health director, or the director's designee, and the peace officer who made the original written application for 72–hour evaluation pursuant to Section 5150 or a person who is designated by the law enforcement agency that employs the peace officer, that the person admitted pursuant to the application has been released unconditionally if all of the following conditions apply:

(a) The peace officer has requested notification at the time he or she makes the application for 72–hour evaluation.

(b) The peace officer has certified in writing at the time he or she made the application that the person has been referred to the facility under circumstances which, based upon an allegation of facts regarding actions witnessed by the officer or another person, would support the filing of a criminal complaint.

(c) The notice is limited to the person's name, address, date of admission for 72–hour evaluation, date of certification for intensive treatment, and date of release.

If a police officer, law enforcement agency, or designee of the law enforcement agency, possesses any record of information obtained pursuant to the notification requirements of this section, the officer, agency, or designee shall destroy that record two years after receipt of notification. *(Added by Stats.1983, c. 755, § 2. Amended by Stats.1988, c. 1517, § 2; Stats.2015, c. 455 (S.B.804), § 21, eff. Jan. 1, 2016.)*

Cross References

Evaluation defined for purposes of this Part, see Welfare and Institutions Code § 5008.
Intensive treatment defined for purposes of this Part, see Welfare and Institutions Code § 5008.
Peace officer defined for purposes of this Part, see Welfare and Institutions Code § 5008.

§ 5251. Notice of certification; signatories

(a) For a person to be certified under this article, a notice of certification shall be signed by two people.

(1) The first person shall be the professional person, or his or her designee, in charge of the agency or facility providing evaluation services. A designee of the professional person in charge of the agency or facility shall be a physician or a licensed psychologist who has a doctoral degree in psychology and at least five years of postgraduate experience in the diagnosis and treatment of emotional and mental disorders.

(2) The second person shall be a physician or psychologist who participated in the evaluation. The physician shall be, if possible, a board certified psychiatrist. The psychologist shall be licensed and have at least five years of postgraduate experience in the diagnosis and treatment of emotional and mental disorders.

(b) If the professional person in charge, or his or her designee, is the physician who performed the medical evaluation or a psychologist, the second person to sign may be another physician or psychologist unless one is not available, in which case a licensed clinical social worker, licensed marriage and family therapist, licensed professional clinical counselor, or registered nurse who participated in the evaluation shall sign the notice of certification. *(Added by Stats.1982, c. 1598, § 4. Amended by Stats.1998, c. 1013 (A.B.1439), § 2; Stats.2017, c. 184 (A.B.191), § 1, eff. Jan. 1, 2018.)*

Cross References

Evaluation defined for purposes of this Part, see Welfare and Institutions Code § 5008.
Waiver of presence of physician, licensed psychologist or other professional person, see Welfare and Institutions Code § 5276.1.

§ 5252. Necessity for, and form of, notice of certification

A notice of certification is required for all persons certified for intensive treatment pursuant to Section 5250 or 5270.15, and shall be in substantially the following form (strike out inapplicable section):

The authorized agency providing evaluation services in the County of ________ has evaluated the condition of:

Name ________________________________

Address ________________________________

Age ________________________________

Sex ________________________________

Marital status ________________________________

We the undersigned allege that the above-named person is, as a result of mental disorder or impairment by chronic alcoholism:

(1) A danger to others.

(2) A danger to himself or herself.

(3) Gravely disabled as defined in paragraph (1) of subdivision (h) or subdivision (*l*) of Section 5008 of the Welfare and Institutions Code.

The specific facts which form the basis for our opinion that the above-named person meets one or more of the classifications indicated above are as follows:

(certifying persons to fill in blanks) ________________________________

____

____

[Strike out all inapplicable classifications.]

The above-named person has been informed of this evaluation, and has been advised of the need for, but has not been able or willing to accept treatment on a voluntary basis, or to accept referral to, the following services:

____

____

____

____

____

We, therefore, certify the above-named person to receive intensive treatment related to the mental disorder or impairment by chronic alcoholism beginning this __ day of ________,
(Month)
19__, in the intensive treatment facility herein named ________________

____
(Date)

Signed ________________________________

Signed ________________________________

Countersigned ________________________________
(Representing facility)

I hereby state that I delivered a copy of this notice this day to the above-named person and that I informed him or her that unless judicial review is requested a certification review hearing will be held within four days of the date on which the person is certified for a period of intensive treatment and that an attorney or advocate will visit him or her to provide assistance in preparing for the hearing or to answer questions regarding his or her commitment or to provide other assistance. The court has been notified of this certification on this day.

Signed ________________

(Added by Stats.1982, c. 1598, § 4. Amended by Stats.1983, c. 319, § 1; Stats.1988, c. 1517, § 3.)

Cross References

Court defined for purposes of this Part, see Welfare and Institutions Code § 5008.
Delivery of copy of certification notice, see Welfare and Institutions Code § 5253.
Evaluation defined for purposes of this Part, see Welfare and Institutions Code § 5008.
Gravely disabled defined for purposes of this Part, see Welfare and Institutions Code § 5008.

Habeas corpus, right of review by, see Welfare and Institutions Code § 5275 et seq.
Intensive treatment defined for purposes of this Part, see Welfare and Institutions Code § 5008.
Referral defined for purposes of this Part, see Welfare and Institutions Code § 5008.
Right to counsel, see Welfare and Institutions Code §§ 5226, 5276, 5302.
Right to counsel in criminal cases, see Const. Art. 1, § 15; Penal Code § 686.

§ 5253. Delivery of copy of certification notice; designation of any other person to be informed

A copy of the certification notice shall be personally delivered to the person certified, the person's attorney, or the attorney or advocate designated in Section 5252. The person certified shall also be asked to designate any person who is to be sent a copy of the certification notice. If the person certified is incapable of making this designation at the time of certification, he or she shall be asked to designate a person as soon as he or she is capable. *(Added by Stats.1982, c. 1598, § 4. Amended by Stats.1983, c. 319, § 2.)*

Cross References

Suicidal persons, second notice of certification, see Welfare and Institutions Code § 5261.

§ 5254. Certification review hearing; notice of entitlement; time; issues; rights of person certified

The person delivering the copy of the notice of certification to the person certified shall, at the time of delivery, inform the person certified that he or she is entitled to a certification review hearing, to be held within four days of the date on which the person is certified for a period of intensive treatment in accordance with Section 5256 unless judicial review is requested, to determine whether or not probable cause exists to detain the person for intensive treatment related to the mental disorder or impairment by chronic alcoholism. The person certified shall be informed of his or her rights with respect to the hearing, including the right to the assistance of another person to prepare for the hearing or to answer other questions and concerns regarding his or her involuntary detention or both. *(Added by Stats.1982, c. 1598, § 4. Amended by Stats.1983, c. 319, § 3; Stats.1988, c. 1517, § 4.)*

Cross References

Intensive treatment defined for purposes of this Part, see Welfare and Institutions Code § 5008.

§ 5254.1. Judicial review by habeas corpus; notice of right; explanation of term; right to counsel

The person delivering the copy of the notice of certification to the person certified shall, at the time of delivery, inform the person certified of his or her legal right to a judicial review by habeas corpus, and shall explain that term to the person certified, and inform the person of his or her right to counsel, including court-appointed counsel pursuant to Section 5276. *(Added by Stats.1982, c. 1598, § 4.)*

Cross References

Advice as to right of counsel, see Welfare and Institutions Code §§ 5226, 5276, 5302.
Appointment of public defender or other attorney, see Welfare and Institutions Code §§ 5276, 5302, 5365.
Confinement of outpatient pending proceeding for revocation of outpatient status, rights and notice of rights, see Welfare and Institutions Code § 5308.
Court defined for purposes of this Part, see Welfare and Institutions Code § 5008.
Habeas corpus, right of review by, see Welfare and Institutions Code § 5275 et seq.
Right to counsel in criminal cases, see Const. Art. 1, § 15, cl. 3; Penal Code § 686.

§ 5255. Discussion of commitment process with person certified; assistance

As soon after the certification as practicable, an attorney or patient advocate shall meet with the person certified to discuss the commitment process and to assist the person in preparing for the certification review hearing or to answer questions or otherwise assist the person as is appropriate. *(Added by Stats.1982, c. 1598, § 4.)*

Cross References

Determinations, according to law, public employee's exemption from liability, see Government Code § 856.
Procedures on certification review hearing following withdrawal of request for judicial review, see Welfare and Institutions Code § 5276.2.

§ 5256. Necessity and time for certification review hearing

(a) When a person is certified for intensive treatment pursuant to Section 5250 or 5270.15, a certification review hearing shall be held unless judicial review has been requested as provided in Sections 5275 and 5276. The certification review hearing shall be within four days of the date on which the person is certified for a period of intensive treatment unless postponed by request of the person or * * * their attorney or advocate. * * *

(b) When a person has not been certified for intensive treatment pursuant to Section 5250 and remains detained pursuant to Section 5150, a certification review hearing shall be held within seven days of the date the person was initially detained pursuant to Section 5150, unless judicial review has been requested as provided in Sections 5275 and 5276. The professional person in charge of the facility designated by the county for evaluation and treatment, or an individual designated by the county if the person is not in a designated facility, shall inform the detained person of their rights with respect to the hearing, such as the right to the assistance of another person, including the county patients' rights advocate, to prepare for the hearing, shall answer questions and address concerns regarding involuntary detention, and shall inform them of their rights pursuant to Section 5254.1. An attorney or county patients' rights advocate shall meet with the person to discuss the commitment process and to assist the person in preparing for the certification review hearing or to answer questions or otherwise assist the person as appropriate. The certification review hearing shall be conducted in accordance with Sections 5256.1, 5256.2, 5256.3, 5256.4, 5256.5, 5256.6, and 5256.7 and the detained person shall be considered a person certified. *(Added by Stats.1982, c. 1598, § 4. Amended by Stats.1983, c. 319, § 4; Stats.1988, c. 1517, § 5; Stats.2022, c. 960 (A.B.2275), § 3, eff. Jan. 1, 2023.)*

Cross References

Intensive treatment defined for purposes of this Part, see Welfare and Institutions Code § 5008.
Notice of entitlement to hearing, see Welfare and Institutions Code § 5254.
Procedures on certification review hearing following withdrawal of request for judicial review, see Welfare and Institutions Code § 5276.2.
Report of operation of division, see Welfare and Institutions Code § 5402.

§ 5256.1. Conduct of hearing; commissioner, referee, or certification review hearing officer; qualifications; location of hearing

The certification review hearing shall be conducted by either a court-appointed commissioner or a referee, or a certification review hearing officer. The certification review hearing officer shall be either a state qualified administrative law hearing officer, a physician and surgeon, a licensed psychologist, a registered nurse, a lawyer, a certified law student, a licensed clinical social worker, a licensed marriage and family therapist, or a licensed professional clinical counselor. Licensed psychologists, licensed clinical social workers, licensed marriage and family therapists, licensed professional clinical counselors, and registered nurses who serve as certification review hearing officers shall have had a minimum of five years' experience in mental health. Certification review hearing officers shall be selected from a list of eligible persons unanimously approved by a panel composed of the local mental health director, the county public defender, and the county counsel or district attorney designated by the county board of supervisors. No employee of the county mental health program or of any facility designated by the county and approved by the State Department of Social Services as a facility for 72–hour treatment and evaluation may serve as a certification review hearing officer.

The location of the certification review hearing shall be compatible with, and least disruptive of, the treatment being provided to the person certified. In addition, hearings conducted by certification review officers shall be conducted at an appropriate place at the facility where the person certified is receiving treatment. *(Added by Stats.1982, c. 1598, § 4. Amended by Stats.1983, c. 319, § 5; Stats.1987, c. 139, § 1; Stats.2002, c. 1013 (S.B.2026), § 97; Stats. 2011, c. 381 (S.B.146), § 43; Stats.2012, c. 438 (A.B.1468), § 11, eff. Sept. 22, 2012.)*

Cross References

Court defined for purposes of this Part, see Welfare and Institutions Code § 5008.
Evaluation defined for purposes of this Part, see Welfare and Institutions Code § 5008.
Procedures on certification review hearing following withdrawal of request for judicial review, see Welfare and Institutions Code § 5276.2.

§ 5256.2. Evidence; presentation

At the certification review hearing, the evidence in support of the certification decision shall be presented by a person designated by the director of the facility. In addition, either the district attorney or the county counsel may, at his or her discretion, elect to present evidence at the certification review hearing. *(Added by Stats.1982, c. 1598, § 4.)*

Cross References

Procedures on certification review hearing following withdrawal of request for judicial review, see Welfare and Institutions Code § 5276.2.

§ 5256.3. Presence of certified person at certification review hearing; necessity; waiver

The person certified shall be present at the certification review hearing unless he or she, with the assistance of his or her attorney or advocate, waives his or her right to be present at a hearing. *(Added by Stats.1982, c. 1598, § 4.)*

Cross References

Procedures on certification review hearing following withdrawal of request for judicial review, see Welfare and Institutions Code § 5276.2.

§ 5256.4. Rights of certified person at certification review hearing; manner of conducting hearing; notification of family members; admission and consideration of evidence

(a) At the certification review hearing, the person certified shall have the following rights:

(1) Assistance by an attorney or advocate.

(2) To present evidence on his or her own behalf.

(3) To question persons presenting evidence in support of the certification decision.

(4) To make reasonable requests for the attendance of facility employees who have knowledge of, or participated in, the certification decision.

(5) If the person has received medication within 24 hours or such longer period of time as the person conducting the hearing may designate prior to the beginning of the hearing, the person conducting the hearing shall be informed of that fact and of the probable effects of the medication.

(b) The hearing shall be conducted in an impartial and informal manner in order to encourage free and open discussion by participants. The person conducting the hearing shall not be bound by rules of procedure or evidence applicable in judicial proceedings.

(c) Reasonable attempts shall be made by the mental health facility to notify family members or any other person designated by the patient, of the time and place of the certification hearing, unless the patient requests that this information not be provided. The patient shall be advised by the facility that is treating the patient that he or she has the right to request that this information not be provided.

(d) All evidence which is relevant to establishing that the person certified is or is not as a result of mental disorder or impairment by chronic alcoholism, a danger to others, or to himself or herself, or gravely disabled, shall be admitted at the hearing and considered by the hearing officer.

(e) Although resistance to involuntary commitment may be a product of a mental disorder, this resistance shall not, in itself, imply the presence of a mental disorder or constitute evidence that a person meets the criteria of being dangerous to self or others, or gravely disabled. *(Added by Stats.1982, c. 1598, § 4. Amended by Stats.1986, c. 872, § 3.)*

Cross References

Gravely disabled defined for purposes of this Part, see Welfare and Institutions Code § 5008.
Procedures on certification review hearing following withdrawal of request for judicial review, see Welfare and Institutions Code § 5276.2.

§ 5256.5. Termination of involuntary detention upon finding of lack of probable cause; certified person voluntarily remaining at facility

If at the conclusion of the certification review hearing the person conducting the hearing finds that there is not probable cause to believe that the person certified is, as a result of a mental disorder or impairment by chronic alcoholism, a danger to others, or to himself or herself, or gravely disabled, then the person certified may no longer be involuntarily detained. Nothing herein shall prohibit the person from remaining at the facility on a voluntary basis or the facility from providing the person with appropriate referral information concerning mental health services. *(Added by Stats.1982, c. 1598, § 4.)*

Cross References

Gravely disabled defined for purposes of this Part, see Welfare and Institutions Code § 5008.
Procedures on certification review hearing following withdrawal of request for judicial review, see Welfare and Institutions Code § 5276.2.
Referral defined for purposes of this Part, see Welfare and Institutions Code § 5008.

§ 5256.6. Detention of certified person for involuntary care, protection and treatment upon finding of probable cause

If at the conclusion of the certification review hearing the person conducting the hearing finds that there is probable cause that the person certified is, as a result of a mental disorder or impairment by chronic alcoholism, a danger to others, or to himself or herself, or gravely disabled, then the person may be detained for involuntary care, protection, and treatment related to the mental disorder or impairment by chronic alcoholism pursuant to Sections 5250 and 5270.15. *(Added by Stats.1982, c. 1598, § 4. Amended by Stats.1988, c. 1517, § 6.)*

Cross References

Gravely disabled defined for purposes of this Part, see Welfare and Institutions Code § 5008.

Procedures on certification review hearing following withdrawal of request for judicial review, see Welfare and Institutions Code § 5276.2.

§ 5256.7. Notification of decision at conclusion of certification review hearing; request for release; right to fill; hearing

The person certified shall be given oral notification of the decision at the conclusion of the certification review hearing. As soon thereafter as is practicable, the attorney or advocate for the person certified and the director of the facility where the person is receiving treatment shall be provided with a written notification of the decision, which shall include a statement of the evidence relied upon and the reasons for the decision. The attorney or advocate shall notify the person certified of the certification review hearing decision and of his or her rights to file a request for release and to have a hearing on the request before the superior court as set forth in Article 5 (commencing with Section 5275). A copy of the decision and the certification made pursuant to Section 5250 or 5270.15 shall be submitted to the superior court. *(Added by Stats.1982, c. 1598, § 4. Amended by Stats.1983, c. 319, § 6; Stats.1988, c. 1517, § 7.)*

Cross References

Court defined for purposes of this Part, see Welfare and Institutions Code § 5008.

Procedures on certification review hearing following withdrawal of request for judicial review, see Welfare and Institutions Code § 5276.2.

§ 5256.8. Limitation on certification review hearing requirement

The requirement that there is a certification review hearing in accordance with this article shall apply only to persons certified for intensive treatment on or after January 1, 1983. *(Added by Stats.1982, c. 1598, § 4.)*

Cross References

Intensive treatment defined for purposes of this Part, see Welfare and Institutions Code § 5008.

Procedures on certification review hearing following withdrawal of request for judicial review, see Welfare and Institutions Code § 5276.2.

§ 5257. Termination of involuntary commitment; remaining at facility on a voluntary basis; referral information; limitation on involuntary detainment

(a) During the period of intensive treatment pursuant to Section 5250 or 5270.15, the person's involuntary detention shall be terminated and the person shall be released only if the psychiatrist directly responsible for the person's treatment believes, as a result of the psychiatrist's personal observations, that the person certified no longer is, as a result of mental disorder or impairment by chronic alcoholism, a danger to others, or to himself or herself, or gravely disabled. However, in those situations in which both a psychiatrist and psychologist have personally evaluated or examined a person who is undergoing intensive treatment and there is a collaborative treatment relationship between the psychiatrist and the psychologist, either the psychiatrist or psychologist may authorize the release of the person, but only after they have consulted with one another. In the event of a clinical or professional disagreement regarding the early release of a person who is undergoing intensive treatment, the person may not be released unless the facility's medical director overrules the decision of the psychiatrist or psychologist opposing the release. Both the psychiatrist and psychologist shall enter their findings, concerns, or objections into the person's medical record. If any other professional person who is authorized to release the person believes the person should be released during the designated period of intensive treatment, and the psychiatrist directly responsible for the person's treatment objects, the matter shall be referred to the medical director of the facility for the final decision. However, if the medical director is not a psychiatrist, he or she shall appoint a designee who is a psychiatrist. If the matter is referred, the person shall be released during the period of intensive treatment only if the psychiatrist making the final decision believes, as a result of the psychiatrist's personal observations, that the person certified no longer is, as a result of mental disorder or impairment by chronic alcoholism, a danger to others, or to himself or herself, or gravely disabled. Nothing herein shall prohibit the person from remaining at the facility on a voluntary basis or prevent the facility from providing the person with appropriate referral information concerning mental health services.

(b) A person who has been certified for a period of intensive treatment pursuant to Section 5250 shall be released at the end of 14 days unless the patient either:

(1) Agrees to receive further treatment on a voluntary basis.

(2) Is certified for an additional 14 days of intensive treatment pursuant to Article 4.5 (commencing with Section 5260).

(3) Is certified for an additional 30 days of intensive treatment pursuant to Article 4.7 (commencing with Section 5270.10).

(4) Is the subject of a conservatorship petition filed pursuant to Chapter 3 (commencing with Section 5350).

(5) Is the subject of a petition for postcertification treatment of a dangerous person filed pursuant to Article 6 (commencing with Section 5300).

(c) The amendments to this section made by Assembly Bill 348 of the 2003-04 Regular Session [1] shall not be construed to revise or expand the scope of practice of psychologists, as defined in Chapter 6.6 (commencing with Section 2900) of Division 2 of the Business and Professions Code. *(Added by Stats.1982, c. 1598, § 4. Amended by Stats.1985, c. 1288, § 7, eff. Sept. 30, 1985; Stats.1988, c. 1517, § 8; Stats.2003, c. 94 (A.B.348), § 3.)*

[1] See Stats.2003, c. 94 (A.B.348), § 3.

Cross References

Additional detention pending petition for temporary conservatorship, see Welfare and Institutions Code § 5352.3.

Additional intensive treatment of suicidal persons, see Welfare and Institutions Code § 5260 et seq.

Gravely disabled defined for purposes of this Part, see Welfare and Institutions Code § 5008.

Intensive treatment defined for purposes of this Part, see Welfare and Institutions Code § 5008.

Postcertification treatment defined for purposes of this Part, see Welfare and Institutions Code § 5008.

Referral defined for purposes of this Part, see Welfare and Institutions Code § 5008.

Similar provision, see Welfare and Institutions Code § 5264.

§ 5257.5. Care coordination plan

(a) A care coordination plan shall be developed by, at a minimum, the individual, the facility, the county behavioral health department, the health care payer, if different from the county, and any other individuals designated by the individual as appropriate, and shall be provided to the individual before their discharge. The care coordination plan shall include a first followup appointment with an appropriate behavioral health professional. The appointment information shall be provided to the individual before their release. In no event may the individual be involuntarily held based on the requirements of this subdivision beyond when they would otherwise qualify for release. All care and treatment after release shall be voluntary.

(b) For purposes of care coordination and to schedule a followup appointment, the health plan, mental health plan, primary care provider, or other appropriate provider to whom the individual has been referred pursuant to subdivision (a) shall make a good faith effort to contact the referred individual no fewer than three times, either by email, telephone, mail, or in-person outreach, whichever method or methods is most likely to reach the individual.

(c) The requirement to develop a care coordination plan under this section shall take effect immediately, without waiting for the department to create a model care coordination plan, as required pursuant to Section 5402.5. *(Added by Stats.2022, c. 867 (A.B.2242), § 3, eff. Jan. 1, 2023.)*

§ 5258. Limitation on total period of detention

After the involuntary detention has begun, the total period of detention, including intervening periods of voluntary treatment, shall not exceed the total maximum period during which the person could have been detained, if the person had been detained continuously on an involuntary basis, from the time of initial involuntary detention. *(Added by Stats.1982, c. 1598, § 4. Amended by Stats.1988, c. 1517, § 9.)*

§ 5259. Permitting person certified for intensive treatment to leave facility for short periods during involuntary additional treatment

Nothing in this article shall prohibit the professional person in charge of a treatment facility, or his or her designee, from permitting a person certified for intensive treatment to leave the facility for short periods during the person's involuntary additional treatment. *(Added by Stats.1982, c. 1598, § 4.)*

Cross References

Intensive treatment defined for purposes of this Part, see Welfare and Institutions Code § 5008.

§ 5259.1. Detention in violation of this article; civil damages

Any individual who is knowingly and willfully responsible for detaining a person in violation of the provisions of this article is liable to that person in civil damages. *(Added by Stats.1982, c. 1598, § 4.)*

Cross References

Determinations according to law, public employees' exemption from liability, see Government Code § 856.
Exemption from liability, see Welfare and Institutions Code §§ 5154, 5173, 5267, 5278, 5306.

§ 5259.2. Compliance with preference for one of two or more treatment facilities

Whenever a county designates two or more facilities to provide treatment, and the person to be treated, his or her family, conservator, or guardian expresses a preference for one of these facilities, the professional person certifying the person to be treated shall attempt, if administratively possible, to comply with the preference. *(Added by Stats.1982, c. 1598, § 4.)*

§ 5259.3. Immunity from civil or criminal liability for release

(a) Notwithstanding Section 5113, if the provisions of Section 5257 have been met, the professional person in charge of the facility providing intensive treatment, his or her designee, the professional person designated by the county, the medical director of the facility or his or her designee described in Section 5257, the psychiatrist directly responsible for the person's treatment, or the psychologist shall not be held civilly or criminally liable for any action by a person released before the end of 14 days pursuant to this article.

(b) The professional person in charge of the facility providing intensive treatment, his or her designee, the professional person designated by the county, the medical director of the facility or his or her designee described in Section 5257, the psychiatrist directly responsible for the person's treatment, or the psychologist shall not be held civilly or criminally liable for any action by a person released at the end of the 14 days pursuant to this article.

(c) The attorney or advocate representing the person, the court-appointed commissioner or referee, the certification review hearing officer conducting the certification review hearing, and the peace officer responsible for the detainment of the person shall not be civilly or criminally liable for any action by a person released at or before the end of 14 days pursuant to this article.

(d) The amendments to this section made by Assembly Bill 348 of the 2003–04 Regular Session [1] shall not be construed to revise or expand the scope of practice of psychologists, as defined in Chapter 6.6 (commencing with Section 2900) of Division 2 of the Business and Professions Code. *(Added by Stats.1982, c. 1598, § 4. Amended by Stats.1983, c. 319, § 7; Stats.1985, c. 1288, § 8, eff. Sept. 30, 1985; Stats.2003, c. 94 (A.B.348), § 4; Stats.2013, c. 567 (S.B.364), § 10.)*

[1] Stats.2003, c. 94 (A.B.348), § 4.

Cross References

Court defined for purposes of this Part, see Welfare and Institutions Code § 5008.
Determinations according to law, public employees' exemption from liability, see Government Code § 856.
Intensive treatment defined for purposes of this Part, see Welfare and Institutions Code § 5008.
Liability for excessive detention, see Welfare and Institutions Code §§ 5259.1, 5265.
Liability for false application, see Welfare and Institutions Code § 5203.
Peace officer defined for purposes of this Part, see Welfare and Institutions Code § 5008.
Similar provisions, see Welfare and Institutions Code §§ 5154, 5173, 5267, 5278, 5306.

ARTICLE 4.5. ADDITIONAL INTENSIVE TREATMENT OF SUICIDAL PERSONS

§ 5260. Confinement for further intensive treatment; conditions

At the expiration of the 14–day period of intensive treatment any person who, as a result of mental disorder or impairment by chronic alcoholism, during the 14–day period or the 72 hour evaluation period, threatened or attempted to take his or her own life or who was detained for evaluation and treatment because he or she threatened or attempted to take his or her own life and who continues to present an imminent threat of taking his or her own life, may be confined for further intensive treatment pursuant to this article for an additional period not to exceed 14 days.

This further intensive treatment may occur only under the following conditions:

(a) The professional staff of the agency or facility providing intensive treatment services has analyzed the person's condition and has found that the person presents an imminent threat of taking his or her own life.

(b) The person has been advised of, but has not accepted, voluntary treatment.

(c) The facility providing additional intensive treatment is equipped and staffed to provide treatment, is designated by the county to provide that intensive treatment, and agrees to admit the person.

(d) The person has, as a result of mental disorder or impairment by chronic alcoholism, threatened or attempted to take his or her own life during the 14–day period of intensive treatment or the 72–hour evaluation period or was detained for evaluation and treatment because he or she threatened or attempted to take his or her own life. *(Added by Stats.1968, c. 1374, p. 2650, § 33.5, operative July 1, 1969. Amended by Stats.2017, c. 218 (S.B.565), § 1, eff. Jan. 1, 2018.)*

Cross References

Administration of antipsychotic medication to persons subject to detention, see Welfare and Institutions Code § 5332.
Certification for intensive treatment, see Welfare and Institutions Code § 5250 et seq.
Consumers placed on involuntary psychiatric hold or Lanterman–Petris–Short conservatorship, notification to clients' rights advocate, see Welfare and Institutions Code § 4696.3.
Detention for evaluation and treatment, see Welfare and Institutions Code § 5150 et seq.
Evaluation defined for purposes of this Part, see Welfare and Institutions Code § 5008.
Intensive treatment defined for purposes of this Part, see Welfare and Institutions Code § 5008.

§ 5261. Second notice of certification; necessity; signing

(a) For a person to be certified under this article, a second notice of certification shall be signed by the professional person in charge of the facility providing the 14–day intensive treatment under Article 4 (commencing with Section 5250) to the person and by a physician, if possible a board-qualified psychiatrist, or a licensed psychologist who has a doctoral degree in psychology and at least five years of postgraduate experience in the diagnosis and treatment of emotional and mental disorders. The physician or psychologist who signs shall have participated in the evaluation and finding referred to in subdivision (a) of Section 5260.

(b) If the professional person in charge is the physician who performed the medical evaluation and finding, or a psychologist, the second person to sign may be another physician or psychologist unless one is not available, in which case a social worker, licensed marriage and family therapist, licensed professional clinical counselor, or registered nurse who participated in the evaluation and finding shall sign the notice of certification. *(Added by Stats.1968, c. 1374, p. 2651, § 33.5, operative July 1, 1969. Amended by Stats.1969, c. 722, p. 1426, § 15, eff. Aug. 8, 1969, operative July 1, 1969; Stats.1978, c. 391, p. 1243, § 4; Stats.2017, c. 184 (A.B.191), § 2, eff. Jan. 1, 2018.)*

Cross References

Certification notice, see Welfare and Institutions Code § 5253.
Evaluation defined for purposes of this Part, see Welfare and Institutions Code § 5008.
Intensive treatment defined for purposes of this Part, see Welfare and Institutions Code § 5008.

§ 5262. Form of second notice of certification

A second notice of certification for imminently suicidal persons is required for all involuntary 14-day intensive treatment, pursuant to this article, and shall be in substantially the following form:

To the Superior Court of the State of California
for the County of ....

The authorized agency providing 14-day intensive treatment, County of ...., has custody of: ....

Name ....
Address ....
Age ....
Sex ....
Marital status ....
Religious affiliation ....

The undersigned allege that the above-named person presents an imminent threat of taking his own life.

This allegation is based upon the following facts:.................
....
....
....
....

This allegation is supported by the accompanying affidavits signed by ....

The above-named person has been informed of this allegation and has been advised of, but has not been able or willing to accept referral to, the following services:
....
....
....
....
....

We, therefore, certify the above-named person to receive additional intensive treatment for no more than 14 days beginning this ... day of ...., 19..., in the intensive treatment
(Month)
facility herein named ....

We hereby state that a copy of this notice has been delivered this day to the above-named person and that he has been clearly advised of his continuing legal right to a judicial review by habeas corpus, and this term has been explained to him.

....
(Date)
Signed ....
Countersigned ....
Representing intensive treatment facility

(Added by Stats.1968, c. 1374, p. 2651, § 33.5, operative July 1, 1969.)

Cross References

Certification for intensive treatment, form of notice of certification, see Welfare and Institutions Code § 5252.
Copies of second notice of certification for imminently suicidal persons, filing and delivery, see Welfare and Institutions Code § 5263.
Court defined for purposes of this Part, see Welfare and Institutions Code § 5008.
Habeas corpus, right of review by, see Welfare and Institutions Code § 5275 et seq.
Informing person of rights, see Welfare and Institutions Code §§ 5226, 5254.1.
Intensive treatment defined for purposes of this Part, see Welfare and Institutions Code § 5008.
Referral defined for purposes of this Part, see Welfare and Institutions Code § 5008.

§ 5263. Copies of second notice of certification for imminently suicidal persons; filing; delivery; designation of person to be informed

Copies of the second notice of certification for imminently suicidal persons, as set forth in Section 5262, shall be filed with the court and personally delivered to the person certified. A copy shall also be sent to the person's attorney, to the district attorney, to the public defender, if any, and to the facility providing intensive treatment.

The person certified shall also be asked to designate any person who is to be sent a copy of the certification notice. If the person certified is incapable of making such a designation at the time of certification, he or she shall be asked to designate such person as soon as he or she is capable. *(Added by Stats.1968, c. 1374, p. 2652, § 33.5, operative July 1, 1969. Amended by Stats.1971, c. 1593, p. 3339, § 373, operative July 1, 1973; Stats.1977, c. 1252, p. 4569, § 559, operative July 1, 1978; Stats.1982, c. 1598, § 5; Stats.1983, c. 319, § 8.)*

Cross References

Court defined for purposes of this Part, see Welfare and Institutions Code § 5008.

Intensive treatment defined for purposes of this Part, see Welfare and Institutions Code § 5008.

§ 5264. Duration of certification; release; exceptions

(a) A certification for imminently suicidal persons shall be for no more than 14 days of intensive treatment, and shall terminate only as soon as the psychiatrist directly responsible for the person's treatment believes, as a result of the psychiatrist's personal observations, that the person has improved sufficiently for him or her to leave, or is prepared to voluntarily accept treatment on referral or to remain on a voluntary basis in the facility providing intensive treatment. However, in those situations in which both a psychiatrist and psychologist have personally evaluated or examined a person who is undergoing intensive treatment and there is a collaborative treatment relationship between the psychiatrist and psychologist, either the psychiatrist or psychologist may authorize the release of the person, but only after they have consulted with one another. In the event of a clinical or professional disagreement regarding the early release of a person who is undergoing intensive treatment, the person may not be released unless the facility's medical director overrules the decision of the psychiatrist or psychologist opposing the release. Both the psychiatrist and psychologist shall enter their findings, concerns, or objections into the person's medical record. If any other professional person who is authorized to release the person believes the person should be released before 14 days have elapsed, and the psychiatrist directly responsible for the person's treatment objects, the matter shall be referred to the medical director of the facility for the final decision. However, if the medical director is not a psychiatrist, he or she shall appoint a designee who is a psychiatrist. If the matter is referred, the person shall be released before 14 days have elapsed only if the psychiatrist believes, as a result of the psychiatrist's personal observations, that the person has improved sufficiently for him or her to leave, or is prepared to accept voluntary treatment on referral or to remain in the facility providing intensive treatment on a voluntary basis.

(b) Any person who has been certified for 14 days of intensive treatment under this article and to whom Section 5226.1 is not applicable, or with respect to whom the criminal charge has been dismissed under Section 5226.1, shall be released at the end of the 14 days unless any of the following applies:

(1) The patient agrees to receive further treatment on a voluntary basis.

(2) The patient has been recommended for conservatorship pursuant to Chapter 3 (commencing with Section 5350).

(3) The patient is a person to whom Article 6 (commencing with Section 5300) of this chapter is applicable.

(c) The amendments to this section made by Assembly Bill 348 of the 2003-04 Regular Session [1] shall not be construed to revise or expand the scope of practice of psychologists, as defined in Chapter 6.6 (commencing with Section 2900) of Division 2 of the Business and Professions Code. *(Added by Stats.1968, c. 1374, p. 2652, § 33.5, operative July 1, 1969. Amended by Stats.1969, c. 722, p. 1426, § 16, eff. Aug. 8, 1969, operative July 1, 1969; Stats.1985, c. 1288, § 9, eff. Sept. 30, 1985; Stats.2003, c. 94 (A.B.348), § 5.)*

[1] Stats.2003, c. 94 (A.B.348), § 5.

Cross References

Intensive treatment defined for purposes of this Part, see Welfare and Institutions Code § 5008.
Referral defined for purposes of this Part, see Welfare and Institutions Code § 5008.
Similar provision, see Welfare and Institutions Code § 5257.

§ 5265. Liability for excessive detention

Any individual who is knowingly and willfully responsible for detaining a person for more than 14 days in violation of the provisions of Section 5264 is liable to that person in civil damages. *(Added by Stats.1968, c. 1374, p. 2652, § 33.5, operative July 1, 1969.)*

Cross References

Determinations according to law, public employees' exemption from liability, see Government Code § 856.
Exemption from liability, see Welfare and Institutions Code §§ 5154, 5173, 5259.3, 5267, 5278, 5306.

§ 5266. Preference for treatment facility

Whenever a county designates two or more facilities to provide intensive treatment and the person to be treated, his family, conservator or guardian expresses a preference for one such facility, the professional person certifying the person to be treated shall attempt, if administratively possible, to comply with the preference. *(Added by Stats.1968, c. 1374, p. 2652, § 33.5, operative July 1, 1969.)*

Cross References

Intensive treatment defined for purposes of this Part, see Welfare and Institutions Code § 5008.

§ 5267. Exemption from liability

(a) Notwithstanding Section 5113, if the provisions of Section 5264 have been met, the professional person in charge of the facility providing intensive treatment, his or her designee, the medical director of the facility or his or her designee described in Section 5264, the psychiatrist directly responsible for the person's treatment, or the psychologist shall not be held civilly or criminally liable for any action by a person released before the end of 14 days pursuant to this article.

(b) The professional person in charge of the facility providing intensive treatment, his or her designee, the medical director of the facility or his or her designee described in Section 5264, the psychiatrist directly responsible for the person's treatment, or the psychologist shall not be held civilly or criminally liable for any action by a person released at the end of 14 days pursuant to this article.

(c) The amendments to this section made by Assembly Bill 348 of the 2003-04 Regular Session [1] shall not be construed to revise or expand the scope of practice of psychologists, as defined in Chapter 6.6 (commencing with Section 2900) of Division 2 of the Business and Professions Code. *(Added by Stats.1968, c. 1374, p. 2653, § 33.5, operative July 1, 1969. Amended by Stats.1985, c. 1288, § 10, eff. Sept. 30, 1985; Stats.2003, c. 94 (A.B.348), § 6.)*

[1] Stats.2003, c. 94 (A.B.348), § 6.

Cross References

Determinations according to law, public employees' exemption from liability, see Government Code § 856.
Intensive treatment defined for purposes of this Part, see Welfare and Institutions Code § 5008.
Liability for excessive detention, see Welfare and Institutions Code §§ 5259.1, 5265.
Liability for false application, see Welfare and Institutions Code § 5203.
Similar provisions, see Welfare and Institutions Code §§ 5154, 5173, 5259.3, 5278, 5306.

§ 5268. Leaves of absence during confinement

Nothing in this article shall prohibit the professional person in charge of an intensive treatment facility, or his designee, from permitting a person certified for intensive treatment to leave the facility for short periods during the person's involuntary intensive treatment. *(Added by Stats.1968, c. 1374, p. 2653, § 33.5, operative July 1, 1969.)*

Cross References

Intensive treatment defined for purposes of this Part, see Welfare and Institutions Code § 5008.

ARTICLE 4.7. ADDITIONAL INTENSIVE TREATMENT

§ 5270.10. Legislative intent

It is the intent of the Legislature to reduce the number of gravely disabled persons for whom conservatorship petitions are filed and who are placed under the extensive powers and authority of a temporary conservator simply to obtain an additional period of treatment without the belief that a conservator is actually needed and without the intention of proceeding to trial on the conservatorship petition. This change will substantially reduce the number of conservatorship petitions filed and temporary conservatorships granted under this part which do not result in either a trial or a conservatorship. *(Added by Stats.1988, c. 1517, § 10.)*

Cross References

Consumers placed on involuntary psychiatric hold or Lanterman–Petris–Short conservatorship, notification to clients' rights advocate, see Welfare and Institutions Code § 4696.3.

Habeas corpus, request for release, see Welfare and Institutions Code § 5275.

§ 5270.12. Counties; application of article; monitoring of compliance

This article shall be operative only in those counties in which the county board of supervisors, by resolution, authorizes its application and, by resolution, makes a finding that any additional costs incurred by the county in the implementation of this article are funded either by new funding sufficient to cover the costs incurred by the county resulting from this article, or funds redirected from cost savings resulting from this article, or a combination thereof, so that no current service reductions will occur as a result of the enactment of this article. Compliance with this section shall be monitored by the State Department of Health Care Services as part of its review and approval of mental health plans and performance contracts. *(Added by Stats.1988, c. 1517, § 10. Amended by Stats.2012, c. 34 (S.B.1009), § 84, eff. June 27, 2012.)*

§ 5270.15. Certification for additional treatment; conditions; certification review hearings; notification; monitoring and early termination of certification

(a) Upon the completion of a 14–day period of intensive treatment pursuant to Section 5250, the person may be certified for an additional period of not more than 30 days of intensive treatment under both of the following conditions:

(1) The professional staff of the agency or facility treating the person has found that the person remains gravely disabled as a result of a mental disorder or impairment by chronic alcoholism.

(2) The person remains unwilling or unable to accept treatment voluntarily.

(b) A person certified for an additional 30 days pursuant to this article shall be provided a certification review hearing in accordance with Section 5256 unless a judicial review is requested pursuant to Article 5 (commencing with Section 5275).

(1) Reasonable attempts shall be made by the mental health facility to notify family members or any other person designated by the patient at least 36 hours before the certification review hearing, of the time and place of the certification hearing, unless the patient requests that this information not be provided. The patient shall be advised by the facility that is treating the patient that he or she has the right to request that this information not be provided.

(2) The professional staff of the agency or facility providing intensive treatment shall analyze the person's condition at intervals not to exceed 10 days, to determine whether the person continues to meet the criteria established for certification under this section, and shall daily monitor the person's treatment plan and progress. Termination of this certification before the 30th day shall be made pursuant to Section 5270.35. *(Added by Stats.1988, c. 1517, § 10. Amended by Stats.2017, c. 218 (S.B.565), § 2, eff. Jan. 1, 2018; Stats.2018, c. 92 (S.B.1289), § 225, eff. Jan. 1, 2019.)*

Cross References

Administration of antipsychotic medication to persons subject to detention, see Welfare and Institutions Code § 5332.

Certification review hearing, submission of copy of decision and certification made pursuant to this section, see Welfare and Institutions Code § 5256.7.

Detention beyond 14-day period of intensive treatment, see Welfare and Institutions Code § 5270.55.

Detention of certified person for involuntary care, protection and treatment upon finding of probable cause, see Welfare and Institutions Code § 5256.6.

Intensive treatment defined for purposes of this Part, see Welfare and Institutions Code § 5008.

Necessity and form of notice of certification, see Welfare and Institutions Code § 5252.

Particular persons, weapons restrictions, see Welfare and Institutions Code § 8103.

Right to refuse antipsychotic medication, see Welfare and Institutions Code § 5325.2.

Termination of involuntary commitment, see Welfare and Institutions Code § 5257.

Unconditional release from intensive treatment, notice, destruction of records, see Welfare and Institutions Code § 5250.1.

§ 5270.20. Second notice of certification; signature by professional person in charge of facility; requirements

(a) For a person to be certified under this article, a second notice of certification shall be signed by the professional person in charge of the facility providing intensive treatment to the person and by either a physician who shall, if possible, be a board-qualified psychiatrist, or a licensed psychologist who has a doctoral degree in psychology and at least five years of postgraduate experience in the diagnosis and treatment of emotional and mental disorders. The physician or psychologist who signs shall have participated in the evaluation and finding referred to in subdivision (a) of Section 5270.15.

(b) If the professional person in charge is the physician who performed the medical evaluation and finding, or a psychologist, the second person to sign may be another physician or psychologist unless one is not available, in which case a social worker, licensed marriage and family therapist, licensed professional clinical counselor, or registered nurse who participated in the evaluation and finding shall sign the notice of certification. *(Added by Stats.1988, c. 1517, § 10. Amended by Stats.2017, c. 184 (A.B.191), § 3, eff. Jan. 1, 2018.)*

Cross References

Evaluation defined for purposes of this Part, see Welfare and Institutions Code § 5008.
Intensive treatment defined for purposes of this Part, see Welfare and Institutions Code § 5008.

§ 5270.25. Requirement of second notice for involuntary intensive treatment; form

A second notice of certification is required for all involuntary intensive treatment, pursuant to this article, and shall be in substantially the form indicated in Section 5252. *(Added by Stats.1988, c. 1517, § 10.)*

Cross References

Intensive treatment defined for purposes of this Part, see Welfare and Institutions Code § 5008.

§ 5270.30. Second notice of certification; filing; delivery; designation of recipient

Copies of the second notice of certification as set forth in Section 5270.25, shall be filed with the court and personally delivered to the person certified. A copy shall also be sent to the person's attorney, to the district attorney, to the public defender, if any, and to the facility providing intensive treatment.

The person certified shall also be asked to designate any individual who is to be sent a copy of the certification notice. If the person certified is incapable of making the designation at the time of certification, that person shall be given another opportunity to designate when able to do so. *(Added by Stats.1988, c. 1517, § 10.)*

Cross References

Court defined for purposes of this Part, see Welfare and Institutions Code § 5008.
Intensive treatment defined for purposes of this Part, see Welfare and Institutions Code § 5008.

§ 5270.35. Certification; length of intensive treatment; termination; release of patient

(a) A certification pursuant to this article shall be for no more than 30 days of intensive treatment, and shall terminate only as soon as the psychiatrist directly responsible for the person's treatment believes, as a result of the psychiatrist's personal observations, that the person no longer meets the criteria for the certification, or is prepared to voluntarily accept treatment on a referral basis or to remain on a voluntary basis in the facility providing intensive treatment. However, in those situations in which both a psychiatrist and psychologist have personally evaluated or examined a person who is undergoing intensive treatment and there is a collaborative treatment relationship between the psychiatrist and the psychologist, either the psychiatrist or psychologist may authorize the release of the person but only after they have consulted with one another. In the event of a clinical or professional disagreement regarding the early release of a person who is undergoing intensive treatment, the person may not be released unless the facility's medical director overrules the decision of the psychiatrist or psychologist opposing the release. Both the psychiatrist and psychologist shall enter their findings, concerns, or objections into the person's medical record. If any other professional person who is authorized to release the person believes the person should be released before 30 days have elapsed, and the psychiatrist directly responsible for the person's treatment objects, the matter shall be referred to the medical director of the facility for the final decision. However, if the medical director is not a psychiatrist, he or she shall appoint a designee who is a psychiatrist. If the matter is referred, the person shall be released before 30 days have elapsed only if the psychiatrist believes, as a result of the psychiatrist's personal observations, that the person no longer meets the criteria for certification, or is prepared to voluntarily accept treatment on referral or to remain on a voluntary basis in the facility providing intensive treatment.

(b) Any person who has been certified for 30 days of intensive treatment under this article, shall be released at the end of 30 days unless one or more of the following is applicable:

(1) The patient agrees to receive further treatment on a voluntary basis.

(2) The patient is the subject of a conservatorship petition filed pursuant to Chapter 3 (commencing with Section 5350).

(3) The patient is the subject of a petition for postcertification treatment of a dangerous person filed pursuant to Article 6 (commencing with Section 5300).

(c) The amendments to this section made by Assembly Bill 348 of the 2003–04 Regular Session [1] shall not be construed to revise or expand the scope of practice of psychologists, as defined in Chapter 6.6 (commencing with Section 2900) of Division 2 of the Business and Professions Code. *(Added by Stats.1988, c. 1517, § 10. Amended by Stats.2003, c. 94 (A.B.348), § 7.)*

[1] Stats.2003, c. 94 (A.B.348), § 7.

Cross References

Intensive treatment defined for purposes of this Part, see Welfare and Institutions Code § 5008.
Postcertification treatment defined for purposes of this Part, see Welfare and Institutions Code § 5008.
Referral defined for purposes of this Part, see Welfare and Institutions Code § 5008.

§ 5270.40. Knowing and willful detention of a person; civil damages

Any individual who is knowingly and willfully responsible for detaining a person for more than 30 days in violation of the provisions of Section 5270.35 is liable to that person in civil damages. *(Added by Stats.1988, c. 1517, § 10.)*

§ 5270.45. Preference for one facility

Whenever a county designates two or more facilities to provide intensive treatment and the person to be treated, his or her family, conservator, or guardian expresses a preference for one facility, the professional person certifying the person to be treated shall attempt, if administratively possible, to comply with the preference. *(Added by Stats.1988, c. 1517, § 10.)*

Cross References

Intensive treatment defined for purposes of this Part, see Welfare and Institutions Code § 5008.

§ 5270.50. Release of person prior to end of 30 days; criminal and civil liability; officers of the court

(a) Notwithstanding Section 5113, if the provisions of Section 5270.35 have been met, the professional person in charge of the facility providing intensive treatment, his or her designee, and the professional person directly responsible for the person's treatment shall not be held civilly or criminally liable for any action by a person released before or at the end of 30 days pursuant to this article.

(b) The attorney or advocate representing the person, the court-appointed commissioner or referee, the certification review hearing officer conducting the certification review hearing, or the peace officer responsible for detaining the person shall not be civilly or criminally liable for any action by a person released at or before the end of the 30 days of intensive treatment pursuant to this article. *(Added by Stats.1988, c. 1517, § 10. Amended by Stats.2016, c. 703 (A.B.2881), § 23, eff. Jan. 1, 2017.)*

Cross References

Intensive treatment defined for purposes of this Part, see Welfare and Institutions Code § 5008.

§ 5270.55. Detention beyond 14–day period of intensive treatment; evaluation; appointment of conservator; additional certification; hearing

(a) Whenever it is contemplated that a gravely disabled person may need to be detained beyond the end of the 14–day period of intensive treatment and prior to proceeding with an additional 30–day certification, the professional person in charge of the facility shall cause an evaluation to be made, based on the patient's current condition and past history, as to whether it appears that the person, even after up to 30 days of additional treatment, is likely to qualify for appointment of a conservator. If the appointment of a conservator appears likely, the conservatorship referral shall be made during the 14–day period of intensive treatment.

(b) If it appears that with up to 30 days additional treatment a person is likely to reconstitute sufficiently to obviate the need for appointment of a conservator, then the person may be certified for the additional 30 days.

(c) * * * When a conservatorship referral has not been made during the 14–day period and * * * it appears during the 30–day certification that the person is likely to require the appointment of a conservator, or when a conservatorship referral has not been made during the initial 30–day period and it appears during a second consecutive 30–day period of intensive treatment approved by a court pursuant to Section 5270.70 that the person is likely to require the appointment of a conservator, then the conservatorship referral shall be made to allow sufficient time for conservatorship investigation and other related procedures. If a temporary conservatorship is obtained, it shall run concurrently with and not consecutively to the 30–day certification period. The conservatorship hearing shall be held by the 30th day of the certification period. The maximum involuntary detention period for gravely disabled persons pursuant to Sections 5150, 5250, and 5270.15 shall be limited to 77 days. * * * This section * * * does not prevent a person from exercising * * * their right to a hearing as stated in Sections 5275 and 5353. *(Added by Stats.1988, c. 1517, § 10. Amended by Stats.2001, c. 854 (S.B.205), § 77; Stats.2022, c. 619 (S.B.1227), § 1, eff. Jan. 1, 2023.)*

Cross References

Conservatorship investigation defined for purposes of this Part, see Welfare and Institutions Code § 5008.
Evaluation defined for purposes of this Part, see Welfare and Institutions Code § 5008.
Intensive treatment defined for purposes of this Part, see Welfare and Institutions Code § 5008.
Referral defined for purposes of this Part, see Welfare and Institutions Code § 5008.

§ 5270.65. Permission for certified person to leave facility

Nothing in this article shall prohibit the professional person in charge of an intensive treatment facility, or a designee, from permitting a person certified for intensive treatment to leave the facility for short periods during the person's intensive treatment. *(Added by Stats.1988, c. 1517, § 10.)*

Cross References

Intensive treatment defined for purposes of this Part, see Welfare and Institutions Code § 5008.

§ 5270.70. Petition seeking approval for additional involuntary intensive treatment; notification of family or designated person; hearing and order; admissibility of findings in subsequent civil proceeding; 30-day limitation

(a) If, after 15 days of the 30–day period of intensive treatment pursuant to this article, but at least 7 days before expiration of the 30 days, the professional staff of the agency or facility treating the person finds that the person remains gravely disabled as a result of a mental disorder or impairment by chronic alcoholism and the person remains unwilling or unable to accept treatment voluntarily, the professional person in charge of the facility providing intensive treatment to the person may file a petition in the superior court for the county in which the facility providing intensive treatment is located, seeking approval for up to an additional 30 days of intensive treatment. The court shall immediately appoint the public defender or other attorney to represent the person in the hearing under this section, if that person does not already have counsel to represent them in the proceedings.

(b) Reasonable attempts shall be made by the mental health facility to notify family members or any other person designated by the patient of the time and place of the judicial review, unless the patient requests that this information not be provided. The patient shall be advised by the facility that is treating the patient that the patient has the right to request that this information not be provided.

(c)(1) The court shall either deny the petition or order an evidentiary hearing to be held within two court days after the petition is filed. The court may order that the person be held for up to an additional 30 days of intensive treatment if, at the evidentiary hearing, the court finds all of the following, based on the evidence presented:

(A) That the person, as a result of mental disorder or impairment by chronic alcoholism, is gravely disabled.

(B) That the person had been advised of the existence of, and has not accepted, voluntary treatment.

(C) That the facility providing intensive treatment is equipped and staffed to provide the required treatment and is designated by the county to provide intensive treatment [1]

(D) That the person is likely to benefit from continued treatment.

(2) If the court does not make all of the findings required by paragraph (1), the person shall be released no later than the expiration of the original 30–day period.

(d) A finding under this section shall not be admissible in evidence in any civil proceeding without the consent of the person who was the subject of the finding.

(e) In no event may a person be held beyond the original 30–day period of intensive treatment unless a court has determined that an additional period of up to 30 days of treatment is required, regardless of whether or not the court hearing has been set. *(Added by Stats.2022, c. 619 (S.B.1227), § 2, eff. Jan. 1, 2023.)*

[1] So in chaptered copy.

ARTICLE 5. JUDICIAL REVIEW

Section
5275. Habeas corpus; request for release.
5276. Jurisdiction and venue; counsel; order for evidentiary hearing; findings; release.
5276.1. Waiver of presence of physician, licensed psychologist, or other professional person; reception of certification of records.

§ 5275. Habeas corpus; request for release

Every person detained * * * under this part shall have a right to a hearing by writ of habeas corpus for * * * their release after they or * * * any person acting on * * * their behalf has made a request for release to either (a) the person delivering the copy of the notice of certification to the person certified at the time of the delivery, or (b) to any member of the treatment staff of the facility providing intensive treatment, at any time during * * * treatment pursuant to * * * this part.

Any person delivering a copy of the certification notice or any member of the treatment staff to whom a request for release is made shall promptly provide the person making the request for * * * their signature or mark a copy of the form set forth below. The person delivering the copy of the certification notice or the member of the treatment staff, as the case may be, shall fill in * * * their own name and the date, and, if the person signs by mark, shall fill in the person's name, and shall then deliver the completed copy to the professional person in charge of the intensive treatment facility, or * * * their designee, notifying * * * them of the request. As soon as possible, the person notified shall inform the superior court for the county in which the facility is located of the request for release.

Any person who intentionally violates this section is guilty of a misdemeanor.

The form for a request for release shall be substantially as follows:

(Name of the facility) ___ day of ____ 19__

I, ____ (member of the treatment staff, or person delivering the copy of the certification notice), have today received a request for the release of ____ (name of patient) from the undersigned patient on the patient's own behalf or from the undersigned person on behalf of the patient.

____
Signature or mark of patient making request for release

____
Signature or mark of person making request on behalf of patient

(Added by Stats.1967, c. 1667, p. 4074, § 36, operative July 1, 1969. Amended by Stats.1968, c. 1374, p. 2653, § 35, operative July 1, 1969; Stats.1969, c. 722, p. 1427, § 16.1, eff. Aug. 8, 1969, operative July 1, 1969; Stats.1988, c. 1517, § 11; Stats.2022, c. 960 (A.B.2275), § 4, eff. Jan. 1, 2023.)

Cross References

Certification review hearing, see Welfare and Institutions Code § 5256.
Confinement of outpatient pending proceeding for revocation of outpatient status, rights and notice of rights, see Welfare and Institutions Code § 5308.
Court defined for purposes of this Part, see Welfare and Institutions Code § 5008.
Detention by temporary conservator, right to review, see Welfare and Institutions Code § 5353.
Habeas corpus after commitment to state hospital, see Welfare and Institutions Code § 7250.
Habeas corpus proceedings in general, see Penal Code § 1473 et seq.
Information as to right to review by habeas corpus, see Welfare and Institutions Code § 5254.1.
Intensive treatment defined for purposes of this Part, see Welfare and Institutions Code § 5008.
Liability for intentional and unjustifiable interference with inmates' right to judicial determination of legality of confinement, see Government Code § 855.2.
Misdemeanor, see Penal Code §§ 17, 19, 19.2.
Notice of right to file request for release and to have hearing on request, see Welfare and Institutions Code § 5256.7.
Report of operation of division, see Welfare and Institutions Code § 5402.

Research References

5 Witkin, California Criminal Law 4th Criminal Trial § 813 (2021), Termination of Outpatient Status.

§ 5276. Jurisdiction and venue; counsel; order for evidentiary hearing; findings; release

Judicial review shall be in the superior court for the county in which the facility providing intensive treatment is located or in the county in which the 72–hour evaluation was conducted if the patient or a person acting in his or her behalf informs the professional staff of the evaluation facility (in writing) that judicial review will be sought. No patient shall be transferred from the county providing evaluation services to a different county for intensive treatment if the staff of the evaluation facility has been informed in writing that a judicial review will be sought, until the completion of the judicial review. The person requesting to be released shall be informed of his or her right to counsel by the member of the treatment staff and by the court; and, if he or she so elects, the court shall immediately appoint the public defender or other attorney to assist him or her in preparation of a petition for the writ of habeas corpus and, if he or she so elects, to represent him or her in the proceedings. The person shall pay the costs of the legal service if he or she is able.

Reasonable attempts shall be made by the mental health facility to notify family members or any other person designated by the patient, of the time and place of the judicial review, unless the patient requests that this information not be provided. The patient shall be advised by the facility that is treating the patient that he or she has the right to request that this information not be provided.

The court shall either release the person or order an evidentiary hearing to be held within two judicial days after the petition is filed. If the court finds, (a) that the person requesting release is not, as a result of mental disorder or impairment by chronic alcoholism, a danger to others, or to himself or herself, or gravely disabled, (b) that he or she had not been advised of, or had accepted, voluntary treatment, or (c) that the facility providing intensive treatment is not equipped and staffed to provide treatment, or is not designated by the county to provide intensive treatment he or she shall be released immediately. *(Added by Stats.1967, c. 1667, p. 4074, § 36, operative July 1, 1969. Amended by Stats.1968, c. 1374, p. 2654, § 37, operative July 1, 1969; Stats.1969, c. 722, p. 1428, § 17, eff. Aug. 8, 1969, operative July 1, 1969; Stats.1970, c. 1627, p. 3443, § 16; Stats.1971, c. 776, p. 1527, § 2; Stats.1986, c. 872, § 4.)*

Cross References

Advice as to right of counsel, see Welfare and Institutions Code §§ 5226, 5254.1, 5302.
Appointment of public defender or other attorney, see Welfare and Institutions Code §§ 5302, 5365.
Certification for intensive treatment, informing a person certified of right to counsel, see Welfare and Institutions Code § 5254.1.
Certification review hearing unless judicial review requested, see Welfare and Institutions Code § 5256.
Court defined for purposes of this Part, see Welfare and Institutions Code § 5008.
Evaluation defined for purposes of this Part, see Welfare and Institutions Code § 5008.
Finding under this section as evidence, see Welfare and Institutions Code § 5277.
Intensive treatment defined for purposes of this Part, see Welfare and Institutions Code § 5008.
Public defender, see Government Code § 27700 et seq.
Report of operation of division, see Welfare and Institutions Code § 5402.

Right to counsel in criminal cases, see Const. Art. 1, § 15, cl. 3; Penal Code § 686.
Writ of habeas corpus, see Penal Code § 1473 et seq.

§ 5276.1. Waiver of presence of physician, licensed psychologist, or other professional person; reception of certification of records

The person requesting release may, upon advice of counsel, waive the presence at the evidentiary hearing of the physician, licensed psychologist who meets the requirements of the first paragraph of Section 5251, or other professional person who certified the petition under Section 5251 and of the physician, or licensed psychologist who meets the requirements of the second paragraph of Section 5251, providing intensive treatment. In the event of such a waiver, such physician, licensed psychologist, or other professional person shall not be required to be present at the hearing if it is stipulated that the certification and records of such physicians, licensed psychologists, or other professional persons concerning the mental condition and treatment of the person regarding release will be received in evidence. *(Added by Stats.1971, c. 1162, p. 2221, § 2. Amended by Stats.1980, c. 1206, p. 4067, § 2.)*

Cross References

Intensive treatment defined for purposes of this Part, see Welfare and Institutions Code § 5008.

§ 5276.2. Certification review hearing upon withdrawal of request for judicial review; procedures

In the event that the person, or anyone acting on his or her behalf, withdraws the request for judicial review, a certification review hearing shall be held within four days of the withdrawal of the request, and the procedures in Sections 5255 to 5256.8, inclusive, shall be applicable. *(Added by Stats.1982, c. 1598, § 6.)*

§ 5277. Findings as evidence

A finding under Section 5276 shall not be admissible in evidence in any civil or criminal proceeding without the consent of the person who was the subject of the finding. *(Added by Stats.1967, c. 1667, p. 4074, § 36, operative July 1, 1969. Amended by Stats.1969, c. 722, p. 1428, § 18, eff. Aug. 8, 1969, operative July 1, 1969.)*

§ 5278. Exemption from liability

Individuals authorized under this part to detain a person for 72–hour treatment and evaluation pursuant to Article 1 (commencing with Section 5150) or Article 2 (commencing with Section 5200), or to certify a person for intensive treatment pursuant to Article 4 (commencing with Section 5250) or Article 4.5 (commencing with Section 5260) or Article 4.7 (commencing with Section 5270.10) or to file a petition for post-certification treatment for a person pursuant to Article 6 (commencing with Section 5300) shall not be held either criminally or civilly liable for exercising this authority in accordance with the law. *(Added by Stats.1967, c. 1667, p. 4074, § 36, operative July 1, 1969. Amended by Stats.1968, c. 1374, p. 2654, § 39, operative July 1, 1969; Stats.1969, c. 722, p. 1428, § 19, eff. Aug. 8, 1969, operative July 1, 1969; Stats.1988, c. 1517, § 12.)*

Cross References

Determinations according to law, public employees' exemption from liability, see Government Code § 856.
Evaluation defined for purposes of this Part, see Welfare and Institutions Code § 5008.
Intensive treatment defined for purposes of this Part, see Welfare and Institutions Code § 5008.
Liability for excessive detention, see Welfare and Institutions Code §§ 5259.1, 5265.
Liability for false application, see Welfare and Institutions Code § 5203.
Postcertification treatment defined for purposes of this Part, see Welfare and Institutions Code § 5008.
Similar provisions, see Welfare and Institutions Code §§ 5154, 5173, 5259.3, 5267, 5306.

ARTICLE 6. POSTCERTIFICATION PROCEDURES FOR IMMINENTLY DANGEROUS PERSONS

Section

§ 5300. Additional confinement; duration; grounds; necessity of and amenability to treatment

(a) At the expiration of the 14–day period of intensive treatment, a person may be confined for further treatment pursuant to the provisions of this article for an additional period, not to exceed 180 days if one of the following exists:

(1) The person has attempted, inflicted, or made a serious threat of substantial physical harm upon the person of another after having been taken into custody, and while in custody, for evaluation and treatment, and who, as a result of a mental health disorder, presents a demonstrated danger of inflicting substantial physical harm upon others.

(2) The person had attempted, or inflicted physical harm upon the person of another, that act having resulted in the person being taken into custody and who presents, as a result of a mental health disorder, a demonstrated danger of inflicting substantial physical harm upon others.

(3) The person had made a serious threat of substantial physical harm upon the person of another within seven days of being taken into custody, that threat having at least in part resulted in the person being taken into custody, and the person presents, as a result of a mental health disorder, a demonstrated danger of inflicting substantial physical harm upon others.

(b) A commitment to a licensed health facility under this article places an affirmative obligation on the facility to provide treatment for the underlying causes of the person's mental health disorder.

(c) Amenability to treatment is not required for a finding that a person is a person as described in paragraph (1), (2), or (3) of subdivision (a). Treatment programs need only be made available to these persons. Treatment does not mean that the treatment must be successful or potentially successful, and it does not mean that the person must recognize the person's problem and willingly participate in the treatment program. *(Added by Stats.1967, c. 1667, p. 4074, § 36, operative July 1, 1969. Amended by Stats.1968, c. 1374, p. 2655, § 41, operative July 1, 1969; Stats.1982, c. 1563, § 1; Stats.1983, c. 754, § 2; Stats.2019, c. 9 (A.B.46), § 22, eff. Jan. 1, 2020.)*

Cross References

Additional intensive treatment of suicidal persons, see Welfare and Institutions Code § 5260 et seq.
Certification for intensive treatment, see Welfare and Institutions Code § 5250 et seq.
Commitment of juvenile court wards, see Welfare and Institutions Code § 6551.
Consumers placed on involuntary psychiatric hold or Lanterman–Petris–Short conservatorship, notification to clients' rights advocate, see Welfare and Institutions Code § 4696.3.
Criminal matters, forwarding information to department of justice, see Welfare and Institutions Code § 5328.2.
Custody defined for purposes of this Article, see Welfare and Institutions Code § 5300.5.
Evaluation defined for purposes of this Part, see Welfare and Institutions Code § 5008.
Examination of prisoner by physician and remand to hospital, see Penal Code § 4011.6.
Intensive treatment defined for purposes of this Part, see Welfare and Institutions Code § 5008.
Termination of involuntary commitment, exception for imminently dangerous persons, see Welfare and Institutions Code § 5257.

Research References

5 Witkin, California Criminal Law 4th Criminal Trial § 802 (2021), Where Defendant Has Not Recovered.
3 Witkin, California Criminal Law 4th Punishment § 69 (2021), Right to Refuse Treatment.
3 Witkin, California Criminal Law 4th Punishment § 171 (2021), Commitment and Treatment.
3 Witkin, California Criminal Law 4th Punishment § 775 (2021), Right to Refuse Antipsychotic Medication.

§ 5300.5. "Custody" defined; necessity of conviction; demonstrated danger; determination

For purposes of this article:

(a) "Custody" shall be construed to mean involuntary detainment under the provisions of this part uninterrupted by any period of unconditioned release from a licensed health facility providing involuntary care and treatment.

(b) Conviction of a crime is not necessary for commitment under this article.

(c) Demonstrated danger may be based on assessment of present mental condition, which is based upon a consideration of past behavior of the person within six years prior to the time the person attempted, inflicted, or threatened physical harm upon another, and other relevant evidence. *(Added by Stats.1982, c. 1563, § 2. Amended by Stats.1983, c. 754, § 2.5.)*

§ 5301. Petition; time; contents; form; affidavits

(a) At any time during the 14–day intensive treatment period the professional person in charge of the licensed health facility, or his or her designee, may ask the public officer required by Section 5114 to present evidence at proceedings under this article to petition the superior court in the county in which the licensed health facility providing treatment is located for an order requiring the person to undergo an additional period of treatment on the grounds set forth in Section 5300. This petition shall summarize the facts that support the contention that the person falls within the standard set forth in Section 5300. The petition shall be supported by affidavits describing in detail the behavior that indicates that the person falls within the standard set forth in Section 5300.

(b) Copies of the petition for postcertification treatment and the affidavits in support thereof shall be served upon the person named in the petition on the same day as they are filed with the clerk of the superior court.

(c) The petition shall be in the following form:

Petition for Postcertification Treatment of a Dangerous Person

I, _________, (the professional person in charge of the _________ intensive treatment facility) (the designee of _________ the professional person in charge of the _________, treatment facility) in which _________ has been under treatment pursuant to the certification by _________ and _________, hereby petition the court for an order requiring _________ to undergo an additional period of treatment, not to exceed 180 days, pursuant to the provisions of Article 6 (commencing with Section 5300) of Chapter 2 of Part 1 of Division 5 of the Welfare and Institutions Code. This petition is based upon my allegation that (a) _________ has attempted, inflicted, or made a serious threat of substantial physical harm upon the person of another after having been taken into custody, and while in custody, for evaluation, and that, by reason of mental health disorder, presents a demonstrated danger of inflicting substantial physical harm upon others, or that (b) _________ had attempted or inflicted physical harm upon the person of another, that act having resulted in his or her being taken into custody, and that he or she presents, as a result of mental health disorder, a demonstrated danger of inflicting substantial physical harm upon others, or that (c) _________ had made a serious threat of substantial physical harm upon the person of another within seven days of being taken into custody, that threat having at least in part resulted in his or her being taken into custody, and that he or she presents, as a result of mental health disorder, a demonstrated danger of inflicting substantial physical harm upon others.

My allegation is based upon the following facts:

____
____
____
____
____
____
____

This allegation is supported by the accompanying affidavits signed by _________.

Signed ____________________

(d) The courts may receive the affidavits in evidence and may allow the affidavits to be read to the jury and the contents thereof considered in rendering a verdict, unless counsel for the person named in the petition subpoenas the treating professional person. If the treating professional person is subpoenaed to testify, the public officer, pursuant to Section 5114, shall be entitled to a continuance of the hearing or trial. *(Added by Stats.1967, c. 1667, p. 4074, § 36, operative July 1, 1969. Amended by Stats.1968, c. 1374, p. 2656, § 42, operative July 1, 1969; Stats.1982, c. 1563, § 3; Stats.1983, c. 754, § 2.7; Stats.2014, c. 144 (A.B.1847), § 90, eff. Jan. 1, 2015.)*

Cross References

Court defined for purposes of this Part, see Welfare and Institutions Code § 5008.

Custody defined for purposes of this Article, see Welfare and Institutions Code § 5300.5.
Evaluation defined for purposes of this Part, see Welfare and Institutions Code § 5008.
Intensive treatment defined for purposes of this Part, see Welfare and Institutions Code § 5008.
Postcertification treatment defined for purposes of this Part, see Welfare and Institutions Code § 5008.

§ 5302. Attorney for patient; appointment; jury trial

At the time of filing of a petition for postcertification treatment the court shall advise the person named in the petition of his right to be represented by an attorney and of his right to demand a jury trial. The court shall assist him in finding an attorney, or, if need be, appoint an attorney if the person is unable to obtain counsel. The court shall appoint the public defender or other attorney to represent the person named in the petition if the person is financially unable to provide his own attorney. The attorney shall advise the person of his rights in relation to the proceeding and shall represent him before the court. *(Added by Stats.1967, c. 1667, p. 4074, § 36, operative July 1, 1969. Amended by Stats.1968, c. 1374, p. 2657, § 43.5, operative July 1, 1969; Stats.1969, c. 722, p. 1428, § 20, eff. Aug. 8, 1969, operative July 1, 1969; Stats.1970, c. 1627, p. 3443, § 17.)*

Cross References

Advice as to right of counsel, see Welfare and Institutions Code §§ 5226, 5254.1, 5276.
Appointment of public defender or other attorney, see Welfare and Institutions Code §§ 5276, 5365.
Court defined for purposes of this Part, see Welfare and Institutions Code § 5008.
Postcertification treatment defined for purposes of this Part, see Welfare and Institutions Code § 5008.
Public defender, see Government Code § 27700 et seq.
Right to counsel in criminal cases, see Const. Art. 1, § 15, cl. 3; Penal Code § 686.

§ 5303. Time for hearing; due process; jury trial; continuation of treatment

The court shall conduct the proceedings on the petition for postcertification treatment within four judicial days of the filing of the petition and in accordance with constitutional guarantees of due process of law and the procedures required under Section 13 of Article 1 of the Constitution of the State of California.

If at the time of the hearing the person named in the petition requests a jury trial, such trial shall commence within 10 judicial days of the filing of the petition for postcertification treatment unless the person's attorney requests a continuance, which may be for a maximum of 10 additional judicial days. The decision of the jury must be unanimous in order to support the finding of facts required by Section 5304.

Until a final decision on the merits by the trial court the person named in the petition shall continue to be treated in the intensive treatment facility until released by order of the superior court having jurisdiction over the action, or unless the petition for postcertification treatment is withdrawn. If no decision has been made within 30 days after the filing of the petition, not including extensions of time requested by the person's attorney, the person shall be released. *(Added by Stats.1967, c. 1667, p. 4074, § 36, operative July 1, 1969. Amended by Stats.1968, c. 1374, p. 2657, § 44, operative July 1, 1969.)*

Cross References

Cost reimbursement to county furnishing services from county of residence, see Welfare and Institutions Code § 5110.
Court defined for purposes of this Part, see Welfare and Institutions Code § 5008.
Intensive treatment defined for purposes of this Part, see Welfare and Institutions Code § 5008.
Jury trial, see Const. Art. 1, § 16.
Postcertification treatment defined for purposes of this Part, see Welfare and Institutions Code § 5008.

§ 5303.1. Hearing or jury trial; appointment of forensic psychiatrist or psychologist; testimony; waiver of presence of professional or designee and physician; reception of documents

For the purposes of any hearing or jury trial held pursuant to this article, the judge of the court in which such hearing or trial is held may appoint a psychiatrist or psychologist with forensic skills. Such psychiatrist or psychologist shall personally examine the person named in the petition. Such a forensic psychiatrist or psychologist shall testify at the hearing or jury trial concerning the mental condition of the person named in the petition and the threat of substantial physical harm to other beings such person presents, and neither the professional person or his designee who petitioned for the additional period of treatment nor of the physicians providing intensive treatment shall be required, unless the person named in the petition chooses to subpoena such persons, to be present at the hearing or jury trial.

If a psychiatrist or psychologist with forensic skills is not appointed pursuant to this section the person named in the petition may, upon advice of counsel, waive the presence at the hearing or at the jury trial of the professional person or his designee who petitioned for the additional period of treatment and the physicians providing intensive treatment. In the event of such waiver, such professional person, his designee, or other physicians shall not be required to be present at the hearing if it is stipulated that the certification, supporting affidavit and records of such physicians concerning the mental condition of the person named in the petition will be received in evidence. *(Added by Stats.1971, c. 1162, p. 2221, § 3. Amended by Stats.1975, c. 960, p. 2244, § 5.)*

Cross References

Affidavits, see Code of Civil Procedure § 2009 et seq.
Compelling the attendance of witnesses, see Penal Code § 1326 et seq.
Court defined for purposes of this Part, see Welfare and Institutions Code § 5008.
Intensive treatment defined for purposes of this Part, see Welfare and Institutions Code § 5008.
Jury trial, see Const. Art. 1, § 16.
Right to counsel, see Const. Art. 1, § 15, cl. 3; Penal Code § 686.
Subpoena, see Code of Civil Procedure §§ 1985 et seq., 1986.

§ 5304. Remand for additional treatment; duration; new petition

(a) The court shall remand a person named in the petition for postcertification treatment to the custody of the State Department of State Hospitals or to a licensed health facility designated by the county of residence of that person for a further period of intensive treatment, not to exceed 180 days from the date of court judgment, if the court or jury finds that the person named in the petition for postcertification treatment has done any of the following:

(1) Attempted, inflicted, or made a serious threat of substantial physical harm upon the person of another after having been taken into custody, and while in custody, for evaluation and treatment, and who, as a result of mental health disorder, presents a demonstrated danger of inflicting substantial physical harm upon others.

(2) Attempted or inflicted physical harm upon the person of another, that act having resulted in his or her being taken into custody, and who, as a result of mental health disorder, presents a demonstrated danger of inflicting substantial physical harm upon others.

(3) Expressed a serious threat of substantial physical harm upon the person of another within seven days of being taken into custody, that threat having at least in part resulted in his or her being taken into custody, and who presents, as a result of mental health disorder, a demonstrated danger of inflicting substantial physical harm upon others.

(b) The person shall be released from involuntary treatment at the expiration of 180 days unless the public officer, pursuant to Section 5114, files a new petition for postcertification treatment on the grounds that he or she has attempted, inflicted, or made a serious threat of substantial physical harm upon another during his or her period of postcertification treatment, and he or she is a person who by reason of mental health disorder, presents a demonstrated danger of inflicting substantial physical harm upon others. The new petition for postcertification treatment shall be filed in the superior court in which the original petition for postcertification was filed.

(c) The county from which the person was remanded shall bear any transportation costs incurred pursuant to this section. *(Added by Stats.1983, c. 754, § 4. Amended by Stats.2012, c. 440 (A.B.1488), § 62, eff. Sept. 22, 2012; Stats.2014, c. 144 (A.B.1847), § 91, eff. Jan. 1, 2015.)*

Cross References

Court defined for purposes of this Part, see Welfare and Institutions Code § 5008.

Custody defined for purposes of this Article, see Welfare and Institutions Code § 5300.5.

Evaluation defined for purposes of this Part, see Welfare and Institutions Code § 5008.

Intensive treatment defined for purposes of this Part, see Welfare and Institutions Code § 5008.

Postcertification treatment defined for purposes of this Part, see Welfare and Institutions Code § 5008.

§ 5305. Outpatient status; qualifications; notice of outpatient treatment plan; effective date of plan; hearing; outpatient supervision; reports

(a) Any person committed pursuant to Section 5300 may be placed on outpatient status if all of the following conditions are satisfied:

(1) In the evaluation of the superintendent or professional person in charge of the licensed health facility, the person named in the petition will no longer be a danger to the health and safety of others while on outpatient status and will benefit from outpatient status.

(2) The county behavioral health director advises the court that the person named in the petition will benefit from outpatient status and identifies an appropriate program of supervision and treatment.

(b) After actual notice to the public officer, pursuant to Section 5114, and to counsel of the person named in the petition, to the court and to the county behavioral health director, the plan for outpatient treatment shall become effective within five judicial days unless a court hearing on that action is requested by any of the aforementioned parties, in which case the release on outpatient status shall not take effect until approved by the court after a hearing. This hearing shall be held within five judicial days of the actual notice required by this subdivision.

(c) The county behavioral health director shall be the outpatient supervisor of persons placed on outpatient status under this section. The county behavioral health director may delegate outpatient supervision responsibility to a designee.

(d) The outpatient treatment supervisor shall, when the person is placed on outpatient status at least three months, submit at 90-day intervals to the court, the public officer, pursuant to Section 5114, and counsel of the person named in the petition and to the supervisor or professional person in charge of the licensed health facility, when appropriate, a report setting forth the status and progress of the person named in the petition. Notwithstanding the length of the outpatient status, a final report shall be submitted by the outpatient treatment supervisor at the conclusion of the 180-day commitment setting forth the status and progress of the person. *(Added by Stats.1967, c. 1667, p. 4074, § 36, operative July 1, 1969. Amended by Stats.1968, c. 1374, p. 2658, § 45.5, operative July 1, 1969; Stats.1982, c. 1563, § 5; Stats.2015, c. 455 (S.B.804), § 22, eff. Jan. 1, 2016.)*

Cross References

Court approval for subsequent release require after approval of confinement, see Welfare and Institutions Code § 5308.

Court defined for purposes of this Part, see Welfare and Institutions Code § 5008.

Evaluation defined for purposes of this Part, see Welfare and Institutions Code § 5008.

§ 5306. Exemption from liability

(a) Notwithstanding Section 5113, if the provisions of Section 5309 have been met, the superintendent, the professional person in charge of the hospital providing 90-day involuntary treatment, the medical director of the facility or his or her designee described in subdivision (a) of Section 5309, and the psychiatrist directly responsible for the person's treatment shall not be held civilly or criminally liable for any action by a person released before the end of a 90-day period pursuant to this article.

(b) The superintendent, the professional person in charge of the hospital providing 90-day involuntary treatment, the medical director of the facility or his or her designee described in subdivision (a) of Section 5309, and the psychiatrist directly responsible for the person's treatment shall not be held civilly or criminally liable for any action by a person released at the end of a 90-day period pursuant to this article. *(Added by Stats.1967, c. 1667, p. 4074, § 36, operative July 1, 1969. Amended by Stats.1968, c. 1374, p. 2659, § 46, operative July 1, 1969; Stats.1985, c. 1288, § 11, eff. Sept. 30, 1985.)*

Cross References

Determination according to law, public employees' exemption from liability, see Government Code § 856.

Liability for excessive detention, see Welfare and Institutions Code §§ 5259.1, 5265.

Liability for false application, see Welfare and Institutions Code § 5203.

Similar provisions, see Welfare and Institutions Code §§ 5154, 5173, 5259.3, 5267, 5278.

§ 5306.5. Request for outpatient status revocation; copy of request; hearing; order for confinement and revocation

(a) If at any time during the outpatient period, the outpatient treatment supervisor is of the opinion that the person receiving treatment requires extended inpatient treatment or refuses to accept further outpatient treatment and supervision, the county behavioral health director shall notify the superior court in either the county that approved outpatient status or in the county where outpatient treatment is being provided of that opinion by means of a written request for revocation of outpatient status. The county behavioral health director shall furnish a copy of this request to the counsel of the person named in the request for revocation and to the public officer, pursuant to Section 5114, in both counties if the request is made in the county of treatment, rather than the county of commitment.

(b) Within 15 judicial days, the court where the request was filed shall hold a hearing and shall either approve or disapprove the request for revocation of outpatient status. If the court approves the request for revocation, the court shall order that the person be confined in a state hospital or other treatment facility approved by the county behavioral health director. The court shall transmit a copy of its order to the county behavioral health director or a designee and to the Director of State Hospitals. When the county of treatment and the county of commitment differ and revocation occurs in the county of treatment, the court shall enter the name of the committing county and its case number on the order of revocation and shall send a copy of the order to the committing court and the public officer, pursuant to Section 5114, and counsel of the person named in the request for revocation in the county of commitment. *(Added by Stats.1982, c. 1563, § 6. Amended by Stats.2012, c. 24 (A.B.1470), § 125, eff. June 27, 2012; Stats.2015, c. 455 (S.B.804), § 23, eff. Jan. 1, 2016.)*

Cross References

Court defined for purposes of this Part, see Welfare and Institutions Code § 5008.

§ 5307. Petition for hearing to determine whether outpatient should be continued on such status; notice; body attachment order of confinement

If at any time during the outpatient period the public officer, pursuant to Section 5114, is of the opinion that the person is a danger to the health and safety of others while on outpatient status, the public officer, pursuant to Section 5114, may petition the court for a hearing to determine whether the person shall be continued on outpatient status. Upon receipt of the petition, the court shall calendar the case for further proceedings within 15 judicial days and the clerk shall notify the person, the county behavioral health director, and the attorney of record for the person of the hearing date. Upon failure of the person to appear as noticed, if a proper affidavit of service and advisement has been filed with the court, the court may issue a body attachment for that person. If, after a hearing in court the judge determines that the person is a danger to the health and safety of others, the court shall order that the person be confined in a state hospital or other treatment facility that has been approved by the county behavioral health director. *(Added by Stats.1982, c. 1563, § 7. Amended by Stats.2015, c. 455 (S.B.804), § 24, eff. Jan. 1, 2016.)*

Cross References

Court defined for purposes of this Part, see Welfare and Institutions Code § 5008.

§ 5308. Confinement of outpatient pending proceeding for revocation of outpatient status; taking into custody and transporting outpatient; notice; review; subsequent release

Upon the filing of a request for revocation of outpatient status under Section 5306.5 or 5307 and pending the court's decision on revocation, the person subject to revocation may be confined in a state hospital or other treatment facility by the county behavioral health director when it is the opinion of that director that the person will now be a danger to self or to another while on outpatient status and that to delay hospitalization until the revocation hearing would pose a demonstrated danger of harm to the person or to another. Upon the request of the county behavioral health director or a designee, a peace officer shall take, or cause to be taken, the person into custody and transport the person to a treatment facility for hospitalization under this section. The county behavioral health director shall notify the court in writing of the admission of the person to inpatient status and of the factual basis for the opinion that immediate return to inpatient treatment was necessary. The court shall supply a copy of these documents to the public officer, pursuant to Section 5114, and counsel of the person subject to revocation.

A person hospitalized under this section shall have the right to judicial review of the detention in the manner prescribed in Article 5 (commencing with Section 5275) of Chapter 2 and to an explanation of rights in the manner prescribed in Section 5252.1.

Nothing in this section shall prevent hospitalization pursuant to the provisions of Section 5150, 5250, 5350, or 5353.

A person whose confinement in a treatment facility under Section 5306.5 or 5307 is approved by the court shall not be released again to outpatient status unless court approval is obtained under Section 5305. *(Added by Stats.1982, c. 1563, § 8. Amended by Stats.2015, c. 455 (S.B.804), § 25, eff. Jan. 1, 2016.)*

Cross References

Court defined for purposes of this Part, see Welfare and Institutions Code § 5008.
Custody defined for purposes of this Article, see Welfare and Institutions Code § 5300.5.
Peace officer defined for purposes of this Part, see Welfare and Institutions Code § 5008.

§ 5309. Release prior to expiration of commitment period; grounds; plan for unconditional release; notice; effective date; approval after hearing

(a) Nothing in this article shall prohibit the superintendent or professional person in charge of the hospital in which the person is being involuntarily treated from releasing him or her from treatment prior to the expiration of the commitment period when, the psychiatrist directly responsible for the person's treatment believes, as a result of his or her personal observations, that the person being involuntarily treated no longer constitutes a demonstrated danger of substantial physical harm to others. If any other professional person who is authorized to release the person, believes the person should be released prior to the expiration of the commitment period, and the psychiatrist directly responsible for the person's treatment objects, the matter shall be referred to the medical director of the facility for the final decision. However, if the medical director is not a psychiatrist, he or she shall appoint a designee who is a psychiatrist. If the matter is referred, the person shall be released prior to the expiration of the commitment period only if the psychiatrist making the final decision believes, as a result of his or her personal observations, that the person being involuntarily treated no longer constitutes a demonstrated danger of substantial physical harm to others.

(b) After actual notice to the public officer, pursuant to Section 5114, and to counsel of the person named in the petition, to the court, and to the county mental health director, the plan for unconditional release shall become effective within five judicial days unless a court hearing on that action is requested by any of the aforementioned parties, in which case the unconditional release shall not take effect until approved by the court after a hearing. This hearing shall be held within five judicial days of the actual notice required by this subdivision. *(Added by Stats.1982, c. 1563, § 9. Amended by Stats.1985, c. 1288, § 12, eff. Sept. 30, 1985.)*

Cross References

Court defined for purposes of this Part, see Welfare and Institutions Code § 5008.

ARTICLE 7. LEGAL AND CIVIL RIGHTS OF PERSONS INVOLUNTARILY DETAINED

Section

§ 5325. List of rights; posting; waiver

Each person involuntarily detained for evaluation or treatment under provisions of this part, and each person admitted as a voluntary patient for psychiatric evaluation or treatment to any health facility, as defined in Section 1250 of the Health and Safety Code, in which psychiatric evaluation or treatment is offered, shall have the following rights, a list of which shall be prominently posted in the predominant languages of the community and explained in a language or modality accessible to the patient in all facilities providing those services, and otherwise brought to his or her attention by any additional means as the Director of Health Care Services may designate by regulation. Each person committed to a state hospital shall also have the following rights, a list of which shall be prominently posted in the predominant languages of the community and explained in a language or modality accessible to the patient in all facilities providing those services and otherwise brought to his or her attention by any additional means as the Director of State Hospitals may designate by regulation:

(a) To wear his or her own clothes; to keep and use his or her own personal possessions including his or her toilet articles; and to keep and be allowed to spend a reasonable sum of his or her own money for canteen expenses and small purchases.

(b) To have access to individual storage space for his or her private use.

(c) To see visitors each day.

(d) To have reasonable access to telephones, both to make and receive confidential calls or to have such calls made for them.

(e) To have ready access to letterwriting materials, including stamps, and to mail and receive unopened correspondence.

(f) To refuse convulsive treatment including, but not limited to, any electroconvulsive treatment, any treatment of the mental condition which depends on the induction of a convulsion by any means, and insulin coma treatment.

(g) To refuse psychosurgery. Psychosurgery is defined as those operations currently referred to as lobotomy, psychiatric surgery, and behavioral surgery, and all other forms of brain surgery if the surgery is performed for the purpose of any of the following:

(1) Modification or control of thoughts, feelings, actions, or behavior rather than the treatment of a known and diagnosed physical disease of the brain.

(2) Modification of normal brain function or normal brain tissue in order to control thoughts, feelings, actions, or behavior.

(3) Treatment of abnormal brain function or abnormal brain tissue in order to modify thoughts, feelings, actions or behavior when the abnormality is not an established cause for those thoughts, feelings, actions, or behavior.

Psychosurgery does not include prefrontal sonic treatment wherein there is no destruction of brain tissue. The Director of Health Care Services and the Director of State Hospitals shall promulgate appropriate regulations to assure adequate protection of patients' rights in such treatment.

(h) To see and receive the services of a patient advocate who has no direct or indirect clinical or administrative responsibility for the person receiving mental health services.

(i) Other rights, as specified by regulation.

Each patient shall also be given notification in a language or modality accessible to the patient of other constitutional and statutory rights which are found by the State Department of Health Care Services and the State Department of State Hospitals to be frequently misunderstood, ignored, or denied.

Upon admission to a facility each patient, involuntarily detained for evaluation or treatment under provisions of this part, or as a voluntary patient for psychiatric evaluation or treatment to a health facility, as defined in Section 1250 of the Health and Safety Code, in which psychiatric evaluation or treatment is offered, shall immediately be given a copy of a State Department of Health Care Services prepared patients' rights handbook. Each person committed to a state hospital, upon admission, shall immediately be given a copy of a State Department of State Hospitals prepared patients' rights handbook.

The State Department of Health Care Services and the State Department of State Hospitals shall prepare and provide the forms specified in this section. The State Department of Health Care Services shall prepare and provide the forms specified in Section 5157.

The rights specified in this section may not be waived by the person's parent, guardian, or conservator. *(Added by Stats.1972, c. 1055, p. 1940, § 3, operative July 1, 1973. Amended by Stats.1974, c. 1534, p. 3459, § 1; Stats.1976, c. 1109, p. 4992, § 1.5; Stats.1977, c. 1252, p. 4570, § 561, operative July 1, 1978; Stats.1977, c. 1021, p. 3060, § 2; Stats.1978, c. 429, p. 1454, § 206, eff. July 17, 1978, operative July 1, 1978; Stats.1981, c. 841, p. 3231, § 2; Stats.2012, c. 448 (A.B.2370), § 52; Stats.2012, c. 457 (S.B.1381), § 52; Stats.2012, c. 34 (S.B.1009), § 85, eff. June 27, 2012.)*

Cross References

Conservatees, retention of rights specified in this section, see Welfare and Institutions Code § 5357.
Convulsive treatment, conditions for administering, see Welfare and Institutions Code § 5326.7.
Developmentally disabled persons in state hospital or community care facility, rights, see Welfare and Institutions Code § 4503.
Discrimination or retaliation against participants in judicial proceedings prohibited, see Welfare and Institutions Code § 5550.
Evaluation defined for purposes of this Part, see Welfare and Institutions Code § 5008.
State Department of Mental Health, see Welfare and Institutions Code § 4000 et seq.

Research References

5 Witkin, California Criminal Law 4th Criminal Trial § 813 (2021), Termination of Outpatient Status.
3 Witkin, California Criminal Law 4th Punishment § 775 (2021), Right to Refuse Antipsychotic Medication.

§ 5325.1. Same rights and responsibilities guaranteed others; discrimination by programs or activities receiving public funds; additional rights

Persons with mental illness have the same legal rights and responsibilities guaranteed all other persons by the Federal Constitution and laws and the Constitution and laws of the State of California, unless specifically limited by federal or state law or regulations. No otherwise qualified person by reason of having been involuntarily detained for evaluation or treatment under provisions of this part or having been admitted as a voluntary patient to any health facility, as defined in Section 1250 of the Health and Safety Code, in which psychiatric evaluation or treatment is offered shall be excluded from participation in, be denied the benefits of, or be subjected to discrimination under any program or activity, which receives public funds.

It is the intent of the legislature that persons with mental illness shall have rights including, but not limited to, the following:

(a) A right to treatment services which promote the potential of the person to function independently. Treatment should be provided in ways that are least restrictive of the personal liberty of the individual.

(b) A right to dignity, privacy, and humane care.

(c) A right to be free from harm, including unnecessary or excessive physical restraint, isolation, medication, abuse, or neglect. Medication shall not be used as punishment, for the convenience of staff, as a substitute for program, or in quantities that interfere with the treatment program.

(d) A right to prompt medical care and treatment.

(e) A right to religious freedom and practice.

(f) A right to participate in appropriate programs of publicly supported education.

(g) A right to social interaction and participation in community activities.

(h) A right to physical exercise and recreational opportunities.

(i) A right to be free from hazardous procedures. *(Added by Stats.1978, c. 1320, p. 4319, § 1.)*

Cross References

Evaluation defined for purposes of this Part, see Welfare and Institutions Code § 5008.
Rights of developmentally disabled persons in state hospital or community care facility, see Welfare and Institutions Code § 4503.
Violation of patient's rights, penalties, see Welfare and Institutions Code § 5326.9.

§ 5325.2. Persons subject to detention pursuant to §§ 5150, 5250, 5260, 5270.15; right to refuse antipsychotic medication

Any person who is subject to detention pursuant to Section 5150, 5250, 5260, or 5270.15 shall have the right to refuse treatment with antipsychotic medication subject to provisions set forth in this chapter. *(Added by Stats.1991, c. 681 (S.B.665), § 2.)*

Cross References

Antipsychotic medication defined for purposes of this Part, see Welfare and Institutions Code § 5008.

§ 5325.3. Administration of antipsychotic medications; signature not required; written records of informed consent; implementation

(a) For purposes of administering antipsychotic medications to a person admitted as a voluntary patient, as described in Section 850 of Title 9 of the California Code of Regulations, or any successor regulation, who consents to receiving those medications, as part of specialty mental health services covered under Medi-Cal or as part of community mental health services, a health facility, or a facility that has a community residential treatment program pursuant to Article 1 (commencing with Section 5670) of Chapter 2.5 of Part 2, shall not be required to obtain the signature of that patient.

(b) For a patient described in subdivision (a), the facility shall maintain a written record containing both of the following:

(1) A notation that the information about informed consent to antipsychotic medications as described in subdivisions (a) to (f), inclusive, of Section 851 of Title 9 of the California Code of Regulations, or any successor regulations, has been discussed with the patient by the prescribing physician.

(2) A notation that the patient understands the nature and effect of the antipsychotic medications and consents to the administration of those medications.

(c) For purposes of this section, "health facility" has the same meaning as set forth in Section 1250 of the Health and Safety Code, except for subdivisions (c), (d), (e), (g), (h), (k), and (m) of that section.

(d)(1) Notwithstanding Chapter 3.5 (commencing with Section 11340) of Part 1 of Division 3 of Title 2 of the Government Code, the State Department of Health Care Services may implement, interpret, or make specific this section, in whole or in part, by means of information notices or other similar instructions, without taking any further regulatory action. The notice or other similar instruction shall supersede Section 852 of Title 9 of the California Code of Regulations.

(2) The department may amend, adopt, or repeal regulations for purposes of implementing this section in accordance with the requirements of Chapter 3.5 (commencing with Section 11340) of Part 1 of Division 3 of Title 2 of the Government Code. *(Added by Stats.2022, c. 47 (S.B.184), § 58, eff. June 30, 2022.)*

§ 5326. Denial of rights; cause; record

The professional person in charge of the facility or state hospital or his or her designee may, for good cause, deny a person any of the rights under Section 5325, except under subdivisions (g) and (h) and the rights under subdivision (f) may be denied only under the conditions specified in Section 5326.7. To ensure that these rights are denied only for good cause, the Director of Health Care Services and Director of State Hospitals shall adopt regulations specifying the conditions under which they may be denied. Denial of a person's rights shall in all cases be entered into the person's treatment record. *(Added by Stats.1967, c. 1667, p. 4074, § 36, operative July 1, 1969. Amended by Stats.1971, c. 1593, p. 3341, § 376, operative July 1, 1973; Stats.1973, c. 959, p. 1804, § 1; Stats.1974, c. 1534, p. 3460, § 2; Stats.1976, c. 1109, p. 4993, § 2; Stats.1977, c. 1252, p. 4571, § 562, operative July 1, 1978; Stats.1981, c. 841, p. 3232, § 3; Stats.2012, c. 34 (S.B.1009), § 86, eff. June 27, 2012.)*

Cross References

Rights of developmentally disabled persons in state hospital or community care facility, see Welfare and Institutions Code § 4503.

§ 5326.1. Reports; number of persons denied rights; availability of information

Quarterly, each local mental health director shall furnish to the Director of Health Care Services, the facility reports of the number of persons whose rights were denied and the right or rights which were denied. The content of the reports from facilities shall enable the local mental health director and Director of Health Care Services to identify individual treatment records, if necessary, for further analysis and investigation. These quarterly reports, except for the identity of the person whose rights are denied, shall be available, upon request, to Members of the State Legislature, or a member of a county board of supervisors.

Notwithstanding any other provision of law, information pertaining to denial of rights contained in the person's treatment record shall be made available, on request, to the person, his or her attorney, his or her conservator or guardian, the local mental health director, or his or her designee, or the Patients' Rights program of the State Department of Health Care Services. The information may include consent forms, required documentation for convulsive treatment, documentation regarding the use of restraints and seclusion, physician's orders, nursing notes, and involuntary detention and conservatorship papers. The information, except for the identity of the person whose rights are denied, shall be made available to the Members of the State Legislature or a member of a county board of supervisors. *(Added by Stats.1976, c. 1109, p. 4993, § 2.5. Amended by Stats.1977, c. 1252, p. 4571, § 563, operative July 1, 1978; Stats.1981, c. 841, p. 3233, § 4; Stats.1983, c. 101, § 169; Stats.2012, c. 34 (S.B.1009), § 87, eff. June 27, 2012.)*

§ 5326.15. Reports; persons receiving treatment; categories

(a) Quarterly, any doctor or facility which administers convulsive treatments or psychosurgery, shall report to the local mental health director, who shall transmit a copy to the Director of Health Care Services, the number of persons who received such treatments wherever administered, in each of the following categories:

(1) Involuntary patients who gave informed consent.

(2) Involuntary patients who were deemed incapable of giving informed consent and received convulsive treatment against their will.

(3) Voluntary patients who gave informed consent.

(4) Voluntary patients deemed incapable of giving consent.

(b) Quarterly, the State Department of State Hospitals shall report to the Director of Health Care Services the number of persons who received such treatments wherever administered, in each of the following categories:

(1) Involuntary patients who gave informed consent.

(2) Involuntary patients who were deemed incapable of giving informed consent and received convulsive treatment against their will.

(3) Voluntary patients who gave informed consent.

(4) Voluntary patients deemed incapable of giving consent.

(c) Quarterly, the Director of Health Care Services shall forward to the Medical Board of California any records or information received from these reports indicating violation of the law, and the regulations which have been adopted thereto. *(Added by Stats.1976, c. 1109, p. 4994, § 3. Amended by Stats.1977, c. 1252, p. 4572, § 564, operative July 1, 1978; Stats.1989, c. 886, § 102; Stats.1992, c. 713 (A.B.3564), § 41, eff. Sept. 15, 1992; Stats.2012, c. 34 (S.B.1009), § 88, eff. June 27, 2012.)*

§ 5326.2. Voluntary informed consent; information to be given to patient

To constitute voluntary informed consent, the following information shall be given to the patient in a clear and explicit manner:

(a) The reason for treatment, that is, the nature and seriousness of the patient's illness, disorder or defect.

(b) The nature of the procedures to be used in the proposed treatment, including its probable frequency and duration.

(c) The probable degree and duration (temporary or permanent) of improvement or remission, expected with or without such treatment.

(d) The nature, degree, duration, and the probability of the side effects and significant risks, commonly known by the medical profession, of such treatment, including its adjuvants, especially noting the degree and duration of memory loss (including its irreversibility) and how and to what extent they may be controlled, if at all.

(e) That there exists a division of opinion as to the efficacy of the proposed treatment, why and how it works and its commonly known risks and side effects.

(f) The reasonable alternative treatments, and why the physician is recommending this particular treatment.

(g) That the patient has the right to accept or refuse the proposed treatment, and that if he or she consents, has the right to revoke his or her consent for any reason, at any time prior to or between treatments. *(Added by Stats.1976, c. 1109, p. 4994, § 3.5.)*

Cross References

Penalty for violation of this section to § 5326.8, see Welfare and Institutions Code § 5326.9.

Violation of section by physician as unprofessional conduct, see Business and Professions Code § 2256.

§ 5326.3. Written consent form; contents

The State Department of Health Care Services and State Department of State Hospitals shall promulgate a standard written consent form, setting forth clearly and in detail the matters listed in Section 5326.2, and any further information with respect to each item as deemed generally appropriate to all patients.

The treating physician shall utilize the standard written consent form and in writing supplement it with those details which pertain to the particular patient being treated. *(Added by Stats.1974, c. 1534, p. 3460, § 3. Amended by Stats.1976, c. 1109, p. 4995, § 4; Stats.1977, c. 1252, p. 4572, § 565, operative July 1, 1978; Stats.2012, c. 34 (S.B.1009), § 89, eff. June 27, 2012.)*

Cross References

Developmentally disabled persons refusing psychosurgery, see Welfare and Institutions Code § 4503.

§ 5326.4. Supplemented written consent form; oral explanation by physician; entry on record

The treating physician shall then present to the patient the supplemented form specified under Section 5326.3 and orally, clearly, and in detail explain all of the above information to the patient. The treating physician shall then administer the execution by the patient of the total supplemented written consent form, which shall be dated and witnessed.

The fact of the execution of such written consent form and of the oral explanation shall be entered into the patient's treatment record, as shall be a copy of the consent form itself. Should entry of such latter information into the patient's treatment record be deemed by any court an unlawful invasion of privacy, then such consent form shall be maintained in a confidential manner and place.

The consent form shall be available to the person, and to his or her attorney, guardian, and conservator and, if the patient consents, to a responsible relative of the patient's choosing. *(Added by Stats.1974, c. 1534, p. 3462, § 4. Amended by Stats.1976, c. 1109, p. 4995, § 5.)*

Cross References

Court defined for purposes of this Part, see Welfare and Institutions Code § 5008.

Inspection of public records, other exemptions from disclosure, see Government Code § 6276.30.

§ 5326.5. Written informed consent; definition; when given

(a) For purposes of this chapter, "written informed consent" means that a person knowingly and intelligently, without duress or coercion, clearly and explicitly manifests consent to the proposed therapy to the treating physician and in writing on the standard consent form prescribed in Section 5326.4.

(b) The physician may urge the proposed treatment as the best one, but may not use, in an effort to gain consent, any reward or threat, express or implied, nor any other form of inducement or coercion, including, but not limited to, placing the patient in a more restricted setting, transfer of the patient to another facility, or loss of the patient's hospital privileges. Nothing in this subdivision shall be construed as in conflict with Section 5326.2. No one shall be denied any benefits for refusing treatment.

(c) A person confined shall be deemed incapable of written informed consent if that person cannot understand, or knowingly and intelligently act upon, the information specified in Section 5326.2.

(d) A person confined shall not be deemed incapable of refusal solely by virtue of being diagnosed as having a mental health disorder.

(e) Written informed consent shall be given only after 24 hours have elapsed from the time the information in Section 5326.2 has been given. *(Added by Stats.1974, c. 1534, p. 3463, § 5. Amended by Stats.1976, c. 1109, p. 4995, § 6; Stats.2014, c. 144 (A.B.1847), § 92, eff. Jan. 1, 2015.)*

§ 5326.55. Personal involvement in treatment; committee members; review of cases

Persons who serve on review committees shall not otherwise be personally involved in the treatment of the patient whose case they are reviewing. *(Added by Stats.1976, c. 1109, p. 4996, § 6.5.)*

§ 5326.6. Psychosurgery; conditions for performing; responsible relative; refusal to consent

Psychosurgery, wherever administered, may be performed only if:

(a) The patient gives written informed consent to the psychosurgery.

(b) A responsible relative of the person's choosing and with the person's consent, and the guardian or conservator if there is one, has read the standard consent form as defined in Section 5326.4 and has been given by the treating physician the information required in Section 5326.2. Should the person desire not to inform a relative or should such chosen relative be unavailable this requirement is dispensed with.

(c) The attending physician gives adequate documentation entered in the patient's treatment record of the reasons for the procedure, that all other appropriate treatment modalities have been exhausted and that this mode of treatment is definitely indicated and is the least drastic alternative available for the treatment of the patient at the time. Such statement in the treatment record shall be signed by the attending and treatment physician or physicians.

(d) Three physicians, one appointed by the facility and two appointed by the local mental health director, two of whom shall be either board-certified or eligible psychiatrists or board-certified or eligible neurosurgeons, have personally examined the patient and unanimously agree with the attending physicians' determinations pursuant to subdivision (c) and agree that the patient has the capacity to give informed consent. Such agreement shall be documented in the patient's treatment record and signed by each such physician.

Psychosurgery shall in no case be performed for at least 72 hours following the patient's written consent. Under no circumstances shall psychosurgery be performed on a minor.

As used in this section and Sections 5326.4 and 5326.7 "responsible relative" includes the spouse, parent, adult child, or adult brother or sister of the person.

The giving of consent to any of the treatments covered by this chapter may not be construed as a waiver of the right to refuse treatment at a future time. Consent may be withdrawn at any time. Such withdrawal of consent may be either oral or written and shall be given effect immediately.

Refusal of consent to undergo a psychosurgery shall be entered in the patient's treatment record. *(Added by Stats.1976, c. 1109, p. 4996, § 7.)*

Cross References

Rights of developmentally disabled persons in state hospitals or community care facilities, see Welfare and Institutions Code § 4503.

§ 5326.7. Convulsive treatment; involuntary patients; conditions for administering

Subject to the provisions of subdivision (f) of Section 5325, convulsive treatment may be administered to an involuntary patient, including anyone under guardianship or conservatorship, only if:

(a) The attending or treatment physician enters adequate documentation in the patient's treatment record of the reasons for the procedure, that all reasonable treatment modalities have been carefully considered, and that the treatment is definitely indicated and is the least drastic alternative available for this patient at this time. Such statement in the treatment record shall be signed by the attending and treatment physician or physicians.

(b) A review of the patient's treatment record is conducted by a committee of two physicians, at least one of whom shall have personally examined the patient. One physician shall be appointed by the facility and one shall be appointed by the local mental health director. Both shall be either board-certified or board-eligible psychiatrists or board-certified or board-eligible neurologists. This review committee must unanimously agree with the treatment physician's determinations pursuant to subdivision (a). Such agreement shall be documented in the patient's treatment record and signed by both physicians.

(c) A responsible relative of the person's choosing and the person's guardian or conservator, if there is one, have been given the oral explanation by the attending physician as required by Section 5326.2. Should the person desire not to inform a relative or should such chosen relative be unavailable, this requirement is dispensed with.

(d) The patient gives written informed consent as defined in Section 5326.5 to the convulsive treatment. Such consent shall be for a specified maximum number of treatments over a specified maximum period of time not to exceed 30 days, and shall be revocable at any time before or between treatments. Such withdrawal of consent may be either oral or written and shall be given effect immediately. Additional treatments in number or time, not to exceed 30 days, shall require a renewed written informed consent.

(e) The patient's attorney, or if none, a public defender appointed by the court, agrees as to the patient's capacity or incapacity to give written informed consent and that the patient who has capacity has given written informed consent.

(f) If either the attending physician or the attorney believes that the patient does not have the capacity to give a written informed consent, then a petition shall be filed in superior court to determine the patient's capacity to give written informed consent. The court shall hold an evidentiary hearing after giving appropriate notice to the patient, and within three judicial days after the petition is filed. At such hearing the patient shall be present and represented by legal counsel. If the court deems the above-mentioned attorney to have a conflict of interest, such attorney shall not represent the patient in this proceeding.

(g) If the court determines that the patient does not have the capacity to give written informed consent, then treatment may be performed upon gaining the written informed consent as defined in Sections 5326.2 and 5326.5 from the responsible relative or the guardian or the conservator of the patient.

(h) At any time during the course of treatment of a person who has been deemed incompetent, that person shall have the right to claim regained competency. Should he do so, the person's competency must be reevaluated according to subdivisions (e), (f), and (g). *(Added by Stats.1976, c. 1109, p. 4997, § 8.)*

Cross References

Conservatorship and guardianship for developmentally disabled persons, see Health and Safety Code § 416 et seq.

Court defined for purposes of this Part, see Welfare and Institutions Code § 5008.

§ 5326.75. Convulsive treatment; other than involuntary patients; condition to administer

Convulsive treatment for all other patients including but not limited to those voluntarily admitted to a facility, or receiving the treatment in a physician's office, clinic or private home, may be administered only if:

(a) The requirements of subdivisions (a), (c), and (d) of Section 5326.7 are met.

(b) A board-certified or board-eligible psychiatrist or a board-certified or board-eligible neurologist other than the patient's attending or treating physician has examined the patient and verifies that the patient has the capacity to give and has given written informed consent. Such verification shall be documented in the patient's treatment record and signed by the treating physician.

(c) If there is not the verification required by subdivision (b) of this section or if the patient has not the capacity to give informed consent, then subdivisions (b), (e), (f), (g), and (h) of Section 5326.7 shall also be met. *(Added by Stats.1976, c. 1109, p. 4998, § 8.5.)*

§ 5326.8. Convulsive treatment; minors; conditions to perform

Under no circumstances shall convulsive treatment be performed on a minor under 12 years of age. Persons 16 and 17 years of age shall personally have and exercise the rights under this article.

Persons 12 years of age and over, and under 16, may be administered convulsive treatment only if all the other provisions of this law are complied with and in addition:

(a) It is an emergency situation and convulsive treatment is deemed a lifesaving treatment.

(b) This fact and the need for and appropriateness of the treatment are unanimously certified to by a review board of three board-eligible or board-certified child psychiatrists appointed by the local mental health director.

(c) It is otherwise performed in full compliance with regulations promulgated by the Director of State Hospitals under Section 5326.95.

(d) It is thoroughly documented and reported immediately to the Director of Health Care Services. *(Added by Stats.1976, c. 1109, p. 4998, § 9. Amended by Stats.1977, c. 1252, p. 4572, § 566, operative July 1, 1978; Stats.2012, c. 34 (S.B.1009), § 90, eff. June 27, 2012.)*

Cross References

Emergency defined for purposes of this Part, see Welfare and Institutions Code § 5008.

§ 5326.85. Refusal of convulsive treatment; entry on record

No convulsive treatment shall be performed if the patient, whether admitted to the facility as a voluntary or involuntary patient, is deemed to be able to give informed consent and refuses to do so. The physician shall indicate in the treatment record that the treatment was refused despite the physician's advice and that he has explained to the patient the patient's responsibility for any untoward consequences of his refusal. *(Added by Stats.1976, c. 1109, p. 4999, § 9.5.)*

§ 5326.9. Violations; investigation; notice; authorized actions; intentional violation by physician of §§ 5326.2 to 5326.8; violations of §§ 5325, 5325.1

(a) Any alleged or suspected violation of the rights described in Chapter 2 (commencing with Section 5150) shall be investigated by the local director of mental health, or his or her designee. Violations of Sections 5326.2 to 5326.8, inclusive, concerning patients involuntarily detained for evaluation or treatment under this part, or as a voluntary patient for psychiatric evaluation or treatment to a health facility, as defined in Section 1250 of the Health and Safety Code, in which psychiatric evaluation or treatment is offered, shall also be investigated by the Director of Health Care Services, or his or her designee. Violations of Sections 5326.2 to 5326.8, inclusive, concerning persons committed to a state hospital shall also be investigated by the Director of State Hospitals, or his or her designee. If it is determined by the local director of mental health, the Director of Health Care Services, or the Director of State Hospitals that a right has been violated, a formal notice of violation shall be issued.

(b) Either the local director of mental health or the Director of Health Care Services, upon issuing a notice of violation, may take any or all of the following action:

(1) Assign a specified time period during which the violation shall be corrected.

(2) Referral to the Medical Board of California or other professional licensing agency. Such board shall investigate further, if warranted, and shall subject the individual practitioner to any penalty the board finds necessary and is authorized to impose.

(3) Revoke a facility's designation and authorization under Section 5404 to evaluate and treat persons detained involuntarily.

(4) Refer any violation of law to a local district attorney or the Attorney General for prosecution in any court with jurisdiction.

(c) The Director of State Hospitals, upon issuing a notice of violation, may take any or all of the following actions:

(1) Assign a specified time period during which the violation shall be corrected.

(2) Make a referral to the Medical Board of California or other professional licensing agency. The board or agency shall investigate further, if warranted, and shall subject the individual practitioner to any penalty the board finds necessary and is authorized to impose.

(3) Refer any violation of law to a local district attorney or the Attorney General for prosecution in any court with jurisdiction.

(d) Any physician who intentionally violates Sections 5326.2 to 5326.8, inclusive, shall be subject to a civil penalty of not more than five thousand dollars ($5,000) for each violation. The penalty may be assessed and collected in a civil action brought by the Attorney General in a superior court. Such intentional violation shall be grounds for revocation of license.

(e) Any person or facility found to have knowingly violated the provisions of the first paragraph of Section 5325.1 or to have denied without good cause any of the rights specified in Section 5325 shall pay a civil penalty, as determined by the court, of fifty dollars ($50) per day during the time in which the violation is not corrected, commencing on the day on which a notice of violation was issued, not to exceed one thousand dollars ($1,000), for each and every violation, except that any liability under this provision shall be offset by an amount equal to a fine or penalty imposed for the same violation under the provisions of Sections 1423 to 1425, inclusive, or 1428 of the Health and Safety Code. These penalties shall be deposited in the general fund of the county in which the violation occurred. The local district attorney or the Attorney General shall enforce this section in any court with jurisdiction. Where the State Department of Public Health, under the provisions of Sections 1423 to 1425, inclusive, of the Health and Safety Code, determines that no violation has occurred, the provisions of paragraph (4) of subdivision (b) shall not apply.

(f) The remedies provided by this subdivision shall be in addition to and not in substitution for any other remedies which an individual may have under law. *(Added by Stats.1976, c. 1109, p. 4999, § 10. Amended by Stats.1977, c. 1252, p. 4573, § 567, operative July 1, 1978; Stats.1978, c. 429, p. 1455, § 207, eff. July 17, 1978, operative July 1, 1978; Stats.1981, c. 841, p. 3233, § 5; Stats.1989, c. 886, § 103; Stats.2012, c. 34 (S.B.1009), § 91, eff. June 27, 2012; Stats.2013, c. 23 (A.B.82), § 35, eff. June 27, 2013.)*

Cross References

Attorney General, generally, see Government Code § 12500 et seq.
Court defined for purposes of this Part, see Welfare and Institutions Code § 5008.
Department of Health Care Services, generally, see Health and Safety Code § 100100 et seq.
Referral defined for purposes of this Part, see Welfare and Institutions Code § 5008.

§ 5326.91. Committee reviewal of convulsive treatments; records; immunity of members

In any facility in which convulsive treatment is performed on a person whether admitted to the facility as an involuntary or voluntary patient, the facility will designate a qualified committee to review all such treatments and to verify the appropriateness and need for such treatment. The local mental health director shall establish a postaudit review committee for convulsive treatments administered anywhere other than in any facility as defined in Section 1250 of the Health and Safety Code in which psychiatric evaluation or treatment is offered. Records of these committees will be subject to availability in the same manner as are the records of other hospital utilization and audit committees and to other regulations. Persons serving on these review committees will enjoy the same immunities as other persons serving on utilization, peer review, and audit committees of health care facilities. *(Added by Stats.1976, c. 1109, p. 4999, § 11. Amended by Stats.1977, c. 1252, p. 4573, § 568, operative July 1, 1978; Stats.2012, c. 34 (S.B.1009), § 92, eff. June 27, 2012.)*

Cross References

Evaluation defined for purposes of this Part, see Welfare and Institutions Code § 5008.

§ 5326.95. Regulations by director; standards for excessive use of convulsive treatment

The Director of State Hospitals shall adopt regulations to carry out the provisions of this chapter, including standards defining excessive use of convulsive treatment, which shall be developed in consultation with the State Department of Health Care Services and the County Behavioral Health Directors Association of California. *(Added by Stats.1976, c. 1109, p. 5000, § 12. Amended by Stats.1977, c. 1252, p. 4574, § 569, operative July 1, 1978; Stats.2012, c. 34 (S.B.1009), § 93, eff. June 27, 2012; Stats.2015, c. 455 (S.B.804), § 26, eff. Jan. 1, 2016.)*

Cross References

Administrative rules and regulations, see Government Code § 11340.

§ 5327. Rights of involuntarily detained persons

Every person involuntarily detained under provisions of this part or under certification for intensive treatment or postcertification treatment in any public or private mental institution or hospital, including a conservatee placed in any medical, psychiatric or nursing facility, shall be entitled to all rights set forth in this part and shall retain all rights not specifically denied him under this part. *(Added by Stats.1967, c. 1667, p. 4074, § 36, operative July 1, 1969.)*

Cross References

Intensive treatment defined for purposes of this Part, see Welfare and Institutions Code § 5008.
Postcertification treatment defined for purposes of this Part, see Welfare and Institutions Code § 5008.

§ 5328. Confidential information and records; disclosure; consent

(a) All information and records obtained in the course of providing services under Division 4 (commencing with Section 4000), Division 4.1 (commencing with Section 4400), Division 4.5 (commencing with Section 4500), Division 5 (commencing with Section 5000), Division 6 (commencing with Section 6000), or Division 7 (commencing with Section 7100), to either voluntary or involuntary recipients of services are confidential. Information and records obtained in the course of providing similar services to either voluntary or involuntary recipients before 1969 are also confidential. Information and records shall be disclosed only in any of the following cases:

(1) In communications between qualified professional persons in the provision of services or appropriate referrals, or in the course of conservatorship proceedings. The consent of the patient, or the patient's guardian or conservator, shall be obtained before information or records may be disclosed by a professional person employed by a facility to a professional person not employed by the facility who does not have the medical or psychological responsibility for the patient's care.

(2) If the patient, with the approval of the physician and surgeon, licensed psychologist, social worker with a master's degree in social

work, licensed marriage and family therapist, or licensed professional clinical counselor, who is in charge of the patient, designates persons to whom information or records may be released, except that this article does not compel a physician and surgeon, licensed psychologist, social worker with a master's degree in social work, licensed marriage and family therapist, licensed professional clinical counselor, nurse, attorney, or other professional person to reveal information that has been given to the person in confidence by members of a patient's family. This paragraph does not authorize a licensed marriage and family therapist or licensed professional clinical counselor to provide services or to be in charge of a patient's care beyond the therapist's or counselor's lawful scope of practice.

(3) To the extent necessary for a recipient to make a claim, or for a claim to be made on behalf of a recipient for aid, insurance, or medical assistance to which the recipient may be entitled.

(4) If the recipient of services is a minor, ward, dependent, or conservatee, and the recipient's parent, guardian, guardian ad litem, conservator, or authorized representative designates, in writing, persons to whom records or information may be disclosed, except that this article does not compel a physician and surgeon, licensed psychologist, social worker with a master's degree in social work, licensed marriage and family therapist, licensed professional clinical counselor, nurse, attorney, or other professional person to reveal information that has been given to the person in confidence by members of a patient's family.

(5) For research, provided that the Director of Health Care Services, the Director of State Hospitals, the Director of Social Services, or the Director of Developmental Services designates by regulation, rules for the conduct of research and requires the research to be first reviewed by the appropriate institutional review board or boards. The rules shall include, but need not be limited to, the requirement that all researchers shall sign an oath of confidentiality as follows:

____

Date

As a condition of doing research concerning persons who have received services from ____ (fill in the facility, agency, or person), I, ____, agree to obtain the prior informed consent of those persons who have received services to the maximum degree possible as determined by the appropriate institutional review board or boards for protection of human subjects reviewing my research, and I further agree not to divulge any information obtained in the course of that research to unauthorized persons, and not to publish or otherwise make public any information regarding persons who have received services such that the person who received services is identifiable.

I recognize that the unauthorized release of confidential information may make me subject to a civil action under provisions of the Welfare and Institutions Code.

(6) To the courts, as necessary to the administration of justice.

(7) To governmental law enforcement agencies as needed for the protection of federal and state elective constitutional officers and their families.

(8) To the Senate Committee on Rules or the Assembly Committee on Rules for the purposes of legislative investigation authorized by the committee.

(9) If the recipient of services who applies for life or disability insurance designates in writing the insurer to which records or information may be disclosed.

(10) To the attorney for the patient in any and all proceedings upon presentation of a release of information signed by the patient, except that when the patient is unable to sign the release, the staff of the facility, upon satisfying itself of the identity of the attorney, and of the fact that the attorney does represent the interests of the patient, may release all information and records relating to the patient, except that this article does not compel a physician and surgeon, licensed psychologist, social worker with a master's degree in social work, licensed marriage and family therapist, licensed professional clinical counselor, nurse, attorney, or other professional person to reveal information that has been given to the person in confidence by members of a patient's family.

(11) Upon written agreement by a person previously confined in or otherwise treated by a facility, the professional person in charge of the facility or the professional person's designee may release any information, except information that has been given in confidence by members of the person's family, requested by a probation officer charged with the evaluation of the person after the person's conviction of a crime if the professional person in charge of the facility determines that the information is relevant to the evaluation. The agreement shall only be operative until sentence is passed on the crime of which the person was convicted. The confidential information released pursuant to this paragraph shall be transmitted to the court separately from the probation report and shall not be placed in the probation report. The confidential information shall remain confidential except for purposes of sentencing. After sentencing, the confidential information shall be sealed.

(12)(A) Between persons who are trained and qualified to serve on multidisciplinary personnel teams pursuant to subdivision (d) of Section 18951. The information and records sought to be disclosed shall be relevant to the provision of child welfare services or the investigation, prevention, identification, management, or treatment of child abuse or neglect pursuant to Chapter 11 (commencing with Section 18950) of Part 6 of Division 9. Information obtained pursuant to this paragraph shall not be used in any criminal or delinquency proceeding. This paragraph does not prohibit evidence identical to that contained within the records from being admissible in a criminal or delinquency proceeding, if the evidence is derived solely from means other than this paragraph, as permitted by law.

(B) As used in this paragraph, "child welfare services" means those services that are directed at preventing child abuse or neglect.

(13) To county patients' rights advocates who have been given knowing voluntary authorization by a client or a guardian ad litem. The client or guardian ad litem, whoever entered into the agreement, may revoke the authorization at any time, either in writing or by oral declaration to an approved advocate.

(14) To a committee established in compliance with Section 14725.

(15) In providing information as described in Section 7325.5. This paragraph does not permit the release of any information other than that described in Section 7325.5.

(16) To the county behavioral health director or the director's designee, or to a law enforcement officer, or to the person designated by a law enforcement agency, pursuant to Sections 5152.1 and 5250.1.

(17) If the patient gives consent, information specifically pertaining to the existence of genetically handicapping conditions, as defined in Section 125135 of the Health and Safety Code, may be released to qualified professional persons for purposes of genetic counseling for blood relatives upon request of the blood relative. For purposes of this paragraph, "qualified professional persons" means those persons with the qualifications necessary to carry out the genetic counseling duties under this paragraph as determined by the genetic disease unit established in the State Department of Health Care Services under Section 125000 of the Health and Safety Code. If the patient does not respond or cannot respond to a request for permission to release information pursuant to this paragraph after reasonable attempts have been made over a two-week period to get a response, the information may be released upon request of the blood relative.

(18) If the patient, in the opinion of the patient's psychotherapist, presents a serious danger of violence to a reasonably foreseeable

victim or victims, then any of the information or records specified in this section may be released to that person or persons and to law enforcement agencies and county child welfare agencies as the psychotherapist determines is needed for the protection of that person or persons. For purposes of this paragraph, "psychotherapist" has the same meaning as provided in Section 1010 of the Evidence Code.

(19)(A) To the designated officer of an emergency response employee, and from that designated officer to an emergency response employee regarding possible exposure to HIV or AIDS, but only to the extent necessary to comply with the federal Ryan White Comprehensive AIDS Resources Emergency Act of 1990 (Public Law 101–381; 42 U.S.C. Sec. 201).

(B) For purposes of this paragraph, "designated officer" and "emergency response employee" have the same meaning as these terms are used in the federal Ryan White Comprehensive AIDS Resources Emergency Act of 1990 (Public Law 101–381; 42 U.S.C. Sec. 201).

(C) The designated officer shall be subject to the confidentiality requirements specified in Section 120980 of the Health and Safety Code, and may be personally liable for unauthorized release of any identifying information about the HIV results. Further, the designated officer shall inform the exposed emergency response employee that the employee is also subject to the confidentiality requirements specified in Section 120980 of the Health and Safety Code, and may be personally liable for unauthorized release of any identifying information about the HIV test results.

(20)(A) To a law enforcement officer who personally lodges with a facility, as defined in subparagraph (B), a warrant of arrest or an abstract of a warrant showing that the person sought is wanted for a serious felony, as defined in Section 1192.7 of the Penal Code, or a violent felony, as defined in Section 667.5 of the Penal Code. The information sought and released shall be limited to whether or not the person named in the arrest warrant is presently confined in the facility. This subparagraph shall be implemented with minimum disruption to health facility operations and patients, in accordance with Section 5212. If the law enforcement officer is informed that the person named in the warrant is confined in the facility, the officer may not enter the facility to arrest the person without obtaining a valid search warrant or the permission of staff of the facility.

(B) For purposes of subparagraph (A), a facility means all of the following:

(i) A state hospital, as defined in Section 4001.

(ii) A general acute care hospital, as defined in subdivision (a) of Section 1250 of the Health and Safety Code, solely with regard to information pertaining to a person with mental illness subject to this section.

(iii) An acute psychiatric hospital, as defined in subdivision (b) of Section 1250 of the Health and Safety Code.

(iv) A psychiatric health facility, as described in Section 1250.2 of the Health and Safety Code.

(v) A mental health rehabilitation center, as described in Section 5675.

(vi) A skilled nursing facility with a special treatment program for individuals with mental illness, as described in Sections 51335 and 72445 to 72475, inclusive, of Title 22 of the California Code of Regulations.

(21) Between persons who are trained and qualified to serve on multidisciplinary personnel teams pursuant to Section 15610.55. The information and records sought to be disclosed shall be relevant to the prevention, identification, management, or treatment of an abused elder or dependent adult pursuant to Chapter 13 (commencing with Section 15750) of Part 3 of Division 9.

(22)(A) When an employee is served with a notice of adverse action, as defined in Section 19570 of the Government Code, all of the following information and records may be released:

(i) All information and records that the appointing authority relied upon in issuing the notice of adverse action.

(ii) All other information and records that are relevant to the adverse action, or that would constitute relevant evidence as defined in Section 210 of the Evidence Code.

(iii) The information described in clauses (i) and (ii) may be released only if both of the following conditions are met:

(I) The appointing authority has provided written notice to the consumer and the consumer's legal representative or, if the consumer has no legal representative or if the legal representative is a state agency, to the clients' rights advocate, and the consumer, the consumer's legal representative, or the clients' rights advocate has not objected in writing to the appointing authority within five business days of receipt of the notice, or the appointing authority, upon review of the objection, has determined that the circumstances on which the adverse action is based are egregious or threaten the health, safety, or life of the consumer or other consumers and without the information the adverse action could not be taken.

(II) The appointing authority, the person against whom the adverse action has been taken, and the person's representative, if any, have entered into a stipulation that does all of the following:

(ia) Prohibits the parties from disclosing or using the information or records for any purpose other than the proceedings for which the information or records were requested or provided.

(ib) Requires the employee and the employee's legal representative to return to the appointing authority all records provided to them under this paragraph, including, but not limited to, all records and documents from any source containing confidential information protected by this section, and all copies of those records and documents, within 10 days of the date that the adverse action becomes final, except for the actual records and documents or copies thereof that are no longer in the possession of the employee or the employee's legal representative because they were submitted to the administrative tribunal as a component of an appeal from the adverse action.

(ic) Requires the parties to submit the stipulation to the administrative tribunal with jurisdiction over the adverse action at the earliest possible opportunity.

(B) For purposes of this paragraph, the State Personnel Board may, before any appeal from adverse action being filed with it, issue a protective order, upon application by the appointing authority, for the limited purpose of prohibiting the parties from disclosing or using information or records for any purpose other than the proceeding for which the information or records were requested or provided, and to require the employee or the employee's legal representative to return to the appointing authority all records provided to them under this paragraph, including, but not limited to, all records and documents from any source containing confidential information protected by this section, and all copies of those records and documents, within 10 days of the date that the adverse action becomes final, except for the actual records and documents or copies thereof that are no longer in the possession of the employee or the employee's legal representatives because they were submitted to the administrative tribunal as a component of an appeal from the adverse action.

(C) Individual identifiers, including, but not limited to, names, social security numbers, and hospital numbers, that are not necessary for the prosecution or defense of the adverse action, shall not be disclosed.

(D) All records, documents, or other materials containing confidential information protected by this section that have been submitted or otherwise disclosed to the administrative agency or other person as a component of an appeal from an adverse action shall, upon proper motion by the appointing authority to the administrative tribunal, be placed under administrative seal and shall not, thereafter, be subject to disclosure to any person or entity except upon the issuance of an order of a court of competent jurisdiction.

(E) For purposes of this paragraph, an adverse action becomes final when the employee fails to answer within the time specified in Section 19575 of the Government Code, or, after filing an answer, withdraws the appeal, or, upon exhaustion of the administrative appeal or of the judicial review remedies as otherwise provided by law.

(23) To the person appointed as the developmental services decisionmaker for a minor, dependent, or ward pursuant to Section 319, 361, or 726.

(24) During the provision of emergency services and care, as defined in Section 1317.1 of the Health and Safety Code, the communication of patient information between a physician and surgeon, licensed psychologist, social worker with a master's degree in social work, licensed marriage and family therapist, licensed professional clinical counselor, nurse, emergency medical personnel at the scene of an emergency or in an emergency medical transport vehicle, or other professional person or emergency medical personnel at a health facility licensed pursuant to Chapter 2 (commencing with Section 1250) of Division 2 of the Health and Safety Code.

(25) To a business associate or for health care operations purposes, in accordance with Part 160 (commencing with Section 160.101) and Part 164 (commencing with Section 164.102) of Subchapter C of Subtitle A of Title 45 of the Code of Federal Regulations.

(26) To authorized personnel who are employed by the California Victim Compensation Board for the purposes of verifying the identity and eligibility of individuals claiming compensation pursuant to the Forced or Involuntary Sterilization Compensation Program described in Chapter 1.6 (commencing with Section 24210) of Division 20 of the Health and Safety Code. The California Victim Compensation Board shall maintain the confidentiality of any information or records received from the department in accordance with Part 160 (commencing with Section 160.101) and Part 164 (commencing with Section 164.102) of Subchapter C of Subtitle A of Title 45 of the Code of Federal Regulations and this section. Public disclosure of aggregated claimant information or the annual report required under subdivision (b) of Section 24211 of the Health and Safety Code is not a violation of this section.

(27) To parties to a judicial or administrative proceeding as permitted by law, and who satisfy the requirements under Part 164 (commencing with Section 164.512(e)) of Subchapter C of Subtitle A of Title 45 of the Code of Federal Regulations, except that this paragraph shall not be construed to affect any rights or privileges provided under law of any party or nonparty.

(b) Notwithstanding subdivision (a), patient information and records shall, as necessary, be provided to and discussed with district attorneys for purposes of commitment, recommitment, or petitions for release proceedings for patients committed under Sections 1026, 1370, 1600, 2962, and 2972 of the Penal Code and Section 6600 of this code, unless otherwise prohibited by law.

(c) The amendment of paragraph (4) of subdivision (a) enacted at the 1970 Regular Session of the Legislature does not constitute a change in, but is declaratory of, the preexisting law.

(d) This section is not limited by Section 5150.05 or 5332. *(Added by Stats.1972, c. 1058, p. 1960, § 2, operative July 1, 1973. Amended by Stats.1974, c. 486, p. 1120, § 2, eff. July 11, 1974; Stats.1975, c. 1258, p. 3300, § 6; Stats.1977, c. 1252, p. 4574, § 570, operative July 1, 1978; Stats.1978, c. 69, p. 190, § 5; Stats.1978, c. 432, p. 1502, § 12, eff. July 17, 1978, operative July 1, 1978; Stats.1978, c. 1345, p. 4397, § 1; Stats.1979, c. 373, p. 1396, § 364; Stats.1979, c. 244, p. 529, § 1; Stats.1980, c. 676, p. 2036, § 332; Stats.1981, c. 841, p. 3234, § 6; Stats.1982, c. 234, § 6, eff. June 2, 1982; Stats.1982, c. 1141, § 7; Stats.1982, c. 1415, § 1, eff. Sept. 27, 1982; Stats.1983, c. 755, § 3; Stats.1983, c. 1174, § 1.5; Stats.1985, c. 1121, § 3; Stats.1985, c. 1194, § 1; Stats.1985, c. 1324, § 1.7; Stats.1991, c. 534 (S.B.1088), § 6; Stats.1996, c. 1023 (S.B.1497), § 464, eff. Sept. 29, 1996; Stats.1996, c. 111 (S.B.2082), § 2; Stats.1998, c. 148 (A.B.302), § 1; Stats.2001, c. 37 (A.B.213), § 1; Stats.2001, c. 506 (A.B.1424), § 8.5; Stats.2002, c. 552 (A.B.2735), § 1; Stats.2004, c. 406 (S.B.1819), § 2; Stats.2010, c. 551 (A.B.2322), § 2, eff. Sept. 29, 2010; Stats.2011, c. 381 (S.B.146), § 44; Stats.2011, c. 471 (S.B.368), § 13.5; Stats.2012, c. 34 (S.B. 1009), § 94, eff. June 27, 2012, operative July 1, 2012; Stats.2015, c. 455 (S.B.804), § 27, eff. Jan. 1, 2016; Stats.2017, c. 323 (A.B.1119), § 1, eff. Jan. 1, 2018; Stats.2017, c. 513 (S.B.241), § 3.5, eff. Jan. 1, 2018; Stats.2018, c. 92 (S.B.1289), § 226, eff. Jan. 1, 2019; Stats.2021, c. 77 (A.B.137), § 33, eff. July 16, 2021; Stats.2022, c. 47 (S.B.184), § 59, eff. June 30, 2022; Stats.2022, c. 589 (A.B.2317), § 12, eff. Jan. 1, 2023; Stats.2022, c. 738 (A.B.204), § 14, eff. Sept. 29, 2022.)*

Cross References

Access to records for purposes of appeal, see Welfare and Institutions Code § 4726.

Administration of antipsychotic medication to persons subject to detention, see Welfare and Institutions Code § 5332.

Administrative rules and regulations, see Government Code § 11340.

Closure of Division of Juvenile Justice, continuation of services for state hospital patients referred by division, see Welfare and Institutions Code § 1732.10.

Conservatees, change to more restrictive placement, written notice notwithstanding this section, see Welfare and Institutions Code § 5358.

Court defined for purposes of this Part, see Welfare and Institutions Code § 5008.

Department of Health Care Services, generally, see Health and Safety Code § 100100 et seq.

Determination of probable cause to take person into custody or cause person to be taken into custody, limits imposed on application of this section, see Welfare and Institutions Code § 5150.05.

Developmentally disabled persons, similar provisions, see Welfare and Institutions Code § 4514.

Duties of board, outreach, review of applications for victim compensation, see Health and Safety Code § 24211.

Elder death review teams, confidentiality and disclosure of information, see Penal Code § 11174.8.

Emergency defined for purposes of this Part, see Welfare and Institutions Code § 5008.

Evaluation defined for purposes of this Part, see Welfare and Institutions Code § 5008.

Felonies, definition and penalties, see Penal Code §§ 17, 18.

Forensic Conditional Release Program, notice to local law enforcement notwithstanding this section, see Welfare and Institutions Code § 4360.

Inspection of public records, see Government Code § 6250 et seq.

Inspection of public records, other exemptions from disclosure, see Government Code § 6276.30.

Interagency child death review team, disclosure of records and other information, see Penal Code § 11174.32.

Investigation of alternatives to conservatorship, recommendations of conservatorship, report of investigation, service of report, see Welfare and Institutions Code § 5354.

Lanterman–Petris–Short Act, consideration of historical course of disorder, application of this section, see Welfare and Institutions Code § 5008.2.

Mental health services recipients, information about and records of as confidential, see Welfare and Institutions Code § 5540.

Patient access to health records, see Health and Safety Code § 123110.

Physician-patient privilege, see Evidence Code § 990 et seq.

Pre-petition screening, application of this section, see Welfare and Institutions Code § 5202.

Psychotherapist-patient privilege, see Evidence Code § 1010 et seq.

Record of disclosures, see Welfare and Institutions Code § 5328.6.

Record of persons who died while residing in state hospitals or developmental centers, confidentiality, see Welfare and Institutions Code § 4015.

Referral defined for purposes of this Part, see Welfare and Institutions Code § 5008.

Referrals between facilities, providers, and other organizations, legislative intent, see Welfare and Institutions Code § 5013.

Search warrants, see Penal Code § 1523 et seq.

Sexually violent predators, conditional release program, terms and conditions, see Welfare and Institutions Code § 6608.8.

State Personnel Board, generally, see Const. Art. 7, § 2 et seq.; Government Code § 18650 et seq.

Research References

3 Witkin, California Criminal Law 4th Punishment § 165 (2021), Updated, Replacement, and Additional Evaluations.

§ 5328.01. Confidential information and records; disclosure to law enforcement agencies; consent; court orders

Notwithstanding Section 5328, all information and records made confidential under the first paragraph of Section 5328 shall also be disclosed to governmental law enforcement agencies investigating evidence of a crime where the records relate to a patient who is confined or has been confined as a mentally disordered sex offender or pursuant to Section 1026 or 1368 of the Penal Code and the records are in the possession or under the control of any state hospital serving the mentally disabled, as follows:

(a) In accordance with the written consent of the patient; or

(b) If authorized by an appropriate order of a court of competent jurisdiction in the county where the records are located compelling a party to produce in court specified records and specifically describing the records being sought, when the order is granted after an application showing probable cause therefor. In assessing probable cause, the court shall do all of the following:

(1) Weigh the public interest and the need for disclosure against the injury to the patient, to the physician-patient relationship, and to the treatment services.

(2) Determine that there is a reasonable likelihood that the records in question will disclose material information or evidence of substantial value in connection with the investigation or prosecution.

(3) Determine that the crime involves the causing of, or direct threatening of, the loss of life or serious bodily injury.

(4) In granting or denying a subpoena, the court shall state on the record the reasons for its decision and the facts which the court considered in making such a ruling.

(5) If a court grants an order permitting disclosure of such records, the court shall issue all orders necessary to protect, to the maximum extent possible, the patient's privacy and the privacy and confidentiality of the physician-patient relationship.

(6) Any records disclosed pursuant to the provisions of this subdivision and any copies thereof shall be returned to the facility at the completion of the investigation or prosecution unless they have been made a part of the court record.

(c) A governmental law enforcement agency applying for disclosure of patient records under this subdivision may petition the court for an order, upon a showing of probable cause to believe that delay would seriously impede the investigation, which requires the ordered party to produce the records forthwith.

(d) Records obtained by a governmental law enforcement agency pursuant to this section shall not be disseminated to any other agency or person unless such dissemination relates to the criminal investigation for which the records were obtained by the governmental law enforcement agency. The willful dissemination of any record in violation of this paragraph shall constitute a misdemeanor.

(e) If any records obtained pursuant to this section are of a patient presently receiving treatment at the state hospital serving the mentally disabled, the law enforcement agency shall only receive copies of the original records. *(Added by Stats.1985, c. 1036, § 1.)*

Cross References

Court defined for purposes of this Part, see Welfare and Institutions Code § 5008.

Misdemeanors, definition and penalties, see Penal Code §§ 17, 19, 19.2.

§ 5328.02. Confidential information and records; disclosure to youth authority and adult correctional agency

Notwithstanding Section 5328, all information and records made confidential under the first paragraph of Section 5328 shall also be disclosed to the Youth Authority and Adult Correctional Agency or any component thereof, as necessary to the administration of justice. *(Added by Stats.1980, c. 1117, p. 3608, § 26.)*

§ 5328.03. Confidential information and records; disclosure to parent or guardian; minor removed from physical custody of parent or guardian

(a)(1) Notwithstanding Section 5328 of this code, Section 3025 of the Family Code, or paragraph (2) of subdivision (c) of Section 56.11 of the Civil Code, a psychotherapist who knows that a minor has been removed from the physical custody of his or her parent or guardian pursuant to Article 6 (commencing with Section 300) to Article 10 (commencing with Section 360), inclusive, of Chapter 2 of Part 1 of Division 2 shall not release mental health records of the minor patient and shall not disclose mental health information about that minor patient based upon an authorization to release those records or the information signed by the minor's parent or guardian. This restriction shall not apply if the juvenile court has issued an order authorizing the parent or guardian to sign an authorization for the release of the records or information after finding that such an order would not be detrimental to the minor patient.

(2) Notwithstanding Section 5328 of this code or Section 3025 of the Family Code, a psychotherapist who knows that a minor has been removed from the physical custody of his or her parent or guardian pursuant to Article 6 (commencing with Section 300) to Article 10 (commencing with Section 360), inclusive, of Chapter 2 of Part 1 of Division 2 shall not allow the parent or guardian to inspect or obtain copies of mental health records of the minor patient. This restriction shall not apply if the juvenile court has issued an order authorizing the parent or guardian to inspect or obtain copies of the mental health records of the minor patient after finding that such an order would not be detrimental to the minor patient.

(b) For purposes of this section, the following definitions apply:

(1) "Mental health records" means mental health records as defined by subdivision (b) of Section 123105 of the Health and Safety Code.

(2) "Psychotherapist" means a provider of health care as defined in Section 1010 of the Evidence Code.

(c)(1) When the juvenile court has issued an order described in paragraph (1) of subdivision (a), the parent or guardian seeking the release of the minor's mental health records or information about the minor shall present a copy of the court order to the psychotherapist before any records or information may be released pursuant to the signed authorization.

(2) When the juvenile court has issued an order described in paragraph (2) of subdivision (a), the parent or guardian seeking to inspect or obtain copies of the mental health records of the minor patient shall present a copy of the court order to the psychotherapist and shall comply with subdivisions (a) and (b) of Section 123110 of the Health and Safety Code before the parent or guardian is allowed to inspect or obtain copies of the mental health records of the minor patient.

(d) Nothing in this section shall be construed to prevent or limit a psychotherapist's authority under subdivision (a) of Section 123115 of the Health and Safety Code to deny a parent's or guardian's written request to inspect or obtain copies of the minor patient's mental health records, notwithstanding the fact that the juvenile court has issued an order authorizing the parent or guardian to sign an authorization for the release of the mental health records or information about that minor patient, or to inspect or obtain copies of the minor patient's health records. Liability for a psychotherapist's decision not to release records, not to disclose information about the minor patient, or not to allow the parent or guardian to inspect or obtain copies of the mental health records pursuant to the authority of subdivision (a) of Section 123115 of the Health and Safety Code shall be governed by that section.

(e) Nothing in this section shall be construed to impose upon a psychotherapist a duty to inquire or investigate whether a child has been removed from the physical custody of his or her parent or guardian pursuant to Article 6 (commencing with Section 300) to Article 10 (commencing with Section 360), inclusive, of Chapter 2 of Part 1 of Division 2 when a parent or guardian presents the minor's psychotherapist with an order authorizing the parent or guardian to sign an authorization for the release of information or the mental health records regarding the minor patient or authorizing the parent or guardian to inspect or obtain copies of the mental health records of the minor patient. *(Added by Stats.2012, c. 657 (S.B.1407), § 3. Amended by Stats.2013, c. 76 (A.B.383), § 209.)*

Cross References

Disclosure of minor's mental health records, minor removed from custody of parent or guardian, see Civil Code § 56.106.

Minor removed from physical custody of parent or guardian, mental health records, psychotherapist duty not to permit inspection or obtaining of copies, see Health and Safety Code § 123116.

§ 5328.04. Disclosure of confidential information and records to social worker, probation officer, foster care public health nurse, or other person with custody of minor; evidence; psychotherapy notes excluded

(a) Notwithstanding Section 5328, information and records made confidential under that section may be disclosed to a county social worker, a probation officer, a foster care public health nurse acting pursuant to Section 16501.3, or any other person who is legally authorized to have custody or care of a minor, for the purpose of coordinating health care services and medical treatment, as defined in subdivision (b) of Section 56.103 of the Civil Code, mental health services, or services for developmental disabilities, for the minor.

(b) Information disclosed under subdivision (a) shall not be further disclosed by the recipient unless the disclosure is for the purpose of coordinating health care services and medical treatment, or mental health or developmental disability services, for the minor and only to a person who would otherwise be able to obtain the information under subdivision (a) or any other law.

(c) Information disclosed pursuant to this section shall not be admitted into evidence in any criminal or delinquency proceeding against the minor. Nothing in this subdivision shall prohibit identical evidence from being admissible in a criminal proceeding if that evidence is derived solely from lawful means other than this section and is permitted by law.

(d) Nothing in this section shall be construed to compel a physician and surgeon, licensed psychologist, social worker with a master's degree in social work, licensed marriage and family therapist, licensed professional clinical counselor, nurse, attorney, or other professional person to reveal information, including notes, that has been given to him or her in confidence by the minor or members of the minor's family.

(e) The disclosure of information pursuant to this section is not intended to limit disclosure of information when that disclosure is otherwise required by law.

(f) Nothing in this section shall be construed to expand the authority of a social worker, probation officer, foster care public health nurse, or custodial caregiver beyond the authority provided under existing law to a parent or a patient representative regarding access to confidential information.

(g) As used in this section, "minor" means a minor taken into temporary custody or for whom a petition has been filed with the court, or who has been adjudged a dependent child or ward of juvenile court pursuant to Section 300 or 601.

(h) Information and records that may be disclosed pursuant to this section do not include psychotherapy notes, as defined in Section 164.501 of Title 45 of the Code of Federal Regulations. *(Added by Stats.2008, c. 700 (A.B.2352), § 2. Amended by Stats.2011, c. 381 (S.B.146), § 45; Stats.2015, c. 535 (S.B.319), § 2, eff. Jan. 1, 2016.)*

Cross References

Court defined for purposes of this Part, see Welfare and Institutions Code § 5008.

Disclosure of minor's medical information, mental health condition, see Civil Code § 56.103.

§ 5328.05. Confidential information and records; elder abuse or neglect; consent; staff requirements

(a) Notwithstanding Section 5328, information and records may be disclosed when an older adult client, in the opinion of a designee of a human service agency serving older adults through an established multidisciplinary team, presents signs or symptoms of elder abuse or neglect, whether inflicted by another or self-inflicted, the agency designee to the multidisciplinary team may, with the older adult's consent, obtain information from other county agencies regarding, and limited to, whether or not a client is receiving services from any other county agency.

(b) The information obtained pursuant to subdivision (a) shall not include information regarding the nature of the treatment or services provided, and shall be shared among multidisciplinary team members for multidisciplinary team activities pursuant to this section.

(c) The county agencies which may cooperate and share information under this section shall have staff designated as members of an established multidisciplinary team, and include, but not be limited to, the county departments of public social services, health, mental health, and alcohol and drug abuse, the public guardian, and the area agencies on aging.

(d) The county patient's rights advocate shall report any negative consequences of the implementation of this exception to confidentiality requirements to the local mental health director. *(Added by Stats.1990, c. 654 (S.B.2488), § 1.)*

Cross References

Fundamental rights of residents of residential care facilities, see Health and Safety Code § 1569.261 et seq.

§ 5328.06. Disclosure of information and records to protection and advocacy agency for rights of people with mental disabilities and mental illness

(a) Notwithstanding Section 5328, information and records shall be disclosed to the protection and advocacy agency established in this state to fulfill the requirements and assurances of the federal Protection and Advocacy for the Mentally Ill Individuals Amendments Act of 1991, contained in Chapter 114 (commencing with Section 10801) of Title 42 of the United States Code, for the protection and advocacy of the rights of people with mental disabilities, including people with mental illness, as defined in Section 10802(4) of Title 42 of the United States Code.

(b) Access to information and records to which subdivision (a) applies shall be in accord with Division 4.7 (commencing with Section 4900). *(Added by Stats.1991, c. 534 (S.B.1088), § 8. Amended by Stats.2003, c. 878 (S.B.577), § 10.)*

§ 5328.1. Information to patient's family; patient authorization; liability for damages

(a) Upon request of a member of the family of a patient, or other person designated by the patient, a public or private treatment facility shall give the family member or the designee notification of the patient's diagnosis, the prognosis, the medications prescribed, the side effects of medications prescribed, if any, and the progress of the patient, if, after notification of the patient that this information is requested, the patient authorizes its disclosure. If, when initially informed of the request for notification, the patient is unable to authorize the release of such information, notation of the attempt shall be made into the patient's treatment record, and daily efforts shall be made to secure the patient's consent or refusal of authorization. However, if a request for information is made by the spouse, parent, child, or sibling of the patient and the patient is unable to authorize the release of such information, the requester shall be given notification of the patient's presence in the facility, except to the extent prohibited by federal law.

(b) Upon the admission of any mental health patient to a 24-hour public or private health facility licensed pursuant to Section 1250 of the Health and Safety Code, the facility shall make reasonable attempts to notify the patient's next of kin or any other person designated by the patient, of the patient's admission, unless the patient requests that this information not be provided. The facility shall make reasonable attempts to notify the patient's next of kin or any other person designated by the patient, of the patient's release, transfer, serious illness, injury, or death only upon request of the family member, unless the patient requests that this information not be provided. The patient shall be advised by the facility that he or she has the right to request that this information not be provided.

(c) No public or private entity or public or private employee shall be liable for damages caused or alleged to be caused by the release of information or the omission to release information pursuant to this section.

Nothing in this section shall be construed to require photocopying of a patient's medical records in order to satisfy its provisions. *(Added by Stats.1969, c. 722, p. 1430, § 22, eff. Aug. 8, 1969, operative July 1, 1969. Amended by Stats.1970, c. 1627, p. 3447, § 22; Stats.1980, c. 924, p. 2932, § 1; Stats.1983, c. 1174, § 2.)*

Cross References

Record of disclosures, see Welfare and Institutions Code § 5328.6.

§ 5328.15. Authorized disclosure of confidential information and records

All information and records obtained in the course of providing services under Division 5 (commencing with Section 5000), Division 6 (commencing with Section 6000), or Division 7 (commencing with Section 7100), to either voluntary or involuntary recipients of services shall be confidential. Information and records may be disclosed, however, notwithstanding any other law, as follows:

(a) To authorized licensing personnel who are employed by, or who are authorized representatives of, the State Department of Public Health, and who are licensed or registered health professionals, and to authorized legal staff or special investigators who are peace officers who are employed by, or who are authorized representatives of the State Department of Social Services, as necessary to the performance of their duties to inspect, license, and investigate health facilities and community care facilities and to ensure that the standards of care and services provided in such facilities are adequate and appropriate and to ascertain compliance with the rules and regulations to which the facility is subject. The confidential information shall remain confidential except for purposes of inspection, licensing, or investigation pursuant to Chapter 2 (commencing with Section 1250) of, and Chapter 3 (commencing with Section 1500) of, Division 2 of the Health and Safety Code, or a criminal, civil, or administrative proceeding in relation thereto. The confidential information may be used by the State Department of Public Health or the State Department of Social Services in a criminal, civil, or administrative proceeding. The confidential information shall be available only to the judge or hearing officer and to the parties to the case. Names which are confidential shall be listed in attachments separate to the general pleadings. The confidential information shall be sealed after the conclusion of the criminal, civil, or administrative hearings, and shall not subsequently be released except in accordance with this subdivision. If the confidential information does not result in a criminal, civil, or administrative proceeding, it shall be sealed after the State Department of Public Health or the State Department of Social Services decides that no further action will be taken in the matter of suspected licensing violations. Except as otherwise provided in this subdivision, confidential information in the possession of the State Department of Public Health or the State Department of Social Services shall not contain the name of the patient.

(b) To any board which licenses and certifies professionals in the fields of mental health pursuant to state law, when the Director of State Hospitals has reasonable cause to believe that there has occurred a violation of any provision of law subject to the jurisdiction of that board and the records are relevant to the violation. The information shall be sealed after a decision is reached in the matter of the suspected violation, and shall not subsequently be released except in accordance with this subdivision. Confidential information in the possession of the board shall not contain the name of the patient.

(c) To a protection and advocacy agency established pursuant to Section 4901, to the extent that the information is incorporated within any of the following:

(1) An unredacted facility evaluation report form or an unredacted complaint investigation report form of the State Department of Social Services. The information shall remain confidential and subject to the confidentiality requirements of subdivision (f) of Section 4903.

(2) An unredacted citation report, unredacted licensing report, unredacted survey report, unredacted plan of correction, or unredacted statement of deficiency of the State Department of Public Health, prepared by authorized licensing personnel or authorized representatives as described in subdivision (a). The information shall remain confidential and subject to the confidentiality requirements of subdivision (f) of Section 4903. *(Added by Stats.1980, c. 695, p. 2095, § 1. Amended by Stats.1982, c. 1141, § 9; Stats.1985, c. 994, § 2; Stats.2012, c. 440 (A.B.1488), § 63, eff. Sept. 22, 2012; Stats.2012, c. 664 (S.B.1377), § 3; Stats.2014, c. 442 (S.B.1465), § 14, eff. Sept. 18, 2014; Stats.2015, c. 303 (A.B.731), § 582, eff. Jan. 1, 2016.)*

Cross References

Department of Health Care Services, generally, see Health and Safety Code § 100100 et seq.

Inspection of public records, other exemptions from disclosure, see Government Code § 6276.30.

Peace officer defined for purposes of this Part, see Welfare and Institutions Code § 5008.

§ 5328.2. Criminal matters; information to Department of Justice

Notwithstanding Section 5328, movement and identification information and records regarding a patient who is committed to the department, state hospital, or any other public or private mental health facility approved by the county behavioral health director for observation or for an indeterminate period as a mentally disordered sex offender, or for a person who is civilly committed as a sexually violent predator pursuant to Article 4 (commencing with Section 6600) of Chapter 2 of Part 2 of Division 6, or regarding a patient who is committed to the department, to a state hospital, or any other public or private mental health facility approved by the county behavioral health director under Section 1026 or 1370 of the Penal Code or receiving treatment pursuant to Section 5300 of this code, shall be forwarded immediately without prior request to the Department of Justice. Except as otherwise provided by law, information automatically reported under this section shall be restricted to name, address, fingerprints, date of admission, date of discharge, date of escape or return from escape, date of any home leave, parole or leave of absence and, if known, the county in which the person will reside upon release. The Department of Justice may in turn furnish information reported under this section pursuant to Section 11105 or 11105.1 of the Penal Code. It shall be a misdemeanor for recipients furnished with this information to in turn furnish the information to any person or agency other than those specified in Section 11105 or 11105.1 of the Penal Code. *(Added by Stats.1970, c. 1627, p. 3447, § 22.5. Amended by Stats.1972, c. 1377, p. 2857, § 121; Stats.1977, c. 691, p. 2231, § 4; Stats.1983, c. 754, § 5; Stats.1984, c. 1415, § 4; Stats.1997, c. 818 (A.B.1303), § 6; Stats.2015, c. 455 (S.B.804), § 28, eff. Jan. 1, 2016.)*

Cross References

Department of Justice, see Government Code § 15000 et seq.
Inspection of public records, other exemptions from disclosure, see Government Code § 6276.30.
Misdemeanor, see Penal Code §§ 17, 19, 19.2.
Record of disclosures, see Welfare and Institutions Code § 5328.6.

§ 5328.3. Notice of disappearance of patient

(a) When a voluntary patient would otherwise be subject to the provisions of Section 5150 of this part and disclosure is necessary for the protection of the patient or others due to the patient's disappearance from, without prior notice to, a designated facility and his or her whereabouts is unknown, notice of the disappearance may be made to relatives and governmental law enforcement agencies designated by the physician in charge of the patient or the professional person in charge of the facility or his or her designee.

(b)(1) When an involuntary patient is gravely disabled, as defined in subparagraph (B) of paragraph (1) of subdivision (h) of Section 5008, and the patient has disappeared from a designated facility, or is transferred between state hospitals, notice of the disappearance or transfer shall be made to the court initially ordering the patient's commitment pursuant to Section 1370 of the Penal Code, the district attorney for the county that ordered the commitment, and governmental law enforcement agencies designated by the physician in charge of the patient or the professional person in charge of the facility or his or her designee. This notice shall be made within 24 hours of the patient's disappearance or transfer from the facility.

(2) A designated facility shall not permit the release of an involuntary patient who is gravely disabled, as defined in subparagraph (B) of paragraph (1) of subdivision (h) of Section 5008, without prior written authorization of the court pursuant to paragraph (2) of subdivision (d) of Section 5358. The court may approve the pending release without a hearing unless a party notified pursuant to subdivision (d) of Section 5358 objects to the pending release within 10 days after receiving notice. This paragraph does not apply to the transfer of persons between state hospitals. *(Added by Stats.1970, c. 1627, p. 3447, § 22.6. Amended by Stats.1995, c. 593 (A.B.145), § 2.)*

Cross References

Court defined for purposes of this Part, see Welfare and Institutions Code § 5008.
Record of disclosures, see Welfare and Institutions Code § 5328.6.

§ 5328.4. Crimes against person by or upon patient; release of information

The physician in charge of the patient, or the professional person in charge of the facility or his or her designee, when he or she has probable cause to believe that a patient while hospitalized has committed, or has been the victim of, murder, manslaughter, mayhem, aggravated mayhem, kidnapping, carjacking, robbery, assault with intent to commit a felony, arson, extortion, rape, forcible sodomy, forcible oral copulation, unlawful possession of a weapon as provided in any provision listed in Section 16590 of the Penal Code, or escape from a hospital by a mentally disordered sex offender as provided in Section 6330 of the Welfare and Institutions Code, shall release information about the patient to governmental law enforcement agencies.

The physician in charge of the patient, or the professional person in charge of the facility or his or her designee, when he or she has probable cause to believe that a patient, while hospitalized has committed, or has been the victim of assault or battery may release information about the patient to governmental law enforcement agencies.

This section shall be limited solely to information directly relating to the factual circumstances of the commission of the enumerated offenses and shall not include any information relating to the mental state of the patient or the circumstances of his or her voluntary or involuntary admission, commitment, or treatment.

This section shall not be construed as an exception to or in any other way affecting the provisions of Article 7 (commencing with Section 1010) of Chapter 4 of Division 8 of the Evidence Code. *(Added by Stats.1978, c. 160, p. 391, § 2. Amended by Stats.1989, c. 897, § 46; Stats.1993, c. 610 (A.B.6), § 32, eff. Oct. 1, 1993; Stats.1993, c. 611 (S.B.60), § 36, eff. Oct. 1, 1993; Stats.2010, c. 178 (S.B.1115), § 101, operative Jan. 1, 2012.)*

Law Revision Commission Comments

Section 5328.4 is amended to reflect nonsubstantive reorganization of the statutes governing control of deadly weapons. [38 Cal.L.Rev.Comm. Reports 217 (2009)].

Cross References

Felonies, definition and penalties, see Penal Code §§ 17, 18.
Inspection of public records, other exemptions from disclosure, see Government Code § 6276.30.
Record of disclosures, see Welfare and Institutions Code § 5328.6.

§ 5328.5. Confidential information and records; disclosure; elder abuse or dependent adult abuse

Information and records described in Section 5328 may be disclosed in communications relating to the prevention, investigation, or treatment of elder abuse or dependent adult abuse pursuant to Chapter 11 (commencing with Section 15600) and Chapter 13 (commencing with Section 15750), of Part 3 of Division 9. *(Added by Stats.1987, c. 1166, § 1, eff. Sept. 26, 1987.)*

§ 5328.6. Record of disclosures

When any disclosure of information or records is made as authorized by the provisions of Section 11878 or 11879 of the Health and Safety Code, subdivision (a) or (d) of Section 5328, Sections 5328.1, 5328.3, or 5328.4, the physician in charge of the patient or the professional person in charge of the facility shall promptly cause to be entered into the patient's medical record: the date and circumstances under which such disclosure was made; the names and relationships to the patient if any, of persons or agencies to whom such disclosure was made; and the specific information disclosed. *(Added by Stats.1970, c. 1627, p. 3448, § 23.5. Amended by Stats. 1975, c. 1108, p. 2685, § 3; Stats.1980, c. 676, p. 2038, § 333.)*

§ 5328.7. Consent forms; record of forms used; copy for patient

Signed consent forms by a patient for release of any information to which such patient is required to consent under the provisions of Sections 11878 or 11879 of the Health and Safety Code or subdivision (a) or (d) of Section 5328 shall be obtained for each separate use with the use specified, the information to be released, the name of the agency or individual to whom information will be released indicated on the form and the name of the responsible individual who has authorization to release information specified. Any use of this form shall be noted in the patient file. Patients who sign consent forms shall be given a copy of the consent form signed. *(Added by Stats.1975, c. 1108, p. 2685, § 4. Amended by Stats.1980, c. 676, p. 2038, § 334.)*

§ 5328.8. Death of patient; release of patient's medical record to medical examiner, forensic pathologist, or coroner

(a) The State Department of State Hospitals, the physician in charge of the patient, or the professional person in charge of the facility or his or her designee, shall release the patient's medical record to a medical examiner, forensic pathologist, or coroner, upon request, when a patient dies from any cause, natural or otherwise, while hospitalized in a state mental hospital. Except for the purposes included in paragraph (8) of subdivision (b) of Section 56.10 of the Civil Code, a medical examiner, forensic pathologist, or coroner shall not disclose any information contained in the medical record obtained pursuant to this subdivision without a court order or authorization pursuant to paragraph (4) of subdivision (c) of Section 56.11 of the Civil Code.

(b) A health facility, as defined in Section 1250 of the Health and Safety Code, a health or behavioral health facility or clinic, and the physician in charge of the patient shall release the patient's medical record to a medical examiner, forensic pathologist, or coroner, upon request, when a patient dies from any cause, natural or otherwise. Except for the purposes included in paragraph (8) of subdivision (b) of Section 56.10 of the Civil Code, a medical examiner, forensic pathologist, or coroner shall not disclose any information contained in the medical record obtained pursuant to this subdivision without a court order or authorization pursuant to paragraph (4) of subdivision (c) of Section 56.11 of the Civil Code.

(c) For purposes of this section, a reference to a "medical examiner, forensic pathologist, or coroner" means a coroner or deputy coroner, as described in subdivision (c) of Section 830.35 of the Penal Code, or a licensed physician who currently performs official autopsies on behalf of a county coroner's office or a medical examiner's office, whether as a government employee or under contract to that office. *(Added by Stats.1977, c. 498, p. 1624, § 2. Amended by Stats.1978, c. 69, p. 192, § 6; Stats.1979, c. 373, p. 1398, § 365; Stats.1982, c. 1141, § 8; Stats.2012, c. 24 (A.B.1470), § 127, eff. June 27, 2012; Stats.2016, c. 690 (A.B.2119), § 3, eff. Jan. 1, 2017.)*

Cross References

Coroner, duties, see Government Code § 27460 et seq.
Inspection of public records, other exemptions from disclosure, see Government Code § 6276.30.

§ 5328.9. Disclosure to employer; conditions; disclosure to patient; notice of nondisclosure to superior court

If at such time as a patient's hospital records are required by an employer to whom the patient has applied for employment, such records shall be forwarded to a qualified physician or psychiatrist representing the employer upon the request of the patient unless the physician or administrative officer responsible for the patient deems the release of such records contrary to the best interest of the patient.

If the physician or administrative officer responsible for a patient deems the release of such records contrary to the best interest of the patient, he shall notify the patient within five days. In the event that the disclosure of the patient's records to the patient himself would not serve his best interests, the physician or administrative officer in question shall render formal notice of his decision to the superior court of the county in which the patient resides. *(Added by Stats.1972, c. 1058, p. 1961, § 3.)*

Cross References

Court defined for purposes of this Part, see Welfare and Institutions Code § 5008.
Inspection of public records, other exemptions from disclosure, see Government Code § 6276.30.

§ 5329. Statistical data

Nothing in this chapter shall be construed to prohibit the compilation and publication of statistical data for use by government or researchers under standards set by the Director of State Hospitals. *(Added by Stats.1967, c. 1667, p. 4074, § 36, operative July 1, 1969. Amended by Stats.1968, c. 1374, p. 2660, § 49, operative July 1, 1969; Stats.1973, c. 142, p. 417, § 70.5, eff. June 30, 1973, operative July 1, 1973; Stats.1977, c. 1252, p. 4576, § 571, operative July 1, 1978; Stats.1978, c. 429, p. 1455, § 209, eff. July 17, 1978, operative July 1, 1978; Stats.1982, c. 1141, § 10; Stats.2012, c. 440 (A.B.1488), § 64, eff. Sept. 22, 2012.)*

§ 5330. Action for damages

(a) Any person may bring an action against an individual who has willfully and knowingly released confidential information or records concerning him or her in violation of this chapter, or of Chapter 1 (commencing with Section 11860) of Part 3 of Division 10.5 of the Health and Safety Code, for the greater of the following amounts:

(1) Ten thousand dollars ($10,000).

(2) Three times the amount of actual damages, if any, sustained by the plaintiff.

(b) Any person may bring an action against an individual who has negligently released confidential information or records concerning him or her in violation of this chapter, or of Chapter 1 (commencing with Section 11860) of Part 3 of Division 10.5 of the Health and Safety Code, for both of the following:

(1) One thousand dollars ($1,000). In order to recover under this paragraph, it shall not be a prerequisite that the plaintiff suffer or be threatened with actual damages.

(2) The amount of actual damages, if any, sustained by the plaintiff.

(c) Any person may, in accordance with Chapter 3 (commencing with Section 525) of Title 7 of Part 2 of the Code of Civil Procedure, bring an action to enjoin the release of confidential information or records in violation of this chapter, and may in the same action seek damages as provided in this section.

(d) In addition to the amounts specified in subdivisions (a) and (b), the plaintiff shall recover court costs and reasonable attorney's fees as determined by the court. *(Added by Stats.1967, c. 1667, p. 4074, § 36, operative July 1, 1969. Amended by Stats.1975, c. 1108, p. 2685, § 5; Stats.1980, c. 676, p. 2038, § 335; Stats.1998, c. 738 (S.B.2098), § 1, eff. Sept. 22, 1998.)*

Cross References

Court defined for purposes of this Part, see Welfare and Institutions Code § 5008.
Damages for torts in general, see Civil Code § 3333.
Exemplary damages, see Civil Code § 3294.
Injunction, see Civil Code § 3420 et seq.; Code of Civil Procedure § 525 et seq.
Preventive relief, see Civil Code § 3420 et seq.

§ 5331. Evaluation on competency; effect; statement of California law

No person may be presumed to be incompetent because he or she has been evaluated or treated for mental disorder or chronic alcoholism, regardless of whether such evaluation or treatment was voluntarily or involuntarily received. Any person who leaves a public or private mental health facility following evaluation or treatment for mental disorder or chronic alcoholism, regardless of whether that evaluation or treatment was voluntarily or involuntarily received, shall be given a statement of California law as stated in this paragraph.

Any person who has been, or is, discharged from a state hospital and received voluntary or involuntary treatment under former provisions of this code relating to inebriates or the mentally ill shall, upon request to the state hospital executive director or the State Department of State Hospitals, be given a statement of California law as stated in this section unless the person is found to be incompetent under proceedings for conservatorship or guardianship.

(Added by Stats.1967, c. 1667, p. 4074, § 36, operative July 1, 1969. Amended by Stats.1968, c. 1374, p. 2660, § 50, operative July 1, 1969; Stats.1971, c. 1593, p. 3342, § 378, operative July 1, 1973; Stats.1977, c. 1252, p. 4572, § 572, operative July 1, 1978; Stats.2012, c. 24 (A.B.1470), § 128, eff. June 27, 2012.)

Cross References

Burden of proof of insanity, see Evidence Code § 522.
Conservatorship, see Probate Code § 1800 et seq.
Conservatorship and guardianship for developmentally disabled persons, see Health and Safety Code § 416 et seq.
Conservatorship for gravely disabled persons, see Welfare and Institutions Code § 5350 et seq.
Disabilities of conservatee, see Welfare and Institutions Code §§ 5356, 5357.
Evaluation defined for purposes of this Part, see Welfare and Institutions Code § 5008.
Firearms, possession by mental patients, see Welfare and Institutions Code § 8100 et seq.
Guardians, appointment, see Probate Code § 2250.
Legal disability not imposed by evaluation proceedings, see Welfare and Institutions Code § 5005.
Presumption of competence after termination of conservatorship, see Welfare and Institutions Code § 5368.
Public guardian, see Government Code § 27430 et seq.
Rights of conservatees, right to contract, see Welfare and Institutions Code § 5357.

§ 5332. Administration of antipsychotic medication to persons subject to detention; consideration of treatment alternatives; internal procedures at hospitals; acquisition of person's medication history; emergency procedures

(a) Antipsychotic medication, as defined in subdivision (*l*) of Section 5008, may be administered to any person subject to detention pursuant to Section 5150, 5250, 5260, or 5270.15, if that person does not refuse that medication following disclosure of the right to refuse medication as well as information required to be given to persons pursuant to subdivision (c) of Section 5152 and subdivision (b) of Section 5213.

(b) If any person subject to detention pursuant to Section 5150, 5250, 5260, or 5270.15, and for whom antipsychotic medication has been prescribed, orally refuses or gives other indication of refusal of treatment with that medication, the medication shall be administered only when treatment staff have considered and determined that treatment alternatives to involuntary medication are unlikely to meet the needs of the patient, and upon a determination of that person's incapacity to refuse the treatment, in a hearing held for that purpose.

(c) Each hospital in conjunction with the hospital medical staff or any other treatment facility in conjunction with its clinical staff shall develop internal procedures for facilitating the filing of petitions for capacity hearings and other activities required pursuant to this chapter.

(d) When any person is subject to detention pursuant to Section 5150, 5250, 5260, or 5270.15, the agency or facility providing the treatment shall acquire the person's medication history, if possible.

(e) In the case of an emergency, as defined in subdivision (m) of Section 5008, a person detained pursuant to Section 5150, 5250, 5260, or 5270.15 may be treated with antipsychotic medication over his or her objection prior to a capacity hearing, but only with antipsychotic medication that is required to treat the emergency condition, which shall be provided in the manner least restrictive to the personal liberty of the patient. It is not necessary for harm to take place or become unavoidable prior to intervention. *(Added by Stats.1991, c. 681 (S.B.665), § 3. Amended by Stats.2001, c. 506 (A.B.1424), § 9.)*

Cross References

Antipsychotic medication defined for purposes of this Part, see Welfare and Institutions Code § 5008.
Emergency defined for purposes of this Part, see Welfare and Institutions Code § 5008.
Report of operation of division, see Welfare and Institutions Code § 5402.

Research References

3 Witkin, California Criminal Law 4th Punishment § 775 (2021), Right to Refuse Antipsychotic Medication.

§ 5333. Capacity hearings; representation by advocate or counsel; petition; notice

(a) Persons subject to capacity hearings pursuant to Section 5332 shall have a right to representation by an advocate or legal counsel. "Advocate," as used in this section, means a person who is providing mandated patients' rights advocacy services pursuant to Chapter 6.2 (commencing with Section 5500), and this chapter. If the State Department of State Hospitals provides training to patients' rights advocates, that training shall include issues specific to capacity hearings.

(b) Petitions for capacity hearings pursuant to Section 5332 shall be filed with the superior court. The director of the treatment facility or his or her designee shall personally deliver a copy of the notice of the filing of the petition for a capacity hearing to the person who is the subject of the petition.

(c) The mental health professional delivering the copy of the notice of the filing of the petition to the court for a capacity hearing shall, at the time of delivery, inform the person of his or her legal right to a capacity hearing, including the right to the assistance of the patients' rights advocate or an attorney to prepare for the hearing and to answer any questions or concerns.

(d) As soon after the filing of the petition for a capacity hearing is practicable, an attorney or a patients' rights advocate shall meet with the person to discuss the capacity hearing process and to assist the person in preparing for the capacity hearing and to answer questions or to otherwise assist the person, as is appropriate. *(Added by Stats.1991, c. 681 (S.B.665), § 4. Amended by Stats.2012, c. 24 (A.B.1470), § 129, eff. June 27, 2012.)*

Cross References

Court defined for purposes of this Part, see Welfare and Institutions Code § 5008.
Destruction of court records, notice, retention periods, see Government Code § 68152.

§ 5334. Capacity hearings; time for hearing; location; hearing officer; determination; notification; appeal; habeas corpus

(a) Capacity hearings required by Section 5332 shall be heard within 24 hours of the filing of the petition whenever possible. However, if any party needs additional time to prepare for the hearing, the hearing shall be postponed for 24 hours. In case of hardship, hearings may also be postponed for an additional 24 hours, pursuant to local policy developed by the county mental health director and the presiding judge of the superior court regarding the scheduling of hearings. The policy developed pursuant to this subdivision shall specify procedures for the prompt filing and processing of petitions to ensure that the deadlines set forth in this section are met, and shall take into consideration the availability of advocates and the treatment needs of the patient. In no event shall hearings be held beyond 72 hours of the filing of the petition. The person who is the subject of the petition and his or her advocate or counsel shall receive a copy of the petition at the time it is filed.

(b) Capacity hearings shall be held in an appropriate location at the facility where the person is receiving treatment, and shall be held in a manner compatible with, and the least disruptive of, the treatment being provided to the person.

(c) Capacity hearings shall be conducted by a superior court judge, a court-appointed commissioner or referee, or a court-appointed hearing officer. All commissioners, referees, and hearing officers shall be appointed by the superior court from a list of attorneys unanimously approved by a panel composed of the local mental health director, the county public defender, and the county counsel or district attorney designated by the county board of supervisors. No employee of the county mental health program or of any facility designated by the county and approved by the department as a facility for 72-hour treatment and evaluation may serve as a hearing officer. All hearing officers shall receive training in the issues specific to capacity hearings.

(d) The person who is the subject of the capacity hearing shall be given oral notification of the determination at the conclusion of the capacity hearing. As soon thereafter as is practicable, the person, his or her counsel or advocate, and the director of the facility where the person is receiving treatment shall be provided with written notification of the capacity determination, which shall include a statement of the evidence relied upon and the reasons for the determination. A copy of the determination shall be submitted to the superior court.

(e) (1) The person who is the subject of the capacity hearing may appeal the determination to the superior court or the court of appeal.

(2) The person who has filed the original petition for a capacity hearing may request the district attorney or county counsel in the county in which the person is receiving treatment to appeal the determination to the superior court or the court of appeal, on behalf of the state.

(3) Nothing shall prohibit treatment from being initiated pending appeal of a determination of incapacity pursuant to this section.

(4) Nothing in this section shall be construed to preclude the right of a person to bring a writ of habeas corpus pursuant to Section 5275, subject to the provisions of this chapter.

(f) All appeals to the superior court pursuant to this section shall be subject to de novo review. *(Added by Stats.1991, c. 681 (S.B.665), § 5.)*

Cross References

Administration of psychiatric medication without consent prohibited, county jail inmates, involuntary medication procedures, see Penal Code § 2603.
Court defined for purposes of this Part, see Welfare and Institutions Code § 5008.
Destruction of court records, notice, retention periods, see Government Code § 68152.
Evaluation defined for purposes of this Part, see Welfare and Institutions Code § 5008.
Report of operation of division, see Welfare and Institutions Code § 5402.

§ 5336. Capacity hearings; effect of determination

Any determination of a person's incapacity to refuse treatment with antipsychotic medication made pursuant to Section 5334 shall remain in effect only for the duration of the detention period described in Section 5150 or 5250, or both, or until capacity has been restored according to standards developed pursuant to subdivision (c) of Section 5332, or by court determination, whichever is sooner. *(Added by Stats.1991, c. 681 (S.B.665), § 6.)*

Cross References

Antipsychotic medication defined for purposes of this Part, see Welfare and Institutions Code § 5008.
Court defined for purposes of this Part, see Welfare and Institutions Code § 5008.

§ 5337. Persons determined at certification review hearing to be danger to others; right to file petition for post certification

Notwithstanding Section 5257, nothing shall prohibit the filing of a petition for post certification pursuant to Article 6 (commencing with Section 5300) for persons who have been determined to be a danger to others at a certification review hearing. *(Added by Stats.1991, c. 681 (S.B.665), § 7.)*

ARTICLE 8. COMMUNITY CONTROLLED SUBSTANCES TREATMENT SERVICES

§ 5340. Legislative intent

It is the intention of the Legislature by enacting this article to provide legal procedures for the custody, evaluation, and treatment of users of controlled substances. The enactment of this article shall not be construed to be evidence that a person subject to its provisions is [1] has a mental health disorder, or evidence that the Legislature considers that those persons have a mental health disorder. *(Added by Stats.1970, c. 1502, p. 2986, § 1. Amended by Stats.1984, c. 1635, § 99; Stats.2014, c. 144 (A.B.1847), § 93, eff. Jan. 1, 2015.)*

[1] So in chaptered copy.

Cross References

Controlled substance addicts, see Health and Safety Code § 11550 et seq.
Controlled substances defined, see Welfare and Institutions Code § 5341; Health and Safety Code § 11019.
Evaluation defined for purposes of this Part, see Welfare and Institutions Code § 5008.

§ 5341. "Controlled substances" defined

As used in this article, "controlled substances" means those substances referred to in Division 10 (commencing with Section 11000) of the Health and Safety Code. *(Added by Stats.1984, c. 1635, § 101.)*

§ 5342. Construction

Where other applicable sections of this part contain the phrase "a danger to himself or herself or others, or gravely disabled," such sections shall be deemed to refer to the condition of danger to self or others or grave disability as a result of the use of controlled substances, rather than by mental disorder, as such. *(Added by Stats.1970, c. 1502, p. 2987, § 1. Amended by Stats.1984, c. 1635, § 102.)*

Cross References

Gravely disabled defined for purposes of this Part, see Welfare and Institutions Code § 5008.

§ 5343. Laws applicable

Notwithstanding any other provision of law, if any person is a danger to others or to himself or herself, or gravely disabled, as a result of the use of controlled substances, he or she shall be subject, insofar as possible, to the provisions of Articles 1 (commencing with Section 5150), 2 (commencing with Section 5200), 4 (commencing with Section 5250), 5 (commencing with Section 5275), and 7 (commencing with Section 5325) of this chapter, except that any custody, evaluation and treatment, or any procedure pursuant to such provisions shall only be related to and concerned with the problem of the person's use of controlled substances. *(Added by Stats.1970, c. 1502, p. 2987, § 1. Amended by Stats.1984, c. 1635, § 103.)*

Cross References

Controlled substances,
Addicts, see Health and Safety Code § 11550 et seq.
Definition, see Welfare and Institutions Code § 5341; Health and Safety Code § 11019.
Evaluation defined for purposes of this Part, see Welfare and Institutions Code § 5008.

Treatment of addicts for addiction, see Health and Safety Code § 11215 et seq.

§ 5344. Expenditures

Any expenditure for the custody, evaluation, treatment, or other procedures for services rendered a person pursuant to this article shall be considered an expenditure made under the provisions of Part 2 (commencing with Section 5600) of this division, and shall be paid as are other expenditures pursuant to that part. No person shall be admitted to a state hospital for care and treatment of his or her use of controlled substances prior to screening and referral by an agency designated in the county Short–Doyle plan to provide the services. *(Added by Stats.1970, c. 1502, p. 2987, § 1. Amended by Stats.1984, c. 1635, § 104.)*

Cross References

Evaluation defined for purposes of this Part, see Welfare and Institutions Code § 5008.

Referral defined for purposes of this Part, see Welfare and Institutions Code § 5008.

ARTICLE 9. THE ASSISTED OUTPATIENT TREATMENT DEMONSTRATION PROJECT ACT OF 2002

§ 5345. Short title; definitions

(a) This article shall be known, and may be cited, as Laura's Law.

(b) "Assisted outpatient treatment" shall be defined as categories of outpatient services that have been ordered by a court pursuant to Section 5346 or 5347. *(Added by Stats.2002, c. 1017 (A.B.1421), § 2.)*

Cross References

Adult and older adult mental health system of care, funding, see Welfare and Institutions Code § 5813.5.

Court defined for purposes of this Part, see Welfare and Institutions Code § 5008.

§ 5346. Assisted outpatient treatment; orders; petitions; right to counsel; hearings; treatment plan; involuntary detention; continued treatment; habeas corpus

(a) In any county or group of counties where services are available as provided in Section 5348, a court may order a person who is the subject of a petition filed pursuant to this section to obtain assisted outpatient treatment if the court finds, by clear and convincing evidence, that the facts stated in the verified petition filed in accordance with this section are true and establish that all of the requisite criteria set forth in this section are met, including, but not limited to, each of the following:

(1) The person is 18 years of age or older.

(2) The person is suffering from a mental illness as defined in paragraphs (2) and (3) of subdivision (b) of Section 5600.3.

(3) There has been a clinical determination that, in view of the person's treatment history and current behavior, at least one of the following is true:

(A) The person is unlikely to survive safely in the community without supervision and the person's condition is substantially deteriorating.

(B) The person is in need of assisted outpatient treatment in order to prevent a relapse or deterioration that would be likely to result in grave disability or serious harm to the person or to others, as defined in Section 5150.

(4) The person has a history of lack of compliance with treatment for the person's mental illness, in that at least one of the following is true:

(A) The person's mental illness has, at least twice within the last 36 months, been a substantial factor in necessitating hospitalization, or receipt of services in a forensic or other mental health unit of a state correctional facility or local correctional facility, not including any period during which the person was hospitalized or incarcerated immediately preceding the filing of the petition.

(B) The person's mental illness has resulted in one or more acts of serious and violent behavior toward themselves or another, or threats, or attempts to cause serious physical harm to themselves or another within the last 48 months, not including any period in which the person was hospitalized or incarcerated immediately preceding the filing of the petition.

(5) The person has been offered an opportunity to participate in a treatment plan by the director of the local mental health department, or the director's designee, provided the treatment plan includes all of the services described in Section 5348, and the person continues to fail to engage in treatment.

(6) Participation in the assisted outpatient treatment program would be the least restrictive placement necessary to ensure the person's recovery and stability.

(7) It is likely that the person will benefit from assisted outpatient treatment.

(b)(1) A petition for an order authorizing assisted outpatient treatment may be filed by the county behavioral health director, or the director's designee, in the superior court in the county in which the person who is the subject of the petition is present or reasonably believed to be present.

(2) A request may be made only by any of the following persons to the county mental health department for the filing of a petition to obtain an order authorizing assisted outpatient treatment:

(A) A person 18 years of age or older with whom the person who is the subject of the petition resides.

(B) A person who is the parent, spouse, or sibling or child 18 years of age or older of the person who is the subject of the petition.

(C) The director of a public or private agency, treatment facility, charitable organization, or licensed residential care facility providing mental health services to the person who is the subject of the petition in whose institution the subject of the petition resides.

(D) The director of a hospital in which the person who is the subject of the petition is hospitalized.

(E) A licensed mental health treatment provider who is either supervising the treatment of, or treating for a mental illness, the person who is the subject of the petition.

(F) A peace officer, parole officer, or probation officer assigned to supervise the person who is the subject of the petition.

(G) A judge of a superior court before whom the person who is the subject of the petition appears.

(3) Upon receiving a request pursuant to paragraph (2), the county behavioral health director shall conduct an investigation into the appropriateness of filing of the petition. The director shall file the petition only if the director determines that there is a reasonable likelihood that all the necessary elements to sustain the petition can be proven in a court of law by clear and convincing evidence.

(4) The petition shall state all of the following:

(A) Each of the criteria for assisted outpatient treatment as set forth in subdivision (a).

(B) Facts that support the petitioner's belief that the person who is the subject of the petition meets each criterion, provided that the hearing on the petition shall be limited to the stated facts in the verified petition, and the petition contains all the grounds on which the petition is based, in order to ensure adequate notice to the person who is the subject of the petition and that person's counsel.

(C) That the person who is the subject of the petition is present, or is reasonably believed to be present, within the county where the petition is filed.

(D) That the person who is the subject of the petition has the right to be represented by counsel in all stages of the proceeding under the petition, in accordance with subdivision (c).

(5)(A) The petition shall be accompanied by an affidavit of a licensed mental health treatment provider designated by the local mental health director who shall state, if applicable, either of the following:

(i) That the licensed mental health treatment provider has personally examined the person who is the subject of the petition no more than 10 days prior to the submission of the petition, the facts and reasons why the person who is the subject of the petition meets the criteria in subdivision (a), that the licensed mental health treatment provider recommends assisted outpatient treatment for the person who is the subject of the petition, and that the licensed mental health treatment provider is willing and able to testify at the hearing on the petition.

(ii) That, no more than 10 days prior to the filing of the petition, the licensed mental health treatment provider, or the provider's designee, has made appropriate attempts to elicit the cooperation of the person who is the subject of the petition, but has not been successful in persuading that person to submit to an examination, that the licensed mental health treatment provider has reason to believe that the person who is the subject of the petition meets the criteria for assisted outpatient treatment, and that the licensed mental health treatment provider is willing and able to examine the person who is the subject of the petition and testify at the hearing on the petition.

(B) An examining mental health professional in their affidavit to the court shall address the issue of whether the defendant has capacity to give informed consent regarding psychotropic medication.

(c) The person who is the subject of the petition shall have the right to be represented by counsel at all stages of a proceeding commenced under this section. If the person so elects, the court shall immediately appoint the public defender or other attorney to assist the person in all stages of the proceedings. The person shall pay the cost of the legal services if able to do so.

(d)(1) Upon receipt by the court of a petition submitted pursuant to subdivision (b), the court shall fix the date for a hearing at a time not later than five days from the date the petition is received by the court, excluding Saturdays, Sundays, and holidays. The petitioner shall promptly cause service of a copy of the petition, together with written notice of the hearing date, to be made personally on the person who is the subject of the petition, and shall send a copy of the petition and notice to the county office of patient rights, and to the current health care provider appointed for the person who is the subject of the petition, if the provider is known to the petitioner. Continuances shall be permitted only for good cause shown. In granting continuances, the court shall consider the need for further examination by a physician or the potential need to provide expeditiously assisted outpatient treatment. Upon the hearing date, or upon any other date or dates to which the proceeding may be continued, the court shall hear testimony. If it is deemed advisable by the court, and if the person who is the subject of the petition is available and has received notice pursuant to this section, the court may examine in or out of court the person who is the subject of the petition who is alleged to be in need of assisted outpatient treatment. If the person who is the subject of the petition does not appear at the hearing, and appropriate attempts to elicit the attendance of the person have failed, the court may conduct the hearing in the person's absence. If the hearing is conducted without the person present, the court shall set forth the factual basis for conducting the hearing without the person's presence. The person who is the subject of the petition shall maintain the right to appear before the court in person, but may appear by videoconferencing means if they choose to do so.

(2) The court shall not order assisted outpatient treatment unless an examining licensed mental health treatment provider, who has personally examined, and has reviewed the available treatment history of, the person who is the subject of the petition within the time period commencing 10 days before the filing of the petition, testifies at the hearing. An examining mental health professional may appear before the court by videoconferencing means.

(3) If the person who is the subject of the petition has refused to be examined by a licensed mental health treatment provider, the court may request that the person consent to an examination by a licensed mental health treatment provider appointed by the court. If the person who is the subject of the petition does not consent and the court finds reasonable cause to believe that the allegations in the petition are true, the court may order any person designated under Section 5150 to take into custody the person who is the subject of the petition and transport the person, or cause the person to be transported, to a hospital for examination by a licensed mental health treatment provider as soon as is practicable. Detention of the person who is the subject of the petition under the order may not exceed 72 hours. If the examination is performed by another licensed mental health treatment provider, the examining licensed mental health treatment provider may consult with the licensed mental health treatment provider whose affirmation or affidavit accompanied the petition regarding the issues of whether the allegations in the petition are true and whether the person meets the criteria for assisted outpatient treatment.

(4) The person who is the subject of the petition shall have all of the following rights:

(A) To adequate notice of the hearings to the person who is the subject of the petition, as well as to parties designated by the person who is the subject of the petition.

(B) To receive a copy of the court-ordered evaluation.

(C) To counsel. If the person has not retained counsel, the court shall appoint a public defender.

(D) To be informed of the right to judicial review by habeas corpus.

(E) To be present at the hearing unless the person waives the right to be present.

(F) To present evidence.

(G) To call witnesses on the person's behalf.

(H) To cross-examine witnesses.

(I) To appeal decisions, and to be informed of the right to appeal.

(5)(A) If after hearing all relevant evidence, the court finds that the person who is the subject of the petition does not meet the criteria for assisted outpatient treatment, the court shall dismiss the petition.

(B) If after hearing all relevant evidence, the court finds that the person who is the subject of the petition meets the criteria for assisted outpatient treatment, and there is no appropriate and feasible less restrictive alternative, the court may order the person who is the subject of the petition to receive assisted outpatient treatment for an initial period not to exceed six months. In fashioning the order, the court shall specify that the proposed treatment is the least restrictive treatment appropriate and feasible for the person who is the subject of the petition. The order shall state the categories of assisted outpatient treatment, as set forth in Section 5348, that the person who is the subject of the petition is to receive, and the court may not order treatment that has not been recommended by the examining licensed mental health treatment provider and included in the written treatment plan for assisted outpatient treatment as required by subdivision (e). If the person has executed an advance health care directive pursuant to Chapter 2 (commencing with Section 4650) of Part 1 of Division 4.7 of the Probate Code, any directions included in the advance health care directive shall be considered in formulating the written treatment plan.

(C) The court may conduct status hearings with the person and the treatment team to receive information regarding progress related to the categories of treatment listed in the treatment plan and may inquire about medication adherence.

(6) If the person who is the subject of a petition for an order for assisted outpatient treatment pursuant to subparagraph (B) of paragraph (5) refuses to participate in the assisted outpatient treatment program, the court may order the person to meet with the assisted outpatient treatment team designated by the director of the assisted outpatient treatment program. The treatment team shall attempt to gain the person's cooperation with treatment ordered by the court. The person may be subject to a 72–hour hold pursuant to subdivision (f) only after the treatment team has attempted to gain the person's cooperation with treatment ordered by the court, and has been unable to do so.

(e) Assisted outpatient treatment shall not be ordered unless the licensed mental health treatment provider recommending assisted outpatient treatment to the court has submitted to the court a written treatment plan that includes services as set forth in Section 5348, and the court finds, in consultation with the county behavioral health director, or the director's designee, all of the following:

(1) That the services are available from the county, or a provider approved by the county, for the duration of the court order.

(2) That the services have been offered to the person by the local director of mental health, or the director's designee, and the person has been given an opportunity to participate on a voluntary basis, and the person has failed to engage in, or has refused, treatment.

(3) That all of the elements of the petition required by this article have been met.

(4) That the treatment plan will be delivered to the county behavioral health director, or to the director's appropriate designee.

(f) If, in the clinical judgment of a licensed mental health treatment provider, the person who is the subject of the petition has failed or has refused to comply with the treatment ordered by the court, and, in the clinical judgment of the licensed mental health treatment provider, efforts were made to solicit compliance, and, in the clinical judgment of the licensed mental health treatment provider, the person may be in need of involuntary admission to a hospital for evaluation, the provider may request that persons designated under Section 5150 take into custody the person who is the subject of the petition and transport the person, or cause the person to be transported, to a hospital, to be held up to 72 hours for examination by a licensed mental health treatment provider to determine if the person is in need of treatment pursuant to Section 5150. Any continued involuntary retention in a hospital beyond the initial 72–hour period shall be pursuant to Section 5150. If at any time during the 72–hour period the person is determined not to meet the criteria of Section 5150, and does not agree to stay in the hospital as a voluntary patient, the person shall be released and any subsequent involuntary detention in a hospital shall be pursuant to Section 5150. Failure to comply with an order of assisted outpatient treatment alone may not be grounds for involuntary civil commitment or a finding that the person who is the subject of the petition is in contempt of court.

(g) If the director of the assisted outpatient treatment program determines that the condition of the patient requires further assisted outpatient treatment, the director shall apply to the court, prior to the expiration of the period of the initial assisted outpatient treatment order, for an order authorizing continued assisted outpatient treatment for a period not to exceed 180 days from the date of the order. The procedures for obtaining an order pursuant to this subdivision shall be in accordance with subdivisions (a) to (f), inclusive. The period for further involuntary outpatient treatment authorized by a subsequent order under this subdivision may not exceed 180 days from the date of the order.

(h)(1) At intervals of not less than 60 days during an assisted outpatient treatment order, the director of the outpatient treatment program shall file an affidavit with the court that ordered the outpatient treatment affirming that the person who is the subject of the order continues to meet the criteria for assisted outpatient treatment. At these times, the person who is the subject of the order shall have the right to a hearing on whether or not the person still meets the criteria for assisted outpatient treatment if they disagree with the director's affidavit. The burden of proof shall be on the director.

(2) When making the affidavit pursuant to paragraph (1), the director of the outpatient treatment program shall also report to the court on adherence to prescribed medication.

(i) During each 60–day period specified in subdivision (h), if the person who is the subject of the order believes that they are being wrongfully retained in the assisted outpatient treatment program against their wishes, the person may file a petition for a writ of habeas corpus, thus requiring the director of the assisted outpatient treatment program to prove that the person who is the subject of the order continues to meet the criteria for assisted outpatient treatment.

(j) A person ordered to undergo assisted outpatient treatment pursuant to this article, who was not present at the hearing at which the order was issued, may immediately petition the court for a writ of habeas corpus. Treatment under the order for assisted outpatient treatment may not commence until the resolution of that petition.

(k) This section shall become operative on July 1, 2021. *(Added by Stats.2020, c. 140 (A.B.1976), § 2, eff. Jan. 1, 2021, operative July 1, 2021. Amended by Stats.2021, c. 426 (S.B.507), § 1, eff. Jan. 1, 2022; Stats.2022, c. 828 (S.B.1035), § 1, eff. Jan. 1, 2023.)*

Cross References

Assisted outpatient treatment defined for purposes of this Article, see Welfare and Institutions Code § 5345.
Burden of proof, generally, see Evidence Code § 500 et seq.
Care system for older adults with severe mental illness, volunteering for benefits, see Welfare and Institutions Code § 5801.
Court defined for purposes of this Part, see Welfare and Institutions Code § 5008.
Court-ordered evaluation defined for purposes of this Part, see Welfare and Institutions Code § 5008.
Department of Health Care Services, generally, see Health and Safety Code § 100100 et seq.
Effect of mental competency finding on criminal process, options upon finding defendant mentally incompetent, see Penal Code § 1370.01.
Evaluation defined for purposes of this Part, see Welfare and Institutions Code § 5008.
Peace officer defined for purposes of this Part, see Welfare and Institutions Code § 5008.

§ 5346.5. Assisted outpatient treatment; eligible conservatee

(a) In a county or group of counties where services are available, as provided in Section 5348, and in accordance with the requirements of Section 5346, a court may order a person who is the subject of a petition filed pursuant to this section to obtain assisted outpatient treatment if the court finds, by clear and convincing evidence, both of the following:

(1) The facts stated in the verified petition filed in accordance with this section are true.

(2) The person meets the definition of an eligible conservatee as set forth in this section.

(b) An "eligible conservatee" is a person who is a conservatee under this part who is the subject of a pending petition to terminate a conservatorship, who meets the criteria of Section 5346, and who, if the petition were granted, would benefit from assisted outpatient treatment to reduce the risk of deteriorating mental health while living independently. *(Added by Stats.2021, c. 426 (S.B.507), § 2, eff. Jan. 1, 2022.)*

§ 5347. Voluntary treatment; settlement agreements

(a) In a county or group of counties where services are available pursuant to Section 5348, a person who is determined by the court to be subject to subdivision (a) of Section 5346 may voluntarily enter into an agreement for services under this section.

(b)(1) After a petition for an order for assisted outpatient treatment is filed, but before the conclusion of the hearing on the petition, the person who is the subject of the petition, or the person's legal counsel with the person's consent, may waive the right to an assisted outpatient treatment hearing for the purpose of obtaining treatment under a settlement agreement, provided that an examining licensed mental health treatment provider states that the person can survive safely in the community. The settlement agreement may not exceed 180 days in duration and shall be agreed to by all parties.

(2) The settlement agreement shall be in writing, be approved by the court, and include a treatment plan developed by the community-based program that will provide services that provide treatment in the least restrictive manner consistent with the needs of the person who is the subject of the petition.

(3) Either party may request that the court modify the treatment plan at any time during the 180–day period.

(4) The court shall designate the appropriate county department to monitor the person's treatment under, and compliance with, the settlement agreement. If the person fails to comply with the treatment according to the agreement, the designated county department shall notify the counsel designated by the county and the person's counsel of the person's noncompliance.

(5) A settlement agreement approved by the court pursuant to this section shall have the same force and effect as an order for assisted outpatient treatment pursuant to Section 5346.

(6) At a hearing on the issue of noncompliance with the agreement, the written statement of noncompliance submitted shall be prima facie evidence that a violation of the conditions of the agreement has occurred. If the person who is the subject of the petition denies any of the facts as stated in the statement, they have the burden of proving by a preponderance of the evidence that the alleged facts are false.

(c) This section shall become operative on July 1, 2021. *(Added by Stats.2020, c. 140 (A.B.1976), § 4, eff. Jan. 1, 2021, operative July 1, 2021.)*

Cross References

Assisted outpatient treatment defined for purposes of this Article, see Welfare and Institutions Code § 5345.

Court defined for purposes of this Part, see Welfare and Institutions Code § 5008.

Prima facie evidence, see Evidence Code § 602.

§ 5348. Services offered; involuntary medication; report

(a) For purposes of subdivision (e) of Section 5346, a county or group of counties that chooses to provide assisted outpatient treatment services pursuant to this article shall offer assisted outpatient treatment services, including, but not limited to, all of the following:

(1) Community–based, mobile, multidisciplinary, highly trained mental health teams that use high staff-to-client ratios of no more than 10 clients per team member for those subject to court-ordered services pursuant to Section 5346.

(2) A service planning and delivery process that includes the following:

(A) Determination of the numbers of persons to be served and the programs and services that will be provided to meet their needs. The local director of mental health shall consult with the sheriff, the police chief, the probation officer, the mental health board, contract agencies, and family, client, ethnic, and citizen constituency groups as determined by the director.

(B) Plans for services, including outreach to families whose severely mentally ill adult is living with them, design of mental health services, coordination and access to medications, psychiatric and psychological services, substance abuse services, supportive housing or other housing assistance, vocational rehabilitation, and veterans' services. Plans shall also contain evaluation strategies that shall consider cultural, linguistic, gender, age, and special needs of minorities and those based on any characteristic listed or defined in Section 11135 of the Government Code in the target populations. Provision shall be made for staff with the cultural background and linguistic skills necessary to remove barriers to mental health services as a result of having limited-English-speaking ability and cultural differences. Recipients of outreach services may include families, the public, primary care physicians, and others who are likely to come into contact with individuals who may be suffering from an untreated severe mental illness who would be likely to become homeless if the illness continued to be untreated for a substantial period of time. Outreach to adults may include adults voluntarily or involuntarily hospitalized as a result of a severe mental illness.

(C) Provision for services to meet the needs of persons who are physically disabled.

(D) Provision for services to meet the special needs of older adults.

(E) Provision for family support and consultation services, parenting support and consultation services, and peer support or self-help group support, if appropriate.

(F) Provision for services to be client-directed and that employ psychosocial rehabilitation and recovery principles.

(G) Provision for psychiatric and psychological services that are integrated with other services and for psychiatric and psychological collaboration in overall service planning.

(H) Provision for services specifically directed to seriously mentally ill young adults 25 years of age or younger who are homeless or at significant risk of becoming homeless. These provisions may include continuation of services that still would be received through other funds had eligibility not been terminated as a result of age.

(I) Services reflecting special needs of women from diverse cultural backgrounds, including supportive housing that accepts children, personal services coordinator therapeutic treatment, and substance treatment programs that address gender-specific trauma and abuse in the lives of persons with mental illness, and vocational rehabilitation programs that offer job training programs free of gender bias and sensitive to the needs of women.

(J) Provision for housing for clients that is immediate, transitional, permanent, or all of these.

(K) Provision for clients who have been suffering from an untreated severe mental illness for less than one year, and who do not require the full range of services, but who are at risk of becoming homeless unless a comprehensive individual and family support services plan is implemented. These clients shall be served in a manner that is designed to meet their needs.

(3) Each client shall have a clearly designated mental health personal services coordinator who may be part of a multidisciplinary treatment team that is responsible for providing or ensuring needed services. Responsibilities include complete assessment of the client's needs, development of the client's personal services plan, linkage with all appropriate community services, monitoring of the quality

and followthrough of services, and necessary advocacy to ensure each client receives those services that are agreed to in the personal services plan. Each client shall participate in the development of their personal services plan, and responsible staff shall consult with the designated conservator, if one has been appointed, and, with the consent of the client, shall consult with the family and other significant persons as appropriate.

(4) The individual personal services plan shall ensure that persons subject to assisted outpatient treatment programs receive age-appropriate, gender-appropriate, and culturally appropriate services, to the extent feasible, that are designed to enable recipients to:

(A) Live in the most independent, least restrictive housing feasible in the local community, and, for clients with children, to live in a supportive housing environment that strives for reunification with their children or assists clients in maintaining custody of their children, as is appropriate.

(B) Engage in the highest level of work or productive activity appropriate to their abilities and experience.

(C) Create and maintain a support system consisting of friends, family, and participation in community activities.

(D) Access an appropriate level of academic education or vocational training.

(E) Obtain an adequate income.

(F) Self–manage their illnesses and exert as much control as possible over both the day-to-day and long-term decisions that affect their lives.

(G) Access necessary physical health care and maintain the best possible physical health.

(H) Reduce or eliminate serious antisocial or criminal behavior, and thereby reduce or eliminate their contact with the criminal justice system.

(I) Reduce or eliminate the distress caused by the symptoms of mental illness.

(J) Have freedom from dangerous addictive substances.

(5) The individual personal services plan shall describe the service array that meets the requirements of paragraph (4) and, to the extent applicable to the individual, the requirements of paragraph (2).

(b) A county that provides assisted outpatient treatment services pursuant to this article also shall offer the same services on a voluntary basis.

(c) Involuntary medication shall not be allowed absent a separate order by the court pursuant to Sections 5332 to 5336, inclusive.

(d) A county that operates an assisted outpatient treatment program pursuant to this article shall provide data to the State Department of Health Care Services and, based on the data, the department shall report to the Legislature on or before May 1 of each year in which the county provides services pursuant to this article. The report shall include, at a minimum, an evaluation of the effectiveness of the strategies employed by each program operated pursuant to this article in reducing homelessness and hospitalization of persons in the program and in reducing involvement with local law enforcement by persons in the program. The evaluation and report shall also include any other measures identified by the department regarding persons in the program and all of the following, based on information that is available:

(1) The number of persons served by the program and, of those, the number who are able to maintain housing and the number who maintain contact with the treatment system.

(2) The number of persons in the program with contacts with local law enforcement, and the extent to which local and state incarceration of persons in the program has been reduced or avoided.

(3) The number of persons in the program participating in employment services programs, including competitive employment.

(4) The days of hospitalization of persons in the program that have been reduced or avoided.

(5) Adherence to prescribed treatment by persons in the program.

(6) Other indicators of successful engagement, if any, by persons in the program.

(7) Victimization of persons in the program.

(8) Violent behavior of persons in the program.

(9) Substance abuse by persons in the program.

(10) Type, intensity, and frequency of treatment of persons in the program.

(11) Extent to which enforcement mechanisms are used by the program, when applicable.

(12) Social functioning of persons in the program.

(13) Skills in independent living of persons in the program.

(14) Satisfaction with program services both by those receiving them, and by their families, when relevant.

(e) This section shall become operative on July 1, 2021. *(Added by Stats.2020, c. 140 (A.B.1976), § 6, eff. Jan. 1, 2021, operative July 1, 2021.)*

Cross References

Adult and older adult mental health system of care, funding, see Welfare and Institutions Code § 5813.5.
Assisted outpatient treatment defined for purposes of this Article, see Welfare and Institutions Code § 5345.
Court defined for purposes of this Part, see Welfare and Institutions Code § 5008.
Effect of mental competency finding on criminal process, options upon finding defendant mentally incompetent, see Penal Code § 1370.01.
Evaluation defined for purposes of this Part, see Welfare and Institutions Code § 5008.

§ 5349. Implementation; opt out resolution; funding

(a) A county or group of counties that does not wish to implement this article may opt out of the requirements of this article by a resolution passed by the governing body that state the reasons for opting out and any facts or circumstances relied on in making that decision. To the extent otherwise permitted under state and federal law, counties that implement this article may pay for the provision of services under Sections 5347 and 5348 using funds distributed to the counties from the Mental Health Subaccount, the Mental Health Equity Subaccount, and the Vehicle License Collection Account of the Local Revenue Fund, funds from the Mental Health Account and the Behavioral Health Subaccount within the Support Services Account of the Local Revenue Fund 2011, funds from the Mental Health Services Fund when included in county plans pursuant to Section 5847, and any other funds from which the Controller makes distributions to the counties for those purposes. Compliance with this section shall be monitored by the State Department of Health Care Services as part of the review and approval of city, county, or group of county performance contracts.

(b) In lieu of the resolution to opt out pursuant to subdivision (a), a county may elect to implement this article in combination with one or more counties pursuant to the implementation provisions of subdivision (d).

(c) A county or group of counties implementing this article shall not reduce existing voluntary mental health programs serving adults or children's mental health programs as a result of implementation.

(d) If multiple counties choose to provide services pursuant to Section 5348, those counties shall execute a memorandum of understanding (MOU) that shall include, but not be limited to, a process for designating the lead county for an individual receiving services pursuant to the MOU for the following purposes:

(1) Making the finding set forth in subdivision (d) of Section 5346.

(2) Ensuring that services are provided and determining where they are provided.

(3) Determining the county incurring financial responsibility, as applicable, for an individual receiving services.

(4) Ensuring that appropriate followup care is in place upon an individual's release from the treatment program.

(e) This section shall become operative on July 1, 2021. *(Added by Stats.2020, c. 140 (A.B.1976), § 8, eff. Jan. 1, 2021, operative July 1, 2021.)*

§ 5349.1. Training and education program

(a) A county or group of counties that implements this article, shall, in consultation with the State Department of Health Care Services, client and family advocacy organizations, and other stakeholders, develop a training and education program for purposes of improving the delivery of services to mentally ill individuals who are, or who are at risk of being, involuntarily committed under this part. This training shall be provided to mental health treatment providers contracting with participating counties and to other individuals, including, but not limited to, mental health professionals, law enforcement officials, and certification hearing officers involved in making treatment and involuntary commitment decisions.

(b) The training shall include both of the following:

(1) Information relative to legal requirements for detaining a person for involuntary inpatient and outpatient treatment, including criteria to be considered with respect to determining if a person is considered to be gravely disabled.

(2) Methods for ensuring that decisions regarding involuntary treatment, as provided for in this part, direct patients toward the most effective treatment. Training shall include an emphasis on each patient's right to provide informed consent to assistance.

(c) This section shall become operative on July 1, 2021. *(Added by Stats.2020, c. 140 (A.B.1976), § 10, eff. Jan. 1, 2021, operative July 1, 2021.)*

CHAPTER 3. CONSERVATORSHIP FOR GRAVELY DISABLED PERSONS

§ 5350. Appointment; procedure

A conservator of the person, of the estate, or of the person and the estate may be appointed for a person who is gravely disabled as a result of a mental health disorder or impairment by chronic alcoholism.

The procedure for establishing, administering, and terminating a conservatorship under this chapter shall be the same as that provided in Division 4 (commencing with Section 1400) of the Probate Code, except as follows:

(a) A conservator may be appointed for a gravely disabled minor.

(b)(1) Appointment of a conservator under this part, including the appointment of a conservator for a person who is gravely disabled, as defined in subparagraph (A) of paragraph (1) of subdivision (h) of Section 5008, shall be subject to the list of priorities in Section 1812 of the Probate Code unless the officer providing conservatorship investigation recommends otherwise to the superior court.

(2) In appointing a conservator, as defined in subparagraph (B) of paragraph (1) of subdivision (h) of Section 5008, the court shall consider the purposes of protection of the public and the treatment of the conservatee. Notwithstanding any other provision of this section, the court shall not appoint the proposed conservator if the court determines that appointment of the proposed conservator will not result in adequate protection of the public.

(c) No conservatorship of the estate pursuant to this chapter shall be established if a conservatorship or guardianship of the estate exists under the Probate Code. When a gravely disabled person already has a guardian or conservator of the person appointed under the Probate Code, the proceedings under this chapter shall not terminate the prior proceedings but shall be concurrent with and superior thereto. The superior court may appoint the existing guardian or conservator of the person or another person as conservator of the person under this chapter.

(d)(1) The person for whom conservatorship is sought shall have the right to demand a court or jury trial on the issue of whether * * * the person is gravely disabled. Demand for court or jury trial shall be made within five days following the hearing on the conservatorship petition. If the proposed conservatee demands a court or jury trial before the date of the hearing as provided for in Section 5365, the demand shall constitute a waiver of the hearing.

(2) Court or jury trial shall commence within 10 days of the date of the demand, except that the court shall continue the trial date for a period not to exceed 15 days upon the request of counsel for the proposed conservatee. Failure to commence the trial within that period of time is grounds for dismissal of the conservatorship proceedings.

(3) This right shall also apply in subsequent proceedings to reestablish conservatorship.

(e)(1) Notwithstanding subparagraph (A) of paragraph (1) of subdivision (h) of Section 5008, a person is not "gravely disabled" if that person can survive safely without involuntary detention with the help of responsible family, friends, or others who are both willing and able to help provide for the person's basic personal needs for food, clothing, or shelter.

(2) However, unless they specifically indicate in writing their willingness and ability to help, family, friends, or others shall not be considered willing or able to provide this help.

(3) The purpose of this subdivision is to avoid the necessity for, and the harmful effects of, requiring family, friends, and others to publicly state, and requiring the court to publicly find, that no one is willing or able to assist a person with a mental health disorder in providing for the person's basic needs for food, clothing, or shelter.

(4) This subdivision does not apply to a person who is gravely disabled, as defined in subparagraph (B) of paragraph (1) of subdivision (h) of Section 5008.

(f) Conservatorship investigation shall be conducted pursuant to this part and shall not be subject to Section 1826 or Chapter 2 (commencing with Section 1850) of Part 3 of Division 4 of the Probate Code.

(g) Notice of proceedings under this chapter shall be given to a guardian or conservator of the person or estate of the proposed conservatee appointed under the Probate Code.

(h) As otherwise provided in this chapter. *(Added by Stats.1967, c. 1667, p. 4074, § 36, operative July 1, 1969. Amended by Stats.1969, c. 722, p. 1430, § 23, eff. Aug. 8, 1969, operative July 1, 1969; Stats.1970, c. 68, p. 82, § 1; Stats.1970, c. 1627, p. 3448, § 24; Stats.1971, c. 776, p. 1529, § 4; Stats.1972, c. 574, p. 981, § 1; Stats.1978, c. 1294, p. 4244, § 4; Stats.1979, c. 730, p. 2533, § 145, operative Jan. 1, 1981; Stats.1986, c. 322, § 1; Stats.1989, c. 999, § 2; Stats.1995, c. 593 (A.B.145), § 3; Stats.2006, c. 799 (A.B.2858), § 2; Stats.2014, c. 144 (A.B.1847), § 94, eff. Jan. 1, 2015; Stats.2022, c. 960 (A.B.2275), § 5, eff. Jan. 1, 2023.)*

Law Revision Commission Comments

Section 5350 is amended to correct the references to the Probate Code in view of the guardianship-conservatorship revision. [14 Cal.L.Rev.Comm.Reports 958 (1978)].

Cross References

Conservatorship investigation defined for purposes of this Part, see Welfare and Institutions Code § 5008.
Consumers placed on involuntary psychiatric hold or Lanterman–Petris–Short conservatorship, notification to clients' rights advocate, see Welfare and Institutions Code § 4696.3.
Court defined for purposes of this Part, see Welfare and Institutions Code § 5008.
Gravely disabled defined for purposes of this Chapter, see Welfare and Institutions Code § 5008.
Gravely disabled minor defined, see Welfare and Institutions Code § 5585.25.
Procedure for confinement of outpatient pending proceeding for revocation of outpatient status as not preventing hospitalization under other sections, see Welfare and Institutions Code § 5308.

Research References

5 Witkin, California Criminal Law 4th Criminal Trial § 846 (2021), Return to Court.

§ 5350.1. Purpose

The purpose of conservatorship, as provided for in this article, is to provide individualized treatment, supervision, and placement. *(Added by Stats.1978, c. 1294, p. 4244, § 5.)*

§ 5350.2. Notification of family members or other designated persons; time and place of hearing

Reasonable attempts shall be made by the county mental health program to notify family members or any other person designated by the person for whom conservatorship is sought, of the time and place of the conservatorship hearing. The person for whom the conservatorship is sought shall be advised by the facility treating the person that he or she may request that information about the time and place of the conservatorship hearing not be given to family members, in those circumstances where the proposed conservator is not a family member. The request shall be honored by the mental health program. Neither this section nor Section 5350 shall be interpreted to allow the proposed conservatee to request that any proposed conservator not be advised of the time and place of the conservatorship hearing. *(Added by Stats.1986, c. 872, § 5. Amended by Stats.1987, c. 56, § 183.)*

§ 5350.5. Referral of conservatee for assessment to determine if conservatee has treatable mental illness and is unwilling or unable to accept voluntary treatment; counsel; filing of copy with court

(a) If a conservatorship has already been established under the Probate Code, the court, in a proceeding under the Probate Code, after an evidentiary hearing attended by the conservatee, unless the conservatee waives presence, and the conservatee's counsel, may refer the conservatee, in consultation with a licensed physician or licensed psychologist satisfying the conditions of subdivision (c) of Section 2032.020 of the Code of Civil Procedure providing assessment or treatment to the conservatee, for an assessment by the local mental health system or plan to determine if the conservatee has a treatable mental illness, including whether the conservatee is gravely disabled as a result of a mental disorder or impairment by chronic alcoholism, and is unwilling to accept, or is incapable of accepting, treatment voluntarily. If the conservatee cannot afford counsel, the court shall appoint counsel for him or her pursuant to Section 1471 of the Probate Code.

(b) The local mental health system or plan shall file a copy of the assessment with the court that made the referral for assessment in a proceeding under the Probate Code. *(Added by Stats.2016, c. 819 (A.B.1836), § 1, eff. Jan. 1, 2017.)*

§ 5351. Investigating agencies; provision of services

In each county or counties acting jointly under the provisions of Article 1 (commencing with Section 6500) of Chapter 5 of Division 7 of Title 1 of the Government Code, the governing board shall designate the agency or agencies to provide conservatorship investigation as set forth in this chapter. The governing board may designate that conservatorship services be provided by the public guardian or agency providing public guardian services. *(Added by Stats.1967, c. 1667, p. 4074, § 36, operative July 1, 1969. Amended by Stats.1968, c. 1374, p. 2660, § 51.5, operative July 1, 1969; Stats.1986, c. 335, § 1.)*

Cross References

Conservatorship investigation defined for purposes of this Part, see Welfare and Institutions Code § 5008.

§ 5352. Recommendation; petition; temporary conservator; procedure

When the professional person in charge of an agency providing comprehensive evaluation or a facility providing intensive treatment determines that a person in his or her care is gravely disabled as a result of mental disorder or impairment by chronic alcoholism and is unwilling to accept, or incapable of accepting, treatment voluntarily, he or she may recommend conservatorship to the officer providing conservatorship investigation of the county of residence of the person prior to his or her admission as a patient in such facility.

The professional person in charge of an agency providing comprehensive evaluation or a facility providing intensive treatment, or the professional person in charge of providing mental health treatment at a county jail, or his or her designee, may recommend conservatorship for a person without the person being an inpatient in a facility providing comprehensive evaluation or intensive treatment, if both of the following conditions are met: (a) the professional person or another professional person designated by him or her has examined and evaluated the person and determined that he or she is gravely disabled; (b) the professional person or another professional person designated by him or her has determined that future examination on an inpatient basis is not necessary for a determination that the person is gravely disabled.

If the officer providing conservatorship investigation concurs with the recommendation, he or she shall petition the superior court in the county of residence of the patient to establish conservatorship.

Where temporary conservatorship is indicated, the fact shall be alternatively pleaded in the petition. The officer providing conservatorship investigation or other county officer or employee designated by the county shall act as the temporary conservator. *(Added by Stats.1967, c. 1667, p. 4074, § 36, operative July 1, 1969. Amended by Stats.1968, c. 1374, p. 2661, § 52, operative July 1, 1969; Stats.1969, c. 722, p. 1430, § 24, eff. Aug. 8, 1969, operative July 1, 1969; Stats.1970, c. 35, p. 56, § 1; Stats.1970, c. 1627, p. 3449, § 24.1; Stats.1972, c. 692, p. 1274, § 1; Stats.1979, c. 730, p. 2534, § 146, operative Jan. 1, 1981; Stats.2018, c. 458 (S.B.931), § 1, eff. Jan. 1, 2019.)*

Law Revision Commission Comments

Section 5352 is amended to delete the references to the Probate Code in view of the revision of guardianship–conservatorship law. Under Section 5350 of the Welfare and Institutions Code, the procedure for establishing, administering, and terminating conservatorship under this chapter is the same as that provided in Division 4 (commencing with Section 1400) of the Probate Code. [14 Cal.L.Rev.Comm. Reports 958 (1978)].

Cross References

Conservatorship investigation defined for purposes of this Part, see Welfare and Institutions Code § 5008.
Court defined for purposes of this Part, see Welfare and Institutions Code § 5008.
Evaluation defined for purposes of this Part, see Welfare and Institutions Code § 5008.
Gravely disabled defined for purposes of this Chapter, see Welfare and Institutions Code § 5008.
Intensive treatment defined for purposes of this Part, see Welfare and Institutions Code § 5008.

§ 5352.1. Temporary conservatorship

(a) The court may establish a temporary conservatorship for a period not to exceed 30 days and appoint a temporary conservator, on the basis of the comprehensive report of the officer providing conservatorship investigation filed pursuant to Section 5354, or on the basis of an affidavit of the professional person who recommended conservatorship stating the reasons for * * * their recommendation, if the court is satisfied that the comprehensive report or affidavit shows the necessity for a temporary conservatorship.

(b) Except as provided in this section, a temporary conservatorship shall expire automatically * * * after 30 days, unless prior to that date the court * * * conducts a hearing on the issue of whether or not the proposed conservatee is gravely disabled, as defined in subdivision (h) of Section 5008.

(c) If the proposed conservatee demands a court or jury trial on the issue of whether * * * they are gravely disabled, the court may extend the temporary conservatorship until the date of the disposition of the issue by the court or jury trial, provided that the extension * * * does not exceed 180 days. *(Added by Stats.1969, c. 722, p. 1431, § 24.05, eff. Aug. 8, 1969, operative July 1, 1969. Amended by Stats.1971, c. 776, p. 1530, § 5; Stats.1972, c. 574, p. 981, § 2; Stats.2008, c. 179 (S.B.1498), § 238; Stats.2022, c. 996 (S.B.1394), § 1, eff. Jan. 1, 2023.)*

Cross References

Conservatorship investigation defined for purposes of this Part, see Welfare and Institutions Code § 5008.
Court defined for purposes of this Part, see Welfare and Institutions Code § 5008.
Gravely disabled defined for purposes of this Chapter, see Welfare and Institutions Code § 5008.

§ 5352.2. Public guardian; bond and oath

Where the duly designated officer providing conservatorship investigation is a public guardian, his official oath and bond as public guardian are in lieu of any other bond or oath on the grant of temporary letters of conservatorship to him. *(Added by Stats.1970, c. 566, p. 1138, § 1.)*

Cross References

Conservatorship investigation defined for purposes of this Part, see Welfare and Institutions Code § 5008.

Public guardian, see Government Code § 27430 et seq.

§ 5352.3. Additional detention pending filing petition; maximum involuntary detention for gravely disabled

If the professional person in charge of the facility providing intensive treatment recommends conservatorship pursuant to Section 5352, the proposed conservatee may be held in that facility for a period not to exceed three days beyond the designated period for intensive treatment if the additional time period is necessary for a filing of the petition for temporary conservatorship and the establishment of the temporary conservatorship by the court. The involuntary detention period for gravely disabled persons pursuant to Sections 5150, 5250, and 5170.15 shall not exceed 47 days unless continuance is granted. *(Added by Stats.1970, c. 1627, p. 3449, § 24.5. Amended by Stats.1988, c. 1517, § 13.)*

Cross References

Certification for fourteen days of intensive treatment, see Welfare and Institutions Code § 5250 et seq.

Court defined for purposes of this Part, see Welfare and Institutions Code § 5008.

Gravely disabled defined for purposes of this Chapter, see Welfare and Institutions Code § 5008.

Intensive treatment defined for purposes of this Part, see Welfare and Institutions Code § 5008.

§ 5352.4. Appeal of judgment establishing conservatorship; continuation of conservatorship; exception

If a conservatee appeals the court's decision to establish conservatorship, the conservatorship shall continue unless execution of judgment is stayed by the appellate court. *(Added by Stats.1972, c. 574, p. 982, § 4.)*

Cross References

Court defined for purposes of this Part, see Welfare and Institutions Code § 5008.

§ 5352.5. Initiation of proceedings; reimbursement

(a) Conservatorship proceedings may be initiated for any person committed to a state hospital or local mental health facility or placed on outpatient treatment pursuant to Section 1026 or 1370 of the Penal Code or transferred pursuant to Section 4011.6 of the Penal Code upon recommendation of the medical director of the state hospital, or a designee, or professional person in charge of the local mental health facility, or a designee, or the local mental health director, or a designee, to the conservatorship investigator of the county of residence of the person prior to his or her admission to the hospital or facility or of the county in which the hospital or facility is located. The initiation of conservatorship proceedings or the existence of a conservatorship shall not affect any pending criminal proceedings. The custody status of a person who is subject to the conservatorship investigation shall not be the sole reason for not scheduling an investigation by the conservatorship investigator.

(b) Subject to the provisions of Sections 5150 and 5250, conservatorship proceedings may be initiated for any person convicted of a felony who has been transferred to a state hospital under the jurisdiction of the State Department of State Hospitals pursuant to Section 2684 of the Penal Code by the recommendation of the medical director of the state hospital to the conservatorship investigator of the county of residence of the person or of the county in which the state hospital is located.

(c) Subject to the provisions of Sections 5150 and 5250, conservatorship proceedings may be initiated for any person committed to the Department of Corrections and Rehabilitation, Division of Juvenile Justice, or on parole from a facility of the Department of Corrections and Rehabilitation, Division of Juvenile Justice, by the Chief Deputy Secretary for Juvenile Justice or a designee, to the conservatorship investigator of the county of residence of the person or of the county in which the facility is situated.

(d) The county mental health program providing conservatorship investigation services and conservatorship case management services for any persons except those transferred pursuant to Section 4011.6 of the Penal Code shall be reimbursed for the expenditures made by it for the services pursuant to the Short–Doyle Act (commencing with Section 5600) at 100 percent of the expenditures. Each county Short–Doyle plan shall include provision for the services in the plan. *(Added by Stats.1975, c. 1258, p. 3302, § 7. Amended by Stats.1977, c. 1252, p. 4572, § 572, operative July 1, 1978; Stats.1977, c. 691, p. 2231, § 5; Stats.1978, c. 429, p. 1455, § 209.5, eff. July 17, 1978, operative July 1, 1978; Stats.1986, c. 933, § 2; Stats.2012, c. 24 (A.B.1470), § 130, eff. June 27, 2012; Stats.2018, c. 458 (S.B.931), § 2, eff. Jan. 1, 2019.)*

Cross References

Conservatorship investigation defined for purposes of this Part, see Welfare and Institutions Code § 5008.

Felonies, definition and penalties, see Penal Code §§ 17, 18.

§ 5352.6. Individualized treatment plan; development; goals; progress review; termination of conservatorship by court

Within 10 days after conservatorship of the person has been established under the provisions of this article, there shall be an individualized treatment plan unless treatment is specifically found not to be appropriate by the court. The treatment plan shall be developed by the Short–Doyle Act community mental health service, the staff of a facility operating under a contract to provide such services in the individual's county of residence, or the staff of a health facility licensed pursuant to Chapter 2 (commencing with Section 1250) of Division 2 of the Health and Safety Code to provide inpatient psychiatric treatment. The person responsible for developing the treatment plan shall encourage the participation of the client and the client's family members, when appropriate, in the development, implementation, revision, and review of the treatment plan. The individualized treatment plan shall specify goals for the individual's treatment, the criteria by which accomplishment of the goals can be judged, and a plan for review of the progress of treatment. The goals of the treatment plan shall be equivalent to reducing or eliminating the behavioral manifestations of grave disability. If a treatment plan is not developed as provided herein then the matter shall be referred to the court by the Short–Doyle Act community mental health service, or the staff of a facility operating under a contract to provide such services, or the conservator, or the attorney of record for the conservatee.

When the progress review determines that the goals have been reached and the person is no longer gravely disabled, a person designated by the county shall so report to the court and the conservatorship shall be terminated by the court.

If the conservator fails to report to the court that the person is no longer gravely disabled as provided herein, then the matter shall be referred to the court by the Short–Doyle Act community mental health service, or the staff of a facility operating under a contract to provide such services, or the attorney of record for the conservatee. *(Added by Stats.1978, c. 1294, p. 4244, § 6. Amended by Stats.1986, c. 872, § 6.)*

Cross References

Community mental health service, see Welfare and Institutions Code § 5602.

Court defined for purposes of this Part, see Welfare and Institutions Code § 5008.

Gravely disabled defined for purposes of this Chapter, see Welfare and Institutions Code § 5008.

§ 5353. Temporary conservator; arrangements pending determination of conservatorship; powers; residence of conservatee; sale or relinquishment of property

A temporary conservator under this chapter shall determine what arrangements are necessary to provide the person with food, shelter, and care pending the determination of conservatorship. He shall give preference to arrangements which allow the person to return to his home, family or friends. If necessary, the temporary conservator may require the person to be detained in a facility providing intensive treatment or in a facility specified in Section 5358 pending the determination of conservatorship. Any person so detained shall have the same right to judicial review set forth in Article 5 (commencing with Section 5275) of Chapter 2 of this part.

The powers of the temporary conservator shall be those granted in the decree, but in no event may they be broader than the powers which may be granted a conservator.

The court shall order the temporary conservator to take all reasonable steps to preserve the status quo concerning the conservatee's previous place of residence. The temporary conservator shall not be permitted to sell or relinquish on the conservatee's behalf any estate or interest in any real or personal property, including any lease or estate in real or personal property used as or within the conservatee's place of residence, without specific approval of the court, which may be granted only upon a finding based on a preponderance of the evidence that such action is necessary to avert irreparable harm to the conservatee. A finding of irreparable harm as to real property may be based upon a reasonable showing that such real property is vacant, that it cannot reasonably be rented, and that it is impossible or impractical to obtain fire or liability insurance on such property. *(Added by Stats.1967, c. 1667, p. 4074, § 36, operative July 1, 1969. Amended by Stats.1968, c. 1374, p. 2661, § 53, operative July 1, 1969; Stats.1969, c. 722, p. 1431, § 24.1, eff. Aug. 8, 1969, operative July 1, 1969; Stats.1971, c. 776, p. 1530, § 6; Stats.1972, c. 574, p. 982, § 3; Stats.1977, c. 1237, p. 4157, § 5; Stats.1978, c. 1268, p. 4116, § 2.)*

Cross References

Court defined for purposes of this Part, see Welfare and Institutions Code § 5008.
Intensive treatment defined for purposes of this Part, see Welfare and Institutions Code § 5008.
Procedure for confinement of outpatient pending proceeding for revocation of outpatient status as not preventing hospitalization under other sections, see Welfare and Institutions Code § 5308.

§ 5354. Investigation of alternatives to conservatorship; recommendations of conservatorship; report of investigation, necessity, contents, transmittal, use; service of report

(a) The officer providing conservatorship investigation shall investigate all available alternatives to conservatorship and shall recommend conservatorship to the court only if no suitable alternatives are available. This officer shall render to the court a written report of investigation prior to the hearing. The report to the court shall be comprehensive and shall contain all relevant aspects of the person's medical, psychological, financial, family, vocational, and social condition, and information obtained from the person's family members, close friends, social worker, or principal therapist. The report shall also contain all available information concerning the person's real and personal property. The facilities providing intensive treatment or comprehensive evaluation shall disclose any records or information which may facilitate the investigation. If the officer providing conservatorship investigation recommends either for or against conservatorship, * * * the officer shall set forth all alternatives available, including all less restrictive alternatives. A copy of the report shall be transmitted to the individual who originally recommended conservatorship, to the person or agency, if any, recommended to serve as conservator, and to the person recommended for conservatorship. The court may receive the report in evidence and may read and consider the contents thereof in rendering its judgment.

(b) Notwithstanding Section 5328, when a court with jurisdiction over a person in a criminal case orders an evaluation of the person's mental condition pursuant to Section 5200, and that evaluation leads to a conservatorship investigation, the officer providing the conservatorship investigation shall serve a copy of the report required under subdivision (a) upon the defendant or the defendant's counsel. Upon the prior written request of the defendant or the defendant's counsel, the officer providing the conservatorship investigation shall also submit a copy of the report to the court hearing the criminal case, the district attorney, and the county probation department. The conservatorship investigation report and the information contained in that report, shall be kept confidential and shall not be further disclosed to anyone without the prior written consent of the defendant. After disposition of the criminal case, the court shall place all copies of the report in a sealed file, except as follows:

(1) The defendant and the defendant's counsel may retain their copy.

(2) If the defendant is placed on probation status, the county probation department may retain a copy of the report for the purpose of supervision of the defendant until the probation is terminated, at which time the probation department shall return its copy of the report to the court for placement into the sealed file. *(Added by Stats.1967, c. 1667, p. 4074, § 36, operative July 1, 1969. Amended by Stats.1974, c. 833, p. 1795, § 1; Stats.1978, c. 1294, p. 4245, § 7; Stats.1982, c. 1598, § 7; Stats.2014, c. 734 (A.B.2190), § 4, eff. Jan. 1, 2015; Stats.2022, c. 960 (A.B.2275), § 6, eff. Jan. 1, 2023.)*

Cross References

Conservatorship investigation defined for purposes of this Part, see Welfare and Institutions Code § 5008.
Court defined for purposes of this Part, see Welfare and Institutions Code § 5008.
Effect of mental competency finding on criminal process, options upon finding defendant mentally incompetent, see Penal Code § 1370.01.
Evaluation defined for purposes of this Part, see Welfare and Institutions Code § 5008.
Intensive treatment defined for purposes of this Part, see Welfare and Institutions Code § 5008.
State summary criminal history information, persons entitled to receive, restrictions on use, see Penal Code § 11105.1.

§ 5354.5. Acceptance or rejection of position as conservator; recommendation of substitute; public guardian

Except as otherwise provided in this section, the person recommended to serve as conservator shall promptly notify the officer providing conservatorship investigation whether he or she will accept the position if appointed. If notified that the person or agency recommended will not accept the position if appointed, the officer providing conservatorship investigation shall promptly recommend another person to serve as conservator.

The public guardian shall serve as conservator of any person found by a court under this chapter to be gravely disabled, if the court recommends the conservatorship after a conservatorship investigation, and if the court finds that no other person or entity is willing and able to serve as conservator. *(Added by Stats.1967, c. 1667, p. 4074, § 36, operative July 1, 1969. Amended by Stats.1986, c. 872, § 6.5.)*

Cross References

Conservatorship investigation defined for purposes of this Part, see Welfare and Institutions Code § 5008.
Court defined for purposes of this Part, see Welfare and Institutions Code § 5008.
Gravely disabled defined for purposes of this Chapter, see Welfare and Institutions Code § 5008.

§ 5355. Designation of conservator; conflicts of interest; public guardian

If the conservatorship investigation results in a recommendation for conservatorship, the recommendation shall designate the most suitable person, corporation, state or local agency or county officer, or employee designated by the county to serve as conservator. No person, corporation, or agency shall be designated as conservator whose interests, activities, obligations or responsibilities are such as to compromise his or her or their ability to represent and safeguard the interests of the conservatee. Nothing in this section shall be construed to prevent the State Department of State Hospitals from serving as guardian pursuant to Section 7284, or the function of the conservatorship investigator and conservator being exercised by the same public officer or employee.

When a public guardian is appointed conservator, his or her official bond and oath as public guardian are in lieu of the conservator's bond and oath on the grant of letters of conservatorship. No bond shall be required of any other public officer or employee appointed to serve as conservator. *(Added by Stats.1967, c. 1667, p. 4074, § 36, operative July 1, 1969. Amended by Stats.1970, c. 566, p. 1138, § 2; Stats.1971, c. 1593, p. 3343, § 378.5; Stats.1971, c. 955, p. 1861, § 10; Stats.1973, c. 142, p. 417, § 71, eff. June 30, 1973, operative July 1, 1973; Stats.1974, c. 1060, p. 2284, § 9; Stats.1977, c. 1252, p. 4577, § 574, operative July 1, 1978; Stats.2012, c. 24 (A.B.1470), § 131, eff. June 27, 2012.)*

Cross References

Conservatorship investigation defined for purposes of this Part, see Welfare and Institutions Code § 5008.
Public guardian, see Government Code § 27430 et seq.

§ 5356. Investigation report; recommendations; agreement to serve as conservator

The report of the officer providing conservatorship investigation shall contain his or her recommendations concerning the powers to be granted to, and the duties to be imposed upon the conservator, the legal disabilities to be imposed upon the conservatee, and the proper placement for the conservatee pursuant to Section 5358. Except as provided in this section, the report to the court shall also contain an agreement signed by the person or agency recommended to serve as conservator certifying that the person or agency is able and willing to serve as conservator. The public guardian shall serve as conservator of any person found by a court under this chapter to be gravely disabled, if the court recommends the conservatorship after a conservatorship investigation, and if the court finds that no other person or entity is willing and able to serve as conservator. *(Added by Stats.1967, c. 1667, p. 4074, § 36, operative July 1, 1969. Amended by Stats.1980, c. 681, p. 2066, § 1; Stats.1986, c. 872, § 7.)*

Cross References

Conservatorship investigation defined for purposes of this Part, see Welfare and Institutions Code § 5008.
Court defined for purposes of this Part, see Welfare and Institutions Code § 5008.
Gravely disabled defined for purposes of this Chapter, see Welfare and Institutions Code § 5008.

§ 5357. Conservator; general and special powers; disability of conservatee

All conservators of the estate shall have the general powers specified in Chapter 6 (commencing with Section 2400) of Part 4 of Division 4 of the Probate Code and shall have the additional powers specified in Article 11 (commencing with Section 2590) of Chapter 6 of Part 4 of Division 4 of the Probate Code as the court may designate. The report shall set forth which, if any, of the additional powers it recommends. The report shall also recommend for or against the imposition of each of the following disabilities on the proposed conservatee:

(a) The privilege of possessing a license to operate a motor vehicle. If the report recommends against this right and if the court follows the recommendation, the agency providing conservatorship investigation shall, upon the appointment of the conservator, so notify the Department of Motor Vehicles.

(b) The right to enter into contracts. The officer may recommend against the person having the right to enter specified types of transactions or transactions in excess of specified money amounts.

(c) The disqualification of the person from voting pursuant to Section 2208 of the Elections Code.

(d) The right to refuse or consent to treatment related specifically to the conservatee's being gravely disabled. The conservatee shall retain all rights specified in Section 5325.

(e) The right to refuse or consent to routine medical treatment unrelated to remedying or preventing the recurrence of the conservatee's being gravely disabled. The court shall make a specific determination regarding imposition of this disability.

(f) The disqualification of the person from possessing a firearm pursuant to subdivision (e) of Section 8103. *(Added by Stats.1967, c. 1667, p. 4074, § 36, operative July 1, 1969. Amended by Stats.1969, c. 722, p. 1431, § 25, eff. Aug. 8, 1969, operative July 1, 1969; Stats.1976, c. 905, p. 2078, § 1; Stats.1978, c. 1363, p. 4531, § 14; Stats.1979, c. 730, p. 2535, § 147, operative Jan. 1, 1981; Stats.1984, c. 1562, § 3; Stats.1990, c. 180 (S.B.2138), § 1; Stats.1994, c. 923 (S.B.1546), § 268.)*

Law Revision Commission Comments

Section 5357 is amended to revise the cross-references to the Probate Code in view of the revision of guardianship–conservatorship law in the Probate Code. [14 Cal.L.Rev.Comm. Reports 958 (1978)].

Cross References

Competence of former conservatee, see Welfare and Institutions Code § 5368.
Conservatorship investigation defined for purposes of this Part, see Welfare and Institutions Code § 5008.
Contract powers, loss by person whose incapacity judicially determined, see Civil Code § 40.
Court defined for purposes of this Part, see Welfare and Institutions Code § 5008.
Drivers' license,
Mental defect, effect, see Vehicle Code § 12805 et seq.
Statement in application, see Vehicle Code § 12800.
Firearms,
Certificate for possession, see Welfare and Institutions Code § 8103.
Mental patient, see Welfare and Institutions Code § 8100 et seq.
Gravely disabled defined for purposes of this Chapter, see Welfare and Institutions Code § 5008.
Restriction on disabilities imposed upon person complained against, see Welfare and Institutions Code § 5005.

§ 5358. Placement of conservatee; treatment

(a)(1) When ordered by the court after the hearing required by this section, a conservator appointed pursuant to this chapter shall place his or her conservatee as follows:

(A) For a conservatee who is gravely disabled, as defined in subparagraph (A) of paragraph (1) of subdivision (h) of Section 5008, in the least restrictive alternative placement, as designated by the court.

(B) For a conservatee who is gravely disabled, as defined in subparagraph (B) of paragraph (1) of subdivision (h) of Section 5008, in a placement that achieves the purposes of treatment of the conservatee and protection of the public.

(2) The placement may include a medical, psychiatric, nursing, or other state-licensed facility, or a state hospital, county hospital, hospital operated by the Regents of the University of California, a United States government hospital, or other nonmedical facility approved by the State Department of Health Care Services or an agency accredited by the State Department of Health Care Services, or in addition to any of the foregoing, in cases of chronic alcoholism, to a county alcoholic treatment center.

(b) A conservator shall also have the right, if specified in the court order, to require his or her conservatee to receive treatment related specifically to remedying or preventing the recurrence of the conservatee's being gravely disabled, or to require his or her conservatee to receive routine medical treatment unrelated to remedying or preventing the recurrence of the conservatee's being gravely disabled. Except in emergency cases in which the conservatee faces loss of life or serious bodily injury, no surgery shall be performed upon the conservatee without the conservatee's prior consent or a court order obtained pursuant to Section 5358.2 specifically authorizing that surgery.

(c)(1) For a conservatee who is gravely disabled, as defined in subparagraph (A) of paragraph (1) of subdivision (h) of Section 5008, if the conservatee is not to be placed in his or her own home or the home of a relative, first priority shall be to placement in a suitable facility as close as possible to his or her home or the home of a relative. For the purposes of this section, suitable facility means the least restrictive residential placement available and necessary to achieve the purpose of treatment. At the time that the court considers the report of the officer providing conservatorship investigation specified in Section 5356, the court shall consider available placement alternatives. After considering all the evidence the court shall determine the least restrictive and most appropriate alternative placement for the conservatee. The court shall also determine those persons to be notified of a change of placement. The fact that a person for whom conservatorship is recommended is not an inpatient shall not be construed by the court as an indication that the person does not meet the criteria of grave disability.

(2) For a conservatee who is gravely disabled, as defined in subparagraph (B) of paragraph (1) of subdivision (h) of Section 5008, first priority shall be placement in a facility that achieves the purposes of treatment of the conservatee and protection of the public. The court shall determine the most appropriate placement for the conservatee. The court shall also determine those persons to be notified of a change of placement, and additionally require the conservator to notify the district attorney or attorney representing the originating county prior to any change of placement.

(3) For any conservatee, if requested, the local mental health director shall assist the conservator or the court in selecting a placement facility for the conservatee. When a conservatee who is receiving services from the local mental health program is placed, the conservator shall inform the local mental health director of the facility's location and any movement of the conservatee to another facility.

(d)(1) Except for a conservatee who is gravely disabled, as defined in subparagraph (B) of paragraph (1) of subdivision (h) of Section 5008, the conservator may transfer his or her conservatee to a less restrictive alternative placement without a further hearing and court approval. In any case in which a conservator has reasonable cause to believe that his or her conservatee is in need of immediate more restrictive placement because the condition of the conservatee has so changed that the conservatee poses an immediate and substantial danger to himself or herself or others, the conservator shall have the right to place his or her conservatee in a more restrictive facility or hospital. Notwithstanding Section 5328, if the change of placement is to a placement more restrictive than the court-determined placement, the conservator shall provide written notice of the change of placement and the reason therefor to the court, the conservatee's attorney, the county patient's rights advocate and any other persons designated by the court pursuant to subdivision (c).

(2) For a conservatee who is gravely disabled, as defined in subparagraph (B) of paragraph (1) of subdivision (h) of Section 5008, the conservator may not transfer his or her conservatee without providing written notice of the proposed change of placement and the reason therefor to the court, the conservatee's attorney, the county patient's rights advocate, the district attorney of the county that made the commitment, and any other persons designated by the court to receive notice. If any person designated to receive notice objects to the proposed transfer within 10 days after receiving notice, the matter shall be set for a further hearing and court approval. The notification and hearing is not required for the transfer of persons between state hospitals.

(3) At a hearing where the conservator is seeking placement to a less restrictive alternative placement pursuant to paragraph (2), the placement shall not be approved where it is determined by a preponderance of the evidence that the placement poses a threat to the safety of the public, the conservatee, or any other individual.

(4) A hearing as to placement to a less restrictive alternative placement, whether requested pursuant to paragraph (2) or pursuant to Section 5358.3, shall be granted no more frequently than is provided for in Section 5358.3. *(Added by Stats.1967, c. 1667, p. 4074, § 36, operative July 1, 1969. Amended by Stats.1968, c. 1374, p. 2661, § 54, operative July 1, 1969; Stats.1971, c. 1593, p. 3343, § 379, operative July 1, 1973; Stats.1973, c. 523, p. 1011, § 1; Stats.1976, c. 905, p. 2078, § 2; Stats.1977, c. 1252, p. 4576, § 575, operative July 1, 1978; Stats.1980, c. 681, p. 2067, § 2; Stats.1986, c. 872, § 8; Stats.1990, c. 180 (S.B.2138), § 2; Stats.1995, c. 593 (A.B.145), § 4; Stats.2012, c. 34 (S.B.1009), § 98, eff. June 27, 2012; Stats.2013, c. 23 (A.B.82), § 36, eff. June 27, 2013.)*

Cross References

Conservatorship investigation defined for purposes of this Part, see Welfare and Institutions Code § 5008.
Court defined for purposes of this Part, see Welfare and Institutions Code § 5008.
Emergency defined for purposes of this Part, see Welfare and Institutions Code § 5008.
Evaluation defined for purposes of this Part, see Welfare and Institutions Code § 5008.
Gravely disabled defined for purposes of this Chapter, see Welfare and Institutions Code § 5008.
Voluntary admission to,
County hospital upon application of conservator, see Welfare and Institutions Code § 6004.
State hospital upon application of conservator, see Welfare and Institutions Code § 6002.
State mental hospital or institution, see Welfare and Institutions Code § 6000.

Research References

3 Witkin, California Criminal Law 4th Punishment § 775 (2021), Right to Refuse Antipsychotic Medication.

§ 5358.1. Nonliability of conservator, public guardian or peace officer for action by conservatee

Neither a conservator, temporary conservator, or public guardian appointed pursuant to this chapter, nor a peace officer acting pursuant to Section 5358.5, shall be held civilly or criminally liable for any action by a conservatee. *(Added by Stats.1972, c. 574, p. 982, § 5.)*

Cross References

Peace officer defined for purposes of this Part, see Welfare and Institutions Code § 5008.

§ 5358.2. Medical treatment of conservatee; court order; emergencies

If a conservatee requires medical treatment and the conservator has not been specifically authorized by the court to require the conservatee to receive medical treatment, the conservator shall, after notice to the conservatee, obtain a court order for that medical treatment, except in emergency cases in which the conservatee faces loss of life or serious bodily injury. The conservatee, if he or she chooses to contest the request for a court order, may petition the court for hearing which shall be held prior to granting the order. *(Added by Stats.1976, c. 905, p. 2079, § 3. Amended by Stats.1990, c. 180 (S.B.2138), § 3.)*

Cross References

Court defined for purposes of this Part, see Welfare and Institutions Code § 5008.

Emergency defined for purposes of this Part, see Welfare and Institutions Code § 5008.

§ 5358.3. Petition to contest rights denied conservatee or powers granted conservator; subsequent petitions; voting rights

Section operative until Jan. 1, 2024. See, also, § 5358.3 operative Jan. 1, 2024.

(a) At any time, a conservatee or any person on * * * the conservatee's behalf with the consent of the conservatee or * * * the conservatee's counsel, may petition the court for a hearing to contest the rights denied under Section 5357 or the powers granted to the conservator under Section 5358. However, after the filing of the first petition for hearing pursuant to this section, no further petition for rehearing shall be submitted for a period of six months.

(b) A request for hearing pursuant to this section shall not affect the right of a conservatee to petition the court for a rehearing as to their status as a conservatee pursuant to Section 5364. A hearing pursuant to this section shall not include trial by jury. If a person's right to vote is restored, the court shall so notify the county elections official pursuant to subdivision (c) of Section 2210 of the Elections Code.

(c) This section shall remain in effect only until January 1, 2024, and as of that date is repealed. *(Added by Stats.1976, c. 905, p. 2079, § 4. Amended by Stats.1978, c. 1363, p. 4531, § 15; Stats.1994, c. 923 (S.B.1546), § 269; Stats.2022, c. 807 (A.B.2841), § 13, eff. Jan. 1, 2023.)*

Repeal

For repeal of this section, see its terms.

Cross References

Court defined for purposes of this Part, see Welfare and Institutions Code § 5008.

§ 5358.3. Petition to contest rights denied conservatee or powers granted conservator; subsequent petitions; voting rights

Section operative Jan. 1, 2024. See, also, § 5358.3 operative until Jan. 1, 2024.

(a) At any time, a conservatee or any person on the conservatee's behalf with the consent of the conservatee or the conservatee's counsel, may petition the court for a hearing to contest the rights denied under Section 5357 or the powers granted to the conservator under Section 5358. However, after the filing of the first petition for hearing pursuant to this section, no further petition for rehearing shall be submitted for a period of six months.

(b) A request for hearing pursuant to this section shall not affect the right of a conservatee to petition the court for a rehearing as to their status as a conservatee pursuant to Section 5364. A hearing pursuant to this section shall not include trial by jury. If a person's right to vote is restored, the court shall provide notice to the Secretary of State pursuant to Section 2211.5 of the Elections Code.

(c) This section shall become operative on January 1, 2024. *(Added by Stats.2022, c. 807 (A.B.2841), § 14, eff. Jan. 1, 2023, operative Jan. 1, 2024.)*

Cross References

Court defined for purposes of this Part, see Welfare and Institutions Code § 5008.

§ 5358.5. Conservatee leaving facility without approval; return to facility or removal to county designated treatment facility; request to peace officer

When any conservatee placed into a facility pursuant to this chapter leaves the facility without the approval of the conservator or the person in charge of the facility, or when the conservator appointed pursuant to this chapter deems it necessary to remove his conservatee to the county designated treatment facility, the conservator may take the conservatee into custody and return him to the facility or remove him to the county designated treatment facility. A conservator, at his discretion, may request a peace officer to detain the conservatee and return such person to the facility in which he was placed or to transfer such person to the county designated treatment facility, pursuant to Section 7325 of the Welfare and Institutions Code. Such request shall be in writing and accompanied by a certified copy of the letters of conservatorship showing the person requesting detention and transfer to be the conservator appointed pursuant to this chapter as conservator of the person sought to be detained. Either the conservator or his assistant or deputy may request detention under this section. Whenever possible, persons charged with apprehension of persons pursuant to this section shall dress in plain clothes and shall travel in unmarked vehicles. *(Added by Stats.1972, c. 574, p. 982, § 6. Amended by Stats.1974, c. 833, p. 1796, § 2.)*

Cross References

Peace officer defined for purposes of this Part, see Welfare and Institutions Code § 5008.

§ 5358.6. Outpatient treatment for conservatee; agreement of person in charge of facility; progress report

Any conservator who places his or her conservatee in an inpatient facility pursuant to Section 5358, may also require the conservatee to undergo outpatient treatment. Before doing so, the conservator shall obtain the agreement of the person in charge of a mental health facility that the conservatee will receive outpatient treatment and that the person in charge of the facility will designate a person to be the outpatient supervisor of the conservatee. The person in charge of these facilities shall notify the county mental health director or his or her designee of such agreement. At 90-day intervals following the commencement of the outpatient treatment, the outpatient supervisor shall make a report in writing to the conservator and to the person in charge of the mental health facility setting forth the status and progress of the conservatee. *(Added by Stats.1975, c. 960, p. 2244, § 6. Amended by Stats.1980, c. 681, p. 2067, § 3.)*

§ 5358.7. Challenge by conservatee of placement or conditions of confinement; place of judicial review; place of return upon release

When any conservatee challenges his or her placement or conditions of confinement pursuant to Section 1473 of the Penal Code or Section 7250 of the Welfare and Institutions Code, notwithstanding the continuing jurisdiction of the court which appointed the conservators, judicial review shall be in the county where the conservatorship was established or in the county in which the conservatee is placed or confined. If the conservatee is released as a result of the hearing, he or she shall be returned to the county where the conservatorship originated. *(Added by Stats.1986, c. 226, § 1.)*

Cross References

Court defined for purposes of this Part, see Welfare and Institutions Code § 5008.

§ 5359. Alternative placement

A conservator appointed under this chapter shall find alternative placement for his conservatee within seven days after he is notified by the person in charge of the facility serving the conservatee that the conservatee no longer needs the care or treatment offered by that facility.

If unusual conditions or circumstances preclude alternative placement of the conservatee within seven days, the conservator shall find such placement within 30 days.

If alternative placement cannot be found at the end of the 30-day period the conservator shall confer with the professional person in charge of the facility and they shall then determine the earliest practicable date when such alternative placement may be obtained. *(Added by Stats.1967, c. 1667, p. 4074, § 36, operative July 1, 1969. Amended by Stats.1968, c. 1374, p. 2662, § 55, operative July 1, 1969; Stats.1980, c. 676, p. 2039, § 336.)*

§ 5360. Recommendations of officer providing conservatorship investigation

The officer providing conservatorship investigation shall recommend, in his report to the court, for or against imposition of a disability set forth in Section 5357 on the basis of the determination of the professional person who recommended conservatorship pursuant to Section 5352.

The officer providing conservatorship investigation shall recommend in his report any of the additional powers of a conservator set forth in Section 2591 of the Probate Code if the needs of the individual patient or his estate require such powers. In making such determination, the officer providing conservatorship investigation shall consult with the professional person who recommended conservatorship pursuant to Section 5352. *(Added by Stats.1967, c. 1667, p. 4074, § 36, operative July 1, 1969. Amended by Stats.1969, c. 722, p. 1432, § 27, eff. Aug. 8, 1969, operative July 1, 1969; Stats.1979, c. 730, p. 2535, § 148, operative Jan. 1, 1981.)*

Law Revision Commission Comments

Section 5360 is amended to correct the cross-reference to the Probate Code in view of the revision of guardianship-conservatorship law. [14 Cal.L.Rev. Comm. Reports 958 (1978)].

Cross References

Conservatorship investigation defined for purposes of this Part, see Welfare and Institutions Code § 5008.

Court defined for purposes of this Part, see Welfare and Institutions Code § 5008.

§ 5361. Termination; power and authority over estate; reappointment; opinion of physicians or psychologists; release or detention of conservatee; care coordination plan

(a) Conservatorship initiated pursuant to this chapter shall automatically terminate one year after the appointment of the conservator by the superior court. The period of service of a temporary conservator shall not be included in the one-year period. When the conservator has been appointed as conservator of the estate, the conservator shall, for a reasonable time, continue to have * * * the authority over the estate that the superior court, on petition by the conservator, * * * deems necessary for (1) the collection of assets or income that accrued during the period of conservatorship, but were uncollected before the date of termination, (2) the payment of expenses that accrued during period of conservatorship and of which the conservator was notified prior to termination, but were unpaid before the date of termination, and (3) the completion of sales of real property when the only act remaining at the date of termination is the actual transfer of title.

(b) If, upon the termination of an initial or a succeeding period of conservatorship, the conservator determines that conservatorship is still required, * * * the conservator may petition the superior court for * * * reappointment as conservator for a succeeding one-year period. The petition shall include the opinion of two physicians or licensed psychologists who have a doctoral degree in psychology and at least five years of postgraduate experience in the diagnosis and treatment of emotional and mental disorders that the conservatee is still gravely disabled as a result of mental disorder or impairment by chronic alcoholism. * * * If the conservator is unable to obtain the opinion of two physicians or psychologists, * * * the conservator shall request that the court appoint them.

* * * (c)(1) A facility in which a conservatee is placed shall release the conservatee at * * * the conservatee's request when the conservatorship terminates. A petition for reappointment filed by the conservator or a petition for appointment filed by a public guardian shall be transmitted to the facility at least 30 days before the automatic termination date. The facility may detain the conservatee after the end of the termination date only if the conservatorship proceedings have not been completed and the court orders the conservatee to be held until the proceedings have been completed.

(2) A care coordination plan shall be developed by, at a minimum, the individual, the facility, the county behavioral health department, the health care payer, if different from the county, and other individuals designated by the individual as appropriate, and shall be provided to the conservatee prior to their release. The care coordination plan shall include a first followup appointment with an appropriate behavioral health professional. The appointment information shall be provided to the individual before the individual is released. In no event may the individual be involuntarily held based on the requirements of this paragraph beyond when they would otherwise qualify for release. All care and treatment after release shall be voluntary.

(3) For purposes of care coordination and to schedule a followup appointment, the health plan, mental health plan, primary care provider, or other appropriate provider to whom an individual leaving a facility has been referred pursuant to paragraph (2) of subdivision (c) shall make a good faith effort to contact the referred individual no less than three times, either by email, telephone, mail, or in-person outreach, whichever method or methods are most likely to reach the individual.

(4) The requirement to develop a care coordination plan under this subdivision shall take effect immediately, without waiting for the department to create a model care coordination plan, as required pursuant to Section 5402.5. *(Added by Stats.1967, c. 1667, p. 4074, § 36, operative July 1, 1969. Amended by Stats.1968, c. 1374, p. 2662, § 56, operative July 1, 1969; Stats.1969, c. 722, p. 1432, § 28, eff. Aug. 8, 1969, operative July 1, 1969; Stats.1976, c. 110, p. 171, § 1, eff. April 9, 1976; Stats.1978, c. 1294, p. 4246, § 8; Stats.1979, c. 245, p. 534, § 2; Stats.2022, c. 867 (A.B.2242), § 4, eff. Jan. 1, 2023.)*

Cross References

Court defined for purposes of this Part, see Welfare and Institutions Code § 5008.

Gravely disabled defined for purposes of this Chapter, see Welfare and Institutions Code § 5008.

§ 5362. Notice of impending termination; petition for reappointment; court hearing or jury trial; decree of termination

(a) The clerk of the superior court shall notify each conservator, his or her conservatee and the person in charge of the facility in which the person resides, and the conservatee's attorney, at least 60 days before the termination of the one-year period. If the conservator is a private party, the clerk of the superior court shall also notify the mental health director and the county officer providing conservatorship investigation pursuant to Section 5355, at least 60 days before the termination of the one-year period. Notification shall be delivered pursuant to Section 1215 of the Probate Code. The notification shall be in substantially the following form:

In the Superior Court of the State of California for the County of _____

The people of the State of California Concerning _____ No. _____

Notice of Termination of Conservatorship

The people of the State of California to _____ _____:

(conservatee, conservatee's attorney, conservator, and professional person in charge of the facility in which the conservatee resides, county mental health director, and county officer providing conservatorship investigation.)

The one-year conservatorship established for _____ pursuant to Welfare and Institutions Code Section _____ on _____ will terminate on _____. If the conservator, _____, wishes to reestablish conservatorship for another year he or she must petition the court by _____. Subject to a request for a court hearing by jury trial the judge may, on his or her own motion, accept or reject the conservator's petition.

If the conservator petitions to reestablish conservatorship the conservatee, the professional person in charge of the facility in which he or she resides, the conservatee's attorney, and, if the conservator is a private party, the county mental health director and the county officer providing conservatorship investigation shall be notified. If any of them request it, there shall be a court hearing or a jury trial, whichever is requested, on the issue of whether the conservatee is still gravely disabled and in need of conservatorship. If the private conservator does not petition for reappointment, the county officer providing conservatorship investigation may recommend another conservator. Such a petition shall be considered a petition for reappointment as conservator.

Clerk of the Superior Court
by _______________________
Deputy

(b) Subject to a request for a court hearing or jury trial, the judge may, on his or her own motion, accept or reject the conservator's petition.

If the conservator does not petition to reestablish conservatorship at or before the termination of the one-year period, the court shall issue a decree terminating conservatorship. The decree shall be delivered to the conservator and his or her conservatee pursuant to Section 1215 of the Probate Code and shall be accompanied by a statement of California law as set forth in Section 5368. *(Added by Stats.1967, c. 1667, p. 4074, § 36, operative July 1, 1969. Amended by Stats.1968, c. 1374, p. 2662, § 56.5, operative July 1, 1969; Stats.1969, c. 722, p. 1432, § 28.1, eff. Aug. 8, 1969, operative July 1, 1969; Stats.1978, c. 1294, p. 4246, § 9; Stats.1982, c. 1598, § 8; Stats.1983, c. 464, § 4; Stats.1985, c. 1239, § 5; Stats.2017, c. 319 (A.B.976), § 148, eff. Jan. 1, 2018.)*

Cross References

Conservatorship investigation defined for purposes of this Part, see Welfare and Institutions Code § 5008.
Court defined for purposes of this Part, see Welfare and Institutions Code § 5008.
Gravely disabled defined for purposes of this Chapter, see Welfare and Institutions Code § 5008.

§ 5363. Ratification of acts beyond term

In the event the conservator continues in good faith to act within the powers granted him in the original decree of conservatorship beyond the one-year period, he may petition for and shall be granted a decree ratifying his acts as conservator beyond the one-year period. The decree shall provide for a retroactive appointment of the conservator to provide continuity of authority in those cases where the conservator did not apply in time for reappointment. *(Added by Stats.1967, c. 1667, p. 4074, § 36, operative July 1, 1969.)*

§ 5364. Petition for rehearing on status as conservatee; notice of voter registration right

Section operative until Jan. 1, 2024. See, also, § 5364 operative Jan. 1, 2024.

(a) At any time, the conservatee may petition the superior court for a rehearing as to their status as a conservatee. However, after the filing of the first petition for rehearing pursuant to this section, no further petition for rehearing shall be submitted for a period of six months. If the conservatorship is terminated pursuant to this section, the court shall, in accordance with subdivision (c) of Section 2210 of the Elections Code, notify the county elections official that the person's right to register to vote is restored.

(b) This section shall remain in effect only until January 1, 2024, and as of that date is repealed. *(Added by Stats.1967, c. 1667, p. 4074, § 36, operative July 1, 1969. Amended by Stats.1976, c. 905, p. 2080, § 5; Stats.1978, c. 1363, p. 4532, § 16; Stats.1994, c. 923 (S.B.1546), § 270; Stats.2022, c. 807 (A.B.2841), § 15, eff. Jan. 1, 2023.)*

Repeal

For repeal of this section, see its terms.

Cross References

Court defined for purposes of this Part, see Welfare and Institutions Code § 5008.

§ 5364. Petition for rehearing on status as conservatee; notice of voter registration right

Section operative Jan. 1, 2024. See, also, § 5364 operative until Jan. 1, 2024.

(a) At any time, the conservatee may petition the superior court for a rehearing as to their status as a conservatee. However, after the filing of the first petition for rehearing pursuant to this section, no further petition for rehearing shall be submitted for a period of six months. If the conservatorship is terminated pursuant to this section, the court shall provide notice to the Secretary of State pursuant to Section 2211.5 of the Elections Code.

(b) This section shall become operative on January 1, 2024. *(Added by Stats.2022, c. 807 (A.B.2841), § 16, eff. Jan. 1, 2023, operative Jan. 1, 2024.)*

Cross References

Court defined for purposes of this Part, see Welfare and Institutions Code § 5008.

§ 5365. Time for hearing petitions; attorney

A hearing shall be held on all petitions under this chapter within 30 days of the date of the petition. The court shall appoint the public defender or other attorney for the conservatee or proposed conservatee within five days after the date of the petition. *(Added by Stats.1967, c. 1667, p. 4074, § 36, operative July 1, 1969. Amended by Stats.1970, c. 509, p. 997, § 1; Stats.1970, c. 1627, p. 3449, § 25; Stats.1971, c. 776, p. 1530, § 7; Stats.1972, c. 574, p. 983, § 7.)*

Cross References

Advice as to right of counsel, see Welfare and Institutions Code §§ 5226, 5254.1, 5276, 5302.
Appointment of public defender or other attorney, see Welfare and Institutions Code §§ 5276, 5302.
Conservatorship for gravely disabled persons, appointment, demand for trial as waiver of hearing, see Welfare and Institutions Code § 5350.
Court defined for purposes of this Part, see Welfare and Institutions Code § 5008.

§ 5365.1. Waiver of presence of professionals and physicians; reception of documents

The conservatee or proposed conservatee may, upon advice of counsel, waive the presence at any hearing under this chapter of the physician or other professional person who recommended conservatorship pursuant to Section 5352 and of the physician providing evaluation or intensive treatment. In the event of such a waiver, such physician and professional persons shall not be required to be present at the hearing if it is stipulated that the recommendation and records of such physician or other professional person concerning the mental condition and treatment of the conservatee or proposed conservatee will be received in evidence. *(Added by Stats.1971, c. 1162, p. 2221, § 4.)*

Cross References

Evaluation defined for purposes of this Part, see Welfare and Institutions Code § 5008.
Intensive treatment defined for purposes of this Part, see Welfare and Institutions Code § 5008.

§ 5366.1. Detention for evaluation; persons detained under court commitment or upon application of local health officer; disposition

(a) Any person detained as of June 30, 1969, under court commitment, in a private institution, a county psychiatric hospital, facility of the Veterans Administration, or other agency of the United States government, community mental health service, or detained in a state hospital or facility of the Veterans Administration upon application of a local health officer, pursuant to former Section 5567 or Sections 6000 to 6019, inclusive, as they read immediately preceding July 1, 1969, may be detained, after January 1, 1972, for a period no longer than 180 days, except as provided in this section.

(b) Any person detained pursuant to this section on the effective date of this section shall be evaluated by the facility designated by the county and approved by the State Department of Health Care Services pursuant to Section 5150 as a facility for 72–hour treatment and evaluation. The evaluation shall be made at the request of the person in charge of the institution in which the person is detained. If in the opinion of the professional person in charge of the evaluation and treatment facility or his or her designee, the evaluation of the person can be made by the professional person or his or her designee at the institution in which the person is detained, the person shall not be required to be evaluated at the evaluation and treatment facility, but shall be evaluated at the institution where he or she is detained, or other place to determine if the person is a danger to others, himself or herself, or gravely disabled as a result of mental disorder.

(c) Any person evaluated under this section shall be released from the institution in which he or she is detained immediately upon completion of the evaluation if in the opinion of the professional person in charge of the evaluation and treatment facility, or his or her designee, the person evaluated is not a danger to others, or to himself or herself, or gravely disabled as a result of mental disorder, unless the person agrees voluntarily to remain in the institution in which he or she has been detained.

(d) If in the opinion of the professional person in charge of the facility or his or her designee, the person evaluated requires intensive treatment or recommendation for conservatorship, the professional person or his or her designee shall proceed under Article 4 (commencing with Section 5250) of Chapter 2, or under Chapter 3 (commencing with Section 5350), of Part 1 of Division 5.

(e) If it is determined from the evaluation that the person is gravely disabled and a recommendation for conservatorship is made, and if the petition for conservatorship for the person is not filed by June 30, 1972, the court commitment or detention under a local health officer application for the person shall terminate and the patient shall be released unless he or she agrees to accept treatment on a voluntary basis. *(Added by Stats.1971, c. 1459, p. 2875, § 2. Amended by Stats.1973, c. 142, p. 418, § 72.5, eff. June 30, 1973, operative July 1, 1973; Stats.1977, c. 1252, p. 4578, § 577, operative July 1, 1978; Stats.2012, c. 34 (S.B.1009), § 99, eff. June 27, 2012; Stats.2013, c. 23 (A.B.82), § 37, eff. June 27, 2013.)*

Cross References

Court defined for purposes of this Part, see Welfare and Institutions Code § 5008.
Detention in private institution, see Welfare and Institutions Code § 6007.
Evaluation defined for purposes of this Part, see Welfare and Institutions Code § 5008.
Gravely disabled defined for purposes of this Chapter, see Welfare and Institutions Code § 5008.
Intensive treatment defined for purposes of this Part, see Welfare and Institutions Code § 5008.

§ 5367. Effect of conservatorship on prior commitment

Conservatorship established under this chapter shall supersede any commitment under former provisions of this code relating to inebriates or the mentally ill. *(Added by Stats.1967, c. 1667, p. 4075, § 36, operative July 1, 1969. Amended by Stats.1968, c. 1374, p. 2664, § 58, operative July 1, 1969.)*

§ 5368. Effect of conservatorship on presumption of competence

A person who is no longer a conservatee shall not be presumed to be incompetent by virtue of his having been a conservatee under the provisions of this part. *(Added by Stats.1967, c. 1667, p. 4074, § 36, operative July 1, 1969.)*

Cross References

Burden of proof of insanity, see Evidence Code § 522.
Disabilities of conservatee, see Welfare and Institutions Code §§ 5356, 5357.
Drivers' license, statement in application, see Vehicle Code § 12800.
Firearms, possession by mental patients, see Welfare and Institutions Code § 8100 et seq.
Legal disability not imposed by evaluation proceedings, see Welfare and Institutions Code § 5005.
Public guardian, see Government Code § 27430 et seq.

§ 5369. Conservatee with criminal charges pending; recovery of competence

When a conservatee who has criminal charges pending against him and has been found mentally incompetent under Section 1370 of the Penal Code recovers his mental competence, the conservator shall certify that fact to the court, sheriff, and district attorney of the county in which the criminal charges are pending and to the defendant's attorney of record.

The court shall order the sheriff to immediately return the defendant to the court in which the criminal charges are pending. Within two judicial days of the defendant's return, the court shall hold a hearing to determine whether the defendant is entitled to be admitted to bail or released upon his own recognizance pending conclusion of criminal proceedings. *(Added by Stats.1974, c. 1511, p. 3323, § 13, eff. Sept. 27, 1974.)*

Cross References

Court defined for purposes of this Part, see Welfare and Institutions Code § 5008.

§ 5370. Conservatorship proceeding for one charged with offense

Notwithstanding any other provision of law, a conservatorship proceeding may be initiated pursuant to this chapter for any person who has been charged with an offense, regardless of whether action is pending or has been initiated pursuant to Section 1370 of the Penal Code. *(Added by Stats.1974, c. 1511, p. 3323, § 14, eff. Sept. 27, 1974.)*

§ 5370.1. Appointment of counsel for private conservator with insufficient funds

The court in which a petition to establish a conservatorship is filed may appoint the county counsel or a private attorney to represent a private conservator in all proceedings connected with the conservatorship, if it appears that the conservator has insufficient funds to obtain the services of a private attorney. Such appointments of the county counsel, however, may be made only if the board of supervisors have, by ordinance or resolution, authorized the county counsel to accept them. *(Added by Stats.1975, c. 960, p. 2245, § 8. Amended by Stats.1980, c. 415, p. 818, § 1.)*

Cross References

County counsel, duty to represent county in mental health proceedings, see Government Code § 27646.

Court defined for purposes of this Part, see Welfare and Institutions Code § 5008.

§ 5370.2. Protection and advocacy agency; services to be provided under contract; coordination with the advocates; plan to provide patients' rights advocacy services; reviews and investigations

(a) The State Department of State Hospitals and the State Department of Health Care Services shall contract with a single nonprofit agency that meets the criteria specified in subdivision (b) of Section 5510 to conduct the activities specified in paragraphs (1) to (5), inclusive. These two state departments shall enter into a memorandum of understanding to ensure the effective management of the contract and the required activities affecting county patients' rights programs:

(1) Provide patients' rights advocacy services for, and conduct investigations of alleged or suspected abuse and neglect of, including deaths of, persons with mental disabilities residing in state hospitals.

(2) Investigate and take action as appropriate and necessary to resolve complaints from or concerning recipients of mental health services residing in licensed health or community care facilities regarding abuse, and unreasonable denial, or punitive withholding of rights guaranteed under this division that cannot be resolved by county patients' rights advocates.

(3) Provide consultation, technical assistance, and support to county patients' rights advocates in accordance with their duties under Section 5520.

(4) Conduct program review of patients' rights programs.

(5) Make patients' rights advocacy training materials readily accessible to all county patients' rights advocates online. The training materials shall include, but are not limited to, the topics described in Section 5512.

(b) The services shall be provided in coordination with the appropriate mental health patients' rights advocates.

(c)(1) The contractor shall develop a plan to provide patients' rights advocacy services for, and conduct investigations of alleged or suspected abuse and neglect of, including the deaths of, persons with mental disabilities residing in state hospitals.

(2) The contractor shall develop the plan in consultation with the statewide organization of mental health patients' rights advocates, the statewide organization of mental health clients, and the statewide organization of family members of persons with mental disabilities, and the statewide organization of county mental health directors.

(3) In order to ensure that persons with mental disabilities have access to high quality advocacy services, the contractor shall establish a grievance procedure and shall advise persons receiving services under the contract of the availability of other advocacy services, including services provided by the protection and advocacy agency specified in Section 4901 and the county patients' rights advocates specified in Section 5520.

(d) This section does not restrict or limit the authority of the department to conduct the reviews and investigations it deems necessary for personnel, criminal, and litigation purposes.

(e) The State Department of State Hospitals and the State Department of Health Care Services shall jointly contract on a multiyear basis for a contract term of up to five years. *(Added by Stats.1992, c. 722 (S.B.485), § 25, eff. Sept. 15, 1992. Amended by Stats.1995, c. 546 (S.B.361), § 2; Stats.2010, c. 717 (S.B.853), § 138, eff. Oct. 19, 2010; Stats.2012, c. 34 (S.B.1009), § 100, eff. June 27, 2012; Stats.2018, c. 237 (A.B.2316), § 2, eff. Jan. 1, 2019.)*

Cross References

Mental health advocacy, county advocates, county verification of advocates' review of training materials, see Welfare and Institutions Code § 5524.

§ 5371. Conflict of interest in evaluation of conservatee; independent conduct of investigation and administration of conservatorship

No person upon whom a duty is placed to evaluate, or who, in fact, does evaluate a conservatee for any purpose under this chapter shall have a financial or other beneficial interest in the facility where the conservatee is to be, or has been placed.

Conservatorship investigation and administration shall be conducted independently from any person or agency which provides mental health treatment for conservatees, if it has been demonstrated that the existing arrangement creates a conflict of interest between the treatment needs of the conservatee and the investigation or administration of the conservatorship. The person or agency responsible for the mental health treatment of conservatees shall execute a written agreement or protocol with the conservatorship investigator and administrator for the provision of services to conservatees. The agreement or protocol shall specify the responsibilities of each person or agency who is a party to the agreement or protocol, and shall specify a procedure to resolve disputes or conflicts of interest between agencies or persons. *(Added by Stats.1975, c. 960, p. 2245, § 9. Amended by Stats.1986, c. 335, § 2.)*

Cross References

Conservatorship investigation defined for purposes of this Part, see Welfare and Institutions Code § 5008.

§ 5372. Ex parte communications; prohibitions; exemption

(a) The provisions of Section 1051 of the Probate Code shall apply to conservatorships established pursuant to this chapter.

(b) The Judicial Council shall, on or before January 1, 2008, adopt a rule of court to implement this section.

(c) Subdivision (a) of this section shall become operative on January 1, 2008. *(Added by Stats.2006, c. 492 (S.B.1716), § 5.)*

Cross References

Court defined for purposes of this Part, see Welfare and Institutions Code § 5008.

CHAPTER 4. ADMINISTRATION

Section

§ 5400. Director; administrative duties; rules and regulations

(a) The Director of Health Care Services shall administer this part and shall adopt rules, regulations, and standards as necessary. In developing rules, regulations, and standards, the Director of Health Care Services shall consult with the County Behavioral Health Directors Association of California, the California Behavioral Health Planning Council, and the office of the Attorney General. Adoption of these standards, rules, and regulations shall require approval by the County Behavioral Health Directors Association of California by majority vote of those present at an official session.

(b) Wherever feasible and appropriate, rules, regulations, and standards adopted under this part shall correspond to comparable rules, regulations, and standards adopted under the Bronzan–McCorquodale Act. These corresponding rules, regulations, and standards shall include qualifications for professional personnel.

(c) Regulations adopted pursuant to this part may provide standards for services for persons with chronic alcoholism that differ from the standards for services for persons with mental health disorders. *(Added by Stats.1967, c. 1667, p. 4074, § 36, operative July 1, 1969. Amended by Stats.1969, c. 722, p. 1432, § 30, eff. Aug. 8, 1969, operative July 1, 1969; Stats.1971, c. 1593, p. 3344, § 381, operative July 1, 1973; Stats.1977, c. 1252, p. 4579, § 579, operative July 1, 1978; Stats.1985, c. 1232, § 22, eff. Sept. 30, 1985; Stats.2012, c. 34 (S.B.1009), § 101, eff. June 27, 2012; Stats.2014, c. 144 (A.B.1847), § 96, eff. Jan. 1, 2015; Stats.2015, c. 455 (S.B.804), § 30, eff. Jan. 1, 2016; Stats.2017, c. 511 (A.B.1688), § 3, eff. Jan. 1, 2018.)*

Cross References

Attorney General, generally, see Government Code § 12500 et seq.
Bronzan–McCorquodale Act, see Welfare and Institutions Code § 5600 et seq.
Department of Mental Health, general administration, powers and duties, see Welfare and Institutions Code § 4000 et seq.

§ 5402. Report of operation of division

(a) The State Department of Health Care Services shall collect data quarterly and publish * * *, on or before May 1 of each year, a report including quantitative, deidentified information concerning the operation of this division * * *. The report shall include an evaluation of the effectiveness of achieving the legislative intent of this part pursuant to Section 5001. Based on information that is available from each county, the report shall include all of the following information:

(1) The number of persons in designated and approved facilities admitted or detained for 72–hour evaluation and treatment, admitted for 14–day and 30–day periods of intensive treatment, and admitted for 180–day postcertification intensive treatment * * * in each county.

(2) The number of persons transferred to mental health facilities pursuant to Section 4011.6 of the Penal Code * * * in each county.

(3) The number of persons for whom temporary conservatorships are established * * * in each county.

(4) The number of persons for whom conservatorships are established in each county.

(5) The number of persons admitted or detained either once, between two and five times, between six and eight times, and greater than eight times for each type of detention, including 72–hour evaluation and treatment, 14–day and 30–day periods of intensive treatment, and 180–day postcertification intensive treatment.

(6) The clinical outcomes for individuals identified in paragraphs (1) to (4), inclusive.

(7) The services provided or offered to individuals identified in paragraphs (1) to (4), inclusive. Data pertaining to services provided or offered to individuals placed on each type of hold shall include, but not be limited to, assessment, evaluation, medication treatment, crisis intervention, and psychiatric and psychological treatment services. Data pertaining to services shall specify payer information or funding used to pay for services.

(8) The waiting periods for individuals prior to receiving an evaluation in a designated and approved facility pursuant to Section 5150 or 5151 and waiting periods for individuals prior to receiving treatment services in a designated facility, including the reasons for waiting periods. The waiting period shall be calculated from the date and time when the hold began and end on the date and time when the individual received an evaluation or received evaluation and treatment services in a designated facility.

(9) If the source of admission is an emergency department, the date and time of service and release from emergency care.

(10) Demographic data of those receiving care, including age, sex, gender identity, race, ethnicity, primary language, sexual orientation, veteran status, and housing status, to the extent those data are available.

(11) The number of all county-contracted beds.

(12) The number and outcomes of all of the following:

(A) The certification review hearings held pursuant to Section 5256.

(B) The petitions for writs of habeas corpus filed pursuant to Section 5275.

(C) The judicial review hearings held pursuant to Section 5276.

(D) The petitions for capacity hearings filed pursuant to Section 5332.

(E) The capacity hearings held pursuant to Section 5334 in each superior court.

(13) Analysis and evaluation of the efficacy of mental health assessments, detentions, treatments, and supportive services provided both under this part and subsequent to release.

(14) Recommendations for improving mental health assessments, detentions, treatments, and supportive services provided both under this part and subsequent to release.

(15) An assessment of the disproportionate use of detentions and conservatorships on various groups, including an assessment of use by the race, ethnicity, gender identity, age group, veteran status, housing status, and Medi-Cal enrollment status of detained and conserved persons. This assessment shall evaluate disproportionate use at the county, regional, and state levels.

(16) An explanation for the absence of any data required pursuant to this section that are not included in the report.

(17) Beginning with the report due May 1, 2025, the report shall also include the progress that has been made on implementing recommendations from prior reports issued under this subdivision.

(b)(1) Each * * * county behavioral health director, each designated and approved facility providing services to persons pursuant to this division, and each other entity involved in implementing Section 5150 shall provide accurate and complete data in a form and manner, and in accordance with timelines, prescribed by the department * * *. County behavioral health agencies and designated and approved facilities shall provide the data specified in paragraphs (1) to (11), inclusive, of subdivision (a), and any other information, records, and reports that the department deems necessary for the purposes of this section. Data shall be submitted on a quarterly basis, or more frequently, as required by the department. The department shall not have access to any patient name identifiers.

(2) All data submitted to the department by each county behavioral health director and each designated and approved facility shall be transmitted in a secure manner in compliance with all applicable state and federal requirements, including, but not limited to, Section 164.312 of Title 45 of the Code of Federal Regulations.

(c) Information published pursuant to * * * subdivision (a) shall not contain * * * data that may lead to the identification of patients receiving services under this division and shall contain statistical data only. Data published by the department shall be deidentified in compliance with subdivision (b) of Section 164.514 of Title 45 of the Code of Federal Regulations.

(d) The Judicial Council shall provide the department, by October 1 of each year, with data from each superior court to complete the report described in this section, including the number and outcomes of certification review hearings held pursuant to Section 5256, petitions for writs of habeas corpus filed pursuant to Section 5275, judicial review hearings held pursuant to Section 5276, petitions for capacity hearings filed pursuant to Section 5332, and capacity hearings held pursuant to Section 5334 in each superior court. The department shall not have access to any patient name identifiers.

(e) The department shall make the * * * report publicly available * * * on the department's internet website.

(f)(1) The department may impose a plan of correction against a facility that fails to submit data timely or as required pursuant to this section.

(2) The department may impose a plan of correction against a county that fails to submit data timely or as required pursuant to this section.

(g) Notwithstanding Chapter 3.5 (commencing with Section 11340) of Part 1 of Division 3 of Title 2 of the Government Code, the department may implement, interpret, or make specific this section, in whole or in part, by means of information notices, provider bulletins, or other similar instructions, without taking any further regulatory action.

(h) The department may enter into exclusive or nonexclusive contracts, or amend existing contracts, on a bid or negotiated basis for purposes of administering or implementing the requirements of this section. Contracts entered into or amended pursuant to this section shall be exempt from Chapter 6 (commencing with Section 14825) of Part 5.5 of Division 3 of Title 2 of the Government Code, Section 19130 of the Government Code, and Part 2 (commencing with Section 10100) of Division 2 of the Public Contract Code, and shall be exempt from the review or approval of any division of the Department of General Services. *(Added by Stats.1975, c. 960, p. 2245, § 10. Amended by Stats.1977, c. 1252, p. 4580, § 581, operative July 1, 1978; Stats.1988, c. 1517, § 14; Stats.1991, c. 89 (A.B.1288), § 52, eff. June 30, 1991; Stats.1991, c. 611 (A.B.1491), § 33, eff. Oct. 7, 1991; Stats.2012, c. 34 (S.B.1009), § 102, eff. June 27, 2012; Stats.2022, c. 539 (S.B.929), § 1, eff. Jan. 1, 2023.)*

Operative Effect

For conditions rendering the provisions of Stats.1991, c. 89 (A.B.1288), inoperative "in the event of a determination by the Commission on State Mandates . . . or a final judicial determination . . . that any provision of this act is a state-mandated local program requiring state reimbursement to a local agency or school district within the meaning of Section 6 of Article XIII B of the California Constitution", see Stats. 1991, c. 89 (A.B.1288), § 209, as amended by Stats.1993, c. 728 (A.B.1728), § 6.

Cross References

Evaluation defined for purposes of this Part, see Welfare and Institutions Code § 5008.

Intensive treatment defined for purposes of this Part, see Welfare and Institutions Code § 5008.

§ 5402.2. Master plan for utilization of state hospital facilities; levels of care

The Director of State Hospitals shall develop a master plan for the utilization of state hospital facilities identifying levels of care. The level of care shall be either general acute care, skilled nursing care, subacute, intermediate care, or residential care. *(Added by Stats. 1988, c. 1517, § 15. Amended by Stats.2012, c. 24 (A.B.1470), § 133, eff. June 27, 2012.)*

§ 5402.5. Model care coordination plan

(a) On or before December 1, 2023, the State Department of Health Care Services shall convene a stakeholder group to create a model care coordination plan to be followed when discharging those held under temporary holds pursuant to Section 5152 or a conservatorship. The stakeholder group shall include, at a minimum, the County Behavioral Health Directors Association of California, the California Chapter of the American College of Emergency Physicians, the California Hospital Association, Medi-Cal managed care plans, private insurance plans, other organizations representing the various facilities where individuals may be detained under temporary holds or a conservatorship, other appropriate entities or agencies as determined by the department, and advocacy organizations representing those who have been involuntarily detained or conserved, as well as individuals who have been detained or conserved.

(b) The model care coordination plan and process shall outline who will be on the care team and how the communication will occur to coordinate care. It shall specify that the care coordination is a shared responsibility between, at a minimum, the county, the facility, and the health care payer, if different from the county. The model care coordination plan shall, at a minimum, also address the following:

(1) The roles of each entity to ensure continuity of services and care for all individuals exiting involuntary holds, including how referrals will be made and appointments will be scheduled pursuant to subdivision (d) of Section 5008. This shall include all of the following:

(A) Identification of county resources, programs, and contact information to facilitate referrals for individuals exiting involuntary holds or intensive treatment, including, but not limited to, suicide prevention, substance use disorder treatment, Medi-Cal Enhanced Care Management, Full Service Partnerships, assisted outpatient treatment, early psychosis intervention services, and resources published pursuant to Section 5013.

(B) Hospital aftercare and discharge planning processes pursuant to Sections 1262 and 1262.5 of the Health and Safety Code.

(C) Hospital policies and procedures in compliance with nationally accepted accreditation standards to reduce the risk of suicide, including, but not limited to, screening and assessing patients for suicidal ideation and suicidal risk, developing a safety plan with patients at risk for suicide, and following written policies and procedures addressing the care, counseling, and followup care at discharge for patients at risk for suicide.

(2) A requirement that the care coordination plan for an individual exiting a temporary hold or a conservatorship include a detailed plan that includes a scheduled first appointment with the health plan, the mental health plan, a primary care provider, or another appropriate provider to whom the person has been referred.

(3) County procedures and contact information for the availability of designated persons for the purpose of conducting an assessment pursuant to Section 5150. Designated individuals shall be available on a 24–hours-per-day, seven-days-per-week basis in order to ensure that individuals are released from the hold as soon as possible after it is determined they no longer require detention. In no event may the individual be involuntarily held beyond when they would otherwise qualify for release.

(4) County procedures for facilities and professional persons to request designation to perform assessments and evaluations, pursuant to Sections 5151 and 5152.

(5) County procedures and contact information facilities are required to use to obtain an assessment and evaluation of an individual, pursuant to Sections 5151 and 5152.

(6) Defined expectations for information sharing, including notification of and transmittal of applications pursuant to Section 5150 and plans to periodically convene to identify and resolve challenges.

(c)(1) Each county mental health department shall ensure that a care coordination plan that ensures continuity of services and care in the community for all individuals exiting holds or a conservatorship pursuant to this part is established.

(2) All facilities designated by the counties for evaluation and treatment under this part shall implement the model care coordination plan on or before August 1, 2024.

(3) Notwithstanding Chapter 3.5 (commencing with Section 11340) of Part 1 of Division 3 of Title 2 of the Government Code, the State Department of Health Care Services may implement Section 5402.5 by means of all-county letters, plan letters, plan or provider bulletins, or similar instructions, without taking any further regulatory action. *(Added by Stats.2022, c. 867 (A.B.2242), § 5, eff. Jan. 1, 2023.)*

§ 5403. Regulations; approval by California Conference of Local Mental Health Directors

(a) From July 1, 1991 to June 30, 1993, inclusive, regulations promulgated by the department shall not be subject to the approval of the California Conference of Local Mental Health Directors. The impact of this subdivision on regulatory timing shall be included in the department's report to the Legislature on September 30, 1992.

(b) The department shall continue to involve the conference in the development of all regulations which affect local mental health programs prior to the promulgation of those regulations pursuant to the Administrative Procedure Act. *(Added by Stats.1991, c. 89 (A.B.1288), § 55, eff. June 30, 1991. Amended by Stats.1991, c. 611 (A.B.1491), § 34, eff. Oct. 7, 1991.)*

Operative Effect

For conditions rendering the provisions of Stats.1991, c. 89 (A.B.1288), inoperative "in the event of a determination by the Commission on State Mandates . . . or a final judicial determination . . . that any provision of this act is a state-mandated local program requiring state reimbursement to a local agency or school district within the meaning of Section 6 of Article XIII B of the California Constitution", see Stats. 1991, c. 89 (A.B.1288), § 209, as amended by Stats.1993, c. 728 (A.B.1728), § 6.

§ 5404. Designation of evaluation and treatment facilities; encouragement of use; continuation of regulations

(a) Each county may designate facilities, which are not hospitals or clinics, as 72–hour evaluation and treatment facilities and as 14–day intensive treatment facilities if the facilities meet those requirements as the Director of Health Care Services may establish by regulation. The Director of Health Care Services shall encourage the use by counties of appropriate facilities, which are not hospitals or clinics, for the evaluation and treatment of patients pursuant to this part.

(b) All regulations relating to the approval of facilities designated by the county for 72–hour treatment and evaluation and 14–day intensive treatment facilities, heretofore adopted by the State Department of Mental Health, or a successor, shall remain in effect and shall be fully enforceable by the State Department of Health Care Services with respect to any facility or program required to be approved as a facility for 72–hour treatment and evaluation and 14–day intensive treatment facilities, unless and until readopted, amended, or repealed by the Director of Health Care Services. The State Department of Health Care Services shall succeed to and be vested with all duties, powers, purposes, functions, responsibilities, and jurisdiction of the State Department of Mental Health, or a successor, as they relate to approval of facilities for 72–hour treatment and evaluation and 14–day intensive treatment facilities. *(Added by Stats.1975, c. 960, p. 2245, § 11. Amended by Stats.1977, c. 1252, p. 4581, § 584, operative July 1, 1978; Stats.2012, c. 34 (S.B.1009), § 103, eff. June 27, 2012; Stats.2013, c. 23 (A.B.82), § 38, eff. June 27, 2013.)*

Cross References

Evaluation defined for purposes of this Part, see Welfare and Institutions Code § 5008.

Intensive treatment defined for purposes of this Part, see Welfare and Institutions Code § 5008.

Violation of rights of patients, penalties as including revocation of facility's designation and authorization, see Welfare and Institutions Code § 5326.9.

§ 5405. Facilities licensed on or after January 1, 2003; criminal record checks; denial, suspension or revocation of license for certain criminal offenses; additional considerations; director review

(a) This section shall apply to each facility licensed by the State Department of Health Care Services, or its delegated agent, on or after January 1, 2003. For purposes of this section, "facility" means psychiatric health facilities, as defined in Section 1250.2 of the Health and Safety Code, licensed pursuant to Chapter 9 (commencing with Section 77001) of Division 5 of Title 22 of the California Code of Regulations, psychiatric residential treatment facilities, as defined in Section 1250.10 of the Health and Safety Code, licensed pursuant to Section 4081 of the Welfare and Institutions Code, and mental health rehabilitation centers licensed pursuant to Chapter 3.5 (commencing with Section 781.00) of Division 1 of Title 9 of the California Code of Regulations.

(b)(1)(A) Prior to the initial licensure or first renewal of a license on or after January 1, 2003, of any person to operate or manage a facility specified in subdivision (a), the applicant or licensee shall submit fingerprint images and related information pertaining to the applicant or licensee to the Department of Justice for purposes of a criminal record check, as specified in paragraph (2), at the expense of the applicant or licensee. The Department of Justice shall provide the results of the criminal record check to the State Department of Health Care Services. The State Department of Health Care Services may take into consideration information obtained from or provided by other government agencies. The State Department of Health Care Services shall determine whether the applicant or licensee has ever been convicted of a crime specified in subdivision (c). The applicant or licensee shall submit fingerprint images and related information each time the position of administrator, manager, program director, or fiscal officer of a facility is filled and prior to actual employment for initial licensure or an individual who is initially hired on or after January 1, 2003. For purposes of this subdivision, "applicant" and "licensee" include the administrator, manager, program director, or fiscal officer of a facility.

(B) Commencing July 1, 2013, upon the employment of, or contract with or for, any direct care staff, the direct care staff person or licensee shall submit fingerprint images and related information pertaining to the direct care staff person to the Department of Justice for purposes of a criminal record check, as specified in paragraph (2), at the expense of the direct care staff person or licensee. The Department of Justice shall provide the results of the criminal record check to the State Department of Health Care Services. The State Department of Health Care Services shall determine whether the direct care staff person has ever been convicted of a crime specified in subdivision (c). The State Department of Health Care Services shall notify the licensee of these results. No direct client contact by the trainee or newly hired staff, or by any direct care contractor shall occur prior to clearance by the State Department of Health Care Services unless the trainee, newly hired employee, contractor, or employee of the contractor is constantly supervised.

(C) Commencing July 1, 2013, any contract for services provided directly to patients or residents shall contain provisions to ensure that the direct services contractor submits to the Department of Justice fingerprint images and related information pertaining to the direct services contractor for submission to the State Department of Health Care Services for purposes of a criminal record check, as specified in paragraph (2), at the expense of the direct services contractor or licensee. The Department of Justice shall provide the results of the criminal record check to the State Department of Health Care Services. The State Department of Health Care Services shall determine whether the direct services contractor has ever been convicted of a crime specified in subdivision (c). The State Department of Health Care Services shall notify the licensee of these results.

(2) If the applicant, licensee, direct care staff person, or direct services contractor specified in paragraph (1) has resided in California for at least the previous seven years, the applicant, licensee, direct care staff person, or direct services contractor shall only submit one set of fingerprint images and related information to the Department of Justice. The Department of Justice shall charge a fee sufficient to cover the reasonable cost of processing the fingerprint submission. Fingerprints and related information submitted pursuant to this subdivision include fingerprint images captured and transmitted electronically. When requested, the Department of Justice shall forward one set of fingerprint images to the Federal Bureau of Investigation for the purpose of obtaining any record of previous convictions or arrests pending adjudication of the applicant, licensee, direct care staff person, or direct services contractor. The results of a criminal record check provided by the Department of Justice shall contain every conviction rendered against an applicant, licensee, direct care staff person, or direct services contractor, and every offense for which the applicant, licensee, direct care staff person, or direct services contractor is presently awaiting trial, whether the person is incarcerated or has been released on bail or on * * * their own recognizance pending trial. The State Department of the Health Care Services shall request subsequent arrest notification from the Department of Justice pursuant to Section 11105.2 of the Penal Code.

(3) An applicant and any other person specified in this subdivision, as part of the background clearance process, shall provide information as to whether or not the person has any prior criminal convictions, has had any arrests within the past 12–month period, or has any active arrests, and shall certify that, to the best of * * * their knowledge, the information provided is true. This requirement is not intended to duplicate existing requirements for individuals who are required to submit fingerprint images as part of a criminal background clearance process. Every applicant shall provide information on any prior administrative action taken against * * * them by any federal, state, or local government agency and shall certify that, to the best of * * * their knowledge, the information provided is true. An applicant or other person required to provide information pursuant to this section that knowingly or willfully makes false statements, representations, or omissions may be subject to administrative action, including, but not limited to, denial of * * * their application or exemption or revocation of any exemption previously granted.

(c)(1) The State Department of Health Care Services shall deny any application for any license, suspend or revoke any existing license, and disapprove or revoke any employment or contract for direct services, if the applicant, licensee, employee, or direct services contractor has been convicted of, or incarcerated for, a felony defined in subdivision (c) of Section 667.5 of, or subdivision (c) of Section 1192.7 of, the Penal Code, within the preceding 10 years.

(2) The application for licensure or renewal of any license shall be denied, and any employment or contract to provide direct services shall be disapproved or revoked, if the criminal record of the person includes a conviction in another jurisdiction for an offense that, if committed or attempted in this state, would have been punishable as one or more of the offenses referred to in paragraph (1).

(d)(1) The State Department of Health Care Services may approve an application for, or renewal of, a license, or continue any employment or contract for direct services, if the person has been convicted of a misdemeanor offense that is not a crime upon the person of another, the nature of which has no bearing upon the duties for which the person will perform as a licensee, direct care staff person, or direct services contractor. In determining whether to approve the application, employment, or contract for direct services, the department shall take into consideration the factors enumerated in paragraph (2).

(2) Notwithstanding subdivision (c), if the criminal record of a person indicates any conviction other than a minor traffic violation, the State Department of Health Care Services may deny the application for license or renewal, and may disapprove or revoke any employment or contract for direct services. In determining whether or not to deny the application for licensure or renewal, or to disapprove or revoke any employment or contract for direct services, the department shall take into consideration the following factors:

(A) The nature and seriousness of the offense under consideration and its relationship to the person's employment, duties, and responsibilities.

(B) Activities since conviction, including employment or participation in therapy or education, that would indicate changed behavior.

(C) The time that has elapsed since the commission of the conduct or offense and the number of offenses.

(D) The extent to which the person has complied with any terms of parole, probation, restitution, or any other sanction lawfully imposed against the person.

(E) Any rehabilitation evidence, including character references, submitted by the person.

(F) Employment history and current employer recommendations.

(G) Circumstances surrounding the commission of the offense that would demonstrate the unlikelihood of repetition.

(H) The granting by the Governor of a full and unconditional pardon.

(I) A certificate of rehabilitation from a superior court.

(e) Denial, suspension, or revocation of a license, or disapproval or revocation of any employment or contract for direct services specified in subdivision (c) and paragraph (2) of subdivision (d) are not subject to appeal, except as provided in subdivision (f).

(f) After a review of the record, the director may grant an exemption from denial, suspension, or revocation of any license, or disapproval of any employment or contract for direct services, if the crime for which the person was convicted was a property crime that did not involve injury to any person and the director has substantial and convincing evidence to support a reasonable belief that the person is of such good character as to justify issuance or renewal of the license or approval of the employment or contract.

(g) A plea or verdict of guilty, or a conviction following a plea of nolo contendere shall be deemed a conviction within the meaning of this section. The State Department of Health Care Services may deny any application, or deny, suspend, or revoke a license, or disapprove or revoke any employment or contract for direct services based on a conviction specified in subdivision (c) when the judgment of conviction is entered or when an order granting probation is made suspending the imposition of sentence.

(h)(1) For purposes of this section, "direct care staff" means any person who is an employee, contractor, or volunteer who has contact with other patients or residents in the provision of services. Administrative and licensed personnel shall be considered direct care staff when directly providing program services to participants.

(2) An additional background check shall not be required pursuant to this section if the direct care staff or licensee has received a prior criminal history background check while working in a mental health rehabilitation center, psychiatric residential treatment facility, or psychiatric health facility licensed by the State Department of Health Care Services, and provided the department has maintained continuous subsequent arrest notification on the individual from the Department of Justice since the prior criminal background check was initiated.

(3) When an application is denied on the basis of a conviction pursuant to this section, the State Department of Health Care Services shall provide the individual whose application was denied with notice, in writing, of the specific grounds for the proposed denial. *(Added by Stats.2002, c. 642 (A.B.1454), § 1. Amended by Stats.2003, c. 62 (S.B.600), § 327; Stats.2006, c. 902 (S.B.1759), § 20; Stats.2012, c. 34 (S.B.1009), § 104, eff. June 27, 2012; Stats.2012, c. 439 (A.B.1471), § 20, eff. Sept. 22, 2012; Stats.2013, c. 23 (A.B.82), § 39, eff. June 27, 2013; Stats.2022, c. 589 (A.B.2317), § 13, eff. Jan. 1, 2023.)*

Cross References

Court defined for purposes of this Part, see Welfare and Institutions Code § 5008.
Felonies, definition and penalties, see Penal Code §§ 17, 18.
Misdemeanors, definition and penalties, see Penal Code §§ 17, 19 and 19.2.

Part 1.5

CHILDREN'S CIVIL COMMITMENT AND MENTAL HEALTH TREATMENT ACT OF 1988

CHAPTER 1. GENERAL PROVISIONS

§ 5585. Title

This part shall be known as the Children's Civil Commitment and Mental Health Treatment Act of 1988. *(Added by Stats.1988, c. 1202, § 2.)*

§ 5585.10. Legislative intent and purposes

This part shall be construed to promote the legislative intent and purposes of this part as follows:

(a) To provide prompt evaluation and treatment of minors with mental health disorders, with particular priority given to seriously emotionally disturbed children and adolescents.

(b) To safeguard the rights to due process for minors and their families through judicial review.

(c) To provide individualized treatment, supervision, and placement services for gravely disabled minors.

(d) To prevent severe and long-term mental disabilities among minors through early identification, effective family service interventions, and public education. *(Added by Stats.1988, c. 1202, § 2. Amended by Stats.2014, c. 144 (A.B.1847), § 99, eff. Jan. 1, 2015.)*

Cross References

Gravely disabled minor defined, see Welfare and Institutions Code § 5585.25.

§ 5585.20. Application of part; conflicting provisions

This part shall apply only to the initial 72 hours of mental health evaluation and treatment provided to a minor. Notwithstanding the provisions of the Lanterman-Petris-Short Act (Part 1 (commencing with Section 5000)), unless the context otherwise requires, the definitions and procedures contained in this part shall, for the initial 72 hours of evaluation and treatment, govern the construction of state law governing the civil commitment of minors for involuntary treatment. To the extent that this part conflicts with any other * * * law, it is the intent of the Legislature that this part shall apply. Evaluation and treatment of a minor beyond the initial 72 hours shall be pursuant to the Lanterman-Petris-Short Act (Part 1 (commencing with Section 5000)). *(Added by Stats.1988, c. 1202, § 2. Amended by Stats.2022, c. 960 (A.B.2275), § 7, eff. Jan. 1, 2023.)*

§ 5585.21. Regulations

The Director of Health Care Services may promulgate regulations as necessary to implement and clarify the provisions of this part as they relate to minors. *(Added by Stats.1988, c. 1202, § 2. Amended by Stats.2012, c. 34 (S.B.1009), § 111, eff. June 27, 2012; Stats.2013, c. 23 (A.B.82), § 40, eff. June 27, 2013.)*

Cross References

Director of Mental Health, see Welfare and Institutions Code §§ 4004, 4005.

§ 5585.22. Educational materials and training curriculum

The Director of Health Care Services, in consultation with the County Behavioral Health Directors Association of California, may develop the appropriate educational materials and a training curriculum, and may provide training as necessary to ensure that those persons providing services pursuant to this part fully understand its purpose. *(Added by Stats.1988, c. 1202, § 2. Amended by Stats.2012, c. 34 (S.B.1009), § 112, eff. June 27, 2012; Stats.2015, c. 455 (S.B.804), § 31, eff. Jan. 1, 2016.)*

Cross References

Director of Mental Health, see Welfare and Institutions Code §§ 4004, 4005.

§ 5585.25. "Gravely disabled minor" defined

"Gravely disabled minor" means a minor who, as a result of a mental disorder, is unable to use the elements of life that are essential to health, safety, and development, including food, clothing, and shelter, even though provided to the minor by others. Intellectual disability, epilepsy, or other developmental disabilities, alcoholism, other drug abuse, or repeated antisocial behavior do not, by themselves, constitute a mental disorder. *(Added by Stats.1988, c. 1202, § 2. Amended by Stats.2012, c. 448 (A.B.2370), § 53; Stats.2012, c. 457 (S.B.1381), § 53.)*

CHAPTER 2. CIVIL COMMITMENT OF MINORS

§ 5585.50. Custody and placement of minor in facility; notice to parent or legal guardian; probable cause application; civil liability for intentional false statement

(a) When any minor, as a result of mental disorder, is a danger to others, or to himself or herself, or gravely disabled and authorization for voluntary treatment is not available, a peace officer, member of the attending staff, as defined by regulation, of an evaluation facility designated by the county, or other professional person designated by the county may, upon probable cause, take, or cause to be taken, the minor into custody and place him or her in a facility designated by the county and approved by the State Department of Health Care Services as a facility for 72–hour treatment and evaluation of minors.

The facility shall make every effort to notify the minor's parent or legal guardian as soon as possible after the minor is detained.

(b) The facility shall require an application in writing stating the circumstances under which the minor's condition was called to the attention of the officer, member of the attending staff, or professional person, and stating that the officer, member of the attending staff, or professional person has probable cause to believe that the minor is, as a result of mental disorder, a danger to others, or to himself or herself, or gravely disabled and authorization for voluntary treatment is not available. If the probable cause is based on the statement of a person other than the officer, member of the attending staff, or professional person, the person shall be liable in a civil action for intentionally giving a statement which he or she knows to be false. *(Added by Stats.1988, c. 1202, § 2. Amended by Stats.2012, c. 34 (S.B.1009), § 113, eff. June 27, 2012; Stats.2013, c. 23 (A.B.82), § 41, eff. June 27, 2013.)*

§ 5585.52. Clinical evaluation; parent or legal guardian involvement

Any minor detained under the provisions of Section 5585.50 shall receive a clinical evaluation consisting of multidisciplinary professional analyses of the minor's medical, psychological, developmental, educational, social, financial, and legal conditions as may appear to constitute a problem. This evaluation shall include a psychosocial evaluation of the family or living environment, or both. Persons providing evaluation services shall be properly qualified professionals with training or supervised experience, or both, in the diagnosis and treatment of minors. Every effort shall be made to involve the minor's parent or legal guardian in the clinical evaluation. *(Added by Stats.1988, c. 1202, § 2.)*

§ 5585.53. Additional treatment; treatment plan; least restrictive placement alternative; consultation and consent; involuntary treatment

If, in the opinion of the professional person conducting the evaluation as specified in Section 5585.52, the minor will require additional mental health treatment, a treatment plan shall be written and shall identify the least restrictive placement alternative in which the minor can receive the necessary treatment. The family, legal guardian, or caretaker and the minor shall be consulted and informed as to the basic recommendations for further treatment and placement requirements. Every effort shall be made to obtain the consent of the minor's parent or legal guardian prior to treatment and placement of the minor. Inability to obtain the consent of the minor's parent or legal guardian shall not preclude the involuntary treatment of a minor who is determined to be gravely disabled or a danger to himself or herself or others. Involuntary treatment shall only be allowed in accordance with the provisions of the Lanterman–Petris–Short Act (Part 1 (commencing with Section 5000)). *(Added by Stats.1988, c. 1202, § 2.)*

§ 5585.55. Involuntary treatment; confinement with adults

The minor committed for involuntary treatment under this part shall be placed in a mental health facility designated by the county and approved by the State Department of Health Care Services as a facility for 72–hour evaluation and treatment. Except as provided for in Section 5751.7, each county shall ensure that minors under 16 years of age are not held with adults receiving psychiatric treatment under the provisions of the Lanterman–Petris–Short Act (Part 1 (commencing with Section 5000)). *(Added by Stats.1988, c. 1202, § 2. Amended by Stats.2012, c. 34 (S.B.1009), § 114, eff. June 27, 2012; Stats.2013, c. 23 (A.B.82), § 42, eff. June 27, 2013.)*

§ 5585.57. Aftercare plan

A mentally ill minor, upon being considered for release from involuntary treatment, shall have an aftercare plan developed. The plan shall include educational or training needs, provided these are necessary for the minor's well-being. *(Added by Stats.1988, c. 1202, § 2.)*

§ 5585.58. Funding

This part shall be funded under the Bronzan–McCorquodale Act pursuant to Part 2 (commencing with Section 5600), as part of the county performance contract. *(Added by Stats.1988, c. 1202, § 2. Amended by Stats.1993, c. 1245 (S.B.282), § 8, eff. Oct. 11, 1993.)*

§ 5585.59. Legally emancipated minors

For the purposes of this part, legally emancipated minors requiring involuntary treatment shall be considered adults and this part shall not apply. *(Added by Stats.1988, c. 1202, § 2.)*

Cross References

Emancipation of minors, see Family Code § 7000 et seq.

Part 6

EDAPT FUNDING PILOT PROGRAM

Section

§ 5950. Early Diagnosis and Preventive Treatment (EDAPT) Program Fund; definitions

(a) There is hereby established the Early Diagnosis and Preventive Treatment (EDAPT) Program Fund within the State Treasury. Moneys from private or other sources may be deposited into the fund and used for purposes of this part. General Fund moneys shall not be deposited into the fund.

(b) When the Department of Finance has determined that the total amount of the moneys in the fund established pursuant to subdivision (a) has reached or exceeded one million two hundred thousand dollars ($1,200,000), the Controller shall distribute all of the moneys in the fund to the Regents of the University of California for the purpose of providing reimbursement to an EDAPT program for services provided to persons who are referred to that program, but whose private health benefit plan does not cover the full range of required services.

(c) Funds distributed pursuant to this part shall not be used to pay for services normally covered by the patient's private health benefit plan and shall only be used to augment private health benefit plan coverage to provide the patient with the full range of necessary services.

(d) For purposes of this part, the following definitions shall apply:

(1) "EDAPT program" means an Early Diagnosis and Preventive Treatment program and refers to a program that utilizes integrated systems of care to provide early intervention, assessment, diagnosis, a treatment plan, and necessary services for individuals with severe mental illness and children with severe emotional disturbance using an interdisciplinary team of physicians, clinicians, advocates, and staff who coordinate care on an outpatient basis.

(2) "Private health benefit plan" means a program or entity that provides, arranges, pays for, or reimburses the cost of health benefits, but does not include coverage provided through the Medi–Cal system. *(Added by Stats.2016, c. 547 (A.B.38), § 2, eff. Jan. 1, 2017.)*

Repeal

For repeal of Part 6, see Welfare and Institutions Code § 5952.

§ 5951. Reports from the Regents of the University of California

(a) If the Regents of the University of California accept moneys from the fund established pursuant to this part, or accept federal funds distributed by the State Department of Health Care Services as described in subdivision (b), the regents shall report, on or after January 1, 2022, but prior to January 1, 2023, to the health committees of both houses of the Legislature all of the following:

(1) Evidence as to whether the early psychosis approach reduces the duration of untreated psychosis, reduces the severity of symptoms, improves relapse rates, decreases the use of inpatient care in comparison to standard care, supports educational and career progress, and reduces the cost of treatment in comparison to standard treatment methodologies.

(2) The number of patients with private health benefit plans served by an EDAPT program in the 12 months prior to the implementation of this part.

(3) The number of patients with private health benefit plans served by an EDAPT program that has received funding pursuant to this part.

(4) The number of patients participating in an EDAPT program that has received funding pursuant to this part who are considered stabilized, as a percentage of patients served.

(5) The number of patients participating in an EDAPT program that has received funding pursuant to this part who need services beyond those provided in the program and the nature of those services.

(6) Any other information the regents deem necessary.

(b) If the State Department of Health Care Services distributes federal funds to the Regents of the University of California for the purpose of supporting an EDAPT program, the regents shall issue the report described in subdivision (a), to the extent permitted by federal law.

(c) A report to be submitted pursuant to this section shall be submitted in compliance with Section 9795 of the Government Code. *(Added by Stats.2016, c. 547 (A.B.38), § 2, eff. Jan. 1, 2017.)*

Repeal

For repeal of Part 6, see Welfare and Institutions Code § 5952.

§ 5952. Duration of part

This part shall remain in effect only until January 1, 2023, and as of that date is repealed, unless a later enacted statute, that is enacted before January 1, 2023, deletes or extends that date. *(Added by Stats.2016, c. 547 (A.B.38), § 2, eff. Jan. 1, 2017.)*

Part 7

BEHAVIORAL HEALTH SERVICES AND SUPPORTS

CHAPTER 1. BEHAVIORAL HEALTH CONTINUUM INFRASTRUCTURE PROGRAM

§ 5960. Establishment of Behavioral Health Continuum Infrastructure Program

The department may establish the Behavioral Health Continuum Infrastructure Program pursuant to this chapter if the Legislature appropriates funds for this purpose. *(Added by Stats.2021, c. 143 (A.B.133), § 355, eff. July 27, 2021.)*

Repeal

For repeal of Chapter 1, see Welfare and Institutions Code § 5960.45.

§ 5960.05. Award of competitive grants

If the department establishes the program pursuant to this chapter, the department may award competitive grants to qualified entities to construct, acquire, and rehabilitate real estate assets or to invest in needed mobile crisis infrastructure to expand the community continuum of behavioral health treatment resources to build new capacity or expand existing capacity for short-term crisis stabilization, acute and subacute care, crisis residential, community-based mental health residential, substance use disorder residential, peer respite, mobile crisis, community and outpatient behavioral health services, and other clinically enriched longer term treatment and rehabilitation options for persons with behavioral health disorders in the least restrictive and least costly setting. *(Added by Stats.2021, c. 143 (A.B.133), § 355, eff. July 27, 2021.)*

Repeal

For repeal of Chapter 1, see Welfare and Institutions Code § 5960.45.

§ 5960.1. Determination of methodology and distribution of grant funds

Except as provided in Section 5960.15, the department shall determine the methodology and distribution of the grant funds appropriated for the program pursuant to Section 5960.05 to those entities it deems qualified. *(Added by Stats.2021, c. 143 (A.B.133), § 355, eff. July 27, 2021.)*

Repeal

For repeal of Chapter 1, see Welfare and Institutions Code § 5960.45.

§ 5960.15. Conditions for receipt of grant funds

An entity shall meet all of the following conditions in order to receive grant funds pursuant to Section 5960.05, to the extent applicable and as required by the department:

(a) Provide matching funds or real property.

(b) Expend funds to supplement and not supplant existing funds to construct, acquire, and rehabilitate real estate assets.

(c) Report data to the department within 90 days of the end of each quarter for the first five years.

(d) Operate services in the financed facility for the intended purpose for a minimum of 30 years. *(Added by Stats.2021, c. 143 (A.B.133), § 355, eff. July 27, 2021.)*

Repeal

For repeal of Chapter 1, see Welfare and Institutions Code § 5960.45.

§ 5960.2. Implementation of chapter

(a) This chapter shall be implemented only if, and to the extent that, the department determines that federal financial participation under the Medi–Cal program, including but not limited to the increased federal funding available pursuant to Section 9813 of the federal American Rescue Plan Act of 2021 (Pub. Law 117–2),[1] is not jeopardized.

(b) Notwithstanding Chapter 3.5 (commencing with Section 11340) of Part 1 of Division 3 of Title 2 of the Government Code, the department may implement, interpret, or make specific this chapter, in whole or in part, by means of information notices or other similar instructions, without taking any further regulatory action. *(Added by Stats.2021, c. 143 (A.B.133), § 355, eff. July 27, 2021.)*

[1] For public law sections classified to the U.S.C.A., see USCA–Tables.

Repeal

For repeal of Chapter 1, see Welfare and Institutions Code § 5960.45.

§ 5960.25. Contracts

For purposes of implementing this chapter, the department may enter into exclusive or nonexclusive contracts, or amend existing contracts, on a bid or negotiated basis. Contracts entered into or amended pursuant to this section shall be exempt from Chapter 6 (commencing with section 14825) of Part 5.5 of Division 3 of Title 2 of the Government Code, Section 19130 of the Government Code, Part 2 (commencing with Section 10100) of Division 2 of the Public Contract Code, and the State Administrative Manual, and shall be exempt from the review or approval of any division of the Department of General Services. *(Added by Stats.2021, c. 143 (A.B.133), § 355, eff. July 27, 2021.)*

Repeal

For repeal of Chapter 1, see Welfare and Institutions Code § 5960.45.

§ 5960.3. Facility projects

(a) Notwithstanding any other law, a facility project funded by a grant pursuant to this chapter shall be deemed consistent and in conformity with any applicable local plan, standard, or requirement, and allowed as a permitted use, within the zone in which the structure is located, and shall not be subject to a conditional use permit, discretionary permit, or to any other discretionary reviews or approvals.

(b) Notwithstanding any other law, the California Environmental Quality Act (Division 13 (commencing with Section 21000) of the Public Resources Code) shall not apply to a project, including a phased project, funded by a grant pursuant to this chapter if, where applicable, all of the following applicable requirements are satisfied:

(1) The project is not acquired by eminent domain.

(2) The project applicant demonstrates that the project is, and will continue to be, licensed by and in good standing with the department or other state licensing entity at the time of, and for the duration of, occupancy. The project shall be in decent, safe, and sanitary condition at the time of occupancy.

(3) The project applicant requires all contractors and subcontractors performing work on the facility project to pay prevailing wages for any proposed rehabilitation, construction, or major alterations in accordance with Chapter 1 (commencing with Section 1720) of Part 7 of Division 2 of the Labor Code.

(4) The project applicant obtains an enforceable commitment that all contractors and subcontractors performing work on the project will use a skilled and trained workforce for any proposed rehabilitation, construction, or major alterations in accordance with Chapter 2.9 (commencing with Section 2600) of Part 1 of Division 2 of the Public Contract Code.

(5) The project applicant submits to the lead agency a letter of support, or other durable documentary proof for the project, from a county, city, or other local public entity for any new proposed construction, major alteration work, or rehabilitation.

(6) The project applicant demonstrates that not less than ninety-five percent of the total cost of any new construction, facility acquisition, or rehabilitation project is paid for with public funds, private non-profit funds, or philanthropic funds.

(7) The project applicant demonstrates that the project expands the availability of behavioral health treatment services in the subject jurisdiction.

(8) The project applicant demonstrates that there are long-term covenants and restrictions that require the project to be used to provide behavioral health treatment for no less than 30 years, and those covenants and restrictions may not be amended or extinguished by a subsequent title holder, owner, or operator.

(9) The project does not result in any increase in the existing onsite development footprint of structures or improvements.

(c) If a project applicant determines that a project is not subject to the California Environmental Quality Act pursuant to this section, and the lead agency for the project publicly concurs in that determination, the project applicant shall file a notice of exemption with the Office of Planning and Research and the county clerk of the county in which the project is located in the manner specified in subdivisions (b) and (c) of Section 21152 of the Public Resources Code. *(Added by Stats.2021, c. 143 (A.B.133), § 355, eff. July 27, 2021.)*

Repeal

For repeal of Chapter 1, see Welfare and Institutions Code § 5960.45.

§ 5960.35. Definitions

(a) The following definitions shall apply to this chapter:

(1) "Department" means the State Department of Health Care Services.

(2) "Program" means the Behavioral Health Continuum Infrastructure Program authorized by this chapter.

(b) The following provisions shall apply to the implementation of this chapter:

(1) "Low–rent housing project," as defined in Section 1 of Article XXXIV of the California Constitution, does not apply to any facility project pursuant to this section that meets any one of the following criteria:

(A) The development is privately owned housing, receiving no ad valorem property tax exemption, other than exemptions granted pursuant to subdivision (f) or (g) of Section 214 of the Revenue and Taxation Code, not fully reimbursed to all taxing entities, and not more than 49 percent of the dwellings, apartments, or other living accommodations of the development may be occupied by persons of low income.

(B) The development is privately owned housing, is not exempt from ad valorem taxation by reason of any public ownership, and is not financed with direct long-term financing from a public body.

(C) The development is intended for owner-occupancy, which may include a limited-equity housing cooperative as defined in Section 50076.5 of the Health and Safety Code, or cooperative or condominium ownership, rather than for rental-occupancy.

(D) The development consists of newly constructed, privately owned, one-to-four family dwellings not located on adjoining sites.

(E) The development consists of existing dwelling units leased by the state public body from the private owner of these dwelling units.

(F) The development consists of the rehabilitation, reconstruction, improvement or addition to, or replacement of, dwelling units of a previously existing low-rent housing project, or a project previously or currently occupied by lower income households, as defined in Section 50079.5 of the Health and Safety Code.

(G) The development consists of the acquisition, rehabilitation, reconstruction, improvement, or any combination thereof, of a development which, prior to the date of the transaction to acquire, rehabilitate, reconstruct, improve, or any combination thereof, was subject to a contract for federal or state public body assistance for the purpose of providing affordable housing for low-income households and maintains, or enters into, a contract for federal or state public body assistance for the purpose of providing affordable housing for low-income households.

(2) "Tribal entity" shall mean a federally recognized Indian tribe, tribal organization, or urban Indian organization, as defined in Section 1603 of Title 25 of the United States Code. *(Added by Stats.2021, c. 143 (A.B.133), § 355, eff. July 27, 2021.)*

Repeal

For repeal of Chapter 1, see Welfare and Institutions Code § 5960.45.

§ 5960.4. Severability

The provisions of this chapter are severable. If any provision of this chapter or its application is held invalid, that invalidity shall not affect other provisions or applications that can be given effect without the invalid provision or application. *(Added by Stats.2021, c. 143 (A.B.133), § 355, eff. July 27, 2021.)*

Repeal

For repeal of Chapter 1, see Welfare and Institutions Code § 5960.45.

§ 5960.45. Duration of chapter

This chapter shall remain in effect only until January, 1, 2027, and as of that date is repealed. *(Added by Stats.2021, c. 143 (A.B.133), § 355, eff. July 27, 2021.)*

CHAPTER 2. CHILDREN AND YOUTH BEHAVIORAL HEALTH INITIATIVE ACT

§ 5961. Short title; administration; purpose; components; implementation

(a) This chapter shall be known, and may be cited, as the Children and Youth Behavioral Health Initiative Act.

(b) The Children and Youth Behavioral Health Initiative shall be administered by the California Health and Human Services Agency and its departments, as applicable.

(c) The initiative is intended to transform California's behavioral health system into an innovative ecosystem in which all children and youth 25 years of age and younger, regardless of payer, are screened, supported, and served for emerging and existing behavioral health needs.

(d) Subject to an appropriation by the Legislature for this purpose, the initiative shall include, but need not be limited to, all of the following components:

(1) A behavioral health services and supports virtual platform, as described in Section 5961.1.

(2) School–linked partnership, capacity, and infrastructure grants to qualified entities to support implementation of the initiative for behavioral health services in schools and school-linked settings, as described in Section 5961.2.

(3) Incentive payments to qualifying Medi–Cal managed care plans to implement interventions that increase access to preventive, early intervention, and behavioral health services by school-affiliated behavioral health providers for children in publicly funded childcare and preschool and TK–12 children in public schools, as described in Section 5961.3.

(4) Development and maintenance of a statewide fee schedule for school-linked outpatient mental health and substance use disorder treatment, as described in Section 5961.4.

(5) Development and expansion of evidence-based behavioral health programs, as described in Section 5961.5.

(6) Funding targeted to qualified entities serving individuals 25 years of age and younger through the Behavioral Health Continuum Infrastructure Program, as described in Chapter 1 (commencing with Section 5960).

(7) A comprehensive, and culturally and linguistically proficient, public education and social change campaign in support of the initiative.

(8) Investments for behavioral health workforce, education, and training to foster broad behavioral health capacity in support of the initiative, including a multiyear plan to launch and implement a statewide school behavioral health counselor system pursuant to Chapter 1.5 (commencing with Section 127825) of Part 3 of Division 107 of the Health and Safety Code.

(9) Funding targeted to qualified entities serving individuals 25 years of age and younger through the Mental Health Student Services Act, as described in Chapter 3 (commencing with Section 5886) of Part 4.

(e) Each component of the initiative shall be implemented only if, and to the extent that, the State Department of Health Care Services determines that federal financial participation under the Medi–Cal program is not jeopardized.

(f) For purposes of implementing this chapter, the California Health and Human Services Agency, the State Department of Health Care Services, and the Office of Statewide Health Planning and Development may enter into exclusive or nonexclusive contracts, or amend existing contracts, on a bid or negotiated basis. Contracts entered into or amended pursuant to this chapter shall be exempt from Chapter 6 (commencing with Section 14825) of Part 5.5 of Division 3 of Title 2 of the Government Code, Section 19130 of the Government Code, Part 2 (commencing with Section 10100) of Division 2 of the Public Contract Code, and the State Administrative Manual, and shall be exempt from the review or approval of any division of the Department of General Services.

(g) Notwithstanding Chapter 3.5 (commencing with Section 11340) of Part 1 of Division 3 of Title 2 of the Government Code, the State Department of Health Care Services and the Office of Statewide Health Planning and Development may implement, interpret, or make specific this chapter, in whole or in part, by means of plan letters, information notices, provider bulletins, or other similar instructions, without taking any further regulatory action.

(h) The Legislature finds and declares that this chapter is a state law within the meaning of Section 1621(d) of Title 8 of the United States Code. *(Added by Stats.2021, c. 143 (A.B.133), § 355, eff. July 27, 2021.)*

§ 5961.1. Behavioral health services and supports virtual platform

(a) As a component of the initiative, the State Department of Health Care Services shall procure and oversee a vendor to establish and maintain a behavioral health services and supports virtual platform that integrates behavioral health screenings, application-based supports, and direct behavioral health services to children and youth 25 years of age and younger, regardless of payer.

(b) Any virtual platform established or procured shall include access in all Medi–Cal threshold languages and shall be culturally appropriate to accommodate the diversity of the population and shall be accessible by telephone.

(c) The virtual platform may provide behavioral health services and supports, including, but not limited to, the following:

(1) Regular, automated behavioral health screenings.

(2) Short–term individual counseling, group counseling, and behavioral health peer and coaching supports.

(3) Interactive education, self-monitoring tools, application-based games, video and book suggestions, automated cognitive behavioral therapy, and mindful exercises designed to build skills and enhance wellbeing.

(4) Access to behavioral health peers, coaches, and licensed clinicians.

(5) Referrals to an individual's commercial health insurance, Medi–Cal managed care plan, county behavioral health, school-linked counselor, or community-based organizations, or other resources for higher-level behavioral health services.

(6) Statewide e-consult service to allow primary care pediatric and family practice providers to receive asynchronous support and consultation to manage behavioral health conditions for their patients. *(Added by Stats.2021, c. 143 (A.B.133), § 355, eff. July 27, 2021.)*

§ 5961.2. Award of competitive grants; purposes; eligibility; allowable activities

(a) As a component of the initiative, the State Department of Health Care Services, or its contracted vendor, may award competitive grants to entities it deems qualified for the following purposes:

(1) To build partnerships, capacity, and infrastructure supporting ongoing school-linked behavioral health services for children and youth 25 years of age and younger.

(2) To expand access to licensed medical and behavioral health professionals, counselors, peer support specialists, community health workers, and behavioral health coaches serving children and youth.

(3) To build a statewide, community-based organization provider network for behavioral health prevention and treatment services for children and youth, including those attending institutions of higher education.

(4) To enhance coordination and partnerships with respect to behavioral health prevention and treatment services for children and youth via appropriate data sharing systems.

(b) Subject to subdivision (c), entities eligible to receive grants pursuant to this section may include counties, city mental health authorities, tribal entities, local educational agencies, institutions of higher education, publicly funded childcare and preschools, health care service plans, community-based organizations, and behavioral health providers.

(c) The department shall determine the eligibility criteria, grant application process, and methodology for the distribution of funds appropriated for the purposes described in this section to those entities it deems qualified.

(d) The department shall ensure that grant distribution includes, but is not limited to, rural, urban, and suburban regions and geographic distribution among different age cohorts. Allowable activities shall include, but not be limited to, the following:

(1) Addressing behavioral health disparities while providing linguistically and culturally competent services for children and youth who lack access to adequate behavioral health services or otherwise are difficult to reach.

(2) Supporting administrative costs, including planning, project management, training, and technical assistance.

(3) Linking plans, counties, and school districts with local social services and community-based organizations.

(4) Implementing telehealth equipment and virtual systems in schools or near schools.

(5) Implementing data-sharing tools, information technology interfaces, or other technology investments designed to connect to behavioral health services.

(e) Of the funds appropriated for purposes of this section to institutions of higher education, at least two-thirds shall be reserved for California Community Colleges.

(f) For purposes of this section, the following definitions shall apply:

(1) "Comprehensive risk contract" has the same meaning as set forth in Section 438.2 of Title 42 of the Code of Federal Regulations.

(2) "Health care service plan" has the same meaning as described in subdivision (f) of Section 1345 of the Health and Safety Code.

(3) "Institution of higher education" means the California Community Colleges, the California State University, or the University of California.

(4) "Local educational agency" means a school district, county office of education, charter school, the California Schools for the Deaf, and the California School for the Blind.

(5) "Tribal entity" means a federally recognized Indian tribe, tribal organization, or urban Indian organization. *(Added by Stats. 2021, c. 143 (A.B.133), § 355, eff. July 27, 2021.)*

§ 5961.3. Incentive payments to qualifying Medi Cal managed care plans; interventions, goals, and metrics; modification of requirements

(a) As a component of the initiative, the State Department of Health Care Services shall make incentive payments to qualifying Medi–Cal managed care plans that meet predefined goals and metrics developed pursuant to subdivision (b) associated with targeted interventions that increase access to preventive, early intervention and behavioral health services by school-affiliated behavioral health providers for K–12 children in schools.

(b) The department, in consultation with the State Department of Education, Medi–Cal managed care plans, county behavioral health departments, local educational agencies, and other affected stakeholders, shall develop the interventions, goals, and metrics used to determine a Medi–Cal managed care plan's eligibility to receive the incentive payments described in this section. Higher incentive payments may be made for activities that increase Medi–Cal reimbursable services provided to children and youth, to reduce health equity gaps, and for services provided to children and youth living in transition, are homeless, or are involved in the child welfare system. Interventions, goals, and metrics include, but are not limited to, the following:

(1) Local planning efforts to review existing plans and documents that articulate children and youth needs in the area; compile data; map existing behavioral health providers and resources; identify gaps, disparities, and inequities; and convene stakeholders and develop a framework for a robust and coordinated system of social, emotional, and behavioral health supports for children and youth.

(2) Providing technical assistance to increase coordination and partnerships between schools and health care plans to build an integrated continuum of behavioral health services using contracts, a memorandum of understanding, or other agreements.

(3) Developing or piloting behavioral health wellness programs to expand greater prevention and early intervention practices in school settings, such as Mental Health First Aid and Social and Emotional Learning.

(4) Expanding the workforce by using community health workers or peers to expand the surveillance and early intervention of behavioral health issues in school-age children 0 to 25 years of age, inclusive.

(5) Increasing telehealth in schools and ensure students have access to technological equipment.

(6) Implementing school-based suicide prevention strategies.

(7) Improving performance and outcomes-based accountability for behavioral health access and quality measures through local student behavioral health dashboards or public reporting.

(8) Increasing access to substance use disorder prevention, early intervention, and treatment.

(c)(1) For each Medi–Cal managed care rating period, as defined in paragraph (3) of subdivision (a) of Section 14105.945, that the department implements this section, the department shall determine the amount of incentive payment earned by each qualifying Medi–Cal managed care plan.

(2) Any incentive payments that are eligible for federal financial participation pursuant to subdivision (e) shall be made in accordance with the requirements for incentive arrangements in Section 438.6(b)(2) of Title 42 of the Code of Federal Regulations and any associated federal guidance.

(d) Incentive payments made pursuant to this section shall be used to supplement and not supplant existing payments to Medi–Cal managed care plans. In addition to developing new collaborative initiatives, incentive payments shall be used to build on existing school-based partnerships between schools and applicable Medi–Cal plans, including Medi–Cal behavioral health delivery systems.

(e) The department shall seek any necessary federal approvals to claim federal financial participation for the incentive payments to qualifying Medi–Cal managed care plans described in this section. If federal approval is obtained for one or more Medi–Cal managed care rating periods, the department shall implement this section only to the extent that federal financial participation is available in that applicable rating period. If federal approval is not obtained for one or more Medi–Cal managed care rating periods, the department may make incentive payments to qualifying Medi–Cal managed care plans as described in this section on a state-only funding basis during the applicable rating period, but only to the extent sufficient funds are appropriated to the department for this purpose and the department determines that federal financial participation for the Medi–Cal program is not otherwise jeopardized as a result.

(f)(1) The department may modify any requirement specified in this section to the extent that it deems the modification necessary to meet the requirements of federal law or regulations, to obtain or maintain federal approval, or to ensure that federal financial participation is available or not otherwise jeopardized. The department shall not propose any modification pursuant to this subdivision until the Department of Finance has reviewed and approved a fiscal impact statement.

(2) If the department, after consulting with the State Department of Education, Medi–Cal managed care plans, county behavioral health departments, local educational agencies, and other affected stakeholder entities, determines that the potential modification would be consistent with the goals of this section, the modification may be made in consultation with the Department of Finance and the department shall execute a declaration stating that this determination has been made. The department shall post the declaration on its internet website.

(3) The department shall notify entities consulted in paragraph (2), the Joint Legislative Budget Committee, the Senate Committees on Appropriations, Budget and Fiscal Review, and Health, and the Assembly Committees on Appropriations, Budget, and Health, within 10 business days of that modification or adjustment.

(4) The department shall work with the affected entities and the Legislature to make the necessary statutory changes.

(g) For purposes of this section, the following definitions apply:

(1) "Comprehensive risk contract" has the same meaning as set forth in Section 438.2 of Title 42 of the Code of Federal Regulations.

(2) "Local educational agency" means a school district, county office of education, charter school, the California Schools for the Deaf, and the California School for the Blind.

(3) "Medi–Cal managed care plan" means an individual, organization, or entity that enters into a comprehensive risk contract with the department to provide covered full-scope health care services to enrolled Medi–Cal beneficiaries pursuant to any provision of Chapter 7 (commencing with Section 14000) or Chapter 8 (commencing with Section 14200) of Part 3 of Division 9.

(4) "Medi–Cal behavioral health delivery system" has the meaning described in subdivision (i) of Section 14184.101. *(Added by Stats.2021, c. 143 (A.B.133), § 355, eff. July 27, 2021.)*

§ 5961.4. School-linked outpatient mental health or substance use disorder treatment; statewide fee schedule; provider network; reimbursement; implementation

(a) As a component of the initiative, the State Department of Health Care Services shall develop and maintain a school-linked statewide fee schedule for outpatient mental health or substance use disorder treatment provided to a student 25 years of age or younger at a schoolsite.

(b) The department shall develop and maintain a school-linked statewide provider network of schoolsite behavioral health counselors.

(c)(1) Commencing January 1, 2024, and subject to subdivision (d), each Medi–Cal managed care plan and Medi–Cal behavioral health delivery system, as applicable, shall reimburse providers of medically necessary outpatient mental health or substance use disorder treatment provided at a schoolsite to a student 25 years of age or younger who is an enrollee of the plan or delivery system, in accordance with paragraph (2), but only to the extent the Medi–Cal managed care plan or Medi–Cal behavioral delivery system is financially responsible for those schoolsite services under its approved managed care contract with the department.

(2) Providers of medically necessary schoolsite services described in this section shall be reimbursed, at a minimum, at the fee schedule rate or rates developed pursuant to subdivision (a), regardless of network provider status.

(d) This section shall be implemented only to the extent that the department obtains any necessary federal approvals, and federal financial participation under the Medi–Cal program is available and not otherwise jeopardized.

(e) This section does not relieve a local educational agency or institution of higher education from requirements to accommodate or provide services to students with disabilities pursuant to any applicable state and federal law, including, but not limited to, the federal Individuals with Disabilities Education Act (20 U.S.C. Sec. 1400 ct seq.), Part 30 (commencing with Section 56000) of Division 4 of Title 2 of the Education Code, Chapter 26.5 (commencing with Section 7570) of Division 7 of Title 1 of the Government Code, and Chapter 3 (commencing with Section 3000) of Division 1 of Title 5 of the California Code of Regulations.

(f) For purposes of this section, the following definitions shall apply:

(1) "Comprehensive risk contract" has the same meaning as set forth in Section 438.2 of Title 42 of the Code of Federal Regulations.

(2) "Institution of higher education" means the California Community Colleges, the California State University, or the University of California.

(3) Local educational agency" means a school district, county office of education, charter school, the California Schools for the Deaf, and the California School for the Blind.

(4) "Medi–Cal behavioral health delivery system" has the meaning described in subdivision (i) of Section 14184.101.

(5) "Medi–Cal managed care plan" means any individual, organization, or entity that enters into a comprehensive risk contract with the department to provide covered full-scope health care services to enrolled Medi–Cal beneficiaries pursuant to any provision of Chapter 7 (commencing with Section 14000) or Chapter 8 (commencing with Section 14200) of Part 3 of Division 9.

(6) "Schoolsite" has the meaning described in paragraph (6) of subdivision (b) of Section 1374.722 of the Health and Safety Code. *(Added by Stats.2021, c. 143 (A.B.133), § 355, eff. July 27, 2021.)*

§ 5961.5. Development and selection of evidence-based interventions and community-defined promising practices

(a) As a component of the initiative, the State Department of Health Care Services shall develop and select evidence-based interventions and community-defined promising practices to improve outcomes for children and youth with, or at high risk for, behavioral health conditions.

(b) Prior to selecting the evidence-based interventions, as described in subdivision (a), the department shall establish a workgroup comprised of subject matter experts and affected stakeholders to consider evidence-based interventions based on robust evidence for effectiveness, impact on racial equity, and sustainability.

(c) The department, or its contracted vendor, shall provide competitive grants to entities it deems qualified to support the implementation of the evidence-based interventions and community-defined promising practices developed pursuant to subdivision (a).

(d) Subject to subdivision (e), entities eligible to receive grants pursuant to this section may include Medi-Cal behavioral health delivery systems, city mental health authorities, tribal entities, health care service plans, Medi-Cal managed care plans, community-based organizations, and behavioral health providers. * * *

(e) The department shall determine the eligibility criteria, grant application process, and methodology for the distribution of funds appropriated for the purposes described in this section * * * to those entities it deems qualified.

(f) As a condition of funding, grant recipients shall share standardized data, in a manner and form determined by the department.

(g) For purposes of this section, "Medi-Cal behavioral health delivery system" shall have the same meaning as specified in subdivision (i) of Section 14184.101. *(Added by Stats.2021, c. 143 (A.B.133), § 355, eff. July 27, 2021. Amended by Stats.2022, c. 47 (S.B.184), § 61, eff. June 30, 2022.)*

Part 8

THE COMMUNITY ASSISTANCE, RECOVERY, AND EMPOWERMENT ACT

CHAPTER 1. GENERAL PROVISIONS

§ 5970. Short title

This part shall be known, and may be cited, as Community Assistance, Recovery, and Empowerment (CARE) Act. *(Added by Stats.2022, c. 319 (S.B.1338), § 7, eff. Jan. 1, 2023.)*

§ 5970.5. Implementation of part; timeline

This part shall be implemented as follows, with technical assistance and continuous quality improvement, pursuant to Section 5983:

(a) A first cohort of counties, which shall include the Counties of Glenn, Orange, Riverside, San Diego, Stanislaus, and Tuolumne, and the City and County of San Francisco, shall begin no later than October 1, 2023, unless the county is provided additional time pursuant to paragraph (2) of subdivision (c).

(b) A second cohort of counties, representing the remaining population of the state, shall begin no later than December 1, 2024, unless the county is provided additional time pursuant to paragraph (2) of subdivision (c).

(c)(1) The department shall issue guidelines under which counties can apply for, and be provided, additional time to implement this part. The guidelines shall not be subject to the Administrative Procedure Act (Chapter 3.5 (commencing with Section 11340) of Part 1 of Division 3 of Title 2 of the Government Code).

(2) The department shall approve implementation delay for the first or second cohort if the county experiences a state or local emergency and the delay of the provision of the CARE process is necessary as a result of the emergency.

(3) The department shall only grant extensions once and no later than December 1, 2025.

(d) This part shall become operative only upon the department, in consultation with county stakeholders, developing a CARE Act allocation to provide state financial assistance to counties to implement the care process in this act. *(Added by Stats.2022, c. 319 (S.B.1338), § 7, eff. Jan. 1, 2023.)*

§ 5971. Definitions governing construction of part

Unless the context otherwise requires, the following definitions shall govern the construction of this part.

(a) "CARE agreement" means a voluntary settlement agreement entered into by the parties. A CARE agreement includes the same elements as a CARE plan to support the respondent in accessing community-based services and supports.

(b) "CARE plan" means an individualized, appropriate range of community-based services and supports, as set forth in this part, which include clinically appropriate behavioral health care and stabilization medications, housing, and other supportive services, as appropriate, pursuant to Section 5982.

(c) "CARE process" means the court and related proceedings to implement the CARE Act.

(d) "Counsel" means the attorney representing the respondent, provided pursuant to Section 5980, or chosen by the respondent, in CARE Act proceedings and matters related to CARE agreements and CARE plans.

(e) "County behavioral health agency" means the local director of mental health services described in Section 5607, the local behavioral health director, or both as applicable, or their designee.

(f) "Court-ordered evaluation" means an evaluation ordered by a superior court pursuant to Section 5977.

(g) "Department" means the State Department of Health Care Services.

(h) "Graduation plan" means a voluntary agreement entered into by the parties at the end of the CARE program that includes a strategy to support a successful transition out of court jurisdiction and that may include a psychiatric advance directive. A graduation plan includes the same elements as a CARE plan to support the respondent in accessing community-based services and supports. The graduation plan shall not place additional requirements on the local government entities and is not enforceable by the court.

(i) "Homeless outreach worker" means a person who engages people experiencing homelessness to assess for unmet needs, offer information, services, or other assistance, or provide care coordination.

(j) "Indian health care provider" means a health care program operated by the Indian Health Service, an Indian tribe, a tribal organization, or urban Indian organization (I/T/U) as those terms are defined in Section 4 of the Indian Health Care Improvement Act (25 U.S.C. Sec. 1603).

(k) "Licensed behavioral health professional" means either of the following:

(1) A licensed mental health professional, as defined in subdivision (j) of Section 4096.

(2) A person who has been granted a waiver of licensure requirements by the department pursuant to Section 5751.2.

(*l*) "Parties" means the petitioner, respondent, the county behavioral health agency in the county where proceedings under this part are pending, and other parties added by the court pursuant to paragraph (4) of subdivision (d) of Section 5977.1.

(m) "Petitioner" means the entity who files the CARE Act petition with the court. Additionally, if the petitioner is a person listed in Section 5974 other than the director of a county behavioral health agency, or their designee, the petitioner shall have the right to file a petition with the court, but at the initial hearing the court shall substitute the director of a county behavioral health agency, or their designee, of the county in which the proceedings are filed as petitioner. The petitioner who filed the petition may, at the court's discretion and in furtherance of the interests of the respondent, retain rights as described in subparagraph (A) of paragraph (7) of subdivision (b) of Section 5977.

(n) "Psychiatric advance directive" means a legal document, executed on a voluntary basis by a person who has the capacity to make medical decisions, that allows a person with mental illness to protect their autonomy and ability to self-direct care by documenting their preferences for treatment in advance of a mental health crisis.

(*o*) "Respondent" means the person who is subject to the petition for the CARE process.

(p) "Stabilization medications" means medications included in the CARE plan that primarily consist of antipsychotic medications, to reduce symptoms of hallucinations, delusions, and disorganized thinking. Stabilization medications may be administered as long-acting injections if clinically indicated. Stabilization medications shall not be forcibly administered.

(q) "Supporter" means an adult, designated pursuant to Chapter 4 (commencing with Section 5980), who assists the person who is the subject of the petition, which may include supporting the person to understand, make, communicate, implement, or act on their own life decisions during the CARE process, including a CARE agreement, a CARE plan, and developing a graduation plan. A supporter shall not act independently. *(Added by Stats.2022, c. 319 (S.B.1338), § 7, eff. Jan. 1, 2023.)*

CHAPTER 2. PROCESS

Section

§ 5972. Criteria for individuals qualifying for CARE process

An individual shall qualify for the CARE process only if all of the following criteria are met:

(a) The person is 18 years of age or older.

(b) The person is currently experiencing a severe mental illness, as defined in paragraph (2) of subdivision (b) of Section 5600.3 and has a diagnosis identified in the disorder class: schizophrenia spectrum and other psychotic disorders, as defined in the most current version of the Diagnostic and Statistical Manual of Mental Disorders. This section does not establish respondent eligibility based upon a psychotic disorder that is due to a medical condition or is not primarily psychiatric in nature, including, but not limited to, physical health conditions such as traumatic brain injury, autism, dementia, or neurologic conditions. A person who has a current diagnosis of substance use disorder as defined in paragraph (2) of subdivision (a) of Section 1374.72 of the Health and Safety Code, but who does not meet the required criteria in this section shall not qualify for the CARE process.

(c) The person is not clinically stabilized in on-going voluntary treatment.

(d) At least one of the following is true:

(1) The person is unlikely to survive safely in the community without supervision and the person's condition is substantially deteriorating.

(2) The person is in need of services and supports in order to prevent a relapse or deterioration that would be likely to result in grave disability or serious harm to the person or others, as defined in Section 5150.

(e) Participation in a CARE plan or CARE agreement would be the least restrictive alternative necessary to ensure the person's recovery and stability.

(f) It is likely that the person will benefit from participation in a CARE plan or CARE agreement. *(Added by Stats.2022, c. 319 (S.B.1338), § 7, eff. Jan. 1, 2023.)*

§ 5973. Place of proceedings

(a) Proceedings under this part may be commenced in any of the following:

(1) The county in which the respondent resides.

(2) The county where the respondent is found.

(3) The county where the respondent is facing criminal or civil proceedings.

(b) If the respondent does not reside in the county in which proceedings are initiated under this subdivision, as determined in accordance with Section 244 of the Government Code, except as provided in subdivision (e) of Section 5982, and this part is operative in the respondent's county of residence, the proceeding shall, with the respondent's consent, be transferred to the county of residence as soon as reasonably feasible. Should the respondent not consent to the transfer, the proceedings shall continue in the county where the respondent was found. *(Added by Stats.2022, c. 319 (S.B.1338), § 7, eff. Jan. 1, 2023.)*

§ 5974. Adult persons who may file a petition to initiate CARE process

The following adult persons may file a petition to initiate the CARE process:

(a) A person with whom the respondent resides.

(b) A spouse, parent, sibling, child, or grandparent or other individual who stands in loco parentis to the respondent.

(c) The director of a hospital, or their designee, in which the respondent is hospitalized, including hospitalization pursuant to Section 5150 or 5250.

(d) The director of a public or charitable organization, agency, or home, or their designee, who has, within the previous 30 days, provided or who is currently providing behavioral health services to the respondent or in whose institution the respondent resides.

(e) A licensed behavioral health professional, or their designee, who is, or has been within the previous 30 days, either supervising the treatment of, or treating the respondent for a mental illness.

(f) A first responder, including a peace officer, firefighter, paramedic, emergency medical technician, mobile crisis response worker, or homeless outreach worker, who has had repeated interactions with the respondent in the form of multiple arrests, multiple detentions and transportation pursuant to Section 5150, multiple attempts to engage the respondent in voluntary treatment, or other repeated efforts to aid the respondent in obtaining professional assistance.

(g) The public guardian or public conservator, or their designee, of the county in which the respondent is present or reasonably believed to be present.

(h) The director of a county behavioral health agency, or their designee, of the county in which the respondent resides or is found.

(i) The director of county adult protective services, or their designee, of the county in which the respondent resides or is found.

(j) The director of a California Indian health services program, California tribal behavioral health department, or their designee.

(k) The judge of a tribal court that is located in California, or their designee.

(*l*) The respondent. *(Added by Stats.2022, c. 319 (S.B.1338), § 7, eff. Jan. 1, 2023.)*

§ 5975. Petition; development of form; contents;

The Judicial Council shall develop a mandatory form for use to file a CARE process petition with the court and any other forms necessary for the CARE process. The petition shall be signed under the penalty of perjury and contain all of the following:

(a) The name of the respondent and, if known, the respondent's address.

(b) The petitioner's relationship to the respondent.

(c) Facts that support the petitioner's assertion that the respondent meets the CARE criteria in Section 5972.

(d) Either of the following:

(1) An affidavit of a licensed behavioral health professional, stating that the licensed behavioral health professional or their designee has examined the respondent within 60 days of the submission of the petition, or has made multiple attempts to examine, but has not been successful in eliciting the cooperation of the respondent to submit to an examination, within 60 days of the petition, and that the licensed behavioral health professional had determined that the respondent meets, or has reason to believe, explained with specificity in the affidavit, that the respondent meets the diagnostic criteria for CARE proceedings.

(2) Evidence that the respondent was detained for a minimum of two intensive treatments pursuant to Article 4 (commencing with Section 5250) of Chapter 2 of Part 1, the most recent one within the previous 60 days. *(Added by Stats.2022, c. 319 (S.B.1338), § 7, eff. Jan. 1, 2023.)*

§ 5975.1. Vexatious litigant

Notwithstanding Section 391 of the Code of Civil Procedure, if a person other than the respondent files a petition for CARE Act proceedings that is without merit or is intended to harass or annoy the respondent, and the person has previously filed a pleading in CARE Act proceedings that was without merit or was intended to harass or annoy the respondent, the petition shall be grounds for the court to determine that the person is a vexatious litigant for the purposes of Title 3A (commencing with Section 391) of Part 2 of the Code of Civil Procedure. *(Added by Stats.2022, c. 319 (S.B.1338), § 7, eff. Jan. 1, 2023.)*

§ 5976. Rights of respondent

The respondent shall:

(a) Receive notice of the hearings.

(b) Receive a copy of the court-ordered evaluation.

(c) Be entitled to be represented by counsel at all stages of a proceeding commenced under this chapter, regardless of the ability to pay.

(d) Be allowed to have a supporter, as described in Section 5982.

(e) Be present at the hearing unless the respondent waives the right to be present.

(f) Have the right to present evidence.

(g) Have the right to call witnesses.

(h) Have the right to cross-examine witnesses.

(i) Have the right to appeal decisions, and to be informed of the right to appeal. *(Added by Stats.2022, c. 319 (S.B.1338), § 7, eff. Jan. 1, 2023.)*

§ 5976.5. Hearings; time and place; public; confidential information; notice of rights

(a) Notwithstanding any other law, and except as otherwise provided in this section, a hearing held under this part is presumptively closed to the public.

(b) The respondent may demand that the hearing be public and be held in a place suitable for attendance by the public.

(c) The respondent may request the presence of any family member or friend without waiving the right to keep the hearing closed to the rest of the public.

(d) A request by any other party to the proceeding to make the hearing public may be granted if the judge conducting the hearing finds that the public interest in an open hearing clearly outweighs the respondent's interest in privacy.

(e) All reports, evaluations, diagnoses, or other information related to the respondent's health shall be confidential.

(f) Before commencing a hearing, the judge shall inform the respondent of their rights under this section. *(Added by Stats.2022, c. 319 (S.B.1338), § 7, eff. Jan. 1, 2023.)*

§ 5977. Review of petition; hearing; initial appearance; dismissal

(a)(1) The court shall promptly review the petition to determine if the petitioner has made a prima facie showing that the respondent is, or may be, a person described in Section 5972.

(2) If the court finds that the petitioner has not made a prima facie showing that the respondent is, or may be, a person described in Section 5972, the court may dismiss the case without prejudice subject to consideration of Section 5975.1.

(3) If the court finds that the petitioner has made a prima facie showing that the respondent is, or may be, a person described in Section 5972, the court shall do one of the following:

(A) If the petitioner is the director of a county behavioral health agency, or their designee, the court shall do the following:

(i) Set the matter for an initial appearance on the petition within 14 court days.

(ii) Appoint a qualified legal services project, as defined in Sections 6213 to 6214.5, inclusive, of the Business and Professions Code, to represent the respondent. If no legal services project has agreed to accept these appointments, a public defender shall be appointed to represent the respondent. Unless replaced by respondent's own counsel, appointed counsel shall represent the respondent in any proceeding under this part, and shall represent the individual, as needed, in matters related to CARE agreements and CARE plans, including appeals.

(iii) Determine if the petition includes all of the following information, or order the county to submit a report within 14 court days that addresses all the following:

(I) A determination as to whether the respondent meets, or is likely to meet, the criteria for the CARE process.

(II) The outcome of efforts made to voluntarily engage the respondent prior to the filing of the petition.

(III) Conclusions and recommendations about the respondent's ability to voluntarily engage in services.

(iv) Order the county behavioral health director or their designee to provide notice to the respondent, the appointed counsel, and the county behavioral health agency in the county where the respondent resides, if different from the county where the CARE process has commenced.

(B) If the petitioner is a person other than the director of a county behavioral health agency, or their designee, the court shall order a county agency, or their designee, as determined by the court, to investigate, as necessary, and file a written report with the court within 14 court days and provide notice to the respondent and petitioner that a report has been ordered. The written report shall include all of the following:

(i) A determination as to whether the respondent meets, or is likely to meet, the criteria for the CARE process.

(ii) The outcome of efforts made to voluntarily engage the respondent during the 14–day report period.

(iii) Conclusions and recommendations about the respondent's ability to voluntarily engage in services.

(4) If, upon a request by the county, the court finds that the county agency is making progress to engage the respondent, the court may, in its discretion, grant the county no more than 30 additional days to continue to work with, engage, and enroll the individual in voluntary treatment and services. The county shall provide notice to the respondent and petitioner that an extension for filing a report has been granted.

(5) Upon receipt of the report described in subparagraph (B) of paragraph (3), the court shall, within five days, take one of the following actions:

(A) If the court determines that voluntary engagement with the respondent is effective, and that the individual has enrolled or is likely to enroll in voluntary behavioral health treatment, the court shall dismiss the matter.

(B) If the court determines that county's report does not support the petition's prima facie showing that the respondent is a person described in Section 5972, the court shall dismiss the matter. This section shall not prevent a county behavioral health agency from continuing to voluntarily engage with individuals who do not meet CARE criteria, but who are in need of services and supports.

(C) If the court determines that county's report does support the petition's prima facie showing that the respondent is, or may be, a person described in Section 5972, and engagement with the county was not effective, the court shall do all of the following:

(i) Set an initial appearance on the petition within 14 court days.

(ii) Appoint a qualified legal services project, as defined in Sections 6213 to 6214.5, inclusive, of the Business and Professions Code or, if no legal services project has agreed to accept these appointments, a public defender to represent the respondent for all purposes related to this part, including appeals, unless the respondent has retained their own counsel. Unless replaced by respondent's own counsel, appointed counsel shall represent the respondent in any proceeding under this part, and shall represent the individual, as needed, in matters related to CARE agreements and CARE plans.

(iii) Order the county to provide notice of the hearing to the petitioner, the respondent, the appointed counsel, the county behavioral health agency in the county where the respondent resides, and, if different, the county where the CARE court proceedings have commenced.

(b) At the initial appearance on the petition, all of the following shall apply:

(1) The court shall permit the respondent to substitute their own counsel.

(2) Petitioner shall be present. If the petitioner is not present, the matter may be dismissed.

(3) Respondent may waive personal appearance and appear through counsel. If the respondent does not waive personal appearance and does not appear at the hearing, and the court makes a finding on the record that reasonable attempts to elicit the attendance of the respondent have failed, the court may conduct the hearing in the respondent's absence if the court makes a finding on the record that conducting the hearing without the participation or presence of the respondent would be in the respondent's best interest.

(4) A representative from the county behavioral health agency shall be present.

(5) A supporter may be appointed.

(6) If the respondent self-identifies that they are enrolled in a federally recognized Indian tribe or otherwise receiving services from an Indian health care provider, a tribal court, or a tribal organization, a representative from the program, the tribe, or the tribal court shall be allowed to be present, subject to the consent of the respondent. The tribal representative shall be entitled to notice by the county of the initial appearance.

(7)(A) If the petitioner is a person described in Section 5974 other than the director of a county behavioral health agency, or their designee, the court shall issue an order relieving the petitioner and appointing the director of the county behavioral health agency or their designee as the substitute petitioner.

(B) If the petitioner who is relieved pursuant to this paragraph is described in subdivision (a) or (b) of Section 5974, all of the following apply:

(i) The petitioner shall have the right to participate in the initial hearing to determine the merits of the petition, pursuant to subparagraphs (A) and (B) of paragraph (8).

(ii) The court may, in its discretion, assign ongoing rights of notice.

(iii) The court may, additionally, allow for participation and engagement in the respondent's CARE proceedings if the respondent consents.

(iv) The petitioner may file a new petition with the court, pursuant to Section 5974, if the matter is dismissed and there is a change in circumstances.

(C) If the petitioner who is relieved pursuant this paragraph is described in Section 5974, other than persons described in subparagraph (a) or (b) of that section, the court shall not assign ongoing rights to the entity that originally filed the CARE petition, other than the right to make a statement at the hearing on the merits of the petition as provided in subparagraphs (A) and (B) of paragraph (8).

(8)(A) The court shall set a hearing on the merits of the petition within 10 days, at which time the court shall determine by clear and convincing evidence if the respondent meets the CARE criteria in Section 5972. In making this determination, the court shall consider all evidence properly before it, including the report from the county required pursuant to paragraph (3) of subdivision (a) and any additional evidence presented by the parties, including the petition submitted by the petitioner who is relieved.

(B) The hearing on the merits of the petition may be conducted concurrently with the initial appearance on the petition upon stipulation of the petitioner and respondent and agreement by the court.

(c)(1) If, at the hearing on the merits of the petition, the court finds, by clear and convincing evidence, that the respondent does not meet the CARE criteria in Section 5972, the court shall dismiss the case without prejudice, unless the court makes a finding, on the record, that the initial petitioner's filing was not in good faith.

(2) If, at the hearing on the merits of the petition, the court finds that the petitioner has shown by clear and convincing evidence that the respondent meets the CARE criteria in Section 5972, the court shall order the county behavioral health agency to work with the respondent, the respondent's counsel, and the supporter to engage in behavioral health treatment and determine if the parties will be able to enter into a CARE agreement. The court shall set a case management hearing within 14 days.

(3) If the respondent is enrolled in a federally recognized Indian tribe, the respondent shall provide notice of the case management hearing to the tribe, subject to the consent of the respondent. *(Added by Stats.2022, c. 319 (S.B.1338), § 7, eff. Jan. 1, 2023.)*

§ 5977.1. Case management hearing; clinical evaluation; clinical evaluation hearing; CARE plan review hearing; issuance of order approving CARE plan

(a)(1) At the case management hearing, the court shall hear evidence as to whether the parties have entered, or are likely to enter, into a CARE agreement.

(2) If the court finds that the parties have entered, or are likely to enter, into a CARE agreement, the court shall do both of the following:

(A) Approve the terms of the CARE agreement or modify the terms of the CARE agreement and approve the agreement as modified by the court.

(B) Continue the matter and set a progress hearing for 60 days.

(b) If the court finds that the parties have not entered into a CARE agreement, and are not likely to enter into a CARE agreement, the court shall order the county behavioral health agency, through a licensed behavioral health professional, to conduct a clinical evaluation of the respondent, unless there is an existing clinical evaluation of the respondent completed within the last 30 days and the parties stipulate to the use of that evaluation. The evaluation shall address, at a minimum, the following:

(1) A clinical diagnosis of the respondent.

(2) Whether the respondent has the legal capacity to give informed consent regarding psychotropic medication.

(3) Any other information as ordered by the court or that the licensed behavioral health professional conducting the evaluation determines would help the court make future informed decisions about the appropriate care and services the respondent should receive.

(4) An analysis of recommended services, programs, housing, medications, and interventions that support the recovery and stability of the respondent.

(c)(1) The court shall set a clinical evaluation hearing to review the evaluation within 21 days. The court shall order the county to file the evaluation with the court and provide the evaluation to the respondent's counsel no later than five days prior to the scheduled clinical evaluation hearing. The clinical evaluation hearing may be continued for a maximum of 14 days upon stipulation of the respondent and the county behavioral health agency, unless there is good cause for a longer extension.

(2) At the clinical evaluation review hearing, the court shall review the evaluation and any other evidence from the county behavioral health agency and the respondent. The county behavioral health agency and the respondent may present evidence and call witnesses, including the person who conducted the evaluation. Only relevant and admissible evidence that fully complies with the rules of evidence may be considered by the court.

(3) At the conclusion of the hearing, the court shall make orders as follows:

(A) If the court finds by clear and convincing evidence, after review of the evaluation and other evidence, that the respondent meets the CARE criteria, the court shall order the county behavioral health agency, the respondent, and the respondent's counsel and supporter to jointly develop a CARE plan within 14 days.

(B) If the court finds, in reviewing the evaluation, that clear and convincing evidence does not support that the respondent meets the CARE criteria, the court shall dismiss the petition.

(4) If the respondent is a self-identified American Indian or Alaska Native individual, as defined in Sections 1603(13), 1603(28), and 1679(a) of Title 25 of the United States Code, has been determined eligible as an Indian under Section 136.12 of Title 42 of the Code of Federal Regulations, or is otherwise receiving services from an Indian health care provider or tribal court, the county behavioral health agency shall use best efforts to meaningfully consult with and incorporate the Indian health care provider or tribal court available to the respondent to develop the CARE plan.

(5) The evaluation and all reports, documents, and filings submitted to the court shall be confidential.

(6) The date for the hearing to review and consider approval of the proposed CARE plan shall be set not more than 14 days from the date of the order to develop a CARE plan, unless the court finds good cause for an extension. The party requesting an extension of time for the CARE plan review hearing shall provide notice to the opposing party and their counsel of the request for extension of time, and the court's order if the request is granted.

(d)(1) At the CARE plan review hearing, the parties shall present their plans to the court. The county behavioral health agency or the respondent, or both, may present a proposed CARE plan.

(2) After consideration of the plans proposed by the parties, the court shall adopt the elements of a CARE plan that support the recovery and stability of the respondent. The court may issue any orders necessary to support the respondent in accessing appropriate services and supports, including prioritization for those services and

supports, subject to applicable laws and available funding pursuant to Section 5982. These orders shall constitute the CARE plan.

(3) A court may order medication if it finds, upon review of the court-ordered evaluation and hearing from the parties, that, by clear and convincing evidence, the respondent lacks the capacity to give informed consent to the administration of medically necessary stabilization medication. To the extent the court orders medically necessary stabilization medication, the medication shall not be forcibly administered and the respondent's failure to comply with a medication order shall not result in a penalty, including, but not limited to, contempt or termination of the CARE plan pursuant to Section 5979.

(4) If the proposed CARE plan includes services and supports, such as housing, provided directly or indirectly through another local governmental entity, that local entity may agree to provide the service or support, or the court may consider a motion by either of the parties to add the local entity as a party to the CARE proceeding. If the local entity agrees to provide the service or support, it may request to be added as a party by the court.

(5) If, after presentation of the CARE plan or plans, the court determines that additional information is needed, including from a licensed behavioral health professional, the court shall order a supplemental report to be filed by the county behavioral health agency for which the court may grant a continuance of no more than 14 days, unless there is good cause for a longer extension.

(6) If there is no CARE plan because the parties have not had sufficient time to complete it, the court may grant a continuance of no more than 14 days, unless there is good cause for a longer extension.

(e) The issuance of an order approving a CARE plan pursuant to paragraph (2) of subdivision (d) begins the CARE process timeline, which shall not exceed one year. *(Added by Stats.2022, c. 319 (S.B.1338), § 7, eff. Jan. 1, 2023.)*

Cross References

Behavioral health care, evaluation and health care services provided pursuant to a CARE agreement or CARE plan approved by the court, department guidance on compliance, see Health and Safety Code § 1374.723.

Coverage for evaluation and health care services provided pursuant to a CARE agreement or CARE plan approved by the court, see Insurance Code § 10144.54.

§ 5977.2. Status review hearing; report; contents

(a)(1) At intervals set by the court, but not less frequently than 60 days after the court orders the CARE plan, the court shall hold a status review hearing. The county behavioral health agency shall file with the court and serve on the respondent, and the respondent's counsel and supporter, a report not fewer than five court days prior to the review hearing with the following information:

(A) Progress the respondent has made on the CARE plan.

(B) What services and supports in the CARE plan were provided, and what services and supports were not provided.

(C) Any issues the respondent expressed or exhibited in adhering to the CARE plan.

(D) Recommendations for changes to the services and supports to make the CARE plan more successful.

(2) The respondent shall be permitted to respond to the report submitted by the county behavioral health agency and to the county behavioral health agency's testimony. The respondent shall be permitted to introduce their own information and recommendations.

(3) Subject to applicable law, intermittent lapses or setbacks described in this section of the report shall not impact access to services, treatment, or housing.

(b) The county behavioral health agency or the respondent may request, or the court upon its own motion may set, a hearing to occur at any time during the CARE process to address a change of circumstances. *(Added by Stats.2022, c. 319 (S.B.1338), § 7, eff. Jan. 1, 2023.)*

Cross References

Behavioral health care, evaluation and health care services provided pursuant to a CARE agreement or CARE plan approved by the court, department guidance on compliance, see Health and Safety Code § 1374.723.

Coverage for evaluation and health care services provided pursuant to a CARE agreement or CARE plan approved by the court, see Insurance Code § 10144.54.

§ 5977.3. One-year status hearing; report; contents; conditions for involuntary reappointment of respondent to program

(a)(1) In the 11th month of the program timeline, the court shall hold a one-year status hearing. Not fewer than five court days prior to the one-year status hearing, the county behavioral health agency shall file a report with the court and shall serve the report on the respondent and the respondent's counsel and supporter. The report shall include the following information:

(A) Progress the respondent has made on the CARE plan including a final assessment of the respondent's stability.

(B) What services and supports in the CARE plan were provided, and what services and supports were not provided, over the life of the program.

(C) Any issues the respondent expressed or exhibited in adhering to the CARE plan.

(D) Recommendations for next steps, including what ongoing and additional services would benefit the respondent that the county behavioral health agency can facilitate or provide.

(2) At an evidentiary hearing, the respondent shall be permitted to respond to the report submitted by the county behavioral health agency and to the county behavioral health agency's testimony. Respondent shall be permitted to introduce their own information and recommendations. The respondent shall have the right at the hearing to call witnesses and to present evidence as to whether the respondent agrees with the report. The respondent may request either to be graduated from the program or to remain in the program.

(3) The court shall issue an order as follows:

(A) If the respondent elects to be graduated from the program, the court shall order the county behavioral health agency and the respondent to work jointly on a graduation plan. The court shall schedule a hearing in the 12th month after adoption of the CARE plan for presentation of the graduation plan. The court shall review the voluntary graduation plan and recite the terms on the record. The graduation plan shall not place additional requirements on local government entities and is not enforceable by the court, except that the graduation plan may, at respondent's election, include a psychiatric advance directive, which shall have the force of law. Upon completion of the hearing, the respondent shall be officially graduated from the program.

(B) If the respondent elects to remain in the CARE process, respondent may request any amount of time, up to and including one additional year. The court may permit the ongoing voluntary participation of the respondent if the court finds both of the following:

(i) The respondent did not successfully complete the CARE plan.

(ii) The respondent would benefit from continuation of the CARE plan.

(C) The court shall issue an order permitting the respondent to continue in the CARE plan or denying respondent's request to remain in the CARE plan, and state its reasons on the record.

(b) The respondent may be involuntarily reappointed to the program only if the court finds, by clear and convincing evidence, that all of the following conditions apply:

(1) The respondent did not successfully complete the CARE process.

(2) All services and supports required through the CARE process were provided to the respondent.

(3) The respondent would benefit from continuation in the CARE process.

(4) The respondent currently meets the requirements in Section 5972.

(c) A respondent may only be reappointed to the CARE process once, for up to one additional year. *(Added by Stats.2022, c. 319 (S.B.1338), § 7, eff. Jan. 1, 2023.)*

Cross References

Behavioral health care, evaluation and health care services provided pursuant to a CARE agreement or CARE plan approved by the court, department guidance on compliance, see Health and Safety Code § 1374.723.

Coverage for evaluation and health care services provided pursuant to a CARE agreement or CARE plan approved by the court, see Insurance Code § 10144.54.

§ 5977.4. Conduct of proceedings; adoption of rules for implementation

(a) In all CARE Act proceedings, the judge shall control the proceedings during the hearings with a view to the expeditious and effective ascertainment of the jurisdictional facts and the ascertainment of all information relative to the present condition and future welfare of the respondent. Except when there is a contested issue of fact or law, the proceedings shall be conducted in an informal nonadversarial atmosphere with a view to obtaining the maximum cooperation of the respondent, all persons interested in the respondent's welfare, and all other parties, with any provisions that the court may make for the disposition and care of the respondent. All evaluations and reports, documents, and filings submitted to the court pursuant to CARE Act proceedings shall be confidential.

(b) The hearings described in this chapter shall occur in person unless the court, in its discretion, allows a party or witness to appear remotely through the use of remote technology. The respondent shall have the right to be in person for all hearings.

(c) Consistent with its constitutional rulemaking authority, the Judicial Council shall adopt rules to implement the policies and provisions in this section and in Sections 5977, 5977.1, 5977.2, and 5977.3 to promote statewide consistency, including, but not limited to, what is included in the petition form packet, the clerk's review of the petition, and the process by which counsel will be appointed. *(Added by Stats.2022, c. 319 (S.B.1338), § 7, eff. Jan. 1, 2023.)*

§ 5978. Individuals who may be referred to CARE Act proceedings

(a) A court may refer an individual from assisted outpatient treatment, as well as from conservatorship proceedings pursuant Chapter 3 (commencing with Section 5350) of Part 1 of Division 5 (LPS conservatorship) to CARE Act proceedings. If the individual is being referred from assisted outpatient treatment, the county behavioral health director or their designee shall be the petitioner. If the individual is being referred from LPS conservatorship proceedings, the conservator shall be the petitioner pursuant to Section 5974.

(b) A court may refer an individual from misdemeanor proceedings pursuant to Section 1370.01 of the Penal Code. *(Added by Stats.2022, c. 319 (S.B.1338), § 7, eff. Jan. 1, 2023.)*

CHAPTER 3. ACCOUNTABILITY

§ 5979. Conditions for termination of respondent's participation in CARE process; failure of county or local government to comply with part; appeal

(a)(1) If, at any time during the proceedings, the court determines by clear and convincing evidence that the respondent is not participating in the CARE process, after the respondent receives notice, or is not adhering to their CARE plan, after the respondent receives notice, the court may terminate the respondent's participation in the CARE process.

(2) To ensure the respondent's safety, the court may utilize existing legal authority pursuant to Article 2 (commencing with Section 5200) of Chapter 2 of Part 1. The court shall provide notice to the county behavioral health agency and the Office of the Public Conservator and Guardian if the court utilizes that authority.

(3) If the respondent was timely provided with all of the services and supports required by the CARE plan, the fact that the respondent failed to successfully complete their CARE plan, including reasons for that failure, shall be a fact considered by the court in a subsequent hearing under the Lanterman-Petris-Short Act (Part 1 (commencing with Section 5000)), provided that the hearing occurs within six months of the termination of the CARE plan and shall create a presumption at that hearing that the respondent needs additional intervention beyond the supports and services provided by the CARE plan.

(4) The respondent's failure to comply with an order shall not result in a penalty outside of this section, including, but not limited to, contempt or a failure to appear.

(5) The respondent's failure to comply with a medication order shall not result in any penalty, including under this section.

(b)(1) If, at any time during the CARE process, the court finds that the county or other local government entity is not complying with court orders, the court shall report that finding to the presiding judge of the superior court or their designee.

(2)(A) The presiding judge or their designee shall issue an order to show cause why the local government entity should not be fined as set forth in this section. The time set for hearing shall be no earlier than 15 days after the date of the order. The scheduled date of the hearing shall allow adequate time for notice of the hearing to be served upon the local government entity.

(B) The presiding judge, or their designee, shall consider the matter on the record established at the hearing. If the presiding judge or their designee finds, by clear and convincing evidence, that the local government entity has substantially failed to comply with this part, or with lawful orders issued by a court under this part, the presiding judge or their designee may issue an order imposing a fine under this section.

(C) A fine under this section shall be in an amount of up to one thousand dollars ($1,000) per day, not to exceed $25,000 for each individual violation identified in the order imposing fines.

(D)(i) Funds collected pursuant to this subdivision shall be deposited in the CARE Act Accountability Fund, which is hereby created in the State Treasury. Upon appropriation, the department shall administer the funds annually, and shall issue guidance, as necessary, to local government entities, pursuant to subdivision (b) of Section 5984, regarding the distribution and conditions associated with the administered funds.

(ii) All moneys in the fund shall be allocated and distributed to the local government entity that paid the fines, to be used by that entity to serve individuals who have schizophrenia spectrum or other psychotic disorders and who are experiencing, or are at risk of, homelessness, criminal justice involvement, hospitalization, or conservatorship.

(3) If, after notice and hearing as set forth in paragraph (2), the presiding judge or their designee finds, by clear and convincing evidence, that the local government entity is persistently noncompliant with this part, or with lawful orders issued by a court under this part, the presiding judge or their designee may appoint a special master to secure court-ordered care for the respondent at the local government entity's cost. The presiding judge, or their designee, shall not make an order under this paragraph unless they have received five or more reports under paragraph (1) pertaining to the same local government entity within a one-year period.

(4) In determining the application of the remedies available under this section, the court shall consider whether there are any mitigating circumstances impairing the ability of the local government entity to fully comply with the requirements of this part, or with court orders issued under this part. The court may consider whether the local government entity is making a good faith effort to come into substantial compliance or is facing substantial undue hardships.

(c) Either the respondent or the county behavioral health agency may appeal an adverse court determination. *(Added by Stats.2022, c. 319 (S.B.1338), § 7, eff. Jan. 1, 2023.)*

CHAPTER 4. SUPPORTER AND COUNSEL

Section

§ 5980. Volunteer supporters; training; duties

(a) Subject to appropriation, the department, in consultation with disability rights groups, county behavioral health and aging agencies, individuals with lived expertise, families, racial justice experts, and other appropriate stakeholders, shall provide optional training and technical resources for volunteer supporters on the CARE process, community services and supports, supported decisionmaking, people with behavioral health conditions, trauma-informed care, family psychoeducation, and psychiatric advance directives. The department may consult with other state and national public and nonprofit agencies and organizations and the Judicial Council to align supported decisionmaking training with best practices for persons with mental illnesses, intellectual and developmental disabilities, other disabilities, and older adults. The department may enter into a technical assistance and training agreement for this purpose, pursuant to Section 5984.

(b) The supporter shall do all of the following:

(1) Offer the respondent a flexible and culturally responsive way to maintain autonomy and decisionmaking authority over their own life by developing and maintaining voluntary supports to assist them in understanding, making, communicating, and implementing their own informed choices.

(2) Strengthen the respondent's capacity to engage in and exercise autonomous decisionmaking and prevent or remove the need to use more restrictive protective mechanisms, such as conservatorship.

(3) Assist the respondent with understanding, making, and communicating decisions and expressing preferences throughout the CARE process. *(Added by Stats.2022, c. 319 (S.B.1338), § 7, eff. Jan. 1, 2023.)*

§ 5981. Presence of supporter at meetings, proceedings, hearing, or specific communications; intended behavior and authority of supporter

(a) Notwithstanding any other provision of this part, the respondent may have a supporter present in any meeting, judicial proceeding, status hearing, or communication related to any of the following:

(1) An evaluation.

(2) Development of a CARE agreement or CARE plan.

(3) Establishing a psychiatric advance directive.

(4) Development of a graduation plan.

(b) A supporter is intended to do all the following:

(1) Support the will and preferences of the respondent to the best of their ability and to the extent reasonably possible.

(2) Respect the values, beliefs, and preferences of the respondent.

(3) Act honestly, diligently, and in good faith.

(4) Avoid, to the greatest extent possible, and disclose to the court, the respondent, and the respondent's counsel, minimize, and manage, conflicts of interest. A court may remove a supporter because of any conflict of interest with the respondent, and shall remove the supporter if the conflict cannot be managed in such a way to avoid any possible harm to the respondent.

(c) Unless explicitly authorized by the respondent with capacity to make that authorization, a supporter shall not do either of the following:

(1) Make decisions for, or on behalf of, the respondent, except when necessary to prevent imminent bodily harm or injury.

(2) Sign documents on behalf of the respondent.

(d) In addition to the obligations in this section, a supporter shall be bound by all existing obligations and prohibitions otherwise applicable by law that protect people with disabilities and the elderly from fraud, abuse, neglect, coercion, or mistreatment. This section does not limit a supporter's civil or criminal liability for prohibited conduct against the respondent, including liability for fraud, abuse, neglect, coercion, or mistreatment, including liability under the Elder Abuse and Dependent Adult Civil Protection Act (Chapter 11 (commencing with Section 15600) of Part 3 of Division 9), including, but not limited to, Sections 15656 and 15657.

(e) The supporter shall not be subpoenaed or called to testify against the respondent in any proceeding relating to this part, and the supporter's presence at any meeting, proceeding, or communication shall not waive confidentiality or any privilege. *(Added by Stats.2022, c. 319 (S.B.1338), § 7, eff. Jan. 1, 2023.)*

§ 5981.5. Funding for legal counsel; contracts or grants

(a) The Legal Services Trust Fund Commission at the State Bar shall provide funding to qualified legal services projects, as defined in Sections 6213 to 6214.5, inclusive, of the Business and Professions Code, to be used to provide legal counsel appointed pursuant to subdivision (c) of Section 5976, for representation in CARE Act proceedings, matters related to CARE agreements and CARE plans, and to qualified support centers, as defined in subdivision (b) of Section 6213 of, and Section 6215 of, the Business and Professions Code, for training, support, and coordination.

(b) For purposes of implementing this part, the Legal Services Trust Fund Commission may enter into exclusive or nonexclusive contracts, or amend existing contracts, on a bid or negotiated basis, or award grants, provided that they make a finding that both of the following are satisfied:

(1) The state agency will retain control over the distribution of funds to the contractor or grantee.

(2) The contract or grant includes provisions to ensure transparency, accountability, and oversight in delivering the services, including

measurement of outcomes established pursuant to Sections 5984, 5985, and 5986. *(Added by Stats.2022, c. 319 (S.B.1338), § 7, eff. Jan. 1, 2023.)*

CHAPTER 5. CARE PLAN

§ 5982. Plan coverage; prioritization of participants for bridge housing; full service partnership; services and supports subject to available funding and applicable statutes, regulations, and guidelines on program eligibility; county of responsibility

(a) The CARE plan may include only the following:

(1) Behavioral health services funded through the 1991 and 2011 Realignment, Medi-Cal behavioral health, health care plans and insurers, and services supported by the Mental Health Services Act pursuant to Part 3 (commencing with Section 5800).

(2) Medically necessary stabilization medications, to the extent not described in paragraph (1).

(3) Housing resources funded through the No Place Like Home Program (Part 3.9 (commencing with Section 5849.1) of Division 5 of the Welfare and Institutions Code); California Housing Accelerator (Chapter 6.6 (commencing with Section 50672) of Part 2 of Division 31 of the Health and Safety Code); the Multifamily Housing Program (Chapter 6.7 (commencing with Section 50675) of Part 2 of Division 31 of the Health and Safety Code); the Homeless Housing, Assistance, and Prevention Program (Chapter 6 (commencing with Section 50216) of Part 1 of Division 31 of the Health and Safety Code); the Encampment Resolution Funding Program (Chapter 7 (commencing with Section 50250) of Part 1 of Division 31 of the Health and Safety Code); the Project Roomkey and Rehousing Program pursuant to Provision 22 of Item 5180–151–0001 of the Budget Act of 2021 (Ch. 21, Stats. 2021); the Community Care Expansion Program (Chapter 20 (commencing with Section 18999.97) of Part 6 of Division 9 of the Welfare and Institutions Code); the CalWORKs Housing Support Program (Article 3.3 (commencing with Section 11330) of Chapter 2 of Part 3 of Division 9 of the Welfare and Institutions Code); the CalWORKs Homeless Assistance pursuant to clause (i) of subparagraph (A) of paragraph (2) of subdivision (f) of Section 11450 of Article 6 of Chapter 2 of Part 3 of Division 9 of the Welfare and Institutions Code; the Housing and Disability Advocacy Program (Chapter 17 (commencing with Section 18999) of Part 6 of Division 9 of the Welfare and Institutions Code); the Home Safe Program (Chapter 14 (commencing with Section 15770) of Part 3 of Division 9 of the Welfare and Institutions Code); the Bringing Families Home Program (Article 6 (commencing with Section 16523) of Chapter 5 of Part 4 of Division 9 of the Welfare and Institutions Code); the Transitional Housing Placement program for nonminor dependents (Article 4 (commencing with Section 16522) of Chapter 5 of Part 4 of Division 9 of the Welfare and Institutions Code); the Transitional Housing Program-Plus pursuant to subdivision (s) of Section 11400 and paragraph (2) of subdivision (a) of Section 11403.2 of Article 5 of Chapter 2 of Part 3 of Division 9 of the Welfare and Institutions Code and Article 4 (commencing with Section 16522) of Chapter 5 of Part 4 of Division 9 of the Welfare and Institutions Code; the Behavioral Health Continuum Infrastructure Program (Chapter 1 (commencing with Section 5960) of Part 7 of Division 5 of the Welfare and Institutions Code); the Behavioral Health Bridge Housing Program; HUD–Veterans Affairs Supportive Housing Program (Section 8(*o*)(19) of the United States Housing Act of 1937 [42 U.S.C. Section 1437f(*o*)(19)]); Supportive Services for Veteran Families (Section 604 of the Veterans' Mental Health and Other Care Improvements Act of 2008 [38 U.S.C. Sec. 2044]); HUD Continuum of Care program (Section 103 of the McKinney-Vento Homeless Assistance Act [42 U.S.C. Sec. 11302]); the Emergency Solutions Grant (Subtitle B of Title IV of the McKinney-Vento Homeless Assistance Act [42 U.S.C. Secs. 11371–11378]); HUD Housing Choice Voucher program (Section 8 of the United States Housing Act of 1937 [42 U.S.C. Sec. 1437f]); the Emergency Housing Vouchers (Section 3202 of the American Rescue Plan Act of 2021 [Public Law 117–2];[1] Section 8(*o*) of the United States Housing Act of 1937 [42 U.S.C. Sec. 1437f(*o*)]); HOME Investment Partnerships Program (Title II of the Cranston-Gonzalez National Affordable Housing Act [42 U.S.C. Sec. 12721 et seq.]); the Community Development Block Grant Program (Title 1 of the Housing and Community Development Act of 1974 [42 U.S.C. Sec. 5301 et seq.]); housing supported by the Mental Health Services Act pursuant to Part 3 (commencing with Section 5800); community development block grants; and other state and federal housing resources.

(4) Social services funded through Supplemental Security Income/State Supplementary Payment (SSI/SSP), Cash Assistance Program for Immigrants (CAPI), CalWORKs, California Food Assistance Program, In-Home Supportive Services program, and CalFresh.

(5) Services provided pursuant to Part 5 (commencing with Section 17000) of Division 9.

(b) Individuals who are CARE process participants shall be prioritized for any appropriate bridge housing funded by the Behavioral Health Bridge Housing program.

(c) If the county behavioral health agency elects not to enroll the respondent into a full service partnership, as defined in Section 3620 of Title 9 of the California Code of Regulations, the court may request information on the reasons for this and any barriers to enrollment.

(d) All CARE plan services and supports ordered by the court are subject to available funding and all applicable federal and state statutes and regulations, contractual provisions, and policy guidance governing initial and ongoing program eligibility. In addition to the resources funded through programs listed in subdivision (a), the State Department of Health Care Services may identify other adjacent covered Medi-Cal services, including, but not limited to, enhanced care management and available community supports, which may be suggested, although not ordered, by the court, subject to all applicable federal and state statutes, regulations, contractual provisions, and policy guidance.

(e) This section does not prevent a county or other local government entity from recommending their own services that are their own responsibility not listed in subdivision (a) or (c). Any such recommendation is not required by this section and shall be made at the request of the county for the purposes of Section 6 of Article XIII B, and Sections 6 and 36 of Article XIII of the California Constitution.

(f)(1) For respondents who are Medi-Cal beneficiaries, the county in which the respondent resides is the county of responsibility as defined in Section 1810.228 of Title 9 of the California Code of Regulations.

(2) If a proceeding commences in a county where the respondent is found or is facing criminal or civil proceedings that is different than the county in which the respondent resides, the county in which the respondent is found or is facing criminal or civil proceedings shall not delay proceedings under this part and is the responsible county behavioral health agency for providing or coordinating all components of the CARE agreement or CARE plan.

(3) The county in which the respondent resides, as defined in paragraph (1), shall be responsible for the costs of providing all CARE agreement or CARE plan behavioral health services, as defined in paragraph (1) of subdivision (a).

(4) In the event of a dispute over responsibility for any costs of providing components of the CARE agreement or CARE plan, the impacted counties shall resolve the dispute in accordance with the arbitration process established in Section 1850.405 of Title 9 of the California Code of Regulations for county mental health plans, including for respondents who are not Medi-Cal beneficiaries, and pursuant to any related guidance issued pursuant to subdivision (b) of Section 5984. *(Added by Stats.2022, c. 319 (S.B.1338), § 7, eff. Jan. 1, 2023.)*

1 For public law sections classified to the U.S.C.A., see USCA–Tables.

Cross References

Behavioral health care, evaluation and health care services provided pursuant to a CARE agreement or CARE plan approved by the court, department guidance on compliance, see Health and Safety Code § 1374.723.
Coverage for evaluation and health care services provided pursuant to a CARE agreement or CARE plan approved by the court, see Insurance Code § 10144.54.

CHAPTER 6. TECHNICAL ASSISTANCE AND ADMINISTRATION

§ 5983. Duties of California Health and Human Services Agency or designated department; training and technical assistance for county agencies, judges, and counsel

(a) The California Health and Human Services Agency, or a designated department within the agency, shall do both of the following:

(1) Engage an independent, research-based entity, as described in Section 5986, to advise on the development of data-driven process and outcome measures to guide the planning, collaboration, reporting, and evaluation of the CARE Act pursuant to this part.

(2) Convene a working group to provide coordination and ongoing engagement with, and support collaboration among, relevant state and local partners and other stakeholders throughout the phases of county implementation to support the successful implementation of the CARE Act. The working group shall meet no more than quarterly. The working group shall meet during the implementation and shall end no later than December 31, 2026.

(b) The department shall provide training and technical assistance to county behavioral health agencies to support the implementation of this part, including training regarding the CARE process, CARE agreement and plan services and supports, supported decisionmaking, the supporter role, trauma-informed care, elimination of bias, psychiatric advance directives, family psychoeducation, and data collection.

(c) The Judicial Council, in consultation with the department, other relevant state entities, and the County Behavioral Health Directors Association, shall provide training and technical assistance to judges to support the implementation of this part, including training regarding the CARE process, CARE agreement and plan services and supports, working with the supporter, supported decisionmaking, the supporter role, the family role, trauma-informed care, elimination of bias, best practices, and evidence-based models of care for people with severe behavioral health conditions.

(d) The department, in consultation with other relevant state departments and the California Interagency Council on Homelessness, shall provide training to counsel regarding the CARE process and CARE agreement and plan services and supports. *(Added by Stats.2022, c. 319 (S.B.1338), § 7, eff. Jan. 1, 2023.)*

Cross References

Implementation of part, timeline, see Welfare and Institutions Code § 5970.5.

§ 5984. Contracts; implementation

(a) For purposes of implementing this part, the California Health and Human Services Agency and the department may enter into exclusive or nonexclusive contracts, or amend existing contracts, on a bid or negotiated basis. Contracts entered into or amended pursuant to this part shall be exempt from Chapter 6 (commencing with Section 14825) of Part 5.5 of Division 3 of Title 2 of the Government Code, Section 19130 of the Government Code, Part 2 (commencing with Section 10100) of Division 2 of the Public Contract Code, and the State Administrative Manual, and shall be exempt from the review or approval of any division of the Department of General Services.

(b) Notwithstanding Chapter 3.5 (commencing with Section 11340) of Part 1 of Division 3 of Title 2 of the Government Code, the California Health and Human Services Agency and the department may implement, interpret, or make specific this part, in whole or in part, by means of plan letters, information notices, provider bulletins, or other similar instructions, without taking any further regulatory action. *(Added by Stats.2022, c. 319 (S.B.1338), § 7, eff. Jan. 1, 2023.)*

§ 5985. Annual CARE Act report; development of reporting schedule; report contents

(a) The department shall develop, in consultation with county behavioral health agencies, other relevant state or local government entities, disability rights groups, individuals with lived experience, families, counsel, racial justice experts, and other appropriate stakeholders, an annual CARE Act report. The department shall post the annual report on its internet website.

(b) County behavioral health agencies and any other state or local governmental entity, as identified by the department, shall provide data related to the CARE Act participants, services, and supports to the department. The department shall determine the data measures and specifications, and shall publish them via guidance issues pursuant to subdivision (b) of Section 5984.

(c) Each county behavioral health department and any other state and local governmental entity, as identified by the department, shall provide the required data to the department, in a format and frequency as directed by the department.

(d)(1) In consultation with the Judicial Council, the department shall develop an annual reporting schedule for the submission of CARE Act data from the trial courts.

(2) Data from the trial courts shall be submitted to the Judicial Council, which shall aggregate the data and submit it to the department consistent with the reporting schedule developed pursuant to paragraph (1).

(3) On an annual basis to be determined by the Judicial Council and consistent with the annual reporting schedule developed pursuant to paragraph (1), the trial courts shall report to the Judicial Council the following data related to CARE Act petitions:

(A) The number of petitions submitted pursuant to Section 5975.

(B) The number of initial appearances on the petition set pursuant to paragraph (3) of subdivision (a) of Section 5977.

(C) The total number of hearings held pursuant to this part.

(e) The annual report shall include process measures to examine the scope of impact and monitor the performance of CARE Act model implementation. The report shall include, at a minimum, all of the following:

(1) The demographics of participants, including, but not limited to, the age, sex, race, ethnicity, disability, languages spoken, sexual orientation, gender identity, housing status, veteran status, immigration status, health coverage status, including Medi-Cal enrollment status, and county of residence, to the extent statistically relevant data is available.

(2) The services and supports ordered, the services and supports provided, and the services and supports ordered but not provided.

(3) The housing placements of all participants during the program and at least one year following the termination of the CARE plan, to the extent administrative data are available to report the latter. Placements include, but are not limited to, transition to a higher level of care, independent living in the person's own house or apartment, community-based housing, community-based housing with services, shelter, and no housing.

(4) Treatments continued and terminated at least one year following termination of the CARE plan, to the extent administrative data are available.

(5) Substance use disorder rates and rates of treatment among active CARE plan participants and former participants at least one year following termination of the CARE plan, to the extent administrative data are available to report the latter.

(6) Detentions and other Lanterman-Petris-Short Act involvement for participants with an active CARE plan and for former participants at least one year following termination of the CARE plan, to the extent administrative data are available to report the latter.

(7) Criminal justice involvement of participants with an active CARE plan and for former participants at least one year following termination of the CARE plan, to the extent administrative data are available to report the latter.

(8) Deaths among active participants and for former participants at least one year following termination of the CARE plan, along with causes of death, to the extent administrative data are available.

(9) The number, rates, and trends of petitions resulting in dismissal and hearings.

(10) The number, rates, and trends of supporters.

(11) The number, rates, and trends of voluntary CARE agreements.

(12) The number, rates, and trends of ordered and completed CARE plans.

(13) Statistics on the services and supports included in CARE plans, including court orders for stabilizing medications.

(14) The rates of adherence to medication.

(15) The number, rates, and trends of psychiatric advance directives created for participants with active CARE plans.

(16) The number, rates, and trends of developed graduation plans.

(17) Outcome measures to assess the effectiveness of the CARE Act model, such as improvement in housing status, including gaining and maintaining housing, reductions in emergency department visits and inpatient hospitalizations, reductions in law enforcement encounters and incarceration, reductions in involuntary treatment and conservatorship, and reductions in substance use.

(18) A health equity assessment of the CARE Act to identify demographic disparities based on demographic data in paragraph (1), and to inform disparity reduction efforts.

(f)(1) The report shall include, at a minimum, information on the effectiveness of the CARE Act model in improving outcomes and reducing disparities, homelessness, criminal justice involvement, conservatorships, and hospitalization of participants. The annual report shall include process measures to examine the scope of impact and monitor the performance of CARE Act model implementation, such as the number and source of petitions filed for CARE Court; the number, rates, and trends of petitions resulting in dismissal and hearings; the number, rates, and trends of supporters; the number, rates, and trends of voluntary CARE agreements; the number, rates, and trends of ordered and completed CARE plans; the services and supports included in CARE plans, including court orders for stabilizing medications; the rates of adherence to medication; the number, rates, and trends of psychiatric advance directives; and the number, rates, and trends of developed graduation plans. The report shall include outcome measures to assess the effectiveness of the CARE Act model, such as improvement in housing status, including gaining and maintaining housing; reductions in emergency department visits and inpatient hospitalizations; reductions in law enforcement encounters and incarceration; reductions in involuntary treatment and conservatorship; and reductions in substance use. The annual report shall examine these data through the lens of health equity to identify racial, ethnic, and other demographic disparities and inform disparity reduction efforts.

(2) Data shall be stratified by age, sex, race, ethnicity, languages spoken, disability, sexual orientation, gender identity, housing status, veteran status, immigration status, health coverage source, and county, to the extent statistically relevant data is available. Information released or published pursuant to this section shall not contain data that may lead to the identification of respondents or information that would otherwise allow an individual to link the published information to a specific person. Data published by the department shall be deidentified in compliance with Section 164.514(a) and (b) of Title 45 of the Code of Federal Regulations.

(g) The outcomes shall be presented to relevant state oversight bodies, including, but not limited to, the California Interagency Council on Homelessness. *(Added by Stats.2022, c. 319 (S.B.1338), § 7, eff. Jan. 1, 2023.)*

§ 5986. Independent evaluation; methodology and contents; reports to Legislature

(a) An independent, research-based entity shall be retained by the department to develop, in consultation with county behavioral health agencies, county CARE courts, racial justice experts, and other appropriate stakeholders, including providers and CARE court participants, an independent evaluation of the effectiveness of the CARE Act. The independent evaluation shall employ statistical research methodology and include a logic model, hypotheses, comparative or quasi-experimental analyses, and conclusions regarding the extent to which the CARE Act model is associated, correlated, and causally related with the performance of the outcome measures included in the annual reports. The independent evaluation shall include results from a survey conducted of program participants. The independent evaluation shall highlight racial, ethnic, and other demographic disparities, and include causal inference or descriptive analyses regarding the impact of the CARE Act on disparity reduction efforts.

(b) The department shall provide a preliminary report to the Legislature three years after the implementation date of the CARE Act and a final report to the Legislature five years after the implementation date of CARE Act. The department shall post the preliminary and final reports on its internet website.

(c) Each county behavioral health department, each county CARE court, and any other state or local governmental entity, as determined by the department, shall provide the required data to the department, in a format and frequency as directed by the department.

(d) A report to be submitted pursuant to this section shall be submitted in compliance with Section 9795 of the Government Code. *(Added by Stats.2022, c. 319 (S.B.1338), § 7, eff. Jan. 1, 2023.)*

§ 5987. Exemption from liability

A county, or an employee or agent of a county, shall not be held civilly or criminally liable for any action by a respondent in the CARE process, except when the act or omission of a county, or the employee or agent of a county, constitutes gross negligence, recklessness, or willful misconduct. This section does not limit any immunity provided under any other law. *(Added by Stats.2022, c. 319 (S.B.1338), § 7, eff. Jan. 1, 2023.)*

Division 6

ADMISSIONS AND JUDICIAL COMMITMENTS

Part 1

ADMISSIONS

CHAPTER 1. VOLUNTARY ADMISSIONS TO MENTAL HOSPITALS AND INSTITUTIONS

§ 6000. Requirements for admission; prohibition on admission commencing July 1, 2012

(a) Pursuant to applicable rules and regulations established by the State Department of State Hospitals or the State Department of Developmental Services, the medical director of a state hospital may receive in that hospital, as a boarder and patient, a person who is a suitable person for care and treatment in that hospital, upon receipt of a written application for the admission of the person into the hospital for care and treatment made in accordance with the following requirements:

(1) In the case of an adult, the application shall be made voluntarily by the person, at a time when he or she is in a condition of mind as to render him or her competent to make it or, if he or she is a conservatee with a conservator of the person or person and estate who was appointed under Chapter 3 (commencing with Section 5350) of Part 1 of Division 5 with the right as specified by court order under Section 5358 to place his or her conservatee in a state hospital, by his or her conservator.

(2) In the case of a minor, the application shall be made by his or her parents, or by the parent, guardian, conservator, or other person entitled to his or her custody to a mental hospital as may be designated by the Director of State Hospitals or the Director of Developmental Services to admit minors on voluntary applications. If the minor has a conservator of the person, or the person and the estate, appointed under Chapter 3 (commencing with Section 5350) of Part 1 of Division 5, with the right as specified by court order under Section 5358 to place the conservatee in a state hospital the application for the minor shall be made by his or her conservator.

(b) A person received in a state hospital shall be deemed a voluntary patient.

(c) Upon the admission of a voluntary patient to a state hospital the medical director shall immediately forward to the office of the State Department of State Hospitals or the State Department of Developmental Services the record of the voluntary patient, showing the name, residence, age, sex, place of birth, occupation, civil condition, date of admission of the patient to the hospital, and other information as required by the rules and regulations of the department.

(d) The charges for the care and keeping of a person with a mental health disorder in a state hospital shall be governed by the provisions of Article 4 (commencing with Section 7275) of Chapter 3 of Division 7 relating to the charges for the care and keeping of persons with mental health disorders in state hospitals.

(e) A voluntary adult patient may leave the hospital or institution at any time by giving notice of his or her desire to leave to a member of the hospital staff and completing normal hospitalization departure procedures. A conservatee may leave in a like manner if notice is given by his or her conservator.

(f) A minor who is a voluntary patient may leave the hospital or institution after completing normal hospitalization departure procedures after notice is given to the superintendent or person in charge by the parents, or the parent, guardian, conservator, or other person entitled to the custody of the minor, of their desire to remove him or her from the hospital.

(g) No person received into a state hospital, private mental institution, or county psychiatric hospital as a voluntary patient during his or her minority shall be detained therein after he or she reaches the age of majority. A person, after attaining the age of majority, may apply for admission into the hospital or institution for care and treatment in the manner prescribed in this section for applications by an adult.

(h) The State Department of State Hospitals or the State Department of Developmental Services shall establish rules and regulations necessary to carry out properly the provisions of this section.

(i) Commencing July 1, 2012, the department shall not admit any person to a developmental center pursuant to this section. *(Added by Stats.1967, c. 1667, p. 4107, § 37, operative July 1, 1969. Amended by Stats.1968, c. 1374, p. 2675, § 86, operative July 1, 1969; Stats.1969, c. 722, p. 1442, § 47, eff. Aug. 8, 1969, operative July 1, 1969; Stats.1971, c. 1593, p. 3356, § 414, operative July 1, 1973; Stats.1973, c. 546, p. 1067, § 55, eff. Sept. 17, 1973; Stats.1977, c. 1252, p. 4597, § 634, operative July 1, 1978; Stats.1978, c. 429, p. 1461, § 219, eff. July 17, 1978, operative July 1, 1978; Stats.1979, c. 730, p. 2536, § 149, operative Jan. 1, 1981; Stats.1980, c. 676, p. 2041, § 340; Stats.2012, c. 24 (A.B.1470), § 137, eff. June 27, 2012; Stats.2012, c. 25 (A.B.1472), § 18, eff. June 27, 2012; Stats.2014, c. 144 (A.B.1847), § 106, eff. Jan. 1, 2015.)*

Law Revision Commission Comments

Section 6000 is amended to add the references to a conservator of a minor since a conservator may be appointed for the person of a married minor under the Probate Code as well as under the Welfare and Institutions Code. Prob. Code § 1800. [14 Cal.L.Rev.Comm. Reports 958 (1978)].

Cross References

Admission of developmentally disabled person to be upon application of parent or conservator, see Welfare and Institutions Code § 4825.
Department of Developmental Services, see Welfare and Institutions Code § 4400 et seq.
Insurance, intentional submission of false or fraudulent claims, adjournment of criminal proceedings under this Division, see Penal Code § 550.
State hospitals for developmentally disabled, see Welfare and Institutions Code § 7500 et seq.
State hospitals for mentally disordered, see Welfare and Institutions Code § 7200 et seq.
Voluntary application for mental health services by minors under juvenile court jurisdiction, see Welfare and Institutions Code § 6552.

Research References

3 Witkin, California Criminal Law 4th Punishment § 617 (2021), Felony Involving Public Transit Vehicle.
3 Witkin, California Criminal Law 4th Punishment § 618 (2021), Designated Felonies Within Ten-Year Period.

§ 6000.5. Admission of developmentally disabled person to hospital for developmentally disabled

Pursuant to Section 6000, the medical director of a state hospital for the developmentally disabled may receive in such hospital, as a boarder and patient, any developmentally disabled person as defined in Section 4512 who has been referred in accordance with Sections 4652, 4653, and 4803. *(Added by Stats.1973, c. 546, p. 1068, § 56, eff. Sept. 17, 1973. Amended by Stats.1979, c. 373, p. 1398, § 367.)*

§ 6001. Admissions to neuropsychiatric institutes

Admissions to the Langley Porter Neuropsychiatric Institute or to the Neuropsychiatric Institute, U.C.L.A. Medical Center, may be on a voluntary basis after approval by the medical superintendent of the clinic or institute, as the case may be. *(Added by Stats.1967, c. 1667, p. 4107, § 37, operative July 1, 1969.)*

Cross References

Langley Porter Neuropsychiatric Institute, see Welfare and Institutions Code § 7600.
Neuropsychiatric Institute, U.C.L.A. Medical Center, see Welfare and Institutions Code § 7700.

§ 6002. Persons eligible for admission; application; record; departure

(a) The person in charge of a private institution, hospital, or clinic that is conducted for, or includes a department or unit conducted for, the care and treatment of persons who have mental health disorders may receive therein as a voluntary patient a person with a mental health disorder who is a suitable person for care and treatment in the institution, hospital, or clinic who voluntarily makes a written application to the person in charge for admission into the institution, hospital, or clinic and who is, at the time of making the application, mentally competent to make the application. A conservatee, with a conservator of the person, or person and estate, appointed under Chapter 3 (commencing with Section 5350) of Part 1 of Division 5, with the right as specified by court order under Section 5358 to place his conservatee, may be admitted upon written application by his or her conservator.

(b) After the admission of a voluntary patient to a private institution, hospital, or clinic, the person in charge shall forward to the office of the State Department of State Hospitals a record of the voluntary patient showing all information required by rule by the department.

(c) A voluntary adult patient may leave the hospital, clinic, or institution at any time by giving notice of his or her desire to leave to a member of the hospital staff and completing normal hospitalization departure procedures. A conservatee may leave in a like manner if notice is given by his or her conservator. *(Added by Stats.1967, c. 1667, p. 4107, § 37, operative July 1, 1969. Amended by Stats.1969, c. 722, p. 1444, § 47.1, eff. Aug. 8, 1969, operative July 1, 1969; Stats.1970, c. 516, p. 1006, § 9; Stats.1971, c. 1593, p. 3358, § 416, operative July 1, 1973; Stats.1977, c. 1252, p. 4599, § 635, operative July 1, 1978; Stats.2014, c. 144 (A.B.1847), § 107, eff. Jan. 1, 2015.)*

Cross References

Voluntary application for mental health services by minors under juvenile court jurisdiction, see Welfare and Institutions Code § 6552.

§ 6002.10. Inpatient psychiatric treatment; admission procedures for minors; criteria

A facility licensed under Chapter 2 (commencing with Section 1250) of Division 2 of the Health and Safety Code, to provide inpatient psychiatric treatment, excluding state hospitals and county hospitals, shall establish admission procedures for minors who meet the following criteria:

(a) The minor is 14 years of age or older, and is under 18 years of age.

(b) The minor is not legally emancipated.

(c) The minor is not detained under Sections 5585.50 and 5585.53.

(d) The minor is not voluntarily committed pursuant to Section 6552.

(e) The minor has not been declared a dependent of the juvenile court pursuant to Section 300 or a ward of the court pursuant to Section 602.

(f) The minor's admitting diagnosis or condition is either of the following:

(1) A mental health disorder only. Although resistance to treatment may be a product of a mental health disorder, the resistance shall not, in itself, imply the presence of a mental health disorder or constitute evidence that the minor meets the admission criteria. A minor shall not be considered to have a mental health disorder solely for exhibiting behaviors specified under Sections 601 and 602.

(2) A mental health disorder and a substance abuse disorder. *(Added by Stats.1989, c. 1375, § 2. Amended by Stats.2014, c. 144 (A.B.1847), § 108, eff. Jan. 1, 2015.)*

§ 6002.15. Explanation of treatment to parent or guardian; notification to minor of minor's rights

(a) Prior to accepting the written authorization for treatment, the facility shall assure that a representative of the facility has given a full explanation of the treatment philosophy of the facility, including, where applicable, the use of seclusion and restraint, the use of medication, and the degree of involvement of family members in the minor's treatment to the parent, guardian or other person entitled to the minor's custody. This explanation shall be given orally and in writing, and shall be documented in the minor's treatment record upon completion.

(b) As part of the admission process, the professional person responsible for the minor's admission shall affirm in writing that the minor meets the admission criteria as specified above.

(c) Upon admission, a facility specified in Section 6002.10 shall do all of the following:

(1) Inform the minor in writing of the availability of an independent clinical review of his or her further inpatient treatment. The notice shall be witnessed and signed by an appropriate representative of the facility.

(2) Within one working day, notify the patients' rights advocate, as defined in Article 2 (commencing with Section 5540) of Chapter 5.2, regarding the admission of the minor.

(3) Provide all minors with a booklet promulgated by the State Department of Health Care Services outlining the specific rights of minors in mental health facilities. The booklet shall include the phone number of the local advocate and the hours that he or she may be reached. *(Added by Stats.1989, c. 1375, § 2.5. Amended by Stats.2012, c. 34 (S.B.1009), § 212, eff. June 27, 2012.)*

§ 6002.20. Minor's request for independent clinical review; notification of patients' rights advocate; advocate's responsibilities

(a) If the minor requests an independent clinical review of his or her continued inpatient treatment, the patients' rights advocate shall be notified of the request, as soon as practical, but no later than one working day. The role of the advocate shall be to provide information and assistance to the minor relating to the minor's right to obtain an independent clinical review to determine the appropriateness of placement within the facility. The advocate shall conduct his or her activities in a manner least disruptive to patient care in the facility. Nothing in this section shall be construed to limit, or expand, rights and responsibilities the advocate has pursuant to other provisions of law.

(b) An independent review may be requested up to 10 days after admission. At any time the minor may rescind his or her request for a review. *(Added by Stats.1989, c. 1375, § 3.)*

§ 6002.25. Independent clinical review; neutral licensed psychiatrist; list of reviewers

The independent clinical review shall be conducted by a licensed psychiatrist with training and experience in treating psychiatric adolescent patients, who is a neutral party to the review, having no direct financial relationship with the treating clinician, nor a personal or financial relationship with the patient, or his or her parents or guardian. Nothing in this section shall prevent a psychiatrist affiliated with a health maintenance organization, as defined in subdivision (b) of Section 1373.10 of the Health and Safety Code, from providing the independent clinical review where the admitting, treating, and reviewing psychiatrists are affiliated with a health maintenance organization that predominantly serves members of a prepaid health care service plan. The independent clinical reviewer shall be assigned, on a rotating basis, from a list prepared by the facility, and submitted to the county behavioral health director prior to March 1, 1990, and annually thereafter, or more frequently when necessary. The county behavioral health director shall, on an annual basis, or at the request of the facility, review the facility's list of independent clinical reviewers. The county behavioral health director shall approve or disapprove the list of reviewers within 30 days of submission. If there is no response from the county behavioral health director, the facility's list shall be deemed approved. If the county behavioral health director disapproves one or more of the persons on the list of reviewers, the county behavioral health director shall notify the facility in writing of the reasons for the disapproval. The county behavioral health director, in consultation with the facility, may develop a list of one or more additional reviewers within 30 days. The final list shall be mutually agreeable to the county behavioral health director and the facility. Sections 6002.10 to 6002.40, inclusive, shall not be construed to prohibit the treatment of minors prior to the existence of an approved list of independent clinical reviewers. The independent clinical reviewer may be an active member of the medical staff of the facility who has no direct financial relationship, including, but not limited to, an employment or other contract arrangement with the facility except for compensation received for the service of providing clinical reviews. *(Added by Stats.1989, c. 1375, § 4. Amended by Stats.2015, c. 455 (S.B.804), § 47, eff. Jan. 1, 2016.)*

§ 6002.30. Independent clinical review; information to be considered; timing and procedure

(a) All reasonably available clinical information which is relevant to establishing whether the minor meets the admission criteria pursuant to subdivision (d) of Section 6002.35 shall be considered by the psychiatrist conducting the review. In considering the information presented, the psychiatrist conducting the review shall privately interview the minor, and shall consult the treating clinician to review alternative treatment options which may be suitable for the minor's mental disorder.

(b) If the minor has received medication while an inpatient, the person conducting the review shall be informed of that fact and of the probable effects of the medication. The person presenting the clinical information in favor of inpatient treatment shall also inform the psychiatrist conducting the review of the proposed treatment plan for the minor, and, if known, whether the minor has had any previous independent clinical review at any facility, and the results of that service.

(c) The standard of review shall be whether the minor continues to have a mental disorder, whether further inpatient treatment is reasonably likely to be beneficial to the minor's mental disorder, or whether the placement in the facility represents the least restrictive, most appropriate available setting, within the constraints of reasonably available services, facilities, resources, and financial support, in which to treat the minor.

(d) The review shall take place within five days of the request.

(e) At the review, the minor shall have the right to be present, to be assisted by the advocate, and to question persons recommending inpatient treatment. If the minor is unwilling to attend, the review shall be held in his or her absence with the advocate representing the minor.

(f) The location of the independent clinical review shall be compatible with, and least disruptive of, the treatment being provided to the minor. Independent clinical reviews shall be conducted at the facility where the minor is treated. The review shall be situated in a location which ensures privacy.

(g) The independent clinical review shall be held in an informal setting so as to minimize the anxiety of both parents and minors and promote cooperation and communication among all interested parties. All parties shall make a reasonable effort to speak in terms the minor can understand and shall explain any terminology with which he or she may not be familiar.

(h) The review may be closed to anyone other than the minor, his or her parents or legal guardian, a representative of the facility, the minor's advocate, the psychiatrist conducting the review and the person presenting information in favor of, or opposition to, the inpatient treatment. The person conducting the review shall have discretion to limit the number of participants and shall keep participants to the minimum time necessary to relate the needed information.

(i) No party shall have legal representation in the review process.

(j) If any of the parties to the independent clinical review do not comprehend the language used at the independent clinical review, it shall be the responsibility of the psychiatrist conducting the independent clinical review to retain an interpreter. *(Added by Stats.1989, c. 1375, § 5.)*

§ 6002.35. Record of review; decision

(a) It shall be the responsibility of the psychiatrist conducting the independent clinical review to keep a record of the proceeding.

(b) After considering all the clinical information, the psychiatrist conducting the review shall render a binding decision. If he or she determines that further inpatient treatment is reasonably likely to be beneficial to the minor's disorder and placement in the facility represents the least restrictive, most appropriate available setting in which to treat the minor, the minor's inpatient treatment shall be authorized.

(c) If the psychiatrist conducting the review determines that the admission criteria have been met, this determination shall terminate when the minor is discharged from the facility.

(d) If the psychiatrist conducting the clinical review determines that further inpatient treatment in the facility is not reasonably likely to be beneficial to the minor's mental disorder or does not represent the least restrictive, most appropriate available setting in which to treat the minor, the minor shall be released from the facility to a custodial parent or guardian on the same day the determination was made. Except as provided in Section 43.92 of the Civil Code, upon the minor's release, neither the attending psychiatrist, any licensed health professional providing treatment to the minor in the facility, the psychiatrist who releases the minor pursuant to this section, nor the facility in which the minor was admitted or treated shall be civilly or criminally liable for any conduct of the released minor, a parent, legal guardian, or other persons entitled to custody of the minor. *(Added by Stats.1989, c. 1375, § 6.)*

§ 6002.40. Treatment costs covered by private insurer or county; legislative intent; monitoring compliance

(a) For any insurance contracts entered into after January 1, 1990, where any private insurer, certified medical plan, or private health service plan is liable to pay or reimburse a professional provider or institutional provider for the costs of medically necessary mental health services provided to the patient, the costs of the clinical review required by Sections 6002.10 to 6002.40, inclusive, including, but not limited to, the costs of the interpreter, if any, and the costs of the patients' rights advocate, shall be borne by the insurer, certified medical plan, or the health service plan. Payments to providers for the costs of the independent clinical review shall be made promptly.

For Medi–Cal eligible patients placed in these private facilities, the costs of the clinical review required by Sections 6002.10 to 6002.40, inclusive, including the costs of the patients rights advocate, shall be borne by the county.

(b) The Legislature intends that Sections 6002.10 to 6002.40, inclusive, affect only the rights of minors confined in private mental health facilities on the consent of their parents or guardians, where the costs of treatment are paid or reimbursed by a private insurer or private health service plan.

(c) Mental health facilities shall summarize on an annual basis, information including, but not limited to, the number of minors admitted by diagnosis, length of stay, and source of payment, the number of requests for an independent clinical review by diagnosis, source of payment, and outcome of the independent clinical review and submit this information to the State Department of Health Care Services. The State Department of Public Health shall monitor compliance of this section during an inspection of the facility pursuant to Sections 1278 and 1279 of the Health and Safety Code. *(Added by Stats.1989, c. 1375, § 6.5. Amended by Stats.1992, c. 711 (A.B.2874), § 147, eff. Sept. 15, 1992; Stats.1992, c. 713 (A.B.3564), § 48, eff. Sept. 15, 1992; Stats.2012, c. 34 (S.B.1009), § 213, eff. June 27, 2012.)*

Cross References

Department of Health Care Services, generally, see Health and Safety Code § 100100 et seq.

§ 6003. County psychiatric hospital

As used in this article, "county psychiatric hospital" means the hospital, ward, or facility provided by the county pursuant to the provisions of Section 7100. *(Added by Stats.1967, c. 1667, p. 4107, § 37, operative July 1, 1969.)*

Cross References

Similar provision, see Welfare and Institutions Code § 7101.

§ 6003.1. County psychiatric health facility

As used in this article, county psychiatric health facility means a 24–hour acute care facility provided by the county pursuant to the provisions in Sections 5404 and 7100. *(Added by Stats.1978, c. 1234, p. 3988, § 6. Amended by Stats.1996, c. 245 (A.B.2616), § 3, eff. July 22, 1996.)*

§ 6003.2. County psychiatric hospital interchangeable with psychiatric health facility

Wherever in this article the term "county psychiatric hospital" appears, such term shall be interchangeable with the term "psychiatric health facility." *(Added by Stats.1978, c. 1234, p. 3988, § 7.)*

§ 6004. County psychiatric hospital; persons eligible for admission

The superintendent or person in charge of the county psychiatric hospital may receive, care for, or treat in the hospital any person who voluntarily makes a written application to the superintendent or person in charge thereof for admission into the hospital for care, treatment, or observation, and who is a suitable person for care, treatment, or observation, and who in the case of an adult person is in such condition of mind, at the time of making application for admission, as to render him competent to make such application. In the case of a minor person, the application shall be made by his parents, or by the parent, guardian, or other person entitled to his custody. A conservatee, with a conservator of the person, or person and estate, appointed under Chapter 3 (commencing with Section 5350) of Part 1 of Division 5, with the right as specified by court order under Section 5358 to place his conservatee, may be admitted upon written application by his conservator. *(Added by Stats.1967, c. 1667, p. 4107, § 37, operative July 1, 1969. Amended by Stats.1969, c. 722, p. 1444, § 47.2, eff. Aug. 8, 1969, operative July 1, 1969; Stats.1970, c. 516, p. 1007, § 10.)*

Cross References

Similar provision, see Welfare and Institutions Code § 7102.
Voluntary application for mental health services by minors under juvenile court jurisdiction, see Welfare and Institutions Code § 6552.

§ 6005. Departure from county psychiatric hospital

A voluntary adult patient may leave the hospital or institution at any time by giving notice of his desire to leave to any member of the hospital staff and completing normal hospitalization departure procedures. A conservatee may leave in a like manner if notice is given by his conservator.

A minor person who is a voluntary patient may leave the hospital or institution after completing normal hospitalization departure procedures after notice is given to the superintendent or person in charge by the parents, or the parent, guardian, or other person entitled to the custody of the minor, of their desire to remove him from the hospital. *(Added by Stats.1967, c. 1667, p. 4107, § 37, operative July 1, 1969.)*

§ 6006. Rights of voluntary patients

A person admitted as a voluntary patient to a state hospital, a private mental institution, or a county psychiatric hospital shall have the following rights in addition to the right to leave such hospital as specified in this chapter:

(a) He shall receive such care and treatment as his condition requires for the full period that he is a patient;

(b) He shall have the full patient rights specified in Article 7 (commencing with Section 5325) of Chapter 2 of Part 1 of Division 5 of this code. *(Added by Stats.1967, c. 1667, p. 4107, § 37, operative July 1, 1969. Amended by Stats.1968, c. 1374, p. 2676, § 87, operative July 1, 1969.)*

§ 6007. Detention in private institution; evaluation; release or further proceedings

(a) Any person detained pursuant to this section shall be evaluated by the facility designated by the county and approved by the State Department of Health Care Services pursuant to Section 5150 as a facility for 72–hour treatment and evaluation. The evaluation shall be made at the request of the person in charge of the private institution in which the person is detained or by one of the physicians who signed the certificate. If in the opinion of the professional person in charge of the evaluation and treatment facility or his or her designee, the evaluation of the person can be made by the professional person or his or her designee at the private institution in which the person is detained, the person shall not be required to be evaluated at the evaluation and treatment facility, but shall be evaluated at the private institution to determine if the person is a danger to others, himself or herself, or gravely disabled as a result of mental disorder.

(b) Any person evaluated under this section shall be released from the private institution immediately upon completion of the evaluation if in the opinion of the professional person in charge of the evaluation and treatment facility, or his or her designee, the person evaluated is not a danger to others, or to himself or herself, or gravely disabled as a result of mental disorder, unless the person agrees voluntarily to remain in the private institution.

(c) If in the opinion of the professional person in charge of the facility or his or her designee, the person evaluated requires intensive treatment or recommendation for conservatorship, the professional person or his or her designee shall proceed under Article 4 (commencing with Section 5250) of Chapter 2, or under Chapter 3 (commencing with Section 5350), of Part 1 of Division 5. *(Added by Stats.1969, c. 722, p. 1445, § 48, eff. Aug. 8, 1969, operative July 1, 1969. Amended by Stats.1971, c. 1593, p. 3358, § 416, operative July 1, 1973; Stats.1977, c. 1252, p. 4599, § 636, operative July 1, 1978; Stats.2012, c. 34 (S.B.1009), § 214, eff. June 27, 2012; Stats.2013, c. 23 (A.B.82), § 52, eff. June 27, 2013.)*

§ 6008. Admission of conservatee to United States government hospital; departure

For the purposes of this part, a person who is a conservatee with a conservator of the person or of the person and estate appointed under Chapter 3 (commencing with Section 5350) of Part 1 of Division 5 with the right as specified by court order under Section 5358 to place his conservatee in a hospital of the United States government, may be admitted to such a hospital upon written application made by his conservator. A conservatee so admitted to such a hospital may leave the hospital at any time after his conservator gives notice to a member of the hospital staff that the conservatee is leaving and normal hospitalization departure procedures are completed by the conservator or by the conservator and conservatee. *(Added by Stats.1969, c. 722, p. 1445, § 48.1, eff. Aug. 8, 1969, operative July 1, 1969. Amended by Stats.1970, c. 516, p. 1007, § 11.)*

Part 2

JUDICIAL COMMITMENTS

CHAPTER 1. DEFINITIONS, CONSTRUCTION AND STANDARD FORMS

Section

§ 6250. "A person subject to judicial commitment" defined; effect on other laws; liberal construction

(a) As used in this part, "a person subject to judicial commitment" means a person who may be judicially committed under this part as a mentally disordered sex offender pursuant to Article 1 (commencing with Section 6331), a sexually violent predator pursuant to Article 4 (commencing with Section 6600), or a person with intellectual disabilities pursuant to Article 2 (commencing with Section 6500) of Chapter 2.

(b) Nothing in this part shall be held to change or interfere with the provisions of the Penal Code and other laws relating to persons with mental health disorders who are charged with a crime or to persons who are found to be not guilty by reason of insanity.

(c) This part shall be liberally construed so that, as far as possible and consistent with the rights of persons subject to commitment, those persons shall be treated, not as criminals, but as sick persons. *(Added by Stats.1969, c. 722, p. 1446, § 49.1, eff. Aug. 8, 1969, operative July 1, 1969. Amended by Stats.1970, c. 1502, p. 2987, § 6; Stats.1979, c. 373, p. 1399, § 368; Stats.1995, c. 762 (S.B.1143), § 2; Stats.1995, c. 763 (A.B.888), § 2; Stats.2012, c. 448 (A.B.2370), § 54; Stats.2012, c. 457 (S.B.1381), § 54; Stats.2014, c. 144 (A.B.1847), § 109, eff. Jan. 1, 2015.)*

Cross References

Commitment of mentally disordered persons charged with crime, see Welfare and Institutions Code § 6825.
Discharged patient mentally deficient or affected with chronic harmless mental disorder, recommitment, see Welfare and Institutions Code § 7362.
Inquiry into the competence of the defendant before trial or after conviction, see Penal Code § 1367 et seq.
Judicially committed defined for purposes of this Division, see Welfare and Institutions Code § 5008.1.
Not guilty by reason of insanity, proceedings, see Penal Code § 1026 et seq.
Prohibition of judicial commitment, mentally disordered persons and persons impaired by chronic alcoholism, see Welfare and Institutions Code § 5002.
Return of judicially committed nonresidents, see Welfare and Institutions Code § 4119.
Statutory construction,
Amended statutes, see Government Code § 9605.
Amendment of repealed statutes, see Government Code § 9609.
Court's duties, see Code of Civil Procedure § 1858; Evidence Code § 310.
Intention of legislature, see Code of Civil Procedure § 1859.
Natural rights preferred, see Code of Civil Procedure § 1866.
Repeal of repealing statutes, see Government Code § 9607.
Temporary suspension of law, see Government Code § 9611.

Research References

3 Witkin, California Criminal Law 4th Punishment § 153 (2021), In General.

§ 6251. Petition; form

Wherever, on the basis of a petition, provision is made in this code for issuing and delivering an order for examination and detention directing that a person be apprehended and taken before a judge of a superior court for a hearing and examination on an allegation of being a person subject to judicial commitment, the petition shall be in substantially the following form:

In the Superior Court of the State of California
For the County of ____

____
The People)
For the Best Interest and Protection of)
______________________________)
as a __________________________)
and Concerning) Petition
______________________________ and)
______________________________)
Respondents)
______________________________)

____, residing at ____ (tel. ______), being duly sworn deposes and says: That there is now in the county in the City or Town of ______ a person named ______, who resides at ______, and who is believed to be a ______. That the person is ___ years of age; that __ the person is ___ (sex) and that __ the person is ____ (single, married, widowed, or divorced); and that ____ occupation is ______.

That the facts because of which petitioner believes that the person is a ______ are as follows: That __ the person, at ____ in the county, on the ______ day of ______, 20___,

____

That petitioner's interest in and case is ______________

____

That petitioner believes that said person is ____ as defined in Section ______.

That the persons responsible for the care, support, and maintenance of the ____, and their relationship to the person are, so far as known to the petitioner, as follows:
(Give names, addresses, and relationship of persons named as respondents) Wherefore, petitioner prays that examination be made to determine the state of the mental health of ____, alleged to be ____, and that such measures be taken for the best interest and protection of said ____, in respect to the person's supervision, care and treatment, as may be necessary and provided by law.

____
Petitioner

Subscribed and sworn to before me this ____ day of ______, 20__.

______________________________, Clerk of the Court
By ______________________________ Deputy

(Added by Stats.1967, c. 1667, p. 4107, § 37, operative July 1, 1969. Amended by Stats.1968, c. 1374, p. 2679, § 93, operative July 1, 1969; Stats.2002, c. 784 (S.B.1316), § 619.)

Law Revision Commission Comments

Section 6251 is amended to reflect elimination of the county clerk's role as ex officio clerk of the superior court. See former Gov't Code § 26800 (county clerk acting as clerk of superior court). The powers, duties, and responsibilities formerly exercised by the county clerk as ex officio clerk of the court are delegated to the court administrative or executive officer, and the county clerk is relieved of those powers, duties, and responsibilities. See Gov't Code §§ 69840 (powers, duties, and responsibilities of clerk of court and deputy clerk of court), 71620 (trial court personnel). [32 Cal.L.Rev.Comm. Reports 563 (2002)].

Cross References

Petition for commitment of mentally retarded, see Welfare and Institutions Code § 6502.

Use of form in proceedings for judicial commitment of mentally disordered sex offenders, see Welfare and Institutions Code § 6302.

§ 6252. Order for examination or detention; form

Wherever provision is made in this code for a judge of a superior court to issue and deliver an order for examination or detention directing that a person be apprehended and taken before a judge of a superior court for a hearing and examination on an allegation of being a person subject to judicial commitment, the order for examination or detention shall be in substantially the following form:

The People)
For the Best Interest and Protection of)
....................................) Order
as a ....) for
and Concerning) Examination
....................................) Detention
Respondents)

The People of the State of California ....
....

(peace officer)

The petition for .... having been presented this day to me, a Judge of the Superior Court in and for the County of ...., State of California, from which it appears that there is now in this county, at ...., a person by the name of ...., who is a ....

And it satisfactorily appears to me that said person is sufficiently .... that examination should be made and hearing held, if demanded, to determine the supervision, treatment, care or restraint, if any, necessary for his best interest and protection, and the protection of the people.

I do hereby appoint .... and .... as medical examiners to make a personal examination of ...., the person alleged to be ...., and to report thereon to the court, pursuant to Section .... of the Welfare and Institutions Code.

* Now, therefore, you are commanded to notify said ...., to submit to an examination .... on or before the .... day of ...., that thereafter he may be taken before a judge of the superior court in this county for examination and hearing to determine the measures to be taken for the best interest and protection of said ...., as a ...., as provided by law.

* And it affirmatively appearing to me that said person is sufficiently .... that he is likely to injure himself or others if not immediately hospitalized or detained, you are therefore commanded to forthwith detain said ...., or cause him to be detained for examination and hearing, pending the further order of the judge, at ...., and there be cared for in a humane manner as a .... and provided with any medical treatment deemed necessary to his physical well-being.

* And it satisfactorily appearing to me that said person has failed or has refused to appear for examination when notified by order of this court, you are therefore commanded to forthwith detain said .... or cause him to be detained for examination and hearing, pending the further order of the judge, at ...., and there be cared for in a humane manner as a ....

I hereby direct that a copy of this order, together with a copy of the said petition be delivered to said person and his representative, if any, at the time of his notification; and I further direct that this order may be served at any hour of the night.

Witness my hand, this .... day of ...., 19.....

....
Judge of the Superior Court

* Strike out when not applicable.

Return of Order

I hereby certify that I received the above order for examination or detention, and on the .... day of ...., 19...., served it by notifying and delivering to said .... personally, and to his representatives, if any, to wit, ..., a copy of the order and of the petition,* or by apprehending said person and causing h.. to be detained for examination and hearing and for humane care as an alleged .... at ....; until further ordered and directed by the judge.

* I hereby certify that prior to the service of the above order for detention and the apprehension of .... I served notice on the person and his representative, if any, as required under Article 2 (commencing with Section 5200) of Chapter 2 of Part 1 of Division 5 of the Welfare and Institutions Code.

Dated ...., 19....

....
Signature of officer

* Strike out when not applicable. *(Added by Stats.1967, c. 1667, p. 4107, § 37, operative July 1, 1969. Amended by Stats.1968, c. 1374, p. 2680, § 94, operative July 1, 1969.)*

Cross References

Use of form for order of examination and detention of mentally disordered sex offenders, see Welfare and Institutions Code § 6302.

§ 6253. Certificate of medical examiners; form

Wherever provision is made in this code for court-appointed medical examiners to make and sign a certificate showing the facts of an examination in the case of a person alleged to be subject to judicial commitment, the certificate shall be in substantially the following form:

In the Superior Court of the State of California
for the County of ....

The People	)	
For the Best Interest and Protection of	)	
.................................,	)	Certificate
as a .... and	)	of Medical
Concerning ....,	)	Examiners
and ....,	)	
Respondents	)	

We, Dr. .... and Dr. ...., medical examiners in the County of ...., duly appointed and certified as such, do hereby certify under our hands that we have examined ...., alleged to be a ...., and have attended before a judge of said court at the hearing on the petition concerning said person, and have heard the testimony of all witnesses, and, as a result of the examination, have testified under oath before the court to the following facts concerning the alleged ....:

Name ....

Address ....

Age .... Sex ....

Occupation .... Marital status ....
(Single, married, widowed, divorced)

Religious belief ....

Pertinent case history ....
....
....

General physical condition ....
....

Present mental status ....
....
....

Laboratory reports (if any) ....
....

Tentative diagnosis of mental health ....
....
....

Recommendation for disposition or supervision, treatment and care
....
....
....

Reasons for the recommendation ....
....
....
....

Date ....

....
Medical Examiner

....
Medical Examiner

(Added by Stats.1967, c. 1667, p. 4107, § 37, operative July 1, 1969.)

Cross References

Certification of medical examiners, see Welfare and Institutions Code § 6750.

§ 6254. Order for care, hospitalization or commitment; form

Wherever provision is made in this code for an order of commitment by a superior court, the order of commitment shall be in substantially the following form:

In the Superior Court of the State of California
For the County of ______

______________________		
The People	}	
For the Best Interest and Protection of ______________	}	
as a ______________,	}	
	}	Order for Care,
and Concerning	}	Hospitalization,
______________ and	}	or Commitment
______________, Respondents	}	
______________________	}	

The petition dated ______, alleging that ______, having been presented to this court on the ______ day of ______, 20__, and an order of detention issued thereon by a judge of the superior court of this county, and a return of the said order:

And it further appearing that the provisions of Sections 6250 to 6254, inclusive, of the Welfare and Institutions Code have been complied with;

And it further appearing that Dr. ______ and Dr. ______, two regularly appointed and qualified medical examiners of this county, have made a personal examination of the alleged ______, and have made and signed the certificate of the medical examiners, which certificate is attached hereto and made a part hereof;

Now therefore, after examination and certificate made as aforesaid, the court is satisfied and believes that ______ is a ______ and is so ______.

It is ordered, adjudged, and decreed:

That ______ is a ______ and that _he

* (a) Be cared for and detained in ______, a county psychiatric hospital, a community mental health service, or a licensed hospital for the care of persons with mental health disorders until the further order of the court, or

* (b) Be cared for at ______, until the further order of the court, or

* (c) Be committed to the State Department of State Hospitals for placement in a state hospital, or

* (d) Be committed to a facility of the Department of Veterans Affairs or other agency of the United States, to wit: ______ at ______.

It is further ordered and directed that ______ of this county, take, convey, and deliver ______ to the proper authorities of the hospital or establishment designated herein to be cared for as provided by law.

Dated this ______ day of ______, 20__.

____
Judge of the Superior Court

* Strike out when not applicable.

(Added by Stats.1967, c. 1667, p. 4107, § 37, operative July 1, 1969. Amended by Stats.1968, c. 1374, p. 2682, § 95, operative July 1, 1969; Stats.1971, c. 1593, p. 3359, § 417, operative July 1, 1973; Stats.1977, c. 1252, p. 4600, § 637, operative July 1, 1978; Stats.1988, c. 113, § 22, eff. May 25, 1988, operative July 1, 1988; Stats.2012, c. 440 (A.B.1488), § 65, eff. Sept. 22, 2012; Stats.2013, c. 76 (A.B.383), § 210; Stats. 2014, c. 144 (A.B.1847), § 110, eff. Jan. 1, 2015.)

Law Revision Commission Comments

Section 6254 is amended to delete the reference to former Section 1663 of the Probate Code which has been repealed. A court-ordered commitment to a United States government hospital is made pursuant to Section 5358 of the Welfare & Institutions Code. See also Welf. & Inst. Code §§ 4123 (transfer to federal institution), 5008(c) (intensive treatment in United States government hospital), 5366.1 (detention of person in facility of Veterans Administration or other agency of United States government), 6008 (conservatee admitted to hospital of United States government). [19 Cal.L.Rev.Comm.Reports 1099 (1988)].

Cross References

County psychiatric hospitals, see Welfare and Institutions Code § 7100 et seq.
State hospitals for the mentally disordered, see Welfare and Institutions Code § 7200 et seq.

CHAPTER 2. COMMITMENT CLASSIFICATION

Section

Section

§ 6300. Definitions

Section 6300 was repealed by Stats.1981, c. 928, p. 3485, § 2. For continued application to certain sex offenders, see §§ 3 and 4 of that act.

As used in this article, "mentally disordered sex offender" means any person who by reason of mental defect, disease, or disorder, is predisposed to the commission of sexual offenses to such a degree that he is dangerous to the health and safety of others. Wherever the term "sexual psychopath" is used in any code, such term shall be construed to refer to and mean a "mentally disordered sex offender." *(Added by Stats.1967, c. 1667, p. 4107, § 37, operative July 1, 1969.)*

Cross References

Procedure governing handling of mentally disordered person charged with public offense, see Welfare and Institutions Code § 6825.

Research References

3 Witkin, California Criminal Law 4th Punishment § 137 (2021), In General.

§ 6300.1. Treatment by prayer

Section 6300.1 was repealed by Stats.1981, c. 928, p. 3485, § 2. For continued application to certain sex offenders, see Historical and Statutory Notes under Welfare and Institutions Code § 6300.

No person who is being treated by prayer in the practice of the religion of any well-recognized church, sect, denomination or organization, shall be ordered detained or committed under this chapter unless the court shall determine that he is or would likely become dangerous to himself or to the person or property of others, or unless being a minor, his parent or guardian having custody of his person shall consent to such detention or commitment. *(Added by Stats. 1969, c. 722, p. 1446, § 49.2, eff. Aug. 8, 1969, operative July 1, 1969.)*

Cross References

Exemption from medical or psychiatric treatment, reliance on faith healing, see Welfare and Institutions Code § 7104.

§ 6300.2. Patient rights

Section 6300.2 was repealed by Stats.1981, c. 928, p. 3485, § 2. For continued application to certain sex offenders, see Historical and Statutory Notes under Welfare and Institutions Code § 6300.

Any person admitted to a state hospital as a mentally disordered sex offender shall have the full patient rights specified in Article 7 (commencing with Section 5325) of Chapter 2 of Part 1 of Division 5. *(Added by Stats.1972, c. 574, p. 983, § 8.)*

Cross References

"Mentally disordered sex offender" defined for purposes of this Article, see Welfare and Institutions Code § 6300.

§ 6301. Application of article

Section 6301 was repealed by Stats.1981, c. 928, p. 3485, § 2. For continued application to certain sex offenders, see Historical and Statutory Notes under Welfare and Institutions Code § 6300.

This article shall not apply to any person sentenced to death. This article shall not apply to any person convicted of an offense the punishment for which may be death until after a sentence other than death has been imposed, at which time this article shall apply to such person and he may be certified to the superior court as provided in Section 6302. *(Added by Stats.1967, c. 1667, p. 4107, § 37, operative July 1, 1969. Amended by Stats.1976, c. 1101, p. 4973, § 1.)*

§ 6302. Certification for hearing and examination after conviction

Section 6302 was repealed by Stats.1981, c. 928, p. 3485, § 2. For continued application to certain sex offenders, see Historical and Statutory Notes under Welfare and Institutions Code § 6300.

(a) General provisions; failure to register under Penal Code § 290. When a person is convicted of any sex offense, the trial judge, on his own motion, or on motion of the prosecuting attorney, or on application by affidavit by or on behalf of the defendant, if it appears to the satisfaction of the court that there is probable cause for believing such a person is a mentally disordered sex offender within the meaning of this chapter, may adjourn the proceeding or suspend the sentence, as the case may be, and may certify the person for hearing and examination by the superior court of the county to determine whether the person is a mentally disordered sex offender within the meaning of this article.

As used in this section the term "sex offense" means any offense for which registration is required by Section 290 of the Penal Code; or any felony or misdemeanor which is shown by clear proof or the stipulation of the defendant to have been committed primarily for purposes of sexual arousal or gratification.

When an affidavit is filed under (a) it shall be substantially in the form specified for the affidavit in Section 6251 of this code. The title and body of the affidavit shall refer to such person as "an alleged mentally disordered sex offender" and shall state fully the facts upon which the allegation that the person is a mentally disordered sex offender is based. If the person is then before the court or is in custody, the court may order that the person be detained in a place of safety until the issue and service of an order for examination and detention as provided by this article.

(b) Child under 14; misdemeanor. When a person is convicted of a sex offense involving a child under 14 years of age and it is a misdemeanor, and the person has been previously convicted of a sex offense in this or any other state, the court shall adjourn the proceeding or suspend the sentence, as the case may be, and shall certify the person for hearing and examination by the superior court of the county to determine whether the person is a mentally disordered sex offender within the meaning of this article.

(c) Child under 14; felony. When a person is convicted of a sex offense involving a child under 14 years of age and it is a felony, the court shall adjourn the proceeding or suspend the sentence, as the case may be, and shall certify the person for hearing and examination by the superior court of the county to determine whether the person is a mentally disordered sex offender within the meaning of this article.

(d) Certification; statement. When the court certifies the person for hearing and examination by the superior court of the county to determine whether the person is a mentally disordered sex offender, the court shall transmit to the superior court its certification to that effect, accompanied by a statement of the court's reasons for finding that there is probable cause for believing such person is a mentally disordered sex offender within the meaning of this article in cases certified under (a), or a statement of the facts making such certification mandatory under (b) or (c).

The judge or justice presiding in such court, whenever it is deemed necessary or advisable, may issue and deliver to some peace officer for service, an order directing that the person be apprehended and taken before a judge of the superior court for a hearing and examination to determine whether the person is a mentally disordered sex offender. The officer shall thereupon apprehend and detain the person until a hearing and examination can be had. At the time of the apprehension a copy of the affidavit if one was filed, the certification, accompanied by the court's statement, and the warrant shall be personally delivered to the person and copies thereof shall also be delivered to the superior court to which the person was certified and to the district attorney of the county.

The order for examination and detention shall be substantially in the form provided by Section 6252 of this code. *(Added by Stats.1967, c. 1667, p. 4107, § 37, operative July 1, 1969. Amended by Stats.1976, c. 1101, p. 4973, § 2.)*

Cross References

Felonies, definition and penalties, see Penal Code §§ 17, 18.
"Mentally disordered sex offender" defined for purposes of this Article, see Welfare and Institutions Code § 6300.
Misdemeanors, definition and penalties, see Penal Code §§ 17, 19 and 19.2.

§ 6303. Service of notice; form

Section 6303 was repealed by Stats.1981, c. 928, p. 3485, § 2. For continued application to certain sex offenders, see Historical and Statutory Notes under Welfare and Institutions Code § 6300.

At the time of service of the petition and order for examination or detention, the officer making the service shall also deliver to each person served a copy of a notice which shall read substantially as follows:

The petition which accompanies this notice has been filed in the Superior Court in and for the County of ......, alleging that ...... is a ....

*...... is notified to present himself at the time and place designated in the attached order to submit to an examination into the state of his mental health. He is permitted to be accompanied by one or more of his relatives or friends to the place of examination. If he fails or refuses to appear for such examination, the court may issue an order for his forthwith detention for such examination.

*...... has been affirmatively alleged to be likely to injure himself or others if not immediately hospitalized or detained. The court has therefore issued the attached order for detention and for examination and hearing before the court. ...... has the right to a hearing, to bring in witnesses and to have compulsory process therefor, and to be represented by an attorney.

If ...... or a relative, friend, counsel or representative desires to be heard by the court, he must within four days after service of this notice file a request for a hearing with the clerk of the Superior Court in and for the County of ....

* Strike out when not applicable. *(Added by Stats.1967, c. 1667, p. 4107, § 37, operative July 1, 1969.)*

§ 6304. Certification; form

Section 6304 was repealed by Stats.1981, c. 928, p. 3485, § 2. For continued application to certain sex offenders, see

Historical and Statutory Notes under Welfare and Institutions Code § 6300.

Whenever a person is certified to the superior court for hearing and examination under Section 6302 the certification may be made in substantially the following form:

(Title of court and cause)

Order Adjoining Proceedings and Certifying Alleged Mentally Disordered Sex Offender to the Superior Court

Upon the court's own motion, the motion of the prosecuting attorney, application by or on behalf of the defendant (strike the conditions not applicable), it appearing to the satisfaction of the court that the above-named defendant has been convicted of a criminal offense, to wit, violation of . . . . . . of the State of California, and that there is probable cause for believing that said defendant is a mentally disordered sex offender within the meaning of Article 1 of Chapter 2 of Part 2 of Division 6 of the Welfare and Institutions Code of the State of California, as amended, in that—he is a person who by reason of mental defect, disease, or disorder, is predisposed to the commission of sexual offenses to such a degree that he is dangerous to the health and safety of others.

Now, therefore, the above proceeding is adjourned and it is hereby ordered that the above-named defendant is certified to the Superior Court of the State of California, in and for the County of . . . . . . for hearing and examination by said court to determine whether said defendant is a mentally disordered sex offender within the meaning of said Article 1 of Chapter 2 of Part 2 of Division 6 of the Welfare and Institutions Code of the State of California, as amended. The above-named defendant shall be taken before said court, as provided in Section 6305 of said code, on the . . . . day of . . . ., 19. ., at the hour of . . . . .* A copy of this certification of said defendant to said superior court shall be delivered to said defendant.

Dated this . . . . . . day of . . . . . ., 19. . .

. . . .
Judge

* This sentence may be included if such date and hour have been set by the superior court upon the request of the certifying judge. *(Added by Stats.1967, c. 1667, p. 4107, § 37, operative July 1, 1969.)*

Cross References

"Mentally disordered sex offender" defined for purposes of this Article, see Welfare and Institutions Code § 6300.

§ 6305. Advice as to allegation and rights; time and place of hearing; notice; attorney

Section 6305 was repealed by Stats.1981, c. 928, p. 3485, § 2. For continued application to certain sex offenders, see Historical and Statutory Notes under Welfare and Institutions Code § 6300.

The person certified or alleged to be a mentally disordered sex offender shall be taken before a judge of the superior court of the county. The judge shall then inform him that he is certified or alleged to be a mentally disordered sex offender, and inform him of his rights to make a reply and to produce witnesses in relation thereto. The judge shall by order fix such time and place for the hearing and examination in open court as will give reasonable opportunity for the filing of the probation officer's report as provided in Section 6306, and for the production and examination of witnesses. If, however, the person is too ill to appear in court, or if appearance in court would be detrimental to the mental or physical health of the person, the judge may hold the hearing at the bedside of the person. The order shall be entered at length in the minute book of the court or shall be signed by the judge and filed, and a certified copy thereof served on the person. The judge shall order that notice of the apprehension of the person and of the hearing of mentally disordered sex offender be served on the district attorney of the county and on such relatives of the person known to be residing in the county as the judge deems necessary or proper.

If the alleged mentally disordered sex offender has no attorney, an attorney shall be appointed to represent the person in the manner prescribed by Section 6314. In a county where there is no public defender, the court shall fix the compensation to be paid by the county for such services if the court determines that the person is not financially able to employ counsel. *(Added by Stats.1967, c. 1667, p. 4107, § 37, operative July 1, 1969. Amended by Stats.1976, c. 1101, p. 4974, § 2.5.)*

Cross References

"Mentally disordered sex offender" defined for purposes of this Article, see Welfare and Institutions Code § 6300.

§ 6306. Probation officer; reference; report

Section 6306 was repealed by Stats.1981, c. 928, p. 3485, § 2. For continued application to certain sex offenders, see Historical and Statutory Notes under Welfare and Institutions Code § 6300.

The court shall refer the matter to the probation officer, along with a copy of the certification accompanied by the certifying court's statement, and the name and address of each psychiatrist or clinical psychologist appointed pursuant to Section 6307, to investigate and report to the court within a specified time, upon the circumstances surrounding the crime and the prior record and history of the person. The report shall include the criminal record, if any, of the person, obtained from the State Bureau of Criminal Identification and Investigation. The probation officer shall furnish to the psychiatrists and clinical psychologists pertinent information concerning the circumstances surrounding the crime and the prior record and history of the person. *(Added by Stats.1967, c. 1667, p. 4107, § 37, operative July 1, 1969. Amended by Stats.1970, c. 516, p. 1007, § 12; Stats.1980, c. 1206, p. 4067, § 3.)*

§ 6307. Appointment of psychologists or psychiatrists; contest of commitment

Section 6307 was repealed by Stats.1981, c. 928, p. 3485, § 2. For continued application to certain sex offenders, see Historical and Statutory Notes under Welfare and Institutions Code § 6300.

The judge shall appoint not less than two nor more than three certified clinical psychologists, each of whom shall have a doctoral degree in psychology and at least five years of postgraduate experience in the diagnosis of emotional and mental disorders, or psychiatrists, each of whom shall be a holder of a valid and unrevoked physician's and surgeon's certificate and have directed his professional practice primarily to the diagnosis and treatment of mental and nervous disorders for a period of not less than five years to make a personal examination of the alleged mentally disordered sex offender, directed toward ascertaining whether the person is a mentally disordered sex offender.

If the proposed commitment is contested by either the defendant or the people, one of the clinical psychologists or psychiatrists so appointed may be designated by the defendant, and one by the people. *(Added by Stats.1967, c. 1667, p. 4107, § 37, operative July 1, 1969. Amended by Stats.1970, c. 685, p. 1313, § 1; Stats.1976, c. 1101, p. 4975, § 3; Stats.1978, c. 391, p. 1242, § 3.)*

Cross References

"Mentally disordered sex offender" defined for purposes of this Article, see Welfare and Institutions Code § 6300.

§ 6308. Psychiatrists and psychologists; report and testimony

Section 6308 was repealed by Stats.1981, c. 928, p. 3485, § 2. For continued application to certain sex offenders, see

Historical and Statutory Notes under Welfare and Institutions Code § 6300.

Each psychiatrist or psychologist so appointed shall file with the court a separate written report of the result of his examination, together with his conclusions and recommendations and his opinion as to whether or not the person would benefit by care and treatment in a state hospital. At the hearing each psychiatrist or psychologist shall hear the testimony of all witnesses, and shall testify as to the result of his examination, and to any other pertinent facts within his knowledge, unless the person upon the advice of counsel waives the presence of the psychiatrists or psychologist and it is stipulated that their respective reports may be received in evidence. *(Added by Stats.1967, c. 1667, p. 4107, § 37, operative July 1, 1969. Amended by Stats.1968, c. 1206, p. 2287, § 4, operative July 1, 1969; Stats.1976, c. 1101, p. 4975, § 4.)*

§ 6309. Examination of psychiatrists or psychologists

Section 6309 was repealed by Stats.1981, c. 928, p. 3485, § 2. For continued application to certain sex offenders, see Historical and Statutory Notes under Welfare and Institutions Code § 6300.

Any psychiatrist or psychologist so appointed by the court may be called by either party to the proceeding or by the court itself and when so called shall be subject to all legal objections as to competency and bias and as to qualification as an expert. When called by the court, or by either party to the proceeding, the court may examine the psychiatrist or psychologist, as deemed necessary, but either party shall have the same right to object to the questions asked by the court and the evidence adduced as though the psychiatrist or psychologist were a witness for the adverse party. When the psychiatrist is called and examined by the court the parties may cross-examine him in the order directed by the court. When called by either party to the proceeding the adverse party may examine him the same as in the case of any other witness called by such party. *(Added by Stats.1967, c. 1667, p. 4107, § 37, operative July 1, 1969. Amended by Stats.1976, c. 1101, p. 4976, § 5.)*

Cross References

Calling and examining court-appointed expert, see Evidence Code § 732.
Cross-examination of expert witness, see Evidence Code § 721.
Examination of witnesses generally, see Evidence Code § 765.
Opinion testimony, see Evidence Code § 801 et seq.
Witnesses, generally, see Evidence Code § 700 et seq.

§ 6310. Fees of psychiatrists or psychologists

Section 6310 was repealed by Stats.1981, c. 928, p. 3485, § 2. For continued application to certain sex offenders, see Historical and Statutory Notes under Welfare and Institutions Code § 6300.

The psychiatrists or psychologists so appointed by the court shall be allowed such fees not exceeding one hundred fifty dollars ($150) per day, prorated by the court when services are rendered for less than a full day. The fees allowed shall be paid by the county in which the hearing is held. *(Added by Stats.1967, c. 1667, p. 4107, § 37, operative July 1, 1969. Amended by Stats.1969, c. 1140, p. 2209, § 1; Stats.1975, c. 926, p. 2043, § 1; Stats.1976, c. 1101, p. 4976, § 6.)*

§ 6311. Other expert evidence

Section 6311 was repealed by Stats.1981, c. 928, p. 3485, § 2. For continued application to certain sex offenders, see Historical and Statutory Notes under Welfare and Institutions Code § 6300.

The provisions of this article relating to psychiatrists appointed by the court shall not be deemed or construed to prevent any party to a proceeding under this article from producing any other expert evidence as to the mental condition of the alleged mentally disordered sex offender. *(Added by Stats.1967, c. 1667, p. 4107, § 37, operative July 1, 1969.)*

Cross References

Expert witnesses, generally, see Evidence Code § 720 et seq.
"Mentally disordered sex offender" defined for purposes of this Article, see Welfare and Institutions Code § 6300.
Testimony of expert witnesses, see Evidence Code § 801 et seq.
Witnesses, generally, see Evidence Code § 700 et seq.

§ 6312. Examination of other witnesses

Section 6312 was repealed by Stats.1981, c. 928, p. 3485, § 2. For continued application to certain sex offenders, see Historical and Statutory Notes under Welfare and Institutions Code § 6300.

The judge shall also cause to be examined as a witness any other person whom he believes to have knowledge of the mental condition of the alleged mentally disordered sex offender, or of the financial condition of the alleged mentally disordered sex offender and of any person liable for his support. *(Added by Stats.1967, c. 1667, p. 4107, § 37, operative July 1, 1969.)*

Cross References

Examination of witnesses, generally, see Evidence Code § 765 et seq.
"Mentally disordered sex offender" defined for purposes of this Article, see Welfare and Institutions Code § 6300.

§ 6313. Attendance of witnesses; fees and expenses

Section 6313 was repealed by Stats.1981, c. 928, p. 3485, § 2. For continued application to certain sex offenders, see Historical and Statutory Notes under Welfare and Institutions Code § 6300.

The judge may, for any hearing, order the clerk of the court to issue subpoenas and compel the attendance of witnesses from any place within the boundaries of this state, as provided by law for the trial of a criminal case.

All witnesses, other than psychiatrists or psychologists appointed by the court, attending a hearing upon a subpoena issued under this section shall be entitled to the same fees and expenses as in criminal cases, to be paid upon the same conditions and in like manner. *(Added by Stats.1967, c. 1667, p. 4107, § 37, operative July 1, 1969. Amended by Stats.1976, c. 1101, p. 4976, § 7.)*

Cross References

Evidence, means of production, see Code of Civil Procedure § 1985 et seq.
Fees and expenses of witnesses in criminal cases, see Penal Code § 1329.
Witnesses, generally, see Evidence Code § 700 et seq.

§ 6314. Presence at hearing; attorney; public defender

Section 6314 was repealed by Stats.1981, c. 928, p. 3485, § 2. For continued application to certain sex offenders, see Historical and Statutory Notes under Welfare and Institutions Code § 6300.

The alleged mentally disordered sex offender shall be present at the hearing; and if he has no attorney, the judge shall appoint the public defender or other counsel to represent him unless the defendant affirmatively, knowingly and intelligently demands to act as his own attorney. *(Added by Stats.1967, c. 1667, p. 4107, § 37, operative July 1, 1969. Amended by Stats.1976, c. 1101, p. 4976, § 8.)*

Cross References

Counsel, right of accused to, see Cal. Const. Art. 1, § 15, cl. 3; Penal Code § 686.

"Mentally disordered sex offender" defined for purposes of this Article, see Welfare and Institutions Code § 6300.

§ 6315. Hearing; findings; return to original court

Section 6315 was repealed by Stats.1981, c. 928, p. 3485, § 2. For continued application to certain sex offenders, see Historical and Statutory Notes under Welfare and Institutions Code § 6300.

If, upon the hearing, the person is found by the superior court not to be a mentally disordered sex offender, the superior court shall return the person to the court in which the case originated for such disposition as that court may deem necessary and proper. *(Added by Stats.1967, c. 1667, p. 4107, § 37, operative July 1, 1969. Amended by Stats.1970, c. 685, p. 1313, § 2.)*

Cross References

"Mentally disordered sex offender" defined for purposes of this Article, see Welfare and Institutions Code § 6300.

§ 6316. Return to criminal court for further disposition or commitment to hospital or other facility for care and treatment

Section 6316 was repealed by Stats.1981, c. 928, p. 3485, § 2. For continued application to certain sex offenders, see Historical and Statutory Notes under Welfare and Institutions Code § 6300.

(a)(1) If, after examination and hearing, the court finds that the person is a mentally disordered sex offender and that the person could benefit by treatment in a state hospital, or other treatment facility the court in its discretion has the alternative to return the person to the criminal court for further disposition, or may make an order committing the person to the department for confinement in a state hospital, or may commit the person to the county mental health director for confinement in an appropriate public or private treatment facility, approved by such director or may place the person on outpatient status under Title 15 (commencing with Section 1600) of Part 2 of the Penal Code. A copy of such commitment shall be personally served upon such person within five days after the making of such order.

If after examination and hearing, the court finds that the person is a mentally disordered sex offender but will not benefit by care or treatment in a state hospital or other treatment facility the court shall then cause the person to be returned to the court in which the criminal charge was tried to await further action with reference to such criminal charge. Such court shall resume the proceedings and shall impose sentence or make such other suitable disposition of the case as the court deems necessary.

The court shall transmit a copy of its order to the county mental health director or a designee and to the Director of Mental Health in all cases where a person is found to be a mentally disordered sex offender.

(2) Prior to making such order, the court shall order the county mental health director or a designee to evaluate the person and to submit to the court within 15 judicial days of such order a written recommendation as to whether the person should be committed to a state hospital or to another treatment facility approved by the county mental health director or be placed on outpatient status under the provisions of Title 15 (commencing with Section 1600) of Part 2 of the Penal Code. No such person shall be admitted to a state hospital or other treatment facility or placed on outpatient status without having been evaluated by the county mental health director or a designee.

(3) If the person is committed or transferred to a state hospital pursuant to this article, the committing court may, upon receiving the written recommendation of the medical director of the state hospital and the county mental health director that the person be transferred to a public or private treatment facility approved by the county mental health director, order the person transferred to such facility. If the person is committed or transferred to a public or private treatment facility approved by the county mental health director, the committing court may, upon receiving the written recommendation of the county mental health director or a designee, transfer the person to a state hospital or to another public or private treatment facility approved by the county mental health director. Where either the defendant, or the prosecutor chooses to contest either kind of order of transfer, a petition may be filed in the court for a hearing, which shall be held if the court determines that sufficient grounds exist. At such hearing, the prosecuting attorney or the defendant may present evidence bearing on the order of transfer. The court shall use the same standards used in conducting probation revocation hearings pursuant to Section 1203.2 of the Penal Code.

Prior to making an order for transfer under this section, the court shall notify the person, the prosecuting attorney, attorney of record for the person, and the county mental health director or a designee.

(b) During the time the person is confined in a state hospital or other treatment facility as an inpatient under the provisions of this article, the medical director of the facility shall, at six-month intervals, submit a report in writing to the court, and the county mental health director of the county of commitment or a designee concerning the person's progress toward recovery. The court shall supply a copy of the report to the prosecutor and the defense attorney. *(Added by Stats.1967, c. 1667, p. 4107, § 37, operative July 1, 1969. Amended by Stats.1970, c. 685, p. 1313, § 3; Stats.1971, c. 1593, p. 3360, § 418, operative July 1, 1973; Stats.1975, c. 1274, p. 3399, § 9; Stats.1976, c. 1101, p. 4976, § 9; Stats.1977, c. 164, p. 633, § 1, eff. June 29, 1977, operative July 1, 1977; Stats.1977, c. 691, p. 2232, § 5.5; Stats.1978, c. 1291, p. 4229, § 5; Stats.1980, c. 547, p. 1525, § 19.)*

Cross References

"Mentally disordered sex offender" defined for purposes of this Article, see Welfare and Institutions Code § 6300.

Outpatient status of mentally disordered criminal offenders, actual custody and credit toward maximum term of commitment or extended commitment, see Penal Code § 1600.5.

§ 6316.1. Maximum term of commitment; notice; hearing; statement

Section 6316.1 was repealed by Stats.1981, c. 928, p. 3485, § 2. For continued application to certain sex offenders, see Historical and Statutory Notes under Welfare and Institutions Code § 6300.

(a) In the case of any person found to be a mentally disordered sex offender who committed a felony on or after July 1, 1977, the court shall state in the commitment order the maximum term of commitment, and the person may not be kept in actual custody longer than the maximum term of commitment, except as provided in Section 6316.2. For the purposes of this section, "maximum term of commitment" shall mean the longest term of imprisonment which could have been imposed for the offense or offenses of which the defendant was convicted, including the upper term of the base offense and any additional terms for enhancements and consecutive sentences which could have been imposed less any applicable credits as defined by Section 2900.5 of the Penal Code and disregarding any credits which could have been earned under Sections 2930 to 2932, inclusive, of the Penal Code.

(b) In the case of a person found to be a mentally disordered sex offender who committed a felony prior to July 1, 1977, who could have been sentenced under Section 1168 or 1170 of the Penal Code if the offense were committed after July 1, 1977, the Board of Prison Terms shall determine the maximum term of commitment which could have been imposed under subdivision (a), and the person may not be kept in actual custody longer than the maximum term of commitment, except as provided in Section 6316.2.

In fixing a term under this section, the board shall utilize the upper term of imprisonment which could have been imposed for the offense or offenses of which the defendant was convicted, increased by any additional terms which could have been imposed based on matters which were found to be true in the committing court. However, if at least two of the members of the board after reviewing the person's file determine that a longer term should be imposed for the reasons specified in Section 1170.2 of the Penal Code, a longer term may be imposed following the procedures and guidelines set forth in Section 1170.2 of the Penal Code, except that any hearings deemed necessary by the board shall be held before April 1, 1978. Within 90 days of July 1, 1977, or of the date the person is received by the State Department of Mental Health, whichever is later, the Board of Prison Terms shall provide each person committed pursuant to Section 6316 with the determination of his maximum term of commitment or shall notify such person that he will be scheduled for a hearing to determine his term.

Within 20 days following the determination of the maximum term of commitment the board shall provide the person committed, the prosecuting attorney, the committing court, and the State Department of Mental Health with a written statement setting forth the maximum term of commitment, the calculations, the statements, the recommendations, and any other materials considered in determining the maximum term.

(c) In the case of a person found to be a mentally disordered sex offender who committed a misdemeanor, whether before or after July 1, 1977, the maximum term of commitment shall be the longest term of county jail confinement which could have been imposed for the offense or offenses of which the defendant was convicted, and the person may not be kept in actual custody longer than this maximum term. The provisions of this subdivision shall be applied retroactively.

(d) Nothing in this section limits the power of the State Department of Mental Health or of the committing court to release the person, conditionally or otherwise, for any period of time allowed by any other provision of law. *(Added by Stats.1977, c. 164, p. 633, § 2, eff. June 29, 1977, operative July 1, 1977. Amended by Stats.1979, c. 373, p. 1399, § 369; Stats.1979, c. 255, p. 570, § 63.)*

Cross References

Felonies, definition and penalties, see Penal Code §§ 17, 18.
"Mentally disordered sex offender" defined for purposes of this Article, see Welfare and Institutions Code § 6300.
Misdemeanors, definition and penalties, see Penal Code §§ 17, 19 and 19.2.

§ 6316.2. Commitment beyond maximum term; procedure

Section 6316.2 was repealed by Stats.1981, c. 928, p. 3485, § 2. For continued application to certain sex offenders, see Historical and Statutory Notes under Welfare and Institutions Code § 6300.

(a) A person may be committed beyond the term prescribed by Section 6316.1 only under the procedure set forth in this section and only if such person meets all of the following:

(1) The "sex offense" as defined in subdivision (a) of Section 6302 of which the person has been convicted is a felony, whether committed before or after July 1, 1977, or is a misdemeanor which was committed before July 1, 1977.

(2) Suffers from a mental disease, defect, or disorder, and as a result of such mental disease, defect, or disorder, is predisposed to the commission of sexual offenses to such a degree that he presents a substantial danger of bodily harm to others.

(b) If during a commitment under this part, the Director of Mental Health has good cause to believe that a patient is a person described in subdivision (a), the director may submit such supporting evaluations and case file to the prosecuting attorney who may file a petition for extended commitment in the superior court which issued the original commitment. Such petition shall be filed no later than 90 days before the expiration of the original commitment. Such petition shall state the reasons for the extended commitment, with accompanying affidavits specifying the factual basis for believing that the person meets each of the requirements set forth in subdivision (a).

(c) At the time of filing a petition, the court shall advise the patient named in the petition of his right to be represented by an attorney and of his right to a jury trial. The rules of discovery in criminal cases shall apply.

(d) The court shall conduct a hearing on the petition for extended commitment. The trial shall be by jury unless waived by both the patient and the prosecuting attorney. The trial shall commence no later than 30 days prior to the time the patient would otherwise have been released by the State Department of Mental Health.

(e) The patient shall be entitled to the rights guaranteed under the Federal and State Constitutions for criminal proceedings. All proceedings shall be in accordance with applicable constitutional guarantees. The State Controller shall reimburse the counties for all expenses of transportation, care and custody of the patient and all trial and related costs. The state shall be represented by the Attorney General or the district attorney with the consent of the Attorney General. If the patient is indigent, the State Public Defender shall be appointed. The State Public Defender may provide for representation of the patient in any manner authorized by Section 15402 of the Government Code. Appointment of necessary psychologists or psychiatrists shall be made in accordance with this article and Penal Code and Evidence Code provisions applicable to criminal defendants who have entered pleas of not guilty by reason of insanity or asserted diminished capacity defenses.

(f) If the court or jury finds that the patient is a person described in subdivision (a), the court may order the patient committed to the State Department of Mental Health in a treatment facility. A commitment or a recommitment under Section 6316.1 shall be for a period of two years from the date of termination of the previous commitment.

(g) A person committed under this section to the State Department of Mental Health shall be eligible for outpatient release as provided in this article.

(h) Prior to termination of a commitment under this section, a petition for recommitment may be filed to determine whether the person remains a person described in subdivision (a). Such recommitment proceeding shall be conducted in accordance with the provisions of this article.

(i) Any commitment to the State Department of Mental Health under this article places an affirmative obligation on the department to provide treatment for the underlying causes of the person's mental disorder.

(j) Amenability to treatment is not required for a finding that any person is a person as described in subdivision (a), nor is it required for treatment of such person. Treatment programs need only be made available to such person. Treatment does not mean that the treatment be successful or potentially successful, nor does it mean that the person must recognize his or her problem and willingly participate in the treatment program.

(k) The person committed pursuant to this section shall be confined in a state hospital unless released as an outpatient as provided in Section 6325.1. The Director of Mental Health may, with the consent of the Director of Corrections, transfer the person to a treatment unit in the Department of Corrections for confinement and treatment if the person is not amenable for treatment in existing hospital programs or is in need of stricter security and custody measures than are available within the state hospitals. The treatment unit shall be designated by the Director of Corrections. A person transferred under this section shall be entitled to a hearing by the State Department of Mental Health to determine whether he may be confined and treated in a state hospital.

The person shall be entitled to be present at the hearing, to ask and answer questions, to speak on his own behalf, and to offer relevant evidence. The hearing shall be held before any transfer to the Department of Corrections unless the person is already in the custody of the Director of Corrections or the need for transfer becomes immediate making a hearing before transfer impractical.

Any person transferred to the Department of Corrections pursuant to this section shall be entitled to treatment of a kind and quality similar to that which he would receive if confined by the State Department of Mental Health. He shall be treated in a unit at a level of staffing that will enable him to receive the equivalent quality of care and therapy that would be received in a similar state hospital program.

(*l*) The provisions of Section 6327 shall apply to a commitment ordered pursuant to this section. *(Added by Stats.1977, c. 164, p. 634, § 3, eff. June 29, 1977, operative July 1, 1977. Amended by Stats.1978, c. 1036, p. 3198, § 1, eff. Sept. 25, 1978; Stats.1978, c. 1039, p. 3225, § 2; Stats.1979, c. 991, p. 3373, § 1; Stats.1979, c. 992, p. 3377, § 1, eff. Sept. 22, 1979; Stats.1979, c. 992, p. 3379, § 2, eff. Sept. 22, 1979, operative Jan. 1, 1980.)*

Cross References

Attorney General, generally, see Government Code § 12500 et seq.
Department of Corrections and Rehabilitation, generally, see Penal Code § 5000 et seq.
Felonies, definition and penalties, see Penal Code §§ 17, 18.
Misdemeanors, definition and penalties, see Penal Code §§ 17, 19 and 19.2.
Outpatient status of mentally disordered criminal offenders, actual custody and credit toward maximum term of commitment or extended commitment, see Penal Code § 1600.5.
State Controller, generally, see Government Code § 12402 et seq.

Research References

1 Witkin California Criminal Law 4th Introduction to Crimes § 25 (2021), Other Valid Statutes.
3 Witkin, California Criminal Law 4th Punishment § 247 (2021), Punishment for Disease or Status.

§ 6318. Demand for trial; date; finding or verdict

Section 6318 was repealed by Stats.1981, c. 928, p. 3485, § 2. For continued application to certain sex offenders, see Historical and Statutory Notes under Welfare and Institutions Code § 6300.

If a person ordered under Section 6316 to be committed as a mentally disordered sex offender to the department for placement in a state hospital for care and treatment or to the county mental health director for placement in an appropriate facility, or any friend in his behalf, is dissatisfied with the order of the judge so committing him, he may, within 15 days after the making of such order, demand that the question of his being a mentally disordered sex offender be tried by a judge or by a jury in the superior court of the county in which he was committed. Thereupon the court shall set the case for hearing at a date, or shall cause a jury to be summoned and to be in attendance at a date stated, not less than five nor more than 10 days from the date of the demand for a court or jury trial. The court shall adjudge whether the person is a mentally disordered sex offender, or if it is a trial by jury the judge shall submit to the jury the question: Are you convinced to a moral certainty and beyond a reasonable doubt that the defendant is a mentally disordered sex offender? *(Added by Stats.1967, c. 1667, p. 4107, § 37, operative July 1, 1969. Amended by Stats.1970, c. 685, p. 1314, § 4; Stats.1975, c. 1274, p. 3400, §11; Stats.1976, c. 1101, p. 4977, § 11.)*

Cross References

Jury trial,
Conservatorship for gravely disabled, see Welfare and Institutions Code §§ 5350, 5362.
Constitutional right to, see Cal. Const. Art. 1, § 16.
"Mentally disordered sex offender" defined for purposes of this Article, see Welfare and Institutions Code § 6300.

§ 6319. Stay of proceedings

Section 6319 was repealed by Stats.1981, c. 928, p. 3485, § 2. For continued application to certain sex offenders, see Historical and Statutory Notes under Welfare and Institutions Code § 6300.

Proceedings under this article under the order for commitment to the department for placement in a state hospital or to a county mental health director for placement in an appropriate facility shall not be stayed, pending the proceedings for determining the question of whether the person is a mentally disordered sex offender by a judge or jury, except upon the order of a superior court judge, with provision made therein for such temporary care and custody of the person as the judge deems necessary. If the superior court judge, by the order granting the stay, commits the person to the custody of any person other than a peace officer, he may, by such order, require a bond for his appearance at the trial. *(Added by Stats.1967, c. 1667, p. 4107, § 37, operative July 1, 1969. Amended by Stats.1975, c. 1274, p. 3400, § 12.)*

Cross References

"Mentally disordered sex offender" defined for purposes of this Article, see Welfare and Institutions Code § 6300.

§ 6320. Duties of district attorney

Section 6320 was repealed by Stats.1981, c. 928, p. 3485, § 2. For continued application to certain sex offenders, see Historical and Statutory Notes under Welfare and Institutions Code § 6300.

At the trial the petition and its allegations that the person is a mentally disordered sex offender shall be presented by the district attorney of the county. *(Added by Stats.1967, c. 1667, p. 4107, § 37, operative July 1, 1969.)*

Cross References

District attorney, see Government Code § 26500.
Duties of district attorney in mental health proceedings, see Government Code § 26530.
"Mentally disordered sex offender" defined for purposes of this Article, see Welfare and Institutions Code § 6300.

§ 6321. Trial; verdict; court order

Section 6321 was repealed by Stats.1981, c. 928, p. 3485, § 2. For continued application to certain sex offenders, see Historical and Statutory Notes under Welfare and Institutions Code § 6300.

The trial shall be had as provided by law for the trial of criminal causes, and if tried before a jury the person shall be discharged unless a verdict that he is a mentally disordered sex offender is found unanimously by the jury. If the judge adjudges or the verdict of the jury is that he is a mentally disordered sex offender the judge shall adjudge that fact and make an order similar to the original order for commitment to the department for placement in a state hospital or to a county mental health director for placement in an appropriate facility. The order committing the person to the department for placement in a state hospital or other facility shall be presented to the superintendent of the state hospital or other facility or other representative of the department to whom the person is committed. *(Added by Stats.1967, c. 1667, p. 4107, § 37, operative July 1, 1969. Amended by Stats.1975, c. 1274, p. 3401, § 13; Stats.1976, c. 1101, p. 4978, § 12.)*

Cross References

"Mentally disordered sex offender" defined for purposes of this Article, see Welfare and Institutions Code § 6300.
Trial by court, see Code of Civil Procedure § 631 et seq.
Verdict,
Generally, see Code of Civil Procedure § 624 et seq.
Polling jurors as to, see Code of Civil Procedure § 618.
Three-fourths of jury to render, see Cal. Const. Art. 1, § 16.

§ 6322. Execution of writ; fees; expenses

Section 6322 was repealed by Stats.1981, c. 928, p. 3485, § 2. For continued application to certain sex offenders, see Historical and Statutory Notes under Welfare and Institutions Code § 6300.

The sheriff of any county wherein an order is made by the court committing a person for an indeterminate period to a state hospital or other facility or returning such person to the court, or any other peace officer designated by the court, shall execute the writ of commitment or order of return, and receive as compensation therefor such fees as are now or may hereafter be provided by law for the transportation of prisoners to the state prison, which shall be payable in the same manner.

The expense of transporting a person to a county facility or state hospital temporarily for an observation placement under this article and returning such person to the court is a charge upon the county in which the court is situated. *(Added by Stats.1967, c. 1667, p. 4107, § 37, operative July 1, 1969. Amended by Stats.1975, c. 1274, p. 3401, § 14.)*

Cross References

Expenses for transporting persons to state institutions, see Government Code § 26749.

§ 6323. Delivery of documents

Section 6323 was repealed by Stats.1981, c. 928, p. 3485, § 2. For continued application to certain sex offenders, see Historical and Statutory Notes under Welfare and Institutions Code § 6300.

Certified copies of the affidavit, certification from the trial court, order for examination or detention, order for hearing and examination, report of the probation officer and of the court-appointed psychiatrists, and the order of commitment for an indeterminate period shall be delivered to the person transporting the mentally disordered sex offender to the state hospital or other facility, and shall be delivered by that person to the officer in charge of the hospital or other facility. *(Added by Stats.1967, c. 1667, p. 4107, § 37, operative July 1, 1969. Amended by Stats.1970, c. 685, p. 1314, § 5; Stats.1975, c. 1274, p. 3401, § 15.)*

Cross References

"Mentally disordered sex offender" defined for purposes of this Article, see Welfare and Institutions Code § 6300.

§ 6324. Applicable laws

Section 6324 was repealed by Stats.1981, c. 928, p. 3485, § 2. For continued application to certain sex offenders, see Historical and Statutory Notes under Welfare and Institutions Code § 6300.

The provisions of Section 4025 and of Article 4 (commencing with Section 7275) of Chapter 3 of Division 7 relative to the property and care and support of persons in state hospitals, the liability for such care and support, and the powers and duties of the State Department of Mental Health and all officers and employees thereof in connection therewith shall apply to persons committed to state hospitals or to other facilities pursuant to this article the same as if such persons were expressly referred to in Section 4025 and Article 4 (commencing with Section 7275) of Chapter 3 of Division 7. *(Formerly § 5516, added by Stats.1965, c. 391, p. 1651, § 5, eff. May 25, 1965. Amended by Stats.1967, c. 1620, p. 3863, § 6, eff. Aug. 30, 1967. Renumbered § 6324 and amended by Stats.1968, c. 1374, p. 2664, § 60, operative July 1, 1969. Amended by Stats.1973, c. 142, p. 423, § 79.4, eff. June 30, 1973, operative July 1, 1973; Stats.1975, c. 1274, p. 3401, § 16; Stats.1977, c. 1252, p. 4601, § 638, operative July 1, 1978.)*

§ 6325. Certification as to recovery; return to court; probation; credit for hospitalization time

Section 6325 was repealed by Stats.1981, c. 928, p. 3485, § 2. For continued application to certain sex offenders, see Historical and Statutory Notes under Welfare and Institutions Code § 6300.

(a) Whenever a person who is committed to a state hospital or other treatment facility under the provisions of this article or placed on outpatient status under Title 15 (commencing with Section 1600) of Part 2 of the Penal Code has been treated to such an extent that in the opinion of the medical director of the state hospital or other facility or the outpatient treatment supervisor under Title 15 (commencing with Section 1600) of Part 2 of the Penal Code, the person will not benefit by further care and treatment and is not a danger to the health and safety of others, the medical director or person in charge of the facility or county mental health director or a designee where the person is on outpatient status, shall file with the committing court a certification of that opinion including therein a report, diagnosis, and recommendation concerning the persons's future care, supervision, or treatment.

(b) Whenever a person who is committed to a state hospital or other treatment facility under the provisions of this article or who is placed on outpatient status under Title 15 (commencing with Section 1600) of Part 2 of the Penal Code has not recovered, and in the opinion of the medical director of the state hospital or other facility or of the county mental health director where the patient is on outpatient status the person is still a danger to the health and safety of others, the director shall file with the committing court a certification of that opinion, including therein a report, diagnosis and recommendation concerning the person's future care, supervision or treatment.

(c) The court shall transmit a copy of the opinion certified under subdivision (a) or (b) to the county mental health director or a designee and shall give notice of the hearing date to the county mental health director or a designee and to the Director of Mental Health.

Upon the expiration of the time for making a motion pursuant to Section 6325.2, upon the denial of such motion, or upon the entry of a finding that the person is no longer a mentally disordered sex offender after a hearing pursuant to Section 6327, the committing court shall order the return of the person to the committing court. The committing court shall thereafter cause the person to be returned to the court in which the criminal charge was tried to await further action with reference to such criminal charge.

Such court shall resume the proceedings, upon the return of the person to the court, and after considering all the evidence before it may place the person on probation upon such terms as may be required to protect the public if the criminal charge permits such probation and the person is otherwise eligible for probation. In any case, where the person is sentenced on a criminal charge, the time the person spent under indeterminate commitment as a mentally disordered sex offender shall be credited by the court or community release board against such sentence. The court in which the criminal case was tried shall notify the county mental health director or a designee and the Director of Mental Health of the outcome of the criminal proceedings. *(Added by Stats.1967, c. 1667, p. 4107, § 37, operative July 1, 1969. Amended by Stats.1975, c. 1274, p. 3402, § 17; Stats.1976, c. 1101, p. 4979, § 13.1; Stats.1978, c. 1291, p. 4230, § 7; Stats.1980, c. 547, p. 1529, § 21.)*

Cross References

"Mentally disordered sex offender" defined for purposes of this Article, see Welfare and Institutions Code § 6300.

Research References

5 Witkin, California Criminal Law 4th Criminal Trial § 813 (2021), Termination of Outpatient Status.

3 Witkin, California Criminal Law 4th Punishment § 178 (2021), Former Statute: Scope and Repeal.

§ 6325.1. Authority to place committed person on outpatient status

Section 6325.1 was repealed by Stats.1981, c. 928, p. 3485, § 2. For continued application to certain sex offenders, see Historical and Statutory Notes under Welfare and Institutions Code § 6300.

A person committed pursuant to Section 6316.2 may be placed on outpatient status as provided in Title 15 (commencing with Section 1600) of Part 2 of the Penal Code. *(Added by Stats.1980, c. 547, p. 1527, § 23.)*

§ 6325.2. Motion for new examination; time; hearing; court order

Section 6325.2 was repealed by Stats.1981, c. 928, p. 3485, § 2. For continued application to certain sex offenders, see Historical and Statutory Notes under Welfare and Institutions Code § 6300.

When a person is returned to the committing court pursuant to Section 6325, either party may move for a new examination and hearing pursuant to Sections 6306 through 6318, inclusive, within five days of the person's arrival. The motion may be granted if the moving party shows by affidavit the existence of facts which establish that the opinion certified under subdivision (a) or (b) of Section 6325 was an abuse of discretion. Such hearing shall be set to commence within 30 days of the person's return to court. If the opinion certified was under subdivision (a) of Section 6325, and a new hearing is granted upon motion of the people, the person shall be entitled to be admitted to bail or released on his own recognizance in the manner provided by law for criminal cases. If, at the conclusion of a hearing pursuant to this section, the person is found to remain a mentally disordered sex offender who could benefit by treatment in the state hospital or other mental health facility, the court may direct that the previous order of commitment remain in full force and effect. *(Formerly § 6325.1, added by Stats.1976, c. 1101, p. 4979, § 13.5. Renumbered § 6325.2 and amended by Stats.1977, c. 691, p. 2233, § 8.)*

Cross References

"Mentally disordered sex offender" defined for purposes of this Article, see Welfare and Institutions Code § 6300.

§ 6325.3. Authority to place committed person on outpatient status

Section 6325.3 was repealed by Stats.1981, c. 928, p. 3485, § 2. For continued application to certain sex offenders, see Historical and Statutory Notes under Welfare and Institutions Code § 6300.

A person committed to a state hospital or other treatment facility under the provisions of Section 6316 or 6321 may be placed on outpatient status from such commitment as provided in Title 15 (commencing with Section 1600) of Part 2 of the Penal Code. *(Added by Stats.1980, c. 547, p. 1528, § 24.)*

§ 6325.5. Certification of no recovery and continued menace; release upon probation or other court disposition

Section 6325.5 was repealed by Stats.1981, c. 928, p. 3485, § 2. For continued application to certain sex offenders, see Historical and Statutory Notes under Welfare and Institutions Code § 6300.

If the opinion so certified is under subdivision (b) of Section 6325, the person may not be released until such time as probation is granted or such other disposition as the court may deem necessary and proper is made of the case. *(Added by Stats.1973, c. 346, p. 770, § 1.)*

§ 6327. Persons committed for indeterminate period; report; return to court; hearing; recommitment; subsequent hearings; recovery and return to criminal court

Section 6327 was repealed by Stats.1981, c. 928, p. 3485, § 2. For continued application to certain sex offenders, see Historical and Statutory Notes under Welfare and Institutions Code § 6300.

After a person has been committed to the State Department of Mental Health for placement in a state hospital or to a county mental health director for placement in a treatment facility as a mentally disordered sex offender and has been confined or released on outpatient status pursuant to Title 15 (commencing with Section 1600) of Part 2 of the Penal Code for a period of not less than six months from the date of the order of commitment, the committing court may upon its own motion or on motion by or on behalf of the person committed, require the medical director of the state hospital or other facility or the outpatient supervisor, as appropriate, to forward to the committing court and to the county mental health director or a designee, within 30 days an opinion under subdivision (a) or (b) of Section 6325, including therein a report, diagnosis, and recommendation concerning the person's future care, supervision, or treatment. After receipt of the report, the committing court may order the return of the person to the court for a hearing as to whether the person is still a mentally disordered sex offender within the meaning of this article.

The court shall give notice of the hearing date to the county mental health director or a designee and to the Director of Mental Health.

The hearing shall be conducted substantially in accordance with Sections 6306 to 6314, inclusive. If, after the hearing, the judge finds that the person has not recovered from the mental disorder and is still a danger to the health and safety of others, the judge shall order the person returned to the State Department of Mental Health or county mental health director under the prior order of commitment. The court shall transmit a copy of its order to the county mental health director or a designee and to the Director of Mental Health. A subsequent hearing may not be held under this section until the person has been confined or on outpatient status for an additional period of six months from the date of return to the department or county mental health director. If the court finds that the person has recovered from the mental disorder to such an extent that the person is no longer a danger to the health and safety of others, or that the person will not benefit by further care and treatment in the hospital or other facility and is not a danger to the health and safety of others, the committing court shall thereafter cause the person to be returned to the court in which the criminal charge was tried to await further action with reference to such criminal charge. The court in which the criminal charge was tried shall notify the county mental health director or a designee and the Director of Mental Health of the outcome of the criminal proceedings. *(Added by Stats.1967, c. 1667, p. 4107, § 37, operative July 1, 1969. Amended by Stats.1971, c. 1593, p. 3362, § 420, operative July 1, 1973; Stats.1975, c. 1274, p. 3405, § 19; Stats.1976, c. 1101, p. 4980, § 15; Stats.1977, c. 1252, p. 4602, § 639, operative July 1, 1978; Stats.1979, c. 991, p. 3376, § 3; Stats.1980, c. 547, p. 1528, § 25.)*

Cross References

"Mentally disordered sex offender" defined for purposes of this Article, see Welfare and Institutions Code § 6300.

§ 6328. Privileges of persons confined

Section 6328 was repealed by Stats.1981, c. 928, p. 3485, § 2. For continued application to certain sex offenders, see

Historical and Statutory Notes under Welfare and Institutions Code § 6300.

The superintendent of a state hospital or other facility may extend to any person confined therein pursuant to this article such of the privileges granted to other patients of the hospital or facility as are not incompatible with his detention or unreasonably conducive to his escape from custody. *(Added by Stats.1967, c. 1667, p. 4107, § 37, operative July 1, 1969. Amended by Stats.1975, c. 1274, p. 3405, § 20.)*

§ 6329. District attorney; appearance for people

Section 6329 was repealed by Stats.1981, c. 928, p. 3485, § 2. For continued application to certain sex offenders, see Historical and Statutory Notes under Welfare and Institutions Code § 6300.

The district attorney of the county may appear on behalf of the people at any of the hearings held pursuant to this article. *(Added by Stats.1967, c. 1667, p. 4107, § 37, operative July 1, 1969.)*

§ 6330. Escape; punishment

Section 6330 was repealed by Stats.1981, c. 928, p. 3485, § 2. For continued application to certain sex offenders, see Historical and Statutory Notes under Welfare and Institutions Code § 6300.

Every person committed to a state hospital or state institution or other public or private mental health facility as a mentally disordered sex offender, who escapes from or who escapes while being conveyed to or from such county facility, state hospital or state institution, is punishable by imprisonment in the state prison; or in the county jail not to exceed one year. *(Added by Stats.1967, c. 1667, p. 4107, § 37, operative July 1, 1969. Amended by Stats.1975, c. 1274, p. 3406, § 21; Stats.1976, c. 1139, p. 5174, § 345; Stats.1976, c. 1101, p. 5180, § 16.)*

Cross References

Escapes,
Aiding or abetting, see Penal Code §§ 109, 4534.
Attempts, see Penal Code § 4530 et seq.
Juvenile delinquents, institutions for, see Welfare and Institutions Code §§ 1152, 7325 et seq.
Mentally disordered, see Welfare and Institutions Code § 7325 et seq.
"Mentally disordered sex offender" defined for purposes of this Article, see Welfare and Institutions Code § 6300.
Payment of costs of trial of person charged with escape or attempt to escape, see Welfare and Institutions Code § 4117.

Research References

California Jury Instructions - Criminal 7.30, Escape Without Force or Violence—Defined.

§ 6331. Operative effect of article; application to persons already committed; amendment of section

Article 1 was repealed by Stats.1981, c. 928, § 2. For continued application to certain sex offenders, see Historical and Statutory Notes under Welfare and Institutions Code § 6300.

This article shall become inoperative the day after the election at which the electors adopt this section, except that the article shall continue to apply in all respects to those already committed under its provisions.

The provisions of this section shall not be amended by the Legislature except by statute passed in each house by rollcall vote entered in the journal, two-thirds of the membership concurring, or by a statute that becomes effective only when approved by the electors. *(Added by Initiative Measure, approved by the people, June 8, 1982.)*

Research References

1 Witkin California Criminal Law 4th Introduction to Crimes § 124 (2021), Constitutional Provisions and Statutes.

§ 6332. Outpatient status; actual custody and credit toward maximum term of commitment or term of extended commitment; time spent in locked facilities

Article 1 was repealed by Stats.1981, c. 928, § 2. For continued application to certain sex offenders, see Historical and Statutory Notes under Welfare and Institutions Code § 6300.

For a person committed as a mentally disordered sex offender, whose term of commitment has been extended pursuant to former Section 6316.2, and who is placed on outpatient status pursuant to Section 1604 of the Penal Code, time spent on outpatient status, except when placed in a locked facility at the direction of the outpatient supervisor, shall not count as actual custody and shall not be counted toward the person's maximum term of commitment or toward the person's term of extended commitment. *(Added by Stats.1993–94, 1st Ex.Sess., c. 9 (S.B.39), § 3.)*

Cross References

"Mentally disordered sex offender" defined for purposes of this Article, see Welfare and Institutions Code § 6300.

ARTICLE 2. PERSONS WITH INTELLECTUAL DISABILITIES

§ 6500. "Dangerousness to self or others" and "Developmental disability" defined; commitment of persons dangerous to self or others or in acute crisis; counsel; duty of district attorney or county counsel; expiration of commitment order

(a) For purposes of this article, the following definitions shall apply:

(1) "Dangerousness to self or others" shall include, but not be limited to, a finding of incompetence to stand trial pursuant to the provisions of Chapter 6 (commencing with Section 1367) of Title 10 of Part 2 of the Penal Code when the defendant has been charged with murder, mayhem, aggravated mayhem, a violation of Section

207, 209, or 209.5 of the Penal Code in which the victim suffers intentionally inflicted great bodily injury, robbery perpetrated by torture or by a person armed with a dangerous or deadly weapon or in which the victim suffers great bodily injury, carjacking perpetrated by torture or by a person armed with a dangerous or deadly weapon or in which the victim suffers great bodily injury, a violation of subdivision (b) of Section 451 of the Penal Code, a violation of paragraph (1) or (2) of subdivision (a) of former Section 262 or paragraph (2) or (3) of subdivision (a) of Section 261 of the Penal Code, a violation of Section 288 of the Penal Code, any of the following acts when committed by force, violence, duress, menace, fear of immediate and unlawful bodily injury on the victim or another person: a violation of paragraph (1) or (2) of subdivision (a) of former Section 262 of the Penal Code, a violation of Section 264.1, 286, or 287 of, or former Section 288a of, the Penal Code, or a violation of subdivision (a) of Section 289 of the Penal Code; a violation of Section 459 of the Penal Code in the first degree, assault with intent to commit murder, a violation of Section 220 of the Penal Code in which the victim suffers great bodily injury, a violation of Section 18725, 18740, 18745, 18750, or 18755 of the Penal Code, or if the defendant has been charged with a felony involving death, great bodily injury, or an act that poses a serious threat of bodily harm to another person.

(2) "Developmental disability" shall have the same meaning as defined in subdivision (a) of Section 4512.

(b)(1) A person with a developmental disability may be committed to the State Department of Developmental Services for residential placement other than in a developmental center or state-operated community facility, as provided in subdivision (a) of Section 6509, if the person is found to be a danger to self or others.

(A) An order of commitment made pursuant to this paragraph shall expire automatically one year after the order of commitment is made.

(B) This paragraph does not prohibit any party enumerated in Section 6502 from filing subsequent petitions for additional periods of commitment. If subsequent petitions are filed, the procedures followed shall be the same as with the initial petition for commitment.

(2) A person with a developmental disability shall not be committed to the State Department of Developmental Services for placement in a developmental center or state-operated community facility pursuant to this article unless the person meets the criteria for admission to a developmental center or state-operated community facility pursuant to paragraph (2), (3), (4), (5), or (7) of subdivision (a) of Section 7505 and is dangerous to self or others, or as a result of an acute crisis, or the person currently is a resident of a state developmental center or state-operated community facility pursuant to an order of commitment made pursuant to this article prior to July 1, 2012, and is being recommitted pursuant to paragraph (4) of this subdivision.

(3) If the person with a developmental disability is in the care or treatment of a state hospital, developmental center, or other facility at the time a petition for commitment is filed pursuant to this article, proof of a recent overt act while in the care and treatment of a state hospital, developmental center, or other facility is not required in order to find that the person is a danger to self or others.

(4) If subsequent petitions are filed with respect to a resident of a developmental center or a state-operated community facility committed prior to July 1, 2012, the procedures followed and criteria for recommitment shall be the same as with the initial petition for commitment.

(5) In any proceedings conducted under the authority of this article, the person alleged to have a developmental disability shall be informed of their right to counsel by the court and, if the person does not have an attorney for the proceedings, the court shall immediately appoint the public defender or other attorney to represent them. The person shall pay the cost for the legal services if the person is able to do so. At any judicial proceeding under this article, allegations that a person has a developmental disability and is dangerous to self or others, or as a result of an acute crisis, shall be presented by the district attorney for the county unless the board of supervisors, by ordinance or resolution, delegates this authority to the county counsel. The regional center shall inform the clients' rights advocate, as described in Section 4433, when a petition is filed under this section and when a petition expires. The clients' rights advocate for the regional center may attend any judicial proceedings to assist in protecting the individual's rights.

(c)(1) An order of commitment made pursuant to this article with respect to a person described in paragraph (3) of subdivision (a) of Section 7505 shall expire automatically one year after the order of commitment is made. This section does not prohibit a party enumerated in Section 6502 from filing subsequent petitions for additional periods of commitment. If subsequent petitions are filed, the procedures followed shall be the same as with an initial petition for commitment.

(2) An order of commitment made pursuant to this article on or after July 1, 2012, with respect to the admission to a developmental center or state-operated community facility of a person described in paragraph (2), (4), or (7) of subdivision (a) of Section 7505 shall expire automatically six months after the earlier of the order of commitment pursuant to this section or the order of a placement in a developmental center pursuant to Section 6506, unless the regional center, prior to the expiration of the order of commitment, notifies the court in writing of the need for an extension. The required notice shall state facts demonstrating that the individual continues to be in acute crisis, as defined in paragraph (1) of subdivision (d) of Section 4418.7, and the justification for the requested extension, and shall be accompanied by the comprehensive assessment and plan described in subdivision (e) of Section 4418.7. An order granting an extension shall not extend the total period of commitment beyond one year, including a placement in a developmental center pursuant to Section 6506. If, prior to expiration of one year, the regional center notifies the court in writing of facts demonstrating that, due to circumstances beyond the regional center's control, the placement cannot be made prior to expiration of the extension, and the court determines that good cause exists, the court may grant one further extension of up to 30 days. The court may also issue any orders the court deems appropriate to ensure that necessary steps are taken to ensure that the individual can be safely and appropriately transitioned to the community in a timely manner. The required notice shall state facts demonstrating that the regional center has made significant progress implementing the plan described in subdivision (e) of Section 4418.7 and that extraordinary circumstances exist beyond the regional center's control that have prevented the plan's implementation. This paragraph does not preclude the individual or a person acting on the person's behalf from making a request for release pursuant to Section 4800, or counsel for the individual from filing a petition for habeas corpus pursuant to Section 4801. Notwithstanding subdivision (a) of Section 4801, for purposes of this paragraph, judicial review shall be in the superior court of the county that issued the order of commitment pursuant to this section.

(3) An order of commitment made pursuant to this article on or after January 1, 2020, with respect to the admission to an institution for mental disease, as described in subparagraph (C) of paragraph (9) of subdivision (a) of Section 4648, shall expire automatically six months after the earlier of the order of commitment pursuant to this section, the order of a placement in an institution for mental disease pursuant to Section 6506, or the date the regional center placed the individual in the institution for mental disease, unless the regional center notifies the court in writing of the need for an extension. The required notice shall state facts demonstrating that the individual continues to be in acute crisis, as defined in paragraph (1) of subdivision (d) of Section 4418.7, and the justification for the requested extension, and shall be accompanied by the comprehensive

assessment and plan described in clause (v) of subparagraph (C) of paragraph (9) of subdivision (a) of Section 4648. An order granting an extension shall not extend the total period of commitment beyond one year, including a placement in an institution for mental disease pursuant to Section 6506. If, prior to expiration of one year, the regional center notifies the court in writing of facts demonstrating that, due to circumstances beyond the regional center's control, the placement cannot be made prior to expiration of the extension, and the court determines that good cause exists, the court may grant one further extension of up to 30 days. The court may also issue any orders the court deems appropriate in order for necessary steps to be taken to ensure that the individual can be safely and appropriately transitioned to the community in a timely manner. The required notice shall state facts demonstrating that the regional center has made significant progress implementing the plan described in clause (v) of subparagraph (C) of paragraph (9) of subdivision (a) of Section 4648 and that extraordinary circumstances exist beyond the regional center's control that have prevented the plan's implementation. This paragraph does not preclude the individual or any person acting on their own behalf from making a request for release pursuant to Section 4800, or counsel for the individual from filing a petition for habeas corpus pursuant to Section 4801. Notwithstanding subdivision (a) of Section 4801, for purposes of this paragraph, judicial review shall be in the superior court of the county that issued the order of commitment pursuant to this section. *(Formerly § 6500.1, added by Stats.1970, c. 351, p. 765, § 3. Amended by Stats.1971, c. 1593, p. 3363, § 421.1, operative July 1, 1973; Stats.1975, c. 694, p. 1651, § 27; Stats.1977, c. 1252, p. 4603, § 641, operative July 1, 1978; Stats.1977, c. 695, p. 2248, § 7; Stats.1978, c. 429, p. 1462, § 220. Renumbered § 6500 and amended by Stats.1978, c. 1319, p. 4316, § 2. Amended by Stats.1989, c. 897, § 47; Stats.1993, c. 610 (A.B.6), § 33, eff. Oct. 1, 1993; Stats.1993, c. 611 (S.B.60), § 37, eff. Oct. 1, 1993; Stats.1994, c. 224 (S.B.1436), § 10; Stats.1996, c. 1075 (S.B.1444), § 20; Stats.1996, c. 1076 (S.B.1391), § 5; Stats.2010, c. 178 (S.B. 1115), § 102, operative Jan. 1, 2012; Stats.2012, c. 25 (A.B.1472), § 19, eff. June 27, 2012; Stats.2012, c. 439 (A.B.1471), § 21, eff. Sept. 22, 2012; Stats.2013, c. 25 (A.B.89), § 11, eff. June 27, 2013; Stats.2018, c. 423 (S.B.1494), § 127, eff. Jan. 1, 2019; Stats.2018, c. 884 (S.B.175), § 1, eff. Sept. 28, 2018; Stats.2018, c. 884 (S.B.175), § 1.5, eff. Sept. 28, 2018, operative Jan. 1, 2019; Stats.2019, c. 28 (S.B.81), § 31, eff. June 27, 2019; Stats.2021, c. 76 (A.B.136), § 54, eff. July 16, 2021; Stats.2021, c. 626 (A.B.1171), § 74, eff. Jan. 1, 2022.)*

Validity

This section was held unconstitutional in the decision of People v. Bailie (App. 3 Dist., 2006) 50 Cal.Rptr.3d 761, 144 Cal.App.4th 841.

Law Revision Commission Comments

Section 6500 is amended to reflect nonsubstantive reorganization of the statutes governing control of deadly weapons. [38 Cal.L.Rev.Comm. Reports 217 (2009)].

Cross References

Felonies, definition and penalties, see Penal Code §§ 17, 18.
Roster of judicially committed retarded persons, see Welfare and Institutions Code § 4509.

Research References

5 Witkin, California Criminal Law 4th Criminal Trial § 848 (2021), Developmental Disability.

§ 6501. Persons charged with violent felonies; placement

If a person is charged with a violent felony, as described in Section 667.5 of the Penal Code, and the individual has been committed to the State Department of Developmental Services pursuant to Section 1370.1 of the Penal Code or Section 6500 for placement in a secure treatment facility, as described in subdivision (e) of Section 1370.1 of the Penal Code, the department shall give priority to placing the individual at Porterville Developmental Center prior to placing the individual at any other secure treatment facility. *(Added by Stats. 1999, c. 146 (A.B.1107), § 29, eff. July 22, 1999. Amended by Stats.2012, c. 25 (A.B.1472), § 20, eff. June 27, 2012.)*

Cross References

Department of Developmental Services, see Welfare and Institutions Code § 4400 et seq.
Felonies, definition and penalties, see Penal Code §§ 17, 18.

§ 6502. Petition

A petition for the commitment of a person with a developmental disability to the State Department of Developmental Services who has been found incompetent to stand trial pursuant to Chapter 6 (commencing with Section 1367) of Title 10 of Part 2 of the Penal Code when the defendant has been charged with one or more of the offenses identified or described in Section 6500, may be filed in the superior court of the county that determined the question of mental competence of the defendant. All other petitions may be filed in the county in which that person is physically present. A petition for the commitment of a person with a developmental disability to the State Department of Developmental Services who is in acute crisis, as defined in paragraph (1) of subdivision (d) of Section 4418.7, may be filed in the superior court of the county that determined the question of acute crisis or the county in which the acute crisis home is located. The following persons may request the person authorized to present allegations pursuant to Section 6500 to file a petition for commitment:

(a) The parent, guardian, conservator, or other person charged with the support of the person with a developmental disability.

(b) The probation officer.

(c) The Department of Corrections and Rehabilitation, Division of Juvenile Justice.

(d) Any person designated for that purpose by the judge of the court.

(e) The Secretary of the Department of Corrections and Rehabilitation.

(f) The regional center director or the director's designee.

The request shall state the petitioner's reasons for supposing the person to be eligible for admission thereto, and shall be verified by affidavit. *(Added by Stats.1967, c. 1667, p. 4107, § 37, operative July 1, 1969. Amended by Stats.1969, c. 624, p. 1263, § 4; Stats.1971, c. 1593, p. 3364, § 423, operative July 1, 1973; Stats.1977, c. 1252, p. 4603, § 642, operative July 1, 1978; Stats.1978, c. 1319, p. 4317, § 4; Stats.1979, c. 730, p. 2537, § 150, operative Jan. 1, 1981; Stats.1992, c. 722 (S.B.485), § 30, eff. Sept. 15, 1992; Stats.2012, c. 25 (A.B.1472), § 21, eff. June 27, 2012; Stats.2021, c. 76 (A.B.136), § 55, eff. July 16, 2021.)*

Law Revision Commission Comments

Section 6502 is amended to add the reference to a conservator in subdivision (a). [14 Cal.L.Rev.Comm. Reports 959 (1978)].

Cross References

Department of Developmental Services, see Welfare and Institutions Code § 4400 et seq.
Department of Mental Health, see Welfare and Institutions Code § 4000 et seq.
Director of corrections, generally, see Penal Code § 5050 et seq.
District attorneys, see Government Code § 26500 et seq.
Probation officers, see Penal Code § 1203.5; Government Code §§ 27770, 27772.

Youth Authority, generally, see Welfare and Institutions Code § 1700 et seq.

§ 6503. Time and place of hearing

The court shall fix a time and place for the hearing of the petition. The time for the hearing shall be set no more than 60 days after the filing of the petition. The court may grant a continuance only upon a showing of good cause. The hearing may, in the discretion of the court, be held at any place which the court deems proper, and which will give opportunity for the production and examination of witnesses. *(Added by Stats.1967, c. 1667, p. 4107, § 37, operative July 1, 1969. Amended by Stats.1980, c. 859, p. 2690, § 3.)*

Cross References

Time of expiration of orders for care, custody and treatment pending hearing, see Welfare and Institutions Code § 6506.

§ 6504. Notice of hearing

In all cases the court shall require due notice of the hearing of the petition to be given to the person alleged to have a developmental disability. Whenever a petition is filed, the court shall require such notice of the hearing of the petition as it deems proper to be given to any parent, guardian, conservator, or other person charged with the support of the person mentioned in the petition. *(Added by Stats.1967, c. 1667, p. 4107, § 37, operative July 1, 1969. Amended by Stats.1978, c. 1319, p. 4317, § 5; Stats.1979, c. 730, p. 2537, § 151, operative Jan. 1, 1981; Stats.2012, c. 25 (A.B.1472), § 22, eff. June 27, 2012.)*

Law Revision Commission Comments

Section 6504 is amended to add the reference to a conservator. [14 Cal.L.Rev.Comm. Reports 959 (1978)].

Cross References

Director of Corrections, generally, see Penal Code § 5050 et seq.
Youth Authority, generally, see Welfare and Institutions Code § 1700 et seq.

§ 6504.5. Examination; report

(a) Wherever a petition is filed pursuant to this article, the court shall appoint the director of a regional center for the developmentally disabled established under Division 4.5 (commencing with Section 4500), or the designee of the director, to examine the person alleged to have a developmental disability.

(b) Within 15 judicial days after his or her appointment, the regional center director or designee shall submit to the court in writing a report containing his or her evaluation of the person alleged to have a developmental disability. If the person is an individual described in paragraph (2) of subdivision (a) of Section 7505, the report shall include the results of the assessment conducted pursuant to subdivision (b) of Section 4418.7. The report shall contain a recommendation of a facility or facilities in which the alleged developmentally disabled person may be placed. The report shall include any comprehensive assessment, or updated assessment, conducted by the regional center pursuant to paragraph (2) of subdivision (c) of Section 4418.25.

(c) The report shall include a description of the least restrictive residential placement necessary to achieve the purposes of treatment. In determining the least restrictive residential placement, consideration shall be given to public safety. If placement into or out of a developmental center is recommended, the regional center director or designee simultaneously shall submit the report to the executive director of the developmental center or his or her designee. The executive director of the developmental center or his or her designee may, within 15 days of receiving the regional center report, submit to the court a written report evaluating the ability of the developmental center to achieve the purposes of treatment for this person and whether the developmental center placement can adequately provide the security measures or systems required to protect the public health and safety from the potential dangers posed by the person's known behaviors.

(d) The reports prepared by the regional center director and developmental center director, if applicable, shall also address suitable interim placements for the person as provided for in Section 6506. *(Added by Stats.1978, c. 1319, p. 4317, § 5.5. Amended by Stats.1996, c. 1076 (S.B.1391), § 6; Stats.2012, c. 25 (A.B.1472), § 23, eff. June 27, 2012; Stats.2014, c. 30 (S.B.856), § 22, eff. June 20, 2014.)*

Cross References

Consideration of reports, determination of placement of committed mentally retarded person, see Welfare and Institutions Code § 6509.

§ 6505. Order for apprehension

Whenever the court considers it necessary or advisable, it may cause an order to issue for the apprehension and delivery to the court of the person alleged to have a developmental disability, and may have the order executed by a peace officer. *(Added by Stats.1967, c. 1667, p. 4107, § 37, operative July 1, 1969. Amended by Stats.2012, c. 448 (A.B.2370), § 56; Stats.2012, c. 457 (S.B.1381), § 56.)*

Cross References

Counselor in mental health, as peace officer, see Welfare and Institutions Code § 6778.
Peace officer, definition, see Penal Code §§ 7, 830 et seq.

§ 6506. Custody, care and treatment pending hearing; order of court; expiration

Pending the hearing, the court may order that the alleged dangerous person alleged to have a developmental disability may be left in the charge of his or her parent, guardian, conservator, or other suitable person, or placed in a state developmental center, in the county psychiatric hospital, or in any other suitable placement as determined by the court. Prior to the issuance of an order under this section, the regional center and developmental center, if applicable, shall recommend to the court a suitable person or facility to care for the person alleged to have a developmental disability. The determination of a suitable person or facility shall be the least restrictive option that provides for the person's treatment needs and that has existing security systems or measures in place to adequately protect the public safety from any known dangers posed by the person. In determining whether the public safety will be adequately protected, the court shall make the finding required by subparagraph (D) of paragraph (1) of subdivision (a) of Section 1370.1 of the Penal Code.

Pending the hearing, the court may order that the person receive necessary habilitation, care, and treatment, including medical and dental treatment.

Orders made pursuant to this section shall expire at the time set for the hearing pursuant to Section 6503. If the court upon a showing of good cause grants a continuance of the hearing on the matter, it shall order that the person be detained pursuant to this section until the hearing on the petition is held. *(Added by Stats.1967, c. 1667, p. 4107, § 37, operative July 1, 1969. Amended by Stats.1978, c. 1319, p. 4317, § 6; Stats.1979, c. 730, p. 2537, § 152, operative Jan. 1, 1981; Stats.1980, c. 859, p. 2690, § 4; Stats.1996, c. 1076 (S.B.1391), § 7; Stats.2012, c. 25 (A.B.1472), § 24, eff. June 27, 2012.)*

Law Revision Commission Comments

Section 6506 is amended to add the reference to a conservator. [14 Cal.L.Rev.Comm. Reports 959 (1978)].

§ 6507. Witnesses

The court shall inquire into the condition or status of the person alleged to have a developmental disability. For this purpose it may by subpoena require the attendance before it of a physician who has made a special study of developmental disabilities and is qualified as a medical examiner, and of a clinical psychologist, or of two such physicians, or of two such psychologists, to examine the person and testify concerning his or her developmental disability. The court may also by subpoena require the attendance of such other persons as it deems advisable, to give evidence. *(Added by Stats.1967, c. 1667, p. 4107, § 37, operative July 1, 1969. Amended by Stats.2012, c. 25 (A.B.1472), § 25, eff. June 27, 2012.)*

Cross References

Appointment of expert witnesses by court, see Evidence Code § 730 et seq.
Cross-examination of expert witness, see Evidence Code § 721.
Subpoena, see Code of Civil Procedure § 1985.
Witnesses, generally, see Evidence Code § 720 et seq.

§ 6508. Fees and expenses of psychologist, physician and witnesses

Each psychologist and physician shall receive for each attendance mentioned in Section 6507 the sum of five dollars ($5) for each person examined, together with his necessary actual expenses occasioned thereby, and other witnesses shall receive for such attendance such fees and expenses as the court in its discretion allows, if any, not exceeding the fees and expenses allowed by law in other cases in the superior court.

Any fees or traveling expenses payable to a psychologist, physician, or witness as provided in this section and all expenses connected with the execution of any process under the provisions of this article, which are not paid by the parent, guardian, conservator, or person charged with the support of the person with the supposed developmental disability, shall be paid by the county treasurer of the county in which the person resides, upon the presentation to the treasurer of a certificate of the judge that the claimant is entitled thereto. *(Added by Stats.1967, c. 1667, p. 4107, § 37, operative July 1, 1969. Amended by Stats.1979, c. 730, p. 2538, § 153, operative Jan. 1, 1981; Stats.2012, c. 25 (A.B.1472), § 26, eff. June 27, 2012.)*

Law Revision Commission Comments

Section 6508 is amended to add the reference to a conservator. [14 Cal.L.Rev.Comm. Reports 959 (1978)].

Cross References

Claims against county, see Government Code § 29700 et seq.

§ 6509. Order of commitment; least restrictive placement; change of placement; hearings

(a) If the court finds that the person has a developmental disability, and is a danger to self or to others, or is in acute crisis, as defined in paragraph (1) of subdivision (d) of Section 4418.7, the court may make an order that the person be committed to the State Department of Developmental Services for suitable treatment and habilitation services. For purposes of this section, "suitable treatment and habilitation services" means the least restrictive residential placement necessary to achieve the purposes of treatment. Care and treatment of a person committed to the State Department of Developmental Services may include placement in any of the following:

(1) A licensed community care facility, as defined in Section 1502 of the Health and Safety Code, or a health facility, as defined in Section 1250 of the Health and Safety Code, other than a developmental center or state-operated facility.

(2) A property used to provide Stabilization, Training, Assistance and Reintegration (STAR) services operated by the department if the person meets the criteria for admission pursuant to paragraph (2) of subdivision (a) of Section 7505.

(3) The secure treatment program at Porterville Developmental Center, if the person meets the criteria for admission pursuant to paragraph (3) of subdivision (a) of Section 7505.

(4) Canyon Springs Community Facility, if the person meets the criteria for admission pursuant to paragraph (4), (5), or (6) of subdivision (a) of Section 7505.

(5) On or after July 1, 2019, the acute crisis center at Porterville Developmental Center, if the person meets the criteria for admission pursuant to paragraph (7) of subdivision (a) of Section 7505.

(6) Any other appropriate placement permitted by law.

(b)(1) The court shall hold a hearing as to the available placement alternatives and consider the reports of the regional center director or designee and the developmental center director or designee submitted pursuant to Section 6504.5. After hearing all the evidence, the court shall order that the person be committed to the placement that the court finds to be the most appropriate and least restrictive alternative. If the court finds that release of the person can be made subject to conditions that the court deems proper and adequate for the protection and safety of others and the welfare of the person, the person shall be released subject to those conditions.

(2) The court, however, may commit a person with a developmental disability who is not a resident of this state under Section 4460 for the purpose of transportation of the person to the state of legal residence pursuant to Section 4461. The State Department of Developmental Services shall receive the person committed to it and shall place the person in the placement ordered by the court.

(c) If the person has at any time been found mentally incompetent pursuant to Chapter 6 (commencing with Section 1367) of Title 10 of Part 2 of the Penal Code arising out of a complaint charging a felony offense specified in Section 290 of the Penal Code, the court shall order the State Department of Developmental Services to give notice of that finding to the designated placement facility and the appropriate law enforcement agency or agencies having local jurisdiction at the site of the placement facility.

(d) For persons residing in the secure treatment program at the Porterville Developmental Center, at the person's annual individual program plan meeting the team shall determine if the person should be considered for transition from the secure treatment program to an alternative placement. If the team concludes that an alternative placement is appropriate, the regional center, in coordination with the developmental center, shall conduct a comprehensive assessment and develop a proposed plan to transition the individual from the secure treatment program to the community. The transition plan shall be based upon the individual's needs, developed through the individual program plan process, and shall ensure that needed services and supports will be in place at the time the individual moves. Individual supports and services shall include, when appropriate for the individual, wrap-around services through intensive individualized support services. The clients' rights advocate for the regional center shall be notified of the individual program plan meeting and may participate in the meeting unless the consumer objects on their own behalf. The individual's transition plan shall be provided to the court as part of the notice required pursuant to subdivision (e).

(e) If the State Department of Developmental Services decides that a change in placement is necessary, it shall notify, in writing, the court of commitment, the district attorney, the attorney of record for the person, and the regional center of its decision at least 15 days in advance of the proposed change in placement. The court may hold a hearing and either approve or disapprove of the change or take no action, in which case the change shall be deemed approved. At the request of the district attorney or of the attorney for the person, a hearing shall be held. *(Added by Stats.1967, c. 1667, p. 4107, § 37, operative July 1, 1969. Amended by Stats.1969, c. 624, p. 1264, § 5; Stats.1971, c. 1593, p. 3364, § 424, operative July 1, 1973; Stats.1977, c. 1252, p. 4603, § 643, operative July 1, 1978; Stats.1978, c. 1319, p. 4318, § 7; Stats.1980, c. 676, p. 2042, § 341; Stats.1996, c. 1026 (A.B.2104), § 4; Stats.1996, c. 1076 (S.B.1391), § 8.5; Stats.2012, c. 25 (A.B.1472), § 27, eff. June 27, 2012; Stats.2013, c. 25 (A.B.89),*

§ 12, eff. June 27, 2013; Stats.2014, c. 30 (S.B.856), § 23, eff. June 20, 2014; Stats.2017, c. 18 (A.B.107), § 25, eff. June 27, 2017; Stats.2018, c. 92 (A.B.1289), § 228, eff. Jan. 1, 2019; Stats.2018, c. 884 (S.B.175), § 2, eff. Sept. 28, 2018; Stats.2019, c. 28 (S.B.81), § 32, eff. June 27, 2019; Stats.2021, c. 76 (A.B.136), § 56, eff. July 16, 2021; Stats.2021, c. 85 (A.B.135), § 17, eff. July 16, 2021.)

Cross References

Certificate of medical examiners, see Welfare and Institutions Code § 6253.
Community care facilities, see Health and Safety Code § 1500 et seq.
Delivery and execution of order of commitment of mentally retarded person, see Welfare and Institutions Code §§ 6740, 6741.
Department of Developmental Services, see Welfare and Institutions Code § 4400 et seq.
Felonies, definition and penalties, see Penal Code §§ 17, 18.
Patients admitted to state hospital subject to provisions of this section, see Welfare and Institutions Code § 7507.
State hospitals for developmentally disabled, admissions, application of this section, see Welfare and Institutions Code § 7507.

§ 6510. Payment of expenses on dismissal of petition

In case of the dismissal of the petition, the court may, if it considers the petition to have been filed with malicious intent, order the petitioner to pay the expenses in connection therewith, and may enforce such payment by such further orders as it deems necessary. *(Added by Stats.1967, c. 1667, p. 4107, § 37, operative July 1, 1969.)*

§ 6510.5. Individuals who cannot safely be served in a developmental center; prohibition on court ordered placement

Under no circumstances shall the court order placement of a person described in this article or a dangerous person committed pursuant to Section 1370.1 of the Penal Code to a developmental center if the department has specifically notified the court in writing that the individual cannot be safely served in that developmental center. *(Added by Stats.2012, c. 25 (A.B.1472), § 28, eff. June 27, 2012.)*

Research References

5 Witkin, California Criminal Law 4th Criminal Trial § 848 (2021), Developmental Disability.

§ 6511. Contriving to have person adjudged to have a developmental disability

Any person who knowingly contrives to have any person adjudged to have a developmental disability under the provisions of this article, unlawfully or improperly, is guilty of a misdemeanor. *(Added by Stats.1967, c. 1667, p. 4107, § 37, operative July 1, 1969. Amended by Stats.2012, c. 25 (A.B.1472), § 29, eff. June 27, 2012.)*

Cross References

Misdemeanor,
Defined, see Penal Code § 17.
Punishment, see Penal Code §§ 19, 19.2.

§ 6512. Juvenile court proceedings

If, when a boy or girl is brought before a juvenile court under the juvenile court law, it appears to the court, either before or after adjudication, that the person has a developmental disability, or if, on the conviction of any person of a crime by any court, it appears to the court that the person has a developmental disability, the court may adjourn the proceedings or suspend the sentence, as the case may be, and direct some suitable person to take proceedings under this article against the person before the court, and the court may order that, pending the preparation, filing, and hearing of the petition, the person before the court be detained in a place of safety, or be placed under the guardianship of some suitable person, on his entering into a recognizance for the appearance of the person upon trial or under conviction when required. If, upon the hearing of the petition, or upon a subsequent hearing, the person upon trial or under conviction is not found to have a developmental disability, the court may proceed with the trial or impose sentence, as the case may be. *(Added by Stats.1967, c. 1667, p. 4107, § 37, operative July 1, 1969. Amended by Stats.2012, c. 25 (A.B.1472), § 30, eff. June 27, 2012.)*

Cross References

Juvenile court,
Jurisdiction, see Welfare and Institutions Code §§ 300 et seq., 601.
Proceedings, see Welfare and Institutions Code § 650 et seq.

§ 6513. Payment of costs of judicial proceedings

(a) The State Department of Developmental Services shall pay for the costs, as defined in this section, of judicial proceedings, including commitment, placement, or release, under this article under both of the following conditions:

(1) The judicial proceedings are in a county where a state hospital or developmental center maintains a treatment program for persons with intellectual disabilities who are a danger to themselves or others.

(2) The judicial proceedings relate to a person with an intellectual disability who is at the time residing in the state hospital or developmental center located in the county of the proceedings.

(b) The appropriate financial officer or other designated official in a county described in subdivision (a) may prepare a statement of all costs incurred by the county in the investigation, preparation for, and conduct of the proceeding, including any costs of the district attorney or county counsel and any public defender or court-appointed counsel representing the person, and including any costs incurred by the county for the guarding or keeping of the person while away from the state hospital and for transportation of the person to and from the hospital. The statement shall be certified by a judge of the superior court and shall be sent to the State Department of Developmental Services. In lieu of sending statements after each proceeding, the statements may be held and submitted quarterly for the preceding three-month period. *(Added by Stats.1980, c. 644, p. 1810, § 1. Amended by Stats.1996, c. 1076 (S.B.1391), § 9; Stats. 2001, c. 176 (S.B.210), § 55; Stats.2012, c. 448 (A.B.2370), § 57; Stats.2012, c. 457 (S.B.1381), § 57.)*

Cross References

Department of Developmental Services, see Welfare and Institutions Code § 4400 et seq.

ARTICLE 3. JUVENILE COURT WARDS

§ 6550. Doubt as to mental health or condition of minor; procedure under this article

If the juvenile court, after finding that the minor is a person described by Section 300, 601, or 602, is in doubt concerning the state of mental health or the mental condition of the person, the court may continue the hearing and proceed pursuant to this article. *(Added by Stats.1969, c. 722, p. 1447, § 52, eff. Aug. 8, 1969, operative July 1, 1969. Amended by Stats.1989, c. 1360, § 163.)*

§ 6551. Commitment to county facility

(a) If the court is in doubt as to whether the person has a mental health disorder or an intellectual disability, the court shall order the person to be taken to a facility designated by the county and approved by the State Department of Health Care Services as a facility for 72–hour treatment and evaluation. Thereupon, Article 1 (commencing with Section 5150) of Chapter 2 of Part 1 of Division 5 applies, except that the professional person in charge of the facility shall make a written report to the court concerning the results of the evaluation of the person's mental condition. If the professional person in charge of the facility finds the person is, as a result of a mental health disorder, in need of intensive treatment, the person may be certified for not more than 14 days of involuntary intensive treatment if the conditions set forth in subdivision (c) of Section 5250 and subdivision (b) of Section 5260 are complied with. Thereupon, Article 4 (commencing with Section 5250) of Chapter 2 of Part 1 of Division 5 shall apply to the person. The person may be detained pursuant to Article 4.5 (commencing with Section 5260), or Article 4.7 (commencing with Section 5270.10), or Article 6 (commencing with Section 5300) of Part 1 of Division 5 if that article applies.

(b) If the professional person in charge of the facility finds that the person has an intellectual disability, the juvenile court may direct the filing in any other court of a petition for the commitment of a minor as an intellectually disabled person to the State Department of Developmental Services for placement in a state hospital. In that case, the juvenile court shall transmit to the court in which the petition is filed a copy of the report of the professional person in charge of the facility in which the minor was placed for observation. The court in which the petition for commitment is filed may accept the report of the professional person in lieu of the appointment, or subpoenaing, and testimony of other expert witnesses appointed by the court, if the laws applicable to the commitment proceedings provide for the appointment by court of medical or other expert witnesses or may consider the report as evidence in addition to the testimony of medical or other expert witnesses.

(c) If the professional person in charge of the facility for 72–hour evaluation and treatment reports to the juvenile court that the minor is not affected with a mental health disorder requiring intensive treatment or an intellectual disability, the professional person in charge of the facility shall return the minor to the juvenile court on or before the expiration of the 72–hour period and the court shall proceed with the case in accordance with the Juvenile Court Law.

(d) Expenditure for the evaluation or intensive treatment of a minor under this section shall be considered an expenditure made under Part 2 (commencing with Section 5600) of Division 5 and shall be reimbursed by the state as are other local expenditures pursuant to that part.

(e) The jurisdiction of the juvenile court over the minor shall be suspended during the time that the minor is subject to the jurisdiction of the court in which the petition for postcertification treatment of an imminently dangerous person or the petition for commitment of an intellectually disabled person is filed or under remand for 90 days for intensive treatment or commitment ordered by the court. *(Added by Stats.1969, c. 722, p. 1447, § 53, eff. Aug. 8, 1969, operative July 1, 1969. Amended by Stats.1971, c. 1593, p. 3364, § 425, operative July 1, 1973; Stats.1977, c. 1252, p. 4604, § 644, operative July 1, 1978; Stats.1988, c. 1517, § 16; Stats.2012, c. 448 (A.B.2370), § 58; Stats.2012, c. 457 (S.B.1381), § 58; Stats.2012, c. 34 (S.B.1009), § 215, eff. June 27, 2012; Stats.2013, c. 23 (A.B.82), § 53, eff. June 27, 2013; Stats.2014, c. 144 (A.B.1847), § 111, eff. Jan. 1, 2015.)*

Cross References

Department of Developmental Services, see Welfare and Institutions Code § 4400 et seq.
Juvenile court proceedings, see Welfare and Institutions Code § 650 et seq.
Mental health evaluations, recommendations, and dispositional procedures for minors, see Welfare and Institutions Code § 710 et seq.
State hospitals for the developmentally disabled, see Welfare and Institutions Code § 7500 et seq.
Temporary placement of minor at diagnostic and treatment center, see Welfare and Institutions Code § 704.

§ 6552. Voluntary application for mental health services; authority; reception at facility; return to court

A minor who has been declared to be within the jurisdiction of the juvenile court may, with the advice of counsel, make voluntary application for inpatient or outpatient mental health services in accordance with Section 5003. Notwithstanding the provisions of subdivision (b) of Section 6000, Section 6002, or Section 6004, the juvenile court may authorize the minor to make such application if it is satisfied from the evidence before it that the minor suffers from a mental disorder which may reasonably be expected to be cured or ameliorated by a course of treatment offered by the hospital, facility, or program in which the minor wishes to be placed; and that there is no other available hospital, program, or facility which might better serve the minor's medical needs and best interest. The superintendent or person in charge of any state, county, or other hospital facility or program may then receive the minor as a voluntary patient. Applications and placements under this section shall be subject to the provisions and requirements of the Short-Doyle Act (Part 2 (commencing with Section 5600) * * * of Division 5), which are generally applicable to voluntary admissions. The juvenile court shall review the application for judicial authorization of the voluntary application for admission to a psychiatric residential treatment facility pursuant to Section 361.23 or 727.13, as applicable.

If the minor is accepted as a voluntary patient, the juvenile court may issue an order to the minor and to the person in charge of the hospital, facility, or program in which the minor is to be placed that should the minor leave or demand to leave the care or custody thereof prior to the time * * * they are discharged by the superintendent or person in charge, they shall be returned forthwith to the juvenile court for a further dispositional hearing pursuant to the juvenile court law.

The provisions of this section shall continue to apply to the minor until the termination or expiration of the jurisdiction of the juvenile court. *(Added by Stats.1976, c. 445, p. 1179, § 4, eff. July 10, 1976. Amended by Stats.2022, c. 589 (A.B.2317), § 15, eff. Jan. 1, 2023.)*

ARTICLE 4. SEXUALLY VIOLENT PREDATORS

Section

§ 6600. Definitions

As used in this article, the following terms have the following meanings:

(a)(1) "Sexually violent predator" means a person who has been convicted of a sexually violent offense against one or more victims and who has a diagnosed mental disorder that makes the person a danger to the health and safety of others in that it is likely that he or she will engage in sexually violent criminal behavior.

(2) For purposes of this subdivision any of the following shall be considered a conviction for a sexually violent offense:

(A) A prior or current conviction that resulted in a determinate prison sentence for an offense described in subdivision (b).

(B) A conviction for an offense described in subdivision (b) that was committed prior to July 1, 1977, and that resulted in an indeterminate prison sentence.

(C) A prior conviction in another jurisdiction for an offense that includes all of the elements of an offense described in subdivision (b).

(D) A conviction for an offense under a predecessor statute that includes all of the elements of an offense described in subdivision (b).

(E) A prior conviction for which the inmate received a grant of probation for an offense described in subdivision (b).

(F) A prior finding of not guilty by reason of insanity for an offense described in subdivision (b).

(G) A conviction resulting in a finding that the person was a mentally disordered sex offender.

(H) A prior conviction for an offense described in subdivision (b) for which the person was committed to the Division of Juvenile Facilities, Department of Corrections and Rehabilitation pursuant to Section 1731.5.

(I) A prior conviction for an offense described in subdivision (b) that resulted in an indeterminate prison sentence.

(3) Conviction of one or more of the crimes enumerated in this section shall constitute evidence that may support a court or jury determination that a person is a sexually violent predator, but shall not be the sole basis for the determination. The existence of any prior convictions may be shown with documentary evidence. The details underlying the commission of an offense that led to a prior conviction, including a predatory relationship with the victim, may be shown by documentary evidence, including, but not limited to, preliminary hearing transcripts, trial transcripts, probation and sentencing reports, and evaluations by the State Department of State Hospitals. Jurors shall be admonished that they may not find a person a sexually violent predator based on prior offenses absent relevant evidence of a currently diagnosed mental disorder that makes the person a danger to the health and safety of others in that it is likely that he or she will engage in sexually violent criminal behavior.

(4) The provisions of this section shall apply to any person against whom proceedings were initiated for commitment as a sexually violent predator on or after January 1, 1996.

(b) "Sexually violent offense" means the following acts when committed by force, violence, duress, menace, fear of immediate and unlawful bodily injury on the victim or another person, or threatening to retaliate in the future against the victim or any other person, and that are committed on, before, or after the effective date of this article and result in a conviction or a finding of not guilty by reason of insanity, as defined in subdivision (a): a felony violation of Section 261, 262, 264.1, 269, 286, 287, 288, 288.5, or 289 of, or former Section 288a of, the Penal Code, or any felony violation of Section 207, 209, or 220 of the Penal Code, committed with the intent to commit a violation of Section 261, 262, 264.1, 286, 287, 288, or 289 of, or former Section 288a of, the Penal Code.

(c) "Diagnosed mental disorder" includes a congenital or acquired condition affecting the emotional or volitional capacity that predisposes the person to the commission of criminal sexual acts in a degree constituting the person a menace to the health and safety of others.

(d) "Danger to the health and safety of others" does not require proof of a recent overt act while the offender is in custody.

(e) "Predatory" means an act is directed toward a stranger, a person of casual acquaintance with whom no substantial relationship exists, or an individual with whom a relationship has been established or promoted for the primary purpose of victimization.

(f) "Recent overt act" means any criminal act that manifests a likelihood that the actor may engage in sexually violent predatory criminal behavior.

(g) Notwithstanding any other provision of law and for purposes of this section, a prior juvenile adjudication of a sexually violent offense may constitute a prior conviction for which the person received a determinate term if all of the following apply:

(1) The juvenile was 16 years of age or older at the time he or she committed the prior offense.

(2) The prior offense is a sexually violent offense as specified in subdivision (b).

(3) The juvenile was adjudged a ward of the juvenile court within the meaning of Section 602 because of the person's commission of the offense giving rise to the juvenile court adjudication.

(4) The juvenile was committed to the Division of Juvenile Facilities, Department of Corrections and Rehabilitation for the sexually violent offense.

(h) A minor adjudged a ward of the court for commission of an offense that is defined as a sexually violent offense shall be entitled to specific treatment as a sexual offender. The failure of a minor to receive that treatment shall not constitute a defense or bar to a determination that any person is a sexually violent predator within the meaning of this article. *(Added by Stats.1995, c. 763 (A.B.888), § 3. Amended by Stats.1996, c. 462 (A.B.3130), § 4, eff. Sept. 13, 1996; Stats.1999, c. 350 (S.B.786), § 3, eff. Sept. 7, 1999; Stats.1999, c. 995 (S.B.746), § 2.2; Stats.2000, c. 643 (A.B.2849), § 1; Stats.2006, c. 337 (S.B.1128), § 53, eff. Sept. 20, 2006; Initiative Measure (Prop. 83, § 24, approved Nov. 7, 2006, eff. Nov. 8, 2006); Stats.2014, c. 442 (S.B.1465), § 15, eff. Sept. 18, 2014; Stats.2018, c. 423 (S.B.1494), § 128, eff. Jan. 1, 2019.)*

Cross References

Confidential information and records, disclosure, consent, see Welfare and Institutions Code § 5328.
Felonies, definition and penalties, see Penal Code §§ 17, 18.
Invalidity of sentence enhancements imposed pursuant to Penal Code § 667.5 prior to January 1, 2020, identification of persons serving enhanced sentences, review and resentencing, waiver of resentencing hearing, see Penal Code § 1171.1.
Parole violations, exceptions to specified responses, see Penal Code § 3000.03.
Sex offenders, mandatory registration, see Penal Code § 290 et seq.

Research References

West's California Judicial Council Forms CR–173, Order for Commitment (Sexually Violent Predator).
California Jury Instructions - Criminal 4.19, Commitment as Sexually Violent Predator.
California Jury Instructions - Criminal 16.160.1, Persuading, Luring or Transporting Minors Under 14 Years of Age.
6 Witkin, California Criminal Law 4th Criminal Judgment § 195 (2021), No Proper Ground.
5 Witkin, California Criminal Law 4th Criminal Trial § 707 (2021), Technical or Specialized Terms.
5 Witkin, California Criminal Law 4th Criminal Trial § 810 (2021), In General.
1 Witkin California Criminal Law 4th Defenses § 9 (2021), In General.
1 Witkin California Criminal Law 4th Introduction to Crimes § 23 (2021), Sex Offender Statutes.
3 Witkin, California Criminal Law 4th Punishment § 139B (2021), (New) Three Tier System.
3 Witkin, California Criminal Law 4th Punishment § 153 (2021), In General.
3 Witkin, California Criminal Law 4th Punishment § 154 (2021), Definitions.
3 Witkin, California Criminal Law 4th Punishment § 160 (2021), Evidentiary Rules.
3 Witkin, California Criminal Law 4th Punishment § 162 (2021), Evidence.
3 Witkin, California Criminal Law 4th Punishment § 163 (2021), Discovery.
3 Witkin, California Criminal Law 4th Punishment § 169 (2021), Jury Instructions.
3 Witkin, California Criminal Law 4th Punishment § 170 (2021), Requisite Finding.
3 Witkin, California Criminal Law 4th Punishment § 176 (2021), California Cases.
3 Witkin, California Criminal Law 4th Punishment § 178 (2021), Former Statute: Scope and Repeal.
3 Witkin, California Criminal Law 4th Punishment § 399 (2021), Prior Felony in Another Jurisdiction.
3 Witkin, California Criminal Law 4th Punishment § 400 (2021), In General.
3 Witkin, California Criminal Law 4th Punishment § 404 (2021), Dual Use of Prior Conviction.
3 Witkin, California Criminal Law 4th Punishment § 417 (2021), Theft.
3 Witkin, California Criminal Law 4th Punishment § 429A (2021), (New) Where Third Strike is Not Serious or Violent Felony.
3 Witkin, California Criminal Law 4th Punishment § 445 (2021), Answer.
3 Witkin, California Criminal Law 4th Punishment § 719 (2021), Remaining Effects of Conviction.
3 Witkin, California Criminal Law 4th Punishment § 752 (2021), Discretionary Conditions.

§ 6600.05. Mental health facility; Coalinga State Hospital; alternate facilities

(a) Coalinga State Hospital shall be used whenever a person is committed to a secure facility for mental health treatment pursuant to this article and is placed in a state hospital under the direction of the State Department of State Hospitals unless there are unique circumstances that would preclude the placement of a person at that facility. If a state hospital is not used, the facility to be used shall be located on a site or sites determined by the Secretary of the Department of Corrections and Rehabilitation and the Director of State Hospitals. In no case shall a person committed to a secure facility for mental health treatment pursuant to this article be placed at Metropolitan State Hospital or Napa State Hospital.

(b) The State Department of State Hospitals shall be responsible for operation of the facility, including the provision of treatment. *(Added by Stats.1996, c. 197 (A.B.3483), § 20, eff. July 22, 1996. Amended by Stats.1997, c. 294 (S.B.391), § 40, eff. Aug. 18, 1997; Stats.1998, c. 961 (S.B.1976), § 2, eff. Sept. 29, 1998; Stats.2001, c. 171 (A.B.430), § 29.5, eff. Aug. 10, 2001; Stats.2012, c. 24 (A.B.1470), § 138, eff. June 27, 2012.)*

§ 6600.1. Victims under the age of 14; sexually violent offense

If the victim of an underlying offense that is specified in subdivision (b) of Section 6600 is a child under the age of 14, the offense shall constitute a "sexually violent offense" for purposes of Section 6600. *(Added by Stats.1996, c. 461 (S.B.2161), § 3. Amended by Initiative Measure (Prop. 83, § 25, approved Nov. 7, 2006, eff. Nov. 8, 2006).)*

Cross References

Sexually violent offense defined for purposes of this Article, see Welfare and Institutions Code § 6600.

Research References

3 Witkin, California Criminal Law 4th Punishment § 154 (2021), Definitions.

§ 6601. Persons in custody; determination as potential sexually violent predator; prerelease evaluations; petition for commitment

(a)(1) When the Secretary of the Department of Corrections and Rehabilitation determines that an individual who is in custody under the jurisdiction of the Department of Corrections and Rehabilitation, who is either serving a determinate prison sentence or whose parole has been revoked, and who is not in custody for the commission of a new offense committed while the individual was serving an indeterminate term in a state hospital as a sexually violent predator, may be a sexually violent predator, the secretary shall, at least six months prior to that individual's scheduled date for release from prison, refer the person for evaluation in accordance with this section. However, if the inmate was received by the department with less than nine months of their sentence to serve, or if the inmate's release date is modified by judicial or administrative action, the secretary may refer the person for evaluation in accordance with this section at a date that is less than six months prior to the inmate's scheduled release date.

(2) When an individual is in custody under the jurisdiction of the Department of Corrections and Rehabilitation for the commission of a new offense committed while the individual was serving an indeterminate term in a state hospital as a sexually violent predator, the Secretary of the Department of Corrections and Rehabilitation shall, at least six months prior to the individual's scheduled date for release from prison, refer the person directly to the State Department of State Hospitals for a full evaluation of whether the person still meets the criteria in Section 6600. However, if the inmate was received by the department with less than nine months of their

sentence to serve, or if the inmate's release date is modified by judicial or administrative action, the secretary may refer the person for evaluation in accordance with this section at a date that is less than six months prior to the inmate's scheduled release date. The evaluation shall be conducted in accordance with subdivisions (c) to (g), inclusive. If both evaluators concur that the person has a diagnosed mental disorder so that the person is likely to engage in acts of sexual violence without appropriate treatment and custody, the Director of State Hospitals shall forward a request for a court order no less than 20 calendar days prior to the scheduled release date of the person to the county designated in subdivision (i) authorizing a transfer of the individual from the Department of Corrections and Rehabilitation to the State Department of State Hospitals to continue serving the remainder of the individual's original indeterminate commitment as a sexually violent predator if the original petition has not been dismissed. If the petition has previously been dismissed, the Director of State Hospitals shall forward a request for a new petition to be filed for commitment to the county designated in subdivision (i) no less than 20 calendar days prior to the scheduled release date of the person consistent with subdivision (d).

(3) A petition may be filed under this section if the individual was in custody pursuant to a determinate prison term, parole revocation term, or a hold placed pursuant to Section 6601.3, at the time the petition is filed. A petition shall not be dismissed on the basis of a later judicial or administrative determination that the individual's custody was unlawful, if the unlawful custody was the result of a good faith mistake of fact or law. This paragraph applies to any petition filed on or after January 1, 1996.

(b) The person shall be screened by the Department of Corrections and Rehabilitation and the Board of Parole Hearings based on whether the person has committed a sexually violent predatory offense and on a review of the person's social, criminal, and institutional history. This screening shall be conducted in accordance with a structured screening instrument developed and updated by the State Department of State Hospitals in consultation with the Department of Corrections and Rehabilitation. If as a result of this screening it is determined that the person is likely to be a sexually violent predator, the Department of Corrections and Rehabilitation shall refer the person to the State Department of State Hospitals for a full evaluation of whether the person meets the criteria in Section 6600.

(c) The State Department of State Hospitals shall evaluate the person in accordance with a standardized assessment protocol, developed and updated by the State Department of State Hospitals, to determine whether the person is a sexually violent predator as defined in this article. The standardized assessment protocol shall require assessment of diagnosable mental disorders, as well as various factors known to be associated with the risk of reoffense among sex offenders. Risk factors to be considered shall include criminal and psychosexual history, type, degree, and duration of sexual deviance, and severity of mental disorder.

(d) Pursuant to subdivision (c), the person shall be evaluated by two practicing psychiatrists or psychologists, or one practicing psychiatrist and one practicing psychologist, designated by the Director of State Hospitals. If both evaluators concur that the person has a diagnosed mental disorder so that the person is likely to engage in acts of sexual violence without appropriate treatment and custody, the Director of State Hospitals shall forward a request for a petition for commitment under Section 6602 to the county designated in subdivision (i). Copies of the evaluation reports and any other supporting documents shall be made available to the attorney designated by the county pursuant to subdivision (i) who may file a petition for commitment.

(e) If one of the professionals performing the evaluation pursuant to subdivision (d) does not concur that the person meets the criteria specified in subdivision (d), but the other professional concludes that the person meets those criteria, the Director of State Hospitals shall arrange for further examination of the person by two independent professionals selected in accordance with subdivision (g).

(f) If an examination by independent professionals pursuant to subdivision (e) is conducted, a petition to request commitment under this article shall only be filed if both independent professionals who evaluate the person pursuant to subdivision (e) concur that the person meets the criteria for commitment specified in subdivision (d). The professionals selected to evaluate the person pursuant to subdivision (g) shall inform the person that the purpose of their examination is not treatment but to determine if the person meets certain criteria to be involuntarily committed pursuant to this article. It is not required that the person appreciate or understand that information.

(g) An independent professional who is designated by the Secretary of the Department of Corrections and Rehabilitation or the Director of State Hospitals for purposes of this section shall not be a state government employee, shall have at least five years of experience in the diagnosis and treatment of mental disorders, and shall include psychiatrists and licensed psychologists who have a doctoral degree in psychology. The requirements set forth in this section also shall apply to professionals appointed by the court to evaluate the person for purposes of any other proceedings under this article.

(h)(1) If the State Department of State Hospitals determines that the person is a sexually violent predator as defined in this article, the Director of State Hospitals shall forward a request for a petition to be filed for commitment under this article to the county designated in subdivision (i) no less than 20 calendar days prior to the scheduled release date of the person. Copies of the evaluation reports and any other supporting documents shall be made available to the attorney designated by the county pursuant to subdivision (i) who may file a petition for commitment in the superior court.

(2) If a hold is placed pursuant to Section 6601.3 and the State Department of State Hospitals determines that the person is a sexually violent predator as defined in this article, the Director of State Hospitals shall forward a request for a petition to be filed for commitment under this article to the county designated in subdivision (i) no less than 20 calendar days prior to the end of the hold.

(3) The person shall have no right to enforce the time limit set forth in this subdivision and shall have no remedy for its violation.

(i) If the county's designated counsel concurs with the recommendation, a petition for commitment shall be filed in the superior court of the county in which the person was convicted of the offense for which the person was committed to the jurisdiction of the Department of Corrections and Rehabilitation. The petition shall be filed, and the proceedings shall be handled, by either the district attorney or the county counsel of that county. A person's subsequent conviction for an offense that is not a sexually violent offense committed while in the custody of the Department of Corrections and Rehabilitation or the State Department of State Hospitals that occurs prior to the resolution of a petition filed pursuant to this section shall not change jurisdiction for the petition from the county in which the person was convicted of the offense for which the person was committed to the jurisdiction of the Department of Corrections and Rehabilitation. If a person is convicted of a subsequent sexually violent offense committed while in the custody of the Department of Corrections and Rehabilitation or the State Department of State Hospitals that occurs prior to the resolution of a petition filed pursuant to this section a subsequent petition for commitment as a sexually violent predator pursuant to this section shall be filed in the superior court of the county in which the person was convicted of the subsequent sexually violent offense. The county board of supervisors shall designate either the district attorney or the county counsel to assume responsibility for proceedings under this article.

(j) An order issued by a judge pursuant to Section 6601.5, finding that the petition, on its face, supports a finding of probable cause to believe that the individual named in the petition is likely to engage in sexually violent predatory criminal behavior upon release, shall toll that person's parole pursuant to paragraph (4) of subdivision (a) of Section 3000 of the Penal Code, if that individual is determined to be a sexually violent predator.

(k) The attorney designated by the county pursuant to subdivision (i) shall notify the State Department of State Hospitals of its decision regarding the filing of a petition for commitment pursuant to subdivision (d) within 15 days of making that decision. *(Added by Stats.2008, c. 601 (S.B.1546), § 3, eff. Sept. 30, 2008, operative contingent. Amended by Stats.2010, c. 710 (S.B.1201), § 4, operative contingent; Stats.2011, c. 359 (S.B.179), § 3, operative Jan. 1, 2013; Stats.2014, c. 442 (S.B.1465), § 16, eff. Sept. 18, 2014; Stats.2016, c. 878 (A.B.1906), § 1, eff. Jan. 1, 2017; Stats.2018, c. 821 (A.B.2661), § 1, eff. Jan. 1, 2019; Stats.2021, c. 383 (S.B.248), § 1, eff. Jan. 1, 2022.)*

Cross References

Department of Corrections and Rehabilitation, generally, see Penal Code § 5000 et seq.
Department of Finance, generally, see Government Code § 13000 et seq.
Diagnosed mental disorder defined for purposes of this Article, see Welfare and Institutions Code § 6600.
Predatory defined for purposes of this Article, see Welfare and Institutions Code § 6600.
Sexually violent predator defined for purposes of this Article, see Welfare and Institutions Code § 6600.

Research References

3 Witkin, California Criminal Law 4th Punishment § 153 (2021), In General.
3 Witkin, California Criminal Law 4th Punishment § 155 (2021), Effect of Reversal of Conviction.
3 Witkin, California Criminal Law 4th Punishment § 156 (2021), In General.
3 Witkin, California Criminal Law 4th Punishment § 157 (2021), Validity of Evaluator's Recommendation.
3 Witkin, California Criminal Law 4th Punishment § 165 (2021), Updated, Replacement, and Additional Evaluations.
3 Witkin, California Criminal Law 4th Punishment § 170 (2021), Requisite Finding.

§ 6601.3. Order to remain in custody beyond scheduled release date for evaluation; maximum time; good cause

(a) Upon a showing of good cause, the Board of Parole Hearings may order that a person referred to the State Department of State Hospitals pursuant to subdivision (b) of Section 6601 remain in custody for no more than 45 days beyond the person's scheduled release date for full evaluation pursuant to subdivisions (c) to (i), inclusive, of Section 6601.

(b) For purposes of this section, good cause means circumstances where there is a recalculation of credits or a restoration of denied or lost credits by any custodial agency or court, a resentencing by a court, the receipt of the prisoner into custody, or equivalent exigent circumstances that result in there being less than 45 days prior to the person's scheduled release date for the full evaluation described in subdivisions (c) to (i), inclusive, of Section 6601. *(Added by Stats.1998, c. 19 (S.B.536), § 1, eff. April 14, 1998. Amended by Stats.2000, c. 41 (S.B.451), § 1, eff. June 26, 2000; Stats.2010, c. 710 (S.B.1201), § 5; Stats.2012, c. 24 (A.B.1470), § 140, eff. June 27, 2012; Stats.2016, c. 878 (A.B.1906), § 2, eff. Jan. 1, 2017.)*

Cross References

Disposition of mentally disordered male prisoners upon discharge, order to remain in custody beyond scheduled release date for evaluation, see Penal Code § 2963.

Research References

3 Witkin, California Criminal Law 4th Punishment § 156 (2021), In General.

§ 6601.5. Review of petition for likelihood of sexually violent predatory criminal behavior upon release

Upon filing of the petition and a request for review under this section, a judge of the superior court shall review the petition and determine whether the petition states or contains sufficient facts that, if true, would constitute probable cause to believe that the individual named in the petition is likely to engage in sexually violent predatory criminal behavior upon his or her release. If the judge determines that the petition, on its face, supports a finding of probable cause, the judge shall order that the person be detained in a secure facility until a hearing can be completed pursuant to Section 6602. The probable cause hearing provided for in Section 6602 shall commence within 10 calendar days of the date of the order issued by the judge pursuant to this section. *(Added by Stats.1998, c. 19 (S.B.536), § 2, eff. April 14, 1998. Amended by Stats.2000, c. 41 (S.B.451), § 2, eff. June 26, 2000.)*

Cross References

Predatory defined for purposes of this Article, see Welfare and Institutions Code § 6600.
Tolling of parole period for persons subject to sexually violent predator proceedings, see Penal Code § 3000.

Research References

3 Witkin, California Criminal Law 4th Punishment § 153 (2021), In General.
3 Witkin, California Criminal Law 4th Punishment § 159 (2021), In General.

§ 6602. Probable cause hearing; right to counsel; custody requirements; continuances

(a) A judge of the superior court shall review the petition and shall determine whether there is probable cause to believe that the individual named in the petition is likely to engage in sexually violent predatory criminal behavior upon his or her release. The person named in the petition shall be entitled to assistance of counsel at the probable cause hearing. Upon the commencement of the probable cause hearing, the person shall remain in custody pending the completion of the probable cause hearing. If the judge determines there is not probable cause, he or she shall dismiss the petition and any person subject to parole shall report to parole. If the judge determines that there is probable cause, the judge shall order that the person remain in custody in a secure facility until a trial is completed and shall order that a trial be conducted to determine whether the person is, by reason of a diagnosed mental disorder, a danger to the health and safety of others in that the person is likely to engage in acts of sexual violence upon his or her release from the jurisdiction of the Department of Corrections and Rehabilitation or other secure facility.

(b) The probable cause hearing shall not be continued except upon a showing of good cause by the party requesting the continuance.

(c) The court shall notify the State Department of State Hospitals of the outcome of the probable cause hearing by forwarding to the department a copy of the minute order of the court within 15 days of the decision. *(Added by Stats.1995, c. 763 (A.B.888), § 3. Amended by Stats.1996, c. 4 (A.B.1496), § 4, eff. Jan. 25, 1996; Stats.1998, c. 19 (S.B.536), § 3, eff. April 14, 1998; Stats.1998, c. 961 (S.B.1976), § 4, eff. Sept. 29, 1998; Stats.2000, c. 41 (S.B.451), § 3, eff. June 26, 2000; Stats.2012, c. 24 (A.B.1470), § 141, eff. June 27, 2012.)*

Cross References

Danger to the health and safety of others defined for purposes of this Article, see Welfare and Institutions Code § 6600.
Department of Corrections and Rehabilitation, generally, see Penal Code § 5000 et seq.
Diagnosed mental disorder defined for purposes of this Article, see Welfare and Institutions Code § 6600.
Predatory defined for purposes of this Article, see Welfare and Institutions Code § 6600.

Research References

3 Witkin, California Criminal Law 4th Punishment § 156 (2021), In General.
3 Witkin, California Criminal Law 4th Punishment § 159 (2021), In General.
3 Witkin, California Criminal Law 4th Punishment § 160 (2021), Evidentiary Rules.

3 Witkin, California Criminal Law 4th Punishment § 170 (2021), Requisite Finding.
3 Witkin, California Criminal Law 4th Punishment § 172 (2021), Petition Initiated by Department of Mental Health.

§ 6602.5. State hospital placement; probable cause determination; identification of persons who have not had a probable cause hearing

(a) No person may be placed in a state hospital pursuant to the provisions of this article until there has been a determination pursuant to Section 6601.3 or 6602 that there is probable cause to believe that the individual named in the petition is likely to engage in sexually violent predatory criminal behavior.

(b) The State Department of State Hospitals shall identify each person for whom a petition pursuant to this article has been filed who is in a state hospital on or after January 1, 1998, and who has not had a probable cause hearing pursuant to Section 6602. The State Department of State Hospitals shall notify the court in which the petition was filed that the person has not had a probable cause hearing. Copies of the notice shall be provided by the court to the attorneys of record in the case. Within 30 days of notice by the State Department of State Hospitals, the court shall either order the person removed from the state hospital and returned to local custody or hold a probable cause hearing pursuant to Section 6602.

(c) In no event shall the number of persons referred pursuant to subdivision (b) to the superior court of any county exceed 10 in any 30–day period, except upon agreement of the presiding judge of the superior court, the district attorney, the public defender, the sheriff, and the Director of State Hospitals.

(d) This section shall be implemented in Los Angeles County pursuant to a letter of agreement between the Department of State Hospitals, the Los Angeles County district attorney, the Los Angeles County public defender, the Los Angeles County sheriff, and the Los Angeles County Superior Court. The number of persons referred to the Superior Court of Los Angeles County pursuant to subdivision (b) shall be governed by the letter of agreement. *(Added by Stats.1998, c. 19 (S.B.536), § 4, eff. April 14, 1998. Amended by Stats.1998, c. 961 (S.B.1976), § 5, eff. Sept. 29, 1998; Stats.2012, c. 24 (A.B.1470), § 142, eff. June 27, 2012.)*

Cross References

Predatory defined for purposes of this Article, see Welfare and Institutions Code § 6600.

Research References

3 Witkin, California Criminal Law 4th Punishment § 171 (2021), Commitment and Treatment.

§ 6603. Trial by jury; right to counsel; continuance; examination by expert or professional; access to records; unanimous verdict; requesting DNA testing

(a) A person subject to this article is entitled to a trial by jury, to the assistance of counsel, to the right to retain experts or professional persons to perform an examination on the person's behalf, and to have access to all relevant medical and psychological records and reports. If the person is indigent, the court shall appoint counsel to assist that person and, upon the person's request, assist the person in obtaining an expert or professional person to perform an examination or participate in the trial on the person's behalf. Any right that may exist under this section to request DNA testing on prior cases shall be made in conformity with Section 1405 of the Penal Code.

(b) The attorney petitioning for commitment under this article has the right to demand that the trial be before a jury.

(c) To continue a trial, written notice shall be filed and served on all parties to the proceeding, together with affidavits or declarations detailing specific facts showing that a continuance is necessary.

(1) All moving and supporting papers shall be served and filed at least 10 court days before the hearing, except as provided in paragraph (2). The moving and supporting papers served shall be a copy of the papers filed or to be filed with the court.

(2) If the written notice is served by mail, the 10–day period of notice before the hearing shall be increased as follows:

(A) Five calendar days if the place of mailing and the place of address are within the State of California.

(B) Ten calendar days if either the place of mailing or the place of address is outside the State of California, but within the United States.

(C) Twenty calendar days if either the place of mailing or the place of address is outside the United States.

(D) Two calendar days if the notice is served by facsimile transmission, express mail, or another method of delivery providing for overnight delivery.

(3) All papers opposing a continuance motion noticed pursuant to this subdivision shall be filed with the court and a copy shall be served on each party at least four court days before the hearing. All reply papers shall be served on each party at least two court days before the hearing. A party may waive the right to have documents served in a timely manner after receiving actual notice of the request for continuance.

(4) If a party makes a motion for a continuance that does not comply with the requirements described in this subdivision, the court shall hold a hearing on whether there is good cause for the failure to comply with those requirements. At the conclusion of the hearing, the court shall make a finding whether good cause has been shown and, if it finds that there is good cause, shall state on the record the facts proved that justify its finding. If the moving party is unable to show good cause for the failure to give notice, the motion for continuance shall not be granted.

(5) Continuances shall be granted only upon a showing of good cause. The court shall not find good cause solely based on the convenience of the parties or a stipulation of the parties. At the conclusion of the motion for continuance, the court shall make a finding whether good cause has been shown and, if it finds that there is good cause, shall state on the record the facts proved that justify its finding.

(6) In determining good cause, the court shall consider the general convenience and prior commitments of all witnesses. The court shall also consider the general convenience and prior commitments of each witness in selecting a continuance date if the motion is granted. The facts as to inconvenience or prior commitments may be offered by the witness or by a party to the case.

(7) Except as specified in paragraph (8), a continuance shall be granted only for the period of time shown to be necessary by the evidence considered at the hearing on the motion. If a continuance is granted, the court shall state on the record the facts proved that justify the length of the continuance.

(8) For purposes of this subdivision, "good cause" includes, but is not limited to, those cases in which the attorney assigned to the case has another trial or probable cause hearing in progress. A continuance granted pursuant to this subdivision as the result of another trial or hearing in progress shall not exceed 10 court days after the conclusion of that trial or hearing.

(d)(1) If the attorney petitioning for commitment under this article determines that updated evaluations are necessary in order to properly present the case for commitment, the attorney may request the State Department of State Hospitals to perform updated evaluations. If one or more of the original evaluators is no longer available to testify for the petitioner in court proceedings, the attorney petitioning for commitment under this article may request the State Department of State Hospitals to perform replacement evaluations. When a request is made for updated or replacement evaluations, the State Department of State Hospitals shall perform the requested evaluations and forward them to the petitioning attorney and to the counsel for the person subject to this article. However, updated or replacement evaluations shall not be performed except as necessary to update one or more of the original evaluations or to replace the evaluation of an evaluator who is no longer available to testify for the petitioner in court proceedings. These updated or replacement evaluations shall include review of available medical and psychological records, including treatment records, consultation with current treating clinicians, and interviews of the person being evaluated, either voluntarily or by court order. If an updated or replacement evaluation results in a split opinion as to whether the person subject to this article meets the criteria for commitment, the State Department of State Hospitals shall conduct two additional evaluations in accordance with subdivision (f) of Section 6601.

(2) For purposes of this subdivision, "no longer available to testify for the petitioner in court proceedings" means that the evaluator is no longer authorized by the Director of State Hospitals to perform evaluations regarding sexually violent predators as a result of any of the following:

(A) The evaluator has failed to adhere to the protocol of the State Department of State Hospitals.

(B) The evaluator's license has been suspended or revoked.

(C) The evaluator is unavailable pursuant to Section 240 of the Evidence Code.

(D) The independent professional or state employee who has served as the evaluator has resigned or retired and has not entered into a new contract to continue as an evaluator in the case, unless this evaluator, in the evaluator's most recent evaluation of the person subject to this article, opined that the person subject to this article does not meet the criteria for commitment.

(e) This section does not prevent the defense from presenting otherwise relevant and admissible evidence.

(f) If the person subject to this article or the petitioning attorney does not demand a jury trial, the trial shall be before the court without a jury.

(g) A unanimous verdict shall be required in any jury trial.

(h) The court shall notify the State Department of State Hospitals of the outcome of the trial by forwarding to the department a copy of the minute order of the court within 72 hours of the decision.

(i) This section does not limit any legal or equitable right that a person may have to request DNA testing.

(j) Subparagraph (D) of paragraph (2) of subdivision (d) does not affect the authority of the State Department of State Hospitals to conduct two additional evaluations when an updated or replacement evaluation results in a split opinion.

(k)(1) Notwithstanding any other law, the evaluator performing an updated evaluation shall include with the evaluation a statement listing all records reviewed by the evaluator pursuant to subdivision (d). The court shall issue a subpoena, upon the request of either party, for a certified copy of these records. The records shall be provided to the attorney petitioning for commitment and the counsel for the person subject to this article. The attorneys may use the records in proceedings under this article and shall not disclose them for any other purpose.

(2) This subdivision does not affect the right of a party to object to the introduction at trial of all or a portion of a record subpoenaed under paragraph (1) on the ground that it is more prejudicial than probative pursuant to Section 352 of the Evidence Code or that it is not material to the issue of whether the person subject to this article is a sexually violent predator, as defined in subdivision (a) of Section 6600, or to any other issue to be decided by the court. If the relief is granted, in whole or in part, the record or records shall retain any confidentiality that may apply under Section 5328 of this code and Section 1014 of the Evidence Code.

(3) This subdivision does not affect any right of a party to seek to obtain other records regarding the person subject to this article.

(4) Except as provided in paragraph (1), this subdivision does not affect any right of a committed person to assert that records are confidential under Section 5328 of this code or Section 1014 of the Evidence Code. *(Added by Stats.1995, c. 763 (A.B.888), § 3. Amended by Stats.1998, c. 961 (S.B.1976), § 6, eff. Sept. 29, 1998; Stats.2000, c. 420 (S.B.2018), § 2, eff. Sept. 13, 2000; Stats.2001, c. 323 (A.B.1142), § 2, eff. Sept. 24, 2001; Stats.2007, c. 208 (S.B.542), § 1; Stats.2012, c. 440 (A.B.1488), § 66, eff. Sept. 22, 2012; Stats. 2012, c. 790 (S.B.760), § 1, eff. Sept. 29, 2012; Stats.2015, c. 576 (S.B.507), § 1, eff. Jan. 1, 2016; Stats.2019, c. 606 (A.B.303), § 1, eff. Jan. 1, 2020.)*

Cross References

Sexually violent predator defined for purposes of this Article, see Welfare and Institutions Code § 6600.

Research References

5 Witkin, California Criminal Law 4th Criminal Trial § 179 (2021), When Counsel is Not Required.
3 Witkin, California Criminal Law 4th Punishment § 161 (2021), In General.
3 Witkin, California Criminal Law 4th Punishment § 161B (2021), (New) Continuance.
3 Witkin, California Criminal Law 4th Punishment § 163 (2021), Discovery.
3 Witkin, California Criminal Law 4th Punishment § 165 (2021), Updated, Replacement, and Additional Evaluations.
3 Witkin, California Criminal Law 4th Punishment § 176 (2021), California Cases.

§ 6603.3. Attorneys prohibited from disclosing identifying information of a victim or witness; exceptions; violations; pro se parties

(a)(1) Except as provided in paragraph (2), no attorney may disclose or permit to be disclosed to a person subject to this article, family members of the person subject to this article, or any other person, the name, address, telephone number, or other identifying information of a victim or witness whose name is disclosed to the attorney pursuant to Section 6603 and Chapter 1 (commencing with Section 2016.010) of Part 4 of Title 4 of the Code of Civil Procedure, unless specifically permitted to do so by the court after a hearing and showing of good cause.

(2) Notwithstanding paragraph (1), an attorney may disclose or permit to be disclosed, the name, address, telephone number, or other identifying information of a victim or witness to persons employed by the attorney or to a person hired or appointed for the purpose of assisting the person subject to this article in the preparation of the case, if that disclosure is required for that preparation. Persons provided this information shall be informed by the attorney that further dissemination of the information, except as provided by this section, is prohibited.

(3) A willful violation of this subdivision by an attorney, persons employed by an attorney, or persons appointed by the court is a misdemeanor.

(b) If the person subject to this article is acting as his or her own attorney, the court shall endeavor to protect the name, address, telephone number, or other identifying information of a victim or witness by providing for contact only through a private investigator licensed by the Department of Consumer Affairs and appointed by the court or by imposing other reasonable restrictions, absent a showing of good cause as determined by the court. *(Added by Stats.2008, c. 155 (A.B.2410), § 1.)*

Cross References

Misdemeanors, definition and penalties, see Penal Code §§ 17, 19 and 19.2.

Research References

3 Witkin, California Criminal Law 4th Punishment § 164 (2021), Restrictions on Disclosure of Identity of Victims and Witnesses.

§ 6603.5. Employees or agents prohibited from disclosing identifying information of victims of sex offenses; exceptions

No employee or agent of the Department of Corrections and Rehabilitation, the Board of Parole Hearings, or the State Department of State Hospitals shall disclose to any person, except to employees or agents of each named department, the prosecutor, the respondent's counsel, licensed private investigators hired or appointed for the respondent, or other persons or agencies where authorized or required by law, the name, address, telephone number, or other identifying information of a person who was involved in a civil commitment hearing under this article as the victim of a sex offense except where authorized or required by law. *(Added by Stats.2008, c. 155 (A.B.2410), § 2. Amended by Stats.2009, c. 35 (S.B.174), § 33; Stats.2012, c. 440 (A.B.1488), § 67, eff. Sept. 22, 2012.)*

Cross References

Department of Corrections and Rehabilitation, generally, see Penal Code § 5000 et seq.

Research References

3 Witkin, California Criminal Law 4th Punishment § 164 (2021), Restrictions on Disclosure of Identity of Victims and Witnesses.

§ 6603.7. Court orders may identify sex offense victim as Jane Doe or John Doe

(a) Except as provided in Section 6603.3, the court, at the request of the victim of a sex offense relevant in a proceeding under this article, may order the identity of the victim in all records and during all proceedings to be either Jane Doe or John Doe, if the court finds that the order is reasonably necessary to protect the privacy of the person and will not unduly prejudice the party petitioning for commitment under this article or the person subject to this article.

(b) If the court orders the victim to be identified as Jane Doe or John Doe pursuant to subdivision (a), and if there is a jury trial, the court shall instruct the jury at the beginning and at the end of the trial that the victim is being so identified only for the purposes of protecting his or her privacy. *(Added by Stats.2008, c. 155 (A.B. 2410), § 3.)*

Research References

3 Witkin, California Criminal Law 4th Punishment § 164 (2021), Restrictions on Disclosure of Identity of Victims and Witnesses.

§ 6604. Burden of proof; commitment for treatment; term; facilities

The court or jury shall determine whether, beyond a reasonable doubt, the person is a sexually violent predator. If the court or jury is not satisfied beyond a reasonable doubt that the person is a sexually violent predator, the court shall direct that the person be released at the conclusion of the term for which he or she was initially sentenced, or that the person be unconditionally released at the end of parole, whichever is applicable. If the court or jury determines that the person is a sexually violent predator, the person shall be committed for an indeterminate term to the custody of the State Department of State Hospitals for appropriate treatment and confinement in a secure facility designated by the Director of State Hospitals. The facility shall be located on the grounds of an institution under the jurisdiction of the Department of Corrections and Rehabilitation. *(Added by Stats.1995, c. 763 (A.B.888), § 3. Amended by Stats.2000, c. 420 (S.B.2018), § 3, eff. Sept. 13, 2000; Stats.2006, c. 337 (S.B.1128), § 55, eff. Sept. 20, 2006; Initiative Measure (Prop. 83, § 27, approved Nov. 7, 2006, eff. Nov. 8, 2006); Stats.2012, c. 24 (A.B.1470), § 143, eff. June 27, 2012.)*

Cross References

Department of Corrections and Rehabilitation, generally, see Penal Code § 5000 et seq.

Sexually violent predator defined for purposes of this Article, see Welfare and Institutions Code § 6600.

Research References

West's California Judicial Council Forms CR–173, Order for Commitment (Sexually Violent Predator).

California Jury Instructions - Criminal 4.19, Commitment as Sexually Violent Predator.

3 Witkin, California Criminal Law 4th Punishment § 161 (2021), In General.

3 Witkin, California Criminal Law 4th Punishment § 168 (2021), Effect of Delay in Trial.

3 Witkin, California Criminal Law 4th Punishment § 171 (2021), Commitment and Treatment.

3 Witkin, California Criminal Law 4th Punishment § 177 (2021), Challenges to Indeterminate Term.

§ 6604.1. Indeterminate term of commitment

(a) The indeterminate term of commitment provided for in Section 6604 shall commence on the date upon which the court issues the initial order of commitment pursuant to that section.

(b) The person shall be evaluated by two practicing psychologists or psychiatrists, or by one practicing psychologist and one practicing psychiatrist, designated by the State Department of State Hospitals. The provisions of subdivisions (c) to (i), inclusive, of Section 6601 shall apply to evaluations performed for purposes of extended commitments. The rights, requirements, and procedures set forth in Section 6603 shall apply to all commitment proceedings. *(Added by Stats.1998, c. 19 (S.B.536), § 5, eff. April 14, 1998. Amended by Stats.1998, c. 961 (S.B.1976), § 7, eff. Sept. 29, 1998; Stats.2000, c. 420 (S.B.2018), § 4, eff. Sept. 13, 2000; Stats.2006, c. 337 (S.B.1128), § 56, eff. Sept. 20, 2006; Initiative Measure (Prop. 83, § 28, approved Nov. 7, 2006, eff. Nov. 8, 2006); Stats.2012, c. 440 (A.B.1488), § 68, eff. Sept. 22, 2012.)*

Research References

3 Witkin, California Criminal Law 4th Punishment § 171 (2021), Commitment and Treatment.

§ 6604.9. Annual examination of mental condition; report; filing of report with court; petition for conditional release or unconditional discharge

(a) A person found to be a sexually violent predator and committed to the custody of the State Department of State Hospitals shall have a current examination of his or her mental condition made at least once every year. The report shall be in the form of a declaration and shall be prepared by a professionally qualified person. The person may retain or, if he or she is indigent and so requests, the court may appoint, a qualified expert or professional person to examine him or her, and the expert or professional person shall have access to all records concerning the person.

(b) The annual report shall include consideration of whether the committed person currently meets the definition of a sexually violent predator and whether conditional release to a less restrictive alternative, pursuant to Section 6608, or an unconditional discharge, pursuant to Section 6605, is in the best interest of the person and conditions can be imposed that would adequately protect the community.

(c) The State Department of State Hospitals shall file this periodic report with the court that committed the person under this article. A copy of the report shall be served on the prosecuting agency involved in the initial commitment and upon the committed person.

(d) If the State Department of State Hospitals determines that either: (1) the person's condition has so changed that the person no longer meets the definition of a sexually violent predator and should, therefore, be considered for unconditional discharge, or (2) conditional release to a less restrictive alternative is in the best interest of the person and conditions can be imposed that adequately protect the community, the director shall authorize the person to petition the court for conditional release to a less restrictive alternative or for an unconditional discharge. The petition shall be filed with the court and served upon the prosecuting agency responsible for the initial commitment.

(e) The court, upon receipt of the petition for conditional release to a less restrictive alternative, shall consider the petition using procedures described in Section 6608.

(f) The court, upon receiving a petition for unconditional discharge, shall order a show cause hearing, pursuant to the provisions of Section 6605, at which the court may consider the petition and any accompanying documentation provided by the medical director, the prosecuting attorney, or the committed person. *(Added by Stats. 2013, c. 182 (S.B.295), § 1. Amended by Stats.2014, c. 71 (S.B.1304), § 189, eff. Jan. 1, 2015.)*

Research References

3 Witkin, California Criminal Law 4th Punishment § 171 (2021), Commitment and Treatment.
3 Witkin, California Criminal Law 4th Punishment § 172 (2021), Petition Initiated by Department of Mental Health.
3 Witkin, California Criminal Law 4th Punishment § 173 (2021), Petition Initiated by Committed Person.

§ 6605. Petition for unconditional discharge; procedure for show cause hearing; effect of ruling against committed person; judicial review of commitment

(a)(1) The court, upon receiving a petition for unconditional discharge, shall order a show cause hearing at which the court can consider the petition and any accompanying documentation provided by the medical director, the prosecuting attorney, or the committed person.

(2) If the court at the show cause hearing determines that probable cause exists to believe that the committed person's diagnosed mental disorder has so changed that he or she is not a danger to the health and safety of others and is not likely to engage in sexually violent criminal behavior if discharged, then the court shall set a hearing on the issue.

(3) At the hearing, the committed person shall have the right to be present and shall be entitled to the benefit of all constitutional protections that were afforded to him or her at the initial commitment proceeding. The attorney designated by the county pursuant to subdivision (i) of Section 6601 shall represent the state and shall have the right to demand a jury trial and to have the committed person evaluated by experts chosen by the state. The committed person also shall have the right to demand a jury trial and to have experts evaluate him or her on his or her behalf. The court shall appoint an expert if the person is indigent and requests an appointment. The burden of proof at the hearing shall be on the state to prove beyond a reasonable doubt that the committed person's diagnosed mental disorder remains such that he or she is a danger to the health and safety of others and is likely to engage in sexually violent criminal behavior if discharged. Where the person's failure to participate in or complete treatment is relied upon as proof that the person's condition has not changed, and there is evidence to support that reliance, the jury shall be instructed substantially as follows:

"The committed person's failure to participate in or complete the State Department of State Hospitals Sex Offender Commitment Program (SOCP) are facts that, if proved, may be considered as evidence that the committed person's condition has not changed. The weight to be given that evidence is a matter for the jury to determine."

(b) If the court or jury rules against the committed person at the hearing conducted pursuant to subdivision (a), the term of commitment of the person shall run for an indeterminate period from the date of this ruling and the committed person may not file a new petition until one year has elapsed from the date of the ruling. If the court or jury rules for the committed person, he or she shall be unconditionally released and unconditionally discharged.

(c) If the State Department of State Hospitals has reason to believe that a person committed to it as a sexually violent predator is no longer a sexually violent predator, it shall seek judicial review of the person's commitment pursuant to the procedures set forth in Section 7250 in the superior court from which the commitment was made. If the superior court determines that the person is no longer a sexually violent predator, he or she shall be unconditionally released and unconditionally discharged. *(Added by Stats.1995, c. 763 (A.B.888), § 3. Amended by Stats.2006, c. 337 (S.B.1128), § 57, eff. Sept. 20, 2006; Initiative Measure (Prop. 83, § 29, approved Nov. 7, 2006, eff. Nov. 8, 2006); Stats.2009, c. 61 (S.B.669), § 1; Stats.2012, c. 24 (A.B.1470), § 144, eff. June 27, 2012; Stats.2013, c. 182 (S.B.295), § 2.)*

Cross References

Burden of proof, generally, see Evidence Code § 500 et seq.
Danger to the health and safety of others defined for purposes of this Article, see Welfare and Institutions Code § 6600.
Diagnosed mental disorder defined for purposes of this Article, see Welfare and Institutions Code § 6600.
Sexually violent predator defined for purposes of this Article, see Welfare and Institutions Code § 6600.

Research References

3 Witkin, California Criminal Law 4th Punishment § 171 (2021), Commitment and Treatment.
3 Witkin, California Criminal Law 4th Punishment § 172 (2021), Petition Initiated by Department of Mental Health.
3 Witkin, California Criminal Law 4th Punishment § 173 (2021), Petition Initiated by Committed Person.

§ 6606. Program of treatment; standards; protocol; model; patients who chose not to participate in a specific course of offender treatment

(a) A person who is committed under this article shall be provided with programming by the State Department of State Hospitals which shall afford the person with treatment for his or her diagnosed mental disorder. Persons who decline treatment shall be offered the opportunity to participate in treatment on at least a monthly basis.

(b) Amenability to treatment is not required for a finding that any person is a person described in Section 6600, nor is it required for treatment of that person. Treatment does not mean that the treatment be successful or potentially successful, nor does it mean that the person must recognize his or her problem and willingly participate in the treatment program.

(c) The programming provided by the State Department of State Hospitals in facilities shall be consistent with current institutional standards for the treatment of sex offenders, and shall be based on a structured treatment protocol developed by the State Department of State Hospitals. The protocol shall describe the number and types of treatment components that are provided in the program, and shall specify how assessment data will be used to determine the course of treatment for each individual offender. The protocol shall also specify measures that will be used to assess treatment progress and changes with respect to the individual's risk of reoffense.

(d) Notwithstanding any other provision of law, except as to requirements relating to fire and life safety of persons with mental illness, and consistent with information and standards described in subdivision (c), the State Department of State Hospitals is authorized to provide the programming using an outpatient/day treatment model, wherein treatment is provided by licensed professional clinicians in living units not licensed as health facility beds within a secure facility setting, on less than a 24–hour a day basis. The State Department of State Hospitals shall take into consideration the unique characteristics, individual needs, and choices of persons committed under this article, including whether or not a person needs antipsychotic medication, whether or not a person has physical medical conditions, and whether or not a person chooses to participate in a specified course of offender treatment. The State Department of State Hospitals shall ensure that policies and procedures are in place that address changes in patient needs, as well as patient choices, and respond to treatment needs in a timely fashion. The State Department of State Hospitals, in implementing this subdivision, shall be allowed by the State Department of Public Health to place health facility beds at Coalinga State Hospital in suspense in order to meet the mental health and medical needs of the patient population. Coalinga State Hospital may remove all or any portion of its voluntarily suspended beds into active license status by request to the State Department of Public Health. The facility's request shall be granted unless the suspended beds fail to comply with current operational requirements for licensure.

(e) The department shall meet with each patient who has chosen not to participate in a specific course of offender treatment during monthly treatment planning conferences. At these conferences the department shall explain treatment options available to the patient, offer and re-offer treatment to the patient, seek to obtain the patient's cooperation in the recommended treatment options, and document these steps in the patient's health record. The fact that a patient has chosen not to participate in treatment in the past shall not establish that the patient continues to choose not to participate. *(Added by Stats.1995, c. 763 (A.B.888), § 3. Amended by Stats.2005, c. 80 (A.B.131), § 20, eff. July 19, 2005; Stats.2012, c. 24 (A.B.1470), § 145, eff. June 27, 2012.)*

Cross References

Department of Health Care Services, generally, see Health and Safety Code § 100100 et seq.

Diagnosed mental disorder defined for purposes of this Article, see Welfare and Institutions Code § 6600.

Research References

3 Witkin, California Criminal Law 4th Punishment § 171 (2021), Commitment and Treatment.

3 Witkin, California Criminal Law 4th Punishment § 176 (2021), California Cases.

§ 6607. Determination that future predatory acts unlikely; report and recommendation of conditional release; judicial hearing

(a) If the Director of State Hospitals determines that the person's diagnosed mental disorder has so changed that the person is not likely to commit acts of predatory sexual violence while under supervision and treatment in the community, the director shall forward a report and recommendation for conditional release in accordance with Section 6608 to the county attorney designated in subdivision (i) of Section 6601, the attorney of record for the person, and the committing court.

(b) When a report and recommendation for conditional release is filed by the Director of State Hospitals pursuant to subdivision (a), the court shall set a hearing in accordance with the procedures set forth in Section 6608. *(Added by Stats.1995, c. 763 (A.B.888), § 3. Amended by Stats.2012, c. 440 (A.B.1488), § 69, eff. Sept. 22, 2012.)*

Cross References

Diagnosed mental disorder defined for purposes of this Article, see Welfare and Institutions Code § 6600.

Predatory defined for purposes of this Article, see Welfare and Institutions Code § 6600.

Research References

3 Witkin, California Criminal Law 4th Punishment § 171 (2021), Commitment and Treatment.

§ 6608. Petition for conditional release; hearing procedures; petition for unconditional discharge

(a) A person who has been committed as a sexually violent predator shall be permitted to petition the court for conditional release with or without the recommendation or concurrence of the Director of State Hospitals. If a person has previously filed a petition for conditional release without the concurrence of the director and the court determined, either upon review of the petition or following a hearing, that the petition was frivolous or that the committed person's condition had not so changed that * * * the person would not be a danger to others in that it is not likely that * * * the person will engage in sexually violent criminal behavior if placed under supervision and treatment in the community, the court shall deny the subsequent petition unless it contains facts upon which a court could find that the condition of the committed person had so changed that a hearing was warranted. Upon receipt of a first or subsequent petition from a committed person without the concurrence of the director, the court shall endeavor whenever possible to review the petition and determine if it is based upon frivolous grounds and, if so, shall deny the petition without a hearing. The person petitioning for conditional release under this subdivision shall be entitled to assistance of counsel in all hearings under this section. The person petitioning for conditional release shall serve a copy of the petition on the State Department of State Hospitals at the time the petition is filed with the court.

(b) The procedure for a conditional release hearing in a case where the county of domicile has not yet been determined shall be as follows:

(1) If the court deems the petition not frivolous pursuant to subdivision (a), the court shall give notice to the attorney designated in subdivision (i) of Section 6601, the retained or appointed attorney for the committed person, and the Director of State Hospitals of its intention to set a conditional release hearing. The person petitioning for conditional release, the Director of State Hospitals, and the designated attorney of the county of commitment shall notify the court within 30 court days of receipt of this notice if it appears that a county other than the county of commitment may be the county of domicile.

(2) If no county other than the county of commitment appears to be the county of domicile, the court shall determine, consistent with Section 6608.5, that the county of commitment is the county of domicile.

(3) If it appears or there are allegations that one or more counties, other than the county of commitment, may be the county of domicile, the court shall set a hearing to determine the county of domicile, consistent with the provisions of Section 6608.5. The court shall, at least 30 court days prior to the hearing, give notice of the domicile hearing to the persons listed in paragraph (1) and to the designated attorney for any county that is alleged to be the county of domicile. Persons listed in this paragraph and paragraph (1) may, at least 10 court days prior to the hearing, file and serve declarations, documentary evidence, and other pleadings, that are specific only to the issue of domicile. The court may, consistent with Section 6608.5, decide the issue of domicile solely on the pleadings, or additionally permit, in the interests of justice, argument and testimony.

(4) After determining the county of domicile pursuant to paragraph (2) or (3), the court shall set a date for a conditional release hearing and shall give notice of the hearing at least 30 court days before the hearing to the persons described in paragraph (1) and the designated attorney for the county of domicile.

(5)(A) If the county of domicile is different than the county of commitment, the designated attorney for the county of domicile and the designated attorney for the county of commitment may mutually agree that the designated attorney for the county of domicile will represent the state at the conditional release hearing. If the designated attorneys do not make this agreement, the designated attorney for the county of commitment will represent the state at the conditional release hearing.

(B) At least 20 court days before the conditional release hearing, the designated attorney for the county of commitment shall give notice to the parties listed in paragraph (1) and to the court whether the state will be represented by the designated attorney of the county of domicile or the designated attorney of the county of commitment.

(C) The designated attorney for the county of domicile and the designated attorney for the county of commitment should cooperate with each other to ensure that all relevant evidence is submitted on behalf of the state. No attorney other than the designated attorney for the county representing the state shall appear on behalf of the state at the conditional release hearing.

(6) The court's determination of a county of domicile shall govern the current and any subsequent petition for conditional release under this section.

(7) For the purpose of this subdivision, the term "county of domicile" shall have the same meaning as defined in Section 6608.5.

(8) For purposes of this section, the term "designated attorney of the county of commitment" means the attorney designated in subdivision (i) of Section 6601 in the county of commitment.

(9) For purposes of this section, the term "designated attorney for the county of domicile" means the attorney designated in subdivision (i) of Section 6601 in the county of domicile.

(c) The proceedings for a conditional release hearing in a case where the court has previously determined the county of domicile shall be as follows:

(1) If the court determines, pursuant to subdivision (a), that the petition is not frivolous, the court shall give notice of the hearing date at least 30 days prior to the hearing to the designated attorneys for the county of domicile and the county of commitment, the retained or appointed attorney for the petitioner, and the Director of State Hospitals.

(2) Representation of the state at the conditional release hearing shall be pursuant to paragraph (5) of subdivision (b).

(d)(1) If a committed person has been conditionally released by a court to a county other than the county of domicile, and the jurisdiction of the person has been transferred to that county, pursuant to subdivision (g) of Section 6608.5, the notice specified in paragraph (1) of subdivision (c) shall be given to the designated attorney of the county of placement, who shall represent the state in any further proceedings.

(2) The term "county of placement" means the county where the court has placed a person who is granted conditional release.

(e) If the petition for conditional release is made without the consent of the director of the treatment facility, no action shall be taken on the petition by the court without first obtaining the written recommendation of the director of the treatment facility.

(f) A hearing upon the petition shall not be held until the person who is committed has been under commitment for confinement and care in a facility designated by the Director of State Hospitals for not less than one year from the date of the order of commitment. A hearing upon the petition shall not be held until the community program director designated by the State Department of State Hospitals submits a report to the court that makes a recommendation as to the appropriateness of placing the person in a state-operated forensic conditional release program.

(g) The court shall hold a hearing to determine whether the person committed would be a danger to the health and safety of others in that it is likely that * * * <u>the person</u> will engage in sexually violent criminal behavior due to * * * <u>the person's</u> diagnosed mental disorder if under supervision and treatment in the community. The attorney designated pursuant to paragraph (5) of subdivision (b) shall represent the state and may have the committed person evaluated by experts chosen by the state. The committed person shall have the right to the appointment of experts, if * * * <u>the committed person</u> so requests. If the court at the hearing determines that the committed person would not be a danger to others due to * * * <u>the committed person's</u> diagnosed mental disorder while under supervision and treatment in the community, the court shall order the committed person placed with an appropriate forensic conditional release program operated by the state for one year. A substantial portion of the state-operated forensic conditional release program shall include outpatient supervision and treatment. The court shall retain jurisdiction of the person throughout the course of the program, except as provided in subdivision (g) of Section 6608.5.

(h) Before placing a committed person in a state-operated forensic conditional release program, the community program director designated by the State Department of State Hospitals shall submit a written recommendation to the court stating which forensic conditional release program is most appropriate for supervising and treating the committed person. If the court does not accept the community program director's recommendation, the court shall specify the reason or reasons for its order on the record. The procedures described in Sections 1605 to 1610, inclusive, of the Penal Code shall apply to the person placed in the forensic conditional release program.

(i) If the court determines that the person should be transferred to a state-operated forensic conditional release program, the community program director, or * * * <u>their</u> designee, shall make the necessary placement arrangements and, within 30 days after receiving notice of the court's finding, the person shall be placed in the community in accordance with the treatment and supervision plan unless good cause for not doing so is presented to the court.

(j) If the court denies the petition to place the person in an appropriate forensic conditional release program, the person may not file a new application until one year has elapsed from the date of the denial.

(k) In a hearing authorized by this section, the committed person shall have the burden of proof by a preponderance of the evidence, unless the report required by Section 6604.9 determines that conditional release to a less restrictive alternative is in the best interest of the person and that conditions can be imposed that would adequately protect the community, in which case the burden of proof shall be on the state to show, by a preponderance of the evidence, that conditional release is not appropriate.

(*l*) Time spent in a conditional release program pursuant to this section shall not count toward the term of commitment under this article unless the person is confined in a locked facility by the conditional release program, in which case the time spent in a locked facility shall count toward the term of commitment.

(m) After a minimum of one year on conditional release, the committed person, with or without the recommendation or concurrence of the Director of State Hospitals, may petition the court for unconditional discharge. The court shall use the procedures described in subdivisions (a) and (b) of Section 6605 to determine if the person should be unconditionally discharged from commitment on the basis that, by reason of a diagnosed mental disorder, * * * <u>the person</u> is no longer a danger to the health and safety of others in that it is not likely that * * * <u>the person</u> will engage in sexually violent criminal behavior. *(Added by Stats.1995, c. 763 (A.B.888), § 3. Amended by Initiative Measure (Prop. 83, § 30, approved Nov. 7, 2006, eff. Nov. 8, 2006); Stats.2007, c. 571 (A.B.1172), § 3; Stats.2012, c. 24 (A.B.1470), § 146, eff. June 27, 2012; Stats.2013, c. 182 (S.B.295),*

§ 3; Stats.2014, c. 877 (A.B.1607), § 1, eff. Jan. 1, 2015; Stats.2022, c. 880 (S.B.1034), § 1, eff. Jan. 1, 2023.)

Cross References

Burden of proof, generally, see Evidence Code § 500 et seq.
Danger to the health and safety of others defined for purposes of this Article, see Welfare and Institutions Code § 6600.
Diagnosed mental disorder defined for purposes of this Article, see Welfare and Institutions Code § 6600.
Sexually violent predator defined for purposes of this Article, see Welfare and Institutions Code § 6600.

Research References

3 Witkin, California Criminal Law 4th Punishment § 171 (2021), Commitment and Treatment.
3 Witkin, California Criminal Law 4th Punishment § 172 (2021), Petition Initiated by Department of Mental Health.
3 Witkin, California Criminal Law 4th Punishment § 173 (2021), Petition Initiated by Committed Person.

§ 6608.1. Release on outpatient status or conditional release; GPS monitoring

A person who is released on outpatient status or granted conditional release pursuant to this article shall be monitored by a global positioning system (GPS) until the person is unconditionally discharged. *(Added by Stats.2022, c. 104 (A.B.1641), § 1, eff. Jan. 1, 2023.)*

§ 6608.5. Conditional release; placement in county of domicile; considerations for recommending a specific placement for community outpatient treatment; placement restrictions with respect to schools

(a) * * * After a judicial determination that a person would not be a danger to the health and safety of others in that it is not likely that the person will engage in sexually violent criminal behavior due to the person's diagnosed mental disorder while under supervision and treatment in the community, a person who is conditionally released pursuant to this article shall be placed in the county of * * * domicile of the person prior to the person's incarceration, unless both of the following conditions are satisfied:

(1) The court finds that extraordinary circumstances require placement outside the county of domicile as set forth in Section 6608.6.

(2) The designated county of placement was given prior notice and an opportunity to comment on the proposed placement of the committed person in the county, according to procedures set forth in Section 6609.1.

(b)(1) For the purposes of this section, "county of domicile" means the county where the person has * * * their true, fixed, and permanent home and principal residence and to which * * * the person has manifested the intention of returning whenever * * * the person is absent. For the purposes of determining the county of domicile, the court shall consider information found on a California driver's license, California identification card, recent rent or utility receipt, printed personalized checks or other recent banking documents showing that person's name and address, or information contained in an arrest record, probation officer's report, trial transcript, or other court document. If no information can be identified or verified, the county of domicile of the individual shall be considered to be the county in which the person was arrested for the crime for which * * * the person was last incarcerated in the state prison or from which * * * the person was last returned from parole.

(2) In a case where the person committed a crime while being held for treatment in a state hospital, or while being confined in a state prison or local jail facility, the county wherein that facility was located shall not be considered the county of domicile unless the person resided in that county prior to being housed in the hospital, prison, or jail.

(c) For the purposes of this section, "extraordinary circumstances" means circumstances that would inordinately limit the department's ability to effect conditional release of the person in the county of domicile in accordance with Section 6608 or any other provision of this article, and the procedures described in Sections 1605 to 1610, inclusive, of the Penal Code.

(d)(1) The counsel for the committed individual, the sheriff or the chief of police of the locality for placement, and the county counsel and the district attorney of the county of domicile, or their designees, shall * * * provide assistance and consultation in the department's process of locating and securing housing within the county for persons committed as sexually violent predators who are about to be conditionally released under Section 6608. Upon notification by the department of a person's potential or expected conditional release under Section 6608, the counsel for the committed individual, the sheriff or the chief of police of the locality for placement, and the county counsel and the district attorney of the county of domicile, or their designees, shall * * * provide appropriate contact information for their respective office to the department, at least 60 days before the date of the potential or expected release.

(2) The department shall convene a committee with the participants listed in paragraph (1) for the purpose of obtaining relevant assistance and consultation information in order to secure suitable housing for the person to be conditionally released.

(3) The court may order a status conference to evaluate the department's progress in locating and securing housing and in obtaining relevant assistance and consultation information from the participants listed in paragraph (1). The court may sanction any of the participants listed in paragraph (1) for failure to appear at the status conference unless the participant shows good cause for their failure to appear.

(4) This subdivision does not require the participants listed in paragraph (1) to perform a housing site assessment.

(e) In recommending a specific placement for community outpatient treatment, the department or its designee shall consider all of the following:

(1) The concerns and proximity of the victim or the victim's next of kin.

(2) The age and profile of the victim or victims in the sexually violent offenses committed by the person subject to placement. For purposes of this subdivision, the "profile" of a victim includes, but is not limited to, gender, physical appearance, economic background, profession, and other social or personal characteristics.

(f) Notwithstanding any other law, a person released under this section shall not be placed within one-quarter mile of any public or private school providing instruction in kindergarten or any of grades 1 to 12, inclusive, if either of the following conditions exist:

(1) The person has previously been convicted of a violation of Section 288.5 of, or subdivision (a) or (b), or paragraph (1) of subdivision (c) of Section 288 of, the Penal Code.

(2) The court finds that the person has a history of improper sexual conduct with children.

* * *

(g)(1) Except as provided in paragraph (2), if the committed person is ordered to be conditionally released in a county other than the county of commitment due to an extraordinary circumstances pursuant to Section 6608.6, the court shall order that jurisdiction of the person and all records related to the case be transferred to the court of the county of placement. Upon transfer of jurisdiction to the county of placement, the designated attorney of the county of placement shall represent the state in all further proceedings.

(2) The designated attorney of the county of commitment shall serve written notice upon the designated attorney for the county of placement within 15 court days of an order to place a committed

person in the county of placement. The designated attorney of the county of placement may file an affidavit with the court in the county of commitment objecting to the transfer of jurisdiction within 15 court days after receiving the notice. If the affidavit objecting to the transfer of jurisdiction is timely filed, the court shall not transfer jurisdiction. If an affidavit objecting to the transfer of jurisdiction is not timely filed, paragraph (1) shall apply.

(3) For the purpose of this section, "county of placement" means the county where the court orders the committed person to be placed for conditional release.

(4) For the purpose of this section, "designated attorney of the county of placement" means the attorney designated in subdivision (*l*) of Section 6601 in the county of placement.

(5) This section shall not be construed to negate or in any way affect the decision of the court of the county of commitment to conditionally release the committed person in the county of placement. *(Added by Stats.2004, c. 222 (A.B.493), § 1, eff. Aug. 12, 2004. Amended by Stats.2005, c. 162 (A.B.893), § 1; Stats.2005, c. 486 (S.B.723), § 1.5; Stats.2014, c. 877 (A.B.1607), § 2, eff. Jan. 1, 2015; Stats.2017, c. 39 (A.B.255), § 1, eff. Jan. 1, 2018; Stats.2022, c. 880 (S.B.1034), § 2, eff. Jan. 1, 2023.)*

Cross References

Sexually violent offense defined for purposes of this Article, see Welfare and Institutions Code § 6600.

Sexually violent predator defined for purposes of this Article, see Welfare and Institutions Code § 6600.

Research References

3 Witkin, California Criminal Law 4th Punishment § 173 (2021), Petition Initiated by Committed Person.

3 Witkin, California Criminal Law 4th Punishment § 174 (2021), Placement on Conditional Release.

§ 6608.6. County of domicile; petition for finding of extraordinary circumstances

(a) A court may make a finding of extraordinary circumstances only after the committed person's county of domicile has petitioned the court to make this finding.

(b) The court may grant the county of domicile's petition and make a finding of extraordinary circumstances only after all of the following have occurred:

(1) The county of domicile has demonstrated to the court that the county of domicile has engaged in an exhaustive housing search with meaningful and robust participation from the participants listed in subdivision (d) of Section 6608.5 in both committee conferences and status conferences. The county of domicile shall provide the court with declarations from the county of domicile and all the participants attesting to the exhaustive housing search.

(2)(A) The county of domicile has provided at least one alternative placement county for consideration and has noticed the district attorney, or district attorneys, of the alternative placement county, or counties, and the department regarding the county of domicile's intention to petition for a finding of extraordinary circumstance.

(B) The county of domicile shall indicate, if applicable, how the committed person has a community connection to a proposed alternative placement county, including whether the committed person has previously resided, been employed, or has next of kin in a proposed alternative placement county.

(3) The county of domicile has provided the declarations and community connection information required by paragraphs (1) and (2) to the department and to the district attorney of a proposed alternative placement county.

(4) The department and the district attorney of a proposed alternative placement county have had an opportunity to be heard at a hearing, which shall be noticed no fewer than 30 days before the date of the hearing.

(c)(1) If the court finds that extraordinary circumstances require the placement to occur outside the county of domicile, the court shall state its findings on the record and the grounds supporting its findings.

(2) Extraordinary costs associated with a housing placement inside the county of domicile shall not be grounds for a finding of extraordinary circumstances.

(d) A court shall not order a search of alternative housing placements outside of the county of domicile until after the court has granted a petition finding that extraordinary circumstances exist.

(e) The Judicial Council shall report to the Legislature on an annual basis the instances in which a court issues a finding of extraordinary circumstances and shall detail the court's findings and grounds supporting the findings, as stated by the court pursuant to subdivision (c). The annual report required by this subdivision shall be submitted in compliance with Section 9795 of the Government Code.

(f) Notwithstanding any other law, a court may order the placement of the committed person in an alternative placement county upon stipulation between the domicile county and the alternative placement county. *(Added by Stats.2022, c. 880 (S.B.1034), § 3, eff. Jan. 1, 2023.)*

§ 6608.7. Interagency agreements or contracts for services related to supervision or monitoring of sexually violent predators conditionally released into community

The State Department of State Hospitals may enter into an interagency agreement or contract with the Department of Corrections and Rehabilitation or with local law enforcement agencies for services related to supervision or monitoring of sexually violent predators who have been conditionally released into the community under the forensic conditional release program pursuant to this article. *(Added by Stats.2005, c. 137 (S.B.383), § 1. Amended by Stats.2014, c. 442 (S.B.1465), § 17, eff. Sept. 18, 2014.)*

Cross References

Department of Corrections and Rehabilitation, generally, see Penal Code § 5000 et seq.

Sexually violent predator defined for purposes of this Article, see Welfare and Institutions Code § 6600.

§ 6608.8. Persons proposed for community outpatient treatment under forensic conditional release program; terms and conditions

(a) For any person who is proposed for community outpatient treatment under the forensic conditional release program, the department shall provide to the court a copy of the written contract entered into with any public or private person or entity responsible for monitoring and supervising the patient's outpatient placement and treatment program. This subdivision does not apply to subcontracts between the contractor and clinicians providing treatment and related services to the person.

(b) The terms and conditions of conditional release shall be drafted to include reasonable flexibility to achieve the aims of conditional release, and to protect the public and the conditionally released person.

(c) The court in its discretion may order the department to, notwithstanding Section 4514 or 5328, provide a copy of the written terms and conditions of conditional release to the sheriff or chief of police, or both, that have jurisdiction over the proposed or actual placement community.

(d)(1) Except in an emergency, the department or its designee shall not alter the terms and conditions of conditional release without the prior approval of the court.

(2) The department shall provide notice to the person committed under this article and the district attorney or designated county counsel of any proposed change in the terms and conditions of conditional release.

(3) The court on its own motion, or upon the motion of either party to the action, may set a hearing on the proposed change. The hearing shall be held as soon as is practicable.

(4) If a hearing on the proposed change is held, the court shall state its findings on the record. If the court approves a change in the terms and conditions of conditional release without a hearing, the court shall issue a written order.

(5) In the case of an emergency, the department or its designee may deviate from the terms and conditions of the conditional release if necessary to protect public safety or the safety of the person. If a hearing on the emergency is set by the court or requested by either party, the hearing shall be held as soon as practicable. The department, its designee, and the parties shall endeavor to resolve routine matters in a cooperative fashion without the need for a formal hearing.

(e) Notwithstanding any provision of this section, including, but not limited to, subdivision (d), matters concerning the residential placement, including any changes or proposed changes in the residence of the person, shall be considered and determined pursuant to Section 6609.1. *(Added by Stats.2006, c. 339 (A.B.1683), § 1. Amended by Stats.2007, c. 302 (S.B.425), § 20.)*

§ 6609. Conditional release program; requests for information on participants; time for compliance

Within 10 days of a request made by the chief of police of a city or the sheriff of a county, the State Department of State Hospitals shall provide the following information concerning each person committed as a sexually violent predator who is receiving outpatient care in a conditional release program in that city or county: name, address, date of commitment, county from which committed, date of placement in the conditional release program, fingerprints, and a glossy photograph no smaller than 3 ⅛ x 3 ⅛ inches in size, or clear copies of the fingerprints and photograph. *(Added by Stats.1996, c. 462 (A.B.3130), § 7, eff. Sept. 13, 1996. Amended by Stats.2014, c. 442 (S.B.1465), § 18, eff. Sept. 18, 2014.)*

Cross References

Sexually violent predator defined for purposes of this Article, see Welfare and Institutions Code § 6600.

Research References

3 Witkin, California Criminal Law 4th Punishment § 173 (2021), Petition Initiated by Committed Person.

§ 6609.1. Community outpatient treatment or petition for release or unconditional discharge of sexually violent predators; notice requirements; agency comments and statements; other notice requirements concerning recommitment recommendations or review of commitment status; parole arrangement; time limits; subsequent notice

(a)(1) When the State Department of State Hospitals makes a recommendation to the court for community outpatient treatment for any person committed as a sexually violent predator, or when a person who is committed as a sexually violent predator pursuant to this article has petitioned a court pursuant to Section 6608 for conditional release under supervision and treatment in the community pursuant to a conditional release program, or has petitioned a court pursuant to Section 6608 for subsequent unconditional discharge, and the department is notified, or is aware, of the filing of the petition, and when a community placement location is recommended or proposed, the department shall notify the sheriff or chief of police, or both, the district attorney, or the county's designated counsel, that have jurisdiction over the following locations:

(A) The community in which the person may be released for community outpatient treatment.

(B) The community in which the person maintained his or her last legal residence as defined by Section 3003 of the Penal Code.

(C) The county that filed for the person's civil commitment pursuant to this article.

(2) The department shall also notify the Sexually Violent Predator Parole Coordinator of the Department of Corrections and Rehabilitation, if the person is otherwise subject to parole pursuant to Article 1 (commencing with Section 3000) of Chapter 8 of Title 1 of Part 3 of the Penal Code. The department shall also notify the Department of Justice.

(3) The notice shall be given when the department or its designee makes a recommendation under subdivision (e) of Section 6608 or proposes a placement location without making a recommendation, or when any other person proposes a placement location to the court and the department or its designee is made aware of the proposal.

(4) The notice shall be given at least 30 days prior to the department's submission of its recommendation to the court in those cases in which the department recommended community outpatient treatment under Section 6607, or in which the department or its designee is recommending or proposing a placement location, or in the case of a petition or placement proposal by someone other than the department or its designee, within 48 hours after becoming aware of the petition or placement proposal.

(5) The notice shall state that it is being made under this section and include all of the following information concerning each person committed as a sexually violent predator who is proposed or is petitioning to receive outpatient care in a conditional release program in that city or county:

(A) The name, proposed placement address, date of commitment, county from which committed, proposed date of placement in the conditional release program, fingerprints, and a glossy photograph no smaller than 3 ⅛ by 3 ⅛ inches in size, or clear copies of the fingerprints and photograph.

(B) The date, place, and time of the court hearing at which the location of placement is to be considered and a proof of service attesting to the notice's mailing in accordance with this subdivision.

(C) A list of agencies that are being provided this notice and the addresses to which the notices are being sent.

(b) Those agencies receiving the notice referred to in paragraphs (1) and (2) of subdivision (a) may provide written comment to the department and the court regarding the impending release, placement, location, and conditions of release. All community agency comments shall be combined and consolidated. The written comment shall be filed with the court at the time that the comment is provided to the department. The written comment shall identify differences between the comment filed with the court and that provided to the department, if any. In addition, a single agency in the community of the specific proposed or recommended placement address may suggest appropriate, alternative locations for placement within that community. A copy of the suggested alternative placement location shall be filed with the court at the time that the suggested placement location is provided to the department. The State Department of State Hospitals shall issue a written statement to the commenting agencies and to the court within 10 days of receiving the written comments with a determination as to whether to adjust the release location or general terms and conditions, and explaining the basis for its decision. In lieu of responding to the individual community agencies or individuals, the department's statement responding to the community comment shall be in the form of a public statement.

(c) The agencies' comments and department's statements shall be considered by the court which shall, based on those comments and statements, approve, modify, or reject the department's recommendation or proposal regarding the community or specific address to which the person is scheduled to be released or the conditions that shall apply to the release if the court finds that the department's recommendation or proposal is not appropriate.

(d)(1) When the State Department of State Hospitals makes a recommendation to pursue recommitment, makes a recommendation not to pursue recommitment, or seeks a judicial review of commitment status pursuant to subdivision (f) of Section 6605, of any person committed as a sexually violent predator, it shall provide written notice of that action to the sheriff or chief of police, or both, and to the district attorney, that have jurisdiction over the following locations:

(A) The community in which the person maintained his or her last legal residence as defined by Section 3003 of the Penal Code.

(B) The community in which the person will probably be released, if recommending not to pursue recommitment.

(C) The county that filed for the person's civil commitment pursuant to this article.

(2) The State Department of State Hospitals shall also notify the Sexually Violent Predator Parole Coordinator of the Department of Corrections and Rehabilitation, if the person is otherwise subject to parole pursuant to Article 1 (commencing with Section 3000) of Chapter 8 of Title 1 of Part 3 of the Penal Code. The State Department of State Hospitals shall also notify the Department of Justice. The notice shall be made at least 15 days prior to the department's submission of its recommendation to the court.

(3) Those agencies receiving the notice referred to in this subdivision shall have 15 days from receipt of the notice to provide written comment to the department regarding the impending release. At the time that the written comment is made to the department, a copy of the written comment shall be filed with the court by the agency or agencies making the comment. Those comments shall be considered by the department, which may modify its decision regarding the community in which the person is scheduled to be released, based on those comments.

(e)(1) If the court orders the release of a sexually violent predator, the court shall notify the Sexually Violent Predator Parole Coordinator of the Department of Corrections and Rehabilitation. The Department of Corrections and Rehabilitation shall notify the Department of Justice, the State Department of State Hospitals, the sheriff or chief of police or both, and the district attorney, that have jurisdiction over the following locations:

(A) The community in which the person is to be released.

(B) The community in which the person maintained his or her last legal residence as defined in Section 3003 of the Penal Code.

(2) The Department of Corrections and Rehabilitation shall make the notifications required by this subdivision regardless of whether the person released will be serving a term of parole after release by the court.

(f) If the person is otherwise subject to parole pursuant to Article 1 (commencing with Section 300) of Chapter 8 of Title 1 of Part 3 of the Penal Code, to allow adequate time for the Department of Corrections and Rehabilitation to make appropriate parole arrangements upon release of the person, the person shall remain in physical custody for a period not to exceed 72 hours or until parole arrangements are made by the Sexually Violent Predator Parole Coordinator of the Department of Corrections and Rehabilitation, whichever is sooner. To facilitate timely parole arrangements, notification to the Sexually Violent Predator Parole Coordinator of the Department of Corrections and Rehabilitation of the pending release shall be made by telephone or facsimile and, to the extent possible, notice of the possible release shall be made in advance of the proceeding or decision determining whether to release the person.

(g) The notice required by this section shall be made whether or not a request has been made pursuant to Section 6609.

(h) The time limits imposed by this section are not applicable when the release date of a sexually violent predator has been advanced by a judicial or administrative process or procedure that could not have reasonably been anticipated by the State Department of State Hospitals and where, as the result of the time adjustments, there is less than 30 days remaining on the commitment before the inmate's release, but notice shall be given as soon as practicable.

(i) In the case of any subsequent community placement or change of community placement of a conditionally released sexually violent predator, notice required by this section shall be given under the same terms and standards as apply to the initial placement, except in the case of an emergency where the sexually violent predator must be moved to protect the public safety or the safety of the sexually violent predator. In the case of an emergency, the notice shall be given as soon as practicable, and the affected communities may comment on the placement as described in subdivision (b).

(j) The provisions of this section are severable. If any provision of this section or its application is held invalid, that invalidity shall not affect other provisions or applications that can be given effect without the invalid provision or application. *(Added by Stats.1996, c. 462 (A.B.3130), § 8, eff. Sept. 13, 1996. Amended by Stats.1998, c. 19 (S.B.536), § 6, eff. April 14, 1998; Stats.1998, c. 961 (S.B.1976), § 9, eff. Sept. 29, 1998; Stats.1999, c. 83 (S.B.966), § 201; Stats.2002, c. 139 (A.B.1967), § 1; Stats.2004, c. 425 (A.B.2450), § 1; Stats.2007, c. 571 (A.B.1172), § 4; Stats.2012, c. 440 (A.B.1488), § 70, eff. Sept. 22, 2012.)*

Cross References

Department of Corrections and Rehabilitation, generally, see Penal Code § 5000 et seq.
Sexually violent predator defined for purposes of this Article, see Welfare and Institutions Code § 6600.
Sexually violent predators, conditional release program, terms and conditions, see Welfare and Institutions Code § 6608.8.

§ 6609.2. Notice of recommendation regarding disposition of sexually violent predator; immunity

(a) When any sheriff or chief of police is notified by the State Department of State Hospitals of its recommendation to the court concerning the disposition of a sexually violent predator pursuant to subdivision (a) or (b) of Section 6609.1, that sheriff or chief of police may notify any person designated by the sheriff or chief of police as an appropriate recipient of the notice.

(b) A law enforcement official authorized to provide notice pursuant to this section, and the public agency or entity employing the law enforcement official, shall not be liable for providing or failing to provide notice pursuant to this section. *(Added by Stats.1996, c. 462 (A.B.3130), § 9, eff. Sept. 13, 1996. Amended by Stats.1998, c. 19 (S.B.536), § 7, eff. April 14, 1998; Stats.1998, c. 961 (S.B.1976), § 10, eff. Sept. 29, 1998; Stats.2012, c. 440 (A.B.1488), § 71, eff. Sept. 22, 2012.)*

Cross References

Sexually violent predator defined for purposes of this Article, see Welfare and Institutions Code § 6600.

§ 6609.3. Notice to witnesses, victims, or next of kin

(a) At the time a notice is sent pursuant to subdivisions (a) and (b) of Section 6609.1, the sheriff, chief of police, or district attorney notified of the release shall also send a notice to persons described in Section 679.03 of the Penal Code who have requested a notice, informing those persons of the fact that the person who committed the sexually violent offense may be released together with information identifying the court that will consider the conditional release, recommendation regarding recommitment, or review of commitment status pursuant to subdivision (f) of Section 6605. When a person is approved by the court to be conditionally released, notice of the community in which the person is scheduled to reside shall also be given only if it is (1) in the county of residence of a witness, victim, or family member of a victim who has requested notice, or (2) within 100 miles of the actual residence of a witness, victim, or family member of a victim who has requested notice. If, after providing the witness, victim, or next of kin with the notice, there is any change in the release date or the community in which the person is to reside, the sheriff, chief of police, or the district attorney shall provide the witness, victim, or next of kin with the revised information.

(b) At the time a notice is sent pursuant to subdivision (c) of Section 6609.1 the Department of Corrections shall also send a notice to persons described in Section 679.03 of the Penal Code who have requested a notice informing those persons of the fact that the person who committed the sexually violent offense has been released.

(c) In order to be entitled to receive the notice set forth in this section, the requesting party shall keep the sheriff, chief of police, and district attorney who were notified under Section 679.03 of the Penal Code, informed of his or her current mailing address. *(Added by Stats.1996, c. 462 (A.B.3130), § 10, eff. Sept. 13, 1996. Amended by Stats.1998, c. 19 (S.B.536), § 8, eff. April 14, 1998; Stats.1998, c. 961 (S.B.1976), § 11, eff. Sept. 29, 1998.)*

Cross References

Department of Corrections and Rehabilitation, generally, see Penal Code § 5000 et seq.
Sexually violent offense defined for purposes of this Article, see Welfare and Institutions Code § 6600.

§ 6625. Editorial Note

Stats.1953, c. 110, p. 844, § 1, repealed Stats.1913, c. 363, p. 775. The 1953 act, by § 2, repealed § 6625. The same act, by § 3, stated that § 2 became operative only if § 6625, codifying Chapter 363 of the Statutes of 1913 was added to the code at the 1953 regular session. The 1913 act was not codified, hence § 2 did not become operative.

Division 7

MENTAL INSTITUTIONS

CHAPTER 2. STATE HOSPITALS FOR THE MENTALLY DISORDERED

ARTICLE 6. ESCAPES

§ 7326. Assisting escape; offense

Any person who willfully assists any judicially committed or remanded patient of a state hospital or other public or private mental health facility to escape, to attempt to escape therefrom, or to resist being returned from a leave of absence shall be punished by imprisonment pursuant to subdivision (h) of Section 1170 of the Penal Code, a fine of not more than ten thousand dollars ($10,000), or both such imprisonment and fine; or by imprisonment in a county jail for a period of not more than one year, a fine of not more than two thousand dollars ($2,000), or both such imprisonment and fine. *(Added by Stats.1967, c. 1667, p. 4146, § 40, operative July 1, 1969. Amended by Stats.1969, c. 1021, p. 1989, § 1; Stats.1970, c. 79, p. 92, § 1; Stats.1976, c. 1139, p. 5174, § 346, operative July 1, 1977; Stats.1981, c. 1054, p. 4071, § 5; Stats.1983, c. 1092, § 420, eff. Sept. 27, 1983, operative Jan. 1, 1984; Stats.2011, c. 15 (A.B.109), § 624, eff. April 4, 2011, operative Oct. 1, 2011.)*

Cross References

Judicially committed defined for purposes of this Division, see Welfare and Institutions Code § 5008.1.

Research References

2 Witkin, California Criminal Law 4th Crimes Against Governmental Authority § 103 (2021), Assisting Escape.

Division 8

MISCELLANEOUS

CHAPTER 3. FIREARMS

§ 8100. Possession, purchase or receipt by person receiving inpatient treatment for a mental disorder or who has communicated a threat of physical violence to a psychotherapist; violation

(a) A person shall not have in his or her possession or under his or her custody or control, or purchase or receive, or attempt to purchase or receive, any firearms whatsoever or any other deadly weapon, if on or after January 1, 1992, he or she has been admitted to a facility and is receiving inpatient treatment and, in the opinion of the attending health professional who is primarily responsible for the patient's treatment of a mental disorder, is a danger to self or others, as specified by Section 5150, 5250, or 5300, even though the patient has consented to that treatment. A person is not subject to the prohibition in this subdivision after he or she is discharged from the facility.

(b)(1) A person shall not have in his or her possession or under his or her custody or control, or purchase or receive, or attempt to purchase or receive, any firearms whatsoever or any other deadly weapon for a period of five years if, on or after January 1, 2014, he or she communicates to a licensed psychotherapist, as defined in subdivisions (a) to (e), inclusive, of Section 1010 of the Evidence Code, a serious threat of physical violence against a reasonably identifiable victim or victims. The five-year period shall commence from the date that the licensed psychotherapist reports to the local law enforcement agency the identity of the person making the communication. The prohibition provided for in this subdivision shall not apply unless the licensed psychotherapist notifies a local law enforcement agency of the threat by that person. The person, however, may own, possess, have custody or control over, or receive or purchase any firearm if a superior court, pursuant to paragraph (3) and upon petition of the person, has found, by a preponderance of the evidence, that the person is likely to use firearms or other deadly weapons in a safe and lawful manner.

(2) Upon receipt of the report from the local law enforcement agency pursuant to subdivision (c) of Section 8105, the Department of Justice shall notify by certified mail, return receipt requested, a person subject to this subdivision of the following:

(A) That he or she is prohibited from possessing, having custody or control over, receiving, or purchasing any firearm or other deadly weapon for a period of five years commencing from the date that the licensed psychotherapist reports to the local law enforcement agency the identity of the person making the communication. The notice shall state the date when the prohibition commences and ends.

(B) That he or she may petition a court, as provided in this subdivision, for an order permitting the person to own, possess, control, receive, or purchase a firearm.

(3)(A) Any person who is subject to paragraph (1) may petition the superior court of his or her county of residence for an order that he or she may own, possess, have custody or control over, receive, or purchase firearms. At the time the petition is filed, the clerk of the court shall set a hearing date and notify the person, the Department of Justice, and the district attorney. The people of the State of California shall be the respondent in the proceeding and shall be represented by the district attorney. Upon motion of the district attorney, or upon its own motion, the superior court may transfer the petition to the county in which the person resided at the time of the statements, or the county in which the person made the statements. Within seven days after receiving notice of the petition, the Department of Justice shall file copies of the reports described in Section 8105 with the superior court. The reports shall be disclosed upon request to the person and to the district attorney. The district attorney shall be entitled to a continuance of the hearing to a date of not less than 14 days after the district attorney is notified of the hearing date by the clerk of the court. The court, upon motion of the petitioner establishing that confidential information is likely to be discussed during the hearing that would cause harm to the person, shall conduct the hearing in camera with only the relevant parties present, unless the court finds that the public interest would be better served by conducting the hearing in public. Notwithstanding any other provision of law, declarations, police reports, including criminal history information, and any other material and relevant evidence that is not excluded under Section 352 of the Evidence Code, shall be admissible at the hearing under this paragraph.

(B) The people shall bear the burden of showing by a preponderance of the evidence that the person would not be likely to use firearms in a safe and lawful manner.

(C) If the court finds at the hearing that the people have not met their burden as set forth in subparagraph (B), the court shall order that the person shall not be subject to the five-year prohibition in this section on the ownership, control, receipt, possession, or purchase of firearms, and that person shall comply with the procedure described in Chapter 2 (commencing with Section 33850) of Division 11 of Title 4 of Part 6 of the Penal Code for the return of any firearms. A copy of the order shall be submitted to the Department of Justice. Upon receipt of the order, the Department of Justice shall delete any reference to the prohibition against firearms from the person's state mental health firearms prohibition system information.

(D) If the district attorney declines or fails to go forward in the hearing, the court shall order that the person shall not be subject to the five-year prohibition required by this subdivision on the ownership, control, receipt, possession, or purchase of firearms, and that person shall comply with the procedure described in Chapter 2 (commencing with Section 33850) of Division 11 of Title 4 of Part 6 of the Penal Code for the return of any firearms. A copy of the order shall be submitted to the Department of Justice. Upon receipt of the order, the Department of Justice shall, within 15 days, delete any reference to the prohibition against firearms from the person's state mental health firearms prohibition system information.

(E) Nothing in this subdivision shall prohibit the use of reports filed pursuant to this section to determine the eligibility of a person to own, possess, control, receive, or purchase a firearm if the person is the subject of a criminal investigation, a part of which involves the ownership, possession, control, receipt, or purchase of a firearm.

(c) "Discharge," for the purposes of this section, does not include a leave of absence from a facility.

(d) "Attending health care professional," as used in this section, means the licensed health care professional primarily responsible for the person's treatment who is qualified to make the decision that the person has a mental disorder and has probable cause to believe that the person is a danger to self or others.

(e) "Deadly weapon," as used in this section and in Sections 8101, 8102, and 8103, means any weapon, the possession or concealed carrying of which is prohibited by any provision listed in Section 16590 of the Penal Code.

(f) "Danger to self," as used in subdivision (a), means a voluntary person who has made a serious threat of, or attempted, suicide with the use of a firearm or other deadly weapon.

(g) A violation of subdivision (a) of, or paragraph (1) of subdivision (b) of, this section shall be a public offense, punishable by imprisonment pursuant to subdivision (h) of Section 1170 of the Penal Code, or in a county jail for not more than one year, by a fine not exceeding one thousand dollars ($1,000), or by both that imprisonment and fine.

(h) The prohibitions set forth in this section shall be in addition to those set forth in Section 8103.

(i) Any person admitted and receiving treatment prior to January 1, 1992, shall be governed by this section, as amended by Chapter 1090 of the Statutes of 1990, until discharged from the facility. *(Added by Stats.1967, c. 1667, p. 4183, § 42, operative July 1, 1969. Amended by Stats.1985, c. 1324, § 2; Stats.1990, c. 9 (A.B.497), § 15; Stats.1990, c. 1090 (S.B.2050), § 4; Stats.1991, c. 951 (A.B.664), § 9; Stats.1991, c. 952 (A.B.1904), § 5; Stats.1992, c. 1326 (A.B.3552), § 16; Stats.2010, c. 178 (S.B.1115), § 103, operative Jan. 1, 2012; Stats.2011, c. 15 (A.B.109), § 626, eff. April 4, 2011, operative Jan. 1, 2012; Stats.2013, c. 747 (A.B.1131), § 1.)*

Law Revision Commission Comments

Subdivision (e) of Section 8100 is amended to reflect nonsubstantive reorganization of the statutes governing control of deadly weapons. [38 Cal.L.Rev.Comm. Reports 217 (2009)].

Cross References

Certificate of eligibility requirement for agents or employees who handle, sell, or deliver firearm precursor parts, prohibition against specified agents or employees handling firearm precursor parts, see Penal Code § 30447.
Concealed weapons, unlawful possession thereof, see Penal Code § 12020 et seq.
Custodial or transportation officers, notification to state or local agency of restrictions on firearm possession, see Penal Code § 832.17.
License to carry a concealed weapon, denial or revocation, persons within prohibited class described in this section, see Penal Code § 26150.
License to sell firearms at retail, forfeiture upon delivery of firearms to persons in prohibited classes under this section, see Penal Code § 26700.
Notification to agencies employing or taking applications for peace officers authorized to carry firearms, see Penal Code §§ 832.15, 832.16.
Permits, denial to issue, refusal to renew, and automatic revocation, alarm companies, see Business and Professions Code §§ 7596.8, 7596.81, 7596.83.
Person prohibited from owning or possessing firearm also prohibited from owning or possessing firearm precursor part, penalties, exemptions, see Penal Code § 30405.
Processing firearm purchaser information, background check, delay of transfer of firearm to purchaser following receipt of information about purchaser, see Penal Code § 28220.
Prohibited persons, attempt to acquire or report acquisition or ownership of firearm, notice to local law enforcement agency and county department of mental health, see Penal Code § 29880.

Research References

2 Witkin, California Criminal Law 4th Crimes Against Public Peace and Welfare § 194 (2021), Furnishing Erroneous Firearm Purchaser Information.
2 Witkin, California Criminal Law 4th Crimes Against Public Peace and Welfare § 196 (2021), Transfers to Specified Persons.
2 Witkin, California Criminal Law 4th Crimes Against Public Peace and Welfare § 202 (2021), License to Manufacture.
2 Witkin, California Criminal Law 4th Crimes Against Public Peace and Welfare § 204 (2021), Punishment.
2 Witkin, California Criminal Law 4th Crimes Against Public Peace and Welfare § 207 (2021), Exempt Persons.
2 Witkin, California Criminal Law 4th Crimes Against Public Peace and Welfare § 210 (2021), Unlawful Acts Involving Ammunition.
2 Witkin, California Criminal Law 4th Crimes Against Public Peace and Welfare § 232 (2021), Nature and Scope of Statutes.
2 Witkin, California Criminal Law 4th Crimes Against Public Peace and Welfare § 239 (2021), Misdemeanants.
2 Witkin, California Criminal Law 4th Crimes Against Public Peace and Welfare § 245 (2021), In General.
2 Witkin, California Criminal Law 4th Crimes Against Public Peace and Welfare § 246 (2021), Persons Prohibited from Possession.
2 Witkin, California Criminal Law 4th Crimes Against Public Peace and Welfare § 247 (2021), Confiscation of Firearm or Weapon.
2 Witkin, California Criminal Law 4th Crimes Against Public Peace and Welfare § 250 (2021), Punishment.
2 Witkin, California Criminal Law 4th Crimes Against Public Peace and Welfare § 253A (2021), (New) Carrying Unloaded Firearm that is Not Handgun in Incorporated Area or Other Public Place.
2 Witkin, California Criminal Law 4th Crimes Against Public Peace and Welfare § 257 (2021), Firearms.
2 Witkin, California Criminal Law 4th Crimes Against Public Peace and Welfare § 263 (2021), Nuisances.

§ 8101. Supplying, selling, giving, or allowing possession or control of firearms or deadly weapons; persons described in § 8100 or 8103; punishment

(a) Any person who shall knowingly supply, sell, give, or allow possession or control of a deadly weapon to any person described in Section 8100 or 8103 shall be punishable by imprisonment pursuant to subdivision (h) of Section 1170 of the Penal Code, or in a county jail for a period of not exceeding one year, by a fine of not exceeding onc thousand dollars ($1,000), or by both the fine and imprisonment.

(b) Any person who shall knowingly supply, sell, give, or allow possession or control of a firearm to any person described in Section 8100 or 8103 shall be punished by imprisonment pursuant to subdivision (h) of Section 1170 of the Penal Code for two, three, or four years.

(c) "Deadly weapon," as used in this section has the meaning prescribed by Section 8100. *(Added by Stats.1967, c. 1667, p. 4183, § 42, operative July 1, 1969. Amended by Stats.1969, c. 1021, p. 1989, § 2; Stats.1970, c. 79, p. 93, § 3; Stats.1976, c. 1139, p. 5174, § 348, operative July 1, 1977; Stats.1983, c. 1092, § 421, eff. Sept. 27, 1983, operative Jan. 1, 1984; Stats.1984, c. 1562, § 13; Stats.1985, c. 1324, § 3; Stats.1994, c. 451 (A.B.2470), § 12; Stats.1993–94, 1st Ex.Sess., c. 33 (S.B.36), § 12, eff. Nov. 30, 1994; Stats.2011, c. 15 (A.B.109), § 627, eff. April 4, 2011, operative Oct. 1, 2011.)*

Cross References

Felony, see Penal Code §§ 17, 18.
Misdemeanor, see Penal Code §§ 17, 19, 19.2.

Research References

2 Witkin, California Criminal Law 4th Crimes Against Public Peace and Welfare § 196 (2021), Transfers to Specified Persons.
2 Witkin, California Criminal Law 4th Crimes Against Public Peace and Welfare § 245 (2021), In General.
3 Witkin, California Criminal Law 4th Punishment § 621 (2021), P.C. 1203.

§ 8102. Confiscation and custody of firearms or other deadly weapons; procedure for return of weapon; notice; destruction of weapon

(a) Whenever a person, who has been detained or apprehended for examination of his or her mental condition or who is a person described in Section 8100 or 8103, is found to own, have in his or her possession or under his or her control, any firearm whatsoever, or any other deadly weapon, the firearm or other deadly weapon shall be confiscated by any law enforcement agency or peace officer, who shall retain custody of the firearm or other deadly weapon.

"Deadly weapon," as used in this section, has the meaning prescribed by Section 8100.

(b)(1) Upon confiscation of any firearm or other deadly weapon from a person who has been detained or apprehended for examination of his or her mental condition, the peace officer or law enforcement agency shall issue a receipt describing the deadly weapon or any firearm and listing any serial number or other identification on the firearm and shall notify the person of the procedure for the return, sale, transfer, or destruction of any firearm or other deadly weapon which has been confiscated. A peace officer or law enforcement agency that provides the receipt and notification described in Section 33800 of the Penal Code satisfies the receipt and notice requirements.

(2) If the person is released, the professional person in charge of the facility, or his or her designee, shall notify the person of the procedure for the return of any firearm or other deadly weapon which may have been confiscated.

(3) Health facility personnel shall notify the confiscating law enforcement agency upon release of the detained person, and shall make a notation to the effect that the facility provided the required notice to the person regarding the procedure to obtain return of any confiscated firearm.

(4) For purposes of this subdivision, the procedure for the return, sale, or transfer of confiscated firearms includes the procedures described in this section and the procedures described in Chapter 2 (commencing with Section 33850) of Division 11 of Title 4 of Part 6 of the Penal Code.

(5) In lieu of destroying a firearm that has been confiscated pursuant to this section that is a nuisance, unclaimed, abandoned, or otherwise subject to destruction, a law enforcement agency may retain or transfer the firearm as provided in Section 34005 of the Penal Code.

(c) Upon the release of a person as described in subdivision (b), the confiscating law enforcement agency shall have 30 days to initiate a petition in the superior court for a hearing to determine whether the return of a firearm or other deadly weapon would be likely to result in endangering the person or others, and to send a notice advising the person of his or her right to a hearing on this issue. The law enforcement agency may make an ex parte application stating good cause for an order extending the time to file a petition. Including any extension of time granted in response to an ex parte request, a petition shall be filed within 60 days of the release of the person from a health facility.

(d) If the law enforcement agency does not initiate proceedings within the 30–day period, or the period of time authorized by the court in an ex parte order issued pursuant to subdivision (c), it shall make the weapon available for return upon compliance with all applicable requirements, including the requirements specified in Chapter 2 (commencing with Section 33850) of Division 11 of Title 4 of Part 6 of the Penal Code.

(e) The law enforcement agency shall inform the person that he or she has 30 days to respond to the court clerk to confirm his or her desire for a hearing, and that the failure to respond will result in a default order forfeiting the confiscated firearm or weapon. For a confiscated firearm, the period of forfeiture is 180 days pursuant to Section 33875 of the Penal Code, unless the person contacts the law enforcement agency to facilitate the sale or transfer of the firearm to a licensed dealer pursuant to Section 33870 of the Penal Code. For the purpose of this subdivision, the person's last known address shall be the address provided to the law enforcement officer by the person at the time of the person's detention or apprehension.

(f) If the person responds and requests a hearing, the court clerk shall set a hearing, no later than 30 days from receipt of the request. The court clerk shall notify the person and the district attorney of the date, time, and place of the hearing.

(g) If the person does not respond within 30 days of the notice, the law enforcement agency may file a petition for order of default, allowing the law enforcement agency to destroy the firearm in 180 days from the date the court enters default unless the person contacts the law enforcement agency to facilitate the sale or transfer of the firearm to a licensed dealer pursuant to Section 33870 of the Penal Code.

(h) If, after a hearing, the court determines that the return of the firearm or other deadly weapon would likely endanger the person or others, the law enforcement agency may destroy the firearm within 180 days from the date that the court makes that determination, unless the person contacts the law enforcement agency to facilitate the sale or transfer of the firearm to a licensed dealer pursuant to Section 33870 of the Penal Code. *(Added by Stats.1967, c. 1667, p. 4183, § 42, operative July 1, 1969. Amended by Stats.1979, c. 250, p. 540, § 1; Stats.1979, c. 730, p. 2548, § 174.5, operative Jan. 1, 1981; Stats.1985, c. 1324, § 3.5; Stats.1989, c. 921, § 1, eff. Sept. 27, 1989; Stats.1991, c. 866 (A.B.363), § 8; Stats.1993, c. 606 (A.B.166), § 22, eff. Oct. 1, 1993; Stats.1995, c. 328 (A.B.633), § 1; Stats.2000, c. 254 (S.B.2052), § 2; Stats.2001, c. 159 (S.B.662), § 192; Stats.2013, c. 747 (A.B.1131), § 2.)*

Law Revision Commission Comments

Section 8102 is amended to add the reference to a conservator. [14 Cal.L.Rev.Comm. Reports 962 (1978)].

Cross References

Peace officer defined, see Welfare and Institutions Code § 5008.

Search warrants, grounds for issuance, firearm or deadly weapon owned by, in possession of, or in custody and control of person described in this section, see Penal Code § 1524.

Research References

2 Witkin, California Criminal Law 4th Crimes Against Public Peace and Welfare § 247 (2021), Confiscation of Firearm or Weapon.

4 Witkin, California Criminal Law 4th Illegally Obtained Evidence § 111 (2021), Statutory Grounds.

§ 8103. Particular persons; weapons restrictions; lifetime firearm prohibition; violations; punishment; reports in electronic format

(a)(1) A person who after October 1, 1955, has been adjudicated by a court of any state to be a danger to others as a result of a mental disorder or mental illness, or who has been adjudicated to be a mentally disordered sex offender, shall not purchase or receive, or attempt to purchase or receive, or have in his or her possession, custody, or control a firearm or any other deadly weapon unless there has been issued to the person a certificate by the court of adjudication upon release from treatment or at a later date stating that the person may possess a firearm or any other deadly weapon without endangering others, and the person has not, subsequent to the issuance of the certificate, again been adjudicated by a court to be a danger to others as a result of a mental disorder or mental illness.

(2) The court shall notify the Department of Justice of the court order finding the individual to be a person described in paragraph (1) as soon as possible, but not later than one court day after issuing the order. The court shall also notify the Department of Justice of any certificate issued as described in paragraph (1) as soon as possible, but not later than one court day after issuing the certificate.

(b)(1) A person who has been found, pursuant to Section 1026 of the Penal Code or the law of any other state or the United States, not guilty by reason of insanity of murder, mayhem, a violation of Section 207, 209, or 209.5 of the Penal Code in which the victim suffers intentionally inflicted great bodily injury, carjacking or robbery in which the victim suffers great bodily injury, a violation of Section 451 or 452 of the Penal Code involving a trailer coach, as defined in Section 635 of the Vehicle Code, or any dwelling house, a violation of paragraph (1) or (2) of subdivision (a) of Section 262 or paragraph (2) or (3) of subdivision (a) of Section 261 of the Penal Code, a violation of Section 459 of the Penal Code in the first degree, assault with intent to commit murder, a violation of Section 220 of the Penal Code in which the victim suffers great bodily injury, a violation of Section 18715, 18725, 18740, 18745, 18750, or 18755 of the Penal Code, or of a felony involving death, great bodily injury, or an act which poses a serious threat of bodily harm to another person, or a violation of the law of any other state or the United States that includes all the elements of any of the above felonies as defined under California law, shall not purchase or receive, or attempt to purchase or receive, or have in his or her possession or under his or her custody or control any firearm or any other deadly weapon.

(2) The court shall notify the Department of Justice of the court order finding the person to be a person described in paragraph (1) as soon as possible, but not later than one court day after issuing the order.

(c)(1) A person who has been found, pursuant to Section 1026 of the Penal Code or the law of any other state or the United States, not guilty by reason of insanity of any crime other than those described in subdivision (b) shall not purchase or receive, or attempt to purchase or receive, or have in his or her possession, custody, or control, any firearm or any other deadly weapon unless the court of commitment has found the person to have recovered sanity, pursuant to Section 1026.2 of the Penal Code or the law of any other state or the United States.

(2) The court shall notify the Department of Justice of the court order finding the person to be a person described in paragraph (1) as soon as possible, but not later than one court day after issuing the order. The court shall also notify the Department of Justice when it finds that the person has recovered his or her sanity as soon as possible, but not later than one court day after making the finding.

(d)(1) A person found by a court to be mentally incompetent to stand trial, pursuant to Section 1370 or 1370.1 of the Penal Code or the law of any other state or the United States, shall not purchase or receive, or attempt to purchase or receive, or have in his or her possession, custody, or control, any firearm or any other deadly weapon, unless there has been a finding with respect to the person of restoration to competence to stand trial by the committing court, pursuant to Section 1372 of the Penal Code or the law of any other state or the United States.

(2) The court shall notify the Department of Justice of the court order finding the person to be mentally incompetent as described in paragraph (1) as soon as possible, but not later than one court day after issuing the order. The court shall also notify the Department of Justice when it finds that the person has recovered his or her competence as soon as possible, but not later than one court day after making the finding.

(e)(1) A person who has been placed under conservatorship by a court, pursuant to Section 5350 or the law of any other state or the United States, because the person is gravely disabled as a result of a mental disorder or impairment by chronic alcoholism, shall not purchase or receive, or attempt to purchase or receive, or have in his or her possession, custody, or control, any firearm or any other deadly weapon while under the conservatorship if, at the time the conservatorship was ordered or thereafter, the court that imposed the conservatorship found that possession of a firearm or any other deadly weapon by the person would present a danger to the safety of the person or to others. Upon placing a person under conservatorship, and prohibiting firearm or any other deadly weapon possession by the person, the court shall notify the person of this prohibition.

(2) The court shall notify the Department of Justice of the court order placing the person under conservatorship and prohibiting firearm or any other deadly weapon possession by the person as described in paragraph (1) as soon as possible, but not later than one court day after placing the person under conservatorship. The notice shall include the date the conservatorship was imposed and the date the conservatorship is to be terminated. If the conservatorship is subsequently terminated before the date listed in the notice to the Department of Justice or the court subsequently finds that possession of a firearm or any other deadly weapon by the person would no longer present a danger to the safety of the person or others, the court shall notify the Department of Justice as soon as possible, but not later than one court day after terminating the conservatorship.

(3) All information provided to the Department of Justice pursuant to paragraph (2) shall be kept confidential, separate, and apart from all other records maintained by the Department of Justice, and shall be used only to determine eligibility to purchase or possess firearms or other deadly weapons. A person who knowingly furnishes that information for any other purpose is guilty of a misdemeanor. All the information concerning any person shall be destroyed upon receipt by the Department of Justice of notice of the termination of conservatorship as to that person pursuant to paragraph (2).

(f)(1)(A) A person who has been (i) taken into custody as provided in Section 5150 because that person is a danger to himself, herself, or to others, (ii) assessed within the meaning of Section 5151, and (iii) admitted to a designated facility within the meaning of Sections 5151 and 5152 because that person is a danger to himself, herself, or others, shall not own, possess, control, receive, or purchase, or attempt to own, possess, control, receive, or purchase, any firearm for a period of five years after the person is released from the facility.

(B) A person who has been taken into custody, assessed, and admitted as specified in subparagraph (A), and who was previously taken into custody, assessed, and admitted as specified in subparagraph (A) one or more times within a period of one year preceding the most recent admittance, shall not own, possess, control, receive, or purchase, or attempt to own, possess, control, receive, or purchase, any firearm for the remainder of his or her life.

(C) A person described in this paragraph, however, may own, possess, control, receive, or purchase, or attempt to own, possess, control, receive, or purchase any firearm if the superior court has, pursuant to paragraph (5), found that the people of the State of California have not met their burden pursuant to paragraph (6).

(2)(A)(i) For each person subject to this subdivision, the facility shall, within 24 hours of the time of admission, submit a report to the Department of Justice, on a form prescribed by the Department of Justice, containing information that includes, but is not limited to, the identity of the person and the legal grounds upon which the person was admitted to the facility.

(ii) Any report submitted pursuant to this paragraph shall be confidential, except for purposes of the court proceedings described in this subdivision and for determining the eligibility of the person to own, possess, control, receive, or purchase a firearm.

(B) Facilities shall submit reports pursuant to this paragraph exclusively by electronic means, in a manner prescribed by the Department of Justice.

(3) Prior to, or concurrent with, the discharge, the facility shall inform a person subject to this subdivision that he or she is prohibited from owning, possessing, controlling, receiving, or purchasing any firearm for a period of five years or, if the person was previously taken into custody, assessed, and admitted to custody for a 72–hour hold because he or she was a danger to himself, herself, or to others during the previous one-year period, for life. Simultaneously, the facility shall inform the person that he or she may request a hearing from a court, as provided in this subdivision, for an order permitting the person to own, possess, control, receive, or purchase a firearm. The facility shall provide the person with a copy of the most recent "Patient Notification of Firearm Prohibition and Right to Hearing Form" prescribed by the Department of Justice. The Department of Justice shall update this form in accordance with the requirements of this section and distribute the updated form to facilities by January 1, 2020. The form shall include information regarding how the person was referred to the facility. The form shall include an authorization for the release of the person's mental health records, upon request, to the appropriate court, solely for use in the hearing conducted pursuant to paragraph (5). A request for the records may be made by mail to the custodian of records at the facility, and shall not require personal service. The facility shall not submit the form on behalf of the person subject to this subdivision.

(4) The Department of Justice shall provide the form upon request to any person described in paragraph (1). The Department of Justice shall also provide the form to the superior court in each county. A person described in paragraph (1) may make a single request for a hearing at any time during the five-year period or period of the lifetime prohibition. The request for hearing shall be made on the form prescribed by the department or in a document that includes equivalent language.

(5) A person who is subject to paragraph (1) who has requested a hearing from the superior court of his or her county of residence for an order that he or she may own, possess, control, receive, or purchase firearms shall be given a hearing. The clerk of the court shall set a hearing date and notify the person, the Department of Justice, and the district attorney. The people of the State of California shall be the plaintiff in the proceeding and shall be represented by the district attorney. Upon motion of the district attorney, or on its own motion, the superior court may transfer the hearing to the county in which the person resided at the time of his or her detention, the county in which the person was detained, or the county in which the person was evaluated or treated. Within seven days after the request for a hearing, the Department of Justice shall file copies of the reports described in this section with the superior court. The reports shall be disclosed upon request to the person and

to the district attorney. The court shall set the hearing within 60 days of receipt of the request for a hearing. Upon showing good cause, the district attorney shall be entitled to a continuance not to exceed 30 days after the district attorney was notified of the hearing date by the clerk of the court. If additional continuances are granted, the total length of time for continuances shall not exceed 60 days. The district attorney may notify the county behavioral health director of the hearing who shall provide information about the detention of the person that may be relevant to the court and shall file that information with the superior court. That information shall be disclosed to the person and to the district attorney. The court, upon motion of the person subject to paragraph (1) establishing that confidential information is likely to be discussed during the hearing that would cause harm to the person, shall conduct the hearing in camera with only the relevant parties present, unless the court finds that the public interest would be better served by conducting the hearing in public. Notwithstanding any other law, declarations, police reports, including criminal history information, and any other material and relevant evidence that is not excluded under Section 352 of the Evidence Code shall be admissible at the hearing under this section.

(6) The people shall bear the burden of showing by a preponderance of the evidence that the person would not be likely to use firearms in a safe and lawful manner.

(7) If the court finds at the hearing set forth in paragraph (5) that the people have not met their burden as set forth in paragraph (6), the court shall order that the person shall not be subject to the five-year prohibition or lifetime prohibition, as appropriate, in this section on the ownership, control, receipt, possession, or purchase of firearms, and that person shall comply with the procedure described in Chapter 2 (commencing with Section 33850) of Division 11 of Title 4 of Part 6 of the Penal Code for the return of any firearms. A copy of the order shall be submitted to the Department of Justice. Upon receipt of the order, the Department of Justice shall delete any reference to the prohibition against firearms from the person's state mental health firearms prohibition system information.

(8) If the district attorney declines or fails to go forward in the hearing, the court shall order that the person shall not be subject to the five-year prohibition or lifetime prohibition required by this subdivision on the ownership, control, receipt, possession, or purchase of firearms. A copy of the order shall be submitted to the Department of Justice. Upon receipt of the order, the Department of Justice shall, within 15 days, delete any reference to the prohibition against firearms from the person's state mental health firearms prohibition system information, and that person shall comply with the procedure described in Chapter 2 (commencing with Section 33850) of Division 11 of Title 4 of Part 6 of the Penal Code for the return of any firearms.

(9) This subdivision does not prohibit the use of reports filed pursuant to this section to determine the eligibility of persons to own, possess, control, receive, or purchase a firearm if the person is the subject of a criminal investigation, a part of which involves the ownership, possession, control, receipt, or purchase of a firearm.

(10) If the court finds that the people have met their burden to show by a preponderance of the evidence that the person would not be likely to use firearms in a safe and lawful manner and the person is subject to a lifetime firearm prohibition because the person had been admitted as specified in subparagraph (A) of paragraph (1) more than once within the previous one-year period, the court shall inform the person of his or her right to file a subsequent petition no sooner than five years from the date of the hearing.

(11) A person subject to a lifetime firearm prohibition is entitled to bring subsequent petitions pursuant to this subdivision. A person shall not be entitled to file a subsequent petition, and shall not be entitled to a subsequent hearing, until five years have passed since the determination on the person's last petition. A hearing on subsequent petitions shall be conducted as described in this subdivision, with the exception that the burden of proof shall be on the petitioner to establish by a preponderance of the evidence that the petitioner can use a firearm in a safe and lawful manner. Subsequent petitions shall be filed in the same court of jurisdiction as the initial petition regarding the lifetime firearm prohibition.

(g)(1)(i) [1]A person who has been certified for intensive treatment under Section 5250, 5260, or 5270.15 shall not own, possess, control, receive, or purchase, or attempt to own, possess, control, receive, or purchase, any firearm for a period of five years.

(ii) [2]Any person who meets the criteria contained in subdivision (e) or (f) who is released from intensive treatment shall nevertheless, if applicable, remain subject to the prohibition contained in subdivision (e) or (f).

(2)(A) For each person certified for intensive treatment under paragraph (1), the facility shall, within 24 hours of the certification, submit a report to the Department of Justice, on a form prescribed by the department, containing information regarding the person, including, but not limited to, the legal identity of the person and the legal grounds upon which the person was certified. A report submitted pursuant to this paragraph shall only be used for the purposes specified in paragraph (2) of subdivision (f).

(B) Facilities shall submit reports pursuant to this paragraph exclusively by electronic means, in a manner prescribed by the Department of Justice.

(3) Prior to, or concurrent with, the discharge of each person certified for intensive treatment under paragraph (1), the facility shall inform the person of that information specified in paragraph (3) of subdivision (f).

(4) A person who is subject to paragraph (1) may petition the superior court of his or her county of residence for an order that he or she may own, possess, control, receive, or purchase firearms. At the time the petition is filed, the clerk of the court shall set a hearing date within 60 days of receipt of the petition and notify the person, the Department of Justice, and the district attorney. The people of the State of California shall be the respondent in the proceeding and shall be represented by the district attorney. Upon motion of the district attorney, or on its own motion, the superior court may transfer the petition to the county in which the person resided at the time of his or her detention, the county in which the person was detained, or the county in which the person was evaluated or treated. Within seven days after receiving notice of the petition, the Department of Justice shall file copies of the reports described in this section with the superior court. The reports shall be disclosed upon request to the person and to the district attorney. The district attorney shall be entitled to a continuance of the hearing to a date of not less than 30 days after the district attorney was notified of the hearing date by the clerk of the court. If additional continuances are granted, the total length of time for continuances shall not exceed 60 days. The district attorney may notify the county behavioral health director of the petition, and the county behavioral health director shall provide information about the detention of the person that may be relevant to the court and shall file that information with the superior court. That information shall be disclosed to the person and to the district attorney. The court, upon motion of the person subject to paragraph (1) establishing that confidential information is likely to be discussed during the hearing that would cause harm to the person, shall conduct the hearing in camera with only the relevant parties present, unless the court finds that the public interest would be better served by conducting the hearing in public. Notwithstanding any other law, any declaration, police reports, including criminal history information, and any other material and relevant evidence that is not excluded under Section 352 of the Evidence Code, shall be admissible at the hearing under this section. If the court finds by a preponderance of the evidence that the person would be likely to use firearms in a safe and lawful manner, the court may order that the person may own, control, receive, possess, or purchase firearms, and that person shall comply with the procedure described in Chapter 2

(commencing with Section 33850) of Division 11 of Title 4 of Part 6 of the Penal Code for the return of any firearms. A copy of the order shall be submitted to the Department of Justice. Upon receipt of the order, the Department of Justice shall delete any reference to the prohibition against firearms from the person's state mental health firearms prohibition system information.

(h)(1) For all persons identified in subdivisions (f) and (g), facilities shall report to the Department of Justice as specified in those subdivisions, except facilities shall not report persons under subdivision (g) if the same persons previously have been reported under subdivision (f).

(2) Additionally, all facilities shall report to the Department of Justice upon the discharge of persons from whom reports have been submitted pursuant to subdivision (f) or (g). However, a report shall not be filed for persons who are discharged within 31 days after the date of admission.

(i) Every person who owns or possesses or has under his or her custody or control, or purchases or receives, or attempts to purchase or receive, any firearm or any other deadly weapon in violation of this section shall be punished by imprisonment pursuant to subdivision (h) of Section 1170 of the Penal Code or in a county jail for not more than one year.

(j) "Deadly weapon," as used in this section, has the meaning prescribed by Section 8100.

(k) Any notice or report required to be submitted to the Department of Justice pursuant to this section shall be submitted in an electronic format, in a manner prescribed by the Department of Justice.

(*l*) This section shall become operative on January 1, 2020. *(Added by Stats.2018, c. 861 (A.B.1968), § 2, eff. Jan. 1, 2019, operative Jan. 1, 2020.)*

1 So in enrolled bill.

2 So in enrolled bill.

Cross References

Certificate of eligibility requirement for agents or employees who handle, sell, or deliver firearm precursor parts, prohibition against specified agents or employees handling firearm precursor parts, see Penal Code § 30447.
Custodial or transportation officers, notification to state or local agency of restrictions on firearm possession, see Penal Code § 832.17.
Felonies, definition and penalties, see Penal Code §§ 17, 18.
Inspection of public records, other exemptions from disclosure, see Government Code § 6276.30.
License to carry a concealed weapon, denial or revocation, persons within prohibited class described in this section, see Penal Code § 26150.
License to sell firearms at retail, forfeiture upon delivery of firearms to persons in prohibited classes under this section, see Penal Code § 26700.
Misdemeanor, see Penal Code §§ 17, 19, 19.2.
Notification to agencies employing or taking applications for peace officers authorized to carry firearms, see Penal Code §§ 832.15, 832.16.
Penalty for possession of loaded firearms or enumerated prohibited weapons within State Capitol, legislative offices, etc., prosecution not precluded under this section, see Penal Code § 171c.
Permits, denial to issue, refusal to renew, and automatic revocation, alarm companies, see Business and Professions Code §§ 7596.8, 7596.81, 7596.83.
Person prohibited from owning or possessing firearm also prohibited from owning or possessing firearm precursor part, penalties, exemptions, see Penal Code § 30405.
Processing firearm purchaser information, background check, delay of transfer of firearm to purchaser following receipt of information about purchaser, see Penal Code § 28220.
Prohibited persons, attempt to acquire or report acquisition or ownership of firearm, notice to local law enforcement agency and county department of mental health, see Penal Code § 29880.
Retention of title of firearms or ammunition acquired by bequest or intestate succession, see Penal Code § 12020.

Research References

2 Witkin, California Criminal Law 4th Crimes Against Public Peace and Welfare § 194 (2021), Furnishing Erroneous Firearm Purchaser Information.
2 Witkin, California Criminal Law 4th Crimes Against Public Peace and Welfare § 202 (2021), License to Manufacture.
2 Witkin, California Criminal Law 4th Crimes Against Public Peace and Welfare § 232 (2021), Nature and Scope of Statutes.
2 Witkin, California Criminal Law 4th Crimes Against Public Peace and Welfare § 245 (2021), In General.
2 Witkin, California Criminal Law 4th Crimes Against Public Peace and Welfare § 246 (2021), Persons Prohibited from Possession.

§ 8104. Records necessary to identify persons coming within § 8100 or 8103; availability to Department of Justice

The State Department of State Hospitals shall maintain in a convenient central location and shall make available to the Department of Justice those records that the State Department of State Hospitals has in its possession that are necessary to identify persons who come within Section 8100 or 8103. Upon request of the Department of Justice, the State Department of State Hospitals shall make these records available to the Department of Justice in electronic format within 24 hours of receiving the request. The Department of Justice shall make these requests only with respect to its duties with regard to applications for permits for, or to carry, or the possession, purchase, or transfer of, explosives as defined in Section 12000 of the Health and Safety Code, devices defined in Section 16250, 16530, or 16640 of the Penal Code, in subdivisions (a) to (d), inclusive, of Section 16520 of the Penal Code, or in subdivision (a) of Section 16840 of the Penal Code, machineguns as defined in Section 16880 of the Penal Code, short-barreled shotguns or short-barreled rifles as defined in Sections 17170 and 17180 of the Penal Code, assault weapons as defined in Section 30510 of the Penal Code, and destructive devices as defined in Section 16460 of the Penal Code, or to determine the eligibility of a person to acquire, carry, or possess a firearm, explosive, or destructive device by a person who is subject to a criminal investigation, a part of which involves the acquisition, carrying, or possession of a firearm by that person. These records shall not be furnished or made available to any person unless the department determines that disclosure of any information in the records is necessary to carry out its duties with respect to applications for permits for, or to carry, or the possession, purchase, or transfer of, explosives, destructive devices, devices as defined in Section 16250, 16530, or 16640 of the Penal Code, in subdivisions (a) to (d), inclusive, of Section 16520 of the Penal Code, or in subdivision (a) of Section 16840 of the Penal Code, short-barreled shotguns, short-barreled rifles, assault weapons, and machineguns, or to determine the eligibility of a person to acquire, carry, or possess a firearm, explosive, or destructive device by a person who is subject to a criminal investigation, a part of which involves the acquisition, carrying, or possession of a firearm by that person. *(Added by Stats.1972, c. 1377, p. 2858, § 123, operative July 1, 1973. Amended by Stats.1977, c. 1252, p. 4627, § 707, operative July 1, 1978; Stats.1982, c. 1409, § 2; Stats.1984, c. 1562, § 15; Stats.1988, c. 1269, § 6; Stats.1990, c. 1090 (S.B.2050), § 5; Stats.1992, c. 1326 (A.B.3552), § 18; Stats.2010, c. 178 (S.B.1115), § 105, operative Jan. 1, 2012; Stats.2012, c. 440 (A.B.1488), § 75, eff. Sept. 22, 2012; Stats.2013, c. 747 (A.B.1131), § 4.)*

Law Revision Commission Comments

Section 8104 is amended to reflect nonsubstantive reorganization of the statutes governing control of deadly weapons. [38 Cal.L.Rev.Comm. Reports 217 (2009)].

§ 8105. Submission of information identifying certain persons receiving inpatient treatment for mental disorders; use of information

(a) The Department of Justice shall request each public and private mental hospital, sanitarium, and institution to submit to the department information the department deems necessary to identify those persons who are subject to the prohibition specified by subdivision (a) of Section 8100, in order to carry out its duties in relation to firearms, destructive devices, and explosives.

(b) Upon request of the Department of Justice pursuant to subdivision (a), each public and private mental hospital, sanitarium, and institution shall submit to the department information the department deems necessary to identify those persons who are subject to the prohibition specified by subdivision (a) of Section 8100, in order to carry out its duties in relation to firearms, destructive devices, and explosives.

(c) A licensed psychotherapist shall report to a local law enforcement agency, within 24 hours, in a manner prescribed by the Department of Justice, the identity of a person subject to the prohibition specified by subdivision (b) of Section 8100. Upon receipt of the report, the local law enforcement agency, on a form prescribed by the Department of Justice, shall notify the department electronically, within 24 hours, in a manner prescribed by the department, of the person who is subject to the prohibition specified by subdivision (b) of Section 8100.

(d) All information provided to the Department of Justice pursuant to this section shall be kept confidential, separate, and apart from all other records maintained by the department. The information provided to the Department of Justice pursuant to this section shall be used only for any of the following purposes:

(1) By the department to determine eligibility of a person to acquire, carry, or possess firearms, destructive devices, or explosives.

(2) For the purposes of the court proceedings described in subdivision (b) of Section 8100, to determine the eligibility of the person who is bringing the petition pursuant to paragraph (3) of subdivision (b) of Section 8100.

(3) To determine the eligibility of a person to acquire, carry, or possess firearms, destructive devices, or explosives who is the subject of a criminal investigation, or who is the subject of a petition for the issuance of a gun violence restraining order issued pursuant to Division 3.2 (commencing with Section 18100) of Title 2 of Part 6 of the Penal Code, if a part of the investigation involves the acquisition, carrying, or possession of firearms, explosives, or destructive devices by that person.

(e) Reports shall not be required or requested under this section if the same person has been previously reported pursuant to Section 8103 or 8104.

(f) This section shall become operative on January 1, 2016. *(Added by Stats.2014, c. 872 (A.B.1014), § 7, eff. Jan. 1, 2015, operative Jan. 1, 2016.)*

§ 8106. Data reported pursuant to this chapter relating to prohibition of ownership and possession of firearm and ammunition; availability to researchers; identifying information

Individual data required to be reported to the Department of Justice pursuant to this chapter related to prohibition of ownership and possession of a firearm and ammunition shall be available to researchers affiliated with the California Firearm Violence Research Center at UC Davis following approval by the institution's governing institutional review board, when required. At the department's discretion, and subject to Section 14240 of the Penal Code, the data may be provided to any other nonprofit bona fide research institution accredited by the United States Department of Education or the Council for Higher Education Accreditation for the study of the prevention of violence, following approval by the institution's governing institutional review board or human subjects committee, when required, for academic and policy research purposes. Material identifying individuals shall only be provided for research or statistical activities and shall not be transferred, revealed, or used for purposes other than research or statistical activities, and reports or publications derived therefrom shall not identify specific individuals. Reasonable costs to the department associated with the department's processing of that data may be billed to the researcher. If a request for data or letter of support for research using the data is denied, the department shall provide a written statement of the specific reasons for the denial. *(Added by Stats.2021, c. 253 (A.B.173), § 13, eff. Sept. 23, 2021.)*

§ 8108. Civil liability of health professionals; immunity

Mental hospitals, health facilities, or other institutions, or treating health professionals or psychotherapists who provide reports subject to this chapter shall be civilly immune for making any report required or authorized by this chapter. This section is declaratory of existing law. *(Added by Stats.1991, c. 951 (A.B.664), § 11.)*

Division 9

PUBLIC SOCIAL SERVICES

Part 2

ADMINISTRATION

CHAPTER 9. PENALTIES

§ 10980. Unlawful acts; penalties; exceptions to criminal prosecution for overpayment or overissuance of benefits

(a) Any person who, willfully and knowingly, with the intent to deceive, makes a false statement or representation or knowingly fails to disclose a material fact in order to obtain aid under the provisions of this division or who, knowing he or she is not entitled thereto, attempts to obtain aid or to continue to receive aid to which he or she is not entitled, or to receive a larger amount than that to which he or she is legally entitled, is guilty of a misdemeanor, punishable by imprisonment in a county jail for a period of not more than six months, by a fine of not more than five hundred dollars ($500), or by both imprisonment and fine.

(b) Any person who knowingly makes more than one application for aid under the provisions of this division with the intent of establishing multiple entitlements for any person for the same period or who makes an application for that aid for a fictitious or nonexistent person or by claiming a false identity for any person is guilty of a felony, punishable by imprisonment pursuant to subdivision (h) of Section 1170 of the Penal Code for a period of 16 months, two years, or three years, by a fine of not more than five thousand dollars ($5,000), or by both that imprisonment and fine; or by imprisonment in a county jail for a period of not more than one year, or by a fine of not more than one thousand dollars ($1,000), or by both imprisonment and fine.

(c) Whenever any person has, willfully and knowingly, with the intent to deceive, by means of false statement or representation, or by failing to disclose a material fact, or by impersonation or other fraudulent device, obtained or retained aid under the provisions of this division for himself or herself or for a child not in fact entitled thereto, the person obtaining this aid shall be punished as follows:

(1) If the total amount of the aid obtained or retained is nine hundred fifty dollars ($950) or less, by imprisonment in a county jail for a period of not more than six months, by a fine of not more than five hundred dollars ($500), or by both imprisonment and fine.

(2) If the total amount of the aid obtained or retained is more than nine hundred fifty dollars ($950), by imprisonment pursuant to subdivision (h) of Section 1170 of the Penal Code for a period of 16 months, two years, or three years, by a fine of not more than five thousand dollars ($5,000), or by both that imprisonment and fine; or by imprisonment in a county jail for a period of not more than one year, by a fine of not more than one thousand dollars ($1,000), or by both imprisonment and fine.

(d) Any person who knowingly uses, transfers, acquires, or possesses blank authorizations to participate in the federal Supplemental Nutrition Assistance Program in any manner not authorized by Chapter 10 (commencing with Section 18900) of Part 6 with the intent to defraud is guilty of a felony, punishable by imprisonment pursuant to subdivision (h) of Section 1170 of the Penal Code for a period of 16 months, two years, or three years, by a fine of not more than five thousand dollars ($5,000), or by both that imprisonment and fine.

(e) Any person who counterfeits or alters or knowingly uses, transfers, acquires, or possesses counterfeited or altered authorizations to participate in the federal Supplemental Nutrition Assistance Program or to receive CalFresh benefits or electronically transferred benefits in any manner not authorized by the former federal Food Stamp Act of 1964 (Public Law 88–525 [1] and all amendments thereto) or the federal Food and Nutrition Act of 2008 (7 U.S.C. Sec. 2011 et seq.) or the federal regulations pursuant to the act is guilty of forgery.

(f) Any person who fraudulently appropriates CalFresh benefits, electronically transferred benefits, or authorizations to participate in the federal Supplemental Nutrition Assistance Program with which he or she has been entrusted pursuant to his or her duties as a public employee is guilty of embezzlement of public funds.

(g) Any person who knowingly uses, transfers, sells, purchases, or possesses CalFresh benefits, electronically transferred benefits, or authorizations to participate in the federal Supplemental Nutrition Assistance Program in any manner not authorized by Chapter 10 (commencing with Section 18900) of Part 6, or by the former federal Food Stamp Act of 1977 (Public Law 95–113 and all amendments thereto) or the federal Food and Nutrition Act of 2008 (7 U.S.C. Sec. 2011 et seq.) (1) is guilty of a misdemeanor if the face value of the benefits or the authorizations to participate is nine hundred fifty dollars ($950) or less, and shall be punished by imprisonment in a county jail for a period of not more than six months, by a fine of not more than five hundred dollars ($500), or by both imprisonment and fine, or (2) is guilty of a felony if the face value of the CalFresh benefits or the authorizations to participate exceeds nine hundred fifty dollars ($950), and shall be punished by imprisonment pursuant to subdivision (h) of Section 1170 of the Penal Code for a period of 16 months, two years, or three years, by a fine of not more than five thousand dollars ($5,000), or by both that imprisonment and fine, or by imprisonment in a county jail for a period of not more than one year, or by a fine of not more than one thousand dollars ($1,000), or by both imprisonment and fine.

(h)(1) If the violation of subdivision (f) or (g) is committed by means of an electronic transfer of benefits, in addition and consecutive to the penalties for the violation, or attempted violation, of those subdivisions, the court shall impose the following punishment:

(A) If the electronic transfer of benefits exceeds fifty thousand dollars ($50,000), an additional term pursuant to subdivision (h) of Section 1170 of the Penal Code of one year.

(B) If the electronic transfer of benefits exceeds one hundred fifty thousand dollars ($150,000), an additional term pursuant to subdivision (h) of Section 1170 of the Penal Code of two years.

(C) If the electronic transfer of benefits exceeds one million dollars ($1,000,000), an additional term pursuant to subdivision (h) of Section 1170 of the Penal Code of three years.

(D) If the electronic transfer of benefits exceeds two million five hundred thousand dollars ($2,500,000), an additional term pursuant to subdivision (h) of Section 1170 of the Penal Code of four years.

(2) In any accusatory pleading involving multiple charges of violations of subdivision (f) or (g), or both, committed by means of an electronic transfer of benefits, the additional terms provided in paragraph (1) may be imposed if the aggregate losses to the victims from all violations exceed the amounts specified in this paragraph and arise from a common scheme or plan.

(i) A person who is punished by an additional term of imprisonment under another law for a violation of subdivision (f) or (g) shall not receive an additional term of imprisonment under subdivision (h).

(j)(1) A person shall not be subject to criminal prosecution, under this section or under any other law, for an overpayment or overissuance of benefits, obtained under the California Work Opportunity and Responsibility to Kids (CalWORKs) program (Chapter 2 (commencing with Section 11200) of Part 3) or the CalFresh program (Chapter 10 (commencing with Section 18900) of Part 6), for any month in which the county human services agency was in receipt of any Income and Eligibility Verification System (IEVS) data match information indicating any potential for an overpayment or an overissuance and for which the county human services agency has not provided to the person a timely and adequate notice of action for the collection of the overpayment or the overissuance.

(2)(A) For purposes of paragraph (1), the county human services agency shall be deemed to be in receipt of IEVS data match information indicating any potential for an overpayment or an overissuance following 45 days from the date of the county human services agency's possession of that information.

(B) Notwithstanding subparagraph (A), if the county human services agency does not complete the required actions for an IEVS data match for a CalFresh or CalWORKs applicant or recipient within 45 days of receipt of information pursuant to Section 272.8 of Title 7 of, or Section 205.56 of Title 45 of, the Code of Federal Regulations, or their successors, but is authorized to exceed the 45–day period due to exceptions provided under those regulations or under any other federal law, the county human services agency shall be deemed, for purposes of paragraph (1), to be in receipt of IEVS data match information indicating any potential for an overpayment or an overissuance following the combined total of 45 days and the authorized delay from the date of the county human services agency's possession of that information. *(Added by Stats.1984, c. 1448, § 2. Amended by Stats.1985, c. 568, § 1, eff. Sept. 13, 1985; Stats.1998, c. 902 (A.B.2772), § 11; Stats.1998, c. 903 (A.B.131), § 2.5; Stats.1999, c. 83 (S.B.966), § 202; Stats.2002, c. 1022 (A.B.444), § 23.5, eff. Sept. 28, 2002; Stats.2009–2010, 3rd Ex.Sess., c. 28 (S.B.18), § 56, eff. Jan. 25, 2010; Stats.2011, c. 15 (A.B.109), § 629, eff. April 4, 2011, operative Oct. 1, 2011; Stats.2011, c. 227 (A.B.1400), § 37.5; Stats. 2012, c. 162 (S.B.1171), § 204; Stats.2012, c. 43 (S.B.1023), § 112, eff. June 27, 2012; Stats.2017, c. 390 (S.B.360), § 1, eff. Jan. 1, 2018.)*

[1] For public law sections classified to the U.S.C.A., see USCA–Tables.

Cross References

Felonies, definition and penalties, see Penal Code §§ 17, 18.
Judgment and execution, food stamp fraud, see Penal Code § 1203.049.
Misdemeanors, definition and penalties, see Penal Code §§ 17, 19, 19.2.

Public social services, eligibility to provide in-home support services, additional criminal conviction exclusions, see Welfare and Institutions Code § 12305.87.
Trial court initial sentencing, specific enhancement, see Penal Code § 1170.11.
Willfully and Knowingly defined, see Penal Code § 117.

Research References

2 Witkin, California Criminal Law 4th Crimes Against Governmental Authority § 61 (2021), Effect of Special Statute.
2 Witkin, California Criminal Law 4th Crimes Against Governmental Authority § 156 (2021), In General.
2 Witkin, California Criminal Law 4th Crimes Against Governmental Authority § 157 (2021), Misuse, Forgery, or Embezzlement.
2 Witkin, California Criminal Law 4th Crimes Against Governmental Authority § 162 (2021), Demand for Restitution as Prerequisite to Prosecution.
1 Witkin California Criminal Law 4th Introduction to Crimes § 75 (2021), General Principles.
1 Witkin California Criminal Law 4th Introduction to Crimes § 84 (2021), Distinction: Reenactment.

Part 3

AID AND MEDICAL ASSISTANCE

CHAPTER 2. CALIFORNIA WORK OPPORTUNITY AND RESPONSIBILITY TO KIDS ACT

ARTICLE 7. ENFORCEMENT

§ 11480. Receipt or use of aid for purpose other than support

Any person other than a needy child, who willfully and knowingly receives or uses any part of an aid grant paid pursuant to this chapter for a purpose other than support of the needy children and the caretaker involved, is guilty of a misdemeanor. *(Added by Stats.1965, c. 1784, p. 4018, § 5.)*

Cross References

Misdemeanor, generally, see Penal Code §§ 17, 19, 19.2.

Research References

2 Witkin, California Criminal Law 4th Crimes Against Governmental Authority § 157 (2021), Misuse, Forgery, or Embezzlement.

§ 11481. Prosecution for contributing to delinquency of minor

If the district attorney, during the course of any investigation made by him pursuant to this article, determines that any person has committed any act or has omitted the performance of any duty, which act or omission causes or tends to cause or encourage any child receiving aid under this chapter to come within the provisions of Sections 300, 601, or 602 of this code, the district attorney shall prosecute such person under the provisions of Section 272 of the Penal Code. *(Added by Stats.1965, c. 1784, p. 4018, § 5. Amended by Stats.1979, c. 373, § 379.)*

Cross References

Duties of district attorney, see Government Code § 26500.

Research References

4 Witkin, California Criminal Law 4th Introduction to Criminal Procedure § 19 (2021), In General.

§ 11481.5. Welfare fraud hotline pilot project; effectiveness evaluation

The department shall evaluate the effectiveness of a 24-hour welfare fraud hotline pilot project, to assess greater public involvement and assistance in welfare fraud detection. *(Added by Stats. 1984, c. 1448, § 3.5.)*

Cross References

Fraud, nature of, see Civil Code §§ 1571 to 1574.

§ 11482. False representation to obtain aid; unlawfully receiving or attempting to receive aid

Any person other than a needy child, who willfully and knowingly, with the intent to deceive, makes a false statement or representation or knowingly fails to disclose a material fact to obtain aid, or who, knowing he or she is not entitled thereto, attempts to obtain aid or to continue to receive aid to which he or she is not entitled, or a larger amount than that to which he or she is legally entitled, is guilty of a misdemeanor, except as specified in Section 11482.5 and shall be subject to prosecution under the provisions of Chapter 9 (commencing with Section 10980) of Part 2. *(Added by Stats.1965, c. 1784, p. 4018, § 5. Amended by Stats.1983, c. 1235, § 1; Stats.1984, c. 1448, § 4.)*

Cross References

Affirmation in lieu of oath, see Code of Civil Procedure § 2015.6.
Annual redetermination, false statement, see Welfare and Institutions Code § 11265.
False affirmation by applicant for public assistance, see Welfare and Institutions Code § 11054.
Misdemeanors, definition and penalties, see Penal Code §§ 17, 19 and 19.2.
Obtaining money etc., by false or fraudulent representation, see Penal Code § 484.
Overpayments, suits to recover overpayments to be brought by county counsel, see Welfare and Institutions Code § 11004.

Research References

2 Witkin, California Criminal Law 4th Crimes Against Governmental Authority § 61 (2021), Effect of Special Statute.
2 Witkin, California Criminal Law 4th Crimes Against Governmental Authority § 156 (2021), In General.
2 Witkin, California Criminal Law 4th Crimes Against Governmental Authority § 161 (2021), Relationship to Other Crimes.
1 Witkin California Criminal Law 4th Defenses § 257 (2021), Effect of Amendment to Accusatory Pleading.

§ 11482.5. Applications claiming multiple entitlements, false identity, or for fictitious or nonexistent persons; punishment

Any person who knowingly makes more than one application for aid with the intent of establishing multiple entitlements for any person for the same period, or who makes an application for aid by claiming a false identity for any person or by making an application for a fictitious or nonexistent person, is guilty of a felony and shall be subject to prosecution under the provisions of Chapter 9 (commencing with Section 10980) of Part 2. *(Added by Stats.1983, c. 1235, § 2. Amended by Stats.1984, c. 1448, § 5.)*

Cross References

Felonies, definition and penalties, see Penal Code §§ 17, 18.

Research References

2 Witkin, California Criminal Law 4th Crimes Against Governmental Authority § 156 (2021), In General.

§ 11483. Fraud in obtaining aid; punishment; restitution

Except as specified in Section 11483.5, whenever any person has, by means of false statement or representation or by impersonation or other fraudulent device, obtained aid for a child not in fact entitled thereto, the person obtaining such aid shall be subject to prosecution under the provisions of Chapter 9 (commencing with Section 10980) of Part 2.

When the allegation is limited to failure to report not more than two thousand dollars ($2,000) of income or resources, or the failure to report the presence of an additional person or persons in the household, all actions necessary to secure restitution shall be brought against persons in violation of Section 10980. The action for restitution may be satisfied by sending a registered letter requesting restitution to the last address at which the person was receiving public assistance. *(Added by Stats.1965, c. 1784, p. 4018, § 5. Amended by Stats.1970, c. 693, p. 1322, § 1; Stats.1977, c. 165, p. 679, § 95, eff. June 29, 1977, operative July 1, 1977; Stats.1979, c. 373, § 380; Stats.1979, c. 1170, § 12; Stats.1979, c. 1171, § 1; Stats.1983, c. 1092, § 422, eff. Sept. 27, 1983, operative Jan. 1, 1984; Stats.1983, c. 711, § 4; Stats.1984, c. 1448, § 6.)*

Cross References

Fraud, nature of, see Civil Code §§ 1571 to 1574.
Overpayments, suits to recover overpayments to be brought by county counsel, see Welfare and Institutions Code § 11004.
Recovery of assistance paid parents when gainfully employed or possessed of sufficient assets, see Family Code § 17402.
Theft by false or fraudulent representation or pretense, see Penal Code § 484.
Time of commencing criminal actions, tolling or extension of time periods, revival of cause of action, see Penal Code § 803.

Research References

2 Witkin, California Criminal Law 4th Crimes Against Governmental Authority § 25 (2021), Prohibited Compromises.
2 Witkin, California Criminal Law 4th Crimes Against Governmental Authority § 61 (2021), Effect of Special Statute.
2 Witkin, California Criminal Law 4th Crimes Against Governmental Authority § 156 (2021), In General.
2 Witkin, California Criminal Law 4th Crimes Against Governmental Authority § 162 (2021), Demand for Restitution as Prerequisite to Prosecution.
6 Witkin, California Criminal Law 4th Criminal Appeal § 17 (2021), Reviewable Claims.
5 Witkin, California Criminal Law 4th Criminal Trial § 466 (2021), Proper Grounds.
1 Witkin California Criminal Law 4th Defenses § 252 (2021), Discovery of Crime: Statutory Provisions.
1 Witkin California Criminal Law 4th Introduction to Crimes § 76 (2021), Illustrations: Special Statute is Controlling.
1 Witkin California Criminal Law 4th Introduction to Crimes § 77 (2021), Illustrations: Special Statute is Not Controlling.
3 Witkin, California Criminal Law 4th Punishment § 417 (2021), Theft.

§ 11483.5. Obtaining aid by applications claiming multiple entitlements, false identity, or for fictitious or nonexistent persons; punishment

Any person who obtains more than one aid payment for any person as a result of knowingly making more than one application for aid with the intent of establishing multiple entitlements for that person during the same period, or who obtains aid for any person by making an application claiming a false identity or by making an application for a fictitious or nonexistent person, is guilty of a felony, and shall be subject to prosecution under the provisions of Chapter 9 (commencing with Section 10980) of Part 2. *(Added by Stats.1983, c. 1235, § 3. Amended by Stats.1984, c. 1448, § 7.)*

Cross References

Felonies, definition and penalties, see Penal Code §§ 17, 18.

Research References

2 Witkin, California Criminal Law 4th Crimes Against Governmental Authority § 156 (2021), In General.

§ 11484. Public assistance fraud; cooperation of agencies to assist in investigation and prevention

On request, all state, county, and local agencies shall cooperate with an investigator of an agency whose primary function is to detect, prevent, or prosecute public assistance fraud, by providing all information on hand relative to the location and prosecution of any person who has, by means of false statement or representation or by impersonation or other fraudulent device, obtained aid, or attempted to obtain aid for an individual under this chapter. That information is subject to confidentiality requirements under Chapter 5 (commencing with Section 10850) of Part 2. For purposes of this section, "information" shall not include taxpayer return information as defined in Section 19549 of the Revenue and Taxation Code, unless disclosure of this information is expressly authorized pursuant to Article 2 (commencing with Section 19501) of Chapter 7 of Part 10.2 of the Revenue and Taxation Code. *(Added by Stats.2000, c. 808 (A.B.1358), § 128, eff. Sept. 28, 2000.)*

Cross References

Fraud, nature of, see Civil Code §§ 1571 to 1574.
Theft by false or fraudulent representation or pretense, see Penal Code § 484.

CHAPTER 7. BASIC HEALTH CARE

ARTICLE 3. ADMINISTRATION

§ 14107. Fraudulent claims; intent; punishment; other enforcement remedies

(a) Any person, including any applicant or provider as defined in Section 14043.1, or billing agent, as defined in Section 14040.1, who engages in any of the activities identified in subdivision (b) is punishable by imprisonment as set forth in subdivisions (c), (d), and (e), by a fine not exceeding three times the amount of the fraud or improper reimbursement or value of the scheme or artifice, or by both this fine and imprisonment.

(b) The following activities are subject to subdivision (a):

(1) A person, with intent to defraud, presents for allowance or payment any false or fraudulent claim for furnishing services or merchandise under this chapter or Chapter 8 (commencing with Section 14200).

(2) A person knowingly submits false information for the purpose of obtaining greater compensation than that to which he or she is legally entitled for furnishing services or merchandise under this chapter or Chapter 8 (commencing with Section 14200).

(3) A person knowingly submits false information for the purpose of obtaining authorization for furnishing services or merchandise under this chapter or Chapter 8 (commencing with Section 14200).

(4) A person knowingly and willfully executes, or attempts to execute, a scheme or artifice to do either of the following:

(A) Defraud the Medi–Cal program or any other health care program administered by the department or its agents or contractors.

(B) Obtain, by means of false or fraudulent pretenses, representations, or promises, any of the money or property owned by, or under the custody or control of, the Medi–Cal program or any other health care program administered by the department or its agents or contractors, in connection with the delivery of or payment for health care benefits, services, goods, supplies, or merchandise.

(c) A violation of subdivision (a) is punishable by imprisonment in a county jail, or in the state prison for two, three, or five years.

(d) If the execution of a scheme or artifice to defraud as defined in paragraph (4) of subdivision (b) is committed under circumstances likely to cause or that do cause two or more persons great bodily injury, as defined in Section 12022.7 of the Penal Code, or serious bodily injury, as defined in paragraph (4) of subdivision (f) of Section 243 of the Penal Code, a term of four years, in addition and consecutive to the term of imprisonment imposed in subdivision (c), shall be imposed for each person who suffers great bodily injury or serious bodily injury.

The additional terms provided in this subdivision shall not be imposed unless the facts showing the circumstances that were likely to cause or that did cause great bodily injury or serious bodily injury to two or more persons are charged in the accusatory pleading and admitted or found to be true by the trier of fact.

(e) If the execution of a scheme or artifice to defraud, as defined in paragraph (4) of subdivision (b) results in a death which constitutes a second degree murder, as defined in Section 189 of the Penal Code, the offense shall be punishable, upon conviction, pursuant to subdivision (a) of Section 190 of the Penal Code.

(f) Any person, including an applicant or provider as defined in Section 14043.1, or billing agent, as defined in Section 14040.1, who has engaged in any of the activities subject to fine or imprisonment under this section, shall be subject to the asset forfeiture provisions for criminal profiteering.

(g) Pursuant to Section 923 of the Penal Code, the Attorney General may convene a grand jury to investigate and indict for any of the activities subject to fine, imprisonment, or asset forfeiture under this section.

(h) The enforcement remedies provided under this section are not exclusive and shall not preclude the use of any other criminal or civil remedy. However, an act or omission punishable in different ways by this section and other provisions of law shall not be punished under more than one provision, but the penalty to be imposed shall be determined as set forth in Section 654 of the Penal Code. *(Added by Stats.1969, c. 562, p. 1189, § 1. Amended by Stats.1976, c. 1139, p. 5174, § 349, operative July 1, 1977; Stats.1977, c. 1036, p. 3103, § 4, eff. Sept. 23, 1977; Stats.1980, c. 947, p. 2990, § 1; Stats.2000, c. 322 (A.B.1098), § 27.)*

Cross References

Abuse of elderly or dependent adults suspected at care facilities, local ombudsman and local law enforcement, duty to report to certain state agencies, see Welfare and Institutions Code § 15630.

Attorney General, generally, see Government Code § 12500 et seq.

Department defined for purposes of this Chapter, see Welfare and Institutions Code § 14062.

Department of insurance, reported violation of state law concerning illegally provided medical services, license revocation of physician or surgeon, see Business and Professions Code § 2417.

Fraud, nature of, see Civil Code §§ 1571 to 1574.

Medi–Cal defined for purposes of this Chapter, see Welfare and Institutions Code § 14063.

Powers and duties of grand jury, investigation of matters of criminal nature, presentation by Attorney General, see Penal Code § 923.

Time of commencing criminal actions, tolling or extension of time periods, revival of cause of action, see Penal Code § 803.

Research References

2 Witkin, California Criminal Law 4th Crimes Against Governmental Authority § 158 (2021), False Medi-Cal Claim.

2 Witkin, California Criminal Law 4th Crimes Against Governmental Authority § 161 (2021), Relationship to Other Crimes.

1 Witkin California Criminal Law 4th Introduction to Crimes § 77 (2021), Illustrations: Special Statute is Not Controlling.

3 Witkin, California Criminal Law 4th Punishment § 207 (2021), Definitions.

§ 14107.2. Kickbacks, bribes or rebates; punishment

(a) Any person who solicits or receives any remuneration, including, but not restricted to, any kickback, bribe, or rebate, directly or indirectly, overtly or covertly, in cash or in valuable consideration of any kind, either:

(1) In return for the referral, or promised referral, of any individual to a person for the furnishing or arranging for the furnishing of any service or merchandise for which payment may be made, in whole or in part, under this chapter or Chapter 8 (commencing with Section 14200); or

(2) In return for the purchasing, leasing, ordering, or arranging for or recommending the purchasing, leasing, or ordering of any goods, facility, service or merchandise for which payment may be made, in whole or in part, under this chapter or Chapter 8 (commencing with Section 14200), is punishable upon a first conviction by imprisonment in a county jail for not longer than one year or imprisonment pursuant to subdivision (h) of Section 1170 of the Penal Code, or by a fine not exceeding ten thousand dollars ($10,000), or by both that imprisonment and fine. A second or subsequent conviction shall be punishable by imprisonment pursuant to subdivision (h) of Section 1170 of the Penal Code.

(b) Any person who offers or pays any remuneration, including, but not restricted to, any kickback, bribe, or rebate, directly or indirectly, overtly or covertly, in cash or in valuable consideration of any kind, either:

(1) To refer any individual to a person for the furnishing or arranging for furnishing of any service or merchandise for which payment may be made, in whole or in part, under this chapter or Chapter 8 (commencing with Section 14200); or

(2) To purchase, lease, order, or arrange for or recommend the purchasing, leasing, or ordering of any goods, facility, service, or merchandise for which payment may be made, in whole or in part, under this chapter or Chapter 8 (commencing with Section 14200), is punishable upon a first conviction by imprisonment in a county jail for not longer than one year or pursuant to subdivision (h) of Section 1170 of the Penal Code, or by a fine not exceeding ten thousand dollars ($10,000), or by both that imprisonment and fine. A second or subsequent conviction shall be punishable by imprisonment pursuant to subdivision (h) of Section 1170 of the Penal Code.

(c) Subdivisions (a) and (b) shall not apply to the following:

(1) Any amount paid by an employer to an employee, who has a bona fide employment relationship with that employer, for employment with provision of covered items or services.

(2) A discount or other reduction in price obtained by a provider of services or other entity under this chapter or Chapter 8 (commencing with Section 14200), if the reduction in price is properly disclosed and reflected in the costs claimed or charges made by the provider or entity under this chapter or Chapter 8 (commencing with Section 14200). This paragraph shall not apply to consultant pharmaceutical services rendered to nursing facilities nor to all categories of intermediate care facilities for the developmentally disabled.

(3) The practices or transactions between a federally qualified health center, as defined in Section 1396d(*l*)(2)(B) of Title 42 of the

United States Code, and any individual or entity shall be permitted only to the extent sanctioned or permitted by federal law.

(4) The provision of nonmonetary remuneration in the form of hardware, software, or information technology and training services, as described in subsections (x) and (y) of Section 1001.952 of Title 42 of the Code of Federal Regulations, as amended October 4, 2007, as published in the Federal Register (72 Fed. Reg. 56631, 56644), and subsequently amended versions.

(d) For purposes of this section, "kickback" means a rebate or anything of value or advantage, present or prospective, or any promise or undertaking to give any rebate or thing of value or advantage, with a corrupt intent to unlawfully influence the person to whom it is given in actions undertaken by that person in his or her public, professional, or official capacity.

(e) The enforcement remedies provided under this section are not exclusive and shall not preclude the use of any other criminal or civil remedy. *(Added by Stats.1980, c. 947, p. 2991, § 2. Amended by Stats.1989, c. 731, § 11; Stats.1990, c. 1329 (S.B.1524), § 17, eff. Sept. 26, 1990; Stats.2006, c. 772 (A.B.2282), § 2; Stats.2007, c. 130 (A.B.299), § 247; Stats.2008, c. 290 (A.B.55), § 2, eff. Sept. 25, 2008; Stats.2009, c. 140 (A.B.1164), § 206; Stats.2011, c. 15 (A.B.109), § 630, eff. April 4, 2011, operative Oct. 1, 2011.)*

Cross References

Department of insurance, reported violation of state law concerning illegally provided medical services, license revocation of physician or surgeon, see Business and Professions Code § 2417.

Research References

2 Witkin, California Criminal Law 4th Crimes Against Governmental Authority § 46 (2021), Other Persons.
2 Witkin, California Criminal Law 4th Crimes Against Governmental Authority § 160 (2021), Illegal Payment for Referral or Services.
2 Witkin, California Criminal Law 4th Crimes Against Public Peace and Welfare § 394 (2021), Unlawful Referral of Patients.

§ 14107.3. Knowing and willful charging of sum in addition to amount owed as a precondition to providing services or merchandise; punishment

Any person who knowingly and willfully charges, solicits, accepts, or receives, in addition to any amount payable under this chapter, any gift, money, contribution, donation, or other consideration as a precondition to providing services or merchandise to a Medi–Cal beneficiary for any service or merchandise in the Medi–Cal program's scope of benefits in addition to a claim submitted to the Medi–Cal program under this chapter or Chapter 8 (commencing with Section 14200), except either:

(1) To collect payments due under a contractual or legal entitlement pursuant to subdivision (b) of Section 14000; or

(2) To bill a long-term care patient or representative for the amount of the patient's share of the cost; or

(3) As provided under Section 14019.3, is punishable upon a first conviction by imprisonment in the county jail for not longer than one year or pursuant to subdivision (h) of Section 1170 of the Penal Code, or by a fine not to exceed ten thousand dollars ($10,000), or both such imprisonment and fine. A second or subsequent conviction shall be punishable by imprisonment pursuant to subdivision (h) of Section 1170 of the Penal Code. *(Added by Stats.1980, c. 947, p. 2992, § 3. Amended by Stats.2011, c. 15 (A.B.109), § 631, eff. April 4, 2011, operative Oct. 1, 2011.)*

Cross References

Medi–Cal defined for purposes of this Chapter, see Welfare and Institutions Code § 14063.

Research References

2 Witkin, California Criminal Law 4th Crimes Against Governmental Authority § 160 (2021), Illegal Payment for Referral or Services.

§ 14107.4. Cost reports; fraud; punishment; certification as correct; definition

(a) Any person who, with the intent to defraud, certifies as true and correct any cost report, submitted by a hospital to a state agency for reimbursement pursuant to Section 14170, who knowingly fails to disclose in writing on the cost report any significant beneficial interest, as defined in subdivision (d), which the owners of the provider, or members of the provider governing board, or employees of the provider, or independent contractor of the provider, have in the contractors or vendors to the providers, is guilty of a public offense.

(b) Any person who, with the intent to defraud, knowingly causes any material false information to be included in any cost report submitted by a hospital to a state agency for reimbursement pursuant to Section 14170 shall be guilty of an offense punishable by imprisonment pursuant to subdivision (h) of Section 1170 of the Penal Code, or by a fine not exceeding ten thousand dollars ($10,000), or by a fine and imprisonment, or by imprisonment in the county jail not exceeding one year, or by a fine not exceeding five thousand dollars ($5,000), or by both a fine and imprisonment.

(c) The provider's chief executive officer shall certify that any cost report submitted by a hospital to a state agency for reimbursement pursuant to Section 14170 shall be true and correct. In the case of a hospital which is operated as a unit of a coordinated group of health facilities and under common management, either the hospital's chief executive officer or administrator, or the chief financial officer of the operating region of which the hospital is a part, shall certify to the accuracy of the report.

(d) As used in this section, "significant beneficial interest" means any financial interest that is equal to or greater than twenty-five thousand dollars ($25,000) of ownership interest or 5 percent of the whole ownership or any other contractual or compensatory arrangement with vendors or contractors or immediate family members of vendors or contractors. "Immediate family" means spouse, son, daughter, father, mother, father-in-law, mother-in-law, daughter-in-law, or son-in-law. Interests held by these persons specified in subdivision (a) and members of these person's [1] immediate family should be combined and included as a single interest.

(e) Any person who violates the provisions of subdivision (a) is punishable by imprisonment in the county jail for a period not to exceed one year or pursuant to subdivision (h) of Section 1170 of the Penal Code, or by fine not to exceed five thousand dollars ($5,000), or by both such fine and imprisonment. *(Added by Stats.1984, c. 1465, § 2. Amended by Stats.2011, c. 15 (A.B.109), § 632, eff. April 4, 2011, operative Oct. 1, 2011.)*

[1] So in enrolled bill.

Cross References

Fraud, nature of, see Civil Code §§ 1571 to 1574.

CHAPTER 8. PREPAID PLANS

ARTICLE 4. ENROLLMENT AND DISENROLLMENT

Section

§ 14409. Misrepresentations; penalties; misdemeanor

(a) No prepaid health plan, marketing representative, or marketing organization shall in any manner misrepresent itself, the plans it represents, or the Medi–Cal program. A violation of this section shall include, but is not limited to, all of the following:

(1) False or misleading claims that marketing representatives are employees or representatives of the state, county, or anyone other than the prepaid health plan or the organization by whom they are reimbursed.

(2) False or misleading claims that the prepaid health plan is recommended or endorsed by any state or county agency, or by any other organization which has not certified its endorsement in writing to the prepaid health plan.

(3) False or misleading claims that the state or county recommends that a Medi–Cal beneficiary enroll in a prepaid health plan.

(4) Claims that a Medi–Cal beneficiary will lose their benefits under the Medi–Cal program or any other health or welfare benefits to which they are legally entitled, if they do not enroll in a prepaid health plan.

(b) Violations of this article or regulations adopted by the department pursuant to this article shall result in one or more of the following sanctions that are appropriate to the specific violation, considering the nature of the offense and frequency of occurrence within the prepaid health plan:

(1) Revocation of one or more permitted methods of marketing.

(2) Termination of authorization for a plan to provide application assistance.

(3) Refusal of the department to accept new enrollments for a period specified by the department.

(4) Refusal of the department to accept enrollments submitted by a marketing representative or organization.

(5) Forfeiture by the plan of all or part of the capitation payments for persons enrolled as a result of such violations.

(6) Requirement that the prepaid health plan in violation of this article personally contact each enrollee enrolled to explain the nature of the violation and inform the enrollee of their right to disenroll.

(7) Application of sanctions as provided in Section 14197.7.

(8) Temporarily suspend capitation payments for beneficiaries enrolled in violation of this article, or regulations adopted thereunder, until the prepaid health plan is in substantial compliance with the statutory and regulatory requirements.

(c) Any marketing representative who violates subdivision (a) while engaged in door-to-door solicitation is guilty of a misdemeanor, and shall be subject to a fine of five hundred dollars ($500) or imprisonment in a county jail for six months, or both. *(Added by Stats.1974, c. 983, p. 2044, § 13. Amended by Stats.1977, c. 1036, p. 3115, § 35, eff. Sept. 23, 1977; Stats.1981, c. 702, p. 2524, § 7; Stats.1992, c. 1056 (A.B.3463), § 6, eff. Sept. 29, 1992; Stats.2000, c. 93 (A.B.2877), § 98, eff. July 7, 2000; Stats.2012, c. 797 (S.B.1529), § 27; Stats.2019, c. 465 (A.B.1642), § 9, eff. Jan. 1, 2020.)*

Cross References

Dental health plans, marketing materials, materials to be submitted to department, see Welfare and Institutions Code § 14459.6.
Department defined for purposes of this Chapter, see Welfare and Institutions Code § 14260.
Department defined for purposes of this Division, see Welfare and Institutions Code § 10054.
Marketing defined for purposes of this Chapter, see Welfare and Institutions Code § 14263.
Marketing organization defined for purposes of this Chapter, see Welfare and Institutions Code § 14264.
Marketing representative defined for purposes of this Chapter, see Welfare and Institutions Code § 14265.
Medi–Cal beneficiary defined for purposes of this Chapter, see Welfare and Institutions Code § 14252.
Misdemeanors, definition and penalties, see Penal Code §§ 17, 19, 19.2.
Prepaid health plan defined for purposes of this Chapter, see Welfare and Institutions Code § 14251.
Regulations defined for purposes of this Division, see Welfare and Institutions Code § 10060.
Soliciting and advertising, nature of plan, operation, ownership by a professional, construction, see Health and Safety Code § 1395.

CHAPTER 11. ELDER ABUSE AND DEPENDENT ADULT CIVIL PROTECTION ACT

ARTICLE 3. MANDATORY AND NONMANDATORY REPORTS OF ABUSE

Section

§ 15630. Mandated reporters; known or suspected abuse; telephone or Internet reports; failure to report; impeding or inhibiting report; penalties

(a) A person who has assumed full or intermittent responsibility for the care or custody of an elder or dependent adult, whether or not they receive compensation, including administrators, supervisors, and any licensed staff of a public or private facility that provides care or services for elder or dependent adults, or any elder or dependent adult care custodian, health practitioner, clergy member, or employee of a county adult protective services agency or a local law enforcement agency, is a mandated reporter.

(b)(1) A mandated reporter who, in their professional capacity, or within the scope of their employment, has observed or has knowledge of an incident that reasonably appears to be physical abuse, as defined in Section 15610.63, abandonment, abduction, isolation, financial abuse, or neglect, or is told by an elder or dependent adult that they have experienced behavior, including an act or omission, constituting physical abuse, as defined in Section 15610.63, abandonment, abduction, isolation, financial abuse, or neglect, or reasonably suspects that abuse, shall report the known or suspected instance of abuse by telephone or through a confidential internet reporting tool, as authorized by Section 15658, immediately or as soon as practicably possible. If reported by telephone, a written report shall be sent, or an internet report shall be made through the confidential internet reporting tool established in Section 15658, within two working days.

(A) If the suspected or alleged abuse is physical abuse, as defined in Section 15610.63, and the abuse occurred in a long-term care facility, except a state mental health hospital or a state developmental center, the following shall occur:

(i) If the suspected abuse results in serious bodily injury, a telephone report shall be made to the local law enforcement agency immediately, but also no later than within two hours of the mandated reporter observing, obtaining knowledge of, or suspecting the physical abuse, and a written report shall be made to the local ombudsman, the corresponding licensing agency, and the local law enforcement agency within two hours of the mandated reporter observing, obtaining knowledge of, or suspecting the physical abuse.

(ii) If the suspected abuse does not result in serious bodily injury, a telephone report shall be made to the local law enforcement agency within 24 hours of the mandated reporter observing, obtaining knowledge of, or suspecting the physical abuse, and a written report shall be made to the local ombudsman, the corresponding licensing agency, and the local law enforcement agency within 24 hours of the mandated reporter observing, obtaining knowledge of, or suspecting the physical abuse.

(iii) When the suspected abuse is allegedly caused by a resident with a physician's diagnosis of dementia, and there is no serious bodily injury, as reasonably determined by the mandated reporter, drawing upon their training or experience, the reporter shall report to the local ombudsman or law enforcement agency by telephone, immediately or as soon as practicably possible, and by written report, within 24 hours.

(iv) When applicable, reports made pursuant to clauses (i) and (ii) shall be deemed to satisfy the reporting requirements of the federal Elder Justice Act of 2009, as set out in Subtitle H of the federal Patient Protection and Affordable Care Act (Public Law 111–148),[1] Section 1418.91 of the Health and Safety Code, and Section 72541 of Title 22 of the California Code of Regulations. When a local law enforcement agency receives an initial report of suspected abuse in a long-term care facility pursuant to this subparagraph, the local law enforcement agency may coordinate efforts with the local ombudsman to provide the most immediate and appropriate response warranted to investigate the mandated report. The local ombudsman and local law enforcement agencies may collaborate to develop protocols to implement this subparagraph.

(B) Notwithstanding the rulemaking provisions of Chapter 3.5 (commencing with Section 11340) of Part 1 of Division 3 of Title 2 of the Government Code, or any other law, the department may implement subparagraph (A), in whole or in part, by means of all-county letters, provider bulletins, or other similar instructions without taking regulatory action.

(C) If the suspected or alleged abuse is abuse other than physical abuse, and the abuse occurred in a long-term care facility, except a state mental health hospital or a state developmental center, a telephone report and a written report shall be made to the local ombudsman or the local law enforcement agency.

(D) With regard to abuse reported pursuant to subparagraph (C), the local ombudsman and the local law enforcement agency shall, as soon as practicable, except in the case of an emergency or pursuant to a report required to be made pursuant to clause (v), in which case these actions shall be taken immediately, do all of the following:

(i) Report to the State Department of Public Health any case of known or suspected abuse occurring in a long-term health care facility, as defined in subdivision (a) of Section 1418 of the Health and Safety Code.

(ii) Report to the State Department of Social Services any case of known or suspected abuse occurring in a residential care facility for the elderly, as defined in Section 1569.2 of the Health and Safety Code, or in an adult day program, as defined in paragraph (2) of subdivision (a) of Section 1502 of the Health and Safety Code.

(iii) Report to the State Department of Public Health and the California Department of Aging any case of known or suspected abuse occurring in an adult day health care center, as defined in subdivision (b) of Section 1570.7 of the Health and Safety Code.

(iv) Report to the Division of Medi-Cal Fraud and Elder Abuse any case of known or suspected criminal activity.

(v) Report all cases of known or suspected physical abuse and financial abuse to the local district attorney's office in the county where the abuse occurred.

(E)(i) If the suspected or alleged abuse or neglect occurred in a state mental hospital or a state developmental center, and the suspected or alleged abuse or neglect resulted in any of the following incidents, a report shall be made immediately, but no later than within two hours of the mandated reporter observing, obtaining knowledge of, or suspecting abuse, to designated investigators of the State Department of State Hospitals or the State Department of Developmental Services, and to the local law enforcement agency:

(I) A death.

(II) A sexual assault, as defined in Section 15610.63.

(III) An assault with a deadly weapon, as described in Section 245 of the Penal Code, by a nonresident of the state mental hospital or state developmental center.

(IV) An assault with force likely to produce great bodily injury, as described in Section 245 of the Penal Code.

(V) An injury to the genitals when the cause of the injury is undetermined.

(VI) A broken bone when the cause of the break is undetermined.

(ii) All other reports of suspected or alleged abuse or neglect that occurred in a state mental hospital or a state developmental center shall be made immediately, but no later than within two hours of the mandated reporter observing, obtaining knowledge of, or suspecting abuse, to designated investigators of the State Department of State Hospitals or the State Department of Developmental Services, or to the local law enforcement agency.

(iii) When a local law enforcement agency receives an initial report of suspected or alleged abuse or neglect in a state mental hospital or a state developmental center pursuant to clause (i), the local law enforcement agency shall coordinate efforts with the designated investigators of the State Department of State Hospitals or the State Department of Developmental Services to provide the most immediate and appropriate response warranted to investigate the mandated report. The designated investigators of the State Department of State Hospitals or the State Department of Developmental Services and local law enforcement agencies may collaborate to develop protocols to implement this clause.

(iv) Except in an emergency, the local law enforcement agency shall, as soon as practicable, report any case of known or suspected criminal activity to the Division of Medi-Cal Fraud and Elder Abuse.

(v) Notwithstanding any other law, a mandated reporter who is required to report pursuant to Section 4427.5 shall not be required to report under clause (i).

(F) If the abuse has occurred in any place other than a long-term care facility, a state mental hospital, or a state developmental center, the report shall be made to the adult protective services agency or the local law enforcement agency.

(2)(A) A mandated reporter who is a clergy member who acquires knowledge or reasonable suspicion of elder or dependent adult abuse during a penitential communication is not subject to paragraph (1). For purposes of this subdivision, "penitential communication" means a communication that is intended to be in confidence, including, but not limited to, a sacramental confession made to a clergy member who, in the course of the discipline or practice of their church, denomination, or organization is authorized or accustomed to hear those communications and under the discipline tenets, customs, or practices of their church, denomination, or organization, has a duty to keep those communications secret.

(B) This subdivision shall not modify or limit a clergy member's duty to report known or suspected elder and dependent adult abuse if they are acting in the capacity of a care custodian, health practitioner, or employee of an adult protective services agency.

(C) Notwithstanding this section, a clergy member who is not regularly employed on either a full-time or part-time basis in a long-term care facility or does not have care or custody of an elder or dependent adult shall not be responsible for reporting abuse or neglect that is not reasonably observable or discernible to a reasonably prudent person having no specialized training or experience in elder or dependent care.

(3)(A) A mandated reporter who is a physician and surgeon, a registered nurse, or a psychotherapist, as defined in Section 1010 of the Evidence Code, shall not be required to report, pursuant to paragraph (1), an incident if all of the following conditions exist:

(i) The mandated reporter has been told by an elder or dependent adult that they have experienced behavior constituting physical abuse, as defined in Section 15610.63, abandonment, abduction, isolation, financial abuse, or neglect.

(ii) The mandated reporter is unaware of any independent evidence that corroborates the statement that the abuse has occurred.

(iii) The elder or dependent adult has been diagnosed with a mental illness or dementia, or is the subject of a court-ordered conservatorship because of a mental illness or dementia.

(iv) In the exercise of clinical judgment, the physician and surgeon, the registered nurse, or the psychotherapist, as defined in Section 1010 of the Evidence Code, reasonably believes that the abuse did not occur.

(B) This paragraph shall not impose upon mandated reporters a duty to investigate a known or suspected incident of abuse and shall not lessen or restrict any existing duty of mandated reporters.

(4)(A) In a long-term care facility, a mandated reporter shall not be required to report as a suspected incident of abuse, as defined in Section 15610.07, an incident if all of the following conditions exist:

(i) The mandated reporter is aware that there is a proper plan of care.

(ii) The mandated reporter is aware that the plan of care was properly provided or executed.

(iii) A physical, mental, or medical injury occurred as a result of care provided pursuant to clause (i) or (ii).

(iv) The mandated reporter reasonably believes that the injury was not the result of abuse.

(B) This paragraph shall neither require a mandated reporter to seek, nor preclude a mandated reporter from seeking, information regarding a known or suspected incident of abuse before reporting. This paragraph shall apply only to those categories of mandated reporters that the State Department of Public Health determines, upon approval by the Division of Medi-Cal Fraud and Elder Abuse and the state long-term care ombudsman, have access to plans of care and have the training and experience necessary to determine whether the conditions specified in this section have been met.

(c)(1) Any mandated reporter who has knowledge, or reasonably suspects, that types of elder or dependent adult abuse for which reports are not mandated have been inflicted upon an elder or dependent adult, or that their emotional well-being is endangered in any other way, may report the known or suspected instance of abuse.

(2) If the suspected or alleged abuse occurred in a long-term care facility other than a state mental health hospital or a state developmental center, the report may be made to the long-term care ombudsman program. Except in an emergency, the local ombudsman shall report any case of known or suspected abuse to the State Department of Public Health and any case of known or suspected criminal activity to the Division of Medi-Cal Fraud and Elder Abuse, as soon as is practicable.

(3) If the suspected or alleged abuse occurred in a state mental health hospital or a state developmental center, the report may be made to the designated investigator of the State Department of State Hospitals or the State Department of Developmental Services or to a local law enforcement agency. Except in an emergency, the local law enforcement agency shall report any case of known or suspected criminal activity to the Division of Medi-Cal Fraud and Elder Abuse, as soon as is practicable.

(4) If the suspected or alleged abuse occurred in a place other than a place described in paragraph (2) or (3), the report may be made to the county adult protective services agency.

(5) If the conduct involves criminal activity not covered in subdivision (b), it may be immediately reported to the appropriate law enforcement agency.

(d) If two or more mandated reporters are present and jointly have knowledge or reasonably suspect that types of abuse of an elder or a dependent adult for which a report is or is not mandated have occurred, and there is agreement among them, the telephone report or internet report, as authorized by Section 15658, may be made by a member of the team selected by mutual agreement, and a single report may be made and signed by the selected member of the reporting team. Any member who has knowledge that the member designated to report has failed to do so shall thereafter make the report.

(e) A telephone report or internet report, as authorized by Section 15658, of a known or suspected instance of elder or dependent adult abuse shall include, if known, the name of the person making the report, the name and age of the elder or dependent adult, the present location of the elder or dependent adult, the names and addresses of family members or any other adult responsible for the elder's or dependent adult's care, the nature and extent of the elder's or dependent adult's condition, the date of the incident, and any other information, including information that led that person to suspect elder or dependent adult abuse, as requested by the agency receiving the report.

(f) The reporting duties under this section are individual, and no supervisor or administrator shall impede or inhibit the reporting duties, and no person making the report shall be subject to any sanction for making the report. However, internal procedures to facilitate reporting, ensure confidentiality, and apprise supervisors and administrators of reports may be established, provided they are not inconsistent with this chapter.

(g)(1) Whenever this section requires a county adult protective services agency to report to a law enforcement agency, the law enforcement agency shall, immediately upon request, provide a copy of its investigative report concerning the reported matter to that county adult protective services agency.

(2) Whenever this section requires a law enforcement agency to report to a county adult protective services agency, the county adult protective services agency shall, immediately upon request, provide to that law enforcement agency a copy of its investigative report concerning the reported matter.

(3) The requirement to disclose investigative reports pursuant to this subdivision shall not include the disclosure of social services records or case files that are confidential, nor shall this subdivision allow disclosure of any reports or records if the disclosure would be prohibited by any other state or federal law.

(h) Failure to report, or impeding or inhibiting a report of, physical abuse, as defined in Section 15610.63, abandonment, abduction, isolation, financial abuse, or neglect of an elder or dependent adult, in violation of this section, is a misdemeanor, punishable by not more than six months in the county jail, by a fine of not more than one thousand dollars ($1,000), or by both that fine and imprisonment. A mandated reporter who willfully fails to report, or impedes or inhibits a report of, physical abuse, as defined in Section 15610.63, abandonment, abduction, isolation, financial abuse, or neglect of an elder or dependent adult, in violation of this section, if that abuse results in death or great bodily injury, shall be punished by not more than one year in a county jail, by a fine of not more than five thousand dollars ($5,000), or by both that fine and imprisonment. If a mandated reporter intentionally conceals their failure to report an incident known by the mandated reporter to be abuse or severe neglect under this section, the failure to report is a continuing offense until a law enforcement agency specified in paragraph (1) of subdivision (b) of Section 15630 discovers the offense.

(i) For purposes of this section, "dependent adult" has the same meaning as that term is defined in Section 15610.23. *(Added by Stats.1994, c. 594 (S.B.1681), § 7. Amended by Stats.1995, c. 813 (A.B.1836), § 1; Stats.1998, c. 946 (S.B.2199), § 8; Stats.1998, c. 980 (A.B.1780), § 1; Stats.1999, c. 236 (A.B.739), § 1; Stats.2002, c. 54 (A.B.255), § 9; Stats.2004, c. 823 (A.B.20), § 19; Stats.2005, c. 163 (A.B.1188), § 2; Stats.2008, c. 481 (A.B.2100), § 1; Stats.2011, c. 373 (S.B.718), § 1; Stats.2012, c. 24 (A.B.1470), § 202, eff. June 27, 2012; Stats.2012, c. 660 (S.B.1051), § 4, eff. Sept. 27, 2012; Stats.2012, c. 659 (A.B.40), § 2; Stats.2012, c. 660 (S.B.1051), § 4.5, eff. Sept. 27, 2012, operative Jan. 1, 2013; Stats.2013, c. 76 (A.B.383), § 223; Stats.2013, c. 673 (A.B.602), § 3; Stats.2021, c. 85 (A.B.135), § 66, eff. July 16, 2021; Stats.2021, c. 554 (S.B.823), § 14, eff. Jan. 1, 2022.)*

[1] For public law sections classified to the U.S.C.A., see USCA–Tables.

Cross References

Abandonment defined for purposes of this Chapter, see Welfare and Institutions Code § 15610.05.
Abduction defined for purposes of this Chapter, see Welfare and Institutions Code § 15610.06.
Adult protective services agency defined for purposes of this Chapter, see Welfare and Institutions Code § 15610.13.
Adult protective services defined for purposes of this Chapter, see Welfare and Institutions Code § 15610.10.
Authority to investigate complaints and carry out random inspections, refusal to permit inspection, oversight of home care aides, cross-reporting of abuse to law enforcement, see Health and Safety Code § 1796.52.
Authorization for disclosure of medical information, compelled and other permitted disclosures, see Civil Code § 56.10.
Bureau of Medi-Cal Fraud, powers and duties, see Government Code § 12528.
Care custodian defined for purposes of this Chapter, see Welfare and Institutions Code § 15610.17.
Clergy member defined for purposes of this Chapter, see Welfare and Institutions Code § 15610.19.
Confidential information and records, disclosure, consent, see Welfare and Institutions Code § 4514.
Department defined for purposes of this Division, see Welfare and Institutions Code § 10054.
Department of Health Care Services, generally, see Health and Safety Code § 100100 et seq.
Elder defined for purposes of this Chapter, see Welfare and Institutions Code § 15610.27.
Employees of mandated reporters, signed statements as prerequisite to employment, acknowledgment of knowledge and agreed compliance with this section, see Welfare and Institutions Code § 15659.
False report of criminal offense, exemption from criminal liability for persons who are required by statute to report abuse, see Penal Code § 148.5.
Financial abuse defined for purposes of this Chapter, see Welfare and Institutions Code § 15610.30.
Fundamental rights of residents of residential care facilities, see Health and Safety Code § 1569.261 et seq.
Health practitioner defined for purposes of this Chapter, see Welfare and Institutions Code § 15610.37.
Isolation defined for purposes of this Chapter, see Welfare and Institutions Code § 15610.43.
Licensed educational psychologists, unprofessional conduct, grounds for refusal to issue, or suspension or revocation of license, see Business and Professions Code § 4989.54.
Licensed professional clinical counselors, unprofessional conduct, see Business and Professions Code § 4999.90.
Local law enforcement agency defined for purposes of this Chapter, see Welfare and Institutions Code § 15610.45.
Long-term care facility defined for purposes of this Chapter, see Welfare and Institutions Code § 15610.47.
Marriage and family therapists, violation of this section as unprofessional conduct, see Business and Professions Code § 4982.
Misdemeanors, definition and penalties, see Penal Code §§ 17, 19, 19.2.
Neglect defined for purposes of this Chapter, see Welfare and Institutions Code § 15610.57.
Protection and advocacy agency, private nonprofit corporations, conformance with requirements of federal law, see Welfare and Institutions Code § 4901.
Reasonable suspicion defined for purposes of this Chapter, see Welfare and Institutions Code § 15610.65.
Reports of incidents of alleged abuse or suspected abuse of residents, see Health and Safety Code § 1418.91.
Senior and Disability Justice Act, see Penal Code § 368.6.
Services defined for purposes of this Division, see Welfare and Institutions Code § 10053.
Social workers, unprofessional conduct, effect on licensee or registrant, see Business and Professions Code § 4992.3.

Research References

2 Witkin, California Criminal Law 4th Sex Offenses and Crimes Against Decency § 186 (2021), Report of Abuse.

§ 15630.1. Mandated reporter of suspected financial abuse of an elder or dependent adult; definitions and reporting requirements; power of attorney

(a) As used in this section, "mandated reporter of suspected financial abuse of an elder or dependent adult" means all officers and employees of financial institutions.

(b) As used in this section, the term "financial institution" means any of the following:

(1) A depository institution, as defined in Section 3(c) of the Federal Deposit Insurance Act (12 U.S.C. Sec. 1813(c)).

(2) An institution-affiliated party, as defined in Section 3(u) of the Federal Deposit Insurance Act (12 U.S.C. Sec. 1813(u)).

(3) A federal credit union or state credit union, as defined in Section 101 of the Federal Credit Union Act (12 U.S.C. Sec. 1752), including, but not limited to, an institution-affiliated party of a credit union, as defined in Section 206(r) of the Federal Credit Union Act (12 U.S.C. Sec. 1786(r)).

(c) As used in this section, "financial abuse" has the same meaning as in Section 15610.30.

(d)(1) Any mandated reporter of suspected financial abuse of an elder or dependent adult who has direct contact with the elder or dependent adult or who reviews or approves the elder or dependent adult's financial documents, records, or transactions, in connection with providing financial services with respect to an elder or dependent adult, and who, within the scope of his or her employment or professional practice, has observed or has knowledge of an incident, that is directly related to the transaction or matter that is within that scope of employment or professional practice, that reasonably appears to be financial abuse, or who reasonably suspects that abuse, based solely on the information before him or her at the time of reviewing or approving the document, record, or transaction in the case of mandated reporters who do not have direct contact with the elder or dependent adult, shall report the known or suspected instance of financial abuse by telephone or through a confidential Internet reporting tool, as authorized pursuant to Section 15658, immediately, or as soon as practicably possible. If reported by telephone, a written report shall be sent, or an Internet report shall be made through the confidential Internet reporting tool established in Section 15658, within two working days to the local adult protective services agency or the local law enforcement agency.

(2) When two or more mandated reporters jointly have knowledge or reasonably suspect that financial abuse of an elder or a dependent adult for which the report is mandated has occurred, and when there is an agreement among them, the telephone report or Internet report, as authorized by Section 15658, may be made by a member of the reporting team who is selected by mutual agreement. A single report may be made and signed by the selected member of the reporting team. Any member of the team who has knowledge that the member designated to report has failed to do so shall thereafter make that report.

(3) If the mandated reporter knows that the elder or dependent adult resides in a long-term care facility, as defined in Section 15610.47, the report shall be made to the local ombudsman or local law enforcement agency.

(e) An allegation by the elder or dependent adult, or any other person, that financial abuse has occurred is not sufficient to trigger the reporting requirement under this section if both of the following conditions are met:

(1) The mandated reporter of suspected financial abuse of an elder or dependent adult is aware of no other corroborating or independent evidence of the alleged financial abuse of an elder or dependent adult. The mandated reporter of suspected financial abuse of an elder or dependent adult is not required to investigate any accusations.

(2) In the exercise of his or her professional judgment, the mandated reporter of suspected financial abuse of an elder or dependent adult reasonably believes that financial abuse of an elder or dependent adult did not occur.

(f) Failure to report financial abuse under this section shall be subject to a civil penalty not exceeding one thousand dollars ($1,000) or if the failure to report is willful, a civil penalty not exceeding five thousand dollars ($5,000), which shall be paid by the financial institution that is the employer of the mandated reporter to the party bringing the action. Subdivision (h) of Section 15630 shall not apply to violations of this section.

(g)(1) The civil penalty provided for in subdivision (f) shall be recovered only in a civil action brought against the financial institution by the Attorney General, district attorney, or county counsel. No action shall be brought under this section by any person other than the Attorney General, district attorney, or county counsel. Multiple actions for the civil penalty may not be brought for the same violation.

(2) Nothing in the Financial Elder Abuse Reporting Act of 2005 shall be construed to limit, expand, or otherwise modify any civil liability or remedy that may exist under this or any other law.

(h) As used in this section, "suspected financial abuse of an elder or dependent adult" occurs when a person who is required to report under subdivision (a) observes or has knowledge of behavior or unusual circumstances or transactions, or a pattern of behavior or unusual circumstances or transactions, that would lead an individual with like training or experience, based on the same facts, to form a reasonable belief that an elder or dependent adult is the victim of financial abuse as defined in Section 15610.30.

(i) Reports of suspected financial abuse of an elder or dependent adult made by an employee or officer of a financial institution pursuant to this section are covered under subdivision (b) of Section 47 of the Civil Code.

(j)(1) A mandated reporter of suspected financial abuse of an elder or dependent adult is authorized to not honor a power of attorney described in Division 4.5 (commencing with Section 4000) of the Probate Code as to an attorney-in-fact, if the mandated reporter of suspected financial abuse of an elder or dependent adult makes a report to an adult protective services agency or a local law enforcement agency of any state that the principal may be subject to financial abuse, as described in this chapter or as defined in similar laws of another state, by that attorney-in-fact or person acting for or with that attorney-in-fact.

(2) If a mandated reporter of suspected financial abuse of an elder or dependent adult does not honor a power of attorney as to an attorney-in-fact pursuant to paragraph (1), the power of attorney shall remain enforceable as to every other attorney-in-fact also designated in the power of attorney about whom a report has not been made.

(3) For purposes of this subdivision, the terms "principal" and "attorney-in-fact" shall have the same meanings as those terms are used in Division 4.5 (commencing with Section 4000) of the Probate Code. *(Added by Stats.2005, c. 140 (S.B.1018), § 4, operative Jan. 1, 2007. Amended by Stats.2011, c. 372 (S.B.33), § 1; Stats.2011, c. 373 (S.B.718), § 2.5; Stats.2017, c. 408 (A.B.611), § 1, eff. Jan. 1, 2018.)*

Cross References

Abuse of an elder or a dependent adult defined for purposes of this Chapter, see Welfare and Institutions Code § 15610.07.
Adult protective services agency defined for purposes of this Chapter, see Welfare and Institutions Code § 15610.13.
Adult protective services defined for purposes of this Chapter, see Welfare and Institutions Code § 15610.10.
Attorney General, generally, see Government Code § 12500 et seq.
Dependent adult defined for purposes of this Chapter, see Welfare and Institutions Code § 15610.23.
Elder defined for purposes of this Chapter, see Welfare and Institutions Code § 15610.27.
Local law enforcement agency defined for purposes of this Chapter, see Welfare and Institutions Code § 15610.45.
Senior and Disability Justice Act, see Penal Code § 368.6.
Services defined for purposes of this Division, see Welfare and Institutions Code § 10053.

§ 15630.2. Mandated reporter of suspected financial abuse of an elder or dependent adult; broker-dealers and investment advisors; definitions and reporting requirements; power of attorney; delay of requested disbursement or transaction

(a) For purposes of this section, the following terms have the following definitions:

(1) "Financial abuse" has the same meaning as in Section 15610.30.

(2) "Broker-dealer" has the same meaning as in Section 25004 of the Corporations Code.

(3) "Investment adviser" has the same meaning as in Section 25009 of the Corporations Code.

(4) "Mandated reporter of suspected financial abuse of an elder or dependent adult" means a broker-dealer or an investment adviser.

(b)(1) Any mandated reporter of suspected financial abuse of an elder or dependent adult who has direct contact with the elder or dependent adult or who reviews or approves the elder or dependent adult's financial documents, records, or transactions, in connection with providing financial services with respect to an elder or dependent adult, and who, within the scope of their employment or professional practice, has observed or has knowledge of an incident that is directly related to the transaction or matter that is within that scope of employment or professional practice, that reasonably appears to be financial abuse, or who reasonably suspects that abuse, based solely on the information before them at the time of reviewing or approving the document, record, or transaction in the case of mandated reporters who do not have direct contact with the elder or dependent adult, shall report the known or suspected instance of financial abuse by telephone or through a confidential internet reporting tool, as authorized pursuant to Section 15658, immediately, or as soon as practicably possible. If reported by telephone, a written report shall be sent, or an internet report shall be made through the confidential internet reporting tool established in Section 15658, within two working days to the local adult protective services agency, the local law enforcement agency, and the Department of * * * Financial Protection and Innovation.

(2) When two or more mandated reporters jointly have knowledge or reasonably suspect that financial abuse of an elder or a dependent adult for which the report is mandated has occurred, and when there is an agreement among them, the telephone report or internet report, as authorized by Section 15658, may be made by a member of the reporting team who is selected by mutual agreement. A single report may be made and signed by the selected member of the reporting team. Any member of the team who has knowledge that the member designated to report has failed to do so shall thereafter make that report.

(3) If the mandated reporter knows that the elder or dependent adult resides in a long-term care facility, as defined in Section 15610.47, the report shall be made to the local ombudsman, local law enforcement agency, and the Department of * * * Financial Protection and Innovation.

(c) An allegation by the elder or dependent adult, or any other person, that financial abuse has occurred is not sufficient to trigger the reporting requirement under this section if both of the following conditions are met:

(1) The mandated reporter of suspected financial abuse of an elder or dependent adult is aware of no other corroborating or independent evidence of the alleged financial abuse of an elder or dependent adult. The mandated reporter of suspected financial abuse of an elder or dependent adult is not required to investigate any accusations.

(2) In the exercise of their professional judgment, the mandated reporter of suspected financial abuse of an elder or dependent adult reasonably believes that financial abuse of an elder or dependent adult did not occur.

(d) Failure to report financial abuse under this section shall be subject to a civil penalty not exceeding one thousand dollars ($1,000) or if the failure to report is willful, a civil penalty not exceeding five thousand dollars ($5,000), which shall be paid by the employer of the mandated reporter of suspected financial abuse of an elder or dependent adult to the party bringing the action. Subdivision (h) of Section 15630 shall not apply to violations of this section.

(e) The civil penalty provided for in subdivision (d) shall be recovered only in a civil action brought against the broker-dealer or investment adviser by the Attorney General, district attorney, or county counsel. An action shall not be brought under this section by any person other than the Attorney General, district attorney, or county counsel. Multiple actions for the civil penalty may not be brought for the same violation.

(f) As used in this section, "suspected financial abuse of an elder or dependent adult" occurs when a person who is required to report under subdivision (b) observes or has knowledge of behavior or unusual circumstances or transactions, or a pattern of behavior or unusual circumstances or transactions, that would lead an individual with like training or experience, based on the same facts, to form a reasonable belief that an elder or dependent adult is the victim of financial abuse as defined in Section 15610.30.

(g) Reports of suspected financial abuse of an elder or dependent adult made pursuant to this section are covered under subdivision (b) of Section 47 of the Civil Code.

(h)(1) A mandated reporter of suspected financial abuse of an elder or dependent adult who makes a report pursuant to this section may notify any trusted contact person who had previously been designated by the elder or dependent adult to receive notification of any known or suspected financial abuse, unless the trusted contact person is suspected of the financial abuse. This authority does not affect the ability of the mandated reporter to make any other notifications otherwise permitted by law.

(2) A mandated reporter of suspected financial abuse of an elder or dependent adult shall not be civilly liable for any notification made in good faith and with reasonable care pursuant to this subdivision.

(i)(1) A mandated reporter of suspected financial abuse of an elder or dependent adult is authorized to not honor a power of attorney described in Division 4.5 (commencing with Section 4000) of the Probate Code as to an attorney-in-fact, if the mandated reporter of suspected financial abuse of an elder or dependent adult makes a report to an adult protective services agency or a local law enforcement agency of any state that the principal may be subject to financial abuse, as described in this chapter or as defined in similar laws of another state, by that attorney-in-fact or person acting for or with that attorney-in-fact.

(2) If a mandated reporter of suspected financial abuse of an elder or dependent adult does not honor a power of attorney as to an attorney-in-fact pursuant to paragraph (1), the power of attorney shall remain enforceable as to every other attorney-in-fact also designated in the power of attorney about whom a report has not been made.

(3) For purposes of this subdivision, the terms "principal" and "attorney-in-fact" have the same meanings as those terms are used in Division 4.5 (commencing with Section 4000) of the Probate Code.

(j)(1) A mandated reporter of suspected financial abuse of an elder or dependent adult may temporarily delay a requested disbursement from, or a requested transaction involving, an account of an elder or dependent adult or an account to which an elder or dependent adult is a beneficiary if the mandated reporter meets all of following conditions:

(A) They have a reasonable belief, after initiating an internal review of the requested disbursement or transaction and the suspected financial abuse, that the requested disbursement or transaction may result in the financial abuse of an elder or dependent adult.

(B) Immediately, but no later than two business days after the requested disbursement or transaction is delayed, they provide written notification of the delay and the reason for the delay to all parties authorized to transact business on the account, unless a party is reasonably believed to have engaged in suspected financial abuse of the elder or dependent.

(C) Immediately, but no later than two business days after the requested disbursement or transaction is delayed, they notify the local county adult protective services agency, local law enforcement agency, and the Department of * * * Financial Protection and Innovation about the delay.

(D) They provide any updates relevant to the report to the local adult protective services agency, the local law enforcement agency, and the Department of * * * Financial Protection and Innovation.

(2) Any delay of a requested disbursement or transaction authorized by this subdivision shall expire upon either of the following, whichever is sooner:

(A) A determination by the mandated reporter that the requested disbursement or transaction will not result in financial abuse of the elder or dependent adult provided that the mandated reporter first consults with the local county adult protective services agency, local law enforcement agency, and the Department of * * * Financial Protection and Innovation, and receives no objection from those entities.

(B) Fifteen business days after the date on which the mandated reporter first delayed the requested disbursement or transaction, unless the adult protective services agency, local law enforcement agency, or the Department of * * * Financial Protection and Innovation requests that the mandated reporter extend the delay, in which case the delay shall expire no more than 25 business days after the date on which the mandated reporter first delayed the requested disbursement or transaction, unless sooner terminated by the adult protective services agency, local law enforcement agency, the Department of * * * Financial Protection and Innovation, or an order of a court of competent jurisdiction.

(3) A court of competent jurisdiction may enter an order extending the delay of the requested disbursement or transaction or may order other protective relief based on the petition of the adult protective services agency, the mandated reporter who initiated the delay, or any other interested party.

(4) A mandated reporter of suspected financial abuse of an elder or dependent adult shall not be civilly liable for any temporary disbursement delay or transaction made in good faith and with reasonable care on an account pursuant to this subdivision.

(k) Notwithstanding any provision of law, a local adult protective services agency, a local law enforcement agency, and the Department of * * * Financial Protection and Innovation may disclose to a mandated reporter of suspected financial abuse of an elder or dependent adult or their employer, upon request, the general status or final disposition of any investigation that arose from a report made by that mandated reporter of suspected financial abuse of an elder or dependent adult pursuant to this section. *(Added by Stats.2019, c. 272 (S.B.496), § 1, eff. Jan. 1, 2020. Amended by Stats.2022, c. 452 (S.B.1498), § 210, eff. Jan. 1, 2023.)*

§ 15631. Nonmandated reporters; known or suspected abuse

(a) Any person who is not a mandated reporter under Section 15630, who knows, or reasonably suspects, that an elder or a dependent adult has been the victim of abuse may report that abuse to a long-term care ombudsman program or local law enforcement agency, or both the long-term care ombudsman program and local law enforcement agency when the abuse is alleged to have occurred in a long-term care facility.

(b) Any person who is not a mandated reporter under Section 15630, who knows, or reasonably suspects, that an elder or a dependent adult has been the victim of abuse in any place other than a long-term care facility may report the abuse to the county adult protective services agency or local law enforcement agency. *(Added by Stats.1994, c. 594 (S.B.1681), § 9. Amended by Stats.2012, c. 659 (A.B.40), § 3.)*

Cross References

Adult protective services agency defined for purposes of this Chapter, see Welfare and Institutions Code § 15610.13.
Adult protective services defined for purposes of this Chapter, see Welfare and Institutions Code § 15610.10.
Dependent adult defined for purposes of this Chapter, see Welfare and Institutions Code § 15610.23.
Elder defined for purposes of this Chapter, see Welfare and Institutions Code § 15610.27.
False report of criminal offense, exemption from criminal liability for persons who are required by statute to report abuse, see Penal Code § 148.5.
Local law enforcement agency defined for purposes of this Chapter, see Welfare and Institutions Code § 15610.45.
Long-term care facility defined for purposes of this Chapter, see Welfare and Institutions Code § 15610.47.
Long-term care ombudsman defined for purposes of this Chapter, see Welfare and Institutions Code § 15610.50.
Services defined for purposes of this Division, see Welfare and Institutions Code § 10053.

§ 15632. Physician-patient privilege; psychotherapist-patient privilege

(a) In any court proceeding or administrative hearing, neither the physician-patient privilege nor the psychotherapist-patient privilege applies to the specific information reported pursuant to this chapter.

(b) Nothing in this chapter shall be interpreted as requiring an attorney to violate his or her oath and duties pursuant to Section 6067 or subdivision (e) of Section 6068 of the Business and Professions Code, and Article 3 (commencing with Section 950) of Chapter 4 of Division 8 of the Evidence Code. *(Added by Stats.1994, c. 594 (S.B.1681), § 11.)*

ARTICLE 8. PROSECUTION OF ELDER AND DEPENDENT ADULT ABUSE CASES

§ 15656. Subjecting elder or dependent adults to great bodily harm or death; unjustifiable physical pain or mental suffering; theft or embezzlement; penalties

(a) Any person who knows or reasonably should know that a person is an elder or dependent adult and who, under circumstances or conditions likely to produce great bodily harm or death, willfully causes or permits any elder or dependent adult to suffer, or inflicts unjustifiable physical pain or mental suffering upon him or her, or having the care or custody of any elder or dependent adult, willfully causes or permits the person or health of the elder or dependent adult to be injured, or willfully causes or permits the elder or dependent adult to be placed in a situation such that his or her person or health is endangered, is punishable by imprisonment in the county jail not exceeding one year, or in the state prison for two, three, or four years.

(b) Any person who knows or reasonably should know that a person is an elder or dependent adult and who, under circumstances or conditions other than those likely to produce great bodily harm or death, willfully causes or permits any elder or dependent adult to suffer, or inflicts unjustifiable physical pain or mental suffering on him or her, or having the care or custody of any elder or dependent adult, willfully causes or permits the person or health of the elder or dependent adult to be injured or willfully causes or permits the elder or dependent adult to be placed in a situation such that his or her person or health may be endangered, is guilty of a misdemeanor.

(c) Any caretaker of an elder or a dependent adult who violates any provision of law prescribing theft or embezzlement, with respect to the property of that elder or dependent adult, is punishable by imprisonment in the county jail not exceeding one year, or in the state prison for two, three, or four years when the money, labor, or real or personal property taken is of a value exceeding nine hundred fifty dollars ($950), and by a fine not exceeding one thousand dollars ($1,000), or by imprisonment in the county jail not exceeding one year, or by both that imprisonment and fine, when the money, labor, or real or personal property taken is of a value not exceeding nine hundred fifty dollars ($950).

(d) As used in this section, "caretaker" means any person who has the care, custody, or control of or who stands in a position of trust with, an elder or a dependent adult.

(e) Conduct covered in subdivision (b) of Section 15610.57 shall not be subject to this section. *(Added by Stats.1994, c. 594 (S.B.1681), § 23. Amended by Stats.2004, c. 886 (A.B.2611), § 2; Stats.2009–2010, 3rd Ex.Sess., c. 28 (S.B.18), § 57, eff. Jan. 25, 2010.)*

Cross References

Dependent adult defined for purposes of this Chapter, see Welfare and Institutions Code § 15610.23.
Elder defined for purposes of this Chapter, see Welfare and Institutions Code § 15610.27.
Fundamental rights of residents of residential care facilities, see Health and Safety Code § 1569.261 et seq.
Mental suffering defined for purposes of this Chapter, see Welfare and Institutions Code § 15610.53.
Misdemeanors, definition and penalties, see Penal Code §§ 17, 19, 19.2.
Revocable transfer on death deed, additional penalties and remedies, application of this section, see Probate Code § 5698.
Supporter in CARE process, presence of supporter at meetings, proceedings, hearing, or specific communications, intended behavior and authority, see Welfare and Institutions Code § 5981.

Research References

2 Witkin, California Criminal Law 4th Crimes Against Governmental Authority § 25 (2021), Prohibited Compromises.
2 Witkin, California Criminal Law 4th Sex Offenses and Crimes Against Decency § 179 (2021), Nature of Offense.
2 Witkin, California Criminal Law 4th Sex Offenses and Crimes Against Decency § 180 (2021), Infliction of Unjustifiable Pain or Suffering.
2 Witkin, California Criminal Law 4th Sex Offenses and Crimes Against Decency § 181 (2021), Injury to Health by Caretaker.
2 Witkin, California Criminal Law 4th Sex Offenses and Crimes Against Decency § 182 (2021), Theft, Embezzlement, Forgery, Fraud, or Identity Theft.

Part 5

COUNTY AID AND RELIEF TO INDIGENTS

CHAPTER 5. TERMINATION AND RECOVERY OF ASSISTANCE

§ 17410. Fraudulent claims; intent; punishment

Any person who with the intent to defraud, buys or receives a voucher, invoice, or similar document issued for services or merchandise under this part without furnishing such services or merchandise is punishable either by imprisonment in the county jail for a period of not more than one year, by a fine of not exceeding one thousand dollars ($1,000), or by both that imprisonment and fine, or by imprisonment pursuant to subdivision (h) of Section 1170 of the Penal Code for a period of not more than one year, by a fine of not exceeding ten thousand dollars ($10,000), or by both that imprisonment and fine. *(Added by Stats.1972, c. 370, p. 691, § 1. Amended by Stats.2011, c. 15 (A.B.109), § 633, eff. April 4, 2011, operative Oct. 1, 2011.)*

Cross References

Services defined for purposes of this Division, see Welfare and Institutions Code § 10053.

Research References

2 Witkin, California Criminal Law 4th Crimes Against Governmental Authority § 159 (2021), False General Assistance Claim.

CALIFORNIA RULES OF COURT

Title 2

TRIAL COURT RULES

Division 4

COURT RECORDS

Chapter 1

GENERAL PROVISIONS

Rule 2.400. Court records

(a) Removal of records

Only the clerk may remove and replace records in the court's files. Unless otherwise provided by these rules or ordered by the court, court records may only be inspected by the public in the office of the clerk and released to authorized court personnel or an attorney of record for use in a court facility. No original court records may be used in any location other than a court facility, unless so ordered by the presiding judge or his or her designee.

(b) Original documents filed with the clerk; duplicate documents for temporary judge or referee

(1) All original documents in a case pending before a temporary judge or referee must be filed with the clerk in the same manner as would be required if the case were being heard by a judge, including filing within any time limits specified by law and paying any required fees. The filing party must provide a filed-stamped copy to the temporary judge or referee of each document relevant to the issues before the temporary judge or referee.

(2) If a document must be filed with the court before it is considered by a judge, the temporary judge or referee must not accept or consider any copy of that document unless the document has the clerk's file stamp or is accompanied by a declaration stating that the original document has been submitted to the court for filing.

(3) If a document would ordinarily be filed with the court after it is submitted to a judge or if a party submits an ex parte application, the party that submits the document or application to a temporary judge or referee must file the original with the court no later than the next court day after the document or application was submitted to the temporary judge or referee and must promptly provide a filed-stamped copy of the document or application to the temporary judge or referee.

(4) A party that has submitted a document to a temporary judge or referee must immediately notify the temporary judge or referee if the document is not accepted for filing by the court or if the filing is subsequently canceled.

(c) Return of exhibits

(1) The clerk must not release any exhibit except on order of the court. The clerk must require a signed receipt for a released exhibit.

(2) If proceedings are conducted by a temporary judge or a referee outside of court facilities, the temporary judge or referee must keep all exhibits and deliver them, properly marked, to the clerk at the conclusion of the proceedings, unless the parties file, and the court approves, a written stipulation providing for a different disposition of the exhibits. On request of the temporary judge or referee, the clerk must deliver exhibits filed or lodged with the court to the possession of the temporary judge or referee, who must not release them to any person other than the clerk, unless the court orders otherwise.

(d) Access to documents and exhibits in matters before temporary judges and referees

(1) Documents and exhibits in the possession of a temporary judge or referee that would be open to the public if filed or lodged with the court must be made available during business hours for inspection by any person within a reasonable time after request and under reasonable conditions.

(2) Temporary judges and referees must file a statement in each case in which they are appointed that provides the name, telephone number, and mailing address of a person who may be contacted to obtain access to any documents or exhibits submitted to the temporary judge or referee that would be open to the public if filed or lodged with the court. The statement must be filed at the same time as the temporary judge's or referee's certification under rule 2.831(b), 3.904(a), or 3.924(a). If there is any change in this contact information, the temporary judge or referee must promptly file a revised statement with the court.

(e) Definition

For purposes of this rule, "court facility" consists of those areas within a building required or used for court functions. *(Formerly Rule 243, adopted, eff. Jan. 1, 1949. As amended, eff. July 1, 1993. Renumbered Rule 2.400 and amended, eff. Jan. 1, 2007. As amended, eff. Jan. 1, 2008; Jan. 1, 2009; Jan. 1, 2010.)*

Advisory Committee Comment

Subdivision (b)(1). Rules 2.810 and 2.830 provide definitions of temporary judges appointed by the court and temporary judges requested by the parties, respectively.

Subdivision (d)(1). Public access to documents and exhibits in the possession of a temporary judge or referee should be the same as if the case were being heard by a judge. Documents and exhibits are not normally available to the public during a hearing or when needed by the judge for hearing or decision preparation. A temporary judge or referee may direct that access to documents and exhibits be available by scheduled appointment.

Chapter 3

SEALED RECORDS

Rule 2.550. Sealed records

(a) Application

(1) Rules 2.550–2.551 apply to records sealed or proposed to be sealed by court order.

(2) These rules do not apply to records that are required to be kept confidential by law.

(3) These rules do not apply to discovery motions and records filed or lodged in connection with discovery motions or proceedings. However, the rules do apply to discovery materials that are used at trial or submitted as a basis for adjudication of matters other than discovery motions or proceedings.

(b) Definitions

As used in this chapter:

(1) "Record." Unless the context indicates otherwise, "record" means all or a portion of any document, paper, exhibit, transcript, or other thing filed or lodged with the court, by electronic means or otherwise.

(2) "Sealed." A "sealed" record is a record that by court order is not open to inspection by the public.

(3) "Lodged." A "lodged" record is a record that is temporarily placed or deposited with the court, but not filed.

(c) Court records presumed to be open

Unless confidentiality is required by law, court records are presumed to be open.

(d) Express factual findings required to seal records

The court may order that a record be filed under seal only if it expressly finds facts that establish:

(1) There exists an overriding interest that overcomes the right of public access to the record;

(2) The overriding interest supports sealing the record;

(3) A substantial probability exists that the overriding interest will be prejudiced if the record is not sealed;

(4) The proposed sealing is narrowly tailored; and

(5) No less restrictive means exist to achieve the overriding interest.

(e) Content and scope of the order

(1) An order sealing the record must:

(A) Specifically state the facts that support the findings; and

(B) Direct the sealing of only those documents and pages, or, if reasonably practicable, portions of those documents and pages, that contain the material that needs to be placed under seal. All other portions of each document or page must be included in the public file.

(2) Consistent with Code of Civil Procedure sections 639 and 645.1, if the records that a party is requesting be placed under seal are voluminous, the court may appoint a referee and fix and allocate the referee's fees among the parties. *(Formerly Rule 243.1, adopted, eff. Jan. 1, 2001. As amended, eff. Jan. 1, 2004. Renumbered Rule 2.550 and amended, eff. Jan. 1, 2007. As amended, eff. Jan. 1, 2016.)*

Advisory Committee Comment

This rule and rule 2.551 provide a standard and procedures for courts to use when a request is made to seal a record. The standard is based on *NBC Subsidiary (KNBC–TV), Inc. v. Superior Court* (1999) 20 Cal.4th 1178. These rules apply to civil and criminal cases. They recognize the First Amendment right of access to documents used at trial or as a basis of adjudication. The rules do not apply to records that courts must keep confidential by law. Examples of confidential records to which public access is restricted by law are records of the family conciliation court (Family Code, § 1818(b)), in forma pauperis applications (Cal. Rules of Court, rules 3.54 and 8.26), and search warrant affidavits sealed under *People v. Hobbs* (1994) 7 Cal.4th 948. The sealed records rules also do not apply to discovery proceedings, motions, and materials that are not used at trial or submitted to the court as a basis for adjudication. (See *NBC Subsidiary, supra,* 20 Cal.4th at pp. 1208–1209, fn. 25.)

Rule 2.550(d)–(e) is derived from *NBC Subsidiary*. That decision contains the requirements that the court, before closing a hearing or sealing a transcript, must find an "overriding interest" that supports the closure or sealing, and must make certain express findings. (*Id.* at pp. 1217–1218.) The decision notes that the First Amendment right of access applies to records filed in both civil and criminal cases as a basis for adjudication. (*Id.* at pp. 1208–1209, fn. 25.) Thus, the *NBC Subsidiary* test applies to the sealing of records.

NBC Subsidiary provides examples of various interests that courts have acknowledged may constitute "overriding interests." (See *id.* at p. 1222, fn. 46.) Courts have found that, under appropriate circumstances, various statutory privileges, trade secrets, and privacy interests, when properly asserted and not waived, may constitute "overriding interests." The rules do not attempt to define what may constitute an "overriding interest," but leave this to case law.

Research References

West's California Judicial Council Forms SH–020, Motion to Place Documents Under Seal Under Code of Civil Procedure Section 367.3.
West's California Judicial Council Forms SH–020–INFO, Instructions for Motion to Place Documents Under Seal Under Code of Civil Procedure Section 367.3.
West's California Judicial Council Forms SH–022, Declaration in Support of Motion to Place Documents Under Seal Under Code of Civil Procedure Section 367.3.
West's California Judicial Council Forms SH–025, Order on Motion to Place Documents Under Seal Under Code of Civil Procedure Section 367.3.
6 Witkin, California Criminal Law 4th Criminal Appeal § 53D (2021), (New) Procedure for Sealing Record Not Filed in Trial Court.
6 Witkin, California Criminal Law 4th Criminal Appeal § 53E (2021), (New) Procedure for Unsealing Record.

Rule 2.551. Procedures for filing records under seal

(a) Court approval required

A record must not be filed under seal without a court order. The court must not permit a record to be filed under seal based solely on the agreement or stipulation of the parties.

(b) Motion or application to seal a record

(1) *Motion or application required*

A party requesting that a record be filed under seal must file a motion or an application for an order sealing the record. The motion or application must be accompanied by a memorandum and a declaration containing facts sufficient to justify the sealing.

(2) *Service of motion or application*

A copy of the motion or application must be served on all parties that have appeared in the case. Unless the court orders otherwise, any party that already has access to the records to be placed under seal must be served with a complete, unredacted version of all papers as well as a redacted version. Other parties must be served with only the public redacted version. If a party's attorney but not the party has access to the record, only the party's attorney may be served with the complete, unredacted version.

(3) *Procedure for party not intending to file motion or application*

(A) A party that files or intends to file with the court, for the purposes of adjudication or to use at trial, records produced in discovery that are subject to a confidentiality agreement or protective order, and does not intend to request to have the records sealed, must:

(i) Lodge the unredacted records subject to the confidentiality agreement or protective order and any pleadings, memorandums, declarations, and other documents that disclose the contents of the records, in the manner stated in (d);

(ii) File copies of the documents in (i) that are redacted so that they do not disclose the contents of the records that are subject to the confidentiality agreement or protective order; and

(iii) Give written notice to the party that produced the records that the records and the other documents lodged under

(i) will be placed in the public court file unless that party files a timely motion or application to seal the records under this rule.

(B) If the party that produced the documents and was served with the notice under (A)(iii) fails to file a motion or an application to seal the records within 10 days or to obtain a court order extending the time to file such a motion or an application, the clerk must promptly transfer all the documents in (A)(i) from the envelope, container, or secure electronic file to the public file. If the party files a motion or an application to seal within 10 days or such later time as the court has ordered, these documents are to remain conditionally under seal until the court rules on the motion or application and thereafter are to be filed as ordered by the court.

(4) *Lodging of record pending determination of motion or application*

The party requesting that a record be filed under seal must lodge it with the court under (d) when the motion or application is made, unless good cause exists for not lodging it or the record has previously been lodged under (3)(A)(i). Pending the determination of the motion or application, the lodged record will be conditionally under seal.

(5) *Redacted and unredacted versions*

If necessary to prevent disclosure, any motion or application, any opposition, and any supporting documents must be filed in a public redacted version and lodged in a complete, unredacted version conditionally under seal. The cover of the redacted version must identify it as "Public—Redacts materials from conditionally sealed record." The cover of the unredacted version must identify it as "May Not Be Examined Without Court Order—Contains material from conditionally sealed record."

(6) *Return of lodged record*

If the court denies the motion or application to seal, the moving party may notify the court that the lodged record is to be filed unsealed. This notification must be received within 10 days of the order denying the motion or application to seal, unless otherwise ordered by the court. On receipt of this notification, the clerk must unseal and file the record. If the moving party does not notify the court within 10 days of the order, the clerk must (1) return the lodged record to the moving party if it is in paper form or (2) permanently delete the lodged record if it is in electronic form.

(c) References to nonpublic material in public records

A record filed publicly in the court must not disclose material contained in a record that is sealed, conditionally under seal, or subject to a pending motion or an application to seal.

(d) Procedure for lodging of records

(1) A record that may be filed under seal must be transmitted to the court in a secure manner that preserves the confidentiality of the records to be lodged. If the record is transmitted in paper form, it must be put in an envelope or other appropriate container, sealed in the envelope or container, and lodged with the court.

(2) The materials to be lodged under seal must be clearly identified as "CONDITIONALLY UNDER SEAL." If the materials are transmitted in paper form, the envelope or container lodged with the court must be labeled "CONDITIONALLY UNDER SEAL."

(3) The party submitting the lodged record must affix to the electronic transmission, the envelope, or the container a cover sheet that:

(A) Contains all the information required on a caption page under rule 2.111; and

(B) States that the enclosed record is subject to a motion or an application to file the record under seal.

(4) On receipt of a record lodged under this rule, the clerk must endorse the affixed cover sheet with the date of its receipt and must retain but not file the record unless the court orders it filed.

(e) Order

(1) If the court grants an order sealing a record and if the sealed record is in paper format, the clerk must substitute on the envelope or container for the label required by (d)(2) a label prominently stating "SEALED BY ORDER OF THE COURT ON *(DATE)*," and must replace the cover sheet required by (d)(3) with a filed-endorsed copy of the court's order. If the sealed record is in electronic form, the clerk must file the court's order, maintain the record ordered sealed in a secure manner, and clearly identify the record as sealed by court order on a specified date.

(2) The order must state whether—in addition to the sealed records—the order itself, the register of actions, any other court records, or any other records relating to the case are to be sealed.

(3) The order must state whether any person other than the court is authorized to inspect the sealed record.

(4) Unless the sealing order provides otherwise, it prohibits the parties from disclosing the contents of any materials that have been sealed in anything that is subsequently publicly filed.

(f) Custody of sealed records

Sealed records must be securely filed and kept separate from the public file in the case. If the sealed records are in electronic form, appropriate access controls must be established to ensure that only authorized persons may access the sealed records.

(g) Custody of voluminous records

If the records to be placed under seal are voluminous and are in the possession of a public agency, the court may by written order direct the agency instead of the clerk to maintain custody of the original records in a secure fashion. If the records are requested by a reviewing court, the trial court must order the public agency to deliver the records to the clerk for transmission to the reviewing court under these rules.

(h) Motion, application, or petition to unseal records

(1) A sealed record must not be unsealed except on order of the court.

(2) A party or member of the public may move, apply, or petition, or the court on its own motion may move, to unseal a record. Notice of any motion, application, or petition to unseal must be filed and served on all parties in the case. The motion, application, or petition and any opposition, reply, and supporting documents must be filed in a public redacted version and a sealed complete version if necessary to comply with (c).

(3) If the court proposes to order a record unsealed on its own motion, the court must give notice to the parties stating the reason for unsealing the record. Unless otherwise ordered by the court, any party may serve and file an opposition within 10 days after the notice is provided and any other party may file a response within 5 days after the filing of an opposition.

(4) In determining whether to unseal a record, the court must consider the matters addressed in rule 2.550(c)–(e).

(5) The order unsealing a record must state whether the record is unsealed entirely or in part. If the court's order unseals only part of the record or unseals the record only as to certain persons, the order must specify the particular records that are unsealed, the particular persons who may have access to the record, or both. If, in addition to the records in the envelope, container, or secure electronic file, the court has previously ordered the sealing order, the register of actions, or any other court records relating to the case to be sealed, the unsealing order must state whether these additional records are unsealed. *(Formerly Rule 243.2, adopted, eff. Jan. 1, 2001. As amended, eff. Jan. 1, 2004. Renumbered Rule 2.551 and amended, eff. Jan. 1, 2007. As amended, eff. Jan. 1, 2016; Jan. 1, 2017.)*

Research References

West's California Judicial Council Forms SH–020, Motion to Place Documents Under Seal Under Code of Civil Procedure Section 367.3.
West's California Judicial Council Forms SH–020–INFO, Instructions for Motion to Place Documents Under Seal Under Code of Civil Procedure Section 367.3.
West's California Judicial Council Forms SH–022, Declaration in Support of Motion to Place Documents Under Seal Under Code of Civil Procedure Section 367.3.
West's California Judicial Council Forms SH–025, Order on Motion to Place Documents Under Seal Under Code of Civil Procedure Section 367.3.
6 Witkin, California Criminal Law 4th Criminal Appeal § 53B (2021), (New) Definitions.
6 Witkin, California Criminal Law 4th Criminal Appeal § 131 (2021), Confidential Material.

Chapter 5

NAME CHANGE PROCEEDINGS UNDER ADDRESS CONFIDENTIALITY PROGRAM

Rule 2.575. Confidential information in name change proceedings under address confidentiality program

(a) Definitions

As used in this chapter, unless the context or subject matter otherwise requires:

(1) "Confidential name change petitioner" means a petitioner who is a participant in the address confidentiality program created by the Secretary of State under chapter 3.1 (commencing with section 6205) of division 7 of title 1 of the Government Code.

(2) "Record" means all or a portion of any document, paper, exhibit, transcript, or other thing that is filed or lodged with the court.

(3) "Lodged" means temporarily placed or deposited with the court but not filed.

(b) Application of chapter

The rules in this chapter apply to records filed in a change of name proceeding under Code of Civil Procedure section 1277(b) by a confidential name change petitioner who alleges any of the following reasons or circumstances as a reason for the name change:

(1) The petitioner is seeking to avoid domestic violence, as defined in Family Code section 6211.

(2) The petitioner is seeking to avoid stalking, as defined in Penal Code section 646.9.

(3) The petitioner is, or is filing on behalf of, a victim of sexual assault, as defined in Evidence Code section 1036.2.

(c) Confidentiality of current name of the petitioner

The current legal name of a confidential name change petitioner must be kept confidential by the court as required by Code of Civil Procedure section 1277(b)(3) and not be published or posted in the court's calendars, indexes, or register of actions, or by any means or in any public forum. Only the information concerning filed records contained on the confidential cover sheet prescribed under (d) may be entered into the register of actions or any other forum that is accessible to the public.

(d) Special cover sheet omitting names of the petitioner

To maintain the confidentiality provided under Code of Civil Procedure section 1277(b) for the petitioner's current name, the petitioner must attach a completed *Confidential Cover Sheet—Name Change Proceeding Under Address Confidentiality Program (Safe at Home)* (form NC–400) to the front of the petition for name change and every other document filed in the proceedings. The name of the petitioner must not appear on that cover sheet.

(e) Confidentiality of proposed name of the petitioner

To maintain the confidentiality provided under Code of Civil Procedure section 1277(b) for the petitioner's proposed name, the petitioner must not include the proposed name on the petition for name change or any other record in the proceedings. In any form that requests the petitioner's proposed name, the petitioner and the court must indicate that the proposed name is confidential and on file with the Secretary of State under the provisions of the Safe at Home address confidentiality program. *(Adopted, eff. Jan. 1, 2010.)*

Research References

West's California Judicial Council Forms NC–400, Confidential Cover Sheet—Name Change Proceeding Under Address Confidentiality Program (Safe at Home).
West's California Judicial Council Forms NC–400–INFO, Information Sheet for Name Change Proceedings Under Address Confidentiality Program (Safe at Home).
West's California Judicial Council Forms NC–425, Order on Application to File Documents Under Seal in Name Change Proceeding Under Address Confidentiality Program (Safe at Home).

Rule 2.576. Access to name of the petitioner

(a) Termination of confidentiality

The current name of a confidential name change petitioner must remain confidential until a determination is made that:

(1) Petitioner's participation in the address confidentiality program has ended under Government Code section 6206.7; or

(2) The court finds by clear and convincing evidence that the allegations of domestic violence or stalking in the petition are false.

(b) Procedure to obtain access

A determination under (a) must be made by noticed motion, with service by mail on the confidential name change petitioner in care of the Secretary of State's address confidentiality program as stated in Government Code section 6206(a)(5)(A). *(Adopted, eff. Jan. 1, 2010.)*

Research References

West's California Judicial Council Forms NC–425, Order on Application to File Documents Under Seal in Name Change Proceeding Under Address Confidentiality Program (Safe at Home).

Rule 2.577. Procedures for filing confidential name change records under seal

(a) Court approval required

Records in a name change proceeding may not be filed under seal without a court order. A request by a confidential name change petitioner to file records under seal may be made under the procedures in this chapter. A request by any other petitioner to file records under seal must be made under rules 2.550–2.573.

(b) Application to file records in confidential name change proceedings under seal

An application by a confidential name change petitioner to file records under seal must be filed at the time the petition for name change is submitted to thc court. The application must be made on the *Application to File Documents Under Seal in Name Change Proceeding Under Address Confidentiality Program (Safe at Home)* (form NC–410) and be accompanied by a *Declaration in Support of Application to File Documents Under Seal in Name Change Proceeding*

Under Address Confidentiality Program (Safe at Home) (form NC–420), containing facts sufficient to justify the sealing.

(c) Confidentiality

The application to file under seal must be kept confidential by the court until the court rules on it.

(d) Procedure for lodging of petition for name change

(1) The records that may be filed under seal must be lodged with the court. If they are transmitted on paper, they must be placed in a sealed envelope. If they are transmitted electronically, they must be transmitted to the court in a secure manner that preserves the confidentiality of the documents to be lodged.

(2) If the petitioner is transmitting the petition on paper, the petitioner must complete and affix to the envelope a completed *Confidential Cover Sheet—Name Change Proceeding Under Address Confidentiality Program* (*Safe at Home*) (form NC–400) and in the space under the title and case number mark it "CONDITIONALLY UNDER SEAL." If the petitioner is transmitting the petition electronically, the first page of the electronic transmission must be a completed *Confidential Cover Sheet—Name Change Proceeding Under Address Confidentiality Program* (*Safe at Home*) (form NC–400) with the space under the title and case number marked "CONDITIONALLY UNDER SEAL."

(3) On receipt of a petition lodged under this rule, the clerk must endorse the cover sheet with the date of its receipt and must retain but not file the record unless the court orders it filed.

(4) If the court denies the application to seal, the moving party may notify the court that the lodged record is to be filed unsealed. This notification must be received within 10 days of the order denying the motion or application to seal, unless otherwise ordered by the court. On receipt of this notification, the clerk must unseal and file the record. If the moving party does not notify the court within 10 days of the order, the clerk must (1) return the lodged record to the moving party if it is in paper form or (2) permanently delete the lodged record if it is in electronic form.

(e) Consideration of application to file under seal

The court may order that the record be filed under seal if it finds that all of the following factors apply:

(1) There exists an overriding interest that overcomes the right of public access to the record;

(2) The overriding interest supports sealing the record;

(3) A substantial probability exists that the overriding interest will be prejudiced if the record is not sealed;

(4) The proposed order to seal the record is narrowly tailored; and

(5) No less restrictive means exist to achieve the overriding interest.

(f) Order

(1) The order may be issued on *Order on Application to File Documents Under Seal in Name Change Proceeding Under Address Confidentiality Program (Safe at Home)* (form NC–425).

(2) Any order granting the application to seal must state whether the declaration in support of the application, the order itself, and any other record in the proceeding are to be sealed as well as the petition for name change.

(3) For petitions transmitted in paper form, if the court grants an order sealing a record, the clerk must strike out the notation required by (d)(2) on the *Confidential Cover Sheet* that the matter is filed "CONDITIONALLY UNDER SEAL," add a notation to that sheet prominently stating "SEALED BY ORDER OF THE COURT ON *(DATE)*," and file the documents under seal. For petitions transmitted electronically, the clerk must file the court's order, maintain the record ordered sealed in a secure manner, and clearly identify the record as sealed by court order on a specified date.

(4) If the court grants the application to file under seal and issues an order under (e), the petition and any associated records may be filed under seal and ruled on by the court immediately.

(5) The order must identify any person other than the court who is authorized to inspect the sealed records.

(g) Custody of sealed records

Sealed records must be securely filed and kept separate from the public file in the case. If the sealed records are in electronic form, appropriate access controls must be established to ensure that only authorized persons may access the sealed records.

(h) Motion, application, or petition to unseal record

(1) A sealed record may not be unsealed except by order of the court.

(2) Any member of the public seeking to unseal a record or a court proposing to do so on its own motion must follow the procedures described in rule 2.551(h). *(Adopted, eff. Jan. 1, 2010. As amended, eff. Jan. 1, 2016; Jan. 1, 2017.)*

Research References

West's California Judicial Council Forms NC–400–INFO, Information Sheet for Name Change Proceedings Under Address Confidentiality Program (Safe at Home).

West's California Judicial Council Forms NC–410, Application to File Documents Under Seal in Name Change Proceeding Under Address Confidentiality Program (Safe at Home).

West's California Judicial Council Forms NC–420, Declaration in Support of Publication to File Documents Under Seal in Name Change Proceeding Under Address Confidentiality Program (Safe at Home).

West's California Judicial Council Forms NC–425, Order on Application to File Documents Under Seal in Name Change Proceeding Under Address Confidentiality Program (Safe at Home).

Chapter 6

OTHER SEALED OR CLOSED RECORDS

Rule

Rule 2.580. Request for delayed public disclosure

In an action in which the prejudgment attachment remedy under Code of Civil Procedure section 483.010 et seq. is sought, if the plaintiff requests at the time a complaint is filed that the records in the action or the fact of the filing of the action be made temporarily unavailable to the public under Code of Civil Procedure section 482.050, the plaintiff must file a declaration stating one of the following:

(1) "This action is on a claim for money based on contract against a defendant who is not a natural person. The claim is not secured within the meaning of Code of Civil Procedure section 483.010(b)."—or—

(2) "This action is on a claim for money based on contract against a defendant who is a natural person. The claim arises out of the defendant's conduct of a trade, business, or profession, and the money, property, or services were not used by the defendant primarily for personal, family, or household purposes. The claim is not secured within the meaning of Code of Civil Procedure section 483.010(b)." *(Formerly Rule 243.3, adopted, eff. Jan. 1, 2001. Renumbered Rule 2.580, eff. Jan. 1, 2007.)*

Rule 2.585. Confidential in-camera proceedings

(a) Minutes of proceedings

If a confidential in-camera proceeding is held in which a party is excluded from being represented, the clerk must include in the minutes the nature of the hearing and only such references to writings or witnesses as will not disclose privileged information.

(b) Disposition of examined records

Records examined by the court in confidence under (a), or copies of them, must be filed with the clerk under seal and must not be disclosed without court order. *(Formerly Rule 243.4, adopted, eff. Jan. 1, 2001. Renumbered Rule 2.585, eff. Jan. 1, 2007.)*

Division 8

TRIALS

Chapter 2

CONDUCT OF TRIAL

Rule 2.1030. Communications from or with jury

(a) Preservation of written jury communications

The trial judge must preserve and deliver to the clerk for inclusion in the record all written communications, formal or informal, received from the jury or from individual jurors or sent by the judge to the jury or individual jurors, from the time the jury is sworn until it is discharged.

(b) Recording of oral jury communications

The trial judge must ensure that the reporter, or any electronic recording system used instead of a reporter, records all oral communications, formal or informal, received from the jury or from individual jurors or communicated by the judge to the jury or individual jurors, from the time the jury is sworn until it is discharged. *(Formerly Rule 231, adopted eff. Jan. 1, 1990. Renumbered Rule 2.1030 and amended, eff. Jan. 1, 2007.)*

Rule 2.1031. Juror note–taking

Jurors must be permitted to take written notes in all civil and criminal trials. At the beginning of a trial, a trial judge must inform jurors that they may take written notes during the trial. The court must provide materials suitable for this purpose. *(Adopted, eff. Jan. 1, 2007.)*

Rule 2.1032. Juror notebooks in complex civil cases

A trial judge should encourage counsel in complex civil cases to include key documents, exhibits, and other appropriate materials in notebooks for use by jurors during trial to assist them in performing their duties. *(Adopted, eff. Jan. 1, 2007.)*

Rule 2.1033. Juror questions

A trial judge should allow jurors to submit written questions directed to witnesses. An opportunity must be given to counsel to object to such questions out of the presence of the jury. *(Adopted, eff. Jan. 1, 2007.)*

Rule 2.1035. Preinstruction

Immediately after the jury is sworn, the trial judge may, in his or her discretion, preinstruct the jury concerning the elements of the charges or claims, its duties, its conduct, the order of proceedings, the procedure for submitting written questions for witnesses as set forth in rule 2.1033 if questions are allowed, and the legal principles that will govern the proceeding. *(Adopted, eff. Jan. 1, 2007.)*

Research References

5 Witkin, California Criminal Law 4th Criminal Trial § 673 (2021), Nature of Instructions.

Rule 2.1036. Assisting the jury at impasse

(a) Determination

After a jury reports that it has reached an impasse in its deliberations, the trial judge may, in the presence of counsel, advise the jury of its duty to decide the case based on the evidence while keeping an open mind and talking about the evidence with each other. The judge should ask the jury if it has specific concerns which, if resolved, might assist the jury in reaching a verdict.

(b) Possible further action

If the trial judge determines that further action might assist the jury in reaching a verdict, the judge may:

(1) Give additional instructions;

(2) Clarify previous instructions;

(3) Permit attorneys to make additional closing arguments; or

(4) Employ any combination of these measures. *(Adopted, eff. Jan. 1, 2007.)*

Research References

California Jury Instructions-Civil, 8th Edition 15.60, Deadlocked Jury Admonition.

Chapter 4

JURY INSTRUCTIONS

Rule 2.1055. Proposed jury instructions

(a) Application

(1) This rule applies to proposed jury instructions that a party submits to the court, including:

(A) "Approved jury instructions," meaning jury instructions approved by the Judicial Council of California; and

(B) "Special jury instructions," meaning instructions from other sources, those specially prepared by the party, or approved instructions that have been substantially modified by the party.

(2) This rule does not apply to the form or format of the instructions presented to the jury, which is a matter left to the discretion of the court.

(b) Form and format of proposed instructions

(1) All proposed instructions must be submitted to the court in the form and format prescribed for papers in the rules in division 2 of this title.

(2) Each set of proposed jury instructions must have a cover page, containing the caption of the case and stating the name of the party

proposing the instructions, and an index listing all the proposed instructions.

(3) In the index, approved jury instructions must be identified by their reference numbers and special jury instructions must be numbered consecutively. The index must contain a checklist that the court may use to indicate whether the instruction was:

(A) Given as proposed;

(B) Given as modified;

(C) Refused; or

(D) Withdrawn.

(4) Each set of proposed jury instructions filed on paper must be bound loosely.

(c) Format of each proposed instruction

Each proposed instruction must:

(1) Be on a separate page or pages;

(2) Include the instruction number and title of the instruction at the top of the first page of the instruction; and

(3) Be prepared without any blank lines or unused bracketed portions, so that it can be read directly to the jury.

(d) Citation of authorities

For each special instruction, a citation of authorities that support the instruction must be included at the bottom of the page. No citation is required for approved instructions.

(e) Form and format are exclusive

No local court form or rule for the filing or submission of proposed jury instructions may require that the instructions be submitted in any manner other than as prescribed by this rule. *(Formerly Rule 229, adopted, eff. Jan. 1, 1949. As amended, eff. April 1, 1962; July 1, 1988; Jan. 1, 2003; Jan. 1, 2004; Aug. 26, 2005. Renumbered Rule 2.1055 and amended, eff. Jan. 1, 2007. As amended, eff. Jan. 1, 2016.)*

Advisory Committee Comment

This rule does not preclude a judge from requiring the parties in an individual case to transmit the jury instructions to the court electronically.

Research References

6 Witkin, California Criminal Law 4th Criminal Appeal § 129 (2021), Normal Record.

Title 3

CIVIL RULES

Division 15

TRIAL

Chapter 7

JURY INSTRUCTIONS

Rule 3.1560. Application

The rules on jury instructions in chapter 4 of division 8 of title 2 of these rules apply to civil cases. *(Adopted, eff. Jan. 1, 2007.)*

Chapter 8

SPECIAL VERDICTS

Rule 3.1580. Request for special findings by jury

Whenever a party desires special findings by a jury, the party must, before argument, unless otherwise ordered, present to the judge in writing the issues or questions of fact on which the findings are requested, in proper form for submission to the jury, and serve copies on all other parties. *(Formerly Rule 230, adopted, eff. Jan. 1, 1949. Renumbered Rule 3.1580 and amended, eff. Jan. 1, 2007.)*

Chapter 9

STATEMENT OF DECISION

Rule 3.1590. Announcement of tentative decision, statement of decision, and judgment

(a) Announcement and service of tentative decision

On the trial of a question of fact by the court, the court must announce its tentative decision by an oral statement, entered in the minutes, or by a written statement filed with the clerk. Unless the announcement is made in open court in the presence of all parties that appeared at the trial, the clerk must immediately serve on all parties that appeared at the trial a copy of the minute entry or written tentative decision.

(b) Tentative decision not binding

The tentative decision does not constitute a judgment and is not binding on the court. If the court subsequently modifies or changes its announced tentative decision, the clerk must serve a copy of the modification or change on all parties that appeared at the trial.

(c) Provisions in tentative decision

The court in its tentative decision may:

(1) State that it is the court's proposed statement of decision, subject to a party's objection under (g);

(2) Indicate that the court will prepare a statement of decision;

(3) Order a party to prepare a statement of decision; or

(4) Direct that the tentative decision will become the statement of decision unless, within 10 days after announcement or service of the tentative decision, a party specifies those principal controverted issues as to which the party is requesting a statement of decision or makes proposals not included in the tentative decision.

(d) Request for statement of decision

Within 10 days after announcement or service of the tentative decision, whichever is later, any party that appeared at trial may request a statement of decision to address the principal controverted issues. The principal controverted issues must be specified in the request.

(e) Other party's response to request for statement of decision

If a party requests a statement of decision under (d), any other party may make proposals as to the content of the statement of decision within 10 days after the date of request for a statement of decision.

(f) Preparation and service of proposed statement of decision and judgment

If a party requests a statement of decision under (d), the court must, within 30 days of announcement or service of the tentative decision, prepare and serve a proposed statement of decision and a proposed judgment on all parties that appeared at the trial, unless the court has ordered a party to prepare the statement. A party that has been ordered to prepare the statement must within 30 days after the announcement or service of the tentative decision, serve and submit to the court a proposed statement of decision and a proposed judgment. If the proposed statement of decision and judgment are not served and submitted within that time, any other party that appeared at the trial may within 10 days thereafter: (1) prepare, serve, and submit to the court a proposed statement of decision and judgment or (2) serve on all other parties and file a notice of motion for an order that a statement of decision be deemed waived.

(g) Objections to proposed statement of decision

Any party may, within 15 days after the proposed statement of decision and judgment have been served, serve and file objections to the proposed statement of decision or judgment.

(h) Preparation and filing of written judgment when statement of decision not prepared

If no party requests or is ordered to prepare a statement of decision and a written judgment is required, the court must prepare and serve a proposed judgment on all parties that appeared at the trial within 20 days after the announcement or service of the tentative decision or the court may order a party to prepare, serve, and submit the proposed judgment to the court within 10 days after the date of the order.

(i) Preparation and filing of written judgment when statement of decision deemed waived

If the court orders that the statement of decision is deemed waived and a written judgment is required, the court must, within 10 days of the order deeming the statement of decision waived, either prepare and serve a proposed judgment on all parties that appeared at the trial or order a party to prepare, serve, and submit the proposed judgment to the court within 10 days.

(j) Objection to proposed judgment

Any party may, within 10 days after service of the proposed judgment, serve and file objections thereto.

(k) Hearing

The court may order a hearing on proposals or objections to a proposed statement of decision or the proposed judgment.

(*l*) Signature and filing of judgment

If a written judgment is required, the court must sign and file the judgment within 50 days after the announcement or service of the tentative decision, whichever is later, or, if a hearing was held under (k), within 10 days after the hearing. An electronic signature by the court is as effective as an original signature. The judgment constitutes the decision on which judgment is to be entered under Code of Civil Procedure section 664.

(m) Extension of time; relief from noncompliance

The court may, by written order, extend any of the times prescribed by this rule and at any time before the entry of judgment may, for good cause shown and on such terms as may be just, excuse a noncompliance with the time limits prescribed for doing any act required by this rule.

(n) Trial within one day

When a trial is completed within one day or in less than eight hours over more than one day, a request for statement of decision must be made before the matter is submitted for decision and the statement of decision may be made orally on the record in the presence of the parties. *(Formerly Rule 232, adopted, eff. Jan. 1, 1949. As amended, eff. Jan. 1, 1969; July 1, 1973; Jan. 1, 1982; Jan. 1, 1983. Renumbered Rule 3.1590 and amended, eff. Jan. 1, 2007. As amended, eff. Jan. 1, 2010; Jan. 1, 2016.)*

Rule 3.1591. Statement of decision, judgment, and motion for new trial following bifurcated trial

(a) Separate trial of an issue

When a factual issue raised by the pleadings is tried by the court separately and before the trial of other issues, the judge conducting the separate trial must announce the tentative decision on the issue so tried and must, when requested under Code of Civil Procedure section 632, issue a statement of decision as prescribed in rule 3.1590; but the court must not prepare any proposed judgment until the other issues are tried, except when an interlocutory judgment or a separate judgment may otherwise be properly entered at that time.

(b) Trial of issues by a different judge

If the other issues are tried by a different judge or judges, each judge must perform all acts required by rule 3.1590 as to the issues tried by that judge and the judge trying the final issue must prepare the proposed judgment.

(c) Trial of subsequent issues before issuance of statement of decision

A judge may proceed with the trial of subsequent issues before the issuance of a statement of decision on previously tried issues. Any motion for a new trial following a bifurcated trial must be made after all the issues are tried and, if the issues were tried by different judges, each judge must hear and determine the motion as to the issues tried by that judge. *(Formerly Rule 232.5, adopted, eff. Jan. 1, 1975. As amended, eff. Jan. 1, 1982; Jan. 1, 1985. Renumbered Rule 3.1591 and amended, eff. Jan. 1, 2007.)*

Division 16

POST-TRIAL

Rule 3.1600. Notice of intention to move for new trial

(a) Time for service of memorandum

Within 10 days after filing notice of intention to move for a new trial in a civil case, the moving party must serve and file a memorandum in support of the motion, and within 10 days thereafter any adverse party may serve and file a memorandum in reply.

(b) Effect of failure to serve memorandum

If the moving party fails to serve and file a memorandum within the time prescribed in (a), the court may deny the motion for a new trial without a hearing on the merits. *(Formerly Rule 203, as amended, eff. April 1, 1962; Jan. 1, 1984; Jan. 1, 1987. Renumbered Rule 236.5, and amended, eff. Jan. 1, 2003. Renumbered Rule 3.1600 and amended, eff. Jan. 1, 2007.)*

Rule 3.1602. Hearing of motion to vacate judgment

A motion to vacate judgment under Code of Civil Procedure section 663 must be heard and determined by the judge who presided at the trial; provided, however, that in case of the inability or death of such judge or if at the time noticed for the hearing thereon he is absent from the county where the trial was had, the motion may be heard and determined by another judge of the same court. *(Formerly Rule 236, adopted, eff. Jan. 1, 1949. Renumbered Rule 3.1602 and amended, eff. Jan. 1, 2007.)*

Title 4

CRIMINAL RULES

Division 1

GENERAL PROVISIONS

Rule

Rule 4.1. Title

The rules in this title may be referred to as the Criminal Rules. *(Adopted, eff. Jan. 1, 2007.)*

Research References

4 Witkin, California Criminal Law 4th Introduction to Criminal Procedure § 9 (2021), Rules of Court.

Rule 4.2. Application

The Criminal Rules apply to all criminal cases in the superior courts unless otherwise provided by a statute or rule in the California Rules of Court. *(Adopted, eff. Jan. 1, 2007.)*

Rule 4.3. Reference to Penal Code

All statutory references are to the Penal Code unless stated otherwise. *(Adopted, eff. Jan. 1, 2007.)*

Research References

4 Witkin, California Criminal Law 4th Introduction to Criminal Procedure § 9 (2021), Rules of Court.

Division 2

PRETRIAL

Chapter 1

PRETRIAL PROCEEDINGS

Rule

Rule 4.100. Arraignments

At the arraignment on the information or indictment, unless otherwise ordered for good cause, and on a plea of not guilty, including a plea of not guilty by reason of insanity;

(1) The court must set dates for:

(A) Trial, giving priority to a case entitled to it under law; and

(B) Filing and service of motions and responses and hearing thereon;

(2) A plea of not guilty must be entered if a defendant represented by counsel fails to plead or demur; and

(3) An attorney may not appear specially. *(Formerly Rule 227.4, adopted, eff. Jan. 1, 1985. As amended, eff. June 6, 1990. Renumbered Rule 4.100 and amended, eff. Jan. 1, 2001. As amended, eff. Jan. 1, 2007.)*

Advisory Committee Comment

Cross reference: Penal Code section 987.1.

Research References

4 Witkin, California Criminal Law 4th Introduction to Criminal Procedure § 9 (2021), Rules of Court.
4 Witkin, California Criminal Law 4th Pretrial Proceedings § 255 (2021), In General.
4 Witkin, California Criminal Law 4th Pretrial Proceedings § 257 (2021), In General.
4 Witkin, California Criminal Law 4th Pretrial Proceedings § 297 (2021), Refusal or Failure to Enter Plea.

Rule 4.101. Bail in criminal cases

The fact that a defendant in a criminal case has or has not asked for a jury trial must not be taken into consideration in fixing the amount of bail and, once set, bail may not be increased or reduced by reason of such fact. *(Formerly Rule 801. Renumbered Rule 4.101, eff. Jan. 1, 2001. As amended, eff. Jan. 1, 2007.)*

Research References

4 Witkin, California Criminal Law 4th Pretrial Proceedings § 98 (2021), In General.

Rule 4.102. Uniform bail and penalty schedules—traffic, boating, fish and game, forestry, public utilities, parks and recreation, business licensing

The Judicial Council of California has established the policy of promulgating uniform bail and penalty schedules for certain offenses in order to achieve a standard of uniformity in the handling of these offenses.

In general, bail is used to ensure the presence of the defendant before the court. Under Vehicle Code sections 40512 and 13103, bail may also be forfeited and forfeiture may be ordered without the necessity of any further court proceedings and be treated as a conviction for specified Vehicle Code offenses. A penalty in the form of a monetary sum is a fine imposed as all or a portion of a sentence imposed.

To achieve substantial uniformity of bail and penalties throughout the state in traffic, boating, fish and game, forestry, public utilities, parks and recreation, and business licensing cases, the trial court judges, in performing their duty under Penal Code section 1269b to annually revise and adopt a schedule of bail and penalties for all misdemeanor and infraction offenses except Vehicle Code infractions, must give consideration to the Uniform Bail and Penalty Schedules approved by the Judicial Council. The Uniform Bail and Penalty Schedule for infraction violations of the Vehicle Code will be established by the Judicial Council in accordance with Vehicle Code section 40310. Judges must give consideration to requiring additional bail for aggravating or enhancing factors.

After a court adopts a countywide bail and penalty schedule, under Penal Code section 1269b, the court must, as soon as practicable, mail or e-mail a copy of the schedule to the Judicial Council with a report stating how the revised schedule differs from the council's uniform traffic bail and penalty schedule, uniform boating bail and penalty schedule, uniform fish and game bail and penalty schedule, uniform forestry bail and penalty schedule, uniform public utilities bail and penalty schedule, uniform parks and recreation bail and penalty schedule, or uniform business licensing bail and penalty schedule.

The purpose of this uniform bail and penalty schedule is to:

(1) Show the standard amount for bail, which for Vehicle Code offenses may also be the amount used for a bail forfeiture instead of further proceedings; and

(2) Serve as a guideline for the imposition of a fine as all or a portion of the penalty for a first conviction of a listed offense where a fine is used as all or a portion of the penalty for such offense. The amounts shown for the misdemeanors on the boating, fish and game, forestry, public utilities, parks and recreation, and business licensing bail and penalty schedules have been set with this dual purpose in mind.

Unless otherwise shown, the maximum penalties for the listed offenses are six months in the county jail or a fine of $1,000, or both. The penalty amounts are intended to be used to provide standard fine amounts for a first offense conviction of a violation shown where a fine is used as all or a portion of the sentence imposed.

Note:
Courts may obtain copies of the Uniform Bail and Penalty Schedules by contacting:
Criminal Justice Services
Judicial Council of California
455 Golden Gate Avenue
San Francisco, CA 94102–3688

or
www.courts.ca.gov/7532.htm

(Formerly Rule 850, adopted, eff. Jan. 1, 1965. As amended, eff. Jan. 1, 1970; Jan. 1, 1971; July 1, 1972; Jan. 1, 1973; Jan. 1, 1974; July 1, 1975; July 1, 1979; July 1, 1980; July 1, 1981; Jan. 1, 1983; July 1, 1984; July 1, 1986; Jan. 1, 1989; Jan. 1, 1993; Jan. 1, 1995; Jan. 1, 1997. Renumbered Rule 4.102 and amended, eff. Jan. 1, 2001. As amended, eff. July 1, 2004; Jan. 1, 2007; July 1, 2013; Jan. 1, 2016; Jan. 1, 2018.)

Research References

2 Witkin, California Criminal Law 4th Crimes Against Public Peace and Welfare § 266 (2021), Infractions.
4 Witkin, California Criminal Law 4th Pretrial Proceedings § 94 (2021), On Arrest.

Rule 4.103. Notice to appear forms

(a) Traffic offenses

A printed or electronic notice to appear that is issued for any violation of the Vehicle Code other than a felony or for a violation of an ordinance of a city or county relating to traffic offenses must be prepared and filed with the court on *Automated Traffic Enforcement System Notice to Appear* (form TR–115), *Traffic/Nontraffic Notice to Appear* (form TR–130), *Electronic Traffic/Nontraffic Notice to Appear* (4–inch format) (form TR–135), or *Electronic Traffic/Nontraffic Notice to Appear* (3–inch format) (form TR–145), and must comply with the requirements in the current version of the Judicial Council's instructions, *Notice to Appear and Related Forms* (form TR–INST).

(b) Nontraffic offenses

A notice to appear issued for a nontraffic infraction or misdemeanor offense that is prepared on *Nontraffic Notice to Appear* (form TR–120), *Traffic/Nontraffic Notice to Appear* (form TR–130), *Electronic Traffic/Nontraffic Notice to Appear* (4–inch format) (form TR–135), or *Electronic Traffic/Nontraffic Notice to Appear* (3–inch format) (form TR–145), and that complies with the requirements in the current version of the Judicial Council's instructions, *Notice to Appear and Related Forms* (form TR–INST), may be filed with the court and serve as a complaint as provided in Penal Code section 853.9 or 959.1.

(c) Corrections

Corrections to citations previously issued on *Continuation of Notice to Appear* (form TR–106), *Continuation of Citation* (form TR–108), *Automated Traffic Enforcement System Notice to Appear* (form TR–

115), *Nontraffic Notice to Appear* (form TR–120), *Traffic/Nontraffic Notice to Appear* (form TR–130), *Electronic Traffic/Nontraffic Notice to Appear* (4–inch format) (form TR–135), or *Electronic Traffic/Nontraffic Notice to Appear* (3–inch format) (form TR–145) must be made on a *Notice of Correction and Proof of Service* (form TR–100).

(d) Electronic citation forms

A law enforcement agency that uses an electronic citation device to issue notice to appear citations on the Judicial Council's *Electronic Traffic/Nontraffic Notice to Appear* (4–inch format) (form TR–135) or *Electronic Traffic/Nontraffic Notice to Appear* (3–inch format) (form TR–145) must submit to the Judicial Council an exact printed copy of the agency's current citation form that complies with the requirements in the most recent version of the Judicial Council's instructions, *Notice to Appear and Related Forms* (form TR–INST). *(Adopted, eff. Jan. 1, 2004. As amended, eff. Jan. 1, 2007; June 26, 2015.)*

Research References

4 Witkin, California Criminal Law 4th Pretrial Proceedings § 51 (2021), Citation, Promise, and Release.
4 Witkin, California Criminal Law 4th Pretrial Proceedings § 52 (2021), Appearance, Bail Forfeiture, or Trial.
4 Witkin, California Criminal Law 4th Pretrial Proceedings § 53 (2021), Failure to Appear.

Rule 4.104. Procedures and eligibility criteria for attending traffic violator school

(a) Purpose

The purpose of this rule is to establish uniform statewide procedures and criteria for eligibility to attend traffic violator school.

(b) Authority of a court clerk to grant a request to attend traffic violator school

(1) *Eligible offenses*

Except as provided in (2), a court clerk is authorized to grant a request to attend traffic violator school when a defendant with a valid driver's license requests to attend an 8–hour traffic violator school under Vehicle Code sections 41501(a) and 42005 for any infraction under divisions 11 and 12 (rules of the road and equipment violations) of the Vehicle Code if the violation is reportable to the Department of Motor Vehicles.

(2) *Ineligible offenses*

A court clerk is not authorized to grant a request to attend traffic violator school for a misdemeanor or any of the following infractions:

(A) A violation that carries a negligent operator point count of more than one point under Vehicle Code section 12810 or one and one-half points or more under Vehicle Code section 12810.5(b)(2);

(B) A violation that occurs within 18 months after the date of a previous violation and the defendant either attended or elected to attend a traffic violator school for the previous violation (Veh. Code, §§ 1808.7 and 1808.10);

(C) A violation of Vehicle Code section 22406.5 (tank vehicles);

(D) A violation related to alcohol use or possession or drug use or possession;

(E) A violation on which the defendant failed to appear under Vehicle Code section 40508(a) unless the failure-to-appear charge has been adjudicated and any fine imposed has been paid;

(F) A violation on which the defendant has failed to appear under Penal Code section 1214.1 unless the civil monetary assessment has been paid;

(G) A speeding violation in which the speed alleged is more than 25 miles over a speed limit as stated in Chapter 7 (commencing with section 22348) of Division 11 of the Vehicle Code; and

(H) A violation that occurs in a commercial vehicle as defined in Vehicle Code section 15210(b).

(c) Judicial discretion

(1) A judicial officer may in his or her discretion order attendance at a traffic violator school in an individual case as permitted under Vehicle Code section 41501(a) or 42005 or for any other purpose permitted by law. A defendant having a class A, class B, or commercial class C driver's license may request to attend traffic violator school if the defendant was operating a vehicle requiring only a noncommercial class C or class M license. The record of conviction after completion of traffic violator school by a driver who holds a class A, class B, or commercial class C license must not be reported as confidential. A defendant charged with a violation that occurs in a commercial vehicle, as defined in Vehicle Code section 15210(b), is not eligible to attend traffic violator school under Vehicle Code sections 41501 or 42005 in lieu of adjudicating an offense, to receive a confidential conviction, or to avoid violator point counts.

(2) A defendant who is otherwise eligible for traffic violator school is not made ineligible by entering a plea other than guilty or by exercising his or her right to trial. A traffic violator school request must be considered based on the individual circumstances of the specific case. The court is not required to state on the record a reason for granting or denying a traffic violator school request. *(Formerly Rule 851, adopted, eff. Jan. 1, 1997. As amended, eff. Jan. 1, 1998; July 1, 2001; Jan. 1, 2003; Sept. 20, 2005. Renumbered Rule 4.104 and amended, eff. Jan. 1, 2007. As amended, eff. July 1, 2011; Jan. 1, 2013.)*

Advisory Committee Comment

Subdivision (c)(1). Rule 4.104(c)(1) reflects that under Vehicle Code sections 1808.10, 41501, and 42005, the record of a driver with a class A, class B, or commercial class C license who completes a traffic violator school program is not confidential and must be reported to and disclosed by the Department of Motor Vehicles for purposes of Title 49 of the Federal Code of Regulations and to insurers for underwriting and rating purposes.

Subdivision (c)(2). Rule 4.104(c)(2) reflects court rulings in cases where defendants wished to plead not guilty and have the court order attendance of traffic violator school if found guilty after trial. A court has discretion to grant or not grant traffic violator school. (*People v. Schindler* (1993) 20 Cal.App.4th 431, 433; *People v. Levinson* (1984) 155 Cal.App.3d Supp. 13, 21.) However, the court may not arbitrarily refuse to consider a request for traffic violator school because a defendant pleads not guilty. (*Schindler*, supra, at p. 433; *People v. Wozniak* (1987) 197 Cal.App.3d Supp. 43, 44; *People v. Enochs* (1976) 62 Cal.App.3d Supp. 42, 44.) If a judicial officer believes that a defendant's circumstances indicate that a defendant would benefit from attending school, such attendance should be authorized and should not be affected by the order in which the plea, explanation, and request for traffic violator school are presented. (*Enochs*, supra, at p. 44.) A court is not required to state its reasons for granting or denying traffic violator school following a defendant's conviction for a traffic violation. (*Schindler*, supra, at p. 433.)

Research References

2 Witkin, California Criminal Law 4th Crimes Against Public Peace and Welfare § 265 (2021), In General.

Rule 4.105. Appearance without deposit of bail in infraction cases

(a) Application. This rule applies to any infraction for which the defendant has received a written notice to appear.

(b) Appearance without deposit of bail. Except as provided in (c), courts must allow a defendant to appear for arraignment and trial without deposit of bail.

(c) Deposit of bail.

(1) Courts must require the deposit of bail when the defendant elects a statutory procedure that requires the deposit of bail.

(2) Courts may require the deposit of bail when the defendant does not sign a written promise to appear as required by the court.

(3) Courts may require a deposit of bail before trial if the court determines that the defendant is unlikely to appear as ordered

without a deposit of bail and the court expressly states the reasons for the finding.

(4) In determining the amount of bail set under (2) and (3), courts must consider the totality of the circumstances.

(d) Notice. Courts must inform defendants of the option to appear in court without the deposit of bail in any instructions or other materials courts provide for the public that relate to bail for infractions, including any website information, written instructions, courtesy notices, and forms.

(e) Local Website Information. The website for each trial court must include a link to the traffic self-help information posted at: *http://www.courts.ca.gov/selfhelp-traffic.htm*. *(Adopted, eff. June 8, 2015. As amended, eff. Dec. 1, 2015; Jan. 1, 2017.)*

Advisory Committee Comment

Subdivision (a). The rule is intended to apply only to an infraction violation for which the defendant has received a written notice to appear and has appeared by the appearance date or an approved extension of that date. The rule does not apply to postconviction matters or cases in which the defendant seeks an appearance in court after a failure to appear or pay.

Subdivision (c). This subdivision takes into account the distinct statutory purposes and functions that bail and related considerations serve in infraction cases, including, for example, the posting and forfeiting of bail in uncontested cases and the use of bail to satisfy later judgments, as distinguished from felony and most misdemeanor cases.

Subdivision (c)(1). Various statutory provisions authorize infraction defendants who have received a written notice to appear to elect to deposit bail in lieu of appearing in court or in advance of the notice to appear date. (See, e.g., Veh. Code, §§ 40510 [authorizing defendants to deposit bail before the notice to appear date]; 40519(a) [authorizing defendants who have received a written notice to appear to declare the intention to plead not guilty and deposit bail before the notice to appear date for purposes of electing to schedule an arraignment and trial on the same date or on separate dates]; 40519(b) [authorizing defendants who have received a written notice to appear to deposit bail and plead not guilty in writing in lieu of appearing in person]; and 40902 [authorizing trial by written declaration].)

This rule is not intended to modify or contravene any statutorily authorized alternatives to appearing in court. (See, e.g., Pen. Code, §§ 853.5, 853.6; Veh. Code, §§ 40510, 40512, and 40512.5 [authorizing defendants to post and forfeit bail in lieu of appearing for arraignment].) The purpose of this rule is to clarify that if the defendant declines to use a statutorily authorized alternative, courts must allow the defendant to appear *without* prior deposit of bail as provided above.

Subdivision (c)(2). As used in this subdivision, the phrase "written promise to appear as required by the court" refers to a signed promise, made by a defendant who has appeared in court, to return to court on a future date and time as ordered by the court.

Subdivision (c)(3). In exercising discretion to require deposit of bail on a particular case, courts should consider, among other factors, whether previous failures to pay or appear were willful or involved adequate notice.

Subdivision (c)(4). In considering the "totality of the circumstances" under this subdivision, courts may consider whether the bail amount would impose an undue hardship on the defendant.

Research References

4 Witkin, California Criminal Law 4th Pretrial Proceedings § 52 (2021), Appearance, Bail Forfeiture, or Trial.

4 Witkin, California Criminal Law 4th Pretrial Proceedings § 58 (2021), Filing and Bail.

Rule 4.106. Failure to appear or failure to pay for a *Notice to Appear* issued for an infraction offense

(a) Application

This rule applies to infraction offenses for which the defendant has received a written notice to appear and has failed to appear or failed to pay.

(b) Definitions

As used in this rule, "failure to appear" and "failure to pay" mean failure to appear and failure to pay as defined in section 1214.1(a).

(c) Procedure for consideration of good cause for failure to appear or pay

(1) A notice of a civil assessment under section 1214.1(b) must inform the defendant of his or her right to petition that the civil assessment be vacated for good cause and must include information about the process for vacating or reducing the assessment.

(2) When a notice of civil assessment is given, a defendant may, within the time specified in the notice, move by written petition to vacate or reduce the assessment.

(3) When a court imposes a civil assessment for failure to appear or pay, the defendant may petition that the court vacate or reduce the civil assessment without paying any bail, fines, penalties, fees, or assessments.

(4) A petition to vacate an assessment does not stay the operation of any order requiring the payment of bail, fines, penalties, fees, or assessment unless specifically ordered by the court.

(5) The court must vacate the assessment upon a showing of good cause under section 1214.1(b)(1) for failure to appear or failure to pay.

(6) If the defendant does not establish good cause, the court may still exercise its discretion under section 1214.1(a) to reconsider:

(A) Whether a civil assessment should be imposed; and

(B) If so, the amount of the assessment.

(7) In exercising its discretion, the court may consider such factors as a defendant's due diligence in appearing or paying after notice of the assessment has been given under section 1214.1(b)(1) and the defendant's financial circumstances.

(d) Procedure for unpaid bail referred to collection as delinquent debt in unadjudicated cases

(1) When a case has not been adjudicated and a court refers it to a comprehensive collection program as provided in section 1463.007(b)(1) as delinquent debt, the defendant may schedule a hearing for adjudication of the underlying charge(s) without payment of the bail amount.

(2) The defendant may request an appearance date to adjudicate the underlying charges by written petition or alternative method provided by the court.

Alternatively, the defendant may request or the court may direct a court appearance.

(3) A court may require a deposit of bail before adjudication of the underlying charges if the court finds that the defendant is unlikely to appear as ordered without a deposit of bail and the court expressly states the reasons for the finding. The court must not require payment of the civil assessment before adjudication.

(e) Procedure for failure to pay or make a payment under an installment payment plan

(1) When a defendant fails to pay a fine or make a payment under an installment plan as provided in section 1205 or Vehicle Code sections 40510.5, 42003, or 42007, the court must permit the defendant to appear by written petition to modify the payment terms. Alternatively, the defendant may request or the court may direct a court appearance.

(2) The court must not require payment of bail, fines, penalties, fees, or assessments to consider the petition.

(3) The petition to modify the payment terms does not stay the operation of any order requiring the payment of bail, fines, penalties, fees, or assessments unless specifically ordered by the court.

(4) If the defendant petitions to modify the payment terms based on an inability to pay, the procedures stated in rule 4.335 apply.

(5) If the petition to modify the payment terms is not based on an inability to pay, the court may deny the defendant's request to modify

the payment terms and order no further proceedings if the court determines that:

(A) An unreasonable amount of time has passed; or

(B) The defendant has made an unreasonable number of requests to modify the payment terms.

(f) Procedure after a trial by written declaration in absentia for a traffic infraction.

When the court issues a judgment under Vehicle Code section 40903 and a defendant requests a trial de novo within the time permitted, courts may require the defendant to deposit bail.

(g) Procedure for referring a defendant to the Department of Motor Vehicles (DMV) for license suspension for failure to pay a fine

Before a court may notify the DMV under Vehicle Code sections 40509(b) or 40509.5(b) that a defendant has failed to pay a fine or an installment of bail, the court must provide the defendant with notice of and an opportunity to be heard on the inability to pay. This notice may be provided on the notice required in rule 4.107, the civil assessment notice, or any other notice provided to the defendant. *(Adopted, eff. Jan. 1, 2017.)*

Advisory Committee Comment

Subdivision (a). The rule is intended to apply only to an infraction offense for which the defendant (1) has received a written notice to appear and (2) has failed to appear by the appearance date or an approved extension of that date or has failed to pay as required.

Subdivision (c)(3). Circumstances that indicate good cause may include, but are not limited to, the defendant's hospitalization, incapacitation, or incarceration; military duty required of the defendant; death or hospitalization of the defendant's dependent or immediate family member; caregiver responsibility for a sick or disabled dependent or immediate family member of the defendant; or an extraordinary reason, beyond the defendant's control, that prevented the defendant from making an appearance or payment on or before the date listed on the notice to appear.

Subdivision (e)(1). A court may exercise its discretion to deny a defendant's request to modify the payment terms. If the court chooses to grant the defendant's request, the court may modify the payment terms by reducing or suspending the base fine, lowering the payments, converting the remaining balance to community service, or otherwise modifying the payment terms as the court sees fit.

Subdivision (g). A hearing is not required unless requested by the defendant or directed by the court.

Research References

West's California Judicial Council Forms CR–320, Can't Afford to Pay Fine: Traffic and Other Infractions.

West's California Judicial Council Forms CR–321, Can't Afford to Pay Fine: Traffic and Other Infractions (Court Order).

West's California Judicial Council Forms TR–320, Can't Afford to Pay Fine: Traffic and Other Infractions.

West's California Judicial Council Forms TR–321, Can't Afford to Pay Fine: Traffic and Other Infractions (Court Order).

4 Witkin, California Criminal Law 4th Pretrial Proceedings § 53 (2021), Failure to Appear.

Rule 4.107. Mandatory reminder notice—traffic procedures

(a) Mandatory reminder notice

(1) Each court must send a reminder notice to the address shown on the *Notice to Appear*, unless the defendant otherwise notifies the court of a different address.

(2) The court may satisfy the requirement in paragraph (1) by sending the notice electronically, including by e-mail or text message, to the defendant. By providing an electronic address or number to the court or to a law enforcement officer at the time of signing the promise to appear, a defendant consents to receiving the reminder notice electronically at that electronic address or number.

(3) The failure to receive a reminder notice does not relieve the defendant of the obligation to appear by the date stated in the *Notice to Appear*.

(b) Minimum information in reminder notice

In addition to information obtained from the *Notice to Appear*, the reminder notice must contain at least the following information:

(1) An appearance date and location;

(2) Whether a court appearance is mandatory or optional;

(3) The total bail amount and payment options;

(4) The notice about traffic school required under Vehicle Code section 42007, if applicable;

(5) Notice that a traffic violator school will charge a fee in addition to the administrative fee charged by the court;

(6) The potential consequences for failure to appear, including a driver's license hold or suspension, a civil assessment of up to $300, a new charge for failure to appear, a warrant of arrest, or some combination of these consequences, if applicable;

(7) The potential consequences for failure to pay a fine, including a driver's license hold or suspension, a civil assessment of up to $300, a new charge for failure to pay a fine, a warrant of arrest, or some combination of these consequences, if applicable;

(8) The right to request an ability-to-pay determination;

(9) Notice of the option to pay bail through community service (if available) and installment plans (if available);

(10) Contact information for the court, including the court's website;

(11) Information regarding trial by declaration, informal trial (if available), and telephone or website scheduling options (if available); and

(12) Correction requirements and procedures for correctable violations. *(Adopted, eff. Jan. 1, 2017.)*

Advisory Committee Comment

Subdivision (a)(2). The court may provide a means for obtaining the defendant's consent and designated electronic address or number on its local website. Because notices to appear state the website address for the superior court in each county, this location may increase the number of defendants who become aware and take advantage of this option. To obtain the defendant's electronic address or number at the time of signing the promise to appear, the court may need to collaborate with local law enforcement agencies.

Subdivision (b). While not required, some local court websites may provide information about local court processes and local forms related to the information on the reminder notice. If in electronic form, the reminder notice should include direct links to any information and forms on the local court website. If in paper form, the reminder notice may include the website addresses for any information and forms on the local court website.

Research References

4 Witkin, California Criminal Law 4th Pretrial Proceedings § 52 (2021), Appearance, Bail Forfeiture, or Trial.

Rule 4.108. Installment payment agreements

(a) Online interface for installment payment agreements

(1) A court may use an online interface to enter into installment payment agreements with traffic infraction defendants under Vehicle Code sections 40510.5 and 42007.

(2) Before entering into an installment payment agreement, an online interface must provide defendants with the Advisement of Rights stated in Attachment 1 of *Online Agreement to Pay and Forfeit Bail in Installments* (form TR-300 (online)), and *Online Agreement to Pay Traffic Violator School Fees in Installments* (form TR-310 (online)).

(b) Alternative mandatory forms

(1) The Judicial Council has adopted the following alternative mandatory forms for use in entering into installment payment agreements under Vehicle Code sections 40510.5 and 42007:

(A) *Agreement to Pay and Forfeit Bail in Installments* (form TR-300); and *Online Agreement to Pay and Forfeit Bail in Installments* (form TR-300 (online)); and

(B) *Agreement to Pay Traffic Violator School Fees in Installments* (form TR-310); and *Online Agreement to Pay Traffic Violator School Fees in Installments* (form TR-310 (online)).

(2) Forms TR-300 (online) and TR-310 (online) may be used only in online interfaces for installment payment agreements as provided in subdivision (a). *(Adopted, eff. Jan. 1, 2017.)*

Rule 4.110. Time limits for criminal proceedings on information or indictment

Time limits for criminal proceedings on information or indictment are as follows:

(1) The information must be filed within 15 days after a person has been held to answer for a public offense;

(2) The arraignment of a defendant must be held on the date the information is filed or as soon thereafter as the court directs; and

(3) A plea or notice of intent to demur on behalf of a party represented by counsel at the arraignment must be entered or made no later than seven days after the initial arraignment, unless the court lengthens time for good cause. *(Formerly Rule 227.3, adopted, eff. Jan. 1, 1985. As amended, eff. June 6, 1990. Renumbered Rule 4.110, and amended, eff. Jan. 1, 2001. As amended, eff. Jan. 1, 2007.)*

Research References

4 Witkin, California Criminal Law 4th Pretrial Proceedings § 200 (2021), Procedure.
4 Witkin, California Criminal Law 4th Pretrial Proceedings § 253 (2021), Time and Place.
4 Witkin, California Criminal Law 4th Pretrial Proceedings § 283 (2021), Form and Procedure.
4 Witkin, California Criminal Law 4th Pretrial Proceedings § 293 (2021), Time and Form.

Rule 4.111. Pretrial motions in criminal cases

(a) Time for filing papers and proof of service

Unless otherwise ordered or specifically provided by law, all pretrial motions, accompanied by a memorandum, must be served and filed at least 10 court days, all papers opposing the motion at least 5 court days, and all reply papers at least 2 court days before the time appointed for hearing. Proof of service of the moving papers must be filed no later than 5 court days before the time appointed for hearing.

(b) Failure to serve and file timely points and authorities

The court may consider the failure without good cause of the moving party to serve and file a memorandum within the time permitted as an admission that the motion is without merit. *(Formerly Rule 227.5, adopted, eff. Jan. 1, 1985. Renumbered Rule 4.111, eff. Jan. 1, 2001. As amended, eff. Jan. 1, 2007; Jan. 1, 2010.)*

Research References

4 Witkin, California Criminal Law 4th Introduction to Criminal Procedure § 8 (2021), Practice.

Rule 4.112. Readiness conference

(a) Date and appearances

The court may hold a readiness conference in felony cases within 1 to 14 days before the date set for trial. At the readiness conference:

(1) All trial counsel must appear and be prepared to discuss the case and determine whether the case can be disposed of without trial;

(2) The prosecuting attorney must have authority to dispose of the case; and

(3) The defendant must be present in court.

(b) Motions

Except for good cause, the court should hear and decide any pretrial motion in a criminal case before or at the readiness conference. *(Subd. (a) formerly Rule 227.6, adopted, eff. Jan. 1, 1985. Subd. (b) formerly § 10.1, Standards of Judicial Administration, adopted, eff. Jan. 1, 1985. Renumbered Rule 4.112 and amended, eff. Jan. 1, 2001. As amended, eff. Jan. 1, 2005; Jan. 1, 2007.)*

Research References

5 Witkin, California Criminal Law 4th Criminal Trial § 380 (2021), In General.
4 Witkin, California Criminal Law 4th Introduction to Criminal Procedure § 8 (2021), Practice.

Rule 4.113. Motions and grounds for continuance of criminal case set for trial

Motions to continue the trial of a criminal case are disfavored and will be denied unless the moving party, under Penal Code section 1050, presents affirmative proof in open court that the ends of justice require a continuance. *(Formerly Rule 227.7, adopted, eff. Jan. 1, 1985. Renumbered Rule 4.113, eff. Jan. 1, 2001. As amended, eff. Jan. 1, 2007.)*

Research References

5 Witkin, California Criminal Law 4th Criminal Trial § 382 (2021), Policies Involved.
4 Witkin, California Criminal Law 4th Jurisdiction and Venue § 15 (2021), Criminal Departments and Divisions.

Rule 4.114. Certification under Penal Code section 859a

When a plea of guilty or no contest is entered under Penal Code section 859a, the magistrate must:

(1) Set a date for imposing sentence; and

(2) Refer the case to the probation officer for action as provided in Penal Code sections 1191 and 1203. *(Formerly Rule 227.9, adopted, eff. Jan. 1, 1985. Renumbered Rule 4.114 and amended, eff. Jan. 1, 2001. As amended, eff. Jan. 1, 2007.)*

Research References

4 Witkin, California Criminal Law 4th Pretrial Proceedings § 144 (2021), By Plea of Guilty or Nolo Contendere.

Rule 4.115. Criminal case assignment

(a) Master calendar departments

To ensure that the court's policy on continuances is firm and uniformly applied, that pretrial proceedings and trial assignments are handled consistently, and that cases are tried on a date certain, each court not operating on a direct calendaring system must assign all criminal matters to one or more master calendar departments. The presiding judge of a master calendar department must conduct or supervise the conduct of all arraignments and pretrial hearings and conferences, and assign to a trial department any case requiring a trial or dispositional hearing.

(b) Trial calendaring and continuances

Any request for a continuance, including a request to trail the trial date, must comply with rule 4.113 and the requirement in section 1050 to show good cause to continue a hearing in a criminal proceeding. Active management of trial calendars is necessary to minimize the number of statutory dismissals. Accordingly, courts should avoid calendaring or trailing criminal cases for trial to the last day permitted for trial under section 1382. Courts must implement calendar management procedures, in accordance with local conditions and needs, to ensure that criminal cases are assigned to trial departments before the last day permitted for trial under section 1382. *(Formerly § 10, Standards of Judicial Administration, adopted, eff. Jan. 1, 1985. Renumbered Rule 4.115 and amended, eff. Jan. 1, 2001. As amended, eff. Jan. 1, 2007; Jan. 1, 2008.)*

Advisory Committee Comment

Subdivision (b) clarifies that the "good cause" showing for a continuance under section 1050 applies in all criminal cases, whether or not the case is in the 10–day grace period provided for in section 1382. The Trial Court Presiding Judges Advisory Committee and Criminal Law Advisory Committee observe that the "good cause" requirement for a continuance is separate and distinct from the "good cause" requirement to avoid dismissals under section 1382. There is case law stating that the prosecution is not required to show good cause to avoid a dismissal under section 1382 during the 10–day grace period because a case may not be dismissed for delay during that 10–day period. (See, e.g., *Bryant v. Superior Court* (1986) 186 Cal.App.3d 483, 488.) Yet, both the plain language of section 1050 and case law show that there must be good cause for a continuance under section 1050 during the 10–day grace period. (See, e.g., section 1050 and *People v. Henderson* (2004) 115 Cal. App.4th 922, 939–940.) Thus, a court may not dismiss a case during the 10–day grace period under section 1382, but the committees believe that the court must deny a request for a continuance during the 10–day grace period that does not comply with the good cause requirement under section 1050.

The decision in *Henderson* states that when the prosecutor seeks a continuance but fails to show good cause under section 1050, the trial court "must nevertheless postpone the hearing to another date within the statutory period." (115 Cal.App.4th at p. 940.) That conclusion, however, may be contrary to the plain language of section 1050, which requires a court to deny a continuance if the moving party fails to show good cause. The conclusion also appears to be dicta, as it was not a contested issue on appeal. Given this uncertainty, the rule is silent as to the remedy for failure to show good cause for a requested continuance during the 10–day grace period. The committees note that the remedies under section 1050.5 are available and, but for the *Henderson* dicta, a court would appear to be allowed to deny the continuance request and commence the trial on the scheduled trial date.

Research References

4 Witkin, California Criminal Law 4th Jurisdiction and Venue § 15 (2021), Criminal Departments and Divisions.

Rule 4.116. Certification to juvenile court

(a) Application

This rule applies to all cases not filed in juvenile court in which the person charged by an accusatory pleading appears to be under the age of 18, except when jurisdiction over the child has been transferred from the juvenile court under Welfare and Institutions Code section 707.

(b) Procedure to determine whether certification is appropriate

If an accusatory pleading is pending, and it is suggested or it appears to the court that the person charged was under the age of 18 on the date the offense is alleged to have been committed, the court must immediately suspend proceedings and conduct a hearing to determine the true age of the person charged. The burden of proof of establishing the age of the accused person is on the moving party. If, after examination, the court is satisfied by a preponderance of the evidence that the person was under the age of 18 on the date the alleged offense was committed, the court must immediately certify the matter to the juvenile court and state on the certification order:

(1) The crime with which the person named is charged;

(2) That the person was under the age of 18 on the date of the alleged offense;

(3) The date of birth of the person;

(4) The date of suspension of criminal proceedings; and

(5) The date and time of certification to juvenile court.

(c) Procedure on certification

If the court determines that certification to the juvenile court is appropriate under (b), copies of the certification, the accusatory pleading, and any police reports must immediately be transmitted to the clerk of the juvenile court. On receipt of the documents, the clerk of the juvenile court must immediately notify the probation officer, who must immediately investigate the matter to determine whether to commence proceedings in juvenile court.

(d) Procedure if child is in custody

If the person is under the age of 18 and is in custody, the person must immediately be transported to the juvenile detention facility. *(Formerly Rule 241.2, adopted, eff. Jan. 1, 1991. As amended, eff. July 1, 1991. Renumbered Rule 4.116 and amended, eff. Jan. 1, 2001. As amended, eff. Jan. 1, 2007; May 22, 2017.)*

Rule 4.117. Qualifications for appointed trial counsel in capital cases

(a) Purpose

This rule defines minimum qualifications for attorneys appointed to represent persons charged with capital offenses in the superior courts. These minimum qualifications are designed to promote adequate representation in death penalty cases and to avoid unnecessary delay and expense by assisting the trial court in appointing qualified counsel. Nothing in this rule is intended to be used as a standard by which to measure whether the defendant received effective assistance of counsel.

(b) General qualifications

In cases in which the death penalty is sought, the court must assign qualified trial counsel to represent the defendant. The attorney may be appointed only if the court, after reviewing the attorney's background, experience, and training, determines that the attorney has demonstrated the skill, knowledge, and proficiency to diligently and competently represent the defendant. An attorney is not entitled to appointment simply because he or she meets the minimum qualifications.

(c) Designation of counsel

(1) If the court appoints more than one attorney, one must be designated lead counsel and meet the qualifications stated in (d) or (f), and at least one other must be designated associate counsel and meet the qualifications stated in (e) or (f).

(2) If the court appoints only one attorney, that attorney must meet the qualifications stated in (d) or (f).

(d) Qualifications of lead counsel

To be eligible to serve as lead counsel, an attorney must:

(1) Be an active member of the State Bar of California;

(2) Be an active trial practitioner with at least 10 years' litigation experience in the field of criminal law;

(3) Have prior experience as lead counsel in either:

(A) At least 10 serious or violent felony jury trials, including at least 2 murder cases, tried to argument, verdict, or final judgment; or

(B) At least 5 serious or violent felony jury trials, including at least 3 murder cases, tried to argument, verdict, or final judgment;

(4) Be familiar with the practices and procedures of the California criminal courts;

(5) Be familiar with and experienced in the use of expert witnesses and evidence, including psychiatric and forensic evidence;

(6) Have completed within two years before appointment at least 15 hours of capital case defense training approved for Minimum Continuing Legal Education credit by the State Bar of California; and

(7) Have demonstrated the necessary proficiency, diligence, and quality of representation appropriate to capital cases.

(e) Qualifications of associate counsel

To be eligible to serve as associate counsel, an attorney must:

(1) Be an active member of the State Bar of California;

(2) Be an active trial practitioner with at least three years' litigation experience in the field of criminal law;

(3) Have prior experience as:

Ct. Rules

(A) Lead counsel in at least 10 felony jury trials tried to verdict, including 3 serious or violent felony jury trials tried to argument, verdict, or final judgment; or

(B) Lead or associate counsel in at least 5 serious or violent felony jury trials, including at least 1 murder case, tried to argument, verdict, or final judgment;

(4) Be familiar with the practices and procedures of the California criminal courts;

(5) Be familiar with and experienced in the use of expert witnesses and evidence, including psychiatric and forensic evidence;

(6) Have completed within two years before appointment at least 15 hours of capital case defense training approved for Minimum Continuing Legal Education credit by the State Bar of California; and

(7) Have demonstrated the necessary proficiency, diligence, and quality of representation appropriate to capital cases.

(f) Alternative qualifications

The court may appoint an attorney even if he or she does not meet all of the qualifications stated in (d) or (e) if the attorney demonstrates the ability to provide competent representation to the defendant. If the court appoints counsel under this subdivision, it must state on the record the basis for finding counsel qualified. In making this determination, the court must consider whether the attorney meets the following qualifications:

(1) The attorney is an active member of the State Bar of California or admitted to practice *pro hac vice* under rule 9.40;

(2) The attorney has demonstrated the necessary proficiency, diligence, and quality of representation appropriate to capital cases;

(3) The attorney has had extensive criminal or civil trial experience;

(4) Although not meeting the qualifications stated in (d) or (e), the attorney has had experience in death penalty trials other than as lead or associate counsel;

(5) The attorney is familiar with the practices and procedures of the California criminal courts;

(6) The attorney is familiar with and experienced in the use of expert witnesses and evidence, including psychiatric and forensic evidence;

(7) The attorney has had specialized training in the defense of persons accused of capital crimes, such as experience in a death penalty resource center;

(8) The attorney has ongoing consultation support from experienced death penalty counsel;

(9) The attorney has completed within the past two years before appointment at least 15 hours of capital case defense training approved for Minimum Continuing Legal Education credit by the State Bar of California; and

(10) The attorney has been certified by the State Bar of California's Board of Legal Specialization as a criminal law specialist.

(g) Public defender appointments

When the court appoints the Public Defender under Penal Code section 987.2, the Public Defender should assign an attorney from that office or agency as lead counsel who meets the qualifications described in (d) or assign an attorney that he or she determines would qualify under (f). If associate counsel is designated, the Public Defender should assign an attorney from that office or agency who meets the qualifications described in (e) or assign an attorney he or she determines would qualify under (f).

(h) Standby or advisory counsel

When the court appoints standby or advisory counsel to assist a self-represented defendant, the attorney must qualify under (d) or (f).

(i) Order appointing counsel

When the court appoints counsel to a capital case, the court must complete *Order Appointing Counsel in Capital Case* (form CR–190), and counsel must complete *Declaration of Counsel for Appointment in Capital Case* (form CR–191). *(Adopted, eff. Jan. 1, 2003. As amended, eff. Jan. 1, 2004; Jan. 1, 2007.)*

Research References

West's California Judicial Council Forms CR–190, Order Appointing Counsel in Capital Case.
West's California Judicial Council Forms CR–191, Declaration of Counsel for Appointment in Capital Case.
5 Witkin, California Criminal Law 4th Criminal Trial § 187 (2021), In General.
5 Witkin, California Criminal Law 4th Criminal Trial § 193 (2021), In General.
5 Witkin, California Criminal Law 4th Criminal Trial § 308 (2021), Nature of Participation.
4 Witkin, California Criminal Law 4th Pretrial Proceedings § 147 (2021), Mandatory Representation in Capital Case.

Rule 4.119. Additional requirements in pretrial proceedings in capital cases

(a) Application

This rule applies only in pretrial proceedings in cases in which the death penalty may be imposed.

(b) Checklist

Within 10 days of counsel's first appearance in court, primary counsel for each defendant and the prosecution must each acknowledge that they have reviewed *Capital Case Attorney Pretrial Checklist* (form CR–600) by signing and submitting this form to the court. Counsel are encouraged to keep a copy of this checklist.

(c) Lists of appearances, exhibits, and motions

(1) Primary counsel for each defendant and the prosecution must each prepare the lists identified in (A)–(C):

(A) A list of all appearances made by that party during the pretrial proceedings. *Capital Case Attorney List of Appearances* (form CR–601) must be used for this purpose. The list must include all appearances, including ex parte appearances; the date of each appearance; the department in which it was made; the name of counsel making the appearance; and a brief description of the nature of the appearance. A separate list of Penal Code section 987.9 appearances must be maintained under seal for each defendant.

(B) A list of all exhibits offered by that party during the pretrial proceedings. *Capital Case Attorney List of Exhibits* (form CR–602) must be used for this purpose. The list must indicate whether the exhibit was admitted in evidence, refused, lodged, or withdrawn.

(C) A list of all motions made by that party during the pretrial proceedings, including ex parte motions. *Capital Case Attorney List of Motions* (form CR–603) must be used for this purpose. The list must indicate if a motion is awaiting resolution.

(2) In the event of any substitution of attorney during the pretrial proceedings, the relieved attorney must provide the lists of all appearances, exhibits, and motions to substituting counsel within five days of being relieved.

(3) No later than 21 days after the clerk notifies trial counsel that it must submit the lists to the court, counsel must submit the lists to the court and serve on all parties a copy of all the lists except the list of Penal Code section 987.9 appearances. Unless otherwise provided by local rule, the lists must be submitted to the court in electronic form.

(d) Electronic recordings presented or offered into evidence

Counsel must comply with the requirements of rule 2.1040 regarding electronic recordings presented or offered into evidence, including any such recordings that are part of a digital or electronic presentation. *(Adopted, eff. April 25, 2019.)*

Advisory Committee Comment

Subdivision (b). *Capital Case Attorney Pretrial Checklist* (form CR–600) is designed to be a tool to assist pretrial counsel in identifying and fulfilling all their record preparation responsibilities. Counsel are therefore encouraged to keep a copy of this form and to use it to monitor their own progress.

Subdivision (c)(1). To facilitate preparation of complete and accurate lists, counsel are encouraged to add items to the lists at the time appearances or motions are made or exhibits offered.

Subdivision (c)(3). Rule 8.613(d) requires the clerk to notify counsel to submit the lists of appearances, exhibits, and motions.

Research References

West's California Judicial Council Forms CR–600, Capital Case Attorney Pretrial Checklist (Criminal).
West's California Judicial Council Forms CR–601, Captal Case Attorney List of Appearances (Criminal).
West's California Judicial Council Forms CR–602, Capital Case Attorney List of Exhibits (Criminal).
West's California Judicial Council Forms CR–603, Capital Case Attorney List of Motions (Criminal).
West's California Judicial Council Forms CR–604, Capital Case Attorney List of Jury Instructions (Criminal).
West's California Judicial Council Forms CR–605, Capital Case Attorney Trial Checklist (Criminal).
5 Witkin, California Criminal Law 4th Criminal Trial § 187 (2021), In General.
4 Witkin, California Criminal Law 4th Pretrial Proceedings § 147 (2021), Mandatory Representation in Capital Case.

Rule 4.130. Mental competency proceedings

(a) Application

(1) This rule applies to proceedings in the superior court under Penal Code section 1367 et seq. to determine the mental competency of a criminal defendant.

(2) The requirements of subdivision (d)(2) apply only to a formal competency evaluation ordered by the court under Penal Code section 1369(a).

(3) The requirements of subdivision (d)(2) do not apply to a brief preliminary evaluation of the defendant's competency if:

(A) The parties stipulate to a brief preliminary evaluation; and

(B) The court orders the evaluation in accordance with a local rule of court that specifies the content of the evaluation and the procedure for its preparation and submission to the court.

(b) Initiation of mental competency proceedings

(1) The court must initiate mental competency proceedings if the judge has a reasonable doubt, based on substantial evidence, about the defendant's competence to stand trial.

(2) The opinion of counsel, without a statement of specific reasons supporting that opinion, does not constitute substantial evidence. The court may allow defense counsel to present his or her opinion regarding the defendant's mental competency in camera if the court finds there is reason to believe that attorney-client privileged information will be inappropriately revealed if the hearing is conducted in open court.

(3) In a felony case, if the judge initiates mental competency proceedings prior to the preliminary examination, counsel for the defendant may request a preliminary examination as provided in Penal Code section 1368.1(a)(1), or counsel for the People may request a determination of probable cause as provided in Penal Code section 1368.1(a)(2) and rule 4.131.

(c) Effect of initiating mental competency proceedings

(1) If mental competency proceedings are initiated, criminal proceedings are suspended and may not be reinstated until a trial on the competency of the defendant has been concluded and the defendant is found mentally competent at a trial conducted under Penal Code section 1369, at a hearing conducted under Penal Code section 1370(a)(1)(G), or at a hearing following a certification of restoration under Penal Code section 1372.

(2) In misdemeanor cases, speedy trial requirements are tolled during the suspension of criminal proceedings for mental competency evaluation and trial. If criminal proceedings are later reinstated and time is not waived, the trial must be commenced within 30 days after the reinstatement of the criminal proceedings, as provided by Penal Code section 1382(a)(3).

(3) In felony cases, speedy trial requirements are tolled during the suspension of criminal proceedings for mental competency evaluation and trial. If criminal proceedings are reinstated, unless time is waived, time periods to commence the preliminary examination or trial are as follows:

(A) If criminal proceedings were suspended before the preliminary hearing had been conducted, the preliminary hearing must be commenced within 10 days of the reinstatement of the criminal proceedings, as provided in Penal Code section 859b.

(B) If criminal proceedings were suspended after the preliminary hearing had been conducted, the trial must be commenced within 60 days of the reinstatement of the criminal proceedings, as provided in Penal Code section 1382(a)(2).

(d) Examination of defendant after initiation of mental competency proceedings

(1) On initiation of mental competency proceedings, the court must inquire whether the defendant, or defendant's counsel, seeks a finding of mental incompetence.

(2) Any court-appointed experts must examine the defendant and advise the court on the defendant's competency to stand trial. Experts' reports are to be submitted to the court, counsel for the defendant, and the prosecution. The report must include the following:

(A) A brief statement of the examiner's training and previous experience as it relates to examining the competence of a criminal defendant to stand trial and preparing a resulting report;

(B) A summary of the examination conducted by the examiner on the defendant, including a summary of the defendant's mental status, a diagnosis under the most recent version of the *Diagnostic and Statistical Manual of Mental Disorders,* if possible, of the defendant's current mental health disorder or disorders, and a statement as to whether symptoms of the mental health disorder or disorders which motivated the defendant's behavior would respond to mental health treatment;

(C) A detailed analysis of the competence of the defendant to stand trial using California's current legal standard, including the defendant's ability or inability to understand the nature of the criminal proceedings or assist counsel in the conduct of a defense in a rational manner as a result of a mental health disorder;

(D) A summary of an assessment—conducted for malingering or feigning symptoms, if clinically indicated—which may include, but need not be limited to, psychological testing;

(E) Under Penal Code section 1369, a statement on whether treatment with antipsychotic or other medication is medically appropriate for the defendant, whether the treatment is likely to restore the defendant to mental competence, a list of likely or potential side effects of the medication, the expected efficacy of the medication, possible alternative treatments, whether it is medically appropriate to administer antipsychotic or other medication in the county jail, and whether the defendant has capacity to make decisions regarding antipsychotic or other medication. If an examining psychologist is of the opinion that a referral to a psychiatrist is necessary to address these issues, the psychologist must inform the court of this opinion and his or her recommendation that a psychiatrist should examine the defendant;

(F) A list of all sources of information considered by the examiner, including legal, medical, school, military, regional center, employment, hospital, and psychiatric records; the evaluations of other experts; the results of psychological testing; police reports; criminal history; the statement of the defendant; statements of any witnesses to the alleged crime; booking information, mental health screenings, and mental health records following the alleged crime; consultation with the prosecutor and defendant's attorney; and any other collateral sources considered in reaching his or her conclusion;~~and~~

(G) If the defendant is charged with a felony offense, a recommendation, if possible, for a placement or type of placement or treatment program that is most appropriate for restoring the defendant to competency; and

(H) If the defendant is charged only with a misdemeanor offense, an opinion based on present clinical impressions and available historical data as to whether the defendant, regardless of custody status, appears to be gravely disabled, as defined in Welfare and Institutions Code section 5008(h)(1)(A).

(3) Statements made by the defendant during the examination to experts appointed under this rule, and products of any such statements, may not be used in a trial on the issue of the defendant's guilt or in a sanity trial should defendant enter a plea of not guilty by reason of insanity.

(e) Trial on mental competency

(1) Regardless of the conclusions or findings of the court-appointed expert, the court must conduct a trial on the mental competency of the defendant if the court has initiated mental competency proceedings under (b).

(2) At the trial, the defendant is presumed to be mentally competent, and it is the burden of the party contending that the defendant is not mentally competent to prove the defendant's mental incompetence by a preponderance of the evidence.

(3) In addition to the testimony of the experts appointed by the court under (d), either party may call additional experts or other relevant witnesses.

(4) After the presentation of the evidence and closing argument, the trier of fact is to determine whether the defendant is mentally competent or mentally incompetent.

(A) If the matter is tried by a jury, the verdict must be unanimous.

(B) If the parties have waived the right to a jury trial, the court's findings must be made in writing or placed orally in the record.

(f) Posttrial procedure

(1) If the defendant is found mentally competent, the court must reinstate the criminal proceedings.

(2) If the defendant in a felony case is found to be mentally incompetent under section 1370 or the defendant in any criminal action is found to be mentally incompetent under section 1370.1 due to a developmental disability, the criminal proceedings remain suspended and the court ~~must~~ either:

(A) Must issue an order committing the person for restoration treatment under the provisions of the governing statute; or

(B) In the case of a person eligible for commitment under ~~Penal Code~~ sections 1370~~or 1370.01~~, if the person is found incompetent due to a mental disorder, may consider placing the ~~committed~~ person on a program of diversion under section 1001.36 in lieu of commitment.

(3) If the defendant is found to be mentally incompetent in a misdemeanor case under section 1370.01, the criminal proceedings remain suspended, and the court may dismiss the case under section 1385 or conduct a hearing to consider placing the person on a program of diversion under section 1001.36.

(g) ~~Diversion of a person eligible for commitment under section 1370 or 1370.01~~Reinstatement of felony proceedings under section 1001.36(d)

~~(1) After the court finds that the defendant is mentally incompetent and before the defendant is transported to a facility for restoration under section 1370(a)(1)(B)(i), the court may consider whether the defendant may benefit from diversion under Penal Code section 1001.36. The court may set a hearing to determine whether the defendant is an appropriate candidate for diversion. When determining whether to exercise its discretion to grant diversion under this section, the court may consider previous records of participation in diversion under section 1001.36.~~

~~(2) The maximum period of diversion after a finding that the defendant is incompetent to stand trial is the lesser of two years or the maximum time for restoration under Penal Code section 1370(c)(1) (for felony offenses) or 1370.01(c)(1) (for misdemeanor offenses).~~

~~(3) The court may not condition a grant of diversion for defendant found to be incompetent on either:~~

~~(A) The defendant's consent to diversion, either personally, or through counsel; or~~

~~(B) A knowing and intelligent waiver of the defendant's statutory right to a speedy trial, either personally, or through counsel.~~

~~(4) A finding that the defendant suffers from a mental health disorder or disorders rendering the defendant eligible for diversion, any progress reports concerning the defendant's treatment in diversion, or any other records related to a mental health disorder or disorders that were created as a result of participation in, or completion of, diversion or for use at a hearing on the defendant's eligibility for diversion under this section, may not be used in any other proceeding without the defendant's consent, unless that information is relevant evidence that is admissible under the standards described in article I, section 28(f)(2) of the California Constitution.~~

~~(5)~~If a defendant eligible for commitment under section 1370 is granted diversion under section 1001.36, and during the period of diversion~~,~~ the court determines that criminal proceedings should be reinstated under ~~Penal Code~~ section 1001.36(d), the court must, under ~~Penal Code~~ section 1369, appoint a psychiatrist, licensed psychologist, or any other expert the court may deem appropriate, to examine the defendant and return a report~~,~~ opining on the defendant's competence to stand trial. The expert's report must be provided to counsel for the People and to the defendant's counsel.

(1) On receipt of the evaluation report, the court must conduct an inquiry into the defendant's current competency, under the procedures set forth in (h)(2) of this rule.

(2) If the court finds by a preponderance of the evidence that the defendant is mentally competent, the court must hold a hearing as set forth in Penal Code section 1001.36(d).

~~(C)~~(3) If the court finds by a preponderance of the evidence that the defendant is mentally incompetent, criminal proceedings must remain suspended, and the court must order that the defendant be committed~~, under Penal Code section 1370 (for felonies) or 1370.01 (for misdemeanors),~~ and placed for restoration treatment.

~~(D)~~(4) If the court concludes, based on substantial evidence, that the defendant is mentally incompetent and is not likely to attain competency within the time remaining before the defendant's maximum date for returning to court, and has reason to believe the defendant may be gravely disabled, within the meaning of Welfare and Institutions Code section 5008(h)(1), the court may, instead of issuing a commitment order under ~~Penal Code~~ sections 1370~~or 1370.01~~, refer the matter to the conservatorship investigator of the county of commitment to initiate conservatorship proceedings for the defendant under Welfare and Institutions Code section 5350 et seq.

~~(6) If the defendant performs satisfactorily and completes diversion, the case must be dismissed under the procedures stated in Penal Code section 1001.36, and the defendant must no longer be deemed incompetent to stand trial.~~

(h) Posttrial hearings on competence under section 1370

(1) If, at any time after the court has declared a defendant incompetent to stand trial, and counsel for the defendant, or a jail medical or mental health staff provider, provides the court with substantial evidence that the defendant's psychiatric symptoms have changed to such a degree as to create a doubt in the mind of the judge as to the defendant's current mental incompetence, the court may appoint a psychiatrist or a licensed psychologist to examine the defendant and, in an examination with the court, opine as to whether the defendant has regained competence.

(2) On receipt of ~~the~~an evaluation report under (h)(1) or an evaluation by the State Department of State Hospitals under Welfare and Institutions Code section 4335.2, the court must direct the clerk to serve a copy on counsel for the People and counsel for the defendant. If, in the opinion of the appointed expert or the department's expert, the defendant has regained competence, the court must conduct a hearing~~,~~ as if a certificate of restoration of competence had been filed under ~~Penal Code~~section 1372(a)(1), except that a presumption of competency does not apply. At the hearing, the court may consider any evidence, presented by any party, ~~which~~that is relevant to the question of the defendant's current mental competency.

(A) At the conclusion of the hearing, if the court finds that it has been established by a preponderance of the evidence that the defendant is mentally competent, the court must reinstate criminal proceedings.

(B) At the conclusion of the hearing, if the court finds that it has not been established by a preponderance of the evidence that the defendant is mentally competent, criminal proceedings must remain suspended.

(C) The court's findings on the defendant's mental competency must be stated on the record and recorded in the minutes. *(Adopted, eff. Jan. 1, 2007. As amended, eff. Jan. 1, 2018; Jan. 1, 2020; Sept. 1, 2020; May 13, 2022.)*

Advisory Committee Comment

The case law interpreting Penal Code section 1367 et seq. established a procedure for judges to follow in cases where there is a concern whether the defendant is legally competent to stand trial, but the concern does not necessarily rise to the level of a reasonable doubt based on substantial evidence. Before finding a reasonable doubt as to the defendant's competency to stand trial and initiating competency proceedings under Penal Code section 1368 et seq., the court may appoint an expert to assist the court in determining whether such a reasonable doubt exists. As noted in *People v. Visciotti* (1992) 2 Cal.4th 1, 34–36, the court may appoint an expert when it is concerned about the mental competency of the defendant, but the concern does not rise to the level of a reasonable doubt, based on substantial evidence, required by Penal Code section 1367 et seq. Should the results of this examination present substantial evidence of mental incompetency, the court must initiate competency proceedings under (b).

Once mental competency proceedings under Penal Code section 1367 et seq. have been initiated, the court is to appoint at least one expert to examine the defendant under (d). Under no circumstances is the court obligated to appoint more than two experts. (Pen. Code, § 1369(a).) The costs of the experts appointed under (d) are to be paid for by the court as the expert examinations and reports are for the benefit or use of the court in determining whether the defendant is mentally incompetent. (See Cal. Rules of Court, rule 10.810, function 10.)

Subdivision (d)(3), which provides that the defendant's statements made during the examination cannot be used in a trial on the defendant's guilt or a sanity trial in a not guilty by reason of sanity trial, is based on the California Supreme Court holdings in *People v. Arcega* (1982) 32 Cal.3d 504 and *People v. Weaver* (2001) 26 Cal.4th 876.

Although the court is not obligated to appoint additional experts, counsel may nonetheless retain their own experts to testify at a trial on the defendant's competency. (See *People v. Mayes* (1988) 202 Cal.App.4th 908, 917–918.) These experts are not for the benefit or use of the court, and their costs are not to be paid by the court. (See Cal. Rules of Court, rule 10.810, function 10.)

Both the prosecution and the defense have the right to a jury trial. (See *People v. Superior Court (McPeters)* (1995) 169 Cal.App.3d 796.) Defense counsel may waive this right, even over the objection of the defendant. (*People v. Masterson* (1994) 8 Cal.4th 965, 970.)

Either defense counsel or the prosecution (or both) may argue that the defendant is not competent to stand trial. (*People v. Stanley* (1995) 10 Cal.4th 764, 804 [defense counsel may advocate that defendant is not competent to stand trial and may present evidence of defendant's mental incompetency regardless of defendant's desire to be found competent].) If the defense declines to present evidence of the defendant's mental incompetency, the prosecution may do so. (Pen. Code, § 1369(b)(2).) If the prosecution elects to present evidence of the defendant's mental incompetency, it is the prosecution's burden to prove the incompetency by a preponderance of the evidence. (*People v. Mixon* (1990) 225 Cal.App.3d 1471, 1484, fn. 12.)

Should both parties decline to present evidence of defendant's mental incompetency, the court may do so. In those cases, the court is not to instruct the jury that a party has the burden of proof. "Rather, the proper approach would be to instruct the jury on the legal standard they are to apply to the evidence before them without allocating the burden of proof to one party or the other." (*People v. Sherik* (1991) 229 Cal.App.3d 444, 459–460.)

Research References

5 Witkin, California Criminal Law 4th Criminal Trial § 826 (2021), In General.
5 Witkin, California Criminal Law 4th Criminal Trial § 828 (2021), Judge Expresses Doubt as to Competency.
5 Witkin, California Criminal Law 4th Criminal Trial § 832 (2021), What Proceedings Are Suspended.
5 Witkin, California Criminal Law 4th Criminal Trial § 833 (2021), What Proceedings Are Not Suspended.
5 Witkin, California Criminal Law 4th Criminal Trial § 836 (2021), Appointment of Experts.
5 Witkin, California Criminal Law 4th Criminal Trial § 837 (2021), Statements Made by Defendant.
5 Witkin, California Criminal Law 4th Criminal Trial § 838 (2021), Presentation of Evidence.
5 Witkin, California Criminal Law 4th Criminal Trial § 839 (2021), Burden of Proof.
5 Witkin, California Criminal Law 4th Criminal Trial § 841 (2021), Determination.
5 Witkin, California Criminal Law 4th Criminal Trial § 843 (2021), In General.
4 Witkin, California Criminal Law 4th Introduction to Criminal Procedure § 9 (2021), Rules of Court.

Rule 4.131. Probable cause determinations under section 1368.1(a)(2)

(a) Notice of a request for a determination of probable cause

The prosecuting attorney must serve and file notice of a request for a determination of probable cause on the defense at least 10 court days before the time appointed for the proceeding.

(b) Judge requirement

A judge must hear the determination of probable cause unless there is a stipulation by both parties to having the matter heard by a subordinate judicial officer.

(c) Defendant need not be present

A defendant need not be present for a determination of probable cause to proceed.

(d) Application of section 861

The one-session requirement of section 861 does not apply.

(e) Transcript

A transcript of the determination of probable cause must be provided to the prosecuting attorney and counsel for the defendant consistent with the manner in which a transcript is provided in a preliminary examination. *(Adopted, eff. Jan. 1, 2019.)*

Research References

5 Witkin, California Criminal Law 4th Criminal Trial § 833 (2021), What Proceedings Are Not Suspended.

Chapter 2

CHANGE OF VENUE

Rule 4.150. Change of venue: application and general provisions

(a) Application

Rules 4.150 to 4.155 govern the change of venue in criminal cases under Penal Code section 1033.

(b) General provisions

When a change of venue has been ordered, the case remains a case of the transferring court. Except on good cause to the contrary, the court must follow the provisions below:

(1) Proceedings before trial must be heard in the transferring court.

(2) Proceedings that are not to be heard by the trial judge must be heard in the transferring court.

(3) Postverdict proceedings, including sentencing, if any, must be heard in the transferring court.

(c) Appellate review

Review by the Court of Appeal, either by an original proceeding or by appeal, must be heard in the appellate district in which the transferring court is located. *(Formerly Rule 840, adopted, eff. March 4, 1972. Renumbered Rule 4.150 and amended, eff. Jan. 1, 2001. As amended, eff. Jan. 1, 2006; Jan. 1, 2007.)*

Advisory Committee Comment

Subdivision (b)(1). This subdivision is based on Penal Code section 1033(a), which provides that all proceedings before trial are to be heard in the transferring court, except when a particular proceeding must be heard by the trial judge.

Subdivision (b)(2). This subdivision addresses motions heard by a judge other than the trial judge, such as requests for funds under Penal Code section 987.9 or a challenge or disqualification under Code of Civil Procedure section 170 et seq.

Subdivision (b)(3). Reflecting the local community interest in the case, (b)(3) clarifies that after trial the case is to return to the transferring court for any posttrial proceedings. There may be situations where the local interest is outweighed, warranting the receiving court to conduct posttrial hearings. Such hearings may include motions for new trial where juror testimony is necessary and the convenience to the jurors outweighs the desire to conduct the hearings in the transferring court.

Subdivision (c). This subdivision ensures that posttrial appeals and writs are heard in the same appellate district as any writs that may have been heard before or during trial.

Research References

6 Witkin, California Criminal Law 4th Criminal Writs § 14 (2021), Proper Court to Determine Petition.
4 Witkin, California Criminal Law 4th Introduction to Criminal Procedure § 9 (2021), Rules of Court.
4 Witkin, California Criminal Law 4th Jurisdiction and Venue § 72 (2021), In General.
4 Witkin, California Criminal Law 4th Jurisdiction and Venue § 74 (2021), Orders.

Rule 4.151. Motion for change of venue

(a) Motion procedure

A motion for change of venue in a criminal case under Penal Code section 1033 must be supported by a declaration stating the facts supporting the application. Except for good cause shown, the motion must be filed at least 10 days before the date set for trial, with a copy served on the adverse party at least 10 days before the hearing. At the hearing counter declarations may be filed.

(b) Policy considerations in ruling on motion

Before ordering a change of venue in a criminal case, the transferring court should consider impaneling a jury that would give the defendant a fair and impartial trial. *(Formerly Rule 841, adopted, eff. March 4, 1972. Renumbered Rule 4.151 and amended, eff. Jan. 1, 2001. As amended, eff. Jan. 1, 2006; Jan. 1, 2007.)*

Advisory Committee Comment

Rule 4.151(b) is not intended to imply that the court should attempt to impanel a jury in every case before granting a change of venue.

Research References

4 Witkin, California Criminal Law 4th Jurisdiction and Venue § 72 (2021), In General.

Rule 4.152. Selection of court and trial judge

When a judge grants a motion for change of venue, he or she must inform the presiding judge of the transferring court. The presiding judge, or his or her designee, must:

(1) Notify the Administrative Director of the change of venue. After receiving the transferring court's notification, the Administrative Director, in order to expedite judicial business and equalize the work of the judges, must advise the transferring court which courts would not be unduly burdened by the trial of the case.

(2) Select the judge to try the case, as follows:

(A) The presiding judge, or his or her designee, must select a judge from the transferring court, unless he or she concludes that the transferring court does not have adequate judicial resources to try the case.

(B) If the presiding judge, or his or her designee, concludes that the transferring court does not have adequate judicial resources to try the case, he or she must request that the Chief Justice of California determine whether to assign a judge to the transferring court. If the Chief Justice determines not to assign a judge to the transferring court, the presiding judge, or his or her designee, must select a judge from the transferring court to try the case. *(Formerly Rule 842, adopted, eff. March 4, 1972. Renumbered Rule 4.152 and amended, eff. Jan. 1, 2001. As amended, eff. Jan. 1, 2006; Jan. 1, 2016.)*

Research References

4 Witkin, California Criminal Law 4th Jurisdiction and Venue § 74 (2021), Orders.

Rule 4.153. Order on change of venue

After receiving the list of courts from the Administrative Director, the presiding judge, or his or her designee, must:

(1) Determine the court in which the case is to be tried. In making that determination, the court must consider, under Penal Code section 1036.7, whether to move the jury rather than to move the pending action. In so doing, the court should give particular consideration to the convenience of the jurors.

(2) Transmit to the receiving court a certified copy of the order of transfer and any pleadings, documents, or other papers or exhibits necessary for trying the case.

(3) Enter the order for change of venue in the minutes of the transferring court. The order must include the determinations in (1). *(Formerly Rule 843, adopted, eff. March 4, 1972. Renumbered Rule 4.153, eff. Jan. 1, 2001. As amended, eff. Jan. 1, 2006; Jan. 1, 2016.)*

Advisory Committee Comment

Rules 4.152 and 4.153 recognize that, although the determination of whether to grant a motion for change of venue is judicial in nature, the selection of the receiving court and the decision whether the case should be tried by a judge of the transferring court are more administrative in nature. Thus, the rules provide that the presiding judge of the transferring court is to make the latter decisions. He or she may delegate those decisions to the trial judge, the supervising judge of the criminal division, or any other judge the presiding judge deems appropriate. If, under the particular facts of the case, the latter decisions are both judicial and administrative, those decisions may be more properly made by the judge who heard the motion for change of venue.

Research References

4 Witkin, California Criminal Law 4th Jurisdiction and Venue § 74 (2021), Orders.

Rule 4.154. Proceedings in the receiving court

The receiving court must conduct the trial as if the case had been commenced in the receiving court. If it is necessary to have any of the original pleadings or other papers before the receiving court, the transferring court must transmit such papers or pleadings. If, during the trial, any original papers or pleadings are submitted to the receiving court, the receiving court is to file the original. After sentencing, all original papers and pleadings are to be retained by the transferring court. *(Formerly Rule 844, adopted, eff. March 4, 1972. Renumbered Rule 4.154, eff. Jan. 1, 2001. As amended, eff. Jan. 1, 2006.)*

Research References

4 Witkin, California Criminal Law 4th Jurisdiction and Venue § 74 (2021), Orders.

Rule 4.155. Guidelines for reimbursement of costs in change of venue cases—criminal cases

(a) General

Consistent with Penal Code section 1037, the court in which an action originated must reimburse the court receiving a case after an order for change of venue for any ordinary expenditure and any extraordinary but reasonable and necessary expenditure that would not have been incurred by the receiving court but for the change of venue.

(b) Reimbursable ordinary expenditures—court related

Court-related reimbursable ordinary expenses include:

(1) For prospective jurors on the panel from which the jury is selected and for the trial jurors and alternates seated:

(A) Normal juror per diem and mileage at the rates of the receiving court. The cost of the juror should only be charged to a change of venue case if the juror was not used in any other case on the day that juror was excused from the change of venue case.

(B) If jurors are sequestered, actual lodging, meals, mileage, and parking expenses up to state Board of Control limits.

(C) If jurors are transported to a different courthouse or county, actual mileage and parking expenses.

(2) For court reporters:

(A) The cost of pro tem reporters, even if not used on the change of venue trial, but not the salaries of regular official reporters who would have been paid in any event. The rate of compensation for pro tem reporters should be that of the receiving court.

(B) The cost of transcripts requested during trial and for any new trial or appeal, using the folio rate of the receiving court.

(C) The cost of additional reporters necessary to allow production of a daily or expedited transcript.

(3) For assigned judges: The assigned judge's per diem, travel, and other expenses, up to state Board of Control limits, if the judge is assigned to the receiving court because of the change of venue case, regardless of whether the assigned judge is hearing the change of venue case.

(4) For interpreters and translators:

(A) The cost of the services of interpreters and translators, not on the court staff, if those services are required under Evidence Code sections 750 through 754. Using the receiving court's fee schedule, this cost should be paid whether the services are used in a change of venue trial or to cover staff interpreters and translators assigned to the change of venue trial.

(B) Interpreters' and translators' actual mileage, per diem, and lodging expenses, if any, that were incurred in connection with the trial, up to state Board of Control limits.

(5) For maintenance of evidence: The cost of handling, storing, or maintaining evidence beyond the expenses normally incurred by the receiving court.

(6) For services and supplies: The cost of services and supplies incurred only because of the change of venue trial, for example, copying and printing charges (such as for juror questionnaires), long-distance telephone calls, and postage. A pro rata share of the costs of routine services and supplies should not be reimbursable.

(7) For court or county employees:

(A) Overtime expenditures and compensatory time for staff incurred because of the change of venue case.

(B) Salaries and benefit costs of extra help or temporary help incurred either because of the change of venue case or to replace staff assigned to the change of venue case.

(c) Reimbursable ordinary expenses—defendant related

Defendant-related reimbursable ordinary expenses include the actual costs incurred for guarding, keeping, and transporting the defendant, including:

(1) Expenses related to health care: Costs incurred by or on behalf of the defendant such as doctors, hospital expenses, medicines, therapists, and counseling for diagnosis, evaluation, and treatment.

(2) Cost of food and special clothing for an in-custody defendant.

(3) Transportation: Nonroutine expenses, such as transporting an in-custody defendant from the transferring court to the receiving court. Routine transportation expenses if defendant is transported by usual means used for other receiving court prisoners should not be reimbursable.

(d) Reimbursable ordinary expenditures—defense expenses

Reimbursable ordinary expenses related to providing defense for the defendant include:

(1) Matters covered by Penal Code section 987.9 as determined by the transferring court or by a judge designated under that section.

(2) Payment of other defense costs in accordance with policies of the court in which the action originated, unless good cause to the contrary is shown to the trial court.

(3) Unless Penal Code section 987.9 applies, the receiving court may, in its sound discretion, approve all trial-related expenses including:

(A) Attorney fees for defense counsel and, if any, co-counsel and actual travel-related expenses, up to state Board of Control limits, for staying in the county of the receiving court during trial and hearings.

(B) Paralegal and extraordinary secretarial or office expenditures of defense counsel.

(C) Expert witness costs and expenses.

(D) The cost of experts assisting in preparation before trial or during trial, for example, persons preparing demonstrative evidence.

(E) Investigator expenses.

(F) Defense witness expenses, including reasonable-and-necessary witness fees and travel expenses.

(e) Extraordinary but reasonable-and-necessary expenses

Except in emergencies or unless it is impracticable to do so, a receiving court should give notice before incurring any extraordinary expenditures to the transferring court, in accordance with Penal Code section 1037(d). Extraordinary but reasonable-and-necessary expenditures include:

(1) Security-related expenditures: The cost of extra security precautions taken because of the risk of escape or suicide or threats of, or the potential for, violence during the trial. These precautions might include, for example, extra bailiffs or correctional officers, special transportation to the courthouse for trial, television monitoring, and security checks of those entering the courtroom.

(2) Facility remodeling or modification: Alterations to buildings or courtrooms to accommodate the change of venue case.

(3) Renting or leasing of space or equipment: Renting or leasing of space for courtrooms, offices, and other facilities, or equipment to accommodate the change of venue case.

(f) Nonreimbursable expenses

Nonreimbursable expenses include:

(1) Normal operating expenses including the overhead of the receiving court, for example:

(A) Salary and benefits of existing court staff that would have been paid even if there were no change of venue case.

(B) The cost of operating the jail, for example, detention staff costs, normal inmate clothing, utility costs, overhead costs, and jail construction costs. These expenditures would have been incurred whether or not the case was transferred to the receiving court. It is, therefore, inappropriate to seek reimbursement from the transferring court.

(2) Equipment that is purchased and then kept by the receiving court and that can be used for other purposes or cases.

(g) Miscellaneous

(1) Documentation of costs: No expense should be submitted for reimbursement without supporting documentation, such as a claim, invoice, bill, statement, or time sheet. In unusual circumstances, a declaration under penalty of perjury may be necessary. The declaration should describe the cost and state that it was incurred because of the change of venue case. Any required court order or approval of costs also should be sent to the transferring court.

(2) Timing of reimbursement: Unless both courts agree to other terms, reimbursement of all expenses that are not questioned by the transferring court should be made within 60 days of receipt of the claim for reimbursement. Payment of disputed amounts should be made within 60 days of the resolution of the dispute. *(Formerly § 4.2, Standards of Judicial Administration, adopted, eff. July 1, 1989. As amended, eff. Jan. 1, 1998. Renumbered Rule 4.162 and amended, eff. Jan. 1, 2001. Renumbered Rule 4.155 and amended, eff. Jan. 1, 2006. As amended, eff. Jan. 1, 2007; Sept. 1, 2017.)*

Research References

4 Witkin, California Criminal Law 4th Introduction to Criminal Procedure § 9 (2021), Rules of Court.

Division 3

TRIALS

Rule 4.200. Pre-voir dire conference in criminal cases

(a) The conference

Before jury selection begins in criminal cases, the court must conduct a conference with counsel to determine:

(1) A brief outline of the nature of the case, including a summary of the criminal charges;

(2) The names of persons counsel intend to call as witnesses at trial;

(3) The People's theory of culpability and the defendant's theories;

(4) The procedures for deciding requests for excuse for hardship and challenges for cause;

(5) The areas of inquiry and specific questions to be asked by the court and by counsel and any time limits on counsel's examination;

(6) The schedule for the trial and the predicted length of the trial;

(7) The number of alternate jurors to be selected and the procedure for selecting them; and

(8) The procedure for making objections pursuant to Code of Civil Procedure 231.7(b).

The judge must, if requested, excuse the defendant from then disclosing any defense theory.

(b) Written questions

The court may require counsel to submit in writing, and before the conference, all questions that counsel requests the court to ask of prospective jurors. This rule applies to questions to be asked either orally or by written questionnaire. The *Juror Questionnaire for Criminal Cases* (form MC–002) may be used. *(Formerly Rule 228.1, adopted, eff. June 6, 1990. Renumbered Rule 4.200, eff. Jan. 1, 2001. As amended, eff. Jan. 1, 2006; Jan. 1, 2007; March 14, 2022.)*

Advisory Committee Comment

This rule is to be used in conjunction with standard 4.30.

Research References

5 Witkin, California Criminal Law 4th Criminal Trial § 569 (2021), Pre-Voir Dire Conference.
4 Witkin, California Criminal Law 4th Introduction to Criminal Procedure § 9 (2021), Rules of Court.

Rule 4.201. Voir dire in criminal cases

To select a fair and impartial jury, the judge must conduct an initial examination of the prospective jurors orally, or by written questionnaire, or by both methods. The *Juror Questionnaire for Criminal Cases* (form MC–002) may be used. After completion of the initial examination, the court must permit counsel to conduct supplemental questioning as provided in Code of Civil Procedure section 223. *(Formerly Rule 228.2, adopted, eff. June 6, 1990. Renumbered Rule 4.201 and amended, eff. Jan. 1, 2001. As amended, eff. Jan. 1, 2006.)*

Advisory Committee Comment

Although Code of Civil Procedure section 223 creates a preference for nonsequestered voir dire (*People v. Roldan* (2005) 35 Cal.4th 646, 691), a judge may conduct sequestered voir dire on questions concerning media reports of the case and on any other issue deemed advisable. (See, e.g., Cal. Stds. Jud. Admin., std. 4.30(a)(3).) To determine whether such issues are present, a judge may consider factors including the charges, the nature of the evidence that is anticipated to be presented, and any other relevant factors. To that end, a judge should always inform jurors of the possibility of sequestered voir dire if the voir dire is likely to elicit answers that the juror may believe are sensitive in nature. It should also be noted that when written questionnaires are used, jurors must be advised of the right to request a hearing in chambers on sensitive questions rather than answering them on the questionnaire. (*Copley Press Inc. v. Superior Court* (1991) 228 Cal.App.3d 77, 87.)

Rule 4.202. Statements to the jury panel

Prior to the examination of prospective jurors, the trial judge may, in his or her discretion, permit brief opening statements by counsel to the panel. *(Adopted, eff. Jan. 1, 2013.)*

Research References

5 Witkin, California Criminal Law 4th Criminal Trial § 566 (2021), In General.

Rule 4.210. Traffic court—trial by written declaration

(a) Applicability

This rule establishes the minimum procedural requirements for trials by written declaration under Vehicle Code section 40902. The procedures established by this rule must be followed in all trials by written declaration under that section.

(b) Procedure

(1) *Definition of due date*

As used in this subdivision, "due date" means the last date on which the defendant's appearance is timely.

(2) *Extending due date*

If the clerk receives the defendant's written request for a trial by written declaration by the appearance date indicated on the *Notice to Appear*, the clerk must, within 15 calendar days after receiving the defendant's written request, extend the appearance date 25 calendar days and must give or mail notice to the defendant of the extended due date on the *Request for Trial by Written Declaration* (form TR–205) with a copy of the *Instructions to Defendant* (form TR–200) and any other required forms.

(3) *Election*

The defendant must file a *Request for Trial by Written Declaration* (form TR–205) with the clerk by the appearance date indicated on the *Notice to Appear* or the extended due date as provided in (2). The *Request for Trial by Written Declaration* (form TR–205) must be filed in addition to the defendant's written request for a trial by written declaration, unless the defendant's request was made on the election form.

(4) *Bail*

The defendant must deposit bail with the clerk by the appearance date indicated on the *Notice to Appear* or the extended due date as provided in (2).

(5) *Instructions to arresting officer*

If the clerk receives the defendant's *Request for Trial by Written Declaration* (form TR–205) and bail by the due date, the clerk must deliver or mail to the arresting officer's agency *Notice and Instructions to Arresting Officer* (form TR–210) and *Officer's Declaration* (form TR–235) with a copy of the *Notice to Appear* and a specified return date for receiving the officer's declaration. After receipt of the officer's declaration, or at the close of the officer's return date if no officer's declaration is filed, the clerk must submit the case file with all declarations and other evidence received to the court for decision.

(6) *Court decision*

After the court decides the case and returns the file and decision, the clerk must immediately deliver or mail the *Decision and Notice of Decision* (form TR–215) to the defendant and the arresting agency.

(7) *Trial de novo*

If the defendant files a *Request for New Trial (Trial de Novo)* (form TR–220) within 20 calendar days after the date of delivery or mailing of the *Decision and Notice of Decision* (form TR–215), the clerk must set a trial date within 45 calendar days of receipt of the defendant's written request for a new trial. The clerk must deliver or mail to the defendant and to the arresting officer's agency the *Order and Notice to Defendant of New Trial (Trial de Novo)* (form TR–225). If the defendant's request is not timely received, no new trial may be held and the case must be closed.

(8) *Case and time standard*

The clerk must deliver or mail the *Decision and Notice of Decision* (form TR–215) within 90 calendar days after the due date. Acts for which no specific time is stated in this rule must be performed promptly so that the *Decision and Notice of Decision* can be timely delivered or mailed by the clerk. Failure of the clerk or the court to comply with any time limit does not void or invalidate the decision of the court, unless prejudice to the defendant is shown.

(c) Due dates and time limits

Due dates and time limits must be as stated in this rule, unless changed or extended by the court. The court may extend any date, but the court need not state the reasons for granting or denying an extension on the record or in the minutes.

(d) Ineligible defendants

If the defendant requests a trial by written declaration and the clerk or the court determines that the defendant is not eligible for a trial by written declaration, the clerk must extend the due date 25 calendar days and notify the defendant by mail of the determination and due date.

(e) Noncompliance

If the defendant does not comply with this rule (including submitting the required bail amount, signing and filing all required forms, and complying with all time limits and due dates), the court may deny a trial by written declaration and may proceed as otherwise provided by statute and court rules.

(f) Evidence

Testimony and other relevant evidence may be introduced in the form of a *Notice to Appear* issued under Vehicle Code section 40500; a business record or receipt; a sworn declaration of the arresting officer; and, on behalf of the defendant, a sworn declaration of the defendant.

(g) Fines, assessments, or penalties

The statute and the rules do not prevent or preclude the court from imposing on a defendant who is found guilty any lawful fine, assessment, or other penalty, and the court is not limited to imposing money penalties in the bail amount, unless the bail amount is the maximum and the only lawful penalty.

(h) Additional forms and procedures

The clerk may approve and prescribe forms, time limits, and procedures that are not in conflict with or not inconsistent with the statute or this rule.

(i) Forms

The following forms are to be used to implement the procedures under this rule:

(1) *Instructions to Defendant* (form TR–200)

(2) *Request for Trial by Written Declaration* (form TR–205)

(3) *Notice and Instructions to Arresting Officer* (form TR–210)

(4) *Officer's Declaration* (form TR–235)

(5) *Decision and Notice of Decision* (form TR–215)

(6) *Request for New Trial (Trial de Novo)* (form TR–220)

(7) *Order and Notice to Defendant of New Trial (Trial de Novo)* (form TR–225)

(j) Local forms

A court may adopt additional forms as may be required to implement this rule and the court's local procedures not inconsistent with this rule. *(Formerly Rule 828, adopted, eff. Jan. 1, 1999. As amended, eff. Jan. 1, 2000; July 1, 2000. Renumbered Rule 4.210 and amended, eff. Jan. 1. 2007.)*

Research References

5 Witkin, California Criminal Law 4th Criminal Trial § 668 (2021), Minor Vehicle Offenses.

4 Witkin, California Criminal Law 4th Introduction to Criminal Procedure § 9 (2021), Rules of Court.

Rule 4.230. Additional requirements in capital cases

(a) Application

This rule applies only in trials in cases in which the death penalty may be imposed.

(b) Checklist

Within 10 days of counsel's first appearance in court, primary counsel for each defendant and the prosecution must each acknowledge that they have reviewed *Capital Case Attorney Trial Checklist* (form CR–605) by signing and submitting this form to the court. Counsel is encouraged to keep a copy of this checklist.

(c) Review of daily transcripts by counsel during trial

During trial, counsel must call the court's attention to any errors or omissions they may find in the daily transcripts. The court must periodically ask counsel for lists of any such errors or omissions and may hold hearings to verify them. Immaterial typographical errors that cannot conceivably cause confusion are not required to be brought to the court's attention.

(d) Lists of appearances, exhibits, motions, and jury instructions

(1) Primary counsel for each defendant and the prosecution must each prepare the lists identified in (A)–(D).

(A) A list of all appearances made by that party. *Capital Case Attorney List of Appearances* (form CR–601) must be used for this purpose. The list must include all appearances, including ex parte appearances, the date of each appearance, the department in which it was made, the name of counsel making the appearance, and a brief description of the nature of the appearance. A separate list of Penal Code section 987.9 appearances must be maintained under seal for each defendant. In the event of any substitution of attorney at any stage of the case, the relieved attorney must provide the list of all appearances to substituting counsel within five days of being relieved.

(B) A list of all exhibits offered by that party. *Capital Case Attorney List of Exhibits* (form CR–602) must be used for this purpose. The list must indicate whether the exhibit was admitted in evidence, refused, lodged, or withdrawn.

(C) A list of all motions made by that party, including ex parte motions. *Capital Case Attorney List of Motions* (form CR–603) must be used for this purpose.

(D) A list of all jury instructions submitted in writing by that party. *Capital Case Attorney List of Jury Instructions* (form CR–604) must be used for this purpose. The list must indicate whether the instruction was given, given as modified, refused, or withdrawn.

(2) No later than 21 days after the imposition of a sentence of death, counsel must submit the lists to the court and serve on all parties a copy of all the lists except the list of Penal Code section 987.9 appearances. Unless otherwise provided by local rule, the lists must be submitted to the court in electronic form.

(e) Electronic recordings presented or offered into evidence

Counsel must comply with the requirements of rule 2.1040 regarding electronic recordings presented or offered into evidence, including any such recordings that are part of a digital or electronic presentation.

(f) Copies of audio and visual aids

Primary counsel must provide the clerk with copies of any audio or visual aids not otherwise subject to the requirements of (e) that are used during jury selection or in presentations to the jury, including digital or electronic presentations. If a visual aid is oversized, a photograph of that visual aid must be provided in place of the original. For digital or electronic presentations, counsel must supply both a copy of the presentation in its native format and printouts showing the full text of each slide or image. Photographs and printouts provided under this subdivision must be on 8–1/2 by 11 inch paper. *(Adopted, eff. April 25, 2019.)*

Advisory Committee Comment

Subdivision (b). *Capital Case Attorney List of Appearances* (form CR–601), *Capital Case Attorney List of Exhibits* (form CR–602), *Capital Case Attorney List of Motions* (form CR–603), and *Capital Case Attorney List of Jury Instructions* (form CR–604) must be used to comply with the requirements in this subdivision.

Subdivision (d). To facilitate preparation of complete and accurate lists, counsel are encouraged to add items to the lists at the time appearances or motions are made, exhibits are offered, or jury instructions are submitted.

Research References

West's California Judicial Council Forms CR–600, Capital Case Attorney Pretrial Checklist (Criminal).

West's California Judicial Council Forms CR–601, Captal Case Attorney List of Appearances (Criminal).

West's California Judicial Council Forms CR–602, Capital Case Attorney List of Exhibits (Criminal).

West's California Judicial Council Forms CR–603, Capital Case Attorney List of Motions (Criminal).

West's California Judicial Council Forms CR–604, Capital Case Attorney List of Jury Instructions (Criminal).

West's California Judicial Council Forms CR–605, Capital Case Attorney Trial Checklist (Criminal).

6 Witkin, California Criminal Law 4th Criminal Appeal § 132 (2021), Complete Record in Capital Case.

6 Witkin, California Criminal Law 4th Criminal Appeal § 141 (2021), Special Requirements in Death Penalty Cases.

Division 4

SENTENCING

Rule 4.305. Notification of appeal rights in felony cases

After imposing sentence or making an order deemed to be a final judgment in a criminal case on conviction after trial, or after imposing sentence following a revocation of probation, except where the revocation is after the defendant's admission of violation of probation, the court must advise the defendant of his or her right to appeal, of the necessary steps and time for taking an appeal, and of the right of an indigent defendant to have counsel appointed by the reviewing court. *(Formerly Rule 250, adopted, eff. Jan. 1, 1972. As amended, eff. July 1, 1972; Jan. 1, 1977. Renumbered Rule 470 and amended, eff. Jan. 1, 1991. Renumbered Rule 4.305 and amended, eff. Jan. 1, 2001. As amended, eff. Jan. 1, 2007; Jan. 1, 2013.)*

Research References

6 Witkin, California Criminal Law 4th Criminal Appeal § 36 (2021), Nature of Rule.
6 Witkin, California Criminal Law 4th Criminal Appeal § 102 (2021), Changes in Rules.
6 Witkin, California Criminal Law 4th Criminal Appeal § 206 (2021), In General.
6 Witkin, California Criminal Law 4th Criminal Judgment § 154 (2021), Notification of Appeal Rights.

Rule 4.306. Notification of appeal rights in misdemeanor and infraction cases

After imposing sentence or making an order deemed to be a final judgment in a misdemeanor case on conviction after trial or following a revocation of probation, the court must orally or in writing advise a defendant not represented by counsel of the right to appeal, the time for filing a notice of appeal, and the right of an indigent defendant to have counsel appointed on appeal. This rule does not apply to infractions or when a revocation of probation is ordered after the defendant's admission of a violation of probation. *(Formerly Rule 535, adopted, eff. July 1, 1981. Renumbered Rule 4.306 and amended, eff. Jan. 1, 2001. As amended, eff. Jan. 1, 2007.)*

Research References

6 Witkin, California Criminal Law 4th Criminal Appeal § 102 (2021), Changes in Rules.
6 Witkin, California Criminal Law 4th Criminal Appeal § 206 (2021), In General.
6 Witkin, California Criminal Law 4th Criminal Judgment § 154 (2021), Notification of Appeal Rights.

Rule 4.310. Determination of presentence custody time credit

At the time of sentencing, the court must cause to be recorded on the judgment or commitment the total time in custody to be credited on the sentence under Penal Code sections 2900.5, 2933.1(c), and 2933.2(c). On referral of the defendant to the probation officer for an investigation and report under Penal Code section 1203(b) or 1203(g), or on setting a date for sentencing in the absence of a referral, the court must direct the sheriff, probation officer, or other appropriate person to report to the court and notify the defendant or defense counsel and prosecuting attorney within a reasonable time before the date set for sentencing as to the number of days that defendant has been in custody and for which he or she may be entitled to credit. Any challenges to the report must be heard at the time of sentencing. *(Formerly Rule 252, adopted, eff. Jan. 1, 1977. Renumbered Rule 472 and amended, eff. Jan. 1, 1991. Renumbered Rule 4.310, and amended, eff. Jan. 1, 2001. As amended, eff. July 1, 2004; Jan. 1, 2007.)*

Research References

3 Witkin, California Criminal Law 4th Punishment § 464 (2021), Credit for All Days of Custody.

Rule 4.315. Setting date for execution of death sentence

(a) Open session of court; notice required

A date for execution of a judgment of death under Penal Code section 1193 or 1227 must be set at a public session of the court at which the defendant and the People may be represented.

At least 10 days before the session of court at which the date will be set, the court must mail notice of the time and place of the proceeding by first-class mail, postage prepaid, to the Attorney General, the district attorney, the defendant at the prison address, the defendant's counsel or, if none is known, counsel who most recently represented the defendant on appeal or in postappeal legal proceedings, and the executive director of the California Appellate Project in San Francisco. The clerk must file a certificate of mailing copies of the notice. The court may not hold the proceeding or set an execution date unless the record contains a clerk's certificate showing that the notices required by this subdivision were timely mailed.

Unless otherwise provided by statute, the defendant does not have a right to be present in person.

(b) Selection of date; notice

If, at the announced session of court, the court sets a date for execution of the judgment of death, the court must mail certified copies of the order setting the date to the warden of the state prison and to the Governor, as required by statute; and must also, within five days of the making of the order, mail by first-class mail, postage prepaid, certified copies of the order setting the date to each of the persons required to be given notice by (a). The clerk must file a certificate of mailing copies of the order. *(Formerly Rule 490, adopted, eff. July 1, 1989. As amended, eff. July 1, 1990. Renumbered Rule 4.315, eff. Jan. 1, 2001. As amended, eff. Jan. 1, 2007.)*

Research References

6 Witkin, California Criminal Law 4th Criminal Judgment § 178 (2021), Order of Execution.

Rule 4.320. Records of criminal convictions (Gov. Code, §§ 69844.5, 71280.5)

(a) Information to be submitted

In addition to the information that the Department of Justice requires from courts under Penal Code section 13151, each trial court must also report, electronically or manually, the following information, in the form and manner specified by the Department of Justice:

(1) Whether the defendant was represented by counsel or waived the right to counsel; and

(2) In the case of a guilty or nolo contendere plea, whether:

(A) The defendant was advised of and understood the charges;

(B) The defendant was advised of, understood, and waived the right to a jury trial, the right to confront witnesses, and the privilege against self–incrimination; and

(C) The court found the plea was voluntary and intelligently made.

For purposes of this rule, a change of plea form signed by the defendant, defense counsel if the defendant was represented by counsel, and the judge, and filed with the court is a sufficient basis for the clerk or deputy clerk to report that the requirements of (2) have been met.

(b) Certification required

The reporting clerk or a deputy clerk must certify that the report submitted to the Department of Justice under Penal Code section 13151 and this rule is a correct abstract of the information contained in the court's records in the case. *(Formerly Rule 895, adopted, eff. July 1, 1998. Renumbered Rule 4.320 and amended, eff. Jan. 1, 2001. As amended, eff. Jan. 1, 2007.)*

Rule 4.325. Ignition interlock installation orders: "interest of justice" exceptions

If the court finds that the interest of justice requires an exception to the Vehicle Code sections 14601(e), 14601.1(d), 14601.4(c), or 14601.5(g) requirements for installation of an ignition interlock device under Vehicle Code section 23575, the reasons for the finding must be stated on the record. *(Formerly Rule 530, adopted, eff. Jan. 1, 1995. Renumbered Rule 4.325 and amended, eff. Jan. 1, 2001. As amended, eff. July 1, 2001.)*

Research References

2 Witkin, California Criminal Law 4th Crimes Against Public Peace and Welfare § 290 (2021), Ignition Interlock Device.

Rule 4.330. Misdemeanor hate crimes

(a) Application

This rule applies to misdemeanor cases where the defendant is convicted of either (1) a substantive hate crime under section 422.6 or (2) a misdemeanor violation and the facts of the crime constitute a hate crime under section 422.55.

(b) Sentencing consideration

In sentencing a defendant under (a), the court must consider the goals for hate crime sentencing stated in rule 4.427(e). *(Adopted, eff. Jan. 1, 2007.)*

Research References

4 Witkin, California Criminal Law 4th Introduction to Criminal Procedure § 9 (2021), Rules of Court.

Rule 4.335. Ability-to-pay determinations for infraction offenses

(a) Application

This rule applies to any infraction offense for which the defendant has received a written *Notice to Appear*.

(b) Required notice regarding an ability-to-pay determination

Courts must provide defendants with notice of their right to request an ability-to-pay determination and make available instructions or other materials for requesting an ability-to-pay determination.

(c) Procedure for determining ability to pay

(1) The court, on request of a defendant, must consider the defendant's ability to pay.

(2) A defendant may request an ability-to-pay determination at adjudication, or while the judgment remains unpaid, including when a case is delinquent or has been referred to a comprehensive collection program.

(3) The court must permit a defendant to make this request by written petition 6 unless the court directs a court appearance. The request must include any information or documentation the defendant wishes the court to consider in connection with the determination. The judicial officer has the discretion to conduct the review on the written record or to order a hearing.

(4) Based on the ability-to-pay determination, the court may exercise its discretion to:

(A) Provide for payment on an installment plan (if available);

(B) Allow the defendant to complete community service in lieu of paying the total fine (if available);

(C) Suspend the fine in whole or in part;

(D) Offer an alternative disposition.

(5) A defendant ordered to pay on an installment plan or to complete community service may request to have an ability-to-pay determination at any time during the pendency of the judgment.

(6) If a defendant has already had an ability-to-pay determination in the case, a defendant may request a subsequent ability-to-pay determination only based on changed circumstances. *(Adopted, eff. Jan. 1, 2017.)*

Advisory Committee Comment

Subdivision (b). This notice may be provided on the notice required by rule 4.107, the notice of any civil assessment under section 1214.1, a court's website, or any other notice provided to the defendant.

Subdivision(c)(1). In determining the defendant's ability to pay, the court should take into account factors including: (1) receipt of public benefits under Supplemental Security Income (SSI), State Supplementary Payment (SSP), California Work Opportunity and Responsibility to Kids (CalWORKS), Federal Tribal Temporary Assistance for Needy Families (Tribal TANF), Supplemental Nutrition Assistance Program, California Food Assistance Program, County Relief, General Relief (GR), General Assistance (GA), Cash Assistance Program for Aged, Blind, and Disabled Legal Immigrants (CAPI), In Home Supportive Services (IHSS), or Medi-Cal; and (2) a monthly income of 125 percent or less of the current poverty guidelines, updated periodically in the Federal Register by the U.S. Department of Health and Human Services under 42 U.S.C. § 9902(2).

Subdivision (c)(4). The amount and manner of paying the total fine must be reasonable and compatible with the defendant's financial ability. Even if the defendant has not demonstrated an inability to pay, the court may still exercise discretion. Regardless of whether the defendant has demonstrated an inability to pay, the court in exercising its discretion under this subdivision may consider the severity of the offense, among other factors. While the base fine may be suspended in whole or in part in the court's discretion, this subdivision is not intended to affect the imposition of any mandatory fees.

Research References

West's California Judicial Council Forms CR–320, Can't Afford to Pay Fine: Traffic and Other Infractions.
West's California Judicial Council Forms CR–321, Can't Afford to Pay Fine: Traffic and Other Infractions (Court Order).
West's California Judicial Council Forms TR–320, Can't Afford to Pay Fine: Traffic and Other Infractions.
West's California Judicial Council Forms TR–321, Can't Afford to Pay Fine: Traffic and Other Infractions (Court Order).
1 Witkin California Criminal Law 4th Introduction to Crimes § 86 (2021), In General.

Rule 4.336. Confidential Can't Afford to Pay Fine Forms

(a) Use of request and order forms

(1) A court uses the information on *Can't Afford to Pay Fine: Traffic and Other Infractions* (form TR–320/CR–320) to determine an infraction defendant's ability to pay under rule 4.335.

(2) A court may use *Can't Afford to Pay Fine: Traffic and Other Infractions (Court Order)* (form TR–321/CR–321) to issue an order in response to an infraction defendant's request for an ability-to-pay determination under rule 4.335.

(b) Confidential request form

Can't Afford to Pay Fine: Traffic and Other Infractions (form TR–320/CR–320), the information it contains, and any supporting documentation are confidential. The clerk's office must maintain the form and supporting documentation in a manner that will protect and preserve their confidentiality. Only the parties and the court may access the form and supporting documentation.

(c) Optional request and order forms

Can't Afford to Pay Fine: Traffic and Other Infractions (form TR–320/CR–320) and *Can't Afford to Pay Fine: Traffic and Other Infractions (Court Order)* (form TR–321/CR–321) are optional forms under rule 1.35. *(Adopted, eff. April 1, 2018.)*

Research References

1 Witkin California Criminal Law 4th Introduction to Crimes § 86 (2021), In General.

Division 5

FELONY SENTENCING LAW

Rule

Rule 4.401. Authority

The rules in this division are adopted under Penal Code section 1170.3 and under the authority granted to the Judicial Council by the Constitution, article VI, section 6, to adopt rules for court administration, practice, and procedure. *(Formerly Rule 401, adopted, eff. July 1, 1977. Renumbered Rule 4.401, eff. Jan. 1, 2001. As amended, eff. Jan. 1, 2007.)*

Research References

5 Witkin, California Criminal Law 4th Criminal Trial § 520 (2021), Upper Term Sentence Under Determinate Sentencing Law.

4 Witkin, California Criminal Law 4th Introduction to Criminal Procedure § 9 (2021), Rules of Court.

3 Witkin, California Criminal Law 4th Punishment § 313 (2021), In General.

Rule 4.403. Application

These rules apply to criminal cases in which the defendant is convicted of one or more offenses punishable as a felony by (1) a determinate sentence imposed under Penal Code part 2, title 7, chapter 4.5 (commencing with section 1170) and (2) an indeterminate sentence imposed under section 1168(b) only if it is imposed relative to other offenses with determinate terms or enhancements. *(Formerly Rule 403, adopted, eff. July 1, 1977. Renumbered Rule 4.403 and amended, eff. Jan. 1, 2001. As amended, eff. July 1, 2003; Jan. 1, 2007; Jan. 1, 2018.)*

Advisory Committee Comment

The operative portions of section 1170 deal exclusively with prison sentences; and the mandate to the Judicial Council in section 1170.3 is limited to criteria affecting the length of prison sentences, sentences in county jail under section 1170(h), and the grant or denial of probation.

Research References

3 Witkin, California Criminal Law 4th Punishment § 313 (2021), In General.

Rule 4.405. Definitions

As used in this division, unless the context otherwise requires:

(1) "These rules" means the rules in this division.

(2) "Base term" is the determinate or indeterminate sentence imposed for the commission of a crime, not including any enhancements that carry an additional term of imprisonment.~~determinate term in prison or county jail under section 1170(h) selected from among the three possible terms prescribed by statute; the determinate term in prison or county jail under section 1170(h) prescribed by statute if a range of three possible terms is not prescribed; or the indeterminate term in prison prescribed by statute.~~

(3) When a person is convicted of two or more felonies, the "principal term" is the greatest determinate term of imprisonment imposed by the court for any of the crimes, including any term imposed for applicable count-specific enhancements.

(4) When a person is convicted of two or more felonies, the "subordinate term" is the determinate term imposed for an offense, plus any count-specific enhancements applicable to the offense ordered to run consecutively to the principal term.

~~(3)~~(5) "Enhancement" means an additional term of imprisonment added to the base term.

(6) "Offense" means the offense of conviction unless a different meaning is specified or is otherwise clear from the context. The term "instant" or "current" is used in connection with "offense" or "offense of conviction" to distinguish the violation for which the defendant is being sentenced from an enhancement, prior or subsequent offense, or from an offense before another court.

~~(4)~~(7) "Aggravation," or "circumstances in aggravation" ~~"mitigation," or "circumstances in mitigation"~~means factors that justify the imposition of the upper prison term referred to in ~~Penal Code~~ section 1170(b) and 1170.1, or factors that the court may consider in exercising discretion authorized by statute and under these rules including imposing the middle term instead of a low term, denying probation, ordering consecutive sentences, or determining whether to exercise discretion pursuant to section 1385(c).~~that the court may consider in its broad sentencing discretion authorized by statute and under these rules.~~

(8) "Mitigation" or "circumstances in mitigation" means factors that the court may consider in its broad sentencing discretion authorized by statute and under these rules.

~~(5)~~(9) "Sentence choice" means the selection of any disposition of the case that does not amount to a dismissal, acquittal, or grant of a new trial.

~~(6)~~(10) "Section" means a section of the Penal Code.

~~(7)~~(11) "Imprisonment" means confinement in a state prison or county jail under section 1170(h).

~~(8)~~(12) "Charged" means charged in the indictment or information.

~~(9)~~(13) "Found" means admitted by the defendant or found to be true by the trier of fact upon trial.

~~(10)~~(14) "Mandatory supervision" means the period of supervision defined in section 1170(h)(5)(A), (B).

~~(11)~~(15) "Postrelease community supervision" means the period of supervision governed by section 3451 et seq.

~~(12)~~(16) "Risk/needs assessment" means a standardized, validated evaluation tool designed to measure an offender's actuarial risk factors and specific needs that, if successfully addressed, may reduce the likelihood of future criminal activity.

~~(13)~~(17) "Evidence-based practices" means supervision policies, procedures, programs, and practices demonstrated by scientific research to reduce recidivism among individuals under probation, parole, or postrelease supervision.

~~(14)~~(18) "Community-based corrections program" means a program consisting of a system of services for felony offenders under local supervision dedicated to the goals stated in section 1229(c)(1)–(5).

~~(15)~~(19) "Local supervision" means the supervision of an adult felony offender on probation, mandatory supervision, or postrelease community supervision.

~~(16)~~(20) "County jail" means local county correctional facility. *(Formerly Rule 405, adopted, eff. July 1, 1977. As amended, eff. July 28, 1977; Jan. 1, 1991. Renumbered Rule 4.405, eff. Jan. 1, 2001. As amended, eff. July 1, 2003; Jan. 1, 2007; May 23, 2007; Jan. 1, 2017; Jan. 1, 2018; March 14, 2022.)*

Advisory Committee Comment

The Legislature amended the determinate sentencing law to require courts to order imposition of a sentence or enhancement not to exceed the middle term unless factors in aggravation justify imposition of the upper term and are stipulated to by the defendant or found true beyond a reasonable doubt at trial by the jury or by the judge in a court trial. (See Sen. Bill 567; Stats. 2021, ch. 731.) However, in determining whether to impose the upper term for a criminal offense, the court may consider as an aggravating factor that a defendant has suffered one or more prior convictions, based on certified records of conviction. This exception may not be used to select the upper term of an enhancement.

The court may exercise its judicial discretion in imposing the middle term or low term and must state the facts and reasons on the record for choosing the sentence imposed. In exercising this discretion between the middle term and the low term, the court may rely on aggravating factors that have not been stipulated to by the defendant or proven beyond a reasonable doubt. (*People v. Black* (2007) 41 Cal.4th 799.)

The Legislature also amended the determinate sentencing law to require courts to order imposition of the low term when the court finds that certain factors contributed to the commission of the crime unless the court finds that it would not be in the interests of justice to do so because the aggravating factors outweigh the mitigating factors. (Pen. Code, § 1170(b)(6).)

Research References

5 Witkin, California Criminal Law 4th Criminal Trial § 533 (2021), Sandoval Case.
1 Witkin California Criminal Law 4th Introduction to Crimes § 28 (2021), Revised Sentencing Procedure.
3 Witkin, California Criminal Law 4th Punishment § 313 (2021), In General.
3 Witkin, California Criminal Law 4th Punishment § 317 (2021), In General.
3 Witkin, California Criminal Law 4th Punishment § 323 (2021), In General.
3 Witkin, California Criminal Law 4th Punishment § 333 (2021), In General.
3 Witkin, California Criminal Law 4th Punishment § 339 (2021), In General.
3 Witkin, California Criminal Law 4th Punishment § 344 (2021), Nature and Scope.
3 Witkin, California Criminal Law 4th Punishment § 384 (2021), In General.
3 Witkin, California Criminal Law 4th Punishment § 623 (2021), Unusual Circumstances Justifying Probation.

Rule 4.406. Reasons

(a) How given

If the sentencing judge is required to give reasons for a sentence choice, the judge must state in simple language the primary factor or factors that support the exercise of discretion. The statement need not be in the language of the statute or these rules. It must be delivered orally on the record. The court may give a single statement explaining the reason or reasons for imposing a particular sentence or the exercise of judicial discretion, if the statement identifies the sentencing choices where discretion is exercised and there is no impermissible dual use of facts.

(b) When reasons required

Sentence choices that generally require a statement of a reason include, but are not limited to:

(1) Granting probation when the defendant is presumptively ineligible for probation;

(2) Denying probation when the defendant is presumptively eligible for probation;

~~(3) Declining to commit an eligible juvenile found amenable to treatment to the Department of Corrections and Rehabilitation, Division of Juvenile Justice;~~

~~(4)~~(3) Selecting a term for either an offense or an enhancemen~~t one of the three authorized terms in prison or county jail under section 1170(h) referred to in section 1170(b) for either a base term or an enhancement~~;

~~(5)~~(4) Imposing consecutive sentences;

~~(6)~~(5) Imposing full consecutive sentences under section 667.6(c) rather than consecutive terms under section 1170.1(a), when the court has that choice;

~~(7)~~(6) Waiving a restitution fine;

~~(8)~~(7) Granting relief under section 1385; and

~~(9)~~(8) Denying mandatory supervision in the interests of justice under section 1170(h)(5)(A). *(Formerly Rule 406, adopted, eff. Jan. 1, 1991. Renumbered Rule 4.406 and amended, eff. Jan. 1, 2001. As amended, eff. July 1, 2003; Jan. 1, 2006; Jan. 1, 2007; May 23, 2007; Jan. 1, 2017; Jan. 1, 2018; March 14, 2022.)*

Advisory Committee Comment

This rule is not intended to expand the statutory requirements for giving reasons, and is not an independent interpretation of the statutory requirements.

The court is not required to separately state the reasons for making each sentencing choice so long as the record reflects the court understood it had discretion on a particular issue and its reasons for making the particular choice. For example, if the court decides to deny probation and impose the upper term of punishment, the court may simply state: "I am denying probation and imposing the upper term because of the extensive losses to the victim and because the defendant's record is increasing in seriousness." It is not necessary to state a reason after exercising each decision.

The court must be mindful of impermissible dual use of facts in stating reasons for sentencing choices. For example, the court is not permitted to use a reason to impose a greater term if that reason also is either (1) the same as an enhancement that will be imposed, or (2) an element of the crime. The court should not use the same reason to impose a consecutive sentence and to impose an upper term of imprisonment. (*People v. Avalos* (1984) 37 Cal.3d 216, 233.) It is not improper to use the same reason to deny probation and to impose the upper term. (*People v. Bowen* (1992) 11 Cal.App.4th 102, 106.)

Whenever relief is granted under section 1385, the court's reasons for exercising that discretion must be stated orally on the record and entered in the minutes if requested by a party or if the proceedings are not recorded electronically or reported by a court reporter. (Pen. Code, § 1385(a).) Although no legal authority requires the court to state reasons for denying relief, such a statement may be helpful in the appellate review of the exercise of the court's discretion.

Research References

2 Witkin, California Criminal Law 4th Crimes Against Public Peace and Welfare § 178 (2021), Discretion of Court in Felony Cases.
3 Witkin, California Criminal Law 4th Punishment § 339 (2021), In General.
3 Witkin, California Criminal Law 4th Punishment § 341 (2021), When Statement is Required.
3 Witkin, California Criminal Law 4th Punishment § 343 (2021), Adequacy of Statement.

Rule 4.408. Listing of factors not exclusive; sequence not significant

(a) The listing of factors in these rules for making discretionary sentencing decisions is not exhaustive and does not prohibit a trial judge from using additional criteria reasonably related to the decision being made. Any such additional criteria must be stated on the record by the sentencing judge.

(b) The order in which criteria are listed does not indicate their relative weight or importance. *(Formerly Rule 408, adopted, eff. July 1, 1977. Renumbered Rule 4.408, eff. Jan. 1, 2001. As amended, eff. Jan. 1, 2007; Jan. 1, 2018.)*

Advisory Committee Comment

The variety of circumstances presented in felony cases is so great that no listing of criteria could claim to be all-inclusive. (Cf., Evid. Code, § 351.)

The court may impose a sentence or enhancement exceeding the middle term only if the facts underlying the aggravating factor were stipulated to by the defendant or found true beyond a reasonable doubt at trial by the jury or by the judge in a court trial. (Pen. Code, § 1170(b)(2).)

However, in determining whether to impose the upper term for a criminal offense, the court may consider as an aggravating factor that a defendant has suffered one or more prior convictions, based on certified records of conviction. This exception may not be used to select the upper term of an enhancement. (Pen. Code, § 1170(b)(3).)

The Legislature also amended the determinate sentencing law to require courts to order imposition of the low term when the court finds that certain factors contributed to the commission of the crime unless the court finds that it would not be in the interests of justice to do so because the aggravating factors outweigh the mitigating factors. (Pen. Code, § 1170(b)(6).)

Research References

3 Witkin, California Criminal Law 4th Punishment § 315 (2021), Sentencing Proceeding.
3 Witkin, California Criminal Law 4th Punishment § 323 (2021), In General.
3 Witkin, California Criminal Law 4th Punishment § 333 (2021), In General.
3 Witkin, California Criminal Law 4th Punishment § 341 (2021), When Statement is Required.
3 Witkin, California Criminal Law 4th Punishment § 385 (2021), Criteria for Decision.
3 Witkin, California Criminal Law 4th Punishment § 457 (2021), Discretion of Trial Judge.

Rule 4.409. Consideration of relevant factors

Relevant factors enumerated in these rules must be considered by the sentencing judge, and will be deemed to have been considered unless the record affirmatively reflects otherwise. *(Formerly Rule 409, adopted, eff. July 1, 1977. Renumbered Rule 4.409, eff. Jan. 1, 2001. As amended, eff. Jan. 1, 2007; Jan. 1, 2018.)*

Advisory Committee Comment

Relevant factors are those applicable to the facts in the record of the case; not all factors will be relevant to each case. The judge's duty is similar to the duty to consider the probation officer's report. Section 1203.

In deeming the sentencing judge to have considered relevant factors, the rule applies the presumption of Evidence Code section 664 that official duty has been regularly performed. (See *People v. Moran* (1970) 1 Cal.3d 755, 762 [trial court presumed to have considered referring eligible defendant to California Youth Authority in absence of any showing to the contrary, citing Evidence Code section 664].)

Research References

3 Witkin, California Criminal Law 4th Punishment § 333 (2021), In General.

Rule 4.410. General objectives in sentencing

(a) General objectives of sentencing include:

(1) Protecting society;

(2) Punishing the defendant;

(3) Encouraging the defendant to lead a law-abiding life in the future and deterring him or her from future offenses;

(4) Deterring others from criminal conduct by demonstrating its consequences;

(5) Preventing the defendant from committing new crimes by isolating him or her for the period of incarceration;

(6) Securing restitution for the victims of crime;

(7) Achieving uniformity in sentencing; and

(8) Increasing public safety by reducing recidivism through community-based corrections programs and evidence-based practices.

(b) Because in some instances these objectives may suggest inconsistent dispositions, the sentencing judge must consider which objectives are of primary importance in the particular case. The sentencing judge should be guided by statutory statements of policy, the criteria in these rules, and any other facts and circumstances relevant to the case. *(Formerly Rule 410, adopted, eff. July 1, 1977. Renumbered Rule 4.410, eff. Jan. 1, 2001. As amended, eff. July 1, 2003; Jan. 1, 2007; Jan. 1, 2017; Jan. 1, 2018.)*

Advisory Committee Comment

Statutory expressions of policy include:

Section 1170(a)(1), which expresses the policies of uniformity, proportionality of terms of imprisonment to the seriousness of the offense, and the use of imprisonment as punishment. It also states that "the purpose of sentencing is public safety achieved through punishment, rehabilitation, and restorative justice."

Sections 17.5, 1228, and 3450, which express the policies promoting reinvestment of criminal justice resources to support community-based corrections programs and evidence-based practices to improve public safety through a reduction in recidivism.

Research References

3 Witkin, California Criminal Law 4th Punishment § 313 (2021), In General.
3 Witkin, California Criminal Law 4th Punishment § 359 (2021), P.C. 12022.53: Personal Use of Firearm in Specified Felonies.
3 Witkin, California Criminal Law 4th Punishment § 412 (2021), Procedure.

Rule 4.411. Presentence investigations and reports

(a) When required

As provided in subdivision (b), the court must refer the case to the probation officer for:

(1) A presentence investigation and report if the defendant:

(A) Is statutorily eligible for probation or a term of imprisonment in county jail under section 1170(h); or

(B) Is not eligible for probation but a report is needed to assist the court with other sentencing issues, including the determination of the proper amount of restitution fine;

(2) A supplemental report if a significant period of time has passed since the original report was prepared.

(b) Waiver of the investigation and report

The parties may stipulate to the waiver of the probation officer's investigation and report in writing or in open court and entered in the minutes, and with the consent of the court. In deciding whether to consent to the waiver, the court should consider whether the information in the report would assist in the resolution of any current or future sentencing issues, or would assist in the effective supervision of the person. A waiver under this section does not affect the requirement under section 1203c that a probation report be created when the court commits a person to state prison. *(Formerly Rule 418, adopted, eff. July 1, 1977. Renumbered Rule 411 and amended, eff. Jan. 1, 1991. Renumbered Rule 4.411, eff. Jan. 1, 2001. As amended, eff. Jan. 1, 2006; Jan. 1, 2007; Jan. 1, 2015; Jan. 1, 2018.)*

Advisory Committee Comment

Section 1203 requires a presentence report in every felony case in which the defendant is eligible for probation. Subdivision (a) requires a presentence report in every felony case in which the defendant is eligible for a term of imprisonment in county jail under section 1170(h).

When considering whether to waive a presentence investigation and report, courts should consider that probation officers' reports are used by (1) courts in determining the appropriate term of imprisonment in prison or county jail under section 1170(h); (2) courts in deciding whether probation is appropriate, whether a period of mandatory supervision should be denied in the interests of justice under section 1170(h)(5)(A), and the appropriate length and conditions of probation and mandatory supervision; (3) the probation department in supervising the defendant; and (4) the Department of Corrections and Rehabilitation, Division of Adult Operations, in deciding on the type of facility and program in which to place a defendant.

Subdivision (a)(2) is based on case law that generally requires a supplemental report if the defendant is to be resentenced a significant time after the original sentencing, as, for example, after a remand by an appellate court, or after the apprehension of a defendant who failed to appear at sentencing. The rule is not intended to expand on the requirements of those cases.

The rule does not require a new investigation and report if a recent report is available and can be incorporated by reference and there is no indication of changed circumstances. This is particularly true if a report is needed only for the Department of Corrections and Rehabilitation because the defendant has waived a report and agreed to a prison sentence. If a full report was prepared in another case in the same or another jurisdiction within the preceding six months, during which time the defendant was in custody, and that report is available to the Department of Corrections and Rehabilitation, it is unlikely that a new investigation is needed.

This rule does not prohibit pre-conviction, pre-plea reports as authorized by section 1203.7.

Research References

3 Witkin, California Criminal Law 4th Punishment § 627 (2021), Waiver.
3 Witkin, California Criminal Law 4th Punishment § 629 (2021), Effect of Defendant's Ineligibility.
3 Witkin, California Criminal Law 4th Punishment § 630 (2021), In General.

Rule 4.411.5. Probation officer's presentence investigation report

(a) Contents

A probation officer's presentence investigation report in a felony case must include at least the following:

(1) A face sheet showing at least:

(A) The defendant's name and other identifying data;

(B) The case number;

(C) The crime of which the defendant was convicted, and any enhancements which were admitted or found true;

(D) Any factors in aggravation including whether the factors were stipulated to by the defendant, found true beyond a reasonable doubt at trial by a jury, or found true beyond a reasonable doubt by a judge in a court trial;

~~(D)~~(E) The date of commission of the crime, the date of conviction, and any other dates relevant to sentencing;

~~(E)~~(F) The defendant's custody status; and

~~(F)~~(G) The terms of any agreement on which a plea of guilty was based.

(2) The facts and circumstances of the crime and the defendant's arrest, including information concerning any co-defendants and the status or disposition of their cases. The source of all such information must be stated.

(3) A summary of the defendant's record of prior criminal conduct, including convictions as an adult and sustained petitions in juvenile delinquency proceedings. Records of an arrest or charge not leading to a conviction or the sustaining of a petition may not be included unless supported by facts concerning the arrest or charge.

(4) Any statement made by the defendant to the probation officer, or a summary thereof, including the defendant's account of the circumstances of the crime.

(5) Information concerning the victim of the crime, including:

(A) The victim's statement or a summary thereof, if available;

(B) Any physical or psychological injuries suffered by the victim;

(C) The amount of the victim's monetary loss, and whether or not it is covered by insurance; and

(D) Any information required by law.

(6) Any relevant facts concerning the defendant's social history, including those categories enumerated in section 1203.10, organized under appropriate subheadings, including, whenever applicable, "Family," "Education," "Employment and income," "Military," "Medical/psychological," "Record of substance abuse or lack thereof," and any other relevant subheadings. This includes:

(A) ~~f~~Facts relevant to whether the defendant may be suffering from sexual trauma, traumatic brain injury, posttraumatic stress disorder, substance abuse, or mental health problems as a result of his or her U.S. military service; and

(B) Factors listed in section 1170(b)(6) and whether the current offense is connected to those factors.

(7) Collateral information, including written statements from:

(A) Official sources such as defense and prosecuting attorneys, police (subsequent to any police reports used to summarize the crime), probation and parole officers who have had prior experience with the defendant, and correctional personnel who observed the defendant's behavior during any period of presentence incarceration; and

(B) Interested persons, including family members and others who have written letters concerning the defendant.

(8) The defendant's relevant risk factors and needs as identified by a risk/needs assessment, if such an assessment is performed, and such other information from the assessment as may be requested by the court.

(9) An evaluation of factors relating to disposition. This section must include:

(A) A reasoned discussion of the defendant's suitability and eligibility for probation, and, if probation is recommended, a proposed plan including recommendations for the conditions of probation and any special need for supervision;

(B) If a prison sentence or term of imprisonment in county jail under section 1170(h) is recommended or is likely to be imposed, a reasoned discussion of aggravating and mitigating factors affecting the sentence length;

(C) If denial of a period of mandatory supervision in the interests of justice is recommended, a reasoned discussion of the factors prescribed by rule 4.415(b);

(D) If a term of imprisonment in county jail under section 1170(h) is recommended, a reasoned discussion of the defendant's suitability for specific terms and length of period of mandatory supervision, including the factors prescribed by rule 4.415(c); and

(E) A reasoned discussion of the defendant's ability to make restitution, pay any fine or penalty that may be recommended, or satisfy any special conditions of probation that are proposed.

Discussions of factors (A) through (D) must refer to any sentencing rule directly relevant to the facts of the case, but no rule may be cited without a reasoned discussion of its relevance and relative importance.

(10) Any mitigating factors pursuant to section 1385(c).

~~(10)~~(11) The probation officer's recommendation. When requested by the sentencing judge or by standing instructions to the probation department, the report must include recommendations concerning the length of any prison or county jail term under section 1170(h) that may be imposed, including the base term, the imposition of concurrent or consecutive sentences, and the imposition or striking of the additional terms for enhancements charged and found.

~~(11)~~(12) Detailed information on presentence time spent by the defendant in custody, including the beginning and ending dates of the period or periods of custody; the existence of any other sentences imposed on the defendant during the period of custody; the amount of good behavior, work, or participation credit to which the defendant is entitled; and whether the sheriff or other officer holding custody, the prosecution, or the defense wishes that a hearing be held for the purposes of denying good behavior, work, or participation credit.

~~(12)~~(13) A statement of mandatory and recommended restitution, restitution fines, and other fines, fees, assessments, penalties, and costs to be assessed against the defendant; ~~including chargeable probation services and attorney fees under section 987.8 when appropriate, findings concerning the defendant's ability to pay, and~~a recommendation whether any restitution order should become a judgment under section 1203(j) if unpaid~~.~~; and, when appropriate, any finding concerning the defendant's ability to pay.

(14) Information pursuant to section 29810(c):

(A) Whether the defendant has properly complied with Penal Code section 29810 by relinquishing firearms identified by the probation officer's investigation or declared by the defendant on the Prohibited Persons Relinquishment Form, and

(B) Whether the defendant has timely submitted a completed Prohibited Persons Relinquishment Form.

(b) Format

The report must be on paper 8–½ by 11 inches in size and must follow the sequence set out in (a) to the extent possible.

(c) Sources

The source of all information must be stated. Any person who has furnished information included in the report must be identified by name or official capacity unless a reason is given for not disclosing the person's identity. *(Formerly Rule 419, adopted, eff. July 1, 1981. Renumbered Rule 411.5 and amended eff. Jan. 1, 1991. Renumbered Rule 4.411.5, eff. Jan. 1, 2001. As amended, eff. July 1, 2003; Jan. 1, 2007; Jan. 1, 2015; Jan. 1, 2017; Jan. 1, 2018; March 14, 2022.)*

Research References

3 Witkin, California Criminal Law 4th Punishment § 631 (2021), Required Contents.

3 Witkin, California Criminal Law 4th Punishment § 632 (2021), Improper Contents.

Rule 4.412. Reasons—agreement to punishment as an adequate reason and as abandonment of certain claims

(a) Defendant's agreement as reason

It is an adequate reason for a sentence or other disposition that the defendant, personally and by counsel, has expressed agreement that it be imposed and the prosecuting attorney has not expressed an objection to it. The agreement and lack of objection must be recited on the record. This section does not authorize a sentence that is not otherwise authorized by law.

(b) Agreement to sentence abandons section 654 claim

By agreeing to a specified term in prison or county jail under section 1170(h) personally and by counsel, a defendant who is sentenced to that term or a shorter one abandons any claim that a component of the sentence violates section 654's prohibition of double punishment, unless that claim is asserted at the time the agreement is recited on the record. *(Formerly Rule 412, adopted, eff. Jan. 1, 1991. Renumbered Rule 4.412 and amended, eff. Jan. 1, 2001. As amended, eff. Jan. 1, 2007; Jan. 1, 2017.)*

Advisory Committee Comment

Subdivision (a). This subdivision is intended to relieve the court of an obligation to give reasons if the sentence or other disposition is one that the defendant has accepted and to which the prosecutor expresses no objection. The judge may choose to give reasons for the sentence even though not obligated to do so.

Judges should also be aware that there may be statutory limitations on "plea bargaining" or on the entry of a guilty plea on the condition that no more than a particular sentence will be imposed. Such limitations appear, for example, in sections 1192.5 and 1192.7.

Subdivision (b). This subdivision is based on the fact that a defendant who, with the advice of counsel, expresses agreement to a specified term of imprisonment normally is acknowledging that the term is appropriate for his or her total course of conduct. This subdivision applies to both determinate and indeterminate terms.

Research References

3 Witkin, California Criminal Law 4th Punishment § 270 (2021), Where Defendant Agrees to Sentence.

3 Witkin, California Criminal Law 4th Punishment § 343 (2021), Adequacy of Statement.

Rule 4.413. Grant of probation when defendant is presumptively ineligible for probation

(a) Consideration of eligibility

The court must determine whether the defendant is eligible for probation. In most cases, the defendant is presumptively eligible for probation; in some cases, the defendant is presumptively ineligible; and in some cases, probation is not allowed.

(b) Probation in cases when defendant is presumptively ineligible

If the defendant comes under a statutory provision prohibiting probation "except in unusual cases where the interests of justice would best be served," or a substantially equivalent provision, the court should apply the criteria in (c) to evaluate whether the statutory limitation on probation is overcome; and if it is, the court should then apply the criteria in rule 4.414 to decide whether to grant probation.

(c) Factors overcoming the presumption of ineligibility

The following factors may indicate the existence of an unusual case in which probation may be granted if otherwise appropriate:

(1) *Factors relating to basis for limitation on probation*

A factor or circumstance indicating that the basis for the statutory limitation on probation, although technically present, is not fully applicable to the case, including:

(A) The factor or circumstance giving rise to the limitation on probation is, in this case, substantially less serious than the circumstances typically present in other cases involving the same probation limitation, and the defendant has no recent record of committing similar crimes or crimes of violence; and

(B) The current offense is less serious than a prior felony conviction that is the cause of the limitation on probation, and the defendant has been free from incarceration and serious violation of the law for a substantial time before the current offense.

(2) *Factors limiting defendant's culpability*

A factor or circumstance not amounting to a defense, but reducing the defendant's culpability for the offense, including:

(A) The defendant participated in the crime under circumstances of great provocation, coercion, or duress not amounting to a defense, and the defendant has no recent record of committing crimes of violence;

(B) The crime was committed because of a mental condition not amounting to a defense, and there is a high likelihood that the defendant would respond favorably to mental health care and treatment that would be required as a condition of probation; and

(C) The defendant is youthful or aged, and has no significant record of prior criminal offenses.

(3) Results of risk/needs assessment

Along with all other relevant information in the case, the court may consider the results of a risk/needs assessment of the defendant, if one was performed. The weight of a risk/needs assessment is for the court to consider in its sentencing discretion. *(Formerly Rule 413, adopted, eff. Jan. 1, 1991. Renumbered Rule 4.413, eff. Jan. 1, 2001. As amended, eff. July 1, 2003; Jan. 1, 2007; Jan. 1, 2018.)*

Advisory Committee Comment

Subdivision (c)(3). Standard 4.35 of the California Standards of Judicial Administration provides courts with additional guidance on using the results of a risk/needs assessment at sentencing.

Research References

3 Witkin, California Criminal Law 4th Punishment § 621 (2021), P.C. 1203.
3 Witkin, California Criminal Law 4th Punishment § 623 (2021), Unusual Circumstances Justifying Probation.
3 Witkin, California Criminal Law 4th Punishment § 624 (2021), Procedure.

Rule 4.414. Criteria affecting probation

Criteria affecting the decision to grant or deny probation include facts relating to the crime and facts relating to the defendant.

(a) Facts relating to the crime

Facts relating to the crime include:

(1) The nature, seriousness, and circumstances of the crime as compared to other instances of the same crime;

(2) Whether the defendant was armed with or used a weapon;

(3) The vulnerability of the victim;

(4) Whether the defendant inflicted physical or emotional injury;

(5) The degree of monetary loss to the victim;

(6) Whether the defendant was an active or a passive participant;

(7) Whether the crime was committed because of an unusual circumstance, such as great provocation, which is unlikely to recur;

(8) Whether the manner in which the crime was carried out demonstrated criminal sophistication or professionalism on the part of the defendant; and

(9) Whether the defendant took advantage of a position of trust or confidence to commit the crime.

(b) Facts relating to the defendant

Facts relating to the defendant include:

(1) Prior record of criminal conduct, whether as an adult or a juvenile, including the recency and frequency of prior crimes; and whether the prior record indicates a pattern of regular or increasingly serious criminal conduct;

(2) Prior performance and present status on probation, mandatory supervision, postrelease community supervision, or parole;

(3) Willingness to comply with the terms of probation;

(4) Ability to comply with reasonable terms of probation as indicated by the defendant's age, education, health, mental faculties, history of alcohol or other substance abuse, family background and ties, employment and military service history, and other relevant factors;

(5) The likely effect of imprisonment on the defendant and his or her dependents;

(6) The adverse collateral consequences on the defendant's life resulting from the felony conviction;

(7) Whether the defendant is remorseful; and

(8) The likelihood that if not imprisoned the defendant will be a danger to others.

(c) Suitability for probation

In determining the suitability of the defendant for probation, the court may consider factors in aggravation and mitigation, whether or not the factors have been stipulated to by the defendant or found true beyond a reasonable doubt at trial by a jury or the judge in a court trial. *(Formerly Rule 414, adopted, eff. July 1, 1977. As amended, eff. Jan. 1, 1991. Renumbered Rule 4.414, eff. Jan. 1, 2001. As amended, eff. July 1, 2003; Jan. 1, 2007; Jan. 1, 2017; March 14, 2022.)*

Advisory Committee Comment

The sentencing judge's discretion to grant probation is unaffected by the Uniform Determinate Sentencing Act (section 1170(a)(3)).

The decision whether to grant probation is normally based on an overall evaluation of the likelihood that the defendant will live successfully in the general community. Each criterion points to evidence that the likelihood of success is great or small. A single criterion will rarely be determinative; in most cases, the sentencing judge will have to balance favorable and unfavorable facts.

Under criteria (b)(3) and (b)(4), it is appropriate to consider the defendant's expressions of willingness to comply and his or her apparent sincerity, and whether the defendant's home and work environment and primary associates will be supportive of the defendant's efforts to comply with the terms of probation, among other factors.

Research References

3 Witkin, California Criminal Law 4th Punishment § 601 (2021), Nature and Purpose.
3 Witkin, California Criminal Law 4th Punishment § 639 (2021), Criteria Affecting Grant or Denial of Probation.

Rule 4.415. Criteria affecting the imposition of mandatory supervision

(a) Presumption

Except where the defendant is statutorily ineligible for suspension of any part of the sentence, when imposing a term of imprisonment in county jail under section 1170(h), the court must suspend execution of a concluding portion of the term to be served as a period of mandatory supervision unless the court finds, in the interests of justice, that mandatory supervision is not appropriate in a particular case. Because section 1170(h)(5)(A) establishes a statutory presumption in favor of the imposition of a period of mandatory supervision in all applicable cases, denials of a period of mandatory supervision should be limited.

(b) Criteria for denying mandatory supervision in the interests of justice

In determining that mandatory supervision is not appropriate in the interests of justice under section 1170(h)(5)(A), the court's determination must be based on factors that are specific to a particular case or defendant. Factors the court may consider include:

(1) Consideration of the balance of custody exposure available after imposition of presentence custody credits;

(2) The defendant's present status on probation, mandatory supervision, postrelease community supervision, or parole;

(3) Specific factors related to the defendant that indicate a lack of need for treatment or supervision upon release from custody; and

(4) Whether the nature, seriousness, or circumstances of the case or the defendant's past performance on supervision substantially outweigh the benefits of supervision in promoting public safety and the defendant's successful reentry into the community upon release from custody.

(c) Criteria affecting conditions and length of mandatory supervision

In exercising discretion to select the appropriate period and conditions of mandatory supervision, factors the court may consider include:

(1) Availability of appropriate community corrections programs;

(2) Victim restitution, including any conditions or period of supervision necessary to promote the collection of any court-ordered restitution;

(3) Consideration of length and conditions of supervision to promote the successful reintegration of the defendant into the community upon release from custody;

(4) Public safety, including protection of any victims and witnesses;

(5) Past performance and present status on probation, mandatory supervision, postrelease community supervision, and parole;

(6) The balance of custody exposure after imposition of presentence custody credits;

(7) Consideration of the statutory accrual of post-sentence custody credits for mandatory supervision under section 1170(h)(5)(B) and sentences served in county jail under section 4019(a)(6);

(8) The defendant's specific needs and risk factors identified by a risk/needs assessment, if available; and

(9) The likely effect of extended imprisonment on the defendant and any dependents.

(d) Statement of reasons for denial of mandatory supervision

Notwithstanding rule 4.412(a), when a court denies a period of mandatory supervision in the interests of justice, the court must state the reasons for the denial on the record. *(Adopted, eff. Jan. 1, 2015. As amended, eff. Jan. 1, 2017; Jan. 1, 2018.)*

Advisory Committee Comment

Penal Code section 1170.3 requires the Judicial Council to adopt rules of court that prescribe criteria for the consideration of the court at the time of sentencing regarding the court's decision to "[d]eny a period of mandatory supervision in the interests of justice under paragraph (5) of subdivision (h) of Section 1170 or determine the appropriate period of and conditions of mandatory supervision."

Subdivision (a). Penal Code section 1170(h)(5)(A): "Unless the court finds, in the interests of justice, that it is not appropriate in a particular case, the court, when imposing a sentence pursuant to paragraph (1) or (2) of this subdivision, shall suspend execution of a concluding portion of the term for a period selected at the court's discretion." Under *People v. Borynack* (2015) 238 Cal.App.4th 958, review denied, courts may not impose mandatory supervision when the defendant is statutorily ineligible for a suspension of part of the sentence.

Subdivisions (b)(3), (b)(4), and (c)(3). The Legislature has declared that "[s]trategies supporting reentering offenders through practices and programs, such as standardized risk and needs assessments, transitional community housing, treatment, medical and mental health services, and employment, have been demonstrated to significantly reduce recidivism among offenders in other states." (Pen. Code, § 17.7(a).)

Subdivision (c)(7). Under Penal Code section 1170(h)(5)(B), defendants serving a period of mandatory supervision are entitled to day-for-day credits: "During the period when the defendant is under such supervision, unless in actual custody related to the sentence imposed by the court, the defendant shall be entitled to only actual time credit against the term of imprisonment imposed by the court." In contrast, defendants serving terms of imprisonment in county jails under Penal Code section 1170(h) are entitled to conduct credits under Penal Code section 4019(a)(6).

Subdivision (c)(8). Standard 4.35 of the California Standards of Judicial Administration provides courts with additional guidance on using the results of a risk/needs assessment at sentencing.

Research References

3 Witkin, California Criminal Law 4th Punishment § 310 (2021), County Jail Sentence and Realignment Legislation.

Rule 4.420. Selection of term of imprisonment <u>for offense</u>

(a) When a ~~sentence~~judgment of imprisonment is imposed, or the execution of a ~~sentence~~<u>judgment</u> of imprisonment is ordered suspended, the sentencing judge must<u>, in their sound discretion, order imposition of a sentence not to exceed the middle term, except as otherwise provided in paragraph (b).</u>~~select the upper, middle, or lower term on each count for which the defendant has been convicted, as provided in section 1170(b) and these rules.~~

<u>**(b)** The court may only choose an upper term when (1) there are circumstances in aggravation of the crime that justify the imposition of an upper term, and (2) the facts underlying those circumstances have been (i) stipulated to by the defendant, (ii) found true beyond a reasonable doubt at trial by a jury, or (iii) found true beyond a reasonable doubt by the judge in a court trial.</u>

<u>**(c)** Notwithstanding paragraphs (a) and (b), the court may consider the fact of the defendant's prior convictions based on a certified record of conviction without it having been stipulated to by the defendant or found true beyond a reasonable doubt at trial by a jury or the judge in a court trial. This exception does not apply to the use of the record of a prior conviction in selecting the upper term of an enhancement.</u>

~~**(b)**~~<u>**(d)**</u> In <u>selecting between the middle and lower terms of imprisonment,</u> ~~exercising his or her discretion in selecting one of the three authorized terms of imprisonment referred to in section 1170(b),~~the sentencing judge may consider circumstances in aggravation or mitigation, and any other factor reasonably related to the sentencing decision. <u>The court may consider factors in aggravation and mitigation, whether or not the factors have been stipulated to by the defendant or found true beyond a reasonable doubt at trial by a jury or the judge in a court trial.</u> The relevant circumstances may be obtained from the case record, the probation officer's report, other reports and statements properly received, statements in aggravation or mitigation, and any evidence introduced at the sentencing hearing.

<u>**(e)** Notwithstanding section 1170(b)(1), and unless the court finds that the aggravating circumstances outweigh the mitigating circumstances such that imposition of the lower term would be contrary to the interests of justice, the court must order imposition of the lower term if any of the following was a contributing factor in the commission of the offense:</u>

<u>(1) The defendant has experienced psychological, physical, or childhood trauma, including, but not limited to, abuse, neglect, exploitation, or sexual violence;</u>

<u>(2) The defendant is a youth, or was a youth as defined under section 1016.7(b) at the time of the commission of the offense; or</u>

<u>(3) Prior to the instant offense, or at the time of the commission of the offense, the defendant is or was a victim of intimate partner violence or human trafficking.</u>

<u>**(f)** Paragraph (e) does not preclude the court from imposing the lower term even if there is no evidence of the circumstances listed in paragraph (e).</u>

~~**(c)**~~<u>**(g)**</u> To comply with section 1170(b)(<u>5</u>), a fact charged and found as an enhancement may be used as a reason for imposing a particular term only if the court has discretion to strike the punishment for the enhancement and does so. The use of a fact of an enhancement to impose the upper term of imprisonment is an adequate reason for striking the additional term of imprisonment, regardless of the effect on the total term.

~~**(d)**~~<u>**(h)**</u> A fact that is an element of the crime on which punishment is being imposed may not be used to impose a particular term.

~~**(e)**~~<u>**(i)**</u> The reasons for selecting one of the three authorized terms of imprisonment referred to in section 1170(b) must be stated orally on the record. *(Formerly Rule 439, adopted, eff. July 1, 1977. As amended, eff. July 28, 1977. Renumbered Rule 420 and amended, eff. Jan. 1, 1991. Renumbered Rule 4.420, eff. Jan. 1, 2001. As amended, eff. Jan. 1, 2007; May 23, 2007; Jan. 1, 2008; Jan. 1, 2017; Jan. 1, 2018; March 14, 2022.)*

Advisory Committee Comment

It is not clear whether the reasons stated by the judge for selecting a particular term qualify as "facts" for the purposes of the rule prohibition on dual use of facts. Until the issue is clarified, judges should avoid the use of reasons that may constitute an impermissible dual use of facts. For example, the court is not permitted to use a reason to impose a greater term if that reason also is either (1) the same as an enhancement that will be imposed, or (2) an element of the crime. The court should not use the same reason to impose a consecutive sentence as to impose an upper term of imprisonment. (*People v. Avalos* (1984) 37 Cal.3d 216, 233.) It is not improper to use the same reason to deny probation and to impose the upper term. (*People v. Bowen* (1992) 11 Cal.App.4th 102, 106.)

The rule makes it clear that a fact charged and found as an enhancement may, in the alternative, be used as a factor in aggravation.

People v. Riolo (1983) 33 Cal.3d 223, 227 (and note 5 on 227) held that section 1170.1(a) does not require the judgment to state the base term (upper, middle, or lower) and enhancements, computed independently, on counts that are subject to automatic reduction under the one-third formula of section 1170.1(a).

Even when sentencing is under section 1170.1, however, it is essential to determine the base term and specific enhancements for each count independently, in order to know which is the principal term count. The principal term count must be determined before any calculation is made using the one-third formula for subordinate terms.

In addition, the base term (upper, middle, or lower) for each count must be determined to arrive at an informed decision whether to make terms consecutive or concurrent; and the base term for each count must be stated in the judgment when sentences are concurrent or are fully consecutive (i.e., not subject to the one-third rule of section 1170.1(a)).

Case law suggests that in determining the "interests of justice" the court should consider the constitutional rights of the defendant and the interests of society represented by the people; the defendant's background and prospects, including the presence or absence of a record; the nature and circumstances of the crime and the defendant's level of involvement; the factors in aggravation and mitigation including the specific factors in mitigation of Penal Code section 1170(b)(6); and the factors that would motivate a "reasonable judge" in the exercise of their discretion. The court should not consider whether the defendant has simply pled guilty, factors related to controlling the court's calendar, or antipathy toward the statutory scheme. (See *People v. Romero* (1996) 13 Cal.4th 947; *People v. Dent* (1995) 38 Cal.App.4th 1726; *People v. Kessel* (1976) 61 Cal.App.3d 322; *People v. Orin* (1975) 13 Cal.3d 937.)

Research References

5 Witkin, California Criminal Law 4th Criminal Trial § 520 (2021), Upper Term Sentence Under Determinate Sentencing Law.
3 Witkin, California Criminal Law 4th Punishment § 315 (2021), Sentencing Proceeding.
3 Witkin, California Criminal Law 4th Punishment § 317 (2021), In General.
3 Witkin, California Criminal Law 4th Punishment § 319 (2021), Fact of Enhancement.
3 Witkin, California Criminal Law 4th Punishment § 320 (2021), Element of Crime.
3 Witkin, California Criminal Law 4th Punishment § 321 (2021), Exception: Facts About Probation.
3 Witkin, California Criminal Law 4th Punishment § 341 (2021), When Statement is Required.
3 Witkin, California Criminal Law 4th Punishment § 347 (2021), Power to Strike Enhancements.

Rule 4.421. Circumstances in aggravation

Circumstances in aggravation include factors relating to the crime and factors relating to the defendant.

(a) Factors relating to the crime

Factors relating to the crime, whether or not charged or chargeable as enhancements include that:

(1) The crime involved great violence, great bodily harm, threat of great bodily harm, or other acts disclosing a high degree of cruelty, viciousness, or callousness;

(2) The defendant was armed with or used a weapon at the time of the commission of the crime;

(3) The victim was particularly vulnerable;

(4) The defendant induced others to participate in the commission of the crime or occupied a position of leadership or dominance of other participants in its commission;

(5) The defendant induced a minor to commit or assist in the commission of the crime;

(6) The defendant threatened witnesses, unlawfully prevented or dissuaded witnesses from testifying, suborned perjury, or in any other way illegally interfered with the judicial process;

(7) The defendant was convicted of other crimes for which consecutive sentences could have been imposed but for which concurrent sentences are being imposed;

(8) The manner in which the crime was carried out indicates planning, sophistication, or professionalism;

(9) The crime involved an attempted or actual taking or damage of great monetary value;

(10) The crime involved a large quantity of contraband; and

(11) The defendant took advantage of a position of trust or confidence to commit the offense.

(12) The crime constitutes a hate crime under section 422.55 and:

(A) No hate crime enhancements under section 422.75 are imposed; and

(B) The crime is not subject to sentencing under section 1170.8.

(b) Factors relating to the defendant

Factors relating to the defendant include that:

(1) The defendant has engaged in violent conduct that indicates a serious danger to society;

(2) The defendant's prior convictions as an adult or sustained petitions in juvenile delinquency proceedings are numerous or of increasing seriousness;

(3) The defendant has served a prior term in prison or county jail under section 1170(h);

(4) The defendant was on probation, mandatory supervision, postrelease community supervision, or parole when the crime was committed; and

(5) The defendant's prior performance on probation, mandatory supervision, postrelease community supervision, or parole was unsatisfactory.

(c) Other factors

Any other factors statutorily declared to be circumstances in aggravation or that reasonably relate to the defendant or the circumstances under which the crime was committed. *(Formerly Rule 421, adopted, eff. July 1, 1977. As amended, eff. Jan. 1, 1991. Renumbered Rule 4.421, eff. Jan. 1, 2001. As amended, eff. Jan. 1, 2007; May 23, 2007; Jan. 1, 2017; Jan. 1, 2018.)*

Advisory Committee Comment

Courts may not impose a sentence greater than the middle term except when aggravating factors justifying the imposition of the upper term have been stipulated to by the defendant or found true beyond a reasonable doubt at trial by the jury or the judge in a court trial. These requirements do not apply to consideration of aggravating factors for the lower or middle term. If the court finds that any of the factors listed in section 1170(b)(6)(A–C) were a contributing factor to the commission of the offense, the court must impose the lower term (see rule 4.420(e)) unless the court finds that the aggravating factors outweigh the mitigating factors to such a degree that imposing the lower term would be contrary to the interests of justice. In this instance, since the court is not addressing the imposition of the upper term, the court may consider factors in aggravation that have not been stipulated to by the defendant or found true beyond a reasonable doubt at trial by the jury or the judge in a court trial.

In determining whether to impose the upper term for a criminal offense, the court may consider as an aggravating factor that a defendant has suffered one or more prior convictions, based on a certified record of conviction. This exception may not be used to select the upper term of an enhancement.

This rule does not deal with the dual use of the facts; the statutory prohibition against dual use is included, in part, in the comment to rule 4.420.

Refusal to consider the personal characteristics of the defendant in imposing sentence may raise serious constitutional questions. The California Supreme Court has held that sentencing decisions must take into account "the nature of the offense and/or the offender, with particular regard to the degree of danger both present to society." (*In re Rodriguez* (1975) 14 Cal.3d 639, 654, quoting *In re Lynch* (1972) 8 Cal.3d 410, 425.) In *Rodriguez* the court released petitioner from further incarceration because "it appears that neither the circumstances of his offense *nor his personal characteristics* establish a danger to society sufficient to justify such a prolonged period of imprisonment." (*Id.* at p. 655, fn. omitted, italics added.) "For the determination of sentences, justice generally requires . . . that there be taken into account the circumstances of the offense together with the character and propensities of the offender." (*Pennsylvania ex rel. Sullivan v. Ashe* (1937) 302 U.S. 51, 55, quoted with approval in *Gregg v. Georgia* (1976) 428 U.S. 153, 189.)

Other statutory factors in aggravation are listed, for example, in sections 422.76, 1170.7, 1170.71, 1170.8, and 1170.85, and may be considered to impose the upper term if stipulated to by the defendant or found true beyond a reasonable doubt at trial by a jury or the judge in a court trial.

Research References

2 Witkin, California Criminal Law 4th Crimes Against Public Peace and Welfare § 130 (2021), Drug Treatment Centers, Detoxification Facilities, and Homeless Shelters.
5 Witkin, California Criminal Law 4th Criminal Trial § 519 (2021), Recidivism Exception to Apprendi-Blakely Rule.
5 Witkin, California Criminal Law 4th Criminal Trial § 528 (2021), Juvenile Delinquency Determinations.
4 Witkin, California Criminal Law 4th Pretrial Proceedings § 250 (2021), Aggravating Facts for Sentencing Purposes.
3 Witkin, California Criminal Law 4th Punishment § 308L (2021), (New) Consideration of Aggravating and Mitigating Factors.
3 Witkin, California Criminal Law 4th Punishment § 323 (2021), In General.
3 Witkin, California Criminal Law 4th Punishment § 325 (2021), Use of Violence or Weapon.
3 Witkin, California Criminal Law 4th Punishment § 326 (2021), Victim's Status.
3 Witkin, California Criminal Law 4th Punishment § 327 (2021), Multiple Victims.
3 Witkin, California Criminal Law 4th Punishment § 328 (2021), Defendant's Role.
3 Witkin, California Criminal Law 4th Punishment § 329 (2021), Interference With Judicial Process.
3 Witkin, California Criminal Law 4th Punishment § 330 (2021), Value or Quantity.
3 Witkin, California Criminal Law 4th Punishment § 331 (2021), Other Factors.
3 Witkin, California Criminal Law 4th Punishment § 332 (2021), Factors Relating to Defendant.
3 Witkin, California Criminal Law 4th Punishment § 337 (2021), General Rule: No Consideration of Dismissed Charges.
3 Witkin, California Criminal Law 4th Punishment § 343 (2021), Adequacy of Statement.
3 Witkin, California Criminal Law 4th Punishment § 355 (2021), In General.
3 Witkin, California Criminal Law 4th Punishment § 359 (2021), P.C. 12022.53: Personal Use of Firearm in Specified Felonies.
3 Witkin, California Criminal Law 4th Punishment § 631 (2021), Required Contents.

Rule 4.423. Circumstances in mitigation

Circumstances in mitigation include factors relating to the crime and factors relating to the defendant.

(a) Factors relating to the crime

Factors relating to the crime include that:

(1) The defendant was a passive participant or played a minor role in the crime;

(2) The victim was an initiator of, willing participant in, or aggressor or provoker of the incident;

(3) The crime was committed because of an unusual circumstance, such as great provocation, that is unlikely to recur;

(4) The defendant participated in the crime under circumstances of coercion or duress, or the criminal conduct was partially excusable for some other reason not amounting to a defense;

(5) The defendant, with no apparent predisposition to do so, was induced by others to participate in the crime;

(6) The defendant exercised caution to avoid harm to persons or damage to property, or the amounts of money or property taken were deliberately small, or no harm was done or threatened against the victim;

(7) The defendant believed that he or she had a claim or right to the property taken, or for other reasons mistakenly believed that the conduct was legal;

(8) The defendant was motivated by a desire to provide necessities for his or her family or self; and

(9) The defendant suffered from repeated or continuous physical, sexual, or psychological abuse inflicted by the victim of the crime, and the victim of the crime, who inflicted the abuse, was the defendant's spouse, intimate cohabitant, or parent of the defendant's child; and the abuse does not amount to a defense.

(10) If a firearm was used in the commission of the offense, it was unloaded or inoperable.

(b) Factors relating to the defendant

Factors relating to the defendant include that:

(1) The defendant has no prior record, or has an insignificant record of criminal conduct, considering the recency and frequency of prior crimes;

(2) The defendant was suffering from a mental or physical condition that significantly reduced culpability for the crime;

(3) The defendant experienced psychological, physical, or childhood trauma, including, but not limited to, abuse, neglect, exploitation, or sexual violence and it was a factor in the commission of the crime;

(4) The commission of the current offense is connected to the defendant's prior victimization or childhood trauma, or mental illness as defined by section 1385(c);

(5) The defendant is or was a victim of intimate partner violence or human trafficking at the time of the commission of the offense, and it was a factor in the commission of the offense;

(6) The defendant is under 26 years of age, or was under 26 years of age at the time of the commission of the offense;

(7) The defendant was a juvenile when they committed the current offense;

~~(3)~~(8) The defendant voluntarily acknowledged wrongdoing before arrest or at an early stage of the criminal process;

~~(4)~~(9) The defendant is ineligible for probation and but for that ineligibility would have been granted probation;

(10) Application of an enhancement could result in a sentence over 20 years;

(11) Multiple enhancements are alleged in a single case;

(12) Application of an enhancement could result in a discriminatory racial impact;

(13) An enhancement is based on a prior conviction that is over five years old;

~~(5)~~(14) The defendant made restitution to the victim; and

~~(6)~~(15) The defendant's prior performance on probation, mandatory supervision, postrelease community supervision, or parole was satisfactory.

(c) Other factors

Any other factors statutorily declared to be circumstances in mitigation or that reasonably relate to the defendant or the circumstances under which the crime was committed. *(Formerly Rule 423, adopted, eff. July 1, 1977. As amended, eff. Jan. 1, 1991; July 1, 1993. Renumbered Rule 4.423, eff. Jan. 1, 2001. As amended, eff. Jan. 1, 2007; May 23, 2007; Jan. 1, 2017; Jan. 1, 2018; March 14, 2022.)*

Advisory Committee Comment

See comment to rule 4.421.

This rule applies both to mitigation for purposes of section 1170(b) and to circumstances in mitigation justifying the court in striking the additional punishment provided for an enhancement.

Some listed circumstances can never apply to certain enhancements; for example, "the amounts taken were deliberately small" can never apply to an excessive taking under section 12022.6, and "no harm was done" can never apply to infliction of great bodily injury under section 12022.7. In any case, only the facts present may be considered for their possible effect in mitigation.

See also rule 4.409; only relevant criteria need be considered.

Since only the fact of restitution is considered relevant to mitigation, no reference to the defendant's financial ability is needed. The omission of a comparable factor from rule 4.421 as a circumstance in aggravation is deliberate.

Research References

2 Witkin, California Criminal Law 4th Crimes Against Public Peace and Welfare § 130 (2021), Drug Treatment Centers, Detoxification Facilities, and Homeless Shelters.

1 Witkin California Criminal Law 4th Defenses § 114 (2021), Sentencing Entrapment or Manipulation.

3 Witkin, California Criminal Law 4th Punishment § 308L (2021), (New) Consideration of Aggravating and Mitigating Factors.

3 Witkin, California Criminal Law 4th Punishment § 333 (2021), In General.

3 Witkin, California Criminal Law 4th Punishment § 334 (2021), Factors Relating to the Crime.

3 Witkin, California Criminal Law 4th Punishment § 335 (2021), Listed Factors.

3 Witkin, California Criminal Law 4th Punishment § 336 (2021), Alcoholism or Drug Addiction.

3 Witkin, California Criminal Law 4th Punishment § 359 (2021), P.C. 12022.53: Personal Use of Firearm in Specified Felonies.

3 Witkin, California Criminal Law 4th Punishment § 631 (2021), Required Contents.

Rule 4.424. Consideration of applicability of section 654

Before determining whether to impose either concurrent or consecutive sentences on all counts on which the defendant was convicted, the court must determine whether the proscription in section 654 against multiple punishments for the same act or omission requires a stay of execution of the sentence imposed on some of the counts. If a stay of execution is required due to the prohibition against multiple punishments for the same act, the court has discretion to choose which act or omission will be punished and which will be stayed. *(Formerly Rule 424, adopted, eff. Jan. 1, 1991. Renumbered Rule 4.424, eff. Jan. 1, 2001. As amended, eff. Jan. 1, 2007; Jan. 1, 2011; March 14, 2022.)*

Validity

A former version of this rule was held to be invalid in the decision of People v. Alford (App. 3 Dist. 2010) 103 Cal.Rptr.3d 898, 180 Cal.App.4th 1463, review denied.

Research References

3 Witkin, California Criminal Law 4th Punishment § 384 (2021), In General.

Rule 4.425. Factors affecting concurrent or consecutive sentences

Factors affecting the decision to impose consecutive rather than concurrent sentences include:

(a) Facts relating to crimes

Facts relating to the crimes, including whether or not:

(1) The crimes and their objectives were predominantly independent of each other;

(2) The crimes involved separate acts of violence or threats of violence; or

(3) The crimes were committed at different times or separate places, rather than being committed so closely in time and place as to indicate a single period of aberrant behavior.

(b) Other facts and limitations

Any circumstances in aggravation or mitigation, whether or not the factors have been stipulated to by the defendant or found true beyond a reasonable doubt at trial by a jury or the judge in a court trial, may be considered in deciding whether to impose consecutive rather than concurrent sentences, except:

(1) A fact used to impose the upper term;

(2) A fact used to otherwise enhance the defendant's sentence in prison or county jail under section 1170(h); and

(3) A fact that is an element of the crime.~~may not be used to impose consecutive sentences.~~ *(Formerly Rule 425, adopted, eff. July 1, 1977. As amended, eff. Jan. 1, 1991. Renumbered Rule 4.425, eff. Jan. 1, 2001. As amended, eff. Jan. 1, 2007; Jan. 1, 2017; Jan. 1, 2018; March 14, 2022.)*

Advisory Committee Comment

The sentencing judge should be aware that there are some cases in which the law mandates consecutive sentences.

Research References

3 Witkin, California Criminal Law 4th Punishment § 385 (2021), Criteria for Decision.

3 Witkin, California Criminal Law 4th Punishment § 435 (2021), Dual Use of Prior Conviction.

3 Witkin, California Criminal Law 4th Punishment § 457 (2021), Discretion of Trial Judge.

Rule 4.426. Violent sex crimes

(a) Multiple violent sex crimes

When a defendant has been convicted of multiple violent sex offenses as defined in section 667.6, the sentencing judge must determine whether the crimes involved separate victims or the same victim on separate occasions.

(1) *Different victims*

If the crimes were committed against different victims, a full, separate, and consecutive term must be imposed for a violent sex crime as to each victim, under section 667.6(d).

(2) *Same victim, separate occasions*

If the crimes were committed against a single victim, the sentencing judge must determine whether the crimes were committed on separate occasions. In determining whether there were separate occasions, the sentencing judge must consider whether, between the commission of one sex crime and another, the defendant had a reasonable opportunity to reflect on his or her actions and nevertheless resumed sexually assaultive behavior. A full, separate, and consecutive term must be imposed for each violent sex offense committed on a separate occasion under section 667.6(d).

(b) Same victim, same occasion; other crimes

If the defendant has been convicted of multiple crimes, including at least one violent sex crime, as defined in section 667.6, or if there have been multiple violent sex crimes against a single victim on the same occasion and the sentencing court has decided to impose consecutive sentences, the sentencing judge must then determine whether to impose a full, separate, and consecutive sentence under section 667.6(c) for the violent sex crime or crimes instead of including the violent sex crimes in the computation of the principal and subordinate terms under section 1170.1(a). A decision to impose a fully consecutive sentence under section 667.6(c) is an additional sentence choice that requires a statement of reasons separate from those given for consecutive sentences, but which may repeat the same reasons. The sentencing judge is to be guided by the criteria listed in rule 4.425, which incorporates rules 4.421 and 4.423, as well as any other reasonably related criteria as provided in rule 4.408. *(Formerly Rule 426, adopted, eff. Jan. 1, 1991. Renumbered Rule 4.426, eff. Jan. 1, 2001. As amended, eff. July 1, 2003; Jan. 1, 2007.)*

Advisory Committee Comment

Section 667.6(d) requires a full, separate, and consecutive term for each of the enumerated violent sex crimes that involve separate victims, or the same victim on separate occasions. Therefore, if there were separate victims or the court found that there were separate occasions, no other reasons are required.

If there have been multiple convictions involving at least one of the enumerated violent sex crimes, the court may impose a full, separate, and consecutive term for each violent sex crime under section 667.6(c). (See *People v. Coleman* (1989) 48 Cal.3d 112, 161.) A fully consecutive sentence under section 667.6(c) is a sentence choice, which requires a statement of reasons. The court may not use the same fact to impose a sentence under section 667.6(c) that was used to impose an upper term. (See rule 4.425(b).) If the court selects the upper term, imposes consecutive sentences, and uses section 667.6(c), the record must reflect three sentencing choices with three separate statements of reasons, but the same reason may be used for sentencing under section 667.6(c) and to impose consecutive sentences. (See *People v. Belmontes* (1983) 34 Cal.3d 335, 347–349.)

Research References

3 Witkin, California Criminal Law 4th Punishment § 341 (2021), When Statement is Required.
3 Witkin, California Criminal Law 4th Punishment § 457 (2021), Discretion of Trial Judge.
3 Witkin, California Criminal Law 4th Punishment § 458 (2021), Separate Occasions.

Rule 4.427. Hate crimes

(a) Application

This rule is intended to assist judges in sentencing in felony hate crime cases. It applies to:

(1) Felony sentencing under section 422.7;

(2) Convictions of felonies with a hate crime enhancement under section 422.75; and

(3) Convictions of felonies that qualify as hate crimes under section 422.55.

(b) Felony sentencing under section 422.7

If one of the three factors listed in section 422.7 is pled and proved, a misdemeanor conviction that constitutes a hate crime under section 422.55 may be sentenced as a felony. The punishment is imprisonment in state prison or county jail under section 1170(h) as provided by section 422.7.

(c) Hate crime enhancement

If a hate crime enhancement is pled and proved, the punishment for a felony conviction must be enhanced under section 422.75 unless the conviction is sentenced as a felony under section 422.7.

(1) The following enhancements apply:

(A) An enhancement of a term in state prison as provided in section 422.75(a). Personal use of a firearm in the commission of the offense is an aggravating factor that must be considered in determining the enhancement term.

(B) An additional enhancement of one year in state prison for each prior felony conviction that constitutes a hate crime as defined in section 422.55.

(2) The court may strike enhancements under (c) if it finds mitigating circumstances under rule 4.423, or pursuant to section 1385(c) and states those mitigating circumstances on the record.

(3) The punishment for any enhancement under (c) is in addition to any other punishment provided by law.

(d) Hate crime as aggravating factor

If the defendant is convicted of a felony, and the facts of the crime constitute a hate crime under section 422.55, that fact must be considered a circumstance in aggravation in determining the appropriate punishment under rule 4.421 unless:

(1) The court imposed a hate crime enhancement under section 422.75; or

(2) The defendant has been convicted of an offense subject to sentencing under section 1170.8.

(e) Hate crime sentencing goals

When sentencing a defendant under this rule, the judge must consider the principal goals for hate crime sentencing.

(1) The principal goals for hate crime sentencing, as stated in section 422.86, are:

(A) Punishment for the hate crime committed;

(B) Crime and violence prevention, including prevention of recidivism and prevention of crimes and violence in prisons and jails; and

(C) Restorative justice for the immediate victims of the hate crimes and for the classes of persons terrorized by the hate crimes.

(2) Crime and violence prevention considerations should include educational or other appropriate programs available in the community, jail, prison, and juvenile detention facilities. The programs should address sensitivity or similar training or counseling intended to reduce violent and antisocial behavior based on one or more of the following actual or perceived characteristics of the victim:

(A) Disability;

(B) Gender;

(C) Nationality;

(D) Race or ethnicity;

(E) Religion;

(F) Sexual orientation; or

(G) Association with a person or group with one or more of these actual or perceived characteristics.

(3) Restorative justice considerations should include community service and other programs focused on hate crime prevention or diversity sensitivity. Additionally, the court should consider ordering payment or other compensation to programs that provide services to violent crime victims and reimbursement to the victim for reasonable costs of counseling and other reasonable expenses that the court finds are a direct result of the defendant's actions. *(Adopted, eff. Jan. 1, 2007. As amended, eff. Jan. 1, 2017; March 14, 2022.)*

Advisory Committee Comment

Multiple enhancements for prior convictions under subdivision (c)(1)(B) may be imposed if the prior convictions have been brought and tried separately. (Pen. Code, § 422.75(d).)

In order to impose the upper term based on section 422.75, the fact of the enhancement pursuant to sections 422.55 or 422.6 must be stipulated to by the defendant or found true beyond a reasonable doubt at trial by the jury or the judge in a court trial.

Any enhancement alleged pursuant to this section may be dismissed pursuant to section 1385(c).

Research References

3 Witkin, California Criminal Law 4th Punishment § 326 (2021), Victim's Status.

3 Witkin, California Criminal Law 4th Punishment § 373 (2021), Hate Crimes.

Rule 4.428. Factors affecting imposition of enhancements

(a) Enhancements punishable by one of three terms

If an enhancement is punishable by one of three terms, the court must, in its sound discretion, order imposition of a sentence not to exceed the middle term, unless there are circumstances in aggravation that justify the imposition of a term of imprisonment exceeding the middle term, and the facts underlying those circumstances have been stipulated to by the defendant, or have been found true beyond a reasonable doubt at trial by the jury or by the judge in a court trial.~~, in its discretion, impose the term that best serves the interest of justice and state the reasons for its sentence choice on the record at the time of sentencing. In exercising its discretion in selecting the appropriate term, the court may consider factors in mitigation and aggravation as described in these rules or any other factor authorized by rule 4.408.~~

(b) Striking or dismissing enhancements under section 1385

If the court has discretion under section 1385(a) to strike an enhancement in the interests of justice, the court also has the authority to strike the punishment for the enhancement under section 1385(~~c~~b). In determining whether to strike the entire enhancement or only the punishment for the enhancement, the court may consider the effect that striking the enhancement would have on the status of the crime as a strike, the accurate reflection of the defendant's criminal conduct on his or her record, the effect it may have on the award of custody credits, and any other relevant consideration.

(c) Dismissing enhancements under section 1385(c)

(1) The court shall exercise the discretion to dismiss an enhancement if it is in the furtherance of justice to do so, unless the dismissal is prohibited by initiative statute.

(2) In exercising its discretion under section 1385(c), the court must consider and afford great weight to evidence offered by the defendant to prove that any of the mitigating circumstances in section 1385(c) are present.

(A) Proof of the presence of one or more of these circumstances weighs greatly in favor of dismissing the enhancement, unless the court finds that dismissal of the enhancement would endanger public safety.

(B) The circumstances listed in 1385(c) are not exclusive.

(C) "Endanger public safety" means there is a likelihood that the dismissal of the enhancement would result in physical injury or other serious danger to others.

(3) If the court dismisses the enhancement pursuant to 1385(c), then both the enhancement and its punishment must be dismissed. *(Formerly Rule 428, adopted, eff. Jan. 1, 1991. As amended, eff. Jan. 1, 1998. Renumbered Rule 4.428, eff. Jan. 1, 2001. As amended, eff. July 1, 2003; Jan. 1, 2007; May 23, 2007; Jan. 1, 2008; Jan. 1, 2011; Jan. 1, 2018; March 14, 2022.)*

Advisory Committee Comment

Case law suggests that in determining the "furtherance of justice" the court should consider the constitutional rights of the defendant and the interests of society represented by the people; the defendant's background and prospects, including the presence or absence of a record; the nature and circumstances of the crime and the defendant's level of involvement; the factors in aggravation and mitigation including the specific factors in mitigation of section 1385(c); and the factors that would motivate a "reasonable judge" in the exercise of their discretion. The court should not consider whether the defendant has simply pled guilty, factors related to controlling the court's calendar, or antipathy toward the statutory scheme. (See *People v. Romero* (1996) 13 Cal.4th 947; *People v. Dent* (1995) 38 Cal.App.4th 1726; *People v. Kessel* (1976) 61 Cal.App.3d 322; *People v. Orin* (1975) 13 Cal.3d 937.)

How to afford great weight to a mitigating circumstance is not further explained in section 1385. The court is not directed to give conclusive weight to the mitigating factors, and must still engage in a weighing of both mitigating and aggravating factors. A review of case law suggests that the court can find great weight when there is an absence of "substantial evidence of countervailing considerations of sufficient weight to overcome" the presumption of dismissal when the mitigating factors are present. (*People v. Martin* (1996) 42 Cal.3d 437.) In exercising this discretion, the court may rely on aggravating factors that have not been stipulated to by the defendant or proven beyond a reasonable doubt at trial by a jury or a judge in a court trial. (*People v. Black* (2007) 41 Cal.4th 799.)

Research References

3 Witkin, California Criminal Law 4th Punishment § 341 (2021), When Statement is Required.

3 Witkin, California Criminal Law 4th Punishment § 347 (2021), Power to Strike Enhancements.

Rule 4.431. Proceedings at sentencing to be reported

All proceedings at the time of sentencing must be reported. *(Formerly Rule 431, adopted, eff. July 1, 1977. Renumbered Rule 4.431, eff. Jan. 1, 2001. As amended, eff. Jan. 1, 2007.)*

Advisory Committee Comment

Reporters' transcripts of the sentencing proceedings are required on appeal (rule 8.320, except in certain cases under subdivision (d) of that rule), and when the defendant is sentenced to prison (section 1203.01).

Research References

3 Witkin, California Criminal Law 4th Punishment § 315 (2021), Sentencing Proceeding.

Rule 4.433. Matters to be considered at time set for sentencing

(a) In every case, at the time set for sentencing under section 1191, the sentencing judge must hold a hearing at which the judge must:

(1) Hear and determine any matters raised by the defendant under section 1201;

(2) Determine whether a defendant who is eligible for probation should be granted or denied probation, unless consideration of probation is expressly waived by the defendant personally and by counsel; and

(3) Determine whether to deny a period of mandatory supervision in the interests of justice under section 1170(h)(5)(A).

(b) If the imposition of a sentence is to be suspended during a period of probation after a conviction by trial, the trial judge must identify and state circumstances that would justify imposition of one of the three authorized terms of imprisonment referred to in section 1170(b), or any enhancement, if probation is later revoked. The circumstances identified and stated by the judge must be based on evidence admitted at the trial or other circumstances properly considered under rule 4.420(b).

(c) If a sentence of imprisonment is to be imposed, or if the execution of a sentence of imprisonment is to be suspended during a period of probation, the sentencing judge must:

(1) Determine, under section 1170(b), whether to impose one of the three authorized terms of imprisonment referred to in section 1170(b), or any enhancement, and state on the record the reasons for imposing that term;

(2) Determine whether any additional term of imprisonment provided for an enhancement charged and found will be stricken;

(3) Determine whether the sentences will be consecutive or concurrent if the defendant has been convicted of multiple crimes;

(4) Determine any issues raised by statutory prohibitions on the dual use of facts and statutory limitations on enhancements, as required in rules 4.420(c) and 4.447; and

(5) Pronounce the court's judgment and sentence, stating the terms thereof and giving reasons for those matters for which reasons are required by law.

(d) All these matters must be heard and determined at a single hearing unless the sentencing judge otherwise orders in the interests of justice.

(e) When a sentence of imprisonment is imposed under (c) or under rule 4.435, the sentencing judge must inform the defendant:

(1) Under section 1170(c) of the parole period provided by section 3000 to be served after expiration of the sentence, in addition to any period of incarceration for parole violation;

(2) Of the period of postrelease community supervision provided by section 3456 to be served after expiration of the sentence, in addition to any period of incarceration for a violation of postrelease community supervision; or

(3) Of any period of mandatory supervision imposed under section 1170(h)(5)(A) and (B), in addition to any period of imprisonment for a violation of mandatory supervision. *(Formerly Rule 433, adopted, eff. July 1, 1977. As amended, eff. July 28, 1977; Jan. 1, 1979. Renumbered Rule 4.433, eff. Jan. 1, 2001. As amended, eff. July 1, 2003; Jan. 1, 2007; May 23, 2007; Jan. 1, 2008; Jan. 1, 2017; Jan. 1, 2018.)*

Advisory Committee Comment

This rule summarizes the questions that the court is required to consider at the time of sentencing, in their logical order.

Subdivision (a)(2) makes it clear that probation should be considered in every case, without the necessity of any application, unless the defendant is statutorily ineligible for probation.

Under subdivision (b), when imposition of sentence is to be suspended, the sentencing judge is not to make any determinations as to possible length of a term of imprisonment on violation of probation (section 1170(b)). If there was a trial, however, the judge must state on the record the circumstances that would justify imposition of one of the three authorized terms of imprisonment based on the trial evidence.

Subdivision (d) makes it clear that all sentencing matters should be disposed of at a single hearing unless strong reasons exist for a continuance.

Research References

3 Witkin, California Criminal Law 4th Punishment § 315 (2021), Sentencing Proceeding.

3 Witkin, California Criminal Law 4th Punishment § 317 (2021), In General.

Rule 4.435. Sentencing on revocation of probation, mandatory supervision, and postrelease community supervision

(a) When the defendant violates the terms of probation, mandatory supervision, or postrelease community supervision or is otherwise subject to revocation of supervision, the sentencing judge may make any disposition of the case authorized by statute. In deciding whether to permanently revoke supervision, the judge may consider the nature of the violation and the defendant's past performance on supervision.

(b) On revocation and termination of supervision under section 1203.2, when the sentencing judge determines that the defendant will be committed to prison or county jail under section 1170(h):

(1) If the imposition of sentence was previously suspended, the judge must impose judgment and sentence after considering any findings previously made and hearing and determining the matters enumerated in rule 4.433(c). The length of the sentence must be based on circumstances existing at the time supervision was granted, and subsequent events may not be considered in selecting the base term or in deciding whether to strike the additional punishment for enhancements charged and found.

(2) If the execution of sentence was previously suspended, the judge must order that the judgment previously pronounced be in full force and effect and that the defendant be committed to the custody of the Secretary of the Department of Corrections and Rehabilitation or local county correctional administrator or sheriff for the term prescribed in that judgment. *(Formerly Rule 435, adopted, eff. July 1, 1977. As amended, eff. Jan. 1, 1991. Renumbered Rule 4.435, eff. Jan. 1, 2001. As amended, eff. July 1, 2003; Jan. 1, 2006; Jan. 1, 2007; Jan. 1, 2017; Jan. 1, 2018.)*

Advisory Committee Comment

Subdivision (a) makes it clear that there is no change in the court's power, on finding cause to revoke and terminate supervision under section 1203.2(a), to continue the defendant on supervision.

The restriction of subdivision (b)(1) is based on *In re Rodriguez* (1975) 14 Cal.3d 639, 652: "[T]he primary term must reflect the circumstances existing at the time of the offense."

A judge imposing imprisonment on revocation of probation will have the power granted by section 1170(d) to recall the commitment on his or her own motion within 120 days after the date of commitment, and the power under section 1203.2(e) to set aside the revocation of probation, for good cause, within 30 days after the court has notice that execution of the sentence has commenced.

Consideration of conduct occurring after the granting of probation should be distinguished from consideration of preprobation conduct that is discovered after the granting of an order of probation and before sentencing following a revocation and termination of probation. If the preprobation conduct affects or nullifies a determination made at the time probation was granted, the preprobation conduct may properly be considered at sentencing following revocation and termination of probation. (See *People v. Griffith* (1984) 153 Cal.App.3d 796, 801.) While *People v. Griffith* refers only to probation, this rule likely will apply to any form of supervision.

Research References

3 Witkin, California Criminal Law 4th Punishment § 704 (2021), Length of Sentence.

3 Witkin, California Criminal Law 4th Punishment § 713 (2021), In General.

Rule 4.437. Statements in aggravation and mitigation

(a) Time for filing and service

Statements in aggravation and mitigation referred to in section 1170(b) must be filed and served at least four days before the time set for sentencing under section 1191 or the time set for pronouncing judgment on revocation of probation under section 1203.2(c) if imposition of sentence was previously suspended.

(b) Combined statement

A party seeking consideration of circumstances in aggravation or mitigation may file and serve a statement under section 1170(b) and this rule.

(c) Contents of statement

A statement in aggravation or mitigation must include:

(1) A summary of evidence that the party relies on as circumstances justifying the imposition of a particular term; and

(2) Notice of intention to dispute facts or offer evidence in aggravation or mitigation at the sentencing hearing. The statement must generally describe the evidence to be offered, including a description of any documents and the names and expected substance of the testimony of any witnesses. No evidence in aggravation or mitigation may be introduced at the sentencing hearing unless it was described in the statement, or unless its admission is permitted by the sentencing judge in the interests of justice.

(d) Support required for assertions of fact

Assertions of fact in a statement in aggravation or mitigation must be disregarded unless they are supported by the record in the case, the probation officer's report or other reports properly filed in the case, or other competent evidence.

(e) Disputed facts

In the event the parties dispute the facts on which the conviction rested, the court must conduct a presentence hearing and make appropriate corrections, additions, or deletions in the presentence probation report or order a revised report. *(Formerly Rule 437, adopted, eff. July 1, 1977. As amended, eff. July 28, 1977; Jan. 1, 1991. Renumbered Rule 4.437, eff. Jan. 1, 2001. As amended, eff. Jan. 1, 2007; May 23, 2007.)*

Advisory Committee Comment

Section 1170(b)(4) states in part:

"At least four days prior to the time set for imposition of judgment, either party or the victim, or the family of the victim if the victim is deceased, may submit a statement in aggravation or mitigation to dispute facts in the record or the probation officer's report, or to present additional facts."

This provision means that the statement is a document giving notice of intention to dispute evidence in the record or the probation officer's report, or to present additional facts.

The statement itself cannot be the medium for presenting new evidence, or for rebutting competent evidence already presented, because the statement is a unilateral presentation by one party or counsel that will not necessarily have any indicia of reliability. To allow its factual assertions to be considered in the absence of corroborating evidence would, therefore, constitute a denial of due process of law in violation of the United States (14th Amend.) and California (art. I, § 7) Constitutions.

The requirement that the statement include notice of intention to rely on new evidence will enhance fairness to both sides by avoiding surprise and helping to ensure that the time limit on pronouncing sentence is met. This notice may include either party's intention to provide evidence to prove or contest the existence of a factor in mitigation that would require imposition of the low term for the underlying offense or dismissal of an enhancement.

Research References

3 Witkin, California Criminal Law 4th Punishment § 318 (2021), Statements in Aggravation and Mitigation.

Rule 4.447. Sentencing of enhancements

(a) Enhancements resulting in unlawful sentences

Except pursuant to section 1385(c), ~~A~~a court may not strike or dismiss an enhancement solely because imposition of the term is prohibited by law or exceeds limitations on the imposition of multiple enhancements. Instead, the court must:

(1) Impose a sentence for the aggregate term of imprisonment computed without reference to those prohibitions or limitations; and

(2) Stay execution of the part of the term that is prohibited or exceeds the applicable limitation. The stay will become permanent once the defendant finishes serving the part of the sentence that has not been stayed.

(b) Multiple enhancements

Notwithstanding section 1385(c), ~~I~~if a defendant is convicted of multiple enhancements of the same type, the court must either sentence each enhancement or, if authorized, strike the enhancement or its punishment. While the court may strike an enhancement, the court may not stay an enhancement except as provided in (a) or as authorized by section 654. *(Formerly Rule 447, adopted, eff. July 1, 1977. As amended, eff. July 28, 1977; Jan. 1, 1991. Renumbered Rule 4.447 and amended, eff. Jan. 1, 2001. As amended, eff. July 1, 2003; Jan. 1, 2007; Jan. 1, 2018; March 14, 2022.)*

Advisory Committee Comment

Subdivision (a). Statutory restrictions may prohibit or limit the imposition of an enhancement in certain situations. (See, for example, sections 186.22(b)(1), 667(a)(2), 667.61(f), 1170.1(f) and (g), 12022.53(e)(2) and (f), and Vehicle Code section 23558.)

Section 1385(c) requires that in the furtherance of justice certain enhancements be dismissed unless dismissal is prohibited by any initiative statute.

Present practice of staying execution is followed to avoid violating a statutory prohibition or exceeding a statutory limitation, while preserving the possibility of imposition of the stayed portion should a reversal on appeal reduce the unstayed portion of the sentence. (See *People v. Gonzalez* (2008) 43 Cal.4th 1118, 1129–1130; *People v. Niles* (1964) 227 Cal.App.2d 749, 756.)

Only the portion of a sentence or component thereof that exceeds a limitation is prohibited, and this rule provides a procedure for that situation. This rule applies to both determinate and indeterminate terms.

Subdivision (b). A court may stay an enhancement if section 654 applies. (See *People v. Bradley* (1998) 64 Cal.App.4th 386; *People v. Haykel* (2002) 96 Cal.App.4th 146, 152.)

Research References

3 Witkin, California Criminal Law 4th Punishment § 346 (2021), Sentencing Procedure.

3 Witkin, California Criminal Law 4th Punishment § 379 (2021), Aggravated White Collar Crime.

Rule 4.451. Sentence consecutive to or concurrent with indeterminate term or term in other jurisdiction

(a) When a defendant is sentenced under section 1170 and the sentence is to run consecutively to or concurrently with a sentence imposed under section 1168(b) in the same or another proceeding, the judgment must specify the determinate term imposed under section 1170 computed without reference to the indeterminate sentence, must order that the determinate term be served consecutively to or concurrently with the sentence under section 1168(b), and must identify the proceedings in which the indeterminate sentence was imposed. The term under section 1168(b), and the date of its completion or date of parole or postrelease community supervision, and the sequence in which the sentences are deemed or served, will be determined by correctional authorities as provided by law.

(b) When a defendant is sentenced under sections 1168 or 1170 and the sentence is to run consecutively to or concurrently with a sentence imposed by a court of the United States or of another state or territory, the judgment must specify the term imposed under sections 1168(b) or 1170 computed without reference to the sentence imposed by the other jurisdiction, must identify the other jurisdiction and the proceedings in which the other sentence was imposed, and must indicate whether the sentences are imposed concurrently or consecutively. If the term imposed is to be served consecutively to the term imposed by the other jurisdiction, the court must order that the California term be served commencing on the completion of the sentence imposed by the other jurisdiction. *(Formerly Rule 451, adopted, eff. July 1, 1977. As amended, eff. Jan. 1, 1979. Renumbered Rule 4.451, eff. Jan. 1, 2001. As amended, eff. July 1, 2003; Jan. 1, 2007; Jan. 1, 2018.)*

Advisory Committee Comment

Subdivision (a). The provisions of section 1170.1(a), which use a one-third formula to calculate subordinate consecutive terms, can logically be applied only when all the sentences are imposed under section 1170. Indeterminate sentences are imposed under section 1168(b). Since the duration of the indeterminate term cannot be known to the court, subdivision (a) states the only feasible mode of sentencing. (See *People v. Felix* (2000) 22 Cal.4th 651, 654–657; *People v. McGahuey* (1981) 121 Cal.App.3d 524, 530–532.)

Subdivision (b). On the authority to sentence consecutively to the sentence of another jurisdiction and the effect of such a sentence, see *In re Helpman* (1968) 267 Cal.App.2d 307 and cases cited at page 310, footnote 3. The mode of sentencing required by subdivision (b) is necessary to avoid the illogical conclusion that the total of the consecutive sentences will depend on whether the other jurisdiction or California is the first to pronounce judgment.

Research References

3 Witkin, California Criminal Law 4th Punishment § 392 (2021), Indeterminate Term Consecutive to Determinate Term.

3 Witkin, California Criminal Law 4th Punishment § 393 (2021), California Term Consecutive to Non-California Term.

Rule 4.452. Determinate sentence consecutive to prior determinate sentence

(a) If a determinate sentence is imposed under section 1170.1(a) consecutive to one or more determinate sentences imposed previously in the same court or in other courts, the court in the current case must pronounce a single aggregate term, as defined in section 1170.1(a), stating the result of combining the previous and current sentences. In those situations:

(1) The sentences on all determinately sentenced counts in all the cases on which a sentence was or is being imposed must be combined as though they were all counts in the current case.

(2) The court in the current case must make a new determination of which count, in the combined cases, represents the principal term, as defined in section 1170.1(a). The principal term is the term with the greatest punishment imposed including conduct enhancements. If two terms of imprisonment have the same punishment, either term may be selected as the principal term.

(3) Discretionary decisions of courts in previous cases may not be changed by the court in the current case. Such decisions include the decision to impose one of the three authorized terms of imprisonment referred to in section 1170(b), making counts in prior cases concurrent with or consecutive to each other, or the decision that circumstances in mitigation or in the furtherance of justice justified striking the punishment for an enhancement. However, if a previously designated principal term becomes a subordinate term after the resentencing, the subordinate term will be limited to one-third the middle base term as provided in section 1170.1(a).

(4) If all previously imposed sentences and the current sentence being imposed by the second or subsequent court are under section 1170(h), the second or subsequent court has the discretion to specify whether a previous sentence is to be served in custody or on mandatory supervision and the terms of such supervision, but may not, without express consent of the defendant, modify the sentence on the earlier sentenced charges in any manner that will (i) increase the total length of the sentence imposed by the previous court; (ii) increase the total length of the custody portion of the sentence imposed by the previous court; (iii) increase the total length of the mandatory supervision portion of the sentence imposed by the previous court; or (iv) impose additional, more onerous, or more restrictive conditions of release for any previously imposed period of mandatory supervision.

(5) If the second or subsequent court imposes a sentence to state prison because the defendant is ineligible for sentencing under section 1170(h), the jurisdiction of the second or subsequent court to impose a prison sentence applies solely to the current case. The defendant must be returned to the original sentencing court for potential resentencing on any previous case or cases sentenced under section 1170(h). The original sentencing court must convert all remaining custody and mandatory supervision time imposed in the previous case to state prison custody time and must determine whether its sentence is concurrent with or consecutive to the state prison term imposed by the second or subsequent court and incorporate that sentence into a single aggregate term as required by this rule. (A)(4) does not apply—and the consent of the defendant is not required—for this conversion and resentencing.

(6) In cases in which a sentence is imposed under the provisions of section 1170(h) and the sentence has been imposed by courts in two or more counties, the second or subsequent court must determine the county or counties of incarceration or supervision, including the order of service of such incarceration or supervision. To the extent reasonably possible, the period of mandatory supervision must be served in one county and after completion of any period of incarceration. In accordance with rule 4.472, the second or subsequent court must calculate the defendant's remaining custody and supervision time.

(7) In making the determination under (a)(6), the court must exercise its discretion after consideration of the following factors:

(A) The relative length of custody or supervision required for each case;

(B) Whether the cases in each county are to be served concurrently or consecutively;

(C) The nature and quality of treatment programs available in each county, if known;

(D) The nature and extent of the defendant's current enrollment and participation in any treatment program;

(E) The nature and extent of the defendant's ties to the community, including employment, duration of residence, family attachments, and property holdings;

(F) The nature and extent of supervision available in each county, if known;

(G) The factors listed in rule 4.530(f); and

(H) Any other factor relevant to such determination.

(8) If after the court's determination in accordance with (a)(6) the defendant is ordered to serve only a custody term without supervision in another county, the defendant must be transported at such time and under such circumstances as the court directs to the county where the custody term is to be served. The defendant must be transported with an abstract of the court's judgment as required by section 1213(a), or other suitable documentation showing the term imposed by the court and any custody credits against the sentence. The court may order the custody term to be served in another county without also transferring jurisdiction of the case in accordance with rule 4.530.

(9) If after the court's determination in accordance with (a)(6) the defendant is ordered to serve a period of supervision in another county, whether with or without a term of custody, the matter must be transferred for the period of supervision in accordance with provisions of rule 4.530(f), (g), and (h). *(Formerly Rule 452, adopted, eff. Jan. 1, 1991. Renumbered Rule 4.452, eff. Jan. 1, 2001. As amended, eff. July 1, 2003; Jan. 1, 2007; May 23, 2007; Jan. 1, 2017; Jan. 1, 2018; July 1, 2019; Jan. 1, 2021.)*

Advisory Committee Comment

The restrictions of (a)(3) do not apply to circumstances where a previously imposed base term is made a consecutive term on resentencing. If the court selects a consecutive sentence structure, and since there can be only one principal term in the final aggregate sentence, if a previously imposed full base term becomes a subordinate consecutive term, the new consecutive term normally will become one-third the middle term by operation of law (section 1170.1(a)).

Research References

3 Witkin, California Criminal Law 4th Punishment § 391 (2021), Separate Proceedings Imposing Consecutive Sentences.
3 Witkin, California Criminal Law 4th Punishment § 465 (2021), Calculation of Credits Where Sentence is Altered.

Rule 4.472. Determination of presentence custody time credit

At the time of sentencing, the court must cause to be recorded on the judgment or commitment the total time in custody to be credited on the sentence under sections 2900.5, 2933.1(c), 2933.2(c), and 4019. On referral of the defendant to the probation officer for an investigation and report under section 1203(b) or 1203(g), or on setting a date for sentencing in the absence of a referral, the court must direct the sheriff, probation officer, or other appropriate person to report to the court and notify the defendant or defense counsel and prosecuting attorney within a reasonable time before the date set for sentencing as to the number of days that defendant has been in custody and for which he or she may be entitled to credit. Any challenges to the report must be heard at the time of sentencing. *(Formerly Rule 252, adopted, eff. Jan. 1, 1977. Renumbered Rule 472 and amended, eff. Jan. 1, 1991. Renumbered Rule 4.472 and amended, eff. Jan. 1, 2001. As amended, eff. July 1, 2003; Jan. 1, 2007; Jan. 1, 2017.)*

Research References

3 Witkin, California Criminal Law 4th Punishment § 391 (2021), Separate Proceedings Imposing Consecutive Sentences.

Ct. Rules

3 Witkin, California Criminal Law 4th Punishment § 464 (2021), Credit for All Days of Custody.

Rule 4.480. Judge's statement under section 1203.01

A sentencing judge's statement of his or her views under section 1203.01 respecting a person sentenced to the Department of Corrections and Rehabilitation, Division of Adult Operations is required only in the event that no probation report is filed. Even though it is not required, however, a statement should be submitted by the judge in any case in which he or she believes that the correctional handling and the determination of term and parole should be influenced by information not contained in other court records.

The purpose of a section 1203.01 statement is to provide assistance to the Department of Corrections and Rehabilitation, Division of Adult Operations in its programming and institutional assignment and to the Board of Parole Hearings with reference to term fixing and parole release of persons sentenced indeterminately, and parole and postrelease community supervision waiver of persons sentenced determinately. It may amplify any reasons for the sentence that may bear on a possible suggestion by the Secretary of the Department of Corrections and Rehabilitation or the Board of Parole Hearings that the sentence and commitment be recalled and the defendant be resentenced. To be of maximum assistance to these agencies, a judge's statements should contain individualized comments concerning the convicted offender, any special circumstances that led to a prison sentence rather than local incarceration, and any other significant information that might not readily be available in any of the accompanying official records and reports.

If a section 1203.01 statement is prepared, it should be submitted no later than two weeks after sentencing so that it may be included in the official Department of Corrections and Rehabilitation, Division of Adult Operations case summary that is prepared during the time the offender is being processed at the Reception–Guidance Center of the Department of Corrections and Rehabilitation, Division of Adult Operations. *(Formerly § 12, Standards of Judicial Administration, adopted, eff. Jan. 1, 1973. As amended, eff. July 1, 1978. Renumbered California Rules of Court, Rule 4.480, and amended, eff. Jan. 1. 2001. As amended, eff. July 1, 2003; Jan. 1, 2006; Jan. 1, 2007; Jan. 1, 2017.)*

Research References

6 Witkin, California Criminal Law 4th Criminal Judgment § 175 (2021), State Prison Sentence.

4 Witkin, California Criminal Law 4th Introduction to Criminal Procedure § 9 (2021), Rules of Court.

Division 6

POSTCONVICTION, POSTRELEASE, AND WRITS

Chapter 1

POSTCONVICTION

Rule 4.510. Reverse remand

(a) Minor prosecuted under Welfare and Institutions Code section 602(b) or 707(d) and convicted of offense listed in Welfare and Institutions Code section 602(b) or 707(d) (Penal Code, § 1170.17)

If the prosecuting attorney lawfully initiated the prosecution as a criminal case under Welfare and Institutions Code section 602(b) or 707(d), and the minor is convicted of a criminal offense listed in those sections, the minor must be sentenced as an adult.

(b) Minor convicted of an offense not listed in Welfare and Institutions Code section 602(b) or 707(d) (Penal Code, § 1170.17)

(1) If the prosecuting attorney lawfully initiated the prosecution as a criminal case and the minor is convicted of an offense not listed in Welfare and Institutions Code section 602(b) or 707(d), but one that would have raised the presumption of unfitness under juvenile court law, the minor may move the court to conduct a postconviction fitness hearing.

(A) On the motion by the minor, the court must order the probation department to prepare a report as required in rule 5.768.

(B) The court may conduct a fitness hearing or remand the matter to the juvenile court for a determination of fitness.

(C) The minor may receive a disposition hearing under the juvenile court law only if he or she is found to be fit under rule 5.772. However, if the court and parties agree, the minor may be sentenced in adult court.

(D) If the minor is found unfit, the minor must be sentenced as an adult, unless all parties, including the court, agree that the disposition be conducted under juvenile court law.

(2) If the minor is convicted of an offense not listed in Welfare and Institutions Code section 602(b) or 707(d), but one for which the minor would have been presumed fit under the juvenile court law, the minor must have a disposition hearing under juvenile court law, and consistent with the provisions of Penal Code section 1170.19, either in the trial court or on remand to the juvenile court.

(A) If the prosecuting attorney objects to the treatment of the minor as within the juvenile court law and moves for a fitness hearing to be conducted, the court must order the probation department to prepare a report as required by rule 5.768.

(B) The court may conduct a fitness hearing or remand the matter to the juvenile court for a determination of fitness.

(C) If found to be fit under rule 5.770, the minor will be subject to a disposition hearing under juvenile court law and Penal Code section 1170.19.

(D) If the minor is found unfit, the minor must be sentenced as an adult, unless all parties, including the court, agree that the disposition be conducted under juvenile court law.

(3) If the minor is convicted of an offense that would not have permitted a fitness determination, the court must remand the matter to juvenile court for disposition, unless the minor requests sentencing in adult court and all parties, including the court, agree.

(4) Fitness hearings held under this rule must be conducted as provided in title 5, division 3, chapter 14, article 2. *(Adopted, eff. Jan. 1, 2001. As amended, eff. Jan. 1, 2007.)*

Research References

4 Witkin, California Criminal Law 4th Introduction to Criminal Procedure § 9 (2021), Rules of Court.

3 Witkin, California Criminal Law 4th Punishment § 91 (2021), Commitment Procedure.

Rule 4.530. Intercounty transfer of probation and mandatory supervision cases

(a) Application

This rule applies to intercounty transfers of probation and mandatory supervision cases under Penal Code section 1203.9.

(b) Definitions

As used in this rule:

(1) "Transferring court" means the superior court of the county in which the supervised person is supervised on probation or mandatory supervision.

(2) "Receiving court" means the superior court of the county to which transfer of the case and probation or mandatory supervision is proposed.

(c) Motion

Transfers may be made only after noticed motion in the transferring court.

(d) Notice

(1) If transfer is requested by the probation officer of the transferring county, the probation officer must provide written notice of the date, time, and place set for hearing on the motion to:

(A) The presiding judge of the receiving court or his or her designee;

(B) The probation officer of the receiving county or his or her designee;

(C) The prosecutor of the transferring county;

(D) The victim (if any);

(E) The supervised person; and

(F) The supervised person's last counsel of record (if any).

(2) If transfer is requested by any other party, the party must first request in writing that the probation officer of the transferring county notice the motion. The party may make the motion to the transferring court only if the probation officer refuses to do so. The probation officer must notify the party of his or her decision within 30 days of the party's request. Failure by the probation officer to notify the party of his or her decision within 30 days is deemed a refusal to make the motion.

(3) If the party makes the motion, the motion must include a declaration that the probation officer has refused to bring the motion, and the party must provide written notice of the date, time, and place set for hearing on the motion to:

(A) The presiding judge of the receiving court or his or her designee;

(B) The probation officers of the transferring and receiving counties or their designees;

(C) The prosecutor of the transferring county;

(D) The supervised person; and

(E) The supervised person's last counsel of record (if any).

Upon receipt of notice of a motion for transfer by a party, the probation officer of the transferring county must provide notice to the victim, if any.

(4) Notice of a transfer motion must be given at least 60 days before the date set for hearing on the motion.

(5) Before deciding a transfer motion, the transferring court must confirm that notice was given to the receiving court as required by (1) and (3).

(e) Comment

(1) No later than 10 days before the date set for hearing on the motion, the receiving court may provide comments to the transferring court regarding the proposed transfer.

(2) Any comments provided by the receiving court must be in writing and signed by a judge and must state why transfer is or is not appropriate.

(3) Before deciding a transfer motion, the transferring court must state on the record that it has received and considered any comments provided by the receiving court.

(f) Factors

The transferring court must consider at least the following factors when determining whether transfer is appropriate:

(1) The permanency of the supervised person's residence. As used in this subdivision, "residence" means the place where the supervised person customarily lives exclusive of employment, school, or other special or temporary purpose. A supervised person may have only one residence. The fact that the supervised person intends to change residence to the receiving county, without further evidence of how, when, and why this is to be accomplished, is insufficient to transfer supervision;

(2) The availability of appropriate programs for the supervised person, including substance abuse, domestic violence, sex offender, and collaborative court programs;

(3) Restitution orders, including whether transfer would impair the ability of the receiving court to determine a restitution amount or impair the ability of the victim to collect court-ordered restitution; and

(4) Victim issues, including:

(A) The residence and places frequented by the victim, including school and workplace; and

(B) Whether transfer would impair the ability of the court, law enforcement, or the probation officer of the transferring county to properly enforce protective orders.

(g) Transfer

(1) If the transferring court determines that the permanent residence of the supervised person is in the county of the receiving court, the transferring court must transfer the case unless it determines that transfer would be inappropriate and states its reasons on the record.

(2) To the extent possible, the transferring court must establish any amount of restitution owed by the supervised person before it orders the transfer.

(3) Transfer is effective the date the transferring court orders the transfer. Upon transfer of the case, the receiving court must accept the entire jurisdiction over the case.

(4) The orders for transfer must include an order committing the supervised person to the care and custody of the probation officer of the receiving county.

(5) Upon transfer of the case, the transferring court must transmit the entire original court file to the receiving court in all cases in which the supervisee is the sole defendant, except the transferring court shall not transfer (A) exhibits or (B) any records of payments. If transfer is ordered in a case involving more than one defendant, the transferring court must transmit certified copies of the entire original court file, except exhibits and any records of payments, to the receiving court upon transfer of the case.

(6) A certified copy of the entire court file may be electronically transmitted if an original paper court file does not exist. Upon receipt of an electronically transmitted certified copy of the entire court file from the transferring court, the receiving court must deem it an original file.

(7) Upon transfer the probation officer of the transferring county must transmit, at a minimum, any court orders, probation or mandatory supervision reports, and case plans to the probation officer of the receiving county.

(8) Upon transfer of the case, the probation officer of the transferring county must notify the supervised person of the transfer order. The supervised person must report to the probation officer of the receiving county no later than 30 days after transfer unless the transferring court orders the supervised person to report sooner. If the supervised person is in custody at the time of transfer, the supervised person must report to the probation officer of the

receiving county no later than 30 days after being released from custody unless the transferring court orders the supervised person to report sooner. Any jail sentence imposed as a condition of probation or mandatory supervision prior to transfer must be served in the transferring county unless otherwise authorized by law.

(9) Upon transfer of the case, only the receiving court may certify copies from the case file.

(h) Court–ordered debt

(1) In accordance with Penal Code section 1203.9(d) and (e):

(A) If the transferring court has ordered the defendant to pay fines, fees, forfeitures, penalties, assessments, or restitution, the transfer order must require that those and any other amounts ordered by the transferring court that are still unpaid at the time of transfer be paid by the defendant to the collection program for the transferring court for proper distribution and accounting once collected.

(B) The receiving court and receiving county probation department may not impose additional local fees and costs.

(C) Upon approval of a transferring court, a receiving court may elect to collect all of the court-ordered payments from a defendant attributable to the case under which the defendant is being supervised.

(2) Policies and procedures for implementation of the collection, accounting, and disbursement of court-ordered debt under this rule must be consistent with Judicial Council fiscal procedures available at *www.courts.ca.gov*. *(Adopted, eff. July 1, 2010. As amended, eff. Nov. 1, 2012; Feb. 20, 2014; Jan. 1, 2017; Jan. 1, 2021; March 14, 2022.)*

Advisory Committee Comment

Subdivision (g)(5) requires the transferring court to transmit the entire original court file, except exhibits and any records of payments, to the court of the receiving county in all cases in which the supervisee is the sole defendant. Before transmitting the entire original court file, transferring courts should consider retaining copies of the court file in the event of an appeal or a writ. In cases involving more than one defendant, subdivision (g)(5) requires the transferring court to transmit certified copies of the entire original court file to ensure that transferring courts are able to properly adjudicate any pending or future codefendant proceedings. Only documents related to the transferring defendant must be transmitted to the receiving court.

Subdivision (g)(7) clarifies that any jail sentence imposed as a condition of probation or mandatory supervision before transfer must be served in the transferring county unless otherwise authorized by law. For example, Penal Code section 1208.5 authorizes the boards of supervisors of two or more counties with work furlough programs to enter into agreements to allow work-furlough-eligible persons sentenced to or imprisoned in one county jail to transfer to another county jail.

Subdivision (h) requires defendants still owing fines, fees, forfeitures, penalties, assessments, or restitution to pay the transferring court's collection program. In counties where the county probation department collects this court-ordered debt, the term "collection program" is intended to include the county probation department.

Research References

West's California Judicial Council Forms CR–250, Notice and Motion for Transfer.
West's California Judicial Council Forms CR–251, Order for Transfer.
West's California Judicial Council Forms CR–252, Receiving Court Comment Form.
4 Witkin, California Criminal Law 4th Introduction to Criminal Procedure § 9 (2021), Rules of Court.
3 Witkin, California Criminal Law 4th Punishment § 603 (2021), Supervision of Probationer.

Chapter 2

POSTRELEASE

Rule 4.541. Minimum contents of supervising agency reports

(a) Application

This rule applies to supervising agency petitions for revocation of formal probation, parole, mandatory supervision under Penal Code section 1170(h)(5)(B), and postrelease community supervision under Penal Code section 3455.

(b) Definitions

As used in this rule:

(1) "Supervised person" means any person subject to formal probation, parole, mandatory supervision under Penal Code section 1170(h)(5)(B), or community supervision under Penal Code section 3451.

(2) "Formal probation" means the suspension of the imposition or execution of a sentence and the order of conditional and revocable release in the community under the supervision of a probation officer.

(3) "Court" includes any hearing officer appointed by a superior court and authorized to conduct revocation proceedings under Government Code section 71622.5.

(4) "Supervising agency" includes the county agency designated by the board of supervisors under Penal Code section 3451.

(c) Minimum contents

Except as provided in (d), a petition for revocation of supervision must include a written report that contains at least the following information:

(1) Information about the supervised person, including:

(A) Personal identifying information, including name and date of birth;

(B) Custody status and the date and circumstances of arrest;

(C) Any pending cases and case numbers;

(D) The history and background of the supervised person, including a summary of the supervised person's record of prior criminal conduct; and

(E) Any available information requested by the court regarding the supervised person's risk of recidivism, including any validated risk-needs assessments;

(2) All relevant terms and conditions of supervision and the circumstances of the alleged violations, including a summary of any statement made by the supervised person, and any victim information, including statements and type and amount of loss;

(3) A summary of any previous violations and sanctions; and

(4) Any recommended sanctions.

(d) Subsequent reports

If a written report was submitted as part of the original sentencing proceeding or with an earlier revocation petition, a subsequent report need only update the information required by (c). A subsequent report must include a copy of the original report if the original report is not contained in the court file.

(e) Parole and Postrelease Community Supervision Reports

In addition to the minimum contents described in (c), a report filed by the supervising agency in conjunction with a petition to revoke parole or postrelease community supervision must include the reasons for that agency's determination that intermediate sanctions without court intervention as authorized by Penal Code sections 3000.08(f) or 3454(b) are inappropriate responses to the alleged violations. *(Adopted, eff. Oct. 28, 2011. As amended, eff. Nov. 1, 2012; July 1, 2013.)*

Advisory Committee Comment

Subdivision (c). This subdivision prescribes minimum contents for supervising agency reports. Courts may require additional contents in light of local customs and needs.

Subdivision (c)(1)(D). The history and background of the supervised person may include the supervised person's social history, including family, education, employment, income, military, medical, psychological, and substance abuse information.

Subdivision (c)(1)(E). Penal Code section 3451(a) requires postrelease community supervision to be consistent with evidence-based practices, including supervision policies, procedures, programs, and practices demonstrated by scientific research to reduce recidivism among supervised persons. "Evidence-based practices" refers to "supervision policies, procedures, programs, and practices demonstrated by scientific research to reduce recidivism among individuals under probation, parole, or postrelease supervision." (Pen. Code, § 3450(b)(9).)

Subdivision (e). Penal Code sections 3000.08(d) and 3454(b) authorize supervising agencies to impose appropriate responses to alleged violations of parole and postrelease community supervision without court intervention, including referral to a reentry court under Penal Code section 3015 or flash incarceration in a county jail. Penal Code sections 3000.08(f) and 3455(a) require the supervising agency to determine that the intermediate sanctions authorized by sections 3000.08(d) and 3454(b) are inappropriate responses to the alleged violation *before* filing a petition to revoke parole or postrelease community supervision.

Research References

3 Witkin, California Criminal Law 4th Punishment § 687A (2021), (New) Uniform Revocation Procedure.
3 Witkin, California Criminal Law 4th Punishment § 802 (2021), In General.
3 Witkin, California Criminal Law 4th Punishment § 803 (2021), Petition.
3 Witkin, California Criminal Law 4th Punishment § 805A (2021), (New) in General.
3 Witkin, California Criminal Law 4th Punishment § 805B (2021), (New) Petition and Report.

Chapter 3

HABEAS CORPUS

Article 1

GENERAL PROVISIONS

Rule

Rule 4.545. Definitions

In this chapter, the following definitions apply:

(1) A "petition for writ of habeas corpus" is the petitioner's initial filing that commences a proceeding.

(2) An "order to show cause" is an order directing the respondent to file a return. The order to show cause is issued if the petitioner has made a prima facie showing that he or she is entitled to relief; it does not grant the relief requested. An order to show cause may also be referred to as "granting the writ."

(3) The "return" is the respondent's statement of reasons that the court should not grant the relief requested by the petitioner.

(4) The "denial" is the petitioner's pleading in response to the return. The denial may be also referred to as the "traverse."

(5) An "evidentiary hearing" is a hearing held by the trial court to resolve contested factual issues.

(6) An "order on writ of habeas corpus" is the court's order granting or denying the relief sought by the petitioner.

(7) The definitions in rule 8.601 also apply to this chapter. *(Adopted, eff. April 25, 2019.)*

Research References

6 Witkin, California Criminal Law 4th Criminal Writs § 67 (2021), Overview.
6 Witkin, California Criminal Law 4th Criminal Writs § 76 (2021), In General.
6 Witkin, California Criminal Law 4th Criminal Writs § 84 (2021), In General.

Article 2

NONCAPITAL HABEAS CORPUS PROCEEDINGS IN THE SUPERIOR COURT

Rule

Rule 4.550. Habeas corpus application

This article applies to habeas corpus proceedings in the superior court under Penal Code section 1473 et seq. or any other provision of law authorizing relief from unlawful confinement or unlawful conditions of confinement, except for death penalty-related habeas corpus proceedings, which are governed by rule 4.560 et seq. *(Adopted, eff. Jan. 1, 2002. As amended, eff. Jan. 1, 2007; April 25, 2019.)*

Research References

6 Witkin, California Criminal Law 4th Criminal Writs § 67 (2021), Overview.
6 Witkin, California Criminal Law 4th Criminal Writs § 76 (2021), In General.
6 Witkin, California Criminal Law 4th Criminal Writs § 84 (2021), In General.
4 Witkin, California Criminal Law 4th Introduction to Criminal Procedure § 9 (2021), Rules of Court.

Rule 4.551. Habeas corpus proceedings

(a) Petition; form and court ruling.

(1) Except as provided in (2), the petition must be on the *Petition for Writ of Habeas Corpus* (form HC–001).

(2) For good cause, a court may also accept for filing a petition that does not comply with (a)(1). A petition submitted by an attorney need not be on the Judicial Council form. However, a petition that is not on the Judicial Council form must comply with Penal Code section 1474 and must contain the pertinent information specified in the *Petition for Writ of Habeas Corpus* (form HC–001), including the information required regarding other petitions, motions, or applications filed in any court with respect to the conviction, commitment, or issue.

(3)(A) On filing, the clerk of the court must immediately deliver the petition to the presiding judge or his or her designee. The court must rule on a petition for writ of habeas corpus within 60 days after the petition is filed.

(B) If the court fails to rule on the petition within 60 days of its filing, the petitioner may file a notice and request for ruling.

(i) The petitioner's notice and request for ruling must include a declaration stating the date the petition was filed and the date of the notice and request for ruling, and indicating that the petitioner has not received a ruling on the petition. A copy of the original petition must be attached to the notice and request for ruling.

(ii) If the presiding judge or his or her designee determines that the notice is complete and the court has failed to rule, the presiding judge or his or her designee must assign the petition to a judge and calendar the matter for a decision without appearances within 30 days of the filing of the notice and request for ruling. If the judge assigned by the presiding judge rules on the petition before the date the petition is calendared for decision, the matter may be taken off calendar.

(4) For the purposes of (a)(3), the court rules on the petition by:

(A) Issuing an order to show cause under (c);

Ct. Rules

(B) Denying the petition for writ of habeas corpus; or

(C) Requesting an informal response to the petition for writ of habeas corpus under (b).

(5) The court must issue an order to show cause or deny the petition within 45 days after receipt of an informal response requested under (b).

(b) Informal response

(1) Before passing on the petition, the court may request an informal response from:

(A) The respondent or real party in interest; or

(B) The custodian of any record pertaining to the petitioner's case, directing the custodian to produce the record or a certified copy to be filed with the clerk of the court.

(2) A copy of the request must be sent to the petitioner. The informal response, if any, must be served on the petitioner by the party of whom the request is made. The informal response must be in writing and must be served and filed within 15 days. If any informal response is filed, the court must notify the petitioner that he or she may reply to the informal response within 15 days from the date of service of the response on the petitioner. If the informal response consists of records or copies of records, a copy of every record and document furnished to the court must be furnished to the petitioner.

(3) After receiving an informal response, the court may not deny the petition until the petitioner has filed a timely reply to the informal response or the 15–day period provided for a reply under (b)(2) has expired.

(c) Order to show cause

(1) The court must issue an order to show cause if the petitioner has made a prima facie showing that he or she is entitled to relief. In doing so, the court takes petitioner's factual allegations as true and makes a preliminary assessment regarding whether the petitioner would be entitled to relief if his or her factual allegations were proved. If so, the court must issue an order to show cause.

(2) On issuing an order to show cause, the court must appoint counsel for any unrepresented petitioner who desires but cannot afford counsel.

(3) An order to show cause is a determination that the petitioner has made a showing that he or she may be entitled to relief. It does not grant the relief sought in the petition.

(d) Return

If an order to show cause is issued as provided in (c), the respondent may, within 30 days thereafter, file a return. Any material allegation of the petition not controverted by the return is deemed admitted for purposes of the proceeding. The return must comply with Penal Code section 1480 and must be served on the petitioner.

(e) Denial

Within 30 days after service and filing of a return, the petitioner may file a denial. Any material allegation of the return not denied is deemed admitted for purposes of the proceeding. Any denial must comply with Penal Code section 1484 and must be served on the respondent.

(f) Evidentiary hearing; when required

Within 30 days after the filing of any denial or, if none is filed, after the expiration of the time for filing a denial, the court must either grant or deny the relief sought by the petition or order an evidentiary hearing. An evidentiary hearing is required if, after considering the verified petition, the return, any denial, any affidavits or declarations under penalty of perjury, and matters of which judicial notice may be taken, the court finds there is a reasonable likelihood that the petitioner may be entitled to relief and the petitioner's entitlement to relief depends on the resolution of an issue of fact. The petitioner must be produced at the evidentiary hearing unless the court, for good cause, directs otherwise.

(g) Reasons for denial of petition

Any order denying a petition for writ of habeas corpus must contain a brief statement of the reasons for the denial. An order only declaring the petition to be "denied" is insufficient.

(h) Extending or shortening time

On motion of any party or on the court's own motion, for good cause stated in the order, the court may shorten or extend the time for doing any act under this rule. A copy of the order must be mailed to each party. *(Formerly Rule 260, adopted and amended, eff. Jan. 1, 1982. Renumbered Rule 4.500, eff. Jan. 1, 2001. Renumbered Rule 4.551 and amended, eff. Jan. 1, 2002. As amended, eff. Jan. 1, 2004; Jan. 1, 2007; Jan. 1, 2009; Jan. 22, 2019.)*

Advisory Committee Comment

The court must appoint counsel on the issuance of an order to show cause. (*In re Clark* (1993) 5 Cal.4th 750, 780 and *People v. Shipman* (1965) 62 Cal.2d 226, 231–232.) The Court of Appeal has held that under Penal Code section 987.2, counties bear the expense of appointed counsel in a habeas corpus proceeding challenging the underlying conviction. (*Charlton v. Superior Court* (1979) 93 Cal.App.3d 858, 862.) Penal Code section 987.2 authorizes appointment of the public defender, or private counsel if there is no public defender available, for indigents in criminal proceedings.

Research References

West's California Judicial Council Forms HC–003, Petition for Writ of Habeas Corpus—Penal Commitment (Mental Health).
West's California Judicial Council Forms HC–004, Notice and Request for Ruling.
5 Witkin, California Criminal Law 4th Criminal Trial § 270 (2021), Habeas Corpus Proceeding.
6 Witkin, California Criminal Law 4th Criminal Writs § 67 (2021), Overview.
6 Witkin, California Criminal Law 4th Criminal Writs § 68 (2021), In General.
6 Witkin, California Criminal Law 4th Criminal Writs § 75 (2021), Informal Response and Determination of Petition.
6 Witkin, California Criminal Law 4th Criminal Writs § 76 (2021), In General.
6 Witkin, California Criminal Law 4th Criminal Writs § 83 (2021), Appointed Counsel.
6 Witkin, California Criminal Law 4th Criminal Writs § 84 (2021), In General.
6 Witkin, California Criminal Law 4th Criminal Writs § 88 (2021), Form of Return.
6 Witkin, California Criminal Law 4th Criminal Writs § 91 (2021), Nature.
6 Witkin, California Criminal Law 4th Criminal Writs § 95 (2021), Where Return is Filed in Superior Court.

Rule 4.552. Habeas corpus jurisdiction

(a) Proper court to hear petition

Except as stated in (b), the petition should be heard and resolved in the court in which it is filed.

(b) Transfer of petition

(1) The superior court in which the petition is filed must determine, based on the allegations of the petition, whether the matter should be heard by it or in the superior court of another county.

(2) If the superior court in which the petition is filed determines that the matter may be more properly heard by the superior court of another county, it may nonetheless retain jurisdiction in the matter or, without first determining whether a prima facie case for relief exists, order the matter transferred to the other county. Transfer may be ordered in the following circumstances:

(A) If the petition challenges the terms of a judgment, the matter may be transferred to the county in which judgment was rendered.

(B) If the petition challenges the conditions of an inmate's confinement, it may be transferred to the county in which the petitioner is confined. A change in the institution of confinement that effects a change in the conditions of confinement may constitute good cause to deny the petition.

(C) If the petition challenges the denial of parole or the petitioner's suitability for parole and is filed in a superior court other than the court that rendered the underlying judgment, the court in which the petition is filed should transfer the petition to the superior court in which the underlying judgment was rendered.

(3) The transferring court must specify in the order of transfer the reason for the transfer.

(4) If the receiving court determines that the reason for transfer is inapplicable, the receiving court must, within 30 days of receipt of the case, order the case returned to the transferring court. The transferring court must retain and resolve the matter as provided by these rules.

(c) Single judge must decide petition

A petition for writ of habeas corpus filed in the superior court must be decided by a single judge; it must not be considered by the appellate division of the superior court. *(Adopted, eff. Jan. 1, 2002. As amended, eff. Jan. 1, 2006; Jan. 1, 2007; Jan. 1, 2012.)*

Advisory Committee Comment

Subdivision (b)(2)(C). This subdivision is based on the California Supreme Court decision in *In re Roberts* (2005) 36 Cal.4th 575, which provides that petitions for writ of habeas corpus challenging denial or suitability for parole should first be adjudicated in the trial court that rendered the underlying judgment.

Research References

6 Witkin, California Criminal Law 4th Criminal Writs § 14 (2021), Proper Court to Determine Petition.

4 Witkin, California Criminal Law 4th Introduction to Criminal Procedure § 9 (2021), Rules of Court.

Article 3

DEATH PENALTY–RELATED HABEAS CORPUS PROCEEDINGS IN THE SUPERIOR COURT

Rule

Rule 4.560. Application of article

This article governs procedures for death penalty-related habeas corpus proceedings in the superior courts. *(Adopted, eff. April 25, 2019.)*

Research References

6 Witkin, California Criminal Law 4th Criminal Writs § 67C (2021), (New) Rules and Forms.

Rule 4.561. Superior court appointment of counsel in death penalty–related habeas corpus proceedings

(a) Purpose

This rule, in conjunction with rule 4.562, establishes a mechanism for superior courts to appoint qualified counsel to represent indigent persons in death penalty-related habeas corpus proceedings. This rule governs the appointment of counsel by superior courts only, including when the Supreme Court or a Court of Appeal has transferred a habeas corpus petition without having appointed counsel for the petitioner. It does not govern the appointment of counsel by the Supreme Court or a Court of Appeal.

(b) Prioritization of oldest judgments

In the interest of equity, both to the families of victims and to persons sentenced to death, California courts, whenever possible, should appoint death penalty-related habeas corpus counsel first for those persons subject to the oldest judgments of death.

(c) List of persons subject to a judgment of death

The Habeas Corpus Resource Center must maintain a list of persons subject to a judgment of death, organized by the date the judgment was entered by the sentencing court. The list must indicate whether death penalty-related habeas corpus counsel has been appointed for each person and, if so, the date of the appointment. The list must also indicate for each person whether a petition is pending in the Supreme Court.

(d) Notice of oldest judgments without counsel

(1) Within 30 days of the effective date of this rule, the Habeas Corpus Resource Center must identify the persons on the list required by (c) with the 25 oldest judgments of death for whom death penalty-related habeas corpus counsel have not been appointed.

(2) The Habeas Corpus Resource Center must notify the presiding judges of the superior courts in which these 25 judgments of death were entered that these are the oldest cases in which habeas corpus counsel have not been appointed. The Habeas Corpus Resource Center will send a copy of the notice to the administrative presiding justice of the appellate district in which the superior court is located.

(3) The presiding judge must identify the appropriate judge within the court to make an appointment and notify the judge that the case is among the oldest cases in which habeas corpus appointments are to be made.

(4) If qualified counsel is available for appointment to a case for which a petition is pending in the Supreme Court, the judge must provide written notice to the Supreme Court that counsel is available for appointment.

(5) On entry of an order appointing death penalty-related habeas corpus counsel, the appointing court must promptly send a copy of the appointment order to the Habeas Corpus Resource Center, which must update the list to reflect that counsel was appointed, and to the clerk/executive officer of the Supreme Court, the Attorney General, and the district attorney. The court must also send notice to the Habeas Corpus Resource Center, clerk/executive officer of the Supreme Court, Attorney General, and district attorney if, for any reason, the court determines that it does not need to make an appointment.

(6) When a copy of an appointment order, or information indicating that an appointment is for any reason not required, has been received by the Habeas Corpus Resource Center for 20 judgments, the center will identify the next 20 oldest judgments of death in cases in which death penalty-related habeas corpus counsel have not been appointed and send out a notice identifying these 20 judgments, and the procedures required by paragraphs (3) through (6) of this subdivision must be repeated.

(7) The presiding judge of a superior court may designate another judge within the court to carry out his or her duties in this subdivision.

(e) Appointment of counsel

(1) After the court receives a notice under (d)(2) and has made the findings required by Government Code section 68662, the

appropriate judge must appoint a qualified attorney or attorneys to represent the person in death penalty-related habeas corpus proceedings.

(2) The superior court must appoint an attorney or attorneys from the statewide panel of counsel compiled under rule 4.562(d)(4); an entity that employs qualified attorneys, including the Habeas Corpus Resource Center, the local public defender's office, or alternate public defender's office; or if the court has adopted a local rule under 4.562(g), an attorney determined to be qualified under that court's local rules. The court must at this time also designate an assisting entity or counsel, unless the appointed counsel is employed by the Habeas Corpus Resource Center.

(3) When the court appoints counsel to represent a person in a death penalty-related habeas corpus proceeding under this subdivision, the court must complete and enter an *Order Appointing Counsel in Death Penalty–Related Habeas Corpus Proceeding* (form HC–101). *(Adopted, eff. April 25, 2019.)*

Research References

6 Witkin, California Criminal Law 4th Criminal Writs § 67C (2021), (New) Rules and Forms.

Rule 4.562. Recruitment and determination of qualifications of attorneys for appointment in death penalty–related habeas corpus proceedings

(a) Purpose

This rule provides for a panel of attorneys from which superior courts may appoint counsel in death penalty-related habeas corpus proceedings.

(b) Regional habeas corpus panel committees

Each Court of Appeal must establish a death penalty-related habeas corpus panel committee as provided in this rule.

(c) Composition of regional habeas corpus panel committees

(1) The administrative presiding justice of the Court of Appeal appoints the members of each committee. Each committee must be composed of:

(A) One justice of the Court of Appeal to serve as the chair of the committee;

(B) A total of three judges from among those nominated by the presiding judges of the superior courts located within the appellate district; and

(C) A total of three attorneys from among those nominated by the entities in the six categories below. At least two of those appointed must have experience representing a petitioner in a death penalty-related habeas corpus proceeding.

(i) An attorney nominated by the Habeas Corpus Resource Center;

(ii) An attorney nominated by the California Appellate Project–San Francisco;

(iii) An attorney nominated by the appellate project with which the Court of Appeal contracts;

(iv) An attorney nominated by any of the federal public defenders' offices of the federal districts in which the participating courts are located;

(v) An attorney nominated by any of the public defenders' offices in a county where the participating courts are located; and

(vi) An attorney nominated by any entity not listed in this subparagraph, if the administrative presiding justice requests such a nomination.

(2) Each committee may also include advisory members, as authorized by the administrative presiding justice.

(3) The term of the chair and committee members is three years. Terms are staggered so that an approximately equal number of each committee's members changes annually. The administrative presiding justice has the discretion to remove or replace a chair or committee member for any reason.

(4) Except as otherwise provided in this rule, each committee is authorized to establish the procedures under which it is governed.

(d) Regional habeas corpus panel committee responsibilities

The committee has the following responsibilities:

(1) *Support superior court efforts to recruit applicants*

Each committee must assist the participating superior courts in their efforts to recruit attorneys to represent indigent petitioners in death penalty-related habeas corpus proceedings in the superior courts.

(2) *Accept applications*

Each committee must accept applications from attorneys who seek to be included on the panel of attorneys qualified for appointment in death penalty-related habeas corpus proceedings in the superior courts.

(A) The application must be on a *Declaration of Counsel re Minimum Qualifications for Appointment in Death Penalty–Related Habeas Corpus Proceedings* (form HC–100).

(B) Except as provided in (C), each committee must accept applications from attorneys whose principal place of business is within the appellate district and from only those attorneys.

(C) In addition to accepting applications from attorneys whose principal place of business is in its district, the First Appellate District committee must also accept applications from attorneys whose principal place of business is outside the state.

(3) *Review qualifications*

Each committee must review the applications it receives and determine whether the applicant meets the minimum qualifications stated in this division to represent persons in death penalty-related habeas corpus proceedings in the superior courts.

(4) *Provide names of qualified counsel for statewide panel*

(A) If a committee determines by a majority vote that an attorney is qualified to represent persons in death penalty-related habeas corpus proceedings in the superior court, it must include the name of the attorney on a statewide panel of qualified attorneys.

(B) Committees will provide to the Habeas Corpus Resource Center the names of attorneys who the committees determine meet the minimum qualifications. The Habeas Corpus Resource Center must consolidate the names into a single statewide panel, update the names on the panel at least quarterly, and make the most current panel available to superior courts on its website.

(C) Unless removed from the panel under (d)(6), an attorney included on the panel may remain on the panel for up to six years without submitting a renewed application.

(D) Inclusion on the statewide panel does not entitle an attorney to appointment by a superior court, nor does it compel an attorney to accept an appointment.

(5) *Match qualified attorneys to cases*

Each committee must assist a participating superior court in matching one or more qualified attorneys from the statewide panel to a person for whom counsel must be appointed under Government Code section 68662, if the court requests such assistance.

(6) *Remove attorneys from panel*

Suspension or disbarment of an attorney will result in removal of the attorney from the panel. Other disciplinary action, or a finding that counsel has provided ineffective assistance of counsel, may result in a reevaluation of the attorney's inclusion on the panel by the committee that initially determined the attorney to have met minimum qualifications.

(e) Consolidated habeas corpus panel committees

The administrative presiding justices of two or more Courts of Appeal may elect, following consultation with the presiding judges of the superior courts within their respective appellate districts, to operate a single committee to collectively fulfill the committee responsibilities for the superior courts in their appellate districts.

(f) Recruitment of qualified attorneys

The superior courts in which a judgment of death has been entered against an indigent person for whom habeas corpus counsel has not been appointed must develop and implement a plan to identify and recruit qualified counsel who may apply to be appointed.

(g) Local rule

A superior court may, by adopting a local rule, authorize appointment of qualified attorneys who are not members of the statewide panel. The local rule must establish procedures for submission and review of a *Declaration of Counsel re Minimum Qualifications for Appointment in Death Penalty–Related Habeas Corpus Proceedings* (form HC–100) and require attorneys to meet the minimum qualifications under rule 8.652(c). *(Adopted, eff. April 25, 2019.)*

Advisory Committee Comment

Subdivisions (d) and (f). In addition to the responsibilities identified in subdivisions (d) and (f), courts and regional committees are encouraged to support activities to expand the pool of attorneys that are qualified to represent petitioners in death penalty-related habeas corpus proceedings. Examples of such activities include providing mentoring and training programs and encouraging the use of supervised counsel.

Research References

West's California Judicial Council Forms HC–100, Declaration of Counsel Re Minimum Qualifications for Appointment in Dealth Penalty-Related Habeas Corpus Proceedings.

6 Witkin, California Criminal Law 4th Criminal Writs § 67C (2021), (New) Rules and Forms.

Rule 4.571. Filing of petition in the superior court

(a) Petition

(1) A petition and supporting memorandum must comply with this rule and, except as otherwise provided in this rule, with rules 2.100–2.117 relating to the form of papers.

(2) A memorandum supporting a petition must comply with rule 3.1113(b), (c), (f), (h), (i), and (*l*).

(3) The petition and supporting memorandum must support any reference to a matter in the supporting documents or declarations, or other supporting materials, by a citation to its index number or letter and page and, if applicable, the paragraph or line number.

(b) Supporting documents

(1) The record prepared for the automatic appeal, including any exhibits admitted in evidence, refused, or lodged, and all briefs, rulings, and other documents filed in the automatic appeal are deemed part of the supporting documents for the petition.

(2) The petition must be accompanied by a copy of any petition, excluding exhibits, pertaining to the same judgment and petitioner that was previously filed in any state court or any federal court, along with any order in a proceeding on such a petition that disposes of any claim or portion of a claim.

(3) If the petition asserts a claim that was the subject of a hearing, the petition must be accompanied by a certified transcript of that hearing.

(4) If any supporting documents have previously been filed in the same superior court in which the petition is filed and the petition so states and identifies the documents by case number, filing date and title of the document, copies of these documents need not be included in the supporting documents.

(5) Rule 8.486(c)(1) governs the form of any supporting documents accompanying the petition.

(6) If any supporting documents accompanying the petition or any subsequently filed paper are sealed, rules 2.550 and 2.551 govern. Notwithstanding rule 8.45(a), if any supporting documents accompanying the petition or any subsequently filed papers are confidential records, rules 8.45(b), (c), and 8.47 govern, except that rules 2.550 and 2.551 govern the procedures for making a motion or application to seal such records.

(7) When other laws establish specific requirements for particular types of sealed or confidential records that differ from the requirements in this subdivision, those specific requirements supersede the requirements in this subdivision.

(c) Filing and service

(1) If the petition is filed in paper form, an original and one copy must be filed, along with an original and one copy of the supporting documents.

(2) A court that permits electronic filing must specify any requirements regarding electronically filed petitions as authorized under rules 2.250 et seq.

(3) Petitioner must serve one copy of the petition and supporting documents on the district attorney, the Attorney General, and on any assisting entity or counsel.

(d) Noncomplying filings

The clerk must file an attorney's petition not complying with this rule if it otherwise complies with the rules of court, but the court may notify the attorney that it may strike the petition or impose a lesser sanction if the petition is not brought into compliance within a stated reasonable time of not less than five court days.

(e) Ruling on the petition

(1) The court must rule on the petition within 60 days after the petition is filed with the court or transferred to the court from another superior court.

(2) For purposes of this subdivision, the court rules on a petition by:

(A) Requesting an informal response to the petition;

(B) Issuing an order to show cause; or

(C) Denying the petition.

(3) If the court requests an informal response, it must issue an order to show cause or deny the petition within 30 days after the filing of the reply, or if none is filed, after the expiration of the time for filing the reply under rule 4.573(a)(3). *(Adopted eff. April 25, 2019.)*

Research References

6 Witkin, California Criminal Law 4th Criminal Writs § 67C (2021), (New) Rules and Forms.

Rule 4.572. Transfer of petitions

Unless the court finds good cause for it to consider the petition, a petition subject to this article that is filed in a superior court other than the court that imposed the sentence must be transferred to the court that imposed the sentence within 21 days of filing. The court in which the petition was filed must enter an order with the basis for its transfer or its finding of good cause for retaining the petition. *(Adopted eff. April 25, 2019.)*

Ct. Rules

Research References

6 Witkin, California Criminal Law 4th Criminal Writs § 67C (2021), (New) Rules and Forms.

Rule 4.573. Proceedings after the petition is filed

(a) Informal response and reply

(1) If the court requests an informal written response, it must serve a copy of the request on the district attorney, the Attorney General, the petitioner and on any assisting entity or counsel.

(2) The response must be served and filed within 45 days of the filing of the request, or a later date if the court so orders. One copy of the informal response and any supporting documents must be served on the petitioner and on any assisting entity or counsel. If the response and supporting documents are served in paper form, two copies must be served on the petitioner.

(3) If a response is filed, the court must notify the petitioner that a reply may be served and filed within 30 days of the filing of the response, or a later date if the court so orders. The court may not deny the petition until that time has expired.

(4) If a reply is filed, the petitioner must serve one copy of the reply and any supporting documents on the district attorney, the Attorney General, and on any assisting entity or counsel.

(5) The formatting of the response, reply, and any supporting documents must comply with the applicable requirements for petitions in rule 4.571(a) and (b). The filing of the response, reply, and any supporting documents must comply with the requirements for petitions in rule 4.571(c)(1) and (2).

(6) On motion of any party or on the court's own motion, for good cause stated in the order, the court may extend the time for a party to perform any act under this subdivision. If a party requests extension of a deadline in this subdivision, the party must explain the additional work required to meet the deadline.

(b) Order to show cause

If the petitioner has made the required prima facie showing that petitioner is entitled to relief, the court must issue an order to show cause. An order to show cause does not grant the relief sought in the petition. *(Adopted eff. April 25, 2019.)*

Research References

6 Witkin, California Criminal Law 4th Criminal Writs § 67C (2021), (New) Rules and Forms.

Rule 4.574. Proceedings following an order to show cause

(a) Return

(1) Any return must be served and filed within 45 days after the court issues the order to show cause, or a later date if the court so orders.

(2) The formatting of the return and any supporting documents must comply with the applicable requirements for petitions in rule 4.571(a) and (b). The filing of the return and any supporting documents must comply with the requirements for petitions in rule 4.571(c)(1) and (2).

(3) A copy of the return and any supporting documents must be served on the petitioner and on any assisting entity or counsel. If the return is served in paper form, two copies must be served on the petitioner.

(4) Any material allegation of the petition not controverted by the return is deemed admitted for purposes of the proceeding.

(b) Denial

(1) Unless the court orders otherwise, within 30 days after the return is filed, or a later date if the court so orders, the petitioner may serve and file a denial.

(2) The formatting of the denial and any supporting documents must comply with the applicable requirements for petitions in rule 4.571(a) and (b). The filing of the denial and any supporting documents must comply with the requirements for petitions in rule 4.571(c)(1) and (2).

(3) A copy of the denial and any supporting documents must be served on the district attorney, the Attorney General, and on any assisting entity or counsel.

(4) Any material allegation of the return not controverted in the denial is deemed admitted for purposes of the proceeding.

(c) Ruling on the petition

Within 60 days after filing of the denial, or if none is filed, after the expiration of the deadline for filing the denial under (b)(1), the court must either grant or deny the relief sought by the petition or set an evidentiary hearing.

(d) Evidentiary hearing

(1) An evidentiary hearing is required if, after considering the verified petition, the return, any denial, any affidavits or declarations under penalty of perjury, exhibits, and matters of which judicial notice may be taken, the court finds there is a reasonable likelihood that the petitioner may be entitled to relief and the petitioner's entitlement to relief depends on the resolution of an issue of fact.

(2) The court must assign a court reporter who uses computer-aided transcription equipment to report all proceedings under this subdivision.

(A) All proceedings under this subdivision, whether in open court, in conference in the courtroom, or in chambers, must be conducted on the record with a court reporter present. The court reporter must prepare and certify a daily transcript of all proceedings.

(B) Any computer-readable transcript produced by court reporters under this subdivision must conform to the requirements of Code of Civil Procedure section 271.

(3) Rule 3.1306(c) governs judicial notice.

(e) Additional briefing

The court may order additional briefing during or following the evidentiary hearing.

(f) Submission of cause

For purposes of article VI, section 19, of the California Constitution, a death penalty-related habeas corpus proceeding is submitted for decision at the conclusion of the evidentiary hearing, if one is held. If there is supplemental briefing after the conclusion of the evidentiary hearing, the matter is submitted when all supplemental briefing is filed with the court.

(g) Extension of deadlines

On motion of any party or on the court's own motion, for good cause stated in the order, the court may extend the time for a party to perform any act under this rule. If a party requests extension of a deadline in this rule, the party must explain the additional work required to meet the deadline. *(Adopted eff. April 25, 2019. As amended, eff. Sept. 1, 2021.)*

Research References

6 Witkin, California Criminal Law 4th Criminal Writs § 67C (2021), (New) Rules and Forms.

Rule 4.575. Decision on death penalty-related habeas corpus petition

On decision of the initial petition, the court must prepare and file a statement of decision specifying its order and explaining the factual and legal basis for its decision. The clerk of the court must serve a copy of the decision on the petitioner, the district attorney, the Attorney General, the clerk/executive officer of the Supreme Court, the clerk/executive officer of the Court of Appeal, and on any assisting entity or counsel. *(Adopted eff. April 25, 2019.)*

Research References

6 Witkin, California Criminal Law 4th Criminal Writs § 67C (2021), (New) Rules and Forms.

Rule 4.576. Successive petitions

(a) Notice of intent to dismiss

Before dismissing a successive petition under Penal Code section 1509(d), a superior court must provide notice to the petitioner and an opportunity to respond.

(b) Certificate of appealability

The superior court must grant or deny a certificate of appealability concurrently with the issuance of its decision denying relief on a successive death penalty-related habeas corpus petition. Before issuing its decision, the superior court may order the parties to submit arguments on whether a certificate of appealability should be granted. If the superior court grants a certificate of appealability, the certificate must identify the substantial claim or claims for relief shown by the petitioner and the substantial claim that the requirements of Penal Code section 1509(d) have been met. The superior court clerk must send a copy of the certificate to the petitioner, the Attorney General, the district attorney, the clerk/executive officer of the Court of Appeal and the district appellate project for the appellate district in which the superior court is located, the assisting counsel or entity, and the clerk/executive officer of the Supreme Court. The superior court clerk must send the certificate of appealability to the Court of Appeal when it sends the notice of appeal under rule 8.392(c). *(Adopted eff. April 25, 2019.)*

Research References

6 Witkin, California Criminal Law 4th Criminal Writs § 67C (2021), (New) Rules and Forms.

Rule 4.577. Transfer of files

Counsel for the petitioner must deliver all files counsel maintained related to the proceeding to the attorney representing petitioner in any appeal taken from the proceeding. *(Adopted eff. April 25, 2019.)*

Research References

6 Witkin, California Criminal Law 4th Criminal Writs § 67C (2021), (New) Rules and Forms.

Ct. Rules

Division 7

MISCELLANEOUS

Rule 4.601. Judicial determination of factual innocence form

(a) Form to be confidential

Any *Certificate of Identity Theft: Judicial Finding of Factual Innocence* (form CR–150) that is filed with the court is confidential. The clerk's office must maintain these forms in a manner that will protect and preserve their confidentiality.

(b) Access to the form

Notwithstanding (a), the court, the identity theft victim, the prosecution, and law enforcement agencies may have access to the *Certificate of Identity Theft: Judicial Finding of Factual Innocence* (form CR–150). The court may allow access to any other person on a showing of good cause. *(Adopted, eff. Jan. 1, 2002. As amended, eff. Jan. 1, 2007.)*

Research References

2 Witkin, California Criminal Law 4th Crimes Against Property § 214 (2021), Procedures for Victims of Identity Theft.

4 Witkin, California Criminal Law 4th Introduction to Criminal Procedure § 9 (2021), Rules of Court.

Rule 4.700. Firearm relinquishment procedures for criminal protective orders

(a) Application of rule

This rule applies when a court issues a criminal protective order under Penal Code section 136.2 during a criminal case or as a condition of probation under Penal Code section 1203.097(a)(2) against a defendant charged with a crime of domestic violence as defined in Penal Code section 13700 and Family Code section 6211.

(b) Purpose

This rule is intended to:

(1) Assist courts issuing criminal protective orders to determine whether a defendant subject to such an order owns, possesses, or controls any firearms; and

(2) Assist courts that have issued criminal protective orders to determine whether a defendant has complied with the court's order to relinquish or sell the firearms under Code of Civil Procedure section 527.9.

(c) Setting review hearing

(1) At any hearing where the court issues a criminal protective order, the court must consider all credible information, including information provided on behalf of the defendant, to determine if there is good cause to believe that the defendant has a firearm within his or her immediate possession or control.

(2) If the court finds good cause to believe that the defendant has a firearm within his or her immediate possession or control, the court must set a review hearing to ascertain whether the defendant has complied with the requirement to relinquish the firearm as specified in Code of Civil Procedure section 527.9. Unless the defendant is in custody at the time, the review hearing should occur within two court days after issuance of the criminal protective order. If circumstances warrant, the court may extend the review hearing to occur within 5 court days after issuance of the criminal protective order. The court must give the defendant an opportunity to present information at the review hearing to refute the allegation that he or she owns any firearms. If the defendant is in custody at the time the criminal protective order is issued, the court should order the defendant to appear for a review hearing within two court days after the defendant's release from custody.

(3) If the proceeding is held under Penal Code section 136.2, the court may, under Penal Code section 977(a)(2), order the defendant to personally appear at the review hearing. If the proceeding is held under Penal Code section 1203.097, the court should order the defendant to personally appear.

(d) Review hearing

(1) If the court has issued a criminal protective order under Penal Code section 136.2, at the review hearing:

(A) If the court finds that the defendant has a firearm in or subject to his or her immediate possession or control, the court must consider whether bail, as set, or defendant's release on own recognizance is appropriate.

(B) If the defendant does not appear at the hearing and the court orders that bail be revoked, the court should issue a bench warrant.

(2) If the criminal protective order is issued as a condition of probation under Penal Code section 1203.097, and the court finds at the review hearing that the defendant has a firearm in or subject to his or her immediate possession or control, the court must proceed under Penal Code section 1203.097(a)(12).

(3) In any review hearing to determine whether a defendant has complied with the requirement to relinquish firearms as specified in Code of Civil Procedure section 527.9, the burden of proof is on the prosecution. *(Adopted, eff. July 1, 2010. As amended, eff. Jan. 22, 2019.)*

Advisory Committee Comment

When issuing a criminal protective order under Penal Code section 136. 2 or 1203.097(a)(2), the court is required to order a defendant "to relinquish any firearm in that person's immediate possession or control, or subject to that person's immediate possession or control . . ." (Code Civ. Proc., § 527.9(b).) Mandatory Judicial Council form CR–160, *Criminal Protective Order—Domestic Violence,* includes a mandatory order in bold type that the defendant "must surrender to local law enforcement or sell to a licensed gun dealer any firearm owned or subject to his or her immediate possession or control within 24 hours after service of this order and must file a receipt with the court showing compliance with this order within 48 hours of receiving this order."

Courts are encouraged to develop local procedures to calendar review hearings for defendants in custody beyond the two-court-day time frame to file proof of firearms relinquishment with the court under Code of Civil Procedure section 527.9.

Research References

2 Witkin, California Criminal Law 4th Crimes Against Public Peace and Welfare § 242 (2021), Subjects of Protective and Restraining Orders.
4 Witkin, California Criminal Law 4th Introduction to Criminal Procedure § 9 (2021), Rules of Court.

Title 8

APPELLATE RULES

Division 1

RULES RELATING TO THE SUPREME COURT AND COURTS OF APPEAL

Chapter 1

GENERAL PROVISIONS

Article 2

SERVICE, FILING, FILING FEES, FORM, AND PRIVACY

Rule 8.25. Service, filing, and filing fees

(a) Service

(1) Before filing any document, a party must serve one copy of the document on the attorney for each party separately represented, on each unrepresented party, and on any other person or entity when required by statute or rule.

(2) The party must attach to the document presented for filing a proof of service showing service on each person or entity required to be served under (1), or, if using an electronic filing service provider's automatic electronic document service, the party may have the electronic filing service provider generate a proof of service. The proof must name each party represented by each attorney served.

(b) Filing

(1) A document is deemed filed on the date the clerk receives it.

(2) Unless otherwise provided by these rules or other law, a filing is not timely unless the clerk receives the document before the time to file it expires.

(3) A brief, an application to file an amicus curiae brief, an answer to an amicus curiae brief, a petition for rehearing, an answer to a petition for rehearing, a petition for transfer of an appellate division case to the Court of Appeal, an answer to such a petition for transfer, a petition for review, an answer to a petition for review, or a reply to an answer to a petition for review is timely if the time to file it has not expired on the date of:

(A) Its mailing by priority or express mail as shown on the postmark or the postal receipt; or

(B) Its delivery to a common carrier promising overnight delivery as shown on the carrier's receipt.

(4) The provisions of (3) do not apply to original proceedings.

(5) If the clerk receives a document by mail from an inmate or a patient in a custodial institution after the period for filing the document has expired but the envelope shows that the document was mailed or delivered to custodial officials for mailing within the period for filing the document, the document is deemed timely. The clerk must retain in the case file the envelope in which the document was received.

(c) Filing fees

(1) Unless otherwise provided by law, any document for which a filing fee is required under Government Code sections 68926 or 68927 must be accompanied at the time of filing by the required fee or an application for a waiver of court fees under rule 8.26.

(2) Documents for which a filing fee may be required under Government Code sections 68926 or 68927 include:

(A) A notice of appeal in a civil case. For purposes of this rule, "notice of appeal" includes a notice of cross-appeal;

(B) A petition for a writ within the original civil jurisdiction of the Supreme Court or Court of Appeal;

(C) A petition for review in a civil case in the Supreme Court;

(D) The following where the document is the first document filed in the Court of Appeal or Supreme Court by a party other than the appellant or petitioner in a civil case. For purposes of this rule, a "party other than the appellant" does not include a respondent who files a notice of cross-appeal.

(i) An application or an opposition or other response to an application;

(ii) A motion or an opposition or other response to a motion;

(iii) A respondent's brief;

(iv) A preliminary opposition to a petition for a writ, excluding a preliminary opposition requested by the court unless the court has notified the parties that it is considering issuing a peremptory writ in the first instance;

(v) A return (by demurrer, verified answer, or both) after the court issues an alternative writ or order to show cause;

(vi) Any answer to a petition for review in the Supreme Court; and

(vii) Any brief filed in the Supreme Court after the Court grants review.

(3) If a document other than the notice of appeal or a petition for a writ is not accompanied by the filing fee or an application for a waiver of court fees under rule 8.26, the clerk must file the document and must promptly notify the filing party in writing that the court may strike the document unless, within the stated time of not less than 5 court days after the notice is sent, the filing party either:

(A) Pays the filing fee; or

(B) Files an application for a waiver under rule 8.26 if the party has not previously filed such an application.

(4) If the party fails to take the action specified in a notice given under (3), the reviewing court may strike the document, but may vacate the striking of the document for good cause. *(Formerly Rule 40.1, adopted, eff. Jan. 1, 2005. Renumbered Rule 8.25 and amended, eff. Jan. 1, 2007. As amended, eff. Jan. 1, 2009; July 1, 2010; Jan. 1, 2011; Oct. 28, 2011; July 1, 2012; Jan. 1, 2018; Jan. 1, 2021.)*

Advisory Committee Comment

Subdivision (a). Code of Civil Procedure sections 1010.6-1013a describe generally permissible methods of service. *Information Sheet for Proof of Service (Court of Appeal)* (form APP–009–INFO) provides additional information about how to serve documents and how to provide proof of service. In the Supreme Court and the Courts of Appeal, registration with the court's electronic filing service provider is deemed to show agreement to accept service electronically at the email address provided, unless a party affirmatively opts out of electronic service under rule 8.78(a)(2)(B). This procedure differs from the procedure for electronic service in the superior courts, including their appellate divisions. See rules 2.250–2.261.

Subdivision (b) In general, to be filed on time, a document must be received by the clerk before the time for filing that document expires. There are, however, some limited exceptions to this general rule. For example, (5) provides that if the clerk receives a document by mail from a custodial institution after the deadline for filing the document has expired but the envelope shows that the document was mailed or delivered to custodial officials for mailing before the deadline expired, the document is deemed timely. This provision applies to notices of appeal as well as to other documents mailed from a custodial institution and reflects the "prison-delivery" exception articulated by the California Supreme Court in *In re Jordan* (1992) 4 Cal.4th 116 and *Silverbrand v. County of Los Angeles* (2009) 46 Cal.4th 106.

Note that if a deadline runs from the date of filing, it runs from the date that the document is actually received and deemed filed under (b)(1); neither (b)(3) nor (b)(5) changes that date. Nor do these provisions extend the date of finality of an appellate opinion or any other deadline that is based on finality, such as the deadline for the court to modify its opinion or order rehearing. Subdivision (b)(5) is also not intended to limit a criminal defendant's appeal rights under the case law of constructive filing. (See, e.g., *In re Benoit* (1973) 10 Cal.3d 72.)

Subdivision (b)(3). This rule includes applications to file amicus curiae briefs because, under rules 8.200(c)(4) and 8.520(f)(5), a proposed amicus curiae brief must accompany the application to file the brief.

Subdivision (c). Government Code section 68926 establishes fees in civil cases for filing a notice of appeal, filing a petition a for a writ within the original civil jurisdiction of the Supreme Court or a Court of Appeal, and for a party other than appellant or petitioner filing its first document in such an appeal or writ proceeding in the Supreme Court or a Court of Appeal. Government Code section 68927 establishes fees for filing a petition for review in a civil case in the Supreme Court and for a party other than the petitioner filing its first document in a civil case in the Supreme Court. These statutes provide that fees may not be charged in appeals from, petitions for writs involving, or petitions for review from decisions in juvenile cases or proceedings to declare a minor free from parental custody or control, or proceedings under the Lanterman–Petris–Short Act (Part 1 (commencing with Section 5000) of Division 5 of the Welfare and Institutions Code).

Subdivision (c)(2)(A) and (D). Under rule 8.100(f), "notice of appeal" includes a notice of a cross-appeal and a respondent who files a notice of cross-appeal in a civil appeal is considered an appellant and is required to pay the fee for filing a notice of appeal under Government Code section 68926.

A person who files an application to file an amicus brief is not a "party" and therefore is not subject to the fees applicable to a party other than the appellant or petitioner.

Subdivision (c)(3). Rule 8.100 establishes the procedures applicable when an appellant in a civil appeal fails to pay the fee for filing a notice of appeal or the deposit for the clerk's transcript that must also be paid at that time.

Research References

6 Witkin, California Criminal Law 4th Criminal Appeal § 102 (2021), Changes in Rules.

3 Witkin, California Criminal Law 4th Punishment § 54 (2021), Access to Civil Courts.

Rule 8.26. Waiver of fees and costs

(a) Application form

An application for initial waiver of court fees and costs in the Supreme Court or Court of Appeal must be made on *Request to Waive Court Fees* (form FW–001) or, if the application is made for the benefit of a (proposed) ward or conservatee, on *Request to Waive Court Fees (Ward or Conservatee)* (form FW–001–GC). The clerk must provide *Request to Waive Court Fees* (form FW–001) or *Request to Waive Court Fees (Ward or Conservatee)* (form FW–001–GC) and the *Information Sheet on Waiver of Fees and Costs (Supreme Court, Court of Appeal, or Appellate Division)* (form APP–015/FW–015–INFO) without charge to any person who requests any fee waiver application or states that he or she is unable to pay any court fee or cost.

(b) Filing the application

(1) *Appeals*

(A) The appellant should submit any application for initial waiver of court fees and costs for an appeal with the notice of appeal in the superior court that issued the judgment or order being appealed. For purposes of this rule, a respondent who files a notice of cross-appeal is an "appellant."

(B) A party other than the appellant should submit any application for initial waiver of the court fees and costs for an appeal at the time the fees are to be paid to the court.

(2) *Writ proceedings*

(A) The petitioner should submit the application for waiver of the court fees and costs for a writ proceeding with the writ petition.

(B) A party other than the petitioner should submit any application for initial waiver of the court fees and costs at the time the fees for filing its first document in the writ proceeding are to be paid to the reviewing court.

(3) *Petitions for review*

(A) The petitioner should submit the application for waiver of the court fees and costs for a petition for review in the Supreme Court with the petition.

(B) A party other than the petitioner should submit any application for initial waiver of the court fees and costs at the time the fees for filing its first document in the proceeding are to be paid to the Supreme Court.

(c) Procedure for determining application

The application must be considered and determined as required by Government Code section 68634.5. An order from the Supreme Court or Court of Appeal determining the application for initial fee waiver or setting a hearing on the application in the Supreme Court or Court of Appeal may be made on *Order on Court Fee Waiver (Court of Appeal or Supreme Court)* (form APP–016/FW–016) or, if the application is made for the benefit of a (proposed) ward or conservatee, on *Order on Court Fee Waiver (Court of Appeal or Supreme Court) (Ward or Conservatee)* (form APP–016–GC/FW–016–GC).

(d) Application granted unless acted on by the court

The application for initial fee waiver is deemed granted unless the court gives notice of action on the application within five court days after the application is filed.

(e) Court fees and costs waived

Court fees and costs that must be waived on granting an application for initial waiver of court fees and costs in the Supreme Court or Court of Appeal include:

(1) The fee for filing the notice of appeal and the fee required for a party other than the appellant filing its first document under Government Code section 68926;

(2) The fee for filing an original proceeding and the fee required for a party other than the petitioner filing its first document under Government Code section 68926;

(3) The fee for filing a petition for review and the fee required for a party other than the petitioner filing its first document under Government Code section 68927; and

(4) Any court fee for telephonic oral argument.

(f) Denial of the application

If an application is denied, the applicant must pay the court fees and costs or submit the new application or additional information requested by the court within 10 days after the clerk gives notice of the denial.

(g) Confidential Records

(1) No person may have access to an application for an initial fee waiver submitted to the court except the court and authorized court personnel, any persons authorized by the applicant, and any persons authorized by order of the court. No person may reveal any information contained in the application except as authorized by law or order of the court. An order granting access to an application or financial information may include limitations on who may access the information and on the use of the information after it has been released.

(2) Any person seeking access to an application or financial information provided to the court by an applicant must make the request by motion, supported by a declaration showing good cause as to why the confidential information should be released. *(Adopted, eff. July 1, 2009. As amended, eff. Oct. 28, 2011; Sept. 1, 2015.)*

Advisory Committee Comment

Subdivision (a). The waiver of court fees and costs is called an "initial" waiver because, under Government Code section 68630 and following, any such waiver may later be modified, terminated, or retroactively withdrawn if the court determines that the applicant was not or is no longer eligible for a waiver. The court may, at a later time, order that the previously waived fees be paid.

Subdivision (b)(1). If an applicant is requesting waiver of both Court of Appeal fees, such as the fee for filing the notice of appeal, and superior court fees, such as the fee for preparing, certifying, copying, and transmitting the clerk's transcript, the clerk of the superior court may ask the applicant to provide two signed copies of *Request to Waive Court Fees* (form FW–001).

Subdivision (e). The parties in an appeal may also ask the superior court to waive the deposit required under Government Code section 68926.1 and the fees under rule 8.122 for preparing, certifying, copying, and transmitting the clerk's transcript to the reviewing court and to the requesting party.

Research References

West's California Judicial Council Forms FW–001, Request to Waive Court Fees (Also Available in Spanish).

Rule 8.29. Service on nonparty public officer or agency

(a) Proof of service

When a statute or this rule requires a party to serve any document on a nonparty public officer or agency, the party must file proof of such service with the document unless a statute permits service after the document is filed, in which case the proof of service must be filed immediately after the document is served on the public officer or agency.

(b) Identification on cover

When a statute or this rule requires a party to serve any document on a nonparty public officer or agency, the cover of the document must contain a statement that identifies the statute or rule requiring service of the document on the public officer or agency in substantially the following form: "Service on [insert name of the officer or agency] required by [insert citation to the statute or rule]."

(c) Service on the Attorney General

In addition to any statutory requirements for service of briefs on public officers or agencies, a party must serve its brief or petition on the Attorney General if the brief or petition:

(1) Questions the constitutionality of a state statute; or

(2) Is filed on behalf of the State of California, a county, or an officer whom the Attorney General may lawfully represent in:

(A) A criminal case;

(B) A case in which the state or a state officer in his or her official capacity is a party; or

(C) A case in which a county is a party, unless the county's interest conflicts with that of the state or a state officer in his or her official capacity.

(Formerly Rule 44.5, adopted, eff. Jan. 1, 2004. As amended, eff. July 1, 2004. Renumbered Rule 8.29 and amended, eff. Jan. 1, 2007.)

Advisory Committee Comment

Rule 8.29 refers to statutes that require a party to serve documents on a nonparty public officer or agency. For a list of examples of such statutory requirements, please see the *Civil Case Information Statement* (form APP–004).

Rule 8.32. Address and other contact information of record; notice of change

(a) Address and other contact information of record

In any case pending before the court, the court will use the mailing address, telephone number, fax number, and e-mail address that an attorney or unrepresented party provides on the first document filed in that case as the mailing address, telephone number, fax number, and e-mail address of record unless the attorney or unrepresented party files a notice under (b).

(b) Notice of change

(1) An attorney or unrepresented party whose mailing address, telephone number, fax number, or e-mail address changes while a case is pending must promptly serve and file a written notice of the change in the reviewing court in which the case is pending.

(2) The notice must specify the title and number of the case or cases to which it applies. If an attorney gives the notice, the notice must include the attorney's California State Bar number.

(c) Multiple addresses or other contact information

If an attorney or an unrepresented party has more than one mailing address, telephone number, fax number, or e-mail address, only one mailing address, telephone number, fax number, or e-mail address for that attorney or unrepresented party may be used in a given case. *(Formerly Rule 40.5, adopted, eff. Jan. 1, 2005. Renumbered Rule 8.32 and amended, eff. Jan. 1, 2007. As amended, eff. Jan. 1, 2008; July 1, 2008; Jan. 1, 2013.)*

Rule 8.36. Substituting parties; substituting or withdrawing attorneys

(a) Substituting parties

Substitution of parties in an appeal or original proceeding must be made by serving and filing a motion in the reviewing court. The clerk of that court must notify the superior court of any ruling on the motion.

(b) Substituting attorneys

A party may substitute attorneys by serving and filing in the reviewing court a substitution signed by the party represented and the new attorney. In all appeals and in original proceedings related to a superior court proceeding, the party must also serve the superior court.

(c) Withdrawing attorney

(1) An attorney may request withdrawal by filing a motion to withdraw. Unless the court orders otherwise, the motion need be served only on the party represented and the attorneys directly affected.

(2) The proof of service need not include the address of the party represented. But if the court grants the motion, the withdrawing attorney must promptly provide the court and the opposing party with the party's current or last known address and telephone number.

(3) In all appeals and in original proceedings related to a superior court proceeding, the reviewing court clerk must notify the superior court of any ruling on the motion.

(4) If the motion is filed in any proceeding pending in the Supreme Court after grant of review, the clerk/executive officer of the Supreme Court must also notify the Court of Appeal of any ruling on the motion. *(Formerly Rule 48, adopted, eff. Jan. 1, 2005. Renumbered Rule 8.36, eff. Jan. 1, 2007. As amended, eff. Jan. 1, 2018.)*

Rule 8.40. Cover requirements for documents filed in paper form

(a) Cover color

(1) As far as practicable, the covers of briefs and petitions filed in paper form must be in the following colors:

Appellant's opening brief or appendix	green
Respondent's brief or appendix	yellow
Appellant's reply brief or appendix	tan
Joint appendix	white
Amicus curiae brief	gray
Answer to amicus curiae brief	blue
Petition for rehearing	orange
Answer to petition for rehearing	blue
Petition for original writ	red
Answer (or opposition) to petition for original writ	red
Reply to answer (or opposition) to petition for original writ	red
Petition for transfer of appellate division case to Court of Appeal	white
Answer to petition for transfer of appellate division case to Court of Appeal	blue
Petition for review	white
Answer to petition for review	blue
Reply to answer to petition for review	white
Opening brief on the merits	white
Answer brief on the merits	blue
Reply brief on the merits	white

(2) In appeals under rule 8.216, the cover of a combined respondent's brief and appellant's opening brief filed in paper form must be yellow, and the cover of a combined reply brief and respondent's brief filed in paper form must be tan.

(3) A paper brief or petition not conforming to (1) or (2) must be accepted for filing, but in case of repeated violations by an attorney or party, the court may proceed as provided in rule 8.204(e)(2).

(b) Cover information

(1) Except as provided in (2), the cover—or first page if there is no cover—of every document filed in a reviewing court must include the name, mailing address, telephone number, fax number (if available), e-mail address (if available), and California State Bar number of each attorney filing or joining in the document, or of the party if he or she is unrepresented. The inclusion of a fax number or e-mail address on any document does not constitute consent to service by fax or e-mail unless otherwise provided by law.

(2) If more than one attorney from a law firm, corporation, or public law office is representing one party and is joining in the document, the name and State Bar number of each attorney joining in the document must be provided on the cover. The law firm, corporation, or public law office representing each party must designate one attorney to receive notices and other communication in the case from the court by placing an asterisk before that attorney's name on the cover and must provide the contact information specified under (1) for that attorney. Contact information for the other attorneys from the same law firm, corporation, or public law office is not required but may be provided. *(Formerly Rule 44, adopted, eff. Jan. 1, 2005. As amended, eff. Jan. 1, 2006. Renumbered Rule 8.40 and amended, eff. Jan. 1, 2007. As amended, eff. Jan. 1, 2011; Jan. 1, 2013; Jan. 1, 2016; Jan. 1, 2020.)*

Research References

6 Witkin, California Criminal Law 4th Criminal Writs § 69 (2021), Format in Reviewing Court.

6 Witkin, California Criminal Law 4th Criminal Writs § 90 (2021), Where Return is Filed in Reviewing Court.

Rule 8.41. Protection of privacy in documents and records

The provisions on protection of privacy in rule 1.201 apply to documents and records under these rules. *(Adopted, eff. Jan. 1, 2017.)*

Research References

6 Witkin, California Criminal Law 4th Criminal Appeal § 53A (2021), (New) in General.

Rule 8.42. Requirements for signatures of multiple parties on filed documents

When a document to be filed in paper form, such as a stipulation, requires the signatures of multiple parties, the original signature of at least one party must appear on the document filed in the reviewing court; the other signatures may be in the form of copies of the signed signature page of the document. Electronically filed documents must comply with the relevant provisions of rule 8.77. *(Adopted, eff. Jan. 1, 2014. As amended, eff. Jan. 1, 2016.)*

Rule 8.44. Number of copies of filed documents

(a) Documents filed in the Supreme Court

Except as these rules provide otherwise, the number of copies of every brief, petition, motion, application, or other document that must be filed in the Supreme Court and that is filed in paper form is as follows:

(1) An original of a petition for review, an answer, a reply, a brief on the merits, an amicus curiae brief, an answer to an amicus curiae brief, a petition for rehearing, or an answer to a petition for rehearing and either

(A) 13 paper copies; or

(B) 8 paper copies and one electronic copy;

(2) Unless the court orders otherwise, an original of a petition for a writ within the court's original jurisdiction, an opposition or other response to the petition, or a reply; and either:

(A) 10 paper copies; or

(B) 8 paper copies and one electronic copy;

(3) Unless the court orders otherwise, an original and 2 copies of any supporting document accompanying a petition for writ of habeas corpus, an opposition or other response to the petition, or a reply;

(4) An original and 8 copies of a petition for review to exhaust state remedies under rule 8.508, an answer, or a reply, or an amicus curiae letter under rule 8.500(g);

(5) An original and 8 copies of a motion or an opposition or other response to a motion; and

(6) An original and 1 copy of an application, including an application to extend time, or any other document.

(b) Documents filed in a Court of Appeal

Except as these rules provide otherwise, the number of copies of every brief, petition, motion, application, or other document that must be filed in a Court of Appeal and that is filed in paper form is as follows:

(1) An original and 4 paper copies of a brief, an amicus curiae brief, or an answer to an amicus curiae brief. In civil appeals, for briefs other than petitions for rehearing or answers thereto, 1 electronic copy or, in case of undue hardship, proof of delivery of 4 paper copies to the Supreme Court, as provided in rule 8.212(c) is also required;

(2) An original of a petition for writ of habeas corpus filed under rule 8.380 by a person who is not represented by an attorney and 1 set of any supporting documents;

(3) An original and 4 copies of any other petition, an answer, opposition or other response to a petition, or a reply;

(4) Unless the court orders otherwise, an original and 1 copy of a motion or an opposition or other response to a motion;

(5) Unless the court provides otherwise by local rule or order, 1 set of any separately bound supporting documents accompanying a document filed under (3) or (4);

(6) An original and 1 copy of an application, other than an application to extend time, or any other document; and

(7) An original and 1 copy of an application to extend time. In addition, 1 copy for each separately represented and unrepresented party must be provided to the court.

(c) Electronic copies of paper documents

Even when filing a paper document is permissible, a court may provide by local rule for the submission of an electronic copy of the paper document either in addition to the copies of the document required to be filed under (a) or (b) or as a substitute for one or more of these copies. The local rule must provide for an exception if it would cause undue hardship for a party to submit an electronic copy. *(Adopted, eff. Jan. 1, 2007. As amended, eff. Jan. 1, 2007; Jan. 1, 2011; Jan. 1, 2013; Jan. 1, 2014; Jan. 1, 2016; Jan. 1, 2020.)*

Advisory Committee Comment

The initial sentence of this rule acknowledges that there are exceptions to this rule's requirements concerning the number of copies. See, for example, rule 8.150, which specifies the number of copies of the record that must be filed.

Information about electronic submission of copies of documents can be found on the web page for the Supreme Court at: *www.courts.ca.gov/appellatebriefs* or for the Court of Appeal District in which the brief is being filed at: *www.courts.ca.gov/courtsofappeal.*

Note that submitting an electronic copy of a document under this rule or under a local rule adopted pursuant to subdivision (c) does not constitute filing a document electronically under rules 8.70–8.79 and thus does not substitute for the filing of the original document with the court in paper format.

Research References

6 Witkin, California Criminal Law 4th Criminal Appeal § 153 (2021), Requirement.

6 Witkin, California Criminal Law 4th Criminal Writs § 69 (2021), Format in Reviewing Court.

6 Witkin, California Criminal Law 4th Criminal Writs § 90 (2021), Where Return is Filed in Reviewing Court.

Article 3

SEALED AND CONFIDENTIAL RECORDS

Rule

Rule 8.45. General provisions

(a) Application

The rules in this article establish general requirements regarding sealed and confidential records in appeals and original proceedings in the Supreme Court and Courts of Appeal. Where other laws establish specific requirements for particular types of sealed or confidential records that differ from the requirements in this article, those specific requirements supersede the requirements in this article.

(b) Definitions

As used in this article:

(1) "Record" means all or part of a document, paper, exhibit, transcript, or other thing filed or lodged with the court by electronic means or otherwise.

(2) A "lodged" record is a record temporarily deposited with the court but not filed.

(3) A "sealed" record is a record that is closed to inspection by the public or a party by order of a court under rules 2.550–2.551 or rule 8.46.

(4) A "conditionally sealed" record is a record that is filed or lodged subject to a pending application or motion to file it under seal.

(5) A "confidential" record is a record that, in court proceedings, is required by statute, rule of court, or other authority except a court order under rules 2.550–2.551 or rule 8.46 to be closed to inspection by the public or a party.

(6) A "redacted version" is a version of a filing from which all portions that disclose material contained in a sealed, conditionally sealed, or confidential record have been removed.

(7) An "unredacted version" is a version of a filing or a portion of a filing that discloses material contained in a sealed, conditionally sealed, or confidential record.

(c) Format of sealed and confidential records

(1) Unless otherwise provided by law or court order, sealed or confidential records that are part of the record on appeal or the supporting documents or other records accompanying a motion, petition for a writ of habeas corpus, other writ petition, or other filing in the reviewing court must be kept separate from the rest of a clerk's or reporter's transcript, appendix, supporting documents, or other

records sent to the reviewing court and in a secure manner that preserves their confidentiality.

(A) If the records are in paper format, they must be placed in a sealed envelope or other appropriate sealed container. This requirement does not apply to a juvenile case file but does apply to any record contained within a juvenile case file that is sealed or confidential under authority other than Welfare and Institutions Code section 827 et seq.

(B) Sealed records, and if applicable the envelope or other container, must be marked as "Sealed by Order of the Court on (*Date*)."

(C) Confidential records, and if applicable the envelope or other container, must be marked as "Confidential (*Basis*)—May Not Be Examined Without Court Order." The basis must be a citation to or other brief description of the statute, rule of court, case, or other authority that establishes that the record must be closed to inspection in the court proceeding.

(D) The superior court clerk or party transmitting sealed or confidential records to the reviewing court must prepare a sealed or confidential index of these materials. If the records include a transcript of any in-camera proceeding, the index must list the date and the names of all parties present at the hearing and their counsel. This index must be transmitted and kept with the sealed or confidential records.

(2) Except as provided in (3) or by court order, the alphabetical and chronological indexes to a clerk's or reporter's transcript, appendix, supporting documents, or other records sent to the reviewing court that are available to the public must list each sealed or confidential record by title, not disclosing the substance of the record, and must identify it as "Sealed" or "Confidential"—May Not Be Examined Without Court Order."

(3) Records relating to a request for funds under Penal Code section 987.9 or other proceedings the occurrence of which is not to be disclosed under the court order or applicable law must not be bound together with, or electronically transmitted as a single document with, other sealed or confidential records and must not be listed in the index required under (1)(D) or the alphabetical or chronological indexes to a clerk's or reporter's transcript, appendix, supporting documents to a petition, or other records sent to the reviewing court.

(d) Transmission of and access to sealed and confidential records

(1) A sealed or confidential record must be transmitted in a secure manner that preserves the confidentiality of the record.

(2) Unless otherwise provided by (3)—(5) or other law or court order, a sealed or confidential record that is part of the record on appeal or the supporting documents or other records accompanying a motion, petition for a writ of habeas corpus, other writ petition, or other filing in the reviewing court must be transmitted only to the reviewing court and the party or parties who had access to the record in the trial court or other proceedings under review and may be examined only by the reviewing court and that party or parties. If a party's attorney but not the party had access to the record in the trial court or other proceedings under review, only the party's attorney may examine the record.

(3) Except as provided in (4), if the record is a reporter's transcript or any document related to any in-camera hearing from which a party was excluded in the trial court, the record must be transmitted to and examined by only the reviewing court and the party or parties who participated in the in-camera hearing.

(4) A reporter's transcript or any document related to an in-camera hearing concerning a confidential informant under Evidence Code sections 1041–1042 must be transmitted only to the reviewing court.

(5) A probation report must be transmitted only to the reviewing court and to appellate counsel for the People and the defendant who was the subject of the report. *(Adopted, eff. Jan. 1, 2014. As amended, eff. Jan. 1, 2016; Jan. 1, 2019.)*

Advisory Committee Comment

Subdivision (a). Many laws address sealed and confidential records. These laws differ from each other in a variety of respects, including what information is closed to inspection, from whom it is closed, under what circumstances it is closed, and what procedures apply to closing or opening it to inspection. It is very important to determine if any such law applies with respect to a particular record because where other laws establish specific requirements that differ from the requirements in this article, those specific requirements supersede the requirements in this article.

Subdivision (b)(5). Examples of confidential records are records in juvenile proceedings (Welf. & Inst. Code, § 827 and California Rules of Court, rule 8.401), records of the family conciliation court (Fam. Code, § 1818(b)), fee waiver applications (Gov. Code, § 68633(f)), and court-ordered diagnostic reports (Penal Code, § 1203.03). This term also encompasses records closed to inspection by a court order other than an order under rules 2.550–2.551 or 8.46, such as situations in which case law, statute, or rule has established a category of records that must be closed to inspection and a court has found that a particular record falls within that category and has ordered that it be closed to inspection. Examples include discovery material subject to a protective order under Code of Civil Procedure sections 2030.090, 2032.060, or 2033.080 and records closed to inspection by court order under *People v. Marsden* (1970) 2 Cal.3d 118 or *Pitchess v. Superior Court* (1974) 11 Cal.3d 531. For more examples of confidential records, please see appendix 1 of the *Trial Court Records Manual* at *www.courts.ca.gov/documents/trial-court-records-manual.pdf*.

Subdivisions (c) and (d). The requirements in this rule for format and transmission of and access to sealed and confidential records apply only unless otherwise provided by law. Special requirements that govern transmission of and/or access to particular types of records may supersede the requirements in this rule. For example, rules 8.619(g) and 8.622(e) require copies of reporters' transcripts in capital cases to be sent to the Habeas Corpus Resource Center and the California Appellate Project in San Francisco, and under rules 8.336(g)(2) and 8.409(e)(2), in non-capital felony appeals, if the defendant—or in juvenile appeals, if the appellant or the respondent—is not represented by appellate counsel when the clerk's and reporter's transcripts are certified as correct, the clerk must send that counsel's copy of the transcripts to the district appellate project.

Subdivision (c)(1)(C). For example, for juvenile records, this mark could state "Confidential—Welf. & Inst. Code, § 827" or "Confidential—Juvenile Case File"; for a fee waiver application, this mark could state "Confidential—Gov. Code, § 68633(f)" or "Confidential—Fee Waiver Application"; and for a transcript of an in-camera hearing under *People v. Marsden* (1970) 2 Cal.3d 118, this mark could say "Confidential—*Marsden* Hearing."

Subdivision (c)(2). Subdivision (c)(2) requires that, with certain exceptions, the alphabetical and chronological indexes to the clerk's and reporter's transcripts, appendixes, and supporting documents must list any sealed and confidential records but identify them as sealed or confidential. The purpose of this provision is to assist the parties in making—and the court in adjudicating—motions to unseal sealed records or to provide confidential records to a party. To protect sealed and confidential records from disclosure until the court issues an order, however, each index must identify sealed and confidential records without disclosing their substance.

Subdivision (c)(3). Under certain circumstances, the Attorney General has a statutory right to request copies of documents filed under Penal Code section 987.9(d). To facilitate compliance with such requests, this subdivision requires that such documents not be bound with other confidential documents.

Subdivision (d). See rule 8.47(b) for special requirements concerning access to certain confidential records.

Subdivision (d)(2) and (3). Because the term "party" includes any attorney of record for that party, under rule 8.10(3), when a party who had access to a record in the trial court or other proceedings under review or who participated in an in-camera hearing—such as a *Marsden* hearing in a criminal or juvenile proceeding—is represented by appellate counsel, the confidential record or transcript must be transmitted to that party's appellate counsel. Under rules 8.336(g)(2) and 8.409(e)(2), in non-capital felony appeals, if the defendant—or in juvenile appeals, if the appellant or the respondent—is not represented by appellate counsel when the clerk's and reporter's transcripts are certified as correct, the clerk must send the copy of the transcripts that would go to appellate counsel, including confidential records such as transcripts of *Marsden* hearings, to the district appellate project.

Subdivision (d)(5). This rule limits to whom a copy of a probation report is transmitted based on the provisions of Penal Code section 1203.05, which limit who may inspect or copy probation reports.

Research References

6 Witkin, California Criminal Law 4th Criminal Appeal § 53A (2021), (New) in General.
6 Witkin, California Criminal Law 4th Criminal Appeal § 53B (2021), (New) Definitions.
6 Witkin, California Criminal Law 4th Criminal Appeal § 53C (2021), (New) in General.
6 Witkin, California Criminal Law 4th Criminal Appeal § 53G (2021), (New) Confidential Records.
6 Witkin, California Criminal Law 4th Criminal Appeal § 53H (2021), (New) Format of Sealed and Confidential Records.
6 Witkin, California Criminal Law 4th Criminal Appeal § 53–I (2021), (New) Transmission and Access to Sealed and Confidential Records.
6 Witkin, California Criminal Law 4th Criminal Appeal § 128 (2021), In General.
6 Witkin, California Criminal Law 4th Criminal Appeal § 129 (2021), Normal Record.
6 Witkin, California Criminal Law 4th Criminal Appeal § 131 (2021), Confidential Material.
6 Witkin, California Criminal Law 4th Criminal Appeal § 132 (2021), Complete Record in Capital Case.
6 Witkin, California Criminal Law 4th Criminal Writs § 69 (2021), Format in Reviewing Court.
6 Witkin, California Criminal Law 4th Criminal Writs § 75 (2021), Informal Response and Determination of Petition.

Rule 8.46. Sealed records

(a) Application

This rule applies to sealed records and records proposed to be sealed on appeal and in original proceedings, but does not apply to confidential records.

(b) Record sealed by the trial court

If a record sealed by order of the trial court is part of the record on appeal or the supporting documents or other records accompanying a motion, petition for a writ of habeas corpus, other writ petition, or other filing in the reviewing court:

(1) The sealed record must remain sealed unless the reviewing court orders otherwise under (e). Rule 8.45 governs the form and transmission of and access to sealed records.

(2) The record on appeal or supporting documents filed in the reviewing court must also include:

(A) The motion or application to seal filed in the trial court;

(B) All documents filed in the trial court supporting or opposing the motion or application; and

(C) The trial court order sealing the record.

(c) Record not sealed by the trial court

A record filed or lodged publicly in the trial court and not ordered sealed by that court must not be filed under seal in the reviewing court.

(d) Record not filed in the trial court; motion or application to file under seal

(1) A record not filed in the trial court may be filed under seal in the reviewing court only by order of the reviewing court; it must not be filed under seal solely by stipulation or agreement of the parties.

(2) To obtain an order under (1), a party must serve and file a motion or application in the reviewing court, accompanied by a declaration containing facts sufficient to justify the sealing. At the same time, the party must lodge the record under (3), unless good cause is shown not to lodge it.

(3) To lodge a record, the party must transmit the record to the court in a secure manner that preserves the confidentiality of the record to be lodged. The record must be transmitted separately from the rest of a clerk's or reporter's transcript, appendix, supporting documents, or other records sent to the reviewing court with a cover sheet that complies with rule 8.40(b) if the record is in paper form or rule 8.74(a)(9) if the record is in electronic form, and that labels the contents as "CONDITIONALLY UNDER SEAL." If the record is in paper format, it must be placed in a sealed envelope or other appropriate sealed container.

(4) If necessary to prevent disclosure of material contained in a conditionally sealed record, any motion or application, any opposition, and any supporting documents must be filed in a redacted version and lodged in a complete unredacted version conditionally under seal. The cover of the redacted version must identify it as "Public—Redacts material from conditionally sealed record." In juvenile cases, the cover of the redacted version must identify it as "Redacted version—Redacts material from conditionally sealed record." The cover of the unredacted version must identify it as "May Not Be Examined Without Court Order—Contains material from conditionally sealed record." Unless the court orders otherwise, any party that had access to the record in the trial court or other proceedings under review must be served with a complete, unredacted version of all papers as well as a redacted version.

(5) On receiving a lodged record, the clerk must note the date of receipt on the cover sheet and retain but not file the record. The record must remain conditionally under seal pending determination of the motion or application.

(6) The court may order a record filed under seal only if it makes the findings required by rule 2.550(d)–(e).

(7) If the court denies the motion or application to seal the record, the lodging party may notify the court that the lodged record is to be filed unsealed. This notification must be received within 10 days of the order denying the motion or application to seal, unless otherwise ordered by the court. On receipt of this notification, the clerk must unseal and file the record. If the lodging party does not notify the court within 10 days of the order, the clerk must (1) return the lodged record to the lodging party if it is in paper form, or (2) permanently delete the lodged record if it is in electronic form.

(8) An order sealing the record must direct the sealing of only those documents and pages or, if reasonably practical, portions of those documents and pages, that contain the material that needs to be placed under seal. All other portions of each document or page must be included in the public file.

(9) Unless the sealing order provides otherwise, it prohibits the parties from disclosing the contents of any materials that have been sealed in anything that is subsequently publicly filed.

(e) Challenge to an order denying a motion or application to seal a record

Notwithstanding the provisions in (d)(1)—(2), when an appeal or original proceeding challenges an order denying a motion or application to seal a record, the appellant or petitioner must lodge the subject record labeled as conditionally under seal in the reviewing court as provided in (d)(3)—(5), and the reviewing court must maintain the record conditionally under seal during the pendency of the appeal or original proceeding. Once the reviewing court's decision on the appeal or original proceeding becomes final, the clerk must (1) return the lodged record to the lodging party if it is in paper form, or (2) permanently delete the lodged record if it is in electronic form.

(f) Unsealing a record in the reviewing court

(1) A sealed record must not be unsealed except on order of the reviewing court.

(2) Any person or entity may serve and file a motion, application, or petition in the reviewing court to unseal a record.

(3) If the reviewing court proposes to order a record unsealed on its own motion, the court must send notice to the parties stating the reason for unsealing the record. Unless otherwise ordered by the court, any party may serve and file an opposition within 10 days after the notice is sent, and any other party may serve and file a response within 5 days after an opposition is filed.

(4) If necessary to prevent disclosure of material contained in a sealed record, the motion, application, or petition under (2) and any opposition, response, and supporting documents under (2) or (3) must be filed in both a redacted version and a complete unredacted version. The cover of the redacted version must identify it as "Public—Redacts material from sealed record." In juvenile cases, the cover of the redacted version must identify it as "Redacted version—Redacts material from sealed record." The cover of the unredacted version must identify it as "May Not Be Examined Without Court Order—Contains material from sealed record." Unless the court orders otherwise, any party that had access to the sealed record in the trial court or other proceedings under review must be served with a complete, unredacted version of all papers as well as a redacted version. If a party's attorney but not the party had access to the record in the trial court or other proceedings under review, only the party's attorney may be served with the complete, unredacted version.

(5) In determining whether to unseal a record, the court must consider the matters addressed in rule 2.550(c)–(e).

(6) The order unsealing a record must state whether the record is unsealed entirely or in part. If the order unseals only part of the record or unseals the record only as to certain persons, the order must specify the particular records that are unsealed, the particular persons who may have access to the record, or both.

(7) If, in addition to the record that is the subject of the sealing order, a court has previously ordered the sealing order itself, the register of actions, or any other court records relating to the case to be sealed, the unsealing order must state whether these additional records are unsealed.

(g) Disclosure of nonpublic material in public filings prohibited

(1) Nothing filed publicly in the reviewing court—including any application, brief, petition, or memorandum—may disclose material contained in a record that is sealed, lodged conditionally under seal, or otherwise subject to a pending motion to file under seal.

(2) If it is necessary to disclose material contained in a sealed record in a filing in the reviewing court, two versions must be filed:

(A) A public redacted version. The cover of this version must identify it as "Public—Redacts material from sealed record." In juvenile cases, the cover of the redacted version must identify it as "Redacted Version—Redacts material from sealed record."

(B) An unredacted version. If this version is in paper format, it must be placed in a sealed envelope or other appropriate sealed container. The cover of this version, and if applicable the envelope or other container, must identify it as "May Not Be Examined Without Court Order—Contains material from sealed record." Sealed material disclosed in this version must be identified as such in the filing and accompanied by a citation to the court order sealing that material.

(C) Unless the court orders otherwise, any party who had access to the sealed record in the trial court or other proceedings under review must be served with both the unredacted version of all papers as well as the redacted version. Other parties must be served with only the public redacted version. If a party's attorney but not the party had access to the record in the trial court or other proceedings under review, only the party's attorney may be served with the unredacted version.

(3) If it is necessary to disclose material contained in a conditionally sealed record in a filing in the reviewing court:

(A) A public redacted version must be filed. The cover of this version must identify it as "Public—Redacts material from conditionally sealed record." In juvenile cases, the cover of the redacted version must identify it as "Redacted version—Redacts material from conditionally sealed record."

(B) An unredacted version must be lodged. The filing must be transmitted in a secure manner that preserves the confidentiality of the filing being lodged. If this version is in paper format, it must be placed in a sealed envelope or other appropriate sealed container. The cover of this version, and if applicable the envelope or other container, must identify it as "May Not Be Examined Without Court Order—Contains material from conditionally sealed record." Conditionally sealed material disclosed in this version must be identified as such in the filing.

(C) Unless the court orders otherwise, any party who had access to the conditionally sealed record in the trial court or other proceedings under review must be served with both the unredacted version of all papers as well as the redacted version. Other parties must be served with only the public redacted version.

(D) If the court denies the motion or application to seal the record, the party who filed the motion or application may notify the court that the unredacted version lodged under (B) is to be filed unsealed. This notification must be received within 10 days of the order denying the motion or application to seal, unless otherwise ordered by the court. On receipt of this notification, the clerk must unseal and file the lodged unredacted version. If the party who filed the motion or application does not notify the court within 10 days of the order, the clerk must (1) return the lodged unredacted version to the lodging party if it is in paper form, or (2) permanently delete the lodged unredacted version if it is in electronic form.

(Formerly Rule 12.5, adopted, eff. Jan. 1, 2002. As amended, eff. July 1, 2002; Jan. 1, 2004; Jan. 1, 2006. Renumbered Rule 8.160 and amended, eff. Jan. 1, 2007. Renumbered Rule 8.46, eff. Jan. 1, 2010. As amended, eff. Jan. 1, 2014; Jan. 1, 2016; Jan. 1, 2019; Jan. 1, 2020.)

Advisory Committee Comment

This rule and rules 2.550–2.551 for the trial courts provide a standard and procedures for courts to use when a request is made to seal a record. The standard is based on *NBC Subsidiary (KNBC–TV), Inc. v. Superior Court* (1999) 20 Cal.4th 1178. The sealed records rules apply to civil and criminal cases. They recognize the First Amendment right of access to documents used at trial or as a basis of adjudication. Except as otherwise expressly provided in this rule, motions in a reviewing court relating to the sealing or unsealing of a record must follow rule 8.54.

Subdivision (e). This subdivision is not intended to expand the availability of existing appellate review for any person aggrieved by a court's denial of a motion or application to seal a record.

Research References

6 Witkin, California Criminal Law 4th Criminal Appeal § 53A (2021), (New) in General.
6 Witkin, California Criminal Law 4th Criminal Appeal § 53B (2021), (New) Definitions.
6 Witkin, California Criminal Law 4th Criminal Appeal § 53C (2021), (New) in General.
6 Witkin, California Criminal Law 4th Criminal Appeal § 53D (2021), (New) Procedure for Sealing Record Not Filed in Trial Court.
6 Witkin, California Criminal Law 4th Criminal Appeal § 53E (2021), (New) Procedure for Unsealing Record.
6 Witkin, California Criminal Law 4th Criminal Appeal § 53F (2021), (New) Filings Disclosing Material in Sealed or Conditionally Sealed Records.
6 Witkin, California Criminal Law 4th Criminal Appeal § 53G (2021), (New) Confidential Records.
6 Witkin, California Criminal Law 4th Criminal Appeal § 131 (2021), Confidential Material.
6 Witkin, California Criminal Law 4th Criminal Appeal § 132 (2021), Complete Record in Capital Case.
6 Witkin, California Criminal Law 4th Criminal Writs § 69 (2021), Format in Reviewing Court.
6 Witkin, California Criminal Law 4th Criminal Writs § 75 (2021), Informal Response and Determination of Petition.

Rule 8.47. Confidential records

(a) Application

This rule applies to confidential records but does not apply to records sealed by court order under rules 2.550–2.551 or rule 8.46 or to conditionally sealed records under rule 8.46. Unless otherwise provided by this rule or other law, rule 8.45 governs the form and transmission of and access to confidential records.

(b) Records of *Marsden* hearings and other in-camera proceedings

(1) This subdivision applies to reporter's transcripts of and documents filed or lodged by a defendant in connection with:

(A) An in-camera hearing conducted by the superior court under *People v. Marsden* (1970) 2 Cal.3d 118; or

(B) Another in-camera hearing at which the defendant was present but from which the People were excluded in order to prevent disclosure of information about defense strategy or other information to which the prosecution was not allowed access at the time of the hearing.

(2) Except as provided in (3), if the defendant raises a *Marsden* issue or an issue related to another in-camera hearing covered by this rule in a brief, petition, or other filing in the reviewing court, the following procedures apply:

(A) The brief, including any portion that discloses matters contained in the transcript of the in-camera hearing, and other documents filed or lodged in connection with the hearing, must be filed publicly. The requirement to publicly file this brief does not apply in juvenile cases; rule 8.401 governs the format of and access to such briefs in juvenile cases.

(B) The People may serve and file an application requesting a copy of the reporter's transcript of, and documents filed or lodged by a defendant in connection with, the in-camera hearing.

(C) Within 10 days after the application is filed, the defendant may serve and file opposition to this application on the basis that the transcript or documents contain confidential material not relevant to the issues raised by the defendant in the reviewing court. Any such opposition must identify the page and line numbers of the transcript or documents containing this irrelevant material.

(D) If the defendant does not timely serve and file opposition to the application, the reviewing court clerk must send to the People a copy of the reporter's transcript of, and documents filed or lodged by a defendant in connection with, the in-camera hearing.

(3) A defendant may serve and file a motion or application in the reviewing court requesting permission to file under seal a brief, petition, or other filing that raises a *Marsden* issue or an issue related to another in-camera hearing covered by this subdivision, and requesting an order maintaining the confidentiality of the relevant material from the reporter's transcript of, or documents filed or lodged in connection with, the in-camera hearing.

(A) Except as otherwise provided in this rule, rule 8.46(d) governs a motion or application under this subdivision.

(B) The declaration accompanying the motion or application must contain facts sufficient to justify an order maintaining the confidentiality of the relevant material from the reporter's transcript of, or documents filed or lodged in connection with, the in-camera hearing and sealing of the brief, petition, or other filing.

(C) At the time the motion or application is filed, the defendant must:

(i) File a public redacted version of the brief, petition, or other filing that he or she is requesting be filed under seal. The cover of this version must identify it as "Public—Redacts material from conditionally sealed record." The requirement to publicly file the redacted version does not apply in juvenile cases; rule 8.401 generally governs access to filings in juvenile cases. In juvenile cases, the cover of the redacted version must identify it as "Redacted version—Redacts material from conditionally sealed record."

(ii) Lodge an unredacted version of the brief, petition, or other filing that he or she is requesting be filed under seal. The filing must be transmitted in a secure manner that preserves the confidentiality of the filing being lodged. If this version is in paper format, it must be placed in a sealed envelope or other appropriate sealed container. The cover of the unredacted version of the document, and if applicable the envelope or other container, must identify it as "May Not Be Examined Without Court Order—Contains material from conditionally sealed record." Conditionally sealed material disclosed in this version must be identified as such in the filing.

(D) If the court denies the motion or application to file the brief, petition, or other filing under seal, the defendant may notify the court that the unredacted brief, petition, or other filing lodged under (C)(ii) is to be filed unsealed. This notification must be received within 10 days of the order denying the motion or application to file the brief, petition, or other filing under seal, unless otherwise ordered by the court. On receipt of this notification, the clerk must unseal and file the lodged unredacted brief, petition, or other filing. If the defendant does not notify the court within 10 days of the order, the clerk must (1) return the lodged unredacted brief, petition, or other filing to the defendant if it is in paper form, or (2) permanently delete the lodged unredacted brief, petition, or other filing if it is in electronic form.

(c) Other confidential records

Except as otherwise provided by law or order of the reviewing court:

(1) Nothing filed publicly in the reviewing court—including any application, brief, petition, or memorandum—may disclose material contained in a confidential record, including a record that, by law, a party may choose be kept confidential in reviewing court proceedings and that the party has chosen to keep confidential.

(2) To maintain the confidentiality of material contained in a confidential record, if it is necessary to disclose such material in a filing in the reviewing court, a party may serve and file a motion or application in the reviewing court requesting permission for the filing to be under seal.

(A) Except as otherwise provided in this rule, rule 8.46(d) governs a motion or application under this subdivision.

(B) The declaration accompanying the motion or application must contain facts sufficient to establish that the record is required by law to be closed to inspection in the reviewing court and to justify sealing of the brief, petition, or other filing.

(C) At the time the motion or application is filed, the party must:

(i) File a redacted version of the brief, petition, or other filing that he or she is requesting be filed under seal. The cover of this version must identify it as "Public—Redacts material from conditionally sealed record," In juvenile cases, the cover of this version must identify it as "Redacted version—Redacts material from conditionally sealed record."

(ii) Lodge an unredacted version of the brief, petition, or other filing that he or she is requesting be filed under seal. The filing must be transmitted in a secure manner that preserves the confidentiality of the filing being lodged. If this version is in paper format, it must be placed in a sealed envelope or other appropriate sealed container. The cover of the unredacted version of the document, and if applicable the envelope or other container, must identify it as "May Not Be Examined Without Court Order—Contains material from conditionally sealed record." Material from a confidential record disclosed in this version must be identified and accompanied by a citation to the statute, rule of court, case, or other authority establishing that the record is required by law to be closed to inspection in the reviewing court.

(D) If the court denies the motion or application to file the brief, petition, or other filing under seal, the party who filed the motion or application may notify the court that the unredacted brief, petition, or other filing lodged under (C)(ii) is to be filed unsealed. This notification must be received within 10 days of the order denying the motion or application to file the brief, petition, or other filing under seal, unless otherwise ordered by the court. On receipt of this notification, the clerk must unseal and file the lodged unredacted brief, petition, or other filing. If the party who filed the motion or application does not notify the court within 10 days of the order, the clerk must (1) return the lodged unredacted brief, petition, or other filing to the lodging party if it is in paper form, or (2) permanently delete the lodged unredacted brief, petition, or other filing if it is in electronic form.

(Adopted, eff. Jan. 1, 2014. As amended, eff. Jan. 1, 2016; Jan. 1, 2019.)

Advisory Committee Comment

Subdivisions (a) and (c). Note that there are many laws that address the confidentiality of various records. These laws differ from each other in a variety of respects, including what information is closed to inspection, from whom it is closed, under what circumstances it is closed, and what procedures apply to closing or opening it to inspection. It is very important to determine if any such law applies with respect to a particular record because this rule applies only to confidential records as defined in rule 8.45, and the procedures in this rule apply only "unless otherwise provided by law." Thus, where other laws establish specific requirements that differ from the requirements in this rule, those specific requirements supersede the requirements in this rule. For example, although Penal Code section 1203.05 limits who may inspect or copy probation reports, much of the material contained in such reports—such as the factual summary of the offense(s); the evaluations, analyses, calculations, and recommendations of the probation officer; and other nonpersonal information—is not considered confidential under that statute and is routinely discussed in openly filed appellate briefs (see *People v. Connor* (2004) 115 Cal.App.4th 669, 695–696). In addition, this rule does not alter any existing authority for a court to open a confidential record to inspection by the public or another party to a proceeding.

Subdivision (c)(1). The reference in this provision to records that a party may choose be kept confidential in reviewing court proceedings is intended to encompass situations in which a record may be subject to a privilege that a party may choose to maintain or choose to waive.

Subdivision (c)(2). Note that when a record has been sealed by court order, rule 8.46(g)(2) requires a party to file redacted (public) and unredacted (sealed) versions of any filing that discloses material from the sealed record; it does not require the party to make a motion or application for permission to do so. By contrast, this rule requires court permission before redacted (public) and unredacted (sealed) filings may be made to prevent disclosure of material from confidential records.

Research References

6 Witkin, California Criminal Law 4th Criminal Appeal § 53A (2021), (New) in General.
6 Witkin, California Criminal Law 4th Criminal Appeal § 53G (2021), (New) Confidential Records.
6 Witkin, California Criminal Law 4th Criminal Appeal § 53–I (2021), (New) Transmission and Access to Sealed and Confidential Records.

Article 4

APPLICATIONS AND MOTIONS; EXTENDING AND SHORTENING TIME

Rule 8.50. Applications

(a) Service and filing

Except as these rules provide otherwise, parties must serve and file all applications in the reviewing court, including applications to extend the time to file records, briefs, or other documents, and applications to shorten time. For good cause, the Chief Justice or presiding justice may excuse advance service.

(b) Contents

The application must state facts showing good cause-or making an exceptional showing of good cause, when required by these rules-for granting the application and must identify any previous application filed by any party.

(c) Disposition

Unless the court determines otherwise, the Chief Justice or presiding justice may rule on the application. *(Formerly Rule 43, adopted, eff. Jan. 1, 2005. Renumbered Rule 8.50 and amended, eff. Jan. 1, 2007. As amended, eff. Jan. 1, 2016.)*

Advisory Committee Comment

Rule 8.50 addresses applications generally. Rules 8.60, 8.63, and 8.68 address applications to extend or shorten time.

Subdivision (a). A party other than the appellant or petitioner who files an application or opposition to an application may be required to pay a filing fee under Government Code sections 68926 or 68927 if the application or opposition is the first document filed in the appeal or writ proceeding in the reviewing court by that party. See rule 8.25(c).

Subdivision (b). An exceptional showing of good cause is required in applications in certain juvenile proceedings under rules 8.416, 8.450, 8.452, and 8.454.

Research References

West's California Judicial Council Forms App–006, Application for Extension of Time to File Brief (Civil Case).
West's California Judicial Council Forms App–012, Stipulation of Extension of Time to File Brief (Civil Case).
West's California Judicial Council Forms CR–126, Application for Extension of Time to File Brief (Criminal Case).
West's California Judicial Council Forms JV–816, Application for Extension of Time to File Brief (Juvenile Delinquency).
West's California Judicial Council Forms JV–817, Application for Extension of Time to File Brief (Juvenile Dependency).

Rule 8.54. Motions

(a) Motion and opposition

(1) Except as these rules provide otherwise, a party wanting to make a motion in a reviewing court must serve and file a written motion stating the grounds and the relief requested and identifying any documents on which the motion is based.

(2) A motion must be accompanied by a memorandum and, if it is based on matters outside the record, by declarations or other supporting evidence.

(3) Any opposition must be served and filed within 15 days after the motion is filed.

(b) Disposition

(1) The court may rule on a motion at any time after an opposition or other response is filed or the time to oppose has expired.

(2) On a party's request or its own motion, the court may place a motion on calendar for a hearing. The clerk must promptly send each party a notice of the date and time of the hearing.

(c) Failure to oppose motion

A failure to oppose a motion may be deemed a consent to the granting of the motion. *(Formerly Rule 41, adopted, eff. Jan. 1, 2005. Renumbered Rule 8.54 and amended, eff. Jan. 1, 2007.)*

Advisory Committee Comment

Subdivision (a). A party other than the appellant or petitioner who files a motion or opposition to a motion may be required to pay a filing fee under Government Code sections 68926 or 68927 if the motion or opposition is the first document filed in the appeal or writ proceeding in the reviewing court by that party. See rule 8.25(c).

Subdivision (c). Subdivision (c) provides that a "failure to oppose a motion" may be deemed a consent to the granting of the motion. The provision is not intended to indicate a position on the question whether there is an implied right to a hearing to oppose a motion to dismiss an appeal.

Rule 8.57. Motions before the record is filed

(a) Motion to dismiss appeal

A motion to dismiss an appeal before the record is filed in the reviewing court must be accompanied by a certificate of the superior court clerk, a declaration, or both, stating:

(1) The nature of the action and the relief sought by the complaint and any cross-complaint or complaint in intervention;

(2) The names, addresses, and telephone numbers of all attorneys of record—stating whom each represents—and unrepresented parties;

(3) A description of the judgment or order appealed from, its entry date, and the service date of any written notice of its entry;

(4) The factual basis of any extension of the time to appeal under rule 8.108;

(5) The filing dates of all notices of appeal and the courts in which they were filed;

(6) The filing date of any document necessary to procure the record on appeal; and

(7) The status of the record preparation process, including any order extending time to prepare the record.

(b) Other motions

Any other motion filed before the record is filed in the reviewing court must be accompanied by a declaration or other evidence necessary to advise the court of the facts relevant to the relief requested. *(Formerly Rule 42, adopted, eff. Jan. 1, 2005. Renumbered Rule 8.57 and amended, eff. Jan. 1, 2007.)*

Rule 8.60. Extending time

(a) Computing time

The Code of Civil Procedure governs computing and extending the time to do any act required or permitted under these rules.

(b) Extending time

Except as these rules provide otherwise, for good cause—or on an exceptional showing of good cause, when required by these rules—the Chief Justice or presiding justice may extend the time to do any act required or permitted under these rules.

(c) Application for extension

(1) An application to extend time must include a declaration stating facts, not mere conclusions, and must be served on all parties. For good cause, the Chief Justice or presiding justice may excuse advance service.

(2) The application must state:

(A) The due date of the document to be filed;

(B) The length of the extension requested;

(C) Whether any earlier extensions have been granted and, if so, their lengths and whether granted by stipulation or by the court; and

(D) Good cause—or an exceptional showing of good cause, when required by these rules—for granting the extension, consistent with the factors in rule 8.63(b).

(d) Relief from default

For good cause, a reviewing court may relieve a party from default for any failure to comply with these rules except the failure to file a timely notice of appeal or a timely statement of reasonable grounds in support of a certificate of probable cause.

(e) No extension by superior court

Except as these rules provide otherwise, a superior court may not extend the time to do any act to prepare the appellate record.

(f) Notice to party

(1) In a civil case, counsel must deliver to his or her client or clients a copy of any stipulation or application to extend time that counsel files. Counsel must attach evidence of such delivery to the stipulation or application, or certify in the stipulation or application that the copy has been delivered.

(2) In a class action, the copy required under (1) need be delivered to only one represented party.

(3) The evidence or certification of delivery under (1) need not include the address of the party notified. *(Formerly Rule 45, adopted, eff. Jan. 1, 2005. Renumbered Rule 8.60 and amended, eff. Jan. 1, 2007.)*

Advisory Committee Comment

Subdivisions (b) and (c): An exceptional showing of good cause is required in applications in certain juvenile proceedings under rules 8.416, 8.450, 8.452, and 8.454.

Research References

West's California Judicial Council Forms App–006, Application for Extension of Time to File Brief (Civil Case).
West's California Judicial Council Forms App–012, Stipulation of Extension of Time to File Brief (Civil Case).
West's California Judicial Council Forms CR–126, Application for Extension of Time to File Brief (Criminal Case).
West's California Judicial Council Forms JV–816, Application for Extension of Time to File Brief (Juvenile Delinquency).
West's California Judicial Council Forms JV–817, Application for Extension of Time to File Brief (Juvenile Dependency).
6 Witkin, California Criminal Law 4th Criminal Appeal § 3 (2021), In General.
6 Witkin, California Criminal Law 4th Criminal Appeal § 13 (2021), Strict Compliance.
6 Witkin, California Criminal Law 4th Criminal Appeal § 28 (2021), Filing Notice of Appeal and Request for Certificate.
6 Witkin, California Criminal Law 4th Criminal Appeal § 96 (2021), Normal Time.
6 Witkin, California Criminal Law 4th Criminal Appeal § 98 (2021), General Rule.

Rule 8.63. Policies and factors governing extensions of time

(a) Policies

(1) The time limits prescribed by these rules should generally be met to ensure expeditious conduct of appellate business and public confidence in the efficient administration of appellate justice.

(2) The effective assistance of counsel to which a party is entitled includes adequate time for counsel to prepare briefs or other documents that fully advance the party's interests. Adequate time also allows the preparation of accurate, clear, concise, and complete submissions that assist the courts.

(3) For a variety of legitimate reasons, counsel may not always be able to prepare briefs or other documents within the time specified in the rules of court. To balance the competing policies stated in (1) and (2), applications to extend time in the reviewing courts must demonstrate good cause—or an exceptional showing of good cause, when required by these rules—under (b). If good cause is shown, the court must extend the time.

(b) Factors considered

In determining good cause—or an exceptional showing of good cause, when required by these rules—the court must consider the following factors when applicable:

(1) The degree of prejudice, if any, to any party from a grant or denial of the extension. A party claiming prejudice must support the claim in detail.

(2) In a civil case, the positions of the client and any opponent with regard to the extension.

(3) The length of the record, including the number of relevant trial exhibits. A party relying on this factor must specify the length of the record. In a civil case, a record containing one volume of clerk's transcript or appendix and two volumes of reporter's transcript is considered an average-length record.

(4) The number and complexity of the issues raised. A party relying on this factor must specify the issues.

(5) Whether there are settlement negotiations and, if so, how far they have progressed and when they might be completed.

(6) Whether the case is entitled to priority.

(7) Whether counsel responsible for preparing the document is new to the case.

(8) Whether other counsel or the client needs additional time to review the document.

(9) Whether counsel responsible for preparing the document has other time-limited commitments that prevent timely filing of the document. Mere conclusory statements that more time is needed because of other pressing business will not suffice. Good cause requires a specific showing of other obligations of counsel that:

(A) Have deadlines that as a practical matter preclude filing the document by the due date without impairing its quality; or

(B) Arise from cases entitled to priority.

(10) Illness of counsel, a personal emergency, or a planned vacation that counsel did not reasonably expect to conflict with the due date and cannot reasonably rearrange.

(11) Any other factor that constitutes good cause in the context of the case. *(Formerly Rule 45.5, adopted, eff. Jan. 1, 2005. Renumbered Rule 8.63 and amended, eff. Jan. 1, 2007.)*

Advisory Committee Comment

An exceptional showing of good cause is required in applications in certain juvenile proceedings under rules 8.416, 8.450, 8.452, and 8.454.

Research References

West's California Judicial Council Forms App–006, Application for Extension of Time to File Brief (Civil Case).
West's California Judicial Council Forms App–012, Stipulation of Extension of Time to File Brief (Civil Case).
West's California Judicial Council Forms CR–126, Application for Extension of Time to File Brief (Criminal Case).
West's California Judicial Council Forms JV–816, Application for Extension of Time to File Brief (Juvenile Delinquency).
West's California Judicial Council Forms JV–817, Application for Extension of Time to File Brief (Juvenile Dependency).
6 Witkin, California Criminal Law 4th Criminal Appeal § 3 (2021), In General.
6 Witkin, California Criminal Law 4th Criminal Appeal § 4 (2021), Factors Considered.

Rule 8.66. Tolling or extending time because of public emergency

(a) Emergency tolling or extensions of time

If made necessary by the occurrence or danger of an earthquake, fire, public health crisis, or other public emergency, or by the destruction of or danger to a building housing a reviewing court, the Chair of the Judicial Council, notwithstanding any other rule in this title, may:

(1) Toll for up to 30 days or extend by no more than 30 days any time periods specified by these rules; or

(2) Authorize specified courts to toll for up to 30 days or extend by no more than 30 days any time periods specified by these rules.

(b) Applicability of order

(1) An order under (a)(1) must specify the length of the tolling or extension and whether the order applies throughout the state, only to specified courts, or only to courts or attorneys in specified geographic areas, or applies in some other manner.

(2) An order under (a)(2) must specify the length of the authorized tolling or extension.

(c) Renewed orders

If made necessary by the nature or extent of the public emergency, with or without a request, the Chair of the Judicial Council may renew an order issued under this rule prior to its expiration. An order may be renewed for additional periods not to exceed 30 days per renewal. *(Formerly Rule 45.1, adopted, eff. Jan. 1, 2005. Renumbered Rule 8.66 and amended, eff. Jan. 1, 2007. As amended, eff. April 4, 2020.)*

Advisory Committee Comment

The Chief Justice of California is the Chair of the Judicial Council (see rule 10.2).

Any tolling ordered under this rule is excluded from the time period specified by the rules. (See *Woods v. Young* (1991) 53 Cal.3d 315, 326, fn. 3 ["Tolling may be analogized to a clock that is stopped and then restarted. Whatever period of time that remained when the clock is stopped is available when the clock is restarted, that is, when the tolling period has ended."].)

The tolling and extension of time authorized under this rule include and apply to all rules of court that govern finality in both the Supreme Court and the Courts of Appeal.

Research References

6 Witkin, California Criminal Law 4th Criminal Appeal § 28 (2021), Filing Notice of Appeal and Request for Certificate.
6 Witkin, California Criminal Law 4th Criminal Appeal § 96 (2021), Normal Time.

Rule 8.68. Shortening time

For good cause and except as these rules provide otherwise, the Chief Justice or presiding justice may shorten the time to do any act required or permitted under these rules. *(Adopted, eff. Jan. 1, 2007.)*

Article 5

E–FILING

Rule 8.70. Application, construction, and definitions

(a) Application

Notwithstanding any other rules to the contrary, the rules in this article govern filing and service by electronic means in the Supreme Court and the Courts of Appeal.

(b) Construction

The rules in this article must be construed to authorize and permit filing and service by electronic means to the extent feasible.

(c) Definitions

As used in this article, unless the context otherwise requires:

(1) "The court" means the Supreme Court or a Court of Appeal.

(2) A "document" is any writing submitted to the reviewing court by a party or other person, including a brief, a petition, an appendix, or a motion. A document is also any writing transmitted by a trial court to the reviewing court, including a notice or a clerk's or reporter's transcript, and any writing prepared by the reviewing court, including an opinion, an order, or a notice. A document may be in paper or electronic form.

(3) "Electronic service" is service of a document on a party or other person by either electronic transmission or electronic notification. Electronic service may be performed directly by a party or other person, by an agent of a party or other person including the party or other person's attorney, through an electronic filing service provider, or by a court.

(4) "Electronic transmission" means the sending of a document by electronic means to the electronic service address at or through which a party or other person has authorized electronic service.

(5) "Electronic notification" means the notification of a party or other person that a document is served by sending an electronic message to the electronic service address at or through which the party or other person has authorized electronic service, specifying the exact name of the document served and providing a hyperlink at which the served document can be viewed and downloaded.

(6) "Electronic service address" means the electronic address at or through which a party or other person has authorized electronic service.

(7) An "electronic filer" is a person filing a document in electronic form directly with the court, by an agent, or through an electronic filing service provider.

(8) "Electronic filing" is the electronic transmission to a court of a document in electronic form for filing. Electronic filing refers to the activity of filing by the electronic filer and does not include the court's actions upon receipt of the document for filing, including processing and review of the document and its entry into the court's records.

(9) An "electronic filing service provider" is a person or entity that receives an electronic document from a party or other person for retransmission to the court or for electronic service on other parties, or both. In submitting electronic filings, the electronic filing service provider does so on behalf of the electronic filer and not as an agent of the court.

(10) An "electronic signature" is an electronic sound, symbol, or process attached to or logically associated with an electronic record and executed or adopted by a person with the intent to sign a document or record created, generated, sent, communicated, received, or stored by electronic means.

(11) A "secure electronic signature" is a type of electronic signature that is unique to the person using it, capable of verification, under the sole control of the person using it, and linked to data in such a manner that if the data are changed, the electronic signature is invalidated. *(Adopted, eff. July 1, 2010. As amended, eff. Jan. 1, 2011; Jan. 1, 2012; Jan. 1, 2017; Jan. 1, 2022.)*

Advisory Committee Comment

Subdivision (c)(3). The definition of "electronic service" has been amended to provide that a party may effectuate service not only by the electronic transmission of a document, but also by providing electronic notification of where a document served electronically may be located and downloaded. This amendment is intended to expressly authorize electronic notification as an alternative means of service. This amendment is consistent with the amendment of Code of Civil Procedure section 1010.6, effective January 1, 2011, to authorize service by electronic notification. (See Stats. 2010, ch. 156 (Sen. Bill 1274).) The amendments change the law on electronic service as understood by the appellate court in *Insyst, Ltd. v. Applied Materials, Inc.* (2009) 170 Cal.App.4th 1129, which interpreted the rules as authorizing only electronic transmission as an effective means of electronic service.

Subdivision (c)(10). The definition of electronic signature is based on the definition in the Uniform Electronic Transactions Act, Civil Code section 1633.2.

Subdivision (c)(11). The definition of secure electronic signature is based on the first four requirements of a "digital signature" set forth in Government Code section 16.5(a), specifically the requirements stated in section 16.5(a)(1)–(4). The section 16.5(a)(5) requirement of conformance to regulations adopted by the Secretary of State does not apply to secure electronic signatures.

Rule 8.71. Electronic filing

(a) Mandatory electronic filing

Except as otherwise provided by these rules, the *Supreme Court Rules Regarding Electronic Filing*, or court order, all parties are required to file all documents electronically in the reviewing court.

(b) Self-represented parties

(1) Self-represented parties are exempt from the requirement to file documents electronically.

(2) A self-represented party may agree to file documents electronically. By electronically filing any document with the court, a self-represented party agrees to file documents electronically.

(3) In cases involving both represented and self-represented parties, represented parties are required to file documents electronically; however, in these cases, each self-represented party may file documents in paper form.

(c) Trial courts

Trial courts are exempt from the requirement to file documents electronically, but are permitted to file documents electronically.

(d) Excuse for undue hardship or significant prejudice

A party must be excused from the requirement to file documents electronically if the party shows undue hardship or significant prejudice. A court must have a process for parties, including represented parties, to apply for relief and a procedure for parties excused from filing documents electronically to file them in paper form.

(e) Applications for fee waivers

The court may permit electronic filing of an application for waiver of court fees and costs in any proceeding in which the court accepts electronic filings.

(f) Effect of document filed electronically

(1) A document that the court, a party, or a trial court files electronically under the rules in this article has the same legal effect as a document in paper form.

(2) Filing a document electronically does not alter any filing deadline.

(g) Paper documents

When it is not feasible for a party to convert a document to electronic form by scanning, imaging, or another means, the court may allow that party to file the document in paper form. *(Adopted, eff. Jan. 1, 2017. As amended, eff. Jan. 1, 2020.)*

Rule 8.72. Responsibilities of court and electronic filer

(a) Responsibilities of court

(1) The court will publish, in both electronic form and print form, the court's electronic filing requirements.

(2) If the court is aware of a problem that impedes or precludes electronic filing, it must promptly take reasonable steps to provide notice of the problem.

(b) Responsibilities of electronic filer

Each electronic filer must:

(1) Take all reasonable steps to ensure that the filing does not contain computer code, including viruses, that might be harmful to the court's electronic filing system and to other users of that system;

(2) Furnish one or more electronic service addresses, in the manner specified by the court, at which the electronic filer agrees to accept receipt and filing confirmations under rule 8.77 and, if applicable, at which the electronic filer agrees to receive electronic service; and

(3) Immediately provide the court and all parties with any change to the electronic filer's electronic service address. *(Formerly Rule 8.74, adopted, eff. July 1, 2010. Renumbered Rule 8.72 and amended, eff. Jan. 1, 2017. As amended, eff. Jan. 1, 2020; Jan. 1, 2021.)*

Advisory Committee Comment

Subdivision (b)(1). One example of a reasonable step an electronic filer may take is to use a commercial virus scanning program. Compliance with this subdivision requires more than an absence of intent to harm the court's electronic filing system or other users' systems.

Rule 8.73. Contracts with electronic filing service providers

(a) Right to contract

(1) The court may contract with one or more electronic filing service providers to furnish and maintain an electronic filing system for the court.

(2) If the court contracts with an electronic filing service provider, the court may require electronic filers to transmit the documents to the provider.

(3) If the court contracts with an electronic service provider or the court has an in-house system, the provider or system must accept filing from other electronic filing service providers to the extent the provider or system is compatible with them.

(b) Provisions of contract

The court's contract with an electronic filing service provider may allow the provider to charge electronic filers a reasonable fee in addition to the court's filing fee. Whenever possible, the contract should require that the electronic filing service provider agree to waive a fee that normally would be charged to a party when the court orders that the fee be waived for that party. The contract may also allow the electronic filing service provider to make other reasonable requirements for use of the electronic filing system.

(c) Transmission of filing to court

An electronic filing service provider must promptly transmit any electronic filing and any applicable filing fee to the court.

(d) Confirmation of receipt and filing of document

(1) An electronic filing service provider must promptly send to an electronic filer its confirmation of the receipt of any document that the filer has transmitted to the provider for filing with the court.

(2) The electronic filing service provider must send its confirmation to the filer's electronic service address and must indicate the date and time of receipt, in accordance with rule 8.77.

(3) After reviewing the documents, the court must arrange to promptly transmit confirmation of filing or notice of rejection to the electronic filer in accordance with rule 8.77.

(e) Ownership of information

All contracts between the court and electronic filing service providers must acknowledge that the court is the owner of the contents of the filing system and has the exclusive right to control the system's use. *(Formerly Rule 8.75, adopted, eff. July 1, 2010. As amended, eff. Jan. 1, 2011. Renumbered Rule 8.73 and amended, eff. Jan. 1, 2017.)*

Rule 8.74. Format of electronic documents

(a) Formatting requirements applicable to all electronic documents

(1) *Text-searchable portable document format*: Electronic documents must be in text-searchable portable document format (PDF) while maintaining the original document formatting. In the limited circumstances in which a document cannot practicably be converted to a text-searchable PDF, the document may be scanned or converted to non-text-searchable PDF. An electronic filer is not required to use a specific vendor, technology, or software for creation of a searchable-format document, unless the electronic filer agrees to such use. The software for creating and reading electronic documents must be in the public domain or generally available at a reasonable cost. The printing of an electronic document must not result in the loss of document text, formatting, or appearance. The electronic filer is responsible for ensuring that any document filed is complete and readable.

(2) *Pagination*: The electronic page counter for the electronic document must match the page number for each page of the document. The page numbering of a document filed electronically must begin with the first page or cover page as page 1 and thereafter be paginated consecutively using only arabic numerals (e.g., 1, 2, 3). The page number for the cover page may be suppressed and need not appear on the cover page. When a document is filed in both paper form and electronic form, the pagination in both versions must comply with this paragraph.

(3) *Bookmarking*: An electronic bookmark is a descriptive text link that appears in the bookmarks panel of an electronic document. Each electronic document must include an electronic bookmark to each heading, subheading, and the first page of any component of the document, including any table of contents, table of authorities, petition, verification, memorandum, declaration, certificate of word count, certificate of interested entities or persons, proof of service, exhibit, or attachment. Each electronic bookmark must briefly describe the item to which it is linked. For example, an electronic bookmark to a heading must provide the text of the heading, and an electronic bookmark to an exhibit or attachment must include the letter or number of the exhibit or attachment and a brief description of the exhibit or attachment. An electronic appendix must have bookmarks to the indexes and to the first page of each separate exhibit or attachment. Exhibits or attachments within an exhibit or attachment must be bookmarked. All bookmarks must be set to retain the reader's selected zoom setting.

(4) *Protection of sensitive information*: Electronic filers must comply with rules 1.201, 8.45, 8.46, 8.47, and 8.401 regarding the protection of sensitive information, except for those requirements exclusively applicable to paper form.

(5) *Size and multiple files*: An electronic filing may not be larger than 25 megabytes. This rule does not change the limitations on word count or number of pages otherwise established by the California Rules of Court for documents filed in the court. Although certain provisions in the California Rules of Court require volumes of no more than 300 pages (see, e.g., rules 8.124(d)(1), 8.144(b)(6), 8.144(g)), an electronic filing may exceed 300 pages so long as its individual components comply with the 300–page volume requirement and the electronic filing does not exceed 25 megabytes. If a document exceeds the 25–megabyte file-size limitation, the electronic filer must submit the document in more than one file, with each file 25 megabytes or less. The first file must include a master chronological and alphabetical index stating the contents for all files. Each file must have a cover page stating (a) the file number for that file and the total number of files for that document, (b) the volumes contained in that file, and (c) the page numbers contained in that file. (For example: File 2 of 4, Volumes 3–4, pp. 301–499.) In addition, each file must be paginated consecutively across all files in the document, including the cover pages for each file. (For example, if the first file ends on page 300, the cover of the second file must be page 301.) If a multiple-file document is submitted to the court in both electronic form and paper form, the cover pages for each file must be included in the paper documents.

(6) *Manual Filing*:

(A) When an electronic filer seeks to file an electronic document consisting of more than 10 files, or when the document cannot or should not be electronically filed in multiple files, or when electronically filing the document would cause undue hardship, the document must not be electronically filed but must be manually filed with the court on an electronic medium such as a flash drive, DVD, or compact disc (CD). When an electronic filer files with the court one or more documents on an electronic medium, the electronic filer must electronically file, on the same day, a "manual filing notification" notifying the court and the parties that one or more documents have been filed on electronic media, explaining the reason for the manual filing. The electronic media must be served on the parties in accordance with the requirements for service of paper documents. To the extent practicable, each document or file on electronic media must comply with the format requirements of this rule.

(B) Electronic media files such as audio or video must be manually filed. Audio files must be filed in .wav or mp3 format. Video files must be filed in .avi or mp4 format.

(C) If manually filed, photographs must be filed in .jpg, .png, .tif, or .pdf format.

(D) If an original electronic media file is converted to a required format for manual filing, the electronic filer must retain the original.

(7) *Page size*: All documents must have a page size of 8–1/2 by 11 inches.

(8) *Color*: An electronic document with a color component may be electronically filed or manually filed on electronic media, depending on its file size. An electronic document must not have a color cover.

(9) *Cover or first-page information*:

(A) Except as provided in (B), the cover—or first page, if there is no cover—of every electronic document filed in a reviewing court must include the name, mailing address, telephone number, fax number (if available), email address (if available), and California State Bar number of each attorney filing or joining in the document, or of the party if he or she is unrepresented. The inclusion of a fax number or email address on any electronic document does not constitute consent to service by fax or email unless otherwise provided by law.

(B) If more than one attorney from a law firm, corporation, or public law office is representing one party and is joining in the document, the name and State Bar number of each attorney joining in the electronic document must be provided on the cover. The law firm, corporation, or public law office representing each party must designate one attorney to receive notices and other communication in the case from the court by placing an asterisk before that attorney's name on the cover and must provide the contact information specified under (A) for that attorney. Contact information for the other attorneys from the same law firm, corporation, or public law office is not required but may be provided.

(b) Additional formatting requirements applicable to documents prepared for electronic filing in the first instance in a reviewing court

(1) *Font*: The font style must be a proportionally spaced serif face. Century Schoolbook is preferred. A sans-serif face may be used for headings, subheadings, and captions. Font size must be 13–points, including in footnotes. Case names must be italicized or underscored. For emphasis, italics or boldface may be used or the text may be underscored. Do not use all capitals (i.e., ALL CAPS) for emphasis.

(2) *Spacing*: Lines of text must be 1.5 spaced. Footnotes, headings, subheadings, and quotations may be single-spaced. The lines of text must be unnumbered.

(3) *Margins*: The margins must be set at 1–1/2 inches on the left and right and 1 inch on the top and bottom. Quotations may be block-indented.

(4) *Alignment*: Paragraphs must be left-aligned, not justified.

(5) *Hyperlinks*: Hyperlinks to legal authorities and appendixes or exhibits are encouraged but not required. However, if an electronic filer elects to include hyperlinks in a document, the hyperlink must be active as of the date of filing, and if the hyperlink is to a legal authority, it should be formatted to standard citation format as provided in the California Rules of Court.

(c) Additional formatting requirements for certain electronic documents

(1) *Brief*: In addition to compliance with this rule, an electronic brief must also comply with the contents and length requirements stated in rule 8.204(a) and (c). The brief need not be signed. The cover must state:

(A) The title of the brief;

(B) The title, trial court number, and Court of Appeal number of the case;

(C) The names of the trial court and each participating trial judge; and

(D) The name of the party that each attorney on the brief represents.

(2) *Request for judicial notice or request, application, or motion supported by documents*: When seeking judicial notice of matter not already in the appellate record, or when a request, application, or motion is supported by matter not already in the appellate record, the electronic filer must attach a copy of the matter to the request, application, or motion, or an explanation of why it is not practicable to do so. The request, application, or motion and its attachments must comply with this rule.

(3) *Appendix*: The format of an appendix must comply with this rule and rule 8.144 pertaining to clerks' transcripts.

(4) *Agreed statement and settled statement*: The format for an agreed statement or a settled statement must comply with this rule and rule 8.144.

(5) *Reporter's transcript and clerk's transcript*: The format for an electronic reporter's transcript must comply with Code of Civil Procedure section 271 and rule 8.144. The format for an electronic clerk's transcript must comply with this rule and rule 8.144.

(6) *Exhibits*: Electronic exhibits must be submitted in files no larger than 25 megabytes, rather than as individual documents.

(7) *Sealed and confidential records*: Under rule 8.45(c)(1), electronic records that are sealed or confidential must be filed separately from publicly filed records. If one or more pages are omitted from a record and filed separately as a sealed or confidential record, an omission page or pages must be inserted in the publicly filed record at the location of the omitted page or pages. The omission page or pages must identify the type of page or pages omitted. Each omission page must be paginated consecutively with the rest of the publicly filed record. Each single omission page or the first omission page in a range of omission pages must be bookmarked and must be listed in any indexes included in the publicly filed record. The PDF counter for each omission page must match the page number of the page omitted from the publicly filed record. Separately–filed sealed or confidential records must comply with this rule and rules 8.45, 8.46, and 8.47.

(d) Other formatting rules

This rule prevails over other formatting rules. *(Formerly Rule 8.76, adopted, eff. July 1, 2010. As amended, eff. Jan. 1, 2011. Renumbered*

Rule 8.74 and amended, eff. Jan. 1, 2017. As amended, eff. Jan. 1, 2020.)

Advisory Committee Comment

Subdivision (a)(1). If an electronic filer must file a document that the electronic filer possesses only in paper form, use of a scanned image is a permitted means of conversion to PDF, but optical character recognition must be used, if possible. If a document cannot practicably be converted to a text-searchable PDF (e.g., if the document is entirely or substantially handwritten, a photograph, or a graphic such as a chart or diagram that is not primarily text based), the document may be converted to a non-text-searchable PDF file.

Subdivision (a)(3). An electronic bookmark's brief description of the item to which it is linked should enable the reader to easily identify the item. For example, if a declaration is attached to a document, the bookmark to the declaration might say "Robert Smith Declaration," and if a complaint is attached to a declaration as an exhibit, the bookmark to the complaint might say "Exhibit A, First Amended Complaint filed 8/12/17."

Subdivision (b). Subdivision (b) governs documents prepared for electronic filing in the first instance in a reviewing court and does not apply to previously created documents (such as exhibits), whose formatting cannot or should not be altered.

Subdivision (c)(7). In identifying the type of pages omitted, the omission page might say, for example, "probation report" or "*Marsden* hearing transcript."

Rule 8.75. Requirements for signatures on documents

(a) Documents signed under penalty of perjury

When a document must be signed under penalty of perjury, the document is deemed to have been signed by the declarant if filed electronically, provided that either of the following conditions is satisfied:

(1) The declarant has signed the document using an electronic signature (or a secure electronic signature if the declarant is not the electronic filer) and declares under penalty of perjury under the laws of the State of California that the information submitted is true and correct; or

(2) The declarant, before filing, has physically signed a printed form of the document. By electronically filing the document, the electronic filer certifies that the original signed document is available for inspection and copying at the request of the court or any other party. In the event this second method of submitting documents electronically under penalty of perjury is used, the following conditions apply:

(A) At any time after the electronic version of the document is filed, any other party may serve a demand for production of the original signed document. The demand must be served on all other parties but need not be filed with the court.

(B) Within five days of service of the demand under (A), the party or other person on whom the demand is made must make the original signed document available for inspection and copying by all other parties.

(C) At any time after the electronic version of the document is filed, the court may order the electronic filer to produce the original signed document for inspection and copying by the court. The order must specify the date, time, and place for the production and must be served on all parties.

(b) Documents not signed under penalty of perjury

(1) If a document does not require a signature under penalty of perjury, the document is deemed signed by the electronic filer.

(2) When a document to be filed electronically, such as a stipulation, requires the signatures of multiple persons, the document is deemed to have been signed by those persons if filed electronically, provided that either of the following procedures is satisfied:

(A) The parties or other persons have signed the document using a secure electronic signature; or

(B) The electronic filer has obtained all the signatures either in the form of an original signature on a printed form of the document or in the form of a copy of the signed signature page of the document. The electronic filer must maintain the original signed document and any copies of signed signature pages and must make them available for inspection and copying as provided in (a)(2)(B). The court and any party may demand production of the original signed document and any copies of the signed signature pages as provided in (a)(2)(A)–(C). By electronically filing the document, the electronic filer indicates that all persons whose signatures appear on it have signed the document and that the filer has possession of the signatures of all those persons in a form permitted by this rule.

(c) Judicial signatures

If a document requires a signature by a court or a judicial officer, the document may be electronically signed in any manner permitted by law. *(Formerly Rule 8.77, adopted eff. July 1, 2010. As amended, eff. Jan. 1, 2014. Renumbered Rule 8.75, eff. Jan. 1, 2017. As amended, eff. Jan. 1, 2022.)*

Advisory Committee Comment

The requirements for electronic signatures that are compliant with the rule do not impair the power of the courts to resolve disputes about the validity of a signature.

Rule 8.76. Payment of filing fees

(a) Use of credit cards and other methods

The court may permit the use of credit cards, debit cards, electronic fund transfers, or debit accounts for the payment of filing fees associated with electronic filing, as provided in Government Code section 6159 and other applicable law. The court may also authorize other methods of payment.

(b) Fee waivers

Eligible persons may seek a waiver of court fees and costs, as provided in Government Code section 68634.5 and rule 8.26. *(Formerly Rule 8.78, adopted, eff. July 1, 2010. Renumbered Rule 8.76, eff. Jan. 1, 2017.)*

Advisory Committee Comment

Subdivision (b). A fee charged by an electronic filing service provider under rule 8.73(b) is not a court fee that can be waived under Government Code section 68634.5 and rule 8.26.

Rule 8.77. Actions by court on receipt of electronically submitted document; date and time of filing

(a) Confirmation of receipt and filing of document

(1) *Confirmation of receipt*

When the court receives an electronically submitted document, the court must arrange to promptly send the electronic filer confirmation of the court's receipt of the document, indicating the date and time of receipt by the court.

(2) *Filing*

If the electronically submitted document received by the court complies with filing requirements, the document is deemed filed on the date and time it was received by the court as stated in the confirmation of receipt.

(3) *Confirmation of filing*

When the court files an electronically submitted document, the court must arrange to promptly send the electronic filer confirmation that the document has been filed. The filing confirmation must indicate the date and time of filing as specified in the confirmation of receipt, and must also specify:

(A) Any transaction number associated with the filing; and

(B) The titles of the documents as filed by the court.

(4) *Transmission of confirmations*

The court must arrange to send receipt and filing confirmation to the electronic filer at the electronic service address that the filer furnished to the court under rule 8.72(b)(2). The court or the electronic filing service provider must maintain a record of all receipt and filing confirmations.

(5) *Filer responsible for verification*

In the absence of confirmation of receipt and filing, there is no presumption that the court received and filed the document. The electronic filer is responsible for verifying that the court received and filed any document that the electronic filer submitted to the court electronically.

(b) Notice of rejection of document for filing

If the clerk does not file a document because it does not comply with applicable filing requirements, the court must arrange to promptly send notice of the rejection of the document for filing to the electronic filer. The notice must state the reasons that the document was rejected for filing.

(c) Document received after close of business

A document that is received electronically by the court after 11:59 p.m. is deemed to have been received on the next court day.

(d) Delayed delivery

If a filer fails to meet a filing deadline imposed by court order, rule, or statute because of a failure at any point in the electronic transmission and receipt of a document, the filer may file the document on paper or electronically as soon thereafter as practicable and accompany the filing with a motion to accept the document as timely filed. For good cause shown, the court may enter an order permitting the document to be filed nunc pro tunc to the date the filer originally sought to transmit the document electronically.

(e) Endorsement

(1) The court's endorsement of a document electronically filed must contain the following: "Electronically filed by [Name of Court], on ___ (date)," followed by the name of the court clerk.

(2) The endorsement required under (1) has the same force and effect as a manually affixed endorsement stamp with the signature and initials of the court clerk.

(3) A record on appeal, brief, or petition in an appeal or original proceeding that is filed and endorsed electronically may be printed and served on the appellant or respondent in the same manner as if it had been filed in paper form. *(Formerly Rule 8.79, adopted, eff. July 1, 2010. As amended, eff. Jan. 1, 2011; Jan. 1, 2012. Renumbered Rule 8.77 and amended, eff. Jan. 1, 2017. As amended, eff. Jan. 1, 2020; Jan. 1, 2021.)*

Rule 8.78. Electronic service

(a) Authorization for electronic service; exceptions

(1) A document may be electronically served under these rules:

(A) If electronic service is provided for by law or court order; or

(B) If the recipient agrees to accept electronic services as provided by these rules and the document is otherwise authorized to be served by mail, express mail, overnight delivery, or fax transmission.

(2) A party indicates that the party agrees to accept electronic service by:

(A) Serving a notice on all parties that the party accepts electronic service and filing the notice with the court. The notice must include the electronic service address at which the party agrees to accept service; or

(B) Registering with the court's electronic filing service provider and providing the party's electronic service address. Registration with the court's electronic filing service provider is deemed to show that the party agrees to accept service at the electronic service address that the party has provided, unless the party serves a notice on all parties and files the notice with the court that the party does not accept electronic service and chooses instead to be served paper copies at an address specified in the notice.

(3) A document may be electronically served on a nonparty if the nonparty consents to electronic service or electronic service is otherwise provided for by law or court order. All provisions of this rule that apply or relate to a party also apply to any nonparty who has agreed to or is otherwise required by law or court order to accept electronic service or to electronically serve documents.

(b) Maintenance of electronic service lists

When the court orders or permits electronic service in a case, it must maintain and make available electronically to the parties an electronic service list that contains the parties' current electronic service addresses as provided by the parties that have been ordered to or have consented to electronic service in the case.

(c) Service by the parties

Notwithstanding (b), parties are responsible for electronic service on all other parties in the case. A party may serve documents electronically directly, by an agent, or through a designated electronic filing service provider.

(d) Change of electronic service address

(1) A party whose electronic service address changes while the appeal or original proceeding is pending must promptly file a notice of change of address electronically with the court and must serve this notice electronically on all other parties.

(2) A party's election to contract with an electronic filing service provider to electronically file and serve documents or to receive electronic service of documents on the party's behalf does not relieve the party of its duties under (1).

(e) Reliability and integrity of documents served by electronic notification

A party that serves a document by means of electronic notification must:

(1) Ensure that the documents served can be viewed and downloaded using the hyperlink provided;

(2) Preserve the document served without any change, alteration, or modification from the time the document is posted until the time the hyperlink is terminated; and

(3) Maintain the hyperlink until the case is final.

(f) Proof of service

(1) Proof of electronic service may be by any of the methods provided in Code of Civil Procedure section 1013a, with the following exceptions:

(A) The proof of electronic service does not need to state that the person making the service is not a party to the case.

(B) The proof of electronic service must state:

(i) The electronic service address of the person making the service, in addition to that person's residence or business address;

(ii) The date of the electronic service, instead of the date and place of deposit in the mail;

(iii) The name and electronic service address of the person served, in place of that person's name and address as shown on the envelope; and

(iv) That the document was served electronically, in place of the statement that the envelope was sealed and deposited in the mail with postage fully prepaid.

(2) Proof of electronic service may be in electronic form and may be filed electronically with the court.

(3) The party filing the proof of electronic service must maintain the printed form of the document bearing the declarant's original signature and must make the document available for inspection and copying on the request of the court or any party to the action or proceeding in which it is filed, in the manner provided in rule 8.75.

(g) Electronic delivery by court and electronic service on court

(1) The court may deliver any notice, order, opinion, or other document issued by the court by electronic means.

(2) A document may be electronically served on a court if the court consents to electronic service or electronic service is otherwise provided for by law or court order. A court indicates that it agrees to accept electronic service by:

(A) Serving a notice on all parties that the court accepts electronic service. The notice must include the electronic service address at which the court agrees to accept service; or

(B) Adopting a local rule stating that the court accepts electronic service. The rule must indicate where to obtain the electronic service address at which the court agrees to accept service. *(Formerly Rule 8.80, adopted, eff. July 1, 2010. Renumbered Rule 8.71 and amended, eff. Jan. 1, 2011. As amended, eff. Jan. 1, 2016. Renumbered Rule 8.78 and amended, eff. Jan. 1, 2017. As amended, eff. Jan. 1, 2020; Jan. 1, 2021.)*

Advisory Committee Comment

In the Supreme Court and the Courts of Appeal, registration with the court's electronic filing service provider is deemed to show agreement to accept service electronically at the email address provided, unless a party affirmatively opts out of electronic service under rule 8.78(a)(2)(B). This procedure differs from the procedure for electronic service in the superior courts, including their appellate divisions. See rules 2.250–2.261.

Rule 8.79. Court order requiring electronic service

(a) Court order

(1) The court may, on the motion of any party or on its own motion, provided that the order would not cause undue hardship or significant prejudice to any party, order some or all parties to do either or both of the following:

(A) Serve all documents electronically, except when personal service is required by statute or rule; or

(B) Accept electronic service of documents.

(2) The court will not:

(A) Order a self-represented party to electronically serve or accept electronic service of documents; or

(B) Order a trial court to electronically serve documents.

(3) If the reviewing court proposes to make an order under (1) on its own motion, the court must mail notice to the parties. Any party may serve and file an opposition within 10 days after the notice is mailed or as the court specifies.

(b) Serving in paper form

When it is not feasible for a party to convert a document to electronic form by scanning, imaging, or another means, the court may allow that party to serve the document in paper form. *(Formerly Rule 8.73, adopted, eff. July 1, 2010. As amended, eff. Jan. 1, 2011. Renumbered Rule 8.79 and amended, eff. Jan. 1, 2017.)*

Article 6

PUBLIC ACCESS TO ELECTRONIC APPELLATE COURT RECORDS

Rule

Rule 8.80. Statement of purpose

(a) Intent

The rules in this article are intended to provide the public with reasonable access to appellate court records that are maintained in electronic form, while protecting privacy interests.

(b) Benefits of electronic access

Improved technologies provide courts with many alternatives to the historical paper-based record receipt and retention process, including the creation and use of court records maintained in electronic form. Providing public access to appellate court records that are maintained in electronic form may save the courts and the public time, money, and effort and encourage courts to be more efficient in their operations. Improved access to appellate court records may also foster in the public a more comprehensive understanding of the appellate court system.

(c) No creation of rights

The rules in this article are not intended to give the public a right of access to any record that they are not otherwise entitled to access. The rules do not create any right of access to sealed or confidential records. *(Adopted, eff. Jan. 1, 2016.)*

Advisory Committee Comment

The rules in this article acknowledge the benefits that electronic court records provide but attempt to limit the potential for unjustified intrusions into the privacy of individuals involved in litigation that can occur as a result of remote access to electronic court records. The proposed rules take into account the limited resources currently available in the appellate courts. It is contemplated that the rules may be modified to provide greater electronic access as the courts' technical capabilities improve and with the knowledge gained from the experience of the courts in providing electronic access under these rules.

Subdivision (c). Rules 8.45–8.47 govern sealed and confidential records in the appellate courts.

Rule 8.81. Application and scope

(a) Application

The rules in this article apply only to records of the Supreme Court and Courts of Appeal.

(b) Access by parties and attorneys

The rules in this article apply only to access to court records by the public. They do not limit access to court records by a party to an action or proceeding, by the attorney of a party, or by other persons or entities that are entitled to access by statute or rule. *(Adopted, eff. Jan. 1, 2016.)*

Rule 8.82. Definitions

As used in this article, the following definitions apply:

(1) "Court record" is any document, paper, exhibit, transcript, or other thing filed in an action or proceeding; any order, judgment, or opinion of the court; and any court minutes, index, register of actions, or docket. The term does not include the personal notes or preliminary memoranda of justices, judges, or other judicial branch personnel.

(2) "Electronic record" is a court record that requires the use of an electronic device to access. The term includes both a record that has been filed electronically and an electronic copy or version of a record that was filed in paper form.

Ct. Rules

(3) "The public" means an individual, a group, or an entity, including print or electronic media, or the representative of an individual, a group, or an entity.

(4) "Electronic access" means computer access to court records available to the public through both public terminals at the courthouse and remotely, unless otherwise specified in the rules in this article.

(5) Providing electronic access to electronic records "to the extent it is feasible to do so" means that electronic access must be provided to the extent the court determines it has the resources and technical capacity to do so.

(6) "Bulk distribution" means distribution of multiple electronic records that is not done on a case-by-case basis. *(Adopted, eff. Jan. 1, 2016.)*

Rule 8.83. Public access

(a) General right of access

All electronic records must be made reasonably available to the public in some form, whether in electronic or in paper form, except sealed or confidential records.

(b) Electronic access required to extent feasible

(1) Electronic access, both remote and at the courthouse, will be provided to the following court records, except sealed or confidential records, to the extent it is feasible to do so:

(A) Dockets or registers of actions;

(B) Calendars;

(C) Opinions; and

(D) The following Supreme Court records:

i. Results from the most recent Supreme Court weekly conference;

ii. Party briefs in cases argued in the Supreme Court for at least the preceding three years;

iii. Supreme Court minutes from at least the preceding three years.

(2) If a court maintains records in civil cases in addition to those listed in (1) in electronic form, electronic access to these records, except those listed in (c), must be provided both remotely and at the courthouse, to the extent it is feasible to do so.

(c) Courthouse electronic access only

If a court maintains the following records in electronic form, electronic access to these records must be provided at the courthouse, to the extent it is feasible to do so, but remote electronic access may not be provided to these records:

(1) Any reporter's transcript for which the reporter is entitled to receive a fee; and

(2) Records other than those listed in (b)(1) in the following proceedings:

(A) Proceedings under the Family Code, including proceedings for dissolution, legal separation, and nullity of marriage; child and spousal support proceedings; child custody proceedings; and domestic violence prevention proceedings;

(B) Juvenile court proceedings;

(C) Guardianship or conservatorship proceedings;

(D) Mental health proceedings;

(E) Criminal proceedings;

(F) Civil harassment proceedings under Code of Civil Procedure section 527.6;

(G) Workplace violence prevention proceedings under Code of Civil Procedure section 527.8;

(H) Private postsecondary school violence prevention proceedings under Code of Civil Procedure section 527.85;

(I) Elder or dependent adult abuse prevention proceedings under Welfare and Institutions Code section 15657.03; and

(J) Proceedings to compromise the claims of a minor or a person with a disability.

(d) Remote electronic access allowed in extraordinary cases

Notwithstanding (c)(2), the presiding justice of the court, or a justice assigned by the presiding justice, may exercise discretion, subject to (d)(1), to permit remote electronic access by the public to all or a portion of the public court records in an individual case if (1) the number of requests for access to documents in the case is extraordinarily high and (2) responding to those requests would significantly burden the operations of the court. An individualized determination must be made in each case in which such remote electronic access is provided.

(1) In exercising discretion under (d), the justice should consider the relevant factors, such as:

(A) The privacy interests of parties, victims, witnesses, and court personnel, and the ability of the court to redact sensitive personal information;

(B) The benefits to and burdens on the parties in allowing remote electronic access; and

(C) The burdens on the court in responding to an extraordinarily high number of requests for access to documents.

(2) The following information must be redacted from records to which the court allows remote access under (d): driver's license numbers; dates of birth; social security numbers; Criminal Identification and Information and National Crime Information numbers; addresses, e-mail addresses, and phone numbers of parties, victims, witnesses, and court personnel; medical or psychiatric information; financial information; account numbers; and other personal identifying information. The court may order any party who files a document containing such information to provide the court with both an original unredacted version of the document for filing in the court file and a redacted version of the document for remote electronic access. No juror names or other juror identifying information may be provided by remote electronic access. Subdivision (d)(2) does not apply to any document in the original court file; it applies only to documents that are made available by remote electronic access.

(3) Five days' notice must be provided to the parties and the public before the court makes a determination to provide remote electronic access under this rule. Notice to the public may be accomplished by posting notice on the court's website. Any person may file comments with the court for consideration, but no hearing is required.

(4) The court's order permitting remote electronic access must specify which court records will be available by remote electronic access and what categories of information are to be redacted. The court is not required to make findings of fact. The court's order must be posted on the court's website and a copy sent to the Judicial Council.

(e) Access only on a case-by-case basis

With the exception of the records covered by (b)(1), electronic access to an electronic record may be granted only when the record is identified by the number of the case, the caption of the case, the name of a party, the name of the attorney, or the date of oral argument, and only on a case-by-case basis.

(f) Bulk distribution

Bulk distribution may be provided only of the records covered by (b)(1).

(g) Records that become inaccessible

If an electronic record to which electronic access has been provided is made inaccessible to the public by court order or by operation of law, the court is not required to take action with respect to any copy of the record that was made by a member of the public before the record became inaccessible. *(Adopted, eff. Jan. 1, 2016.)*

Advisory Committee Comment

The rule allows a level of access by the public to all electronic records that is at least equivalent to the access that is available for paper records and, for some types of records, is much greater. At the same time, it seeks to protect legitimate privacy concerns.

Subdivision (b). Courts should encourage availability of electronic access to court records at public off-site locations.

Subdivision (c). This subdivision excludes certain records (those other than the register, calendar, opinions, and certain Supreme Court records) in specified types of cases (notably criminal, juvenile, and family court matters) from remote electronic access. The committees recognized that while these case records are public records and should remain available at the courthouse, either in paper or electronic form, they often contain sensitive personal information. The court should not publish that information over the Internet. However, the committees also recognized that the use of the Internet may be appropriate in certain individual cases of extraordinary public interest where information regarding a case will be widely disseminated through the media. In such cases, posting of selected nonconfidential court records, redacted where necessary to protect the privacy of the participants, may provide more timely and accurate information regarding the court proceedings, and may relieve substantial burdens on court staff in responding to individual requests for documents and information. Thus, under subdivision (d), if the presiding justice makes individualized determinations in a specific case, certain records in individual cases may be made available over the Internet.

Subdivision (d). Courts must send a copy of the order permitting remote electronic access in extraordinary cases to: Legal Services, Judicial Council of California, 455 Golden Gate Avenue, San Francisco, CA 94102–3688.

Subdivisions (e) and (f). These subdivisions limit electronic access to records (other than the register, calendars, opinions, and certain Supreme Court records) to a case-by-case basis and prohibit bulk distribution of those records. These limitations are based on the qualitative difference between obtaining information from a specific case file and obtaining bulk information that may be manipulated to compile personal information culled from any document, paper, or exhibit filed in a lawsuit. This type of aggregate information may be exploited for commercial or other purposes unrelated to the operations of the courts, at the expense of privacy rights of individuals.

Rule 8.84. Limitations and conditions

(a) Means of access

Electronic access to records required under this article must be provided by means of a network or software that is based on industry standards or is in the public domain.

(b) Official record

Unless electronically certified by the court, a court record available by electronic access is not the official record of the court.

(c) Conditions of use by persons accessing records

Electronic access to court records may be conditioned on:

(1) The user's consent to access the records only as instructed; and

(2) The user's consent to monitoring of access to its records.

The court must give notice of these conditions, in any manner it deems appropriate. Access may be denied to a member of the public for failure to comply with either of these conditions of use.

(d) Notices to persons accessing records

The court must give notice of the following information to members of the public accessing its records electronically, in any manner it deems appropriate:

(1) The identity of the court staff member to be contacted about the requirements for accessing the court's records electronically.

(2) That copyright and other proprietary rights may apply to information in a case file, absent an express grant of additional rights by the holder of the copyright or other proprietary right. This notice must advise the public that:

(A) Use of such information in a case file is permissible only to the extent permitted by law or court order; and

(B) Any use inconsistent with proprietary rights is prohibited.

(3) Whether electronic records are the official records of the court. The notice must describe the procedure and any fee required for obtaining a certified copy of an official record of the court.

(4) That any person who willfully destroys or alters any court record maintained in electronic form is subject to the penalties imposed by Government Code section 6201.

(e) Access policy

A privacy policy must be posted on the California Courts public-access website to inform members of the public accessing its electronic records of the information collected regarding access transactions and the uses that may be made of the collected information. *(Adopted, eff. Jan. 1, 2016.)*

Rule 8.85. Fees for copies of electronic records

The court may impose fees for the costs of providing copies of its electronic records, under Government Code section 68928. *(Adopted, eff. Jan. 1, 2016.)*

Article 7

PRIVACY

Rule 8.90. Privacy in opinions

(a) Application

(1) This rule provides guidance on the use of names in appellate court opinions.

(2) Reference to juveniles in juvenile court proceedings is governed by rule 8.401(a).

(3) Where other laws establish specific privacy-protection requirements that differ from the provisions in this rule, those specific requirements supersede the provisions in this rule.

(b) Persons protected

To protect personal privacy interests, in all opinions, the reviewing court should consider referring to the following people by first name and last initial or, if the first name is unusual or other circumstances would defeat the objective of anonymity, by initials only:

(1) Children in all proceedings under the Family Code and protected persons in domestic violence-prevention proceedings;

(2) Wards in guardianship proceedings and conservatees in conservatorship proceedings;

(3) Patients in mental health proceedings;

(4) Victims in criminal proceedings;

(5) Protected persons in civil harassment proceedings under Code of Civil Procedure section 527.6;

(6) Protected persons in workplace violence-prevention proceedings under Code of Civil Procedure section 527.8;

(7) Protected persons in private postsecondary school violence-prevention proceedings under Code of Civil Procedure section 527.85;

(8) Protected persons in elder or dependent adult abuse-prevention proceedings under Welfare and Institutions Code section 15657.03;

(9) Minors or persons with disabilities in proceedings to compromise the claims of a minor or a person with a disability;

(10) Persons in other circumstances in which personal privacy interests support not using the person's name; and

(11) Persons in other circumstances in which use of that person's full name would defeat the objective of anonymity for a person identified in (1)–(10). *(Adopted, eff. Jan. 1, 2017.)*

Advisory Committee Comment

Subdivision (b)(1)–(9) lists people in proceedings under rule 8.83 for which remote electronic access to records—except dockets or registers of actions, calendars, opinions, and certain Supreme Court records—may not be provided. If the court maintains these records in electronic form, electronic access must be provided at the courthouse only, to the extent it is feasible to do so. (Cal. Rules of Court, rule 8.83(c).) Subdivision (b)(1)–(9) recognizes the privacy considerations of certain persons subject to the proceedings listed in rule 8.83(c). Subdivision (b)(10) recognizes people in circumstances other than the listed proceedings, such as witnesses, in which the court should consider referring to a person by first name and last initial, or, if the first name is unusual or other circumstances would defeat the objective of protecting personal privacy interests, by initials. Subdivision (b)(11) recognizes people in circumstances other than the listed proceedings, such as relatives, in which the court should consider referring to a person by first name and last initial or by initials if the use of that person's full name would identify another person whose personal privacy interests support remaining anonymous.

Chapter 3

CRIMINAL APPEALS

Article 1

TAKING THE APPEAL

Rule 8.300. Appointment of appellate counsel by the Court of Appeal

(a) Procedures

(1) Each Court of Appeal must adopt procedures for appointing appellate counsel for indigents not represented by the State Public Defender in all cases in which indigents are entitled to appointed counsel.

(2) The procedures must require each attorney seeking appointment to complete a questionnaire showing the attorney's California State Bar number, date of admission, qualifications, and experience.

(b) List of qualified attorneys

(1) The Court of Appeal must evaluate the attorney's qualifications for appointment and, if the attorney is qualified, place the attorney's name on a list to receive appointments in appropriate cases.

(2) Each court's appointments must be based on criteria approved by the Judicial Council or its designated oversight committee.

(c) Demands of the case

In matching counsel with the demands of the case, the Court of Appeal should consider:

(1) The length of the sentence;

(2) The complexity or novelty of the issues;

(3) The length of the trial and of the reporter's transcript; and

(4) Any questions concerning the competence of trial counsel.

(d) Evaluation

The court must review and evaluate the performance of each appointed counsel to determine whether counsel's name should remain on the list at the same level, be placed on a different level, or be deleted from the list.

(e) Contracts to perform administrative functions

(1) The court may contract with an administrator having substantial experience in handling appellate court appointments to perform any of the duties prescribed by this rule.

(2) The court must provide the administrator with the information needed to fulfill the administrator's duties. *(Formerly Rule 76.5, adopted, eff. Jan. 1, 2005. Renumbered Rule 8.300 and amended, eff. Jan. 1, 2007.)*

Advisory Committee Comment

Subdivision (b). The "designated oversight committee" referred to in subdivision (b)(2) is currently the Appellate Indigent Defense Oversight Advisory Committee. The criteria approved by this committee can be found on the judicial branch's public website at *www.courts.ca.gov/4206.htm*.

Research References

6 Witkin, California Criminal Law 4th Criminal Appeal § 2 (2021), Appellate Rules.

6 Witkin, California Criminal Law 4th Criminal Appeal § 40 (2021), Selection and Compensation.

4 Witkin, California Criminal Law 4th Introduction to Criminal Procedure § 9 (2021), Rules of Court.

Rule 8.304. Filing the appeal; certificate of probable cause

(a) Notice of appeal

(1) To appeal from a judgment or an appealable order of the superior court in a felony case—other than a judgment imposing a sentence of death—the defendant or the People must file a notice of appeal in that superior court. To appeal after a plea of guilty or nolo contendere or after an admission of probation violation, the defendant must also comply with (b).

(2) As used in (1), "felony case" means any criminal action in which a felony is charged, regardless of the outcome. A felony is "charged" when an information or indictment accusing the defendant of a felony is filed or a complaint accusing the defendant of a felony is certified to the superior court under Penal Code section 859a. A felony case includes an action in which the defendant is charged with:

(A) A felony and a misdemeanor or infraction, but is convicted of only the misdemeanor or infraction;

(B) A felony, but is convicted of only a lesser offense; or

(C) An offense filed as a felony but punishable as either a felony or a misdemeanor, and the offense is thereafter deemed a misdemeanor under Penal Code section 17(b).

(3) If the defendant appeals, the defendant or the defendant's attorney must sign the notice of appeal. If the People appeal, the attorney for the People must sign the notice.

(4) The notice of appeal must be liberally construed. Except as provided in (b), the notice is sufficient if it identifies the particular judgment or order being appealed. The notice need not specify the court to which the appeal is taken; the appeal will be treated as taken to the Court of Appeal for the district in which the superior court is located.

(b) Appeal from a judgment of conviction after plea of guilty or nolo contendere or after admission of probation violation

(1) *Appeal requiring a certificate of probable cause*

(A) To appeal from a superior court judgment after a plea of guilty or nolo contendere or after an admission of probation violation on grounds that affect the validity of the plea or admission, the defendant must file in that superior court—with the notice of appeal required by (a)—the written statement required by Penal Code section 1237.5 for issuance of a certificate of probable cause.

(B) Within 20 days after the defendant files a written statement under Penal Code section 1237.5, the superior court must sign and file either a certificate of probable cause or an order denying the certificate.

(2) *Appeal not requiring a certificate of probable cause*

To appeal from a superior court judgment after a plea of guilty or nolo contendere or after an admission of probation violation on grounds that do not affect the validity of the plea or admission, the defendant need not file the written statement required by Penal Code section 1237.5 for issuance of a certificate of probable cause. No certificate of probable cause is required for an appeal based on or from:

(A) The denial of a motion to suppress evidence under Penal Code section 1538.5;

(B) The sentence or other matters occurring after the plea or admission that do not affect the validity of the plea or admission; or

(C) An appealable order for which, by law, no certificate of probable cause is required.

(3) *Appeal without a certificate of probable cause*

If the defendant does not file the written statement required by Penal Code section 1237.5 or the superior court denies a certificate of probable cause, the appeal will be limited to issues that do not require a certificate of probable cause.

(c) Notification of the appeal

(1) When a notice of appeal is filed, the superior court clerk must promptly send a notification of the filing to the attorney of record for each party, any unrepresented defendant, the district appellate project, the reviewing court clerk, each court reporter, and any primary reporter or reporting supervisor. The notification must specify whether the defendant filed a statement under (b)(1)(A) and, if so, whether the superior court filed a certificate or an order denying a certificate under (b)(1)(B).

(2) The notification must show the date it was sent, the number and title of the case, and the dates that the notice of appeal and any certificate or order denying a certificate under (b)(1)(B) were filed. If the information is available, the notification must also include:

(A) The name, address, telephone number, e-mail address, and California State Bar number of each attorney of record in the case;

(B) The name of the party each attorney represented in the superior court; and

(C) The name, address, telephone number and e-mail address of any unrepresented defendant.

(3) The notification to the reviewing court clerk must also include a copy of the notice of appeal, any certificate filed under (b)(1), and the sequential list of reporters made under rule 2.950.

(4) A copy of the notice of appeal is sufficient notification under (1) if the required information is on the copy or is added by the superior court clerk.

(5) The sending of a notification under (1) is a sufficient performance of the clerk's duty despite the discharge, disqualification, suspension, disbarment, or death of the attorney.

(6) Failure to comply with any provision of this subdivision does not affect the validity of the notice of appeal. *(Formerly Rule 30, adopted, eff. Jan. 1, 2004. Renumbered Rule 8.304 and amended, eff. Jan. 1, 2007. As amended, eff. July 1, 2007; Jan. 1, 2016; Jan. 1, 2022.)*

Advisory Committee Comment

Subdivision (a). Penal Code section 1235(b) provides that an appeal from a judgment or appealable order in a "felony case" is taken to the Court of Appeal, and Penal Code section 691(f) defines "felony case" to mean "a criminal action in which a felony is charged." Rule 8.304(a)(2) makes it clear that a "felony case" is an action in which a felony is charged *regardless of the outcome of the action*. Thus the question whether to file a notice of appeal under this rule or under the rules governing appeals to the appellate division of the superior court (rule 8.800 et seq.) is answered simply by examining the accusatory pleading: if that document charged the defendant with at least one count of felony (as defined in Pen. Code, § 17(a)), the Court of Appeal has appellate jurisdiction and the appeal must be taken under this rule *even if the prosecution did not result in a punishment of imprisonment in a state prison*.

It is settled case law that an appeal is taken to the Court of Appeal not only when the defendant is charged with and convicted of a felony, but also when the defendant is charged with both a felony and a misdemeanor (Pen. Code, § 691(f)) but is convicted of only the misdemeanor (e.g., *People v. Brown* (1970) 10 Cal.App.3d 169); when the defendant is charged with a felony but is convicted of only a lesser offense (Pen. Code, § 1159; e.g., *People v. Spreckels* (1954) 125 Cal.App.2d 507); and when the defendant is charged with an offense filed as a felony but punishable as either a felony or a misdemeanor, and the offense is thereafter deemed a misdemeanor under Penal Code section 17(b) (e.g., *People v. Douglas* (1999) 20 Cal.4th 85; *People v. Clark* (1971) 17 Cal.App.3d 890).

Trial court unification did not change this rule: after as before unification, "Appeals in felony cases lie to the [C]ourt of [A]ppeal, regardless of whether the appeal is from the superior court, the municipal court, or the action of a magistrate. *Cf.* Cal. Const. art. VI, § 11(a) [except in death penalty cases, Courts of Appeal have appellate jurisdiction when superior courts have original jurisdiction 'in causes of a type within the appellate jurisdiction of the [C]ourts of [A]ppeal on June 30, 1995']." *(Recommendation on Trial Court Unification: Revision of Codes* (July 1998) 28 Cal. Law Revision Com. Rep. (1998) pp. 455–456.)

Subdivision (b).

Subdivision (b)(1) reiterates the requirement stated in Penal Code section 1237.5(a) that to challenge the validity of a plea or the admission of a probation violation on appeal under Penal Code section 1237(a), the defendant must file both a notice of appeal and the written statement required by section 1237.5(a) for the issuance of a certificate of probable cause. (See *People v. Mendez* (1999) 19 Cal.4th 1084, 1098 [probable cause certificate requirement is to be applied strictly].)

Subdivision (b)(2) identifies exceptions to the certificate-of-probable-cause requirement, including an appeal that challenges the denial of a motion to suppress evidence under Penal Code section 1538.5 (see *People v. Stamps* (2020) 9 Cal.5th 685, 694) and an appeal that does not challenge the validity of the plea or the admission of a probation violation (see, e.g., *id.* at pp. 694–698 [appeal based on a postplea change in the law]; *People v. Arriaga* (2014) 58 Cal.4th 950, 958–960 [appeal from the denial of a motion to vacate a conviction based on inadequate advisement of potential immigration consequences under Penal Code section 1016.5]; and *People v. French* (2008) 43 Cal.4th 36, 45–46 [appeal that challenges a postplea sentencing issue that was not resolved by, and as a part of, the negotiated disposition]).

Subdivision (b)(2)(C) clarifies that no certificate of probable cause is required for an appeal from an order that, by law, is appealable without a certificate. (See, e.g., Pen. Code, § 1473.7.)

Subdivision (b)(3) makes clear that if a defendant raises on appeal an issue that requires a certificate of probable cause, but the defendant does not file the written statement required by Penal Code section 1237.5 or the superior court denies the certificate, then the appeal is limited to issues, such as those identified in subdivision (b)(2), that do not require a certificate of probable cause. (See *Mendez, supra* 19 Cal.4th at pp. 1088–1089.)

Research References

West's California Judicial Council Forms CR–120, Notice of Appeal—Felony (Defendant).

6 Witkin, California Criminal Law 4th Criminal Appeal § 10 (2021), In General.

6 Witkin, California Criminal Law 4th Criminal Appeal § 11 (2021), Exceptions.

6 Witkin, California Criminal Law 4th Criminal Appeal § 12 (2021), Criticisms of Relaxed Compliance.

6 Witkin, California Criminal Law 4th Criminal Appeal § 13 (2021), Strict Compliance.

6 Witkin, California Criminal Law 4th Criminal Appeal § 20 (2021), General Rule.

6 Witkin, California Criminal Law 4th Criminal Appeal § 21 (2021), In General.

6 Witkin, California Criminal Law 4th Criminal Appeal § 27 (2021), In General.

6 Witkin, California Criminal Law 4th Criminal Appeal § 28 (2021), Filing Notice of Appeal and Request for Certificate.
6 Witkin, California Criminal Law 4th Criminal Appeal § 41 (2021), Duties of Trial Attorney.
6 Witkin, California Criminal Law 4th Criminal Appeal § 90 (2021), Written or Printed Notice Must be Filed.
6 Witkin, California Criminal Law 4th Criminal Appeal § 91 (2021), Notification by Clerk.
6 Witkin, California Criminal Law 4th Criminal Appeal § 92 (2021), In General.
6 Witkin, California Criminal Law 4th Criminal Appeal § 94 (2021), Specification of Sentence or Verdict.
6 Witkin, California Criminal Law 4th Criminal Appeal § 132 (2021), Complete Record in Capital Case.
6 Witkin, California Criminal Law 4th Criminal Appeal § 138 (2021), In General.
6 Witkin, California Criminal Law 4th Criminal Appeal § 163 (2021), New Matter on Appeal.
6 Witkin, California Criminal Law 4th Criminal Writs § 101 (2021), Appeal and Petition for Review.

Rule 8.308. Time to appeal

(a) Normal time

Except as provided in (b) or as otherwise provided by law, a notice of appeal and any statement required by Penal Code section 1237.5 must be filed within 60 days after the rendition of the judgment or the making of the order being appealed. Except as provided in rule 8.66, no court may extend the time to file a notice of appeal.

(b) Cross-appeal

If the defendant or the People timely appeals from a judgment or appealable order, the time for any other party to appeal from the same judgment or order is either the time specified in (a) or 30 days after the superior court clerk sends notification of the first appeal, whichever is later.

(c) Premature notice of appeal

A notice of appeal filed before the judgment is rendered or the order is made is premature, but the reviewing court may treat the notice as filed immediately after the rendition of judgment or the making of the order.

(d) Late notice of appeal

The superior court clerk must mark a late notice of appeal "Received [date] but not filed," notify the party that the notice was not filed because it was late, and send a copy of the marked notice of appeal to the district appellate project. *(Formerly Rule 30.1, adopted, eff. Jan. 1, 2004. As amended, eff. Jan. 1, 2005. Renumbered Rule 8.308 and amended, eff. Jan. 1, 2007. As amended, eff. July 1, 2007; Jan. 1, 2008; July 1, 2010; Jan. 1, 2016.)*

Advisory Committee Comment

Subdivision (c). The subdivision requires the clerk to send a copy of a late notice of appeal, marked with the date it was received but not filed, to the appellate project for the district; that entity is charged with the duty, among others, of dealing with indigent criminal appeals that suffer from procedural defect, but it can do so efficiently only if it is promptly notified of such cases.

Subdivision (d). See rule 8.25(b)(5) for provisions concerning the timeliness of documents mailed by inmates or patients from custodial institutions.

Research References

6 Witkin, California Criminal Law 4th Criminal Appeal § 28 (2021), Filing Notice of Appeal and Request for Certificate.
6 Witkin, California Criminal Law 4th Criminal Appeal § 90 (2021), Written or Printed Notice Must be Filed.
6 Witkin, California Criminal Law 4th Criminal Appeal § 96 (2021), Normal Time.
6 Witkin, California Criminal Law 4th Criminal Appeal § 98 (2021), General Rule.
6 Witkin, California Criminal Law 4th Criminal Appeal § 101 (2021), Communicated Desire to Appeal.
6 Witkin, California Criminal Law 4th Criminal Appeal § 102 (2021), Changes in Rules.
6 Witkin, California Criminal Law 4th Criminal Appeal § 104 (2021), Premature Filing is Excusable.
6 Witkin, California Criminal Law 4th Criminal Appeal § 105 (2021), Conditional Notice Attached to Motion.
6 Witkin, California Criminal Law 4th Criminal Writs § 110 (2021), Time to Apply.

Rule 8.312. Stay of execution and release on appeal

(a) Application

Pending appeal, the defendant may apply to the reviewing court:

(1) For a stay of execution after a judgment of conviction or an order granting probation; or

(2) For bail, to reduce bail, or for release on other conditions.

(b) Showing

The application must include a showing that the defendant sought relief in the superior court and that the court unjustifiably denied the application.

(c) Service

The application must be served on the district attorney and on the Attorney General.

(d) Interim relief

Pending its ruling on the application, the reviewing court may grant the relief requested. The reviewing court must notify the superior court under rule 8.489 of any stay that it grants. *(Formerly Rule 30.2, adopted, eff. Jan. 1, 2004. Renumbered Rule 8.312 and amended, eff. Jan. 1, 2007. As amended, eff. Jan. 1, 2009.)*

Advisory Committee Comment

Subdivision (a). The remedy of an application for bail under (a)(2) is separate from but consistent with the statutory remedy of a petition for habeas corpus under Penal Code section 1490. (*In re Brumback* (1956) 46 Cal.2d 810, 815, fn. 3.)

An order of the Court of Appeal denying bail or reduction of bail, or for release on other conditions, is final on filing. (See rule 8.366(b)(2)(A).)

Subdivision (d). The first sentence of (d) recognizes the case law holding that a reviewing court may grant bail or reduce bail, or release the defendant on other conditions, pending its ruling on an application for that relief. (See, e.g., *In re Fishman* (1952) 109 Cal.App.2d 632, 633; *In re Keddy* (1951) 105 Cal.App.2d 215, 217.) The second sentence of the subdivision requires the reviewing court to notify the superior court under rule 8.489 when it grants either (1) a stay to preserve the status quo pending its ruling on a stay application or (2) the stay requested by that application.

Research References

6 Witkin, California Criminal Law 4th Criminal Appeal § 108 (2021), Power and Procedure.
6 Witkin, California Criminal Law 4th Criminal Appeal § 116 (2021), Procedure.
6 Witkin, California Criminal Law 4th Criminal Appeal § 117 (2021), Power and Condition.
6 Witkin, California Criminal Law 4th Criminal Appeal § 118 (2021), Procedure.

Rule 8.316. Abandoning the appeal

(a) How to abandon

An appellant may abandon the appeal at any time by filing an abandonment of the appeal signed by the appellant or the appellant's attorney of record.

(b) Where to file; effect of filing

(1) If the record has not been filed in the reviewing court, the appellant must file the abandonment in the superior court. The filing effects a dismissal of the appeal and restores the superior court's jurisdiction.

(2) If the record has been filed in the reviewing court, the appellant must file the abandonment in that court. The reviewing court may dismiss the appeal and direct immediate issuance of the remittitur.

(c) Clerk's duties

(1) The clerk of the court in which the appellant files the abandonment must immediately notify the adverse party of the filing or of the order of dismissal. If the defendant abandons the appeal, the clerk must notify both the district attorney and the Attorney General.

(2) If the appellant files the abandonment in the superior court, the clerk must immediately notify the reviewing court.

(3) The clerk must immediately notify the reporter if the appeal is abandoned before the reporter has filed the transcript. *(Formerly Rule 30.3, adopted, eff. Jan. 1, 2004. Renumbered Rule 8.316, eff. Jan. 1, 2007.)*

Research References

6 Witkin, California Criminal Law 4th Criminal Appeal § 180 (2021), Voluntary Abandonment or Dismissal.

3 Witkin, California Criminal Law 4th Punishment § 598 (2021), In General.

Article 2

RECORD ON APPEAL

Rule 8.320. Normal record; exhibits

(a) Contents

If the defendant appeals from a judgment of conviction, or if the People appeal from an order granting a new trial, the record must contain a clerk's transcript and a reporter's transcript, which together constitute the normal record.

(b) Clerk's transcript

The clerk's transcript must contain:

(1) The accusatory pleading and any amendment;

(2) Any demurrer or other plea;

(3) All court minutes;

(4) All jury instructions that any party submitted in writing and the cover page required by rule 2.1055(b)(2) indicating the party requesting each instruction, and any written jury instructions given by the court;

(5) Any written communication between the court and the jury or any individual juror;

(6) Any verdict;

(7) Any written opinion of the court;

(8) The judgment or order appealed from and any abstract of judgment or commitment;

(9) Any motion for new trial, with supporting and opposing memoranda and attachments;

(10) The notice of appeal and any certificate of probable cause filed under rule 8.304(b);

(11) Any transcript of a sound or sound-and-video recording furnished to the jury or tendered to the court under rule 2.1040;

(12) Any application for additional record and any order on the application;

(13) And, if the appellant is the defendant:

(A) Any written defense motion denied in whole or in part, with supporting and opposing memoranda and attachments;

(B) If related to a motion under (A), any search warrant and return and the reporter's transcript of any preliminary examination or grand jury hearing;

(C) Any document admitted in evidence to prove a prior juvenile adjudication, criminal conviction, or prison term;

(D) The probation officer's report; and

(E) Any court-ordered diagnostic or psychological report required under Penal Code section 1203.03(b) or 1369.

(c) Reporter's transcript

The reporter's transcript must contain:

(1) The oral proceedings on the entry of any plea other than a not guilty plea;

(2) The oral proceedings on any motion in limine;

(3) The oral proceedings at trial, but excluding the voir dire examination of jurors and any opening statement;

(4) All instructions given orally;

(5) Any oral communication between the court and the jury or any individual juror;

(6) Any oral opinion of the court;

(7) The oral proceedings on any motion for new trial;

(8) The oral proceedings at sentencing, granting or denying of probation, or other dispositional hearing;

(9) And, if the appellant is the defendant:

(A) The oral proceedings on any defense motion denied in whole or in part except motions for disqualification of a judge and motions under Penal Code section 995;

(B) The closing arguments; and

(C) Any comment on the evidence by the court to the jury.

(d) Limited normal record in certain appeals

If the People appeal from a judgment on a demurrer to the accusatory pleading, or if the defendant or the People appeal from an appealable order other than a ruling on a motion for new trial, the normal record is composed of:

(1) *Clerk's transcript*

A clerk's transcript containing:

(A) The accusatory pleading and any amendment;

(B) Any demurrer or other plea;

(C) Any written motion or notice of motion granted or denied by the order appealed from, with supporting and opposing memoranda and attachments;

(D) The judgment or order appealed from and any abstract of judgment or commitment;

(E) Any court minutes relating to the judgment or order appealed from and:

(i) If there was a trial in the case, any court minutes of proceedings at the time the original verdict is rendered and any subsequent proceedings; or

(ii) If the original judgment of conviction is based on a guilty plea or nolo contendere plea, any court minutes of the proceedings at the time of entry of such plea and any subsequent proceedings;

(F) The notice of appeal; and

(G) If the appellant is the defendant, all probation officer reports and any court-ordered diagnostic report required under Penal Code section 1203.03(b).

(2) *Reporter's transcript*

(A) A reporter's transcript of any oral proceedings incident to the judgment or order being appealed; and

(B) If the appeal is from an order after judgment, a reporter's transcript of:

(i) The original sentencing proceeding; and

(ii) If the original judgment of conviction is based on a guilty plea or nolo contendere plea, the proceedings at the time of entry of such plea.

(e) Exhibits

Exhibits admitted in evidence, refused, or lodged are deemed part of the record, but may be transmitted to the reviewing court only as provided in rule 8.224.

(f) Stipulation for partial transcript

If counsel for the defendant and the People stipulate in writing before the record is certified that any part of the record is not required for proper determination of the appeal, that part must not be prepared or sent to the reviewing court. *(Formerly Rule 31, adopted, eff. Jan. 1, 2004. As amended, eff. Jan. 1, 2005. Renumbered Rule 8.320 and amended, eff. Jan. 1, 2007. As amended, eff. Jan. 1, 2008; Jan. 1, 2010; Jan. 1, 2013; Jan. 1, 2014.)*

Advisory Committee Comment

Rules 8.45–8.46 address the appropriate handling of sealed and confidential records that must be included in the record on appeal. Examples of confidential records include Penal Code section 1203.03 diagnostic reports, records closed to inspection by court order under *People v. Marsden* (1970) 2 Cal.3d 118 or *Pitchess v. Superior Court* (1974) 11 Cal.3d 531, in-camera proceedings on a confidential informant, and defense expert funding requests (Pen. Code, § 987.9; *Keenan v. Superior Court* (1982) 31 Cal.3d 424, 430).

Subdivision (d)(1)(E). This rule identifies the minutes that must be included in the record. The trial court clerk may include additional minutes beyond those identified in this rule if that would be more cost-effective.

Rule 8.483 governs the normal record and exhibits in civil commitment appeals.

Research References

6 Witkin, California Criminal Law 4th Criminal Appeal § 122 (2021), Felony.
6 Witkin, California Criminal Law 4th Criminal Appeal § 128 (2021), In General.
6 Witkin, California Criminal Law 4th Criminal Appeal § 129 (2021), Normal Record.
6 Witkin, California Criminal Law 4th Criminal Appeal § 130 (2021), Additional Record.
6 Witkin, California Criminal Law 4th Criminal Appeal § 133 (2021), In General.
6 Witkin, California Criminal Law 4th Criminal Appeal § 134 (2021), Appeal After Probation is Revoked.
6 Witkin, California Criminal Law 4th Criminal Appeal § 135 (2021), Short Record.
6 Witkin, California Criminal Law 4th Criminal Appeal § 148 (2021), Exhibits.
3 Witkin, California Criminal Law 4th Punishment § 599 (2021), Preparation of Record.

Rule 8.324. Application in superior court for addition to normal record

(a) Appeal by the People

The People, as appellant, may apply to the superior court for inclusion in the record of any item that would be part of the normal record in a defendant's appeal.

(b) Application by either party

Either the People or the defendant may apply to the superior court for inclusion in the record of any of the following items:

(1) In the clerk's transcript: any written defense motion granted in whole or in part or any written motion by the People, with supporting and opposing memoranda and attachments;

(2) In the reporter's transcript:

(A) The voir dire examination of jurors;

(B) Any opening statement; and

(C) The oral proceedings on motions other than those listed in rule 8.320(c).

(c) Application

(1) An application for additional record must describe the material to be included and explain how it may be useful in the appeal.

(2) The application must be filed in the superior court with the notice of appeal or as soon thereafter as possible, and will be treated as denied if it is filed after the record is sent to the reviewing court.

(3) The clerk must immediately present the application to the trial judge.

(d) Order

(1) Within five days after the application is filed, the judge must order that the record include as much of the additional material as the judge finds proper to fully present the points raised by the applicant. Denial of the application does not preclude a motion in the reviewing court for augmentation under rule 8.155.

(2) If the judge does not rule on the application within the time prescribed by (1), the requested material—other than exhibits—must be included in the clerk's transcript or the reporter's transcript without a court order.

(3) The clerk must immediately notify the reporter if additions to the reporter's transcript are required under (1) or (2). *(Formerly Rule 31.1, adopted, eff. Jan. 1, 2004. Renumbered Rule 8.324 and amended, eff. Jan. 1, 2007.)*

Research References

6 Witkin, California Criminal Law 4th Criminal Appeal § 128 (2021), In General.
6 Witkin, California Criminal Law 4th Criminal Appeal § 130 (2021), Additional Record.
6 Witkin, California Criminal Law 4th Criminal Appeal § 131 (2021), Confidential Material.
6 Witkin, California Criminal Law 4th Criminal Appeal § 149 (2021), Procedure.

Rule 8.332. Juror–identifying information

(a) Application

A clerk's transcript, a reporter's transcript, or any other document in the record that contains juror-identifying information must comply with this rule.

(b) Juror names, addresses, and telephone numbers

(1) The name of each trial juror or alternate sworn to hear the case must be replaced with an identifying number wherever it appears in any document. The superior court clerk must prepare and keep under seal in the case file a table correlating the jurors' names with their identifying numbers. The clerk and the reporter must use the table in preparing all transcripts or other documents.

(2) The addresses and telephone numbers of trial jurors and alternates sworn to hear the case must be deleted from all documents.

(c) Potential jurors

Information identifying potential jurors called but not sworn as trial jurors or alternates must not be sealed unless otherwise ordered under Code of Civil Procedure section 237(a)(1). *(Formerly Rule 31.3, adopted, eff. Jan. 1, 2004. Renumbered Rule 8.332 and amended, eff. Jan. 1, 2007.)*

Advisory Committee Comment

Rule 8.332 implements Code of Civil Procedure section 237.

Research References

6 Witkin, California Criminal Law 4th Criminal Appeal § 137 (2021), Juror Identifying Information.

Rule 8.336. Preparing, certifying, and sending the record

(a) Immediate preparation when appeal is likely

(1) The reporter and the clerk must begin preparing the record immediately after a verdict or finding of guilt of a felony is announced following a trial on the merits, unless the judge determines that an appeal is unlikely under (2).

(2) In determining the likelihood of an appeal, the judge must consider the facts of the case and the fact that an appeal is likely if the defendant has been convicted of a crime for which probation is prohibited or is prohibited except in unusual cases, or if the trial involved a contested question of law important to the outcome.

(3) A determination under (2) is an administrative decision intended to further the efficient operation of the court and not intended to affect any substantive or procedural right of the defendant or the People. The determination cannot be cited to prove or disprove any legal or factual issue in the case and is not reviewable by appeal or writ.

(b) Appeal after plea of guilty or nolo contendere or after admission of probation violation

In an appeal under rule 8.304(b)(1), the time to prepare, certify, and file the record begins when the court files a certificate of probable cause under rule 8.304(b)(2).

(c) Clerk's transcript

(1) Except as provided in (a) or (b), the clerk must begin preparing the clerk's transcript immediately after the notice of appeal is filed.

(2) Within 20 days after the notice of appeal is filed, the clerk must complete preparation of an original and two copies of the clerk's transcript, one for defendant's counsel and one for the Attorney General or the district attorney, whichever is the counsel for the People on appeal.

(3) On request, the clerk must prepare an extra copy for the district attorney or the Attorney General, whichever is not counsel for the People on appeal.

(4) If there is more than one appealing defendant, the clerk must prepare an extra copy for each additional appealing defendant represented by separate counsel.

(5) The clerk must certify as correct the original and all copies of the clerk's transcript.

(d) Reporter's transcript

(1) Except as provided in (a) or (b), the reporter must begin preparing the reporter's transcript immediately on being notified by the clerk under rule 8.304(c)(1) that the notice of appeal has been filed.

(2) The reporter must prepare an original and the same number of copies of the reporter's transcript as (c) requires of the clerk's transcript, and must certify each as correct.

(3) The reporter must deliver the original and all copies to the superior court clerk as soon as they are certified, but no later than 20 days after the notice of appeal is filed.

(4) Any portion of the transcript transcribed during trial must not be retyped unless necessary to correct errors, but must be repaginated and combined with any portion of the transcript not previously transcribed. Any additional copies needed must not be retyped but, if the transcript is in paper form, must be prepared by photocopying or an equivalent process.

(5) In a multireporter case, the clerk must accept any completed portion of the transcript from the primary reporter one week after the time prescribed by (3) even if other portions are uncompleted. The clerk must promptly pay each reporter who certifies that all portions of the transcript assigned to that reporter are completed.

(e) Extension of time

(1) The superior court may not extend the time for preparing the record.

(2) The reviewing court may order one or more extensions of time for preparing the record, including a reporter's transcript, not exceeding a total of 60 days, on receipt of:

(A) A declaration showing good cause; and

(B) In the case of a reporter's transcript, certification by the superior court presiding judge, or a court administrator designated by the presiding judge, that an extension is reasonable and necessary in light of the workload of all reporters in the court.

(f) Form of record

The clerk's and reporter's transcripts must comply with rules 8.45–8.47, relating to sealed and confidential records, and rule 8.144.

(g) Sending the transcripts

(1) When the clerk and reporter's transcripts are certified as correct, the clerk must promptly send:

(A) The original transcripts to the reviewing court, noting the sending date on each original;

(B) One copy of each transcript to appellate counsel for each defendant represented by separate counsel and to the Attorney General or the district attorney, whichever is counsel for the People on appeal; and

(C) One copy of each transcript to the district attorney or Attorney General if requested under (c)(3).

(2) If the defendant is not represented by appellate counsel when the transcripts are certified as correct, the clerk must send that defendant's counsel's copy of the transcripts to the district appellate project.

(h) Supervision of preparation of record

Each clerk/executive officer of the Court of Appeal, under the supervision of the administrative presiding justice or the presiding justice, must take all appropriate steps to ensure that superior court clerks and reporters promptly perform their duties under this rule. This provision does not affect the superior courts' responsibility for the prompt preparation of appellate records. *(Formerly Rule 32, adopted, eff. Jan. 1, 2004. Renumbered Rule 8.336 and amended, eff. Jan. 1, 2007. As amended, eff. Jan. 1, 2010; Jan. 1, 2014; Jan. 1, 2016; Jan. 1, 2017; Jan. 1, 2018.)*

Advisory Committee Comment

Subdivision (a). Subdivision (a) implements Code of Civil Procedure section 269(b).

Subdivision (f). Examples of confidential records include Penal Code section 1203.03 diagnostic reports, records closed to inspection by court order under *People v. Marsden* (1970) 2 Cal.3d 118 or *Pitchess v. Superior Court* (1974) 11 Cal.3d 531, in-camera proceedings on a confidential informant, and defense expert funding requests (Pen. Code, § 987.9; *Keenan v. Superior Court* (1982) 31 Cal.3d 424, 430).

Subdivision (g). Under rule 8.71(c), the superior court clerk may send the record to the reviewing court in electronic form.

Research References

6 Witkin, California Criminal Law 4th Criminal Appeal § 28 (2021), Filing Notice of Appeal and Request for Certificate.

6 Witkin, California Criminal Law 4th Criminal Appeal § 122 (2021), Felony.

6 Witkin, California Criminal Law 4th Criminal Appeal § 129 (2021), Normal Record.

6 Witkin, California Criminal Law 4th Criminal Appeal § 138 (2021), In General.

6 Witkin, California Criminal Law 4th Criminal Appeal § 139 (2021), Preparation of Record.

6 Witkin, California Criminal Law 4th Criminal Appeal § 140 (2021), Time Requirements in Felony Cases.

6 Witkin, California Criminal Law 4th Criminal Appeal § 147 (2021), In General.

Rule 8.340. Augmenting or correcting the record in the Court of Appeal

(a) Subsequent trial court orders

(1) If, after the record is certified, the trial court amends or recalls the judgment or makes any other order in the case, including an order affecting the sentence or probation, the clerk must promptly certify and send a copy of the amended abstract of judgment or other order—as an augmentation of the record—to:

(A) The reviewing court, the probation officer, the defendant,

(B) The defendant's appellate counsel for each defendant represented by separate counsel, and the Attorney General or the district attorney, whichever is counsel for the People on appeal; and

(C) The district attorney or Attorney General, whichever is not counsel for the People on appeal, if he or she requested a copy of the clerk's transcript under 8.336(c)(3).

(2) If there is any additional document or transcript related to the amended judgment or new order that any rule or order requires be included in the record, the clerk must send this document or transcript with the amended abstract of judgment or other order. The clerk must promptly copy and certify any such document, and the reporter must promptly prepare and certify any such transcript.

(b) Omissions

(1) If, after the record is certified, the superior court clerk or the reporter learns that the record omits a document or transcript that any rule or order requires to be included, the clerk must promptly copy and certify the document or the reporter must promptly prepare and certify the transcript. Without the need for a court order, the clerk must promptly send the document or transcript—as an augmentation of the record—to all those who are listed under (a)(1).

(c) Augmentation or correction by the reviewing court

At any time, on motion of a party or on its own motion, the reviewing court may order the record augmented or corrected as provided in rule 8.155. The clerk must send any document or transcript added to the record to all those who are listed under (a)(1).

(d) Defendant not yet represented

If the defendant is not represented by appellate counsel when the record is augmented or corrected, the clerk must send that defendant's counsel's copy of the augmentations or corrections to the district appellate project. *(Formerly Rule 32.1, adopted, eff. Jan. 1, 2004. Renumbered Rule 8.340 and amended, eff. Jan. 1, 2007.)*

Advisory Committee Comment

Subdivision (b). The words "or order" in the first sentence of (b) are intended to refer to any court order to include additional material in the record, e.g., an order of the superior court under rule 8.324(d)(1).

Research References

6 Witkin, California Criminal Law 4th Criminal Appeal § 131 (2021), Confidential Material.
6 Witkin, California Criminal Law 4th Criminal Appeal § 136 (2021), Augmenting or Correcting Record by Trial Court.
6 Witkin, California Criminal Law 4th Criminal Appeal § 138 (2021), In General.
6 Witkin, California Criminal Law 4th Criminal Appeal § 147 (2021), In General.
6 Witkin, California Criminal Law 4th Criminal Appeal § 149 (2021), Procedure.

Rule 8.344. Agreed statement

If the parties present the appeal on an agreed statement, they must comply with the relevant provisions of rule 8.134, but the appellant must file an original and, if the statement is filed in paper form, three copies of the statement in superior court within 25 days after filing the notice of appeal. *(Formerly Rule 32.2, adopted, eff. Jan. 1, 2004. Renumbered Rule 8.344 and amended, eff. Jan. 1, 2007. As amended, eff. Jan. 1, 2016.)*

Research References

6 Witkin, California Criminal Law 4th Criminal Appeal § 128 (2021), In General.
6 Witkin, California Criminal Law 4th Criminal Appeal § 135 (2021), Short Record.
6 Witkin, California Criminal Law 4th Criminal Appeal § 139 (2021), Preparation of Record.

Rule 8.346. Settled statement

(a) Application

As soon as a party learns that any portion of the oral proceedings cannot be transcribed, the party may serve and file in superior court an application for permission to prepare a settled statement. The application must explain why the oral proceedings cannot be transcribed.

(b) Order and proposed statement

The judge must rule on the application within five days after it is filed. If the judge grants the application, the parties must comply with the relevant provisions of rule 8.137, but the applicant must deliver a proposed statement to the judge for settlement within 30 days after it is ordered, unless the reviewing court extends the time.

(c) Serving and filing the settled statement

The applicant must prepare, serve, and file in superior court an original and, if the statement is filed in paper form, three copies of the settled statement. *(Formerly Rule 32.3, adopted, eff. Jan. 1, 2004. Renumbered Rule 8.346 and amended, eff. Jan. 1, 2007. As amended, eff. Jan. 1, 2016.)*

Research References

6 Witkin, California Criminal Law 4th Criminal Appeal § 128 (2021), In General.
6 Witkin, California Criminal Law 4th Criminal Appeal § 142 (2021), In General.

Article 3

BRIEFS, HEARING, AND DECISION

Rule

Rule 8.360. Briefs by parties and amici curiae

(a) Contents and form

Except as provided in this rule, briefs in criminal appeals must comply as nearly as possible with rules 8.200 and 8.204.

(b) Length

(1) A brief produced on a computer must not exceed 25,500 words, including footnotes. Such a brief must include a certificate by appellate counsel or an unrepresented defendant stating the number of words in the brief; the person certifying may rely on the word count of the computer program used to prepare the brief.

(2) A typewritten brief must not exceed 75 pages.

(3) The tables required under rule 8.204(a)(1), the cover information required under rule 8.204(b)(10), any Certificate of Interested Entities or Persons required under rule 8.361, a certificate under (1),

any signature block, and any attachment permitted under rule 8.204(d) are excluded from the limits stated in (1) or (2).

(4) A combined brief in an appeal governed by (e) must not exceed double the limit stated in (1) or (2).

(5) On application, the presiding justice may permit a longer brief for good cause.

(c) Time to file

(1) The appellant's opening brief must be served and filed within 40 days after the record is filed in the reviewing court.

(2) The respondent's brief must be served and filed within 30 days after the appellant's opening brief is filed.

(3) The appellant must serve and file a reply brief, if any, within 20 days after the respondent files its brief.

(4) The time to serve and file a brief may not be extended by stipulation, but only by order of the presiding justice under rule 8.60.

(5) If a party fails to timely file an appellant's opening brief or a respondent's brief, the reviewing court clerk must promptly notify the party in writing that the brief must be filed within 30 days after the notice is sent, and that failure to comply may result in one of the following sanctions:

(A) If the brief is an appellant's opening brief:

(i) If the appellant is the People, the court will dismiss the appeal;

(ii) If the appellant is the defendant and is represented by appointed counsel on appeal, the court will relieve that appointed counsel and appoint new counsel;

(iii) If the appellant is the defendant and is not represented by appointed counsel, the court will dismiss the appeal; or

(B) If the brief is a respondent's brief, the court will decide the appeal on the record, the opening brief, and any oral argument by the appellant.

(6) If a party fails to comply with a notice under (5), the court may impose the sanction specified in the notice.

(d) Service

(1) Defendant's appellate counsel must serve each brief for the defendant on the People and the district attorney, and must send a copy of each to the defendant personally unless the defendant requests otherwise.

(2) The proof of service under (1) must state that a copy of the defendant's brief was sent to the defendant, or counsel must file a signed statement that the defendant requested in writing that no copy be sent.

(3) The People must serve two copies of their briefs on the appellate counsel for each defendant who is a party to the appeal and one copy on the district appellate project. If the district attorney is representing the People, one copy of the district attorney's brief must be served on the Attorney General.

(4) A copy of each brief must be served on the superior court clerk for delivery to the trial judge.

(e) When a defendant and the People appeal

When both a defendant and the People appeal, the defendant must file the first opening brief unless the reviewing court orders otherwise, and rule 8.216(b) governs the contents of the briefs.

(f) Amicus curiae briefs

Amicus curiae briefs may be filed as provided in rule 8.200(c). *(Formerly Rule 33, adopted, eff. Jan. 1, 2004. Renumbered Rule 8.360 and amended, eff. Jan. 1, 2007. As amended, eff. Jan. 1, 2011; Jan. 1, 2013; Jan. 1, 2016.)*

Advisory Committee Comment

Subdivision (b). Subdivision (b)(1) states the maximum permissible length of a brief produced on a computer in terms of word count rather than page count. This provision tracks a provision in rule 8.204(c) governing Court of Appeal briefs and is explained in the comment to that provision. The word count assumes a brief using one-and-one-half spaced lines of text, as permitted by rule 8.204(b)(5). Subdivision (b)(3) specifies certain items that are not counted toward the maximum brief length. Signature blocks as referenced in this provision, include not only the signatures, but also the printed names, titles, and affiliations of any attorneys filing or joining in the brief, which may accompany the signature.

The maximum permissible length of briefs in death penalty appeals is prescribed in rule 8.630.

Research References

West's California Judicial Council Forms CR-126, Application for Extension of Time to File Brief (Criminal Case).
6 Witkin, California Criminal Law 4th Criminal Appeal § 153 (2021), Requirement.
6 Witkin, California Criminal Law 4th Criminal Appeal § 154 (2021), Content, Form, and Style.
6 Witkin, California Criminal Law 4th Criminal Appeal § 155 (2021), Length.
6 Witkin, California Criminal Law 4th Criminal Appeal § 156 (2021), Service and Filing.

Rule 8.361. Certificate of interested entities or persons

In criminal cases in which an entity is a defendant, that defendant must comply with the requirements of rule 8.208 concerning serving and filing a certificate of interested entities or persons. *(Adopted, eff. Jan. 1, 2009.)*

Advisory Committee Comment

Under rule 8.208(c), for purposes of certificates of interested entities or persons, an "entity" means a corporation, a partnership, a firm, or any other association but does not include a governmental entity or its agencies or a natural person.

Rule 8.366. Hearing and decision in the Court of Appeal

(a) General application of rules 8.252–8.272

Except as provided in this rule, rules 8.252–8.272 govern the hearing and decision in the Court of Appeal of an appeal in a criminal case.

(b) Finality

(1) Except as otherwise provided in this rule, a Court of Appeal decision in a proceeding under this chapter, including an order dismissing an appeal involuntarily, is final in that court 30 days after filing.

(2) The following Court of Appeal decisions are final in that court on filing:

(A) The denial of an application for bail or to reduce bail pending appeal; and

(B) The dismissal of an appeal on request or stipulation.

(3) If a Court of Appeal certifies its opinion for publication or partial publication after filing its decision and before its decision becomes final in that court, the finality period runs from the filing date of the order for publication.

(4) If an order modifying an opinion changes the appellate judgment, the finality period runs from the filing date of the modification order.

(c) Sanctions

Except for (a)(1), rule 8.276 applies in criminal appeals. *(Formerly Rule 33.1, adopted, eff. Jan. 1, 2004. Renumbered Rule 8.366 and amended, eff. Jan. 1, 2007. As amended, eff. Jan. 1, 2008; Jan. 1, 2009.)*

Advisory Committee Comment

Subdivision (b). As used in subdivision (b)(1), "decision" includes all interlocutory orders of the Court of Appeal. (See Advisory Committee Comment to rule 8.500(a) and (e).) This provision addresses the finality of decisions in criminal appeals. See rule 8.264(b) for provisions addressing the finality of decisions in proceedings under chapter 2, relating to civil appeals, and rule 8.490 for provisions addressing the finality of proceedings under chapter 7, relating to writs of mandate, certiorari, and prohibition.

Research References

6 Witkin, California Criminal Law 4th Criminal Appeal § 2 (2021), Appellate Rules.
6 Witkin, California Criminal Law 4th Criminal Appeal § 118 (2021), Procedure.
6 Witkin, California Criminal Law 4th Criminal Appeal § 196 (2021), Finality of Decision.

Rule 8.368. Hearing and decision in the Supreme Court

Rules 8.500 through 8.552 govern the hearing and decision in the Supreme Court of an appeal in a criminal case. *(Formerly Rule 33.2, adopted, eff. Jan. 1, 2004. Renumbered Rule 8.368 and amended, eff. Jan. 1, 2007.)*

Research References

6 Witkin, California Criminal Law 4th Criminal Appeal § 2 (2021), Appellate Rules.

Chapter 4

HABEAS CORPUS APPEALS AND WRITS

Article 1

HABEAS CORPUS PROCEEDINGS NOT RELATED TO JUDGMENT OF DEATH

Rule 8.380. Petition for writ of habeas corpus filed by petitioner not represented by an attorney

(a) Required Judicial Council form

A person who is not represented by an attorney and who petitions a reviewing court for writ of habeas corpus seeking release from, or modification of the conditions of, custody of a person confined in a state or local penal institution, hospital, narcotics treatment facility, or other institution must file the petition on *Petition for Writ of Habeas Corpus* (form HC–001). For good cause the court may permit the filing of a petition that is not on that form, but the petition must be verified.

(b) Form and content

A petition filed under (a) need not comply with the provisions of rules 8.40, 8.204, or 8.486 that prescribe the form and content of a petition and require the petition to be accompanied by a memorandum. If any supporting documents accompanying the petition are sealed or confidential records, rules 8.45–8.47 govern these documents.

(c) Number of copies

In the Court of Appeal, the petitioner must file the original of the petition under (a) and one set of any supporting documents. In the Supreme Court the petitioner must file an original and, if the petition is filed in paper form, 10 copies of the petition and an original and, if the document is filed in paper form, 2 copies of any supporting document accompanying the petition unless the court orders otherwise. *(Formerly Rule 60, adopted, eff. Jan. 1, 2005. As amended, eff. Jan. 1, 2006. Renumbered Rule 8.380 and amended, eff. Jan. 1, 2007. As amended, eff. Jan. 1, 2009; Jan. 1, 2014; Jan. 1, 2016; Jan. 1, 2018; Jan. 1, 2020.)*

Advisory Committee Comment

Subdivision (b). Examples of confidential records include Penal Code section 1203.03 diagnostic reports, records closed to inspection by court order under *People v. Marsden* (1970) 2 Cal.3d 118 or *Pitchess v. Superior Court* (1974) 11 Cal.3d 531, in-camera proceedings on a confidential informant, and defense expert funding requests (Pen. Code, § 987.9; *Keenan v. Superior Court* (1982) 31 Cal.3d 424, 430).

Research References

West's California Judicial Council Forms HC–001, Petition for Writ of Habeas Corpus.
6 Witkin, California Criminal Law 4th Criminal Appeal § 2 (2021), Appellate Rules.
5 Witkin, California Criminal Law 4th Criminal Trial § 270 (2021), Habeas Corpus Proceeding.
6 Witkin, California Criminal Law 4th Criminal Writs § 67 (2021), Overview.
6 Witkin, California Criminal Law 4th Criminal Writs § 69 (2021), Format in Reviewing Court.
4 Witkin, California Criminal Law 4th Introduction to Criminal Procedure § 9 (2021), Rules of Court.

Rule 8.384. Petition for writ of habeas corpus filed by an attorney for a party

(a) Form and content of petition and memorandum

(1) A petition for habeas corpus filed by an attorney need not be filed on *Petition for Writ of Habeas Corpus* (form HC–001) but must contain the information requested in that form and must be verified. All petitions filed by attorneys, whether or not on form HC–001, must be either typewritten or produced on a computer, and must comply with this rule and rule 8.40(b)–(c) relating to document covers and rule 8.204(a)(1)(A) relating to tables of contents and authorities. A petition that is not on form HC–001 must also comply with the remainder of rule 8.204(a)(b).

(2) Any memorandum accompanying the petition must comply with rule 8.204(a)–(b). Except in habeas corpus proceedings related to sentences of death, any memorandum must also comply with the length limits in rule 8.204(c).

(3) The petition and any memorandum must support any reference to a matter in the supporting documents by a citation to its index number or letter and page.

(b) Supporting documents

(1) The petition must be accompanied by a copy of any petition—excluding exhibits—pertaining to the same judgment and petitioner that was previously filed in any state court or any federal court. If such documents have previously been filed in the same Court of Appeal where the petition is filed or in the Supreme Court and the petition so states and identifies the documents by case name and number, copies of these documents need not be included in the supporting documents.

(2) If the petition asserts a claim that was the subject of an evidentiary hearing, the petition must be accompanied by a certified transcript of that hearing.

(3) Rule 8.486(c)(1) and (2) govern the form of any supporting documents accompanying the petition.

(4) If any supporting documents accompanying the petition are sealed or confidential records, rules 8.45–8.47 govern these documents.

(c) Number of copies

If the petition is filed in the Supreme Court, the attorney must file the number of copies of the petition and supporting documents required by rule 8.44(a). If the petition is filed in the Court of Appeal, the attorney must file the number of copies of the petition and supporting documents required by rule 8.44(b).

(d) Noncomplying petitions

The clerk must file an attorney's petition not complying with (a)–(c) if it otherwise complies with the rules of court, but the court may notify the attorney that it may strike the petition or impose a lesser sanction if the petition is not brought into compliance within a stated reasonable time of not less than five days. *(Formerly Rule 60.5, adopted, eff. Jan. 1, 2006. Renumbered Rule 8.384 and amended, eff. Jan. 1, 2007. As amended, eff. Jan. 1, 2009; Jan. 1, 2014; Jan. 1, 2016; Jan. 1, 2018; Jan. 1, 2020.)*

Advisory Committee Comment

Subdivision (b)(4). Examples of confidential records include Penal Code section 1203.03 diagnostic reports, records closed to inspection by court order under *People v. Marsden* (1970) 2 Cal.3d 118 or *Pitchess v. Superior Court* (1974) 11 Cal.3d 531, in-camera proceedings on a confidential informant, and defense expert funding requests (Pen. Code, § 987.9; *Keenan v. Superior Court* (1982) 31 Cal.3d 424, 430).

Research References

5 Witkin, California Criminal Law 4th Criminal Trial § 270 (2021), Habeas Corpus Proceeding.
6 Witkin, California Criminal Law 4th Criminal Writs § 69 (2021), Format in Reviewing Court.

Rule 8.385. Proceedings after the petition is filed

(a) Production of record

Before ruling on the petition, the court may order the custodian of any relevant record to produce the record or a certified copy to be filed with the court. Sealed and confidential records are governed by rules 8.45–8.47.

(b) Informal response

(1) Before ruling on the petition, the court may request an informal written response from the respondent, the real party in interest, or an interested person. The court must send a copy of any request to the petitioner.

(2) The response must be served and filed within 15 days or as the court specifies. If the petitioner is not represented by counsel in the habeas corpus proceeding, one copy of the informal response and any supporting documents must be served on the petitioner. If the petitioner is represented by counsel in the habeas corpus proceeding, the response must be served on the petitioner's counsel. If the response is served in paper form, two copies must be served on the petitioner's counsel. If the petitioner is represented by court-appointed counsel other than the State Public Defender's Office or Habeas Corpus Resource Center, one copy must also be served on the applicable appellate project.

(3) If a response is filed, the court must notify the petitioner that a reply may be served and filed within 15 days or as the court specifies. The court may not deny the petition until that time has expired.

(c) Petition filed in an inappropriate court

(1) A Court of Appeal may deny without prejudice a petition for writ of habeas corpus that is based primarily on facts occurring outside the court's appellate district, including petitions that question:

(A) The validity of judgments or orders of trial courts located outside the district; or

(B) The conditions of confinement or the conduct of correctional officials outside the district.

(2) A Court of Appeal should deny without prejudice a petition for writ of habeas corpus that challenges the denial of parole or the petitioner's suitability for parole if the issue was not first adjudicated by the trial court that rendered the underlying judgment.

(3) If the court denies a petition solely under (1), the order must state the basis of the denial and must identify the appropriate court in which to file the petition.

(d) Order to show cause

If the petitioner has made the required prima facie showing that he or she is entitled to relief, the court must issue an order to show cause. An order to show cause does not grant the relief sought in the petition.

(e) Return to the superior court

The reviewing court may order the respondent to file a return in the superior court. The order vests jurisdiction over the cause in the superior court, which must proceed under rule 4.551.

(f) Return to the reviewing court

If the return is ordered to be filed in the Supreme Court or the Court of Appeal, rule 8.386 applies and the court in which the return is ordered filed must appoint counsel for any unrepresented petitioner who desires but cannot afford counsel. *(Adopted, eff. Jan. 1, 2009. As amended, eff. Jan. 1, 2012; Jan. 1, 2014; Jan. 1, 2016.)*

Validity

A prior version of this rule that Court of Appeal must deny writ petition under certain circumstances was held unconstitutional in the decision of In re Kler (App. 1 Dist. 2010) 115 Cal.Rptr.3d 889, 188 Cal.App.4th 1399.

Advisory Committee Comment

Subdivision (a). Examples of confidential records include Penal Code section 1203.03 diagnostic reports, records closed to inspection by court order under *People v. Marsden* (1970) 2 Cal.3d 118 or *Pitchess v. Superior Court* (1974) 11 Cal.3d 531, in-camera proceedings on a confidential informant, and defense expert funding requests (Pen. Code, § 987.9; *Keenan v. Superior Court* (1982) 31 Cal.3d 424, 430).

Subdivision (c). Except for subdivision (c)(2), rule 8.385(c) restates former section 6.5 of the Standards of Judicial Administration. Subdivision (c)(2) is based on the California Supreme Court decision in *In re Roberts* (2005) 36 Cal.4th 575, which provides that petitions for writ of habeas corpus challenging denial or suitability for parole should first be adjudicated in the trial court that rendered the underlying judgment. The committee notes, however, that courts of appeal have original jurisdiction in writ proceedings and may, under appropriate circumstances, adjudicate a petition that challenges the denial or suitability of parole even if the petition was not first adjudicated by the trial court that rendered the underlying judgment. (*In re Kler* (2010) 188 Cal.App.4th 1399.) A court of appeal may, for example, adjudicate a petition that follows the court's prior reversal of a denial of parole by the Board of Parole Hearings where the issues presented by the petition directly flow from the court of appeal's prior decision and the limited hearing conducted. (*Id.* at 1404–05.)

Subdivision (d). Case law establishes the specificity of the factual allegations and support for these allegations required in a petition for a writ of habeas corpus (see, e.g., *People v. Duvall* (1995) 9 Cal.4th 464, 474–475, and *Ex parte Swain* (1949) 34 Cal.2d 300, 303–304). A court evaluating whether a petition meeting these requirements makes a prima facie showing asks whether, assuming the petition's factual allegations are true, the petitioner would be entitled to relief (*People v. Duvall*, supra).

Issuing an order to show cause is just one of the actions a court might take on a petition for a writ of habeas corpus. Examples of other actions that a court might take include denying the petition summarily, requesting an informal response from the respondent under (b), or denying the petition without prejudice under (c) because it is filed in an inappropriate court.

Research References

6 Witkin, California Criminal Law 4th Criminal Writs § 75 (2021), Informal Response and Determination of Petition.
6 Witkin, California Criminal Law 4th Criminal Writs § 76 (2021), In General.

6 Witkin, California Criminal Law 4th Criminal Writs § 83 (2021), Appointed Counsel.
6 Witkin, California Criminal Law 4th Criminal Writs § 95 (2021), Where Return is Filed in Superior Court.

Rule 8.386. Proceedings if the return is ordered to be filed in the reviewing court

(a) Application

This rule applies if the Supreme Court orders the return to be filed in the Supreme Court or the Court of Appeal or if the Court of Appeal orders the return to be filed in the Court of Appeal.

(b) Serving and filing return

(1) Unless the court orders otherwise, any return must be served and filed within 30 days after the court issues the order to show cause.

(2) If the return is filed in the Supreme Court, the respondent must file the number of copies of the return and any supporting documents required by rule 8.44(a). If the return is filed in the Court of Appeal, the respondent must file the number of copies of the return and any supporting documents required by rule 8.44(b).

(3) The return and any supporting documents must be served on the petitioner's counsel. If the return is served in paper form, two copies must be served on the petitioner's counsel. If the petitioner is represented for the habeas corpus proceeding by court-appointed counsel other than the State Public Defender's Office or Habeas Corpus Resource Center, one copy must be served on the applicable appellate project.

(c) Form and content of return

(1) The return must be either typewritten or produced on a computer and must comply with Penal Code section 1480 and rules 8.40(b)–(c) and 8.204(a)–(b). Except in habeas corpus proceedings related to sentences of death, any memorandum accompanying a return must also comply with the length limits in rule 8.204(c).

(2) Rule 8.486(c)(1) and (2) govern the form of any supporting documents accompanying the return. The return must support any reference to a matter in the supporting documents by a citation to its index number or letter and page.

(3) Any material allegation of the petition not controverted by the return is deemed admitted for purposes of the proceeding.

(d) Traverse

(1) Unless the court orders otherwise, within 30 days after the respondent files a return, the petitioner may serve and file a traverse.

(2) Any traverse must be either typewritten or produced on a computer and must comply with Penal Code section 1484 and rules 8.40(b)–(c) and 8.204(a)–(b). Except in habeas corpus proceedings related to sentences of death, any memorandum accompanying a traverse must also comply with the length limits in rule 8.204(c).

(3) Rule 8.486(c)(1) and (2) govern the form of any supporting documents accompanying the traverse.

(4) Any material allegation of the return not denied in the traverse is deemed admitted for purposes of the proceeding.

(5) If the return is filed in the Supreme Court, the attorney must file the number of copies of the traverse required by rule 8.44(a). If the return is filed in the Court of Appeal, the attorney must file the number of copies of the traverse required by rule 8.44(b).

(e) Judicial notice

Rule 8.252(a) governs judicial notice in the reviewing court.

(f) Evidentiary hearing ordered by the reviewing court

(1) An evidentiary hearing is required if, after considering the verified petition, the return, any traverse, any affidavits or declarations under penalty of perjury, and matters of which judicial notice may be taken, the court finds there is a reasonable likelihood that the petitioner may be entitled to relief and the petitioner's entitlement to relief depends on the resolution of an issue of fact.

(2) The court may appoint a referee to conduct the hearing and make recommended findings of fact.

(g) Oral argument and submission of the cause

Unless the court orders otherwise:

(1) Rule 8.256 governs oral argument and submission of the cause in the Court of Appeal.

(2) Rule 8.524 governs oral argument and submission of the cause in the Supreme Court. *(Adopted, eff. Jan. 1, 2009. As amended, eff. Jan. 1, 2014; Jan. 1, 2016.)*

Research References

6 Witkin, California Criminal Law 4th Criminal Writs § 90 (2021), Where Return is Filed in Reviewing Court.
6 Witkin, California Criminal Law 4th Criminal Writs § 91 (2021), Nature.

Rule 8.387. Decision in habeas corpus proceedings

(a) Filing the decision

(1) Rule 8.264(a) governs the filing of the decision in the Court of Appeal.

(2) Rule 8.532(a) governs the filing of the decision in the Supreme Court.

(b) Finality of decision in the Court of Appeal

(1) *General finality period*

Except as otherwise provided in this rule, a Court of Appeal decision in a habeas corpus proceeding is final in that court 30 days after filing.

(2) *Denial of a petition for writ of habeas corpus without issuance of an order to show cause*

(A) Except as provided in (B), a Court of Appeal decision denying a petition for writ of habeas corpus without issuance of an order to show cause is final in the Court of Appeal upon filing.

(B) A Court of Appeal decision denying a petition for writ of habeas corpus without issuing an order to show cause is final in that court on the same day that its decision in a related appeal is final if the two decisions are filed on the same day. If the Court of Appeal orders rehearing of the decision in the appeal, its decision denying the petition for writ of habeas corpus is final when its decision on rehearing is final.

(3) *Decision in a habeas corpus proceeding after issuance of an order to show cause*

(A) If necessary to prevent mootness or frustration of the relief granted or to otherwise promote the interests of justice, a Court of Appeal may order early finality in that court of a decision in a habeas corpus proceeding after issuing an order to show cause. The decision may provide for finality in that court on filing or within a stated period of less than 30 days.

(B) If a Court of Appeal certifies its opinion for publication or partial publication after filing its decision and before its decision becomes final in that court, the finality period runs from the filing date of the order for publication.

(c) Finality of decision in the Supreme Court

Rule 8.532(b) governs finality of a decision in the Supreme Court.

(d) Modification of decision

(1) A reviewing court may modify a decision until the decision is final in that court. If the clerk's office is closed on the date of finality, the court may modify the decision on the next day the clerk's office is open.

(2) An order modifying an opinion must state whether it changes the appellate judgment. A modification that does not change the appellate judgment does not extend the finality date of the decision.

If a modification changes the appellate judgment, the finality period runs from the filing date of the modification order.

(e) Rehearing

(1) Rule 8.268 governs rehearing in the Court of Appeal.

(2) Rule 8.536 governs rehearing in the Supreme Court.

(f) Remittitur

(1) A Court of Appeal must issue a remittitur in a habeas corpus proceeding under this chapter except when the court denies the petition without issuing an order to show cause or orders the return filed in the superior court.

(2) A Court of Appeal must also issue a remittitur if the Supreme Court issues a remittitur to the Court of Appeal.

(3) Rule 8.272(b)–(d) governs issuance of a remittitur by a Court of Appeal in habeas corpus proceedings, including the clerk's duties; immediate issuance, stay, and recall of remittitur; and notice of issuance. *(Formerly Rule 8.386, adopted, eff. Jan. 1, 2008. Renumbered Rule 8.387 and amended, eff. Jan. 1, 2009. As amended, eff. Jan. 1, 2014.)*

Advisory Committee Comment

A party may seek review of a Court of Appeal decision in a habeas corpus proceeding by way of a petition for review in the Supreme Court under rule 8.500.

Subdivision (f). Under this rule, a remittitur serves as notice that the habeas corpus proceedings have concluded.

Research References

6 Witkin, California Criminal Law 4th Criminal Writs § 99 (2021), Finality and Further Proceedings in Reviewing Court.

Rule 8.388. Appeal from order granting relief by writ of habeas corpus

(a) Application

Except as otherwise provided in this rule, rules 8.304–8.368 and 8.508 govern appeals under Penal Code section 1506 or 1507 from orders granting all or part of the relief sought in a petition for writ of habeas corpus. This rule does not apply to appeals under Penal Code section 1509.1 from superior court decisions in death penalty-related habeas corpus proceedings.

(b) Contents of record

In an appeal under this rule, the record must contain:

(1) The petition, the return, and the traverse;

(2) The order to show cause;

(3) All court minutes;

(4) All documents and exhibits submitted to the court;

(5) The reporter's transcript of any oral proceedings;

(6) Any written opinion of the court;

(7) The order appealed from; and

(8) The notice of appeal. *(Formerly Rule 39.2, adopted, eff. Jan. 1, 2005. Renumbered Rule 8.388 and amended, eff. Jan. 1, 2007. As amended, eff. April 25, 2019.)*

Research References

6 Witkin, California Criminal Law 4th Criminal Writs § 101 (2021), Appeal and Petition for Review.

Article 2

APPEALS FROM SUPERIOR COURT DECISIONS IN DEATH PENALTY–RELATED HABEAS CORPUS PROCEEDINGS

Rule 8.390. Application

(a) Application

The rules in this article apply only to appeals under Penal Code section 1509.1 from superior court decisions in death penalty-related habeas corpus proceedings.

(b) General application of rules for criminal appeals

Except as otherwise provided in this article, rules 8.300, 8.316, 8.332, 8.340–8.346, and 8.366–8.368 govern appeals subject to the rules in this article. *(Adopted eff. April 25, 2019.)*

Research References

6 Witkin, California Criminal Law 4th Criminal Writs § 67C (2021), (New) Rules and Forms.

Rule 8.391. Qualifications and appointment of counsel by the Court of Appeal

(a) Qualifications

To be appointed by the Court of Appeal to represent an indigent petitioner not represented by the State Public Defender in an appeal under this article, an attorney must:

(1) Meet the minimum qualifications established by rule 8.652 for attorneys to be appointed to represent a person in a death penalty-related habeas corpus proceeding, including being willing to cooperate with an assisting counsel or entity that the court may designate;

(2) Be familiar with appellate practices and procedures in the California courts, including those related to death penalty appeals; and

(3) Not have represented the petitioner in the habeas corpus proceedings that are the subject of the appeal unless the petitioner and counsel expressly request, in writing, continued representation.

(b) Designation of assisting entity or counsel

Either before or at the time it appoints counsel, the court must designate an assisting entity or counsel. *(Adopted eff. April 25, 2019.)*

Research References

6 Witkin, California Criminal Law 4th Criminal Writs § 67C (2021), (New) Rules and Forms.

Rule 8.392. Filing the appeal; certificate of appealability

(a) Notice of appeal

(1) To appeal from a superior court decision in a death penalty-related habeas corpus proceeding, the petitioner or the People must serve and file a notice of appeal in that superior court. To appeal a decision denying relief on a successive habeas corpus petition, the petitioner must also comply with (b).

(2) If the petitioner appeals, petitioner's counsel, or, in the absence of counsel, the petitioner, is responsible for signing the notice of appeal. If the People appeal, the attorney for the People must sign the notice.

(b) Appeal of decision denying relief on a successive habeas corpus petition

(1) The petitioner may appeal the decision of the superior court denying relief on a successive death penalty-related habeas corpus petition only if the superior court or the Court of Appeal grants a certificate of appealability under Penal Code section 1509.1(c).

(2) The petitioner must identify in the notice of appeal that the appeal is from a superior court decision denying relief on a successive petition and indicate whether the superior court granted or denied a certificate of appealability.

(3) If the superior court denied a certificate of appealability, the petitioner must attach to the notice of appeal a request to the Court of Appeal for a certificate of appealability. The request must identify the petitioner's claim or claims for relief and explain how the requirements of Penal Code section 1509(d) have been met.

(4) On receiving the request for a certificate of appealability, the Court of Appeal clerk must promptly file the request and send notice of the filing date to the parties.

(5) The People need not file an answer to a request for a certificate of appealability unless the court requests an answer. The clerk must promptly send to the parties and the assisting entity or counsel copies of any order requesting an answer and immediately notify the parties by telephone or another expeditious method. Any answer must be served on the parties and the assisting entity or counsel and filed within five days after the order is filed unless the court orders otherwise.

(6) The Court of Appeal must grant or deny the request for a certificate of appealability within 10 days of the filing of the request in that court. If the Court of Appeal grants a certificate of appealability, the certificate must identify the substantial claim or claims for relief shown by the petitioner. The clerk must send a copy of the certificate or its order denying the request for a certificate to:

(A) The attorney for the petitioner or, if unrepresented, to the petitioner;

(B) The district appellate project and, if designated, any assisting entity or counsel other than the district appellate project;

(C) The Attorney General;

(D) The district attorney;

(E) The superior court clerk; and

(F) The clerk/executive officer of the Supreme Court.

(7) If both the superior court and the Court of Appeal deny a certificate of appealability, the clerk/executive officer of the Court of Appeal must mark the notice of appeal "Inoperative," notify the petitioner, and send a copy of the marked notice of appeal to the superior court clerk, the clerk/executive officer of the Supreme Court, the district appellate project, and, if designated, any assisting entity or counsel other than the district appellate project.

(c) Notification of the appeal

(1) Except as provided in (2), when a notice of appeal is filed, the superior court clerk must promptly—and no later than five days after the notice of appeal is filed—send a notification of the filing to:

(A) The attorney for the petitioner or, if unrepresented, to the petitioner;

(B) The district appellate project and, if designated, any assisting entity or counsel other than the district appellate project;

(C) The Attorney General;

(D) The district attorney;

(E) The clerk/executive officer of the Court of Appeal;

(F) The clerk/executive officer of the Supreme Court;

(G) Each court reporter; and

(H) Any primary reporter or reporting supervisor.

(2) If the petitioner is appealing from a superior court decision denying relief on a successive petition and the superior court did not issue a certificate of appealability, the clerk must not send the notification of the filing of a notice of appeal to the court reporter or reporters unless the clerk receives a copy of a certificate of appealability issued by the Court of Appeal under (b)(6). The clerk must send the notification no later than five days after the superior court receives the copy of the certificate of appealability.

(3) The notification must show the date it was sent, the number and title of the case, and the dates the notice of appeal was filed and any certificate of appealability was issued. If the information is available, the notification must also include:

(A) The name, address, telephone number, e-mail address, and California State Bar number of each attorney of record in the case; and

(B) The name of the party each attorney represented in the superior court.

(4) The notification to the clerk/executive officer of the Court of Appeal must also include a copy of the notice of appeal, any certificate of appealability or denial of a certificate of appealability issued by the superior court, and the sequential list of reporters made under rule 2.950.

(5) A copy of the notice of appeal is sufficient notification under (1) if the required information is on the copy or is added by the superior court clerk.

(6) The sending of a notification under (1) is a sufficient performance of the clerk's duty despite the discharge, disqualification, suspension, disbarment, or death of the attorney.

(7) Failure to comply with any provision of this subdivision does not affect the validity of the notice of appeal. *(Adopted eff. April 25, 2019.)*

Advisory Committee Comment

Subdivision (b). This subdivision addresses issuance of a certificate of appealability by the Court of Appeal. Rule 4.576(b) addresses issuance of a certificate of appealability by the superior court.

Research References

6 Witkin, California Criminal Law 4th Criminal Writs § 67C (2021), (New) Rules and Forms.

Rule 8.393. Time to appeal

A notice of appeal under this article must be filed within 30 days after the rendition of the judgment or the making of the order being appealed. *(Adopted eff. April 25, 2019.)*

Research References

6 Witkin, California Criminal Law 4th Criminal Writs § 67C (2021), (New) Rules and Forms.

Rule 8.394. Stay of execution on appeal

(a) Application

Pending appeal under this article, the petitioner may apply to the reviewing court for a stay of execution of the death penalty. The application must be served on the People.

(b) Interim relief

Pending its ruling on the application, the reviewing court may grant the relief requested. The reviewing court must notify the superior court under rule 8.489 of any stay that it grants. Notification must also be sent to the clerk/executive officer of the Supreme Court. *(Adopted eff. April 25, 2019.)*

Research References

6 Witkin, California Criminal Law 4th Criminal Writs § 67C (2021), (New) Rules and Forms.

Rule 8.395. Record on appeal

(a) Contents

In an appeal under this article, the record must contain:

(1) A clerk's transcript containing:

(A) The petition;

(B) Any informal response to the petition and any reply to the informal response;

(C) Any order to show cause;

(D) Any reply, return, answer, denial, or traverse;

(E) All supporting documents under rule 4.571, including the record prepared for the automatic appeal and all briefs, rulings, and other documents filed in the automatic appeal;

(F) Any other documents and exhibits submitted to the court, including any transcript of a sound or sound-and-video recording tendered to the court under rule 2.1040 and any visual aids submitted to the court;

(G) Any written communication between the court and the parties, including printouts of any e-mail messages and their attachments;

(H) All court minutes;

(I) Any statement of decision required by Penal Code section 1509(f) and any other written decision of the court;

(J) The order appealed from;

(K) The notice of appeal; and

(L) Any certificate of appealability issued by the superior court or the Court of Appeal.

(2) A reporter's transcript of any oral proceedings.

(b) Stipulation for partial transcript

If counsel for the petitioner and the People stipulate in writing before the record is certified that any part of the record is not required for proper determination of the appeal, that part need not be prepared or sent to the reviewing court.

(c) Preparation of record

(1) The reporter and the clerk must begin preparing the record immediately after the superior court issues the decision on an initial petition under Penal Code section 1509.

(2) If either party appeals from a superior court decision on a successive petition under Penal Code section 1509.1(c):

(A) The clerk must begin preparing the clerk's transcript immediately after the filing of the notice of appeal or, if one is required, the superior court's issuance of a certificate of appealability or the clerk's receipt of a copy of a certificate of appealability issued by the Court of Appeal under rule 8.391(b)(5), whichever is later. If a certificate of appealability is required to appeal the decision of the superior court, the clerk must not begin preparing the clerk's transcript until a certificate of appealability has issued.

(B) The reporter must begin preparing the reporter's transcript immediately on being notified by the clerk under rule 8.392(c) that the notice of appeal has been filed.

(d) Clerk's transcript

(1) Within 30 days after the clerk is required to begin preparing the transcript, the clerk must complete preparation of an original and four copies of the clerk's transcript.

(2) On request, the clerk must prepare an extra copy for the district attorney or the Attorney General, whichever is not counsel for the People on appeal.

(3) The clerk must certify as correct the original and all copies of the clerk's transcript.

(e) Reporter's transcript

(1) The reporter must prepare an original and the same number of copies of the reporter's transcript as (d) requires of the clerk's transcript, and must certify each as correct.

(2) As soon as the transcripts are certified, but no later than 30 days after the reporter is required to begin preparing the transcript, the reporter must deliver the original and all copies to the superior court clerk.

(3) Any portion of the transcript transcribed during superior court habeas corpus proceedings must not be retyped unless necessary to correct errors, but must be repaginated and combined with any portion of the transcript not previously transcribed. Any additional copies needed must not be retyped but, if the transcript is in paper form, must be prepared by photocopying or an equivalent process.

(4) In a multireporter case, the clerk must accept any completed portion of the transcript from the primary reporter one week after the time prescribed by (2) even if other portions are uncompleted. The clerk must promptly pay each reporter who certifies that all portions of the transcript assigned to that reporter are completed.

(f) Extension of time

(1) Except as provided in this rule, rules 8.60 and 8.63 govern requests for extension of time to prepare the record.

(2) On request of the clerk or a reporter showing good cause, the superior court may extend the time prescribed in (d) or (e) for preparing the clerk's or reporter's transcript for no more than 30 days. If the superior court orders an extension, the order must specify the reason justifying the extension. The clerk must promptly send a copy of the order to the reviewing court.

(3) For any further extension, the clerk or reporter must file a request in the reviewing court showing good cause.

(4) A request under (2) or (3) must be supported by:

(A) A declaration showing good cause. The court may presume good cause if the clerk's and reporter's transcripts combined will likely exceed 10,000 pages, not including the supporting documents submitted with the petition, any informal response, reply to the informal response, return, answer, or traverse; and

(B) In the case of a reporter's transcript, certification by the superior court presiding judge or a court administrator designated by the presiding judge that an extension is reasonable and necessary in light of the workload of all reporters in the court.

(g) Form of record

(1) The reporter's transcript must be in electronic form. The clerk is encouraged to send the clerk's transcript in electronic form if the court is able to do so.

(2) The clerk's and reporter's transcripts must comply with rules 8.45–8.47, relating to sealed and confidential records, and rule 8.144.

(h) Sending the transcripts

(1) When the clerk's and reporter's transcripts are certified as correct, the clerk must promptly send:

(A) The original transcripts to the reviewing court, noting the sending date on each original; and

(B) One copy of each transcript to:

(i) Appellate counsel for the petitioner;

(ii) The assisting entity or counsel, if designated, or the district appellate project;

(iii) The Attorney General or the district attorney, whichever is counsel for the People on appeal;

(iv) The district attorney or Attorney General if requested under (d)(2); and

(v) The Governor.

(2) If the petitioner is not represented by appellate counsel when the transcripts are certified as correct, the clerk must send that copy of the transcripts to the assisting entity or counsel, if designated, or the district appellate project.

(i) Supervision of preparation of record

Ct. Rules

The clerk/executive officer of the Court of Appeal, under the supervision of the administrative presiding justice or the presiding justice, must take all appropriate steps to ensure that superior court clerks and reporters promptly perform their duties under this rule. This provision does not affect the responsibility of the superior courts for the prompt preparation of appellate records.

(j) Augmenting or correcting the record in the Court of Appeal

Rule 8.340 governs augmenting or correcting the record in the Court of Appeal, except that copies of augmented or corrected records must be sent to those listed in (h).

(k) Judicial notice

Rule 8.252(a) governs judicial notice in the reviewing court. *(Adopted eff. April 25, 2019.)*

Research References

6 Witkin, California Criminal Law 4th Criminal Writs § 67C (2021), (New) Rules and Forms.

Rule 8.396. Briefs by parties and amici curiae

(a) Contents and form

(1) Except as provided in this rule, briefs in appeals governed by the rules in this article must comply as nearly as possible with rules 8.200 and 8.204.

(2) If, as permitted by Penal Code section 1509.1(b), the petitioner wishes to raise a claim in the appeal of ineffective assistance of trial counsel that was not raised in the superior court habeas corpus proceedings, that claim must be raised in the first brief filed by the petitioner. A brief containing such a claim must comply with the additional requirements in rule 8.397.

(3) If the petitioner is appealing from a decision of the superior court denying relief on a successive death penalty-related habeas corpus petition, the petitioner may only raise claims in the briefs that were identified in the certificate of appealability that was issued and any additional claims added by the Court of Appeal as provided in Penal Code section 1509.1(c).

(b) Length

(1) A brief produced on a computer must not exceed the following limits, including footnotes, except that if the presiding justice permits the appellant to file an opening brief that exceeds the limit set in (1)(A) or (3)(A), the respondent's brief may not exceed the same length:

(A) Appellant's opening brief: 102,000 words.

(B) Respondent's brief: 102,000 words.

(C) Reply brief: 47,600 words.

(2) A brief under (1) must include a certificate by appellate counsel stating the number of words in the brief; counsel may rely on the word count of the computer program used to prepare the brief.

(3) A typewritten brief must not exceed the following limits, except that if the presiding justice permits the appellant to file an opening brief that exceeds the limit set in (1)(A) or (3)(A), the respondent's brief may not exceed the same length:

(A) Appellant's opening brief: 300 pages.

(B) Respondent's brief: 300 pages.

(C) Reply brief: 140 pages.

(4) The tables required under rule 8.204(a)(1), the cover information required under rule 8.204(b)(10), a certificate under (2), any signature block, and any attachment permitted under rule 8.204(d) are excluded from the limits stated in (1) and (3).

(5) A combined brief in an appeal governed by (e) must not exceed double the limit stated in (1) or (3).

(6) On application, the presiding justice may permit a longer brief for good cause.

(c) Time to file

(1) The appellant's opening brief must be served and filed within 210 days after either the record is filed or appellate counsel is appointed, whichever is later.

(2) The respondent's brief must be served and filed within 120 days after the appellant's opening brief is filed.

(3) The appellant must serve and file a reply brief, if any, within 60 days after the filing of respondent's brief.

(4) If the clerk's and reporter's transcripts combined exceed 10,000 pages, the time limits stated in (1) and (2) are extended by 15 days for each 1,000 pages of combined transcript over 10,000 pages, up to 20,000 pages. The time limits in (1) and (2) may be extended further by order of the presiding justice under rule 8.60.

(5) The time to serve and file a brief may not be extended by stipulation, but only by order of the presiding justice under rule 8.60.

(6) If a party fails to timely file an appellant's opening brief or a respondent's brief, the clerk/executive officer of the Court of Appeal must promptly notify the party in writing that the brief must be filed within 30 days after the notice is sent, and that failure to comply may result in sanctions specified in the notice.

(d) Service

(1) The petitioner's appellate counsel must serve each brief for the petitioner on the assisting entity or counsel, the Attorney General, and the district attorney, and must deliver a copy of each to the petitioner unless the petitioner requests otherwise.

(2) The proof of service must state that a copy of the petitioner's brief was delivered to the petitioner or will be delivered in person to the petitioner within 30 days after the filing of the brief, or counsel must file a signed statement that the petitioner requested in writing that no copy be delivered.

(3) The People must serve each of their briefs on the appellate counsel for the petitioner, the assisting entity or counsel, and either the district attorney or the Attorney General, whichever is not representing the People on appeal.

(4) A copy of each brief must be served on the superior court clerk for delivery to the superior court judge who issued the order being appealed.

(e) When the petitioner and the People appeal

When both the petitioner and the People appeal, the petitioner must file the first opening brief unless the reviewing court orders otherwise, and rule 8.216(b) governs the contents of the briefs.

(f) Amicus curiae briefs

Amicus curiae briefs may be filed as provided in rule 8.200(c), except that an application for permission of the presiding justice to file an amicus curiae brief must be filed within 14 days after the last appellant's reply brief is filed or could have been filed under (c), whichever is earlier. *(Adopted eff. April 25, 2019.)*

Advisory Committee Comment

Subdivision (a)(3). This subdivision is intended to implement the sentence in Penal Code section 1509.1(c) providing that "[t]he jurisdiction of the court of appeal is limited to the claims identified in the certificate [of appealability] and any additional claims added by the court of appeal within 60 days of the notice of appeal."

Subdivision (b)(4). This subdivision specifies certain items that are not counted toward the maximum brief length. Signature blocks referred to in this provision include not only the signatures, but also the printed names, titles, and affiliations of any attorneys filing or joining in the brief, which may accompany the signature.

Research References

6 Witkin, California Criminal Law 4th Criminal Writs § 67C (2021), (New) Rules and Forms.

Rule 8.397. Claim of ineffective assistance of trial counsel not raised in the superior court

(a) Application

This rule governs claims under Penal Code section 1509.1(b) of ineffective assistance of trial counsel not raised in the superior court habeas corpus proceeding giving rise to an appeal under this article.

(b) Discussion of claim in briefs

(1) A claim subject to this rule must be raised in the first brief filed by the petitioner.

(2) All discussion of claims subject to this rule must be addressed in a separate part of the brief under a heading identifying this part as addressing claims of ineffective assistance of trial counsel that were not raised in a superior court habeas corpus proceeding.

(3) Discussion of each claim within this part of the brief must be under a separate subheading identifying the claim. Petitioner's brief must include a summary of the claim under the subheading, and each claim must be supported by argument and, if possible, by citation of authority.

(4) This part of the brief may include references to matters:

(A) In the record on appeal prepared under rule 8.395. Any reference to a matter in the record must be supported by a citation to the volume and page number of the record where the matter appears.

(B) Of which the court has taken judicial notice.

(C) In a proffer required under (c). Any reference to a matter in a proffer must be supported by a citation to its index number or letter and page.

(c) Proffer

(1) A brief raising a claim under Penal Code section 1509.1(b) of ineffective assistance of trial counsel not raised in a superior court habeas corpus proceeding must be accompanied by a proffer of any reasonably available documentary evidence supporting the claim that is not in either the record on appeal prepared under rule 8.395 or matters of which the court has taken judicial notice. A brief responding to such a claim must be accompanied by a proffer of any reasonably available documentary evidence the People are relying on that is not in the petitioner's proffer, the record on appeal prepared under rule 8.395, or matters of which the court has taken judicial notice.

(A) If a brief raises a claim that was the subject of an evidentiary hearing, the proffer must include a certified transcript of that hearing.

(B) Evidence may be in the form of affidavits or declarations under penalty of perjury.

(2) The proffer must comply with the following formatting requirements:

(A) The pages must be consecutively numbered.

(B) It must begin with a table of contents listing each document by its title and its index number or letter. If a document has attachments, the table of contents must give the title of each attachment and a brief description of its contents.

(C) If submitted in paper form:

(i) It must be bound together at the end of the brief or in separate volumes not exceeding 300 pages each.

(ii) It must be index-tabbed by number or letter.

(3) The clerk must file any proffer not complying with (2), but the court may notify the filer that it may strike the proffer and the portions of the brief referring to the proffer if the documents are not brought into compliance within a stated reasonable time of not less than five court days.

(4) If any documents in the proffer are sealed or confidential records, rules 8.45–8.47 govern these documents.

(d) Evidentiary hearing

An evidentiary hearing is required if, after considering the briefs, the proffer, and matters of which judicial notice may be taken, the court finds there is a reasonable likelihood that the petitioner may be entitled to relief and the petitioner's entitlement to relief depends on the resolution of an issue of fact. The reviewing court may take one of the following actions:

(1) Order a limited remand to the superior court to consider the claim under Penal Code section 1509.1(b). The order for limited remand vests jurisdiction over the claim in the superior court, which must proceed under rule 4.574(d)(2)–(3) and (e)–(g) and rule 4.575 for death penalty-related habeas corpus proceedings in the superior court. The clerk/executive officer of the Court of Appeal must send a copy of any such order to the clerk/executive officer of the Supreme Court.

(2) Appoint a referee to conduct the hearing and make recommended findings of fact.

(3) Conduct the hearing itself or designate a justice of the court to conduct the hearing.

(e) Procedures following limited remand

(1) If the reviewing court orders a limited remand to the superior court to consider a claim under Penal Code section 1509.1(b), it may stay the proceedings on the remainder of the appeal pending the decision of the superior court on remand. The clerk/executive officer of the Court of Appeal must send a copy of any such stay to the clerk/executive officer of the Supreme Court.

(2) If any party wishes to appeal from the superior court decision on remand, the party must file a notice of appeal as provided in rule 8.392.

(3) If an appeal is filed from the superior court decision on remand, the reviewing court may consolidate this appeal with any pending appeal under Penal Code section 1509.1 from the superior court's decisions in the same habeas corpus proceeding. A copy of any consolidation order must be promptly sent to the superior court clerk. The superior court clerk must then augment the record on appeal to include all items listed in rule 8.395(a) from the remanded proceedings. *(Adopted eff. April 25, 2019.)*

Advisory Committee Comment

Penal Code section 1509.1(b) states when a claim of ineffective assistance of trial counsel not raised in the superior court habeas corpus proceeding may be raised in an appeal under this article.

Research References

6 Witkin, California Criminal Law 4th Criminal Writs § 67C (2021), (New) Rules and Forms.

Rule 8.398. Finality

(a) General rule

Except as otherwise provided in this rule, rule 8.366(b) governs the finality of a Court of Appeal decision in a proceeding under this article.

(b) Denial of certificate of appealability

The Court of Appeal's denial of an application for a certificate of appealability in a proceeding under this article is final in that court on filing. *(Adopted eff. April 25, 2019.)*

Research References

6 Witkin, California Criminal Law 4th Criminal Writs § 67C (2021), (New) Rules and Forms.

Chapter 5

JUVENILE APPEALS AND WRITS

Article 1

GENERAL PROVISIONS

Rule 8.400. Application

The rules in this chapter govern:

(1) Appeals from judgments or appealable orders in:

(A) Cases under Welfare and Institutions Code sections 300, 601, and 602; and

(B) Actions to free a child from parental custody and control under Family Code section 7800 et seq. and Probate Code section 1516.5;

(2) Appeals of orders requiring or dispensing with an alleged father's consent for the adoption of a child under Family Code section 7662 et seq.; and

(3) Writ petitions under Welfare and Institutions Code sections 366.26 and 366.28. *(Formerly Rule 37, adopted, eff. Jan. 1, 2005. As amended, eff. Jan. 1, 2006. Renumbered Rule 8.400 and amended, eff. Jan. 1, 2007. As amended, eff. Jan. 1, 2008; July 1, 2010; Jan. 1, 2017.)*

Research References

West's California Judicial Council Forms JV–291–INFO, Information on Requesting Access to Records for Persons With a Limited Right to Appeal.
West's California Judicial Council Forms JV–800, Notice of Appeal—Juvenile.
West's California Judicial Council Forms JV–805–INFO, Information Regarding Appeal Rights.

Rule 8.401. Confidentiality

(a) References to juveniles or relatives in documents

To protect the anonymity of juveniles involved in juvenile court proceedings:

(1) In all documents filed by the parties in proceedings under this chapter, a juvenile must be referred to by first name and last initial; but if the first name is unusual or other circumstances would defeat the objective of anonymity, the initials of the juvenile may be used.

(2) In opinions that are not certified for publication and in court orders, a juvenile may be referred to either by first name and last initial or by his or her initials. In opinions that are certified for publication in proceedings under this chapter, a juvenile must be referred to by first name and last initial; but if the first name is unusual or other circumstances would defeat the objective of anonymity, the initials of the juvenile may be used.

(3) In all documents filed by the parties and in all court orders and opinions in proceedings under this chapter, if use of the full name of a juvenile's relative would defeat the objective of anonymity for the juvenile, the relative must be referred to by first name and last initial; but if the first name is unusual or other circumstances would defeat the objective of anonymity for the juvenile, the initials of the relative may be used.

(b) Access to filed documents and records

For the purposes of this rule, "filed document" means a brief, petition, motion, application, or other thing filed by the parties in the reviewing court in a proceeding under this chapter; "record on appeal" means the documents referenced in rule 8.407; "record on a writ petition" means the documents referenced in rules 8.450 and 8.454; and "records in the juvenile case file" means all or part of a document, paper, exhibit, transcript, opinion, order, or other thing filed or lodged in the juvenile court.

(1) Except as provided in (2)–(4), a filed document, the record on appeal, or the record on a writ petition may be inspected only by the reviewing court, appellate project personnel, the parties, attorneys for the parties, or other persons the reviewing court may designate.

(2) Access to records in the juvenile case file, including any such records made part of the record on appeal or the record on a writ petition, is governed by Welfare and Institutions Code section 827. A person who is not described in section 827(a)(1)(A)–(P) may not access records in the juvenile case file, including any such records made part of the record on appeal or the record on a writ petition, unless that person petitioned the juvenile court under section 827(a)(1)(Q) and was granted access by order of the juvenile court.

(3) A filed document that protects anonymity as required by (a) may be inspected by any person or entity that is considering filing an amicus curiae brief.

(4) Access to a filed document or items in the record on appeal or the record on a writ petition that are sealed or confidential under authority other than Welfare and Institutions Code section 827 is governed by rules 8.45–8.47 and the applicable statute, rule, sealing order, or other authority.

(c) Access to oral argument

The court may limit or prohibit public admittance to oral argument. *(Adopted, eff. July 1, 2010. As amended, eff. Jan. 1, 2012; Jan. 1, 2014; Sept. 1, 2020.)*

Advisory Committee Comment

Subdivision (b)(2). Welfare and Institutions Code section 827(a)(1)(Q) authorizes a petition by which a person may request access to records in the juvenile case file. The petition process is stated in rule 5.552. The Judicial Council has adopted a mandatory form—*Petition for Access to Juvenile Case File* (form JV–570)—that must be filed in the juvenile court to make the request. This form is available at any courthouse or county law library or online at *www.courts.ca.gov/forms*.

Research References

West's California Judicial Council Forms JV–800, Notice of Appeal—Juvenile.

Article 2

APPEALS

Rule 8.403. Right to appointment of appellate counsel and prerequisites for appeal

(a) Welfare and Institutions Code section 601 or 602 proceedings

In appeals of proceedings under Welfare and Institutions Code section 601 or 602, the child is entitled to court-appointed counsel.

(b) Welfare and Institutions Code section 300 proceedings

(1) Any judgment, order, or decree setting a hearing under Welfare and Institutions Code section 366.26 may be reviewed on appeal following the order at the Welfare and Institutions Code section 366.26 hearing only if:

(A) The procedures in rules 8.450 and 8.452 regarding writ petitions in these cases have been followed; and

(B) The petition for an extraordinary writ was summarily denied or otherwise not decided on the merits.

(2) The reviewing court may appoint counsel to represent an indigent child, parent, or guardian.

(3) Rule 5.661 governs the responsibilities of trial counsel in Welfare and Institutions Code section 300 proceedings with regard to appellate representation of the child. *(Adopted, eff. July 1, 2010. As amended, eff. Jan. 1, 2013.)*

Advisory Committee Comment

The right to appeal in Welfare and Institutions Code section 601 or 602 (juvenile delinquency) cases is established by Welfare and Institutions Code section 800 and case law (see, for example, *In re Michael S.* (2007) 147 Cal.App.4th 1443, *In re Jeffrey M.* (2006) 141 Cal.App.4th 1017 and *In re Sean R.* (1989) 214 Cal.App.3d 662). The right to appeal in Welfare and Institutions Code section 300 (juvenile dependency) cases is established by Welfare and Institutions Code section 395 and case law (see, for example, *In re Aaron R.* (2005) 130 Cal.App.4th 697, and *In re Merrick V.* (2004) 122 Cal.App.4th 235).

Subdivision (b)(1). Welfare and Institutions Code section 366.26(*l*) establishes important limitations on appeals of judgments, orders, or decrees setting a hearing under section 366.26, including requirements for the filing of a petition for an extraordinary writ and limitations on the issues that can be raised on appeal.

Rule 8.404. Stay pending appeal

The court must not stay an order or judgment pending an appeal unless suitable provision is made for the maintenance, care, and custody of the child. *(Adopted, eff. July 1, 2010.)*

Rule 8.405. Filing the appeal

(a) Notice of appeal

(1) To appeal from a judgment or appealable order under these rules, the appellant must file a notice of appeal in the superior court. Any notice of appeal on behalf of the child in a Welfare and Institutions Code section 300 proceeding must be authorized by the child or the child's CAPTA guardian ad litem.

(2) The appellant or the appellant's attorney must sign the notice of appeal.

(3) The notice of appeal must be liberally construed, and is sufficient if it identifies the particular judgment or order being appealed. The notice need not specify the court to which the appeal is taken; the appeal will be treated as taken to the Court of Appeal for the district in which the superior court is located.

(b) Superior court clerk's duties

(1) When a notice of appeal is filed, the superior court clerk must immediately:

(A) Send a notification of the filing to:

(i) Each party other than the appellant, including the child if the child is 10 years of age or older;

(ii) The attorney of record for each party;

(iii) Any person currently awarded by the juvenile court the status of the child's de facto parent;

(iv) Any Court Appointed Special Advocate (CASA) volunteer;

(v) If the court knows or has reason to know that an Indian child is involved, the Indian custodian, if any, and tribe of the child or the Bureau of Indian Affairs, as required under Welfare and Institutions Code section 224.2; and

(vi) The reviewing court clerk; and

(B) Notify the reporter, in a manner providing immediate notice, to prepare a reporter's transcript and deliver it to the clerk within 20 days after the notice of appeal is filed.

(2) The notification must show the name of the appellant, the date it was sent, the number and title of the case, and the date the notice of appeal was filed. If the information is available, the notification must also include:

(A) The name, address, telephone number, e-mail address, and California State Bar number of each attorney of record in the case;

(B) The name of the party that each attorney represented in the superior court; and

(C) The name, address, telephone number and e-mail address of any unrepresented party.

(3) The notification to the reviewing court clerk must also include a copy of the notice of appeal and any sequential list of reporters made under rule 2.950.

(4) A copy of the notice of appeal is sufficient notification if the required information is on the copy or is added by the superior court clerk.

(5) The sending of a notification is a sufficient performance of the clerk's duty despite the discharge, disqualification, suspension, disbarment, or death of the attorney.

(6) Failure to comply with any provision of this subdivision does not affect the validity of the notice of appeal. *(Adopted, eff. July 1, 2010. As amended, eff. Jan. 1, 2016; Jan. 1, 2021.)*

Advisory Committee Comment

Subdivision (a). *Notice of Appeal—Juvenile (California Rules of Court, Rule 8.400)* (form JV–800) may be used to file the notice of appeal required under this rule. This form is available at any courthouse or county law library or online at *www.courts.ca.gov/forms*.

Research References

West's California Judicial Council Forms JV–800, Notice of Appeal—Juvenile.

West's California Judicial Council Forms JV–805–INFO, Information Regarding Appeal Rights.

Rule 8.406. Time to appeal

(a) Normal time

(1) Except as provided in (2) and (3), a notice of appeal must be filed within 60 days after the rendition of the judgment or the making of the order being appealed.

(2) In matters heard by a referee not acting as a temporary judge, a notice of appeal must be filed within 60 days after the referee's order becomes final under rule 5.540(c).

(3) When an application for rehearing of an order of a referee not acting as a temporary judge is denied under rule 5.542, a notice of appeal from the referee's order must be filed within 60 days after that order is served under rule 5.538(b)(3) or 30 days after entry of the order denying rehearing, whichever is later.

(b) Cross-appeal

If an appellant timely appeals from a judgment or appealable order, the time for any other party to appeal from the same judgment or order is either the time specified in (a) or 20 days after the superior court clerk sends notification of the first appeal, whichever is later.

(c) No extension of time; late notice of appeal

Except as provided in rule 8.66, no court may extend the time to file a notice of appeal. The superior court clerk must mark a late notice of appeal "Received [date] but not filed," notify the party that the notice was not filed because it was late, and send a copy of the marked notice of appeal to the district appellate project.

(d) Premature notice of appeal

A notice of appeal is premature if filed before the judgment is rendered or the order is made, but the reviewing court may treat the notice as filed immediately after the rendition of judgment or the making of the order. *(Adopted, eff. July 1, 2010. As amended, eff. July 1, 2010; Jan. 1, 2016.)*

Advisory Committee Comment

Subdivision (c). See rule 8.25(b)(5) for provisions concerning the timeliness of documents mailed by inmates or patients from custodial institutions.

Research References

West's California Judicial Council Forms JV–800, Notice of Appeal—Juvenile.

West's California Judicial Council Forms JV–805–INFO, Information Regarding Appeal Rights.

Rule 8.407. Record on appeal

(a) Normal record: clerk's transcript

The clerk's transcript must contain:

(1) The petition;

(2) Any notice of hearing;

(3) All court minutes;

(4) Any report or other document submitted to the court;

(5) The jurisdictional and dispositional findings and orders;

(6) The judgment or order appealed from;

(7) Any application for rehearing;

(8) The notice of appeal and any order pursuant to the notice;

(9) Any transcript of a sound or sound-and-video recording tendered to the court under rule 2.1040;

(10) Any application for additional record and any order on the application;

(11) Any opinion or dispositive order of a reviewing court in the same case; and

(12) Any written motion or notice of motion by any party, with supporting and opposing memoranda and attachments, and any written opinion of the court.

(b) Normal record: reporter's transcript

The reporter's transcript must contain any oral opinion of the court and:

(1) In appeals from dispositional orders, the oral proceedings at hearings on:

(A) Jurisdiction;

(B) Disposition;

(C) Any motion by the appellant that was denied in whole or in part; and

(D) In cases under Welfare and Institutions Code section 300 et seq., hearings:

(i) On detention; and

(ii) At which a parent of the child made his or her initial appearance.

(2) In appeals from an order terminating parental rights under Welfare and Institutions Code section 300 et seq., the oral proceedings at all section 366.26 hearings.

(3) In all other appeals, the oral proceedings at any hearing that resulted in the order or judgment being appealed.

(c) Application in superior court for addition to normal record

(1) Any party or Indian tribe that has intervened in the proceedings may apply to the superior court for inclusion of any oral proceedings in the reporter's transcript.

(2) An application for additional record must describe the material to be included and explain how it may be useful in the appeal.

(3) The application must be filed in the superior court with the notice of appeal or as soon thereafter as possible, and will be treated as denied if it is filed after the record is sent to the reviewing court.

(4) The clerk must immediately present the application to the trial judge.

(5) Within five days after the application if filed, the judge must order that the record include as much of the additional material as the judge finds proper to fully present the points raised by the applicant. Denial of the application does not preclude a motion in the reviewing court for augmentation under rule 8.155.

(6) If the judge does not rule on the application within the time prescribed by (5), the requested material-other than exhibits-must be included in the clerk's transcript or the reporter's transcript without a court order.

(7) The clerk must immediately notify the reporter if additions to the reporter's transcript are required under (5) or (6).

(d) Agreed or settled statement

To proceed by agreed or settled statement, the parties must comply with rule 8.344 or 8.346, as applicable.

(e) Transmitting exhibits

Exhibits that were admitted in evidence, refused, or lodged may be transmitted to the reviewing court as provided in rule 8.224. *(Formerly Rule 37.1, adopted, eff. Jan. 1, 2005. Renumbered Rule 8.404 and amended, eff. Jan. 1, 2007. Renumbered Rule 8.407 and amended, eff. July 1, 2010. As amended, eff. Jan. 1, 2014; Jan. 1, 2017.)*

Advisory Committee Comment

Rules 8.45–8.47 address the appropriate handling of sealed or confidential records that must be included in the record on appeal. Examples of confidential records include records of proceedings closed to inspection by court order under *People v. Marsden* (1970) 2 Cal.3d 118 and in-camera proceedings on a confidential informant.

Subdivision (a)(4). Examples of the documents that must be included in the clerk's transcript under this provision include all documents filed with the court relating to the Indian Child Welfare Act, including but not limited to all inquiries regarding a child under the Indian Child Welfare Act (*Indian Child Inquiry Attachment* [form ICWA–010(A)]), any *Parental Notification of Indian Status* (form ICWA–020), any *Notice of Child Custody Proceeding for Indian Child* (form ICWA–030) sent, any signed return receipts for the mailing of form ICWA–030, and any responses received to form ICWA–030.

Subdivision (b). Subdivision (b)(1) provides that only the reporter's transcript of a hearing that resulted in the order being appealed must be included in the normal record. This provision is intended to achieve consistent record requirements in all appeals of cases under Welfare and Institutions Code section 300, 601, or 602 and to reduce the delays and expense caused by transcribing proceedings not necessary to the appeal.

Subdivision (b)(1)(A) recognizes that findings made in a jurisdictional hearing are not separately appealable and can be challenged only in an appeal from the ensuing disposition order. The rule therefore specifically provides that a reporter's transcript of jurisdictional proceedings must be included in the normal record on appeal from a disposition order.

Subdivision (b)(1)(C) specifies that the oral proceedings on any motion by the appellant that was denied in whole or in part must be included in the normal record on appeal from a disposition order. Rulings on such motions usually have some impact on either the jurisdictional findings or the subsequent disposition order. Routine inclusion of these proceedings in the record will promote expeditious resolution of appeals of cases under Welfare and Institutions Code section 300, 601, or 602.

Rule 8.408. Record in multiple appeals in the same case

If more than one appeal is taken from the same judgment or related order, only one appellate record need be prepared, which must be filed within the time allowed for filing the record in the latest appeal. *(Formerly Rule 8.406, adopted, eff. Jan. 1, 2007. Renumbered Rule 8.408, eff. July 1, 2010.)*

Rule 8.409. Preparing and sending the record

(a) Application

This rule applies to appeals in juvenile cases except cases governed by rule 8.416.

(b) Form of record

The clerk's and reporter's transcripts must comply with rules 8.45–8.47, relating to sealed and confidential records, and with rule 8.144.

(c) Preparing and certifying the transcripts

Within 20 days after the notice of appeal is filed:

(1) The clerk must prepare and certify as correct an original of the clerk's transcript and one copy each for the appellant, the respondent, the child's Indian tribe if the tribe has intervened, and the child if the child is represented by counsel on appeal or if a recommendation has been made to the Court of Appeal for appointment of counsel for the child under rule 8.403(b)(2) and that recommendation is either pending with or has been approved by the Court of Appeal but counsel has not yet been appointed; and

(2) The reporter must prepare, certify as correct, and deliver to the clerk an original of the reporter's transcript and the same number of copies as (1) requires of the clerk's transcript.

(d) Extension of time

(1) The superior court may not extend the time to prepare the record.

(2) The reviewing court may order one or more extensions of time for preparing the record, including a reporter's transcript, not exceeding a total of 60 days, on receipt of:

(A) A declaration showing good cause; and

(B) In the case of a reporter's transcript, certification by the superior court presiding judge, or a court administrator designated by the presiding judge, that an extension is reasonable and necessary in light of the workload of all reporters in the court.

(e) Sending the record

(1) When the transcripts are certified as correct, the court clerk must immediately send:

(A) The original transcripts to the reviewing court, noting the sending date on each original; and

(B) One copy of each transcript to the appellate counsel for the following, if they have appellate counsel:

(i) The appellant;

(ii) The respondent;

(iii) The child's Indian tribe if the tribe has intervened; and

(iv) The child.

(2) If appellate counsel has not yet been retained or appointed for the appellant or the respondent, or if a recommendation has been made to the Court of Appeal for appointment of counsel for the child under rule 8.403(b)(2) and that recommendation is either pending with or has been approved by the Court of Appeal but counsel has not yet been appointed, when the transcripts are certified as correct, the clerk must send that counsel's copy of the transcripts to the district appellate project. If a tribe that has intervened is not represented by counsel when the transcripts are certified as correct, the clerk must send that counsel's copy of the transcripts to the tribe.

(3) The clerk must not send a copy of the transcripts to the Attorney General or the district attorney unless that office represents a party. *(Formerly Rule 37.2, adopted, eff. Jan. 1, 2005. Renumbered Rule 8.408 and amended, eff. Jan. 1, 2007. Renumbered Rule 8.409 and amended, eff. July 1, 2010. As amended, eff. Jan. 1, 2013; Jan. 1, 2014; Jan. 1, 2015; Jan. 1, 2017; Jan. 1, 2018.)*

Advisory Committee Comment

Subdivision (a). Subdivision (a) calls litigants' attention to the fact that a different rule (rule 8.416) governs the record in appeals from judgments or orders terminating parental rights and in dependency appeals in certain counties.

Subdivision (b). Examples of confidential records include records closed to inspection by court order under *People v. Marsden* (1970) 2 Cal.3d 118 and in-camera proceedings on a confidential informant.

Subdivision (e). Under rule 8.71(c), the superior court clerk may send the record to the reviewing court in electronic form. Subsection (1)(B) clarifies that when a child's Indian tribe has intervened in the proceedings, the tribe is a party who must receive a copy of the appellate record. The statutes that require notices to be sent to a tribe by registered or certified mail return receipt requested and generally be addressed to the tribal chairperson (25 U.S.C. § 1912(a), 25 C.F.R. § 23.11, and Welf. & Inst. Code, § 224.2) do not apply to the sending of the appellate record.

Rule 8.410. Augmenting and correcting the record in the reviewing court

(a) Omissions

If, after the record is certified, the superior court clerk or the reporter learns that the record omits a document or transcript that any rule or order requires to be included, without the need for a motion or court order, the clerk must promptly copy and certify the document or the reporter must promptly prepare and certify the transcript and the clerk must promptly send the document or transcript—as an augmentation of the record—to all those who are listed under 8.409(e).

(b) Augmentation or correction by the reviewing court

(1) On motion of a party or on its own motion, the reviewing court may order the record augmented or corrected as provided in rule 8.155(a) and (c).

(2) If, after the record is certified, the trial court amends or recalls the judgment or makes any other order in the case, the trial court clerk must notify each entity and person to whom the record is sent under rule 8.409(e). *(Adopted, eff. July 1, 2010. As amended, eff. Jan. 1, 2015.)*

Rule 8.411. Abandoning the appeal

(a) How to abandon

An appellant may abandon the appeal at any time by filing an abandonment of the appeal. The abandonment must be authorized by the appellant and signed by either the appellant or the appellant's attorney of record. In a Welfare and Institutions Code section 300 proceeding in which the child is the appellant, the abandonment must be authorized by the child or, if the child is not capable of giving authorization, by the child's CAPTA guardian ad litem.

(b) Where to file; effect of filing

(1) If the record has not been filed in the reviewing court, the appellant must file the abandonment in the superior court. The filing effects a dismissal of the appeal and restores the superior court's jurisdiction.

(2) If the record has been filed in the reviewing court, the appellant must file the abandonment in that court. The reviewing court may dismiss the appeal and direct immediate issuance of the remittitur.

(c) Clerk's duties

(1) If the abandonment is filed in the superior court, the clerk must immediately send a notification of the abandonment to:

(A) Every other party;

(B) The reviewing court; and

(C) The reporter if the appeal is abandoned before the reporter has filed the transcript.

(2) If the abandonment is filed in the reviewing court and the reviewing court orders the appeal dismissed, the clerk must immediately send a notification of the order of dismissal to every party. *(Adopted, eff. July 1, 2010. As amended, eff. Jan. 1, 2016.)*

Advisory Committee Comment

The Supreme Court has held that appellate counsel for an appealing minor has the power to move to dismiss a dependency appeal based on counsel's assessment of the child's best interests, but that the motion to dismiss requires the authorization of the child or, if the child is incapable of giving authorization, the authorization of the child's CAPTA guardian ad litem *(In re Josiah Z.* (2005) 36 Cal.4th 664).

Rule 8.412. Briefs by parties and amici curiae

(a) Contents, form, and length

(1) Rule 8.200 governs the briefs that may be filed by parties and amici curiae.

(2) Except as provided in (3), rule 8.204 governs the form and contents of briefs. Rule 8.216 also applies in appeals in which a party is both appellant and respondent.

(3) Rule 8.360(b) governs the length of briefs.

(b) Time to file

(1) Except in appeals governed by rule 8.416, the appellant must serve and file the appellant's opening brief within 40 days after the record is filed in the reviewing court.

(2) The respondent must serve and file the respondent's brief within 30 days after the appellant's opening brief is filed.

(3) The appellant must serve and file any reply brief within 20 days after the respondent's brief is filed.

(4) In dependency cases in which the child is not an appellant but has appellate counsel, the child must serve and file any brief within 10 days after the respondent's brief is filed.

(5) Rule 8.220 applies if a party fails to timely file an appellant's opening brief or a respondent's brief, but the period specified in the notice required by that rule must be 30 days.

(c) Extensions of time

The superior court may not order any extensions of time to file briefs. Except in appeals governed by rule 8.416, the reviewing court may order extensions of time for good cause.

(d) Failure to file a brief

(1) Except in appeals governed by rule 8.416, if a party fails to timely file an appellant's opening brief or a respondent's brief, the reviewing court clerk must promptly notify the party's counsel or the party, if not represented, in writing that the brief must be filed within 30 days after the notice is sent and that failure to comply may result in one of the following sanctions:

(A) If the brief is an appellant's opening brief:

(i) If the appellant is the county, the court will dismiss the appeal;

(ii) If the appellant is other than the county and is represented by appointed counsel on appeal, the court will relieve that appointed counsel and appoint new counsel;

(iii) If the appellant is other than the county and is not represented by appointed counsel, the court will dismiss the appeal.

(B) If the brief is a respondent's brief, the court will decide the appeal on the record, the opening brief, and any oral argument by the appellant.

(2) If a party fails to comply with a notice under (1), the court may impose the sanction specified in the notice.

(3) Within the period specified in the notice under (1), a party may apply to the presiding justice for an extension of that period for good cause. If an extension is granted beyond the 30–day period and the brief is not filed within the extended period, the court may impose the sanction under (2) without further notice.

(e) Additional service requirements

(1) A copy of each brief must be served on the superior court clerk for delivery to the superior court judge.

(2) A copy of each brief must be served on the child's trial counsel, or, if the child is not represented by trial counsel, on the child's guardian ad litem appointed under rule 5.662.

(3) If the Court of Appeal has appointed counsel for any party:

(A) The county child welfare department and the People must serve two copies of their briefs on that counsel; and

(B) Each party must serve a copy of its brief on the district appellate project.

(4) In delinquency cases the parties must serve copies of their briefs on the Attorney General and the district attorney. In all other cases the parties must not serve copies of their briefs on the Attorney General or the district attorney unless that office represents a party.

(5) The parties must not serve copies of their briefs on the Supreme Court under rule 8.44(b)(1). *(Formerly Rule 37.3, adopted, eff. Jan. 1, 2005. Renumbered Rule 8.412 and amended, eff. Jan. 1, 2007. As amended, eff. July 1, 2007; July 1, 2010; Jan. 1, 2016.)*

Advisory Committee Comment

Subdivision (b). Subdivision (b)(1) calls litigants' attention to the fact that a different rule (rule 8.416(e)) governs the time to file an appellant's opening brief in appeals from judgments or orders terminating parental rights and in dependency appeals in certain counties.

Subdivision (c). Subdivision (c) calls litigants' attention to the fact that a different rule (rule 8.416(f)) governs the showing required for extensions of time to file briefs in appeals from judgments or orders terminating parental rights and in dependency appeals in certain counties.

Research References

West's California Judicial Council Forms App–012, Stipulation of Extension of Time to File Brief (Civil Case).
West's California Judicial Council Forms JV–816, Application for Extension of Time to File Brief (Juvenile Delinquency).
West's California Judicial Council Forms JV–817, Application for Extension of Time to File Brief (Juvenile Dependency).

Rule 8.416. Appeals from all terminations of parental rights; dependency appeals in Orange, Imperial, and San Diego Counties and in other counties by local rule

(a) Application

(1) This rule governs:

(A) Appeals from judgments or appealable orders of all superior courts terminating parental rights under Welfare and Institutions Code section 366.26 or freeing a child from parental custody and control under Family Code section 7800 et seq.; and

(B) Appeals from judgments or appealable orders in all juvenile dependency cases of:

(i) The Superior Courts of Orange, Imperial, and San Diego Counties; and

(ii) Other superior courts when the superior court and the District Court of Appeal with jurisdiction to hear appeals from that superior court have agreed and have adopted local rules providing that this rule will govern appeals from that superior court.

(2) In all respects not provided for in this rule, rules 8.403–8.412 apply.

(b) Form of record

(1) The clerk's and reporter's transcripts must comply with rules 8.45–8.467, relating to sealed and confidential records, and, except as provided in (2) and (3), with rule 8.144.

(2) In appeals under (a)(1)(A), the cover of the record must prominently display the title "Appeal From [Judgment or Order] Terminating Parental Rights Under [Welfare and Institutions Code Section 366.26 or Family Code Section 7800 et seq.]," whichever is appropriate.

(3) In appeals under (a)(1)(B), the cover of the record must prominently display the title "Appeal From [Judgment or Order] Under [Welfare and Institutions Code Section 300 et seq. or Family Code Section 7800 et seq.]," whichever is appropriate.

(c) Preparing, certifying, and sending the record

(1) Within 20 days after the notice of appeal is filed:

(A) The clerk must prepare and certify as correct an original of the clerk's transcript and one copy each for the appellant, the respondent, the district appellate project, the child's Indian tribe if the tribe has intervened, and the child if the child is represented by counsel on appeal or if a recommendation has been made to the Court of Appeal for appointment of counsel for the child under rule 8.403(b)(2) and that recommendation is either pending with or has been approved by the Court of Appeal but counsel has not yet been appointed; and

(B) The reporter must prepare, certify as correct, and deliver to the clerk an original of the reporter's transcript and the same number of copies as (A) requires of the clerk's transcript.

(2) When the clerk's and reporter's transcripts are certified as correct, the clerk must immediately send:

(A) The original transcripts to the reviewing court by the most expeditious method, noting the sending date on each original; and

(B) One copy of each transcript to the district appellate project and to the appellate counsel for the following, if they have appellate counsel, by any method as fast as United States Postal Service express mail:

(i) The appellant;

(ii) The respondent;

(iii) The child's Indian tribe if the tribe has intervened; and

(iv) The child.

(3) If appellate counsel has not yet been retained or appointed for the appellant or the respondent or if a recommendation has been made to the Court of Appeal for appointment of counsel for the child under rule 8.403(b)(2) and that recommendation is either pending with or has been approved by the Court of Appeal but counsel has not yet been appointed, when the transcripts are certified as correct, the clerk must send that counsel's copies of the transcripts to the district appellate project. If a tribe that has intervened is not represented by counsel when the transcripts are certified as correct, the clerk must send that counsel's copy of the transcripts to the tribe.

(d) Augmenting or correcting the record

(1) Except as provided in (2) and (3), rule 8.410 governs any augmentation or correction of the record.

(2) An appellant must serve and file any motion for augmentation or correction within 15 days after receiving the record. A respondent must serve and file any such motion within 15 days after the appellant's opening brief is filed.

(3) The clerk and the reporter must prepare any supplemental transcripts within 20 days, giving them the highest priority.

(4) The clerk must certify and send any supplemental transcripts as required by (c).

(e) Time to file briefs

(1) To permit determination of the appeal within 250 days after the notice of appeal is filed, the appellant must serve and file the appellant's opening brief within 30 days after the record is filed in the reviewing court.

(2) Rule 8.412(b) governs the time for filing other briefs.

(f) Extensions of time

The superior court may not order any extensions of time to prepare the record or to file briefs; the reviewing court may order extensions of time, but must require an exceptional showing of good cause.

(g) Failure to file a brief

Rule 8.412(d) applies if a party fails to timely file an appellant's opening brief or a respondent's brief, but the period specified in the notice required by that rule must be 15 days.

(h) Oral argument and submission of the cause

(1) Unless the reviewing court orders otherwise, counsel must serve and file any request for oral argument no later than 15 days after the appellant's reply brief is filed or due to be filed. Failure to file a timely request will be deemed a waiver.

(2) The court must hear oral argument within 60 days after the appellant's last reply brief is filed or due to be filed, unless the court extends the time for good cause or counsel waive argument.

(3) If counsel waive argument, the cause is deemed submitted no later than 60 days after the appellant's reply brief is filed or due to be filed. *(Formerly Rule 37.4, adopted, eff. Jan. 1, 2005. Renumbered Rule 8.416 and amended, eff. Jan. 1, 2007. As amended, eff. July 1, 2010; Jan. 1, 2015; Jan. 1, 2017; Jan. 1, 2018.)*

Advisory Committee Comment

Subdivision (c). Under rule 8.71(c), the superior court clerk may send the record to the reviewing court in electronic form.

Subdivision (g). Effective January 1, 2007, revised rule 8.416 incorporates a new subdivision (g) to address a failure to timely file a brief in all termination of parental rights cases and in dependency appeals in Orange, Imperial, and San Diego Counties. Under the new subdivision, appellants would not have the full 30–day grace period given in rule 8.412(d) in which to file a late brief, but instead would have the standard 15–day grace period that is given in civil cases. The intent of this revision is to balance the need to determine the appeal within 250 days with the need to protect appellants' rights in this most serious of appeals.

Subdivision (h). Subdivision (h)(1) recognizes certain reviewing courts' practice of requiring counsel to file any request for oral argument within a time period other than 15 days after the appellant's reply brief is filed or due to be filed. The reviewing court is still expected to determine the appeal "within 250 days after the notice of appeal is filed." (*Id.*, subd. (c).)

Research References

West's California Judicial Council Forms JV–817, Application for Extension of Time to File Brief (Juvenile Dependency).

Article 3

WRITS

Rule 8.450. Notice of intent to file writ petition to review order setting hearing under Welfare and Institutions Code section 366.26

(a) Application

Rules 8.450–8.452 and 8.490 govern writ petitions to review orders setting a hearing under Welfare and Institutions Code section 366.26.

(b) Purpose

Rules 8.450–8.452 are intended to encourage and assist the reviewing courts to determine on their merits all writ petitions filed under these rules within the 120–day period for holding a hearing under Welfare and Institutions Code section 366.26.

(c) Who may file

The petitioner's trial counsel, or in the absence of trial counsel, the party, is responsible for filing any notice of intent and writ petition under rules 8.450–8.452. Trial counsel is encouraged to seek assistance from or consult with attorneys experienced in writ procedure.

(d) Extensions of time

The superior court may not extend any time period prescribed by rules 8.450–8.452. The reviewing court may extend any time period but must require an exceptional showing of good cause.

(e) Notice of intent

(1) A party seeking writ review under rules 8.450–8.452 must file in the superior court a notice of intent to file a writ petition and a request for the record.

(2) The notice must include all known dates of the hearing that resulted in the order under review.

(3) The notice must be authorized by the party intending to file the petition and must be signed by that party or by the attorney of record for that party.

(4) The date of the order setting the hearing is the date on which the court states the order on the record orally, or issues an order in writing, whichever occurs first. The notice of intent must be filed according to the following timeline requirements:

(A) If the party was present at the hearing when the court ordered a hearing under Welfare and Institutions Code section 366.26, the notice of intent must be filed within 7 days after the date of the order setting the hearing.

(B) If the party was notified of the order setting the hearing only by mail, the notice of intent must be filed within 12 days after the date the clerk mailed the notification.

(C) If the party was notified of the order setting the hearing by mail, and the notice was mailed to an address outside California but within the United States, the notice of intent must be filed within 17 days after the date the clerk mailed the notification.

(D) If the party was notified of the order setting the hearing by mail, and the notice was mailed to an address outside the United States, the notice of intent must be filed within 27 days after the date the clerk mailed the notification.

(E) If the order was made by a referee not acting as a temporary judge, the party has an additional 10 days to file the notice of intent as provided in rule 5.540(c).

(f) Premature or late notice of intent to file writ petition

(1) A notice of intent to file a writ petition under Welfare and Institutions Code section 366.26 is premature if filed before an order setting a hearing under Welfare and Institutions Code section 366.26 has been made.

(2) If a notice of intent is premature or late, the superior court clerk must promptly:

(A) Mark the notice of intent "Received [date] but not filed;"

(B) Return the marked notice of intent to the party with a notice stating that:

(i) The notice of intent was not filed either because it is premature, as no order setting a hearing under Welfare and Institutions Code section 366.26 has been made, or because it is late; and

(ii) The party should contact his or her attorney as soon as possible to discuss this notice, because the time available to take appropriate steps to protect the party's interests may be short; and

(C) Send a copy of the marked notice of intent and clerk's notice to the party's counsel of record, if applicable.

(g) Sending the notice of intent

(1) When the notice of intent is filed, the superior court clerk must immediately send a copy of the notice to:

(A) The attorney of record for each party;

(B) Each party, including the child if the child is 10 years of age or older;

(C) Any known sibling of the child who is the subject of the hearing if that sibling either is the subject of a dependency proceeding or has been adjudged to be a dependent child of the juvenile court as follows:

(i) If the sibling is under 10 years of age, on the sibling's attorney;

(ii) If the sibling is 10 years of age or over, on the sibling and the sibling's attorney.

(D) The mother, the father, and any presumed and alleged parents;

(E) The child's legal guardian, if any;

(F) Any person currently awarded by the juvenile court the status of the child's de facto parent;

(G) The probation officer or social worker;

(H) Any Court Appointed Special Advocate (CASA) volunteer;

(I) The grandparents of the child, if their address is known and if the parents' whereabouts are unknown; and

(J) If the court knows or has reason to know that an Indian child is involved, the Indian custodian, if any, and tribe of the child or the Bureau of Indian Affairs as required under Welfare and Institutions Code section 224.2.

(2) The clerk must promptly send by first-class mail, e-mail, or fax a copy of the notice of intent and a list of those to whom the notice of intent was sent to:

(A) The reviewing court; and

(B) The petitioner if the clerk sent the notice of intent to the Indian custodian, tribe of the child, or the Bureau of Indian Affairs.

(3) If the party was notified of the order setting the hearing only by mail, the clerk must include the date that the notification was mailed.

(h) Preparing the record

When the notice of intent is filed, the superior court clerk must:

(1) Immediately notify each court reporter, in a manner providing immediate notice, to prepare a reporter's transcript of the oral proceedings at each session of the hearing that resulted in the order under review and deliver the transcript to the clerk within 12 calendar days after the notice of intent is filed; and

(2) Within 20 days after the notice of intent is filed, prepare a clerk's transcript that includes the notice of intent, proof of service, and all items listed in rule 8.407(a).

(i) Sending the record

When the transcripts are certified as correct, the superior court clerk must immediately send:

(1) The original transcripts to the reviewing court by the most expeditious method, noting the sending date on each original, and

(2) One copy of each transcript to each counsel of record and any unrepresented party by any means as fast as United States Postal Service express mail.

(j) Reviewing court clerk's duties

(1) The reviewing court clerk must immediately lodge the notice of intent. When the notice is lodged, the reviewing court has jurisdiction of the writ proceedings.

(2) When the record is filed in the reviewing court, that court's clerk must immediately notify the parties, stating the date on which the 10–day period for filing the writ petition under rule 8.452(c)(1) will expire. *(Formerly Rule 38, adopted, eff. Jan. 1, 2005. As amended, eff. Jan. 1, 2006; July 1, 2006. Renumbered Rule 8.450 and amended, eff. Jan. 1, 2007. As amended, eff. Jan. 1, 2008; Jan. 1, 2009; July 1, 2010; Jan. 1, 2013; Jan. 1, 2017; Jan. 1, 2021.)*

Advisory Committee Comment

Subdivision (d). The case law generally recognizes that the reviewing courts may grant extensions of time under these rules for exceptional good cause. (See, e.g., *Jonathan M. v. Superior Court* (1995) 39 Cal.App.4th 1826, and *In re Cathina W.* (1998) 68 Cal.App.4th 716 [recognizing that a late notice of intent may be filed on a showing of exceptional circumstances not under the petitioner's control].) It may constitute exceptional good cause for an extension of the time to file a notice of intent if a premature notice of intent is returned to a party shortly before the issuance of an order setting a hearing under Welfare and Institutions Code section 366.26.

Subdivision (e)(4). See rule 8.25(b)(5) for provisions concerning the timeliness of documents mailed by inmates or patients from custodial institutions.

Subdivision (f)(1). A party who prematurely attempts to file a notice of intent to file a writ petition under Welfare and Institutions Code section 366.26 is not precluded from later filing such a notice after the issuance of an order setting a hearing under Welfare and Institutions Code section 366.26.

Subdivision (i). Under rule 8.71(c), the superior court clerk may send the record to the reviewing court in electronic form.

Research References

West's California Judicial Council Forms JV–820, Notice of Intent to File Writ Petition and Request for Record to Review Order Setting a Hearing Under Welfare and Institutions Code Section 366.26 (California Rules of Court, Rule 8.450).

Rule 8.452. Writ petition to review order setting hearing under Welfare and Institutions Code section 366.26

(a) Petition

(1) The petition must be liberally construed and must include:

(A) The identities of the parties;

(B) The date on which the superior court made the order setting the hearing;

(C) The date on which the hearing is scheduled to be held;

(D) A summary of the grounds of the petition; and

(E) The relief requested.

(2) The petition must be verified.

(3) The petition must be accompanied by a memorandum.

(b) Contents of the memorandum

(1) The memorandum must provide a summary of the significant facts, limited to matters in the record.

(2) The memorandum must state each point under a separate heading or subheading summarizing the point and support each point by argument and citation of authority.

(3) The memorandum must support any reference to a matter in the record by a citation to the record. The memorandum should explain the significance of any cited portion of the record and note any disputed aspects of the record.

(c) Serving and filing the petition and response

(1) The petition must be served and filed within 10 days after the record is filed in the reviewing court. The petitioner must serve a copy of the petition on:

(A) Each attorney of record;

(B) Any unrepresented party, including the child if the child is 10 years of age or older;

(C) Any known sibling of the child who is the subject of the hearing if that sibling either is the subject of a dependency proceeding or has been adjudged to be a dependent child of the juvenile court as follows:

(i) If the sibling is under 10 years of age, on the sibling's attorney;

(ii) If the sibling is 10 years of age or over, on the sibling and the sibling's attorney.

(D) The child's Court Appointed Special Advocate (CASA) volunteer;

(E) Any person currently awarded by the juvenile court the status of the child's de facto parent; and

(F) If the court sent the notice of intent to file the writ petition to an Indian custodian, tribe, or Bureau of Indian Affairs, then to that Indian custodian, tribe of the child, or the Bureau of Indian Affairs as required under Welfare and Institutions Code section 224.2.

(2) Any response must be served on each of the people and entities listed above and filed:

(A) Within 10 days—or, if the petition was served by mail, within 15 days—after the petition is filed; or

(B) Within 10 days after a respondent receives a request from the reviewing court for a response, unless the court specifies a shorter time.

(d) Order to show cause or alternative writ

If the court intends to determine the petition on the merits, it must issue an order to show cause or alternative writ.

(e) Augmenting or correcting the record in the reviewing court

(1) Except as provided in (2) and (3), rule 8.410 governs any augmentation or correction of the record.

(2) The petitioner must serve and file any request for augmentation or correction within 5 days—or, if the record exceeds 300 pages, within 7 days; or, if the record exceeds 600 pages, within 10 days—after receiving the record. A respondent must serve and file any such request within 5 days after the petition is filed or an order to show cause has issued, whichever is later.

(3) A party must attach to its motion a copy, if available, of any document or transcript that the party wants added to the record. The pages of the attachment must be consecutively numbered, beginning with the number one. If the reviewing court grants the motion, it may augment the record with the copy.

(4) If the party cannot attach a copy of the matter to be added, the party must identify it as required under rules 8.122 and 8.130.

(5) An order augmenting or correcting the record may grant no more than 15 days for compliance. The clerk and the reporter must give the order the highest priority.

(6) The clerk must certify and send any supplemental transcripts as required by rule 8.450(h). If the augmentation or correction is ordered, the time to file any petition or response is extended by the number of additional days granted to augment or correct the record.

(f) Stay

The reviewing court may stay the hearing set under Welfare and Institutions Code section 366.26, but must require an exceptional showing of good cause.

(g) Oral argument

(1) The reviewing court must hear oral argument within 30 days after the response is filed or due to be filed, unless the court extends the time for good cause or counsel waive argument.

(2) If argument is waived, the cause is deemed submitted not later than 30 days after the response is filed or due to be filed.

(h) Decision

(1) Absent exceptional circumstances, the reviewing court must decide the petition on the merits by written opinion.

(2) The reviewing court clerk must promptly notify the parties of any decision and must promptly send a certified copy of any writ or order to the court named as respondent.

(3) If the writ or order stays or prohibits proceedings set to occur within 7 days or requires action within 7 days—or in any other urgent situation—the reviewing court clerk must make a reasonable effort to notify the clerk of the respondent court by telephone or e-mail. The clerk of the respondent court must then notify the judge or officer most directly concerned.

(4) The reviewing court clerk need not give telephonic or e-mail notice of the summary denial of a writ, unless a stay previously issued will be dissolved.

(i) Filing, modification, finality of decision, and remittitur

Rule 8.490 governs the filing, modification, finality of decisions, and remittitur in writ proceedings under this rule. *(Formerly Rule 38.1, adopted, eff. Jan. 1, 2005. As amended, eff. Jan. 1, 2006. Renumbered Rule 8.452 and amended, eff. Jan. 1, 2007. As amended, eff. July 1, 2010; Jan. 1, 2017; Jan. 1, 2018.)*

Advisory Committee Comment

Subdivision (d). Subdivision (d) tracks the second sentence of former rule 39.1B(*l*). (But see *Maribel M. v. Superior Court* (1998) 61 Cal.App.4th 1469, 1471–1476.)

Subdivision (h). Subdivision (h)(1) tracks former rule 39.1B(*o*). (But see *Maribel M. v. Superior Court* (1998) 61 Cal.App.4th 1469, 1471–1476.)

Research References

West's California Judicial Council Forms JV–825, Petition for Extraordinary Writ.

West's California Judicial Council Forms JV–826, Denial of Petition (California Rules of Court, Rules 8.452, 8.456) (Also Available in Spanish).

Rule 8.454. Notice of intent to file writ petition under Welfare and Institutions Code section 366.28 to review order designating specific placement of a dependent child after termination of parental rights

(a) Application

Rules 8.454–8.456 and 8.490 govern writ petitions to review placement orders following termination of parental rights entered on or after January 1, 2005. "Posttermination placement order" as used in this rule and rule 8.456 refers to orders following termination of parental rights.

(b) Purpose

The purpose of this rule is to facilitate and implement Welfare and Institutions Code section 366.28. Delays caused by appeals from court orders designating the specific placement of a dependent child after parental rights have been terminated may cause a substantial detriment to the child.

(c) Who may file

The petitioner's trial counsel, or, in the absence of trial counsel, the party, is responsible for filing any notice of intent and writ petition under rules 8.454–8.456. Trial counsel is encouraged to seek assistance from, or consult with, attorneys experienced in writ procedure.

(d) Extensions of time

The superior court may not extend any time period prescribed by rules 8.454–8.456. The reviewing court may extend any time period, but must require an exceptional showing of good cause.

(e) Notice of intent

(1) A party seeking writ review under rules 8.454–8.456 must file in the superior court a notice of intent to file a writ petition and a request for the record.

(2) The notice must include all known dates of the hearing that resulted in the order under review.

(3) The notice must be authorized by the party intending to file the petition and signed by the party or by the attorney of record for that party.

(4) The notice must be served and filed within 7 days after the date of the posttermination placement order or, if the order was made by a referee not acting as a temporary judge, within 7 days after the referee's order becomes final under rule 5.540(c). The date of the posttermination placement order is the date on which the court states the order on the record orally or in writing, whichever first occurs.

(5) If the party was notified of the posttermination placement order only by mail, the notice of intent must be filed within 12 days after the date that the clerk mailed the notification.

(f) Premature or late notice of intent to file writ petition

(1) A notice of intent to file a writ petition under Welfare and Institutions Code section 366.28 is premature if filed before a date for a posttermination placement order has been made. The reviewing court may treat the notice as filed immediately after the posttermination order has been made.

(2) The superior court clerk must mark a late notice of intent to file a writ petition under section 366.28 "Received [date] but not filed," notify the party that the notice was not filed because it was late, and send a copy of the marked notice to the party's counsel of record, if applicable.

(g) Sending the notice of intent

(1) When the notice of intent is filed, the superior court clerk must immediately send a copy of the notice to:

(A) The attorney of record for each party;

(B) Each party, including the child if the child is 10 years of age or older;

(C) Any known sibling of the child who is the subject of the hearing if that sibling either is the subject of a dependency proceeding or has been adjudged to be a dependent child of the juvenile court as follows:

(i) If the sibling is under 10 years of age, on the sibling's attorney;

(ii) If the sibling is 10 years of age or over, on the sibling and the sibling's attorney;

(D) Any prospective adoptive parent;

(E) The child's legal guardian if any;

(F) Any person currently awarded by the juvenile court the status of the child's de facto parent;

(G) The probation officer or social worker;

(H) The child's Court Appointed Special Advocate (CASA) volunteer, if any; and

(I) If the court knows or has reason to know that an Indian child is involved, the Indian custodian, if any, and tribe of the child or the Bureau of Indian Affairs as required under Welfare and Institutions Code section 224.2.

(2) The clerk must promptly send by first-class mail, e-mail, or fax a copy of the notice of intent and a list of those to whom the notice of intent was sent to:

(A) The reviewing court; and

(B) The petitioner if the clerk sent a copy of the notice of intent to the Indian custodian, tribe of the child, or the Bureau of Indian Affairs.

(3) If the party was notified of the post placement order only by mail, the clerk must include the date that the notification was mailed.

(h) Preparing the record

When the notice of intent is filed, the superior court clerk must:

(1) Immediately notify each court reporter, in a manner providing immediate notice, to prepare a reporter's transcript of the oral proceedings at each session of the hearing that resulted in the order under review and to deliver the transcript to the clerk within 12 calendar days after the notice of intent is filed; and

(2) Within 20 days after the notice of intent is filed, prepare a clerk's transcript that includes the notice of intent, proof of service, and all items listed in rule 8.407(a).

(i) Sending the record

When the transcripts are certified as correct, the superior court clerk must immediately send:

(1) The original transcripts to the reviewing court by the most expeditious method, noting the sending date on each original; and

(2) One copy of each transcript to each counsel of record and any unrepresented party and unrepresented custodian of the dependent child by any means as fast as United States Postal Service express mail.

(j) Reviewing court clerk's duties

(1) The reviewing court clerk must promptly lodge the notice of intent. When the notice is lodged, the reviewing court has jurisdiction over the writ proceedings.

(2) When the record is filed in the reviewing court, that court's clerk must immediately notify the parties, stating the date on which the 10–day period for filing the writ petition under rule 8.456(c)(1) will expire. *(Formerly Rule 38.2, adopted, eff. Jan. 1, 2005. As amended, eff. Jan. 1, 2006; July 1, 2006. Renumbered Rule 8.454 and amended, eff. Jan. 1, 2007. As amended, eff. Jan. 1, 2008; Jan. 1, 2009; July 1, 2010; July 1, 2013; Jan. 1, 2017; Jan. 1, 2021.)*

Advisory Committee Comment

Subdivision (f)(2). See rule 8.25(b)(5) for provisions concerning the timeliness of documents mailed by inmates or patients from custodial institutions.

Subdivision (i). Under rule 8.71(c), the superior court clerk may send the record to the reviewing court in electronic form.

Research References

West's California Judicial Council Forms JV–822, Notice of Intent to File Writ Petition and Request for Record to Review Order Designating or Denying Specific Placement of a Dependent Child After Termination of Parental Rights (California Rules of Court, Rule 8.454).

Rule 8.456. Writ petition under Welfare and Institutions Code section 366.28 to review order designating or denying specific placement of a dependent child after termination of parental rights

(a) Petition

(1) The petition must be liberally construed and must include:

(A) The identities of the parties;

(B) The date on which the superior court made the posttermination placement order;

(C) A summary of the grounds of the petition; and

(D) The relief requested.

(2) The petition must be verified.

(3) The petition must be accompanied by a memorandum.

(b) Contents of memorandum

(1) The memorandum must provide a summary of the significant facts, limited to matters in the record.

(2) The memorandum must state each point under a separate heading or subheading summarizing the point and support each point by argument and citation of authority.

(3) The memorandum must support any reference to a matter in the record by a citation to the record. The memorandum should explain the significance of any cited portion of the record and note any disputed aspects of the record.

(c) Serving and filing the petition and response

(1) The petition must be served and filed within 10 days after the record is filed in the reviewing court. The petitioner must serve the petition on:

(A) Each attorney of record;

(B) Any unrepresented party, including the child if the child is 10 years of age or older;

(C) Any known sibling of the child who is the subject of the hearing if that sibling either is the subject of a dependency proceeding or has been adjudged to be a dependent child of the juvenile court as follows:

(i) If the sibling is under 10 years of age, on the sibling's attorney;

(ii) If the sibling is 10 years of age or over, on the sibling and the sibling's attorney;

(D) Any prospective adoptive parent;

(E) The child's Court Appointed Special Advocate (CASA) volunteer;

(F) Any person currently awarded by the juvenile court the status of the child's de facto parent; and

(G) If the court sent the notice of intent to file the writ petition to an Indian custodian, tribe, or Bureau of Indian Affairs, then to that Indian custodian, tribe, or the Bureau of Indian Affairs as required under Welfare and Institutions Code section 224.2.

(2) Any response must be served on each of the people and entities listed in (1) and filed:

(A) Within 10 days—or, if the petition was served by mail, within 15 days—after the petition is filed; or

(B) Within 10 days after a respondent receives a request from the reviewing court for a response, unless the court specifies a shorter time.

(d) Order to show cause or alternative writ

If the court intends to determine the petition on the merits, it must issue an order to show cause or alternative writ.

(e) Augmenting or correcting the record in the reviewing court

(1) Except as provided in (2) and (3), rule 8.410 governs augmentation or correction of the record.

(2) The petitioner must serve and file any request for augmentation or correction within 5 days—or, if the record exceeds 300 pages, within 7 days; or, if the record exceeds 600 pages, within 10 days—after receiving the record. A respondent must serve and file any such request within 5 days after the petition is filed or an order to show cause has issued, whichever is later.

(3) A party must attach to its motion a copy, if available, of any document or transcript that it wants added to the record. The pages of the attachment must be consecutively numbered, beginning with the number one. If the reviewing court grants the motion, it may augment the record with the copy.

(4) If the party cannot attach a copy of the matter to be added, the party must identify it as required under rules 8.122 and 8.130.

(5) An order augmenting or correcting the record may grant no more than 15 days for compliance. The clerk and the reporter must give the order the highest priority.

(6) The clerk must certify and send any supplemental transcripts as required by rule 8.454(i). If the augmentation or correction is ordered, the time to file any petition or response is extended by the number of additional days granted to augment or correct the record.

(f) Stay

A request by petitioner for a stay of the posttermination placement order will not be granted unless the writ petition shows that implementation of the superior court's placement order pending the reviewing court's decision is likely to cause detriment to the child if the order is ultimately reversed.

(g) Oral argument

(1) The reviewing court must hear oral argument within 30 days after the response is filed or due to be filed, unless the court extends the time for good cause or counsel waive argument.

(2) If argument is waived, the cause is deemed submitted not later than 30 days after the response is filed or due to be filed.

(h) Decision

(1) Absent exceptional circumstances, the reviewing court must review the petition and decide it on the merits by written opinion.

(2) The reviewing court clerk must promptly notify the parties of any decision and must promptly send a certified copy of any writ or order to the court named as respondent.

(3) If the writ or order stays or requires action within 7 days—or in any other urgent situation—the reviewing court clerk must make a reasonable effort to notify the clerk of the respondent court by telephone or e-mail. The clerk of the respondent court must then notify the judge or officer most directly concerned.

(4) The reviewing court clerk need not give telephonic or e-mail notice of the summary denial of a writ, unless a stay previously issued and will be dissolved.

(5) Rule 8.490 governs the filing, modification, finality of decisions, and remittitur in writ proceedings under this rule.

(i) Right to appeal other orders

This section does not affect the right of a parent, a legal guardian, or the child to appeal any order that is otherwise appealable and that is issued at a hearing held under Welfare and Institutions Code section 366.26. *(Formerly Rule 38.3, adopted, eff. Jan. 1, 2005. As amended, eff. Jan. 1, 2006; Feb. 24, 2006. Renumbered Rule 8.456 and amended, eff. Jan. 1, 2007. As amended, eff. July 1, 2010; Jan. 1, 2017; Jan. 1, 2018.)*

Research References

West's California Judicial Council Forms JV–825, Petition for Extraordinary Writ.

West's California Judicial Council Forms JV–826, Denial of Petition (California Rules of Court, Rules 8.452, 8.456) (Also Available in Spanish).

Article 4

HEARING AND DECISION

Rule 8.470. Hearing and decision in the Court of Appeal

Except as provided in rules 8.400–8.456, rules 8.252–8.272 govern hearing and decision in the Court of Appeal in juvenile cases. *(Formerly Rule 38.4, adopted, eff. Jan. 1, 2005. As amended, eff. July 1, 2005. Renumbered Rule 8.470 and amended, eff. Jan. 1, 2007.)*

Rule 8.472. Hearing and decision in the Supreme Court

Rules 8.500–8.552 govern hearing and decision in the Supreme Court in juvenile cases. *(Formerly Rule 38.5, adopted, eff. Jan. 1, 2005. As amended, eff. July 1, 2005. Renumbered Rule 8.472 and amended, eff. Jan. 1, 2007.)*

Rule 8.474. Procedures and data

(a) Procedures

The judges and clerks of the superior courts and the reviewing courts must adopt procedures to identify the records and expedite the processing of all appeals and writs in juvenile cases.

(b) Data

The clerks of the superior courts and the reviewing courts must provide the data required to assist the Judicial Council in evaluating the effectiveness of the rules governing appeals and writs in juvenile cases. *(Formerly Rule 38.6, adopted, eff. Jan. 1, 2005. Renumbered Rule 8.474, eff. Jan. 1, 2007. As amended, eff. Jan. 1, 2016.)*

Chapter 7

WRITS OF MANDATE, CERTIORARI, AND PROHIBITION IN THE SUPREME COURT AND COURT OF APPEAL

Rule 8.485. Application

(a) Writ proceedings governed

Except as provided in (b), the rules in this chapter govern petitions to the Supreme Court and Court of Appeal for writs of mandate, certiorari, or prohibition, or other writs within the original jurisdiction of these courts. In all respects not provided for in these rules, rule 8.204 governs the form and content of documents in the proceedings governed by this chapter.

(b) Writ proceedings not governed

These rules do not apply to proceedings for writs of mandate, certiorari, or prohibition in the appellate division of the superior court under rules 8.930–8.936, writs of supersedeas under rule 8.116, writs of habeas corpus except as provided in rule 8.384, writs to review orders setting a hearing under Welfare and Institutions Code section 366.26, writs under Welfare and Institutions Code section 366.28 to review orders designating or denying a specific placement of a dependent child after termination of parental rights, and writs under rules 8.450–8.456 except as provided in rules 8.452 and 8.456, or writs under rules 8.495–8.498. *(Adopted, eff. Jan. 1, 2009. As amended, eff. July 1, 2012; Jan. 1, 2014.)*

Research References

6 Witkin, California Criminal Law 4th Criminal Writs § 109 (2021), In General.

Rule 8.486. Petitions

(a) Contents of petition

(1) If the petition could have been filed first in a lower court, it must explain why the reviewing court should issue the writ as an original matter.

(2) If the petition names as respondent a judge, court, board, or other officer acting in a public capacity, it must disclose the name of any real party in interest.

(3) If the petition seeks review of trial court proceedings that are also the subject of a pending appeal, the notice "Related Appeal Pending" must appear on the cover of the petition and the first paragraph of the petition must state:

(A) The appeal's title, trial court docket number, and any reviewing court docket number; and

(B) If the petition is filed under Penal Code section 1238.5, the date the notice of appeal was filed.

(4) The petition must be verified.

(5) The petition must be accompanied by a memorandum, which need not repeat facts alleged in the petition.

(6) Rule 8.204(c) governs the length of the petition and memorandum, but, in addition to the exclusions provided in that rule, the verification and any supporting documents are excluded from the limits stated in rule 8.204(c)(1) and (2).

(7) If the petition requests a temporary stay, it must comply with the following or the reviewing court may decline to consider the request for a temporary stay:

(A) The petition must explain the urgency.

(B) The cover of the petition must prominently display the notice "STAY REQUESTED" and identify the nature and date of the proceeding or act sought to be stayed.

(C) The trial court and department involved and the name and telephone number of the trial judge whose order the request seeks to stay must appear either on the cover or at the beginning of the text.

(b) Contents of supporting documents

(1) A petition that seeks review of a trial court ruling must be accompanied by an adequate record, including copies of:

(A) The ruling from which the petition seeks relief;

(B) All documents and exhibits submitted to the trial court supporting and opposing the petitioner's position;

(C) Any other documents or portions of documents submitted to the trial court that are necessary for a complete understanding of the case and the ruling under review; and

(D) A reporter's transcript of the oral proceedings that resulted in the ruling under review.

(2) In exigent circumstances, the petition may be filed without the documents required by (1)(A)–(C) but must include a declaration that explains the urgency and the circumstances making the documents unavailable and fairly summarizes their substance.

(3) If a transcript under (1)(D) is unavailable, the record must include a declaration:

(A) Explaining why the transcript is unavailable and fairly summarizing the proceedings, including the parties' arguments and any statement by the court supporting its ruling. This declaration may omit a full summary of the proceedings if part of the relief sought is an order to prepare a transcript for use by an indigent criminal defendant in support of the petition and if the declaration demonstrates the need for and entitlement to the transcript; or

(B) Stating that the transcript has been ordered, the date it was ordered, and the date it is expected to be filed, which must be a date before any action requested of the reviewing court other than issuance of a temporary stay supported by other parts of the record.

(4) If the petition does not include the required record or explanations or does not present facts sufficient to excuse the failure to submit them, the court may summarily deny a stay request, the petition, or both.

(c) Form of supporting documents

(1) Documents submitted under (b) must comply with the following requirements:

(A) If submitted in paper form, they must be bound together at the end of the petition or in separate volumes not exceeding 300 pages each. The pages must be consecutively numbered.

(B) If submitted in paper form, they must be index-tabbed by number or letter.

(C) They must begin with a table of contents listing each document by its title and its index number or letter. If a document has attachments, the table of contents must give the title of each attachment and a brief description of its contents.

(2) The clerk must file any supporting documents not complying with (1), but the court may notify the petitioner that it may strike or summarily deny the petition if the documents are not brought into compliance within a stated reasonable time of not less than 5 days.

(3) Rule 8.44(a) governs the number of copies of supporting documents to be filed in the Supreme Court. Rule 8.44(b) governs the number of supporting documents to be filed in the Court of Appeal.

(d) Sealed and confidential records

Rules 8.45–8.47 govern sealed and confidential records in proceedings under this chapter.

(e) Service

(1) If the respondent is the superior court or a judge of that court, the petition and one set of supporting documents must be served on any named real party in interest, but only the petition must be served on the respondent.

(2) If the respondent is not the superior court or a judge of that court, both the petition and one set of supporting documents must be served on the respondent and on any named real party in interest.

(3) In addition to complying with the requirements of rule 8.25, the proof of service must give the telephone number of each attorney served.

(4) The petition must be served on a public officer or agency when required by statute or rule 8.29.

(5) The clerk must file the petition even if its proof of service is defective, but if the petitioner fails to file a corrected proof of service within 5 days after the clerk gives notice of the defect the court may strike the petition or impose a lesser sanction.

(6) The court may allow the petition to be filed without proof of service. *(Formerly Rule 56, adopted, eff. Jan. 1, 2005. As amended, eff. July 1, 2005; Jan. 1, 2006; July 1, 2006. Renumbered Rule 8.490 and amended, eff. Jan. 1, 2007. As amended, eff. Jan. 1, 2008. Renumbered Rule 8.486 and amended, eff. Jan. 1, 2009. As amended, eff. July 1, 2009; Jan. 1, 2011; Jan. 1, 2014; Jan. 1, 2016.)*

Advisory Committee Comment

Subdivision (a). Because of the importance of the point, rule 8.486(a)(6) explicitly states that the provisions of rule 8.204(c)—and hence the word-count limits imposed by that rule—apply to a petition for original writ.

Subdivision (d). Examples of confidential records include records of the family conciliation court (Fam. Code, § 1818(b)) and fee waiver applications (Gov. Code, § 68633(f)).

Subdivision (e). Rule 8.25, which generally governs service and filing in reviewing courts, also applies to the original proceedings covered by this rule.

Research References

6 Witkin, California Criminal Law 4th Criminal Writs § 69 (2021), Format in Reviewing Court.
6 Witkin, California Criminal Law 4th Criminal Writs § 90 (2021), Where Return is Filed in Reviewing Court.

Rule 8.487. Opposition and amicus curiae briefs

(a) Preliminary opposition

(1) Within 10 days after the petition is filed, the respondent or any real party in interest, separately or jointly, may serve and file a preliminary opposition.

(2) A preliminary opposition must contain a memorandum and a statement of any material fact not included in the petition.

(3) Within 10 days after a preliminary opposition is filed, the petitioner may serve and file a reply.

(4) Without requesting preliminary opposition or waiting for a reply, the court may grant or deny a request for temporary stay, deny the petition, issue an alternative writ or order to show cause, or notify the parties that it is considering issuing a peremptory writ in the first instance.

(b) Return or opposition; reply

(1) If the court issues an alternative writ or order to show cause, the respondent or any real party in interest, separately or jointly, may serve and file a return by demurrer, verified answer, or both. If the court notifies the parties that it is considering issuing a peremptory writ in the first instance, the respondent or any real party in interest may serve and file an opposition.

(2) Unless the court orders otherwise, the return or opposition must be served and filed within 30 days after the court issues the alternative writ or order to show cause or notifies the parties that it is considering issuing a peremptory writ in the first instance.

(3) Unless the court orders otherwise, the petitioner may serve and file a reply within 15 days after the return or opposition is filed.

(4) If the return is by demurrer alone and the demurrer is not sustained, the court may issue the peremptory writ without granting leave to answer.

(c) Supporting documents

Any supporting documents accompanying a preliminary opposition, return or opposition, or reply must comply with rule 8.486(c)–(d).

(d) Attorney General's amicus curiae brief

(1) If the court issues an alternative writ or order to show cause, the Attorney General may file an amicus curiae brief without the permission of the Chief Justice or presiding justice, unless the brief is submitted on behalf of another state officer or agency.

(2) The Attorney General must serve and file the brief within 14 days after the return is filed or, if no return is filed, within 14 days after the date it was due. For good cause, the Chief Justice or presiding justice may allow later filing.

(3) The brief must provide the information required by rule 8.200(c)(2) and comply with rule 8.200(c)(5).

(4) Any party may serve and file an answer within 14 days after the brief is filed.

(e) Other amicus curiae briefs

(1) This subdivision governs amicus curiae briefs when the court issues an alternative writ or order to show cause.

(2) Any person or entity may serve and file an application for permission of the Chief Justice or presiding justice to file an amicus curiae brief.

(3) The application must be filed no later than 14 days after the return is filed or, if no return is filed, within 14 days after the date it was due. For good cause, the Chief Justice or presiding justice may allow later filing.

(4) The proposed brief must be served on all parties. It must accompany the application and may be combined with it.

(5) The proposed brief must provide the information required by rule 8.200(c)(2) and (3) and comply with rule 8.200(c)(5).

(6) If the court grants the application, any party may file either an answer to the individual amicus curiae brief or a consolidated answer to multiple amicus curiae briefs filed in the case. If the court does not specify a due date, the answer must be filed within 14 days after either the court rules on the last timely filed application to file an amicus curiae brief or the time for filing applications to file an amicus curiae brief expires, whichever is later. The answer must be served on all parties and the amicus curiae. *(Adopted, eff. Jan. 1, 2009. As amended, eff. Jan. 1, 2014; Jan. 1, 2017.)*

Advisory Committee Comment

A party other than the petitioner who files a preliminary opposition under (a) or a return or opposition under (b) may be required to pay a filing fee under Government Code section 68926 if the preliminary opposition, return, or opposition is the first document filed in the writ proceeding in the reviewing court by that party. See rule 8.25(c).

Subdivision (a). Consistent with practice, rule 8.487 draws a distinction between a "preliminary opposition," which the respondent or a real party in interest may file before the court takes any action on the petition ((a)(1)), and a more formal "opposition," which the respondent or a real party in interest may file if the court notifies the parties that it is considering issuing a peremptory writ in the first instance ((b)(1)).

Subdivision (a)(1) allows the respondent or any real party in interest to serve and file a preliminary opposition within 10 days after the petition is filed. The reviewing court retains the power to act in any case without obtaining preliminary opposition ((a)(4)).

Subdivision (a)(3) allows a petitioner to serve and file a reply within 10 days after a preliminary opposition is filed. To permit prompt action in urgent cases, however, the provision recognizes that the reviewing court may act on the petition without waiting for a reply.

Subdivision (a)(4) recognizes that the reviewing court may "grant or deny a request for temporary stay" without requesting preliminary opposition or waiting for a reply.

The several references in rule 8.487 to the power of the court to issue a peremptory writ in the first instance after notifying the parties that it is considering doing so ((a)–(b)) implement the rule of *Palma v. U. S. Industrial Fasteners, Inc.* (1984) 36 Cal.3d 171.

Subdivision (b). Subdivision (b)(2) requires that the return or opposition be served and filed within 30 days after the court issues the alternative writ or order to show cause or notifies the parties that it is considering issuing a peremptory writ in the first instance. To permit prompt action in urgent cases, however, the provision recognizes that the reviewing court may order otherwise.

Subdivision (b)(3) formalizes the common practice of permitting petitioners to file replies to returns and specifies that such a reply must be served and filed within 15 days after the return is filed. To permit prompt action in urgent cases, however, the provision recognizes that the reviewing court may order otherwise.

Subdivision (c). Examples of confidential records include records of the family conciliation court (Fam. Code, § 1818 (b)) and fee waiver applications (Gov. Code, § 68633(f)).

Subdivisions (d) and (e). These provisions do not alter the court's authority to request or permit the filing of amicus briefs or amicus letters in writ proceedings in circumstances not covered by these subdivisions, such as before the court has determined whether to issue an alternative writ or order to show cause or when it notifies the parties that it is considering issuing a peremptory writ in the first instance.

Rule 8.488. Certificate of Interested Entities or Persons

(a) Application

This rule applies in writ proceedings in criminal cases in which an entity is the defendant and in civil cases other than family, juvenile, guardianship, and conservatorship cases.

(b) Compliance with rule 8.208

Each party in a civil case and any entity that is a defendant in a criminal case must comply with the requirements of rule 8.208 concerning serving and filing a certificate of interested entities or persons.

(c) Placement of certificates

(1) The petitioner's certificate must be included in the petition.

(2) The certificates of the respondent and real party in interest must be included in their preliminary opposition or, if no such opposition is filed, in their return, if any.

(3) The certificate must appear after the cover and before the tables.

(4) If the identity of any party has not been publicly disclosed in the proceedings, the party may file an application for permission to file its certificate under seal separately from the petition, preliminary opposition, or return.

(d) Failure to file a certificate

(1) If a party fails to file a certificate as required under (b) and (c), the clerk must notify the party in writing that the party must file the certificate within 10 days after the clerk's notice is sent and that if the party fails to comply, the court may impose one of the following sanctions:

(A) If the party is the petitioner, the court may strike the petition; or

(B) If the party is the respondent or the real party in interest, the court may strike that party's document.

(2) If the party fails to file the certificate as specified in the notice under (1), the court may impose the sanctions specified in the notice. *(Adopted, eff. Jan. 1, 2009. As amended, eff. Jan. 1, 2016.)*

Advisory Committee Comment

The Judicial Council has adopted an optional form, *Certificate of Interested Entities or Persons* (form APP–008), that can be used to file the certificate required by this provision.

Subdivision (a). Under rule 8.208(c), for purposes of certificates of interested entities or persons, an "entity" means a corporation, a partnership, a firm, or any other association, but does not include a governmental entity or its agencies or a natural person.

Research References

West's California Judicial Council Forms App–008, Certificate of Interested Entities or Persons.

Rule 8.489. Notice to trial court

(a) Notice if writ issues

If a writ or order issues directed to any judge, court, board, or other officer, the reviewing court clerk must promptly send a certified copy of the writ or order to the person or entity to whom it is addressed.

(b) Notice by telephone

(1) If the writ or order stays or prohibits proceedings set to occur within 7 days or requires action within 7 days—or in any other urgent situation—the reviewing court clerk must make a reasonable effort to notify the clerk of the respondent court by telephone or e-mail. The clerk of the respondent court must then notify the judge or officer most directly concerned.

(2) The clerk need not give telephonic or e-mail notice of the summary denial of a writ, whether or not a stay previously issued. *(Adopted, eff. Jan. 1, 2009. As amended, eff. Jan. 1, 2017.)*

Research References

6 Witkin, California Criminal Law 4th Criminal Appeal § 108 (2021), Power and Procedure.

Rule 8.490. Filing, finality, and modification of decisions; rehearing; remittitur

(a) Filing and modification of decisions

Rule 8.264(a) and (c) govern the filing and modification of decisions in writ proceedings.

(b) Finality of decision

(1) Except as otherwise ordered by the court, the following decisions regarding petitions for writs within the court's original jurisdiction are final in the issuing court when filed:

(A) An order denying or dismissing such a petition without issuance of an alternative writ, order to show cause, or writ of review; and

(B) An order denying or dismissing such a petition as moot after issuance of an alternative writ, order to show cause, or writ of review.

(2) All other decisions in a writ proceeding are final 30 days after the decision is filed, except as follows:

(A) If necessary to prevent mootness or frustration of the relief granted or to otherwise promote the interests of justice, the court may order early finality in that court of a decision granting a petition for a writ within its original jurisdiction or denying such a petition after issuing an alternative writ, order to show cause, or writ of review. The decision may provide for finality in that court on filing or within a stated period of less than 30 days.

(B) If a Court of Appeal certifies its opinion for publication or partial publication after filing its decision and before the decision becomes final in that court, the 30 days or other finality period ordered under (A) runs from the filing date of the order for publication.

(C) If an order modifying a decision changes the appellate judgment, the 30 days or other finality period ordered under (A) runs from the filing date of the modification order.

(c) Rehearing

(1) Rule 8.268 governs rehearing in the Courts of Appeal.

(2) Rule 8.536 governs rehearing in the Supreme Court.

(d) Remittitur

A Court of Appeal must issue a remittitur in a writ proceeding under this chapter except when the court issues one of the orders listed in (b)(1). Rule 8.272(b)–(d) governs issuance of a remittitur by a Court of Appeal in writ proceedings under this chapter. *(Adopted, eff. Jan. 1, 2009. As amended, eff. Jan. 1, 2014.)*

Advisory Committee Comment

Subdivision (b). This provision addresses the finality of decisions in proceedings relating to writs of mandate, certiorari, and prohibition. See rule 8.264(b) for provisions addressing the finality of decisions in proceedings under chapter 2, relating to civil appeals, and rule 8.366 for provisions addressing the finality of decisions in proceedings under chapter 3, relating to criminal appeals.

Subdivision (b)(1). Examples of situations in which the court may issue an order dismissing a writ petition include when the petitioner fails to comply with an order of the court, when the court recalls the alternative writ, order to show cause, or writ of review as improvidently granted, or when the petition becomes moot.

Subdivision (d). Under this rule, a remittitur serves as notice that the writ proceedings have concluded.

Rule 8.491. Responsive pleading under Code of Civil Procedure section 418.10

If the Court of Appeal denies a petition for writ of mandate brought under Code of Civil Procedure section 418.10(c) and the

Supreme Court denies review of the Court of Appeal's decision, the time to file a responsive pleading in the trial court is extended until 10 days after the Supreme Court files its order denying review. *(Adopted, eff. Jan. 1, 2009.)*

Rule 8.492. Sanctions

(a) Grounds for sanctions

On motion of a party or its own motion, a Court of Appeal may impose sanctions, including the award or denial of costs under rule 8.493, on a party or an attorney for:

(1) Filing a frivolous petition or filing a petition solely to cause delay; or

(2) Committing any other unreasonable violation of these rules.

(b) Notice

The court must give notice in writing if it is considering imposing sanctions.

(c) Opposition

Within 10 days after the court sends such notice, a party or attorney may serve and file an opposition, but failure to do so will not be deemed consent. An opposition may not be filed unless the court sends such notice.

(d) Oral argument

Unless otherwise ordered, oral argument on the issue of sanctions must be combined with any oral argument on the merits of the petition. *(Adopted, eff. Jan. 1, 2009.)*

Rule 8.493. Costs

(a) Award of costs

(1) Except in a criminal or juvenile or other proceeding in which a party is entitled to court-appointed counsel:

(A) Unless otherwise ordered by the court under (B), the prevailing party in an original proceeding is entitled to costs if the court resolves the proceeding by written opinion after issuing an alternative writ, an order to show cause, or a peremptory writ in the first instance.

(B) In the interests of justice, the court may also award or deny costs as it deems proper in the proceedings listed in (A) and in other circumstances.

(2) The opinion or order resolving the proceeding must specify the award or denial of costs.

(b) Procedures for recovering costs

Rule 8.278(b)–(d) governs the procedure for recovering costs under this rule. *(Adopted, eff. Jan. 1, 2009.)*

Division 2

RULES RELATING TO DEATH PENALTY APPEALS AND HABEAS CORPUS PROCEEDINGS

Chapter 1

GENERAL PROVISIONS

Rule 8.601. Definitions

For purposes of this division:

(1) "Appointed counsel" or "appointed attorney" means an attorney appointed to represent a person in a death penalty appeal, death penalty-related habeas corpus proceedings, or an appeal of a decision in death penalty-related habeas corpus proceedings. Appointed counsel may be either lead counsel or associate counsel.

(2) "Lead counsel" means an appointed attorney or an attorney in the Office of the State Public Defender, the Habeas Corpus Resource Center, the California Appellate Project–San Francisco, or a Court of Appeal district appellate project who is responsible for the overall conduct of the case and for supervising the work of associate and supervised counsel. If two or more attorneys are appointed to represent a person jointly in a death penalty appeal, in death penalty-related habeas corpus proceedings, or in both classes of proceedings together, one such attorney will be designated as lead counsel.

(3) "Associate counsel" means an appointed attorney who does not have the primary responsibility for the case but nevertheless has casewide responsibility. Associate counsel must meet the same minimum qualifications as lead counsel.

(4) "Supervised counsel" means an attorney who works under the immediate supervision and direction of lead or associate counsel but is not appointed by the court. Supervised counsel must be an active member of the State Bar of California.

(5) "Assisting counsel or entity" means an attorney or entity designated by the appointing court to provide appointed counsel with consultation and resource assistance. An assisting counsel must be an experienced capital appellate counsel or habeas corpus practitioner, as appropriate. An assisting counsel in an automatic appeal must, at a minimum, meet the qualifications for appointed appellate counsel, including the case experience requirements in rule 8.605(c)(2). An assisting counsel in a habeas corpus proceeding must, at a minimum, meet the qualifications for appointed habeas corpus counsel, including the case experience requirements in rule 8.652(c)(2)(A). Entities that may be designated include the Office of the State Public Defender, the Habeas Corpus Resource Center, the California Appellate Project–San Francisco, and a Court of Appeal district appellate project.

(6) "Trial counsel" means both the defendant's trial counsel and the prosecuting attorney.

(7) "Panel" means a panel of attorneys from which superior courts may appoint counsel in death penalty-related habeas corpus proceedings.

(8) "Committee" means a death penalty-related habeas corpus panel committee that accepts and reviews attorney applications to determine whether applicants are qualified for inclusion on a panel. *(Adopted, eff. April 25, 2019.)*

Advisory Committee Comment

Number (3). The definition of "associate counsel" in (3) is intended to make it clear that, although appointed lead counsel has overall and supervisory responsibility in a capital case, appointed associate counsel also has casewide responsibility.

Research References

6 Witkin, California Criminal Law 4th Criminal Appeal § 2 (2021), Appellate Rules.
6 Witkin, California Criminal Law 4th Criminal Writs § 67 (2021), Overview.
6 Witkin, California Criminal Law 4th Criminal Writs § 67A (2021), (New) in General.
6 Witkin, California Criminal Law 4th Criminal Writs § 67C (2021), (New) Rules and Forms.

4 Witkin, California Criminal Law 4th Introduction to Criminal Procedure § 9 (2021), Rules of Court.
3 Witkin, California Criminal Law 4th Punishment § 599 (2021), Preparation of Record.

Chapter 2

AUTOMATIC APPEALS FROM JUDGMENTS OF DEATH

Article 1

GENERAL PROVISIONS

Rule 8.603. In general

(a) Automatic appeal to Supreme Court

If a judgment imposes a sentence of death, an appeal by the defendant is automatically taken to the Supreme Court.

(b) Copies of judgment

When a judgment of death is rendered, the superior court clerk must immediately send certified copies of the commitment to the Supreme Court, the Attorney General, the Governor, the Habeas Corpus Resource Center, and the California Appellate Project–San Francisco. *(Formerly Rule 34, adopted, eff. Jan. 1, 2004. Renumbered Rule 8.600 and amended, eff. Jan. 1, 2007. As amended, eff. Jan. 1, 2018. Renumbered Rule 8.603 and amended, eff. April 25, 2019.)*

Research References

6 Witkin, California Criminal Law 4th Criminal Appeal § 1 (2021), Appellate Jurisdiction.

Rule 8.605. Qualifications of counsel in death penalty appeals

(a) Purpose

This rule defines the minimum qualifications for attorneys appointed by the Supreme Court in death penalty appeals. These minimum qualifications are designed to promote competent representation and to avoid unnecessary delay and expense by assisting the court in appointing qualified counsel. Nothing in this rule is intended to be used as a standard by which to measure whether the defendant received effective assistance of counsel. An attorney is not entitled to appointment simply because the attorney meets these minimum qualifications.

(b) General qualifications

The Supreme Court may appoint an attorney only if it has determined, after reviewing the attorney's experience, writing samples, references, and evaluations under (c) and (d), that the attorney has demonstrated the commitment, knowledge, and skills necessary to competently represent the defendant. An appointed attorney must be willing to cooperate with an assisting counsel or entity that the court may designate.

(c) Qualifications for appointed appellate counsel

Except as provided in (d), an attorney appointed as lead or associate counsel in a death penalty appeal must satisfy the following minimum qualifications and experience:

(1) *California legal experience*

Active practice of law in California for at least four years.

(2) *Criminal appellate experience*

Either:

(A) Service as counsel of record for either party in seven completed felony appeals, including as counsel of record for a defendant in at least four felony appeals, one of which was a murder case; or

(B) Service as:

(i) Counsel of record for either party in five completed felony appeals, including as counsel of record for a defendant in at least three of these appeals; and

(ii) Supervised counsel for a defendant in two death penalty appeals in which the opening brief has been filed. Service as supervised counsel in a death penalty appeal will apply toward this qualification only if lead or associate counsel in that appeal attests that the supervised attorney performed substantial work on the case and recommends the attorney for appointment.

(3) *Knowledge*

Familiarity with Supreme Court practices and procedures, including those related to death penalty appeals.

(4) *Training*

(A) Within three years before appointment, completion of at least nine hours of Supreme Court-approved appellate criminal defense training, continuing education, or course of study, at least six hours of which involve death penalty appeals. Counsel who serves as an instructor in a course that satisfies the requirements of this rule may receive course participation credit for instruction, on request to and approval by the Supreme Court, in an amount to be determined by the Supreme Court.

(B) If the Supreme Court has previously appointed counsel to represent a person in a death penalty appeal or a related habeas corpus proceeding, and counsel has provided active representation within three years before the request for a new appointment, the court, after reviewing counsel's previous work, may find that such representation constitutes compliance with some or all of this requirement.

(5) *Skills*

Proficiency in issue identification, research, analysis, writing, and advocacy, taking into consideration all of the following:

(A) Two writing samples—ordinarily appellate briefs—written by the attorney and presenting an analysis of complex legal issues;

(B) If the attorney has previously been appointed in a death penalty appeal or death penalty-related habeas corpus proceeding, the evaluation of the assisting counsel or entity in that proceeding;

(C) Recommendations from two attorneys familiar with the attorney's qualifications and performance; and

(D) If the attorney is on a panel of attorneys eligible for appointments to represent indigents in the Court of Appeal, the evaluation of the administrator responsible for those appointments.

(d) Alternative qualifications

The Supreme Court may appoint an attorney who does not meet the California law practice requirement of (c)(1) or the criminal appellate experience requirements of (c)(2) if the attorney has the qualifications described in (c)(3)–(5) and:

(1) The court finds that the attorney has extensive experience in another jurisdiction or a different type of practice (such as civil trials or appeals, academic work, or work for a court or prosecutor) for at least four years, providing the attorney with experience in complex cases substantially equivalent to that of an attorney qualified under (c).

(2) Ongoing consultation is available to the attorney from an assisting counsel or entity designated by the court.

(3) Within two years before appointment, the attorney has completed at least 18 hours of Supreme Court-approved appellate criminal defense or habeas corpus defense training, continuing

Ct. Rules

education, or course of study, at least nine hours of which involve death penalty appellate or habeas corpus proceedings. The Supreme Court will determine in each case whether the training, education, or course of study completed by a particular attorney satisfies the requirements of this subdivision in light of the attorney's individual background and experience. If the Supreme Court has previously appointed counsel to represent a person in a death penalty appeal or a related habeas corpus proceeding, and counsel has provided active representation within three years before the request for a new appointment, the court, after reviewing counsel's previous work, may find that such representation constitutes compliance with some or all of this requirement.

(e) Use of supervised counsel

An attorney who does not meet the qualifications described in (c) or (d) may assist lead or associate counsel, but must work under the immediate supervision and direction of lead or associate counsel.

(f) Appellate and habeas corpus appointment

(1) An attorney appointed to represent a person in both a death penalty appeal and death penalty-related habeas corpus proceedings must meet the minimum qualifications of both (c) or (d) and rule 8.652.

(2) Notwithstanding (1), two attorneys together may be eligible for appointment to represent a person jointly in both a death penalty appeal and death penalty-related habeas corpus proceedings if the Supreme Court finds that one attorney satisfies the minimum qualifications set forth in (c) or (d), and the other attorney satisfies the minimum qualifications set forth in rule 8.652.

(g) Designated entities as appointed counsel

(1) Notwithstanding any other provision of this rule, both the State Public Defender and the California Appellate Project–San Francisco are qualified to serve as appointed counsel in death penalty appeals.

(2) When serving as appointed counsel in a death penalty appeal, the State Public Defender or the California Appellate Project–San Francisco must not assign any attorney as lead counsel unless it finds the attorney qualified under (c)(1)–(5) or the Supreme Court finds the attorney qualified under (d). *(Formerly Rule 76.6, adopted, eff. Jan. 1, 2005. Renumbered Rule 8.605 and amended, eff. Jan. 1, 2007. As amended, eff. April 25, 2019.)*

Research References

6 Witkin, California Criminal Law 4th Criminal Writs § 67A (2021), (New) in General.

Article 2

RECORD ON APPEAL

Rule

Rule 8.608. General provisions

(a) Supervising preparation of record

The clerk/executive officer of the Supreme Court, under the supervision of the Chief Justice, must take all appropriate steps to ensure that superior court clerks and reporters promptly perform their duties under the rules in this article. This provision does not affect the superior courts' responsibility for the prompt preparation of appellate records in capital cases.

(b) Extensions of time

When a rule in this article authorizes a trial court to grant an extension of a specified time period, the court must consider the relevant policies and factors stated in rule 8.63.

(c) Delivery date

The delivery date of a transcript sent by mail is the mailing date plus five days. *(Adopted, eff. April 25, 2019.)*

Research References

6 Witkin, California Criminal Law 4th Criminal Appeal § 4 (2021), Factors Considered.

6 Witkin, California Criminal Law 4th Criminal Appeal § 141 (2021), Special Requirements in Death Penalty Cases.

Rule 8.610. Contents and form of the record

(a) Contents of the record

(1) The record must include a clerk's transcript containing:

(A) The accusatory pleading and any amendment;

(B) Any demurrer or other plea;

(C) All court minutes;

(D) All instructions submitted in writing, the cover page required by rule 2.1055(b)(2) indicating the party requesting each instruction, and any written jury instructions given by the court;

(E) Any written communication, including printouts of any e-mail or text messages and their attachments, between the court and the parties, the jury, or any individual juror or prospective juror;

(F) Any verdict;

(G) Any written opinion of the court;

(H) The judgment or order appealed from and any abstract of judgment or commitment;

(I) Any motion for new trial, with supporting and opposing memoranda and attachments;

(J) Any transcript of a sound or sound-and-video recording furnished to the jury or tendered to the court under rule 2.1040, including witness statements;

(K) Any application for additional record and any order on the application;

(L) Any written defense motion or any written motion by the People, with supporting and opposing memoranda and attachments;

(M) If related to a motion under (L), any search warrant and return and the reporter's transcript of any preliminary examination or grand jury hearing;

(N) Any document admitted in evidence to prove a prior juvenile adjudication, criminal conviction, or prison term;

(O) The probation officer's report;

(P) Any court-ordered diagnostic or psychological report required under Penal Code section 1369;

(Q) Any copies of visual aids provided to the clerk under rule 4.230(f). If a visual aid is oversized, a photograph of that visual aid must be included in place of the original. For digital or electronic presentations, printouts showing the full text of each slide or image must be included;

(R) Each juror questionnaire, whether or not the juror was selected;

(S) The table correlating the jurors' names with their identifying numbers required by rule 8.611;

(T) The register of actions;

(U) All documents filed under Penal Code section 987.2 or 987.9; and

(V) Any other document filed or lodged in the case.

(2) The record must include a reporter's transcript containing:

(A) The oral proceedings on the entry of any plea other than a not guilty plea;

(B) The oral proceedings on any motion in limine;

(C) The voir dire examination of jurors;

(D) Any opening statement;

(E) The oral proceedings at trial;

(F) All instructions given orally;

(G) Any oral communication between the court and the jury or any individual juror;

(H) Any oral opinion of the court;

(I) The oral proceedings on any motion for new trial;

(J) The oral proceedings at sentencing, granting or denying of probation, or other dispositional hearing;

(K) The oral proceedings on any motion under Penal Code section 1538.5 denied in whole or in part;

(L) The closing arguments;

(M) Any comment on the evidence by the court to the jury;

(N) The oral proceedings on motions in addition to those listed above; and

(O) Any other oral proceedings in the case, including any proceedings that did not result in a verdict or sentence of death because the court ordered a mistrial or a new trial.

(3) All exhibits admitted in evidence, refused, or lodged are deemed part of the record, but, except as provided in rule 8.622, may be transmitted to the reviewing court only as provided in rule 8.634.

(4) The superior court or the Supreme Court may order that the record include additional material.

(b) Sealed and confidential records

Rules 8.45–8.47 govern sealed and confidential records in appeals under this chapter.

(c) Juror–identifying information

Any document in the record containing juror-identifying information must be edited in compliance with rule 8.611. Unedited copies of all such documents and a copy of the table required by the rule, under seal and bound together if filed in paper form, must be included in the record sent to the Supreme Court.

(d) Form of record

The clerk's transcript and the reporter's transcript must comply with rules 8.45–8.47, relating to sealed and confidential records, and rule 8.144. *(Formerly Rule 34.1, adopted, eff. Jan. 1, 2004. As amended, eff. Jan. 1, 2005. Renumbered Rule 8.610 and amended, eff. Jan. 1, 2007. As amended, eff. Jan. 1, 2014; Jan. 1, 2016; April 25, 2019.)*

Advisory Committee Comment

Subdivision (a). Subdivision (a) implements Penal Code section 190.7(a).

Subdivision (b). The clerk's and reporter's transcripts may contain records that are sealed or confidential. Rules 8.45–8.47 address the handling of such records, including requirements for the format, labeling, and transmission of and access to such records. Examples of confidential records include Penal Code section 1203.03 diagnostic reports, records closed to inspection by court order under *People v. Marsden* (1970) 2 Cal.3d 118 or *Pitchess v. Superior Court* (1974) 11 Cal.3d 531, in-camera proceedings on a confidential informant, and defense investigation and expert funding requests (Pen. Code, §§ 987.2 and 987.9; *Puett v. Superior Court* (1979) 96 Cal.App.3d 936, 940, fn. 2; *Keenan v. Superior Court* (1982) 31 Cal.3d 424, 430).

Research References

6 Witkin, California Criminal Law 4th Criminal Appeal § 128 (2021), In General.

6 Witkin, California Criminal Law 4th Criminal Appeal § 132 (2021), Complete Record in Capital Case.

6 Witkin, California Criminal Law 4th Criminal Appeal § 137 (2021), Juror Identifying Information.

Rule 8.611. Juror–identifying information

(a) Application

A clerk's transcript, a reporter's transcript, or any other document in the record that contains juror-identifying information must comply with this rule.

(b) Juror names, addresses, and telephone numbers

(1) The name of each trial juror or alternate sworn to hear the case must be replaced with an identifying number wherever it appears in any document. The superior court clerk must prepare and keep under seal in the case file a table correlating the jurors' names with their identifying numbers. The clerk and the reporter must use the table in preparing all transcripts or other documents.

(2) The addresses and telephone numbers of trial jurors and alternates sworn to hear the case must be deleted from all documents.

(c) Potential jurors

Information identifying potential jurors called but not sworn as trial jurors or alternates must not be sealed unless otherwise ordered under Code of Civil Procedure section 237(a)(1). *(Adopted, eff. April 25, 2019.)*

Advisory Committee Comment

Rule 8.611 implements Code of Civil Procedure section 237.

Research References

6 Witkin, California Criminal Law 4th Criminal Appeal § 132 (2021), Complete Record in Capital Case.

6 Witkin, California Criminal Law 4th Criminal Appeal § 137 (2021), Juror Identifying Information.

Rule 8.613. Preparing and certifying the record of preliminary proceedings

(a) Definitions

For purposes of this rule:

(1) The "preliminary proceedings" are all proceedings held before and including the filing of the information or indictment, whether in open court or otherwise, and include the preliminary examination or grand jury proceeding;

(2) The "record of the preliminary proceedings" is the court file and the reporter's transcript of the preliminary proceedings;

(3) The "responsible judge" is the judge assigned to try the case or, if none is assigned, the presiding superior court judge or designee of the presiding judge; and

(4) The "designated judge" is the judge designated by the presiding judge to supervise preparation of the record of preliminary proceedings.

(b) Notice of intent to seek death penalty

In any case in which the death penalty may be imposed:

(1) If the prosecution notifies the responsible judge that it intends to seek the death penalty, the judge must notify the presiding judge and the clerk. The clerk must promptly enter the information in the court file.

(2) If the prosecution does not give notice under (1)—and does not give notice to the contrary—the clerk must notify the responsible judge 60 days before the first date set for trial that the prosecution is presumed to seek the death penalty. The judge must notify the presiding judge, and the clerk must promptly enter the information in the court file.

Ct. Rules

(c) Assignment of judge designated to supervise preparation of record of preliminary proceedings

(1) Within five days after receiving notice under (b), the presiding judge must designate a judge to supervise preparation of the record of the preliminary proceedings.

(2) If there was a preliminary examination, the designated judge must be the judge who conducted it.

(d) Notice to prepare transcript and lists

Within five days after receiving notice under (b)(1) or notifying the judge under (b)(2), the clerk must do the following:

(1) Notify each reporter who reported a preliminary proceeding to prepare a transcript of the proceeding. If there is more than one reporter, the designated judge may assign a reporter or another designee to perform the functions of the primary reporter.

(2) Notify trial counsel to submit the lists of appearances, exhibits, and motions required by rule 4.119.

(e) Reporter's duties

(1) The reporter must prepare an original and five copies of the reporter's transcript in electronic form and two additional copies in electronic form for each codefendant against whom the death penalty is sought. The transcript must include the preliminary examination or grand jury proceeding unless a transcript of that examination or proceeding has already been filed in superior court for inclusion in the clerk's transcript.

(2) The reporter must certify the original and all copies of the reporter's transcript as correct.

(3) Within 20 days after receiving the notice to prepare the reporter's transcript, the reporter must deliver the original and all copies of the transcript to the clerk.

(f) Review by counsel

(1) Within five days after the reporter delivers the transcript, the clerk must deliver the original transcript and the lists of appearances, exhibits, and motions required by rule 4.119 to the designated judge and one copy of the transcript and each list required by rule 4.119 that is not required to be sealed to each trial counsel. If a different attorney represented the defendant or the People in the preliminary proceedings, both attorneys must perform the tasks required by (2).

(2) Each trial counsel must promptly:

(A) Review the reporter's transcript and the lists of appearances, exhibits, and motions to identify any errors or omissions in the transcript;

(B) Review the docket sheets and minute orders to determine whether all preliminary proceedings have been transcribed; and

(C) Review the court file to determine whether it is complete.

(3) Within 21 days after the clerk delivers the transcript and lists under (1), trial counsel must confer regarding any errors or omissions in the reporter's transcript or court file identified by trial counsel during the review required under (2) and determine whether any other proceedings or discussions should have been transcribed.

(g) Declaration and request for corrections or additions

(1) Within 30 days after the clerk delivers the reporter's transcript and lists, each trial counsel must serve and file:

(A) A declaration stating that counsel or another person under counsel's supervision has performed the tasks required by (f), including conferring with opposing counsel; and

(B) Either:

(i) A request for corrections or additions to the reporter's transcript or court file. Immaterial typographical errors that cannot conceivably cause confusion are not required to be brought to the court's attention; or

(ii) A statement that counsel does not request any corrections or additions.

(C) The requirements of (B) may be satisfied by a joint statement or request filed by counsel for all parties.

(2) If a different attorney represented the defendant in the preliminary proceedings, that attorney must also file the declaration required by (1).

(3) A request for additions to the reporter's transcript must state the nature and date of the proceedings and, if known, the identity of the reporter who reported them.

(4) If any counsel fails to timely file a declaration under (1), the designated judge must not certify the record and must set the matter for hearing, require a showing of good cause why counsel has not complied, and fix a date for compliance.

(h) Corrections or additions to the record of preliminary proceedings

If any counsel files a request for corrections or additions:

(1) Within 15 days after the last request is filed, the designated judge must hold a hearing and order any necessary corrections or additions.

(2) If any portion of the proceedings cannot be transcribed, the judge may order preparation of a settled statement under rule 8.346.

(3) Within 20 days after the hearing under (1), the original reporter's transcript and court file must be corrected or augmented to reflect all corrections or additions ordered. The clerk must promptly send copies of the corrected or additional pages to trial counsel.

(4) The judge may order any further proceedings to correct or complete the record of the preliminary proceedings.

(5) When the judge is satisfied that all corrections and additions ordered have been made and copies of all corrected or additional pages have been sent to the parties, the judge must certify the record of the preliminary proceedings as complete and accurate.

(6) The record of the preliminary proceedings must be certified as complete and accurate within 120 days after the presiding judge orders preparation of the record.

(i) Transcript delivered in electronic form

(1) When the record of the preliminary proceedings is certified as complete and accurate, the clerk must promptly notify the reporter to prepare five copies of the transcript in electronic form and two additional copies in electronic form for each codefendant against whom the death penalty is sought.

(2) Each transcript delivered in electronic form must comply with the applicable requirements of rule 8.144 and any additional requirements prescribed by the Supreme Court, and must be further labeled to show the date it was made.

(3) A copy of a sealed or confidential transcript delivered in electronic form must be separated from any other transcripts and labeled as required by rule 8.45.

(4) The reporter is to be compensated for copies delivered in electronic form as provided in Government Code section 69954(b).

(5) Within 20 days after the clerk notifies the reporter under (1), the reporter must deliver the copies in electronic form to the clerk.

(j) Delivery to the superior court

Within five days after the reporter delivers the copies in electronic form, the clerk must deliver to the responsible judge, for inclusion in the record:

(1) The certified original reporter's transcript of the preliminary proceedings and the copies that have not been distributed to counsel; and

(2) The complete court file of the preliminary proceedings or a certified copy of that file.

(k) Extension of time

(1) Except as provided in (2), the designated judge may extend for good cause any of the periods specified in this rule.

(2) The period specified in (h)(6) may be extended only as follows:

(A) The designated judge may request an extension of the period by presenting a declaration to the responsible judge explaining why the time limit cannot be met; and

(B) The responsible judge may order an extension not exceeding 90 additional days; in an exceptional case the judge may order an extension exceeding 90 days, but must state on the record the specific reason for the greater extension.

(*l*) Notice that the death penalty is no longer sought

After the clerk has notified the court reporter to prepare the pretrial record, if the death penalty is no longer sought, the clerk must promptly notify the reporter that this rule does not apply. *(Formerly Rule 34.2, adopted, eff. Jan. 1, 2004. Renumbered Rule 8.613 and amended, eff. Jan. 1, 2007. As amended, eff. Jan. 1, 2017; Jan. 1, 2018; April 25, 2019.)*

Advisory Committee Comment

Rule 8.613 implements Penal Code section 190.9(a). Rules 8.613–8.622 govern the process of preparing and certifying the record in any appeal from a judgment of death; specifically, rule 8.613 provides for the record of the preliminary proceedings in such an appeal.

Subdivision (f). As used in subdivision (f)—as in all rules in this chapter—trial counsel "means both the defendant's trial counsel and the prosecuting attorney." (Rule 8.600(e)(2).)

Subdivision (i). Subdivision (i)(4) restates a provision of former rule 35(b), second paragraph, as it was in effect on December 31, 2003.

Research References

3 Witkin, California Criminal Law 4th Punishment § 599 (2021), Preparation of Record.

Rule 8.616. Preparing the trial record

(a) Clerk's duties

(1) The clerk must promptly—and no later than five days after the judgment of death is rendered:

(A) Notify the reporter to prepare the reporter's transcript; and

(B) Notify trial counsel to submit the lists of appearances, exhibits, and motions required by rule 4.230.

(2) The clerk must prepare an original and eight copies of the clerk's transcript and two additional copies for each codefendant sentenced to death. The clerk is encouraged to send the clerk's transcript in electronic form if the court is able to do so.

(3) The clerk must certify the original and all copies of the clerk's transcript as correct.

(b) Reporter's duties

(1) The reporter must prepare an original and five copies of the reporter's transcript in electronic form and two additional copies in electronic form for each codefendant sentenced to death.

(2) Any portion of the transcript transcribed during trial must not be retyped unless necessary to correct errors, but must be repaginated and combined with any portion of the transcript not previously transcribed. Any additional copies needed must not be retyped but, if the transcript is in paper form, must be prepared by photocopying or an equivalent process.

(3) The reporter must certify the original and all copies of the reporter's transcript as correct and deliver them to the clerk.

(c) Sending the record to trial counsel

Within 30 days after the judgment of death is rendered, the clerk must deliver one copy of the clerk's and reporter's transcripts and one copy of each list of appearances, exhibits, and motions required by rule 4.230 that is not required to be sealed to each trial counsel. The clerk must retain the original transcripts and any remaining copies. If counsel does not receive the transcripts within that period, counsel must promptly notify the superior court.

(d) Extension of time

(1) On request of the clerk or a reporter and for good cause, the superior court may extend the period prescribed in (c) for no more than 30 days. For any further extension the clerk or reporter must file a request in the Supreme Court, showing good cause.

(2) A request under (1) must be supported by a declaration explaining why the extension is necessary. The court may presume good cause if the clerk's and reporter's transcripts combined will likely exceed 10,000 pages.

(3) If the superior court orders an extension under (1), the order must specify the reason justifying the extension. The clerk must promptly send a copy of the order to the Supreme Court. *(Formerly Rule 35, adopted, eff. Jan. 1, 2004. Renumbered Rule 8.616, eff. Jan. 1, 2007. As amended, eff. Jan. 1, 2016; April 25, 2019.)*

Advisory Committee Comment

Rule 8.616 implements Penal Code section 190.8(b).

Research References

6 Witkin, California Criminal Law 4th Criminal Appeal § 141 (2021), Special Requirements in Death Penalty Cases.

Rule 8.619. Certifying the trial record for completeness

(a) Review by counsel after trial

(1) When the clerk delivers the clerk's and reporter's transcripts and the lists of appearances, exhibits, motions, and jury instructions required by rule 4.230 to trial counsel, each counsel must promptly:

(A) Review the docket sheets, minute orders, and the lists of appearances, exhibits, motions, and jury instructions to determine whether the reporter's transcript is complete; and

(B) Review the court file to determine whether the clerk's transcript is complete.

(2) Within 21 days after the clerk delivers the transcripts and lists under (1), trial counsel must confer regarding any errors or omissions in the reporter's transcript or clerk's transcript identified by trial counsel during the review required under (1).

(b) Declaration and request for additions or corrections

(1) Within 30 days after the clerk delivers the transcripts, each trial counsel must serve and file:

(A) A declaration stating that counsel or another person under counsel's supervision has performed the tasks required by (a), including conferring with opposing counsel; and

(B) Either:

(i) A request to include additional materials in the record or to correct errors that have come to counsel's attention. Immaterial typographical errors that cannot conceivably cause confusion are not required to be brought to the court's attention; or

(ii) A statement that counsel does not request any additions or corrections.

(2) The requirements of (1)(B) may be satisfied by a joint statement or request filed by counsel for all parties.

(3) If the clerk's and reporter's transcripts combined exceed 10,000 pages, the time limits stated in (a)(2) and (b)(1) are extended by three days for each 1,000 pages of combined transcript over 10,000 pages.

Ct. Rules

(4) A request for additions to the reporter's transcript must state the nature and date of the proceedings and, if known, the identity of the reporter who reported them.

(5) If any counsel fails to timely file a declaration under (1), the judge must not certify the record and must set the matter for hearing, require a showing of good cause why counsel has not complied, and fix a date for compliance.

(c) Completion of the record

If any counsel files a request for additions or corrections:

(1) The clerk must promptly deliver the original transcripts to the judge who presided at the trial.

(2) Within 15 days after the last request is filed, the judge must hold a hearing and order any necessary additions or corrections. The order must require that any additions or corrections be made within 10 days of its date.

(3) The clerk must promptly—and in any event within five days—notify the reporter of an order under (2). If any portion of the proceedings cannot be transcribed, the judge may order preparation of a settled statement under rule 8.346.

(4) The original transcripts must be augmented or corrected to reflect all additions or corrections ordered. The clerk must promptly send copies of the additional or corrected pages to trial counsel.

(5) Within five days after the augmented or corrected transcripts are filed, the judge must set another hearing to determine whether the record has been completed or corrected as ordered. The judge may order further proceedings to complete or correct the record.

(6) When the judge is satisfied that all additions or corrections ordered have been made and copies of all additional or corrected pages have been sent to trial counsel, the judge must certify the record as complete and redeliver the original transcripts to the clerk.

(7) The judge must certify the record as complete within 30 days after the last request to include additional materials or make corrections is filed or, if no such request is filed, after the last statement that counsel does not request any additions or corrections is filed.

(d) Transcript delivered in electronic form

(1) When the record is certified as complete, the clerk must promptly notify the reporter to prepare five copies of the transcript in electronic form and two additional copies in electronic form for each codefendant sentenced to death.

(2) Each copy delivered in electronic form must comply with the applicable requirements of rule 8.144 and any additional requirements prescribed by the Supreme Court, and must be further labeled to show the date it was made.

(3) A copy of a sealed or confidential transcript delivered in electronic form must be separated from any other transcripts and labeled as required by rule 8.45.

(4) The reporter is to be compensated for copies delivered in electronic form as provided in Government Code section 69954(b).

(5) Within 10 days after the clerk notifies the reporter under (1), the reporter must deliver the copies in electronic form to the clerk.

(e) Extension of time

(1) The court may extend for good cause any of the periods specified in this rule.

(2) An application to extend the period to review the record under (a) or the period to file a declaration under (b) must be served and filed within the relevant period.

(3) If the court orders an extension of time, the order must specify the justification for the extension. The clerk must promptly send a copy of the order to the Supreme Court.

(f) Sending the certified record

(1) When the record is certified as complete, the clerk must promptly send one copy of the clerk's transcript and one copy of the reporter's transcript:

(A) To each defendant's appellate counsel and each defendant's habeas corpus counsel. If either counsel has not been retained or appointed, the clerk must keep that counsel's copies until counsel is retained or appointed.

(B) To the Attorney General, the Habeas Corpus Resource Center, and the California Appellate Project in San Francisco.

(2) The reporter's transcript must be in electronic form. The clerk is encouraged to send the clerk's transcript in electronic form if the court is able to do so.

(g) Notice of delivery

When the clerk sends the record to the defendant's appellate counsel, the clerk must serve a notice of delivery on the clerk/executive officer of the Supreme Court. *(Formerly Rule 35.1, adopted, eff. Jan. 1, 2004. Renumbered Rule 8.619 and amended, eff. Jan. 1, 2007. As amended, eff. Jan. 1, 2017; Jan. 1, 2018; April 25, 2019.)*

Advisory Committee Comment

Rule 8.619 implements Penal Code section 190.8(c)–(e).

Subdivision (d)(4) restates a provision of former rule 35(b), second paragraph, as it was in effect on December 31, 2003.

Research References

3 Witkin, California Criminal Law 4th Punishment § 600 (2021), Certification of Record.

Rule 8.622. Certifying the trial record for accuracy

(a) Request for corrections or additions

(1) Within 90 days after the clerk delivers the record to defendant's appellate counsel:

(A) Any party may serve and file a request for corrections or additions to the record. Immaterial typographical errors that cannot conceivably cause confusion are not required to be brought to the court's attention. Items that a party may request to be added to the clerk's transcript include a copy of any exhibit admitted in evidence, refused, or lodged that is a document in paper or electronic format. The requesting party must state the reason that the exhibit needs to be included in the clerk's transcript. Parties may file a joint request for corrections or additions.

(B) Appellate counsel must review all sealed records that they are entitled to access under rule 8.45 and file an application to unseal any such records that counsel determines no longer meet the criteria for sealing specified in rule 2.550(d). Notwithstanding rule 8.46(e), this application must be filed in the trial court and these records may be unsealed on order of the trial court.

(2) A request for additions to the reporter's transcript must state the nature and date of the proceedings and, if known, the identity of the reporter who reported them. A request for an exhibit to be included in the clerk's transcript must specify that exhibit by number or letter.

(3) Unless otherwise ordered by the court, within 10 days after a party serves and files a request for corrections or additions to the record, defendant's appellate counsel and the trial counsel from the prosecutor's office must confer regarding the request and any application to unseal records served on the prosecutor's office.

(4) If the clerk's and reporter's transcripts combined exceed 10,000 pages, the time limits stated in (1), (3), and (b)(4) are extended by 15 days for each 1,000 pages of combined transcript over 10,000 pages.

(b) Correction of the record

(1) If any counsel files a request for corrections or additions, the procedures and time limits of rule 8.619(c)(1)–(5) must be followed.

(2) If any application to unseal a record is filed, the judge must grant or deny the application before certifying the record as accurate.

(3) When the judge is satisfied that all corrections or additions ordered have been made, the judge must certify the record as accurate and redeliver the record to the clerk.

(4) The judge must certify the record as accurate within 30 days after the last request to include additional materials or make corrections is filed.

(c) Copies of the record

(1) When the record is certified as accurate, the clerk must promptly notify the reporter to prepare six copies of the reporter's transcript in electronic form and two additional copies in electronic form for each codefendant sentenced to death.

(2) In preparing the copies, the procedures and time limits of rule 8.619(d)(2)–(5) must be followed.

(d) Extension of time

(1) The court may extend for good cause any of the periods specified in this rule.

(2) An application to extend the period to request corrections or additions under (a) must be served and filed within that period.

(3) If the court orders an extension of time, the order must specify the justification for the extension. The clerk must promptly send a copy of the order to the Supreme Court.

(4) If the court orders an extension of time, the court may conduct a status conference or require the counsel who requested the extension to file a status report on counsel's progress in reviewing the record.

(e) Sending the certified record

When the record is certified as accurate, the clerk must promptly send:

(1) To the Supreme Court: the corrected original record, including the judge's certificate of accuracy. The reporter's transcript must be in electronic form. The clerk is encouraged to send the clerk's transcript in electronic form if the court is able to do so.

(2) To each defendant's appellate counsel, each defendant's habeas corpus counsel, the Attorney General, the Habeas Corpus Resource Center, and the California Appellate Project in San Francisco: a copy of the order certifying the record and a copy of the reporter's transcript in electronic form.

(3) To the Governor: the copies of the transcripts required by Penal Code section 1218, with copies of any corrected or augmented pages inserted. *(Formerly Rule 35.2, adopted, eff. Jan. 1, 2004. Renumbered Rule 8.622 and amended, eff. Jan. 1, 2007. As amended, eff. Jan. 1, 2018; April 25, 2019.)*

Advisory Committee Comment

Rule 8.622 implements Penal Code section 190.8(g).

Research References

6 Witkin, California Criminal Law 4th Criminal Appeal § 132 (2021), Complete Record in Capital Case.

6 Witkin, California Criminal Law 4th Criminal Appeal § 147 (2021), In General.

3 Witkin, California Criminal Law 4th Punishment § 600 (2021), Certification of Record.

Article 3

BRIEFS, HEARING, AND DECISION

Rule 8.630. Briefs by parties and amicus curiae

(a) Contents and form

Except as provided in this rule, briefs in appeals from judgments of death must comply as nearly as possible with rules 8.200 and 8.204.

(b) Length

(1) A brief produced on a computer must not exceed the following limits, including footnotes:

(A) Appellant's opening brief: 102,000 words.

(B) Respondent's brief: 102,000 words. If the Chief Justice permits the appellant to file an opening brief that exceeds the limit set in (1)(A) or (3)(A), respondent's brief may not exceed the length of appellant's opening brief approved by the Chief Justice.

(C) Reply brief: 47,600 words.

(D) Petition for rehearing and answer: 23,800 words each.

(2) A brief under (1) must include a certificate by appellate counsel stating the number of words in the brief; counsel may rely on the word count of the computer program used to prepare the brief.

(3) A typewritten brief must not exceed the following limits:

(A) Appellant's opening brief: 300 pages.

(B) Respondent's brief: 300 pages. If the Chief Justice permits the appellant to file an opening brief that exceeds the limit set in (1)(A) or (3)(A), respondent's brief may not exceed the length of appellant's opening brief approved by the Chief Justice.

(C) Reply brief: 140 pages.

(D) Petition for rehearing and answer: 70 pages each.

(4) The tables required under rule 8.204(a)(1), the cover information required under rule 8.204(b)(10), a certificate under (2), any signature block, and any attachment permitted under rule 8.204(d) are excluded from the limits stated in (1) and (3).

(5) On application, the Chief Justice may permit a longer brief for good cause. An application in any case in which the certified record is filed in the California Supreme Court on or after January 1, 2008, must comply with rule 8.631.

(c) Time to file

(1) Except as provided in (2), the times to file briefs in an appeal from a judgment of death are as follows:

(A) The appellant's opening brief must be served and filed within 210 days after the record is certified as complete or the superior court clerk delivers the completed record to the defendant's appellate counsel, whichever is later. The clerk/executive officer of the Supreme Court must promptly notify the defendant's appellate counsel and the Attorney General of the due date for the appellant's opening brief.

(B) The respondent's brief must be served and filed within 120 days after the appellant's opening brief is filed. The clerk/executive officer of the Supreme Court must promptly notify the defendant's appellate counsel and the Attorney General of the due date for the respondent's brief.

(C) If the clerk's and reporter's transcripts combined exceed 10,000 pages, the time limits stated in (A) and (B) are extended by 15 days for each 1,000 pages of combined transcript over 10,000 pages.

(D) The appellant must serve and file a reply brief, if any, within 60 days after the respondent files its brief.

(2) In any appeal from a judgment of death imposed after a trial that began before January 1, 1997, the time to file briefs is governed by rule 8.360(c).

(3) The Chief Justice may extend the time to serve and file a brief for good cause.

(d) Supplemental briefs

Supplemental briefs may be filed as provided in rule 8.520(d).

(e) Amicus curiae briefs

Amicus curiae briefs may be filed as provided in rule 8.520(f).

(f) Briefs on the court's request

The court may request additional briefs on any or all issues.

(g) Service

(1) The Supreme Court Policy on Service of Process by Counsel for Defendant governs service of the defendant's briefs.

(2) The Attorney General must serve two paper copies or one electronic copy of the respondent's brief on each defendant's appellate counsel and, for each defendant sentenced to death, one copy on the California Appellate Project in San Francisco.

(3) A copy of each brief must be served on the superior court clerk for delivery to the trial judge.

(h) Judicial notice

To obtain judicial notice by the Supreme Court under Evidence Code section 459, a party must comply with rule 8.252(a). *(Formerly Rule 36, adopted, eff. Jan. 1, 2004. Renumbered Rule 8.630 and amended, eff. Jan. 1, 2007. As amended, eff. Jan. 1, 2008; Jan. 1, 2011; Jan. 1, 2016; Jan. 1, 2018.)*

Advisory Committee Comment

Subdivision (b). Subdivision (b)(1) states the maximum permissible lengths of briefs produced on a computer in terms of word count rather than page count. This provision tracks a provision in rule 8.204(c) governing Court of Appeal briefs and is explained in the comment to that provision. Each word count assumes a brief using one-and-one-half spaced lines of text, as permitted by rule 8.204(b)(5).

Subdivision (b)(4) specifies certain items that are not counted toward the maximum brief length. Signature blocks, as referenced in this provision includes not only the signatures, but also the printed names, titles, and affiliations of any attorneys filing or joining in the brief, which may accompany the signature.

Subdivision (g). Subdivision (g)(1) is a cross-reference to Policy 4 of the Supreme Court Policies Regarding Cases Arising From Judgments of Death.

Research References

6 Witkin, California Criminal Law 4th Criminal Appeal § 153 (2021), Requirement.
6 Witkin, California Criminal Law 4th Criminal Appeal § 154 (2021), Content, Form, and Style.
6 Witkin, California Criminal Law 4th Criminal Appeal § 155 (2021), Length.
6 Witkin, California Criminal Law 4th Criminal Appeal § 156 (2021), Service and Filing.
6 Witkin, California Criminal Law 4th Criminal Appeal § 197 (2021), Rehearing in Court Rendering Decision.

Rule 8.631. Applications to file overlength briefs in appeals from a judgment of death

(a) Cases in which this rule applies

This rule applies in appeals from a judgment of death in which the certified record is filed in the California Supreme Court on or after January 1, 2008.

(b) Policies

(1) The brief limits set by rule 8.630 are substantially higher than for other appellate briefs in recognition of the number, significance, and complexity of the issues generally presented in appeals from judgments of death and are designed to be sufficient to allow counsel to prepare adequate briefs in the majority of such appeals.

(2) In a small proportion of such appeals, counsel may not be able to prepare adequate briefs within the limits set by rule 8.630. In those cases, necessary additional briefing will be permitted.

(3) A party may not file a brief that exceeds the limit set by rule 8.630 unless the court finds that good cause has been shown in an application filed within the time limits set in (d).

(c) Factors considered

The court will consider the following factors in determining whether good cause exists to grant an application to file a brief that exceeds the limit set by rule 8.630:

(1) The unusual length of the record. A party relying on this factor must specify the length of each of the following components of the record:

(A) The reporter's transcript;

(B) The clerk's transcript; and

(C) The portion of the clerk's transcript that is made up of juror questionnaires.

(2) The number of codefendants in the case and whether they were tried separately from the appellant;

(3) The number of homicide victims in the case and whether the homicides occurred in more than one incident;

(4) The number of other crimes in the case and whether they occurred in more than one incident;

(5) The number of rulings by the trial court on unusual, factually intensive, or legally complex motions that the party may assert are erroneous and prejudicial. A party relying on this factor must briefly describe the nature of these motions;

(6) The number of rulings on objections by the trial court that the party may assert are erroneous and prejudicial;

(7) The number and nature of unusual, factually intensive, or legally complex hearings held in the trial court that the party may assert raise issues on appeal; and

(8) Any other factor that is likely to contribute to an unusually high number of issues or unusually complex issues on appeal. A party relying on this factor must briefly specify those issues.

(d) Time to file and contents of application

(1) An application to file a brief that exceeds the limits set by rule 8.630 must be served and filed as follows:

(A) For an appellant's opening brief or respondent's brief:

(i) If counsel has not filed an application requesting an extension of time to file the brief, no later than 45 days before the brief is due.

(ii) If counsel has filed an application requesting an extension of time to file the brief, within the time specified by the court in its order regarding the extension of time.

(B) For an appellant's reply brief:

(i) If counsel has not filed an application requesting an extension of time to file the brief, no later than 30 days before the brief is due.

(ii) If counsel has filed an application requesting an extension of time to file the brief, within the time specified by the court in its order regarding the extension of time.

(2) After the time specified in (1), an application to file a brief that exceeds the applicable limit may be filed only under the following circumstances:

(A) New authority substantially affects the issues presented in the case and cannot be adequately addressed without exceeding the applicable limit. Such an application must be filed within 30 days of finality of the new authority; or

(B) Replacement counsel has been appointed to represent the appellant and has determined that it is necessary to file a brief that exceeds the applicable limit. Such an application must be filed within the time specified by the court in its order setting the deadline for replacement counsel to file the appellant's brief.

(3) The application must:

(A) State the number of additional words or typewritten pages requested.

(B) State good cause for granting the additional words or pages requested, consistent with the factors in (c). The number of additional words or pages requested must be commensurate with the good cause shown. The application must explain why the factors identified demonstrate good cause in the particular case. The application must not state mere conclusions or make legal arguments regarding the merits of the issues on appeal.

(C) Not exceed 5,100 words if produced on a computer or 15 pages if typewritten.

(Adopted, eff. Jan. 1, 2008.)

Advisory Committee Comment

Subdivision (a). In all cases in which a judgment of death was imposed after a trial that began after January 1, 1997, the record filed with the Supreme Court will be the record that has been certified for accuracy under rule 8.622. In cases in which a judgment of death was imposed after a trial that began before January 1, 1997, the record filed with the Supreme Court will be the certified record under rule 8.625.

Subdivision (c)(1)(A). As in guideline 8 of the Supreme Court's Guidelines for Fixed Fee Appointments, juror questionnaires generally will not be taken into account in considering whether the length of the record is unusual unless these questionnaires are relevant to an issue on appeal. A record of 10,000 pages or less, excluding juror questionnaires, is not considered a record of unusual length; 70 percent of the records in capital appeals filed between 2001 and 2004 were 10,000 pages or less, excluding juror questionnaires.

Subdivision (c)(1)(E). Examples of unusual, factually intensive, or legally complex motions include motions to change venue, admit scientific evidence, or determine competency.

Subdivisions (c)(1)(E)–(I). Because an application must be filed before briefing is completed, the issues identified in the application will be those that the party anticipates may be raised on appeal. If the party does not ultimately raise all of these issues on appeal, the party is expected to have reduced the length of the brief accordingly.

Subdivision (c)(1)(I). Examples of unusual, factually intensive, or legally complex hearings include jury composition proceedings and hearings to determine the defendant's competency or sanity, whether the defendant is mentally retarded, and whether the defendant may represent himself or herself.

Subdivision (d)(1)A)(ii). To allow the deadline for an application to file an overlength brief to be appropriately tied to the deadline for filing that brief, if counsel requests an extension of time to file a brief, the court will specify in its order regarding the request to extend the time to file the brief, when any application to file an overlength brief is due. Although the order will specify the deadline by which an application must be filed, counsel are encouraged to file such applications sooner, if possible.

Subdivision (d)(3). These requirements apply to applications filed under either (d)(1) or (d)(2).

Research References

6 Witkin, California Criminal Law 4th Criminal Appeal § 155 (2021), Length.

Rule 8.634. Transmitting exhibits; augmenting the record in the Supreme Court

(a) Application

Except as provided in (b), rule 8.224 governs the transmission of exhibits to the Supreme Court.

(b) Time to file notice of designation

No party may file a notice designating exhibits under rule 8.224(a) until the clerk/executive officer of the Supreme Court notifies the parties of the time and place of oral argument.

(c) Augmenting the record in the Supreme Court

At any time, on motion of a party or on its own motion, the Supreme Court may order the record augmented or corrected as provided in rule 8.155. *(Formerly Rule 36.1, adopted, eff. Jan. 1, 2003. As amended, eff. Jan. 1, 2004. Renumbered Rule 8.634 and amended, eff. Jan. 1, 2007. As amended, eff. Jan. 1, 2018.)*

Research References

6 Witkin, California Criminal Law 4th Criminal Appeal § 132 (2021), Complete Record in Capital Case.

6 Witkin, California Criminal Law 4th Criminal Appeal § 149 (2021), Procedure.

6 Witkin, California Criminal Law 4th Criminal Appeal § 151 (2021), Correction by Order of Appellate Court.

Rule 8.638. Oral argument and submission of the cause

(a) Application

Except as provided in (b), rule 8.524 governs oral argument and submission of the cause in the Supreme Court unless the court provides otherwise in its Internal Operating Practices and Procedures or by order.

(b) Procedure

(1) The appellant has the right to open and close.

(2) Each side is allowed 45 minutes for argument.

(3) Two counsel may argue on each side if, within 10 days after the date of the order setting the case for argument, they notify the court that the case requires it. *(Formerly Rule 36.2, adopted, eff. Jan. 1, 2003. As amended, eff. Jan. 1, 2004. Renumbered Rule 8.638 and amended, eff. Jan. 1, 2007.)*

Research References

6 Witkin, California Criminal Law 4th Criminal Appeal § 158 (2021), In General.

Rule 8.642. Filing, finality, and modification of decision; rehearing; remittitur

Rules 8.532 through 8.540 govern the filing, finality, and modification of decision, rehearing, and issuance of remittitur by the Supreme Court in an appeal from a judgment of death. *(Formerly Rule 36.3, adopted, eff. Jan. 1, 2004. Renumbered Rule 8.642 and amended, eff. Jan. 1, 2007.)*

Research References

6 Witkin, California Criminal Law 4th Criminal Appeal § 2 (2021), Appellate Rules.

Chapter 3

DEATH PENALTY–RELATED HABEAS CORPUS PROCEEDINGS

Rule

Rule 8.652. Qualifications of counsel in death penalty-related habeas corpus proceedings

(a) Purpose

This rule defines the minimum qualifications for attorneys to be appointed by a court to represent a person in a habeas corpus proceeding related to a sentence of death. These minimum qualifications are designed to promote competent representation in habeas corpus proceedings related to sentences of death and to avoid unnecessary delay and expense by assisting the courts in appointing qualified counsel. Nothing in this rule is intended to be used as a standard by which to measure whether a person received effective assistance of counsel. An attorney is not entitled to appointment simply because the attorney meets these minimum qualifications.

(b) General qualifications

An attorney may be included on a panel, appointed by the Supreme Court, or appointed by a court under a local rule as provided in rule 4.562, only if it is determined, after reviewing the attorney's experience, training, writing samples, references, and evaluations, that the attorney meets the minimum qualifications in this rule and has demonstrated the commitment, knowledge, and skills necessary to competently represent a person in a habeas corpus proceeding related to a sentence of death. An appointed attorney must be willing to cooperate with an assisting counsel or entity that the appointing court designates.

(c) Qualifications for appointed habeas corpus counsel

An attorney included on a panel, appointed by the Supreme Court, or appointed by a court under a local rule as provided in rule 4.562, must satisfy the following minimum qualifications:

(1) *California legal experience*

Active practice of law in California for at least five years.

(2) *Case experience*

The case experience identified in (A), (B), or (C).

(A) Service as counsel of record for a petitioner in a death penalty-related habeas corpus proceeding in which the petition has been filed in the California Supreme Court, a Court of Appeal, or a superior court.

(B) Service as:

(i) Supervised counsel in two death penalty-related habeas corpus proceedings in which the petition has been filed. Service as supervised counsel in a death penalty-related habeas corpus proceeding will apply toward this qualification only if lead or associate counsel in that proceeding attests that the attorney performed substantial work on the case and recommends the attorney for appointment; and

(ii) Counsel of record for either party in a combination of at least five completed appeals, habeas corpus proceedings, or jury trials in felony cases, including as counsel of record for a petitioner in at least two habeas corpus proceedings, each involving a serious felony in which the petition has been filed. Service as counsel of record in an appeal where counsel did not file a brief, or in a habeas corpus proceeding where counsel did not file a petition, informal response, or a return, does not satisfy any part of this combined case experience. The combined case experience must be sufficient to demonstrate proficiency in investigation, issue identification, and writing.

(C) Service as counsel of record for either party in a combination of at least eight completed appeals, habeas corpus proceedings, or jury trials in felony cases, including as counsel of record for a petitioner in at least two habeas corpus proceedings, each involving a serious felony in which the petition has been filed. Service as counsel of record in an appeal where counsel did not file a brief, or in a habeas corpus proceeding where counsel did not file a petition, informal response, or a return, does not satisfy any part of this combined case experience. The combined case experience must be sufficient to demonstrate proficiency in investigation, issue identification, and writing.

(3) *Knowledge*

Familiarity with the practices and procedures of the California courts and the federal courts in death penalty-related habeas corpus proceedings.

(4) *Training*

(A) Within three years before being included on a panel, appointed by the Supreme Court, or appointed by a court under a local rule as provided in rule 4.562, completion of at least 15 hours of appellate criminal defense or habeas corpus defense training approved for Minimum Continuing Legal Education credit by the State Bar of California, at least 10 hours of which address death penalty-related habeas corpus proceedings.

(B) Counsel who serves as an instructor in a course that satisfies the requirements of this rule may receive course participation credit for instruction, on request to and approval by the committee, the Supreme Court, or a court appointing counsel under a local rule as provided in rule 4.562, in an amount to be determined by the approving entity.

(C) If the attorney has previously represented a petitioner in a death penalty-related habeas corpus proceeding, the committee, the Supreme Court, or the court appointing counsel under a local rule as provided in rule 4.562, after reviewing counsel's previous work, may find that such representation constitutes compliance with some or all of this requirement.

(5) *Skills*

Demonstrated proficiency in issue identification, research, analysis, writing, investigation, and advocacy. To enable an assessment of the attorney's skills:

(A) The attorney must submit:

(i) Three writing samples written by the attorney and presenting analyses of complex legal issues. If the attorney has previously served as lead counsel of record for a petitioner in a death penalty-related habeas corpus proceeding, these writing samples must include one or more habeas corpus petitions filed by the attorney in that capacity. If the attorney has previously served as associate or supervised counsel for a petitioner in a death penalty-related habeas corpus proceeding, these writing samples must include the portion of the habeas corpus petition prepared by the attorney in that capacity. If the attorney has not served as lead counsel of record for a petitioner in a death penalty-related habeas corpus proceeding, these writing samples must include two or more habeas corpus petitions filed by the attorney as counsel of record for a petitioner in a habeas corpus proceeding involving a serious felony; and

(ii) Recommendations from two attorneys familiar with the attorney's qualifications and performance.

(B) The committee, the Supreme Court, or the court appointing counsel under a local rule as provided in rule 4.562, must obtain and review:

(i) If the attorney has previously been appointed in a death penalty appeal or death penalty-related habeas corpus proceeding, the evaluation of the assisting counsel or entity in those proceedings; and

(ii) If the attorney is on a panel of attorneys eligible for appointments to represent indigent appellants in the Court of Appeal, the evaluation of the administrator responsible for those appointments.

(d) Alternative experience

An attorney who does not meet the experience requirements of (c)(1) and (2) may be included on a panel or appointed by the Supreme Court if the attorney meets the qualifications described in (c)(3) and (5), excluding the writing samples described in (c)(5)(A)(i), and:

(1) The committee or the Supreme Court finds that the attorney has:

(A) Extensive experience as an attorney at the Habeas Corpus Resource Center or the California Appellate Project–San Francisco, or in another jurisdiction or a different type of practice (such as civil trials or appeals, academic work, or work for a court or as a prosecutor), for at least five years, providing the attorney with experience in complex cases substantially equivalent to that of an attorney qualified under (c)(1) and (2); and

(B) Demonstrated proficiency in issue identification, research, analysis, writing, investigation, and advocacy. To enable an assessment of the attorney's skills, the attorney must submit three writing samples written by the attorney and presenting analyses of complex legal issues, including habeas corpus petitions filed by the attorney, if any.

(2) Ongoing consultation is available to the attorney from an assisting counsel or entity designated by the court.

(3) Within two years before being included on a panel or appointed by the Supreme Court, the attorney has completed at least 18 hours of appellate criminal defense or habeas corpus defense training approved for Minimum Continuing Legal Education credit by the State Bar of California, at least 10 hours of which involve death penalty-related habeas corpus proceedings. The committee or the Supreme Court will determine whether the training completed by an attorney satisfies the requirements of this subdivision in light of the attorney's individual background and experience.

(e) Attorneys without trial experience

If an evidentiary hearing is ordered in a death penalty-related habeas corpus proceeding and an attorney appointed under (c) or (d) to represent a person in that proceeding lacks experience in conducting trials or evidentiary hearings, the attorney must associate with an attorney who has such experience.

(f) Use of supervised counsel

An attorney who does not meet the qualifications described in (c) or (d) may assist lead or associate counsel, but must work under the immediate supervision and direction of lead or associate counsel.

(g) Appellate and habeas corpus appointment

(1) An attorney appointed to represent a person in both a death penalty appeal and death penalty-related habeas corpus proceedings must meet the minimum qualifications of both (c) or (d) and rule 8.605.

(2) Notwithstanding (1), two attorneys together may be eligible for appointment to represent a person jointly in both a death penalty appeal and death penalty-related habeas corpus proceedings if it is determined that one attorney satisfies the minimum qualifications stated in (c) or (d) and the other attorney satisfies the minimum qualifications stated in rule 8.605.

(h) Entities as appointed counsel

(1) Notwithstanding any other provision of this rule, the Habeas Corpus Resource Center and the California Appellate Project–San Francisco are qualified to serve as appointed counsel in death penalty-related habeas corpus proceedings.

(2) When serving as appointed counsel in a death penalty-related habeas corpus proceeding, the Habeas Corpus Resource Center or the California Appellate Project–San Francisco must not assign any attorney as lead counsel unless it finds the attorney is qualified under (c) or (d).

(i) Attorney appointed by federal court

Notwithstanding any other provision of this rule, a court may appoint an attorney who is under appointment by a federal court in a death penalty-related habeas corpus proceeding for the purpose of exhausting state remedies in the California courts if the court finds that the attorney has the commitment, proficiency, and knowledge necessary to represent the person competently in state proceedings. Counsel under appointment by a federal court is not required to also be appointed by a state court in order to appear in a state court proceeding. *(Adopted, eff. April 25, 2019.)*

Research References

6 Witkin, California Criminal Law 4th Criminal Writs § 67A (2021), (New) in General.

6 Witkin, California Criminal Law 4th Criminal Writs § 67C (2021), (New) Rules and Forms.

Division 4

RULES RELATING TO THE SUPERIOR COURT APPELLATE DIVISION

Chapter 1

GENERAL RULES APPLICABLE TO APPELLATE DIVISION PROCEEDINGS

Rule 8.800. Application of division and scope of rules

(a) Application

The rules in this division apply to:

(1) Appeals in the appellate division of the superior court; and

(2) Writ proceedings, motions, applications, and petitions in the appellate division of the superior court.

(b) Scope of rules

The rules in this division apply to documents filed and served electronically as well as in paper form, unless otherwise provided. *(Adopted, eff. Jan. 1, 2009. As amended, eff. Jan. 1, 2016.)*

Research References

West's California Judicial Council Forms App–101–INFO, Information on Appeal Procedures for Limited Civil Cases.

West's California Judicial Council Forms CR–131–INFO, Information on Appeal Procedures for Misdemeanors.

6 Witkin, California Criminal Law 4th Criminal Appeal § 1 (2021), Appellate Jurisdiction.

6 Witkin, California Criminal Law 4th Criminal Appeal § 206 (2021), In General.

4 Witkin, California Criminal Law 4th Illegally Obtained Evidence § 468 (2021), Review by Appeal (Misdemeanor).

4 Witkin, California Criminal Law 4th Illegally Obtained Evidence § 479 (2021), Misdemeanor Prosecution: Appeal from Order Granting Motion.

Rule 8.802. Construction

(a) Construction

The rules in this division must be construed to ensure that the proceedings they govern will be justly and speedily determined.

(b) Terminology

As used in this division:

(1) "Must" is mandatory;

(2) "May" is permissive;

(3) "May not" means is not permitted to;

(4) "Will" expresses a future contingency or predicts action by a court or person in the ordinary course of events, but does not signify a mandatory duty; and

(5) "Should" expresses a preference or a nonbinding recommendation.

(c) Construction of additional terms

In the rules:

(1) Each tense (past, present, or future) includes the others;

(2) Each gender (masculine, feminine, or neuter) includes the others;

(3) Each number (singular or plural) includes the other; and

(4) The headings of divisions, chapters, articles, rules, and subdivisions are substantive. *(Adopted, eff. Jan. 1, 2009.)*

Rule 8.803. Definitions

As used in this division, unless the context or subject matter otherwise requires:

(1) "Action" includes special proceeding.

(2) "Case" includes action or proceeding.

(3) "Civil case" means a case prosecuted by one party against another for the declaration, enforcement, or protection of a right or the redress or prevention of a wrong. Civil cases include all cases except criminal cases.

(4) "Unlimited civil cases" and "limited civil cases" are defined in Code of Civil Procedure section 85 et seq.

(5) "Criminal case" means a proceeding by which a party charged with a public offense is accused and brought to trial and punishment.

(6) "Rule" means a rule of the California Rules of Court.

(7) "Local rule" means every rule, regulation, order, policy, form, or standard of general application adopted by a court to govern practice and procedure in that court or by a judge of the court to govern practice or procedure in that judge's courtroom.

(8) "Presiding judge" includes the acting presiding judge or the judge designated by the presiding judge.

(9) "Judge" includes, as applicable, a judge of the superior court, a commissioner, or a temporary judge.

(10) "Person" includes a corporation or other legal entity as well as a natural person.

(11) "Appellant" means the appealing party.

(12) "Respondent" means the adverse party.

(13) "Party" is a person appearing in an action. Parties include both self-represented persons and persons represented by an attorney of record. "Party," "applicant," "petitioner," or any other designation of a party includes the party's attorney of record.

(14) "Attorney" means a member of the State Bar of California.

(15) "Counsel" means an attorney.

(16) "Prosecuting attorney" means the city attorney, county counsel, or district attorney prosecuting an infraction or misdemeanor case.

(17) "Complaint" includes a citation.

(18) "Service" means service in the manner prescribed by a statute or rule.

(19) "Declaration" includes "affidavit."

(20) "Trial court" means the superior court from which an appeal is taken.

(21) "Reviewing court" means the appellate division of the superior court.

(22) "Judgment" includes any judgment or order that may be appealed.

(23) "Attach" or "attachment" may refer to either physical attachment or electronic attachment, as appropriate.

(24) "Copy" or "copies" may refer to electronic copies, as appropriate.

(25) "Cover" includes the cover page of a document filed electronically.

(26) "Written" and "writing" include electronically created written materials, whether or not those materials are printed on paper. *(Formerly Rule 8.804, adopted, eff. Jan. 1, 2009. As amended, eff. Jan. 1, 2014. Renumbered Rule 8.803 and amended, eff. Jan. 1, 2016.)*

Advisory Committee Comment

Item (18). See rule 1.21 for general requirements relating to service, including proof of service.

Rule 8.804. Requirements for signatures on documents

Except as otherwise provided, or required by order of the court, signatures on electronically filed documents must comply with the requirements of rule 8.77. *(Adopted, eff. Jan. 1, 2016.)*

Rule 8.805. Amendments to rules and statutes

(a) Amendments to rules

Only the Judicial Council may amend these rules, except the rules in division 5, which may be amended only by the Supreme Court. An amendment by the Judicial Council must be published in the advance pamphlets of the Official Reports and takes effect on the date ordered by the Judicial Council.

(b) Amendments to statutes

In these rules, a reference to a statute includes any subsequent amendment to the statute. *(Adopted, eff. Jan. 1, 2009.)*

Rule 8.806. Applications

(a) Service and filing

Except as these rules provide otherwise, parties must serve and file all applications, including applications to extend time to file records, briefs, or other documents and applications to shorten time. Applications to extend the time to prepare the record on appeal may be filed in either the trial court or the appellate division. All other applications must be filed in the appellate division. For good cause, the presiding judge of the court where the application was filed, or his or her designee, may excuse advance service.

(b) Contents

The application must:

(1) State facts showing good cause to grant the application; and

(2) Identify any previous applications relating to the same subject filed by any party in the same appeal or writ proceeding.

(c) Envelopes

If any party or parties in the case are served in paper form, an application must be accompanied by addressed, postage-prepaid envelopes for the clerk's use in mailing copies of the order on the application to those parties.

(d) Disposition

Unless the court determines otherwise, the presiding judge of the court in which the application was filed, or his or her designee, may rule on the application. *(Adopted, eff. Jan. 1, 2009. As amended, eff. Jan. 1, 2016.)*

Advisory Committee Comment

Subdivision (a). See rule 1.21 for the meaning of "serve and file," including the requirements for proof of service.

Subdivisions (a) and (d). These provisions permit the presiding judge to designate another judge, such as the trial judge, to handle applications.

Rule 8.808. Motions

(a) Motion and opposition

(1) Except as these rules provide otherwise, to make a motion in the appellate division a party must serve and file a written motion, stating the grounds and the relief requested and identifying any documents on which it is based.

(2) A motion must be accompanied by a memorandum and, if it is based on matters outside the record, by declarations or other supporting evidence.

(3) Any opposition to the motion must be served and filed within 15 days after the motion is filed.

(b) Disposition

(1) The court may rule on a motion at any time after an opposition or other response is filed or the time to oppose has expired.

(2) On a party's request or its own motion, the appellate division may place a motion on calendar for a hearing. The clerk must promptly send each party a notice of the date and time of the hearing. *(Adopted, eff. Jan. 1, 2009.)*

Advisory Committee Comment

Subdivision (a)(1). See rule 1.21 for the meaning of "serve and file," including the requirements for proof of service.

Subdivision (b). Although a party may request a hearing on a motion, a hearing will be held only if the court determines that one is needed.

Research References

6 Witkin, California Criminal Law 4th Criminal Appeal § 206 (2021), In General.

Rule 8.809. Judicial notice

(a) Motion required

(1) To obtain judicial notice by a reviewing court under Evidence Code section 459, a party must serve and file a separate motion with a proposed order.

(2) The motion must state:

(A) Why the matter to be noticed is relevant to the appeal;

(B) Whether the matter to be noticed was presented to the trial court and, if so, whether judicial notice was taken by that court;

(C) If judicial notice of the matter was not taken by the trial court, why the matter is subject to judicial notice under Evidence Code section 451, 452, or 453; and

(D) Whether the matter to be noticed relates to proceedings occurring after the order or judgment that is the subject of the appeal.

(b) Copy of matter to be judicially noticed

If the matter to be noticed is not in the record, the party must serve and file a copy with the motion or explain why it is not practicable to do so. The pages of the copy of the matter or matters to be judicially noticed must be consecutively numbered, beginning with the number 1. *(Adopted, eff. Jan. 1, 2011. As amended, eff. Jan. 1, 2013; Jan. 1, 2015.)*

Rule 8.810. Extending time

(a) Computing time

The Code of Civil Procedure governs computing and extending the time to do any act required or permitted under these rules.

(b) Extension by trial court

(1) For good cause and except as these rules provide otherwise, the presiding judge of the trial court, or his or her designee, may extend the time to do any act to prepare the record on appeal.

(2) The trial court may not extend:

(A) The time to do an act if that time—including any valid extension—has expired; or

(B) The time for a court reporter to prepare a transcript.

(3) Notwithstanding anything in these rules to the contrary, the trial court may grant an initial extension to any party to do any act to prepare the record on appeal on an ex parte basis.

(c) Extension by appellate division

For good cause and except as these rules provide otherwise, the presiding judge of the appellate division, or his or her designee, may extend the time to do any act required or permitted under these rules, except the time to file a notice of appeal.

(d) Application for extension

(1) An application to extend time, including an application requesting an extension of time to prepare a transcript from either a court reporter or a person preparing a transcript of an official electronic recording, must be served on all parties. For good cause, the presiding judge of the appellate division, or his or her designee, may excuse advance service.

(2) The application must include a declaration stating facts, not mere conclusions, that establish good cause for granting the extension. For applications filed by counsel or self-represented litigants, the facts provided to establish good cause must be consistent with the policies and factors stated in rule 8.811.

(3) The application must state:

(A) The due date of the document to be filed;

(B) The length of the extension requested; and

(C) Whether any earlier extensions have been granted and, if so, their lengths.

(e) Notice to party

(1) In a civil case, counsel must deliver to his or her client or clients a copy of any stipulation or application to extend time that counsel files. Counsel must attach evidence of such delivery to the stipulation or application or certify in the stipulation or application that the copy has been delivered.

(2) The evidence or certification of delivery under (1) need not include the address of the party notified. *(Adopted, eff. Jan. 1, 2009. As amended, eff. March 1, 2014.)*

Advisory Committee Comment

Subdivision (b)(1). This provision permits the presiding judge to designate another judge, such as the trial judge, to handle applications to extend time.

Research References

6 Witkin, California Criminal Law 4th Criminal Appeal § 98 (2021), General Rule.

6 Witkin, California Criminal Law 4th Criminal Appeal § 208 (2021), Notice of Appeal.

Rule 8.811. Policies and factors governing extensions of time

(a) Policies

(1) The time limits prescribed by these rules should generally be met to ensure expeditious conduct of appellate business and public confidence in the efficient administration of appellate justice.

Ct. Rules

(2) The effective assistance of counsel to which a party is entitled includes adequate time for counsel to prepare briefs or other documents that fully advance the party's interests. Adequate time also allows the preparation of accurate, clear, concise, and complete submissions that assist the courts.

(3) For a variety of legitimate reasons, counsel or self-represented litigants may not always be able to prepare briefs or other documents within the time specified in the rules of court. To balance the competing policies stated in (1) and (2), applications to extend time in the appellate division must demonstrate good cause under (b). If good cause is shown, the court must extend the time.

(b) Factors considered

In determining good cause, the court must consider the following factors when applicable:

(1) The degree of prejudice, if any, to any party from a grant or denial of the extension. A party claiming prejudice must support the claim in detail.

(2) In a civil case, the positions of the client and any opponent with regard to the extension.

(3) The length of the record, including the number of relevant trial exhibits. A party relying on this factor must specify the length of the record.

(4) The number and complexity of the issues raised. A party relying on this factor must specify the issues.

(5) Whether there are settlement negotiations and, if so, how far they have progressed and when they might be completed.

(6) Whether the case is entitled to priority.

(7) Whether counsel responsible for preparing the document is new to the case.

(8) Whether other counsel or the client needs additional time to review the document.

(9) Whether counsel or a self-represented party responsible for preparing the document has other time-limited commitments that prevent timely filing of the document. Mere conclusory statements that more time is needed because of other pressing business will not suffice. Good cause requires a specific showing of other obligations of counsel or a self-represented party that:

(A) Have deadlines that as a practical matter preclude filing the document by the due date without impairing its quality; or

(B) Arise from cases entitled to priority.

(10) Illness of counsel or a self-represented party, a personal emergency, or a planned vacation that counsel or a self-represented party did not reasonably expect to conflict with the due date and cannot reasonably rearrange.

(11) Any other factor that constitutes good cause in the context of the case. *(Adopted, eff. Jan. 1, 2009.)*

Rule 8.812. Relief from default

For good cause, the presiding judge of the appellate division, or his or her designee, may relieve a party from a default for any failure to comply with these rules, except the failure to file a timely notice of appeal. *(Adopted, eff. Jan. 1, 2009.)*

Research References

6 Witkin, California Criminal Law 4th Criminal Appeal § 214 (2021), Relief from Default.

Rule 8.813. Shortening time

For good cause and except as these rules provide otherwise, the presiding judge of the appellate division, or his or her designee, may shorten the time to do any act required or permitted under these rules. *(Adopted, eff. Jan. 1, 2009.)*

Rule 8.814. Substituting parties; substituting or withdrawing attorneys

(a) Substituting parties

Substitution of parties in an appeal or original proceeding must be made by serving and filing a motion in the appellate division. The clerk of the appellate division must notify the trial court of any ruling on the motion.

(b) Substituting attorneys

A party may substitute attorneys by serving and filing in the appellate division a stipulation signed by the party represented and the new attorney.

(c) Withdrawing attorney

(1) An attorney may request withdrawal by filing a motion to withdraw. Unless the court orders otherwise, the motion need be served only on the party represented and the attorneys directly affected.

(2) The proof of service need not include the address of the party represented. But if the court grants the motion, the withdrawing attorney must promptly provide the court and the opposing party with the party's current or last known address, e-mail address, and telephone number.

(3) In all appeals and in original proceedings related to a trial court proceeding, the appellate division clerk must notify the trial court of any ruling on the motion. *(Adopted, eff. Jan. 1, 2009. As amended, eff. Jan. 1, 2016.)*

Rule 8.815. Form of filed documents

Except as these rules provide otherwise, documents filed in the appellate division may be either produced on a computer or typewritten and must comply with the relevant provisions of rule 8.883(c). *(Adopted, eff. Jan. 1, 2020.)*

Rule 8.816. Address and other contact information of record; notice of change

(a) Address and other contact information of record

(1) Except as provided in (2), the cover—or first page if there is no cover—of every document filed in the appellate division must include the name, mailing address, telephone number, fax number (if available), e-mail address (if available), and California State Bar number of each attorney filing or joining in the document, or of the party if he or she is unrepresented. The inclusion of a fax number or e-mail address on any document does not constitute consent to service by fax or e-mail unless otherwise provided by law.

(2) If more than one attorney from a law firm, corporation, or public law office is representing one party and is joining in the document, the name and State Bar number of each attorney joining in the document must be provided on the cover. The law firm, corporation, or public law office representing each party must designate one attorney to receive notices and other communication in the case from the court by placing an asterisk before that attorney's name on the cover and need must provide the contact information specified under (1) for that attorney. Contact information for the other attorneys from the same law firm, corporation, or public law office is not required but may be provided.

(3) In any case pending before the appellate division, the appellate division will use the mailing address, telephone number, fax number, and e-mail address that an attorney or unrepresented party provides on the first document filed in that case as the mailing address, telephone number, fax number, and e-mail address of record unless the attorney or unrepresented party files a notice under (b).

(b) Notice of change

(1) An attorney or unrepresented party whose mailing address, telephone number, fax number, or e-mail address changes while a

case is pending must promptly serve and file a written notice of the change in the appellate division in which the case is pending.

(2) The notice must specify the title and number of the case or cases to which it applies. If an attorney gives the notice, the notice must include the attorney's California State Bar number.

(c) Multiple addresses or other contact information

If an attorney or unrepresented party has more than one mailing address, telephone number, fax number, or e-mail address, only one mailing address, telephone number, fax number, and e-mail address may be used in a given case. *(Adopted, eff. Jan. 1, 2009. As amended, eff. Jan. 1, 2013.)*

Research References

West's California Judicial Council Forms MC–040, Notice of Change of Address or Other Contact.

Rule 8.817. Service and filing

(a) Service

(1) Before filing any document, a party must serve, by any method permitted by the Code of Civil Procedure, one copy of the document on the attorney for each party separately represented, on each unrepresented party, and on any other person or entity when required by statute or rule.

(2) The party must attach to the document presented for filing a proof of service showing service on each person or entity required to be served under (1). The proof must name each party represented by each attorney served.

(b) Filing

(1) A document is deemed filed on the date the clerk receives it.

(2) Unless otherwise provided by these rules or other law, a filing is not timely unless the clerk receives the document before the time to file it expires.

(3) A brief, a petition for rehearing, or an answer to a petition for rehearing is timely if the time to file it has not expired on the date of:

(A) Its mailing by priority or express mail as shown on the postmark or the postal receipt; or

(B) Its delivery to a common carrier promising overnight delivery as shown on the carrier's receipt.

(4) The provisions of (3) do not apply to original proceedings.

(5) If the clerk receives a document by mail from an inmate or a patient in a custodial institution after the period for filing the document has expired but the envelope shows that the document was mailed or delivered to custodial officials for mailing within the period for filing the document, the document is deemed timely. The clerk must retain in the case file the envelope in which the document was received. *(Adopted, eff. Jan. 1, 2009. As amended, eff. July 1, 2010.)*

Advisory Committee Comment

Subdivision (a). Subdivision (a)(1) requires service "by any method permitted by the Code of Civil Procedure." The reference is to the several permissible methods of service provided in Code of Civil Procedure sections 1010–1020. *What Is Proof of Service?* (form APP–109–INFO) provides additional information about how to serve documents and how to provide proof of service.

Subdivision (b). In general, to be filed on time, a document must be received by the clerk before the time for filing that document expires. There are, however, some limited exceptions to this general rule. For example, (5) provides that if the superior court clerk receives a document by mail from a custodial institution after the deadline for filing the document has expired but the envelope shows that the document was mailed or delivered to custodial officials for mailing before the deadline expired, the document is deemed timely. This provision reflects the "prison-delivery" exception articulated by the California Supreme Court in *In re Jordan* (1992) 4 Cal. 4th 116 and *Silverbrand v. County of Los Angeles* (2009) 46 Cal.4th 106.

Note that if a deadline runs from the date of filing, it runs from the date that the document is actually received and deemed filed under (b)(1); neither (b)(3) nor (b)(5) changes that date. Nor do these provisions extend the date of finality of an appellate opinion or any other deadline that is based on finality, such as the deadline for the court to modify its opinion or order rehearing. Subdivision (b)(5) is also not intended to limit a criminal defendant's appeal rights under the case law of constructive filing. (See, e.g., *In re Benoit* (1973) 10 Cal.3d 72.)

Research References

6 Witkin, California Criminal Law 4th Criminal Appeal § 206 (2021), In General.

3 Witkin, California Criminal Law 4th Punishment § 54 (2021), Access to Civil Courts.

Rule 8.818. Waiver of fees and costs

(a) Applications for waiver of fees and costs

(1) *Appeals*

(A) If the trial court previously issued an order granting a party's request to waive court fees and costs in a case, and that fee waiver is still in effect, all of the court fees for an appeal to the appellate division in that case that are listed in (d) are waived by that order, and the party is not required to file a new application for waiver of court fees and costs for an appeal to the appellate division in that case.

(B) If the trial court did not previously issue an order granting a party's request to waive court fees and costs in a case or an order that was previously issued is no longer in effect, an application for initial waiver of court fees and costs for an appeal must be made on *Request to Waive Court Fees* (form FW–001). The appellant should file the application with the notice of appeal in the trial court that issued the judgment or order being appealed. The respondent should file any application at the time the fees are to be paid to the court.

(2) *Writ Proceedings*

To request the waiver of fees and costs in a writ proceeding, the petitioner must complete *Request to Waive Court Fees* (form FW–001). The petitioner should file the application with the writ petition.

(3) *Forms*

The clerk must provide *Request to Waive Court Fees* (form FW–001) and *Information Sheet on Waiver of Fees and Costs (Supreme Court, Court of Appeal, Appellate Division)* (form APP–015/FW–015–INFO) without charge to any person who requests any fee waiver application or states that he or she is unable to pay any court fee or cost.

(b) Procedure for determining application

The application must be considered and determined as required by Government Code section 68634.5. An order determining the application for initial fee waiver or setting a hearing on the application may be made on *Order on Court Fee Waiver (Superior Court)* (form FW–003).

(c) Application granted unless acted on by the court

The application for initial fee waiver is deemed granted unless the court gives notice of action on the application within five court days after the application is filed.

(d) Court fees and costs waived.

Court fees and costs that must be waived upon granting an application for initial waiver of court fees and costs are listed in rule 3.55. The court may waive other necessary court fees and costs itemized in the application upon granting the application, either at the outset or upon later application.

(e) Denial of the application

If an application is denied, the applicant must pay the court fees and costs or submit the new application or additional information requested by the court within 10 days after the clerk gives notice of the denial.

(f) Confidential Records

(1) No person may have access to an application for an initial fee waiver submitted to the court except the court and authorized court personnel, any person authorized by the applicant, and any persons authorized by order of the court. No person may reveal any information contained in the application except as authorized by law or order of the court. An order granting access to an application or financial information may include limitations on who may access the information and on the use of the information after it has been released.

(2) Any person seeking access to an application or financial information provided to the court by an applicant must make the request by motion, supported by a declaration showing good cause as to why the confidential information should be released. *(Adopted, eff. July 1, 2009. As amended, eff. July 1, 2015.)*

Advisory Committee Comment

Subdivision (a)(1)(B). The waiver of court fees and costs is called an "initial" waiver because, under Government Code section 68630 and following, any such waiver may later be modified, ended, or retroactively withdrawn if the court determines that the applicant was not or is no longer eligible for a waiver. The court may, at a later time, order that the previously waived fees be paid.

Research References

West's California Judicial Council Forms FW–001, Request to Waive Court Fees (Also Available in Spanish).

Rule 8.819. Sealed records

Rule 8.46 governs records sealed by court order under rules 2.550–2.551 and records proposed to be sealed in the appellate division. *(Adopted, eff. Jan. 1, 2010.)*

Research References

6 Witkin, California Criminal Law 4th Criminal Appeal § 53A (2021), (New) in General.

Chapter 3

APPEALS AND RECORDS IN MISDEMEANOR CASES

Article 1

TAKING APPEALS IN MISDEMEANOR CASES

Rule 8.850. Application of chapter

The rules in this chapter apply only to appeals in misdemeanor cases. In postconviction appeals, misdemeanor cases are cases in which the defendant was convicted of a misdemeanor and was not charged with any felony. In preconviction appeals, misdemeanor cases are cases in which the defendant was charged with a misdemeanor but was not charged with any felony. A felony is "charged" when an information or indictment accusing the defendant of a felony is filed or a complaint accusing the defendant of a felony is certified to the superior court under Penal Code section 859a. *(Adopted, eff. Jan. 1, 2009.)*

Advisory Committee Comment

Chapters 1 and 4 of this division also apply in appeals from misdemeanor cases. The rules that apply in appeals in felony cases are located in chapter 3 of division 1 of this title.

Penal Code section 1466 provides that an appeal in a "misdemeanor or infraction case" is to the appellate division of the superior court, and Penal Code section 1235(b), in turn, provides that an appeal in a "felony case" is to the Court of Appeal. Penal Code section 691(g) defines "misdemeanor or infraction case" to mean "a criminal action in which a misdemeanor or infraction is charged *and does not include a criminal action in which a felony is charged* in conjunction with a misdemeanor or infraction" (emphasis added), and section 691(f) defines "felony case" to mean "a criminal action in which a felony is charged *and includes a criminal action in which a misdemeanor or infraction is charged in conjunction with a felony*" (emphasis added).

As rule 8.304 from the rules on felony appeals provides, the following types of cases are felony cases, not misdemeanor cases: (1) an action in which the defendant is charged with a felony and a misdemeanor, but is convicted of only the misdemeanor; (2) an action in which the defendant is charged with felony, but is convicted of only a lesser offense; or (3) an action in which the defendant is charged with an offense filed as a felony but punishable as either a felony or a misdemeanor, and the offense is thereafter deemed a misdemeanor under Penal Code section 17(b). Rule 8.304 makes it clear that a "felony case" is an action in which a felony is charged *regardless of the outcome of the action*. Thus the question of which rules apply—these rules governing appeals in misdemeanor cases or the rules governing appeals in felony cases—is answered simply by examining the accusatory pleading: if that document charged the defendant with at least one count of felony (as defined in Penal Code, section 17(a)), the Court of Appeal has appellate jurisdiction and the appeal must be taken under the rules on felony appeals *even if the prosecution did not result in a punishment of imprisonment in a state prison.*

It is settled case law that an appeal is taken to the Court of Appeal not only when the defendant is charged with and convicted of a felony, but also when the defendant is charged with both a felony and a misdemeanor (Pen. Code, § 691(f)) but is convicted of only the misdemeanor (e.g., *People v. Brown* (1970) 10 Cal.App.3d 169); when the defendant is charged with a felony but is convicted of only a lesser offense (Pen. Code, § 1159; e.g., *People v. Spreckels* (1954) 125 Cal.App.2d 507); and when the defendant is charged with an offense filed as a felony but punishable as either a felony or a misdemeanor, and the offense is thereafter deemed a misdemeanor under Penal Code section 17(b) (e.g., *People v. Douglas* (1999) 20 Cal.4th 85; *People v. Clark* (1971) 17 Cal.App.3d 890).

Trial court unification did not change this rule: after as before unification, "Appeals in felony cases lie to the [C]ourt of [A]ppeal, regardless of whether the appeal is from the superior court, the municipal court, or the action of a magistrate. *Cf.* Cal. Const. art. VI, § 11(a) [except in death penalty cases, Courts of Appeal have appellate jurisdiction when superior courts have original jurisdiction 'in causes of a type within the appellate jurisdiction of the [C]ourts of [A]ppeal on June 30, 1995 . . .']." ("Recommendation on Trial Court Unification" (July 1998) 28 *Cal. Law Revision Com. Rep.* 455–56.)

Research References

6 Witkin, California Criminal Law 4th Criminal Appeal § 2 (2021), Appellate Rules.

6 Witkin, California Criminal Law 4th Criminal Appeal § 206 (2021), In General.

4 Witkin, California Criminal Law 4th Introduction to Criminal Procedure § 9 (2021), Rules of Court.

Rule 8.851. Appointment of appellate counsel

(a) Standards for appointment

(1) On application, the appellate division must appoint appellate counsel for a defendant who was represented by appointed counsel in the trial court or establishes indigency and who:

(A) Was convicted of a misdemeanor and is subject to incarceration or a fine of more than $500 (including penalty and other assessments), or who is likely to suffer significant adverse collateral consequences as a result of the conviction; or

(B) Is charged with a misdemeanor and the appeal is a critical stage of the criminal process.

(2) On application, the appellate division may appoint counsel for any other indigent defendant charged with or convicted of a misdemeanor.

(3) For applications under (1)(A), a defendant is subject to incarceration or a fine if the incarceration or fine is in a sentence, is a condition of probation, or may be ordered if the defendant violates probation.

(b) Application; duties of trial counsel and clerk

(1) If defense trial counsel has reason to believe that the client is indigent and will file an appeal or is a party in an appeal described in (a)(1)(B), counsel must prepare and file in the trial court an application to the appellate division for appointment of counsel.

(2) If the defendant was represented by appointed counsel in the trial court, the application must include trial counsel's declaration to that effect. If the defendant was not represented by appointed counsel in the trial court, the application must include a declaration of indigency in the form required by the Judicial Council.

(3) Within 15 court days after an application is filed in the trial court, the clerk must send it to the appellate division. A defendant may, however, apply directly to the appellate division for appointment of counsel at any time after the notice of appeal is filed.

(4) The appellate division must grant or deny a defendant's application for appointment of counsel within 30 days after the application is filed.

(c) Defendant found able to pay in trial court

(1) If a defendant was represented by appointed counsel in the trial court and was found able to pay all or part of the cost of counsel in proceedings under Penal Code section 987.8 or 987.81, the findings in those proceedings must be included in the record or, if the findings were made after the record is sent to the appellate division, must be sent as an augmentation of the record.

(2) In cases under (1), the appellate division may determine the defendant's ability to pay all or part of the cost of counsel on appeal, and if it finds the defendant able, may order the defendant to pay all or part of that cost. *(Adopted, eff. Jan. 1, 2009. As amended, eff. March 1, 2014; Sept. 1, 2020.)*

Advisory Committee Comment

Request for Court-Appointed Lawyer in Misdemeanor Appeal (form CR-133) may be used to request that appellate counsel be appointed in a misdemeanor case. If the defendant was not represented by the public defender or other appointed counsel in the trial court, the defendant must use *Defendant's Financial Statement on Eligibility for Appointment of Counsel and Reimbursement and Record on Appeal at Public Expense* (form CR-105) to show indigency. These forms are available at any courthouse or county law library or online at *www.courts.ca.gov/forms*.

Subdivision (a)(1)(B). In *Gardner v. Appellate Division of Superior Court* (2019) 6 Cal.5th 998, the California Supreme Court addressed what constitutes a critical stage of the criminal process. The court provided the analysis for determining whether a defendant has a right to counsel in confrontational proceedings other than trial, and held that the pretrial prosecution appeal of an order granting the defendant's motion to suppress evidence was a critical stage of the process at which the defendant, who was represented by appointed counsel in the trial court, had a right to appointed counsel as a matter of state constitutional law.

Research References

West's California Judicial Council Forms CR-133, Request for Court-Appointed Lawyer in Misdemeanor Appeal.
6 Witkin, California Criminal Law 4th Criminal Appeal § 51 (2021), Misdemeanor Appeal.
6 Witkin, California Criminal Law 4th Criminal Appeal § 206 (2021), In General.
5 Witkin, California Criminal Law 4th Criminal Trial § 178 (2021), When Counsel is Required.

Rule 8.852. Notice of appeal

(a) Notice of appeal

(1) To appeal from a judgment or an appealable order of the trial court in a misdemeanor case, the defendant or the People must file a notice of appeal in the trial court. The notice must specify the judgment or order—or part of it—being appealed.

(2) If the defendant appeals, the defendant or the defendant's attorney must sign the notice of appeal. If the People appeal, the attorney for the People must sign the notice.

(3) The notice of appeal must be liberally construed in favor of its sufficiency.

(b) Notification of the appeal

(1) When a notice of appeal is filed, the trial court clerk must promptly send a notification of the filing to the attorney of record for each party and to any unrepresented defendant. The clerk must also send or deliver this notification to the appellate division clerk.

(2) The notification must show the date it was sent or delivered, the number and title of the case, the date the notice of appeal was filed, and whether the defendant was represented by appointed counsel.

(3) The notification to the appellate division clerk must also include a copy of the notice of appeal.

(4) A copy of the notice of appeal is sufficient notification under (1) if the required information is on the copy or is added by the trial court clerk.

(5) The sending of a notification under (1) is a sufficient performance of the clerk's duty despite the discharge, disqualification, suspension, disbarment, or death of the attorney.

(6) Failure to comply with any provision of this subdivision does not affect the validity of the notice of appeal. *(Adopted, eff. Jan. 1, 2009. As amended, eff. Jan. 1, 2016.)*

Advisory Committee Comment

Notice of Appeal (Misdemeanor) (form CR-132) may be used to file the notice of appeal required under this rule. This form is available at any courthouse or county law library or online at *www.courts.ca.gov/forms*.

Subdivision (a). The only orders that a defendant can appeal in a misdemeanor case are (1) orders granting or denying a motion to suppress evidence (Penal Code section 1538.5(j)); and (2) orders made after the final judgment that affects the substantial rights of the defendant (Penal Code section 1466).

Research References

West's California Judicial Council Forms CR-132, Notice of Appeal (Misdemeanor).
6 Witkin, California Criminal Law 4th Criminal Appeal § 91 (2021), Notification by Clerk.
6 Witkin, California Criminal Law 4th Criminal Appeal § 92 (2021), In General.
6 Witkin, California Criminal Law 4th Criminal Appeal § 208 (2021), Notice of Appeal.
4 Witkin, California Criminal Law 4th Illegally Obtained Evidence § 479 (2021), Misdemeanor Prosecution: Appeal from Order Granting Motion.

Rule 8.853. Time to appeal

(a) Normal time

A notice of appeal must be filed within 30 days after the rendition of the judgment or the making of the order being appealed. If the defendant is committed before final judgment for insanity or narcotics addiction, the notice of appeal must be filed within 30 days after the commitment.

(b) Cross-appeal

If the defendant or the People timely appeal from a judgment or appealable order, the time for any other party to appeal from the same judgment or order is either the time specified in (a) or 15 days after the trial court clerk sends notification of the first appeal, whichever is later.

(c) Premature notice of appeal

A notice of appeal filed before the judgment is rendered or the order is made is premature, but the appellate division may treat the notice as filed immediately after the rendition of the judgment or the making of the order.

(d) Late notice of appeal

The trial court clerk must mark a late notice of appeal "Received [date] but not filed" and notify the party that the notice was not filed because it was late. *(Adopted, eff. Jan. 1, 2009. As amended, eff. July 1, 2010; Jan. 1, 2016.)*

Advisory Committee Comment

Subdivision (d). See rule 8.817(b)(5) for provisions concerning the timeliness of documents mailed by inmates or patients from custodial institutions.

Research References

West's California Judicial Council Forms CR–132, Notice of Appeal (Misdemeanor).

6 Witkin, California Criminal Law 4th Criminal Appeal § 90 (2021), Written or Printed Notice Must be Filed.

6 Witkin, California Criminal Law 4th Criminal Appeal § 96 (2021), Normal Time.

6 Witkin, California Criminal Law 4th Criminal Appeal § 102 (2021), Changes in Rules.

6 Witkin, California Criminal Law 4th Criminal Appeal § 104 (2021), Premature Filing is Excusable.

6 Witkin, California Criminal Law 4th Criminal Appeal § 208 (2021), Notice of Appeal.

4 Witkin, California Criminal Law 4th Illegally Obtained Evidence § 479 (2021), Misdemeanor Prosecution: Appeal from Order Granting Motion.

Rule 8.854. Stay of execution and release on appeal

(a) Application

Pending appeal, the defendant may apply to the appellate division:

(1) For a stay of execution after a judgment of conviction or an order granting probation; or

(2) For bail for release from custody, to reduce bail for release from custody, or for release on other conditions.

(b) Showing

The application must include a showing that the defendant sought relief in the trial court and that the court unjustifiably denied the application.

(c) Service

The application must be served on the prosecuting attorney.

(d) Interim relief

Pending its ruling on the application, the appellate division may grant the relief requested. The appellate division must notify the trial court of any stay that it grants. *(Adopted, eff. Jan. 1, 2009.)*

Advisory Committee Comment

Subdivision (c). As defined in rule 8.804, the "prosecuting attorney" may be the city attorney, county counsel, district attorney, or state Attorney General, depending on what government agency filed the criminal charges.

Research References

6 Witkin, California Criminal Law 4th Criminal Appeal § 206 (2021), In General.

Rule 8.855. Abandoning the appeal

(a) How to abandon

An appellant may abandon the appeal at any time by filing an abandonment of the appeal signed by the appellant or the appellant's attorney of record.

(b) Where to file; effect of filing

(1) The appellant must file the abandonment in the appellate division.

(2) If the record has not been filed in the appellate division, the filing of an abandonment effects a dismissal of the appeal and restores the trial court's jurisdiction.

(3) If the record has been filed in the appellate division, the appellate division may dismiss the appeal and direct immediate issuance of the remittitur.

(c) Clerk's duties

(1) The appellate division clerk must immediately notify the adverse party of the filing or of the order of dismissal.

(2) If the record has not been filed in the appellate division, the clerk must immediately notify the trial court.

(3) If a reporter's transcript has been requested, the clerk must immediately notify the reporter if the appeal is abandoned before the reporter has filed the transcript. *(Adopted, eff. Jan. 1, 2009.)*

Advisory Committee Comment

Abandonment of Appeal (Misdemeanor) (form CR–137) may be used to file an abandonment under this rule. This form is available at any courthouse or county law library or online at *www.courtinfo.ca.gov/forms.*

Research References

West's California Judicial Council Forms CR–137, Abandonment of Appeal (Misdemeanor).

6 Witkin, California Criminal Law 4th Criminal Appeal § 215 (2021), Abandonment and Dismissal.

Article 2

RECORD IN MISDEMEANOR APPEALS

Rule

Rule 8.860. Normal record on appeal

(a) Contents

Except as otherwise provided in this chapter, the record on an appeal to a superior court appellate division in a misdemeanor criminal case must contain the following, which constitute the normal record on appeal:

(1) A record of the written documents from the trial court proceedings in the form of one of the following:

(A) A clerk's transcript under rule 8.861 or 8.867; or

(B) If the court has a local rule for the appellate division electing to use this form of the record, the original trial court file under rule 8.863.

(2) If an appellant wants to raise any issue that requires consideration of the oral proceedings in the trial court, the record on appeal must include a record of the oral proceedings in the form of one of the following:

(A) A reporter's transcript under rules 8.865–8.867 or a transcript prepared from an official electronic recording under rule 8.868;

(B) If the court has a local rule for the appellate division permitting this form of the record, an official electronic recording of the proceedings under rule 8.868; or

(C) A statement on appeal under rule 8.869.

(b) Stipulation for limited record

If, before the record is certified, the appellant and the respondent stipulate in writing that any part of the record is not required for proper determination of the appeal and file that stipulation in the trial court, that part of the record must not be prepared or sent to the appellate division. *(Adopted, eff. Jan. 1, 2009. As amended, eff. July 1, 2009.)*

Research References

West's California Judicial Council Forms CR–134, Notice Regarding Record on Appeal (Misdemeanor).

6 Witkin, California Criminal Law 4th Criminal Appeal § 96 (2021), Normal Time.

6 Witkin, California Criminal Law 4th Criminal Appeal § 209 (2021), Normal Record on Appeal.

Rule 8.861. Contents of clerk's transcript

Except in appeals covered by rule 8.867 or when the parties have filed a stipulation under rule 8.860(b) that any of these items is not required for proper determination of the appeal, the clerk's transcript must contain:

(1) The complaint, including any notice to appear, and any amendment;

(2) Any demurrer or other plea;

(3) All court minutes;

(4) Any jury instructions that any party submitted in writing, the cover page required by rule 2.1055(b)(2), and any written jury instructions given by the court;

(5) Any written communication between the court and the jury or any individual juror;

(6) Any verdict;

(7) Any written findings or opinion of the court;

(8) The judgment or order appealed from;

(9) Any motion or notice of motion for new trial, in arrest of judgment, or to dismiss the action, with supporting and opposing memoranda and attachments;

(10) Any transcript of a sound or sound-and-video recording furnished to the jury or tendered to the court under rule 2.1040; and

(11) The notice of appeal; and

(12) If the appellant is the defendant:

(A) Any written defense motion denied in whole or in part, with supporting and opposing memoranda and attachments;

(B) If related to a motion under (A), any search warrant and return;

(C) Any document admitted in evidence to prove a prior juvenile adjudication, criminal conviction, or prison term. If a record was closed to public inspection in the trial court because it is required to be kept confidential by law, it must remain closed to public inspection in the appellate division unless that court orders otherwise;

(D) The probation officer's report; and

(E) Any court-ordered psychological report required under Penal Code section 1369. *(Adopted, eff. Jan. 1, 2009. As amended, eff. Jan. 1, 2010.)*

Advisory Committee Comment

Rule 8.862(c) addresses the appropriate handling of probation officers' reports that must be included in the clerk's transcript under (12)(D).

Research References

6 Witkin, California Criminal Law 4th Criminal Appeal § 210 (2021), Transcripts.

Rule 8.862. Preparation of clerk's transcript

(a) When preparation begins

Unless the original court file will be used in place of a clerk's transcript under rule 8.863, the clerk must begin preparing the clerk's transcript immediately after the notice of appeal is filed.

(b) Format of transcript

The clerk's transcript must comply with rule 8.144.

(c) Probation officer's reports

A probation officer's report included in the clerk's transcript under rule 8.861(12)(D) must appear in only the copies of the appellate record that are sent to the reviewing court, to appellate counsel for the People, and to appellate counsel for the defendant who was the subject of the report or to the defendant if he or she is self-represented. If the report is in paper form, it must placed in a sealed envelope. The reviewing court's copy of the report, and if applicable, the envelope, must be marked "CONFIDENTIAL—MAY NOT BE EXAMINED WITHOUT COURT ORDER—PROBATION OFFICER REPORT."

(d) When preparation must be completed

Within 20 days after the notice of appeal is filed, the clerk must complete preparation of an original clerk's transcript for the appellate division, one copy for the appellant, and one copy for the respondent. If there is more than one appellant, the clerk must prepare an extra copy for each additional appellant who is represented by separate counsel or self-represented.

(e) Certification

The clerk must certify as correct the original and all copies of the clerk's transcript. *(Adopted, eff. Jan. 1, 2009. As amended, eff. July 1, 2009; Jan. 1, 2010; Jan. 1, 2016.)*

Advisory Committee Comment

Rule 8.872 addresses when the clerk's transcript is sent to the appellate division in misdemeanor appeals.

Research References

6 Witkin, California Criminal Law 4th Criminal Appeal § 210 (2021), Transcripts.

Rule 8.863. Trial court file instead of clerk's transcript

(a) Application

If the court has a local rule for the appellate division electing to use this form of the record, the original trial court file may be used instead of a clerk's transcript. This rule and any supplemental provisions of the local rule then govern unless the trial court orders otherwise after notice to the parties.

(b) When original file must be prepared

Within 20 days after the filing of the notice of appeal, the trial court clerk must put the trial court file in chronological order, number the pages, and attach a chronological index and a list of all attorneys of record, the parties they represent, and any unrepresented parties.

(c) Copies

The clerk must send a copy of the index to the appellant and the respondent for use in paginating their copies of the file to conform to the index. If there is more than one appellant, the clerk must prepare an extra copy of the index for each additional appellant who is represented by separate counsel or self-represented. *(Adopted, eff. Jan. 1, 2009. As amended, eff. July 1, 2009.)*

Advisory Committee Comment

Rule 8.872 addresses when the original file is sent to the appellate division in misdemeanor appeals.

Research References

6 Witkin, California Criminal Law 4th Criminal Appeal § 210 (2021), Transcripts.

Rule 8.864. Record of oral proceedings

(a) Appellant's election

The appellant must notify the trial court whether he or she elects to proceed with or without a record of the oral proceedings in the trial court. If the appellant elects to proceed with a record of the oral proceedings in the trial court, the notice must specify which form of the record of the oral proceedings in the trial court the appellant elects to use:

(1) A reporter's transcript under rules 8.865–8.867 or a transcript prepared from an official electronic recording of the proceedings under rule 8.868(b). If the appellant elects to use a reporter's transcript, the clerk must promptly send a copy of appellant's notice making this election and the notice of appeal to each court reporter;

(2) An official electronic recording of the proceedings under rule 8.868(c). If the appellant elects to use the official electronic recording itself, rather than a transcript prepared from that recording, the appellant must attach a copy of the stipulation required under rule 8.868(c); or

(3) A statement on appeal under rule 8.869.

(b) Time for filing election

The notice of election required under (a) must be filed no later than the following:

(1) If no application for appointment of counsel is filed, 20 days after the notice of appeal is filed; or

(2) If an application for appointment of counsel is filed before the period under (A) expires, either 10 days after the court appoints counsel to represent the defendant on appeal or denies the application for appointment of counsel or 20 days after the notice of appeal is filed, whichever is later.

(c) Failure to file election

If the appellant does not file an election within the time specified in (b), rule 8.874 applies. *(Adopted, eff. Jan. 1, 2009. As amended, eff. Jan. 1, 2010; March 1, 2014; Jan. 1, 2016.)*

Advisory Committee Comment

Notice Regarding Record of Oral Proceedings (Misdemeanor) (form CR-134) may be used to file the election required under this rule. This form is available at any courthouse or county law library or online at *www.courtinfo.ca gov/forms*. To assist parties in making an appropriate election, courts are encouraged to include information about whether the proceedings were recorded by a court reporter or officially electronically recorded in any information that the court provides to parties concerning their appellate rights.

Research References

6 Witkin, California Criminal Law 4th Criminal Appeal § 210 (2021), Transcripts.

Rule 8.865. Contents of reporter's transcript

(a) Normal contents

Except in appeals covered by rule 8.867, when the parties have filed a stipulation under rule 8.860(b), or when, under a procedure established by a local rule adopted pursuant to (b), the trial court has ordered that any of these items is not required for proper determination of the appeal, the reporter's transcript must contain:

(1) The oral proceedings on the entry of any plea other than a not guilty plea;

(2) The oral proceedings on any motion in limine;

(3) The oral proceedings at trial, but excluding the voir dire examination of jurors and any opening statement;

(4) Any jury instructions given orally;

(5) Any oral communication between the court and the jury or any individual juror;

(6) Any oral opinion of the court;

(7) The oral proceedings on any motion for new trial;

(8) The oral proceedings at sentencing, granting or denying probation, or other dispositional hearing;

(9) If the appellant is the defendant, the reporter's transcript must also contain:

(A) The oral proceedings on any defense motion denied in whole or in part except motions for disqualification of a judge;

(B) Any closing arguments; and

(C) Any comment on the evidence by the court to the jury.

(b) Local procedure for determining contents

A court may adopt a local rule that establishes procedures for determining whether any of the items listed in (a) is not required for proper determination of the appeal or whether a form of the record other than a reporter's transcript constitutes a record of sufficient completeness for proper determination of the appeal. *(Adopted, eff. Jan. 1, 2009. As amended, eff. March 1, 2014.)*

Advisory Committee Comment

Subdivision (b). Both the United States Supreme Court and the California Supreme Court have held that, where the State has established a right to appeal, an indigent defendant convicted of a criminal offense has a constitutional right to a "'record of sufficient completeness' to permit proper consideration of [his] claims." (*Mayer v. Chicago* (1971) 404 U.S. 189, 193–194; *March v. Municipal Court* (1972) 7 Cal.3d 422, 427–428.) The California Supreme Court has also held that an indigent appellant is denied his or her right under the Fourteenth Amendment to the competent assistance of counsel on appeal if counsel fails to obtain an appellate record adequate for consideration of appellant's claims of errors (*People v. Barton* (1978) 21 Cal.3d 513, 518–520).

The *Mayer* and *March* decisions make clear, however, that the constitutionally required "record of sufficient completeness" does not necessarily mean a complete verbatim transcript; other forms of the record, such as a statement on appeal, or a partial transcript may be sufficient. The record that is necessary depends on the grounds for the appeal in the particular case. Under these decisions, where the grounds of appeal make out a colorable need for a complete transcript, the burden is on the State to show that only a portion of the transcript or an alternative form of the record will suffice for an effective appeal on those grounds. The burden of overcoming the need for a verbatim reporter's transcript appears to be met where a verbatim recording of the proceedings is provided. (*Mayer, supra,* 404 U.S. at p. 195; cf. *Eyrich v. Mun. Court* (1985) 165 Cal.App.3d 1138, 1140 ["Although use of a court reporter is one way of obtaining a verbatim record, it may also be acquired through an electronic recording when no court reporter is available"].)

Some courts have adopted local rules that establish procedures for determining whether only a portion of a verbatim transcript or an alternative form of the record will be sufficient for an effective appeal, including (1) requiring the appellant to specify the points the appellant is raising on appeal; (2) requiring the appellant and respondent to meet and confer about the content and form of the record; and (3) holding a hearing on the content and form of the record. Local procedures can be tailored to reflect the methods available in a particular court for making a record of the trial court proceedings that is sufficient for an effective appeal.

Research References

6 Witkin, California Criminal Law 4th Criminal Appeal § 210 (2021), Transcripts.

Rule 8.866. Preparation of reporter's transcript

(a) When preparation begins

(1) Unless the court has adopted a local rule under rule 8.865(b) that provides otherwise, the reporter must immediately begin preparing the reporter's transcript if the notice sent to the reporter by the clerk under rule 8.864(a)(1) indicates either:

(A) That the defendant was represented by appointed counsel at trial; or

(B) That the appellant is the People.

(2) If the notice sent to the reporter by the clerk under rule 8.864(a)(1) indicates that the appellant is the defendant and that the defendant was not represented by appointed counsel at trial:

(A) Within 10 days after the date the clerk sent the notice under rule 8.864(a)(1), the reporter must file with the clerk the estimated cost of preparing the reporter's transcript.

(B) The clerk must promptly notify the appellant and his or her counsel of the estimated cost of preparing the reporter's transcript. The notification must show the date it was sent.

(C) Within 10 days after the date the clerk sent the notice under (B), the appellant must do one of the following:

(i) Deposit with the clerk an amount equal to the estimated cost of preparing the transcript;

(ii) File a waiver of the deposit signed by the reporter;

(iii) File a declaration of indigency supported by evidence in the form required by the Judicial Council;

(iv) File a certified transcript of all of the proceedings required to be included in the reporter's transcript under rule 8.865. The transcript must comply with the format requirements of rule 8.144;

(v) Notify the clerk by filing a new election that he or she will be using a statement on appeal instead of a reporter's transcript. The appellant must prepare, serve, and file a proposed statement on appeal within 20 days after serving and filing the notice and must otherwise comply with the requirements for statements on appeal under rule 8.869; or

(vi) Notify the clerk by filing a new election that he or she now elects to proceed without a record of the oral proceedings in the trial court; or

(vii) Notify the clerk that he or she is abandoning the appeal by filing an abandonment in the reviewing court under rule 8.855.

(D) If the trial court determines that the appellant is not indigent, within 10 days after the date the clerk sends notice of this determination to the appellant, the appellant must do one of the following:

(i) Deposit with the clerk an amount equal to the estimated cost of preparing the transcript;

(ii) File with the clerk a waiver of the deposit signed by the reporter;

(iii) File a certified transcript of all of the proceedings required to be included in the reporter's transcript under rule 8.865. The transcript must comply with the format requirements of rule 8.144;

(iv) Notify the clerk by filing a new election that he or she will be using a statement on appeal instead of a reporter's transcript. The appellant must prepare, serve, and file a proposed statement on appeal within 20 days after serving and filing the notice and must otherwise comply with the requirements for statements on appeal under rule 8.869;

(v) Notify the clerk by filing a new election that he or she now elects to proceed without a record of the oral proceedings in the trial court; or

(vi) Notify the clerk that he or she is abandoning the appeal by filing an abandonment in the reviewing court under rule 8.855.

(E) The clerk must promptly notify the reporter to begin preparing the transcript when:

(i) The clerk receives the required deposit under (C)(i) or (D)(i);

(ii) The clerk receives a waiver of the deposit signed by the reporter under (C)(ii) or (D)(ii); or

(iii) The trial court determines that the appellant is indigent and orders that the appellant receive the transcript without cost.

(b) Format of transcript

The reporter's transcript must comply with rule 8.144.

(c) Copies and certification

The reporter must prepare an original and the same number of copies of the reporter's transcript as rule 8.862 requires of the clerk's transcript and must certify each as correct.

(d) When preparation must be completed

(1) The reporter must deliver the original and all copies to the trial court clerk as soon as they are certified but no later than 20 days after the reporter is required to begin preparing the transcript under (a). Only the presiding judge of the appellate division or his or her designee may extend the time to prepare the reporter's transcript (see rule 8.810).

(2) If the appellant deposited with the clerk an amount equal to the estimated cost of preparing the transcript and the appeal is abandoned or dismissed before the reporter has filed the transcript, the reporter must inform the clerk of the cost of the portion of the transcript that the reporter has completed. The clerk must pay that amount to the reporter from the appellant's deposited funds and refund any excess deposit to the appellant.

(e) Multi-reporter cases

In a multi-reporter case, the clerk must accept any completed portion of the transcript from the primary reporter one week after the time prescribed by (d) even if other portions are uncompleted. The clerk must promptly pay each reporter who certifies that all portions of the transcript assigned to that reporter are completed.

(f) Notice when proceedings were not reported or cannot be transcribed

(1) If any portion of the oral proceedings to be included in the reporter's transcript was not reported or cannot be transcribed, the trial court clerk must so notify the parties in writing. The notice must:

(A) Indicate whether the identified proceedings were officially electronically recorded under Government Code section 69957; and

(B) Show the date it was sent.

(2) Within 15 days after this notice is sent by the clerk, the appellant must serve and file a notice with the court stating whether the appellant elects to proceed with or without a record of the identified proceedings. When the party elects to proceed with a record of these oral proceedings:

(A) If the clerk's notice under (1) indicates that the proceedings were officially electronically recorded under Government Code section 69957, the appellant's notice must specify which form of the record listed in rule 8.864(a) other than a reporter's transcript the appellant elects to use. The appellant must comply with the requirements applicable to the form of the record elected.

(B) If the clerk's notice under (1) indicates that the proceedings were not officially electronically recorded under Government Code section 69957, the appellant must prepare, serve, and file a proposed statement on appeal within 20 days after serving and filing the notice.

(Adopted, eff. Jan. 1, 2009. As amended, eff. March 1, 2014; Jan. 1, 2016; Jan. 1, 2017; Jan. 1, 2018; March 5, 2018.)

Advisory Committee Comment

Subdivision (a). If the appellant was not represented by the public defender or other appointed counsel in the trial court, the appellant must use *Defendant's Financial Statement on Eligibility for Appointment of Counsel and Reimbursement and Record on Appeal at Public Expense* (form CR–105) to show indigency. This form is available at any courthouse or county law library or online at www.courts.ca.gov/forms.

Subdivisions (a)(2)(C)(iv) and (a)(2)(D)(iii). Sometimes a party in a trial court proceeding will purchase a reporter's transcripts of all or part of the proceedings before any appeal is filed. In recognition of the fact that such transcripts may already have been purchased, this rule allows an appellant, in lieu of depositing funds for a reporter's transcript, to deposit with the trial court a certified transcript of the proceedings necessary for the appeal. Subdivisions (a)(2)(C)(iv) and (a)(2)(D)(iii) make clear that the certified transcript may be filed in lieu of a deposit for a reporter's transcript only where the certified transcript contains all of the proceedings required under rule 8.865 and the transcript complies with the format requirements of rule 8.144.

Research References

6 Witkin, California Criminal Law 4th Criminal Appeal § 210 (2021), Transcripts.

Rule 8.867. Limited normal record in certain appeals

(a) Application and additions

This rule establishes a limited normal record for certain appeals. This rule does not alter the parties' right to request that exhibits be transmitted to the reviewing court under rule 8.870 nor preclude either an application in the superior court under (e) for additions to the limited normal record or a motion in the reviewing court for augmentation under rule 8.841.

(b) Pretrial appeals of rulings on motions under Penal Code section 1538.5

If before trial either the defendant or the People appeal a ruling on a motion under Penal Code section 1538.5 for the return of property or the suppression of evidence, the normal record is composed of:

(1) *Record of the documents filed in the trial court*

A clerk's transcript or original trial court file containing:

(A) The complaint, including any notice to appear, and any amendment;

(B) The motion under Penal Code section 1538.5, with supporting and opposing memoranda, and attachments;

(C) The order on the motion under Penal Code section 1538.5;

(D) Any court minutes relating to the order; and

(E) The notice of appeal.

(2) *Record of the oral proceedings in the trial court*

If an appellant wants to raise any issue that requires consideration of the oral proceedings in the trial court, a reporter's transcript, a transcript prepared under rule 8.868, an official electronic recording under rule 8.868, or a statement on appeal under rule 8.869 summarizing any oral proceedings incident to the order on the motion under Penal Code section 1538.5.

(c) Appeals from judgments on demurrers or certain appealable orders

If the People appeal from a judgment on a demurrer to the complaint, including any notice to appear, or if the defendant or the People appeal from an appealable order other than a ruling on a motion for new trial or a ruling covered by (a), the normal record is composed of:

(1) *Record of the documents filed in the trial court*

A clerk's transcript or original trial court file containing:

(A) The complaint, including any notice to appear, and any amendment;

(B) Any demurrer or other plea;

(C) Any motion or notice of motion granted or denied by the order appealed from, with supporting and opposing memoranda and attachments;

(D) The judgment or order appealed from and any abstract of judgment or commitment;

(E) Any court minutes relating to the judgment or order appealed from and

(i) If there was a trial in the case, any court minutes of proceedings at the time the original verdict is rendered and any subsequent proceedings; or

(ii) If the original judgment of conviction is based on a guilty plea or nolo contendere plea, any court minutes of the proceedings at the time of entry of such plea and any subsequent proceedings;

(F) The notice of appeal; and

(G) If the appellant is the defendant, all probation officer reports.

(2) *Record of the oral proceedings in the trial court*

If an appellant wants to raise any issue which requires consideration of the oral proceedings in the trial court:

(A) A reporter's transcript, a transcript prepared under rule 8.868, an official electronic recording under rule 8.868, or a statement on appeal under rule 8.869 summarizing any oral proceedings incident to the judgment or order being appealed.

(B) If the appeal is from an order after judgment, a reporter's transcript, a transcript prepared under rule 8.868, an official electronic recording under rule 8.868, or a statement on appeal under rule 8.869 summarizing any oral proceedings from:

(i) The original sentencing proceeding; and

(ii) If the original judgment of conviction is based on a guilty plea or nolo contendere plea, the proceedings at the time of entry of such plea.

(d) Appeals of the conditions of probation

If a defendant's appeal of the judgment contests only the conditions of probation, the normal record is composed of:

(1) *Record of the documents filed in the trial court*

A clerk's transcript or original trial court file containing:

(A) The complaint, including any notice to appear, and any amendment;

(B) The judgment or order appealed from and any abstract of judgment or commitment;

(C) Any court minutes relating to the judgment or order appealed from and:

(i) If there was a trial in the case, any court minutes of proceedings at the time the original verdict is rendered and any subsequent proceedings; or

(ii) If the original judgment of conviction is based on a guilty plea or nolo contendere plea, any court minutes of the proceedings at the time of entry of such plea and any subsequent proceedings;

(D) The notice of appeal; and

(E) All probation officer reports.

(2) *Record of the oral proceedings in the trial court*

If an appellant wants to raise any issue that requires consideration of the oral proceedings in the trial court, a reporter's transcript, a transcript prepared under rule 8.868, an official electronic recording under rule 8.868, or a statement on appeal under rule 8.869 summarizing any oral proceedings from:

(A) The sentencing proceeding; and

(B) If the judgment of conviction is based on a guilty plea or nolo contendere plea, the proceedings at the time of entry of such plea.

(e) Additions to the record

Either the People or the defendant may apply to the superior court for inclusion in the record under (b), (c), or (d) of any item that would ordinarily be included in the clerk's transcript under rule 8.861 or a reporter's transcript under rule 8.865.

(1) An application for additional record must describe the material to be included and explain how it may be useful in the appeal.

(2) The application must be filed in the superior court with the notice of appeal or as soon thereafter as possible, and will be treated as denied if it is filed after the record is sent to the reviewing court.

(3) The clerk must immediately present the application to the trial judge.

(4) Within five days after the application is filed, the judge must order that the record include as much of the additional material as the judge finds proper to fully present the points raised by the applicant. Denial of the application does not preclude a motion in the reviewing court for augmentation under rule 8.841.

(5) If the judge does not rule on the application within the time prescribed by (4), the requested material—other than exhibits—must be included in the clerk's transcript or the reporter's transcript without a court order.

(6) The clerk must immediately notify the reporter if additions to the reporter's transcript are required under (4) or (5). *(Adopted, eff. Jan. 1, 2009. As amended, eff. Jan. 1, 2013; March 1, 2014.)*

Advisory Committee Comment

Subdivisions (b)(1)(D), (c)(1)(E), and (d)(1)(C). These provisions identify the minutes that must be included in the record. The trial court clerk may include additional minutes beyond those identified in these subdivisions if that would be more cost-effective.

Subdivisions (c)(1)(G) and (d)(1)(E). Rule 8.862(c) addresses the appropriate handling of probation officers' reports that must be included in the clerk's transcript.

Research References

6 Witkin, California Criminal Law 4th Criminal Appeal § 209 (2021), Normal Record on Appeal.

Rule 8.868. Record when trial proceedings were officially electronically recorded

(a) Application

This rule applies only if:

(1) The trial court proceedings were officially recorded electronically under Government Code section 69957; and

(2) The electronic recording was prepared in compliance with applicable rules regarding electronic recording of court proceedings.

(b) Transcripts from official electronic recording

Written transcripts of an official electronic recording may be prepared under rule 2.952. A transcript prepared and certified as provided in that rule is prima facie a true and complete record of the oral proceedings it purports to cover, and satisfies any requirement in these rules or in any statute for a reporter's transcript of oral proceedings.

(c) Use of official recording as record of oral proceedings

If the court has a local rule for the appellate division permitting this, on stipulation of the parties or on order of the trial court under rule 8.869(d)(6), the original of an official electronic recording of the trial court proceedings, or a copy made by the court, may be transmitted as the record of these oral proceedings without being transcribed. Such an electronic recording satisfies any requirement in these rules or in any statute for a reporter's transcript of these proceedings.

(d) Contents

Except in appeals when either the parties have filed a stipulation under rule 8.860(b) or the trial court has ordered that any of these items is not required for proper determination of the appeal, rules 8.865 and 8.867 govern the contents of a transcript of an official electronic recording.

(e) When preparation begins

(1) If the appellant files an election under rule 8.864 to use a transcript of an official electronic recording or a copy of the official electronic recording as the record of the oral proceedings, unless the trial court has a local rule providing otherwise, preparation of a transcript or a copy of the recording must begin immediately if either:

(A) The defendant was represented by appointed counsel at trial; or

(B) The appellant is the People.

(2) If the appellant is the defendant and the defendant was not represented by appointed counsel at trial:

(A) Within 10 days after the date the defendant files the election under rule 8.864(a)(1), the clerk must notify the appellant and his or her counsel of the estimated cost of preparing the transcript or the copy of the recording. The notification must show the date it was sent.

(B) Within 10 days after the date the clerk sent the notice under (A), the appellant must do one of the following:

(i) Deposit with the clerk an amount equal to the estimated cost of preparing the transcript or the copy of the recording;

(ii) File a declaration of indigency supported by evidence in the form required by the Judicial Council;

(iii) Notify the clerk by filing a new election that he or she will be using a statement on appeal instead of a transcript or copy of the recording. The appellant must prepare, serve, and file a proposed statement on appeal within 20 days after serving and filing the notice and must otherwise comply with the requirements for statements on appeal under rule 8.869;

(iv) Notify the clerk by filing a new election that he or she now elects to proceed without a record of the oral proceedings in the trial court; or

(v) Notify the clerk that he or she is abandoning the appeal by filing an abandonment in the reviewing court under rule 8.855.

(C) If the trial court determines that the appellant is not indigent, within 10 days after the date the clerk sends notice of this determination to the appellant, the appellant must do one of the following:

(i) Deposit with the clerk an amount equal to the estimated cost of preparing the transcript or the copy of the recording;

(ii) Notify the clerk by filing a new election that he or she will be using a statement on appeal instead of a reporter's transcript. The appellant must prepare, serve, and file a proposed statement on appeal within 20 days after serving and filing the notice and must otherwise comply with the requirements for statements on appeal under rule 8.869;

(iii) Notify the clerk by filing a new election that he or she now elects to proceed without a record of the oral proceedings in the trial court; or

(iv) Notify the clerk that he or she is abandoning the appeal by filing an abandonment in the reviewing court under rule 8.855.

(D) Preparation of the transcript or the copy of the recording must begin when:

(i) The clerk receives the required deposit under (B)(i) or (C)(i); or

(ii) The trial court determines that the defendant is indigent and orders that the defendant receive the transcript or the copy of the recording without cost.

(f) Notice when proceedings were not officially electronically recorded or cannot be transcribed

(1) If any portion of the oral proceedings to be included in the transcript was not officially electronically recorded under Government Code section 69957 or cannot be transcribed, the trial court clerk must so notify the parties in writing. The notice must:

(A) Indicate whether the identified proceedings were reported by a court reporter; and

(B) Show the date it was sent.

(2) Within 15 days after this notice is sent by the clerk, the appellant must serve and file a notice with the court stating whether the appellant elects to proceed with or without a record of the identified oral proceedings. When the party elects to proceed with a record of these oral proceedings:

(A) If the clerk's notice under (1) indicates that the proceedings were reported by a court reporter, the appellant's notice must specify which form of the record listed in rule 8.864(a) other than an official electronic recording or a transcript prepared from an official electronic recording the appellant elects to use. The appellant must comply with the requirements applicable to the form of the record elected.

(B) If the clerk's notice under (1) indicates that the proceedings were not reported by a court reporter, the appellant must prepare, serve, and file a proposed statement on appeal within 20 days after serving and filing the notice.

(Adopted, eff. Jan. 1, 2009. As amended, eff. July 1, 2010; March 1, 2014; Jan. 1, 2016.)

Advisory Committee Comment

Subdivision (d). If the appellant was not represented by the public defender or other appointed counsel in the trial court, the appellant must use *Defendant's Financial Statement on Eligibility for Appointment of Counsel and Reimbursement and Record on Appeal at Public Expense* (form CR–105) to show indigency. This form is available at any courthouse or county law library or online at www.courts.ca.gov/forms.

Research References

6 Witkin, California Criminal Law 4th Criminal Appeal § 209 (2021), Normal Record on Appeal.

Rule 8.869. Statement on appeal

(a) Description

A statement on appeal is a summary of the trial court proceedings that is approved by the trial court. An appellant can elect under rule 8.864 to use a statement on appeal as the record of the oral proceedings in the trial court, replacing the reporter's transcript.

(b) Preparing the proposed statement

(1) If the appellant elects under rule 8.864 to use a statement on appeal, the appellant must prepare, serve, and file a proposed statement within 20 days after filing the record preparation election.

(2) Appellants who are not represented by an attorney must file their proposed statement on *Proposed Statement on Appeal (Misdemeanor)* (form CR–135). For good cause, the court may permit the filing of a statement that is not on form CR–135.

(3) If the appellant does not serve and file a proposed statement within the time specified in (1), rule 8.874 applies.

(c) Contents of the proposed statement on appeal

A proposed statement prepared by the appellant must contain:

(1) A statement of the points the appellant is raising on appeal. The appeal is then limited to those points unless the appellate division determines that the record permits the full consideration of another point.

(A) The statement must specify the intended grounds of appeal by clearly stating each point to be raised but need not identify each particular ruling or matter to be challenged.

(B) If one of the grounds of appeal is insufficiency of the evidence, the statement must specify how it is insufficient.

(2) A summary of the trial court's rulings and the sentence imposed on the defendant.

(3) A condensed narrative of the oral proceedings that the appellant believes necessary for the appeal.

(A) The condensed narrative must include a concise factual summary of the evidence and the testimony of each witness that is relevant to the points which the appellant states under (1) are being raised on appeal. Any evidence or portion of a proceeding not included will be presumed to support the judgment or order appealed from.

(B) If one of the points which the appellant states under (1) is being raised on appeal is a challenge to the giving, refusal, or modification of a jury instruction, the condensed narrative must include any instructions submitted orally and not in writing and must identify the party that requested the instruction and any modification.

(d) Review of the appellant's proposed statement

(1) Within 10 days after the appellant files the proposed statement, the respondent may serve and file proposed amendments to that statement.

(2) No later than 10 days after either the respondent files proposed amendments or the time to do so expires, a party may request a hearing to review and correct the proposed statement. No hearing will be held unless ordered by the trial court judge, and the judge will not ordinarily order a hearing unless there is a factual dispute about a material aspect of the trial court proceedings.

(3) Except as provided in (6), if no hearing is ordered, no later than 10 days after the time for requesting a hearing expires, the trial court judge must review the proposed statement and any proposed amendments filed by the respondent and take one of the following actions:

(A) If the proposed statement does not contain material required under (c), the trial court judge may order the appellant to prepare a new proposed statement. The order must identify the additional material that must be included in the statement to comply with (c) and the date by which the new proposed statement must be served and filed. If the appellant does not serve and file a new proposed statement as directed, rule 8.874 applies.

(B) If the trial court judge does not issue an order under (A), the trial court judge must either:

(i) Make any corrections or modifications to the statement necessary to ensure that it is an accurate summary of the evidence and the testimony of each witness that is relevant to the points which the appellant states under (c)(1) are being raised on appeal; or

(ii) Identify the necessary corrections and modifications and order the appellant to prepare a statement incorporating these corrections and modifications.

(4) If a hearing is ordered, the court must promptly set the hearing date and provide the parties with at least 5 days' written notice of the hearing date. No later than 10 days after the hearing, the trial court judge must either:

(A) Make any corrections or modifications to the statement necessary to ensure that it is an accurate summary of the evidence and the testimony of each witness that is relevant to the points which the appellant states under (c)(1) are being raised on appeal; or

(B) Identify the necessary corrections and modifications and order the appellant to prepare a statement incorporating these corrections and modifications.

(5) The trial court judge must not eliminate the appellant's specification of grounds of appeal from the proposed statement.

(6) If the trial court proceedings were reported by a court reporter or officially electronically recorded under Government Code section 69957 and the trial court judge determines that it would save court time and resources, instead of correcting a proposed statement on appeal:

(A) If the court has a local rule for the appellate division permitting the use of an official electronic recording as the record of the oral proceedings, the trial court judge may order that the original of an official electronic recording of the trial court proceedings, or a copy made by the court, be transmitted as the record of these oral proceedings without being transcribed. The court will pay for any copy of the official electronic recording ordered under this subdivision; or

(B) If the court has a local rule permitting this, the trial court judge may order that a transcript be prepared as the record of the oral proceedings. The court will pay for any transcript ordered under this subdivision.

(e) Review of the corrected or modified statement

(1) If the trial court judge makes any corrections or modifications to the proposed statement under (d), the clerk must serve copies of the corrected or modified statement on the parties. If under (d) the trial court judge orders the appellant to prepare a statement incorporating corrections and modifications, the appellant must serve and file the corrected or modified statement within the time ordered by the court. If the appellant does not serve and file a corrected or modified statement as directed, rule 8.874 applies.

(2) Within 10 days after the corrected or modified statement is served on the parties, any party may serve and file proposed modifications or objections to the statement.

(3) Within 10 days after the time for filing proposed modifications or objections under (2) has expired, the judge must review the corrected or modified statement and any proposed modifications or objections to the statement filed by the parties. The procedures in (d)(3) or (4) apply if the judge determines that further corrections or modifications are necessary to ensure that the statement is an accurate summary of the evidence and the testimony of each witness relevant to the points which the appellant states under (c)(1) are being raised on appeal.

(f) Certification of the statement on appeal

If the trial court judge does not make or order any corrections or modifications to the proposed statement under (d)(3), (d)(4), or (e)(3) and does not order either the use of an official electronic recording or preparation of a transcript in lieu of correcting the proposed statement under (d)(6), the judge must promptly certify the statement.

(g) Extensions of time

For good cause, the trial court may grant an extension of not more than 15 days to do any act required or permitted under this rule. *(Adopted, eff. Jan. 1, 2009. As amended, eff. July 1, 2009; March 1, 2014.)*

Advisory Committee Comment

Rules 8.806, 8.810, and 8.812 address applications for extensions of time and relief from default.

Subdivision (b)(2). *Proposed Statement on Appeal (Misdemeanor)* (form CR–135) is available at any courthouse or county law library or online at *www.courts.ca.gov/forms*.

Subdivision (d). Under rule 8.804, the term "judge" includes a commissioner or a temporary judge.

Subdivisions (d)(3)(B), (d)(4), and (f). The judge need not ensure that the statement as modified or corrected is complete, but only that it is an accurate summary of the evidence and testimony relevant to the issues identified by the appellant.

Research References

West's California Judicial Council Forms CR–136, Order Concerning Appellant's Proposed Statement on Appeal (Misdemeanor).

6 Witkin, California Criminal Law 4th Criminal Appeal § 211 (2021), In General.

6 Witkin, California Criminal Law 4th Criminal Appeal § 212 (2021), Procedure.

Ct. Rules

Rule 8.870. Exhibits

(a) Exhibits deemed part of record

Exhibits admitted in evidence, refused, or lodged are deemed part of the record, but may be transmitted to the appellate division only as provided in this rule.

(b) Notice of designation

(1) Within 10 days after the last respondent's brief is filed or could be filed under rule 8.882, if the appellant wants the appellate division to consider any original exhibits that were admitted in evidence, refused, or lodged, the appellant must serve and file a notice in the trial court designating such exhibits.

(2) Within 10 days after a notice under (1) is served, any other party wanting the appellate division to consider additional exhibits must serve and file a notice in trial court designating such exhibits.

(3) A party filing a notice under (1) or (2) must serve a copy on the appellate division.

(c) Request by appellate division

At any time, the appellate division may direct the trial court or a party to send it an exhibit.

(d) Transmittal

Unless the appellate division orders otherwise, within 20 days after the first notice under (b) is filed or after the appellate division directs that an exhibit be sent:

(1) The trial court clerk must put any designated exhibits in the clerk's possession into numerical or alphabetical order and send them to the appellate division. The trial court clerk must also send a list of the exhibits sent. If the exhibits are not transmitted electronically, the trial court clerk must send two copies of the list. If the appellate division clerk finds the list correct, the clerk must sign and return a copy to the trial court clerk.

(2) Any party in possession of designated exhibits returned by the trial court must put them into numerical or alphabetical order and send them to the appellate division The party must also send a list of the exhibits sent. If the exhibits are not transmitted electronically, the party must send two copies of the list. If the appellate division clerk finds the list correct, the clerk must sign and return a copy to the party.

(e) Return by appellate division

On request, the appellate division may return an exhibit to the trial court or to the party that sent it. When the remittitur issues, the appellate division must return all exhibits not transmitted electronically to the trial court or to the party that sent them. *(Adopted, eff. Jan. 1, 2009. As amended, eff. Jan. 1, 2016.)*

Research References

6 Witkin, California Criminal Law 4th Criminal Appeal § 209 (2021), Normal Record on Appeal.

Rule 8.871. Juror-identifying information

(a) Applicability

In a criminal case, a clerk's transcript, a reporter's transcript, or any other document in the record that contains juror-identifying information must comply with this rule.

(b) Juror names, addresses, and telephone numbers

(1) The name of each trial juror or alternate sworn to hear the case must be replaced with an identifying number wherever it appears in any document. The trial court clerk must prepare and keep under seal in the case file a table correlating the jurors' names with their identifying numbers. The clerk and the reporter must use the table in preparing all transcripts or other documents.

(2) The addresses and telephone numbers of trial jurors and alternates sworn to hear the case must be deleted from all documents.

(c) Potential jurors

Information identifying potential jurors called but not sworn as trial jurors or alternates must not be sealed unless otherwise ordered under Code of Civil Procedure section 237(a)(1). *(Adopted, eff. Jan. 1, 2009.)*

Advisory Committee Comment

This rule implements Code of Civil Procedure section 237.

Research References

6 Witkin, California Criminal Law 4th Criminal Appeal § 209 (2021), Normal Record on Appeal.

Rule 8.872. Sending and filing the record in the appellate division

(a) When the record is complete

(1) If the appellant elected under rule 8.864 to proceed without a record of the oral proceedings in the trial court, the record is complete when the clerk's transcript is certified as correct or, if the original trial court file will be used instead of the clerk's transcript, when that original file is ready for transmission as provided under rule 8.863(b).

(2) If the appellant elected under rule 8.864 to proceed with a record of the oral proceedings in the trial court, the record is complete when the clerk's transcript is certified as correct or the original file is ready for transmission as provided in (1) and:

(A) If the appellant elected to use a reporter's transcript, the certified reporter's transcript is delivered to the court under rule 8.866;

(B) If the appellant elected to use a transcript prepared from an official electronic recording, the transcript has been prepared under rule 8. 868;

(C) If the parties stipulated to the use of an official electronic recording of the proceedings, the electronic recording has been prepared under rule 8.868; or

(D) If the appellant elected to use a statement on appeal, the statement on appeal has been certified by the trial court or a transcript or an official electronic recording has been prepared under rule 8.869(d)(6).

(b) Sending the record

When the record is complete, the clerk must promptly send:

(1) The original record to the appellate division;

(2) One copy of the clerk's transcript or index to the original court file and one copy of any record of the oral proceedings to each appellant who is represented by separate counsel or is self-represented; and

(3) One copy of the clerk's transcript or index to the original court file and one copy of any record of the oral proceedings to the respondent.

(c) Filing the record

On receipt, the appellate division clerk must promptly file the original record and send notice of the filing date to the parties. *(Adopted, eff. Jan. 1, 2009. As amended, eff. Jan. 1, 2016.)*

Research References

6 Witkin, California Criminal Law 4th Criminal Appeal § 200 (2021), In General.

6 Witkin, California Criminal Law 4th Criminal Appeal § 209 (2021), Normal Record on Appeal.

Rule 8.873. Augmenting or correcting the record in the appellate division

(a) Subsequent trial court orders

If, after the record is certified, the trial court amends or recalls the judgment or makes any other order in the case, including an order affecting the sentence or probation, the clerk must promptly certify and send a copy of the amended abstract of judgment or other order as an augmentation of the record to all those who received the record under rule 8. 872(b). If there is any additional document or transcript related to the amended judgment or new order that any rule or order requires be included in the record, the clerk must send these documents or transcripts with the amended abstract of judgment or other order. The clerk must promptly copy and certify any such document and the reporter must promptly prepare and certify any such transcript.

(b) Omissions

If, after the record is certified, the trial court clerk or the reporter learns that the record omits a document or transcript that any rule or order requires to be included, the clerk must promptly copy and certify the document or the reporter must promptly prepare and certify the transcript. Without the need for a court order, the clerk must promptly send the document or transcript as an augmentation of the record to all those who received the record under rule 8.872(b).

(c) Augmentation or correction by the appellate division

At any time, on motion of a party or on its own motion, the appellate division may order the record augmented or corrected as provided in rule 8.841. *(Adopted, eff. Jan. 1, 2009.)*

Research References

6 Witkin, California Criminal Law 4th Criminal Appeal § 209 (2021), Normal Record on Appeal.

Rule 8.874. Failure to procure the record

(a) Notice of default

If a party fails to do any act required to procure the record, the trial court clerk must promptly notify that party in writing that it must do the act specified in the notice within 15 days after the notice is sent and that, if it fails to comply, the appellate division may impose the following sanctions:

(1) When the defaulting party is the appellant:

(A) If the appellant is the defendant and is represented by appointed counsel on appeal, the appellate division may relieve that appointed counsel and appoint new counsel; or

(B) If the appellant is the People or the appellant is the defendant and is not represented by appointed counsel, the appellate division may dismiss the appeal.

(2) When the defaulting party is the respondent:

(A) If the respondent is the defendant and is represented by appointed counsel on appeal, the appellate division may relieve that appointed counsel and appoint new counsel; or

(B) If the respondent is the People or the respondent is the defendant and is not represented by appointed counsel, the appellate division may proceed with the appeal on the record designated by the appellant.

(b) Sanctions

If the party fails to take the action specified in a notice given under (a), the trial court clerk must promptly notify the appellate division of the default and the appellate division may impose the sanction specified in the notice. If the appellate division dismisses the appeal, it may vacate the dismissal for good cause. If the appellate division orders the appeal to proceed on the record designated by the appellant, the respondent may obtain relief from default under rule 8.812. *(Adopted, eff. March 1, 2014. As amended, eff. Jan. 1, 2016.)*

Research References

6 Witkin, California Criminal Law 4th Criminal Appeal § 212 (2021), Procedure.

6 Witkin, California Criminal Law 4th Criminal Appeal § 213A (2021), (New) Failure to Procure Record.

Chapter 4

BRIEFS, HEARING, AND DECISION IN LIMITED CIVIL AND MISDEMEANOR APPEALS

Rule 8.880. Application

Except as otherwise provided, the rules in this chapter apply to both civil and misdemeanor appeals in the appellate division. *(Adopted, eff. Jan. 1, 2009.)*

Research References

6 Witkin, California Criminal Law 4th Criminal Appeal § 206 (2021), In General.

Rule 8.881. Notice of briefing schedule

When the record is filed, the clerk of the appellate division must promptly send a notice to each appellate counsel or unrepresented party giving the dates the briefs are due. *(Adopted, eff. Jan. 1, 2009. As amended, eff. Jan. 1, 2016.)*

Research References

6 Witkin, California Criminal Law 4th Criminal Appeal § 217 (2021), In General.

Rule 8.882. Briefs by parties and amici curiae

(a) Briefs by parties

(1) The appellant must serve and file an appellant's opening brief within:

(A) 30 days after the record—or the reporter's transcript, after a rule 8.845 election in a civil case—is filed in the appellate division; or

(B) 60 days after the filing of a rule 8.845 election in a civil case, if the appeal proceeds without a reporter's transcript.

(2) Any respondent's brief must be served and filed within 30 days after the appellant files its opening brief.

(3) Any appellant's reply brief must be served and filed within 20 days after the respondent files its brief.

(4) No other brief may be filed except with the permission of the presiding judge.

(5) Instead of filing a brief, or as part of its brief, a party may join in a brief or adopt by reference all or part of a brief in the same or a related appeal.

(b) Extensions of time

(1) Except as otherwise provided by statute, in a civil case, the parties may extend each period under (a) by up to 30 days by filing one or more stipulations in the appellate division before the brief is due. Stipulations must be signed by and served on all parties. If the stipulation is filed in paper form, the original signature of at least one party must appear on the stipulation filed in the appellate division; the signatures of the other parties may be in the form of fax copies of the signed signature page of the stipulation. If the stipulation is electronically filed, the signatures must comply with the requirements of rule 8.77.

(2) A stipulation under (1) is effective on filing. The appellate division may not shorten such a stipulated extension.

(3) Before the brief is due, a party may apply to the presiding judge of the appellate division for an extension of the time period for filing a brief under (a). The application must show that there is good cause to grant an extension under rule 8.811(b). In civil appeals, the application must also show that:

(A) The applicant was unable to obtain—or it would have been futile to seek—the extension by stipulation; or

(B) The parties have stipulated to the maximum extension permitted under (1) and the applicant seeks a further extension.

(4) A party need not apply for an extension or relief from default if it can file its brief within the time prescribed by (c). The clerk must file a brief submitted within that time if it otherwise complies with these rules.

(c) Failure to file a brief

(1) If a party in a civil appeal fails to timely file an appellant's opening brief or a respondent's brief, the appellate division clerk must promptly notify the party in writing that the brief must be filed within 15 days after the notice is sent and that if the party fails to comply, the court may impose one of the following sanctions:

(A) If the brief is an appellant's opening brief, the court may dismiss the appeal; or

(B) If the brief is a respondent's brief, the court may decide the appeal on the record, the appellant's opening brief, and any oral argument by the appellant.

(2) If the appellant in a misdemeanor appeal fails to timely file an opening brief, the appellate division clerk must promptly notify the appellant in writing that the brief must be filed within 30 days after the notice is sent and that if the appellant fails to comply, the court may impose one of the following sanctions:

(A) If the appellant is the defendant and is represented by appointed counsel on appeal, the court may relieve that appointed counsel and appoint new counsel; or

(B) In all other cases, the court may dismiss the appeal.

(3) If the respondent in a misdemeanor appeal fails to timely file a brief, the appellate division clerk must promptly notify the respondent in writing that the brief must be filed within 30 days after the notice is sent and that if the respondent fails to comply, the court may impose one of the following sanctions:

(A) If the respondent is the defendant and is represented by appointed counsel on appeal, the court may relieve that appointed counsel and appoint new counsel; or

(B) In all other cases, the court may decide the appeal on the record, the appellant's opening brief, and any oral argument by the appellant.

(4) If a party fails to comply with a notice under (1), (2), or (3), the court may impose the sanction specified in the notice.

(d) Amicus curiae briefs

(1) Within 14 days after the appellant's reply brief is filed or was required to be filed, whichever is earlier, any person or entity may serve and file an application for permission of the presiding judge to file an amicus curiae brief. For good cause, the presiding judge may allow later filing.

(2) The application must state the applicant's interest and explain how the proposed amicus curiae brief will assist the court in deciding the matter.

(3) The application must also identify:

(A) Any party or any counsel for a party in the pending appeal who:

(i) Authored the proposed amicus brief in whole or in part; or

(ii) Made a monetary contribution intended to fund the preparation or submission of the brief; and

(B) Every person or entity who made a monetary contribution intended to fund the preparation or submission of the brief, other than the amicus curiae, its members, or its counsel in the pending appeal.

(4) The proposed brief must be served and must accompany the application and may be combined with it.

(5) The Attorney General may file an amicus curiae brief without the presiding judge's permission, unless the brief is submitted on behalf of another state officer or agency; but the presiding judge may prescribe reasonable conditions for filing and answering the brief.

(e) Service and filing

(1) Copies of each brief must be served as required by rule 8.817.

(2) Unless the court provides otherwise by local rule or order in the specific case, only the original brief, with proof of service, must be filed in the appellate division.

(3) A copy of each brief must be served on the trial court clerk for delivery to the judge who tried the case.

(4) A copy of each brief must be served on a public officer or agency when required by rule 8.817.

(5) In misdemeanor appeals:

(A) Defendant's appellate counsel must serve each brief for the defendant on the People and must send a copy of each brief to the defendant personally unless the defendant requests otherwise;

(B) The proof of service under (A) must state that a copy of the defendant's brief was sent to the defendant, or counsel must file a signed statement that the defendant requested in writing that no copy be sent; and

(C) The People must serve two copies of their briefs on the appellate counsel for each defendant who is a party to the appeal.

(Adopted, eff. Jan. 1, 2009. As amended, eff. Jan. 1, 2009; Jan. 1, 2010; Jan. 1, 2013; March 1, 2014; Jan. 1, 2016; Jan. 1, 2018; Jan. 1, 2021.)

Advisory Committee Comment

Subdivision (a). Note that the sequence and timing of briefing in appeals in which a party is both appellant and respondent (cross-appeals) are governed by rule 8.884. Typically, a cross-appellant's combined respondent's brief and opening brief must be filed within the time specified in (a)(2) for the respondent's brief.

Subdivision (b). Extensions of briefing time are limited by statute in some cases. For example, under Public Resources Code section 21167.6(h) in cases under section 21167 extensions are limited to one 30–day extension for the opening brief and one 30–day extension for "preparation of responding brief."

Research References

West's California Judicial Council Forms App–106, Application for Extension of Time to File Brief (Limited Civil Case).

6 Witkin, California Criminal Law 4th Criminal Appeal § 217 (2021), In General.

Rule 8.883. Contents and form of briefs

(a) Contents

(1) Each brief must:

(A) State each point under a separate heading or subheading summarizing the point and support each point by argument and, if possible, by citation of authority; and

(B) Support any reference to a matter in the record by a citation to the volume and page number of the record where the matter appears.

(2) An appellant's opening brief must:

(A) State the nature of the action, the relief sought in the trial court, and the judgment or order appealed from;

(B) State that the judgment appealed from is final or explain why the order appealed from is appealable; and

(C) Provide a summary of the significant facts limited to matters in the record.

(b) Length

(1) A brief produced on a computer must not exceed 6,800 words, including footnotes. Such a brief must include a certificate by appellate counsel or an unrepresented party stating the number of words in the brief. The person certifying may rely on the word count of the computer program used to prepare the brief.

(2) A brief produced on a typewriter must not exceed 20 pages.

(3) The information listed on the cover, any table of contents or table of authorities, the certificate under (1), and any signature block are excluded from the limits stated in (1) or (2).

(4) On application, the presiding judge may permit a longer brief for good cause. A lengthy record or numerous or complex issues on appeal will ordinarily constitute good cause. If the court grants an application to file a longer brief, it may order that the brief include a table of contents and a table of authorities.

(c) Form

(1) A brief may be reproduced by any process that produces a clear, black image of letter quality. All documents filed must have a page size of 8 ½ by 11 inches. If filed in paper form, the paper must be white or unbleached and of at least 20–pound weight. Both sides of the paper may be used if the brief is not bound at the top.

(2) Any conventional font may be used. The font may be either proportionally spaced or monospaced.

(3) The font style must be roman; but for emphasis, italics or boldface may be used or the text may be underscored. Case names must be italicized or underscored. Headings may be in uppercase letters.

(4) Except as provided in (11), the font size, including footnotes, s, must not be smaller than 13–point.

(5) The lines of text must be at least one-and-a-half-spaced. Headings and footnotes may be single-spaced. Quotations may be block-indented and single-spaced. Single-spaced means six lines to a vertical inch.

(6) The margins must be at least 1½ inches on the left and right and 1 inch on the top and bottom.

(7) The pages must be consecutively numbered.

(8) The cover—or first page if there is no cover—must include the information required by rule 8.816(a)(1).

(9) If filed in paper form, the brief must be bound on the left margin, except that briefs may be bound at the top if required by a local rule of the appellate division. If the brief is stapled, the bound edge and staples must be covered with tape.

(10) The brief need not be signed.

(11) If the brief is produced on a typewriter:

(A) A typewritten original and carbon copies may be filed only with the presiding judge's permission, which will ordinarily be given only to unrepresented parties proceeding in forma pauperis. All other typewritten briefs must be filed as photocopies.

(B) Both sides of the paper may be used if a photocopy is filed; only one side may be used if a typewritten original and carbon copies are filed.

(C) The type size, including footnotes, must not be smaller than standard pica, 10 characters per inch. Unrepresented incarcerated litigants may use elite type, 12 characters per inch, if they lack access to a typewriter with larger characters.

(d) Noncomplying briefs

If a brief does not comply with this rule:

(1) The reviewing court clerk may decline to file it, but must mark it "received but not filed" and return it to the party; or

(2) If the brief is filed, the presiding judge may with or without notice:

(A) Order the brief returned for corrections and refiling within a specified time;

(B) Strike the brief with leave to file a new brief within a specified time; or

(C) Disregard the noncompliance.

(Adopted, eff. Jan. 1, 2009. As amended, eff. Jan. 1, 2011; Jan. 1, 2013; Jan. 1, 2014; Jan. 1, 2016.)

Advisory Committee Comment

Subdivision (b). Subdivision (b)(1) states the maximum permissible lengths of briefs produced on a computer in terms of word count rather than page count. This provision tracks a provision in rule 8.204(c) governing Court of Appeal briefs and is explained in the comment to that provision. Subdivision (b)(3) specifies certain items that are not counted toward the maximum brief length. Signature blocks, as referenced in this provision, include not only the signatures, but also the printed names, titles, and affiliations of any attorneys filing or joining in the brief, which may accompany the signature.

Research References

6 Witkin, California Criminal Law 4th Criminal Appeal § 217 (2021), In General.

Rule 8.884. Appeals in which a party is both appellant and respondent

(a) Briefing sequence and time to file briefs

In an appeal in which any party is both an appellant and a respondent:

(1) The parties must jointly—or separately if unable to agree—submit a proposed briefing sequence to the appellate division within 20 days after the second notice of appeal is filed.

(2) After receiving the proposal, the appellate division must order a briefing sequence and prescribe briefing periods consistent with rule 8.882(a).

(b) Contents of briefs

(1) A party that is both an appellant and a respondent must combine its respondent's brief with its appellant's opening brief or its reply brief, if any, whichever is appropriate under the briefing sequence that the appellate division orders under (a).

(2) A party must confine a reply brief to points raised in its own appeal.

(3) A combined brief must address the points raised in each appeal separately but may include a single summary of the significant facts. *(Adopted, eff. Jan. 1, 2009. As amended, eff. Jan. 1, 2009.)*

Research References

6 Witkin, California Criminal Law 4th Criminal Appeal § 217 (2021), In General.

Rule 8.885. Oral argument

(a) Calendaring and sessions

(1) Unless otherwise ordered, and except as provided in (2), all appeals in which the last reply brief was filed or the time for filing this brief expired 45 or more days before the date of a regular appellate division session must be placed on the calendar for that session by the appellate division clerk. By order of the presiding judge or the division, any appeal may be placed on the calendar for oral argument at any session.

(2) Oral argument will not be set in appeals under *People v. Wende* (1979) 25 Cal.3d 436 where no arguable issue is raised.

(b) Oral argument by videoconference

(1) Oral argument may be conducted by videoconference if:

(A) It is ordered by the presiding judge of the appellate division or the presiding judge's designee on application of any party or on the court's own motion. An application from a party requesting that oral argument be conducted by videoconference must be filed within 10 days after the court sends notice of oral argument under (c)(1); or

(B) A local rule authorizes oral argument to be conducted by videoconference consistent with these rules.

(2) If oral argument is conducted by videoconference:

(A) Each judge of the appellate division panel assigned to the case must participate in the entire oral argument either in person at the superior court that issued the judgment or order that is being appealed or by videoconference from another court.

(B) Unless otherwise allowed by local rule or ordered by the presiding judge of the appellate division or the presiding judge's designee, all the parties must appear at oral argument in person at the superior court that issued the judgment or order that is being appealed.

(C) The oral argument must be open to the public at the superior court that issued the judgment or order that is being appealed. If provided by local rule or ordered by the presiding judge of the appellate division or the presiding judge's designee, oral argument may also be open to the public at any of the locations from which a judge of the appellate division is participating in oral argument.

(D) The appellate division must ensure that:

(i) During oral argument, the participants in oral argument are visible and their statements are audible to all other participants, court staff, and any members of the public attending the oral argument;

(ii) Participants are identified when they speak; and

(iii) Only persons who are authorized to participate in the proceedings speak.

(E) A party must not be charged any fee to participate in oral argument by videoconference if the party participates from the superior court that issued the judgment or order that is being appealed or from a location from which a judge of the appellate division panel is participating in oral argument.

(c) Notice of argument

(1) Except for appeals covered by (a)(2), as soon as all parties' briefs are filed or the time for filing these briefs has expired, the appellate division clerk must send a notice of the time and place of oral argument to all parties. The notice must be sent at least 20 days before the date for oral argument. The presiding judge may shorten the notice period for good cause; in that event, the clerk must immediately notify the parties by telephone or other expeditious method.

(2) If oral argument will be conducted by videoconference under (b), the clerk must specify, either in the notice required under (1) or in a supplemental notice sent to all parties at least 5 days before the date for oral argument, the location from which each judge of the appellate division panel assigned to the case will participate in oral argument.

(d) Waiver of argument

(1) Parties may waive oral argument in advance by filing a notice of waiver of oral argument within 7 days after the notice of oral argument is sent.

(2) The court may vacate oral argument if all parties waive oral argument.

(3) If the court vacates oral argument, the court must notify the parties that no oral argument will be held.

(4) If all parties do not waive oral argument, or if the court rejects a waiver request, the matter will remain on the oral argument calendar. Any party who previously filed a notice of waiver may participate in the oral argument.

(e) Conduct of argument

Unless the court provides otherwise:

(1) The appellant, petitioner, or moving party has the right to open and close. If there are two or more such parties, the court must set the sequence of argument.

(2) Each side is allowed 10 minutes for argument. The appellant may reserve part of this time for reply argument. If multiple parties are represented by separate counsel, or if an amicus curiae—on written request—is granted permission to argue, the court may apportion or expand the time.

(3) Only one counsel may argue for each separately represented party. *(Adopted, eff. Jan. 1, 2009. As amended, eff. Jan. 1, 2010; Jan. 1, 2020.)*

Advisory Committee Comment

Subdivision (a). Under rule 10.1108, the appellate division must hold a session at least once each quarter, unless no matters are set for oral argument that quarter, but may choose to hold sessions more frequently.

Research References

West's California Judicial Council Forms App–108, Notice of Waiver of Oral Argument (Limited Civil Case).
West's California Judicial Council Forms CR–138, Notice of Waiver of Oral Argument (Misdemeanor).
6 Witkin, California Criminal Law 4th Criminal Appeal § 217 (2021), In General.

Rule 8.886. Submission of the cause

(a) When the cause is submitted

(1) Except as provided in (2), a cause is submitted when the court has heard oral argument or approved its waiver and the time has expired to file all briefs and papers, including any supplemental brief permitted by the court. The appellate division may order the cause submitted at an earlier time if the parties so stipulate.

(2) For appeals that raise no arguable issues under *People v. Wende* (1979) 25 Cal.3d 436, the cause is submitted when the time has expired to file all briefs and papers, including any supplemental brief permitted by the court.

(b) Vacating submission

The court may vacate submission only by an order stating its reasons and setting a timetable for resubmission. *(Adopted, eff. Jan. 1, 2009. As amended, eff. Jan. 1, 2020.)*

Research References

6 Witkin, California Criminal Law 4th Criminal Appeal § 218 (2021), Decision.

Rule 8.887. Decisions

(a) Written opinions

Appellate division judges are not required to prepare a written opinion in any case but may do so when they deem it advisable or in the public interest. A decision by opinion must identify the participating judges, including the author of the majority opinion and of any concurring or dissenting opinion, or the judges participating in a "by the court" opinion.

(b) Filing the decision

The appellate division clerk must promptly file all opinions and orders of the court and on the same day send copies (by e-mail where permissible under rule 2.251) showing the filing date to the parties and, when relevant, to the trial court.

(c) Opinions certified for publication

(1) Opinions certified for publication must comply to the extent practicable with the *California Style Manual*.

(2) When the opinion is certified for publication, the clerk must immediately send:

(A) Two paper copies and one electronic copy to the Reporter of Decisions in a format approved by the Reporter.

(B) One copy to the Court of Appeal for the district. The copy must bear the notation "This opinion has been certified for publication in the Official Reports. It is being sent to assist the Court of Appeal in deciding whether to order the case transferred to the court on the court's own motion under rules 8.1000–8.1018." The clerk/executive officer of the Court of Appeal must promptly file that copy or make a docket entry showing its receipt. *(Adopted, eff. Jan. 1, 2009. As amended, eff. Jan. 1, 2011; March 1, 2014; Jan. 1, 2018; Jan. 1, 2019.)*

Research References

6 Witkin, California Criminal Law 4th Criminal Appeal § 218 (2021), Decision.

Rule 8.888. Finality and modification of decision

(a) Finality of decision

(1) Except as otherwise provided in this rule, an appellate division decision, including an order dismissing an appeal involuntarily, is final 30 days after the decision is sent by the court clerk to the parties.

(2) If the appellate division certifies a written opinion for publication or partial publication after its decision is filed and before its decision becomes final in that court, the finality period runs from the date the order for publication is sent by the court clerk to the parties.

(3) The following appellate division decisions are final in that court when filed:

(A) The denial of a petition for writ of supersedeas;

(B) The denial of an application for bail or to reduce bail pending appeal; and

(C) The dismissal of an appeal on request or stipulation.

(b) Modification of judgment

(1) The appellate division may modify its decision until the decision is final in that court. If the clerk's office is closed on the date of finality, the court may modify the decision on the next day the clerk's office is open.

(2) An order modifying a decision must state whether it changes the appellate judgment. A modification that does not change the

appellate judgment does not extend the finality date of the decision. If a modification changes the appellate judgment, the finality period runs from the date the modification order is sent by the court clerk to the parties.

(c) Consent to increase or decrease in amount of judgment

If an appellate division decision conditions the affirmance of a money judgment on a party's consent to an increase or decrease in the amount, the judgment is reversed unless, before the decision is final under (a), the party serves and files a copy of a consent in the appellate division. If a consent is filed, the finality period runs from the filing date of the consent. The clerk must send one filed-endorsed copy of the consent to the trial court with the remittitur. *(Adopted, eff. Jan. 1, 2009. As amended, eff. Jan. 1, 2016; Jan. 1, 2019.)*

Research References

6 Witkin, California Criminal Law 4th Criminal Appeal § 199 (2021), Hearing After Appeal in Misdemeanor Case.
6 Witkin, California Criminal Law 4th Criminal Appeal § 218 (2021), Decision.

Rule 8.889. Rehearing

(a) Power to order rehearing

(1) On petition of a party or on its own motion, the appellate division may order rehearing of any decision that is not final in that court on filing.

(2) An order for rehearing must be filed before the decision is final. If the clerk's office is closed on the date of finality, the court may file the order on the next day the clerk's office is open.

(b) Petition and answer

(1) A party may serve and file a petition for rehearing within 15 days after the following, whichever is later:

(A) The decision is sent by the court clerk to the parties;

(B) A publication order restarting the finality period under rule 8.888(a)(2), if the party has not already filed a petition for rehearing, is sent by the court clerk to the parties;

(C) A modification order changing the appellate judgment under rule 8.888(b) is sent by the court clerk to the parties; or

(D) A consent is filed under rule 8.888(c).

(2) A party must not file an answer to a petition for rehearing unless the court requests an answer. The clerk must promptly send to the parties copies of any order requesting an answer and immediately notify the parties by telephone or another expeditious method. Any answer must be served and filed within 8 days after the order is filed unless the court orders otherwise. A petition for rehearing normally will not be granted unless the court has requested an answer.

(3) The petition and answer must comply with the relevant provisions of rule 8.883.

(4) Before the decision is final and for good cause, the presiding judge may relieve a party from a failure to file a timely petition or answer.

(c) No extensions of time

The time for granting or denying a petition for rehearing in the appellate division may not be extended. If the court does not rule on the petition before the decision is final, the petition is deemed denied.

(d) Effect of granting rehearing

An order granting a rehearing vacates the decision and any opinion filed in the case. If the appellate division orders rehearing, it may place the case on calendar for further argument or submit it for decision. *(Adopted, eff. Jan. 1, 2009. As amended, eff. Jan. 1, 2019.)*

Research References

West's California Judicial Council Forms CR-131-INFO, Information on Appeal Procedures for Misdemeanors.
6 Witkin, California Criminal Law 4th Criminal Appeal § 218 (2021), Decision.

Rule 8.890. Remittitur

(a) Proceedings requiring issuance of remittitur

An appellate division must issue a remittitur after a decision in an appeal.

(b) Clerk's duties

(1) If an appellate division case is not transferred to the Court of Appeal under rule 8.1000 et seq., the appellate division clerk must:

(A) Issue a remittitur immediately after the Court of Appeal denies transfer or the period for granting transfer under rule 8.1008(a) expires if there will be no further proceedings in the appellate division;

(B) Send the remittitur to the trial court with a filed-endorsed copy of the opinion or order; and

(C) Return to the trial court with the remittitur all original records, exhibits, and documents sent nonelectronically to the appellate division in connection with the appeal, except any certification for transfer under rule 8.1005, the transcripts or statement on appeal, briefs, and the notice of appeal.

(2) If an appellate division case is transferred to a Court of Appeal under rule 8.1000 et seq., on receiving the Court of Appeal remittitur, the appellate division clerk must issue a remittitur and return documents to the trial court as provided in rule 8.1018.

(c) Immediate issuance, stay, and recall

(1) The appellate division may direct immediate issuance of a remittitur only on the parties' stipulation or on dismissal of the appeal on the request or stipulation of the parties under rule 8.825(b)(2).

(2) On a party's or its own motion or on stipulation, and for good cause, the court may stay a remittitur's issuance for a reasonable period or order its recall.

(3) An order recalling a remittitur issued after a decision by opinion does not supersede the opinion or affect its publication status.

(d) Notice

The remittitur is deemed issued when the clerk enters it in the record. The clerk must immediately send the parties notice of issuance of the remittitur, showing the date of entry. *(Adopted, eff. Jan. 1, 2009. As amended, eff. Jan. 1, 2011; March 1, 2014; Jan. 1, 2016.)*

Research References

6 Witkin, California Criminal Law 4th Criminal Appeal § 200 (2021), In General.
6 Witkin, California Criminal Law 4th Criminal Appeal § 219 (2021), Remittitur.

Rule 8.891. Costs and sanctions in civil appeals

(a) Right to costs

(1) Except as provided in this rule, the prevailing party in a civil appeal is entitled to costs on appeal.

(2) The prevailing party is the respondent if the appellate division affirms the judgment without modification or dismisses the appeal. The prevailing party is the appellant if the appellate division reverses the judgment in its entirety.

(3) If the appellate division reverses the judgment in part or modifies it, or if there is more than one notice of appeal, the appellate division must specify the award or denial of costs in its decision.

(4) In the interests of justice, the appellate division may also award or deny costs as it deems proper.

(b) Judgment for costs

(1) The appellate division clerk must enter on the record and insert in the remittitur judgment awarding costs to the prevailing party under (a).

(2) If the clerk fails to enter judgment for costs, the appellate division may recall the remittitur for correction on its own motion or on a party's motion made not later than 30 days after the remittitur issues.

(c) Procedure for claiming or opposing costs

(1) Within 30 days after the clerk sends notice of issuance of the remittitur, a party claiming costs awarded by the appellate division must serve and file in the trial court a verified memorandum of costs under rule 3.1700(a)(1).

(2) A party may serve and file a motion in the trial court to strike or tax costs claimed under (1) in the manner required by rule 3.1700.

(3) An award of costs is enforceable as a money judgment.

(d) Recoverable costs

(1) A party may recover only the costs of the following, if reasonable:

(A) Filing fees;

(B) The amount the party paid for any portion of the record, whether an original or a copy or both, subject to reduction by the appellate division under subdivision (e);

(C) The cost to produce additional evidence on appeal;

(D) The costs to notarize, serve, mail, and file the record, briefs, and other papers;

(E) The cost to print and reproduce any brief, including any petition for rehearing or review, answer, or reply;

(F) The cost to procure a surety bond, including the premium, the cost to obtain a letter of credit as collateral, and the fees and net interest expenses incurred to borrow funds to provide security for the bond or to obtain a letter of credit, unless the trial court determines the bond was unnecessary; and

(G) The fees and net interest expenses incurred to borrow funds to deposit with the superior court in lieu of a bond or undertaking, unless the trial court determines the deposit was unnecessary.

(2) Unless the court orders otherwise, an award of costs neither includes attorney's fees on appeal nor precludes a party from seeking them under rule 3.1702.

(e) Sanctions

(1) On motion of a party or its own motion, the appellate division may impose sanctions, including the award or denial of costs, on a party or an attorney for:

(A) Taking a frivolous appeal or appealing solely to cause delay; or

(B) Committing any unreasonable violation of these rules.

(2) A party's motion under (1) must include a declaration supporting the amount of any monetary sanction sought and must be served and filed before any order dismissing the appeal but no later than 10 days after the appellant's reply brief is due. If a party files a motion for sanctions with a motion to dismiss the appeal and the motion to dismiss is not granted, the party may file a new motion for sanctions within 10 days after the appellant's reply brief is due.

(3) The court must give notice in writing if it is considering imposing sanctions. Within 10 days after the court sends such notice, a party or attorney may serve and file an opposition, but failure to do so will not be deemed consent. An opposition may not be filed unless the court sends such notice.

(4) Unless otherwise ordered, oral argument on the issue of sanctions must be combined with oral argument on the merits of the appeal. *(Adopted, eff. Jan. 1, 2009. As amended, eff. Jan. 1, 2011; Jan. 1, 2013.)*

Advisory Committee Comment

Subdivision (d). "Net interest expenses" in subdivisions (d)(1)(F) and (G) means the interest expenses incurred to borrow the funds that are deposited minus any interest earned by the borrower on those funds while they are on deposit.

Subdivision (d)(1)(D), allowing recovery of the "costs to notarize, serve, mail, and file the record, briefs, and other papers," is intended to include fees charged by electronic filing service providers for electronic filing and service of documents.

Research References

West's California Judicial Council Forms App–101–INFO, Information on Appeal Procedures for Limited Civil Cases.

Chapter 5

APPEALS IN INFRACTION CASES

Article 1

TAKING APPEALS IN INFRACTION CASES

Rule

Rule 8.900. Application of chapter

The rules in this chapter apply only to appeals in infraction cases. An infraction case is a case in which the defendant was convicted only of an infraction and was not charged with any felony. A felony is "charged" when an information or indictment accusing the defendant of a felony is filed or a complaint accusing the defendant of a felony is certified to the superior court under Penal Code section 859a. *(Adopted, eff. Jan. 1, 2009.)*

Advisory Committee Comment

Chapter 1 of this division also applies in appeals from infraction cases. Chapters 3 and 4 of this division apply to appeals in misdemeanor cases. The rules that apply in appeals in felony cases are located in chapter 3 of division 1 of this title.

Penal Code section 1466 provides that an appeal in a "misdemeanor or infraction case" is to the appellate division of the superior court, and Penal Code section 1235(b), in turn, provides that an appeal in a "felony case" is to the Court of Appeal. Penal Code section 691(g) defines "misdemeanor or infraction case" to mean "a criminal action in which a misdemeanor or infraction is charged *and does not include a criminal action in which a felony is charged* in conjunction with a misdemeanor or infraction" (emphasis added), and section 691(f) defines "felony case" to mean "a criminal action in which a felony is charged *and includes a criminal action in which a misdemeanor or infraction is charged in conjunction with a felony*" (emphasis added).

As rule 8.304 from the rules on felony appeals makes clear, a "felony case" is an action in which a felony is charged *regardless of the outcome of the action*. Thus the question of which rules apply—these appellate division rules or the rules governing appeals in felony cases—is answered simply by examining the accusatory pleading: if that document charged the defendant with at least one count of felony (as defined in Penal Code, section 17(a)), the Court of Appeal has appellate jurisdiction and the appeal must be taken under the rules on felony appeals *even if the prosecution did not result in a punishment of imprisonment in a state prison*.

It is settled case law that an appeal is taken to the Court of Appeal not only when the defendant is charged with and convicted of a felony, but also when the defendant is charged with both a felony and a misdemeanor (Pen. Code, § 691(f)) but is convicted of only the misdemeanor (e.g., *People v. Brown*

(1970) 10 Cal.App.3d 169); when the defendant is charged with a felony but is convicted of only a lesser offense (Pen. Code, § 1159; e.g., *People v. Spreckels* (1954) 125 Cal.App.2d 507); and when the defendant is charged with an offense filed as a felony but punishable as either a felony or a misdemeanor, and the offense is thereafter deemed a misdemeanor under Penal Code section 17(b) (e.g., *People v. Douglas* (1999) 20 Cal.4th 85; *People v. Clark* (1971) 17 Cal.App.3d 890).

Trial court unification did not change this rule: after as before unification, "Appeals in felony cases lie to the [C]ourt of [A]ppeal, regardless of whether the appeal is from the superior court, the municipal court, or the action of a magistrate. *Cf.* Cal. Const. art. VI, § 11(a) [except in death penalty cases, Courts of Appeal have appellate jurisdiction when superior courts have original jurisdiction 'in causes of a type within the appellate jurisdiction of the [C]ourts of [A]ppeal on June 30, 1995 . . .']." ("Recommendation on Trial Court Unification" (July 1998) 28 *Cal. Law Revision Com. Rep.* 455–56.)

Research References

West's California Judicial Council Forms CR–141–INFO, Information on Appeal Procedures for Infractions.

6 Witkin, California Criminal Law 4th Criminal Appeal § 2 (2021), Appellate Rules.

6 Witkin, California Criminal Law 4th Criminal Appeal § 206 (2021), In General.

4 Witkin, California Criminal Law 4th Introduction to Criminal Procedure § 9 (2021), Rules of Court.

Rule 8.901. Notice of appeal

(a) Notice of appeal

(1) To appeal from a judgment or an appealable order in an infraction case, the defendant or the People must file a notice of appeal in the trial court that issued the judgment or order being appealed. The notice must specify the judgment or order—or part of it—being appealed.

(2) If the defendant appeals, the defendant or the defendant's attorney must sign the notice of appeal. If the People appeal, the attorney for the People must sign the notice.

(3) The notice of appeal must be liberally construed in favor of its sufficiency.

(b) Notification of the appeal

(1) When a notice of appeal is filed, the trial court clerk must promptly send a notification of the filing to the attorney of record for each party and to any unrepresented defendant. The clerk must also send or deliver this notification to the appellate division clerk.

(2) The notification must show the date it was sent or delivered, the number and title of the case, and the date the notice of appeal was filed.

(3) The notification to the appellate division clerk must also include a copy of the notice of appeal.

(4) A copy of the notice of appeal is sufficient notification under (1) if the required information is on the copy or is added by the trial court clerk.

(5) The sending of a notification under (1) is a sufficient performance of the clerk's duty despite the discharge, disqualification, suspension, disbarment, or death of the attorney.

(6) Failure to comply with any provision of this subdivision does not affect the validity of the notice of appeal. *(Adopted, eff. Jan. 1, 2009. As amended, eff. Jan. 1, 2016.)*

Advisory Committee Comment

Notice of Appeal and Record on Appeal (Infraction) (form CR–142) may be used to file the notice of appeal required under this rule. This form is available at any courthouse or county law library or online at *www.courts.ca.gov/forms.*

Research References

West's California Judicial Council Forms CR–142, Notice of Appeal and Record on Appeal.

6 Witkin, California Criminal Law 4th Criminal Appeal § 208 (2021), Notice of Appeal.

Rule 8.902. Time to appeal

(a) Normal time

A notice of appeal must be filed within 30 days after the rendition of the judgment or the making of the order being appealed. If the defendant is committed before final judgment for insanity or narcotics addiction, the notice of appeal must be filed within 30 days after the commitment.

(b) Cross-appeal

If the defendant or the People timely appeals from a judgment or appealable order, the time for any other party to appeal from the same judgment or order is either the time specified in (a) or 30 days after the trial court clerk sends notification of the first appeal, whichever is later.

(c) Premature notice of appeal

A notice of appeal filed before the judgment is rendered or the order is made is premature, but the appellate division may treat the notice as filed immediately after the rendition of the judgment or the making of the order.

(d) Late notice of appeal

The trial court clerk must mark a late notice of appeal "Received [date] but not filed" and notify the party that the notice was not filed because it was late. *(Adopted, eff. Jan. 1, 2009. As amended, eff. July 1, 2010; Jan. 1, 2016.)*

Research References

6 Witkin, California Criminal Law 4th Criminal Appeal § 208 (2021), Notice of Appeal.

Advisory Committee Comment

Subdivision (d). See rule 8.817(b)(5) for provisions concerning the timeliness of documents mailed by inmates or patients from custodial institutions.

Rule 8.903. Stay of execution on appeal

(a) Application

Pending appeal, the defendant may apply to the appellate division for a stay of execution after a judgment of conviction.

(b) Showing

The application must include a showing that the defendant sought relief in the trial court and that the court unjustifiably denied the application.

(c) Service

The application must be served on the prosecuting attorney.

(d) Interim relief

Pending its ruling on the application, the appellate division may grant the relief requested. The appellate division must notify the trial court of any stay that it grants. *(Adopted, eff. Jan. 1, 2009.)*

Advisory Committee Comment

Subdivision (c). Under rule 8.804, the prosecuting attorney means the city attorney, county counsel, or district attorney prosecuting the infraction.

Research References

6 Witkin, California Criminal Law 4th Criminal Appeal § 206 (2021), In General.

Rule 8.904. Abandoning the appeal

(a) How to abandon

An appellant may abandon the appeal at any time by filing an abandonment of the appeal signed by the appellant or the appellant's attorney of record.

(b) Where to file; effect of filing

(1) The appellant must file the abandonment in the appellate division.

(2) If the record has not been filed in the appellate division, the filing of an abandonment effects a dismissal of the appeal and restores the trial court's jurisdiction.

(3) If the record has been filed in the appellate division, the appellate division may dismiss the appeal and direct immediate issuance of the remittitur.

(c) Clerk's duties

(1) The appellate division clerk must immediately notify the adverse party of the filing or of the order of dismissal.

(2) If the record has not been filed in the appellate division, the clerk must immediately notify the trial court.

(3) If a reporter's transcript has been requested, the clerk must immediately notify the reporter if the appeal is abandoned before the reporter has filed the transcript. *(Adopted, eff. Jan. 1, 2009.)*

Advisory Committee Comment

Abandonment of Appeal (Infraction) (form CR–145) may be used to file an abandonment under this rule. This form is available at any courthouse or county law library or online at *www.courts.ca.gov/forms*.

Research References

West's California Judicial Council Forms CR–145, Abandonment of Appeal (Infraction).

6 Witkin, California Criminal Law 4th Criminal Appeal § 215 (2021), Abandonment and Dismissal.

Article 2

RECORD IN INFRACTION APPEALS

Rule

Rule 8.910. Normal record on appeal

(a) Contents

Except as otherwise provided in this chapter, the record on an appeal to a superior court appellate division in an infraction criminal case must contain the following, which constitute the normal record on appeal:

(1) A record of the written documents from the trial court proceedings in the form of one of the following:

(A) A clerk's transcript under rule 8.912 or 8.920; or

(B) If the court has a local rule for the appellate division electing to use this form of the record, the original trial court file under rule 8.914.

(2) If an appellant wants to raise any issue that requires consideration of the oral proceedings in the trial court, the record on appeal must include a record of the oral proceedings in the form of one of the following:

(A) A statement on appeal under rule 8.916;

(B) If the court has a local rule for the appellate division permitting this form of the record, an official electronic recording of the proceedings under rule 8.917; or

(C) A reporter's transcript under rules 8.918–8.920 or a transcript prepared from an official electronic recording under rule 8.917.

(b) Stipulation for limited record

If before the record is certified, the appellant and the respondent stipulate in writing that any part of the record is not required for proper determination of the appeal and file the stipulation in the trial court, that part of the record must not be prepared or sent to the appellate division. *(Adopted, eff. Jan. 1, 2009. As amended, eff. Jan. 1, 2010.)*

Research References

West's California Judicial Council Forms CR–142, Notice of Appeal and Record on Appeal.

6 Witkin, California Criminal Law 4th Criminal Appeal § 209 (2021), Normal Record on Appeal.

Rule 8.911. Prosecuting attorney's notice regarding the record

If the prosecuting attorney does not want to receive a copy of the record on appeal, within 10 days after the notification of the appeal under rule 8.901(b) is sent to the prosecuting attorney, the prosecuting attorney must serve and file a notice indicating that he or she does not want to receive the record. *(Adopted, eff. Jan. 1, 2009. As amended, eff. Jan. 1, 2016.)*

Rule 8.912. Contents of clerk's transcript

Except in appeals covered by rule 8.920 or when the parties have filed a stipulation under rule 8.910(b) that any of these items is not required for proper determination of the appeal, the clerk's transcript must contain:

(1) The complaint, including any notice to appear, and any amendment;

(2) Any demurrer or other plea;

(3) All court minutes;

(4) Any written findings or opinion of the court;

(5) The judgment or order appealed from;

(6) Any motion or notice of motion for new trial, in arrest of judgment, or to dismiss the action, with supporting and opposing memoranda and attachments;

(7) Any transcript of a sound or sound-and-video recording tendered to the court under rule 2.1040;

(8) The notice of appeal; and

(9) If the appellant is the defendant:

(A) Any written defense motion denied in whole or in part, with supporting and opposing memoranda and attachments; and

(B) If related to a motion under (A), any search warrant and return. *(Adopted, eff. Jan. 1, 2009.)*

Research References

6 Witkin, California Criminal Law 4th Criminal Appeal § 210 (2021), Transcripts.

Rule 8.913. Preparation of clerk's transcript

(a) When preparation begins

Unless the original court file will be used in place of a clerk's transcript under rule 8.914, the clerk must begin preparing the clerk's transcript immediately after the notice of appeal is filed.

(b) Format of transcript

The clerk's transcript must comply with rule 8.144.

(c) When preparation must be completed

Within 20 days after the notice of appeal is filed, the clerk must complete preparation of an original clerk's transcript for the appellate division and one copy for the appellant. If there is more than one appellant, the clerk must prepare an extra copy for each additional appellant who is represented by separate counsel or self-represented. If the defendant is the appellant, a copy must also be prepared for the prosecuting attorney unless the prosecuting attorney has notified the court under rule 8.911 that he or she does not want to receive the record. If the People are the appellant, a copy must also be prepared for the respondent.

(d) Certification

The clerk must certify as correct the original and all copies of the clerk's transcript. *(Adopted, eff. Jan. 1, 2009.)*

Advisory Committee Comment

Rule 8.922 addresses when the clerk's transcript is sent to the appellate division in infraction appeals.

Research References

6 Witkin, California Criminal Law 4th Criminal Appeal § 210 (2021), Transcripts.

Rule 8.914. Trial court file instead of clerk's transcript

(a) Application

If the court has a local rule for the appellate division electing to use this form of the record, the original trial court file may be used instead of a clerk's transcript. This rule and any supplemental provisions of the local rule then govern unless the trial court orders otherwise after notice to the parties.

(b) When original file must be prepared

Within 20 days after the filing of the notice of appeal, the trial court clerk must put the trial court file in chronological order, number the pages, and attach a chronological index and a list of all attorneys of record, the parties they represent, and any unrepresented parties.

(c) Copies

The clerk must send a copy of the index to the appellant for use in paginating his or her copy of the file to conform to the index. If there is more than one appellant, the clerk must prepare an extra copy of the index for each additional appellant who is represented by separate counsel or self-represented. If the defendant is the appellant, a copy must also be prepared for the prosecuting attorney unless the prosecuting attorney has notified the court under rule 8.911 that he or she does not want to receive the record. If the People are the appellant, a copy must also be prepared for the respondent. *(Adopted, eff. Jan. 1, 2009.)*

Advisory Committee Comment

Rule 8.922 addresses when the original file is sent to the appellate division in infraction appeals.

Rule 8.915. Record of oral proceedings

(a) Appellant's election

The appellant must notify the trial court whether he or she elects to proceed with or without a record of the oral proceedings in the trial court. If the appellant elects to proceed with a record of the oral proceedings in the trial court, the notice must specify which form of the record of the oral proceedings in the trial court the appellant elects to use:

(1) A statement on appeal under rule 8.916;

(2) If the court has a local rule for the appellate division permitting this, an official electronic recording of the proceedings under rule 8.917(c). The appellant must attach to the notice a copy of the stipulation required under rule 8.917(c); or

(3) A reporter's transcript under rules 8.918–8.920 or a transcript prepared from an official electronic recording of the proceedings under rule 8.917(b). If the appellant elects to use a reporter's transcript, the clerk must promptly send a copy of appellant's notice making this election and the notice of appeal to each court reporter.

(b) Time for filing election

The notice of election required under (a) must be filed with the notice of appeal.

(c) Failure to file election

If the appellant does not file an election within the time specified in (b), rule 8.924 applies. *(Adopted, eff. Jan. 1, 2009. As amended, eff. Jan. 1, 2010; March 1, 2014; Jan. 1, 2016.)*

Advisory Committee Comment

Notice of Appeal and Record of Oral Proceedings (Infraction) (form CR–142) may be used to file the election required under this rule. This form is available at any courthouse or county law library or online at *www.courtinfo.ca.gov/forms*. To assist appellants in making an appropriate election, courts are encouraged to include information about whether the proceedings were recorded by a court reporter or officially electronically recorded in any information that the court provides to parties concerning their appellate rights.

Rule 8.916. Statement on appeal

(a) Description

A statement on appeal is a summary of the trial court proceedings that is approved by the trial court.

(b) Preparing the proposed statement

(1) If the appellant elects under rule 8.915 to use a statement on appeal, the appellant must prepare and file a proposed statement within 20 days after filing the record preparation election. If the defendant is the appellant and the prosecuting attorney appeared in the case, the defendant must serve a copy of the proposed statement on the prosecuting attorney. If the People are the appellant, the prosecuting attorney must serve a copy of the proposed statement on the respondent.

(2) Appellants who are not represented by an attorney must file their proposed statements on *Proposed Statement on Appeal (Infraction)* (form CR–143). For good cause, the court may permit the filing of a statement that is not on form CR–143.

(3) If the appellant does not serve and file a proposed statement within the time specified in (1), rule 8.924 applies.

(c) Contents of the proposed statement on appeal

A proposed statement prepared by the appellant must contain:

(1) A statement of the points the appellant is raising on appeal. The appeal is then limited to those points unless the appellate division determines that the record permits the full consideration of another point.

(A) The statement must specify the intended grounds of appeal by clearly stating each point to be raised but need not identify each particular ruling or matter to be challenged.

(B) If one of the grounds of appeal is insufficiency of the evidence, the statement must specify how it is insufficient.

(2) A summary of the trial court's rulings and the sentence imposed on the defendant.

(3) A condensed narrative of the oral proceedings that the appellant believes necessary for the appeal. The condensed narrative must include a concise factual summary of the evidence and the testimony of each witness that is relevant to the points which the appellant states under (1) are being raised on appeal. Any evidence

or portion of a proceeding not included will be presumed to support the judgment or order appealed from.

(d) Review of the appellant's proposed statement

(1) Within 10 days after the appellant files the proposed statement, the respondent may serve and file proposed amendments to that statement.

(2) No later than 10 days after the respondent files proposed amendments or the time to do so expires, a party may request a hearing to review and correct the proposed statement. No hearing will be held unless ordered by the trial court judge, and the judge will not ordinarily order a hearing unless there is a factual dispute about a material aspect of the trial court proceedings.

(3) Except as provided in (6), if no hearing is ordered, no later than 10 days after the time for requesting a hearing expires, the trial court judge must review the proposed statement and any proposed amendments filed by the respondent and take one of the following actions:

(A) If the proposed statement does not contain material required under (c), the trial court judge may order the appellant to prepare a new proposed statement. The order must identify the additional material that must be included in the statement to comply with (c) and the date by which the new proposed statement must be served and filed. If the appellant does not serve and file a new proposed statement as directed, rule 8.924 applies.

(B) If the trial court judge does not issue an order under (A), the trial court judge must either:

(i) Make any corrections or modifications to the statement necessary to ensure that it is an accurate summary of the evidence and the testimony of each witness that is relevant to the points which the appellant states under (c)(1) are being raised on appeal; or

(ii) Identify the necessary corrections and modifications and order the appellant to prepare a statement incorporating these corrections and modifications.

(4) If a hearing is ordered, the court must promptly set the hearing date and provide the parties with at least 5 days' written notice of the hearing date. No later than 10 days after the hearing, the trial court judge must either:

(A) Make any corrections or modifications to the statement necessary to ensure that it is an accurate summary of the evidence and the testimony of each witness that is relevant to the points which the appellant states under (c)(1) are being raised on appeal; or

(B) Identify the necessary corrections and modifications and order the appellant to prepare a statement incorporating these corrections and modifications.

(5) The trial court judge must not eliminate the appellant's specification of grounds of appeal from the proposed statement.

(6) If the trial court proceedings were reported by a court reporter or officially electronically recorded under Government Code section 69957 and the trial court judge determines that it would save court time and resources, instead of correcting a proposed statement on appeal:

(A) If the court has a local rule for the appellate division permitting the use of an official electronic recording as the record of the oral proceedings, the trial court judge may order that the original of an official electronic recording of the trial court proceedings, or a copy made by the court, be transmitted as the record of these oral proceedings without being transcribed. The court will pay for any copy of the official electronic recording ordered under this subdivision; or

(B) If the court has a local rule permitting this, the trial court judge may order that a transcript be prepared as the record of the oral proceedings. The court will pay for any transcript ordered under this subdivision.

(e) Review of the corrected or modified statement

(1) If the trial court judge makes any corrections or modifications to the proposed statement under (d), the clerk must serve copies of the corrected or modified statement on the parties. If under (d) the trial court judge orders the appellant to prepare a statement incorporating corrections and modifications, the appellant must serve and file the corrected or modified statement within the time ordered by the court. If the prosecuting attorney did not appear at the trial, no copy of the statement is to be sent to or served on the prosecuting attorney. If the appellant does not serve and file a corrected or modified statement as directed, rule 8.924 applies.

(2) Within 10 days after the statement is served on the parties, any party may serve and file proposed modifications or objections to the statement.

(3) Within 10 days after the time for filing proposed modifications or objections under (2) has expired, the judge must review the corrected or modified statement and any proposed modifications or objections to the statement filed by the parties. The procedures in (d)(3) or (d)(4) apply if the judge determines that further corrections or modifications are necessary to ensure that the statement is an accurate summary of the evidence and the testimony of each witness relevant to the points which the appellant states under (c)(1) are being raised on appeal.

(f) Certification of the statement on appeal

If the trial court judge does not make or order any corrections or modifications to the proposed statement under (d)(3), (d)(4), or (e)(3) and does not direct the preparation of a transcript in lieu of correcting the proposed statement under (d)(6), the judge must promptly certify the statement.

(g) Extensions of time

For good cause, the trial court may grant an extension of not more than 15 days to do any act required or permitted under this rule. *(Adopted, eff. Jan. 1, 2009. As amended, eff. July 1, 2009; March 1, 2014.)*

Advisory Committee Comment

Rules 8.806, 8.810, and 8.812 address applications for extensions of time and relief from default.

Subdivision (b)(2). *Proposed Statement on Appeal (Infraction)* (form CR–143) is available at any courthouse or county law library or online at *www.courts.ca.gov/forms*.

Subdivision (d). Under rule 8.804, the term "judge" includes a commissioner or a temporary judge.

Subdivisions (d)(3)(B), (d)(4), and (f). The judge need not ensure that the statement as modified or corrected is complete, but only that it is an accurate summary of the evidence and testimony relevant to the issues identified by the appellant.

Research References

West's California Judicial Council Forms CR–143, Proposed Statement on Appeal (Infraction).

West's California Judicial Council Forms CR–144, Order Concerning Appellant's Proposed Statement on Appeal (Infraction).

6 Witkin, California Criminal Law 4th Criminal Appeal § 211 (2021), In General.

Rule 8.917. Record when trial proceedings were officially electronically recorded

(a) Application

This rule applies only if:

(1) The trial court proceedings were officially recorded electronically under Government Code section 69957; and

(2) The electronic recording was prepared in compliance with applicable rules regarding electronic recording of court proceedings.

(b) Transcripts from official electronic recording

Written transcripts of official electronic recordings may be prepared under rule 2.952. A transcript prepared and certified as provided in that rule is prima facie a true and complete record of the oral proceedings it purports to cover, and satisfies any requirement in these rules or in any statute for a reporter's transcript of oral proceedings.

(c) Use of official recording as record of oral proceedings

If the court has a local rule for the appellate division permitting this, on stipulation of the parties or on order of the trial court under rule 8.916(d)(6), the original of an official electronic recording of the trial court proceedings, or a copy made by the court, may be transmitted as the record of these oral proceedings without being transcribed. This official electronic recording satisfies any requirement in these rules or in any statute for a reporter's transcript of these proceedings.

(d) Contents

Except in appeals when either the parties have filed a stipulation under rule 8.910(b) or the trial court has ordered that any of these items is not required for proper determination of the appeal, rules 8.918 and 8.920 govern the contents of a transcript of an official electronic recording.

(e) When preparation begins

(1) If the appellant is the People, preparation of a transcript or a copy of the recording must begin immediately after the appellant files an election under rule 8.915(a) to use a transcript of an official electronic recording or a copy of the official electronic recording as the record of the oral proceedings.

(2) If the appellant is the defendant:

(A) Within 10 days after the date the appellant files the election under rule 8.915(a), the clerk must notify the appellant and his or her counsel of the estimated cost of preparing the transcript or the copy of the recording. The notification must show the date it was sent.

(B) Within 10 days after the date the clerk sent the notice under (A), the appellant must do one of the following:

(i) Deposit with the clerk an amount equal to the estimated cost of preparing the transcript or the copy of the recording;

(ii) File a declaration of indigency supported by evidence in the form required by the Judicial Council; or

(iii) Notify the clerk by filing a new election that he or she will be using a statement on appeal instead of a transcript or copy of the recording. The appellant must prepare, serve, and file a proposed statement on appeal within 20 days after serving and filing the notice and must otherwise comply with the requirements for statements on appeal under rule 8.869;

(iv) Notify the clerk by filing a new election that he or she now elects to proceed without a record of the oral proceedings in the trial court; or

(v) Notify the clerk that he or she is abandoning the appeal by filing an abandonment in the reviewing court under rule 8.904.

(C) If the trial court determines that the appellant is not indigent, within 10 days after the date the clerk sends notice of this determination to the appellant, the appellant must do one of the following:

(i) Deposit with the clerk an amount equal to the estimated cost of preparing the transcript or the copy of the recording;

(ii) Notify the clerk by filing a new election that he or she will be using a statement on appeal instead of a reporter's transcript. The appellant must prepare, serve, and file a proposed statement on appeal within 20 days after serving and filing the notice and must otherwise comply with the requirements for statements on appeal under rule 8.869;

(iii) Notify the clerk by filing a new election that he or she now elects to proceed without a record of the oral proceedings in the trial court; or

(iv) Notify the clerk that he or she is abandoning the appeal by filing an abandonment in the reviewing court under rule 8.904.

(D) Preparation of the transcript or the copy of the recording must begin when:

(i) The clerk receives the required deposit under (B)(i) or (C)(i); or

(ii) The trial court determines that the defendant is indigent and orders that the defendant receive the transcript or the copy of the recording without cost.

(f) Notice when proceedings were not officially electronically recorded or cannot be transcribed

(1) If any portion of the oral proceedings to be included in the transcript were not officially electronically recorded under Government Code section 69957 or cannot be transcribed, the trial court clerk must so notify the parties in writing. The notice must:

(A) Indicate whether the identified proceedings were reported by a court reporter; and

(B) Show the date it was sent.

(2) Within 15 days after this notice is sent by the clerk, the appellant must serve and file a notice with the court stating whether the appellant elects to proceed with or without a record of the identified proceedings. When the party elects to proceed with a record of these oral proceedings:

(A) If the clerk's notice under (1) indicates that the proceedings were reported by a court reporter, the appellant's notice must specify which form of the record listed in rule 8.915(a) other than an official electronic recording or a transcript prepared from an official electronic recording the appellant elects to use. The appellant must comply with the requirements applicable to the form of the record elected.

(B) If the clerk's notice under (1) indicates that the proceedings were not reported by a court reporter, the appellant must prepare, serve, and file a proposed statement on appeal within 20 days after serving and filing the notice.

(Adopted, eff. Jan. 1, 2009. As amended, eff. July 1, 2010; March 1, 2014; Jan. 1, 2016.)

Advisory Committee Comment

Subdivision (d). The appellant must use *Defendant's Financial Statement on Eligibility for Appointment of Counsel and Reimbursement and Record on Appeal at Public Expense* (form CR–105) to show indigency. This form is available at any courthouse or county law library or online at *www.courtinfo.ca.gov/forms*.

Research References

6 Witkin, California Criminal Law 4th Criminal Appeal § 209 (2021), Normal Record on Appeal.

Rule 8.918. Contents of reporter's transcript

(a) Normal contents

Except in appeals covered by rule 8.920, when the parties have filed a stipulation under rule 8.910(b), or when, under a procedure established by a local rule adopted pursuant to (b), the trial court has ordered that any of these items is not required for proper determination of the appeal, the reporter's transcript must contain:

(1) The oral proceedings on the entry of any plea other than a not guilty plea;

(2) The oral proceedings on any motion in limine;

(3) The oral proceedings at trial, but excluding any opening statement;

(4) Any oral opinion of the court;

(5) The oral proceedings on any motion for new trial;

(6) The oral proceedings at sentencing or other dispositional hearing;

(7) If the appellant is the defendant, the reporter's transcript must also contain:

(A) The oral proceedings on any defense motion denied in whole or in part except motions for disqualification of a judge; and

(B) The closing arguments.

(b) Local procedure for determining contents

A trial court may adopt a local rule that establishes procedures for determining whether any of the items listed in (a) is not required for proper determination of the appeal or whether a form of the record other than a reporter's transcript constitutes a record of sufficient completeness for proper determination of the appeal. *(Adopted, eff. Jan. 1, 2009. As amended, eff. March 1, 2014.)*

Advisory Committee Comment

Subdivision (b). Both the United States Supreme Court and the California Supreme Court have held that, where the State has established a right to appeal, an indigent defendant convicted of a criminal offense has a constitutional right to a "'record of sufficient completeness' to permit proper consideration of [his] claims." (*Mayer v. Chicago* (1971) 404 U.S. 189, 193–194; *March v. Municipal Court* (1972) 7 Cal.3d 422, 427–428.) The California Supreme Court has also held that an indigent appellant is denied his or her right under the Fourteenth Amendment to the competent assistance of counsel on appeal if counsel fails to obtain an appellate record adequate for consideration of appellant's claims of errors (*People v. Barton* (1978) 21 Cal.3d 513, 518–520).

The *Mayer* and *March* decisions make clear, however, that the constitutionally required "record of sufficient completeness" does not necessarily mean a complete verbatim transcript; other forms of the record, such as a statement on appeal or a partial transcript, may be sufficient. The record that is necessary depends on the grounds for the appeal in the particular case. Under these cases, where the grounds of appeal make out a colorable need for a complete transcript, the burden is on the State to show that only a portion of the transcript or an alternative form of the record will suffice for an effective appeal on those grounds. The burden of overcoming the need for a verbatim reporter's transcript appears to be met where a verbatim recording of the proceedings is provided. (*Mayer, supra,* 404 U.S. at p. 195; cf. *Eyrich v. Mun. Court* (1985) 165 Cal.App.3d 1138, 1140 ["Although use of a court reporter is one way of obtaining a verbatim record, it may also be acquired through an electronic recording when no court reporter is available."].)

Some courts have adopted local rules that establish procedures for determining whether only a portion of a verbatim transcript or an alternative form of the record will be sufficient for an effective appeal, including: (1) requiring the appellant to specify the points the appellant is raising on appeal; (2) requiring the appellant and respondent to meet and confer about the content and form of the record; and (3) holding a hearing on the content and form of the record. Local procedures can be tailored to reflect the methods available in a particular court for making a record of the trial court proceedings that is sufficient for an effective appeal.

Research References

6 Witkin, California Criminal Law 4th Criminal Appeal § 210 (2021), Transcripts.

Rule 8.919. Preparation of reporter's transcript

(a) When preparation begins

(1) Unless the court has adopted a local rule under rule 8.920(b) that provides otherwise, the reporter must immediately begin preparing the reporter's transcript if the notice sent to the reporter by the clerk under rule 8.915(a)(3) indicates that the appellant is the People.

(2) If the notice sent to the reporter by the clerk under rule 8.915(a)(3) indicates that the appellant is the defendant:

(A) Within 10 days after the date the clerk sent the notice under rule 8.915(a)(3), the reporter must file with the clerk the estimated cost of preparing the reporter's transcript; and

(B) The clerk must promptly notify the appellant and his or her counsel of the estimated cost of preparing the reporter's transcript. The notification must show the date it was sent.

(C) Within 10 days after the date the clerk sent the notice under (B), the appellant must do one of the following:

(i) Deposit with the clerk an amount equal to the estimated cost of preparing the transcript;

(ii) File a waiver of the deposit signed by the reporter;

(iii) File a declaration of indigency supported by evidence in the form required by the Judicial Council;

(iv) File a certified transcript of all of the proceedings required to be included in the reporter's transcript under rule 8.918. The transcript must comply with the format requirements of rule 8.144;

(v) Notify the clerk by filing a new election that he or she will be using a statement on appeal instead of a reporter's transcript. The appellant must prepare, serve, and file a proposed statement on appeal within 20 days after serving and filing the notice and must otherwise comply with the requirements for statements on appeal under rule 8.916;

(vi) Notify the clerk by filing a new election that he or she now elects to proceed without a record of the oral proceedings in the trial court; or

(vii) Notify the clerk that he or she is abandoning the appeal by filing an abandonment in the reviewing court under rule 8.904.

(D) If the trial court determines that the appellant is not indigent, within 10 days after the date the clerk sends notice of this determination to the appellant, the appellant must do one of the following:

(i) Deposit with the clerk an amount equal to the estimated cost of preparing the transcript;

(ii) File with the clerk a waiver of the deposit signed by the reporter;

(iii) File a certified transcript of all of the proceedings required to be included in the reporter's transcript under rule 8.918. The transcript must comply with the format requirements of rule 8.144;

(iv) Notify the clerk by filing a new election that he or she will be using a statement on appeal instead of a reporter's transcript. The appellant must prepare, serve, and file a proposed statement on appeal within 20 days after serving and filing the notice and must otherwise comply with the requirements for statements on appeal under rule 8.916;

(v) Notify the clerk by filing a new election that he or she now elects to proceed without a record of the oral proceedings in the trial court; or

(vi) Notify the clerk that he or she is abandoning the appeal by filing an abandonment in the reviewing court under rule 8.904.

(E) The clerk must promptly notify the reporter to begin preparing the transcript when:

(i) The clerk receives the required deposit under (C)(i) or (D)(i); or

(ii) The clerk receives a waiver of the deposit signed by the reporter under (C)(ii) or (D)(ii); or

(iii) The trial court determines that the defendant is indigent and orders that the defendant receive the transcript without cost.

(b) Format of transcript

The reporter's transcript must comply with rule 8.144.

(c) Copies and certification

The reporter must prepare an original and the same number of copies of the reporter's transcript as rule 8.913(c) requires of the clerk's transcript and must certify each as correct.

(d) When preparation must be completed

The reporter must deliver the original and all copies to the trial court clerk as soon as they are certified but no later than 20 days after the reporter is required to begin preparing the transcript under (a). Only the presiding judge of the appellate division or his or her designee may extend the time to prepare the reporter's transcript (see rule 8.810).

(3) [1]If the appellant deposited with the clerk an amount equal to the estimated cost of preparing the transcript and the appeal is abandoned or dismissed before the reporter has filed the transcript, the reporter must inform the clerk of the cost of the portion of the transcript that the reporter has completed. The clerk must pay that amount to the reporter from the appellant's deposited funds and refund any excess deposit to the appellant.

(e) Multi-reporter cases

In a multi-reporter case, the clerk must accept any completed portion of the transcript from the primary reporter one week after the time prescribed by (d) even if other portions are uncompleted. The clerk must promptly pay each reporter who certifies that all portions of the transcript assigned to that reporter are completed.

(f) Notice when proceedings cannot be transcribed

(1) If any portion of the oral proceedings to be included in the reporter's transcript was not reported or cannot be transcribed, the trial court clerk must so notify the parties in writing. The notice must:

(A) Indicate whether the identified proceedings were officially electronically recorded under Government Code section 69957; and

(B) Show the date it was sent.

(2) Within 15 days after this notice is sent by the clerk, the appellant must serve and file a notice with the court stating whether the appellant elects to proceed with or without a record of the identified proceedings. When the party elects to proceed with a record of these oral proceedings:

(A) If the clerk's notice under (1) indicates that the proceedings were officially electronically recorded under Government Code section 69957, the appellant's notice must specify which form of the record listed in rule 8.915(a) other than a reporter's transcript the appellant elects to use. The appellant must comply with the requirements applicable to the form of the record elected.

(B) If the clerk's notice under (1) indicates that the proceedings were not officially electronically recorded under Government Code section 69957, the appellant must prepare, serve, and file a proposed statement on appeal within 20 days after serving and filing the notice.

(Adopted, eff. Jan. 1, 2009. As amended, eff. March 1, 2014; Jan. 1, 2016; Jan. 1, 2017; Jan. 1, 2018.)

1 Subd. (d)(3) was adopted at the Sept. 14–15, 2017 Judicial Council meeting. At the Nov. 17, 2017 Judicial Council meeting, subd. (d)(2) was deleted, as was the paragraph (1) designation, however, no indication as to whether subd. (d)(3) should be retained or deleted was provided, therefore it is retained here with its current designation.

Advisory Committee Comment

Subdivision (a). The appellant must use *Defendant's Financial Statement on Eligibility for Appointment of Counsel and Reimbursement and Record on Appeal at Public Expense* (form CR–105) to show indigency. This form is available at any courthouse or county law library or online at *www.courts.ca.gov/forms*.

Subdivisions (a)(2)(C)(iv) and (a)(2)(D)(iii). Sometimes a party in a trial court proceeding will purchase a reporter's transcripts of all or part of the proceedings before any appeal is filed. In recognition of the fact that such transcripts may already have been purchased, this rule allows an appellant, in lieu of depositing funds for a reporter's transcript, to deposit with the trial court a certified transcript of the proceedings necessary for the appeal. Subdivisions (a)(2)(C)(iv) and (a)(2)(D)(iii) make clear that the certified transcript may be filed in lieu of a deposit for a reporter's transcript only where the certified transcript contains all of the proceedings required under rule 8.865 and the transcript complies with the format requirements of rule 8.144.

Research References

6 Witkin, California Criminal Law 4th Criminal Appeal § 210 (2021), Transcripts.

Rule 8.920. Limited normal record in certain appeals

If the People appeal from a judgment on a demurrer to the complaint, including any notice to appear, or if the defendant or the People appeal from an appealable order other than a ruling on a motion for new trial, the normal record is composed of:

(1) *Record of the documents filed in the trial court*

A clerk's transcript or original trial court file containing:

(A) The complaint, including any notice to appear, and any amendment;

(B) Any demurrer or other plea;

(C) Any motion or notice of motion granted or denied by the order appealed from, with supporting and opposing memoranda and attachments;

(D) The judgment or order appealed from and any abstract of judgment;

(E) Any court minutes relating to the judgment or order appealed from and

(i) If there was a trial in the case, any court minutes of proceedings at the time the original judgment is rendered and any subsequent proceedings; or

(ii) If the original judgment of conviction is based on a guilty plea or nolo contendere plea, any court minutes of the proceedings at the time of entry of such plea and any subsequent proceedings; and

(F) The notice of appeal.

(2) *Record of the oral proceedings in the trial court*

If an appellant wants to raise any issue that requires consideration of the oral proceedings in the trial court:

(A) A reporter's transcript, a transcript prepared under rule 8.917, an official electronic recording under rule 8.917, or a statement on appeal under rule 8.916 summarizing any oral proceedings incident to the judgment or order being appealed.

(B) If the appeal is from an order after judgment, a reporter's transcript, a transcript prepared under rule 8.917, an official electronic recording under rule 8.917, or a statement on appeal under rule 8.916 summarizing any oral proceedings from:

(i) The original sentencing proceeding; and

(ii) If the original judgment of conviction is based on a guilty plea or nolo contendere plea, the proceedings at the time of entry of such plea.

(Adopted, eff. Jan. 1, 2009. As amended, eff. Jan. 1, 2013.)

Advisory Committee Comment

Subdivision (1)(E). This rule identifies the minutes that must be included in the record. The trial court clerk may include additional minutes beyond those identified in this rule if that would be more cost-effective.

Rule 8.921. Exhibits

(a) Exhibits deemed part of record

Exhibits admitted in evidence, refused, or lodged are deemed part of the record but may be transmitted to the appellate division only as provided in this rule.

(b) Notice of designation

(1) Within 10 days after the last respondent's brief is filed or could be filed under rule 8.927, if the appellant wants the appellate division to consider any original exhibits that were admitted in evidence, refused, or lodged, the appellant must serve and file a notice in the trial court designating such exhibits.

(2) Within 10 days after a notice under (1) is served, any other party wanting the appellate division to consider additional exhibits must serve and file a notice in trial court designating such exhibits.

(3) A party filing a notice under (1) or (2) must serve a copy on the appellate division.

(c) Request by appellate division

At any time the appellate division may direct the trial court or a party to send it an exhibit.

(d) Transmittal

Unless the appellate division orders otherwise, within 20 days after notice under (b) is filed or after the appellate division directs that an exhibit be sent:

(1) The trial court clerk must put any designated exhibits in the clerk's possession into numerical or alphabetical order and send them to the appellate division. The trial court clerk must also send a list of the exhibits sent. If the exhibits are not transmitted electronically, the trial court clerk must send two copies of the list. If the appellate division clerk finds the list correct, the clerk must sign and return a copy to the trial court clerk.

(2) Any party in possession of designated exhibits returned by the trial court must put them into numerical or alphabetical order and send them to the appellate division. The party must also send a list of the exhibits sent. If the exhibits are not transmitted electronically, the party must send two copies of the list. If the appellate division clerk finds the list correct, the clerk must sign and return a copy to the party.

(e) Return by appellate division

On request, the appellate division may return an exhibit to the trial court or to the party that sent it. When the remittitur issues, the appellate division must return all exhibits not transmitted electronically to the trial court or to the party that sent them. *(Adopted, eff. Jan. 1, 2009. As amended, eff. Jan. 1, 2016.)*

Rule 8.922. Sending and filing the record in the appellate division

(a) When the record is complete

(1) If the appellant elected under rule 8.915 to proceed without a record of the oral proceedings in the trial court, the record is complete when the clerk's transcript is certified as correct or, if the original trial court file will be used instead of the clerk's transcript, when that original file is ready for transmission as provided under rule 8.914(b).

(2) If the appellant elected under rule 8.915 to proceed with a record of the oral proceedings in the trial court, the record is complete when the clerk's transcript is certified as correct or the original file is ready for transmission as provided in (1) and:

(A) If the appellant elected to use a reporter's transcript, the certified reporter's transcript is delivered to the court under rule 8.919;

(B) If the appellant elected to use a transcript prepared from an official electronic recording, the transcript has been prepared under rule 8.917;

(C) If the parties stipulated to the use of an official electronic recording of the proceedings, the electronic recording has been prepared under rule 8.917; or

(D) If the appellant elected to use a statement on appeal, the statement on appeal has been certified by the trial court or a transcript or copy of an official electronic recording has been prepared under rule 8.916(d)(6).

(b) Sending the record

When the record is complete, the clerk must promptly send:

(1) The original record to the appellate division;

(2) One copy of the clerk's transcript or index to the original court file and one copy of any record of the oral proceedings to each appellant who is represented by separate counsel or is self-represented;

(3) If the defendant is the appellant, one copy of the clerk's transcript or index to the original court file and one copy of any record of the oral proceedings to the prosecuting attorney unless the prosecuting attorney has notified the court under rule 8.911 that he or she does not want to receive the record; and

(4) If the People are the appellant, a copy of the clerk's transcript or index to the original court file and one copy of any record of the oral proceedings to the respondent.

(c) Filing the record

On receipt, the appellate division clerk must promptly file the original record and send notice of the filing date to the parties. *(Adopted, eff. Jan. 1, 2009. As amended, eff. Jan. 1, 2016.)*

Rule 8.923. Augmenting or correcting the record in the appellate division

(a) Subsequent trial court orders

If, after the record is certified, the trial court amends or recalls the judgment or makes any other order in the case, including an order affecting the sentence or probation, the clerk must promptly certify and send a copy of the amended abstract of judgment or other order as an augmentation of the record to all those who received the record under rule 8.872(b). If there is any additional document or transcript related to the amended judgment or new order that any rule or order requires be included in the record, the clerk must send these documents or transcripts with the amended abstract of judgment or other order. The clerk must promptly copy and certify any such document and the reporter must promptly prepare and certify any such transcript.

(b) Omissions

If, after the record is certified, the trial court clerk or the reporter learns that the record omits a document or transcript that any rule or order requires to be included, the clerk must promptly copy and certify the document or the reporter must promptly prepare and certify the transcript. Without the need for a court order, the clerk must promptly send the document or transcript as an augmentation of the record to all those who received the record under rule 8.922(b).

(c) Augmentation or correction by the appellate division

At any time, on motion of a party or on its own motion, the appellate division may order the record augmented or corrected as provided in rule 8.841. *(Adopted, eff. Jan. 1, 2009.)*

Rule 8.924. Failure to procure the record

(a) Notice of default

If a party fails to do any act required to procure the record, the trial court clerk must promptly notify that party in writing that it must do the act specified in the notice within 15 days after the notice is sent and that, if it fails to comply, the reviewing court may impose the following sanctions:

(1) If the defaulting party is the appellant, the court may dismiss the appeal or, if the default relates only to procurement of the record of the oral proceedings, may proceed on the clerk's transcript or other record of the written documents from the trial court proceedings; or

(2) If the defaulting party is the respondent, the court may proceed with the appeal on the record designated by the appellant.

(b) Sanctions

If the party fails to take the action specified in a notice given under (a), the trial court clerk must promptly notify the appellate division of the default and the appellate division may impose the sanction specified in the notice. If the appellate division dismisses the appeal, it may vacate the dismissal for good cause. If the appellate division orders the appeal to proceed on the record designated by the appellant, the respondent may obtain relief from default under rule 8.812. *(Adopted, eff. March 1, 2014. As amended, eff. Jan. 1, 2016.)*

Article 3

BRIEFS, HEARING, AND DECISION IN INFRACTION APPEALS

Rule

Rule 8.925. General application of chapter 4

Except as provided in this article, rules 8.880–8.890 govern briefs, hearing, and decision in the appellate division in infraction cases. *(Adopted, eff. Jan. 1, 2009.)*

Rule 8.926. Notice of briefing schedule

When the record is filed, the clerk of the appellate division must promptly send, to each appellate counsel or unrepresented party, a notice giving the dates the briefs are due. *(Adopted, eff. Jan. 1, 2009. As amended, eff. Jan. 1, 2016.)*

Rule 8.927. Briefs

(a) Time to file briefs

(1) The appellant must serve and file an appellant's opening brief within 30 days after the record is filed in the appellate division.

(2) Any respondent's brief must be served and filed within 30 days after the appellant files its opening brief.

(3) Any appellant's reply brief must be served and filed within 20 days after the respondent files its brief.

(4) No other brief may be filed except with the permission of the presiding judge.

(5) Instead of filing a brief, or as part of its brief, a party may join in a brief or adopt by reference all or part of a brief in the same or a related appeal.

(b) Failure to file a brief

(1) If the appellant fails to timely file an opening brief, the appellate division clerk must promptly notify the appellant in writing that the brief must be filed within 20 days after the notice is sent and that if the appellant fails to comply, the court may dismiss the appeal.

(2) If the respondent fails to timely file a brief, the appellate division clerk must promptly notify the respondent in writing that the brief must be filed within 20 days after the notice is sent and that if the respondent fails to comply, the court will decide the appeal on the record, the appellant's opening brief, and any oral argument by the appellant.

(3) If a party fails to comply with a notice under (1) or (2), the court may impose the sanction specified in the notice.

(c) Service and filing

(1) Copies of each brief must be served as required by rule 8.25.

(2) Unless the appellate division provides otherwise by local rule or order in the specific case, only the original brief, with proof of service, must be filed in the appellate division.

(3) A copy of each brief must be served on the trial court clerk for delivery to the judge who tried the case.

(4) A copy of each brief must be served on a public officer or agency when required by rule 8.29. *(Adopted, eff. Jan. 1, 2009. As amended, eff. March 1, 2014; Jan. 1, 2016.)*

Research References

6 Witkin, California Criminal Law 4th Criminal Appeal § 217 (2021), In General.

Ct. Rules

Rule 8.928. Contents and form of briefs

(a) Contents

(1) Each brief must:

(A) State each point under a separate heading or subheading summarizing the point and support each point by argument and, if possible, by citation of authority; and

(B) Support any reference to a matter in the record by a citation to the volume and page number of the record where the matter appears.

(2) An appellant's opening brief must:

(A) State the nature of the action, the relief sought in the trial court, and the judgment or order appealed from;

(B) State that the judgment appealed from is final or explain why the order appealed from is appealable; and

(C) Provide a summary of the significant facts limited to matters in the record.

(b) Length

(1) A brief produced on a computer must not exceed 5,100 words, including footnotes. Such a brief must include a certificate by appellate counsel or an unrepresented party stating the number of words in the brief. The person certifying may rely on the word count of the computer program used to prepare the brief.

(2) A brief produced on a typewriter must not exceed 15 pages.

(3) The information listed on the cover, any table of contents or table of authorities, the certificate under (1), and any signature block are excluded from the limits stated in (1) or (2).

(4) On application, the presiding judge may permit a longer brief for good cause. A lengthy record or numerous or complex issues on appeal will ordinarily constitute good cause.

(c) Form

(1) A brief may be reproduced by any process that produces a clear, black image of letter quality. All documents filed must have a page size of 8 ½ by 11 inches. If filed in paper form, the paper must be white or unbleached and of at least 20–pound weight. Both sides of the paper may be used if the brief is not bound at the top.

(2) Any conventional font may be used. The font may be either proportionally spaced or monospaced.

(3) The font style must be roman; but for emphasis, italics or boldface may be used or the text may be underscored. Case names must be italicized or underscored. Headings may be in uppercase letters.

(4) Except as provided in (11), the font size, including footnotes, must not be smaller than 13–point.

(5) The lines of text must be unnumbered and at least one-and-a-half-spaced. Headings and footnotes may be single-spaced. Quotations may be block-indented and single-spaced. Single-spaced means six lines to a vertical inch.

(6) The margins must be at least 1½ inches on the left and right and 1 inch on the top and bottom.

(7) The pages must be consecutively numbered.

(8) The cover—or first page if there is no cover—must include the information required by rule 8.816(a)(1).

(9) If filed in paper form, the brief must be bound on the left margin, except that briefs may be bound at the top if required by a local rule of the appellate division. If the brief is stapled, the bound edge and staples must be covered with tape.

(10) The brief need not be signed.

(11) If the brief is produced on a typewriter:

(A) A typewritten original and carbon copies may be filed only with the presiding justice's permission, which will ordinarily be given only to unrepresented parties proceeding in forma pauperis. All other typewritten briefs must be filed as photocopies.

(B) Both sides of the paper may be used if a photocopy is filed; only one side may be used if a typewritten original and carbon copies are filed.

(C) The type size, including footnotes, must not be smaller than standard pica, 10 characters per inch. Unrepresented incarcerated litigants may use elite type, 12 characters per inch, if they lack access to a typewriter with larger characters.

(d) Noncomplying briefs

If a brief does not comply with this rule:

(1) The reviewing court clerk may decline to file it, but must mark it "received but not filed" and return it to the party; or

(2) If the brief is filed, the presiding judge may with or without notice:

(A) Order the brief returned for corrections and refiling within a specified time;

(B) Strike the brief with leave to file a new brief within a specified time; or

(C) Disregard the noncompliance.

(Adopted, eff. Jan. 1, 2009. As amended, eff. Jan. 1, 2011; Jan. 1, 2013; Jan. 1, 2014; March 1, 2014; Jan. 1, 2016.)

Advisory Committee Comment

Subdivision (b). Subdivision (b)(1) states the maximum permissible lengths of briefs produced on a computer in terms of word count rather than page count. This provision tracks a provision in rule 8.204(c) governing Court of Appeal briefs and is explained in the comment to that provision. Subdivision (b)(3) specifies certain items that are not counted toward the maximum brief length. Signature blocks, as referenced in this provision include not only the signatures, but also the printed names, titles, and affiliations of any attorneys filing or joining in the brief, which may accompany the signature.

Rule 8.929. Oral argument

(a) Calendaring and sessions

Unless otherwise ordered, all appeals in which the last reply brief was filed or the time for filing this brief expired 45 or more days before the date of a regular appellate division session must be placed on the calendar for that session by the appellate division clerk. By order of the presiding judge or the appellate division, any appeal may be placed on the calendar for oral argument at any session.

(b) Oral argument by videoconference

(1) Oral argument may be conducted by videoconference if:

(A) It is ordered by the presiding judge of the appellate division or the presiding judge's designee on application of any party or on the court's own motion. An application from a party requesting that oral argument be conducted by videoconference must be filed within 10 days after the court sends notice of oral argument under (c)(1); or

(B) A local rule authorizes oral argument to be conducted by videoconference consistent with these rules.

(2) If oral argument is conducted by videoconference:

(A) Each judge of the appellate division panel assigned to the case must participate in the entire oral argument either in person at the superior court that issued the judgment or order that is being appealed or by videoconference from another court.

(B) Unless otherwise allowed by local rule or ordered by the presiding judge of the appellate division or the presiding judge's designee, all of the parties must appear at oral argument in person at the superior court that issued the judgment or order that is being appealed.

(C) The oral argument must be open to the public at the superior court that issued the judgment or order that is being appealed. If provided by local rule or ordered by the presiding judge of the appellate division or the presiding judge's designee, oral argument may also be open to the public at any of the locations from which a judge of the appellate division is participating in oral argument.

(D) The appellate division must ensure that:

(i) During oral argument, the participants in oral argument are visible and their statements are audible to all other participants, court staff, and any members of the public attending the oral argument;

(ii) Participants are identified when they speak; and

(iii) Only persons who are authorized to participate in the proceedings speak.

(E) A party must not be charged any fee to participate in oral argument by videoconference if the party participates from the superior court that issued the judgment or order that is being appealed or from a location from which a judge of the appellate division panel is participating in oral argument.

(c) Notice of argument

(1) As soon as all parties' briefs are filed or the time for filing these briefs has expired, the appellate division clerk must send a notice of the time and place of oral argument to all parties. The notice must be sent at least 20 days before the date for oral argument. The presiding judge may shorten the notice period for good cause; in that event, the clerk must immediately notify the parties by telephone or other expeditious method.

(2) If oral argument will be conducted by videoconference under (b), the clerk must specify, either in the notice required under (1) or in a supplemental notice sent to all parties at least 5 days before the date for oral argument, the location from which each judge of the appellate division panel assigned to the case will participate in oral argument.

(d) Waiver of argument

Parties may waive oral argument.

(e) Conduct of argument

Unless the court provides otherwise:

(1) The appellant, petitioner, or moving party has the right to open and close. If there are two or more such parties, the court must set the sequence of argument.

(2) Each side is allowed 5 minutes for argument. The appellant may reserve part of this time for reply argument. If multiple parties are represented by separate counsel, or if an amicus curiae—on written request—is granted permission to argue, the court may apportion or expand the time.

(3) Only one counsel may argue for each separately represented party. *(Adopted, eff. Jan. 1, 2009. As amended, eff. Jan. 1, 2010.)*

Advisory Committee Comment

Subdivision (a). Under rule 10.1108, the appellate division must hold a session at least once each quarter, unless no matters are set for oral argument that quarter, but may choose to hold sessions more frequently.

Research References

West's California Judicial Council Forms CR–141–INFO, Information on Appeal Procedures for Infractions.

Chapter 6

WRIT PROCEEDINGS

Rule

Rule 8.930. Application

(a) Writ proceedings governed

Except as provided in (b), the rules in this chapter govern proceedings in the appellate division for writs of mandate, certiorari, or prohibition, or other writs within the original jurisdiction of the appellate division, including writs relating to a postjudgment enforcement order of the small claims division. In all respects not provided for in this chapter, rule 8.883, regarding the form and content of briefs, applies.

(b) Writ proceedings not governed

The rules in this chapter do not apply to:

(1) Petitions for writs of supersedeas under rule 8.824;

(2) Petitions for writs relating to acts of the small claims division other than a postjudgment enforcement order; or

(3) Petitions for writs not within the original jurisdiction of the appellate division. *(Adopted, eff. Jan. 1, 2009. As amended, eff. Jan. 1, 2016.)*

Advisory Committee Comment

Information on Writ Proceedings in Misdemeanor, Infraction, and Limited Civil Cases (form APP–150–INFO) provides additional information about proceedings for writs in the appellate division of the superior court. This form is available at any courthouse or county law library or online at *www.courts.ca.gov/forms*.

Subdivision (b)(1). The superior courts, not the appellate divisions, have original jurisdiction in habeas corpus proceedings (see Cal. Const., art. VI, § 10). Habeas corpus proceedings in the superior courts are governed by rules 4.550 et seq.

Subdivision (b)(2). A petition that seeks a writ relating to an act of the small claims division other than a postjudgment enforcement order is heard by a single judge of the appellate division (see Code Civ. Proc. § 116.798(a)) and is governed by rules 8.970 et seq.

Research References

West's California Judicial Council Forms App–150–INFO, Information on Writ Proceedings in Misdemeanor, Infraction, and Limited Civil Cases.
West's California Judicial Council Forms App–151, Petition for Writ (Misdemeanor, Infraction, or Limited Civil Case).

Rule 8.931. Petitions filed by persons not represented by an attorney

(a) Petitions

A person who is not represented by an attorney and who petitions the appellate division for a writ under this chapter must file the petition on *Petition for Writ (Misdemeanor, Infraction, or Limited Civil Case)* (form APP–151). For good cause the court may permit an unrepresented party to file a petition that is not on form APP–151, but the petition must be verified.

(b) Contents of supporting documents

(1) The petition must be accompanied by an adequate record, including copies of:

(A) The ruling from which the petition seeks relief;

(B) All documents and exhibits submitted to the trial court supporting and opposing the petitioner's position;

(C) Any other documents or portions of documents submitted to the trial court that are necessary for a complete understanding of the case and the ruling under review; and

(D) A reporter's transcript, a transcript of an electronic recording or, if the court has a local rule permitting this, an electronic recording of the oral proceedings that resulted in the ruling under review.

(2) In extraordinary circumstances, the petition may be filed without the documents required by (1)(A)–(C) but must include a declaration that explains the urgency and the circumstances making the documents unavailable and fairly summarizes their substance.

(3) If a transcript or electronic recording under (1)(D) is unavailable, the record must include a declaration:

(A) Explaining why the transcript or electronic recording is unavailable and fairly summarizing the proceedings, including the parties' arguments and any statement by the court supporting its ruling. This declaration may omit a full summary of the proceedings if part of the relief sought is an order to prepare a transcript for use by an indigent criminal defendant in support of the petition and if the declaration demonstrates the need for and entitlement to the transcript; or

(B) Stating that the transcript or electronic recording has been ordered, the date it was ordered, and the date it is expected to be filed, which must be a date before any action requested of the appellate division other than issuance of a temporary stay supported by other parts of the record.

(4) If the petition does not include the required record or explanations or does not present facts sufficient to excuse the failure to submit them, the court may summarily deny a stay request, the petition, or both.

(c) Form of supporting documents

(1) Documents submitted under (b) must comply with the following requirements:

(A) If submitted in paper form, they must be bound together at the end of the petition or in separate volumes not exceeding 300 pages each. The pages must be consecutively numbered.

(B) If submitted in paper form, they must be index-tabbed by number or letter.

(C) They must begin with a table of contents listing each document by its title and its index number or letter. If a document has attachments, the table of contents must give the title of each attachment and a brief description of its contents.

(2) The clerk must file any supporting documents not complying with (1), but the court may notify the petitioner that it may strike or summarily deny the petition if the documents are not brought into compliance within a stated reasonable time of not less than five days.

(3) Unless the court provides otherwise by local rule or order, only one set of the supporting documents needs to be filed in support of a petition, an answer, an opposition, or a reply.

(d) Service

(1) The petition and one set of supporting documents must be served on any named real party in interest, but only the petition must be served on the respondent.

(2) The proof of service must give the telephone number of each attorney or unrepresented party served.

(3) The petition must be served on a public officer or agency when required by statute or rule 8.29.

(4) The clerk must file the petition even if its proof of service is defective, but if the petitioner fails to file a corrected proof of service within five days after the clerk gives notice of the defect the court may strike the petition or impose a lesser sanction.

(5) The court may allow the petition to be filed without proof of service. *(Adopted, eff. Jan. 1, 2009. As amended, eff. Jan. 1, 2009; Jan. 1, 2011; Jan. 1, 2014; Jan. 1, 2016; Jan. 1, 2018.)*

Advisory Committee Comment

Subdivision (a). *Petition for Writ (Misdemeanor, Infraction, or Limited Civil Case)* (form APP–151) is available at any courthouse or county law library or online at *www.courts.ca.gov/forms*.

Subdivision (b). Rule 2.952 addresses the use of electronic recordings and transcripts of such recordings as the official record of proceedings.

Subdivision (d). Rule 8.25, which generally governs service and filing in appellate divisions, also applies to the original proceedings covered by this rule.

Rule 8.932. Petitions filed by an attorney for a party

(a) General application of rule 8.931

Except as provided in this rule, rule 8.931 applies to any petition for an extraordinary writ filed by an attorney.

(b) Form and content of petition

(1) A petition for an extraordinary writ filed by an attorney may, but is not required to be, filed on *Petition for Writ (Misdemeanor, Infraction, or Limited Civil Case)* (form APP–151).

(2) The petition must disclose the name of any real party in interest.

(3) If the petition seeks review of trial court proceedings that are also the subject of a pending appeal, the notice "Related Appeal Pending" must appear on the cover of the petition, and the first paragraph of the petition must state the appeal's title and any appellate division docket number.

(4) The petition must be verified.

(5) The petition must be accompanied by a memorandum, which need not repeat facts alleged in the petition.

(6) Rule 8.883(b) governs the length of the petition and memorandum, but the verification and any supporting documents are excluded from the limits stated in rule 8.883(b)(1) and (2).

(7) If the petition requests a temporary stay, it must explain the urgency. *(Adopted, eff. Jan. 1, 2009.)*

Rule 8.933. Opposition

(a) Preliminary opposition

(1) Within 10 days after the petition is filed, the respondent or any real party in interest, separately or jointly, may serve and file a preliminary opposition.

(2) An opposition must contain a memorandum and a statement of any material fact not included in the petition.

(3) Within 10 days after an opposition is filed, the petitioner may serve and file a reply.

(4) Without requesting opposition or waiting for a reply, the court may grant or deny a request for temporary stay, deny the petition, issue an alternative writ or order to show cause, or notify the parties that it is considering issuing a peremptory writ in the first instance.

(b) Return or opposition; reply

(1) If the court issues an alternative writ or order to show cause, the respondent or any real party in interest, separately or jointly, may serve and file a return by demurrer, verified answer, or both. If the court notifies the parties that it is considering issuing a peremptory writ in the first instance, the respondent or any real party in interest may serve and file an opposition.

(2) Unless the court orders otherwise, the return or opposition must be served and filed within 30 days after the court issues the alternative writ or order to show cause or notifies the parties that it is considering issuing a peremptory writ in the first instance.

(3) Unless the court orders otherwise, the petitioner may serve and file a reply within 15 days after the return or opposition is filed.

(4) If the return is by demurrer alone and the demurrer is not sustained, the court may issue the peremptory writ without granting leave to answer.

(c) Form of preliminary opposition, return, or opposition

Any preliminary opposition, return, or opposition must comply with rule 8.931(c). If it is filed by an attorney, it must also comply with rule 8.932(b)(3)–(7). *(Adopted, eff. Jan. 1, 2009. As amended, eff. Jan. 1, 2014.)*

Rule 8.934. Notice to trial court

(a) Notice if writ issues

If a writ or order issues directed to any judge, court, or other officer, the appellate division clerk must promptly send a certified copy of the writ or order to the person or entity to whom it is directed.

(b) Notice by telephone

(1) If the writ or order stays or prohibits proceedings set to occur within seven days or requires action within seven days—or in any other urgent situation—the appellate division clerk must make a reasonable effort to notify the clerk of the respondent court by telephone. The clerk of the respondent court must then notify the judge or officer most directly concerned.

(2) The clerk need not give notice by telephone of the summary denial of a writ, whether or not a stay previously issued. *(Adopted, eff. Jan. 1, 2009.)*

Rule 8.935. Filing, finality, and modification of decisions; rehearing; remittitur

(a) Filing of decision

(1) The appellate division clerk must promptly file all opinions and orders of the court and on the same day send copies (by e-mail where permissible under rule 2.251) showing the filing date to the parties and, when relevant, to the trial court.

(2) A decision must identify the participating judges, including the author of any majority opinion and of any concurring or dissenting opinion, or the judges participating in a "by the court" decision.

(b) Finality of decision

(1) Except as otherwise ordered by the court, the following appellate division decisions regarding petitions for writs within the court's original jurisdiction are final in the issuing court when filed:

(A) An order denying or dismissing such a petition without issuance of an alternative writ, order to show cause, or writ of review; and

(B) An order denying or dismissing such a petition as moot after issuance of an alternative writ, order to show cause, or writ of review.

(2) Except as otherwise provided in (3), all other appellate division decisions in a writ proceeding are final 30 days after the decision is sent by the court clerk to the parties.

(3) If necessary to prevent mootness or frustration of the relief granted or to otherwise promote the interests of justice, an appellate division may order early finality in that court of a decision granting a petition for a writ within its original jurisdiction or denying such a petition after issuing an alternative writ, order to show cause, or writ of review. The decision may provide for finality in that court on filing or within a stated period of less than 30 days.

(c) Modification of decisions

Rule 8.888(b) governs the modification of appellate division decisions in writ proceedings.

(d) Rehearing

Rule 8.889 governs rehearing in writ proceedings in the appellate division.

(e) Remittitur

Except as provided in rule 8.1018 for cases transferred to the Courts of Appeal, the appellate division must issue a remittitur after the court issues a decision in a writ proceeding except when the court issues one of the orders listed in (b)(1). Rule 8.890(b)–(d) govern issuance of a remittitur in these proceedings, including the clerk's duties, immediate issuance, stay, and recall of remittitur, and notice of issuance. *(Adopted, eff. Jan. 1, 2009. As amended, eff. Jan. 1, 2014; Jan. 1, 2019.)*

Advisory Committee Comment

Subdivision (b). This provision addresses the finality of decisions in proceedings relating to writs of mandate, certiorari, and prohibition. See rule 8.888(a) for provisions addressing the finality of decisions in appeals.

Subdivision (b)(1). Examples of situations in which the appellate division may issue an order dismissing a writ petition include when the petitioner fails to comply with an order of the court, when the court recalls the alternative writ, order to show cause, or writ of review as improvidently granted, or when the petition becomes moot.

Subdivision (d). Under this rule, a remittitur serves as notice that the writ proceedings have concluded.

Research References

6 Witkin, California Criminal Law 4th Criminal Appeal § 219 (2021), Remittitur.

Rule 8.936. Costs

(a) Entitlement to costs

Except in a criminal proceeding or other proceeding in which a party is entitled to court-appointed counsel, the prevailing party in an original proceeding is entitled to costs if the court resolves the proceeding after issuing an alternative writ, an order to show cause, or a peremptory writ in the first instance.

(b) Award of costs

(1) In the interests of justice, the court may award or deny costs as it deems proper.

(2) The opinion or order resolving the proceeding must specify the award or denial of costs.

(3) Rule 8.891(b)–(d) governs the procedure for recovering costs under this rule. *(Adopted, eff. Jan. 1, 2009.)*

Research References

West's California Judicial Council Forms App–150–INFO, Information on Writ Proceedings in Misdemeanor, Infraction, and Limited Civil Cases.
West's California Judicial Council Forms App–151, Petition for Writ (Misdemeanor, Infraction, or Limited Civil Case).

Ct. Rules

Division 5

RULES RELATING TO APPEALS AND WRITS IN SMALL CLAIMS CASES

Chapter 2

WRIT PETITIONS

Rule 8.970. Application

(a) Writ proceedings governed

Except as provided in (b), the rules in this chapter govern proceedings under Code of Civil Procedure section 116.798(a) for writs of mandate, certiorari, or prohibition, relating to an act of the small claims division, other than a postjudgment enforcement order. In all respects not provided for in this chapter, rule 8.883, regarding the form and content of briefs, applies.

(b) Writ proceedings not governed

The rules in this chapter do not apply to:

(1) Proceedings under Code of Civil Procedure section 116.798(c) for writs relating to a postjudgment enforcement order of the small claims division, which are governed by rules 8.930–8.936.

(2) Proceedings under Code of Civil Procedure section 116.798(b) for writs relating to an act of a superior court in a small claims appeal, which are governed by rules 8.485–8.493. *(Adopted, eff. Jan. 1, 2016.)*

Advisory Committee Comment

Code of Civil Procedure section 116.798 provides where writs in small claims actions may be heard.

The Judicial Council form *Information on Writ Proceedings in Small Claims Actions* (form SC– 300–INFO) provides additional information about proceedings for writs in small claims actions in the appellate division of the superior court. This form is available at any courthouse or county law library or online at *www.courts.ca.gov/forms*.

Research References

West's California Judicial Council Forms SC–300, Petition for Writ (Small Claims).
West's California Judicial Council Forms SC–300 INFO, Information on Writ Proceedings in Small Claims Cases.

Rule 8.971. Definitions

The definitions in rule 1.6 apply to these rules unless the context or subject matter requires otherwise. In addition, the following definitions apply to these rules:

(1) "Writ" means an order telling the small claims court to do something that the law says it must do, or not do something the law says it must not do. The various types of writs covered by this chapter are described in statutes beginning at section 1067 of the Code of Civil Procedure.

(2) "Petition" means a request for a writ.

(3) "Petitioner" means the person asking for the writ.

(4) "Respondent" and "small claims court" mean the court against which the writ is sought.

(5) "Real party in interest" means any other party in the small claims court case who would be affected by a ruling regarding the request for a writ. *(Adopted, eff. Jan. 1, 2016.)*

Rule 8.972. Petitions filed by persons not represented by an attorney

(a) Petitions

(1) A person who is not represented by an attorney and who requests a writ under this chapter must file the petition on a *Petition for Writ (Small Claims)* (form SC–300). For good cause the court may permit an unrepresented party to file a petition that is not on that form, but the petition must be verified.

(2) If the petition raises any issue that would require the appellate division judge considering it to understand what was said in the small claims court, it must include a statement that fairly summarizes the proceedings, including the parties' arguments and any statement by the small claims court supporting its ruling.

(3) The clerk must file the petition even if it is not verified but if the party asking for the writ fails to file a verification within five days after the clerk gives notice of the defect, the court may strike the petition.

(b) Contents of supporting documents

(1) The petition must be accompanied by copies of the following:

(A) The small claims court ruling from which the petition seeks relief;

(B) All documents and exhibits submitted to the small claims court supporting and opposing the petitioner's position; and

(C) Any other documents or portions of documents submitted to the small claims court that are necessary for a complete understanding of the case and the ruling under review.

(2) If the petition does not include the required documents or does not present facts sufficient to excuse the failure to submit them, the appellate division judge may summarily deny a stay request, the petition, or both.

(c) Form of supporting documents

(1) Documents submitted under (b) must comply with the following requirements:

(A) They must be attached to the petition. The pages must be consecutively numbered.

(B) They must each be given a number or letter.

(2) The clerk must file any supporting documents not complying with (1), but the court may notify the petitioner that it may strike or summarily deny the petition if the documents are not brought into compliance within a stated reasonable time of not less than five days.

(d) Service

(1) The petition and all its attachments, and a copy of *Information on Writ Proceedings in Small Claims Cases* (form SC–300–INFO) must be served personally or by mail on all the parties in the case, and the petition must be served on the small claims court.

(2) The petitioner must file a proof of service at the same time the petition is filed.

(3) The clerk must file the petition even if its proof of service is defective but if the party asking for the writ fails to file a corrected proof of service within five days after the clerk gives notice of the defect, the court may strike the petition or allow additional time to file a corrected proof of service.

(4) The court may allow the petition to be filed without proof of service. *(Adopted, eff. Jan. 1, 2016. As amended, eff. Jan. 1, 2018.)*

Advisory Committee Comment

Subdivision (a). *Petition for Writ (Small Claims)* (form SC–300) and Information on Writ Proceedings in Small Claims Cases (form SC–300–INFO) are available at any courthouse or county law library or online at *www.courts.ca.gov/forms*.

Rule 8.973. Petitions filed by an attorney for a party

(a) General application of rule 8.972

Except as provided in this rule, rule 8.972 applies to any petition for an extraordinary writ filed by an attorney under this chapter.

(b) Form and content of petition

(1) A petition for an extraordinary writ filed by an attorney may, but is not required to be, filed on *Petition for Writ (Small Claims)* (form SC–300). It must contain all the information requested in that form.

(2) The petition must disclose the name of any real party in interest.

(3) If the petition seeks review of small claims court proceedings that are also the subject of a pending appeal, the notice "Related Appeal Pending" must appear on the cover of the petition, and the first paragraph of the petition must state the appeal's title and any appellate division docket number.

(4) The petition must be verified.

(5) The petition must be accompanied by a memorandum, which need not repeat facts alleged in the petition.

(6) Rule 8.883(b) governs the length of the petition and memorandum, but the verification and any supporting documents are excluded from the limits stated in rule 8.883(b)(1) and (2).

(7) If the petition requests a temporary stay, it must explain the urgency. *(Adopted, eff. Jan. 1, 2016.)*

Rule 8.974. Opposition

(a) Preliminary opposition

(1) The respondent and real party in interest are not required to file any opposition to the petition unless asked to do so by the appellate division judge.

(2) Within 10 days after the petition is filed, the respondent or any real party in interest may serve and file a preliminary opposition.

(3) A preliminary opposition should contain any legal arguments the party wants to make as to why the appellate division judge should not issue a writ and a statement of any material facts not included in the petition.

(4) Without requesting opposition, the appellate division judge may grant or deny a request for temporary stay, deny the petition, issue an alternative writ or order to show cause, or notify the parties that the judge is considering issuing a peremptory writ in the first instance.

(b) Return or opposition; reply

(1) If the appellate division judge issues an alternative writ or order to show cause, the respondent or any real party in interest, individually or jointly, may serve and file a return (which is a response to the petition) by demurrer, verified answer, or both. If the appellate division judge notifies the parties that he or she is considering issuing a peremptory writ in the first instance, the respondent or any real party in interest may serve and file an opposition.

(2) Unless the appellate division judge orders otherwise, the return or opposition must be served and filed within 30 days after the appellate division judge issues the alternative writ or order to show cause or notifies the parties that it is considering issuing a peremptory writ in the first instance.

(3) Unless the appellate division judge orders otherwise, the petitioner may serve and file a reply within 15 days after the return or opposition is filed.

(4) If the return is by demurrer alone and the demurrer is not sustained, the appellate division judge may issue the peremptory writ without granting leave to answer.

(c) Form of preliminary opposition, return, or opposition

Any preliminary opposition, return, or opposition must comply with rule 8.931(c). If it is filed by an attorney, it must also comply with rule 8.932(b)(3)—(7). *(Adopted, eff. Jan. 1, 2016.)*

Rule 8.975. Notice to small claims court

(a) Notice if writ issues

If a writ or order issues directed to any judge, court, or other officer, the appellate division clerk must promptly send a certified copy of the writ or order to the person or entity to whom it is directed.

(b) Notice by telephone

(1) If the writ or order stays or prohibits proceedings set to occur within seven days or requires action within seven days—or in any other urgent situation—the appellate division clerk must make a reasonable effort to notify the clerk of the respondent small claims court by telephone. The clerk of the respondent small claims court must then notify the judge or officer most directly concerned.

(2) The appellate division clerk need not give notice by telephone of the summary denial of a writ, whether or not a stay was previously issued. *(Adopted, eff. Jan. 1, 2016.)*

Rule 8.976. Filing, finality, and modification of decisions; remittitur

(a) Filing of decision

The appellate division clerk must promptly file all opinions and orders in proceedings under this chapter and on the same day send copies (by e-mail where permissible under rule 2.251) showing the filing date to the parties and, when relevant, to the small claims court.

(b) Finality of decision

(1) Except as otherwise ordered by the appellate division judge, the following decisions regarding petitions for writs under this chapter are final in the issuing court when filed:

(A) An order denying or dismissing such a petition without issuance of an alternative writ, order to show cause, or writ of review; and

(B) An order denying or dismissing such a petition as moot after issuance of an alternative writ, order to show cause, or writ of review.

(2) Except as otherwise provided in (3), all other decisions in a writ proceeding under this chapter are final 30 days after the decision is sent by the court clerk to the parties.

(3) If necessary to prevent mootness or frustration of the relief granted or to otherwise promote the interests of justice, a judge in the appellate division may order early finality of a decision granting a petition for a writ under this chapter or denying such a petition after issuing an alternative writ, order to show cause, or writ of review. The decision may provide for finality on filing or within a stated period of less than 30 days.

(c) Modification of decisions

Rule 8.888(b) governs the modification of decisions in writ proceedings under this chapter.

(d) Remittitur

The appellate division must issue a remittitur after the judge issues a decision on in a writ proceeding under this chapter except when the judge issues one of the orders listed in (b)(1). The remittitur is deemed issued when the clerk enters it in the record. The clerk must immediately send the parties notice of issuance of the remittitur, showing the date of entry. *(Adopted, eff. Jan. 1, 2016. As amended, eff. Jan. 1, 2019.)*

Advisory Committee Comment

Subdivision (b)(1). Examples of situations in which the appellate division judge may issue an order dismissing a writ petition include when the petitioner fails to comply with an order, when the judge recalls the alternative writ, order to show cause, or writ of review as improvidently granted, or when the petition becomes moot.

Rule 8.977. Costs

(a) Entitlement to costs

The prevailing party in an original proceeding is entitled to costs if the appellate division judge resolves the proceeding after issuing an alternative writ, an order to show cause, or a peremptory writ in the first instance.

(b) Award of costs

(1) In the interests of justice, the appellate division judge may award or deny costs as the court deems proper.

(2) The opinion or order resolving the proceeding must specify the award or denial of costs.

(3) Rule 8.891(b)–(d) governs the procedure for recovering costs under this rule. *(Adopted, eff. Jan. 1, 2016.)*

Research References

West's California Judicial Council Forms SC–300, Petition for Writ (Small Claims).

West's California Judicial Council Forms SC–300 INFO, Information on Writ Proceedings in Small Claims Cases.

Title 10

JUDICIAL ADMINISTRATION RULES

Division 4

TRIAL COURT ADMINISTRATION

Chapter 13

TRIAL COURT MANAGEMENT OF CRIMINAL CASES

Rule 10.950. Role of presiding judge, supervising judge, criminal division, and master calendar department in courts having more than three judges

The presiding judge of a court having more than three judges may designate one or more departments primarily to hear criminal cases. Two or more departments so designated must be the criminal division. The presiding judge may designate supervising judges for the criminal division, but retains final authority over all criminal and civil case assignments. *(Formerly Rule 227.1, adopted, eff. Jan. 1, 1985. Renumbered Rule 10.950 and amended, eff. Jan. 1, 2007.)*

Research References

4 Witkin, California Criminal Law 4th Introduction to Criminal Procedure § 9 (2021), Rules of Court.
4 Witkin, California Criminal Law 4th Jurisdiction and Venue § 15 (2021), Criminal Departments and Divisions.

Rule 10.951. Duties of supervising judge of the criminal division

(a) Duties

In addition to any other duties assigned by the presiding judge or imposed by these rules, a supervising judge of the criminal division must assign criminal matters requiring a hearing or cases requiring trial to a trial department.

(b) Arraignments, pretrial motions, and readiness conferences

The presiding judge, supervising judge, or other designated judge must conduct arraignments, hear and determine any pretrial motions, preside over readiness conferences, and, where not inconsistent with law, assist in the disposition of cases without trial.

(c) Mental health case protocols

The presiding judge, supervising judge, or other designated judge, in conjunction with the justice partners designated in rule 10.952, is encouraged to develop local protocols for cases involving offenders with mental illness or co-occurring disorders to ensure early identification of and appropriate treatment for offenders with mental illness or co-occurring disorders with the goals of reducing recidivism, responding to public safety concerns, and providing better outcomes for those offenders while using resources responsibly and reducing costs.

(d) Additional judges

To the extent that the business of the court requires, the presiding judge may designate additional judges under the direction of the supervising judge to perform the duties specified in this rule.

(e) Courts without supervising judge

In a court having no supervising judge, the presiding judge performs the duties of a supervising judge. *(Formerly Rule 227.2, adopted, eff. Jan. 1, 1985. Renumbered Rule 10.951 and amended, eff. Jan. 1, 2007. As amended, eff. Jan. 1, 2008; Jan. 1, 2014.)*

Research References

5 Witkin, California Criminal Law 4th Criminal Trial § 380 (2021), In General.
4 Witkin, California Criminal Law 4th Jurisdiction and Venue § 15 (2021), Criminal Departments and Divisions.

Rule 10.952. Meetings concerning the criminal court system

The supervising judge or, if none, the presiding judge must designate judges of the court to attend regular meetings to be held with the district attorney; public defender; representatives of the local bar, probation department, parole office, sheriff department, police departments, and Forensic Conditional Release Program (CONREP); county mental health director or his or her designee; county alcohol and drug programs director or his or her designee; court personnel; and other interested persons to identify and eliminate problems in the criminal court system and to discuss other problems of mutual concern. *(Formerly Rule 227.8, adopted, eff. Jan. 1, 1985. Renumbered Rule 10.952 and amended, eff. Jan. 1, 2007. As amended, eff. Jan. 1, 2014; Jan. 1, 2015.)*

Research References

4 Witkin, California Criminal Law 4th Introduction to Criminal Procedure § 5 (2021), Procedure in Criminal Courts.
4 Witkin, California Criminal Law 4th Jurisdiction and Venue § 15 (2021), Criminal Departments and Divisions.

Rule 10.953. Procedures for disposition of cases before the preliminary hearing

(a) Disposition before preliminary hearing

Superior courts having more than three judges must, in cooperation with the district attorney and defense bar, adopt procedures to facilitate dispositions before the preliminary hearing and at all other stages of the proceedings. The procedures may include:

(1) Early, voluntary, informal discovery, consistent with part 2, title 6, chapter 10 of the Penal Code (commencing with section 1054); and

(2) The use of superior court judges as magistrates to conduct readiness conferences before the preliminary hearing and to assist, where not inconsistent with law, in the early disposition of cases.

(b) Case to be disposed of under rule 4.114

Pleas of guilty or no contest resulting from proceedings under (a) must be disposed of as provided in rule 4.114. *(Formerly Rule 227.10, adopted, eff. Jan. 1, 1985. As amended, eff. June 6, 1990; Jan. 1, 1991; July 1, 2001. Renumbered Rule 10.953 and amended, eff. Jan. 1, 2007.)*

Chapter 14

MANAGEMENT OF SELF–HELP CENTERS

Rule

Rule 10.960. Court self-help centers

(a) Scope and application

This rule applies to all court-based self-help centers whether the services provided by the center are managed by the court or by an entity other than the court.

(b) Purpose and core court function

Providing access to justice for self-represented litigants is a priority for California courts. The services provided by court self-help centers facilitate the timely and cost-effective processing of cases involving self-represented litigants and improve the delivery of justice to the public. Court programs, policies, and procedures designed to assist self-represented litigants and effectively manage cases involving self-represented litigants at all stages must be incorporated and budgeted as core court functions.

(c) Staffing

Court self-help centers provide assistance to self-represented litigants. A court self-help center must include an attorney and other qualified staff who provide information and education to self-represented litigants about the justice process, and who work within the court to provide for the effective management of cases involving self-represented litigants.

(d) Neutrality and availability

The information and education provided by court self-help centers must be neutral and unbiased, and services must be available to all sides of a case.

(e) Guidelines and procedures

The Advisory Committee on Providing Access and Fairness must recommend to the council updates to the *Guidelines for the Operation of Self–Help Centers in California Trial Courts* as needed. It should, in collaboration with judges, court executives, attorneys, and other parties with demonstrated interest in services to self-represented litigants, develop and disseminate guidelines, procedures and best practices for the operation of court self-help centers. The guidelines and procedures must address the following topics:

(1) Location and hours of operation;

(2) Scope of services;

(3) Attorney qualifications;

(4) Other staffing qualifications and supervision requirements;

(5) Language access;

(6) Contracts with entities other than the court that provide self-help services;

(7) Use of technology;

(8) Ethics;

(9) Efficiency of operation; and

(10) Security.

(f) Budget and funding

A court must include in its annual budget funding necessary for operation of its self-help center. In analyzing and making recommendations on the allocation of funding for a court self-help center, Judicial Council staff will consider the degree to which individual courts have been successful in meeting the guidelines and procedures for the operation of the self-help center. *(Adopted, eff. Jan. 1, 2008. As amended, eff. Feb. 20, 2014; Jan. 1, 2015; Jan. 1, 2016.)*

CALIFORNIA SUPREME COURT

SUPREME COURT POLICIES REGARDING CASES ARISING FROM JUDGMENTS OF DEATH

Policy 1. Stays of Execution

The court will consider a motion for a stay of execution only if such a motion is made in connection with a petition for a writ of habeas corpus filed in this court, or to permit certiorari review by the United States Supreme Court.

Policy 2. Withdrawal of Counsel

In the absence of exceptional circumstances—for example, when an appointed counsel becomes mentally or physically incapacitated—the court will consider a motion to withdraw as attorney of record only if appropriate replacement counsel is ready and willing to accept appointment for the balance of the representation for which the withdrawing attorney has been appointed (i.e., appellate representation, habeas corpus/executive clemency representation, or both). *(As amended, eff. Jan. 22, 1998.)*

Policy 3. Standards Governing Filing of Habeas Corpus Petitions and Compensation of Counsel in Relation to Such Petitions

The Supreme Court promulgates these standards as a means of implementing the following goals with respect to petitions for writs of habeas corpus relating to capital cases: (i) ensuring that potentially meritorious habeas corpus petitions will be presented to and heard by this court in a timely fashion; (ii) providing appointed counsel some certainty of payment for authorized legal work and investigation expenses; and (iii) providing this court with a means to monitor and regulate expenditure of public funds paid to counsel who seek to investigate and file habeas corpus petitions.

For these reasons, effective June 6, 1989, all petitions for writs of habeas corpus arising from judgments of death, whether the appeals therefrom are pending or previously resolved, are governed by these standards:

1. Timeliness standards

1–1. Appellate counsel in a capital case shall take and maintain detailed, understandable and computerized transcript notes and shall compile and maintain a detailed list of potentially meritorious habeas corpus issues that have come to appellate counsel's attention. In addition, if appellate counsel's appointment does not include habeas corpus representation, until separate counsel is appointed for that purpose, appellate counsel shall preserve evidence that comes to the attention of appellate counsel if that evidence appears relevant to a potential habeas corpus investigation. If separate "post-conviction" habeas corpus/executive clemency counsel (hereafter "habeas corpus" counsel) is appointed, appellate counsel shall deliver to habeas corpus counsel copies of the list of potentially meritorious habeas corpus issues, copies of the transcript notes, and any preserved evidence relevant to a potential habeas corpus investigation, and thereafter shall update the issues list and transcript notes as warranted. Appellate counsel shall consult with and work cooperatively with habeas corpus counsel to facilitate timely investigation, and timely preparation and filing (if warranted) of a habeas corpus petition by habeas corpus counsel.

Habeas corpus counsel in a capital case shall have a duty to investigate factual and legal grounds for the filing of a petition for a writ of habeas corpus. The duty to investigate is limited to investigating potentially meritorious grounds for relief that come to counsel's attention in the course of reviewing appellate counsel's list of potentially meritorious habeas corpus issues, the transcript notes prepared by appellate counsel, the appellate record, trial counsel's existing case files, and the appellate briefs, and in the course of making reasonable efforts to discuss the case with the defendant, trial counsel and appellate counsel. The duty to investigate does not impose on counsel an obligation to conduct, nor does it authorize the expenditure of public funds for, an unfocused investigation having as its object uncovering all possible factual bases for a collateral attack on the judgment. Instead, counsel has a duty to investigate potential habeas corpus claims only if counsel has become aware of information that might reasonably lead to actual facts supporting a potentially meritorious claim. All petitions for writs of habeas corpus should be filed without substantial delay.

1–1.1. A petition for a writ of habeas corpus will be presumed to be filed without substantial delay if it is filed within 180 days after the final due date for the filing of appellant's reply brief on the direct appeal or within 36 months after appointment of habeas corpus counsel, whichever is later.

1–1.2. A petition filed more than 180 days after the final due date for the filing of appellant's reply brief on the direct appeal, or more than 36 months after appointment of habeas corpus counsel, whichever is later, may establish absence of substantial delay if it alleges with specificity facts showing the petition was filed within a reasonable time after petitioner or counsel (a) knew, or should have known, of facts supporting a claim and (b) became aware, or should have become aware, of the legal basis for the claim.

Official Note No. 1: The amendments to standards 1–1.1 and 1–1.2, effective July 17, 2002, changing "90 days" to "180 days," shall apply to all petitions for a writ of habeas corpus arising from a judgment of death that were pending before the Supreme Court on July 17, 2002, and to all such petitions filed after that date.

Official Note No. 2: The amendments to standards 1–1.1 and 1–1.2, effective November 30, 2005, changing "24 months" to "36 months," shall apply to all petitions for a writ of habeas corpus arising from a judgment of death that were pending before the Supreme Court on November 30, 2005, and to all such petitions filed after that date.

1–2. If a petition is filed after substantial delay, the petitioner must demonstrate good cause for the delay. A petitioner may establish good cause by showing particular circumstances sufficient to justify substantial delay.

1–3. Any petition that fails to comply with these requirements may be denied as untimely.

1–4. The court may toll the 180–day period of presumptive timeliness for the filing of a capital-related habeas corpus petition (which begins to run from the final due date to file the appellant's reply brief in the appeal) when it authorizes the appellant to file supplemental briefing. The court will not toll before the 180–day presumptive timeliness period begins to run or after it has finished running.

Ordinarily, the court will toll the 180–day presumptive timeliness period only when the appellant is represented by the same counsel on appeal and also for related habeas corpus/executive clemency proceedings.

If the court determines that it will toll such 180–day presumptive timeliness period, it will so provide in its order authorizing the appellant to file supplemental briefing.

When the court provides for tolling of the 180–day presumptive timeliness period in its order authorizing the appellant to file supplemental briefing, it will determine a reasonable period of time for the appellant to devote to whatever supplemental briefing is authorized, add that period of time to the final due date to file the appellant's reply brief in the appeal, and indicate the new date by which the appellant may file a presumptively timely habeas corpus petition.

Other than under these circumstances, the court will not toll, or otherwise extend, the period in which to file a presumptively timely capital-related habeas corpus petition.

2. Compensation standards

2–1. This court's appointment of appellate counsel for a person under a sentence of death is for the following: (i) pleadings and proceedings related to preparation and certification of the appellate record; (ii) representation in the direct appeal before the California Supreme Court; (iii) preparation and filing of a petition for a writ of certiorari, or an answer thereto, in the United States Supreme Court and, if certiorari is granted, preparation and filing of a brief or briefs on the merits and preparation and presentation of oral argument; and (iv) representation in the trial court relating to proceedings pursuant to Penal Code section 1193.

This court's appointment of habeas corpus counsel for a person under a sentence of death shall be made simultaneously with appointment of appellate counsel or at the earliest practicable time thereafter. The appointment of habeas corpus counsel is for the following: (i) investigation, and preparation and filing (if warranted), of a habeas corpus petition in the California Supreme Court, including any informal briefing and evidentiary hearing ordered by the court and any petition to exhaust state remedies; (ii) representation in the trial court relating to proceedings pursuant to Penal Code section 1227; and (iii) representation in executive clemency proceedings before the Governor of California.

Absent prior authorization by this court, this court will not compensate counsel for the filing of any other motion, petition, or pleading in any other California or federal court or court of another state. Counsel who seek compensation for representation in another court should secure appointment by, and compensation from, that court.

2–2. Habeas corpus counsel should expeditiously investigate potentially meritorious bases for filing a petition for a writ of habeas corpus. If the timing of separate appointments permits, this investigation should be done concurrently with appellate counsel's review of the appellate record and briefing on appeal, and in any event, in cooperation with appellate counsel.

2–2.1. In all cases in which counsel was appointed on or after the October 12, 1997, enactment of Senate Bill No. 513 (Stats. 1997, ch. 869), counsel, without prior authorization of the court, may incur expenses up to a total of $25,000 for habeas corpus investigation, and may submit claims to the court for reimbursement up to that amount. Investigative expenses include travel associated with habeas corpus investigation, and services of law clerks, paralegals, and others serving as habeas corpus investigators. The reasonable cost of photocopying defense counsel's trial files is not considered an investigative expense, and will be separately reimbursed. The court will reimburse counsel for expenses up to $25,000 that were reasonably incurred pursuant to the duty to investigate as described in standard 1–1, but it will not authorize counsel to expend, nor will it reimburse counsel for, habeas corpus investigation expenses exceeding $25,000 before the issuance of an order to show cause. This policy applies to both hourly ("time and costs") and fixed fee appointments.

The policy described in the foregoing paragraph shall also apply to those cases in which counsel was appointed prior to October 12, 1997 (the enactment of Sen. Bill No. 513), and in which, by January 22, 1998, the effective date of the above-described policy, the defendant has not filed a habeas corpus petition in this court and no more than 90 days [now 180 days] have passed since the final due date for the filing of the appellant's reply brief on direct appeal.

As to those cases in which, by January 1, 2008 (the effective date of Assem. Bill No. 1248 [1]), the defendant has not filed a capital-related habeas corpus petition in this court and the date by which to file a presumptively timely petition has not yet passed, counsel may be reimbursed up to $50,000 for those investigative services and expenses incurred on or after that date. Such investigative funding for expenses incurred after January 1, 2008, also is available in those cases in which a presumptively timely petition has been filed by January 1, 2008, but petitioner's reply to the informal response has not been filed and the time to do so (with any extensions of time) has not passed as of that date.

2–2.2. In all cases in which counsel was appointed on an hourly basis prior to October 12, 1997, and in which, by January 22, 1998, either a petition for a writ of habeas corpus has been filed in this court, or more than 90 days have passed since the final due date for the filing of the appellant's reply brief on direct appeal, requests by appointed counsel for authorization to incur, and reimbursement of, investigation expenses shall be governed by the following standards (2–2.3 through 2–4.4):

2–2.3. Without prior authorization of the court, counsel may incur expenses up to a total of $3,000 for habeas corpus investigation relating to a death penalty judgment, and may submit claims to the court for reimbursement up to that amount. The court will reimburse counsel for expenses up to $3,000 that were reasonably incurred pursuant to the duty to investigate as described in standard 1–1.

2–2.4. If after incurring $3,000 in investigation expenses (or if $3,000 in reimbursement for investigation funds previously has been granted on behalf of the same defendant/petitioner with regard to the same underlying death penalty judgment), counsel determines it is necessary to incur additional expenses for which he or she plans to seek reimbursement from the court, counsel must seek and obtain prior authorization from the court. As a general rule, the court will *not* reimburse counsel for expenses exceeding $3,000, without prior authorization of the court. Requests by appointed counsel for prior authorization to incur investigation expenses shall be governed by the following standards.

2–3. Counsel shall file with this court a "Confidential request for authorization to incur expenses to investigate potential habeas corpus issues," showing good cause why the request was not filed on or before the date the appellant's opening brief on appeal was filed.

2–4. The confidential request for authorization to incur expenses shall set out:

2–4.1. The issues to be explored;

2–4.2. Specific facts that suggest there may be an issue of possible merit;

2–4.3. An itemized list of the expenses requested for each issue of the proposed habeas corpus petition; and

2–4.4. (a) An itemized listing of all expenses previously sought from, and/or approved by any court of this state and/or any federal court in connection with any habeas corpus proceeding or investigation concerning the same judgment and petitioner; (b) A statement summarizing the status of any proceeding or investigation in any court of this state and/or any federal court concerning the same judgment and petitioner; and (c) A copy of any related petition previously filed in any trial and/or lower appellate court of this state and/or any federal court concerning the same judgment and petitioner.

2–5. Counsel generally will not be awarded compensation for fees and expenses relating to matters that are clearly not cognizable in a petition for a writ of habeas corpus.

2–6. When a petition is pending in this court to exhaust claims presented in a federal habeas corpus petition, a request by counsel for investigative funds to bolster or augment claims already presented in the petition normally will be denied absent a showing of strong justification for the request. A request for investigative funds may be granted if the petitioner demonstrates that he or she has timely discovered new and potentially meritorious areas of investigation not previously addressed in the petitioner's federal or state petitions. This has been the internal operating policy of the court since December 16, 1992.

2–7. Each request for fees relating to a habeas corpus petition must be accompanied by: (a) An itemized listing of all fees previously sought from, and/or approved by any court of this state and/or any federal court in connection with any habeas corpus proceeding or investigation concerning the same judgment and petitioner; (b) A statement summarizing the status of any proceeding or investigation in any court of this state and/or any federal court concerning the same judgment and petitioner; and (c) A copy of any related petition previously filed in any trial and/or lower appellate court of this state and/or any federal court concerning the same judgment and petitioner.

2–8. In a case in which the court orders an evidentiary hearing, and counsel and the court do not enter into a "fixed fee and expenses agreement" covering the evidentiary hearing (see "Guideline 10" of the "Guidelines for Fixed Fee Appointments, on Optional Basis, to Automatic Appeals and Related Habeas Corpus Proceedings in the California Supreme Court"), requests for reimbursement of necessary and reasonable expenses incurred in preparation for and presentation of the evidentiary hearing shall be governed by the following standards:

2–8.1. Counsel may incur "incidental" expenses (i.e., travel to and from the evidentiary hearing and related hearings before the referee, meals and lodging during the hearing, telephone charges, photocopying, etc.) without prior approval, and the court will reimburse counsel for such itemized, reasonable and necessarily incurred expenses pursuant to the court's "Payment Guidelines for Appointed Counsel Representing Indigent Criminal Appellants in the California Supreme Court," part III ("Necessary Expenses").

2–8.2. Counsel should seek and obtain from this court prior approval for all investigation and witness expenses, including, but not limited to, investigator fees and costs, expert fees and costs, and expert witness fees and costs.

2–8.3. Counsel may submit requests for reimbursement of expenses every 60 days to this court, and will be reimbursed for necessary and reasonable expenses consistently with part III of the "Payment Guidelines," *supra*.

(As amended, eff. Sept. 28, 1989; Sept. 19, 1990; Jan. 27, 1992; Dec. 21, 1992; July 29, 1993; Dec. 22, 1993; June 20, 1996; Jan. 22, 1997; Jan. 22, 1998; Feb. 4, 1998; Jan. 16, 2002; July 17, 2002; July 26, 2002; Nov. 20, 2002; Nov. 30, 2005; Jan. 1, 2008.)

1 Stats.2007, c. 738.

Policy 4. Service of Process by Counsel for Defendant

Consistently with longstanding practice and court policy, except as specified below, counsel for the defendant must serve his or her client, any separate counsel of record in any matter related to the same judgment, counsel of record for every other party, the trial court, the assisting entity or attorney for counsel for the defendant and any separate counsel of record, and trial counsel, with a copy of each motion, request for extension of time, brief, petition or other public document filed in this court or in the trial court on the client's behalf, including any supporting declaration, with attached proof of service. A declaration submitted in support of any motion or request may refer to and incorporate by reference matters set forth in a current "confidential 60–day status report" simultaneously provided only to this court. Counsel also must serve any additional person or entity as requested by this court.

Counsel for the defendant need not serve (1) trial counsel with any matter upon or after the filing in this court of the certified record on appeal; (2) the trial court with any extension-of-time request related to appellate briefing; and (3) the trial court or trial counsel with any matter related to habeas corpus briefing.

If counsel for the defendant elects to serve the defendant personally with the document, counsel may indicate on the proof of service the date by which counsel will so serve the defendant (not to exceed 30 calendar days), and counsel shall thereafter notify the court in writing that the defendant has been served. In the alternative, counsel for the defendant need not serve the defendant with any specific document to be filed if counsel for the defendant attaches to the proof of service for that specific document (1) a declaration by the defendant stating that he or she does not wish to be served with that specific document, and (2) a declaration by counsel for the defendant stating that he or she has described to the defendant the substance and purpose of that specific document. *(Adopted, eff. Aug. 23, 2001. As amended, eff. Dec. 19, 2001.)*

PAYMENT GUIDELINES FOR APPOINTED COUNSEL REPRESENTING INDIGENT CRIMINAL APPELLANTS IN THE CALIFORNIA SUPREME COURT

Section

I. Introduction

The California Supreme Court determines the compensation of appointed counsel representing indigent criminal appellants. The guidelines set forth below are a general statement of the factors considered by the court in determining appropriate compensation for the time devoted to indigent criminal appeals (and related habeas corpus representation) and the reasonable and necessary expenses incurred by appointed counsel. In reviewing these guidelines, counsel should bear in mind the following:

A. Although most of the guidelines apply routinely, the application of others, such as the reimbursement of travel expenses or of the cost of expert witnesses and investigators, depends on the circumstances of each case.

B. The rates in the guidelines are subject to periodic change. These include the hourly compensation of appointed counsel, mileage and per diem rates for travel, and rates for the reimbursement of the cost of services by others.

C. For the most current information concerning these matters, and the payment guidelines generally, counsel are encouraged to contact the California Appellate Project (CAP). CAP is the appointed counsel administrator that assists private counsel with automatic appeals. CAP's address and telephone number are as follows:

California Appellate Project
101 Second Street, Suite 600
San Francisco, CA 94105
(415) 495–0500

(Revised, eff. Sept. 19, 1990. As amended, eff. Jan. 1, 1997; Jan. 22, 1998.)

II. Reasonable Compensation

A. Compensation rate The compensation rate for members of the State Bar of California who are appointed as counsel in indigent criminal appeals is the same allowable-hour rate appointed counsel received or was eligible to receive in the Court of Appeal, except for automatic appeals and/or related habeas corpus/executive clemency proceedings, for which the rate is $145 per allowable hour.

B. "Allowable hours" The compensation rate is multiplied by the number of "allowable hours" of appellate work to determine a reasonable sum for compensation. Benchmarks for "allowable hours" in capital cases (i.e., an estimate of the time an attorney experienced in the handling of criminal appeals might devote to the various stages of capital litigation) are set out below, in part II. subpart *I*.3.

C. Recording of hours Appointed counsel should record the number of hours devoted to the following phases of appellate work:

1. Record review
2. Record correction
3. Motions and applications
4. Sixty–day status reports
5. Researching and writing opening brief
6. Researching and writing reply brief
7. Researching and writing supplemental brief(s)
8. Investigating and writing habeas corpus petition
9. Reply to response(s) to habeas corpus petition
10. Evidentiary hearing
11. Oral argument (includes preparation)
12. Post–oral argument representation
13. Rehearing petition or opposition
14. Certiorari petition or opposition (and briefing and argument in the United States Supreme Court after grant of certiorari; see post, subpart *I*.3.(i))
15. Client communication
16. Travel
17. Other services (specify)

D. Factors considered by the court The following factors are considered by the court in determining the number of allowable hours:

1. Whether the billed hours are within the benchmarks, or whether there exists good cause to depart from the benchmarks.
2. Length of the record.
3. Complexity and novelty of the legal issues.
4. Quality of work.

E. Exceptional procedural matters Counsel should provide the court with an explanation of the time spent on exceptional procedural matters, such as repeated applications for augmentation of the record on appeal.

F. Travel time Travel time will be compensated to the extent that the time could not reasonably be spent working on the case.

G. Circumstances warranting additional compensation If counsel believes there exist extraordinary circumstances that justify compensation beyond that set out in these guidelines, counsel should bring such factors to the attention of the court at the time a claim for payment of compensation and expenses is presented. Counsel's showing of justification should be commensurate with the extent to which he or she seeks to exceed the benchmarks.

H. Submission of payment requests Counsel may submit a request for payment of compensation and expenses every 90 days.

I. Special rules for capital cases The following rules apply to capital cases only:

1. *Delay in certification of record or filing of brief* If delay in the certification of the record on appeal or in the filing of the appellant's opening brief (AOB) is due to a lack of diligence on the part of appointed counsel, payment of compensation will be deferred until the record is certified or the AOB is filed.

2. *Forms and reports* Counsel must submit a cumulative hours compensation form and the most recent status report with every request for payment. The cumulative hours compensation form will be provided by the court or may be obtained from CAP. Counsel should retain a copy of each cumulative hours compensation form submitted. These forms will facilitate completion of the data form for automatic appeals, which must accompany the request for final payment for services rendered in this court. Note that although a request for payment may be submitted every 90 days, a current status report must be submitted every 60 days.

3. *"Allowable hours" benchmarks* The court, after consultation with representatives of a cross-section of the criminal justice bar, has established the following benchmarks for the various stages of capital representation:

(i) APPEAL

Reading the record and producing detailed, understandable and computerized transcript notes: 40 pp./hr.

Record correction: 20–120 hrs.

Client communication: 15–30 hrs.

Appellant's opening brief (AOB): 260–600 hrs.

Appellant's reply brief (ARB): 55–160 hrs.

Oral argument: 40–80 hrs.

Supplemental briefs: 20–80 hrs.

Rehearing petition: 25–75 hrs.

Certiorari petition: 40–75 hrs.

Briefing and argument in the United States Supreme Court after grant of certiorari: Counsel shall seek compensation for such services from the United States Supreme Court. Should that court deny compensation for such services, this court will authorize reasonable compensation for such services up to a maximum of $6,000.

(ii) HABEAS CORPUS

a. Investigation and Presentation of Petition

(For cases in which appellate counsel also handles habeas corpus responsibilities):

Client communication related to habeas corpus investigation: Up to 60 hours, as follows: Up to 30 hrs. in the first year after appointment; and up to 15 hrs. per year thereafter.

Investigate and present habeas corpus *petition*: 140–400 hrs.

(For cases in which separate appointed counsel handles habeas corpus responsibilities):

Client communication related to habeas corpus investigation: Up to 70 hours, as follows: Up to 40 hrs. in the first year after appointment; and up to 15 hrs. per year thereafter.

Record review: 50 pp./hr.

Investigate and present habeas corpus petition: 180–500 hrs.

For all cases:

Informal reply: 50–120 hrs.

Traverse: 50–120 hrs.

b. Habeas Corpus Evidentiary Hearing

Preparation: 150– 600 hrs.

Evidentiary hearing: 72–144 hrs. (i.e., 3–6 days)

Post-hearing litigation before the referee: 75–125 hrs.

These benchmarks apply collectively to all counsel, appointed and supervised, who are engaged in work related to a habeas corpus evidentiary hearing, and are not multiplied, or otherwise increased, by virtue of the fact that more than one attorney is participating in this work.

c. Post–Hearing Briefs in the Supreme Court

Brief on the merits, response brief, and supplemental brief: 50–150 hrs.

d. Habeas Corpus Proceedings Returnable in Superior Court Following Order to Show Cause on Alleged Mental Retardation of Condemned Inmate

The "allowable hours" benchmark ranges for habeas corpus proceedings after issuance of an order to show cause, including any traverse to the return, and preparation for, or presentation at, an evidentiary hearing, as set forth in Payment Guideline II, subpart *I*.3.(ii), apply to all habeas corpus proceedings following an order to show cause issued by the Supreme Court, including any order to show cause returnable to the superior court regarding a condemned inmate's alleged mental retardation and resulting ineligibility for the death penalty within the meaning of *Atkins v. Virginia* (2002) 536 U.S. 304.

Before requesting compensation from the Supreme Court for attorney fees related to such *Atkins* litigation in superior court, appointed counsel first must obtain the superior court's recommendation for payment of the incurred hours. However, the superior court's recommendation is not binding on the Supreme Court, which will, in all cases, exercise independent review concerning attorney fees recommended for payment by the superior court.

These requirements apply to all such fee requests, for *Atkins* litigation in superior court, pending before the Supreme Court on or after March 5, 2012.

(iii) EXECUTIVE CLEMENCY

Representation in executive clemency proceedings before the Governor of California: 40–80 hrs.

These benchmarks are guidelines for the expected hours in "typical" cases, and are neither ceilings nor floors for fees in any given case. The court will continue to monitor its fee payment data to determine whether adjustment of the benchmarks is warranted in the future. Counsel is advised to review the benchmarks carefully, and to bear the following in mind throughout the course of representation (i.e., at each "stage" of the litigation):

a. *The "lower range" of the benchmarks* A case that has a relatively short record (i.e., 3,000–6,000 pages), and that raises standard (albeit fact–specific) issues already resolved in prior cases, should generally produce hours near or below the "lower range" of the benchmarks. Based on experience, the court expects a substantial percentage of cases to be completed under the lower range of the benchmarks.

Counsel should determine at an early stage of representation whether the case meets the description of a "lower range" case. If counsel has such a case, and submits a fee request substantially exceeding the lower range of the benchmarks for any particular stage of the litigation, he or she must include in each request a detailed explanation of why fees exceeding the lower range of the benchmarks should be awarded. The court will award fees substantially exceeding the appropriate benchmark range only if it is convinced that on the facts of the case, such fees are warranted.

b. *The "upper range" of the benchmarks* Based on experience, the court anticipates a number of cases will produce fee hours at or near the upper range of the benchmarks, and occasionally, over that range. The following important caveats apply in such cases:

The upper range of the benchmarks is generally reserved for those cases with relatively long records (i.e., 10,000 or more pages), *and* that raise novel or difficult issues. The mere fact that the record may be long does *not* indicate that "upper range" or "over-benchmark" hours will be appropriate in any or each stage of the litigation.

If a case does not meet the above description of an "upper range" or "over-benchmark" case, counsel should not expect to receive "upper range" or "over-benchmark" fees. In order to secure such fees in a case not otherwise meeting the above description, counsel must include in the request a detailed explanation of why the fees requested should be awarded. The court will award fees near or exceeding the appropriate benchmark range only if it is convinced that on the facts of the case, such fees are warranted.

4. *Second counsel "override"* In cases in which appointed counsel deems it necessary to associate with second counsel, and the court approves the association, the court may in its discretion, and on a showing of good cause, approve compensation to appointed counsel for hours incurred exceeding the "appeal" through "habeas corpus briefing" benchmarks by 5–15 percent. As a general rule the court will allow the full 15 percent override in cases in which counsel divides the hours fairly evenly for the stage for which fees are sought. If counsel divides the work less evenly, the override will be diminished accordingly. The court will continue to monitor the cases to determine whether the 15 percent ceiling should be increased. *(Revised, eff. Sept. 19, 1990. As amended, eff. Dec. 22, 1993; Sept. 1, 1995; Jan. 1, 1997; Jan. 22, 1998; Feb. 4, 1998; Aug. 25, 2004; Oct. 1, 2005; Nov. 30, 2005; July 1, 2006; Oct. 1, 2007; March 5, 2012.)*

III. Necessary Expenses

A. Items not qualifying as expenses The hourly fee should cover all overhead related to a case, *including secretarial services, word processing, and the like*. Expenses listed below will be reimbursed to the extent they are itemized, reasonable, and necessarily incurred during the course of the appeal, and otherwise comply with the court's procedures (see below, part III.B). Note that these guidelines apply not only to appointed counsel, but to those persons, including experts and investigators, who assist appointed counsel with the appeal.

B. Prior approval Prior approval is required for extraordinary expenses, such as for out-of-state travel, expert witnesses and investigators. *In capital cases*, expense requests are governed by the court's "Standards Governing Filing of Habeas Corpus Petitions and Compensation of Counsel in Relation to Such Petitions," published in the Official Reports advance sheet pamphlets. (See *id.*, std. 2–1 et seq.)

C. Reimbursable expenses In general, when making a request for reimbursement, counsel must itemize *all* expenses, and must provide in the request the original receipts for the following: (i) travel expenses (airfare, car rental, hotel bills, etc.) over $47 per day; (ii) telephone and copying expenses over $50 and $100 per month, respectively (see below); and (iii) all other single transactions that exceed $100. Counsel should keep all receipts in the event documentation is later required.

1. *Photocopying* The cost of photocopying will be reimbursed, at not more than 10 cents per page, whether the copying is done inside or outside counsel's office. If counsel represents that photocopying was billed at 10 cents per page or less, receipts will not be required unless the expenses are in excess of $100 per month.

In addition to investigative expenses as set forth in the "Supreme Court Policies Regarding Cases Arising From Judgments of Death," Policy 3, standard 2–2.1, counsel appointed to handle habeas corpus/executive clemency representation will be reimbursed the reasonable cost of photocopying defense counsel's trial files, at the rate of not more than 10 cents per page, after filing of the certified record on appeal. Counsel must provide a receipt or invoice showing the number of pages copied, and the cost per page. Reimbursement will not be paid for photocopying of items already contained in the record on appeal, such as daily transcripts or exhibits.

2. *Postage and delivery costs* Expenses for express mail/messenger service will be reimbursed only on a showing that use of express mail/messenger service was necessary and reasonable.

3. *Telephone charges* Receipts will not be required unless the expenses are in excess of $50 per month.

4. *Travel expenses*

a. The court will determine the reasonableness and necessity of travel expenses on a case-by-case basis. Counsel are cautioned that travel expenses are not considered necessary when the purpose of a trip may reasonably be accomplished in another way, such as by telephone or correspondence. Further, counsel should use the least expensive alternative means of travel. For motor vehicles, the mileage rate is the prevailing amount established by the Administrative Office of the Courts.

b. When travel is required by appointed counsel or a person authorized to assist appointed counsel, reasonable and necessary meals and lodging may be claimed, to the extent allowed under State Board of Control rules. Counsel should contact CAP for further information.

c. Some of the lesser known provisions of the Board of Control rules are as follows:

(1) The per diem allowance does not apply for trips of 25 miles or less.

(2) Lunch is not covered unless the travel period is 24 hours or more.

(3) The cost of collision coverage in a contract for a rental car is not covered.

5. *Computerized legal research* The reasonable cost of computerized legal research (as opposed to the costs of installation and monthly access fees), when the use is specifically attributable to the case, will be reimbursed to the extent reasonably and necessarily incurred. Counsel must explain in writing the specific nature of the computer expenses (e.g., Shepard's, Autocite, issue searches, etc.), and must explain why computerized research was more efficient than the same research performed "manually."

6. *Services of law clerks, paralegals, and State Bar members*

a. Counsel shall be reimbursed for the compensation of the following individuals at a rate not to exceed the following:

(1) Law clerks who are not members of the State Bar of California at $40 per allowable hour.

(2) Paralegals at $40 per allowable hour.

(3) Members of the State Bar of California, who are not appointed to the case, at the rate of $98 per allowable hour.

b. Reimbursement of the compensation for all persons performing legal services, other than appointed counsel, shall be subject to the following conditions:

(1) In submitting a claim for reimbursement, counsel shall describe with specificity the legal services and number of hours of work performed by each other person so the court can evaluate the reasonableness of the services and expenses as part of appointed counsel's overall claim. *It is expected that the hours devoted to legal services by nonappointed counsel, and any "exceptionally high" hours attributed to law clerks and paralegals* (i.e., hours exceeding 30 percent of the benchmark hours for appointed counsel for any given stage), *will reduce the hours that appointed counsel will devote to those services.*

(2) Appointed counsel shall not delegate to others those functions that require the ability and experience for which counsel was appointed.

(3) Appointed counsel shall supervise and have full responsibility for the services performed by others.

7. *Services of investigators and experts*

a. An investigator or expert shall be compensated at a rate not to exceed the maximum rates listed below. Counsel must establish that use of an expert's services is reasonably necessary under the facts of the case. Counsel seeking to use the services of multiple experts relating to a single or common issue must demonstrate a compelling necessity for such use of multiple experts. In addition, counsel must include in the request for reimbursement a representation that the rate requested

(1) does not exceed the investigator's or expert's customary rates for the services performed, and

(2) does not exceed local prevailing rates for the services performed.

b. The maximum rates are as follows

(1) Investigators, $55–90 per hour.

(2) Penalty phase consultants, $60–125 per hour.

(3) Psychiatrists and other medically licensed mental health experts, $200–350 per hour.

(4) Other forensic experts, $125–225 per hour.

(5) Psychologists (Ph.D.'s), $150–275 per hour.

(6) Attorneys serving as experts, $125–145 per hour. (*Note:* Until an order to show cause is issued, *or* the People submit an expert declaration in their informal opposition to a habeas corpus petition, the court will not approve payment for attorney "expert opinion" in the form of declarations, etc.)

(7) Any expert listed above testifying at a court proceeding, eight times the hourly rate per day or four times the hourly rate per half day.

c. In exceptional circumstances, when the need for services at a greater rate of compensation is documented and prior authorization is obtained from the Supreme Court, compensation beyond the maximum may be paid.

8. *Proceedings returnable in superior court following order to show cause on alleged mental retardation of condemned inmate*

In proceedings pending in superior court pursuant to an order to show cause issued by the California Supreme Court, and returnable before the superior court, regarding a condemned inmate's alleged mental retardation and resulting ineligibility for the death penalty within the meaning of *Atkins v. Virginia* (2002) 536 U.S. 304 (see also *In re Hawthorne* (2005) 35 Cal.4th 40), the following practices apply to requests by counsel appointed in the California Supreme Court for the reimbursement of investigation services and expenses incurred in superior court for experts, investigators and law clerks/paralegals:

a. The superior court in which the *Atkins*-related proceedings are pending makes only a *recommendation* for pre-authorization to incur, and payment of, the expenses of investigators, experts, and other service providers for whom reimbursement is sought by appointed counsel. Thereafter, the Supreme Court independently determines, pursuant to its time-and-costs Payment Guidelines and the Policy 3 compensation standards (see Supreme Ct. Policies Regarding Cases Arising From Judgments of Death), whether the recommended funding is reasonable and, to the extent found reasonable, authorizes appointed counsel to incur such expenses and reimburses appointed counsel, as appropriate.

This provision will apply to all such funding requests pending before the Supreme Court on or after March 5, 2012.

b. Appointed counsel may engage experts, investigators and law clerks/paralegals either in the locality where counsel's offices are situated or in the locality where the superior court proceedings are being held, at counsel's option.

c. The California Supreme Court will pay for investigation services and expenses at the rate prevailing where the services are engaged, if otherwise permissible within the maximum hourly rates and other applicable provisions set forth within these payment guidelines.

(Revised, eff. Sept. 19, 1990. As amended, eff. Sept. 1, 1995; Jan. 1, 1997; Jan. 22, 1998; Jan. 16, 2002; Oct. 1, 2005; July 1, 2006; July 23, 2008; Aug. 27, 2008; March 5, 2012.)

IV. Fee and Expense Disallowances

The court will provide reasons in writing for fee disallowances of $1,000 or more, and expense disallowances of $500 or more. *(Revised, eff. Sept. 19, 1990.)*

V. Court Action Upon Nonperformance of Work, and Reimbursement of Fees Upon Authorized Withdrawal of Appointed Counsel

A. Nonperformance of counsel. In the rare circumstance in which appointed counsel ceases work on a case and refuses to complete the work with reasonable diligence, the court has had, and will continue to exercise as appropriate, the following nonexclusive options: The court may enforce its legal rights; the court may refer the matter to the State Bar; and finally, the court may institute contempt proceedings to enforce its orders.

B. Authorized withdrawal of counsel. In the event that the court permits appointed counsel to withdraw before completion of counsel's duties in a case, the court will, as appropriate under the circumstances, authorize payment to counsel for legal work completed. Alternatively, the court may, as appropriate under the circumstances, order counsel to reimburse the court for fees paid, less a credit for work performed that is determined by the court to be of value to the court. *(Adopted, eff. July 30, 1997.)*

GUIDELINES FOR FIXED FEE APPOINTMENTS, ON OPTIONAL BASIS, TO AUTOMATIC APPEALS AND RELATED HABEAS CORPUS PROCEEDINGS IN THE CALIFORNIA SUPREME COURT

Section

Introduction

Presently, appointed counsel in automatic appeals are compensated on a "time and costs" basis, under the Payment Guidelines for Appointed Counsel Representing Indigent Criminal Appellants in the California Supreme Court (as revised) (hereafter Payment Guidelines). Under the Payment Guidelines, appointed counsel must submit a detailed and lengthy cumulative hours compensation form with every request for payment of fees and reimbursement of expenses. Moreover, "allowable hours" benchmarks limit the fees available for each stage of the capital representation; other provisions limit or exclude reimbursement for expenses. Requests for prior approval of extraordinary expenses are governed by the Supreme Court Policies Regarding Cases Arising From Judgments of Death (as revised).

In an effort to provide appointed counsel in capital cases greater predictability, consistency and control over compensation and expenses, and to reduce administrative burdens on both counsel and the Court, the Court has adopted an optional fixed fee and expenses payment system.

The categories of fixed fees set out below in Guidelines 1, 1.1, and 1.2 establish the compensation and responsibilities of appointed counsel for all services and "incidental expenses" (habeas corpus investigation expenses are separately provided for in Guideline 2):

(1) In cases in which counsel is appointed to represent the defendant both on appeal and in related habeas corpus/executive clemency proceedings, fixed fee compensation is for: (a) the direct appeal, through the filing of a certiorari petition to the United States Supreme Court, or an answer thereto (but not including any briefs or appearances in the United States Supreme Court after grant of certiorari or any briefs or appearances on remand to the California Supreme Court, which work would be compensated under the terms and limitations of the Payment Guidelines); (b) state habeas corpus investigation, and preparation and filing (if warranted) of a state habeas corpus petition and informal reply, and any subsequent habeas corpus petition, including any petition to exhaust state remedies, in the California Supreme Court (but not including any traverse, habeas corpus evidentiary hearing or post-hearing briefs in the California Supreme Court, which work would be compensated under the terms and limitations of the Payment Guidelines); (c) any trial court proceedings under Penal Code sections 1193 and 1227 to

set an execution date; and (d) representation in executive clemency proceedings before the Governor of California. (See Cal. Supreme Ct., Policies Regarding Cases Arising From Judgments of Death, *supra*. Compensation Stds., std. 2–1.)

(2) In cases in which counsel is appointed to represent the defendant on appeal only, fixed fee compensation is for: (a) the direct appeal, through the filing of a certiorari petition to the United States Supreme Court, or an answer thereto (but not including any briefs or appearances in the United States Supreme Court after grant of certiorari or any briefs or appearances on remand to the California Supreme Court, which work would be compensated under the terms and limitations of the Payment Guidelines); and (b) any trial court proceedings under Penal Code section 1193 to set an execution date. (See Cal. Supreme Ct., Policies Regarding Cases Arising From Judgments of Death, *supra*, Compensation Stds., std. 2–1.)

(3) In cases in which counsel is appointed to represent the defendant in habeas corpus/executive clemency proceedings only, fixed fee compensation is for: (a) state habeas corpus investigation, and preparation and filing (if warranted) of a state habeas corpus petition and informal reply, and any subsequent habeas corpus petition, including any petition to exhaust state remedies, in the California Supreme Court (but not including any traverse, habeas corpus evidentiary hearing or post-hearing briefs in the California Supreme Court, which work would be compensated under the terms and limitations of the Payment Guidelines); (b) any trial court proceedings under Penal Code section 1227 to set an execution date; and (c) representation in executive clemency proceedings before the Governor of California. (See Cal. Supreme Ct., Policies Regarding Cases Arising From Judgments of Death, *supra*, Compensation Stds., std. 2–1.) *(Adopted, eff. Jan. 1, 1994. As amended, eff. Sept. 1, 1995; Jan. 22, 1998; Feb. 4, 1998.)*

1. Fixed Fee Categories for Cases in Which Counsel is Appointed to Handle the Appeal and Related Habeas Corpus/Executive Clemency Proceedings

Category I: $160,000

A. An appeal from a judgment based on a guilty plea and penalty phase; or

B. An appeal from a judgment on remand following a reversal limited to penalty.

C. Caveat: An appeal from a judgment on limited remand for a new hearing on the automatic motion to modify the death verdict (Pen. Code, § 190.4, subd. (e)) likely will be valued well below $160,000. (See also Guideline 4 [Case Evaluation], *post*.)

Category II: $231,000

A. An appeal from a judgment on remand following a reversal limited to the special circumstance finding(s) and penalty; or

B. An appeal otherwise in category I(A) or I(B) that presents a more complex case, in the Court's view, by reason of, but not limited to, one or more of the following factors: The combined record on appeal is 4,000 or more pages; there was more than one homicide victim, and the homicides occurred in more than one incident; there were numerous pretrial and/or penalty phase motions; there were multiple defendants and/or appellants; or

C. An initial appeal or an appeal from a judgment on remand following a reversal of guilt, in which the combined record on appeal is under 6,000 pages.

Category III: $283,000

A. An initial appeal or an appeal from a judgment on remand following a reversal of guilt, in which the combined record on appeal is between 6,000 and 12,000 pages; or

B. An appeal otherwise in category II(A) or II(C) that presents a more complex case, in the Court's view, by reason of, but not limited to, one or more of the following factors: The combined record on appeal is 5,000 or more pages; there was more than one homicide victim, and the homicides occurred in more than one incident; there were numerous pretrial and/or penalty phase motions; there were multiple defendants and/or appellants.

Category IV: $322,000

A. An initial appeal or an appeal from a judgment on remand following a reversal of guilt, in which the combined record on appeal is 12,000 or more pages; or

B. An appeal otherwise in category III(A) that presents a more complex case, in the Court's view, by reason of, but not limited to, one or more of the following factors: The combined record on appeal is 10,000 or more pages; there was more than one homicide victim, and the homicides occurred in more than one incident; there were numerous pretrial and/or penalty phase motions; there were multiple defendants and/or appellants.

Category V: $368,000 base fee

Exceptional cases that occur infrequently, involve many victims and incidents, and have a combined record on appeal of 25,000 or more pages. In this category, appointed counsel may present a justification at the outset for a fixed fee higher than the base fee. *(Adopted, eff. Jan. 1, 1994. As amended, eff. Sept. 1, 1995; Jan. 1, 1997; Jan. 22, 1998; Oct. 1, 2005; July 1, 2006; Oct. 1, 2007.)*

1.1. Fixed Fee Categories for Cases in Which Counsel is Appointed to Handle the Appeal Only

Category I: $65,000

A. An appeal from a judgment based on a guilty plea and penalty phase; or

B. An appeal from a judgment on remand following a reversal limited to penalty.

C. Caveat: An appeal from a judgment on limited remand for a new hearing on the automatic motion to modify the death verdict (Pen. Code, § 190.4, subd. (e)) likely will be valued well below $65,000. (See also Guideline 4 [Case Evaluation], *post*.)

Category II: $136,000

A. An appeal from a judgment on remand following a reversal limited to the special circumstance finding(s) and penalty; or

B. An appeal otherwise in category I(A) or I(B) that presents a more complex case, in the Court's view, by reason of, but not limited to, one or more of the following factors: The combined record on appeal is 4,000 or more pages; there was more than one homicide victim, and the homicides occurred in more than one incident; there were numerous pretrial and/or penalty phase motions; there were multiple defendants and/or appellants; or

C. An initial appeal or an appeal from a judgment on remand following a reversal of guilt, in which the combined record on appeal is under 6,000 pages.

Category III: $178,000

A. An initial appeal or an appeal from a judgment on remand following a reversal of guilt, in which the combined record on appeal is between 6,000 and 12,000 pages; or

B. An appeal otherwise in category II(A) or II(C) that presents a more complex case, in the Court's view, by reason of, but not limited to, one or more of the following factors: The combined record on appeal is 5,000 or more pages; there was more than one homicide victim, and the homicides occurred in more than one incident; there were numerous pretrial and/or penalty phase motions; there were multiple defendants and/or appellants.

Category IV: $219,000

A. An initial appeal or an appeal from a judgment on remand following a reversal of guilt, in which the combined record on appeal is 12,000 or more pages; or

B. An appeal otherwise in category III(A) that presents a more complex case, in the Court's view, by reason of, but not limited to, one or more of the following factors: The combined record on appeal is 10,000 or more pages; there was more than one homicide victim, and the homicides occurred in more than one incident; there were numerous pretrial and/or penalty phase motions; there were multiple defendants and/or appellants.

Category V: $263,000 base fee

Exceptional cases that occur infrequently, involve many victims and incidents, and have a combined record on appeal of 25,000 or more pages. In this category, appointed counsel may present a justification at the outset for a fixed fee higher than the base fee. *(Adopted, eff. Jan. 22, 1998. As amended, eff. Oct. 1, 2005; July 1, 2006; Oct. 1, 2007.)*

1.2. Fixed Fee Categories for Cases in Which Counsel is Appointed to Handle Habeas Corpus/Executive Clemency Proceedings Only

Category I: $85,000, plus an additional fixed fee calculated at the rate of $145 for every 50 pages of transcript in the combined record on appeal.

A. Habeas corpus representation related to a case that would fall within Fixed Fee Guideline 1.1, Categories I or II.

B. Habeas corpus representation related to a case that would fall within Fixed Fee Guideline 1.1, Categories III, IV, or V, but that, for case-specific reasons, is of below-average complexity.

Category II: $110,000, plus an additional fixed fee calculated at the rate of $145 for every 50 pages of transcript in the combined record on appeal.

A. Habeas corpus representation related to a case that would fall within Fixed Fee Guideline 1.1, Categories III, IV, or V.

B. Habeas corpus representation related to a case that would fall within Fixed Fee Guideline 1.1, Categories I or II, but that, for case-specific reasons, nevertheless is of average complexity.

Category III: $127,000, plus an additional fixed fee calculated at the rate of $145 for every 50 pages of transcript in the combined record on appeal, for cases of above-average complexity.

For cases of exceptional complexity, appointed counsel may present a justification at the outset for a fixed fee higher than the $127,000 base fee. (Adopted, eff. Jan. 22, 1998. As amended, eff. Oct. 1, 2005; Nov. 30, 2005; July 1, 2006; Oct. 1, 2007.)

1.3. Factors Affecting Fee Categories

The California Supreme Court considers four factors in determining the fee in fixed fee appointments in capital proceedings: *complexity, difficulty, extraordinary costs*, and *time–intensiveness*. The case-specific issues that influence the applicability of these factors often overlap, but examples of such issues include the following:

- Multiple defendants
- Motion for change of venue
- Joint or separate trials with co-defendants
- Multiple homicides or multiple incidents (including multiple victims in separate incidents)
- Mistrials and re–trial(s)
- Substitution of trial counsel: additional trial proceedings or phases (e.g., grand jury, competency phase, sanity phase)
- Multiple special circumstances
- Prior convictions or unadjudicated criminal conduct admitted at penalty phase
- Prosecution's use of informants
- Extensive litigation of the admissibility of evidence
- Forensic testing, analysis, and evidence (e.g., DNA, hair, fingerprint, blood, ballistics) introduced at trial or necessary for habeas investigation
- Mentally ill, mentally impaired, or mentally retarded capital defendants
- Non–English–speaking or foreign national capital defendant
- Non–English–speaking witnesses
- Minimal guilt and/or penalty phase investigation done for trial
- Investigation requirements in multiple locations and/or out of the state or country
- Extended elapsed time since offenses/trial
- Necessity of expert witnesses
- Necessity of using some fees to cover investigative and incidental expenses
- Length of record
- Number of trial witnesses

(Adopted, eff. Nov. 30, 2005.)

1.4. Suggested Format and Contents of Fixed Fee Requests

Counsel may submit requests for consideration of a case for a particular fixed fee category. Lengthy letters are not necessary or encouraged. Letters for the most complex cases should not exceed seven pages. A suggested format that will assist the Court in making a fixed fee determination includes the following elements:

Fixed fee request: An opening paragraph stating the fee category and base fee requested, plus additional amounts sought for transcript length and cases of exceptional complexity.

Short summary of the case: This paragraph should not extensively reiterate the facts of the case or the procedural history.

Discussion of the applicability of the four factors to this particular case: An explanation of why the appointed case is particularly complex, difficult, costly, and/or time-intensive. *(Adopted, eff. Nov. 30, 2005.)*

2. Incidental and Investigative Expenses

All incidental expenses for the direct appeal and habeas corpus/executive clemency representation are included in the fixed fee. Incidental expenses include photocopying, postage, telephone charges, computerized legal research, travel (other than for habeas corpus investigation) and services of law clerks and paralegals (other than for habeas corpus investigation). In addition to the agreed-upon fixed fee, counsel may also incur up to $25,000 in habeas corpus investigative expenses, without prior Court authorization, subject to the Court's Payment Guidelines, *supra*, part III, subpart C, paragraphs 1–7, inclusive ("Reimbursable expenses"). Investigative expenses include travel associated with habeas corpus investigation, and services of law clerks, paralegals, and others serving as habeas corpus investigators. Counsel will be reimbursed for all such habeas corpus investigative expenses that were reasonably incurred, up to $25,000. The Court will not authorize or reimburse habeas corpus investigative expenses exceeding $25,000 prior to the issuance of an order to show cause.

As to those cases in which, by January 1, 2008 (the effective date of Assem. Bill No. 1248 [1]), the defendant has not filed a capital-related habeas corpus petition in this court and the date by which to file a presumptively timely petition has not yet passed, counsel may be reimbursed up to $50,000 for those investigative services and expenses incurred on or after that date. Such investigative funding for expenses incurred after January 1, 2008, also is available in those cases in which a presumptively timely petition has been filed by January 1, 2008, but petitioner's reply to the informal response has not been filed and the time to do so (with any extensions of time) has not passed as of that date. (See also Cal. Supreme Ct., Policies

Regarding Cases Arising From Judgments of Death, *supra.*, Timeliness Stds., std. 1–1, & Compensation Stds., std. 2–2.1.) *(Adopted, eff. Jan. 1, 1994. As amended, eff. Sept. 1, 1995; Jan. 22, 1998; Jan. 1, 2008.)*

1 Stats.2007, c. 738.

3. Requests for Additional Fees

In extraordinary and unique situations, the Court will entertain requests for additional fees based on exceptional circumstances (e.g., circumstances that were unforeseeable at the time of the appointment of counsel on a fixed fee basis). In such situations, counsel shall have the burden of proof to justify any additional fees. *(Adopted, eff. Jan. 1, 1994.)*

4. Case Evaluation

There will be agreement on the fixed fee prior to the appointment of counsel. (See also, Guideline 6 [Conversion From Time and Costs Appointment to Fixed Fee], *post.*) Initially, applicant counsel selected to consider an appointment to a specific automatic appeal and/or habeas corpus/executive clemency proceedings will have the option of investigating that case for purposes of proposing a fixed fee pursuant to these alternative guidelines, rather than the traditional time and costs method. At any given time, there will be only one set of applicant counsel investigating a specific automatic appeal and/or habeas corpus/executive clemency proceedings for purposes of a possible appointment. Applicant counsel are encouraged to consult with trial counsel, examine any available transcript "dailies" prepared during the trial or other proceedings, and examine any available materials normally found in the clerk's transcript. Counsel are also encouraged to examine additional materials and information that may be available from the California Appellate Project in San Francisco.

Using these alternative guidelines, applicant counsel opting to be appointed on a fixed fee basis will propose a category and hence a fee for all services and expenses in the case. The Court's concurrence is required for any such appointment.

Discussions with applicant counsel regarding proposals for fixed fee appointments shall be conducted through the Automatic Appeals Monitor.

The fixed fee encompasses counsel's investigative costs in reviewing the case for purposes of considering an appointment. If counsel's proposal for a fixed fee is not accepted by the Court, counsel will not be reimbursed for those investigative costs; however, counsel may request an appointment to that case pursuant to the traditional time and costs method of the Payment Guidelines. *(Adopted, eff. Jan. 1, 1994. As amended, eff. Jan. 22, 1998.)*

5. Progress Payments

Until appointed appellate counsel files the appellant's opening brief or appointed habeas corpus counsel files a petition, a current status report must be filed every 60 days. Other than reimbursement for habeas corpus investigative expenses, documentation and itemization of hours and expenses by appointed counsel are not required under these alternative fixed fee guidelines.

Counsel appointed for both the direct appeal and habeas corpus/executive clemency proceedings will receive progress payments after specified stages of representation as follows: (i) one-sixth of the fixed amount shortly after counsel is appointed; (ii) one-sixth after counsel (a) submits to the assisting entity or counsel (e.g., the Habeas Corpus Resource Center, the California Appellate Project, or other assisting counsel) detailed, understandable and computerized transcript notes, a list of potentially meritorious habeas corpus issues, and a draft first request for correction of the record (and, if appropriate, any motion for augmentation and/or settled statement), and (b) files this first request; (iii) one-sixth after certification of the record and filing of the record in this court (one-half of this progress payment will be advanced upon request after the trial court's order disposing of the consolidated motion to augment, correct, and settle the record on appeal); (iv) one-sixth after counsel (a) files a confidential declaration that he or she has made reasonable efforts to consult with defendant and trial counsel about potential habeas corpus issues, (b) submits to the assisting entity or counsel a detailed outline of potential habeas corpus issues to be investigated, and (c) files the appellant's opening brief (one-quarter of this progress payment will be advanced upon request after counsel's submission to the assisting entity or counsel of a complete draft of the statement of the case and statement of the facts portion of the appellant's opening brief; one-quarter after submission of a complete draft of the guilt phase and special circumstance issues portion of the appellant's opening brief; and one-quarter after submission of a complete draft of the penalty phase issues portion of the appellant's opening brief [counsel may request these advances before progress payment (iii) has been paid in full]); (v) one-sixth after counsel (a) submits to the assisting entity or counsel a draft reply brief, (b) files a reply brief, and (c) files a confidential declaration that counsel has substantially completed the habeas corpus investigation (to the extent possible given funding provided therefor), and has submitted for review to the assisting entity or counsel a draft habeas corpus petition with necessary exhibits and declarations (or, in the alternative, that counsel has submitted for review to the assisting entity or counsel a draft declaration indicating that all potential leads have been substantially pursued to the extent possible given funding provided therefor, and that it appears that no habeas corpus petition will be filed) (one-half of this progress payment will be advanced upon request after the following: (a) the Attorney General files the respondent's brief, and (b) counsel files a confidential declaration that counsel has completed approximately one-half of the anticipated habeas corpus investigation, and has submitted to the assisting entity or counsel a detailed outline of the remainder of the planned investigation); (vi) one-sixth, less $10,000, after counsel files a habeas corpus petition in this court on behalf of counsel's client, and after oral argument and submission of the matter on the direct appeal (except that if counsel files no petition, counsel must instead file a confidential declaration indicating that all potential leads have been pursued to the extent possible given funding provided therefor, and that no habeas corpus petition will be filed, after which counsel will receive no sixth progress payment, except upon a showing that in view of work performed, full or partial payment is warranted); and finally (vii) the sum of $10,000 after completion of representation in executive clemency proceedings before the Governor of California. With each request for payment except for those set forth above in (i), (vi), and (vii), counsel shall provide to the court a statement from the assisting entity or counsel that counsel's submission to the entity or counsel substantially complies with the conditions set forth for payment.

Counsel appointed for the direct appeal only will receive progress payments after specified stages of representation as follows: (i) one-sixth of the fixed amount shortly after counsel is appointed; (ii) one-sixth after counsel (a) submits to the assisting entity or counsel (e.g., the Habeas Corpus Resource Center, the California Appellate Project, or other assisting counsel) detailed, understandable and computerized transcript notes, and a draft first request for correction of the record (and, if appropriate, any motion for augmentation and/or settled statement), and (b) files this first request; (iii) one-sixth after certification of the record and filing of the record in this court (one-half of this progress payment will be advanced upon request after the trial court's order disposing of the consolidated motion to augment, correct, and settle the record on appeal); (iv) one-sixth after counsel files the appellant's opening brief (one-quarter of this progress payment will be advanced upon request after counsel's submission to the assisting entity or counsel of a complete draft of the statement of the case and statement of the facts portion of the appellant's opening brief; one-quarter after submission of a complete draft of the guilt phase and special circumstance issues portion of the appellant's opening brief; and one-quarter after submission of a complete draft of the penalty phase issues portion of

Ct. Rules

the appellant's opening brief [counsel may request these advances before progress payment (iii) has been paid in full]); (v) one-sixth after counsel (a) submits to the assisting entity or counsel a draft of the appellant's reply brief, and (b) files the reply brief; and (vi) one-sixth after oral argument and submission of the matter on the direct appeal. With each request for payment except for those set forth above in (i) and (vi), counsel shall provide to the court a statement from the assisting entity or counsel that counsel's submission to the entity or counsel substantially complies with the conditions set forth for payment.

Counsel whose appointment is limited to habeas corpus/executive clemency proceedings will receive progress payments after specified stages of representation as follows: (i) one-fifth of the fixed amount shortly after counsel is appointed; (ii) one-fifth after counsel files a confidential declaration that counsel has reviewed the record on appeal and the detailed transcript notes and list of potentially meritorious habeas corpus issues provided by appointed counsel on the direct appeal, has made reasonable efforts to consult with defendant, appellate counsel and trial counsel, and has submitted to the assisting entity or counsel (e.g., the Habeas Corpus Resource Center, the California Appellate Project, or other assisting counsel) a detailed outline of potential habeas corpus issues to be investigated; (iii) one-fifth after counsel files a confidential declaration that counsel has completed approximately one-half of the anticipated habeas corpus investigation, and has submitted to the assisting entity or counsel a detailed outline of the remainder of the planned investigation; (iv) one-fifth after counsel files a confidential declaration that counsel has submitted for review to the assisting entity or counsel a draft habeas corpus petition with necessary exhibits and declarations (or, in the alternative, that counsel has submitted for review to the assisting entity or counsel a draft declaration indicating that all potential leads have been pursued to the extent possible given funding provided therefor, and that no habeas corpus petition will be filed) (one-half of this progress payment will be advanced upon request after counsel files a confidential declaration that counsel has completed the habeas corpus investigation to the extent possible given the funding provided therefor); (v) one-fifth, less $10,000, after counsel files a habeas corpus petition in this court on behalf of his or her client (except that if counsel files no petition, counsel must instead file a confidential declaration indicating that all potential leads have been pursued to the extent possible given funding provided therefor, and that no habeas corpus petition will be filed, after which counsel will receive no fifth progress payment, except upon a showing that in view of work performed, full or partial payment is warranted); and finally (vi) $10,000 after completion of representation in executive clemency proceedings before the Governor of California. With each request for payment except for those set forth above in (i), (v), and (vi), counsel shall provide to the court a statement from the assisting entity or counsel that counsel's submission to the entity or counsel substantially complies with the conditions set forth for payment.

Under limited circumstances (e.g., a delay in the certification of the record not due to a lack of diligence on the part of appointed counsel), the court will authorize partial payments before completion of the relevant stage(s) of representation.

In the event the proceedings terminate prior to the completion of all of the stages set forth in the progress payment schedule (as a result, for example, of the death of the defendant), appointed counsel shall memorialize all work completed and the court shall determine and pay an appropriate sum to compensate counsel for work performed prior to the termination of the proceedings. *(Adopted, eff. Jan. 1, 1994. As amended effective Jan. 22, 1998; Feb. 4, 1998; March 21, 2002.)*

6. Conversion from Time and Costs Appointment to Fixed Fee

Counsel appointed to an automatic appeal and/or habeas corpus/executive clemency proceedings under the traditional time and costs basis of the Payment Guidelines are encouraged to consider converting their method of compensation pursuant to this optional, fixed fee payment system. Any such conversion must take into account any payments previously made to counsel, and must be approved by the Court. Ordinarily, conversion will not be approved after the filing of the appellant's opening brief, or, in the case of habeas corpus/executive clemency counsel, after six months following counsel's appointment, whichever is later.

Counsel approved by the Court for an appointment to his/her first automatic appeal and/or habeas corpus/executive clemency proceedings should carefully consider an initial appointment under the time and costs basis of the Payment Guidelines. A conversion to a fixed fee appointment pursuant to these alternative guidelines may be more appropriate after such counsel has become familiar with the case. *(Adopted, eff. Jan. 1, 1994. As amended, eff. Jan. 22, 1998.)*

7. Second Counsel

The Court encourages association with second counsel. Unlike the procedure under the traditional time and costs appointment scheme of the Payment Guidelines, the fixed fees provided by this optional payment system are intended to adequately compensate appointed counsel and any associate counsel. Hence, the Court will not recognize a "second counsel override" in fixed fee cases. *(Adopted, eff. Jan. 1, 1994.)*

8. Valuation and Length of Record on Appeal

In determining the length of the combined record on appeal as part of the process whereby a case may be valued within a fixed fee category, the Court will take into consideration whether an unusual proportion of the record is comprised of jury voir dire and/or preliminary hearing transcript. When appropriate, the Court may treat the combined record as having a reduced length. Moreover, consistent with this court's historical practice, when determining the appropriate fixed fee category, the Court will not include, in determining the size of the combined record on appeal, the juror questionnaires completed by actual or prospective jurors. *(Adopted, eff. Jan. 1, 1994. As amended, eff. July 18, 2001.)*

9. Applicability of Supreme Court Policies Regarding Cases Arising From Judgments of Death

The Supreme Court Policies Regarding Cases Arising From Judgments of Death, as amended, apply to all automatic appeals and habeas corpus/executive clemency proceedings in which counsel has opted for a fixed fee pursuant to these alternative guidelines. However, standard 2–2.2 of the Compensation Standards, through standard 2–4.4 of the Compensation Standards (governing authorization to incur, and reimbursement of, habeas corpus investigation expenses), shall not apply to fixed fee cases. *(Adopted, eff. Jan. 1, 1994. As amended, eff. Jan. 22, 1998.)*

10. Fixed Legal Fees and Expenses for Evidentiary Hearings

In a case in which the Court orders an evidentiary hearing, counsel may elect to enter a fixed legal fee and expenses agreement covering (i) preparation for the evidentiary hearing, (ii) presentation of the evidentiary hearing, (iii) post-hearing litigation before the referee, and (iv) post-hearing briefs and proceedings in this Court.

(1) FIXED LEGAL FEE AND EXPENSE CATEGORIES. The Court and counsel for petitioner will agree to fix legal fees and expenses within one of the following categories.

Each agreement shall specify one fixed dollar sum covering *all* legal fees and *all* expenses—"incidental" and investigative—(e.g., photocopying, postage, telephone charges, travel, computerized legal research, services of law clerks and paralegals, services of and witness fees for investigators and experts, and any other witness expenses).

The fixed sum agreement shall also specify separately a dollar amount for the "legal fee component" and the "expenses component" of the fixed sum.

Category A: $68,500 ($60,000 legal fees; $8,500 expenses)

A matter presenting a single issue or limited issues expected to require minimal additional investigation, minimal or no services of experts, and to consume 1–2 hearing days.

Category A(1): $74,000 ($60,000 legal fees; $14,000 expenses)

A matter otherwise within Category A, but which is expected to require significant additional investigation and use of experts.

Category B: $108,000 ($94,000 legal fees; $14,000 expenses)

A matter expected to require significant additional investigation and/or significant use of experts, and to consume 3–4 hearing days.

Category B(1): $115,000 ($94,000 legal fees; $21,000 expenses)

A matter otherwise within Category B, but which is expected to require substantial additional investigation and use of experts.

Category C: $156,000 ($135,000 legal fees; $21,000 expenses)

A matter expected to require substantial additional investigation and/or services of experts, and to consume 5–6 hearing days.

Category C(1): $165,000 ($135,000 legal fees; $30,000 expenses)

A matter otherwise within Category C, but which is expected to require substantial additional investigation and use of experts.

Category D: $202,500 *base sum* ($167,500 base amount for legal fees; $35,000 base amount for expenses)

A matter that is expected to require substantial additional investigation and services of experts, and to consume 7 or more hearing days. In this category, counsel may present justification at the outset for a fixed sum higher than the base amount.

(2) REQUESTS FOR ADDITIONAL LEGAL FEES. In extraordinary and unique situations, the Court will entertain requests for additional fees based on exceptional circumstances, as set out *ante*, Fixed Fee Appointment Guideline 3.

(3) CASE EVALUATION. A fixed fee and expenses agreement shall be reached within 60 days after the Court issues its order appointing a referee. Discussions with applicant counsel regarding proposals for such an agreement shall be conducted through the Automatic Appeals Monitor.

(4) FIXED LEGAL FEE AND EXPENSE PAYMENTS.

Fixed legal fee payments. Counsel shall be entitled to be paid one-fourth of the *legal fee component* of the amount set out in the fixed legal fee and expenses agreement upon the filing of the Court's order making the fixed legal fee and expenses appointment. Thereafter, counsel will receive, on written request (but without the necessity of providing an itemization of hours), a one-fourth progress payment of the legal fee component after (i) the evidentiary hearing commences, (ii) the post-hearing litigation before the referee is completed, and (iii) the post-hearing briefing in this Court is completed. Under limited circumstances (e.g., substantial delay not due to lack of diligence on the part of counsel), the Court will authorize partial payments before completion of the aforementioned stages.

Expense payments. Every 30 days, counsel may request reimbursement from this Court for all necessary and reasonable expenses, up to the amount set out in the fixed legal fee and expenses agreement. Reimbursement shall be governed by and calculated in accordance with the Court's Payment Guidelines, *supra*, part III ("Necessary Expenses"). *(Adopted, eff. Jan. 22, 1997. As amended, eff. Jan. 22, 1998; Oct. 1, 2005; July 1, 2006; Oct. 1, 2007; March 5, 2012.)*

11. Court Action Upon Nonperformance of Work, and Reimbursement of Fees Upon Authorized Withdrawal of Appointed Counsel

The provisions of "Guideline V" of the "Payment Guidelines for Appointed Counsel Representing Indigent Criminal Appellants in the California Supreme Court" apply as well to counsel appointed on a "fixed fee" basis. *(Adopted, eff. July 30, 1997.)*

12. Reimbursement for Photocopying Defense Counsel's Trial Files

In addition to investigative expenses as set forth in the "Supreme Court Policies Regarding Cases Arising From Judgments of Death," Policy 3, standard 2–2.1, counsel appointed to handle habeas corpus/executive clemency representation will be reimbursed the reasonable cost of photocopying defense counsel's trial files, at the rate of not more than 10 cents per page, after filing of the certified record on appeal. Counsel must provide a receipt or invoice showing the number of pages copied, and the cost per page. Reimbursement will not be paid for photocopying of items already contained in the record on appeal, such as daily transcripts or exhibits. *(Adopted, eff. Jan. 16, 2002.)*

SUPREME COURT RULES REGARDING ELECTRONIC FILING

Rule

Rule 1. Application; Electronic Filing System

These rules govern electronic filing in the Supreme Court under California Rules of Court, rules 8.70—8.79. The court's electronic filing system (EFS) is operated by ImageSoft TrueFiling (TrueFiling).

Rule 2. Documents Subject to Electronic Filing

Rules 3 and 4 identify the documents that must or may be filed electronically in the Supreme Court. Except as provided in this rule, no document other than those identified in rules 3 and 4 may be filed electronically in the Supreme Court. In certain circumstances, including but not limited to natural disasters, public health emergencies, and other situations substantially affecting the court's operations, the Supreme Court may direct the Clerk/Executive Officer of the Supreme Court to accept or require electronic filing of any document and/or to modify the requirements of rule 5 regarding the filing of paper copies. If the court so directs, the Clerk must promptly make reasonable efforts to provide adequate notice to affected parties and counsel, including identifying the type of documents that may or must be electronically filed and the duration of the expanded electronic procedures.

Rule 3. Mandatory Electronic Filing

(a) Documents that Attorneys Must File Electronically. Pursuant to California Rules of Court, rule 8.71, effective September 1, 2017, unless the court grants a motion for an excuse under rule 6, all attorneys representing a party in a matter before the court must file the documents listed in this subdivision electronically through the court's EFS.

(1) *Documents in Proceedings Under Rules 8.495-8.498, 8.500-8.508, 9.13, and 9.60.* All documents filed before the court issues its decision to grant or deny review, including:

(A) Petitions for review; answers, replies;

(B) Applications to permit the filing of a petition, answer, reply, or attachment that exceeds the length limits set by California Rules of Court, rule 8.504(d);

(C) Applications to extend the time to file an answer or reply;

(D) Motions for relief from default for failure to timely file a petition, answer, or reply;

(E) All other applications and motions in these proceedings filed before the court issues its decision to grant or deny review; and

(F) Any correspondence filed in connection with the documents in (A)—(E).

(G) Amicus curiae letters under California Rules of Court, rule 8.500(g) and requests for depublication and related documents under California Rules of Court, rule 8.1125 may be filed electronically on a voluntary basis. (See Rule 4.)

(2) *Documents in proceedings under rules 8.380-8.385.* All documents filed before the court issues an order to show cause or its ruling on the petition, including:

(A) Petitions for writ of habeas corpus; informal responses, replies;

(B) Applications to permit the filing of a petition, informal response, reply, or attachment that exceeds the length limits set by California Rules of Court, rule 8.204(c);

(C) Applications to extend the time to file an informal response or reply;

(D) Motions for relief from default for failure to timely file an informal response, or reply;

(E) All other applications and motions in these proceedings filed before the court issues an order to show cause or its ruling on the petition; and

(F) Any correspondence filed in connection with the documents in (A) – (E).

(3) *Documents in proceedings under rules 8.485-8.486, and 9.13.* All documents filed before the court issues an alternative writ or its ruling on the petition, including:

(A) Petitions; preliminary responses, replies, and accusations against an attorney;

(B) Applications to permit the filing of a petition, preliminary response, reply, or attachment that exceeds the length limits set by California Rules of Court, rule 8.204(c);

(C) Applications to extend the time to file a preliminary response or reply;

(D) Motions for relief from default for failure to timely file a preliminary response, reply, or accusation against an attorney;

(E) All other applications and motions in these proceedings filed before the court issues an alternative writ or its ruling on the petition; and

(F) Any correspondence filed in connection with the documents in (A) – (E).

(4) *Documents in matters arising from a judgment of death.* All documents filed in these matters. For purposes of this subdivision:

(A) Matters arising from a judgment of death include:

(i) Automatic appeals under California Rules of Court, rules 8.600–8.642;

(ii) Habeas corpus proceedings in the court under California Rules of Court, rules 8.380-8.388 that involve a challenge to the validity of the petitioner's death judgment, including proceedings before any referee appointed by the court to conduct a hearing following the court's issuance of an order to show cause; and;

(iii) Other original writ proceedings in the court under California Rules of Court, rules 8.485-8.493 that relate to an automatic appeal or a habeas corpus proceeding challenging the validity of the death judgment, including proceedings on petitions for a writ of mandate under Penal Code section 1405, subdivision (k).

(B) Matters arising from a judgment of death do not include:

(i) Habeas corpus proceedings on petitions challenging only a capital inmate's conditions of confinement; and

(ii) Proceedings under California Rules of Court, rules 8.500–8.552 that relate to an automatic appeal or a habeas corpus proceeding challenging the validity of the death judgment, including petitions for review from lower court decisions regarding Penal Code section 1054.9 motions. These proceedings are governed by subdivision (a)(1) of this rule.

(C) A superior court judge who is appointed by the court as a referee in a proceeding under (A)(ii) is not considered a trial court for purposes of exemption from mandatory e-filing under California Rules of Court, rule 8.71(c).

(3) *Other Documents on Order of the Court.* Any other document on order of the court.

(b) Application to New and Pending Cases. Electronic filing of the documents listed in (a) is mandatory as of September 1, 2017, including documents filed in cases commenced before that date.

Rule 4. Voluntary Electronic Filing

(a) Individuals or Entities Exempt from Mandatory Electronic Filing. Pursuant to California Rules of Court, rule 8.71(b) and (c), electronic filing is voluntary for:

(1) Self-represented litigants; and

(2) Trial courts.

(b) Amicus Curiae Letters and Requests for Depublication. Amicus curiae letters under California Rules of Court, rule 8.500(g) and requests for depublication and related documents under California Rules of Court, rule 8.1125 may be filed electronically on a voluntary basis.

Rule 5. Submission of Paper Copies of Electronically Filed Documents

(a) Documents in Proceedings Under Rules 8.380-8.385, 8.485-8.486, 8.495-8.498, 8.500-8.508, 9.13, and 9.60. Unless otherwise ordered by the court:

(1) For each electronically filed document in these proceedings, the filer must also submit to the court one unbound paper copy of the document.

(2) The paper copy must be mailed, delivered to a common carrier, or delivered to the court within two court days after the document is filed electronically with the court. If the filing requests an immediate stay, the paper copy must be delivered to court by the close of business the next court day after the document is filed electronically.

(b) Documents in Matters Arising from a Judgment of Death. Unless otherwise ordered by the court:

(1) For each electronically filed document in these matters, the filer must also submit to the court one unbound paper copy of the document.

(2) The paper copy must be mailed, delivered to a common carrier, or delivered to the court within two court days after the document is filed electronically with the court.

Rule 6. Excuse from Electronic Filing

(a) Motion Requesting Excuse. A party wanting to be excused from the requirement to file a document electronically must file a motion in the court requesting to be excused. The motion must comply with California Rules of Court, rule 8.54 and must specify whether the party is requesting to be excused from electronically filing all documents or only a particular document or documents.

(b) Grounds for Excuse. Pursuant to California Rules of Court, rule 8.71(d), the court will grant an excuse on a satisfactory showing that:

(1) The party will suffer undue hardship if required to file electronically;

(2) The party will suffer significant prejudice if required to file electronically; or

(3) It is not feasible for the party to convert a particular document to electronic form by scanning, imaging, or another means.

Rule 7. Registration of Electronic Filers

(a) Obligation to Register. Unless the court excuses the filer from this obligation under rule 6, every filer who is required or voluntarily chooses to file a document electronically under these rules must register as a TrueFiling user and obtain a username and password for access to TrueFiling. Registration with and access to the EFS is through the TrueFiling website at https://www.truefiling.com.

(b) Registered Users' Responsibilities. A registered TrueFiling user is responsible for all documents filed under the user's registered username and password. The registered user must also comply with the requirements of California Rules of Court, rule 8.32 regarding the duty to provide address and other contact information, and notice of any changes.

Rule 8. Signatures

Use of a registered TrueFiling user's username and password to electronically file a document is the equivalent of placing the registered user's electronic signature on the document.

Rule 9. Service

(a) Electronic Service. In addition to the ways identified in California Rules of Court, rule 8.78 that a recipient may agree to accept electronic service, a recipient is deemed to have agreed to electronic service in a matter before this court if the recipient agreed to electronic service in the same matter in the Court of Appeal.

(b) Service by the Court. Documents prepared by the court will be served on EFS users through the EFS or by electronic notification.

(c) Service of Paper Copies. When service of a document is required to be made on a person or entity that has not consented to electronic service, the server must comply with California Rules of Court, rule 8.25 regarding service of paper copies.

Rule 10. Format and Size of Electronically Filed Documents

(a) Format.

(1) *Text Searchable Format.* All documents filed electronically must be in text-searchable PDF (portable document format), or other searchable format approved by the court, while maintaining original document formatting. If an electronic filer must file a document the filer possesses only in paper format, the filer must convert the document to an electronic document that complies with this rule by scanning or other means. It is the filer's responsibility to ensure that any document filed is complete and readable. Except as otherwise specified in this rule, electronically filed documents must comply with the content and form requirements of the California Rules of Court applicable to the particular document, with the exception of those provisions dealing exclusively with requirements for paper documents.

(2) *Pagination* The page numbering of document filed electronically must comply with California Rules of Court, rule 8.74(b)(3).

(3) *Electronic Bookmarks.* Each document must include in the bookmarks panel of the electronic document a descriptive link (hereafter referred to as an electronic bookmark), to each heading, subheading and to the first page of any component of the document, including any table of contents, table of authorities, petition, verification, points and authorities, declaration, certificate of word count, certificate of interested entities or persons, proof of service, tab, exhibit, or attachment. Each electronic bookmark to a tab, exhibit, or attachment must include the letter or number of the tab, exhibit, or attachment and a description of the tab, exhibit, or attachment.

(b) Size.

(1) An electronic filing may not be larger than 25 megabytes. This rule does not change the length limitations established by the California Rules of Court for petitions, answers, replies, briefs or any other document filed in the court.

(2) If a document exceeds the size limitation in (1), a party must submit the document in multiple files.

(A) These files must be paginated consecutively across all files in the document, including the cover pages required by (B).

(B) Each file must have a cover page that includes the following information:

(i) The total number of files constituting document;

(ii) The number of this file within the document;

(iii) The total number of pages in the document; and

(iv) The page numbers of the document contained in this file.

(C) The cover pages required by (B) must be included in the paper copies of the document submitted to the court under rule 5.

Rule 11. Privacy Protection

(a) Personal Identifiers. Electronic filers must comply with California Rules of Court, rule 1.201 regarding exclusion or redaction of personal identifiers from all documents filed with the court. Neither TrueFiling nor the Clerk of the Court has any responsibility to review documents for compliance with these requirements.

(b) Sealed and Confidential Records. Electronic filers must comply with California Rules of Court, rules 8.45–8.47 regarding sealed and confidential records, with the exception of those requirments [1] exclusively applicable to paper filings.

[1] So in original.

Rule 12. Fees

(a) Collection of Filing Fees. For electronic filings, TrueFiling is designated as the court's agent for collection of filing fees required by law and any associated credit card or bank charges or convenience fees.

(b) Vendor Fees. Pursuant to California Rules of Court, rule 8.73 and TrueFiling's contract with the court, in addition the filing fees required by law, TrueFiling will assess fees for each electronic filing in accordance with the schedule posted on the TrueFiling Web site, as approved by the court. These fees will be considered recoverable costs under rule 8.278(d)(1)(D).

(c) Exemption from Vendor Fees. The following are exempt from the fees charged for electronic filing under (b):

(1) *Parties with Fee Waivers.* A party who has been granted a fee waiver by the court who chooses to file documents electronically.

(2) *Government Officers and Entities.* The persons and entities identified in Government Code section 6103.

Rule 13. Technical Failure of Electronic Filing System

The court is not responsible for malfunctions or errors occurring in the electronic transmission or receipt of electronically filed documents. The initial point of contact for anyone experiencing difficulty with TrueFiling is the toll-free telephone number posted on the TrueFiling Web site. California Rules of Court, rule 8.77, governs if a filer fails to meet a filing deadline imposed by court order, rule, or statute because of a failure at any point in the electronic transmission and receipt of a document. A motion under California Rules of Court, rule 8.77(d) to accept the document as timely filed must comply with rule 8.54.

CONSTITUTION OF THE UNITED STATES

ARTICLE I—THE CONGRESS

Section 9, Clause 2. Suspension of Habeas Corpus

The Privilege of the Writ of Habeas Corpus shall not be suspended, unless when in Cases of Rebellion or Invasion the public Safety may require it.

Section 9, Clause 3. Bills of Attainder and Ex Post Facto Laws

No Bill of Attainder or ex post facto Law shall be passed.

ARTICLE II—THE PRESIDENT

Section 2, Clause 1. Commander in Chief; Reprieves and Pardons

Section 2. The President shall be Commander in Chief of the Army and Navy of the United States, and of the Militia of the several States, when called into the actual Service of the United States; he may require the Opinion, in writing, of the principal Officer in each of the executive Departments, upon any Subject relating to the Duties of their respective Offices, and he shall have Power to grant Reprieves and Pardons for Offenses against the United States, except in Cases of Impeachment.

ARTICLE III—THE JUDICIARY

Section 2, Clause 2. Supreme Court, Original and Appellate Jurisdiction

In all Cases affecting Ambassadors, other public Ministers and Consuls, and those in which a State shall be Party, the supreme Court shall have original Jurisdiction. In all the other Cases before mentioned, the supreme Court shall have appellate Jurisdiction, both as to Law and Fact, with such Exceptions, and under such Regulations as the Congress shall make.

Section 2, Clause 3. Criminal Trial by Jury

The Trial of all Crimes, except in Cases of Impeachment, shall be by Jury; and such Trial shall be held in the State where the said Crimes shall have been committed; but when not committed within any State, the Trial shall be at such Place or Places as the Congress may by Law have directed.

ARTICLE IV—STATES—RECIPROCAL RELATIONSHIP BETWEEN STATES AND WITH UNITED STATES

Section 2, Clause 1. Privileges and Immunities

Section 2. The Citizens of each State shall be entitled to all Privileges and Immunities of Citizens in the several States.

Section 2, Clause 2. Extradition

A person charged in any State with Treason, Felony, or other Crime, who shall flee from Justice, and be found in another State, shall on Demand of the executive Authority of the State from which he fled, be delivered up, to be removed to the State having Jurisdiction of the Crime.

ARTICLE VI—DEBTS VALIDATED—SUPREME LAW OF LAND—OATH OF OFFICE

Clause 2. Supreme Law of Land

This Constitution, and the Laws of the United States which shall be made in Pursuance thereof; and all Treaties made, or which shall be made, under the Authority of the United States, shall be the supreme Law of the Land; and the Judges in every State shall be bound thereby, any Thing in the Constitution or Laws of any State to the Contrary notwithstanding.

AMENDMENT IV—SEARCHES AND SEIZURES; WARRANTS

The right of the people to be secure in their persons, houses, papers, and effects, against unreasonable searches and seizures, shall not be violated, and no Warrants shall issue, but upon probable cause, supported by Oath or affirmation, and particularly describing the place to be searched, and the persons or things to be seized.

AMENDMENT V—GRAND JURY; DOUBLE JEOPARDY; SELF-INCRIMINATION; DUE PROCESS; TAKINGS

No person shall be held to answer for a capital, or otherwise infamous crime, unless on a presentment or indictment of a Grand Jury, except in cases arising in the land or naval forces, or in the Militia, when in actual service in time of War or public danger; nor shall any person be subject for the same offence to be twice put in jeopardy of life or limb; nor shall be compelled in any criminal case to be a witness against himself, nor be deprived of life, liberty, or property, without due process of law; nor shall private property be taken for public use, without just compensation.

AMENDMENT VI—JURY TRIAL FOR CRIMES, AND PROCEDURAL RIGHTS

In all criminal prosecutions, the accused shall enjoy the right to a speedy and public trial, by an impartial jury of the State and district wherein the crime shall have been committed, which district shall have been previously ascertained by law, and to be informed of the nature and cause of the accusation; to be confronted with the witnesses against him; to have compulsory process for obtaining witnesses in his favor, and to have the Assistance of Counsel for his defence.

AMENDMENT VIII—EXCESSIVE BAIL, FINES, PUNISHMENTS

Excessive bail shall not be required, nor excessive fines imposed, nor cruel and unusual punishments inflicted.

AMENDMENT XIV—CITIZENSHIP; PRIVILEGES AND IMMUNITIES; DUE PROCESS; EQUAL PROTECTION; APPORTIONMENT OF REPRESENTATION; DISQUALIFICATION OF OFFICERS; PUBLIC DEBT; ENFORCEMENT

Section 1. All persons born or naturalized in the United States, and subject to the jurisdiction thereof, are citizens of the United States and of the State wherein they reside. No State shall make or enforce any law which shall abridge the privileges or immunities of citizens of the United States; nor shall any State deprive any person of life, liberty, or property, without due process of law; nor deny to any person within its jurisdiction the equal protection of the laws.

Section 2. Representatives shall be apportioned among the several States according to their respective numbers, counting the whole number of persons in each State, excluding Indians not taxed. But when the right to vote at any election for the choice of electors for President and Vice President of the United States, Representatives in Congress, the Executive and Judicial officers of a State, or the members of the Legislature thereof, is denied to any of the male inhabitants of such State, being twenty-one years of age, and citizens of the United States, or in any way abridged, except for participation in rebellion, or other crime, the basis of representation therein shall be reduced in the proportion which the number of such male citizens shall bear to the whole number of male citizens twenty-one years of age in such State.

Section 3. No person shall be a Senator or Representative in Congress, or elector of President and Vice President, or hold any office, civil or military, under the United States, or under any State, who, having previously taken an oath, as a member of Congress, or as an officer of the United States, or as a member of any State legislature, or as an executive or judicial officer of any State, to support the Constitution of the United States, shall have engaged in insurrection or rebellion against the same, or given aid or comfort to the enemies thereof. But Congress may by a vote of two-thirds of each House, remove such disability.

Section 4. The validity of the public debt of the United States, authorized by law, including debts incurred for payment of pensions and bounties for services in suppressing insurrection or rebellion, shall not be questioned. But neither the United States nor any State shall assume or pay any debt or obligation incurred in aid of insurrection or rebellion against the United States, or any claim for the loss or emancipation of any slave; but all such debts, obligations and claims shall be held illegal and void.

Section 5. The Congress shall have power to enforce, by appropriate legislation, the provisions of this article.

INDEX TO
PENAL CODE
AND SELECTED PENAL PROVISIONS OF:

U.S. Const	**Constitution of the United States**
Const	**Constitution of California**
Bus & P	**Business and Professions Code**
CCP	**Code of Civil Procedure**
Fam	**Family Code**
Gov	**Government Code**
Health & S	**Health and Safety Code**
Ins	**Insurance Code**
Veh	**Vehicle Code**
Welf & I	**Welfare and Institutions Code**

Index

Index

Index

Index

Index

Index

Index

Index

Index

Index

Index

Index

Index

Index

Index

Index

Index

Index

Index

Index

Index

Index

Index

Index

Index

Index

Index

Index

Index

Index

Index

Index

Index

Index

Index

Index

Index

Index

Index

Index

Index

Index

Index

Index

Index

Index

Index

Index

Index

Index

Index

Index

Index

Index

Index

Index

Index

Index

Index

Index

Index

Index

Index

Index

Index

Index

Index

Index

Index

Index

Index

Index

Index

Index

Index

Index

Index